C000111829

ISBN 978-0-365-20153-3
PIBN 10851918

Englisch-Deutsches und Deutsch-Englisches

Wörterbuch

von

Dr. Joseph Leonhard Hilpert.

Mit einer Vorrede von Dr. E. Kärcher.

Zweiter Band

Deutsch-Englisch.

Erste Abtheilung.

A—K.

„Vestigia filo regenda sunt: omnisque via, usque a primis sensuum perceptionibus, certa ratione munienda.“

BACO *in praefatione ad instaurationem magnam.*

Karlsruhe,

G. Braun'sche Hofbuchhandlung.

New-York, bei Wm. *Radde*, № 322. Broadway.

1846.

A

DICTIONARY

OF THE

ENGLISH AND GERMAN, AND THE GERMAN AND ENGLISH LANGUAGE.

BY

Dr. J. L. HILPERT.

WITH A PREFACE BY *Dr. E. KÆRCHER.*

VOL. II.

German and English.

PART. I.

A—K.

»Vestigia filo regenda sunt: omnisque via, usque à primis sensuum perceptionibus, certâ ratione munienda.«

Baco *in praefatione ad instaurationem magnam.*

NEW-YORK:
WILLIAM RADDE, N° 322. BROADWAY.
CARLSRUHE:
TH. BRAUN, BOOKSELLER AND PRINTER TO THE COURT.
1846.

TO

HER MOST EXCELLENT MAJESTY

VICTORIA,

QUEEN OF THE UNITED KINGDOM OF GREAT BRITAIN AND IRELAND,

AND

HIS ROYAL HIGHNESS

PRINCE ALBERT

THIS WORK

IS, WITH THEIR GRACIOUS PERMISSION,

MOST RESPECTFULLY DEDICATED

BY THE PUBLISHER.

Vorrede. *Preface.*

Indem wir dem Publikum nunmehr die beiden Theile von Hilpert's deutsch-englischem Wörterbuche übergeben, möchte es nicht unzweckmäßig, ja gewissermaßen Pflicht seyn, eine Erklärung wegen verspäteter Erscheinung desselben vorauszuschicken.

Als Hilpert im Frühjahre 1833 starb, hatte er zwar das Manuscript des deutsch-englischen Theiles bis beinahe an das Ende des Buchstaben F ausgearbeitet; allein dasselbe war nach näherer Einsicht keineswegs schon zum Drucke reif.

Die Masse des Stoffes, die technische Anordnung des Ganzen, und die möglichst gleichförmige Durchführung desselben, bot für einen Einzelnen so große und so vielfache Schwierigkeiten, daß es dem Verewigten wohl nicht zur Last gelegt werden kann, namentlich bei dem Mangel an ähnlichen Arbeiten, wenn seine Leistungen nicht sofort reif genug zur Veröffentlichung erschienen.

Es mußte daher, wie auch der von der Braun'schen Hofbuchhandlung früher ausgegebene Prospectus besagt, dafür gesorgt werden, daß sein Manuscript noch einmal, und zwar von Mehreren in verschiedener Beziehung durchgesehen und überarbeitet wurde, um ihm den zur Erscheinung erforderlichen Grad von Feile, Abrundung und Erweiterung zu geben.

Dennoch wird der Billige nicht verlangen, daß dieser Theil des Werkes, nämlich die Buchstaben A — F, nach allen Beziehungen in vollkommenem Einklange mit dem übrigen Theile stehen, wiewohl der Unterschied wenig fühlbar seyn, und sich hauptsächlich darauf beschränken dürfte, daß die logische Eintheilung einzelner Artikel in

In laying before the Public the Two Parts of *Hilpert's* German and English Dictionary, it may not be considered out of place, but rather a duty devolving upon us, to explain here the reason of their retarded appearance.

When *Hilpert* died in the spring of the year 1833, he had written the manuscript nearly to the end of the letter *F*; but from a more careful inspection it was found by no means ready for the press.

The mass of matter, the technical arrangement of the whole, and the utmost uniformity of execution presented such great and manifold difficulties for a single person, that, considering at the same time the want of similar works, it can scarcely be preferred as a charge against the departed originator, that his performance did not appear sufficiently mature for immediate publication.

It was therefore necessary, as already stated in the Prospectus published some years ago by Th. Braun, printer and bookseller to the Court, that the late Hilpert's manuscript should be carefully examined and revised, in order to give it the requisite polish and enlargement for its appearance before the Public.

This part of the work however, viz. from the letter *A* to *F* inclusive, cannot of course be expected to be in all points in perfect unison with the rest, although the difference is scarcely perceptible and principally limited to the fact, that the logical division of certain articles in the former portion is less comprehensive, and the phrases given in

dieser vordern Partie weniger erschöpfend, und die ihm beigegebenen Phrasen weniger manchfaltig sind, als in den folgenden Buchstaben.

Eine weitere Verzögerung in Ausarbeitung und Druck des Werkes wurde theils durch den Tod, theils durch Austritt des einen und andern der Mitarbeiter herbeigeführt.

Und je sorgfältiger die Verlagshandlung, sowie Diejenigen, welchen die nächste Leitung des ganzen Unternehmens übertragen war, in Beiziehung neuer Mitarbeiter waren, um so weniger durfte es ihnen auf rasches Erscheinen des Ganzen ankommen, insofern die Gediegenheit desselben darunter in irgend einer Beziehung zu leiden gehabt hätte.

Lieber sollten pekuniäre Opfer gebracht werden, und daß solche in einem sehr bedeutenden Maße gebracht wurden, braucht bei dem nur einigermaßen Geschäftskundigen keiner besondern Versicherung.

Für Herrn L. A. Spearman, der bis zu seinem Tode an dem Werke arbeitete,*) traten später die Herren H. Howe**) und R. H. Whitelocke***) ein. Außerdem hat Herr J. Towler, ein hier privatisirender englischer Gelehrter, uns für einen Theil des Werkes freundliche und willkommene Beihülfe †) geleistet. Und nachdem Herr

*) Er ist auch Verfasser einer durch ihre Klarheit und verständige Anordnung ausgezeichneten Grammatik der englischen Sprache, wovon die erste Auflage im Jahr 1835 und die neueste im Jahr 1844 in der Chr. Fr. Müller'schen Hofbuchhandlung zu Karlsruhe erschienen ist. Von Herrn Spearman rührt die Revision der Buchstaben A — F, und G — M des Manuscripts der Herren Hilpert und Süpfle her, und ebenso die englische Bearbeitung der Synonymen in den Buchstaben A — K.

**) Verfasser der englischen Bearbeitung von Zschokke's Schweizergeschichte. Hr. Howe hat die Buchstaben N — O (Obedienz) und T (bis Türkisch) bearbeitet; sowie die Synonymen von L — S (Schlank).

***) Er hat mehrere sprachliche und Reiseschriften veröffentlicht. Hr. Whitelocke ist der Bearbeiter der Buchstaben O (Obedienziar) und P, R und S, T (von Türkiß an), U und V, und W (bis Wohl), nebst einer Anzahl Wörter in dem Buchstaben Z, sodann sämmtlicher Synonymen in den Buchstaben S. (Schlemmen) bis Z (Schluß).

†) Hr. Towler hat außer dieser Beihülfe die Buchstaben W (von Wohl) bis gegen dem Schluß von Z (Zusammenlauf) bearbeitet.

exemplification are less various, than in the following letters of the alphabet.

A further delay in the composition and printing of the work was caused partly by the death and partly by the withdrawing out of the concern of one or other of the coadjutors.

Considering the care the editors took, as well as those entrusted with the immediate management of the whole undertaking, in the engagement of new and competent writers, the less can it be supposed, that the speedy appearance of the whole would be their object, inasmuch as the solid character of the work might, in some respect, have been thereby impaired.

It was preferable that pecuniary sacrifices should be made, and any one, however slightly acquainted with the editorial and printing departments of a work, will require no particular assurance to be convinced, that such and no inconsiderable ones have been made.

Mr. *L. A. Spearman**, who was engaged in the work until his death, was succeeded, by Mr. *H. Howe*,** and after him came Mr. *R. H. Whitelocke*.*** In addition to these gentlemen Mr. *I. Towler*, an Englishman of literary attainments, residing here and private teacher of his vernacular tongue, has rendered us kind and welcome assistance in one part of the work.†

*Author of an English Grammar for Germans distinguished for its conspicuity and intelligent arrangement; the first edition, appeared in 1835, and the latest in 1844. Published by Müller, Carlsruhe. *Dr. Hilpert's* manuscript from A to F inclusive and that of *Dr. Süpfle* were revised by Mr. *Spearman*, and the English elucidation of the synonyms from A to K is also by him.

**Author of an English translation of Zschokke's History of Switzerland. The letter N, to Obedienz in the letter O, and the letter T as far as the word Türkisch is the work of this gentleman, as also the synonyms from L to the word Schlank in S.

*** Several philological works and Guides for tourists have appeared by him. Mr. *Whitelocke* furnished the manuscript from Obedienziar in the letter O, also the letters P, R, S and T from the word Türkiß, and U, V and as far as the word Wohl in W, together with a number of words in Z. The Synonyms from S (Schlemmen) to the end of Z are got up by him.

† Besides this assistance rendered by Mr. *Towler*, the part from Wohl in W to the word Zusammenlauf in Z is his work.

Dr. Süpfle*) theils durch Rücksicht auf seine Gesundheit, theils wegen anderweitiger Anstellung seine Mitwirkung an demselben aufgeben mußte, übernahm es hauptsächlich Herr v. Killinger, der die englische Sprache seit langer Zeit zu seinem Hauptstudium gemacht hat und in der literarischen Welt (unter dem Namen K. v. Kreling) vortheilhaft bekannt ist, und gleich vom Beginne dieses deutsch-englischen Theiles an beirathend thätig war, die Ausarbeitung des Ganzen in mehrfacher Beziehung, namentlich auch durch stete und für die gleichförmige Durchführung des Werks so wichtige Besprechungen mit den englischen Mitarbeitern, so wie durch reiche Beiträge für beide Sprachen, zu unterstützen und zu fördern.

Auch Herr Mittell, jetzt Geheimer Kabinetssekretär Sr. Königlichen Hoheit des Großherzogs, der durch einen Aufenthalt von mehreren Jahren in England sich die Sprache dieses Landes in nicht gewöhnlichem Grade zu eigen gemacht hat, widmete dem Buche, soweit es ihm seine Berufsgeschäfte gestatteten, fortwährend die möglichste Sorgfalt. Nicht weniger haben wir des Herrn Professors und Hofbibliothekars Graß — Verfassers mehrerer sprachlichen Werke — dankbar zu erwähnen, besonders in Bezug auf die Genauigkeit, die derselbe der letzten Durchsicht der einzelnen Druckbogen angedeihen ließ.

Den vereinten Bemühungen dieser Männer dürfte es nun wohl gelungen seyn, die Hauptrücksicht, welche auch ein deutsch-englisches Wörterbuch haben soll, überall festgehalten zu haben; wir meinen nämlich das Bestreben, das Englische, sowohl für einzelne Wörter als auch ganze Phrasen, so entsprechend und kurz als möglich, und insbesondere, bei aller Classicität der gewählten Ausdrücke, den modernsten Sprach- und eleganten Umgangsgebrauch wiederzugeben, anstatt, wie bisher fast durchgängig in solchen deutsch-englischen Wörterbüchern geschah, alte von Lexikon zu Lexikon vererbte Ausdrücke und Redensarten, bequemer Weise, aufzunehmen und fortzupflanzen und statt der stets lebendig quellenden Sprache dem gebrauchsbedürftigen Publikum eine theilweise abgestorbene und todte Wortmasse zu bieten.

Bei der Aufnahme der einzelnen deutschen Wörter waren wir ferner darauf bedacht, die Masse derselben nicht ungebührlich zu häufen, was sehr leicht gewesen wäre.

*) Von ihm ist, außer der Mitdurchsicht (mit Hrn. Sp.) der Buchstaben A — F (Fuhrmann), die Bearbeitung der Buchstaben F (von Fuhrmann an) bis M (Schluß) und O — R (Ranft).

And after *Dr. Süpfle*,* who was obliged partly in regard to his health and partly on account of a local change in his professional duties to give up his assistance in the composition of the work, the superintendence was undertaken by *Baron von Killinger*, who has long made the English language his principal study, (being also favourably known in the literary world under the assumed name of *K. v. Kreling*) and who from the very commencement of the German and English part of the Dictionary was always ready with his advice and assistance to promote the uniformity of the whole in every respect possible, but particularly by his highly useful conferences with the English writers engaged in the work, and by the rich communications he himself contributed for both languages.

Mr. *Mittell* also, now private secretary to his Royal Highness the Grand Duke of Baden, and who, during several years' residence in England had made himself master of the language of this country in no common degree, uninterruptedly devoted, as much as the duties of his calling allowed, every possible attention to this book. And with no less degree of obligation do we mention the name of Professor *Gratz*, librarian to the Court, and author of several philological works, for his minute care in revising the sheets &c. the last time before taking them to the press.

It is presumed that the united efforts of these gentlemen have everywhere strictly adhered to the chief point, by which any Dictionary of modern languages, and thus also a German and English dictionary, ought to be made available and valued, namely the aiming to render, in the present work, the English construction as corresponding to the German and as concise as possible both in regard to single words and whole passages, and above all to give, without neglecting the classic correctness of the language, the most modern and the most colloquial form to its expressions, instead (as has been heretofore almost universally the case with such German and English dictionaries) of copying and handing down from lexicon to lexicon old terms and forms of speech and of presenting the Public (always craving after words to keep march with the times), in a great measure with an obsolete and a dead mass of

*Besides assisting Mr. *Spearman* in the revision of the part from A to F (Fuhrmann), the letter *F* (from Fuhrmann) to M inclusive, and O to R (Ranft) are his production.

Es sollten hauptsächlich die allgemein gültigen aufgenommen, immerhin aber auch etwas veraltete Wörter, insofern sie in manchen Gegenden oder für manche Gewerbe noch gebräuchlich sind, eher berücksichtigt werden, als neugeprägte, deren Zusammensetzung dem der deutschen Sprache nur einigermaßen Kundigen entweder gar keine Schwierigkeit bietet oder die ihr Daseyn häufig nur auf dem Papiere behaupten; wiewohl auch von letztern solche, welche Lebenskraft und dauernde Aufnahme in den deutschen Sprachschatz zu gewinnen verheißen, nicht vermißt werden dürften.

Die Synonymen, ein für das genauere Verständniß einer Sprache so wichtiger Punkt, wurden, mit Benutzung der besten Hülfsmittel, auf eine Weise berücksichtigt, wie dieß bis jetzt in keinem deutsch-englischen Wörterbuche geschehen ist.

Was aber die logische Anordnung einzelner, namentlich umfassenderer, Artikel betrifft, so war nach des Unterzeichneten Ansicht hier noch Mancherlei und nicht Unbedeutendes zu thun.

Adelung's wiewohl immer noch sehr verdienstliches Werk, das der Unterzeichnete wohl nicht mit Unrecht als Führer des Schwarms ansieht, und das er als Grundlage für die Hauptartikel dieses Werkes benutzte, hat bei der logischen Behandlung der Wortbedeutung durchaus noch nicht jener eben so einfachen als allein zum Ziele führenden Sprachphilosophie gehuldigt, an deren Hand eine Masse von diesem Schriftsteller begangener Irrthümer, oder wenigstens Bequemlichkeitsfehler, wie von selbst vermieden werden konnte.

Wir glauben, ohne Ruhmredigkeit gesagt, daß namentlich von da an, wo kein fremdes Manuscript mehr zu berücksichtigen war, nicht wohl ein etwas umfangreicherer Artikel in unserm Werke gefunden werden dürfte, der auch in dieser Hinsicht nicht wesentliche Veränderungen, die wir für Verbesserungen halten möchten, erfahren hat; besonders ist dies der Fall bei den Zeitwörtern, Präpositionen und Conjunctionen. Adelung hat nämlich häufig den Fehler so vieler, selbst neuerer und neuester Lexikographen begangen — und Diejenigen, die ihn benutzten, nahmen sich wenig Zeit, ihn darin zu verbessern, — daß er gewöhnlich die üblichste, aber jüngste — weil abstrahirteste — Bedeutung des Worts voran stellte, und er hat durch diesen Mißgriff sich die Sache unendlich erschwert und der Brauchbarkeit seines Buches großen Eintrag gethan. Davon gibt jeder

words, in lieu of an overflowing spring of language adapted to their wants.

It was further a consideration of ours in furnishing the single German words, not to heap together an unnecessary and incongruous mass, which might have been done very easily; but principally to introduce those generally adopted, not omitting however such as are, in some measure, obsolete, though still in use in certain districts or among certain artisans, rather than new-fangled ones, whose composition either presents no difficulty at all to those, who are in any degree acquainted with the German language, or whose existence is often only to be maintained upon paper; although such of the latter, as give promise of vitality and of gaining a lasting reception in the German tongue, could not be omitted.

The synonyms, so important for the more intimate understanding of a language, have, by availing ourselves of the best authorities, been treated with a precision and care not to be found in any other German and English dictionary.

But in regard to the logical arrangement of individual articles admitting of an extensive diversity of signification there remained, in the writer's view of the subject, much and of no small importance still to be accomplished.

Adelung in his work, however estimable it may still be, and which the writer of this preface still regards as the 'leader of the host' and has availed himself of as the groundwork for the heads of this work, has by no means, in the logical treatment of the meaning of words, kept strictly to that simple philosophy of language, which alone is the only guide, by which that celebrated lexicographer might have avoided a mass of errors or, to say the least of them, convenient mistakes.

We believe without boasting, that in all those instances where we had no other author to go by, there is scarcely a single article of any consequence to be found in our work, that has not undergone important changes, which we look upon as improvements; this is particularly the case with the verbs, prepositions and conjunctions. *Adelung* has often fallen into the same fault which many others of the more recent and even latest lexicographers have committed (those, who followed him, giving themselves little trouble to correct him in this respect), by generally placing the most common, but most modern — because most abstract — meaning of the

etwas wichtigere Artikel bei ihm Zeugniß. In genauere Erörterung darüber einzugehen, ist jedoch hier nicht der Ort.

Wir haben überall, nach dem Grundsatze, daß in der Regel die breiteste, weiteste und sinnlichere Bedeutung eines Wortes die frühere seyn muß, — insofern die Sprache für etwas Anderes angesehen werden will, als für einen durch blinden Zufall zusammengewehten Haufen willkührlicher Bezeichnungen, — wir haben, sagen wir, überall nach diesem Grundsatze das Einzelne zu ordnen gesucht. Und wenn wir dabei allerdings gerne zugeben, daß dem strengen Beurtheiler immer noch Manches verfehlt und ungenügend erscheinen wird, so glauben wir doch dem Leser die erfreuliche Erfahrung, die sich uns häufig gerade bei den scheinbar schwierigsten Artikeln am unzweideutigsten aufdrängte, nicht vorenthalten zu dürfen, wie leicht und scharf selbst die verwickeltsten Artikel, durch die Anwendung des oben von uns ausgesprochenen Grundsatzes, sich sondern und ordnen ließen: seine Wahrheit, übrigens von gewichtigern Stimmen, als die unsrige ist, schon vielfach ausgesprochen, hatte sich uns bei frühern ähnlichen Studien in den klassischen Sprachen bereits hinlänglich erprobt.

Noch ist ein Punkt übrig, über den wir uns mit dem Publikum etwas genauer zu verständigen für nöthig halten. Wir sprechen von den etymologischen Beisätzen.

Unser Hauptbestreben hierbei war, Dasjenige, was zur Feststellung der Grundbedeutung des betreffenden Wortes als das Wesentlichste erschien, in möglichster Kürze*) anzugeben. Und wiewohl es bei den vielfach noch schwankenden Ansichten, theils über die allgemeinen Grundsätze, welche bei solchen etymologischen Forschungen als maßgebend anzunehmen sind, theils über die Anwendung des Allgemeinen auf das Einzelne, keine kleine Aufgabe ist, hier überall die richtige Mitte zu halten, so wird doch dem Aufmerksamen nicht entgehen, daß auch diesem Gegenstande die möglichste Sorgfalt gewidmet wurde, wenn es gleich vorerst nicht gegeben war, für jedes Wort solche etymologische Schlüssel zu finden.**)

*) Webster behandelt in seinem Wörterbuche der englischen Sprache die Etymologie, dem Zwecke seines Buchs angemessen, ausführlicher; Ad. Wagner in seinem deutsch-englischen Wörterbuche, wenn auch sehr geistreich, doch wohl allzu weitläufig.

**) Dieß ist eine Aufgabe, welcher ein Einzelner kaum gewachsen ist und der nur im Laufe längerer Zeit genügt werden kann.

word at the head of each article, and by this misconception he has involved himself in endless difficulties and greatly injured the utility of his book. Every article of any importance bears evidence to this assertion. But this is not the place to enter into a more minute disquisition of this subject.

It has everywhere been our endeavour to follow the principle, that generally the *broadest*, *widest* and most *palpable* signification of a word ought to take the lead, (inasmuch as language is regarded as something more than a mere heap of arbitrary signs drifted together by chance), it has everywhere been our endeavour, then, to arrange each article according to this principle. And though we are willing to concede, that the severe critic may still find much that may appear faulty and unsatisfactory, yet we consider ourselves bound not to hold back from the reader the pleasant experience, which often forcibly struck us even in parts seemingly the most difficult, how easily and effectually even the most intricate articles were capable of being sifted and arranged according to the above-stated principle: its truth, which, moreover, has been proclaimed by weightier authorities than ours, we had already sufficiently tested in former and similar studies in the classical languages.

There still remains a point, in regard to which we consider it necessary to come to an explanation with the Public.

Our chief aim was, to express in as concise a manner* as possible that which appeared to be most essential for fixing the primary meaning of the word in question. And although in the midst of such varied and still wavering views, partly as regards the general principles to be adopted as the leading ones in such etymological investigations, and partly as to the application of the general idea to the individual, it is no slight task to preserve in every case the due medium, yet an attentive perusal will show that the utmost care has been devoted also to this part, although for the present it was impossible to give such an etymological key for every word.**

**Webster* in his English dictionary has given a more copious elucidation of the etymology of that language, in accordance with the intention of his work; *Ad. Wagner* in his German and English dictionary, although very ingenious, is much too diffuse.

** This is a task almost beyond the province of a single person, and which can only be accomplished with satisfaction in a long course of time.

Dieß ist besonders der Fall bei den Ausdrücken, die dem Seewesen eigenthümlich sind.

Conjecturen, die sich im Felde der Etymologie nur allzuleicht aufdrängen, sollten aber so selten als möglich gewagt werden.

Einen eigenthümlichen Vorzug glauben wir dem Werke durch genauere Bezeichnung der Sylbenbetonung verschafft zu haben. Das Nähere hierüber ist unten aufgeführt.

Und so übergeben wir denn dieses Buch dem geehrten Publikum mit der Ueberzeugung, daß es, bei allen Mängeln, die jedem menschlichen Werke ankleben, keine unwürdige Stelle in der Reihe ähnlicher einnehmen, und Jedem, der es einer genauern Prüfung werth hält, die Ueberzeugung geben wird, daß es sich bei seiner Ausarbeitung darum handelte, nicht blos dem Tagesbedürfnisse zu genügen, sondern auch dem höhern Prinzipe der Wissenschaftlichkeit zu huldigen.

Karlsruhe, im Mai 1845.

Dr. E. Kärcher.

This is particularly the case with expressions peculiar to naval affairs.

Conjectures, however, which but too easily crowd upon the field of etymology, ought to be risked as seldom as possible.

We believe we have rendered this work a peculiar advantage over similar ones by a more careful notification of the accentuation of syllables. This subject will be found more fully elucidated in the 'Introductory Explanations.'

And thus we resign this work into the hands of the honoured Public with the conviction, that, notwithstanding all its defects, which no human work is free from, it will occupy no mean position in the rank of similar productions and that every one, who deigns to bestow upon it a more minute examination, will be convinced that the object of this task was not only to meet the wants of the age, but also to do homage to the higher principle of erudition.

Einleitende Bemerkungen. Introductory Explanations.

Erklärung der vorkommenden Zeichen.

* (im Texte) gewöhnliche oder vertrauliche, nur in der Umgangssprache gebräuchliche Ausdrücke und Redensarten (späterhin immer mit "in fam. lang." ausgedrückt).
* (vorn) bedeutet Fremdwörter.
† gemeine oder niedrige Ausdrücke und Redensarten.
‡ veraltete Wörter und Ausdrücke.
‡ scherzhafte Wörter und launige Ausdrücke, auch solche, die der komischen oder burlesken Sprech- oder Schreibart angehören.
‖ landschaftliche Wörter und Ausdrücke.
— bedeutet das Wort im Anfange des Abschnitts.
= bedeutet gleich.

Bemerkungen über die Pluralbezeichnung.

1) Die auf heit, keit, schaft, ung, inn, ei und von den Fremdwörtern die auf ion ausgehenden Hauptwörter nehmen in der Mehrzahl en an.
2) Mit Ausnahme der auf heit, keit, schaft rc. ausgehenden Hauptwörter, sind alle diejenigen, bei denen keine Pluralbezeichnung angegeben ist, in der Mehrzahl ungebräuchlich.
3) Das Zeichen: *pl.* - bedeutet, daß Einzahl und Mehrzahl gleich sind; z. B. Adler, *m.* [*pl.* -].

Bemerkung über die Stellung der Composita.

Die Composita sind nicht streng in der alphabetischen Reihenfolge, sondern bei den Stammwörtern zu suchen; auch sind die von gleichlautenden — aber nicht gleichbedeutenden Stammwörtern abgeleiteten, mit sehr seltenen Ausnahmen, getrennt aufgeführt.

Erklärung der Bezeichnung [*used with* seyn].

Die Verba intransitiva werden theils mit haben, theils mit seyn conjugirt. Wenn sie mit seyn conjugirt werden, ist immer *used with* (oder *u. w.*) seyn hinzugesetzt worden; wenn sie aber mit haben gebraucht werden, ist, wie bei den andern Verbis, jede Bezeichnung weggeblieben.

Die Zeichen für die Betonung der Sylben

(im Deutschen) sind so eingerichtet, daß
1) nicht nur auf die geschärften und gedehnten Sylben Rücksicht genommen ist, sondern auch auf die zwischen beiden schwebenden, d. h. solche, die in manchen Gegenden auf die eine, in andern auf die andere Art ausgesprochen werden. Die Präpos. an lautet z. B. bald wie ān, bald wie án. Für solche Fälle ist in unserer Tonbezeichnung ein perpendikularer Strich angenommen (ȧn).
2) Sind die gedehnten und geschärften Diphthongen ebenfalls unterschieden, was z. B. von Heinsius, in dessen volksthümlichem Wörterbuche der deutschen Sprache, nicht geschehen ist, so daß bei ihm ein (= hinein) und die Zahl ein ganz gleich betont sind. Ferner haben wir, wie es in der griechischen Sprache Sitte ist, überall den zweiten Buchstaben des Diphthongs accentuirt, also z. B. aúf, aús. Endlich
3) haben wir durch eine sehr einfache Einrichtung bei dem Buchstaben e, neben der Dehnung (ē) und Schärfung (é), auch noch jedesmal angegeben, ob derselbe den geschlossenen oder den breiten (offenen) Ton hat, oder, wie die französische Sprache sich ausdrückt, ob es ein e fermé (é) oder ein e ouvert (è) ist. Diese Unterscheidung findet sich ebenfalls noch in keinem ähnlichen Werke durchgeführt. Wir haben nämlich für das gedehnte und zugleich geschlossene e einen Strich mit einem Acutus (ḗ), für das gedehnte und zugleich offene e einen Strich mit einem Gravis (ḕ) angenommen. Wir schreiben also z. B. hḗben, ḗdel, gḕben, Ḕber.

EXPLANATION OF THE SIGNS MADE USE OF.

* [in the text] familiar or colloquial expressions. In the latter part of the work always expressed by 'in fam. lang.'

* [before a word] signifies foreign words.
† vulgar or low expressions and phrases.
‡ obsolete words.
‡ jocose words and humorous expressions, and such as belong to the comic or burlesque style.
‖ provincialisms.
— signifies the word at the commencement of the paragraph.
= signifies equal to or of the same meaning.

REMARKS ON THE FORMATION OF THE PLURAL.

1) Substantives ending in heit, keit, schaft, ung, inn, ei and foreign words ending in ion form their plural by adding en.
2) With the exception of the Substantives in heit, keit, schaft &c., those Substantives to which no plural is given, are unusual in the plural form.
3) This mark: *pl.* - denotes that the singular and plural are alike, as: Adler, *m.* [*pl.* -].

REMARKS ON THE POSITION OF COMPOUND OR DERIVATIVE WORDS.

Compound or derivative words are not strictly in alphabetical order, but are to be locked for under their primitives or the words from which they are derived; derivatives of simple words, which, though *similarly written*, have *different significations*, are, with few exceptions, separately classified.

EXPLANATION OF THE TERM — *used with* seyn.

Of the *intransitive* Verbs some are conjugated with haben, and some with seyn. Those which are conjugated with seyn are distinguished by *used with* (or *u. w.*) seyn; those which are conjugated with haben, have no peculiar mark of distinction.

THE MARKS FOR THE ACCENTUATION

(of the German words) are so arranged, that
1) not only the short and long sounds are distinguished, but also those which are undecided between the two, that is, such as in some districts are pronounced in one manner and in others in a different. The preposition an, for instance, is pronounced sometimes ān, sometimes án. In such cases we have chosen a perpendicular stroke (ȧn).
2) The long or broad and short or close diphthongs are also distinguished, which has not been done by Heinsius in his „Volksthümliches Wörterbuch der deutschen Sprache", in which he gives ein (= hinein) and the numeral ein precisely the same sound. As in the Greek we have always placed the accent over the last vowel of the diphthong, as: aúf, aús.
3) Lastly, with regard to the vowel e by a simple arrangement, we have given not only the long (ē) and short (é), but also whether it has the close or open sound, or, as it is expressed in French, whether it is an e *fermé* (é), or an e *ouvert* (è). This distinction is not to be found in any similar work. For the long and at the same time close sound we have adopted a stroke with the acute accent (ḗ), for the long and at the same time open sound, a stroke with the grave accent (ḕ). Thus for instance: hḗben, ḗdel, gḕben, Ḕber.

Erklärung der Abkürzungen. Explanation of the Abbreviations.

adj.	=	adjective	Eigenschaftswort, Beiwort.
adv.	„	adverb	Umstandswort.
am.	„	among	unter, bei.
conj.	„	conjunction . . .	Bindewort.
D.	„	Dutch	Holländisch or Niederländisch.
Dan.	„	Danish	Dänisch.
dim	„	diminutive . . .	Verkleinerungswort.
Eng.	„	English	Englisch.
f.	„	feminine . . .	weiblich.
fam.	„	familiar	vertraulich, im gewöhnlichen Umgang.
Fig.	„	figuratively . . .	bildlich or uneigentlich.
Fr.	„	French	Französisch.
G. or *Germ.*	„	German	Deutsch.
Goth.	„	Gothic	Gothisch.
Gr.	„	Greek	Griechisch.
Heb.	„	Hebrew	Hebräisch.
Icel.	„	Icelandic . . .	Isländisch.
Interj.	„	interjection . . .	Empfindungs-, Ausrufungswort.
Ir.	„	Irish or Gaelic .	Irisch or Gaelisch.
ir.	„	irregular	unregelmäßig.
it.	„	item, also . . .	item, auch, ferner.
lang.	„	language . . .	Sprache, Redeweise.
Lat. or *L.*	„	Latin	Lateinisch.
m.	„	masculine . . .	männlich.

n.	=	neuter	sächlich; Neutrum.
Part.	„	participle . . .	Mittelwort, Participium.
pl.	„	plural	Mehrzahl.
Pers.	„	Persian	Persisch.
pop.	„	popular	im vertraulichen Umgang; volksmäßig.
Prep.	„	preposition . . .	Verhältnißwort.
Pron.	„	pronoun	Fürwort.
Prov.	„	proverb or proverbial form of speech	Sprichwort or sprichwörtliche Redensart.
s.	„	substantive . . .	Hauptwort.
Sans.	„	Sanscrit	Sanskrit.
Sax.	„	Saxon or Anglo-Saxon	Sächsisch or Angel-Sächsisch.
Sp.	„	Spanish	Spanisch.
Sw.	„	Swedish	Schwedisch.
Syn.	„	Synonyms	sinnverwandte Wörter.
V.	„	vide or see . . .	Sieh or vide.
v. imp.	„	verb impersonal .	unpersönliches Zeitwort.
v. intr.	„	verb intransitive .	Verbum intransitivum or neutrum.
v. r.	„	verb reflective . .	zurückführendes Zeitwort.
v. tr.	„	verb transitive . .	handelndes Zeitwort.
u. w.	„	used with . . .	gebraucht mit.
W.	„	Welsh	Wallisisch.

A.

A, a, [a vowel] A, a. 1) *n.* A, a. *Fig.* Er weiß weder — noch B zu sagen, he does not know *a* from *b*, he knows nothing at all; [in scripture] Ich bin das — und das O, I am alpha and omega. *Prov.* Wer — sagt, muß auch B sagen, he who begins with a thing, must go on with it. 2) [in music] *a*) [the sixth note of the gamut] A, la. *b*) [the open note of the 2d string of the violin, by which the other strings are tuned and regulated] A. 3) in the Julian calendar, the first of the seven dominical letters. 4) it is improperly used for: zu, at. — fünf Procent, at five per Cent.

Aachen, *n.* [a town in Rhenish Prussia] Aix-la-Chapelle.

Aak, *f.* [*pl.* -e] and *n.* [-es, *pl.* -e] a kind of flat bottomed lighter, employed on the Rhine.

Aal, *m.* [-es, *pl.* -e] 1) [a fish] an eel. Ein sehr großer —, a fausen; ein mittelmäßiger —, a scalling; ein kleiner —, a grig. 2) a kind of cake. 3) [among clothiers] a wrong fold in cloth.

Aal-baum, *m.* fly honeysuckle. —**beere** or **Alantbeere,** *f.* common black currant. —**beerstrauch,** *m.* common black currant bush. —**eidechse,** *f.* eel-lizard. —**fang,** *m.* 1) the act of catching eels, eel-fishing. 2) the season for catching eels. 3) a place for catching eels, eel-fishery. —**fänger,** *m.* eel-catcher. —**fett,** *n.* eel-grease. —**flöße,** *f.* V. —puppe. —**förmig,** *adj.* and *adv.* anguilliform. —**frau,** *f.* V. —mutter. —**gabel,** *f.* eel-spear. —**grundel,** *f.* —**gründling,** *m.* eel-groundling. —**hälter,** *m.* an eel-pond. —**haut,** *f.* eel-skin. —**kasten,** *m.* a kind of trunk used for keeping eels in. —**kirsche,** *f.* black wild service-berry. —**korb,** *m.* V. —reuse. —**krug,** *m.* a large pitcher with holes to keep eels in. —**lege,** *f.* V. —wehr. —**mutter,** *f.* the viviparous blenny. —**pastete,** *f.* eel-pie. —**pricke,** *f.* V. —gabel. —**puppe,** *f.* a bundle of bulrushes with a bait fastened to it, used for catching eels. —**quappe,** *f.* eel-pout. —**quaste,** *f.* a bundle of green twigs used for catching eels. —**raupe,** *f.* V. —quappe. —**reuse,** *f.* a kind of basket used for catching eels, eel-pot. —**schlange,** *f.* V. Meeraal. —**stachel,** *m.* V. —gabel. —**stecher,** *m.* 1) V. —gabel. 2) a person who spears eels. —**streif,** —**streifen,** —**strich,** *m.* 1) a black streak or stripe on the back of an eel. 2) a black streak or stripe on the back of a dun-coloured horse. —**suppe,** *f.* eel-soup. —**teich,** *m.* an eel-pond. —**thierchen,** *n.* an animalcule bred in vinegar and in all other acids. —**wate,** *f.* a net for catching eels. —**wehr,** *n.* a wear for catching eels. —**wels,** *m.* [Buntaal, a fish] the sea-serpent, the sea-eel. —**wurm,** *m.* V. Aalthierchen.

Aalen, *v. intr.* to fish for eels, to sniggle.

Aap, *n.* [-es, *pl.* -en] [a sea term] mizen stay-sail.

Aapenfall, *m.* [-es, *pl.* -fälle] [a sea term] the mizen staysail halliard.

Aar, *m.* [-es, *pl.* -e, also des Aaren and die Aaren] 1) [in poetry] a large bird of prey in general. 2) an eagle. Syn. Aar, Adler. Both mean large birds of prey. But Aar [originally synonymous with Vogel, bird] denotes the entire genus, Adler [from ädel Aar] that species which preys only upon living animals.

Aar-weihe, *m.* and *f.* a kind of kite.

Aaron, V. Aron.

Aas, *n.* [-es, *pl.* Aeser] 1) [properly] any food for animals. 2) [chiefly] carcass, carrion. Ein — [or eine Lockspeise] legen, to lay a bait; ein — an die Angel stecken, to bait a hook. *Fig.* [a term of reproach] carrion. Syn. Aas, Luder. Both are the remains of dead bodies, the former however denotes not only those of beasts but also of men as far as their form is still distinguishable; the latter the remains of beasts only.

Aas-blatter, *f.* a noxious, black and stinking pock. —**fliege,** *f.* [Fleisch- or Schmeißfliege] carrion-fly, dung-fly. —**fräßig,** —**fressend,** —**fressig,** *adj.* and *adv.* feeding on carcasses, carrion. —**geier,** *m.* carrion-kite, horse-kite. —**geruch,** —**gestank,** *m.* any disgustful smell. —**gierig,** *adj.* and *adv.* greedy of carrion. —**grube,** *f.* a pit into which carcasses are thrown. —**haft,** *adj.* and *adv.* like carrion. —**käfer,** *m.* horse-beetle, carrion-beetle, black-fly. —**kopf,** *m.* [in ancient architecture] a kind of ornament, resembling the head of a flayed beast. —**krähe,** *f.* [Nebel- or Rabenkrähe] carrion-crow, gore-crow. —**kuhle,** *f.* V. —grube. —**pflanze,** *f.* [a succulent plant of the Cape of Good Hope] stapelia. —**pocke,** *f.* V. —blatter. —**rabe,** *m.* V. —krähe. —**seite,** *f.* the flesh-side of a hide. —**vogel,** *m.* any bird of prey feeding on carrion, carrion-bird.

Aasen, I. *v. intr.* [among hunters] to browse, to graze [said of deer]. II. *v. tr.* [among tanners] to flesh [a hide].

Aasig, I. *adj.* 1) V. Aashaft. 2) *Fig.* *a*) foul, dirty. *b*) lazy, idle. II. *adv.* 1) V. Aashaft. 2) *Fig.* *a*) foully, dirtily, *b*) lazily, idly.

Áb, [Sw. Dan. D. *af*, perhaps allied to the L. *ab* and the Gr. ἀπό] *adv.* 1) [denoting breach of continuity, disjunction, distance] der Knopf ist —, the button is off; Bajonet —! [words of command among soldiers] unfix bayonets! — und zu, to and fro, off and on, backward and forward; auf und —, up and down; Hut —! hats off! kurz —, short off, abruptly; weit —, far off; wir sind ganz vom Wege —, we are quite out of our way; wir sind noch weit —, we are still at a great distance; einen Thaler auf oder —, a dollar more or less; todt und —, null and void. 2) much used in composition, as: abhold, Abgunst; but chiefly with verbs, as: abkochen, abreisen, absehen, abtrinken; [in conjugating, — always follows the verb, as: ablegen, ich lege —, ich legte —, lege —].

Ábaasen, *v. tr.* V. Aasen II.

Ábächzen, *v. r.* sich —, to pine away, to wear one's self away with sighing and moaning.

Ábackern, *v. tr.* 1) to separate or take off by ploughing. 2) to finish ploughing.

***Abalienation,** *f.* [law term] abalienation, alienation.

***Abalieniren,** *v. tr.* 1) to make over one's property, to alienate. 2) to alienate, to estrange, to make indifferent or averse.

***Ábandon,** *m.* [in commerce, the relinquishing to underwriters all the property saved from loss by shipwreck, capture, or other peril stated in the policy of insurance] abandonment.

***Abandonniren,** *v. tr.* 1) [in commerce] to abandon. 2) to leave with a view never to return, to desert, to abandon. 3) [in war] to give up [a town to an enemy &c.].

Ábänderlich, I. *adj.* alterable. II. *adv.* alterably.

Ábändern, *v. tr.* 1) to make some change in, to alter, to modify. Die Farbe oder Form eines Dinges —, to alter the color or shape of a thing. 2) V. Decliniren. Syn. Aendern, to make otherwise; abändern, to alter a little; verändern, to change entirely; umändern, to change so completely as to produce a new thing.

Ábänderung, *f.* 1) an altering or partial change, alteration, modification. 2) V. Declination.

Ábängsten, Abängstigen, I. *v. tr.* to frighten one, or to extort by frightening. Er hat mir das Geständniß meiner Schuld abgeängstigt, he frightened me into the confession of my guilt. II. *v. r.* sich —, to be in great anxiety.

Ábängstigung, Abängstung, *f.* 1) the act of frightening &c. 2) anxiety, uneasiness, disturbance, trouble, anguish of mind.

Ábarbeiten, I. *v. tr.* 1) to get off by labor. Das Gröbste —, to rough-hew; ein Schiff vom Strande —, to get a ship afloat or off from the ground; ein geentertes Schiff —, to push off an enemy who attempts to board. *Fig.* Sein Tagwerk —, to work out, to finish one's task. 2) to wear out [by labor]. 3) to pay off by labor. Eine Schuld —, to clear a debt by working for one's creditor. II. *v. r.* sich —, to toil hard.

Ábarbeitung, *f.* the act of removing any thing by labor.

Ábärgern, *v. r.* sich —, to weary one's self by vexation.

Ábärndten, Abärnten, Abernten, I. *v. tr.* to clear off a crop by reaping. Ein Feld —, to reap a field. II. *v. intr.* to have done reaping.

Ábart, *f.* [*pl.* -en] 1) [many and different kinds] variety. 2) [in morals, decay of virtue] degeneracy. 3) degenerate race or breed.

Ábarten, *v. intr.* [used with seyn] 1) to degenerate. Pflanzen und Thiere arten ab, wenn sie nicht die gewöhnliche Größe oder Höhe erreichen, plants and animals degenerate, when they do not attain their usual size. 2) [to decline in virtue or other good qualities] to degenerate. V. Ausarten.

Ábartig, I. *adj.* degenerate. II. *adv.* degenerately.

Ábartung, *f.* the degeneracy of plants, manners &c., degeneration, degenerateness.

Ábäschern, Abeschern, I. *v. tr.* to scour [slimy fishes] with ashes. II. *v. r.* sich —, to fatigue one's self by great bodily exertion.

Ábäsen, *v. tr.* [among hunters] to browse.

Ábaßen, *v. tr.* [among hunters] to gnaw [the bark of a tree].

***Abbattirt,** I. *adj.* cast down, depressed, dejected, deject, sad, low-spirited. II. *adv.* dejectedly, low-spiritedly.

Ábästen, *v. tr.* to deprive of branches, to lop [a tree].

Ábästung, *f.* [among foresters] the act of depriving a tree of its branches.

Ábäthmen, *v. tr.* [in metallurgy] to redden a cupel in the fire in order to dry it completely.

Ábätzen, *v. tr.* to remove by caustics.

Ábäugeln, *v. tr.* 1) to ogle, to win by sheep's eyes. 2) [among hunters] to search [the track] with the eye.

***Ábba,** [in scripture] Abba [father, God].

1. **Ábbacken,** I. *v. intr.* [used with seyn] to bake in such a manner, that the crust of the bread separates from the crumb. Das Brod ist abgebacken, the crust of the bread has separated from the crumb. II. *v. tr.* to finish baking. Der Bäcker hat abgebacken, the baker has done baking.

2. **Ábbacken,** *v. tr.* [in diking] to mark a line with small posts.

Ábbaden, I. *v. tr.* to cleanse by bathing. II. *v. intr.* to finish bathing.

Ábbähen, *v. tr.* to foment duly.

Ábbaken, *v. tr.* to mark by beacons.

1. **Ábbalgen**, *v. tr.* to strip off the skin of an animal, to flay, to uncase, to skin. Einen Hasen —, to skin a hare.

2. **Ábbalgen**, *v. r.* sich —, to fatigue one's self by wrestling or boxing.

Ábbalzen, *v. r.* sich —, [among hunters] to grow lean by coupling or pairing.

Ábbamsen, *v. tr.* to beat [a skin].

Ábbangen, I. *v. tr.* to extort by frightening. Er hat mir dieses Versprechen abgebangt, he frightened me into this promise. II. *v. r.* sich —, to weary one's self with anxiety.

Ábbansen, *v. tr.* [in husbandry] to remove sheaves from the barn.

Ábbarbieren, *v. tr.* to shave off.

Ábbasten, *v. tr.* to remove the inner bark of a tree.

Ábbauchen, Abbäuchen, *v. tr.* V. Bäuchen.

Ábbauen, *v. tr.* 1) to pull down, to demolish a building. 2) to finish a building. 3) [in mining] to pay off [with the produce of a mine] the expense of working it. 4) [in mining] Die Zeche ist abgebauet, the pit has been carried to such a depth that the work cannot be carried on any longer.

Ábbaumen, *v. intr.* [with hunters] to descend or light from a tree.

Ábbäumen, *v. tr.* [among weavers] to take from the loom [the web].

Ábbauort, *m.* [-es, *pl.* -e] **Abbaustrecke**, *f.* [*pl.* -n] [in mining] board, stall.

Ábbauung, *f.* 1) the expense of working a mine. 2) the giving over working a mine.

Ábbeeren, *v. tr.* to pick or strip of berries [a shrub, a vine].

Ábbefehlen, *ir. v. tr.* [to revoke a former command] to countermand. V. Abbestellen.

Ábbehalten, *ir. v. tr.* Den Hut —, to keep off the hat, to be or to remain uncovered.

Ábbeißen, *ir.* I. *v. tr.* to bite off, to wear away by biting. Sich die Nägel —, to nibble one's nails. *Fig.* Sich vor Lachen die Zunge —, to laugh immoderately, to burst with laughing; er hat aller Schande den Kopf abgebissen, he is past shame, he is dead to all sense of shame. II. *v. r.* sich —, to weary one's self by biting.

Ábbeizen, *v. tr.* 1) to remove by caustics, to take away with corrosives, aquafortis &c. [a wart]. 2) [with tanners, to steep almost to solution] to macerate.

Ábbekommen, *ir. v. tr.* to partake of, to have a share in, to take part with. *Fig.* Schläge —, to get blows.

† **Ábbelzen**, *v. tr.* to beat soundly, to bang.

† **Ábbengeln**, *v. tr.* to beat down with a stick [walnuts from a tree].

Ábbersten, *ir. v. intr.* [used with seyn] to burst, to crack, to fly, or fall off. Der Firniß ist abgeborsten, the varnish is broken off.

Ábberufen, *ir. v. tr.* to recall, to call home [an envoy &c.].

Ábberufung, *f.* recall, calling home.

Abberufungsschreiben, *n.* letter of recall.

Ábbesolden, *v. tr.* to pay off [a servant &c.].

Ábbestellen, *v. tr.* to countermand [a dinner &c.].

Ábbestellung, *f.* countermand.

Ábbeten, *v. tr.* 1) to say a certain number of prayers. 2) to absolve one's self from any thing by praying. Er hat seine Sünden abgebetet, he has atoned for his sins by praying. 3) to utter in a monotonous manner.

Ábbetteln, *v. tr.* to obtain or to get by begging. Einem Geld —, to beg money of any one.

Ábbeugen, *v. tr.* to bend off, to bend [a twig &c.] aside or downwards.

Ábbewegen, *v. tr.* to move from.

Ábbezahlen, *v. tr.* 1) to pay off. V. Bezahlen. 2) to pay completely.

Ábbiegen, I. *v. tr.* [*ir.* in the sense of abbeugen] V. Abbeugen. II. *v. intr.* to turn aside, to divert.

Ábbieten, *ir. v. tr.* 1) V. Ueberbieten. 2) V. Aufbieten. 3) to bid for the last time [at a public sale].

Ábbild, *n.* [-es] copy, image, portrait.

Ábbilden, *v. tr.* 1) to portray, to copy, to represent in a picture, to paint, to delineate, to draw a likeness of. Er ist abgebildet, wie er leibt und lebt, he is drawn to the life; die Gestalt eines Menschen —, to draw the figure of a man; nach dem Leben —, to draw from the life; in Wachs —, to imboss in wax. 2) *Fig.* to describe, to delineate.

‖ **Ábbildner**, *m.* [-s, *pl.* -] a person, who portrays or draws a likeness of.

Ábbildung, *f.* 1) [the act of representing an object in a picture] representation, drawing. Die — des Gesichts, portrait, portraiture. 2) [the object represented] copy, draught, drawing, picture, painting.

Ábbimsen, *v. tr.* to rub with pumice, or pumice-stone.

Ábbinden, *ir. v. tr.* 1) to unbind, to untie, to loose. 2) to disjoin, to separate by binding. Eine Warze —, to tie off a wart, to wither a wart by tying it tightly; [more commonly in a figurative sense] ein Kalb —, to wean a calf; einen Ochsen —, to geld an ox. 3) [among workmen] to tie or to fasten together. Ein Haus —, [among carpenters] to join the timberwork of a house; ein Faß —, to hoop a cask.

Ábbindung, *f.* the act of untying &c.

Ábbiß, *m.* [Abbisses, *pl.* Abbisse] 1) the act of biting off. 2) the thing bitten off, a bite. *Fig.* Der Teufelsabbiß, [a plant] devil's bit.

Ábbitte, *f.* [*pl.* -n] an excusing, a begging pardon for, deprecation. — thun, to ask, to beg pardon, to crave for pardon; eine öffentliche — thun, to make honorable amends; eine schriftliche —, a deprecatory letter. *Prov.* — ist die beste Buße, deprecation is the best way to repent.

Ábbitten, *ir. v. tr.* 1) to beg pardon for. 2) to gain or obtain by begging.

Ábblasen, *ir.* I. *v. tr.* 1) to remove or to cleanse by blowing. Den Staub —, to blow away the dust; ein Buch —, to blow off the dust from a book. 2) to announce by the blowing of an instrument. Der Wächter bläst die Stunden ab, the night-watch sounds the hours [viz. upon the horn]. 3) [in gunnery] die Kanonen —, to scale the guns [in order to cleanse them]; [in sea language] to blow the pieces off. II. *v. intr.* 1) [among hunters] to sound the retreat. 2) to cease blowing.

Ábblatten, *v. tr.* [in husbandry] to take off the leaves.

Ábblattern, *v. intr.* to get rid of the small pox.

Ábblättern, I. *v. tr.* to strip of the leaves, to divest of leaves. II. *v. r.* sich —, to flake; [in surgery] to exfoliate.

† **Ábbläuen**, *v. tr.* to beat soundly, to cudgel.

Ábbleiben, *ir. v. intr.* [used with seyn] to keep off, to keep at a distance from any thing.

Ábbleichen, I. *ir. v. intr.* [used with seyn] to lose color entirely, to fade. II. *reg. v. tr.* to bleach [linen] sufficiently.

Ábblicken, *v. intr.* [in metallurgy and in trying silver] to cease to shine.

Ábblitzen, *v. intr.* 1) to finish lightening or flashing. 2) [used with seyn] to miss fire [said of guns].

Ábblühen, *v. intr.* [used with seyn, by some with haben] to finish blooming, blowing or flowering, to drop or shed the blossoms. Die Bäume haben abgeblüht, the trees have done blossoming, the trees are no longer clothed with bloom; die Nelken haben abgeblüht, the carnations are no longer in bloom.

Ábbluten, I. *v. intr.* to shed all the blood. II. *v. tr.* to atone for by blood.

Ábblüten, *v. tr.* to strip or to divest of the bloom.

Ábbohnen, V. Bohnen.

Ábbohren, *v. intr.* [in mining] to finish boring.

Ábbohrer, *m.* [-s, *pl.* -] [in mining] an auger or other borer to finish the boring of a hole.

Ábborgen, *v. tr.* to borrow [a book &c.] from any one. *Fig.* Jemanden einen Gedanken —, to take an idea from any one; einem Buche eine Stelle —, to borrow, to copy a passage from a book. V. Borgen, Entlehnen.

Ábborger, *m.* [-s, *pl.* -] borrower.

Ábborgung, *f.* a borrowing.

Ábbrand, *m.* [-es, *pl.* Abbrände] [in metallurgy and mining] the diminution of silver, quicksilver or other metals on the test or in cleansing.

Ábbrändler, *m.* [-s, *pl.* -] [better Abgebrannte] a person that has been burnt out of house and home and therefore goes a begging.

Ábbrassen, *v. tr.* [a sea term] 1) to brace. 2) to fill the sails after they have been braced aback.

Ábbraten, I. *v. tr.* to roast thorougly. Diese Schöpskeule ist wohl abgebraten, this leg of mutton is well done. II. *v. intr.* to finish roasting.

Ábbrauchen, *v. tr.* to wear off, to wear out.

Ábbrauen, *v. intr.* to finish brewing.

Ábbräunen, *v. tr.* to make brown sufficiently. Dieser Braten ist nicht genug abgebräunt, this meat is not roasted brown enough.

1. **Ábbrechen**, *ir.* I. *v. tr.* 1) to part by breaking. Blumen, Früchte —, to crop, to pluck off, to break off flowers, fruits; eine Rose —, to slip off a rose; abgebrochene Stücke, broken pieces, fragments; [in printing] die Ballen —, to knock off the balls; [milit. term] die Glieder —, [to diminish the front] to break off files. *Fig.* Den Soldaten wurde an ihrer Löhnung abgebrochen, the soldiers were cut short of their pay; ich kann mir nichts — lassen, I cannot allow any abatement; an einer Rechnung etwas —, to deduct something from an account; er bricht sich nichts ab, he debars or deprives himself of no conveniencies; eine Rede —, to break off a discourse; eine Arbeit —, to break off, to discontinue, to desist from work; eine Unterhandlung —, to break off a negociation; mit Einem allen Umgang —, to break with one; kurz —, to cut short; wir wollen davon —, let us leave off; lassen Sie uns hier —, [reden wir nicht weiter davon], let us leave off here; sich am Schlafe —, to pinch one's self in sleep; abgebrochene Seufzer, broken sighs; abgebrochene Worte, broken words; abgebrochen, abrupt [an epithet for the lateral line in fishes]; der arme Mann bricht ab, the poor man is in a declining way. 2) to break down, to pull down. Ein Haus —, to pull down a house; ein Gerüst —, to take down a scaffold; die Zelte —, to

strike the tents; ein Lager —, to decamp, or to strike a camp; ein altes Schiff —, [in sea language] to break up a ship. II. *v. intr.* [used with seyn] to be broke or broken off.

2. **Abbrechen**, *ir. v. intr.* to finish breaking or beating [hemp].

Abbrechung, *f.* the act of breaking off or pulling down, [in speaking of crystals, stones] abruption. *Fig.* [in rhetoric] Die plötzliche — [Unterbrechung] eines Redesatzes, apophasis; die — einer Rede [Verschweigung], aposiopesis, aposiopesy.

Abbreiten, *v. tr.* [in copper-works] to flatten, to make flat.

Abbrennen, *ir.* I. *v. intr.* [used with seyn] 1) to be destroyed by fire. Mir ist mein Haus abgebrannt, my house has been consumed with fire, is burnt down. 2) to lose one's house or property by fire. Er ist abgebrannt, he has suffered damage by fire; ein Abgebrannter, one ruined by fire. 3) to cease burning. Das Feuer ist abgebrannt, the fire has gone out. 4) [in pyrotechny] to burn without explosion. Das Zündkraut ist abgebrannt, the powder has flashed in the pan; die Flinte ist abgebrannt, the gun has missed fire. 5) V. Losbrennen. II. *v. tr.* [often reg.] 1) to consume with fire. Ein Haus —, to burn down a house; einen Wald —, to burn up a wood; eine Warze —, to burn away a wart. 2) to set on fire, to light. Ein Feuerwerk —, to let off a fire-work; eine Kanone —, to discharge, to fire, or to fire off a gun. 3) to destroy by excessive heat. Die Sonnenhitze hat alles Gras abgebrannt, the heat of the sun has scorched all the grass. 4) [in various technical terms] *a)* [in brickburning] to heat [the kiln] for the last time. *b)* [in metallurgy] to cleanse the refined silver by fire. *c)* to calcine by heat. Austerschalen, Kalk —, to burn, calcine oyster-shells, limestone. *d)* [among braziers] to give a brighter color [to] brass by aquafortis. *e)* [in forges] to temper iron. *f)* [in iron-plate making] to steep iron-plates in a solution of tin. *g)* [in chimistry] to burn spirit of wine upon certain bodies.

***Abbreviatur**, *f.* [*pl.* -en] abbreviature, abbreviation.

Abbreviaturschrift, *f.* short-hand writing.

***Abbreviren**, *v. tr.* to abbreviate, to abridge [words &c.].

Abbringen, *ir. v. tr.* 1) to get off. Einen Nagel von der Wand —, to get a nail out of the wall; er konnte in der Schnelligkeit seinen Rock nicht —, in the hurry he could not get his coat off. *Fig.* Vom rechten Wege —, to mislead, to lead the wrong way; von einer Meinung —, to divert from an opinion; Einen von seinem Vorhaben —, to divert a man from his purpose; davon lasse ich mich nicht —, I will not be persuaded to another course; Gesetze —, to abrogate, to repeal laws; er hat diese üble Gewohnheit abgebracht, he has put an end to this bad practice; er läßt sich vom Trinken nicht —, he will not leave off drinking. 2) Korn, Heu —, to [illegible] corn, hay. V. Abärndten.

Abbröckeln, I. *v. tr.* to break into small pieces, to crumble. II. *v. intr.* [used with seyn] to fall into small pieces, to crumble. III. *v. r.* sich —, to break or part into small fragments.

Abbröckelung, *f.* the act of breaking or parting into small fragments, crumbling.

Abbrocken, *v. tr.* to break into small pieces, to crumble.

Abbruch, *m.* [-es, *pl.* Abbrüche] 1) the act of breaking off; *Fig.* damage, hurt, injury, loss, harm, detriment. Ein Haus auf den — verkaufen, to sell the materials of a house, that is to be pulled down. *Fig.* Jemand leidet — durch die Verbrennung seines Hauses, a man suffers damage by the burning of his house; — thun, to damage, to hurt; einem Gesetze an seiner vollen Ausdehnung — thun, to derogate a law, to lessen the extent of a law; Einem an seiner Ehre — thun, to injure the reputation of a person, to slander, to impair, to tarnish a reputation, to derogate from one's reputation; sich selbst — thun an &c., to pinch one's self in, to deprive one's self of &c.; — leiden, to suffer abatement or diminution. 2) the thing broken off, a fragment. 3) the place where a house &c. has been pulled down. 4) [in mining] the breaking off stones by proper means. 5) [among letter-founders] the break of a letter.

Abbrüchig, I. *adj.* 1) breaking easily off, brittle. 2) *Fig.* derogatory. II. *adv.* derogatorily.

Abbrühen, *v. tr.* to scald, to parboil. Ein Huhn —, to scald a fowl; wohl — to seeth.

Abbrunften, *v. intr.* [among hunters] to cease rutting [said of deer]. Das Wild hat abgebrunftet, the rutting-season is over.

Abbrüten, *v. intr.* to cease brooding [said of hens].

Abbügeln, *v. tr.* to iron sufficiently [linen].

Abbuhlen, I. *v. tr.* to get by coquettish tricks, or by coaxing. II. *v. r.* sich —, to waste one's strength with women.

Abbürsten, *v. tr.* 1) to brush [a hat &c.]. 2) to brush off or away [the dust from a carpet &c.].

Abbüßen, *v. tr.* to expiate, to atone for. Er hat es mit Geld abgebüßt, he has been fined for it.

Abbüßung, *f.* expiation, atonement.

Abbuttern, *v. intr.* to finish churning.

Abc [pronounce: Abeck], *n.* 1) a b c, alphabet. Zum — gehörig, abecedary; nach dem —, alphabetically. 2) *Fig.* the first rudiments, beginnings. 3) [in printing]. V. Alphabet.

Abc-buch, *n.* an abc, cross-row, hornbook, primer. **—lehrer**, *m.* abecedarian. **—schüler**, **—schütz**, *m.* primer-boy, abecedarian, abece-scholar, alphabetarian. **—tafel**, *f.* an alphabetical board.

***Abcirkeln**, *v. tr.* 1) to measure or delineate by means of compasses. 2) *Fig.* to be ridiculously nice or punctilious in any thing.

***Abconterfeien**, *v. tr.* to portray. Sich — lassen, to sit for one's picture.

***Abcopiren**, *v. tr.* 1) to copy, to transcribe. 2) to sketch, to draw.

Abdachen, I. *v. tr.* 1) [to pull off the roof] to uncover, to unroof [a house]. 2) [in fortification and in gardening] to slope, to scarp. II. *v. intr.* to become declivous towards the sea or a plain.

Abdachig, *adj.* sloping, slope, declivous. Ein —er Berg, a sloping hill.

Abdachung, *f.* 1) the act of unroofing. 2) [in fortification] V. Böschung. 3) a slope, descent, fall, declivity, slanting. Die — der Küste gegen die See, the declension of the shore towards the sea.

Abdämmen, *v. tr.* 1) [water] to dam up, to confine or shut in. 2) [land] to gain land by damming off the water.

Abdämmung, *f.* 1) the act of damming up. 2) V. Damm.

Abdampfen, *v. intr.* [used with seyn] 1) to evaporate. Das Wasser auf der Oberfläche der Erde dampft unmerklich ab, the water on the surface of the earth evaporates imperceptibly. 2) to cease evaporating.

Abdämpfen, *v. tr.* 1) to cause to evaporate. 2) to complete the evaporation of.

Abdampfung, *f.* evaporation.

Abdanken, I. *v. tr.* to dismiss, to discharge. Seinen Haushofmeister —, to discharge one's steward; einen Soldaten —, to discharge a soldier; ein Regiment —, to disband or break up a regiment; ein abgedankter Soldat, a disbanded soldier; das Volk —, [in sea language] to pay off, to discharge the crew; *Fig.* ein Schiff —, [a sea term] to lay up a vessel; Pferde und Wagen —, to part with carriage and horses. II. *v. intr.* to go from a public station, to retire. Der Minister hat abgedankt, the minister has resigned; der Sekretär hat abgedankt, the secretary has asked for his dismission; der Bediente hat abgedankt, the servant has asked for his discharge; der Pfarrer hat abgedankt, the rector has given up his living. *Fig.* Bei einer Leiche —, to thank the persons attending the burial of a deceased person, to preach a funeral sermon [said of a priest]; der Nachtwächter dankt ab, the watchman calls for the last time at break of day. Syn. Abdanken, ein Amt niederlegen. Ein Amt niederlegen is said especially when the resigning or retaining of the post or offfice depends upon the person's own free will. Abdanken is said also of the lowest offices. Of a charge or office one says niederlegen, of a service abdanken. V. Verabschieden, Absetzen, Entlassen.

Abdankung, *f.* 1) dismission, discharge. 2) resignation, abdication. 3) *Fig.* *a)* a valedictory, funeral-sermon, a thanksgiving after the burial. *b)* the last call of a watchman at break of day. *c)* the announcing of the play.

Abdankungsrede, *f.* V. Abdankung 3) *Fig. a.*

Abdarben, *v. r.* Sich or seinem Munde etwas —, to stint one's belly, to pinch one's self, to starve one's body for.

Abdarren, *v. tr.* to dry [malt, corn].

Abdecken, *v. tr.* 1) to strip of the covering, to uncover. Ein Dach —, to uncover a roof; den Tisch —, to remove the cloth, to clear the table, to take away. 2) to flay or flea, to skin.

Abdecker, *m.* [-s, *pl.* -] [a mean person who flays animals that have died of disease] the flayer. V. Schinder.

Abdeckerleder, *n.* hides of animals that have died by disease, morkins.

Abdeckerei, *f.* 1) the act of flaying. 2) a flaying-house, flaying-place. 3) the flayer's dwelling-house.

Abdeichen, *v. tr.* to surround with a dike, to dike.

Abdeichung, *f.* the act of diking.

***Abderite**, *m.* [-n, *pl.* -n] 1) [an inhabitant of Abdera] an Abderite. 2) *Fig.* a fool. Der Abderitenstreich, a piece of folly.

Abderitisch, I. *adj.* foolish, silly. II. *adv.* foolishly, sillily.

Abdicken, V. Verdicken.

Abdielen, *v. tr.* 1) to separate, to partition by deals or boards. 2) to furnish with a floor, to floor [a room].

Abdienen, *v. tr.* 1) to serve for a debt, to pay off a debt by personal service. || 2) to carry off the dishes from the table, to take away.

Abdingen, *ir. v. tr.* 1) to beat down, to cheapen. 2) to dismiss an apprentice.

***Abdisputiren**, V. Abstreiten.

Abdocken, *v. tr.* [with hunters] to unwind.

Abdoppeln, *v. tr.* [with shoemakers] to sew

double, to double-stitch.

Abdorren, *v. intr.* [used with seyn] to dry, to get dry and fall off [said of leaves]. Ein abgedorrtes Glied, a withered, shriveled or dried limb.

Abdörren, *v. tr.* 1) to dry up, to make dry. 2) [in metallurgy] to reduce [the ores of silver] by liquation.

Abdörrung, *f.* the act of drying &c.

Abdörrofen, *m.* [in metallurgy] V. Frischherd.

Abdraht, *m.* tin-shavings, chips of pewter.

Abdrängen, V. Abdringen.

Abdräuen, V. Abdrohen.

Abdrechseln, *v. tr.* to separate or remove by turning on a lathe.

Abdrehen, *v. tr.* 1) to wring or twist off. Einem Huhn den Kopf —, to wring off the head of a fowl. 2) V. Abdrechseln.

Abdreschen, *ir. v. tr.* 1) to thrash. *Fig.* Ein alter abgedroschener Beweis, an old beaten argument; altes abgedroschenes Zeug, old trite stuff; es war ein abgedroschener Handel, it was a privately concerted thing. 2) to finish thrashing. Wir werden bald abgedroschen haben, we shall soon have done thrashing. 3) to clear a debt by thrashing for one's creditor. 4) † *Fig.* to thrash, to maul, to bang. Sie haben ihn tüchtig abgedroschen, they have thrashed him soundly.

Abdrillen, V. Abdringen.

Abdringen, *ir. v. tr.* to exact from, to extort from, to force from. Ich habe ihm diese Gnade abgedrungen, I forced this favor from him.

Abdringung, *f.* extortion, exaction.

Abdrohen, *v. tr.* to get by threatening, to obtain by threats, to extort by menaces.

Abdruck, *m.* [-es, *pl.* Abdrücke] 1) [the act of impressing] impression. Der — eines Siegels in Wachs, the impression of a seal on wax. 2) [the figure or image of any thing made by pressure] impression, copy, stamp, mark. Ein — in Gyps, a plaster cast; 500 Abdrücke von einem Buche fertigen, to print 500 copies of a book; ein — vor der Schrift, [of an engraving or a lithography] a proof impression. *Fig.* Das Kind ist der — seiner Mutter, the child is the image of its mother; die Natur ist der — der Gottheit, nature is the image of the deity. 3) the trigger [in fire-arms]. 4) the act of pulling the trigger.

Abdrucksstange, *f.* the stopper [in fire-arms].

Abdrucken, *v. tr.* 1) to imprint, to impress, to stamp, to make a mark or figure on any thing by pressure. Ein Siegel in Wachs —, to impress a seal on wax; einige Fußstapfen in Lehm abgedruckt, some footsteps printed in the clay. *Fig.* In seinem Gesichte druckt sich die Verzweiflung ab, despair is imprinted on his face; die Gegenstände drucken ihr Bild auf die Organe ab, objects impress their own images upon the organs. 2) to imprint, to impress, to print [a book]. Einen Kupferstich —, to print an engraving.

Abdrücken, I. *v. tr.* 1) to separate or to loosen by pressing. Ein Gewehr —, to discharge or to fire off a gun, to pull the trigger; einen Pfeil —, to let fly an arrow. *Fig.* Es würde ihm das Herz abgedrückt haben, wenn &c., his heart would have burst, if &c. 2) *Fig.* to obtain by soliciting. II. *v. intr.* [a sea term] to set sail, to weigh anchor, to unmoor.

Abdudeln, *v. tr.* to thrum or play badly on a musical instrument, to hum [a tune].

Abdunkeln, *v. tr.* to change to a darker colour.

Abdunsten, *v. intr.* [used with seyn] to pass off in vapor, to evaporate.

Abdunstung, *f.* [the act of flying off in fumes] evaporation.

Abdünsten, *v. tr.* to convert or resolve a fluid into vapor, to dissipate in steam, to evaporate. Die Hitze dünstet das Wasser bei jedem Grade der Temperatur ab, heat evaporates water at every point of temperature.

Abdünstung, *f.* [the conversion of a fluid into vapor] evaporation.

Abdünstungshaus, *n.* [in salt-works] drying house. V. Gradirhaus.

Abdupfen, *v. tr.* to dry by wiping with lint [as, a sore].

Abebenen, *v. tr.* 1) to level, to make even. 2) [among furriers] Einen Pelz —, to clip the hair of a fur.

Abeck, V. Abc.

Abecken, *v. tr.* to deprive of edges or corners.

Abegen, Abeggen, *v. tr.* 1) to take away by harrowing, to harrow off. 2) to harrow sufficiently.

Abeichen, *v. tr.* to measure or to ascertain the contents of a cask or vessel, to gage or gauge.

Abeifern, *v. r.* sich —, to weary one's self by zeal, eagerness or anger.

Abeilen, I. *v. intr.* [used with seyn] V. Forteilen. II. *v. r.* sich —, to tire one's self by hurrying.

Abeisen, I. *v. tr.* to free from ice. II. *v. intr.* [used with haben] to thaw.

Abelmoschus, *m.* [in botany] musk mallow, [and the seed of this plant] abelmusk.

Abend, [either from the ancient verb aben = to go down, to decline, or allied to the Sax. *aftana*=after] *m.* [-s, *pl.* -e] 1) even, [in poetry] eve, [in prose we use generally] evening. Auf den —, in the evening; diesen —, heute —, this evening, to-night; heute — war es voll, we had a full night; gestern —, last night, yester-day evening; vorgestern —, the night before last; morgen —, to-morrow evening; alle —, every evening; — werden, to draw towards evening; es wird —, it grows night, evening draws near, it gets dark; guten —, good evening; zu — essen, to sup; der heilige —, [the evening before a holiday] eve; den — mit einem Freunde zubringen, to spend the evening with a friend; am — schätzt man erst das Haus, at evening's hour we learn our home to prize *Fig.* Der — des Lebens, the evening of life or of one's days. *Prov.* Es ist noch nicht aller Tage —, the success is not yet assured; the evening crowns the day; ist der Tag auch noch so lang, dennoch kommt der —, the longest day must have an end; be the day ever so long, at length comes evensong. 2) the west, occident. Gegen — gelegen, western, occidental.

Abend-andacht, *f.* evening devotion, evening prayers. —**arbeit**, *f.* evening work, evening occupation. —**besuch**, *m.* an evening visit. —**betrachtung**, *f.* evening meditation. —**blatt**, *n.* an evening paper. —**blume**, *f.* [a plant] the marvel of Peru. —**brod**, *n.* supper. *Syn.* V. —essen. —**cirkel**, V. —gesellschaft. —**dämmerung**, *f.* evening twilight, dusk of the evening. —**essen**, *n.* supper, supping. Das —essen zurecht machen, to get supper ready. Syn. Abendessen, Abendmahlzeit, Abendmahl, Abendbrod. Abendessen is the last meal of the day, that which is taken in the evening, *supper*. Abendmahl has become obsolete in the sense of Abendessen, since it has been made use of by the church to denote the Sacrament of the Lord's supper. Abendmahlzeit is a supper of a more festive description. Abendbrod is the supper or last meal of the poorer classes, and is frequently used to express a simple or frugal evening meal. V. Vesperbrod. —**falter**, *m.* the hawk, hawk-moth, sphinx. —**gang**, *m.* [in mining] a lode [load] having a western direction. —**gebet**, *n.* evening prayer. —**gegend**, *f.* the west. —**gesang**, *m.* V. —lied. —**gesellschaft**, *f.* evening party. —**glocke**, *f.* the evening bell; curfew. —**jagd**, *f.* a chase in the evening. —**kost**, *f.* supper, evening meal. —**land**, *n.* a western country. —**länder**, *m.* 1) an inhabitant of a western country. 2) *pl.* *a)* western countries, western regions. *b)* the western nations. —**ländisch**, *adj.* western, westerly, occidental. —**lich**, *adj.* 1) [being at the close of the day] evening. Die —liche Zeit, even, eventide, cockshut; ein —licher Schmaus, an evening feast. 2) western. Die —liche Gegend, the western or occidental country. —**licht**, *n.* the evening light, evening star. —**lied**, *n.* evening song, evening hymn; [in poetry] even song. —**luft**, *f.* the evening air, a westerly breeze. —**lust**, *f.* evening pleasure, pastime or diversion. —**mahl**, *n.* 1) supper. V. —essen. 2) das heilige —mahl, the Lord's supper, the communion, eucharist. Zum —mahl gehen, to go to or to partake of the Lord's supper, to receive the communion, to communicate, ‖ to commune; das —mahl empfangen, genießen, to take the sacrament; das —mahl austheilen, to administer the sacrament of the Lord's supper; der —mahlsgast, —mahlsgenoß, communicant; das —mahlsgebet, communion prayer; der —mahlsgottesdienst, communion service; der —mahlstisch, communion table. Die —**mahlzeit**, supper. *Syn.* V. —essen. —**markt**, *m.* 1) a market held in the evening. 2) the evening before a fair. —**musik**, *f.* a night or evening music, a serenade. —**opfer**, *n.* the evening sacrifice. —**pfauenauge**, *n.* a species of hawkmoth [sphinx ocellata]. —**punkt**, *m.* [in astronomy] the true west. —**regen**, *m.* 1) evening rain or shower. 2) [in the bible, the rainy season which set in a little before harvest] the latter rain. —**roth**, *n.* —**röthe**, *f.* evening red. *Prov.* —roth gut Wetterboth, an evening red and a morning grey, is a sign of a fair day. —**schein**, *m.* V. —dämmerung. —**schicht**, *f.* [in mining] the working hours commencing in the evening. —**schmaus**, *m.* evening banquet, evening feast. —**segen**, *m.* V. —gebet. —**seite**, *f.* west side, western aspect. —**sonne**, *f.* the setting sun. —**ständchen**, *n.* a night music, serenade. V. —musik. —**stern**, *m.* 1) the evening star, Hesperus or Vesper, Venus. 2) *Fig.* the glow-worm. —**stille**, *f.* the calmness of the evening. —**stillstand**, *m.* [in astronomy] the western station. —**stunde**, *f.* evening hour. —**thau**, *m.* the night-dew. —**tisch**, *m.* supper. Ich habe den —tisch bei ihm, I sup with him. —**trunk**, *m.* evening draught. —**uhr**, *f.* western sun-dial. —**unterhaltung**, *f.* evening amusement, evening entertainment, evening diversion. —**viole**, V. Nachtviole. —**vogel**, V. —falter. —**volk**, *n.* people of the west. Die —völker, the western nations. —**wärts**, *adv.* westerly, westward, westwardly. —**weite**, *f.* [in astronomy] the western amplitude. —**wind**, *m.* 1) a west wind, western breeze. 2) evening wind or breeze. —**wolf**, striped hyæna. V. Hyäne. —**zeit**, *f.* even, eventide, cockshut. —**zeitvertreib**, *m.* evening amusement, evening pastime. —**zirkel**, *m.* V. —gesellschaft.

Abends, *adv.* in the evening. Heute —, this evening; gestern —, last night.

Abenteuer, [from the L. of the middle ages *adventura*] *n.* [-s, *pl.* -] an enterprise of hazard, an adventure, an undertaking of chance or danger, a venture, or any odd or strange event. Auf — ausgehen, to go in quest or in search of adventures; ein — bestehen, to hazard upon or to encounter an adventure. SYN. Abenteuer, Begebenheit, Vorfall, Zufall. The word Begebenheit has the most extensive signification. Ebbe und Fluth ist eine Naturbegebenheit, the ebb and flood is an event or occurrence in nature. Ein Vorfall is an event which occurs to individuals; ein Zufall an accident which they could not foresee. Ein Abenteuer is a strange and extraordinary occurrence which happens to individual persons, and connected especially with danger.

Ábenteuerig, I. *adj.* full of hazard, adventurous. Ein —es Unternehmen, an adventurous undertaking. II. *adv.* adventurously.

Ábenteuerlich, I. *adj.* strange, odd. Eine —e Geschichte, an odd story, a wild story; ein —er Mensch, an odd person. II. *adv.* oddly, strangely.

Ábenteuerlichkeit, *f.* 1) adventurousness, adventuresomeness; strangeness, oddity. 2) a strange thing, strange appearance, strange occurrence. 3) quixotism.

Ábenteuern, *v. intr.* to go in quest or in search of adventures.

Ábenteurer, *m.* [-s, *pl.* -] an adventurer, a knight errant, a vagrant.

Áber, I. [Goth. *afar* = behind, allied to after] *adv.* again, once more. Ich habe es ihm tausend und — tausendmal gesagt, I have told it him a thousand and a thousand times. II. [perhaps allied to ober and über] *conj.* [a particle by which the meaning of the foregoing sentence is limited and restrained] but. Sie ist nicht schön, — gütig, she is not handsome, but kind; — doch, — dennoch, but yet; — auch, but also; — sonst, sonst —, oder —, else, or else; — gleichwohl, however, nevertheless; nun —, but now; aber, aber! but alas! III. *subst.* Die Sache hat ein —, there is an exceptionable circumstance in the affair, there is a but in the question; er hat immer ein —, he always has something to object to or to blame, he always contradicts.

Áberacht, *f.* a repeated excommunication, a higher degree of the penalty of the ban.

Áberben, *v. intr.* to get by inheritance from, to inherit from.

Áberglaube, *m.* [-ns] superstition.

Ábergläubig, **Ábergläubisch**, I. *adj.* 1) superstitious. Abergläubische Gebräuche, superstitious rites or observances. 2) bigot, bigoted. Abergläubige Heuchler, bigot hypocrites. II. *adv.* 1) superstitiously. 2) bygotedly.

Áberglaubigkeit, *f.* superstitiousness.

Áberkennen, *ir. v. tr.* to take away by a juridical sentence, to abjudicate, to set aside.

Áberklaue, *f.* V. Afterklaue.

Ábermahlig, *adj.* iterated, repeated.

Ábermahls [Abermahl], *adv.* again, once more, afresh, anew, repeatedly.

Ábername, *m.* V. Schimpfname, Uebername.

Áberraten, V. Abärndten.

Áberobern, *v. tr.* to conquer from.

Áberraute, *f.* [better Stabwurz] southernwood.

Ábersaat, *f.* a second sowing.

Ábersinn, *m.* [-es] pertinacity, obstinacy, stubbornness.

Ábersinnig, I. *adj.* obstinate, stubborn. II. *adv.* obstinately, stubbornly.

Áberwitz, *m.* [-es] 1) false wit 2) craziness, imbecillity of mind, derangement.

Áberwitzig, I. *adj.* weakened, or impaired in intellect, crazy, cracked, disordered in mind, deranged. SYN. Aberwitzig, wahnwitzig. The man is called aberwitzig who utters incongruous nonsense; wahnwitzig he who has entirely lost the use of his reasoning faculties. II. *adv.* nonsensically, crazily.

Ábeschern, V. Abäschern.

Ábessen, *ir.* I. *v. tr.* to eat off, to clear by eating, to consume by eating. Einen Knochen —, to pick a bone; ich habe euch nichts abgegessen, I have not been fed by you. II. *v. intr.* to finish eating. Haben Sie abgegessen? have you done dining or supping?

Ábfachen, *v. tr.* 1) to divide into compartments. 2) to arrange in sets or ranks [according to some method founded on natural distinctions], to class.

Ábfachung, *f.* 1) division into compartments. 2) distribution into sets, sorts or ranks, classification.

Ábfadmen, V. Fadmen.

Ábfahen, V. Abfangen.

Ábfahren, *ir.* I. *v. tr.* 1) to take off by driving a wheel over a thing, to break. Einen Eckstein —, to break a corner-stone by driving a carriage against it. 2) to carry away upon wheels, to carry. 3) to pay or compensate by means of driving. 4) to make a road by constant driving, 5) to overwork, to overdrive. 6) to measure a road by driving a carriage over it. 7) to save time by driving a shorter road. Wir haben zwei Meilen abgefahren, we have cut off two miles by driving the shorter road. 8) to wear out by constant driving. Die Heerstraße ist abgefahren, the high-road is worn out.

II. *v. intr.* [used with seyn] 1) to set off, to be conveyed by land or water, to depart, to sail. *Fig.* Er ist übel abgefahren, he was sadly disappointed. 2) to fly off in an oblique direction, to glance. *Fig.* Solche Leiden fahren an ihm ab, he is proof against such hardships. 3) = fehl fahren. Er ist von dem rechten Wege abgefahren, he has driven out of the right road.

Ábfahrt, *f.* [*pl.* -en] 1) [moving from or leaving a place] departure. 2) the place of departure. 3) [a law term] V. Abzug.

Abfahrts-flagge, *f.* a flag hoisted when a ship is near its departure, the blue peter. —**geld**, *n.* 1) [a law term] money paid to government by persons emigrating. 2) money given to a journeyman, when he sets off for the first time to seek employment. —**ort**, *m.* [a sea term] departure. —**recht**, *n.* [a law term] V. Abzugsrecht. —**schuß**, *m.* [a sea term] signal gun fired at departing.

Ábfall, *m.* [-es, *pl.* Abfälle] 1) the act of falling off, fall. Der — des Laubes, the fall of the leaf. 2) the descent of land or water, fall. Der — eines Flusses [= Wehr], waste wear, waste wier. 3) that which falls off, or is thrown away, refuse. Der — von gekalkten Häuten, [among tanners] screws; der — von Seide, waste silk; der — auf einem Zimmerwerfte, [a sea term] the chips and useless pieces of timber on a shipwright's wharf. 4) [in water-works] superfluous water and the pipe which carries it off, a wastepipe. 5) *Fig.* *a*) the act of forsaking or abandoning, the falling away. Der — von einer Partei, the desertion from a party; der — einer Provinz, the defection or revolt of a province; der — von der Religion, apostasy. *b*) diminution or decay, decline. In — kommen, to decline, to go to decay. *c*) [sea terms] *α*) V. Ausschießen. *β*) V. Krumelingen. *γ*) [the departure of a ship from its true course] deflection. *d*) [in mining] the becoming of a worse quality [said of ores]. *e*) a falling away, decay, fading [said of colours]. *f*) opposition of things or qualities, contrast. 6) [in horology] V. Hemmung. SYN. Abfall, Empörung. Abfall is a revolt or falling off only of a part, of one or more provinces from the main body of the state; Empörung an open and forcible rising against civil or political authority, insurrection. V. Abtrünnigkeit.

Abfallsröhre, *f.* [in water-works] a pipe which carries off superfluous water, a waste-pipe.

Ábfallen, *ir.* I. *v. intr.* [used with seyn] 1) to fall off, to drop. Früchte fallen ab, wenn sie reif sind, fruits fall off when ripe. *Fig.* Vom Fleische —, to lose flesh, to fall away, to become lean or emaciated, 2) *Fig* Von Einem —, to fall off from one, to forsake him, to quit his party; ein abgefallener Bassa, a revolted pashaw; von der Religion —, to apostatize, to turn apostate, to backslide; ein Abgefallener, an apostate, a renegade; die Erze fallen ab, [in mining] the ores become of worse quality; † dabon fällt nicht viel ab, it is an unprofitable business. 3) *Fig.* *a*) [in mining] to take another direction [said of lodes]. *b*) [with hunters] to fly from a tree [said of feathered game]. *c*) V. Abstechen [said of colors]. *d*) [a sea term] V. Abhalten. Das — von dem Striche, falling to leeward, sagging.

II. *v. r.* sich —, to break by falling.

Ábfällig, *adj.* and *adv.* 1) that which falls off. —es Obst, fruits fallen off. *Fig.* —e [= verfallene] Zinsen, rents that are due; —e Meinung, a different opinion; — werden, to desert; von der Religion — werden, to apostatize; Einen — machen, to induce one to desert, to make one desert. 2) inclining down-ward, sloping. Eine —e Küste, a shelving coast; die —e Seite des platten Daches, [in building] inclined plane of a flat roof.

Ábfälligkeit, *f.* 1) fall, declivity. 2) *Fig.* apostasy.

Ábfalzen, *v. tr.* 1) [among joiners and carpenters] to rabbet, to make rabbets. 2) [among tanners] V. Abaasen.

Ábfangen, *ir. v. tr.* 1) to catch a thing away from another. 2) [in mining] to support by beams and props. 3) [among hunters] Einen Hirsch, eine Sau —, to stab a stag, a wild boar [to kill a stag or a wild boar with a cutlass or hanger]; fangt ihn ab! do him!

Ábfärben, I. *v. tr.* to die, to colour thoroughly. II. *v. intr.* 1) to part with colour. Das Tuch färbt ab, the cloth parts with its colour, the colour comes off. 2) to finish dying.

Ábfäseln, *v. intr.* and *v. r.* to lose filaments, to unravel.

Ábfasern, *v. tr.* to free from fibres. Bohnen —, to string beans.

Ábfaßen, *v. intr.* [among joiners] to round off sharp edges with a plane.

Ábfassen, *v. tr.* 1) to sort, to separate. Getreide —, to measure corn. 2) to seize or take hold of. Der Verbrecher wurde in seinem Hause abgefaßt, the criminal was arrested in his house. 3) [among blacksmiths] to bend [a piece of iron]. 4) *Fig.* to compose, to draw up, to write in due form. Eine Predigt —, to compose a sermon; eine Schrift, ein Testament —, to draw up a deed, a will; eine gut abgefaßte oder gut geschriebene Rede, a speech well penned.

Ábfasser, *m.* [-s, *pl.* -] he that writes or draws up, an author.

Ábfassung, *f.* 1) the act of composing, drawing up, writing, penning. 2) the style in which any thing is written.

Ábfasten, I. *v. intr.* to atone for by fasting. II. *v. r.* sich —, to become weak by fasting. Abgefastet, pinched with hunger.

Ábfaulen, *v. intr.* [used with seyn] to rot off.

Ábfäumen, *v. tr.* to take off the froth, to skim. *Fig.* Abgefäumt [† abgefeimt] practised, cunning; ein abgefäumter Schelm, an arch-rogue, an arrant knave; abgefäumte Bosheit, crafty malice.

Ábfechten, I. *ir. v. tr.* 1) to get any thing by fighting. 2) V. Abbetteln. II. *v. r.* sich —, to fatigue one's self with fighting, to tire with fighting. *Fig.* Sich im Sprechen mit den Händen —, to gesticulate violently in speaking.

Ábfedern, I. *v. tr.* 1) to free or cleanse from feathers [a coat &c.]. 2) to strip of the feathers, to pluck. II. *v. intr.* to shed the feathers, to moult, to mew.

Ábfegen, *v. tr.* to cleanse by sweeping. Den Staub —, to dust. *Fig.* [in medicine] Abfegende Mittel, abstergent medicines, detergents.

Ábfegung, *f.* the act of cleansing and sweeping.

Ábfeiern, V. Abvieren.

Ábfeilen, *v. tr.* 1) to file, to file off, to cut with a file. Einen Zahn —, to file off a tooth. 2) to perfect by filing. Eine Klinge —, [among cutlers] to rub a blade.

Ábfeilicht, *n.* file-dust, filings. V. Feilspäne.

Ábfeilraspel, *f.* a great rasp used in filing.

Ábfeilschen, V. Abkaufen, Abhandeln, Abmarkten.

Ábfeimen, V. Abfäumen.

Ábfeinen, *v. tr.* to refine [sugar].

† **Ábfenstern**, V. Ausschelten.

Ábfertigen, *v. tr.* 1) to finish, to complete [a work]. 2) to dispatch, to send or to send away. Er fertigte einen Boten an seinen Gesandten in Frankreich ab, he dispatched a messenger to his envoy in France. *Fig.* Einen kurz —, to be short with any one.

Ábfertigung, *f.* 1) the act of the finishing or dispatching. 2) *Fig.* the act of being short with any one.

Ábfetten, I. *v. tr.* 1) to take off the grease. 2) to make greasy. II. *v. intr.* to part with grease.

Ábfeuern, I. *v. tr.* to fire off, to shoot. Eine Pistole —, to discharge a pistol; eine Kanone —, to fire a cannon. II. *v. intr.* [in smelting-houses] to cease heating, to let the fire go out.

Ábfiedeln, *v. tr.* 1) to play awkwardly on a fiddle, to scrape. 2) to separate by rubbing.

Ábfiedern, I. *v. tr.* [with glaziers] to break off the ends or sides of glass with a grossing-iron. II. *v. intr.* to shed the feathers, to moult, to mew.

Ábfinden, *ir.* I. *v. tr.* to satisfy the claims of a person. Einen Gläubiger —, to pay a creditor; Einen —, to quit scores with any one; eine Tochter —, to make a settlement on a daughter; abgefundene Kinder, portioned children; abgefundene Prinzen, princes having an appanage. II. *v. r.* sich —, to come to terms with one, to come to an agreement. Er hat sich mit seinen Gläubigern abgefunden, he has settled with his creditors. Syn. Abfinden, befriedigen. A person is said to be abgefunden, when by the acceptance of a compensation he loses all right to further claim, whether the compensation be to his satisfaction or not; befriedigt, when he is satisfied with his equivalent, and has no longer the wish to make further claim.

Ábfindung, *f.* the act of satisfying the claims of others.

Abfindungsgeld, *n.* money given to get clear of all claims.

Ábfingern, *v. tr.* 1) to number, to count on the fingers. *Fig.* † Das läßt sich leicht —, that is easy to be guessed. 2) to finger [a musical instrument].

Ábfinnen, *v. tr.* [among blacksmiths and locksmiths] to thin the edges of iron by hammering.

Ábfischen, I. *v. tr.* 1) to clear [a pond] from fish. 2) *Fig.* † to skim or take the best of any thing. Einem etwas —, to trick any one out of a thing. II. *v. intr.* to cease fishing.

Ábfitzen, *v. tr.* [among masons] to smooth [a wall].

Ábflachen, *v. tr.* to level, to slope. V. Abebenen, Abdachen.

Ábflammen, *v. tr.* [among curriers] to tallow [a hide].

Ábflattern, *v. intr.* [used with seyn] to flutter or fly away. *Fig.* Er ist abgeflattert, he is off.

Ábflauen, *v. tr.* [in mining] Erz —, [to wash ore] to buddle.

Ábflaufaß, *n.* [-fasses, *pl.* -fässer] [in mining] buddle.

Ábflauherd, *m.* [-es, *pl.* -e] [in mining] buddling-dish.

Ábflecken, *v. intr.* to stain, to make stains.

Ábfledern, *v. tr.* [in husbandry] to cleanse corn with a goosewing.

Ábfleischen, *v. tr.* [among curriers] to flesh [a hide].

Ábfleischmesser, *n.* [-s, *pl.* -] a fleshing knife.

Ábfleischung, *f.* the act of fleshing a hide.

Ábflenzen, *v. tr.* to divest a whale of its fat.

Ábfliegen, *v. intr.* [used with seyn] 1) to fly off, to fly away. 2) to fly off = to separate suddenly.

Ábfließen, *ir. v. intr.* [used with seyn] to flow downwards.

Ábflößen, *v. tr.* 1) to cause to be conveyed by water, to float [timber]. Ein Floß —, to float a raft down a river. 2) to cream [milk].

Ábflöten, *v. tr.* 1) to play a tune on the flute. 2) V. Abflößen 2.

Ábflug, *m.* 1) V. Abstecher. 2) [the act of flying off] flight.

Abflugsort, *m.* the place from which the flight is taken [as with birds of passage &c.].

Ábflügeln, I. *v. tr.* [in botany] to deprive [winged seeds] of wings. II. *v. intr.* [used with seyn] to go away suddenly.

Ábfluß, *m.* [Abflusses, *pl.* Abflüsse] 1) the flowing or running down. 2) a channel for water, a passage for water, a gutter, a waste-pipe.

Ábfodern, **Ábfordern**, *v. tr* to request, to seek to obtain by words, to ask. Einem Geld —, to ask money of any one; etwas — lassen, to send for a thing; Einem Rechnung —, to call any one to account. *Fig.* Von der Welt abgefordert werden, to be called to one's last account, to die.

Ábfoderung, *f.* 1) the act of asking or requesting. 2) the act of recalling, revocation.

Abfoderungsbrief, *m.* letter of revocation.

Ábfohlen, *v. intr.* to have done foaling.

Ábfolgen, [only used with lassen] *v. intr.* — lassen, to let have, to deliver up. V. Verabfolgen, Ausfolgen.

Ábfolgung, *f.* handing, delivering, delivery.

Ábfoltern, *v. tr.* to extort a confession &c. from any one by inflicting bodily torture; *Fig.* to wrest or wring from by menace or duress, to extort. Er hat es mir abgefoltert, he extorted it from me.

Ábfordern, V. Abfodern.

Ábforderung, *f.* V. Abfoderung.

Ábform, *f.* [*pl.* -en] [the matrix in which any thing is cast or receives its form] mould, die, frame.

Ábformen, *v. tr.* 1) to form, to model, to mould. 2) [among bookbinders] to give the cover of a book its due form. 3) [among shoemakers] to beat [a shoe] off from the last.

Ábforschen, *v. tr.* to get by inquiring, by searching, to elicit by cross-questioning.

Ábfragen, *v. tr.* to inquire into facts and circumstances by interrogating, to examine. Ich werde ihm sein Geheimniß —, I shall pump out his secret. *Prov.* So fragt man dem Bauer die Künste ab, thus one gets things out of a fool.

Ábfressen, *ir. v. tr.* to separate by eating, to eat off, to clear by eating. Der Krebs hat seine Nase abgefressen, the cancer has eaten away his nose; Scheidwasser frißt das Kupfer ab, nitric acid corrodes copper. *Fig.* Es wird ihm das Herz —, it will break his heart.

Ábfrieren, *ir. v. intr.* [used with seyn] to freeze off, to freeze. Die Nase ist ihm abgefroren, his nose is frozen off.

Ábfrohnen, **Ábfröhnen**, *v. tr.* 1) to pay off a debt by menial labor or service. 2) to perform the labor or service imposed by statute.

† **Ábfuchteln**, *v. tr.* to strike with the flat side of a sword, to beat soundly.

Ábfügen, *v. tr.* 1) [among glaziers] V. Abfiedern. 2) [among joiners] to smooth with a plane.

Ábfuhre, *f.* [*pl.* -n] the act of carrying away upon wheels, conveyance, carriage.

Ábführarbeit, *f.* [*pl.* -en] [among wire-drawers] all the work to be done in wire-drawing.

Ábführeisen, *n.* [-s] [among wiredrawers] drawing plate.

Ábführen, I. *v. tr.* 1) to carry, to carry away. Getreide nach Frankreich —, to convey corn to France; Einen ins Gefängniß —, to carry any one to goal; vom rechten Wege —, to lead astray; *Fig.* to mislead. 2) [in medicine] to void by any of the excretory passages, to evacuate. Die Feuchtigkeiten —, to expel the humors; Unreinigkeiten aus dem Körper —, to purge; der durch den Harn abgeführte Stoff, matter voided by urine; der Schleim, der durch die Nase abgeführt wird, the pituite secerned from the nose; abführend, opening, laxative, aperient; abführende Mittel, detergents; abführende Mittel gebrauchen, to purge, to take physic. 3) *Fig.* *a*) to pay off [a debt &c.]. *b*) to check, to rebuke, to chide, to reprove, to snub. 4) [among wire-drawers] to draw [wire] smaller and smaller. II. *v. r.* sich —, [to go as if afraid to be seen] to sneak or slink away, to take one's self off.

Ábführlatwerge, *f.* a laxative electuary.

Ábführmittel, *n.* [-s, *pl.* -] [in medicine] an evacuant, a detergent, an aperient, a laxative, a purge.

Ábführtisch, *m.* V. Ziehbank.

Ábführung, *f.* 1) the act of carrying away; *Fig.* the act of paying off. 2) [in medicine] a purgative, a purge.

Abführungsmittel, *n.* V. Abführmittel.

Ábführweg, *m.* [-es, *pl.* -e] [in anatomy] an excretory passage. Abführwege, excretories.

Ábfüllen, V. Abfohlen.

Ábfüllen, *v. tr.* to take from a cask or vessel. Wein —, to draw off wine.

Ábfurchen, *v. tr.* to furrow, to divide by furrows; to plough off.

Ábfuttern, **Ábfüttern**, *v. tr.* 1) to feed sufficiently [the cattle]. 2) to give the last feed at night [jocosely said of men] † to give any one a feed or blow-out.

Ábfütterung, *f.* 1) the act of feeding. 2) jocosely said of a repast, to which all the acquaintance of a person is invited; † feed.

Ábgabe, *f.* [*pl.* -n] 1) [the act of giving, or transferring from one to another] delivery, deliverance. 2) a tax, duty, tribute, impost, or custom.

Ábgabeln, *v. tr.* to take away with a fork.

† **Ábgaffen**, V. Absehen.

Ábgähren, *ir. v. intr.* to cease fermenting.

Ábgang, *m.* [-es, *pl.* Abgänge] 1) [the act of going away from a place] departure. Der — eines Boten, the setting out of a messenger; der — der Post, the starting of the mail; der — einer Leibesfrucht, an abortion, a miscarriage; der — eines Schauspielers von der Bühne [at the close of an act], exit. *Fig.* Der — [when leaving the stage entirely] eines Schauspielers von der Bühne, retirement from the stage; der — aus diesem Leben, departure from this life, decease, death. 2) *Fig.* *a*) sale, market, vent. Diese Waare hat guten —, this commodity sells well. *b*) diminution, decay, declension from prosperity, decline of fortune. In — kommen, gerathen, to decay; in — der Nahrung kommen, to lose customers; der — an Etwas, the want of something, the decay of something. *c*) [cessation of use] disuse. Diese Gewohnheit, dieses Gesetz ist in — gekommen, this custom, this law has fallen into disuse. *d*) diminution, deduction, loss; [with goldsmiths] washings, [among other workmen] scrapings, shreds, chips, chippings, filings, shavings, waste. *e*) [in commerce] V. Tara. *f*) [in printing] waste-paper.

Abgangs-loch, *n.* [in husbandry] an opening at the bottom of a hive. **—rechnung**, *f.* V. Tararechnung.

Ábgängig, *adj.* 1) missing. 2) saleable, vendible. 3) tending to a worse state, decaying, declining.

Ábgänglein, *n.* [-s] V. Abgängsel.

Ábgängling, *m.* [-s, *pl.* -e] 1) shreds, clippings, chippings. 2) [in medicine] a miscarriage, an abortion.

Ábgängsel, *n.* [-s] 1) waste or refuse matter. 2) an abortion.

† **Ábgärben**, *v. tr.* V. Abgerben.

Ábgäschen, *v. intr.* to cease fermenting or foaming.

Ábgaukeln, *v. tr.* to obtain by juggling.

Ábgeben, *ir.* I. *v. tr.* 1) to give, to put into another's hand. Einen Brief auf der Post —, to drop a letter at the post-office; wollen Sie diesen Brief für mich auf der Post —? will you put this letter into the post-office for me? eine Botschaft —, to deliver a message; Zoll —, to pay duties, tolls, customs; einen Wechsel auf Einen —, [in commerce] to draw, or to pass a draft upon any one; sein Amt —, V. Aufgeben; die Siegel —, to quit the seals [said of the lord privy-seal]; dieser Bezirk hat so und so viel Mann zum Militär abzugeben or zu stellen, this district has to furnish so many men to the army, this district is obliged to furnish a contingent of so many men; einen Soldaten von einem Regiment zu einem andern &c. —, to transfer a soldier from one regiment to another &c.; Einem etwas von seinem Ueberflusse —, to share one's superfluities with any one. *Fig.* Einem eins — or versetzen, to hit any one, to give him one. Er hat ihm eins abgegeben, he hit him, he gave him a cutting reply. Syn. Abgeben, Abliefern. The latter is generally used in speaking of important things. I have delivered the money, ich habe das Geld abgeliefert, and the book abgegeben. 2) *Fig.* to serve for, to be good for. Er würde einen guten Soldaten —, he would make a good soldier; einen Zeugen —, to bear witness; einen Beweis —, to afford a proof; einen Narren —, to play the fool. 3) *Fig.* Es wird etwas —, it is probable that we shall have something [as: rain, a dispute]; es wird nichts dabei —, we shall have no profit by it. II. *v. intr.* [at cards] to deal for the last time. III. *v. r.* sich mit Einem —, to have intercourse, to meddle, to be familiar with one; sich mit Versemachen —, to deal in poetry; sich mit Kohlentragen —, to follow the business of a coal-porter. Syn. V. Befassen.

Ábgebot, *n.* V. Aufgebot.

Ábgebrochenheit, *f.* abruptness.

Ábgehen, *ir.* I. *v. intr.* [used with seyn] to go or move from, to depart. Die Briefpost geht jeden Tag ab, the mail goes every day; der Postwagen geht um sechs Uhr ab, the stage coach starts at six o' clock; er ist nach Berlin abgegangen, he has gone to Berlin; ein Schiff geht regelmäßig nach London ab, a ship goes regularly to London; er ist abgegangen, he made his exit [from the stage]; vom rechten Wege —, to go astray, to miss the road. *Fig.* Vom Pfade der Tugend —, to wander from the path of virtue; die Leibesfrucht ging ihr ab, she aborted, she miscarried; es ging schwarze Oeffnung von ihm ab, he voided dark-coloured matter; — lassen, to send off, to dispatch; einen Brief — lassen, to send off a letter; da die Briefe abgingen, when the letters went off; von einer Sache —, to swerve, to go from one's subject; von eines Andern Meinung — [abweichen], to differ from any one in opinion; hievon kann ich nicht —, I must insist upon that; die Farbe geht ab, the colour fades; das Feuer — lassen, to let the fire go out; diese Waare geht gut ab, this commodity sells well, is of a quick sale; dieser Atlas geht erstaunlich ab, this satin takes wonderfully; ich lasse keinen Heller davon —, I will not abate one farthing on it; Etwas von seiner Forderung — lassen, to allow, to yield some abatement; davon geht ab, [in commerce] discount of; für Tara muß zehn und für gut Gewicht ein Prozent —, [in commerce] you must discount ten per Cent for tare, and one per Cent for tret; er läßt sich nichts —, he does not deny himself any thing; es gehen mir fünf Thaler ab, I want, I miss five dollars; es geht schlecht ab, it does not speed; it sticks by me; es wird nicht gut —, it will not end well; übel —, to have an ill issue; von der Bühne gänzlich or für immer —, [of an actor] to retire from the stage, to take leave of the stage; mit Tode —, to depart this life, to go off, to die. *Prov.* Es geht ab wie Pech am Aermel, it speeds like a lame horse.

II. *v. tr.* [used with haben] 1) to wear off by walking [viz. one's shoes]. 2) to measure by walking. III. *v. r.* sich —, to tire by walking. Syn. Abgehen, weggehen, fortgehen. Abgehen is used especially when regard is had to the place whence the person removed, and to which he before belonged; weggehen and fortgehen in reference merely to the removal. Speaking of an actor's going off the stage at the end of a scene, one says, er ist abgegangen; but of the going away of the candle snuffer, er ist weggegangen. Fortgehen expresses a moving forwards, and is used not only in opposition to being in a state of rest, but also to going backwards.

Ábgeigen, *v. tr.* [in contempt] to tweedle, to scrape.

Ábgeißeln, *v. tr.* 1) to seperate by scourging. 2) to scourge, to whip, to lash soundly.

Ábgeizen, *v. tr.* to deprive of by avarice. Sich etwas —, to stint one's self from avarice.

Ábgekürzt, *part.* of Abkürzen, abridged; [in botany] short [said of the calix]; [in heraldry] couped [in distinction from erased].

Ábgelben, I. *v. tr.* to yellow sufficiently. II. *v. intr.* to part with yellow.

Ábgelebt, *part.* of Ableben. 1) broken down with age, weakened by age, decrepit, debilitated by excesses. 2) deceased, defunct. V. Ableben.

Ábgelebtheit, *f.* decrepitness, decrepitude, debility produced by excesses, premature old age.

Ábgeledigt, *adj.* [in heraldry] couped [said of pendants &c.].

Ábgelegen, *part.* of Abliegen. 1) distant, out of the way, remote, retired. Der abgelegene Spaziergang, a sequestered walk. 2) reposed, settled [said of wine that has lain long].

Ábgelegenheit, *f.* distance, remoteness.

Ábgemessenheit, *f.* exactness, regularity, formality.

Ábgeneigt, *part.* of Abneigen. 1) inclined, bent downwards. Eine —e Fläche, an inclined plane. 2) *Fig.* not favourably disposed, disinclined, averse, reluctant, unfavourable, not kind. Syn. V. Abhold, Ungeneigt. [NB. Abgeneigt is the most usual.]

Ábgeneigtheit, *f.* 1) disaffection, dislike, unfriendliness, disinclination, reluctance, repugnance. 2) enmity, malevolence, ill-will.

Ábgenutzt, *part.* of Abnutzen. worn out. Nicht —, unworn. *Fig.* Ein —er Witz, a trite wit.

Ábgenutztheit, *f.* attriteness.

Ábgeordnet, *part.* of Abordnen. Der —e, ein —er [-en, *pl.* die -en, without the article -e] deputy, legate, delegate, commissary. Syn. Abgeordnete, Abgesandte. Abgesandte are only such as are sent by one prince or state to the court of another on particular occasions; Abgeordnete those who are deputed by separate bodies of the citizens and invested with power to transact business as their representatives.

Ábgerben, *v. tr.* 1) to take off by tanning. 2) to curry [a hide] sufficiently; † *Fig.* to cudgel, to bang, to thump.

Ábgeredet, *part.* of Abreden. concerted, agreed upon. —er Maaßen, according to agreement; ein —er Handel, a concerted thing.

Ábgesandt, *part.* of Absenden. Der —e, ein —er [-en, *pl.* die -en, without the article -e] 1) [= Bote] a messenger. 2) envoy, deputy, delegate. Ein heimlicher —er, an emissary; ein geistlicher —er, a missionary. Syn. V. Abgeordnete. 3) ambassador. [V. Gesandte.]

Ábgesang, *m.* [-es, *pl.* Abgesänge] [in the Romish church] V. Collecte.

Ábgescharrte, *n.* [-n] scrapings.

Ábgeschieden, *adj. part.* of Abscheiden. 1) dead, deceased, departed, defunct. Der —e Geist, a shade. 2) retired, secluded, sequestered.

Ábgeschiedenheit, *f.* retiredness, seclusion.

Ábgeschliffen, *part.* of Abschleifen, polished; *Fig.* refined, polite. —e Sitten, polite or elegant manners.

Ábgeschliffenheit, *f.* refinement, politeness, elegance of manners.

Ábgeschmackt, I. *adj.* insipid, flat, dull, stale, absurd. II. *adv.* absurdly, nonsensically.

Ábgeschmacktheit, *f.* nonsense, absurdity.

Ábgesehen, *part.* of Absehen. — von, [in logic] in the abstract, abstractively, abstractedly from.

Ábgespannt, *part.* of Abspannen, weakened, enervated, slackened; relaxed, atonic [said of a muscle, nerve].

Ábgespanntheit, *f.* [in medicine] defect of muscular power, relaxation, debility, atony.

Ábgestalten, *v. tr.* to delineate, to picture.

Ábgestorben, *part.* of Absterben, *adj.* and *adv. Fig.* Er ist der Gesellschaft ganz —, he is absolutely lost to society.

Ábgestorbenheit, *f.* 1) want of feeling, apathy. 2) *Fig.* indifference, alienation of heart from temporal pleasures. Die — für die Welt, deadness to the world.

Ábgestumpft, *part.* of Abstumpfen, 1) blunted. 2) *Fig.* dull.

Ábgestumpftheit, *f.* dullness.

Ábgewähren, *v. tr.* [in mining] to discharge [in the counterbook].

Ábgewichen, *part.* of Abweichen. V. Verwichen.

Ábgewinnen, *ir. v. tr.* to win, to gain from any body. Einem den Vortheil —, to gain or get the better of any one; die Engländer gewonnen den Spaniern den Vortheil ab, the English got the better of the Spaniards; den Vorzug —, to get the advantage, to gain upon, to prevail against; Einem ein Geheimniß —, to pump a secret out of one; den Wind —, [a sea term] to gain the wind, to get to windward; einer Sache Geschmack —, to get a taste for a thing.

Ábgewöhnen, *v. tr.* 1) to destroy the force of habit by disuse, to disaccustom, to cause to abandon, to cause to reform. Einem üble Gewohnheiten —, to break one of ill habits or practices; sich den Trunk —, to leave off drinking. Syn. V. Entwöhnen. 2) V. Entwöhnen.

Ábgezogen, *part.* of Abziehen. —e Begriffe, [in logic] abstract ideas.

Ábgezogenheit, *f.* V. Abgeschiedenheit.

Ábgieren, *v. tr.* 1) to get by longing. 2) [a sea term] *a)* Ein Schiff —, to shear off. *b)* to get sea-room.

Ábgießen, *ir. v. tr.* 1) to pour gently the upper part of a liquor from one vessel into another. Wein —, to decant wine. 2) to form by melting a metal, and pouring it into a mold, to cast, [seldom] to found.

Ábgießer, *m.* [-s, *pl.* -] a founder, or caster.

Ábgießung, *f.* 1) pouring off, decanting. 2) founding, casting.

Ábgift, *f.* [a law term] a rent.

Ábgipfeln, *v. tr.* to top [a tree].

Ábgirren, *v. tr.* to get from one by coaxing.

Ábgischen, **Abgischten**, V. Abgäschen.

Ábgittern, *v. tr.* to separate by bars.

Ábglanz, *m.* [-es] reflected splendour, reflection. Der — der Sonne im Wasser, the reflection of the sun in the water. *Fig.* Das Weib ist der — des Mannes, the woman is the image of the man.

Ábglätten, *v. tr.* 1) to polish, to smooth. 2) *Fig.* to refine, to make elegant of manners, to polish.

Ábgleichen, *v. tr.* to make equal. Rechnungen —, to equalise accounts.

Ábgleichfeile, *f.* [*pl.* -n] [with some workmen] a kind of smoothing file.

Ábgleichstange, *f.* [*pl.* -n] [in horology] adjusting tool.

Ábgleichung, *f.* the act of equalising or making equal, equalisation.

Abgleichungswaage, *f.* [in coining] adjusting-scale.

Ábgleiten, *ir. v. intr.* [used with seyn] to slip or glide off.

Ábglimmen, *ir. v. intr.* [used with seyn] to cease glowing, to cease burning.

† **Ábglitschen**, V. Abgleiten.

Ábglühen, I. *v. tr.* to heat through. Wein —, to mull wine; abgeglühtes Eisen, redhot iron. II. *v. intr.* to cease to glow.

Ábgott, *m.* [-es, *pl.* Abgötter] [a pagan deity] an idol. *Fig.* Dieß Mädchen ist der — der Familie, this girl is the idol of the family. Syn. Abgott, Götze, Götzenbild. Abgott is any thing consecrated as an object of worship, also a person loved and honored to adoration, as: „The prince was the Abgott (idol) of the people", or any thing on which we set our affections to an excessive and sinful degree, as our money &c. Götze that which is worshipped as a deity, but is not God; Götzenbild the image, form or representation of a false God.

Abgottschlange, *f.* great boa, boa constrictor.

Ábgötter, **Ábgötterer**, *m.* [-s, *pl.* -] a worshipper of idols, idolater.

Abgötterei, *f.* the worship of idols, idolatry. — treiben, to worship idols, to idolatrize, to commit idolatry.

Ábgöttern, *v. intr.* to worship idols, to idolatrize.

Ábgöttinn, *f.* a female idol. *Fig.* Sie war seine —, she was his idol, the darling of his heart.

Ábgöttisch, I. *adj.* idolatrous, idolish. II. *adv.* idolatrously. Seine Kinder — lieben, to idolize one's children.

Ábgraben, *ir. v. tr.* 1) to lower [a hillock] by digging. 2) to separate or mark by a ditch. Einen Weg —, to furnish a road with a ditch. 3) to deprive of by digging. 4) to drain by a ditch or ditches. Einen Sumpf —, to ditch a swamp; einen Teich —, to drain a pond.

Ábgrabung, *f.* digging off &c.

Ábgrämeln, **Ábgrämen**, *v. r.* sich —, to waste or consume by grief, to wear away with grief; to pine one's self away.

Ábgrasen, *v. tr.* to graze [a meadow].

Ábgrasung, *f.* the act of grazing.

Ábgreifen, *ir. v. tr.* to wear by handling. Ein abgegriffener Hut, a worn out hat.

Ábgrenzen, *v. tr.* to fix the limits [borders, frontiers] of.

Ábgrund, *m.* [-es, *pl.* Abgründe] a precipice, an abyss, a gulf; [in sea language] an eddy of water, a race or whirlpool. Er stürzte sich mit seinem Pferde in den —, he leapt with his horse into the abyss. *Fig.* Der — der Zeit, the abyss, the precipice of time; der — des Elends, the abyss of misery.

Ábgründen, *v. tr.* [among joiners] to groove, to channel, to flute.

Ábgrünen, *v. intr.* 1) to cease to be verdant. 2) to part with green.

† **Ábgucken**, I. *v. tr.* to learn from any one by looking at him by stealth. II. *v. r.* sich —, to become tired by gazing.

Ábgunst, *f.* V. Mißgunst.

Ábgünstig, *adj.* V. Mißgünstig.

Ábgurgeln, *v. tr.* 1) to kill by cutting the throat. 2) to sing with full throat. 3) V. Ableiern *Fig.*

Ábgürten, *v. tr.* to ungird, to ungirth [a horse].

Ábgürtung, *f.* ungirding, ungirthing.

Ábguß, *m.* [Abgusses, *pl.* Abgüsse] 1) the act of pouring from one vessel into another, decanting. 2) the act of casting, or founding. 3) cast, copy. 4) the receptacle for the fluid which oozes from the tobacco at the bottom of a tobacco-pipe.

Ábgüten, V. Abfinden.

Ábhaaren, *v. intr.* to part with hair [said of a fur].

Ábhaben, *ir. v. tr.* 1) to have a part of. Er will etwas —, he comes in for a share. 2) not to carry appendant to the body, not to wear. Den Hut —, to have the hat off.

Ábhacken, *v. tr.* to hack or chop off, to cut off or down. Einem die Finger —, to chop off one's fingers.

Ábhacker, *m.* [-s, *pl.* -] one who chops off.

Ábhadern, *v. tr.* to extort by contention and dispute.

Ábhäften, **Ábhaften**, *v. tr.* to unhook, to unclasp, to unfix.

Ábhageln, I. *v. imp.* to cease hailing. II. *v. tr.* to beat down by hailing. Es hat die Blüthen abgehagelt, the hail has beaten off the blossoms.

Ábhägen, *v. tr.* to separate by a hedge, to hedge, to fence off [a field, a garden].

Ábhagern, *v. intr.* [used with seyn] to lose flesh, to fall away. V. Abmagern.

Ábhägung, *f.* 1) the act of hedging, fencing. 2) inclosure.

Ábhäkeln, **Ábhaken**, *v. tr.* to unhook.

Ábhalftern, *v. tr.* to unhalter [a horse].

Ábhalsen, *v. tr.* 1) to cut off the throat. 2) [among hunters] to uncouple [dogs].

Ábhalt, *m.* [-es] V. Abhaltung.

Ábhalten, *ir.* I. *v. tr.* to hold off, to keep at a distance. Die Kinder vom Feuer —, to keep the children at a distance from the fire; sie hielt die Hunde ab, she kept the dogs off; einen Streich —, to ward off, to parry a blow; jeden Zutritt der Kälte abhaltend, excluding all entrance of cold; den Regen mittelst eines dichten Daches —, to shut out rain by a tight roof; ein Regenschirm, der den Regen abhält, an umbrella that keeps off, sheds rain. *Fig.* Sie haben mich abgehalten, weiter fortzuschreiten, you detained me from proceeding any further; er soll mich davon nicht —, he shall not keep me from it; was hält euch ab? what hinders you? er läßt sich durch Nichts —, he sticks at nothing; lassen Sie sich nicht —, do not let yourself be stopped or disturbed. II. *v. intr.* [a sea term] to edge away. Auf ein Schiff —, to bear up to or away for a ship; vom Lande —, to bear off from the land; halt ab! bear away! bear up! halt nicht ab! don't fall off! keep her to! luff! ganz — und mit dem Winde gehen, to bear away large; von einer Bank oder Klippe —, to keep aloof from any rock or shoal, to give it a good birth.

Ábhalter, *m.* [-s, *pl.* -] [a sea term, a rope used to keep a heavy body steady while hoisting or lowering] a guy.

Ábhaltung, *f.* 1) the act of holding off, keeping off, hindering, stopping. 2) *Fig.* hinderance, impediment, occupation.

Ábhämmern, *v. tr.* to separate by hammering.

Ábhandeln, *v. tr.* 1) to buy, to purchase, to bargain for. 2) to beat down in bargaining. Etwas von einem Preise —, to beat down the price [of any commodity]. 3) to discourse on, to debate. Einen Gegenstand —, to treat of a subject, to discuss a subject. 4) [a law term] V. Verhandeln.

Abhänden, **Abhánden**, *adv.* [used with seyn and kommen] not at hand, lost. — seyn, not to be at hand; — kommen, to be lost.

Ábhändler, *m.* [-s, *pl.* -] he that discusses

a matter or treats of a subject, discusser.

Ábhandlung, *f.* [the treating of a subject] treatise, discussion.

Ábhang, *m.* [-es, *pl.* Abhänge] descent of land, slope, declivity. Der — eines Berges, declivity of a hill; ein jäher —, a precipitous declivity, a cliff; ein sanfter —, [in fortification] rampe.

Ábhangen, *ir. v. intr.* 1) V. Herabhangen, Herunterhangen. 2) to incline, to have a steep declivity, to hang. Die Straße hangt gegen Norden ab, the road declines to the north. 3) to hang at a distance, to hang off. 4) *Fig.* [to be connected with any thing, as the cause of its existence, or of its operations and effects] to depend. Die Vegetation hangt von der Wärme und Feuchtigkeit ab, vegetation depends on heat and moisture; die Ruhe der Gesellschaft hangt von guten Gesetzen ab, the peace of society depends on good laws; in Hinsicht des Athmens hangen wir von der Luft ab, we depend on air for respiration; es hangt von mir ab, it depends on or upon me; diese Frage hangt von einem einzigen Punkte ab, this question hangs on a single point. *Syn.* V. Ankommen.

Ábhängen, *v. tr.* 1) to hang off, to unhang. Die Gewichte einer Uhr —, to take off the weights of a clock; die gedruckten Bogen von den Trockenleinen —, [among printers] to take down the sheets. 2) [in forges] to stop the action of the bellows.

Ábhängig, I. *adj.* 1) declivous, declivitous, sloping. 2) *Fig.* depending, dependent. Wir sind von Gott und seiner Vorsehung —, we are dependent on God and his providence. II. *adv.* slopingly.

Ábhängigkeit, *f.* 1) declivity, slope. 2) *Fig.* dependence, dependency. Die — des Kindes von seinen Eltern, the dependence of a child on his parents.

Ábhängling, *m.* [-s, *pl.* -e] [in contempt] a dependent, depender.

Ábhären, *v. tr.* [among tanners] to strip [a hide] of hair.

Ábharken, *v. tr.* to take off with a rake.

Ábhärmen, *v. r.* sich —, to pine away, to consume by grief. Wir härmen uns über den Verlust von Freunden oder Vermögen ab, we grieve at the loss of friends or property.

Ábhärten, *v. tr.* to make hard or more hard, to harden. Den Stahl —, to temper steel. *Fig.* Abgehärtet, inured to fatigue, hardy; sich —, to make one's self hardy, callous; sich gegen ein Clima —, to inure one's self to a climate; sich gegen die Empfindungen des Mitleids —, to harden one's self against impressions of pity; ein abgehärteter Sünder, an obdurate, hardened sinner.

Ábhärtung, *f.* 1) the act of hardening. 2) *Fig.* [firmness of body derived from laborious exercises] hardiness.

Ábharzen, *v. tr.* to free [a tree] from resin.

Ábhaschen, I. *v. tr.* to snatch from a person. II. *v. r.* sich —, to tire one's self by snatching or catching at a thing.

Ábhaspeln, *v. tr.* 1) to reel off, to wind off, to unwind [yarn] from the reel. 2) *Fig.* to perform negligently.

Ábhauben, *v. tr.* [among hunters] to unhood [a hawk].

Ábhauchen, *v. tr.* 1) to blow away [the dust]. 2) to breathe or utter softly.

Ábhauen, *ir. v. tr.* 1) to cut off, to chop off, to cut down. Bäume —, to fell trees; Einem den Kopf —, to behead one. Abgehauen, hewed down; ein abgehauener Baum, a stick of timber, a log; das Abhauen, the act of hewing down &c., beheading. 2) to switch, to lash.

Ábhäufeln, *v. tr.* to divide into small heaps.

Ábhaufen, *v. tr.* to divide into heaps.

Ábhäuten, I. *v. tr.* 1) to skin, to flay. Einen Ochsen —, to flay an ox. 2) to strip off the pellicle [cuticle]. II. *v. intr.* to cast off the slough or skin.

Ábheben, *ir.* I. *v. tr.* to throw or bring down from an elevation, to lift off, to take off. Den Deckel —, to take off the cover; den Rahm von der Milch —, to skim the cream from the milk; eine Kanone von der Lafette —, to dismount a cannon; den Tisch [die Speisen] —, to clear the table, to take away; eine Karte —, [at cards] to cut a card; eine Karte —, um zu sehen, wer gibt, to cut for the deal; wer hebt ab? whose cut is it. II. *v. intr.* || auf Etwas —, = abzielen, to aim at a thing, to have a thing in view.

Ábhebung, *f.* the act of heaving off; cutting [said of cards].

Ábhecheln, *v. intr.* to finish hackling.

Ábheften, *v. tr.* to loosen, to unloose, to untie, to unhook, to unclasp.

Ábheilen, I. *v. tr.* to cause to heal and fall off [a scab]. II. *v. intr.* to heal and fall off.

Ábheischen, V. Abfordern.

Ábhelfen, *ir. v. tr.* 1) to help down. 2) *Fig.* to help, to remedy, to change for the better. Einem Fehler —, to correct a fault; Beschwerden —, to redress grievances; dem ist nicht abzuhelfen, it is past remedy.

Ábhelflich, *adj.* remediable.

Ábhelflichkeit, *f.* remediableness.

Ábhellen, I. *v. tr.* to make clear, to purify, to clarify, to clear. Wein —, to clarify, to fine wine. II. *v. r.* sich —, to clarify, to clear up.

Ábhenken, V. Abhängen.

Ábherzen, *v. tr.* Einen —, to hug and kiss any one heartily.

Ábhetzen, *v. tr.* 1) to tire or fatigue by hunting. Abgehetzte Dachshunde, jaded terriers; Einen Hirsch —, to run down a stag. 2) to get or obtain by harassing.

Ábheucheln, *v. tr.* to obtain from one by hypocrisy.

Ábheuern, *v. tr.* to hire from. V. Abmiethen.

Ábheulen, I. *v. tr.* to utter with howling. II. *v. r.* sich —, to weary one's self with howling.

Ábhexen, *v. tr.* to get from any one by witchcraft.

Ábhinken, *v. intr.* [u. w. seyn] to limp away.

Ábhobeln, *v. tr.* 1) to smooth with a plane, to plane; [among tawers] to rub. 2) *Fig.* to polish.

Ábhocken, **Ábhucken**, *v. tr.* to put down from the back or shoulders [a burden].

Ábhold [also abhóld], *adv.* disinclined, averse, unfavourable. Einem — seyn, to be averse to any one, to bear ill will to any one; dem Frieden —, averse to peace. V. Abgeneigt, Ungeneigt.

Ábholen, *v. tr.* 1) to go and bring, to fetch. Ich will ihn —, I will go for him; ich will Sie bei Ihrem Vater —, I will call for you at your father's; der Wagen wird mich —, the carriage will come for me; — lassen, to send for. 2) [a sea term] Ein Schiff vom Strande, to haul a ship off from the shore, to get it off from the ground.

Ábholung, *f.* the act of fetching off, calling away.

Ábholz, *n.* V. Abraum.

Ábholzen, *v. tr.* to clear from wood. Das —, die Abholzung eines Schlages, the second cutting of a wood.

Ábholzig, *adj.* and *adv.* deficient or weak in timber [said of trees].

Ábhorchen, *v. tr.* to learn by listening, to overhear.

Ábhören, *v. tr.* 1) to learn by hearing. Was hörst du dir davon ab? what do you learn by hearing that? V. Ablernen. *Fig.* Rechnungen —, to audit accounts. 2) [a law term] to examine, to interrogate [a witness]. Zeugen gegen einander —, to confront witnesses. SYN. Abhören, verhören. Abhören is said only of the witnesses, verhören as well of the accused as of the witnesses. Both words may be used when speaking of witnesses, with this distinction; that, they are said to be verhört when their evidence in general is heard, and abgehört when their whole deposition is taken or they are examined as to the entire knowledge they have of a thing.

Ábhörung, *f.* 1) the act of hearing. 2) trial, examination.

Ábhub, *m.* [-es] 1) offal, remains; broken meat. 2) the act of cutting [the cards at dealing]. 3) [in mining] scoria.

Abhubkiste, *f.* [in mining] rake.

Ábhucken, V. Abhocken.

Ábhügeln, *v. tr.* to clear of a hillock.

Ábhuld, *f.* V. Abgeneigtheit.

Ábhülfe, *f.* redress, relief, remedy. — bringen, — leisten, to remedy, to render assistance, to redress, to relieve.

Ábhülflich, V. Abhelflich.

Ábhülsen, *v. tr.* to blanch, to shell, || to hud.

Ábhumpeln, *v. intr.* [u. w. seyn] to limp away.

Ábhungern, I. *v. tr.* to starve, to famish. Abgehungert seyn, to be pinched for want of food, to be emaciated, to be half-starved. II. *v. r.* sich —, to starve, to stint one's self in food.

† **Ábhuren**, *v. r.* sich —, to exhaust one's self by whoring.

Ábhüten, *v. tr.* to graze, to feed [a meadow].

Ábhütten, *v. tr.* [in mining] to break.

Ábhütung, *f.* feeding, grasing.

Ábicht, *adj.* and *adv.* [among hatters] turned, being the wrong side.

Ábichten, *v. tr.* [among clothiers] to card on the wrong side.

Ábirren, *v. intr.* [used with seyn] to deviate, to err, to stray.

Ábirrung, *f.* deviation, aberration, aberrance, aberrancy; [in optics, the deviation of the rays of light when inflected by a lens or speculum] aberration. Newtons —, Newtonian aberration [arising from the unequal refrangibility of the rays of light]; [in astronomy] die — eines Sternes, eines Planeten, aberration of a star, of a planet.

† **Ábjachtern**, *v. r.* sich —, to weary one's self by running.

Ábjagen, I. *v. tr.* 1) to rescue, to recover. Einem etwas wieder —, to rescue [retrieve, recover] something from one. 2) to overdrive, to overcourse, to override, to founder [a horse]. Ein abgejagtes Pferd, a jaded horse. II. *v. intr.* [among sportsmen] to leave off hunting.

Ábjammern, *v. tr.* to get from one by lamenting.

Ábjochen, *v. tr.* to unyoke.

Ábkalben, *v. intr.* to finish calving.

Ábkälten, *v. tr.* 1) to cool, to make cool. 2) *Fig.* to slacken, to relax, to relent. V. Erkälten.

Ábkämmen, *v. tr.* 1) to comb off. 2) *Fig.*

[a military term] to shoot off the upper part of a wall, or parapet.

Ábkämpfen, *v. tr.* 1) to get by fighting. 2) [among sportsmen] to drive away by fighting [said of harts in the rutting season].

Ábkanten, *v. tr.* to take off the corners and edges, to round off.

Ábkanzeln, *v. tr.* 1) to mention from the pulpit. 2) to reprimand from the pulpit. † *Fig.* Einen —, to rebuke any one.

Ábkappen, *v. tr.* 1) to take off the cap or hood. Den Falken —, to unhood the hawk. 2) to cut off, to chop off, to lop off. Das — [der Aeste &c.], the pruning, lopping off of branches &c. 3) to rebuke, to give a severe reprimand, or a harsh answer. Wie ich ihn abgekappt habe, how I have put him down.

Ábkargen, *v. tr.* to deprive by stinginess, to pinch, to stint. Sich selbst etwas —, to pinch one's self of something.

Ábkarten, *v. tr.* to concert clandestinely, to plot. Ein abgekarteter Handel, a concerted game.

Ábkauf, *m.* [-s] 1) the act of buying, or purchasing from another. 2) [the thing bought] purchase.

Ábkaufen, I. *v. tr.* to buy or purchase from. *Fig.* Eine Strafe —, to redeem by the payment of a fine. II. *v. r.* sich —, V. Loskaufen.

Ábkäufer, *m.* [-s, *pl.* -] a purchaser, buyer.

Ábkäuflich, *adj.* purchasable, redeemable.

Ábkehlen, *v. tr.* 1) V. Abstechen. 2) [among joiners] to groove, to channel, to flute.

Ábkehr, *f.* V. Abneigung.

Ábkehren, I. *v. tr.* 1) to turn away [the face], to avert [the eyes]. 2) to brush [a hat]. 3) to wear out by sweeping. Ein abgekehrter Besen, a broom worn to the stump. II. *v. r.* sich —, to avert one's self, to remove, to retire.

Ábkehrer, *m.* [-s, *pl.* -] a brusher, a sweeper.

Ábkehricht, *n.* [-s] sweepings.

Ábkehrung, *f.* 1) the act of turning away, averting. 2) the act of brushing, sweeping.

Ábkeifen, *ir.* I. *v. tr.* to get, to obtain by chiding or scolding. II. *v. r.* sich —, to weary one's self by chiding.

Ábkeltern, I. *v. tr.* to press [grapes]. II. *v. intr.* to finish pressing.

Ábketteln, *v. tr.* [among hosiers] to fasten the stitches duly.

Ábketten, *ir. v. tr.* to unchain, unfasten [a dog].

Ábkichern, *v. r.* sich —, to tire one's self by tittering.

Ábkimmen, *v. tr.* [among coopers] to chop off the chime.

Ábkindern, *v. intr.* to cease child-bearing.

Ábkippen, I. *v. tr.* [einen Nagel], to cut off [the head or point of a nail]. II. *v. intr.* to fall from the edge.

Ábkitzeln, *v. tr.* to tickle thoroughly, to weary by tickling.

Ábklaffen, *v. intr.* to gape, to stand gaping. Die Thür klafft ab, the door is a-jar.

Ábklagen, *v. tr.* to get by lamenting.

Ábklammern, *v. tr.* to rid of pegs, to unpeg [linen fastened to a clothes-line].

Ábklang, *m.* [-es, *pl.* Abklänge] dissonance.

Ábklappen, *v. tr.* to let down the leaf [of a table].

Ábklären, I. *v. tr.* to clear, to clarify, to fine [any liquor]. II. *v. r.* sich —, to clarify.

Ábklärung, *f.* clarification, fining.

Abklärungsmittel, *n.* any ingredient used in fining wine &c.

Ábklatschen, *v. tr.* 1) [among letter-founders &c.] to impress [forms in liquid metal]. 2) to slap [a child].

Ábklauben, *v. tr.* to pick off, to pluck off. Das Fleisch von einem Knochen —, to pick a bone.

Ábkleiden, *v. tr.* 1) to partition. Ein Zimmer —, to separate a room by a partition. 2) [a sea term] Die Taue —, to take off the service.

Ábkleidung, *f.* 1) partition, erection of a partition wall. 2) part divided from the rest, division.

Ábklemmen, *v. tr.* to pinch off, to squeeze off.

Ábklopfen, *v. tr.* 1) to beat off, to clean by beating. † *Fig.* Einen —, to beat a person soundly. 2) [in printing] to strike off a proof sheet.

Ábklötzen, *v. tr.* to saw off a log.

Ábknappen, *v. tr.* 1) to break off in little bits. 2) *Fig.* to withhold through parsimony, to stint. Einem an der Kost —, to stint a person in his meals; sich Etwas —, to deprive one's self of necessaries; am Lohne —, to curtail wages.

Ábknaupeln, *v. tr.* to pick off [with the teeth], to gnaw.

Ábknausern, *v. tr.* to withhold through parsimony, to stint.

Ábkneifen, *ir. v. tr.* [a sea term] to haul the wind, to ply or turn to windward.

Ábkneipen, *r.* and *ir. v. tr.* to pinch off, to nip off.

Ábknicken, *v. tr.* 1) to break, to snap off. 2) [among sportsmen] to stab [a hart &c.]; to break or wring off the neck [of a hare].

Ábknöpfen, *v. tr.* to unbutton and take off.

Ábknüpfen, *v. tr.* to unbind, to loose, to untie, to undo.

Ábknuppern, *v. tr.* to pick off, to pluck off.

Ábkochen, I. *v. tr.* to boil, to decoct. Ein abgekochter Trank, a decoction. II. *v. intr.* 1) to finish cooking. 2) [used with seyn] to be separated by boiling.

Ábkohlen, *v. tr.* [among carpenters] to mark with a blackened string.

Ábköhlen, V. Abhütten.

Ábkohler, *m.* [-s, *pl.* -] [in mining] breaker.

Ábkomme, *m.* V. Abkömmling, Nachkomme.

Ábkommen, *ir. v. intr.* [u. w. seyn] 1) to get off, to deviate. Vom Wege —, to miss the road, to lose the way; [among sportsmen] von der Fährte —, to get off the scent, to be thrown out, to be at fault; auf der zum Durchsägen bezeichneten Linie bleiben, ohne davon abzukommen, to keep in the line marked to be sawn, without wriggling on either side. *Fig.* Er kann nicht —, he is detained by business; können Sie wohl eine Viertelstunde —? can you spare a quarter of an hour? — können, to be able to get away, to be disengaged; von seinem Zwecke —, to deviate from one's purpose; mit Verlust —, to come off a loser. 2) *Fig.* to grow out of use, to fall into disuse, to become obsolete.

Ábkommen, *n.* [-s, *pl.* -] agreement, accommodation, composition; ein — mit Einem treffen, to come to an agreement, to settle or compound with one.

Ábkommenschaft, *f.* offspring, descent, posterity. V. Nachkommenschaft.

Ábkömmling, *m.* [-s, *pl.* -e] descendant, offspring. V. Nachkömmling.

Ábkommniß, *n.* [-sses, *pl.* -sse] [in mining] 1) deviation of a vein from the principal lode. 2) the vein of ore which deviates from the principal lode.

Ábköpfen, *v. tr.* 1) to top, to lop, to head [trees]. Einen Nagel —, to point a nail. 2) to head, to behead, to decapitate.

Ábkopiren, *v. tr.* to copy.

Ábkoppeln, *v. tr.* to uncouple [dogs].

Ábkosen, *v. tr.* to get by wheedling, coaxing, courting, or fawning, to wheedle or coax out of.

Ábkrächzen, I. *v. tr.* to utter groaning. II. *v. r.* sich —, 1) to wear one's self out with groaning. 2) to caw, to croak [as a raven].

Ábkräften, *v. tr.* to weaken.

Ábkramen, *v. tr.* to clear [a table &c.].

Ábkrämpeln, I. *v. tr.* to card thoroughly. II. *v. intr.* to finish carding.

Ábkrämpen, *v. tr.* [among hatters] to take down the flap, to uncock [a hat].

Ábkränkeln, *v. intr.* [used with seyn] to be weakened by illness.

Ábkranken, *v. intr.* [u. w. seyn] to be weakened by long illness.

Ábkränken, I. *v. tr.* to waste by grief. II. *v. r.* sich —, to pine.

Ábkratzen, *v. tr.* 1) to take away by scraping, to scrape off, to scratch off. † 2) *Fig.* *a*) to go off, to run away. *b*) to play awkwardly on a fiddle, to scrape.

Ábkratzung, *f.* the act of scratching or scraping off.

Ábkrauten, *v. tr.* [in husbandry] to rid of noxious plants, to weed [a vineyard].

1. **Ábkreischen**, *v. tr.* [in printing] to cleanse.

2. **Ábkreischen**, I. *v. tr.* to proclaim by bawling. II. *v. r.* sich —, to tire one's self with bawling.

Ábkreisen, *v. tr.* to separate by a circle.

Ábkreisend, *adj.* eccentric, eccentrical.

Ábkriechen, *v. intr.* [used with seyn] to creep away.

1. **Ábkriegen**, *v. tr.* 1) to get, to obtain a share of. † *Fig.* Etwas —, to get a reprimand or to be punished. 2) to remove by force, to get off. Seine Stiefeln nicht — können, not get his boots off.

2. **Ábkriegen**, *v. tr.* to acquire by war, to obtain by arms.

Ábkröschen, *v. tr.* 1) to roast. 2) [in printing] to clarify [linseed-oil].

Ábkrümeln, *v. intr.* [used with seyn] to break off in crumbs, to fall off in small pieces, to crumb or crumble.

Ábkühlen, I. *v. tr.* to allay heat. Das Eis kühlt das Wasser ab, ice cools water; das Glas nach und nach [im Kühlofen, Temperirofen] —, [in glassworks] to anneal the glass; das Gewitter kühlt die Luft ab, the thunder storm cools the air. *Fig.* Dieses Ereigniß hat meinen Eifer abgekühlt, this event has cooled my zeal or ardour; dies wird ihren Muth —, this will cool their courage. II. *v. intr.* [used with seyn] to become less hot, to cool. III. *v. r.* sich —, to grow cool. Das Wetter fängt an sich abzukühlen, the weather begins to cool.

Ábkühlfaß, *n.* [-sses, *pl.* -fässer] [in metallurgy] a cooling vat or cooler.

Ábkühlrinne, *f.* [*pl.* -n] [in metallurgy] cooling channel.

Ábkühlung, *f.* cooling, refreshing, [in chimistry] refrigeration.

Abkühlungsmittel, *n.* [in medicine] refrigerant.

Abkümmern, *v. r.* sich —, to wear one's self away with grief, to pine away.

Abkünden, Abkündigen, *v. tr.* 1) to publish [from a high place, from the pulpit], to proclaim, to make known, to notify, to announce. Ein Brautpaar —, to publish the bans of matrimony. 2) [a law term] to resign, to give up.

Abkündigung, *f.* 1) the act of proclaiming, publication, proclamation, the act of publishing bans. 2) [a law term] the act of giving up a claim, resignation.

Abkunft, *f.* 1) descent, birth, family, race, extraction, origin. Er ist von guter —, he is well born, or of a good family, gentle; von edler —, of noble birth or extraction; von gemeiner —, low-born, base-born. V. Herkunft, Abstammung. 2) [sometimes it is used for] accommodation, agreement. V. Abkommen.

Abküpfeln, *v. tr.* to cut off, [as exuberances] to lop. Den Weinstock —, to prune a vine.

Abküpfen, *v. tr.* to cut off, [as the extreme part of any thing] to lop.

Abkuppen, Abkupfen, *v. tr.* to top, to lop.

Abkürzen, *v. tr.* 1) to abridge, to shorten. Ein Wort —, to abbreviate a word; es läßt sich nicht —, [in mathematics] it is not reducible; sich das Leben —, to shorten one's life. 2) to lessen, to diminish. Jemands Lohn —, to curtail one's wages.

Abkürzer, *m.* [-s, *pl.* -] an abbreviator, abridger, epitomiser, or epitomist.

Abkürzung, *f.* 1) abridgement, shortening. Die — beim Schreiben, abbreviation, abbreviature, short-hand; die — der Brüche, [in arithmetic] reduction of fractions. 2) defalcation, deduction, diminution.

Abkürzungszeichen, *n.* abbreviature.

Abküssen, V. Abherzen.

Abkutschen, *v. intr.* [used with seyn] to drive away in a coach.

Ablachen, *v. r.* sich —, to laugh one's fill, to split one's sides with laughing, to tire with laughing.

Abladen, *ir. v. tr.* 1) to unlade, to unload, to discharge, to disburden. 2) *Fig.* to overthrow, to overturn.

Ablader, *m.* [-s, *pl.* -] an unloader, discharger.

Abladerlohn, *m.* fee for unloading.

Ablage, *f.* [*pl.* -n] 1) the act of giving an account, or bringing in one's accounts. 2) [a law term] a compensation made by parents to children in lieu of their inheritance. 3) a place of deposit.

Ablager, *n.* [-s, *pl.* -] 1) the act of alighting or putting up. 2) a place for rest, a resting-place. 3) [a law term] the privilege of the liege-lord of reposing and refreshing himself in convents and in the houses of his tenants.

Ablagern, *v. intr.* to separate from and encamp in another place.

Ablammen, *v. intr.* to have done yeaning.

Ablanden, *v. intr.* to shove off from the land, to weigh anchor, to set sail, to stand or put out to sea. = abländen.

Ablang, *adj.* and *adv.* somewhat long, longish. — rund, oblongly round.

Ablangen, *v. tr.* to reach, to fetch. Er kann es —, it is within his reach.

Áblängen, *v. tr.* 1) [in mining] to dig lengthwise. 2) [in carpentry] to hew lengthwise.

Ablaschen, *v. tr.* [with foresters] to point out a way through a forest by blazing the trees.

Ablaß, *m.* [-sses, *pl.* Ablässe] 1) the act of letting off, or draining a liquid body. 2) a sluice, a watergate, a floodgate. 3) [in mining] a drain, or watercourse. 4) indulgence, pardon, remission. Vollkommener —, plenary indulgence.

Ablaßbrief, *m.* letter of indulgence, of pardon. —**geld**, *n.* shrove money. —**horn**, *n.* a piece of horn used by shoemakers in paring the soles. —**kanzellei**, *f.* [an office at the court of Rome] penitentiary. —**kirche**, *f.* [a church where indulgences are to be had on certain days] station. —**kram**, *m.* sale of the pope's indulgences. —**krämer**, *m.* one that sells the pope's indulgences, a pardonner. —**pfennig**, V. —geld. —**prediger**, *m.* a preacher [seller] of indulgences. —**woche**, *f.* the week of Corpus Christi day.

Ablassen, *ir.* I. *v. tr.* 1) to let off, to let go, to slacken, to relax. Den Bogen —, to unbend the bow; einen Teich —, to let off a pond [for taking the fish]; einen Graben —, [in fortification] to saigner a mote; ein Faß Wein —, to broach, to tap a cask of wine; Wein —, to rack wine; ein Schiff —, to launch a vessel; einen Brief —, to send a letter. 2) to give up, to give over. Einem etwas —, to give over, to cede any one a thing; ich kann es so wohlfeil nicht —, I cannot afford it so cheap. 3) [among shoemakers] to pare [a sole].

II. *v. intr.* to cease from, to desist, to leave off, to give over. Syn. *a*) Ablassen, abtreten, überlassen. Ueberlassen signifies — not to prevent another's taking possession of a thing. Abtreten expresses a distinct declaration that one resigns a thing or right. Ablassen is to part with in the way of exchange or sale, and therefore only made use of with regard to saleable things. Of resigning a crown one says abtreten, but not ablassen. *b*) Ablassen, unterlassen, einhalten, aufhören, abstehen. Ablassen signifies to discontinue to do what one has till now done. Unterlassen does not comprehend this last idea. The virtuous man unterläßt das Böse [forbears to do evil]; the wicked one, reforming, läßt vom Bösen ab [ceases to do evil]. One says that a person läßt ab [leaves off] without further determining whether he will at a future time continue; that he hält ein [stops] with the intention of recommencing; and that he hört auf [ceases] not, immediately at least, to continue. Abstehen conveys the idea of desisting from a thing that we intended to do, or from a claim to which we believe that we have a right.

***Ablativ**, *m.* [-es, *pl.* -e] [in grammar] the ablative case.

Ablatten, *v. tr.* to take away the laths.

Ablauben, *v. tr.* to strip of the foliage, to unleave [a vine].

Ablauerer, *m.* [-s, *pl.* -] a lurker, an eaves-dropper.

Ablauern, *v. tr.* to obtain by watching or waylaying; to discover by secret observation. *Fig.* Die Gelegenheit —, to watch for an opportunity.

Ablauf, *m.* [-es] 1) the running or flowing off, away, or down. Der — des Meeres, the ebb, or ebbing of the sea. *Fig.* Vor — [mit —] des Jahres, before the end [with the end] of the year; der — einer Frist, the expiration of a term; der — eines Wechsels, time of payment; der — des Mondes, wane of the moon. 2) channel, outlet, vent, gutter, kennel, conduit; [in ships] —rinne, channels at the sides to allow the water to run off the decks, scupper-holes. 3) [in architecture] shafferoon.

Ablaufröhre, *f.* a waste-pipe, tunnel.

Ablaufen, *ir.* I. *v. intr.* [used with seyn] 1) to run or flow down, to run off, to go off. Ablaufendes Wasser, [a sea term] V. Ebbe; ein Schiff — lassen [vom Stapel laufen lassen], to launch a vessel; das Licht lauft ab, the candle runs; die Spulen sind abgelaufen, [among clothiers] the spools are empty; einen Brief — lassen, to dispatch a letter; die Uhr ist abgelaufen, the watch has run down; der Wechsel ist abgelaufen, the bill of exchange has become due; wie wird das —? what will be the end of it? gut oder übel —, to have a good or bad issue; dieß wird nimmer gut —, this will never turn out well; Einen — lassen, to fit one with a smart reply. 2) to lean from a right line, to decline. 3) [in sea language] Vor dem Winde — [abfallen], to bring the wind aft.

II. *v. r.* sich —, to grow weary by running, to tire with running.

III. *v. tr.* [u. w. haben] 1) to wear off by running. *Prov.* Sich die Hörner —, to sow one's wild oats, to ged rid of the impetuosity of temper; to grow wise by experience. *Fig.* Das habe ich längst an den Schuhen abgelaufen, I have known that long ago; sich die Hacken nach etwas —, to give one's self much trouble for attaining a thing. 2) to outrun. Einen im Wettlaufen —, to gain the prize in a race, to beat any one in running. *Fig.* Einem den Rang —, to outdo any one, to get the start of any one.

Abläufer, *m.* [-s, *pl.* -] 1) that which runs off. 2) [among clothiers] a large spool become empty. 3) [among weavers] a thread out of its place. 4) [a sea term] V. Speigat.

Ablaugen, *v. tr.* 1) to impregnate with lye. 2) to wash out or rinse the lye.

Abläugnen, *v. tr.* to deny, to disown, to abnegate. Er läugnet es steif und fest ab, he denies through thick and thin.

Abläugnung, *f.* the act of denying, abnegation.

Abläugnungseid, *m.* oath of abnegation.

Ablauschen, *v. tr.* to gain or to learn by listening, to overhear, to eaves-drop. Einen Vortheil —, to get a profit by listening.

† **Ablausen**, *v. tr.* 1) to louse, to take off lice. 2) *Fig.* to fleece, to cheat. Einem etwas —, to trick, to chouse, to do one out of a thing.

Abläuterfaß, *n.* [-sses, *pl.* -fässer] [in metallurgy] a kind of washing tub.

Abläuterkiste, *f.* [*pl.* -n] [in mining] a washing trunk.

Abläutern, *v. tr.* 1) to clarify, to filter, to clear, to refine, to purify, to fine. Wein —, to rack wine; Zucker —, to refine sugar. 2) [in mining] to buddle the ore.

Ableben, *v. intr.* to decease, to die [it is only used in the past part.]. Abgelebt [used with seyn], worn out by age, very old. V. Abgelebt.

Ableben, *n.* [—s] decease, death. Nach meines Vaters —, after my father's death.

Ablecken, *v. tr.* to lick a thing off [one's fingers].

Abledern, *v. tr.* 1) to skin. 2) † *Fig.* to beat, to thrash, to belabour, to drub.

Ableeren, *v. tr.* to clear, to empty. Den Tisch —, to clear the table.

Ablegen, I. *v. tr.* 1) to lay by, to lay away, to lay aside, to lay apart, to put, to put down, to take off. Eine Last —, to put down a load; die Handschuhe —, to take off one's gloves; die Kleider —, to put off one's clothes, to undress; abgelegte Kleider, left off clothes; sie legte ihren Schleier ab, she laid aside her veil; eine Form —, [in printing] to distribute the letters of a form; eine Karte —, to discard. *Fig.* eine Schuld —, to pay a debt; eine Predigt —, to deliver a sermon; einen Besuch —, to pay a visit; Rechenschaft —, to give an account, to render an account, to account for; Rechnung —, to give in an account, to bring in one's accounts, to submit them to examination; einen Eid —, to take an oath; dieser Mönch hat seine Gelübde abgelegt, this monk has taken the vows; ein Zeugniß —, to bear witness, to depose; einen Titel —, to quit a title; die Sterblichkeit —, to die. 2) to leave off [a coat &c.]. *Fig.* eine üble Gewohnheit —, to leave off, to throw off an ill habit. 3) [in gardening] to plant or set [carnations]. 4) [among foresters and in mining] to pay off.

II *v. intr.* 1) to bring forth [said of animals and in contempt of the clandestine parturition of an unmarried woman]. 2) [a sea term] to move from the shore, to remove into the roads. 3) *Fig.* to decline, to decay. V. Abnehmen.

Ábleger, *m.* [-s, *pl.* -] 1) a layer of a plant. V. Absenker. 2) a new swarm of bees.

Áblegespahn, *m.* [-es, *pl.* -spähne] [in printing] distributing rule.

Áblegung, *f.* the act of laying aside &c.

Áblehn, *n.* [-s, *pl.* -] appanage.

1. || **Áblehnen**, *v. tr.* to borrow. V. Ableihen, Abborgen, Borgen, Entlehnen.

2. **Áblehnen**, *v. tr.* 1) to transfer from a leaning position to another. Ein Brett von der Wand —, to remove a board from against the wall. 2) *Fig.* to decline, to refuse. Sie lehnten das Anerbieten ab, they declined the offer; eine Gerichtsbarkeit —, to decline a jurisdiction. Syn. Ablehnen, ausschlagen, verbitten. One says ausschlagen a proposition when one bluntly rejects it; ablehnen when some ground is given for the rejection. Ablehnen is therefore the more polite expression. Verbitten contains at the same time a request that we may be held excused for not accepting a proposition.

Áblehnung, *f.* the act of declining.

Áblelern, *v. tr.* 1) to perform a tune on the lyre. 2) *Fig.* to utter in a monotonous and disagreeable manner.

Ábleihen, *ir. v. tr.* to take from another upon credit, to borrow from.

Ábleihung, *f.* the act of borrowing.

Ábleinen, *v. tr.* to take off from the clothesline.

Ábleisten, *v. tr.* [with shoemakers] to take off from the last.

Ábleiten, *v. tr.* 1) to derive, to divert, to turn from its natural course, to lead away. Wasser —, to drain or turn off water; einen Fluß —, to divert a river from its usual channel; die Feuchtigkeiten im Körper —, to draw the humors from one part of the body to another; vom rechten Wege —, to guide a wrong way, to mislead, to misguide. 2) to deduce or draw, [as from a root] or cause. Ein Wort —, to derive a word.

Ábleiter, *m.* [-s, *pl.* -] a conductor of lightning.

Ábleitung, *f.* 1) a drawing from, or turning aside from a natural course or channel, derivation. Die — von Feuchtigkeiten im Körper, [in medicine] a drawing of humours from one part of the body to another, derivation, revulsion, antispasis; Feuchtigkeiten ableitende Mittel, antispastic medicines. 2) [in grammar] the drawing or tracing of a word from its root or original, derivation, etymology. 3) [the thing reduced or derived] derivation.

Ableitungs-kunst, *f.* the art of deducing or deriving words from their original, etymology. —schirm, *m.* an umbrella provided with a conductor of lightning. —silbe, *f.* a particle added to adjectives and substantives on account of derivation [as, ig, isch, heit, keit &c., freudig, kindisch, Menschheit, Lieblichkeit].

Áblenken, I. *v. tr.* to turn off from any direction, to divert, to avert. Ein Pferd von dem Wege —, to turn a horse from the road; einen Stoß —, to parry a thrust; die Gedanken von ernsthaften Gegenständen —, to turn off or divert the thoughts from serious objects; einen Verdacht von sich —, to remove or avert a suspicion. II. *v. intr.* to turn away, to deviate, to depart from. Von der Sache —, to deviate or ramble from the subject.

Áblenkung, *f.* the act of turning off &c.

Ablenkungsangriff, *m.* [in war] the act of drawing the enemy off from some design by threatening or attacking a distant part, diversion.

Áblernen, *v. tr.* to learn by looking and observing, to imitate. Einem etwas —, to learn a thing from any one by seeing and observing how it is done. Syn. Ablernen, absehen, abhören. One says that a person has abgelernt a thing from another, when he by narrowly observing how the other does it has contrived to do the like. This is the most usual expression. Absehen and abhören are merely two branches of ablernen. For instance, I say, ich sehe ab a trick from a juggler, when by close inspection I comprehend how he does it; ich lerne ab, when by practice I learn to do it as he does. One says of a person who in the theatre catches a melody from the singer, er hört dem Sänger eine Arie ab.

Áblesen, *ir. v. tr.* 1) to gather [fruits], to pick off. Das Ungeziefer —, to rid of vermin; Steine vom Acker —, to pick the stones in a field, to rid a field of stones; man hat abgelesen, [of a vineyard] the crop of grapes is gathered, the vintage is over. 2) to read aloud, to recite. Jährlich zweimal abzulesen, to be read twice a year; der Prediger hat seine Predigt nicht hergesagt, er hat sie abgelesen, the preacher did not recite his sermon, but read it from the book. 3) V. Zerlesen.

Ábleser, *m.* [-s, *pl.* -] 1) gatherer. 2) reciter.

Ábleugnen, V. Abläugnen.

Áblichten, *v. tr.* to make clear or bright.

Ábliebeln, *v. r.* sich —, to weaken one's self by much caressing.

Áblieben, I. *v. tr.* [among sportsmen] to caress and encourage a young hound when he has got the right scent. II. *v. r.* V. Abliebeln.

Áblieferer, *m.* [-s, *pl.* -] he who delivers up or in, bearer.

Abliefern, *v. tr.* to deliver up or in.

Áblieferung, *f.* the act of delivering up or in, delivery.

Ablieferungsschein, *m.* certificate of delivery. V. Lieferungsschein.

Ábliegen, *ir.* I. *v. intr.* [u. w. seyn] 1) to lie at a distance, [in sea language] to be distant. Der abgelegene Weg, by-path. 2) to lie for a given time. Abgelegener Wein, wine that has lain long, become mellow by age. II. *v. tr.* [u. w. haben] to rub off by lying down. III. *v. r.* sich —, to part or wear off by lying; = sich wund liegen, [of a bed-ridden person] to become sore by lying. Der Hund liegt sich die Haare ab, the dog loses its hair by much lying.

Áblisten, *v. tr.* to get, to obtain by tricks and cunning. Einem etwas —, to trick, to chouse any one out of a thing.

Áblocken, *v. tr.* 1) to decoy, to entice away, to lure away. 2) *Fig.* to get by flattery or coaxing, to draw out. Geheimnisse —, to pump out secrets; Einem sein Geheimniß —, to draw out a secret from one; Einem sein Geld —, to flatter any one out of his money; Einem Thränen —, to draw tears from one.

Áblockern, *v. tr.* to get loose and separate.

Áblohnen, *v. tr.* to pay off, to discharge.

Áblörschen, *v. tr.* [in mining] to sink a pit not far below the surface.

Áblöschen, *v. tr.* 1) to cool, to quench, to extinguish. Kalk —, [in building] to slake lime. 2) to rub out, to wipe off. Eine Rechnung —, to sponge out a reckoning.

Áblösen, I. *v. tr.* 1) to take off, to detach. Einen Strick —, to untie or undo a cord; ein Glied vom Körper —, to cut off, or to amputate a limb; eine Schildwache —, to relieve a sentinel; die Mannschaft in den Trancheen —, [in military affairs] to relieve the trenches; die Wache —, [in sea language] to set the watch; ablösende Mittel, [in medicine] solvent medicines, resolvents, pectorals. *Fig.* Eine Rente —, to buy off an annuity; ein Pfand —, to redeem or recover a pledge or pawn. 2) [in printing] to unlock. II. *v. r.* sich —, 1) to succeed by turns. Sich einander —, to relieve one another, to perform alternately or in turns, to alternate. 2) to part, to become disunited, to separate; sich —, to peel off, to drop off.

Áblöslich, *adj.* and *adv.* 1) what may be loosened or untied. 2) *Fig.* redeemable, recoverable.

Áblösung, *f.* 1) the act of taking off, loosening, untying, relieving, relief. Die — eines Gliedes vom Körper, amputation; die — eines Knotens, the loosening, untying or undoing of a knot. 2) *Fig.* [in law] ransom.

Áblöthen, *v. tr.* to unsolder.

Áblubern, V. Abledern.

Áblügen, *ir. v. tr.* to get by lying, to gain by telling a lie.

† **Áblugsen**, *v. tr.* 1) to perceive by lurking. 2) to get by roguery, to swindle out of.

Ábmachen, *v. tr.* 1) to undo, to loose, to loosen, to untie. 2) *Fig.* to settle, to arrange, to complete. Ein Geschäft —, to wind-up an affair; heute Nacht wollen wir die Sache —, this night we'll finish the business; gleich —, to cut short in an instant; abgemacht [among merchants] in order.

Ábmagern, *v. intr.* [u. w. seyn] to grow lean, to fall away. Den Falken — lassen, [in falconry] to unfatten a bird.

Ábmagerung, *f.* emaciation, wasting of the body.

Ábmähen, *v. tr.* to mow, to mow off, to cut down [grass].

1. **Ábmahlen**, *v. tr.* [past participle abgemahlen] to grind completely.

2. **Ábmahlen**, *v. tr.* [from Mahl, a mark] to mark out [as a field, the channel of a river].

3. **Ábmahlen**, *v. tr.* 1) to paint, to portray. Einen —, to draw one's picture. 2) *Fig.* to describe, to represent, to depict. Einen nach dem Leben —, to describe any one to the life.

Ábmahnen, *v. tr.* to advise to the contrary, to dissuade from, to dehort from.

Ábmahnung, *f.* dehortation, dissuasion.

Abmahnungsschreiben, *n.* dehortatory letter.

Ábmaischen, V. Abmeischen.

Ábmangeln, I. *v. tr.* to mangle thoroughly. II. *v. intr.* to finish mangling.

Ábmärgeln, V. Abmergeln.

Ábmarken, *v. tr.* to mark off [a piece of ground].

Ábmarkten, *v. tr.* to bargain down, to beat down.

Ábmarsch, *m.* [-es, *pl.* Abmärsche] the marching off, march, departure [of soldiers].

Ábmarschiren, *v. intr.* [u. w. seyn] 1) to depart, to decamp. 2) to march off. Sie sind heute abmarschirt, they marched off to-day.

Ábmartern, *v. tr.* 1) to torment, to excruciate, to torture, to worry, to plague, to vex. 2) to extort.

Ábmaß, *n.* [-es] **Ábmaße**, *f.* dimension.

Ábmäßigen, *v. tr.* to change the external qualities or accidents of any thing, to modify.

Ábmatten, I. *v. tr.* 1) to harass, to tire, to weary, to fatigue. Durch Arbeit —, to tire with labour; durch Hunger —, to enervate with fasting; sie waren ganz abgemattet, they were quite spent. 2) [among metallists] to dull [metals]. Abgemattetes Kohl, [in metallurgy] coal-dust. II. *v. r.* sich —, to spend one's self, to overweary one's self.

Ábmattung, *f.* 1) the act of harassing, tiring, or wearying. 2) weariness, lassitude, fatigue.

Ábmeiern, *v. tr.* to expel from or turn out of a farm.

Ábmeischen, I. *v. tr.* to mash thoroughly. II. *v. intr.* to have done mashing.

Ábmeißeln, *v. tr.* 1) to chisel off. 2) to smooth with a chisel. 3) to model with a chisel, to chisel out.

Ábmergeln, *v. tr.* to emaciate, to enervate.

Ábmerken, *v. tr.* to learn by imperceptible observation, to observe, to discover, to penetrate.

Ábmessen, *ir. v. tr.* 1) to measure off [as land]. Einen Acker —, to survey a field. 2) to give or take the quantity required or demanded. Drei Ellen von einem Zeug —, to measure and cut off three ells of a stuff; einen Vers —, to scan a verse; das — der Verse, scanning, scansion. *Fig.* Seine Schritte —, to walk slowly and considerately, to act with great circumspection; eine Sache nach einer andern —, to measure a thing by another; er mißt Andere nach sich ab, he judges of others by himself, he measures other people's corn by his own bushel; seine Neigungen nach seinem Vortheil —, to suit one's inclinations to one's interest; die Zeit abmessend, apportioning the time; das ist nicht abzumessen, there is no standard for it.

Ábmesser, *m.* [-s, *pl.* -] a measurer, surveyor.

Ábmessung, *f.* 1) measurement, mensuration. 2) *Fig.* proportioning &c.

Ábmetzen, *v. tr.* [among millers] to take a peck of any grain instead of payment.

Ábmiethen, *v. tr.* to hire from, to take in hire, to rent, to farm.

Ábmiether, *m.* [-s, *pl.* -] hirer, lessee.

Ábmisten, *v. tr.* to clear away dung.

Ábmitteln, V. Vermitteln.

Ábmodeln, *v. tr.* to form according to a model, to copy.

Ábmoosen, *v. tr.* to clear of moss, to free from moss. Einen Stein —, to scrape off the moss from a stone.

Ábmoosung, *f.* a freeing from moss, emuscation.

Ábmühen, *v. r.* sich —, to fatigue, to exert one's self. Er hat sich abgemüht, he exerted himself.

Ábmüßigen, I. *v. tr.* 1) to extort. V. Abnöthigen. Einem eine Erklärung —, to extort or force a declaration from any one. 2) to find time, leisure. Die Zeit —, to spare time from business; einen —, to withhold one from occupations, to disturb one. II. *v. r.* sich —; wenn ich mich — kann, if I can find leisure, if business will permit me.

Ábnageln, *v. tr.* [a sea term] to drive the treenails into a ship's sides or bottom.

Ábnagen, *v. tr.* to gnaw off. Einen Knochen —, to gnaw or pick a bone. *Fig.* der Kummer nagt ihm das Herz ab, his heart is consumed with grief, sorrow preys upon his heart.

Ábnagung, *f.* the act of gnawing off; picking.

Ábnähen, *v. tr.* to quilt, to embroider.

Ábnahme, *f.* [*pl.* -n] 1) the act of taking off or down. V. Abnehmung. Die — eines Gliedes, amputation. *Fig.* Die — einer Rechnung, audit. 2) *Fig.* [= Verminderung] diminution, decrease, decay, abatement, decrement. Die — der Kräfte, a decrease of strength; die — der Einkünfte, a decrease of revenue; die — des Handels, the decline of commerce; in — gerathen, to decay, to fail, to decline. 3) = Abgang. Die — der Waaren, sale of merchandise. Syn. Abnahme, Verfall. Verfall signifies such a degree of diminution or decay, that the thing is no longer what is was, and cannot by any amendment or reparation be placed in its original state. Abnahme only such degree of decline, that the thing does not cease to be what it was, nor is incapable of being placed in its former condition.

Ábnarben, *v. tr.* [among curriers] to scrape [a skin].

Ábnarren, *v. tr.* to get, to obtain by pranks and tricks.

Ábnaschen, *v. tr.* to nibble daintily.

Ábnehmen, *ir.* I. *v. tr.* 1) to take off, to take down or away. Den Hut —, to take off one's hat; die Maske —, to pull off the mask; einem Pferde die Hufeisen —, to unshoe a horse; die Ruderpinne —, [in sea language] to unship the tiller; Einem eine Last —, to take off a burden; Früchte —, to gather, or pluck fruits; das Joch —, to unyoke; den Rahm von der Milch —, to cream, to skim milk; die gedruckten Bogen —, [in printing] to take down the sheets; den Bart —, to shave the beard; den Schafen die Wolle —, to shear, to fleece the sheep; Einem den Fuß —, to cut off any one's foot, ein Glied —, to amputate a limb; ein Kalb —, *fig.* to wean a calf; die Karten — [= abheben], to cut. *Fig.* Einem Waaren —, to take or buy commodities from any one; eine Rechnung —, to audit an account; Einem einen Eid —, to take any one's oath; [among sportsmen] die Hunde —, to call off the dogs [when they get on a wrong scent]. 2) [in knitting, to contract the size of a stocking by taking two meshes into one] to narrow. 3) *Fig.* [= vermuthen, bemerken] to judge, to conclude, to measure. Dieß ist leicht abzunehmen, this is very easy to be seen; so viel ich — kann, for aught I perceive; sie konnten es aus seinem Betragen —, you might judge of it by his demeanour.

II. *v. intr.* to diminish, to grow less, to decrease. Die Höhe der Ströme nimmt ab, the streams are subsiding from their banks; der Mond nimmt ab, the moon wanes; beim abnehmenden Monde, at the wane of the moon; die Tage nehmen ab, the days are getting shorter, decreasing in length; die Hitze nimmt ab, the heat abates; seine Kräfte nehmen täglich ab, his strength fails daily; mein Gesicht nimmt ab, my eyesight fails; er nimmt zusehends ab, he wastes away sensibly.

Ábnehmer, *m.* [-s, *pl.* -] a buyer, purchaser, employer, consumer, customer, or chapman.

Ábneigen, I. *v. tr.* to incline, to decline, to bend downwards. II. *v. intr.* 1) to avert, to turn aside. 2) *Fig.* to render averse.

Ábneigung, *f.* 1) declination. 2) *Fig.* disinclination, repugnance, aversion, averseness, dislike. Eine große — gegen das schöne Geschlecht haben, to bear a great aversion for the fair sex; die —, die wir von Natur aus gegen die Arbeit haben, the repugnancy which we naturally have to labour; die natürliche —, antipathy.

Ábnicken, *v. tr.* [among sportsmen] to give [a hart &c.] a stab through the neck.

Ábnießeln, *v. tr.* [in mining] to wear out.

Ábnießen, *ir. v. tr.* [a law term] to have the usufruct of an estate.

Ábnieten, *v. tr.* to unrivet.

Ábnippen, *v. tr.* to taste any liquor.

Ábnöthigen, *v. tr.* to force, to extort, to wring from, to draw from.

Ábnützen, **Ábnutzen**, I. *v. tr.* 1) to waste, to wear out by use. Einen Anzug —, to wear out a suit of clothes; ein abgenutzter Besen, a broom worn to the stump. 2) [a law term] to have the use or the usufruct of &c. II. *v. r.* sich —, to wear out.

Ábnützer, *m.* [-s, *pl.* -] [a law term] usufructuary.

Ábnutzung, *f.* 1) wearing out, wasting. Die — der Schiffsgeräthschaften, [a sea term] wear and tear. 2) [a law term] usufruct.

Ábböden, *v. tr.* to deprive [a forest] of game.

Ábbödung, *f.* destruction of game.

Ábohrfeigen, *v. a.* Einen —, to box any one's ears well.

* **Abolíren**, *v. tr.* [a law term] to abolish.

* **Abolitión**, *f.* [a law term] abolition.

* **Abolitionsbrief**, *m.* a mandate of abolition.

* **Abominábel**, *adj.* V. Abscheulich.

* **Abónnement**, *n.* subscription.

* **Abonnént**, *m.* [-en, *pl.* -en] a subscriber.

* **Abonníren**, *v. r.* sich auf etwas —, to subscribe to a thing.

Ábordnen, *v. tr.* 1) to depute, to delegate, to constitute. 2) to arrange, dispose or order otherwise.

Ábordner, *m.* [-s, *pl.* -] [he that deputes another to parliament &c.] constituent.

Ábordnung, *f.* delegation, depntātion, constitution.

Ábort, *m.* [-es] a remote place, a privy.

* **Abortíren**, *v. tr.* to bring forth untimely, to abort, miscarry, to cast young. V. Mißgebären.

* **Abortíva**, *n.* and *pl.* abortives.

* **Abórtus**, *m.* abortion, miscarriage.

Ábpachten, *v. tr.* to farm, to lease, to rent from.

Ábpachter, *m.* [-s, *pl.* Abpächter] a farmer, lessee.

Ábpacken, *v. tr.* to unpack, to unlade, to unload, to discharge.

Ábpassen, *v. tr.* to measure with compasses, to square, to proportion. *Fig.* Die Gelegenheit —, to watch the opportunity; etwas übel —, to take one's time ill; sie hätten es nicht besser — können, they could not have seized a better opportunity; man muß ihn —, one must keep an eye upon him; Einen —, to lay wait for any one.

* **Abpatrouilliren**, *v. tr.* to send patrols over a tract of country occupied by the enemy.

Ábpeitschen, *v. tr.* 1) to whip off [an apple from a tree]. 2) to lash, to scourge, to whip, to flog soundly.

Ábpelzen, *v. tr.* 1) [among curriers] to beat a skin. † 2) *Fig.* to cudgel, to thump, to thrash. V. Abbamsen.

Ábpfählen, *v. tr.* to mark out with pales.

Ábpfänden, *v. tr.* to seize by law, to distrain.

Ábpflöcken, *v. tr.* to mark out with pegs.

Ábpflücken, *v. tr.* to pluck, to gather. Einen Vogel —, to pluck a bird.

Ábpflügen, *v. tr.* 1) to plough off, to divide by ploughing. 2) to finish ploughing. 3) to pay off [a debt] by ploughing for one's creditor. 4) to mark by ploughing.

Ábpicken, *v. tr.* to peck off; to snatch away by pecking.

Ábplacken, I. *v. tr.* to extort by vexations. II. *v. r.* sich —, to weary one's self by toil, to harass one's self.

Ábplagen, I. *v. tr.* to get by urgent and unceasing sollicitations, to obtain by dint of importuning, by tormenting. II. *v. r.* sich —, to weary one's self by toil.

† **Ábplärren**, *v. tr.* to utter with roaring, to bawl.

Ábplätten, I. *v. tr.* to smooth with an iron, to iron. Einen Draht —, [among goldsmiths] to flatten a wire with an iron. II. *v. intr.* to finish ironing.

Ábplattung, *f.* Die — der Erde, the oblateness of the earth.

Ábplaudern, V. Abschwatzen.

Ábplatzen, *v. intr.* [u. w. seyn] to loosen by bursting.

Ábplätzen, *v. tr.* 1) to cause to burst. 2) [among foresters] to blaze [trees sold]. 3) [with carpenters and coopers] to cut down [trees bought]. 4) [in coppermills] V. Abkühlen, Ablöschen.

Ábplündern, V. Plündern.

Ábpochen, *v. tr.* [in metallurgy] to separate by stamping; † *Fig.* to obtain by threats. Einem etwas —, to bully any one out of a thing, to get it by threats, to hector one out of a thing.

Ábpölen, V. Abhären.

Ábposaunen, *v. tr.* to perform on the trumpet.

Ábprägen, *v. tr.* 1) to coin, to mint, to stamp. 2) *Fig.* to represent, to copy, to stamp.

Ábprallen, *v. intr.* [u. w. seyn] to fly back, to rebound, to recoil.

Ábprallung, *f.* rebounding, recoiling, resilience. [mechanics] —swinkel, the angle of reflection.

Ábpredigen, *v. r.* sich —, to weary one's self by preaching.

Ábprellen, *v. tr.* to make rebound.

Ábpressen, *v. tr.* 1) to separate by pressing. 2) to press sufficiently. Sie pressen ihre Kleider beständig ab, they keep their clothes constantly in press. *Fig.* Einem etwas —, to force, exact, or extort a thing from one. V. Erpressen.

Ábpressung, *f.* 1) pressing. 2) *Fig.* exaction, extortion. V. Erpressung.

Ábprotzen, *v. tr.* [in gunnery] to take a cannon from the limbers. Abgeprotzt, unlimbered.

Ábprozessiren, *v. tr.* to get by litigation from.

Ábprügeln, *v. tr.* to beat, to thump, to maul, to cudgel, to thrash.

Ábpuffen, *v. tr.* 1) to separate by striking with the fist. Ein Kalb —, [among butchers] to skin a calf. † 2) to buffet, to beat. 3) [in chimistry.] V. Verpuffen.

Ábpusten, *v. tr.* to cleanse by blowing. Den Staub —, to blow away the dust.

Ábputzen, *v. tr.* to clean, to cleanse. Schuhe —, to wipe, to clean shoes; Geschirre —, to scour, to cleanse, to polish utensils; ein Pferd —, to rub down a horse; das Licht —, to snuff the candle; eine Mauer —, to smooth or finish down a wall; ein Haus —, to smooth the walls of a house; die Taue —, [a sea term] to cut off the loose strands or ends from the hempen cables. † *Fig.* Einen wacker —, to reprimand any one severely.

Ábquälen, *v. tr.* 1) to torment out of, to teaze from. 2) to plague very much, to harass, to worry.

‖ **Ábquellen**, *v. tr.* [= Absieden] to boil. Abgequellte Kartoffeln, boiled potatoes.

Ábquerlen, *v. tr.* to beat up, to mill [chocolate].

Ábquetschen, *v. tr.* 1) to separate by crushing, to crush off, to squeeze off. 2) to get, to obtain by squeezing.

Ábquicken, *v. tr.* [in metallurgy and in chimistry] 1) to refine the gold-ore by means of mercury. 2) to cool the refined silver.

Ábquieken, *v. tr.* to utter in a whining or squeaking tone.

Ábracadabra, *n.* [the name of a Syrian deity; a cabalistic word, which being written in the form of an inverted cone was used as a charm against certain diseases] Abracadabra.

Ábrädeln, *v. tr.* to cut by means of a little wheel. Teig —, to cut paste with the jagging-iron.

Ábrädern, I. *v. tr.* to separate by a wheel. II. *v. intr. Fig.* [used with seyn] Ich bin ganz abgerädert vom langen Fahren, I am almost jolted to death with travelling.

Ábraffen, *v. tr.* 1) to take away quickly, to take from the surface. 2) [in husbandry] to make up into sheaves [reaped corn].

Ábrafft, *m.* [-es] the corn, flour, grit, which is taken away clandestinely in mills.

Ábraham, [a name of men] Abraham. *Prov.* In —s Schooße sitzen, to enjoy wealth and affluence.

Abrahamsbaum, *m.* the officinal chaste-tree.

Ábrahmen, *v. tr.* to fleet cream or skim milk. Abgerahmte Milch, skim-milk, ‖ old milk.

Ábrainen, *v. tr.* to separate by marks, to border or fix the boundary of [a field] by landmarks.

Ábrändeln, **Ábränden**, *v. tr.* 1) to take away the border or margin to round off the edge. Geld —, to clip money. 2) to border, to edge duly.

Ábranften, *v. tr.* to rid of the border or edge.

Ábranken, *v. tr.* to prune [a vine].

Ábrappen, *v. tr.* Die Trauben —, to pick the grapes of the stalk.

Ábrasen, *v. tr.* to graze, to eat off, to browse or crop the grass.

Ábraspeln, *v. tr.* to rasp off, to smooth by rasping.

Ábrathen, *ir. v. tr.* 1) to dissuade, to dehort. Einem abrathen, to advise any one to the contrary; man hat ihm diese Reise abgerathen, or man hat ihm von dieser Reise abgerathen, they dissuaded him from undertaking this journey; der Minister rieth dem Fürsten diese Maßregel ab, the minister dissuaded the prince from adopting this measure; er rieth ihm von seinem Vorhaben ab, he dissuaded him from his purpose. 2) to hit upon by accident, to guess.

Ábrathung, *f.* dissuasion, dehortation.

Abrathungsschreiben, *n.* dehortatory letter.

Ábrauben, V. Rauben.

Ábrauchen, *v. intr.* [in chimistry] to fly off in vapours or fumes, to evaporate.

Ábräuchern, *v. tr.* to dry in smoke, to smoke duly.

Ábrauchschale, *f.* [*pl.* -n] [in chimistry] a vessel for evaporating [fluids &c.].

Ábraufen, I. *v. tr.* to pull off, to tear off. II. *v. r.* sich —, to exhaust one's self with scuffling.

Ábraum, *m.* 1) [among foresters] chips of wood. 2) [in mining] shelf. 3) [in building] rubbish.

Ábräumen, *v. tr.* 1) to take away, to remove, to clear. Den Tisch —, to clear the table, to take away; die Teller &c. —, to take away, to remove the plates &c.; ein Gesims —, to take down things from the shelves. 2) [among foresters] to remove the trees which are cut down, to clear or thin a forest.

Ábraupen, *v. tr.* to rid or clear of caterpillars.

Abráxas, *m.* [the name given by the heretic Basilides to God and Jesus Christ, worshipped under the figure of Isis, Osiris, and other Egyptian gods, as also under the figure of animals, with the head of a cock, a lion &c., the body of a man, and the tail of a serpent. This word was employed as a talisman] Abrasax, Abraxas.

Ábrechen, *v. tr.* 1) to clear with a rake, to rake. 2) to rake off.

Ábrechnen, *v. tr.* 1) to deduct. 2) to settle accounts, to make up accounts. Mit Einem —, to settle with one; wir haben mit einander abgerechnet, we have passed accounts with one another.

Ábrechnung, *f.* 1) deduction, discount. 2) settlement, adjustment, liquidation. — halten, to balance accounts; auf —, on account.

Ábrechte, *f.* [among clothiers] the wrong side of cloth.

Ábrechten, *v. tr.* 1) to get by a lawsuit. 2) [among clothiers] to dress the wrong side of cloth.

Abrèchts, *adv.* V. Verkehrt.

Ábrecken, *v. tr.* [in making ironplate] to stretch duly.

Ábrede, *f.* [*pl.* -n] 1) the thing agreed on, or concerted, an agreement, an accord. — nehmen, to concert together, to make an agreement, an appointment; ich werde mich an unsere — halten, I shall keep or stick to our agreement. 2) denial, contradiction. Ich bin es nicht in —, I do not deny it, I do not disown it.

Ábreden, I. *v. tr.* 1) to concert, to agree upon. Ein abgeredeter Handel, a concerted affair; abgeredeter Maßen, according to contract, as agreed to. 2) V. Abrathen. II. *v. r.* sich —, to fatigue one's self by talking.

Ábregeln, *v. tr.* to adjust by rule or method, to regulate.

Ábregnen, I. *v. tr.* to beat off [the flowers] by rain. II. *v. imp.* to cease to rain. Es hat abgeregnet, is has done raining.

Ábreiben, *ir.* I. *v. tr.* 1) to rub, to rub off. Den Koth von den Schuhen —, to scrape one's shoes. Die Saiten —, to scour catguts. 2) to rub duly or thoroughly. Farben —, to grind colours. 3) to wear out by rubbing. Die Farben eines Gemähldes [beim Putzen] —, to efface the colours of a painting; das —, attrition; das Abgeriebenseyn, attriteness, attrition. II. *v. r.* sich —, to wear by rubbing. Ein Tau reibt sich ab, a cable chafes.

Ábreibung, *f.* attrition.

Ábreichen, *v. tr.* to attain any thing distant, to reach. Wenn ich es — kann, if it is within my reach; (der Hut hängt zu hoch) ich kann ihn nicht —, I cannot reach it down.

Ábreifen, I. *v. tr.* 1) [among locksmiths] to

take away the sharp edges. 2) to unhoop. II. *v. intr.* [used with seyn] to grow quite ripe. Das Obst — lassen, to let the fruit get ripe, or ripen.

Ábreihen, *v. tr.* to take from a string, to unstring.

Ábreise, *f.* a going away, departure.

Ábreisen, *v. tr.* to depart, to set off. Als er abgereist war, when he had departed, had gone away; im Begriffe abzureisen, on the point of setting out.

Ábreißen, *ir.* I. *v. tr.* 1) to pull off, tear off, pluck off, or break off. Einen Zweig —, to slip off a twig; reiß es ab, rend it off; Planken von der Seite eines Schiffes —, to rip off planks from a ship's side; einer Taube den Kopf —, to pull off a pigeon's head; ein Haus —, to pull down a building. *Fig.* Doch ich will nicht das ganze Reich —, [1. Kings, xi] I will not rend away all the kingdom. 2) to wear out, to wear away, to wear off. Ein abgerissener Mensch, a ragged fellow. 3) to sketch. Eine Landschaft —, to trace off a landscape. II. *v. intr.* [u. w. seyn] to tear, to break. *Fig.* Meine Geduld ist abgerissen, my patience is gone, at an end.

Ábreißer, *m.* [-s, *pl.* -] 1) one who pulls off, tears off. 2) an instrument for sketching or tracing lines or figures.

Ábreißung, *f.* 1) the act of pulling from, avulsion. 2) [in music] a sudden stop.

Ábreiten, *ir.* I. *v. intr.* [u. w. seyn] to ride away, to set off on horseback. II. *v. tr.* [u. w. haben] 1) to tear off, to destroy, to wear out by riding [one's breeches]. Ein Hufeisen —, to cast or throw a shoe. 2) to measure a distance by riding it. 3) to manage, to break or break in a horse. Ein auf der Schule abgerittenes [ein zugerittenes] Pferd, a managed, or broken horse. 4) to harass by riding. Ein Pferd —, to override a horse. 5) V. Zurücklegen. Er hat zehn Meilen in einer Stunde abgeritten, he rode ten miles in the hour. III. *v. r.* sich —, 1) to fatigue one's self by riding. 2) to chafe one's self by riding.

Ábrennen, *ir.* I. *v. intr.* to run away. II. *v. r.* sich —, to fatigue one's self by running. III. *v. tr.* 1) to run off, to push off. 2) to leave behind in running, to overrun, to outrun.

Ábrichten, *v. tr.* to regulate, to adjust. Das Stabeisen —, [in forges] to straighten hammered iron; die Schienen —, to bend tires; ein Brett —, [among joiners] to level a board with a plane; den Boden —, [among coopers] to smooth the heads of a cask; die Ecken eines Kistchens glatt —, [among cabinet-makers] to smooth the corners of a box; die Mauer —, [among masons] to level a wall. *Fig.* Ein Pferd —, to break or rough-ride a horse; einen Hund —, to break or train a dog; einen Falken —, to man a hawk; auf Karten oder Taschenspielerkünste —, to teach tricks; er ist gut darauf abgerichtet, he understands his part well, he knows his cue; das — eines Füllens, the breaking in of a foal.

Abricht-hammer, *m.* [in forges] a hammer for straightening hammered iron. —**peitsche**, *f.* [in manege] shammbrie, horsewhip. —**stab**, —**stock**, *m.* [in forges] an anvil for straightening hammered iron.

Ábriegeln, *v. tr.* to bolt up, to fasten with a bolt. V. Verriegeln.

Ábrieseln, *v. intr.* [u. w. seyn] to drizzle down, to glide gently down.

Ábriffeln, *v. tr.* to pull off with a flax-comb. *Fig.* Einen —, to reprimand any one severely.

Ábrinden, *v. tr.* to take off the bark, to bark, to rind, to peel. Abgerindet, unbarked.

Ábrindern, *v. intr.* to cease longing for the bull [said of cows].

Ábrindig, *adj.* Das Brod ist —, the crust of the bread is detached from the crumb. V. Abgebacken, in Abbacken.

1. **Ábringen**, *v. tr.* to unring, to deprive of a ring or rings.

2. **Ábringen**, *ir.* I. *v. tr.* 1) to get, to obtain by wrestling. 2) to separate by wrestling. 3) to wring sufficiently [as linen]. Sich die Hände —, to wring one's hands. II. *v. r.* sich —, 1) to weary one's self by wrestling. 2) sich — im Todeskampfe, to struggle or writhe in agony.

Ábrinnen, *ir. v. intr.* [u. w. seyn] to run off, to run or flow down.

Ábrispen, *v. intr.* to fall out of the panicles [said of oats].

Ábriß, *m.* [-sses, *pl.* Abrisse] the first draught, delineation, sketch. Einen — von etwas nehmen, to take off a thing; ein — der Geschichte, an epitome, epitomy of history.

Ábritt, *m.* [-es, *pl.* -e] the riding away on horseback.

* **Abrogiren**, *v. tr.* to abrogate, to repeal, to annul, to abolish [a law].

Ábrohren, *v. tr.* 1) to rid, to clear of reeds. 2) to cover with reeds. Abgerohrt, reeded.

Ábrollen, I. *v. intr.* [used with seyn] 1) to roll away, to roll down, to run down. 2) to finish mangling. II. *v. tr.* [u. w. haben] 1) to roll away. 2) to separate by rolling. 3) to unroll, to unfold. 4) to mangle, to calender sufficiently [linen].

Ábrosten, *v. intr.* [used with seyn] to rust off.

Ábrösten, *v. tr.* to roast thoroughly.

Ábröthen, I. *v. intr.* to part with red. II. *v. tr.* to dye red.

Ábrotten, *v. intr.* [u. w. seyn] to rot off [said of corn].

Ábrücken, *v. tr.* to remove, to move off, to withdraw. Eine Leiter —, to make a ladder heel.

Ábrudern, *v. intr.* [u. w. seyn] to row off.

Ábruf, *m.* V. Abrufung.

Ábrufen, *ir.* I. *v. tr.* 1) to publish aloud, to proclaim, to cry. Die Stunden —, to cry the hours about the streets [said of a watchman]. 2) to call off, to call away. Einen — lassen, to send for one; einen Gesandten —, to recall an envoy; die Hunde —, [among sportsmen] to call off the hounds. 3) to reach by calling. Es läßt sich —, it is within call. II. *v. intr.* to call for the last time. Der Nachtwächter ruft ab, the night-watch calls for the last time. III. *v. r.* sich —, to tire one's self by calling.

Ábrufung, *f.* the act of calling off, call, recall, avocation.

Abrufungs-brief, *m.* —**schreiben**, *n.* avocatory letter, order of recall. —**schuß**, *m.* signal of recall [made by a gun].

Ábrühren, *v. tr.* to stir up or about, to beat up. Die Suppe mit einem Ei —, to beat up an egg in the broth.

Ábrunden, **Ábründen**, *v. tr.* to make round, to round. *Fig.* Einen Redesatz —, to round a period.

Ábrupfen, *v. tr.* to pluck off, to pluck. Blätter —, to pick off leaves. *Fig.* [falsche Spieler] haben ihn abgerupft, have fleeced him.

Ábrüsten, *v. tr.* to take down a scaffold.

Ábrutschen, *v. intr.* [used with seyn] 1) to slip or slide off or down, to glide down. † 2) to take one's departure in a shabby manner. *Fig.* [in contempt] to die.

Ábrütteln, *v. tr.* to shake off.

Ábsäbeln, *v. tr.* to cut off [with a sword or sabre]. Einem den Kopf —, to cut off any one's head.

Ábsacken, I. *v. tr.* 1) to take the sacks off, to unload, to disburden. Einen Esel —, to take the bags from an ass. 2) to divide into sacks. II. *v. intr.* [a sea term] Auf einem Fluß —, to drop down a river with the tide, to sag with the stream.

Ábsäen, *v. tr.* 1) [among curriers] to besprinkle a hide with unbolted meal. 2) V. Besäen.

Ábsage, *f.* 1) countermanding, counter-order. 2) a disowning [of friendship, of a right]. 3) a defiance, a challenge.

Absagebrief, *m.* 1) a letter of renunciation or a countermanding. 2) a declaration of enmity, challenge, letter of defiance.

Ábsagen, I. *v. tr.* to countermand, to counterorder, to revoke, to retract. Eine Einladung —, to disinvite one; einen Besuch — lassen, to send an excuse. II. *v. intr.* 1) to renounce, to give up. Der Welt —, to forsake the world; der Wollust, dem Satan —, to renounce the flesh and the devil; seinem Glauben —, to abjure one's faith. 2) to denounce friendship, to break with one, to declare hostility. Ein abgesagter Feind, a sworn, declared, mortal or deadly enemy.

Ábsägen, *v. tr.* to saw off. Die Wankanten oder Schillstücke von dem Holze —, [a sea term] to take off the slabs.

Ábsägung, *f.* a sawing off.

Ábsahnen, *v. tr.* [to take off the cream] to skim [milk].

Ábsatteln, I. *v. tr.* to take off the saddle from a horse. Ein Pferd —, to unsaddle a horse. *Fig.* Das Pferd hat ihn abgesattelt, the horse has thrown him off. II. *v. intr.* to alight from one's horse.

Ábsatz, *m.* [-es, *pl.* Absätze] 1) stop, pause, intermission. Ein Glas ohne — austrinken, to empty a glass at one draught. 2) sale, vent. Schnellen — haben, to have ready or quick sale. 3) the place, where a straight line is interrupted. Der — an einem Berge, break, shelf; der — an einem Weinstocke, articulation in a vine; der — an einem Rohre, knot; der — an einer Mauer, settle; der — an einer Treppe &c., landing-place, the stair-head; der — an einem Fahrschachte, [in mining] a shamble; der — an Schuhen, Stiefeln, the heel; der — in einem Liede, stanza, stave; der — in Versen, cadence; der — in der Musik, a stop or intermission in music, a pause [marked thus 𝄐]; der — in einem Buche oder im Drucken, break; die Absätze in einer Rede, the pauses of a discourse; der — in Capiteln &c., paragraph [§]; in Absätzen, at intervals, intermittingly. 4) the act of pausing in music, pause.

Absatz-draht, *m.* cobler's thread used for heels on shoes and boots. —**holz**, *n.* wood used for making a sort of heels. —**kuchen**, *m.* chips of leather used for making heels. —**leder**, *n.* heelband. —**pflock**, *m.* heeltap. —**zwecke**, *pl.* heelpegs. —**macher**, —**schneider**, *m.* heel-maker. —**ort**, *m.* pegging-awl.

Ábsätzig, *adj.* intermissive. Ein —er Ort, [in mining] a start, or leap.

Ábsäubern, *v. tr.* to cleanse, to clean.

† **Ábsaufen**, *ir.* I. *v. tr.* v. Abtrinken. II. *v. r.* sich —, to ruin one's self by drinking.

Ábsäugeln, diminutive of Absaugen.

Ábsaugen, *ir. v. tr.* 1) to suck off. 2) to weaken by sucking.

Ábsäugen, *v. tr.* 1) to suckle to the fill. 2) to wean a child. 3) [in gardening] to graft by approach, to inarch.

Ábschaben, *v. tr.* to scrape off, to shave off, to rub off, to abrade, [a sea term] to grave [a ship]. Die Rinde von dem Brode —, to chip bread; Wurzeln —, to scrape roots; ein abgeschabtes Tuch, a worn-out, or thread-bare cloth; das —, the act of rubbing off, abrasion.

Ábschabsel, *n.* [-s, *pl.* -] shaving, paring. Das — von Lammsfellen, lambskin paring or shreds.

Ábschach, *m.* [= Doppelt Schach] check to the king and queen at the same time.

† **Ábschachern**, *v. tr.* 1) [in contempt] to chop, to barter. 2) to beat down in bargaining.

Ábschachteln, *v. tr.* to rub or polish with shave-glass, to smooth.

Ábschaffen, I. *v. tr.* to remove, to part with, to give up. Seine Bedienten —, to dismiss one's servants; Pferde und Wagen —, to part with carriage and horses; er hat seine Hunde abgeschafft, he has rid himself of his dogs; Soldaten —, to disband troops; Gesetze —, to abrogate, abolish, annul, or repeal laws; Mißbräuche —, to reform, to abolish abuses. Syn. Abschaffen, Abstellen. Abstellen is said generally of bad customs only; abschaffen both of good and indifferent. Abuses are abgestellt and abgeschafft; useful and unhurtful practices merely abgeschafft and not abgestellt. II. *v. r.* sich —, V. Abarbeiten.

Ábschaffung, *f.* 1) discharging, dismission. 2) abrogation, abolition, abolishment, reforming.

Ábschacken, *v. tr.* [a sea term] to fleet a tackle.

Ábschäkern, *v. tr.* to get by toying, joking.

Ábschälen, I. *v. tr.* to divest of the bark or husk, to decorticate, to peel. Obst —, to pare fruits; Grüne Nüsse —, to shell walnuts; Mandeln —, to blanch almonds; eine Pomeranze —, to peel an orange; einen Baum —, to bark a tree. II. *v. r.* sich —, to peel. V. Schälen.

Ábschalmen, *v. tr.* [among foresters] to blaze [a tree].

Ábschälung, *f.* peeling, paring, blanching, barking, decortication.

Ábschärfen, *v. tr.* 1) to take away the sharp edges, to dull the edge or point, to blunt. Einen Karnieß —, to chamfer a cornice; eine Ecke —, [among bookbinders] to pare the cover of a book. 2) to form to an edge, to sharpen. 3) [among sportsmen] to cut off.

Ábschärfmesser, *n.* [-s, *pl.* -] [among shoemakers and glovers] a paring knife.

Ábscharren, *v. tr.* to take away by scraping, to cleanse by scraping, to scrape or scratch off, to grate off.

Ábscharricht, **Ábscharrsel**, *n.* [-s] shavings.

Ábschatten, *v. tr.* 1) to shadow out, to adumbrate. 2) to shadow, to delineate faintly. 3) to take a profile, shade. Eine Person —, to take the shade of a person.

Ábschattiren, *v. tr.* to adumbrate, to shadow out. V. Schattiren.

Ábschattung, *f.* 1) adumbration, sciagraphy. 2) V. Schattenbild.

Ábschätzen, *v. tr.* 1) to estimate, to appraise. 2) V. Herabsetzen [not much used].

Ábschätzung, *f.* 1) estimation, appraisement. 2) V. Herabsetzung [not much used].

Ábschauen, I. *v. intr.* to look down. II. *v. tr.* V. Absehen.

Ábschauern, *v. tr.* to partition off.

Ábschaufeln, *v. tr.* to remove, to clean with a shovel.

Ábschaukeln, I. *v. tr.* 1) to take away by swinging. 2) to throw down by swinging. II. *v. r.* sich —, to tire by swinging.

Ábschaum, *m.* [-es] scum, dross. *Fig.* Der — des Volks, the dregs, the refuse of the people. Syn. Abschaum, Hefe. When used with regard to men both words signify the most despicable part of them. Abschaum, however, refers to moral depravity generally and in all classes of society, Hefe to the lowest only. Thus, the most depraved part of the lowest people is called contemptibly die Hefe des Volkes [the dregs of the people]; but a profligate vilain, be his rank high or low, belongs to the Abschaum des menschlichen Geschlechtes [scum of mankind].

Ábschäumen, *v. tr.* to scum, to skim.

Ábschäumung, *f.* scumming, skimming.

Ábscheeren, V. Abscheren.

Ábscheiden, I. *ir. v. tr.* 1) to separate, to divide, to part. V. Scheiden. Gold von Kupfer —, to part gold and copper. 2) [a law term] to give children their portion and to exclude them from all future pretensions. II. *v. intr.* [u. w. seyn] to depart. Von der Welt —, to depart this life, to die; die Abgeschiedenen, the deceased, the departed; er führt ein abgeschiedenes Leben, he leads a solitary life. V. Abgeschieden.

Ábscheiden, *n.* death, decease.

Ábscheider, *m.* [-s, *pl.* -] refiner; [in metallurgy] one, who parts gold and silver with aqua fortis.

Ábscheidung, *f.* separating, parting.

Abscheidungsthätigkeit, *f.* that agency in the animal economy that consists in secreting the nutritive parts from aliment.

‡ **Ábschein**, [-es] V. Abglanz.

Ábschelfern, V. Abschälen.

Ábschenken, *v. tr.* 1) to measure out liquor. 2) to pour out the concluding draught. 3) = aufhören zu säugen. Ein Kind —, to wean a child.

Ábscheren, *ir. v. tr.* to shave, to shear. Die Wolle am Halse und Kopfe eines Schafes —, [in husbandry] to beard or to bard wool.

Ábscheren, *v. tr.* to separate by a partition.

Ábscherzen, *v. tr.* to get, to obtain by jesting [joking].

Ábscheu, *m.* [-es] 1) abhorrence, abhorrency, detestation, abomination, aversion, loathing. — vor etwas haben, to abhor a thing; mein — wird durch euch vermehrt, my horror encreases from what you preach; mit — erfüllt, abhorrent. 2) [the object of abhorrence] abhorring, abomination. Ein — seyn, to be an abomination, to be detested.

Ábscheuchen, *v. tr.* to fright away, to scare off.

Ábscheuern, I. *v. tr.* to scour off, to clear away. † *Fig.* to reprimand. II. *v. r.* sich —, to wear off.

Abscheúlich, I. *adj.* 1) abominable, detestable, horrid, horrible. Ein —er Mensch, an abandoned wretch; ein —er Gestank, an abominable stink. † 2) very great, vast, enormous, prodigious. II. *adv.* 1) abominably, † 2) vastly, prodigiously.

Abscheúlichkeit, *f.* horribleness, abominableness, atrocity, enormity, blackness, loathsomeness, ghastliness.

Ábschichten, *v. tr.* 1) V. Schichten. 2) [a law term] to exclude a person from future inheritance by the present payment of a certain sum.

Ábschicken, *v. tr.* to send away, to dispatch. Einen eignen Bothen —, to dispatch an express; einen Brief mit der Post —, to send a letter by the post.

Ábschickung, *f.* sending away, dispatch, despatch.

Ábschieben, *ir.* I. *v. tr.* 1) to shove off, push off, move off. Einen Tisch von der Wand —, to remove a table from the wall. *Fig.* Etwas von sich —, to exonerate, to exculpate one's self; er will es von sich — und mir zuschieben, he wishes to clear himself and lay it at my door. 2) to separate by shoving. 3) [at nine-pins] Einen —, to carry more pins than another. 4) [at nine-pins] to diminish by carrying pins [a debt]. II. *v. intr.* to lose the young teeth [applied to cattle and sheep]. Die Füllenzeichen —, to lose the colt's teeth.

Ábschied, *m.* [-es, *pl.* -e] 1) dismission, discharge. Einem seinen — geben, to dismiss, to discharge, to discard one; einem Regimente den — geben, to disband a regiment; einem Soldaten den — geben, to discharge a soldier; seinen — verlangen, to ask one's dismission, to solicit the discharge, to tender, to give in one's resignation. *Fig.* Der — aus diesem Leben, departure from this life, death. 2) letters testimonial, a certificate. 3) the decision of an assembly, of a judge, and the writing which contains this decision, ein gerichtlicher —, a decree; Reichs —, recess. 4) leave, farewell, adieu. — nehmen, to take leave, to bid farewell [adieu], to shake hands. † *Fig.* Hinter der Thüre — nehmen, to go away without bidding farewell, to take French leave, to make off. V. Abdankung, Entlassung.

Abschieds-nehmen, *n.* leave-taking. —s**audienz**, *f.* audience of leave. —s**besuch**, *m.* farewell-visit. —s**brief**, *m.* 1) letter of discharge, discharge. 2) letters testimonial, certificate. 3) farewell-letter. —s**kuß**, *m.* parting-kiss. —s**predigt**, *f.* valedictory sermon. —s**rede**, *f.* farewell speech. —s**schmaus**, *m.* valedictory dinner or supper, parting treat. —s**trunk**, *m.* parting-cup.

Ábschiefern, *v. tr.* and *v. r.* sich —, to split off, to peel off in thin flakes, or scales.

Ábschielen, *v. tr.* to learn a thing from another by looking by stealth and observing how it is done. V. Absehen.

Ábschienen, *v. tr.* 1) to secure by splints, to splint. 2) [a broken leg &c.] to take off the splints. 3) [in mining] to measure out a mine.

Ábschiener, *m.* [-s, *pl.* -] V. Markscheider.

Ábschießen, *ir.* I. *v. tr.* 1) to shoot, to shoot off, to discharge, to let fly. Ein Feuergewehr —, to shoot off, to fire, to discharge fire-arms; einen Pfeil —, to shoot, or to let fly an arrow. 2) to strike off or down by shooting, to shoot. Den Vogel —, to hit, to shoot, bring down the bird; eine Hand &c. —, to shoot off a hand &c. 3) to surpass in shooting, to excel in shooting. Einen —, to outshoot any one. II. *v. intr.* to make an end of shooting, [among sportsmen] to cease shooting. 2) [used with seyn] to shoot down, slide or slip down; to fall rapidly, to precipitate. Hier schießt das Wasser stromweise ab, here the water rushes down in torrents. 3) to lose colour, to fade.

Ábschießung, *f.* the act of shooting, discharging &c.

Ábschiffen, I. *v. tr.* to transport or convey in a ship, to ship off, to carry away on board of a ship. II. *v. intr.* to set sail. Bei schönem oder schlechtem Wetter —, to sail with fair or foul weather.

Ábschildern, *v. tr.* 1) to picture, to paint, to draw. 2) *Fig.* to describe in words, to draw, to picture, to depict, to depaint.

Ábschilderung, *f.* 1) painting. 2) *Fig.* picture, description in words.

Ábschinden, *ir. v. tr.* 1) to strip of the skin, to skin, to flay, to excoriate. Sich den Arm —, to tear one's arm; einem Ochsen die Haut — [abziehen], to flay an ox; das Geschirr hat das Pferd abgeschunden, the harness has galled the horse; die Karren haben im Vorbeifahren diesen Baum abgeschunden, the carts in passing have peeled the tree. 2) *Fig.* to harrass, to excess.

Ábschirren, *v. tr.* to unharness, to ungear [horses].

Ábschlachten, I. *v. tr.* to slaughter animals for food, for market, to kill, to slay, to butcher. II. *v. intr.* to finish slaughtering.

Ábschlacken, *v. tr.* to rid of slacks.

Ábschlaffen, *v. tr.* to slacken, to relax.

Ábschlag, *m.* [-es, *pl.* Abschläge] 1) the thing beaten, or hewen off, chips, fragments; [among foresters] V. Abraum. Abschläge [among letter founders] matrices. 2) rebound, rebounding. Der — einer Kugel, the rebound of a ball. 3) a future account. Auf —, on account, in part payment; auf — geben, to give before-hand, by anticipation; auf — nehmen, to take before-hand. 4) diminution, abatement. — des Preises, a lessening, sinking of the price. 5) [in building] reduct. 6) a fall, outlet, vent [of a pond]. 7) refusal.

Abschlags-anleihe, *f.* a loan on condition that every year part of the stock be repaid, annuity. —zahlung, *f.* payment on account.

Ábschlageisen, *n.* [-s, *pl.* -] V. Schmiedeeisen.

Ábschlagen, *ir.* I. *v. tr*) 1. to separate by beating, knocking or hewing. Abgeschlagenes Obst, windfall; Früchte —, to beat down corn; einem den Kopf, die Hand —, to strike off, to sever one's head, hand; ein Gerüst —, to take down a scaffold; ein Zelt —, to strike a tent; [in printing] das Format —, to unlock; eine Presse —, to break down; [in sea language] die Segel —, to unbend the sails; [among furriers] ein Stück Pelzwerk —, to clip a piece of a fur. 2) to give another direction by beating. Den Feind —, to repel or repulse the enemy; einen Teich —, to drain a pond; das Wasser —, to lead off the water; sein Wasser —, to make water, to piss, to stale. 3) *Fig.* to deny what is solicited or required, to refuse. Einem etwas —, to refuse, deny; er hat es rund abgeschlagen, he has given a flat refusal. 4) to strike off a copy. Eine Münze in Blei —, to impress, to stamp a coin in lead. 5) to beat well. Das Eierweiß mit dem Quirl —, to beat the white of an egg with a mill; † Einen —, to beat any one soundly, to maul him. 6) to diminish, to lessen. II. *v. r.* sich —, to depart from a place, to remove from a place. Ich schlug mich rechts vom Wege ab, I left the road, and turned to the right; das Wild schlägt sich ab, [among sportsmen] the game flies, runs away [when it separates from its kind]. III. *v. intr.* 1) to abate, to fall. Der Preis schlägt ab, the price falls; das Brod schlägt ab, the bread diminishes in price; das Getreide schlägt ab, the price of corn falls; die Kälte schlägt ab, the cold abates. *Fig.* Die Kuh schlägt ab, the cow gives less milk than before. 2) to fly back, to rebound. Die Kugel schlägt ab, the ball rebounds. Syn. Abschlagen, verweigern, versagen. Abschlagen refers to a wish or request; versagen, and verweigern to the thing wished for or requested. One says: I begged him to lend me a hundred florins, but my request he has abgeschlagen [denied], and the hundred florins verweigert or versagt [refused]. It is less usual to say versagen a wish, verweigern a request.

Ábschlagewisch, *m.* [-es, *pl.* -e] a wisp of straw used in saltworks for cleansing the saltpans.

Ábschlägig, *adj.* 1) easily broken, brittle. —e Stücke, fragments, splinters. 2) containing a refusal. Eine —e Antwort, a refusal, repulse, denial; eine —e Antwort bekommen, to be refused, to meet with a repulse.

Ábschläglich, *adj.* and *adv.* paid on account, before-hand. Eine —e Bezahlung, a before-hand payment, a payment on account.

Ábschlämmen, V. Abschlemmen.

Ábschleichen, I. *v. tr.* to obtain by cunning. V. Ablisten. II. *v. intr.* [u. w. seyn] to sneak off, withdraw, disappear, to steal or slink away. III. *v. r* sich —, V. Sich wegschleichen.

1. **Ábschleifen**, [von schleifen] *ir.* I. *v. tr.* 1) to take off by grinding. Die Spitze des Messers —, to grind off the point of the knife; den Rost —, to do away, to get out, to fetch off the rust. 2) to smooth, to polish. Eine Klinge —, to rub a blade; eine Marmorplatte —, to polish a marble-plate; einen Spiegel —, to polish a plate-glass; einen Degen —, to furbish a sword; *Fig.* die gute Gesellschaft hat ihn abgeschliffen, good company has rubbed the rust off him; abgeschliffene Sitten, polished manners. II. *v. r.* Sich —, to improve one's manners.

2. **Ábschleifen**, [von schleifen] *reg. v. tr.* 1) to wear out [by dragging &c.]. 2) to carry away on a sledge.

Ábschleifer, *m.* [-s, *pl.* -] [in grinding or polishing mills] he who polishes [marble-plates &c.], grinder.

Ábschleifsel, *n.* [-s] that which falls off in grinding, refuse.

1. **Ábschleifung**, *f.* grinding off; grinding, sharpening; furbishing, polishing.

2. **Ábschleifung**, *f.* wearing off; carrying away on a sledge.

Ábschleimen, I. *v. tr.* to rid of slime. Fische —, to soak or water fishes; Zucker —, to clarify sugar. II. *v. r.* sich —, to lose slime.

Ábschleißen, *ir. v. tr.* 1) to wear out by use. V. Abnützen. 2) to pull down.

Ábschlemmen, *v. tr.* to clear of mud, to remove the mud.

Ábschlendern, *v. intr.* [u. w. seyn] to retire slowly, to saunter away.

Ábschlenkern, *v. tr.* to fling away, to shake off.

Ábschleppen, I. *v. tr.* 1) to wear out by dragging. 2) to carry off clandestinely. II. *v. r.* sich —, to tire one's self by dragging, moving or carrying heavy things.

Ábschlichten, *v. tr.* to smooth off. [among tawers] Die Felle —, to cleanse hides with the sleeking knife; [among joiners] ein Brett — to plane a board; das Holz —, [a sea term] to dub timber.

Ábschließen, *ir. v. tr.* 1) to separate from others by locking up [a prisoner]. *Fig.* sich von der Welt —, to retire from the world. 2) to lock. Die Thür —, to lock the door; ein Schloß —, to turn the key. 3) *Fig.* to close, to conclude. Eine Rechnung —, to close, to balance, to settle, to wind up an account; einen Handel —, to conclude a bargain, to make or strike a bargain, to agree. ‡ 4) to unchain, to unfetter [a prisoner].

Ábschließend, *adj.* definitive.

Ábschließlich, *adv.* 1) definitively. 2) positively, decidedly.

Ábschließung, *f.* the act of separating by locking up &c. V. Abschluß.

Ábschlingern, *v. tr.* [a sea term] to roll away the masts.

Ábschlüpfen, *v. intr.* [u. w. seyn] 1) to slip off. 2) V. Entschlüpfen.

Ábschlürfen, *v. tr.* to sip off [the cream from a pot of milk].

Ábschluß, *m.* [-es, *pl.* Abschlüsse] Der — des Friedens, conclusion of peace, conclusion; der — einer Rechnung, the closing of an account.

Abschlußrechnung, *f.* statement, balance of account.

Ábschmack, *m.* [-es] bad taste.

Ábschmaddern, V. Abschmieren.

Ábschmähen, I. *v. tr.* to reproach severely, to rail, to inveigh. II. *v. r.* sich —, to tire one's self with reproaching, with railing.

Ábschmälen, V. Ausschmälen.

Ábschmarotzen, *v. tr.* to get, to obtain by parasitism or sponging.

† **Ábschmatzen**, V. Abherzen.

Ábschmausen, I. *v. tr.* 1) to eat up. 2) to eat out of house and home. II. *v. intr.* to finish rioting [banquetting]. III. *v. r.* sich —, to tire one's self with banquetting and reveling.

Ábschmecken, I. *v. tr.* to taste, to judge of a thing by tasting. II. *v. intr.* to have a bad taste [only used in the participle].

Ábschmeckend, *adj.* ill tasted, ill flavoured. — werden, [said of meat and fish] to become tainted.

Ábschmeicheln, *v. tr.* to obtain by flattery. Er hat es mir abgeschmeichelt, he has coaxed or cajoled me out of it.

† **Ábschmeißen**, V. Abwerfen.

Ábschmelzen, I. *reg. v. tr.* 1) to melt off, to separate by melting. 2) [in metallurgy] to part. 3) to melt sufficiently [butter &c.]. 4) to clarify by melting. II. *ir. v. intr.* [used with seyn] to melt, to fall off in consequence of melting.

† **Ábschmieren**, I. *v. tr.* 1) to grease sufficiently [a wheel &c.]. † 2) *Fig.* *a*) to copy, to transcribe negligently, to scrawl. *b*) to thrash, to beat, to cudgel soundly. II. *v. intr.* to part with grease, or smear.

† **Ábschmierer**, *m.* [-s] one who transcribes negligently, a scrawler, scribbler.

Ábschmunzeln, *v. tr.* to obtain by smirking and smiling.

Ábschmutzen, *v. tr.* to part with dirt, to soil. Die frisch gedruckten Bogen schmutzen ab, the newly printed sheets soil or maculate.

Ábschnäbeln, *v. r.* sich —, to tire with billing, with kissing.

Ábschnallen, *v. tr.* to loosen from buckles, to unbuckle, to take off after unbuckling.

Ábschnappen, I. *v. intr.* [used with seyn] to slip, get loose. Das Schloß ist abgeschnappt, the lock is slipt. II. *v. tr.* 1) to let off, to let loose [by slackening the spring] Die Thür —, to snap the door. † 2) *Fig.* to die.

Ábschnattern, *v. tr.* to utter chatteringly.

‖ **Ábschnautzen**, *v. tr.* Einen —, to snub any one.

Ábschnäutzen, V. Schnäutzen.

Ábschneiden, *ir.* I. *v. tr.* 1) to separate by cutting, to cut off, to sever, to abscind, [in gardening] to prune. Einen Finger —, to cut off a finger; die großen Haare, welche über das Ende des Tuches herausstehen, —, [among clothiers] to beard a stuff; Einem den Kopf —, to cut off any one's head; sich die Nägel —, to pare one's nails; die Flügel —, to clip the wings; ein Glied —, to amputate a limb: das Korn —, to cut the corn; einem Schafe die Wolle —, to shear a sheep; sich die Kehle —, to cut one's throat. *Fig.* Den Lebensfaden —, to cut the thread of life, to kill; Einem die Hoffnung —, to deprive any one of hope, to bid him despair; einen Buchstaben oder eine Silbe —, [in grammar] to cut off a letter or syllable; das Wasser —, to dig off the water; die Zufuhr —, to cut off provisions, to intercept the passage of provisions; einer Armee den Rückzug —, to cut off an army's retreat; die Gelegenheit —, to deprive of an opportunity, to prevent the occasion; jede Ausflucht —, to preclude any evasion; Einem seine Ehre —, to hurt [wound, blast] any one's reputation. 2) to shape or form by cutting. Ein Muster —, [among milliners] to cut out a pattern. 3) [among clothiers] to cut off the notches of a score or tally = to settle accounts. II. *v. r.* 1) sich —, to be at an end. Die Erze schneiden sich ab, [in mining] the veins disappear suddenly, they make a start or leap. 2) to contrast. Die Umrisse dieses Gebirges schneiden sich scharf am Himmel ab, these hills print a hard outline on the sky. III. *v. intr.* to make a contrast, to differ.

Ábschneider, *m.* [-s, *pl.* -] he that cuts off, cutter.

Ábschneideln, *v. tr.* [in gardening] V. Abschneiden.

Ábschneidlinie, *f.* [*pl.* -n] [in printing] cutting-line.

Ábschneidung, *f.* a cutting off &c.; [in surgery] abscision [applied to the soft parts of the body].

Ábschnellen, I. *v. tr.* to let fly with a jerk. Einen Pfeil —, to fling a dart. II. *v. intr.* [u. w. seyn] to spring off, to fly off with a jerk, to snap.

Ábschneien, *v. imp.* to cease snowing.

Ábschneuzen, *v. tr.* to snuff, to poll or top [a candle].

Ábschnippen, Abschnippeln, Abschnippseln, *v. tr.* to clip off.

Ábschnipperling, [-es] **Ábschnipsel**, *m.* [-s] clippings.

Ábschnitt, *m.* [-es, *pl.* -e] 1) the act of cutting off; [among clothiers] notching = settling of accounts. 2) a part cut off, [commonly in a figurative sense]. *a*) [in mathem., a figure contained between a chord and an arch of the circle] segment. *b*) [in coining] exerque. *c*) [in fortif.] intrenchment, retirade. *d*) [a figure in poetry] pause in a verse, caesura, cesura, cesure. *e*) [a small and distinct part of a writing or book] section. *f*) [in history] paragraph. *g*) [any thing cut out in paper to direct the cutting of cloth &c.] pattern. *h*) [in commerce] appoint.

Abschnitts-schein, *m.* check, V. Schnittschein. —slinie, *f.* [among printers] cutting-line. —swinkel, *m.* angle of a segment.

Ábschnittlein, Ábschnitzel, *n.* [-s] shred, chip, shaving, cutting, clipping, snipping. Die Abschnitzel vom gewalzten Silber, [in coining] sizel.

Ábschnitzeln, Abschnitzen, *v. tr.* 1) to cut away by little and little, to pare, to whittle. 2) to carve.

Ábschnüren, *v. tr.* 1) to unlace. 2) to measure out with the line. 3) to lay out by the line. 4) to separate with a line. Eine Warze —, to tie off a wart.

Ábschnurren, I. *v. tr.* to get [obtain] by begging. II. *v. intr.* [u. w. seyn] to rattle off [said of spools].

Ábschöpfen, *v. tr.* to scum, to skim, to take off. Die Milch —, to skim the milk.

Ábschoß, *m.* [-sses] [a law term] tax, duty paid for removing with one's property from one country or jurisdiction to another; also a duty paid for an inheritance, legacy tax. V. Abzugsgeld and Nachsteuer.

Abschoß-pflichtig, *adj.* liable to pay the above duty. —pflichtigkeit, *f.* liableness to pay the above duty. —recht, V. Abfahrtsrecht.

Ábschrägen, *v. tr.* to slope.

Ábschrägung, *f.* 1) the act of sloping. 2) slope.

Ábschrammen, I. *v. tr.* to separate by scratching. II. *v. intr.* [u. w. seyn] to sneak off, away in silence.

Ábschrapen, V. Abschaben.

Ábschrauben, *v. tr.* to unscrew, screw off.

Ábschrecken, *v. tr.* 1) to scare or fright away [game from a field]. Ein wolkiger Himmel kann Einen von einer Reise —, a cloudy sky may deter a man from undertaking a journey; er läßt sich leicht —, he is easily dispirited; er läßt sich durch nichts —, he is not to be discouraged. 2) to extort by terror. 3) to sprinkle with a liquid any thing hot. 4) [in cookery] Einen Fisch mit Essig —, um ihn blau zu machen, to sprinkle a fish with vinegar in order to turn the skin blue in boiling.

Ábschreiben, *ir. v. tr.* 1) to copy, to transcribe. Einen Brief —, to copy a letter. 2) to wear off by writing. Eine Feder —, to dull or blunt a pen [by writing]; ich habe mir fast die Finger abgeschrieben, I have almost worn my fingers out with writing. 3) to pay off a debt by writing for one's creditor. 4) to order by writing the contrary to what was ordered before. Einen Besuch —, to countermand a visit; einen Termin —, to put off a term. 5) [in commerce] to deduct, to write off; eine Summe —, to take out or to write off, to credit a sum in the books; eine böse Schuld —, to balance the account of a bad debt; in der Bank —, [in commerce] to assign in banco.

Abschreibe-gebühr, *f.*, —geld, *n.* copy money.

Ábschreiber, *m.* [-s, *pl.* -] copier, copist, transcriber.

Abschreiberei, *f.* [in contempt] the act of copying, transcribing.

Ábschreibung, *f.* copying, transcription.

Ábschreien, *ir.* I. *v. tr.* 1) to cry, to proclaim. 2) to get by dint of crying. 3) to reach in crying. II. *v. r.* sich —, to tire one's self by crying. Das Kind wird sich ganz —, this child will squall itself to death; sich die Kehle —, to scream till one's throat is sore, to bawl till one grows hoarse.

Ábschreiten, *ir.* I. *v. tr.* to measure off by steps, to step, to pace [a garden &c.]. II. *v. intr.* [used with seyn] to pace or stride away. *Fig.* to deviate, to digress. Von dem Wege der Tugend —, to swerve from the path of virtue.

Ábschreitend, *part. adj.* digressive.

Ábschricken, *v. tr.* (a sea term) to pay out, to ease off a little. Das um das Gangspill laufende Ankertau oder auch die Kabelaring —, to surge at the windlass or capstern.

Ábschrift, *f.* [*pl.* -en] copy, transcript; [in commerce] duplicate. Eine — nehmen, to draw a copy; eine beglaubigte —, a certified copy.

Ábschriftlich, *adv.* in manner of a copy, transcriptively.

‡ **Ábschröcken**, V. Abschrecken.

Ábschröpfen, *v. tr.* 1) [in husb.] to cut off [the points of corn] with a sickle. V. Abschroten. 2) to remove by cupping. *Fig.* Einen —, to strip any one. V. Aussaugen.

Ábschrote, *f.* V. Schrotmeißel.

Ábschroten, *v. tr.* 1) to roll down [a barrel]. 2) [among different workmen] to separate, to divide; [among carpenters] to saw off with a large double saw; [among pinmakers] to clip [the wire]; [among smiths and locksmiths] to hew [a piece of iron on the chisel]. 3) to bronze. 4) [in mills] to grind sufficiently. 5) to turn or lead off [the course of a spring]. 6) to slope sufficiently [a ditch &c.].

Ábschultern, *v. tr.* to take from the shoulder

Ábschuppen, I. *v. tr.* to scale, to unscale, to strip of scales. Einen Fisch —, to scale a fish. II. *v. r.* sich —, to peel off in thin particles, to scale, to flake.

Ábschüppen, *v. tr.* to take off with a shovel, to shovel off.

Ábschuppern, V. Abschuppen II.

Ábschur, *f.* V. Schur.

Ábschurfen, Ábschürfen, *v. tr.* to take off the scurf.

Ábschurren, I. *v. tr.* to wear off by scraping. II. *v. intr.* to go away rustling.

Ábschuß, *m.* [-sses, *pl.* -schüsse] 1) the rushing down [of the water], fall. 2) slope, declivity. 3) fading [said of colours].

Ábschüssig, I. *adj.* declivous, sloping, bending; shelving, steep. II. *adv.* slopingly, slopewise, steepy, aslope.

Ábschüssigkeit, *f.* declivity, steepness, shelvingness.

Ábschütteln, *v. tr.* 1) to throw down by a violent motion, to shake off. Obst —, to shake off fruit; den Staub von den Füßen —, to shake off the dust from the feet. *Fig.* Das Joch eines Tirannen —, to shake off the yoke of a tyrant; die Sorgen —, to shake off cares; solche Sachen lassen sich nicht —, things of that kind are not arranged, settled in a hurry. 2) to shake violently. *Fig.* Einen —, to reprimand any one severely.

Ábschütten, *v. tr.* 1) to pour off, to throw off. 2) to pour down.

Ábschüttsel, *n.* [-s] windfall.

Ábschützen, *v. tr.* [in hydrost.] 1) to stop by a flood-gate. 2) to let off by opening the flood-gate. Einen Teich —, to drain a pond.

Ábschwächen, V. Entkräften.

Ábschwämmen, V. Abschwemmen.

Ábschwänzeln, *v. tr.* to get by fawning and coaxing.

Ábschwären, *ir. v. intr.* [used with seyn] to be separated by a sore. Der Nagel ist ihm abgeschworen, his nail is festered away.

Ábschwärmen, I. *v. intr.* 1) to swarm for the last time [said of bees]. 2) to withdraw swarming. II. *v. r.* sich —, to fatigue one's self by reveling and rioting.

Ábschwarten, *v. tr.* 1) to peel off the sward, skin [of bacon &c.]. 2) [in saw-mills] to saw off the slabs.

Ábschwärzen, *v. tr.* 1) to blacken thoroughly [leather &c.]. 2) *Fig.* to calumniate [not used]. II. *v. intr.* to part with black. Dieses Tuch schwärzt ab, the black comes off this cloth.

Ábschwatzen, *v. tr.* 1) to obtain by talk. Einem etwas —, to talk any one out of a thing. 2) to deny by idle talk. 3) to discuss amply.

Ábschwefeln, *v. tr.* 1) to clear of sulphur. 2) to impregnate sufficiently with sulphur [a straw-hat &c.].

Ábschweif, [-es, *pl.* -e] V. Abschweifung.

Ábschweifen, I. *v. tr.* 1) to rinse, to wash

[linen &c.]. **Die Seidengehäuſe —**, to steep the cods or balls of the silk worm in scalding water in order to wind them off the more easily. 2) [among joiners] V. **Ausſchweifen**. II. *v. intr.* [u. w. ſeyn] to depart from the main design of a discourse or argument, to digress. **Von einem Gegenſtande —**, to deviate or ramble from one's subject; **ich bin von meinem Gegenſtande abgeſchweift**, I have launched out of my subject.

Ábſchweifend, *adj.* digressive.

Ábſchweifung, *f.* 1) the act of quitting the right way, deviation, digression. 2) a short voyage or journey, a trip. 3) a passage deviating from the main design of a discourse, digression.

Ábſchwelgen, I. *v. intr.* to have done rioting. II. *v. r.* **ſich —**, to weaken one's self by debauchery.

Ábſchwemmen, *v. tr.* 1) to cause to pass by swimming, to float. 2) to clean by water. **Die Pferde —**, to ride the horses into the water. 3) to wash away, to wash off.

Ábſchwenden, *v. tr.* to lay waste, to destroy. **Einen Wald —**, to burn down a wood; **eine Haide —**, to burn up a heath; **Äcker —**, to burn fields.

Ábſchwenken, I. *v. tr.* to cleanse by rinsing. II. *v. r.* **ſich —**, to turn aside, to wheel aside or off.

Ábſchwimmen, *ir.* I. *v. intr.* [u. w. ſeyn] 1) to swim off or away. **Der Kahn iſt abgeſchwommen**, the boat has gone adrift. 2) to move or to be conveyed on water, to swim, to float. II. *v. r.* **ſich —**, to tire one's self by violent swimming.

Ábſchwinden, *v. intr.* to waste away, to dwindle away.

Ábſchwinden, *n.* **Ábſchwindung**, *f.* V. **Abzehrung, Auszehren, Auszehrung, Schwindſucht**.

Ábſchwingen, *ir.* I. *v. tr.* to shake off, to clean by shaking. **Hafer —**, to winnow oats. II. *v. r.* **ſich —**, to leap down. **Sich vom Pferde —**, to leap from the horse, to alight, to dismount nimbly.

Ábſchwitzen, *v. tr.* 1) to remove or clear by sweating. **Die Felle —**, [among curriers] to heap the hides or skins. † *Fig.* 2) to atone, to expiate by sweating. II. *v. r.* **ſich —**, to sweat one's self, to weaken one's self by sweating. III. *v. intr.* to have done sweating.

Ábſchwören, *ir. v. tr.* 1) to take an oath of. 2) to abjure, forswear, renounce. **Seine Religion —**, to forswear one's religion, to revolt from one's religion; **ſeine Irrthümer —**, to revoke one's errors. 3) to deny by an oath. **Einen Diebſtahl —**, to take an oath of not having committed a theft.

Ábſchwörung, *f.* abjuration.

Ábſchwung, *m.* [-s] the leaping down.

Ábſciſſe, *f.* [in mathematics] abscise, abscissa.

Ábſegeln, I. *v. intr.* [used with ſeyn] to sail away, to set sail, to put to sea. † *Fig.* **Er iſt in die Ewigkeit abgeſegelt**, he has launched into eternity. II. *v. tr.* 1) to take down the sails of a windmill. 2) [a sea term] **Den Maſt —**, to carry away a mast.

Ábſehbar, *adj.* and *adv.* 1) within reach of the eyes, within sight. 2) *Fig.* imaginable, conceivable.

Ábſehen, *ir. v. tr.* 1) to look off, to turn away or avert one's eyes from something. *Fig.* **Abgeſehen von**, abstractedly from, in the abstract. 2) to reach with the eyes. **Eine Allee, deren Ende nicht abzuſehen iſt**, an avenue the end of which is lost to the view, out of sight. *Fig.* **Es iſt ſchwer abzuſehen, warum er es that**, it is difficult to conceive why he did it; **ſo viel ich — kann**, for ought I see or perceive; **die Zeit, Gelegenheit —**, to watch for an opportunity. 3) *Fig.* to aim at. **Auf etwas abgeſehen ſeyn**, to have some design, some object in view, to aim at a thing; **es war auf dein Beſtes abgeſehen**, I had your interest in view. 4) *Fig.* to learn or know by looking on. **Einem etwas —**, to learn a thing from a person by seeing and observing how he does it; **Einem einen Handgriff —**, to catch a knack from any one; **ich that Alles, was ich ihm nur an den Augen — konnte**, I anticipated his wishes as much as possible.

Ábſehen, *n.* [-s] 1) the act of looking away &c. 2) *Fig.* aim, design, view, purpose, intention. V. **Abſicht**. **Sein — auf etwas haben oder richten**, to aim at a thing, to have it in view; **ich habe es in dem — gethan**, I did it with that view, or in that intention. 3) the sight upon the barrel of a gun or upon an optical or geometrical instrument. 4) [in geometry and astronomy] the label, index or ruler moveable about the centre of an astrolabe, Alidade, Alhidade. 5) [of pregnant women] **Ein — an etwas nehmen**, to take fright at some sudden sight so as to influence the appearance of the child they bear.

Ábſeide, *f.* floss-silk.

Ábſeifen, *v. tr.* [among silk-throwers] to cleanse from soap, to wash out the soap.

Ábſeigen, V. **Abſeihen**.

Ábſeigern, *v. tr.* [in min.] 1) to measure the depth of a shaft with a plumb-line. 2) [in metallurgy] to complete the liquidation of or parting the silver and copper.

Ábſeihen, *v. tr.* to purify by filtration, to filter, to strain.

Ábſeihung, *f.* filtration, straining.

Ábſein, V. **Abſeyn**.

Ábſeite, *f.* [*pl.* -n] 1) [in building] the wing of an edifice, aisle [of a church]. 2) the reverse [of a coin].

Abſeiten, *prep.* [a law term] from any one's side. **— meiner**, for my part, as for me.

Abſeits, *adv.* aside, apart.

Ábſenden, *ir. v. tr.* 1) to send, send away. **Einen Brief mit der Poſt —**, to send a letter by the post; **der König ſandte einen Botſchafter an den Madrider Hof ab**, the king dispatched an envoy to the court of Madrid. 2) [in poetry] to throw, to fling, to cast.

Ábſender, *m.* [-s, *pl.* -] dispatcher; [in commerce] dispatcher, consigner.

Ábſendung, *f.* sending, dispatching.

Abſendungstag, *m.* day when any thing is dispatched or sent away.

Ábſengen, *v. tr.* to burn slightly or superficially, to singe off.

Ábſengung, *f.* the act of burning slightly or singeing off.

Ábſenken, *v. tr.* 1) to cause to fall, to sink. 2) [in gardening and husb.] to set slips or layers, to practise arcuation. **Reben —**, to provine; **Nelken —**, to lay carnations. 3) [in mining] to sink, to delve. **Einen Schacht — (abteufen)**, to sink a shaft.

Ábſenkung, *f.* laying, setting.

Ábſenker, *m.* [-s, *pl.* -] [in gardening and husb.] a layer of a plant.

Ábſetzen, I. *v. tr.* and *intr.* 1) to set down, put down. **Eine Laſt —**, to put down a burden; **einen Tiſch von der Wand —**, to remove a table from the wall; **ſetzt ab!** [a word of command with soldiers] as you were! **er trank es aus, ohne abzuſetzen**, he drank it off without taking breath; **abgeſetzt**, [in music] staccato. 2) to lodge in any place, to deposit. **Er ſetzte ſie in ſeinem Wagen ab**, he set her down in his carriage; **der Wagen ſetzte einen Reiſenden bei dem Gaſthofe ab**, the coach dropped a passenger at the inn. 3) to throw down. **Das Pferd hat ſeinen Reiter abgeſetzt**, the horse has thrown its rider. 4) to bring forth, to give birth to clandestinely. 5) [in mining] to separate by beating. 6) [in forges] = **abziehen**. 7) [among clothiers] = **abſtreichen**. 8) to break off, to interrupt, to discontinue. 9) *Fig.* *a*) to depose, to degrade. **Einen König —**, to dethrone or depose a king; **einen Beamten —**, to dismiss, discharge, depose, remove, degrade [a public functionary], to cashier [an officer]. *b*) to sell, to vend. **Waaren —**, to sell goods, to dispose of goods. *c*) to wean [a calf &c.]. *d*) to contrast [colours]. **Einen Schrank grün —**, [among house-painters] to edge a chest with green. *e*) [in printing] to finish composing. II. *v. intr.* 1) to change [in mining]. **Der Gang ſetzt ab**, the vein deviates from its direct course. 2) to contrast [said of colours]. III. *v. imp.* to result, to be a consequence of. † **Es wird Schläge dabei —**, it will come to blows.

Ábſetzer, *m.* [-s, *pl.* -] one who sets down, puts down something.

Ábſetzferkel, *n.* [-s, *pl.* -] a pig newly weaned.

Ábſetztiſch, *m.* [-es, *pl.* -e] 1) a kind of sideboard. 2) [among clothiers] a table on which the cloth is brushed.

Ábſetzung, *f.* 1) the act of setting down &c. 2) deposition, degradation, removal.

Ábſeufzen, *v. r.* **ſich —**, to tire or enfeeble one's self by sighing.

Ábſeyn, *ir. v. intr.* 1) to be separated, to be absent. [The handle of a pitcher] **iſt ab**, is off; **der Garten iſt nicht weit von der Landſtraße ab**, the garden is not far from the highroad. 2) [a law term] to be abolished. **Dies ſoll nichtig, todt und —**, this shall be null and void. ‖ 3) to omit or neglect. V. **Verfehlen, Unterlaſſen**.

Ábſeyn, *n.* [-s] V. **Abweſenheit**.

Ábſicht, *f.* [-en] 1) the act of looking on an object. *Fig.* **In — auf**, in regard to, with a view to; **in aller —**, in all respects, in every respect; **in der nämlichen —**, in the same view. 2) *Fig.* view, intention, purpose. **Meine — iſt**, my intention is; **eine — auf etwas haben**, to have a design upon, to aim at, intend; **er hat —en auf ſie**, he has a design upon her; **es iſt der — gemäß**, it answers the purpose; **ſeine — erreichen**, to obtain one's end, to hit one's aim, to gain the point; **das Geſetz entſpricht der — der &c.**, the law reaches the intention of the &c.; **ich werde ſehen, was ihre — iſt**, I will see what they will be at; **ſeine — iſt, Ihnen zu gefallen**, his end is to please you; **ohne —**, unintentionally, undesignedly. SYN. **Abſicht, Zweck, Endzweck**. That which is, or can be, used to any thing else, is a means to it, and of this it is said, that it has **einen Zweck** [end], but only he has **die Abſicht** [intention], who designedly makes use of the means to gain an end. The watch is a means of ascertaining the time, it has therefore this **Zweck** [end], but only he, who looks at it for the purpose of ascertaining the time, has this **Zweck** [aim], and this **Abſicht** [intention]. The watch itself has not the **Abſicht**.

Ábſichten, *v. tr.* to sift off.

Ábſichtlich, I. *adj.* designed, intended, intentional. **Eine —e Beleidigung**, a premeditated offence. II. *adv.* designedly, intentionally.

Ábſichtlos, *adv.* undesignedly.

Ábſichtloſigkeit, *f.* undesignedness.

Ábſichtsvoll, *adj.* full of designs.

Ábſickern, *v. intr.* [u. w. ſeyn] to fall in drops,

to trickle down.

Ábſieben, *v. tr.* to sift off [the chaff].

Ábſiechen, *v. intr.* [u. w. ſeyn] to languish, to consume, pine away [by sickness].

Ábſieden, *ir. v. intr.* 1) to seeth, to boil. Einen Trank —, to make a decoction; Eier —, to poach, boil eggs. 2) to clean by seething. V. Kochen, Abkochen, ‖ Abquellen and Sieden.

Ábſingen, *ir.* I. *v. tr.* to recite singing, to carol, to chant. II. *v. r.* ſich —, to fatigue one's self by singing. III. *v. intr.* to sing for the last time.

Ábſingung, *f.* singing, chanting, carolling.

Ábſinken, *v. intr.* [used with ſeyn] to sink down.

Ábſintern, V. Abſickern.

Abſinth, V. Wermuth.

Ábſitzen, *ir.* I. *v. intr.* 1) to sit at a distance. Weit vom Fenſter —, to sit away from the window. 2) [u. w. ſeyn] to alight, to dismount. Er ſaß ab, he alighted from his horse. II. *v. tr.* 1) to atone, to diminish by sitting. Eine Schuld —, to pay off a debt by sitting in prison. 2) to sit out a given time. 3) [among clothiers] to take off from the growme or tenter. III. *v. r.* ſich —, to tire one's self by sitting.

Ábſocken, *v. intr.* [used with ſeyn], [in saltworks] to trickle down.

Ábſod, V. Abſud.

Ábſohlen, *v. intr.* [in min.] to wear out [ropes].

Ábſolden, *v. tr.* to pay off.

* **Abſolút**, I. *adj.* [not relative, not limited, positive] absolute Der —e Raum, absolute vacuum; Eine —e Wahrheit, a positive truth. II. *adv.* absolutely.

* **Abſolutión**, *f.* the remission of sins, absolution.

* **Abſolutórium**, *n.* [-s] [a law term] acquittal.

* **Abſolvíren**, *v. tr.* 1) to absolve, to acquit. Ab Inſtantia —, [a law term] to set free a defendant, for want of sufficient evidence against him. 2) to remit sin, to absolve. 3) to dispatch. 4) to end, to finish [one's studies].

Ábſonderbar, *adj.* separable.

Ábſonderlich, I. *adj.* 1) separate, secluded. 2) Abſónderlich, particular, peculiar, especial, singular. Ein —er Menſch, a strange, odd fellow. V. Beſonder. II. *adv.* 1) separately. 2) particularly, especially. V. Beſonders.

Ábſonderling, *m.* [-s, *pl.* -e] separatist, nonconformist.

Ábſondern, I. *v. tr.* 1) to divide from the rest, to separate. Einen Hof in zwei Theile —, to partition a yard [by a wall &c.]; die Engel werden die Böſen von den Gerechten —, the angels shall sever the wicked from among the just. 2) V. Abſtrahiren. Die Galle &c., welche abgeſondert wird, [in animal economy] bile &c., which is secreted or secerned; ein Kind —, [a law term] to pay off an heir. II. *v. r.* ſich —, 1) to separate. Die ſchlechten Säfte müſſen ſich —, the noxious humours must be secreted; ſich von der Geſellſchaft —, to seclude one's self, to withdraw from the world; to live by one's self; er lebt abgeſondert, he lives retired. 2) [in commerce] to dissolve partnership.

Ábſonderung, *f.* 1) separation, segregation. 2) [in animal economy] secretion.

Abſonderungs-vermögen, *n.* 1) abstractive faculty, abstraction. 2) secretive power. —zeichen, *n.* mark of distinction.

Ábſonnig, *adj.* removed from the sun, shady.

* **Abſorbíren**, *v. intr.* 1) [in medicine] to imbibe, to absorb. Abſorbirende Mittel, absorbents. 2) *Fig.* to waste wholly, to absorb, to consume.

Ábſorgen, *v. r.* ſich —, to wear out with care.

Ábſpähnen, *v. tr.* [among carpenters] to plane off, to take off shavings.

Ábſpalten, I. *v. intr.* [u. w. ſeyn; *part.* of the pret. abgeſpalten] to split and separate. II. *v. tr.* [u. w. haben; *part.* of the pret. abgeſpaltet] to separate by splitting, to cleave, to split off.

Ábſpaltung, *f.* 1) the act of separating by splitting. 2) the thing split off.

Ábſpänen, *v. tr.* to wean [a child, a calf]. V. Spänen, Entwöhnen.

Ábſpannen, *v. tr.* 1) to unbend, to loose, to relax. Die Pferde —, to unteam, to take off the horses; die Ochſen —, to unyoke the oxen; einen Bogen &c. —, to unbend a bow &c.; die Saiten —, to let down the strings, to slacken the strings; eine Trommel —, to unbrace a drum; den Hahn am Gewehre —, to uncock. Abgeſpannte Saiten, slackened strings. *Fig.* Den Geiſt —, to relax one's mind. Uebermäßiger Kummer ſpannt den Geiſt ab, excessive grief enfeebles the mind. ‡ 2) *Fig.* to alienate one's customers &c. 3) to reach in spanning.

Ábſpannung, *f.* 1) remission. 2) unbending, relaxation.

Ábſpänſtig, *adj.* alienate, alienated. — machen, to alienate; einem Manne ſeine Frau — machen, to seduce a man's wife; — werden, to turn disloyal, to desert.

Ábſparen, *v. tr.* to deprive of any thing by sparing, to spare, to stint. Ich will es mir am Munde —, I will pinch myself in my food for it.

Ábſpeiſen, I. *v. tr.* 1) to take away by eating, to consume by eating. 2) to entertain, to feed. 3) *Fig.* to feed with words and promises. Einen mit leeren Worten —, to put any one off with fair words; to sprinkle any one with court-holywater; glaubt nicht, daß ich mich auf dieſe Art — laſſe, you must not think to put me off thus. II. *v. intr.* to finish dinner or supper. Abgeſpeiſet haben, to have done dining or supping.

Ábſperren, *v. tr.* to seclude, to shut out, to debar.

Ábſperrung, *f.* seclusion.

Ábſpiegeln, *v. tr.* to reflect as from a mirror.

Ábſpiegelung, *f.* 1) the act of reflecting [as from a mirror]. 2) the thing so reflected.

Ábſpielen, I. *v. tr.* 1) to perform on an instrument. Ein Lied —, to play a tune. 2) to play, to act, to perform, to the end. 3) to separate by playing on an instrument. 4) to pay off a debt by playing [at cards &c.]. II. *v. intr.* to finish playing. III. *v. r.* ſich —, to tire one's-self by playing.

Ábſpindeln, *v. tr.* to take from the spindle.

Ábſpinnen, *ir. v. tr.* 1) to clear by spinning. *Fig.* Sich die Finger —, to wear out one's fingers by spinning. 2) to pay off [a debt] by spinning [for one's creditor].

Ábſpitzen, *v. tr.* 1) to divest of the point. Eine Feder —, to nib a pen. 2) to cut off with a point. † 3) *Fig.* es auf einen —, V. Abſehen.

Ábſplittern, I *v. tr.* and II. *v. intr.* [u. w. haben and w. ſeyn] to splint, to splinter, to break off in splinters. III. *v. r.* ſich —, to come off in splinters.

‡ **Ábſprache**, *f.* V. Abrede.

Ábſprechen, *ir. v. tr.* 1) to deprive any one of something by one's decision. Die Aerzte haben ihm das Leben abgeſprochen, the physicians have given him over; Einem alle Hoffnung —, to bid any one give over all hopes, to take all hope from any one. 2) to deprive of by a judicial sentence. Das Leben —, to condemn, to sentence to death. 3) to speak sufficiently of a thing, to talk over or discuss a thing with any one. V. Beſprechen. II. *v. intr.* 1) to judge and decide precipitately. Er ſpricht gern ab, he is in the habit of prejudging. 2) to object in a disputation, to oppose.

Ábſprechend, **Abſprecheriſch**, *adj.* positive, dogmatical, magisterial, decisive.

Ábſprecher, *m.* [-s] overhasty decider.

Abſprecherei, *f.* [in contempt] the act of deciding overhastily, of prejudging.

Ábſpreizen, *v. tr.* to prop [with timber]. [In mining] Einen Schacht —, to provide a shaft with props.

Ábſprengen, I. *v. tr.* to cause to break off suddenly. Einen Felſen —, to blast a rock with gunpowder; ein Hufeiſen —, to cast a horse's shoe. II. *v. intr.* [u. w. ſeyn] to hasten away; [on horseback] to gallop off.

Ábſprießen, V. Abſproſſen.

Ábſpringen, *ir.* I. *v. intr.* [u. w. ſeyn] 1) to crack off, to fly off, to come off. Die Farbe ſpringt ab, the paint cracks off; die Saite iſt abgeſprungen, the string has snapped. 2) to move with a leap or bound. Vom Pferde —, to alight; der Ball ſprang von der Wand ab, the ball rebounded from the wall. *Fig.* Springen Sie nicht ab, do not prevaricate, stick to the point; nachdem er es mir verſprochen hatte, wollte er wieder —, he promised it me and afterwards wanted to retract; von einer Partei —, to forsake or desert a party suddenly; abſpringend, desultory. II. *v. r.* ſich —, to tire one's self by running and jumping.

Ábſpritzen, *v. intr.* to spurt back. Das Blut ſpritzte von der Wand ab, the blood spurted back from the wall.

Ábſproß, [-ſſes, *pl.* -ſſen] V. Abſprößling.

Ábſproſſen, *v. intr.* [u. w. ſeyn] to descend.

Ábſprößling, *m.* [-s, *pl.* -e] V. Nachkomme.

Ábſpruch, *m.* [-es, *pl.* -ſprüche] 1) the act of depriving any one by judicial sentence. 2) [a law term] the final sentence.

Ábſprung, *m.* [-es, *pl.* -ſprünge] 1) a spring, a jump, a leap, a bound. 2) a sudden quitting or leaving a place. 3) [among sportsmen] the place from which an animal makes a spring, the point from which it takes off. *Fig.* Abſprünge machen, to run from one thing to another; dieß iſt ein großer —, here is a great falling off; — von Jahren, disparity of years.

Abſprungswinkel, *m.* [in mathematics] angle of reflection.

Ábſpulen, *v. tr.* 1) to unwind from the spool [yarn]. 2) to complete spooling.

Ábſpülen, *v. tr.* 1) to cleanse by rinsing. Flaſchen —, to wash out bottles. Die Gläſer —, to rinse glasses; die Schüſſeln —, to wash up the dishes; die Räder eines Wagens —, to wash, to mop the wheels of a carriage. 2) to wash off, to wash away. Der Fluß ſpület ſeine Ufer ab, the river gradually washes away its banks.

Ábſpuler, *m.* [-s *pl.* -] he that unwinds yarn from the spool.

Ábſpülicht, *n.* [-s] dish-water, hog-wash, swill.

Ábſpülung, *f.* 1) washing, rinsing. 2) washing away.

Ábſtählen, *v. tr.* 1) to steel, to harden. *Fig.* Sich gegen das Gefühl des Schmerzes —, to harden one's self against all sense of pain; gegen das Wetter abgeſtählt, hardened to the weather. 2) [among dyers] to try the broth, in which cloth &c. is to be dyed, by dipping a little piece of cloth into it and exposing it to the air.

‖**Ábſtähren**, *v. intr.* to cease desiring the ram [said of ewes].

Ábſtamm, V. Stamm.

Ábſtammeln, *v. tr.* V. Herſtammeln.

Ábſtammen, *v. intr.* [used with ſeyn] to be descended, to be derived. Von königlichem Geblüte —, to be of or descended from royal blood; dieß Wort ſtammt von keinem andern ab, this word is derived from no other.

Ábſtammung, *f.* descent, derivation. Er iſt von vornehmer —, he is of high extraction.

Abſtammungstafel, *f.* genealogical table.

Ábſtämmen, *v. tr.* [among foresters] to cut down, to fell [trees].

Ábſtämmling, V. Abkömmling.

Ábſtämpeln, V Abſtempeln.

Ábſtampfen, I. *v. tr.* 1) to separate by stamping. 2) to stamp, to pound sufficiently. 3) to wear by stamping. II. *v. intr.* to finish stamping. III. *v. r.* ſich —, to tire by stamping. Er ſtampfte ſich ab vor Zorn, he stamped with rage.

Ábſtand, *m.* [-es, *pl.* -ſtände] 1) [an interval or space between two objects] distance. Der — der Sonne von der Erde, [in astronomy] the distance of the sun from the earth, der — vom Scheitel, zenith distance; der geringſte, der weiteſte — eines Planeten von der Erde, the perihelion, the apogee; der — des Mittelpunktes einer elliptiſchen Planetenbahn vom Brennpunkte, eccentricity; der — zwiſchen mir und ihm iſt zu groß, the distance between me and him is too great. 2) [a law term] act of desisting from any claim, recession. — thun, [in com.] to abandon [a ship]; — leiſten, to give a compensation [for a claim].

Abſtands-geld, *n.* money paid to a person, who desists from any claim. —**meſſung**, *f.* [in mechan.] apomecometry. V. Fernmeßkunde. —**winkel**, *m.* [the angle contained under lines supposed to be drawn from the centres of the sun and a given planet to the centre of the earth] angle of elongation.

Ábſtänder, *m.* [-s, *pl.* -] [among foresters] a dead tree.

Ábſtändig, *adj.* [among foresters] —es Holz, dead [dry] wood; die Eichen fangen an — zu werden, the oaks are beginning to decay, are on the decline.

Ábſtapeln, *v. tr.* to take down from a stack.

Ábſtatten, *v. tr.* 1) to execute, to discharge. Einen Beſuch —, to pay a visit; Einem ſeine Schuldigkeit —, to pay one's debt; *Fig.* to pay one's respects to another; Dank —, to give, to render, to return thanks; einen Gruß —, to deliver a compliment. 2) [a law term for ausſtatten] to endow, to portion.

Ábſtattung, *f.* the act of performing, discharging; endowing.

Ábſtaub, *m.* [-es] dust flying about.

Ábſtäuben, *v. tr.* to free from dust, to dust [a table &c.].

‖**Ábſtaubern**, **Abſtöbern**, V. Abſtäuben.

Ábſtäubung, *f.* dusting.

Ábſtäuber, *m.* [-s, *pl.* -] a person that frees from dust. 2) that which frees from dust, duster.

Ábſtäupen, *v. tr.* to scourge soundly.

Ábſtecheiſen, *n.* [-s, *pl.* -] 1) [among pewterers] a scraper. 2) [in fortif.] a narrow spade, a shovel.

Ábſtechen, *ir.* I. *v. tr.* 1) to separate with a pointed instrument. Heu —, to unload hay; den Ring —, to get the ring with the lance (in running at the ring); Raſen —, to cut green sods; ein Schwein —, to stick a pig. 2) to surpass any one in thrusting, shooting. *Fig.* Einen —, (at cards) to trump any one. 3) to draw off by a pointed instrument. Einen Teich —, to drain, to draw a pond. *Fig.* Wein —, to draw wine. 4) to copy by means of a pointed instrument. Eine Zeichnung —, to engrave a drawing; ein Muſter —, to prick a pattern upon paper. 5) to mark out with poles or stakes placed in the ground. Ein Lager —, to mark the place for a camp; einen Bauplatz —, [more usual abſtecken], to mark out the groundplot. 6) [a sea term] to get the wind or weathergage of a ship. II. *v. intr.* 1) [u. w. ſeyn], [in sea language] to sheer off. 2) [u. w. haben] to make a contrast. Sie ſticht gegen euch ab, she is the set off to you; dieſe Farben ſtechen gut [gegen einander] ab, these colours contrast well, set off well; ſein Frohſinn ſticht von ihrer [or gegen ihre] Traurigkeit ſehr ab, his gaiety contrasts very much with her melancholy; dieſe Charaktere ſtechen ſcharf gegen einander ab, these characters are strongly contrasted.

Ábſtecher, *m.* [-s, *pl.* -] 1) a person, who separates with a pointed instrument &c. 2) a tool of clothiers. 3) a short voyage or journey, a trip, an excursion. 4) *Fig.* digression.

Abſtech-grube, *f.* [in metallurgy] a pit for the metal which is let out of the dam of the furnace by a channel made in sand. —**herd**, V. —grube. —**meſſer**, *n.* butchering-knife. —**pflug**, *m.* [in husbandry] breast plough.

Ábſtechung, V. Abſtich.

Ábſtecken, *v. tr.* 1) to unpin. 2) to mark with poles or sticks. Die Mauern einer Stadt —, to mark out the walls of a town; ein Lager —, to pitch a field with poles, to trace out an encampment by fixing poles; die Grenzen —, to mark out the boundaries; eine Straße —, to lay out a street; das —, the laying out by a line. 3) *Fig.* V. Entwöhnen.

Abſteck-eiſen, *n.* an iron stake. —**leine**, *f.* a line used in marking out a space. —**pfahl**, *m.* a pole or picket used in marking out a space. —**ſchnur**, *f.* V. —leine.

Ábſtehen, *ir.* I. *v. intr.* [used with ſeyn and haben] to be at a distance, to stand off. Parallellinien ſtehen überall gleich weit von einander ab, [in Geom.] parallel lines are every where equidistant from each other; abſtehend, [in botany] expanding. 2) to decay, to spoil [said of things], to die [said of animals, and of plants]. Das Bier iſt abgeſtanden, the beer has grown stale, it is palled; der Donner macht die Milch abſtehen, the thunder turns the milk; die Fiſche ſind abgeſtanden, the fishes are dead; abgeſtandenes Holz, dead wood. 3) to stand no longer and to go away. Der Jäger ſteht ab, the hunter leaves his stand; das Geflügel ſteht ab, [among sportsmen] the game flies from a tree. 4) *Fig.* to desist. Von ſeiner Forderung —, to desist from one's claim; ich will von meiner Bemerkung —, I will withdraw or retract my observation or assertion; ich will von allem weiteren Verfahren gegen ihn —, I will drop all farther proceedings against him; von einer übeln Gewohnheit —, to leave off a bad habit; von einem Gute —, to give up, to relinquish an estate; er ſtand ihm ab, he did not stand by him, he abandoned him. II. *v. tr.* [u. w. haben] to give up, to resign, to relinquish, to yield, to cede. Stehen Sie mir Ihre Uhr ab, let me have your watch, V. Abtreten; ein Amt —, to resign an office; V. Abtreten, Niederlegen. III. *v. r.* ſich —, to tire with standing.

Ábſteher, *m.* [-s, *pl.* -] one who cedes or yields any thing.

Ábſtehlen, *ir. v. tr.* to steal from, to rob of. *Fig.* Dem lieben Gott die Tage —, to spend one's time in doing nothing; einem etwas —, to learn a thing of any one by stealth.

Ábſteifen, I. *v. tr.* 1) to stiffen. Einen Hemdkragen —, to starch a shirt collar. 2) [in build. and mining] to prop. II. *v. intr.* [u. w. ſeyn] to grow stiff, to stiffen.

Ábſteigen, *ir. v. intr.* [used with ſeyn] 1) to come down, to descend. Ich ſah ſie, als ſie abſtiegen, I saw them as they alighted; vom Pferde, vom Wagen —, to dismount from a horse, to alight from a coach; von einem Berge —, to descend a hill. *Fig.* Die —de Linie, the descending line; [in astron.] —de Zeichen, descending signs; der —de Knoten, descending node. 2) to stop at an inn. Sie ſtiegen im König von Preußen ab, they put up at the king of Prussia.

Abſteige-haus, *n.* —**quartier**, *n.* —**wohnung**, *f.* house of accommodation.

Ábſteigern, *v. tr.* [at sales by auction] Einen —, to outbid any one, to bid higher than an other.

Ábſteigung, *f.* 1) the act of alighting, lighting, descending, descent. 2) *Fig.* a) [in astron.] descension. Die gerade —, [astron. term.] right descension; die ſchiefe —, oblique descension. b) [in fortif.] a narrow passage leading from the covert way to the ditch, descent.

Ábſteinen, *v. tr.* to mark out with landmarks [fields belonging to a town &c.].

Ábſteinigen, *v. tr.* to knock off or down with stones [walnuts].

Ábſtellen, *v. tr.* 1) to put away, to remove. Stellen Sie die Laſt ein wenig ab, put down the burden for a moment; den Tiſch ein wenig von der Wand —, to remove the table a little from the wall. *Fig.* Ein Geſetz —, to repeal, abolish or abrogate a law; Beſchwerden —, to redress grievances; ich werde dieſen Unfug —, I will put an end to, remedy this abuse; ſein böſes Leben —, to leave off one's ill courses. 2) [among brewers] to season the beer.

Ábſteller, *m.* [-s, *pl.* -] 1) he that abolishes, abolisher. 2) [among brewers] beer more seasoned.

Ábſtellung, *f.* abolishing, leaving off &c.

Abſtellungsmittel, *n.* means of abolishing any thing, or by which a thing is remedied.

Ábſtemmen, *v. tr.* [among joiners] to take off with the mortise chisel.

Ábſtempeln, I. *v. tr.* [among bookbind.] to flourish. II. *v. intr.* to finish stamping.

Ábſteppen, *v. tr.* to quilt [a coat].

Ábſterben, *ir. v. intr.* [u. w. ſeyn] 1) to die [said of men, plants]. Ein abgeſtorbenes Glied, a dead limb; dieſer Baum ſtirbt ab, this tree is decaying; ein abgeſtorbener Baum, a dead tree. *Fig.* Der Welt —, to withdraw from the world, to lose all relish for or of pleasures. Handel und Wandel ſind abgeſtorben, trade and commerce have decayed. 2) to become extinct. Meine Familie iſt abgeſtorben, my family is extinct. V. Ausſterben. 3) *Fig.* [in mining] to become narrower or of a worse quality [said of a vein].

Ábſterben, *n.* [-s] decease, death.

Ábſteuer, *f.* [*pl.* -n] V. Abzugsgeld.

Ábſteuern, *v. tr.* and *intr.* to steer off or away.

Ábſtich, *m.* [-es, *pl.* -e] 1) [in metallurgy] the metal that is let out of the dam of the furnace. 2) [in sewing] a pattern pricked off on paper.

3) *Fig.* contrast, set off.

Ábsticken, *v. tr.* to copy in embroidery.

Ábstimmen, I. *v. tr.* 1) to tune properly [a fiddle &c.]. 2) to lower or tune down. 3) to outvote. 4) to vote against any one. II. *v. intr.* 1) to vote. Ueber etwas —, to put a thing to the vote. 2) to be dissonant in sound. —de Töne, discordant tones. *Fig.* to disagree, to differ in opinion, to dissent.

Ábstimmig, *adj.* 1) dissonant, discordant. 2) *Fig.* dissenting.

Ábstimmung, *f.* 1) voting, [of sounds] discordance, dissonance. 2) vote.

Ábstochern, *v. tr.* to separate by picking.

Ábstöbern, *v. tr.* 1) V. Abstäuben. 2) V. Abstoppeln.

Ábstöckeln, *v. tr.* to beat off or down with a switch or stick [walnuts].

Ábstocken, I. *v. tr.* V. Ablegen. II. *v. intr.* [u. w. seyn] to separate from putrefaction, to rot off.

Ábstöhnen, *v. r.* sich —, to tire with groaning.

Ábstoppeln, *v. tr.* to gather any thing thinly scattered, to glean.

Ábstoßeisen, *n.* V. Schroteisen.

Ábstoßen, *ir.* I. *v. tr.* 1) to separate or remove by a thrust or push. Einen Kahn vom Ufer —, to push or shove off a boat from the shore, to get clear of the shore: sich die Haut —, to knock off one's skin; Einem den Hut —, to knock off any one's hat; einem Missethäter das Genick oder das Herz —, = den Gnadenstoß geben, to give the finishing blow or stroke to a person executed. *Fig.* Es wird ihm das Herz —, it will break his heart. *Prov.* Er hat sich die Hörner noch nicht abgestoßen, he has not yet sown his wild oats 2) [among joiners, carpenters, masons] Eine Fuge —, to shoot a joint; die untere Kante an einem Brette schief —, [among organ builders] to cut a board slopingly; die Kanten einer Staffel —, to hew off, to round off the edges of a step; einen Stein —, to hew off a stone. 3) [in husbandry] Kälber —, to wean calves; die Lammszähne —, to lose the milkteeth; die Bienen —, to kill the bees and take their honey. 4) [in music] Die Töne —, to perform the notes in a distinct and detached manner; abgestoßen, staccato. 5) [in commerce] eine Schuld —, to pay a debt; Waaren —, to sell, vend commodities. 6) *Fig.* to repel approach by raising aversion or dislike. Eine abstoßende Miene, a forbidding air. 7) [in physics] V. Zurückstoßen. 8) to thrust sufficiently. [in metallurgy] Eine Grube —, to fill a pit with ashes, and to thrust them in. II. *v. intr.* to shove off from the land, to bear off. III. *v. r.* sich —, to wear out, to rub off. Das Kleid hat sich abgestoßen, the coat is worn out, threadbare.

Ábstottern, V. Herstottern.

* **Abstráct**, I. *adj.* 1) [in logic, an epithet applied to whatever is separated from any other thing by an operation of the mind, termed abstraction] abstract. Ein —er Begriff, an abstract idea [as virtue, honour]; — [abgesondert] betrachtet, considered in the abstract, abstractly. 2) [separate, existing in the mind only] abstract. Ein —er Gegenstand, an abstract subject; eine —e Frage, an abstract question. II. *s.* V. Conspan.

Abstractión, *f.* [in logic] abstraction.

Abstractionsvermögen, *n.* V. Absonderungsvermögen.

Abstráctum, *n.* [-s] abstract.

Ábstrafen, *v. tr.* to punish, to chastise, to correct.

Ábstrafung, *f.* punishment, chastisement, correction.

† **Abstrahíren**, *v. tr.* 1) [in logic] to abstract. Abstrahirend, abstractive. 2) to concede, to yield up. Von etwas —, to give a thing over. V. Abstehen.

Ábstrahl, *m.* [-es, *pl.* -en] a reflected ray.

Ábstrahlen, *v. intr.* to reflect.

Abstrahlungswinkel, V. Absprungswinkel.

Ábstrebekraft, *n.* [*pl.* -kräfte] [in physics] centrifugal force [of the planets &c.].

Ábstreben, *v. intr.* to exert one's self to get rid of any thing.

Ábstreichbaum, *m.* V. Streichbaum.

Ábstreicheisen, *n.* V. Streicheisen.

Ábstreichen, *ir.* I. *v. tr.* 1) to strike off or away. Das Korn im Scheffel —, to strike corn; das Fell —, [among tanners] to scrape a skin. 2) [in metall., to take away the slag which rises at the top of the melted iron] to skim, to scum. 3) to strike sufficiently. Ein Scheermesser —, to strap a razor; † Einen —, to whip any one soundly. 4) [among sportsmen] Ein Feld —, to beat a field for larks; eine Flur —, to fly over a plain in all directions, to scour a plain in search of prey. II. *v. intr.* [used with seyn and haben] 1) [among sportsmen] to quit the nest [said of birds]. 2) [among anglers] to finish spawning.

Ábstreifbar, *adj.* and *adv.* capable of being stript off.

Ábstreifeln, *diminut.* of Abstreifen.

Ábstreifen, I. *v. tr.* to separate with the hand by stripping, to strip, to strip off. Blätter —, to strip off leaves, to unleave; Bohnen —, to unstring beans; einen Hasen —, to strip a hare; einen Aal —, to skin an eel; einen Fuchs —, to flay a fox; die Handschuhe —, to draw off one's gloves; ein Pferd streift den Zaum ab, a horse slips his bridle; die Kugel streifte ihm den Hut ab, the bullet carried his hat off. II. *v. intr.* to glance [as an arrow from a tree].

Ábstreifer, *m.* [-s, *pl.* -] 1) one who strips off. 2) V. Abstecher.

Ábstreiten, *ir. v. tr.* 1) to obtain by dispute. 2) to deprive of &c. by a lawsuit, to obtain by litigation. 3) to dispute, to contest. Dieß lasse ich mir nicht —, this shall not be disputed me, I won't be argued out of this.

Ábstrich, *m.* [-es, *pl.* -e] 1) that which is skimmed off the surface of any thing with the hand or an instrument. 2) [in metallurgy the scum of lead that arises in purifying silver with lead] litharge.

Abstrichblei, *n.* the lead obtained by remelting the dross which has been skimmed off.

Ábstricken, *v. tr.* 1) to clear [a needle] by knitting off the meshes. 2) to finish knitting. 3) to loosen [a dog that is fastened by a cord]. || 4) *Fig.* to steal cunningly.

Ábstriegeln, *v. tr.* to curry [a horse]. † *Fig.* Einen —, to curry, to thrash, to lick any one.

Ábströmen, I. *v. intr.* [used with seyn] 1) to be carried away by the stream, to flow off rapidly. *Fig.* V. sich verlaufen. 2) [a sea term] to be carried away by currents. II. *v. tr.* 1) to float down a stream [timber &c.]. 2) to separate by streaming.

Ábstrossen, *v. tr.* [in mining] to dig or work by gradation.

Abstückeln, **Abstücken**, *v. tr.* to separate in pieces, to crumble.

Ábstudieren, *v. r.* sich —, to overstudy one's self, to fatigue or hurt one's self by too severe study.

Ábstufen, I. *v. tr.* 1) [in mining] to break off [ore] piece-meal. 2) to mark at regular intervals. *Fig.* to form shades or nice differences, to diversify by gradation. II. *v. intr.* to diminish gradually.

Ábstufung, *f.* gradation, graduation. V. Gradation, Nuance.

Ábstülpen, *v. tr.* Den Hut —, to uncock a hat, to let down the flap.

Ábstümpfen, **Abstumpfen**, I. *v. tr.* to take off, to dull the edge or point. Ein Messer —, to blunt a knife; einem Pferde den Schwanz —, to dock a horse; [in mathematics] ein abgestumpfter Kegel, a truncate cone. *Fig.* Die Sinne —, to deaden the senses; das Gesicht —, to dull the sight; das beständige Saufen hat ihn, hat seinen Verstand ganz abgestumpft, continual drunkeness has completely stupefied him; es wird seinen Geist —, it will take off the edge of his wit. II. *v. r.* sich —, to make insensible, dull.

Ábstürmen, I. *v. tr.* 1) to separate by a storm, 2) to obtain by bullying. II. *v. intr.* 1) [u. w. haben] to cease storming. 2) [u. w. seyn] to go away in a hurry, to rush out.

Ábsturz, *m.* [-es, *pl.* -stürze] 1) rapid downfall [of water]. 2) precipice, steep.

Ábstürzen, I. *v. intr.* to fall headlong, to precipitate. II. *v. tr.* 1) to precipitate, to throw headlong. 2) to break off by falling down. Sich den Hals —, to break one's neck. 3) to throw down by a quick motion.

Ábstutzen, *v. tr.* 1) to cut short, to clip. Einem Pferde den Schwanz —, to dock the tail of a horse; einem Pferde die Mähnen —, to hog the mane of a horse; einem Pferde oder Hunde die Ohren —, to crop the ears of a horse or dog; die Flügel —, to clip the wings; Bäume —, to top, crop or lop trees; abgestutzt, [in herald.] truncated. Ein abgestutztes Blatt, [in botany] a truncated leaf. 2) [among cloth-shearers] to give the first sheering to the cloth.

Ábstützen, *v. tr.* [a sea term] to shore or shore up [a ship on the stocks].

Ábsuchen, *v. tr.* 1) to search and take. Die Raupen vom Baume —, to pick caterpillars from a tree; die Läuse —, to louse. 2) to search duly. Der Hühnerhund sucht ein Feld ab, [among sportsmen] the pointer ranges over a field in quest of game, quarters a field.

Ábsud, *m.* [-es, *pl.* -süde] a preparation extracted by boiling water, decoction, decocture. Ein starker — von China, a strong decoction of Peruvian bark.

Ábsudeln, *v. tr.* to transcribe, to copy, to take off negligently.

Ábsumpfen, *v. tr.* 1) to dry up a swamp or march, to drain. 2) [in metallurgy] to break down the cupels.

* **Absúrd**, I. *adj.* inconsistent with reason, absurd, foolish. II. *adv.* absurdly, foolishly.

* **Absurditä́t**, *f.* [*pl.* -en] absurdity, foolishness.

Ábsüßen, *v. tr.* 1) to sweeten, to edulcorate, to dulcorate a medicine. 2) [in chimistry and metallurgy] to edulcorate, to purify. Absüßend, edulcorative.

Ábt, *m.* [-es, *pl.* Aebte] abbot. Ein infulirter —, a mitred abbot; ein gefürsteter —, an abbot prince, an abbot sovereign. *Prov.* Wie der —, so die Mönche, like abbot, like monks; den — reiten lassen, to be merry without constraint.

Ábtafeln, *v. intr.* to finish dining, to have done dining, to rise from table.

Ábtäfeln, V. Täfeln.

Ábtakeln, *v. tr.* [a sea term] to unrig, to dismantle a ship. Die Masten —, to strip the masts.

Ábtändeln, *v. tr.* to obtain by toying.

Ábtanzen, *v. tr.* I. 1) to take off in dancing. 2) to wear off by dancing. Sich die Sohlen —, to wear out the soles of one's shoes by dancing. II. *v. intr.* 1) to dance off. 2) to finish dancing. III. *v. r.* sich —, to tire one's self by dancing.

Ábtauchen, I. *v. intr.* V. Untertauchen. II. *v. tr.* to cleanse by dipping.

Ábtaumeln, *v. intr.* [used with seyn] to reel off, to stagger away.

Ábtausch, *m.* [-es] exchange, barter, swap.

Ábtauschen, *v. tr.* to exchange, to barter, to swap.

Ábtauschung, *f.* exchanging.

Abtei, *f.* 1) abbey, the residence of an abbot. 2) abbotship, the state of an abbot. 3) abbacy, the dignity, right and privileges of an abbot.

Abteilich, *adj.* belonging to an abbey, abbatical.

Ábteufen, *v. tr.* [in mining] Einen Schacht —, to sink a shaft or a pit.

Ábthauen, I. *v. intr.* [u. w. seyn] to separate by thawing. II. *v. tr.* [u. w. haben] to cause to thaw off.

Ábtheil, *m.* [-es, *pl.* -e] appanage.

Ábtheilen, *v. tr.* to divide. Eine Summe Geldes —, to divide a sum of money; einen Wärmemesser in seine Grade —, to graduate a thermometer; die Gottesgelahrtheit wird in &c. abgetheilt, divinity is divided into &c.; in Klassen —, to form or to range into classes, to class, classify; die Zimmer eines Hauses —, to dispose the rooms of a house. 2) [a law term] to pay off children. V. Abschichten, Abfinden. Mit Einem —, to settle accounts with one; ein abgetheilter [better abgetheiligter] Prinz, an appanaged prince.

Ábtheilung, *f.* 1) the act of dividing, division, partition. Die — in Klassen, classification; die — in Grade, graduation. 2) the part which is separated by dividing, division. Die Abtheilung eines Gartens, the compartments of a garden; die — eines Heeres, einer Flotte, a division of an army, or a fleet; die —en in einem Hause, the partitions; die Amphitheater bedurften keiner —en, amphitheatres needed no compartitions; die — in einer Schrift, the section of a book or writing; die — einer Rede, the part or division of a discourse.

Abtheilungszeichen, *n.* hyphen.

Abthön, *m.* V. Frauenhaar.

Ábthun, *ir. v. tr.* 1) to take off, to put off, to lay aside. Den Hut —, [better abnehmen] to take off the hat, to uncover. *Fig.* Eine Rechnung —, to close or settle an account; eine Schuld —, to pay, clear a debt; einen Streit —, to end a quarrel; dies ist eine abgethane Sache, 't is a settled thing; einen Besuch —, to dispatch a visit. 2) to kill, to put to death. Ein Schwein —, to stick a pig; einen Uebelthäter —, to execute a malefactor, to put a malefactor to death; mit dem Schwert —, to put to the sword. Syn. Abthun, beilegen, schlichten. Abthun is used to signify merely that an affair is ended or settled, without any reference to its having been previously disputed. Thus one can say not only einen Streit abthun, settle a dispute, but also an account or debt. Beilegen and schlichten refer to a disputed matter which is adjusted by compromise.

Ábtiefen, V. Abteufen.

Ábtilgen, V. Tilgen. *Fig.* Eine Schuld —, to clear a debt.

Aebtinn, *f.* the wife of a protestant abbot.

Aebtissinn, *f.* abbess.

Aebtlich, *adj.* belonging to an abbot.

Ábtoben, I. *v. tr.* Einem etwas —, to obtain a thing from any one by bullying. II. *v. intr.* V. Austoben.

Ábtödten, *v. tr.* to kill. *Fig.* Unsere sinnlichen Begierden —, to mortify our sensual appetites.

Ábtödtung, *f.* mortification [of desires &c.].

Ábtönen, *v. intr.* to deviate from the right tone.

Ábtrab, [-es] [in milit. affairs] a detachment.

Ábtraben, *v. intr.* [u. w. seyn] to move, or march off on a trot. † *Fig.* Er mußte —, he was obliged to take himself off.

Ábtrag, *m.* [-es, *pl.* -träge] 1) the act of paying. Der — einer Schuld, the payment of a debt. 2) the sum given in discharge of a debt, payment. 3) [a law term] amends, compensation, reparation. 4) detriment, hurt [in commerce]. Einem — thun, to prejudice any one.

Ábtragen, *ir.* I. *v. tr.* 1) to separate by taking down, carrying away; to carry away or off, to remove. Ein Gebäude —, to pull down, to take down a building; einen Hügel —, to level or lower a hill; den Tisch —, to clear the table; den Leithund [among sportsmen] to carry away the limer from the trace [in order that he may find it again]. 2) [in mathem.] to sketch, to copy. 3) to pay, to discharge. Schulden —, to clear off debts; Steuern, Zoll —, to pay taxes, tolls; eine Schuld der Dankbarkeit —, to pay a debt of gratitude. 4) to wear out [one's clothes &c.]. II. *v. r.* sich —, Die Bäume haben sich abgetragen, the trees are exhausted and yield no fruit, have ceased bearing. Syn. Abtragen, Bezahlen. Abtragen does not necessarily mean to pay in money, but also in any other thing. Bezahlen properly speaking signifies to pay in money only. The farmer trägt seinen Pacht ab [discharges his rent], by payment in kind or in money; er bezahlt ihn ab, when he pays it in money.

Ábträger, *m.* [-s, *pl.* -] [among brickmakers] one who carries the moulded bricks to the hacks.

Ábtragung, *f.* the act off carrying off, pulling down, leveling. V. Abtragen.

Ábtrampeln, I. *v. tr.* 1) to wear off by trampling. 2) to obtain by trampling. II. *v. intr.* [u. w. seyn] to tramp off. III. *v. r.* sich —, to stamp violently.

Ábtrauern, I. *v. intr.* 1) to cease wearing mourning. 2) to put on half mourning. II. *v. r.* sich —, to waste away or pine away with grief.

Ábträufeln, **Abtraufen**, *v. intr.* to trickle down.

Ábtreibemittel, *n.* [-s, *pl.* -] a drug having the power of causing an abortion, abortive.

Ábtreiben, *ir. v. tr.* 1) to drive off, drive away. Wilde Thiere von einem Walde —, to expel wild beasts from a forest; den Feind —, to repel the enemy; Einen von einem Kaufe —, to get the better of any one in a purchase, by outbidding him or otherwise; dieser zudringliche Mensch läßt sich nicht —, this obtrusive fellow is not to be rebuffed. 2) [among sportsmen] Ein Dickicht —, to beat or drive the game out of a thicket in the direction of the hunters placed on the outside. 3) [among foresters] einen Wald —, to cut down, to fell a wood or forest. 4) to overdrive, to jade [a horse]. 5) *Fig.* Ein Kind —, to cause an abortion; —de Mittel, abortive draughts. 6) [in metallurgy] to refine [gold, silver], to purify from other metals. II. *v. intr.* [u. w. seyn] 1) [a sea term] to make leeway, to drive or fall to leeward. 2) to be carried out of the right course, to drift [said of a ship].

Ábtreiber, *m.* [-s, *pl.* -] [in metallurgy] one who refine's metals.

Ábtreibung, *f.* the act of driving off. V. Abtreiben. Das —smittel, V. Abtreibemittel.

Ábtrennbar, *adj.* capable of being separated, separable. V. Abtrennen.

Ábtrennen, *v. tr.* 1) to separate, disjoin, disunite, dismember. 2) to rip, to unstitch, to unsew. Den Besatz vom Kleide —, to rip off the trimming of a gown.

Ábtrennung, *f.* separation, dismemberment, the act of ripping.

Ábtreppen, *v. tr.* [among masons] Eine Mauer —, to build a wall in the form of stairs

Ábtreten, *ir.* I. *v. tr.* 1) to tread off, tread down, to trample. 2) to wear off by treading. Ein abgetretener Absatz, a worn off heel. 3) to mark by treading, to form by treading. Einen Weg —, to tread a path, to beat a path. 4) to yield, to give up. Die Krone —, to abdicate the crown; Jupiter tritt seinen Donner dem Gott der Liebe ab, Jove resigns his thunder to the god of love; ein Land —, to cede a country; ein Recht —, to make over or relinquish a right to another; sein Besitzthum einem andern —, to transfer one's estate to another; ein Zahlungsunfähiger, der seine Güter seinen Gläubigern abgetreten hat, an absolvent who has yielded up his estates to be divided among his creditors, a cessionary bankrupt; einen Pachtvertrag —, to assign a lease.

II. *v. intr.* [used with seyn] 1) to withdraw, to retire, to retreat. Einen — heißen, to bid one retire; der Schauspieler trat ab, the actor made his exit. 2) *Fig.* Von der Bühne —, to go off the stage; vom Schauplatz des Lebens —, to depart this life, to die; von einer Meinung —, to quit an opinion; von einer Religion —, to depart from one's religion. 2) to alight, to stop at an inn &c.

Ábtreter, *m.* [-s, *pl.* -] one who gives up a right.

Ábtretung, *f.* 1) the act of treading off. 2) wearing off. 3) cession, resignment, abdication, resignation. 4) alighting. 5) putting up [at]. 6) making his exit &c.

Ábtrieb, *m.* [-es, *pl.* -e] 1) the act of driving off. 2) [among foresters] felling, cutting down [trees]. 3) [a law term] the prior right of purchase, the refusal.

Ábtriefen, *v. intr.* [u. w. seyn] to trickle down, to drip, to drop. † *Fig.* Es wird dabei auch für mich etwas — [or abfallen], I hope to profit a little by it.

Ábtrifft, *f.* [*pl.* -en] 1) [a sea term] deflection, lee way, drift. 2) [in husbandry] the right of pasturage.

Ábtrillern, *v. tr.* to utter with a shaking or quavering voice. Ein Liedchen —, to hum a tune.

Ábtrinken, *ir.* I. *v. tr.* 1) to drink off the surface, to sip off. 2) to finish by drinking; der Thee ist schon abgetrunken, the tea-pot has been drained. 3) to drink at an innkeeper's for the sum he owes one; II. *v. r.* sich —, to weaken one's self by drinking.

Ábtrippeln, I. *v. intr.* [u. w. seyn] to trip off or away. II. *v. r.* sich —, to bustle or trip busily about.

Ábtritt, *m.* [-es, *pl.* -e] 1) the act of going off, of retiring [not used]. Seinen — nehmen, to go off, to retire, to withdraw, to retreat. *Fig.* Der — von einer Kirche, the departing from one's religion, apostasy; wir haben ihm 100 Thaler für den — gegeben, we have paid him a hundred dollars for resigning his right. 2) *Fig.* departure, death, decease. 3) alighting [on a journey]. Seinen — bei Einem nehmen, to alight at any one's house. 4) [in mining] a stepping place, a step, a landing place, shambles. 5) a privy, necessaryhouse, watercloset. 6) [among hunters] the sprigs or grass that the stag beats down in passing by, abature; das —smerkmahl, the footing or track of deer on the grass, foiling.

Ábtrocknen, I. *v. tr.* to wipe off, to dry. Sich die Hände —, to dry one's hands; den Tisch —, to wipe the table; trocknet eure Thränen ab, dry up your tears; Wäsche —, to air linen. II. *v. intr.* [u. w. seyn] 1) to dry or to grow dry; die Straße trocknet an einem hellen und windigen Tage schnell ab, the road dries fast on a clear windy day. 2) to wither and fall off.

† **Ábtrollen**, *v. intr.* [u. w. seyn] to walk off with short quick steps.

Ábtrommeln, I. *v. tr.* 1) to beat on the drum [a march]. 2) to publish by drumming. 3) [in husbandry] to dislodge bees by beating with a stick on the hive. II. *v. intr.* to finish drumming.

Ábtrompeten, I. *v. tr.* 1) to perform on the trumpet. 2) to publish by sound of trumpet, to trumpet. II. *v. intr.* to finish trumpeting.

Ábtröpfeln, **Ábtropfen**, *v. intr.* to drop off, to drip, to trickle down. Die Heringe — lassen, to let the herrings drain [after taking them out of the brine].

Ábtropfbank, *f.* [*pl.* -bänke] drainer.

Ábtropfpfanne, *f.* [*pl.* -n] 1) [in paper-mills] dropping-board. 2) [among paste-board makers] drainer.

Ábtropftrog, *m.* [-es, *pl.* -tröge] [among tallowchandlers] dropping-board.

Ábtrotzen, *v. tr.* to extort from, to hector out. Einem sein Geld —, to hector or bully any one out of his money.

Ábtrümmern, *v. intr.* [used with seyn] to fall off in fragments, to crumble away.

Ábtrumpfen, *v. tr.* 1) [among carpenters] to frame trimmers at right angles to the joists. 2) [at cards] to trump, to take with a trump card. † *Fig.* Einen —, to snap any one up, to take any one up short.

Ábtrünnig, *adj.* faithless, disloyal, recreant, apostate. — werden, to desert, to revolt; er ist seinen Versprechungen — geworden, he has proved faithless to his promises; von der Religion — werden, to apostatize, to backslide, to revolt, to depart from one's religion; — machen, to debauch, to seduce, draw off. Der Abtrünnige, deserter, revolter, apostate, renegade, recreant.

Ábtrünnigkeit, *f.* disloyalty, desertion, revolt, apostacy, defection.

Ábtruppen, I. *v. tr.* to dismiss soldiers from duty. II. *v. intr.* [u. w. seyn] to march off in troops.

Ábtummeln, *v. tr.* to knock up, to tire, to fatigue [a horse]. *Fig.* Sich —, to fatigue one's self by bustling.

Ábtünchen, V. Tünchen.

Ábtupfen, *v. tr.* to dry up, to desiccate.

Ábtuschen, *v. tr.* [a drawing] to copy with Indian ink.

Áburtheilen, ‡ **Aburtheln**, I. *v. tr.* to deprive of by a judicial sentence, to give a verdict against. Einem ein Gut —, to dispossess or turn any one out of possession, of an estate. II. *v. intr.* 1) to decide finally. Der Gerichtshof urtheilte zu Gunsten des Beklagten ab, the court decided in favour of the defendant. 2) to prejudicate. Sie haben Unrecht, über eine Sache —, die Sie nicht verstehen, you are wrong to pronounce so decided an opinion upon a thing with which you are not acquainted.

* **Abus**, **Abusus**, *m.* V. Mißbrauch.

Ábverdienen, *v. intr.* 1) to get by service from any one, to gain by labour, to earn. 2) to clear by service. Eine Schuld —, to clear a debt by working for one's creditor.

Ábverlangen, V. Abfodern.

Ábvieren, *v. tr.* 1) to square [a stone]. Einen Balken —, [among carpenters] to square a beam. 2) *Fig.* to polish, to refine, to make elegant of manners. 3) [a sea term] to veer. — und anholen, to veer and haul.

Ábvierung, *f.* the act of squaring [a stone, beam &c.].

Ábvisiren, *v. tr.* [in practic. mathem.] 1) to measure the height of an object by the level, to estimate the dimensions of a tree [before it is felled]. 2) to measure the contents of a cask or other vessel with a gauge, to gauge.

* **Ábvotiren**, *v. tr.* 1) to outvote. 2) to vote against. V. Abstimmen.

Ábwachen, *v. r.* sich —, to fatigue one's self by watching.

Ábwackeln, I. *v. tr.* to shake off. † *Fig.* Einen —, to bang any one. II. *v. intr.* [used with seyn] to go off totteringly.

Ábwage, *f.* [in physics] 1) the mutual difference between a height and a depth. 2) the distance between the resistance and the fulcrum or point of suspension in a lever.

Ábwägekunst, *f.* [Nivellirkunst] art of leveling.

Ábwägen, *v. tr.* 1) to determine the weight of an object by the scales, to weigh. Alle Dinge nach Freuden und Leiden —, to weigh all things by pleasure and sorrow; seine Worte auf der Goldwage —, to weigh one's words well. 2) to ascertain how much higher or lower any given point on the surface of the earth is than another. Das Abwägen, [in mathem.] leveling. 3) to give by weight, to weigh out.

Ábwägung, *f.* the act of 1) weighing, 2) leveling.

Ábwäger, *m.* [-s, *pl.* -] level. V. Niveleur.

Ábwägungskunst, *f.* V. Nivelirkunst.

Ábwalken, *v. tr.* 1) to full, to mill [cloth]. † 2) *Fig.* to drub soundly.

Ábwalzen, I. *v. tr.* to separate by a roller. II. *v. r.* sich —, to tire one's self by waltzing.

Ábwälzen, *v. tr.* to roll off, to roll away, to roll down. *Fig.* Eine Beschuldigung von sich —, to exculpate one's self and throw the blame on others; er wälzt Alles von sich ab, he shakes or throws every thing off his own shoulders.

† **Ábwamsen**, *v. tr.* to beat, to drub, to thrush soundly.

Ábwandelbar, *adj.* [in gram.] capable of being conjugated, declinable.

Ábwandeln, I. *v. tr.* 1) [in gram.] to conjugate or to decline. 2) [law term and ||] ein Verbrechen —, to pronounce sentence of punishment for a crime. *Fig.* Einen Fehler — [V. Abbüßen], to atone for a fault. II. *v. intr.* [u. w. seyn] to wander away.

Ábwandelung, *f.* [in gram.] conjugation, declension.

Ábwandern, I. *v. intr.* [u. w. seyn] to walk off, to depart, to wander away. II. *v. r.* sich —, to tire one's self with walking.

Ábwärmen, *v. tr.* 1) to warm through, [in metallurgy] to heat the furnace [in order to dry it]. 2) [in glass works] to diminish slowly the heat of a furnace.

Ábwarnen, *v. tr.* to warn from, to caution against.

Ábwarten, *v. tr.* 1) to await, to wait for, to stay for, to attend the coming, to await the termination of any thing. Er kann nichts —, he cannot wait for any thing, he is always in a hurry; wir wollen den Sturm —, let us wait till the storm is over; ich kann es nicht —, I cannot await the issue of it. 2) to attend to, to look to or after, to fix the mind upon. Ein Geschäft —, to attend to, to mind a business, to apply one's self to a business; einen Kranken —, to tend, to take care of a sick person.

Ábwärts, *adv.* downward, downwards, [in sea language] offward. Wir segelten auf dem Strom —, we sailed down the stream; — des Flusses, down the river.

Ábwartung, *f.* 1) waiting or staying for a thing. 2) attending, minding, tending.

Ábwäsche, *f.* 1) the act of washing or cleansing. 2) the set of vessels washed at once.

Ábwaschen, *ir.* I. *v. tr.* 1) to wash away, to wash off, to lave, to bathe, to cleanse. Die Hände —, to wash one's hands. *Fig.* Eine Sünde durch Reue —, to wash away a sin by repentance. 2) to wear out by washing. 3) to clear by washing. II. *v. r.* sich —, 1) to wash one's self. 2) to tire with washing.

Ábwaschbecken, *n.* [-s, *pl.* -] basin, washhandbasin, laver.

Ábwaschfaß, *n.* [-fasses, *pl.* -fässer] laver, washing tub.

Ábwaschung, *f.* washing, bathing, [in chimistry and liturgy] ablution.

Ábwässern, *v. tr.* 1) to drain, to rid of superfluous water [a swamp]. 2) to steep in water, to soak [herrings]. 3) *Fig.* [among carpenters] to slope [a piece of timber] so as to cause the water to run off.

Ábwässerung, *f.* 1) the act of draining. 2) soaking, steeping in water. 3) [among carpenters] a slope [in windows, doors, beams], to turn off water.

Ábweben, *v. tr.* 1) to finish weaving. 2) V. Abwickeln.

Ábwechseln, I. *v. tr.* 1) to get by changing or by exchange. 2) to cause to succeed by turns. Die Stimme —, to modulate the voice. 3) [among carpenters] V. Abtrumpfen. II. *v. intr.* to do, to perform, to use by turns. Sie wechseln ab, they relieve one another; der Koch wechselt mit den Speisen ab, the cook varies his dishes. 2) to follow, to take place alternately. Ebbe und Fluth wechseln mit einander ab, the ebb and flood tides alternate with each other; —de Blätter, Zweige, [in botany] alternate leaves, branches. Diese beiden Heerführer befehligten abwechselnd das Heer, these two generals commanded the army alternately. Glück und Unglück wechseln mit einander ab, good and bad luck come by turns; —de Fieber, intermitting fevers; —de Witterung, changeable weather.

Ábwechselung, *f.* 1) change, exchange, variation, variety. 2) the reciprocal succession of things in time or place; the act of following and being followed in succession, alternation. Die — von Tag und Nacht, the alternation of day and night; — in eine Landschaft durch Berge, Ebenen und Bäume bringen, to diversify a landscape with mountains, plains and trees; die — beim Choralgesang, alternation; die — der Jahreszeiten, the vicissitude of the seasons; zur —, for a change, by way of variety.

Ábweg, *m.* [-es, *pl.* -e] 1) by-way, by-path. Diese Straße hat viele Abwege, this road has many by-roads. 2) a wrong way. *Fig.* Auf Abwege gerathen, to get off the right path, to follow bad courses; Abwege suchen, to seek shifts, evasions. V. Ausflüchte.

Ábwegs, Abwégs, *adv.* out of the way.

Ábwegig, *adj.* and *adv.* situated out of the high road.

Ábwegsam, *adj.* and *adv.* out of the way, devious.

Ábwehen, I. *v. tr.* to blow off, to blow away or down. Fliegen —, to flap off flies. II. *v. intr.* 1) to blow from. Der Wind wehet vom Lande ab, the breeze comes from the land. 2) to cease blowing [in sea language]. Es hat abgeweht, the storm has blown over, has subsided, the weather clears up.

Ábwehr, *f.* 1) that which defends from an attack &c., fence, defence. 2) the act of defending one's self against a blow. Die — eines Stoßes, the warding off or parrying of a thrust or blow.

Abwehrmittel, *n.* [against disease, infection &c.] preventive, preservative.

Ábwehren, *v. tr.* to keep off, to fend off. Einen Stoß —, to ward off or parry a blow &c.; Fliegen —, to keep off, to flap away flies. *Fig.* Ein Uebel —, to avert, to turn away, to prevent some evil; er läßt sich nicht —, he is not to be kept from it, he won't be rebuffed.

1. **Ábweichen**, [from weich, soft] I. *v. tr.* 1) to separate or detach by mollifying [a plaster]. 2) to soften, to drench sufficiently, to macerate. Die Häute —, [among curriers] to soak the skins. II. *v. intr.* [u. w. seyn] to become soft and fall off.

2. **Ábweichen**, [from weichen] *ir. v. intr.* 1) to deviate [from the common track or path], to decline. Alle Körper, die in einem Kreise bewegt werden, haben einen beständigen Hang, vom Mittelpunkt abzuweichen, all bodies, moving circularly, have a perpetual tendency to recede from the centre; die Sterne weichen vom Gleicher ab, [in astronomy] the stars decline from the equator. —de Sonnenuhren, declining dials. 2) to differ, to vary. Von der allgemeinen Gewohnheit —, not to follow the general custom; von der Wahrheit —, to depart from truth; er weicht keinen Finger breit ab, he will not abate an inch of it; wir weichen sehr von einander ab, we differ widely; ein —des Zeitwort, an irregular verb; eine —de Aussprache, a different, varying pronunciation. 3) to pass. Der Termin ist abgewichen, the term has elapsed. Im abgewichenen Jahre, last year. Nicht abweichend, 1) undeviating. 2) regular.

Ábweichen, *n.* [-s] diarrhœa, looseness [of bowels].

1. **Ábweichung**, *f.* the act of separating or detaching by mollifying &c., the act of softening, maceration. V. 1. Abweichen.

2. **Ábweichung**, *f.* a turning aside from the right way, course or line, deviation. Die — eines fallenden Körpers, [in physics] the deviation of a falling body; die — der Magnetnadel, the variation or declination of the compass or needle; die — eines Sterns, [in astron.] the distance of a star from the equinoctial line or equator, the declination of a star; die — eines Planeten, [in astronomy] an irregularity in the motion of a planet, whereby it deviates from the aphelion or apogee, anomaly; die — zweier Linien, the divergence of two lines; die — der Lichtstrahlen, the deflection of the rays of light; [by Newton it is called] inflection. *Fig.* Die — von der Regel, the deviation from the rule, anomaly.

Abweichungs-compaß, *m.* declinator, azimuth-compass. —finder, *m.* V. —zeiger. —kreis, *m.* [in astronomy] circle of declination. —tafel, *f.* table of declinations. —zeiger, *m.* [in dialing] declinator, declinatory.

Ábweiden, *v. tr.* 1) to graze, to feed on. Das Rindvieh weidet die Wiese ab, the cattle graze the meadow. 2) to place cattle to feed. Der Hirt weidet das Feld ab, the shepherd grazes the field [puts the sheep in it].

Ábweifen, *v. tr.* to wind off on a reel [yarn].

Ábweinen, I. *v. tr.* 1) to obtain by dint of weeping. 2) to expiate by tears. II. *v. r.* sich —, to tire one's self by weeping, or to cry one's eyes out.

Ábweisen, *ir. v. tr* [from weisen] 1) to turn away, to refuse. Einen —, to dismiss or send away any one without complying with his request or accepting his offer; Einen kurz —, to send any one about one's business; etwas —, to reject something; abgewiesen werden, to be turned away, to be repulsed, to meet with a rebuff; den Feind —, to drive off, to repel, to repulse the enemy. 2) Vor Gericht —, [a law term] to nonsuit. 3) Einen Wechsel —, to dishonour, not accept a bill.

Ábweisestock, *m.* [-es, *pl.* -stöcke] V. Prallstein.

Ábweisung, *f.* a turning away, refusal. 1) Die — vor Gericht, [a law term] nonsuit; er hat einen —sbescheid erhalten, he was non-suited. 2) [in commerce] Die — eines Wechsels, dishonouring, non-acceptance of a bill.

Ábweißen, [from weiß, white] I. *v. tr.* to white-wash, to whiten. II. *v. intr.* to part with white.

Ábweite, *f.* [*pl.* -n] distance.

Ábwelken, *v. intr.* [u. w. seyn] 1) to wither and fall off. 2) *Fig.* to pine away, to wear away, to fade.

Ábwendbar, *adj.* capable of being prevented or hindered, preventable.

Ábwendbarkeit, *f.* possibility of being prevented.

Ábwenden, *reg.* and *ir.* I. *v. tr.* 1) to turn off or away, to turn from, to avert. Die Augen von einem Gegenstand —, to avert the eyes from an object; einen Hieb, Streich —, to ward, ward off, to parry a blow. 2) to keep off, to divert or prevent, to avert. Ein sich nahendes Unglück —, to avert an approaching calamity; das wolle Gott —! God forbid! *Fig.* Das Gemüth von etwas —, to turn or divert one's mind from a thing. II. *v. r.* sich —, 1) to turn away, to avert. 2) *Fig.* sich — von Einem, to leave, to abandon any one.

Ábwendig, *adj.* and *adv.* alienated, estranged, averse. — machen, to turn off, to alienate; Einem die Kunden — machen, to entice any one's customers away; Einen von seinem Vorhaben — machen, to divert or dissuade any one from his purpose; Einem die Gattin — machen, to seduce any one's wife.

Ábwendung, *f.* 1) a turning off or away, a turning from, averting. Die — eines Stoßes, [in fencing] parade, ward, guard. 2) *Fig.* die — des Gemüths, alienation of affections.

Ábwerfen, *ir.* I. *v. tr.* 1) to cast off, to throw, to throw off. Aepfel —, to knock down apples [with stones &c. from the tree]; das Pferd hat den Reiter abgeworfen, the horse has thrown its rider; die Hörner —, [among hunters] to shed the horns; die Schlange wirft ihre Haut ab, the serpent casts its skin; die Aeste eines Baumes —, to cut off the boughs of a tree; Brücken —, to pull down bridges; Junge —, to whelp; [in metall.] die Schlacken —, to throw off the slags; das überflüssige Zinn —, to melt off the superfluous tin from tinned iron plate; *Fig.* das Joch —, to shake off the yoke. 2) [at dice, at ninepins] to surpass in casting, throwing. Er hat mich abgeworfen, he has thrown more than I. 3) *Fig.* to bring in, to yield. Diese Stelle wirft nur hundert Pfund Sterling ab, this place yields only a hundred pounds a year. 4) *Fig.* [in the form of a *v. r.*] Sich mit einem —, to fall out with one. II. *v. intr.* 1) to finish whelping. 2) [among hunters] to shed the horns completely. 3) to finish playing at ninepins. Er wird —, he will throw last.

Ábwerfung, *f.* the act of casting off &c.

Ábwesend, *adj.* and *adv.* absent. Sprech Gutes von den Abwesenden, speak well of the absent. *Prov.* Die Abwesenden haben immer Unrecht, those who are absent are always in the wrong. Ein von seinem Amt, Besitzthum oder Vaterland Abwesender, absentee. *Fig.* Geistes—, absent [of mind], lost in thought, heedless.

Ábwesenheit, *f.* absence. Die — von dem Orte, wo ein Verbrechen begangen wurde, [a law term] alibi; die — [oder das Alibi] beweisen, to prove an alibi; der —svormund [a law term] curator of an absentee. *Fig.* absence of mind, heedlessness.

Ábwetten, *v. tr.* to get something from any one by betting. Er hat mir zehn Thaler abgewettet, he won a bet of ten dollars from me.

Ábwettern, I. *v. tr.* [among carpenters] to cut slantwise. II. *v. intr.* 1) to cease thundering and lightening. 2) *Fig.* to cease scolding.

Ábwetzen, *v. tr.* 1) to take off by whetting. Den Rost von einer Klinge —, to rub off the rust of a blade. 2) to whet, to sharpen [a knife]. 3) to wear out by whetting.

Ábwichsen, *v. tr.* 1) to polish with wax [mahogony] or with blacking [a pair of boots]. 2) *Fig.* to beat, to cane.

Ábwickeln, *v. tr.* to unwind, to unroll. V. Abwinden. Einen Knaul —, to unwind a clew.

Ábwiegen, V. Abwägen.

Ábwimmern, *v. tr.* to get by whining.

Ábwimpeln, *v. tr.* to lower the pendant [from the mast head].

Ábwinde, *f.* [*pl.* -n] a frame [turning upon an axis and upon which yarn is wound into skeins from the spindle], a reel.

Ábwinden, *ir. v. tr.* 1) to unwind, to wind off, to reel off. 2) to let down by means of a pulley. Die Stücke aus einem Schiffe —, to lower the guns out of a ship with the gun-tackle.

Ábwinken, *v. intr.* Einem —, 1) to call off or warn a person from a thing by a nod or beck; 2) to deny or refuse any one something by shaking one's head.

Ábwinseln, I. *v. tr.* to get by whining. II. *v. r.* sich —, to tire by whining.

Ábwirken, I. *v. tr.* 1) to work off. Den Teig —, to knead well the dough. 2) to finish working or weaving. 3) [in salt-houses] to finish the boiling. 4) [among hunters] to flay, to skin. Die Haut —, to strip or divest of the skin.

Ábwischen, I. *v. tr.* to wipe off, to wipe. Den Staub —, to dust or wipe away the dust; die Hände —, to wipe one's hands [with a napkin or towel]. II. *v. r.* sich —, to clean one's self by wiping.

Ábwischer, *m.* [-s, *pl.* -] 1) one who wipes any thing, a wiper. 2) the thing used for wiping, a wiper, duster, dusting-cloth. 3) a lamb's skin [used in rubbing parchment].

Ábwischlumpen, *m.* [-s, *pl.* -] dish-clout, dusting-clout or cloth, rubber, duster.

Ábwittern, I. *v. tr.* to find out by the scent, to scent. II. *v. intr.* 1) [u. w. haben] to cease thundering and lightening. V. Abwettern. 2) [u. w. seyn] to be dissolved by the action of the atmosphere. V. Verwittern.

Ábwölfen, *v. intr.* to finish whelping [said of a she-wolf].

Ábwollen, *v. tr.* to strip a hide of its wool [among curriers].

Ábwuchern, *v. tr.* to get by usury.

Ábwürdigen, *v. tr.* to reduce from a higher to a lower state, to degrade. Eine Münze —, to reduce a coin.

Ábwürdigung, *f.* V. Herabwürdigung.

Ábwurf, *m.* [-es, *pl.* Abwürfe] 1) a throwing down. 2) [at ninepins and dice] the last throw. 3) the thing thrown down or away.

Ábwürfeln, *v. tr.* 1) to win at dice. 2) to throw more than another [who had thrown before]. 3) V. Abwiegen.

Ábwürfig, *adj.* [said of a horse] inclined to kick and throw its rider.

Ábwürgen, *v. tr.* 1) to strangle, to choke. 2) *Fig.* to kill, to butcher. *Prov.* Einen unter der Maske der Freundschaft —, to cut any one's throat with a feather.

Ábwürgung, *f.* 1) the act of strangling or choking, strangulation. 2) *Fig.* killing.

Ábwürzen, *v. tr.* to season [meat]. *Fig.* Einen —, to reprimand any one, to turn off with a short answer, to snub any one.

Ábwüthen, I. *v. intr.* to cease raging II. *v. r.* sich —, to tire one's self by raging.

Ábwurzeln, *v. tr.* 1) to uproot. 2) to cut off the roots.

Abyssinien, *n.* [-s] Abyssinia.

Abyssinier, *m.* [-s, *pl.* -] Abyssinian.

Abyssinisch, *adj.* Abyssinian.

Ábzählen, *v. tr.* 1) to number, to count, to tell, or name one by one, or by small numbers. *Fig.* Ich kann mir dieß an den Fingern —, I can readily conceive this; I can easily guess it. 2) to separate by numbering.

Ábzählung, *f.* counting, telling.

Ábzahlen, *v. tr.* to pay, to discharge. Eine Rechnung —, to discharge an account. *Fig.* Einen —, to reprimand any one.

Ábzahlung, *f.* paying, discharging.

Ábzahnen, I. *v. intr.* to shed the milk-teeth. II. *v. tr.* [among joiners] to take off with the tooth plane.

Ábzahnung, *f.* the shedding of milk-teeth.

Ábzanken, I. *v. tr.* 1) to obtain by quarreling. 2) to reprimand any one sharply or roughly, to scold any one. II. *v. r.* sich —, to tire or fatigue one's self with quarreling.

Ábzapfen, *ir. v. tr.* 1) to draw, to draw off, to tap [wine, cider &c.]; einen Wassersüchtigen —, to tap a dropsical person; Blut —, to draw blood. *Fig.* Einen —, to cheat any one impudently.

Ábzapfer, *m.* [-s, *pl.* -] 1) one who draws liquors from a cask &c., a tapster. 2) [in surgery] a catheter.

Ábzapfung, *f.* 1) the act of tapping or drawing wine or any other liquor from a cask &c. 2) [in surgery] tapping, paracentesis.

Ábzappeln, I. *v. intr.* to sprawl about, to withdraw sprawling. II. *v. r.* sich —, to tire with sprawling.

Ábzasern, I. *v. tr.* to take off the fibres [of a root &c.]. II. *v. r.* sich —, to part with threads or fibres. V. Abfasern.

Ábzaubern, *v. tr.* to obtain by witchcraft, by the power of charms.

Ábzäumen, *v. tr.* to unbridle [a horse].

Ábzäumung, *f.* unbridling.

Ábzäunen, *v. tr.* 1) to fence in or off. 2) Einem etwas von seinem Gute —, to encroach by enclosing or hedging off a part of any one's estate.

Ábzausen, I. *v. tr.* 1) to separate by hauling and pulling about. 2) to disorder, to tumble, to pull or haul about, to tousel. II. *v. r.* sich —, to tire with pulling about.

Ábzechen, V. Abtrinken.

Ábzehnten, I. *v. tr.* 1) to gather or levy the tithes [of a field &c.]. 2) to satisfy the claims of a person by paying tithe, to pay tithe to any one. II. *v. intr.* to pay tithe. Er hat abgezehntet, he has paid his tithes.

Ábzehren, I. *v. tr.* 1) to diminish by eating and drinking. Eine Schuldforderung —, to pay one's self by living at the debtor's expense. 2) to exhaust, to consume slowly, to extenuate, to emaciate. Diese Krankheit hat ihn ganz abgezehrt, this illness has quite reduced him; der Kummer zehrt ihn ab, he pines away with sorrow; eine abzehrende Krankheit, a wasting disease, atrophy. II. *v. r.* sich —, to consume or waste away. III. *v. intr.* to grow lean, to pine, to emaciate.

Ábzehrung, *f.* 1) the growing lean, falling away, emaciation. 2) V. Auszehrung.

Ábzeichen, *n.* [-s, *pl.* -] 1) a mark or sign of distinction. 2) a mark on the body [as a harelip, a wart, a mole &c.].

Ábzeichnen, I. *v. tr.* 1) to mark, to mark out [a plot of ground &c.]. 2) to draw, to sketch [the figure of a man]. Die Gestalt der Erde —, to delineate the form of the earth; eine Figur —, to design or draw a figure; mit Kreide —, to chalk; eine Festung —, to take or draw the plan of a fortress. II. *v. r.* sich —, to be traced against. Die Umrisse dieses Gebirgs zeichnen sich schwach am Himmel ab, the outlines of these hills are faintly traced against the sky.

Ábzeichnung, *f.* 1) the act of drawing, designing, delineating. — mit Kreide, chalking. 2) draught, drawing, design, delineation, sketch.

Ábzerren, *v. tr.* to pull away from, to tear off, to wrest or to wring from.

Ábzetteln, *v. tr.* to unwarp a woof.

Ábziehen, *ir. v. tr.* 1) to separate by drawing or pulling off, to draw off, to pull off, to take off. Die Handschuhe —, to pull off one's gloves; die Kleider —, to pull off one's clothes; den Hut —, to take off, to pull off one's hat; einen Ring vom Finger —, to take a ring off one's finger; die Haut —, to strip off the skin, to skin, to flay; einem Kalbe die Haut —, to flay a calf; Mandeln —, to blanch almonds; die Larve —, to unmask; einen Bogen —, [in printing] to take off a proof, to work off a sheet; eine Kupferplatte —, to draw off an impression; *Fig.* das Wasser von einem Sumpfe —, to draw off the water from a marsh or bog, to drain a marsh or bog; einen Teich —, to drain a pond; von den Hefen —, to rack off; Wein, Bier &c. —, to draw off wine, beer &c., to rack wine; Branntwein —, to distill brandy [from wine &c.]; abgezogene Wasser, distilled waters; Kräuter —, to distill herbs. 2) [among several workmen] Ein Fell —, [among furriers] to scrape the fleshside completely, to pare a hide; die Arbeit —, [among joiners] to smooth the work with the spoke-shave; die Farbe —, [among dyers] to boil the colour out of a dyed stuff; die Stücke, welche zusammengelöthet werden sollen, —, [among braziers] to take off with a file the unevenness of the pieces which are to be sodered, to smooth them; ein Scheermesser —, to set, or to strap a razor; ein Gewicht —, to fix the standard of a weight, to size it; das Leder —, [among shoemakers] to rub the leather with pumice-stone; die Suppe mit einem Ei —, [in cooking] to dress the soup with the yellow of an egg. 3) to subtract, to deduct [in arithmetic]. Die Frachtkosten —, to deduct the charges of freight; einige Schillinge an einer Rechnung —, to defalcate some shillings from an account; Einem von seinem Lohne —, to diminish, to lessen any one's wages. 4) *Fig.* to abstract. [in logic] Ein abgezogener Begriff, an abstract idea. V. Abstrahiren.

II. *v. r.* sich —, 1) to weaken one's self by drawing or pulling. 2) [in printing] to lose colour. 3) V. Zurückziehen.

III. *v. intr.* [u. w. seyn] 1) to withdraw, to retire, to march off. Heimlich —, to slink or sneak away; von der Wache —, to come off guard, to be relieved; mit Schande —, to get off with disgrace; leer —, to withdraw without having obtained any thing; mit einer langen Nase —, *Prov.* to be disappointed in one's design. 2) to leave service. Die Kammerjungfer ist aus ihrem Dienste abgezogen, the lady's maid has left her place. 3) V. Wegziehen.

Abzieh-blase, *f.* [in distilling] a still, alembic. **—bogen**, *m.* [in printing, beim Wiederdruck] tympan sheet. **—bürste**, *f.* [in printing] letter brush. **—eisen**, *n.* 1) [among tanners] scraper. 2) [in husbandry] a hatchel or hitchel, a flaxcomb. **—feile**, *f.* [an iron tool used by wiredrawers] smoothing-file. **—flasche**, *f.* [a chimical vessel] cucurbit. **—klinge**, *f.* V. Zugklinge. **—leder**, *n.* razor-strap. **—muskel**, *m.* [in anatomy] abducent muscle, abductor. **—pflug**, *m.* [in husbandry] draining-plough. **—stein**, *m.* a hone. **—zahl**, *f.* [in arithmetic] subtrahend. **—zeug**, *n.* utensils used in distillery.

Ábzieher, *m.* [-s, *pl.* -] 1) a person who draws off &c. 2) a person who departs &c. 3) V. Abziehmuskel.

Ábziehung, *f.* 1) drawing off, deduction &c. 2) *Fig.* [in logic] abstraction.

Abziehungsvermögen, *n.* V. Abstractionsvermögen, Absonderungsvermögen.

Ábzielen, *v. intr.* to tend towards. Auf etwas —, to aim at, to tend to something; es war auf eine Schelmerei abgezielt, he had some roguery in view.

Ábzirkeln, *v. tr.* 1) to measure with compasses. 2) *Fig.* to define with great precision.

Ábzirkelung, *f.* measuring with compasses.

Ábzucht, *f.* [*pl.* Abzüchte] 1) a breed [of horses, sheep]. 2) wastewell, common-sewer, canal, [in metallurgy] a channel, conduit [under the furnace].

Ábzug, *m.* [-es, *pl.* Abzüge] 1) the act retiring, retreating, departure. Der — ein Bedienten, the going off of a servant; zum blasen, [milit. term.] to sound the retreat. 2) [act of deducting] deduction. Nach — der Koste deducting all charges. 3) [that which is drawn or deducted] [in arithm.] deduction, defalcatio abatement. Ohne —, clear, nett; [in metallurg slag, scum; [in printing] proof sheet = Probebogen. 4) the trigger [of a gun]. V. Abdruck. 5) issue, a flowing, a current. Das Wasser hat keinen —, the water has no fall; der Rauch hat nen —, the smoke has no issue.

Abzugs-bogen, *m.* [in printing = Probebogen, Correkturbogen] proof sheet. **—faß**, [among wax-chandlers] a copper-bottomed to draw the melted wax from the boiler. **—flagge**, *f.* [among sailers] a flag hoisted at pa ing, the blue peter. —freiheit, *f.* [a law-term] the liberty of quitting one's country and settling in another, without paying a tax [Abzugsgeld] for doing so. —geld, *n.* the duty, which emigrants pay for exporting their goods and chattels. —graben, *m.* a trench or ditch to draw off stagnant water, a watercourse, drain. —kupfer, *n.* copper obtained by melting the scoria or slags. —predigt, *f.* V. Abschiedspredigt. —recht, *n.* [a law term] 1) the right of any government to exact a tax from persons emigrating. 2) the right of any government to deduct a part of any property that is sent abroad. —schlackenblei, *n.* [in metall.] lead procured from slags of lead. —schmaus, *m.* V. Abschiedsschmaus. —schnalle, *f.* a detent or stop that lifts up the minute wheel. —zahl, *f.* [in arithm.] [the number, from which the subtrahend is to be taken] minuend. —zeit, *f.* 1) the time when any one quits his residence. 2) the term at which servants leave their places, hirings. —zoll, *m.* V. Abzugsgeld.

Abzupfen, *v. tr.* to pluck, to pull off.

Abzwacken, *v. tr.* 1) to nip off, to pinch off. 2) *Fig.* to squeeze out of any one, to extort from any one.

Abzwecken, I. *v. intr.* [auf etwas —] to aim at, to tend to. II. *v. tr.* to loose from pegs, to unpeg.

Abzwicken, *v. tr.* to nip off, to pinch off. *Fig.* V. Abzwacken.

Abzwingen, *v. tr.* to obtain by force, to extort from, to wring from. Einem ein Versprechen —, to extort a promise from any one; abgezwungen, extorted.

Abzwirnen, *v. tr.* to wind off [thread].

*Acacie, *f.* [*pl.* -n] acacia. Acacienbaum, the common acacia, the locust-tree.

*Academie, *f.* [*pl.* -n] 1) a school or seminary of learning, an academy. Eine Militär—, a military academy. 2) university or college. 3) a society of men united for the promotion of arts and sciences, an academy.

*Academiker, *m.* [-s, *pl.* -] 1) the member of an academy for promoting arts and sciences, academian, academician, academist. 2) a student in a university or college, an academian, a collegian.

*Academisch, *adj.* academic, academical. Ein —er Bürger, [a student in a university] an academian, a collegian.

*Acajounuß, *f.* [*pl.* -nüsse] cashew-nut.

*Accapariren, *v. tr.* to forestall, to engross.

*Accent, *m.* [-es, *pl.* -e] accent. 1) [in grammar] [a mark or character used in writing to direct the stress of the voice in pronunciation]. 2) [a particular stress or force of voice upon certain syllables and words, which distinguishes them from the others]. 3) [the modulation of the voice in reading or speaking].

*Accentuation, *f.* accentuation.

*Accentuiren, *v. tr.* to accent, to accentuate.

*Accept, *m.* [-es, *pl.* -e] [in commerce] acceptance. —geschäfte machen, to effect acceptances for account of a third person.

*Acceptant, *m.* [-en, *pl.* -en] [in commerce] acceptor. V. Annehmer.

*Acceptiren, *v. tr.* [in commerce] to agree or promise to pay, to accept, to honour. V. Annehmen.

*Acceptirung, *f.* [in commerce] acceptance. V. Annehmung, Annahme.

*Accessist, *m.* [-en, *pl.* -en] any candidate or aspirant for a vacancy practising unpaid, especially in public offices.

*Accessit and Accéssit, *n.* [-s, *pl.* -e] second or next best prise or premium.

*Accessorisch, *adj.* accessory.

*Acceß, *m.* [-sses] 1) access, admittance. V. Zugang, Zutritt. 2) [in medicine] accession, fit. V. Anwandlung.

*Accidenz or Áccidenz, *n.* [*pl.* —ien] perquisite. —ien, perquisites, emoluments.

Accidenzarbeit, *f.* [in printing] accidental or casual work.

*Accise, *f.* excise. —nehmen, auflegen, to excise.

Accis-amt, *n.* excise office. —bar, *adj.* excisable. —barkeit, *f.* liability to pay excise duty. —bedienter, *m.* excise-man, † shark. —einnehmer, *m.* collector of excise. —frei, *adj.* not liable or subject to excise duty, free from excise. —freiheit, *f.* exemption or immunity from excise. —stube, *f.* excise office. —vergehen, *n.* offence against the law of excise. —zettel, *m.* excise bill.

*Acclimatisirung, *f.* acclimatisation.

*Acclimatisirt, *adj.* acclimated.

*Accolade, *f.* [in printing] brace.

*Accommodiren, *v. r.* sich —, to accommodate or reconcile one's self to.

*Accompágnement, *n.* [-s] [in music] accompaniment.

*Accompagniren, *v. tr.* [in music] to accompany.

*Accompagnist, *m.* [-en, *pl.* -en] accompanist.

Accórd, *m.* [-es, *pl.* -e] 1) [in music] accord. 2) agreement, compact, convention, indenture. Einen — machen oder treffen, to make an agreement; eine Festung mit — einnehmen, to take a fortress by capitulation; auf — unternehmen, [a building &c.] to undertake by contract.

*Accordiren, I. *v. intr.* 1) [in music] to accord. 2) [in law] to agree. Der Fallirte hat mit seinen Gläubigern accordirt, the bankrupt has compromised or compounded with his creditors. II. *v. tr.* 1) to make to agree, to accord. 2) to consent to, to grant.

*Accouchement, *n.* [-s] 1) obstetrics, midwifery. 2) parturition, delivery, childbirth, childbed.

*Accoucheur, *m.* [-s, *pl.* -e] obstetrician, man-widwife.

*Accouchiren, *v. tr.* to deliver, to assist women in parturition. V. Entbinden.

Accouchir-kunst, *f.* V. Entbindungskunst. —zange, *f.* V. Entbindungszange.

*Accreditiren, *v. tr.* 1) to accredit [an envoy]. 2) [in commerce] to open a credit.

*Accurat, I. *adj.* accurate, exact, punctual. II. *adv.* accurately, exactly. V. Genau.

*Accuratésse, *f.* accuracy, exactness, niceness. V. Genauigkeit.

*Áccusativ, *m.* [-s, *pl.* -e] [in grammar] accusative.

Ách, *interj.* [an exclamation expressive of pain, joy, pity or surprise] ah, oh, O! — ja, oh! yes, yes indeed, alas; — welch' ein unglücklicher Tag! alas the day!

*Achat, *m.* [-s, *pl.* -e] [class of gems] agate.

Achat-artig, *adj.* [like agate] agatized. —breccie, *f.* V. Trümmer-Achat. —dattel, *f.* porphyry-shell. —en, *adj.* agaty. —kiesel, *m.* aegyptilla. —muschel, *f.* an agatized shell. —onyx, *m.* agate-onyx. —tute, *f.* agate stamper.

Áchel, *f.* V. Granne.

Achillenkraut, *n.* V. Schafgarbe.

Achillesflechse, *f.* [*pl.* -n] [in anatomy] tendon-achilles.

*Achromátisch, *adj.* [in optics] achromatic. —es Teleskop, achromatic telescope [an invention of Dollond].

*Achronisch, *adj.* [in astronomy] acronic, acronical.

Áchse, *f.* [*pl.* -n] [allied to the Gr. ἄξων, the L. *axis* and *ago* and the Ice. *aka*, *to ride*, *to move*] 1) axle, axle-tree. 2) *Fig.* [often used for] a carriage. Güter auf der — verführen, to convey goods by land, land carriage. 3) [in mathematics, a straight line, real or imaginary, passing through a body, on which it revolves] axis. Die Erd—, the axis of the earth; [in mechanics] die — der Schwingung [des Pendels], the axis of oscillation; die — eines Kegelschnitts, the axis of a conic section; die — der Strahlenbrechung, [in optics] axis of refraction.

Achsen-blech, *n.* clout. —büchse, *f.* box. —eisen, *n.* V. —blech. —futter, *n.* axle-bed. —geld, *n.* wheelage. —neigung, *f.* [in astronomy] obliquity of the ecliptic. —nagel, *m.* linch-pin, axle-pin. —riegel, *m.* transom of a gun-carriage. —ring, *m.* iron-ring. —schiene, *f.* V. —blech. —schraube, *f.* axle-nut. —stoß, *m.* washer, hurter.

Áchsel, *f.* [*pl.* -n] [Sax. *eaxle*, W. *asgell* = *wing*, allied either to the Ice. *aka*, *to ride*, *to move*, or to the W. *ucho*, *high*] joint which connects the arm to the body, the shoulder. Die —n zucken, to shrug the shoulders; auf die —n klopfen, to slap upon the shoulders; auf die —n nehmen, to take upon the shoulders; *Fig.* das will ich auf meine —n nehmen, I'll take that on my shoulders, that I will be answerable for; auf die leichte — nehmen, to take a thing lightly, to pay little regard to a difficulty, to be easy about a thing; Einen über die — ansehen, to look down upon any one, to slight any one, to despise, to hold any one cheap; *Prov.* auf beiden —n tragen, to serve the time, to temporize, to serve two masters, to trim, to be Jack of both sides; er trägt auf beiden —n, he holds with the hounds and runs with the hares.

Achsel-ader, *f.* [in anatomy] axillary vein. —band, *n.* shoulder-knot. —bein, *n.* shoulder-bone. —blutader, *f.* [in anatomy] the axillary-vein. —drüsen, *pl.* [in anatomy] axillary glands. —fleck, *m.* shoulderpiece of a shirt, gusset. —grube, *f.* axilla, arm-pit, arm-hole. —hembe, *n.* a shift without sleeves. —kleid, *n.*, —tuch, *n.* [in catholic churches] amice. —knochen, *m.* V. —bein. —naht, *f.* a seam upon the shoulder-piece of a gown &c. —nerve, *f.* [in anatomy] axillary nerve. —ranke, *f.* [in botany] axillary tendril. —röhre, *f.* V. —bein. —schlagader, *f.* [in anatomy] axillary artery. —schnur, *f.* shoulder-strap. —schnüre, *pl.* shoulder-points. —seil, *n.* V. Tragseil. —streifen, *m.* V. —fleck. —träger, *m.* *Fig.* a time-server, a hypocrite. —trägerei, *f.* *fig.* hypocrisy, timeserving. —troddel, *f.* shoulder-knot, epaulette. —tuch, *n.* V. —kleid. —zucken, *n.* shrug, shrugging. —zucker, *m.* 1) one, who shrugs his shoulders. 2) [among letter founders] the shoulder of a letter.

Áchseln, *v. intr.* to serve the time, to play the hypocrite.

Áchsen, *v. tr.* to provide with axle-trees.

1. Ácht, [a cardinal number] eight. — und zwanzig, eight and twenty, twenty eight. [as a substant.] Die —e, the eight [figure or number]; — Tage, eight days, a sennight; eine römische

—, a Roman eight (VIII); ein Stück von —en, a piece of eight [a Span. coin = 8 reals]; mit —en fahren, to drive with eight horses; zwei —en werfen, to throw two eights [at dice]; zum —en, V. Achtens.

Acht-äugig, *adj.* octonocular. —bätzner, *m.* a coin in Switzerland [about eleven pence]. —beinig, *adj.* eight-legged. —blättrig, —blumig, *adj.* [in botan.] octopetalous. —draht, *m.* a sort of coarse cloth. —eck, *n.* octagon. —eckig, *adj.* octagonal, octangular. —fach, eight-fold, octuple. —fältig, *adj.* V. —fach. —flach, *n.* [in geometry] octaëdron. —füßig, *adj.* 1) eight-footed. 2) eight-feet long. —groschenstück, *n.* a piece of eight groshen [about a shilling]. —halb, *adj.* seven and a half. Ein Kind von —halb Jahren, a child seven years and a half of age. —hundertste, *adj.* eight hundredth. —jährig, *adj.* 1) of eight years, eight years old. 2) lasting eight years, octennial. —jährlich, *adj.* happening every eight years. —kantig, *adj.* having eight edges. —klang, V. Oktave. —mahl, *adv.* eight times. —mahlig, *adj.* repeated eight times. —mann, *m.* one of a college or sodality of eight men. —männerig, *adj.* [in botany] octandric. —monatig, *adj.* and *adv.* lasting eight months. —monatlich, *adj.* and *adv.* occurring every eight months. —pfenniger, *m.* piece of eight farthings. —pfünder, *m.* [in gunnery] eight-pounder. —pfündig, *adj.* of eight pounds. —säulig, *adj.* octostyle. —seitig, *adj.* octoëdrical. —schildig, *adj.* [in herald.] having eight quarterings in the coat of arms. —silbe, *m.* a word of eight syllables. —silbig, *adj.* octosyllabic. —spännig, *adj.* yoked with eight horses, drawn by eight horses. Er fuhr —spännig aus, he drove out in a carriage and eight. —strahl, *m.* [in nat. history] a star-fish with eight rays. —stündig, *adj.* and *adv.* lasting eight hours. —stündlich, *adj.* and *adv.* every eight hour. —stündner, *m.* [in mining] one that works for eight hours. —tägig, *adj.* of eight days. —täglich, *adj.* and *adv.* every sennight. —theil, *m.* and *n.* the eighth part. —theilig, *adj.* consisting of eight parts, octopartite. —ton, *m.* V. Oktave. —wöchentlich, *adj.* occurring every eight weeks. —wöchig, *adj.* lasting eight weeks. —zeilig, *adj.* of eight lines.

2. Ácht, *f.* [probably allied to Aug, Auge, *eye*] care, attention. Auf etwas — geben, to attend to, to give heed to, to mind, to take care of, to pay attention to, to watch, to have an eye upon, to beware of; gebt auf den Mann —, mind that man; aus der — lassen, to overlook, to forget, to slight, to neglect; etwas in — nehmen, to take care of, to look to, to keep carefully, to observe, to remember a thing; sich in — nehmen, to take care, to be prudent, cautious, careful; nehmen Sie sich in —, take heed, take care, have a care of yourself; nehmen Sie sich vor diesem Hunde in —, beware of this dog. Syn. Acht geben, Acht haben, aufmerken, beobachten. Aufmerken signifies merely to direct one's thoughts to any thing, in order to obtain a distinct perception of it. Acht geben and Acht haben join also the idea of paying attention with the design to derive profit or supposed profit from the thing to which the thoughts are turned. Beobachten signifies a higher degree of attention, an especial heedfulness and consideration. Acht geben is a single act, Acht haben a continued state.

3. Ácht, *f.* [probably allied to ἔχθος = Haß, hatred, Haß being also used formerly instead of Acht] outlawry, ban. In die — erklären, to outlaw, to proscribe, to put under the ban; von der — befreien, to remove the ban.

Achts-erklärung, *f.* proscription, outlawry. —fällig, *adj.* outlawed; —schatz, *m.* [a law term] money by which a person frees himself from outlawry; —schilling, *m.* V. —schatz.

‖ Ácht, *adj.* V. Echt.

Áchtbar, *adj.* estimable, respectable, honourable, honoured, worshipful.

Áchtbarkeit, *f.* dignity, respectability.

Áchte, I. *adj.* eighth. Der — Tag, the eighth day. II. *f.* [in music] octave.

Áchtehalb, V. Achthalb.

Áchtel, *n.* [-s, *pl.* -] 1) the eighth part, the eighth. Drei —, three eighths. 2) [in music] quaver, or eighth part of a semibreve. 3) the eighth part of an aic. 4) Ein Buch im — [better in —form or —größe] a book in octavo.

Achtel-form, *f.*, —größe, *f.* V. Achtel. In —, in octavo. —kreis, *m.* [in astronomy] octant.

Áchteln, *v. tr.* to divide into eight parts.

Áchten, I. *v. tr.* 1) to mind, regard, to fix the mind upon, to attend to. Auf etwas —, to take care of a thing, to mind it; kein Mensch achtet auf deinen Kummer, nobody cares for or heeds thy grief. 2) to think, to judge, to be of opinion, to deem. Er achtet für klug, zu schweigen, he deems it prudent, to be silent; wofür —, to repute; ich achte es für eine Schande, I hold it for a disgrace; ich achte es für eine große Ehre, I take it as a great honour; ich achte es für verloren, I look upon it as lost. 3) to estimate, to value, to esteem. Etwas hoch —, to esteem highly, to set a high value on something. 4) to esteem, to prize, to regard with some degree of reverence. Die Gesetze —, to respect the laws; ich achte Ihren Bruder, I respect your brother; kein Ansehen der Person —, to respect no person; Gott achtet kein Ansehen der Person, God is no respecter of persons; er ist gar nicht geachtet, he is not at all respected; er achtet weder Ehre noch Schande, he is past all sense of shame. II. *v. r.* sich —, to comply with, to conform to, to obey; wornach man sich zu — hat, which ought to be observed. Syn. Achten, merken. Auf etwas merken requires the thoughts to be directed with a greater degree of exertion towards an object to observe it accurately and distinctly. Auf etwas achten, on the contrary, means simply, not to be distracted, to collect one's thoughts, otherwise one would neither see nor hear any thing at all of the thing in question, nor receive any impression from it.

Ächten, *v. tr.* to outlaw, to prescribe, to put under the ban. Ein Geächteter, an outlaw.

Áchtens, *adv.* eighthly, in the eighth place.

Áchtender, *m.* [-s, *pl.* -] [among hunters] a stag having antlers with eight starts or branches.

Áchtenswerth, Áchtenswürdig, *adj.* respectable, esteemable, estimable.

Áchter, *m.* [-s, *pl.* -] 1) eight [the number]. 2) any thing, having eight parts.

Ächter, *m.* [-s, *pl.* -] = Geächteter, an outlaw.

Áchterlei, *adj.* of eight different sorts.

Áchtgeber, *m.* [-s, *pl.* -] one who attends to.

Áchthaber, *m.* V. Aufpasser.

Áchtlos, I. *adj.* unmindful, careless, negligent. II. *adv.* carelessly, negligently.

Áchtlosigkeit, *f.* inattention, negligence, carelessness.

Áchtsam, I. *adj.* careful, heedful, mindful, attentive. II. *adv.* carefully, attentively. Syn. Achtsam, aufmerksam, bedachtsam. A person is said to be aufmerksam when he directs his mind to a thing, to comprehend and retain it in his memory; achtsam when he does so with a view to profit by it; he is bedachtsam, who considers well before he resolves upon an action, who weighs the consequences of what he is about to do, in order to be assured that they may not be injurious.

Áchtsamkeit, *f.* carefulness, heedfulness, mindfulness, attention, attentiveness.

Áchtung, *f.* 1) the act of attending or heeding, attention. — [Acht] auf etwas geben, to attend to something; [military term] —! attention! 2) esteem, regard. Aus — für die Damen, in deference to the ladies; ein Mann von keiner —, a man of no esteem; alle — aus den Augen setzen, to lay aside all respect; seine — bezeigen, to pay one's duty or respects. 3) a complying with, obeying. Zu eurer Nachricht und — [Nachachtung], to your rule and guidance.

Ächtung, *f.* proscription.

Áchtzehn, [the number] eighteen. —er, *m.* a person or thing to which the number eighteen is attached; what was grown in 18 (1818) [as wine &c.]. —te, *adj.* eighteenth. —tel, *n.* the eighteenth part, the eighteenth. —tens, *adv.* in the eighteenth place.

Áchtzehnender, *m.* [-s, *pl.* -] [among hunters] a stag with antlers of eighteen starts or branches.

Áchtzig, [a cardinal number] eighty, fourscore. —er, *m.* 1) a member of a sodality of eighty. 2) an octogenarian. 3) what was grown or made in 1780 [as wine &c.]. —jährig, *adj.* eighty years old, octogenary. —ste, *adj* eightieth. Der —ste, the eightieth. —stel, *n.* the eightieth part.

Ächzen, *v. intr.* to groan.

Ackelei, V. Akelei.

Ácker, *m.* [-s, *pl.* Äcker] [diminut. Äckerchen, Äckerlein] [Persic *ackar*, L. *ager*, Gr. ἀγρός, Eng. *acre*] 1) [a piece of arable or meadow land, Ackerfeld, Wiesenfeld] a field. Den — bauen or bestellen, to till the field. 2) [ground, considered with relation to its vegetative qualities] soil. Ein fetter —, a fat soil. 3) [a quantity of land] an acre = Morgen. Syn. Acker, Feld, Land. Land signifies any portion of the solid superficial part of the earth, in contradistinction to that which consists of water, without any regard to its agricultural properties. One says: wir steigen ans Land — we land. Feld is productive land, whether actually cultivated or not, as: Brachfeld, Winterfeld — fallow land. Acker means land actually under tillage, as: Weizen Acker, Gersten Acker — wheat field, barley field.

Acker-andorn, *m.* V. Andorn. —arbeit, *f.* labour in the fields, agriculture —baldrian, *m.* great wild valerian, —bau, *m.* agriculture, husbandry, tillage. Den —bau betreffend, agricultural. —bauer, *m.* tiller, husbandman, farmer. —baugesellschaft, *f.* agricultural society. —beere, *f.* V. Brombeere. —beet, *n.* a strip of ground between two furrows, a ridge. —bestellung, *f.* tillage, cultivation. —bohne, *f.* V. Saubohne. —buch, *n.* V. Lagerbuch. —bürger, *m.* inhabitant of a town, who practises agriculture, a farmer. —distel, *f.* common thistle. —drossel, *f.* the rose-coloured thrush. —ehrenpreis, *m.* germander-speedwell or chickweed. —eichel, *f.* V. Erdnuß. —erde, *f.* soil. —fadenkraut, *n.* a species of cudweed. —feld, *n.* a field of arable land. —filzkraut, *n.* V. —fadenkraut. —fleischblume, *f.* purplecow-wheat. —frauenmantel, *m.* V. —ohmkraut. —frohn, *m.* V. Flurschütz. —fuchsschwanz, *m.* field fox-tail, grass. —galle, *f.* a tract of barren soil in a field. —gänsedistel, *f.* corn sow-thistle —gauchheil, *n.* red pimpernel, the shepherd's weather-glass. —gaul, *m.* a farm-horse. —gefilde, *n.* [in poetry] fields. —geld, *n* 1) land-rent, contribution levied on arable land. 2) money paid for tilling. —geräthe, n. agricultural implements, farming utensils. —gericht, n. court of agriculture. —gesetz, n. [with the Romans: lex agraria] agrarian law. —gras, n. V. —hornkraut. —grindkraut, n. meadow-scabious. —hahnenfuß, m. corn crow-foot. —hauhechel, f. rest-harrow. —heu, n. hay from a fallow field. —hof, m. a farm, farm-house, farm-yard. —holunder, m. dwarf-elder. —hornkraut, n. mouse-ear, chickweed. —huhn, n. a partridge. —kamille, f. corn-camomile. —kannenkraut, n. common horse-tail, corn horse-tail. —klee, m. horned or yellow medic. —klette, f. prickly-parsnip. —knecht, m a farmer's man, ploughman, hind. —knoblauch, m. wild garlic. —kohl, m. 1) coleseed. 2) field cabbage. 3) wild mustard. 4) wild radish. 5) common nipple-wort. —krähe, f. the rook. —kraut, n. brook-lime. —krebs, m. V. Erdgrille. —kuhweizen, m. V. —fleischblume. —kummet, n. a collar for a farm-horse. —land, n. arable land. —lattich, m. V. —baldrian. —leine, f. a cord or a line used for guiding horses at a plough. —lerche, f. V. Feldlerche. —lohn, m. money paid for ploughing. —männchen, n. [= weiße Bachstelze] white water-wagtail. —mann, —smann, m. [pl. —leute] ploughman, husbandman, tiller, cultivator, agriculturist. Syn. Ackermann, Landwirth, Bauer. Ackermann is he whose principal business is husbandry, he may reside in the town or in the country. The Landwirth and Bauer are those engaged in agriculture and live altogether in the country, but are distinct in as much as the word Bauer signifies also the station of peasant, whereas, the Landwirth may be at the same time a nobleman. —mähre, f. a plough-mare, jade. —maß, n. a measure, by which a field is measured. —maus, f. V. Feldmaus. —mauseohr, n. mouse-ear, scorpion-grass. —menning, m. V. Odermennig. —messer, n. a sort of plough [invented in Italy for ploughing fields without the use of draught-cattle]. —mohn, m. rough poppy, smooth poppy. —münze, f. 1) mountain-calamint. 2) corn-mint. —neft, field balm or calamint. —nelkengras, n. —nägelein, n. a kind of grass. —nessel, f. 1) common dead-nettle. 2) nettle hemp or hemp-leaved dead-nettle. —nuß, f. V Erdnuß. —nußwasser, n. a water drawn from the tuberous lathyrus. —ohmkraut, n. percepier. —pferd, n. farm-horse. —rain, m. a ridge as landmark between two fields. —raute, f. common fumitory or earth-smoke. —reich, adj. rich in fields. —rettig, m. V. —kohl 4. —ried, n a boggy and reedy place on a field. —riedgras, n. turfy, hair-grass, great corn-grass. —ringelblume, f. common marigold. —rittersporn, m. lark's spur, the lark's heel. —ruhrkraut, n. a species of cudweed. —salat, m. V. —baldrian. —saudistel, f. V. —gänsedistel. —sauerampfer, m. common sorrel. —schmiele, f. V. —straußgras. —schnecke, f. V. Feldschnecke. —scholle, f. V. Erdscholle. —schwarzkümmel, m. V. Feldschwarzkümmel. —schwertel, m corn-flag. —senf, m. charlock. —spargel, f. pearl wort. —steinsame, m. painting-root. —sternkraut, n. V. —waldmeister. —sternmeier, V. —waldmeister. —straußgras, n. silky bent-grass, corn-bent, fair panicled corn-grass. —trappe, m. bustard. —trespe, f. corn breme-grass. —vieh, n. cattle used for agriculture. —viole, f. V. Frauenspiegel. —vogel, m. V. Feldlaufer. —wage, f. a level for measuring the depth of the furrows. —waldmeister, m. wood-roof. —walze, f. a large roller. —weg, m. a field-way. —werbel, m. V. Erdgrille, Maulwurfsgrille. —werkzeug, n. V. —zeug —wespe, f. field-wasp. —wiese, f. V. Feldwiese. —winde, f. cornbind. —windhalm, m. V. —straußgras. —wurm, m. V. Engerling. —wurz, f. 1) sweet-cane, sweet-grass. 2) V. Blutwurz. —zeit, f. the ploughing season. —zeug, n. ploughing utensils. —zins, m. the rent paid for land. —zwiebel, f. the star of Bethlehem.

Äckern, v. tr. to plough, to till.

Äckerer, m [-s, pl. -] V. Ackermann.

*Acronisch, adj. [in astron.] acronic, acronical.

*Acróstichon, f. [-s] [in poetry] acrostic [a poem, in which the initial letters of the lines form the name of a person or a thing].

*Áct, m. [-es, pl. -e] 1) act, action, performance. 2) act [of a play]. V. Aufzug.

*Ácte, f. [pl. -n] 1) act, decree, law. Eine Parlaments—, an act of parliament. 2) public papers, legal documents, acts, judicial acts, deeds, rolls. Die —nkammer, f. office of the rolls, das —nstück, a judicial act, a legal document.

*Acteur, m. [-s, pl. -e] an actor, a [stage-] player.

*Áctie, f. [pl. -n] a share in the capital stock of a company, or in the public funds, an action, a share. Actien, actions, stocks, funds, shares; Inhaber von —n, stockholder, shareholder; ich will Ihnen meine Tunnelactien verkaufen, I will sell you my share in the Tunnel; der —nhändler, m. stock-jobber, stock-broker, actionist.

*Action, f. 1) an action, a fight, battle, engagement. 2) the gestures used in declamation, action.

*Actionär, m. [-s, pl. -e] 1) [a proprietor of stock in a trading company &c.] actionary, actionist, 2) shareholder, stockholder.

*Activ and Áctiv, adj. 1) busy, constantly engaged in action, active. 2) actual, effective [said of military service]. —handel, m. active commerce; Großbrittanien führt einen —, China einen Passivhandel, the commerce of Great-Britain is active, that of China is passive; —schulden, pl. f. active debts; —s und Passivschulden, assets and debts.

*Áctivum, n. [in gramm.] verb active.

*Actrice, f. [pl. -n] actress, female [stage-] player.

*Actuär, m. [-s, pl. -e] actuary, clerk, registrar.

*Áctus, m. public act.

*Acústik, f. [the science of sounds] acoustics.

*Acústisch, adj. acoustic.

*Adāgio, n. [in music] adagio.

Ádam, m. Adam Fig. Der alte —, original sin; den alten — ausziehen, to put off the old man, to amend one's life.

Adams=apfel, m. Adam's-apple. —feige, f. Egyptian fig, sycamore.

Ádansonie, f. [pl. -n] [in botany] sour-gourd.

*Addiren and Áddiren, v tr. to add, to sum up, to cast up.

*Addition and Áddition, f. addition.

*Addreßbuch, Addresse &c., V. Adresse &c.

Adē, [‡ and poet.] adv. and n. adieu. Einem — sagen, to bid any one farewell or adieu.

Ádel, m. [-s] [allied to the ancient Atta = Vater, father or to Adel = Geschlecht, race, family] 1) nobility, nobleness. Einer von —, a nobleman; von altem —, of ancient nobility, stock; von gutem —, of a noble extraction. Fig. — der Seele, nobility of mind; der [die Würde] des Lebens, nobleness of life. 2) the persons of high rank, nobility. Prov. Tugend vor altem — geht, — mit Tugend nur besteht, birth is much, but breeding is more; gentility without ability is worse than plain beggary.

Adel=beere, f. V. Elsebeere. —bursche, m. a Dutch sea-cadet. —esche, f. V. Vogelbeerbaum. —fisch, m. a sort of trout. —herrisch, adj. V. Aristokratisch. —herrschaft, f. V. Aristokratie. —herrscher, m. V. Aristokrat. —schaft, f. 1) V. Adelstand. 2) the nobility. —sbrief, m. a charter, a patent of nobility. —sfreund, m. V. Aristokrat. —sgewalt, f. the power of the nobility. —skunde, f. the knowledge of the rights and privileges of the nobility. —stand, m. nobility. Einen in den —stand erheben, to knight any one. Einen in den hohen — erheben, to raise any one to the nobility. —stolz, m. the pride of nobility, haughtiness. —sucht, f. a longing after dignities attached to nobility. —süchtig, adj. longing after dignities attached to nobility. —thum, n. the state and the privileges of the nobility. —wildprett or Edelwild, n. [among hunters] deer.

Ádelbert, m. [a name of men] Ethelbert.

Ádelheid, f. [a name of women] Adelina, Alice, Assy.

Ádelig, adj. 1) noble. 2) belonging or relating to a nobleman. Von —er Geburt, of noble birth or extraction; die —en, the nobility.

Ádeline and Adeline, f. [a name of women] Adelina.

Adeln, v. tr. to ennoble, to nobilitate, to make noble. Tugend adelt, virtue ennobles; das —, the act of making noble, nobilitation.

Adépt, m. [-s, pl. -en] alchymist, adept.

Áder, f. [pl. -n] [Sax. Aeddre, Ice. Aedr; its primitive sense is probably a tube] 1) vein, a cylindrical blood-vessel. Die goldne —, hemorrhoidal vein, hemorrhoids, the piles; Einem die — öffnen oder schlagen, zur — lassen, to open a vein, to bleed or blood a person, to let any one blood; ich habe zur — gelassen, I have got myself bled, I have been bled. Fig. Eine dichterische —, a poetical vein; es ist keine gute — an ihm, there is no good about him, he is a downright rascal. 2) [in mines] a seam, a vein of metal, coal &c., of water in the earth, vein, variegation; — im Holze, vein, grain, streak; — im Stein, vein, cloud; die —n im Marmor, the veins of the marble; Goldadern, veins of gold; Wasseradern, veins of water; Basalt—, a vein of basalt, a dike.

Ader=balg, m. V. Erdnuß —binde, f. a bandage or ligature to tie up a vein. —bruch, m. [in surgery] varicocele. —förmig, adj. and adv. veined, veiny, in form of a vein. —gebäude, n. system of the veins or arteries. —geflecht, —gewebe, n. plexus of veins. —geschwulst, f. [in veterinary art] a swollen vein. —gewächs, n. [a tough concretion of grumous blood in the arteries] polypus. —haut, f. [in anatomy] the second coat of the eye, choroid. —häutchen, n. [in anatomy] chorion. —knoten, —kropf, m. [in surgery] varix. —laß, m. bleeding, blood-letting, phlebotomy, venesection. —laßbäuschchen, n a compress or bolster applied after blood-letting. —laßbecken, n. bleeding-basin. —laßbinde, f. bandage, fillet, swath. —laßeisen, n. fleam, lancet. —laßkunst, f. art of letting blood, phlebotomy. —laßschnäpper, m. V. —laßeisen. —laßtafel, f. a table of the days proper for bleeding on or of the veins proper to bleed in certain diseases. —laßverband, m. ligature. —laßzeit, f. season for letting blood. —laßzeug, n. bleeding-instruments, bleeding-case, —lehre, *f.* [in medicine] angiology. —los, *adj.* [in botany] not veined, not nerved. —mennig or Odermennig, *m.* agrimony or liver-wort. —messer, *n.* V. Pulsmesser. —presse, *f.* [in surgery] tourniquet. —reich, *adj.* full of veins, veined. —rippig, *adj.* [in botany] nerved. —schlag, *m.* [poetic] pulse. —schwamm, *m.* morel, moril. —staar, *m.* a cataract of the choroid. —strang, *m.* V. Adergeflecht. —system, *n.* V. Adergebäude. —wasser, [in anat.] the lymph mixed with blood.

Äderchen, *n.* [-s, *pl.* -] a little vein.

Äderig, *adj.* veiny, veined, streaked.

Ädern, *v. tr.* to mark with veins, to vein, to streak [wood]. Eine wohlgeäderte Bildsäule, a well-veined statue.

*Adjectiv, *n.* [-s, *pl.* -e] [in gramm.] adjective.

*Adjeu and Adieu, adieu, good bye. — sagen, to bid farewell.

*Adjúnct, *m.* [-s, *pl.* -en] assistant, associate in office, a deputy.

*Adjungiren, *ir. v. tr.* to give as an assistant, to join, to associate.

*Adjutánt, *m.* [-en, *pl.* -en] adjutant, aid-de-camp.

Adler, *m.* [-s, *pl.* -] the eagle [a well known bird of prey]. Der weibliche —, eagless; ein junger —, eaglet. *Prov.* — fangen keine Fliegen, a goshawk beats not a bunting. [in heraldry one of the bearings] eagle. Ein doppelter —, an eagle with two heads. [in astronomy] a northern constellation. Syn. V. Aar.

Adler-ähnlich, *adj.* eagle-like. —auge, *n. Fig.* a piercing and discerning eye, eagle-eye. —äugig, *adj.* eagle-eyed, discerning, sharp-sighted, sharpsightedness. —beere, *f.* V. Arlesbeere. —blick, *m.* V. —auge. —blume, *f.* V. Akelei. —bohne, *f.* a sort of kidney-beans. —eile, *f.* eagle-speed. —eule, *f.* eagle-owl. —fisch, *m.* [a fish] sea-eagle. —fittig, —flug, *m.* [in poetry] wing of an eagle, flight of an eagle. Mit —fittigen, im —fluge, eaglewinged. —holz, *n.* agalloch, agallochum. —kraut, *n.* female fern. —nase, *f.* an aquiline or Roman nose. V. Habichtsnase. —orden, *m.* order of the eagle. Der schwarze —orden, the order of the black eagle [of Prussia]. —saumfarn, *m.* a species of fern. —schnelle, *f.* eagle-speed. —schwinge, *f.* [in poetry] a wing of an eagle. —sklaue, *f.* the talons or pounce of an eagle. —stein, *m.* eaglestone, etite. —zange, *f.* [in metallurgy] great pincers.

*Administratión, *f.* administration, government.

Administriren, *v. tr.* to administer.

*Admirál, *m.* [-s, *pl.* Admiräle] admiral.

Admiral-schaft, *f.* office of an admiral, admiralship. —schaft machen, [a sea term] to sail in company with other ships. —schiff, *n.* admiral's-ship, the flagship. —sflagge, the flag of the admiral.

*Admiralität, *f.* admiralty, navy office. Das —sgericht, *n.* admiralty-court, court of admiralty.

Adolf, *m.* [a name of men] Adolphus.

Adónis, Adonis.

Adonisblume, V. Feuerröschen.

*Adoptión, *f.* adoption.

*Adoptiren, *v. tr.* to adopt. *Fig.* Eines Andern Meinungen —, to adopt the opinions of another.

*Adoptivkind, *n.* [-es, *pl.* -er] an adopted or adoptive child.

*Adoptivvater, *m.* [-s, *pl.* -väter] an adoptive father.

*Adrèsse, *f.* [*pl.* -n] 1) address. *a*) a written or formal application. Dank—, an address of thanks. *b*) direction. Geben Sie mir Ihre —, give me your address or direction; die — eines Briefes, the direction or superscription of a letter. 2) letter of recommendation.

Adreß-buch, *n.* directory. —comptoir, *n.* intelligence office, advertising office. —haus, *n.* V. Leihhaus. —kalender, *m.* V. Adreßbuch.

*Adressiren, I. *v. tr.* 1) [to direct in writing, as a letter] to address, to direct. Ein Schreiben an Einen —, to direct a letter to any one, er adressirte einen Brief an den Sprecher, he addressed, he forwarded a letter to the speaker. 2) [in commerce] to consign. Das Schiff war an einen Kaufmann in Baltimore adressirt, the ship was consigned to a merchant at Baltimore. II. *v. r.* sich —, to apply to, to address one's self to any one.

Adriátisch, *adj.* Adriatic. Das —e Meer, Adriatic sea, the Adriatic.

*Adrittura, *f.* [in commerce] direct.

*Advént, *m.* [-s] advent.

Advents-vogel, *m.* embergoose. —zeit, *f.* advent-season.

*Adventurinstein, *m.* [-s, *pl.* -e] adventurine.

*Advèrbium, *n.* [*pl.* Adverbien] [in gramm.] adverb. Adverbialisch, adverbial.

*Advis, *m.* [-es, *pl.* -e] advice, notice. V. Bericht.

Advis-brief, *m.* letter of advice. —jacht, *f.* —boot, *n.* advice-boat, a packet-boat, a cutter.

*Advocát, *m.* [-en, *pl.* -en] an advocate, a pleader, lawyer, counsel, counsellor, barrister at law, attorney. Die —engebühren, lawyer's fees; der —enstreich, a lawyer's trick.

*Advocatúr, *f.* [*pl.* -en] advocation, advocateship, advocacy.

*Advociren, *v. intr.* to follow the law, to practise as an advocate.

*Aerométer, *m.* [-s, *pl.* -] [in nat. hist.] aërometer.

*Aerometrie, *f.* [in nat. hist.] aëromotry.

*Aeronaút, *m.* [-en, *pl.* -en] aëronant.

*Aeronaútik, *f.* aëronautics, aërostation.

*Aerostát, *m.* [-en, *pl.* -en] air-balloon, aërostat.

*Aerostátik, *f.* aërostatics.

Äfern, Äffern, *v. tr.* [obsolete] to stir up again, to repeat.

*Affäre, *f.* [*pl.* -n] affair, matter, concern.

Äffchen, *n.* [-s, *pl.* -] [*dimin.* of Affe] little monkey. V. Affe.

Affe, *m.* [-n, *pl.* -n] *dimin.* das Aeffchen. 1) an ape, a monkey. Ein großer —, baboon; ein kleiner —, marmoset, pug. *Prov.* Affen bleiben Affen, wenn man sie auch in Sammt kleidet, an ape 's an ape, a varlet 's a varlet, tho' they be clad in silk or scarlet; je höher die Affen steigen, desto lächerlicher sie sich zeigen, the higher the ape goes, the more he shews his tail. 2) *Fig.* an ape, a silly fellow. [in drawing] V. Storchschnabel. [in mechanics] a crane.

Affen-art, *f.* a species of apes. —artig, I. *adj.* apish. II. *adv.* apishly. —baum, *m.* Ethiopian sourgourd, monkey's bread, adansonia. —beere, *f.* 1) black-berried heath, crow-berry, crake-berry. 2) cran-berry, moor-berry. —bezoar, *m.* monkey bezoar. —bild, *n.* figure of an ape, monkey's face. —brodbaum, *m.* V. Affenbaum. —gesicht, *n.* ape's face. —haft, *adj.* V. Affenartig. —könig, *m.* a species of monkeys, aquiqui. —liebe, *f. Fig.* a blind fondness, especially of parents for their children. —mäßig [äffisch], I. *adj.* apish. II. *adv.* apishly. —nase, *f.* a flat nose, pug-nose. —nasig, *adj.* flat-nosed, pug-nosed. —posse, *f.* monkey trick. —schädel, *m.* the skull of an ape. —spiel, —werk, *n.* apishness, apish tricks, foolery. —stein, *m.* bezoar. —weibchen, *n.* a she-ape. —wurm, *m.* Guinea-worm.

*Affèct, *m.* [-es, *pl.* -e] emotion, passion, affection.

*Affectatión, *f.* affectation.

*Affectiren, *v. tr.* to affect, to pretend [friendship &c.].

*Affectirt, *adj.* conceited, affected. Das —e Wesen, conceitedness, affectation.

Affectlos, *adj.* passionless, dispassionate, unimpassioned, wanting affection.

Affèctlosigkeit, *f.* apathy.

Äffen, *v. tr.* to deceive, to hoax, to chouse, to trick, to banter, to delude, to fool, to make a fool of. Laß dich nicht von ihm —, don't let him make a fool of you.

Äfferei, *f.* 1) apish behaviour, monkey tricks, mimickry. 2) delusion, mockery, banter.

*Affettuóso, *adv.* [in music] affettuoso.

*Affiche, *f.* [*pl.* -n] a bill posted up, a handbill.

*Afficiren, *v. tr.* to affect, to touch, to act upon

*Affiliatión, *f.* affiliation.

*Affiliren, *v. tr.* [in free-masonry] to affiliate.

Äffinn, *f.* she-ape, she-monkey.

Äffisch, I. *adj* apish, monkey-like. II. *adv.* apishly.

*Affodill, *m.* [-s] Affodille, *f.* [a plant] daffodil.

Affodill-lilie, *f.* day-lily, asphodel-lily. —wurz, *f.* affodil.

Äfholder, *m.* [-s, *pl.* -] guelder-rose, water-elder.

Äfrica, *n.* Africa.

Africáner, *m.* [-s, *pl.* -] an African.

Africánisch, *adj.* African.

Äfrusch, V. Stabwurz.

1. Äfter, [V. Aber I.] I. [anciently a prep., now only used in composition, and signifying] after, behind, similar, approaching to, inferior, not genuine; hence II. *subst. m.* [-s] any thing worthless, waste matter, shreds, parings, clippings in general. [in metallurgy] residuum. [among butchers] tripe, gut, chitterlings. [in agriculture] V. Aftergetreide.

After-alabaster, *m.* alabaster-stone, alabastrites. —anwalt, *m.* a substitute attorney. —arzt, *m.* an ignorant physician, a quack. —belehnen, *v. tr.* only used in the part. as ein Afterbelehnter, V. Afterlehnsmann. —biene, *f.* American ant, mutille. —bier, *n.* small bier. —blatt, *n.* [in botany] stipule. —bürge, *m.* [a law term] second bail. —christ, *m.* false christian. —dolde, *f.* [in botany] cyme. —drohne, *f.* a small imperfect drone. —erbe, *m.* after-heir, substitute heir. —falke, *m.* the greater shrike. —flügel, *m.* bastard-wing. —geburt, *f.* after-birth, secundine. —gefälle, *n.* [in mining] sump. —gelehrsamkeit, *f.* a pretended learning. —gelehrte, *m.* a pretender to learning. —getreide, *n.* V. Afterkorn. —glaube, *m.* V. Aberglaube. —gold, *n.* false gold. —

granit, *m.* a sort of granite. —größe, *f.* pretended, false, empty greatness. —hase, *m.* V. Meerschwein. —heu, V. Grummet. —holz, *n.* windfallen wood. —holzkäfer, *m.* V. Holzbock. —hüfner, *m.* V. Afterlehnsmann. —kameel, *n.* the sheep of Peru, Llama. —kaninchen, *n.* Guinea pig. —kegel, *m.* [in geom.] conoid. —kegelartig, *adj.* [in geom.] conoidical, conoidic. —kind, *n.* 1) a posthumous child, [in law] a child born after its father has made his will. 2) a spurious child, a bastard. —kiel, *m.* [in ship building] false keel. —klaue, *f.* [among hunters] hindclaw, dewclaw. —könig, *m.* 1) a pretended king, pretender, a mock-king. 2) vice-roy. —kohle, *f.* erdige —, earth-coal, earthy brown coal; holzige —, bituminous or carbonated wood, fibrous brown coal. —kohlen, *f. pl.* small coals, cinders, dust of coals. —korn, *n.* [in husb.] spur. —kugel, *f.* [in geom.] spheroid, oblate spheroid. —leder, *n.* [among shoemakers] 1) chips of leather. 2) heel-piece inside. —lehn, *n.* [a law term] arriere fee or fief. —lehnsherr, *m.* [a law term] mesne-lord. —lehnsmann, *m.* [a law term] under-feudatory, arriere vassal. —lehre, *f.* erroneous doctrine. —leuchtkäfer, *m.* oilbeetle. —mehl, *n.* coarse flour, pollard. —miethe, *f.* underletting, subletting. —miethsmann, undertenant, subtenant. —moose, *n. pl.* the flags. —pacht, *m.* underlease, subtenure. —papst, *m.* antipope, pretended pope. —raupe, *f.* tenthredo, sawfly. —raupentödter, *m.* V. Raupentödter. —rede, *f.* calumny, slander. —reden, *v. intr.* to backbite, to calumniate. —sabbath, *m.* [in the bible transl. by Luther, Luke IV. 1] the second sabbath after the first. —schanze, *f.* V. Feldschanze. —schein, = falscher Schein. —schlacke, *f.* [in metall.] twice refined slag. —schlag, *m.* V. Abraum. —schörl, *m.* thumerstone, axinite. —segel, *n.* V. Afterschlag. —spinne, *f.* a sort of spider. —sprache, *f.* a barbarous language. —stein, *m.* a false stone. —theologe, *m.* atheologian. —thrum, *f.* V. Afterdrohre. —topas, *m.* Bohemian brown topas. —weise, *m.* philosophaster. —weisel, *m.* V. Drohnenweisel. —weisheit, *f.* philosophism. —witz, *m.* V. Aberwitz.

2. Äfter, *m.* [-s, *pl.* -] 1) the hinderpart of an animal, the fundament, backside, breech; chiefly for the rectum of horses, game &c. 2) [among saddlers] the back part of a saddle, cantle. 3) *pl.* -n, [among hunters] = Afterklauen.

After-blutfluß, *m.* V. [fließende] Hämorrhoiden. —darm, *m.* the rectum. —finnen, —floßfedern, *f.* [in nat. hist.] the anal fins. —geschirr, *n.* V. Hintergeschirr. —kriecher, *m.* a sort of gadfly. —welt, *f.* V. Nachwelt. —wind, *m.* [a sea term] wind from abaft. —wurm, *m.* ascaris, *pl.* ascarides. —zeit, *f.* the time to come, the future. —zwang, *m.* tenesmus.

Agat, Agatstein, *m.* V. Achatstein.

Age, *f.* [*pl.* -n] [allied to the L. *acus*, *husk*, *chaff*, and to Axt, *axe* and Ecke, *corner*] the awn or beard of corn or flax.

*Ägäisch, *adj.* Aegean, Egaean. Das —e Meer, the Aegean or Egaean sea.

Agelei, *f.* V. Akelei.

Agelholz, *n.* [-es, *pl.* -hölzer] V. Adlerholz.

*Agende, *f.* [*pl.* -n] agenda, a ritual or liturgy.

*Agent, *m.* [-en, *pl.* -en] an agent, factor.

*Agentschaft, Agentur, *f.* agency, agentship.

*Aggregat, *n.* [-s, *pl.* -e] the aggregate.

*Ägide, *f.* 1) the shield of Pallas [Aegis]. 2) *Fig.* shelter, protection.

Ägidius, *m.* [a name of men] Giles.

*Agio, *n.* [-s] [in commerce] agio.

*Agiotage, *f.* [*pl.* -n] stock-jobbing, stock-bubbling.

*Agioteur, *m.* [-s, *pl.* -e] stock-jobber.

*Agiren, *v. tr.* 1) to act, to play. 2) to mimick, to ridicule by a burlesque imitation.

Aglarkraut, *n.* [-es, *pl.* -kräuter] V. Ackerhauhechel or Stachelkraut.

Aglaster, *f.* V. Elster.

Aglei, V. Akelei.

*Agnate, *m.* [-n, *pl.* -en] [any male relation by the father's side] agnate. Die —n, agnati.

Agnes, *f.* [a name of women] Agnes.

*Agonie, *f.* agony.

*Agraffe, *f.* [*pl.* -n] [a hook for fastening] a clasp, catch.

*Agrest, *m.* verjuice.

*Agrimonie, *f.* V. Odermennig.

Agter, *adv.* [in sea language] aft, abaft.

Agtstein, *m.* [-es, *pl.* -e] [from the ancient aiston, *to burn*] V. Bernstein.

Ägypten, *n.* [-s] Egypt.

Ägypter, *m.* [-s, *pl.* -] Egyptian.

Ägyptisch, *adj.* Egyptian.

Ah, *interj.* [an exclamation denoting joy, admiration, surprise] oh. Aha! [Haha] [a word intimating surprise and content] ha!

Ahlbeere, *f.* [*pl.* -n] V. Aantbeere and Aalbeere.

Ahle, *f.* [*pl.* -n] [allied to *ac*-us, to Age, Axt, Ecke, V. Age] [an iron instrument used by shoemakers, sadlers &c.] an awl, [in printing] a bodkin.

Ahlenmacher [—schmied] *m.* an awlmaker.

Ahlkirsche, *f.* [*pl.* -n] 1) V. Traubenkirsche. 2) V. Heckenkirsche. 3) the fruit of the common bird-cherrytree. V. Faulbeere.

Ahm, *f.* [*pl.* -en] [allied to Eimer, which see] 1) [a liquid measure] an ame [awme or awn], a tierce. 2) [a sea term] the ship's draught marked on her sternpost.

Ahmen, *v. tr.* to gage [gauge] a cask.

Ahmer, *m.* [-s, *pl.* -] gager.

Ahmig, *adj.* and *adv.* containing a tierce.

Ahn, [allied to the L. *anus*, old woman, and to the Sax. *eanian*, to bring forth] I. *f.* [*pl.* -en] grandmother. II. *m.* [-s, *pl.* -en] 1) grandfather, grandsire. 2) forefather, ancestor, [in poetry] grandsire.

Ahn-frau, —mutter, Altermutter, [in poetry] Ahnin, *f.* grandam, grandmother. —herr, —vater, *m.* 1) grandsire, grandfather. 2) forefather, ancestor, predecessor. V. 2. Ahnen.

Ahnden, *v. tr.* [from the ancient Ande, *mind, spirit*, D. Aande; *breath*; so that ahnden, signifies properly *to remember*] to resent, to punish. Ein solches Verfahren ist immer geahndet worden, such proceedings have always been resented.

Ahndung, *f.* resentment, punishment.

Ahndungsfrei, free from resentment or punishment.

Ähneln, *v. intr.* to be somewhat like to, to resemble in some measure.

1. Ahnen, *v. intr.* [V. Ahnden] to have a presentiment or foreboding of something. Es ahnt mir, my heart forebodes; es ahnt mir nichts Gutes, my mind misgives me.

2. Ahnen, [*pl.* of Ahn] ancestors, forefathers, progenitors. Adelige —, noble ancestors; von vierzehn —, of fourteen descents.

Ahnen-probe, *f.* the proof of nobility or gentility [in having the required number of noble ancestors]. —reihe, *f.* line of ancestors. —recht, *n.* a prerogative founded upon ancestry. —stolz, *m.* I. *subst. m.* pride of ancestry. II. *adj.* proud of ancestry. —zahl, *f.* a prescribed number of ancestors.

Ahnlich, *adj.* and *adv.* like the ancestors.

Ähnlich, *adj.* [either instead of angleich, i. e. ziemlich gleich, pretty like or similar, or allied to the Sax. *anen*, to approach] like, resembling. Dies sieht ihm —, this is just like him; sie sieht ihm etwas —, she somewhat resembles him; die in einem Gemählde ausgedrückten Züge sind dem Original —, the features represented in a picture resemble the original; was thäten Sie in einem —en Falle? what would you do in a like case, or under similar circumstances? [in mathem.] —e Figuren, similar figures, plane figures; —e Glieder [einer Gleichung], equal terms [of an equation]; [in logic] —e Begriffe, Ausdrücke, analogical ideas, analogous expressions.

Ähnlichen, *v. intr.* 1) to have likeness to, to resemble, to bear similitude. 2) *v. tr.* to make like to. 3) *v. r.* sich —, to make one's self like to.

Ähnlichgleich, *adj.* [in geom.] similar.

Ähnlichkeit, *f.* 1) likeness, similitude, similarity, resemblance. Eine auffallende —, a striking resemblance. 2) analogy. Der —sbeweis, *m.* the argument by analogy; das —sgesetz, *n.* the law of analogy; der —sgrund, *m.* analogism; die —sregel, *f.* analogy; der —sschluß, *m.* analogism.

Ahnung, *f.* a secret anticipation of something future, a presage, a foreboding, a presentiment.

Ahnungs-vermögen, *n.* the faculty of presaging. —voll, *adj.* presageful. —los, *adj.* having no presentiment.

Ahorn, *m.* [-s, *pl.* -e] the maple, mapletree.

Ahorn-laus, *f.* the maple aphis. —zucker, *m.* maple-sugar.

Ahornen, *adj.* maple, made of maple, belonging to maple.

1. Ähre, *f.* [better Eern, Ehrn or Hern] [*pl.* -n] entrance-hall of a house.

2. Ähre, *f.* [*pl.* -n] [Sax. *aechir*, Allemannic *ahir*, allied to Age, Axt, Ecke, V. Age] 1) the spike of grass or corn, an ear of corn. Eine Weizen —, an ear of wheat. —n lesen, to glean. 2) [in botany] the spike.

Aehren-bekränzt, *adj.* crowned with ears of corn. —farn, *m.* a name for plants resembling ears or spikes. —fisch, *m.* atherine. —förmig, *adj.* like ears of corn or spikes. —frucht, *f.* grain. —gebund, *n.* V. Wirrbund. —kranz, *m.* a wreath consisting of ears of corn. —lese, *f.* gleaning. —leser, *m.* —leserinn, *f.* gleaner. —sammler, *m.* V. Aehrenleser. —sieb, *n.* a sieve by which thrashed corn is separated from ears or spikes. —stein, *m.* asbest with chaffy filaments. —stoppler, *m.* gleaner. —weiderich, *m.* purplespiked loose-strife, common or purple willow-herb.

1. Ähren, I. *v. tr.* to glean. II. *v. intr.* to ear, to shoot into ears.

‡2. Ähren, *v. tr.* to plough. V. Ackern.

Ährig, *adj.* having ears or spikes [used only in composition, as] lang—, having long ears or spikes.

Ai, *m.* [-s, *pl.* -e] [in nat. hist.] the ai or three-toed sloth [found in South-America]. V. Faulthier.

Aichen, *v. intr.* V. Eichen.

||**Aisch, Eisch**, *adj.* and *adv.* ugly, hideous.

Akelei, *f.* 1) the columbine [a plant]. 2) [better Ukelei] bleak [a fish]. 3) whitlow [in surgery] V. Wurm.

Alabáster, *m.* [-s] alabaster.

Alabaster-bild, *n.* an alabaster figure. — —**bruch**, *m.* an alabaster quarry. —**brust**, *f.* a bosom as white as alabaster. —**gyps**, *m.* plaster of Paris made of alabaster. —**stein**, *m.* alabaster-stone, alabaster. —**tute**, *f.* the wax-stamper.

Alabásterer, *m.* [-s, *pl.* -] an artist, who works in alabaster.

Alabástern, *adj.* made of alabaster, as white as alabaster.

Alant, *m.* [-s, *pl.* -e] 1) [a fish] the chub, cheven. 2) [a plant] elecampane, inula.

Alant-beere, *f.* the black currant [a shrub]. —**bier**, *n.* elecampane-beer. —**blede**, *m.* a sort of carp [cyprinus bipunctatus]. —**öl**, *n.* an oil extracted from the root of the elecampane. —**wein**, *m.* elecampane-wine.

***Alárm**, *m.* [-s] alarm, tumult. V. Lärm. Das—wort, *n.* [in military affairs] the countersign.

***Alarmiren**, *v. tr.* to alarm, to disturb. V. Lärmen and Beunruhigen.

***Alatérn**, *m.* evergreen privet, alaternus.

Alaun, *m.* [-s, *pl.* -e] alum. Der natürliche oder gebiegene—, rock alum; der gebrannte —, burnt alum; der künstliche—, artificial alum, English alum.

Alaun-artig, *adj.* alumish. —**bad**, *n.* a bath of alum water. —**bereiter**, *m.* alum-maker. —**bereitung**, *f.* the manufacturing of alum. —**bergwerk**, *n.* alum quarry or pit. —**blumen**, *pl.* the flowers of alum. —**bruch**, *m.* alum quarry or pit. —**brühe**, *f.* [among tawers] aluminous water. —**erde**, *f.* alum-earth. —**erz**, *m.* alum-ore. —**faß**, *n.* a cooler [made of deal boards, in which the alum is made to strike or shoot]. —**gar**, *adj.* [among curriers] dressed with alum. —**geist**, *m.* sulphuric acid diluted with water. —**gerber**, *m.* a tanner, who dresses the skin with alum and tallow. —**grube**, *f.* V. Alaunbruch. —**haltig**, *adj.* containing alum, aluminous. —**haufen**, *m.* a heap of alum-ores. —**holz**, *n.* aluminous pit-coal. —**hütte**, *f.* alum-house. —**kessel**, *m.* alum boiler. —**kies**, *m.* aluminous pyrites. —**lauge**, *f.* aluminous lie. —**leder**, *n.* alum leather, white leather. —**mehl**, *n.* slam [which sinks to the bottom of the settler]. —**mine**, *f.* —**mutter**, *f.* alum-ore. —**pfanne**, *f.* V. —kessel. —**quelle**, *f.* an aluminous spring. —**sieder**, *m.* alum boiler. —**siederei**, *f.* the art of manufacturing alum, and the place where it is manufactured. —**stein**, *m.* alum-stone. —**wasser**, *n.* alum water. —**werk**, *n.* alum-work. —**zucker**, *m.* saccharine alum.

Alaunen, *v. tr.* to prepare, to dress with alum, to steep in alum water.

Alaunicht, *adj.* alumish.

Alaunig, *adj.* aluminous.

Alb, *f.* [a high grassy hill] alp.

Albanien, *n.* [-s] Albania.

Albanier, *m.* [-s, *pl.* -]—inn, *f.* an Albanian.

Albanisch, *adj.* Albanian.

Albanus, Alban, *m.* [a name of men] Alban.

***Albatroß**, *n.* [-sses, *pl.* -sse] albatros.

1. **Albe, Albele, Alber**, *f.* [allied to the L. *albus*, *white*] white poplar-tree.

2. **Albe**, *f.* alb. V. Meßhemd and Chorhemd.

Alberich, *m.* [a name of men] Alberick, Aubry.

1. **Albern**, [seems to be allied to fahl, and *albus*] I. *adj.* silly, simple, foolish, sottish, absurd, awkward, uncouth. Ein —er Mensch, a foolish fellow, a simpleton, a changeling; ein —er Streich, a silly trick; —es Zeug, nonsense. II. *adv.* sillily, foolishly &c. —reden, to talk nonsense.

||2. **Albern**, *v. intr.* to act foolishly.

3. **Albern**, *f.* V. Weißpappel and Schwarzpappel.

Albernheit, *f.* silliness, simpleness, sottishness, absurdity, absurdness, folly, foolishness.

Albert, Albrecht, [a name of men] Albert.

Albertsthaler, *m.* [-s, *pl.* -] a dollar, worth about 2 florins or 3 s. 4 d.

***Albinos**, *pl.* [white offspring of black parents] albinos.

Albion, *n.* [-s] [an ancient name of England still used in poetry] Albion.

***Albus**, *m.* V. Weißpfennig.

***Alcali**, *n.* [in chimistry] alkali.

***Alcalisch**, *adj.* alkaline.

***Alcalisiren**, *v. tr.* [in chimistry] to alkalize.

Alchemille, *f.* [*pl.* -n] V. Löwenfuß.

***Alchimie**, *f.* alchymy.

***Alchimist**, *m.* [-en, *pl.* -en] alchymist.

***Alchimistisch**, I. *adj.* alchymic, alchymical, alchymistical, alchymistic. II. *adv.* alchymically.

***Alcohol**, *m.* [-s] alcohol.

***Alcoholisiren**, *v. tr.* to alcoholize.

***Alcoholisirung**, *f.* alcoholization.

***Alcoran**, V. Alkoran.

Aldermann, V. Altermann.

Alexandrien, [a city of this name] Alexandria.

Alexandriner, Alexandrinischer Vers, *m.* [a kind of verse, peculiar to modern poetry] Alexandrine, Alexandrian.

Alexia, *f.* [a name of women] Alice.

Alfanzerei, *f.* foolery, foppery, silly tricks. —treiben, to play off foolish tricks, to play the fool.

***Alfresco**, *adv.* —mahlen, to paint in fresco.

***Alfrescomahlerei**, *f.* [a method of painting in relief with watercolours on fresh plaster or on a wall laid with mortar not yet dry] fresco.

Alfried, *m.* [a name of men] Alfred.

***Algebra**, *f.* algebra.

***Algebraisch**, I. *adj.* algebraic, algebraical, ‡ cossic. —e Größen, algebraic quantities; —e Gleichungen, algebraic equations; die —e krumme Linie, algebraic curve. II. *adv.* by algebra.

***Algebraist**, *m.* [-en, *pl.* -en] algebraist.

Algier, [a city and government on the coast of Africa] Algiers.

Algierisch, *adj.* Algerine.

Algierer, *m.* [-s, *pl.* -] [a native of Algiers] an Algerine.

***Alicantwein**, *m.* [-es, *pl.* -e] alicantwine.

***Alimentengeld**, *n.* [-es, *pl.* -er] [a law term] an allowance made for the support of any one, but particularly of a woman, legally separated from her husband, alimony.

***Alimentation**, *f.* alimentation.

***Alimentiren**, *v. tr.* to maintain. V. Unterhalten, Ernähren.

Alizari, *m.* Adrianople-red.

Alk, *m.* [-es, *pl.* -e] auk, penquin, razorbill. Der kleine —, the little auk.

Alkahest, *n.* [-es] [a universal dissolvent] alkahest.

Alkannablätter, *pl.* alcanna-leaves. —öl, *n.* alcanna-oil; —wurzel, *f.* alcanna-root.

***Alkoran**, *m.* [-s] the koran, alkoran.

***Alkoven**, *m.* [-s, *pl.* -] an alcove, a bed-chamber.

All, [Goth. *all*, Sax. *eal*, Eng. *all* and *whole*, allied to the Gr. ὅλος, Shemitic *kol* from *kalah*, *to be ended or completed*] I. *n.* [-s] the universe, world. Das weite —, the vast universe.

II. *adv.* 1) all done, all gone, all consumed. Die Häute alle machen, [with curriers] to pile the hides; der Wein ist alle, the wine is at an end; das Geld ist alle, the money is spent; alle machen, to exhaust, dissipate; alle werden, to be spent. 2) entirely, wholly, completely. 3) [in composition enlarges the meaning and adds force to a word].

All-anerkannt, *adj.* all-acknowledged. —**barmherzig**, *adj.* all-merciful. —**bekannt**, *adj.* notorious. —**belebend**, *adj.* all-cheering. —**bereits**, *adv.* already. V. Bereits. —**da**, *adv.* there. V. Da. —**dieweil**, V. Weil. —**dort**, V. Dort. —**durchwaltend**, *adj.* all-pervading. —**entscheidend**, *adj.* all-deciding. —**erbarmend**, *adj.* all-merciful. —**erbarmer**, *m.* the All-merciful. —**erfreuend**, *adj.* all-cheering. —**erleuchtend**, *adj.* all-enlightening. —**ernährend**, *adj.* nourishing all. —**erschaffend**, *adj.* all-creating, omnific. —**geber**, *m.* God, giver of all things. —**gebietend**, *adj.* all-commanding. —**gefürchtet**, *adj.* all-dreaded. —**gegenwart**, *f.* omnipresence, ubiquity. —**gegenwärtig**, *adj.* omnipresent. —**geliebt**, *adj.* all-beloved. —**gemach**, *adv.* by little and little, by degrees, gradually. —**genugsam**, *adj.* [in theology] all-sufficient. —**gepriesen**, *adj.* all-praised. —**gerecht**, *adj.* all-just. Der—gerechte, the all-righteous, God. —**gewalt**, *f.* omnipotence, omnipotency. —**gewaltig**, *adj.* omnipotent, most powerful. —**gnädig**, *adj.* all-gracious. —**götterei**, *f.* pantheism. —**götterer**, *m.* pantheist. —**göttstempel**, *m.* pantheon. —**gut**, *n.* [a plant] all-good, good Henry, English mercury. —**gütig**, *adj.* all-bounteous, all-bountiful, all-good, all-kind. —**heil**, *n.* all-heal, panacea, catholicon. —**herrschend**, *adj.* all-commanding, all-ruling. —**hier**, *adv.* here, in this place. V. Hier. —**jährlich**, I. *adj.* annual. II. *adv.* annually, yearly. —**kundig**, *adj.* all-knowing, omniscient. —**liebend**, *adj.* all-loving. —**macht**, *f.* almightiness, omnipotence. —**mächtig**, *adj.* almighty, omnipotent, allpowerful. —**mählig**, *adv.* softly, gently, by little and little, gradually. Es wird —mählig Nacht, night is drawing on. V. —gemach. —**mutter**, *f.* [the common mother of mankind] nature. —**nachthuend**, *adj.* all-imitating. —**schreibekunst**, *f.* pasigraphy. —**sehend**, *adj.* all-seeing, all-beholding, all-viewing. Der —sehende Gott, *m.* all-seer. —**tag**, *m.* V. Wochentag. —**tägig**, *adj.* and *adv.* happening every day, daily. Eine —tägige Beschäftigung, daily occupation; ein —tägiges Fieber, a quotidian fever, ague. —**täglich**, *adj.* and *adv.* 1) daily, quotidian, every day. Ein —tägliches Kleid or Alltagskleid, every day coat. 2) *Fig.* common, ordinary, trifling, unimportant, trivial, trite. —tägliche Dinge, common things; —tägliche Betrachtungen, commonplace reflexions. —**täglichkeit**, *f.* commonness, vulgarity, meanness. —**tags-**, [in compositions] common, commonplace, ordinary, trite, as: —**tagsbegebenheit**, *f.* every-day occurrence. —**tagsbemerkung**, *f.* a commonplace observation. —tagsgeschichte, *f.* a tale of every day. —tagsgesicht, *n.* unmeaning, every-day face. —tagsleben, *n.* every-day life. —tagsmensch, *m.* commonplace fellow. —tagswitz, *m.* common-place wit. —umfassend, *adj.* all-embracing, comprehensive. —umschließend, *adj.* all-surrounding. —vater, *m.* father of all, God. Adam, unser—vater, Adam, our common progenitor. —verderbend, *adj.* all-devastating, all-blasting. —verflucht, *adj.* cursed by all. —verhüllend, *adj.* all-dimming. —vermögend, *adj.* all-efficient, all-powerful. —vernichtung, *f.* destruction of all things. —verschlingend, *adj.* all-devouring. —versöhnend, *adj.* all-reconciling. —versöhner, *m.* one, who reconciles all. —verwüstend, *adj.* all-devastating, all-destroying. —verzehrend, *adj.* all-consuming. —vollkommen, *adj.* all-perfect. —vollkommenheit, *f.* all-perfectness. —waltend, *adj.* all-governing. —weise, *adj.* all-wise. —weisheit, *f.* infinite wisdom, omniscience, omnisciency. —wissend, *adj.* omniscient, all-conscious, all-knowing. —wissenheit, *f.* omniscience, boundless knowledge. —wisserei, *f.* a superficial knowledge of all things. —wo, *adv.* where. V. Wo. —zerstörend, *adj.* all-destroying.

*Allée, *f.* [*pl.* -n] an alley, a walk or road planted with trees, an avenue.

*Allegationsregel, *f.* [*pl.* -n] [a rule of arithmetic] alligation.

*Allegiren, *v. tr.* to alledge. V. Anführen.

*Allegorie, *f.* [*pl.* -en] allegory.

*Allegórisch, I. *adj.* allegoric, allegorical. II. *adv.* allegorically.

*Allegorisiren, *v. tr.* to allegorize.

*Allegrétto, *adv.* [in music] allegretto.

*Allégro, *n.* and *adv.* [in music] allegro.

Allein, I. *adj.* 1) [without the presence of another, applied to a person or a thing] without company, alone. Es ist nicht gut, daß der Mensch — sey, it is not good, that man should be alone; und als sie — waren, and when they were alone or by themselves; laß mich —, leave me. 2) [with the exclusion of all others] alone. Gott — kann es thun, God alone can do that; er lebt —, he lives by himself, or alone. II. *conj.* 1) but. Ich wartete eine ganze Stunde, — er kam nicht, I waited a whole hour, but he did not come; [joined with: nicht] nicht —, sondern, not only, but. 2) [in composition].

Allein-besitz, *m.* exclusive possession. —friede, *m.* V. Separatfriede. —gespräch, *n.* monologue, soliloquy. —gesang, *m.* V —sang. —nützig, *adj.* [opposed to gemeinnützig] useful or advantageous to one alone. —rede, *f.* monologue, soliloquy. —sang, *m.* a solo. —sänger, *m.* one who sings a solo, solo singer. —spiel, *n.* a solo. —spieler, *m.* one who plays a solo. —verkauf, *m.* V. —handel. —handel, *m.* monopoly. —handel treiben, to monopolize. —händler, *m.* monopolist. —herrscher, *m.* monarch. —herrschaft, *f.* monarchy.

Alleinig, *adj.* only. Der —e Gott, the one God. Syn. V. Einsam.

Allemal, *adv.* always, ever, at all times, at any time, every time. Ein für —, once for all.

Allemande, *f.* [*pl.* -n] [a German or Suabian dance and the music to such dance] allemande.

Alemánnen, *pl.* [a name of an ancient people in Germany] Alemanni; ein Alemanne, an Almain.

Allemánnien, Alemanien, *f.* [an ancient name of Germany] Alemannia.

Állenfalls, *adv.* 1) at all events, at any rate. 2) perhaps, by accident, by chance. Wenn ich ihn — nicht sehen sollte, in case I should not see him.

Állenfallsig, *adj.* casual, eventual.

Állenthalben and Allenthálben, *adv.* every where, in all places, all over.

Áller, Álle, Álles, a declinable word of number, signifying the whole number or entire thing or all the parts or particulars of which it is composed. It is used alone or joined with a substantive or a pronoun. Alle Beide, both of them; alle Menschen, all men, every body; vor allen Dingen, before all things; alle Welt redet davon, every body talks of it; auf alle Weise, in every way; ohne alle Ursache, without any reason; mit aller Gewalt aufdringen, to obtrude forcibly upon any one; in aller Eile, with all possible speed; alle Jahre, every year; alle drei Tage, every third day; [sometimes in the form of a substantive] sie Alle, all of them; so sind sie Alle, so are they all; das macht Alles wieder gut, that makes amends for all; er hat sein Alles verloren, he has lost his all; wenn das Alles ist, if that be all; Alle für Einen, [in commerce] in solido, all together and one for all; mein All, mein Alles, my all; Alles in Einem seyn, to be all in all; unser Alles ist auf dem Spiel, our all is at stake; *Prov.* wer es Allen recht machen will, der soll noch geboren werden, one cannot please every one; wer Alles will, bekommt nichts, all grasp, all lose.

Aller-bester, *adj.* the very best, the best of all. —christlichst, *adj.* [a title of the kings of France] most christian. —durchlauchtigster, *adj.* [a title given to an emperor or king] most serene, most high, most illustrious. —erst, *adv.* 1) first of all. Zu —erst, first and foremost, originally. 2) just now. V. Erst. —erster, —erste, —erstes, *adj.* first of all. —getreuester, *adj.* [a title of the king of Portugal] most faithful. —gewürz, *n.* all-spice. —gnädigst, I. *adj.* most gracious. II. *adv.* most graciously. —hand, *adj.* of all sorts, of all kinds. —hand Weine, a variety of wines. —heiligen, all-hallow, all-hallows, all-saints, all-saints-day. —heiligenholz, *n.* a sort of log-wood or brasil wood of All-saints-bay. —heiligste, *n.* 1) [in scripture] holy of holies, sanctuary. 2) V. Monstranz. —heiligster, *adj.* [a title given to the pope] most holy. —höchst, *adj.* highest, most high. —höchster, *adj.* most high. —höchste, *m.* The Most-high. —liebst, *adj.* and *adv.* most charming, delightful, extremely amiable, very engaging. —liebster, *adj.* dearest, most beloved. —mannsharnisch, *m.* [a plant] the long rooted garlic. †—mannshure, *f.* common prostitute. —maßen, I. *adv.* in every way, quite, entirely. ‡II. *conj.* since, whereas. —meist, *adv.* especially, particularly, chiefly, most of all. —meister, —meiste, —meistes, *adj.* most. —nächst, *adv.* hard by, close by, next to. —nächster, —nächste, —nächstes, *adj.* next, the very next. —neuester, —neueste, —neuestes, *adj.* newest of all. —séelen, [viz. the festival] all-souls-day. —seits, *adv.* 1) on every side, from all parts. 2) altogether, all of them. —wärts, *adv* every where. †—weltshure, *f.* V. —mannshure.

Állerdings and Allerdíngs, *adv.* quite, entirely, perfectly, by all means, undoubtedly, indeed, certainly, really, surely, sure enough, to be sure. Es ist — nicht so, it is certainly not so.

Állerlei, I. *adj.* various, of all kinds. II. *n.* hodge-podge, salmagundi.

Állesammt, *adv.* altogether.

Állewege u. Allewége, *adv.* 1) every where. 2) quite, completely. || and ‡ 3) always.

Álleweile, *adv.* just now.

Állezeit, *adv.* always, every time.

Állgemein u. Allgeméin, I. *adj.* [common to all or to the greatest number] general. Ein —er Gebrauch, a common custom; eine —e Meinung, a general opinion; göttliche Gesetze sind —, divine laws are universal; das —e Beste, the general good; eine —e Krankheit, an epidemic disease; ein —es Mittel, a universal remedy, a panacea, a catholicon; ein —er Begriff, Ausdruck, [in logic] a general idea, a general term; aus einer besondern Thatsache einen —en Schluß ziehen, to draw a general inference from a particular fact; im —en, in general, generally; die Menschen im —en, the run or generality of mankind; das —e und das Besondere, [in log.] the abstract and the concrete; — machen, to generalize. II. *adv.* universally, generally.

Allgeméinheit, *f.* 1) universality, generality. 2) the quality of being common, or belonging to all.

*Alliánz, *f.* [*pl.* -en] alliance, confederacy, league.

*Alligatión, *f.* [a rule of arithmet.] alligation.

*Alligíren, *v. tr.* to alligate.

*Alliíren, *v. tr.* to ally. Ein Alliirter, an ally; die Alliirten, the allies.

*Alliteratión, *f.* [a repetition of and play upon the same letter] alliteration.

Allmánde or Allménde, *f.* [*pl.* -n] the common, common land. V. also Gemeindegut, Gemeinstück, Gemeintrift, Gemeinweide.

Allód (eigentl. Állod) and Allódium, *n.* V. Allodialgut.

Allodiál, *adj.* allodial. Der —erbe, [a law term] heir to a freehold; das —gut, free-hold estate, allodium.

*Alludíren, *v. intr.* to allude.

*Allusión, *f.* [in rhetoric] allusion.

*Alluvión, *f.* alluvion, alluvium.

Állzu, *adv.* too, too much.

Allzu-fruchtbar, *adj.* over-fruitful. —groß, *adj.* too great, over-great. —zärtlich, *adj.* over-fond. —gleich, *adv.* [for: alle zugleich] all together, all at once. —mal, *adv.* [for: alle insgesammt] all together, one and all.

*Almadíe, *f.* [*pl.* -en] almade [a small African canoe, formed of the bark of a tree].

Almágra, *n.* Spanish brown-red.

Álmanach, *m.* [-s, *pl.* -e] almanack, annual.

Almandínrubin, *m.* [-s, *pl.* -en] almendine.

Álmei, *m.* [in metall.] white tutty.

Álmer, *f.* V. Faulbaum.

Álmosen, *n.* [-s, *pl.* -] [from the Gr. ἐλεημοσύνη] alms, charity, [seldom] alms-deed. Um ein — bitten, to ask charity, to ask alms, to beg; — geben, to bestow charity upon, to give alms to; — austheilen, to distribute alms; Leute, die von — leben, alms-men, alms-people, paupers, eleemosynaries; — sammeln, to collect alms; — betreffend, eleemosynary. *Prov.* — geben, armet nicht, the giving of alms empoverishes not; —, das vom Herzen kommt, dem Geber wie dem Nehmer frommt; giving to the Poor encreases our store.

Almosen-amt, *n.* almonry. —einnehmer, *m.* a collector of alms. —büchse, *f.* V. —kasten. —geld, *n.* charity money, poor-money, poor's-rates. —genosse, *m.* —mann, *m.* alms-man, pauper. —kasten, *m.* alms-box, poor's-box. —korb, *m.* alms-basket. —pfleger, *m.* almoner, overseer of the poor. —sammler, *m.* a gatherer of alms. —sammlung, *f.* gathering of alms. —stock, *m.* alms-box, poor's-box.

Almosenier, [Almosenpfleger] *m.* [-s, *pl.* -e] almoner, overseer of the poor.

Aloe, *f.* [*pl.* -n] aloes. Mit — versetzt, aloetic, aloetical.

Aloe-Auszug [—extract], *m.* [in medic.] aloes. —holz, *n.* aloes-wood. Das Paradies—holz, calambac, tambac, agillochum, xylo-aloes. —mittel, *n.*, —latwerge, *f.* aloetic.

Álse, *f.* [*pl.* -n] [a fish] alose, the shad.

1. Álp, *m.* [-es, *pl.* -e] [appears to be allied to Elf, Elfe] the night-mare, incubus.

Alp-mährchen, *n.* a fairy-tale. —männchen, hobgoblin. —schoß, *m.* a fairy-stone. —zopf, *m.* plica.

2. Álp, 1) V. Alpen. 2) a name given to a hilly tract of land, as: die schwäbische Alp [a hilly part of Suabia].

Alp-balsam, *m.* the dwarf rosebay. —forelle, *f.* char. —hahn, *m.* V. Auerhahn. —hof, *m.* a farm upon the mountains. —horn, *n.* alpine horn. —kirscher, *pl* the common bird-cherry tree. —kraut, *n.* 1) hemp-agrimony. 2) woody nightshade, bitter-sweet. —maus, *f.* V. Murmelthier. —meier, *m.* a farmer on the Alps. —rabe, *m.* hermit-crow, solitary sparrow. —ranken, *pl.* 1) V. —kraut. 2) missletoe. —rauch, *m.* V. Erdrauch. —raute, *f.* V. Stabwurz. —rose, *f.* rhododendron. —volk, *n.* the people of the Alps.

Álpen, *pl.* 1) [any high mountains but chiefly the high mountains covered with snow in Switzerland on the borders of Italy and in some parts of Germany] the Alps. Jenseits der —, beyond the Alps, transalpine; diesseits der —, on this side the Alps, cisalpine. 2) [in Switzerland] pasturages on the hills or on the Alps.

Alpen-ampfer, *m.* Alpine-dock, monk's rhubarb. —balsam, *m.* V. Alprose. —bärlapp, *m.* cypress-moss, heath-moss. —beifuß, *m.* mountain wormwood. —bewohner, *m.* [*f.*—inn], *pl.* the inhabitants of the Alps, mountaineers. —birke, *f.* dwarf birchtree. —bockkäfer, *m.* a species of goat chafer [cerambyx alpinus]. —eis, *n.* Alpine ice. —gänsedistel, *f.* Alpine sowthistle. —gebirge, *n* the Alps. —geld, *n.* a certain tax paid in Switzerland. —günsel, *m.* V. Berggünsel. —habichtskraut, *n.* Alpine hawkweed. —hahnenfuß, *m.* a species of crowfoot (ranunculus alpestris). —heckenkirsche, *f.* red-berried upright honeysuckle. —heerde, *f.* a herd of cattle on the Alps. —huflattich, *m.* a species of colt's foot (tusilago alpina). —kiefer, *f.* wild mountain-pine, mountain-pine tree. —klee, *m.* Alpine trefoil. —krähe, *f.* Alpine crow. —kraut, *n.* Alpine stachys. —maus, *f.* V. Murmelthier. —mohn, *m.* Alpine poppy. —ratte, *f.* V. Murmelthier. —salz, *n.* Alpine salt. —scharte, *f.* Alpine sawwort. —schmetterling, *m.* a species of butterfly (papilio Apollo). —schnee, *m.* Alpine snow. —schwalbe, *f.* V. Mauerschwalbe. —sinau, *n.* Alpine lady-mantle. —strandläufer, *m.* [a species of sandpiper] dunlin. —volk, *n.* inhabitants of the Alps. —wegebreit, —wegerich, *m.* Alpine plantain.

Álpler, *m.* [-s] a Swiss cowherd.

* Álpha, *n.* [the first letter in the Greek alphabet] alpha. Ich bin das — und das Omega, [Rev. I.] I am alpha and omega [the beginning and the end].

* Alphabét, *n.* [-s, *pl.* -e] 1) alphabet. 2) [in printing] three and twenty printed sheets.

Alphabetschloß, *n.* a letter-keyed lock.

* Alphabétisch, I. *adj.* alphabetic, alphabetical. II. *adv.* alphabetically. — ordnen, to alphabet.

Álraun and Alraún, *f.* [-s, *pl.* -e] [a plant] mandrake, mandragora.

Álraune and Alraúne, *f.* [*pl.* -n] [= *wise woman*, from *all* and the ancient word *runa* = *to know*] 1) a priestess of the ancient Germans. 2) a witch, a sorceress.

Áls, *conj.* [probably from also] 1) [in the sense of a comparison] than, as, like. Er ist reicher — ich, he is richer than I; süßer — Honig, sweeter than honey; so roth — eine Rose, as red as a rose; er handelt — ein rechtschaffener Mann, he acts as an honest man; — ein Held, like a hero; ich stand vor ihm — ein anderer Goliath, I stood before him like an other Goliath; — ob, — wenn, as if; — ob, — wenn ich es nicht wüßte, as if I did not know it. 2) [denoting an exception] but, except. Sie hat keinen Reichthum — ihre Tugend, she has no riches but her virtue; nichts —, nothing but. 3) [in an explanatory sense] as, namely, to wit, for instance, such as. Das Thierreich wurde von ihm in sechs Klassen abgetheilt, — Säugethiere &c., the animal kingdom was divided by him into six classes, namely into mammalia &c. 4) [under a particular consideration] as. Der König von Preußen — Kurfürst von Brandenburg, the king of Prussia as elector of Brandenburg; ich — Vater, I as father. 5) [as mere copulative] as. Sowohl —, sowohl — auch, as well as; sowohl er — ich, he as well as I. 6) [noting time] — dieses geschah, when this happened. 7) [noting a cause with zu in the first member of the sentence and daß in the second] Er ist zu billig, — daß er es verlangte, he is too reasonable to demand it.

Álsbald and Alsbáld, *adv.* as soon as, directly, immediately, presently, forthwith.

Alsdánn, *adv*, then.

Álse, *f.* V. Alose.

Álsen, *m.* V. Wermuth.

* Al Ségno, *adv.* [in music] al segno.

Álso, [from all and so] 1) for: so. 2) *adv.* [in this manner, after this or that manner, in this wise] thus, so. Er sprach —, he spoke thus; die Sache verhält sich —, the thing stands thus. 3) *conj.* consequently, therefore, then. — wenn er das nächste Mal kommt, lassen Sie ihn nicht vor, therefore, the next time he comes, deny him admittance; Sie haben mir es versprochen, halten Sie es —, you gave me your promise, keep it then; laß uns —, let us then.

‡ Álsobald, V. Alsbald.

‡ Álsofort, V. Sofort, sogleich.

Álster, *f.* V. Elster.

1. Ált, älter, älteste, *adj.* and *adv.* [allied to the old word alen = wachsen] [of long continuance, not young, not new, not modern, long practised, decayed by time] old. Wie — ist er? how old is he? er ist 80 Jahre —, he is 80 years old; ein —er Rock, an old coat; —e Gebräuche, old customs; eine —e Mode, an old fashion, an antique fashion; die —en Römer, the ancient Romans; vor —en Zeiten, of old, in days of yore; —es Bier, stale beer; —er Speck, rusty bacon; eine —e Jungfer, an old maid, a stale virgin; ein —er Junggeselle, an old bachelor; —er Aberglaube, inveterate superstition; die —e Geschichte, ancient history; das —e Testament, the old testament; das ist etwas —es, that is something old; ich bleibe beim —en, I am still for the old thing; er ist noch immer der —e, he is still the same; nimm dich in Acht, —er! take care, old man! or [as a term of endearment] my old fellow! die —en, the ancients [the Greeks and Romans]; die Kleidung der —en, the dress of the ancients; unsere —en, our forefathers, ancestors. *Fig.* — thun, to give one's self a knowing air. *Prov.* Wie die —en sungen, so zwitschern die Jungen, as the old cock crows so crows the young; —er Freund, —er Wein, —es Geld, führen den Preis in aller Welt, friends, like wine, are better for being old.

Alt-backen, *adj.* —backenes Brod, stale bread. —baum, *m.* V. Traubenkirsche. —bekannt, *adj.* long-known. —britisch, *adj.* old English. —binder, *m.* a cooper. —deutsch, *adj.* old German. —flicker, *m.* a mender of old shoes [clothes &c.], a cobbler. —fränkisch, = —modisch, —väterisch, I. *adj.* old-fashioned, old, antiquated, antique, II. *adv.* in an antique manner. —förmig, *adj.* having an old form, old-fashioned. —gebacken, V. —backen. —gelehrsamkeit, *f.* philology. —gelehrte, *m.* philologer. —gesell, *m.* head journeyman, foreman. —gläubig, *adj.* addicted to the old doctrine, orthodox. —gläubigkeit, *f.* orthodoxy. —gothisch, *adj.* 1) Gothic. 2) *Fig.* antique, old-fashioned, Gothic. —griechisch, *adj.* ancient Greek. —herkömmlich, *adj.* being an old custom. ‖—herr, *m.* alderman. —jagdbar, *adj.* [among hunters] full grown [said of a stag eight years old]. —klug, *adj.* knowing, cunning, intelligent or knowing beyond one's years. —knecht, *m.* V. —gesell. —krieger, *m.* a veteran soldier, a veteran. —lapper, *m.* V. Altflicker. —lehrig, *adj.* V. Altgläubig. —meister, *m.* the senior master. *Fig.* Goethe ist der —meister der deutschen Dichter, Goethe is the head of the German poets; —modisch, *adj.* V. —fränkisch. —römisch, *adj.* ancient Roman. —soldat, *m.* V. —krieger. —stadt, *f.* the old town. —testamentlich, *adj.* founded on the old testament. —vater, *m.* grand-father, senior; die —väter der ersten Kirche, the Fathers. V. Kirchenväter. —väterisch, *adj.* V. —fränkisch. —vertraut, *adj.* intimate, of old acquaintance. —vordern, *pl.* the ancestors. —wasser, *n.* the water remaining in what was formerly the bed of the river. *Fig.* —weibersommer, *m.* the warm sunny days in the latter months of the year, Indian summer.

2. Ált, *m.* [-s] [in music] counter, counter-tenor. Der hohe —, the first or upper alto; der tiefe —, the lower alto.

Alt-geige, *f.* V. Bratsche. —sänger, *m.* altist, counter tenor. —sängerinn, *f.* altista. —schlüssel, *m.* [in music] counter-tenor or alto clef. —stimme, *f.* counter tenor, altista.

3. Ált, *m.* V. Alant.

* Altán and Áltan, *m.* [-es, *pl.* -e] a balcony, a flat roof to walk on.

* Altár, [and in poetry] Áltar, [-s, *pl* -äre] altar, communion table. Das Sakrament des Altars, the sacrament of the communion.

Altar-diener, *m.* [Altarist] he, that ministers at the altar. —bekleidung, *f.* V. Altartuch. —blatt, *n.* altar piece. —buch, *n.* agenda. —gemählde, *n.* V. Altarblatt. —geräth, *n.* altar furniture. —geschirre, *n. pl.* sacred vessels, altar plate. —kerze, *f.* a wax taper on the altar. —recht, *n.* [a law term in the Roman church] a kind of tenure. —stück, *n.* altar piece. —stufe, *f.* the step of an altar. —tuch, *n.* altar-cloth.

Álte, *m.* [-n, *pl.* -n] the chub, a fish.

Älte, *f.* oldness, old-age.

Älteln, *v. intr.* 1) to grow elderly, oldish, to be elderly. 2) to grow stale, to fade, to wither.

Älten, *v. intr.* to grow old.

Áltentheil, *n.* [-es, *pl.* -e] V. Ausgedinge.

Álter, *n.* [-s, *pl.* -] 1) age. *a*) [the whole duration of a being]. Das gewöhnliche — eines Menschen ist siebenzig Jahre, the usual age of a man is seventy years; das — eines Pferdes, eines Baumes, the age of a horse, of a tree. *b*) [that part of the duration of a being, which is between its beginning and any given time]. Er ist in meinem —, he is of my age. *Fig.* Das — des Monats, [in astronomy] [the number of days elapsed since the last new moon] the age of the moon. *c*) [a certain period of human life, marked by a difference of state] Das Jugend—, the age of youth; das männliche —, the age of manhood; das hohe —, great age, old age, oldness; das mittlere —, middle-age; das blühende —, the prime of life; die sieben — des Menschen, the seven ages of man or stages of life. *d*) [the latter part of life, or long continued duration] = oldness, old age. Die Augen Israels waren dunkel geworden vor —, [Gen. XLVIII] the eyes of Israel were dim with age. *Prov.* Das — ist des Todes Vorbote, grey hairs are death's blossoms; — schützt vor Thorheit nicht, age is not proof against folly. *e*) [the period, when a person is enabled by law to do certain acts for himself] Das unmündige —, non-age, under-age, minority. *f*) [mature years, ripeness of strength or discretion] Das mündige — erreicht haben, to be of age, of full age, to have come to one's majority. *g*) [a peculiar period of time as distinguished from others] Das goldene — der Welt, the golden age. 2) existence from old times. Das — einer Familie, the antiquity of a family; das — eines Rechts, ancientness of a right. 3) [priority in office &c.] Nach dem — im Amte vorrücken, to advance in office by seniority; vor —s, von —s her, in old times, of old, in days of yore, anciently, formerly.

Alters-erlaß, *m.* [a law term] dispensation of age [venia aetatis]. —folge, *f.* seniority. —genoß, *m.* one of the same age, contemporary. —pflege, *f.* gerocomy [in medic.]. —reife, *f.* puberty. —schwäche, *f.* weakness of old age.

Älter, *adj.* [comp. of alt] older, elder, more ancient.

***Alteratiōn**, *f.* 1) consternation. 2) emotion, anger, chagrin, indignation.

***Alterīren**, *v. r.* sich —, 1) to fret, to be vexed. 2) to become much moved or affected.

Älterlich, *adj.* V. Elterlich.

Ältermann, *m.* [-es, *pl.* -männer] senior, elder.

Ältermutter, *f.* [*pl.* -mütter] V. Eltermutter.

Ältern, *v. intr.* to grow old.

Ältern, *pl.* V. Eltern.

***Alternatīv**, *adv.* alternately.

***Alternatīve**, *f.* [*pl.* -n] alternative. Es gibt hier keine —, there is no alternative.

***Alternīren**, *v. intr.* to alternate. Ebbe und Fluth alterniren mit einander, the ebb and flood tides alternate with each other.

Alterthum, *n.* [-s, *pl.* -thümer] antiquity. *a*) [ancient times, former ages, times long since past] Cicero war der beredteste Redner des —s, Cicero was the most eloquent orator of antiquity. *b*) [great age, the quality of being ancient] = ancientness. Das — einer Bildsäule, the antiquity of a statue. *c*) [the people of ancient times] Die Weissagungen des —s, the predictions of antiquity; Der gute Geschmack des —s, the good taste of the ancients. *d*) [the remains of ancient times; in this sense it is almost always used in the plural]. Das heidnische —, the ages of paganism; römische Alterthümer, Roman antiquities; Liebhaberei für Alterthümer, antiquarianism.

Alterthums-forscher, *m.* antiquary, antiquarian. —kenner, *m.* —kundige, *m.* one versed in antiquity, antiquary. —kunde, *f.* archeology. —stück, *n.* an antique.

Älterthümler, *m.* [-s, *pl.* -] antiquary, antiquarian.

Älterthümlich, *adj.* antiquarian. Das —e Ansehen einer Sache, antiqueness of a thing.

Ältervater, *m.* [-s, *pl.* -väter] V. Eltervater.

Älteste, [sup. of alt] oldest, eldest, most ancient. Mein —r Bruder, my eldest brother; der —, eldest, senior; die Aeltesten [New-Test.], the elders; das Aeltestenrecht, the right of seniority.

***Althēa**, *f.* V. Heilwurz.

*Althea-staude, *f.* great flowered lavatera. —strauch, *m.* Syrina mellow.

Altist, *m.* [-en, *pl.* -en] V. Altsänger.

Altistinn, *f.* V. Altsängerinn.

Ältlich, *adj.* elderly, oldish. —e Leute, elderly people.

***Alúmnus**, *m.* [*pl.* -nen] pupil, scholar, especially one educated in a seminary.

***Alýsse**, *f.* [*pl.* -n] [a plant] mad-wort.

*Alyssen-andorn, *m.* plaited leaved white horehound. —kraut, *n.* 1) mad-wort. 2) red dead-nettle, nettle-hemp, narrow leaved allheal, or iron-wort.

Ám, *prep.* [a contraction for: an dem] 1) Ochsen — Pfluge, oxen at plough; — Halse aufhängen, to hang by the neck; — Wege, by the way; nahe — Hause, near the house, close by the house; — Hofe leben, to live at court; — Tage liegen, to be evident, manifest; eine Wunde — Haupte, a wound on the head; arm — Geiste, poor in spirit; — Leben, alive; — Ende, at last, at length; — heutigen Tage, this very day; — dritten Tage, on the third day; Frankfurt — Main, Frankfort on the Main. 2) [before adverbs expressing the highest degree] — ersten, first of all, in the first place; — besten, best, the best of all; — nächsten, nearest, the nearest, next; — meisten, most, the most; hier lebt man — angenehmsten, one lives here the most pleasantly.

***Amálgama**, *n.* [in chimistry] amalgam.

***Amalgamatiōn**, *f.* [in chimistry] amalgamation.

***Amalgamīren**, *v. a.* [in chimistry] to amalgamate.

Amālie or **Ámalie**, [name of woman] Amelia.

***Amanuénsis**, *m.* copist, clerk, amanuensis.

***Amaránth**, *m.* 1) amaranth, amaranthus, flower gentle, flower amour. 2) [a colour inclining to purple] amaranth.

***Amaránthen**, *adj.* amaranthine.

*Amaranthen-baum, *m.* amaranth plant.

***Amarèlle**, *f.* [*pl.* -n] 1) the morello cherry. 2) [a sort of apricot] the turkey.

***Amazōne**, *f.* [*pl.* -n] 1) Amazon, 2) *Fig.* an Amazon, virago.

*Amazonen-ammer, *f.* amazon bunting, —fluß, *m.* [a river in South-America] the Amazon [more correctly] Maranon. —kleid, *n.* a lady's riding-dress or habit. —land, *n.* Amazonia. —stein, *m.* the common fieldspar, a kind of the common nephrite. —strom, *m.* V. —fluß.

Ámbachtslehen, *n.* [-s, *pl.* -] [a law term] a fief, wherewith the liege-lord invests a person, who has the management of his affairs.

***Ambassāde**, *f.* [*pl.* -n] embassy.

***Ambassadeūr**, *m.* [-s, *pl.* -e] ambassador, or embassador.

***Ambassadeūrinn**, **Ambassadrice**, *f.* ambassadress or embassadress [mostly used in some jocose sense].

***Ámbe**, *f.* [*pl.* -n] two numbers [in a lottery].

Ámber, *m.* [-s] 1) indurated fæces of the spermaceti whale, ambergris. Grauer —, ambergris; flüssiger —, liquid amber. 2) formerly the name of the fossil resin, amber. Gelber —, [= Bernstein] yellow amber.

Amber-baum, *m.* maple leaved liquid amber, or sweet gum. —duft, *m.* fragrance, sweet perfume. —fisch, *m.* spermaceti whale. —forster, *m.* = Amberfisch. —geruch, *m.* the fragrant odours of the ambergris. —kraut, *n.* wild basil. —staude, *f.* amber-tree.

***Ambiguitāt**, *f.* [*pl.* -en] V. Zweideutigkeit.

***Ambīren**, *v. intr.* to sue for an office [as the ancient Romans were wont to do].

***Ambitiōn**, *f.* V. Ehrgeiz.

Ámboß, *m.* [-es, *pl.* -e] [from an and bossen or botten, = *beat*] 1) anvil, stiddy. Ein zweispitziger —, a rising anvil. *Prov.* Ein tüchtiger — achtet schwere Schläge nicht, a good anvil fears not the hammer. 2) *Fig.* [in anatomy] [the longest and strongest of the bones in the ear] incus.

Amboß-schmied, *m.* a blacksmith. —stock, *m.* the stock of an anvil.

***Ámbra**, *m.* V. Amber.

***Ambrōsia**, *f.* ambrosia. V. Götterspeise.

Ambrosia-kraut, *n.* V. Götterkraut. —mandeln, *f. pl.* a species of almonds [amygdalæ ambrosianæ].

***Ambrōsisch**, *adj.* ambrosial, ambrosian, ambrosiac. —e Thaue, ambrosial dews.

***Ambrosiānisch**, *adj.* Ambrosian. Der —e Kirchengebrauch, [a formula of worship in the church of Milan, instituted by St. Ambrose in the fourth century] the Ambrosian office, or ritual.

***Ambulānce**, *f.* [*pl.* -n] a field-hospital.

Ámeise, *f.* [*pl.* -n] [the a is probably the article and meise, Eng. [pis-] *mire*, allied to the Ice. *mira*, = *bite*, *sting*] ant, emmet, pis-mire, ‡ mire. Die weiße —, white ant, termite.

Ameisen-bär, *m.* 1) ant-bear, ant-eater. 2) the little black bear. —bad, *n.* a kind of medicated bath, saturated with ants. —drossel, *f.* a species of thrush [turdus formicivorus]. —ei, *n.* ant-egg. —fresser, *m.* ant-bear, ant-eater. —haufen, *m.* V. —nest. —jäger, *m.* 1) V. —fresser. 2) V. Pfefferkäfer. —löwe, *m.* the lion-ant, myrmeleon. —natter, *f.* a species of snake [coluber cenchoa]. —nest, *n.* ant-hill. —puppe, *f.* V. —ei. —säure, *f.* [in chimistry] formic acid.

***Amelioratiōn**, *f.* [*pl.* -en] V. Verbesserung.

Ámelkorn, *n.* [-es, *pl.* -körner] a sort of spelt or German wheat.

Ámelmehl, *n.* [-s] starch.

***Ámen**, amen, so be it. *Prov.* So wahr als — im Gebete, sure as amen in the lord's prayer.

Amérika, *n.* America.

Amerikāner, *m.* [*pl.* -s, *pl.* -] an American.

Amerikānisch, *adj.* American, Columbian.

***Amethýst**, *m.* [-es, *pl.* -e] amethyst, violet quarz. —enfarbig, *adj.* amethystine.

***Amiánth**, *m.* [-es] amianthus, earth-flax, flexible asbestus.

***Amidam**, *n.* V. Amelmehl, Stärke.

Ámmann, *m.* [-s, *pl.* -männer] [chiefly in Switzerland, a civil officer invested with a certain branch of the executive government, magistrate, justice of the peace] an Amman.

Ámmeister, *m.* [-s, *pl.* -] chief magistrate.

Ámme, *f.* [*pl.* -n] [allied to the D. ammen, = *nourish*] nurse, wet-nurse.

Ammen-mährchen, *n.* a nursery tale. —milch, *f.* the milk of a nurse. —stube, *f.* nursery.

Ámmei, *m.* bull-wort, or bishop's weed.

Ammeisaamen, *m.* seed of the bull-wort or bishop's weed.

Ámmer, *f.* [*pl.* -n] 1) V. Goldammer. 2) [a species of cherry] the morello. 3) —n, *pl.* hot ashes, embers.

* Ammoniák, *m.* [-s] ammoniac, ammony.

Ammoniak-gummi, *m.* gum-ammoniac, —salz, *n.* ammoniac, sal-ammoniac. V. Salmiak.

Ámmonshorn, *n.* [-s, *pl.* -hörner] ammonite, serpent stone.

* Ammunitión, *f.* military stores or provisions for attack and defence, ammunition.

Ammunitions-schiff, *n.* store-ship.

* Ámor, *m.* [-s] the God of Love, Cupid.

* Amortisatión, *f.* V. Tilgung.

Amortisations-schein, *m.* V. Tilgungsschein. —casse, *f.* V. Tilgungscasse.

Ámpel, *f.* [*pl.* -n] V. Lampe.

Ámpfer, *m.* [-s] [allied to the D. amper, = *sour*] sorrel. V. Sauerampfer.

Ampfer-baum, *m.* sorrel-tree. —kraut, *n.* common sorrel.

* Amphíbien, [in zoology] *pl.* of Amphibium, amphibials, amphibia.

Amphibienhaft, *adj.* amphibious. Das —e, *n.* amphibiousness.

* Ámphibiolíth, *m.* [-en, *pl.* -en] [in nat. hist.] amphibiolite.

* Amphíbium, *n.* [-s, *pl.* -bien] amphibial, amphibium.

* Amphibráchys, *m.* [in poetry] amphibrach [υ - υ].

Amphibrachysmacer, *m.* [in poetry] amphimacer [- υ -].

* Amphictyónen, *m. pl.* amphictyons.

* Ámphitheater, *n.* [-s, *pl.* -] amphitheatre.

* Amputatión, *f.* [in surgery] amputation.

* Amputíren, *v. tr.* [in surg.] to amputate.

Ámsel, *f.* [*pl.* -n] [allied to the Engl. *ousel*, Sax. *osle*] the black-bird, ousel. Die italienische —, the solitary thrush.

Amsel-fisch, *m.* V. Meeramsel. —möve, *f.* black tern, or sea-crow.

Ámsig, *adj.* V. Emsig.

Ámt, *n.* [-es, *pl.* Aemter] [anciently Ambacht; allied to the L. *ambactus*] 1) charge, office, employment. Er hat ein gutes — bekommen, he has got a good place or appointment; Einem ein — verleihen, to confer a place on any one; Einem ein — übertragen, to admit any one into an office, to appoint to a place or office; ein — antreten, to enter upon an office; ein — bekleiden, to fill an office; Kraft meines —es, by virtue of my office. *Prov.* Was deines —es nicht ist, da laß deinen Vorwitz, meddle not with what does not concern you. 2) [in a more limited sense] *a*) an ecclesiastical function, sacred ministry, service [in the Rom. and protestant church]. Das Hoch—, [in the Romish church] high mass, grand mass; das Hoch— halten, to say high mass. *b*) the administration of justice; *it.* the district over which the jurisdiction of an amman extends. *c*) a board, court, council and the place, where business is transacted. V. Post—, Kammer—, Zoll—. *d*) a company, corporation. Das Tischler—, the joiners' company. 3) the house in which the amman resides.

Amt-frei, *adj.* V. Privat. Ein —freier Mann, a private person, one not in any public employment: seine —freie Stellung erlaubte ihm, sich nach Laune zu beschäftigen, his being free of all public duties allowed him to occupy himself according to his fancy. —geld, *n.* [a law-term] money paid for certain fiefs. —haus, *n.* office, court, the house of the amman. —lich, 1) *adj.* official; 2) *adv.* officially. —los, *adj.* and *adv.* 1) without employment, out of place or office [of a public functionary]. 2) private, independent of office. —losigkeit, *f.* 1) the state of being out of office. 2) independency of office. —mann, *m.* [in Germany] 1) an officer, who is invested with the jurisdiction of a certain district, amman. 2) one who is intrusted with the administration of a public domain, a steward, a bailiff. —männinn, *f.* the wife of an amman or steward. —mannschaft, *f.* the dignity and office or the jurisdiction of an amman. —meister, *m.* the head or chief of a guild or corporation. —sactuar, *m.* the actuary or clerk of an amman or steward. —salter, *n.* seniority in office. —sansehen, *n.* official authority. —santritt, *m.* the entering upon office. —sarbeit, *f.* official duty. —sbauer, *m.* peasant attached to a public domain, or living within a certain jurisdiction. —sbefehl, *m.* the order of an amman. —sbeförderung, *f.* promotion to an office. —sbericht, *m.* official reports, return. —sbescheid, *m.* decree, sentence, or decision of an amman. —sbesetzung, *f.* right of nominating to, or giving away a place. Die —sbesetzung kommt dem Fürsten zu, the nomination to this office belongs to the prince, or is in his gift. —sbewerber, *m.* a candidate for an office. —sbezirk, *m.* limit of a jurisdiction, a jurisdiction. —sblatt, *n.* any paper printed by authority, official paper. —sbote, *m.* a messenger belonging to a certain jurisdiction. —sbrauch, *m.* the custom in a certain office. —sbrief, *m.* official letter. —sbruder, *m.* a colleague. —sbuch, *n.* the court-roll. —sdiener, *m.* servitor attached to the jurisdiction of an amman, or to a public domain. —sdorf, *n.* village belonging to a jurisdiction or a public domain. —seid, *m.* oath taken upon entering into office. —seifer, *m.* official zeal. —seinkünfte, [used only in the plural] emoluments proceeding from any office. —sertrag, *m.* 1) the emoluments of an office. 2) the revenues or rents of a domain. —sfolge, *f.* 1) order of succession in office. 2) a kind of hue and cry. 3) obedience due to the amman. —sfolge leisten, to obey the orders of an amman. —sfolger, *m.* successor in office. —sfrohn, *m.* V. —sdiener, Büttel. —sfrohne, *f.* statute labour or service due to a public domain by the peasantry. —sführung, *f.* the administration or conducting of an office. —sgebühr, *f.* fees of office. —sgebührlich, *adj.* official. —sgefälle, *pl.* 1) the fees, the perquisites of an office. 2) the domain revenues. —sgehülfe, *m.* assistant, adjunct. —sgenosse, *m.* colleague, associate, joint commissioner. —sgericht, *n.* a tribunal or court of justice, over which the amman presides. —sgeschäft, *n.* official duty, business. *Fig.* and ‡—sgesicht, *n.* official face, grave air, solemn air. —sgewalt, *f.* the power and authority belonging to an office. —shauptmann, *m.* the chief officer, prefect, or provost of a jurisdiction. —shauptmannschaft, *f.* the dignity or jurisdiction of a prefect. —shelfer, *m.* an associate in office. —hoheit, *f.* the seigniory of an amman. —skammer, *f.* an office, to which belongs the administration of the domains. —skanzlei, *f.* the chancery or office of an amman or steward. —skasse, *f.* treasury of a jurisdiction. —skeller, *m.* administrator or steward of the revenues or finances of a jurisdiction. —skleid, *n.* —skleidung, *f.* V. Ornat, Pontificalia. —sknecht, *m.* V. —sdiener. —skosten, *pl.* fees paid to an amman for the administration of justice, expenses of a law-suit, costs of suit. —slade, *f.* a box or chest for the papers and money of a corporation. —sname, *m.* title adherent to an office. —spflege, *f.* the office, or jurisdiction of an amman or steward. —spfleger, *m.* the administrator of the revenues of a jurisdiction. —spflicht, *f.* official duty. —sphysikus, *m.* the physician attached to a jurisdiction. —srath, *m.* counsel to a jurisdiction. —sregistratur, *f.* board of rolls of a jurisdiction. —srichter, *m.* a judge. —ssache, *f.* any official business. —ssaß, *m.* any one belonging to or residing in the jurisdiction of an amman. —sschaffner, *m.* V. —skeller. —sschösser, *m.* the auditor or accountant of the revenues of a domain. —sschreiben, *n.* V. —sbrief. —sschreiber, *m.* the clerk or recorder in a public office. —sschultheiß, *m.* the mayor or magistrate of a town or village situated within the jurisdiction of an amman. —ssiegel, *n.* the seal of office. —sstadt, *f.* 1) the town in which the amman resides. 2) a town attached to an amman's jurisdiction. —sstube, *f.* the apartment in which official business is transacted, amman's office. —stag, *m.* the court-day, audience-day. —sthätigkeit, *f.* activity in official duty. —stracht, *f.* official dress, robes of office. —sverrichtung, *f.* official functions. —sversammlung, *f.* an assembly of all the magistrates of the different villages or towns in the jurisdiction of an amman. —svertreter, *m.* a substitute in office, a deputy. —sverwalter, *m.* the steward of a public domain. —sverweser, *m.* deputy administrator of any office, jurisdiction or public domain. —svogt, *m.* 1) the administrator of a public domain. 2) the justice or judge of a public domain. 3) servitor of such a judge. —svogtei, *f.* the dignity of an administrator of a public domain and the district under his administration.

Ámtchen, *n.* [-s, *pl.* -] *dimin.* of Amt. *Prov.* — bringt Käppchen, no employment without profit; kein — ohne ein Schlämpchen, no office without its vexations.

Ámten, † and ‡ Amtiren, *v. intr.* to officiate, to discharge an office.

* Amulét, *n.* [-s, *pl.* -e] amulet.

* Amüsíren, *v. r.* sich —, V. Ergetzen.

* Amüsánt, *adj.* V. Ergetzlich.

Án, [Goth. *ana*, Eng. *on*, Fr. *en*; originally synonymous with in] I. *prep.* [with the dative case, denotes nearness, closeness, contiguity, or the presence of a thing, chiefly] 1) [when you may ask: wo? (where?)] — einem Orte wohnen, to live at a place; das Haus steht — einem Flusse, the house stands by a river; — einer Kirche vorbei gehen, to pass by a church; — dem Ufer, upon the shore; — der Themse, on the Thames; dicht — der Mauer, close by the wall; — der Wand hängen, to hang on the wall; Frankfurt — der Oder, Francfort on the Oder. 2) [when you may ask: wann? (when?)] — einem Sonntage, on a sunday; — dem Abend, in the evening. 3) [when you may ask: woran? (on or in what?)] Er hat viele Fehler — sich, he is subject to many faults; er geht — Krücken, he walks with crutches; er starb — einem Fieber, he died of a fever; er zweifelt — der Wahrheit dieser Geschichte, he doubts the truth of this story; wir zweifeln — einer Thatsache, we doubt of a fact. 4) [when you may ask: an wem? (here a word is omitted)]. Es ist [scil. die Reihe] — Ihnen, it is your turn; — meiner Stelle [Statt], in my place; es ist [sc. die Zeit] — dem, it is about the time; es ist [sc. die Zeit] — dem, daß ich gehen muß, it is about time for me to go.

II. [with the accusative, it denotes progression, direction or motion] 1) [when you may ask: wohin? (where to?)] Eine Kette — die Füße befestigen, to fasten a chain to the feet; er lehnt sich — eine Mauer, he leans against a wall; Etwas — eine Wand befestigen, to fasten something against a wall; er griff ihr — die Hand, he seized her hand; bis — die Schultern, up to the shoulders; — das Feuer setzen, to put to the fire; — die Thüre klopfen, to knock at the door. 2) [when you may ask: an wen? an was? (to whom? to what?)] Er hat seine Tochter — einen Edelmann verheirathet, he married his daughter to a nobleman; sich — eine spärliche Kost gewöhnen, to accustom one's self to a spare diet; — das Licht bringen, to bring to light; — eine Sache denken, to think of a thing; — Etwas glauben, to believe in a thing; bis — das Ende, to the end. 3) [when you may ask: bis wann (till when or what time?)] Vom Morgen bis — den Abend, from morning till evening. 4) [= ungefähr] nearly, about. Es kostet mich — die zehn Thaler, it costs me about ten dollars; — zweitausend Mann, nearly two thousand men. 5) [= für, for] So viel — Macherlohn, so much for the charge of making. 6) [= anfangend, beginning] Es ging — ein Schreien, they commenced screaming, a cry was set up.

III. *adv.* Von nun —, from this moment, henceforth; von Stund' —, from this time forward; oben —, uppermost, at the top; unten —, below, at the bottom; er wohnt neben —, he lives close to; berg —, up hill; himmel —, towards heaven; — und für sich betrachtet, abstractedly, abstractly; von Kindheit —, from childhood.

Ánaaßen, Ánäsen, *v. tr.* [am. sportsmen] to bait, to attract by a bait.

* **Anabaptíst**, *m.* [-en, *pl.* -en] anabaptist.

* **Anachorét**, *m.* [-s, *pl.* -en] anchoret, anchorite.

* **Anachronísmus**, *m.* [*pl.* -men] anachronism.

* **Anagrámm**, *n.* [-es, *pl.* -e] anagram [thus: Galenus becomes Angelus].

* **Analékten**, *pl.* analects.

* **Analōg** and **Analōgisch**, *adj.* analogous. Es ist — mit &c., it is analogous to &c.

* **Analogíe**, *f.* [*pl.* -en] analogy. Es findet eine — zwischen Pflanzen und Thieren statt, there is an analogy between plants and animals; eine Pflanze hat einige — mit einem Thiere, a plant has some analogy to or with an animal; alle diese Nennwörter werden durch — mit andern Wörtern derselben Art gebildet, all these nouns are formed by analogy with other words of a like kind.

* **Analȳse**, *f.* [*pl.* -n] analysis. 1) the separation of a compound body into its parts, a resolving. Eine — des Wassers, der Luft, an analysis of water, air. 2) a consideration of any thing in its separate parts [it is opposed to Synthesis]. 3) [in mathem.] the resolving of algebraic operations. Die — der endlichen oder unendlichen Größen, the analysis of finites or of infinites. 4) [in logic] the tracing of things to their source, and the resolving of knowledge into its original principles.

* **Analysíren**, *v. tr.* to analyse.

* **Analȳtik**, *f.* analytics.

* **Analȳtisch**, *adj.* analytic, analytical. Ein —es Experiment in der Scheidekunst, an analytical experiment in chimistry.

* **Ananas**, *f.* ananas, pine-apple. Die wilde —, wild ananas.

Ananas-birn, *f.* pine-apple-pear. —**haus**, *n.* a pinery. —**vogel**, *m.* the humming bird. —**wein**, *m.* pine-apple-wine.

Ánankern, *v. tr.* 1) to fasten by means of anchors, to anchor. 2) [in building] to fasten a beam to the purlins with cramps.

* **Anapäst**, *m.* [-es, *pl.* -e] [in poetry] anapest [*v v* -].

* **Anápher**, *f.* [*pl.* -n] [a figure in rhet.] anaphora.

* **Anarchíe**, *f.* anarchy.

* **Anárchisch**, *adj.* anarchic, anarchical.

Ánarbeiten, *v. tr.* to join by means of work.

* **Anathém**, *n.* [-es, *pl.* -e] anathema.

* **Anathematisíren**, *v. tr.* to anathematize.

* **Anatomíe**, *f.* anatomy. 1) the act of dividing any thing, corporeal or intellectual, for the purpose of examining its parts. 2) the act of dissecting the different parts of an animal body. 3) the doctrine of the structure of the body learned by dissection. 4) a house, which contains the anatomical theatre.

* **Anatōmiker**, *m.* [-s, *pl.* -] anatomist.

* **Anatomíren**, *v. tr.* to anatomize.

* **Anatōmisch**, I. *adj.* anatomical. II. *adv.* anatomically.

Ánätzen, *v. tr.* to begin to etch.

Ánäugeln, *v. tr.* to look on a person amorously, to ogle.

Ánbacken, I. *v. intr.* [u. w. seyn] to cleave, to stick, to adhere by baking. II. *v. tr.* to make to stick or to adhere by baking.

Ánbannen, *v. tr.* to bewitch, to charm, to fascinate. Er ist wie angebannt an seine Arbeit, an seine Bücher, he is bound to his work, to his books, as it were, by a spell.

Ánbau, *m.* [-es] 1) the first cultivation or bringing into order of an untilled piece of land. 2) cultivation, culture, in general. Das Land wird oft durch — besser, land is often made better by cultivation. *Fig.* Der — der Künste, the cultivation of the arts; der — des Geistes, the culture of the mind. 3) the act of settling, building. Der — eines Dorfes, the constructing of a village. 4) a building added to another, as, for instance, an additional wing, or outhouse added to the principal building.

Ánbaubar, *adj.* capable of being tilled, cultivable.

Ánbauen, I. *v. tr.* 1) to commence cultivating. 2) to cultivate, to till [in general]. Einen Acker —, to cultivate, to till a field. *Fig.* Eine Sprache —, to cultivate a language; seinen Geist —, to cultivate one's mind. 3) to build, to construct [a village &c.]. 4) to add by building. Einen Flügel an einem Hause —, to add a wing to a house. II. *v. r.* sich —, to settle. Sie bauten sich an der Mündung des Po an, they settled at the mouth of the river Po.

Ánbauer, *m.* [-s, *pl.* -] settler, cultivator, planter, colonist.

Ánbaulich, *adj.* and *adv.* easy to cultivate, cultivable.

Ánbefehlen, *ir. v. tr.* 1) to enjoin, to command, to order, to direct, to instruct. 2) to recommend.

Ánbeginn, *m.* [-s] the beginning. Im — der Welt, in the very commencement of the world; der — des Tages, the dawn.

Ánbehalten, *ir. v. tr.* to keep on. Ich will die Kleider —, die ich anhabe, I will keep on the clothes which I have on my back.

‡ **Ánbei** and **Anbey**, *adv.* jointly, withal. — folgt &c., annexed, enclosed to this, subjoined, joined to this, you receive &c. V. Hiebei.

Ánbeißen, *ir.* I. *v. tr.* to begin to bite, to bite at or off. Einen Apfel —, to bite a piece off an apple, to bite into an apple. II. *v. intr.* to bite at, to nibble at; [of a fish] to bite or nibble at, to take the bait. *Fig.* [to engage or embark in any thing] to close with, to bite at the hook. Man bot ihm einen Antheil bei dieser Unternehmung an, aber er wollte nicht —, they offered him a share in this speculation, but he would not swallow the bait.

Ánbelangen, V. Anlangen, Betreffen.

Ánbelfern, Ánbellen, *v. tr.* to bark at, to yelp at. Ein anderer Hund bellt laut den Himmel an, another hound against the welkin vollies out his voice. † Einen —, to bawl at any one.

Ánbequemen, I. *v. tr.* to fit, to adapt, to accommodate. II. *v. r.* sich —, to accommodate one's self to; sich den Umständen —, to accommodate one's self, to conform, to yield to circumstances.

Ánberahmen, Ánberaumen, *v. tr.* [a law term] to fix, set or appoint [a stated time].

Ánberaumung, *f.* the setting, fixing or appointing of a certain time, term.

‡ **Ánberegt**, *adj.* and *adv.* for: erwähnt, angeführt.

Ánberg, *m.* [-es, *pl.* -e] a small hill or hillock, contiguous to and forming part of the foot of a mountain.

Ánbeten, *v. tr.* to adore, to worship. *Fig.* [to love in the highest degree] to adore, to doat upon. Er liebt sie nicht blos, er betet sie an, he not only loves, but idolizes her.

Ánbetenswerth, Ánbetenswürdig, I. *adj.* adorable. II. *adv.* adorably.

Ánbeter, *m.* [-s, *pl.* -] adorer, worshipper. Die — der Sonne, worshippers of the sun. *Fig.* adorer, admirer. Dieses Mädchen hat viele —, this girl has many admirers.

Ánbetracht, V. Betracht.

Ánbetreffen, *ir. v. intr.* V. Betreffen.

Ánbetreffend, V. Betreffend.

Ánbetteln, I. *v. tr.* Einen —, to ask alms or charity of any one. II. *v. r.* sich —, to get into a place, or in favour with any one by dint of mean entreaties or supplications, to insinuate one's self in a begging manner.

Ánbetung, *f.* adoration, worship. *Fig.* [love in the highest degree, profound reverence] adoration, a doating fondness.

Anbetungs-werth, —würdig, I. *adj.* adorable. II. *adv.* adorably. —**würdigkeit**, *f.* adorableness.

Ánbezielen, *v. tr.* [a law term] V. Anberaumen.

Ánbiegen, *ir. v. tr.* 1) to bend to or towards. Ein Reis an einen Pfahl —, to bend and fasten a shoot to a post. 2) to subjoin, to annex. Aus angebogenem Aufsatz, by the annexed treatise.

Ánbieten, *ir.* I. *v. tr.* 1) to offer. Einem seine Dienste —, to offer one's self to serve another, to make a tender of one's services to any one, to proffer one's services to any one; dem Feinde eine Schlacht —, to offer battle to the enemy; er hat ihr seine Hand angeboten, he offered her his hand [in marriage]. II. *v. intr.* [at an auction] to bid first. III. *v. r.* sich —, to offer one's self, to offer; er bietet sich an, zu gehen, he offers to go; sobald sich eine gute Gelegenheit anbietet [better darbietet], as soon as a good opportunity offers or presents itself. Syn. Anbieten, Antragen, Erbieten, Anerbieten. Erbieten and anerbieten are said only of persons, not of things. Anbieten and antragen are used with reference as well to things as persons. Anbieten can be used in speaking of weighty and important, as well as of trifling and unimportant things. One says, for instance: Jemanden ein Amt anbieten [to offer any one an office or situation], seine Dienste anbieten [to tender one's services], ein Glas Wein anbieten [to offer a glass of wine]. Antragen, on the contrary, is used when speaking only of more important concerns, as: Einem ein Amt antragen [to proffer an office or appointment], seine Tochter zur Ehe antragen [to offer one's daughter in marriage].

Anbinden, *ir.* I. *v. tr.* to tie to, to bind to. Ein Pferd an einen Baum —, to tie a horse to a tree; ein Buch an das andere —, to bind two books together, one book to another. *Fig.* Er ist so angebunden, daß er nicht eine Stunde frei hat, he is so occupied that he has not an hour to himself; Kälber — [better abbinden], to wean calves; Einen an seinem Geburtstage —, to make any one a present on his birth-day. *Fig.* Einem einen Bären —, to contract a debt, to run in debt with any one; *it.* to put trick upon, to humbug a person, to make any one believe something. II. *v. intr. Fig.* Mit Einem —, to engage in a quarrel, to pick a quarrel with any one, to banter or jeer any one; kurz angebunden seyn, to be irritable, choleric or irascible, to be hot-brained, to grow easily angry, to be short with any one.

Anbindekalb, *n.* Anbindling, *m.* a weaned calf.

Anbiß, *m.* [-bisses, *pl.* -bisse] 1) the act of biting at and the place where any one has bitten, a bite. 2) a bit to eat. 3) [especially used of fish] a bait. 4) [= Imbiß] breakfast, luncheon.

Anbißkraut, *n.* devil's bit.

Anblaffen, V. Anbellen.

Anblasen, *ir. v. tr.* 1) to blow at, to blow upon, to breathe at, to breathe upon. Der Wind bläst uns an, the wind blows upon us. 2) to excite by blowing upon. Das Feuer —, to blow up the fire. *Fig.* Das Feuer der Zwietracht —, to foment discord, to sow dissension. 3) to announce by blowing. Einen —, to receive, or announce the arrival of any one by sound of trumpet; die Jagd —, to announce the beginning of the chase by blowing the hunting-horn. 4) to fill with air, to blow up [a bladder].

Anblatt, *n.* [-es] [a plant] toothwort.

Anblatten, *v. tr.* [am. carpent.] to join together with clamps, to clamp.

Anblatten, *n.* [-s] square clamp, square joint.

Anbläuen, *v. tr.* to make blue, to blue.

Anblecken, *v. tr.* to show one's teeth at, to grind the teeth at.

Anblick, *m.* [-es, *pl.* -e] 1) [the act of seeing] look, view, sight, aspect. Beim ersten —e, at first sight; sie flieht seinen —, she flies his sight. 2) [any thing perceived by the sight] sight. Ein erbarmenswerther —, a pitiful sight; ein schrecklicher —, a dreadful spectacle.

Anblicken, *v. tr.* to look at or upon, to view. Einen starr —, to gaze, to stare at, to look fixedly upon any one; er blickte die Menge wüthend an, he cast a furious look upon the crowd; oberflächlich — [or hinsehen], to glance at.

Anblinken, I. *v. tr.* V. Anblinzen. II. *v. intr.* to shine upon.

Anblinzen, **Anblinzeln**, *v. tr.* to leer at, to wink at.

Anblitzen, *v. tr.* to glance at, to dart a look or glance upon any one, to look at with a rapid cast of the eye. Einen mit dem Spiegel —, to dazzle any one by throwing on him the rays of the sun reflected from a mirror.

Anblöken, *v. tr.* to bleat at.

Anblümen, *v. tr.* V. Besäen.

Anbohren, *v. tr.* to bore, to pierce, to perforate. Ein Faß —, to broach, to tap a cask.

Anbolzen, *v. tr.* to fasten or secure with a bolt or an iron-pin [one piece of timber to another], to bolt.

Anborden, *v. tr.* V. Entern.

Anborsten, *v. intr.* [am. sportsmen] to bristle, to erect the bristles [said of the wild boar].

Anbot, *n.* [-es] 1) offer. 2) first bid [at an auction]. 3) order, command, bidding.

Anbrassen, *v. tr.* V. Brassen.

Anbrausen, I. *v. intr.* [n. w. seyn and kommen] to approach or come on in a boisterous, blustering manner. II. *v. tr.* to attack in a boisterous manner, to rush on, to assail with harsh language.

Anbrechen, *ir.* I. *v. intr.* [n. w. seyn] 1) to begin to break. *Fig.* to begin to rot. Angebrochenes Obst, unsound, decaying fruit. 2) *Fig.* to break forth, to appear. Die Nacht bricht an, the night is coming on, is drawing near; bei — der Nacht, at night-fall; der Tag bricht an, the day breaks, it dawns; bei — dem Tage, at break of day, at day-break. II. *v. tr.* to begin to break. Ein Brod —, to make the first cut in a loaf; ein Faß Bier —, to broach a cask of beer; eine angebrochene Flasche Wein, a bottle of wine that has been opened and partly emptied. *Fig.* Einen Geldsack —, to break in upon a bag of money.

Anbrennen, *ir.* I. *v. intr.* 1) [n. w. seyn] to begin to burn, to catch fire, to take fire, to kindle. Das Holz will nicht —, the wood will not take fire; das Stroh brennt leicht an, straw kindles easily. *Fig.* † and ‡ Er ist angebrannt, *a*) he has fallen in love, is smitten; *b*) he is flushed [with strong drink], half seas over. 2) to be partly burned or consumed. Das Licht ist angebrannt, the candle is partly burnt. 3) [in cookery] to adhere in consequence of being burnt, to be burnt. II. *v. tr.* to light. Ein Feuer —, to kindle or light a fire; ein Haus —, to set a house on fire, to fire it. 2) to begin to burn. 3) to mark by burning. Ein Pferd —, to mark a horse by burning. 4) [in cookery] to affect with heat, so as to give the food a disagreeable taste, to burn. Die Köchin hat den Brei angebrannt, the cook has burnt the pap. Angebrannt riechen, to smell of burning.

Anbringbar, I. *adj.* saleable, vendible, marketable. II. *adv.* saleably.

Anbringen, *ir. v. tr.* 1) to bring to a place. Ich kann diese Stiefeln nicht —, I cannot get on these boots. 2) to fix in a proper place. Eine an der Wand angebrachte Bank, a bench fixed to the wall; ein in einer Mauer angebrachter Altar, an altar constructed in a wall. 3) [am. hunt.] Die Schweißhunde —, to set the bloodhounds or retrievers on the trace of wounded game [in order to recover it]; einen Stoß —, to hit any one; ein wohl angebrachter Stoß, a home thrust. *Fig. a*) to dispose of. Ich habe mein Geld gut angebracht, I have placed my money well; Waaren —, to vend, to sell commodities; eine Tochter —, to dispose of a daughter; *it.* to get her a place, to marry her; wie werden Sie Ihren Sohn —? how will you dispose of your son? how will you settle him? *b*) to utter or give utterance to something at a seasonable time, to express seasonably. Erlauben Sie mir, ein Wort anzubringen, give me leave to put in a word; einen Scherz —, to crack a joke; eine Klage [vor Gericht] —, to complain, to inform against, to lay a complaint or information; er hat es vor Gericht angebracht, he has denounced it to the court. SYN. Anbringen, Anklagen. Anbringen conveys merely the idea of laying an information, anklagen includes also that there is evidence or proof to substantiate a charge.

Anbringegeld, *n.* a premium or bounty given to the person who enlists a recruit.

Anbringer, *m.* [-s, *pl.* -] informer, accusant, complainant.

Anbruch, *m.* [-es, *pl.* -brüche] 1) the act of beginning to break. Einen — machen, to begin to dig a mine, to open a mine. *Fig.* Der — des Tages, the break of day, day-break, dawn; der — der Nacht, the coming on or drawing on of night, night-fall. 2) the piece first broken off, the first cut. 3) the place where a break or opening is first made. 4) [in mineral., the manner, in which a mineral or a stone breaks, and by which its texture is displayed] fracture. Ein glatter —, a smooth fracture. 5) *Fig.* [a distemper in sheep] the rot.

Anbrüchig, *adj.* [commencing to rot or spoil] unsound, decayed, tainted, rotten. — werden, to grow rotten; —es Obst, unsound fruit; die Hitze macht das Fleisch —, the hot weather taints the meat; der Wein ist — geworden, the wine is turned; ein —er Zahn, a decayed tooth.

Anbrühen, *v. tr.* to pour hot water upon, to scald, to infuse in hot water.

Anbrüllen, *v. tr.* to bellow or low at, to roar at. *Fig.* Einen —, to bawl at, to vociferate against any one.

Anbrummen, *v. tr.* to growl, to snarl at. *Fig.* Einen —, to scold any one in a grumbling tone.

Anbrüten, *v. tr.* to begin to brood, to commence sitting eggs.

Anchorn, *f.* V. Ahorn.

* **Anchove**, *f.* [*pl.* -n] [a small fish] anchovy.

Anchovebirne, *f.* anchovy-pear.

Anciennität, *f.* [*pl.* -en] seniority in office, eldership. V. Amtsalter.

Andacht, *f.* 1) the act of thinking devoutly on the Supreme Being and religious matters, devotion, devoutness. 2) the attention paid to religious discourses, devotion, devoutness. 3) prayer to the Supreme Being, devotion, devoutness. Morgen- und Abendandachten, morning and evening devotions, morning and evening prayers; seine — verrichten or halten, to say one's prayers, to attend to one's devotion.

Andachtslos, *adj.* and *adv.* undevout, destitute of devotion, devoutless. —losigkeit, *f.* devoutlessness. —sbuch, *n.* a manual of devotion, prayer-book. —seifer, *m.* fervour of devotion. —sort, *m.* a place of devotion. —sreise, *f.* V. Wallfahrt. —sstunde, *f.* an hour of devotion. —sübung, *f.* devotional exercise; acts of devotion, performance of religious duties. —svoll, *adj.* full of devotion, devout, pious.

Andächtelei, *f.* bigotry, superstitious or hypocritical devotion.

Andächteln, *v. intr.* to be over-pious, to affect devotion.

Andächtelnd, *adj.* over-pious, bigot.

Andächtig, I. *adj.* 1) attentive. 2) devout, pious. *a*) yielding a solemn and reverential attention to God in religious exercises, particularly in prayer. Der, die —e, devotee. *b*) expressing devotion. II. *adv.* 1) attentively. 2) devoutly. Er betete —, he was devoutly engaged in prayer.

Ándächtler, *m.* [-s, *pl.* -] [a person superstitiously or formally devout] devotionalist, devotionist, false devotee.

Ándächtlerisch, *adj.* bigot, bigoted.

Ándämmen, *v. tr.* to swell a river by damming it up.

Ándampfen, *v. intr.* to adhere to any thing in evaporating.

* **Andánte**, *n.* [in music] andante.

Ándauern, *v. intr.* V. Dauern.

Ándenken, *ir. v. tr.* to bear any thing in mind, remember, recollect [used only in the participle of the present tense]. —d, remembering, recollecting.

Ándenken, *n.* [-s, *pl.* -] 1) reminiscence, recollection, remembrance, memory. Das schmerzende —, a painful remembrance; in noch allzu frischem —, too green in remembrance; schreibseligen —s, of scribbling memory; Hr. N. seligen —s, the late Mr. N., or of blessed memory. 2) [a token, by which any one is kept in memory] remembrance, token, keepsake. Ein süßes —, a love-toy, love-token.

Ánder, [Goth. *anthar*, Ice. *annar*; appears to be allied to the L. *alter*] der, die, das andere or andre, *adj.* [not the same, different, not the one, not this, but the contrary] other. Einer muß dem —n helfen, the one must assist the other; das —e Mal, the second time; die —e Seite, the wrong side [of cloth]; das —e Ufer, the opposite shore; —e Leute, others, other people; eines und das —e, one thing and the other; wir haben eine Regierungsform, Frankreich hat eine —, we have one form of government, France has another; Einer oder der —, some body or other; kein —er, nobody else; einen Tag um den —n, every other day; das ist ganz etwas —es, that is quite different, that 's quite another thing; Eines um das —e, by turns, alternately; einmal über das —e, again and again, repeatedly; er macht eine Dummheit über or um die —e, he commits one folly upon the other or after an other; ein Jahr in's —e gerechnet, reckoning one year with an other; —e Kleider anziehen, to shift one's clothes; macht das —en weiß, I am not to be bubbled or humbugged. *Prov.* —er Stand, —e Sitten, the clerk forgets that ever he was a sexton; was du von —n ungern hast, damit thu' Keinem Ueberlast, or was du nicht willst daß dir geschieht, das thu' auch einem —n nicht; do as you would be done by; frage nicht nach —er Sachen, achte deiner eignen Sachen, meddle with your own affairs; wer sich auf —e verläßt, ist verlassen genug, for what thou canst do thyself, rely not on others; Heil dem, den —er Mißgeschick bewahren lehrt sein eigenes Glück, it is good to learn at other men's cost.

Änderbar, I. *adj.* alterable, changeable. II. *adv.* alterably, changeably.

Ánderlei, *adj.* and *adv.* of another kind.

Ändern, I. *v. tr.* to alter, to change. Ein Kleid —, to alter a coat; die Kleider —, to change or shift one's clothes; eine Meinung —, to alter an opinion; klag' nicht um das, was nicht zu — steht, cease to lament for what you cannot help; eine Verfassung —, to reform a constitution [form of government]; seine Gesinnung —, to change one's mind. II. *v. r.* sich —, 1) = abwechseln, to alter, to change, to vary. Das Wetter ändert sich fast täglich, the weather changes almost daily. 2) = sich bessern, to change for the better, to mend. Sich geändert haben, to be altered, to be changed, to have mended. Syn. V. Abändern.

Ándernfalls, *adv.* otherwise, in the contrary case.

Ánderntheils, *adv.* on the other hand.

Ánders, I. *adv.* otherwise, differently, in another way, in another manner. — als ich erwartete, otherwise, than I expected; nicht —, not otherwise, exactly so, just so; nichts — als, nothing but, nothing else but; Niemand —, no one else, nobody else; irgendwo —, somewhere else; — werden, to become different, to alter, to change; Sie müssen — werden [= sich bessern], you must amend yourself; sich — besinnen, to change one's mind; ich weiß es —, I know it better; ich konnte nicht —, ich mußte weinen, I could not help weeping. II. *conj.* for: nämlich. Wenn —, wo —, if, provided; wenn Sie — zu Hause sind, provided you be at home; wenn — nicht, unless.

Anders-wo, *adv.* elsewhere, otherwhere, somewhere else; er bewies, daß er —wo war, he proved an alibi [a law term]. —**woher**, *adv.* from elsewhere, from another place. —**wohin**, *adv.* to another place, towards some other place, elsewhere.

Ánderseits, *adv.* on the other side.

Anderthalb or **Anderhalb**, [an indeclinable word of number] one and a half. — Pfund, one pound and a half; — Fuß lang, sesquipedal, sesquipedalian.

Ánderthalbig, *adj.* [in mathem.] sesquialteral. Ein —es Verhältniß, [in math.] sesquialter, a sesquialteral proportion (2:3=6:9); das —e Verhältniß, [in arithm.] sesquiduplicate ratio.

Änderung, *f.* alteration. 1) [the act of altering] = change. Eine — der Grundsätze, a change of principles. 2) [the change made] Eine — treffen, to make an alteration.

Ánderwärts, *adv.* ‡ **Ánderwärtig**, *adj.* in another place; else-where.

Ánderweit, *adv.* **Ánderweitig**, *adj.* in another place, at another time, otherwise, done in another manner, further. Anderweitige Hülfe erwarten, to expect assistance from another quarter.

Ándeuten, *v. tr.* 1) to declare by some sign, to signify; to give to understand. Das deutet einen langen Winter an, that indicates a long winter; das deutet nichts Gutes an, that presages nothing good. 2) = eröffnen, to notify, to intimate, to insinuate. Es wurde ihm angedeutet, it was intimated to him. 3) = befehlen, to order, to enjoin. Man hat ihm angedeutet, die Stadt zu verlassen, it was signified or intimated to him to leave the town.

Ándeuter, *m.* [in gramm.] V. Artikel.

Ándeutung, *f.* notification, intimation, insinuation, hint.

Ándichten, *v. tr.* to impute, to charge, to attribute falsely.

Ándichtung, *f.* false imputation.

Ándienen, *v. tr.* [in commerce] to announce [the average to the insurers].

Ándonnern, I. *v. intr.* to thunder at, to knock at violently. II. *v. tr.* 1) to assail with a thundering voice. 2) to stun with noise, to din.

Ándorn, [i. e. somewhat resembling a thorn] *m.* [-s] 1) common white horehound. 2) red dead nettle, nettle hemp. 3) downy stachys. 4) stinking or black horehound. 5) small-flowered motherwort.

Ándorren, *v. intr.* [u. w. seyn] to dry on any thing and to adhere to it.

Ándörren, *v. tr.* to begin to dry [fruit].

Ándrang, *m.* [-es] 1) the act of pressing forward. *Fig.* [in medecine] congestion. 2) crowd, press.

Ándrängen, I. *v. tr.* to press, or to press to, to crowd. II. *v. r.* sich —, to exert one's self to get near any object. Sich an die Großen —, to court importunely and meanly the favour of the great.

Ándräuen, *v. tr.* V. Androhen.

Andréas, [a name of men] Andrew.

Andreas-kreuz, *n.* 1) St. Andrew's cross, Scotch-cross. [in herald.] Ein abgelediglес —, saltier. 2) [a plant] common ascyrum or St. Andrew's cross. —**kraut**, *n.* V. —kreuz 2. —**orden**, *m.* the order of St. Andrew [in Russia]. —**tag**, *m.* [a festival] St. Andrew's day.

Ándrechseln, *v. tr.* to fit or adapt one thing to another by means of a turner's lathe. Dieses Kleid sitzt so gut, als ob es ihm angedrechselt wäre, this coat fits exceedingly well.

Ándrehen, *v. tr.* 1) to fix by turning or twisting. Die Wand —, [a sea term] to set up the shrouds of the top mast. *Fig.* Einem eine Nase —, to impose upon, to humbug any one. 2) V. Andrechseln.

Ándreschen, I. *v. tr.* to begin to thrash, to give the first stroke with the flail. II. *v. intr.* to beat against the wall with the flail.

Ándrillen, *v. tr.* V. Andrehen.

* **Ándrienne**, *f.* a kind of gown.

Ándringen, *ir. v. intr.* [u. w. seyn] to press on, to urge forward, to advance impetuously. Die Türken drangen von allen Seiten an, the Turks pressed on from all sides.

Ándringlich, I. *adj.* pressing or urging in request or demand, urgent in sollicitation, forward, importunate, over-officious, indiscreetly curious. II. *adv.* importunately.

* **Androgyn**, *m.* V. Zwitter.

Ándrohen, *v. tr.* to threaten, to threaten with, to menace.

Ándrohung, *f.* threatening, threat, menace.

Ándrucken, *v. tr.* to print something afterwards and add it to what was printed before, to print in addition to.

Ándruck, *m.* [-s, *pl.* -drücke] 1) the act of joining one thing to another thing by printing. 2) the thing, so joined on.

Ándrücken, *v. tr.* to press close to, to press against. Einen an or wider die Wand —, to squeeze any one against the wall.

Ánduften, *v. intr.* to exhale a fragrant odour.

‡ **Ándurch**, *adv.* thereby. = Dadurch.

Áneifern, *v. tr.* to incite, to stimulate, to spur on, to animate, to urge.

Áneignen, *v. tr.* to appropriate. Sich die Meinungen eines Andern —, to adopt the opinions of another; sich die Verdienste eines Andern —, to attribute to one's self the merits of another.

Áneignung, *f.* the act of appropriating something to one's self.

Aneinánder, *adv.* together. V. Einander. Die —fügung, *f.* junction, joining; —hangend, coherent, continual.

Anekdōte, *f.* [*pl.* -n] anecdote.

Anekdotenartig, I. *adj.* anecdotical. II. *adv.* anecdotically.

Ánekeln, *v. tr.* to be loathsome, to disgust. Jede Speise ekelt ihn an, he loathes every meat. *Fig.* Es ekelt mich an, it disgusts me.

* **Anemométer**, *m.* [-s, *pl.* -] = Windschnelligkeitsmesser, [in physics] anemometer.

Anemōne, *f.* [*pl.* -n] anemone, anemony, wind-flower, pass-rose.

* **Anemoscop**, *m.* [-s, *pl.*-e] = Windrichtungszeiger, [in physics] anemoscope.

Anempfehlen, *ir. v. tr.* to recommend to. V. Empfehlen.

Anerbe, 1) *m.* [-n, *pl.*-n] the next heir, heir-apparent. 2) *n.* [-s] the hereditary portion, heritage, inheritance.

Anerben, *v. intr.* [u. w. seyn] to inherit. Angeerbt. *Fig.* angeerbte Krankheit, inherited disease; das Laster ist angeerbt, vice is inborn; angeerbter Stolz, hereditary pride.

Anerbieten, *ir. v. tr.* to offer. V. Anbieten.

Anerbieten, *n.* an offer made, proffer, tender. Ein — annehmen, to close with an offer.

Anerbung, *f.* inheritance.

Anerkennen, *ir. v. tr.* 1) to own, to acknowledge. Das Daseyn Gottes —, to acknowledge the being of a God, or the existence of God; einen Sohn —, to acknowledge a son; einen Anspruch —, to allow a claim; die Wahrheit eines Satzes —, to allow the truth of a proposition; die Wahrheit einer Beschuldigung —, to avow one's self guilty or one's guilt; nicht —, to disown, to disavow; die Klage —, to plead guilty. 2) to recognize.

Anerkennbar, Anerkenntlich, *adj.* recognisable.

Anerkennung, *f.* 1) acknowledgement [of one's signature &c.], acceptation [of a draft or bill of exchange]. 2) recognition.

Anerkennungsgeld, *n.* [a law term] acknowledgement money [a sum paid by tenants on the death of their landlords, as an acknowledgement of their new lords].

Anerkenntniß, *n.* [-sses, *pl.* -sse] clear perception.

Anerle, *f.* 1) great maple. 2) common or small maple.

Anerringen, *v. tr.* to acquire by toil. V. Erringen.

Anerschaffen, *ir. v. tr.* to impart in creating, or at the moment of creation. Gott hat dem Menschen den Trieb der Ehre —, sein Ebenbild —, God has implanted in man the desire of glory, impressed on him his own likeness.

Anerschaffen, *part.* innate.

Anerschlichen, *part.* and *adj.* subreptitiously acquired.

‡ **Anerwogen**, *conj.* considering, since.

Anerziehen, *ir. v. tr.* 1) V. Aufziehen. 2) to communicate, to inculcate by education.

Anessen, I. *ir. v. tr.* to commence eating [a cake &c.], to take away by eating, to nibble. II. *v. r.* sich —, to eat to satiety, to stuff one's belly well.

Anfabeln, *v. tr.* V. Andichten.

Anfächeln, *v. tr.* to agitate the air towards any one with a fan, to fan. *Poet.* Ein sanftes Lüftchen fächelte uns an, a gentle breeze played upon us.

Anfachen, *v. tr.* to blow into a flame; to set on fire, to kindle, to inflame. *Fig.* Die Liebe —, to inflame love; es fachte sein Leben an, it reanimated him; die Flamme des Krieges —, to enkindle the flames of war; den Zorn Eines —, to exasperate a person, to kindle the anger of any one.

Anfächern, *v. tr.* V. Anfächeln.

Anfädeln, *v. tr.* to string, to thread [pearls &c.]. V. Aufreihen.

‡ **Anfahen**, *v. intr.* V. Anfangen.

Anfahrbar, *adj.* [of a coast] accessible, easy of approach to ships.

Anfahren, *ir.* I. *v. intr.* 1) [u. w. seyn] to come near to, to advance with a ship or carriage, to drive near to, to arrive at. Die Flotte fuhr an die Insel an, the fleet put in, touched at the island, the fleet came to anchor near the island; er kam mit Vieren angefahren, he came driving up with his coach and four; bei dem Hause eines Freundes —, to stop or arrive at the house of a friend; angefahren kommen, to arrive in a ship or carriage. 2) to drive, fly or rush against. An einen Stein —, to drive or strike against a stone. 3) [in mining] to go to work, to descend the shaft. II. *v. tr.* 1) to convey or transport [goods &c.] to a place either by land or by water. 2) *Fig.* to assail with harsh language, to snub any one, to use any one roughly. Einen Bedienten hart —, to rattle a servant sharply.

Anfahrschacht, *m.* [-es, *pl.* -e] [in mining] a shaft which miners descend in going to their work.

Anfahrt, *f.* [*pl.*-en] 1) arrival at any place by water or by land. 2) [in mining] the going to work. 3) V. Anfurt.

Anfall, *m.* [-es, *pl.*-fälle] 1) the fall against something. Der — [or Fall] eines Baumes an or gegen die Mauer, the falling of a tree against the wall. 2) a falling on, an attack, assault, shock. Er widerstand dem —, he withstood the shock. *Fig.* Ein — von Schlag, a fit or attack of apoplexy; ein Fieber—, an accession of fever; Anfälle von Verrücktheit, fits of insanity or lunacy; ist ein neuer — zu fürchten? is a relapse to be expected? ein — von Ekel, Uebelkeit, a rising of the stomach, a fit of squeamishness; so manchen — fühlt' ich schon von Freuden und von Schmerzen, I've felt so many quirks of joy and grief. 3) an acquisition by chance, accession to an inheritance. 4) the place or the thing, on which any thing falls. Die Anfälle am Vogelherde, dry sticks on the fowling-floor, on which birds alight, perching-sticks.

Anfallen, *ir.* I. *v. intr.* [u. w. seyn] 1) to fall towards or against any thing. *Fig.* Es ist ihm ein großes Gut angefallen, a great estate has fallen to him. 2) to approach suddenly. Die Vögel fallen gern auf diesen Baum an, the birds are fond of lighthing or perching on this tree. II. *v. tr.* 1) to attack, to assail. Eine Stadt —, to assault a town; ein Land —, to invade a country; [among hunters] die Fährte muthig —, to be eager on the scent. *Fig.* Es hat ihn eine Krankheit angefallen, he has been seized with a fit of sickness; er fiel mich mit Schimpfworten an, he assailed me with abusive words. Syn. Anfallen, Angreifen. Anfallen conveys the idea of a more sudden and violent attack than Angreifen. Whoever first injures or uses any violence to another, greift ihn an [assails him]. The wolf fällt die Schaafe an [attacks the sheep].

Anfällig, *adj.* and *adv.* —e Güter, property which is to fall into any one's possession, of which he has the reversion.

Anfallsrecht, *n.* [-es, *pl.* -e] right of inheriting, right of future possession or enjoyment, reversion.

Anfälschen, *v. tr.* V. Andichten.

Anfalzen, *v. tr.* [among joiners] to join a board into another by a rabbet, to rabbet.

Anfang, *m.* [-s, *pl.*-fänge] beginning, commencement. Der — der Feindseligkeiten im Jahr 1792, the commencement of hostilities in 1792; der — eines Feldzuges, the opening of a campaign; im —e (Eingange) einer Rede, in the entrance of a discourse; der — einer Predigt, the exordium, the beginning of a sermon; der — eines Buches, Weges &c., the commencement of a book, of a road &c.; den — mit etwas machen, to set about or begin a thing; er hat die ersten Anfänge dieser Wissenschaft inne, he knows the first rudiments or elements of this science. *Prov.* Aller — ist schwer, beginnings are always hard; guter — ist halbe Arbeit, well begun is half done, a good beginning makes a good ending.

Anfangs-los, *adj.* and *adv.* without a beginning. **—sbuch**, *n.* rudimental book, primer. **—sbuchstabe**, *m.* initial letter, capital. **—seindruck**, *m.* the first impression any thing makes in the mind. **—sgründe**, *pl.* the first rules or principles of an art or science, rudiments, elements. Die —sgründe der Erdmeßkunst, Musik, Mahlerei, the elements of geometry, of music, of painting. **—slehre**, *f.* V. —sgründe. **—spunkt**, *m.* the point of beginning. **—sschule**, *f.* a school, in which rudiments are taught. V. Elementarschule. **—stag**, *m.* the day of beginning. **—szeile**, *f.* initial line.

Anfangen, *ir.* I. *v. tr.* 1) to begin, to commence. Das Lied —, to begin the song; einen Prozeß —, to institute a suit; einen Feldzug, to open a campaign; die lateinische Sprachlehre —, to begin with the Latin grammar; ein Geschäft mit einem kleinen Kapitale —, to begin business with a small capital; etwas —, to set about any thing, to go about a thing; einen Handel —, to set up as a merchant; eine eigene Haushaltung or einen eigenen Haushalt —, to set up for one's self, to commence keeping house for one's self; ein anderes Leben —, to change one's manner of life, to turn over a new leaf; er ist glücklich in Allem, was er anfängt, he succeeds in every thing he undertakes; eine Unterhandlung —, to enter into a negociation; Händel mit Einem —, to pick a quarrel with any one. 2) to do, to perform in any exigency. Was fange ich an? what shall I do, what am I to do? was ist dabei anzufangen? what is to be done in this case? was sollen wir —, um unsere Schande zu verbergen? how shall we contrive to hide our shame? 3) to do with, to employ. Es ist nichts mit diesem eigensinnigen Menschen anzufangen, I can do nothing with this obstinate fellow; ich will es anders mit ihm —, I'll go another way to work with him; Müßiggänger wissen nicht, was sie mit ihrer Zeit — sollen, idle men don't know what to do with their time, or how to spend their time.

II. *v. intr.* to begin, to commence. Thränen fingen an zu fließen, tears begun to flow; — zu lachen, zu weinen, to set up a laugh, to fall a laughing, a weeping.

III. *v. r.* sich —, [seldom used, better as an intransitive verb, without sich] to begin. Das Lied fängt sich mit einem Chore an, the song begins with a chorus; das Wort fängt sich mit einem Z an, the word begins with a Z. Syn. Anfangen, Anheben, Beginnen, Angehen. Anfangen comprehends the idea of beginning in its widest signification, and is used as well in regard to things that exist in time as in space, as: er fing an zu reden [he began to speak]; hier fängt sein Acker an [his field commences here]. Beginnen and Anheben are used only when speaking of things which exist in time, and of actions. Beginnen, therefore, denotes also to undertake. Angehen has the same signification as Anfangen, but is used mostly only in familiar style.

Anfänger, *m.* [-s, *pl.*-] **—inn**, *f.* 1) one who commences any thing, beginner. Der — eines Streites, the author of a quarrel. 2) [the person, who begins, one who first enters upon any art, science or business, one who is in rudiments, often implying want of experience] beginner. Ein — seyn, to be young in one's business; für einen — ist dieses gut geschrieben, for a beginner, this is well written; ein — in Künsten or Wissenschaften, a tyro, novice; ein junger —, one who has not long been established in business, a young beginner.

Anfängerei, *f.* [*pl.*-en] the work, the skill of a beginner.

Anfänglich, I. *adj.* beginning, incipient, original. Wir wollen bei dem —en Plane bleiben, we will keep to the original plan. II. *adv.* in the beginning, at first, originally. Er wollte — hingehen, aber &c., he intended to go there at first, but &c.

Anfangs, *adv.* in the beginning, at first. Gleich —, at the very beginning.

Anfärben, *v. tr.* 1) to colour, to paint. 2) to adulterate by colouring [wine &c.].

Anfassen, *v. tr.* 1) to take or to lay hold of, to seize. Mit der Hand —, to seize with the hand; mit den Zähnen —, to take hold with the teeth; dieses Gefäß ist ganz rund, man kann es nirgends —, this vessel is quite round, there is no laying hold of it. 2) V. Anreihen, Auffassen.

Anfaßbar, *adj.* what may be taken or laid hold of, seizable.

Anfaulen, *v. intr.* [u. w. seyn] to begin to rot.

Anfechtbar, *adj* and *adv.* liable to be called in question, controverted or contested, disputable, controvertible.

Anfechten, *v. tr.* [used only in a fig. sense] 1) to attack. Jemandes Meinungen —, to combat, to attack the opinions of another; einen aufgestellten Satz —, to combat a proposition; der Sachwalter focht jeden Punkt an, the advocate contested every point; ein Urtheil —, to controvert a sentence; ein Testament —, to contest a will, to call a will in question; einen guten Namen —, to assault a character; er ist vom Podagra angefochten [heimgesucht] worden, he has had a fit or attack of the gout. 2) to tempt, to entice. Vom Satan angefochten, tempted by Satan. 3) to move, to agitate, to disturb, to disquiet. Laßt euch dieß nicht —, don't be uneasy about that, don't let this disturb you; laßt euch diese Fehler nicht —, never trouble yourselves about these faults.

Anfechter, *m.* [-s, *pl.* -] one who contests any thing.

Anfechtung, *f.* 1) the act of attacking or combating [opinions, an assertion &c.]. 2) [that which is offered to the mind as a motive to ill] temptation. = Versuchung.

Anfeilen, 1) to begin filing, to file a little. 2) to produce by filing. Eine neue Spitze —, to file a new point.

Anfeilschen, *v. tr.* and *intr.* to ask the price of a commodity; to chaffer, to cheapen.

Anfeinden, *v. tr.* to treat any one with enmity, to show enmity to any one, to bear ill-will towards any one. Einen bei Einem —, to set any one against another.

Anfeindung, *f.* the act of treating any one with enmity, bearing ill-will, enmity, hatred.

Anfertigen, *v. tr.* 1) to make, to arrange, to compose, to manufacture. Eine Liste —, to draw up a list. V. Verfertigen. 2) [a law term] to send to.

Anfesseln, *v. tr.* to fasten with a chain, to enchain, to fetter. *Fig.* Er fesselt Wind und Stürme an, he enchains wind and storms; er ist an seinen Schreibtisch wie angefesselt, he is nailed or chained, as it were, to his desk.

Anfesselung, *f.* enchaining, fettering.

Anfetten, *v. tr.* to make fat, to mix with fat or grease, to baste.

Anfeuchten, *v. tr.* 1) to moisten, to wet, to water. 2) [am. hunt.] to piss against a tree [said of wolves, foxes &c.]. 3) [am. potters] to free from moisture, to dry earthen ware in a heated furnace.

Anfeuchtpinsel, *m.* [am. gilders] a brush for moistening. **Anfeuchtungsgrube**, *f.* [in papermills] a pit, wherein rags are moistened.

Anfeuern, *v. tr.* to kindle or light a fire, to set on fire, to make hot, to cause to be hot. [in fireworks] to lay a train, to prime. Den Ofen —, [in metall.] to heat the furnace. *Fig.* Den Geist —, to fire the genius; entmuthigte Truppen —, to animate or encourage dispirited troops; dieß hat seinen Muth angefeuert [or befeuert], this spurred on his courage; angefeuert von hochfliegenden Gedanken, inflamed with thoughts of high design; die Ruhmbegierde feuerte euch zu jenen Thaten an, the desire of fame quickened you in the pursuit of those actions.

Anfilzen, *v. tr.* [am. hatters] to put the felt upon the block.

Anfirnissen, *v. tr.* to varnish. V. Firnissen.

Anflammen, I. *v. tr.* to kindle, to inflame, to fire. *Fig.* Einen —, to inflame, to incite, to animate any one; den Zorn Eines —, to provoke the anger of any one, to exasperate any one. II. *v. intr.* to take fire, to be kindled, to fire. *Fig.* to be inflamed with passion. [In this sense Entflammen would be better.]

Anflattern, *v intr.* to strike against something in fluttering. Angeflattert kommen, to advance or come on fluttering.

Anflechten, *ir. v. tr.* to join to by plaiting or twisting.

Anflecken, *v. tr.* [am. shoemak.] to cover with a piece of leather, to patch.

Anflehen, *v. tr.* to implore, to supplicate [mercy &c.]. Einen — um &c., to entreat any one earnestly for &c.

Anfleher, *m.* [-s, *pl.*-] [a law term] one that sues, a suitor.

Anflehung, *f.* imploration, entreaty, supplication.

Anfletschen, *v. tr.* to show the teeth to, to growl at. V. Anblecken.

Anflicken, *v. tr.* to add by patching, to patch to. *Fig.* Er hat noch etwas an seine Rede angeflickt, he has yet added something to his discourse; sich überall —, to intrude one's self every where.

Anfliegen, *ir. v. intr.* [u. w. seyn] 1) to approach flying. Angeflogen kommen, to come flying; angeflogen, [in mineralogy] disseminated. *Fig.* Die Farben auf diesem Gemählde sind wie angeflogen, the colouring of this picture is laid on very thin; die Krankheit ist ihm wie angeflogen, he has been taken ill suddenly; es fliegt ihm Alles an, he gets all without pains. 2) to strike against something in flying. Die Kanonenkugel flog an den Mast an, the canon-ball hit the mast; [in forestry] Das Nadelholz fliegt an, the winged seed of fir scatters, takes and grows.

Anfliehen, *ir. v. intr.* to have recourse to.

Anfließen, *ir. v. intr.* [u. w. seyn] 1) to flow towards. 2) to touch in flowing. Der Fluß fließt an die Stadtmauer an, the river washes the town-walls. 3) to swell [said of a river].

Anflößen, *v. tr.* 1) to transport to a place by floating, by means of a raft. 2) *Fig.* to wash or to carry earth or other substances to a shore or bank.

Anflößung, *f.* alluvion. 1) the gradual washing or carrying of earth or other substances to a shore or bank. 2) the earth or substances thus added.

Anflößungsrecht, *n.* [in law] the right, the owner of the land thus augmented has to the alluvial earth. = Anwachsungsrecht.

Anfluchen, *v. tr.* Einen —, to imprecate evil upon one, to call for mischief or injury to fall upon one, to invoke evil on any one, to pray that a curse or calamity may fall upon any one.

Anflug, *m.* [-s, *pl.* -flüge] 1) the act of flying to or against. Der — des Falken, the flight or soaring of the hawk; ein — von Röthe auf ihren Wangen, a blush on her cheeks. *Fig.* Ein — von Gelehrsamkeit, a smattering or tincture of learning. 2) [gleichsam etwas Angeflogenes] [am. foresters] *a*) a plantation or nursery consisting of young pines and firs grown from the seed. *b*) [in miner.] disseminated mineral. *c*) [in salpetre houses] the efflorescence of salpetre.

Anfluß, *m.* [-sses, *pl.* -flüsse] 1) a flowing towards. 2) swelling, or rising of water. Der Ab- und — des Meeres, the ebb and flood. 3) V. Anflößung.

Anflüstern, *v. tr.* to address whisperingly. Einen —, to whisper to any one.

Anfluten, *v. intr.* [u. w. seyn] to approach flowing [said of high water], to touch in flowing.

Anfodern and **Anfordern**, *v. tr.* to claim, to demand as due.

Anfoderer, *m.* [-s, *pl.* -] an importunate creditor, who urges for payment, a dun.

Anfoderung, *f.* claim, a calling on another for something due or supposed to be due. Eine — auf Etwas or an Einen machen, to make claim, to lay claim to a thing, to claim from any one.

Anformen, *v. tr.* 1) to put on a form. Einen Hut —, to put a hat upon the block. 2) to give a particular form or shape to any thing. Die Natur hat ihm eine eigenthümlich gebildete Stirn angeformt, nature has given him a forehead of peculiar form or conformation.

Anfrage, *f.* [*pl.* -n] inquiry, asking, question. Wegen einer Sache, in einer Sache or über eine Sache — thun, to inquire about or after a thing, to make inquiry about a thing.

Anfragen, *v. intr.* [to put a question with a view to an answer] to interrogate, to ask, to inquire, to question. Um Etwas — bei Einem, to inquire after a thing of any one.

Anfrager, *m.* [-s, *pl.* -] one who asks a question, an inquirer.

Anfressen, *ir.* I. *v. tr.* 1) [to eat a small portion off] to gnaw, to nibble. Die Ratten haben einen Laib Brod angefressen, the rats have gnawed a loaf. 2) to eat, to corrode. Der Rost frißt das Eisen an, rust corrodes iron. II. *v. r.* † sich —, to fill one's self with food, to eat one's fill, to grow fat by food, to fatten.

Anfrieren, *ir. v. intr.* [u. w. seyn] to freeze to. Der Stein ist an die Erde angefroren, the stone is frozen to the earth.

Anfrischen, *v. tr.* to refresh, to freshen. Das Alaunbad wieder —, [am. dyers] to refresh the dye with alum; die Thonerde —, [in sugar houses] to wet the clay for the second time. *Fig.* *a*) to refresh, to recreate, [to bring back to its former state] to restore; [in metall.] to revive. *b*) to animate, to incite, to stimulate. Einen zu Etwas —, to incite any one to a thing; die schlafenden Geistesfähigkeiten —, to arouse the dormant faculties.

Anfrischofen, *m.* [in forges] refining furnace.

Anfrischer, *m.* [-s, *pl.*-] [in forges] refiner.

Anfuge, *f.* [*pl.* -n] a leaf, clause or additional piece added to another writing, a rider. In der —, enclosed or subjoined.

Anfugen, *v. tr.* [am. Joiners] to shoot.

Anfügen, I. *v. tr.* to add, to join to, to subjoin, to annex. Das angefügte Verzeichniß, the annexed list. II. *v. r.* sich —, to lie close to, to cling to.

Anfühlen, I. *v. tr.* to feel, to touch, to handle. Fühlen Sie dieses Stück Seidenzeug an, feel this piece of silk. II. *v. r.* sich —, to be perceptible to the touch, to feel. Etwas fühlt sich weich, hart, rauh an, something feels soft, hard, rough.

Anführbar, *adj.* and *adv.* that may be alledged, adducible.

Anfuhr, *f.* [*pl.* -en] the act of transporting or carrying to a place.

Anführen, *v. tr.* 1) to lead, to conduct or to guide [by the hand] to a place; *it.* to bring or carry to a place. V. Anfahren. *Fig.* to cite or quote, to alledge [a passage &c.]. Die Autorität eines Richters —, to alledge the authority of a judge; falsch —, to misquote; einen Beweis —, to adduce an argument. 2) to conduct as head or commander, to lead. Ich werde das Heer —, I shall lead the army; eine Meute —, [with huntsmen] to hunt a pack of dogs. *Fig. a)* to guide, to instruct and direct; [am. print.] to instruct. Seine Kinder zur Tugend —, to guide one's children to virtue; zur Handlung —, to bring any one up for trade; Einen zum Zeichnen —, to teach any one drawing. *b)* to deceive, to impose on, to take in, to cheat, to trick, to dupe.

Anführe=geld, *f.* [am. print.] money paid to the teacher. **—gespahn**, *m.* [am. printers] teacher.

Anführer, *m.* [-s, *pl.* -] 1) a leader, guide, conductor, director. Die —inn, a conductress, directress or instructress. Er war der — dieses Tumultes, he was the ringleader of this tumult. 2) a chief, a commander, general. Keines der beiden Heere hatte einen guten —, neither army had a good commander.

Anführerstelle, *f.* the office of a commander, or chief.

Anführerei, *f.* imposition, deception, hoaxing.

Anführung, *f.* 1) leading, direction, command. 2) [the act of citing a passage from a book &c., also the passage or words quoted] citation, quotation.

Anführungszeichen, *n.* [am. print., Gänsefüßchen, Gänseaugen, Hasenöhrchen] sign of quotation („ “).

Anfüllen, *v. tr.* to fill [a bottle with wine &c.]. Ein Zimmer mit Leuten —, to cram a room with people; Einen —, sich — [with too much eating &c.] to fill with drink and food beyond satiety, to cram, to stuff, to gorge.

Anfüllung, *f.* filling, cramming.

Anfunkeln, I. *v. intr.* to shoot a dazzling light or to glare on. II. *v. tr.* to look with glaring eyes upon any one.

Anfurt, *f.* [*pl.* -en] a landing place, a quay.

Anfußen, *v. intr.* to get a footing; [of birds] to light.

Angabe, *f.* [*pl.* -n] 1) [in commerce] giving some goods, ready money &c. in part payment. 2) a first plan, sketch, projection, design. 3) declaration, assertion, averment. Nach seiner — fehlt ein Gulden, according to him there is a florin wanting. 4) [better das Angeben] act of charging with a crime, denunciation, accusation. 5) earnest, earnest money. 6) a minute and particular account, statement.

Angabeln, *v. tr.* 1) to pitch with a fork, to fork up. 2) † *Fig.* to possess one's self of, to seize, to make one's self master of.

Angaffen, *v. tr.* to gape at, to stare at [a person &c.].

Angaffer, *m.* [-s, *pl.* -] gaper, starer.

Angähnen, *v. tr.* to gape or yawn at. *Poet.* Der Abgrund gähnt uns an, the abyss yawns at us.

Angällen, *v. tr.* 1) to mix with bile. 2) to make bitter.

Angatten, *v. tr.* to give, to bestow in marriage. Der Tochter einen Mann —, to marry a daughter, to bestow her upon any one.

Angattung, *f.* giving in marriage. *Fig.* union, connection, conjunction.

Angebäude, *n.* [-s, *pl.* -] a building attached to another.

Angebbar, *adj.* declarable.

Angebeliste, *f.* [*pl.* -n] [in commerce] manifest [of a ship's cargo].

Angeben, *ir.* I. *v. tr.* 1) to give in advance, to give an earnest, to give on account. Die Karten —, to deal cards. 2) to give [goods] in part payment. Er kaufte für 50 Thaler, bezahlte aber nur 30 und gab eine Uhr an, he bought for the value of 50 dollars, but paid only 30 ready money and gave a watch for the rest. 3) to mention, to declare, to specify, to tell, to indicate. St. Peter gibt nicht an &c., St. Peter does not specify &c.; Gründe —, to show cause or reason; geben Sie einen guten Grund dafür an, yield me a good reason for it; sein Spiel —, [at cards] to call one's game; das Bild —, [in weaving] to tell the pattern; den Ton —, [in music] to give the tone, [*fig.*] to take the lead. *Fig.* to sketch, to project. Was wird er nun —? what will he do now? [sometimes in a bad sense] was hat er angegeben? what has he committed or perpetrated? 4) to denounce, to accuse, to inform against, to bear a charge against, to delate. Sich —, to accuse one's self. II. *v. intr.* [at cards] 1) to deal first. 2) to follow suit. Syn. V. Anklagen.

Angeber, *m.* [-s, *pl.* -] 1) one, who makes the first plan or sketch, the beginner, former or mover of any thing, author. 2) [at cards] one who deals first. 3) accuser, informer, impeacher, delator.

Angeberei, *f.* the vile trade of denouncing or informing.

Angeberisch, *adj.* and *adv.* 1) inventive, ready at expedients. 2) acting as an informer.

Angebinde, *n.* [-s, *pl.* -] a birth-day present.

Angeblich, *adj.* and *adv.* pretended. Ein —es Recht, a pretended right or title; —er Maßen, in the manner stated, alluded to; [in math.] eine —e Größe, a nominal quantity; dieser Fremde ist — ein Kaufmann, this stranger is, according to his own account, or is given out to be, a merchant.

Angeboren, *adj.* and *adv.* implanted by nature, innate. —e Leidenschaften, inborn passions; —e Zuneigung, inbred affection; —e Begriffe, innate ideas.

Angebot, *n.* [-es, *pl.* -e] 1) the act of bidding first. V. Das Anbieten. 2) the first offer or bid [at a sale by action].

Angeburt, *f.* [the native state or properties of any thing] nature.

Angedeihen, *v. intr.* [n. w. seyn and chiefly with lassen] to bestow, or confer upon. Einem Ehre oder Gunst — lassen, to impart honour or favour to any one; Einem die Vorrechte eines Bürgers — lassen, to confer on any one the privileges of a citizen.

Angedenken, *n.* [-s, *pl.* -] V. Andenken.

Angefälle, *n.* [-s, *pl.* -] 1) [in law] a contingent inheritance, an inheritance in reversion or [in general] an inheritance. 2) V. Anwartschaft.

Angehänge, Angehenke, *n.* [-s, *pl.* -] something appended, or any thing hanging by way of ornament, a bob, a pendant, or something worn as a remedy or preservative against evil or mischief, an amulet.

Angehäufe, *n.* [-s, *pl.* -] 1) a heap, mass. 2) aggregate. Ein Haus ist ein — von Steinen, Holz &c., a house is an aggregate of stones, timber. &c.

Angehen, *ir.* I. *v. tr.* to approach, to advance towards. Noch ist nichts angegangen, [am. hunters] no game came yet in sight. *Fig. a)* Einen — [= sich an ihn wenden], Einen mit Bitten —, to supplicate or entreat any one, to solicit any one pressingly, to importune any one. *b)* to concern, to regard, to relate to. Was geht es mich an? what's that to me? angehend, concerning; mich angehend, as for me; was geht mich das Gerede der Leute an? what do I mind people's talk? dieß geht mich nichts an, that does not touch or concern me; es geht ihn an, it is his concern; es geht mich mit an, I have a share in it; er geht mich nichts an, he is not related to me. II. *v. intr.* 1) to begin, to commence. [in husb.] Die Bäume gehen an, the trees begin to take root and to thrive; bei —der Nacht, in the dusk, at nightfall; ein —der Schüler, Soldat, a young scholar, a young soldier, a raw recruit; [am. hunters] ein —des Schwein, a three-year-old wild boar. 2) to begin to burn, take fire. Unser Haus geht auch an, our house is catching too. 3) to begin to putrify or to rot. Angegangen, a little touched, or trained. 4) to be put on. Der Rock geht nicht an, the coat goes not on. *Fig. a)* [= möglich seyn] So geht es nicht an, it will not do so; das geht recht gut an, this may be done very well; in so weit es — wird, as far as it is possible, feasible. *b)* to be supportable, tolerable, passable. Es geht noch an, it is passable, tolerable; der Verlust wird noch —, the loss will not be great; die Hitze geht noch an, the heat can yet be endured. V. Anfangen.

Angehends, *adv.* V. Anfänglich.

Angehenke, *n.* V. Angehänge.

Angehör, *n.* [-s] [the thing possessed] property.

Angehören, *v. intr.* 1) to be the property of, to belong, to appertain. Das Haus gehört mir an, the house belongs to me. 2) to be related. Das Kind gehört mir an, this child is related to me.

Angehörig, *adj.* and *adv.* belonging to; [sometimes as a subst.] Die —en, the relations; meine —en, my family; sie ist eine —e von mir, she is related to me, is a relation of mine.

Angeifern, *v. tr.* to slabber.

Angeißeln, *v. tr.* to urge on with a scourge.

Angeklagte, *m.* and *f.* [-n, *pl.* -n] V. Anklagen.

Angel, [allied to the Lat. *ango* and *angulus*, and the Gr. *ἀγκύλος*] *f.* [*pl.* -n] 1) *a)* in general a point, any thing pointed. Die —n der Bienen, the stings of bees. *b)* tongue [of a sword blade &c.] 2) the hook or joint, on which a door or gate turns, hinge. Die —n am Preßgestell, [am. print.] hinges. *Prov.* Zwischen Thür und — stecken, to be at a pinch, to be in a sad dilemma. *Fig.* [in poetry] pole of the earth or of the world. 3) a fishing-hook, an angle.

Angel-band, *n.* an iron band on doors and windows, by which the door or gate is supported in the hinges. **—draht**, *m.* V. Angelhaken. **—fisch**, *m.* V. Stachelroche. **—fischer**, *m.* angler. **—fischerei**, *f.* angling. **—förmig**, *adj.* and *adv.* in the form of a hook. **—haken**, *m.* 1) hook. 2) fishing-hook. **—kreis**, *m.* the polar circle. **—leine**, *f.* a line. **—maus**, *f.* the shrew. **—mund**, *m.* V. Gerberbaum. **—platz**, *m.* a place [fit] for angling. **—punkt**, *m.* the pole of the earth or of the world. **—ruthe**, *f.* 1) angling-rod, fishing-rod. 2) angle. **—schiff**, *n.* a fisher-boat used for angling. **—schnur**, *f* [angling-] line. **—stange**, *f.* a fishing-rod. **—stern**, *m.* [in poetry for Polarstern] polar-star. **—tugend**, *f.* cardinal virtue. **—weit**, *adj.* and *adv.* wide open, as far open as the hinge will allow a door to go. Er riß bei der Annäherung seines Herrn die Thüre —weit auf, he threw the door wide open on the approach of his master.

Angelangen, *v. tr.* [u. w. seyn] to arrive. V. also Anlangen.

Angeld, *n.* [-es, *pl.* -er] earnest, earnest-money.

Angelegen, V. Anliegen.

Angelegenheit, *f.* concern, business, affair. Mische dich nicht in die häuslichen —en einer Familie, intermeddle not in the private concerns of a family; in Handels—en, in the affairs of trade; Staats—en, state affairs. Syn. Angelegenheit, Geschäfte. Geschäft [from schaffen] denotes any business or occupation in which any one is, or ought to be engaged. Angelegenheit [from anliegen, am Herzen liegen] signifies an affair or concern which is the object or means of obtaining the object of one's wish or desire.

Angelegentlich, I. *adj.* pressing, urgent, earnest, important. Ein —er Wunsch, an ardent wish; ein —es Geschäft, an important business. II. *adv.* pressingly, urgently, earnestly. Ich bitte Sie sehr —, I entreat you earnestly.

Angeler, *m.* [-s, *pl.* -] 1) [one that fishes with an angle] angler. *Fig.* a person that angles for the hearts of people &c. 2) a species of water-fowl.

Angelika, 1) [a name of woman] Angelica. 2) *f. a)* [in botany] angelica. V. Engelwurz. *b)* [an instrument of music] angelot.

Angeln, I. *v. tr.* to catch fish with an angle. *Fig.* Herzen —, to angle for hearts; der Satan angelt nach Seelen, Satan fishes for souls. II. *v. intr.* to fish with an angle, to angle.

Angeloben, *v. tr.* to promise solemnly.

Angelöbniß, *n.* [-nisses, *pl.* -nisse] the act of promising solemnly, the thing so promised, a solemn promise, or vow.

Angelotte, *f.* V. Engelotte.

Angelsachse, *m.* [-n, *pl.* -n] an Anglo-Saxon.

Angelsächsisch, *adj.* Anglo-Saxon. Das Angelsächsische, the Anglo-Saxon.

Angemessen, I. *adj.* conformable, suitable, consistent, fitting. Seine Schreibart ist seinem Charakter vollkommen —, his way of writing is perfectly conformable with his character; die Größe des Verbrechens fordert eine —e Strafe, the magnitude of the crime requires a proportional or proportionate punishment; ein dem Gebete —es heiliges Leben, a holiness of life suitable to prayers, with or in conformity; Mittel, dem Zwecke —, means accommodated to the end; Mittel, die dem Gegenstande völlig —sind, means adequate to the object. II. *adv.* conformably, suitably. Seinem Stande — leben, to live suitably to one's station.

Angemessenheit, *f.* conformity, suitableness, fitness, answerableness.

Angenehm, I. *adj.* 1) pleasing to a receiver, acceptable, welcome 2) pleasing [either to the mind or to the senses] agreeable. —e Manieren, agreeable manners; Obst, das einen —en Geschmack hat, fruit agreeable to the taste; ein —er Geruch, a sweet smell; er ist bei Jedermann —, every body likes him; sich bei Jemanden — machen, to make one's self liked by any one, to render one's self agreeable to any one; er hat ein sehr —es Betragen, he has very agreeable, engaging manners. II. *adv.* 1) acceptably. 2) agreeably.

Anger, [probably allied to eng; in Dan. Eng signifies meadow] *m.* [-s, *pl.* -] 1) a grassy place, a green. 2) a grassy ridge between two fields. V. Rain.

Anger-blume, *f.* daisy. V. Maaslieb, Gänseblümchen. **—kraut**, *n.* common knot-grass.

Angerling, *m.* [-s, *pl.* -e] common mushroom or champignon.

Angerling, *m.* V. Engerling.

Angesehen, I. *adj.* 1) regarded with esteem, respectable. 2) [holding a distinguished rank in society] honourable, distinguished. II. *adv.* honourably. III. *conj.* seeing, considering.

Angesessen, [from Ansitzen] *adj.* residing, resident. Er ist in Berlin —, he lives or is resident in Berlin.

Angesicht, *n.* [-s] 1) [a nobler word for Gesicht] face, visage 2) *Fig.* presence, sight. Vor meinem —, before my face; im —e der ganzen Welt, in the face of the whole world; ich will es ihm ins — sagen, I will tell it him to his face.

Angesichts, *adv.* 1) in the face. Er that es — der Gesellschaft, he did it in presence of the company. 2) upon the spot, immediately.

Angewandt, *part.* of Anwenden. Die —e Mathematik, practical mathematics.

Angewinnen, *ir. v. tr.* 1) to win, to win from. 2) to acquire.

Angewöhnen, I. *v. tr.* to accustom, to habituate or inure. Er hat mir das Spielen angewöhnt, he gave me the taste for gaming. II. *v. r.* sich etwas —, to accustom, to use one's self to a thing.

Angewohnheit, *f.* [commonly in a bad sense] custom, habit, habitude.

Angieren, *v. tr.* to look greedily.

Angießen, *ir. v. tr.* 1) to pour at or against. 2) to join by casting. Das Kleid paßt, als wenn es angegossen wäre, the coat fits like a glove. 3) to pour to. Der Leim ist zu dick, man muß Wasser —, the glue is too thick, we must pour some water to it. 4) to water a little [plants &c.]. *Fig.* ‖ and † to calumniate, to blacken. Er hat ihn garstig angegossen, he aspersed him foully.

Angift, *f.* V. Angeld.

Angirren, *v. tr.* to coo at. *Fig.* Sie girrt ihn zärtlich an, she looks at him tenderly sighing.

* **Anglaise**, *f.* [*pl.* -n] an English dance.

Anglanz, *m.* [-s] glare cast on a body.

Anglänzen, *v. tr.* to cast a glare [on any thing]. *Fig.* Das Glück glänzt ihn an, fortune favours him.

Angleichen, *v. tr.* to convert into a like substance, to assimilate.

Angleichung, *f.* assimilation.

Angleiten, *ir. v. intr.* [u. w. seyn] to glide towards, to slip against.

Angler, *m.* V. Angeler.

* **Anglicism**, *m.* [*pl.* -en] anglicism.

* **Anglikänisch**, *adj.* Anglic, Anglican, English. Die —e Kirche, the church of England.

Angliedern, *v. tr.* to joint.

Anglimmen, *ir.* [with some authors *reg.*] *v. intr.* [u. w. seyn] to begin to burn. [also in a fig. sense] Der Schwamm war angeglimmt or angeglommen, the tinder had caught fire.

* **Anglisiren**, *v. tr.* 1) to anglicise. 2) *Fig.* to dock the tail of a horse.

Anglitschen, V. Angleiten.

* **Anglomane**, *n.* [-n, *pl.* -n] an Angloman.

* **Anglomanie**, *f.* anglomanie.

† **Anglotzen**, *v. tr.* to stare at.

Anglühen, I. *v. intr.* [u. w. seyn] to begin to glow. II. *v. tr.* 1) [= glühend machen] to heat to a glow. Wein anglühen or Glühwein machen, to mull wine. 2) *Poet.* [= glutroth färben] to dye with glowing colours. Die Morgensonne glüht die Berggipfel an, the morning-sun crimsons the summits of the mountains. 3) to look at with glowing eyes.

Angränzen, V. Angrenzen.

Angrauen, *v. tr.* to inspire dread, fear. Das Grab grauete mich an, the grave awed me.

Angrausen, *v. tr.* to look at with a terrible look.

Angreifen, *ir.* I. *v. tr.* 1) to touch, to handle. Mit den Händen —, to feel with the hands. *Prov.* Wer Pech angreift, besudelt sich, touch pitch, and you will be defiled; [in a more limited sense] to lay hands on, to seize. Einen Verbrecher — [better ergreifen], to seize a criminal, to lay hold of him. *Fig. a)* to engage in, to undertake. Eine Sache verkehrt —, to go the wrong way to work. *b)* to do, to work. 2) to attack, to assault. Syn. V. Anfallen. Ein Volk —, to assail a nation; der —de Theil, aggressor; angreifend, offensive. *a)* [= befallen] Er ist von einer Krankheit angegriffen worden, he has been seized by a fit of sickness. *b)* to attack with abuse, to bring into disrepute, to assail. Jemands guten Namen —, to attack, to defile, to tarnish any one's reputation. *c)* to begin a controversy with, to attempt to overthrow by criticism. Jemands Meinungen —, to attack any one's opinions. *d)* to begin to make use of. Ich habe meine Vorräthe bis jetzt noch nicht angegriffen, I have not as yet touched my stores. *e)* to make a visible impression on. Die Salpetersäure greift das Kupfer an, nitric acid corrodes copper; eine Feile greift es nicht an [dringt nicht ein], a file will not touch it. *Fig.* [= beschädigen] Kleine Schrift greift die Augen an, small print hurts the eyes. *f)* to weaken, to enfeeble. Unmäßigkeit greift den Körper und die Verdauungsorgane an, intemperance enfeebles the body, and debilitates the organs of digestion; Kälte greift die Nerven an, cold affects the nerves.

II. *v. r.* sich —, 1) to put in action, to bring into active operation, to exert. Ich habe mich heute im Singen zu sehr angegriffen, I made too great exertions in singing to day. † and ‡ 2) to be liberal, munificent, generous. Er hat sich bei diesem Mittagessen sehr angegriffen, he spent a great deal of money for that dinner.

Angreifer, *m.* [-s, *pl.* -] the person, who attacks, chiefly one that attacks first, aggressor, assaulter, invader.

Angreifisch, I. *adj.* tempting, inciting. II. *adv.* temptingly.

Angreiflich, *adj.* and *adv.* that may be touched or handled, touchable, tangible.

Angreifung, *f.* V. [the more us. word] Angriff.

Angreifungsweise, *adv.* V. Angriffsweise.

Angrenzen, *v. intr.* to be contiguous to, to border on or upon, to confine on. Europa grenzt an Asien an, Europe borders on Asia; England grenzt an Schottland an, England confines on Scotland; angrenzend, lying adjacent to, contiguous; die —den Felder, the bordering or adjacent fields.

Angrenzer, *m.* [-s, *pl.*-] borderer.

Angriff, *m.* [-es, *pl.* -e] 1) the act of handling, touching 2) a falling on with force or violence, or with calumny, satire or criticism, attack. Einen — auf Einen thun or machen, to assault any one; den — thun, to come to the charge; zum —e blasen, to sound the charge; den ersten — aushalten or abhalten, to stand the first brunt or shock; [among weavers] the upper end of the web 3) [sometimes for] the handle. Der — am Deckel, [among printers] thumb-piece.

Angriffs-bündniß, *n.* an offensive alliance. —krieg, *m.* an offensive war. —waffe, *f.* one of the offensive arms which are used in attacks; die —waffen, offensive arms. —weise, I. *f.* manner of attack. II. *adv.* offensively. —weise zu Werke gehen, to keep one's self on the offensive.

Angrinsen, *v. intr.* to grin on. Narren grinsen einander an, fools grin on fools.

|| **Angrölen**, *v. tr.* to bawl at.

Angrunzen, *v. tr.* to grunt at.

Angst, [French *angoisse*, Engl. *anguish*, allied to the Lat. *ango*, to the Gr. *ἄγχω*, to the Germ. engen] I. *f.* [*pl.* Aengste] anguish, anxiety [in pl. only used in the dative case]. In Aengsten seyn, to be in a state of alarm, to be seized with anguish; ich bin in tödtlicher —, in tödtlichen Aengsten gewesen, I was in an agony of fear; aber sie hörten Moses nicht vor —, [Ex. VI.] and they harkened not to Moses for anguish of spirit. II. [without any case or indeclin.] impressed with anguish, with fear or apprehension, afraid [only used with seyn, machen, werden]. Es ist mir — vor dem Tode, I am afraid of death; Ihre Krankheit hat mir sehr — gemacht, your illness caused me great alarm; es wurde uns — bei dem Feuerlärm, we felt alarmed at the cry of fire; Einem — machen, to alarm any one, to put any one in fear.

Angst-ausruf, *m.* cry of anguish, scream. —erregend, *adj.* alarming. Seine Krankheit verschlimmerte sich in einem —erregenden Grade, his illness increased in an alarming degree. —fieber, *n.* a fever caused by fear. —gefühl, *n.* sensation of anguish. —geheul, *n.* [the cry of any one in distress] howling. —geschrei, *n.* cry of anguish, shriek. —gestöhne, *n.* [a deep mournful sound, uttered in anguish] groan. —ruf, *m.* cry of anguish, scream. —schweiß, cold sweat. —traum, *m.* an alarming dream. —tropfen, *m.* V. —schweiß. —voll, *adj.* and *adv.* full of anguish, painful.

Angsten, I. *v. tr.* to fill with anguish by the prospect of evil, to disturb with terror, to alarm. II. *v. r.* sich — über &c., to be alarmed at &c.

1. **Angster**, *m.* [-s, *pl.*-] a Swiss farthing.

2. || **Angster**, [allied to *angustus*] *m.* [-s, *pl.*-] a kind of bottle.

Angsthaft, *adj.* and *adv.* V. Aengstlich.

Angstig, *adj.* and *adv.* full of anguish, oppressed with anguish.

Angstigen, *v. tr.* to anguish. V. Aengsten. Er ängstigte mich, he alarmed me; ich ängstige mich über &c., I feel an alarm at &c.; ängstige dich nicht über die Zukunft, do not distress yourself or fret about the future.

‡ **Angstiglich**, V. Aengstlich.

Ängstlich, I. *adj.* anxious. 1) [full of solicitude, unquiet] —e Gedanken, anxious thoughts. 2) [very careful, solicitous] —, zu gefallen, anxious to please; eine —e Ordnung, an anxious order. II. *adv.* anxiously, solicitously, carefully.

Ängstlichkeit, *f.* 1) anxiety, fear, timidity. 2) anxiousness, anxious care, solicitude.

Angucken, *v. tr.* to look at.

* **Angurie**, *f.* [*pl.* -n] the water melon.

Angurren, *v. tr.* to coo at. V. Angirren.

Angurten, *v. tr.* to gird on [a sword &c.], to girth on [a saddle].

Anguß, *m.* [-sses, *pl.* -güsse] a thing cast or founded on to another.

Angusturarinde, *f.* angustura-bark.

Anhaben, *ir. v. intr.* to have on, to wear. Er sah einen Menschen, der hatte kein hochzeitliches Kleid an, [Math. XXII.] he saw a man, who had not on a wedding garment; er hatte weder Schuhe noch Strümpfe an, he had neither shoes nor stockings on. *Fig.* Einem etwas —, to get or gain the better of any one, to obtain the advantage over any one. Man kann ihm nichts —, es ist ihm nichts anzuhaben, one cannot gain any advantage over him, he is not to be out done; sie konnten ihm nichts —, they could not get any hold upon him.

Anhacken, *v. tr.* to begin to chop at. Einen Garten —, to commence hoeing a garden.

Anhaften, *v. intr.* to adhere, to stick to. Das Pflaster will nicht —, the plaster will not hold.

Anhäften, V. Anheften.

Anhäkeln, I. *v. tr.* to fasten with a clasp, to clasp. II. *v. r.* sich —, to cling.

Anhaken, I. *v. tr.* 1) to fasten with a hook, to hook. 2) to seize and draw near with a hook. Etwas mit dem Bootshaken —, to hook any thing with a boat-hook; ein Schiff hakt ein anderes an, a ship grapples another ship. II. *v. r.* sich —, to catch. Das Kleid hat sich an etwas angehakt [= ist an einem Haken &c. hängen geblieben] the gown has caught or hooked on something. III. *v. intr.* to be fastened by a hook, to be hooked.

Anhalftern, *v. tr.* to fasten by a halter [a horse &c.]

Anhall, *m.* [-s, *pl.* -e] return of sound, resound.

Anhallen, I. *v. intr.* and *tr.* to sound. II. *v. intr.* to resound.

Anhalsen, *v. intr.* [among hunters] to couple [the dogs].

Anhalt, *m.* [-es, *pl.* -e] 1) the act of stopping. Machen wir einen kleinen —? shall we make a little stay [on a journey]? 2) [something which may be seized for support] hold.

Anhalts-seil, *n.* [a sea term] relieving tackle. —talje, *f.* [a sea term] V. Einholtalje.

Anhalten, *ir.* I. *v. tr.* 1) to hold to. *Fig.* Einen zu Etwas —, to keep any one to any thing; Einen zu seiner Arbeit —, to keep any one to his work; Einen zum Bezahlen —, to urge any one for payment, to dun any one; Jemanden zur Erfüllung seines Versprechens —, to hold any one to his promise. 2) to hinder from progressive motion, to put an end to the motion of any thing, to stop. Mit dem Zaum — [a horse], to rein in; die Pferde —, to hold in the horses; einen Wagen —, to stop a carriage; einen Dieb —, to stop a thief. *Fig.* Ein —des Arzneimittel, an astringent. II. *v. r.* sich —, to seize and to cling to. Halte dich an dem Zweige des Baumes an, hold on by the branch of the tree; sich fest —, to keep fast hold, to hold on. III. *v. intr.* 1) to cease to go forward, to stop. Wir wollen im Kaiser —, we will stop or alight or put up at the Emperor; bei einem guten Freunde —, to stop and turn in at the house of a friend; durchreisen, ohne anzuhalten, to go through without stopping; ein Pferd, das schön anhält [sich beim Anhalten schön stellt], a horse that stops well. *Fig.* Der Wagen hält an, the carriage stands still. 2) to persevere, to hold on, to continue. Es war —der Westwind, the wind settled in the west; eine —de Krankheit, a lasting disease. 3) [to make a request, to solicit] to apply. Bei dem Könige um ein Amt —, to apply to the king for an office; er hielt um diese Stelle an, he sued for that employment; um ein Frauenzimmer —, to ask for a lady, to woo, to court her, to solicit her in marriage.

Anhalten, *n.* [-s] solicitation.

Anhalter, *m.* [-s, *pl.*-] 1) he that holds to. 2) that wich holds. 3) a thing to hold by.

Anhaltsam, *adj.* and *adv.* uninterrupted, constant, persevering.

Anhaltsamkeit, *f.* perseverance, constancy.

Anhämmern, I. *v. tr.* to fasten to by hammering. II. *v. intr.* to beat with a hammer, to knock with force at. *Fig.* Er hämmerte an die Thüre an, he knocked with force at the door.

Anhang, *m.* [-es, *pl.* -hänge] 1) any thing that adheres, sticks or cleaves to; [among hunters] snow, hoarfrost, rain that hangs on the bushes. 2) *Fig.* *a*) [those, who follow a leader or a party] adherents, followers, partisans. *b*) appendix. Der — eines Buches, a supplement or short treatise added to a book; — zu einem Testamente, codicil to a will.

Anhangen, *ir. v. intr.* [u. w. seyn] to hang on. Die Lunge hing an den Rippen an, the lungs adhered to the ribs. *Fig.* [u. w. haben] Jene Besorgnisse, welche den Furchtsamen —, those apprehensions, which hang on the timorous; Einem —, [= ergeben seyn] to adhere, to hold to, to be attached; einer Partei, einer Kirche —, to adhere to a party, to a church or creed; Einige hangen euch an, some stick to you; das — des Eisens an den Magnet, the cohesion of the iron to the loadstone.

Anhängen, *reg.* I. *v. tr.* to hang or to attach to, to append. Ein Siegel an eine Urkunde —, to append, to affix a seal to a dead; die Hängematten —, [in sea language] to sling the hammocks. *Prov.* Niemand will der Katze die Schellen —, who shall hang the bell about the cat's neck? [i. e. be the first to take a hazardous step]. *Fig.* *a*) to add, to subjoin, to annex, Einem Worte eine Silbe —, to affix a syllable to a word; die angehängte Silbe, der angehängte Buchstabe, affix. *b*) to give to, to bestow upon [said in contempt]. Er hat ihr Alles angehängt, he has squandered away all his fortune upon her; Einem eine Krankheit —, to infect any one, to taint any one with a disease; Einem einen Spottnamen —, to give any one a nick-name; Einem Etwas —, to tarnish or blemish any one's reputation or character, to put a slur upon any one. II. *v. r.* sich —, to stick, to cling to. Wo der Thau sich anhängt, where the dew hangs; das hängt sich an wie Vogelleim, that sticks like bird-lime; der Kuchen hängt sich in der Pfanne an, the cake adheres to the pan. *Fig.* [in contempt] to adhere to any one.

Anhänger, *m.* [-s, *pl.*-] —inn, *f.* a follower or partisan, an adherent. Ein — der Vernunft, a retainer to reason.

Anhängerei, *f.* [mostly in a contemptuous sense] the act of adhering to a party, a leader, a creed &c.

Anhängig, *adj.* and *adv.* adherent, sticking, uniting [as glue, wax &c.]. *Fig.* *a*) belonging to, appendant to. Das Haus mit Allem, was dem — ist, the house with all its appertenances. *b*) [a law term] — seyn, to be pending; einen Prozeß — machen, to commence a law suit, to bring an action against any one.

Ánhänglich, *adj.* and *adv.* attached to [a friend &c.].

Ánhänglichkeit, *f.* attachment, close adherence or affection, fidelity. Die — an eine Partei, attachment to a party.

Ánhängsel, *n.* [-s, *pl.*-] V. Angehänge.

Ánhaspen, Ánhäspen, *v. tr.* to fasten with hooks [chiefly in mining].

Ánhauch, *m.* [-s, *pl.*-e] 1) [breeze, air in gentle motion] breath. — des Windes, a breath of wind. 2) *Fig.* *a*) breath [of flowers], sensation, inspiration. *b*) Ein zarter — von Roth färbte ihre Wange, a slight tint of red coloured her cheek.

Ánhauchen, *v. tr.* 1) to breathe on or upon [a glass &c.]. Die Finger an einem kalten Tage —, to blow one's fingers on a cold day. 2) *Fig.* to inspire.

Ánhauchen, *n.* [-s] afflation.

Ánhauen, *ir. v. tr.* 1) to strike upon. Die Pferde —, to whip the horses in order to impel them to greater speed. 2) to cut a little of. Einen Baum —, to cut out some splinters from a tree [to mark a tree that is to be felled]. 3) to begin to hew or cut. Einen Wald —, to begin to fell trees in a forest; einen Ochsen —, [among butchers] to begin to cut up an ox; [in angling] einen Fisch mit der Angel —, to give a jerk with the angling-rod [when the fish has taken the bait].

Ánhäufeln, *v. tr.* to form small heaps round something.

Ánhäufen, I. *v. tr.* to heap up, to pile up. *Fig.* Schätze —, to accumulate or amass riches. II. *v. r.* sich —, to accumulate. Oeffentliches Unglück häuft sich an, public evils accumulate, public calamity increases.

Ánhäufer, *m.* [-s, *pl.*-] accumulator.

Ánhäufung, *f.* accumulation. Eine — von Erde, an accumulation of earth; die Steine wachsen durch —, [in nat. hist.] stones increase by accretion. *Fig.* Eine — von Uebeln, an accumulation of evils.

Ánheben, *ir.* I. *v. tr.* to heave or lift towards. *Fig.* to begin, to commence. II. *v. intr.* to begin, to take rise, to commence [sometimes in the form of a *v. r.*]. Er hub also an und sprach, he began thus and said; hier hebt ein neuer Zeitabschnitt in der Geschichte an, here begins a new period in history. V. Anfangen.

Ánheften, *v. tr.* to fix or fasten in any manner to. Einen ans Kreuz —, to crucify any one; ein Stück Leinwand an ein anderes —, to stitch, sew, or pin a piece of linen to another, to baste a piece of linen to another; ein Buch an das andere —, to stitch, sew or bind one book to another.

Ánheilen, I. *v. tr.* to join to by healing, to consolidate. II. *v. intr.* [u. w. seyn] to be united by healing, to consolidate.

Ánheim, *adv.* V. Heim, [commonly used in law with the words fallen, geben, stellen]. — fallen, to fall to, to fall into the possession of; nach dem Tode des Königs fiel die Krone seinem ältesten Sohne —, on the death of the king, the crown devolved on his eldest son; — geben, to put into any one's hand. *Fig.* to leave for consideration. Ich stelle es Ihrem Urtheile —, I leave it to your judgement; er stellte die Sache dem Senate —, he referred it to the senate.

Ánheischig, *adj.* Sich zu etwas — machen, to pledge or engage one's self to any thing.

Ánhelfen, *ir. v. intr.* Einem —, to assist, to aid or to help any one by furnishing means to effect a purpose, to obtain an employ &c.

Ánhenken, V. Anhängen [in a lit. sense].

‡**Anhér**, *adv.* for her.

‡**Anhérkunft**, *f.* arrival.

Ánhetzen, *v. tr.* 1) to begin to hunt. Wild —, [among hunters] to hound game. 2) to set on [a dog]. *Fig.* to incite, to instigate. Man hetzt ihn gegen mich an, they irritate him against me.

Ánhetzer, *m.* [-s, *pl.*-] —inn, *f.* an inciter, an instigator, an abettor, a setter on.

Anhetzeréi, *f.* inciting, instigation, setting on.

Ánheucheln, *v. tr.* to feign, to pretend any thing. Sich eine sanfte Miene —, to put on a mild air.

Ánheulen, *v. tr.* to howl at [the moon &c.].

‡**Ánheut**, V. Heut.

Ánhexen, *v. tr.* to inflict by witchcraft, to bewitch.

Ánhieb, *m.* [-es, *pl.* -e] 1) the commencement of felling wood. 2) the place, where wood is felled.

Ánhöhe, *f.* [*pl.*-n] a rising ground, a hill of moderate elevation, an eminence. Eine —, welche die Gegend beherrscht, a commanding ground.

Ánholen, *v. tr.* to draw or pull with force to a place; [in sea lang.] to haul. Die Schoten —, to haul at or to tally the sheets; die Bolinen —, to haul taught the bowlines.

Ánholtau, *n.* tow-rope, halser or hawser [of a small boat], painter.

Ánhören, *v. tr.* 1) to listen to, to hearken to, to give heed to what is uttered. Hört mich geduldig an, hear me patiently; sein Bruder ist die einzige Person, die er anhört, his brother is the only person, he attends to; das Wort Gottes mit Aufmerksamkeit —, to attend to the word of God. 2) to learn, to perceive by the ear. Es ist ihm [an seiner Aussprache] leicht anzuhören, daß er ein Engländer ist, it is easy to hear from his pronunciation that he is an Englishman.

Ánhörung, *f.* hearing.

Ánhosen, *v. r.* sich —, to put on one's breeches, or trowsers.

Ánhüpfen, *v. intr.* [u. w. seyn and sometimes with kommen] to approach jumping.

Ánhusten, *v. tr.* 1) to cough at. 2) to make signs to by coughing.

* **Änigmátisch**, *adj.* enigmatic, enigmatical, obscure, ambiguous.

Anill, *m.* V. Indigopflanze.

* **Animálisch**, *adj.* V. Thierisch.

* **Animalität**, *f.* V. Thierheit.

* **Aníme**, *n.* gum anime.

* **Animíren**, *v. tr.* V. Anreizen.

* **Animosität**, *f.* [*pl.*-en] animosity.

* **Animóso**, *adv.* [in music] animoso.

* **Ánis**, *m.* [-es] anise.

Anis=apfel, *m.* fennel-apple. —**balsam**, *m.* a balm obtained from the anise-seed oil. —**bau**, *m.* the culture of anise. —**blatt**, *n.* an exotic [limonia acidissima]. —**branntwein**, *m.* anise-seed spirit or cordial, anisette. —**brod**, *n.* a sort of bread made of sugar and anise-seed. —**feld**, *n.* a field planted with anise. —**geruch**, *m.* the smell of anise-seed. —**geschmack**, *m.* the taste peculiar to anise-seed. —**holz**, *n.* 1) common spindle-tree. 2) alligator-pear. —**kerbel**, *m.* 1) aromatic chaerophyllum. 2) sweet-scented cicely or myrrh. —**korn**, *n.* 1) a grain of anise-seed. 2) a grain of anise-seed covered with sugar. —**kuchen**, *m.* a cake baked with anise-seed. —**öl**, *n.* anise-seed oil. —**same**, *m.* anise-seed. —**wasser**, *n.* water prepared with anise-seed. —**zucker**, *m.* little sweet-cakes prepared with anise-seed oil.

Ánjagen, I. *v. tr.* 1) to begin to hunt. 2) to hound. Einen Hirsch —, [am. hunters] to emprime a stag. 3) to drive, to impel to greater speed. V. Anhetzen 2. II. *v. intr.* [u. w. seyn] angejagt kommen, to approach with the greatest speed.

‡**Anjétzo, Anjetzt**, V. Jetzt.

‡ and † **Ánjetzund, Ánjetzunder**, V. Jetzt.

Ánjochen, *v. tr.* to put to the yoke, to yoke [oxen].

Ánkämmen, *v. tr.* to adjust with a comb [hair], to comb smooth.

Ánkämpfen, *v. intr.* to struggle against or with. Jakob verstand es nicht, gegen verzweifelte Zufälligkeiten anzukämpfen, James knew not how to wrestle with desperate contingencies.

Ánkarren, I. *v. tr.* 1) to convey on a cart. Steine —, to cart stones. 2) to touch in driving a cart. II. *v. intr.* [u. w. seyn] angekarrt kommen, to come near in or with a cart.

Ánkauf, *m.* [-es, *pl.* -käufe] 1) buying. 2) [the thing bought] purchase, bargain.

Ánkaufen, I. *v. tr.* to buy, to purchase [books &c.]. II. *v. r.* sich —, to buy land, to settle at a place.

1. **Ánke**, *f.* [allied to Angel, engen = krümmen] [*pl.*-n] [am. metallists] a table of brass with cavities used for working buttons or knobs into a round projecting form.

2. **Ánke**, *f.* [*pl.*-n] lake-trout.

3. **Ánke**, *f.* [unguentum?] [in Switzerland and in some parts of South-Germany] butter.

Anken=blume, *f.* V. Butterblume. —**butter**, *f.* and || *m.* butter churned in May. —**milch**, *f.* butter-milk.

Ánke, *f.* V. Ente.

Ánkehren, *v. tr.* 1) to sweep towards. 2) to sweep on or upon. 3) V. Einkehren.

Ánkeilen, *v. tr.* to fasten by wedges, to wedge.

Ánkel, [allied to Angel, engen = krümmen] *m.* [-s, *pl.*-] the ancle. V. Knöchel.

1. **Ánker**, [Dutch *Anker*, Swed. *Ankare*, old French *anche*] *m.* [-s, *pl.* -] [a measure of liquids] an anker.

Ankerfäßchen, *n.* a cask holding an anker.

2. **Ánker**, [Lat. *ancora*, allied to *ango*, engen = krümmen] *m.* [-s, *pl.*-] an anchor. Ein kleiner — für kleine Schiffe, grapnel; den — werfen, auswerfen or fallen lassen, to cast anchor, to let go the anchor, to anchor; sich vor — legen, vor — gehen, to anchor; vor — liegen, to lie or ride at anchor; die [den] — lichten, to weigh anchor; einen Sturm vor — aushalten, to ride out a storm; vor — treiben, to drag the anchor, to drive; das Schiff treibt vor —, or der — schleppt, the anchor comes home; der — hängt, the anchor is a-trip, a-peak; einen — schuhen or bekleiden, to shoe an anchor; den — kappen, to cut the cable; einen — am Ringe fest machen, to clinch a cable; einen — fischen, to sweep for an anchor. *Prov.* Ein Schiff steht an zwei —n fester als an einem, good riding at two anchors men have told, for if one break, the other may hold. 2) *Fig.* [that which gives stability or security, that on which we place dependence for safety] anchor. Welche Hoffnung wir haben, als einen sichern und festen —, [Heb. VI] which hope we have as an anchor [of the soul], both sure and steadfast.

3) [in architect.] a cramp, cramp-iron [serving to hold together pieces of timber, stones &c.]. 4) [am. silk-weavers] a kind of spools.

Anker-ambos, *m.* an anvil on which anchors are shaped. —**arm**, *m.* the arm of an anchor. —**auge**, *n.* eye. —**balken**, *m.* cat-heads. —**baum**, *m.* clinch-bolt. —**blume**, *f.* an exotic [rheria]. —**boje**, *f.* a buoy fastened to an anchor. —**fest**, *adj.* and *adv.* suitable for anchoring, hold by an anchor. Ein —fester Grund, anchor-ground, good anchorage. —**fliege**, *f.*, —**flügel**, *m.* fluke, palm. —**flott**, *n.* V. —boje. —**förmig**, *adj.* and *adv.* like an anchor. —**fütterung**, *f.* lining of the bow. —**geld**, *n.* anchorage. —**grund**, *m.* anchor-ground, anchorage. Schlechter —grund, foul ground. —**haken**, *m.* cat-hook. —**hammer**, *m.* a great hammer, —**hals**, *m.* the throat. —**hände**, *pl.* flukes. —**helm**, *m.* the shank or beam. —**holz**, *n.* 1) the stock. 2) [in carpentry] the wooden part of a cramp. —**kreuz**, *n.* the crown. —**krücke**, *f.* the stock. —**loch**, *n.* hawse-hole. —**los**, *adj.* unmoored, adrift. Das Schiff ist —los, the vessel drags the anchors. —**nüsse**, *pl. f.* nuts of an anchor. —**platz**, *m.* an anchoring place, anchorage, anchor-ground. —**recht**, *n.* 1) the privilege of anchoring. 2) [a duty imposed on ships for anchoring in a harbour] anchorage. —**ring**, *m.* ring. —**ruthe**, *f.*, —**schaft**, *m.* the shank or beam of an anchor. —**schaufel**, *f.* V. —fliege. —**scheuer**, *f.* V. —fütterung. —**schmied**, *m.* anchor-smith. —**schmiede**, *f.* a forge or smithy in which anchors are made. —**schuh**, *m.* the shoe. —**seil**, *n.* V. —tau. —**spitze**, *f.* the bill. —**stange**, *f.* V. —ruthe. —**stelle**, *f.* V. —platz. —**stich**, *m.* [in seaman's language] clinch. —**stock**, *m.* the stock. —stocksbanden, hooks of the stock. —**talje**, *f.* the fish-takle. —**tau**, *n.* the cable. Das —tau zusammenlegen, to coil the cable; das —tau in den Küssen verwahren, to freshen the hawse; ein —tau trensen, to worm a cable; das —tau schwebt, the cable surges; die —taus Länge, [in seaman's lang.] cable's length; das —tauwerk, ground-tackle. —**wächter**, *m.* V. —boje. —**winde**, *f.* windlass, capstan. —**zeichen**, *n.* V. boje. —**zoll**, *m.* V. —geld.

Ankerben, *v. tr.* 1) to begin to notch. 2) to mark by notches.

Ankern, *v. intr.* to anchor, to cast anchor, to come to anchor. Wir ankerten auf der Höhe der Insel Wight, we anchored off the Isle of Wight. *Fig.* || Nach Etwas —, to hanker after.

Anketteln, *v. tr.* 1) to fasten with little chains. 2) [am. stocking-weavers] to chain. 3) [am. sempstresses, to make chain-work] to chain.

Anketten, *v. tr.* to fasten with a chain, to chain. *Fig.* Sich an Einen —, to stick to any one.

Ankind, *n.* [-es, *pl.* -er] [a law term] an adoptive child.

Ankinden, *v. tr.* [a law-term] to adopt [a child].

Ankinder, *m.* [-s, *pl.* -] [a law term] one who adopts, adopter.

Ankindung, *f.* [a law term] adoption, affiliation.

Ankirren, *v. tr.* to tame. *Fig.* to allure [commonly in a bad sense].

Ankitten, *v. tr.* to fix to by cement, to cement to.

Anklaffen, **Ankläffen**, *v. tr.* to yelp at.

Anklaffern, V. Anklaffen.

Anklagbar, *adj.* and *adv.* accusable. — wegen &c., accusable of &c.

Anklage, *f.* [*pl.* -n] 1) [the act of accusing] accusation, arraignment, [against a public officer] impeachment. 3) the charge with an offence or crime or the written declaration containing the charge, accusation; indictment.

Anklageschrift, *f.* accusation, bill of indictment.

Anklagen, *v. tr.* 1) to inform against. A. hat den B. angeklagt, A. informed against B. 2) to accuse [any one of a crime &c.]. Einen des Diebstahls —, to charge any one with theft. *Fig.* Sich wegen &c. —, to blame one's self for &c. Syn. Anklagen, Verklagen, Belangen, Beschuldigen, Angeben. Anklagen is used generally only of a criminal charge or accusation, Verklagen also in civil cases. Man verklagt Jemanden, that the authorities may oblige him to perform some thing or pay what he is indebted to me; man klagt Jemanden an, in order that he may be punished. Belangen appears to be used only in more trifling offences. When the complaint is laid before the proper authorities, in order that the accused person may be punished or compelled to give satisfaction, it is called Anklagen; if the charge is made without the above intention and not in a judicial way, it is merely Beschuldigen. We may often Beschuldigen Einen eines Verbrechens [impute a crime to a person], without the slightest intention ihn anzuklagen [to accuse him judicially]. Angeben signifies merely to inform against, and does not include, as anklagen, the idea that the informant undertakes to produce proof of the guilt, or that he requires the punishment of the offender. V. Anbringen.

Ankläger, *m.* [-s, *pl.* -] —inn, *f.* accuser, accusant, informer.

Anklägerisch, *adj.* and *adv.* 1) prone to accuse. 2) [law term] —erseits, on the part of the accuser or complainant.

Anklammern, I. *v. tr.* to fasten with cramps or grappling irons, to cramp to. II. *v. r.* sich —, to clasp. Sich an Einen —, to attach one's self to a person.

Anklang, *m.* [-es, *pl.* -klänge] 1) the beginning of a sound, followed by other sounds. *Fig.* Sein Vorschlag fand den allgemeinsten —, his proposal found the most general approbation; ein — dieser Stimmung gab sich in dem von den Unzufriedenen versuchten Aufstande kund, the opinions of the people showed themselves in this rising. 2) a sound produced by the collision of sounding bodies. 3) [in music] accord. 4) the sounding of the notes of the scale, intonation.

Anklappern, *v. intr.* to rattle at [a door &c.].

Anklatschen, I. *v. intr.* to begin to clap. II. *v. tr.* 1) to clap at. 2) to make to adhere by clapping, to clap to.

Ankleben, I. *v. intr.* to stick, to cling, to adhere, to hold to. Das Papier klebt an der Wand an, the paper cleaves to the wall. *Fig.* Einem —, to adhere to, to hold or to cleave to any one; das dem Menschen —de Recht auf Freiheit, the inherent right of man to liberty. II. *v. tr.* to make to cleave or cling. Einen Comödienzettel —, to set up, stick up or post up a play-bill; angeklebt, posted up.

Anklecken, **Anklecksen**, *v. tr.* 1) to cast on as a stain or blot. 2) *Fig.* *a*) to add or subjoin clumsily. *b*) to dawb on.

Ankleiben, *v. tr.* V. Ankleben.

Ankleiden, I. *v. tr.* to put clothes on, to dress. II. *v. r.* sich —, to put on one's clothes, to dress one's self, to dress. Er kleidete sich zum Mittag(s)essen an, he dressed himself for dinner. Syn. Anziehen, Ankleiden, Anlegen. Sich ankleiden signifies always the putting on of the entire clothing, to dress one's self; Anziehen and anlegen are said not only when speaking of the whole, but also of the individual parts of which the dress is composed. Anziehen [from an and ziehen] is said only of such parts of dress as are drawn on to the body; anlegen [from an and legen] properly speaking only of such as are laid on. Boots and stockings are angezogen [drawn on]; a sword, buckles &c. are not angezogen, but angelegt [put on]. As however, those parts of dress which are not angezogen as a covering, but merely angelegt, are for the most part ornamental, anlegen has obtained also the signification of ornamenting, and is then used of such parts of dress as are angezogen, when these are especially costly and ornamental, or when we wish to express anziehen [to dress or clothe] in a more serious and pompous manner: er hat heute seine besten Kleider angelegt. Trauer anlegen [to put on mourning]. Der Fürst wird gleich erscheinen; er will nur erst andere Kleider anlegen.

Ankleidezimmer, *n.* dressing-room; [in theatres] tiring-room; [in a church] the vestry or revestiary.

Ankleider, *m.* [-s, *pl.* -] [a person who is employed in putting on clothes and adorning another] dresser.

Ankleistern, *v. tr.* to fix with paste, to paste, to paste to or on. Ein Papier an die Wand —, to paste up a paper on the wall.

Anklemmen, *v. tr.* to pinch or squeeze against.

Anklettern, *v. tr.* *Fig.* Sie kletterte sich an ihn an, she stuck to him like burs.

Anklimmen, *v. tr.* to climb up to.

Anklingeln, I. *v. intr.* to pull or ring the bell, to tingle. *Fig.* Bei Einem —, to sift or to sound any one. II. *v. tr.* Einen —, to make a signal with a small bell to a person [as church-wardens do, who go about the church, during the sermon, and collect alms from the congregation].

Anklingen, I. *ir. v. intr.* 1) to begin to sound. 2) [in music] to accord in sound. II. *reg. v. tr.* to make to tingle.

Anklitschen, V. Anklatschen.

Anklopfen, I. *v. intr.* to knock at, to knock. An die or an der Thüre —, to rap at the door, to knock. Syn. V. Anpochen. *Fig.* Bei Jemand —, to sound or sift any one. II. *v. tr.* to fix by beating. Ein Bild an die Wand —, to nail up a picture against the wall.

Anklopfring, *m.* a ring fastened to a door, serving as knocker.

Anklopfer, *m.* [-s, *pl.* -] 1) he that knocks at a door, knocker. 2) a kind of hammer fastened to a door, a knocker.

† **Anklotzen**, V. Anglotzen.

Anknallen, *v. tr.* to drive [horses] by cracking the whip.

Anknebeln, *v. tr.* to fasten to any thing with a short stick.

Ankneipen, I. *v. tr.* to pinch at, to touch with the fingers or with pincers. II. *v. r.* sich —. Der Krebs kneipt sich an, the crab takes hold with its claws, holds fast by them.

Anknöpfen, *v. tr.* to fix to by buttoning.

Anknüpfen, *v. tr.* to fix to by tying a k… to knot, to tie [a thread &c.]. *Fig.* Ein Gespr… wieder —, to resume a discourse.

Anknurren, *v. tr.* to snarl or growl at.

Anködern, *v. tr.* 1) to allure by means o… bait [fish &c.]. 2) to put any bait [as worms &c.] … a hook, line &c., to furnish with a bait, to ba…

Anköderung, *f.* the act of baiting.

Ankollern, *v. intr.* [u. w. seyn] to touch … something in rolling.

Ankommen, *ir. v. intr.* [u. w. seyn] to co…

or go near a place, to approach, to come up. Da kommt er an, there he comes; er mag nur —, let him come up. 2) to come to or reach a place, to arrive. Die Post kommt um zwei Uhr an, the post arrives at two o' clock; es ist heute ein Brief für mich angekommen, I received a letter to-day. 3) *Fig. a)* to meet with a reception. Bei mir kommt er nicht an he shall not come to me; bei Einem wohl oder übel —, to be well or ill received by any one; da wird er schön —, he will meet with a fine reception; hier ist kein Ankommen [used as a subst.], no access is to be had here. *b)* to attain an end. Bei einer Sache gut oder schlecht —, to meet with good or ill success, to fare well or ill; †Sie kommen blind an, you are mistaken. *c)* to obtain a place or office, to be promoted. Gut oder schlecht —, to be well or ill placed, settled, established &c.; †er ist bei Hofe angekommen, he has got a place at court. *d)* to be felt, to appear. Es kommt mir leicht, schwer, hart oder sauer an, it is easy or hard to me. *e)* [joined with auf and frequently with lassen] to wait for or await any thing that will happen or be done, to depend upon, to signify. Es darauf — lassen, to run the hazard, to risk, to venture; Alles aufs Glück — lassen, to leave every thing to chance; es kommt auf Sie an, it depends on or upon you; ich lasse es auf Sie —, I leave it to you, to your disposition, I rely on your decision; es kommt auf unser Leben an, our life is at stake; hier kommt es bloß aufs Geld an, here is nothing required but money; es soll mir darauf nicht —, I shall not stick at this; es kommt mir auf ein wenig Geld nicht an, I do not mind a little money; es kommt auf zehn Thaler an, it concerns ten dollars, it is a matter of &c.; es kommt mir auf eine Woche nicht an, I shall not stand for a week, a week more or less does not signify. 4) [sometimes *v. tr.*] to befall. *Fig.* Was ist ihm angekommen [angestoßen]? what has befallen him? der Schlaf kam mir [mich] an, I became sleepy or drowsy; es kam mir [mich] Furcht, Schrecken &c. an, I was seized or struck with fear, with terror &c.; es kam mir [mich] die Lust an, I took a fancy to. Syn. Ankommen, Anlangen, Eintreffen. Anlangen refers to the distance and to the way that a person or thing had to make in order to be present at a certain distant place. Ankommen has reference merely to the place of arrival. Eintreffen comprehends also the idea of arriving at the proper time and at the proper place. — Ankommen [auf etwas], Abhängen [von etwas]. Ankommen is used only when the cause upon which any thing depends, is something accidental or contingent. One can say: die Fortdauer unserer Seele nach dem Tode hängt von der göttlichen Güte ab [the continuance of our soul after death depends upon the divine goodness]; but not: kommt auf die göttliche Güte an.

Ankömmling, *m.* [-s, *pl.* -e] a new comer, a stranger.

Anköpfen, *v. tr.* [am. pinmakers] to head [a pin].

Anköpfer, *m.* [-s, *pl.* -] [among pinmakers] header.

Ankoppeln, *v. tr.* to couple [dogs &c.].

Ankörnen, *v. tr.* to attract by corn [birds &c.], to allure, to bait. *Fig.* to allure.

Ankrächzen, *v. tr.* 1) to caw or croak at. 2) to announce by cawing or croaking.

Ankrähen, *v. tr.* 1) to crow at. 2) to announce by crowing.

Ankrallen, I. *v. tr.* to touch, to seize with claws. II. *v. r.* sich —, to take hold with, to hold on by the claws.

Ankratzen, I. *v. tr.* to grate at, to scratch on. Seinen Namen an die Wand —, to scratch one's name on the wall. II. *v. intr.* to produce on a body by grating or scratching. An der Thüre — or kratzen, to scratch at the door.

Ankreiden, *v. tr.* to note with chalk, to chalk up [a score on a table &c.]. Der Wirth hat ihm schon eine artige Rechnung or Zeche angekreidet, the landlord has scored his up a handsome reckoning.

Ankreischen, *v. tr.* V. Anschreien.

Ankreuzen, *v. tr.* to mark with crosses.

Ankriechen, *ir. v. intr.* [u. w. seyn] to creep near, at or to. Angekrochen kommen, to approach creeping.

†Ankriegen, *v. tr.* to get on [a coat &c.].

Ankritzeln, *v. tr.* to scribble on.

‖Ankuken, V. Ansehen.

Ankünden, V. Ankündigen.

Ankündigen, *v. tr.* to publish, to proclaim, to give notice, to announce, to intimate, to advertise. Den Krieg —, to declare war; man hat angekündigt, daß das Parlament im November zusammenkommen würde, it was given out that parliament would assemble in November; ein Schauspiel —, to give out a play.

Ankündiger, *m.* [-s, *pl.* -] an announcer, a proclaimer, [also of things, viz. the title of a periodical publication] advertiser.

Ankündigung, *f.* 1) [the act of giving notice] announcement, publication, proclamation, declaration, intimation. 2) [the thing published] publication. Oeffentliche —, advertisement.

Ankunft, *f.* the coming to, or reaching of a place, arrival. Die — eines Freundes, the arrival of a friend; die — des Messias, the coming or advent of the Messiah.

Ankünsteln, *v. tr.* to produce on a thing by artificial effort or refinement.

Ankuppeln, *v. tr.* to couple [dogs &c.]. †*Fig.* Einem eine Person —, to procure any one a person in marriage.

Ankürzen, *v. tr.* [in heraldry, used only in the part.] Angekürzt, V. Angestückt.

Ankutschen, *v. intr.* [u. w. seyn, and kommen] to arrive in a coach.

Anlächeln, *v. tr.* to smile on or upon.

Anlachen, *v. tr.* to look at laughing, to smile upon. *Fig.* Das Glück lacht ihn an, fortune favours or smiles on him.

Anlacher, Anlächler, *m.* [-s, *pl.* -] he that smiles upon.

Anlage, *f.* [*pl.* -n] 1) the act of laying on, [in a figurative sense] *a)* the act of laying on taxes or of assessing each citizen &c. in due proportion, assessment, imposition, impost, tax, duty. V. Auflage. Eine — machen, ausschreiben, to impose a tax. *b)* the act of laying out [a street &c.]. Die — eines Gartens machen, to lay out a garden; die — eines Feldes zu Wald [die Einforstung], afforestation. 2) something added. *a)* [= Beilage *y*]. Aus der — werden Sie ersehen, by the annexed you will see. *b)* the cheek-piece of a gun-stock. 3) [something laid on] Die erste — [eines Gemähldes, die Skizze], rough sketch or draft [draught]; die neuen —n bei Heidelberg, the new walks and pleasure grounds near Heidelberg; Anlagen, improvements. *Fig. a)* gift of nature, natural ability, talent, disposition. Er hat keine — zur Dichtkunst, he has no talent for poetry; er hat keine —n dazu, his talents do not lie that way; — zur Schwindsucht, disposition to consumption. *b)* a stock or capital, a fund. Syn. Anlagen, Naturgaben. Anlagen are only such talents or dispositions as render us in an eminent degree capable of acquiring certain accomplishments or perfections, they require exercise and improvement if we wish to arrive at the perfections to which they are the Anlagen. A man may have great Anlagen [talents] for music and yet not become a great musician, if he does not devote himself to the study of it. Naturgaben are endowments or qualities for which we are entirely indebted to nature, without any assistance from art or industry.

Anlallen, *v. tr.* to address in infantine language.

Anlandbar, *adj.* and *adv.* accessible [said of a shore]. Ein —er Ort, a landing-place.

Anlände, *f.* [*pl.* -n] the landing-place.

Anländen, V. Anlanden II.

Anlanden, I. *v. intr.* [u. w. seyn] to come to shore, to land, to disembark. Wir landeten in Havre an, we arrived at Havre. II. *v. tr.* to push to the shore.

Anlangen, I. *v. intr.* [u. w. seyn] 1) to come to, to arrive. Zu Pferde, zu Fuße —, to arrive on horseback, on foot; der Gesandte ist in London angelangt, the ambassador has arrived in London; der Brief ist an Ort und Stelle angelangt, the letter has reached its place of destination. II. *v. tr.* to concern, to relate to. Was mich anlangt, as for me; die Russen —d, with respect or as to the Russians. Syn. Anlangen, Angehen, Betreffen. Anlangen expresses only the reference or relation which one thing has to another; Angehen and Betreffen intimate also an interest or concern which the one has in the other; that the one is affected in some way by the other. Betreffen generally in a disagreeable manner, Angehen in any way.

Anlappen, *v. tr.* 1) to patch to. 2) [among hunters] to spread the toils.

Anlarven, *v. intr.* to fix a mask to.

Anlaschen, *v. tr.* 1) [among foresters] to mark [trees that are to be felled, by paring off a part of the bark], to blaze. 2) [among shoemakers] to put a new strap to a shoe.

Anlaß, *m.* [-sses, *pl.* -lässe] 1) the act of swelling water [without a plural]. 2) *Fig. a)* appearance, likelihood, probability. Es hat allen — dazu, it is very likely, there is every probability of it. *b)* cause, occasion, motive, inducement. — geben, to induce, to occasion; zu einem Gerüchte — geben, to raise a report, to be the author of a rumour. Dieser Vorfall hat zu dem seltsamen Gerüchte — gegeben, daß &c., this event gave occasion to the strange report, that &c.; — zum Lachen geben, to give subject for laughter.

Anlassen, *ir.* I. *v. tr.* 1) to suffer, to stay on, to leave on, to keep on [his coat &c.], not to take off. Ich ließ den Rock an, I kept on my coat. 2) to let loose, to let go. Einen Hund —, to set a dog on; einen Teich —, to let water into a pond; eine Mühle —, to set a mill a-going; die Bälge —, [in forges] to set the bellows a-going. 3) [am. metallists] die Metalle —, to anneal metals; blau —, [steel springs &c.] to blue. V. Anlaufen. 4) to receive with harsh words, to rebuke. Einen übel —, to snub any one; seine Dienstleute hart —, to rattle off one's servants sharply. II. *v. r.* sich —, to have the appearance, to appear. Es läßt sich zum Kriege an, there is an appearance of war; das Wetter läßt sich zum Regen an, it looks as if it would rain; der Knabe läßt sich gut an, he is a hopeful boy; die Sache läßt sich gut an, it promises fair.

Anlauf, *m.* [-es, *pl.* -läufe] 1) the act of running to or up to a thing, start. Einen — nehmen, to take a run, to take a spring or start in order to leap. *Fig.* * and ‡ Er nimmt jedesmal einen gewaltigen —, ehe er seine Meinung von sich gibt, he has a great deal to do or he must make a great exertion, before he can get out what he wishes to say. 2) the swelling of water. Der — der See gegen das Ufer, V. Brandung. 3) any thing that rises in an oblique direction. [in archit., a concave part or ring of a column, lying below the flat member] apophyge, apophygy.

Anlaufen, *ir. v. intr.* [u. w. seyn] 1) to begin to run, to start. 2) to run up, to run up to. Eine Reiterschaar auf den Feind — lassen, to order a troop to rush on the enemy; sie kamen angelaufen, they flocked together; ein wildes Schwein — lassen, [am. hunt.] to let a wild boar run against a boar-spear; das Wild läuft an, [am. hunters] the game comes within gun-shot. *Fig.* Uebel —, to be disappointed; er ist schön angelaufen, he has met with a fine reception; Einen — lassen, to treat any one as he deserves. 3) [to be covered, as it were, with something] to lose lustre or brightness [said of shining bodies], to become dull. Der Spiegel läuft an, the looking-glass tarnishes; Stahl blau — lassen, to make steel blue; vom Roste —, to get rusty; vom Schimmel —, to get mouldy. 4) [among printers] to rut. 5) to rise. Die Fläche läuft sanft an, the plain rises with a gentle slope; der Fluß läuft an, the river swells; der Fluß ist durch den Regen angelaufen, the river is swollen by the rain; die Füße sind ihm angelaufen, his feet are swelled or inflamed. *Fig.* Seine Schulden laufen täglich höher an, his debts increase daily more and more.

II. *v. tr.* to run against [used only in a figurative sense]. Einen —, to importune any one; sie liefen ihn häufig an, they applied frequently and urgently to him.

Anläuten, I. *v. tr.* to ring the bell as a signal for commencing work [chiefly in mining]. II. *v. intr.* Bei Einem —, to ring the bell at any one's house. *Fig.* Er läutete bei ihm hierüber ganz sachte an, he sounded him gently upon this matter.

Anlecken, *v. tr.* to lick. Der Hund leckt mich an, the dog licks me.

Anlegen, I. *v. tr.* 1) to lay against, to put against, to put to. Eine Leiter an die Wand —, to apply a ladder to the wall; Holz —, to add fuel to the fire; Feuer an ein Haus —, to set fire to a house [in order to fire it]; ein Kind —, to put a child to the breast; einen Hund —, to enchain a dog; einem Menschen Fesseln —, to fetter any one; das Gewehr —, to aim or take aim with a gun, to present a firelock; [among coopers] einem Fasse Reife —, to bind a cask with hoops; ein Faß —, to hoop a cask; [in seamen's language] das Schiff —, or mit dem Schiffe —, to go close to the shore; [in seamen's language] die Wand —, to fix the shrouds over the mastheads by their eyes or collar; [among paint.] die ersten schwachen Farben —, to paint slightly. *Fig.* Steuern —, to lay on, or to impose taxes; er hat es auf das Reichwerden angelegt, he aims to be rich; er hat es darauf angelegt, he aims at; es auf ein Räuschchen —, to be in a drinking mood. 2) to put on [a coat &c.]. Kleider —, to dress one's self; eine tiefe Trauer —, to put on a mourning apparel, to go into mourning; Staatskleider —, to put on rich garments, court-dress, full dress; Syn. V. Ankleiden. Hand —, to put the hand to work, to take in hand. *Fig.* Hand — [= anfangen], to set to work; er hat Hand an sich selbst gelegt [= er hat sich selbst umgebracht], he laid violent hands on himself; die letzte Hand —, to put the finishing stroke to. 3) *Fig.* *a*) to employ, to make use of. Seine Zeit gut — [or better: anwenden], to employ one's time well; Geld —, to lay out money; sein Geld sicher —, to place one's money on good security; sein Geld in Ländereien —, to realise one's money, to convert it into land; sein Geld auf Zinsen —, to put out one's money at interest, to put one's money to use; Geld in Waaren —, to vest or invest money in goods; sein ganzes Vermögen in den öffentlichen Fonds —, to vest all one's property in the public funds. *b*) to begin, to lay the foundation. Einen Garten —, to lay out a garden; Ländereien zu Wald —, to afforest land; eine Stadt —, to found a city; ein Gebäude —, to lay the foundation of a building; eine Colonie —, to plant or settle a colony; die Griechen legten Colonien im südlichen Italien und Frankreich an, the Greeks colonized the south of Italy and of France; ein Schiff —, [a sea term] to lay a ship on the stocks; [at whist] was muß ich —? what am I to mark up? *c*) to grow fat, to fatten [said of animals].

II. *v. r.* sich —, 1) to lean against. Das Kind legt sich an die Brust an, the child leans against the breast. 2) to attach to, to fix to, to stick to. Der Kuchen legt sich an die Pfanne an, the cake adheres to the pan. 3) to put on clothes, to dress one's self. 4) *Fig.* to connect one's self with.

III. *v. intr.* [in seamen's lang.] Mit dem Schiffe —, to go close to the shore; bei einem Schiffe —, to lay a ship alongside of another; zur Ladung —, to lay [a ship] alongside of any place to take in her cargo or lading. Syn. Anlegen, Errichten, Stiften. An order is gestiftet, as: Benedict hat den Orden der Benedictiner gestiftet; a manufactory is angelegt; an academy is errichtet, as far as relates to the building of it, and gestiftet in as much as founder is immortalized by it.

Anlegeschloß, *n.* padlock. —spähne, *pl.* [in printing] scale-boards. —stege, *pl.* [in printing] head-sides and foot-sticks.

Anlehen, *n.* [-s] V. Anleihe.

Anlehne, *f.* [*pl.* -n] a thing to lean upon, a back of a chair.

1. **Anlehnen**, *v. tr.* to lean against, to lean upon. Sich an die Wand —, to lean against the wall; die Thür —, to leave the door upon the latch. *Fig.* Das Heer lehnte sich an den Fluß an, the army was drawn up with the river in its rear.

2. **Anlehnen**, V. Lehnen, Leihen, Anleihen, Herleihen.

Anlehnpunkt, *m.* [-es, *pl.* -e] any point or object to lean one's self against. *Fig.* [in milit. aff.] appui.

Anlehren, *v. tr.* 1) to teach, to instruct. 2) [among workmen] to apprentice.

Anleihe, *f.* [*pl.* -n] 1) the act of lending. 2) loan. Oeffentliche —, government-loan.

Anleihen, *v. tr.* to lend.

Anleimen, *v. tr.* to glue on, to agglutinate.

Anleiten, *v. tr.* to guide or to lead to. [in husb.] Die Hopfenranken —, to train the tendrils of hops, to furnish hops with poles. *Fig.* Seine Kinder zur Tugend —, to guide one's children to virtue; zu Künsten und Wissenschaften —, to instruct in arts and sciences.

Anleiter, *m.* [-s, *pl.* -] leader, guider, guide.

Anleitung, *f.* leading, guidance, direction, instruction, conduct. Nach — ihrer Vernunft, as reason directs them. 2) a treatise which instructs how to acquire an art or a science, a guide, a key. Eine — zur englischen Sprache, instructions for learning the English language.

Anlenken, *v. tr.* to direct to. Die Pferde, den Wagen an das Haus —, to drive the horses, the carriage towards or up to the house.

Anlernen, *v. tr.* to acquire by study. V. Erlernen.

Anleuchten, *v. tr.* to let light fall upon a thing, to cast light upon.

Anliegen, *ir. v. intr.* 1) to lie close or near to. Diese Bretter liegen nicht genau aneinander an, these boards don't join well; sein Garten liegt an dem meinigen an, his garden adjoins mine; der Rock liegt nicht gut an, the coat does not fit well, does not sit close enough; die —de Gegend, the bordering or adjacent country; —s des Schreiben, the inclosed letter; [in seamen's language] wo liegt das Schiff an? how does the ship lie, how is her head? seewärts —, to stand for the offing. 2) *Fig.* *a*) to be solicitous or careful. [particularly the part. Angelegen] Sie ließen es sich angelegen seyn, des Königs Ehre vor &c. zu bewahren, they were solicitous to preserve the king's honour from &c.; er läßt sich diese Sache sehr angelegen seyn, he is very careful about it, he bestows great care upon it, he treats it with earnest attention. *b*) Einem —, to petition any one earnestly, to solicit or to press any one.

Anliegen, *n.* [-s] 1) the act of lying close to [without a plural]. 2) *Fig.* *a*) concern, care, solicitude. *b*) a latent desire, a latent wish.

Anliegenheit, *f.* V. Anliegen *n.* 2. *b*)

Anlispeln, *v. tr.* 1) to address any one lispingly. 2) *poet.* [said of the wind] to blow gently upon.

Anloben, *v. tr.* to praise. V. Anpreisen.

Anlocken, *v. tr.* to allure, to entice, to decoy, to inveigle. *Fig.* Bewunderer —, to attract admirers; durch Liebkosungen —, to draw on by caresses; eine —de Gegend, an attractive landscape.

Anlocker, *m.* [-s, *pl.* -] allurer, enticer, inveigler. Die —inn, a coquette, a flirt.

Anlockung, *f.* allurement, enticement.

Anlodern, I. *v. intr.* [u. w. seyn] to begin to blaze or to flame [also in a figurative sense]. II. *v. tr.* to make to blaze, or to flame.

Anlöthen, *v. tr.* 1) to solder or soder to. 2) *Fig.* to unite with.

Anludern, *v. tr.* [among hunters] to allure by a bait [birds and other animals].

Anlügen, *v. tr.* 1) to tell lies concerning &c., to belie, to calumniate by false reports. Einem Etwas —, to belie any one. 2) V. Belügen.

Anluven, *v. intr.* [a sea term] to bring a ship's head closer to the wind, to luff. Luv an! luff!

Anmachen, *v. r.* 1) to fix, to fasten, or join to. *Fig.* Er weiß sich anzumachen, he knows how to insinuate himself. 2) to produce, to cause, to effect. Feuer —, to light or kindle a fire. 3) to mix with a liquid, to supply with moisture. Farben —, to temper colours; sie machen Lehm mit englischem Blute an, they temper clay with blood of Englishmen; * in der Kunst, den Salat anzumachen, übertrifft ihn Niemand, nobody can beat him in making a salad. 4) to adulterate [liquors].

Anmächtigen, *v. r.* sich —, to usurp, to appropriate to one's self by force.

Anmahlen, *v. tr.* 1) to paint on. 2) to paint [a wall &c.]. Sich das Gesicht —, to paint.

Anmahnen, *v. tr.* 1) to exhort, to incite by words or advice. Einen zu Etwas —, to exhort any one to. 2) to put in mind, to force to remember, to remind.

Anmahnung, *f.* exhortation, incitement to that which is good or commendable.

Anmahnungsschreiben, *n.* [in law] monitory.

Anmarsch, *m.* [-es, *pl.* -märsche] march

ing on. Der — eines Heeres, the advance of an army.

Anmarschiren, *v. intr.* [u. w. seyn] to march on, to advance.

Anmaschen, *v. tr.* [among hunters] die Netze —, to string the nets or toils.

Anmaßen, *v. r.* sich —, to assume, to arrogate. Sich eine gesetzwidrige Gewalt —, to assume unwarrantable powers; der Papst maßte sich die Herrschaft über die Könige an, the pope arrogated dominion over kings; hierin maßen wir uns an, besser als Gott selbst zu sehen, was &c., in that we presume to see better than God himself, what &c.; er maßte sich an, der erste Dichter des Jahrhunderts zu seyn, he claims to be the best poet of the age; sich eine Gewalt —, to usurp a power. SYN. Anmaßen [sich], Bemächtigen [sich]. Anmaßen always denotes, to appropriate a thing in an unlawful manner; bemächtigen signifies also, to take possession of in a lawful way, when the thing belongs to no one else, or no one has the right to prevent our taking possession of it. Sich bemächtigen is said only of material things, anmaßen also of immaterial, of rights &c. Cäsar bemächtigte sich des öffentlichen Schatzes [seized the public treasures], and maßte sich die Herrschaft über das römische Reich an [usurped the sovereign authority over the Roman empire].

Anmaßend, *adj.* Sein —es Wesen, his assuming air; ein —es Betragen, an arrogant behaviour; ein —er junger Mensch, a self-sufficient youth.

Anmaßlich, I. *adj.* 1) assumed, arrogated, pretended to, claimed. Sein —es Recht, his pretended right. 2) arrogant, assuming, pretending, arrogative, presumptuous. Ein —er [better: anmaßender] Mensch, an arrogant, presumptuous fellow. II. *adv.* presumptuously, arrogantly.

Anmaßlichkeit, *f.* pretence, pretension.

Anmaßung, *f.* usurpation, assumption, arrogation, pretension, presumption. Es dürfte weder — noch Zweifelsucht seyn, Beider Meinungen in Zweifel zu ziehen, it may not be presumptive or sceptical to doubt of both opinions.

Anmaßungsgeist, *m.* arrogance, presumption, conceitedness. —voll, *adj.* very arrogant or presumptuous, conceited, haughty.

Anmästen, I. *v. tr.* to make fat, to fatten. II. *v. r.* sich —, to fatten [one's self].

Anmauern, *v. tr.* 1) to join by masonry, to wall to. 2) to add by masonry.

Anmaulen, *v. tr.* to grumble [mutter] against any one, to pout at.

Anmelden, *v. tr.* to announce, to give notice. Sich —, to present one's self; sich — lassen, to send in one's name; ich habe Sie angemeldet, I have told my master that you are here.

Anmelken, *v. tr.* to begin to milk.

Anmengen, *v. tr.* to mix or mingle together, to blend.

Anmerkebuch, *n.* [-es, *pl.* -bücher] table-book, memorandum-book, note-book.

Anmerken, I. *v. intr.* to make a remark, to observe. II. *v. tr.* 1) to mark, to note, to put down, to write down. Man hat alle seine Sachen angemerkt, they have noted down, taken an inventory of all his things. 2) to observe, to perceive, to see. Man merkte ihm den Rausch an, one could perceive that he was tipsy.

Anmerkenswerth, I. *adj.* worthy of note, remarkable. II. *adv.* remarkably.

Anmerker, *m.* [-s, *pl.* -] 1) he that observes, marks or notes. 2) annotator.

Anmerklich, I. *adj.* 1) remarkable. 2) perceivable. II. *adv.* 1) remarkably. 2) perceivably.

Anmerkung, *f.* 1) remark, observation. 2) note, annotation, comment, illustration. Scott's —en über die heilige Schrift, the comments of Scott on the scriptures. SYN. Anmerkung, Bemerkung. The derivation of the word Anmerkung [from an and merken], gives us the idea of thoughts being added to others, whether our own or those of another. Thus, the notes by which a text is explained or the remarks that are subjoined, are denominated Anmerkungen. The thoughts which observations made during a journey through France might give occasion to, might be published under the title of „Bemerkungen über den gegenwärtigen Zustand von Frankreich" [„Observations on the present state of France"]. In this instance one could not say Anmerkungen.

Anmerkungs-werth, —würdig, V. Anmerkenswerth.

Anmessen, *ir. v. tr.* to measure, to take measure. Einem ein Kleid —, to take any one's measure for a coat, to take the measure of a coat, to measure any one for &c. *Fig.* to adapt, to fit or suit, to apportion. Dieses Wort ist dem Gegenstande vollkommen angemessen, this word is very well adapted to the subject.

Anmieneln, *v. tr.* to look at fondly.

Anmischen, *v. tr.* to mix, mix up.

‡ **Anmit**, V. Hiemit.

Anmurren, *v. tr.* to murmur at, to grumble at.

Anmuth, *f.* 1) pleasingness, pleasantness, sweetness, agreeableness, charm. Die — eines Thales, pleasantness of a valley; die — eines Ortes, einer Aussicht, the amenity of a place, of a prospect. 2) grace, gracefulness, graciousness. Sie singt mit —, she sings gracefully.

Anmuth-los, I. *adj.* 1) unpleasant. 2) ungracious. II. *adv.* 1) unpleasantly. 2) ungraciously. —reich, I. *adj.* very pleasant or gracious. II. *adv* very pleasantly or graciously. —voll, *adj.* 1) attractive, pleasant, sweet, charming. 2) graceful. Ein —volles Wesen, a graceful air.

Anmuthen, V. Zumuthen, Ansinnen.

Anmuthig, I. *adj.* 1) pleasant, agreeable, sweet, charming. Eine —e Gegend, a pleasant landscape; eine —e Abwechslung von Berg und Thal, a sweet interchange of hill and valley; eine —e Erzählung, a pleasant story. 2) graceful, gracious. Eine —e Gestalt, a graceful figure. II. *adv.* 1) pleasantly, sweetly. 2) gracefully, graciously.

Anmuthiglich, *adv.* pleasantly.

Anmuthung, V. Zumuthung.

Anna, **Anne**, [-s, -ns, *pl.* -n] and *dimin.* Annchen, Ännchen [a name of women] Ann, Nancy, Nanny.

Annadeln, *v. tr.* to pin to or on.

Annageln, *v. tr.* to nail, nail to or on, to fasten with nails. Eine Planke —, to fasten a plank with nails. *Fig.* Wie angenagelt, as if nailed to the spot.

Annagen, *v. tr.* to begin to gnaw at, to gnaw, to fret.

Annahen, **Annähern**, I. *v. tr.* V. Nähern, Anrücken. II. *v. intr.* [u. w. seyn] to approach, to draw near. Das neue Jahr naht rasch an [heran], the new year is nearing or approaching fast. III. *v. r.* sich —, to approach. Sich heimlich —, to creep on, to steal on or near.

Annähen, *v. tr.* to sew on or to. Ein Stück Zeug an ein anderes —, to sew one piece of cloth or stuff on to another; einen Block —, [in seamen's language] to fix or seize a block.

Annahme, *f.* [*pl.* -n] the act of taking or accepting. Die — an Kindes Statt, adoption; die — eines Wechsels, [in commerce] acceptance; in der gewöhnlichen — des Wortes, in the usual acceptation of the word; — eines Beweissatzes, the admission of a position.

Annahung, **Annäherung** [the more usual word], *f.* approach, approaching, approximation. Gegenseitige — befördert das Entstehen der Freundschaft, mutual advances tend to form friendship.

Annäherungsgraben, *m.* [in a siege] approaches, parallels, trenches.

* **Annalen**, *pl.* annals, the books containing annals. Die — des Tacitus, the annals of Tacitus.

Annalenschreiber, *m.* annalist.

* **Annalist**, *m.* [-en, *pl.* -en] V. Annalenschreiber.

Annässen, *v. tr.* to moisten a little, to wet, to damp.

* **Annaten**, *pl.* the first fruits, annats.

Annchen, **Ännchen**, V. Anna.

‡ **Annebst**, V. Nebst.

Annehmbar, *adj.* and *adv.* that may be accepted, acceptable [said of the stipulations of a treaty &c.].

Annehmen, *ir.* I. *v. tr.* to take or receive what is offered. Ein Geschenk —, to accept a present; Geld —, to take money; [in a more figurative sense] die Sau nimmt den Jäger an, the sow assaults the huntsman; die Hunde nehmen die Fährte an, [among hunters] the hounds take scent; der Magen nimmt die Speisen nicht an, the stomach ejects or casts up meat; ein Zeug nimmt die Farbe an, a stuff takes the die. *Fig.* *a*) [bei sich aufnehmen] Einen Bedienten —, to take into one's service, to engage a servant; Einen an Kindes Statt —, to adopt any one. *b*) [sich etwas gefallen lassen] Einen Antrag —, to accept or to close with an offer; Jemands Entschuldigung —, to admit of or to accept of any one's excuse; ich nahm Ihre matten Entschuldigungen an, I took your weak excuses; ein ehrlicher Mann kann selbst eines Schurken Rath —, an honest man can take even a knave's advice; guten Rath —, to take good advice; Besuche —, to receive or to see company; einen Wechsel —, to accept a bill of exchange; eine Herausforderung —, to take up a challenge. *c*) to admit as true, to let pass undisputed, to take or receive as one's own. Ich nehme diesen Satz nicht an, I do not admit or grant this position; eines Andern Meinung —, to adopt the opinion of another; Etwas ohne Einschränkung —, to concede something without limitation; als ausgemacht —, to take for granted; ich nahm es für Scherz an, I took it for a joke; Sie werden dieß doch nicht für Ernst —, you will not take it in earnest. *d*) to take or take upon one, to assume. Eine Gestalt —, to assume a shape; üble Gewohnheiten —, to contract vicious habits; die christliche Religion —, to embrace the christian religion; den Schein —, to pretend; eine angenommene Freundlichkeit, an assumed or affected friendliness.

II. *v. r* sich [einer Sache] —, to take care of, to interest one's self for; sich einer Person —, to interest one's self for a person, to embrace the interests of, to protect a person.

Annehmen, *n.* [-s] acceptance. V. Annahme.

Annehmenswerth, **Annehmenswürdig**, *adj.* and *adv.* that may be accepted, acceptable.

Annehmer, *m.* [-s, *pl.* -] [one who accepts, (in commerce) he that accepts a bill of exchange] acceptor, accepter.

Annehmlich, *adj.* 1) acceptable. 2) agreeable, pleasant. V. Angenehm.

Annehmlichkeit, *f.* 1) acceptableness. 2) agreeableness, pleasantness. 3) [that which gives security from want, and furnishes moderate enjoyment] comfort. Die —en des Lebens, the comforts of life. Syn. Annehmlichkeiten, Reize. Reize refers more especially to the exterior natural beauties, which belong to a female person; under Annehmlichkeiten are generally understood, such amiable qualities or agreeable accomplishments as she may have acquired by art and industry.

Anneigen, I. *v. tr.* to incline to. II. *v. r.* sich —, to incline one's self to [chiefly in a figurative sense]. Sich Einem —, to insinuate one's self in any one's favour. V. Zuneigen. III. *v. intr.* to incline and approach nearer together, to converge. —de Linien, [in mathem.] convergent lines; —de Strahlen, [in optics] converging rays.

Annesteln, *v. tr.* to lace, to tie with points.

Annetzen, *v. tr.* to wet, to moisten a little, to damp.

Annetzpinsel, *m.* a brush used by masons.

Annicken, *v. tr.* 1) to nod to. 2) to greet by nodding.

Annieten, *v. tr.* to rivet, to rivet to. *Fig.* Er ist an diesen Fleck wie angenietet, he is riveted, as it were, to the spot.

Annisten, *v. intr.* to build or make a nest, to nest, to nestle against any thing. Die Schwalben nisten an den Häusern an, the swallows build against the houses.

Anniversarien, *n. pl.* [stated days returning with the revolution of the year] anniversaries.

‡ **Annoch**, *adv.* V. Noch.

* **Annomination**, *f.* [the use of words nearly alike in sound, but of different meanings] annomination, a paronomasy [as: ihr Berge, berget mich vor meinen Verfolgern!].

* **Annonce**, *f.* [*pl.* -n] V. Anzeige or Ankündigung.

* **Annonciren**, V. Ankündigen.

* **Annuität**, *f.* [*pl.* -en] [a sum of money, payable yearly, to continue for a given number of years; an annual income, charged on the person of the grantor] annuity.

* **Annulliren**, *v. tr.* to annul, to abolish, to abrogate, to nullify [used appropriately of laws &c.]. V. Abschaffen.

Anöhren, *v. tr.* to provide with a ring or an eye. Einen Topf —, to furnish a pot with an ear or handle.

Anölen, *v. tr.* to moisten with oil, to anoint.

* **Anomalie**, *f.* [*pl.* -en] anomaly, irregularity, deviation from the common rule.

* **Anomalisch**, *adj.* anomalous, irregular.

* **Anomalistisch**, *adj.* anomalistic, anomalistical. Das —e Jahr, [in astronomy] anomalistic year.

* **Anonym**, **Anonymisch**, *adj.* anonymous, wanting a name.

* **Anonymus**, *m.* 1) an anonymous writer. 2) a nameless fellow.

Anordnen, *v. tr.* 1) to order = to bid, to direct, to command. Er hat es also angeordnet, he has commanded it thus. 2) to put in proper order, to order, to regulate, to arrange. Gott hat Alles weise angeordnet, God has wisely ordained every thing; ein Fest —, to order a feast; Truppen zu einer Schlacht —, to draw up troops in order of battle; der Baumeister hat die Zimmer dieses Hauses gut angeordnet, the architect has disposed the apartments of this house well.

Anordner, *m.* [-s, *pl.* -] 1) an orderer, arranger, director. 2) [sometimes for] a compiler or editor.

Anordnung, *f.* 1) ordering, bidding, direction. 2) ordering, disposition, regulation, arrangement. Er hat verschiedene —en gemacht, he has made various arrangements; er hat in seinem Testamente verschiedene —en wegen seines Leichenbegängnisses gemacht, he left in his will various directions respecting his funeral.

Anpacken, *v. tr.* 1) to lay hold of violently or roughly, to seize, to grasp. Ich wurde von Räubern angepackt, I was attacked by robbers; mein Pudel hat ihn angepackt, my poodle flew at him. *Fig.* Einen —, to fall upon any one with unfriendly words, to attack any one. 2) to pack to.

Anpappen, *v. tr.* to paste on or to.

Anpassen, I. *v. intr.* to fit, to suit, to be suitable. Sein Rock paßt gut an, his coat fits well. II. *v. tr.* to fit, to suit, to adapt. Einen Rock —, to fit a coat. *Fig.* die Vorräthe dem Bedürfnisse —, to adapt one's provisions to one's wants; einen Deckel auf eine Schachtel —, to fit a lid on a box; dieses Wort ist dem Gegenstande sehr gut angepaßt, this word is very well adapted to the subject.

Anpassend, *adj.* fit, suitable, congruous.

Anpassung, *f.* the act of making suitable, adaptation.

Anpaßlich, I. *adj.* fit, suitable. II. *adv.* fitly, suitably, properly.

Anpatschen, *v. intr.* [u. w. seyn] to plash against.

Anpechen, V. Anpichen.

Anpeitschen, I. *v. intr.* to strike with a whip against. II. *v. tr.* to drive forward by whipping, to lash on.

Anpfahlen, *v. tr.* to fasten or support with pales or stakes, to fasten to a pale or stake [trees &c.].

Anpfeifen, *ir.* I. *v. tr.* to whistle at, to call by whistling. II. *v. intr.* [u. w. seyn] Angepfiffen kommen, to approach whistling.

Anpflanzen, *v. tr.* 1) to begin to prepare for crops, to cultivate. 2) to plant, to set. Ein Feld mit Taback —, to plant a field with tobacco.

Anpflanzer, *m.* [-s, *pl.* -] a planter, a settler.

Anpflanzung, *f.* 1) planting, cultivation. 2) plantation. —en, improvements.

Anpflöcken, *v. tr.* to peg to, to fasten with pegs.

Anpflügen, I. *v. tr.* 1) to begin to plough, to plough a little. 2) to join by ploughing. II. *v. intr.* to drive against something in ploughing.

Anpfropfen, *v. tr.* 1) to add by grafting, to ingraft. 2) *Fig.* to fill, to glut, to cram.

Anpichen, I. *v. tr.* 1) to pitch [a ship]. 2) to fasten with pitch to. II. *v. intr. Fig.* to stick to, to adhere to. Diesem Küchlein picht noch die Eierschale an, the shell still sticks to this chicken.

Anpicken, I. *v. tr.* to pick or peck at. II. *v. intr.* to begin to pick or peck.

Anpinseln, *v. tr.* 1) to paint grossly, to dawb. 2) *Fig.* to set in the worst light.

Anpissen, *v. tr.* to piss against [a wall &c.]. Ihr Hund hat mich angepißt, your dog has pissed upon me.

Anplappern, *v. tr.* to address any one in a prattling manner.

† **Anplärren**, *v. tr.* to bawl at.

Anplatschen, *v. tr.* [u. w. seyn] to plash against.

Anplätschern, *v. intr.* to dabble at, to wet by little dips or strokes.

Anplatzen, *v. intr.* [u. w. seyn] 1) to begin to burst. 2) to burst against. *Fig.* † and ‡ Da kam er unerwartet mit seiner Nachricht angeplatzt, he unexpectedly burst out with his news.

Anplätzen, *v. tr.* [among foresters] to blaze [a tree].

Anplaudern, *v. tr.* to address any one in a chattering, babbling manner.

Anpochen, *v. tr.* to knock at. An die Thür —, to rap or thump at the door. Syn. Anpochen, Anklopfen. Anpochen denotes a more violent knocking than anklopfen. One can anklopfen at a door softly, but not anpochen without a loud noise.

Anpoltern, *v. intr.* 1) [u. w. haben] to rattle at, to knock at. 2) [u. w. seyn and comm. with kommen] angepoltert kommen, to come on or to approach in a blustering manner.

Anposaunen, I. *v. tr.* 1) to announce by sound of trumpet. 2) *Fig.* to advertise in an extolling manner. Ein Buch in den Zeitungen —, to puff a book in the newspapers. II. *v. intr.* anposaunt kommen, to come near, to approach with sounds of trumpets.

Anprall, *m.* [-es, *pl.* -e] 1) the act of bounding or flying against. 2) a bruise, a contusion.

Anprallen, *v. intr.* [u. w. seyn] to bound against, to fly against, to strike against.

Anprasseln, *v. intr.* [u. w. seyn] to strike or beat against with a rustling, crackling noise.

Anpredigen, *v. tr.* to preach at, to tutor. *Fig.* Er predigt ihm tagtäglich einen geordneten Lebenswandel an, he preaches to him every day, to follow an orderly course of life.

Anpreisen, *v. tr.* to praise to another, to recommend, to cry up, to set forth, to vaunt. Syn. Anpreisen, Preisen, Empfehlen. Preisen signifies simply to praise or extol the good qualities of a person or thing. Anpreisen expresses also an intention to incline the person, to whom we praise a thing, favorably towards t. Empfehlen contains the same intention, with this difference, that we may [empfehlen] endeavour to incline a person favorably towards the thing we praise, from other motives than merely on account of its intrinsic worth. A merchant preist seine Waaren an [praises his goods], tries to convince us of their real value or goodness, in order to induce us to purchase them; but he can empfehlen [recommend] goods of an inferior quality on account of their cheapness.

Anpreißlich, I. *adj.* recommendable. II. *adv.* recommendably.

Anprellen, *v. tr.* to cause to bound against, to throw against. Einen Ball wider die Wand —, to throw a ball against the wall.

Anpressen, *v. tr.* to squeeze or press against.

Anprickeln, *v. tr.* to drive, to impel by pricking.

Anproben, * **Anprobiren**, *v. tr.* to try on, to put on [clothes] for trial.

Anpudern, *v. tr.* to sprinkle with hair-powder.

† **Anpuffen**, *v. intr.* [u. w. seyn] to pop against.

Anpunkten, *v. tr.* to mark with dots, to dot.

Anpusten, I. *v. tr.* 1) to blow, to breath upon. 2) to blow [the fire &c.]. II. *v. intr.* ‡ [u. w. seyn] Angepustet kommen, to come near or to approach puffing and blowing.

Anputz, *m.* [-s] 1) the act of dressing. Sie

braucht eine Stunde zu ihrem —e, she requires an hour to dress. 2) ornamental clothing, dress, finery.

Anputzen, *v. tr.* to put on rich garments, to adorn, to embellish, to dress.

Anquaken, Anquäken, Anquiken, *v. tr.* to croak at. *Fig.* to address any one in a croaking, whining tone.

Anqualmen, I. *v. intr.* [u. w. seyn] to smoke or to send vapours at. II. *v. tr.* to cause to smoke at. Eine ganze Wolke von Rauch qualmte uns an, a whole cloud of smoke came rolling towards us; Einen mit Tabakswolken —, to blow the fume of tabacco into any one's face, to smoke in any one's face.

Anquerlen, *v. tr.* to mix together, to beat up by means of a twirling-stick.

Anquetschen, *v. tr.* to squeeze to.

Anquicken, *v. tr.* [in metallurgy] to mix quicksilver with gold or silver, to amalgamate.

Anquickung, *f.* [in metallurgy] amalgamation.

Anracken, *v. tr.* [a sea term] to fasten [the yards] with a parrel.

Anraffen, *v. tr.* to draw by snatching.

Anrainen, *v. intr.* to border upon.

Anraken, V. Raken.

Anrammen, *v. tr.* to fasten by ramming.

Anranken, I. *v. r.* sich —, to catch and hold on by means of tendrils, to clasp, to creep. Der sich anrankende Epheu, the clasping ivy. II. *v. intr.* to fasten by means of tendrils.

Anraspeln, *v. tr.* to begin to rasp, to rasp a little.

Anrasseln, I. *v. tr.* to rattle at. II. *v. intr.* [u. w. seyn] = angerasselt kommen, to come near or approach with a loud noise or rattling.

Anrath, *m.* [-es] V. Das Anrathen.

Anrathen, *v. tr.* to give counsel to, to advise. Ich rathe Ihnen an, vorsichtig zu seyn bei &c., I advise you to be cautious of &c.

Anrathen, *n.* [-s] counsel, advice.

Anräthig, *adj.* and *adv.* giving counsel, advising.

Anrauchen, I. *v. intr.* 1) to smoke at or against. 2) to be seasoned by smoke. Diese Speise ist angeraucht, this meat is seasoned by smoking, is smoked. II. *v. tr.* 1) to begin to smoke. Eine Pfeife —, to light a tabacco pipe. Eine neue Pfeife —, to smoke the first time out of a new pipe. 2) Einen —, to blow the fume of tabacco into any one's face. 3) to be coloured by smoke. Eine Pfeife —, to give a dark colour to a tabacco pipe by smoking.

Anräuchern, I. *v. tr.* 1) to apply smoke to, [but chiefly] to perfume a thing. 2) to smoke a little [a ham]. II. *v. intr.* to begin to be smoked.

Anräumen, *v. tr.* to clear away, to remove.

Anrauschen, *v. intr.* [u. w. seyn] to come near with a rushing noise. Angerauscht kommen, to rush on.

Anrechen, *v. tr.* to rake towards or against a thing.

Anrechnen, *v. tr.* to charge to account, to reckon. Wie viel rechnen Sie dafür an? how much do you charge for that. *Fig.* Sie rechnen es hoch an, you rate it very high; er rechnete es ihm als eine Wohlthat an, he accounted it to him for a benefit; ich rechne es seiner Unwissenheit an, I impute it to his ignorance; er rechnet den schlimmen Erfolg mir an, he attributes the bad success to me.

Anrecht, *n.* [-es, *pl.* -e] a right to claim or demand, a title to any thing. Der Fürst hatte ein Anrecht auf den Thron, the prince had a claim to the throne.

Anrecken, *v. tr.* to join to a thing by stretching.

Anrede, *f.* 1) [Das Anreden] a speaking to a person, address. 2) [a formal manner of speech] address. Der Präsident hielt eine kurze —, the president made a short address; eine — an den Gerichtshof halten, to address the court; Radziwill hielt eine — an das polnische Heer, Radziwill harangued the Polish army.

Anrede-fall, *m.* [in grammar] vocative. —**tag**, *m.* [am. printers] day on which a printer is engaged.

Anreden, *v. tr.* 1) to speak to, to apply to by words, to address. Er redete mich auf der Straße an, he accosted me in the streets; [am. printers] einen Buchdrucker —, to propose to a printer to engage himself for the next six months. 2) Einem etwas —, to persuade any one to take, to buy &c. any thing. V. Aufschwatzen.

Anrege, *f.* V. Anregung.

Anregen, *v. tr.* 1) to put in motion, to give spirit or vigour, to animate, to stimulate or incite, to stir up. Einen zu etwas —, to incite any one to a thing. 2) to bring to mind by a slight mention or remote allusion, to hint. † Angeregter Maßen, as mentioned before.

Anregung, *f.* 1) incitation, stimulation, incitement. 2) the act of mentioning slighty, of hinting. Bringe keine Frage über Gerichtsbarkeit in —, stir not questions of jurisdiction; er brachte diese Angelegenheit bei dem Minister wiederholt in —, he repeatedly reminded the minister, or put him in mind, of this concern.

Anreiben, *ir. v. tr.* 1) to begin to rub. 2) to impart by rubbing. 3) to add by rubbing.

Anreichern, *v. tr.* [in metallurgy] to purify or enrich ores by fusion.

Anreifen, [from Reif] *v. intr.* [u. w. seyn] to begin to rime.

Anreihen, I. *v. tr.* 1) to file on a string, to string [pearls &c.]. V. also Aufreihen. *Fig.* Daran lassen sich viele Folgerungen —, from this may be deduced many inferences. 2) to sew to slightly, to baste on. Eine Bonnette —, [a sea-term] to lace on a bonnet. II. *v. r.* sich —, to rank with.

Anreihnadel, *f.* [*pl.* -n] a needle used for filing or stringing dried fruit &c. on a string.

Anreinen, V. Anrainen.

Anreißen, *ir. v. tr.* 1) to begin to tear. 2) to take off, to break in upon. 3) to chalk out, to sketch, to draw. 4) [among chair-makers] to mark with an awl.

Anreißer, *m.* [-s, *pl.* -] 1) one that begins to tear or to break in upon. 2) [among goldsmiths] a scraper.

Anreiten, *ir.* I. *v. intr.* [u. w. seyn] 1) to come near on horseback, to ride near; [also with kommen] Er kam an die Kirche angeritten, he rode up to the church. 2) to ride against. II. *v. tr.* 1) Ein Pferd —, to ride a horse for the first time, to break a horse. 2) Einen —, to ride up to any one; seine Schwadron ritt muthig gegen den Feind an, his troop courageously charged the enemy.

Anreiz, *m.* [-es, *pl.* -e] incitement, motive, impulse, [Americ.] stimulus. Die Liebe zum Gelde ist ein mächtiger — zu &c., the love of money is a powerful incentive to &c.

Anreizen, *v. tr.* to move to action by impulse or influence, to incite, to stimulate. Einen zum Bösen —, to entice any one to evil, to entice any one to do evil, to instigate any one to do evil; sie bot alle Künste der Gefallsucht auf, ihn zur Liebe anzureizen, she made use of all her coquettish arts, to kindle in him the flame of love; Einen zu einem Verbrechen —, to abet any one; eine Person, die eine andere zu einem Verbrechen anreizt, abettor.

Anreizung, *f.* 1) the act of inciting, incitation, incitement. 2) V. Anreiz.

Anreizungsmittel, *n.* incentive, provocative, stimulant.

Anrennen, *ir.* [with some authors *reg.*] I. *v. intr.* [u. w. seyn and kommen] 1) to advance or to approach running. Angerannt kommen, to come running; gegen Einen —, to run a tilt at any one, [to set out from the barrier at a race] to start. 2) to run against, to begin to run. *Fig.* Er ist schön angerannt, [ironically] he met with a fine reception; übel —, to meet with an ill reception or ill success. II. *v. tr.* 1) to rush upon, to assail. Die ein [or auf ein] Rudel Hirsche anrennenden Jagdhunde, [among hunters] running riot. 2) to run any one against [a wall &c.].

Anrichte, *f.* [*pl.* -n] V. Anrichttisch.

Anrichten, *v. tr.* to prepare or fit for use, to dress, [especially] to dress or serve up dinner. Die Fische —, to dress fish; das Holz —, [among carpenters] to dress timber; das Kupfer [in metallurgy] to prepare the copper for liquation. *Fig.* to cause, to produce. Unheil —, to do mischief; Sie haben da etwas Schönes angerichtet, you have made a precious piece of work of it.

Anricht-kunst, *f.* the act of dressing or serving up a dinner. —**löffel**, *m.* [a large spoon] a ladle. —**schüssel**, *f.* [a broad open vessel, used for serving up meat and various kinds of food at table] a dish. —**tisch**, *m.* [a table on which meat is prepared for use] the dresser, a side-board.

Anrichter, *m.* [-s, *pl.* -] 1) one who dresses, dresser. 2) [a large spoon used in kitchens] a ladle.

Anrichtung, *f.* 1) the act of dressing or fitting for use. 2) [in horology] detents.

Anriechen, *ir. v. tr.* 1) to smell at. Eine Blume —, to smell at a flower. 2) to perceive by smelling, to know by the smell. Man riecht ihm den Wein an, one can perceive the smell of wine on him, one can smell that he has been drinking. 3) to emit a smell. Diese Speise &c. riecht mich sehr gut an, this dish &c. has a very agreeable or savorous smell.

Anringeln, *v. tr.* to fasten by small rings.

Anringen, *v. tr.* 1) to fasten by rings. 2) to furnish with rings, to ring. II. *ir. v. intr.* to struggle for. Er hat muthig gegen sein böses Schicksal angerungen, he boldly struggled against his evil fortune. V. Ankämpfen.

Anrinnen, *ir. v. intr.* [u. w. seyn] 1) to run near [said of fluids]. 2) to run against [said of fluids].

Anritt, *m.* [-es, *pl.* -e] 1) to approach on horseback. 2) the first trial of riding. 3) [formerly] the whole equipment, accoutrements of a cavalier.

Anritzen, *v. tr.* 1) to make a little scratch in a thing. 2) to mark by scratches.

Anrollen, I. *v. intr.* 1) [u. w. seyn and chiefly in the past part. of rollen] to approach rolling. Wir sahen die Lawine angerollt kommen, we saw the avalanche coming rolling on; wir sprachen eben von ihm, als er [in seiner Kutsche] anrollte or angerollt kam, we were just speaking of him, when he drove up in his carriage. 2) to roll against. II. *v. tr.* 1) to cause to roll against. 2) [am. hunt.] Die Hunde rollen das Wild an, the hounds open at the game, without pursuing it.

Anrosten, *v. intr.* [u. w. seyn] 1) to rust on. Der Ring ist an die Stange angerostet, the ring is rusted fast on to the pole. 2) to begin to rust. Diese Klinge ist etwas angerostet, this blade is a little touched by the rust.

Anrötheln, *v. tr.* [among dyers, carpenters &c.] to mark with red chalk.

Anrotzen, *v. tr.* to bespatter or sprinkle with snot.

Anrüchig, Anrüchtig, *adj.* and *adv.* not reputable, not in esteem, not honourable, notorious, ill-famed. —e Gesellschaft, disreputable company.

Anrüchigkeit, *f.* disreputation, want of good name or reputation, ill name.

Anrücken, I. *v. intr.* [u. w. seyn] to approach, to draw near or nigh. Der Feind rückt an, the enemy advances, approaches. *Fig.* Die Zeit rückt an, time approaches; der Tag rückt an, the day approaches or draws on. II. *v. tr.* to bring or to move near to. Rücken Sie den Tisch näher an die Bank an, push the table nearer to the bench.

Anrudern, I. *v. intr.* [u. w. seyn, also with kommen] 1) to approach by means of rowing. An das Ufer —, to row ashore; an das Schiff —, to row aboard; [sea term] angerudert! give way! 2) [in seaman's language] to row against. II. *v. tr.* Das Schiff an das Land —, to row the boat ashore.

Anruf, *m.* [-es, *pl.* -e] 1) the act of calling or appealing to. Als er auf den — der Schildwache nicht stehen blieb, schoß sie ihr Gewehr auf ihn ab, not standing when challenged, the sentry fired on him. 2) [in law] an action upon appeal.

Anrufen, *n.* [-s] V. Anruf and Anrufung.

Anrufen, *ir. v. tr.* 1) to call to. Die Schildwachen haben Befehl, nach 10 Uhr die Leute anzurufen, the sentries have ordres to challenge people after ten o'clock. 2) to call, to invoke or appeal to. Einen um Schutz —, to call upon any one for protection; laßt uns Gott in der Sprache seiner Kirche —, let us call on God in the voice of his church; alle Götter anrufend, die droben herrschen, imploring all the gods that reign above; ich rufe aber Gott an zum Zeugen [2. Cor. 1.], I call God for a record; ein höheres Gericht —, to appeal.

Anrufer, *m.* [-s, *pl.* -] 1) one that calls to, invokes or appeals. 2) [in law, one who removes a cause from a lower to a higher tribunal] appellant.

Anrufung, *f.* 1) the act of calling to. 2) invocation; [in law] appeal.

Anrufungs-gericht, *n.* court of appeals. —rath, *m.* a judge of a court of appeals.

Anrühmen, *v. tr.* to praise, to speak in favour of, to commend.

Anrühren, *v. tr.* 1) to feel with the hand, to handle, to touch. *Fig.* Den guten Namen eines Andern —, to hurt the reputation of another. 2) *Fig.* [in law] to mention. 3) to mix by stirring. Mörtel —, to mix or plash mortar; angerührte Farben, water colours.

Anrührung, *f.* 1) touching, handling. 2) mixing.

An's, [*abbrev. and instead of* an das] Bis — Ende, to the very end; bis — Knie, up to one's knee.

Ansäbeln, *v. tr.* to cut roughly.

Ansacken, I. *v. tr.* to lay hold of, to seize. II. *v. r.* † sich —, to fill, to glut, to eat one's fill.

Ansäen, *v. tr.* 1) to sow [a field]. 2) [among tanners and furriers] to sprinkle with meal [a hide or skin].

Ansage, *f.* 1) the act of making known, notification, intimation [without a plural]. Die — bei einem Reichstage, proposition, matter submitted for the deliberation of the diet. 2) an errand, a message.

Ansage-zettel, *m.* a bill notifying something.

Ansagen, *v. tr.* 1) to bring word, to notify. 2) to announce, to publish, to proclaim. Eine Versammlung —, to call a meeting; ein Schauspiel —, to give out a play; zu Rathe —, to summon to a council; zur Wache —, to warn for guard; sich — lassen, to send in or up one's name; sag an! speak!

Ansägen, *v. tr.* to begin to saw.

Ansager, *m.* [-s, *pl.* -] messenger, summoner.

Ansammeln, I. *v. tr.* to gather, to accumulate, to collect together. II. *v. r.* sich —, to collect, to increase, to gather. Die Wolken sammeln sich im Westen an, the clouds are gathering in the west.

Ansäßig, *adj.* and *adv.* having gained a permanent residence or inhabitancy, domiciled, domiciliated. Er ist hier —, er hat sich hier — gemacht, he is domiciled or has settled himself here.

Ansäßigkeit, *f.* a state of being domiciled.

Ansatz, *m.* [-es, *pl.* -sätze] 1) the act of putting or setting to or near. 2) mode of bringing one thing near another; [in music] the method of placing the mouth to a wind-instrument so as to produce tone, and the power of producing a tone. Dieser Flötenspieler hat einen vortrefflichen —, this fluteplayer has an excellent embouchure. 3) *Fig.* *a*) a disposition, inclination, propensity. — zur Träumerei, disposition to reverie. Er hat einen — von Wassersucht, he has a disposition to dropsy. *b*) rate [in an account]. 4) a thing put or set to. *a*) the mouth-piece of a wind-instrument. *b*) [a sea term] the headpiece of the stem. *c*) a tube of metal adjoined to a horn or trumpet [to raise or lower the tone]. *d*) [in gunnery] the reinforce. *e*) [in anatomy] Der — eines Knochens, epiphysis, epiphysy. *f*.) [in botany, an excrescence from the theca of the mosci] apophysis.

Ansatz-größe, *f.* [in mathematics, an infinitely small quantity] a differential. —rechnung, *f.* [in mathematics] a differential calculus or method.

Ansäuern, *v. tr.* to sour a little [a piece of dough]. V. Einsäuern.

† **Ansaufen**, *v. r.* sich —, to drink to the fill or to get drunk.

Ansaugen, [commonly] *ir.* I. *v. tr.* to begin to suck. II. *v. r.* sich —, 1) to fill with sucking. 2) to fasten by sucking. Der Blutigel hat sich angesaugt, the leech has taken.

Ansäuseln, *v. tr.* to blow or breathe gently upon [said of any calm and soft wind, and figuratively of other things].

Ansausen, *v. intr.* to come near, to approach roaring, blustering or boisterously. Die Truppen hielten Stand, obwol die Kugeln von allen Seiten angesaust kamen, the troops stood their ground, in spite of the balls which came whistling round them; er kam, wie der Sturmwind, angesaust, he came rattling on like a hurricane.

Anschaben, *v. tr.* 1) to begin to scrape. 2) to add to by scraping.

Anschachern, *v. tr.* [in contempt] to buy.

Anschaffen, *v. tr.* I. *reg.* to provide, to procure, [in commerce] to remit. Vorräthe —, to buy provisions; sich Kleider —, to furnish one's self with clothes; er muß sich Stiefel und Schuhe selbst —, he must find himself in boots and shoes. II. *ir.* to create with, to create in. Angeschaffen, inborn, innate, native. Das Anschaffen, 1) the act of providing or making provision. 2) the act of creating with or in.

Anschaffer, *m.* [-s, *pl.* -] 1) provider, purveyor, provisor, furnisher. 2) [in commerce] remitter.

Anschaffung, *f.* provision, [in commerce] remittance

Anschäften, *v. tr.* 1) to provide with a shaft, stock, handle or leg. Ein Gewehr —, to stock a gun; ein Paar Stiefel —, to put new legs to a pair of boots. 2) [among carpenters] to nail the joists to the sleepers.

Anschälen, *v. tr.* to begin to peel or pare [an apple].

Anschalmen, V. Anlaschen.

Anschanzen, *v. tr.* [in mining] to dispose all for working.

Anscharen, *v. intr.* [in mining] to unite in one lode.

Anschärfen, *v. tr.* to rub or touch lightly in passing, to graze.

Anscharren, *v. tr.* 1) to begin to scrape. 2) to draw near by raking or scraping.

Anschauen, *v. tr.* 1) to direct the eyes to an object; to look at. 2) to view. *Fig.* *a*) to contemplate [in theol.]. Das Anschauen Gottes in jenem Leben, the intuitive vision of God. *b*) to perceive by the mind [in philosophy]. Eine anschauende Erkenntniß, an intuitive knowledge; der eine anschauende Erkenntniß aller Dinge hat, who sees all things intuitively.

Anschauenswerth, Anschauenswürdig, *adj.* and *adv.* that which is worth of being looked at or contemplated.

Anschauer, *m.* [-s, *pl.* -] a looker on.

Anschaufeln, *v. tr.* to throw against by means of a shovel, to shovel up.

Anschaukeln, I. *v. intr.* 1) to begin to swing. 2) to strike against any thing by moving up and down. II. *v. tr.* to cause to strike against by swinging or moving up and down.

Anschaulich, I. *adj.* 1) that which may be viewed, visible, evident. Einem etwas — machen, to give any one a clear idea of a thing. 2) *Fig.* = anschauend, V. Anschauen. II. *adv.* 1) visibly. 2) *Fig.* intuitively.

Anschäumen, *v. intr.* [u. w. seyn] to foam or froth against any thing. *Fig.* Er schäumt gegen seine Bande [Fesseln] an, he foams against his fetters.

Anschauung, *f.* 1) the act of looking at any thing, view. Dieser Reisende hat uns das Resultat seiner —en und Erlebnisse im Morgenlande mitgetheilt, this traveller has communicated to us the result of all he saw and experienced in the East. 2) *Fig.* *a*) contemplation, meditation. *b*) intuition, perception.

Anschauungs-vermögen, *n.* power of intuition, intuitive power. —werth, —würdig, *adj.* V. Anschauenswerth.

Anscheeren, V. Anscheren.

Anschein, *m.* [-es, *pl.* -] 1) external show, appearance. Sein Betragen hat einen — von Tugend, his conduct has an appearance of virtue; der — der Großmuth, semblance of generosity; mit einem —e von Freundschaft, with a show of friendship; nach dem —e urtheilen, to judge by appearances. 2) probability, likelihood, appearance. Es ist aller — dazu, there is every appearance of it; allem —e nach, in all likelihood.

Ánscheinen, *ir.* I. *v. tr.* to shine upon. Die Sonne scheint Einen an, the sun shines upon one. II. *v. intr. Fig.* to have the appearance of, to appear [commonly as a part. of the present tense]. Eine —de Gefahr, an apparent danger.

Ánscheinlich, I. *adj.* apparent, seeming. II. *adv.* apparently, seemingly, in appearance.

Ánscheinung, *f.* 1) the act of shining upon. 2) V. Anschein.

Ánschellen, *v. tr.* to ring at, to ring the bell at any place.

Ánschere, *f.* [*pl.* -n] [among weavers] the warp.

1. **Ánscheren**, *v. tr.* 1) [am. weavers] to warp. 2) [am. rope-makers] Ein Tau —, to warp a rope.

2. **Ánscheren**, *ir. v. tr.* to begin to shear, to shear a little.

Ánscherpfahl, *m.* [-es, *pl.* -pfähle] [among rope-makers] warping-post. Ein großer eiserner Haken an einem —e, durch welchen die Kabelgarn fahren, warping-hook.

Ánschichten, *v. tr.* to put in layers at the side of a thing.

Ánschicken, *v. r.* sich —, to make one's self ready, to get ready, to prepare. Er schickt sich zu einer langen Reise an, he is preparing for a long voyage; es schickt sich Alles dazu an, every thing seems disposed for it; er schickt sich gut dazu an, he goes the right way to work.

Ánschieben, *ir.* I. *v. tr.* to shove towards or against any thing. Einen Tisch an die Wand —, to shove a table against the wall. II. *v. intr.* 1) to begin to push [especially in playing at nine-pins]. Ich schiebe an, I bowl first. 2) *Fig.* * and ‡ Angeschoben kommen, to approach hastily or hurriedly, to push one's way forward.

Anschiebetisch, *m.* a table, that may be lengthened.

Ánschieber, *m.* [-s, *pl.* -] 1) one that shoves one thing against an another, [in playing at nine-pins] he that bowls first. 2) a thing that is shoved against [viz. a piece used for lengthening a table].

Ánschielen, *v. tr.* to squint at, to look askance at or upon.

Ánschienen, V. Beschienen.

Ánschießen, *ir.* I. *v. tr.* 1) to wound by shooting. [am. hunt.] V. Anschweißen. *Fig.* † and ‡ Angeschossen seyn, to be in love, to be smitten, to be tipsy, to have a little touch of folly. 2) Ein Gewehr —, to fire a gun for the first time, to handsel a gun; das neue Jahr —, to usher in the new year by firing. 3) [am. workmen] to join to, to shoot. Den Aermel an den Rock —, [am. tailors] to sew the sleeve to the coat; ein Brod an das andere —, [am. bakers] to put one loaf near to the other in the oven. 4) [am. printers] to print to. II. *v. intr* 1) to begin shooting. Wer schießt an? who shoots first? 2) to shoot against. 3) [u. w. seyn] Angeschossen kommen, to approach swiftly, to rush on. Das Wasser schießt an, the water shoots forth. 4) to run or rush against. 5) [in chimistry] to crystallize. Metalle schießen zu Kristallen an, metals shoot into crystals; der Vitriol schießt leicht an, wenn er feucht wird, vitriol is apt to sprout with moisture; das — der Salze, crystallization of salt.

Anschieß-kessel, *m.* [among sugar refiners] the filler. —**pinsel**, *m.* a brush used by gilders.

Ánschiffen, *v. intr.* [u. w. seyn and sometimes with kommen] 1) to approach with a ship. An das Land —, to bear in with the land; an eine Insel —, to touch at an island; wir schifften zu Calais an, we landed at Calais. 2) to strike against a rock &c. with a ship; an Sandbänke —, to ground on sands. 3) to bring in a ship. Eine Schiffsladung Stückgüter —, to land a cargo of dry goods.

Ánschilden, *v. tr.* [in gardening] to scutcheon-graft.

Ánschimmeln, *v. intr.* [u. w. seyn] to begin to grow mouldy.

Ánschimmern, *v. intr.* to glimmer or shine faintly upon.

Ánschimpfen, *v. tr.* to address with reproachful language, to abuse.

Ánschirren, *v. tr.* to put on the furniture of a horse for draught. Pferde —, to harness horses.

Ánschlag, *m.* [-es, *pl.* -schläge] 1) the act of striking against something, or of applying one thing to another [without a plural]. — an eine Glocke, a striking upon a bell; der — einer Orgel, stop of an organ; der — der Wellen [an steile Klippen oder Küsten], surf; eine Flinte im —e halten, to present a musket, to level a musket, to take aim at with a musket; im —e seyn or liegen, to have in one's eye, to aim at, to have pointed at. *Fig* Ein Haus im —e, a house put up for sale. 2) the thing, which is to be applied to another, as the butt-end of a gun; a paper written or printed and posted in some public place, advertising something, an advertisement or hand-bill posted up. 3) *Fig.* *a*) calculation, computation, estimation, valuation. Anschläge über die Kosten eines zu erbauenden Hauses machen, to calculate, to compute the expenses of a house to be build; in — bringen, to take into account [in estimates], to consider. Zeit und Kosten sollten dabei in — gebracht werden, time and expense ought to be considered. *b*) a design formed against another, plot, contrivance. Der geheime —, machination; einen — machen, to contrive; einen — auf Einen machen, to practise on or upon any one; sie machten Anschläge auf mein Verderben, they plotted my ruin. 4) the thing that strikes against another, and the place it touches in striking, as [in mills] the mill-clack, mill-clapper; [am. print. = Immbamen] leather-strap or thing that catches the frame when it is opened; [among joiners] rabbet of the frame of a window or door; [am. tailors] a thread used for basting the linings loosely on the cloth. 5) a kind of play among children, tig or tag.

Anschlag-faden, *m.* [am. tail. and sempstresses] a thread used for basting. —**zettel**, *m.* an advertisement or hand-bill posted up.

Ánschlagen, *ir.* I. *v. tr.* 1) to strike against something. Die Bäume —, [among foresters] to blaze trees; das Gewehr —, to apply a gun to the cheek, to level or present a musket [in this sense commonly as a verb intrans.]. Schlagt an! [with soldiers] present! 2) to fasten to by striking, to fasten on, to nail on. Eine Bekanntmachung —, to post up an advertisement; einen Comödienzettel —, to set a play [bill] on a post, a wall &c.; ein Schloß an eine Thür —, to nail a lock on a door; ein Segel —, [in seamen's lang.] to bend a sail to its yard. *Fig.* Ein Haus —, to advertise the proposed sale of a house, to put up a house for sale. 3) [am. workmen &c.] Einen Aermel &c. —, [among tailors and sempstresses] to baste on a sleeve &c.; die Tücher —, [among clothiers] to hook cloth on a tenter, to tenter cloth; ein Tau —, [in seamen's language] to splice a rope; einen Block —, to seize a block; [in husbandry] Die Bienen schlagen Junge an, the bees deposit their eggs in the cells. 4) to produce by striking. Feuer —, to strike fire; einen Ton auf einem Flügel —, to strike a tone on a piano-forte; die Uhr schlägt die Stunden an, the clock strikes the hours. 5) *Fig.* to estimate, to rate, to value. Das ist zu hoch angeschlagen, that is taxed, rated too high.

II. *v. intr.* 1) to begin to strike. 2) to strike against something. An die Glocke —, to strike the bell. Die Wellen schlagen an die Küsten an, the waves lash the shores; die Wellen schlugen an die Seite des Schiffes an, the waves dashed against the side of the ship. 3) to give a sound. Die Hunde schlagen an, [among hunt.] the hounds challenge; die Vögel schlagen an, the birds sing. 4) to begin to spoil [said of fruit]. 5) *Fig.* to produce the effect desired or intended, to take effect. Die angewandten Mittel schlugen an, the means employed proved effectual; faule Erde schlägt am besten in Weinbergen an, putrid earth takes best in vineyards; Essen und Trinken schlägt gut bei ihm an, eating and drinking takes well with him; es will nichts mehr bei ihm —, he is past mending.

Ánschlagen, *n.* [-s] [= die Bewegung des die Küste bespülenden Wassers] ripple.

Ánschläger, *m.* [-s, *pl.* -] 1) he that strikes. 2) a thing that strikes; [small pieces of loose wood in certain instruments of music] jacks. 3) *Fig.* projector, speculator.

Ánschlägig, [commonly Anschlägisch, Anschläglich] *adj.* and *adv.* designing, scheming, inventive. Er hat einen —en Kopf, he is fruitful in expedients.

Ánschlämmen, V. Anschlemmen.

Ánschleichen, *ir.* I. *v. intr.* [u. w. seyn, commonly w. kommen] to come on or approach slowly and secretly, to creep or steal near. II. *v. r.* sich —, to creep or sneak up to. *Fig.* Dieser Fehler hat sich bei mir so angeschlichen, I got this habit by degrees, this fault stole on me insensibly.

1. **Ánschleifen**, [from schleifen] *ir. v. tr.* 1) to begin to grind or polish. 2) to produce by grinding or sharpening. Eine Spitze —, to grind to a point.

2. **Ánschleifen**, [from schleifen] *v. tr.* 1) to carry upon a sledge, to bring on a sledge. 2) to fasten to by means of a slip-knot.

Ánschlemmen, I. *v. r.* sich —, to collect, to fill, to choke up by the alluvion of mud. II. *v. tr.* 1) to increase by the alluvion of mud. 2) to fill with mud.

Ánschlendern, *v. intr.* [u. w. seyn and with kommen] to come near or to approach sauntering.

Ánschlenkern, *v. tr.* to throw at, to splash at. V. Anschleudern.

Ánschleppen, *v. tr.* to drag to a place.

Ánschleudern, I. *v. tr.* to fling at or against. Er schleuderte einen Stein an das Fenster an, he flung a stone at the window. II. *v. intr.* [u. w. seyn] to be flung or thrown with violence at or against. Der Wagen fiel um und wir schleuderten an einen Baum an [or wurden an einen Baum angeschleudert], the carriage upset and we were thrown against a tree.

Ánschlichten, *v. tr.* 1) to lay up smooth and even against a wall &c. 2) [am. weavers] to spread over [the warp] with weaver's starch.

‖ **Ánschlicken**, *v. intr.* [u. w. seyn] V. Anschlämmen.

Ánschließen, *ir.* I. *v. tr.* to fasten to with a lock. *Fig.* Die angeschlossene Schrift, the annexed writing. II. *v. r.* sich —, to attach one's self to, to join. Sich an Andere —, to join others; sich eng an Einen —, to unite one's self with any one in close connection, to join with any one closely. III. *v. intr.* to fit close, to close, to shut. Der Rock schließt zu sehr an, schließt nicht genug an, that coat sits too close, does not sit close enough; angeschlossen! [word of command with cavalry] draw closer! rechts angeschlossen! close to the right; — [in equitation], to sit closely, to have a firm seat.

Anschlingen, *ir.* I. *v. tr.* to fasten to with a noose. II. *v. r.* sich —, to join one's self closely with any one.

Anschlitzen, *v. tr.* to make a small slit or split in a thing.

Anschloßen, **Anschlossen**, *v. imp.* to hail against. Es schlosset an die Fenster an, the hail beats against the windows.

Anschluß, *m.* [-sses, *pl.* -schlüsse] 1) the act of fastening to by a lock. *Fig.* the adding by inclosure. 2) the thing added or enclosed. Durch den — or aus dem —e &c., by the inclosure &c.

Anschmachten, *v. tr.* to look at in a languishing manner.

Anschmauchen, *v. tr.* 1) to begin to smoke. 2) to blow the smoke of tobacco &c. against.

Anschmauchung, *f.* the act of blowing the smoke against any thing.

Anschmecken, *v. tr.* to perceive by the palate, to taste. *Fig.* Die Hunde schmecken an, the dogs scent [the game].

Anschmeicheln, I. *v. tr.* to persuade by flattering. II. *v. r.* sich —, to insinuate by flattery. Sich an Einen —, to insinuate one's self into a man's favour.

† **Anschmeißen**, *ir.* I. *v. intr.* 1) to fling or throw at. 2) to begin to cast or throw. II. *v. tr.* to move by flinging or throwing against a thing. Den Ball an die Wand —, to throw or fling the ball against the wall. 2) [said of flies &c.] to void excrement against a wall &c.

Anschmelzen, I. *v. tr.* 1) to begin to melt or smelt. 2) to fasten to by melting or smelting. II. *ir. v. intr.* [u. w. seyn] 1) to begin to melt, to become liquid. 2) to adhere by melting.

Anschmettern, I. *v. intr.* [u. w. seyn] to strike or knock against with violence. II. *v. tr.* to dash against. Einen Stein an die Wand —, to throw a stone with violence against the wall.

Anschmieden, *v. tr.* 1) to join or fasten to by forging or hammering. Ein Stück Eisen an das andere —, to hammer two pieces of redhot iron together. 2) to fasten to by fetters or with a chain.

Anschmiegen, I. *v. tr.* to bend to, to draw near to, to join closely. *Fig.* Die Worte den Begriffen —, to adapt the words to the ideas. II. *v. r.* sich —, to cling to, to lie close to. *Fig.* to be obsequious, to yield to. Sich Jemandes Laune —, to comply with any one's humour, to humour any one.

Anschmiegsam, *adj.* and *adv.* pliant, supple.

Anschmieren, *v. tr.* to smear, to daub. Sich eine Salbe —, to smear one's self with a salve. *Fig.* *a*) to paint coarsely, to daub. *b*) to add to by scribbling. *c*) to press or force upon. † Einem etwas —, to put a trick upon any one, to cheat any one into a thing; † Einen —, to cheat, to impose upon, to take any one in. *d*) to adulterate [wine &c.].

Anschminken, *v. tr.* to deck with artificial colours, to paint [the face], to rouge.

Anschmitzen, *v. tr.* 1) to strike with a whiplash [horses]. || 2) to besmear a little.

Anschmollen, *v. tr.* to pout at or upon.

Anschmoren, *v. intr.* [u. w. seyn] to begin to stew.

Anschmücken, V. Schmücken.

Anschmunzeln, *v. tr.* Einen —, to smile and fawn upon any one.

Anschmutzen, *v. tr.* to soil, to bedaub, to daub over.

Anschnäbeln, *v. tr.* to peck at.

Anschnallen, *v. tr.* to fasten with a buckle, to buckle on. *Fig.* † and students' cant. Sich etwas —, to get or obtain, to get hold of something.

Anschnalzen, *v. tr.* to make a signal to by smacking.

Anschnarchen, *v. tr.* 1) to snore at. 2) *Fig.* to snarl at, to growl at.

† **Anschnarcher**, *m.* [-s, *pl.* -] snap-short.

Anschnattern, *v. tr.* to address chattering.

Anschnauben, I. *v. intr.* [u. w. seyn and kommen] to approach or come on breathing hard, to near puffing and blowing. II. *v. tr.* to assail with angry and menacing words. Einen —, to snub any one.

Anschnaufen, **Anschnauzen**, V. Anschnauben, Anfahren.

Anschneidemesser, *n.* [-s, *pl.* -] carving-knife.

Anschneiden, *ir. v. tr.* 1) to begin to cut. Ein Brod —, to make the first cut in a loaf. 2) to add or fit by cutting. 3) to mark by cutting. Etwas auf dem Kerbholze —, to notch or score something. *Fig.* to charge in reckoning, to charge to account.

Anschneien, *v. imp.* to snow against. Es schneiet das Haus an, the snow drives or drifts against the house.

Anschnellen, I. *v. tr.* to jerk against, to fling quickly at. II. *v. intr.* 1) [u. w. seyn] to fly against. 2) † Angeschnellt kommen, to approach quickly.

Anschnieben, I. *v. intr.* [u. w. seyn and kommen] V. Anschnauben. II. *v. tr.* to snub any one.

|| **Anschniepeln**, *v. r.* sich —, to dress with great care, to pay particular regard to one's dress.

Anschnippen, V. Anschnellen.

Anschnitt, *m.* [-es, *pl.* -e] 1) the act of making the first cut in a thing, especially the act of notching a tally. *Fig.* the act of charging to account. 2) a part cut off first from the rest. Der — eines Brodes, the first cut of a loaf. 3) the place where any thing is begun to be cut. 4) the opening made by cutting. Die —e auf einem Kerbholze, the scores, notches or nicks on a tally.

Anschnitt-buch, *n.* [in mining] a book of accounts. —schere, *f.* small-scissars [used in glass-houses].

Anschnitzeln, **Anschnitzen**, *v. tr.* 1) to begin to carve. 2) to produce by carving. Eine Spitze an die Bleifeder —, or der Bleifeder eine Spitze —, to cut a pencil to a point.

Anschnüffeln, V. Beschnüffeln.

Anschnüren, *v. tr.* to fasten with a lace or cord, to lace to. Einen Mantel hinter den Sattel —, to fasten a cloak on behind the saddle.

Anschnurren, *v. tr.* 1) to purr at [said of cats]. 2) to snarl at.

Anschobern, *v. tr.* to pile against as a rick.

Anschönen, *v. r.* sich —, to deck one's self with external ornaments, to dress one's self smartly or dashingly.

* **Anschove**, *f.* [*pl.* -en] [a small fish] anchovy. V. Sardelle.

Anschrammen, *v. tr.* 1) to scratch a little. 2) to mark by scratching.

Anschrauben, *v. tr.* to fasten to with screws, to screw on. Ein Schloß an die Thür —, to screw a lock on the door; Einem die Daumenstöcke —, to apply thumb-screws to any one.

Anschrecken, *v. tr.* [am. hunt.] to startle an animal by calling or whistling so as to make it stop, to stop [a stag &c.] by frightening or startling. Einen —, to frighten any one by one's appearance.

Anschreiben, *ir. v. tr.* 1) to write on [the door &c.]. 2) to write down, to note down, to put to the reckoning, to score up. Einem Etwas auf seine Rechnung —, to put to any one's account, to charge any one with any thing; Einen als Schuldner —, [in commerce] to bring any one in one's books. *Fig.* Gut bei Einem angeschrieben seyn, to stand or to be in favour with any one; er ist schlecht or übel bei mir angeschrieben, I have no good opinion of him, I do not like him.

Anschreiben, *n.* [-s] 1) the act of writing on or down [without a plural]. 2) a letter, a written message, especially a letter addressed by authorities to persons under their control.

Anschreiber, *m.* [-s, *pl.* -] he that writes down, he that keeps the reckoning.

Anschreibetafel, *f.* [*pl.* -n] 1) a table to write upon. 2) memorandum book, a note-book.

Anschreien, *v. tr.* 1) to cry to, to call out to. Einen um Hülfe —, to cry out to any one for help; ein Schiff —, to hail a ship. 2) to proclaim, to cry the beginning of any thing. Ein Jagen —, [among hunters] to halloo.

Anschreiten, *ir. v. intr.* [u. w. seyn and comm. with kommen] to approach with long steps or strides, to stride on.

Anschrote, *f.* [*pl.* -n] [among clothiers] the list of cloth, wale, selvedge.

Anschroten, *v. tr.* 1) to roll on or near [a cask &c.]. 2) to edge, to border, [among clothiers] to form the list or wale.

Anschrumpfen, *v. intr.* [u. w. seyn] to begin to shrink.

Anschub, *m.* [-es, *pl.* -schübe] 1) the first shove or throw, the first bowl [at nine-pins]. 2) a piece joined or added to any thing by shoving or pushing [an additional leaf of a table &c.].

Anschuhen, I. *v. tr.* 1) to put shoes to. Ein Paar Stiefel —, to foot a pair of boots. *Fig.* Pfähle —, to tip staves or piles with iron. 2) to put shoes on. Einen —, to shoe or put shoes on to any one. II. *v. r.* sich —, to put one's shoes on. Ich habe mich angeschuhet, I have put on my shoes.

Anschuldigen, *v. tr.* to charge, to accuse. Einen einer Sache — or beschuldigen or anklagen, to impute a thing to, to accuse any one of a thing; Einen eines Diebstahls — or beschuldigen or anklagen, to charge a man with theft.

Anschuldigung, *f.* 1) the act of charging with a crime or offence, accusation. 2) charge, accusation.

|| **Anschuppen**, *v. tr.* to push against. V. Anstoßen, Anschieben.

Anschüppen, *v. tr.* to throw against by means of a shovel, to shovel up or against.

Anschur, *f.* V. Anschere.

Anschüren, *v. tr.* to kindle, stir. Das Feuer —, to trim, to stir the fire. *Fig.* to stir up, to excite.

Anschuß, *m.* [-sses, *pl.* -schüsse] 1) the act of wounding by shot. 2) the act of shooting first. Wer hat den —? who has the first shot? 3) the act of approaching suddenly, rushing on or shooting forth. Der — des Wassers, the rush of water. 4) [among hunters] the place where game has been found. 5) [in chimistry] the act of crystallizing, and the mass or body formed by the process of crystallizing, crystallization. 6) a rheumatic attack. 7) Anschüsse, grumous milk in the breasts of suckling mothers.

Anschüssig, *adj.* and *adv.* subject to fluxions.

Anschutt, *f.* [*pl.* -en] 1) [the earth added to a shore or bank by the force of water, as by a current or by waves] alluvion, alluvium. 2) a right the owner of the land thus augmented has to the alluvial earth.

Anschütteln, *v. tr.* to bring near to by shaking.

Anschütten, *v. tr.* to pour or throw on or against. Das Getreide an die Wand —, to heap up corn against the wall. 2) to pour to. 3) to fill by pouring or heaping up.

Anschützen, *v. tr.* [in watermills and mines] to raise the water by means of a sluice and to let it fall on the wheels.

Anschwämmen, V. Anschwemmen.

Anschwängern, *v. tr.* to make pregnant, to impregnate; [in chimistry, to infuse particles of one thing into another, by mixing, digestion &c.] to impregnate, to saturate.

Anschwängerung, *f.* [in chimistry] impregnation, saturation.

Anschwanken, I. *v. intr.* [u. w. seyn and commonly w. kommen] to approach wavering.

Anschwänzeln, *v. intr.* [u. w. seyn and with kommen] to come near wagging the tail, fawning [said of dogs]. *Fig.* to come on in an affected riggling manner.

Anschwänzen, *v. tr.* to tack to.

Anschwären, *ir. v. intr.* [u. w. seyn] to adhere, to cleave to by festering.

Anschwärmen, *v. intr.* 1) [u. w. seyn and kommen] to approach swarming, or in swarms. 2) to begin to swarm [said of bees].

Anschwärzen, *v. tr.* to blacken. *Fig.* Einen —, to slander or calumniate any one; einen guten Namen —, to asperse a character.

Anschwärzer, *m.* [-s, *pl.* -] calumniator, slanderer.

Anschwatzen, *v. tr.* to press upon by talking. Einem schlechte Waaren &c. — or aufschwatzen, to persuade, to talk any one into buying bad goods.

Anschweben, *v. intr.* [u. w. seyn and comm. w. kommen] to approach hovering or with light steps.

Anschwefeln, *v. tr.* to fumigate with sulphur. V. Schwefeln.

Anschweiden, V. Anschwöden.

Anschweif, *m.* [-es, *pl.* -e] [in lace making] warp.

Anschweif-rahmen, *m.* [in lace-making] a frame used for warping. — **rolle**, *f.* [in lace-making] a spool used in warping.

Anschweifen, *v. tr.* [among lace-makers] to warp.

Anschweißen, *v. tr.* 1) to weld Ein Stück Eisen an das andere —, to join or weld two pieces of redhot iron together. 2) [among hunters] to wound by shot.

Anschwellen, *ir.* I. *v. intr* [u. w. seyn] to swell. Ein angeschwollenes Gesicht, a swollen face; der Fluß schwillt an, the river swells; die Wogen schwellen an, the waves arise. II. *reg. v. tr.* to swell. Der Regen schwellt den Fluß an, the rain swells the river; der Wind schwellt die Segel an, the wind swells or bellies the sails; das — der Töne, [in music] the swell of sounds.

Anschwemmen, *v. tr.* 1) to float to a place. Der Fluß hat vieles Holz angeschwemmt, the river has floated up a quantity of wood. 2) to form by a current of water, to form by alluvion. Angeschwemmter Boden, alluvial soil; angeschwemmtes Erz, alluvial ores.

Anschwemmung, *f.* [a gradual washing or carrying of earth or other substances to a shore or bank; the earth thus added] alluvion.

Anschwemmungsrecht, *n.* a right the owner of the land augmented by alluvion has to the alluvial earth.

Anschwimmen, *ir. v. intr.* [u. w. seyn, also w. kommen] to swim to, to approach swimming. Er schwamm an das Ufer an, er kam an das Ufer angeschwommen, he swam ashore.

Anschwindeln, *v. tr.* to make a little giddy.

Anschwingen, *ir. v. tr.* to throw against in swinging, to swing at or against.

Anschwirren, *v. intr.* [u. w. seyn and frequently with kommen] to approach whirring.

Anschwöden, *v. tr.* [among tawers] die Felle —, to macerate with chalk the flesh-side of hides.

Anschwung, *m.* [-es] 1) the act of swinging against. 2) the state of being thrown against by swinging.

Ansegeln, *v. intr.* 1) [u. w. seyn and commonly w. kommen] to sail near, to approach sailing. 2) to sail against. An eine Sandbank —, to strike a sand-bank in sailing.

Ansehen, *ir. v. tr.* to direct the eyes on, to look at, to regard. Er sah ihn mit Wohlgefallen an, he looked on him with a friendly regard; er sah mich mit Verachtung an, he looked on me with scorn; sehen Sie mich recht an, look at me well. *Fig.* Er that Alles, was er ihm nur an den Augen — [or absehen] konnte, he did every thing he saw the other wished, he anticipated all his wishes; das ist schön anzusehen, this is a fine sight; sieh nur an, was &c., see! look! what &c.; man sieht ihm keine Noth an, he does not appear to be in want. *Fig.* *a*) to bear, to sustain. Länger kann ich es nicht mit —, I cannot stand it any longer; ich kann es wol noch mit —, I can yet bear or sustain it, I can yet pay the expences. *b*) to regard, to mind. Die Person —, to have respect to a person; er sieht die Gefahr nicht an, he does not regard the danger. *c*) to consider, to esteem [but only used in the part. Angesehen]. Angesehen seyn, to be considered; ein angesehener Mann, a man of consequence; ein sehr angesehener Mann, a man of great note, of high standing; ein angesehener Bürger, a citizen of note; die angesehensten Jungfrauen unseres Landes, the best regarded virgins of our country; er ist bei Jedermann wohl angesehen, every one likes him. *d*) to consider, to regard, to think. Ich werde es für eine große Ehre —, I shall look on it as a great honour; er sah mich für einen Andern an, he took me for another; ich sehe ihn für meinen Freund an, I think him to be my friend; er sieht sich für einen geschickten Mann an, he thinks himself an able man. *e*) Auf etwas angesehen [better: abgesehen] seyn, to aim at. Ist es darauf angesehen? is that aimed at? es ist auf eine Heirath angesehen, they have a marriage in view. V. Absehen. *f*) [rather obsolete] to look at with displeasure, to animadvert on. Ich werde ihn dafür —, I shall reprove him for it, I shall punish him for it.

Ansehen, *n.* [-s] 1) the act of looking at, regard [without a plural]. Es ist des —s nicht werth, it is not worth looking at. 2) external appearance, look, view. Ich kenne ihn vom or von —, I know him by sight; [in mineral.] das — der Mineralien, the aspect of minerals; das — der Oberfläche, aspect of the surface; das — des Bruchs, aspect of the fracture; das — der verschiedenen Absonderungsverhältnisse und ihrer Erscheinungen, aspect of the different concretions. 3) *Fig.* *a*) external show, appearance. Das äußere —, outward appearance, outside; es hat ganz das —, als würde es regnen, it has every appearance of rain; allem — nach, in all likelihood, to all appearance; es gewinnt ein schlechtes —, it begins to look very ill. *b*) consideration, claim to notice or regard. Herr N. war ein Mann von sehr geringem — unter ihnen, Mr. N. was a man of very little esteem among them; ein Mann von großem — in der Gesellschaft, a man of great consequence in society; eine obrigkeitliche Person von großem — in der Stadt, a magistrate of great authority in the city; die Tugend steht in keinem — bei Hofe, virtue is in no request at court; sich ein — geben, to assume airs; er gibt sich ein —, he puts on airs; vor Gott gilt kein — der Person, God has no respect of persons, God is no respecter of persons.

Ansehnlich, I. *adj.* considerable, important, or moderately large [according to the subject]. Dieser Herr hat eine —e Besitzung in Irland, this gentleman has a considerable estate in Ireland; man erwartete eine —e Hülfe von den Alliirten, considerable aid was expected from the allies; eine —e Summe Geldes, a considerable sum of money; eine —e Menge Zuhörer, a respectable audience; ein —er Mann, a portly man, a good looking man. II. *adv.* considerably.

Ansehnlichkeit, *f.* considerableness.

Ansehung, *f.* the act of looking at, regard [without a plural, commonly with in]. *Fig.* In —, in consideration or regard of, with respect to, as for. In — seiner habe ich &c., in reference to him I have &c.; in — seines Fleißes, in consideration of his diligence. Syn. In Ansehung, In Absicht, In Rücksicht, In Betrachtung, In Hinsicht. In Absicht denotes the aim, the object in doing a thing; in Ansehung, that which induces us, the motive for doing a thing; in Rücksicht, denotes the motive which induces us to do a thing, only as far as it arises from circumstances already passed or at present existing, and not with a view to any thing future, in which case, it would be proper to say: in Hinsicht. I did it in Absicht [with a view] to his being better provided for, and I procured this for him in Ansehung [on account] of my friend's intercession. But I did it also in Rücksicht [in regard] of his family. In Betrachtung conveys the idea of greater reflection. In Betrachtung [in consideration] of his numerous family, I took all possible pains to assist him.

† **Anseichen**, *v. tr.* to bepiss, to piss at or against.

Anseilen, *v. tr.* [among hunters] to attach by a cord or leash.

Ansengen, I. *v. tr.* to singe a little. II. *v. intr.* [u. w. seyn] to be singed a little. Die Kleider sind angesengt, the clothes are burnt a little.

Ansenkeln, *v. tr.* to fasten with a lacing-string or lace.

Ansetzblatt, *n.* [-es, *pl.* -blätter] [in print.] fly-leaf.

Ansetzblech, *n.* [-es, *pl.* -e] [in metallurgy] an iron-plate used for closing the refining furnace.

Ansetzen, I. *v. tr.* 1) to put or set to or near. Den Topf an das Feuer —, to put the pot near the fire; die Feder —, to put pen to paper, or to set one's self to write, to take pen in hand; das Eisen —, [in mining] to begin to work; den Mineur —, [in fortif.] to fix the miner. 2) to put one thing to another. Schröpfköpfe —, to apply cupping glasses, to cup; Blutegel —, to apply leeches; einen Aermel —, [among tailors] to sew a sleeve to; die Ladung eines Geschützes —, [in gunn.] to ram down the charge in a gun; die Ladung einer Kanone —, [in seamen's lang.]

to ram home; die Deckel an die Bücher —, [am. bookbinders] to glue the covers to the books; die Wand —, [a sea term] to set up the shrouds. *Fig.* a) to put down in reckoning, to reckon. Wie haben Sie mir das angesetzt? at what rate have you put it down to me? how much did you charge it me? statt fünf habt Ihr mir zehn angesetzt, instead of five you scored or charged me ten. b) to rate, to tax. Er ist in der Steuerliste mit 5000 Gulden steuerbarem Vermögen angesetzt, his taxable property is rated at 5000 florins; er ist zu hoch, zu nieder angesetzt, he is taxed too high, too low. c) to settle, to fix, to appoint. Einen Tag zu Etwas —, to appoint a day for a thing. 3) to put or set in a place. Essig —, to prepare vinegar; der Fluß setzt Land an, the river carries earth to a shore or bank; durch das — neuen Stoffes, by the apposition of new matter.

II. *v. r.* sich —, 1) to sit down near any thing. 2) *Fig.* a) to fix one's self, to establish one's residence, to settle. b) to adhere, to stick. Der Teig setzt sich an dem Hafen an, the dough sticks to the dish; es setzt sich Weinstein an das Weinfaß an, tartar sticks to the wine-cask.

III. *v. intr.* 1) to prepare for taking a leap, to take a run. 2) to thrive, to prosper. Die Kirschbäume setzen an, the cherry-trees set; die Kuh setzt gut an, the cow grows fat. 3) to conceive [said of some animals]. Die Stute hat angesetzt, the mare is stinted. 4) to continue, to hold on. Das Erz setzt an, [in mining] the ore continues.

Ansetzer, [-s, *pl.* -] [a sea term] driving-bolt, drive-bolt. Der — der Kanone, V. Stampfer.

Ansetzung, *f.* the act of putting or setting to or near.

Anseufzen, *v. tr.* to look at sighing.

Ansichhalten, *n.* [-s] the act of keeping the countenance, of refraining from expressing any passion by an unchanged countenance, command of temper, restraint of passions, forbearance.

Ansicht, *f.* [*pl.* -en] 1) the act of looking at. Bei — Ihres Briefes, at the sight of your letter. 2) [sight of something distant] prospect, view. Die — des Meeres, the prospect of the sea; dieses Haus hat or gibt eine schöne —, this house yields a fine prospect; Ansichten, *pl.* sights, prospects; —en von London, views of London; eine — von der Seite, side-view. *Fig.* manner of seeing or understanding, opinion. Dies ist meine —, that's my opinion; dies sind meine —en von der Politik, welche &c., these are my views of the policy, which &c.

Ansichts-seite, *f.* fore-part, front. —tafel, *f.* V. Tabelle.

Ansichtig, *adv.* [used only in conjunction with werden and the gen. case and more commonly with the accusat.] having a sight of any thing. Eines — werden, to see, to behold, to descry any one; sobald die Räuber mich or meiner — wurden, as soon as the robbers had a sight of me.

|| **Ansiedel**, *n.* [-s] a small farm, landed property, also a family estate. V. Stammgut, Bauergut.

Ansiedelei, *f.* [more usual: Ansiedelung 2] a colony, settlement.

Ansiedeln, I. *v. r.* sich —, to settle [at the mouth of a river &c.]. Englische Puritaner siedelten sich in Neu-England an, English Puritans colonized New-England. II. *v. tr.* to plant or establish a colony in, to colonize. Die Griechen siedelten das südliche Italien an, the Greeks colonized the South of Italy.

Ansiedelung, *f.* 1) the act of settling, colonization. 2) a colony, settlement. Die Ansiedelungen der Engländer in Indien, the English colonies or settlements in the Indies.

Ansieden, *ir. v. tr* to begin to boil something. [in metall.] Die Metalle —, to mix a metal with lead by smelting.

Ansiedler, *m.* [-s, *pl.* -] a settler, colonist.

Ansiegeln, *v. tr.* to fasten with sealing wax, to seal.

Ansillen, *v. tr.* [among fowlers] to attach to a leather-strap, to tether.

Ansingen, *ir. v. tr.* Einen —, to address a song to any one.

Ansinken, *ir. v. intr.* [u. w. seyn] to fall against something in sinking down.

Ansinnen, *ir. v. tr.* 1) to desire or require [something wrong or unreasonable]. Einem etwas —, to desire any thing of a person; was sinnt man uns an? what is required of us? 2) [in feudal law] V. Muthen.

Ansinnen, *n.* [-s] **Ansinnung**, *f.* 1) a request to obtain something wrong or unreasonable, desire. 2) [sometimes the object of desire, that which is desired] desire.

Ansintern, *v. intr.* [u. w. seyn] [in mines] to adhere, to coagulate, to be joined or held in contact in form of stalactites.

Ansitz, *m.* [-es, *pl.* -e] [in law] 1) a settled abode. 2) landed property.

Ansitzarbeit, *f.* [in mining] the beginning of the work in the mines.

Ansitzen, *ir.* I. *v. intr.* to sit near any thing. Er saß hart an der Wand an, he sat close to the wall. *Fig.* to stick, to adhere, to cleave, to hold to. Angesessen, settled, having a settled abode. 2) [in mining] to begin the work in the mines. II. *v. r.* sich —, to get by sitting. Er hat sich auf der Grasbank den Schnupfen angesessen, he caught a cold in his head by sitting on a seat covered with turf.

Ansitzer, *m.* [-s, *pl.* -] [in mining] a miner that begins the work in the mines.

Ansod, *m.* V. Ansud.

‡ **Ansónst**, V. Sonst.

Anspalten, I. *v. intr.* [u. w. seyn] [*part.* angespalten] to begin to split. Das Brett ist angespalten, the board is split a little. II. *v. tr.* [*part.* angespaltet] to cause to split a little.

Anspangen, *v. tr.* to fasten with a buckle or a clasp.

Anspann, *m.* [-es, *pl.* -e] 1) draught-cattle, a team. 2) [in feudal law] service due to the landlord that must be performed by draught-cattle.

Anspannen, *v. tr.* 1) to strain, to stretch. Ein Seil —, to stretch or tighten a rope; die Segel —, to bend the sails. *Fig.* Die Kräfte —, to exert one's powers or faculties; alle Kräfte —, to strain every nerve; den Geist —, to exert the mind, to strain one's wit; sein Geist ist immer angespannt, his mind is always on the stretch. 2) to put to [as horses to a carriage &c.]. Die Ochsen an den Pflug —, to yoke the oxen to the plough; es ist angespannt, the horses are put to. *Fig.* † Einen zu etwas —, to set any one a task.

Anspänner, *m.* [-s, *pl.* -] 1) [in feudal law] a farmer that is owner of draught-cattle. 2) one that keeps a horse at the disposal of the magistrates.

Anspännergut, *n.* [in feudal law] a farm whose owner is obliged to keep draught-cattle and to perform the service due to the landlord.

Anspeien, *v. tr.* Einen —, to spit at or upon any one [as a mark of contempt], to vomit upon.

Ansperren, *v. tr.* to fasten or fix to.

Anspicken, *v. tr.* to lard. *Fig.* to fill, to store. Ein angespickter Beutel, a purse well stored.

Anspielen, I. *v. intr.* 1) to begin to play. Ich spiele an, I play first. 2) *Fig.* to hint at by remote suggestions, to allude to. Er spielte auf einen gewissen Doctor an, he glanced at a certain doctor; anspielend, allusive. II. *v. tr.* Eine Karte —, [at cards] to lead a card; der Herr hat Carreau angespielt, this gentleman has led diamonds.

Anspieler, *m.* [-s, *pl.* -] one who commences to play or plays first, [in some games] the one who serves the ball, [at cards] the one who leads.

Anspielung, *f.* 1) the act of alluding. 2) allusion, hint.

Anspießen, *v. tr.* to spit, to thrust through with a spear or spit. Einen Braten —, to put meat upon a spit, to spit meat; Frösche —, to spit frogs.

Anspinnen, *ir.* I. *v. tr.* 1) to begin to spin. *Fig.* to contrive, to devise, to plan [in a bad sense]. Böses —, to devise evil, to hatch mischief; Verrath —, to plot treason. 2) to join by spinning [a thread &c.]. *Fig.* Eine Erzählung an eine andere —, to make a narration coherent with another, to join one tale with another. II. *v. r.* 1) sich an etwas —, as: die Spinne spinnt sich ans Fenster an, the spider spins or fastens its web on to the window. 2) sich —, to arise or originate by degrees. Es spann sich unter ihnen eine enge Freundschaft an, a strict friendship was bred by degrees among them.

Anspitzen, *v. tr.* to furnish with a point. Einen Bleistift —, to point a lead-pencil; wieder —, to new-point. Ein Seil —, to splice a rope.

Ansplittern, I. *v. intr.* [u. w. seyn] 1) to begin to splinter. 2) to be shivered or to be driven against any thing as a splinter. II. *v. tr.* to cause to splinter or to shiver.

Anspornen, *v. tr.* to prick with the spur, to drive with the spur, to set spurs to, to spur [a horse]. *Fig.* to spur, to incite, to urge forward. Der Ehrgeiz spornt ihn an, ambition spurs him on; Leute zu ihrer Pflicht —, to spur people to their duty.

Anspötteln, *v. tr.* to jeer, to treat with scoffs.

Ansprache, *f.* [*pl.* -n] 1) a speaking to, address. 2) [without a plural] *Fig.* sound, tone. Diese Geige hat eine gute —, the violin sounds easily; die Tasten eines Klaviers zur — bringen, to arrange the keys of a piano-forte so as to produce tone.

Ansprechen, *ir.* I. *v. intr.* 1) to emit a sound, to sound. Dieses Klavier spricht leicht an, this piano-forte sounds easily, has an easy touch; eine Orgelpfeife — lassen, to voice the pipe of an organ. 2) to call on without the intention of staying. Bei einem Freunde — [= einsprechen or vorsprechen], to call on, to look in upon a friend. II. *v. tr.* 1) to speak first to, to address, to accost. *Fig.* a) to make impression on, to please. Dieser Vorschlag spricht mich an, I am pleased with this proposal; seine Schreibart spricht das Herz an, his style of writing touches the heart, goes to the heart; sie hat nichts Ansprechendes in ihrem Aeußeren, she has nothing interesting in her appearance. b) to demand, claim or require, to ask or request. Rechte und Privilegien —, to assert rights and privileges; eine Mitgift —, to ask a dowry; Einen um etwas —, to request a thing of any one. 2) to name, to give a name or epithet to, to denominate. Im ersten Jahre wird der Hirsch Hirschkalb und im zweiten Jahre Spießer angesprochen, [among hunters] the buck is called the first year a fawn, the second year a pricket.

Anspreiten, *v. tr.* 1) to spread against something. 2) to spread asunder and fasten.

Anspreizen, I. *v. tr.* to extend or spread against something. II. *v. r.* sich —, to place one's feet firmly against any thing.

Ansprengen, I. *v. tr.* 1) to begin to blow up or blast [a rock &c.]. 2) to drive against by explosion. 3) to sprinkle, to besprinkle, to wet [linen &c.]. 4) to cause to run or to spring forward. Ein Pferd zum Galopp —, to put a horse into a gallop. 5) to ride against in full speed. Einen [auf Einen] —, to gallop against any one. II. *v. intr.* [u. w. seyn and sometimes angesprengt kommen] to approach in full gallop.

Anspringen, *ir.* I. *v. intr.* [u. w. seyn] 1) to begin to spring [said of a mast &c.]. Das Glas ist angesprungen, the glass is cracked a little. 2) [u. w. haben] to leap or spring first. 3) [u. w. seyn] to leap or spring, to fly against, to leap at. 4) [u. w. seyn and kommen] to approach leaping or springing.

Anspritzen, I. *v. tr.* 1) to squirt at. Ein Haus mit Koth —, to splash a house. 2) to sprinkle with a squirt. II. *v. intr.* [u. w. seyn] to be thrown against, to be squirted at. Der Koth ist an den Wagen angespritzt, the dirt splashed up against the carriage.

Anspruch, *m.* [-es, *pl.* -sprüche] 1) the state of emitting a sound [said of instruments]. 2) a speaking to, address. 3) [am. hunters] naming, calling, V. Ansprechen 4. 4) [a demand of a right or supposed right] claim. — auf etwas machen, to lay claim to any thing; — auf etwas haben, to have a claim or title to a thing; — auf etwas machen, etwas in — nehmen, to lay claim to, or put in a claim to a thing; einen — beweisen, to clear a title; ein von Zeit zu Zeit erneuerter —, [in law] a continual claim; er macht große Ansprüche auf Gelehrsamkeit, he pretends very much, or makes great pretensions to learning; in jenen Ländern, welche auf Freiheit — machen, in those countries that pretend to freedom; ihre dünkelhaften Ansprüche zu begünstigen, to favour their arrogant pretensions; er ist voller Ansprüche, he behaves arrogantly.

Anspruchsfrei, *adj.* and *adv.* free from claims. —los, I. *adj.* unassuming, unpretending. II. *adv.* unassumingly. —reich, I. *adj.* pretending. II. *adv.* pretendingly. —sklage, *f.* [in law] a petitory action. —swappen, [in heraldry] escutcheon of pretence. —voll, I. *adj.* behaving arrogantly, assuming. II. *adv.* assumingly.

Ansprüchig, *adj.* and *adv.* 1) having a claim or a title to. 2) that which is claimed or demanded.

Ansprudeln, I. *v. tr.* to sputter at. Einen —, to sputter into any one's face. II. *v. intr.* [u. w. seyn] to strike or touch something in bubbling, to bubble or spout against.

Ansprühen, *v. tr.* to spurt, to sputter at. Er sprüht Einen immer an, wenn er spricht, he always sputters in one's face, when he speaks; ich stand so nahe am Amboß, daß mich die Funken immerfort ansprühten, I stood so near the anvil, that the sparks continually flew against me.

Ansprung, *m.* [-es, *pl.* -sprünge] the act of beginning to run or to leap, [in manage] the act of bringing a horse to a galopp. *Fig.* *a)* [in medicine for] Anfall. *b)* [in medicine, a disease of children] milk-scab.

Anspucken, *v. tr.* V. Anspeien.

Anspulen, *v. tr.* [among weavers and spinners] to spool [a thread].

Anspülen, I. *v. intr.* to flow against. Das Wasser spült an das Haus an, the water washes the house. II. *v. tr.* to wash or carry to a shore or bank. Der Fluß spült Land an, the river washes or carries earth to a shore or bank; die angespülte Erde, alluvion, alluvium.

Anspülung, *f.* [a gradual washing or carrying of earth or other substances to a shore or bank; the earth thus added] alluvion, alluvium.

Anstacheln, *v. tr.* 1) to fasten with a prick, to fix to a prick. 2) to prick, to goad on. Ochsen —, to drive oxen with a goad.

Anstählen, *v. tr.* to steel the top [of a tool &c.]

Anstalt, *f.* [*pl.* -en] 1) the act of preparing, or previously fitting any thing to any purpose, preparation. 2) previous disposition, preparatory measure, arrangement. Wir haben —en zu einer Gesellschaft gemacht, we have made arrangements for receiving company; die —en zu unserer Reise, the preparatives for our journey or voyage; er trifft —en zu einer langen Reise, he prepares for a long journey; —en zum Kriege, preparations for war. 3) institution, establishment. Oeffentliche —en, public institutions; eine Erziehungs—, an institution for education, an academy, school, seminary; eine Taubstummen—, an institution for deaf and dumb.

Anstammeln, *v. tr.* to address stammering.

Anstammen, *v. intr.* to impart by inheritance [used only in the participle]. Ein angestammtes Besitzthum, an ancestral estate, hereditary estate; angestammte Rechte, ancestral rights.

Anstampfen, *v. tr.* 1) to begin to stamp or to strike the foot forcibly downwards. 2) to fix to by stamping [among pinmakers]. Die Köpfe —, to head pins.

Anstand, *m.* [-es] 1) [among hunters] a place where a hunter waits for game standing, stand, station. Auf dem —e seyn, to lie upon the catch. 2) putting off or deferring, delay. Von meiner Seite soll es keinen — haben [= ich will keinen Aufenthalt machen], I will not be the cause of any delay; — begehren, to request a delay; der — der Gerichte [better: Gerichtsferien], vacation; mit einer Zahlung im —e seyn, to be in arrear. 3) what renders manners dignified, graceful and agreeable; a fine demeanour or deportment, a pleasing address. Sie hat den — einer Göttinn, einen göttlichen —, she has a goddess-like deportment; viel —, much good grace; — hatten alle ihre Schritte, grace was in all her steps. 4) [*pl.* Anstände] doubt, hesitation, scruple. — nehmen, to hesitate, to balance; ich werde keinen — nehmen, ihm zu sagen, daß &c., I would not have the slightest hesitation in telling him, that &c.; Anstände gegen eine Rechnung beibringen, to make objections to an account. V. Betragen.

Anstandsbrief, *m.* [in law] letter of respite.

Anständig, I. *adj.* 1) becoming, fit, suitable, congruous, proper, seemly, decent. Er spricht mit einer —en Dreistigkeit, he speaks with becoming boldness; eine sehr —e Kleidung, a dress very becoming, very decent. 2) fitting, suiting. Es ist seiner Würde nicht —, it is unbecoming his dignity; …… noch ist es —, das Fest zu verlängern, …… nor fits it to prolong the feast; dieses ist mir nicht —, that does not suit me or answer my turn. II. *adv.* fitly, suitably, decently, properly, conveniently. Syn. Anständig, Wohlanständig, Schicklich. A female ought always be dressed anständig, for decency's sake; her dress should be wohlanständig, suitable to her rank and station; and schicklich in conformity to circumstances. A dress which leaves the body too much exposed is unanständig; one that is below one's condition, is gegen den Wohlstand [or die Wohlanständigkeit], and it would be unschicklich to appear amongst a company of mourners in a coloured dress. Anständigkeit has its immutable laws, wohlanständig has its rules, and Schicklichkeit depends frequently upon established custom.

Anständigkeit, *f.* 1) propriety of behaviour, decency, decorum. 2) the state of any thing that fits or suits us, fitness, suitableness, conveniency.

Anstandsvoll, I. *adj.* graceful. Ein —er Gang, a graceful walk. II. *adv.* gracefully.

Anstängeln, *v. tr.* to furnish with poles. Den Hopfen —, to pole hops.

Anstapeln, I. *v. tr.* to pile up [wood &c. against a wall &c.]. II. *v. intr.* † [u. w. seyn and frequently with kommen] to approach stalking.

Anstärken, *v. tr.* to starch a little [linen &c.]

Anstarren, *v. tr.* to stare at, to gaze at, to look at as in astonishment. *Poet.* Sie starrte den weiten Himmel an, she gazed the ample sky.

Anstarrer, *m.* [-s, *pl.* -] starer, gazer.

Anstatt [An Statt], *conj.* and *prep.* [with the genitive case] instead of. Er aber, — die Befehle seines Herrn zu vollziehen, weigerte den Gehorsam, but he instead of executing the commands of his master, refused obedience; — dieses zu thun, lief er fort, instead of doing this, he ran away; — meiner, instead of me; — seiner, in lieu of him; [sometimes it is divided into an Statt] er hat es an meiner Statt gethan, he did it instead of me. V. Statt.

Anstauben, I. *v. intr.* [u. w. seyn] 1) to stick to [as dust]. 2) to become a little dusty. II. *v. tr.* Der feine Sand dieser Spaziergänge staubt die Kleider über und über an, the fine sand of these walks completely covers the clothes with dust.

Anstäuben, *v. tr.* to sprinkle with dust, to bedust.

Anstaunen, *v. tr.* to look at or to view as in astonishment, to stare at, to gaze at.

Anstaunenswerth, **Anstaunenswürdig**, *adj.* and *adv.* having qualities of exciting astonishment, worthy of astonishment.

Anstechen, *ir.* I. *v. tr.* 1) to prick, to drive with a goad. Ochsen —, to goad oxen. 2) to fix by the point, to prick. Das Futter [an den Zeug] glatt —, to stitch down the lining. 3) to begin to prick or to pierce a thing in order to draw the liquor; to open [as a store]. Ein Faß Wein —, to broach or to tap a cask of wine. *Fig.* † and ‡ Angestochen seyn, to be tipsy. II *v. intr.* † [u. w. seyn and kommen] Komm mir damit nicht angestochen, do not take it into your head to talk to me of it.

Ansteckärmel, *m.* [-s, *pl.* -] sham-sleeves.

Ansteckbohrer, *m.* [-s, *pl.* -] tap-borer.

Ansteckegift, *n.* [-es, *pl.* -e] [such particles or atoms, as are supposed to arise from distempered putrifying poisonous bodies, by which persons are affected at a distance] miasma, contagion.

Anstecken, *v. tr.* 1) to stick on, to put on. Den Ring an den Finger —, to put the ring on the finger; den Braten an den Bratspieß —, to put the meat on the spit; ein Paar Kaninchen an den Bratspieß —, to spit a couple of rabbits. 2) to fasten with pins, to pin. Einen Rock —, to pin a gown. 3) [= anzünden] to set on fire. Ein Licht —, to light a candle; ein Haus —, to set fire to a house, to set a house on fire. 4) to communicate something bad. Einen —, to taint with disease, to infect. Die Pest, die Blattern, bösartige Fieber, stecken gesunde Personen an, persons in health are infected by the contagion of the plague, of small pox, of malignant fevers; mit der Lustseuche —, to infect with venereal poison, to clap; angesteckt werden, to become infected; von den Masern angesteckt werden, to catch the measles; eine —de Krankheit, a contagious disease; —de Fieber, infectious or pestilential fevers; sein —der Athem, his poisonous breath. *Fig.* Von Irrthümern angesteckt, infected with errors; von Furcht angesteckt, tainted with fear; Kummer sowohl als Freude steckt an, grief as well as joy is infectious; Tollheit steckt an, madness is catching. 5) to begin to stick, to fix, [in mining] to begin to fasten with poles.

Ánstecker, *m.* [-s, *pl.* -] one that puts on, pins, lights or fixes any thing.

Ánsteckung, *f.* contagion, infection. Durch —, by contagion, by infection, infectiously.

Ansteckungsstoff, *m.* the effluvium or infectious matter exhaled from the person of one diseased, infection, contagion.

Ánstehen, *ir v. intr.* 1) to stand near or close to [a wall &c.]. *Fig. a)* to become, to be suitable, to be fit. *b)* to please, to like. Das steht mir gar nicht an, I do not like it, it does not suit me at all; es steht mir an, I am pleased with it. *c)* to stop for a time, to delay. Lassen Sie es bis morgen —, put it off till to-morrow; die Ausführung eines Planes — lassen, to defer the execution of a design; er ließ es lange —, he put it off a long while. *d)* to stop or pause respecting decision or action, to hesitate. Er stand an, ob er das Anerbieten annehmen sollte oder nicht, he hesitated whether to accept the offer or not; ich stehe an or bin im Zweifel, ob ich gehen soll, I doubt whether I shall go. *e)* [in law] to be appointed or fixed. Dazu steht ein Termin an, there is a court-day fixed for it. 3) to join in company as a partner, to participate. Wollen Sie mit mir —? will you associate with me? SYN. Anstehen, sich Bedenken, sich Besinnen. A person who is undetermined steht lange an [hesitates awhile], before he makes a purchase; a timid person besinnt sich lange [considers and doubts] because he is afraid of being cheated; a prudent man bedenkt sich lange [deliberates long] because he considers whether it will be advantageous to him.

Ánsteifen, I. *v. tr.* to stiffen a little [as linen &c.]. II. *v. r.* sich —, to stem against with the feet. *Fig.* Er hat sich aus Leibeskräften, mit seltener Hartnäckigkeit, wider diese Maßregel angesteift, he set himself with singular obstinacy against this measure.

Ánsteigen, *ir. v. intr.* 1) [u. w. seyn] to move upwards, to ascend, to mount, to rise, to go up, to step up. Das Gebirge steigt sanft an, the mountains rise gently. eine sanft —de Anhöhe, a gentle eminence. 2) † and ‡ [u. w. seyn and kommen] to approach with long and slow strides, to strut or stalk on.

Ánstellen, I. *v. tr.* 1) to place or to set to or near, to put one thing to another. Die Leiter an die Mauer —, to lean or put the ladder against the wall. *Fig.* Treiber —, [in hunting] to post drivers or beaters; Einen —, to appoint, depute or elect any one to an office or employment; Arbeiter —, to employ workmen; Beamte —, to appoint officers; angestellt, in place; er ist gut angestellt, he has got a good place. 2) to prepare, to adjust to any use, to make ready for any purpose. Bier —, to set beer to work; Branntwein —, to prepare for a distillation of brandy; die Blauküpe —, [among dyers] to make ready the vat. *Fig. a)* to carry into effect. Eine Reise —, to begin or undertake a journey, to set out on a journey; ein Fest —, to order a feast; Versuche —, to make experiments; eine Klage —, to institute or commence a suit, to complain; eine Vergleichung —, to draw a parallel; eine Vergleichung zwischen Gründen und Beweisen —, to compare reasons with arguments; Betrachtungen über den Zustand Frankreichs —, to contemplate the state of France. *b)* to order, to arrange [sometimes in a bad sense]. Wer hat das angestellt? who has been the author of it? who has done it? er hat etwas angestellt, he has done some mischief.

II. *v. r.* sich —, 1) [among hunters] to post or place one's self. Sich auf Wild —, to be on the look out for game, to lie on the catch. *Fig.* to behave, to conduct one's self. Sich ungeschickt bei einer Sache —, to do a thing awkwardly; sich albern —, to play the fool; sich jämmerlich —, to cut a deplorable figure; [sometimes in the sense of: to make a show of] sie stellt sich an, als ob sie lache, she feigns a laugh; sich freundlich —, to assume a kind manner, to feign or pretend kindness; sich ernsthaft —, to affect to be grave; sie ist nicht so tugendhaft, als sie sich anstellt, she is not so virtuous as she affects to be; er stellt sich an, als ob er mich liebe, he pretends love to me.

Ánsteller, *m.* [-s, *pl.* -] employer.

Ánstellig, *adj.* and *adv.* capable of ordering or arranging things well, apt, able. Er ist ein flinker, —er Bursche, he is a quick handy fellow.

Ánstelligkeit, *f.* aptitude. Sein Eifer und seine — in allen Dingen machten ihn zu einem höchst brauchbaren Gehülfen, his zeal and aptitude in every thing made him a very useful assistant.

Ánstellung, *f.* 1) act of ordering, arranging &c. 2) place, situation, employ, charge.

Ánstemmen, *v. tr.* to stem, push or fix against. Die Füße an die Wand —, to stem with the feet against the wall.

Ánsterben, *ir. v. intr.* [u. w. seyn] to devolve by death. Das Gut ist mir angestorben, the estate devolved by death on me.

Ánsteuern, *v. tr.* [a sea term] to steer towards.

Ánstich, *m.* [-es, *pl.* -e] the act of piercing or broaching.

Ánsticheln, *v. intr.* to treat with satirical merriment, to rally, to jeer. Auf etwas —, to allude to sarcastically.

Ánsticken, *v. tr.* to join embroidery to, to unite by embroidery.

Ánstieben, V. Anstauben.

Ánstieren, *v. tr.* to stare at. V. Anglotzen.

Ánstiften, *v. tr. Fig.* 1) to cause, to devise, to set on foot. [in a bad sense] Böses, Unheil —, to devise evil, to breed mischief; einen Aufstand —, to plot or stir up an insurrection. 2) to excite, to instigate [commonly in a bad sense]. [in law] to abet. Einen —, to suborn any one; Einen zu etwas —, to set any one on to any thing. Das —, the act of devising or instigating. Ich that es auf — meines Bruders, I did it on the instigation of my brother.

Ánstifter, *m.* [-s, *pl.* -] -inn, *f.* contriver, author, plotter, exciter, instigator, [in law] abettor, suborner.

Ánstiftung, *f.* the act of instigating &c. Die — falscher Zeugen, the subornation of false witnesses.

Ánstimmen, *v. tr.* 1) to begin to sing, to tune. Lasset uns ein fröhliches Lied —, let us join in a joyful song. *Fig.* Stimmet sein Lob an, tune his praise. 2) to sound [a violin &c.].

Ánstimmung, *f.* intonation, tuning.

Ánstinken, *ir. v. intr.* to emit an offensive smell, to stink.

Ánstöhnen, *v. tr.* to groan at.

Ánstolpern, *v. intr.* 1) [u. w. seyn] to stumble against something. 2) [u. w. seyn and kommen] to approach stumbling.

Ánstopfen, I. *v. tr.* 1) to stuff to, to add by stuffing. 2) to fill, to stuff. II. *v. r.* sich —, to stuff one's belly, to cram one's self, to gorge one's self.

Ánstören, *v. tr.* to excite, to instigate, to set on.

Ánstoß, *m.* [-es, *pl.* -stöße] 1) a striking against any thing, stumbling, shock, impulse, impulsion. *Fig.* Er gab den ersten — zur Einführung dieser Maßregel, he gave the first impulse to, or he was the first mover of this measure; durch den — [Druck] einer Flüssigkeit, by the impulse of a fluid. *Fig. a)* an impediment in the speech, hesitation, stammering. *b)* displeasure given, scandal, offence. — geben, to give offence; — nehmen an &c., to be scandalized at &c.; der Stein des —es, stumbling-block, stumbling-stone. Shakespeare ist ein Stein des —es für diese strengen Kritiker, Shakespeare is a stumbling-stone to these rigid critics. *c)* [for Anfall] the first attack of a disease, fit. Ein — vom Fieber, a fit of an ague. 2) [something joined on] *a)* [am. tail.] fine-drawing, rentering. *b)* Der — des Brodes, V. Kleberanft.

Anstoßnaht [or blinde Naht], *f.* [am. tailors] fine-drawing, rentering.

Ánstoßen, *ir.* I. *v. tr.* 1) to strike or push against. Die Gläser —, to touch or jingle the glasses; das Obst ist angestoßen, the fruit is bruised or touched a little. 2) to fasten by beating or pushing hard. 3) to join, to unite by pushing, [among tailors] to fine-draw, renter. 4) *Fig.* [among hunters] to announce the beginning of a thing by blowing. Die Jagd mit dem Hifthorne —, to announce the beginning of the chase by blowing upon the bugle-horn. II. *v. intr.* 1) to push against any thing. Mit den Gläsern —, to touch the glasses; wir wollen auf seine Gesundheit —, we will drink to his health; im Finstern mit dem Kopfe an or wider einen Pfosten —, to knock one's head against a post in the dark; [said also of animals] ein Pferd, das bei jedem Tritte anstößt, a horse that stumbles at every step; das Schiff stieß an eine Sandbank an, the ship struck upon a sandbank. *Fig. a)* Im Reden mit der Zunge —, to have an impediment in one's speech, to hesitate, to stammer. *b)* to commit a fault, to offend against. Es stößt gegen die Regeln der Sprachlehre an, it offends against the rules of grammar; diese Behauptung stößt gegen die Religion und guten Sitten an, this assertion shocks religion and good manners. 2) to border, to confine, to be contiguous or adjacent. Der Acker stößt an die Wiese an, the field borders on or upon the meadow; die Häuser im alten Rom stießen nicht an einander an, the houses in ancient Rome were not contiguous; der —de Wald, the adjacent forest.

Ánstößig, I. *adj.* 1) stumbling almost at every step, tripping. 2) *Fig.* giving offence, offensive, scandalous, offensive to decency and delicacy, shocking. —e Reden, indecent language. II. *adv.* offensively, scandalously shockingly. V. Aergerlich.

Ánstößigkeit, *f.* 1) offensiveness. 2) an offence against delicacy &c., indecency.

Ánstottern, *v. tr.* Einen —, to address any one stutteringly.

Ánstrahlen, *v. tr.* 1) to gleam or shine upon. 2) *Fig.* [and in poetry] to throw or spread light on, to illumine, to beam on. Vom Glanz der Sonne angestrahlt, illumined by the rays of the sun.

Ánstranden, *v. intr.* [u. w. seyn] to strand.

V. Stranden.

Ansträngen, *v. tr.* to tie with or to cords. Die Pferde —, to put the horses into the traces, to put them to the carriage &c.

Anstrebekraft, *f.* [*pl.* -kräfte] [that force which draws or impels a body towards some point as a centre] centripetal force.

Anstreben, *v. intr.* to strive against.

Anstrecken, *v. tr.* 1) to strain, to stretch [a rope &c.]. 2) *Fig.* to strain.

Anstreicheln, *v. tr.* to smooth by stroking.

Anstreichen, *ir.* I. *v. tr.* 1) to spread upon. 2) to colour, to paint. Die Stube weiß —, to whiten, to white-wash a room. *Fig* Einer Sache eine Farbe —, to set a thing in a fair light, to give it a specious appearance, to colour it. 3) to mark with the stroke. Etwas in einem Buche —, to mark something in a book, to underline a passage. *Fig.* Ich werde es ihm —, I'll make him pay for it, I'll punish him for it. II. *v. intr.* to brush lightly the surface of a thing in passing, to touch something lightly in passing.

Anstreicher, *m.* [s-, *pl.* -] painter, house-painter.

Anstreifen, *v. intr.* to brush lightly the surface of a thing in passing, to touch or graze something lightly in passing. Im Vorbeigehen mit dem Arme —, to brush with the arm in passing.

Anstrengen, I. *v. tr.* to extend with great effort, to strain, to stretch. *Fig.* to strain, to put in action. Alle seine Kräfte —, to strain every nerve; seine Stimme —, to strain one's voice; den Geist —, to exert the mind; seinen Kopf —, to strain one's wits; diese Arbeit hat ihn sehr angestrengt, this work fatigued him greatly. II. *v. r.* sich —, to exert one's self, to strain; sich über die Maßen —, to overwork, to harass one's self; strenge dich ein wenig an, um es zu erlangen, stretch a little for it.

Anstreuen, *v. tr.* to strew on or to add by strewing. Salz —, to sprinkle with salt.

Anstrich, *m.* [-es, *pl.* -e] 1) a laying on, painting or colouring. Der — dieses Zimmers ist sehr wohlfeil, the painting of this room is very cheap. 2) the thing painted or to be painted or coloured. *Fig. a*) colour, superficial cover or coating, varnish. Der schlechtesten Sache einen guten — geben, to gloss the foulest cause. *b*) tincture. Einen — von Religion haben, to have a tincture of religion; ein — von Sittlichkeit, an appearance of decency; ein — von Gelehrsamkeit, a smack or smattering of learning; er wußte sich einen — von Gelehrsamkeit zu geben, der &c., he knew how to give himself an air of learning, which &c.; ein — von Schwermuth, a touch or dash of melancholy. 3) [among hunters] the trace of a stag on the dewy grass.

Anstricken, *v. tr.* to add by knitting. Strümpfe —, to foot stockings.

Anstriegeln, *v. tr.* to smooth with a curry-comb.

Anströmen, I. *v. intr.* [u. w. seyn and sometimes w. kommen] 1) to flow or stream near. Das Wasser strömt an, kommt angeströmt, the water streams on, advances rapidly. 2) to touch in streaming. Der Fluß strömt an die Mauer an, the river washes the wall. *Fig.* Es kam eine große Volksmenge angeströmt, a multitude of people came flocking on; von allen Seiten strömten die Schaulustigen an, the gazers flocked from all sides II. *v. tr.* to increase by alluvion. Der Fluß strömt an diese or an dieser Küste Land an, the river washes or carries earth to that shore.

Anstückeln, *v. tr.* to add small pieces to, to piece.

Anstücken, *v. tr.* [especially with tailors and sempstresses] to enlarge by the addition of a piece, to piece.

Anstülpen, *v. tr.* to clap a top or lid on. Stiefel —, to top boots.

Anstürmen, *v. intr.* 1) to approach storming or thundering [sometimes with kommen]. Wie die Windsbraut kam die feindliche Reiterei angestürmt, the enemy's cavalry came thundering on like a hurricane. 2) to storm against or at. An eine Thür —, to knock violently at a door.

Ansturz, *m.* [-es, *pl.* -stürze] a violent motion against or at any thing. Sie widerstehen dem —e stürmischer Meere, they resist the shocks of tempestuous seas; er widerstand dem —e eines ganzen feindlichen Heeres, he withstood the shock of a whole host of foes; der — des Wassers, the rush of waters.

Anstürzen, I. *v. intr.* 1) [u. w. seyn and sometimes with kommen] to rush against. Das Wasser stürzt mit großer Gewalt an den Damm an, the water precipitates itself with great force against the dam; angestürzt kommen, to come rushing on, to rush on. 2) to rush near. II. *v. tr.* to clap to. Erde an eine Mauer —, to throw up earth against a wall.

Anstutzen, *v. tr.* to start at. Einen —, to regard any one with surprise or astonishment.

Anstützen, *v. tr.* to support on, to lean on. Sich —, to support one's self against, to lean against.

Ansuchen, *v. intr.* to solicit, to petition. Um etwas —, to solicit for something; um ein Amt —, to sue for a place; um die Erlaubniß —, to ask permission; er hat darum angesucht, he solicited or requested it; ansuchend, requisitive.

Ansuchen, *n.* [-s] solicitation, request, petition. Auf —, upon the application of; er stellte ein — an den Kanzleihof, he made application to the court of chancery; auf — der Gläubiger &c., at the requisition of the creditors &c.

Ansucher, *m.* [-s, *pl.* -] requester, petitioner, claimant, suitor, plaintiff.

Ansuchung, *f.* V. Ansuchen.

Ansud, *m.* [-es, *pl.* -e] [among dyers] the scouring of the wool.

Ansudeln, *v. tr.* V. Besudeln.

Ansummen, I. *v. r.* sich —, to increase, to augment so as to form great sums, to mount up. II. *v. intr.* 1) to approach humming [sometimes w. kommen]. 2) [u. w. seyn] to strike against in humming.

Ansumsen, V. Ansummen II.

Ansüßen, *v. tr.* to sweeten a little [a drink &c.]. [in chem.] to dulcorate or edulcorate.

Ant, [gr. ἀντί] an inseparable prefix to the words Antlitz and Antwort. V. Ent.

***Antagonist**, *m.* [-s, -en, *pl.* -en] antagonist, adversary.

***Antagonismus**, *m.* [*pl.* -men] antagonism.

Antakeln, *v. tr.* [commonly betakeln, a sea-term] to fit with tackling. Ein Schiff —, to rig a ship.

***Antel**, *n.* V. Anthal.

Antanzen, I. *v. intr.* 1) [u. w. haben] to begin to dance, to lead off. Ich tanze an, I dance first. 2) [u. w. seyn and kommen] to approach dancing. 3) to strike against any thing in dancing. II. *v. tr.* *sich etwas —, to catch by dancing; er hat sich den Schnupfen, die Schwindsucht angetanzt, he caught a cold from dancing, he danced himself into a consumption.

Antappen, I. *v. intr.* to grope at any thing [in the dark, or as a blind person]. II. *v. tr.* to take hold of any one in a coarse or awkward manner.

Antasten, *v. tr.* to touch, to feel with the hand, to handle. *Fig.* Jemandes guten Namen —, to assault or injure a man's reputation; Einen mit Worten —, to attack any one, to inveigh against any one.

Antaumeln, *v. intr.* [u. w. seyn] to approach reeling [comm. with kommen]. Angetaumelt kommen, to come reeling along. 2) to reel against any thing.

***Antecessor**, *m.* [-s, *pl.* -en] antecessor. V. Vorgänger.

***Antedatiren**, *v. tr.* to antedate [a letter &c.].

***Antepenultima**, *f.* the last syllable but two, antepenult.

Anthal, *n.* [-es, *pl.* -e] a Hungarian wine-measure about 35 gallons.

Antheil, *m* [-es, *pl.* -e] 1) [with some authors *n.*] portion, part. — an der Erbschaft, a share of an inheritance; Einer, der — an einer Erbschaft hat, a co heir, a joint heir; an etwas — nehmen, to take a share in a thing; — haben, to have part in, to share, to participate. *Fig.* Zu leiden und zu sterben ist des Menschen —, the lot of man is to suffer and to die; er hat großen — an diesen Begebenheiten gehabt, he bore a great share in these events. 2) *Fig.* fellow feeling, sympathy. — an den Leiden eines Menschen nehmen, to sympathize with, to take an interest in any one's troubles, sorrows or sufferings; seyen Sie überzeugt, daß ich den lebhaftesten — an Ihrem Schicksal nehme, be assured, that I take the most lively interest in your fate.

Antheil=haber [better: Theilhaber], *m.* a sharer of any thing, a partaker, participant. — nehmung, *f.* fellow feeling, sympathy. — schein, *m.* a share of a company's stock. — verschreibung, *f.* V. —schein.

Antheilig, *adj.* and *adv.* having a share of any thing, partaking, participating.

Antheilmäßig, *adj.* and *adv.* according to one's share.

***Anthologie**, *f.* [*pl.* -en] a collection of beautiful passages from authors, anthology. V. Blumenlese.

***Anthropolith**, *m.* [-s, *pl.* -en] a petrifaction of the human body, anthropolite.

***Anthropologie**, *f.* [*pl.* -en] the natural history or physiology of the human species, anthropology.

***Anthropomorphismus**, *m.* [*pl.* -men] the heresy of the anthropomorphites, anthropomorphism.

***Anthropomorphiten**, *pl.* [those who believe a human form in the Supreme Being] anthropomorphites.

***Anthropophag**, *m.* [-s, -en, *pl.* -en] a man-eater, cannibal. Die —en, anthropophagi.

Anthun, *ir. v. tr.* 1) to put on [a coat &c.]. *Fig* [in seamen's language] *a*) to make or make for a port. *b*) to touch on or upon. Er that die Molukken an, he touched at the Moluccas; einen Hafen —, to touch at a port. 2) to do any thing for the benefit or to the injury of another. Einem Böses —, to do evil to any one; Einem Gutes —, to do good to any one; es muß dem Vieh etwas angethan seyn, cattle must be bewitched; sie hat es mir angethan, she has bewitched me; sich Zwang —, to put or lay one's self under constraint; sich den Tod —, to make away with one's self.

* Ántichrist, *m.* [-s, *pl.* -en] [a great adversary of Christ; the man of sin] antichrist.

* Antídotum, *n.* [-s, *pl.* -a] [in medec.] antidote.

Ántiefen, *v. tr.* [a sea term] to sound.

* Ánti-epileptisch, *adj.* [in medecine] anti-epileptic.

* Antik, *adj.* old, ancient, antique.

* Antike, *f.* [*pl.* -n] antique.

* Antikritik, *f.* [*pl.* -en] V. Gegenbeurtheilung.

* Antilópe, *f.* [*pl.* -n] antilope or antelope.

* Antimōnium, *n.* [-s] antimony.

* Antinomie, *f.* [*pl.* -en] [a contradiction between two laws, or between two parts of the same law] antinomy.

* Ántipapistisch, *adj.* and *adv.* antipapal, antipapistic, antipapistical.

* Antipathie, *f.* [*pl.* -en] natural aversion, antipathy.

* Ántiphlogistisch, *adj.* and *adv.* antiphlogistic.

* Ántiphon, *m.* the chant or alternate singing of choirs in cathedrals, antiphon. V. Wechselchor, Gegengesang.

* Antiphrāse, *f.* [*pl.* -n] [the use of words in a sense opposite to their proper meaning] antiphrasis. V. Gegensinn.

* Antiphrástisch, *adv.* antiphrastically.

* Antipōde, *m.* [-n, *pl.* -n] antipode.

Ántippen, *v. tr.* to touch with a point. Mit dem Finger —, to touch with the point of one's finger.

* Antiquār, *m.* [-s, *pl.* -e] 1) antiquary, antiquarian. V. Alterthumsforscher. 2) second-hand bookseller, vender of second-hand books.

* Antiquaschrift, *f.* [*pl.* -en] [in printing] Roman characters.

Antiquitāt, *f.* [*pl.* -en] antiquity.

* Ántiscorbutisch, *adj.* and *adv.* antiscorbutic.

* Ántistrophe, *f.* [*pl.* -n] [among the ancients] antistrophe, antistrophy.

* Antithese, *f.* [*pl.* -n] [in rhetoric] antithesis.

* Antithétisch, *adj.* antithetical.

* Ántitypus, *m.* [a figure corresponding to another figure] antitype.

* Ántivenerisch, *adj.* [in medecine] antaphrodisial, antaphroditic, antivenereal.

Ántlitz, *n.* [-es] face, countenance. V. Angesicht. Ins —, to the teeth; sein — glänzte vor Freude, his countenance beamed with joy.

Antlitzseite, *f.* the facade, face or front [of a palace]. V. Vorderseite.

Ántoben, *v. intr.* [u. w. seyn] 1) to approach blustering and raging [sometimes with kommen]. 2) [u. w. haben] to thunder at [a door &c.].

Ánton, *m.* [a name of men] Anthony.

Antons-feuer, *n.* [a popular name of the erysipela] Anthony's fire. —kreuz, *n.* [in heraldry] St. Anthony's cross.

Ántönen, *v. intr.* to begin to sound.

* Antonomasie, *f.* [the use of the name of some office, profession &c. instead of the true name of the person] autonomasia, antonomasy.

Ántraben, *v. intr.* [u. w. seyn and kommen] to come near trotting.

Ántrag, *m.* [-es, *pl.* -träge] 1) the act of making an offer or proposal. 2) proposal made, offer, proposition. Der König verfügte auf den — seines Ministeriums, daß &c., on the proposition of his ministry the king ordered, that &c.; Anträge thun, to motion, to make proposals; Liebesanträge machen, to make tenders of love; meine Anträge wurden verworfen, my offers were disdained; [in parliament] einen — machen, to make a motion; der — ging durch, the motion was carried through or passed.

Ántragen, *ir.* I. *v. tr.* to carry to a place. *Fig.* to propose, to offer. Einem seine Dienste —, to offer one's self to serve another, to make a tender of one's services to any one; Einem Hülfe —, to offer one's aid to another; es wurde ihm eine vortheilhafte Heirath angetragen, an advantageous match was offered to him. II. *v. intr* to make a proposal, to offer plans. Du trugst auf den Frieden mit uns an, thou didst motion peace with us; es ist darauf angetragen worden, the motion was made. V. Anbieten.

Ántrampeln, Antrampen, Antrappeln, Antrappen, *v. intr.* [u. w. seyn and kommen] to approach trampling.

Ántrauen, *v. tr.* to unite in marriage, to dispose of in marriage. Einem seine Tochter —, to marry one's daughter to any one; sie wurde ihm heimlich angetraut, she was secretly married or united to him.

Ántraufeln, *v. intr.* and *v. tr.* to trickle or fall in small drops.

Ántraufen, *v. intr.* [u. w. seyn] to drop or drip at.

Ántraufen, *v. tr.* to drop or drip at.

Ántreffen, *ir.* I. *v. tr.* 1) to meet with, to find. In Wäldern bist du anzutreffen, in forests thou art found; ich traf ihn zufällig an, I met him by chance; ich traf ihn zufällig auf der Straße an, I lighted on him in the street; nicht anzutreffen, not to be met with. *Fig.* Bei Allen treffe ich Schönheit oder Verstand an, beauty or wit in all I find. 2) *Fig.* to concern, to relate to. II. *v. intr.* to meet and strike against. V. Finden.

Ántreiben, *ir.* I. *v. tr.* 1) [in metallurgy] to begin to refine. 2) to drive, to impel. Die Pferde —, to drive the horses; die —de Kraft, impulsive force. *Fig.* Vom Ehrgeize angetrieben, actuated or incited by ambition; vom Hunger angetrieben, impelled by hunger; wenn die Zeit sie — wird, when time shall prompt them. 2) to drive or force. Einen Reif —, to drive a hoop. Die Planken —, [in sea language] to wring the planks. II. *v. intr.* 1) [u. w. seyn] to drive. Das Eis treibt an die Brücke an, the ice drives against the bridge. 2) [u. w. seyn and kommen] to approach driving.

Antreibeholz, *n.* [in metall.] wood used for the refining furnace.

Ántreiber, *m.* [-s, *pl.* -] driver, inciter, impeller.

Ántreten, *ir.* I. *v. tr.* 1) to put one thing to another by treading [as earth round the foot of a tree, &c.]. 2) *Fig.* *a*) Einen —, to accost or to address any one; Einen um etwas —, to apply to any one for any thing. *b*) to begin, to enter on, to commence. Eine Reise —, to set out upon a journey; ein Amt, ein Gut —, to enter upon an office or upon an estate; eine Erbschaft —, to take possession of an inheritance; die Regierung —, to come to the crown; ein neues Jahr —, to begin a new year; er hat sein zehntes Jahr angetreten, he has entered his tenth year. II. *v. intr.* [u. w. seyn] 1) to step close to [a wall &c.]. Bei einem Freunde —, to call on a friend. 2) [in fencing] to begin to fence, to take one's position. 3) [in dancing] to take one's place. 4) *Fig.* to enter upon an office. Er ist gestern angetreten, he entered upon his office yesterday.

Ántrieb, *m.* [-es, *pl.* -e] 1) the act of driving or impelling, impulse, impulsion [without a plural]. Er hat es auf — seines Weibes gethan, he did it at the instigation of his wife. 2) *Fig.* influence acting on the mind, impulse, impulsion. Auf Jupiters —, by Jove's impulse; aus eigenem —e, of one's own accord; der — des Gewissens, the impulse of conscience; aus natürlichem —e, by instinct. 3) that which impels, impellent.

Ántrinken, *ir.* I. *v. r.* sich —, to drink one's fill, to get drunk. II. *v intr.* to begin to drink.

Ántrippeln, *v. intr.* [u. w. seyn and kommen] to come near trippingly.

Ántritt, *m.* [-es, *pl.* -e] 1) the act of stepping on. [in fencing] the beginning of the fencing. [in manege] amble. V. Paß. *Fig.* a beginning, entering upon or commencing. Obrigkeitliche Personen bei dem —e ihres Amtes, magistrates at their entrance into office; bei dem —e seiner Reise, at his setting out; der — des neuen Jahres, the beginning of the year. 2) a place for stepping on; [among printers] foot-step.

Antritts-lehen, *n.* V. Lehenwaare. —gehör, *n.* [—audienz] the first audience [of an ambassador]. —geld, *n.* entrance-money. V. Einstandsgeld. —mahl, *m.* a dinner given to one's friends &c. on one's entrance into office. —predigt, *f.* an inaugural sermon. —schmaus, *m.* V. —mahl.

Ántrocknen, *v. intr.* [u. w. seyn] 1) to begin to dry, to dry a little. 2) to dry and adhere.

Ántrödeln, *v. intr.* [u. w. seyn and kommen] to approach with slow paces, to come sauntering along.

Ántrommeln, I. *v. intr.* 1) to begin to drum. 2) *Fig.* to drum or thump at a door &c. II. *v. tr.* to proclaim by beat of drum [the break of day, &c.].

Ántrompeten, *v. tr.* 1) to direct the sound of a trumpet towards any one. 2) to publish by sound of trumpet, to trumpet.

Ántröpfeln, V. Antraufen.

Ántropfen, *v. intr.* [u. w. seyn] to trickle, drop or drip on a thing.

Ántrotten, V. Antraben.

Ántüpfen, *v. tr.* to touch with the finger's end.

|| Antvogel, *m.* V. Ente.

Ántwort, *f.* [*pl.* -en] reply, answer. Eine abschlägige —, a refusal, a rebuff; eine spitzige —, a smart reply, repartee; — geben, to make, give or return an answer, to answer; auf — dringen, to entreat instantly for an answer, to urge or insist on an answer. *Prov.* Wie die Frage, so die —, to answer any one in his own language. *Fig.* Ein bitteres Lachen war die —, he answered by a bitter laugh.

Antwort-schreiben, *n.* written answer, reply, letter in answer. —schrift, *f.* [in law] reply.

Ántworten, I. *v. intr.* 1) to answer. Ich habe gerufen und ihr habt nicht geantwortet, I have called and ye have not answered; auf eine Frage —, to answer a question; er antwortete darauf, he replied upon it; schnell, lebhaft or beißend —, to repartee; auf eine Flugschrift —, to answer or return an answer to a pamphlet. 2) *Fig.* to suit with, to answer. V. Zusagen, Entsprechen. II. *v tr.* Etwas, nichts —, to answer any thing, nothing; ich habe ihm auf seinen Brief Folgendes geantwortet, I answered his letter as follows; auf meine ernste Frage antwortete er eine Albernheit, my serious question he answered by some folly. Syn. Antworten, Erwiedern, Versetzen. We erwiedern [reply to or return] a speech, a compliment &c., we erwiedern also actions directed or addressed to us, as a bow &c. We antworten [answer] only a question, request, objection &c. Versetzen is to answer in a verbal contest, and generally contains the idea of some heat and quickness.

Antwortlich, *adv.* in reply.

Anüben, *v. tr.* to obtain by practice, to get by exercise, employment or exertion.

Anverlangen, V. Verlangen or Nachsuchen.

Anvermählen, *v. tr.* to dispose of in marriage, to unite in marriage, to marry.

Anversuchen, *v. tr.* to try on [clothes].

Anvertrauen, *v. tr.* to intrust, to commit to the charge of, with a belief in the fidelity of the person intrusted, to confide. Einem etwas —, to put a person in trust with any thing, to commit a thing to a person; einem Freunde ein Geheimniß —, to confide a secret to a friend; der Fürst vertraut seinem Gesandten eine Unterhandlung an, the prince confides a negotiation to his envoy; sein Vater hat ihn unsrer Sorge anvertraut, his father intrusted him to our care; sich einem Freunde —, to unbosom one's self to a friend; anvertrautes Gut, deposit.

Anverwandt, *adj.* and *adv.* related to, kindred, akin to. Sie ist meine —e, she is a relation of mine. V. Verwandt.

Anverwandtschaft, *f.* 1) relationship, kindred. 2) relatives, kindred.

Anvettern, *v. r.* sich —, to be officious to any one as if related to him.

Anwachs, *m.* [-es] 1) increase, augmentation. Der — eines Landes, the increase of a land [especially by alluvion]. *Fig.* Der — der Schulden, an increase or augmentation of the debts. 2) a thing that grows or is grown to. Junger —, young trees or plants.

Anwachsrecht, *n.* V. Anwachsungsrecht.

Anwachsen, *ir. v. intr.* 1) [u. w. seyn] to become united by growth, to grow to, to grow up. Diese Bäume sind an einander angewachsen, these trees are grown together; die Lunge wächst zuweilen an die Rippenhaut an, the lungs sometimes adhere to the pleura; das Pferd ist angewachsen, [veterinary art] the horse is hide-bound; die angewachsene Haut des Auges, [in anatomy, a membrane of the eye] conjunctiva; angewachsen, [in botany] adnate. 2) to grow, to increase, to augment; der Fluß wächst sehr an, the river swells much; die Wasser wachsen an, the waters rise; die Bäume, die Kinder wachsen an, the trees, the children grow; anwachsend, accrescent. *Fig.* Der Wind wuchs zum Sturme an, the wind grew to a tempest; die Schulden wachsen täglich an, the debts augment every day; die Zahl der Einwohner wächst von Jahr zu Jahr an, the number of inhabitants increases from year to year; [in music] die Töne — lassen, V. Anschwellen.

Anwachsung, *f.* 1) the act of growing to, of increasing. 2) [in architecture] V. Ausladung.

Anwachsungsrecht, *n.* [in law] a right to the alluvial earth.

Anwackeln, *v. intr.* [u. w. seyn and sometimes with kommen] to approach tottering.

Anwählen, *v. tr.* to adopt [a child].

Anwallen, *v. intr.* 1) [u. w. seyn] to be moved near or towards in an undulating manner. 2) [often with kommen] to crowd near. 3) to strike against a thing in bubbling, to bubble against. 4) [u. w. haben] to begin to bubble, to boil.

Anwalt, *m.* [-es, *pl.* -e] one entrusted with the business of another, a substitute, deputy, proxy, agent, attorney, advocate, solicitor.

Anwaltgebühr, *f.* the fees of an agent or attorney.

Anwaltschaft, *f.* agency, deputyship, proctorship, attorneyship.

Anwalzen, I. *v. intr.* 1) to begin to waltz. 2) to waltz against [a stone &c.]. II. *v. tr.* 1) to press close to by a roller. 2) to level with a roller.

Anwälzen, I. *v. tr.* to roll towards [a stone against the wall]. II. *v. intr.* [u. w. seyn] to approach rolling.

‖**Anwand**, *f.* V. Grenze.

Anwandeln, *v. intr.* [u. w. seyn] 1) to walk near. 2) to come on, to befall. Es wandelte mich eine Ohnmacht an, I was seized with a fainting fit. 3) [often u. w. kommen] to walk near with slow steps.

Anwandlung, *f.* a slight attack [as for instance of a disorder], a temporary affection. Die — einer Ohnmacht or eine — von Ohnmacht, a fainting-fit; eine — von Andacht, a fit of devotion; in einer — von Frömmigkeit besuchte er ganz unerwartet die Kirche, in a fit of devotion he went to church quite unexpectedly; eine — von Schwermuth, a fit of melancholy.

Anwandern, *v. intr.* [u. w. seyn and commonly w. kommen] to wander near or to approach a place.

Anwanken, *v. intr.* 1) [u. w. seyn and kommen] to come near tottering. 2) to totter against.

Anwärmen, *v. tr.* [in metallurgy] to begin to heat [a furnace].

Anwarten, *v. intr.* to wait in expectation; [in feudal law] to expect, to succeed any one in the possession and enjoyment of any thing.

Anwarter, *m.* [-s, *pl.* -] an expectant, a candidate.

Anwartschaft, *f.* reversion, expectancy, survival, survivorship. Die — auf eine Stelle, the reversion or expectancy of an office. —spatente, reversionary patents.

Anwartschafter, *m.* V. Anwarter.

Anwartschaftlich, *adj.* and *adv.* reversionary.

Anwäsche, *f.* [in metallurgy] the whole proceeding in washing ores.

Anwaschen, *v. intr.* to begin to wash.

Anwässern, *v. intr.* to moisten a little, to irrigate.

Anwatscheln, *v. intr.* [u. w. seyn and kommen] to approach waddling.

Anweben, *v. tr.* to join on to something else by weaving.

Anwedeln, *v. tr.* 1) to fan. 2) to wag to. Der Hund wedelte mich freundlich an, the dog wagged his tail at me.

Anwehen, *v. tr.* 1) to blow upon. Der Wind weht mich an, the wind blows upon me. *Fig.* Die Schrecken des Todes wehten sie an, the horrors of death seized them; Entsetzen wehete ihn an, horror fell on him. Was hat dich denn auf einmal angeweht [= woher kommt denn diese plötzliche Veränderung deiner Stimmung]? what has come over you all at once? 2) to blow against. Der Wind wehet den Schnee an das Haus an, the wind drives or drifts the snow against the house. II *v intr.* [u. w. seyn] to approach blowing.

Anwehen, *n.* [-s] a blowing or breathing on, afflation.

Anweichen, [from weich] *v. tr.* to soak, to steep a little.

Anweinen, *v. tr.* to address [any one] weeping.

Anweisebank, *f.* V. Girobank.

Anweisen, *ir. v. tr.* 1) to assign, to appoint, to designate. Den Priestern ward ihr Theil angewiesen, the priests had a portion assigned to them; was hat man ihm angewiesen? what was allotted to him? einem Jeden seinen Dienst —, to appoint every one to his service; Holz —, to mark out trees that are to be felled; es wurden ihm zehn Klafter Holz als Theil seiner Besoldung, als Geschenk &c. angewiesen, ten cords of wood were assigned him as part of his salary, as a present &c.; Geld —, to assign money; einen Theil seiner Güter zur Bezahlung seiner Schulden —, to assign part of one's estate for the payment of one's debts; Arbeiter —, to show workmen to a place, to direct them; sich — lassen, to take directions; [in husbandry] den Hopfen stängeln und —, to pole hops and give a direction to the tendrils. 2) to refer to. Er hat mich wegen näherer Auskunft an Sie angewiesen [or gewiesen, or verwiesen], he referred me to you for farther information. 3) to direct, to order, to enjoin, to admonish, to command. Ich bin angewiesen &c., I am ordered &c.; zu etwas —, to direct, to instruct, to guide; seine Kinder zur Tugend —, to guide one's children to virtue.

Anweiser, *m.* [-s, *pl.* -] 1) assigner. 2) director, instructor.

Anweisung, *f.* 1) the act of assigning, allotting, assignment. 2) a check, a draft, a bill of exchange. 3) direction, order, injunction. 4) direction, instruction.

Anweißen, *v. tr.* to white-wash [a room &c.].

Anwelken, I. *v. intr.* [u. w. seyn] to begin to fade or to wither. II. *v. tr.* to cause to wither a little, to fade a little.

Anwelle, *f.* [*pl.* -n] a stay, prop, support.

Anwendbar, *adj.* and *adv.* applicable. Diese Bemerkung ist auf &c. —, this observation is applicable to, applies to &c.; alle —en Mittel erschöpfen, to exhaust all practicable means.

Anwendbarkeit, *f.* applicability, applicableness.

Anwenden, *ir.* and *reg. v. tr.* 1) to use or employ for a particular purpose. Seine Zeit gut —, to employ one's time well; seinen Verstand gut —, to make a good use of one's understanding; sein Geld übel —, to misemploy one's money; alle seine Kräfte —, to exert one's utmost strength; er wandte seine Talente lieber zu einem bedeutenden Werke an, als daß er sie für kleine Arbeiten zersplittert hätte, he employed his talents rather to a work of some consequence, instead of wasting them on trifles. 2) [with the prep. auf] to apply to a subject. Dieser Vers Virgils kann auf ihn angewendet werden or läßt sich auf ihn —, that verse of Virgil can be applied to him; Prophezeihungen auf Ereignisse —, to accommodate prophecies to events; er wandte eben diese Schlüsse auf ihn an, he turned these very reasonings upon him; ein angewandter Begriff, a concrete idea; der angewandte Theil einer Wissenschaft, the practical part of a science; die angewandte Erdmeßkunst, practical geometry; die angewandte Größenlehre, mixed mathematics [as hydrostatics, navigation, optics &c.]. 3) to use or employ well. Es ist bei ihm nicht angewandt, it will be of no use or advantage to him, he does not avail himself of it.

Anwendlich, *adj.* and *adv.* capable of being used, fit or proper for use, employable.

Anwendung, *f.* 1) the act of employing or using a thing for a particular purpose, employment, adhibition; the act of referring something to a particular case, application. Durch eine passende — von Belohnungen und Strafen, by a suitable application of rewards and punishments; durch die —, by practice; ich mache die Bemerkung und überlasse Ihnen die —, I make the remark and leave you to make the application. 2) the application of one thing to another by analogy, accommodation, adaptation. Die — der Worte einer Prophezeihung auf ein künftiges Ereigniß, the accommodation of the words of a prophecy to a future event.

Ánwerben, I. *v. tr.* 1) to engage in public service, to enlist, to enroll. Soldaten —, to engage men for military service, to recruit [soldiers]; sich als Soldat or zum Soldaten — lassen, to enroll one's self as soldier; ein Heer —, to levy an army; der Angeworbene, a recruit. 2) *Fig.* to engage. Er hat mich zu einer Lustfahrt angeworben, he has engaged me for a party of pleasure. II. *v. intr.* [with the prep. um] to woo, to court, to pay one's addresses, to demand in marriage. Er hat um sie angeworben, he wooed her.

Ánwerber, *m.* [-s, *pl.* -] wooer, suitor.

Ánwerden, *ir. v. intr.* [u. w. seyn] to get rid of. Er ist alle seine Waare angeworden, he has sold, has disposed of all his goods.

Ánwerfen, *ir.* I. *v. intr.* 1) to begin to throw [at nine-pins, at dice]. Wer wirft an? who throws first? 2) to throw or cast at. II. *v. tr.* 1) to throw on. Groben Mörtel —, to roughcast. 2) to put on in a hurry [a dressing-gown &c.].

Ánwesen, *n.* [not used] V. Gegenwart. It. [a law-term] V. Zubehör.

Ánwesend, *adj.* and *adv.* being at hand, present. Alle —e, all the persons present, or all present.

Ánwesenheit, *f.* [state of being present] presence.

Ánwettern, *v. intr.* † 1) to thunder at [a door &c.]. 2) [u. w. seyn and kommen] to approach thundering.

Ánwetzen, I. *v. tr.* 1) to begin to whet or to sharpen. 2) to furnish with a point by whetting. Eine Spitze an dem Messer —, to point a knife by whetting. ‖ II. *v. intr.* to rub in passing by.

Ánwichsen, *v. tr.* 1) to smear with blacking [shoes, boots]. 2) to make to adhere by means of wax.

Ánwickeln, *v. tr.* to fasten to something by winding, rolling or swathing.

Ánwidern, *v. intr.* to excite aversion, to offend. Gemeine Manieren widern mich an, I am disgusted with [at] vulgar manners. V. Anekeln.

Ánwiehern, *v. tr.* to neigh or whinny at; * to sneer at.

Ánwimmeln, *v. intr.* [u. w. seyn and kommen] to crowd on or near.

Ánwimmern, I. *v. intr.* [u. w. seyn and kommen] to approach whining. II. *v. tr.* Einen — [gegen Einen —], to address any one whining or in a whining manner or tone.

Ánwinden, *ir. v. tr.* to draw near by a windlass.

Ánwinken, *v. tr.* 1) to wink at or upon. 2) to give [any one] a wink to come near. 3) [in seamen's language] to ease off the sheets of the fore-stay-sails and the jib, in order to go to windward.

Ánwinseln, *v. tr.* to whine at.

Ánwintern, *v. intr.* [u. w. seyn] to come with or like the winter.

Ánwirbeln, I. *v. tr.* to fasten, to fix by turning a peg. II. *v. intr.* [u. w. seyn and sometimes kommen] 1) to approach warbling. 2) to whirl on or forward.

Ánwirken, I. *v. intr.* 1) to begin to work; [in salthouses] to begin to boil salt on the first day of the week. II. *v. tr.* to join to by weaving.

Ánwischen, *v. tr.* to wipe on or against.

Ánwispern, *v. tr.* to whisper to. Sie wisperte mich an, she whispered to me.

Ánwittern, *v. intr.* [u. w. seyn], angewittertes Erz, [in mineralogy] flowers of minerals attached to rocks by exhalation.

Ánwohnen, *v. intr.* 1) to dwell near. Er wohnt an dem Berge an, he lives next or close to the hill; der —de, he that inhabits near a place. 2) [= beiwohnen] einer Versammlung —, to be present at an assembly.

Ánworfeln, I. *v. intr.* to begin to winnow. II. *v. tr.* to throw against a thing with a winnowing shovel.

Ánwuchern, *v. intr.* [u. w. seyn] to grow luxuriantly, to luxuriate [said of plants].

Ánwuchs, *m.* [-es, *pl.* -wüchse] 1) a growing to, an increase by natural growth, augmentation. Der — der Pflanzen, the accretion of plants. 2) a thing grown to. Die Anwüchse der Bäume, Pflanzen, excrescences.

Ánwühlen, *v. intr.* to begin to turn up earth, to root up.

Ánwünschen, *v. tr.* 1) to wish [any one a happy voyage, a happy new year &c.]. Böses —, to wish ill, to imprecate. 2) [a law term] to adopt [a child].

Ánwünschung, *f.* 1) the act of wishing any thing in favour of another, wish. 2) [in law] adoption.

Ánwurf, *m.* [-es, *pl.* -würfe] 1) the act of throwing or casting on. Der — groben Mörtels, rough-casting; der — des Landes durch das Wasser, accretion, atterration. 2) the first throw at dice or at nine-pins, the lead. 3) the thing thrown or cast on. [among several workmen] *a*) [am. lock-smiths] a link [held on by a padlock]. *b*) [am. clothiers and manufacturers of serge] selvage. *c*) [in mints] mill. *d*) [am. tailors and sempstresses] eking-piece.

Anwurfschlüssel, *m.* [in mints, a part of the mill] lever.

Ánwürfeln, *v. intr.* 1) to begin to throw or cast [at dice]. Wer würfelt an? who throws first? who is the first to play? 2) [at dice] to strike against in casting.

Ánwurzeln, *v. intr.* [u. w. seyn] to fix the root, to take root.

Ánwüthen, *v. intr.* [u. w. seyn and kommen] 1) to rush on or near raging. 2) [u. w. haben] to rage against. Er wüthet gegen seine Fesseln an, he rages against his fetters.

Ánzahl, *f.* [an indefinite multitude] number. Auf die — kommt es bei einem Heere nicht immer an, number imports not in an army; sie kamen in großer —, they came in great numbers; nach der — or zahlweise verkaufen, to sell by tale. Syn. Anzahl, Menge. Menge signifies quantity, or multitude considered in the aggregate; Anzahl is applied to any collection considered of units or individually, number.

Ánzahlen, *v. tr.* to begin to pay, to pay, to pay on account.

Ánzählen, *v. tr.* to begin to number or tell.

‖ **Ánzahnen**, *v. tr.* to show the teeth to or at.

Ánzapfen, *v. tr.* to tap, to pierce. Ein Faß Bier —, to broach a cask of beer; ein Faß Wein —, to prick a cask of wine; das Faß ist angezapft, the cask is abroach; das Faß ist zum —, the cask is ready for broaching; einen Wassersüchtigen —, to tap any one for the dropsy. *Fig.* † *a*) Einen —, to pinch or nettle any one. *b*) to get money out of any one, to bleed any one.

Ánzappeln, *v. intr.* [u. w. seyn and kommen] to approach sprawling.

Ánzaubern, *v. tr.* to bring on by witchcraft. Einem eine Krankheit —, to cause any one an illness by witchcraft, to give any one a disease by the power of sorcery.

Ánzäumen, *v. tr.* 1) to bridle [a horse]. V. Aufzäumen. 2) to fasten with a bridle.

Ánzechen, *v. r.* sich —, to drink hard, to drink one's fill, to get tipsy.

Ánzeichen, *n.* [-s, *pl.* -] 1) a sign good or bad, a presage, a prognostic, an omen, an augury. Was wird dieses — bedeuten, what does this prognostic indicate. 2) a sign, a mark. [in med.] die — des Fiebers, the diagnostics of the fever; das ist ein untrügliches —, that is an infallible sign.

Ánzeichnen, *v. tr.* to impress with a token, to mark, to write down, to note. Einem etwas —, to put down something to any one's account; ihre Namen sind hier angezeichnet, their names are pricked here; es wurden sechs Schiffe angezeichnet, six ships were signalled.

Ánzeige, *f.* [*pl.* -n] 1) giving notice, informing, notification, information, intelligence, intimation, notice, news or advice communicated by word or writing. Wir erhielten die — von &c, we received the information from &c.; eine — bei Gericht, a charge or accusation exhibited to a magistrate or court, information, denunciation. 2) that which gives notice, [more generally] a publication intended to give notice, advertisement. Oeffentliche —n, advertisements, news, news-papers. 3) indication, mark, token, sign, symptom.

Anzeige-amt, *n.* V. Adreßcomptoir. —**blatt**, *n.* advertiser. —**brief**, *m.* letter of advice, circular. V. Avisbrief, Benachrichtigungsschreiben [in commerce]. —**weise**, *f.* [in gramm.] the indicative mood.

Ánzeigen, I. *v. tr.* to make known to by word or writing, to communicate, to announce, to notify. Einem etwas —, to inform any one of a thing; er zeigte seinen Verlust öffentlich [in öffentlichen Blättern] an, he advertised his loss; Einen [bei der Obrigkeit] —, to inform against, to denounce any one; [in grammar] —de [hinweisende] Fürwörter, demonstrative pronouns. II. *v. intr.* to be a mark, sign, token or symptom of any thing, to indicate, to presage. Dieß zeigt an, daß &c., this is a sign that &c.; sein Stillschweigen zeigt an, daß &c., his silence proves that &c.; es zeigt Regen an, it indicates the approach of rain; dieser Zufall zeigt uns nichts Gutes an, this accident augurs us no good. V. Entdecken, Eröffnen, Bekannt machen, Offenbaren, Verrathen.

Ánzeiger, *m.* [-s, *pl.* -] 1) one who informs or gives intelligence, informer, advertiser. 2) [a name given to public prints] advertiser. 3) [in mathematics] exponent. Der — [Exponent] eines Verhältnisses, the exponent of a ratio or proportion [thus six is the exponent of the ratio of thirty to five].

Ánzeigung, *f.* 1) the act of giving notice, information &c. 2) indication, mark, sign, token, symptom.

Ánzerren, *v. tr.* to fasten to by pulling, to pull on.

Ánzettel, *m.* V. Anschere.

Ánzetteln, *v. tr.* [among weavers] to warp. *Fig.* Sie haben eine Verschwörung gegen den Staat angezettelt, they have plotted against the state.

Ánzettler, *m.* [-s, *pl.* -] 1) [among weavers] one who warps. 2) *Fig.* contriver, plotter.

Anziehen, *ir.* I. *v. tr.* 1) to begin to draw. Die Pferde ziehen den Wagen an, the horses draw on the carriage; die Glocke —, to pull the bell, to give a pull at the bell, to give a ring. 2) to draw or put on [stockings &c.]. Stiefel —, to pull on boots; sich —, to dress one's self; angezogen, dressed, apparelled; sich schwarz —, to dress in black; andere Kleider —, to shift or change clothes; einen Rock —, to get on a coat; ein frisches Hemd —, to put on a clean shirt; weiße Wäsche — [= sich umkleiden], to shift one's self; sich geschwind und nachlässig —, to huddle on one's clothes. SYN. V. Ankleiden. *Fig.* Den alten Menschen ausziehen und den neuen —, to amend one's ways or our conduct. 3) to draw to, to cause to move towards. Der Magnet zieht das Eisen an, the loadstone attracts iron; die —de Kraft des Bernsteins, the attractive force of amber; [in medicine] —de Mittel, astringents. *Fig.* Eine —de Geschichte, an interesting story; —de Manieren, engaging or winning manners; das —de, attractiveness. 4) [= straff anziehen] Die Zügel —, to draw in the reins; ein Tau &c. —, to stretch or strain, to haul taught a rope &c. 5) *Fig.* *a*) [= groß ziehen] to bring up, to nurse. Schafe —, to breed or raise sheep; junges Holz —, to raise young trees. *b*) to cite or quote. Die angezogene Stelle, the passage quoted, citation, quotation.

II. *v. intr.* 1) [u. w. haben and seyn] *a*) [w. haben] to begin to draw, to draw first. Die Pferde wollten nicht —, allein einige Peitschenhiebe brachten sie dazu, the horses would not draw, till a few cuts of the whip made them; to move [at draughts &c.]. Er läßt mich —, [at chess] he gives me the move. *b*) [w. seyn] *α*) [w. kommen] to draw near or nigh, to draw on, to advance. Der Feind zieht an, the enemy approaches. *β*) *Fig.* to enter into service or office. 2) [w. haben] Der Nagel zieht an, the nail takes; der Leim zieht an, the glue holds well; das Salz zieht an, the salt is growing moist. † *Fig.* Die Prügel ziehen bei ihm an, the blows make him smart.

Anzieher, *m.* [-s, *pl.* -] 1) [an instrument for drawing or putting on] shoeing-horn, boot-hook. 2) [in anatomy] adducent muscle, adductor.

Anziehung, *f.* attraction. V. Anziehen.

Anziehungs-kraft, *f.* the attractive force [of bodies], power of attraction, attraction. —**muskel**, *m.* V. Anzieher 2. —**punkt**, *m.* center of gravity.

Anzirpen, *v. tr.* to chirp at.

Anzischeln, *v. tr.* to address any one whispering.

Anzischen, *v. tr.* to hiss at.

Anzittern, *v. intr.* [u. w. seyn and kommen] to approach trembling.

Anzucht, *f.* [*pl.* -züchte] 1) [without a plural] the act of bringing up, nursing, breeding. 2) sewer, common sewer. 3) V. Zucht [= Race or Raffe].

Anzuckern, *v. tr.* to sprinkle with sugar.

Anzug, *m.* [-es, *pl.* -züge] 1) the act of drawing on, putting on &c. V. Anziehen. Der Feind ist im —e, the enemy is drawing on, approaches; der — des Gesindes, the entering of domestics into service or office. 2) that which is put on, clothes, garments, dress, array, a suit of clothes, costume. Ein eleganter —, an elegant dress or attire; ein prächtiger —, splendid clothes, a full dress. 3) a suit of things belonging to dress. Ein — von Spitzen, a set of lace[s]. 4) an instrument for drawing on or pulling on; [among shoemakers] a shoeing-horn.

Anzugs-geld, *n.* money paid at settling in a place, town &c. —**geschenk**, *n.* entrance money. —**mahl**, *n.* a dinner or entertainment given to one's friends &c. at one's entrance into office. —**predigt**, *f.* inaugural-sermon. —**tag**, *m.* a day appointed for servants to enter into service.

Anzüglich, *adj.* and *adv.* satirical, offensive. —e Reden, abusive language; ein —er Scherz, a cutting joke; ein —er Witz, a poignant wit; — sprechen, to speak sarcastically.

Anzüglichkeit, *f.* 1) offensiveness, satiricalness, poignancy. 2) a taunt. —en, abusive words. Einem —en sagen, to be personal; dieses Buch ist voll —en auf gewisse Personen, this book is full of personalities.

Anzünden, *v. tr.* to set on fire, to make to burn. Ein Feuer —, to kindle or light a fire; ein Licht —, to light a candle; ein Haus —, to fire a house, to set a house on fire, or to set fire to a house. V. Entzünden, Anbrennen.

Anzünder, *m.* [-s, *pl.* -] 1) he that sets on fire &c. [seldom used]. 2) he that lights the candles at a play-house, lamp-lighter.

Anzündung, *f.* kindling; [in chimistry] accension.

Anzupfen, *v. tr.* 1) to begin to pluck. 2) to pluck, to pull quickly, to twitch.

Anzwacken, *v. tr.* to jeer, to treat with scoffs.

Anzwängen, *v. tr.* to bring at or upon a thing by force, to force on or upon.

Anzwecken, *v. tr.* to fasten with tacks [leather &c.]. Absätze —, [among shoemakers] to fasten heels with nails, to peg on.

Anzwicken, *v. tr.* to stretch with pincers. *Fig.* Einen —, to jeer any one.

Anzwirnen, *v. tr.* 1) to join with threads. 2) † and ‡ *Fig.* to excite, to cause.

Anzwitschern, *v. tr.* to chirp at.

Äolsharfe, *f.* [*pl.* -en] Aeolian harp. V. Windharfe.

* **Äonen**, *pl.* [poetical] a space of infinite time or duration, eternity.

* **Aoniden**, *f. pl.* the Muses.

* **Aorist**, *n.* [-s, *pl.* -e] [the name of certain tenses in the grammar of the Greek language] aorist.

* **Apanage**, *f.* [*pl.* -n] [an estate appropriated by a prince to the maintenance of his younger sons, as their patrimony] appanage.

* **Apathie**, *f.* want of feeling, an utter privation of passion, insensibility to pain, a calmness of mind incapable of being ruffled by pleasure, pain or passion, apathy.

* **Apatit**, *m.* [-es] [a variety of phosphate of lime] apatite. Apatitspath, asparagus-stone.

‖ **Apenbeere**, *f.* V. Rauschbeere.

Apenninen, *pl.* [a chain of mountains in Italy] Apennine mountains, Apennines.

* **Apertür**, *f.* [in optics] aperture.

Apfel, *m.* [-s, *pl.* Aepfel] [*diminut.* das Aepfelchen, Aepflein] [Sax. *Apl*, *Aepple*, *Epl*, Swed. *Aeple*, Dan. Ablid and Aeble, Ir. *aval*, Engl. *apple*] 1) [any thing round] V. Adams—, Aug—. 2) [a round fruit] V. Eich—, Erd—, Gall—. 3) [the fruit of the apple-tree] apple. Der kurzstielige —, short-shank; ein rothstreifiger —, redstreak; ein rothfleischiger —, golding [= der Maulbeerapfel], russeting or russetting-apple [= der Rußling]; ein ganz rother —, rose-apple; ein früher, süßer — [= Johannisapfel], sweeting, John-apple, summer-apple. *Prov.* Der — fällt nicht weit vom Stamme, such as the tree is, such is the fruit; such a father, such a son; like sire, like son; auch rothe Aepfel sind wurmstichig, all is not gold that glitters; ich muß in einen sauern — beißen, I must submit to do something which is disagreeable, I must swallow a bitter pill.

Apfel-baum, *m.* apple-tree. —**baumen**, *adj.* and *adv.* made of the wood of the apple-tree. —**baumholz**, *n.* the wood of the apple-tree. —**bein**, *n.* [in anatomy] cheek-bone. —**blech**, *n.* apple-roaster. —**bohrer**, *m.* a species of the curculio [curculio pomorum]. —**brei**, *m.* apple-marmalade. —**dorn**, *m.* wild apple-tree. —**essig**, *m.* vinegar made of sour apples. —**förmig**, *adj.* and *adv.* formed like an apple. —**frau**, *f.* apple-woman. —**grau**, *adj.* 1) apple-grey. Das —graue, the apple-grey colour, [in bot.] pomelegryse. 2) dapple-grey [horse]. —**gröbs**, *m.* apple-core. —**grün**, *adj.* and *adv.* apple-green. —**häuschen**, *n.* apple-core. —**höker**, *m.* apple-monger. —**hökerinn**, *f.* V. —frau. **Apfel-kammer**, *f.* apple-loft. —**kern**, *m.* pippin of an apple. —**koch**, *m.* [in cookery] a kind of apple-tart. —**kreuz**, *n.* [in heraldry] pommeled cross. —**kuchen**, *m.* apple-tart. —**küchlein**, *n.* apple-pie. —**leser**, *m.* apple-gatherer. —**most**, *m.* cider. —**muß**, *n.* V. —brei. —**pfanne**, *f.* a pan used for roasting apples. —**pflaume**, *f.* [a species of plum] imperial plum. —**quitte**, *f.* the wild quince. —**raupe**, *f.* codling moth. —**reis**, *n.* apple-graft. —**rose**, *f.* sweet-briar rose. —**röster**, *m.* apple-roaster. —**rund**, *adj.* and *adv.* round as an apple. —**sauer**, *adj.* and *adv.* sour like an apple. —**säure**, *f.* [in chimist.] malic acid. —**schale**, *f.* apple-paring. —**scheibe**, *f.* apple-slice. —**schildlaus**, *f.* a species of cochineal [coccus mali]. —**schimmel**, *m.* a dapplegrey horse. —**schnecke**, *f.* the thick-lipt cake-shell. —**schnitt** *m.*, —**schnittchen**, *n.* apple-slice. —**sine**, *f.* an orange, china-orange. —**sinenbaum**, *m.* orange-tree. —**stecher**, *m.* apple-corer. —**stiel**, *m.* stalk of an apple. —**torte**, *f.* apple-tart. —**trank**, *m.* a drink made of apples. —**weib**, *n.* V. —frau. —**wein**, *m.* cider. —**wickler**, *m.* V. —raupe. —**wurm**, *m.* V. —raupe.

Äpfel-, V. Apfel-.

Äpfeln, *v. tr.* [used only in the part.] geapfelt, dappled.

* **Aphorismus**, *m.* [*pl.* -men] aphorism.

* **Aphoristisch**, I. *adj.* aphoristic, aphoristical. II. *adv.* aphoristically.

Apiaapfel, *m.* [-s, *pl.* -äpfel] [a kind of small apple] pome-apple.

* **Apodiktisch**, I. *adj.* apodictic, apodictical, demonstrative. II. *adv.* apodictically.

* **Appointement**, *n.* [-s, *pl.* -e] wages, salary.

* **Apokalypse**, *f.* [the name of a book in the New Testament] the apocalypse.

* **Apokalyptisch**, I. *adj.* apocalyptic, apocalyptical. II. *adv.* apocalyptically.

* **Apokryphisch**, I. *adj.* apocryphal. Die —en Bücher, [books, whose authenticity, as inspired writings, is not admitted, and which are therefore not considered a part of the sacred canon of the Scripture as, the Book of Enoch &c.] the apocryphal books, apocrypha. II. *adv.* apocryphally.

* **Apoll**, *m.* [-s, sometimes w. a pl. -e] Apollo.

* **Apologetisch**, I. *adj.* apologetic, apologetical. II. *adv.* apologetically.

* **Apologie**, *f.* [*pl.* -en] apology.

Apologist, *m.* [-en, *pl.* -en] apologist.

* **Apoplektisch**, *adj.* [in medicine] apoplectic, apoplectical.

* **Apoplexie**, *f.* [*pl.* -en] [in medicine] apoplexy.

* **Apostasie**, *f.* [*pl.* -en] apostasy.

* **Apostat**, *m.* [-es, -en, *pl.* -en] an apostate.

* **Apostel**, *m.* [-s, *pl.* -] [a disciple of Christ commissioned to preach the Gospel; this title was also given to persons who first planted the Christian faith]

an apostle.

Apostel-amt, *n.* apostleship. —briefe, *pl.* the writings of the apostles. —geschichte, *f.* [the title of a book in the New Testament] the acts of the apostles. —salbe, *f.* [in veterinary art] a salve composed of twelve ingredients. —schaft, *f.* apostleship. —tag, *m.* the day of an apostle, saint's-day.

*Apostém, *n.* [-es, *pl.* -e] aposteme. V. Geschwür.

Apostem-kraut, *n.* scabious. —röschen, *n.* dandelion.

*Apostólisch, I. *adj.* apostolic, apostolical. Der —e Legat, ablegate; das —e Ansehen, apostolicalness. II. *adv.* apostolically.

*Apostróph, *m.* [-es, *pl.* -e] [in grammar] apostrophe, apostrophy; [the comma used for marking the omission of a letter or letters] an apostrophe.

*Apostrophíren, *v. tr.* [to contract a word by omitting a letter or letters] to apostrophize. *Fig.* V. Anreden.

*Apothéke, *f.* [*pl.* -n] an apothecary's shop.

*Apothéker, *m.* [-s, *pl.* -] apothecary, pharmacopolist.

Apotheker-buch, *n.* dispensatory, pharmacopoeia. —gewicht, *n.* Troy-weight. —kenntniß, *f.* pharmacology. —kunst, *f.* pharmacy. Zur —kunst gehörig, pharmaceutic. —taxe, *f.* the price of drugs fixed by the legal authorities.

*Apotheóse, *f.* [*pl.* -n] deification, apotheosis.

*Apparát, *m.* [-es, *pl.* -e] [things provided as means to some end] apparatus.

‖ Appeldören, *m.* [-s] V. Ahornbaum.

*Appéll, *m.* [-s] a call, recall.

*Appellánt, *m.* [-en, *pl.* -en] [in law, one who appeals] appellant.

*Appellát, *m* [-es, *pl.* -en] [in law] appellee.

*Appellatión, *f.* [in law] appeal.

Appellations-gericht, *n.* court of appeals. —klage, *f.* action upon appeal. —rath, *m.* counsellor of appeals. —schrift, *f.* appellatory libel.

*Appelliren, *v. tr.* [in law] to appeal. Er appellirte von des Papstes Urtheil, he appealed from the Pope's decree.

*Appetít, *m.* [-es] appetite, stomach. — bekommen, to get an appetite; den — schwächen, to blunt the appetite; den — reizen, to whet or provoke the appetite; ohne — essen, to eat without appetite; etwas für den — nehmen, to take a provocative. V. Gelüste, Lust.

Appetítlich, *adj.* exciting appetite, inviting, tempting, nice, delicate.

Áppich, *m.* V. Eppich.

*Apportiren, *v. tr.* [said of dogs] to fetch and carry.

*Appróschen, *f. pl.* [in military art] the parallels.

*Aprikóse and Áprikose, *f.* [*pl.* -n] apricot.

Aprikosen-baum, *m.* apricot-tree. —kern, *m.* kernel of an apricot. —stein, *m.* stone of an apricot.

*April, *m.* [-s] April. *Prov.* Einen in den — schicken, to send any one upon a fool's errand, to make an April fool of any one.

April-glück, *n.* the fickleness of fortune. —narr, *m* April fool. —regen, —schauer, *m.* April shower. —schein, *m.* new moon [in April]. —wetter, *n.* April weather.

*Apside, *f.* [*pl.* -n] [in astronomy, the two points of a planet's orbit, which are at the greatest and least distance from the sun or earth] apsis, *pl.* apsides.

Apsiden-linie, *f.* [the line connecting these points] the line of the apsides.

*Aquamarín, I. *m.* [-s, *pl.* -e] [a mineral] aquamarine, beryl. V. Beryll, *m.* II. *adj.* sea-green.

*Aquatínta, *n.* or *f.* [a method of etching on copper] aquatinta.

*Äquātor, *m.* [-s] V. Gleicher.

*Aquavít, *m.* [-es, *pl.* [mostly in commerce] -e] aqua vitae.

*Äquilibríst, *m.* [-en, *pl.* -en] ropedancer.

*Äquinóctium, *n.* [-s, *pl.* -noctien] V. Nachtgleiche.

Áraber or Arāber, *m.* [-s, *pl.* -] an Arab, Arabian.

*Arabéske, *f.* [*pl.* -n] arabesque or arabesky ornament, moresk-work.

Arābien, *n.* [-s, *pl.* -] Arabia, Araby.

Arābisch, I. *adj.* Arabic, Arabian. Das —e, the Arabic language, the Arabic. II. *adv.* Arabically.

*Arachnologíe, *f.* that part of natural history which treats of spiders.

*Árack, *m.* [-s, *pl.* [mostly in comm.] -e] arrack, rack.

*Aräometer, *m.* [-s, *pl.* -] [in physics] areometer.

*Ärárium, *n.* [-s, *pl.* -rien] public treasury, exchequer.

Árbeit, *f.* [*pl.* -en] [Ice. *erfide*, old Swed. *arfwode*, is said to come from ären = to plough, so that the primary sense would have been field-labour] 1) [the bodily or intellectual exertion] labour. Unsere — ist umsonst, our labour is in vain; von seiner Hände — leben, to live upon one's manual labour. *Prov.* Wie die — so der Lohn, without pains, no gains; [especially among workmen] work, employment. *Fig.* *a*) working, fermenting. Der Wein ist in —, the wine works or ferments. *b*) labour, work, pains, toil. 2) work to be done. Bei der — seyn, to be at work; zur — anstellen, to set on work; den Arbeitern ihre — anweisen, to give the workmen their work; eine mühsame —, a labour of great difficulty, toil; Einem eine — auflegen, to set any one a task; es ist in der —, it is making, it is in hand. *Fig.* In der — seyn, to be upon the anvil. *Prov.* Schmutzige —, blankes Geld, so we have the chink, we'll bear with the stink. 3) work done. Die Früchte seiner — genießen, to enjoy the fruits of one's labour; die zwölf —en des Herkules, the twelve labours of Hercules; erhabene —, embossed or raised work, relief; halberhabene —, bas-relief; ein schönes Stück —, a fine piece of work; gelehrte —en, learned works or performances; eine Geistes—, a work of the brain; er beschäftigt sich mit literarischen —, he is engaged in literary pursuits. V. Beschäftigung, Geschäft, Werk.

Arbeits-ameise, *f.* the neuter or working ant. —beutel, *m.* work-bag, reticule. —biene, *f.* working or common bee, neuter bee. —fähig, *adj.* and *adv.* able to labour or work. —feind, *m.* an enemy to bodily exertion. —frau, *f.* V. Arbeiterinn. —freund, *m.* a lover of bodily exertion. —haus, *n.* work-house, working-house. —kammer, *f.* work-shop. —kästchen, *n.* work-chest. —korb, *m.* work-basket. —leute, *pl.* [of —mann] working people, workmen. —los, *adj.* and *adv.* unemployed, wanting employment, without work, out of work. —losigkeit, *f.* want of employment. —lustig, *adj.* and *adv.* labour-loving. —mann, *m.* workman, labourer, worker —meister, *m.* task-master. —ort, *m.* working place; [in chimistry] laboratory. —preis, *m.* price of labour. —scheu, 1) *adj.* and *adv.* unwilling to work, lazy. 2) *f.* aversion to labour, unwillingness to work, laziness. —schule, *f.* school of industry. —stube, *f.* work-room, work-shop, study. —stunde, *f.* a fixed hour for labouring. Diese Fabrikarbeiter haben täglich 10 —stunden, these operatives work ten hours a day. —tag, *m.* a day on which labour is performed, work-day. —tisch, *m.* work-table. —unfähig, *adj.* and *adv.* unable to labour, incapable of working. —vogt, V. —meister. —voll, *adj.* and *adv.* toilsome. —zeit, *f.* working-time, work-hours. —zeug, *n.* instruments of manual operation, tools. —zimmer, *n.* V. —stube.

Árbeiteln, *v. intr.* to work in a trifling manner.

Árbeiten, I. *v. intr.* 1) to do work, to labour. Nachlässig —, to work carelessly; an Feiertagen ist es nicht erlaubt zu —, it is not lawful to work on holidays; für's Brod —, to labour for subsistence; für Einen — to do any one's work; ich habe nichts zu —, I have no work to do. *Prov.* Man muß — in der Jugend, damit man zu zehren hat im Alter, they must hunger in frost, that will not work in heat; wer nicht arbeitet, soll auch nicht essen, no mill, no meal. 2) to move with difficulty, to labour. Seht, wie wir arbeiten, um hinauf zu klimmen, look how we labour to climb up; sich durch den Schnee —, to work one's way through the snow; [in seamen's language] das Schiff arbeitet, the ship works; [among hunters] to hunt well, to be steady to the scent [said of pointers]. 3) *Fig.* to be in a violent agitation. Der Wein fängt an zu —, the wine begins to work, to ferment. Sein Blut arbeitet, his blood boils.

II. *v. tr.* 1) to form by labour, to work. Den Acker —, to cultivate a field: dieses Denkmal ist von einem berühmten Meister gearbeitet, this monument is executed by a celebrated master; gearbeitetes Eisen, wrought iron; [in manege] Einem Pferde Kopf und Hals in die Höhe — [ein Pferd vorn heraufnehmen], to raise a horse's head, to throw him [it] on his [its] haunches. 2) [among hunt.] to break or discipline [a pointer].

III. *v. r.* sich todt —, to kill one's self with hard working, to work one's self to death; sich krank —, to fall sick by hard labour.

Árbeiter, *m.* [-s, *pl.* -] worker, workman, labourer, manufacturer operative. *Fig.* Ein — im Weinberge des Herrn, one who works in the Lord's vineyard.

Árbeiterinn, *f.* work-woman.

Árbeitsam, I. *adj.* laborious, active, busy, industrious, diligent. II. *adv.* labouriously, industriously.

Árbeitsamkeit, *f.* labouriousness, activity, industry, diligence.

Árbeitselig, *adj.* 1) labour-loving. V. Arbeitslustig. 2) [seldom] toilsome.

‖ Árben, *f.* V. Fichte and Zirbelnuß.

*Arbitrāge, *f.* [in commerce] arbitration.

Arbitragerechnung, *f.* arbitration of exchanges

*Arbitrār, I. *adj.* arbitrary. II. *adv.* arbitrarily.

*Arbūse, *f.* [*pl.* -n] water melon.

*Arcāde, *f.* [*pl.* -n] [in archit.] a long or continued arch, a walk arched above, arcade.

*Arcánum, *n.* [-s, *pl.* -cana] arcanum; [in medicine] nostrum.

Archäológ, *m.* [-en, *pl.* -en] one versed in archeology.

*Archäologíe, *f.* [*pl.* -en] 1) [learning or knowledge, which respects ancient times] archeology. 2) works treating of archeology.

*Archäológisch, *adj.* archeological.

*Archaísmus, *m.* [an ancient or obsolete word or expression] archaism.

Árche, Árke, *f.* [*pl.* -n] [Sax. *earc, erc*, Dan. and Sw. *Ark*, Lat. *arca*] 1) a small close vessel, chest or coffer, an ark. 2) the sounding board of an organ. 3) [a sea term] a trunk or thin covering which cases the ship's pump, in order to preserve it. 4) a vessel, a ship. Die — Noahs, Noah's ark. 5) [in waterworks] trough, channel. 6) [a species of the ark-shell] Noah's ark.

*Árchidiakonat, *n.* [-s, *pl.* -e] archdeaconry.

*Árchidiakonus, *m.* [*pl.* -kone] archdeacon.

*Árchimandrit, *m.* [-s, -en, *pl.* -e] archimandrite.

*Archipélagus, *m.* Archipelago.

*Architékt, *m.* [-s, -en, *pl.* -en] architect.

*Architektónisch, *adj.* architectonic, architectural.

*Architektúr, *f.* [*pl.* -en] [the art of building] architecture, architectonics.

*Architráb, Architráv, *n.* [-en, -s, *pl.* -en] [in architecture] architrave.

*Archív, *n.* [-es, *pl.* -e] 1) [the apartment in which records are kept] archives. 2) archives, = papers which are preserved, as evidences of facts, records.

*Archivár, *m.* [-s, *pl.* -e], Archivárius, *m.* [*pl.* -varien] the keeper of archives or records, archivist; [in the court of chancery] the master of the rolls.

*Archívisch, I. *adj.* authentic. II. *adv.* authentically.

*Archónt, *m.* [-es, -en, *pl.* -en] [in ancient Greece] archont.

*Árctisch, *adj.* V. Arktisch.

*Areál, *n.* V. Flächenraum, Flächeninhalt.

*Areálgröße, *f.* V. Flächengröße.

Arékanuß, *f.* [*pl.* -nüsse] the Indian nut, areca.

Arékapalme, *f.* [*pl.* -n] areca.

‖ Áren, [Ice. *eria*, Swed. *aeria*, Low-Sax. aarden and aren] *v. tr.* to plough.

*Aréna, *f.* [in ancient Rome] arena.

Aréndalstein, *m.* [-es, *pl.* -e] [in mineralogy] acanticone, pistacite, arendalite, manganesian epidote.

*Areopág, *m.* [-es, *pl.* -e] [a sovereign tribunal at Athens] Areopagus.

‖ Áressel, *f.* V. Arlesbeere, Eberesche.

Arg, [perhaps allied to the Lat. *argutus*] *adj.* and *adv.* bad, ill, evil [opposed to good]. —e Früchte, bad fruits; es wird immer ärger, it gets worse and worse. [in a more limited sense] *a*) mischievous, wicked. —e Gedanken haben, to have suspicions; ein —er Schelm, an arrant rogue; ich habe kein —es dabei, I mean no harm; es ist kein — in ihm, there is no deceit in him; die Welt liegt im —en, the world is depraved. *b*) severe. Er verfährt zu — mit ihm, he is too severe with him. *c*) [noting a high degree] Das ist zu —, it is too much.

Ärger, *m.* [-s] vexation, anger. Einem gerechte Ursache zum — geben, to give any one just cause of offence; † seinen — in sich fressen, to devour one's vexation, to stomach one's anger.

Ärgerhaft, *adj.* and *adv.* vexing, vexatious.

Ärgerlich, I. *adj.* 1) fretful, peevish, irritable, angry — seyn, to fret; sie ist über Alles —, she is vexed at every thing. 2) causing trouble, vexatious. Eine —e Sache, an irksome matter; es ist —, betrogen zu werden, it is vexing to be cheated. 3) V. Anstößig. II. *adv.* angrily, fretfully, vexatiously.

Ärgerlichkeit, *f.* 1) vexatiousness, fretfulness. 2) V. Anstößigkeit.

Ärgern, I. *v. tr.* 1) to make angry, to vex, to provoke, to fret. 2) [in scripture] to urge or to incite to ill. 3) to give offence. II. *v. r.* sich —, to fret, to fret one's self, to be vexed. Sich heimlich —, to fret inwardly; ich habe mich darüber geärgert, it has put me out of humour, it has put me in a passion; sich über etwas —, to be offended at.

Ärgerniß, *n.* [-sses, *pl.* -sse] 1) displeasure conceived, anger, offence. Ein — an etwas nehmen, to be scandalized at a thing; dem Volke ein —, an offence unto the people; — geben, to raise a scandal; laßt uns aber Niemand ein — geben, [2. Cor. VI, 3] giving no offence in any thing; er wird an &c. kein — nehmen, he will not be scandalised at &c.; ein öffentliches —, a public scandal; er giebt Jedermann ein — mit seiner schlechten Aufführung, he gives offence to, or shocks every one by his bad conduct. 2) displeasure given, vexation. Er hat mir viel — verursacht, he caused me great uneasiness, he caused me great sorrow or vexation.

Árgheit, *f.* wickedness, malice.

Árglist, *f.* craft, cunning, cunningness. Er handelt ohne —, he acts or deals above board.

Árglistig, I. *adj.* crafty, cunning. Eine —e Frage, a shrewd question. II. *adv.* craftily, cunningly.

Árglos, *adj.* and *adv.* harmless, unsuspecting, suspectless of harm, not false, not treacherous, innocent.

Árglosigkeit, *f.* harmlessness, innocence.

*Argumént, *n.* [-es, *pl.* -e] 1) argument, reason. 2) [in logic, an inference drawn from premises] argument.

*Argumentatión, *f.* argumentation.

*Argumentíren, *v. tr.* [to deduce consequences justly from premises] to reason.

*Árgus, *m.* 1) [fabulous being of antiquity] Argus. *Fig.* Er, sie ist ein wahrer —, he, she is a perfect Argus, has his, her eyes every where. 2) *a*) a species of pheasant [phasianus argus]. *b*) a species of serpents [coluber argus]. *c*) Der doppelte —, [a species of porcelain-shell] argus-shell. *d*) [a fish] ocellate dragonet. *e*) a species of day-butterfly [papilio argus].

Argusaugen, *pl.* 1) the eyes of Argus, extreme vigilance. 2) a species of lizard [lacerta punctata].

Árgwille, *m.* [-ns] ill-will, mischievousness.

Árgwillig, *adj.* and *adv.* mischievous.

Árgwilligkeit, *f.* mischievousness.

Árgwohn, *m.* [-es, *pl.* -e] suspicion. In — seyn or stehen, to be suspected; — hegen, to suspect; — erwecken, to rouse suspicion; böser — [1. Tim. VI, 4], evil surmisings. Syn. Argwohn, Verdacht, Mißtrauen. A suspicion founded on grounds existing in the thing itself, or on objective grounds, is called Verdacht. Is the suspicion subjective, that is, existing merely in our own minds, it is called Argwohn. Thus one says: the circumstance of a person's taking to flight at the time that a certain crime became rumoured, gave rise to the Verdacht that he might have been implicated in it. A jealous husband wirft leicht seinen Argwohn auf [is apt to have suspicion of] his virtuous wife, the cause of his suspicion lying only in his own jealousy.

Árgwohnen, Árgwöhnen, *v. tr.* to suspect.

Árgwöhnig, [better:] Árgwöhnisch, I. *adj.* inclined to suspect, indicating suspicion, suspicious, suspectful. II. *adv.* suspiciously.

Árgwöhnigkeit, *f.* suspiciousness.

*Ariáner, *m.* [-s, *pl.* -] [one who adheres to the doctrine of Arius] Arian.

*Arianísmus, *m.* [*pl.* -men] arianism.

*Árie, *f.* [*pl.* -n] a tune, a short song, air.

*Ariétte, *f.* [*pl.* -n] a little air, arietta.

*Arióso, *adv.* [in music] arioso.

*Aristárch, *m.* [-s, -en, *pl.* -e] an over-scrupulous critic.

*Aristokrát, *m.* [-en, *pl.* -en] aristocrat.

*Aristokratíe, *f.* [*pl.* -en] aristocracy.

*Aristokrátisch, I. *adj.* aristocratic, aristocratical. II. *adv.* aristocratically.

*Aristokratísmus, *m.* aristocraticalness.

*Arithmetík, *f.* V. Rechenkunst.

*Arithmétiker, *m.* [-s, *pl.* -] arithmetician.

*Arithmétisch, I. *adj.* arithmetic, arithmetical. II. *adv.* arithmetically.

Árke, V. Arche.

Árke, *f.* [*pl.* -n] a kind of flat-bottomed boat, employed on the Elb.

Árker, *m.* [-s, *pl.* -] V. Erker.

Árkirsche, *f.* [*pl.* -n] V. Arlesbeere.

*Árktisch, *adj.* northern, arctic.

*Arktúr, *m.* [-s] [in astron., a fixed star of the first magnitude, in the constellation of Bootes] Arcturus.

Árlesbeere, [Arleskirsche, Arkirsche] [*pl.* -n] 1) service berry. V. Speierlingsbeere, Sporapfel. 2) service-tree. V. Speierlingsbaum, Sperberbaum.

Arlesbeerenbaum, *m.* service-tree, white-beam.

1. Árm, [ärmer, ärmste] [formerly *arant*, allied to ἔρημος. Sax. *earm* signified elend] *adj.* and *adv.* 1) poor, indigent, oppressed with want, needy, necessitous. Ein —er, a poor man; die —en, the poor; — machen, to make poor, to impoverish; der Arme [= Almosenmann], pauper. *Prov.* So — wie Hiob, as poor as Job; besser — und frei, als ein voller Kragen und eine Kette am Hals, a poor freedom is better than a rich slavery; der —e ist gar wohl geborgen, er hat für wenig nur zu sorgen, little wealth, little sorrow. *Fig.* Eine —e Sprache, a poor language; — an Geist, destitute of genius, witless; — an Liebe, void of love; — an Trost, comfortless; — an Freuden, void of joy, joyless; [in mining] ein —er Gang, a poor vein; ein —es Erz, a poor ore. 2) poor, unhappy, pitiable. Der —e Mensch! poor man! ein —er Sünder, a delinquent sentenced to death. ‖ *Fig.* Der —e Ritter, [in cookery] small pancake, fritter. *Prov.* —e Ritter backen, to live poorly.

Armen-anstalt, *f.* institution for the relief of the poor. —aufseher, *m.* overseer of the poor. —büchse, *f.* V. —stock. —geld, *n.* money given to relieve the poor, alms. —gift, *n.* V. —geld. —haus, *n.* almshouse, hospital, poorhouse. —kasse, *f.* fund for the relief of the poor. —kasten, *m.* V. —stock. —pflege, *f.* care of the poor. —pfleger, *m.* almoner, overseer of the poor. —recht, *n.* poor's privilege in lawsuits. —schule, *f.* charity-school, charge-house. —schüler, *m.* scholar of a charity-school. —steuer, *f.* poor-rates, tax for the poor. —stock, *m.* poor's box. —vater, *m.* almoner. —vogt, *m.* beadle. —vorsteher, *m.* overseer of the poor.

2. Árm, *m.* [-s, *pl.* -e] [*dimin.* Ärmchen, Ärmlein] [Eng., Dan. and Sw. *arm*, Sax. *Earm*, allied to the Lat. *Ramus*] 1) *a*) [the limbs of some animals] arm; [that part of the foreleg of a horse from

the shoulder to the knee] arm of a horse. *b*) [any extended part shooting or extended from the main body of a thing] arm. Der — des Meeres [Meeresarm], an arm of the sea; die —e eines Flusses, branches of a river. *c*) the slender part of a thing, projecting from a trunk or axis. Die —e an der Wage, beam; die —e am Wagen, shafts; die —e eines Leuchters, the branches of a candlestick; der — eines Schubkarrens, the handle of a wheelbarrow; die —e an einem Lehnstuhle, the arms of an elbow-chair. 2) [of a man] arm [a limb of the human body]; [in heraldry] arm. In —'s [= das] Gewehr! [words of command am. sold.] support arms! *Fig.* Der weltliche —, the secular arm; und wem wird der — des Herrn geoffenbaret? [Isa. LIII] to whom is the arm of the Lord revealed? Einem unter die —e greifen, to aid or help one; sich Einem in die —e werfen, to take refuge with any one.

Arm-ader, *f.* brachial vein. —band, *n.* an armlet, a bracelet. —bein, *n.* V. Achselbein. —binde, *f.* sling. —blutader, *f.* [in anatomy] the brachial vein. —bruch, *m.* a fracture of the arm. —brust, *f.* cross-bow. ‡—bruster, *m.* 1) an archer, a cross-bowman. 2) maker or manufacturer of cross-bows. —bruden, *pl.* braces and bits. —eisen, *n.* a piece of armour for the arm, an armlet. —ende, *n.* [in anatomy] the arm's end. —feile, *f.* [among locksmiths] a rubber. —fläche, *f.* [in anatomy] the surface of some bones. —förmig, *adj.* and *adv.* 1) having the form of an arm. 2) [in botany] brachiate, cross-armed, decussated. —geflecht, *n.* [in anatomy] the brachial plexus. —geige, *f.* viol. —geschmeide, *n.* ornaments for the arms, armlets, bracelets. —handschuh, *m.* a glove for the hand and arm. —harnisch, *m.* a piece of armour for the arm, an armlet. —heber, *m.* [in anatomy, a muscle] levator brachii. —höcker, *m.* [in anatomy] the olecranon, ancon. —höhle, *f.* arm-pit. —kissen, *n.* a cushion to support the elbows. —korb, *m.* a handled basket. —lehne, *f.* elbow-piece, support for the elbows. —leuchter, *m.* 1) chandelier, branched candlestick, girandole. 2) [in botany] the chara. —loch, *n.* 1) [a hole for the arm in a garment] arm-hole. 2) = the arm-pit [Achselgrube]. —los, *adj.* and *adv.* having no arms. —muskel, *m.* [in anat.] brachial muscle. —nerve, *m* [in anat.] brachial nerve. —polster, *m.* a cushion to support the elbows. —ring, *m.* a ring, an ornament for the wrist. —röhre, *f.* V. —bein. —schiene, *f.* 1) armlet, vantbrass. 2) [in anatomy, the greater and lesser bone of the arm] focil major and focil minor. 3) [in surgery] splint. 4) [am. turners] a support for the arm. —schild, *m.* a small shield worn to protect the left arm. —schlagader, *f.* [in anat.] the brachial artery. —schleife, *f.* sleeve-knot. —schloß, *n.* bracelet-lock. —sdick, *adj.* as big as one's arm. —sessel, *m.* arm-chair, elbow-chair. —spange, *f.* bracelet-buckle. —spindel, *f.* [in anatomy] the radius. —stück, *n.* —stück an einem Handschuhe, the arm of a glove. —stuhl, *m.* V. —sessel. —umschlungen, *adj.* and *adv.* cross-armed.

*Armāda, *f.* a fleet of armed ships, a squadron, armada.

*Armadillthier, *n.* [-es, *pl.* -e] [a quadruped peculiar to America] armadillo, latoo; [in zoology] the dasypus.

*Armatūr, *f.* [*pl.* -en] armature, armour.

*Armée, *f.* [*pl.* -n] army. V. Heer.

Ärmel, *m.* [-s, *pl.* -] sleeve [of a shirt &c.]. *Fig.* Einem etwas auf den — heften or binden, to impose a thing upon a person, to pin a story upon any one [upon his sleeve]; etwas aus dem — schütteln, to speak extempore, to extemporize, to speak without previous study or preparation.

Aermel-aufschlag, *m.* the facing of a sleeve, cuff. —band, *n.* —band an einem Hemde, sleeve-band. —besatz, *m.* sleeve-band. —hemde, *n.* a shirt with sleeves. —holz, *n.* [among tailors] sleeve-board. —kleid, *n.* a garment with sleeves. —leibchen, *n.* a corset with sleeves. —mantel, *m.* a cloak with sleeves. —mieder, *n.* V. —leibchen. —muster, *n.* the pattern of a sleeve. —schnitt, *m.* the cut of a sleeve. —schürze, *f.* an apron with arm-holes. —weste, *f.* a waist-coat with sleeves; [worn by soldiers] fatigue-jacket.

1. Ärmen, [unusual] I. *v. intr.* to be poor. II. *v. tr.* to make poor, to impoverish.

2. Ärmen, *v. tr.* to furnish with arms [used only in the part. and in comp., as] langgearmet, having long arms, long-armed.

Arménien, *n.* [-s] [a province in Asia] Armenia.

Arménier, *m.* [-s, *pl.* -] Armenian.

Arménisch, *adj.* Armenian. Der —e Stein, Armenian stone, armenite; der —e Bolus, [a species of clay from Armenia] Armenian bole.

*Armīren, *v. tr.* to arm [the militia &c.], to equip [a vessel].

Ärmlich, I. *adj.* poor, needy. *Fig.* Eine —e Gabe, a paltry gift; das ist ein —es Essen, this is a sorry dinner; er ist ein —er [better: armseliger] Mensch, he is a mean, miserable fellow. II. *adv.* poorly.

Ärmlichkeit, *f.* poorness, poverty.

Ärmling, *m.* [-s, *pl.* -e] false sleeve.

Ärmselig, I. *adj.* 1) poor, needy, beggarly. Ein —es Leben führen, to live poorly. 2) unhappy, wretched, miserable. Ein —er Mensch, a wretched person, a miser. 3) worthless, miserable, pitiful, sorry. Ein —er, erbärmlicher Mensch, a mean, pitiful fellow; ein kleines, —es Haus, a little paltry house; eine —e Stadt, a paltry town. II. *adv.* poorly, wretchedly, miserably, beggarly.

Ärmseligkeit, *f.* 1) poorness, wretchedness, paltriness. 2) a paltry thing.

Ärmuth, *f.* 1) poverty, poorness, indigence, indigency, penury. Ein großer Theil des menschlichen Geschlechts lebt in —, a large portion of the human race lives in indigence. *Fig.* Die — des Geistes, want of genius; — an Trost, want of comfort; die — des Geistes, [in theol.] humility of spirit. *Prov.* — thut weh, poverty is a sharp weapon; — hat Viele an den Galgen gebracht, poverty is the cause of many evils; — schändet nicht, poverty is no sin; — trennt Freundschaft, poverty parteth friends. 2) [somewhat obsolete] the poor, poor people. Der — beistehen, to assist the poor.

Armuthszeugniß, *n.* a certificate of poverty.

Ärnold, *m.* [a name of men] Arnold.

Ärnolf, *m.* [a name of men] Arnulf.

Ärnte, *f.* V. Ernte.

*Arōma, *n.* [-s] aroma.

*Aromátisch, *adj.* aromatic, aromatical.

1. Āron, *m.* [-s] [a name of men] Aaron.

2. Āron, *n.* [-s] V. Arum.

*Arquebusade, *f.* [a distilled liquor applied to a bruise] arquebusade.

*Ärrack, *m.* [-s] V. Arack.

Ärragonien and Arragōnien, *n.* [-s] [a province in Spain] Arragon.

Arragōnier, *m.* [-s, *pl.* -] Arragonian.

Arragōnisch, *adj.* Arragon.

*Arrangemént, *n.* [-s, *pl.* -s] arrangement. V. Arrangīren.

*Arrangīren, *v. tr.* to arrange, to order. Sich —, to come to an agreement; sich mit seinen Gläubigern —, to settle or compound with one's creditors.

*Arrèst, *m.* [-s, *pl.* -e] arrest, arrestation, seizure. *Fig.* [in law] seizure. Mit — belegen, to seize; — auf die Güter eines Fremden, foreign attachment.

Arrestanlegung, *f.* sequestration.

*Arrestánt, *m.* [-en, *pl.* -en] prisoner.

*Arretīren, *v. tr.* to arrest [any one for debt, for crime &c.].

*Arrièrgarde, *f.* [*pl.* -n] the rear-guard.

*Arrōbe, *f.* [*pl.* -n] [a weight in Portugal of 32 pounds; in Spain of 25 pounds] arroba.

*Arrogánt, I. *adj.* arrogant, assuming. II. *adv.* arrogantly.

†Ärsch, *m.* [-es, *pl.* Aersche] [Sw. *ars*, D. Ärs and Eers, perhaps allied to the Gr. οὐρά] arse, breech, backside, bum, fundament, the buttocks.

†Ärsch-backe, *f.* buttock. —fuß, *m.* [a species of colymbus] didapper. V. Taucherente. —leder, *n.* miner's breech-leather, an apron. †—loch, *n.* arse-hole, anus. †—pauker, *m.* whip-arse, whipper. †—wisch, *m.* bum-fodder.

*Arsenāl, *n* [-s, *pl.* -e] a magazine of arms and military stores, whether for land or naval service, arsenal.

*Arsénik, *m.* [-s] arsenic; [= Mäusegift, Rattenpulver] rat's-bane. Gediegener —, yellow sulphuret of arsenic, native orpiment; weißer —, white arsenic, oxyd of arsenic; rother —, red sulphuret of arsenic, realgar.

Arsenik-blei, *n.* arseniate of lead. —blume, —blüthe, *f.* arsenic-bloom, arsenic salt. —butter, *f.* [in chimistry] butter of arsenic, sublimated muriate of arsenic, chloride of arsenic. —erz, *n.* any ore in which arsenic is found. —glas, *n.* twice sublimated arsenic. —haltig, *adj.* and *adv.* [containing arsenic] arsenical. —kalk, *m.* arseniate of lime, pharmacolite. Natürlicher —kalk, V. —blüthe. —kies, *m.* arsenical pyrites, arsenical iron. —kobalt, *m.* arsenical cobalt, white or grey cobalt. —könig, *m.* regulus of arsenic. —leber, *f.* [in chimistry] liver of arsenic. —metall, *n.* V. —könig. —nickel, *n.* copper nickel, sulphurated nickel, arsenical nickel. —nickelblüthe, *f.* arseniate of nickel. —öl, *n.* [in chimistry] oil of arsenic. —rubin, *m.* red orpiment, ruby sulphur, realgar. —sauer, *adj.* and *adv.* containing arsenic acid. —saures Salz, arseniate; —saures Nickel, arseniate of nickel, nickel-ochre. —säure, *f.* arseniac or arsenical acid, arsenic acid; [with a less proportion of oxygen] arsenious acid. —silber, *n.* antimonial silver. —stein, *m.* V. —kies. —vitriol, *m.* [in chimistry] sulphate of arsenic.

*Arsenikālisch, *adj.* and *adv.* arsenic, arsenical, arsenious.

*Arsenīzit, *m.* [-s, *pl.* -e] arsenite.

*Ársis, *f.* [in music, the raising of the hand as applied to the beating of time] arsis.

1. ‖Ärt, *f.* 1) ploughing. 2) cultivated field, arable ground.

Artfeld, *n.* arable field.

2. Árt, *f.* [*pl.* -en] [Low-Sax. Aart, Dan. and Sw. *Art*; appears to be allied to the L. *ars*] 1) kind, species, sort. —en Thiere, Pflanzen, species of

animals, plants; die Fortpflanzung der —, the propagation of the species; vielerlei —en von Thieren, many species of animals; was ist das für eine — Menschen? what sort of people are those? alle —en von Menschen versammelten sich hier, all manner of men assembled here; aus der — schlagen, to degenerate; — läßt nicht von —, that which is bred in the bone, will never out of the flesh; die Vollkommensten in ihrer —, the most perfect in their kind; vortrefflich in seiner —, excellent in its kind; einzig in seiner —, unique; die verschiedenen —en des Bodens, the different kinds of soil; die — des Bodens, the nature of the soil; ein Hund, ein Pferd von guter —, a dog, a horse of a good race or breed; ein Kind von guter —, a good-natured child; von göttlicher —, of divine origin; ich bin nicht von dieser —, *fig.* I am not of that feather. 2) kind, manner, way An seiner —, sich auszudrücken, erkennt man den Mann von Bildung, in his manner of expressing himself we recognize the accomplished man; er ist ein guter Mann nach seiner —, he is a good fellow in his way; die — zu schreiben, manner of writing; auf alle — und Weise, in every possible way; es ist auf gewisse — schon geschehen, it is in a manner done already; auf diese —, in this manner, at this rate. 3) = Art und Weise [that which distinguishes a person or thing from another] characteristic. 4) good breeding, politeness, manners, gentility. Er hat keine —, he has no manners; es ist keine —, mich so lange warten zu lassen, it is not polite to let me wait so long. Syn. Art, Weise. Weise denotes the manner of existing or being, mode; Art is the thing itself, considered in regard to the certain character which distinguishes it from others, species.

Artbegriff, *m.* the idea of kind, specific character.

‖ Ártbar, *adj.* and *adv.* arable. —es Land, arable lands.

* Artefácten, *pl.* artificial productions.

Ártеn, I. *v. intr.* 1) to take after, to resemble. 2) to thrive, to prosper. II. *v. tr.* to modify, to qualify. Geartet, *adj.* Er ist ein gut gearteter Junge, he is a well-behaved lad.

* Artérie, *f.* [*pl.* -n] [in anatomy] artery.

‖ Árthaft, *adj.* and *adv.* arable.

* Artificiéll, *adj.* and *adv.* artificial.

Ártig, *adj.* and *adv.* 1) being of the nature or kind of [used only in composition, as] stein—, stony &c. 2) neat, pretty. Er tanzt recht —, he dances very nicely. 3) agreeable, pleasing. —e Manieren, agreeable manners. 4) well bred, genteel, civil. Ein —er junger Mann, a polite young man; er benimmt sich sehr —, he behaves very politely; er behandelt seine Freunde sehr —, he treats his friends with great courtesy; [ironically] eine —e Frage! an odd question!

Ártigkeit, *f.* 1) neatness, prettiness. 2) agreeableness, pleasingness. 3) genteelness, gentility, politeness. 4) an act of civility, a polite word or expression. —en, civilities, acts of politeness; er sagt ihr viele —en, he tells her many sweet things.

* Artíkel, *m.* [-s, *pl.* -] 1) a limb, a joint or connexion of bones adapted for motion. 2) [in grammar] article. 3) [a particular commodity or substance] article. Salz ist ein nöthiger —, salt is a necessary article. 4) a point of faith, article. V. Glaubens—.

Artikelbrief, *m.* the statutes for the navy.

* Artikulatión, *f.* 1) [in anatomy, the joining or juncture of the bones] articulation 2) [a distinct utterance of syllables and words by the human voice] articulation.

* Artikulíren, *v. tr.* [to utter distinct syllables or words] to articulate.

Ártillerie or Artillerie, *f.* 1) artillery, cannon, great guns, ordnance. 2) gunnery.

* Artillerist, *m.* [-en, *pl.* -en] a cannonier, gunner, artillery-man, an officer appointed to manage artillery.

Ártischocke, *f.* [*pl.* -n] [a plant] artichoke. Der Boden, Käse or Stuhl einer —, the bottom of an artichoke; die Fasern, das Rauhe an dem Käse einer —, the florets.

* Artíst, *m.* [-en, *pl.* -en] an artist [a painter, sculptor &c.].

* Artístisch, *adj.* and *adv.* performed with art, artful.

Ártoffel, *f.* V. [the more usual word] Kartoffel.

Ártung, *f.* modification.

Árum, *m.* [-s] hart-wort.

Arvelen, Árven, *f.* V. Zirbelnuß.

Árzen, Árzten, [a word seldom used] *v. tr.* to cure, to heal.

Arzenei, *f.* [V. Arzt] medicine, physic. Eine bewährte —, a specific; die — wider Krämpfe, antispasmodic [as opium &c.]; eine herzstärkende —, a cordial; —en wider den Husten, pectorals, bechicks. *Fig.* Ein fester Glaube ist die beste — wider jedes Uebel, a firm faith is the best remedy for every evil.

Arzenei-bereiter, *m.* apothecary. —bereitung, *f.* pharmacy. —bereitungskunst, *f.* pharmaceutics, pharmacology. —buch, *n.* dispensatory, pharmacopœia. —büchse, *f.* a box in an apothecary's shop. —formel, *f.* receipt. —gelehrsamkeit, —kunde, —kunst, —wissenschaft, *f.* the science of healing, medical science, medicine, physic. —gelehrte, *m.* physician. —geruch, *m.* a medicinal smell. —geschmack, *m.* a medicinal taste. —gewicht, *n.* V. Apothekergewicht. —glas, *n.* phial. —handel, *m.* dealing or trade in drugs. —händler, *m.* druggist, drugster, pharmacopolist. —handlung, *f.* an apothecary's shop. —kiste, *f.* medicine-chest. —kraftlehre, *f.* dynamiology. —kraut, *n.* a medicinal or physical herb. —kundig, I. *adj.* medicinal. II. *adv.* medicinally. —künstig, *adj.* and *adv.* pharmaceutic, pharmaceutical. —künstler, *m.* one skilled in pharmacy. —laden, *m.* V. Apotheke. — [or Heilmittel-] lehre, *f.* pharmacology. —lehrig, *adj.* and *adv.* pharmaceutic, pharmaceutical. —mittel, *n.* remedy, medicament, physic, medicine. Aeußerliche —mittel, local medicaments; kühlende —mittel, refrigerants. —mittellehre, *f.* V. —lehre. —pflanze, *f.* medicinal herb. —trank, *m.* a medicinal draught, potion, physic-drink. V. Mixtur. —waare, *f.* drugs. —zettel, *m.* receipt, medical prescription.

Arzeneíen, *v. intr.* to be busy with physic, to tamper. V. Medicíniren.

Arzeneilich, I. *adj.* medicinal, medical. II. *adv.* medicinally.

Árzt, *m.* [-es, *pl.* Aerzte] [perhaps from the L. *ars*] physician, doctor, medical man. Der ausübende —, practitioner. *Prov.* Gott hilft, und dem —e dankt man, God heals, and the physician has the thanks.

Arzt-gebühr, *f.* —lohn, *m.* physician's fee.

Árzten, V. Arzen.

Árztlich, I. *adj.* medical. II. *adv.* medically.

Árzung, *f.* the act of healing.

Arzungskosten, *pl.* [chiefly a law-term] the expenses caused by a cure.

Ás, V. Aß.

Ásant, *m.* [-s] a name for two sorts of a concrete resinous juice. Der stinkende —, asafoetida; V. Teufelsdreck; der wohlriechende —, asa dulcis or odorata, benzoin or benjamin.

* Asbést, *m.* [-s, *pl.* -e] [a mineral] asbestus, asbestos.

* Ascariden, *pl.* [in zoology, a genus of intestinal worms] the ascarides.

* Ascendènten, *pl.* ascendants [opposed to descendants].

* Ascét, *m.* [-en, *pl.* -en] an ascetic, a recluse.

* Ascétik, *f.* [in the Roman church] the ascetics.

* Ascétisch, *adj.* and *adv.* ascetic.

‖ Ásch, *m.* [-es, *pl.* Aesche] [appears to be allied to the Gr. ἀσκός, Schlauch] a pot. Ein Milch—, a milk-pot.

Aschkuchen, *m.* pot-cake.

Áschbaum, *m.* V. Esche.

Áschblei, *n.* V. Wismuth.

Ásche, *f.* [appears to be related to the Gr. ἄζη = Dürre &c.] 1) ashes [of wood &c.]. Weiße or glimmende —, embers; zu — verbrennen, to reduce to ashes; diese Feuersbrunst hat das ganze Dorf in — gelegt, this fire laid the whole village in ashes. *Fig.* [the remains of a human body] Jeden Tag besuchte sie seinen Grabhügel und weinte hier über seiner —, every day she visited his grave and wept over his ashes; ich will sterben, wo die — meiner Väter ruht, I'll die where the relics of my fathers repose. 2) [in chimistry, the residue of combustion, in general containing earth and fixed salts] ashes. 3) earthy swinstone.

Aschen-bad, *n.* [in chimistry] ash-bath. —behälter, *n.* V. —fall. —bläser, *m.* V. —zieher. —brod, *n.* cake baked under hot ashes. —brödel, *m.* cinder-wench, cinder-woman, domestic drudge, slut, sloven, scullion; [the name of a well-known personage in an old nursery-tale, in some modern operas &c.] Cinderella. —ente, *f.* V. Bergente. —fall, *m.* ash-hole. —farbe, *f.* V. Aschfarbe. —grube, *f.* V. —fall. —haufen, *m.* a heap of ashes. —herd, *m.* [the lower part of a furnace, a repository for ashes] ash-hole. —krug, *m.* [the vessel in which the remains of burnt bodies were put] urn. —kuchen, *m.* V. —brod. —meise, *f.* V. Aschmeise. —ofen, *m.* V. Aschofen. —pflanze, *f.* 1) [a genus of plants] cineraria. 2) [a plant] mugwort. —sack, *m.* Im —sacke Buße thun, to do penance in sackcloth and ashes. —salz, *n.* alkali, potash or vegetable fixed alkali. —stöber, *m.* the grey stamper [a sort of cornet]. —topf, *m.* 1) pot in which ashes of coal, wood &c. are preserved. 2) *Fig.* V. —krug. —tuch, *n.* bucking-cloth. —wurz, *f.* V. Aschwurz. —zieher, *m.* [in mineralogy] turmalin, shorl.

Ásche, *f.* V. Esche.

Áschente, *f.* [*pl.* -n] the scaup.

Áscher, *m.* [-s, *pl.* -] [a fish] grayling, umber.

Áschericht, *adj.* and *adv.* sprinkled as with ashes.

Aschermittwoch, *m.* Aschermittwoche, *f.* ash-wednesday.

1\. Áschern, *v. tr.* 1) to burn or reduce to ashes. 2) [in the Romish church] to sprinkle with ashes [the heads of penitents]. 3) to boil or macerate with ashes.

2\. Áschern, *v. tr.* V. Abäschern.

Ascherofen, *m.* [-s, *pl.* -öfen] [among potters] ash-furnace.

‖Äschertuch, *n.* V. Aschentuch.

Äschfarbe, *f.* ash-colour.

Äschfarben, Äschgrau, *adj.* ash-coloured, ashy, cineritious, cinereous.

Äschgrube, *f.* [*pl.* -n] V. Aschengrube.

Äschhuhn, *n.* [-es, *pl.* -hühner] brook-ouzel, water-rail.

Äschhühnlein, *n.* [-s, *pl.* -] peep.

Äschicht, *adj.* and *adv.* resembling ashes, ashy.

Äschig, *adj.* and *adv.* full of ashes, ashy.

Äschkraut, *n.* V. Jakobskraut.

Äschkuchen, *m.* [-s, *pl.* -] V. Aschenkuchen.

Äschlauch, Äschlauch, *m.* [-es] shallot or eschalot, scallion.

Äschmeise, *f.* [*pl.* -n] V. Graumeise.

Äschofen, *m* [-s, *pl.* -öfen] [in glass-houses] the furnace, in which the ashes are smelted or calcined.

Äschwurz, Äschwurz, *f.* white dittany.

* Äsculáp, *m.* Aesculapius. *Fig.* [chiefly in a jocose sense] a physician.

Asiát, *m.* [-en, *pl.* -en] Asiátinn, *f.* Asier, *m.* [-s, *pl.* -] Asierinn, *f.* Asiatic.

Äsien, *n.* [-s] Asia. Das nördliche —, northern Asia.

Äsisch, *adj.* Asiatic, Asian.

Aspaláthholz, *n.* [-es, *pl.* -hölzer] Jamaica ebony.

1. Äspe, *f.* [*pl.* -n] a river-fish in Sweden.

2. Äspe, Äspe, *f.* V. Espe.

* Aspèct, *m.* [-s, *pl.* -en] 1) [in astron.] aspect. 2) appearance to the mind, aspect.

Äspenmotte, Äspenmotte, *f.* V. Espenmotte.

Äsperbeere, *f.* V. Kräuselbeere.

* Asphált, *m.* [-s] asphalt, asphaltum, jew's pitch.

Asphodíll, *m.* V. Affodill.

* Asphyxíe, *f.* asphyxy.

* Aspiránt, *m.* [-en, *pl.* -en] aspirant.

* Aspiratión, *f.* [the pronunciation of a letter with a full emission of breath] aspiration.

Äß, Äß, *n.* [-sses, *pl.* -sse] [Sw. *Aes*, Fr. *As*, L. *as*] 1) [a single point on a card or die] ace. 2) [without a plural] [a small weight] grain.

* Assecuránt, *m.* [-en, *pl.* -en] [in commerce] insurer, underwriter.

* Assecuránz, *f.* [in commerce] insurance, assecurance. — storniren, to return the premium of insurance. V. Versicherung.

Assecuranz-compagnie, *f.* insurance company. —comptoir, *n.* insurance office. —conto, *n.* account of insurance. —gesellschaft, *f.* V. —compagnie. —police, *f.* policy of insurance. —prämie, *f.* premium of insurance.

* Assecurát, *m.* [-en, *pl.* -en] assured. V. Versicherter, Versicherte.

* Assecurátor, *m.* [-s, *pl.* -en] insurer, assurer. V. Versicherer.

* Assecuríren, *v. tr.* to insure, to assure. V. Versichern.

Ässel, *f.* [*pl.* -n] [agrees with the L. *asellus*] the wood-louse, thurse-louse, milleped, sow, tiller's-louse.

Äßen, Äßen, [V. Aas] I. *v. intr.* [among hunters and fishers] to feed [said of deer, fowls and large fishes]. II. *v. r.* sich —, to feed.

* Assessor, [-s, *pl.* -en] an inferior officer of justice or a junior officer who sits to assist the judge or senior in office, assessor. V. Beisitzer.

* Assiéntoschiffe, *pl.* assiento-ships.

* Assignát, *n.* [-s, *pl.* -en] assignate.

* Assignatión, *f.* assignation. V. Anweisung.

* Assigníren, *v. tr.* to refer to for payment, to assign. V. Anweisen.

* Assísen, *pl.* [a law term in England, France &c.] assizes. Die — halten, to hold the court of assize.

* Assistént, *m.* [-en, *pl.* -en] side's-man, an assistant.

* Associé, *m.* [-s, *pl.* -s] [in commerce] partner.

* Associíren, *v. r.* sich —, to join in company as a partner, to associate, to enter into partnership.

* Assonánz, *f.* [*pl.* -en] [resemblance of sounds] assonance.

* Assortimént, *n.* [-s, *pl.* -e] [in commerce] assortment [of silks, of calicoes &c.].

* Assortíren, *v. tr.* to furnish with all sorts of commodities, to assort.

Äßung, Äßung, *f.* 1) feeding. 2) food; [of deer] viands.

Assýrien, *n.* [-s] Assyria.

Assýrier, *m.* [-s, *pl.* -] Assyrian.

Assýrisch, *adj.* Assyrian.

Äst, *m.* [-es, *pl.* Aeste] [allied to the L. *hasta*] 1) the branch of a tree, bough, arm. Ein kleiner —, twig, sprig; die abgehauenen Aeste, shrowds. [in anatomy] branch [of veins]. *Fig.* [in genealogy] branch [of a family]. 2) knot in wood.

Ast-blatt, *n.* [in botany] a branch-leaf. —holz, *n.* branch-wood. —knorren, *m.* knot, knast, knurl, knub. —krähe, *f.* V. Nebelkrähe. —kreuz, *n.* [in heraldry] cross raguled. —loch, *n.* knot-hole. —los, *adj.* and *adv.* destitute of boughs or branches, branchless. —moos, *n.* [a genus of mosses] hypnum. —ständig, *adj.* and *adv.* [in botany] growing or springing from a branch. Ein —ständiger Blumenstiel, branch-peduncle. —voll, *adj.* and *adv.* branchy. —werk, *n.* ramage.

Äster, *f.* [*pl.* -n] star-wort, aster. V. Sternkraut, Sternpflanze.

Ästerich, *n.* V. Estrich.

* Asteríscus, *m.* asterisk. Thus (*).

* Asthenie, *f.* debility.

* Asthénisch, *adj.* and *adv.* asthenic.

* Ásthma, *n.* [-s] a shortness of breath, asthma. V. Engbrüstigkeit.

* Asthmátiker, *m.* [-s, *pl.* -] asthmatic. V. Engbrüstige.

* Asthmátisch, *adj.* and *adv.* asthmatic. V. Engbrüstig.

Ästig or Ästig, *adj.* 1) full of boughs or branches, branchy. Ein —er Baum, a branchy tree; —e Wurzeln, ramified roots. 2) knotty. —es Holz, knotty wood.

Äſtling, *m.* [-s, *pl.* -e] brancher; [in falconry] ramage-hawk.

* Astrolabium, *n.* [-s, *pl.* -bien] [in astron.] astrolabe, circumferentor.

* Astrológ, *m.* [-s, -en, *pl.* -en] astrologer. V. Sterndeuter.

* Astrologíe, *f.* astrology. V. Sterndeuterei, Sterndeutekunst. — treiben, to astrologize.

* Astrológisch, I. *adj.* astrologic, astrological. II. *adv.* astrologically.

* Ástrometeorologie, *f.* astrometeorology.

* Ástrométer, *m.* [-s, *pl.* -] astrometer.

* Astronóm, *m.* [-s, -en, *pl.* -en] astronomer. V. Sternkundige.

* Astronomíe, *f.* astronomy. V. Sternkunde. — studiren, to astronomize.

* Astronómisch, I. *adj.* astronomic, astronomical. Das —e Jahr, astronomical year. II. *adv.* astronomically.

* Astroscopíe, *f.* astroscopy.

* Asýl, *n* [-s, *pl.* -e] asylum.

* Asymptóte, *f.* [*pl.* -n] [in mathemat.] asymptote.

* Asýndeton, *n.* [-s] [in rhetoric, a figure which omits the connective] asyndeton.

* A Témpo, *adv.* [a direction in music] a tempo.

* Athanasiáner, *m.* [-s, *pl* -] Athanasim.

* Atheíst, *m.* [-s, -en, *pl.* -en] atheist. V. Gotteslängner.

* Atheisteréi, *f.* 1) atheism. 2) atheisticalness.

* Atheístisch, I. *adj.* atheist, atheistical, atheistic. II. *adv.* atheistically.

Äthem, *m.* [-s] [formerly Odem; Sax. *Aethm, Ethm*, allied to the Gr. ἄημι = wehen. V. Athmen] [the air inhaled and expelled in the respiration of animals] breath. — holen or schöpfen, to fetch breath, to breathe, to respire, to take breath; außer —, out of breath, breathless; laßt mich doch zu — kommen, pray, let me take breath, [also in a figur. sense] give me a little breathing-time; wieder zu — kommen, to breathe again, to recover; viel —, einen langen — haben, to be long-winded; der kurze —, shortness of breath; der schwere —, asthma; den — an sich halten, to hold one's breath; er flucht bei jedem —, he swears at every breath. *Fig.* Seinen — verschwenden, to spend one's breath; er schwatzte, bis ihm der — ausging, he talked himself out of breath; er hat seinen letzten — ausgehaucht [= er ist todt], he has breathed his last.

Athem-bar, *adj.* respirable. —holen, *n.* breathing, respiration. —los, *adj.* breathless. —zäpflein, V. Zäpfchen im Halse. —zug, *m.* breathing, breath, respiration. Bis zum letzten —zuge, to the last gasp.

* Athén, *n.* [-s] Athens.

* Athéner [a better word than] Athenienser, *m.* Athenian.

* Athénisch [a better word than] Atheniensisch, *adj.* Athenian.

* Äther, *m.* [-s] ether.

* Athérisch, *adj.* ethereal, ethereous, aerial.

* Athléte, *m.* [-n, *pl.* -n] athlete.

* Athlétisch, *adj.* athletic. Die —en Spiele, athletic games. *Fig.* Ein —er Körper, an athletic [vigorous] body.

Äthmen, I. *v. intr.* 1) to breathe, to respire. Er athmet, also lebt er, he breathes, then he lives; tief —, to draw a deep breath, to suspire; schwer —, to gasp. 2) *Fig.* to blow softly, to breathe. II. *v. tr.* 1) to breathe Lebensluft —, to breathe vital air. *Fig.* Hier athmet man Freiheit und Frieden, here we breathe liberty and peace. 2) to emit a breathing, to respire. Die Rose athmet einen süßen Wohlgeruch, the rose exhales a fragrant odour; die Blumen — Wohlgerüche, the flowers breathe odours or perfume.

* Atlánten, *pl.* the supporters of a building, atlasses.

* Atlántische Meer, *n.* the Atlantic ocean, the Atlantic.

* Átlas, *m.* 1) [proper name] Atlas. 2) [-ses, *pl.* -se

or Atlanten] [a collection of maps] atlas. 3) [in anat. the first vertebra of the neck] atlas.

Atlasformat, *n.* [in printing] large square folio.

Atlaß, *m.* [-sses, *pl.* -sse] satin.

Atlaß-band, *n.* satin ribbon. —beere, *f.* the fruit of the white beam-tree. —blume, *f.* satin flower. —boden, *m.* [in manufactures of ticking] satin-ground. —erz, *n.* fibrous malachite, fibrous green carbonated copper. —glanz, *m.* the gloss of satin. —grund, *m.* [am. weav.] satin-ground. —holz, *n.* satin-wood. —kies, *m.* a kind of copper. —schmetterling, *m.* a species of butterfly [papilio Menelaus]. —streifen, *m.* a shining streak [in woven stuffs]. —vitriol, *m.* sulphate of magnesia, Epsom salts. —weber, —wirker, *m.* satin-weaver.

Atlassen, *adj.* made of satin, satin. Das —e Kleid, a garment of satin.

*Atmosphäre, *f.* [*pl.* -n] atmosphere. V. Dunstkreis.

*Atmosphärisch, *adj.* atmospheric, atmospherical. Die —e Luft, atmospheric air.

*Ätna, *m.* [mount] Aetna.

*Atom, *m.* [-s, *pl.* -e] [a particle of matter so minute as not to admit of any division] atom.

Atomen-ähnlich, *adj.* atom-like. —lehre, *f.* the doctrine of atoms, atomism.

*Atonie, *f.* atony, debility, relaxation.

*Attestat, *n.* [-es, *pl.* -e] certificate, testimony.

Attich, *m.* [-s] [Lat. *acte*] [a plant] danewort, dwarf-elder, wall-wort.

Attich-beere, *f.* the berry of the dwarf-elder. —saft, *m.* the inspissated juice of the fruit of the dwarf elder.

*Attisch, *adj.* Attic. —er Witz, —es Salz, Attic wit, Attic salt [a poignant, delicate wit, peculiar to the Athenians]; die —e Redensart, atticism.

*Attitüde, *f.* [*pl.* -n] attitude, posture.

*Attraction, *f.* the attractive force of bodies, attraction.

*Attribut, *n.* [-es, *pl* -e] attribute. Macht und Weisheit sind —e des höchsten Wesens, power and wisdom are attributes of the Supreme Being.

‖Atzel, *f.* 1) V. Elster. 2) V. Perrücke.

1. Ätzen, *v. tr.* [appears allied to the L. *acies*] 1) to corrode by acid or caustic substances. 2) [am. engravers] to eat or corrode by nitric acid, to etch.

Ätz-bar, *adj.* that which may be corroded, especially [among engravers] that which may be eaten or corroded by nitric acid or etched. —bild, *n.* V. —zeichnung. —grund, *m.* etching varnish or ground. —kasten, *m.* etching-trough. —kraft, *f.* causticity. —kunst, *f.* the art of etching. —mittel, *n.* corrosive, cauter. —nadel, *f.* a needle used in etching. —pulver, *n.* a caustic powder. —stein, *m.* infernal-stone, lunar-stone. —stoff, *m.* a caustic substance. —wasser, *n.* a caustic water —wiege, *f.* V. —kasten. —zeichnung, *f.* [the impression taken from an etched copper-plate] etching.

2. Ätzen, V. Azen.

Ätzung, V. Azung.

Au, Au weh, *interj.* [an exclamation of grief] oh! o sad!

Auch, *conj.* [Goth. *auk*, D. *oock*, allied to the Goth. *aukan* and the Lat. *augeo*] [noting addition or augmentation] also, too, likewise, even. Aber —, but, but yet; doch —, however, yet; sowohl …, als —, as well … as, both … and; nicht allein, nicht nur …., sondern —, not only …. but also; er ist nicht nur reich, sondern — von guter Herkunft, he is not only rich, but also of good family; wann der Körper krank ist, so ist es — der Geist, when the body is sick, the mind is so likewise; Liebe ist nicht nur freigebig, sondern — verschwenderisch, love is not only liberal, but also prodigal; so oft —, so groß — &c., as often as, as great as &c; — noch, still; wenn Sie 10, — noch 20 Jahre, or — 20 Jahre noch, warten, if you wait 10, or even 20 years; es wäre schändlich, — nur davon zu reden, it were a shame even to speak of it; *it.* [as a sort of expletive] — nicht, neither; so will ich — dieses nicht sagen, neither will I say so much; ich bin der erste nicht, werde — der letzte nicht seyn, neither am I the first, nor shall I be the last; und Sie —, and you too; wir bedürfen Ihres Rathes und — Ihrer Gunst, we have need of your counsel and favour too; ich bin glücklich, ich —, I am happy, so am I; jedermann nennt ihn gelehrt, und er ist es —, every body calls him learned, and that he is; Sie sind — gar zu neugierig, you are far too curious; wer er — sei, whoever he may be; es geschehe — wenn es wolle, whenever it may happen; wo es — sey, wheresoever it be; wäre er — noch so reich, let him be ever so rich; und wenn — schon, wenn — gleich, even though, and although.

*Auction, *f.* [*pl.* -en] auction, public sale, [in America and the Westindies] a vendue. Die öffentliche —, public or open sale; die gerichtliche —, subhastation.

*Auctionator, *m.* [-s, *pl.* -en] auctioneer.

*Audienz, *f.* [*pl.* -en] [admittance to a hearing, public reception to an interview] audience. Zur — gelassen werden, to have audience.

Audienz-saal, *m.*, —zimmer, *n.* presence-chamber, presence.

*Auditor, *m.* [-s, *pl.* -e] a military lawyer and judge in military cases.

*Auditorium, *n.* [-s, *pl.* -ien] auditory. *a*) [a place or apartment where discourses are delivered]. *b*) = an assembly of hearers, an audience, an auditory.

Aue, *f.* [*pl.* -n] [allied to Ach and the Fr. *ève* = *water*] 1) a running water. 2) pasture ground, a green, a meadow. [especially used in poetry] Der Morgen lacht auf Wald und —, the morning smiles on wood and lawn.

Au-garten, *m.* a pleasure garden, a park. —wärter, *m.* park-keeper.

Auerhahn, *m.* [Ur = *wild*] the cock of the wood, wood-grouse. Die Auerhenne, the female of the cock of the wood. —balz, *f.* the act and time of copulation of the wood-grouse.

Auerochs, *m.* [-ochsen, *pl.* -ochsen] ure-ox, buffalo.

Auf, [allied to oben, über; Sax. *up*, D. *op*, Ice. *off*] I. *prep.* [governing the dat. and acc. case] 1) [joined with the dat. case, it denotes existence or presence, a state of rest or motion at or over the surface of any body or place, and when it may be asked wo? worauf? auf welchem?] on, upon. — dem Stuhle sitzen, to sit on the chair; — der Erde liegen, to lie on the ground; sein Kopf ruhte — meiner Brust, his head rested upon my bosom; — dem Lande leben, to live in the country; — der Universität seyn, to be at the university; — dem Markte gekauft, bought at the market; — dem Claviere spielen, to play on the harpsichord; — dieser Welt, in this world; lasset die Vögel sich vermehren — der Erde, [in scripture] let fowls multiply on the earth. *Fig.* Zuweilen beruht es — Zeugnissen, sometimes it rests upon testimony; — der Reise seyn, to be on one's way; — der Jagd seyn, to be a-hunting; — Jemands Seite seyn, to be at any one's side; er hat die Lacher — seiner Seite, he has the laugh on his side; — frischer That ertappt, surprised in the very act; — der Stelle, immediately; es hat nichts — sich, it is no matter; das hat viel — sich, this is of great moment or importance. 2) [joined with the accus. case, noting direction or motion towards any object] to, on, upon. Sich — den Ellbogen stützen, to lean on one's elbow; — Einen zugehen, to walk towards any one; — die Messe reisen, to go to the fair; — die Post gehen, to go to the post-office; — einen Berg steigen, to mount a hill; — die Wache ziehen, to mount guard; — das [auf's] Pferd steigen, to get on horseback; — die Gasse laufen, to run into the street; — die Jagd ausgehen, to go out a shooting. *Fig.* Es geht — zwei [Uhr], it draws towards two; es ist drei Viertel — Eins, it is three quarters past twelve, it wants a quarter to one; — Einen weisen, to point at any one; ich rechnete or zählte — ihn, I counted on him; vertrauet — Gott, throw yourself upon God; — Einen zürnen, to be angry with any one; — seinen Befehl, at his command; — seine Frau eifersüchtig seyn, to be jealous of one's wife; Geld — Bücher wenden, to lay out money in books; sich auf's Trinken legen, to take to drinking; er bekam Briefe — Briefe, he received letters upon letters; — alle Gefahr, at all hazards; bis — weitern Befehl, till further orders; — meine Ehre, upon my honour; — Rechnung, on account; — seine Bitten, at his request; — Einen warten, to wait for a person; — ein Haar, to a hair, to a T; — die Minute, to a minute; nur noch — eine Minute, but for a minute; — den Nachmittag, for the afternoon; — einen Sonntag, on a sunday; — das Essen spazieren gehen, to walk after dinner; das kostet — [better an] 100 Thaler, it costs about or nearly 100 dollars; er war — französische Art gekleidet, he was dressed in or after the French manner or fashion; das heißt — Deutsch, that is in German; — einmahl, at once, suddenly; aufs neue, anew; aufs eheste, as soon as possible.

II. *adv.* [it denotes tendency upwards] 1) up. — und ab, up and down; Berg—, up hill; Treppen —, up stairs; die Sonne ist —, the sun is up; — und nieder [in seamen's lang.] apeak [said of an anchor]; der Wind ist — und nieder, the wind is right down; — und nieder stehende Knie, knees up and down, hanging knees; [in the form of an interj.] up! — denn! up then! — zu Gott, Godward. *Fig.* Einen Gulden — oder ab, a florin more or less; von meiner Jugend —, from my youth upwards; — daß, that, in order that; — daß nicht, lest. 2) [open] Die Thür ist —, the door is open.

III. In composition auf denotes tendency upwards; the act of opening; it moreover implies the signification of something put upon another, of something renewed or repeated, of something finished or consumed, of something kept for future use.

SYN. Auf, Offen. A thing is said to be offen [open], when the ingress and egress are not impeded, the absence of the impediment may be natural or artificial. Auf applies to the obstacle itself, by the absence of which any thing becomes open. A vein which is opened by a lancet is offen, but not auf. When the flood-gates are auf, the sluice is offen.

Aufächzen, I. *v. intr.* to groan, to sigh. II. *v. tr.* to get any one up by groaning or sighing.

Aufackern, *v. tr.* 1) to bring up by ploughing, to plough up [old coins &c.]. 2) to plough again. 3) [am. engravers] to score or scratch the ground of a copper-plate by a needle or similar instrument.

Aufangeln, *v. tr.* to draw up [a fish] with a fishing-hook. *Fig.* * and ‡ Neuigkeiten —, to fish up news.

Aufarbeiten, I. *v. tr.* 1) to expend in any

work [as materials], to work up [timber &c.]. [In a proper and in a figurative sense] Sie haben tüchtig aufgearbeitet, you have finished a good deal of work. 2) to open by labour, to break open [a door &c.]. 3) to hurt by labour [one's hands &c.]. II. *v. r.* sich —, to work one's self up in the world.

Aúfathmen, *v. intr.* to breathe anew. Jetzt athme ich erst wieder auf, now I begin to breathe again.

Aúfätzen, *v. tr.* 1) to open by corrosives. 2) to etch on.

Aufbacken, *ir.* I. *v. intr.* [u. w. seyn] to fasten on or to stick to by baking. II. *v. tr.* 1) to consume in baking [flour]. 2) to renew by baking again [stale bread].

[illegible]fbähen, *v. tr.* to open by fomentation [an abscess &c.].

Aufba[illegible], *v. tr.* to put [a corpse] upon the bier.

Aúfballen, [illegible] *tr.* 1) to heap up in bales [goods]. 2) to open [illegible] pack, or bale.

Aúfbansen, *v. t.* [in husbandry] to lay up.

Aúfbau, *m.* [-es] the [illegible] g or building, erection. Der — eines Hauses, th[illegible] erection of a house.

Aúfbauen, *v. tr.* 1) to erect, to [illegible] raise anew. 2) to build. *Fig.* Luftschlö[illegible], to build castles in the air.

Aúfbauer, *m.* [-s, *pl.* -] erecter, builder.

Aúfbäumeln, *v. r.* sich —, [am. sportsmen] to seat [said of hares].

Aúfbaumen, *v. intr.* [am. sportsmen] to take a tree [of cats &c.].

Aúfbäumen, I. *v. tr.* [in weaving] to wind on the beam. Den Aufzug —, to wind the warp on the beam [before weaving]. II. *v. intr.* and *r.* sich —, 1) to prance, to rear [said of horses]. 2) [in mining] to appear, to make its appearance.

Aúfbauschen, **Aúfblausen**, *v. intr.* to swell up.

Aúfbeben, *v. intr.* [u. w. seyn] to start up tremblingly.

Aúfbefinden, *ir. v. r.* sich —, to be up. Helene befand sich noch nicht auf, Helen was not up yet.

Aúfbehalten, *ir. v. tr.* 1) to keep on [a hat &c.]. 2) to keep, to preserve, to lay up. *Fig.* Behalte deine gütigen Blicke für einsame Stunden auf, preserve thy kind looks for private hours. Syn. Aufbehalten, Aufbewahren. Aufbehalten signifies merely, not to throw away, not to destroy a thing. Aufbewahren implies a certain care bestowed, in order to prevent a thing's being lost or destroyed.

Aúfbeißen, *ir. v. tr.* 1) to bite open, to open by biting. Nüsse —, to crack nuts. *Fig.* Einem eine harte Nuß aufzubeißen geben, to set any one a hard task. 2) to open by corrosives.

Aúfbeizen, *v. tr.* 1) to open by corrosives. 2) to produce [on the skin &c.] by corrosives.

Aúfbellen, I. *v. intr.* to bark [like dogs &c.] II. *v. tr.* to awake by barking.

Aúfbersten, *ir.* I. *v. intr.* [u. w. seyn] to open in chinks, to crack. Die Erde ist aufgeborsten, the earth is cracked. *reg.* II. *v. tr.* to make to open in chinks. Der Frost hat die Erde aufgeberstet, the frost has cracked the earth.

Aúfbetten, *v. tr.* 1) to make a bed anew. 2) to put up a bed.

Aúfbewahren, *v. tr.* to keep, to preserve, to lay up. Die Krone wurde stets im Schlosse von Monza aufbewahrt, the crown was always kept in the castle of Monza; Obst —, to conserve fruits; ich will es für Sie —, I will reserve it for you. *Fig.* Zu großen Dingen aufbewahrt seyn, to be destined to great things; ich weiß nicht, was mir das Schicksal aufbewahrt, I don't know, what fortune has in store for me. Syn. V. Aufbehalten.

Aúfbewahrer, *m.* [-s, *pl.* -] layer up.

Aúfbewahrung, *f.* preservation, reservation, conservation.

Aúfbiegen, *ir. v. tr.* 1) to bend upwards. 2) to bend open, to unfold.

Aúfbieten, *ir. v. tr.* 1) to summon by a public order, to summon into service. Die Milizen —, to call out the militia; das ganze Land —, to raise the country in a mass. *Fig.* Er bot allen seinen Muth zu dieser Unternehmung auf, he summoned all his courage for this enterprise; wir sollten alle unsere Kraft —, we should put forth all our strength; alle Geisteskräfte —, to call forth all the faculties of the mind; er bot Allem auf, seinen Freund von dieser Unternehmung zurückzuhalten, he did all he could to dissuade his friend from this undertaking. 2) to make generally and openly known, to publish. Ein Paar Verlobte —, to bid the bans. 3) to offer for sale. 4) to give warning.

Aúfbinden, *ir. v. tr.* 1) to fasten upon. Einem Pferde das Felleisen —, to fasten the valise on to a horse. *Fig.* Einem etwas —, einen Bären —, to impose on any one, to impose a falsehood on another, to put a hoax upon, to humbug any one. 2) to bind up, to tie up, to truss [one's hair]. Ein Kleid —, to upbind a garment; Strümpfe —, to garter stockings. 3) [am. print.] to tie up. 4) to untie, to unbind, to loosen. Den Verband von einer Wunde —, to take off the dressing from a wound.

Aúfblähen, I. *v. tr.* to puff up, to blow up, to swell. *Fig.* Aufgebläht von ihrem beständigen Glücke, puffed up by their constant success; durch langen Ueberfluß aufgebläht, swollen with long plenty; von Stolz aufgebläht, elated or lifted up with pride. II. *v.* [illegible] —, to puff, to swell; *Fig.* to elate one's se[illegible].

Aúfblasen, *ir.* I. *v. tr.* 1) to blow up, to fill with air, to swell, to blow, to inflate. Einen Hammel —, [among butchers] to blow mutton; eine Blase —, to blow up or to inflate a bladder; die Backen —, to swell the cheeks with wind, to puff; [in botany] aufgeblasen, inflated [an epithet of the petiole or leafstalk, the perianth, the pericarp]; da kommt er, aufgeblasen wie ein kalekutischer Hahn, here he comes, swelled like a turkey-cock. *Fig.* Er ist vom Glück aufgeblasen, he is elated with success; aufgeblasene Jünglinge, conceited youths. 2) to open by blowing. 3) to renew by blowing. Das Feuer —, to blow the fire. 4) to sound on a wind-instrument. 5) to awake by sounding a wind-instrument. II. *v. intr.* to call forth by blowing or sounding a wind-instrument. III. *v. r.* sich —, to swell with wind or air, to puff. *Fig.* Er bläst sich auf, he elates himself.

Aúfblättern, *v. tr.* 1) to open the leaves [of a book]. Eine aufgeblätterte Rose, a full-blown rose. 2) to search for by turning over the leaves of a book. II. *v. r.* sich —, to open [said of a flower].

Aúfblausen, V. Aufbauschen.

Aúfbleiben, *ir. v. intr.* [u. w. seyn] 1) to stay up, to sit up. Warum bleibt Ihr so spät auf? what makes you sit up so late? 2) to remain open [said of a door &c.].

Aúfblick, *m.* [-es, *pl.* -e] 1) a looking up. 2) a glimpse.

Aúfblicken, *v. intr.* 1) to look up. Laßt uns zu Gott —, let us look up to God. 2) to emit a transient gleam or glimpse, to glimpse. 3) to grow light. Der —de Morgen, the dawning morning.

Aúfblinken, *v. intr.* to emit a transient gleam, to glimpse.

Aúfblitzen, *v. intr.* to flash. *Fig.* Zuweilen blitzt ein großer Gedanke in ihnen auf, they flash out sometimes into a greatness of thought; mit einem Male blitzte der Gedanke in ihm auf, all at once the thought flashed across his mind; das — und der Ausbruch eines feurigen Gemüthes, the flash and outbreaking of a fiery mind.

Aúfblöken, *v. tr.* to awake any one by bleating.

Aúfblühen, *v. intr.* [u. w. seyn] to begin to blow, to blossom, to bloom. Eine aufgeblühte Rose, a blown rose. *Fig.* Ein —des Mädchen, a blooming girl; der Handel fängt an wieder aufzublühen, trade begins to revive.

Aúfbohren, *v. tr.* 1) to bore anew. 2) to open by boring.

Aúfbojen, *v. tr.* [a sea term] to buoy up.

Aúfborgen, *v. tr.* to get together or to collect by borrowing. V. Borgen.

Aúfborger, *m.* [-s, *pl.* -] he that collects money by borrowing, borrower.

Aúfbot, *m.* V. Aufgebot.

Aúfbrassen, *v. tr.* [a sea term] V. Brassen.

Aúfbraten, *ir. v. tr.* 1) to roast over or again. 2) to expend in roasting [meat].

Aúfbrauchen, V. Verbrauchen.

Aúfbrauen, *v. tr.* to expend in brewing [malt].

Aúfbrausen, *v. intr.* to bubble and hiss, to effervesce. Das Bier, der Wein brauset auf, the beer, the wine effervesces; [in chimistry] das — eines kohlensauren Salzes mit Salpetersäure, the effervescence of a carbonate with nitric acid. *Fig.* Er braust gleich auf, he gets easily into a passion; ein —der Kopf, a fretful, boisterous spirit.

Aúfbrechen, *ir.* I. *v. intr.* 1) to break open, to open, to burst open. Die Wunden brechen auf, the wounds open; die Knospen brechen auf, the buds open, expand; das Geschwür bricht auf, the aposteme breaks; die Hände brechen auf, the hands chap. 2) to change the place of residence, to break up, to depart. *a)* to set out, to march off [said of an army, of a prince with a great retinue &c.]. Das Russische Heer brach um zwei Uhr Morgens auf, the Russian army decamped at two o'clock in the morning; die Gesellschaft brach auf, the company broke up. *b)* to rise from table. II. *v. tr.* 1) to break open, to open by force [a door, a lock &c.]. 2) [among sportsmen] to eviscerate [a deer &c.]. Eine wilde Katze —, to spread open a wild cat.

Aúfbreiten, *v. tr.* to spread, to spread upon.

Aúfbrennen, *ir.* I. *v. intr.* [u. w. seyn] 1) to burn suddenly. *Fig.* to be inflamed, to be excited to. 2) [am. sportsmen] V. Abbrennen. II. *v. tr.* 1) to consume or use up in burning, to burn out. 2) to consume entirely by fire, to burn up. 3) to burn or impress a mark with a hot iron. Dem Fasse ein Zeichen —, to brand a cask [for the purpose of fixing a mark upon it]. 4) [among washerwomen] Die Wäsche —, to pour hot water upon foul linen, to scald it.

Aúfbringen, *ir. v. tr.* 1) to get on [a hat &c.]. [among weavers] V. Aufziehen. 2) to bring up, to convey upwards, to rear. *Fig.* *a)* [großziehen, davon bringen] Ein Kind —, to bring up a child; sie brachten ihre Jungen ohne &c. auf, they reared their young ones without &c. *b)* [herbei schaffen] Geld —, to procure money; er konnte nur fünf Pfund —, he could but raise five pounds; ein Schiff —, to bring in a prize. c) [vorbringen] Er kann dagegen nichts —, he cannot alledge or produce any thing against it. d) [üblich machen &c.] Eine Mode —, to bring up, to introduce a fashion; einen alten Gebrauch wieder —, to renew an old custom. e) [zornig machen] Einen —, to make any one angry, to fret any one, to raise any one's passion, to exasperate any one; gegen Einen aufgebracht seyn, to be irritated at any one.

Aúfbringer, *m.* [-s, *pl.* -] [a sea term] one who takes a prize, captor.

Aúfbrodeln, *v. intr.* [u. w. seyn] to bubble up.

Aúfbruch, *m.* [-es, *pl.* -brüche] 1) the state of breaking open, opening or of being opened, break. Der — eines Geschwürs, the breaking of an apostema. 2) the setting out, marching off. Der — eines Heeres, the decampment of an army; zum —e blasen, to sound the march. 3) [am. sportsmen] *a*) the act of opening and eviscerating. Der — eines wilden Schweines, the opening, the gutting of a boar. *b*) [the entrails of a deer &c.] numbles. V. Geräusch. 4) [in husb.] breaking [the ploughing of ground after lying long fallow].

Aúfbrühen, *v. tr.* to scald.

Aúfbrüllen, I. *v. intr.* to roar. II. *v. tr.* to awake by roaring.

Aúfbrüsten, I. *v. tr.* to open the breast of a butchered ox &c. [as butchers do]. II. *v. r.* sich —, to strut, to make one's self look big.

Aúfbuden, *v. tr.* 1) to put up booths or stalls. 2) to lay out, to display.

Aúfbügeln, *v. tr.* 1) to pass over afresh with the smoothing iron, to iron again. 2) to raise by ironing.

Aúfbürden, *v. tr.* to burden. *Fig. a*) Einem eine schwere Last —, to impose a hard task on any one; einem Volke unerschwingliche Steuern —, to burden a nation with insupportable taxes; bürde dir nicht mehr auf, als du tragen kannst, burden not thyself above thy power; einem Andern Etwas —, to shift a thing on to another's shoulders. *b*) to charge, to impute to. Einem ein Verbrechen —, to charge any one with a crime.

Aúfbürsten, *v. tr.* 1) to brush up again, to dress or trim by brushing [a hat &c.]. 2) to raise by brushing, to brush up.

Aúfdamen, *v. tr.* Einen Stein —, [at draughts] to king or crown a man.

Aúfdämmen, *v. tr.* to dam up, to confine or shut in water.

Aúfdämmern, *v. tr.* [u. w. seyn] to begin to grow light in the morning, to dawn. Der Tag dämmert auf, the day dawns. *Fig.* to begin to open or expand, to dawn. Die Künste und Wissenschaften fangen an bei diesem Volke aufzudämmern, the arts and sciences are beginning to dawn among this people.

Aúfdampfen, I. *v. intr.* [u. w. seyn] to rise up in smoke or vapour, to reek up. II. *v. tr.* 1) to cause to rise up in smoke or vapour. 2) to consume by smoking.

Aúfdauern, *v. intr.* to sit up, not to go to bed, to watch. V. Aufbleiben, 1.

Aúfdecken, I. *v. tr.* 1) to spread. Das Tischtuch —, to spread the cloth, to lay the tablecloth; den Tisch —, to cover the table with a cloth. 2) to uncover [a bed &c.]. *Fig.* Die Ereignisse haben die Pläne des Ministeriums aufgedeckt, events have disclosed the designs of the ministry; die geheimen Kunstgriffe eines Hofes —, to expose the secret artifices of a court. II. *v. r.* sich —, to divest one's self of the blanket or coverlet.

Aúfdeichen, *v. tr.* to dam up higher, to heighten a dam.

Aúfdichten, *v. tr.* to attribute falsely. V. Andichten.

Aúfdienen, I. *v. tr.* 1) to wait upon. V. Aufwarten. 2) to serve up a meal. V. Auftragen. II. *v. r.* sich —, to rise by serving, or in service.

Aúfdingen, *ir. v. tr.* to bind to a master, to apprentice. Einen Lehrling —, to bind an apprentice; einen jungen Menschen bei einem Schuhmacher —, to indenture a young man to a shoemaker.

Aúfdingung, *f.* the binding as apprentice.

Aúfdocken, *v. tr.* [am. hunters] to wind up [a leading-string].

Aúfdonnern, I. *v. intr.* [u. w. seyn] 1) to thunder, to make a great noise. 2) to open with great noise. II. *v. tr.* 1) to awake by thundering. 2) to thunder up. *Fig.* † and student's cant. Aufgedonnert. Diese Komödiantinn ist immer gewaltig aufgedonnert, this actress is always extravagantly tricked out.

Aúfdoppeln, *v. tr.* [am. shoemakers] to sew the sole to the upper-leather.

Aúfdrängen, I. *v. tr.* to open by pressing, to push open. II. *v. r.* sich Einem —, to force one's self into a person's acquaintance. *Fig.* Einige Gedanken drängen sich uns auf, some thoughts intrude upon us.

Aúfdrechseln, V. Andrechseln.

Aúfdrehen, I. *v. tr.* 1) to fix to by turning on a turner's lathe. 2) to form on a lathe by turning. 3) to open by turning round. Hölzerne Büchsen, die schwer aufzudrehen sind, boxes of wood, that are difficult to screw open; einen Strick —, to untwist a rope; eine Schraube —, to unscrew; die Duchten eines Taues —, [a sea term] to unstrand a rope. II. *v. intr.* [in seamen's lang.] Vor dem Winde —, to spring the luff.

Aúfdreschen, *ir. v. tr.* and *intr.* 1) to thrash out all the stock of corn. 2) to finish thrashing.

Aúfdrieseln, *v. tr.* to untwist, to untwine.

Aúfdringen, *ir.* I. *v. tr.* to force or press on, or upon. Er drang mir einen Brief für Sie auf, he pressed a letter upon me, to deliver to you; Einem eine Wohlthat —, to press a benefit upon any one; dem Volke neue Gesetze —, to obtrude new laws upon the people; er wird diese Lehre der Welt nie —, he will never make the world adopt this doctrine. II. *v. r.* sich —, to enter a place, where one is not desired, to thrust one's self in uninvited or against the will of the company, to obtrude one's self.

Aúfdringlich, I. *adj.* obtrusive, importune. II. *adv.* by way of obtrusion.

Aúfdringlichkeit, *f.* obtrusion, importunity.

Aúfdrucken, *v. tr.* 1) to make a mark or figure on any thing by pressure, to impress, to imprint. Ein Bild auf Wachs oder Thon —, to impress a figure on wax or clay; ein Siegel —, to put the seal to, to clap a seal upon; das Petschaft auf einen Brief —, to seal a letter. 2) to expend in printing [paper].

Aúfdrücken, *v. tr.* 1) to open by pressure. Eine Nuß —, to crack a nut. 2) to fix or fasten to by pressure. Ein Pflaster auf eine Wunde —, to press a plaster to a sore.

Aúfduning, *f.* [a sea term] the looming of the land, land-fall.

Aúfdunsen, I. *v. intr.* [u. w. seyn] to be swelled or puffed up. Ein aufgedunsenes Gesicht, a bloated face; aufgedunsene Backen, blubbered cheeks. *Fig.* Ein aufgedunsener Mensch, a puffed up fellow; eine aufgedunsene Schreibart, a turgid style. II. *v. tr.* to make turgid, to bloat.

Aúfdunsten, *v. intr.* [u. w. seyn] to rise in the shape of vapour, to evaporate.

Aúfdünsten, *v. tr.* to make to rise in the shape of vapour, to evaporate.

Aúfdupfen, *v. tr.* 1) to fasten softly to, to fix to by a soft pressure with a compress; [am. gilders] die Goldblättchen —, to press the gold-leaves down. 2) to remove by a soft pressure with a compress [an abscess].

Aúfduven, *v. tr.* [a sea term] to bear up or away.

Aúfegen, **Aúfeggen**, *v. tr.* 1) to get up by harrowing. 2) to open, to tear open by harrowing.

Aufeinánder, *adv.* one upon another, one after another. — treiben, [in seaman's lang.] to run foul of another ship; — folgende Zeichen, signs following signs.

Aúfeisen, I. *v. tr.* to break the ice [of a pond &c.]. II. *v. intr.* [u. w. seyn or w. haben] to thaw.

Aúfenblatt, *n.* [a plant] 1) double-leaved butcher's broom. 2) heart-leaved uvularia.

Aúfenthalt, *m.* [-es, *pl.* -e] 1) continuance [in a place], abode, residence, stay. Während unseres —es in Paris, during our stay or residence in Paris. 2) a place of continuance, abode, residence. 3) [for: Aufhalt] hinderance for a time, delay, impediment. 4) [in seaman's lang.] demurrage.

Aufenthalts-ort, *m.* V. Aufenthalt 2. **—s-zeit**, *f.* 1) time of continuance in a place. 2) [in seaman's lang.] V. Aufenthalt 4.

Aúferbauen, *v. tr.* to erect, to build up. *Fig.* to edify. V. Erbauen.

Aúferbaulich, *adj.* and *adv.* edifying. V. Erbaulich.

Aúferlegen, *v. tr.* to lay on [as a command], to enjoin [as a duty], to impose. V. Auflegen.

Aúferschallen, V. Erschallen.

Aúferstehen, *ir. v. intr.* to rise, to rise from the dead.

Aúferstehung, *f.* the rising from the dead, resurrection. Die — unsers Heilands, the resurrection of our Saviour; der —stag, resurrection-day.

Aúferwachen, V. Aufwachen, Erwachen.

Aúferwecken, *v. tr.* to resuscitate. Die Todten —, to awake, to resuscitate the dead. V. Erwecken, Aufwecken.

Aúferwecker, *m.* [-s, *pl.* -] he that raises from the dead, our Saviour.

Aúferweckung, *f.* the raising from the dead, resuscitation.

Aúferziehen, *v. tr.* to bring up, to nurse. V. Erziehen.

Aúfessen, *ir. v. tr.* to consume in eating, to eat up.

Aúffächeln, *v. tr.* 1) to fan [the fire]. 2) to open, to expand by fanning.

Aúffachen, V. Anfachen.

Aúffädeln, V. Auffädmen.

Aúffädmen, **Aúffädnen**, *v. tr.* 1) to file on a string. Perlen —, to string pearls. 2) to ravel out. 3) to baste the folds of a gown.

Aúffahen, [obsolete] V. Auffangen.

Aúffahren, *ir.* I. *v. intr.* [u. w. seyn] 1) V. Hinauffahren. 2) [am. miners] to mount, to ascend from a pit. 3) to move or rise up quickly, to start or spring up suddenly. Ich fuhr auf wie von einem schrecklichen Traume, I started as from some dreadful dream. *Fig.* to fly into a passion. Er fährt gleich auf, he gets immediately into a passion; auffahrend, irritable, passionate. 4) to strike upon something in driving, to drive on to something; [in seaman's lang.] to run upon. Auf eine Sandbank —, to strike on a sand-bank. 5) to fly open [said of a door &c.]. II. *v. tr.* 1) to open by driving. Man hat den Weg ganz aufgefahren, the road is quite cut up by driving; die Wagen haben die Landstraße aufgefahren, the carriages have spoiled the high road. 2) to make higher, to raise by carrying or conveying something to, to fill up.

Aúffahrisch, *adj.* and *adv.* irritable, passionate.

Aúffahrt, *f.* [*pl.* -en] 1) the act of ascending. Die — Christi gen Himmel, the ascension of the Christ into heaven. 2) the act of driving upwards. 3) [an eminence or high place before a house &c.] ascent.

Aúffallen, *ir.* I. *v. intr.* [u. w. seyn] 1) to fall upon. Er ist hart aufgefallen, he fell hard; [among sportsmen] Ein Flug Vögel ist auf diesen Baum aufgefallen, a flight of birds settled or lighted on this tree. *Fig. a)* Eine —de Aehnlichkeit, a striking likeness; schöne Werke der Kunst fallen uns bei dem ersten Anblicke auf, fine works of art strike us upon the first view; das ist sehr auffallend, that is very striking or remarkable; ein —des Beispiel, a conspicuous instance. *b)* Das ist sehr auffallend, that is very shocking; dieser Ausdruck ist mir auffallend, I am shocked at this expression. 2) to open by falling. II. *v. tr.* and *v. r.* sich —, to open by falling, to hurt, to wound or to bruise by falling. Sich den Kopf —, to break one's head by a fall.

Aúffällig, *adj.* and *adv.* 1) striking, remarkable. 2) offensive, shocking.

Aúffalten, *v. tr.* 1) to unfold, to undo folds or plaits. 2) [am. clothiers] to lay in proper plaits, to fold [a piece of cloth].

Aúffangeglas, *n.* [-glases, *pl* -gläser] a glass in perspectives which collects the rays of light.

Aúffangen, *ir. v. tr.* to stop and seize in the way, to catch or snap up. Den Ball im Rückpralle —, [at tennis] to take the ball at the rebound; einen Kundschafter —, to intercept a spy; Briefe —, to intercept letters; den Regen in einem Fasse —, to collect the rain in a vessel; um einen Theil des Lichtes aufzufangen, der &c., to intercept some part of light, which &c.; [in seam. lang.] ein Tau —, to get up or hang up a rope. *Fig.* Eines Andern Worte —, to take up, to catch another's words; wo haben Sie das aufgefangen? where did you fish out that? † and * eine Krankheit —, to catch a disease.

Aúffärben, *v. tr.* to dye or colour afresh.

Aúffäseln, *v. tr.* to ravel out.

Aúffasen, **Aúffasern**, *v. tr.* to draw out the threads, to ravel out.

Aúffassen, *v. tr.* to catch up, to take up. Eine gefallene Masche — (aufnehmen), to take up a stitch in knitting. *Fig.* to receive into, to take in. Perlen —, to string beads; das Wasser in ein Glas —, to catch water in a glass; ein Begriff, den wir nicht durch die Sinne —, an idea not received by one's senses; dieser Schauspieler hat seine Rolle gut aufgefaßt, that actor has conceived his part well; Einer, der schnell auffaßt, a man of quick apprehension.

Aúffassung, *f.* apprehension, comprehension.

Auffassungs-kraft, *f.* —**vermögen**, *n.* power of apprehension.

Aúffeilen, *v. tr.* 1) [am. locksmiths] V. Befeilen. 2) to file again, to file anew. 3) to open by filing.

Aúffeuchten, *v. tr.* to wet again.

Aúffiedeln, *v. intr.* and *v. tr.* 1) to play ill on a fiddle, to scrape. 2) to awake by scraping. 3) to play. Fiedelt uns eine lustige Weise auf, play up a merry tune for us.

Aúffindebuch, *n.* [-es, *pl.* -bücher] a book in which things are methodically placed, repertory.

Aúffinden, *ir. v. tr.* to seek and find. Er durchstreifte die Stadt, um mich aufzufinden, he ranged the town to seek me out; die Grenzen der Welt —, to trace out the limits of the world; aufgejagte Feldhühner [after alighting] wieder —, [am. sportsmen] to retrieve partridges.

Aúffirnissen, *v. tr.* to varnish afresh, to varnish up.

Aúffischen, *v. tr.* to fish up. Einen todten Körper —, to fish up a dead body. *Fig.* † and * Wo haben Sie das aufgefischt? where did you fish out that?

Aúfflackern, *v. intr.* [u. w. seyn] to blaze up.

Aúfflammen, I. *v. intr.* [u. w. seyn] to break out into a flame, to flame, to blaze. II. *v. tr.* to kindle into a flame, to inflame.

Aúfflattern, *v. intr.* [u. w. seyn] to flatter upwards.

Aúfflechten, *ir. v. tr.* 1) to plait up, to adorn by plaiting [the hair &c.]. 2) to untwist. Eine Flechte —, to ravel out a twist.

Aúfflicken, *v. tr.* to put a patch upon.

Aúffliegen, *ir. v. intr.* [u. w. seyn] 1) to fly upwards, to soar. Ein Vogel, der auffliegt (aufsteht), [am. sportsmen] a bird that rises from the ground; mit einem Luftballe —, to ascend in an air-balloon; die Mine ist aufgeflogen, the mine blew up; in Rauch —, to fly up in smoke, to vanish into smoke, to come to nothing. 2) to open suddenly or with violence. Die Thüren flogen auf, the doors flew open.

Aúffliehen, *ir. v. intr.* [u. w. seyn] to flee upward.

Aúfflimmern, *v. intr.* 1) to glimmer. 2) [u. w. seyn] to rise in air glimmering.

Aúfflößen, I. *v. tr.* to convey up by floating. II. *v. intr.* [u. w. seyn] to strike against in floating.

Aúfflöten, I. *v. intr.* to play on a flute, to flute. II. *v tr.* 1) to perform on a flute [a tune]. 2) to awake by fluting.

Aúffluchen, *v. tr.* to rouse from sleep by swearing.

Aúfflug, *m.* [-es, *pl.* -flüge] a flying upwards, a soaring, ascent. *Fig.* Ein — der Phantasie, a flight of imagination or fancy.

Aúfflügeln, *v. r.* sich —, to dress one's self up.

Aúffodern, **Aúffordern**, *v. tr.* 1) to call, to invite. Ein Frauenzimmer zum Tanze —, to ask a lady to dance; Einen — (etwas zu thun), to summon; eine Festung —, to summon a fortress; fodere ihn auf, morgen im Tower zu erscheinen, summon him to-morrow to the Tower; Liebe, Pflicht fodern uns zum Abgange auf, love, duty summon us away; ich fodere Sie auf, die Wahrheit zu sagen, I call upon you to speak the truth; Einen zur Erfüllung seines Versprechens —, to claim a man's promise.

Aúffoderung, *f.* summons, challenge.

Auffoderungsschreiben, *n.* summons.

Aúffoderer, *m.* [-s, *pl.* -] summoner.

Aúfforderu, V. Auffodern.

Aúffördern, *v. tr.* to move upwards.

Aúfformen, *v. tr.* 1) to put upon the form. 2) [among hatters] to turn up, to cock.

Aúffragen, *ir. v. tr.* to find out by asking. V. Erfragen.

|| **Aúffrätzen**, *v. tr.* to cause to fester [a sore].

Aúffressen, *ir.* I. *v. tr.* to consume in eating, to eat up [said of beasts and in contempt of men]. Er ist von Tiegern aufgefressen worden, he was devoured by tigers; das Kind ist zum — schön, one could eat that child up, it is so pretty; Einen (sein Vermögen) —, to eat any one out of house and home. *Fig.* † Die Leute — (anfahren), to assail people with harsh language. 2) to eat open, to corrode, to wear away. Das Scheidewasser frißt die Haut auf, aquafortis eats the skin. II. *v. r.* sich —, to fatten, thrive or prosper by eating.

Aúffrieren, *v. intr.* 1) to freeze fast on to any thing. || 2) to thaw.

Aúffrischen, *v. tr.* 1) to refresh [a picture &c.]. Das Alaunbad wieder —, [am. dyers] to refresh the dye with alum. *Fig.* Das Andenken einer Sache —, to refresh the memory of a thing, to rub up the memory of a thing; das Andenken großer Männer —, to revive the memory of great men. 2) *Fig.* to encourage, to animate, to inspirit.

Aúffügen, *v. tr.* to join to. Die Felgen —, [am. wheel-wrights] to join the fellies to the spokes.

Aúfführbar, *adj.* and *adv.* 1) that may be erected. 2) that may be represented.

Aúfführen, I. *v. tr.* 1) to raise, to erect, to set up, to build. Einen Tempel —, to erect a temple. 2) to exhibit, to show. Ein Trauerspiel —, to represent a tragedy; einen Tanz —, to perform a dance; Etwas mit in einer Rechnung —, to set or put something to account; die Wache —, to mount guard; eine Schildwache —, to post a sentry; die Kanonen —, to mount the cannon. II. *v. r.* sich —, to conduct one's self, to behave. Er führt sich gut oder schlecht auf, he behaves well or ill.

Aúfführung, *f.* 1) erection. Die — eines Hauses, the erection or building of a house. 2) exhibition, show. Die — eines Schauspiels, the representation or performance of a play. 3) the mounting of a guard, the posting of a sentry, the mounting of a gun. 4) conduct, behaviour.

Aúffüllen, *v. tr.* 1) to make full, to fill up [a cask of wine &c.]. 2) to fill afresh [a bottle]. 3) to bottle [wine &c.].

Aúffunkeln, *v. intr.* 1) [u. w. haben] to sparkle. 2) [u. w. seyn] to rise in sparks.

Aúffurchen, *v. tr.* to furrow up.

Aúffußen, *v. intr.* to stand on one's feet.

Aúffuttern, *v. tr.* [in archit.] to cover with artificial superficies, to face, to line.

Aúffüttern, *v. tr.* 1) to rear by feeding, to bring up by feeding. 2) to consume or to spend in feeding.

Aúffutterung, *f.* 1) facing, lining. 2) [a sea-term] waterboards or weatherboards [used when a ship is to be careened].

Aúfgabe, *f.* [*pl.* -n] 1) the act of transmitting from one's self to another by hand or speech. Die — eines Briefes, the delivering of a letter [to the post-office]; die — eines Räthsels, the putting of a riddle; unter —, [in commerce] with advice. 2) [that which is appointed for a person to perform] task, exercise. Eine leichte —, an easy task; die — für Schüler, theme; die — in der Größenlehre, problem.

Aúfgabeln, *v. tr.* to take up with a fork, to

raise or pitch with a fork. Heu —, to fork hay. Fig. † and * Wo haben sie diesen Dummkopf aufgegabelt? where have they picked up this blockhead?

Aufgackern, *v. tr.* to rouse from sleep by cackling.

Aufgaffen, *v. intr.* to stare upward.

Aufgähnen, *v. intr.* 1) to gape or yawn aloud. 2) to open in fissures or crevices, to gape.

Aufgähren, *ir. v. intr.* [u. w. haben and seyn] to rise fermenting, [of dough] to rise [also in a fig. sense].

Aufgang, *m.* [-es, *pl.* -gänge] 1) the act of rising or ascending. Der — der Sonne, the rising of the sun, sun-rise; sie begrüßen ihren —, they salute his rise [of the sun]; [in astron., the appearance of any star or planet above the horizon which before was hid beneath it] rising; der — eines Sternes mit — oder Untergang der Sonne, the cosmical or acronycal rising of a star. 2) *Fig.* the act of consuming, spending, consumption. 3) a place that favours the act of mounting aloft, rise, ascent. Ein steiler —, a steep ascent. 4) *Fig.* [the point in the heavens, where the sun is seen to rise] east.

Aufgangspunkt, *m.* [in astronomy] the rising point, orient. Der — im Sommer, im Winter, orient estival, orient hibernal.

‖ **Aufgattern**, *v. tr.* to find out, to pick up.

Aufgeben, *ir. v. tr.* 1) to give or reach upward. 2) to deliver. Einen Brief auf der Post —, to deliver a letter at the post-office. 3) to give up. Eine Sache —, to give up a cause; eine Festung — [better übergeben], to give up, to surrender, to deliver a fortress to an enemy; die Spanier gaben Louisiana auf, the Spaniards gave up Louisiana; eine Bekanntschaft —, to drop an acquaintance; er gab die Fuchsjagd auf, he left off fox-hunting; alle Hoffnung —, to abandon, to give up all hope; ein Amt —, to lay down, to resign an office; einen Anspruch —, to quit a claim; sein Recht —, to give up one's right; der Arzt hat den Kranken aufgegeben, the physician has given over the patient or given the patient over; seinen Entschluß —, to relinquish one's resolution; den Geist —, to give up the ghost, to yield the breath or spirit, to expire, to die. 4) to lay on, to impose. Einem eine Arbeit —, to set any one a task; Einem etwas — [as a problem], to propose; eine Frage —, to propose a question; ein Räthsel —, to put or propose a riddle; ich will euch ein Räthsel —, [Judges XIV.] I will now put forth a riddle to you. 5) [a sea term] V. Aufstehen.

Aufgeber, *m.* [-s, *pl.* -] —inn, *f.* he or she that delivers, gives up or proposes a thing; [in commerce] employer. Der — eines Briefes, the person that puts a letter into the post-office; der — eines Räthsels, one that puts a riddle.

Aufgeblasen, *part. adj.* V. Aufblasen. *Fig.* puffed up, proud.

Aufgeblasenheit, *f.* elation, haughtiness, pride of prosperity.

Aufgebot, *m.* [-es, *pl.* -e] 1) public summons to vassals and subjects to perform a certain service [especially a general proclamation of the sovereign of a country, by which not only his immediate feudatories, but his vassals were summoned to take the field for war], [in France] ban, arriere-ban. 2) the feudatories and vassals thus summoned. 3) [notice of a marriage, proclaimed in a church] ban, the bans.

Aufgehen, *ir.* I. *v. intr.* [u. w. seyn] 1) to go up, to rise. Der Teig geht gut auf, the dough rises well; diese Pflanzen fangen an aufzugehen, these plants begin to shoot. V. Aufkeimen. Die Sonne geht auf, the sun rises; der Mond ist aufgegangen, the moon is up. *Fig.* Von Juda aufgegangen ist unser Herr, [Hebr. VII, 14.] our Lord sprang out of Judea; in Feuer, in Rauch —, to be consumed by fire; es geht mir ein Licht auf, I begin to see clear. 2) to unclose itself, to open. Das Fenster ging auf, the window opened; das Geschwür geht auf, the aposteme breaks; Ihr Band geht auf, your ribbon is untying; das ist nicht zerrissen, die Naht ist nur aufgegangen, that is not torn, it has only come unstitched; das Eis fängt an aufzugehen, the ice begins to dissolve, to be melted; das Wetter geht auf, it is beginning to thaw; [of plants] die —de Rose, the opening rose; die Knospen gehen auf, the buds are opening. *Fig.* das Herz ging mir auf, my heart expanded; die Augen gehen mir nun auf, I begin to see clear now. 3) to be consumed, to be spent. Er läßt viel —, he spends a great deal; Alles für Kleider — lassen, to put every thing upon one's back; — [in arithm.] drei geht nicht in sieben auf, seven cannot be divided by three without a remainder; vier von vier geht auf, four subtracted from four leaves no remainder. 4) to go on, to be put on. Der Hut will nicht —, the hat will not go on.

II *v. tr.* and *r.* sich —, to open by going. Ich habe mir die Füße aufgegangen, my feet are galled by walking.

Aufgeien, *v. tr.* [a sea term] Die Segel —, to brail up or to clue up the sails.

Aufgeigen, I. *v. intr.* to play on a fiddle, to fiddle. *Fig.* † and * to serve any one, to be at his service. II. *v. tr.* 1) to play [a tune] on a fiddle, to fiddle. 2) to rouse from sleep by fiddling.

Aufgeklärt, *adj.* [*part.* from Aufklären] *Fig.* enlightened. Ein —er Verstand, an enlightened understanding; —e Zeiten, enlightened times.

Aufgeklärtheit, *f.* the state of being enlightened.

Aufgeld, *n.* [-es, *pl.* -er] 1) agio, premium, change, exchange, balance. 2) V. Angeld.

Aufgelegt, *adj.* [*part.* from Auflegen] *Fig.* disposed, inclined, in humour. Zum Tanzen —, inclined to dance; wie sind Sie heute —? are you in good or bad humour to-day?

Aufgeleiten, *v. tr.* to guide or lead upward.

Aufgeräumt, *adj.* [*part.* from Aufräumen] put in order, arranged. *Fig.* good-humoured, gay, merry. — seyn, to be of good cheer, in spirits. Syn. Aufgeräumt, Lustig. Aufgeräumt signifies, from its derivation, that the causes of discontent or dissatisfaction are removed, cleared up. He is aufgeräumt who is not ill-humoured, and who takes part in the gayety of a cheerful society. Lustig is he who shows his feeling of pleasure, who breaks out into loud merriment. Aufgeräumt denotes, therefore, a more composed frame of mind than lustig.

Aufgeräumtheit, *f.* cheerfulness, gayety.

Aufgewältigen, *v. tr.* [in mining] to open by working.

Aufgeweckt, *adj.* [*part.* from Aufwecken] awaked, roused. *Fig.* brisk, lively, sprightly, gay, cheerful. Er ist ein —er Kopf, he is a clever fellow. V. Aufgeklärt, Aufgelegt.

Aufgewecktheit, *f.* liveliness, sprightliness.

Aufgießen, *ir. v. tr.* to pour upon, to affuse.

Aufglänzen, *ir. v. intr.* [u. w. haben and seyn] 1) to shine, to glitter. 2) to rise shining.

Aufglätten, *v. tr.* to polish afresh, to rub or polish up.

Aufgleiten, *ir. v. intr.* [u. w. seyn] to glide against.

Aufglimmen, *ir. v. intr.* [u. w. seyn] to glimmer anew.

Aufglitschen, *v. intr.* [u. w. seyn] V. Aufgleiten.

Aufglotzen, *v. intr.* to stare upward.

Aufglühen, *v. intr.* [u. w. seyn] 1) to glow, to begin to glow. 2) to glow afresh. 3) to heat to a glow.

Aufgraben, *ir. v. tr.* 1) to raise by digging. 2) to dig up. Einen Stein —, to dig up a stone. 3) to engrave, to mark by incisions. V. Eingraben. 4) to open by digging, to dig.

Aufgrasen, *v. tr.* to consume in grazing.

Aufgrauen, V. Grauen.

Aufgreifen, *ir. v. tr.* 1) to take up [a thing that is fallen &c.] 2) to seize, to lay hold on. Landstreicher —, to take up vagabonds. *Fig.* Ein Gerücht —, to pick up a report; [in law] Eine Sache —, to end a suit or action by compromise.

Aufgrünen, *v. intr.* [u. w. seyn] to become green. *Fig.* to revive.

‖ **Aufgucken**, *v. intr.* to look up.

Aufgürteln, *v. tr.* and *v. r.* sich —, V. Aufgürten.

Aufgürten, I. *v. tr.* 1) to gird up, to tie up with a girdle. 2) to make fast by a girth, to girth [a saddle on a horse's back]. 3) to ungird [a man], to ungirth [a horse]. Aufgegürtet ihr Kleid, her robe ungirt. II. *v. r.* sich —, to ungird one's self.

Aufguß, *m.* [-sses, *pl.* -güsse] 1) pouring upon, affusion. 2) [the liquor in which plants are steeped, and which is impregnated with their virtues or qualities] infusion.

Aufgußthierchen, *n.* infusory worm.

Aufhaben, *ir. v. tr.* 1) to have on, to wear. Den Hut —, to have the hat on, to be covered. 2) to have open or opened. Er hat den Mund auf, he has his mouth open. 3) to have to do, to have as a task. Was haben Sie auf [= was hat Ihnen Ihr Lehrer aufgegeben]? what has your master given you to do?

Aufhacken, *v. tr.* 1) to open by hewing or hoeing. Das Eis —, to break the ice; [of birds] to peck or pick open [nuts &c.]. 2) to loosen by hoeing [the earth in a garden &c.]. 3) to pick up [food &c.] with the beak, to peck. 4) to hew, to cut entirely. Das Holz —, to hew or cut all the stock of wood, to cut all the wood.

Aufhäften, V. Aufheften.

Aufhäkeln, *v. tr.* to unclasp.

Aufhaken, I. *v. tr.* 1) to unhook. 2) to hook up [a garment &c.]. II. *v. intr.* [am. sportsmen] to draw back the cock of a gun [in order to fire], to cock a gun.

Aufhalsen, *v. tr.* to put or load on a person's neck. *Fig.* Sie halsen ihm Alles auf, they lay all on his neck; einem Andern etwas —, to shift a thing to another; sich —, to incur.

Aufhalt, *m.* [-es, *pl.* -e] 1) the act of stopping, [in manege] stop. Ein halber —, [in manege] half a stop. 2) [hinderance for a time] delay. Von meiner Seite soll die Sache keinen — leiden, the affair shall meet with no impediment on my side. V. Aufenthalt.

Aufhaltring, *m.* a ring fastened to the breeching of a horse.

Aufhalten, *ir.* I. *v. tr.* 1) [to hinder from progressive motion] to stop. Einen Dieb —, to stop a thief; den Feind —, to put a stop to the enemy's progress; das Volk hielt ihn auf, daß er nicht von ihnen ginge, [St. Luc. IV, 42] the people stayed him, that he should not depart from them; der Damm hält den Wasserstrom auf, the dam stops the stream of water; wir wurden durch den Regen aufgehalten, we were detained by the rain; von widrigem Winde aufgehalten, windbound;

halten Sie mich nicht auf, do not detain me. 2) to hold open. Die Hand —, to hold one's hand open [to receive something &c.]; den Hut —, to hold out one's hat [to ask something &c.]. Syn. Aufhalten, Hemmen. Hemmen signifies to stop or impede any motion or movement already commenced; aufhalten, to hinder or prevent any action or motion whether already begun or not. One may say, therefore: Ich hielt meine Thränen lange auf, nachdem sie aber einmal angefangen hatten zu fließen, konnte ich ihren Strom nicht wieder hemmen [I restrained my tears long, but after they had once commenced flowing, I could not stop the stream].

II. v. r. sich —, 1) to live in a place, to dwell. Er hielt sich über ein Jahr in dieser Stadt auf, he remained above a year in this town. 2) to continue long, to dwell. Sich bei einem Gegenstande —, to dwell on a subject [in speaking, debating or writing]. 3) to criticise, to blame, to censure. Sich über seines Nachbars Betragen —, to find fault with one's neighbour's conduct.

Áufhalter, *m.* [-s, *pl.* -] 1) an instrument for stopping. 2) [a part of the harness of a horse] breeching. 3) [a sea term] relieving tackle.

Aufhalterei, *f.* scoffing, censure or blame.

Áufhaltung, *f.* 1) the act of stopping, hindering, hinderance. 2) [in horology] a detent.

Áufhämmern, I. *v. tr.* 1) to open by hammering. 2) to rouse from sleep by hammering. 3) to fasten or fit on something with a hammer. II. *v. intr.* 1) to hammer upon. 2) to strike or beat hard upon something. Zum Gesange —, to knock down for a song.

Áufhängeband, *n.* [-es, *pl.* -bänder] [in anatomy] suspensory ligament.

Áufhängeboden, *m.* [-s, *pl.* -böden] [among printers] hanging room, drying place.

Áufhängen, *v. tr.* [*reg.* and *ir.*] to hang up, to hang upon, to suspend. Einen Dieb —, to hang a thief. *Fig.* Einem eine Krankheit —, to infect any one with a disease; man hat ihm etwas aufgehängt, he has been imposed on; denn Sie können uns Neues für Altes —, for you may palm upon us new for old; um Ihnen das, was er schreibt, für Witz aufzuhängen, to impose upon you what he writes for wit.

Áufhängeschnüre, *f. pl.* [am. printers] lines for hanging the damp sheets on.

Áufharken, *v. tr.* 1) to take up with a rake. 2) to loosen [the earth in fields and gardens] with a rake.

Áufhärten, *v. tr.* to give the necessary twisting to ropes.

Áufhaschen, *v. tr.* to snatch up. *Fig.* to pick up.

Áufhaspeln, *v. tr.* 1) to reel. 2) to raise by reeling. *Fig.* † and ‡ Sich —, to raise one's self, to get up from the ground with great difficulty; sich wieder —, to recover slowly from an illness. 3) to finish reeling. Alles Garn —, to reel all the stock of yarn.]

Áufhauben, *v. tr.* to put on a cap.

Áufhauchen, I. *v. intr.* to breathe upon something. II. *v. tr.* 1) to breathe upward. 2) to breathe open, to open by breathing.

Áufhauen, *ir.* I. *v. tr.* 1) to hew or to cut open. Das Eis —, to break up the ice. 2) to hew entirely. Alles Holz —, to cut up all the stock of wood. 3) to cut again, anew. Eine Feile —, to cut a file anew. 4) to make to rise by beating. II. *v. intr.* 1) to strike upon. 2) [in gunnery] Mit der brennenden Lunte —, to put the port-fire to the priming.

Áufhäufeln, *v. tr.* to form or draw into small heaps.

Áufhäufen, I. *v. tr.* to heap, to heap up, to pile. Erde —, to heap up earth; Holz, Kohlen —, to heap on wood or coal. *Fig.* Schätze —, to heap up, to amass, to accumulate treasures; Vorräthe —, to hoard up provisions. II. *v. r.* sich —, to accumulate, to increase visibly. Die Rückstände häufen sich auf, the arrears increase or run up every day.

Áufheben, *ir.* I. *v. tr.* 1) to raise, lift or take up. Die Hände —, to lift up the hands; die Hand — und schwören, to lift the hand and swear; mit aufgehobenen Händen, with hands upheld; mit aufgehobenen Armen, with uplifted arms; er hob den Kopf auf, he heaved his head; er hob seinen Speer auf gegen &c., he lifted up his spear against; beim — der Füße, in the lift of the feet; die Hand gegen einen Obern —, to lift the hand against a superior, *fig.* to rebel. 2) to lift or take up [a thing from the ground]. Ich kann eine so große Last nicht —, I cannot lift so great a load; etwas Gefallenes —, to take up a thing that is fallen; anbetend fiel ich zu seinen Füßen, er hob mich auf, in adoration at his feet I fell, he raised me up; eine Last —, to lift up a burden. 3) *Fig.* *a*) to reposit for future use, to lay up, to keep, to reserve. Einem etwas aufzuheben geben, to give any one something to keep. *b*) to take, to seize, to take hold of. Einen Verbrecher —, to apprehend, to arrest a criminal; einen Vorposten überfallen und —, to surprise and take prisoner an outpost. *c*) to put an end to. Die Tafel —, [am. great personages] to rise from table; das Lager —, to break up the camp, to strike the tents; die Belagerung —, to raise a siege; eine Versammlung —, to dismiss an assembly; ein Gesetz —, to abolish a law; einen Contract —, to annul a contract; landesherrliche Verordnungen —, to annul ordinances. *Prov.* Aufgeschoben ist nicht aufgehoben, forbearance is no acquittance; all is not lost, that is delayed. *d*) [in arithm.] Einen Bruch —, to reduce a fraction.

II. *v. r.* sich —, 1) to arise, to mount up. V. [sich] Erheben. 2) [in arithmetic] to be reducible [said of fractions]. Syn. Aufheben, Aufnehmen, Aufrichten. Man nimmt auf [one takes up] that which is not intended to lie on the ground, or any thing one is going to carry. Man hebt auf [one raises] a thing to place it in a higher position. Man richtet auf [sets up] that which is to stand upright.

Áufheben, *n.* [-s] Das — von Brüchen, the reduction of fractions. *Fig.* Ein —, viel —s von einer Sache machen, to raise a thing in words or eulogy, to extol a thing; viel —s von Läppereien machen, to make a great ado about trifles.

Áufheber, *m.* [-s, *pl.* -] 1) one that lifts or takes something up. 2) [in anatomy, a term applied to several muscles, which raise some part, as the ear, the tip of the nose] attollent, levator, elevator.

Áufhebung, *f.* the act of lifting or taking up. Die — der Hostie, [in the Romish church] elevation of the host. *Fig.* the act of annulling, abolition, abrogation. Die — einer Schenkung, avoidance of a donation; die — eines Fideicommisses or unveräußerlichen Erbgutes, recovery; die — eines Postens, [a milit. term] the relieving of a post; die — einer Versammlung, the dissolution of an assembly.

Aufhebungs=befehl, *m.* a mandate, a decision of a court, by which something is annulled. **—gericht**, *n.* court of cassation.

Áufhefteln, *v. tr.* 1) to pin or hook up. 2) to unpin, to unhook.

Áufheften, *v. tr.* 1) to pin up [a gown &c.]. 2) to pin to, to fix to. Ein Band —, to sew a ribbon slightly to, to baste a ribbon to. *Fig.* Einem etwas —, to impose upon any one; Einem eine Geschichte —, to palm a story on any one; der Storch fand, daß man ihm etwas aufgeheftet hatte, the stork found he was put upon.

Áufheitern, I. *v. tr.* 1) to clear, to clear up, to brighten, to serene. Die Sonne erschien und heiterte das Wetter auf, the sun appeared and cleared the weather up. 2) *Fig.* to cheer. Eine gute Nachricht heitert das Herz auf, good news cheers the heart. II. *v. r.* sich —, to become free from clouds or fog, to clear. Das Wetter heitert sich auf, the weather clears up; es heitert sich auf, it clears away, it clears off. *Fig.* to grow cheerful, to cheer. Meine Seele heitert sich auf, my soul cheers up.

Aufheiterungsmittel, *n.* means of cheering up, or making gay, diversion.

Áufhelfen, *ir. v. tr.* to help up. Sich —, to raise one's self up with difficulty, to get up with difficulty. *Fig.* Einem Bedrängten —, to help any one in distress; einem Nothleidenden —, to assist, to aid or succour any one that is in need; Einem wieder —, to restore any one's fortune.

Áufhelfer, *m.* [-s, *pl.* -] 1) [= Bettzopf, Bettquast] an instrument [commonly a string or cord] for raising one's self up in bed. 2) *Fig.* he that succours.

Áufhellen, I. *v. tr.* to brighten up, to clear up, to serene. Eine Flüssigkeit —, to clarify a liquid. *Fig.* to enlighten, to illuminate. Den Verstand —, to enlighten the mind or understanding. II. *v. r.* sich —, to clear up, to become fair. Der Himmel hellt sich auf, the sky clears, clears up or brightens. *Fig.* to become clear or free from obscurity. Diese Sache fängt an, sich mir aufzuhellen, or mir klar zu werden, this affair begins to develop itself to me.

Áufhellung, *f.* the act of clearing up and the state of being cleared up. Die — des Himmels, the clearness of the sky. *Fig.* enlightening [of the mind or understanding], illustration, planation, elucidation. Ein Beispiel kann des Gegenstandes — dienen, one example may serve for an elucidation of the subject.

Áufhenken, *v. tr.* V. Aufhängen.

Áufherrschen, V. Auffahren I. 3) *Fig.*

Áufhetzen, *v. tr.* to hunt up, to spring, start. Ein wildes Schwein —, to rear a boar; einen Hirsch —, to rouse up a stag. *Fig.* [in tempt] Einen gegen den Andern —, to set any against another; er hat ihn dazu aufgehetzt, instigated him to it.

Áufhetzer, *m.* [-s, *pl.* -] one that sets a son against another, instigator, incitor.

Áufheulen, I. *v. intr.* to howl aloud. II. *v.* to rouse from sleep by howling.

Áufhin, V. Hinauf.

Áufhissen, *v. tr.* [a sea term] to sway up hoist [the main-sail &c.]. Eine Flagge —, to h a flag; die Stagsegel —, to set the stay-; die Marssegel sind aufgehißt, the top-sail atrip.

Áufhocken, I. *v. tr.* 1) to take upon back or shoulders. 2) to put in heaps. II. *v.* and *r.* to hang on the back of a person.

Áufhöhen, *v. tr.* [in painting] to set off.

Áufholen, *v. tr.* to draw, to pull up, [in men's language]. Ein Takel —, to round in haul taught a [slack] rope; ein Boot —, to h up a boat [to lift it upwards by means of a tackle]; Ruder —, to bear up the helm; ein Schiff der —, *a*) to right a ship after careening. *b*) haul the wind again or to bring a ship to wind.

Áufholer, *m.* [-s, *pl.* -] [a sea term] — Stagsegels, the halliard of a stay-sail; —

Stückpforten, the port-tackle; — des Racks, the barrel-truss; — der Besanbrohks und der Dempgordingen, a kind of girt-line to haul up the mizen-brails; — der Brohktalje, a girt-line to haul up the whip of the throat-brail; — an einem Bullen oder an einem Kiellichter, relieving tackle on the mast of a hulk.

Aúfholzen, *v. intr.* [am. sportsmen] V. Aufbaumen.

Aúfhorchen, *v. intr.* 1) to prick up one's ears. 2) *Fig.* to listen.

1. **Aúfhören**, *v. intr.* to hear or listen attentively.

2. **Aúfhören**, *v. intr.* to leave off, to discontinue, to cease, to end, to finish. Der Sturm hat aufgehört, the storm has ceased or subsided; es hat aufgehört zu regnen, it has done or given over raining; — zu arbeiten, to cease from labour, to rest; sie hörten um sechs Uhr auf zu arbeiten, they left off work at six o'clock; — ein Kleid zu tragen, to leave off wearing a garment; — zu weinen, to cease weeping; — zu feuern, [am. soldiers] to cease firing; er fing bei dem Aeltesten an und hörte bei dem Jüngsten auf, he began at the eldest and left off at the youngest; — zu reden, to leave off speaking; — zu zahlen, [in commerce] to stop payment. V. Endigen.

Aúfhucken, V. Aufhocken.

Aúfhügeln, *v. tr.* to raise to a hillock.

Aúfhüllen, *v. tr.* to uncover. *Fig.* to reveal.

Aúfhüpfen, *v. intr.* to frisk, to skip, to hop, to leap, to jump up, to bound.

Aúfhusten, I. *v. intr.* to cough aloud. II. *v. tr.* 1) to cough up [phlegm &c.]. 2) to rouse from sleep by coughing.

Aúfjagen, *v. intr.* to hunt up, to spring, to start, to rear. [am. sportsmen] Den Hirsch, Damhirsch und Rehbock —, to rouse up the stag and buck; ein wildes Schwein —, to uncouch the boar; einen Fuchs —, to unkennel the fox; den Hasen —, to start the hare; ein Kaninchen —, to bolt the rabbit; die Otter —, to unvent the otter; das Eichhörnchen und den Marder —, to untree the squirrel and the marten; Feldhühner, Schnepfen, Wachteln, Becassinen —, to flush, spring or put up partridges, woodcocks, quails, snipes; Birkhühner, Fasanen und Rallen oder Schnerze —, to spring grouse, pheasants and rails. *Fig.* Einen —, to find any one out.

Aúfjammern, I. *v. intr.* to wail, to moan aloud. II. *v. tr.* to rouse from sleep by moaning.

Aúfjauchzen, I. *v. intr.* to shout. Sie jauchzten laut auf, they gave a great shout. II. *v. tr.* to rouse from sleep by shouts.

Aúfjochen, *v. tr.* to yoke. *Fig.* Einem etwas —, to burden any one with a thing; sie mußten sich diesen Zwingherrn — lassen, they were obliged to submit to the yoke of this oppressor.

Aúfjubeln, I. *v. intr.* to shout. II. *v. tr.* to rouse from sleep by shouts.

Aúfkämmen, *v. tr.* 1) to comb upwards. 2) to comb afresh.

Aúfkappen, *v. tr.* to put on a cap, to cap. Den Falken —, to hood the hawk.

Aúfkarren, I. *v. intr.* to strike against with a car. II. *v. tr.* 1) to raise by conveying with a car earth to. 2) to wear out by drawing a car over.

Aúfkatzen, *v. tr.* [a sea term] Den Anker —, to fish the anchor.

Aúfkauen, *v. intr.* and *tr.* to finish or consume in chewing.

Aúfkauf, *m.* [-es, *pl.* -käufe] the act of buying up or engrossing.

Aúfkaufen, *v. tr.* to buy up, to purchase with a view to sell again, to engross [commodities in a market &c.].

Aúfkäufer, *m.* [-s, *pl.* -] —inn, *f.* a person that buys up, engrosser.

Aúfkegeln, *v. tr.* [in gunnery] to pile up [cannon-balls in conical piles].

Aúfkehren, *v. tr.* 1) to sweep up, to sweep together. 2) [am. goldsmiths] to work on a stamp.

Aúfkehricht, *n.* [-es] sweepings, sweepage, [in mining] scrapings.

Aúfkeimen, *v. intr.* [u. w. seyn] to shoot, to bud, to sprout, to germinate, to begin to vegetate [as a plant or its seed]. *Fig.* Meine —den Hoffnungen, my springing hopes.

Aúfkeltern, *v. tr.* to press all the stock of grapes &c.

Aúfkerben, V. Ankerben 2).

Aúfketzern, *v. tr.* [in mining] to cleave with wedges.

Aúfkippen, I. *v. intr.* [u. w. seyn] to rise up, to tilt up. II. *v. tr.* to turn up, to tilt. Die Bienenstöcke ein wenig —, to tilt the hives a little.

Aúfkitten, *v. tr.* to fasten to by cement, to cement on.

Aúfkitzeln, *v. tr.* to rouse from sleep by tickling.

Aúfklaffen, *v. intr.* 1) to gape, to open in crevices. 2) to shut not close. Die Thüre klafft auf, the door does not shut close.

Aúfklaftern, *v. tr.* to pile wood or other material for measurement and sale by the cord, to cord.

Aúfklagen, I. *v. intr.* to complain, to lament to heaven. II. *v. tr.* to rouse from sleep by lamenting.

Aufklammern, *v. tr.* to fasten on with cramps.

Aúfklappe, *f.* [*pl.* -n] the flap [of a hat], the facings [of a coat].

Aúfklappen, *v. tr.* to raise or bend up the flap [of a hat &c.].

Aúfklappsen, *v. intr.* V. Klappen.

Aúfklären, I. *v. tr.* to clear up, to brighten. Eine Flüssigkeit —, to clarify a liquid. *Fig.* Etwas —, to clear up a thing, that is not understood or misunderstood, to eclaircise it. Die Zeit wird Alles —, time will bring all to light; er, der unsern Verstand aufklärt, he who enlightens our understandings; ein aufgeklärter Verstand, an enlightened mind; aufgeklärte Zeiten, enlightened times; die aufgeklärte Welt, illuminated world; durch Anmerkungen —, to illustrate by notes; ein aufgeklärter Kopf, an unprejudiced mind. II. *v. r.* sich —, to clear, to clear up, off or away. Der Himmel klärt sich auf, the sky clears up or brightens. *Fig.* Sein Gesicht klärte sich auf, his countenance became serene; eine Sache, ein Punkt klärt sich auf, a thing, a point clears up.

Aúfklärer, *m.* [-s, *pl.* -] he that communicates clear views to the mind or enlightens, enlightener.

Aufklärerei, *f.* a mock-enlightening.

Aúfklärling, *m.* [-s, *pl.* -e] an enlightener [in contempt].

Aúfklärung, *f.* the clearing up. *Fig.* an enlightening of the understanding by knowledge, illumination.

Aúfklatschen, I. *v. intr.* [u. w. seyn] to fall upon with a clap. II. *v. tr.* to rouse from sleep by a crack [of a whip].

Aúfklauben, *v. tr.* 1) to pick up, to glean up [peas &c.]. *Fig.* Fehler —, to scan faults, to pick a hole in one's coat. 2) to open by picking with the fingers.

Aúfkleben, I. *v. intr.* to stick to. II. *v. tr.* to paste to. Aufgeklebt, pasted on or up.

Aúfkleiben, V. Aufkleben II.

Aúfkleistern, *v. tr.* to paste up.

Aúfklettern, **Aúfklimmen**, *v. tr.* to climb up. An einem Baume —, to climb a tree.

Aúfklingen, *v. tr.* to rouse from sleep by ringing a bell.

Aúfklinken, *v. tr.* to unlatch [a door].

Aúfklopfen, I. *v. intr.* 1) to beat or strike upon a thing. 2) to knock up. *Fig.* Das —de Herz, the throbbing or beating heart. II. *v. tr.* 1) to open by knocking. Nüsse —, to break open nuts. 2) to loosen by beating. Eine Matratze —, to set a mattrass right again. 3) to rouse from sleep by knocking. Einen —, to knock any one up. 4) to fasten to by knocking. Die Ballen —, [among printers] to knock off the balls.

Aúfklöppeln, *v. tr.* to consume all the thread in making lace.

Aúfknacken, *v. tr.* to crack [nuts, almonds &c.]. *Fig.* and *Prov.* Einem eine harte Nuß aufzuknacken geben, to set any one a hard task.

Aúfknallen, I. *v. intr.* [u. w. seyn] to fly upward with a cracking noise. II. *v. tr.* 1) to open with a sharp sudden noise. 2) to rouse from sleep by making a sharp sudden noise.

Aúfknarren, *v. intr.* [u. w. seyn] to open creaking [said of doors].

Aúfknastern, *v. intr.* [u. w. seyn] to open crackling.

Aúfknattern, *v. intr.* [u. w. seyn] to crackle upward. Brennende Dornen knattern auf, burning thorns fly crackling upwards.

Aúfkneipen, *v. tr.* to open by pinching.

Aúfknicken, V. Aufknacken.

Aúfknieen, I. *v. intr.* to kneel upon a thing. II. *v. tr.* to wear out by kneeling.

Aúfknistern, *v. intr.* [u. w. seyn] to crackle, to crepitate.

Aúfknöpfen, I. *v. tr.* to unbutton [a coat &c.]. II. *v. r.* sich —, to unbutton one's self.

Aúfknüpfen, *v. tr.* 1) to fasten with a knot to some fixed object above. Einen an einen Baum —, to truss any one to a tree; einen Dieb —, to hang a thief; sich —, to hang one's self. *Fig.* Einem etwas — [more usual: aufheften], to impose upon any one, to palm a thing upon any one. 2) to untie, to unknot.

Aúfknurren, I. *v. tr.* to rouse from sleep by snarling. II. *v. intr.* to start up snarling.

Aúfkochen, I. *v. intr.* to boil up. *Fig.* Er kocht leicht auf, his blood is soon up. II. *v. tr.* to boil gently [milk &c.]. 2) to boil again [coffee &c.].

Aúfkommen, I. *v. intr.* [u. w. seyn] 1) to get up, to rise up. *Fig.* to recover from illness. 2) to grow up, to thrive. Hier kommen die Bäume gut auf, the trees grow well here. *Fig.* Zweifel und Besorgnisse — lassen, to give rise or scope to doubts and fears. 2) *Fig.* *a*) to come forward, to prosper. Er hat Verstand, er wird —, he has good sense, he will get on well; er ist sehr aufgekommen, he has succeeded well, he has made his fortune. *b*) to come into use [as a fashion]. Dieser Gebrauch ist nach und nach aufgekommen, this custom has by degrees come into vogue.

Aúfkommen, *n.* [-s] recovery from sickness.

Áufkömmling, *m.* [-es, *pl.* -e] upstart.

Áufkönnen, *ir. v. intr.* to be able to get up, to be able to rise.

Áufköpfen, *v. tr.* [among pinmakers] to head [pins]. Nadeln —, to head needles.

Áufköpfer, *m.* [-s, *pl.* -] [am. pinmakers] one who heads pins, header.

Áufkoppeln, *v. tr.* to uncouple [dogs].

Áufkosten, *v. tr.* to consume by tasting.

Áufkrachen, I. *v. intr.* 1) to fly up cracking or with a crack.. 2) to open cracking. II. *v. tr.* to crack open [nuts &c.].

Áufkrächzen, I. *v. intr.* to croak aloud. II. *v. tr.* to rouse from sleep by croaking.

Áufkrähen, I. *v. intr.* to crow aloud. II. *v. tr.* to rouse from sleep by crowing.

Áufkramen, *v. tr.* and *intr.* 1) to set out articles for sale. 2) to remove lumber or other encumbrances.

Áufkrämpeln, *v. tr.* 1) to card again. 2) to card all the stock of wool.

Áufkrämpen, *v. tr.* to turn up, to cock [a hat].

Áufkratzen, *v. tr.* 1) to open by scratching, to scratch up. Eine Wunde wieder —, to scratch open a wound; [am. tailors and sempstresses] Eine Naht —, to smooth a seam down with the nail 2) to scratch in order to level the nap. Eine baumwollene Decke —, [am. woolen weavers] to raise the wool of a blanket with burs; ein Stück Tuch —, [am. clothiers] to raise the nap of the cloth; die Strümpfe leicht —, [am. stocking weavers] to tease the stockings. *Fig.* † Aufgekratzt seyn, to be in good humour, in high spirits. 3) to play ill on a fiddle, to scrape. 4) [ironically for] to dress, to deck.

Áufkräuseln, I. *v. tr.* to curl, to crisp, to frizzle [as hair]. II. *v. intr.* to curl, to shrink into ringlets.

Áufkrausen, *v. intr.* to curl.

Áufkräusen, *v. tr.* to curl or crisp again.

Áufkreischen, I. *v. intr.* to shriek aloud. II. *v. tr.* to rouse from sleep by shrieks.

Áufkreuzen, V. Ankreuzen.

Áufkriechen, *ir. v. intr.* [u. w. seyn] to creep upward.

† **Áufkriegen**, *v. tr.* 1) to get on, to put on. 2) to get open. 3) [= zu thun bekommen] to get to do, to get as a task. Was haben Sie von Ihrem Lehrer aufgekriegt? what has your master given you to do?

Áufkrimpen, *v. intr.* [a sea term, said of the wind] to veer round against the sun, to turn against the sun.

Áufkrümmen, I. *v. tr.* to bend or curve upward [a wire &c.]. II. *v. r.* sich —, to be bent upward.

Áufkünden, V. Aufkündigen.

Áufkündigen, *v. tr* and *intr.* to give any one warning. Seinem Pächter or Miether —, to give one's tenant warning or notice to quit; Einem den Dienst —, to warn any one to quit; ich habe ihm aufgekündiget, I gave him warning or notice. Einem die Freundschaft —, to renounce any one's friendship, to break with a friend. Syn Aufsagen, Aufkündigen. Aufkündigen seems to be used generally in a more solemn style and of more important concerns than aufsagen, and especially of written contracts or agreements. A lodging is aufgesagt, a sum of money standing out at interest aufgekündigt.

Áufkündigen, *n.* [-s] **Áufkündigung**, *f.* a warning or notice [to quit a lodging, situation &c.].

Aufkündigungs-brief, *m.* —schreiben, *n.* a letter to give any one warning.

Áufkunft, *f.* V. Aufkommen, *n.*

Áufküssen, *v. tr.* 1) to snatch up by kissing. Er küßte ihr die Thränen or ihre Thränen auf, he kissed her tears away. 2) to rouse from sleep with kisses. 3) *Fig* [and in poetry] to open, to expand by soft touches.

Áuflächeln, *v. intr*, to smile.

1. **Áuflachen**, I. *v. intr.* to break or burst out into a laugh, to laugh out. II. *v. tr.* to awake any one by laughing, to laugh any one out of sleep.

2. **Áuflachen**, *v. tr.* [am. forest.] to make an incision in, to tap [resinous trees].

Áufladen, *ir. v. tr.* to load, to put on. Holz —, to load wood. *Fig.* Einem etwas —, to burden any one with a thing.

Áuflader, *m.* [-s, *pl.* -] loader, burdener, packer.

Áuflage, *f.* [*pl.* -n] 1) edition of a book, Die erste, zehnte —, the first edition, the tenth edition; die verbesserte und vermehrte zweite — [Ausgabe] eines Werkes, the corrected and enlarged second edition of a book; eine starke —, a large impression; V. Ausgabe; neue —, re-impression. 2) something laid on or imposed as a tax, impost, duty. Eine — auf das Bier, a duty or tax upon malt-liquor; eine neue —, an additional tax or duty. *Fig* [in law] Eine gerichtliche —, injunction; Einem — thun, to issue a writ against any one 3) a sum collected for a charitable purpose, collection. 4) [among craftsmen] a meeting; [in contempt] a conventicle. Eine — halten, to hold a meeting.

Áuflangen, *v. tr.* to hand up.

Áuflanger, *m.* [-s, *pl.* -] 1) one that reaches up. 2) *Fig.* [a sea term] futtock. Der — in einem Spann, the 2d, 3d &c. futtock; die — der Katz- [Katt-] sporen, futtock-riders; die ersten — der Katzsporen, middle futtock-riders; die oberen — der Katzsporen, upper futtock-riders; verkehrte —, top-timbers.

Áuflärmen, I. *v. intr.* to break out in sudden uproar. II. *v. tr.* to rouse from sleep by making a noise.

Áuflassen, *ir. v. tr.* to leave open. *Fig.* *a*) [in mining] to give up or over. Eine Erzgrube —, to cease to work a mine. *b*) [in feudal law] to resign.

Áuflasten, I. *v. tr.* to lay on, to impose as a burden. Einem etwas —, to burden any one with a thing; Einem Alles —, to lay every thing on another's back. II. *v. intr.* to lie heavy upon.

Áuflauerer, *m.* [-s, *pl.* -] one who waits in ambush for another, waylayer.

Áuflauern, *v. intr.* to watch for, to wait, to lie in ambush for. Einem —, to waylay any one, to lay wait for any one. Syn. V. Aufpassen.

Áuflauf, *m.* [-es, *pl.* -läufe] 1) [in cookery] raised pastry, puff-paste. 2) an augmenting in quantity or amount, increase. Der — der Zinsen, the increase of rents. 3) a tumultuous crowd, a rout, tumult. Der Volks—, [in law] riot; einen — erregen, to raise a tumult.

Áuflaufen, *ir.* I. *v. intr.* [u. w. seyn] 1) to run upward. Der Fluß ist aufgelaufen, the river is swollen; das Wasser läuft auf, the water rises. *Fig.* Die Zinsen laufen auf or schwellen an, the rents increase or run up. 2) to swell, to grow turgid. Die Haut ist aufgelaufen, the skin is bloated; aufgelaufene Augen, inflamed, swollen eyes; der Teig läuft auf, the dough rises. 3) to run on. Das Schiff lief auf eine Sandbank auf, the ship ran on a sandbank. II. *v. tr.* 1) to make sore, to open by running. Sich die Füße —, to make one's feet sore by running. 2) [in forges] to bring up. III. *v. r.* sich —, to open by running against or through.

Áufläufer, *m.* [-s, *pl.* -] 1) [in forges] smelter. || 2) a sort of high raised cake. 3) [a sea term] a sailor-boy, younker.

Áuflauschen, I. *v. intr.* to listen. II. *v. tr.* to learn or catch by listening.

Áufläuten, *v. tr.* to rouse from sleep by ringing bells.

Áuflaviren, *v. tr.* [a sea term] einen Fluß —, to tack or beat up a river &c.

Áufleben, I. *v. intr.* [u. w. seyn] to return to life, to revive. Der Regen macht die Pflanzen wieder —, the rain makes the plants revive. *Fig.* Bei dieser Nachricht lebte ich wieder auf, at this news I acquired fresh life. II. *v. tr.* [am. painters] to refresh [a picture].

Áuflecken, *v. tr.* to lick up, to lap.

Áuflegen, *v. tr.* 1) to lay on. Dem Pferde den Sattel —, to put the saddle upon the horse; Kranken die Hände —, to lay hands on the sick; die Hände bei der Confirmation —, to impose hands in the ceremony of confirmation; das — or die Auflegung der Hände, the laying on of hands, imposition; ein Pflaster auf einen kranken Theil des Körpers —, to apply a plaster to a diseased part of the body; den Elbogen —, to lean one's elbow upon; legt es fest auf, lean it steady upon the rest; man kann eine Muskete eben sowohl aus freier Hand als aufgelegt losschießen, a musket may be shot off as well upon the arm as upon a rest; [in husbandry] dieser Baum hat viel Holz aufgelegt, that tree is full of branches, it has wide spreading branches; † das Thier legt viel Fett auf, this animal grows fat; die Farbe sollte so dünn aufgelegt [aufgetragen] werden, the colouring should be laid on so thin; Roth —, to put on rouge; sie legt auf, she paints. *Fig.* Sich —, to rise in opposition, to resist; Einem eine Last —, to burden any one; Steuern —, to impose taxes; Einem eine Strafe —, to put a punishment on any one; ich habe mich versündiget, was du mir auflegest, will ich tragen, [2. kings XVIII] I have offended, that which thou puttest on me, I will bear; eine Buße —, to enjoin a penance; Einem eine Geldstrafe —, to set a fine upon any one; Stillschweigen —, to impose silence; Einem einen Eid —, to tender an oath to any one; Jemanden eine Verbindlichkeit —, to fasten an obligation upon any one. 2) [gleichsam hinauf-, d. h. höher legen] [in seamen's lang.] Ein Schiff —, to dismantle and lay up a ship. *Fig.* to set the mind in a particular frame, to incline, to dispose [used only in the part. aufgelegt]. Zu etwas aufgelegt seyn, to be disposed to; gut aufgelegt seyn, to be in good humour; er ist schlecht aufgelegt, he is out of humour. 3) to print [a book]. Dieses Wörterbuch ist schon dreimal neu aufgelegt worden, this dictionary has gone through three editions.

Áuflehnen, *v. r.* sich —, 1) to lean on or upon. 2) to rear [as a horse]. V. Aufbäumen. *Fig.* to rebel, to mutiny. Sich gegen die Befehle der königlichen Regierung —, to withstand the orders the king's government; die Leute lehnten sich gegen ihre Offiziere auf, the men rose upon th officers.

Áufleimen, *v. tr.* to glue upon a thing [sheet of paper &c.].

Áufleinen, *v. tr.* to hang up on a clothes-line.

Áuflesen, *ir. v. tr.* to pick up, to gather, to collect, to glean [stones, acorns &c.]. *Fig.*

contempt] Dieser Mensch lieset Witz auf, wie Tauben Erbsen, this fellow picks up wit, as pigeons peas.

Aufleuchten, *v. intr.* 1) to give light upward. 2) to rise shining.

Aufliegen, *ir.* I. *v intr.* to lie, lean or rest upon. Ein Balken, der auf einer Säule aufliegt, a beam, that leans upon a column; [manege] dieses Pferd liegt zu sehr auf dem Gebisse auf, this horse bears too heavy on the bridle, he bores; [in botany] der Staubbeutel ist aufliegend, the anther is incumbent [i. e. obliquely or horizontally attached to the filaments]. *Fig.* Mir liegt noch eine schwere Arbeit auf, I have yet a hard work to do. II. *v. r.* sich —, to lie one's self sore.

Auflockern, *v. tr.* to loosen [the soil &c.]. Das Bett —, to shake up the feather-bed.

Auflodern, *v. intr.* [u. w. seyn] to blaze up. Das Feuer lodert auf, the fire blazes; die Flamme loderte hoch auf, the flame did mount on high. *Fig.* Er lodert schnell auf, sein Zorn lodert augenblicklich auf, he is soon up, his anger is easily kindled.

Auflöffeln, *v. tr.* to take up with a spoon.

Auflösbar, *adj.* and *adv.* dissolvable, resolvable, soluble, dissoluble. Zucker und Eis sind auflösbare Körper, sugar and ice are dissolvable bodies. *Fig.* solvable.

Auflösbarkeit, Auflöslichkeit, *f.* dissolubility.

Auflösen, I. *v. tr.* 1) to loose, to loosen. Einen Knoten —, to loose a knot; ein Band —, to unloose, to untie, to undo a ribbon; eine Form —, [am. printers] to untie a form. *Prov.* Er ist nicht werth, ihm die Schuhriemen aufzulösen, he is not fit to hold a candle to him. 2) to resolve a body into its elements. Metalle, Salze —, [in chim.] to analyze metals. salts. 3) to dissolve, to melt, to liquify. Die Sonne löst das Eis auf, the sun melts the ice; Pflanzensalze lösen die coagulirten Flüssigkeiten im menschlichen Körper auf, vegetable salts resolve the coagulated humours of a human body; ein heilsamer Saft, der die Galle auflöst, a wholesome juice, resolvent of the bile; —de Mittel, [in medic.] dissolvents; das Wasser löst Zucker und Salz auf, a water dissolves sugar and salt; aufgelöstes Opium, a solution of opium. 4) to decompos Fäulniß löst das Fleisch auf, flesh is decomposed by putrefaction. *Fig.* *a*) to dissolve, = to clear, to solve. Zweifel —, to resolve doubts; eine Aufgabe —, to solve a problem. *b*) to analyze. Einen Begriff —, to analyze a notion; die —de Lehrart, analytics; ein Räthsel —, to find out the meaning of an enigma; [in music] einen Mißklang —, to resolve a discord. *c*) to dissolve [das Gemüth &c.]. Aufgelöst in Wonne, dissolved in delight; in Wollust aufgelöst, dissolved in luxury. *d*) to dissolve = to cause to separate Das Parlament —, to dissolve the parliamnet; ein Kriegsheer —, to dismiss an army; eine Ehe —, to dissolve the bonds of matrimony, to separate husband and wife, to dissolve a marriage. Die Bande der Freundschaft —, to dissolve the bonds or ties of friendship; ein Bündniß —, to dissolve a league; eine Genossenschaft —, to dissolve a partnership.

II. *v. r.* sich —, to dissolve, to be melted, or to be converted from a solid to a fluid state. Der Zucker löst sich im Wasser auf, sugar dissolves in water; das Salz löst sich auf, salt dissolves; der Himmel löst sich in Regenschauer auf, the skies relent in showers. *Fig.* *a*) to be freed from obscurity, to be cleared up. Dieser Punkt wird sich schon —, this point will be cleared up in time. *b*) to be dissolved, to loose substance. Sein Schmerz löste sich in Thränen auf, his pain melted into tears.

Auflösemittel, *n.* [in medic.] a remedy supposed to dissolve concretions in the body, dissolvent.

Auflöslich, *adj.* and *adv.* dissolvable [but chiefly in a fig. sense]. Eine —e Aufgabe, a solvable problem.

Auflösung, *f.* 1) the act of loosening [a knot &c.]. Die — der Salze in Wasser und der Metalle in Königswasser, the dissolution of salt in water and of metals in nitro-muriatic acid; die — des Wassers, Oels in seine Bestandtheile, the analysis of water, oil; die — thierischer Körper durch Fäulniß, the dissolution, decomposition of animal bodies by putrefaction; die — gefrorner Feuchtigkeit, the resolution of congelated humidity. *Fig.* Die — einer Ehe, eines Vertrags, einer Gesellschaft, the dissolution of a marriage, of a treaty, of a society; die — von Schwierigkeiten, the resolution of difficulties; die — einer Aufgabe, the solution of a problem; die — von Gleichungen, [in mathem.] the resolution of equations; die — des Unendlichen, the analysis of infinites, differential calculus; die — eines Bruches, the reduction of a fraction; die — der Mißklänge, [in music] the resolution of discords; wir erwarteten unsere augenblickliche —, we expected immediate dissolution, death; er ist seiner — nahe, he is near his dissolution, his end. 2) [in chim., the substance formed by dissolving a body in a menstruum] solution.

Auflösungs-begebenheit, *f.* a final event, conclusion, catastrophe. —**kraft**, *f.* the power of dissolving. —**kunst**, *f.* analytics. —**lehre**, *f.* [in logic, the tracing of things to their source and the resolving of knowledge into its original principles] analysis. —**mittel**, *n.* 1) dissolvents, dissolver. 2) [in medic.] dissolvent.

Auflöthen, *v tr.* 1) to fasten upon by soldering, to solder. 2) to unsolder.

Auflüften, *v. tr.* 1) to lift up a little. 2) to air by lifting up.

Auflügen, *v. tr.* V. Erdichten.

Auflüpfen, *v. tr.* to lift up a little.

Aufmachen, I. *v. tr.* 1) to open [a door, the mouth &c.]. Eine Flasche —, to uncork a bottle; eine Nuß —, to crack a nut; einen Brief —, to break open a letter, to unseal a letter; einen Knoten —, to undo a knot; macht diese Schleife auf, untie that knot; die Dame —, [at draughts] to put a man out of the first row. 2) to raise, to turn up. Machen Sie Ihr Kleid auf, turn up your garment. 3) to put or fasten on to something else. Einen Knopf an einen Stock —, to put a knob on a stick; Vorhänge —, to put up curtains. II. *v. r.* sich —, to get up, to rise, to arise. Wir wollen uns morgen früh —, let us set out early to-morrow. *Fig.* to make one's self ready, to prepare; machet euch auf zur Schlacht, [Jer. XLIX.] rise up to the battle; Schwert, mache dich auf über meinen Hirten, [Zech. XIII.] awake, O sword, against my shepherd; sich auf und davon machen, to decamp, to take flight.

1. **Aufmahlen**, *v. tr.* [*part.* aufgemahlen] to grind all, to finish grinding.

2. **Aufmahlen**, *v. tr.* [*part.* aufgemahlt] 1) to repair by new touches an impaired painting. Ein Gemählde —, to refresh, to touch up a painting. 2) to consume or expend in painting.

Aufmahnen, *v. tr.* 1) to exhort, to encourage. 2) to summon.

Aufmarsch, *m.* [-es, *pl.* -märsche] 1) marching upward. 2) drawing up [said of troops].

Aufmarschiren, *v. intr.* to march up, to march. Die Truppen marschirten vor dem Palaste auf, the troops drew up in front of the palace.

Aufmaß, *n.* [-es, *pl.* -e] overmeasure, the heaping of a measure.

Aufmästen, *v. tr.* to fatten [hogs &c.].

Aufmauern, *v. tr.* 1) to build up with stone or brick, to raise [a wall]. 2) to consume in building.

Aufmeißeln, *v. tr.* 1) to open by means of a chisel 2) to chisel on the surface of any thing [an ornament &c.].

Aufmengsel, *n.* [-s, *pl.* -] medley.

Aufmerken, I. *v. intr.* to attend, to listen, to regard with attention. Merke auf! attend! II. *v. tr.* to mark, to note down. Syn. V. Acht

Aufmerker, *m.* [-s, *pl.* -] one that marks or notes.

Aufmerksam, *adj.* and *adv.* attentive, advertent, heedful, intent, observant, regarding with care. Ein —es Ohr oder Auge, an attentive ear or eye; — seyn auf die Worte eines Sprechenden, to be attentive to the words of a speaker; er sah — zu, he looked on attentively, with fixed attention; er war — auf das, was gesagt wurde, he adverted to what was said; ich hörte seinen Belehrungen — zu, I listened heedfully to his instructions. Syn. V. Achtsam.

Aufmerksamkeit, *f.* 1) attention attentiveness, advertence, advertency, heedfulness. Seine — auf etwas richten, to turn one's mind or attention to a thing; alle mögliche — auf eine Sache verwenden, to apply all one's senses to a thing. 2) [act of civility, or courtesy] attention. Die — gegen einen Fremden, attention to a stranger; ich war ihm für seine vielen —en sehr verbunden, I was very much obliged to him for his many assiduities.

Aufmessen, *ir. v. tr.* to measure out, to lay up in store after measuring. *Fig.* and † Es wurden ihm fünfundzwanzig Stockstreiche aufgemessen, five and twenty lashes were served out to him.

Aufmischen, *v. tr.* 1) to supply by mixing. Ein Faß Wein —, to fill up a cask of wine with some of a different sort. 2) to mix up [at cards]. Die Karten wieder —, und von Neuem geben, to shuffle the cards, and to deal again.

|| **Aufmummeln**, *v. tr.* to munch up [bread &c.].

Aufmunterer, *m.* [-s, *pl.* -] one who arouses, encourager, inciter.

Aufmuntern, *v. tr.* 1) to rouse = to wake from rest. Einen vom Schlafe —, to rouse any one from sleep. *Fig.* Das Gemüth —, to cheer the mind, to exhilarate, to enliven; sich —, to brisk one's self up. 2) to rouse = to excite to thought or action, to encourage, to animate, to incite, to stir up. Zur Tugend —, to excite to virtue; das Lob guter Menschen muntert zur Tugend und zum Heldenmuthe auf, the praise of good men serves as an encouragement to virtue and heroism; eine —de Aussicht, an encouraging prospect.

Aufmunterung, *f.* 1) the act of rousing or encouraging, encouragement. Die — der Wissenschaften, the encouragement of science 2) [that which serves to incite, support, promote or advance] encouragement. Der junge Mann fand wenig —, the young man found little encouragement; die schönen Künste finden wenig — bei einem rohen Volke, the fine arts find little encouragement among a rude people.

Aufmünzen, *v. tr.* to consume all the stock of gold, silver or copper in coining.

Áufmurren, *v. tr.* to rouse from sleep by grumbling.

Áufmuthen, *v. tr.* to animate, to excite, to inspirit, to prompt.

‖ **Áufmutzen**, *v. tr. fig.* to reproach as a fault.

Áufnageln, *v. tr.* to nail on [a board &c.].

Áufnagen, *v. tr.* 1) to gnaw open. 2) to consume in gnawing.

Áufnähen, *v. tr.* 1) to sew on. 2) to expend in sewing [all one's thread].

Áufnahme, *f.* [*pl.* -n] 1) taking up [but chiefly in a fig. sense]. Die — einer Geldsumme, the borrowing of a sum of money; sie haben eine so abschreckende — gefunden, they have found so discouraging a reception; eine gütige —, a gracious reception; die nämlichen Worte fanden eine gütigere —, the same words found a gentler receipt; um — in euer glückliches Land zu flehen, to crave admission in your happy land; die — [better: Annahme] an Kindes Statt, adoption. 2) advance or progress from any state to a better, improvement. In — kommen, to prosper, to thrive, to gain credit; in — bringen, to improve, to forward; Künste und Wissenschaften in — bringen, to promote, to encourage arts and sciences; eine Mode in — bringen, to bring a fashion into vogue.

Aufnahmeschein, *m.* a certificate of admission or matriculation. **Aufnahms-fähig, —würdig**, *adj.* and *adv.* able or worthy to be admitted into a society.

Áufnähren, *v. tr.* 1) to bring up, to nurse. 2) to educate, to instruct.

Áufnaschen, *v. tr.* to consume in eating [dainties], to expend in eating dainties [one's money &c.].

‡ and * **Áufnasen**, *v. r. fig.* to impose on.

Áufnehmen, *ir.* I. *v. tr.* 1) to take up. Syn. V. Aufheben. Etwas von der Erde —, to take up a thing from the ground; einen Stich —, [at cards] to take up a trick; die Bogen — [among print.] to take up the sheets; eine gefallene Masche —, to take up a stitch in knitting. *Fig.* Ich nehme es da wieder auf, wo es die Geschichte endigte, I take it up, where the history discontinued; den Faden seiner Rede wieder —, to resume the thread of one's discourse; eine Fährte —, [am. hunt.] to hit off a scent; ein Hund, der die Kaltfährte gut aufnimmt, a hound that draws dryfoot well. 2) *Fig.* *a*) to measure the superficial contents of lands, grounds, fields by the help of proper instruments, to survey. Seine Güter —, to take a survey of one's lands; die Küsten —, to survey the coasts. *b*) Geld —, to take up, to borrow money; eine Rechnung —, to audit an account; ein Verzeichniß —, to draw up a list, a catalogue. *c*) to admit, to receive. Ich nehme Sie unter die Zahl meiner Freunde auf, I admit you among my friends; wir nahmen diesen Fremden auf, we received this stranger; Einen huldreich —, to receive any one graciously; einen Studenten in ein Collegium —, to admit a student into a college; der Wirth sagte, er könne keine Gäste mehr —, the landlord said he could take in no more lodgers; Einen an Kindes Statt — [better: annehmen], to adopt any one; schattige Haine nahmen uns auf, [in poetry] we entered shadowy groves. *d*) to absorb. Das Wasser nimmt das Salz in sich auf, water absorbs salt. *e*) to receive with good or ill will, to receive with a certain affection of mind. Was der Bassa so gut aufnahm, daß &c., which the bassa took in so good part, that &c.; die Flugschrift wird von einer Classe Menschen gut aufgenommen, the pamphlet is well received among a certain class of people; etwas als Ernst —, to take a thing in earnest; es mit Einem —, to enter into a contest with a person, to cope with any one.

II. *v. intr.* 1) to grow, to thrive. 2) [with hunters] to conceive, to breed.

III. *v. r.* sich —, to thrive, to prosper.

Aufnehmens-werth, —würdig, *adj.* and *adv.* worthy of admission.

Áufnehmer, *m.* [-s, *pl.* -] he that takes up, a receiver.

Áufnehmung, *f.* taking up, receiving &c.

Aufnehmungs-werth, —würdig, *adj.* and *adv.* V. Aufnehmenswerth.

Áufnesteln, *v. tr.* 1) to unlace. 2) to fasten with a lace to some fixed object above. Einen Dieb —, to hang a thief; sich —, to hang one's self.

Áufnicken, *v. intr.* to strike against a thing in nodding.

Áufnieten, *v. tr.* to rivet upon.

Áufnippen, *v. tr.* to consume by sipping, to sip up or away.

Áufnöthigen, *v. tr.* to press upon. Er nöthigte mir einen Brief für Sie auf, he pressed a letter upon me, to deliver to you; Einem eine Wohlthat —, to press a benefit upon any one.

Áufopfern, *v. tr.* to sacrifice, to immolate. *Fig.* Seinem Vortheile Alles —, to sacrifice every thing to one's interest; er opferte seine Freundschaft seinem Eigennutze auf, he made a sacrifice of his friendship to his interest; Einem etwas —, to sacrifice a thing to any one; sich seinen Freunden —, to devote one's self to one's friends; sich dem Vaterlande —, to sacrifice one's life for one's country.

Áufopferung, *f.* sacrifice, immolation. *Fig.* a sacrifice offered up, sacrifice.

Áuforgeln, *v. tr.* 1) to play on the organ. 2) to rouse from sleep by playing on the organ.

Áufpacken, I. *v. tr.* 1) to pack upon, to pack up. *Fig.* *a*) Einem etwas —, to load or burden any one with a thing. *b*) Einen auf der Straße —, to pick any one up in the streets. *c*) Etwas — [= stehlen], to make off with. 2) to unpack. ‡ and † II. *v. intr.* to pack off bag and baggage.

Áufpalmen, *v. r.* sich —, [a sea term] to go aloft hand over hand.

Áufpappen, *v. tr.* 1) to paste upon something. 2) to paste up. Aufgepappt, pasted up. 3) to bring up, to nurse with pap [a child].

1\. **Áufpassen**, *v. tr.* to fit upon. Einen Deckel auf die Dose —, to fit a lid to the box.

2\. **Áufpassen**, *v. intr.* 1) to regard with observation, to attend. Passe auf, was ich dir sage, attend to my words; paß' auf, daß du nicht fällst, take care you don't fall. 2) to watch, to espy. Einem —, to lay wait for any one. Syn. Aufpassen, Auflauern. Auflauern signifies to wait or watch for with an evil intention; aufpassen does not convey this last idea. Man lauert einem auf [one lays wait for a person] to whom one intends some harm; man paßt einem auf [one looks out, watches for a person] one wishes to speak to, when one expects him to pass, without knowing exactly when.

Áufpasser, *m.* [-s, *pl.* -] 1) spy, waylayer. 2) overseer. 3) waiter. [in seaman's language] Der — in der Constabelkammer, in der Hell, the gunner's yeoman, the boatswain's yeoman.

Áufpauken, I. *v. tr.* 1) to perform on the kettle-drum. 2) † *Fig.* to open by beating, striking or knocking. 3) to awake by beating the kettle-drum. II. *v. intr.* † to strike upon with a dull noise.

Áufpauschen, V. Aufbrausen.

Áufpeitschen, I. *v. intr.* to whip soundly. II. *v. tr.* to get any one up by whipping.

† **Áufpelzen**, *v. intr.* to beat on.

Áufpentern, *v. tr.* [a sea term] Den Anker —, to fish the anchor.

Áufpfählen, *v. tr.* to fix on a pale.

Áufpfeifen, *ir.* I. *v. tr.* 1) to perform on a pipe or whistle. 2) to get any one up by whistling. II. *v. intr.* to play upon the pipe. † *Fig.* Einem zu jeder Zeit —, to be always at any one's service.

Áufpflanzen, *v. tr.* to plant [in a fig. sense]. Sein Panier auf &c. —, to plant one's standard on &c.; die Fahnen —, to set up the colours; mit aufgepflanztem Flintenspieße, with fixed bayonet; eine Kanone —, to place a cannon.

Áufpflegen, *v. tr.* to foster [plants &c.].

Áufpflöcken, *v. tr.* to fasten with plugs, to plug up.

Áufpflücken, *v. tr.* to pluck all up.

Áufpflügen, I. *v. intr.* to strike against a thing in ploughing. II. *v. tr.* 1) to plough up [ancient coins &c.]. 2) to open by ploughing.

Áufpfropfen, *v. tr.* to insert [a scion or shoot, or a small cutting of it] into another tree, to ingraft, to imp.

Áufpichen, *v. tr.* to fasten upon with pitch.

Áufpicken, *v. tr.* 1) to peck up, to pick up. 2) to open by picking, to pick open.

Áufplappern, *v. tr.* to awake by prattling, chattering.

Áufplätten, *v. tr.* to iron again [a shirt &c.].

Áufplatzen, *v. intr.* [u. w. seyn] 1) to fly or break open with force or with sudden violence, to burst. 2) to rise bursting, to burst upward.

‖ **Áufplätzen**, *v. tr.* to make to burst.

Áufplaudern, *v. tr.* to awake by prattling.

Áufpochen, *v. tr.* 1) to open by knocking. 2) to awake by loud knocking.

Áufpoltern, *v. tr.* to awake by knocking and loud noise.

Áufposaunen, *v. tr.* to awake by blowing the trump.

Áufprägen, *v. tr.* 1) to stamp on. Das Bildniß des Fürsten ist den Münzen aufgeprägt, the image of the prince is struck on the money. *Fig.* Dem Gesichte dieses Menschen ist der Stempel der Gemeinheit aufgeprägt, vulgarity is stamped on this fellow's countenance. 2) to coin up, to expend in coining [all the stock of gold &c.].

Áufprallen, *v. intr.* [u. w. seyn] 1) to bounce or rebound against. 2) to bounce upward, to open bouncing.

Áufprasseln, *v. intr.* 1) to rise crackling. Das Feuer prasselt auf, the fire mounts crackling on high. 2) to open crackling.

Áufprassen, V. Verprassen.

Áufprellen, *v. tr.* to toss up, to jerk up.

Áufpressen, *v. tr.* 1) to press against. 2) to press afresh [stuffs, cloth]. 3) to produce on any thing by pressure, to stamp, to imprint. 4) to press open. 5) to press all that is to be pressed. Alle Trauben —, to press all the stock of grapes.

Áufproben, *v. tr.* to put on for trial. Einen Hut —, to try on a hat.

† **Áufprobiren**, *v. tr.* V. Aufproben.

Áufprotzen, *v. tr.* to put upon the limbers, to limber up [a cannon].

Áufprügeln, *v. tr.* to make any one get up by beating.

Áufpudern, *v. tr.* 1) to powder well. Er

trug eine stark aufgepuderte Perrücke, he wore a well-powdered wig. 2) to powder again. 3) to consume in powdering.

Aufpumpen, *v. tr.* to heave up.

Aufpusten, *v. tr.* to blow up [a feather &c.].

Aufputz, *m.* [-es] 1) the act of dressing up, adorning, decking, tricking out. 2) ornament, dress, finery, attire, trappings.

Aufputzen, *v. tr.* 1) to deck or decorate, dress up, deck with external ornaments, to adorn. Sich —, to dress one's self; sie putzten ihre Kinder mit schönen Kleidern auf, they tricked up their children in fine clothes; ein Zimmer —, to fit up a room. 2) to brush up, to perk up [among hatters]. Einen alten Rock —, to trim up an old coat.

Aufquaken, *v. tr.* to rouse from sleep by croaking.

Aufquellen, *v. tr.* to cause to swell out in water.

Aufquillen, *ir. v. intr.* [u. w. seyn] 1) to spring or bubble up. 2) to swell in water.

Aufquirlen, *v. tr.* to twirl again.

Aufraffen, I. *v. tr.* to gather up quickly, to snatch up. *Fig.* Neuigkeiten —, to pick up news. II. *v. r.* sich —, 1) to get up, to gather one's self up quickly [after a fall]. 2) to recover [from a loss, from sickness &c.].

Aufragen, *v. intr.* to jut on high, to tower.

Auframmen, *v. tr.* 1) to drive by violence [as with a battering ram]. 2) to open by ramming.

Aufranken, *v. intr.* to climb up by the help of tendrils. Der Epheu rankt an der Mauer auf, the ivy creeps up the wall.

Aufrasseln, I. *v. intr.* 1) [u. w. haben] to rattle aloud. 2) [u. w. seyn] to open rattling. II. *v. tr.* to awake any one by rattling.

Aufrauchen, I. *v. intr.* [u. w. seyn and haben] 1) to send up smoke. 2) to ascend in the shape of smoke. II. *v. tr.* to consume or expend in smoking. Den ganzen Tabacksvorrath —, to smoke up all the store of tobacco.

Aufräuchern, *v. tr.* 1) to consume in perfuming. 2) to season with smoke for future use.

Aufrauhen, *v. tr.* to raise with burs &c. Ein Stück Tuch —, [am. clothiers] to raise the nap of cloth.

Aufräumen, *v. tr.* 1) to clear or put away, to set or place in order, to arrange; [in husb.] to loosen the earth about vines; [in commerce] Einen Laden —, to clear a shop. *Fig. a)* to clear up. Das räumt den Kopf auf, that clears the head, brightens one's ideas. V. Aufgeräumt. *b)* to empty, to plunder. *c)* to make thin, to thin. Das feindliche Geschütz räumte unter unsern Gliedern auf, the enemy's cannon thinned our ranks. 2) to free from any incumbrance, to clear or to cleanse again. Das Zündloch —, to pick the vent or touch-hole [of a gun].

Aufräumer, *m.* [-s, *pl.* -] [am. metallists] a rymer.

Aufrauschen, I. *v. intr.* [u. w. seyn and haben] 1) to rise rustling. 2) to make a rustling sound. II. *v. tr.* to rouse any one from sleep by a rustling noise.

Aufrechen, *v. tr.* 1) to rake together. 2) to rake up, to loosen [the earth] with a rake.

Aufrechnen, *v. tr.* to cast up or balance account, to reckon up.

Aufrechnung, *f.* the act of reckoning up.

Aufrecht, *adj.* and *adv.* upright, erect. — stehen, to stand erect; [in botany] ein —er Stengel, ein —es Blatt, an erect stem, an erect leaf; [in seaman's lang.] ein — stehendes Schiff, a ship on an even keel. *Fig.* — erhalten, to maintain; die Hoffnung erhält unser Gemüth —, hope keeps up our spirits; es wird seine Geduld — erhalten, it will sustain his patience; ihn unter den Uebeln dieser Welt — zu erhalten, to sustain him under the evils of this world.

Aufrechthalten, *n.* [-s] **Aufrechthaltung**, *f.* maintenance, support.

Aufrechthalter, *m.* [-s, *pl.* -] maintainer, supporter.

Aufrecken, *v. tr.* 1) to lift up, to erect to a point. Der gejagte Panther reckt seine lauschenden Ohren auf, the hunted panther pricks her listening ears; er reckt die Ohren auf, he pricks up his ears. 2) to reach forth, to extend and open widely.

Aufreden, *v. tr.* 1) to instigate, to incite. 2) to press upon by persuasion.

Aufregen, *v. tr.* to rouse, to stir. Brausende Winde hatten die See aufgeregt, blustering winds had roused the sea; die Säfte im Körper —, to stir the humours in the body. *Fig.* Die Leidenschaften —, to stir up the passions; Einem die Galle —, to provoke any one's anger; Kraft in Einem —, to stir up vigour in any one; spannt die Sehnen an, regt das Blut auf, stiffen the sinews, summon up the blood; ein Volk zur Empörung —, to rouse a people to rebellion. V. Erregen.

Aufregnen, *v. imp.* to rain upon.

Aufreiben, *ir.* I. *v. tr.* 1) to fret and wear away by friction, to excoriate. Die Haut —, to hurt or break the skin by rubbing, to gall, to fret the skin; der Sattel rieb den Rücken des Pferdes auf, the saddle galled the back of the horse. 2) to apply by rubbing [a salve]. 3) to consume in rubbing. Alle Farben —, to grind all the stock of colours. 4) *Fig.* to destroy, to kill, to slay. Ein Heer wird durch Krankheiten und Hunger aufgerieben, an army is destroyed by disease and hunger; die Pest hat viele Menschen aufgerieben, the plague has carried off a great many people; sie haben sich unter einander selbst aufgerieben, they destroyed each other. 5) to rub afresh. Das Tuch —, [among clothiers] to raise the nap of cloth. 6) to rub upward [among bakers]. Den Teig —, to knead well the dough. 7) to rub up, to cleanse by rubbing. Den Fußboden —, to scrub, to clean up the floor. II. *v. intr.* to rub the surface of one body against that of another.

* **Aufreiber**, *m.* [-s, *pl.* -] [among flutemakers] an auger used for boring flutes.

Aufreichen, *v. tr.* to hand up.

Aufreihen, *v. tr.* to string [pearls &c.]

Aufreißahle, *f.* [*pl.* -n] V. Draufbohrer.

Aufreißen, *ir.* I. *v. intr.* [u. w. seyn] [illegible] in chinks, to rend, to chink. Die Bretter reißen auf, the boards crack, split; seine Kleider sind an den Knieen und Elbogen aufgerissen, he is out at the knees and elbows; aufgerissene Hände, chapped hands. II. *v. tr.* 1) to rend, to tear open, to open with violence. Eine Nath —, to rip up a seam; eine Thüre —, to throw open a door violently; den Acker —, to break up, to plough the field; Ströme reißen den Boden auf, torrents tear the ground; [am. clothiers] das Tuch —, to tease the cloth; das Maul —, to open the mouth wide, to gape. *Fig.* † Er reißt über Alles das Maul auf [= hält sich über Alles auf], he jaws about every thing. 2) *Fig.* Ein Gebäude —, [in architect.] to draw and describe the face or principal side of a building; ein Wappen —, [in heraldry] to sketch or design a coat of arms. III. *v. r.* sich —, 1) to be torn open. 2) to get up or rise suddenly. Ich riß mich schnell aus meinem tiefen Sinnen auf, I roused myself quickly from my reverie.

Aufreiten, *ir.* I. *v. intr.* [u. w. seyn] 1) to ride upward. 2) to draw up [said of cavalry]. II. *v. r.* sich —, to chafe by riding.

Aufreizen, *v. tr.* to incite, to rouse. Die Leidenschaften —, to stir up the passions; Einen zum Zorne —, to stir up, to provoke, to raise any one's anger.

Aufrennen, *ir.* I. *v. intr.* [u. w. seyn] 1) to run upward. 2) to run upon. Mit einem Schiffe —, to run aground. II. [with some authors reg.] *v. tr.* 1) to burst open [a door &c.] by running against. * Er ist so dumm, daß man Thüren mit ihm — kann, he is a true blockhead. 2) to make sore by running.

Aufrichten, I. *v. tr.* to erect, to raise. Den Kopf —, to uprear the head; ein Gebäude —, to erect, to set up, to raise, to rear up a building; einen Mast —, to raise a mast; ein Ehrendenkmahl —, to raise a monument; ein Schiff wieder —, [in seaman's language] to right a ship; aufgerichtet, [in heraldry] saliant. Syn. V. Aufheben. *Fig. a)* [= errichten] Ein Regiment —, to raise a regiment; ein Bündniß —, to contract an alliance. V. Errichten. *b)* to strengthen the mind when depressed and enfeebled, to cheer or relieve from depression, or trouble, to comfort, to console. Syn. Aufrichten, Trösten. Aufrichten and trösten are used according to the degree of depression or affliction which it is intended to relieve, and also according to the magnitude of the evils which have produced the affliction. One would say, speaking of a person who had lost a trifling sum of money, that one tried ihn zu trösten [to console him], but not aufzurichten. On the other hand, a mother who is bowed down with grief at the loss of an only child we should try aufzurichten [to raise, to cheer]. The depressed richtet man auf, and the sorrowful tröstet man.

II. *v. r.* sich —, to get up, to rise, [of ships] to right. Der Todte richtete sich auf und fing an zu reden, [St. Lu. VII] he that was dead, sat up, and began to speak.

Aufrichter, *m.* [-s, *pl.* -] [in anatomy a muscle that erects] erector.

Aufrichtig, *adj.* and *adv.* 1) true, genuine, pure, not adulterated. 2) sincere, undissembling, candid. — reden und handeln, to speak and act sincerely; ein —er Freund, a sincere friend; mit —em Herzen, with a sincere heart; Gott mit —er Seele dienen, to serve God with an upright spirit. Syn. Aufrichtig, Offenherzig, Redlich. Der Offenherzige [the open-hearted man] says all he thinks, and exactly as he thinks; der Aufrichtige [the upright man] does not say every thing, but only what he may say without indiscretion; what he does say, however, is his real opinion. Der Offenherzige is necessarily always aufrichtig, for otherwise he must sometimes conceal his thoughts; der Aufrichtige is not always offenherzig; what he cannot say as he thinks, he rather does not say at all. The reverse of Offenherzigkeit is Zurückhaltung [reserve], of Aufrichtigkeit, Verstellung [dissimulation or concealment]. I do not act aufrichtig, when I pretend to think, what I do not, nor redlich [honestly, fairly] when I conceal what I know and think from any one who has a right to require me to make it known, or when I say or give him to understand the reverse of what I know to be the truth.

Aufrichtigkeit, *f.* 1) pureness, freeness from extraneous or foul admixtures. 2) sincereness, trueness, candidness, uprightness. Sie kennen die — meiner Liebe, you know the sincerity of my love.

Aufriegeln, *v. tr.* to unbolt [a door &c.]. Ein Thor —, to unbar a gate.

Aufringeln, I. *v. tr.* 1) to bend or form into ringlets. Das Haar —, to curl the hair. 2) to uncurl. II. *v. r.* sich —, to shrink into ringlets, to curl, to coil up [of snakes].

Aufringen, *ir.* I. *v. tr.* to put or apply to a ring. II. *v. r.* sich —, to make an effort to get up, to raise one's self up with difficulty [from the ground].

Aufriß, *m.* [-sses, *pl.* -sse] 1) [in architecture, a draught and description of the face or principal side of a building] elevation, [in vulgar language] upright. Der — einer Kirche, the elevation of a church; der geometrische — eines Gebäudes, orthography; der perspektivische — einer alten Kirche, scenography of an old church. 2) [the manner of describing a figure or problem in geometry] construction.

Aufritzen, *v. tr.* to scratch open, to slit [the skin &c.].

Aufröcheln, I. *v. intr.* to rattle in the throat. II. *v. tr.* to rouse from sleep by rattling in the throat.

Aufrocken, *v. tr.* to tie to the distaff [a bunch of flax].

Aufröhren, *v. tr.* to open a choked pipe or tube.

Aufrollen, I. *v. tr.* 1) to roll, to roll up. Sie rollt jeden Abend ihre Locken auf, she puts up her curls every evening; rolle sie in lange Rollen auf, roll them up in long rolls; Fleisch —, to collar meat [to roll it up and bind it close with a string]. 2) to raise [the curtain in theatres]. 3) [to open what is rolled] to unroll. 4) to roll afresh. Servietten —, to press or mangle napkins afresh. II. *v. intr.* [u. w. seyn] to be raised [said of a curtain]. Der Vorhang rollt auf, the curtain rises. III. *v. r.* sich —, to unroll, to unfold, to open.

Aufrosten, *v. intr.* [u. w. seyn] to be fixed to by the rust, to rust on to.

Aufrösten, *v. tr.* to roast again.

Aufrücken, I. *v. intr.* [u. w. seyn] to march in close or regular order, to draw up [said of troops]. *Fig.* Sie rücken nach dem Dienstalter auf, they advance according to seniority. II. *v. tr.* to move or push upward. Den Schleifhamen —, to pull up the drag; die Beete —, [in gardening] to raise the beds in the centre. *Fig.* Einem seine Fehler —, [= vorrücken] to upbraid any one with his faults.

Aufrudern, *v. intr.* [u. w. seyn] 1) to row against the stream. 2) to run against a thing or aground in rowing.

Aufruf, *m.* [-es, *pl.* -e] 1) a calling up, summons or invitation. 2) a writing or publication, proclamation by which any one is summoned or summoned up.

Aufrufen, *ir.* I. *v. tr.* to call up, to bid to rise. Einen am Morgen —, to call any one [up] in the morning. *Fig.* Einen zum Zeugen —, to call any one to witness; sie sind zu &c. aufgerufen, they are summoned or summoned up for &c. II. *v. intr.* to call or cry out, to utter a loud voice.

Aufruhen, *v. intr.* to repose upon, to rest upon.

Aufruhr, *m.* [-s] 1) uproar, tumult, great stir, bustle. Die Welt in — bringen, to set the world in an uproar; sein Blut ist in —, his blood is up. 2) *Fig.* insurrection, sedition, mutiny, rebellion. Einen — erregen, to raise a sedition, to raise a stir; einen — stillen, to appease a tumult; einen — dämpfen, to quash, to put down a rebellion.

Aufruhrsacte, *f.* [in English law] riot act. —**sinn**, *m.* spirit of rebellion. —**stifter**, *m.* one who inflames factions, a firebrand, incendiary, ring-leader. *pl.* die —stifter, kindlers of riot. —**süchtig**, *adj.* and *adv.* disposed to sedition or rebellion.

Aufrühren, *v. tr.* 1) to stir [the lees &c.] Wenn Stürme es [das Meer] —, when worked up by storms. *Fig.* Das Volk —, to raise up the people, to stir up the people to rebellion; die Leidenschaften —, to stir up the passions. 2) *Fig.* to mention again, to stir. Man muß den alten Streit nicht wieder —, one must not revive the old quarrel.

Aufrührend, *adj.* and *adv.* full of tumult or rebellion.

Aufrührer, *m.* [-s, *pl.* -] a rebel, rebeller, insurgent, mutineer. *pl.* die —, seditious men, the mutinous, rioters, mutineers.

Aufrührerisch, **Aufrührisch**, I. *adj.* seditious, mutinous, rebellious. Eine —e Menge, a tumultuous multitude; er veranlaßte diese —en Bewegungen, he made these stirs. II. *adv.* tumultuously, mutinously, seditiously, rebelliously.

Aufrunzeln, *v. tr.* to unwrinkle.

Aufrupfen, *v. tr.* to raise by plucking. [am. hatters] Den Hut —, to rub a hat with the sealskin.

|| **Aufrusseln**, V. Aufrütteln.

Aufrüsten, I. *v. intr.* [among carpenters, masons &c.] to erect a scaffolding [on the side of a building for workmen]. II. *v. tr.* to prepare, to fit up. Ein Zimmer —, to fit up a room.

Aufrutschen, *v. intr.* [u. w. seyn] to slide against any thing.

Aufrütteln, *v. tr.* 1) to rouse by shaking. 2) to shake up. *Fig.* to impel. Er rüttelte ihn aus seiner dumpfen Betäubung auf, he shook him out of his torpor.

Aufs, *abbrev.* for auf das. V. Auf.

Aufsäbeln, *v. tr.* to open with a sabre.

Aufsacken, *v. tr.* to take up a sack or any burden. *Fig.* Einem ein Geschäft —, to burden any one with a business.

Aufsäen, *v. tr.* to sow once more a field, already sown.

Aufsagen, *v. tr.* 1) to say, to rehearse, to repeat. Seine Aufgabe, Lection —, to say one's lesson; Verse —, to recite verses. 2) to revoke, to reverse. Einem die Freundschaft —, to renounce any one's friendship, to break with a friend; Einem den Dienst —, to warn any one away; ohne aufzusagen, without previous notice; Einem die Miethe —, to give one's tenant warning or notice. SYN. V. Aufkündigen.

Aufsägen, *v. tr.* 1) to open with the saw, to saw open. 2) to saw up entirely. Den Holzvorrath —, to saw up all the stock of wood.

Aufsalben, *v. tr.* 1) to salve. 2) to consume by salving.

Aufsalzen, *v. tr.* 1) to sprinkle with salt. 2) to salt afresh.

Aufsammeln, *v. tr.* to gather, to collect [fruit &c.]. *Fig.* Neuigkeiten —, to pick up news.

Aufsammler, *m.* [-s, *pl.* -] gatherer, collector.

Aufsäßig, V. Aufsätzig.

Aufsatteln, *v. tr.* 1) to saddle [a horse]. 2) † *Fig.* to burden with.

Aufsatz, *m.* [-es, *pl.* -sätze] 1) the thing put upon another, especially for ornament. *a)* [an additional tube in waterworks, through which the water of a fountain is to be played] ajutage. *b)* [in archit.] panel. *c)* [in gunnery] a coin or wedge under the breech of a cannon in order to elevate or depress it. *d)* [am. sempstr.] a piece sewed on, lining, stabling. *e)* the covering or ornaments of a woman's head, head-dress. *f)* various ornaments on tables &c. Der Tisch- or Tafel—, a plateau of china &c.; der — an einem Spiegel, the top of a mirror. 2) writing, composition, essay, treatise. Aufsätze, memoirs, essays.

Aufsatzplatte, *f.* [Tischaufsatz] a plateau.

Aufsätzig, *adj.* and *adv.* hostile, inimical, adverse.

Aufsäubern, *v. tr.* 1) to clean up, to cleanse. 2) to cleanse again.

Aufsäuern, *v. tr.* to make sour again.

† **Aufsaufen**, *ir. v. tr.* to consume by drinking immoderately, to drink up.

Aufsaugen, *v. tr.* 1) to suck up. 2) to open by sucking

Aufsäugen, *v. tr.* to bring up, to rear by suckling.

Aufsäuseln, I. *v. intr.* [u. w. seyn and haben] to rise with a gentle gale. II. *v. tr.* to open by a gentle gale.

Aufsausen, I. *v. intr.* [u. w. haben and seyn] to rise blustering, to rise with a rushing sound. II. *v. tr.* to rouse from sleep by blustering.

Aufschaben, *v. tr.* 1) to open by scraping. 2) to scrape up. 3) to scrape again. 4) to scrape entirely away.

Aufschallen, *v. intr.* to sound loudly.

Aufschanzen, *v. tr.* to trench up, to throw up.

Aufschärfen, *v. tr.* 1) to cut open. Einen Hirsch —, [am. hunt.] to open a stag; die Haut —, to scratch the skin. 2) to sharpen again. Den Mühlstein —, [in mills] to notch the millstone afresh.

Aufscharren, *v. tr.* 1) to scratch or scrape up. 2) to open by scraping. 3) to loosen [the earth] by scraping. 4) to heap up by scraping. *Fig.* Geld —, to scrape up a sum of money.

Aufschauen, *v. intr.* to look up. Groß —, to lift up one's eyes in astonishment. *Fig.* to take heed. Aufgeschaut! take care!

Aufschauern, *v. intr.* to shudder.

Aufschaufeln, *v. tr.* to take or heap up with a shovel, to shovel up.

Aufschäumen, *v. intr.* to foam up, to froth. *Fig.* to be violently agitated, to foam.

Aufscheinen, *ir. v. intr.* to shine upon something.

Aufschellen, *v. tr.* to rouse from sleep by ringing a bell.

Aufscheren, *v. tr.* 1) [am. weavers] to warp. 2) [a sea term] to coil up [a rope].

Aufscheuchen, *v. tr.* to scare or frighten up, to rouse, to spring, to rear. Feldhühner —, to flush partridges.

Aufscheuern, I. *v. tr.* 1) to scour up. 2) to scour again. 3) to finish scouring. 4) to fret by scouring. II. *v. r.* sich —, to be worn away by scouring.

Aufschichten, *v. tr.* to pile up. Holz —, to stack wood; Mist —, to pile up dung.

Aufschicken, V. Aufputzen.

Aufschiebbar, *adj.* that may be deferred or put off.

Aufschieben, *ir.* I. *v. tr.* 1) to shove one thing upon another. *Fig.* Die Ausführung eines Planes —, to defer the execution of a design; er schob es auf morgen auf, he put it off till tomorrow; ein Geschäft —, to procrastinate a business; es wurde aufgeschoben, it was postponed; etwas bis auf die Letzt —, to delay a thing to the last. *Prov.* Aufgeschoben ist nicht aufgehoben, omittance is no quittance, all is not lost that is delayed, forbearance is no acquittance. V. Aufheben. 2) to shove open. Ein Fenster —, to lift the sash. II. *v. intr.* to strike against a thing in bowling. Syn. Aufschieben, Verzögern. Man verzögert eine Sache [one delays a thing] which one does not do sufficiently quickly, or not against a certain specified time; man schiebt auf [one puts off] that which one defers or postpones doing till some more convenient future time. A journey is verzögert [delayed] on account of some business which unexpectedly intervened, and aufgeschoben [put off] until such time as that business shall be finished.

Aufschiebering, *m.* ring or runner on an umbrella.

Aufschiebling, *m.* [-s, *pl.* -e] [in building] chantlate.

Aufschielen, *v. intr.* to squint up.

Aufschienen, *v. tr.* to fasten upon as a splint.

Aufschießen, *ir.* I. *v. intr.* [u. w. seyn] 1) to shoot, to shoot up, to grow fast. Wo Unkraut aufschießt, where weeds shoot; er ist schnell aufgeschossen [gewachsen], he has shot up quickly, grown fast. 2) to move swiftly upward, to dart up. II. *v. tr.* 1) to open by shooting. 2) to consume or expend in shooting. 3) [a sea term] Ein Tau —, to coil up a rope; ein Tau mit der oder gegen die Sonne —, to coil a cable with or against the sun.

Aufschiffen, *v. intr.* [u. w. seyn] to run upon a thing in sailing. Auf eine Sandbank —, to get on a sand-bank in sailing.

Aufschimmern, *v. intr.* to glimmer.

Aufschinden, *ir. v. r.* sich —, to rub off one's skin.

Aufschirren, *v. tr.* to harness [a horse].

‖**Aufschlabbern**, *v. tr.* 1) to lap up hastily [said of dogs]. 2) to lap the whole.

Aufschlacken, *v. intr.* [used with seyn] to be changed or reduced wholly to slags.

Aufschlag, *m.* [-es, *pl.* -schläge] 1) the act of striking upon, the act of striking or turning up. Der — einer Karte, the turning up of a card. 2) [in music] the raising of the hand as applied to the beating of time, arsis. 3) a thing turned up. Die vordern Aufschläge an einem Kleide, the facings of a garment; ein Kleid mit Aufschlägen versehen, to face a garment; die Aufschläge an Aermeln, cuffs; die Aufschläge an Stiefeln, the tops of boots. 4) *Fig.* *a*) an additional duty imposed on goods. *b*) the increase of price. 5) [in husb.] a young growth of wood.

Aufschlagbuch, *n.* a book that one may consult.

Aufschlagen, *ir.* I. *v. tr.* 1) to strike upward. Einen Ball —, to drive a ball [with a racket &c.]; eine Karte, einen Tisch —, to turn up a card, a table; ein Kleid —, to face a garment; er trug eine blaue, mit Roth aufgeschlagene Uniform, he wore a blue uniform turned up with red; mit Hermelin aufgeschlagen, [in heraldry] lined with ermine. 2) to raise and set in an upright direction or nearly such. Ein Bett —, to set up a bed; ein Zelt —, to pitch a tent; ein Lager —, to raise or pitch a camp; eine Bude —, to put up a booth or stall; einen Hut —, to turn up a hat; die Ballen —, [am. print.] to knock up the balls. *Fig.* Seine Wohnung an einem Orte —, to settle one's self in a place; schlage hier deine bleibende Wohnung auf, settle here your abode. 3) [= erheben] Die Augen —, to lift up the eyes, to turn up one's eyes; mit aufgeschlagenen Augen, with upcast eyes. *Fig.* Eine helle Lache [ein helles Gelächter] —, to set up a hearty laugh, to break out into loud laughter. 4) to rouse by beating. 5) to join to, to fasten to by striking. Den Schuh —, to put a shoe upon the last, to set a shoe on the last; dem Pferde die Hufeisen —, to shoe the horse; das Salz —, [in saltworks] to heap the salt-baskets; das Wasser —, to throw or conduct water upon the wheels of a machine. 6) to open by striking. Eine Thür —, to break open a door; ein Faß —, to unbung a cask; Nüsse —, to crack nuts; [in sea-lang.] ein Tau —, to untwist a rope. *Fig.* Ein Buch blindlings —, to open a book at random; ein Buch —, to open a book, to seek for information or facts in a book, to consult a book; ein Wort —, to seek for a word; eine Stelle —, to look for a passage. 7) Die Wäsche —, [am. washerwomen] to unfold and lay out linen.

II. *v. intr.* 1) to strike or beat upon. 2) [u. w. seyn] *a*) to fall upon a thing violently. Der Hagel schlägt auf das Dach auf, the hail beats the roof. *b*) [u. w. haben and seyn] to spring up, to be turned up. *Fig.* to rise in price. Der Hafer schlägt auf, the oats rise; der Zucker hat aufgeschlagen, the price of sugar is advanced.

III. *v. r.* sich —, to make sore by striking against a thing or by a fall. Sich den Kopf —, to bruise one's head.

Aufschlage-holz, *n.* [am. tailors] sleeve-board. **—schaufel**, *f.* [in hydraul.] float-board, ladle-board, ladle. **—tisch**, *f.* folding-table.

Aufschläger, *m.* [-s, *pl.* -] he that strikes or beats upon.

Aufschlammen, V. Aufschlemmen 1.

Aufschlängeln, *v. r.* sich —, to wind upward with a serpentine course, to serpentize upward [said of a path &c.].

Aufschlecken, V. Auflecken.

Aufschleiern, V. Entschleiern.

Aufschleifen, V. Anschleifen.

Aufschlemmen, *v. tr.* 1) to raise by adding mud or slime. 2) to open or cleanse a pipe or ditch choked with mud.

Aufschleudern, I. *v. tr.* 1) to fling upward. 2) to open by a cast or throw. II. *v. intr.* [u. w. seyn] 1) to fall violently upon a thing. 2) to be cast or thrown upward.

Aufschlichten, *v. tr.* to pile up. Holz —, to range timber, to stack wood. V. Aufschichten.

Aufschließen, *ir.* I. *v. tr.* to open with a key, to unlock. Ein Schloß —, to open a lock; eine Thür —, to unlock a door; die Form —, [am. print.] to unlock the form. *Fig.* to open, to develop. Die Erde schließt im Frühjahr ihren Schooß auf, the earth opens her lap in spring; ich schloß ihr mein ganzes Herz auf, I unlocked all my heart to her; einem Freunde sein Herz —, to open one's heart to a friend; die geheimen Gedanken des Herzens —, to disclose the secret thoughts of the heart; ein Geheimniß —, to unfold a mystery; eine dunkle Stelle in einem Schriftsteller —, to explain a dark passage in an author. II. *v. r.* sich —, to open. Die Blumen schließen sich im Frühlinge auf, the flowers open or expand in spring.

Aufschließer, *m.* [-s, *pl.* -] he that unlocks, turnkey.

1. **Aufschlingen**, *ir.* I. *v. tr.* 1) to fasten by a noose to some fixed object above. 2) to untwist, to untwine. II. *v. r.* sich —, 1) to twine upward. 2) to be opened, to be loosened.

2. **Aufschlingen**, *ir. v. tr.* to swallow up.

Aufschlitzen, *v. tr.* to rip, to rip up. Einem den Bauch —, to rip any one's belly; die Nase —, to slit the nose; eine Feder —, to split a pen.

Aufschluchzen, *v. intr.* 1) to sob. 2) to rise suddenly and sobbing.

Aufschlucken, *v. tr.* to swallow up.

Aufschlürfen, *v. tr.* to drink by small draughts, to sip up.

Aufschluß, *m.* [-sses, *pl.* -schlüsse] the act of opening. Bei — des Thores, at the opening of the gate. *Fig.* the act of clearing from obscurity and making intelligible, the act of disclosing. Die Ereignisse haben uns über die Pläne des Ministeriums — gegeben, the events have disclosed the designs of the ministry; die Zeit wird uns — darüber geben, time will unfold it; er gab ihm — über eine dunkle Stelle in der Schrift, he explained to him a dark passage in Scripture.

Aufschmauchen, I. *v. intr.* to smoke, to rise like smoke. II. *v. tr.* to consume in smoking.

Aufschmausen, *v. tr.* to consume in feasting, to eat up [all the viands &c.], to expend or dissipate in banqueting [one's fortune].

† **Aufschmeißen**, *ir.* I. *v. tr.* 1) to fling upon something. 2) to fling open. II. *v. intr.* to fling, cast or beat upon.

Aufschmelzen, I. *v. intr. ir.* [u. w. seyn] 1) to melt, to dissolve. 2) to be opened by melting. II. *v. tr. reg.* 1) to liquify, to open by melting. 2) to fasten upon a thing by melting. 3) to melt again. 4) to melt up the whole.

Aufschmettern, I. *v. tr.* 1) to crash open. 2) to open with a crashing sound. II. *v. intr.* [u. w. seyn] 1) to fall violently or with a crash upon. 2) to sound loudly.

Aufschmieden, *v. tr.* 1) to fasten upon by forging or hammering. 2) to consume in forging.

Aufschmieren, *v. tr.* 1) to smear upon, to spread upon. † *Fig.* Einem etwas —, to cheat any one into a bargain. 2) to consume in smearing, or spreading.

Aufschminken, *v. tr.* 1) to paint afresh. 2) to improve by painting. *Fig.* Er suchte sein Betragen aufzuschminken, he tried to gloss over or varnish his conduct.

Aufschmoren, *v. tr.* to stew again.

Aufschmücken, *v. tr.* 1) to adorn, to ornament, to embellish, to dress up, to dress. Sich —, to dress one's self in fine clothes. 2) to adorn anew.

Aufschnäbeln, *v. tr.* 1) to peck up. 2) *Fig.* to chop up.

Aufschnallen, *v. tr.* 1) to buckle upon. 2) to unbuckle.

Aufschnappen, I. *v. tr.* to catch or attempt to seize with the mouth, to snap up. **Fig.* Ein Wort —, to catch up a word. II. *v. intr.* [u. w. seyn] to turn suddenly, to fly up.

Aufschnarchen, I. *v. intr.* to snore aloud. II. *v. tr.* to rouse from sleep by snoring.

Aufschnattern, I. *v. intr.* to commence cackling or chattering. II. *v. tr.* to rouse from sleep by prattling.

Aufschneiden, *ir.* I. *v. tr.* 1) to cut upon. Auf das Kerbholz —, to notch the tally. 2) to cut open. Ein Buch —, to cut open the leaves of a book; den Bauch —, to rip up the belly; einen Fisch —, to gut or draw a fish. 3) to cut, to cut off. Brod —, to cut bread. 4) to cut all that is to be cut. Das Brod ist aufgeschnitten, the bread is all cut up. II. *v. intr.* *Fig.* to rodomontade, to stretch, to shoot with a long bow, † to tip the traveller.

Aufschneider, *m.* [-s, *pl.* -] one that stretches, a rodomontador, rodomontadist.

Aufschneiderei, *f.* stretching, exaggeration.

Áufschneiderisch, *adj.* and *adv.* sallying beyond the truth, stretching.

Áufschneien, *v. imp.* to snow upon.

Áufschneiteln, *v. tr.* [in gardening] to lop, to prune.

Áufschnellen, I. *v. intr.* [u. w. seyn] to fly up with a jerk, to spring. II. *v. tr.* to throw with a jerk.

Áufschniegeln, I. *v. tr.* to dress up, to clothe elegantly. II. *v. r.* sich —, to trick one's self out in fine clothes.

Áufschnitt, *m.* [-s, *pl.* -e] 1) the act of cutting open. 2) [in metall.] assay of gold. 3) [a part cut off] cut. 4) slit, opening.

Áufschnitzeln, *v. tr.* to cut figures or devices on hard materials, to carve.

Áufschnupfen, *v. tr.* to take all the stock of snuff, to consume all the snuff.

Áufschnüren, *v. tr.* 1) to unlace. 2) to fasten with a string upon something, to tie on.

Áufschobern, *v. tr.* to put in stacks. Heu, Stroh—, to cock hay, straw.

Áufschocken, *v. tr.* to put in stacks or heaps.

Áufschöpfen, *v. tr.* to take up with a ladle, to scoop up.

Áufschossen, *v. intr.* [u. w. seyn] to shoot pu, to sprout.

Áufschößling, *m.* [-s, *pl.* -e] 1) shoot, sprout, sprig. 2) a young person grown up suddenly, stripling. 3) *Fig.* an upstart.

Áufschrammen, I. *v. tr.* 1) to scratch [the skin]. 2) to mark by a scratch. II. *v. r.* sich —, to scratch one's skin.

Áufschränken, *v. tr.* to lay crossways and pile up [as boards to dry].

Áufschrauben, *v. tr.* 1) to fasten upon with a screw, to screw on. Einen Flintenstein —, to fix a flint into the jaws [of a gun-lock]. 2) to raise by means of a screw, to screw up. 3) to unscrew.

Áufschrecken, I. *v. tr.* to frighten up, to rouse, to startle. II. *v. intr.* [u. w. seyn] to start.

Áufschrei, *m.* [-es, *pl.* -e] shriek, scream.

Áufschreiben, *ir. v. tr.* to write or set down, to note. Seinen Namen —, to write down one's name; seine Ausgaben —, to enter, write, or register one's expences in a book, to book them.

Áufschreien, *ir* I. *v. intr.* to cry aloud, to cry out, to scream, shriek. Sie schrie laut auf, she gave a shriek. II. *v. tr.* to awake by an outcry or scream.

Áufschreiten, *ir. v. intr.* [u. w. seyn] to march up, draw up.

Áufschricken, *v. tr.* [a sea term] Die Kabelaring —, to surge at the capstern.

Áufschrift, *f.* [*pl.* -en] [that which is written on the top or outside] superscription. Die — eines Briefes, direction, address; die — auf einem Grabmahle, auf Ehrensäulen &c., V. Inschrift.

Áufschroten, *v. tr.* 1) to grind coarsely the whole. 2) *Fig.* to eat up [said of animals]. 3) [am. workmen] *a*) [am. locksmiths] to hew or cut open with a large chisel. *b*) [am. carpenters, joiners] to widen a bore with an auger. 4) to roll or shove up [a cask from a cellar].

Áufschroter, *m.* [-s, *pl.* -] 1) [an instrument for boring large holes] an auger. 2) he that rolls or shoves a cask up from a cellar.

Áufschrunden, *v. intr.* [u. w. seyn] to crack, to open in large slits. Die Hände schrunden auf, the hands chap.

Áufschub, *m.* [-es] a putting off or deferring, deferment, delay. Der Befehl zum —e einer Hinrichtung, respite, reprieve; der König hatte die Gnade, ihm einen — zu bewilligen, the king has been pleased to respite or reprieve him.

Aufschubbefehl, *m.* [in law] reprieve.

Áufschultern, *v. tr.* to put upon the shoulder. Riesen, welche Berge —, giants shouldering mountains. *Fig.* to burden with.

Áufschüppen, *v. tr.* 1) to take up with a shovel. 2) to heap with a shovel.

Áufschüren, *v. tr.* to stir up, to trim [the fire].

Áufschürzen, I. *v. tr.* to tuck up, to gird up [a gown &c.]. Die Segel —, to furl the sails. *Fig.* Ein aufgeschürztes Pferd, a horse shrunk in the flank. II. *v. r.* sich —, to tuck up one's clothes. Sie schürzte sich auf wie eine spartanische Jungfrau, she tucked up her vestment like a Spartan virgin.

Áufschuß, *m.* [-sses, *pl.* -schüsse] a sudden rising or moving upward.

Áufschüsseln, *v. tr.* 1) to put in a dish, to dish. 2) to serve up the dishes. 3) *tr.* and *intr.* *Fig.* to treat well at the table, to feast.

Áufschütteln, *v. tr.* to shake up, to make light by motion or agitation. Sein dreimal aufgeschütteltes Schwanenbett, his thrice driven bed of down.

Áufschütten, *v. tr.* 1) to heap up, to throw up in a heap. 2) to throw upon, to pour upon. Korn —, [in mills] to put corn into the hopper; das Zündkraut auf ein Gewehr —, to prime.

Áufschützen, *v. tr.* [in mills] to dam up the water.

1. **Áufschwämmen**, V. Aufschwemmen.

2. **Áufschwämmen**, *v. tr.* 1) to swell like a sponge. 2) [said of persons] to swell or make turgid, to bloat.

Áufschwänzen, *v. tr.* to tie up, to truss up the tail of a horse.

Áufschwärzen, *v. tr.* to blacken afresh.

Áufschwatzen, *v. tr.* to press [goods &c.] upon any one by talking, to talk any one into taking them.

Áufschweben, *v. intr.* [u. w. seyn] to rise and float in the air.

Áufschwefeln, *v. tr.* to sulphur afresh.

Áufschweifen, V. Aufschwänzen.

Áufschweißen, *v. tr.* [am. smiths] to weld.

Áufschwelgen, *v. tr.* to consume or expend in debaucheries.

Áufschwellen, I. *v. intr. ir.* [u. w. seyn] to extend the parts, to grow turgid, to swell, to tumefy. Ein aufgeschwollenes Bein, a bloated or tumid leg; das Wasser schwillt auf, the water swells, rises. *Fig.* Sein Herz schwillt vor Freude auf, his heart expands with joy. II. *v. tr. reg.* to cause to swell, to swell. Der Wind schwellte die Segel auf, the wind swelled or bellied the sails. *Fig.* to cause to increase, to swell. Einen Band —, to swell or swell up a volume.

Áufschwemmen, *v. tr.* 1) to draw [floated wood] out of a river. 2) to wash or carry earth to a shore or bank.

Áufschwenken, *v. tr.* to brandish, to flourish.

Áufschwingen, *ir.* I. *v. tr.* to raise by swinging, to swing upward. II. *v. r.* sich —, to tower, to mount, to soar. *Fig.* Diese erhabenen Gedanken, die sich über die Wolken —, these sublime thoughts which tower above the clouds.

Áufschwören, *ir. v. tr.* to certify again upon oath. Einen Ritter —, to certify upon oath, that a person has the number of ancestors requisite, to be received into a certain order of knighthood.

Áufschwung, *m.* [-es, *pl.* -schwünge] towering, flight, soar. *Fig.* Der — der Phantasie, a soaring of the imagination; er nimmt einen allzu kühnen —, he takes too bold a flight, he soars a little too high.

Áufsegeln, *v. intr.* [u. w. seyn] 1) to sail up [a river]. 2) to strike against or on in sailing, to sail on to [a sand-bank &c.].

Áufsehen, *ir. v. intr.* 1) to look up. Es schneite so stark, daß man kaum — konnte, it snowed so hard that we could scarcely look up. 2) to turn up one's eyes to.

Áufsehen, *n.* [-s] 1) the act of looking up. 2) *Fig.* attention, wonder, surprize. Das erregt allgemeines —, that creates a great sensation, makes a great noise in the world; er macht viel — in der Welt, he cuts a great figure in the world.

Áufseher, *m.* [-s, *pl.* -] overseer, inspector, surveyor, superintendent, warden.

Aufseheramt, *n.* —stelle, *f.* the office of an inspector, surveyorship.

Áufseigen, *v. tr.* to pour upon in straining.

Áufseisen, *v. tr.* [a sea-term] Die Kabelaring —, to nip the cable.

Áufsetzen, I. *v. tr.* 1) to raise or set in an upright position. Holz —, to stack up wood; Kegel —, to set up wooden pins, nine-pins; Buchstaben —, [am. print.] to set up letters; den Vorbersteven —, [in seamen's lang.] to raise the stem; ein Takel, eine Winde —, [in seamen's lang.] to raise a purchase; ein aufgesetztes Faß, [among coopers] a finished cask. *Fig.* Seinen Kopf —, to be obstinate in or against any thing. 2) to invest with as a covering, to put on or upon. Setze deinen Hut auf, put on your hat, be covered; die Speisen —, to serve up the dishes; den Anker —, [in seamen's lang.] to fish the anchor; die Stangen —, to hoist or sway up the yards. * and ‡ *Fig.* Einem Hörner —, to cuckold any one, to make a man a cuckold [by criminal conversation with his wife]. 3) to fix a thing upon another, [among sempstresses] to sew upon. Einen Fleck auf ein Loch —, to cover or patch a hole with a piece sewed on. 4) to put in order, to arrange. Ein Frauenzimmer —, [among hairdressers] to dress a lady's head; einen Nierenbraten —, [among butchers] to skewer a loin of veal. 5) to put down in writing, to form in writing, to minute down. Eine Rechnung —, to draw a bill, to cast an account; seine Gedanken über eine Sache —, to write down one's opinion concerning any thing; eine Schrift, eine Urkunde —, to draw up a paper, a deed; eine Vorstellung —, to draft a memorial; ein Testament —, to draw a will; eine Predigt —, to compose a sermon.

II. *v. r.* sich —, 1) to sit upright. 2) to put in order one's head-dress. 2) to get on horseback, to mount. V. Aufsitzen.

III. *v. intr.* 1) to seize with the teeth. Das Pferd setzt auf, the horse bites the crib 2) [am. sportsmen] Der Hirsch setzt auf, the stag recovers his antlers.

Áufsetzer, *m.* [-s, *pl.* -] a person that sets up, chiefly a boy that sets up nine-pins; crib-biter [said of a horse].

Áufsetzstunde, *f.* the hour of rest among miners.

Áufseufzen, *v. intr.* to heave or fetch a sigh. Tief —, to heave a profound sigh.

Áufseyn, *ir. v. intr.* [u. w. seyn] 1) to be out of bed, to be or sit up. 2) to be in a certain state of health, good or bad. V. Wohlauf, Uebelauf. 3) to be open [said of a window &c.]. 4) to be spent or consumed.

Aúfsicht, *f.* [*pl.* -en] superintendance, inspection, care. Die — über etwas haben, führen, to have the direction or conducting of a thing, control over a thing; er stand unter der — eines Arztes, he was under the care of a physician; die Eltern sollen die — über ihre Kinder führen, children should be under the control of their parents; ohne —, without control; sich eine — über Einen anmaßen, to usurp a tutorage.

Aúfsieden, *ir.* I. *v. intr.* [u. w. seyn] to rise in bubbles, to boil up. II. *v. tr.* 1) to boil again. 2) to prepare in boiling liquor. Das — des Silbers, blanching.

Aúfsiegeln, V. Entsiegeln.

Aúfsingen, *ir.* I. *v. intr.* to sing to, [in seamen's lang.] to sing out. II. *v. tr.* to awake by singing.

Aúfsitz, *m.* [-es, *pl.* -e] for das Aufsitzen.

Aúfsitzen, *ir.* I. *v. intr* 1) to sit or rest upon, [of birds] to perch, (Nachts) —, to go to roost. 2) [to rise from a lying to a sitting posture] to sit up. Er saß im Bette auf, he sat up in his bed. 3) [= Aufbleiben, not to go to bed], to sit up. Einer, der aufsitzt, watcher. 4) to get on horse-back, to mount. Zum — blasen, [among horsemen] to sound to horse; aufgesessen! [word of command, among horsemen] to horse! der ganze Adel muß —, [anciently in feudal law] all the noblemen must take horse, must rise or prepare for war. *Fig.* Einem aufgesessen [more usual aufsätzig] seyn, to bear ill will to some one. II. *v. r.* sich —, [= sich wund sitzen] to be galled by long sitting.

Aufsitzstange, *f.* perch, roost.

Aúfsorren, *v. tr.* [a sea term] Die Hangematten —, to lash up the hammocks [in order to make a clear passage among decks].

Aúfspalten, I. *v. intr.* [u. w. seyn] to split, to burst, to chink. Ein aufgespaltenes Brett, a cracked board; ein aufgespaltener Felsen, a gaping rock. II. *v. tr.* to split open. Ein Stück Holz —, to cleave a piece of wood; die Kälte spaltet den Boden auf, the ground cleaves by the frost.

Aúfspangen, *v. tr.* to fasten upon with a clasp.

Aúfspannen, *v. tr.* 1) to strain or stretch a thing and to fasten it upon another. Saiten auf ein Tonwerkzeug —, to string an instrument. *Fig.* Gelindere Saiten —, to lower one's tone. V. Aufziehen. 2) to extend, to strain, to stretch. Die Garne, Netze —, [among hunters] to pitch the toils; die Segel —, to set or unfurl the sails; alle Segel —, to set, to make all sail, [*fig.*] to apply one's utmost efforts [to accomplish a design]; den Hahnen an einem Feuergewehre —, to cock a gun; einen Fluß —, to dam up a river.

Aúfsparen, *v. tr.* to reserve for future use, to save, to reserve, to postpone to a future time. Ein Stümpchen Licht —, to save a candle's end; sparen Sie Ihre gütigen Blicke für einsame Stunden auf, reserve your kind looks for private hours.

Aúfspeichern, *v. tr.* to lay up in a granary or barn. Korn —, to lay up corn. *Fig.* Schätze —, to hoard up treasures.

Aúfspeien, *v. tr.* to spit upon.

Aúfspeilern, *v. tr.* to skewer [lamb's-skins &c.].

Aúfspeisen, *v. tr.* to eat up.

Aúfspellen, *v. tr.* to cause to split or cleave.

Aúfsperren, *v. tr.* 1) to open wide. *and † Das Maul —, to gape; Maul und Nase —, to open the mouth in wonder or surprize. 2) [among locksmiths] to open with an instrument. Mit dem Dietrich —, to pick a lock; ein Zimmer mit dem Hauptschlüssel —, to open a room with the master-key.

Aúfspielen, I. *v. intr.* to play a dance, to strike up a dance. II. *v. tr.* 1) to play, to strike up. Einen Marsch —, to strike up a march. 2) to awake by playing upon an instrument. 3) to make sore by playing upon an instrument [one's fingers].

Aúfspießen, *v. tr.* to thrust through, to pierce, to spit. Einen Frosch —, to spit a frog; einen Bissen —, to stick and take up a bit with a fork.

Aúfspindeln, *v. tr.* to put upon the spindle.

Aúfspinnen, *v. tr.* 1) to spin the whole. Allen Flachs —, to spin up all the flax. 2) to make sore by spinning [one's fingers].

Aúfspitzen, *v. intr.* to prick up the ears [said of horses and dogs]. *Fig.* to listen with fixed attention.

Aúfspleißen, *v. tr.* to split, to cleave.

Aúfsplittern, I. *v. tr.* to shiver or splint in opening. II. *v intr.* [u. w. seyn] to fly up in shivers.

Aúfspreiten, *v. tr.* to spread upon.

Aúfspreizen, *v tr.* to open wide, to extend, to stretch. Einen geschlachteten Schöps —, [among butchers] to open and skewer a killed wether.

Aúfsprengen, *v. tr.* 1) to break open with force or sudden violence, to wrench open. Eine Thür —, to burst open a door. 2) to blow up [a ship &c.]. 3) Einen Hirsch —, [among hunters] to rouse up a stag. 4) to scatter small drops upon a thing, to sprinkle.

Aúfsprießen, *ir. v. intr.* [u. w. seyn] 1) to begin to vegetate, to germinate, to sprout, to shoot, to spring up [as a plant or its seed]. Sprich, in welchen glücklichen Feldern die Distel aufsprießt, tell, in what happy fields the thistle springs; wenn das Gras anfängt aufzusprießen, when the grass begins to spring forth. 2) *Fig.* to spring, to arise.

Aúfspringen, *ir. v. intr.* [u. w. seyn] 1) to open quickly and suddenly, to fly or spring open. 2) to break into chaps, chinks or fissures. Die Erde springt vor Kälte auf, the earth cleaves, cracks by frost; die Hände springen auf, the hands chap; aufgesprungene Hände, chapt hands. 3) to spring or leap against any thing, so as to rebound, to bounce. 4) to spring up, to jump, to leap up. Von seinem Throne —d, upstarting from his throne; sie sprang aus dem Bette auf, she sprung out of bed.

Aúfspritzen, I. *v. tr.* 1) to spirt up. 2) to consume or expend in spirting. 3) to open by injections [an abscess &c.]. II. *v. intr.* [u. w. seyn] 1) to spirt up. Der Koth spritzte bis an die Kutschengläser auf, the mud splashed up to the carriage windows. 2) to spirt upon. Die Tinte ist auf meinen Brief aufgespritzt, the ink has spirted on to my letter.

Aúfsprossen, *v. intr.* [u. w. seyn] 1) to shoot, to sprout, to germinate [as a plant or its seed]. 2) to grow, to be augmented by natural process [as animals]. 3) *Fig.* *a*) to increase, to be augmented. *b*) to spring, to rise. V. Aufsprießen.

Aúfsprößling, *m.* [-s, *pl.* -e] 1) [of plants] a shoot, a sprout. 2) [of men] a stripling. 3) *Fig.* an upstart.

Aúfsprudeln, I. *v. intr.* [u. w. seyn] to rise in bubbles, to bubble. Dieser Wein sprudelt im Glase auf, this wine sparkles in the glass. *Fig.* Er sprudelt leicht auf, his blood is soon up. II. *v. tr.* to sputter upward.

Aúfsprühen, I. *v. intr.* [u. w. seyn] to emit sparks upward. II. *v. tr.* to cause to emit sparks upward.

Aúfsprung, *m.* [-es, *pl.* -sprünge] 1) a jump, leap upward, a springing up. 2) a sudden disruption, a violent rending, burst.

Aúfspucken, *v. tr.* to spit upon.

Aúfspulen, *v. tr.* 1) to wind on spools, to spool. Garn —, to wind the thread about the bobbin. 2) to spool the whole.

Aúfspülen, *v. tr.* 1) to wash or carry earth or other substances to a shore &c. 2) to cleanse by ablution, to wash, to wash up [the dishes &c.].

Aúfspunden, **Aufspünden**, *v. tr.* to unbung [a cask].

Aúfspüren, *v. tr.* to find out or discover something intended to be hid, to trace out. Wild —, to track game.

Aúfstacheln, *v. tr.* 1) to take up with a prick, to prick up. 2) to rouse with a goad. *Fig.* Einen —, to goad or spur on, to incite any one, to rouse any one up.

Aúfstaffiren, *v tr.* [am. hatters] to fit up a hat.

Aúfstallen, *v. tr.* to stable oxen &c. in order to fatten them.

Aúfstämmen, V. Aufstemmen.

Aúfstampfen, I. *v. intr.* to stamp the ground. Er stampfte mit dem Fuße auf, he stamped the ground. II. *v. tr.* 1) to strike by pressing the foot hastily downwards, to stamp. 2) to fasten to by stamping. Den Kopf einer Nadel —, [am. pinmakers] to head a pin. 3) to open by stamping. 4) to finish stamping.

Aúfstand, *m.* [-es, *pl.* -stände] 1) the act of standing up, rising, rise, stirring. 2) *Fig.* a sedition, rising, a rebellious commotion, insurrection. Einen — erregen, to raise a stir.

Aúfstapeln, *v. tr.* to pile up. Holz —, to stack up wood, to pile up wood. *Fig.* Schätze —, to hoard up riches.

Aúfstarren, *v. intr.* 1) to stand up, to stare. Sein Haar starrte auf, his hair bristled. 2) to stare up towards.

Aúfstauben, *v. intr.* [u. w. seyn] to rise as dust.

Aúfstäuben, *v. tr.* 1) to send up as dust. 2) to sprinkle with dust.

Aúfstäubern, *v. tr.* 1) to rouse or start. 2) to discover.

Aúfstauchen, *v. tr.* 1) to push or press upon. 2) Ein Stück Eisen —, [among smiths] to shorten a piece of iron by beating it lengthwise. 3) [= in die Höhe stauchen] Den Flachs —, to set up steeped or ruited flax in order to dry it; das Wasser —, to dam up water.

Aúfstaunen, *v. intr.* to look up in amazement.

Aúfstechen, *ir.* I. *v. tr.* 1) to raise or pitch with a pointed instrument [with a fork &c.]. Ein Stück Fleisch —, to fork meat; Heu —, [in husb.] to fork hay. 2) to open by a puncture. Ein Geschwür —, to lance or open an aposteme. *Fig.* Einem den Schwären —, to tell any one an unpleasant truth. 3) to prick or puncture again, to mark by new incisions. Eine Kupferplatte —, [am. engravers] to retouch a copper-plate; eine Spitze —, to pink lace anew. 4) to fasten upon by stitching. 5) to mark with stitches on the surface. 6) [in seamen's language] *a*) Einen Rücken oder Katzenrücken —, to become broken-backed or cambered. *b*) Zwei Taue —, to bend or splice two ropes together. *c*) Die Halsen und Schoten —, to let go tacks and sheets. II. *v. intr.* [a sea-term] Dicht bei dem Winde or in den Wind —, to haul the wind, sail in the wind's eye.

Aúfstecher, *m.* [-s, *pl.* -] one that opens any thing by a puncture.

Aúfstecken, *v. tr.* 1) to pin up [a gown &c.]. Die Haare —, to truss up one's hair. 2) to put upon, to put up. Ein Licht —, to put a candle into a candlestick; mit aufgestecktem [more usual aufgepflanztem] Bajonet, with fixed bayonet; die Nadeln —, [am. pinmakers] to stick the pins [in papers]; eine Flagge —, to set up, to plant a flag; die Flagge im Schau —, [in seamen's language] to hoist the flag with a waft. 3) to fasten upon with pins, to pin. 4) to make up again with pins, to fit up again with pins.

Aúfstecknadel, *f.* a large pin, used for pinning up a gown &c.

Aúfstehen, *ir. v intr.* 1) [u. w. haben] *a*) to stand open. Die Thür steht auf, the door is open. *b*) to stand fast and to be stopped. Der Pfahl steht auf, the pale touches a stone or something and enters the ground no farther. 2) [u. w. seyn] to rise [from the ground &c.]. Vom Tische —, to rise from table; vom Stuhle —, to get up, to rise from a seat; er stand auf, he rose from bed; früh —, to rise, to get up early, to turn out early; da der Tag anbrach, stand der König auf, [Dan. VI] the king arose early; Einer, der früh aufsteht, an early riser; vor Einem —, to rise up to any one; ein Vogel, der [vor dem Hunde] aufsteht, [among sportsmen] a bird that rises from the ground; die Pflanzen und Blumen stehen auf, the stalks of the plants and flowers rise upright again; das Schiff steht auf [in seamen's language] the ship rights. *Fig* Ein Prophet ist aufgestanden, a prophet arose; von einer Krankheit —, to recover; von dem Tode or von den Todten —, to rise from the dead, to arise; wider Einen —, to rise or arise against any one; die Polen standen gegen die Russen auf, the Poles rose against the Russians.

Aúfsteifen, *v. tr.* 1) to stiffen [a hat &c.]. 2) to stiffen, to starch afresh.

Aúfsteigen, *ir. v. intr.* [u. w. seyn] 1) to move upwards, to ascend, to go up, to rise, to arise, to mount. Auf- und absteigen, to step or get up and down; auf das Pferd —, to mount on horseback. 2) to ascend, to mount up, to rise, to arise. Der —de Stengel, [in botany] ascending stem [in distinction from the descending stem]; eine Kitte Hühner, die vor unserer Front aufstieg, brachte unser Fußvolk in Unordnung, a covey of partridges springing in our front, put our infantry in disorder; Dünste steigen von feuchten Stellen auf, vapours arise from humid places; das Aufsteigen der Dünste von der Erde, the ascent of vapours from the earth; das Aufsteigen der Flüssigkeiten in einer gläsernen Röhre, [in nat. hist.] ascent of fluids; der Rauch steigt auf, the smoke rises; es stieg eine Röthe in ihrem Gesichte auf, the blood rose to her cheeks, she blushed; die aus dem Magen —den Dünste, the vaporous ascensions from the stomach; der Wind steigt auf, [in seamen's lang.] the wind begins to blow; die —de Linie, [in genealogy] ascending line; [in anat.] die —de große Pulsader, the ascending part of the aorta; die —den Gefäße, ascending vessels; das Aufsteigen der Mutter, [in med.] hysterics. *Fig.* Ein Gedanke stieg in mir auf, a thought rose within me; die Sonne steigt hinter den Bergen auf, the sun rises from behind the mountains; [in astronomy] —de Zeichen, ascending signs; die —de Breite, ascending latitude; der —de Knoten, ascending node, the northern node [in distinction from the descending node]; [in astrology] aufsteigend, ascendant.

Aúfsteigung, *f.* 1) the act of ascending, arising. 2) [in astronomy, that degree of the equator reckoned from the first of Aries eastward, which rises with a star, or any point in the ecliptic] ascension. Die — ist entweder gerade oder schief, ascension is either right or oblique.

Aufsteigungsunterschied, *m.* [in astron.] ascensional difference [the difference between the right and oblique ascension of the same point on the surface of the sphere].

Aúfstellen, *v. tr.* 1) to set up, put up. Die Bücher [auf das Bücherbret] —, to put the books upon the shelves; diese Waaren sind zum Verkaufe aufgestellt, these goods are put up or exposed to sale; Vieh —, [in husbandry] to stable cattle in order to fatten it; einen Zeugen —, to bring a witness. *Fig.* Ein Beispiel —, to exhibit an example; gefährliche Grundsätze —, to lay down dangerous maxims, principles. 2) to cause to be opened. Eine Mausefalle —, to set a mouse-trap; Netze —, to lay or spread nets.

Aúfstemmen, I. *v. tr.* to force open with a crow-bar. Eine Thür —, to open a door with a crow-bar. II. *v. r.* sich —, to place or put firmly on any thing. Die Elbogen auf den Tisch —, to lean one's elbows upon a table; sich —, to lean upon.

Aúfstempeln, *v. tr.* 1) to stamp. 2) to impress with some mark or figure. 3) to stamp anew.

Aúfsteppen, *v. tr.* [am. sempstresses] to fasten upon by quilting, to quilt.

Aúfsteuern, *v. intr.* [u. w. seyn] to steer upward.

Aúfsticheln, *v. tr.* 1) to open by pricking. 2) to take up by pricking repeatedly.

Aúfsticken, *v. tr.* to embroider upon. Dem Stoffe Blumen —, to embroider flowers upon the stuff.

Aúfstieben, *ir. v. intr.* [u. w. seyn] 1) to rise as dust. 2) [among sportsmen] to rise quickly from the ground [said of larks &c.].

Aúfstieren, *v. intr.* to stare up.

Aúfstiften, V. Anstiften.

Aúfstimmen, *v. tr.* to tune higher.

Aúfstöbern, *v. tr.* [for Auftreiben or Aufjagen] to rouse; [am. hunters] to start [game]. **Fig.* to discover, to find out, to meet with.

Aúfstöhnen, I. *v. intr.* to groan. Schwer —, to fetch a deep groan. II. *v. tr.* to awake by groaning.

Aúfstopfen, *v. tr.* to stuff anew [chairs &c.].

Aúfstoppeln, *v. tr.* to collect things thinly scattered, to gather.

Aúfstören, *v. tr.* 1) to stir, to excite from a state of rest, to rouse up. Der Mann schläft, stört ihn nicht auf, the man is asleep, do not disturb him. 2) [= aufwühlen] Lasset das Gefäß stehen, ihr stört den Satz auf, let the vessel stand, you will disturb the sediment; das Feuer —, to stir the fire. *Fig.* Einen —, to stir any one up.

‖ **Aúfstoß**, *m.* [-es] V. Zufall, Krankheit.

Aúfstoßen, *ir.* I. *v. tr.* 1) to push open [a door &c.]. Sich die Haut —, to gall or fret one's skin. 2) to push upon or against another thing. Den Kopf auf einen Pfosten —, to knock one's head against a post. 3) to push or thrust upward. Den Staub mit den Füßen —, to stamp up the dust. 4) to rouse by a kick. [among sportsmen] Der Hund stößt einen Hasen, wildes Geflügel auf, the dog starts a hare, flushes feathered game. II. *v. intr.* [u. w. seyn] 1) to be pushed upward, to rise. † Der Knoblauch stößt mir auf, the garlick rises in my stomach. [= Gähren] to begin to ferment or to work, to ferment again, to grow thick, to become acid. Der Wein stößt auf, the wine grows thick, becomes acid. 2) to strike upon a thing. Das Schiff stößt auf, the ship is aground; die Galeere stieß auf eine Sandbank auf, the galley struck upon a sand. *Fig.* to fall in the way, to meet with. Ein sonderbarer Mensch ist mir aufgestoßen, I met with an odd fellow; es stößt mir eine Gelegenheit auf, I meet with an opportunity. 3) *Fig.* to grow sick [said of children and domestic animals].

Aúfstoßen, *n.* [-s] rising of the stomach.

Aúfstößig, *adj.* and *adv.* 1) turned sour, acid. 2) growing sick. Die Forellen sind —, the trouts throw up their food. 3) irritated, inimical.

Aúfstrahlen, *v. intr.* 1) to rise radiantly. 2) to emit rays upward.

Aúfstrauben, *v. intr.* to rise and stand erect, to bristle [said of stiff hair and of bristles].

Aúfsträuben, *v. tr.* and *r.* sich —, to erect, to bristle, to stand on end. Vor Entsetzen sträubten sich seine Haare auf, his hair stood on end with horror.

Aúfstreben, *v. intr.* 1) to rise aloft. 2) to use an effort to get up. *Fig.* to aspire after.

Aúfstrecken, *v. tr.* to stretch up.

Aúfstreich, *m.* [-es, *pl.* -e] auction, public sale, outcry. Im —e verkaufen, to sell by auction.

Aufstreicheisen, *n.* a tool used for shearing the cloth against the grain.

Aúfstreicheln, *v. tr.* to rub gently, to stroke upward.

Aúfstreichen, *ir.* I. *v. tr.* 1) to lay on, to spread. Eine Farbe —, to lay on a colour. 2) to stroke upward [the hair &c.]. 3) [among cloth-shearers] to shear the cloth against the grain. 4) to strike up [a march &c.]. II. *v. intr.* V. Aufstreifen.

Aúfstreifeln, **Aúfstreifen**, I. *v. tr.* 1) to turn up, to fold back [the sleeves &c.]. Sich die Aermel —, to tuck up one's sleeves. 2) to open by stripping. Trockene Bohnen —, to unstring dry beans. 3) to gall or fret by grazing a wall &c. Sich die Haut —, to fret or rub off one's skin. II. *v. intr.* to rub or touch lightly in passing. Die Kugel streift auf dem Boden auf, the ball grazes the ground; dieser Mantel ist zu lang, er streift auf der Erde auf, this cloak is too long, it trails on the ground.

Aúfstreiten, *v. tr.* to awake by a loud dispute.

Aúfstreuen, *v. tr.* to strew upon, sprinkle on. Zucker auf den Kuchen —, to sprinkle the cake with sugar.

Aúfstricken, *v. tr.* to consume or expend in knitting [all the cotton &c.].

Aúfstriegeln, *v. tr.* 1) to curry upward. 2) to curry again. † and ‡ *Fig.* Sich —, to dress, to adorn, to trim or rig one's self out.

Aúfströmen, *v. tr.* to wash or carry upon by streaming.

Aúfstücken, *v. tr.* to patch upon.

Aúfstufung, *f.* 1) gradation. 2) [a figure of rhetoric, in which a sentence rises, as it were, step by step] climax.

Aúfstülpen, *v. tr.* to turn up, to cock. Einen Hut —, to cock a hat; die Stiefel —, to top boots; eine aufgestülpte Nase, a cocked up nose.

Aúfstürmen, I. *v. intr.* [u. w. seyn] to storm upward. II. *v. tr.* 1) to drive upward storming. 2) to open by violence.

Aúfstürzen, I. *v. tr.* 1) to clap upon, put on. Den Deckel auf den Topf —, to put the cover upon the pot; die Perrücke, die Haube &c. —, to put on one's wig, cap &c. in a hurry. 2) to set up. II. *v. intr.* to fall violently upon.

Aúfstutzen, I. *v. tr.* to turn up [the brim of a hat]. *Fig.* to trim, to dress, to adorn. Waaren zum Verkaufe —, to trim up things for sale. II. *v. intr.* to look up with confusion.

Aufstützen, I. *v. tr.* 1) to lean upon. 2) to prop. II. *v. r.* sich —, to lean upon a thing.

Aufstutzer, *m.* [-s, *pl.* -] he that turns up, cocks.

Aufstützig, V. Aufstößig.

Aufsuchen, *v. tr.* to seek for, to search for. Einen —, to search for any one, to go in quest of any one; er durchstreifte die Stadt, um mich aufzusuchen, he ranged the town to seek me out; eine Stelle im Buche —, to look after a passage; Einen — lassen, to cause search to be made for any one; Wachteln &c. —, [among sportsmen] to quest for quails &c.

1. **Aufsummen**, *v. tr.* to sum up, to increase. — lassen, to let run up; sich —, to run up.

2. **Aufsummen**, I. *v. intr.* [u. w. seyn] to rise buzzing or humming. II. *v. tr.* to awake by buzzing or humming.

Aufsumsen, *v. tr.* to awake by humming.

Auftafeln, *v. tr.* 1) to bring to table, to serve up [a meal]. 2) [am. clothiers] to fold [a piece of cloth].

Auftakeln, *v. tr.* [a sea term] to rig, to new-rig. Nicht gut aufgetakelt, not rigged ship-shape. *Fig.* [in contempt] Sich —, to dress, to accoutre, to rig one's self out.

Auftaljen, *v. tr.* [a sea term] to bowse.

Auftanzen, I. *v. intr.* 1) to dance by any one's order. 2) *Fig.* to dance attendance. II. *v. tr.* 1) to wear out by dancing. 2) to make sore by dancing.

Auftappen, *v. tr.* [a sea term] to peak the yards.

Auftassen, *v. tr.* [in husbandry] to shock, to stack up piles of sheaves.

Auftaumeln, *v. intr.* [u. w. seyn] to rise up reeling or staggering.

Aufthauen, I. *v. intr.* [u. w. seyn] to thaw. *Fig.* Er thauet auf, he begins to speak again, to grow gay. II. *v. tr.* to thaw [ice, snow &c.].

Aufthauungspunkt, *m.* that degree of heat on the thermometer at which ice thaws.

Aufthun, *ir.* I. *v. tr.* 1) to put upon a thing. Das Essen —, to dish meat [to put it on a dish]. 2) to open [a door &c.]. *Fig.* Den Mund —, to speak; die Ohren —, to hearken, to listen; die Augen —, to see attentively; endlich hat er die Augen aufgethan, at length he has opened his eyes, has seen his mistake. 2) *Fig.* to show, to disclose. II. *v. r.* sich —, 1) to open. Die Blumen thun sich auf, the flowers expand; die Erde thut sich auf, the earth gapes; der Himmel thut sich auf, the sky is clearing up. 2) [a sea term] to loom. Das Land, die Küsten thun sich auf, the land, the coast begins to loom.

Aufthürmen, I. *v. tr.* to raise up like a tower, to pile up. Sie thürmen Berge auf Berge auf, they pile hills upon hills. II. *v. r.* sich —, to tower. *Fig.* Die Wogen thürmen sich auf, the waves run mountain high.

Auftiefen, *v. tr.* [am. coppersmiths] to beat out.

Auftippen, I. *v. intr.* to tip, to tap upon a thing. II. *v. tr.* to awake by tapping.

Auftischen, *v. tr.* to place the meat on the table, to serve up. *Fig.* Alltägliche Geschichten —, to tell trite stories.

Auftoben, I. *v. intr.* [u. w. haben and seyn] to bluster, to roar, to be tumultuous. Die Winde toben auf, the winds bluster. II. *v. tr.* to awake by blustering, roaring.

Auftönen, *v. intr.* to sound loudly.

Auftornen, *v. intr.* [a sea term] V. Aufdrehen.

Auftrag, *m.* [-es, *pl.* -träge] the act of carrying upon, of laying on. Der — der Farben, the laying on of colours. *Fig.* *a*) Der — eines Gutes, eines Lehens, [in law] transmission, conveyance, transference of an estate, of a fief. *b*) something to be told or done, a mandate, order, commission, charge. Einem einen — ertheilen, to give a commission to any one; er richtete seinen — aus, he told his errand or message; er hat den — besorgt, ausgerichtet, he has done the errand, executed the commission.

Auftrags-besorger, *m.* commissioner. —**brief**, *m.* V. —schreiben. —**handel**, *m.* buying and selling on commission. Einen — handel führen, to trade or do business on commission. —**schreiben**, *n.* letters patent or other writing from proper authority, empowering a person to perform some office or execute some business, power of attorney.

Auftragen, *ir.* I. *v. tr.* 1) to carry up. 2) to put or place upon a thing. Die Speisen auf den Tisch —, to serve up meats; laßt das Mittag[s]-essen —, send in dinner, desire dinner to be sent in; kalte Küche —, to spread a cold repast; Farben auf Leinwand —, to apply colours on canvass; die Farbe sollte so dünn aufgetragen werden, the colouring should be laid on so thin; Gold —, [among gilders upon metal] to lay on the gold, to apply the gold; zum Vergolden —, to apply a lay of composition; das Auftragen der Farbe, [am. printers] beating; das Auftragen der Farbe mittelst einer Walze, [am. printers] rolling; einen Riß —, to draw a plan. 3) *Fig.* *a*) to lay on, to charge. Einem eine Arbeit, ein Geschäft —, to charge any one with a task, to commission any one with a business. *b*) [in feudal law] to transfer, to convey [an estate, a fief]. 4) to waste with use. Kleidungsstücke —, to wear out a suit of clothes. II. *v. intr.* to expand, to swell a thing lying upon another.

Auftragewalze, *f.* [in print.] a roller.

Auftrager, *m.* [-s, *pl.* -] 1) one that serves up or in. 2) he that charges another with any thing.

Auftrampeln, I. *v. intr.* 1) to trample upon a thing. 2) to make a great noise by trampling. II. *v. tr.* 1) to fasten, to fix by trampling. 2) to awake by trampling.

Auftrappeln, I. *v. intr.* to trample a little. II. *v. tr.* V. Auftrampeln.

Aufträufeln, I. *v. intr.* [u. w. seyn] to fall in small drops upon a thing, to drop upon. II. *v. tr.* to drop. Tropfen auf Zucker —, to drop on sugar [a liquid medicine &c.].

Auftraufen, *v. intr.* [u. w. seyn] to fall in great drops, or to drop upon a thing.

Auftreffen, *ir. v. intr.* 1) to strike upon a thing, to hit on something. 2) to find any one out of bed, still up, not yet gone to bed.

Auftreiben, *ir.* I. *v. tr.* 1) to drive up, to cause to rise. Einen aus dem Bette —, to drive any one up from his bed; ein wildes Schwein —, [among hunters] to uncouch a wild boar. V. Aufjagen. Die Winde treiben den Leib auf, wind occasions a distension of the belly; den Acker —, [in husbandry] to plough a field again. *Fig.* Geld —, to raise money; ich kann ihn nicht —, I cannot find him. 2) to fasten upon by driving or forcing. Einen Ring auf ein Rad —, to drive a ring upon a wheel. II. *v. intr.* [u. w. seyn] [in seamen's language] 1) to drive or run aground. 2) to fall or drive aboard of a ship, to run foul of another ship.

Auftreiblich, *adj.* and *adv.* that is to be found with some difficulty.

Auftrennen, I. *v. tr.* to unsew, unstitch, to rip open [a seam]. Ein Kleid —, to unseam, to rise a garment. II. *v. intr.* to open, to part, to divide.

Auftreten, *ir.* I. *v. intr.* [u. w. seyn] 1) to set the foot upon the ground. Er kann mit dem kranken Fuße nicht —, he cannot put his bad foot to the ground; behutsam —, to walk with cautious tread. *Fig.* to proceed nicely, cautiously. Er ist sehr empfindlich, Sie müssen leise bei ihm —, he is rather irritable, you must not proceed with him harshly. 2) to step forward, to make one's appearance as an orator &c. Zum ersten Mahle auf der Bühne als Schauspieler —, to make one's first appearance on the stage. 3) Gegen Einen —, to rise against a person, to declare one's self as his enemy, accuser &c.; als Zeuge wider Einen —, to appear at witness against any one. II. *v. tr.* 1) to open by treading. 2) to fasten one thing upon another by treading.

Auftriefen, *v. intr.* [u. w. seyn] to drop, drip upon something.

Auftrieseln, V. Aufdrieseln.

Auftrinken, *v. tr.* 1) to drink, to suck in, to absorb, to imbibe. 2) to drink the whole, to drink up.

Auftritt, *m.* [-es, *pl.* -e] 1) the act of stepping forward, exhibition of the person, exhibition of the character, introduction of a person to the public in a particular character, appearance. Der erste — eines Schauspielers auf der Bühne, the first appearance of an actor on the stage; sein — als Redner, his appearance as an orator; der Ruf eines Mannes hängt von seinem ersten — in der Welt ab, the reputation of a man depends upon the first step he makes in the world. 2) [so much of an act of a play as passes between the same persons in the same place] a scene. *Fig.* Ein lächerlicher —, a ridiculous scene; ein fürchterlicher —, a dreadful event. 3) a thing to step upon, step. Der — an einer Kutsche, step of a coach; der — an einer Brustwehr, the banquette of a parapet.

Auftrittbank, *f.* the treadle of a lace-maker's loom.

Auftrocknen, I. *v. tr.* 1) to dry up. Thränen —, to wipe off tears. 2) to dry for future use. II. *v. intr* [u. w. seyn] 1) to dry, to grow dry. 2) to stick to in drying.

Auftrommeln, I. *v. intr.* to beat, to strike. Auf den Tisch —, to drum on the table. II. *v. tr.* 1) to awake by drumming. 2) to beat up.

Auftrompeten, *v. tr.* 1) to perform on a trumpet. 2) to awake by sounding a trumpet.

Auftröpfeln, I. *v. intr.* [u. w. haben and seyn] to fall in small drops upon something. II. *v. tr.* to let fall in small drops upon something. Auf Zucker —, to drop on sugar.

Auftropfen, *v. intr.* [u. w. seyn] to drop upon.

Auftrüben, *v. tr.* to trouble a liquor by disturbing the sediment.

Auftrumpfen, *v. intr.* to play a high trump. *and ‡ *Fig.* to make a smart reply.

Auftunken, *v. tr.* to eat up sauce &c. by dipping one's bread in it.

Auftupfen, I. *v. intr.* to tap upon something. II. *v. tr.* 1) to take up tapping. 2) to awake by tapping or striking gently.

Auftuschen, *v. tr.* to retouch with Indian ink [a drawing].

Aufwachen, *v. intr.* [u. w. seyn] to awake, to cease to sleep, to rouse or wake up. *Fig.* Der Geist wacht aus seiner Unthätigkeit auf, the mind awakes from its torpor; sein Gewissen wacht auf, his conscience awakes.

Aufwachsen, *ir. v. intr.* [u. w. seyn] to grow, to grow up. *Fig.* In Eitelkeit und Thorheit —, to grow up in vanity and folly.

Aufwagen, *v. r.* sich —, to venture to rise.

Aufwägen, *v. tr.* [with some authors *reg.*, with others *ir.*] to raise with a lever. *Fig.* Eine Sache mit Gold —, to buy a thing at an extravagant rate or exceedingly dear. V. Aufwiegen.

Aufwählen, *v. tr.* [at cards] to draw, to choose.

Aufwallen, *v. intr.* [u. w. seyn] to swell, heave, or be agitated by the action of heat, to rise in bubbles, to bubble. Die Milch wallt auf, the milk bubbles up, wallops. Das — des Meeres, swell of the sea; sein Blut wallt auf, his blood boils. *Fig.* Eine —de Hitze, a transitory heat; sein Herz wallt vor Freude auf, his heart dilates for joy.

Aufwällen, *v. tr.* 1) to boil a little, to give a warm. 2) to form into heaps.

Aufwallung, *f.* boiling, bubbling, ebullition. *Fig.* effervescence, emotion.

Aufwalzen, *v. tr* 1) to wind or roll upon a roll. 2) to open by rolling.

Aufwälzen, *v. tr.* to roll upward. to roll up. *Fig.* Einem ein Geschäft —, to burden any one with a business.

Aufwand, *m.* [-es] [a laying out or expending, that which is used, employed, laid out or consumed] expense. Große Unternehmungen werden nur durch einen großen — von Geld, Zeit und Mühe vollbracht, great enterprises are accomplished only by a great expenditure of money, time and labour; ein großer —, sumptuousness; ein Hang zum —e, a disposition to expensiveness, extravagance; diese Sache erfordert großen —, this affair requires great expense.

Aufwandsgesetz, *n.* sumptuary law.

Aufwandeln, I. *v. intr.* [u. w. seyn] to go or walk upward. II. *v. tr.* [in the Romish church] to raise [the host].

Aufwanken, *v. intr.* [u. w. seyn] 1) to fall upon something in tottering. 2) to rise totteringly.

Aufwärmen, *v. tr.* to warm again, to warm up [meat]. Ein aufgewärmtes Gericht, a second-hand dish. *Fig.* Einen alten Streit —, to renew an old dispute; ein aufgewärmter Witz, a hackneyed or hackney wit.

Aufwarten, *v. intr.* to wait, to be within call, to wait on or upon any one. Den Gästen bei Tische —, to wait on the guests at table; Einem bei Tische mit einem Glase Wein —, to help any one to a glass of wine at table; kann ich Ihnen mit sonst etwas —? do you wish for any thing else? kann ich Ihnen jetzt mit einer Tasse Thee —? will you have a cup of tea now? ||bei einer Hochzeit —, to perform dances at a wedding; der Hund wartet auf, the dog waits. *Fig.* Einem —, to wait on any one, to pay a visit to any one; häufig bei Hofe —, to dance attendance at court. Syn. V. Besuchen.

Aufwartegeld, *n.* —lohn, *m.* wages paid to a waiter.

Aufwärter, *m.* [-s, *pl.* -] waiter, servant.

Aufwärterdienst, *m.* the place or service of a waiter. —lohn, *m.* wages paid to a waiter.

Aufwärterinn, *f.* waiting-maid, waiting-woman, maid.

Aufwärts, *adv.* upward, upwards. — sehen, to look up.

Aufwartsam, *adj.* and *adv.* V. Dienstfertig.

Aufwärtszieher, *m.* [-s, *pl.* -] [in anatomy, a muscle which serves to raise the eye] elevator of the eye.

Aufwartung, *f.* waiting, serving, attendance. Die — bei Einem haben, to wait on any one; er hat jetzt die — bei Hofe, he is now in waiting at court; ||die — bei Hochzeiten, musical performance at weddings. *Fig.* Einem seine — machen, to pay one's respects to any one; ich bin gekommen, um Ihnen meine — zu machen, I am come to pay you my respects.

Aufwasch, *m.* [-es] **Aufwäsche**, *f.* all the kettles, dishes &c. that are to be washed after dinner.

Aufwaschfaß, *n.* —kübel, *m.* washing-tub, wash-tub. —wasser, *n.* dish-water, dish-wash.

Aufwaschen, *ir. v. tr.* 1) to clean by washing, to wash up [the kettles or dishes in the kitchen]. **Fig.* Es ist Ein —, it is but one trouble, it may all be done at the same time. 2) to remove by washing and scouring, to wash away. 3) to consume in washing [all the soap]. 4) to gall or fret by washing. Sich die Hände —, to make one's hands sore by washing.

Aufwäscher, *m* [-s, *pl.* -] **Aufwäscherinn**, *f.* scullion, the scullery-maid.

Aufweben, *v. tr.* 1) to consume or expend in weaving. 2) to unweave.

Aufwechsel, *m* [-s, *pl.* -] V. Aufgeld, Agio.

Aufwecken, *v. tr.* to rouse from sleep, to awake, to awaken. *Fig* Die im Herzen schlafende Liebe weckt man leicht auf, that love which lies dormant in the heart is easily awakened; gute Laune weckt die Gesellschaft auf, good humour enlivens society; ein aufgeweckter Gesell[e], a joyous, jolly fellow.

Aufwecker, *m.* [-s, *pl* -] 1) he that awakes any one out of sleep, awakener. 2) V. Wecker.

Aufwehen, *v. tr.* 1) to blow upwards. Der Wind wehet den Staub auf, the wind raises the dust. 2) to open by blowing. Der Wind wehete das Fenster auf, the wind blew the window open. 3) [= anfachen] Das Feuer zur hellen Flamme —, to blow the fire up to a blaze.

Aufweichen, I. *v. tr.* 1) [to make less hard] to soften, to mollify [wax]. 2) to open by softening or soaking [an abscess]. Ein aufweichendes Pflaster, an emollient plaster. II. *v. intr.* [u. w. seyn] 1) to grow less hard, to soften and to open. 2) to thaw.

Aufweifen, *v. tr.* 1) to reel. 2) to reel up the whole.

Aufweifbürste, *f.* a brush used by goldsmiths.

Aufweinen, I. *v. intr.* 1) to weep aloud. 2) to weep with a look directed upward. II. *v. tr.* to awake by weeping.

Aufweisen, *ir. v. tr.* to show, to exhibit [papers or documents in court &c.]. Seine Vollmacht —, to produce one's power of attorney.

Aufweißen, *v. tr.* to whitewash again [a wall &c.].

||**Aufwelken**, *v. tr.* V. Dörren.

Aufwellen, V. Aufwallen.

Aufwenden, *ir.* [with some authors *reg*] *v. tr.* to lay out, to use, to employ, to expend. Viel Geld —, to spend a great deal of money; Zeit und Mühe —, to expend time and labour.

Aufwerfen, *ir.* I. *v. tr.* 1) to throw or cast upward. Einen Ball —, to toss up a ball; die Erde aus dem Graben —, to throw up the earth from a ditch. Der Maulwurf hat hier [Erde] aufgeworfen, the mole has thrown up the earth here; das Wasser wirft im Kochen Blasen auf, water raises bubbles when boiling. 2) to turn up [one's nose &c.]. Die Nasenlöcher —, to distend the nostrils; aufgeworfene Lippen, pouting lips. 3) to throw upon another thing. *Fig.* Eine Frage —, to start a question; einen Zweifel —, to raise a doubt. 4) to throw up, to raise [a bank]. Eine Schanze —, to throw up a battery; einen Wall —, to cast up a rampart; einen Graben —, to dig a trench. 5) to throw open [a door &c.]. Die Karten —, to throw up the cards. II. *v. r.* sich —, to set up for, to usurp authority. Eumenes, einer der Heerführer Alexanders, warf, nach dem Tode seines Herrn, sich selbst zum Herrn auf, Eumenes, one of Alexander's captains, set up for himself after the death of his master; sich zum Reformator —, to set up for a reformer; sich wider Jemand —, to rise, to rebel against any one.

* and † **Aufwettern**, *v. tr.* to thunder any one out of sleep.

Aufwichsen, *v. tr.* 1) to turn up with wax. Seinen Schnurrbart —, to turn up one's mustachios with wax. † 2) to dress up, to clothe elegantly. † and ‡ 3) *Fig.* to treat splendidly, to feast.

Aufwickeln, *v. tr.* 1) to roll, fold or wind upon. Zwirn, Seide —, to wind up thread, silk; die Haare —, to roll one's hair in curling papers. 2) to unroll, to unfold, to unwind.

Aufwiegelei, *f.* rousing to rebellion, or mutiny.

Aufwiegeln, *v. tr.* to stir up to rebellion. Er wiegelte die Numidier wider ihn auf, he stirred up the Numidians against him; das Volk —, to raise up the people.

Aufwiegen, *ir.* I. *v. intr.* to exceed in gravity, to outweigh. II. *v. tr.* V. Aufwägen. *Fig* Diese Freude wiegt jahrelangen Kummer auf, this joy counterbalances years of sorrow.

Aufwiegler, *m.* [-s, *pl.* -] he that stirs up to rebellion, mutineer, instigator, broiler, firebrand.

Aufwieglervolk, *n.* mutineers.

Aufwieglerei, *f.* attempt or endeavour to stir up to rebellion.

Aufwieglerisch, *adj.* and *adv.* disposed to rebellion, and exerting one's self to stir others up to rebellion.

Aufwiehern, I. *v. intr.* to neigh aloud. II. *v. tr.* to awake by neighing.

Aufwimmern, *v. tr.* to awake by whimpering.

Aufwindeln, *v. tr.* to unswathe [a child].

Aufwinden, *ir.* I. *v. tr.* 1) to wind up [thread, silk &c.]. 2) to raise up by a windlass, to wind up [a weight]. Den Anker —, to heave up the anchor; ein Schiff —, [in seamen's language] to ground a vessel. 3) to open by winding. II. *v. r.* sich —, to wind upward.

Aufwinseln, I. *v. intr.* to utter a moaning sound. Der Hund winselte kläglich auf, the dog whined piteously. II. *v. tr.* to awake by moaning or lamenting.

Aufwippen, V. Wippen.

Aufwirbeln, I. *v. tr.* 1) to unpeg. 2) to whirl up. 3) to awake by beating the drum. II. *v. intr.* [u. w. seyn] to rise whirling.

1. **Aufwirken**, *v. tr.* 1) [among hunters] to cut open. 2) [among bakers] to form the bread.

2. **Aufwirken**, *v. tr.* 1) to consume or expend in weaving or working. 2) to unweave.

Aufwirren, *v. tr.* to disentangle [net work &c.].

Aufwischen, *v. tr.* 1) to wipe up, to wipe away. 2) to wipe upon something.

Aufwittern, *v. tr.* to track by the scent.

Aufwocken, V. Aufrocken.

Aufwogen, *v. intr.* to rise and roll in large waves, to billow. *Fig.* to rise or swell by internal heat.

Aufwölben, *v. tr.* to raise in the shape of a vault.

Aufwolken, *v. tr.* to raise in the shape of a cloud.

Aufwollen, *v. intr.* to wish to rise. Er will gern auf, aber er kann nicht, he wishes to rise, but he cannot.

Aufwühlen, *v. tr.* 1) to root up. 2) to open by rooting. Die Erde —, to turn up earth, to root; die Gräber —, to rake up the graves.

‖**Aufwuhnen**, *v. tr.* V. Aufeisen.

Aufwurf, *m.* [-es, *pl.* -würfe] 1) the act of throwing or casting up. 2) the thing thrown up, especially the earth thrown up in digging.

Aufwürfeln, *v. tr.* to throw the dice upon something.

Aufwürgen, *v. tr.* to devour the whole.

Aufzählen, *v. tr.* to put upon a thing in counting. Geld auf den Tisch —, to pay money down upon the table, to count it out upon the table. *Fig.* to count or tell number by number, to enumerate, to detail. Das Aufzählen von Unglücksfällen, enumeration of disasters.

Aufzanken, *v. tr.* to awake by scolding.

Aufzaubern, *v. tr.* 1) to open by witchcraft. 2) V. Anzaubern.

Aufzäumen, *v. tr.* 1) to bridle [a horse]. *Prov.* Das Pferd bei dem Schwanze —, to turn one's tail to the manger, to begin a thing at the wrong end, to go the wrong way to work. 2) [in cookery] to truss [a fowl &c.].

Aufzechen, *v. tr.* to drink up, to expend every thing in drinking.

Aufzehren, *v. tr.* to consume by eating. Alle Lebensmittel —, to consume all the provisions. *Fig.* Der Gram zehrt ihn auf, he pines or wastes away with sorrow.

Aufzeichnen, *v. tr.* 1) to draw or trace upon something. Eine Blume auf einen Zeug —, to draw a flower upon a stuff. 2) to note, to set down in writing, to write down. Seine Ausgaben —, to book one's expenses; einen Vorfall —, to record an event; die Möbel &c. —, to take an inventory of the furniture &c.

Aufzeichnungsbuch, *n.* [-es, *pl.* -bücher] note-book.

Aufzeigen, *v. tr.* to show, to exhibit [papers, documents in court &c.].

Aufzerren, *v. tr.* 1) to pull up. Einen vom Boden —, to pull any one up from the ground. 2) to pull open.

Aufziehen, *ir.* I. *v. tr.* 1) to open by drawing or pulling. Gestricktes —, to ravel out a piece of knitwork; dieses Pflaster zieht ein Geschwür gut auf, this plaster draws well 2) to put on by drawing and stretching. Saiten [auf ein Tonwerkzeug] —, to string an instrument; die Fäden —, [am. weavers] to warp. *Fig.* Gelindere Saiten —, to lower one's tone, to come down a peg; andere Saiten —, to turn over a new leaf. 3) to paste to, to paste upon. Eine Landkarte —, to paste a map upon canvass. *Fig.* Eine Miene —, to assume, to put on a certain air. 4) to draw up, to raise, to elevate. Den Vorhang —, to draw up the curtain; eine Brücke —, to draw up a bridge; Wasser aus dem Brunnen —, to draw water from a well; ein Segel —, to set a sail; die Sonne zieht die Dünste auf, the sun draws the vapours; eine Uhr —, to wind up a watch, a clock; ein Automat, der sich selbst aufzieht, an automaton which can wind itself up. *Fig.* Pflanzen —, to raise plants; Schafe —, to breed sheep; Kinder —, to bring up, rear up, nurse children; zum Tanze —, to ask any one to dance; Einen —, to raise a humorous laugh at another's expense, to banter or jeer. to play upon any one; er zieht mich mit dem Landleben auf, he rallies me upon a country life; sie zogen ihn auf, they smoked the fellow. Syn. V. Erziehen. 5) [am. goldsmiths] to draw up by beating. 6) to weigh [a ducat &c.]. II. *v. intr.* [u. w. seyn] 1) to draw up. Die Truppen zogen vor dem Palaste auf, the troops drew up in front of the palace; in Parade —, to parade; die Wache zieht auf, the soldiers go upon duty, mount guard. **Fig.* Er zieht lächerlich auf, he cuts a ridiculous figure; prächtig —, to make a grand appearance. 2) to emerge from below the horizon. Es zieht ein Gewitter auf, a thunder-storm is coming on, is drawing near. III. *v. r.* sich —, to rise, arise. Es zieht sich ein Gewitter auf, a storm is rising or getting up.

Aufzieh-brücke, *f.* draw-bridge. V. Zugbrücke. —**hammer**, *m.* a hammer used by metallists for beating out. —**loch**, *n.* in watches and clocks the hole, into which the key is put to wind them up, key-hole.

Aufzieher, *m.* [-s, *pl.* -] 1) he that draws or pulls up; *fig.* he that banters another. 2) [in anatomy] a muscle which serves to raise a part of the body, as the lip or the eye, elevator.

Aufzieherei, *f.* mockery, jeering.

Aufzieren, *v. tr.* to dress up, to trim, to rig.

Aufzittern, *v. intr.* [u. w. seyn] to rise trembling.

Aufzuckern, *v. tr.* to sprinkle with sugar.

Aufzug, *m.* [-es, *pl.* -züge] 1) the act of drawing up or putting up. [= das Aufziehen]. 2) a train marching in ceremonious solemnity, procession. Ein — zu Pferde, a procession of persons on horseback, cavalcade; [in milit. aff.] the drawing up of troops to do duty and mount guard, parade [more properly das Aufziehen]. 3) * [= Anzug] Ein seltsamer —, an odd kind of dress, a strange accoutrement. 4) [among weavers] the warp. 5) the beam of a balance; ‖ [a machine for raising weights] a crane. 6) the act of a play. Ein Trauerspiel in fünf Aufzügen, a tragedy in five acts.

Aufzugs-brücke, *f.* V. Aufziehbrücke. —**geld**, *n.* V. Schleusengeld.

Aufzüglich, *adj.* and *adv.* occasioning a delay.

Aufzupfen, *v. tr.* 1) to ravel out [a ribbon &c.]. 2) to open by plucking.

Aufzürnen, *v. intr.* [u. w. seyn and haben] to start up with anger.

Aufzwängen, *v. tr.* 1) to force upon. 2) to force open.

Aufzwecken, *v. tr.* to fasten upon a thing with tacks, [am. shoemak.] with sparables. Die Hinterflecken —, [among shoemakers] to fasten the heels on with wooden pegs.

Aufzwicken, V. Aufzwecken.

Aufzwingen, *ir. v. tr.* to force upon [aufzwängen]. Die Berghölzer —, [in seamen's lang.] to wring on the wales. *Fig.* Einem eine Wohlthat —, to press a benefit upon any one.

Augapfel, [-s, *pl.* -äpfel] the ball, globe or apple of the eye, eyeball; [the round opening in the middle of the iris] the pupil. *Fig.* a favourite, a beloved object. Dieser Sohn war der — seines Vaters, this son was the darling of his father.

Augbolzen, *m.* [-s, *pl.* -] [in sea language] eyebolt.

Aughäutchen, *n.* [-s, *pl.* -] [in anatomy, the second coat of the eye] the choroid.

Augkrampf, *m.* [-es, *pl.* -krämpfe] [in medicine] a spasm affecting the eye.

Augvorfall, *m.* [-es, *pl.* -fälle] [in medicine] exophthalmia.

Auge, *n.* [-s, *pl.* -n] [Gr. ὄκκος, Lat. *oc-ulus*, Sax. *eage*, Engl. *eye*, Sw. *öga*, Slav. *oko*; seems to be allied to hoch, as it signifies at the same time rund] 1) [the name of certain round or roundish objets] Das — auf einer Pfauenfeder, the eye of a peacock's feather; das — auf einem Würfel, the point, the spot on a die; das — auf einer Karte [Spielkarte], the pip, the point; das — einer Pflanze, the eye, bud, gem of a plant; —n gewinnen, —n bekommen [äugeln], to gem, to bud; das — [Oehr] einer Nadel, the eye of a needle; die —n auf or in dem Käse, the eyes of a cheese; das — an den Stangen des Zaumes, the eye of the bits; [among printers] das — [die Krone, Fläche eines Buchstabens], the eye, face of a letter; [in cookery] das — im Eiweiß, treadle; [in seamen's language] das — des Ankers, V. Ankerauge; das gespießte — an einem Pferdebein, the eye of a hawser, or small cable; das — einer Blockstroppe, the eye of a block-strop; die —n an den beiden Enden der Kabelaring, the eyes in the two ends of the voyol. 2) the eye. [the organ of sight or vision] sight, view [said of animals]. Das rechte —, off-eye [of horses]; die —n betreffend, ocular; so weit man mit den —n sehen kann, within sight; so weit trägt mein — nicht, my sight does not reach so far; in die —n or ins — fallen, to catch the eye; Jemand ins — fassen, to fix one's eyes upon any one; der Herr faßte den Sprecher ins —, the gentleman fixed his eyes upon the speaker; er hatte ein wachsames — auf ihn, he kept a strict eye upon him; Aller —n sind auf euch gerichtet, the eyes of all the world are fixed upon you; große —n machen, to be all astonishment die —n niederschlagen, to abase the eyes; aus den —n verlieren, to lose sight of; ich habe die ganze Nacht kein — zugethan, I did not close my eyes, I did not sleep a wink all night. *Prov.* Was die —n sehen, das glaubt das Herz, seeing is believing; was die —n nicht sehen, kümmert das Herz nicht, what the heart sees not, the heart rues not; gehe mir aus den —n! get out of my sight! avoid my presence! komme mir nicht wieder vor die —n! let me not see your face again! aus den —n, aus dem Sinn, out of sight, out of mind; seldom seen, soon forgotten; unter vier —n, between two persons; vor meinen —n, in my view, before my face; Gnade vor Jemands —n finden, to find favour in any one's eyes. Vier —n sehen besser als zwei, two heads are better than one; das — des Herrn weidet das Pferd, the master's eye makes the horse fat; das — Gottes, the omnipresence, omniscience of God his providence; die —n sind oft größer als der Bauch, better fill a glutton's belly, than his eye. Was Einer im Sinne hat, sieht man ihm in den —n an, in the fore-head and the eye, the index of the mind does lie; * Einem ein Dorn or ein Stachel im — seyn, to raise one's envy; dies ist ihm ein Dorn im —, that's an eye-sore for him; ich bin ihm ein Dorn im —, I am an eye-sore to him; Einen mit scheelen —n ansehen, to look upon any one with an evil eye; mit einem blauen — davonkommen, to come off cheaply; ein — zudrücken [nachsichtig seyn], to wink at, to connive at, to pretend ignorance or blindness; Einem Sand in die —n streuen, to cast a mist before a person's eyes, to dazzle any one; Einem den Daumen aufs — setzen, to keep any one short; †das Kalb in die —n schlagen, to offend any one sensibly. 3) *Fig.* the power of perception, view of the mind, opinion formed by observation, or contemplation]. Und erleuchtete die —n eures Verſtandes, [Eph. 1] the eyes of your understanding being enlightened; etwas aus den —n ſetzen, to forget a thing, to make light of a thing; ein — auf etwas haben or werfen, to have an eye upon, to set one's mind upon a thing; ich habe bei Beſetzung dieſer Stelle meine —n auf Sie geworfen, I have designed you for this place; ſie haben ihren eigenen Vortheil im —, they have an eye to their own advantage; in ihren —n, in their own imagination; in den —n des Volkes, in the people's eyes; in meinen —n, in my opinion.

Augen-achat, m. [in mineral. a species of onyx] V. Katzenauge. —ader, f. [in anat.] salvatella. —ähnlich, adj. and adv. resembling the eye. Mit —ähnlichen Flecken, eyespotted. —arzt, m. oculist. —axe, f. [in optics] the axis of the eye. —bad, n. ophthalmic bath. —bader, m. a basin used for bathing the eyes. —balſam, m. eye-balm. —beſchreibung, f. ophthalmography. —betrug, m. illusion. —binde, f. a binding for the eye. —blende, f. the blinker or blind [on the harness of a horse]. —blick, m. a motion of the eye, twinkle, twinkling. Fig. der jetzige —blick, the present time, the present; jeder —blick, every wink of an eye; in einem —blicke, in the twinkling of an eye, in a trice; der günſtige —blick, the favourable moment; ein —blick zu frühe oder zu ſpät, an instant too soon or too late; auf einen —blick, for a moment, for an instant; helle or lichte —blicke eines Verrückten, [in medicine] the lucid intervals of a deranged man. Prov. Im —blicke kann ſich begeben, was Niemand je gedacht im Leben, it chanceth in an hour, that comes not in seven years. —blicklich, I. adj. momentary, instantaneous. —blickliche Freuden, momentary pleasures. II. adv. instantly, in a moment. —blicks, adv. instantly. —blitz, m. eyeglance, eyeshot. —blöde, —blödigkeit, f. weakness of the eyes. —blutader, f. [in anatomy] ophthalmic artery. —blüthe, f. common pimpernel. —bogen, m. [in anatomy] the iris. —braue, f. the eye brow. Hervorragende —brauen habend, beetle-browed. —brauenäugler, m. [in anatomy] corrugator. —brauenbogen, m. the arch of the eyebrows. —butter, f. gum of the eye. —deckel, m. V. —lied. —diener, m. 1) eye-servant. 2) men-pleaser. —dienſt, m. eye-service. —drüſe, f. [in anatomy] V. Thränendrüſe. —dunkelheit, f. dimness of the eyes. —entzündung, f. inflammation of the eye, ophthalmy. Die trockene —entzündung, oceropthalmia; die harte —entzündung, sclerophthalmia. —fell, n. film of the eye. —feuchtigkeit, f. the aqueous humour of the eye. Die gläſerne or glasartige —feuchtigkeit, the vitreous humour; die kryſtallene —feuchtigkeit, the crystalline lens. —fiſch, m. a species of the blenny [blennius superciliaris]. —fiſtel, f. [in surgery] a fistula of the lacrymal sac, fistula lacrymalis. —flecken, m. the white speck in the eye, haw, dragon albugo. —fluß, m. [in surgery] lippitude. —flüſſig, adj. affected with an ophthalmic fluxion. —forelle, f. an eye-spotted trout. —förmig, adj. and adv. having the form of an eye. —geſchwulſt, m. [in surgery] exophthalmia. —geſchwür, n. [an abscess in the inner canthus of the eye] goat's-eye, egilops. —glas, n. 1) an eyeglass, spectacles. 2) [in telescopes, the glass next the eye] eye glass. —glasſchleifer, m. optician. —grube, f. [in veter. art] the hollow over the eyes of an old horse. —häutchen, n. winking membrane. —höhle, f. the orbit, socket. —höhlenblutader, f. [in anat.] the orbital vein. —höhlennerve, f. [in anat.] ophthalmic or orbital nerve. —höhlenrand, m. [in anat.] the bones which form the orbit of the eye. —höhlenſchlagader, f. [in anat.] the internal orbital artery. —höhlenſpole, f. [in anat.] orbiter externus or internus. —holz, n. V. Paradiesholz. —icht, n. [in mineralogy] tutty. —kitzel, m. sensual gratification of the eye. —knochen, m. cheek-bone. —koralle, f. [in natural history] coral with lamelated star-shaped cavities, white coral. —krampf, m. a spasm affecting the eye. —krankheit, f. a disease of the eye. —krankheitsheilung, f. the cure of the diseases of the eye. —krankheitslehre, f. ophthalmonosology. —kraut, n. V. Schöllkraut. —krebs, m. a cancer in the eye. —leder, n. V. —blende. —lehre, f. ophthalmology. —lehrig, adj. and adv. ophthalmic. —licht, n. 1) the clearness of the eye. 2) the sense of seeing, eyesight. —lied, n. the eyelid. —liederbrand, m. a carbuncle incident to the eyelids. —liederentzündung, f. an inflammation of the eyelids, echinophthalmia. —liederkrampf, m. a spasm affecting the eyelids. —liederkrätze, f. an ulceration and inflammation of the eye with itching, psorophthalmia. —liederlähmung, f. a morbid inversion of the eyelids, phalangosis. —liedhaut, f. membrane of the eyelids. —liedheber, m. a muscle which serves the office of lifting up the eyelid. —liedknorpel, m. [in anat.] tarsus. —liedsband, n. [in anat.] the ligament of the eyelid. —liedsvorfall, m. [in medic.] the falling down of the eyelids. —los, adj. and adv. eyeless. —luſt, f. delight of the eye. —mahl, n. V. —flecken. —marmor, m. eyespotted marble. —maß, n. 1) measure taken merely by the eye. 2) judgment by the eye. Ein gutes —maß haben, to have a correct eye, to be able to judge a distance well. —merk, n. the object, to which the eye is directed. Fig. point, view, aim. Sein —merk auf etwas richten, to aim at a thing. —mittel, n. a medicine for the eyes, ophthalmic. —muskel, m. [in anat.] muscle abductor oculi. —muskelnerve, m. eyestring. —nerve, m. a nerve of the eye. —pappel, f. spiked mallow. —pein, f. a pain in the eye, or a disease of the eye. —pulver, n. 1) powder for the eye [as a remedy]. 2) Fig. very small print. —punkt, m. 1) point of sight; fig. object in view. 2) point of view. —reiz, m. a tickling in the eye. —ring, m. 1) V. —bogen. 2) a ring round the eyes. —rinnen, n. V. —fluß. —roche, m. V. Spiegelroche. —röthe, f. xerophthalmia. —ſalbe, f. eye-salve. —ſchein, m. inspection, view, ocular view, personal observation, autopsy. Etwas in —ſchein nehmen, to take a view of a thing. —ſcheinlich, I. adj. evident, apparent, manifest. Eine —ſcheinliche Gefahr, an imminent danger; ein —ſcheinlicher Beweis, an ocular proof. II. adv. evidently, plainly, clearly, obviously, manifestly. —ſcheinlichkeit, f. evidence, apparentness, manifestness. —ſchießer, m. V. Jungfer or Waſſernymphe. —ſchirm, m. V. Lichtſchirm. —ſchlagader, f. [in anat.] ophthalmic artery. —ſchlange, f. V. Spießſchlange. —ſchleim, m. rheum. —ſchmaus, m. V. —weide. —ſchmerz, m. a pain in the eye. —ſchnecke, f. a kind of eyespotted snail. —ſchwäche, f. weakness of the eye. —ſperre, f. [an instrument used by surgeons in dilating the eye] speculum oculi. —ſpiegel, m. 1) anciently used for Brille. 2) V. —ſperre. 3) V. Alpenſchmetterling. —ſpiel, n. play of the eyes. —ſprache, f. the language of the eyes. —ſproſſe, f. [among sportsmen] brow-antler. —ſtaar, m. an opacity of the crystalline lens or its capsule, cataract. —ſtein, m. 1) every-eye-spotted stone. 2) eye stone. 3) white copperas. —ſtern, m. 1) the pupil. 2) the iris. —ſternerweiterung, f. [in medicine, a disease of the eye, consisting in a preternatural dilation of the pupil, and a consequent dimness] mydriasis. —ſternverlängerung, f. [in medicine, a concretion of the iris of the eye with the cornea, or with the capsule of the crystalline lens] synechia. —täuſchung, f. illusion, deceptive appearance. —treibend, adj. [in botany] gemmiparous. —triefen, n. lippitude, bleeredness. —triefig, adj. and adv. blear-eyed, having sore eyes. —troſt, m. 1) eyebright, the euphrasy of several species. 2) V. Mauſeöhrchen. 3) V. —troſtgras. 4) Fig. an expression of endearment. Ihr Anblick iſt ein wahrer —troſt, a sight of you is good for sore eyes. —troſtgras, n. greater stitchwort. —verdunkelung, f. dimness of sight. —vorfall, m. [in medicine, a protuberance of the eye out of its natural position] exophthalmia. —waſſer, n. 1) eyewater, collyrium. 2) rheum. —waſſerſucht, f. [in medicine, a disease of the eye] hydrophthalmia. —weh, n. pain in the eyes. —weide, f. delight of the eye. —weiß, n. the white of the eye. —weite, f. reach of the eye, extent of vision. —welle, f. V. —achſe. —wimmer, —wimper, m. eyelash. Eingebogene —wimpern, [in medicine] trichiasis. —wink, m. a wink or motion of the eyelid, eyewink. —winkel, m an angle of the eye, canthus. Der größere or innere —winkel, the greater canthus; der kleinere —winkel, the lesser canthus. —winkelgeſchwulſt, f. [in medicine] anchilops. —winkelgeſchwür, n. [in medicine] aegilops. —wölkchen, n. [in medicine] nebula. —wonne, f. V. —luſt. —wurzel, f. the root of the valerian and the dandelion. —zahn, m. eyetooth, canine tooth, cuspidatus. —zauber, m. fascination. —zeuge, m. eye-witness. —zeuge ſeyn von Jemands Verhalten, to witness any one. —zeugniß, n. ocular testimony. —zier, f. 1) beauty of the eyes. 2) [a plant] officinal or garden alkant, or bugloss. —zweig, m. [in anatomy] a branch of the third pair of nerves. —zwiſchenraum, m. the space or interval between the eyes.

Äugeln, I. v. tr. [in gardening] to inoculate, to imp. II. v. intr. 1) [to open and shut the eyes by turns] to twinkle. 2) [among sportsmen] V. Äugen.

Augen, I. v. intr. to gem, to bud. II. v. tr. to mark with spots like eyes.

Äugen, v. intr. [among sportsmen] to eye.

Äugicht, adj. and adv. eye-spotted, ocellated.

Äugig, adj. eyed [a word used chiefly in compositions as blau—, blue-eyed].

Augitporphyr, m. [-s, pl. -e] [in mineral.] augite porphyry.

Äugler, m. [-s, pl. -] one that twinkles. Fig. a flatterer, hypocrite.

* Augment, n. [a letter or syllable added or changed in the tenses of Greek verbs] augment.

Augpunkt, m. [-es, pl. -e] V. Augenpunkt.

Augsburg, n. [-s] Augsburg, Augusta.

Augsburgiſch, adj. Augustan. Die —e Confeſſion, the Augustan confession [drawn up at Augsburg or Augusta by Luther and Melanchthon, in 1530, contains the principles of the Protestants, and their reasons for separating from the Romish church].

Augſprießel, m. [-s, pl. -] V. Augenſproſſe.

|| Augſt, m. [-es, pl. -e] harvest.
Augſtzeit, f. harvest-time.

* Augur, m. [-s, pl. -n] [am. the Romans] augur.

* Auguriren, v. tr. to augur, to predict, to foretell.

Auguſt, m. [-s] [a name of men] Augustus.

Auguſt, m. [-es, pl. -e] 1) [the name of the

Roman Emperor Octavius] Augustus. Das Zeitalter des —, the Augustan age. 2) [the month of] August, harvest-month.

Augustsapfel, *m.* summer white calville. Der rothe —apfel, summer red calville —eiche, *f.* V. Steineiche. —hafer, *m.* hasty oats. —hopfen, *m.* hasty hops. —kirsche, *f.* a sour or tart cherry, agriot. —linde, *f.* V. Speckliade. —monat, *m.* August. —schein, *m.* [in astron.] harvest-moon. —schwamm, *m.* the yellow agaric.

Auguste, *f.* [-ns, *pl.* -n] [a name of women] Augusta.

Augustin and **Augustin**, *m.* [-s, *pl.* -e] [a name of men] Austin.

Augustiner, *m.* [-s, *pl.* -] Austin friar.

Augustiner-kloster, *n.* a monastery of Austin friars or nuns. —mönch, *m.* V. Augustiner. —nonne, *f.* [Augustinerinn] Austin nun. —orden, *m.* order of Austin friars or nuns.

Auhirsch, Auenhirsch, *m.* [-es, *pl.*-e] [among sportsmen] a stag that often visits fields and plains.

Aurikel, *f.* [*pl.* -n] [a plant] auricula, bear's-ear.

***Auripigment**, *n.* [-s] a yellow kind of arsenic, orpiment.

***Aurora**, *f.* [-'s, *poet.* -rens] the rising light of the morning, the dawn of day, morning twilight, aurora.

Aus, [Goth. *us, ut, uta*, Sax. *ut*, Engl. *out*, probably allied to the Lat. *ex*] I. *prep.* [it governs the third case, and denotes *a*) a proceeding from a place or the interior of a place; a proceeding as from ancestors, from a country] out of. Er führte ihn — dem Zimmer, he led him out of the apartment; — dem Wege gehen, to go or stand out of the way; — dem Theater kommen, to come from the play; er kommt — Berlin, he comes from Berlin; er schrieb mir von Paris —, he wrote me from Paris; er ist — Rom, he is a native of Rome; — der alten Familie Ranudo, of the ancient family Ranudo; das Wasser kommt — der Erde hervor, water issues from the earth; Pflanzen wachsen — der Erde, plants grow out of the earth; etwas — dem Hause nehmen, to take any thing out of the house; Einen — dem Graben ziehen, to draw any one out of the ditch; sie wachsen — Kirchthürmen heraus, they grow out of steeples; — der Scheide, from the scabbard; — dem Horaz, out of Horace; — demselben Munde, out of the same mouth; — einer Hand in die andere, from hand to hand; er wurde — unserer Mitte gewählt, he was chosen from among us; — dem Innersten des Herzens, from the inmost soul; — der Mode, out of fashion. *b*) [to denote the material out of which any thing is taken, or of which it is made] Ein Bild — Stein, an image of stone; — Wasser Wein machen, to make wine of water; — Nichts wird nichts, of nothing comes nothing. *Fig.* — Freunden können Feinde werden, friends can become foes; ich mache mir — dieser Sache nichts, I don't care about this affair; — was für Macht [= vermittelst welcher], by what authority; ich weiß es — Erfahrung, I know it by experience; ich ersehe — dem Briefe, I see by the letter; — Liebe, out of love; — Freundschaft, out of friendship; er zahlte mich — eigenen Mitteln, he paid me out of his own funds; — Neid, — Ehrgeiz, out of envy, out of ambition; er tadelt ihn — Haß, he blames him through hatred; — vielen Ursachen, on many accounts; — blossem Verdachte, upon mere suspicion; — Mangel an Gelde, for want of money; — Gehorsam gegen Sie, in obedience to you.

II. *adv.* 1) [denoting the end of any thing, commonly in connection with seyn] out. Die Kirche ist —, church is over; die Zeit ist —, the time is out or up, expired, passed; es ist — mit ihm, it is all over with him, he is undone; höre mich —, hear me out. 2) [sometimes used for heraus and hinaus] *Fig.* Er weiß weder — noch ein, he is at his wit's end; Jahr —, Jahr ein, year by year. 3) — is much used in many compound words, in most of which we observe the sense of a proceeding from a place, or a finishing, ending.

Ausächzen, I. *v. intr.* to cease groaning. II. *v. tr.* Sein Leben —, to breathe one's last.

Ausackern, *v. tr.* to bring out of the ground by ploughing, to plough up or out.

Ausädern, *v. tr.* to pluck the veins out.

Ausäffen, *v. tr.* to mock, to deride.

Ausangeln, *v. tr.* to empty [a pond &c. of fish] by angling.

Ausantworten, *v. tr.* to put into another's hand or power, to deliver up or over.

Ausarbeiten, I. *v. tr.* 1) to make hollow by cutting or engraving, to hollow out. 2) to get out a thing by working. Einen Stein aus der Erde —, to dig a stone out of the earth, to dig up a stone; [among butchers] einen Ochsen —, to flay an ox. 3) to work with labour, to finish off, to polish to the degree of excellence intended. Eine Predigt —, to compose a sermon; eine ausgearbeitete Rede, an elaborate discourse. 4) *Fig.* to perfect by working, to improve by successive operations; [am. hunt.] to blood [young foxhounds &c.]. II. *v. intr.* to cease working. *Fig.* Der Wein hat ausgearbeitet, the wine has done working or fermenting. Syn. Ausarbeiten, Bearbeiten. Bearbeiten denotes merely that one is occupied with, or working at a thing, in order to give it a greater degree of perfection. Ausarbeiten includes also the idea of perfecting or completing. One says: ausarbeiten [to complete, to finish] a sermon, and bearbeiten [elaborate] a certain subject in it.

Ausarbeitung, *f.* 1) perfecting, finishing, elaboration. 2) a composition, intended to prove or illustrate a particular subject, essay, treatise.

Ausart, *f.* [*pl.* -en] the thing degenerated, degeneration.

Ausarten, *v. intr.* [u. w. seyn] to degenerate. Pflanzen und Thiere arten aus, plants and animals degenerate. *Fig.* Die Menschen, die Sitten arten aus, men, manners degenerate.

Ausartung, *f.* degeneration, degeneracy. Die — einer Pflanze, the degeneracy of a plant. *Fig.* Die — der Menschen in neuerer Zeit, the degeneracy of men in modern times.

Ausarzeneien, *v. intr.* to cease to take or use physic.

Ausästen, *v. tr.* to prune [a tree].

Ausathmen, I. *v. intr.* to throw out the breath from the lungs, to respire air. II. *v. tr.* to breathe out, to respire. *Fig.* Den letzten Seufzer —, to breathe the last, to expire, to die.

Ausätzen, *v. tr.* 1) to corrode, to eat, to wear away. 2) to eat through. 3) to hollow, to excavate.

Ausbacken, *ir.* I. *v. tr.* 1) to bake sufficiently. 2) [in cookery] to bake in butter [fish, frogs &c.]. II. *v. intr.* to finish baking, to have done baking.

Ausbaden, I. *v. intr.* to bathe enough, to have done bathing. II. *v. tr.* **Fig.* to suffer, pay or atone for. Er muß es —, he must smart for it.

Ausbähen, *v. tr.* to dry, to dry up.

Ausbalgen, Ausbälgen, *v. tr.* 1) to skin, to flay [an animal]. 2) to stuff [birds &c.].

Ausballen, *v. tr.* to unpack [goods].

Ausbalzen, V. Aussalzen 2.

Ausbannen, *v. tr.* to banish. V. Verbannen. *Fig.* Den Teufel —, to exorcise the devil [to cast him out, to drive him from a person by prayers or other ceremonies].

Ausbau, *m.* [-es, *pl.* -e] the act of finishing a building.

Ausbauchen, Ausbäuchen, I. *v. tr.* to work into a round projecting form. Die Porzellangefäße —, [in manufactories of porcelain] to hollow out the stuff, das Sohlenleder —, [among shoemakers] to mould the sole of a shoe. II. *v. r.* and *intr.* sich —, to become protuberant, to belly, to bunch. Die Mauer baucht aus, the wall batters.

Ausbauen, I. *v. tr.* to finish the inside of a building, to make it habitable. II. *v. intr.* to cease building. Das Haus ist jetzt vollkommen ausgebaut und kann jeden Augenblick bezogen werden, the house is now completely finished and can be inhabited at any moment.

Ausbauer, *m.* [-s, *pl.* -] he that finishes a building.

Ausbechern, [in famil. lang.] V. Austrinken.

Ausbedingen, *ir. v. tr.* to condition for. Sich etwas —, to reserve or make a reservation of something to one's self.

Ausbeeren, *v. tr.* 1) to pick out berries [the tainted ones from bunches of grapes &c.]. 2) to deprive of the berries [the springes &c.].

Ausbehalten, V. Ausbedingen.

Ausbeichten, I. *v. tr.* to confess. II. *v. intr.* to finish confession.

Ausbeinen, *v. tr.* to deprive of bones, to bone.

Ausbeißen, *ir.* I. *v. tr.* to bite out. Ein ausgebissenes Blatt, [in botany] an erose leaf. 2) to drive or force out from a place by biting. † and **Fig.* Einen —, to work any one out of favour, to displace him. II. *v. intr.* 1) to cease to bite or to scold. 2) [in mining] to protuberate.

Ausbeizen, *v. tr.* 1) to remove by caustic or corrosive remedies. 2) to purify by fretting or macerating.

Ausbelfern, *v. intr.* to cease quarreling, or scolding.

Ausbellen, *v. intr.* to cease barking.

Ausbersten, *ir. v. intr.* [u. w. seyn] to burst and fall out.

Ausberstung, *f.* V. Ausbruch 1.

‖**Ausbescheiden**, V. Ausbedingen.

‖**Ausbeschied**, *m.* [-es, *pl.* -e] the thing conditioned for, reserved to one's self, reservation.

Ausbessern, *v. tr.* to mend, to repair. Einen Zaun —, to make up a hedge or fence; ein Schiff —, to repair a ship; die Takelage —, to refit the rigging of a ship; plump —, to patch, to botch; einen Rock —, to piece up, to mend a coat; die Vergoldung —, [among gilders] to mend the leaf-gold.

Ausbesserung, *f.* mending, repair, reparation.

Ausbesserungskosten, *pl.* costs of repair.

Ausbeten, *v. tr.* and *v. intr.* to finish praying.

Ausbetten, *v. tr.* 1) to fit out with a bed. 2) to take out of bed. 3) to shift one's bed to some other place.

Ausbeugen, V. Ausbiegen.

Ausbeute, *f.* [*pl.* -n] profit, gain, [in mining] share.

Ausbeuteln, *v. tr.* to shake out of a bag. Das Mehl —, [in mills] to bolt meal. † and *

Fig. Einen —, to drain any one's purse, to fleece any one; sich —, to spend one's money; ich bin arg ausgebeutelt worden, I have been regularly fleeced.

Ausbezahlen, *v. tr.* to pay that which is to be paid.

Ausbiegen, *ir.* I. *v. tr.* to bend, to bow, to inflect. Reben —, to bow vines. II. *v. intr.* to turn aside, to turn out of the way. *Fig.* Jemandes Fragen —, to elude any one's inquiries.

Ausbieten, *ir.* I. *v. tr.* to offer for sale. Waaren —, to set goods to sale. II. *v. tr.* and *intr.* 1) to outbid. 2) to give notice to quit. Einen [or Einem] Pächter —, to give warning to one's tenant.

Ausbildbar, *adj.* and *adv.* susceptible of perfection, that may be advanced in good qualities, improvable.

Ausbilden, *v. tr.* to perfect the form of any thing [commonly in a fig. sense]. Tanzen und Fechten bilden den Körper aus, dancing and fencing render the body active and supple; Talente —, to cultivate talents; den Verstand —, to cultivate one's understanding; den Geist —, to improve, to give a degree of perfection to the mind; eine Sprache —, to improve, to refine a language; ausgebildet, accomplished.

Ausbilder, *m.* [-s, *pl.* -] cultivator, improver.

Ausbildung, *f.* improvement, cultivation. Die — der Naturanlagen, des Geistes, the cultivation of talents, the improvement of the mind; die — einer Sprache, the refinement of a language.

Ausbinden, *ir. v. tr.* 1) to untie and take out. 2) to select [used only in the derivative: Ausbund]. 3) to untie, to unbind, to free from any fastening. Das Rindvieh —, to loose the cattle. 4) [in printing] to tie up.

Ausbitten, *ir. v. tr.* to beg for, to ask for, to apply for. Das bitte ich mir aus, I beg to be excused, I must decline that; ich bitte mir aus, daß Sie dabei sind, I request your presence; darf ich mir &c. —? may I request &c.?

Ausblänken, *v. tr.* to polish. V. Auspoliren.

Ausblasen, *ir.* I. *v. tr.* 1) to empty [an egg &c.] by blowing. 2) to publish by sound of trumpet. *Fig.* Sein Lob —, sich —, to sound one's own praise. 3) to finish blowing [a march &c.]. 4) to perfect by blowing [a flute &c.]. 5) to breathe out. Die Seele —, to expire, to die. 6) to extinguish by a current of air, to blow out [a candle]. *Fig.* Einem das Lebenslicht —, to deprive any one of life. II. *v. intr.* 1) to cease blowing. 2) † to cease breathing, to breathe one's last, to die.

Ausbleiben, *ir. v. intr.* [u. w. seyn] 1) to stay out. Sie sind länger ausgeblieben, als &c., they stayed out longer, than &c.; das ungehorsame —, [in law] contempt of court, default of appearance. *Fig.* Die Quellen sind ausgeblieben, the springs failed; das Fieber ist ihm ausgeblieben, the fever has left him; der Puls bleibt ihm aus, his pulse stops. 2) *Fig.* *a*) not to take place. Deine Strafe wird nicht —, thou shalt not escape or avoid punishment. *b*) to be left out. Wenn ein Wort oder mehrere ausgeblieben sind, if a word or more be left out.

Ausbleichen, I. *v. tr.* to take out by bleaching [the colour of a stuff]. II. *v. intr.* to cease bleaching, [*ir.* u. w. seyn] to grow pale. Die Farbe ist ausgeblichen [verblichen], the colour has faded.

Ausbleien, *v. tr.* [plombiren] to fill with lead [a hollow tooth &c.].

Ausblitz, *m.* [-es, *pl.* -e] lightning.

Ausblitzen, *v. intr.* to cease lightning. Es hat ausgeblitzt, it lightens no more.

Ausblitzung, *f.* V. Ausblitz.

Ausblöken, *v. intr.* to cease bleating.

Ausblühen, *v. intr.* 1) to cease blooming, or blossoming. 2) *Fig.* to fade, to decay.

Ausblumen, *v. tr.* to decorate or deck out with flowers.

Ausbluten, I. *v. intr.* 1) to cease bleading. 2) to shed all the blood. II. *v. tr.* to send forth with the blood. Sein Leben — [verbluten], to lose one's life with one's blood, to die from loss of blood.

Ausböden, *v. tr.* [among coopers] to bottom [a vat].

Ausbogen, *v. tr.* [among sempstr.] to slope [a ruff for the neck &c.].

Ausbohlen, *v. tr.* to cover with planks on the inside, to plank on the inside, to line with planks.

Ausbohren, I. *v. tr.* 1) to hollow with a gimblet or borer. Eine Kanone —, to bore a cannon; einen Schlüssel —, to drill a key; kugelförmig —, [among watchmakers] to chamfer. 2) to remove by means of a boring instrument. Den Spund —, to unbung a cask, to tap a vessel. II. *v. intr.* 1) to cease boring. 2) to bore sufficiently.

Ausborgen, *v. tr* to lend out [money &c.].

Ausbracken, *v. tr.* [in husb.] to turn out as useless, as refuses.

Ausbraten, *ir.* I. *v. tr.* 1) to roast sufficiently. 2) to roast out of. Alles Fett aus einer Gans —, to roast out all the fat out of a goose. II. *v. intr* [u. w. seyn] 1) to be roasted sufficiently. 2) to drip by roasting.

Ausbrauchen, *v. tr.* 1) to use up. 2) to cease using, to use no more.

Ausbrauen, I. *v. tr.* 1) to brew well, to perfect in brewing. 2) to extract in brewing. II. *v. intr.* to finish brewing.

Ausbrausen, I. *v. intr.* 1) to cease to bluster or to roar. Der Wind hat ausgebraust, the wind roars no more. 2) to be past fermenting. *Fig.* Ausgebraust haben, to have done fuming and fretting.

Ausbrechen, *ir.* I. *v. tr.* 1) to break out, to force out, to take out. Einen Zahn —, to draw a tooth; einen Baum —, to lop or to prune a tree; Bohnen —, to slip beans out of the skin. Die Bienen —, to separate a hive; [among hunters] V. Auswählen; [in husbandry] die Füllenzähne —, to lose the colt's teeth. 2) to vomit up or out [bile &c.]. 3) [= austrecken, ausdehnen] Die gar gemachten Felle —, [among tawers] to soften the skins upon the boards. II. *v. intr.* [u. w. seyn] 1) to break loose, to escape from confinement by violence. Aus dem Gefängnisse —, to break out of a prison; Feuer bricht aus, a fire breaks out; der Angstschweiß brach ihm aus, he sweated for fear. *Fig.* Ein Fieber bricht aus, a fever breaks out; es ist ein Aufruhr in dieser Stadt ausgebrochen, a sedition has broken out in this town; in Thränen —, to burst into tears; in ein Gelächter —, to burst into laughter, to set up a laugh; in Entzücken —, to break forth in raptures; — lassen, to make appear, to show with impetuosity. 2) to be broken out.

Ausbrecheisen, *n.* [among tanners] an iron tool used for softening the skins.

Ausbrecher, *m.* [-s, *pl.* -] V. Brechbetel.

Ausbreiten, I. *v. tr.* 1) to spread, to extend. Die Arme —, to stretch out the arms; das Tischtuch —, to lay the table-cloth; die stattlichen Bäume breiten ihre Aeste aus, the stately trees spread their branches; die Flügel —, to stretch out the wings; ein Adler mit ausgebreiteten Flügeln, [in heraldry] an eagle displayed; das Gras — [in hay-making], to spread the grass; das Weißblech —, to spread the tin; Metallplatten —, to extend metal-plates by hammering; ausgebreitet, [in bot.] divaricate; ein ausgebreiteter Ast, a divaricate branch. *Fig.* Sie breiten seinen Ruhm aus, they spread abroad his fame; seine Herrschaft —, to extend one's dominion; ein Geheimniß —, to divulge a secret; ein Gerücht —, to circulate a report; die Wahrheit —, to propagate truth; ausgebreitete Gelehrsamkeit, great or extensive learning. II. *v. r* sich —, to spread. Rußland breitet sich bis an die Gränzen von China aus, Russia extends to the borders of China; Pflanzen, die sich —, sind selten groß, plants, that spread much, are seldom tall. sich ausbreitend, [in botany] spreading. *Fig.* Dieses Gerücht hat sich schon ausgebreitet [verbreitet], this report has already spread abroad, eine Geschichte, die sich weit ausgebreitet hat, a story extensively circulated; ich könnte mich über diesen Gegenstand —, I might enlarge on this topic; sich über wichtige Gegenstände —, to expatiate on important topics, der Fuchs breitet sich über die Anmuth des Raben aus, the fox expatiates upon the gracefulness of the raven; sich weitläufig über etwas —, to dilate, to amplify on &c. Syn. Ausbreiten, Verbreiten. Verbreiten signifies to spread or expand a thing which was till then enclosed in a less, over a greater space. Ausbreiten refers to the greater number of places which a thing occupies. Thus one may say without distinction: Der Geruch hat sich in dem ganzen Zimmer ausgebreitet and verbreitet [the smell has spread over the whole room]; the former refers only to all the different parts of the room, in which the smell is perceived, the latter at the same time to the spot where it was first perceived within a smaller space. One may therefore also say: eine ausgebreitete Gelehrsamkeit [extensive learning], ein ausgebreiteter Ruhm [wide-spread fame], but not: eine verbreitete Gelehrsamkeit, ein verbreiteter Ruhm.

Ausbreitung, *f.* spreading, extension. Die leichte — des Flügels eines Vogels, the easy expansion of the wing of a bird. *Fig.* Die — des Glaubens, the propagating of religion.

Ausbreitungssucht, *f.* proselytism.

Ausbrennen, *reg.* [with some authors *ir.*] I. *v. tr.* 1) to subject the inside of any thing to the action of fire. Einen Zahn —, to cauterize, to sear a tooth; Goldtressen —, to burn gold-lace; ein Kamin —, to burn out a chimney [in order to clean it]; eine Kanone — [ausflammen], to scale a gun. 2) to perfect by burning. Die Ziegel gut —, to bake the bricks sufficiently; gut ausgebrannte Ziegel, bricks well baked. 3) to d[...] excessively, to bake. Die große Sommerh[...] brennt den Boden aus, the great heat of the summer scorches the ground. II. *v. intr.* 1) [...] finish burning. 2) [u. w. seyn and haben] *a*) to b[...] burnt up, to be consumed entirely by fire. [...] to cease to burn. Das Feuer — lassen, to let the fire burn out. *c*) [among brickmakers] to heat the kiln for the last time.

Ausbringen, *ir. v. tr.* 1) to bring out. D[...] Boot — [aussetzen], [in seamen's lang.] to hoist out the boat; den Anker mit dem Boote —, [in seamen's lang.] to boat the anchor; Silber —, [in mining] to melt silver; einen Teich —, [in husb.] to cleanse a pond; junge Hühner —, to hatch chickens; ich kann meine Handschuhe nicht —, I cannot get my gloves off. *Fig.* Ein Gerücht —, to circulate a report; ein Geheimniß —, to divulge a secret; eine Gesundheit —, to drink a health, to give a toast; ich kann diesen Thaler nicht —, I cannot pay this dollar away, nobod[...]

will take it. 2) [among printers] to drive out, to keep out.

Ausbringer, *m.* [-s, *pl.*-] *f.* —inn, divulger.

Ausbröckeln, *v. r.* sich —, to fall into crumbles out of a thing.

Ausbruch, *m.* [-es, *pl.* -brüche] 1) the act of breaking out, or bursting forth from inclosure or confinement. Der — eines feuerspeienden Berges, the eruption of a volcano; der — des Feuers, the breaking out of a fire. *Fig.* Der — einer Krankheit, the breaking out of a disease; beim —e des Krieges, upon the breaking out of war; ein — des Zornes, a burst of passion; die Ausbrüche [der Lüsternheit &c.], the lashings out; zum — kommen, einen — gewinnen, to break out. 2) the thing broken out; [thence] the name of a wine in Hungary made of the juice which oozes from unpressed grapes. Ofener —, Melnecker —, unpressed wine from Buda, from Melneck.

Ausbruchsfieber, *n.* a fever preceding the breaking out of a disease.

Ausbrüchig, *adj.* and *adv.* generally known, notorious. — machen, to make public.

Ausbrühen, *v. tr.* [to burn the inside of a thing with hot liquor in order to cleanse it] to scald [a cask &c.].

Ausbrüllen, I. *v. intr.* 1) to cease bellowing or roaring. Der Sturm hat ausgebrüllt, the storm roars no longer. 2) *v. intr.* and *r.* to bellow one's fill. †II. *v. tr.* to publish bellowing.

Ausbrunften, *v. intr.* to cease to rut.

Ausbrüsten, *v. tr.* [am. butchers] to take out the pluck of an ox &c.

Ausbrüten, I. *v. tr.* to produce by brooding. Junge —, to hatch young; Eier —, to brood. *Fig.* Böses —, to hatch mischief. II. *v. intr.* to cease hatching or brooding.

Ausbuchsen, Ausbüchsen, *v. tr.* to furnish with a box. Ein Rad —, to box a wheel.

Ausbuckeln, *v. tr.* 1) to hammer smooth the unevennesses [of a kettle &c.]. 2) to stud [a shield &c.].

Ausbügeln, I. *v. tr.* 1) to iron out [wrong folds &c.]. 2) to iron sufficiently. II. *v. intr.* to finish ironing.

Ausbühnen, *v. tr.* [in mining] Die Schachte or Schächte — [auszimmern, austonnen], to line the shafts or pits of a mine.

Ausbund, *m.* [-es] something supremely excellent or bad, a pattern. Sie ist ein — von Tugend, she is a paragon of virtue; er ist der — aller schönen Geister, he is the brooch of all witty men; ein — aller Schelme, an arrant-knave, an arch-rogue; ein — von Bosheit, exquisite malice.

‡**Ausbündig**, *adj.* and *adv.* supremely excellent.

‖**Ausbürgen**, *v. tr.* to redeem a pledge.

‖**Ausbürger**, *m.* [-s, *pl.*-] 1) a stranger, a foreigner. 2) an inhabitant of the suburb. 3) a non resident citizen.

Ausbürsten, *v. tr.* to sweep with a brush, to brush. Bürstet meinen Hut aus, whisk off the dust of my hat, brush my hat; den Staub —, to brush away the dust, to dust.

Ausbuschen, *v. tr.* 1) to clear of small wood. 2) to pull up, to weed.

Ausbüßen, I. *v. tr.* 1) to mend, to repair. Netze, Garne —, [among hunters] to mend nets, toils. 2) to atone for, to expiate. Er hat es ausgebüßt, he paid for it. II. *v. intr.* to atone for all.

Ausbuttern, I. *v. tr.* to get by churning. Viel Butter —, to get a great deal of butter by churning. II. *v. intr.* to cease churning.

***Auscuriren**, *v. tr.* to cure thoroughly. V. Ausheilen.

Ausdahlen, *v. intr.* to cease dallying, toying and wantoning.

Ausdämmen, *v. tr.* to raise [a current of water] by a dam.

Ausdampfen, I. *v. intr.* 1) [u. w. seyn] to pass off in vapour, to evaporate. 2) [u. w. haben] *a*) to cease smoking *b*) to steam sufficiently. II. *v. tr.* to empty by smoking.

Ausdämpfen, *v. tr.* 1) to dissipate in fumes, steam or minute particles, to evaporate. 2) to drive out by means of smoke. Füchse —, [am. hunters] to unkennel foxes by smoke. 3) to put out, to extinguish.

Ausdämpfung, *f.* 1) the act of dissipating in fumes, evaporation. 2) the thing evaporated.

Ausdärmen, *v. tr.* to disembowel, to embowel, to eviscerate.

Ausdauer, *f.* perseverance in enterprise, constancy, holding out, [of horses] bottom.

Ausdauern, I. *v. intr.* to last to the end, to hold out. Ausdauernd, lasting, of good bottom [said of racers]; [in botany] —de Pflanzen, perennials. *Fig.* to hold out, to persevere. Der Geist muß bei Dingen —, the mind must abide upon things. II. *v. tr.* to bear without sinking under the pressure, to endure.

Ausdehnbar, *adj.* and *adv.* capable of being extended, extensible, extendible, distensible, expansible, dilatable.

Ausdehnbarkeit, *f.* the capacity of being expanded. Die — der Luft, the expansive quality of the air, the dilatability, expansibility of the air; die — des Goldes, the ductility of gold; die — der Fibern, the extensibility of the fibres; die — einer Blase, the distensibility of a bladder.

Ausdehnen, I. *v. tr.* to stretch in any direction, to spread in breath, to expand or dilate in size, to extend. Metallplatten unter dem Hammer —, to extend metal plates by hammering; Leder —, to stretch leather; die Luft dehnt die Lunge aus, the air dilates the lungs; die Luft wird durch Verdünnung ausgedehnt, air is dilated by rarefaction; eine Luftmasse wird durch Verdünnung ausgedehnt, a volume of air is enlarged by rarefaction; eine Blase —, to distend a bladder; ausgedehnt, [in mathematics] occupying a portion of space; [in philosophy] consisting of separable parts; die —de Kraft der Hitze, des Feuers, the expansive force of heat or fire; widernatürlich —, to distend unnaturally. *Fig.* Sein Geschwätz —, to protract one's idle talk; eine Schriftstelle zu weit —, to stretch a text; sie sind geneigt, ihre Vorrechte zu weit auszudehnen, they are apt, to overstrain their privileges; ein ausgedehnter Wirkungskreis, an extensive sphere of operations, seine Mildthätigkeit selbst auf die Heiden —, to extend one's charity even to the heathens. II. *v. r.* sich —, to stretch, to extend. *Fig.* Ein Feld, das sich weit ausdehnt, an extensive field.

Ausdehnung, *f.* 1) a stretching, extension. Die — der Metalle durch die Hitze, the expansion of metals by heat. *Fig.* Die — eines Vorrechtes, the extension of a privilege; die — einer Rede, amplification. 2) [the state of being extended] extension. Die — des Herzens, [in med.] the expansion of the heart, diastole, diastoly. 3) dimension, extension. Nach allen Punkten der —, in all dimensions.

Ausdehnungskraft, *f.* 1) expansive force. 2) dilatability. —**vermögen**, *n.* expansive force.

Ausdeichen, *v. tr.* to surround with a dike, to dike [a moor &c.].

Ausdenken, *ir.* I. *v. tr.* 1) to find or get out by thinking, to invent, to contrive. Einen Betrug —, to think on a deceit; das ist gut ausgedacht, this is well imagined. 2) to think to the end. Das ist ein Gedanke, den ich mir nicht auszudenken getraue, that is a thought which I dare not trust to follow out. II. *v. intr.* to cease to think. III. *v. r.* sich —, to weary one's self with thinking.

Ausdeuten, *v. tr.* to interpret, to explain, to expound. Joseph deutete den Traum des Pharao aus, Joseph interpreted the dream of Pharaoh; eine Stelle in der Schrift —, to expound a text of Scripture.

1. **Ausdichten**, I. *v. tr.* to find out or to devise by imagination. II. *v. tr.* and *intr.* to finish a poem, to finish making poetry.

2. **Ausdichten**, *v. tr.* to join firmly, to make tight. Ein Schiff —, to secure a ship against the entrance of water, to calk it.

Ausdielen, *v. tr.* to board [a room &c.].

Ausdienen, *v. intr.* 1) to serve the time fixed, to serve out. [also as a *v. tr.*] Seine Zeit, seine Jahre —, to serve one's time; er hat seine Zeit ausgedient, he is out of his time; ausgedient, retired from service. 2) to become unfit for active service. Ausgedient, unfit for service; ein Ausgedienter, *a*) a veteran, *b*) an invalid.

Ausdingen, *ir. v. tr.* 1) V. Ausbedingen. 2) to hire out. 3) V. Ausmiethen.

Ausdocken, *v. tr.* [among hunters] Das Hängeseil — [es von der Docke ablaufen lassen], to slip a dog from the leading-string or leash.

Ausdonnern, I. *v. imp.* to cease thundering. Es hat ausgedonnert, it has done thundering, the thunder has ceased. II. *v. intr.* to cease to speak with a thundering voice. III. *v. tr.* to pronounce with a thundering voice.

Ausdorren, *v. intr.* [u. w. seyn] to scorch, to dry up. Die Haut dorrt aus und wird trocken, the skin grows parched and dry; ausgedorrtes Land, barren, arid ground.

Ausdörren, *v. tr.* to dry up, to parch.

Ausdrängen, *v. tr.* to force out of a place or society. V. Verdrängen.

Ausdrechseln, I. *v. tr.* 1) to hollow by turning on a lathe. 2) to complete or finish on a lathe, *Fig.* to elaborate, to finish with a forced exactness. II. *v. intr.* to cease turning on a lathe.

Ausdrehen, I. *v. tr.* 1) to wind or wrest out of a place. Einem den Stock aus der Hand —, to wrench the stick out of any one's hand. 2) to hollow by turning on a lathe. II. *v. intr.* V. Ausdrechseln.

Ausdreschen, *ir.* I. *v. tr.* 1) to thrash out. 2) to empty by thrashing. 3) to thrash out sufficiently. 4) to get or obtain by thrashing. II. *v. intr.* to finish thrashing.

Ausdrieseln, V. Ausfädeln.

Ausdringen, *ir.* I. *v. intr.* [u. w. seyn] to press out. II. *v. tr.* V. Abdringen.

Ausdrohen, *v. intr.* to cease threatening.

Ausdrommeten, V. Austrompeten.

Ausdruck, *m.* [-es, *pl.* -drücke] expression. *a*) [the act of uttering, declaring or representing]. Ein — des allgemeinen Wunsches, an expression of public will. *b*) [a phrase or mode of speech]. Ein seltsamer —, an odd expression; der veraltete —, archaism; Kunstausdrücke, terms of arts; in allgemeinen Ausdrücken, in general terms. *c*) [in rhetoric &c., elocution, diction, the peculiar manner of utterance, suited to the subject and sentiment]. *d*) [in painting, a natural and lively representation of the subject]. Der — im Auge, im Gesichte, the expression of the eye, of the countenance; der — einer besondern Handlung oder Leidenschaft, the expression of a particular action or passion. *e*) [in music, the tone, grace or modulation of voice or sound suited to any particular subject, that manner which gives life and reality to ideas and sentiments]. *f*) [on the stage, a distinct, sonorous and pleasing enunciation, accompanied with action suited to the subject].

Ausdruck[s]=arm, *adj.* and *adv.* wanting expression or expressions. —[s]art, *f.* the manner of expressing one's self. —[s]leer, *adj.* and *adv.* without expression, void of expression. —[s]los, *adj.* and *adv.* void of expression. —[s]unfähig, *adj.* and *adv.* unable to express one's self. —[s]voll, I. *adj.* expressive, representing with force, emphatical. Das Ausdruck[s]=volle, expressiveness; das —svolle seines Auges, seiner Gesichtszüge oder der Töne, the expressiveness of his eye or of his features, or of sounds. II. *adv.* expressively.

Ausdrucken, I. *v. tr.* 1) to take off by impression, to express. Die Wörter ganz —, to print the whole words, to print them at length without abbreviation; das Siegel ist gut ausgedruckt, the seal is well impressed, has made a good impression. *Fig.* Die Bedingungen in dieser Urkunde sind gut ausgedruckt, the covenants in this deed are well expressed; durch Zeichen —, to express by signs; er druckt seine Ideen oder seine Meinung mit Bestimmtheit aus, he expresses his ideas or his meaning with precision; seine Absichten waren in sehr verständlichen Worten ausgedruckt, his views were expressed in very intelligible terms; ein niedergeschlagener Blick kann Demuth, Scham oder Schuld —, a downcast look may express humility, shame or guilt. 2) to print completely. Das Buch ist noch immer nicht ausgedruckt, the book is not yet entirely printed. II. *v.r.* sich —, to express one's self. Sich deutlich —, to express one's self plainly, intelligibly; sich fein oder zierlich —, to atticize. III. *v. intr.* [in printing] to finish the printing, finish the impression.

Ausdrücken, *v. tr.* 1) to press or squeeze out. Den Saft der Weintrauben oder Aepfel —, to express the juice of grapes or of apples; einen Schwamm —, to strain a sponge; eine Citrone —, to squeeze a lemon; einen Pinsel —, [in painting] to clean a paint-brush [against the edge of a pallet]. 2) to put out, to extinguish by squeezing, to squeeze out. 3) to expand by pressing or squeezing. 4) V. Ausdrucken.

Ausdrücker, *m.* [-s, *pl.* -] [am. tanners] V. Streichmesser.

Ausdrücklich and **Ausdrücklich**, I. *adj.* 1) plain, clear, express. Mit —en Worten, in express terms or words; eine —e Erklärung, an explicit declaration. 2) intentional, designed, intended. II. *adv.* 1) in direct terms, expressly, plainly, explicitly. 2) purposely, intentionally, designedly, by design.

Ausdrucksam, I. *adj.* expressive. II. *adv.* expressively.

|| **Ausdrusch**, *m.* [-es] 1) the act of thrashing out. 2) that which is thrashed out.

Ausduften, I *v. intr.* 1) [u. w. seyn] to ascend as a fume or vapour. 2) [u. w. haben] to cease to ascend as vapour. II. *v. tr.* V. Ausdüften.

Ausdüften, *v. tr.* 1) to emit, to send out, to exhale. Die Rose düftet Wohlgeruch aus, the rose exhales a fragrant odour. 2) to fill with exhalations.

Ausdulden, I. *v. intr.* 1) to suffer to the end. 2) to cease to suffer. Er hat ausgedultet, he suffers no more. II. *v. tr.* to endure suffering.

Ausdunst, *m.* [-es, *pl.* -dünste] that which is exhaled, exhalation.

Ausdünstbar, *adj.* and *adv.* evaporable, transpirable.

Ausdunsten, *v. intr.* [u. w. seyn] 1) to escape and be dissipated, either in visible vapour or in particles too minute to be visible, to evaporate. 2) to perspire, to transpire.

Ausdünsten, *v. tr.* 1) to exhale, to emit by the pores, to perspire, to transpire. 2) to evaporate.

Ausdünstung, *f.* 1) evaporation, exhalation, perspiration, transpiration. 2) [that which is exhaled] exhalation. Der Geruch der Pflanzen entsteht durch unsichtbare —en, the smell of plants is caused by invisible exhalations; die schädlichen —en kranker Körper, the noxious exhalations, effluvia of diseased bodies; die unmerkliche —, imperceptible exhalation.

Ausdünstungsmesser, *m.* [an instrument to measure the quantity of exhalation from a humid surface in a given time] an evaporometer, atmometer.

Ausecken, *v. tr.* to cut into angles.

Ausegen, **Auseggen**, I. *v. tr.* to harrow up. II. *v. intr.* to finish harrowing.

Auseilen, *v. intr.* [u. w. seyn] to go or walk out hastily.

Auseinander, *adv.* 1) separately, into parts, asunder; [military term] —! disperse! 2) much used in composition with verbs, as:

Auseinander=bringen, *ir. v. tr.* to separate. —fahren, *ir. v. intr.* [u. w. seyn] Auseinanderfahrende Strahlen, [in optics] divergent rays; das Auseinanderfahren von Linien, divergence of lines. —fallen, *ir. v. intr.* to fall asunder, [of rays] to diverge. —fliegen, *ir. v. intr.* [u. w. seyn] to separate flying, to fly asunder. —gehen, *ir. v. intr.* [u. w. seyn] to go asunder. Die Gesellschaft ging auseinander, the society broke up. —legen, *v. tr.* to lay or put apart. Eine Maschine —legen, to take a machine to pieces. —nehmen, *ir v. tr.* to take [a machine &c.] in pieces or asunder. —rücken, *v. tr.* to move or push asunder. —setzen, I. *v. tr.* to put or set asunder. *Fig.* Eine Sache —setzen, to analyze, to expound a thing; er setzte die besonderen Umstände auseinander, he stated and explained the particulars. II. *v. r.* sich —, to sit down separately. *Fig. a*) to separate, to break up [a partnership]. *b*) to come to a compromise of differences, to agree. —setzung, *f.* exposition, explication, analysis. —sperren, *v. tr.* to fix apart. Die Beine —sperren, to plant the legs asunder, to straddle. —wirren, *v. tr.* to disentangle. —ziehen, *ir. v. tr.* to stretch, to lengthen.

Auseisen, *v. tr.* to get or take out of the ice.

Auseitern, *v. intr.* 1) [u. w. seyn] to issue from a body as pus. 2) [u. w. haben] to cease festering, or suppurating. Die Wunde hat ausgeeitert, the wound suppurates no longer.

Ausempfinden, *v. tr.* and *intr.* to cease to feel.

Auserkiesen, V. Auserkören.

Auserkoren, *adj.* select, chosen, elect.

Auserkören, **Auserküren**, *v. tr.* [used only in the part. of the preterit] to choose, to elect, to select. Er hat mich auserkoren, he has chosen me.

Auserlesen, *v. tr.* to choose, to select. —e Soldaten, picked troops; —e Speisen, choice, exquisite meats; —e Gesellschaften, select societies; —e Gedichte, excellent poems.

Ausernten, *v intr.* to finish the harvest.

Auserschallen, V. Erschallen.

Ausersehen, *ir. v. tr.* to choose, to select, or distinguish for a particular purpose. Er hat ihn —, he made choice of him; Einen zu etwas —, to designate any one for something.

Aussersinnen, V. Ersinnen.

Auserwählen, *v. tr.* to choose, to select, to elect. Auserwählt, choice, select; Viele sind berufen, aber Wenige sind auserwählet, [Math. XX] many are called, but few chosen; die Auserwählten, the elect.

Auserzählen, I. *v. tr.* to tell to the end. II. *v. intr.* to finish the tale. III. *v. r.* sich —, to tell all the stories that are in one's knowledge, to relate all one knows.

Ausessen, *ir. v. tr.* to empty by eating. Die Suppe —, to eat all the soup. *Fig.* — müssen, was ein Anderer eingebrockt hat, to pay for the faults of another.

Ausfachen, *v. tr.* to furnish with divisions and compartments.

Ausfächsern, *v. tr.* [in husbandry] to lay a stock or scion of a vine in the ground for propagation, to provine. Einen Weinstock —, to propagate a vine.

Ausfädeln, I. *v. tr.* to unravel. Leinwand —, to unweave linen cloth. II. *v. intr.* to unravel.

Ausfahren, *ir.* I. *v. tr.* 1) to deepen or wear out a road by driving. Die Gleise sind so stark ausgefahren, the ruts are so deep. 2) to hollow or excavate lengthwise. Die Fensterrahmen mit Ruthen —, [am. joiners] to rabbet a window frame. 3) to carry out, to export [corn &c.]. 4) to surpass in driving. II. *v. intr.* [u. w. seyn] 1) to ride abroad in a coach, to take a drive. Sie ist ausgefahren, she is taking a drive; der Ort, von dem wir zuerst ausfuhren, the place from whence we first set out; [of ships] to put to sea, to leave the harbour or roadstead. 2) [= herausfahren]. Aus der Grube —, [in mining] to get out of the pit; der Teufel ist aus dem Besessenen ausgefahren, the devil has gone out of the person possessed; die Seele ist ihm ausgefahren, he gave up the ghost, he expired. 3) to move or fly out of a place, to slip. Das Schermesser fuhr mir aus, the razor slipt out of my hand. 4) to appear in eruptions as pustules, to break out, *it.* to have pustules or an efflorescence on the skin. Im Gesichte ausgefahren seyn, to have pimples in the face. 5) *Fig.* Gegen Einen —, to fly into a violent passion with any one.

Ausfahrt, *f.* [*pl.* -en] 1) a driving out or riding abroad, drive, ride. 2) *a*) door-way, gate-way, out-gate. *b*) [in mining] getting out of the pit.

Ausfall, *m.* [-es, *pl.* -fälle] 1) the falling out, shedding. Der — der Bärmutter, [in medicine] the falling of the womb. 2) [in fencing and fighting] a pass, passade, passado; [in military affairs] sally. Die Spanier machten Ausfälle, sallies were made by the Spaniards; einen — thun, to sally out. *Fig.* a falling on with words or writing, with calumny, satire or criticism; seine Ausfälle auf Andersdenkende, his attacks upon dissenters. 3) the produce of the field. 4) *Fig.* the sum of money wanting. Es war ein — von mehr als tausend Thalern vorhanden, there was a deficit of more than a thousand dollars. 5) *Fig.* result. 6) [in fortification = Ausfallthor] sally-port.

Ausfallthor, *n.* V. Ausfall 6.

Ausfallen, *ir.* I. *v. intr.* [u. w. seyn] 1) to fall

out of a place. Die Zähne fangen an, ihm auszufallen, he begins to shed teeth; die Haare sind ihm ausgefallen, his hair has fallen off; alle Haare fallen mir aus, all my hair comes out; das Ausfallen der Haare, [in medic.] the fox-evil or scurf, alopecy. *Fig.* *a*) to degenerate. Die Nelken fallen aus, the carnations degenerate. *b*) not to take place; to remain undone. 2) [hervorgehen] *a*) [in military affairs] to sally out. *b*) [in fencing and fighting] to make a pass, to pass. Auf Einen —, to make a pass at any one. 3) to meet with a certain conclusion. Es ist anders ausgefallen, it took a different turn; die Sache fiel nach meinem Wunsche aus, the thing fell out to my mind; gut —, to have success, to turn out well; die Wahl fiel unglücklich für ihn aus, the choice went against him; das Urtheil fiel zu Gunsten der Angeklagten aus, the verdict went for the accused; die Sache ist zu unserm Vortheile ausgefallen, the affair turned out to our advantage; es wird zu seiner Schande —, it will turn to his shame; der Sommerweizen ist dieses Jahr gut ausgefallen, summer-wheat has prospered well this year. II. *v. tr.* to displace by falling. Sich den Arm —, to dislocate one's arm by a fall.

Aúsfalten, *v. tr.* to unfold.

1. **Aúsfalzen**, *v. tr* 1) [among bookbinders] to fold up. 2) [am. joiners] to rabbet.

2. **Aúsfalzen**, *v. intr.* to cease paring [said only of the cock of the wood].

Aúsfangen, *ir. v. tr.* to empty by catching. Einen Teich —, to fish out a pond, to catch all the fish in it.

Aúsfärben, *v. tr.* V. Ausmahlen.

Aúsfaseln, **Aúsfasen**, I. *v. intr.* to ravel. II. *v. r.* sich —, to unravel, to be unwoven. III. *v. tr.* to ravel out.

Aúsfasern, *v. tr.* V. Ausfaseln.

Aúsfasten, *v. intr.* to cease fasting or abstaining from food.

Aúsfaulen, *v. intr.* [u. w. seyn] 1) to rot inwardly. 2) to rot and fall out.

Aúsfechten, *ir.* I. *v. tr.* to fight out. Einen Streit —, to fight out a quarrel, to decide it with arms. *Fig.* Sie mögen ihren Streit selbst mit einander —, they may settle the dispute between themselves. II. *v. intr.* to cease fighting.

Aúsfechter, *m.* [-s, *pl.* -] champion.

Aúsfedern, *v. tr.* to remove the feathers.

Aúsfegen, *v. tr.* to sweep out, to sweep, to cleanse by sweeping.

Aúsfehmen, *v. tr.* [in agricultural affairs] to take up from the mast [swine &c.]

Aúsfeiern, *v. tr.* to keep as a holiday, to cease from work till the end of a fixed time.

Aúsfeilen, *v. tr.* 1) to file the inside of a thing. 2) to remove by filing, to file out [rust &c.] 3) to perfect by filing. *Fig.* to finish with great diligence, to elaborate. Eine Rede —, to polish or file a discourse.

† and ‡ **Aúsfenstern**, *v. tr.* to reprimand severely.

Aúsferkeln, *v. intr.* to finish pigging, to cease to farrow.

Aúsfertigen, *v. tr.* to finish completely [any thing]. Einen Befehl —, to expedite an order; eine Schrift —, to draw up a paper or writing; einen Wechsel —, to make out, to draw a bill of exchange; eine Urkunde, einen Pachtcontrakt —, to execute a deed, a lease; || Ein Kind —, to portion a child.

Aúsfertiger, *m.* [-s, *pl.* -] he that expedites an order.

Aúsfertigung, *f.* 1) the act of expediting. Die — einer Urkunde, the execution of a deed. 2) dispatch, order, execution. || 3) the portioning of a child.

Ausfertigungstag, *m.* [that addition to a writing which specifies the year, month and day when it was given or executed] date.

Aúsfesten, *v. tr.* to fix thoroughly.

Aúsfetten, *v. tr.* Die Wolle —, [among dyers] to scour the wool, in order to remove the grease.

Aúsfeuchten, *v. tr.* to dry up. *Fig.* V. Ausmergeln.

Aúsfeuern, I. *v. tr.* to warm thoroughly. Ein Faß —, [among coopers] to burn out a cask. II. *v. intr.* 1) to cease firing. 2) *Fig.* to strike out, to kick [said of horses].

Aúsfiedeln, *v. intr.* to cease fiddling.

Aúsfiedern, *v. tr.* [in mining] to fill up with iron wedges.

Aúsfilzen, *v. tr.* 1) to border with felt. 2) [am. saddlers and pouchmakers] to stuff with hair. † 3) *Fig.* to reprimand severely. Einen —, to give any one a rebuke.

Aúsfindbar, *adj.* and *adv.* that may be found out, discoverable.

Aúsfinden, *ir.* I. *v. tr.* to search for and discover, to look out. Er durchstreifte die Stadt, um mich auszufinden, he ranged the town, to seek me out. *Fig.* Eine Wahrheit —, to find out a truth. II. *v. r.* sich —, V. Herausfinden.

Aúsfindig, *adv.* [used only with machen] — machen, to discover, to find out; Einen — machen, to find any one out; mache Genossen von gutem Rufe —, look out associates of good reputation; den Verfasser einer Flugschrift — machen, to trace out the author of a pamphlet; ein Mittel — machen, to find out, to devise an expedient; Mittel — zu machen suchen, to look out for expedients. Syn. Ausfindig machen, Finden. Finden signifies to find or discover only what was lost or hid, the discovery may be made by mere accident. Ausfindig machen signifies to find out what was not before known, and what required considerable pains and thought to discover.

Aúsfindlich, *adj.* and *adv.* that may be found out, discoverable.

Aúsfirnissen, *v. tr.* to varnish the inside of a thing.

Aúsfischen, I. *v. tr.* 1) to draw out or up, to fish up [a human body when sunk]. *Fig.* Geheime Nachrichten —, to find out or pump out secret news. 2) to empty by fishing [a pond]. II. *v. intr.* to cease fishing. Ausgefischt haben, to have done fishing.

Aúsflackern, *v. intr.* 1) [u. w. haben] to flare to the end. 2) [u. w. seyn] to go out flaring.

Aúsflammen, *v. tr* [in pyrotechnics] to dry or clean by means of a flaming fire. Ein Stück —, [in seamen's language] to scale a gun.

Aúsflattern, *v. intr.* [u. w. seyn] to flutter out. *Fig.* to flutter abroad, to go out.

Aúsflechten, *ir.* I. *v. tr.* 1) to furnish the inside of a thing with a twist, to line with wicker-work. 2) to twist or plait duly or completely. 3) to untwist a thing twisted with another. *Fig.* II. *v. r.* sich —, to extricate one's self from &c.

Aúsfleischen, *v. tr.* to strip off the flesh. Die Felle —, [am. tawers] to flesh the hides. *Fig.* Ein ausgefleischter [more usual eingefleischter] Teufel, a devilish fellow, a devil incarnate.

Ausfleischmesser, *n.* [am. tanners] fleshing-knife.

Aúsflicken, *v. tr.* to mend, to piece up [a garment &c.]. Ein ausgeflickter Rock, a patched coat; plump —, to botch.

Aúsfliegen, *ir. v. intr.* [u. w. seyn] 1) to fly out of a place, to leave the nest. *Fig.* Er ist erst ausgeflogen, he has left home for the first time. 2) to go or walk out, to take the air, to make a little excursion [on foot, on horseback or in a carriage].

Aúsfließen, *ir. v. intr.* 1) [u. w. seyn] to flow or run out of any place, to issue, to emanate. Das Bier fließt aus, the beer runs out; der Saft ist ausgeflossen, the sap has oozed out. 2) to cease to flow.

Aúsflimmern, *v. intr.* 1) to cease to glisten or glitter. 2) to go out glisteningly.

Aúsflöhen, *v. tr.* to flea. † Sich —, to flea one's self.

Aúsflöten, *v. intr.* to cease fluting.

Aúsflucht, *f.* [*pl.* -flüchte] 1) the act of fleeing out of a place, flight. *it. Fig.* V. Ausflug. Bei seiner ersten —, at his first setting-out. 2) the place from which bees fly out. 3) *Fig.* escape, evasion, excuse, subterfuge, shift. Eine kahle —, a shuffling excuse; Ausflüchte suchen, to seek excuses; ohne Ausflüchte, without any ifs and ands, without prevarication. *Prov.* Immer eine — bereit haben, to have always a hole to creep out at. Syn. V. Ausrede.

Aúsflüchten, *v. intr.* to flee out of a place or country.

Aúsflüchtig, I. *adj.* containing evasion, evasive. II. *adv.* evasively.

Aúsflug, *m.* [-es, *pl.* -flüge] 1) a flying out of a place, flight. *Fig.* Es ist mein erster —, it is my first setting-out; ich werde einen — auf das Land machen, I shall take a trip into the country; als ich von einem kurzen —e auf Weihnachten zurückkam, coming home after a short Christmas ramble. 2) that which flies out. Der junge —, the young birds flying out. 3) the place to which a flight is directed. V. Flugloch. 4) [among sportsmen] the place to which the deer are hunted out to.

Aúsfluß, *m.* [-sses, *pl.* -flüsse] 1) a flowing or issuing out, discharge, effluence, effluxion, issue. Der — des Eiters aus einem Geschwüre, the efflux of matter from an abscess. 2) a passage out, outlet, issue. Der — der Elbe, the mouth of the Elbe. 3) that which flows out, discharge, efflux, effluxion, effluvium. Ein — aus der Nase, a defluxion of the nose or head in catarrh; ein dünner wässeriger —, a thin serous discharge; ein eiteriger —, a purulent discharge; die wohlriechenden Ausflüsse der Rosen, the fragrant exhalations of the roses; das Licht ist ein — der Sonne, light is an emanation of the sun. *Fig.* Weisheit ist ein — der Gottheit, wisdom is an emanation of the deity.

Aúsflüstern, I. *v intr.* to cease whispering. II. *v. tr.* to put about, to spread or circulate whispering.

Aúsflut, *f.* [*pl.* -en] [in mining] channel, groove

Aúsfluten, *v. intr.* 1) [u. w. seyn] to stream out in floods. 2) [u. w. haben] to cease to stream out in floods.

Aúsfoderer, *m.* [-s, *pl.* -] [one who invites to a single combat] challenger.

Aúsfodern, *v. tr.* 1) [to call to a contest, to call or invite to answer for an offence by duel] to challenge. 2) [at cards] Trumpf —, to play a trump.

Aúsfoderung, *f.* [a calling upon any one to fight in single combat] challenge.

Ausfoderungsbrief, *m.* a challenge.

Ausfohlen, Ausfüllen, *v. intr.* to cease foaling. Die Stute hat ausgefohlt, the mare foals no more, is past foaling.

Ausfolgen, *v. tr.* to deliver, to deliver up, to give up. Belieben Sie dem Ueberbringer diß die &c. auszufolgen, be pleased to deliver up to the bearer of this the &c.; einen Gefangenen — lassen, to deliver up a prisoner.

Ausfoppen, *v. tr.* to rally.

Ausfordern, V. Ausfodern.

Ausfördern, *v. tr.* to remove or get out of. Erz —, [in mining] to dig the ore.

Ausformen, *v. tr.* to perfect the form of any thing.

Ausforschen, *v. tr.* 1) to search for, to seek to find Die Wahrheit —, to sift out the truth; einen Fremden —, to search out a stranger; Jemands Meinungen und Absichten —, to feel or feel out any one's opinions or designs; Einen wegen einer Sache —, to feel any one's pulse about a business; Einen ganz —, to tent any one to the quick. 2) Einen —, to sound or pump any one, to sift any one.

Ausforscher, *m.* [-s, *pl.* -] he that searches for a thing.

Ausfragen, *v. tr.* 1) to ask after, to inquire, to question, to seek by request. Die Wohnung eines Menschen —, to ask after the lodgings of a person. 2) Einen —, to sound any one, to feel out any one's opinions &c.

Ausfragerei, *f.* sounding, pumping.

Ausfransen, I. *v. tr.* to cut out the border of a thing like fringes. II. *v. r.* sich —, V. [sich] Ausfaseln.

Ausfressen, *ir.* I. *v. tr.* 1) to empty by eating, to eat up. Das Wild hat diesen Acker ausgefressen, the game has completely eaten up the crop of this field. *Fig.* Der Krieg frißt das Land aus, war wastes the country. 2) to hollow by eating, excavate by eating. II. *v. intr.* to cease eating. Die Pferde haben ausgefressen, the horses have done eating. III. *v. r.* sich —, to fatten by eating.

Ausfrieren, *ir. v. intr.* 1) [u. w. seyn] to freeze through and through. Der Teich ist fast ganz ausgefroren, the pond is almost frozen to the bottom. 2) to impair by freezing. Die ganze Kraft des Weines ist ausgefroren, the frost has taken out all the strength of the wine. 3) [u. w. haben] to cease to freeze.

Ausfrischen, *v. tr.* to refresh the inside. Einen Hund —, [among hunters] to purge a dog.

Ausfuchteln, *v. tr.* to beat any one soundly with the flat of a sword.

Ausfühlen, *v. tr.* to try by feeling. *Fig.* to feel, to feel out, to sound.

Ausführbar, *adj.* and *adv.* [that may be performed or done] performable, practicable, feasible, achievable.

Ausführbarkeit, *f.* practicableness, practicability, feasibility.

Ausfuhre, Ausfuhr, *f.* exportation [of wine &c.].

Ausfuhr-handel, *m.* export-trade. —**waare**, *f.* a commodity actually conveyed from one country to another in traffic, export. —**waaren**, exports. —**zoll**, *m.* duty paid on the exportation of goods.

Ausführen, *v. tr.* 1) to carry out, [but appropriately] to convey or transport in traffic, to export. Wir führen Salz nach der Schweiz aus, we export salt to Switzerland; aus Persien führt man auf Kameelen Waaren nach Syrien aus, goods are exported on camels from Persia to Syria; —de Mittel, [in medicine] evacuants; einen Hund —, [among hunters] to lead out a dog [in order to use exercise]. 2) [gleichsam bis ans Ende führen] *Fig.* *a)* to carry into complete effect. Einen Bau —, to erect, to finish a building; einen Anschlag —, to execute, to accomplish a design; einen Plan —, to prosecute a scheme; ein unternommenes Werk —, to execute a work undertaken; ich kann es nicht —, I have not the means of accomplishing it, I cannot afford it; ein Gemählde —, to finish a picture; eine Geschichte umständlich —, to prosecute a story in all its circumstances; eine Materie —, to pursue a subject; eine Schilderung —, to amplify a description; der Hauptcharakter in diesem Stück ist gut ausgeführt, the principal character in this play is well drawn. *b)* to carry on to a final close by necessary proofs. Seine Sache vor Gericht —, to prosecute one's cause in court; seine Sache in einer Schrift —, to evidence one's cause in a writing.

Ausführenswerth, Ausführungswürdig, *adj.* and *adv.* that which deserves to be performed or accomplished or executed.

Ausführer, *m.* [-s, *pl.* -] exporter. *Fig.* achiever, accomplisher.

Ausführlich, *adj.* and *adv.* full, detailed, expressing the whole. Eine —e Beschreibung, a full description; eine —e Erzählung, an ample narrative; er erzählte die Geschichte —, he related the story in detail; wo der Schriftsteller —er wird, where the author treats more largely; ich schrieb Ihnen —, I wrote to you at large; ich bin bei Untersuchung des &c. sehr — zu Werke gegangen, I have been very particular in examining the &c.

Ausführlichkeit, *f.* fulness, copiousness, amplification. Die — einer Erzählung, the detail of a story.

Ausführung, *f.* 1) the act of carrying out, of exporting or leading out. Die — böser Säfte, the evacuation of noxious humours 2) *Fig.* Die — eines Vorhabens, the execution of a design; die — einer That, the performance of an action, achievement; die weitere — eines Gegenstandes, amplification; in — bringen, to bring into practise, to carry into execution. 3) *Fig.* the thing evidenced or evinced; a writing containing evidence.

Ausführungs-gang, *m.* [in anatomy] 1) excretory. 2) pancreatic duct. —**weg**, *m.* [in anat.] excretory duct, emunctory. —**würdig**, V. Ausführenswerth.

1. **Ausfüllen**, *v. tr.* 1) to fill, to fill up. Einen Graben mit Steinen —, to fill up a ditch with stones; eine Mauer —, [in masoury] to fill up the cavities in a wall; eine Bresche —, [in milit. aff.] to make up a breach. *Fig.* Suche das Leben mit nützlichen Beschäftigungen auszufüllen, seek to fill up life with useful employments; die Zeit —, to fill up the time; Jemands Stelle —, to supply any one's place. 2) to pour the contents of a vessel &c. into another. Ein Gefäß —, to empty a vessel.

2. **Ausfüllen**, V. Ausfohlen.

Ausfüllung, *f.* 1) a making full, filling. 2) [in architect. to give more fulness to any thing, painture &c.] a thing that serves to set any thing off.

Ausfüllungs-band, *n.* [in anat.] a name of several ligaments. —**wort**, *n.* expletive.

Ausfunkeln, *v. intr.* 1) [u. w. seyn] to sparkle with light, to glisten. 2) [u. w. haben] to cease to sparkle with light. Die Sterne haben ausgefunkelt, the stars twinkle no longer.

Ausfurchen, *v. tr.* to make furrows in, to furrow.

Ausfuttern, *v. tr.* to cover on the inside. Ein Kleid mit Seide —, to line a garment with silk; mit Pelz —, to line with fur.

Ausfüttern, I. *v. tr.* 1) to furnish with provender. 2) to feed well, to fatten. 3) to feed or fodder for a certain period. 4) to empty by feeding [the corn-bin &c.]. Wir haben unsern ganzen Hafervorrath ausgefüttert, we have used up all our oats. II. *v. intr.* Der Kutscher hat ausgefüttert, the coachman has done feeding his horses.

Ausfutterung, *f.* 1) the act of covering on the inside, of lining. 2) [in seamen's language] Die — der Stückpforten, half-ports; die — des Gangspills, whelps.

Ausgabe, *f.* [*pl.* -n] 1) the act of putting into another's hand, of giving or delivering. Die — der Zeitungen, der Briefe auf der Post, the distribution of newspapers, of letters at the post-office. 2) the thing delivered to another, especially the money expended; expenditure, disbursement. Ein kluger Mann beschränkt seine —n auf sein Einkommen, a prudent man limits his expenses by his income; die —n für Lebensunterhalt und Kleidung, the charges of victuals and clothes; die Einnahmen und —n dieses ausgedehnten Landes, the receipts and expenditures of this extensive country; die jährlichen —n übersteigen die Einnahme, the annual disbursements exceed the income. 3) edition [of a book]. Die zweite, dritte —, the second, third edition; [sometimes any single book or set of books printed according to the original] copy.

Ausgabe-buch, *n.* a book or register of expenditures. —**geld**, *n.* [better Ausgebegeld] money destined for daily disbursements. —**rechnung**, *f.* an account of expenditures. —**verzeichniß**, *n.* 1) a list of expenditures. 2) a list of the several editions of a book published successively.

Ausgabeln, *v. tr.* to take out with a fork.

Ausgaffen, *v. intr.* to cease gaping.

Ausgähnen, *v. intr.* to cease gaping or yawning.

Ausgähren, *ir. v. intr.* [u. w. seyn] 1) to ferment sufficiently. 2) to cease fermenting. Das Bier hat ausgegohren, the beer has done fermenting.

Ausgallen, *v. tr.* to take out the gall [of a fish].

Ausgang, *m* [-es, *pl.* -gänge] 1) the going out or abroad, issuing, walking out of a house, outgoing, egression. Du sollst Aus- und Eingang haben, [du kannst gehen und kommen] thou shalt have egress and regress. *Fig.* — der Waaren, exportation of goods; der — Christi vom Vater, [in theology] the proceeding of Christ from God the father. 2) the close or conclusion. Der — des Jahres, des Sommers, the end of the year, of the summer; der — eines Wortes, the ending or termination of a word; der — [die Entwickelung] eines Schauspiels, the conclusion, final event of a play, catastrophe; ein günstiger — des Krieges, a prosperous issue of the war; einen guten — nehmen, to turn out well or successfully, to prove successful; die wird nimmer einen guten — nehmen, that will never turn to good; der —, [in printing] the end of a break. 3) passage out, outlet, issue. Eine Gasse die keinen — hat [die Sackgasse], a street that has no passage out, blind-alley; dem Wasser einen — verschaffen, to give the water an outlet. *Fig.* Es sucht sich einen —, it labours for a vent. Syn. **Ausgang, Erfolg.** Ausgang signifies the termination of an action or series of actions considered only as an event, without reference to a cause. Erfolg de notes the issue not merely as an event, but as the effect produced by some preceding act or cause. We made a journey which, in other respects, turned out to our satisfaction, but which einen schlechten Ausgang nahm [had an unlucky termination], being afterwards attacked by robbers and plundered. Here we could not use Erfolg; for the being robbed was not the effect of the journey. If any one by travelling has improved his health, we may say that the journey has had for him einen glücklichen Erfolg. Thus we say: Die Krankheit nahm einen traurigen Ausgang, der Kranke starb, weil alle angewandte Rettungsmittel ohne Erfolg geblieben waren [the disease had a melancholy issue, the patient died, every remedy having been employed without effect].

Ausgangs-fest, *n.* festival of the Jews in commemoration of their going out of Egypt. —lehre, *f.* [in theology] the doctrine of the proceeding of Christ from God the father, and of the proceeding of the holy Ghost from God the father and God the son. —pforte, *f.* out-gate. —stück, *n.* [in music] finale. —zoll, *m.* V. Ausfuhrzoll.

Aúsgärben, V. Ausgerben.

Aúsgäschen, *v. intr.* to cease to froth.

Aúsgäten, *v. tr.* to weed [noxious plants].

Aúsgattern, *v. tr.* to find out, to discover. V. Auskundschaften, Erlauern.

Aúsgaunern, *v. intr.* to cease to cheat.

Aúsgebegeld, V. Ausgabegeld.

Aúsgeben, *ir.* I. *v. tr.* 1) to put into another's hand, to give out, to deliver. Briefe, Zeitungen —, to deliver letters, to distribute newspapers; die Karten —, to distribute cards, to deal; das — der Karten, the deal; das — verlieren, to lose the deal; ein Buch —, to publish a book; einen Befehl —, to give out, to issue an order; das Losungswort [die Parole] —, [in milit. aff.] to give the word; eine Tochter —, to marry a daughter 2) to lay out, to disburse, to spend. Geld für Nahrung und Kleidung —, to expend money for food and clothing, er hatte fünfzig Pfund ausgegeben, he spent fifty pounds; falsches Geld —, to pass or issue counterfeit money. 3) to give out for, to declare to be. Eine Nachricht für wahr —, to publish news as true; er gab sich für den Prinzen Florizel aus, he gave himself out for the prince or to be the prince Florizel; sie gab es für einen Knaben aus, she passed it for a boy; er gibt sich für einen Gelehrten aus, he pretends to be a scholar. II. *v. r.* sich —, to spend all one has. Ich habe mich ausgegeben, I have spent all my money. III. *v. intr.* 1) to be fruitful, to bear. Viel —, to yield a great deal; die Weinlese hat dieses Jahr nicht ausgegeben, the vintage has fallen short this year. 2) to exhibit as a product or result. 3) [among sportsmen] to sound. Das Horn gibt gut aus, the hunting-horn sounds loudly; der Hund gibt gut aus, the hound gives mouth or tongue well.

Aúsgeber, *m.* [-s, *pl.* -] 1) distributer. 2) steward. 3) [in commerce] the drawer of a bill of exchange.

Aúsgeberinn, *f.* house-keeper, cateress.

Aúsgebot, *n.* [-es, *pl.* -e] 1) a setting out to sale. 2) the first bidding.

Aúsgebreitet, [*part.* of Ausbreiten] *adj.* and *adv.* *Fig.* extensive. V. Verbreitet.

Aúsgeburt, *f.* [*pl.* -en] production. *Fig.* Eine neue — seines Hirns, a new production of his brain; eine — der Hölle, a diabolical scheme.

Aúsgecken, I. *v. tr.* V. Aushöhnen. II. *v. intr.* 1) to cease deriding. 2) to cease playing the fool.

Aúsgedinge, *n.* [-s, *pl.* -] [in some parts of Germany] a certain sum of money, cattle, free lodgings or provisions, for which a landlord or farmer disposing of his property stipulates for with his successor, over and above the purchase-money.

Aúsgehen, *ir.* I. *v. intr.* [u. w. seyn] 1) to go out, to go abroad, to walk out of a house &c. Er ist ausgegangen, he has gone out; der Herr vom Hause ist ausgegangen, the master of the house has gone out; an einem Orte viel aus- und eingehen, to frequent a place; im vorigen Jahre sind 30,000 Centner Salz ausgegangen, last year 30,000 cwt. of salt was exported; ausgehende Waaren, exports. *Fig.* Auf etwas —, to go in pursuit of something, to have something in view, to aim at, to tend to something; auf eine Unternehmung —, to go on an expedition, to go out; auf den Bettel —, to go a-begging; auf Straßenraub —, to go on the highway, to rob on the highway, to pad; leer —, to come away empty-handed, to get nothing; ungestraft —, to come off with impunity; frei —, to pay nothing; einen Befehl — lassen, to give out, to issue an order; ein Buch in Druck — lassen, to publish, to edit a book; der heilige Geist geht von Gott dem Vater und Gott dem Sohne aus, the holy Ghost proceeds from God the father and from God the son. 2) to stand out, or project. Ein —der Winkel, [in fortification, the angle advancing its point towards the field or country] saliant or sortant angle. 3) to be removed from an object. Diese Farbe geht leicht aus, this colour fades dies; dieser Flecken wird nicht leicht —, this stain will not easily come out; die Stiefel wollen nicht —, the boots will not come off. 4) [ausfallen] Die Haare gehen mir aus, my hair comes off. 5) *Fig.* to come to an end, to become extinct. Das Licht, das Feuer geht aus, the candle, the fire goes out; die Lampe ist ausgegangen, the lamp is extinct; die Seele, der Athem geht ihm aus, he breathes his last, he goes off, he dies; viele Pflanzen gehen jährlich aus, many plants die annually; das Geld geht mir aus, I am out of money; die Vorräthe gingen uns aus, our provisions fell short; die Geduld geht ihm aus, his patience forsakes him. 6) to end, to terminate. Das Ausgehende eines Ganges, [in mining] the head [end] of a load; Wörter, die auf *a* —, words ending in *a*; wie wird diese Sache —, how will this affair turn out; wir wissen nicht, wie die Sache — wird, we know not what will be the issue.

II. *v. tr.* 1) to find out by going. Ein Wild —, [am. hunters] to go in search of a head of game; Feldhühner —, to walk up partridges; einen Gang —, [in mining] to explore a load. 2) to measure by going. Einen Garten —, to pace a garden. 3) to widen by treading. Die Schuhe —, to widen one's shoes by walking.

Aúsgeifern, *v. intr.* 1) to slaver. 2) to cease slavering.

Aúsgeigen, I. *v. tr.* to play to the end [a piece of music on the violin]. II. *v. intr.* to cease fiddling.

Aúsgeißeln, *v. tr.* to scourge soundly.

Aúsgeizen, *v. tr.* [in husbandry] to thin out the leaves, to rid of superfluous tendrils, sprouts &c. Den Taback —, to pluck off the superfluous leaves of the tobacco plants.

Aúsgelassen, [*part.* of Auslassen] I. *adj.* 1) using licence, indulging freedom to excess, unrestrained, wild, frolicksome, romping, given to pranks, gay, wanton. 2) extravagant. Die —e Freude, exultation. II. *adv.* frolicksomely, gayly, wantonly.

Aúsgelassenheit, *f.* 1) gayety, frolicksomeness, wantonness, wild pranks. 2) extravagance, excess.

Aúsgeleiten, *v. tr.* to accompany out of a place.

Aúsgemacht, [*part.* of Ausmachen] *adj.* and *adv.* decided, determined, fixed, settled. Eine —e Wahrheit, an undeniable truth; ein —er Schurke, an arrant rogue, a confirmed rascal.

Aúsgenießen, *ir. v. tr.* to enjoy wholly or to the end.

Aúsgenommen, [*part.* of Ausnehmen] except, excepted, with the exception. Einer —, except one.

Aúsgerben, *v. tr.* to curry fully or entirely. †*Fig.* to beat, to thrash soundly, bang, belabour.

Aúsgesprenge, *n.* [-s, *pl.* -] report, rumour.

Aúsgeuden, I. *v. tr.* to spend lavishly. II. *v. intr.* to cease to lavish.

Aúsgewachsen, [*part.* of Auswachsen] V. Buckelig.

Aúsgewanderte, *m.* and *f.* [-n, *pl.* -n] emigrant. V Auswandern.

Aúsgezeichnet, [*part.* of Auszeichnen] I. *adj.* distinguished, eminent, transcendent, noted, famous, celebrated. —e Männer, distinguished men; —e Talente, Tugenden, Dienste, distinguished talents, virtues, services. II. *adv.* eminently, transcendently, famously.

Aúsgiebig, V. Ergiebig.

Aúsgießen, *ir.* I. *v. tr.* 1) to pour out, to effuse. Das Wasser —, to pour out the water. *Fig.* Seinen Zorn —, to give one's anger vent; seinen Zorn über Einen —, to wreak one's anger upon any one; sein Herz vor einem Freunde —, to unbosom one's self to a friend. 2) to fill with a liquid substance. Ein Loch mit Blei —, to fill a hole with molten lead. 3) to extinguish, to quench with any liquor. Das Feuer mit Wasser —, to put out the fire with water. II. *v. r.* sich —, *Fig.* 1) to unbosom one's self. 2) to spread. Todesblässe goß sich über sein Antlitz aus, a deadly paleness spread over his face, he grew deadly pale. III. *v. intr.* [am. hunters] to lose a great deal of blood, to bleed much.

Aúsgießung, *f.* 1) pouring out, effusion. 2) filling up with a liquid substance.

Aúsgipfeln, *v. tr.* to lop, to head [a tree].

Aúsgipsen, *v. tr.* to plaster.

Aúsglätten, *v. tr.* 1) to smooth, to take out by smoothing. Die Falten in einem Kleide —, to take the creases out of a garment by ironing &c. 2) V Auspoliren.

Aúsgleichbar, *adj.* compensable.

Aúsgleichen, *ir* I. *v. tr.* to make equal, to compensate. Die Schrötlinge — [justiren], [in coining] to size the blanks or planchets for coining; Rechnungen —, to equalize, to adjust, to settle or balance accounts; alle Rechnungen mit Jemand ausgeglichen haben, [gut Freund mit ihm seyn] to be upon the square with any one; den Schaden —, to compensate the loss; die Mißverständnisse sind ausgeglichen, the differences are adjusted; der Tod gleicht Alles aus, death reconciles all things. II. *v. r.* sich —, to come to a compromise of differences, to agree.

Aúsgleicher, *m.* [-s, *pl.* -] 1) adjuster. 2) [in mints] the comptroller.

Aúsgleichung, *f.* balance, compensation. Ausgleichungsmünze, *f.* odd-money. Ausgleichwage, *f.* adjusting-scales. V. Justirwage.

Aúsgleiten, *ir. v. tr* [u. w. seyn] [not to tread firmly] to slip, to slide out. Er glitt mit dem Fuße aus und fiel, his foot slipped and he fell. *Fig.* Der Mann glitt auf Fortunens Eise aus, the man slidddered upon Fortune's ice.

Aúsglimmen, *v. intr.* [with some authors *ir.*] 1) [u. w. haben] to cease to burn faintly. 2) [u. w. seyn] to go out gradually.

|| **Aúsglitschen**, V. Ausgleiten.

† **Aúsglotzen**, *v. intr.* to cease staring.

Aúsglucken, *v. intr.* to cease to cluck [said of hens].

Aúsglühen, I. *v. tr.* to heat thorougly. Metalle —, to anneal metals; Eisen —, to anneal iron. II. *v. intr.* to cease glowing.

Aúsglüher, *m.* [-s, *pl.* -] [in mints] boiler.

Aúsgraben, *ir.* I. *v. tr.* 1) to dig out, to dig up. Einen Stein —, to dig up a stone; einen Schatz —, to dig out a treasure; eine Leiche, einen Leichnam —, to disinter a dead body, to untomb a corpse; das Ausgraben eines Todten, exhumation; einen Dachs —, [among sportsmen] to unearth a badger. 2) to excavate, to dig. Einen Teich —, to dig a pond. 3) to grave, to engrave. II. *v intr.* to cease or finish digging.

Aúsgräten, *v. tr.* to rid or deprive of bones, to bone [a fish].

Aúsgreifen, I. *v. tr.* 1) to select from many, to pick out, to cull. 2) to feel, to touch, to handle. † Ein Mädchen —, to feel a girl indecently. 3) to wear out the inside of a thing by handling, touching, feeling. II. *v. intr.* to go a good pace, to stretch out [said of horses].

Aúsgriebsen, **Ausgröbsen**, *v. tr.* to rid apples or pears of the core.

Aúsgrollen, *v. intr.* to cease to bear ill will against any one.

Aúsgrößern, *v. tr.* [among combmakers] to round the teeth of a comb.

Aúsgrübeln, *v. tr.* to get to the bottom of a thing by dint of scoutinizing.

Aúsgründen, *v. tr.* 1) [am. joiners] to gutter, to groove, to flute. 2) [in sculpture] to form in relievo, to raise. 3) *Fig.* V. Ergründen.

Aúsgrünen, *v. intr.* to cease to be verdant.

Aúsgurgeln, I. *v. tr.* 1) to throw out by gargling. 2) to gargle. II *v. intr.* to cease to produce sounds from the throat.

Aúsgurren, *v. intr.* to cease cooing.

Aúsguß, *m.* [-sses, *pl.* -güsse] 1) the act of pouring out, effusion. 2) that which is poured out, effusion. 3) outlet for liquids, conduit, sink.

Ausguß-kelle, *f.* [in metallurgy] a ladle. —pfännchen, *n.* [in metall.] ingot-mould.

Aúshaaren, *v. intr.* to part with hair [said of a fur].

Aúshaben, *v. intr.* not to have on. Ich hatte die Stiefel aus, I had my boots off.

Aúshacken, *v. tr.* 1) to dig up [with a hoe]. Gesträuch —, to grub up shrubs; Einem die Augen —, to pick out any one's eyes from envy or hatred. *Prov.* Keine Krähe hackt der andern die Augen aus, ask my fellow whether I be a thief. 2) [am. butchers] to hew in pieces, to cut in pieces, to cut meat for sale. 3) to cut out into points and edges, to cut into figures, to scallop. 4) [among coopers] Die Faßdauben —, to rough-hew the staves.

Aúshacker, *m.* [-s, *pl.* -] 1) he that grubs up. 2) [am. coopers] a workman that rough-hews the staves. 3) [am. shoemakers and mantuamakers] a tool used for scalloping.

Aúshadern, *v. intr.* to cease quarrelling.

Aúshageln, *v. imp.* to cease hailing.

Aúshäkeln, *v. tr.* to hook out.

Aúshaken, *v. tr.* to hook out.

Aúshalftern, *v. tr.* to unhalter. Ein Pferd, das sich aushalftert, a horse that unhalters itself.

Aúshallen, *v. intr.* 1) to sound at a distance. 2) to sound to the end. 3) to cease sounding.

Aúshalten, *ir.* I. *v. intr.* 1) [in music] to hold on or sustain a note, to dwell on a note; ausgehalten, tenuto. 2) to last, to endure, to continue, to hold out, not to yield. Es ist mit ihm nicht auszuhalten, there is no dealing with him; ich kann es hier nicht länger —, I cannot abide here any longer; das Aushalten, perseverance; die Besatzung hielt noch immer aus, the garrison still held out; im Unglücke —, to hold up under misfortunes. II. *v. tr* 1) to bear, to endure, to sustain. Die Metalle können einen gewissen Grad von Hitze —, ohne zu schmelzen, metals endure a certain degree of heat, without melting; eine Strafe —, to suffer a punishment; ich kann die Hitze nicht —, I cannot stand the heat; den Anfall, Angriff —, to stand the shock; eine Belagerung —, to stand, to hold out a siege; den Sturm —, to weather out the storm; die Probe —, to stand the test. 2) to hold to the end [in a figurative sense]. Seine Lehrzeit —, to serve out one's apprenticeship. 3) [in forestry] to separate, to sever from the rest.

Aushaltungszeichen, Aushaltzeichen, *n.* [in music] the pause [𝄐].

Aúshalter, *m.* [-s, *pl.* -] [in music] a note which must be held on or sustained.

Aúshämmern, I. *v. tr.* to beat out with the hammer. II. *v. intr.* to cease hammering.

Aúshandeln, I. *v. tr.* to conclude a bargain. II. *v. intr.* to cease to traffick.

Aúshändigen, *v. tr.* to deliver over, to transfer, to give or pass from one to another. V. Einhändigen.

Aúshang, *m.* [-s] goods hung out or exposed to sale.

Aúshangen, *ir. v. intr.* to be suspended in open view, to be hung out.

Aúshängen, I. *v. tr.* 1) to hang out, to suspend in open view, to exhibit to notice. Ein Schild —, to hang out a sign; eine Flagge —, to set up a flag; ein Placat &c. —, to post a bill, a citation &c. [in some public place &c.]. *Fig.* Er hängt Wohlwollen und Menschenliebe aus, he makes a show of benevolence and humanity. 2) das Ruder —, [in seamen's language] to unhang the rudder. II. *v. r.* sich —, to come unhinged.

Aushänge-bogen, *m.* [in printing] proof-sheet. —schild, *n.* a sign of an inn or public house &c. *Fig.* Titel sind oft täuschende —schilder, titles often deceive.

Aúshären, *v. tr.* to free from hair.

Aúsharken, *v. tr.* to clean with a rake.

Aúshärmen, *v. r.* sich —, to cease to grieve.

Aúsharnen, I *v. tr.* to eject in urining or pissing. II. *v. intr.* to cease urining or making water.

Aúsharren, *v. intr.* to persevere, to be steadfast or constant in any course, to continue. Das —, perseverance.

Aúshärten, *v. tr.* to harden thoroughly.

Aúshaspeln, I. *v. tr.* to reel out. II. *v. intr.* to cease reeling.

Aúshaspen, **Aúshäspen**, *v. tr.* to unhinge [a door &c.].

Aúshau, *m.* [-es, *pl.* -e] the act of hewing or cutting out. Der — der Zweige eines Baumes, lopping, pruning.

Aúshauch, *m.* [-es] 1) the act of breathing out. 2) [the thing breathed out] breath, fume. *Fig.* Der — lieblich duftender Kräuter, the exhalation of fragrant plants.

Aúshauchen, I. *v. intr.* 1) to breathe out. 2) to cease breathing, to expire. II. *v. tr.* to eject by breathing, to breathe out; den letzten Athem —, to breathe one's last, to expire. *Poet.* Die Rose haucht Wohlgerüche aus, the rose exhales or breathes perfume.

Aúshauen, *ir. v. tr.* 1) to remove the inner part of a thing by hewing or cutting. 2) to hollow by hewing. Einen Trog —, to cut out a trough. 3) [to form or shape with an edged instrument] to hew out, to cut out. Ein Grabmahl —, to hew out a tomb-stone; in einem Walde Gänge —, to cut out a wood into walks. 4) to remove a part by cutting. Einen Baum —, to prune a tree; einen Wald — [ausschneiden], to thin the trees of a wood. 5) [am. butchers] to hew or cut into pieces, to cut for sale. Einen Ochsen —, to cut up an ox for sale. 6) to strike with a rod or whip for punishment. Einen mit Ruthen —, to flog or whip any one.

Aushaustempel, *m.* stamp.

Aúshäuten, I. *v. tr.* to flay [a calf &c.]. Einen Hasen —, to skin a hare. II. *v. r.* sich —, to shed or throw off the skin.

Aúsheben, *ir v. tr.* 1) to heave out, to lift out, to take out. Eine Thür, ein Fenster —, to unhinge a door, a window; die Form — [aus der Presse heben], [in printing] to lift out the form; einen Baum —, to grub up a tree; Blumen aus den Töpfen —, to take flowers out of the pots; Vögel —, to take out of the nest [the young birds]; Wein —, to draw wine out of a cask with the siphon or crane; [among clockmakers] to lift up the detents every hour; [among printers] to empty the stick into the galley. *Fig.* [= auswählen, auslesen] to select from many, to pick out. Soldaten —, to levy men; der Ausgehobene, a recruit; von einer Verhandlung nur die wichtigsten Umstände —, to copy or to relate only the most important particulars of a transaction. 2) to put out of its proper place, particularly to put out of joint. Sich den Arm —, to dislocate one's arm.

Aushebespan, *m.* [in print.] setting-rule. V. Setzlinie.

Aúsheber, *m.* [-s, *pl.* -] 1) [in gardening] an instrument for lifting up trees dug up. 2) [in horology] ratch.

Aúshecheln, *v. tr.* 1) to hatchel. Das Werg —, to clean [flax or hemp] from the tow; den Flachs —, to hatchel flax. *Fig.* Einen —, to censure, to blame, to lash any one. 2) to hatchel sufficiently.

Aúshecken, I. *v. tr.* to produce young from eggs, to hatch. *Fig.* [in contempt] Böses —, to hatch mischief; was für tolle Gedanken haben Sie da ausgeheckt? what strange thoughts have you been brewing? II. *v. intr.* 1) to cease hatching. Die Vögel haben ausgeheckt, the birds hatch no longer. 2) to finish hatching.

Aúsheilen, I. *v. intr.* [u. w. seyn] to heal perfectly. Die Wunde ist ausgeheilt —, the wound has healed up. II. *v. tr.* to heal or cure perfectly.

Aúsheimisch, *adj.* and *adv.* foreign.

Aúsheitern, I. *v. tr.* to cheer [the heart &c.]. V. Erheitern. II. *v. r.* sich —, to clear up. Das Wetter heitert sich aus, the weather clears up; es heitert sich aus, it clears away or off. V. Aufheitern.

Aúsheizen, *v. tr.* to warm thorougly.

Aúshelfen, *ir. v. intr.* to help out, to assist. Einem in der Noth mit Gelde —, to accommodate any one with money in time of distress; hilft mir oft aus, he frequently supplies me;

kann Ihnen —, I can fit you.

Aushellen, I. *v tr.* to clear [liquors &c.] Die Veränderung des Windes hat den Himmel ausgehellt, the change of wind has cleared the sky. II. *v. r.* sich —, to clear up. Es hellt sich aus, it clears away. V. Aufhellen.

Aushemmen, *v. tr.* [to take away the drag-chain] to unlock [a wheel].

Ausheuken, V. Aushängen.

Ausheucheln, *v. intr.* to cease dissembling.

‖**Ausheuern**, *v. tr.* 1) to hire, to hire out, to let, to lease. Er hat seinen Garten ausgeheuert, he has hired out his garden. 2) Einen —, to dispossess any one of his lease by paying a higher rent to the owner, to outbid.

Ausheulen, I. *v. intr.* to cease howling. II. *v. r.* sich —, to howl one's fill.

Aushieb, *m.* [-es, *pl.* -e] 1) that which is hewn or cut out. 2) [in mints] a piece of refined silver hewn off by the assay master for an assay.

Aushiebmeißel, *m.* hewing-chisel.

Aushinken, *v intr.* 1) [u. w. seyn] to hobble out of a place, to limp abroad. 2) [u. w. haben] to cease limping.

Aushobeln, *v. tr.* 1) to plane. 2) to plane off.

† **Aushocken**, *v. tr.* to find out by meditation, to strike out by thinking.

Aushoffen, *v. intr.* to leave off hoping.

Aushöhlen, *v. tr.* to cut, scoop, dig or wear out the inner part of any thing and make it hollow Einen Baumstamm —, to excavate the trunk of a tree; Bäume —, to hollow trees; die Erde —, to excavate the earth; eine Säule —, to form flutes or channels in a column, to flute, to channel, to groove or to chamfer a column; den Rand eines Gimses —, to groove the edge of a moulding; ein ausgehöhlter Felsen, a hollow rock.

Aushöhlung, *f.* 1) [the act of excavating or hollowing] excavation. Die — einer Säule, the fluting, channeling or chamfering of a column. 2) [a hollow or cavity formed by removing the inferior substance] excavation, hole. Die — auf einer Armbrust, the gutter of a cross-bow; —en, die sie selbst gemacht haben, excavations of their own forming.

Aushöhnen, *v. tr.* to mock, to treat with scorn by laughter. Sie höhnten ihn aus, they derided him.

Aushöken, Aushökern, *v. tr.* to retail small articles [cheese, butter, nuts, apples &c.]

Ausholen, I. *v. intr.* 1) to lift or stretch out the arm in order to throw or strike. 2) to prepare for leaping or running. Zu einem Sprunge —, to take a run in order to leap. *Fig.* Um diese Geschichte verständlicher zu machen, müssen wir weiter —, for the better understanding of this story we must fetch it or resume it a little higher, we must trace it up higher; er holt in seiner Erzählung weit aus, he goes far back in his narration. II. † and * *v. tr.* [in a figurative sense] to pump, to sound [a person]. Einen —, to sift any one.

Ausholer, *m.* [-s, *pl.* -] 1) [in seamen's language] the top-rope of the jib-boom Der — der Blinde, sprit-sail halliard; der — der Schiebblinde, sprit-sail top-sail-halliard; der — des Klüvers, tack of the jib. 2) † and * a person that pumps or sounds another.

Ausholzen, *v. tr.* Einen Wald —, to thin a forest.

Aushölzen, *v. tr.* [am. shoemakers] to pare, to slope [wooden heels].

Aushorchen, *v. tr.* to spy or explore by listening.

Aushören, *v. tr.* and *intr.* to hear to the end.

Aushub, *m.* [-es] levy [of troops]. Ein neuer — Soldaten, fresh recruits.

Aushubmeißel, V. Aushiebmeißel.

Aushülfe, *f.* 1) help, assistance, aid. 2) aid, aider.

Aushüllen, V. Enthüllen.

Aushülsen, *v. tr.* to unhusk, to shell, to peel. Bohnen —, to slip beans out of their skin; Erbsen —, to husk pease.

Aushungern, *v. tr.* to exhaust by hunger, to famish. Ausgehungert, hunger-starved; eine Festung —, to famish a fortress; ein Land —, to starve a country.

† **Aushunzen**, *v. tr.* to reprimand, to abuse.

Aushüpfen, *v. intr.* 1) [u. w. seyn] to spring, to leap out of a place. 2) [u. w. haben] to cease leaping or springing.

† **Aushuren**, *v. intr.* 1) to cease whoring. 2) [only used in the past part. with seyn] exhausted by whoring.

Aushusten, I. *v. tr.* to cough up, to expectorate. Schleim —, to cough up phlegm. II. *v. intr.* to cease coughing.

Aushüten, I. *v. tr.* V. Abhüten. II. *v. intr.* to cease heeding or watching.

Ausjagen, I. *v. tr.* to drive out, to expel, to force to leave. Die wilden Thiere aus einem Walde —, to expel wild beasts from a forest. *Fig.* *Einem den Angstschweiß —, to disturb any one with terror, to fill any one with anxiety by the prospect of evil, to alarm any one. II. *v. intr.* 1) [u. w. seyn] to ride out with great quickness. 2) [u. w. haben] to finish hunting. Er hat ausgejagt, he has done hunting.

Ausjammern, I. *v. intr.* to cease lamenting or wailing. II. *v. tr.* Seinen Schmerz —, to give way to one's grief. III. *v. r.* sich —; 1) to grieve violently. 2) to cease lamenting or wailing.

Ausjäten, V. Ausgäten.

Ausjauchzen, I. *v. tr.* to publish shouting. II. *v. intr.* to cease shouting.

Ausjochen, *v. tr.* to unjoke [oxen].

Ausjubeln, I. *v. intr.* to cease shouting. II. *v. r.* sich —, to shout one's fill.

Ausjungen, *v. intr.* to cease breeding.

Auskalben, *v. intr.* to cease calving. Die Kühe haben ausgekalbt, the cows have done calving.

Auskälbern, *v. intr.* to cease frisking.

Auskälten, *v. intr.* [u. w. seyn] to be penetrated with cold.

Auskämmen, *v. tr.* 1) to remove by combing, to comb out. 2) to comb [one's hair].

Auskämmekamm, *m.* [among combmakers] a large comb.

‖**Auskampeln**, *v. intr.* to cease quarrelling.

Auskämpfen, I. *v. tr.* to fight out. Seine Sache —, to fight out one's cause. II. *v. intr.* to cease wrestling or contending.

Auskargen, *v. intr.* to cease to be parsimonious.

Auskarren, I. *v. tr.* to remove in a cart. Erde aus dem Garten —, to cart earth out of the garden. II. *v. intr.* to cease carting.

Auskasteien, *v. r.* sich —, to cease chastizing one's body.

Auskauen, I. *v. tr.* 1) Den Saft —, to draw out the juice by chewing. 2) [in sea language] Das Werg —, to work out the oakum. II. *v. intr.* to finish chewing.

Auskauf, *m.* [-es, *pl.* -käufe] 1) the act of buying up all. 2) the outbidding [of another purchaser].

Auskaufen, I. *v. tr.* 1) Einen —, to buy all the commodities a person offers for sale. * *Fig.* Die Zeit —, to employ time well, to make a good use of time; die Gelegenheit —, to improve the occasion, *Prov* [otherwise: die Gelegenheit am Schopf ergreifen] to take occasion by the forelock. 2) to anticipate in buying. II. *v. intr.* to cease purchasing.

Auskegeln, I *v. intr.* to cease playing at nine-pins. II. *v. tr.* 1) to dislocate the bone of the foreleg [said of horses]. 2) to play for any thing at nine-pins. Wir wollen eine Flasche Wein —, let us play for a bottle of wine.

Auskehlen, *v. tr.* to chamfer, to channel, to flute [a column].

Auskehren, *v tr.* 1) to remove with a broom or brush. Den Staub —, to brush, wipe or sweep away the dust. 2) to clean with a broom or brush. Einen Hut — [more usual: abbürsten, ausbürsten], to brush a hat; das Zimmer —, to sweep the room.

Auskehricht, Auskehrig, *n.* [-es] sweepings.

Auskeifen, I. *v. tr.* to scold, to chide. II. *v. intr.* to cease scolding or chiding.

Auskeilen, I. *v. tr.* to provide with wedges. *Fig.* Der Gang keilet den Berg aus or keilet sich aus, [in mining] the load makes a start or leap [it disappears suddenly]. II. *v. intr.* to end in a point.

Auskeimen, *v. intr.* 1) [u. w. seyn] to begin to vegetate, to germinate, to sprout, to bud, to shoot 2) [u. w. haben] to cease germinating.

Auskellen, *v. tr.* to throw out with a ladle, to lade out.

Auskeltern, I. *v. tr.* to press by means of the wine-press. Weintrauben —, to press grapes. II. *v. intr.* to finish the pressing of grapes.

Auskerben, *v. tr.* [to cut in small hollows] to notch. Ein ausgekerbtes Blatt, [in botany] a notched leaf; ein ausgekerbter Sparren, [in heraldry] chevron engrailed or ingrailed.

Auskernen, *v. tr.* 1) to take out the kernel, pippins, seeds &c. Nüsse —, to shell nuts. 2) *Fig.* [somewhat unusual] to pick out, to select, to cull.

Auskesseln, I. *v. tr.* to form in the shape of a kettle. II. *v. intr.* [in mining] to take or get the shape of a kettle.

Ausketzern, *v. tr.* [in mining] to make clefts into a rock, in order to apply coins or wedges.

Auskeuchen, *v. intr.* to cease panting.

Auskeulen, *v. tr.* to beat with a club.

Auskichern, *v. intr.* to cease tittering.

Auskielen, I. *v. intr.* [obsolete] to produce feathers or quills [said of birds]. II. *v. tr.* to provide with quills.

Auskindern, *v. intr.* [unusual expression] to finish child-bearing.

Auskippen, *v. tr.* to make a selection by means of a pair of scales.

Auskitten, *v. tr.* to fill up with cement.

Auskläffen, *v. intr.* to finish barking or yelping.

Ausklaftern, *v. tr.* to measure out [wood] by the cord.

Ausklagbar, *adj.* and *adv.* [in law] demandable.

Ausklagen, I. *v. tr.* [in law] to seek, to ask for, to sue for, to demand. Capital und Zinsen einer Schuld —, to demand principal and interest of a debt; Einen —, to sue any one at law for a thing. II. *v. intr.* 1) to finish complaining. Er hat ausgeklagt, he has done complaining. 2) to cease sueing at law. III. *v. r.* sich —, to give full vent to one's grievances. Lassen Sie den armen Mann sich —, suffer the poor man give full vents to his complaints.

Aúsklappern, *v. intr.* to cease clappering or rattling.

Aúsklären, I. *v. tr.* to clear or cleanse fully. Ausgeklärtes Mehl, flour. II. *v. r.* sich —, to clear up. Das Wetter klärt sich aus, the weather clears up.

Aúsklatschen, I. *v. tr.* 1) to slap [a child &c.]. 2) to explode with the clapping of hands. Ein Stück —, to explode a play on the stage. 3) to beat out by flapping. Einem die Augen —, to beat out any one's eyes by flapping. 4) *Fig.* [to publish secrets or trifles without discretion] to blab. II. *v. intr.* to cease blabbing.

Aúsklauben, *v. tr.* to pick out with the fingers [nuts from the shells]. Die Erze —, to cull the ores. *Fig.* to find out, to discover by study, [sometimes in contempt] to contrive. Lassen Sie ihn die Sache —, let him study out the thing.

Aúskleben, *v. tr.* Eine Schachtel mit Papier —, to line a box with paper; eine Wand mit Lehm —, to cover a wall with loam, to loam a wall.

Aúskleiden, *v. tr.* 1) [to divest of clothes] to undress. Sich —, to put off one's clothes. 2) to dress in the clothes of another, to disguise. Syn. Auskleiden, Entkleiden. Auskleiden signifies properly to undress, to put off the garments in which one is clothed; Entkleiden has a more general signification, and means to put away any clothing or covering whatever. When a female lays aside an apron which she before had on; this is ein Entkleiden, but not ein Auskleiden. Speaking of trees that the winter has robbed of their foliage, one may say: sie stehen entkleidet da, but not ausgekleidet. As Entkleiden has a more extended signification than Auskleiden, entkleidet only, is used for bare or naked, and not ausgekleidet, especially in a figurative sense. One says: Die Wahrheit gefällt auch von allem fremden Schmuck entkleidet [the truth pleases even when deprived of all foreign ornament, i. e. the naked truth], here one could not say ausgekleidet.

Aúskleistern, *v. tr.* to paste on the inside. Einen Kasten mit Papier —, to line a chest with paper.

Aúsklimpern, *v. intr.* to cease thrumming on a piano &c.

Aúsklingeln, I. *v. tr.* 1) to publish by ringing a bell. 2) to disgrace by clinking, ringing or jingling. II. *v. intr.* to cease ringing.

Aúsklingen, *ir. v. intr.* 1) to cease clinking. 2) to sound sufficiently, to give out sufficient tone.

Aúsklopfen, I. *v. tr.* 1) to remove by beating. Den Staub aus den Kleidern —, to beat the clothes, eine [runzelige] Haut, ein [runzeliges] Fell glatt —, to beat a hide smooth. 2) to clean by beating or knocking. Einen Teppich —, to beat a carpet; Einem den Rock —, to beat any one's coat. † *Fig.* Einem die Jacke oder das Fell —, to dust any one's jacket, to give any one a good drubbing. II. *v. intr.* to cease beating or knocking.

Aúsklügeln, *v. tr.* to strike out by thinking, to excogitate.

Aúsknebeln, *v. tr.* to free from a clog.

Aúskneten, I. *v. tr.* to knead fully. V. Auswirken. II. *v. intr.* to cease kneading.

Aúsknien, I. *v. tr.* to hollow, to wear out by kneeling. II. *v. intr.* 1) to kneel for a fixed time. 2) to cease kneeling.

Aúsknistern, *v. intr.* to cease crackling.

Aúsknöpfen, *v. tr.* to unbutton and take out.

Aúsknurren, *v. intr.* 1) to snarl one's fill. 2) to cease snarling.

Aúskobern, *v. tr.* to take out of a basket.

Aúskochen, I. *v. tr.* 1) to extract the juice or quality of any thing by boiling, to boil. 2) to clean by boiling. 3) [= durchkochen] to boil thoroughly. II. *v. intr.* 1) [u. w. seyn] to boil away or over. Die Milch ist halb ausgekocht, the milk is half boiled away or boiled over. 2) [u. w. haben] to cease boiling. Ausgekocht haben, to have done boiling or cooking [dressing] the victuals.

Aúskollern, *v. intr.* 1) to cease rolling [said of a bowl]. 2) to roll to the end. 3) to cast the staggers [said of horses].

Aúskommen, *ir. v. intr.* 1) to come out of a place. Er kommt gar nicht aus, he never goes out, he is always at home; die jungen Hühner fangen schon an auszukommen, the chickens begin already to peep out of the shell; die jungen Hühner sind schon ausgekommen, the chickens are already hatched. *Fig.* to come out, to become public, to get wind. Die Sache kam aus, the affair came out; die That kam aus [wurde ruchbar], the fact leaked out. 2) to arise, to break out. In meinem Hause ist ein Feuer ausgekommen, a fire broke out in my house. 3) [as it were hinaus oder zu Ende kommen] *Fig.* *a*) to answer the purpose, to do. Er wird mit dieser Entschuldigung nicht —, this excuse will not do, will not serve his purpose. *b*) to live in concord or without contention. Die Eltern und Kinder kommen gut mit einander aus, the parents and children agree well together; ich will schon mit ihm —, I will get on with him well enough. *c*) to have enough of any thing, to make a thing do. Mit diesem Gelde werde ich nicht —, this money will not be sufficient for me; er kann damit nicht —, he cannot subsist upon it; damit können wir —, this will be enough for us to live on. Syn. Auskommen, Bekanntwerden. Bekanntwerden is said of any thing which comes to the knowledge of others; Auskommen only of that which it was intended should be kept secret.

Aúskommen, *n.* [-s] 1) competence, subsistence. Sein — haben, to have a competence to live, to subsist on; sein gutes — haben, to enjoy a competency or independence, to be well off; ein nothdürftiges — haben, to have a bare subsistence; ein artiges —, Zufriedenheit, an elegant sufficiency, content. 2) peaceable intercourse. Mit ihm ist kein —, there is no dealing with him, no getting on with him; Lassen Sie uns denn dieses — treffen, let us come to some agreement. 3) means for the attainment of an end. Ein — treffen, to find ways and means.

Aúskömmlich, *adj.* and *adv.* affording subsistence.

Aúskönnen, *ir. v. intr.* to be able to go out of a place.

Aúskoppeln, *v. tr.* to uncouple [hounds].

‖ **Aúskören**, V. Küren.

Aúskörnen, **Auskörnern**, *v. tr.* to pick the corns or grains out of a thing. *Fig.* to pick out, to select, to choose.

Aúskosen, I. *v. intr.* to cease caressing. II. *v. r.* sich —, to caress sufficiently, to caress one's fill.

Aúskosten, I. *v. tr* 1) to select by tasting. Einen Wein —, to taste wine. 2) to taste sufficiently or thoroughly. 3) to consume by tasting. II. *v. intr.* to have done tasting.

Aúsköthen, *v. r.* sich —, to sprain the fetlock joint.

† **Aúskotzen**, V. Ausspeien.

Aúskrächzen, I. *v. tr.* to eject croaking. II. *v. intr.* 1) to cease croaking. 2) to croak enough.

Aúskragen, *v. tr.* [in building] to make to project. Eine —de Mauer, a projecting wall.

Aúskrähen, I. *v. tr.* to publish or to announce by crowing. II. *v. intr.* 1) to cease crowing. 2) to crow sufficiently.

‖ **Aúskrakeelen**, *v. intr.* to cease quarrelling or kicking up a row.

Aúskrallen, *v. tr.* to pull or tear out with the claws.

Aúskramen, I. *v. tr.* to place in a situation to invite purchasers, to expose [goods] to sale. *Fig.* to se. to view ostentatiously, to display. Seine Gelehrsamkeit —, to make a parade of one's learning; das Auskramen unseres eigenen Werthes, the boastful display of our own worth. II. *v. intr.* to cease rummaging.

Aúskrämpeln, I. *v. tr.* 1) to remove by carding. 2) to card [wool] sufficiently. II. *v. intr.* to finish carding.

Aúskränkeln, *v. intr.* to cease to be sickly.

Aúskranken, *v. intr.* to cease to sicken.

Aúskränken, *v. tr.* and *r.* Einem, sich die Seele —, to plague a person, to plague one's self to death.

‖ **Aúskrätschen**, *v. tr.* Die Beine —, to part the legs wide, to straddle.

Aúskratzen, I. *v. tr.* to scratch out, to scrape out. Einem die Augen —, to scratch out any one's eyes; ein Wort oder einen Namen —, to scrape out, to erase a word or a name; einen Fleck —, to rub out a stain. II. *v. intr.* 1) to cease scratching or scraping. † 2) to stretch out in full gallop.

‖ **Aúskrauseisen**, *n.* [-s, *pl.* -] [am. saddlers] pricking teeth.

Aúskrauten, *v. tr.* to weed, to hoe.

Aúskrebsen, I. *v. tr.* Einen Bach —, to catch all the craw-fishes in a brook. † and ‡ *Fig.* to find out by careful disquisition. II. *v. intr.* to cease catching craw-fish.

Aúskreischen, I. *v. tr.* to express in a shrill manner, to shrill forth. II. *v. intr.* to cease to cry with a shrill voice.

Aúskriechen, *ir.* I *v. intr.* [u. w. seyn] to creep out of a place. Die jungen Vögel kriechen bald aus, the young birds are almost hatched; der Wind kriecht aus und ein, [in sea language] the wind chops about, is variable. II. *v. tr.* Alle Winkel —, to creep into every corner.

1. † and * **Aúskriegen**, *v. tr.* to get off or out, to put off. Ich kann meine Stiefel nicht —, I cannot get off or pull off my boots.

2. **Aúskriegen**, *v. intr.* to cease waging or making war.

Aúskröbsen, V. Ausgriebsen.

Aúskrücken, *v. tr.* to take out [of an oven] with the oven-rake.

Aúskrümeln, I. *v. tr.* to crumble [bread &c.] II. *v. intr.* to finish crumbling.

Aúskugeln, *v. tr.* to vote by ballot.

Aúskühlen, I. *v. intr.* [u. w. seyn] to cool thoroughly. II. *v. tr.* to make cool, to cool thoroughly [a room, an oven &c.].

Aúskümmern, *v. intr.* and *r.* sich —, to cease grieving.

Aúskunden, *v. tr.* to pry into, to explore. V. Auskundschaften, Erkunden.

Aúskünden, *v. tr.* to publish by authority, to proclaim.

Áuskundigen, V. Auskunden.

Áuskündigen, V. Auskünden.

Áuskundschaften, *v. tr.* to search for making discovery, to explore. Moses sandte mich aus, das Land auszukundschaften, [Josh. XIV] Moses sent me to espy out the land; den Feind —, to reconnoitre the enemy.

Áuskundschafter, *m.* [-s, *pl.*-] a spy, prier, informer.

Áuskunft, *f.* [*pl.* -künfte] 1) the issue, event, end. 2) means, resource. Ich weiß keine — mehr, I know no farther resource. 3) information, intelligence. — geben, to give intelligence, to inform; er konnte keine — über diese Sache geben, he could not clear up that matter.

Auskunfts-buch, *n.* a book which gives intelligence. **—mittel**, *n.* means, expedient, resource. Dies war das einzige —mittel, this was the only means.

Áuskünsteln, *v. tr.* to invent, to contrive by art.

‖**Áusküren**, V. Küren.

***Áuskutriren**, V. Austheilen.

Áusküssen, *v. intr.* 1) to kiss one's fill. 2) to cease kissing.

‖and †**Áuskutschen**, *v. intr.* [u. w. seyn] to drive out, to take a ride or drive in a coach.

‖**Áuslabbern**, *v. intr.* to cease twattling or gabbling.

Áuslächeln, *v. intr.* to cease smiling.

Áuslachen, I. *v. tr.* to laugh at. Ausgelacht werden, to be laughed at. Syn. V. Belachen. II. *v. intr.* 1) to laugh out, to laugh without restraint, to laugh one's fill. 2) to cease laughing.

Auslachens-werth, **—würdig**, I. *adj.* laughable, ridiculous. II. *adv.* laughably, ridiculously.

Áusladen, *ir.* I. *v. tr.* 1) to take out [as a cargo], to unload [as a ship], to discharge. Waaren —, to discharge goods. V. Löschen. 2) Ein Gewehr —, to take the charge out of a gun. 3) [in architect.] to make to project. † II. *v. r.* sich —, to clear one's bowels.

Auslade-ort, *m.* place where goods are discharged. **—zeug**, *n.* V. Kugelzieher.

Áuslader, *m.* [-s, *pl.*-] 1) he that unloads or discharges goods, a discharger, a lighterman. 2) [in electricity, an instrument for discharging a Leyden phial, jar &c., by opening a communication between the two surfaces] discharger.

Áusladung, *f.* 1) an unloading [as of a ship], discharge. Die — einer Schiffsladung, the discharge of a cargo. 2) a thing that projects. Die — eines Zapfens, eines Pflocks, the shoulder of a tenon, of a pin; die —, [in architect.] projection, projecture.

Áuslage, *f.* [*pl.* -n] 1) the act of paying for others, in expectation of reimbursement. Ich werde die nöthigen —n machen, I shall make the necessary advances. 2) the money advanced, disbursement. Einem die — wieder erstatten, to reimburse any one his expenses; es lohnt die —n nicht, it does not quit cost, it is not worth the money. 3) a place for laying out things, a bench or form where any thing is set to sale, stall.

Áuslagern, *v. intr.* [u. w. seyn] to lie for a time on the stilling. Ausgelagerter Wein, settled wine, wine that has lain a sufficient time.

Áuslammen, *v. intr.* to have done lambing.

Áusland, *n.* [-es] foreign country. Er versendet viele Waaren ins —, he sends much merchandise abroad.

Auslandssucht, *f.* V. Ausländerei.

Áuslanden, *v. tr.* V. Ausschiffen.

Áusländer, *m.* [-s, *pl.*-] [—inn, *f.*] a foreigner, alien.

Ausländeréi, *f.* a partiality to every thing belonging to other countries.

Áusländisch, *adj.* and *adv.* foreign, outlandish, alien; [produced in a distant country, coming from another country] foreign. —e Waaren, foreign commodities; eine —e Pflanze, an exotic plant.

Áuslangen, *v. intr.* 1) to suffice, to be enough, to be sufficient. Dieses Geld langt nicht aus, this money is not sufficient, will not go far enough. 2) to have sufficient. Ich lange mit diesem Gelde nicht aus, with this money I shall not have enough. *Fig.* Du wirst mit dieser Entschuldigung nicht —, your excuse will not be admitted or allowed, your excuse will not do.

Áuslängen, *v. tr.* to stretch, to extend.

Áuslappern, *v. tr.* to lap up.

Áuslärmen, I. *v. intr.* to cease making a noise. II. *v. r.* sich —, to get tired of making a noise.

Áuslassen, *ir.* I. *v. tr.* 1) to permit to wander at large, to let out of a place. Das Vieh aus dem Stalle —, to let the cattle go out of the stall. *Fig.* Einen Befehl —, to give out, to issue an order; seine Gedanken —, to express or tell one's mind; seine Gedanken über etwas —, to utter or vent one's thoughts about any thing; seinen Zorn —, to give way to one's anger; seinen Zorn an Einem —, to wreak one's anger upon any one; des Himmels Königinn ließ ihre Wuth also aus, the queen of heaven did thus her fury vent; seine Wuth an Jemand —, der sich nicht vertheidigen kann, *Prov.* to pour water on a drowned mouse; ausgelassen, unrestrained, wanton. 2) to leave out, to omit. Ein Wort oder einen Namen beim Schreiben —, to leave out a word or name in writing. 3) to let out, to widen. Ein Kleid —, to let out a garment. 4) to melt [butter, grease &c.]. II. *v. r.* sich —, to express one's mind. Er hat sich nicht weiter ausgelassen, he was not farther explicit.

Áuslassung, *f.* 1) the act of letting out. *Fig.* the act of giving vent to &c. 2) the act of leaving out a word, passage &c., omission. 3) the word, passage left out or omitted. Durch —en, by retrenchings. 4) [in grammar] elision.

Auslassungszeichen, *n.* apostrophe. Mit einem — versehen, to apostrophize.

Áuslauben, *v. tr.* 1) to adorn with leaves. 2) to thin out the superfluous foliage.

Áuslauern, I. *v. tr.* V. Erlauern. II. *v. intr.* to cease lurking.

Áuslauf, *m.* [-es, *pl.* -läufe] 1) the act of running out. Der — des Wassers, the efflux or effluxion of water. Der — [das Auslaufen] eines Schiffes, setting sail, sailing, departure. 2) the projecting of the parts of a whole. *a*) [in archit.] *α*) projection, projecture. *β*) sally. *b*) [in gunn.] the distance of the ornaments from the bore of a cannon. 3) that which runs out. *Fig.* [in salt-works] the profit. 4) the place from which any thing runs out, and at which one runs out.

Auslaufkarren, *m.* [in mining] wheel-barrow.

‖**Áusläufeln**, **Ausläufen**, *v. tr.* to unhusk beans or pease, to slip them out of their pods.

Áuslaufen, *ir.* I. *v. intr.* 1) [u. w. seyn] to run out of a place, to sail out. Die Flotte läuft heute aus, the fleet puts to sea to-day; ich habe den ganzen Tag — müssen, I have been obliged to be running out the whole day. 2) [u. w. seyn] to be moved out of a place, to flow out. Der Sand in der Sanduhr ist ausgelaufen, the sand in the hour glass has all run out; das größte Gefäß läuft aus, wenn &c., the largest vessel runs out, if &c.; der Wein, das Bier läuft aus, the wine, the beer leaks out of the cask; man hat in diesem Keller allen Wein — lassen, all the wine in this cellar has been staved; [in husb.] die Erbsen oder Bohnen laufen aus, the pease or beans drop from the pods. 3) [u. w. seyn] to extend in a certain direction. Wurzeln oder Aeste laufen weit aus, roots or boughs extend or branch far out; die Pflanzen laufen aus, the plants run into suckers; in gerade Linien —, to run out in right lines; [in printing] diese Schrift läuft weiter aus als die andere, this type takes up more room, extends farther than the other; [in archit.] —, to jut, to project; die auslaufenden Theile eines Gebäudes, the projecting parts, or projections of a building. 4) [u. w. seyn] to cease running, to run out [said of a thing]. Die Sanduhr ist ausgelaufen, the hour-glass has run out. *Fig.* to come to an end. Das Jahr läuft aus, the year is coming to a close. V. Ablaufen. 5) [u. w. haben] to cease running [said of man or beast]. II. *v. r.* sich —, 1) to exercise the body by running. 2) to wear out by running or by friction. Das Zapfenloch hat sich ausgelaufen, the mortise is worn out. III. *v. tr.* [in mining] to carry the ores out of the pit.

Áusläufer, *m.* [-s, *pl.*-] 1) errand-boy, runner. Der — in einer Buchdruckerei, the printer's devil. 2) a shoot, sprig, runner. 3) a spur [of a mountain].

Áusläufern, V. Ausläufeln.

Áusläufisch, *adj.* and *adv.* addicted to run out, to walk abroad.

Áuslaufung, *f.* 1) the act of running out. 2) [in archit.] V. Auslauf.

Áuslaugen, *v. tr.* 1) to draw out, to extract [from ashes &c.] by means of lye. Salz —, [in chimistry] to extract salts by lixiviation; die durch — erzielten Salze [Laugensalze], lixivial or lixivious salts; ausgelaugte Asche, buck-ashes. 2) to penetrate with lye. Neue Fässer —, to wash new casks with lye.

Áuslauschen, I. *v. tr.* to discover by listening. II. *v. intr.* to cease listening.

Áuslausen, *v. tr.* to clean from lice, to louse. † *Fig.* Einen —, to drain any one's purse.

Áusläuten, *v. tr.* 1) *a*) to publish, to proclaim by ringing a bell. Einen Todten —, to announce the death of a person by tolling a bell. *b*) to signify the conclusion of any thing by ringing the bells. 2) to finish ringing the bells.

Áusläutern, V. Auslichten.

Áusleben, *v. intr.* 1) to live to the end of a certain period. 2) to cease to live. Er hat ausgelebt, he is dead.

Áuslechzen, *v. intr.* to cease to suffer from drought.

1. **Áuslecken**, *v. tr.* to get out of a thing by licking. Den Honig —, to lick up all the honey; die Katze leckt die Milch aus, the cat laps up all the milk.

2. **Áuslecken**, *v. intr.* [u. w. seyn] to leak out. Das Fäßchen ist bis zur Hälfte ausgeleckt, the cask has leaked half out.

Áusledern, *v. tr.* 1) to line with leather. Eine Pumpe —, to line a pump with leather. †2) *Fig.* to beat, to drub.

Áusleeren, *v. tr.* [to deprive of the contents] to empty [a vessel &c.]. Ein Zimmer —, to empty, to clear out a room; die Gedärme —, to evacuate the bowels; ein Pferd —, [in veter. art] to drench a horse; *Einem den Beutel —, *Fig.* to drain any one's purse.

Áusleerung, *f.* 1) the act of emptying, evacuation. 2) [discharges by stool or other natural means] evacuation.

Ausleerungsmittel, *n.* a medicine which procures evacuations, an evacuant.

Áuslegen, I. *v. tr.* 1) to spread on a surface, to lay out. Leinwand —, to expose cloth [to the rays of the sun] on a bleachery; Waaren —, to expose goods to sale, to put up goods to sale; [in seamen's lang.] das Schiff hat ausgelegt, the ship has hawled out into the roadstead. 2) [as it were hinauslegen] Die Soldaten —, to change the quarters of the soldiers. *Fig. a*) to furnish for others, to pay or lay out for others, in expectation of reimbursement, to advance [money]. *b*) to grant for temporary use, to lend. Sein Geld auf Zinsen —, to lend one's money upon interest. 3) to inlay, [among cabinetmakers] to veneer. Mit Gold ausgelegt, inlaid with gold; die ausgelegte Arbeit, veneering. 4) *Fig.* to explain, to expound. Eine Stelle der Schrift —, to expound a text of Scripture; die Kunst, die Schrift auszulegen, the art of expounding the Scriptures, hermeneutic theology; einen Traum —, to interpret a dream; etwas zum Besten —, to put the best construction on a thing; eine Sache irrig —, to put a false construction on a thing; man legte es ihm als Eigendünkel aus, he was taxed with presumption for it. SYN. Auslegen, Erklären, Deuten. Both auslegen and erklären denote, to explain or make clear what is obscure; with this difference, that auslegen refers only to the signs, erklären to the signification of the signs, or to the thing itself not considered as a sign. Auslegen signifies, to put the proper construction on the signs, erklären to explain whatever may be obscure or unintelligible in their meaning. Thus, speaking of the construction of a sentence or passage we should use auslegen; of the sense of an obscure passage, erklären. Deuten signifies to construe in a certain way, to point at something. One says of a person: er habe uns unser Stillschweigen übel gedeutet [he put a bad construction on our silence], looking upon it as a sign of coldness or enmity. II. *v. intr.* and *r.* [in fencing] to take one's position

Auslege-holz, —städchen, *n.* [among cabinetmakers] inlay, veneer.

Áusleger, *m.* [-s, *pl.* -] 1) [in seamen's lang.] Der — der Besan auf Schmacken, a small boom to extend the bottom of a kind of ring-tail in smacks, an outrigger; der — auf Schmacken und Kuffen, a boom used for a bowsprit in small vessels. 2) an explainer, an expositor, a commentator, an interpreter. Jeder ist der beste — seiner Worte, every one understands his own words best, or can explain his own meaning best.

Áuslegerei, *f.* false interpretation or construction.

Áuslegung, *f.* [of goods &c.] exposition, explanation, interpretation, exegesis. *Fig. a*) Die — von Träumen, the interpretation of dreams, oneirocritics; die buchstäbliche —, the literal acceptation. *b*) [the sense given by an interpreter] explanation, interpretation. Man findet verschiedene —en derselben Stelle der Schrift, we find various interpretations of the same passage of Scripture; die wahre —, the true construction. *c*) [a discourse intended to explain or illustrate a subject] exegesis.

Auslegungs-art, *f.* manner or way of interpreting the sense of a word, discourse &c. **—kunde, —kunst, —wissenschaft**, *f.* the art of interpretation, hermeneutics.

Áuslehnen, V. Ausleihen.

Áuslehren, I. *v. tr.* to finish teaching, *it.* to teach thorougly. II. *v. intr.* to cease to teach, to have done teaching.

Áusleiden, *ir. v. intr.* 1) to suffer to the end. 2) to cease to suffer. Er hat ausgelitten, he suffers no more, his sufferings are at an end.

Áusleihen, *ir. v. tr.* [to grant for temporary use] to lend. Geld auf Zinsen —, to lend money upon interest.

Áusleiher, *m.* [-s, *pl.* -] —inn, *f.* [one who lends] lender.

Áuslenken, *v. tr.* to turn off or out of the way, to strike into another path. Dem Postwagen muß jedes Gefährt —, every carriage must get out of the way of, must give place to, the mail-coach.

Áuslernen, *v. intr.* 1) to finish learning, to obtain experience in any thing. Ausgelernt, practised, experienced; ein ausgelernter Schalk, a cunning blade, an arrant knave; der Mensch lernt niemals aus, we are never too old to learn. 2) to finish the time of learning, to conclude the apprenticeship. Er hat erst in einem Jahre ausgelernt, he has one year more to serve his master; er hat ausgelernt, he has served his time, he is out of his time.

Áuslese, *f.* [*pl.* -n] selection.

Áuslesen, *ir*, I. *v. tr.* 1) to take by way of preference from two or more things offered, to make choice of, to choose, to pick out, to select. Blumen —, to cull flowers; die Lumpen —, [in papermills] to sort the rags; die geleimten Papierblätter —, [am. cardmakers] to sort the sheets. 2) to clean by picking away any thing useless and noxious. Erbsen —, to pick pease; einen Salat —, to pick a salad; die [f. s.] Zwiebelfische —, [in printing] to pick up the pies. 3) to read to the end. Ein Buch —, to peruse, read a book out or through. 4) [in colleges or universities] to read one's lectures to the end. II. *v. intr.* to have done reading, to cease to read.

Áusleser, *m.* [-s, *pl.* -] -inn, *f.* a picker, a chooser, a selector, a sorter.

Áusleuchten, *v. intr.* 1) to light any one out of a place. **Fig.* Einem —, to turn any one out of doors, to show him the door. 2) to cease to light.

Áusleuen, *v. tr.* [in seamen's lang.] to unload by means of a boom and tackle. Steinkohlen —, to whip up coals.

Áuslichten, *v. tr.* to thin [a wood]. Einen Baum —, to cut some boughs or branches off, to lop, to prune a tree.

Áusliefern, *v. tr.* to put into another's hand or power, to deliver over. Einen Verbrecher der Obrigkeit or an die Obrigkeit —, to deliver over a criminal to the magistrate.

Áuslieferer, *m.* [-es, *pl.* -] a deliverer,

Áuslieferung, *f.* [a giving or passing from one to another] delivery.

Auslieferungs-liste, *f.* [among booksellers] a list of those houses to which a bookseller gives permission to his agent [in Leipsic &c.] to deliver works published by him, in his name and on his account. **—vertrag**, *m.* an agreement between some states for the delivery of deserters, a cartel.

Áusliegen, *ir. v. intr.* 1) to improve by lying for a sufficient length of time. Ausgelegener Wein, wine that has lain a considerable time. 2) V. Auslegen II.

Áuslieger, *m.* [-s, *pl.* -] [in seamen's lang.] 1) a vessel lying out in the roadstead, a guardship. 2) an out rigger, a jib-boom. V. Klüverbaum.

‖ **Áusloben**, *v. tr.* to promise.

Áuslochen, *v. tr.* 1) to fetch out of a hole. 2) [am. carpenters &c.] to furnish with a mortise.

Áuslöchern, *v. tr.* to furnish with holes.

Áuslocken, V. Herauslocken.

Áusloden, *v. intr.* V. Loden.

Áuslodern, *v. intr.* [u. w. seyn and haben] to cease to blaze.

Áuslöffeln, *v. tr.* to empty by means of a spoon.

Áuslohen, *v. tr.* [in pyrotechnics] to scale.

Áuslohnen, Auslöhnen, *v. tr.* Die Arbeiter —, to pay the wages of the workmen.

Áuslöschen, *ir.* I. *v. tr.* 1) to put out, to extinguish, to quench. Das Feuer, das Licht —, to extinguish the fire, the candle. 2) [to efface any thing written] to obliterate. II. *v. intr.* [u. w. seyn] 1) to become extinct, to go out. Das Feuer, das Licht lischt aus, the fire, the candle goes out. **Fig.* Er lischt aus wie ein Licht, he goes off like the snuff of a candle. 2) to be effaced, blotted out or erased. Die Schrift ist ausgelöscht, the writing has become illegible.

Áuslöscher, *m.* [-s, *pl.* -] 1) [he that extinguishes] extinguisher, quencher. 2) [a hollow conical utensil to be put on a candle to extinguish it] extinguisher.

Áuslöschlich, *adj.* and *adv.* extinguishable, quenchable; that may be effaced.

Áuslosen, *v. tr.* 1) to draw out by lot. Soldaten —, to ballot soldiers. 2) to dispose of [an estate &c.] by a lottery or raffle.

Áuslösen, I. *v. tr.* 1) to loosen the inside of a thing and take it out. 2) to take out, to draw out, to get out. [am. sportsmen] Die Lerchen —, to get the larks out of the nooses or the net. 3) to relieve from forfeiture or captivity by paying a price, to redeem. Einen Gefangenen —, to ransom a captive; ich kann es für mich nicht —, [Ruth IV] I cannot redeem it for myself. II. *v. r.* sich —, to redeem one's self.

Áusloser, *m.* [-s, *pl.* -] he that disposes any thing by a lottery or raffle.

Áuslosung, *f.* [in law] V. Losung.

Áuslösung, *f.* 1) the act of taking or drawing out, of redeeming or ransoming, redemption. 2) price paid for the redemption of a person or thing, ransom. 3) [in horology] ratch.

Áuslotsen, *v. tr.* to carrry [a ship] out to to pilot [a ship] out of a harbour or river.

Áuslüften, *v. tr.* [to expose to the air, to access to the open air] to air, to ventilate. Kle[ider] —, to air clothes; ein Zimmer —, to ventila[te a] room.

Áusmachen, *v. tr.* 1) to get out, to [take] out. Nüsse —, to shell nuts; Bohnen —, [to] unhusk beans; Mandeln —, to blanch [to ... or peel] almonds; einen Flecken —, to fetch [out] a stain. 2) to get for another, to procure. [Ei]nem einen Dienst, eine Wohnung —, to p[rocure] any one an office, a lodging. 3) to find o[ut, to] discover. Wild —, [am. sportsmen] to di[s]cover. 4) to settle finally or ultimately, to f[inish,] to bring to an end, to put an end to, to d[ecide]. Einen Streit —, to make up a quarrel; [einen] Rechtshandel —, to terminate a lawsuit; [was] haben Sie mit ihm auszumachen? what hav[e you] to do with him? etwas mit Einem —, to [settle] a thing with any one; die Sache mit dem D[egen] —, to try the matter by the sword; was hat [man] in dieser Versammlung ausgemacht? what [was] arranged, what agreed upon in this assem[bly?] ausgemacht, decided, determined, certain; [aus]gemacht! agreed! ich nehme es als ausgem[acht] an, I take it for granted; ein ausgemachter S[pie]ler, a professed gamester; er ist ein ausgema[ch]ter Narr, Schelm, he is a decided fool, a rog[ue] lar knave 5) to put out, to make extinct. Das Licht —, to extinguish the candle. * 6) to reprimand, to rebuke. 7) to form or compose, to constitute. Leib und Seele machen den Menschen aus, body and soul constitute man; sinnliches Vergnügen macht das Glück eines großen Theiles des menschlichen Geschlechtes aus, sensual pleasure makes the happiness of a great part of mankind; die Steuern machen eine große Summe aus, the taxes come to a large sum; es macht sehr wenig aus, it amounts to very little; das macht nichts aus, it imports nothing, it is no matter. V. Abthun, Beilegen, Entscheiden, Schlichten.

Ausmagern, I. *v. intr.* [u. w. seyn] to grow lean. II. *v. tr.* to make lean. V. Abmagern.

Ausmähen, *v. tr.* to mow here and there in the middle.

1. **Ausmahlen**, [*part.* ausgemahlen] I. *v. tr.* 1) to separate all the farinaceous parts from corn by grinding. Das Getreide zu sehr —, to grind the corn too much, to get too much flour and a small quantity of bran by grinding corn. 2) to grind corn &c. to the end or to grind it fully. 3) Das Wasser aus einem Teiche —, to drain a pond by a mill. II. *v. intr.* to finish grinding [corn &c.].

2. **Ausmahlen**, [*part.* ausgemahlt] I. *v. tr.* 1) to perfect or complete in painting. Ein Gemählde —, to finish a picture. 2) to represent in colours. Kupferstiche, Landkarten &c., to illuminate, to colour prints, maps &c. *Fig.* Dieses Wort ist zu gut, um ihre Bosheit auszumahlen, this word is too good to paint sufficiently, to give an adequate idea of her wickedness. 3) to paint. Ein Zimmer —, to paint a room. II. *v. intr.* to finish painting, to have done painting.

3. **Ausmahlen**, *v. tr.* [seldom used] to mark out [a field &c.]. Einen Platz zu einem Garten —, to set out, to designate a place for a garden.

Ausmangeln, **Ausmangen**, I. *v. tr.* 1) to mangle, to calender sufficiently. 2) to extend with a rolling-pin. Den Teig —, to roll the paste. II. *v. intr.* to finish mangling or calendering.

Ausmann, *m.* [-es, *pl* Ausleute] V. Ausbürger 3.

Ausmärgeln, V. Ausmergeln.

Ausmarken, *v. tr.* 1) to mark out [a field &c.]. 2) to set out by marks or boundaries.

Ausmarkten, *v. intr.* to cease haggling.

Ausmärker, *m.* [-s, *pl.* -] a person possessing property within the boundary of a town, village &c. to which he does not belong or of which he has not the freedom.

Ausmarsch, *m.* [-es, *pl.* -märsche] 1) the marching out [of a place or country]. 2) departure [said of troops].

* **Ausmarschiren**, *v. intr.* to march out [said of troops].

Ausmartern, I. *v. tr.* to draw out by torturing. *Fig.* Einem die Seele —, to torment any one to death. II. *v. intr.* 1) to cease torturing. 2) to torture sufficiently.

Ausmästen, *v. tr.* to fatten completely. Ein ausgemästetes Schwein, a fatted hog.

Ausmatratzen, *v. tr.* [am. saddlers] to stuff with hair [a chair, a cushion &c.].

Ausmauern, *v. tr.* to line with stones or masonry [a ditch, a draw-well &c.].

† **Ausmaulen**, *v. intr.* to cease to sulk.

‖ **Ausmausen**, — **mausern**, — **maußern**, I. *v. tr.* to empty [any one's pocket &c.] by stealing. II. *v. intr.* to cease to steal. III. *v. r.* [of birds] sich —, to have done mewing.

Ausmeißeln, *v. tr.* 1) to deepen with the chisel, to scoop out with a gouge, to gouge. 2) to shape or form by chiseling, to chisel. *Fig.* Ein ausgemeißelter Redesatz, an elaborate period, a well turned period.

Ausmelken, I. *v. tr.* to drain by milking, to milk dry [a cow]. II. *v. intr.* to cease milking, *it.* to milk sufficiently.

Ausmergeln, *v. tr.* to deprive of force, strength or vigour, to exhaust. Sinnenlust mergelt den Körper aus, voluptuous indulgences enervate the body; ein Grundstück —, to wear land out of heart. *Fig.* Einen ganz —, to suck any one's marrow.

Ausmerken, *v. tr.* to recognize by chosen marks, to mark or distinguish well.

Ausmerzen, *v. tr.* to pick out what is bad, to reject, to remove. Die Schafe —, to separate the poor or unsound sheep from the sound; eine Stelle aus einer Schrift —, to abridge a passage in a writing.

Ausmessen, *ir. v. tr.* 1) to take the dimensions of, to measure out [a garden, a field &c.]. Ein Schiff —, to gauge a ship. 2) to sell by measure. 3) [in mining] V. Austreiben.

Ausmesser, *m.* [-s, *pl.* -] he that measures out, measurer.

Ausmessung, *f.* the measuring, the gauging.

Ausmetzen, *v. tr.* [among millers] to take the multure.

* **Ausmeubliren**, V. Ausmöbeln.

Ausmiethen, *v. tr.* 1) to hire out, to hire, to let, to lease. Er hat sein Haus ausgemiethet, he has let his house. 2) to dislodge by offering a higher rent. 3) Einen —, to take a lodging for somebody in another house.

Ausmindern, *v. tr.* [seldom used] to assign to the lowest bidder.

Ausminderer, *m.* [-s, *pl.* -] 1) he that assigns any thing to the lowest bidder. 2) a crier [employed at auctions].

Ausmisten, *v. tr.* to clear of dung. Den Stall —, to cast the dung out of the stable.

Ausmitteln, *v. tr.* 1) to ascertain, to find out. 2) to settle, to fix. Die Kosten —, to determine the expenses.

Ausmittler, *m.* [-s, *pl.* -] he that finds out or settles something.

* **Ausmöbeln**, *v. tr.* to furnish, to fit up [a house or room].

* **Ausmöbler**, *m.* [-s, *pl.* -] one who fits out, a furnisher.

Ausmodeln, *v. tr.* to model completely.

Ausmoosen, *v. tr.* to rid of moss.

Ausmünzen, *v. tr.* to mint, to coin. Gold —, to coin gold.

Ausmurmeln, *v. intr.* to cease to mutter, to murmur sufficiently.

Ausmüssen, *v. intr.* to be obliged to leave a place or country. Er muß aus [viz. gehen], he must go out.

Ausmustern, *v. tr.* 1) to reject, to discard. Die Dienstunfähigen —, to discard the invalids; ausgemusterte Pferde, cast horses. † 2) Einen —, to call any one names, to abuse any one. * 3) to dress up, to adorn.

Ausnagen, I. *v. tr.* to gnaw the inside of any thing. II. *v. intr.* to gnaw to the end, to gnaw thoroughly.

Ausnähen, I. *v. tr.* to form work in gold, silk &c. by the needle on muslin &c. into figures, to adorn with raised figures of needlework. Mit Gold und Seide —, to embroider with gold or silk; ausgenähte Arbeit, variegated needlework, embroidery. II. *v. intr.* 1) to cease to sew. 2) [said of sempstr.] to do needlework in the houses of customers, to go out to work.

Ausnahme, *f.* [*pl.* -n] 1) the act of excepting, exception. Eine — machen, to make an exception; mit — von zwei Leuten, with the exception of two persons; etwas ohne — behaupten, to maintain a thing generally, without restriction; die — [das Ausgenommenseyn] von einer öffentlichen Last, the exemption from a public burden. 2) [that which is excepted] exception. *Prov* Keine Regel ohne —, there is no rule without an exception.

Ausnahm[e]-gesetz, *n.* a law which suspends for a time certain existing laws. —[s]-los, *adj.* and *adv.* without exception. —[s]-weise, *adv.* by exception.

Ausnarren, *v. intr.* to cease playing the fool or acting as a fool.

Ausnaschen, I. *v. tr.* to nibble out the inside or contents of a thing. II. *v. intr.* to cease eating sweatmeats.

Ausnebeln, *v. imp.* to cease being misty.

Ausnecken, *v. intr.* to cease rallying or bantering.

Ausnehmen, *ir.* I. *v. tr.* 1) to take out of a place. Vögel —, to take birds out of the nest; einen Zahn —, to extract, to draw a tooth; Waaren —, to take off commodities; er nimmt Alles auf Borg aus, he takes every thing on credit. 2) to eviscerate, to gut, to draw [a swine, fish, poultry &c.]. 3) *Fig.* to except, to exclude. Keinen ausgenommen, nobody excepted; Alle waren in diese Sache verwickelt, Einer ausgenommen, all were involved in this affair, except one. II. *v. r.* sich —, to have a particular appearance. Dieses Zeug nimmt sich gut aus, this stuff looks well; diese Bäume nehmen sich sehr gut aus, these trees yield a fine prospect; diese Farbe nimmt sich sehr gut aus, this colouring has a very good effect.

Ausnehmend, —**nehmlich**, *adj.* and *adv.* distinguished, uncommon. Ausnehmend reich, mächtig, exceedingly rich, powerful; er liebt sie —, he loves her exceedingly, he doats on her.

Ausneigen, *v. tr.* to empty [a vessel] by tilting.

Ausnicken, *v. intr.* to cease to nod.

Ausniesen, I. *v. tr.* to eject by sneezing. II. *v. intr.* to cease sneezing.

Ausnippen, I. *v. tr.* to empty [a glass] by sipping. II. *v. intr.* to cease to sip.

‖ **Ausnutscheln**, —**nutschen**, *v. tr.* to suck out.

Ausnutzen, *v. tr.* to wear sufficiently, to wear to the end.

Ausöden, *v. tr.* to make desert, to desolate.

Ausöhsen, *v. tr.* Ein Boot —, [in seamen's lang.] to bale a boat, to free a boat from water.

Ausölen, *v. tr.* to oil on the inside.

Auspachten, *v. tr.* 1) to let, to lease, to hire out [a farm &c.]. 2) Einen —, to oust any one out of his farm by offering a higher rent.

Auspacken, *v. tr.* to open any thing bound together, to unpack. Einen Ballen —, to open a bale; Waaren —, to unpack goods.

Auspappen, I. *v. tr.* 1) to line [a chest &c.] with pasting paper. 2) [with nurses] to eat up. II. *v. intr.* 1) to cease pasting. 2) [with nurses] to cease eating.

* **Ausparíren**, *v. tr.* to parry. Einen Stoß —, [in fencing] to parry a thrust; einen Schlag —, to ward off a blow.

Áuspaschen, I. *v. tr.* to raffle for. II. *v. intr.* to cease raffling.

Áuspatschen, *v. tr.* [in famil. language] to slap [any one] soundly.

Áuspauken, I. *v. tr.* to proclaim by sound of drum, to drum out. II. *v. intr.* to cease drumming.

Áuspauschen, *v. tr.* [in mining] to bruise [minerals = to bruise them, to reduce them to a coarse powder].

Áuspeilen, *v. tr.* [in seamen's lang.] to sound. Den Grund —, to sound the bottom.

Áuspeitschen, *v. tr.* 1) to drive out, to expel by whipping. Einem Kinde die Unarten —, to whip a child out of his tricks. 2) to beat out with a whip.

Áuspfählen, *v. tr.* 1) to set with pales on the inside. 2) to set out with pales.

Áuspfänden, *v. tr* Einen —, to seize any one's goods for debt, to distrain any one's goods and chattels.

Áuspfänder, *m.* [-s, *pl.* -] distrainer.

Áuspfändung, *f.* distraining, seizing for debt.

Áuspfarren, *v. tr.* to separate from a parish.

Áuspfeifen, *ir.* I. *v. tr.* 1) to condemn by hissing, to explode. Einen Schauspieler —, to hiss a player [off the stage]; ein Stück —, to condemn a play with the catcall, to explode a play on the stage 2) to whistle to the end. II. *v. intr.* to have done whistling, to cease whistling.

Auspfeifenswerth, —**würdig**, *adj.* and *adv.* that which deserves to be condemned by hissing.

Áuspfeifer, *m.* [-s, *pl.* -] he that condemns by hissing, hisser.

Áuspflanzen, *v. tr.* V. Verpflanzen.

Áuspflastern, *v. tr.* to pave the inside of any place. Einen Hof —, to pave a court.

Áuspflöcken, *v. tr.* to mark out, to set out with pegs.

Áuspflücken, *v. tr.* 1) to pluck out. Die überflüssigen Blätter an einem Weinstocke —, to thin out the leaves of a vine. 2) to displace by plucking. Die Federn —, to pluck off the feathers; die Kabelgarne alter Taue —, [in seamen's lang.] to untwist or draw asunder old ropes. 3) to make void by plucking. Ein Blumenbeet —, to deprive a flower-bed of flowers.

Áuspflügen, I. *v. tr.* 1) to plough up [stones &c.]. 2) to finish, to perfect by ploughing. II. *v. intr.* to cease ploughing.

Áuspfunden, *v. tr.* [seldom used] to sell by the pound.

Áuspfützen, *v. tr.* [in mining] to raise from any depth, to draw.

Áuspichen, *v. tr.* to pitch on the inside. Ein Faß —, to pitch a cask. **Fig.* Ein ausgepichter Magen, a stomach that digests well every kind of food and drink.

* **Auspicien**, *pl.* 1) auspices, auguries, omens. Unter günstigen —, auspiciously. 2) protection, favour shown, auspices.

Áuspicken, *v. tr.* to take out with the bill or beak, to peck out. Die Saamenkörner aus den Ähren —, to pick the seeds out of the ears.

Áuspinseln, I. *v. tr.* 1) to efface by a stroke of the brush [something badly painted]. 2) to brush on the inside. II. *v. intr.* to cease pencilling.

Áuspipen, *v. intr.* to cease piping.

Áuspissen, V. Ausharnen.

Áusplagen, I. *v. tr.* to get out by teazing. II. *v. intr.* to cease to tease.

Áusplappern, I. *v. tr.* [in famil. lang.] [to publish secrets or trifles without discretion] to blab out. Ein Geheimniß —, to vent or blab out a secret. II. *v. intr.* to cease blabbing or tattling. III. *v. r.* sich —, to exhaust one's self by prattling.

Áusplatten, *v. tr.* to pave with flat stones [the floor of a church &c.].

Áusplätten, V. Ausbügeln.

Áusplatzen, *v. intr.* 1) [u. w. seyn] [to suffer a violent disruption] to burst. In ein lautes Gelächter —, to burst into a loud laugh; mit dem Geheimniß —, to let out the secret. 2) [u. w. haben] to cease bursting.

Áusplätzen, *v. tr.* to cause to burst.

Áusplauderer, *m.* [-s, *pl.* -] a blabber, a prattler.

Áusplaudern, I. *v. tr.* [to publish secrets or trifles without discretion] to blab out. Ein Geheimniß —, to vent or blab out a secret. II. *v. r.* sich —, to prattle one's fill. III. *v. intr.* to cease prattling.

Áusplünderer, *m.* [-s, *pl.* -] a plunderer, a pillager.

Áusplündern, *v. tr.* to plunder. Sie plündern Häuser aus, they rob houses; eine Stadt —, to sack, to pillage a town.

Áusplünderung, *f.* plundering, pillaging, sacking.

Áuspochen, I. *v. tr.* 1) to decry or reject with noise, to explode [an actor &c.]. 2) [am. sportsmen] Einen Marder —, to untree a marten-cat. II. *v. intr.* to cease knocking.

* **Áuspoliren**, *v tr.* to polish, to burnish.

Áuspolstern, *v. tr.* 1) to stuff on the inside. Einen Wagen —, to quilt a coach. 2) to stuff [a chair &c.].

Áuspoltern, *v. intr.* to cease to bluster.

Áusposaunen, *v. tr.* to publish, to proclaim by sound of trumpet. **Fig.* Homer posaunet des Achilles Lob aus, Homer trumpets forth Achilles' praise; seinen eigenen Ruhm —, to sound one's own trumpet; sein Lob —, to be the trumpet of one's own praises; Nachrichten —, to blazon news.

Áusprägen, *v. tr.* 1) to mint, to coin [silver &c.]. 2) to stamp distinctly. *Fig.* Die größte Gemeinheit ist in seinem Gesichte ausgeprägt, the greatest meanness is stamped on his countenance.

Áusprahlen, *v. intr.* to cease boasting.

Áusprassen, *v. intr.* to cease revelling.

Áuspredigen, *v. intr.* to preach to the end, to finish preaching. *Fig.* to cease lecturing, tutoring. Haben Sie bald ausgepredigt? have you nearly finished your preaching?

Áuspreisen, *v. tr.* to praise, to extol duly.

Áuspressen, *v. tr.* 1) to press out, to squeeze out. Trauben —, to squeeze out grapes; von ausgepreßten süßen Kernen, from sweet kernels pressed; den Saft der Aepfel —, to express the juice of apples. *Fig.* Geld von Einem —, to extort money from any one; einen Seufzer —, to heave a sigh; seine Beredtsamkeit preßte den Zuhörern Thränen aus, his eloquence drew tears from the audience. 2) to stamp distinctly.

Áusproben, *v. tr.* 1) to taste [wine &c.]. 2) to empty by tasting.

Áusprüfen, I. *v. tr* 1) to choose, to select by trying or proving. 2) to try or prove thoroughly. II. *v. intr.* to cease to try or prove.

Áusprügeln, I. *v. tr.* 1) to expel or drive out by cudgelling or drubbing. 2) to cudgel, to drub soundly. II. *v. intr.* to cease to cudgel or drub.

Áuspudern, *v. tr.* 1) to powder thoroughly. 2) to empty by powdering.

Áuspuffen, *v. tr.* to drive or force out with blows.

Áuspumpen, I. *v. tr.* 1) [to raise or throw out by means of a pump] to pump, pump out [water]. 2) to empty by pumping. II. *v. intr.* to cease pumping, to pump sufficiently.

Áuspunkten, **Áuspunktiren**, *v. tr.* to explore by divination.

Áuspunschen, *v. intr.* to cease to drink punch.

Áuspusten, *v. tr.* to blow out [a candle].

Áusputz, *m.* [-es, *pl.* -e] the act of cleansing and the thing which is used for cleansing.

Áusputzen, *v. tr.* 1) to clean out, to cleanse on the inside. Ein Geschirr —, to cleanse a vessel; [in gardening] Bäume —, to prune trees. † and ** Fig.* Einen —, to reprimand any one severely. 2) [among workmen] to polish, to gloss. 3) to snuff out [a candle]. 4) to deck or decorate, to adorn. Eine Braut — [more usual and better: aufschmücken or herausputzen], to dress up a bride; ein Zimmer —, to decorate a room; sich —, to dress one's self smartly.

Áusputzer, *m.* [-s, *pl.* -] 1) dresser. 2) † and ** Fig.* a reproof, severe reprimand. Einem einen — geben, to give any one a wipe, to reprimand any one severely, to give any one a dressing.

Áusquaken, *v. intr.* to cease croaking.

Áusquälen, I. *v. tr.* 1) to get out by tormenting. 2) to torment, to vex. II. *v. intr.* to cease tormenting. III. *v. r.* sich —, to cease to torment one's self.

Áusqualmen, *v. intr.* 1) to emit fumes, to vapour. 2) to cease vapouring.

* **Áusquartieren**, *v. tr.* Soldaten —, to change the quarters of soldiers.

Áusquetschen, *v. tr.* to squeeze out [the juice of lemons &c.].

Áusrädeln, —**räden**, —**rädern**, —**raiden**, *v. tr.* to get out by sifting.

* **Áusradiren**, *v. tr.* to rub or scrape out, to erase [letters or characters written or engraved]. Ein Wort —, to erase, to scrape out a word.

Áusraffen, *v. tr.* [in print.] to raff out.

Áusrahmen, *v. tr.* to take [an embroidery &c.] out of the frame.

Áusraiden, V. Ausrädeln.

Áusrammeln, *v. intr.* to cease bucking [said of hares and rabbits].

Áusrammen, *v. tr.* to drive in piles, to strenghten with piles, to pilot.

Áusrändeln, *v tr.* to furnish with a small carved border.

Áusranden, **Áusrändern**, *v. tr.* to furnish with a carved border. Ausgerandet, [in botany] crenate; ein ausgerandetes Blatt, a crenate leaf; eine ausgerandete Blumenkrone, ein ausgerandeter Honigkelch, a crenate corolla, nectary.

Áusrandung, *f.* 1) the act of furnishing any thing with a carved border. 2) [in nat. hist.] a margin shaped like a flat arch.

* **Áusrangiren**, *v. tr.* V. Ausreihen 1), Ausschießen.

Áusranken, *v. intr.* [u. w. seyn] to spread with tendrils.

‖ and † **Áusrappeln**, *v. intr* 1) to cease making a noise. 2) to cease roving in mind.

Áusrasen, *v. intr.* 1) to burst forth raving. 2) to cease raving, to rave sufficiently, to rave out.

Fig. Er hat ausgeraset, his fire is spent; er hat noch nicht ausgeraset [*prov.* er hat sich die Hörner noch nicht abgelaufen], he has not yet sown his wild oats.

Ausrasseln, *v. tr.* and *v. intr.* to cease rattling.

Ausrasten, *v. intr* to rest sufficiently.

Ausrauben, I. *v. tr.* to rob [a house]. II. *v. intr.* to cease robbing.

Ausrauchen, I. *v. intr.* to cease smoking, to smoke sufficiently, to smoke to the end. II. *v. tr.* 1) to drive out, to expel by smoke Die Füchse —, to smoke the foxes out [of their earths]. 2) to empty by smoking. Eine Pfeife —, to smoke a pipe out.

Ausräuchern, I. *v. tr.* 1) to smoke, to fumigate, to perfume. Ein Zimmer —, to fumigate a room. 2) to smoke, to dry in smoke. Fleisch —, to fume meat; ein gut ausgeräucherter Schinken, a well smoked ham. II. *v. intr.* to cease to smoke.

Ausraufen, *v. tr.* to pluck out, pull out. Flachs, in der Blüthe ausgerauft, flax pulled in the bloom; er raufte sich die Haare aus, he tore his hair.

Ausräumen, *v. tr.* 1) to take or put away, to remove, to clear away. Die Diebe hatten Alles ausgeräumt, the robbers had cleared off every thing. 2) to make empty, to free from any thing contained. Ein Zimmer —, to evacuate a room. Einen Brunnen —, to cleanse a well; sich die Ohren —, to pick one's ears. 3) to enlarge [a hole &c.].

Ausräumer, *m.* [-s, *pl.* -] -inn, *f.* he that removes, clears away or empties, cleanser.

Ausräumung, *f.* clearing, removing, evacuating &c.

‖**Ausraupen**, *v. tr.* to rid of caterpillars.

Ausräuspern, I. *v. tr.* to hawk up [phlegm]. II. *v. r.* sich —, to make an effort to force up phlegm with noise, to hawk.

Ausrechen, *v. tr.* to remove with a rake, to rake.

Ausrechnen, *v. tr.* to calculate, to compute, to reckon [the expenses of building a house &c.] Eine Sonnenfinsterniß —, to calculate an eclipse of the sun. V. Berechnen.

Ausrechnen *n.* [-s], **Ausrechnung**, *f.* calculation, computation.

Ausrechner, *m.* [-s, *pl.* -] a calculator, reckoner, computer, caster up of accounts &c.

Ausrechten, *v. intr.* to cease contending.

Ausrecken, *v. tr.* to stretch, to extend. Die Hände —, to extend the hands; das Leder —, to stretch the leather; sich —, to stretch, [in seamen's lang.] to lengthen.

Ausrede, *f.* [*pl.* -n] 1) [sometimes but unusually for: Aussprache] utterance, delivery, elocution. 2) excuse, evasion, shift, subterfuge, come-off. — n machen, to offer excuses, to evade; eine bessere — suchen, to seek after some better excuse. Syn. Ausrede, Ausflucht, Entschuldigung. The latter is used also when the grounds of excuse are good and sufficient; the two former always denote that the grounds adduced are false and insufficient.

Ausreden, I. *v. intr.* to finish speaking. Lassen Sie mich —, let me speak out, do not interrupt me. II. *v. tr.* 1) V. Aussprechen. 2) to attempt to draw or divert from a measure, to dissuade from. Freunde werden es uns —, friends will persuade us from it; er redete ihm seinen Vorsatz aus, he dissuaded him from his purpose. III. *v. r.* sich — 1) [= nichts mehr zu reden wissen], to be at an end with one's conversational powers, to talk one's self out. Sich mit einem —, to explain one's self with any one, to speak circumstantially with any one concerning an affair. 2) to excuse one's self.

Ausregnen, I. *v. intr.* to cease raining. Es hat ausgeregnet, it has done raining, it is fair. II. *v. tr.* to deepen, to excavate by rain. Ausgeregnete Wege, roads or passes excavated by the rain. III. *v. r.* sich —, Der Himmel hat sich ausgeregnet, the sky has discharged all the rain.

Ausrehden, *v. tr.* [in seamen's lang.] to rig out [a ship].

Ausrehder, *m.* [-s, *pl.* -] V. Rehder.

Ausrehdung, *f.* [in seamen's lang.] 1) the act of rigging out a ship, outfit. 2) rigging.

Ausreiben, *ir.* I. *v. tr.* 1) to rub off, out or away. Den Koth —, to rub off the dirt. 2) to smooth or clean by rubbing. Die Wolle an einem Felle mit dem Rücken des Abfleischmessers —, [among curriers] to clean a skin with the back of the fleshing-knife; die Sohlen und Nähte —, [among shoemakers] to rub up the soles and seams; sich die Augen —, to unglue one's eyes. II. *v. intr.* 1) to cease rubbing. 2) to rub thoroughly.

Ausreibeholz, *n.* —knochen, *m.* [am. shoemakers] burnishing-stick, polisher.

Ausreichen, *v. intr.* 1) to have enough. Wir reichen mit dieser Gattung Tuch aus, we have enough of this sort of cloth. 2) to be sufficient, to be equal to the end or purpose, to be enough, to suffice. Das Geld, welches er mir gab, wird nicht —, the money he gave me will not be sufficient.

Ausreifen, *v. intr.* to ripen completely.

Ausreihen, *v. tr.* 1) to reject, to discard. Pferde — [= ausrangiren], to draft horses. 2) Perlen —, to unstring beads.

Ausreimen, *v. intr.* to cease rhyming, to close a rhyme.

Ausreinigen, *v. tr.* to clean, to cleanse, to purify, to purge.

Ausreisen, *v. intr.* 1) [u. w. seyn] to depart from any place. 2) to set out on a journey. 3) [u. w. haben] to finish travelling. Ausgereiset haben, to have done travelling.

Ausreißen, *ir.* I. *v. tr.* 1) to tear out, to pull out. Einen Zahn —, to draw a tooth; sich die Haare —, to tear one's hair; die Augen —, to pluck out the eyes; wellt ihr mir die Augen —? will you pull my eyes out? eine Pflanze mit der Wurzel —, to pull a plant up by the root. 2) to part or divide by force and violence. Die Fluth hat die Dämme ausgerissen [durchgerissen], the flood has broken the dams. II. *v. intr.* [u. w. seyn] † 1) to run away, to make off. Er riß aus, he scampered off, he betook himself to his heels, he bolted; das Pferd riß aus, the horse ran away. 2) to be torn. Ausgerissene Knopflöcher, worn out button-holes; ausgerissene Deiche, broken down dams or dykes. *Fig.* Meine Geduld reißt aus, my patience is failing.

Ausreißer, *m.* [-s, *pl.* -] 1) he that tears or pulls out. 2) a fugitive, a run-away, a deserter.

Ausreiten, *ir.* I. *v. intr.* [u. w. seyn] to ride out of a place; to ride out, to take a ride. II. *v. tr.* 1) Ein Pferd —, to air a horse. 2) to ride over [a field, meadow &c.]. Man kann diese Wiese in fünf Minuten nicht —, there is no riding across this meadow in five minutes.

‖**Ausreiter**, *m.* [-s, *pl.* -] 1) V. Landreiter. 2) V. Aufseher.

Ausrenken, *v. tr.* to move a bone from its socket, cavity or place of articulation, to put out of joint, to disjoint. Sich den Arm —, to dislocate one's arm.

Ausrenkung, *f.* dislocation.

Ausrennen, *ir.* I. *v. tr.* to knock out in running. Er hat sich ein Auge ausgerannt, he knocked his eye out by running against something. II. *v. intr.* 1) to set out from a barrier; chiefly from the barrier at a race, to start. 2) to cease running.

Ausreudung, *f.* [in seamen's lang.] sea-stores.

Ausreuten, *v. tr.* to root out, to eradicate. Unkraut oder schädliche Pflanzen auf einem Felde —, to extirpate weeds or noxious plants from a field.

Ausrichten, *v. tr.* 1) to make straight, to straighten. Beulen aus einem Gefäße —, to get bruises out of a vessel by hammering; die Strümpfe —, [am. stocking-weavers] to dress the stockings. 2) to bear the charges of, to pay the expenses of. Eine Mahlzeit —, to make a dinner; eine Hochzeit —, to be at the charge of a wedding. 3) to perform, to do, to effect. Einen Auftrag —, to execute a commission; eine Botschaft —, to communicate a message; eine Botschaft an Jemand —, to deliver a message or errand to any one; einen Gruß von Jemand —, to bring compliments from any one; damit ist nichts ausgerichtet, it will prove ineffectual; Sie werden dabei nichts —, you will do no good in it; was haben Sie ausgerichtet? how have you sped? *Prov.* Mit Geld kann man Alles —, money makes the mare to go. 4) [among sportsmen] Das Wild —, to draw a cover. 5) V. Verläumden, *it.* ausschelten, to calumniate.

Ausrichter, *m.* [-s, *pl.* -] 1) he that bears the charges of any thing. 2) [in law] executor.

‖**Ausrichtig**, **Ausrichtsam**, *adj.* and *adv.* dexterous, adroit, quick, ready.

Ausrichtung, *f.* 1) the act of bearing the charges of executing, effecting any thing. 2) a feast, banquet, especially a wedding dinner, a christening feast &c.

Ausriechen, *ir.* I. *v. tr.* to find out by the nose, to smell out, to scent out. II. *v. intr.* 1) to cease to smell. Die Blumen haben ausgerochen, the flowers smell no longer. 2) to smell sufficiently, to cease smelling.

Ausriefen, *v. tr.* to flue or channel duly.

Ausrieseln, **Ausriesen**, *v. intr.* [u. w. seyn] 1) to trickle out of a place. 2) [u. w. haben] to cease trickling or rilling.

Ausrindern, *v. intr.* to want no longer the bull [said of cows].

Ausringen, *ir.* I. *v. tr.* 1) to disjoint, to put out of joint by wrestling. 2) to wring [linen]. Das Wasser aus einem nassen Kleide —, to wring water out of a wet garment. II. *v. intr.* to finish wrestling or struggling. *Fig.* Er hat ausgerungen [= ist nun todt], he is dead. III. *v. r.* sich —, to get suppleness and strength by wrestling.

Ausrinnen, *ir. v. intr.* [u. w. seyn] to run, trickle out [of a vessel &c.].

Ausrippen, *v. tr.* to free from the ribs. Ausgerippte Tabacksblätter, stripped leaves of tobacco.

Ausritt, *m.* [-es, *pl.* -e] a ride out, ride.

Ausritzen, *v. tr.* to furnish the inside of any thing with chinks or fissures.

Ausroden, *v. tr.* to unroot [a stump &c.]; *it.* to prepare for tillage or pasture. Einen Wald —, um einen Weizenacker daraus zu machen, to clear land for wheat; ein Stück Land —, to root land.

Ausroder, *m.* [-s, *pl.* -] he that clears or roots land.

Ausrohren, *v. tr.* [am. masons] to cover with reeds on the inside.

Ausrollen, I. *v. tr.* to unroll, to extend by rolling. II. *v. intr.* 1) to cease to mould with the rolling pin. 2) to cease calendering. 3) to cease rolling, to roll out.

Ausrosten, *v. intr.* [u. w. seyn] to be rust eaten on the inside.

Ausrösten, *v. tr.* to roast thoroughly.

Ausrotten, *v. tr.* to root out, to eradicate, to destroy totally. Das Unkraut —, to exterminate, to extirpate, to eradicate weeds; er rottete die Dornen aus, the thorns he rooted out; was sich ausrotten läßt or ausgerottet werden kann, extirpable. *Fig.* Ein Laster —, to root out a vice; Ketzerei —, to extirpate or exterminate heresy; Irrthümer oder falsche Grundsätze —, to eradicate errors or false principles.

Ausrotter, *m.* [-s, *pl.*-] extirpator, exterminator.

Ausrottung, *f.* extirpation, extermination.

Ausrottungs-krieg, *m.* a war of extermination. —pocken, V. Kuhpocken.

Ausrücken, I. *v. intr.* [u. w. seyn] to march out. Die ganze Garnison rückte aus, the whole garrison was under arms; das Heer rückte um sechs Uhr aus dem Lager aus, the army decamped at six o'clock. II. *v. tr.* V. Herausrücken.

Ausruf, *m.* [-es, *pl.*-e] 1) cry, proclamation. Etwas durch öffentlichen — bekannt machen, to proclaim something. 2) outcry, exclamation, ejaculation. 3) [in grammar, a word expressing outcry] an exclamation, interjection. 4) outcry, sale at public auction.

Ausrufzeichen, *n.* V. Ausrufungszeichen.

Ausrufen, *ir.* I. *v. intr.* 1) to cry out, to utter with a loud voice, to exclaim, to ejaculate. Vor Freude —, to exclaim for joy. 2) to cease crying or calling. II. *v. tr.* to cry, to proclaim. Waaren zum Verkaufe —, to cry goods, to hawk goods; Frieden —, to proclaim peace; Einen zum Könige —, to proclaim any one king; Verlobte — [aufbieten], to publish the bans of marriage.

Ausrufer, *m.* [-s, *pl.*-] 1) one who makes proclamation, one employed to give notice of auctions &c., crier, proclaimer. 2) a crier at public auctions. 3) [one who offers goods for sale by outcry in the streets] a pedlar, hawker.

Ausrufung, *f.* 1) outcry, exclamation, proclamation. 2) the thing cried. Die —en der Verkäufe in den Straßen von Paris und London, the cries of Paris and London. 3) [emphatical utterance] exclamation.

Ausrufungs-gebühr, *f.* public crier's fees. —wort, *n.* V. Ausruf 3). —zeichen, *n.* note of exclamation [!].

Ausruhe, *f.* V. Erholung.

Ausruhen, I. *v. intr.* to rest, to repose Ruhet hier aus, repose you here; ruhet aus von allen euren Arbeiten und Aengsten, rest from all your labours and your fears. II. *v. r.* sich —, to repose one's self.

Ausrühmen, *v. tr.* to extol, to praise publicly.

Ausrühren, *v. tr.* to churn [butter].

Ausrunden, *v. tr.* to form on the inside into a round shape, to round.

Ausrunzeln, *v. tr.* to unwrinkle.

Ausrupfen, *v. tr.* to pull out, to pluck out. Gänsen die Federn —, to pluck geese.

Ausrüsten, *v. tr.* to fit out, to equip, to set out. Schiffe —, to fit out, to arm ships; ein Schiff zu einer langen Seereise —, to fit a ship for a long voyage; einen Kaper —, to fit out a privateer; Truppen zum Kriege —, to equip troops for war; ein Regiment —, to equip a regiment; ein Heer ist gut ausgerüstet, an army is well appointed. *Fig.* Der Mensch ist von seinem Schöpfer mit Vernunft ausgerüstet worden, man is endowed by his maker with reason; Einen mit Kenntnissen —, to furnish any one with knowledge.

Ausrüster, *m.* [-s, *pl.*-] he that fits out or equips; eines Schiffes, he that fits out a ship.

Ausrüstung, *f.* 1) the act of fitting out, equipment. 2) [any thing that is used in equipping] equipment. Die —en eines Heeres, the equipments of an army; die — eines Schiffes, equipage.

Ausrutschen, *v. intr.* [in famil. language] V. Ausgleiten.

Ausrütteln, I. *v. tr.* 1) to shake out. 2) to shake soundly. II. *v. intr.* to cease shaking violently.

Aussaat, *f.* [*pl.* -en] 1) the act of sowing, 2) seed-corn.

Aussäckeln, *v. tr.* V. Ausseckeln.

Aussacken, *v. tr.* 1) to take out of a sack or pocket. 2) to empty a sack or pocket.

Aussäen, I. *v. tr.* to scatter seed, to sow [wheat &c.]. *Fig.* Den Saamen der Zwietracht —, to sow discord. II. *v. intr.* to have done sowing.

Aussage, *f.* [*pl* -n] 1) [an expression of facts, verbal utterance] declaration. Die — eines Zeugen, the declaration of a witness, an evidence; eine eidliche —, a deposition, an affidavit; nach seiner —, according to his declaration or assertion; eine —, wodurch die Wahrheit einer Sache bestätigt wird, a testimony; seiner — nach, according to him, according to his saying; Ihrer — nach ist er ein Schelm, by what you say, he is a knave. 2) [in grammar] predicate.

Aussage-begriff, *m.* [in grammar] predicate. —wort, *n.* [among some grammarians] verb.

Aussagen, *v. tr.* 1) to utter, to express, to pronounce, to enunciate, to declare. Er sagt aus, daß die Geschichte unwahr ist, he declares the story to be false; eidlich etwas —, to give testimony on oath, to depose. 2) to pronounce entirely, to utter to the end, to finish uttering. Ich mag das häßliche Wort nicht —, I don't like to finish or say out the nasty word. 3) [in grammar] to affirm, to declare. Die Zeitwörter sagen etwas von einem Dinge aus, the verbs affirm something of a subject.

Aussägen, I. *v. tr.* to cut out with a saw, to saw out. II. *v. intr.* to finish sawing.

Aussalben, *v. tr.* to salve on the inside.

Aussanden, *v. tr.* to free from sand. Einen Hafen —, to clear a harbour of sand.

Aussatz, *m.* [-es, *pl.* -sätze] 1) [at billiards] the lead. Den — haben, to have the lead. 2) the stake [at play]. Den ganzen — einstreichen, to sweep the stakes. 3) [in medicine] a cutaneous eruption, [among men] leprosy, [among horses] the tetters, [among sheep] the rot, the scab, [among trees] the scurf.

Aussätzig, *adj.* and *adv.* leprous. Der —e, the leper.

Aussäubern, *v. tr.* to clean or cleanse on the inside. Ein Gefäß —, to cleanse a vessel; ein Zimmer —, to scour out, to sweep up a room.

Aussauern, *v. intr.* [u. w. seyn] to lose acidity.

Aussäuern, *v. tr.* to extract the acidity from any thing.

Aussaufen, *ir.* I. *v. tr.* 1) to empty by drinking [a pail &c.]. 2) to drink up entirely. Das Pferd hat den ganzen Kübel Wasser ausgesoffen, the horse has drunk up the whole pail of water. [used correctly only of beasts and vulgarly of men.] II. *v. intr.* to cease drinking [of an animal]. †*Fig.* to cease drunkenness [of men]

Aussaugen, *ir.* [with some authors *reg.*] I. *v. tr.* 1) to suck out, to suck [the juice &c.]. Das Aussaugen, exsuction; [in anatomy] die —den Gefäße, emulgent vessels, emulgents; the emulgent or renal arteries. *Fig.* Einem das Blut —, to drain any one to the last farthing. 2) to exhaust by sucking. Einen Acker —, to wear a field out of heart; Ländereien durch häufiges Abmähen —, to impoverish lands by frequent cropping; Pflanzen, welche die Erde —, plants that soak the earth. *Fig* Einen ganz —, to suck any one's marrow. II. *v. intr.* 1) to suck the full time. 2) to cease to suck.

Aussäugen, I. *v. tr.* to suckle [a child] the full time. II. *v intr.* to cease suckling.

Aussauger, *m.* [-s, *pl.*-] —inn, *f.* 1) he that sucks out. 2) *a*) a parasitical plant. *b*) *Fig.* an oppressor, extortioner.

Aussäumen, I. *v. tr.* to hem entirely. II. *v. intr.* to finish hemming.

Ausschaben, I. *v. tr.* 1) to scrape out. Einen Tintenfleck —, to scratch out, to erase a blot of ink. 2) to hollow by scraping. II. *v. intr.* to have done scraping.

Ausschachern, *v. intr.* to cease chaffering.

Ausschachteln, *v. tr.* 1) to take out of a box. 2) to rub with shave-grass on the inside.

Ausschaffen, I. *v. tr.* 1) to put from its place, to remove. Es wird viel Getreide ausgeschafft, a great deal of corn is exported. 2) to create perfect. II. *v. intr.* 1) to cease removing. 2) to cease creating. ||3) to cease working.

Ausschäften, *v. tr.* [in shipbuilding] to pierce a ship for a given number of guns. Ein auf 110 Stücke ausgeschäftetes Schiff, a vessel pierced for 110 guns.

Ausschalen, *v. tr.* to cover or line with laths, to lath. Die Decke in einem Zimmer —, to lath the ceiling [to support the plastering].

Ausschälen, *v. tr.* to peel, to shell. Nüsse —, to shell nuts; Mandeln —, to blanch almonds, [among butchers] to cut out the lard of slaughtered swine. †and * *Fig.* Einen —, to strip off any one's clothes, to strip or rob any one.

Ausschallen, *v. intr.* to cease sounding.

Ausschalmen, *v. tr.* [among foresters, to set a white mark on a tree by paring off a part of the bark] to blaze.

Ausschämen, I. *v. r.* sich —, to cease being ashamed, to lose all sense of shame. II. *v. t*
* Sich die Augen —, to be much ashamed.

||**Ausschänden**, *v. tr.* to scold at, to chide, to abuse, to injure.

Ausschank, *m.* [-es] retail of liquor.

Ausschärfen, [am. hunters] V. Ausschneiden

Ausscharren, I. *v. tr.* 1) to dig up, to rake or scratch out. Einige wilde Thiere scharren Leichen aus, some wild beasts dig up dead bodies interred. 2) to insult by scraping or shuffling with the feet. II. *v. intr.* 1) Hinten —, to scrape with the feet in making an awkward bow. 2) to cease scraping.

Ausscharten, *v. tr.* [am. furriers] Das Leder —, to indent, to jag the leather.

Ausschartungseisen, *n.* a tool used by furriers for indenting the leather &c.

Ausschatten, **Ausschattiren**, *v. tr.* [in painting, to mark with different gradations of colour] to shade.

Aússchätzen, *v. tr.* [in law] to dispossess.

Aússchauen, V. Aussehen and Hinaussehen.

Aússchaufeln, I. *v. tr.* to lade out, to scoop. Das Wasser aus einem Kahne —, to bale water out of a boat. II. *v. intr.* to cease scooping, lading or baling.

Aússchaukeln, I. *v. tr.* to throw out of a swing. II. *v. intr.* to cease, to have done swinging.

Aússchäumen, I. *v. tr.* to throw out as foam. *Fig.* to throw out with rage or violence, to foam out. Lästerungen —, to foam out defamatory words. II. *v. intr.* to cease foaming or frothing [said of the sea &c.]. *Fig.* to cease foaming, to cease being in rage.

Aússcheiden, I. *ir. v. intr.* to secede. II. *reg.* [with some authors *ir.*] *v. tr.* 1) to sever from the rest, to separate. [in metallurgy] Das Gold vom Silber —, to part gold from silver; die Erze —, to wash the ore. 2) to make the separation of substances in the body, to secern, to secrete. Der Schleim, den die Nase ausscheidet, the pituite secerned from the nose; die —den Gefäße, [in anatomy] the secretory vessels. *Fig.* to reject, to discard.

Aússcheiden, *n.* [-s] secretion.

Aússcheinen, *ir.* I. *v. intr.* to cease shining. II. *v. tr.* to outshine.

Aússcheiteln, *v. tr.* [among clothiers] to wind on the beam.

Aússchellen, I. *v. tr.* to publish by sound of a bell. Einen verlornen Hund — lassen, to have a lost dog cried out by the bell-man. II. *v. intr.* 1) to ring to the end. 2) to cease ringing a bell.

Aússchelten, I. *v. tr.* to chide vehemently, to scold, to rate. Einen wegen &c. —, to rate a person for &c.; sie schalt ihre Diener tüchtig aus, she rattled off her servants sharply. II. *v. intr.* to cease scolding or chiding.

1\. **Aússchenken**, [from schenken = to pour] I. *v. tr.* 1) to pour out [liquids]. 2) to sell [beer &c.] by retail. Wein —, to retail wine. 3) to empty by retailing. II *v. intr.* to cease pouring out or retailing liquors.

2\. **Aússchenken**, [from schenken = to make a present] I. *v. tr.* to give away as a present. II. *v. intr.* to cease making gifts or presents.

Aússcheren, *ir.* I. *v. tr.* 1) to shear in the midst or here and there. 2) [am. clothiers] to shear for the last time. Die Tücher —, to give the last shearing to the cloth. 3) [in seamen's lang.] Ein Tau —, to unreeve a rope. 4) [among foresters] V. Aushauen, 4. † II. *v. intr.* to have done fleecing.

Aússcherzen, *v. intr.* to cease joking or jesting.

Aússcheuchen, *v. tr.* to scare away. V. Fortscheuchen.

Aússcheuern, I. *v. tr.* to remove by scouring, to scour on the inside. Ein Gefäß —, to scour out a vessel. †*Fig.* Einen —, to scold any one, to reprove any one. II. *v. r.* sich —, to be worn out on the inside by rubbing.

Aússchicken, *v. tr.* to send out. Ein Diener, den man mit Aufträgen ausschickt, a servant sent on messages.

Aússchieben, *ir.* I. *v. tr.* 1) to shove out of a place. Das Brod —, [among bakers] to draw [to take from an oven] the bread. 2) to shove asunder. Einen Tisch —, to draw out, to lengthen a table. *Fig.* Sich den Arm —, to disjoint one's arm in bowling or playing at nine-pins. II. *v. intr.* to cease shoving.

Aússchielen, *v. intr.* 1) to squint from out of a place. 2) to cease squinting.

Aússchienen, *v. tr.* to furnish with splints, to splint on the inside.

Aússchießen, *ir.* I. *v. tr.* 1) to put out by shooting. Einem ein Auge —, to shoot out an eye of any one. 2) to empty by shooting. Einen Wald —, to shoot all the game in a forest. 3) to shoot for [a prize &c.]. Einen silbernen Teller —, to shoot for a silver plate. 4) to make better, to improve [a gun] by shooting. 5) to wear out by shooting. 6) to throw out, to draft, to cull out, to garble, to pick. Er schoß drei Guineen aus, die zu leicht waren, he rejected three guineas that were not weight; die Bogen —, [among playing-cardmakers] to sort the sheets; den Ballast —, [in seamen's lang.] to discharge the ballast; die Columnen —, [among printers] to impose the columns. II. *v. intr.* 1) to cease shooting. 2) [u. w. seyn] to shoot out, to sprout. 3) [in seamen's lang.] Der Wind schießt aus, the wind keeps pace with the sun, veers with the sun; das Ausschießen des Vorderstevens, the rake of the stem.

Ausschießbrett, *n.* [in printing] imposing-board.

Aússchießer, *m.* [-s, *pl.* -] [in papermills] he that sorts the paper.

Aússchiffen, I. *v. tr.* to set on shore, to disembark. Truppen —, to land troops from a ship or boat; Geschütz —, to disembark artillery; Güter —, to land goods. II. *v. intr.* to leave a port, to put out [to sea].

1\. **Aússchildern**, [from schildern = to paint, to describe] *v. tr.* to paint, to describe fully.

2\. **Aússchildern**, [from schildern or Schildwache stehen = to be on duty] *v. intr.* 1) to stand sentry one's time. 2) to cease standing sentry, to be relieved.

Aússchilfen, *v. tr.* to free from reeds. Einen Teich —, to cut down the reeds in a pond.

Aússchimmern, *v. intr.* to cease to glimmer.

Aússchimpfen, I. *v. tr.* to treat with reproachful language, to abuse, to revile. II. *v. intr.* to cease abusing.

Aússchinden, *ir. v. tr.* to exhaust by exactions, to fleece.

Aússchirren, *v. tr.* to unharness [the horses].

‖**Aússchlabbern**, *v. tr.* to empty by slabbering, to lick up, to lap.

Aússchlachten, *v. tr.* [among butchers] Ein ausgeschlachtetes Stück Vieh —, the flesh of a slaughtered animal cut up for use or sale.

Aússchlacken, *v. tr.* [in metallurgy] to separate the dross from the metal in melting.

Aússchlafen, *ir.* I. *v. tr.* to get rid of by sleeping. Den Rausch —, to sleep the fumes of wine away, to sleep one's self sober. II. *v. intr.* 1) to sleep sufficiently, to sleep one's fill. 2) to have done or to cease sleeping. *Fig.* *Er hat nicht ausgeschlafen, he is out of humour.

Aússchlag, *m.* [-es, *pl.* -schläge] 1) the act of striking, the first stroke or blow, [in games at ball] the service. 2) putting forth shoots, budding. Ein — aus den Wurzeln, a sprout from the roots. 3) the turn of the scale. Eine Feder gibt der Wage den —, a feather will turn the scale; es wiegt vier Pfund mit —, it weighs four pounds and something over. *Fig.* *a)* [= Entscheidung] Der Sache den — geben, to decide the business; der Schlacht den — geben, to determine the issue of the battle, to turn the scales; die Stimme, die bei Wahlen &c. den — gibt, casting voice, casting vote. *b)* issue, event, consequence, end or ultimate result. 4) a breaking out of humours, an efflorescence or redness on the skin, [as in scarlatina, exanthemata, petechia, vibices, in small pox, measles and fevers] eruption, rash. Mit einem —e verbunden, [in medicine] exanthematic, exanthematous; einen — bekommen, to get a breaking out. 5) [the exterior part or edge of a garment] border. 6) [among upholsterers] a set of tapestry.

Ausschlag-schuppig, *adj.* [in botany] scaly. —sfieber, *n.* [in medicine] an eruptive fever.

Aússchlagen, *ir.* I. *v. tr.* 1) to force out by a blow or by blows, to knock out, to strike out. Einem die Augen —, to beat out any one's eyes; die Erze —, [in mining] to pound the ore. *Fig.* [among foresters] Die Bäume —, to blaze the trees. 2) to extend by beating, to beat. Die Schrötlinge —, [in coining] to flatten the blanchets or blanks. 3) to cover on the inside, to line. Ein Zimmer mit Teppichen —, to hang a room with tapestry; einen Wagen mit Tuch —, to line a carriage with cloth; ein Kleid mit Pelzwerk, mit Seidenzeug —, to face a garment with fur, with silk; mit Pelzwerk ausgeschlagene Aermel, furred sleeves. 4) to unfold, to lay out. Eine Bettstelle —, to undo a bedstead; das Buch war geöffnet und die Karten ausgeschlagen, the book was open and the maps unfolded. 5) to put or turn by, to ward off. [in fencing] Einen Stoß —, to parry a thrust. 6) to stretch out. [in heraldry] Ein Adler mit ausgeschlagener Zunge, an eagle langued. 7) *Fig.* to refuse, to decline. Er schlug das Anerbieten aus, he declined the offer; ich kann weder wählen, wen ich will, noch —, wen ich nicht mag, I may neither choose whom I would, nor refuse whom I dislike; eine Erbschaft —, to give up a succession.

II. *v. intr.* 1) to strike first, to begin to strike; [at tennis] to give service. 2) to strike or lash out with the foot or feet, to kick out, to fling. [in manege] Hinten —, to yerk out behind; ein Pferd, das gern ausschlägt, a horse accustomed to kick, a yerker; er schlug aus, he lashed out his heels. 3) to finish striking. Die Uhr hat elf ausgeschlagen, it struck full eleven o'clock. 4) to incline to one side. Die Wage schlägt aus, the scale is turned. *Fig.* to turn out, to be brought to an issue. Das wird zum Vortheile —, that will turn to account; er schlägt gut aus, he promises well. 5) to begin to grow, or to issue from a stock in the manner of a bud, or as a horn, to bud. Die Bäume fangen an auszuschlagen, the trees begin putting forth shoots; die Rosenstöcke schlagen aus, rose-bushes are budding; Zwiebeln schlagen aus, auch wenn sie hangen, onions, as they hang, will sprout. 6) [u. w. seyn] *a)* (= mit einem krankhaften Ausschlage bedeckt werden) Ausgeschlagen seyn, to have pustules, or an efflorescence on the skin; das Kind schlägt aus, the child is breaking out. *b)* to grow moist or wet by frost; die Wand schlägt aus, the wall becomes wet in thawing weather; die Kälte ist an den Wänden ausgeschlagen, the walls are covered with hoar-frost. 7) to cease to sing [of singing birds]. Die Nachtigallen haben ausgeschlagen, the nightingales have ceased to sing. 8) to break out. Der Funke, der unter der Asche glomm, schlug plötzlich in helle Flammen aus, the spark which was smouldering under the ashes broke suddenly out into a bright flame.

Ausschlageschlägel, *m.* [-s, *pl.* -] [in mining] a hammer used for pounding the ore.

Aússchlämmen, *v. tr.* and *v. intr.* V. Ausschlemmen 1 and 2.

Aússchlauchen, *v. tr.* [among well-diggers] to cleanse [the pipes of an aqueduct].

Aússchlecken, *v. tr.* to lick up. V. Auslecken.

Aússchleichen, I. *v. intr.* [u. w. seyn] to sneak out of a place, to slink away. II. *v. tr.* to search sneaking.

1\. **Aússchleifen**, [from schleifen = to grind] I.

v. tr. 1) to get out by grinding. 2) to grind hollow [a glass &c.]. II. *v. intr.* to finish grinding. III. *v. r.* sich —, to be worn out on the inside by frequent rubbing.

2. **Ausschleifen**, [from schleifen = to drag] *v. tr.* to drag out.

Ausschleimen, *v. tr.* to cleanse of mud. Einen Graben —, to free a ditch of mud.

1. **Ausschlemmen**, [from Schlamm = mud] *v. tr.* to cleanse of mud, to fey.

2. **Ausschlemmen**, [from schlemmen = *fig.* to feast] *v. intr.* to cease feasting, to have done with bacchanals.

Ausschlendern, *v. intr.* to walk sauntering.

Ausschlenkern, I. *v. intr.* [u. w. seyn] to swing out of a vessel. II. *v. tr.* to rinse by swinging.

Ausschleppen, *v. tr.* to drag out of a place.

Ausschleudern, I. *v. tr.* to put out, to force out by flinging. Der Vesuv schleudert Steine aus, Vesuvius casts up stones; ein Auge —, to knock an eye out by flinging. II. *v. intr.* [u. w. seyn] to be flung out of the way.

Ausschlichten, *v. tr.* [in coining] Die Zaine —, to beat out the bars or ingots.

Ausschließen, *ir.* I. *v. tr.* 1) to hinder from entering, to shut out, to lock out, to exclude. Von jeder Küste ausgeschlossen, shut from every coast. *Fig.* to exclude, to debar, to preclude. Die Kirche sollte lasterhafte Menschen von der Gemeine —, the church ought to exclude immoral men from the communion; Einen von der Gemeinschaft der Kirche —, to excommunicate any one; Niemand ist davon ausgeschlossen, none is secluded from it; von der Erbschaft ausgeschlossen, debarred from the succession; er ist von der Thronfolge ausgeschlossen, he is excluded from the right of succession. 2) to loose from fetters. 3) [in printing] to justify [a line]. II. *v. intr.* to finish concluding or forming a final judgment.

Ausschließegeld, *n.* prison-fee.

Ausschließlich, *adj.* and *adv.* exclusive, exclusively. Ein —es Vorrecht, an exclusive privilege; er sandte mir alle Nummern von 78 bis 94 —, he sent me all the numbers from 78 to 94 exclusive; ein Vorrecht — genießen, to enjoy a privilege exclusively.

Ausschließung, *f.* a shutting out, exclusion. *Fig. a)* [the act of debarring from participation in a privilege &c.] exclusion. *b)* exclusion, exception. [in printing] —en, justifiers.

Ausschließungsweise, *adv.* [in a manner which excludes all others] exclusively.

1. **Ausschlingen**, [from schlingen = to swallow] *ir. v. tr.* to eat up or swallow up eagerly.

2. **Ausschlingen**, [from Schlinge = knot] *ir. v. tr.* to disentangle.

Ausschlingern, *v. intr.* [said of ship] to cease rolling.

Ausschloßen, *v. intr.* to cease hailing.

Ausschluchzen, I. *v. intr.* 1) to sob one's fill. 2) to cease sobbing. II. *v. tr.* to utter sobbing.

Ausschlucken, I. *v. tr.* to swallow up eagerly or in large draughts, to gulp down. II. *v. intr.* to cease hickuping.

Ausschlummern, *v. intr.* 1) to slumber one's fill. 2) to cease slumbering.

Ausschlüpfen, *v. intr.* [u. w. seyn] 1) to slip out of, to creep out of a place. Die Küchlein schlüpfen aus, the peepers just break the shell. 2) to fly out of a place. Das Rasirmesser schlüpfte mir aus, the razor slipt out of my hand.

Ausschlürfen, *v. tr.* to empty by sipping, to sip up.

Ausschluß, *m.* [-sses, *pl.* -schlüsse] exclusion, exception. Er hat eine —s, aber keine Wahlstimme, he has an exclusive, but not an elective vote.

Ausschlußweise, *adv.* exclusively.

Ausschmachten, *v. intr.* 1) to languish one's fill. 2) to cease to languish.

Ausschmähen, I. *v. tr.* to scold at, to reprove, to inveigh against. II. *v. intr.* to finish scolding.

Ausschmälen, I. *v. tr.* to reprove, to scold [at]. Einen wegen seiner Fehler —, to chide any one for his faults. II. *v. intr.* to cease chiding or reproving.

Ausschmarotzen, *v. intr.* to cease acting the parasite, to be put out of one's parasitical habits.

Ausschmauchen, I. *v. tr.* 1) to drive out by smoke. Die Füchse —, to smoke the foxes out of their earths. 2) to empty smoking, to smoke out. * and ‡ II. *v. intr.* 1) to smoke one's fill. 2) to cease smoking.

Ausschmausen, I. *v. tr.* to empty, to consume by banqueting. II. *v. intr.* 1) to banquet one's fill. 2) to cease banqueting.

Ausschmeicheln, *v. intr.* to cease flattering.

Ausschmelzen, *ir.* [more properly *reg.*] I. *v. tr.* to melt out, [in metallurgy] to fuse or run metals by means of heat. V. Seigern, Ausseigern. II. *v. intr.* 1) [u. w. seyn] to run out by melting. 2) to melt entirely. 3) [u. w. haben] to cease melting.

Ausschmettern, I. *v. tr.* to force out by throwing or casting, to knock out with violence. II. *v. intr.* to cease thundering or making a loud or terrible noise.

Ausschmieden, I. *v. tr.* 1) to forge or hammer sufficiently. 2) to extend by hammering, to beat out. 3) Einen Gefangenen —, to strike off the irons from a prisoner. 4) *Fig.* Sie schmiedeten diesen Plan miteinander aus, they forged this plan together. II. *v. intr.* to cease forging.

Ausschmieren, *v. tr.* 1) to besmear with soft adhesive matter on the inside, to daub within. 2) *Fig. a)* [in contempt] to compile without discernment. † *b)* to drub, to beat any one.

Ausschmierer, *m.* [-s, *pl.* -] [in contempt] compiler, a scribbler, plagiarist.

Ausschmiererei, *f.* compilation without discernment, plagiarism.

Ausschmollen, *v. intr.* 1) to cease to be sulky, to cease sulking. 2) to sulk sufficiently.

Ausschmoren, I. *v. tr.* to draw out by stewing. II. *v. intr.* [u. w. seyn] to run out in stewing [as: grease].

Ausschmücken, *v. tr.* to adorn, to deck, to decorate, to embellish. Ein Gebäude —, to decorate an edifice; einen Balcon mit Blumen —, to decorate a balcon with flowers; einen Garten mit Gesträuchen —, to embellish a garden with shrubs; eine Braut —, to dress a bride; sich —, to dress one's self up; eine Rede mit Metaphern —, to embellish a speech with metaphors.

Ausschmücker, *m.* [-s, *pl.* -] he that adorns or embellishes, decorator.

Ausschmuggeln, I. *v. tr.* V. Ausschwärzen. II. *v. intr.* to cease, to have done smuggling.

Ausschmunzeln, *v. intr.* to cease smiling.

Ausschnäbeln, I. *v. tr.* to take out with the bill or beak [said of birds, and in contempt of men]. II. *v. r.* sich —, 1) to cease billing or caressing in fondness. 2) to cease kissing.

Ausschnallen, *v. tr.* to loosen from buckles, to unbuckle. Den Küraß —, to unbuckle the cuirass.

Ausschnarchen, *v. intr.* 1) to snore one's fill. 2) to cease snoring.

Ausschnattern, I. [in famil. lang.] *v. tr.* V. Ausplaudern. II. *v. intr.* 1) to cackle or fig. prattle one's fill. 2) to cease cackling or fig. prattling.

Ausschnauben, I. *v. tr.* 1) to get out by blowing the nose. 2) to empty by blowing or breathing. Die Nase —, to blow the nose. II. *v. intr.* to finish blowing or panting, to recover breath. Die Pferde — lassen, to let the horses breathe or get their wind.

Ausschnaufen, V. Ausschnauben II.

Ausschnäuzen, *v. tr.* 1) to get out, to cleanse by blowing the nose. Sich —, to blow one's nose. || 2) to snuff out [the candle].

Ausschneiden, *ir.* I. *v. tr.* 1) to cut out. Ein Stück aus einem Brette —, to cut out a piece from a board, die Zunge —, to cut out the tongue; ein Fleischgewächs —, [in surgery] to cut out, to cut off, to extirpate a wen; ein Hühnerauge —, to cut out a corn: das Ausschneiden der Ballen an den Füßen der Jagdhunde, [among hunters] lawing. 2) to cut out a part, to cut here and there, to thin out by cutting. Bäume —, to prune trees; eine Perücke —, [among hair-dressers] to taper the hair of a wig; die Haare —, to taper the hair out; einen Stier —, to cut, to geld or castrate a bull; Hähne —, to cut capons; das Rähmchen —, [am. printers] to cut out the frisket. 3) to shape or form by cutting, to cut out. Ein Kleid —, to cut out a garment; ein Bild —, to cut out, or to carve an image; nach dem Modelle —, [among joiners] to cut a profile with a sweep; künstlich —, to pink; schräg —, to slope. 4) to jag at the edges. [in botany] Ein ausgeschnittenes Blatt, a crenated leaf. 5) [in commerce] to sell by the ell, to cut out [cloth &c.].

Ausschneidemesser, *n.* cutting-knife.

Ausschneider, *m.* [-s, *pl.* -] 1) he that cuts out. 2) retailer, mercer. 3) gelder.

Ausschneien, *v. intr.* to cease snowing.

Ausschneiteln, [*dim.* of Ausschneiden] *v. tr.* Die Bäume —, to prune trees.

Ausschnellen, *v. intr.* [u. w. seyn] to extend by an elastic impulse, to jerk out.

|| **Ausschnippeln**, **Ausschnippern**, *v. tr.* V. Ausschnitzeln.

Ausschnitt, *m.* [-es, *pl.* -e] 1) the act of cutting out. 2) [in commerce] Auf den — verkaufen, to sell by the ell. 3) that which is cut out, a cut. Ein — des Kreises, Kreis—, sector. 4) an opening made by cutting out. Der runde — [of a gown &c.] slope; der — an einem Barbierbecken, neck of a barber's basin; der — des Fensters [in architecture] aperture of a window.

Ausschnitthandel, *m.* retail. —handlung, *f.* —laden, *m.* a retailer's shop.

Ausschnitzeln, **Ausschnitzen**, *v. tr.* to cut out, to carve. Bilder —, to carve images.

† **Ausschnüffeln**, I. *v. tr.* to smell out. *Fig.* Er schnüffelte ihn aus, he smelt him out. II. *v. intr.* to cease snuffling.

Ausschnupfen, I. *v. tr.* to consume all the snuff. II. *v. intr.* to cease taking snuff.

† **Ausschnuppern**, V. Ausschnüffeln.

Ausschnüren, *v. tr.* 1) to unlace or untie and take out [clothes from a knapsack &c.]. 2) to unlace [a girl &c.].

Ausschöpfen, *v. tr.* 1) to lade [water out of a tub &c.]. Wasser aus einem Kochkessel —, to draw water from a boiler. 2) to empty by lading, to lade out. Einen Brunnen —, to dry a fountain ein Boot —, [in seamen's lang.] to bale out a boat.

Ausſchöpf-kelle, *f.* —löffel, *m.* ladle.

‖ Aúsſchoren, *v. tr.* to thin [a wood].

Aúsſchoſſen, *v. intr.* to put forth shoots, to sprout. Wo Unkraut ausſchoßt, where weeds shoot.

Aúsſchößling, *m.* [-s, *pl.* -e] a shoot, a sucker.

Aúsſchoten, *v. tr.* to strip of the pod or shell. Erbſen —, to shell pease; Bohnen —, to slip beans out of their skin.

Aúsſchramm, *m.* [-s] V. Schramm.

Aúsſchrapen, *v. tr.* [in seamen's lang.] Die Kabelgarne —, to untwist the ends of the strands.

Aúsſchrauben, [with some authors *ir.*] *v. tr.* to screw out, to unscrew.

Aúsſchreiben, *ir.* I. *v. tr.* 1) to write out, to copy, to transcribe, [in contempt]. V. Ausſchmieren 2) *a*). Ein Buch —, to copy passages from a book; den Horaz —, to copy out of Horace; die ausgeſchriebene Stimme, [in music] a part or a piece of the score or partition written by itself. 2) to write at full length. Jemands Namen ganz —, to write any one's name at length. 3) to steal the thoughts or writings of another, to practise literary theft or plagiarism. 4) to write to the end. Eine Seite —, to write to the bottom of a page; warten Sie bis ich meinen Brief ausgeſchrieben habe, wait till I have finished my letter. 5) to publish, to order by letters missive. Einen Landtag —, to call together, to summon to meet, to assemble by summons, to convocate the representatives of the country; Brandſchatzungen —, to exact contributions; Steuern —, to impose, to lay on taxes; einen Bußtag —, to appoint a day of fasting. II. *v. intr.* to cease writing. III. *v. r.* ſich —, to waste or spend one's powers of writing. Dieſer Dichter hat ſich ausgeſchrieben, the imagination of this poet is exhausted by much writing.

Aúsſchreiben, *n.* [-s, *pl.* -] a proclamation. Ein — erlaſſen, to issue a proclamation.

Aúsſchreiber, *m.* [-s, *pl.* -] a plagiary.

Ausſchreiberei, *f.* 1) plagiarism. 2) the thing copied or written out.

Aúsſchreien, *ir.* I. *v. tr.* 1) to proclaim, to name loudly and publicly for giving notice, to cry. Waaren —, to cry goods; ein verlornes Kind —, to cry a lost child. **Fig.* Man ſchreit ihn für reich aus, they give him out to be a rich man. 2) Seine Stimme —, to perfect one's voice by crying. 3) Seine Stimme —, to spoil one's voice by screaming. II. *v. intr.* 1) to utter a loud voice, to call or exclaim with vehemence, to cry. 2) to [illegible] crying. III. *v. r.* ſich —, 1) to cry one's fill. 2) to exhaust one's self with crying, to grow hoarse with crying, to bawl one's throat sore.

Aúsſchreiten, *ir.* I. *v. intr.* 1) [u. w. ſeyn] to step, to step out of a place. 2) to step aside, [in figurative sense] to go too far, to pass the proper bounds, to go over any given limit or measure. 3) to step out, to make a long stride. II. *v. tr.* to measure by steps, to step, to pace.

Aúsſchröpfen, *v. tr.* to get out by scarifying.

Aúsſchrot, *m.* [-es] V. Ausſchrotung.

1. Aúsſchroten, [from ſchroten = nagen] *v. tr.* to gnaw the inner part of any thing.

2. Aúsſchroten, [from ſchroten = wälzen] *v. tr.* 1) to roll or raise by means of a pulley out of a place. Ein Faß aus dem Keller —, to roll a cask out of the cellar. ‖ 2) to sell by the cask.

Aúsſchrotung, *f.* the act of rolling [a cask] out of a place.

Aúsſchuhen, *v. tr.* to take off the shoes.

1. Aúsſchuppen, [from ‖ ſchuppen = ſchnell ſchieben] *v. tr.* to push out.

2. Aúsſchuppen, [from ſchuppen, Schuppe, scale] *v. tr.* to form into scales by cutting. Ausgeſchuppt, [in heraldry] invecked.

Aúsſchüppen, I. *v. tr.* to throw out with a shovel, to shovel out. II. *v. intr.* to cease shovelling.

Aúsſchüren, *v. tr.* [in metallurgy] to draw [to take from the oven] the slags.

Aúsſchürfen, *v. tr.* [in mining, for:] Ausgraben.

‖ Aúsſchurren, *v. intr.* [u. w. ſeyn] V. Ausgleiten.

Aúsſchuß, *m.* [-ſſes, *pl.* -ſchüſſe] 1) the act of picking or separating, culling out. 2) that which is picked, separated or culled out. *a*) refuse, waste matter, dross, garbles. *b*) something culled out on account of superior excellence, the choice, the prime, the pick; [in seamen's language] the second sort of hemp; persons elected or appointed, to whom any matter or business is referred. Ein — der Landſtände, a committee of the states or representatives of the country; ein — der Bürgerſchaft, a committee of citizens.

Ausſchuß-bogen, *m.* —papier, *n.* outside sheet, outside paper.

Aúsſchütteln, *v. tr.* to shake out.

Aúsſchütten, *v. tr.* 1) [ſchüttend herausthun] to pour out. Waſſer —, to pour out water; Sand —, to pour out sand. 2) to empty by pouring. Einen Sack —, to empty a sack. *Fig.* Das Herz —, to pour out the heart; ſein Herz in den Schoß eines Freundes —, to unbosom one's self to a friend; ſich vor Lachen —, to split with laughing. 3) V. Ausfüllen.

Aúsſchwären, *ir. v. intr.* 1) [u. w. ſeyn] to be brought out by suppuration. 2) [u. w. haben] to cease suppurating.

Aúsſchwärmen, *v. intr.* 1) [u. w. ſeyn] *a*) [to rise as bees in a body and quit the hive] to swarm. *b*) *Fig.* to rove, to go out in pursuit of pleasure. 2) [u. w. haben] *a*) to finish swarming. *b*) *Fig.* to sow one's wild oats.

Aúsſchwärzen, *v. tr.* [to export goods without paying the customs] to smuggle.

Aúsſchwatzen, I. *v. tr.* 1) to utter or tell in a thoughtless manner, to publish secrets or trifles without discretion, to blab. 2) Einem etwas —, to talk or persuade any one out of a thing. II. *v. intr.* 1) to talk to the end, to blab out the whole. 2) to finish talking or chattering. III. *v. r.* ſich —, 1) to exhaust one's self by chattering. 2) to prattle or chatter one's fill.

Aúsſchwefeln, *v. tr.* 1) to fumigate with sulphur within. Ein Faß —, to sulphur a cask. 2) to cleanse by applying sulphur to.

Aúsſchweif, *m.* [-es, *pl.* -e] 1) V. Umſchweif (im Reden). 2) [among lace-makers] slope.

Aúsſchweifen, I. *v. tr.* to slope [a garment &c.]. Nach einer Lehre —, [among joiners] to cut a profile with a sweep; ein ausgeſchweiftes Blatt, [in botany] a sinuated leaf. II. *v. intr.* 1) to be immoderate in enjoyment, to indulge to excess any appetite or passion, to be intemperate in sensual gratifications. Ausſchweifend im Eſſen und Trinken, indulging to excess in the use of food or drink; ausſchweifend in der Liebe, lewd; —de Gedanken, extravagant thoughts; ein —des Leben, a libertine life; ein —des Leben führen, to lead a licentious life; ein —der Menſch, a debauchee. 2) [more properly Abſchweifen] to depart or wander from the main subject, design or tenor of a discourse, argument or narration, to digress [used only of speaking and writing].

Aúsſchweifling, *m.* [-s, *pl.* -e] a debauchee, a rake, a libertine.

Aúsſchweifung, *f.* 1) the act of sloping [a garment &c.]. 2) any indulgence of appetite or passion beyond the rules of propriety, intemperance in sensual gratifications, dissoluteness, excess, extravagance, extravagancy. Die — im Eſſen und Trinken, in der Liebe, excess in eating or drinking, debauch, excessive unlawful indulgence of lust, debauchery; große —en begehen, to indulge in great excesses.

Ausſchweifungskreis, *m.* [in astronomy] a circle of excursion.

Aúsſchweißen, I. *v. tr.* [in forges] to cleanse by welding. II. *v. intr.* [among sportsmen] to lose all the blood.

Aúsſchwelgen, *v. intr.* to cease revelling and rioting.

Aúsſchwellen, *ir. v. intr.* [u. w. ſeyn] to swell out of a place.

Aúsſchwemmen, *v. tr.* 1) to wash away. 2) to excavate, to wear out by washing. Der Regen hat die Wege ausgeſchwemmt, the roads are worn out by the rain. 3) to cleanse by the flooding of water. Die Leinwand im fließenden Waſſer — und ſchlagen, [among bleachers] to cleanse and beat the pieces of linen in running water.

Aúsſchwenken, *v. tr.* to rinse [a glass &c.].

Aúsſchwimmen, *ir. v. intr.* [u. w. ſeyn] 1) to swim out of a place. 2) to cease, to have done swimming.

Aúsſchwingen, *ir.* I. *v. tr.* 1) to throw, fling or cast swinging. 2) to cleanse by swinging. Den Flachs —, to rough-dress, to swingle the flax; das Getreide —, to part the corn from the chaff, to winnow corn; Weizen —, to fan wheat. 3) to unfold by shaking. II. *v. intr.* [u. w. ſeyn] to cease to swing, vibrate, or oscillate. Die Spindel ſchwingt aus, [among clockmakers] the ends of the verge cease to play [in the fangs of the balance-wheel].

Aúsſchwirren, *v. intr.* 1) [u. w. ſeyn] to fly out of a place with a quick sharp whirring noise. 2) [u. w. haben] to cease making a quick sharp noise. Die Bogenſehne hat ausgeſchwirrt, the bowstring twangs no more.

Aúsſchwitzen, I. *v. intr.* 1) [u. w. ſeyn] to sweat out, to perspire, to exsude. Das Harz ſchwitzt aus den Bäumen aus, the resin exsudes from the trees; das Ausſchwitzen, exsudation. 2) [u. w. haben] to cease sweating, perspiring or exsuding. II. *v. tr.* to perspire, to exsude. Eine Krankheit —, to sweat out a distemper; die Luſtſeuche —, to sweat for the pox; Fichten ſchwitzen beſtändig Harz aus, firs continually exsude or discharge resin. **Fig.* Etwas —, to forget something.

Aúsſchwören, I. *v. intr.* 1) to swear to the end. 2) to finish swearing. II. *v. tr.* Einen Eid —, to take an oath.

† Aúsſeckeln, I. *v. tr.* V. Ausbeuteln. Geld —, to expend money; ich bin ganz ausgeſeckelt, I am quite out of pocket. II. *v. r.* ſich —, to spend all one has.

Aúsſegeln, I. *v. intr.* [u. w. ſeyn] [in seamen's lang.] to sail out of a place, to get under sail, to put to sea, to depart. II. *v. tr.* [in seamen's lang.] Einen Felſen, eine Sandbank —, to give a good birth to a rock or bank, to keep aloof from it.

Aúsſegnen, *v. tr.* Eine Wöchnerin —, to church a woman.

Aúsſehen, *ir.* I. *v. intr.* 1) V. Hinausſehen. 2) to have the sight or view of remote objects.

Von hier kann man weit —, there is an extended view from this place. 3) to have a particular appearance, to look. Der Kranke sieht jetzt besser aus, the patient looks better than he did; blaß —, to look pale; verdrießlich —, to look vexed or out of humour; Einer, der gut aussieht, a well looking man; die Wolken sehen regnerisch aus, the clouds look rainy; es sieht regnerisch aus, the weather is set in for rain; die ganze Natur sieht düster aus, all nature wears a lowering countenance; er sieht nach einem Spitzbuben aus, he has a hanging look; er sieht nach etwas Vornehmem aus, he looks like a man of rank. *Prov.* — als könnte man nicht fünf zählen, to look as if one could not say bo to a goose. *Fig.* to be in a certain condition. Die Sache sieht schlimm aus, the thing looks ill; dies sieht aus, als wenn er gar keine Freundschaft für mich hätte, this looks as if he had no kindness at all for me; wie sieht es mit ihm or um ihn aus? how is it with him? es sieht schlimm mit ihm or um ihn aus, he is in a bad way.

II. *v. tr.* 1) to see to the end. Ich konnte das Schauspiel nicht —, I could not stay to see the play out. 2) to see and choose. Sich etwas —, to choose something, to make choice of something, to look out something; Einen zu einem Amte —, to choose or designate any one to an office or employment. V. Ausersehen. 3) to fatigue by an exertion of the eyes, to tire by much looking. Sich fast die Augen —, to look one's self almost blind.

Aússehen, *n.* [-s] 1) the act of looking &c. 2) cast of countenance, air of the face, look, mien, figure, appearance. 3) V. Ansehen, Aussicht.

Aússehend, *past part.* and *adj.* Weit —e Plane entwerfen, to form grand designs. designs extensive; das sind sehr weit—e Hoffnungen, these are very remote hopes; wohl —, healthy looking; übel —, sickly looking.

Aússeher, *m.* [-s, *pl.* -] [in seamen's lang.] a look-out. [more usual Ausguck.]

† **Aússeichen**, V. Ausharnen.

Aússeigern, *v. tr.* [in metallurgy] to reduce [the ores of silver] by liquation.

Aússeihen, *v. tr.* 1) to get out by filtration. 2) to purify by filtration, to strain, to defecate [as liquor] by straining, to filtrate.

Aússeimen, *v. tr.* to let the honey when pure and liquid drop or distil from the honey-combs.

Aússein, V. Ausseyn.

Außen, *adv.* 1) without, on the outside, not within, out [opposed to in or within]. — vor dem Hause, on the outside of the house; — vor der Stadt, without the town; das Feuer wird sich einen Weg nach — bahnen, the fire will force its way outwards 2) [in connection with von] from the outside, on the outside. Der Geruch kommt von —, the smell comes from without, manche Früchte scheinen von — &c., the exterior of some fruits seems &c.; ein schönes Haus von —, a fine house on the outside.

Außen=bleiben, *n.* 1) V. Ausbleiben. 2) [= Außerhalbbleiben] the remaining out or outside. —böschung, *f.* [in fortification] counterscarp. — deichsland, *n.* land on the outside of a dam. —ding, *n.* an object exterior to a man [as opposed to that which is within or in his mind]. —ende, *n.* extremity. —gegenstand, *m.* an external object. —gestalt, *f.* outward form. —graben, *m.* [in fortification] avant-fosse. —hafen, *m.* the exterior port —linie, *f.* the outline, contour. Die —linien eines Kopfes, the outlines of a head. *Fig.* the first beginning of any thing. Die —linien einer Wissenschaft, the elements or rudiments of a science. —mensch, *m.* the outward [carnal, corporeal] man. —posten, *m.* [in milit. affairs] an outpost. —rhede, *f.* the exterior road or roadstead. —schein, *m.* outward appearance. Urtheile nicht nach dem —scheine, judge not from the appearance. —schimmer, *m.* external splendour. —seite, *f.* [the external part of a thing] the outside. Geschaffene Wesen sehen nur unsere —seite, created beings see nothing but our outside. —stand [more usual Ausstand], *m.* outstanding debt. —theil, *m.* the external part of a body. —treppe, *f.* a staircase lying open, perron. — wall, *m.* [in fortification] the exterior rampart. —wand, *f.* [the exterior wall of a building] outwall. —welt, *f.* the objects exterior to us [as opposed to those which are within or in our mind]. — werk, *n.* [in fortification] outwork.

Aússenden, *v. tr.* 1) to send out, to send abroad. 2) *Fig.* [in poetry] to send forth, to emit.

Aússengen, *v. tr.* to singe on the inside. *Fig* Von Leidenschaften ausgesengt, consumed by passion.

Außer, I. *prep.* [in connection with the dative case: not within, without] — dem Hause [außerhalb des Hauses], out of the house, out of doors; — der Stadt (außerhalb der Stadt), without town; — dem Schiffe, [in seamen's lang.] without board; — dem Bereiche der Stimme, out of hearing; — dem Gesichte, out of sight. [sometimes in connection with the genitive case] — Landes gehen, to quit one's country, to go abroad; — Landes seyn, to be abroad. *Fig.* *a*) Er ist — sich, he is out of his senses; — sich seyn, to be beside one's self; er ist vor Liebe — sich, he is mad with love; — Athem, out of breath; etwas — Acht lassen, to disregard something; — Gefahr, out of danger; — Dienst, out of place; — der gewöhnlichen Regel, out of the way; — Zweifel, out of doubt; — dem Gesetze, excluded from the benefit of the law, deprived of its protection; Einen — dem Gesetze erklären, to outlaw any one; — der Zeit, out of season; er ist — Stande, das zu thun, he is incapable of doing that, he has it not in his power to do that. *b*) [for: ausgenommen] Alle waren in diese Sache verwickelt — Einem, all were involved in this affair except one or one excepted; — diesen Beiden war Niemand da, there was nobody there, but these two; — diesem, beside that.

II. *conj.* — daß, except that, save that; es kann nicht seyn, — Sie sprechen von einem Andern, it cannot be, unless you speak of another.

Außer=amtlich, *adj.* and *adv.* not official, private. —christlich, *adj.* and *adv.* not professing christianism. —dem, *adv.* beside, besides that, moreover. —ehelich, *adj.* and *adv.* out of wedlock. Ein —eheliches Kind, a child begotten and born out of wedlock, a natural child, a bastard. —europäisch, *adj.* and *adv.* belonging to a nation or country out of Europe. —gerichtlich, *adj.* and *adv.* extrajudicial, extrajudicially. —halb, I. *adv.* abroad, on the outside. —halb ist das Haus schön, the house is handsome on the outside. II. *prep.* [in connection with the genitive case] without, on the outside of. —halb des Hauses, without doors; —halb der Stadt, without the town. —heit, *f.* 1) extreme, extremity. 2) [utmost point, utmost degree] extreme. — kirchlich, *adj.* and *adv.* out of the church, not in connection with the church Die —kirchliche Andacht, private devotion. —ordentlich, I. *adj* 1) außerordentlich, extraordinary [beyond or out of the common order or method]. —ordentliche Uebel erfodern —ordentliche Mittel, extraordinary evils require extraordinary remedies; ein —ordentlicher Gesandter, [sent on a particular occasion] an ambassador extraordinary. 2) außerordentlich, [exceeding the common degree or measure]. Eine —ordentliche Hitze, an extreme heat; eine —ordentliche Freude, an extreme joy; die —ordentlichen Talente Shakespeares, the extraordinary talents of Shakespeare; ein Gebäude von —ordentlicher Größe und Pracht, a building of extraordinary grandeur and magnificence. II. *adv.* extraordinarily. Der Tempel Salomons war —ordentlich prächtig, the temple of Salomon was extraordinarily magnificent; —ordentlich reich, exceedingly rich; —ordentlich heiß, extremely hot; Isaak zitterte —ordentlich, Isaac trembled exceedingly. —sinnlich, *adj.* and *adv.* speculative. —vernünftig, —vernunftlich, *adj.* and *adv.* beyond the limits of reason. —weltlich, *adj.* and *adv.* beyond the limits of the material world, extramundane. — wesentlich, *adj* and *adv.* not essential. —wesentliche Eigenschaften, contingent properties; das Außerwesentliche einer Sache, accidental. — zeitlich, *adj.* and *adv.* unseasonable.

Äußere, [der, die, das] *adj.* exterior, external, outward, outer. Die — Mauer, the outer wall; die — Seite eines Dinges, the outer or external part of a thing; das — Thor, the outer gate; die — Schale einer Zwiebel, the outward coat of an onion; die —n Winkel, [in geometry] external angles; —r Winkel, [in fortification] salient angle, — Gegenstände, external objects; — Ursachen, external causes; der — Mensch, the outward [carnal, fleshly, corporeal] man; ein —r Glanz für eine innere Last, an outward honour for an inward toil; das — Ansehen, the outside, external or outward appearance; das Äußere, outward form, external appearance; ein schönes —, a fair exterior; sein —s, his externals; sein —s verspricht viel, his outside promises much; er hatte ein ernsthaftes —s, he had a solemn appearance; sein —s gefällt mir sehr, I am extremely pleased with his person; die —n Gebräuche der Religion, the externals of religion, the exteriors of religion.

Äußerlich, I. *adj.* external, exterior, outward. —e Arzeneimittel, external remedies; —e Wirkungen, external effects; —er Haß, outward hate; die Trauer ist nur im —en, the mourning is but outward. II. *adv.* outwardly, externally. Welche sie — zu verachten scheinen, which they outwardly seem to despise.

Äußerlichkeit, *f.* external perception, externality. Er sieht nur auf —en, he looks only to external appearances.

Äußern, I. *v. tr.* to utter, to express. Seine Ansichten —, to express one's views; seine Meinung —, to utter one's opinion; seine Gedanken —, to vent one's thoughts; seine Zufriedenheit über etwas —, to speak one's satisfaction about a thing; seine Gesinnungen —, to manifest one's sentiments; er äußerte die Absicht, sein Amt niederzulegen, he intimated his intention of resigning his office. II. *v. r.* sich —, 1) to appear outwardly. Der Aussatz äußert sich auf der Haut, the leprosy appears on the skin; die Blattern äußern sich, the small pox breaks out. 2) to declare in words, to express one's self. Sich über eine Sache —, to speak one's thought about any thing.

Äußerst, *adv* extremely, excessively, exceedingly. — ungeduldig, excessively impatient. Der Wind wehete — stark, the wind blew excessively hard; es ist — schmerzhaft, it is extremely painful; — schön, uncommonly handsome; die Genueser waren — mächtig zur See, the Genoese were exceedingly powerful by sea; Bewegung ist — nöthig zur Gesundheit, exercise is highly requisite to health.

Äußerste, [der, die, das; superl. of Äußere] *adj.* outermost, utmost, extreme. Der — Pu eines Dinges, the extreme point of a thing; die — Reihe, the outermost row; die —n Grenzen eines Landes, the utmost limits, the extremities of a country; die — Tiefe, the utter deep, depth; die —e Gefahr, the utmost peril; die — Armuth des Prinzen, the extreme poverty of the prince; eine Sache von der —n Wichtigkeit, an affair of the last or highest importance; der — Grad des Schmerzes, the extremity of pain; auf das —, to the utmost; sein —s thun, to do one's utmost, to do one's best; das — wagen, to put all to the stake; aufs — bringen, to reduce to extremity; Einen aufs — aufbringen, to excite any one to the utmost; er ist auf das — gebracht, he is put to his last shifts.

Äußerung, *f.* 1) the act of uttering, utterance, expression. Die — seiner Gefühle, the declaration of one's sentiments. 2) [that which is uttered or expressed] expression. Die — des öffentlichen Willens, the expression of the public will; —en der Güte, kindnesses.

Ausſetzen, I. *v. tr.* 1) to cover on the inside. Mit Quadersteinen —, to line with freestones; mit Pfählen —, to face with posts; einen Hof mit Steinen —, to pave a yard. 2) to set out of a place, to remove from one place and put in another. Junge Bäume —, to transplant young trees; Truppen —, to set or put troops on shore or ashore, to land or disembark troops; das Boot —, [in seamen's lang.] to put out the boat; einen Matrosen auf einer wüsten Insel —, to put a sailor ashore on a desolate island, to maroon a sailor; ein Kind —, to expose a child; das Sakrament [die Monstranz] —, [in the Romish church] to expose the sacrament; sich [seinen Ball] —, [at billiards] to give the lead; [at chess or draughts] to move first; die Stimmen —, [in music] to transcribe, to copy the parts from the score; die ausgesetzten Stimmen, the parts or pieces of the score or partition written by themselves. *Fig.* *a*) [in law] Einen —, to deprive any one of actual seizin or possession, to deprive any one of the actual occupancy of a thing, to dispossess any one; einen Pächter auf eine unrechtmäßige Weise —, to disseise a tenant of his leasehold estate. *b*) [to place in a situation to be affected or acted on] to expose. Den Kopf oder die Brust der Luft —, to expose the head or the breast to the air; sich einer heftigen Hitze —, to expose one's self to a violent heat; sich einer Gefahr —, wenn es die Pflicht erheischt, to expose one's self when duty requires it; er setzte sein Weib den Gefahren des Meeres aus, he exposed his wife to the seas; sich einer Beschimpfung —, to expose one's self to insult. *c*) to cause to cease for a time, to suspend. Seine Arbeit —, to lay aside, to discontinue one's work; die Ursachen, wegen denen man das Schauspiel aussetzte, waren schlecht begründet, the reasons for suspending the play were ill founded; es wurde ausgesetzt, it was postponed; laß mich genau die Zeit wissen, wenn die Gerichtshöfe ihre Sitzungen —, let me know the exact time when the courts intermit; arbeiten ohne auszusetzen, to labour without intermission; das Aussetzen des Pulses, intermission of the pulse; ein —des Fieber, an intermittent fever. *d*) to find fault with, to censure, to blame. Er hat an Allem etwas auszusetzen, he finds fault with every thing; an dieser Sache ist nichts auszusetzen, there is nothing to be objected against this thing; daran ist nichts auszusetzen, there is nothing exceptionable in it. *e*) to design for a purpose, to destine to, to grant, to allow, to fix. Er setzte seinem Sohne jährlich hundert Pfund aus, he allowed his son a hundred pounds a year; Jemandem einen Jahrgehalt —, to settle a yearly pension or annuity upon any one; Einem ein Legat —, to bequeath a legacy to any one; einen Tag —, to fix or appoint a day; einen Preis —, to set out, to propose a prize; das Ausgesetzte, allowance, a portion appointed. 3) to set to the end. Einen Bogen —, [among printers] to finish setting or composing a sheet.

II. *v. intr.* 1) [in mining] to appear on the surface. 2) to cease getting teeth [said of sheep].

Aussetzestoß, *m.* [at billiards] the lead.

Aussetzling, *m.* [-s, *pl.* -e] a child exposed.

Ausseufzen, *v. tr.* to utter sighing.

Ausseyn, *ir. v. intr.* 1) to be out, absent or abroad. Er war heute noch nicht aus, he has not yet been out to-day. 2) to be emptied. Das Faß ist aus, the cask is out, is done or finished. 3) to be finished, to be over. Die Predigt ist aus, the sermon is over; das Spiel ist aus, the game is up. 4) to be in a state of extinction. Das Licht, das Feuer ist aus, the candle, the fire is out. *Fig.* Es ist aus mit ihm, it is all over with him, he is going to die, and also, he is completely ruined; es ist mit seinen Hoffnungen aus, there is an end of all his hopes. || and * 5) Auf etwas —, to go after a thing, to be set upon a thing.

Aussicht, *f.* [*pl.* -en] 1) view [of something distant], prospect, [in architecture and in painting] perspective view. Die — auf ferne Gebirge, the view of distant mountains; die Kirche benimmt uns die —, the church obstructs our view; das Haus hat die — nach Süden, the house has a southern aspect [that is, a position which faces or looks to the south]; mein Garten hat die — auf den Fluß, my garden looks towards the river; eine beschränkte —, a confined view; eine weite —, an extended view; die — des Landes von der See, [in seamen's lang.] the perspective view of the land from the sea. *Fig.* Die — auf künftiges Glück, the prospect of future happiness. 2) object of view, prospect, view. Von dieser Stelle hat man eine prachtvolle —, there is a noble prospect from this place; diese Häuser geben eine schöne —, these houses yield a fine prospect. 3) *Fig.* regard to something future, prospect. Man hat die — auf eine gute Erndte, there is a prospect of a good harvest; er hat die —, befördert zu werden, he has a prospect of preferment; er hat schöne —en, he has fine prospects; gute —n, favourable aspects.

Aussichtshaus, *n.* a belvidere.

Aussichten, I. *v. tr.* to sift or bolt, to garble. II. *v. intr.* to cease sifting.

Aussickern, *v. intr.* [u. w. seyn] to percolate as a liquid through the pores of a substance, or through small openings, to ooze, to drip. Der Wein sickert aus dem Fasse aus, the wine oozes out of the cask.

Aussieben, *v. tr.* to get out by sifting, to sift out.

Aussiechen, *v. intr.* to cease being sickly.

Aussieden, *ir.* I. *v. tr.* to seeth or boil out. Das Fett aus dem Fleische —, to extract the fat of meat by boiling; rohes Garn —, to scour raw yarn; Silberstücke —, to blanch pieces of silver. II. *v. intr.* 1) [u. w. seyn] to seeth over. 2) [u. w. haben] to finish seething.

Aussiegen, *v. intr.* to conquer completely.

Aussingen, *ir.* I. *v. tr.* 1) to sing to the end. Ein Lied —, to finish a song. 2) to sing all one knows. 3) to carry out or accompany singing [a corpse &c.]. 4) to perfect by singing. Die Stimme —, to perfect one's voice by singing. 5) to spoil by singing. Eine ausgesungene Stimme, a voice spoilt by too much singing. II. *v. r.* sich —, to lose one's voice by much singing. III. *v. intr.* 1) [in seamen's lang.] to pipe a call, to sing out. 2) to cease singing.

Aussinnen, *ir. v. tr.* to strike or find out by thinking, to devise, to imagine, to excogitate. Ein Mittel —, to contrive a means.

Aussintern, V. Aussickern.

Aussitzen, *ir. v. intr.* 1) to sit on the outside of the house, out of doors. Mit Waaren —, to sit out with commodities. 2) to sit for a given time. Seine Zeit —, to hold out one's time in prison. 3) to finish or cease sitting. Dieses Huhn hat ausgesessen, this hen has done sitting.

Aussöhnbar, *adj.* and *adv.* 1) reconcilable. 2) expiable.

Aussöhnen, I. *v. tr.* 1) to reconcile [contending minds &c.]. Söhne deine starke Seele mit dem Leben aus, reconcile thy mighty soul to life; diese edle Leidenschaft hat meine Gedanken mit &c. ausgesöhnt, this noble passion has reconciled my thoughts to &c.; haben Sie sich mit dem Schauspiele wieder ausgesöhnt? are you reconciled to the play? 2) etwas — [= abbüßen], to expiate, to atone for a thing. II. *v. r.* sich —, [to become reconciled] to reconcile one's self. Sich mit Einem —, to make up a quarrel with any one; söhnt euch aus! make it up! sich mit einem Feinde —, to make one's peace with an enemy.

Aussöhnlich, *adj.* and *adv.* reconcilable.

Aussöhnung, *f.* reconciliation, expiation, atonement, reparation.

Aussommern, **Aussömmern**, V. Ausſonnen.

Aussondern, *v. tr.* 1) to separate one or more things from others, to single out, to single. Die geleimten Papierblätter —, [among playing-card-makers] to sort the sheets. 2) [to take by preference from among others] to select, to choose out, to pick. Ausgesondert, select; ausgesonderte [= auserlesene, vortreffliche] Truppen, select or picked troops.

Aussonnen, *v. tr.* to sun sufficiently. Die Betten —, to expose the beds to the sun, to air them.

Aussoren, *v. tr.* to deprive of natural juice or sap, to dry, to dry up.

Aussorgen, *v. intr.* to cease being anxious or solicitous. *Fig.* Er hat nun ausgesorgt, his cares are at an end, his sorrows are over, he is dead.

Aussorten, **Aussortiren**, *v. tr.* to sort, to separate, to assort, to cull. Die Lumpen —, [in papermills] to sort the rags.

Ausspähen, *v. tr.* to spy out. Einen Ausreißer —, to find out a deserter; einen Dieb —, to detect a thief; er wurde bald ausgespähet, he was soon found out.

Ausspäher, *m.* [-s, *pl.* -] a spy, emissary.

Ausspäherei, *f.* [in contempt] spying.

Ausspalten, I. *v. intr.* 1) [u. w. seyn] to split and fall out. 2) [u. w. haben] *a*) to split to the end. *b*) to have done splitting. II. *v. tr.* to get out or take out by splitting.

Ausspann, *m.* and *f.* 1) baiting place. 2) [in law] V. Ablager, 3.

Ausspannen, *v. tr.* 1) to stretch, to extend. Ein Seil —, to stretch a cord; Tuch —, to tenter cloth; Netze —, to set nets; die Segel —, to set sail. 2) to loosen from the tenters, traces or yoke. Die Pferde —, to take the horses out, to unharness the horses; die Ochsen —, to unyoke the oxen; wir wollen —, let us take the horses out. †*Fig* Einen —, to free any one from some hard task. 3) to measure by the span.

Ausspanneisen, *n.* currier's head-knife.

Ausspänner, *m.* [-s, *pl.* -] 1) he that unyokes &c. 2) [among manufacturers of cloth &c.] a tenter.

Aussparen, *v. tr.* 1) V. Aufsparen. 2) [in

painting] to spare. Die Lichter —, to spare the lights [of a picture or tapestry].

Aússpaßen, v. intr. to cease joking or jesting.

Aússpeichern, v. tr. to clear a ware-house, barn, granary &c.

Aússpeien, ir. I. v. tr. to eject [flame, ashes &c.], to spit [blood &c.]. Der Berg speiet Feuer und Lava aus, the mountain belches flames and lava; die Lunge —, to spit up one's lungs. Fig. to cast out, to throw out in contempt. Lästerungen wider Einen —, to belch out or utter abuse or calumnies against any one, to speak reproachfully of any one; Gift und Galle —, to sputter one's gall, to fret and fume. II. v. intr. [to throw out spittle] to spit. Vor Einem —, [a sign of contempt] to spit out before one's face.

Aússpeilern, v. tr. to skewer.

Aússpeisen, I. v. tr. to empty by eating, to eat up. II. v. intr. to finish eating, dining, to make an end of eating.

|| Aússpellen, V. Ausspalten.

Aússpelzen, v. tr. to separate the husks from the corn by thrashing, riddling or winnowing.

Aússpenden, v. tr. to dispense, to distribute largely. Almosen —, to give alms; spende dein Brod den Hungrigen aus, deal thy bread out to the hungry; seine Segnungen —, to bestow one's blessings; das Abendmahl —, to administer the sacrament; Einer, der Gnaden ausspendet, a dispenser of favours.

Aússpender, m. [-s, pl. -] —inn, f. dispenser, distributor.

Aússpendung, f. distribution, dispensation. Die — des Abendmahls, the administration of the sacrament.

Aússperren, v. tr. 1) to spread apart. Die Beine —, to distend, to spread one's legs; mit ausgesperrten Beinen stehen oder gehen, to stand or walk with the legs far apart, to straddle, to stride; ausgesperrte Aeste, [in botany] divaricate branches. 2) to hinder from entry, to shut out. Einen —, to lock any one out.

Aússpicken, v. tr. to stuff with bacon or pork. Ein ausgespickter Hase, a larded hare. * and ‡ Fig. Einem den Beutel —, to line any one's purse; ein gut ausgespickter [gespickter] Beutel, a purse well furnished with money.

Aússpiel, n. [-es, pl. -e] a playing for a stake or prize, a raffle.

Aússpielen, I. v. tr. 1) to play out. Wer spielte den König aus? [at cards] who played or led the king? haben Sie das Pique ausgespielt? did you play the spade? den Ball —, [at tennis] to serve out the ball; ich werde einen Trumpf —, I shall lead a trump. 2) to dispose of [a house &c.] by a species of lottery [in which several persons stake a small part of the value of the thing, in consideration of the chance of winning it], to raffle. 3) to perfect by playing. Eine Geige —, to perfect or improve a fiddle by playing on it. 4) to play to the end. Die Partie —, to finish the game; ein Stück —, to finish a play. Fig. Er hat seine Rolle ausgespielt, it is over with him; er hat seine Rolle bei Hofe ausgespielt, he is now out of favour at court. II. v. intr. 1) to play or throw first. Sie spielen aus, mein Herr, you are to play, Sir, you lead, you are the eldest hand, Sir; ich muß —, I am to lead. 2) to cease playing. III. v. r. sich —, 1) to exhaust one's self by playing. 2) not to know what to play next.

Aússpießen, v. tr. to take out with a spit or any pointed instrument.

Aússpinnen, ir. I v. tr. 1) to get or obtain by spinning. 2) Fig. a) to spin out. Eine Rede —, to spin out, to lengthen a discourse or speech; durch einen Aufschub um den andern spinnen sie ihr ganzes Leben aus, by one delay after another they spin out their whole lives. b) to excogitate, to strike out by thought, to contrive, to devise [chiefly in a bad sense]. Fein ausgesponnene Lügen, quaint lies. 3) to spin to the end. Fig. Der Faden seines Lebens ist ausgesponnen, the thread of his life is spun out. II. v. intr. 1) to spin to the end. 2) to cease spinning.

* Aússpintisiren, v. tr. to strike out by thought, to excogitate, to contrive.

* Aússpioniren, v. tr. to spy out.

Aússpitzen, v tr. to cut to a point. * Fig. Das ist eine ausgespitzte Lüge, that is a cunning lie.

Aússpötteln, v. tr. to mock or deride a little, to rally.

Aússpotten, I. v. tr. to expose to laughter and contempt, to treat with scorn, to deride, to mock, to ridicule, to laugh at in contempt, to turn to ridicule. II. v. intr. 1) to mock one's fill. 2) to cease deriding or mocking.

Aússprache, f. the act and mode of utterance, pronunciation. Eine gute oder schlechte —, a good or bad pronunciation; die deutliche — der Silben, the distinct articulation of the syllables; es ist fast unmöglich, sich die schottische — abzugewöhnen, it is almost impossible to get rid of the Scottish accent. Syn. Aussprache, Mundart. Die Mundart is the form or idiom of a language, peculiar to a province or country; that peculiarity which distinguishes one dialect or branch of the parent language from another; die Aussprache signifies only the pronunciation which distinguishes a dialect. The Low-German Mundart [dialect, idiom] is distinguished from the High-German, not only by peculiar words, construction, declensions &c. but also by the Aussprache [pronunciation]. We may recognise the Mundart in the writing of an author, whose Aussprache we have never heard.

Aússprechen, ir. I. v. tr. 1) to utter, to pronounce Ein Wort —, to pronounce a word; nicht ausgesprochen werden, to be quiescent or silent [said of a letter]; diese Wörter sind sehr schwer auszusprechen, the utterance of these words is very difficult; deutlich —, to articulate distinctly; das r zu stark aussprechen, to pronounce the letter r with too much force, to whur. 2) to declare in words, to express. Absalon sprach das Todesurtheil über seinen Bruder aus, Absalom pronounced a sentence of death against his brother; seine Zufriedenheit über eine Sache —, to speak one's satisfaction about a thing; sprechen Sie es nur aus, do but speak the word; seine Dankbarkeit —, to express one's gratitude; meine Verlegenheit läßt sich nicht —, I am in a perplexity not to be expressed; [in heraldry] ein Wappen —, [to explain in proper terms the figures or ensigns that belong to a coat of arms] to blazon a coat of arms. 3) to get out by speaking. Sich die Lunge —, to fatigue one's self by speaking. II. v. intr. 1) to speak to the end. 2) to have done speaking. III. v. r. sich —, 1) to exhaust, to fatigue one's self by speaking. 2) Fig. to speak one's mind.

Ausssprecherei, f. a bad pronunciation.

Aússprechlich, adj. and adv. expressible.

Aússpreiten, Ausspreizen, v. tr. to extend, to stretch apart. Die Arme — [better ausbreiten], to extend the arms; die Beine —, to straddle the legs.

Aússprengen, v. tr. 1) to cause to fly or burst out of a place. 2) to scatter in drops, to sprinkle [water &c.]. Fig to noise abroad, to report, to spread. Ein Gerücht —, to circulate a report. 3) [in manege] Ein Pferd —, to put a horse into a gallop.

Aússtreuen, v. tr. to scatter like chaff.

Aússprießen, v. intr. to shoot forth, to sprout.

Aússpringen, ir. I. v. r. sich —, 1) to spring one's fill. Lassen Sie die Kinder sich —, let the children run till they are tired. 2) to fatigue one's self by springing or leaping. II. v. tr. to put out of its proper place by springing or leaping. Sich einen Fuß —, to dislocate or sprain one's foot by springing. III. v. intr. 1) [u. w. seyn] to spring out, to fly off. Es ist ein Stück aus diesem Messer ausgesprungen, a piece has snapped out of this knife; [in fortification] ausspringende Winkel, salient angles. 2) [u. w. haben] to cease springing.

Aússpritzeln, v. tr. to emit in small flying drops, to spurt out.

Aússpritzen, I. v. tr. 1) to spout, to spurt, to spurt out. 2) to put out, to extinguish by spouting. 3) to wash with a syringe, to syringe [a wound &c.]. 4) [in anatomy] Etwas, ein Thier &c. —, to fill the vessels of an animal body with some coloured substance, in order to render visible their figures and ramifications. Die Adern mit Wachs —, to inject the veins with wax; das —, injection. II. v. intr. [u. w. seyn and haben] to spout, to spurt.

Aússprossen, [part. ausgesproßet] v. intr. 1) [u. w. seyn] to put forth shoots, to sprout. 2) [u. w. haben] to finish sprouting.

Aússprößling, m. [-s, pl. -e] a shoot, a sprout.

Aússpruch, m. [-es, pl. -sprüche] final judgment or opinion, in a case which has been under deliberation or discussion. Der Gerichtshof fällte einen — zu Gunsten des Beklagten, the court decided in favour of the defendant; der — eines Gerichtshofes oder Rathes, the decision of a court or council, arret; der — des Richters, sentence; der — der Schiedsrichter, award; der — der Geschwornen, verdict; — eines Orakels, the answer of an oracle; göttliche Aussprüche, divine judgments.

Aússprudeln, I. v. tr. to throw out in flying drops with some noise, to bubble out. Er sprudelte die niedrigsten Beschuldigungen aus, he sputtered out the basest accusations. II. v. intr. 1) to bubble out, to sputter out of a... 2) to cease bubbling or sputtering.

Aússprühen, I. v. intr. to emit small particles of fire, to spark, to sparkle. II. v. tr. to cast or throw out in small particles. Der Berg sprühet Feuer aus, the mountain belches...

Aússprung, m. [-es, pl. -sprünge] the act of springing out of a place, starting.

Aússpucken, I. v. tr. [to eject from the mouth] to spit, to spit out. Blut —, to spit blood. II. v. intr. 1) [to throw out spittle] to spit. 2) Vor Einem —, [as a sign of contempt] to spit out before one's face.

Aússpuken, v. intr. to cease appearing as a spirit. Es hat in diesem Hause ausgespukt, this house is no longer haunted.

Aússpulen, v. intr. 1) to spool to the end. 2) to finish spooling.

Aússpülen, v. tr. 1) to cleanse by washing, to rinse. Ein Glas —, to rinse a glass, to wash out a glass; den Mund —, to wash out the mouth. 2) to hollow, to excavate by washing. Die Strömung hat die Ufer des Flusses ausgespült, the current has undermined the banks of the river.

Ausspülstock, m. [in fulling-mills]

trough.

Ausspünden, *v. tr.* to line with boards.

Ausspüren, *v. tr.* to search for making discovery. Ein Wild —, to track game; den Verfasser einer Flugschrift —, to trace up the author of a pamphlet; einen Dieb oder Diebstahl —, to find out, to detect a thief or a theft; ein Geheimniß —, to find out, to ferret out a secret.

Ausspürer, *m.* [-s, *pl.* -] a tracer, spy.

Ausspürerei, *f.* [in contempt] spying.

* **Ausstaffiren**, *v. tr.* to dress up, to trim, to trick up, off or out.

‖ **Ausstähren**, *v. intr.* to cease desiring the tup.

‖ **Ausstaken**, *v. tr.* [in carpentry] to furnish [a ceiling &c.] with thin narrow slips of wood or laths [to support the plastering].

Ausstallen, I. *v. tr.* to bring out of the stable. II. *v. intr.* V. Ausharnen [said of horses].

Ausstämmen, V. Ausstemmen.

Ausstampfen, I. *v. tr.* to get out by stamping, to stamp out, to beat out [grain &c.]. II. *v. intr.* 1) to stamp one's fill, to stamp to the end. 2) to cease stamping.

Ausstand, *m.* [-es, *pl.* -stände] something outstanding, especially outstanding money.

Ausständer, *m.* [-s, *pl.* -] a sort of hive.

Ausständig, *adj.* outstanding. —e Schulden, outstanding debts.

Ausstänkern, *v. tr.* 1) to fill with a bad smell. 2) *Fig.* to smell out.

Ausstarren, *v. intr.* to cease staring.

Ausstatten, *v. tr* to furnish with a portion, to endow. Eine Tochter —, to portion a daughter; einen Sohn —, to establish, to settle a son. *Fig.* Mit Vernunft ausgestattet, endowed with reason; von der Natur mit Schönheit ausgestattet, endowed by nature with beauty.

Ausstattung, *f.* 1) endowing, portioning, endowment, establishment. 2) portion, dowry. *Fig.* endowment.

Ausstäuben, *v. tr.* to free from dust on the inside. Ein Zimmer —, to dust a room.

Ausstaubern, V. Ausstöbern.

Ausstäupen, *v. tr.* 1) to whip soundly, to [illegible]. 2) to whip publicly, to expel by a public whipping.

Ausstechen, *ir. v. tr.* 1) to get or put out by piercing with some pointed instrument. Torf —, to cut peat; Rasen —, to cut turf; die Philister stachen ihm die Augen aus [Judg. XVII], the Philistines put out his eyes; [in seamen's lang.] ein Tau —, to veer out a cable; dem Anker mehr Tau —, to pay away more cable; stich mehr Ankertau [illegible] away more cable! eine Flasche Wein —, [in familiar lang.] to crack a bottle of wine. **Fig.* to [illegible] gain the better of any one. Einen —, to [illegible] one out, *Prov.* to cut the grass under any [illegible]. Einen Mitbewerber —, to supplant a competitor; er hat alle seine Nebenbuhler ausgestochen, he got the better of all his rivals. 2) to [illegible] by piercing with a pointed instrument, [illegible] out, to hew out. Einen Graben —, to dig a ditch; in Kupfer —, to engrave; in Holz —, [illegible]; Spitzen —, [among washerwomen] to pierce [illegible] when washed [in order to make it look well]. 3) to copy by pricking. Ein Muster —, to prick a pattern.

Ausstecher, *m.* [-s, *pl.* -] [a sea term] a boom [illegible] for a bowsprit in small vessels, a sliding [illegible].

Ausstecken, *v. tr.* 1) to put up to open view, put out; to hang out. Eine Flagge —, to hoist a flag. 2) [to mark by poles or stakes] to set out. Einen Garten —, to set out a garden.

Ausstehen, *ir.* I. *v. intr.* [u. w. seyn and haben] 1) to stand out, to stand in an open place with any thing. Mit Waaren —, to keep a stall. *Fig.* —de Schulden, outstanding [not collected, unpaid] debts; ich habe Geld —, I have money owing me. 2) [u. w. seyn] to stand to the end of a thing. Die ganze Predigt —, to stand during the whole time of the sermon. II. *v. tr.* to undergo, to endure. Mühseligkeiten —, to undergo hardships; eine lange Krankheit —, to go through a long sickness; eine [wundärztliche] Operation —, to go through an operation; eine Strafe —, to bear, to suffer punishment; Kränkungen —, to sustain mortifications; *ich kann diese Person nicht —, I cannot bear, I dislike this person excessively.

Ausstehlen, *ir.* I. *v. tr.* to empty by robbing. Ein Haus —, to rob a house. *Fig.* Einen, ein Buch —, to copy, to transcribe writings of another, to practise literary theft. II. *v. intr.* to cease stealing.

Ausstehlich, *adj.* and *adv.* tolerable, supportable.

Aussteifen, *v. tr.* 1) to make stiff, to stiffen. Ein Kleid —, to stiffen a garment with starch, to starch a garment. 2) [among carpenters &c.] to furnish with stays on the inside, to prop on the inside. Einen Brunnen —, to line a well with boards.

Aussteigen, *ir. v. intr* [u. w. seyn] to walk out; *it.* to step out, to get out of a place. Aus dem Wagen —, to get down or descend, to alight from a coach; er stieg aus, he alighted or got out; aus einem Schiff —, to disembark, to land.

Aussteinen, *v. tr.* 1) to line with stones. 2) to mark by stones. 3) to free from stones. Pflaumen —, to stone prunes.

Ausstellen, *v. tr.* to put in any place; *it.* to offer or present to view. Eine Schildwache —, to set a sentry; die Wache, Wacht —, to set the watch; Gemählde in einer Gallerie —, to expose paintings in a gallery; Waaren zum Verkaufe —, to expose goods to sale; Kunstsachen —, to exhibit specimens of art; zur Schau —, to exhibit, to lay out; eine Leiche —, to lay out a corpse. *Fig.* *a*) [= ausfertigen] Einen Wechsel —, to draw a bill of exchange. *b*) [= preisgeben] Einen der Beschimpfung —, to expose any one to insult. *c*) to censure, to criticise. Er hat an Allem etwas auszustellen, he finds fault with every thing. *d*) to defer, to put off, to postpone. Ein Vorhaben —, to defer the execution of a design.

Aussteller, *m.* [-s, *pl.* -] [*f.* -inn] 1) exposer. 2) *Fig.* [he or she who draws a bill of exchange or an order for the payment of money] drawer.

Ausstellung, *f.* [a setting to public view, a showing or presenting to view] exposition, exhibition. Die — von Gemählden, von Kunstsachen, exposition of paintings, exhibition of specimens of art. *Fig.* *a*) [= Ausfertigung] Die — eines Wechsels, the act of drawing a bill of exchange. *b*) [= Tadel] —en machen, to criticise, to find fault with.

Ausstellungs-saal, *m.* a gallery &c., where paintings &c. are exhibited. —tag, *m.* [in deeds, bills of exchange &c., the time when they are written or drawn] the date.

Ausstemmen, *v. tr.* [among joiners and carpenters] to hollow with a mortise-chisel.

Ausstempeln, *v. tr.* to stamp well.

Aussteppen, *v. tr.* to quilt [a coverlet &c.]

Aussterben, *ir. v. intr.* [u. w. seyn] 1) to become void by the death of its inhabitants. Dieses Haus ist ausgestorben, all the inhabitants of this house are dead; die Stadt ist wie ausgestorben, the town is like a desert. 2) to become extinct, to have no survivor. Die Familie ist ausgestorben, the family has become extinct.

Aussteuer, *f.* 1) portion, dowry, endowment. 2) *Fig.* endowment, gift.

1. **Aussteuern** [from steuern, to portion, to endow], *v. tr.* to furnish with a portion of goods or an estate. Eine Tochter —, to settle a dower on a daughter, to endow her. *Fig.* Der Mensch ist von seinem Schöpfer mit Vernunft ausgesteuert worden, man has been endowed by his maker with reason; von der Natur mit einem besondern Talente ausgesteuert, endowed by nature with a particular talent.

2. **Aussteuern** [from steuern, to steer], *v. intr.* [u. w. seyn] to steer out of a place.

Ausstich, *m.* [-es, *pl.* -e] V. Ausbund, Auswahl.

Aussticheln, I. *v. tr.* to taunt, to sneer or satirize. II. *v. intr.* to cease sneering; *it.* to taunt sufficiently.

Aussticken, I. *v. tr.* to adorn with figures of needle-work or embroidery. II. *v. intr.* to finish embroidering.

Ausstieben, *v. intr.* [u. w. seyn] to fly off like dust.

Ausstiefeln, I. *v. tr.* [unusual term] Einen —, to pull off any one's boots, to take them off, put them off. * and ‡ II. *v. intr.* to walk out.

Ausstieren, *v. intr.* to cease staring.

Ausstillen, I. *v. tr.* V. Aussäugen. II. *v. intr.* to cease nourishing at the breast or nursing, to cease suckling.

Ausstimmen, I. *v. tr.* to tune [a harp] completely. II. *v. intr.* to cease tuning an instrument.

Ausstöbern, *v. tr.* 1) to drive out, to expel like dust, [among sportsmen] to rouse [game] by means of springers or terriers. 2) to search among things covered or sprinkled with dust.

Ausstochern, *v. tr.* to pick [the teeth].

Ausstocken, *v. tr.* to root out by digging, to grub up. Gesträuche —, to cut up shrubs; Bäume —, to stub trees; ein Stück Feld —, to clear a field of the stubs; einen Wald —, to root out a wood, to clear it of stumps.

Ausstoffen, *v. tr.* [unusual word] to make rich or abundant.

Ausstöhnen, *v. intr.* to cease groaning.

Ausstollen, *v. tr.* [among tawers] to stretch [the hides]. Die gar gemachten Felle —, to soften the skins upon the boards.

Ausstopfen, *v. tr.* to stuff [cushions with hair &c.]. Wenn ihr mich nicht mit Stroh ausstopft, unless you stuff me out with straw; ausgestopfte Vögel, stuffed birds.

Ausstören, *v. tr.* to search curiously or impertinently.

Ausstoß, *m.* [-es, *pl.* -stöße] 1) push, thrust, [in fencing, a thrust made by stepping forward and extending the arm] a pass, an allonge [often contracted into lunge]. 2) [in milit. affairs, a charge of coarse powder which is thrown into the bottom of the cartouche to facilitate the explosion of the firework which it contains] chasse.

Ausstoßhobel, *m.* [am. bookbinders] straight-block.

Ausstoßen, *ir.* I. *v. intr.* to make a thrust, to push, to thrust, [in fencing] to make a pass. Auf Einen —, [in fencing] to make a pass at any one. II. *v. tr.* 1) to push, drive or knock out, to get out by thrusting. Ich stieß mir an einem Aste ein Auge aus, I knocked one of my eyes out against a breach; die Marssegel —, [in seamen's lang.] to set the topsails; ein Kalb —, [am. butchers] to strip off the skin of a calf by blows; die Gänge im Garten —, to pare the walks of a garden with a spade; dem Fasse den Boden —, to stave a cask, *fig.* to mar a thing for ever; Einen —, to expel any one from a house, to turn any one out of doors, *fig.* to exclude any one [from a society &c.]. *Fig.* to utter with violence. Gotteslästerungen —, to utter blasphemies; er stieß die niedrigsten Beschuldigungen aus, he sputtered out the basest accusations; Schimpfreden —, to belch out abusive words; Schimpfreden gegen Einen —, to abuse any one; einen entsetzlichen Fluch —, to discharge a terrible oath; er stieß einen derben Fluch aus, he rapped out a great oath; Verwünschungen —, to use imprecations; einen Seufzer —, to heave a sigh; einen Schrei —, to utter a scream. 2) to perfect by pushing or thrusting. Den Teig —, [among bakers] to knead the dough for the last time; das Leder —, [among tanners] to clean the leather [when drawn out of the tan-pit, with the back of the fleshing-knife]; den gewalkten Hut —, [among hatters] to give a fulled hat its form; die Bretter —, [among bookbinders] to straighten the edges of the boards.

Ausstottern, I. *v. intr.* to cease stammering. II. *v. tr.* to utter stammering, to stammer or stutter something out.

Ausstrahlen, I. *v. intr.* to emit rays, to radiate. II. *v. tr.* to emit, to give out [light].

Ausstrecken, I. *v. tr.* to stretch out, to reach forth. Den Arm oder die Hand —, to extend the arm or hand; auf dem Boden ausgestreckt, flat on the ground; das Eisen —, [among smiths] to draw iron by hammering, to draw it out; die Hüte —, [among hatters] to stretch the hats. II. *v. r.* sich —, to stretch, to extend. Sich auf dem Bette —, to stretch one's self out on the bed. *Fig.* to extend in length. Die Ausstreckung, *f.* extension.

Ausstreckmuskel, *m.* [in anatomy] extensor.

Ausstreicheln, I. *v. tr.* to get out by stroking. II. *v. intr.* to cease stroking or caressing.

Ausstreichen, *ir.* I. *v. intr.* 1) [u. w. seyn] to stroll, to ramble, to rove, to roam. 2) [u. w. haben] [in fam. lang.] to make an awkward bow, to scrape. II. *v. tr.* 1) to drive out of a place by striking or flogging. Einen Dieb —, to expel a thief by a public whipping. 2) to make even, to plane, to smooth down. Die falschen Falten oder Striche aus einem Tuche —, to take the creases out of a cloth; die Felle —, [am. tawers] to scrape the hides; [among tanners] to clean the hides with the back of the fleshing knife; die Farbe —, [among printers] to work the ink on the table. 3) to strike off or out. Ein Wort —, to blot out, to erase, to obliterate a word; ganze Zeilen mit der Feder —, to expunge whole lines; einen Namen —, to efface a name; viele Ansätze in einer Rechnung —, to cross or cancel many items in an account. 4) *Fig.* V. Herausstreichen. 5) to paint, to colour on the inside. Ein Zimmer —, to paint a room. 6) to fill up. Die Risse in einer Mauer mit Mörtel —, to fill up the crevices in a wall with mortar.

Ausstreicheisen, *n.* [among cloth-shearers] softening boards.

Ausstreifeln, *v. tr.* to get out by stripping.

Ausstreifen, I. *v. intr.* [u. w. seyn] to rove about, to scour or range about, to straggle. II. *v. tr.* to get out by stripping. Bohnen —, to slip beans out of their skins.

Ausstreiten, *ir.* I. *v. tr.* 1) to contend, contest or dispute to the end, to fight out. 2) Einem etwas —, to argue a person out of a thing. II. *v. intr.* to cease contending or contesting.

Ausstreuen, *v. tr.* [to throw loosely about] to scatter. Den Samen —, to scatter seed, to sow. *Fig.* Den Samen der Zwietracht —, to sow the seeds of discord; falsche Gerüchte —, to circulate or spread false reports.

Ausstrich, *m.* [-s, *pl.* -e] 1) the act of erasing, erasement, erasion. 2) something erased. 3) [in mining] granular-tin, stream-tin.

Ausstricken, I. *v. tr.* to complete or finish knitting a thing. Einen Strumpf —, to finish knitting or to complete a stocking. II. *v. intr.* to cease knitting.

Ausstriegeln, I. *v. tr.* 1) to get out by a currycomb [the dust]. 2) to clean by currying. Ein Pferd —, to curry a horse. † *Fig.* Einen —, to reprimand any one severely. II. *v. intr.* to finish currying.

Ausströmen, I. *v. intr.* 1) [u. w. seyn] to stream forth. 2) [u. w. haben] to cease streaming. II. *v. tr.* to cause to stream forth. *Fig.* to pour forth. London strömt seine Bürger aus, London pours out its citizens.

Ausstückeln, *v. tr.* [in coining] to cut and prepare for the mill.

* Ausstudieren, I. *v. intr.* to finish one's studies at the university. II. *v. tr.* 1) to find out or discover by study, to devise. 2) [= durchstudieren] to study thoroughly.

Ausstufen, *v. tr.* to cut or hew out in steps.

Ausstürmen, *v. intr.* 1) to cease storming or blustering. Es hat ausgestürmt, the storm is over or has subsided. 2) *Fig.* [u. w. seyn] to storm out of a place. 3) [u. w. haben] to storm or rage to the end.

Aussturz, *m.* [-es, *pl.* -stürze] the act of rushing out of a place, rush.

Ausstürzen, I. *v. intr.* [u. w. seyn] to rush out of a place. II. *v. tr.* 1) to throw out, to pour out [water &c.]. Ein Glas Wein —, to swallow down, to throw off a glass of wine. 2) to put out of its proper place by falling. Einen Arm —, sich den Arm —, to dislocate one's arm by falling.

Ausstutzen, *v. tr.* to adorn, to embellish, to dress up.

Ausstützen, *v. tr.* to furnish with props on the inside. Einen Brunnen —, to prop the inside of a well.

Aussuchen, I. *v. tr.* 1) to choose from among a number, to select from many, to pick out. Blumen —, to cull flowers; Reife und Faßdauben für den Markt —, to cull hoops and staves for market; suche den Demüthigsten der verliebten Jugend aus, single the lowliest of the amorous youth; sich ein Ruheplätzchen —, to make choice of a resting place. *Fig.* Ausgesuchte Gesellschaft, choice society; die ausgesuchtesten Speisen, the most exquisite meats; ausgesuchte [more usual: gesuchte or weithergeholte] Ausdrücke, expressions studiously sought, far-fetched; *it.* ausgesuchte [more usual: ausgewählte] Ausdrücke, well chosen or choice expressions. 2) to search thoroughly. Das ganze Haus —, to search the whole house. II. *v. intr.* 1) to search to the end. 2) to cease to search.

|| Aussuckeln, V. Aussaugen.

Aussühnen, V. Aussöhnen.

Aussummen, *v. intr.* 1) [u. w. seyn] to fly humming or buzzing. 2) [u. w. haben] to cease humming or buzzing.

Aussüßen, *v. tr.* [in chimistry, to render substances more mild, by freeing them from acids and salts or other soluble impurities by washing] to edulcorate. Das Aussüßen, edulcoration.

|| Aust, *m.* [-s] 1) V. Ernte. 2) [a genus of insects] the day-fly, ephemera, ephemeron-worm.

Austafeln, *v. intr.* to cease sitting at table, to rise from table.

Austäfeln, *v. tr.* to line with boards within-side. Ein Zimmer —, to wainscot a room.

Austagen, *v. intr.* to cease being light. Es hat ausgetagt, the day is over, the sun is set.

Auständeln, *v. intr.* to cease toying or playing.

Austanzen, I. *v. tr.* to dance to the end. II. *v. intr.* to cease dancing; *it.* to dance sufficiently. Man wird bald ausgetanzt haben, the dancing will soon be over.

* Austapezieren, *v. tr.* to paper [a room].

Austappen, *v. tr.* to search or attempt to find in the dark or as a blind person by feeling, to grope. Wir tappten unsern Weg um Mitternacht aus, we groped our way at midnight.

Austauchen, *v. intr.* 1) [u. w. haben] to finish diving. 2) [= heraus- or auftauchen] [u. w. seyn] to come up after diving.

Austaumeln, *v. intr.* [u. w. seyn] 1) to walk out reeling or staggering. 2) to cease reeling.

Austausch, *m.* [-es, *pl.* -e] [in commerce, the act of giving one thing or commodity for another] exchange, barter. Der — der Waaren, interchange of commodities. *Fig.* Der — der Gedanken, an exchange of thoughts.

Austauschen, *v. tr.* [to give one thing or commodity for another] to exchange, to barter, [in vulgar language] to truck. Ochsen für Korn —, to barter oxen for corn; Pferde —, to exchange horses. *Fig.* Seine Gedanken —, to exchange one's thoughst.

Austeppichen, *v. tr.* to spread or cover with carpets on the inside. Ein Zimmer —, to carpet a room.

Auster, *f.* [*pl.* -n] [Sw. *ostra*, Dan. Oester, Lat. *Ostrea*] an oyster. Marinirte —n, pickled oysters; gebackene —, oyster-pie; —n fangen, to catch oysters, to dredge oysters.

Austerbank, *f.* oysterbed. —dieb, *m.* V. —vogel. —fang, *m.* 1) the act of dredging oysters. 2) the season for taking oysters. 3) the place where they are taken. —fänger, *m.*, —fischer, *m.* oyster-catcher, dredger. —fischerei, V. —fang. —gabel, *f.* oyster-fork. —grund, *m.* V. —bank. —handel, *m.* oyster-trade. —händler, *m.* oyster-man. —händlerin, *f.* oyster-wife, oyster-woman, oyster-wench. —lager, *n.* V. —bank. —laich, *m.* [the spawn of oysters] spat. —mann, *m.* 1) V. —händler. 2) V. —vogel. —messer, *n.* oyster-knife. —nessel, *f.* the wrinkled actinia. —netz, *n.* oyster-dragnet or dredge. —reich, *adj.* and *adv.* abounding in [with] oysters. —schale, *f.* oystershell. —stein, *m.* [an oyster-shell in its fossil state] ostracite. —vogel, *m.* oystercatcher. —weib, *n.* V. —händlerin.

* Austerität, *f.* [*pl.* -en] austerity, severity of manners or life, rigor.

Austhauen, *v. intr.* to cease thawing.

Austheeren, *v. tr.* to tar or pitch on the inside [a cask &c].

Austheilen, *v. tr.* to give or bestow in parts or portions, to deal out, to distribute. Moses theilte Ländereien unter die Stämme Israels aus, Moses distributed lands to the tribes of Israel; Christus theilte die Brode unter seine Jünger aus, Christ distributed the loaves to his disciples; den Soldaten Lebensmittel —, to serve out provisions to the soldiers; Arzneien unter die Armen —, to dispense medicines to the poor; Almosen —, to give alms; das Abendmahl —, to administer the sacrament; Befehle —, to give out, to issue orders; Schläge —, to deal out blows; Gott theilt seine Gnaden nach seinem Wohlgefallen aus, God dispenses his favours according to his good pleasure. Syn. Austheilen, Vertheilen. A thing is vertheilt, when the whole is not given to one, when it is divided among a number, and das Vertheilen has already commenced as soon as an entire thing is separated into two or more parts. Austheilen signifies also to divide or distribute among a number, but das Austheilen does not begin till the share which each is to receive is given over to him. Vertheilen refers to an entire thing which must first be separated, also to a number amongst whom a thing is to be divided; Austheilen denotes a dealing out or distributing of several things, also if they have not originally formed parts of a whole. Thus one does not say: Der Prediger hat das Abendmahl vertheilt, but ausgetheilt.

Austheilung, *f.* distribution. Die — des Abendmahles, administration of the sacrament.

Austheeren, V. Austheeren.

Austhun, I. *v. tr.* 1) to put off. Die Kleider —, to put off one's clothes. 2) to put out [a candle &c.]. Feuer —, to extinguish fire; ein Wort —, to blot out, to erase a word; eine Rechnung —, to cross an account. 3) to put out, to let to hire. Geld auf Zinsen —, to put out money to use, to lend money upon interest; einen Acker —, to let or farm out a field. II. *v. r.* sich —, to undress one's self.

Austiefen, *v. tr.* to deepen, [among coppersmiths] to beat out.

Austilgen, *v. tr.* to destroy utterly, to root out, to extirpate. Unkraut —, to exterminate weeds. *Fig.* Das Laster —, to exterminate vice; durch Reue —, to wash off by repentance.

Austilgung, *f.* extermination, extirpation.

Austippen, *v. tr.* to get out by tipping.

Austoben, I. *v. intr.* to finish roaring, blustering, raging. Der Sturm hat ausgetobt, the storm is over. *Fig.* Sein Schmerz fängt an auszutoben, his pain begins to abate or lessen; sein Zorn hat ausgetobt, his rage is spent, his passion is over. II. *v. tr.* to utter boisterously. Seinen Groll —, to give vent to one's anger.

Austollen, *v. intr.* to cease being noisy, wild, riotous.

Austönen, *v. intr.* 1) to sound to the end. 2) to cease to sound. Die Glocke hat ausgetönt, the bell has done ringing or sounds no more.

Austonnen, *v. tr.* [in mining] Einen Schacht —, to line with boards the shaft of a mine or pit.

†Austorkeln, *v. intr.* 1) [u. w. seyn] to walk out staggering. 2) [u. w. haben] to cease staggering.

Austosen, *v. intr.* V. Austoben.

Austraben, *v. intr.* 1) [u. w. seyn] *a*) to trot out of a place. *b*) to trot as fast as possible. Ein Pferd — lassen, to bring a horse to trot very fast, to put him out to a full trot. 2) [u. w. haben] to leave off trotting.

Austrag, *m.* [-es] 1) decision of a doubtful case, decision of a court. Bis zum — or nach — der Sache, till the matter is decided; vor — der Sache, whilst the cause is pending. 2) [= Ausgang] the end, the issue. 3) [in law] arbitration. Gütlicher —, an amicable accommodation.

Austrags-gericht, Austrägalgericht, a [illegible] court of justice chosen by two or more members of the German confederation for the decision of disputed matters between them. —gerichtlich, *adj.* Das —gerichtliche Urtheil, [illegible] pronounced by such a court; das —gerichtliche Verfahren ist auf diesen Fall nicht anwendbar, this case cannot be decided by such a court.

Austragen, *ir.* I. *v. tr.* 1) to carry out. Briefe —, [von der Post] to deliver letters from the post; Einer, der die Briefe von der Post austrägt, a letter-carrier, postman. *Fig.* Er trägt Geheimnisse und Lappereien aus, he blabs secrets and trifles [he publishes them without discretion]; Mährchen in der Stadt —, to retail gossip about the town; Einen —, to tell tales of any one, to defame any one. **Prov.* Das Bad — müssen, to suffer or pay for the faults of others. 2) to bear to the full time. Ein nicht ausgetragenes Kind, a child born before its time; eine Frau, die ihr Kind die volle Zeit ausgetragen hat, a woman near her time or near her reckoning. 3) [in law] Eine Streitsache durch Schiedsrichter —, to let a disputed matter be decided by arbiters. II. *v. imp* to amount to. Es trägt nur fünfzig Thaler aus, it amounts only to fifty dollars; es trägt sehr wenig aus, it amounts to or yields very little. V. Eintragen.

Austragestempel, *m.* [in metallurgy] the third iron pestle of a stamping-mill.

Austräger, *m.* [-s, *pl.*-] 1) a person that carries out. Der — der Briefe, the letter-carrier, postman; der —, [among tradesmen] light-porter. *Fig.* a tell-tale, a blabber, a blab, a tattler. 2) V. Austragestempel.

Austrägerei, *f.* 1) blabbing, tattling. 2) the thing blabbed, a tale, a report.

Austräglich, V. Einträglich.

*Australien, *n.* [a name given to the countries situated to the South of Asia] Australasia.

Austrällern, *v. intr.* to finish humming or whistling a tune.

Austrampeln, I. *v. tr.* to get out by trampling. II. *v. intr.* to leave off trampling.

Austrauern, *v. intr.* to mourn to the end, to cease wearing, mourning.

Austräufeln, I. *v. intr.* 1) [u. w. seyn] to distil, to drop from in small drops. 2) [u. w. haben] to cease dropping or distilling. II. *v. tr.* to drop or distil from.

Austraufen, I. *v. intr.* 1) [u. w. seyn] to fall in drops, to drop, to distil from. 2) [u. w. haben] to cease dropping. II. *v. tr.* to let fall in drops, to drop from.

Austräumen, I. *v. tr.* to dream to the end. Einen Traum —, to dream out a dream. II. *v. intr.* to dream to the end, to finish dreaming.

Austreiben, *ir.* I. *v. tr.* 1) to drive out. Das Vieh —, to drive out the cattle; wilde Thiere aus einem Walde —, to expel wild beasts from a forest; die Angst treibt ihm den Schweiß aus, he sweats for fear; austreibend, [in medicine] expulsive; Schweiß austreibende Mittel, [in medicine] sudorifics. 2) V. Forttreiben. *Fig.* Den Teufel —, to exorcise a demon [to cast him out or drive him from a person, by prayers or other ceremonies]. II. *v. intr.* 1) to cease driving. 2) [in metallurgy] to let go out the furnace.

Austreibung, *f.* expulsion.

Austrennen, *v. tr.* to rip and take out, to unsew [a sleeve, the lining &c.]

Austreten, *ir.* I. *v. tr.* 1) [to press under the foot] to tread. Weintrauben —, to tread grapes. 2) to widen [one's shoes] by treading or walking. *Fig.* Die Kinderschuhe ausgetreten haben, to be past the spoon. 3) to put out by treading. Eine glühende Kohle —, to tread out a living coal. 4) to wear out by treading. Die Stufen der Treppe sind ganz ausgetreten, the steps of the stair are completely worn out. 5) to sprain, to dislocate [one's foot] by treading. II. *v. intr.* [u. w. seyn] 1) [= antreten] to put out the foot to walk or to march. Alle treten zugleich aus, all step off together. 2) to come forth, to step out. Die, welche aufgerufen werden, müssen —, they who are called, must step out. 3) to leave, to withdraw from. Aus einer Gesellschaft —, to withdraw from a company; von der anglicanischen Kirche —, to secede from the English church. 4) to abscond, to absent one's self in a private manner. Ein austretender Schuldner, an absconding debtor; der Soldat ist ausgetreten, the soldier deserted. 5) to run over the brinks or banks. Der Fluß ist ausgetreten, the river broke out; wenn der Schnee schmilzt, treten die Flüsse aus, when the snow melts, the rivers overflow; ausgetretenes Blut, [in medicine] extravasated blood.

‖ Austreugen, V. Austrocknen.

Austrieb, *m.* [-es, *pl.*-e] V. Trieb.

Austriefen, V. Austraufen.

Austrillern, *v. intr.* to trill to the end, to leave off trilling. Die Lerchen haben ausgetrillert, the larks have ceased to sing.

Austrinken, *ir.* I. *v. tr.* to drink up. Ein Glas Wein —, to drink up a glass of wine; mit einem Schluck —, to drink the whole at a draught, to drink it off at one gulp or swallow. *Fig.* Den Becher des Leidens —, to submit to sufferings and afflictions, to swallow the cup of affliction. II. *v. intr.* to leave off drinking.

Austritt, *m.* [-s] 1) the act of stepping out, leaving or withdrawing &c., [in astronomy] egress. Beim — aus dem Hause, in stepping out of the house; der — der Trabanten des Jupiters, [in astronomy] the emersion of the satellites of Jupiter; der — des Mondes aus dem Schatten der Erde, [in astronomy] the emersion of the moon from the shadow of the earth; der — eines Schuldners, the absconding of a debtor; der — eines Soldaten, desertion of a soldier; der — aus diesem Leben, removal from the present life, departure, decease, death. 2) stepping-place, step. 3) [a frame of wood, iron or stone, in front of a house or other building, encompassed with a balustrade] balcony.

Austrittsbogen, *m.* [in astron.] arc of vision.

Austrocknen, I. *v. intr.* [u. w. seyn] to dry, to dry up. Der Strom trocknet aus, the stream dries or dries up; ausgetrocknetes Holz, dry wood; *fig.* zur Mumie —, to dry like a mummy. II. *v. tr.* to dry up, to dry, to exsiccate wholly, to desiccate. Der Wind trocknet die Erde aus, the wind dries the earth; einen Morast oder Sumpf —, to drain a swamp or marsh; Holz —, to season timber; die Augen —, to dry the eyes; austrocknend, desiccative, exsiccant; —de Mittel, [in surgery] desiccatives, desiccants; ein —des Pflaster, desiccativum.

Austrocknung, *f.* desiccation, exsiccation. Die — eines Geschwürs, desiccation of a sore.

Auströdeln, *v. tr.* to sell as frippery [old clothes &c.].

Austrommeln, I. *v. tr.* 1) to publish by sound of drum. 2) Einen —, to explode any one, to expel by beat of drum, to drum out; die Bienen —, to drum the bees from the hive. II. *v. intr.* 1) to finish drumming. 2) to leave off drumming.

Austrompeten, *v. tr.* to publish by sound of trumpet, to trumpet. **Fig.* Jemands Lob —, to trumpet any one's praise.

Auströpfeln, I. *v. intr.* 1) [u. w. seyn] to trickle out. 2) [u. w. haben] to cease trickling. II. *v. tr.* to drop, to distil.

Austropfen, *v. intr.* to drop or distil from.

Auströpfen, Auströpfeln, *v. tr.* V. Austraufen.

Aústrotten, *v. intr.* V. Austraben.

Aústrotzen, *v. intr.* to cease braving or bidding defiance.

Aústrumpfen, I. *v. tr.* [in archit.] to cut out [joists &c.]. II. *v. intr.* [at cards] to play a trump card, to trump.

Aústünchen, V. Ausweißen.

Aústunken, *v. tr.* 1) to empty [a glass, cup &c.] by soaking bread in it. 2) to soak up [wine &c.] by dipping bread in it.

Aústupfen, V. Austippen.

Aústuschen, *v. tr.* to wash with Indian ink. Eine Zeichnung —, to wash a drawing with Indian ink.

Aúsüben, *v. tr.* 1) to exercise, to practise. Die Heilkunst oder Rechtswissenschaft —, to practise physic or law; ein —der Arzt, a medical practitioner; Macht oder Gewalt —, to exercise authority or power. 2) (= verüben) to do, to practise. Schlechtigkeiten —, to practise wicked works; Verbrechen —, to commit, to perpetrate crimes; Betrügereien —, to commit frauds; Rache an einem —, to take revenge on any one. 3) V. Ausbilden.

Aúsüber, *m.* [-s, *pl.* -] one who exercises or practises, practitioner.

Aúsüblich, I. *adj.* 1) practicable. 2) [not merely speculative] practical. II. *adv.* 1) practicably. 2) practically.

Aúsübung, *f.* 1) [actual performance distinguished from theory] practice. In — bringen, to put in practice. 2) use, exercise, practice. Die — einer Kunst, eines Gewerbes, the exercise of an art or trade.

Aúsverkaufen, *v. intr.* to sell off.

|| **Aúsverschämt**, *adj.* [a colloquial term] shameless. V. Unverschämt, Schamlos.

Aúswachsen, *ir. v. intr.* 1) [u. w. seyn] *a*) to grow out, to shoot out, to sprout. Das Getreide wächst aus, corn begins to bud on the haulm or in the ear. *b*) to attain full growth. Ein ausgewachsener Baum, a full-grown tree. *c*) to grow irregularly [also said of men]. Ausgewachsen [commonly verwachsen] seyn, to have a crooked back, to be crook-backed, hump-backed, to be a cripple. 2) [u. w. haben] to cease growing.

Aúswackeln, I. *v. tr.* to get out or take out by shaking. II. *v. intr.* [u. w. seyn] to walk out waggling.

Aúswagen, *v. r.* sich —, to venture out. Der Kranke darf sich noch nicht —, the patient may not yet trust himself out of the house.

Aúswägen, *ir.* [more properly *reg.*] *v. tr.* 1) to try by the balance, to choose by weight [ducats &c.]. 2) to retail by weight, to weigh out [butter, cheese &c.]

Aúswahl, *f.* [*pl.* -en] 1) [the act of choosing] choice. Eine — treffen, to make a choice; mit — gesammelte Dinge, things choicely collected; — zum Kriegsdienste, conscription, balloting for military service. 2) [the thing chosen, that which is selected in preference to others] choice, selection. Sie hat eine große — von Spitzen in ihrem Laden, she has a great choice of lace in her shop; eine schöne — von Sprüchwörtern, a choice collection of proverbs.

Aúswählen, I. *v. tr.* to choose, to select, to cull, to pick out. Das Beste —, to make a choice of the best; der Auswählende, selector. II. *v. intr.* to have done choosing, making a choice.

Aúswalken, I. *v. tr.* 1) to take out by fulling [stains, &c.]. 2) to full sufficiently. *Fig.* Einen —, to drub any one soundly. II. *v. intr.* to cease fulling.

Aúswallen, *v. intr.* 1) [u. w. seyn] to wander out from a place and go on a pilgrimage. 2) [u. w. haben] to cease to wander.

Aúswalten, *v. intr.* to cease bearing sway, ruling, domineering.

Aúswalzen, I. *v. tr.* 1) to remove by rolling, to roll out. 2) to waltz to the end. II. *v. intr.* to cease waltzing.

Aúswälzen, *v. tr.* to roll out of a place.

|| and † **Aúswamsen**, *v. tr.* to drub, to thrash, to cudgel.

Aúswandeln, *v. intr.* 1) [u. w. seyn] to go out, to walk out. 2) [u. w. haben] to cease walking or wandering.

Aúswanderer, *m.* [-s, *pl.* -] —inn, *f.* an emigrant.

Aúswandern, *v. intr.* 1) [u. w. seyn] to leave a place, to remove from one place to another for the purpose of residence, to emigrate. Sehr viele Deutsche und Schweizer wandern nach Amerika aus, Germans and Swiss emigrate in great numbers to America. 2) [u. w. haben] to leave off travelling.

Aúswanderung, *f.* emigration.

Auswanderungs-geist, *m.* the spirit of emigration. —recht, *n.* the right of emigration. —sucht, *f.* mania of emigration.

Aúswanken, *v. intr.* [u. w. seyn] to walk out staggering.

Aúswannen, *v. tr.* to cleanse by winnowing. Getreide —, to winnow corn.

Aúswärmen, *v. tr.* 1) to warm thoroughly. Sich —, to warm one's self thoroughly. 2) [in metallurgy] to anneal.

Aúswärmer, [-s, *pl.* -] [in metallurgy] he that anneals.

Aúswärmofen, *m.* [-s, *pl.* -] [in metallurgy] nealing-furnace.

Aúswarten, I. *v. tr.* to stay or wait to the end. II. *v. intr.* to cease waiting.

Aúswärtig, *adj.* and *adv.* belonging to a distant place, belonging to another nation or country, relating to or connected with foreign nations. Ein —er Krieg, an external or foreign war; die —en Verhältnisse eines Staates oder Königreiches, the external relations of a state or kingdom; der auswärtige Handel, external trade or commerce; —e Angelegenheiten, foreign affairs; das Büreau der —en Angelegenheiten, the foreign office.

Aúswärts, *adv.* 1) [tending or directed towards the exterior] outward, outwards. — beugen, to bend outwards; — gebogene Schenkel habend, chicken-hammed; die Füße einwärts oder — setzen, to turn one's toes in or out. 2) [beyond the bounds of a country] abroad.

Aúswaschen, *ir.* I. *v. tr.* 1) to remove by washing. Einen Flecken, den Schmutz &c. —, to wash out a stain, dirt &c; das Auswaschen, [in chimistry] ablution. 2) to cleanse by washing, to wash out. Schmutzige Wäsche —, to wash foul linen; ein Gefäß —, to rinse a vessel; eine Wunde —, to bathe a wound. 3) to hollow or wear out by water. Das Wasser wäscht den Damm aus, the water wears away the bank. † 4) *Fig.* to blab, to spread by report, to blow. II. *v. intr.* to cease washing.

Aúswässern, *v. tr.* [to free from salt by soaking in water] to water [herrings &c.].

Aúswässerungslinie, *f.* [*pl.* -n] the water-line or loadwaterline.

Aúsweben, I. *v. tr.* to weave completely. II. *v. intr.* to cease weaving.

Aúswechsel, *m.* [-s] 1) [the act of giving one thing for another] exchange. 2) [the thing given in return for something received, or the thing received in return for what is given] exchange.

Aúswechseln, *v. tr.* to exchange [prisoners &c.]. Banknoten gegen Silber —, to change banknotes for silver; ein Kind —, to change a child, to substitute one child for another.

Aúswechslung, *f.* V. Auswechsel 1).

Auswechslungs-vertrag, *m.* [a writing or agreement between states at war, for the exchange of prisoners] cartel.

Aúsweg, *m.* [-es, *pl.* -e] way-out, opening, issue, outlet, vent. *Fig.* expedient, shift, means devised or employed in an exigency. Einen — suchen, finden, to find out an expedient; dies war der einzige —, this was the only means.

Aúswehen, I. *v. tr.* 1) to get out, to make visible by blowing away the sand or dry earth. 2) to extinguish by a current of air. Das Licht —, to blow out the candle. 3) to blow thoroughly. II. *v. intr.* to cease blowing.

1. **Aúsweichen**, [from weichen] I. *v. tr.* 1) to get out by soaking and softening. 2) to soak through and soften thoroughly. II. *v. intr.* to come out after being soaked and softened.

2. **Aúsweichen**, [from weichen] *ir. v. intr.* [u. w. seyn] to yield, to give way, to give place, to withdraw, to make room for. Einem or der Einem —, to give way to any one, to avoid any one; dem Postwagen müssen alle andere Fuhrwerke —, all other carriages must give way to the mail-coach; er weicht Spielern aus, he avoids gamesters; einem Streiche —, to shun a blow; er wich dem Streiche aus, der seinem Kopfe galt, he evaded the blow aimed at his head; einem Schlage —, to parry a blow, to elude a blow; die Erde weicht unter den Füßen aus, the earth gives under the feet. *Fig.* Jemands Fragen —, to elude any one's questions; dem Gesetze —, to evade or elude the law; eine ausweichende Antwort, an evasive answer; dem Unglücke —, to shun misfortunes; —, [in music] to make a transition from one key to another.

Aúsweichung, *f.* the act of yielding, giving way or making room for; [in music] transition from one key to another; [in astronomy, the recess of a planet from the sun, as it appears to the eye of a spectator on the earth] elongation. *Fig.* eluding, avoiding or shunning, avoidance.

1. **Aúsweiden**, [from Eingeweide = bowels] *v. tr.* [chiefly among sportsmen] to eviscerate, to embowel or disembowel, to gut. Einen Hasen —, to hulk a hare; Schnepfen —, to draw woodcocks.

2. **Aúsweiden**, [from Weide or Waide = pasture] I. *v. tr.* to graze, to feed [a meadow &c.]. II. *v. intr.* to finish grazing, to graze sufficiently.

Aúsweifen, *v. intr.* to cease reeling.

Aúsweinen, I. *v. tr.* 1) to shed tears. 2) to get or bring out by weeping. Sich die Augen —, to cry one's eyes out; seinen Kummer —, to relieve or alleviate one's grief with weeping. II. *v. r.* sich —, to weep one's fill. III. *v. intr.* 1) to weep or cry to the end. 2) to cease weeping.

Aúsweis, *m.* [-weises, *pl.* -weise] statement, proof, evidence. Nach — der Gesetze, [law term] conformable to the law, according to the tenor of the laws.

Aúsweisen, *ir.* I. *v. tr.* 1) to turn out of a place. Einen aus dem Hause —, to turn any one out of doors; Einen [aus dem Lande] —, to expel, banish or exile any one. 2) *Fig.* to make known, to show or prove, to teach, to decide. Die Zeit wird es —, time will show it; die That weiset es aus, the very deed speaks it, proves it; wie es die Gesetze —, according to the purport or tenor of the laws. II. *v. r.* sich —. 1) to become evident. Es wird sich bald —, the end will soon show or discover it. 2) Sich über einen Auftrag —, to prove the legitimacy of one's commission or authority; sich über seinen Aufenthalt —, to give satisfactory proof or information concerning one's domicile.

Auśweissagen, *v. intr.* to cease prophesying.

Auśweißen, **Auśweißeln**, *v. tr.* to whitewash [a room &c.].

Auśweisung, [Ausweis] *f.* 1) the act of turning out of a place, of banishing. 2) proof, evidence. Nach — der Gesetze, in conformity to the laws, according to the tenor of the laws.

Auśweiten, *v. tr.* to make wider, to widen. Schuhe —, to stretch shoes.

Ausweiteholz, *n.* stretching-stick of the glover.

Auśwendig, *adj.* and *adv.* [being on the outside] outer. Die —e Seite, the external part of a thing, the outside; — schön, fair on the outside. *Fig.* Etwas — wissen, to know something by heart; — lernen, to get or learn by heart, to commit to memory, to con [a lesson &c.]; mechanisch — lernen, to learn by rote.

Auśwerfen, *ir.* I. *v. intr.* 1) to throw outward. Das Pferd wirft gut aus, the horse throws his legs well out, steps out well; der Uhrschwengel wirft gut aus, [in horology] the pendulum oscillates well. 2) [at dice] to throw first. Wer wirft aus? who is to lead? II. *v. tr.* 1) to force out by throwing or casting. Einem ein Auge mit einem Steine —, to put or knock out any one's eye by throwing a stone at him, to fling out any one's eye with a stone. 2) to throw and let fall, to throw out. Den Anker —, [in seamen's lang.] to throw over board, to cast anchor, to let go the anchor; das Netz —, to throw the net; das Loth —, [in seamen's lang.] to heave the lead; ein Boot —, [in seamen's lang.] to hoist out a boat; Geld —, to scatter money; Geld unter das Volk —, to throw out money among the people; Schleim —, to expectorate phlegm; Blut —, to spit blood; der Berg wirft Feuer und Asche aus, the mountain belches flames and ashes; ausgeworfene Funken schwimmen auf den Wogen, ejected sparks upon the billows float; das schlechte Geld —, [in counting] to cast out or eject bad money. *Fig.* Einen aus einer Gesellschaft [more usual ausstoßen] —, to exclude, to expel any one from a society; Zahlen, eine Summe —, to set or write out or down numbers, a sum; in Rechnung —, to put or place to account; Einem eine Besoldung —, to appoint any one a salary; Einem einen Jahrgehalt —, to settle an annuity or pension upon any one, to settle so much a year on him. 3) [= entleeren] Einen Graben —, to free a ditch from earth and rubbish, to cleanse it; einen Hasen —, [among sportsmen] to hulk a hare. 4) to castrate, to emasculate. Ein Pferd —, to geld a horse.

Auśwettern, *v. intr.* to cease thundering. *Fig.* to cease blustering, abusing, swearing.

Auśwetzen, *v. tr.* 1) to take out by whetting or grinding. Eine Scharte —, to take out a notch by grinding. **Fig.* to make amends for a fault, an error, to make up, to repair a loss. Einen Schimpf —, to revenge an affront; Sie können diese Scharte nie —, you can never wipe it off. 2) to excavate or wear out by whetting or grinding. 3) to sharpen by whetting.

Auświchsen, *v. tr.* to wax on the inside. †*Fig.* Einen —, to thrash any one.

Auświckeln, *v. tr.* to open what was wrapped or folded, to unwrap. Ein Kind —, to unswathe a child; Garn —, to untangle thread; Papier —, to unroll paper. *Fig.* Sich —, to disentangle or extricate one's self from any thing.

Auświegen, V. Auswägen.

Auświmmern, I. *v. intr.* to cease whimpering. II. *v. tr.* to yield whimpering. Sein Leben —, to yield or give up the ghost whimpering.

Auświndeln, *v. tr.* 1) to unswathe [a child &c.]. 2) [in archit.] V. Ausstaken.

Auświnden, *ir. v. tr.* 1) to get out by turning or winding. Einen in Koth versunkenen Wagen —, to take a carriage out of the mire by means of a windlass; Einem das Schwert oder den Stock —, to wrest or wrench a sword or a cane out of any one's hands. Das Auswinden des Degens, [in fencing] locking. 2) to free from water by wringing. Wäsche —, to wring linen. *Fig.* V. Herauswinden.

Auświnseln, V. Auswimmern.

Auświntern, I. *v. tr.* to winter [plants &c.]. Vieh —, to winter cattle. II. *v. intr* 1) [u. w. seyn] to perish during the winter. Die Saat ist ausgewintert, the seed is destroyed by the severity of the winter. 2) [u. w. haben] Es hat ausgewintert, the winter is over.

Auświpfeln, *v. tr.* to cut off the top. Bäume —, to lop trees.

Auświppen, *v. tr.* to pick out, to select by means of a balance.

Auświrken, I. *v. tr.* 1) to take out by working. Ein Pferd —, to pare a horse's foot; einen Hirsch oder eine Sau —, [among sportsmen] to flay a stag or a wild boar and cut it up; das Salz —, [in saltworks] to take the salt out of the saltpans and put it into baskets. 2) *Fig.* to effect, to bring to pass, to obtain by one's endeavours. Einen Befehl —, to obtain an order; ein Urtheil —, to obtain a sentence; sich Verzeihung —, to procure one's pardon; für Einen Verzeihung —, to get any one's pardon; man hat Gnade bei dem Könige für ihn ausgewirkt, pardon has been obtained for him from the king. 3) to work sufficiently. Den Teig —, [among bakers] to work the dough again. II. *v. intr.* to work or act to the end, to cease working, operating. *Fig.* Die Arznei hat ausgewirkt, the medicine works no longer, has ceased to have any effect.

Auświrkung, *f.* 1) the act of taking out by working, of obtaining &c. 2) improvement by successive operations.

Auświrren, *v. tr.* to unravel, to untwist, to loose, separate or disconnect things which are interwoven or united without order. Einen Strang Zwirn —, to disentangle or untangle a skein of yarn; Netzwerk —, to disentangle network.

Auświschen, *v. tr.* 1) to make clean by wiping, to wipe out. Den Staub —, to sweep away the dust, to dust; eine Kanone —, to sponge a cannon; sich die Augen —, to wipe one's eyes. †*Fig.* Einem die Augen —, to cheat any one; Einen —, to reprimand any one severely. 2) to blot out, to erase so as to destroy or render illegible. Einen Namen, eine Zahl —, to efface a name, a number. *Fig.* 3) Einem etwas or eins —, to hit any one a blow, to slap any one's face, to box any one's ears.

†**Auświscher**, *m.* [-s, *pl.* -] reprimand.

Auświspern, *v. intr.* 1) to whisper to the end. 2) to cease whispering.

Auświttern, I. *v. intr.* 1) [u. w. seyn] *a)* to be acted upon by the weather, to be decomposed by exposure to the atmosphere. *b)* to be exposed to the weather. 2) [u. w. haben] to cease thundering and lightening. II. *v. tr.* 1) to act upon by the air, to decompose. 2) to find out by the nose, to smell out, to scent out [game &c.]. *Fig.* Etwas —, to discover something. III. *v. r.* sich —, 1) to be purified by thundering and lightening [said of the air]. 2) to swarm round the hive in a clear day [said of bees].

Auświtterung, *f.* 1) the acting upon by air or the state of being acted upon by the air or weather, of being decomposed by exposure to the air. *Fig.* the act of smelling out or discovering. 2) [in mining] vapours promoting decomposition.

Auświtzeln, *v. intr.* to cease being witty.

Auświlben, *v. tr.* to arch, to vault within-side. Einen Keller —, to vault a cellar.

Auświlbung, *f.* 1) the act of vaulting &c. 2) a vault, an arch-roof.

Auświlken, I. *v. tr.* to overspread with clouds. Der ausgewölkte Abend, the clouded evening. II. *v. intr.* to become free from clouds. Der Himmel wölkt sich aus, the sky clears up.

Auświllen, *v. intr.* to wish to go out.

1. **Auśwuchern** [from wuchern, to grow luxuriantly], *v. intr.* to spread out luxuriantly [of weeds, plants &c.].

2. **Auśwuchern** [from Wucher, usury] *v. intr.* to leave off usury.

Auśwuchs, *m.* [-wuchses, *pl.* -wüchse] 1) a preternatural germination or budding of a plant [das Auswachsen]. 2) any preternatural enlargement of a plant, or something growing out of a plant, excrescence; [in surgery] a preternatural protuberance growing on any part of the body, excrescence, a humpback, crookback. — der Knochen, exostosis. *Fig.* Auswüchse der Einbildungskraft, excrescences of imagination, extravagancies of a diseased imagination.

Auśwühlen, *v. tr.* to excavate, to form an opening in the earth by digging, to dig with a snout or by other means, to root as swine or moles.

Auśwundern, *v. r.* sich —, to cease wondering.

Auśwünschen, I. *v. intr.* to wish to the end, to cease wishing. II. *v. r.* sich —, to exhaust one's self by wishing.

Auśwurf, *m.* [-es, *pl.* -würfe] 1) the act of throwing outward. *Fig.* Der — des Uhrschwengels, oscillation of the pendulum; der — des Speichels, spitting, expectoration; der — des Blutes, spitting blood; der zertheilende —, [in medic.] diaphoresis; die Auswürfe des Vesuvs, the eruptions of Vesuvius. 2) [in some plays] the first throw or cast. 3) that which is thrown out, matter emitted. Ein dünner wässeriger —, a thin serous discharge; ein eiteriger —, a purulent discharge; der — durch den Unterleib, excrements; die Auswürfe durch den Unterleib betreffend, excrementitious. *Fig.* *a)* any thing vile and worthless, rubbish, trash, scum. Ein — der Menschheit, the refuse of mankind; sie ist der — ihres ganzen Geschlechtes, she is the refuse of all her sex. *b)* [among printers] waste paper, waste sheet.

Auswurfsblatt, *n.* —**bogen**, *m.* [among printers] waste sheet. —**sröhre**, *f.* V. Samenröhre.

Auśwürfeln, I. *v. tr.* to play for a thing with dice, to raffle for. II. *v. intr.* to cease playing at dice.

Auśwürfling, *m.* [-s, *pl.* -e] 1) refuse, trash, rubbish, scum. 2) out-cast.

Auśwürgen, *v. intr.* to cease killing or slaughtering.

Aúswurzeln, I. *v. tr.* to pull up by the roots, to eradicate [weeds &c.]. Er wurzelte die Dornen aus, he rooted out the thorns. *Fig.* extirpate. II. *v. intr.* [u. w. ſeyn] to shoot out into roots, to sprout.

Aúswurzler, *m.* [-s, *pl.* -] he that eradicates &c. *Fig.* [modern word] a Radical.

Aúswüthen, *v. intr.* to rage to the end, to cease raging. Man muß ihn — laſſen, one must let him spend his fury; der Sturm hat ausgewüthet, the storm has ceased.

Aúszacken, *v. tr.* to cut into points, to notch, to jagg, to scallop [a garment &c.]. Den Rand des Papiers —, to indent the edge of paper; [in botany] ein ausgezacktes Blatt, a crenated leaf.

Aúszackern, *v. tr.* to cut into small notches, to notch.

Aúszagen, *v. intr.* to cease being afraid.

Aúszahlen, *v. tr.* to pay, to pay down. Eine Summe Geldes —, to pay away money.

Aúszählen, I. *v. tr.* 1) to sell by the number, by retail. 2) to tell, to number, to count out. II. *v. intr.* to tell or count to the end, to cease telling or counting.

Aúszahler, *m.* [-s, *pl.* -] 1) he that pays down. 2) paymaster, cashier. V. [the more usual word] Zahlmeiſter.

Aúszähneln, *v. tr.* to cut into small notches or teeth, to indent.

Aúszahnen, I. *v. intr.* to cease putting forth teeth, to have done teething. Dieſes Kind hat ausgezahnt, this child has got all its teeth. II. *v. tr.* to furnish with teeth [a comb &c.].

Aúszanken, I. *v. tr.* to scold, to chide vehemently, to rate. II. *v. intr.* to cease rating or scolding.

Aúszapfen, *v. tr.* 1) to take from a cask or vat, to draw, to tap [wine &c.]. 2) to retail [liquids].

Aúszappeln, *v. intr.* to cease sprawling.

Aúszaubern, I. *v. tr.* to draw from, to extort by enchantment. II. *v. intr.* to cease enchanting.

Aúszaudern, *v. intr.* to cease hesitating.

Aúszäumen, *v. tr.* V. Abzäumen.

Aúszäunen, *v. tr.* 1) to furnish with a hedge on the inside. Einen Garten —, to hedge a garden. 2) to fence in.

Aúszauſen, I. *v. tr.* 1) to pull out. Einem die Haare —, to tear any one's hair out. 2) to pull or haul about. II. *v. intr.* to cease pulling and hauling about, to cease tousing.

Aúszechen, I. *v. tr.* to drink off or up. Eine Flaſche Wein —, to drink off a bottle of wine. II. *v. intr.* 1) to carouse one's fill. 2) to cease carousing.

Aúszehenten, **Aúszehnten**, *v. tr.* to tithe, to decimate.

Aúszehenter, **Aúszehnter**, *m.* [-s, *pl.* -] tither.

Aúszehren, *ir.* I. *v. tr.* 1) *Fig.* Einen —, to squander, to consume any one's fortune, to impoverish any one. 2) to waste slowly, to consume. Eine —de Krankheit, a wasting disease, a consumption. II. *v. intr.* [u. w. ſeyn] to waste away slowly, to consume. Er zehrt aus, he is in a consumption or decline; eine —de Perſon, a tabid or consumptive person.

Aúszehrung, *f.* 1) a wasting of flesh, a gradual decay or diminution of the body. 2) [a disease] consumption, pulmonic consumption, decline. Die — haben, to be in a consumption or decline.

Aúszeichnen, I. *v. tr.* 1) to select and mark out. Die Prima im Manuſcripte —, [in printing] to mark out the prima; eine Schmarre im Geſichte zeichnet ihn aus, he is known by a scar in the face; die Bäume — [or anzeichnen], to mark out, to blaze the trees [that are to be felled &c.]. *Fig.* Einen —, to treat any one in a distinguished manner, to distinguish any one; ausgezeichnete Männer, Talente, Tugenden, Dienſte, distinguished men, talents, virtues, services; ausgezeichnete Gelehrſamkeit, eminent learning; ein ausgezeichneter Offizier, an officer of great distinction; ein ausgezeichneter Schriftſteller, a noted or celebrated author. 2) to take a passage or passages from a book or writing, to copy out. Ich habe mir einige wenige offenkundige Unwahrheiten aus der Flugſchrift ausgezeichnet, I have extracted from the pamphlet a few notorious falsehoods. 3) to draw or sketch completely. Einen Umriß —, to finish drawing the outline or contour. *Fig.* Einen Plan —, to complete a plan or scheme. II. *v. r.* ſich —, to distinguish one's self, to signalize one's self. Er zeichnete ſich durch ſeine Talente und ſeinen Muth aus, he distinguished himself by his talents and his courage; der Soldat zeichnet ſich in der Schlacht aus, the soldier signalizes himself in battle; ſich — durch &c., to be distinguished by &c.

Aúszeichnung, *f.* 1) [the act of distinguishing] distinction. 2) [that which confers eminence or superiority] distinction.

Auszeichnens- or **Auszeichnungs-werth**, —**würdig**, *adj.* and *adv.* worthy of distinction.

Aúszeideln, I. *v. tr.* to deprive of honey. Den Bienenſtock —, to empty a hive. II. *v. intr.* to cease depriving of honey.

Aúszeitigen, I. *v. tr.* to cause to ripen. Durch künſtliche Mittel —, to force [fruit &c.]. *Fig.* Erfahrungen zeitigen den Geiſt aus, experience ripens the understanding. II. *v. intr.* [u. w. ſeyn] to ripen or mature fully, to become perfect..

Aúszerren, *v. tr.* to get out by pulling or plucking, to pull or pluck out.

Aúszickeln, *v. intr.* to cease producing young, to cease to kid [said of goats].

Aúsziehen, *ir.* I. *v. tr.* 1) to draw out, to pull out. Unkraut —, to eradicate weeds; einen Zahn —, to extract, to draw a tooth; das Ausziehen eines Zahnes, the extraction of a tooth; ein Knabe kam in großer Haſt, mir die Stiefel auszuziehen, a boy came in a great hurry to pull off my boots; ziehe den Handſchuh aus, take off your glove; ein Kleid —, to get off a garment; er zog ſeine Kleider aus, he stript off his clothes; Einen —, to undress any one, *fig.* to strip any one of all he has; ſie zogen Joſeph ſeinen Rock aus, [Gen. XXXVII] they stript Joseph of his coat; ſich —, to undress one's self, to put off one's clothes. *Fig.* Den alten Menſchen —, to put off the old man; eine Wurzel —, [in arithmetic] to extract a root; die Quadrat- oder Cubikwurzel —, [in arithmetic and algebra] to extract the square root, the cube root; das Ausziehen der Wurzeln, [in arithm. and algebra] the extraction of roots; die Säfte oder Kräfte einer Pflanze —, to extract, to draw out the juices or essence of a plant, to distil; die Farben —, to draw out the colours by soaking, boiling, decocting or by a chemical operation; [in a more figurative sense] ein Zeug, aus dem die Farbe ausgezogen iſt, discoloured stuff; eine Rechnung —, to extract an account; ich habe einige wenige Stellen aus dieſer Flugſchrift ausgezogen, I have extracted from that pamphlet a few passages. 2) to draw out, to lengthen, to stretch by force, to extend. Das Eiſen —, to draw out iron; die Tücher —, [among clothiers] to stretch the cloth. 3) to hollow by drawing. Die Dauben —, [among coopers] to hollow the staves; ein Rohr —, [among gunmakers] to rifle the barrel of a gun.

II. *v. intr.* [u. w. ſeyn] 1) to remove from a place. Er iſt im vorigen Monate ausgezogen, he changed his lodgings last month; das Ausziehen, removal of lodgings. 2) to come forth from a place in a stately or solemn manner. Sie zogen aus, they marched out; ſie zogen in Proceſſion aus, they set out in procession; das Heer zog aus, the army took the field. †3) to turn off, to turn away, to take to one's heels. Einen — machen, to put a man to the run; die Pferde zogen aus, the horses ran at full gallop. 4) [at several games, at chess, drafts &c.] to make the first move. An wem iſt das Ausziehen? who has the first move?

Auszieh-ſcheibe *f.* V. Zieiſcheibe. —**ſtirnrad**, *n.* V. Ziehrad. —**ſtube**, *f.*, —**zimmer**, *n.* 1) dressing-room. 2) [in play-houses] tiring-house, tiring-room.

Aúszieher, [-es, *pl.* -] 1) epitomist, epitomiser. 2) he that makes extracts from proceedings at law &c.

Aúszieren, *v. tr.* to fit up, to adorn, to decorate, to ornament the interior of a thing. Ein Buch mit Kupferſtichen —, to embellish a book with plates. Das Auszieren eines Schiffes mit Flaggen —, [in seaman's language] the dressing of a ship.

Aúszierer, *m.* [-s, *pl.* -] decorator.

Aúszierung, *f.* fitting up, decoration, ornament.

Aúszieffern, *v. tr.* to compute with ciphers.

Aúszimmern, *v. tr.* 1) to cut or frame, to square [timber]. *Fig.* to elaborate. 2) [in mining] Einen Schacht —, to line a shaft.

Aúszinnen, *v. tr.* to cover with tin on the inside, to line with tin. Ein Gefäß —, to tin a vessel.

Aúszirkeln, *v. tr.* to measure with compasses. *Fig.* Seine Handlungen nach &c. —, to square one's actions by &c.; Alles —, to do every thing by rule.

Aúszirpen, *v. intr.* to chirp to the end; to cease chirping.

Aúszischeln, I. *v. tr.* to blab, to circulate whispering. II. *v. intr.* to cease whispering.

Aúszischen, I. *v. tr.* to condemn by hissing, to hiss, to explode. II. *v. intr.* to cease hissing, exploding.

Aúszittern, *v. intr.* to cease trembling.

Aúszitzen, *v. tr.* and *intr.* V. Ausſaugen.

Aúszug, *m.* [-es, *pl.* -züge] 1) the act of removing from a place. Der — aus einer Wohnung, [commonly das Ausziehen] change of lodgings, removal of lodgings; der — der Israeliten aus Aegypten unter Moſes Führung, the departure of the Israelites from Egypt under the conduct of Moses, exodus; der — aus einem Lande, emigration; der — des Heeres, the departure, march of an army. 2) that which is drawn from something. Der — eines Tiſches, [a sliding box in a table, which is drawn at pleasure] drawer. Ein — in der Lotterie, the number drawn in a lottery; der — aus einem Buche, einer Schrift, an extract; der — aus einem Rechnungsbuche, an extract from an account-book; Xiphilen hat einen — aus Dion's Römiſcher Geſchichte gemacht, Xiphilin epitomised Dion's Roman history; Auszüge [from authors], epitomes; in einen — bringen, to abstract; der — [Extract] aus Pflanzen, a vegetable extract; ein — aus Roſen, an extract of roses. 3) *Fig.* [in demises or letting of lands, in sales and auctions] provisional condition, reservation, proviso.

Auszugs=mäßig, *adj.* and *adv.* forming an extract from a book or writing, being an epitome or epitomy. —ſammlung, *f.* 1) a collection of epitomes. 2) a collection of extracts from the best authors. —weiſe, *adv.* in form of an epitome, in epitomes.

Auszupfen, I. *v. tr.* 1) to pull out, to pluck out. Fäden aus einem Zeuge —, to unravel a stuff; ausgezupfte Leinwand, lint. 2) to loosen or separate or disconnect things which are united without order, to clean by plucking, to disentangle. Wolle —, to pick wool. II. *v. intr.* 1) to cease plucking. 2) to finish the plucking of a thing.

Auszürnen, *v. intr.* to cease being angry.

Auszwängen, *v. tr.* to force out.

Auszweifeln, *v. intr.* to cease doubting.

Auszwicken, *v. tr.* to get out, take out by nipping.

Auszwingen, *v. tr.* 1) to force to go out. Einen aus dem Hauſe —, to force any one out of the house. 2) to draw from by force or compulsion. Einem ein Geſtändniß —, to extort a confession of guilt from any one. V. Auspreſſen.

Auszwitſchern, *v. intr.* to cease chirping.

*Authenticität, *f.* authenticity, genuineness [of the Scriptures &c.].

*Authéntiſch, I. *adj.* authentic, authentical. Ein —es Verzeichniß, an authentic register. II. *adv.* authentically.

*Autobiographie, *f.* [*pl.*-en] autobiography.

*Auto da fé, *n.* [in Catholic countries] auto da fé, act of faith.

*Autográphiſch, *adj.* autographic, autographical.

*Autógraphum, *n.* [-s, *pl.* -pha and -phen] autograph, autography.

*Autokrát, *m.* [-en, *pl.* -en] autocrat, autocrater, autocrator.

*Autokratie, *f.* [*pl.* -en] autocrasy.

*Automát, *m.* [-en, *pl.* -en] [a self-moving machine] automaton.

*Autor, *m.* [-s, *pl.* -en] author, writer.

Autorſchaft, *f.* [*pl.*-en] authorship.

*Autoriſation, *f.* authorization.

*Autoriſiren, *v. tr.* [to give authority, warrant or legal power to] to authorize. Der oberſte Gerichtshof iſt autoriſirt, ſowohl bürgerliche als peinliche Sachen zu entſcheiden, the supreme court is empowered to decide all cases, civil as well as criminal.

*Autorität, *f.* [*pl.*-en] 1) [legal power, or a right to command or to act] authority. 2) [precedents, respectable opinions and sayings] authority. 3) *pl.* [the persons or the body exercising power or command] authorities.

*Auxiliartruppen, *pl.* [foreign troops in the service of nations at war] auxiliaries.

*Aval, *n.* [in commerce] surety for payment.

*Avaliren, *v. intr.* [in commerce] to stand security.

*Avance, *f.* [*pl.*-n] money advanced, advance.

*Avancement, *n.* [*pl.*-s] advancement, promotion, preferment. Ein — im Dienſte, an advancement in office.

*Avanciren, I. *v. intr.* to move or go forward, to proceed. Die Truppen avancirten, the troops advanced. II. *v. tr.* [in commerce, to supply beforehand] to advance [money].

*Avantgarde, *f.* [*pl.* -n] 1) [in milit. affairs] the front of an army, van, vanguard. 2) [in marine affairs] the van of a fleet.

*Avarie, *f.* V. Havarie.

*Avers, *m.* [-ſes, *pl.* -ſe] [the face of a coin, opposed to the reverse] the obverse.

*Averſion, *f.* aversion [to any thing].

*Avertiren, *v. tr.* to inform, to advertise, to advise [any one of something].

*Avertiſſement, *n.* [-s, *pl.*-s] [notice given; a publication intended to give notice] advertisement.

*Avis, *m.* *Aviſo, *n.* advise, intelligence. Der —brief, letter of advice; das —ſchiff, advice-boat.

*Aviſen, *pl.* advices, newspapers.

*Aviſiren, *v. tr.* to advise. Einen Wechſel —, [in commerce] to advise of a bill.

*Aviſta, *adv.* [in commerce] at sight.

Axe, *f.* V. Achſe.

*Axiom, *n.* [-s, *pl.* -e] axiom.

*Axiometer, *m.* [-s, *pl.* -] [in seamen's lang.] tell-tale of the tiller.

Axt, *f.* [*pl.* Aexte] an ax, a hatchet. Syn. V. Beil.

Axt=blatt, *n.* the blade or cutting part of an ax or hatchet. —helm, *m.* the neck of an ax or hatchet [in which the helve is fixed]. —ſtiel, *m.* the handle of an ax or hatchet, helve.

Azen, I. *v. intr.* to take food, to feed, to eat. II. *v. tr.* 1) to give food to, to feed. Einen jungen Vogel —, to feed a young bird by putting food into its bill. 2) [to furnish with a bait] to bait.

Aztaube, *f.* V. Locktaube.

*Azeróle, *f.* [*pl.* -n] [a kind of medlar trees, the leaves of which are like parsley] azerole.

*Azimúth, *m.* [-es, *pl.* -e] [in astronomy] azimuth.

*Azimuthál, *adj.* [in astronomy] der Azimuthalkreis, azimuth circle or vertical circle.

Azung, *f.* 1) the act of feeding. 2) food, aliment. 3) a bait.

Azungs=geld, *n.* —koſten, *pl.* [a law term] the costs of nourishing a prisoner during confinement.

*Azúr, *adj.* sky-blue.

*Azúr, *m.* azurestone, azurespar, lapis lazuli. *Fig.* [in poetry] Der — des Himmels, the azure or deep-blue sky.

*Azürn, *adj.* azure.

B.

B, b, [a consonant] b. 1) *n.* B. *Prov.* V. A. 2) [in music] *a*) [the name of the seventh note in the gamut but half a tone flatter] b flat. Das harte — = H, b; dieſes Lied geht aus — Dur, this tune is in the key of B; dieſe Arie geht aus — Moll, this air is in the key of B flat. *b*) a mark denoting a fall or depression of half a tone, a flat. 3) in Chronology it stands for one of the Dominical letters.

Bä, [the cry or appropriate bleating of sheep] baa.

Baake, V. Bake.

1\. Baal, V. Balche.

2\. Baal, *m.* [-s] [an idol among the ancient Chaldeans and Syrians, representing the sun] Baal.

Baals=diener, *m.* a worshipper of the idol Baal. —dienſt, *m.* the worship of the idol Baal. —pfaffe, *m.* a wicked priest.

Baar, *adj.* and *adv.* V. Bar.

Baare, *f.* V. Bahre.

Baars, *m.* V. Börs.

Babbelei, *f.* 1) babble, idle talk, senseless prattle. 2) nonsense, trifles.

Bábbeler, *m.* [-s, *pl.* -] a babbler, an idle talker, an irrational prattler, a prater.

Bábbelhaft, Babbelig, *adj.* and *adv.* talking idly, babbling.

Bábbeln, [Fr. *babiller*, Gr. *βαβάζειν*] *v. intr.* to utter words imperfectly or indistinctly, to talk idly, to babble, to prattle like a child.

Bábylon, *n.* [-s] [ancient capital city of Assyria where the tower of Babel stood] Babylon.

Babylóniſch, *adj.* Babylonian, Babylonic, Babylonish.

*Baccalaureát, *n.* [-en, *pl.* -en] [the degree of a bachelor of arts] baccalaureate, bachelorship.

*Baccalaúreus, *m.* [*pl.* -reen] bachelor.

*Bacchanál, *n.* [-es, *pl.* -e] bacchanals.

*Bacchánt, *m.* [-en, *pl.* -en] bacchanal, bacchanalian. —inn, *f.* a priestess of Bacchus, a bacchant or bacchante, *Fig.* a riotous woman, a reveller, a devotee to Bacchus.

*Bacchántiſch, *adj.* and *adv.* bacchic, drunken, mad with intoxication.

*Bácchus, *m.* [the god of wine] Bacchus.

Bacchus=feſt, *n.* bacchanals. —lied, *m.* bacchanalian song. —ſtab, *m.* thyrsus.

Bách, *m.* [-es, *pl.* Bäche] [allied to the Gr. *πηγή*, and to the old Germ. Ach, Lat. *aqua*] 1) a brook, a rivulet, a beck. 2) a small stream of water collected by rain.

Bach=amſel, *f.* white or collared wagtail. —binſe, *f.* water-bulrush. —blume, *f.* marigold. —bohne, —bunge, *f.* 1) [a species of Veronica] brook-lime, becabunga. 2) broad-leaved brook-lime or water speed-well. —fahrt, *f.* a gutter made by a water-flood, a cartway washed out by torrents, a narrow passage or way, a defile, a ravine. —fiſch, *m.* fish that lives in or frequents brooks. —föhre, —forelle, *f.* the trout. —gräßling, *m.* [a fish] the gudgeon. —holder, —holunder, *m.* the water-elder. —hund, *m.* [among sportsmen] an otter-dog. —krebs, *m.* crayfish, freshwater crawfish. —kreſſe, water-cress. —mücke, *f.* crane-fly. —münze, *f.* brook-mint, water-mint. —reich, *adj.* and *adv.* brooky, rilly. —ſand, *m.* sand found in brooks. —ſchmerle, *f.* [a fish] a sort of loche. —ſtelze, *f.* —vogel, *m.* V. —amſel. —waſſer, *n.* running water. —weide, *f.* the water-willow, osier. —weiſe, *adv.* like a brook, in brooks.

Báche, *f.* [*pl.* -n] [seems to be allied to the Lat. *vacca* (in the middle ages *Baca*), Kuh, so that it originally signified an animal — Thier — in general; in Dutch *bake* signifies a swine in general] [among hunters the female of a wild boar] wild sow.

Bácher, *m.* [-s, *pl.* -] [V. Bache] [among hunters] a two year old wild boar.

Bächlein, *n.* [-s] a rill, rivulet, streamlet.

Báck, *n.* [-es, *pl.* -e] [allied to the Fr. *bac*, and probably to be derived from biegen] [in seamen's language] 1) *a*) fore-castle. *b*) a wooden dish or bowl, to hold the sailor's victuals. *c*) [a number of sailors who eat together] a mess. In —en theilen, to mess. *d*) birth. 2) the back or side of any thing as in Backbord.

Báck, *adv.* [*bak* signifies in Low-Saxon Rücken and hinten] [in seamen's language] towards the back, in the back part, abaft. Das große Marsſegel liegt —, the main top-sail is taken aback; die Segel —legen, —holen oder —braſſen, to back the sails; —liegen, to lay aback.

Back=bord, *m.* larboard. — das Ruder! port the helm! —bug, *m.* larboardside. —ſe gässen, *pl.* castle-crew. —s-geselle, *m.* messmate. —s-meister, *m.* the master of a mess. —piß, *m.* [also Pißback] the manger. —spier, *f.* the outrigger of the boats, guest-rope. —steg, *m.* Der — des Klüverbaums, shrouds of the jib-boom; der — des Bugspriets [Bugsteg], shrouds of the bow-sprit; —stegen eines Bocks, stays of the sheers. —stegsweise, *adv.* on the quarter. —stegswind, *m.* quarter wind or quartering wind. —volk, *n.* [a number of sailors who eat together] a mess. —wache, *f.* larboard-watch.

Back-apfel, —birn &c. V. farther below after Backen.

Backaljau, *m.* [a fish] [-es, *pl.* -e] the common cod.

Bäckchen, *n.* [-s, *pl.* -] [diminut. of Backe] a small cheek.

Backe, *f.* [*pl.* -n] **Backen**, *m.* [-s, *pl.* -] [seems to be allied to biegen, beugen] 1) [the raised side of certain things] Die —n an einem Lehnstuhl, the cheeks of an arm-chair; die Backe or der Backen am Flintenkolben, the cheek-piece of a musket; die —n an dem Bleizuge der Glaser, the cheeks of a glazier's vice; die —n an der Drehbank, the cheeks of a turner's lathe; [in seamen's language] die —n der Masten, the cheeks of a mast; die —n des Schiffs, the bows of a ship; die —n am Kohlschwein, the clamps of the keelson; die —n des Bugspriets, a fiddle or saddle upon the bow-sprit; [in fortification] die —n der Schießscharten, the cheeks or inner parts of the embrasures. 2) [the side of the face below the eyes on each side] the cheek. Mit eingefallenen —n, hollow-cheeked. *Fig.* Ein Apfel mit rothen —n, a rosy-cheeked apple. 3) a protuberant part of some parts of the body as the buttock.

Backen-bart, *m.* whiskers. —bein, *n.* the cheek-bone. —blase, *f.* V. —tasche. —drüse, *f.* [in anatomy] buccanal gland, buccal gland. —grube, *f.* *Dimin.* —grübchen, *n.* a dimple in the cheek. —haube, *f.* a cap with lappets. —knochen, V. —bein. —muskel, *m.* [in anatomy, a muscle of the cheek] buccinator. —nerve, *f.* [in anatomy] a branch of the inferior maxillary nerves. —netz, *n.* [in anatomy] a ganglion formed by a branch of the facial nerve. —puls-ader, *f.* [in anatomy] buccal vein. —riemen, *m.* breeching. —schlag, —streich, *m.* a slap in the face or on the chops, a box on the ear. —stück, *n.* cheek-piece. —tasche, *f.* [the bag which hangs by the mouth of hamsters and of most of the monkey tribe] pouch. —zahn, *m.* cheek-tooth, double-tooth, jaw-tooth, grinder, molar tooth. —zahndrüse, *f.* [in anatomy] molar gland.

‖**Bäcke**, *f.* 1) the act of baking. 2) a batch.

Backen, *ir.* [ich backe, du bäckst, er bäckt, but also reg. du backst, er backt, wir backen &c.; ich backte, gebacken] [is derived by some from bähen = to make warm, by others from the Gr. πήγ-νυμι, *to make compact*] I. *v. intr.* to be baked, to dry and harden in heat, to bake. II. *v. tr.* to bake [bread &c.]. Gebackene Steine [Backsteine], bricks; gebackenes Fleisch, baked meat; in einer Pfanne —, to fry; Gebackenes, fry; Obst backen, to dry fruit; gebackene Fische, fried fish.

Back-apfel, *m.* a sort of apples fit for baking, a baking apple. —birn, *f.* a sort of pears fit for baking, a baking pear. —brett, *n.* board used for baking. —fisch, *m.* 1) fish for frying. 2) ‖ and ‡ *Fig.* a young girl. —fleisch, *n.* a meat pie. —geld, *n.* money paid for baking. —geräth, *n.* the utensils of bakers. —gerechtigkeit, *f.* the privileges of bakers. —haus, *n.* bakehouse. —hecht, *m.* a baking pike. —holz, *n.* wood for baking. —kohle, *f.* [in mining] binding coal, caking coal. —korb, *m.* a basket used for raising bread. —mulde, *f.* a kneading trough. —napf, *m.* V. —korb. —obst, *n.* 1) fruit for baking. 2) baked or dried fruit. —ofen, *m.* an oven [for baking bread]. —ofenhitze, *f.* the heat of a baker's oven. *Fig.* a great heat. —ofenstein, *m.* [in mineral.] trachitic conglomerate. —pfanne, *f.* frying pan. —schaufel, *f.* [a kind of wooden shovel used by bakers] the peel. —schüssel, *f.* V. —korb. —speise, *f.* a pie, pastry, meat &c. in a pie. —stein, *m.* brick. Feuerfeste —steine [for lining furnaces &c.] fire-proof bricks. —stube, *f.* 1) a room for baking. 2) bakehouse. —trog, *m.* a baker's kneading trough, a brake. —werk, *n.* pastry. —zeug, *n.* V. —geräth. —zins, *m.* furnage.

Bäcker, [more properly than Becker] *m.* [-s, *pl.* -] baker.

Bäcker-brod, *n.* bread baked by bakers, bakers' bread. —bursche, —gesell, *m.* a baker's journeyman. —gewerke, *n.* the company of bakers. —knecht, V. —bursche. —schabe, *f.* the cockroach. —stock, *m.* a tally used between bakers and millers.

Bäckerei, *f.* 1) [the trade of a baker] bakery. 2) bakehouse, bakery.

Bäckig, *adj.* and *adv.* having cheeks [only used in composition as bausbäckig, chubby-cheeked, hohlbäckig, hollow-cheeked, rothbäckig, rosy-cheeked, cherry-cheeked &c.].

Bäcksen, *v. tr.* [in seamen's lang.] die Kanonen —, to bowse the guns.

Bad, *n.* [-es, *pl.* Bäder] [seems to be allied to water = Wasser, some derive it from bähen = to make warm] 1) [in some particular meanings]. Ins — [setzen], [among masons] with full mortar; ein trockenes —, a dry bath; das Dampf—, a vapour bath; [in chimistry, in medicine] das nasse —, the wet bath; das Sand—, sand-bath. 2) bath [the liquid or water used for bathing] Ein kaltes oder warmes —, a cold or warm bath; [in Scripture] das — der Taufe, baptism. *Prov.* das — austragen müssen, to suffer for the faults of another; Einem ein schlimmes — zurichten, to speak ill of any one in order to injure him, to create any one trouble; das Kind mit dem Bade aus- or verschütten, to reject the good with the bad. 3) [a natural bath, impregnated with iron, sulphur &c.]. 4) a house for bathing, bath; a room for bathing. 5) a watering-place. In das — reisen, to go to a watering-place. 6) mineral water. Das — brauchen, to take the waters.

Bad[e]-anstalt, *f.* a place for bathing, a bath. —anzug, *m.* bathing-dress, bathing-gown. —arzt, *m.* physician in a watering-place. —ausschlag, *m.* drash got in bathing. —frau, *f.* 1) woman employed in a bath, bathing-woman. 2) midwife. —gast, *m.* one that frequents a watering-place, a visitor of a watering-place. —geld, *n.* money paid for bathing. —haube, *f.* bathing-cap. —haus, *m.* bagnio, hot-house. —hemde, *n.* bathing-shirt or shift. —hose, *f.* bathing-drawers. —kappe, *f.* bathing-cap, oil-case-cap. —kleid, V. —mantel. —knecht, *m.* a man-servant in baths. —kopf, *m.* V. Schröpfkopf. —kraut, *n.* a plant used to medicate baths. —kur, *f.* the use of mineral waters. —lohn, *m.* V. —geld. —magd, *f.* a maidservant in baths. —mantel, *m.* a wide garment for bathing. —meister, *m.* 1) [unusual] bath-keeper. 2) the servant who has the superintendance of the baths. —mulde, *f.* a bathing-vat. —mutter, *f.* midwife. —orden, Orden vom Bade or [more usual] Bathorden, *m.* [in England] the order of the Bath. —ort, *m.* 1) a convenient place for bathing, swimming-place. 2) bathing- or watering-place. —platz, *m.* V. —ort 1). —reise, *f.* a journey to a watering-place. —schiff, *n.* a boat used for bathing. —schraber, —striegel, *m.* strigel. —schwamm, *m.* common spunge. —sinter, —stein, *m.* V. Tropfstein. —stelle, *f.* swimming-place. —stube, *f.* V. —zimmer; morgenländische —stube, hummum. —wanne, *f.* bathing-tub. Eine schuhförmige —wanne, a slipper-bath. —zeit, *f.* the season for bathing at watering-places. —zeug, *n.* articles required for bathing. —zimmer, *n.* bath-room, balneary.

Baden, *v. tr.* [V. Bad] [to wash the body or some part of it in a bath] to bathe. Sich —, to bathe. *Fig.* Sich in Thränen oder Blut —, to bathe in tears or blood; sich in Wollüsten —, to indulge one's self in sensual pleasure. Das Baden, balneation; der Badende, bather.

Baden, *n.* [-s] 1) Baden [Grand-Duchy]. 2) Baden [name of several watering-places in Austria, in the Grand-Duchy of Baden (frequently called Baden-Baden) and in Switzerland].

Badener, *m.* [-s, *pl.* -] —inn, *f.* 1) an inhabitant of the Grand-Duchy of Baden [in this sense with some authors also: Badenser, Badenserinn]. 2) an inhabitant of one of the before-mentioned watering-places.

Badensch, V. Badisch.

Bader, *m.* [-s, *pl.* -] 1) [unusual] the keeper of a bath. 2) a surgeon [of inferior standing], a cupper.

Badergesell, *m.* a cupper's journeyman.

Baderei, *f.* a house for bathing or cupping, bagnio.

***Badian**, *m.* [-s] badiane, Indian anise-seed.

Badisch, *adj.* of the Grand-Duchy of Baden.

Bäffchen, *n.* [-s, *pl.* -] the clergyman's band.

***Bagage**, *f.* [*pl.* -n] baggage, luggage.

***Bagatellen**, *pl.* trifles.

Bagger, *m.* [-s, *pl.* -] 1) one whose business it is to clear out the mud from a place. 2) a machine used for clearing out mud.

Bagger-meister, *m.* the person that superintends the cleaning of a port. —prahmen, *m.* [in seamen's language] a large lighter furnished with wheels and large spoons used for deepening or cleaning a port.

Baggern, *v. tr.* to clear out the mud. Einen Hafen —, to clean a harbour.

Bähen, *v. tr.* [appears to be allied to the Swed. *badda* = to warm] 1) to apply warm lotions or bags stuffed with herbs and other ingredients, to bathe with warm medicated liquors or with flannel steeped in warm water, to foment. Er bähete den Kopf mit Opiaten, um Schlaf zu bewirken, he fomented the head with opiates to procure sleep; eine Wunde —, to bathe a wound; kranke Glieder —, to stupe diseased parts. 2) to dry or heat at the fire. Brod —, to toast bread; gebähtes Brod, a toast.

Bäh[e]-kissen, *n.* a bag stuffed with herbs or other ingredients. —kraut, *n.* a plant used for fomenting. —mittel, *n.* [in med.] [the lotion applied to a diseased part] fomentation. —säckchen, *n.* V. —kissen. —stube, *f.* V. Gerbestube.

Bahn, *f.* [*pl.* -en] [perhaps allied to the Gr. βαίνω = to go] 1) [a way beaten or trodden by the feet of men or beasts or made hard by wheels] path. Die — brechen, to beat a path [as in snow], *fig.* to open the path, to make the beginning, to break the ice. *Fig.* Etwas auf die — bringen, to start something; sie brachten eine neue Frage auf die —, they started a new question. 2) [the way, course or track where a body moves in the atmosphere or in space] path. Die — eines Planeten, [in astronomy] the orbit of a planet; die Mond—, the orbit of the moon; die Sonnen—, ecliptic; die — eines Cometen, the trajectory of a comet;

seinet — entkräfteter Stern, a star disorbed. 3) a place for running &c. Die Reit—, riding-ground, riding-school, manege; die Renn—, [ground, on which a race is run] race-ground, course, career; die Stech—, career; die Kegel—, [a place for playing at nine-pins] bowling-path; die Schlitten—, the road for sleighs or sledges. 4) the level or flat surface of some tools. Die — des Hammers, the face of a hammer; die — des Ambosses, the face of an anvil; die — eines Hobels, the face of a plane; die — eines Hobeleisens, basil of the iron of a plane. 5) Die — (das Blatt) eines Zeuges, the breadth of a stuff.

Bahn=los, —enlos, *adj.* and *adv.* pathless. Ein —loser Wald, a pathless forest. —enschlägel, *m.* [in forges] a great hammer used for repairing the face of a sledge-hammer. —hobeln, *v. tr.* [among coopers] to plane the head of a cask.

Bähnen, I. *v. tr.* [to make a path by treading] to path. Einen Weg —, to beat a path; ein gebahnter Weg, a beaten path. *Fig.* to make way by removing obstacles; es würde unsern Waffen den Weg in Spanien —, it would facilitate the progress of our arms in Spain. II. *v. r.* and *intr.* Es bahnt sich, it becomes level or passable.

Bähnig, *adj.* and *adv.* having level surfaces or faces.

Bähre, *f.* [*pl.* -n] [from the old *peran*, Goth. *bairan*, Dan. bäre, Lat. *ferre* = to bear] 1) a hand-barrow. 2) [Todtenbahre] bier.

Bahrtuch, *n.* [the cloth thrown over a dead body at funerals] pall.

Bai, *f.* [*pl.* -en] [D. *Baye*, probably from biegen, as Bucht] [an arm of the sea extending into the land] bay.

Baisalz, V. Meersalz.

Baier, Baiern, V. Bayer, Bayern.

Baikalít, [-s, *pl.* -en] Baikalstein, *m.* [in mineralogy] baicalit.

Bailbrechen, *v. intr.* [among hunters] to cease barking.

Bailen, *v. intr.* [among hunters] to open.

Baireuth, [-s] Beirut [a town in Bavaria].

Baizen, V. Beizen.

Bajonnét, *n.* [-s, *pl.*-e] bayonet. Die Hülse eines —s, socket of a bayonet; der Einsatz or Griff eines —s, the handle of a bayonet.

Bak, V. Back.

Bäke, *f.* [*pl.* -n] [in seamen's lang.] a beacon, seamark, buoy.

Bakengeld, *n.* beaconage.

‡Bäkel, *m.* [-s, *pl.* -] a stick, a cudgel.

Bäkeljau, *m.* [-s, *pl.*-e] a sort of dried cod-fish.

Bakeljaufischer, *m.* banker.

‖Bäken, *v. tr.* to beat.

*Balance, *f.* [*pl.* -n] balance, equilibrium, equipoise.

*Balanciren, *v. tr.* and *intr.* to poise, to balance.

Balancirstange, *f.* poy.

Balanít, *m.* [-s, *pl.* -en] a petrified acorn shell.

Baláß, *m.* [-sses, *pl.* -e] [Balas-Rubin] balas ruby, spinel, spinel ruby.

Balbier, [incorrect and vulgar] V. Barbier.

Balbieren, [incorr. and vulg.] V. Barbieren.

Bälche, *f.* [allied to fahl, bleich] a pale bluish fish in the lake of Constance, something like the herring, but larger.

*Balcon, *m.* [-s *pl.* -e] balcony, mirador.

Báld, *adv.* [probably allied to wallen = to move, and with the Lat. *valeo*, *validus*] 1) soon = shortly, quickly. Eure Schönheit wird — vergehen, your beauty will soon pass; — nachher, soon after; so — als, as soon as; so — ich ihn ansichtig wurde, as soon as I saw him; nicht so — als, no sooner than; so — als möglich, aufs —este, as soon as may be; komme —, come early; bälder, sooner; aufs bäldeste, the soonest possible; bälder als —, quicker than quick, the sooner the better. *Prov.* Was — reif, hält nicht steif, soon ripe, soon rotten. *Fig.* easily, almost, nearly. Ich wäre — gestorben, I was like to die; *er läßt sich — zu Allem überreden, he allows himself to be easily persuaded. 2) [at one time, at another time] — so, — so, now so, then otherwise.

*Báldachin, *m.* [-s, *pl.* -e] [probably = Wallbach, i. e. a moveable roof] canopy. Bei Prozessionen trägt man einen — über dem Haupte des Priesters, a canopy is borne over the head of the priest at processions.

‖Báldgreis, *m.* [-ses, *pl.* -se] groundsel. V. Kreuzwurz.

Báldig, *adj.* and *adv.* speedy. Eine —e Antwort, a speedy answer; ein —er und glücklicher Ausgang, a soon and prosperous issue; aufs —este, as soon as may be.

Báldrian, *m.* [-s] [a plant] valerian, setwal(l), setwell.

Baldrian=öl, *n.* oil drawn from the valerian. —wurzel, *f.* the root of the valerian.

Báldwin, [a name of men] [-s, *pl.* -e] Baldwin.

Balèster, *m.* [-s, *pl.* -] cross-bow [from which bullets are shot], arbalist.

Bálg, *m.* [-es, *pl.* Bälge] [allied to the Lat. *follis*, and probably from the old *pelkan*, A. S. *belgan* = to swell out] 1) a hollow and soft body which contains another. *a*) the skin of fruits and seeds. Die Bälge an den Weinbeeren, Erbsen, the skins of grapes, pease. *b*) [in botany, the calyx or carol of grasses] glume. *c*) the skin of an animal stript off [without being slit open], pelt. Der — eines Fuchses, the skin of a fox; der Schlangen—, the slough of a serpent. *Fig.* [in contempt of a child] der kleine —, little brat, urchin; der dicke —, paunch. 2) [Blase—] bellows. Syn. Balg, Fell, Haut. Fell signifies a hairy or feathery covering, and is therefore properly applied only to the skin of hairy or feathery animals. Haut is the reticular substance, which is the natural covering of animal bodies, the skin. One says: ein Schaffell [a sheep-skin], and eine Fischhaut [a fish-skin]; the covering of the human body is called eine Haut, that of some animals ein Fell. For this reason the inner integument alone, the hide or skin, even of hairy or feathery animals is called Haut and not Fell. V. Hirnhaut, Knochenhaut. Das Fell [the hairy or feathery covering] of some animals is called Balg. In the language of sportsmen, furriers, and tanners, these words are applied to the skin of particular animals, as: Schaffell, Wildschweinhaut, Fuchsbalg. Skins which are used with the hair on, are called Felle, those from which the hair has been removed, Häute.

Balg=geschwulst, *f.* [in surgery] encysted tumour. —kapsel, *f.* [in botany] follicle. —linse, *f.* —rohr, *n.* V. Balgendiese. —staar, *m.* [in medicine] a milky or fluid cataract. —zug, *m.* [in organs] the stop of the bellows.

Balgen=deckel, *m.* the upper board of a pair of bellows. —diese, —linse, *f.* the nose of a pair of bellows. —luftklappe, *f.* the valve of a pair of bellows. —treter, *m.* the bellows-blower, organ-blower.

‖Bálge, *f.* [*pl.* -n] a tub. V. Balje.

†Bálgen, *v. r.* [appears to be allied to the Gr. βάλλω, πάλλω, and to the Lat. *bellum*] sich —, to wrestle, to struggle, to fight, to scuffle.

Bälgen, *v. r.* sich —, to cast the skin. Die Schlange bälget sich, the serpent casts his slough.

†Bálger, *m.* [-s, *pl.* -] wrestler, boxer.

†Balgereí, *f.* wrestling, fighting, fight, scuffle.

Bálje, *f.* [*pl.* -n] [in seamen's language] a half tub. Die — der Lothlinie [Keil—], a half tub or bucket to hold the plummet and line on the deck ready for sounding; — der Marsfall, a half tub or kind of cage on each side of the quarter deck of several ships, to coil in them the remaining parts of the main-top-halliards and keep them out of the way.

Bálken, *m.* [-s, *pl.* -] [allied to Pfahl and Bohle] 1) [any large piece of timber; the largest, or a principal piece in a building] a beam. Einen — legen, einlegen, ziehen, einziehen, to lay a beam; einen — kantig behauen, to square a beam. **Fig.* Er lügt, daß sich die — biegen, he is a great liar. 2) [in a more limit. sense] *a*) [in seamen's language] Balken [Deck—], beams. Der mittelste — [Segel—], midship-beam; die — der Kuhbrücke, orlop-beams. *b*) [in husbandry] α) the loft of a barn. β) [a ridge of land between furrows] balk. *c*) [among printers] cross-piece. *d*) [the main piece of a plough, in which the plough-tails are fixed, and by which it is drawn] the beam. V. also ‖ Grendel. *e*) [the part of a balance, from the ends of which the scales are suspended = der Wage—] the beam. *f*) [in heraldry] the pale. *g*) [in mathematics] a parallelopiped.

Balken=anker, *m.* [among carpenters or architects] an S. —band, *n.* 1) [in carpentry, a piece of wood in the frame of a building] a key. 2) the bar of a luth. V. also Lautensteg. —decke, *f.* [in architecture] a ceiling formed of timbers. —gesimse, *n.* [in archit.] cornice. —kante, *f.* the face of a beam. —kantig, *adj.* and *adv.* having faces [said of beams]. —keller, *m.* a raftered cellar. —kopf, *m.* the head of a beam. —stein, *m.* [in archit.] corbel, corbet, corbil. —streif, *m.* [in heraldry] fesse. —tracht, *f.* V. Balkwäger. —wage, *f.* steel-yards. V. also Schnellwage. —werk, *n.* the frame of a house or building.

Balk=füllings, *pl.* [in seamen's lang.] small carlings, put between the beams. —wäger, *m.* [in seamen's lang.] clamps of the deckbeams.

1. Báll, *m.* [-es, *pl.* Bälle] [probably allied to wallen, wölben, the Gr. βάλλω, πάλλω, the Lat. *pila* &c.] ball. *a*) [a round body, or a body nearly round] a ball. Ein — zum Spielen [der Spielball], a ball for play; — spielen, to drive a ball, to play at tennis. *b*) = an ivory ball [to play at billiards]. Einen — machen, to drive or to put the ball into the hazard, to pocket a ball; einen — dicht an die Bande legen, ihn colliren, to give a close ball; einen — sprengen, to bound or spring a ball. *c*) = the globe, the earth [Erdball] or any a celestial orb. *d*) [any part of the body that is round or protuberant] V. Ballen.

Ball=förmig, *adj.* and *adv.* round like a ball. —haus, *n.* a tennis-court. —holz, *n.*, a bat. —meister, *m.* master of a tennis-court. —netz, *n.* a racket. —pritsche, *f.* V. —holz. —rose, *f.* the water elder. —schlägel, *m.* V. —holz. —schläger, *m.* a ball-player, cricket-player, tennis or racket player. —spiel, *n* tennis, cricket, rackets. —stock, *m.* V. Billardstock. —stoß, *m.* 1) the driving of a ball. 2) V. Billard. —stoßspiel, *n.* V. Billard. —tafel, *f.* V. Billard. —tafelkugel, *f.* V. Billardkugel. —tafelspiel, *n.* V. Billard. —tafelspieler, *m.* V. Billardspiel. —tafelstock, *m.* V. Billardstock.

2. **Báll**, *m.* [-es, *pl.* Bälle] [allied to wallen, the Gr. βάλλειν &c.] [an entertainment of dancing] a ball. Einen — geben, to give a ball.

Ball=anzug, *m.* ball-dress, full-dress. —fest, *n.* a ball. —gast, *m.* a person invited to a ball. —geber, *m.* the person that gives a ball. —hut, *m.* dress-hat. —kleid, *n.* a gown worn at a ball, ball-dress, a full-dress gown. —schuh, *m.* dress-shoe, ball-shoe.

3. **Báll**, *m.* [-es] [from bellen] [among hunters] the opening [barking] of dogs.

Balläde, *f.* [*pl.* -n] ballad.

Balladen=dichter, *m.* a ballad-writer, ballader. —sänger, *m.* ballad-singer. —verkäufer, *m.* ballad-monger.

Bállast and **Ballást**, *m.* [-es] [probably instead of Baglast, from Bak, Dan. Bag = back, and Last = burthen] [in seamen's language] ballast. Guter —, good ballast [as gravel &c.]; schlechter —, bad ballast [as sand, salt &c.]; grober —, heavy ballast composed of large stones &c.; alter —, old ballast or that which has been already used during a voyage; gewaschener —, washed ballast; den — ausschießen, to unballast; den — einschießen, to ballast; der — schießt über, the ballast shifts; nur mit — beladen seyn, to be in ballast.

Ballásten, *v. tr.* [in seamen's lang.] to ballast [a ship].

Bällchen, *n.* [-s, *pl* -] [dimin. of 1. and 2. Ball and of Ballen] a small ball or bale.

Balleí, *f.* [*pl.* -en] 1) [obsolete = Amt] bailiwick. 2) [a certain benefice belonging to a military order] commandery.

Bállen, *m.* [-s, *pl.* -] [V. 1. Ball] 1) *a*) [a bundle or package of goods in a cloth-cover] a bale. Ein — Waaren, [in commerce] a pack or bale of goods, merchandise. *b*) a fixed quantity of certain wares, fangot. Ein — Papier, ten reams; ein — Leinwand, a bale of linen cloth [consisting of twelve pieces, each of thirty two ells]. 2) a round or nearly round, softly elastic body. 3) a printer's ball [consisting of hair or wool]. Die — benetzen, to bishop the balls, to wet the balls; — machen, to knock up, to make skin-balls; — putzen, to scrape the balls; — reiben, to rub the balls. 4) [in fencing] a button covered with leather at the end of a foil. 5) the ball of the thumb or foot. Einem Hunde die — ausschneiden, [among hunters] to expeditate a dog. 6) [among joiners] the handle of a plane.

Ballen=binder, *m.* a packer. —binderlohn, *m.* [a charge made for packing goods] package. —binderstock, *m.* packing-stick. ‖—degen, *m.* foil [for fencing]. —eisen, *n.* V. —meißel. —fieber, *n.* —gicht, *f.* V. Fußgicht. —holz, *n.* [among printers] ballstock. —knecht, *m.* [among printers] racks. —kreuz, *n.* [in heraldry] V. Kugelstabkreuz. —leder, *n.* [among printers] the leather. —meißel, *m.* [among gunmakers] ripping-chisel. —messer, *n.* [among printers] ball-knife. —waare, *f.* bale-goods. —wälzer, *m.* the dor-beetle. —weise, *adv.* in bales.

Bállen, I. *v. tr.* 1) to form into a ball, to gather into a round mass, to conglobate, to glomerate. Die Faust —, to clench or clutch the hand or fist; eine geballte Wurzel, [in botany] a conglobate root. 2) to make up in a bale, to bale. II. *v. r.* sich —, to conglobate, to ball. Der Schnee ballet sich, the snow balls, sticks.

Ballét, *n.* [-s, *pl.* -e] ballet.

Balletmeister, *m.* a ballet-master.

***Ballíste**, *f.* [*pl.* -n] balista.

***Ballístik**, *f.* [without a plural] ballistics.

***Ballón**, *m.* [-s, *pl.* -s] 1) a foot-ball. 2) a balloon.

***Ballotáde**, *f.* [*pl.* -n] [in manege] ballotade, balotade.

***Ballotáge**, *f.* [*pl.* -n] **Ballótement**, *n.* [-s, *pl.* -s] ballot, balloting.

*1. **Ballotíren**, *v. tr.* to vote by ballot, to ballot.

*2. **Ballotíren**, *v. tr.* to castrate pigs.

Bálsam, *m.* 1) [probably from *balesan*, the Arab. name of the balsam-tree] balm, balsam. 2) balm of Gilead, balsam of Mecca or Syria. 3) any fragrant or valuable ointment, balm. 4) *Fig.* *a*) any fragrant odour. *b*) [any thing, which soothes or mitigates pain] balm.

Balsam=apfel, *m.* balsam-apple. —baum, *m.* balm-tree. —blüte, *f.* 1) blossom of the balsam-tree. 2) any flower breathing perfume. —büchse, *f.* balm-box. —duft, *m.* balsamic-odour. —duftend, *adj.* and *adv.* balmy, breathing perfume. *Poet.* —duftende Flügel, balmy wings. —espe, *f.* V. —pappel. —frucht, *f.* the fruit of the balsam-tree. —geist, *m.* spirit of balsam. —geruch, *m.* 1) the odour of the balm. 2) any fragrant odour. —gewächs, *n.* a plant yielding balm. —harz, *n.* a balsamic resin. —holz, *n.* the fragrant wood of the balm-tree. —kraut, *n.* 1) a balsamic plant. 2) marvel of Peru. —münze, *f.* balm-gentle, balm-mint. —öl, *n.* a balsamic oil. —pappel, *f.* the Tacamahac [a tree]. —pflanze, *f.* a balsamic plant. —schwitzend, *adj.* balsam-sweating. —staude, *f.* —strauch, *m.* balsam-shrub.

Balsāmen, **Balsamíren**, *v. tr.* 1) [to anoint with balm] to balm. 2) to perfume.

Balsamíne, *f.* [*pl.* -n] balsamine, touch-me-not, impatiens.

Balsámisch, *adj.* and *adv* balmy, balsamic, balsamical. *Fig.* Ein —er Schlaf, a balmy sleep; ein —er Hauch, a balmy breath.

Bálse, *f.* [*pl.* -n] a kind of raft.

Bálthasar, [-s] [a name of men] Balthasar.

Báltisch, *adj.* and *adv.* Baltic. Die —en Länder, the Baltic states; das —e Meer, the Baltic.

***Balustrāde**, *f.* [a row of balusters, joined by a rail] balustrade.

Bálz, *f* [also Falz; perhaps from falzen = to double up] [among hunters] the act of pairing and the treading time of the large feathered game, especially of the cock of the mountain.

Balzzeit, *f.* the treading time of the larger birds.

Bálzen, *v. intr.* to pair [said of larger birds and cats].

Bálzer, [-s] V. [the correct word] Balthasar.

***Bambocciāde**, **Bambotschiāde**, *f.* [in painting] a picture of low life.

Bámbus, *m.* [-sses, *pl.* -sse] **Bambusrohr**, *n.* [-s, *pl* -e] 1) [a plant of the reed-kind] bamboo, tabaxir. 2) a bamboo-cane.

Bambus=rohr=zucker, *m.* the juice extracted from the tabaxir [which by the Arabians is called sacar-mambu]. —stock, V. Bambus 2.

‖**Bâmme**, *f.* [*pl.* -n] a slice of bread. Die Butter —, a slice of bread and butter.

†**Bámmel**, (Baumel) *f.* [*pl.* -n] any little round thing that plays loosely at the end of a string &c., a little ornament or pendant that hangs so as to play loosely. An jedem Ohr eine —, at each ear a bob; die Bammeln [Eicheln] an einem Kragen, neck cloth tassels.

Bámmeln, *v. intr.* 1) to bob. 2) to hang and swing, to dangle. *Fig.* † to be executed by the halter. Wenn man die Diebe erhascht, so müssen sie —, if the thieves are taken, they will be hanged.

‖**Báms**, *n.* [-ses, *pl.* -se] [from the same root as Wams] [among saddlers] a well-stuffed pad.

Bámsen, *v. tr.* [among tawers &c.] to beat [the skins &c.].

***Bánco**, *m.* —geld, *n.* banco. V. Bank.

1. **Bánd**, *n.* [-es, *pl.* Bänder and in some significations Bande, and in some technical terms Banden] 1) a tie, a fillet, a bond, a cord, a string, any narrow ligament with which a thing is bound, tied or fastened, or by which a number of things are confined together; any thing bound round or encircling another, a band. Ein — von Stroh, a strawband; ein eisernes —, an iron band; das Weiden— eines Reisigbüschels, a fagot-band; ein Hut—, a hat-band; die Bänder am Sattel [Sattelbänder], the bands of a saddle. [In a more confined sense] *a*) a narrow web of silk &c., which is worn for ornament. Das — von Zwirn [Zwirnband], tape; ein seidenes —, a [silk] riband or ribbon; das gestreifte —, stripe-tape; eine Garnitur Bänder, a set of ribands; mit fliegenden Bändern, with ribands pendent; das blaue oder rothe — eines Ordens, the blue or red riband of an order. *b*) [among coopers, a band of wood or metal used to confine the staves of casks] a hoop. *c*) [in gunnery] the corner-ring of a piece of ordnance, astragal. *d*) [among locksmiths &c.] the ironwork of doors, windows, a holdfast. *e*) [in seamen's lang.] Das — oder der Bügel von Eisen, hoop; die Banden im Bug [Bugbanden], breast-hooks or fore-hooks; die Banden or Bügel des Ankerstocks, the hoops of the anchor-stock. *f*) [among carpenters] a binding-piece, rail. *g*) [in anatomy, a strong compact substance, serving to bind one bone to another] ligament. Die Bänder der Hand, the ligaments of the hand. *h*) [in heraldry] bend. *i*) *pl.* [Bande] ligaments, bonds, chains, fetters, [and *fig.*] imprisonment, captivity. Einem Bande anlegen, to bind any one in chains; er liegt in Banden, he is fettered. *Fig.* [that which binds, restrains, confines or fetters] Hymen's Bande, Hymen's bands; die Bande der Ehe, conjugal ties, matrimonial bonds; die Bande der Finsterniß, the chains of darkness; die schändlichen Bande der Fleischeslust, the shameful ties of flesh; [cause of union, cement which unites, link of connection] die Bande der Zuneigung, Liebe, bonds of affection. 2) [in botany] a species of canary-grass [phalaris picta].

Band=achat, *m.* striped agate. —ader, *f.* [in ancient anatomy] ligaments. —ähnlich, *adj.* and *adv.* like a band or riband. —alabaster, *m.* striped alabaster. —blume, *f.* artificial flower. —bohrer, *m.* [am. carpenters] a brad-awl. —draht, *m.* a sort of wire. —eisen, *n.* hoop-iron. —fest, *adj.* and *adv.* bound, tied or fastened by a band. —frei, —enfrei, *adj.* and *adv.* 1) unfettered. 2) *Fig.* unrestrained, licentious. —fisch, *m.* 1) the ribbon-fish. 2) [a fish] the chaetodon. —förmig, *adj.* and *adv.* having the form of a riband. —gewerk, *n.* a manufacture of ribands. —gras, ribbon-grass. —haken, *m.* [among locksmiths] a hasp. —handel, *m.* riband-trade, mercery. —händler, *m.* one that deals in ribands, mercer. —handlung, *f.* a shop where ribands are sold, mercer's shop. —holz, *n.* wood for hoops. —jaspis, *m.* striped jasper. —kegel, *m.* V. —haken. —kette, *f.* timber-chain, brace. —kiesel, *m.* striped quarz. —kram, *m.* a shop where ribands are sold by retail. —krämer, *m.* he that sells ribands by retail. —laden, *m.* V. —handlung. —macher, *m.* a ribbon-maker, tape-maker. —marmor, *m.* striped marble. —masche, *f.* cockade. —messer, *n.* [among coopers] addize, adz. —motte, *f.* striped moth. —mühle, *f.* a ribbon-maker's loom. —nagel, *m.* [in carpentry] a wooden nail. —natter, *f.* a spe cies of the viper [coluber lemniscatus]. —nudel, *f.* a sort of vermicelli. —quaſt, *f.* a tassel made of ribands. —reif, *m.* [among coopers] a hoop. —roſe, *f.* a knot of ribands having the form of a rose, a rose used as an ornamental tie on a shoe &c. —ſchachtel, *f.* band-box. —ſchleiſe, *f.* a knot of ribands, a bow. —ſtein, *m.* condulated watered agate. —ſtreif, *m.* 1) [in heraldry, an ordinary, which contains a fourth part of the bend or half] a cost. Zwei —ſtreifen, cottises. 2) top-knot. —ſtück, *n.* [in carpentry] prick-post. —ſtuhl, *m.* V. —mühle. —treſſe, *f.* worsted lace. —tute, *f.* [a species of testaceous animals] the listed stamper. —verlängerung, [in surgery, an imperfect luxation] elongation. —waaren, *pl.* small-ware. —weber, *m.* ribbon-weaver. —weberei, *f.* V. —gewerk. —weide, *f.* a water-willow, osier. —werk, *n* all sorts of ribands. —weſen, *n.* [in anatomy] a connection of ligaments. —wirker, *m.* V. —weber. —wurm, *m.* tape-worm. —zwitter, *m.* a sort of tin-ore.

Bänder-blume, *f.* V. Bandblume. —jaspis, *m.* V. Bandjaspis. —lehre, *f.* [in medic.] syndesmology. —ſchuh, *m.* a shoe tied with a string or riband.

2. **Bánd**, *m.* [-es, *pl.* Bände] 1) the binding of a book. 2) a volume, book. Ein Werk in vier Bänden, a work in four volumes.

Bändereich, *adj.* and *adv.* [consisting of many volumes or books] voluminous. Der Verfaſſer eines bändereichen Werkes, a voluminous author.

***Bandáge**, *f.* [*pl.* -n] [a fillet, roller or swath, used in dressing and binding up wounds, ruptures &c.] a bandage. V. also Bruchband.

***Bandagíſt**, *m.* [-en, *pl.* -en] V. Bruchbandmacher.

1. **Bändchen**, **Bändel**, *n.* [-s, *pl.* -] a small band or riband.

2. **Bändchen**, *n.* [-s, *pl.* -] a small-sized volume. Das Werk erſcheint in vier —, the work will be published in four little volumes.

1. **Bánde**, *f.* [*pl.* -n] [allied to Wand, and the French *bande*] 1) the side, edge or border of a thing. Die platte —, [in gardening, in architect.] plat-band; die — eines Schiffes, the side of a ship; [a sea term] ein Schiff auf die — legen, to careen a ship. 2) the cushion of a billiard-table. Einen Ball dicht an die — legen, to give a close ball. 3) a long broad stripe.

2. **Bánde**, *f.* [*pl.* -n] [from binden] a company of persons, united in any common design [most[?] in contempt]. Eine — Räuber [more usual: eine Räuber—], a band, a gang of robbers; eine — Schauſpieler [more usual: eine Schauſpieler—], a company of strolling players; eine — Muſiker [more usual: eine Muſik—], a company, band of musicians.

***Bandelíer**, *n.* [-s, *pl.* -e] a shoulder-belt, bandoleers.

Bänden, *v. tr.* [in seamen's lang.] Ein Segel —, to line a sail at the edges [in order to strengthen it].

Bändern, *v. tr.* 1) to form into long and broad stripes. 2) to furnish with cottises.

Bändig, *adj.* and *adv.* striped.

Bändig, *adj.* and *adv.* [seldom used except in compound words, as: unbändig &c.] tameable, tame. — machen, V. Bändigen.

Bändigen, *v. tr.* to tame [wild beasts &c.]. Wilde Pferde —, to tame wild horses; ein Pferd —, to break a horse. *Fig.* Es iſt nichts Leichtes ihn zu —, it is not easy to check him; bändiget euren Zorn, restrain your anger. Das Bändigen, taming.

Bändiger, *m.* [-s, *pl.* -] -inn, *f.* he or she that tames or subdues, tamer.

***Bandít**, *m.* [-en, *pl.* -en] a bandit, a bravo, an assassin. Banditen, bandits, banditti.

Bánge, *adj.* and *adv.* [allied to the Eng. *bang* = ſchlagen, Goth. *banc, bang* = blow, wound] 1) impressed with fear or apprehension, afraid. Ich habe — vor dem Tode, I am afraid of death; Einen or Einem — machen, to make any one afraid; *es war ihm angſt und —, he was in great trepidation; es war uns — vor ſchlimmen Folgen, we were apprehensive of fatal consequences; es wird uns — bei der nahenden Gefahr, we are alarmed at the approach of danger; laß dir nicht — ſeyn vor der Zukunft, be not solicitous for the future; uns iſt —, aber wir verzagen nicht; [2. Cor. IV.] we are perplexed, but not in despair. 2) [full of solicitude, unquiet] anxious. — Sorgen, Gedanken, anxious cares, thoughts; ich ſtehe hier in —r Erwartung, I stand here in anxious expectation, in great suspense.

Bängel, *m.* V. Bengel.

Bängeln, *v. tr.* V. Bengeln.

Bángen, [V. Bange] I. *v. intr.* and *v. imp.* to be afraid or impressed with fear or apprehension. Mir bangt vor der Zukunft, I am solicitous for the future. II. *v. r.* ſich —, to be afraid of or to long after any thing. III. *v. tr.* to impress with fear or apprehension. *Poet.* Ein —der Traum, a tormenting dream.

Bangenkraut, *n.* V. Schierling.

Bángigkeit, *f.* fear, apprehension, anxiousness, anxiety.

Bänglich, *adj.* and *adv.* being a little afraid, uneasy.

Bángmuth, *m.* [-es] V. [the more usual word] Bangigkeit.

Bángſam, *adj.* and *adv.* V. [the more usual word] Bange.

Baníer, *n.* V. Panier.

Bánjer, *n.* [in seamen's language] a half-deck.

Bánk, *f.* [*pl.* Bänke, and in the sense of a bank for money transactions, die Banken] [probably allied to the L. *pango*, and the Gr. πήγνυμι] 1) [an elevation or rising ground in the sea] a bank. Ein Meer voll von Bänken, a sea full of flats, shoals, shelves or shallows; von einer — abhalten, [in seamen's lang.] to give a shoal or bank a good berth; *fig.* die — am Horizonte, [in seamen's lang.] a cloudy horizon. 2) [in fortification, a little raised way, or foot-bank running along the inside of a parapet] banquette. Ueber — ſchießen, to fire en barbe or à barbette. 3) a layer, a stratum, a bed. 4) [a long seat, usually of board or plank] a bench. Die — ohne Lehne, a form; die Bänke in Schulen, Kirchen, the benches in schools, church benches; die Bänke [Sitzbänke] in einem Boote oder einer Schaluppe, the benches or seats in the stern-sheets of a boat. *Fig.* * Etwas auf die lange — ſchieben, to delay, to put off something; *durch die —, in the gross, upon an average; *etwas durch die — kaufen, to buy any thing by the lump, without distinction, one with another; *ſie taugen durch die — nichts, the whole lot are not worth any thing, they are all bad together. *Prov.* Man liegt ſanfter auf der — als auf einem Purpurbette, lowly sit, richly warm. *Fig. a)* formerly at the diets of the empire of Germany a number of persons sitting on the same bench and forming as it were a whole. Die weltliche —, the secular bench [princes, electors &c.]; die geiſtliche —, the spiritual bench [ecclesiastical dignitaries]. *b)* [in universities] Die — der Rechtsgelehrten, der Theologen &c., the faculty of law, of divinity &c. 5) [among workmen] a working-table or a table used for exposing commodities to sale, as: die Dreh—, a turner's lathe; die Fleiſch—, the shambles. † *Fig.* Einen zur — [Fleiſchbank] hauen, to backbite any one. 6) the table of a banker in gaming-houses. — halten, to keep bank. 7) a collection or stock of money deposited by a number of persons for a particular use; the place where a collection of money is deposited; a common repository of the money of individuals or of companies, a bank; also a house used for a bank. Die engliſche —, the bank of England. 8) [in papermills] a plank. 9) [in heraldry] label.

Bank-antheilsſchein, *m.* [die Bankaktie] bank-stock. —bein, *n.* the leg of a bench. —bohrer, *m.* V. Beinbohrer. —bruch, *m.* bankruptcy. —brüchig, *adj.* and *adv.* bankrupt. Er iſt —brüchig geworden, he became insolvent or bankrupt, he ran bankrupt, he failed; der —brüchige, a bankrupt. —conto, *m.* bank-account. —eiſen, *n.* an iron-band. —geld, *n.* bank-money. —gericht, a kind of court of commerce. —haken, *m.* [among joiners] a hold-fast. —halter, *m.* [Banquier, at some games of hazard] a banker. —hammer, *m.* V. Niethammer. —herr, *m.* [Banquier, one who keeps a bank] a banker. —hobel, *m.* a bench-plane. —horn, *n.* [among locksmiths] a rising anvil. —kiſſen, *n.* a bolster for a bench. —lehne, *f.* the back of a bench or form. —macher, *m.* V. —halter. —meißel, *m.* [am. locksmiths] hewing-chisel. —meiſter, *m.* a master tradesman [especially of the bakers]. —meſſer, *n.* a cleaver, a cleaving-knife. —note, *f.* V. —zettel. —rechnung, *f.* V. —conto. —ſchein, *m.* bank-stock. —ſchlachten, *n.* the selling of meat in public stalls. —ſchneider, *m.* whale-cutter. —ſchreiber, *m.* the clerk of a bank. —weſen, *n.* all things that concern banking business. —zahlung, *f.* a payment made by the means of a bank. —zettel, *m.* bankbill, banknote. —zins, *m.* stallage.

Bänkchen, **Bänklein**, *n.* [-s, *pl.* -] a small bench.

Bänkel-geſang, *m.* the singing of ballads. —ſänger, *m.* 1) [Bänkelreiter] ballad-singer. *Fig.* 2) [in contempt] a bad poet. —ſängerei, *f.* ballad-singing.

***Bankerótt**, *m.* [-es, *pl.* -e] and *adj.* V. Bankbruch and Bankbrüchig.

***Bankerottírer**, *m.* [-s, *pl.* -] a bankrupt. Ein falſcher —, a fraudulent bankrupt.

† **Bánkert**, *m.* [-s, *pl.* -e] [Bank is here probably opposed to Ehebette = marriage-bed] a bastard.

***Bankétt**, *n.* [-s, *pl.* -e] a banquet.

Bánn, *m.* [-es] [from binden] 1) [interdiction or proscription] ban; [expulsion from the communion of a church] excommunication. In den — thun, to put under the ban, to excommunicate, to anathematize. 2) [formerly in law] *a)* a judicial writ. *b)* a citation, a summons. *c)* a mulct. 3) jurisdiction, territory. 4) [formerly] a publication, proclamation.

Bann-brief, *m.* an edict of proscription, ban. —fluch, *m.* excommunication with curses, anathema. —forſt, *m.* [in law] a forest fenced in for game. —grenze, *f.* the bounds of a manorial territory. V. —meile. —gut, *n.* contraband goods. —herr, *m.* V. Gerichtsherr. —kelter, *f.* common winepress [V. —recht]. —leute, *pl.* people under a certain jurisdiction. —ling, *m.* a proscript. —meile, *f.* precinct, boundary. —mühle, *f.* common mill. [V. —recht.] —ofen, *m.* common oven. [V. —recht.] —ort, *m.* retreat. —recht, *n.* the privilege of a manor, according to which all the vassals belonging to it are obliged to make exclusive use of the mill, the winepress, the oven &c. —spruch, *m.* 1) a sentence of proscription. 2) exorcism. —stein, *m.* a landmark. —strahl, *m.* anathema. Den — strahl gegen Einen schleudern, to anathematise any one. —vogt, —wart, *m.* [Flurschütz] a ranger of the fields. —waare, *f.* V. —gut. —wasser, *n.* a forbidden river, water in which it is not permitted to fish &c. —wort, *n.* an exorcising word.

Bánnen, *v. tr.* 1) to confine, to fix in a certain place. 2) to lay [a spirit], to exorcise. Den Teufel in einen Weiberrock —, to lay the devil in a petticoat. 3) formerly for Verbannen.

1. **Bánner**, *m.* [-s, *pl.* -] an exorciser, a conjurer.

2. **Bánner**, *n.* [or Panier] [-s, *pl.* -] [allied either to Fahne and the Lat. *pannus* = Stück Tuch or to binden] [a military ensign] a banner.

Banner=herr, *m.* banneret. —schild, *m.* [in heraldry] a square escutcheon.

* **Banquét**, V. Bankett.

* **Banquettíren**, *v. intr.* to banquet, to feast.

‖ **Bánse, Bánze, Pánse**, *f.* [*pl.* -n], **Bánsen, Pánzen**, *m.* [-s, *pl.* -] [from the old Ban, Pen = Höhe] 1) [in husbandry] the place in the barn in which the sheaves are laid up. 2) a large square basket.

Bánsen, Pánsen, Bánzen, *m.* [-s, *pl.* -] [allied to Wanst] 1) [the first stomach in ruminating quadrupeds] the paunch. 2) a paunch, a belly.

Banz=birne, *f.* a sort of large pears.

Bár, a termination of many nouns, which denotes quality or property of any thing, as: eßbar, eatable, ausführbar, performable &c.

Bār, *adj.* and *adv.* [allied to the Lat. *par*-o, *par*-io, *par*-eo] 1) bare, naked, without covering. 2) *Fig.* *a*) pure. *b*) unmixed. 3) being at hand, ready. Bares Geld, ready money; hundert Thaler —, hundred dollars in cash; — bezahlen, to pay ready money. *Prov.* — Geld lacht, bares Geld ist die Losung, money commands all.

Bar=beinig, *adj.* and *adv.* bare-legged. — —eis, *n.* ice not covered with snow. —frost, *m.* a black frost. —fuß, *adj.* and *adv.* barefoot, bare-footed. —fuß gehen, to walk barefoot. —füßer, —füßermönch, *m.* a Franciscan friar, cordelier. —füßig, *adj.* and *adv.* barefoot. —füßig tanzen, to dance barefoot. —haupt, —häuptig, —kopf, —köpfig, *adj.* and *adv.* bare-headed. —schenkelig, *adj.* and *adv.* bare-

Aufbinden; einen —en ab= or losbinden, to pay off debts. 2) *Fig.* [in astronomy, the name of two constellations in the northern hemisphere] the Greater Bear or Charles's wain, and the Lesser Bear.

Bär=beißig, *adj.* and *adv.* quarrelsome. —bill, *m.* V. —fenchel. —enbeißer, *m.* a dog used for bear-baiting, a bulldog. —endecke, *f.* a bear's skin prepared for use, a bear's skin cover or covering. —endill, *m.* V. —fenchel. —enfang, *m.* 1) bear-catching. 2) a place where bears are fed. —enfell, *n.* bear's skin. —enfenchel, *m.* V. —fenchel. —enfett, *n.* bear's grease. —enführer, *m* 1) a bear-leader. 2) *Fig.* an idle fellow. —enfuß, *m.* 1) the foot of a bear. 2) [a plant] bear's foot, prickly leaved arctopus. —enhaft, *adj.* and *adv.* like a bear. —enhatz, *f.* V. —enhetze. —enhaut, *f.* a bear's skin. †*Fig.* Auf der (faulen) —enhaut liegen, to be idle. *Prov.* Verkaufe nicht eher die —enhaut, als bis der Bär gestochen ist, don't sell the bear's skin before you have caught the bear; never reckon your chickens before they are hatched. —enhäuter, *m.* 1) an idle fellow, a sluggard. 2) a coward, dastard, rogue, lubber, knave. —enhäuterei, *f.* 1) idleness, laziness. 2) cowardice, knavery. —enhäuterisch, I. *adj.* 1) idle, lazy. 2) cowardly, knavish. II. *adv.* 1) idly. 2) cowardly, knavishly. —enhetze, *f.* a bear-baiting. —enhüter, *m.* 1) bear-herd. 2) [a northern constellation] Bootes. —enjagd, *f.* bear-hunting. —enklau, *f.* [the name of several plants] 1) brank ursine, bear's breech. 2) common cow-parsnip. 3) set-wort. —enklaublatt, *n.* 1) the leaf of the brank ursine. 2) *Fig.* [in architecture, an ornament in the capital of a Corinthian pillar] acanthus. —enklaudistel, *f.* [a plant] prickliest thistle. —enklee, *m.* V. Steinklee. —enkoth, *m.* 1) bear's dung. 2) [in metallurgy] the scum which rises at the top of melted silver. —enkraut, *n.* [a plant] lady's-foxglove. —enkrebs, *m.* mother-lobster [cancer arctos]. —enmotte, *f.* bear-fly. —enmütze, V. —mütze. —enohr, *n.* [a genus of plants] arctotis. —enöhrlein, *n.* [a plant] auricula or bear's ear. —enpfeife, *f.* [in organs] drone. —enraupe, *f.* bear-worm. —enschmalz, *n.* V. —enfett. —entanz, *m.* dancing of a bear. —entappe, *f.* 1) the trace or track of a bear. 2) *Fig.* [a plant] V. —lapp. —entatze, *f.* 1) a bear's paw. 2) *Fig.* *a*) a large hand. *b*) [a plant] V. —enklau. —traube, *f.* the trailing arbutus or bear-berry, bear-whortleberry. —enwärter, *m.* the keeper of the bears, bear-ward. —enzwinger, *m.* bear-garden. —fenchel, *m.* [a plant] maldmony or bear's-wort, spignel, Athamanta meum. —lapp, —lappen, *m.* [a plant] earth-moss. —latsche, *f.* cow-hair slipper. —maus, *f.* V. Murmelthier. —muff, *m.*, —muffe, *f.* bear's-skin muff. —mütze, *f.* the high cap of a grenadier, bear-skin cap. —pfeife, *f.* V. —enpfeife. —raupe, *f.* V. —enraupe. —sanikel, *m.* V. —enöhrlein. Der italienische —sanikel, bear's wort. —winde, *f.* [a plant] bear-bind. —winkel, *m.* [a plant] small periwinkle. —wolf, *m.* V. Wehrwolf. —wurz, *f.* [the name of several plants] 1) bear's-wort. 2) mew. 3) meadow sulphur wort or saxifrage. 4) common cow or rutting parsnip. 5) periwinkle. —zeit, *f.* the coupling time of bears.

2. **Bär**, *m.* [-es, *pl.* -e] [probably from the old bären = schlagen] a rammer, a beetle.

3. **Bär**, *m.* [-es, *pl.* -e] [probably to derive from Wehr] [in fortification, a massive perpendicular pile of masonry, whose length is equal to the breadth of the ditch inundation, or any part of a fortification where the water can not be kept in by any other means] batardeau.

* **Barácke**, *f.* [*pl.* -n] a hut for soldiers, a barrack. V. also Feldhütte, Soldatenhütte; *it.* [in contempt] a miserable cot, V. also Knallhütte, a bad lodging.

Baránke, *f.* [*pl.* -n] 1) the skin of a new born lamb. 2) the white and black slink lamb's skin from the Crimea.

* **Barattíren**, *v. tr.* [in commerce] to barter.

* **Barátto**, *m.* [in commerce] barter.

* 1. **Bárbar, Bárber** and [the most usual word] **Bérber**, *m.* [-s, *pl.* -n] 1) an inhabitant of Barbary. 2) a Barbary horse, a barb.

Barbar=falk, *m.* Tunisian falcon.

* 2. **Barbār**, *m.* [-en, *pl.* -en] a barbarian. 1) [among the ancient Greeks and Romans = a foreigner]. 2) [a man in his rude, savage state] a savage. 3) [a cruel, savage, brutal man].

Bárbara, [-s or -ens] [a name of women] Barbara, Bab.

1. **Barbareí** or **Bérbereí**, *f.* Barbary [in northern Africa].

2. **Barbareí**, *f.* 1) any country inhabited by Barbarians. 2) the manners of a barbarian, barbarity, savageness. 3) [*pl.* -en] a barbarous deed.

Barbarésken, *pl.* 1) the pirate-states on the northern coast of Africa, Alger, Tunis, Tripoli and Marocco. 2) the inhabitants of these states, Barbaresques.

Barbārisch, I. *adj.* 1) [contrary to the pure idioms of a particular language] barbaric, barbarous. Das sind —e Ausdrücke, these are barbarous terms or expressions. 2) barbarian, cruel, inhuman. II. *adv.* barbarously. *a*) [contrary to the rules of speech]. *b*) [in a savage, cruel, ferocious or inhuman manner] barbarously, savagely, inhumanly. *Er ist — behandelt worden, he has been most cruelly treated.

Barbarísm, [-s, *pl.* -en] *m.* [an offence against purity of style or language] barbarism.

Bárbarthum, *n.* [-es] V. 2. Barbarei 2).

Bárbe, Bärbchen, V. Barbara.

Bárbe, *f.* [*pl.* -n] [a fish] barb.

Bárbenkraut, *n.* [-es, *pl.* -kräuter] [a plant] winter hedge-mustard.

Bárber, *m.* V. Barbar, 1.

Barbíer, *m.* [-s, *pl.* -e] a barber, shaver, [sometimes] surgeon [of a lower sort or order].

Barbier=becken, *n.* shaving-basin. —beutel, *m.* V. —sack. —gesell, *m.* a barber's-man. —messer, *n.* razor. —riemen, *m.* razor-strap. —sack, *m.* razor-pouch. —schere, *f.* barber's scissors. —stube, *f.* a barber's shop. —zeug, *n.* shaving-instrument, razor-case.

Barbíeren, *v. tr.* [to pare off with a razor] to shave. Sich — lassen, to get one's self shaved. †*Fig* Einen —, to cheat any one in bartering; Einen über den Löffel —, to cheat, to humbug any one.

Bárchent, *m.* [-s, *pl.* -e] [perhaps from Ba = Streif] fustian. Feiner (geköperter) —, dimity.

Barchent=stuhl, *m.* a fustian-weaver's loom. —weber, *m.* fustian-weaver.

Bárchenten, *adj.* and. *adv.* made of fustian, fustian.

Bárde, *m.* [-n, *pl.* -n] [allied to *barritus*, from the old baren = tönen] 1) [a poet and singer among the ancient Celts] bard. 2) [in modern usage especially of epic poets] a poet, bard. Klopstock, der deutsche —, Klopstock, the German bard..

Barden=gesang, *m.* a bardish song. —hain, *m.* [modern word] *fig.* a collection of the choicest poems of the best poets. —thum, *n.* bardism. —wurzel, V. Lendenkraut.

1. **Bāre**, *f.* [*pl.* -n] [instead of Barte] a prepared whalebone.

2. **Bāre**, *f.* [*pl.* -n] [from bar, bären = emporheben] [in seamen's language] a wave, a sea.

Bāren, *v. intr.* [among hunters] to be in heat [said of a she-bear].

Barét, Barétt, *n.* [-s, *pl.* -e] bonnet, cap.

Barett=kram, *m.* hosiery. —krämer, *m.* haberdasher.

Bárg, Bórg, *m.* [-es, *pl.* Bärge, Börge] [allied to *porcus*] [in husbandry a male hog castrated] a barrow.

Bārinn, *f.* V. Bär.

Báriton, *n.* [-s, *pl.* -e] [in music] counter-tenor.

Barkáſſe, *f.* [*pl.* -n] [in seamen's language] a long boat.

Bárke, *f.* [*pl.* -n] [probably from the old bären = tragen] a bark. Eine kleinere —, a barge, a lighter.

Bärme, *f.* [from the old bären = emporheben] barm, yest.

Barmhèrzig, *adj.* and *adv.* [instead of be-armherzig; the Goth. word arman signifies sich erbarmen] 1) merciful, compassionate. Seyd — gegen mich, have pity upon me; die —en Brüder, [in the Romish church] charity-friars. 2) [moving compassion] pitiful.

Barmhèrzigkeit, *f.* mercy, compassion, charity. — zeigen, ausüben, to show mercy, to take compassion.

Bärmutter, [Gebärmutter] *f.* [from the unusual bären = tragen] the womb, matrice, matrix.

Bärmutter-entzündung, *f.* an inflammation of the womb. —krebs [= Mutterkrebs], *m.* a cancer of the womb. —öffnung, *f.* [in surgery] the Cesarean section, hysterotomy.

‖ **Bárn**, *m.* [-s, *pl.* -e] [probably from Barre, allied to wahren] 1) a crib, manger. 2) V. Banse 1. 3) [Bärn, Beeren] a kind of fishing-net.

Barn-beißer, *m.* V. Krippenbeißer. —stein, *m.* V. Backstein.

Bárnabas, [a name of man] Barnaby.

Barnabiten, *pl.* [members of a religious order] Barnabites.

* **Baròk**, *adj.* and *adv.* baroque.

* **Baròkperlen**, *pl.* ragged pearls.

* **Barométer**, *n.* [-s, *pl.* -] barometer.

Barometer-röhre, *f.* barometer tube. —stand, *m.* the height of the barometer.

* **Barométrisch**, *adj.* and *adv.* barometrical. —e Versuche, barometrical experiments.

* **Barōn**, *m.* [-s, *pl.* -e] a baron.

* **Baronèsse**, *f.* [*pl.* -n] [the wife or unmarried daughter of a baron] a baroness.

Barōnchen, *n.* [-s, *pl.* -] [modern word, only used in a jocose way] a little baron.

* **Baronie**, **Baronei**, *f.* [*pl.* -n] barony.

* **Baronisiren**, *v. tr.* [frequently jocose or in contempt] to dub [any one] a baron.

Bárre, *f.* [*pl.* -n] **Bären**, *m.* [-s, *pl.* -] probably from baren or barren = heben, therefore something raised or extended; allied to Sparren] 1) [formerly a piece of wood, iron or other solid matter, long in proportion to its diameter] a bar. 2) [an ingot, lump or wedge, from the mines, run in a mould, and unwrought] a bar [of gold, silver]. 3) the pole of a harpsichord. 4) [in seamen's lang.] *a*) V. Ruderbock. *b*) a rock in the sea, or a bank of sand, gravel or earth, forming a shoal at the mouth of a river or harbour, a bar.

* **Barrière**, *f.* [*pl.* -n] barrier.

Bárs, **Bársch**, *m.* [-es, *pl.* -en] V. Börs.

Bársch, *adj.* and *adv.* [Fr. *brusque*, Eng. *brisk*; in Sw. *barsk* signifies herb] 1) rough to the taste, rough to the ear, harsh. Eine —e Stimme, a harsh voice. 2) rough, rude, harsh. — thun, to look sullen.

Barschaft, *f.* [*pl.* -en] ready money.

Bárt, *m.* [-es, *pl.* Bärte] [allied to *barba*, *barbe* &c. and probably from bären = hervorbringen; therefore originally = something shooting forth] 1) [in several different things] *a*) [in husbandry, the awn or sharp prickles on the ears of corn] beard. *b*) [in natural history] α) the barb [of some species of fish]. β) the wattle of a cock, the barbs. γ) [the threads or hairs of an oyster] beard. *c*) [in botany the down, or pubes, covering the surface of some plants] barb. *d*) [among hunters] the snout of a wild boar. *Fig. a*) [the rays of a comet] the beard [of a comet]. *b*) [among locksmiths] key-bit. *c*) [in seamen's lang.] Der — am Schiff, foul ship. 2) [the hair that grows on the chin, lips and adjacent parts of the face] the beard. Den — scheren, to cut the beard, to shave; sich den — abnehmen lassen, to get one's self shaved. *Prov.* Ein bleicher Mann hat Weiberart, hüte dich vor einem rothen —, a red beard and a black head, catch him with a good trick and take him dead. **Fig.* Etwas in den — murmeln, to mutter; es in seinen — hinein lügen, to lie impudently; Einem etwas in den — sagen, or in den — werfen, to tell any thing to any one's face; frei vom —e, with frankness, ingenuously; um [über] des Kaisers — streiten, to contend for things of no concern to us, to dispute about trifles; Einem einen — machen, [among hunters] to give a person who has missed the game mustachios with gunpowder.

Bart-becken, *n.* shaving basin. —beißer, —beißler, *m.* [a fish] the bearded loche. —faden, *m.* the barb [of some species of fish]. —fisch, *m.* 1) the barbel. 2) a species of the sucker. —fliege, *f.* the beard-fly [musca mystacea]. —geier, V. Lämmergeier. —gerste, *f.* spring-barley. —gras, *n.* the beard grass, andropogon. —grundel, V. Bachkresse and Grundling. —haar, *n.* the hair of the beard. —hafer, *m.* bearded wild oats or haver. —hund, *m.* barbet. —karpfen, *m.* any carp with a barb. —klappe, *f.* [among locksmiths] pincers, nippers. —kratzer, *m.* [jocosely and in contempt] a barber. —läppchen, *n.* gill. —los, *adj.* and *adv.* beardless. —männchen, *n.* 1) the bearded titmouse. 2) the bearded eel. 3) the waved whelk. —messer, *n.* razor. —moos, *n.* the beard moss, phascum, earthmoss. —nelke, *f.* sweet-william, sweet-john. —nuß, *f.* filbert. —putzer, *m.* [mostly jocose or in contempt] shaver, barber. —salbe, *f.* beard-salve. —schwamm, *m.* V. Stachelschwamm. —seife, *f.* shaving-soap. —stern, *m.* a comet. —vogel, *m.* wattle-bird. —zange, *f.* nippers.

1\. **Bárte**, *f.* [*pl.* -n] unprepared whalebone.

2\. **Bárte**, *f.* [*pl.* -n] a broad hatchet.

Bärteln, *v. tr.* Das Tuch —, [among clothiers] to give the first shearing to the cloth.

Bärteltuch, *n.* [among clothiers] cloth of the first shearing.

† **Bárthel**, [a name of men] Bartholomew. *Prov.* Er weiß, wo — Most holt, he knows how to shift for himself, he is a cunning fellow, a sly blade.

Bärtig, *adj.* and *adv.* bearded. *a*) [having a beard as a man]. *b*) [in botany, having parallel hairs or tufts].

‖ **Barútsche**, *f.* [*pl.* -n] a barouche.

Barýt, *m.* baryte. Kohlensaurer —, carbonade of Baryte, rhomboidal Baryt, aerated baryte; schwefelsaurer —, ponderous spar, barytite, heavy spar, sulphate of baryte, barolite; splitteriger — [Barytstein], compact heavy spar or baroselenite, cawk; streifiger —, radiated heavy spar, Bolognese spar, Bolognian stone; körniger —, granular heavy spar.

Baryt-erde, *f.* heavy spar-earth, earthy baroselenite. —spath, *m.* lamellar heavy spar, foliated baroselenite. —stein, *m.* V. Baryt.

* **Basált**, *m.* [-es, *pl.* -e] basalt. Verschluckter —, scorious basalt; von —, basaltic; —förmig, basaltiform.

Basalt-säule, *f.* a column of basalt, basaltine. —tuf, *m.* basaltic tuff.

* **Basaltin**, *m.* [-s, *pl.* -e] [gemeiner Augit] basaltic hornblend, basaltine.

Bäse, *f.* [*pl.* -n] [appears to be allied to the D. Baas = Herr] aunt; cousin; any distant female relation.

Bäsel, [-s] Basil, Basle [a canton and city in Switzerland].

Baselbeere, *f.* V. Berberisbeere.

Bäseler, **Bäsler**, *m.* [-s, *pl.* -] **Bäselerinn**, **Bäslerinn**, *f.* an inhabitant of Basle.

Baselkraut, *n.* climbing night-shade [Basella L.].

* **Basilie**, *f.* [*pl.* -n] **Basilienkraut**, *n.* basil.

* **Basilisk**, *m.* [-en, *pl.* -en] basilisk, cockatrice.

Basilius, [a name of men] Basil.

* **Básin**, *m.* [in commerce] dimity.

* **Bāsis**, *f.* [*pl.* Basen] base; [in architecture] basement, plinth.

Báske, *m.* [-n, *pl.* -n] **Báskinn**, *f.* a Basque. Die Basken, the Basques.

Bäsler, *m.* —inn, *f.* V. Baseler, Baselerinn.

Bäslerisch, *adj.* and *adv.* coming from or belonging to Basle.

* **Básrelief**, *n.* [-s, *pl.* -e] base-relief.

‡ **Báß**, *adv.* [the positive of besser, allied to the provincial batten = to be of use, to serve] 1) well, very, greatly. Die Schwänke seines Narren ergötzten ihn —, he was greatly amused by the jests of his fool. 2) [sometimes for] more.

Báß, *m.* [-sses, *pl.* Bässe] [from the Ital. *basso*] [in music] the bass, the base. Den — spielen oder singen, to play or sing the bass.

Baß-bläser, *m.* bassoonist. —flöte, *f.* courtal. —geige, *f.* base-viol, bass-viol. V. also Contrabaß. Die große —geige, double-bass; die kleine —, violoncello. V. 2 Bassettchen and Kniegeige. †*Prov.* Den Himmel für eine —geige ansehen, to take an owl for an ivy-bush. —pfeife, *f.* bassoon. —posaune, *f.* sackbut. —saite, *f.* base-string. —sänger, *m.* V. Bassist. —schlüssel, *m.* [in music] bass-clef or F cliff. —spieler, *m.* a person playing the base-voice. —stimme, *f.* base-voice.

Bássa, *m.* [-s, in rhyme sometimes Bassen, *pl.* Bassen] bashaw, bassa.

Bassèt, *n.* [-s] basset [a game at cards].

1\. **Bassèttchen**, *n.* [-s, *pl.* -] a beagle.

2\. **Bassèttchen**, *n.* [-s, *pl.* -] V. Baßgeige, [kleine].

* **Bássin**, *n.* [- or -s, *pl.* -s] any reservoir of water, a basin.

Bassist, *m.* [-s or -en, *pl.* -en] a person singing in base-voice, a base.

Bassōn, *m.* [-s, *pl.* -e] bassoon. V. also Fagott.

Bást, *m.* [with some authors] *n.* [-es] [probably from the old fasen = wachsen, and allied to Faser] 1) the inner bark of a tree [liber]. 2) the exterior covering of a plant. 3) [among hunters] the rub. 4) any thing made of the inner bark of trees, or the inner bark made into ropes and mats, bast. Syn. Bast, Borke, Rinde. Rinde signifies the entire exterior covering of a tree, the rind; Borke is the outer bark of large trees, the cortex; Bast signifies only the inner bark or liber, which lies next the wood.

Bast-hanf, *m.* undressed, rough hemp. —hut, *m.* ship-hat, bast-hat, [improperly and incorrectly] Leghorn straw-bonnet. —matte, *f.* bast cover. —schuh, *m.* bast-shoe. —seil, *n.* —strick, *m* bast-rope. —ulme [—ilme], *f.* the soft leaved elm.

* **Básta!** *interj.* enough, basta, stop, avast!

Bástard and **Bastárd**, *m.* [-s, *pl.* -e] bastard. Used frequently in composition and denoting any thing not genuine, of inferior quality, spurious, bastard; especially used of animals or plants, as: —indigo, *m.* amorpha. —wolle, *f.* the wool of sheep of a mixed breed.

* **Báste**, *f.* basto, the ace of clubs at quadrille &c.

* **Bastéi**, *f.* * **Bastion**, *f.* [*pl.* -en] a bastion [formerly called a bulwark].

Básten, *adj.* and *adv.* made of bast.

Básterform, *f.* [*pl.* -en] [in sugarhouses] bastard mould.

* **Bataille**, *f.* [*pl.* -n] battle.

* **Bataillón**, *n.* [-s, *pl.* -e] a battalion.

* **Batáte**, *f.* [*pl.* -n] Spanish potatoe or tuberous-rooted bindweed.

* **Bāthengel**, *m.* [-s, *pl.* -] germander or English treacle [a plant].

Bāthorden, *m.* V. Badorden.

Bāting, *m.* [-s, *pl.* -e] [in seamen's lang.] a frame of two strong pieces of timber on which the cable is fastened, bitts. Die große —, the bitts or main bitts; die kleine —, topsail-sheet bitts, the paul-bitts and the like.

Bātings-balken, *pl.* the cross-piece of the bitts. —bolzen, *pl.* long iron bolts thrust into holes in the bitts [to keep the cable from starting off]. —shölzer, *pl.* the bitts. —sschlag, *m.* a bitter [of the cable]. —sspenen, *pl.* bitt-pins. —sspuhr, *f.* step of the bitt-pins.

* **Batíst**, *m.* [-s, *pl.* -e] [a species of fine white linen] cambric. Roher —, cambric made with half bleached flax.

Batist-blumen, *pl.* cambric flowers. —weber, *m.* cambric weaver.

* **Batterie**, *f.* [*pl.* -n] a battery. *a*) *α*) [in the military art] Eine — errichten, to erect a battery. *β*) a certain nnmber of guns. Eine Fuß—, a brigade of foot artillery; eine reitende —, a troop of horse artillery. *b*) [in seamen's lang., the whole range of cannon placed on both sides of any one deck in a vessel of war] a battery. Die unterste oder erste —, the lower gun deck or the first battery; die obere —, the upper battery; eine halbe —, tier; das Schiff hat eine zu niedrige —, the ship carries her ports too near the surface of the water. *c*) [in electrical apparatus and experiments] Eine elektrische —, an electrical battery.

Batterie-seite, *f.* [in seamen's language] broadside. —steine, *pl.* striking flints.

Bátzen, *m.* [seems to be the same word as *piece* and to come from the old batten = schlagen] [-s, *pl.* -] 1) [an imaginary money of Germany worth four kreutzers, about five farthings] a bat or batz. Das —stück, a coin in Switzerland, worth a Swiss batz. †2) *Fig.* money. Er hat —, he is rich, he has the rhino; ich gebe keinen — dafür, I would not give a farthing for it. ‖3) a coin used as an ornament for the neck of females. ‖4) a patch, botch.

‖ **Bátzen**, *v. tr.* [to mend in a clumsy manner] to botch [a garment].

Bätzner, *m.* [-s, *pl.* -] [only used in composition, as] Der Drei—, a coin of the value of three batz or an English groat; [in the same way or proportion] ein Sechs—, Zehn— &c.

Baú, *m.* [-es, *pl.* -e, commonly die Bauten] 1) the act of building, of cultivating the ground or of working a mine. Der — einer Kirche, eines Hauses, the erection of a church, of a house; der — einer Brücke, the constuction of a bridge; der — des Feldes, Feld—, the cultivation of the ground, agriculture; der — eines Gartens, Garten—, the cultivation of a garden, horticulture; der Berg—, mining, the working of a mine; der Seiden—, the cultivation of silk. 2) [the manner in which the parts of a thing are united or in which a body is formed] structure, fabric, conformation, build. Der — einer Uhr, the mechanism of a watch; der — eines Schiffes, the construction of a vessel; der — des Weltalls, the fabric of the universe; der — der Organe, the conformation of the organs. *Fig.* Der — einer Rede, eines Verses, the structure of a discourse, of a verse. 3) [the thing built or constructed] building, edifice, fabric, structure. Der — [die Höhle] des Dachses, Dachs—, the hole or cover of the badger; der — eines Fuchses, Fuchs—, the earth or hole of a fox; der — eines Kaninchens, Kaninchen—, the burrow of a rabbit. 4) the punishment of working at fortifications, or public buildings. Auf den — [Festungsbau] kommen, to be condemned to work at such fortifications or public works.

Bau-amt, *n.* board of works. —anschlag, *m.* builders' estimate. —arbeit, *f.* building-work. —art, *f.* 1) structure, form, make. 2) mode or style of building, architecture. Die Gothische —art, the Gothic style; die Englische —art, [said of ships], English build; nach englischer —art, English built. —aufseher, *m.* 1) a superintendent of any building. 2) a surveyor or superintendent of the public works. —bar, *adj.* and *adv.* 1) cultivable, arable. 2) that may be built, erected, erigible. —bedarf, *m.* building-materials. —begnadigung, *f.* 1) building-privileges. 2) immunities granted to those who are building. —collegium, *n.* V. —rath, 1. —dienst, *m.* service imposed upon vassals and subjects in assisting at buildings. —fähig, *adj.* and *adv.* fit for plowing and tillage, arable. —feld, *n.* a field in cultivation. —freiheit, *f.* the permission for building. —frohne, *f.* V. —dienst. —gefangene, *m.* a delinquent condemned to work at fortifications &c. —geist, *m.* spirit of building. —geld, *n.* money destined for building. —geräthe, *n.* tools for building. —gericht, *n.* V. —amt. —gerüst, *n.* scaffolding, scaffold. —gewerk, —handwerk, *n.* a trade employed in erecting any building [carpentry, masonry &c.]. —herr, *m.* 1) the owner of a building to be constructed. 2) [in towns or cities] he that superintends public edifices, bridges &c., superintendent of the public works. —hof, *m.* timber-yard. —holz, *n.* timber; *it.* lumber. —kosten, *pl.* expenses of building. —kunst, *f.* 1) [the art of building] architecture. 2) [the science of building] architectonics. —künstig, *adj.* and *adv.* 1) architectural. 2) architectonic. —künstler, *m.* an architect. —land, *n.* arable land. —leute, *pl.* workmen employed in building. —lust, *f.* fondness for building. —lustig, *adj.* and *adv.* fond of building. —materialien, *pl.* V. —bedarf. —meister, *m.* an architect. *—narr, *m.* a person being excessively fond of building. —ordnung, *f.* ordinances concerning building. —rath, *m.* 1) a board of commissioners for public buildings. 2) *a*) a member of such a board. *b*) a title sometimes conferred on architects and engineers. —riß, *m.* the plan for a building. —sache, *f.* a thing belonging to building. —sand, *m.* sand used in building. —schreiber, *m.* clerk of the board of works. —schule, *f.* an academy of architecture. —schutt, *m.* rubbish. —statt, —stätte, —stelle, *f.* 1) building-ground, building-plot. 2) site. Die —stelle des alten Karthago, the site of the ancient Carthago. —stein, *m.* stone for building. —sucht, V. Baulust. —süchtig, V. Baulustig. —verständig, *adj.* and *adv.* skilled in building concerns. —verwalter, *m.* steward of the building concerns. —werk, *n.* a building. —wesen, *n.* the general concerns of building. —würdig, *adj.* and *adv.* [in mining] worth the trouble or expense of working. —wuth, *f.* rage for building. —zierath, *m.* architectural ornament.

Baúch, *m.* [-es, *pl.* Bäuche] [allied to Bug from biegen] 1) the round protuberant part of a body. Der — einer Flasche, the belly of a bottle; der — einer Laute, the belly of a lute; einen — machen, to bunch, to belly out; die Mauer hat einen —, the wall bellies; der — des Schiffes, [in seamen's language] the bottom of a ship; der — des Segels, the belly or foot of a sail. 2) the belly [of men and beasts]. Ein dicker —, a great big belly; seinen — pflegen, to indulge one's belly; welchen der — ihr Gott ist, [Phil. III] whose god is their belly. *Fig.* Faule Bäuche, lazy good-for-nothing fellows. *Prov.* Der — läßt sich nicht mit Worten abspeisen, fair words will not fill a hungry belly, the belly is not filled with fair words; ein hungriger — hat keine Ohren, a hungry belly has no ears; wenn der — voll ist, will das Herz ruhen, when the belly is full, the bones are at rest; voller — studiert nicht gern, fat paunches make lean pates.

Bauch-blasig, V. Herzschlächtig. —blume, *f.* [a genus of plants] lisianthus. —bohrer, *m.* [among joiners] a sort of borer. —bruch, *m.* [in surgery] gastrocele. —compresse, *f.* [in surgery] belly-band, a truss. —deckenschlagader, *f.* [in anatomy] the epigastric artery. —dielen, *pl.* [in seamen's language] the thick stuff and ceiling placed next to the keel over all the floor-timbers. *Fig.* —diener, *m.* one who makes a god of his belly, belly-god, a glutton. *Fig.* —dienerei, *f.* —dienst, *m.* gluttony. —fell, *n.* V. —haut. —fieber, *n.* a gastric fever. —finne, —floße, *f.* ventral fin. —floßer, *m.* abdominal. Die —floßer, [a class of fish] abdominals. —fluß, *m.* a flux of the bowels, lientery. —flüßig, *adj.* and *adv.* affected with a flux of the bowels or lientery, lienteric. —förmig, *adj.* and *adv.* like the belly. —gegend, *f.* [in anatomy] the epigastric region. —geschwulst, *f.* a tumour in the belly. —gordingen, *pl.* [in seamen's language] bunt-lines. —grimmen, *n.* belly-ache, the colic, † the mulligrubs. Ich habe — grimmen, the colic wrings me. —gurt, *m.* 1) [a band or belt] a girdle. Ein lederner —gurt, a leathern girdle. 2) a girth. *a*) belly-band, a truss. *b*) surcingle. 3) V. —gordingen. —gurtriem, —gurtriemen, *m.* the strap of a girth. —gurtschnalle, *f.* the buckle of a girth. —haar, *n.* the hair of the belly. —haut, *f.* [in anatomy, a membrane which covers the whole abdomen on the inside] peritoneum. —hautentzündung, *f.* an inflammation of the peritoneum, peritonitis. —höhle, *f.* [in anatomy] the cavity of the abdomen. —kneipen, *n.* gripes, griping. —krampf, *m.* the colic. —krankheit, *f.* a gastric disease. —linie, *f.* [in anatomy, a concourse of the tendons of the oblique muscles of the abdomen] linea alba. —mündung, *f.* [in anatomy] the bottom of the stomach. —muskel, *m.* [in anatomy] abdominal muscle. —muskelwand, *f.* [in anatomy] a part of the peritoneum. —nähen, *n.* gastroraphy. —naht, *f.* [in surgery] a suture formed by sewing up wounds of the abdomen. —nerv, *m.* —nerve, *f.* [in anatomy] abdominal nerve. —nervenkrank, *adj.* hypochondriac, hypochondriacal. —nervenkrankheit, *f.* hypochondry, hypochondria, hypochondriac complaints. —nervenübel, *n.* any hypochondriac complaint. —öffnung, *f.* V. —schnitt. —rederei, —rednerei, *f.* ventriloquy, ventriloquism. —redner, *m.* gastriloquist, ventriloquist. —riem, —riemen, *m.* 1) a belt or girdle. 2) a girth, belly-band. —ring, *m.* [in anatomy, an oblong tendinous ring in both groins, through which pass the spermatic cords in men, and the round ligaments of the uterus in women] abdominal ring, or inguinal ring. —ründe, *f.* [in architecture] V. Bäuchung. —schmerz, *m.* V. —grimmen. —schnalle, *f.* V. —gurtschnalle. —schnitt, *m.* [in surgery] gastrotomy. —schwellung, *f.* the swelling of the belly in putrid fevers. —sorge, *f.* care of the belly. —speicheldrüse, *f.* abdominal gland. —sprache, *f.* V. —rednerei. —sprecher, *m.* V. —redner. —sprecherei, *f.* V. —rederei. —stich, *m.* [in surgery] tapping, paracentesis, paracentesy. —stück, *n.* 1) [among butchers] meat from the belly of animals. 2) [in seamen's lang.] floor-timber. Das erste or mittelste —stück, the floor-timber amidship; ein flaches or plattes —stück, flat floor-timber; krumme —stücke, the floor-timbers, which are placed between the crotches and the middle floor-timbers; ein eingezogenes —stück, rising floor-timber; die —stücke der Katspuhren, futtock-riders. —übel, *n.* a gastric disease. —wassersucht, *f.* a dropsy or tense elastic swelling of the belly, with fluctuation, from a collection of water, ascites. —wassersüchtig, *adj.* and *adv.* ascitic, ascitical. —weh, *n.* belly-ache. —wirbel, *m.* [in anatomy] abdominal vertebre. —wunde, *f.* a wound in the belly. —würmer, *pl.* ascarides. —zirkel, *m.* double compasses. —zwang, *f.* V. Leibzwang, Stuhlzwang.

Bäuchen, *v. tr.* to make protuberant. V. Ausbäuchen.

Bauchig, **Bäuchig**, *adj.* and *adv.* 1) bellying. Diese Mauer ist —, this wall bellies. 2) bellied. Dick—, bigbellied. 3) [in botany] bellying or bellied. Eine bäuchige Aehre, a bellying spike.

Bäuchung, *f.* [in architecture] the swelling of a column.

1. **Bauen**, *v. tr.* 1) to till, to prepare for crops, to cultivate [land]. Einen Garten —, to cultivate a garden. 2) to work [a mine]. 3) to raise or produce by tillage, to cultivate [corn &c.]. Er baute Weizen, wo früher keiner wuchs, he raised wheat, where none grew before.

2. **Bauen**, [allied to the Gr. ποιέω, φύω; in old G. bowen signified also wohnen] I. *v. tr.* to build, to frame, to construct. Ein Haus —, to build a house; er bauet gerne, he is fond of building; Schiffe —, to build ships; ein Gerüst —, to raise a scaffold; [also said of animals] Nester —, to build nests; wohl gebaut [a person], well made, well shaped. *Fig.* Schlösser in die Luft —, to build castles in the air, to build our hopes on air. *Prov.* — macht leere Beutel, building is a sweet empoverishing; wer am Wege bauet, hat viele Meister, he that builds a house by the highway side, builds it either too high or too low; Narren — Häuser, kluge Leute kaufen sie, fools build houses for wise men to live in. II. *v. intr.* *Fig.* to rely, to count upon. Kann ich auf Sie —? may I trust on you? er baut auf ihre Liebe, he confides in her love; er baut auf Ihre Mitwirkung, he reckons upon your cooperation; wir bauen auf das Wort eines Freundes, we depend on the word of a friend; baue nicht auf sie, do not rely on them; Leute, auf die man — kann, people to be depended upon.

1. **Bauer**, *n.* [with some authors *m.*] [Sw. and Isl. *byr* and *bur*, old Germ. pur and bur = eine Wohnung, habitation; old Engl. *bower* = ein Gemach, closet, chamber, room] [-s, *pl.* -] a cage [for confining birds].

2. **Bauer**, *m.* [-s, *pl.* -n] 1) a cultivator of the soil, a farmer, a husbandman, a peasant, a countryman, a boor, a rustic, a clown. *Prov.* Er geht wie der — in den Thurm, he goes like the bear to the stake; es gibt kein Messer, das schärfer schnitt', als wenn der Bauer zum Edelmann wird, no man looks to be accounted more than a beggar mounted. 2) *Fig.* *a*) an ill-bred man, a rustic, a clown, a churl. *b*) [at chess] a common man, a pawn. *c*) [a card with a soldier painted on it] a knave. *d*) [in seamen's lang.] the lower transom.

Bauer[n]-art, *f.* coarse manners, rusticity. —bengel, *m.* a coarse young rustic or peasant, a sturdy young rustic, a churl, a boor or clown. —brod, *n.* coarse bread. —bursche, *m.* a young peasant or rustic, ‡ a swain. —dill, *m.* V. Bärwurz. —dirne, *f.* a country lass. —eppich, V. Wassereppich. —feind, *m.* an enemy to peasants. —fest, *n.* a country-feast. —flegel, *m.* a churl, a boor. —frau, —s-frau, *f.* a countrywoman, peasant's wife. —freund, *m.* a friend to peasants. —frohne, *f.* feudal service of the peasantry. —gut, *n.* a farm. —haft, *adj.* and *adv.* rustic, boorish. —haus, *n.* a farmhouse. —hochzeit, *f.* a country-wedding. —hof, *m.* a farmhouse. —hund, *m.* a farm-dog. —hütte, *f.* a peasant's cottage, a mean cottage. —junge, *m.* a farmer's boy. —kerl, *m.* a young clown. —kind, *n.* a farmer's child. —kittel, *m.* smock-frock. —kleid, *n.* —kleidung, *f.* country dress, russet. —knecht, *m.* a farmer's man or boy. —knopf, *m.* [a sea term] a single knot. —kost, *f.* countryman's diet, a coarse food. —krieg, *m.* war of the peasantry. —lehen, *n.* —lehne, *f.* a base of land or fief held by a peasant, a base estate, base tenure. —s-leute, *pl.* country-people. —lied, *n.* rustic ballad, peasant-song. —mädchen, *n.* a peasant girl, a country girl. —magd, *f.* a farmer's maid. *—s-mann, *m.* V. Bauer. —meister, *m.* the village magistrate. †—mensch, *n.* a rude girl, a romp, a hoiden. —pfeffer, *m.* the worst sort of pepper. —pferd, *n.* a farmer's horse. —platting, *f.* [in seamen's lang.] foxes, made of nine rope-yarns. —regel, *f.* peasant's proverbs and maxims. —rose, *f.* V. Stockrose. —schaft, *f.* 1) [the body of country people] peasantry. 2) the condition of a peasant. —schenke, *f.* a village alehouse, country alehouse, village gin-shop, country taphouse. †—schinder, *m.* rack-rent. —senf, *m.* field bastard cress, penny cress, or smooth mithridate mustard. —sitte, *f.* the manners of peasants. —spaß, *m.* a low joke. —sprache, *f.* country-dialect. —stand, *m.* V. —schaft. —stolz, *m.* coarse and vulgar pride. —tabak, *m.* common tobacco. —tanz, *m.* the dancing of peasants. —tracht, *f.* country dress, russet. —verstand, *m.* the wit of peasants. —volk, —s-volk, *n.* country people; [in contempt] low, common people. —wagen, *m.* a farmer's cart. —weihrauch, *m.* white resin. —wesen, *n.* —wirthschaft, *f.* 1) husbandry. 2) rural economy.

Bäuerinn, *f.* a country woman, peasant's wife.

Bäuerisch, *adj.* and *adv.* rustic, rural, agrestic. *Fig.* Das —e Wesen, rusticity, clownishness; ein —er Gang, a clownish gait.

Bäuerlich, *adj.* and *adv.* 1) pertaining to husbandry. 2) suiting a countryman. *Fig.* —e Sitten, simple manners.

Baufällig, *adj.* and *adv.* in a state of decay, threatening to fall in, out of repairs [said of a building]. Ein —es Haus, a house in a ruinous state, out of repairs.

Baufälligkeit, *f.* a ruinous state, ruinousness.

Bauhaft, *adj.* and *adv.* that may be worked [said of a mine].

Bauhinie, *f.* [*pl.* -n] [a plant] mountain ebony [Bauhinia].

Baulich, *adj.* and *adv.* [seldom used except in the following and similar phrases] Ein Haus in —em Stande erhalten, to keep a house in repair.

Baum, *m.* [-es, *pl.* Bäume] [Goth. *bagms*, old G. *poum*, Sax. *beam*, *beom* [= Balken], allied to the Gr. φύω, L. *fio*] 1) [in general = Balken] *a*) [mostly in compositions] any thing resembling a tree, having the figure of a tree as: der Heu—, a hay-pole, hay-beam &c. *b*) any large piece of timber, the main piece of a thing as: der — an Webestühlen [Weberbaum], a beam. *c*) Der — an einem Hafen, the bar of a harbour, a boom; aus dem — legen, [in seamen's lang.] to lay out. 2) a tree. Ein Obst—, a fruit tree; ein Apfel—, an apple tree. *Prov.* Den — erkennt man an den Früchten, a tree is known by its fruit, such a tree is, such is the fruit; ist der Baum gefallen, sammelt Jeder Holz, when the tree is fallen, every man goes to it with the hatchet; je größer der Baum, je schwerer der Fall, the greater the tree, the harder the fall; biege den Baum, so lange er jung ist, the tree must be bent whilst it is young; best to bend, while it is a twig; ein hoher — fängt viel Wind, huge winds blow on high hills.

Baum-achat, *m.* [a precious stone] dendrachates. —ähnlich, *adj.* and *adv.* resembling a tree, tree-like. —ähnlich wachsend, arborescent. —ameise, *f.* horse-ant. —artig, *adj.* and *adv.* like a tree. —auster, *f.* V. Holzauster. —bast, *m.* the inner bark of trees. —blüte, *f.* the blossom of trees; *it.* the season in which trees are in blossom. —bohne, *f.* [plants] *a*) connarus, *b*) anagyris. —brand, *m.* the blight. —bruch, *m.* V. —fall. —brüchig, *adj.* and *adv.* V. —fällig. —ente, *f.* the black-billed whistling duck. —eule, *f.* the aluco-owl. —falk, *m.* the hobby. —fall, *m.* windfallen wood. —fällig, *adj.* and *adv.* windfallen. —farn, *m.* common polypody. —flechte, *f.* tree-moss. —floh, *m.* a species of the spring-tail. —flöte, *f.* V. —pfeife. —förmig, *adj.* and *adv.* having the form of a tree. —fraß, *m.* canker. —frosch, *m.* V. Laubfrosch. —frucht, *f.* fruit. —gang, *m.* an avenue of trees. —gans, *f.* tree-goose Die schottische —gans, the barnacle bird. —garten, *m.* an orchard. —gärtner, *m.* nursery-man, nursery-gardener. —geist, *m.* a dryad. —geländer, *n* espalier. —gipfel, *m.* the top of a tree. —grendel, —grindel, *m.* V. Pflugbaum or Pflugsterz. —grille, *f.* 1) the tree-cricket. 2) V. —hacker. —gruppe, *f.* a clump of trees, a bunch of trees. —hacker, —häkel, *m.* the creeper, woodpecker. —harz, *n.* the resin of trees. —haufen, *m.* V. —gruppe. —hippe, *f.* a lopping axe. —hoch, *adj.* and *adv.* as high as a tree, lofty. *Ein —hoher [more usual: —langer] Kerl, a strapping fellow. —holder, *m.* common elder. —holz, *n.* the wood of forest-trees. V Oberholz. —hüpfer, *m* a species of spider [aranea truncorum]. —käfer, *m.* the garden-beetle. —kahn, *m.* [a boat formed of the body or trunk of a tree] a log canoe. —kanne, *f.* a wooden pitcher. —kantig, *adj.* round, uncleft [said of wood]. —klee, *m.* V. Geisklee. —klette, *f.* V. —hacker. —krebs, *m.* V. —fraß. —kunde, *f.* dendrology. —lang, *adj.* V. —hoch. —läufer, *m.* V. —hacker. —laus, *f.* plant-louse, tree-louse. —leiter, *f.* a tree-ladder, double ladder. —lerche, *f.* wood-lark. —lilie, *f.* Italian honey-suckle. —los, *adj.* and *adv.* without a tree. —lunge, *f.* V. —flechte. —malve, *f.* tree-mallow. —marder, *m.* the pine marten. —mast, *f.* forest-mast, mastage. —meißel, *m.* V. Schroteisen. 1. —messer, *m.* [an instrument to measure the height and diameter of a tree] dendrometer. 2. —messer, *n.* a pruning knife. —moos, *n.* tree-moss. —mörder, *m.* climbing staff-tree. —nachtigall, *f.* hedge sparrow, hedge warbler. —nelke, *f.* a species of pink. —nuß, *f.* walnut. —nymphe or —nimfe, *f.* V. —geist. —öl, *n.* sweet oil, olive oil, salad oil. —pappel, *f.* tree-mallow. —pfahl, *m.* a prop, a stay. —pfeife, *f.* [in gardening] a bud [for inoculating]. —pflanzung, *f.* a plantation of trees. —pflaster, *n.* grafting-wax, mummy. —picker, *m.* V. —hacker. —pilz, *m.* V. —schwamm. —räude, *f.* the scurf of trees. —rebe, *f.* the tuberous-rooted ipomea. —reep, *n.* V. —talje. —reich, *adj.* full of trees, abounding in trees, woody. —reihe, *f.* V. —gang. —reiter, *m.* [among hunters] the wild cat. —rinde, *f.* the rind, bark. —rohr, *n.* V. Melonenbaum. —rose, *f.* the water elder. || —rutter, *m.* V. —hacker. —saft, *m.* the juices of trees. —säge, *f.* a large double saw. —salbe, *f.* a glutinous matter applied to injured trees. —sauger, *m.* V. Schmarotzerpflanze. —schatten, *m.* the shade or shadow of trees. —schere, *f.* stock-shears. —schimmel, *m.* the white wash-byssus. —schlag, *m.* [in painting &c.] foliage. —schnecke, *f.* the hedge snail. —schnitt, *m.* lopping, pruning. —schröter, *m.* the stag-beetle. —schule, *f.* a plantation of young trees, a nursery. —schwalbe, *f.* the pied fly-catcher. —schwamm, *m.* agaric. —segel, *n.* V. Giekfegel. —seide, [a sort of stuff] bombasin. —seidenmacher, —seidenweber, *m.* a bombasin-weaver. —specht, *m.* V. Specht and —hacker. —sperling, *m.* V. Weidensperling. —spinne, *f.* a species of spider. —stamm, *m.* the stem, trunk of tree. *Fig.* *—stark, *adj.* and *adv.* robust, vigorous. —steiger, *m.* V. —hacker. —stein, *m.* dendrite. —steinartig, *adj.* and *adv.* dendritic, dendritical. —stock, *m.* stub. —strunk, *m.* the trunk of a tree. —stück, *n.* a grass plot planted with trees, especially fruit-trees. —stütze, *f.* V. —pfahl. —talje, *f.* [a sea term] topping-lift of the main-boom. —tau, *n.* [a sea term] Das —taudes Bootes oder der Schaluppe, guess-warp, guessrope. —umschattet, *adj.* and *adv.* shaded by trees. —wachs, *n.* [am. gardeners, a sort of wax used in grafting and planting trees] mummy. —wanze, *f.* flying bug. —wermuth, *m.* a species of wormwood. —winde, *f.* five-leaved ivy. —wolle, *f.* 1) [a soft downy vegetable substance] cotton. 2) cotton-plant, cotton-shrub. —wollen, *adj.* made of cotton. —wollene Strümpfe, cotton stockings; —wollener Zeug, cotton cloth; —wollenes Garn, spun cotton; ein —wollener Knopf, twist button; —wollener Zwirn, cotton thread. —wollenbaum, *m.* —wollenpflanze, *f.* V. —wolle 2). —wollengarn, *n.* spun cotton, cotton-twist. —wollenpflanzung, *f.* a plantation of cotton-shrubs, a cotton-plantation. —wollensammt, *m.* velveteen, fustian. —wollenstaude, *f.* V. —wolle 2). —wollenstreicher, *m.* one who cards cotton, a carder. —wollenweberei, *f.* a cotton manufactory, cotton-mill. —wollenweide, *f.* the sweet willow. —wollenzeug, *m.* cotton-stuff. —wollicht, *adj.* and *adv.* cottony. *Fig.* soft as cotton. —wurz, *f.* V. Engelsüß. —wurzelsauger, *m.* [a plant] yellow-bird's nest. —zucht, *f.* the business of rearing young trees, the culture of trees.

Baúmannshöhle, *f.* a celebrated cavern in the Hartz mountains.

Bäúmchen, *n.* [-s, *pl.* -] a small tree.

Baúmel, *m.* V. Bammel.

Baúmeln, *v. intr.* V. Bammeln.

Bäúmen, *adj.* and *adv.* [in compositions] from a tree as: Birn—, made of pear-tree.

Bäúmen, *v. r.* V. Baumen III.

Baúmen, I. *v. intr.* 1) to rise like a tree. 2) [among hunters] to ascend a tree, to light upon a tree. Der Marder baumet, the marten-cat is treed. II. *v. tr.* 1) to fasten by means of a tree or large pole [a load of hay, straw &c. upon a cart]. 2) to put on the beam [said of weavers]. III. *v. r.* sich — or bäumen, to rear [said of horses]. Sich bis zum Ueberschlagen —, to rear an end.

Bäúmicht, *adj.* and *adv.* resembling a tree, tree-like.

Bäúmig, *adj.* and *adv.* planted with trees, wooded.

Bäúmlein, V. Bäumchen.

Baúsback, **Paúsback**, *m.* [-s, *pl.* -bäcke] a person with thick puffed cheeks.

|| **Baúsbacken**, **Paúsbacken**, *v. intr.* *Fig.* to talk with ostentation, to vaunt, to boast, to talk big.

Baúsbäckig, **Paúsbäckig**, *adj.* and *adv.* 1) having thick puffed cheeks, or blubbered cheeks, chubcheeked, chubby, chubfaced. 2) *Fig.* talking with ostentation, boasting, vaunting.

Baúsch, *m.* [-es, *pl.* Bäusche] [from bausen, Sw. *bösun*, = to swell up] 1) any thing roundish and prominent, a pad. Sie trägt Bäusche an sich, she is padded. 2) a bolster of soft linen cloth used by surgeons to cover a plaster or dressing, a compress, a pledget. 3) [in saddlery] a bolster. 4) **Fig.* In — und Bogen kaufen, to buy in the lump, in the gross.

Bausch-ähnlich, *adj.* and *adv.* resembling a pad or bolster. —ärmel, *m.* a sleeve made up with pads. —kauf, *m.* V. Bogenfahrt.

Bäúschchen, *n.* [-s, *pl.* -] a little pad or bolster.

Baúschel, *m.* [-s, *pl.* -] a great hammer used in mining.

Baúschen, *v. intr.* to be protuberant and round, to bunch, to swell out in a protuberance.

Baúschig, *adj.* and *adv.* bunchy.

Baúse, *f.* [*pl.* -n] [among painters and sculptors] a sketch.

Baúsen, *v. intr.* to form a bunch or bunches.

Baÿ, V. Bai.

Baÿer, *m.* [-n, *pl.* -n] *f.* -inn, Bavarian. Bayerisch, *adj.* and *adv.* Bavarian. Bayern, *n.* Bavaria.

Bayonnét, V. Bajonnet.

Báxen, *v. r.* sich —, to fight with the fist, to box, to cuff.

Báxer, *m.* [-s, *pl.* -] a boxer, a pugilist.

Bé-, an inseparable preposition, the primitive sense of which is allied to that of bei.

Beábschieden, V. Verabschieden.

Beábsichten, **Beábsichtigen**, *v. tr.* to have in view, to aim at. Den beabsichtigten Zweck erreichen, to attain the end proposed.

Beáchten, *v. tr.* to attend to, to regard with attention. Beachte meine Worte, attend to my words; er benahm sich sehr roh, aber ich beachtete es nicht, his conduct was very rude, but I took no notice of it.

Beachtens-werth, —würdig, *adj.* and *adv.* deserving regard or attention, worthy of notice.

Beáchzen, *v. tr.* to groan for.

Beáckern, *v. tr.* to till, to plough [a field].

Beádern, *v. tr.* to furnish with veins, to ornament with something like veins, to vein.

Beáffen, *v. tr.* to cheat by mockery.

Beámbern, [unusual] *v. tr.* to perfume with ambergris.

Beámte [more properly] Beamtete, *m.* [-n, *pl.* -n] a person in a civil office, an officer, a public functionary; *it.* such military officers, as: quartermasters, surgeons, commissaries, &c. Ein —r, one invested with an office or a commission.

Beámten, *v. tr.* to invest with an office, to commission. Beamtet, in commission, in office, in place.

Beängsten, **Beängstigen**, *v. tr.* to torment, to disturb, to harrass. Bis ins Innerste beängstigt seyn, to be vexed to the soul; sich — wegen &c., to be anxious for, to worry one's self about &c.

Beängstigung, *f.* anguish, anxiety.

Beántlitzen, *v. tr.* to look at, to gaze at.

Beántworten, *v. tr.* to answer [a letter &c.]. Eine Frage —, to reply to a question; er hat den Brief noch nicht beantwortet, he has not yet returned an answer to the letter. *Fig.* Das Feuer der Feinde lebhaft —, to return the enemy's fire with spirit.

Beántworter, *m.* [-s, *pl.* -] answerer, replier.

Beántwortlich, *adj.* [that to which a reply may be made] answerable.

Beántwortung, *f.* 1) answering. 2) an answer, a reply.

Beantwortungsschreiben, *n.* a letter in answer.

Beánwartschaften, *v. tr.* [law term] to bestow on any one a reversion, expectancy, or survivance.

Beárbeitbar, *adj.* and *adv.* that may be elaborated.

Beárbeiten, *v. tr.* 1) to improve or refine by successive operations. Einen Acker, einen Garten —, to cultivate a field, a garden; die Felder werden von Weibern bearbeitet [more usual: bestellt], the lands are laboured by women; Eisen —, to work iron; dieses Metall läßt sich gut —, this metal is very malleable, is easy to be wrought; Wolle oder Seide —, to work wool or silk; bearbeitetes Holz, wrought timber; einen wissenschaftlichen Gegenstand —, to treat a literary subject. **Fig.* Wenn Ihr Einen — wollt, if you would work a man; Einen —, to belabour any one, to beat any one soundly. 2) [= Ausarbeiten] to elaborate. Eine sorgfältig bearbeitete Rede, an elaborate discourse.

Beárbeiter, *m.* [-s, *pl.* -] —inn, *f.* one who works or treats something.

Beárbeitung, *f.* culture [of fields &c.], working, manipulation [of metals &c.]. Die — eines wissenschaftlichen Gegenstandes, the treating or handling of a literary subject.

Beárgwohnen, *v. tr.* to suspect. Einen —, to entertain a suspicion of any one; einer bösen That beargwohnt werden, to be suspected of some evil deed; der Beargwohnte, the suspected person, the person on whom suspicion falls.

Beárten, *v. tr.* [in husb.] to till, to cultivate.

Beáschen, **Beäschen**, *v. tr.* [unusual] to sprinkle with ashes.

Beatrix, [a name of women] [-or, with some authors, Beatricen's] Beatrice.

Beaúfsichtigen, *v. tr.* to survey, to oversee.

Beaúftragen, *v. tr.* to give a commission to, to commission. Einen mit einem Geschäfte —, to charge any one with a business. Beauftragt, charged or commissioned; der Beauftragte, commissioner, commissary, agent.

Beäúgeln, *v. tr.* to look at with fond eyes, to ogle.

Beaúgen, *v. tr.* [to look at by way of examination] to inspect, to view.

Beaúgenscheinigen, *v. tr.* to inspect, to look on, to view or oversee for the purpose of examination.

Beaügenscheinigung, *f.* ocular inspection.

Bebaaken, *v. tr.* [in seamen's lang.] to put up beacons and buoys in, to buoy [a river, a channel &c.].

Bebálsamen, *v. tr.* to balm.

Bebändern, *v. tr.* to adorn with ribands.

Bebärten, Bebärten, *v. tr.* to furnish with a beard.

Bebaüen, *v. tr.* 1) to cover with buildings. Einen Platz — or überbauen, to build upon a place. 2) to cultivate [a garden]. V. Anbauen.

Bebaüer, *m.* [-s, *pl.* -] a builder, cultivator.

Bebäümen, *v. tr.* to plant with trees [seldom used, except in the past part.] Bebäumt. Ein schön bebäumter Platz, a square planted with fine trees.

Bében, *v. intr.* [allied to the L. *pav-eo* and the Gr. φόβος = Furcht &c.] 1) [to be agitated with a vibratory motion] to shake, to tremble. Die Erde bebte, the earth trembled; die Grundfesten der Erde —, [Jes. XXIV, 18] the foundations of the earth do shake; vor Kälte —, to shake or shiver with cold; er bebte wie ein Espenlaub, he quaked like an aspen leaf; der Boden bebte unter seinen Tritten, the ground shrunk before his treading; bebend, tremulous; das Beben der Töne, vibration of sounds. V. Schwingung; eine —de Stimme, a trembling voice. 2) to shake as with fear, to tremble. Vor Angst —, to shrink for fear; ich bebe für dich, I fear for you, I tremble for you; ich bebe vor dir, I fear you, I tremble before you. Syn. Beben, Zittern, Schaudern, Schauern. Das Beben is a more considerable vibratory motion than Zittern and Schaudern. Eine Erderzitterung is less violent than ein Erdbeben. When the ground zittert [shakes] from the discharge of artillery, the windows rattle; but when the ground bebet [quakes], whole buildings are thrown down. Schaudern like Zittern denotes a slight sudden trembling motion, but Schaudern signifies only a shuddering or quivering of the skin, whereas Zittern extends to whole limbs of the animal body. Schauer denotes, a sudden quivering motion of the surface of the body, but of slighter degree than Schauder. Schaudern and Schauder are therefore said of the most violent and disagreeable sensations; Schauern and Schauer of slighter and sometimes even of agreeable sensations.

Béber, *m.* [-s, *pl.* -] a stop of an organ, tremblant.

Beber-esche, *f.* V. Espe.

Bébezug, *m.* [-s, *pl.* -züge] V. Beber.

Bebíldern, *v. tr.* to hang with pictures.

Bebímsen, *v. tr.* to rub with pumice-stone.

Bebínden, *v. tr.* to tie upon, to bind all over.

Bebísamen, *v. tr.* to perfume with musk.

Bébköpfchen, *n.* [-s, *pl.* -] a porcelain figure of a Chinese, mandarina.

Beblásen, *v. tr.* 1) to blow upon. 2) to publish by blowing.

Beblättern, *v. tr.* to furnish with leaves.

Bebléchen, *v. tr.* to cover with tin.

Bebleíen, *v. tr.* to furnish with leads, to lead.

Beblümen, *v. tr.* to cover or embellish with flowers, to flourish. *Poet.* Die beblümten Fluren, the enamelled fields.

Beblúten, *v. tr.* [unusual] to make bloody, to imbue or besmear with blood.

Bebóhlen, *v. tr.* to line with planks.

Bebómben, [unusual] *v. tr.* to bombard.

Bebórden, Bebórten, *v. tr.* to furnish with galloons, to trim with lace.

Bebrämen, *v. tr.* to border, to adorn with a border of ornaments. Ein Kleid —, to border a garment.

Bebrücken, *v. tr.* [unusual] to furnish with a bridge.

Bebrüten, *v. tr.* [seldom used] to brood, to hatch. *Fig.* Der Geizige bebrütet sein Gold, the miser broods over his gold.

Bebürden, *v. tr.* to burden, to load. *Fig.* Ein Volk mit Steuern —, to burden a nation with taxes.

Bebúschen, *v. tr.* to tuft [unusual, except in the past part.] Bebuscht. Ein bebuschter [bebüschter] Ort, a bushy place.

Becassíne, *f.* [*pl.* -n] a snipe.

Bécher, *m.* [-s, *pl.* -] [allied to Becken from biegen] 1) a cup, goblet, beaker, bowl, chalice. Der — zum Würfelspiele, a dice-box. 2) the contents of a cup, glass. Einen — Wein, a cup of wine. 3) [in botany, a little cup or peltated cavity, with a raised rim, which is found on the underside of some algæ] cyphilla, the little cup. 4) [in astronomy, a southern constellation] the cup, crater.

Becher-blume, *f.* burnet. **—flechte**, *f.* the common cup moss. **—förmig**, *adj.* and *adv.* having the form of a cup. **—kraut**, *n.* 1) V. Dickkraut. 2) V. Nebelpflanze. **—schwamm**, *m.* cup mush-room. **—spiel**, *n.* juggler's tricks with goblets. **—stürzer**, *m.* hard drinker, a toper.

Béchern, [in famil. language] *v. intr.* to tipple, to tope. Sie becherten ziemlich lange, they sat long over their cups. Bebechert, tipsy.

Bécken, *n.* [-s, *pl.* -] [V. Becher] 1) a basin. Das Bart—, shaving-basin. 2) cymbal. 3) [that which resembles a basin in containing water, as a pond, a dock for ships] basin. 4) [in anatomy] the pelvis.

Becken-band, *n.* [in anatomy] a ligament of the pelvis. **—blutader**, *f.* [in anatomy] the hypogastric vein. **—förmig**, *adj.* and *adv.* having the form of a basin; [in botany] pitcher-shaped. **—geflecht**, *n.* [in anatomy] the hypogastric ganglion. **—schlagader**, *f.* [in anatomy] the hypogastric artery. **—schläger**, *m.* 1) a tinman. 2) a cymbal-player. **—teich**, *m.* a basin. **—wand**, *f.* [in anat.] a part of the peritoneum.

Bécker, V. Bäcker.

Bedáchen, *v. tr.* to cover with a roof, to roof. Bebacht, roofed.

Bedácht, *m.* [-es] [from bedenken] consideration, deliberation. Mit — reden, to speak considerately or deliberately; — auf etwas nehmen, to take a thing into consideration.

Bedácht, [the past part. of Bedenken] Auf etwas — seyn, to reflect upon any thing.

Bedáchtig, Bedächtlich, Bedáchtsam, *adj.* and *adv.* considerate, advised, circumspect, discreet, deliberate.

Bedächtigkeit, Bedächtlichkeit, Bedáchtsamkeit, *f.* circumspection, caution, prudence, discretion.

Bedánken, *v. r.* 1) Sich bei Einem für etwas —, to thank a person for something; nicht bei mir, bei ihm müssen Sie sich —, not me, but him you must thank. 2) [ironically] Sich —, to decline with thanks. Er kam, um Geld zu entlehnen, allein dafür bedankte ich mich, he came to borrow money, but I begged to decline lending him any.

Bedären, *v. intr.* [a sea term] to fall calm, to becalm.

Bedárf, *m.* [-es] 1) want, need. Der — an Geld, want of money; zum —, for occasion; der — des Staats, Staats—, the necessary expenses of the state. 2) the thing needed or wanted.

Bedaüerlich, *adj.* and *adv.* 1) V. Bedauernswerth. 2) [in law-language] to be regretted. Wegen des höchst —en Ablebens des Fürsten wird Landestrauer angelegt, on account of the much to be lamented demise of the prince a general mourning is ordered.

Bedaüern, *v. tr.* 1) to pity, to commiserate, to compassionate. Einen —, to have compassion for any one. 2) to be uneasy at, to regret. Ich bedaure sehr, daß ich nichts davon gewußt habe, I am very sorry, I regret extremely that I did not know any thing about it. Das Bedauern, regret. Mit wahrem — habe ich erfahren, daß &c., with sincere sorrow I learnt that &c.

Bedauerns-werth, —würdig, Bedauerungs-werth, —würdig, *adj.* and *adv.* deplorable, pitiable. Ein —werther Zustand, a deplorable condition.

Bedéckeln, *v. tr.* to furnish with a cover.

Bedécken, *v. tr.* 1) to cover [a table with a cloth &c.]. Das Haupt —, to cover the head; die Berge sind mit Schnee bedeckt, the hills are covered with snow; der Himmel ist bedeckt, the sky is clouded; ein bedeckter Himmel, a clouded sky; sich —, to put on one's hat; — Sie sich, be covered, cover yourself, put on your hat; bedeckte Gänge, [in gardens] arbours. *Fig.* *a*) to cover = to shelter, to protect, to defend. *b*) [in commerce] to remit, to make remittances, to make provision for. 2) to cover = to conceal by some intervening object. Der bedeckte Weg, [in fortification] the covert-way; dieser Planet wird durch den Mond bedeckt, this planet is obscured by the interposition of the moon. 3) [among hunters &c., to copulate with a female] to cover.

Bedéckung, *f.* 1) the act of covering. 2) that which covers, covering. *Fig.* Er reisete mit einer —, he travelled with an escort; die — einer Flotte, a convoy. 3) [in fortification] epaulment. 4) [in astronomy] occultation [of a star or planet by the interposition of the moon &c.].

Bedeíchen, *v. tr.* to furnish with a pond.

Bedénken, *ir.* I. *v. tr.* 1) to think on with care, to consider, to ponder, to meditate on. Reiflich —, to consider maturely; bedenken Sie wohl or recht, daß &c., don't forget that &c., mind, that &c.; Einem zu — geben, to leave to any one's consideration, to put any one in mind of. 2) to pay attention to, to have regard to, to look close to a thing. Seinen guten Ruf —, to take care of one's reputation; — Sie Ihre Gesundheit, mind your health; man sollte ihre Dienste —, their services ought to be considered. 3) to bear in mind with intent to reward, to assist or be of service. Jemanden im Testamente —, to think of a person in one's will, to give or bequeath a person something by will. II. *v. r.* sich —, 1) to advise with one's self. Sich lange —, to deliberate long; sich anders —, to alter or change one's mind; sich eines Bessern —, to bethink one's self better. Syn. V. Anstehen. 2) to take care of one's own advantage. Er hat sich auch bedacht, he has provided for himself, he has taken care of number one. Syn. Bedenken, Erwägen, Beherzigen. Man bedenkt [we consider well] all the grounds or arguments for and against what we are about to undertake, from the fear that an error might expose us to some danger. As however, there may be many arguments for and against the advantage, feasibility &c. of a resolution, which are of greater or less weight, so erwägt man sie [we balance them] in order to ascertain their respective importance. Beherzigen implies to consider or balance something with lively or deep feelings of interest [for instance: Beherzigen Sie meinen Rath wohl, let my counsel sink deep into your heart].

Bedénken, *n.* [-s, *pl.* -] 1) consideration, reflexion, mature thought, serious deliberation. Die Sache fodert —, the matter or the case requires consideration; etwas in — ziehen, to take a thing into consideration. 2) suspension of opinion or decision, from uncertainty what is proper to be decided, hesitation, doubt, scruple. Ohne —, without hesitation; er aß ohne alles —, he scrupled not to eat; man trägt kein — &c., men make no scruple &c.; — tragen, to consider, to doubt, to hesitate; er trug —, ob er das Anerbieten annehmen sollte oder nicht, he hesitated whether to accept the offer or not; er trug über die Wahl dieser Mittel kein —, he did not scruple at the choice of these means. 3) an opinion given after deliberation. Ein — einholen, to ask an advice; ein theologisches —, the opinion of divines on a point of doctrine; ein ärztliches —, an advice of physicians. Syn. Bedenken, Zweifel. Der Zweifel signifies merely, the hesitating to believe, the fluctuation of the mind respecting the truth of a thing. Die Zweifel become Bedenken as soon as they constitute arguments against the advantage, feasibility &c. of a thing, and afford matter for further thought or consideration.

Bedenk=frist, —zeit, *f.* time for considering.

Bedénklich, *adj.* and *adv.* 1) requiring serious deliberation. Eine —e Sache, a nice point; eine —e Frage, a delicate question; die Sache ist sehr —, the matter requires most mature reflexion. 2) important, as regards the consequences, hazardous, full of risk, suspicious. Ein —es Unternehmen, a hazardous enterprize; ein —er Umstand, a suspicious circumstance; eine —e Lage, a critical situation. 3) [of persons] overconsciencious, too fearful of the consequences, scrupulous.

Bedénklichkeit, *f.* 1) instability of opinion, dubiousness, doubtfulness, scruple, scrupulosity. —en haben, to have scruples, to scruple; mit —en verwirren, to scrupulize. 2) critical condition, hazard.

Bedeúten, I. *v. tr.* 1) to inform, to set right. Er will sich nicht — lassen, he will not let himself be put right, he will not listen to reason. 2) to enjoin, to direct. II. *v. intr.* and *tr.* 1) to have meaning, to signify. Jedes Wort bedeutet etwas, every word expresses something; das Zeichen × bedeutet Vermehrung, the character × indicates multiplication; was soll all dieser Prunk —? what is the meaning of all this parade? die Frage bedeutete &c., the question imported &c.; es bedeutet nichts, it signifies nothing. 2) to indicate something future by that which is seen or known Es bedeutet, daß wir Regen bekommen, it indicates the approach of rain; dieser Vorfall bedeutet nichts Gutes, this accident presages no good; das bedeutet etwas Gutes, that augurs something good. 3) to be of importance. Es hat nichts zu —, 't is of no consequence, it imports nothing, it does not signify, it is no matter.

Bedeútend [*part.* of Bedeuten], **Bedeutsam**, *adj.* and *adv.* 1) significant, significative. Ein sehr —es or bedeutsames Lächeln, a very significant smile. 2) significant, important. Ein —er Mann bei Hof, a man of consideration at court. 3) considerable, important. Ein —er Gewinn, a considerable gain.

Bedeútung [less usual **Bedeútniß**, *n.* -sses, *pl.* -sse], *f.* 1) signification, meaning. Dieses Wort hat viele —en, this word has many significations; die — einer Hieroglyphe, the meaning of a hieroglyphic. 2) indication, sign, prognostication, presage. 3) importance, consequence. Ein Mann von —, a man of consideration; die Zahl ist bei Heeren nicht immer von —, number in armies is not always the most important thing. Syn. Bedeutung, Sinn, Verstand. Sinn and Verstand [sense, meaning] are the ideas and thoughts which are expressed by certain signs, under which, words are also to be understood. On the other hand, a thing that is no thought or idea may be the Bedeutung [signification] but not the Sinn of a sign. Ciphers or characters, whether letters, monograms or hieroglyphics have eine Bedeutung, but only monograms have einen Sinn; the individual letters of our alphabet bedeuten [represent] merely sounds. Sinn and Verstand differ, in as much as Verstand signifies only a connected series of thoughts or ideas expressed by several signs, but Sinn also a single idea.

Bedeutungs=leer, *adj.* and *adv.* insignificant, unimportant. —leere Gebräuche, insignificant rites. —los, *adj.* and *adv.* void of signification or meaning. —lose Worte, insignificant words. —reich, *adj.* and *adv.* having many significations or meanings, significant, significative. —schwer, *adj.* and *adv.* important, weighty, momentous, of great consequence. —voll, *adj.* and *adv.* V. —reich.

Bedielen, *v. tr.* to lay or spread with boards, to cover with boards, to board [a floor].

Bedienen, I. *v. tr.* to wait on, to serve, to attend. Von zahllosen Engeln bedient, ministered by angels numberless; seinen Herrn —, to give attendance to one's master, to wait upon one's master; er mußte sie bei Tische —, they made him wait upon them at table; [among some artists, workmen, shopkeepers &c.] Einen — [* Einem bedient seyn], to work for any one, to serve any one; ich werde Sie sogleich —, I will serve you immediately; ‡ Einem bedient seyn, [in law] to be somebody's counsel; der Pfarrer hat zwei Kirchen zu —, the curate has two churches to serve. *Fig.* Ein Amt —, to fill an office; ein Geschütz —, to serve a piece; [at cards] Farben —, to follow suit; mein Herr, Sie haben nicht bedient, Sir, you have revoked; es ist das erste Mahl, daß ich nicht bedient habe, it is the first time I ever made a revoke. II. *v. r.* sich —, to make use of, to use, to employ. Er bediente sich seiner, um den Frieden zu unterhandeln, he employed him to negociate the peace; sich einer Sache —, to make use of a thing; ich kann mich meiner rechten Hand nicht —, I cannot help myself with my right hand; sich der Gelegenheit —, to profit by the occasion; ich will mich dieser Bewilligung —, I will make use of this concession; — Sie sich selbst, [at table] help yourself.

Bediener, *m.* [-s, *pl.* -] a servant or attendant, a waiter.

Bedienſten, *v. tr.* Einen —, to confer on any one an employment. ‡ Bedienstet. 1) Einem bedienstet seyn, to be in any one's service. 2) having an office or employment. Der Bedienstete, an officer, public officer, place-man.

Bedient, 1) [past part. of bedienen] waited upon, served, attended. Der Bediente, ein Bedienter, a person, who has been waited upon, attended &c. 2) [by contraction, instead of: Ein Bedienender, der Bedienende, a person serving another, any one who attends, waits upon another; lit. Ein as it were einen Dienst Habender, a person holding a service, employment or office] Der Bediente, ein Bedienter, *a*) servant-man or man-servant, footman Seine Bedienten, his attendants. *b*) [a person commissioned to perform any public duty] officer. Ein Zollbedienter, an officer of the customs, a customhouse officer.

Bedienten=kleid, *n.*, —rock, *m.* servant's livery. —stube, *f.*, —zimmer, *n.* servant's room.

Bedienung, *f.* 1) [menial office, low business done at the command of a master] service, attendance. 2) the manner in which service is done. Die — in einem Wirthshause, the accommodations in an inn; die — in diesem Gasthofe ist sehr schlecht, you are badly waited upon in this hotel. 3) a servant, and also the servants collectively. 4) office, employment.

Beding, *m.* [-es, *pl.* -e] V. Bedingung.

Bedingen, *ir.* and *reg. v. tr.* 1) to condition, to stipulate. Es war unter ihnen bedungen, daß &c., it was stipulated between them, that &c. 2) to settle by stipulation. Eine Arbeit —, to agree for the price of a work; eine Waare —, to agree for or on the price of a merchandise; wenn Kaffe zu 15 Schillingen zu bedingen ist, if coffee is to be obtained at 15 shillings; ein Schiff —, V. Verdingen. 3) to provide any thing as the ground of something else or as requisite to another act. Ich bedingte nur, daß &c., I only made it a condition that &c.; [in grammar] ein bedingendes Bindewort, a conditional conjunction; die bedingt zukünftige Zeit, the conditional mood. 4) [in logic and mathematics] to take for granted, to suppose, to lay down as a hypothesis. Die Richtigkeit dieses Satzes bedingt nothwendig die Richtigkeit des weiteren, the truth of this position necessarily presupposes the truth of the following.

Bedingniß, *n.* [-sses, *pl.* -sse] V. Bedingung.

Bedingt, [regular past part. of bedingen, and in this sense never: bedungen] *adj.* and *adv.* 1) conditional, conditionate Ein —es Versprechen, a conditional promise. 2) [in grammar and logic, expressing a condition or supposition] conditional.

Bedingung, *f.* 1) conditioning, stipulating. 2) [terms given or provided, as the ground of something else] condition. Unter der —, on condition, with a proviso; schwere —en, hard conditions.

Bedingungs=weise, *adv.* conditionally.

* **Bedlamit**, *m.* [-en, *pl.* -en] a bedlamite, a madman.

Bedörnen, *v. tr.* to furnish with thorns. *Fig.* Bedornte Wege, thorny ways.

Bedrängen, *v. tr.* to press hard. *Fig.* Bedränge nicht die Moabiter, distress not the Moabites; bedrängt, *adj.* in distress; den Unschuldigen —, to oppress the innocent; von Sorgen bedrängt, harassed out with care.

Bedränger, *m.* [-s, *pl.* -] oppressor.

Bedrängniß, *n.* [-sses, *pl.* -sse] 1) [the act of oppressing] oppression. 2) oppression, distress, affliction, calamity, misery. Noth und — starrt aus deinen Blicken, need and oppression stare within thy eyes. Syn. V. Drangsal, Elend, Jammer, Kreuz, Leiden, Noth, Unglück, Widerwärtigkeit.

Bedrängung, *f.* V. Bedrängniß.

Bedräuen, *v. tr.* in poetry for bedrohen.

Bedrechseln, *v. tr.* 1) to form or shape by turning on a lathe. 2) to turn a little.

Bedrohen, *v. tr.* to menace, to threaten. Die verbündeten Mächte bedrohten Frankreich von jeder Seite mit Krieg, the combined or allied powers menaced France with war on every side; der Geist der Zuchtlosigkeit bedrohte dieses Land mit den Schrecken des Bürgerkrieges, the spirit of insubordination menaced that country with the horrors of civil war.

Bedrohlich, *adj.* and *adv.* threatening, menacing. Bedrohliche Worte, menaces.

Bedrücken, *v. tr.* 1) [rather unusual] to im

print with one's seal. Haben Sie diese Urkunde mit Ihrem Siegel bedruckt? have you put your seal to this document? 2) to print, to fill with printing. Der Bogen ist ganz bedruckt, the sheet is printed quite full; Kattune —, to print cottons.

Bedrücken, *v. tr.* to press much. *Fig.* Ein Volk —, to oppress a nation [with taxes or contributions]; bedrückende Kriege, vexatious wars; vom Unglück bedrückt, oppressed with misfortune, distressed; den die gleiche Noth bedrückte, whom the like necessity pressed.

Bedrücker, *m.* [-s, *pl.* -] oppressor.

Bedrückniß, *f.* [-sses, *pl.* -sse] oppression.

Bedrückung, *f.* 1) [the act of oppressing] oppression. 2) oppression, pressure, affliction, distress.

Bedüften, *v. tr.* to scent, to perfume.

Bedüngen, *v. tr.* to manure with dung, to dung [a field &c.].

Bedünken, *v. imp.* Mich [more properly than mir] bedünkt, methinks, it seems to me, it appears to me, I think. Sich — lassen, to be of opinion. Das Bedünken, opinion; nach meinem — or meines —s, in my opinion.

Bedünsten, *v. intr.* [u. w. seyn] to be covered with vapours.

Bedünsten, *v. tr.* to cover with vapours.

Bedüpfen, *v. tr.* to dab [a sore with lint &c.].

Bedürfen, *ir.* I. *v. intr.* to need, to want, to lack, to require. Die Starken bedürfen des Ärztes nicht, sondern die Kranken, [Math IX.] they that be whole need not a physician, but they that are sick; sie — gewiß mehr der Vernunft, they have sure more lack of reason; ein Heer, welches eines Führers bedarf, an army, that wants a head or a leader; diese Nachricht bedarf der Bestätigung, this news wants confirmation; was er da sagte, bedarf einer Erklärung, what he said, requires or demands some explanation; ich bedarf es nicht, I have no want or need of it, I do not want it. II. *v. imp.* to be wanting. Es bedarf keines Beweises, it requires no proof.

Bedürftlich, *adj.* and *adv.* wanting.

Bedürfniß, *n.* [-sses, *pl.* -sse] 1) want, need, necessity, lack. Das — macht den Menschen kühn, necessity makes men bold; ein natürliches —, a call of nature. 2) the thing wanted, or a thing necessary for some purpose. Er sorgte für alle meine Bedürfnisse, he supplied all my wants; die Bedürfnisse des Lebens, the necessaries of life.

Bedürfnißlos, *adj.* and *adv.* having no wants.

Bedürftig, *adj.* and *adv.* 1) being in want of a thing. 2) needy, poor. Syn. Bedürftig, Dürftig. Dürftig denotes in the most general sense, wanting, destitute; bedürftig limits the sense to the want of a certain thing of which one has need, and is therefore invariably joined with the object needed. Der Dürftige ist einer Unterstützung mit Gelde bedürftig [a destitute person needs pecuniary assistance]; der Mensch kömmt dürftig an Allem auf die Welt, und darum ist er der sorgfältigen Pflege seiner Eltern bedürftig [a man comes into the world destitute of every thing, and therefore needs the fostering care of his parents].

Bedüseln, **Bedüsseln**, *v. tr.* to make tipsy.

Bedutzen, *v. tr.* to confound, to perplex, to disconcert.

Beecken, *v. tr.* [in heraldry] to furnish with angles.

Beegen or **Beeggen**, *v. tr.* to harrow [a field].

Beehren, *v. tr.* to honour. Er beehrte mich mit seinem Besuche, he honoured me with a visit; [in commerce] einen Wechsel —, to honour or accept a bill of exchange.

Beeiden, **Beeidigen**, *v. tr.* 1) [in law] to confirm by an oath. Eine Aussage —, to give evidence or to declare upon oath. 2) to bind by an oath. Einen —, to swear any one; beeidigt, sworn. Das Beeidigen, or die Beeidigung, the act of taking an oath or binding by an oath.

Beeifern, I. *v. tr.* [unusual] to express indignation or displeasure at any thing. II. *v. r.* sich —, to exert one's self with zeal and eagerness, to be zealous. Ich werde mich aufs äußerste —, Ihrer Erwartung zu entsprechen, I will do my best, I will exert myself to the utmost to meet your wishes; sie beeiferten sich, ihn gut zu empfangen, they exerted themselves to give him a good reception.

Beeigenschaften, *v. tr.* to furnish with qualifications, to qualify.

Beeilen, I. *v. tr.* to hurry. — Sie Ihre Abreise, hasten your departure; Ihr müßt Eure Arbeit —, you must hurry on your work. II. *v. r.* sich —, to hasten, to make haste. — Sie sich doch! do but make haste!

Beeinträchtigen, *v. tr.* to injure, to wrong. Einen —, to do any one an injury; wir können sowohl durch Unglück als durch Ungerechtigkeit beeinträchtigt werden, we may receive injury by misfortune as well as by injustice; sie — das Ansehen des Landesherrn, they are a prejudice to the authority of the sovereign; dies kann Sie nicht —, this can not prejudice you, this can not hurt or harm you; des Nachbars Eigenthum —, to encroach on the neighbour's property.

Beeinträchtigung, *f.* 1) the act of injuring, wronging &c. any one. 2) an injury, wrong, hurt, harm, prejudice.

1. **Beeisen**, [from Eis, *ice*] *v. tr.* 1) to cover with ice. Die beeisten Gegenden des Nordens, the icy regions of the north. 2) *Fig.* to be icy or cold. Der beeiste Norden, the icy north.

2. **Beeisen**, [from Eisen, *iron*] *v. tr.* to furnish or arm with iron, to iron.

* **Beelzebub**, *m.* [-s] the chief devil.

Beemsigen, *v. r.* sich —, [unusual] to bestow pains on a thing, to exert one's self.

Been, V. Behen.

Beenden, **Beendigen**, *v. tr.* to end, to finish, to conclude, to put an end to. Eine Reise —, to finish a journey. Das Beendigen, die Beendigung, conclusion.

Beengen, *v. tr.* to narrow, to contract, to cramp, to straiten. Durch diese Möbeln wird der Raum im Zimmer sehr beengt, this furniture takes up much place, contracts the space in the room; wir sitzen hier so beengt, we sit here so cramped. *Fig.* Mein Herz ist beengt, my heart is oppressed with grief.

Beerben, I. *v. intr.* [u. w. seyn] to be provided with an heir [used only in the past part.]. Er ist noch nicht beerbt, he has no issue, no children yet. II. *v. tr.* Einen —, to be any one's heir, to inherit any one's property.

Beerblau, I. *n.* [-es] the blue colour of the whortle-berry. II. *adj.* and *adv.* blue like blueberries.

Beerblume, *f.* [*pl.* -n] climbing nightshade.

Beerchen, **Beerlein**, *n.* [dimin. of Beere] [-s, *pl.* -] a small berry.

Beerden, [more usual:] **Beerdigen**, *v. tr.* to inter, to bury, to inhume [a corpse].

Beerdigung, *f.* the act of interring &c., burial, interment, sepulture, inhumation.

Beerdigungs-feier, *f.* the solemnisation of interment, funeral, burial, obsequies. —feierlichkeit, *f.* funeral ceremony. —kosten, *pl.* funeral expenses.

Beerdolde, *f.* V. Beerendolde.

Beere, *f.* [*pl.* -n] [probably from bären = erzeugen] 1) [a succulent or pulpy fruit, containing naked seeds] berry. 2) much used in composition, as Erd—, strawberry; Heidel—, whortle-berry or bilberry &c.

Beeren-artig, *adj.* and *adv.* like a berry. —dolde, —engelwurz, *f.* [a plant] the berry-bearing angelica. —wanze, *f.* a species of bug or wall-louse.

Beer-gelb, I. *n.* a yellow colour extracted from the unripe berries of the buckthorn. II. *adj.* and *adv.* having the colour of the yellow extracted from the berries of the buckthorn. —grün, I. *n.* a green colour extracted from unripe berries. II. *adj.* and *adv.* green like unripe berries. —heide, *f.* V. Felsenstrauch. —melde, *f.* [a plant] strawberry-blite. —most, —wein, *m.* rape-wine. —raute, *f.* [a plant] a species of rue. —winde, *f.* [a plant] great or hedge bindweed. —wink, *m.* [a plant] small periwinkle.

Beeren, *v. tr.* V. Abbeeren.

Beerlein, V. Beerchen.

Beerzen, *v. tr.* to cover with brass.

† **Beest**, V. Biest.

Beet, *n.* [-es, *pl.* -e] [a plot or level piece of ground in a garden &c., usually a little raised above the adjoining ground] a bed. Das schmale —, [in gardening] platband. —weise, *adv.* in beds.

Beete, *f.* [*pl.* -n] [a plant] beet.

Beeten, *v. tr.* [unusual] to divide into beds.

Befächeln, *v. tr.* to fan.

Befächse[r]n, *v. tr.* to provine. Einen Weinberg —, to lay vines in a vineyard.

Befähigen, *v. tr.* [to make able, to furnish with legal ability or competency] to enable, to authorize. Seine Kenntnisse — ihn vollkommen zu dieser Stelle, his knowledge fits him perfectly for this situation.

Befähigung, *f.* the act of authorizing &c., authorisation, enablement, ability.

Befahrbar, *adj.* and *adv.* fit for passage, passable, practicable, navigable.

‡ 1. **Befahren**, [from Gefahr, *danger*] *v. tr.* to fear, to apprehend. Sie haben dabei nichts zu —, you have nothing to risk in it.

2. **Befahren**, [from fahren, *to drive* &c.] *ir.* *v. tr.* 1) to cross often, to frequent. Eine befahrene Straße, a frequented road. 2) to visit in a carriage or ship. Die Küsten von Frankreich —, to sail along the coasts of France; einen Fluß —, to navigate a river; der St. Lorenzstrom ist im Winter nicht zu —, the St. Lawrence is not navigable in winter; [in mining] eine Grube —, to descend a pit or mine in order to examine the works; [in law] ein Haus —, to take possession of a house; [in seamen's lang.] einen Ort — haben, to be a good pilot for a certain place; befahren Volk, weather-beaten sailors or sailors hardened to the sea, veteran sailors. Die Befahrung [of the sea], navigation.

Befalbeln, *v. tr.* to flounce.

Befallen, *ir.* I. *v. tr.* *Fig.* to befall. Es hat ihn eine Krankheit —, he has been taken ill; von der Cholera —, infected, attacked with the cholera; von einem Sturme — werden, to

17

meet with, to encounter a storm. II. *v. imp.* Es befällt mich ein Unglück, a misfortune befalls me.

Befälzen, *v. tr.* to furnish with a rabbet.

Befangen, *ir. v. tr. Fig.* 1) to entangle, to involve. Er ist mit in dieser Verschwörung —, he is implicated in this conspiracy. 2) to be taken with any thing. Vom Schlafe — seyn, to be oppressed or overcome with sleep, to be drowsy, sleepy. 3) to captivate, to prepossess [commonly used in the past part.] Auf die Handlungen der Fürsten mit einem befangenen Auge sehen, to look upon the actions of princes with a prejudiced eye; — von &c., prejudiced by.

Befangen, *part. adj.* 1) prejudiced. Befangene Leser, biassed readers; ein —er Richter, a partial judge. 2) disconcerted, confused, embarrassed.

Befangenheit, *f.* 1) prejudice, prepossession, bias. 2) confusion, embarrassment.

Befärben, *v. tr.* [among painters] to colour.

Befassen, I. *v. tr.* to touch, to handle. II. *v. r.* Sich mit etwas —, to meddle with any thing, to occupy one's self with a thing; sich mit einem Geschäfte —, to engage, embark in a business; er will sich damit nicht —, he refuses to be concerned in it. Syn. Befassen, Abgeben. Man befaßt sich mit einem Geschäft nicht [one does not engage in or undertake a thing] when one considers it too troublesome or dangerous, man gibt sich nicht damit ab [one does not meddle with it] when one holds it beneath one's notice.

Befechten, *ir. v. tr.* to attack, to assail. *Fig.* Der Advokat befocht jeden Punkt, the advocate contested every point.

Befedern, Befiedern, I. *v. tr.* 1) to cover or fit with feathers, to feather. 2) to pen [a harpsichord]. II. *v. r.* sich —, to get feathers.

Befehden, I. *v. tr.* to make war upon, to war, to be in feud with one another. Dieses Volk befehdet seine Nachbarn unablässig, this people have constant feuds with their neighbours. *Fig.* Eine Lehre —, to attack a doctrine. II. *v. r.* sich —. Sie — sich, they make war one upon the other. Befehdung, *f.* the act of making war upon, &c.

‡**Befehdungsbrief**, *m.* cartel.

Befehl, *m.* [-es, *pl.* -e] 1) a command, order, mandate. Ein ausdrücklicher —, an express command; ein mündlicher, schriftlicher —, a verbal, written order; ein landesherrlicher —, an edict, ordinance; auf — des Königs, by order of the king; einen — ausrichten, to execute an order; bis auf weitern —, till further orders; einen — geben, to give or issue an order; erwarten Sie seine —e, be ready to receive his commands; ertheilt ihnen Eure —e, give them your orders; ich stehe zu Ihrem —e, [in familiar lang.] I am at your command; was ist (steht) zu Ihrem —? what is your pleasure, what are your commands, what do you want? 2) [the right or power of governing with chief or exclusive authority, supreme power, control] command. Die Brigade stand unter seinem —e, he had the brigade under his command; er übernahm den — des Heeres in Polen, he took command of the army in Poland.

Befehls-flagge, *f.* [a sea term] the flag hoisted by the commodore. —**sform**, *f.* [in grammar] the imperative mood [of a verb]. —**shaber**, *m.* a commander [of an army, of the naval force]. Der —shaber einer Division, the commanding officer of a division. —**shaberisch**, *fig.* V. Befehlerisch. —**shaberschaft**, *f.* [the right or power of commanding] command. —**shaberstab**, *m.* the commander's staff. —**shaberstelle**, —**shaberwürde**, *f.* the place or dignity of a commander, command. —**sweise**, I. *f.* [in grammar] the imperative mood [of a verb]. II. *adv.* in the shape of a command. —**swimpel**, *m.* [in seamen's language] a broad pendant. —**swort**, *n.* word of command. —**szettel**, *m.* bulletin.

Befehlen, *ir.* 1) *v. tr.* and *intr.* to command, to bid, to order, to direct, to charge. Befiehl deinen Dienern, give order to thy servants; ich befahl ihm, zu kommen, I bade him [to] come; der General befahl seinen Truppen, vorzurücken, the general ordered his troops to advance; Sie haben kein Recht, mir zu —, you have no right to command me; was — Sie? [in familiar language] what do you please or desire to have, what is your pleasure, what do you want? wie Sie —, as you please! 2) *v. tr.* to commit. Befiehl dem Herrn deine Wege, [Ps. XXXVII.] commit thy way to the Lord; befehlt euch ihm, trust him with yourself; [in familiar language] Gott befohlen, adieu, farewell, good bye.

Befehlerisch, *adj.* and *adv.* imperious, dictatorial, haughty, arrogant, overbearing, domineering. Ein —er Mann, an imperious man.

Befehligen, *v. tr.* 1) to command, to order. Befehligt werden, to receive orders. 2) to command = to lead, to direct. Soult befehligte ein Heer in Spanien, Soult commanded an army in Spain.

Befeilen, *v. tr.* to rub and smooth with a file, to file.

Befeilschen, *v. tr.* to cheapen, to chaffer, to bargain down [goods].

Befeinden, *v. tr.* V. Anfeinden.

Befesten, [more usual] **Befestigen**, *v. tr.* 1) to make fast or close, to fix firmly, to fasten. Ein Bret an die Wand —, to fasten a board to the wall. 2) to fortify [a town &c.]. *Fig.* Da wurden die Gemeinen im Glauben befestigt, [Act. XVI.] so were the churches established in the faith.

Befestigung, *f.* 1) the act of making fast &c., fastening. 2) [the works erected to defend a place] fortification.

Befestigungs-kunst, *f.* [the art or science of fortifying places] fortification. —**pfahl**, *m.* palisade. —**werk**, *n.* any work erected to defend a place [as a parapet, rampart, wall &c.], a fortification.

Befeuchten, *v. tr.* to wet, to moisten, to water. Befeuchtet den trockenen Boden, wet the thirsty ground. Die Befeuchtung, wetting, moistening.

Befeuern, *v. tr. Fig.* [to give spirit or vigour, to infuse courage, or another enlivening passion] to animate. Muthlose Truppen —, to animate dispirited troops; von Liebe befeuert, inflamed by love; ein edler Wetteifer befeuert eure Brust, a noble emulation warms your breast.

Befiedern, V. Befedern.

Befinden, *ir.* I. *v. tr.* to find, to observe, to learn, to hold in opinion, to think, to esteem. Den heißen Erdstrich hat man nunmehr bewohnbar befunden, the torrid zone is now found habitable; der Angeklagte wurde von ihnen schuldig befunden, they found the accused guilty, they brought in a verdict of guilty against the defendant; nach Befinden der Sache, as the thing will prove, as the affair turns out, according to the circumstances. II. *v. r.* sich —, 1) to be in any place or state. Wo befand ich mich zu jener Zeit? where was I at that time? er befindet sich nun in Berlin, he is now at Berlin; sich in Ungewißheit über &c. —, to be in uncertainty with respect to &c.; in welcher traurigen Lage — wir uns! to what a pass are we brought! sich in Verlegenheit —, to be embarrassed. 2) to be [in regard to health]. Sich wohl oder übel —, to be well or ill; wie — Sie sich? how do you do, how are you? wie — Sie sich heute? how do you find yourself to-day? *Fig.* Sich wohl bei einer Sache —, to fare well, to be well off in something; wir wollen sehen, wie er sich dabei — wird, we shall see how it will fare with him. 3) to be [in point of fact], to be as is represented. Die Sache befand sich anders, als ich erwartete, the thing proved otherwise than I expected. Das Befinden, the state of health; sich nach Jemands — erkundigen lassen, to send to enquire after a person's health.

Befindlich, *adj.* and *adv.* being in any place. Es muß dort — seyn, it must be there; irgendwo — seyn, to be somewhere or other; alle in seinem Kabinette —e Seltenheiten, all the curiosities contained in his cabinet.

Befinstern, *v. tr.* to obscure. *Fig.* Den Verstand —, to darken the understanding.

Befirnissen, *v. tr.* to varnish over.

Befischen, *v. tr.* Einen Teich —, to fish in a pond.

Beflammen, *v. tr.* to furnish with flame[s]

1. **Beflecken**, [from Flecken, = *spot, blemish, stain* &c.] *v. tr.* to stain, to spot. Mit Tinte —, to spot with ink, to blot; mit Fett —, to grease; die Kleider —, to spot the clothes; ein mit Blut beflecktes Kleid, a garment stained with blood. *Fig.* Daß das Land mit Blutschulden befleckt wird [Ps. CVI.], that the land was polluted with blood; seine Ehre, seinen guten Namen —, to spot one's honour, one's reputation; Jemands guten Ruf —, to blot, to sully a man's reputation; die Sünde befleckt die Reinheit der Seele, sin stains the purity of the soul; Feigheit befleckt die Ehre, cowardice contaminates honour; befleckte Gedanken, defiled, vitiated, impure, sullied thoughts; Verrath befleckt das Blut, treason taints the blood; sich selbst —, to pollute one's self [to enervate one's body by self pollution]. Das Beflecken, or die Befleckung, spotting, staining. *Fig.* pollution.

2. **Beflecken**, [from Fleck or Flicklappen = *patch*] *v. tr.* 1) to heel-piece [shoes, boots]. 2) to patch.

Befleißen, *ir.* **Befleißigen**, *v. r.* sich —, to bestow pains upon a thing, to endeavour diligently. Sich einer Sache —, to apply one's self to any thing; sich der Weltweisheit —, to study philosophy; sich der Rechtsgelehrsamkeit —, to follow the law; sich der Arzneiwissenschaft —, to study medicine; sich der Gottesgelahrtheit —, to devote one's self to the study of theology; er befleißiget sich der Kürze, he endeavours after briefness or conciseness; er befleißiget sich sehr Ihnen zu gefallen, he is very studious to please you; [less frequently in a bad sense] er befleißiget sich des Bösen, his whole study is mischief.

Befleißigung, *f.* 1) the act of bestowing pains upon a thing. 2) close study, application.

Beflicken, *v. tr.* to patch [a garment &c.].

Befliegen, *ir. v. tr.* to fly upon, to light upon. Beflogen [among sportsmen], fledged.

Befließen, *ir. v. tr.* to flow upon or dis[charge] to. Mit Blut beflossen, stained with blood.

Beflissen, [past part. of Befleißen] *adj.* and *adv.* engaged in the study or pursuit of any thing, studious. Er ist sehr —, seine Besitzungen zu vergrößern, he is very studious to enlarge his possessions; der Rechtswissenschaft —, following the law; der Gottesgelahrtheit Beflissener, student in theology; [seldom in a bad or contemptuous sense] der Vergnügungen —, intent on pl[easures] sams. Befliffentlich, *adv.* carefully, accurately, sedulously.

Beflissenheit, *f.* assiduity, diligence, diligent endeavour.

Beflittern, *v. tr.* 1) to adorn with spangles, to bespangle. *Fig.* Der Himmel ist mit Sternen beflittert, the heaven is bespangled with stars. 2) to dress up with tinsel.

Beflören, *v. tr.* to cover with crape [a hat &c.] *Poet.* Der Gram beflort sein Antlitz, grief clouds his face.

Beflügeln, I. *v. tr.* 1) to furnish with wings, to wing. *Fig.* Wer beflügelt die Stürme? who wings the storms? es wird unsre Thätigkeit —, it will wing our activity; die Liebe beflügelt ihn, love lends him his wings; mit beflügelter Eile, with wingy speed; mit beflügelten Schritten, with rapid or winged steps. 2) [among sportsmen] Einen Wald —, to cut a lane through a forest. *Fig.* II. *v. r.* sich —, to move faster.

Beflügelung, *f.* 1) the act of winging. 2) the wings.

Befolgen, *v. tr.* to follow. *Fig.* to follow = to obey, to observe, to practise, to act in conformity to &c. Die Gebote Christi —, to follow the commands of Christ; gute Diener — die Befehle ihres Herrn, good servants follow the directions of their master; schlechte Beispiele werden eher als gute Regeln befolgt, ill patterns are sure to be followed more than good rules; wir werden Ihren Auftrag genau —, we shall adhere to your order; ein allgemein befolgter Grundsatz, a maxim generally adopted.

Befolgens-werth, **—würdig**, *adj.* and *adv.* deserving to be followed, obeyed or observed.

Befolger, *m.* [-s, *pl.* -] one who follows or obeys, a follower.

Befolgung, *f.* following, obeying or observing, observance, observation.

Befolgungs-werth, **—würdig**, **Befolgewürdig**, *adj.* and *adv.* V. Befolgenswerth.

Beförderer, *m.* [-s, *pl.* -] a promoter, patron. Ein — der Künste und Wissenschaften, a promoter, an encourager of arts and sciences; die — der Tugend, the patrons of virtue; [less usual in a bad sense] der — eines Verbrechens, the abettor of a crime.

Beförderlich, *adj.* furthering, promoting, conducive, conducible. — für das Wohl unsers Vaterlandes, conducive to the good of our country; zu Jemandes Verderben —, accessory to any one's ruin; auf —e Weise, in furtherance.

Befördern, *v. tr.* to send forward, to forward, to expedite. Briefe, Depeschen —, to forward letters, dispatches. *Fig.* *a*) to forward, to accelerate, to quicken, to hasten. Das befördert die Verdauung, that assists the digestion; das Wachsthum einer Pflanze —, to forward, to advance the growth of a plant. *b*) to forward, to promote, to advance. Jemands Plan —, to further or aid any one's design; eine gute Absicht —, to forward a good design. *c*) to advance, to promote, to raise to a higher rank. Einen zu einem Amte —, to prefer any one to a place; sein Gönner wird ihn schon —, his patron will advance him.

Beförderung, *f.* 1) the act of forwarding [goods &c.]. 2). *Fig.* advancement, promotion. Die Beförderungen sollten tauglichen Männern zu Theil werden, all preferments should be conferred upon fit men; die — eines Offiziers, the promotion of an officer.

Beförderungs-alter, *n.* seniority. —**kosten**, *pl.* V. Spesen. —**mittel**, *n.* a means to forward or promote any thing.

Befrachten, *v. tr.* to freight, to load with goods. Ein Schiff nach Amsterdam —, to freight a ship for Amsterdam.

Befrachter, *m.* [-s, *pl.* -] freighter, affreighter.

Befrachtung, *f.* freighting, affreightment.

Befragen, I. *v. tr.* to ask, to interrogate. Einen —, to question or interrogate any one; Einen um Etwas, wegen einer Sache —, to question any one about a thing. II. *v. r.* sich —, to consult with; sich bei Einem [wegen einer Sache] —, to consult with a person, to take any one's advice [about a thing]; *it.* sich —, to ask, to inquire; wenn Sie seine Wohnung auffinden wollen, so müssen Sie sich eben —, you must make inquiries, if you wish to find his lodging; ich befragte mich überall, konnte aber nicht erfahren, ob &c., I consulted everybody, but could not learn, if &c.

Befragung, *f.* questioning, interrogation, inquiry.

Befransen, *v. tr.* to adorn as with fringe, to befringe.

Befreien, *v. tr.* to free, to liberate. Einen aus der Haft, aus dem Gefängnisse —, to free any one from arrest, to liberate any one from imprisonment. *Fig.* Einen aus einer Gefahr —, to rescue any one from danger; unser Land ist von der Wuth der Tiger befreit, our land is freed from the rage of tigers; er befreite ihn aus den Händen des &c., he rescued him out of the hands of &c.; ein Haus von Abgaben —, to exempt a house from rates or taxes; sich von Sorgen —, to get rid of cares. SYN. Befreien, Erlösen, Retten. The removing of an evil from a person or thing, is expressed by Retten, if the evil is only impending or approaching; by Befreien and Erlösen, if it is actually present. When a sick person recovers from a dangerous illness, one may say: der Arzt habe ihn gerettet [the physician has saved him], although he has not yet entirely befreit [freed] him from the disease. Retten is used also of things, but Befreien only of living creatures, and Erlösen, properly speaking, only of persons. Man rettet [one saves] goods from fire and shipwreck, man befreit [one frees] an imprisoned bird, and man erlöset [one ransoms, delivers] a man from captivity.

Befreier, *m.* [-s, *pl.* -], -**inn**, *f.* one, who delivers, releases or rescues, deliverer. Bolivar der —, Bolivar the liberator.

Befreiung, *f.* 1) the act of freeing or delivering, deliverance. *Fig.* Die — aus der Gefahr, rescue from danger. 2) *Fig.* freedom from any service, charge, burden, tax or requisition, to which others are subject, exemption, immunity, privilege.

Befreiungsgeld, *n.* V. Lösegeld.

Befremden, I. *v. intr.* and *v. imp.* to appear strange, to surprise. Dieß befremdet mich von ihm, this astonishes me in him. II *v. r.* sich —, to be astonished, to wonder. Ihre Leichtgläubigkeit befremdet mich, I am surprised at your credulity. Das Befremden, the state of being astonished at something. Er äußerte sein — darüber, he expressed his astonishment; ich kann mein — nicht unterdrücken, daß &c., I cannot help observing, that I think it strange, that &c.

Befremdlich, *adj.* and *adv.* strange, odd, surprising.

Befressen, *ir. v. tr.* to gnaw, to nibble.

Befreunden, I. *v. tr.* 1) to connect by friendship. Sie sind mit einander befreundet, they are connected by friendship. 2) to connect by consanguinity and relationship. Mit Einem befreundet seyn, to be related to any one; der Befreundete, a kinsman, relation, connexion. II. *v. r.* sich —, 1) to make friends with &c. *Fig.* to accustom one's self to a thing. Er befreundete sich bald mit seiner neuen Lage, he soon found himself at home in his new situation. 2) to be united with in friendship. 3) to make affinity with. Und Salomo befreundete sich mit Pharao, [1. kings 3] Salomo made affinity with Pharaoh.

Befreundung, *f.* 1) the act of connecting by friendship or consanguinity. 2) friendly terms: consanguinity, relationship, affinity.

Befrieden, V. Befriedigen.

Befriedigen, *v. tr.* 1) to inclose with a wall, hedge &c., to secure by an enclosure. Einen Garten —, to fence a garden. 2) to make quiet, so as to stop complaint or opposition, to appease, to content. Seine Gläubiger —, to satisfy one's creditors; er ist befriedigt, he is satisfied [paid]; er ist schwer zu —, it is hard to please him, he is difficult to satisfy; eine Leidenschaft —, to satisfy a passion; seinen Stolz —, to gratify one's pride. Befriedigend, satisfactory; —de Zusicherungen, satisfactory assurances. 3) to please to such a degree as that nothing more is desired, to content, to satisfy. Der Erfolg hat unsre Erwartung nicht befriedigt, the issue did not answer our expectation; diese Musik befriedigt Sie nicht, this music does not please you. SYN. V. Abfinden.

Befriedigung, *f.* 1) the act of fencing. 2) the act of contenting, satisfaction. *Fig.* payment. — gewährend, satisfactory. 3) an inclosure, a fence.

Befrieren, *ir. v. intr.* [u. w. seyn, but only in the past part.] to be frozen over. Der Teich ist ganz befroren, the pond is entirely frozen over.

Befröhnen, **Befrohnen**, *v. tr.* 1) to impose feudal labour or service. ‡2) to seize [any one's estate &c.]. ‡3) to arrest [any one].

Befruchten, *v. tr.* to make fruitful, to fecundate [in botany], to impregnate. Das Land —, to fructify, to fertilize the land; ein Ei —, to fecundate an egg; mit Milch —, to milt [said of fish]; der Blumenstaub befruchtet die Narbe, the pollen of flowers fecundates the stigma; [in heraldry] ein befruchteter Baum, a fructed tree.

Befruchtung, *f.* fecundation. Die — der Feigen, caprification; die heimliche oder unmerkliche —, [in botany] cryptogamy.

Befruchtungsboden, *m.* V. Fruchtboden.

Befugen, *v. tr.* to authorize, to give a right to act, to empower [chiefly used in the participle befugt].

Befugniß, *f.* [*pl.* -sse] *n.* [-sses, *pl.* -sse] legal power, authority, warrant, order, permission. Einem — geben or ertheilen, to authorize any one.

Befugt, *part. adj.* 1) authorized, having legal capacity or power. Ein befugter Richter, a competent judge; ein befugter Zeuge, a competent witness. 2) legal, legitimate. SYN. Befugt, Berechtigt. Whoever can do or cause to be done a certain action, without any one's having a right to prevent him, or oblige him to the contrary, he is berechtigt [has a right] to act thus; has he legal grounds for doing so, he is befugt [authorized].

Befühlen, *v. tr.* to feel, to touch, to handle. Befühlen Sie dieses Stück Seidenzeug, feel this piece of silk.

Befund, *m.* [-s] the state in which any thing is found. Nach — der Umstände, as circumstances may prove.

Befunds-bericht, *m.* report, bulletin. —

zettel, *m.* [among physicians] bulletin.

Befurchen, *v. tr.* to make furrows in, to furrow.

Befürchten, *v. tr.* and *intr.* to be in apprehension of evil, to apprehend, to fear. Sie haben nichts zu —, you have nothing to fear.

Befürchtniß, *n.* [-sses, *pl.* -sse] the object of apprehension or fear, fear.

Befürchtung, *f.* apprehension, fear. Meine schlimmsten —en haben sich erfüllt, my worst apprehensions have been fulfilled.

Begabeln, *v. tr.* to hold with a fork.

Begaben, *v. tr.* to settle on as a permanent provision, to furnish with a permanent fund of property, to furnish with a portion of goods or estate. Eine Kirche, ein Collegium —, to endow a church, a college; eine Tochter —, to settle a dower on a daughter; Jemanden mit etwas —, to bestow a thing upon any one. *Fig.* Der Mensch ist mit Vernunft begabt, man is endowed with reason; von der Natur mit einem besondern Talente begabt, gifted by nature with a particular talent. Das Begaben, die Begabung, endowment.

Begäffeln, V. Begaffen.

Begaffen, *v. tr.* to look at gaping, to stare at or upon.

Begaffer, *m.* [-s, *pl.* -] [one who opens his mouth for wonder and stares foolishly] a gaper.

Begähnen, *v. tr.* to yawn at, to express weariness by yawning.

‖ **Begängeln**, *v. r.* sich —, to bedaub or bespatter one's self.

Begängniß, *n.* [-sses, *pl.* -sse] [a distinguishing by solemn rites] celebration [used only in the word Leichenbegängniß].

Begatten, *v. r.* sich —, [to unite in sexual embrace] to couple, to copulate. Laß Wölfe mit Schafen sich —, let wolves match with sheep. Das Begatten, V. Begattung.

Begattung, *f.* copulation, coition.

Begattungs-trieb, *m.* instinct which excites to copulation. **—zeit**, *f.* 1) coupling time. 2) [in botany] time of fecundation.

Begaukeln, *v. tr.* [unusual] to delude, to bewitch.

Begaunern, *v. tr.* [unusual] to deceive by trick or artifice, to juggle.

Begeben, *ir. v. r.* sich —, 1) to go to a place, to resort to, to repair to. Sich in einen schattigen Hain —, to betake one's self to a shady grove; sich nach Hause —, to go home; sich zur Ruhe —, to compose one's self to sleep, to go to bed; er begab sich hinweg, he retired; er begab sich in Cäsars Schutz, he betook himself to Cæsar for his protector; sich zu seinem Regimente —, to join one's regiment; sich unter die Soldaten —, to enlist one's self; sich auf den Weg —, to set out; sich auf die Flucht —, to betake one's self to flight. 2) to happen, to come to pass. Sie sprachen mit einander von allen den Dingen, die sich — hatten, they talked together of all those things which had happened. 3) to give up, to cede, to resign, to renounce. Ich begebe mich meines Rechtes, I divest myself of my right, I yield up my right; Sie müssen sich aller Ihrer Rechte auf meiner Tochter Hand —, you must renounce all pretension to my daughter's hand.

Begebenheit, *f.* **Begebniß**, *n.* [-sses, *pl.* -sse] [that which comes to pass, arrives or happens] event. Eine ungewöhnliche —, an unusual occurrence; die gewöhnlichen —en [Ereignisse] des Lebens, the ordinary occurrences of life. Syn. V. Abenteuer.

Begegnen, *v. intr.* [n. w. seyn] [to approach near, to encounter] to meet. Wie angenehm ist es für Freunde, sich unterwegs zu —, how pleasant it is for friends to meet on the road; noch angenehmer ist es, sich in der Fremde zu —, it is still more pleasant to meet in a foreign country; ich begegnete ihm zufällig auf der Straße, I lighted on him in the street. *Fig. a)* to happen to, to occur to, to come to pass. Das Schlimmste, was mir — kann, the worst that can befall me; es ist ihm ein großes Unglück begegnet, a great misfortune befell him; es begegnete, daß &c., it came to pass that &c. *b)* to prevent by interception or to remove at the beginning or in the outset, to remove in general. Allen Einwürfen —, to obviate all objections; Jemands Zweifeln —, to obviate one's doubts; Jemands Wünschen —, to meet a person's wishes; einem Unglücke —, to prevent a misfortune; dem gefürchteten Ausbruche eines Aufstandes —, to take measures to prevent the dreaded breaking out of a revolt; den Fortschritten einer Krankheit —, to oppose the progress of a disease. *c)* to treat in any manner, to deal with. Einem schlecht —, to deal ill with any one, to use any one ill. *d)* Sich — [in einem Wunsche], to meet or coincide [in a wish]. Ihre sich begegnenden Wünsche, their meeting wishes. Syn. Begegnen, Zusammentreffen. Zusammentreffen, as its derivation denotes, signifies merely a coming together without any reference to the direction in which the things approach one another; Begegnen, on the contrary, denotes, to come together, approaching in opposite or different directions. If two persons set out from the same place, they may fix on an other place where they will zusammentreffen [come together]; if they set out from opposite sides, they may agree on a third place where they will [einander] begegnen [meet one another].

Begegniß, *n.* [-sses, *pl.* -sse] occurrence, circumstance.

Begegnung, *f.* 1) occurrence. 2) prevention. 3) treatment.

Begehen, *ir.* I. *v. tr.* to visit, to inspect [the borders of a tract of land &c.], to enter upon; *it.* ‖ to measure out by walking or by steps, to step. Ein Feld —, to measure out a piece of field by walking; ein Kirchspiel —, to perambulate a parish. *Fig. a)* to distinguish by solemn rites, to honour and distinguish by ceremonies and marks of joy and respect. Ein Fest —, to celebrate a feast; seinen Geburtstag —, to celebrate or to keep one's birthday. *b)* to do, to effect or perpetrate. Verbrechen —, to commit crimes; einen Mord —, to commit a murder. II. *v. r.* sich —, to couple, to copulate.

Begehr, *n.* V. Begehren.

Begehren, *v. tr* and *intr.* 1) to wish for the possession and enjoyment with eagerness. Wer ein Weib ansiehet, ihrer [sie] zu —, [Matth. V.] whosoever looketh on a woman to lust after her; Niemand soll deines Landes —, [Ex. XXXIV.] neither shall any man desire thy land; du sollst nicht — deines Nächsten Haus, thou shalt not covet thy neighbour's house; er hat Alles was sein Herz begehrt, he has all things to his heart's desire; mein Herz begehrte nach ihr, my heart longed for [after] her; [among hunters] der Hirsch begehrt das Wildpret, the stag bellows; die Hirschkuh begehrt nach dem Hirsche, the hind goes to tourn; die Hündinn begehrt nach dem Hunde, the bitch is in heat; der Hirsch begehrt den Jäger, the stag assails the hunter with his horns. 2) to seek to obtain by words, to ask. Was — Sie? what do you ask for, what do you want? was begehrt man von uns? what is required of us? Jemands Tochter zur Ehe —, to solicit any one's daughter in marriage; er begehrt sie zur Frau, he wants her for a wife. Das Begehren, desire, demand, request. Auf Ihr —, at your desire.

Begehrens-werth, —würdig, *adj.* and *adv.* worthy of desire, desirable, appetible.

Begehrig, *adj.* and *adv.* 1) V. Begehrlich. 2) V. Begierlich.

Begehrlich, I. *adj.* eager to obtain, very desirous, covetous. II. *adv.* covetously.

Begehrlichkeit, *f.* covetousness, lustfulness.

Begehrungsklage, *f.* [in law] a petitory action.

Begehrungslos, *adj.* and *adv.* without desires or appetites.

Begehrungstrieb, *m.* [-s, *pl.* -e] the concupiscible appetite.

Begehrungsvermögen, *n.* [-s, *pl.* -] appetitive power or faculty.

Begehung, *f.* 1) celebration. 2) [the act of committing, doing or perpetrating] commission.

Begehungssünde, *f.* sin of commission.

Begeifern, *v. tr.* to slabber. Er hat mich über und über begeifert, he slabbered me all over. *Fig.* to slabber, to attack or pollute by venomous words. Seine gehässige Gemüthsart treibt ihn an, die verdienstvollsten Männer, die schönsten Handlungen zu —, the odious turn of his mind impels him to asperse, to vent out his venom upon the most deserving men, the fairest actions.

‖ **Begeilen**, *v. tr.* to manure, to dung.

Begeistern, *v. tr. Fig.* 1) to infuse or excite spirit in, to inspirit, to animate. 2) to inspire. *a)* [to infuse ideas or poetic spirit] Erato begeistre deines Dichters Seele, Erato thy poet's mind inspire. *b)* [to infuse or suggest ideas or monitions supernaturally] Die Propheten waren begeistert, the prophets have been inspired.

Begeisterung, *f.* 1) inspiration. Göttliche —, divine inspiration; die — Homers, the inspiration of Homer. 2) [heat of imagination, violent passion of the mind, in pursuit of some object] enthusiasm. Eine edle —, a noble enthusiasm; in — gerathen, to get warm or enthusiastic.

Begeisterungsvoll, *adj.* and *adv.* full of enthusiasm, enthusiastic, inspired.

Begeizen, *v. tr.* 1) to be stingy of a thing, to be excessively sparing of something. 2) to envy, to grudge.

Begier, [without a plural] **Begierde**, *f.* [-, *pl.* -n] 1) strong desire, appetite. Die — nach Gewinn, the lust of gain; die — nach Geld, the desire for riches; die — nach Ruhm, the longing after fame; sinnliche Begierden, sensual desires; fleischliche Begierden, carnal lusts, desires, appetence, appetency, concupiscence, lust; unordnete Begierden, inordinate desires. 2) eagerness, anxiousness. Voll —, zu erfahren, ob &c., full of eagerness to know, if &c.

Begierig, *adj.* and *adv.* 1) desiring, very desirous, appetent. — nach Geld, covetous of money; — nach Ehre oder Ruhm seyn, to be desirous of honour or fame. 2) eager, anxious. Ich bin — zu erfahren, ob &c., I am curious to learn, if &c.

Begierigkeit, *f.* V. Begier.

Begierlich, *adj.* and *adv.* having inordinate desires, very desirous.

Begießen, *ir. v. tr.* to moisten with a liquid. Etwas mit Wasser —, to pour water a thing; Pflanzen —, to water plants; begießt den durstigen Boden, wet the thirsty ground; den Braten —, to drip butter or fat upon meat as it turns upon the spit in roasting, to baste roast meat; ein Segel —, [in seamen's language] to wet a sail; ein Stück Eisen mit Blei —, to fix a piece of iron [in a wall &c.] with lead; das — mit Blei, sealing; mit Wachs —, to inject with wax. † *Fig.* Sich die Nase —, sich —, to wet one's whistle, to wet one's throat; *it.* to get drunk.

Begießer, *m.* [-s, *pl.* -] 1) he that moistens with a liquid. 2) V. Gießkanne.

Begiften, *v. tr.* [from Gabe, *gift*] to settle a dower on, to endow.

Beginn, *m.* [-es] the beginning, origin. Beim —e, at the beginning.

Beginnen, [either from gehen, or allied to the old northern word *ginna* = aufdecken, einnehmen, so that it answers to the Lat. *incipere*; or from γίγνομαι, W. is *gin* = Kopf] *ir.* I. *v. intr.* 1) [to have an original or first existence, to take rise] to begin, to commence. Seit die Welt begann, since the world began; und Thränen begannen zu fließen, and tears began to flow; der Frühling beginnt, spring commences. 2) to start, to begin. Mit etwas —, to begin with; er begann mit der lateinischen Sprachlehre, he began with the Latin grammar. II. *v. tr.* 1) [to enter upon first] to begin, to commence. Ein Werk —, to begin a work; seit wann haben Sie das Studium des Englischen begonnen? how long is it since you commenced the study of the English language? 2) to do, to undertake. Was wollt ihr — am Tage der Heimsuchung, [in Scripture] what will you do in the day of visitation? wir wußten nicht, was wir — sollten, we knew not what to do. Das Beginnen, the undertaking. Syn. V. Anfangen.

Beginner, *m.* [-s, *pl.* -] [the person who begins] beginner.

Begipsen, *v. tr.* to overlay with plaster, to plaster [a wall].

Begittern, *v. tr.* to furnish with a grate or trellis, to grate [a window &c.].

Beglänzen, *v. tr.* to throw or spread light on, to surround with splendour.

Begläsen, *v. tr.* 1) to furnish with glasses, looking-glasses or mirrors. Ein Fenster —, to glaze a window. 2) [unusual] to ogle with an eye-glass.

Beglauben, **Beglaubigen**, *v. tr.* 1) to attest [a copy of a record &c.], to give it the evidence of authenticity. Personen — Schriften durch ihre Unterschrift, persons attest writings by subscribing their names; eine Sache mit einem Eide —, to avouch or affirm any thing by oath; eine beglaubigte Abschrift, a certified copy. 2) to accredit [an ambassador, envoy]. II. *v. r.* sich — [more usual: ausweisen], to ascertain or prove one's self to be the person in question, to prove one's identity.

Beglaubiger, *m.* [-s, *pl.* -] 1) one who attests, attester. 2) [an officer authorized to attest contracts and writings of any kind, to give them the evidence of authenticity] a notary.

Beglaubigt, **Beglaubt**, *part. adj.* 1) authentic, authentical. Eine —e Schrift, an authentic paper. 2) having credit, credible.

Beglaubigung, *f.* attestation, notarial attestation, credentials.

Beglaubigungs-amt, *n.* the office of a notary. —brief, *m.* V. —schreiben. —eid, *m.* [in law] attestation by oath. —schein, *m.* a certificate. —schreiben, *n.* credentials, letter of credence.

Begleit, *m.* and *n.* [-es] V. Begleitung.

1\. **Begleiten**, [from Geleit, *conduct, escort, convoy*; instead of beigeleiten] *v. tr.* 1) to go with or attend as a companion or associate on a journey, walk &c., to accompany. Ich begleitete meinen Freund auf einer Reise, I accompanied my friend on a tour; Timokrates begleitete mich zur Belagerung von Troja, Timocrates attended me to the siege of Troy; — Sie ihn an die Thüre, wait on him to the door. *Fig.* Meine besten Wünsche — dich, my best wishes attend thee; die Ausführung dieses Planes ist von vielen Schwierigkeiten begleitet, the execution of this plan is accompanied with many difficulties. 2) *Fig. a)* [in music] to accompany. Mit der Flöte —, to accompany with the flute; einen Sänger —, to play to a person who sings. *b)* [in heraldry] begleitet, accompagnee.

2\. **Begleiten**, [from gleiten, *to glide*] *ir. v. tr.* [unusual] to glide, to slip upon. Er beglitt die Eisfläche mit wunderbarer Schnelligkeit, he glided over the surface of the ice with astonishing rapidity.

Begleiter, *m.* [-s, *pl.* -] one who attends or accompanies, an attendant, companion, follower. Die —inn, *f.* a female companion. *Fig.* Bescheidenheit ist eine —inn des Verdienstes, modesty is an attendant upon merit.

Begleitschaft, *f.* V. Begleitung and Geleite.

Begleitstimme, *f.* [*pl.* -n] the accompanying voice.

Begleitung, *f.* 1) the act of attending, accompanying or going with a companion. 2) an attendant, companion, follower. Die — eines Fürsten, the suite, the retinue, the train of a prince. 3) *Fig.* [in music] the accompanying part, accompaniment.

Begleitungsstimme, *f.* V. Begleitstimme.

Begliedern, *v. tr.* to furnish with limbs or members, to limb. Ein stark begliederter Mann, a stronglimbed man.

Begliederung, *f.* [in painting] limbing.

† **Beglotzen**, *v. tr.* to gaze at or upon.

Beglücken, *v. tr.* to make happy. [in conversational language] — Sie mich mit der Erzählung dieser Sache, do but bless me with the story of it.

Beglücker, *m.* [-s, *pl.* -] he that makes happy. Dieser Fürst ist der — seiner Unterthanen, this prince is the benefactor of his people.

Beglückseligen, *v. tr.* to make happy, to bless.

Beglückt, *adj.* and *adv.* happy, prosperous, fortunate. — durch Frieden und Ueberfluß, blessed with peace and plenty; —, wer fern vom Geräusch der Welt leben darf, happy the man, who can live retired from the bustle of the world.

Beglückwünschen, *v. tr.* [to profess one's joy or pleasure to another on account of an event deemed happy or fortunate] to congratulate, to felicit.

‖ **Begnabbeln**, **Begnabbern**, *v. tr.* to gnaw.

Begnaden and [more usual] **Begnadigen**, *v. tr.* 1) to grace, to favour. Er ist vom Könige mit dieser Auszeichnung begnadiget worden, the king has graciously pleased to confer this distinction upon him. 2) to pardon [a criminal]. Vom Könige begnadigt werden, to obtain the king's full pardon.

Begnader and [more usual] **Begnadiger**, *m.* [-s, *pl.* -] 1) [unusual] one that dispenses favours to any one. 2) one that pardons a criminal, pardoner.

Begnadigung, *f.* 1) pardoning, pardon. 2) favour, grace.

Begnadigungsrecht, *n.* the right of pardoning a criminal.

Begnügen, I. *v. r.* sich —, to content one's self [with any thing]. Sich — lassen mit &c., to be content with &c.; sich mit Wenigem —, to be satisfied with little. II. *v. imp.* V. Genügen.

Begnüglich, *adj.* and *adv.* easily satisfied, moderate.

Begnügsam, *adj.* and *adv.* contented with little, frugal. V. Genügsam.

Begnügsamkeit, *f.* content, contentment, frugality. V. Genügsamkeit.

‖ **Begrabbeln**, *v. tr.* to touch, to feel, to finger.

Begraben, *ir.* I. *v. tr.* to inter, to bury, to inhume [a deceased person]. *Fig.* to bury = to hide in oblivion. † *Prov.* Da liegt der Hund —, there's the rub. Das —, burial, interment, funeral, inhumation. *Fig.* II *v. r.* sich —, to withdraw or conceal in retirement. Sich in einem Kloster —, to bury one's self in a monastery.

Begraber, *m.* [-s, *pl.* -] burier.

Begräbniß, *n.* [-sses, *pl.* -sse] 1) [the act of burying a deceased person] burial, interment, inhumation, obsequies. 2) a sepulchre, a grave.

Begräbniß-feier, *f.* V. Beerdigungsfeier. —feierlichkeit, *f.* V. Beerdigungsfeierlichkeit. —fest, *n.* funeral feast. —gebühr, *f.* V. Leichengebühr. —kosten, *pl.* V. Beerdigungskosten. —lied, *n.* funeral song. —mahl, *n.* V. Leichenmahl. —platz, *m.* burying-place —tuch, *n.* V. Leichentuch.

Begrasen, I. *v. tr.* to cover with grass, to grass. Begraste Hügel, grassy hills. II. *v. r.* sich —, to fatten upon grass.

Begrauen, *v. intr.* [u. w. seyn] to turn, to become grey. [used only in the past part.] begrauet, turned grey, become grey or old.

Begreifen, *ir.* I. *v. tr.* 1) to touch, to handle. Begreifen Sie dieses Stück Seidenzeug, feel this piece of silk, feel of it. *Fig. a)* to comprehend, to include to comprise. England wurde nicht mit in den Frieden begriffen, England was not included in the peace. *b)* to comprehend, to understand, to conceive. Schnell etwas —, to be quick of comprehension; wir können nicht —, auf welche Art der Geist auf den Stoff wirkt, we cannot conceive the manner in which spirit operates upon matter. *c)* In sich —, to contain, to include. Diese Zahl begreift den verzeichneten Artikel nicht in sich, this number does not include the specified article; dieses Wort begreift mehrere Bedeutungen in sich, this word has many significations. *d)* Begriffen seyn, to be engaged in, to be in the act. Ueber der Arbeit begriffen seyn, to be at work; er ist auf einer Reise begriffen, he is travelling, he is on a journey. ‡ 2) to remove, to cure [St. Anthony's fire &c.] by superstitious touching. II. *v. r.* 1) *imp.* to be easily understood. Das begreift sich leicht, that is no difficult matter to comprehend. 2) [unusual] sich —, to recover one's self.

Begreiflich, *adj.* and *adv.* capable of being understood, comprehensible, conceivable by the mind, intelligible. Man konnte ihm nicht — machen, daß &c., he could not be brought to understand, that &c. Syn. V. Deutlich.

Begreiflichkeit, *f.* capability of being understood, comprehensibleness.

Begrenzen, *v. tr.* Die Berge — die Aussicht, the hills terminate the view; jenes Haus begrenzt unsere Aussicht, yonder house determinates or obstructs our view. *Fig.* Seine Wünsche —, to bound one's wishes. Syn. V. Beschränken.

Begrenzung, *f.* 1) the act of bordering or bounding. 2) that which borders or bounds, limits. 3) [the line that terminates the view when extended on the surface of the earth] horizon.

Begriff, *m.* [-es, *pl.* -e] 1) the state of being about to do any thing. Sie waren im —e, sich zu schlagen, they were about to fight, or on the point of fighting; sie waren im —e, aufzubrechen, als &c., they were just preparing to start, when &c 2) V. Inbegriff. 3) [the object of thought, or the notice the mind takes of its perceptions] idea, [in popular language] notion. Helle —e, clear ideas; abstrakte —e, abstract ideas; man kann einen richtigen — von der Gewalt, oder falsche —e von dem Geiste haben, we may have a just notion of power, or false notions respecting spirit; ich kann mir einen vollkommenen — davon machen, I have a perfect idea of it; ich habe keinen — davon, I cannot conceive it, I can form no notion of it. 4) [= Fassungskraft] Er ist von langsamem —e, he is dull of apprehension, he has no quick perception.

Begriff[e]s-leer, *adj.* and *adv.* void of ideas. —**sangabe**, —**sbestimmung**, *f.* definition [of a circle &c.]. Eine —sbestimmung von den Wörtern [or: der Wörter] Tugend, Muth &c. geben, to define the words virtue, courage &c. —**sfach**, *n.* [in logic] category. —**gesellung**, *f.* an association of ideas. —**verwechslung**, *f.* a confounding of ideas.

Begrübeln, *v. tr.* 1) to ruminate upon. 2) to carp at.

Begründen, *v. tr.* 1) to establish by reasons and arguments. Eine Behauptung —, to prove, to make good an assertion; eine Motion [einen Antrag in einer berathenden Versammlung] —, to offer reasons for, to set down the motives or cause of a motion [or proposition made in a deliberative assembly]; seine Meinung ist gut begründet, his opinion is well supported; seine Ansprüche sind nicht gehörig begründet, his claims are not properly founded. 2) to establish, as on something solid or durable, to found [a new doctrine &c.].

Begründer, *m.* [-s, *pl.* -] one that establishes, founder.

Begründniß, *n.* [-sses, *pl.* -sse] **Begründung**, *f.* 1) [the act of establishing, founding] establishment. 2) a reason, argument.

Begrünen, I. *v. tr.* [unusual] to make green, to cover with verdure. Begrünte Felder, verdant fields. II. *v. r.* sich —, to become or grow green or verdant.

Begrüßen, *v. tr.* 1) to address with expressions of kind wishes, to salute in kindness, to greet. [in seamen's lang.] Ein Schiff —, to salute a ship. *Fig.* Die goldene Sonne begrüßt den Morgen, the golden sun salutes the morn. ‡2) Einen um Etwas —, to ask any one's consent to a thing [out of politeness]; er erwartet, daß man ihn darum begrüßt, he expects to be asked for it in a polite manner.

Begrüßung, *f.* 1) greeting, salutation. 2) salute, salutation.

Begrüßungs-formel, *f.* phrase of salutation. —**wort**, *n.* term of salutation.

Begucken, *v. tr.* [in familiar language] to look at inquisitively.

Beguine, Begine, *f.* [*pl.* -n] [name of certain nuns or devout maids] beguine.

Begünstigen, *v. tr.* to regard with kindness, to support, to favour. Die Sache einer Partei —, to favour the cause of a party; das Begünstigen, die Begünstigung &c., a kind act or office, favour. *Fig.* to afford advantages for success, to render successful, to favour. Die Dunkelheit der Nacht begünstigte seine Annäherung, the darkness of the night favoured his approach; heiteres Wetter begünstigte die Reise, fair weather favoured the voyage; unser Vorhaben zu —, to prosper our design.

Begünstiger, *m.* [-s, *pl.* -] favourer. Der — eines Verbrechens, the abettor of a crime.

Begürten, *v. tr.* to bind with a girdle, to begird, to girth.

Begütern, *v. tr.* to make wealthy [used only in the past part.]. Begütert, wealthy, opulent.

Begütigen, *v. tr.* to appease. Durch Liebkosungen oder Schmeicheleien —, to soften by caresses or flattery.

Behaaren, Behären, I. *v. tr.* to cover with hair. Ein behaarter Hund, [among hunters] a hairy dog; behaart, [in botany] pubescent. II. *v. r.* sich —, to get hair.

‖**Behaben**, *v. r.* sich —, to behave [ill].

Behacken, *v. tr.* 1) to hoe [the earth in a garden &c.]. Die Beete —, to hoe the beds. 2) [to clear from weeds] to hoe [cabbages &c.].

Behaftet, [*part.* of the obsolete verb Behaften] *adj.* and *adv.* affected with continued or often repeated pain or infirmities, either of body or mind; suffering grief or distress of any kind. Mit Flüssen —, afflicted with rheumatism; mit Ohnmachten —, subject to fainting; mit der Krätze —, infected with the itch, itchy. *Fig.* Er ist mit der Sucht —, Heirathen zu stiften, he is possessed with the mania of match-making.

Behageln, *v. tr.* to cover with hail, to hail upon. Behagelt, 1) covered with hail. 2) ‖and † dead drunk.

Behagen, *v. imp.* and *intr.* to please, to gratify. Es behagt ihm gar nicht, he does not like it, it does not please him at all; an etwas Behagen finden, to take pleasure in any thing. °Er läßt es sich — [= er macht es sich behaglich, °läßt es sich wohl sein], he takes his ease, he takes it comfortably; das Behagen, comfort; er läßt sich nicht gerne in seinem Behagen stören, he does not like to be troubled in his comforts.

Behaglich, *adj.* and *adv.* pleasing, agreeable, comfortable. Ein sehr —es Leben führen, to live very comfortably.

Behaglichkeit, *f.* comfortableness.

Behaken, *v. tr.* to furnish with hooks.

Behalftern, *v. tr.* to furnish with a halter. Ein Pferd —, to halter a horse.

‖**Behalt**, *m.* [-es] V. [the more usual word] Meinung.

Behaltbar, *adj.* and *adv.* that which may be retained, kept &c. [seldom used in this sense]; *it.* that which may be kept in the memory.

Behalten, *ir. v. tr.* to retain in one's power or possession, not to lose or part with, to keep. Denn ich wollte ihn bei mir —, [Philem. 13] whom I would have retained with me; etwas im Gedächtnisse —, to keep a thing in the memory, to retain, to remember a thing; ich setze die Zahl sieben hin und behalte zwei im Sinne, [in arithmetic] I set down seven and carry two; der Platz behält euren Namen, the place retains your name; er behielt alles dieses bei sich, he kept all this to himself; Fassung —, to keep one's countenance; der Herr weiß &c. die Ungerechten aber zu — zum Tage des Gerichts, zu peinigen, [in Script.] the Lord knoweth &c., and to reserve the unjust unto the day of judgment to be punished. Behalten, *past. part.* [in seamen's language] ein —es Schiff, a ship escaped the danger.

Behälter, ‖**Behalter**, *m.* [-s, *pl.* -] V. Behältniß, 1).

Behältlich, [with some authors] **Behaltlich**, V. Behaltbar.

Behältniß, *n.* [-sses, *pl.* -sse] 1) a place for keeping any thing, a place for preserving any thing in a state desired, as from loss, decay, waste or injury, a conservatory. Das — für Vorräthe, a storehouse; ein Wasser—, a reservoir of water; ein Fisch—, a fishpond; das — der Galle, [in anatomy] gallbladder. 2) *pl.* [in hunting] covert.

Behaltsam, *adj.* and *adv.* retentive. Ein —es Gedächtniß, a retentive memory.

Behaltsamkeit, *f.* the faculty of retaining something in the memory.

‖ and † **Behammeln**, *v. r.* sich —, to bedaggle one's clothes.

Behämmern, *v. tr.* to form or forge with a hammer, to shape by beating, to hammer.

Behandeln, *v. tr.* 1) to handle. *Fig.* *a*) to treat, to discourse on, to discuss, to manage in writing or speaking. Der Schriftsteller hat den Gegenstand mit Gewandtheit or geschickt behandelt, the author has handled the subject with address. *b*) to handle = to treat, to use well or ill. Wie hat man dich behandelt? how wast thou used? 2) to bargain for. Eine Waare —, to chaffer for, to cheapen a commodity; sie — Waaren, kaufen aber nichts, they cheapen goods, but buy nothing; diese Waare ist schon behandelt, the price of this merchandise is already agreed upon.

Behändigen, *v. tr.* to give or transmit with the hand, to hand. Behändige ihm das Buch, hand him the book.

Behandlung, *f.* 1) management, treatment. 2) [in painting, sculpture] management. V. Behandeln.

Behang, *m.* [-es, *pl.* -hänge] 1) that which hangs on a thing. 2) [among hunters] the ears of a sporting-dog, especially of the spaniel or pointer, when large and thin and hanging much below his chaps.

Behangzeit, *f.* [among hunters] the time, when stags lose their hair.

Behangen, *ir v. intr.* [u. w. seyn, and used only joined with bleiben] — bleiben, to continue hanging.

Behangen, [past part. instead of the reg. behängt of behängen] *adj.* Er war mit einer goldenen Kette um den Hals —, a gold chain was suspended from his neck; mit Lumpen —, covered with rags.

Behängen, *v. tr.* to cover or furnish by any thing suspended or fastened to the walls &c., to hang. Ein Zimmer mit Vorhängen oder Gemälden —, to hang an apartment with curtains or pictures; sich mit Bändern, Kränzen —, to deck or adorn one's self with ribands, wreaths; [among hunters] die Hunde — das Wild, the dogs hold fast upon the game; einen Hund —, to leash a pointer. † *Fig.* Er behängt sich mit schlechten Leuten, he keeps bad company.

Behängsel, *n.* [-s, *pl.* -] 1) [mostly in contempt] bawbles or other valueless things with which a person decks himself out. 2) tapestry.

Behären, V. Behaaren.

Beharken, *v. tr.* [in gardening] to hoe [the beds].

Beharnen, *v. tr.* to bepiss.

Beharnischen, *v. tr.* to dress in armour, to harness.

Beharren, *v. intr.* [u. w. seyn and haben] 1) to continue *a*) = to remain in any state or place. *b*) = to persevere, to be steadfast or constant in any course. Bis ans Ende —, to continue to the end. 2) to persevere = to persist. Bei seinem Vorsatze —, to stand to one's resolution; auf seiner Meinung —, to stand to one's opinion; auf Forderungen —, to persist in demands, to insist on demands; das Beharren in einem Fehler, perseverance in a fault.

Behárrlich, *adj.* and *adv.* constant, certain, steady, firmly adherent, persevering, perseverant. Ein —er Fleiß, a constant application; —e Zuneigung, lasting affection; ein Mann, der — bei seinem Vorsatze bleibt, a man constant to his purpose.

Behárrlichkeit, *f.* constancy, persevering, perseverance, resolution. Die — in der Freundschaft, in der Liebe, stability in friendship, constancy in love; mit —, perseveringly; Geduld und — besiegen die größten Schwierigkeiten, patience and perseverance overcome the greatest difficulties.

Behárschen, *v. intr.* [u. w. seyn] 1) to harden, to grow hard. 2) to congeal. Die Wunde ist beharscht, the wound is scabbed over.

Behárzen, *v. tr.* to smear with resin.

Behäuben, *v. tr.* to cover with a cap. Sich —, to put on a cap; die behaubte Lerche, crested or copped lark.

Behauchen, *v. tr.* to breathe upon [a looking glass &c.].

Behauen, *ir. v. tr.* 1) to shape or form by cutting or hewing. Ein Stück Bauholz —, to hew timber; das — [of unevennesses &c.], [in shipbuilding] bearding. 2) to remove a part by cutting, to cut off. Einen Baum —, to lop a tree. 3) [in mining] to assay, to try or prove by hewing.

Behäufeln, Behäufen, *v. tr.* to raise earth about plants. Die Kartoffeln &c. —, to hill potatoes; Pflanzen —, to raise a little mass of earth about plants, to hill plants.

Behauptbar, *adj.* and *adv.* maintainable, warrantable.

Behaupten, I. *v. tr.* 1) to maintain = to support by assertion or argument, to affirm. Eine Meinung —, to maintain an opinion; das Gegentheil —, to affirm the contrary. 2) to maintain = to hold, to keep. Einen Platz —, to maintain a place or post; das Schlachtfeld —, to remain master of the field, to keep the field after a battle. *Fig.* to maintain = to support, to defend. Sein Recht —, to maintain one's right. II. *v. r.* sich —, to keep one's ground, to keep up one's credit, authority, dignity. Syn. Behaupten, Bejahen. Bejahen signifies to affirm, to maintain an opinion only in the affirmative, Behaupten also to maintain in the negative.

Behauptung, *f.* 1) maintaining, assertion. 2) position advanced, affirmation, assertion.

Behausen, I. *v. tr.* to lodge II. *v. r.* sich —, to settle as an inhabitant.

Behäusen, *v. tr.* to cover with a case, to case [a watch] &c.

Behauset, *part. adj.* ‡ 1) possessing a dwelling, habitation or house. 2) settled as an inhabitant.

Behausung, *f.* 1) lodging. 2) a mansion, house, habitation.

Behäuten, *v. tr.* to cover with a skin or with leather.

Beheften, *v. tr.* 1) to fix with hooks or pins. ‡2) V. Betrügen.

Behelf, *m.* [-es, *pl.* -e] 1) means employed in an exigency. Das ist mein letzter —, that is my last resource. [often used in compound words, as Noth— &c.] 2) [in law, a plea offered in extenuation of a fault or irregular deportment] excuse, apology, shift.

Behelfen, *ir. v. r.* sich —, to employ means, to resort to expedients in an exigency. Sich mit Lügen —, to resort, to have recourse to lies, to try to get off by lies; sich kümmerlich — müssen, to have but a scanty allowance, to be pinched, to be put hard to; wir müssen uns — so gut wir können, we must shift as well as we can; ich kann mich ohne dasselbe —, I can make shift without it.

Behelflich, *adj.* and *adv.* [in law] serving for an excuse.

Behellen, [more usual] **Behelligen**, *v. tr.* to molest, to render uneasy, to annoy. Ich will Sie nicht länger mit meinen Besuchen —, I shall no longer molest you with my visits; er behelligte ihn beständig mit seinen Bittgesuchen, he importuned him constantly with his petitions.

Behelligung, *f.* molestation, uneasiness given, disturbance, annoyance.

Behelmen, *v. tr.* to furnish with a helmet. Behelmt, helmed, helmeted.

Behemden, *v. tr.* to furnish with a shift or a shirt, to shirt. Sich —, to put on a shift or a shirt.

* **Behemot**, *n.* [-es, *pl.* -e] [Job. XL] Behemoth.

Behen, Been, *m.* [-s, *pl.* -] [a plant, the root of which is medicinal] behen, ben.

Behen-baum, **—nußbaum**, *m.* smooth bonduc. **—nuß**, *f.* ben or bennut. **—öl**, *n.* the oil extracted from the bennut. **—wurzel**, *f.* the root of the smooth bonduc.

Behende, [Ice. *hentig*, Sw. *handig* and *behaendig*, D. *handig*] I. *adj.* light and quick in motion, moving with ease and celerity, agile, nimble. Ein behender Junge, a nimble boy; er vertraute seinen —n Füßen, he trusted to the nimbleness of his feet. II. *adv.* with agility, with light quick motion, nimbly, adroitly.

Behendigkeit, *f.* lightness and agility in motion, nimbleness.

Behenken, V. [more elegant and usual] Behängen.

Beherbergen, *v. tr.* [to furnish with a temporary habitation] to lodge [a friend &c.]. Er beherbergte ihn eine Nacht, he lodged him for a night.

Beherrschen, I. *v. tr.* 1) to manage with power and authority. Ein Land —, to rule over a country; die Welt —, to sway the world; die Liebe beherrscht sein ganzes Wesen, love sways his whole nature; seine Leidenschaften —, to govern one's passions; er beherrschte seinen Zorn, he suppressed his wrath; seine Neigungen —, to rule one's affections; menschliche Weisheit oder Macht vermag den Gang der Ereignisse nicht zu —, the course of events cannot be controlled by human wisdom or power; sie beherrschte den schwachen Fürsten völlig, she completely ruled the weak-minded prince. 2) to command = to overlook. Die Veste beherrscht den Hafen, the fort commands the harbour; der Thurm beherrscht die Stadt, the tower overlooks the town. II. *v. r.* sich —, to be master of one's self, to have the command or control of one's passions.

Beherrscher, *m* [-s, *pl.* -] ruler, lord, master. Cäsar, der Welt großer und sein eigener —, Cæsar, the world's great master and his own; er ist unumschränkter — seiner Völker, he is the absolute sovereign of his people.

Beherrscherinn, *f.* [a female who governs] mistress, sovereign. *Fig.* Rom war die — der Welt, Rome was mistress of the world.

Beherrschung, *f.* domination, dominion, government, sovereignty.

Beherzen, *v. tr.* to encourage [used only in the part. beherzt].

Beherzigen, *v. tr.* to think or ponder on with care, to take to heart. Eine Sache —, to reflect maturely upon a thing.

Beherzigens-werth, **—würdig**, *adj.* and *adv.* worth reflection, deserving to be considered.

Beherzigung, *f.* consideration, reflection.

Beherzigungs-werth, **—würdig**, *adj.* and *adv.* V. Beherzigenswerth.

Beherzt, [*part.* of Beherzen] *adj.* and *adv.* 1) furnished with a heart [rather unusual in this meaning]. 2) courageous, brave, bold, daring. Ein —er Mann, a courageous man; ein —er Angriff, a bold attack; ein —es Unternehmen, a daring exploit.

Beherztheit, *f.* courage, bravery, intrepidity.

Behetzen, *v. tr.* [in hunting] 1) to harass by dogs. Ein wildes Schwein —, to bait a boar. 2) V. Einhetzen.

Beheucheln, *v. tr.* to deceive by dissembling.

Beheulen, *v. tr.* to bewail, to bemoan, to howl at.

Behexen, *v. tr.* to fascinate, to bewitch, to spell. Sieh, ich bin behext, look, I am bewitched.

Behimmeln, *v. tr.* [used only in the part.] Behimmelt seyn, [in famil. lang.] to be tipsy.

Behindern, *v. tr.* V. Verhindern.

Behinken, *v. tr.* to visit hobbling.

‖ **Behner**, *m.* [-s, *pl.* -] [in gardening] a basket.

Behobeln, *v. tr.* [to smooth with the plane] to plane [a board &c.]. *Fig.* *to refine, to polish.

Behohnlächeln, *v. tr.* [to laugh in scorn] to deride.

Behólfen, [past part. of Behelfen] *adj.* and *adv.* quick, ready, smart. [more usual in compositions, as: Unbeholfen &c.]

Behólfenheit, *f.* quickness, readiness. [more usual in compositions, as: Unbeholfenheit &c.]

Behólzen, Behölzen, Behölzigen, I. *v. tr.* 1) to furnish with wood. Einen Wald —, [am. foresters] to promote the growth of young trees; den Ofen —, [among bakers] to provide the oven with wood. 2) [sometimes improperly for Abholzen] to clear from wood. II. *v. r.* sich —, to grow, to thrive [said of trees]. III. *v. intr* [u. w. seyn] to be covered with wood. Die Insel ist ganz beholzt, the island is wooded all over.

Behólzung, *f.* 1) the act of furnishing with wood. 2) V. Beholzungsgerechtigkeit.

Beholzungsgerechtigkeit, *f.* the liberty of cutting wood in a forest.

‖ **Behör**, *n.* [-s] [and *f.*] appendage, appurtenance.

Behórchen, *v. tr.* Einen —, to listen clandestinely to what any one says, to overhear a person.

Behörde, *f.* [*pl.* -n] 1) that which is necessary and proper. 2) that which is belonging to any thing, appurtenance, appendage. 3) the place, to which any thing belongs, proper place of reference, proper authority, proper office. 4) [in law] office, court, authority. Die Polizei—, police office; die Gerichts-[Justiz-]—, court of justice, judicature, magistracy; die Staats—, supreme authority, government; die Lokal—n, local authorities.

Behören, *v. intr.* V. [the more usual word] Gehören.

Behörig, *adj.* and *adv.* proper. V. [the more usual word] Gehörig.

Behösen, *v. tr.* to furnish with breeches. Ein behoseter [more usual: Hosen tragender] Knabe, a breeched boy.

Behuf, *m.* [-es, *pl.* -e] [allied to haben; Sw.

and Ice. *haefwa*, signifies gestemen] behoof, behalf. Zum —e des &c., in behalf of the &c.; zum — des Hospitals, in behoof of the hospital; zu diesem — ist es gut, it serves to this use or purpose.

Behufen, *v. tr.* to furnish with hoofs. Von allen behuften Thieren ist das Pferd das schönste, of all the hoofed quadrupeds the horse is the most beautiful.

Behufig, *adj.* and *adv.* V. Dienlich.

Behügeln, *v. tr.* [unusual] to raise a little mound of earth about any thing, to hill. Ein behügeltes Land, a hilly country.

Behülflich, *adj.* and *adv.* helpful, useful. Einem bei [in] Bezahlung seiner Schulden — seyn, to help any one to pay his debts; Einem zu etwas — seyn, to help any one to a thing.

Behüllen, *v. tr.* V. Verhüllen.

Behülsen, *v. tr.* to cover with husks.

Behüpfen, *v. tr.* to leap upon.

Behüte, *interject.* V. Behüten 2).

Behüten, *v. tr.* 1) to feed sheep or cattle upon any piece of ground [in this sense also behuten] 2) to guard, to keep. Siehe, ich bin mit dir und will dich —, [Gen. XXVIII] behold, I am with thee to keep thee; Gott behüte mich vor solchem Gedanken, Lord keep me from having any such thought; behüte Gott or Gott behüte, God forbid!

Behüter, *m.* [-s, *pl.* -] he that guards, guardian, protector.

Behutsam, *adj.* and *adv.* cautious, careful, heedful, circumspect. Ein —es Betragen, a prudent behaviour; seid — im Reden, be careful of your conversation.

Behutsamkeit, *f.* heedfulness, caution, carefulness. Mit vieler —, with great circumspection.

Bei, I. *prep.* [Sax., Low-Sax. &c. *bi*, Engl. and D. *by*; is probably derived from the old *bio*, wohnen, with which bin, the Eng. *to be*, is allied] 1) [on the question, whither? it governs the accusative case] — Seite gehen, rufen, nehmen, &c., to go, to call, to take aside; und er kam hart — mich [obsolete] [Dan. 8, 17] and he came close up to me. 2) [on the question, where? *a*)] [noting nearness, presence] by, near — der Kirche, near the church; — Einem sitzen, to sit by any one; — Einem liegen, stehen, wohnen, to lie, stand, live with any one; melden Sie sich — ihm, address yourself to him; sich — Einem bedanken, to render thanks to any one; — Einem anklopfen, to knock at any one's door; die Schlacht — Leipzig, the battle of Leipsic; — dem Flusse, upon the river; — Tische sitzen, to be at table; — der Flasche sitzen, to be engaged at a bottle; — [am] Hofe leben, to live at court; [in seamen's language] — dem Winde segeln, to sail with a scant wind, to sail on a wind; dicht — dem Winde segeln, to sail close hauled, kein Geld — sich haben, to have no money by one or with one; sie gingen Mann — [= neben] Mann, they walked man with man, alongside of each other; — [unter] den Alten, among the ancients; — uns, with us; — den Amerikanern, with or among the Americans. *Fig.* — Sinnen seyn, to be in one's right senses; — sich bleiben, to keep one's temper; nicht — Verstande seyn, to be beside one's self, to be out of one's wits; etwas — sich behalten, to keep a thing by one; dies ist — ihm einerlei, this is all the same with him; — Ihnen [in Bezug auf Sie] verliere ich die Geduld, with you I lose all patience; Einen — Leben erhalten, to keep any one alive; — guter Gesundheit, in good health; — Vermögen seyn, to be well off, in good circumstances; schon — Jahren seyn, to be already advanced in years; — nahe, V. Beinahe; — weitem, by far; — etwas stehen bleiben, [= nicht weiter gehen, als bis zu diesem Punkte] to remain stationary by a thing; — Heller und Pfennig bezahlen, to pay to the last farthing; *— einem Haare, [= beinahe] to a hair; — Gott schwören, [unter Anrufung Gottes] to swear by God; ich schwöre — Allem was heilig ist, I swear by all that is sacred; — meiner Seele, upon my soul, as I hope to be saved; — meiner Ehre, upon my honour; — Lebensgefahr [= so daß Lebensgefahr damit verbunden ist] or Todesstrafe, upon or under pain of death; — Leibe nicht, by no means. *b*) [noting a single part] Einen — der Hand nehmen, to take any one by the hand; Einen —'m Kopfe nehmen, to take any one by the head; *it fig.* to arrest, to seize any one. *Fig.* Einen — seinem Namen nennen, to call any one by his name; — diesen Worten stand er auf, at these words he got up. *c*) [in reference to time = während] — seinen Lebzeiten, in his life-time; — einer halben Stunde, about half an hour; — Tage, in the day time, by day; — Nacht, in the night, by night, at night; — Licht, by candle-light; — Gelegenheit, [= gelegentlich] on occasion; — offenen Fenstern schlafen, to sleep with the windows open; — reiferer Ueberlegung, [= während ich, oder nachdem ich die Sache reifer überlegte] on more mature consideration, on second thoughts. Bei is used in many composed words, in most of which we observe the sense of nearness, closeness or presence.

II. *adv.* [near to, in number or quantity] about. Es fielen an diesem Tage — drei tausend Mann, there fell that day about three thousand men; er wird sich — sechs Wochen daselbst aufhalten, he will stay there about six weeks.

Beián, *adv.* hard by, close by. Er wohnt gleich —, he lodges next door.

Beiarbeiter, *m.* [-s, *pl.* -] an assistant workman.

Beibehalten, *ir. v. tr.* to keep, to retain. Sie haben viel von dieser rohen Methode —, they have retained much of that barbarous method.

Beibehaltung, *f.* keeping, retaining.

Beibiegen, *ir. v. tr.* to bend or inflect one thing towards another. *Fig.* to fold up with another thing, to enclose [a letter]. Aus beigebogenem Schreiben werden Sie ersehen, daß &c., from the enclosed letter you will see, that &c.

Beibinden, *ir. v. tr.* to bind, to tie to. Ein Buch einem andern —, to bind up one book with another.

Beiblatt, *n.* [-es, *pl.* -blätter] supplement [to the newspapers or gazette], a gazette extraordinary.

Beibote, *m.* [-n, *pl.* -n] by-messenger, extra-messenger.

Beibringen, *ir. v. tr.* 1) to bring forward. *Fig.* to bring forward, to present, to offer. Beweise —, to bring forward proofs; einen Zeugen —, to produce a witness [in court]; ein Zeuge wurde beigebracht, um die Thatsache zu beweisen, a witness was adduced to prove the fact; wenn eine Urkunde mit einer Protestation zu Gunsten &c. beigebracht wird, if an instrument be produced with a protestation in favour of &c. 2) to bring on Einen Stoß —, to put in a thrust; Einem einen Schlag —, to hit any one a blow; Einem eine Wunde —, to inflict a wound on any one; Einem ein [Gift-] Pülverchen —, to poison any one; Einem etwas —, to impart something to any one, to inculcate something on any one, to insinuate [to hint, to suggest by remote allusion] to any one; seinen Kindern Grundsätze der Religion und Moral —, to instruct one's children in the principles of religion and morality; sie bringen irrige Begriffe bei, they insinuate wrong ideas; Einem eine böse Meinung von Jemanden —, to injure any one in a person's opinion.

Beibringung, *f.* the act of bringing forward, producing &c.

Beichte, *f.* [*pl.* -n] [for Be-gichte = Bejahung, affirmation, Bekenntniß, avowal, confession; from gehen, jehen, jahen, bejahen] 1) [avowal in general, but especially the act of disclosing sins or faults to a priest] confession. Zur — gehen, to confess, to make confession; Einem — sitzen, to confess any one; der Geistliche hörte die — der Nonnen an, the priest confessed the nuns; sie hat diesem Geistlichen ihre Beichte gethan or abgelegt, she has confessed herself to this priest. 2) a formulary used to confession. *Fig.* * and ‡ Einem [Einen] — hören, to hear a confession.

Beicht=formel, *f.* a formulary used at confession. —**gänger**, *m.* one who confesses, confessor, penitent. —**gebet**, *n.* prayer said before or after confession. —**geld**, *n.* confession-money. —**kind**, V. —gänger. —**pfennig**, *m.* V. —geld. —**schein**, *m.* certificate of confession. —**stuhl**, *m.* a confession-chair, confessional, confessionary. —**tag**, *m.* confession-day. —**vater**, *m.* [one who hears the confessions of others, a priest] confessor. *Prov* Dem —vater, dem Arzte und dem Advocaten darf man nichts verschweigen, hide nothing from thy minister, physician and lawyer. —**zeit**, *f.* time of confession. —**zettel**, *m.* V. —schein.

Beichten, *v. tr.* [to avow, in the Catholic church, to acknowledge sins and faults to a priest] to confess. Einem Priester seine Sünden —, to confess one's self to a priest. *Fig.* * and ‡ Der Spitzbube hat schlimm an uns gehandelt, lassen Sie ihn nur einmal —, the rascal has treated us badly, let him only confess.

Beichter, [more usual: der Beichtende, die Beichtende] *m.* [-s, *pl.* -] [one who confesses] confessor, penitent.

Beichtiger, *m.* 1) V. Beichtvater. Der Pater —, [in monasteries] the father confessor. 2) V. [the more usual] Beichtkind.

Beide, *adj.* [Sax. *badvo*, *butuo*, Dan. badde begge &c.] [two, considered as distinct from others or by themselves, the one and the other] both. Meine —n Schwestern, both my sisters; [it is often used alone, and represents sometimes two members of a sentence] hier sind zwei Bücher, nimm sie —, here are two books, take them both; wir —, both of us; keiner von —n, neither of the two; und machten — einen Bund mit einander [Gen. XXI.], and both of them made a covenant; ich will dir —s geben, I will give you both; man muß —s thun, you must do the one and the other; [it is often placed before the nouns, with which it is connected] —s, Leben und Tod, both life and death; —, Männer und Weiber, both men and women.

Beiderlei, *adv.* both, of both sorts. Landleute — Geschlechts, peasants of both sexes.

Beiderseitig, *adj.* and *adv.* relating to both, reciprocal, mutual. Dieß trug zu ihrer —en Zufriedenheit bei, this contributed to their mutual satisfaction.

Beiderseits, *adv.* on both sides, both. Sie waren — einverstanden, both of them agreed; sie lieben sich —, they love one another mutually.

Beiderwand, *f.* [in commerce] V. Petermann.

Beiding, *n.* 1) an additional thing. 2) by-court.

Beidlebig, *adj.* [having the power of living in two elements, air and water] amphibious. D

—e Thier, amphibium; —e Thiere, amphibials.

Beidrehen, *v. tr.* [sea term] to bring to, to heave to, to lay to.

Beidrucken, *v. tr.* to print to. Die Anmerkungen sind dem Texte beigedruckt, the notes are printed along with the text; sein Siegel —, to set one's seal to.

Beidrücken, *v. tr.* to press one thing near another.

Beidschattig, *adj.* [in geography] die —en Völker, amphiscii, amphiscians.

Beierbe, *m.* [-n, *pl.* -n] joint heir.

|| **Beiern**, *v. tr.* to chime.

Beiessen, *n.* [-s, *pl.* -] a by-dish, a side-dish.

Beifall, *m.* [-s] 1) [the act of approving] approbation. Wir geben den Maßregeln der Regierung unsern —, we approve [of] the measures of the government; es ist gefährlich, sich um den — des Volkes zu bewerben, it is dangerous to court popular applause. 2) [active approbation, or action, in favour of what is approved] approbation, applause. — klatschen, to applaud.

Beifall=gierig, *adj.* and *adv.* covetous of approbation. —klatschen, *n.* applauding, applause, plaudit. —bezeugung, *f.* mark of approbation. Dieser Schauspieler spielte seine Rolle unter den größten —bezeugungen des Publikums, this actor played his part amidst the greatest plaudits of the public. —sruf, *m.* acclamation, applause. —stampfen, *n.* plaudit. —swerth, —swürdig, *adj.* and *adv.* deserving approbation or applause.

Beifallen, *ir. v. intr.* [u. w. seyn] 1) to come into one's memory, to come to one's remembrance. Sein Name fällt mir nicht bei, his name does not occur to me; nun fällt es mir bei, now I recollect it; die nähern Umstände fallen mir jetzt bei, I remember now the particulars; es fällt mir nun ein Mittel bei, now I think of a remedy. 2) to assent to the propriety of a thing, with some degree of pleasure or satisfaction. Jemandem —, to assent to any one's opinion; einer Maßregel —, to approve [of] a measure. 3) to side with. Ein großer Theil des Heeres fiel den Empörern bei, a great part of the army sided with the insurgents.

Beifällig, *adj.* and *adv.* 1) [in law] what is collected. Es ist mir nicht —, it does not occur to me. 2) approving. Eine —e Erklärung, an assenting declaration.

Beifeste, **Beifestung**, *f.* a small fortified place, a citadel.

Beiflechten, *v. tr.* to twist, to plait to be joined or added to.

Beifolgen, *v. intr.* [u. w. seyn] to follow [chiefly used in the part. of the present tense]. Beifolgender Brief, the inclosed letter.

Beifracht, *f.* [*pl.* -en] V. Beilast.

Beifrau, *f.* [*pl.* -n] a woman assisting another woman in her work.

Beifuge, *f.* [*pl.* -n] [chiefly in law and commerce] something added or subjoined. Aus der — werden Sie ersehen, from the enclosed you will see.

Beifügen, *v. tr.* 1) to add, to subjoin. Eine Anmerkung —, to add a remark. 2) to unite at the end, to annex. Einem letzten Willen ein Codicill —, to annex a codicil to a will. Das Beigefügte, V. Beifuge, Beilage.

Beifügig, *adj.* and *adv.* that which may be added or subjoined. Ein —es Wort, an adjective.

Beifügung, *f.* addition.

1\. **Beifuß**, *m.* [-es] [a plant] common wormwood.

Beifußöl, *n.* oil of common wormwood.

2\. **Beifuß**, *m.* [-es] [a sea term] the parrel truss of the main and foresail.

Beigang, *m.* [-es, *pl.* -gänge] [in mining] counter or contra.

Beigeben, *ir. v. tr.* [properly: to give in addition; but especially used in phrases like the following and similar] Er war so mit Geschäften überladen, daß man ihm einen Gehülfen — mußte, he was so much overloaden with business, that they were obliged to give him an assistant; es wurde ihm eine Ehrenwache von zehn Mann beigegeben, a guard of honour consisting of ten soldiers was given to him; er wurde so rasend, daß man ihm einen Wächter — mußte, he became so frantic, that is was deemed necessary to appoint him a watch.

Beigehen, *ir. v. intr.* [u. w. seyn] 1) to be added or annexed [used only in the part. of the present tense]. —den Brief bitte ich Sie an Hrn. N. zu bestellen, the accompanying letter I beg you to deliver to Mr. N. 2) [joined with lassen] to venture, to be bold enough. Keiner seiner Jünger ließ sich —, ihn zu fragen, none of his disciples dared to ask him; wie haben Sie sich beigehen lassen können, meinem ausdrücklichen Befehl zuwiderzuhandeln, how have you dared to act contrary to my express orders.

Beigehülfe, V. Gehülfe.

Beigeschmack, *m.* V. Beischmack.

Beigesellen, I. *v. tr.* to associate. Ich habe mir einen wackern Freund zur Ausführung dieses Unternehmens beigesellt, I took a trusty friend as my associate for the execution of this enterprise. II. *v. r.* sich —, to unite in company, to associate. Ich gesellte mich ihnen bei, I associated with them, I joined them.

Beigethan, *adj.* V. Zugethan.

Beigießen, *ir. v. tr.* to pour to.

Beiglied, *n.* [-s, *pl.* -er] [in archit.] an accessory member.

|| **Beihänden**, *adv.* at hand.

Beiher, *adv.* 1) by the side of. 2) besides. — will ich noch bemerken, daß &c., I will moreover remark, that &c; lassen Sie sich — gesagt seyn, let it be told you by the by!

Beihülfe, *f.* 1) [without a plural] help, aid, assistance. 2) — an Geld, subsidy.

Beikind, *n.* [-es, *pl.* -er] a natural child, a bastard.

Beikirche, *f.* [*pl.* -en] a chapel of ease.

Beiknecht, *m.* [-s, *pl.* -e] a helper to a servant or groom, farmer's second man.

Beikoch, *m.* [-s, *pl.* -köche] under-cook, second cook.

Beikommen, *ir. v. intr.* 1) to come at the same time [used only figurat. and in the part. of the present tense]. Beikommendes Schreiben, the inclosed letter; —des Schreiben wird Ihnen zeigen, the following letter will show you. 2) [u. w. seyn] *a*) to get near, to reach. Ich kann ihm nicht —, I cannot get at him; die Feinde konnten der Stadt nicht —, the enemies could not get near the town; dieser Festung ist nicht beizukommen, this fortress is inaccessible; [in familiar language] seinem Schaden —, to repair one's loss. *b*) to become equal to. Wenige Heerführer kommen Napoleon an Ruhme bei, few generals equal Napoleon in fame; hierin kommen wir den Franzosen nicht bei, in this article we don't come up to the French; nichts in der Welt kommt der Herrlichkeit dieses Schauspiels bei, nothing in the world can match the grandeur of this spectacle; dieß kommt jenen nicht bei, this falls short of that; dieses Tuch kommt jenem bei weitem nicht bei, this cloth is far inferior to that.

Beikraut, *n.* [-es, *pl.* -kräuter] *Fig.* the furniture of a salad, sweet herbs for it.

Beikreis, *m.* [-kreises, *pl.* -kreise] [a little circle, whose centre is in the circumference of a greater circle] an epicycle.

Beil, *n.* [-s, *pl.* -e] [Sax. *bill*, Sw. *bil*, D. *byl*; Old Sw. *bula* signifies spalten] [a small ax with a short handle] a hatchet. Syn. Beil, Axt. The Axt differs from the Beil, in its having a longer handle or helve, which gives it greater power in hewing; the Beil from its shorter handle is better adapted for cutting any thing accurately.

Beil=eisen, *n.* bars of iron. —fertig, *adj.* [a sea term] is said of a ship when every part of her body is built. —förmig, *adj.* having the form of a hatchet. —kraut, *n.* hatchet-vetch. —pflanze, *f.* —strauch, *m.* securidaca. —stein, *m.* [in mineralogy] precious serpentine, axestone, ofite. —träger, *m.* [among the ancient Romans] lictor. —wurzel, *f.* common blue iris.

Beilade, *f.* [*pl.* -n] a small box or drawer in the inside of a larger one.

Beilage, *f.* [*pl.* -n] 1) something added to another. Die — eines Briefes, a writing inclosed in a letter; die — einer Zeitung, the supplement of a gazette. 2) something laid by and kept, a deposit.

Beilageblatt, *n.* V. Beiblatt.

Beilager, *n.* [-s, *pl.* -] the solemnization and consummation of marriage [among persons of high rank].

Beilassen, V. Zulassen.

Beilast, *f.* [*pl.* -en] [in seamen's language] by-fraught.

Beilaufen, *ir. v. intr.* [u. w. seyn] to run by the side.

Beiläufer, *m.* [-s, *pl.* -] a foot-boy, errand-boy, runner. —inn, *f.* an errand-girl.

Beiläufig, I. *adj.* 1) approximative. Nach einer —en Berechnung dürften die Kosten 20 Louisd'ors betragen, on a rough calculation the costs may be some 20 louisd'ors. 2) secondary, occasional, incidental. Es war nur eine —e Frage von mir, it was but an incidental question of mine. II. *adv.* 1) about, near. Es sind — 30 Ballen, there are 30 bales or thereabouts. 2) by the way, by the by. — bemerkt, muß ich Ihnen doch sagen, daß &c., by the way I must tell you, that &c.

Beilegen, I. *v. tr.* 1) to join or unite to. Einem Briefe eine Banknote —, to inclose a banknote in a letter. *Fig.* Wir legen Gott nichts bei, was &c., we attribute nothing to God, that &c.; Lob —, to give praise; wenn er ein Fünkchen von jener Klugheit besitzt, die man ihm beilegt, if he have an atom of that sagacity, ascribed to him; er besitzt alle die Laster, die man ihm beilegt, he has all the vices imputed to him; einen Namen —, to give a name, to surname; beigelegt, [in logic] concrete. 2) to lay up, to lay in a place for preservation, to lodge in the hands of a person for safe keeping or other purpose, to deposit. 3) to compose, to settle, to adjust. Streitigkeiten —, to compose differences. Syn. V. Abthun. II. *v. intr.* 1) [sea term] V. Beidrehen. 2) to try, to lie to. Ein Schiff, welches beiliegt, a ship a-trying [a-try].

Beilegung, *f.* 1) the act of joining or uniting to, of depositing &c. 2) accommodation. Die — von Streitigkeiten, adjustment of differences.

Beilegungs=stück, *n.* a thing, that may be applied to a subject. —**wort**, *n.* [in grammar] an adjective. —**wörtlich**, *adv.* adjectively.

Beileid, *n.* [-s, without a plural] condolence, condoling. Einem sein — bezeigen, to condole with any one; Einem sein — über etwas bezeigen, to condole with any one on a thing.

Beileids=bezeugung, *f.* condolence. —**brief**, *m.*, —**schreiben**, *n.* a letter of condolence.

Beiliegen, *ir. v. intr.* to lie with. Der —de Brief, the inclosed letter.

Beiliegen, *n.* [-s] [in seamen's language] trying, lying to. Das — vor der Fok, trying under the fore-sail.

Beilke, *f.* [*pl.* -n] [comes from Ball and is allied to Billard] truck-board, queck-board.

Beilke=spiel, *n.* trucks, shovel-board, queck-board. V. also Druckspiel. —**stein**, *m.* a metal piece used in playing at trucks. —**tafel**, *f.* truck-table, shovel-board, queck-board. V. also Drucktafel.

Beilken, *v. intr.* to play at trucks.

Beim, [contraction from] bei dem.

Beimagd, *f.* [*pl.* —mägde] second maid-servant.

Beimann, *m.* V. Cicisbeo.

Beimengen, *v. tr.* to mix with.

Beimessen, *ir. v. tr.* to consider as belonging to. Sich —, to attribute to one's self; das Verdienst, welches man dir beimißt, thy merit imputed; sie maßen es seiner Thorheit bei, they imputed it to his folly; sie messen euch die Fehler bei, they lay the faults to your charge; Einem Glauben —, to give credit to a person; wenn ich Gerüchten Glauben — darf, if I may give credit to reports.

Beimessung, *f.* imputation.

Beimischen, *v. tr.* to mingle with something else. Dem Mehle Salz —, to mix flour with salt; diesem Silber ist Kupfer beigemischt, this silver is alloyed with copper. *Fig.* Einer Erzählung seine Bemerkungen —, to add one's remarks to a narration.

Bein, *n.* [-es, *pl.* -e] [from the Gr. *βαίνειν*, to walk, or according to others from the old G. beinen, i. e. binden, so that it signifies a joint, das Gelenk] 1) any bone [used in many compositions by anatomists as Kopfbein, Schulterbein &c.]. Das ungenannte —, [in anatomy, a large irregular bone, situated at the side of the pelvis] os innominatum; aus — gemacht, made of bone. *Fig.* Das geht oder dringt mir durch Mark und —, it cuts or touches me to the quick; † Stein und — schwören, to swear through thick and thin. 2) [the limb of an animal, used in supporting the body in walking and running, properly that part of the limb from the knee to the foot, but in a more general sense, the whole limb, including the thigh, the leg and the foot] leg. Das dicke —, V. Dickbein; die —e über einander schlagen, to cross one's legs; Einem ein — unterschlagen, ein — stellen, ein — vorhalten, to trip any one up, to trip up any one's heels. *Fig.* *Er ist die ganze Nacht auf den —en gewesen, he sat up all night, he was running about all night; *er ist immer auf den —en, his shoes are made of running leather; *sich auf die —e machen, to rise, to move, to set out, to run off, to take to one's heels; *Jemanden —e machen, to make a person move; *ich will euch —e machen, I will make you find your legs; Einem wieder auf die —e helfen, to restore any one to health, to help any one, to relieve any one in distress, to better any one's fortune; er ist nicht gut auf den —en, he is a bad walker, no great pedestrian, *it.* he walks with difficulty; ein Heer auf die —e bringen, to raise an army. 3) *a*) the long or slender support of any thing. Die —e eines Tisches, the legs of a table. *b*) [in mining] staple. SYN. **Bein, Gebein, Knochen.** All the firm hard parts of the animal body are called Knochen, whether individually or in connection with others. Bein, on the contrary, is a single bone which is moved by its own peculiar muscles, as: das Armbein, das Schulterbein &c. The bones of the ribs are therefore not called Rippenbeine, but Rippenknochen. Gebein signifies all the bones of a body collectively, is generally used in higher language, and is said only of the bones of human beings.

Bein=ader, *f.* the vein of the leg. —**ähnlich**, *adj.* resembling a bone, osseous. —**anzug**, *m.* small clothes, stockings, hose, shoes, boots. —**arbeiter**, *m.* a worker in bone. —**artig**, *adj.* and *adv.* resembling a bone or leg, bony, osseous. —**asche**, *f.* bone-ashes. —**bohrer**, *m.* a large auger used by joiners to bore the holes to receive the legs of stools. —**brech**, *m.* 1) V. —gras. 2) the gluebone stone. —**brecher**, *m.* [a fowl of the genus falco or hawk] ospray, the sea-eagle. —**brechgras**, —**brechkraut**, *n.* V. —gras. —**bruch**, *m.* 1) the rupture or disruption of a bone, the fracture of a leg. 2) V. —brech, 2. —**brüchig**, *adj.* and *adv.* having a fractured leg. —**drechsler**, —**dreher**, *m.* a turner in bone. —**dürre**, *adj.* exceedingly meager, lean as a bone. V. [the more usual] klapperdürre. —**erzeugung**, *f.* [the formation of bone in animals] ossification. —**fäule**, —**fäulniß**, *f.* V. —fraß. —**feile**, *f.* [in surgery] raspatory. —**fisch**, *m.* [a genus of fishes] ostracion. —**folter**, *f.* a rack for the legs. —**fraß**, *m.* caries. —**fügung**, *f.* articulation, [in anatomy] symphysis. Die merklich bewegliche —fügung, [in anatomy] diarthrosis; die unmerklich bewegliche —fügung, amphiarthrosis. —**geripp**, —**gerüst**, —**gestell**, *n.* skeleton. —**gewächs**, *n.* [in surgery] exostosis. —**gras**, *n.* Lancashire arthericum or asphodel. —**harnisch**, *m.* armour for the legs, tasses. —**hart**, *adj.* and *adv.* hard as a bone. —**haus**, *n.* charnel-house, ossuary. —**haut**, *f.* [in anatomy] periosteum. —**hebel**, *m.* [in surgery] elevatory. —**heil**, *n.* V. —brech, 2. —**holz**, *n.* 1) fly honey-suckle. 2) Italian honey-suckle. 3) dwarf honey-suckle. 4) common privet. —**kleider**, *pl.* small clothes, breeches, trowsers, pantaloons, [in famil. lang.] inexpressibles. —**knochen**, *m.* a bone in the leg or foot. —**knopf**, *m.* [a protuberance on the end of a bone] condyle. —**krebs**, *m.* V. Knochenkrebs. —**lade**, *f.* [in surgery] a solen or cradle. —**los**, *adj.* boneless. —**mark**, *n.* the marrow of the bones. —**mehl**, *n.* V. —asche. —**muskel**, *m.* a muscle of the leg. —**nerve**, *m.* a nerve of the leg. —**öl**, *n.* an oil extracted from the bones of animals. —**rüstung**, *f.* V. —harnisch. —**säge**, *f.* bone-saw. —**same**, *m.* [a genus of plants] osteospermum. —**schelle**, *f.* an iron or fetter for the leg. —**schiene**, *f.* 1) a splint for a broken leg. 2) cuisse, greaves. —**schwarz**, *n.* bone-black. —**spath**, *m.* [veterinary art] bone-spavin. —**waare**, *f.* bone-toy. —**well**, *n.* V. —brech, 2. —**wuchs**, *m.* V. —erzeugung. —**wunde**, *f.* a wound in the leg.

Beinahe, *adv.* almost, nearly, well nigh. Es ist — Zeit, it is almost time; — zehn Jahre, near upon ten years; ich wäre — gestorben, I was like to die; ich wäre — todtgeschlagen worden, I was near being killed; ich hätte es — vergessen, I had like to have forgotten it; er wäre — verloren gegangen, he had like to have been lost; es ist — dasselbe, it is much the same thing; — am Ende der Woche, about the latter end of the week.

Beiname, *m.* [-n, *pl.* -n] a by-name, epith[et]. Ich meine den Scipio, welcher den —n der „Af[ri]kaner" führte, I mean the Scipio with the s[ur]name of „Africanus"; Alexander, mit dem der Große, Alexander, surnamed the Great; [e]in schimpflicher —, an opprobrious appellation, nickname; Ihr gebt der Tugend den —n Laste[r], you nickname virtue vice; ich bitte Sie, m[ich] mit dergleichen —n zu verschonen, I beg to [be] spared such epithets.

Beinchen, Beinlein, *n.* [-s, *pl.* -] ossicle.

Beineben, Beinebst, *adv.* near.

Beinen, Beinern, *adj.* and *adv.* made of bone.

Beinerven, *pl.* [in anatomy] accessory nerves.

Beinicht, *adj.* and *adv.* resembling bone, hard as bones, bony.

Beinig, *adj.* and *adv.* 1) having bones, bony. 2) [in compos.] legged. Krumm—, bandy-legged; kurzbeinig, short-legged.

Beinlein, V. Beinchen.

Beinöthig, *adj.* and *adv.* necessary.

Beiordnen, *v. tr.* to adjoin. Eine Person ei[]ner andern —, to give any one an assistant.

Beipferd, *n.* [-es, *pl.* -e] a led-horse, [a] horse of reserve.

Beipflichten, *v. intr.* Einem —, to coincid[e] with any one in opinion, to join any one in opin[]ion; ich pflichte seinen Meinungen bei, I assen[t] to his opinions.

Beirath, *m.* [-es] advice.

Beirathen, *v. tr.* to assist with advice.

Beiräthig, *adj.* and *adv.* capable of givin[g] advice. Einem — seyn, to assist any one wit[h] advice.

Beiräumen, V. [the more usual] Aufräumen.

Beirechnen, *v. tr.* to add in reckoning.

Beireihen, *v. tr.* to put in ranks, to rang[e].

Beirücken, I. *v. intr.* to move towards, [to] sit nearer. II. *v. tr.* to add, to communicate.

Beisammen, *adv.* [in company, in the sa[me] place] together. —liegen, leben, to lie togethe[r], to live together.

Beisaß, *m.* [-ssen, *pl.* -ssen] a dweller in a[] town or village, who does not enjoy the free[]dom and all the privileges of the citizens.

Beisatz, *m.* [-es, *pl.* -sätze] an additio[n]. Er vertraute mir das Geheimniß mit dem — an, daß &c., he entrusted the secret to me, add[]ing &c.; [in grammar] apposition.

Beischaffen, V. Herbeischaffen.

Beischießen, *ir. v. tr.* to contribute, to be[ar] a part. Gelder zu einem Geschäft —, to advan[ce] or contribute money towards a business.

Beischiff, *n.* [-es, *pl.* -e] caic, caique, [a] small vessel employed to attend a larger one] a tende[r].

Beischlaf, *m.* [-es] coition, copulation. De[r] uneheliche —, concubinage; unerlaubter —, il[]licit cohabitation.

Beischlafen, V. Beschlafen.

Beischläfer, *m.* [-s, *pl.* -] 1) a man illegall[y] living or cohabiting with a woman. 2) bed-fel[]low. V. [the more usual] Bettgenoß, Schlafcam[e]rad.

Beischläferinn, *f.* concubine. V. also Keb[s]weib.

Beischlag, *m.* [-es, *pl.* -schläge] 1) V. Be[i]schlagung. 2) a forged coin. 3) any thing coun[]terfeit. || and † 4) [a natural child] by-blow. 5) flight of steps to a house.

Beischlagen, *ir.* I. *v. tr.* to add, to supe[r]

add, to bring in farther account. || II. *v. intr.* V. Beistimmen, Beipflichten.

Beischlagung, *f.* the act of adding &c, addition. Mit or unter — der außerordentlichen Kosten, with the addition of the extraordinary expenses.

Beischließen, *ir. v. tr.* 1) to put away and lock up. 2) to add, to inclose. Durch beigeschlossenen Brief, by the inclosed letter.

Beischluß, *m.* [-sses, seldom used in the *pl.* -schlüsse] that which is added or inclosed, inclosure.

Beischlüssel, *m.* V. Nachschlüssel.

Beischmack, *m.* [-es, *pl.* -schmäcke] [a taste left in the mouth] tang. Diese Frucht hat einen sonderbaren —, this fruit has a strange tang; dieses Wasser hat einen salzigen —, this water has a saltish taste.

Beischmelzen, *ir. v. tr.* to melt with.

Beischreiben, *ir. v. tr.* to write by the side of. Ich schrieb es bei, I wrote it on the margin; ich schrieb es meinem Briefe noch bei, I added it to my letter. Das Beischreiben, a second or additional letter.

Beischreiber, *m.* [-s, *pl.* -] an assistant clerk or writer.

Beischrift, *f.* [*pl.* -en] 1) that which is written by the side of something or on the margin. Die — eines Sinnbildes, the motto of a device. 2) an additional written document.

Beischuß, *m.* [-sses, *pl.* -schüsse] V. Beitrag.

Beischüssel, *f.* [*pl.* -n] side-dish.

Beischütten, *v. tr.* to pour to.

Beisegel, V. Leesegel.

Beisein, V. Beiseyn.

Beiseit, Beiseits, *adv.* [on or to one side] aside. 1) Etwas — legen, to lay something aside or apart. 2) to lay something up. Geld — legen, to lay by money. V. Seite.

Beiseitsetzung, *f.* V. Beseitigung.

Beisetzen, *v. tr.* to put near or to any thing. Den Topf —, to put the pot to the fire; eine Leiche —, to entomb a dead body; die Segel —, [in seamen's language] to make sail, to set the sails; viele Segel beigesetzt haben, to crowd sail; einem Briefe auch einige Zeilen —, to add a few lines to a letter; ist Alles gesagt, haben Sie nichts mehr beizusetzen? is every thing said, have you nothing more to add?

Beisetzung, *f.* the act of putting near &c. Die — einer Leiche, entombment, burial.

Beiseyn, *ir. v. intr.* to be present [used only as a noun, joined with in or ohne] In meinem —, before me, in my presence; im — Vieler, in the presence of many persons; ohne Jemands —, without any person being present.

Beisichtig, V. Kurzsichtig.

Beisitz, *m.* [-es, *pl.* -e] 1) presence at a sitting and the right of sitting in any assembly. 2) a seat in the same place.

Beisitzen, *ir. v. intr.* [u. w. seyn] 1) to sit near or by. 2) to sit in a court of law.

Beisitzer, *m.* [-s, *pl.* -] 1) [an inferior officer, who sits to assist the judge] an assessor. 2) V. Beisitz.

Beisitzeramt, *n.* the office of an assessor.

Beisorge, *f.* [*pl.* -n] 1) care, superintendence. || 2) [in law] guardianship.

|| **Beisorger**, *m.* [-s, *pl.* -] [in law] a guardian.

Beispiel, *n.* [-es, *pl.* -e] example. *a*) [instance serving for illustration of a rule or precept, or a particular case or proposition illustrating a general rule, position or truth]. Die Lehrsätze der Trigonometrie und die Regeln der Sprachlehre werden durch —e erläutert, the principles of trigonometry and the rules of grammar are illustrated by examples. *b*) [precedent, in former instance] example. Er hat viele —e von &c. geliefert, he has furnished many examples of &c.; zum —, as for example, for instance. *c*) [precedent, which disposes to imitation] example. —e wirken mehr als Regeln, example has more effect than precept; ein — anführen, to cite an instance; ich will Ihnen hundert —e davon aufweisen, I will bring you a hundred instances of it. *d*) [a pattern in morals or manners] example. Ein — habe ich Euch gegeben, daß Ihr thut wie ich Euch gethan habe, [in Scripture] I have given you an example, that you should do as I have done to you; ein — geben, to set an example; an etwas ein — nehmen, to take a lesson from; an Einem ein — nehmen, to take an example by any one; ein abschreckendes — aufstellen, to make an example; [in law] Andern zum warnenden or abschreckenden —, a warning example to others. *Prov.* Böse —e verderben gute Sitten, bad examples corrupt morals.

Beispiellos, *adj.* and *adv.* without example, unparalleled, unprecedented, matchless. Eine —lose Grausamkeit, unexampled cruelty; eine —los wohlfeile Ausgabe der Werke dieses Schriftstellers, an imprecedented cheap edition of the works of this author; ein —los liederlicher Mensch, an unparalleled debauchee. —**reich**, *adj.* and *adv.* rich in examples, furnishing many examples.

Beispringen, *ir. v. intr.* [u. w. seyn] *Fig.* to give support in time of distress, to succour, to help, to aid, to assist. Einem —, to run to any one's help; Einem im Unglücke —, to succour any one in his adversity.

|| **Beiße**, *f.* 1) V. Beize. 2) V. Krätze.

Beißel, *n.* [-s, *pl.* -] an iron wedge.

Beißelbeere, *f.* V. Berberis.

Beißen, [Sax. *bitan*, D. *byten*, old G. *pizzan*; allied to bitter and beizen] *ir.* I. *v. tr.* 1) [to seize with the teeth, to break or crush with the teeth] to bite. Der Hund hat ihn gebissen, the dog has bitten him; es ist zu hart, ich kann es nicht —, it is too hard, I cannot bite it; die Flöhe haben ihn gebissen, the fleas have bit him; †nichts zu — und zu brocken haben, to have nothing to eat. 2) *Fig.* to torment, to torture. II. *v. intr.* 1) to seize and crush, pierce or wound with the teeth. Der Hund biß nach ihm, the dog snapped at him; auf einen Knochen —, to gnaw at a bone; sich auf die Zunge, auf die Lippen — [also fig.], to bite one's tongue or lips [in order to forbear laughing]; die Zähne zusammen —, to gnash one's teeth; es macht, daß man die Zähne fest zusammen beißt, it makes the teeth set hard one against the other. †*Fig.* Ins Gras —, to bite the dust or ground, to be killed, to die. *Prov.* Ein todter Hund beißt nicht, dead dogs don't bite, when a serpent is dead, his sting hurts not. 2) [u. w. haben] to make to smart. Der Pfeffer beißt auf der Zunge, the pepper bites the tongue; Säuren — im Munde, acids bite the mouth; es beißt mich auf der Haut, my skin itches. *Fig.* ein —der Scherz, a biting jest; ein —der Witz, a poignant wit; eine —de Antwort, a smart reply; das Beißende dieser Ausdrücke, the pungency of these expressions; auf eine —de Weise, sarcastically, mordaciously; eine —de Art, sich auszudrücken, a pungent manner of speech. III. *v. r.* sich —, 1) to bite [one's tongue] by inadvertence. 2) to quarrel [said of dogs].

Beiß-kohl, *m.* V. Beete. —**korb**, *m.* V. Maulkorb. —**rübe**, *f.* V. Beete. —**zahn**, *m.* V. Schneidezahn. —**zange**, *f.* a pair of nippers, pincers. Eine kleine —zange, tweezers.

Beißer, *m.* [-s, *pl.* -] 1) [one who bites] biter [used in compositions as Bullenbeißer, bull-dog &c.]. 2) *Fig.* a quarreller, wrangler.

Beißig, Bissig, *adj.* and *adv.* 1) biting, mordacious. Ein —er Hund, a dog given to biting, a savage dog. 2) *Fig.* quarrelsome.

Beißker, *m.* [-s, *pl.* -] [instead of Beißer] [a fresh water fish] cobitis [cobitis fossilis].

Beistand, *m.* [-es, *pl.* -stände] 1) assistance, aid, help, furtherance, succour. Einem — leisten, to give any one assistance, to give support to any one. 2) an assistant, a helper, second. Der — vor Gericht, counsel; der Geschlechts—, [in law] one without whose knowledge and advice a female is not allowed to transact any legal business.

Beiständer, *m.* [-s, *pl.* -] 1) V. Beistand 2. 2) [in seamen's language] a ship appointed to relieve or assist another in action, a second or consort-ship.

Beiständig, *adj.* and *adv.* assisting, helping, giving support to.

Beistechen, *ir. v. intr.* [in seamen's language] to sail close hauled.

Beistecken, *v. tr.* 1) to put by. *Ich habe vergessen, Geld beizustecken, I have forgotten to take any money with me, to put any in my pocket. 2) *Fig.* to shut up in prison.

Beistehen, *ir. v. intr.* 1) V. Dabeistehen. Die —den, the persons standing by or near. 2) to stand by, to lend aid, to assist. Der Esel hoffte, der Hund würde ihm —, the ass hoped, the dog would stand by him; seinen Freunden mit Rath und That —, to help one's friends with one's advice and purse; einer Frau in Kindesnöthen —, to deliver a woman; Einem in der Todesstunde —, to stand by any one at the hour of death; einem Sterbenden —, to attend a sick person that is dying. 3) [in seamen's language] Alle Segel — lassen, to leave all sails set.

Beisteher, *m.* [-es, *pl.* -] 1) [unusual] a person standing by or near. 2) one that assists another, second.

Beisteuer, *f.* 1) pecuniary aid. Er sprach mich um eine milde — an, he asked charity of me. 2) an additional duty or tax.

Beisteuern, *v. tr.* to assist with money, to contribute, to pay a share. Er steuerte eine größere Summe bei, als jeder Andere, he contributed a greater sum of money than any other; es wurde von allen Seiten beigesteuert, contributions were sent in from all sides.

Beistimmen, *v. intr.* [to express an agreement of the mind to what is alledged or proposed] to assent. Einem —, to adopt any one's opinion; er stimmt mir vollkommen bei, we are of one mind; einer Meinung —, to agree to an opinion; einem Vorschlage —, to accede to a proposition; hierin stimme ich Ihnen vollkommen bei, in this I am perfectly of your opinion, I agree with you exactly.

Beistimmer, *m.* [-s, *pl.* -] assenter.

Beistimmung, *f.* assent, consent.

Beistopfen, *v. tr.* to stuff to.

Beistrich, *m.* [-es, *pl.* -e] comma [,].

Beistrom, *m.* [-es, *pl.* -ströme] the arm of a river.

Beistück, *n.* [-es, *pl.* -e] 1) something added to a greater thing, appendage. 2) V. Nebenstück.

Beithun, *ir.* I. *v. tr.* to lay up, to deposit. *II. *v. r.* sich —, V. Einschmeicheln.

Beitisch, *m.* [*pl.* -es, *pl.* -e] 1) side-board. 2) second table.

Beitrag, *m.* [-es, *pl.* -träge] [that which each individual contributes to the common stock] contribution. Freiwillige Beiträge zu einem Unternehmen, voluntary contributions for some undertaking; seinen — geben, to pay a share, to contribute; der verhältnißmäßige —, quota; jeder Fürst liefert seinen — an Geld und Kriegsvorräthen, every prince furnishes his contingent in money and munition; er hat schätzbare Beiträge zu diesem Buche geliefert, he has furnished valuable materials for that book; Voß und Merian haben Beiträge dazu geliefert, Voss and Merian were the contributors.

Beitrags-fest, *n.* a picknick.

Beitragen, *ir. v. tr.* [to give to a common stock or purpose] to contribute. England trägt mehr bei, als irgend ein Verbündeter, England contributes much more than any other of the allies. *Fig.* to bring near. Es hat zu meinem Glücke beigetragen, it has contributed to [towards] my fortune; dies trug zur Vermehrung meines Schmerzes viel bei, that has added much to my grief; diese Arzneien haben zu seinem Tode beigetragen, these medicines have done much towards causing his death.

Beiträger, *m.* [unusual] [-s, *pl.* -] a contributor.

Beitreiben, *ir. v. tr.* to collect [taxes &c.]. Schulden —, to collect debts.

Beitreten, *ir. v. intr.* [u. w. seyn] *Fig.* to agree, to assent, to accede. Einem Vorschlage —, to accede to a proposition; einer Meinung —, to agree to an opinion. Der König der Niederlande trat dem Vertrage nicht bei, the king of the Netherlands did not accede to the convention.

Beitritt, *m.* [-es] 1) an acceding to and joining, accession. Der — des Königs zum Verbündniß, the king's accession to the confederacy. 2) [among hunters] Den — machen, to overreach [said of stags].

Beitritts-erklärung, *f.* declaration of accession. —**urkunde**, *f.* act of accession.

Beiurtheil, *n.* [-s, *pl.* -e] [in law, an intermediate decree before a final decision] interlocution.

Beivormund, *m.* [-s, *pl.* -münder] [in law] a curator to a minor, in addition to the usual guardian.

Beiwache, *f.* [*pl.* -n] [the guard at night performed by the whole army] bivouac.

Beiwachen, *v. intr.* to bivouac.

Beiwagen, *m.* [-s, *pl.* -] by-waggon or carriage, an extra-carriage, a second waggon. Der Postwagen war mit Reisenden so angefüllt, daß ein — beigegeben werden mußte, the stage-coach was so filled with passengers, that they were obliged to have an extra-chaise.

Beiweg, *m.* [-es, *pl.* -e] by-way.

Beiweib, *n.* [-es, *pl.* -er] V. Kebsweib.

Beiwerfen, *v. tr.* to cast or throw to any thing.

Beiwerk, *n.* [-es, *pl.* -e] 1) secondary work. 2) [in painting, architecture &c.] accessory.

Beiwesen, *n* [-s, *pl.* -] V. Beiwerk 2.

Beiwohnen, *v. intr.* 1) to be present at. Advokaten und Zuschauer wohnen einem Gerichte bei, Lawyers and spectators attend a court; haben Sie der Probe dieser Oper beigewohnt? did you attend the rehearsal of this opera? ich wohnte der Aufführung von Hrn. N.'s Stück bei, I was present at the representation of Mr. N.'s piece; einem Leichenbegängnisse —, to attend a burying; der Messe —, to hear mass; [in law] einer Frau —, to cohabit, to bed with a woman. 2) *Fig.* to be endowed or indued. Es wohnt ihm große Klugheit bei, he is endowed with great sagacity.

Beiwohner, *m* [-s, *pl.* -] [unusual] 1) one that is present at a thing. 2) [in law] one that cohabits with a woman.

Beiwohnung, *f.* 1) presence. 2) [in law] sexual commerce, cohabitation.

Beiwollen, *v. intr.* [in familiar language] Einem —, to wish to get at any one.

Beiwort, *n.* [-es, *pl.* -wörter] [in grammar] an adjective, expressing some real quality of a thing, to which it is applied, or an attributive expressing some quality ascribed to it, an epithet, [in grammar] adjective.

Beiwörtlich, I. *adj.* epithetic. II. *adv.* adjectively.

Beizählen, *v. tr.* to annumerate, to add to a former number, to add to something before mentioned. Man zählt ihn den Reichen bei, he is reckoned among the rich; man darf ihn unbedenklich den Whigs beizählen, you may number him without hesitation to the party of the Whigs.

Beize, *f.* [V. Beizen] 1) [in hunting, catching wild birds by hawks] hawking. 2) maceration. 3) infusion in which any thing is macerated; [the liquor of the tan-vat] ooze; [in metallurgy] lye; [among joiners and cabinetmakers] a colour to tinge wood. Die rothe —, [among tanners] dressing with barley-water and bark between each hide; die fortgesetzte —, [among tanners] gradual preparation.

Beizeichen, *n.* [-s, *pl.* -] 1) a sign or note of distinction added to the principal mark. 2) [in heraldry] rebatement. Wappen mit —, coats of arms rebated; ein Wappen ohne —, a plain coat of arms. 3) [in music] a character not placed at the beginning of a stave, but before the individual notes, such as the marks before incidental flats and sharps &c. 4) [in mythology, painting, sculpture &c., a symbol of office or character] attribute. Der Adler ist ein — des Jupiter, the eagle is an attribute of Jupiter.

Beizen, *v. tr.* [V. Beißen] 1) to catch or attempt to catch [birds] by means of hawks trained for the purpose, and let loose for the prey. Hasen mit Falken —, to hawk at hares. 2) to macerate in water or other fluids. Fleisch in Essig —, to soak meat in vinegar; eine Haut mit Lohe —, to tan a hide; Holz —, to tinge wood; schwarz gebeiztes Holz —, ebonized wood; die Haare —, [am. hatters] to dress the fur.

Beiz-brühe, *f.* [among workmen] a liquor in which any thing is soaked or macerated. —**hund**, *m.* a small dog used in hawking. —**kraft**, *f.* the macerating or corrosive quality of liquors. —**kufe**, —**tenne**, *f.* [am. tanners] tan-vat. —**vogel**, *m.* hawk, falcon. —**wasser**, *n.* V. —brühe. —**wurz**, *f.* V. Küchenschelle.

Beizimmer, *n.* [-s, *pl.* -] a cabinet or closet.

Beizoll, *m.* [-es, *pl.* -zölle] additional duty.

Beizügel, *m.* [-s, *pl.* -] the left or near rein.

Bejagen, *v. tr.* to chase, hunt, sport in a place. Einen Wald —, to hunt a forest.

Bejahen, *v. tr.* to affirm [opposed to deny]. Er bejahte es, he answered in the affirmative. *Prov.* Wer schweigt, bejaht, silence gives consent. Ein —der Satz, [in logic] an affirmative proposition. Syn. V. Behaupten.

Bejahlich, *adv.* affirmatively.

Bejahrt, *adj.* and *adv.* aged, advanced in age, stricken in years.

Bejahung, *f.* 1) affirmation [opposed to negation or denial]. 2) [position declared as true] affirmation.

Bejahungs-satz, *m.* affirmative position. —**weise**, *adv.* affirmatively. —**wort**, *n.* a term of affirmation [as: yes, certainly, to be sure &c.].

Bejammern, *v. tr.* to bewail, to bemoan. Sie — seinen Tod, they deplore his death.

Bejammerns-werth, —**würdig**, *adj.* and *adv.* 1) deplorable, lamentable. 2) [in contempt] deplorable, pitiable. Eine bejammernswerthe Dummheit, a deplorable stupidity. —**würdigkeit**, *f.* deplorableness.

Bejauchzen, *v. tr.* to receive with exultation.

Bejochen, *v. tr.* to yoke.

Bekalken, *v. tr.* 1) to cover with lime. 2) to manure with chalk, to chalk [land].

Bekalmen, *v. tr.* and *intr.* [in seamen's lang.] to becalm. Das Schiff wird durch hohes Land bekalmet or das Schiff bekalmet durch hohes Land, high land becalms a ship.

‖ **Bekämpen**, *v. tr.* [in husbandry] to fence, to inclose with a hedge.

Bekämpfen, *v. tr.* to combat, to fight with. Einen Gegner —, to combat an antagonist; eine Meinung —, to combat an opinion; seine Leidenschaften —, to struggle with, to master one's passions; er bekämpfte seinen Zorn, he got the better of his anger.

‖ **Bekämpung**, *f.* [in husbandry] fence, hedge.

Bekannt, [properly the past participle of Bekennen] *adj.* and *adv.* 1) [that which one knows or what others know] known. Wohl —e Personen, persons well known; allgemein —, notorious; — werden, to come to light, Syn. V. Auskommen; — machen, to bring to light, V. Anzeigen; öffentlich — machen, to publish, to notify, to promulgate. *Fig.* Sich eine or mit einer Sache — machen, to get acquainted with a thing; für — annehmen, to take for granted. 2) familiarly known, acquainted. Mit Einem — seyn, to be acquainted with any one; ich will Sie mit ihm — machen, I'll introduce you to him; — werden, to get acquainted; der, die Bekannte, an acquaintance; er ist ein alter —er von mir, he is an old acquaintance of mine. *Fig.* Ich will Sie mit meinem Vorhaben — machen, I'll get you acquainted with my design; mit dem Kummer — [vertraut], acquainted with grief; er hat sich mit den besten englischen Schriftstellern — gemacht, he is conversant with the best English writers.

Bekanntermaßen, **Bekanntlich**, *adv.* as is known.

Bekanntmachung, *f.* 1) [the act of making known, of publishing] publication, promulgation. 2) publication, proclamation.

Bekanntmachungsamt, *n.* intelligence office.

Bekanntschaft, *f.* 1) [the state of being acquainted with a person or thing] acquaintance. — mit Einem machen, to form an acquaintance with any one. 2) [a person or persons well known] acquaintance. Eine alte —, an old acquaintance.

Bekanten, *v. tr.* 1) to border with lace. Ein Halstuch —, to lace a cravat. 2) [with carpenters] V. Beschlagen.

Bekappen, *v. tr.* 1) to top [a tree]. 2) to finish with a cap, to top. Einen Stiefel —, [with shoemakers] to top a boot. 3) [among sportsmen] Einen Falken —, to hood a hawk.

Bekehrbar, *adj.* and *adv.* he that may be converted, convertible.

Bekehren, I. *v. tr.* to convert. 1) [to bring a person to a different way of thinking] Er ist ganz bekehrt, he is now quite of another opinion. 2) [to ... from a bad life to a good one]. 3) [to change or ... from paganism to christianity] Die Heiden —, convert pagans to christianity; Andere, die ... zu ihrer Religion —, others, whom they proselyte to their religion. Der Bekehrte, a convert

II. *v. r.* sich —, 1) to change for the better. So thut nun Buße und bekehret euch, [in Scripture] repent ye therefore, and be converted. 2) *Fig.* to change one's opinion.

Bekéhrer, *m.* [-s, *pl.* -] a converter.

Bekéhrung, *f.* 1) the act of converting. 2) [in a moral sense] conversion. 3) [a change from paganism to christianity] conversion. Die — der Heiden, the conversion of the Gentiles.

Bekehrungs-anstalt, *f.* a society for propagating the Gospel and converting to the Christian faith, a mission. **—bothe**, *m.* missionary. **—eifer**, *m.* proselytism. **—geist**, *m.* a spirit of converting others. **—gesandte**, *m.* missionary. **—gesandtschaft**, *f.* a mission. **—sucht**, *f.* V. —eifer. **—wesen**, *n.* all that concerns missions.

Bekéilen, *v. tr.* to fasten with wedges.

Bekéimen, *v. intr.* [u. w. seyn] to bud, to put forth gems.

Bekénnen, *ir.* I. *v. tr.* 1) [to acknowledge, to avow] to confess [a crime, a fault, a charge &c.]. Unsere Sünden —, to confess our sins; auf Jemand —, to accuse one's accomplice by confessing one's crime; auch ihre Feinde —, daß sie unschuldig ist, even her enemies avow that she is innocent. 2) [to own or acknowledge, publicly to declare a belief in and adherence to] to confess. Darum, wer mich bekennet vor den Menschen, [in Scripture] whoever shall confess me before men. 3) [at cards] to follow suit. Ich kann nicht —, I have none of that suit; nicht —, to renounce, to revoke. II. *v. r.* sich —, 1) to acknowledge that one has done an act. Sich schuldig —, to own one's guilt; er hat sich zu mir bekannt, he has owned me for his son; sich zu einem Kinde —, to acknowledge a child. 2) publicly to declare a belief in, and adherence to. Einer, der sich zur christlichen Lehre bekennt, a man that professes himself a christian; sich zu einer Religion —, to profess a religion.

Bekénner, *m.* [-s, *pl.* -] 1) he that confesses or he that declares himself of an opinion or religion. Die — der christlichen Religion, the professors of the christian religion; [as a surname] Eduard, der —, Edward the Confessor. 2) confessor = martyr.

Bekénntniß, *n.* [-sses, *pl.* -sse] 1) [the acknowledgement of a crime, fault, or something to one's disadvantage] confession. Ein offenherziges —, a frank avowal. 2) [a formulary in which the articles of faith are comprised, a creed] confession.

Bekenntniß-buch, *n.* a book, which contains confessions. **—feier**, *f.* the sacrament of the Lord's supper. Die —feier begehen, to partake of the sacrament of the Lord's supper.

Bekérben, *v. tr.* to notch [a stick &c.].

Bekérzen, *v. tr.* [unusual] to furnish with waxlights or tapers.

Bekétten, *v. tr.* [unusual] to hang with chains.

Bekíchern, *v. tr.* to titter at.

Bekíelen, *v. tr.* 1) V. Befiedern. 2) to adorn with feathers, to feather.

Bekíesen, *v. tr.* to cover with gravel, to gravel [a walk &c.].

Beklágen, I. *v. tr.* to lament, to bewail, to bemoan [the loss of some object of endearment &c.]. Sein trauriges Schicksal wird allgemein beklagt, his melancholy fate is universally lamented. II. *v. r.* sich —, to complain of. Man beklagt sich sehr über ihn, he is very much complained of; er beklagte sich über die ihm widerfahrene schlechte Behandlung, he complained of the bad treatment which he had been the object of.

Beklagens-werth, **—würdig**, *adj.* and *adv.* deserving pity, pitiable, lamentable.

Beklágt, *part.* of Beklagen. **Beklagte**, *m.* and *f.* [-n, *pl.* -n] ein —er, eine —e, [-en, *pl.* -e] [in law] a defendant.

Beklámmern, *v. tr.* to fasten with cramps, to cramp.

Beklátschen, *v. tr.* 1) [to manifest approbation or praise by striking the hands together] to clap, to applaud. Eine theatralische Aufführung —, to clap or applaud a performance on the stage; dieser Schauspieler wurde eifrig beklatscht, this actor has been applauded very much. Das Beklatschen, clapping. 2) *Einen —, to tell tales of a person. Jungfer A. und Jungfer B. haben die arme Frau Z. arg beklatscht [ausgerichtet], Miss A. and Miss B. have sadly scandalized poor Mrs. Z.

Bekláuben, *v. tr.* 1) to pick with the fingers. 2) to handle with the fingers. Geld —, to finger money.

Beklében, I. *v. intr.* [u. w. seyn] to stick, to adhere; [of plants commonly Bekleiben] to root, to thrive. II. *v. tr.* to paste upon. Eine Schachtel mit Papier —, to line a box with paper.

Beklécken, *v. tr.* to spot, to stain, to bespatter, to dirty. Ein Papier mit Tinte —, to blot a paper; sich —, to bespatter one's clothes. *Fig.* Er bekleckt blos das schöne Papier, he wastes merely the fine paper [said of a scribbler].

Beklécker, *m.* [-s, *pl.* -] he that spots or bespatters. *Fig.* a scribbler.

Bekléckſen, *v. tr.* to spot, to stain. Mit Tinte —, to blot. *Fig.* to fill with worthless writing.

Bekléiben, *v. tr.* V. Bekleben, 1.

Bekléiden, I. *v. tr.* 1) to cover. Den Anker —, [in seamen's language] to shoe the anchor; ein Tau —, [in seamen's language] to serve a rope; das Ankertau —, to serve the cable with keckling, parcelling, mat and foxes; ein Zimmer —, to tapestry or paper a room; den Altar —, to spread the communion-cloth over the altar; eine Wand —, to wainscot a wall or to hang it with tapestry; eine Mauer mit Marmor —, to line a wall with marble; die Thüren und Fenster —, to furnish doors and windows with frames [which inclose them]; einen Schacht mit Brettern und Balken —, [in mining] to line a shaft; die Brustwehren &c. mit Rasen —, [in fortification] to line the parapets with turf; einen Hut —, [among hatters] to trim a hat; die Erde ist mit Grün bekleidet, the earth is clothed with verdure. 2) to cover with dress, to clothe, to dress a person. *Fig.* to clothe, to give to by commission, to invest. Jemanden mit einer geistlichen Würde —, to invest a person with an ecclesiastical dignity; Einen mit einem Amte —, to receive any one into a charge; mit Macht und Ansehen bekleidet, clothed with power and authority; ein Amt —, to hold or fill an office, or to exercise an office; das Amt der ersten obrigkeitlichen Person —, to fill the office of chief magistrate. II. *v. r.* sich —, to dress one's self. *Fig.* to deck one's self, to be covered with. Die Erde bekleidet sich mit jungem Grün, Earth has decked herself with fresh verdure.

Bekléider, *m.* [-s, *pl.* -] he that dresses, clothes, covers &c.

Bekléidung, *f.* 1) the act of clothing, covering, lining, *fig.* investing. 2) any thing which clothes or covers another thing, dress, clothes. Die — der Brustwehren &c. mit Rasen, the lining of parapets with turf; die — der Wände und Mauern der Zimmer, wainscot; die — der Taue, [in seamen's lang.] the serving; die äußere — an einem Schiffe, bulwark; die —, [in painting and sculpture = Draperie] drapery.

Bekléistern, *v. tr.* to cover with something pasted on. Etwas mit Papier —, to line something with paper; die Haare mit Salbe —, to oint the hair. *Fig.* Er bekleisterte die Falschheit des Aeneas mit &c, he coloured the falsehood of Aeneas by &c; seine Fehler mit einer Scheintugend —, to colour one's faults by a show of virtue.

Beklémmen, *v. tr.* [in the past participle often *ir.* beklommen] to press, to pinch. *Fig.* Als wenn es ihr das Herz beklemmte, as if it pressed her heart; es beklemmt mir das Herz, my heart is shrunk with grief; er ist in sehr beklemmten Umständen, he is in great straits, he lives in misery.

Beklémmung, *f.* 1) Die — der Brust &c., [a sense of heaviness or weight in the breast &c.] oppression. 2) [in medical language, uneasiness, unceasing restlessness in sickness] anxiety.

Bekléttern, *v. tr.* to climb [a steep mountain &c.].

Beklínken, *v. tr.* [among carpenters] to assemble or join [one board to another] by a mortise.

Beklínkung, *f.* 1) [among carpenters] the act of joining by a mortise 2) a mortise-joint.

Beklómmen, [*ir.* past participle of Beklemmen] *adj.* and *adv.* *Fig.* uneasy, anxious.

Beklópfen, *v. tr.* 1) to knock or beat repeatedly. 2) to form or shape by beating or knocking.

Beklügeln, *v. tr.* to criticize with too much refinement or subtility. Alles —, to subtilize every thing.

|| **Beklúnkern**, *v. tr.* 1) to furnish with tassels or flaps. 2) to bedraggle [one's garments &c.]. Sich —, to bedraggle one's clothes.

|| **Beknáppern**, *v. tr.* to nibble.

|| **Beknáupeln**, *v. tr.* to pick with the teeth, to gnaw [a bone &c.].

† **Beknáusern**, *v. tr.* to cut short by niggardliness.

Beködern, *v. tr.* to furnish with a bait, to bait [a hook, a trap &c.].

Bekóhlen, *v. tr.* Einen Platz —, [among charcoal-burners] to char coals on a place.

Bekómmen, *ir.* I. *v. tr.* to obtain, to get, to receive. Ich bekam einen Brief von meinem Bruder, I got a letter from my brother; Antworten auf Briefe —, to obtain answers to letters; ich bekam ein Geschenk von ihm, I received a present from him; er bekam Befehle von dem Oberanführer, he has received orders from the commander in chief; Schläge —, to get blows; eine Frau —, to get a wife; die Seeleute bekamen das Land zu Gesichte, the seamen descried land; es ist nichts zu —, there is nothing to be had; es ist nicht zu —, it is not to be had; ich bekam dieses Tuch sehr wohlfeil, I had this cloth very cheap; er bekommt monatlich eine Guinee, he has a guinea a month; er bekommt einen hohen Lohn für seine Dienste, he has high wages for his services; Blüten —, to put forth blossoms or flowers, to bloom, to blossom, to blow, to flower; die Bäume — Laub im Mai, the trees leaf in May; Zähne —, to breed or cut teeth; die Masern oder Blattern —, to catch the measles or small pox; Kinder —, to bear children; Lust zu etwas —, to take a fancy to any thing, to have a mind to something; er bekam Lust zu gehen, he had a mind to go. II. *v. intr.* [u. w. seyn] to suit the body or health. Dieselbe Nahrung bekommt nicht jeder Leibesbeschaffenheit, the same food does not agree with every constitution; das Aderlassen ist ihm sehr gut —, bleeding has done him much good; wohl bekomm's, much good may it do you.

|| **Bekómmlich**, *adj.* and *adv.* commodious.

Bekórken, *v. tr.* to stop [bottles or casks] with corks. Eine Flasche —, to cork a bottle.

Bekö́stigen, *v. tr.* to furnish with food, to feed. Der Meister beköstigt seinen Lehrling, the master diets or boards his apprentice; sie beköstigt zehn Studenten, she boards ten students; wir haben Mehl und Fleisch genug, um das Heer einen Monat zu —, we have flour and meat enough to victual the army a month; sich —, to keep or find one's self in victuals; Sie erhalten freie Wohnung, müssen sich aber selbst —, you shall have free lodging, but you must find yourself in board.

Bekö́stiger, *m.* [unusual] he that boards students &c.

Bekö́stigung, *f.* 1) the act of furnishing with food, boarding 2) food, entertainment, diet, board. Ich gebe ihm jährlich so viel für meine —, I give him so much a year for my board.

†**Bekö́tzen**, I. *v. tr.* V. Bespeien. II. *v. r.* sich —, 1) V. sich bespeien. 2) V. sich erbrechen.

Bekrä́ften, [more usual] **Bekrä́ftigen**, *v. tr.* to corroborate, to strengthen [used only in a figurative sense]. Einen Vertrag —, to confirm a covenant; er bekräftigte seine Gesetze durch sein eigenes Beispiel, he strengthened his laws by his own example; die Nachricht war zweifelhaft, doch wird sie durch neuere Berichte bekräftigt, the news was doubtful, but is confirmed or corroborated by recent advices; eine Aussage mit einem Eide —, to confirm a declaration with an oath.

Bekrä́ftigung, *f.* the act of strengthening or confirming, corroboration, confirmation, averment.

Bekrä́nzen, *v. tr.* to encircle as with a garland, to garland, to wreath. Mit Lorbeer bekränzt, wreathed with laurel.

Bekrä́tzen, *v. tr.* to scratch on the surface of any thing.

‖ **Bekraúen**, *v. tr.* to scratch gently.

Bekraúten, *v. tr.* [in husbandry] to rid of grass or herbs.

Bekraǘtert, *adj.* furnished with herbs.

Bekreíden, *v. tr.* to rub with chalk, to mark with chalk, to chalk [a paper &c.].

Bekreísen, *v. tr.* 1) to surround with a circle, to encircle. 2) [with hunters] Einen Wald —, to beat round a wood in search of game.

Bekreúzen, I. *v. tr.* 1) to furnish with crosses, to mark with crosses, to cross. Ein Wort —, to put a cross before a word. 2) [in gunnery] Die Kanonen — die Einfahrt des Hafens, the cannons command the entry of the harbour by a cross fire. II. *v. r.* sich —, [to make the sign of a cross] to cross one's self.

Bekreúzigen, V. Bekreuzen II.

Bekríechen, *ir. v. tr.* to creep or crawl upon.

Bekríegen, *v. tr.* to make or wage war upon, to war. Sie bekriegten die Franzosen, they made war upon the French.

Bekríttеln, *v. tr.* to pass judgment on with respect to blame, to speak of with disapprobation and contempt, to censure, to find fault with, to carp at. Jemands Betragen —, to criticize any one's conduct; er bekrittelt Alles, he carps at every thing, he is a censorious fellow.

Bekríttler, *m.* [-s, *pl.* -] a censorious critic.

Bekrítzeln, *v. tr.* to scrawl upon. Die Wand —, to scribble over the wall.

Bekrö́nen, *v. tr.* to invest with a crown, to adorn with a crown, to crown. *Fig.* Du hast ihn mit Ehre und Ruhm bekrönt, thou hast crowned him with honour and glory.

Bekrǘmeln, *v. tr.* to strew with small crumbs.

Bekrústen, I. *v. tr.* to furnish with a crust or with a hard coat, to incrust. II. *v. intr.* [u. w. seyn] and *v. r.* sich —, to get a crust, to be incrusted.

Bekrústung, *f.* incrustation.

Bekǘmmern, I. *v. tr.* 1) to give pain of mind to, to grieve, to afflict. Sein Unglück bekümmert mich, I am grieved at his misfortunes; und es bekümmerte ihn in seinem Herzen, [in Scripture] and it grieved him at his heart. ‖ 2) [in law, to take forcible possession of by law] to seize. Jemands Güter —, to seize any one's estate; Schulden halber —, to seize for debt, to distrain. II. *v. r.* sich —, 1) to care for. Er bekümmert sich um nichts, he cares for nothing; — Sie sich um sich, mind your own business; er bekümmert sich um Alles, he meddles with every thing. 2) to grieve, to sorrow. Bekümmert euch nicht über jene Fehler, welche &c., never trouble yourselves about those faults, which &c.

Bekǘmmerniß, *f.* [*pl.* -sse] and *n.* [-sses] grief, pain, affliction.

Bekǘmmert, [past participle of Bekümmern] *adj.* and *adv.* grieved, pained, afflicted. Ein bekümmertes Herz, Gemüth, a grieved heart, mind; — über den Gedanken, die That, grieved at the thought, at [or for] the fact; er ist wegen der Krankheit seines Sohnes sehr —, he is much afflicted about the sickness of his son; um etwas — seyn, to be anxious for or about something.

Bekǘnden, *v. tr.* [in law] to aver.

Bekǘssen, *v. tr.* to kiss repeatedly, to cover with kisses.

Belä́chbar, *adj.* and *adv.* that may justly excite laughter, laughable, ridiculous.

Belä́cheln, *v. tr.* to smile at.

Belä́chen, *v. tr.* to laugh at. Einen lustigen Einfall —, to laugh at a merry conceit; Thorheiten —, to deride follies, to turn them to ridicule, to make sport of them. Syn. Belachen, Auslachen, Verlachen. Auslachen is said only of men, Belachen of things and actions, Verlachen of both. Auslachen and Verlachen convey also an idea of contempt, which is expressed by laughter, to deride. Belachen denotes only the expression of mirth, without any contempt of the cause which excited our laughter.

Belachens=werth, —würdig, *adj.* and *adv.* worthy of laughter, ridiculous. Auf eine —swerthe Weise, ridiculously.

Belä́cken, *v. tr.* to smear over with lacker, to lacker. Ein belackter Tisch, a varnished table.

Belä́den, *ir. v. tr.* to load [a camel or horse, a cart or waggon]. [in husbandry] Beladene Bienen, bees that convey to the hive the pollen of flowers [settled on the hair with which their body is covered]. *Fig.* Ein Volk mit Steuern —, to burden a nation with taxes; sich mit &c. —, to burden one's self with &c.

Belä́dung, *f.* 1) loading. 2) [among cloth-shearers] a heavy piece of lead.

Belä́gerer, *m.* [-s, *pl.* -] beleaguerer, besieger.

Belä́gern, *v. tr.* 1) to lay down. [in husb.] Den Boden mit Schaafen — lassen, to pen sheep on a ground. 2) to lay siege to, to beleaguer, to besiege [a castle or a city &c.]. Die Belagerten, the besieged. *Fig.* Die Schmeichler — stets die Großen, the great are always beset with flatterers.

Belä́gerung, *f.* [investment of a town or fort by an army] siege.

Belagerungs=geschütz, *n.* heavy artillery for sieges. —geschütze, *pl.* battering train. —krone, *f.* [with the ancient Romans] the obsidional crown. —kunst, *f.* the art of besieging towns &c. —park, *m.* a park of artillery used for a siege. —werke, *pl.* [in fortification] approaches [such as parallels, trenches &c.].

Belá́ng, *m.* [-es] 1) amount, sum. 2) importance. Von —e, of weight.

Belá́ngen, *v. tr.* 1) [to touch with the hand extended] to reach. 2) *Fig.* *a*) to relate or belong to, to concern. Was mich belangt, as for me; was das belangt, with respect or regard to that, as for that. *b*) to prosecute by law, to sue. Wenn dich Einer gerichtlich belangt, if any one sue thee at law. Syn. V. Anklagen.

Belá́nger, *m.* [-s, *pl.* -] he that sues a person at law.

Belá́ngreich, *adj.* and *adv.* important, of consequence.

Belä́ppen, *v. tr.* 1) to furnish with rags. [with hunters] Ein Gehölz —, to set up rags round a wood [to frighten or scare game]. ‖ 2) V. Flicken.

‖ **Belä́ssen**, *ir. v. intr.* to leave a thing at rest. Wir wollen es vor der Hand dabei —, we will let that be for the present.

Belä́sten, *v. tr.* to load [an ass, a waggon &c.]. Ein Schiff —, to freight a ship. *Fig.* Ein Gemählde —, to overcharge a picture; Einen —, [in commerce] to charge with debt, to debit. Belastet, [in commerce] charged in debt, debited; den Handel mit Abgaben —, to clog commerce with impositions; mit Sorgen, Schuld oder Schande belastet, loaded with cares, guilt or shame; mit Jahren belastet, burdened with age, advanced in years.

Belä́stern, *v. tr.* to slander, to calumniate.

Belä́stigen, *v. tr.* to burden [a nation with taxes &c.]; V. [the more usual verbs] Beladen and Belasten; *it.* to incommode, to molest, to annoy. Sie belästigten ihn mit unvernünftigen Forderungen, they importuned him with unreasonable demands; Sie — mich, you are a trouble to me; die Hitze belästigte mich sehr, the heat was very oppressive to me.

Belä́tten, *v. tr.* to furnish or cover with laths. Ein Dach —, [with carpenters] to lath a roof.

Belaúbbar, *adj.* and *adv.* that may be stripped of leaves.

Belaúben, I. *v. tr.* 1) to cover with leaves, [in architect.] to foliage. Den Meiler —, [with charcoal-burners] to cover a charcoal-pile with leaves, coal-dust and earth. Belaubt, leafed; ein schön —er Baum, a tree with a luxuriant foliage. 2) to strip of the leaves. Den Wein —, to prune a vine. II. *v. r.* sich —, to leaf. Die Bäume — sich im Mai, the trees leaf in May.

Belaúbung, *f.* 1) the state of producing leaves, of leafing. 2) the act of stripping of leaves. 3) leaves in general, foliage. Ein Baum mit schöner —, a tree of beautiful foliage.

Belaúern, *v. tr.* 1) to observe in ambush, to lurk for, to watch, to lie in wait for. 2) [in familiar language] to deceive, to impose on.

Belaúf, *m.* [-es] amount. Der — der verschiedenen Summen ist fünfzig Thaler, the total of the several sums is fifty dollars.

Belaúfen, *ir.* I. *v. tr.* to visit or to view running, to run over; [with hunters = to impregnate] to line [a bitch]. II. *v. r.* sich —, 1) to couple [said of dogs]. 2) [to compose in the whole] to amount. Die Interessen der verschiedenen Summen — sich auf fünfzig Thaler, the interest on the several sums amounts to fifty dollars.

Belaúschen, *v. tr.* to observe in order to detect, to watch. Sprechen Sie nicht so laut, man belauscht uns, do not speak so loud, we are overheard or somebody is listening.

Belaúscher, *m.* [-s, *pl.* -] he that observes

in order to detect, an eaves-dropper.

† **Belaúsen**, *v. tr.* to free from lice, to louse.

Beláuten, *v. tr.* [unusual] to make known or to celebrate by the ringing of bells. Eine Leiche —, to toll a bell for a funeral, to knoll.

Belében, *v. tr.* to give life to, to vivify. Einen Ertrunkenen —, to restore a drowned person to life; alle belebte Wesen, all animated beings; die Seele belebt den Körper, the soul animates the body; eine Bildsäule —, to animate a statue; Orpheus belebte Eichen und Felsen, Orpheus animated oaks and rocks; das belebende Princip, animator; wieder or von neuem —, to revivify, to reanimate. *Fig.* Der —de Strahl der Sonne, the genial ray of the sun; der Sonne —de Strahlen, the sun's vivifying beams; die —de Kraft des Weines, wine's enlivening power; solche —de Kraft, such quickening power; gute Laune belebt eine Gesellschaft, good humour enlivens a company; die Traurigen — or aufheitern, to enliven the gloomy. V. Belebt.

Beléber, *m.* [-s, *pl.* -] one that gives life, animator, quickener, enlivener.

Belébt, [past participle of Beleben] *adj.* and *adv.* 1) being endowed with animal life, animated. *Fig.* Ein —er Hühnerhof, a crowded poultry yard; eine —e Stadt, a populous city. 2) *Fig.* lively, brisk, vigorous, vivacious. Ein —er junger Mensch, a lively youth; —e Gesichtszüge, animated countenance; ein —es Wesen, lively manners; ein —es Gemählde, an animated picture; dieses Gemählde ist sehr —, there is a great deal of life in this painting.

Belébtheit, *f.* liveliness, animation, vivacity.

Belébung, *f.* [the act of infusing life] animation.

Belebungs-mittel, *n.* a remedy which has the power of restoring to life, a restorative. **—versuch**, *m.* a trial to restore dead or drowned persons to life.

Belécken, *v. tr.* 1) [to pass or draw the tongue over the surface] to lick. Der Hund beleckt eine Wunde, the dog licks a wound; sich die Finger —, to lick one's fingers. 2) * to eat slowly or in small bits, to nibble. † 3) Sich —, to kiss one another repeatedly. Diese beiden Verliebten — sich [or einander] den lieben langen Tag, these lovers are bussing all day long.

Beléderu, *v. tr.* to furnish with leather, to leather.

Belég, *m.* [-es, *pl.* -e] [any official or authoritative paper] a document, voucher. Der Bericht mit allen —en, the report with all the documents.

Belége, *n.* [-s, *pl.* -n] [among tailors] a stripe sewed upon the border of a garment to strengthen it.

Belégen, *v. tr.* to cover or spread over the surface, to overlay. Den Boden mit Teppichen —, to cover the floor with carpets; Cedernholz mit Gold belegt, cedar overlaid with gold; Stahl mit Silber belegt, steel washed with silver; die Hufe —, to shoe the hoofs; die Pflugschar —, to shoe the plough-share; ein Luststück —, [in gardening] to turf a pleasure-ground; mit Marmor —, to face with marble; einen Fußboden mit Dielen —, to board a floor; das Glas —, [in manufactories of looking-glasses] to foliate a looking-glass; [in fam. lang.] ich habe einen Platz belegt, [at a public table or ordinary] I have secured my place; eine belegte Zunge, a furred tongue; [applied to irrational animals] to impregnate; der Hund belegt die Hündinn, the dog lines the bitch; der Hengst belegt die Stute, the stallion covers the mare; eine Stute —, to horse a mare; ein Tau —, [in seamen's lang.] to belay a rope. *Fig.* *a*) to lay on as a tax, toll, duty or penalty. Mit Strafen belegt man diejenigen, welche die Gesetze übertreten, penalties are imposed on those, who violate the laws; einen Verbrecher mit Strafe —, to inflict a punishment on an offender; das Salz mit einer Abgabe —, to lay a duty on salt; Landeigenthum mit einer Steuer —, to lay a tax on land; Jemanden mit einer Geldbuße —, to set a fine upon any one; Jemands Habe mit Arrest —, to seize any one's chattels. *b*) to give an appellation to. Etwas mit einem Namen —, to assign a name to a thing. *c*) to support by documents and vouchers. Die Rechnungen —, to justify or make good accounts by documents or vouchers; seine Behauptungen mit Stellen aus der Schrift —, to maintain or make good one's assertions by passages from the Scripture. *d*) to furnish with people. Eine Stadt mit Besatzung —, to garrison a town; Jemands Haus mit Soldaten —, to quarter soldiers upon any one; eine Grube mit Arbeitern —, [in mining] to employ workmen in a mine. *e*) to lay out, to place. Geld —, to put out money [at interest].

Belégen, [past participle of Beliegen] *adj.* and *adv.* situated. Nordöstlich von &c. —, situated on the North-east of &c.

Beléghölzer, *pl.* [in seamen's lang.] all sorts of belaying pins, cleats, kevels and the like.

Beléhmen, *v. tr.* to cover with loam, to loam.

Beléhnen, *v. tr.* [to invest with a fee or fief] to feoff, to enfeoff. Der Belehnte, feoffee.

Beléhner, *m.* [-s, *pl.* -] [a person who grants a fee] feoffer, feoffor.

Beléhnung, *f.* feoffment, enfeoffment.

Beléhren, I. *v. tr.* to guide by instruction, information or advice. Belehre mich, instruct me; belehrend, serving to instruct or inform, instructive; man hat sie über die Gefahr belehrt, they were advised of the risk or danger; man hat mich eines Andern belehrt, I am otherwise advised; eines Bessern —, to set to rights; ich lasse mich ja gern —, I am quite ready to listen to reason; er ist eines Bessern belehrt worden, he has been disabused; nicht recht von einer or über eine Sache belehrt seyn, to be misinformed of a thing. II. *v. r.* sich —, to improve in knowledge. Er hat sich aus guten Büchern belehrt, he derived instruction from good books; dieß hat mich von Ihrer or über Ihre Rechtlichkeit belehrt, that convinced me of your probity.

Beléhrer, *m.* [-s, *pl.* -] he that imparts knowledge to others by information, instructor.

Beléhrung, *f.* information, instruction. Ich hörte seinen —en aufmerksam zu, I listened heedfully to his instructions.

Beleibt, [past part. of the unusual *v. tr.* beleiben = to furnish with a belly] *adj.* and *adv.* corpulent, lusty. Wohl —, plump, fat; schwer —, bulky, heavy.

Beleibtheit, *f.* corpulence, plumpness, fleshiness. Wohl —, fatness, obesity.

Beleidigen, *v. tr.* [originally = verletzen, now used only figuratively] to offend, to displease. Jemanden schwer —, to insult any one greatly; Mißklänge — die Ohren, discordant sounds are offensive to the ears; ein Anblick, der die Augen beleidiget, an offensive sight, a shocking spectacle or sight; seine Reden — keusche Ohren, his discourses offend chaste ears; mit Worten —, to offend by words; durch Worte oder Thaten beleidiget, offended by words or actions, [in popular lang.] affronted; du beleidigest mich, thou wrongest me; beleidiget seyn von &c., to be wronged by &c.; Einen gröblich —, to outrage any one; —de Worte, offensive words; das Verbrechen der beleidigten Majestät, high treason; sich durch etwas beleidigt finden, to take offence at something; das Beleidigende eines rohen Betragens, the offensiveness of a rude behaviour; er war der Beleidigte, he was the person offended, the injured party; auf eine —de Weise, injuriously.

Beleidiger, *m.* [-s, *pl.* -] a person who offends or has offended, offender.

Beleidigerinn, *f.* offendress.

Beleidigung, *f.* offence, injury, affront. Eine schwere —, a grievous offence; Einem —en zufügen, to give offence to any one; er nahm es für or als eine — auf, he took offence at it; eine — ertragen, * sie einstecken, verschlucken, to bear an injury, to put up with an insult, to pocket an affront, *prov.* to carry coals.

‖ **Beleihen**, *ir. v. tr.* V. Belehnen.

Beleimen, *v. tr.* to join with glue, to glue.

Beleisten, *v. tr.* to furnish with ledges.

Belémmern, *v. tr.* [in seamen's language] to encumber, to cumber.

Belémmerung, *f.* [in seamen's language] any cumbersome goods embarrassing the stowage of the hold, lumber, encumbrance.

* **Belemnít**, *m.* [-s, *pl.* -e] arrow-head, or finger-stone, belemnites.

‖ **Belésen**, *v. tr.* [to separate from any thing useless or noxious, by gleaning out either part] to pick [a salad &c.].

Belésen, [past participle of the unusual verb Belesen = read over, peruse] *adj.* and *adv.* [instructed by reading] read, well-read. — seyn, to be well read in the writers, to be conversant with the writers.

Belésenheit, *f.* acquaintance with books, extensive reading.

Beleúchten, *v. tr.* to supply with light, to illuminate, to illumine. Die Sonne beleuchtet die Erde, the sun enlightens the earth; von der Sonne beleuchtet, illumined by the sun; ein Zimmer —, to light up a room; die Straßen einer Stadt —, to light the streets of a city; die Straßen dieser Stadt sind sehr schlecht beleuchtet, the streets of this town are very badly or scantily lighted; mehrere Hauptstädte Europa's werden jetzt mit Gas beleuchtet, several capitals of Europe are now lighted with gas; bei diesem festlichen Anlasse wurde die ganze Stadt beleuchtet, the whole town was illuminated on this festive occasion; mehrere Häuser waren übrigens sehr ärmlich beleuchtet, several houses were, indeed, but poorly illuminated. [in painting] to throw or spread light upon. Ein Gemählde —, to illumine a picture [to supply it] with the proper light. *Fig.* Einen Gegenstand in allen seinen Verhältnissen und Beziehungen —, to throw light upon a subject in all its relations and bearings; alle Umstände der Rechtssache —, to inquire into all the circumstances of the case; eine Stelle aus der Schrift —, to illustrate a passage of Scripture.

Beleúchter, *m.* [-s, *pl.* -] [one who illumines] enlightener. *Fig.* he that examines, clears up or illustrates [a case or point], illustrator.

Beleúchtung, *f.* the act of supplying with light, illumination. Die — der Straßen einer Stadt, the lighting of the streets of a city; die — eines Gemähldes, the illumining of a picture; die — eines Hauses, einer Stadt, illumination of a house or town [in manifestation of joy]; bei seinem feierlichen Einzuge fand eine allgemeine — der Hauptstadt statt, on his solemn entry a general illumination of the capital took place. *Fig.* examination, disquisition, inquiry, illustration.

† **Bélferer**, *m.* [-s, *pl.* -] yelper [of dogs, espe-

cially small ones] V. Kläffer. *Fig.* a quarrelsome person, a snarler.

† **Bèlferinn**, *f.* a quarrelsome woman, a shrew. V. Widerbellerinn.

† **Bèlfern**, *v. intr.* to yelp [said of dogs, especially of the smaller kind]. *Fig.* to quarrel, to scold. Sie belfert in Einem fort, she never ceases scolding.

Bèlgien, *n.* [-s] Belgium. **Belgier**, *m.* [-s, *pl.* -] —**inn**, *f.* a Belgian. **Belgisch**, *adj.* and *adv.* Belgian.

Belíchtern, *v. tr.* [unusual] 1) to furnish with candles. 2) [in painting] to furnish with lights.

Belíebäugeln, *v. tr.* to view with side-glances, as in fondness, to ogle, to cast a sheep's eye at.

Belíeben, *v. tr.*, *intr.* and *imp.* to desire, to will, to like, to be pleased. — Sie sonst noch etwas? do you wish for any thing else? — Sie jetzt eine Tasse Thee? will you have a cup of tea now? — Sie Schinken? do you choose some ham? nehmen Sie, was Ihnen beliebt, take your choice; was beliebt Ihnen? what's your pleasure? was beliebt? speak your pleasure; diese Speise beliebt mir nicht, I don't like this dish; thun Sie, was Ihnen beliebt, use your pleasure; wie es Ihnen beliebt, as you please, as you choose; es beliebt mir nicht, dahin zu gehen, I have no mind, or no fancy to go there; wem beliebt, der nehme, let every one take, who will; das beliebt Ihnen zu sagen, you are pleased to say so; beliebt's or ‡ geliebt's Gott, if it please God, please God, if God please; er mag gehen oder bleiben, wie es ihm beliebt, he may go or stay, as he likes.

Belíeben, *n.* [-s] will, inclination, pleasure, liking. — an etwas haben, — in or an etwas finden, to take pleasure in any thing; nach —, at pleasure; nach Ihrem —, as you please; ich stelle es in Ihr —, use your pleasure.

Belíebig, *adj.* and *adv.* what is chosen or fixed upon, what pleases. Sie nehmen das ihnen —e Geschlecht und die ihnen —e Gestalt an, they assume what sexes and shapes they please; eine —e Summe Geldes, any sum of money; in —er Größe, of the size you choose; wenn es Ihnen — ist, if it is agreeable to you; nehmen Sie, was Ihnen — ist, take whatever you choose, whatever you have a mind for.

Belíebt, [past part. of Belieben] *adj.* and *adv.* 1) what one likes. In —er or in der Ihnen beliebigen Form, in the form you like or choose. 2) regarded with particular kindness, affection, or preference. Dieses Werk wird in dem so allgemein —en Duodezformat erscheinen, this work will be published in the much liked duodecimo size; ein —er Schriftsteller, a favourite author; ein —er Lustgang, a favourite walk; bei dem Volke —, popular; Demagogen machen sich bei dem gemeinen Volke —, demagogues ingratiate themselves with the populace, seek popularity with the mob; — werden, to grow in favour.

Belíebung, *f.* [unusual] any voluntary contract or agreement.

Belíegen, *ir. v. intr.* V. Belegen (*adj.*) and Liegen.

Belínien, [more usual] **Belinieren**, *v. tr.* to mark with lines, to rule. Papier —, to rule paper.

Belísten, *v. tr.* to trick, to deceive.

Belíttern, *v. tr.* [in mining] to furnish with ladders.

* **Bèlladonna**, *f.* V. Tollkirsche.

Bèlle, *f.* [*pl.* -n] V. Albe 1.

Bèllen, *v. intr.* [originally = tönen; allied to the Lat. *balare*, as also to *pellare* in *ap-pello* &c.; D. *bellen* signifies schellen; V. Bellhammel] 1) [in contempt] to bawl, to clamour. 2) to bark, to bay. *Prov.* Ein Hund, der beißen will, bellt nicht, barking dogs never bite, the greatest barkers bite not sorest.

* **Belletríst**, *m.* [-en, *pl.* -en] —**inn**, *f.* one versed in or who writes polite literature.

* **Belletrístik**, *f.* polite literature, belles-lettres.

* **Belletrístisch**, *adj.* and *adv.* relating to polite literature.

Bèllhammel, *m.* [-s, *pl.* -hämmel] [Bell signifies D. and Eng. die Schelle or Glocke] [a wether or sheep which leads the flock, with a bell on his neck] bell-wether.

Bèllhenne, *f.* [*pl.* -n] the common coot.

Bèllhorn, *m.* [-s, *pl.* -hörner] the Ceilan ribbed partridge shell, the spotted tun.

* **Bellóna**, *f.* [*gen.* der —, or without the article —'s, or, *poet.*, Bellonen's] [the Goddess of war] Bellona.

Belóben, *v. tr.* to mention with approbation, to commend, to praise, to laud. ‡ [in law language] = erwähnen. Sintemalen belobtes Dokument abhanden kam, since the afore-said document is missing; er zeichnete sich so sehr aus, daß er öffentlich belobt wurde, he distinguished himself so much, that public mention was made of his praiseworthy conduct.

Belóbung, *f.* commendation, praise, favourable representation in words.

Belobungs-brief, *m.* V. —schreiben. —**preis**, *m.* the next price to the best. —**schreiben**, *n.* a letter of a superior, expressing approbation.

Belóchen, *v. tr.* [in husbandry] to make holes in, to hole. Fichten —, to make incisions in pines [for the exudation of resin].

Belóhnbar, *adj.* and *adv.* worthy of reward, rewardable, remunerable.

Belóhnen, *v. tr.* 1) to recompense, to pay, to remunerate [for services performed]. 2) to recompense for something good, to reward. Es belohnt die [in familiar language, es verlohnt die or der] Mühe nicht, it is not worth the trouble; Gott belohnt die Gerechten, God rewards the just; schlecht belohnter Häuptling! ill requited chief! 3) [it is sometimes used with a mixture of irony for] to punish. Er ist für seine Treulosigkeit belohnt worden, he has been requited for his faithlessness.

Belóhner, *m.* [-s, *pl.* -] [one that rewards or recompenses] rewarder.

Belóhnung, *f.* 1) the act of recompensing or rewarding, recompense. 2) reward, remuneration. Die — eines Advokaten für seine Bemühung, a lawyer's fee.

Belohnungs-reich, *adj.* and *adv.* rich in rewards. —**süchtig**, *adj.* and *adv.* greedy of reward.

Bèlt, *m.* [-es, *pl.* -e] [in old G. *palz* signifies *girdle*, L. *balteus*] [the name of two straits in the Baltic sea] the Belt. Der große —, der kleine —, the great Belt, the lesser Belt.

‖ and ‡ **Belúgen**, *v. tr.* to view closely.

Belügen, *ir. v. tr.* 1) to lie to, to deceive by lies. Er hat mich belogen, he told me a lie. 2) [to tell lies concerning = über Einen lügen or Lügen aussagen] to belie. Wie können Sie ihn hinter seinem Rücken so —? how can you propagate such lies of him behind his back?

‖ and † **Belúgsen**, *v. tr.* to cheat, to cozen, to defraud.

Belústigen, *v. tr.* to amuse, to divert. Er belustiget sich mit unbedeutenden Dingen, he amuses himself with trifles; sich an einer Sache —, to be diverted with something.

Belústiger, *m.* [-s, *pl.* -] he that amuses or diverts others, diverter, amuser.

Belústigung, *f.* 1) the act of amusing or diverting. 2) [that which amuses, detains or engages the mind, a pleasurable occupation of the senses, or that which furnishes it, as dancing, sports or music] amusement. Die —en der Jugend, the diversions of youth.

* **Bèlvedère** or **Belvedère**, *n.* [a pavilion on the top of an edifice, an artificial eminence in a garden] belvedere.

Bèlzen, *v. tr.* V. Pelzen, Pfropfen.

Bemächtigen, *v. r.* sich —, to get into one's power. Sich einer Stadt —, to take a town; er bemächtigte sich des Thores mit Gewalt, he took possession of the gate by force; wir bemächtigten uns des Königreichs Neapel, we possessed ourselves of the kingdom of Naples; der Herzog von Savoyen bemächtigte sich der französischen Besitzungen, the duke of Savoy made himself master of the French possessions; sich einer Person —, to take any one prisoner; zuletzt — sie sich des Scepters, at last they seize the sceptre. *Fig.* Hoffnung und Zweifel — sich wechselsweise ihrer Seele, hope and doubt alternate seize her soul. Syn. V. Bemeistern and Anmaßen.

1. **Bemáhlen**, [from Mahlen = *to paint*] *v. tr.* 1) [to cover or besmear with colour or colours] to paint [a house &c.]. Schlecht or grob —, to daub; sich —, to paint, to lay colours on the face &c.; man sagt, daß sie sich bemahlt [schminkt], it is said that she paints. 2) to soil with writing [tables, seats &c.].

2. **Bemáhlen**, [from Mahl or Merkzeichen = *mark*] *v. tr.* [to make any sign of distinction] to mark. Einen Ort —, [with hunters] to mark a place.

Bemáhnt, [past part. of the unusual verb bemähnen] *adj.* maned [said of horses and lions].

Bemákeln, *v. tr.* to stain, to maculate.

Bemäkeln, *v. tr.* to criticize. V. Mäkeln.

Bemállen, *v. tr.* [in seamen's language] Ein Stück Holz —, to mould a piece of timber.

Bemánnen, *v. tr.* [to furnish with men] to man [a ship &c.].

‖ and † **Bemánschen**, *v. tr.* to bedaub, touch here and there with soiled hands. Sich —, to bedash one's clothes.

Bemänteln, *v. tr. Fig.* [to use a false covering, to give a specious appearance, to set in a fair light] to cloke, to colour, to palliate. Einen Fehler —, to palliate a fault; sie — nie ihre Laster, they never palliate their vices. Syn. **Bemänteln**, **Beschönigen**. Bemänteln signifies merely to conceal, to cloke what is bad in an action; Beschönigen, to give it a specious appearance.

Bemásten, *v. tr.* to furnish with masts. Ein Schiff —, to fix or place the masts of a ship; bemastet, masted.

Bemáuern, *v. tr.* to surround with a wall or walls, to wall, to immure.

Bemáulkorben, *v. tr.* [unusual] to muzzle [a dog &c.].

† **Bemáusen**, *v. tr.* to pilfer. Einen —, to rob any one of trifles.

Beméhlen, *v. tr.* [unusual] to sprinkle with meal or flour, to meal. Sich —, to sprinkle one's clothes with meal or flour.

‖ **Beméiern**, *v. tr.* 1) to supply with a farmer. Ein Gut —, to place a farmer or steward over an estate. 2) Einen —, to put a farmer in possession of a farm.

Beméißeln, *v. tr.* to work with a chisel, to chisel.

Bemeistern, *v. tr.* to rule, to govern. Seinen Feind —, to overcome one's enemy. *Fig.* Seine Leidenschaften —, to subdue one's passions. [chiefly as *v. r.*] Sich einer Sache —, to get something into one's power; sich einer Festung —, to take a fortress; er bemeisterte sich ihrer Besitzungen, he made himself master of their dominions. *Fig.* Welche Wuth bemeisterte sich Deiner? what fury possessed thee? Kummer bemeistert sich meiner Seele, sorrow seizes my soul. SYN. Sich bemeistern, Sich bemächtigen. Sich bemächtigen signifies merely to get into one's power, to obtain possession of; sich bemeistern signifies sich bemächtigen, with the intention of governing, of making one's self master over.

‡**Bemelden**, *v. tr.* to mention, to cite, to quote. Die bemeldete Sache, the thing aforementioned; bemeldetermaßen, as aforesaid.

Bemengen, *v. r. Fig.* Sich mit einer Sache —, to meddle with something.

Bemerkbar, *adj.* and *adv.* [that may be observed or noticed] observable, noticeable, perceivable. Eine kaum —e Bewegung, a scarcely sensible movement; das ist mit dem bloßen Auge nicht —, that is not perceptible to the naked eye; der Unterschied dieser Umfangsverhältnisse ist nicht —, there is no observable difference between these sizes.

Bemerkbarkeit, *f.* perceptibility.

Bemerken, *v. tr.* 1) to notice, to remark. Ich sah die Gestalt, bemerkte aber nichts Besonderes daran, I saw the figure, but observed nothing peculiar in it; wir bemerken Gegenstände, die an uns vorübergehen oder vor uns stehen, we take notice of objects passing or standing before us; die vorn stehen, sieht der Fürst, indessen er, die hinten sind, kaum bemerkt, those that stand forward are seen by the prince, while those behind are scarce perceived by him; einen Flecken auf der Sonnenscheibe bemerkte er nicht, a spot on the sun's disk did not fall under his observation; Einige beobachten das Betragen Anderer nur, um ihre Fehler zu —, some observe the conduct of others, only in order to remark their faults; man hat bemerkt, it has been observed; ich habe es wohl bemerkt, I have noted it well; Einen — [= ihn grüßen], to take notice of any one; ich grüßte Sie, allein Sie haben mich nicht — wollen, I saluted you, but you would not take notice of me, you seemed to intend to cut me. 2) to observe, to utter or express as a remark, opinion, or sentiment, to remark. Hr. N. bemerkt richtig or macht die richtige Bemerkung, daß kein Mann für seinen Kammerdiener [or seinem Kammerdiener gegenüber] groß erscheint, Mr. N. well observes, that no man appears great to his valet-de-chambre; die bemerkte [= die erwähnte] Sache, the thing mentioned. 3) [= vermerken, auslegen] to receive with a certain affection of the mind. Uebel —, to take ill; bestens —, to take in the best manner.

Bemerkens-werth, **—würdig**, *adj.* and *adv.* worthy of observation, noticeable, remarkable. —werthe Dinge [Merkwürdigkeiten], remarkables, curiosities.

Bemerker, *m.* [-s, *pl.* -] remarker.

Bemerklich, *adj.* and *adv.* that may be observed or noticed. Ein Jeder, dem ein Gegenstand — gemacht wurde, whoever should be pointed to an object; er machte mir —, daß &c., he observed to me, that &c.

Bemerkung, *f.* [the act of observing, taking notice, and the result of seeing or taking cognizance in the mind] observation. —en über etwas machen, to make observations on something; ich habe die — bei mir selbst gemacht, I made the observation in my own mind; ich werde nachher meine —en darüber machen, I shall hereafter observe upon it; mit —en am Rande, with remarks in the margin or marginal notes. SYN. V. Anmerkung.

Bemerkungs-gabe, *f.* the gift of observation. **—geist**, *m.* an observing mind. **—werth**, **—würdig**, *adj.* and *adv.* worthy of observation, noticeable.

Bemisten, *v. tr.* to manure with dung, to dung. Einen Acker —, to manure a field.

Bemitleiden, *v. tr.* to commiserate, to compassionate, to pity.

Bemittelt, [past part. of the obsolete verb bemitteln] *adj.* and *adv.* wealthy, opulent. — seyn, to be well off, to be in good circumstances; ein —er Mann, a warm man.

Bemöbeln, *v. tr.* [unusual] to furnish [a room, a house &c.]. Ein reich bemöbeltes Zimmer, a handsomely furnished room.

Bemöbler, *m.* [-s, *pl.* -] upholsterer.

Bemodern, *v. intr.* [u. w. seyn] to become moldy, to mold.

Bemosen, I. *v. tr.* to cover with moss, to moss. Eine Eiche, deren Zweige vom Alter bemoost waren, an oak whose boughs were mossed with age. II. *v. intr.* [u. w. seyn and the past part.] to be covered with moss. Bemooste Quellen, mossy fountains; bemooste Thürme, moss-grown towers. *Fig.* Ein bemooster Bursche, ein bemoostes Haupt [students' cant], an old student. III. *v. r.* sich —, to cover itself with moss.

Bemörteln, *v. tr.* to cover with mortar. Eine Mauer —, to point a wall.

Bemühen, *v. tr.* and *v. r.* to give occasion of labour to, to trouble. Sich —, to exert one's self; *it.* to trouble one's self, to give one's self trouble. — Sie sich doch nicht, pray, do not give yourself any trouble; sie lachten ihn aus, daß er sich darum bemüht hatte, they called him a fool for his pains; Sie werden sich umsonst —, you will lose your labour; sich um Ehrenstellen —, to run or seek anxiously after honours; sich für Jemand —, to intercede in favour of any one, to interest one's self for any one; Einen um etwas —, [in familiar language] to trouble a person for a thing; darf ich Sie um das Buch —? may I trouble you to reach [or show &c.] me that book? bemüht seyn, to take pains, to try, to endeavour; bei einem Wettrennen bemüht sich Jeder, seinen Gegner zu überrennen, in a race each man endeavours to outstrip his antagonist; [in familiar language, a word of civility or slight regard] wollen Sie sich nicht herein —? won't you please to step in, to walk in?

Bemühen, *n.* [-s], **Bemühung**, *f.* trouble, pains, endeavour. Alle seine Bemühungen waren umsonst, all his exertions or efforts were in vain.

Bemühungsgebühr, *f.* [in commerce] provision, commission.

‖ and † **Bemunkeln**, *v. tr.* to cheat, to deceive.

‡**Bemüßigen**, *v. tr.* to oblige, to compel, to force, to necessitate. Ich bin bemüßiget [or gemüßiget] es zu thun, I am obliged to do it.

Bemuthigen, *v. tr.* [unusual] to inspire with courage, to encourage.

Benachbaren, *v. r.* sich —, [commonly used in the part. benachbart]. Sich mit Jemand —, to become the neighbour of a person; die benachbarten Häuser, the neighbouring houses; die benachbarten Länder oder Völker, the neighbouring countries or nations.

Benachrichten, [better] **Benachrichtigen**, *v. tr.* to inform, to apprize. Jemand —, to give any one notice or intelligence of; Einen —, to send any one word; ein Freund auf dem Lande benachrichtiget mich von seinem Glücke, a friend in the country acquaints me with his success; er benachrichtigte den Befehlshaber von dem, was er gethan hatte, he apprized the commander of what he had done; Jemand von seinen Verlusten —, to advertise, to advise any one of one's losses; ich benachrichtigte sie von seiner Ankunft, I have given her notice of his arrival; wir wurden von &c. benachrichtiget, we received information of &c; Briefe aus Brüssel — uns von dem Anfange der Feindseligkeiten zwischen den Holländern und Belgiern, letters from Brussels inform us of the commencement of hostilities between the Dutch and the Belgians.

Benachrichtiger, *m.* [-s, *pl.* -] [one who advertises] informer, advertiser.

Benachrichtigung, *f.* information, news or advice communicated by word or writing, intelligence.

Benachrichtigungsbrief, *m.* letter of advice.

Benachten, *v. tr.* [unusual] [to involve in darkness, to shroud with the shades of night] to benight.

Benachtheiligen, *v. tr.* to injure, to prejudice, to harm, to hurt. Er benachtheiliget seinen Nachbar durch Verleumdung, he damages his neighbour by calumny; das benachtheiligt &c., that is prejudicial, or detrimental to &c.

Benageln, *v. tr.* 1) to fill or stud with nails, to nail. Benagelte Schuhe, clouted shoes. 2) to fasten with nails, to unite, close or make compact with nails, to nail.

Benagen, *v. tr.* to pick with the teeth. Einen Knochen —, to gnaw a bone; die Mäuse haben das Brod benagt, the mice have nibbled the bread.

Benähen, *v. tr.* to sew upon, to sew round.

Benamen, *v. tr.* [to give an appellation to] to name. Sie benamte das Kind Icabod, she named the child Ichabod.

Benamentlich, *adv.* [in law-language] V. Namentlich.

‖ **Benamsen**, *v. tr.* V. Benamen. Benamset, named, called, designated by the name, ycleped.

Benarben, I. *v. tr.* to mark with a scar, to scar. Die Blattern haben ihm das Gesicht ganz benarbt, the small-pox has quite seamed his face; ganz benarbt, full of scars. II. *v. intr.* [u. w. seyn] and *r.* sich —, to be cicatrized, to cicatrize, to heal up. Eine Wunde im Fleische benarbet sich, wounded flesh cicatrizes.

Benaschen, *v. tr.* to taste or eat privily or by stealth.

Benässen, *v. tr.* to wet. Sich die Finger —, to wet one's fingers.

Benebeln, I. *v. tr.* to wrap in a fog or mist, to fill with fog. Die benebelte Luft, the foggy air. *Fig.* *a*) to cover as with a mist. *b*) to dim the senses or the understanding, to dim. *Der Wein benebelt ihn, the wine dims his senses; benebelt, flustered, tipsy, in the wind, muddled, mellow. II. *v. r.* sich — [in familiar language], to get intoxicated, to get drunk.

‖ **Beneben**, **Benebst**, *adv.* V. Nebst.

***Benedeien**, *v. tr.* to bless, to glorify, to praise.

Benedict, *m.* [-s] [a name of men] Benedict, Benet, Bennet.

Benedicts-kloster, *n.* a Benedictine-convent. **—kraut**, *n.* [a herb] bennet or avens.

Benedictiner, *m.* [-s, *pl.* -], **—mönch**, *m.* a

Benedictine friar. —nonne, *f.* a Benedictine nun. —orden, *m.* [an order of monks] Benedictines; [in the English common law] Black-friars.

*Benediction, *f.* benediction, blessing.

*Benefiziant, *m.* [-en, *pl.* -en] an actor or actress, for whose benefit a play &c. is represented.

*Benefiziat, *m.* [-en, *pl.* -en] beneficiary, incumbent.

*Benefizium, *n.* [-s, *pl.* -fizien] Benefiz, *n.* [-es, *pl.* -e] 1) benefice, advantage, profit. 2) a living.

Benefizvorstellung, *f.* a representation for the benefit of an actor or actress.

Benehmen, *ir.* I. *v. tr.* 1) [as it were wegnehmen] *a*) to take away, to deprive of. Einem die Freiheit —, to deprive any one of his liberty; Einem die Aussicht —, to obstruct any one's view; diese Bäume — die Aussicht auf den Fluß, these trees hinder the prospect of the river; den Muth —, to abate the courage; Einem den Muth —, to discourage or dishearten any one; dies benimmt seiner Ehre nichts, this derogates nothing from his honour; dies benimmt mir den Athem, that takes my breath from me. *b*) to rid, to disencumber. Einem die Mittel zum Entfliehen —, to cut off any one's flight or retreat; dem Weine einen übeln Geschmack —, to take out an unpleasant taste from wine; um dir diese Besorgniß zu —, to rid thee of that care; einem seine Zweifel —, to remove any one's scruples; Einem den Irrthum —, to undeceive any one; das Gehässige —, to remove the odium. 2) [as it were einnehmen] to deprive of sensation. Der Rauch hat ihn benommen, the smoke has stupified him. 3) [as it were abnehmen] [in mints] to size [the planchets or pieces for coining]. II. *v. r.* 1) sich —, to behave, to demean, to deport one's self, to conduct one's self. Er benimmt sich mannhaft, he behaves [himself] manfully; er benimmt sich gut, schlecht, he behaves well, ill. 2) [in law or in official style] to concert measures with any one, to come to an agreement with any one, to have an explanation with any one, to confer with any one [about a thing, wegen einer Sache].

Benehm-schere, *f.* [in mints] a cutter [used for sizing the planchets]. —wage, *f.* a pair of scales for weighing the planchets [after they have been cut and prepared for the mill].

Benehmen, *n.* [-s] 1) behaviour, conduct, demeanour, manners, carriage of one's self with respect to propriety or morals, deportment. Das feine — or das — eines Gebildeten, gentlemanliness. 2) [in law or official style] the concerting measures with any one &c. Sie werden sich hierwegen mit ihm ins — setzen, you will confer with him about this matter.

Benehmlich, *adj.* and *adv.* mannerly, civil.

Beneiden, *v. tr.* to envy [a person, any one's prosperity]. Sie beneidet ihre Schwester um ihre Schönheit, she envies her sister's beauty; er beneidet mir mein Glück, he envies my happiness. *Prov.* Besser beneidet, als beklagt, better be envied than pitied.

Beneidens-werth, —würdig, *adj.* and *adv.* [that may incite envy] enviable. Die Lage von Männern im Amte ist nicht immer —werth, the situation of men in office is not always enviable.

Benennen, *ir. v. tr.* 1) [to give a name to] to denominate, to name, to call. Ich weiß diese Pflanze nicht zu —, I don't know the name of this plant, I don't know what it is called; benannte Zahlen, [in arithmetic] concrete numbers [that express or denote a particular subject, as three men &c.]. 2) to nominate, to appoint. Einen Tag —, to appoint a day.

Benennung, *f.* 1) [the act of naming] denomination. 2) a name or appellation, denomination. Brüche unter einerlei — bringen, [in arithmetic] to bring two or more fractions of different denominations into one denomination.

Benebet, *adj.* [in seamen's lang.] beneaped. Das Schiff ist —, the ship is beneaped [when the water does not flow high enough to float her from a dock or over a bar].

Benetzen, *v. tr.* to wet [one's fingers &c.].

Bengel, *m.* [-s, *pl.* -] 1) a short thick stick of wood, a cudgel. Der Preß—, the bar. †and *2) *Fig.* an ill-bred man, a churl, a clown, a country lout.

Bengel-knopf, *m.* [with printers] the head or a small part of the bar. —scheide, *f.* [with printers] the wooden handle of the bar.

Bengelei, *f.* [vulgar and in familiar language] 1) clownishness, clownery, coarseness or rudeness of behaviour, rustic behaviour, rusticity, incivility. — ist ein vorherrschender Zug dieser jungen Leute, rudeness is a predominant trait of these young people. 2) any act of rudeness or ill-breeding, incivility. Das ist eine rechte —! that's a piece of arrant ill-breeding!

Bengelhaft, *adj.* and *adv.* [vulgar and in familiar language] of coarse manners, ill-bred, clownish. Ein —es Wesen, clownish manners; ein —er Kerl, a rude, coarse fellow.

Bengeln, *v. tr.* ‖ 1) to knock off with a stick [as nuts from a tree]. 2) to clog [a dog &c.].

Benicken, *v. tr.* to affirm or approve by nodding, to nod assent to.

‡Benlemen, *v. tr.* to designate, to fix.

Beniesen, *ir. v. tr.* 1) to sneeze at. 2) to confirm by sneezing.

1. Benjamin, [-s] [a name of men] Benjamin. **Fig.* the nestling. Er ist seines Vaters —, he is his father's darling.

2. Benjamin, *m.* [-s] V. Benzoe.

Benjamin-baum, *m.* benjamin-tree, spice-bush. —harz, *n.* benjamin, gum benjamin, benzoin.

Benippen, I. *v. tr.* [to drink by small draughts] to sip. II. *v. r.* sich —, to get tipsy.

‖ Benne, *f.* [*pl.* -n] a sort of basket.

Benöthigen, *v. intr.* [used only in the past part. and with seyn] to want, to need, to lack, to require. Ich bin seiner Dienste sehr benöthiget, I stand in great need of his services; ich bin Ihres Rathes benöthiget, I want to have your advice; ich bin dieser Dinge dringend benöthiget, I have great need of these things, I cannot spare them.

Benöthigt, *adj.* [past participle of the unusual *v. tr.* benöthigen = nöthig haben] required. Das Benöthigte, the thing wanted, the necessary.

Bensenseide, V. Binsenseide.

Benummern, *v. tr.* to furnish or mark with numbers, to number.

Benutzen and Benützen, *v. tr.* to make use of. Etwas —, to make use of any thing; der Feldherr benutzte seines Feindes Nachlässigkeit zu seinem Vortheile, the general took advantage of his enemy's negligence; eine Gelegenheit —, to embrace an opportunity, to avail one's self of an opportunity; einen Vortheil —, to improve an advantage; benütze den Augenblick, improve the moment.

Benzoe, *f.* benroin, † benjamin.

Benzoe-baum, *m.* the styrax benzoin [a tree of Sumatra]. —sauer, *adj.* benzoic. Ein —saures or —gesäuertes Salz, bensoate. —säure, *f.* —blumen, *pl.* benzoic acid or flowers of benzoin.

Beobachtbar, *adj.* and *adv.* observable.

Beobachten, *v. tr.* 1) to see or behold with attention, to observe. Ich beobachtete eine sonderbare Lufterscheinung, I observed a singular phenomenon; den Lauf der Sterne —, [in seamen's language] to keep the course of the stars; gleichwie dein Auge Andere beobachtet &c., as thine eye observes others &c. 2) to keep or adhere to in practice, to observe. Die Gesetze des Staates —, to observe the laws of the state, seine Pflicht —, to do or perform one's duty; sein Amt —, to perform the duties of one's office, die Fasten —, to keep lent; Stillschweigen —, to keep silence; die zu — den Dinge, observanda. Syn. Beobachten, Wahrnehmen. Wahrnehmen signifies simply, to have knowledge or receive impressions of external objects through the medium or instrumentality of the senses or bodily organs; beobachten conveys, in addition to this signification, the idea of peculiar attention. One would, therefore, say: eine Sache beobachten, when one directs a great degree of attention towards it, in order to discover something in it: etwas wahrnehmen, when one perceives a thing either after attentive observation or when the impression of the object presented to the senses arises of itself, unsought or accidentally. Syn. V. 2. Acht.

Beobachter, *m.* [-s, *pl.* -] —inn, *f.* 1) [one that observes, one who looks to with attention] observer. Er kann dem Auge des —s nicht ganz entgehen, he cannot wholly avoid the eye of the observer; aufmerksame — der Werke der Natur, attentive watchers of the works of nature. 2) [one who keeps any law, custom or rite] observer. Ein strenger — der Formen, a strict observer of the forms; ein — des Sabbaths, an observer of the sabbath.

Beobachtsam, *adj.* and *adv.* [attentively or closely viewing or noticing, giving particular attention] observant. Ein —er or scharf beobachtender Reisender, an observant traveller; er ist ein —er Mann, he is an observing man.

Beobachtung, *f.* 1) [the act of observing or taking notice, notion gained by observing] observation. —en machen, anstellen, to make observations; eine astronomische —, an astronomical observation; nach unseren genauesten —en, to the best of our observation. 2) [the act of keeping or adhering to practice] observance, observation. Die — der Kirchengebräuche oder der Gesetze, the observance of rites or laws.

Beobachtungs-gabe, *f.* a talent for observation. —geist, *m.* a mind or understanding apt to observe attentively. —heer, *n.* army of observation.

Beobhuten, V. Behüten.

Beölen, I. *v. tr.* to smear or rub over with oil, to oil. II. *v. r.* sich —, to bedaub one's clothes with oil. †*Fig.* to get drunk.

Beordern, *v. tr.* to order, to direct, to command. Der Heerführer beorderte seine Truppen vorzurücken, the general ordered his troops to advance.

Bepacken, *v. tr.* to lay on a burden, to charge, to load. Ein Pferd —, to load a horse; unsere Wagen waren sehr schwer bepackt, our carriages were very heavily loaded; sich —, to charge one's self with a load or burden. **Fig.* Mit Aufträgen bepackt, saddled with commissions.

Bepalmen, [seldom used] *v. tr.* to furnish or adorn with palms or branches of the palm. Sein bepalmtes Haupt, his head crowned with palms.

Bepanzern, *v. tr.* to dress in armour, [illegible] harness. Bepanzerte Krieger, harnessed warriors.

Bepáppen, *v. tr.* to cover with paste.

Bepéchen, Bepíchen, *v. tr.* to smear with pitch, to pitch. Sich —, to daub one's clothes with pitch.

Bepélzen, *v. tr.* to cover with fur, to furnish with a fur or with peltry.

Bepérlen, *v. tr.* 1) to adorn with pearls, to pearl. Sich —, to adorn one's self with pearls. 2) *Fig.* to cover or set as with pearls. Die beperlte Rose, the rose spangled with pearls; der Morgenthau beperlt die Fluren, the morning-dew bespangles the fields; der Champagner beperlt sich im Glase, champagne forms beads in the glass.

Bepfählen, *v. tr.* to furnish with pales or pointed stakes, to stake. Einen Weinstock —, to prop a vine.

Bepféffern, *v. tr.* to sprinkle with pepper, to pepper.

Bepféifen, *ir. v. tr.* to pipe at.

Bepférchen, *v. tr.* [in husbandry] Einen Acker —, to pen up sheep on arable land.

Bepflánzen, *v. tr.* to plant [a garden with trees &c.]. *Fig.* Mit Dornen bepflanzte Wege, thorny ways.

Bepflástern, *v. tr.* 1) to pave [a street, a yard &c.]. 2) to plaster [a wound].

Bepflöcken, *v. tr.* to furnish or mark with pegs.

Bepflücken, *v. tr.* to strip of feathers. Gänse —, to plume geese.

Bepflügen, *v. tr.* to plough [a field &c.].

Bepfósten, *v. tr.* to furnish with posts [or pieces of timber set erect].

Bepfröpfen, *v. tr.* to cork. Flaschen —, to stop bottles with corks, to cork them.

Bepfründen, *v. tr.* to provide with a living or benefice. Der Bepfründete, the beneficed clergy-man, an incumbent.

Bepíchen, V. Bepechen.

Bepícken, *v. tr.* to strike with the beak, to peck.

Bepínseln, *v. tr.* 1) to paint with a brush. Eine Wand mit Farben —, to brush a wall with colours. [in contempt] to brush over, to bedaub. Er hat die ganze Wand mit seinen Schmierereien bepinselt, he has bedaubed the entire wall with his paintings. 2) [in contempt] Sich —, to paint, to rouge.

†**Bepíssen**, *v. tr.* to piss upon. Sich —, to soil one's self in pissing.

Beplánken, *v. tr.* to furnish with planks, to plank. Eine Wand —, to line a wall with planks.

‖**Bepláppern**, *v. tr.* to bespeak with great loquacity.

Beplátten, *v. tr.* to furnish with a plate. Mit Silber beplattete [plattirte] Leuchter, plated candlesticks.

Beplätten, *v. tr.* to iron slightly, to smoothe.

Beplaúdern, *v. tr.* to talk over.

Bepólstern, *v. tr.* to stuff with hair. Bepolsterte Sessel, stuffed chairs.

Beprägen, [seldom used] *v. tr.* to impress with some mark or figure, to stamp. Eine Münze mit dem Kopfe des Königs —, to impress coin with the figure of the king's head.

Beprédigen, *v. tr.* to teach, to preach, to sermonise.

Bepréssen, *v. tr.* to impress, to imprint, to stamp.

Bepúdern, *v. tr.* to sprinkle with powder. Eine Perrücke —, to powder a periwig; sich —, *a*) to powder one's head, *b*) to soil one's clothes with powder.

Bepúhsten, V. Bepusten.

Bepúnkten, *v. tr.* to mark with points or dots, to distinguish by points or dots, to dot. Bepunktete [punktirte] Noten, [in music] dotted notes; den Leib —, sich —, to tattoo the body [as Indians do].

Bepúnschen, [seldom used] *v. r.* sich —, to get drunk by drinking punch.

Bepúrpurn, Bepúrpern, *v. tr.* 1) to dress in purple. 2) to colour with purple, to purple.

Bepústen, *v. tr.* to blow repeatedly [on something].

***Bequártiren**, [more usual] **Bequartieren**, *v. tr.* 1) to quarter. Die Soldaten wurden trefflich bequartiert, the soldiers were well quartered. 2) Einen —, to quarter soldiers upon any one.

Bequém, *adj.* and *adv.* [from the old queman = kommen] 1) commodious, convenient, suitable, fit, proper, adopted to its use or purpose. Die —ste Zeit, the most proper time; zur —sten Zeit, most opportunely, seasonably; ich hatte eine —e Gelegenheit, um den Brief abzuschicken, I had an opportunity to send the letter; ein —er Weg, an easy road; ein —er Wagen, an easy carriage; ein —er Aufgang, an easy ascent; ein —es Haus, Zimmer, a commodious house, room; ein — gelegenes Haus, a house commodiously situated; dieses Haus liegt nicht — für einen Handelsmann, this house is not conveniently situated for a tradesman; ein —er Platz zu einem Lager, a place commodious for a camp; — wohnen, to be well accommodated with lodgings; machen Sie es sich —, make yourself comfortable, take your ease; sich's — machen, to serve one's own ease and conveniency; — sitzen, to sit at one's ease; wenn es Ihnen — ist, when it is convenient to you, at your leisure. 2) fond of ease, indolent. Er ist zu — zum Arbeiten, he is too lazy to work.

Bequemlade, *f.* chest of drawers.

Bequémen, I. *v. tr.* to accommodate, to fit, to adopt, to make suitable. *Fig.* Die Wahl der Gegenstände den Gelegenheiten —, to accommodate the subjects to the occasions. V. Anbequemen I. II. *v. r.* sich —, to accommodate. Sich nach den Umständen —, to accommodate one's self to circumstances; sich nach dem Willen eines Andern —, to submit to the will of another; sich [nach] Jemands Laune —, to comply with a man's humour; sich nach der Zeit —, to serve the time. III. *v. imp.* to be convenient or commodious. Es bequemt mir, it is commodious for me.

Bequémheit, *f.* V. Bequemlichkeit.

Bequémlich, *adj.* and *adv.* V. Bequem.

Bequémlichkeit, *f.* 1) commodiousness, convenience, conveniency. Sie können es nach — thun, you can do it at your leisure; die — eines Hauses, the commodiousness of a house. 2) [that which gives ease] convenience. Eine Brille ist eine große — für das Alter, a pair of spectacles is a great convenience for old age; —en [bequeme Dinge], accommodations; die —en des Lebens, the comforts and conveniences of life. 3) love of ease, indisposition to labour, indolence. 4) place of retirement, privy.

Bequemlichkeitsstuhl, *m.* V. Nachtstuhl.

Bequémling, *m.* [-s, *pl.* -e] a person indulging in ease, an indolent person.

Bequícken, *v. tr.* to spread over with a thin coat of tin and quicksilver. Ein Spiegelglas —, to foliate a looking-glass.

Beráhmen, *v. tr.* 1) [in law] to fix, to appoint. V. [the more usual] Anberaumen. 2) to provide [a picture] with a frame.

Beraínen, *v. tr.* to furnish with proper boundaries.

Berándeln, *v. tr.* to furnish with a small edge or margin.

Beránden, *v. tr.* to furnish with an edge or margin. Die Münzen —, to furnish coins with rims.

Berändern, *v. tr.* to edge, to border.

Beránken, *v. tr.* to cover with tendrils.

‖**Beráppen**, *v. tr.* [among masons] to rough-cast. Eine berappte Mauer, a plastered wall.

Berásen, I. *v. intr.* [u. w. seyn] to breed a green turf, to sward. II. *v. tr.* to cover with turfs, to turf. Das berasete Grab, the turfy grave; Brustwehren —, [in fortification] to line parapets with gazon.

Beráspeln, *v. tr.* to shape with a rasp.

Beráthen, *ir.* ‡ I. *v. tr.* to furnish with what is necessary, to endow. Gott berathe Euch, God help you. 2) to give counsel to, to advise, to give support to. Einen wohl —, to counsel any one well; Sie sind schlecht —, you are ill advised. II. *v. r.* sich —, to consult with others, to take counsel. Er berieth sich mit uns, he consulted or conferred with us.

Beráther, *m.* [-s, *pl.* -] he that gives advice or supports, adviser, supporter.

Berathfragen, [seldom used] *v. tr.* to ask advice of, to consult.

Beráthschlagen, I. *v. intr.* to deliberate, as in the case of a single person, or to deliberate in common, to take counsel together, to consult. Ueber eine Sache — [rathschlagen], to consider a case, or of a case; es wird über die Sache berathschlagt, the affair is under consideration. II. *v. r.* sich —, to deliberate or to consult with others, to take advice. Sich mit Jemand über Etwas or wegen einer Sache —, to advise with a person about something; er will sich darüber mit ihr —, he will confer with her, consult with her about it.

Beráthschlagung, Beráthung, *f.* consultation, deliberation.

Beraúben, *v. tr.* to rob [a house &c.]. Einen seines Geldes —, to rob or plunder any one of his money. *Fig.* Jemand seines Vermögens, Lebens, seiner Ehre —, to deprive any one of his property, to take away any one's life, to sully a man's honour; ein Mädchen mit Gewalt der Ehre —, to ravish a girl, to violate her; eine Frauensperson der Jungfrauschaft —, to deprive a woman of her virginity, to deflour her; einen Knaben der Mannheit —, to castrate a boy; einen König der Krone —, to deprive a king of his crown, to dethrone him; Einen seiner bürgerlichen Rechte und Freiheiten —, to disfranchise any one; Ihr beraubtet mich meiner Kinder, [in Scripture] me have ye bereaved of my children; seines Königreiches beraubt, spoiled of his kingdom; [in a more figurative sense] der Hülfe beraubt, aidless, unsupported; des Trostes beraubt, comfortless; Einen seiner Rechte, Genüsse —, to abridge any one of his rights, enjoyments; der Vernunft beraubt, deprived of reason; [in famil. lang.] ich will Sie dieses Vergnügens nicht —, I will not rob you of this pleasure; sich eines Vergnügens —, to deprive one's self of a pleasure.

Beraúbung, *f.* robbing, deprivation, a taking away.

Beraúchen, *v. intr.* [u. w. seyn] to be covered with smoke. [used chiefly in the part. beraucht] Berauchte Wände, smoky walls, walls blackened by smoke, besmoked, soiled with smoke.

Beräuchern, *v. tr.* to apply smoke to, to expose to smoke, to smoke. Den Altar, den Priester, der den Gottesdienst verrichtet, —, to incense the altar, the officiating priest; verpestete Zimmer —, to fumigate infected apartments; Briefe aus verpesteten Gegenden —, to disinfect letters from infected countries by fumigation.

Beraufen, *v. tr.* to pluck, to make bald.

Beraumen, *v. tr.* V. Berahmen 1. and Anberaumen.

Berauschen, I. *v. tr.* 1) to intoxicate, to make drunk. —de Getränke, intoxicating liquors. Berauscht, fuddled, drunk. *Fig.* Ein glücklicher Erfolg kann zuweilen den Nüchternen —, success may sometimes intoxicate a man of sobriety. 2) [with hunters] Der Eber berauscht die Sau, the boar brims the sow. II. *v. r.* sich —, 1) to get drunk. *Fig.* Sich in Vergnügen —, to glut one's self with pleasures. 2) [with hunters] to couple [said of boars and sows].

Berberis, Berberiske, Berberitze, *f.* [*pl.* -n] Berberis-baum, —strauch, *m.* —staude, *f.* [a plant] barberry-tree, pipperidge-bush. —beere, *f.* [a tart berry, the fruit of the barberry-tree] barberry.

Berechen, *v. tr.* to clear with a rake, to rake.

Berechnen, I. *v. tr.* 1) to calculate, to compute, to count, to number, to reckon, to estimate. Die Quantität Wasser —, welche ein Gefäß von gewissen Dimensionen füllen wird, to compute the quantity of water that will fill a vessel of certain dimensions; die Kosten eines Feldzuges —, to compute, to calculate the expenses of a campaign; die Lebens-Jahre, -Tage, -Stunden eines Menschen —, to count the years, days and hours of a man's life; eine Sonnen- oder Monds-finsterniß —, to calculate an eclipse; man hat berechnet, it is computed. *Fig.* Das war nicht berechnet, it was not taken into account. 2) to support by accounts. II. *v. r.* Sich mit Jemand —, to settle accounts with any one.

Berechner, *m.* [-s, *pl.* -] computer, a reckoner, a calculator.

Berechnung, *f.* 1) [the act of computing, numbering, reckoning or estimating] computation. 2) reckoning, calculation.

Berechten, Berechtigen, *v. tr.* 1) to give a right to act, to authorize. Der oberste Gerichtshof ist berechtigt, alle bürgerliche und peinliche Fälle zu untersuchen und zu entscheiden, the supreme court is empowered to try and decide all cases civil and criminal; berechtigt, authorized, empowered; ausschließlich berechtigt, exclusively privileged. Syn. V. Befugt. 2) to give a claim by the possession of suitable qualifications, to entitle. Die Talente eines Offiziers berechtigen ihn, zu befehlen, an officer's talents entitle him to command.

Bereden, I. *v. tr.* 1) [to bring to any particular opinion] to persuade. Man beredet die Leute leicht dessen, was sie wünschen, men are easily persuaded of what they desire; er beredete mich, zu kommen, he prevailed on me to come; er ist nicht leicht zu —, it is not easy to talk him into any thing; man konnte den Kaiser nicht —, an dem Streite Antheil zu nehmen, the emperor could not be induced to take part in the contest. 2) to talk over, to speak of a thing. Wir wollen die Sache späterhin —, we will talk about that another time; sie beredeten vorerst die Ausführbarkeit des Unternehmens, they first weighed the feasibility of the undertaking. 3) Einen —, [seldom used in this sense] to talk ill of any one. II. *v. r.* sich —, to persuade one's self. Sich mit Jemand —, to talk with any one, to consult with any one; da beredete sich Festus mit dem Rath, [in Script.] Festus conferred with the council; er beredete sich darüber mit ihm, he concerted it with him.

Beredsam, *adj.* and *adv.* having the power of persuading, having the power of oratory, eloquent.

Beredsamkeit, *f.* 1) the power of persuasion. 2) [the power of speaking with fluency and elegance] eloquence. 3) [the act or art of speaking well or of speaking according to the rules of rhetoric, in order to persuade] eloquence, oratory. 4) the science of rhetoric. Die — lehren, to teach the science of rhetoric.

Beredt, [past part. of bereden] *adj.* and *adv.* [having the power of oratory] eloquent. Ein —er Prediger, an eloquent preacher. *Fig.* Er hat eine —e Zunge, he has a fluent utterance; ihr Schweigen war —, her silence was expressive; [in astrology] —e Zeichen, the constellations: the twins, the virgin, the water-bearer, the balance and the first fifteen degrees of the archer.

Beregeln, *v. tr.* to judge after rules, to settle by rule, to rule.

Beregnen, *v. tr.* to rain upon.

Bereiben, *ir.* I. *v. tr.* to rub on the surface, to work by rubbing. Einen Pfeifenkopf mit Schachtelhalm —, to rub the bowl of a tobacco-pipe with shave-grass. II. *v. r.* sich —, to rub one's self.

Bereich, *m.* [-es, *pl.* -e] 1) V. Bezirk. 2) stretch, reach, extent, compass. Der — unsers Wissens, the compass of our knowledge; im —e des ganzen menschlichen Wissens, in the whole sphere of human knowledge; außer dem —, out of reach; auf —sweite, within reach.

Bereicherer, *m.* [-s, *pl.* -] enricher. *Fig.* Der — einer Sprache, one that enriches a language.

Bereichern, *v. tr.* to enrich [a nation &c.]. Krieg bereichert selten ein Land, war seldom enriches a country; sich —, to grow rich; sich mit fremdem Gute —, to enrich one's self with others' spoils. *Fig.* Den Geist mit Kenntnissen —, to store the mind with knowledge.

Bereicherung, *f.* enriching, enrichment.

1. **Bereifen**, [from Reif = hoarfrost] *v. tr.* to cover with rime or hoarfrost. Die Dächer sind bereift, the roofs are covered with rime. *Fig.* Sein bereiftes Haupt, his hoary head; [in botany] bereifte Pflanzen, [plants covered with a white pubescence] hoary plants.

2. **Bereifen**, [from Reif = hoop] *v. tr.* to bind or fasten with hoops. Ein Faß —, to hoop a cask.

Bereimen, *v. tr.* to make rhymes upon, to berhyme.

Bereisen, *v. tr.* to journey over, to travel. Die Messen —, to frequent the fairs; fremde Länder —, to visit foreign countries.

Bereit, *adj.* ready, prepared. Wie ein König zur Schlacht —, as a king ready for battle; ich bin —, es zu thun, I am ready or willing to do it; ich bin —, meine Krone zu seinen Füßen zu legen, I'm ready to lay my crown at his feet; sich zu etwas — machen, to prepare for something; — seyn, to be in readiness. *Fig.* Er ist zu Allem —, he is ready for every thing.

1. **Bereiten**, [Ice. *reida*, Swed. *reda*, Low-Sax. reden, V. Geräth] I. *v. tr.* to prepare [a medicine &c.]. Das Essen —, to dress victuals; die Speisen —, to dress meat; man muß ihnen etwas zum Essen —, they must have some meat got ready for them; Leder —, to dress leather; den Boden zur Saat —, to dress the ground to receive the seed. *Fig.* Den Weg —, to open the way; Einem Freude —, to procure, to give joy to any one; Einem eine Ueberraschung —, to prepare a surprise to a person; Einem den Untergang —, to work a man's destruction; Schmerzen, die wir uns selbst —, pains, that we ourselves procure. II. *v. r.* sich —, to prepare. Sich zur Reise —, to prepare for a journey; sich zum Tode —, to prepare for death.

Bereiteisen, *n.* [in sculpture] polisher.

2. **Bereiten**, [from reiten = *to ride*] *ir. v. tr.* 1) to visit riding or on horseback. Ein Feld —, to ride over a field. 2) to break, to manage [a horse]. 3) to furnish with a horse, to mount [used only in the participle] Beritten, mounted; die Dragoner waren gut beritten, the dragoons were well mounted.

1. **Bereiter**, *m.* [-s, *pl.* -] preparer, dresser [in this sense it is used in compound words, as: Leder—, Tuch— &c.].

2. **Bereiter**, *m.* [-s, *pl.* -] 1) a horse-breaker, riding-master, rough-rider. 2) [in compound words] an overseer who has the care to visit the forests &c. on horseback, as: Forst— or Wald— &c.

Bereiterpeitsche, *f.* jockey-whip.

Bereits, [from bereit] *adv.* already. Die Sache ist — vollendet, the business is already completed.

Bereitschaft, *f.* [the state of being ready or fit for any thing] readiness, preparedness. Es ist Alles in —, every thing is ready; in — seyn, to be in readiness; er ist nicht in —, he is not in readiness; sich in — halten, to hold one's self ready or in readiness.

Bereitung, *f.* the act of preparing, dressing, preparation.

Bereitungsart, *f.* the manner of preparing or dressing any thing.

Bereitwillig, *adj.* and *adv.* ready, willing. Ein —er Mensch, a willing man; es macht, daß Untergebene desto —er gehorchen, it makes inferiors the more willingly to obey; sich zu etwas — zeigen, to show one's self ready or disposed to do a thing.

Bereitwilligkeit, *f.* readiness, willingness. Er hat viel — gezeigt, mir zu dienen, he showed great zeal, great promptitude in his wish to serve me.

Berennen, *ir. v. tr.* 1) to visit running. 2) to inclose, to surround, to block up, to lay siege to. Eine Stadt —, to invest a town.

Berenten, *v. tr.* [rather unusual] to furnish with a certain revenue or income. Ein reichlich berentetes Spital, a richly endowed hospital.

Bereuen, *v. tr.* to repent. Ich bereue meine Sünden, I repent my sins; er bereuete es, he repented it; Einer, der bereuet, a penitent; ich werde die Mühe nicht —, die mich meine Versuche kosten, I shall not regret the trouble my experiments cost me; ich bereue, daß ich es nicht gethan habe, I am sorry that I have not done it.

Bereuens-werth, —würdig, *adj.* and *adv.* worthy of repentance.

Bereuung, *f.* [sorrow for any thing past] repentance. Die — der Sünde, sorrow for sin, penitence.

Berg, *m.* [-es, *pl.* -e] [A. S. *beorg*, Ice. *biarg*, Dan. Bierg, Bohem. *wrch*; probably from bären = heben, something borne up, elevated] 1) a mountain, a hill, a mount. Ein hoher —, a high mountain; ein kleiner —, a hill. *Prov.* Je höher der —, je [desto] tiefer das Thal, the higher the mountain, the lower the vale; — und Thal kommen nicht zusammen, aber doch die Menschen, friends may meet, but mountains never greet. *Fig.* Wir sind noch nicht über den —, all is not yet over, do not whistle till you're out of the wood; † da stehen die Ochsen am —e, there's the difficulty, that's the puzzle, there we're brought to a stand, it is there that we're posed; *die Haare standen mir zu —e, my hair stood on end; *goldene —e versprechen, to promise wonders; *er ist über alle —e, he's off, he has made his escape; *hinter dem —e halten, to be reserved, to dissemble. 2) *pl.* [in mining] addle, rubble.

Berg=ab, [bérgab and bergáb] *adv.* down-hill. *Fig.* [in familiar language] Es geht mit ihm —ab, he is going down hill, his affairs are going to the bad, he goes down the wind. —**akademie,** *f.* an institution, where the art and science of mining is taught. —**acker,** *m.* a field situated on a hill, a hanging field. —**ader,** *f.* a metallic vein, lead, lode. —**ahorn,** *m.* 1) V. Maserle. 2) V. [common white] Ahorn. —**alaun,** *m.* V. Alaunstein. —**ammer,** *f.* mountain bunting. —**amsel,** *f.* ring-ouzel, rock-ouzel. —**amt,** *n.* an office or court, which determines the concerns of mines. —**an,** *adv.* uphill. —**andorn,** *m.* downy stachys. —**arbeit,** *f.* work done in mines, mining. —**arbeiter,** *m.* miner. —**aron,** *m.* short-sheathed arum or common dragon. —**art,** *f.* a specimen of stone or other substance, which indicates the presence of ore. —**auf,** *adv.* uphill. —auf steigen, to go uphill. —**auster,** *f.* rock-oyster. —**baldrian,** *m.* mountain-valerian. —**balsam,** *m.* a sort of asphaltum. —**bau,** *m.* 1) the working of mines. 2) the art of mining. —**baukunde,** *f.* the science of mining. —**baukundig,** *adj.* and *adv.* acquainted with the art of mining. —**baukunst,** *f.* V. —baukunde. —**baumwolle,** *f.* cotton from Smyrna. —**beamte,** *m.* an officer, belonging to the mines. —**beschreibung,** *f.* the description of mountains. —**bewohner,** *m.* —**bewohnerinn,** *f.* mountaineer. —**bienenkraut,** *n.* V. Immenblatt. —**binse,** *f.* a species of rush [juncus niveus]. —**blau,** *n.* 1) mountain-blue, malachite, [in chimistry] the blue carbonate of copper. 2) lapis lazuli. 3) [in paint.] ultramarine. —**bock,** *m.* the wild goat, the mountain antelope. —**bohrer,** *m.* V. Erdbohrer. —**braun,** *n.* umber. —**buche,** *f.* V. Hagebuche. —**butter,** *f.* [a species of alum] mountain-butter, stone-butter. —**buttermilch,** *f.* V. —guhr. —**candidat,** *m.* an aspirant to an office or employment in the mining-concerns. —**dachs,** *m.* the marmot. —**distel,** *f.* V. Wegedistel. —**dohle,** *f.* the alpine-crow, the chough. —**dorf,** *n.* a village situated on a hill. —**drossel,** *f.* 1) V. —amsel. 2) the red-wing, wind-thrush. —**dürrwurz,** *f.* a species of cineraria. —**ei,** *n.* [in mineralogy] mountain-egg. —**einsiedler,** *m.* the solitary sparrow. —**elster,** *f.* the great shrike. —**engelwurz,** *f.* a species of angelica. —**ente,** *f.* the scaup duck. —**eppich,** *m.* mountain-parsley. —**eremit,** *m.* V. —einsiedler. —**erle,** *f.* a species of hawthorn [crataegus alpina]. —**erz,** *n.* [in mining] ore. —**esche,** *f.* mountain ash. —**eule,** *f.* the eagle-owl. —**falke,** *m.* the stone-falcon. —**fall,** *m.* V. —sturz. —**fasan,** *m.* V. Auerhahn. —**feld,** *n.* V. —acker. —**fenchel,** *m.* common-dill. —**fertig,** *adj.* and *adv.* [among miners] diseased. —fertig seyn, to be afflicted with a pulmonary consumption. —**feste,** —**festung,** *f.* 1) a fortress situated on a mountain, hill-fort. 2) [in mining] pillar. —**fett,** *n.* 1) V. Erdharz. 2) V. —talg. —**fichte,** *f.* mountain-pine. —**fink,** *m.* the brambling. —**fisch,** *m.* V. Bergerfisch. —**flachs,** *m.* amianthus, earth-flax. —**flecken,** *m.* 1) a small mountain-town. 2) a town inhabited by miners. —**fleisch,** *n.* mountain-flesh, mountain-leather, mountain cork or paper, compact spongy rock-cork. —**flockenblume,** *f.* scabious centaury or great knapweed. —**fluß,** *m.* 1) a mountain river. 2) V. Flußspath. 3) any coloured crystal. —**forelle,** *f.* the charr. —**freiheit,** *f.* 1) the right and freedom of mining. 2) the privileges of a mountain-town. —**fuchs,** *m.* a species of fox. —**gamander,** *m.* V. —polei. —**gang,** *m.* V. —ader. —**gänsedistel,** *f.* a species of sow-thistle. —**gebet,** *n.* a prayer used by miners. —**gebrauch,** *m.* a custom prevailing among miners. —**gegend,** *f.* a mountainous district. —**geist,** *m.* 1) gnome, pigmy, small man. 2) [in mythology] an oread. —**gelb,** *n.* yellow ochre. —**genoß,** *m.* a partner in a mine. —**gericht,** *n.* a court, that decides matters relating to mines. —**gesetz,** *n.* regulation, rule for miners. —**gespenst,** *n.* V. —geist 1). —**gewächs,** *n.* any herb growing on a mountain. —**gezeug,** *n.* every implement used in mining. —**gift,** *n.* arsenic. —**gipfel,** *m.* the top of a mountain. —**glas,** *n.* V. —kristall. —**glasartig,** *adj.* and *adv.* crystalform. —**glasicht,** *adj.* and *adv.* [resembling crystal] crystaline. —**glasig,** *adj.* and *adv.* V. —glasartig. —**gliedkraut,** *n.* a species of iron-wort. —**gott,** *m.* [in mythology] a mountain-god. —**gras,** *n.* 1) sweet vernal-grass. 2) sheep's fescue grass. 3) the fine bent grass. —**grasblume,** *f.* V. —nägelein. —**grün,** *n.* [in mineralogy] mountain-green. Das feinste —grün, Olympian green. —**gruß,** *m.* salutation customary among miners. —**guhr,** *f.* rock milk, agaric mineral. —**günsel,** *m.* alpine bugle. —**gut,** *n.* a mineral, fossil. —**hahn,** *m.* V. Birkhahn. —**hahnenfuß,** *m.* mountain crow-foot. ‖—**halde,** *f.* 1) the declivity of a hill or mountain, hillside, hang. 2) [in mining] a heap of earth thrown out of a mine. —**hase,** *m.* V. Sandhase. —**haspel,** *m.* windlass [in mining]. —**haue,** *f.* a sort of hoe. —**hauer,** *m.* V. —mann. —**hauptmann,** *m.* a director of the mines. —**hauptmannschaft,** *f.* the office of a director of the mines. —**haus,** *n.* a house situated on a hill. —**hauslaub,** *n.* mountain houseleek. —**haut,** *f.* a species of asbestos. —**himbeerbaum,** *m.* the mountain-bramble or cloud-berry. —**himbeere,** *f.* the fruit of the mountain-bramble. —**höhe,** *f.* V. Anhöhe, Berg. —**höhle,** *f.* mountain-cavern. —**holunder,** *m.* the red-berried elder. —**holz,** *n.* 1) rock wood, mountain wood, lignous asbestos. 2) [in seamen's language] wale. Das —holz unter der zweiten Batterie, channel-wale; die —hölzer aufzwingen, to wring the wales up; das große —holz, main wale. —**huhn,** *n.* 1) mountain-partridge. 2) wild hen. —**hund,** *m.* [in mining] a small cart or waggon used for conveying materials out of the mines. —**isop,** *m.* mountain hyssop. —**junge,** *m.* a miner's boy. —**kalk,** *m.* primitive and primary limestone, marble of Paros, of Carrara &c. —**kalkstein,** *m.* transition limestone, mountain-limestone. —**kappe,** *f.* a miner's cap. —**karren,** *m.* a sort of cart with two wheels. —**kater,** *m.* the male of a species of wild cat. —**katze,** *f.* a species of wild cat. —**keller,** *m.* a mountain-cellar. —**kessel,** *m.* a hole, hollow surrounded with hills. —**kette,** *f.* a chain of mountains. —**kicher,** *f.* mountain milk-vetch. —**kiesch,** *m.* V. Feldachat. —**klee,** *m.* V. Alpenklee. —**klette,** *f.* mountain burdock. —**kluft,** *f.* a chasm, precipice. —**knapp,** —**knappe,** *m.* a miner. —**knappschaft,** *f.* 1) the association or body of miners. 2) the meeting of miners. —**knecht,** *m.* a miner's assistant. —**knoblauch,** —**lauch,** *m.* the long-rooted garlick. —**kohle,** *f.* fossil-coal. —**kompaß,** *m.* V. Grubenkompaß. —**kork,** *m.* V. —fleisch. —**krähe,** *f.* the red-legged crow. —**kraut,** *n.* V. —pflanze. —**kresse,** *f.* mountain-cress. —**kristall,** *m.* rock-crystal. Stängeliger —kristall, violet quarz. —**kümmel,** *m.* mountain lazarwort. —**kuppe,** *f.* the top of a mountain. —**land,** *n.* [in husbandry] mountain-land. —**lauch,** *n.* V. Knoblauch. —**läufig,** *adj.* and *adv.* according to the manner of the miners. —**lavendel,** *m.* V. —polei. —**leder,** *n.* 1) a miner's leather or apron. 2) V. —fleisch. —**lehne,** V. —halde 1. —**lerche** *f.* shore lark. —**leute,** *pl.* 1) the miners. 2) mountaineers. —**lilie,** *f.* martagon. —**luft,** *f.* the air on mountains or mountainous countries. —**mann,** *m.* 1) a miner, mine-digger. 2) mountaineer. —**männchen,** *n.* V. —geist 1). —**männisch,** *adj.* and *adv.* relating to miners, practised by miners. —**mannsstand,** *m.* 1) the profession of miners. 2) the corporation of miners. —**mannstreu,** *f.* mountain eryngo. —**markscheider,** *m.* V. Markscheider. —**maus,** *f.* the lemming. —**mehl,** *n.* V. Erdmehl. —**meierkraut,** *n.* the mountain chickweed. —**meise,** *f.* the long-tailed titmouse. —**meister,** *m.* a surveyor of mines or of quarries. —**melisse,** *f.* mountain-balm. —**merle,** *f.* rock-ouzel. —**milch,** *f.* [in mineralogy] rock-milk, agaric mineral. —**mine,** *f.* a mine, pit. —**mittel,** *m.* V. —art. —**münze,** *f.* mountain-balm. —**nägelein,** *n.* —**nelke,** *f.* mountain-avens. —**nimfe,** —**nymphe,** *f.* a mountain nymph, oread. —**öl,** *n.* mineral-oil, rock-oil, petroleum. —**ordnung,** *f.* regulation for the miners. —**papier,** *n.* V. —fleisch. —**paß,** *m.* V. —schlucht. —**pech,** *n.* V. Erdpech. —**pecherde,** *f.* bituminous earth. —**peterlein,** *n.* broad-leaved spignel or black-heart root. —**pfeffer,** *m.* V. Seidelbast. —**pflanze,** *f.* an herb growing on mountains. —**pilz,** *m.* V. Birkenpilz. —**polei,** *m.* poley-mountain. —**prediger,** *m.* a clergyman appointed for the miners. —**predigt,** *f.* 1) a sermon preached to the miners. 2) Christ's sermon on the mount [Matth. V—VII]. —**quendel,** *m.* a species of thyme. —**rath,** *m.* 1) a court or board superintending the mines. 2) the office and title of the members of the above court or board, a counsellor of mines. —**ratte,** —**ratze,** *f.* 1) V. Murmelthier. 2) the fat dormouse. —**raute,** *f.* wild rue. —**recht,** *n.* 1) the right of mining. 2) a law for the mines, miners' code. ‖3) a tax levied upon vineyards. —**rechtlich,** *adj.* and *adv.* founded upon the laws for the mines. —**reigen,** *m.* V. —reihen. —**reihe,** *f.* a range of mountains or hills. —**reihen,** *m.* 1) alpine melody. 2) a miner's song or melody. —**richter,** *m.* a judge or magistrate set over the miners. —**rietgras,** *n.* mountain carex. —**rose,** *f.* 1) mountain-rose. 2) the upright honey-suckle. —**röschen,** *n.* V. —rose 1). —**roth,** *n.* red ochre. —**röthe,** [a plant] *f.* V. Waldmeister. —**röthel,** *m.* V. Rauschgelb. —**rücken,** *m.* the ridge of a mountain. —**ruhrkraut,** *n.* V. Katzenpfötlein. —**rüster,** *f.* V. —ulme. —**ruthe,** *f.* V. Wünschelruthe. —**sache,** *f.* a matter relating to the mines. —**salz,** *n.* V. Steinsalz. —**sanickel,** *m.* V. Bärendöhrlein. —**scharte,** *f.* V. Färberscharte. —**schicht,** *f.* a shift or work done by miners at hours of rest. —**schilf,** *n.* V. —rietgras. —**schlange,** *f.* brown boa or boa with brown body. —**schloß,** *n.* a castle on a mountain. —**schlucht,** *f.* a narrow pass between mountains, a mountain-pass, defile. —**schmiele,** *f.* mountain hair-grass. —**schnepfe,** *f.* V. Waldschnepfe. —**schotte,** *m.* a highlander of Scotland. —**schreiber,** *m.* clerk of the mines. —**schule,** *f.* V. —academie. —**schüssig,** *adj.* and *adv.* mingled with earthy or stony substance. —**schwaden,** *m.* damps in mines. —**schwalbe,** *f.* a species of swallow [hirundo daurica]. —**schwefel,** *m.* sulphur. —**see,** *m.* mountain lake. —**segen,** *m.* rich produce of the mines. —**seife,** *f.* [in mineralogy] mountain-soap. —**seil,** *n.* a strong rope by which every thing is drawn up from the mine. —**sesel,** *m.* long-leaved meadow saxifrage. —**sohle,** *f.* [among miners] the foundation of a mountain. —**sperling,** *m.* the hedge-sparrow. —**spieke,** *f.* V. —baldrian. —**spitze,** *f.* the top of a mountain. —**stadt,** *f.* 1) a mountain-town. 2) a miners' town. —steiger, *m.* V. Steiger. —storch, *m.* V. —falke. —straße, *f.* 1) a road through mountains. 2) the road or district between Darmstadt and Heidelberg [in Germany]. —sträßer, *m.* 1) an inhabitant of the above district between Darmstadt and Heidelberg. 2) a sort of wine that grows on the hills along the road called Bergstraße. —strom, *m.* a mountain stream. —stufe, *f.* mineral in its gangue. —sturz, *m.* the fall of a hill or mine. —sucht, *f.* a pulmonary disorder peculiar to miners. —süchtig, *adj.* and *adv.* affected with a pulmonary disease. —talg, *m.* [in mineral.] mountain tallow. —talk, *m.* V. Talk. —taube, *f.* stock-pigeon. —theer, *m.* mineral or Barbadoes tar, cohesive mineral-pitch, pissasphalt. —theil, *m.* V. Kux. —torf, *m.* mountain peat. —trespe, *f.* wall brome grass. —üblich, *adj.* and *adv.* usual among miners. —uhu, *m.* V. —eule. —ulme, *f.* the common elm. —unschlitt, *n.* vitriol of zinc, white vitriol, sulphate of zinc. —unter, *adv.* V. —ab. —veilchen, *n.* the mountain violet. —vogt, *m.* V. —meister. —volk, *n.* V. —bewohner, *pl.* —wachs, *n.* slate coal, foliated coal, black or common coal. —wand, *f.* 1) [in mining] poor stones. 2) a wall formed by one or more hills or mountains. —wardein, *m.* an assayer of the mines. —wärts, *adv.* towards the hills or mountains. —wasser, *n.* mountain-water. —wegebreit, *m.* the mountain arnica. —weide, *f.* 1) pasture-ground on mountains. 2) a sort of willow grown on hills. —weiderich, *m.* the mountain willow-herb. —wein, *m.* a wine grown on hills. —werk, *n.* [a pit or excavation in earth from which metallic ores &c. are taken by digging] mine. —werkreich, *adj.* and *adv.* rich in mines. —werksgesetz, *n.* V. —gesetz. —werkskunde, *f.* the science of mining. —werkskundig, *adj.* and *adv.* V. —baukundig. Der —werkskundige, metallurgist. —werkssprache, *f.* terms of the art or science of mining. —werkswissenschaft, *f.* V. —baukunde. —wesen, *n.* 1) all affairs connected with mining. 2) V. —werkskunde. —wetter, *n.* damps in the mines. —wolle, *f.* V. —flachs. —wurz, *f.* mountain heath. —zehente, *m.* the tithe of the productions of a mine. —zeitlose, *f.* common meadow-saffron. —ziege, *f.* the female of the wild goat. —zinn, *n.* grain tin. —zinnober, *m.* cinnabar. —zunder, *m.* V. —papier.

Bergamóttbirn, Bergamótte, *f.* [*pl.* -n] [a species of pear] the bergamot.

Bergamottöl, *n.* [essence of] bergamot.

Bèrgen, [old G. perkan, A. S. *beorgan*, Ice. and Sw. *berga*; allied to Pferch; originally = einschließen] *ir. v. tr. Fig.* 1) to hide, to conceal. Sich —, to hide one's self; ein Geheimniß —, to hide a secret; ich kann Ihnen nicht bergen, daß &c., I must openly confess to you, that &c. 2) [to preserve from destruction] to save. Die Güter eines Schiffes —, to save or recover the goods from the sea or things wrecked on the sea-beach; die Segel —, [in seamen's language] to take in the sails; ich bin nun geborgen, I am now safe.

Berge-geld, *n.* —lohn, *m.* [money paid for the preservation of stranded goods] salvage.

Bèrgen, [-s] 1) [a town in the Netherlands] Bergen-op-Zoom. 2) [a town in Norway] Bergen.

Berger-fisch, *m.* a species of cod-fish from Bergen. —thran, *m.* a sort of train-oil from Bergen in Norway.

Bèrger, *m.* [-s, *pl.* -] a person employed in recovering any stores &c. from a wreck on the sea coast.

Bèrgicht, *adj.* and *adv.* mountain-like.

Bèrgig, *adj.* and *adv.* [full of mountains] mountainous. Ein —es Land, a mountainous or hilly country; die —e Beschaffenheit, mountainousness.

Bergmanít, *m.* [-s, *pl.* -e] [in mineralogy] paranthine.

Bèrgung, *f.* [in seamen's language] salvage.

Bericht, *m.* [-es, *pl.* -e] 1) [it is used frequently for] news. Wir haben —e aus Warschau, we have news from Warsaw; günstige —, favourable news or accounts. 2) any written narrative, relation, account, statement of facts, report, also an official report from an officer to his commander or superior. — erstatten, to make report; wer hat über Ihren Prozeß — erstattet? who has reported your law-suit? — von einer [über eine] Sache geben, to give an account of any thing; über die weiteren Umstände einer Verhandlung — erstatten, to relate or report the particulars of a transaction. 3) [in familiar language] notice, information. Der falsche —, false information, misinformation.

Bericht-abstatter, —erstatter, *m.* a reporter, relater. —abstattung, —erstattung, *f.* report, relation. —mäßig, *adj.* and *adv.* having the form of a report or relation. —steller, *m.* a reporter, relater. —zettel, *m.* an official report, as the report of a physician, concerning any person's health, bulletin.

Berichten, *v. tr.* 1) to put in the condition desired, to make suitable or fit. Die Münzstücke —, [in mints] to size the blanks or pieces for coining; einen Falken —, [in falconry] to tame a hawk; ‡ einen Kranken —, to prepare a sick person for death. 2) to give notice to, to acquaint with, to inform, to instruct. Er berichtet ihm alles, was vorfällt, he acquaints him with all that comes to pass; Einen mit Lügen —, to make false reports to, to impose upon any one; Sie sind falsch or irrig berichtet worden, you have been wrongly informed, misinformed. 3) to give an account of, to report. Wer hat über Ihren Prozeß berichtet? who has reported your law-suit?

Berichtigen, *v. tr.* to make accurate. Ein Gewicht —, to adjust a weight to a standard; die Fliegenköpfe —, [with printers] to rectify the turned letters; eine Schuld —, to pay a debt; Rechnungen —, to settle, to pay accounts; die Sache ist berichtigt, the thing is settled, set right, made up, paid; eine Schrift — [corrigiren], to correct a writing; die Druckfehler — [corrigiren], to correct the errors of the press; einem Schüler die Schreibfehler — [corrigiren], to correct the orthographical faults in a schoolboy's exercise; einen Schriftsteller —, to amend an author.

Berichtiger, *m.* [-s, *pl.* -] one that sets right or corrects, as a corrector of the press. Der — einer Druckschrift, [with printers] reader. V. also Corrector.

Berichtigung, *f.* 1) the act of making accurate. Die — eines Buches, die — von Druckfehlern, the correction of a book, of errors of the press. 2) [that which is substituted in the place of what is wrong] correction. Setzen Sie die —en auf den Rand des Berichtigungsbogens, set the corrections in the margin of the proof-sheet.

Berichtigungs-bogen, [Correcturbogen] *m.* [with printers] proof-sheet. —kosten, *pl.* [with printers] the expenses of the correction of the press.

Beriechen, *ir. v. tr.* to smell at. [among hunters] Das Wild —, [said of dogs] to scent the game.

Beriefeln, Beriefen, *v. tr.* to chamfer, to channel, to groove, to flute [a column &c.].

Beriegeln, *v. tr.* to furnish with rails.

Beriemen, *v. tr.* to furnish with [leather-] straps or thongs.

Berieseln, *v. tr.* to drizzle on.

Berill, V. Beryll.

Berinden, I. *v. tr.* to cover with a crust, rind or bark, to crust, to bark. II. *v. intr.* [u. only in the past part. and w. seyn] to be covered with a crust or hard coat, to crust. Etwas Berindetes, something incrusted. III. *v. r.* sich —, to get a crust or bark.

Beringen, *v. tr.* to furnish or fit with a ring. Er ist sehr beringt, he wears a great many rings; eine Stute —, to ring or ringle a mare [to prevent her getting accidently covered].

Berinnen, *ir. v. tr.* to run at or on something [said of fluids].

Beritten, [past participle of Bereiten] *adj.* and *adv.* 1) managed. Ein —es Pferd, a managed or well broken horse. 2) furnished with a horse. Gut—, well mounted; schlecht—, badly mounted.

Beritzen, *v. tr.* to scratch on the surface.

Bèrkan, *m.* [-s, *pl.* -e] [Fr. *barracan, bouracan*, allied to wirren, Werch] [a thick strong stuff] barracan.

Berlin, [-s] [the capital of Prussia] Berlin.

Berline, *f.* [*pl.* -n] [a sort of carriage] a berlin.

Berliner, I. *m.* [-s, *pl.* -] *f.* -inn, an inhabitant of Berlin. II. *adj.* made or invented at Berlin.

Berliner-blau, *n.* Prussian blue. [...]liches —blau, native Prussian blue, blue [...] earth, blue iron-earth. —blausäure [...] Blausäure.

Berlinisch, *adj.* and *adv.* of or from after the Berlin fashion &c.

Berlóken, *pl.* baubles, trinkets [ear [...] watch-seals &c.].

Bèrme, *f.* [*pl.* -n] [Fr. *berme*, allied to Br[...] = Rand] [in fortification, a space of ground, [be]tween the rampart and the moat or foss] berme.

Bermuden, *pl.* [islands in the Westindies] [Ber]mudas.

Bèrnhard, [-s] [a name of men] Bernard

Bernhardiner, *m.* [-s] V. —mönch. Be[rn]hardinerinn, *f.* V. Bernhardinernonne

Bernhardiner-abtei, *f.* [Bernhardsa[btei]] an abbey of Bernardins. —kloster, *n.* [Bern]hardskloster] a convent of Bernardins. —kr[ebs] *m.* the soldier or soldier's crab. —mönch [...] a monk of the order of Bernardins. Die [Bern]hardinermönche [Bernhardiner] Bernardi[ns] —nonne, *f.* a nun of the order of Bernardi[ns] —orden, *m.* the order of Bernardins.

Bèrnstein, *m.* [-s, *pl.* -e] [from the ol[d ...]nen = brennen] amber.

Bernstein-ähnlich, *adj.* and *adv* [resem]bling amber. —arbeit, *f.* any thing m[ade of] amber. —arbeiter, *m.* a worker in a[mber] —artig, *adj.* and *adv.* resembling amber. [am]ber. —auster, *f.* the amber bowlshell. —a[us]zug, *m.* an extract of amber. —fang, *m.* fishing for, or collecting of amber. —fäng[er] *m.* a person that fishes for amber. —geist [...] spirit of amber. —koralle, *f.* a bead of [am]ber. —öl, *n.* oil of amber. —salz, *n.* V [...]säure. —sauer, *adj.* and *adv.* [in chimistry] sauers Salz, succinate; —saures Laug[e] succinate of potash; —saurer Kalk, succin[ate of] lime; —saures Natron, succinate of sod[a] saures Eisen, oxidated succinate of iron; [oxy]dirtes säuerlich —saures Eisen, oxidated a[...]lous succinate of iron; oxydirtes ungesätt[igtes] saures Eisen, oxidated succinate of iron [with] excess of oxide. —säure, *f.* [in chimistry] [succi]nic acid.

Bèrnsteinen, Bernsteinern, *adj.* and [*adv.*] [consisting of amber] amber. Die —en Kor[allen] amber-beads.

Bernthaler, *m.* [-s, *pl.* -] a dollar coined at Bern.

***Berrden**, V. Behacken.

Berohren, *v. tr.* to cover [a wall &c.] with reeds.

Beröhren, *v. tr.* to furnish with pipes.

Berösten, *v. intr.* [u. w. seyn] to gather rust, to rust.

Berötheln, *v. tr.* to mark with red chalk.

Berschling, V. Börs.

Bersing, V. Wirsching.

|| **Berst**, *m.* [-es, *pl.* -e] a disruption, crack.

Bersten, [Sw. *brista*; allied to brechen] *ir. v. intr.* [u. w. seyn] [to fly or break open with force, or with sudden violence, to suffer a violent disruption] to burst. Die Mauer ist geborsten, the wall has cracked. *Fig.* Vor Neid —, to burst with envy; vor Lachen —, to burst, to split one's sides with laughing. Syn. Bersten, Platzen. Platzen is used to signify the sudden rupture of a thing by internal force; Bersten is said when the rupture has an exterior cause.

Berst-gras, —kraut, *n.* the acute carex.

Berstig, *adj.* and *adv.* burst, split, cracked.

Bertha, [-s] [a name of women] Bertha.

1. **Bertram**, [-s] [a name of men] Bertram.

2. **Bertram**, *m.* [-s] {probably corrupted from the Greek πυρεθρον = eine hitzige Pflanze] 1) Spanish chamomile or pellitory. 2) common sneezewort. 3) marsh selinum. 4) shrubby Chrysanthemum.

Bertrambaum, *m.* prickly ash.

Berüchtigen, *v. tr.* to bring into evil report, to defame, to slander [used only in the past part. berüchtigt].

Berüchtigt, *adj.* and *adv.* known to disadvantage, ill-spoken of, ill-famed, ill-renowned. Ein —er Mensch, a notorious man. Syn. Berüchtigt, Berrufen, Berschrieen. Berrufen has the most general signification, and is used both in a good and bad sense. It signifies merely that a thing is generally known and much talked of. Berüchtigt and Berschrieen are said only of such things as are ill-famed. The latter, however, is milder and does not always contain the idea of the disadvantageous opinion's being justly founded.

Berücken, *v. tr.* to draw the net over an animal and catch it, to insnare. Einen Vogel —, to snare a bird. *Fig. a)* to come suddenly upon, to surprise [seldom used in this sense]. Die Nacht, der Regen berückte sie, the night overtook them, they were caught in the rain. *b)* to take by wiles, stratagems or deceit, to insnare, to entrap, to inveigle. Sie berückte ihn ganz und gar mit ihren Liebkosungen, she completely insnared him with her coaxing and caressing; sich — lassen, to fall into the snare or trap, to let one's self be caught.

Berücksichtigen, *v. tr.* to have regard to, to respect.

Berückung, *f.* insnaring, inveigling &c.

Berückungskunst, *f.* the art of insnaring.

Berudern, *v. tr.* 1) [unusual] to furnish with rudders or oars. 2) to pass over rowing.

Beruf, *m.* [-es, *pl.* -e] 1) call, invitation. Der Geistliche bekam den — &c., the clergyman got a call. *Fig. a)* divine vocation or summons. Er folgte seinem —e und wurde Missionär, he followed his inward call and became a missionary. [in a more extensive sense] call, vocation. Ich habe keinen — dazu, this is none of my business; er hatte keinen — zum Soldatenleben, he was never intended for a soldier's life; ‡ei, Heinz, 's ist mein —, why, Hal, 't is my vocation. *b)* calling, vocation, profession, trade. Es ist mein — nicht, it is not my business. || 2) [in law] V. Anruf.

Berufs-kraut, *n.* the name of several plants used by superstitious people for delivering from the power of charms or spells. **—sarbeit**, *f.* V. —geschäft. **—sfach**, *n.* profession. Die gewöhnlichen drei —sfächer, the three professions [law, physic and divinity]. **—sgeschäft**, *n.* professional concerns, the usual business of one's calling. **—smäßig**, *adj.* and *adv.* according to one's calling or vocation. **—spflicht**, *f.* the duties incumbent on one's vocation or profession. **—srecht**, *n.* [in law] patronage. **—sthätig**, *adj.* and *adv.* pursuing one's profession with assiduity. **—streue**, *f.* the strict adherence to the duties of a station, office or function; *it.* fidelity and exactitude in the discharge of the duties of a station &c. **—swand**, *f.* [a plant] procumbent asperugo.

Berufen, *ir.* I. *v. tr.* 1) to invite to come or be present, to call, to convoke, to direct or order to meet. Der Präsident berief den Congreß, the president called together or convoked the congress; der König berief seinen Rath, the king called his council together. *Fig. a)* to call = to appoint, to designate as for an office, duty or employment. *b)* [in theology] to call = to invite or draw in union with Christ. Viele sind berufen, aber Wenige auserwählt, [in Script.] many are called, but few chosen. 2) to bring into evil report, to defame, to slander [used chiefly in the past part. berufen]. 3) V. Beschreien 3. II. *v. r.* sich —, 1) sich auf etwas —, to refer [one's self] to something; er beruft sich auf seine Krankheit, he pleads sickness; sie berief sich auf ihre Schwangerschaft, she pretended her pregnancy; ich berufe mich auf Sie, I appeal to you; sich auf seine Unschuld —, to protest one's innocence; er ist sehr dreist, sich auf mich zu —, ich kenne ihn nicht, he is very bold in making use of my name, I don't know him; in solchen Fällen ist es gut, sich auf einen vertrauten Freund zu —, in such cases it is good to refer to some friend of trust. 2) [to refer to a superior judge or court for the decision or revision of any cause] to appeal. V. Anrufen, Appelliren.

Berufen, [past part. of berufen] *adj.* and *adv.* 1) having a call or vocation. 2) known to disadvantage, ill-famed, notorious, famous.

Berufer, *m.* [-s, *pl.* -] V. Anrufer.

Berufung, *f.* V. Beruf, Anrufung or Appellation.

Beruhen, *v. intr.* [u. w. haben] 1) [w. lassen] to leave a thing at rest, or as it is. Wir wollen es dabei — lassen, let us break off or stop here, let it go no farther, let us leave it as it is; er ließ die Sache auf sich —, he abandoned the affair, he let it rest, he desistet from it. 2) [to be connected with any thing, as the cause of its existence or of its operation and effects] to depend on or upon. Der Friede der Gesellschaft beruht auf guten Gesetzen, the peace of society depends on good laws; das Pflanzenwachsthum beruht auf Wärme und Feuchtigkeit, vegetation depends upon heat and moisture; es beruht zuweilen auf einem Zeugnisse, sometimes it rests upon a testimony; es beruht nur auf Muthmaßungen, it is founded merely on conjectures; es beruht nur auf Ihnen, ob &c., it depends entirely upon you, whether &c.

Beruhigen, I. *v. tr.* to make quiet [also in a figur. sense]. Ein —des Mittel, [in medic.] a calming remedy; die Säfte —, [in medic.] to still the humours; er beruhiget die Elemente, he calms or quiets the elements; das Gemüth —, to tranquillize, to still, to appease, to becalm or to pacify the mind; die letzte Nachricht hat mein Gemüth beruhigt, the last news has eased my mind; ein beruhigtes Gemüth, an easy mind; die tobenden Leidenschaften —, to allay the tumult of the passions; Jemanden über seine Besorgnisse —, to compose any one's fears; hierüber kann ich Sie vollkommen —, I assure you, you may make yourself perfectly easy about that; der Gedanke, daß &c., beruhigt mich sehr, I am much consoled by the thought that &c.; ein —der Gedanke, a consoling or comforting thought. II. *v. r.* sich —, to become quiet or calm. [also in a figur. sense] Lasse seinem Gemüthe Zeit, sich wieder zu —, let his spirits settle; beruhige dich, make your mind easy; ich kann mich dabei nicht —, I cannot acquiesce in it, I cannot rest satisfied with it; so lassen Sie sich doch —, compose yourself!

Beruhigung, *f.* 1) the act of quieting, calming, appeasing. Die — der Säfte, [in medicine] stilling of humours. 2) calm, quiet, stillness, tranquillity, ease. 3) [the thing that calms or comforts] calmer, comfort, consolation. — in Leiden oder in der Noth, consolation under afflictions or distress.

Beruhigungs-grund, *m.* a reason or argument for being easy, quiet. **—mittel**, *n.* any thing that makes calm or quiet, calmer, quieter.

Berühmen, ‡I. *v. tr.* to praise, to laud. Er berühmte ihn wegen seiner löblichen Handlungen, he lauded him on account of his praiseworthy actions. II. *v. r.* Sich einer Sache —, to boast of a thing.

Berühmt, [past part. of the *v. tr.* berühmen] *adj.* and *adv.* celebrated in fame and public report, renowned, famous. Ein —er Schauspieler, a famous actor; ein —er Krieger, a renowned warrior; ein —er Schriftsteller, a celebrated author; eine —e That, a deed of renown; er ist — wegen seiner Gelehrsamkeit, he is famous for erudition, Aristides war wegen seiner Gelehrsamkeit und Weisheit —, Aristides was famed for learning and wisdom; eine —e Familie, an illustrious family or race; sich — machen, to get fame, to render one's self famous; sich — machen durch &c., to signalize one's self by &c.; welt- —, universally known; weit—, far-famed.

Berühmtheit, *f.* celebrity, fame, renown.

Berühren, *v. tr.* to touch [a thing with one's fingers &c.]. Er ist so groß, daß er die Decke berührt, he is so tall, that he touches the ceiling; diese zwei Steine — sich, these two stones touch one another; zwei Kugeln — sich nur in Punkten, two spheres touch only at points; zwei Körper — sich, wenn &c., two bodies come in contact, when &c.; zwei Körper, die sich —, two contiguous bodies; sich berührend, [in botany] contiguous [said of cotyledons]. *Fig.* Dies berührten deine letzten Worte nur, this thy last words touched only; er berührte es or diese Sache oberflächlich, he touched upon it, he mentioned it slightly; man muß diese Saite nicht —, one must not touch upon that string; berührter Maßen [in deeds &c.] as before mentioned. Syn. Berühren, Betasten. Berühren conveys the idea of touching or feeling only by the smallest possible point of contact; Betasten on the contrary, gives us the idea of a greater surface, or several points of the body coming in contact, and takes place more with the flat of the hand, berühren only with the points of the fingers.

Berührig, *adj.* and *adv.* V. [the more usual] Rührig.

Berührung, *f.* 1) the act of touching. 2) [the state of being touched] touching, touch, contact; [in botany] contiguousness; [in astronomy] appulse. In — kommen [in a proper as well as in a figurative sense], to come in contact.

Berührungs-linie, [in mathem.] contingent line, tangent line. **—punkt**, *m.* point of contact. *Fig.* Ich habe keine —punkte mit ihm or wir haben keinen —punkt mit einander, there is no connection between us. —**winkel**, *m.* [in mathem.] angle of contact.

Berümpfen, *v. tr.* to wrinkle up the nose at.

Berunzeln, *v. tr.* to wrinkle, to corrugate. Ein berunzeltes Geſicht, a furrowed countenance; ein berunzeltes Blatt Papier, a rumpled sheet of paper.

Berupfen, *v. tr.* to pluck [a goose &c.]. *Fig.* [in fam. lang.] to fleece. Sie haben ihn arg berupft, they have fleeced him well, cleaned him well out.

Berußen, I. *v. tr.* to blacken with soot, to foul with soot. Sich —, to besmut one's clothes. II. *v. intr.* [u. w. ſeyn] to get sooty. Die Wände ſind berußt, the walls are blackened with soot, are all sooty.

Berütze, *f.* V. Berberis.

Beryll, *m.* [-s, *pl.* -e] [a mineral] beryl, aquamarine. Blätteriger —, cyanite, disthene; ſchörlartiger —, beryl shorliforme.

Beſaamen, V. Beſamen.

||**Beſabbern**, V. Begeifern.

Beſacken, *v. tr.* to load with sacks. Sich —, [in a proper as well as in a figurative sense] to fill one's pockets, to grow rich, to thrive.

Beſäen, *v. tr.* to sow [a field &c.]. *Fig.* Mit Sternen beſäet, sowed with stars.

Beſage, *adv.* [obsolete, except in law, in deeds &c.]. according to. — ſeiner Erklärung, according to his declaration.

Beſagen, *v. tr.* to say, to mention. Auf beſagte Weiſe, in the aforesaid manner. *Fig.* [u. w. haben] [to be of weight, of moment or consequence] to signify, to be of moment and consequence = to prove, to affirm. Das beſagt die Unterſchrift zur Genüge, that is sufficiently attested by the signature; es beſagt nichts, it is of no consequence, it does not signify.

Beſägen, *v. tr.* to shape by sawing.

Beſaiten, *v. tr.* to furnish with cords, to string. Beſaitete Tonwerkzeuge, stringed instruments; das Beſaiten, stringing.

Beſalben, *v. tr* [to smear with an unctuous substance] to anoint. Sich —, to besmear one's self. †Einen —, to cheat any one.

Beſalzen, *v. tr.* to sprinkle with salt, to salt.

Beſamen, I. *v. tr.* to strew or cover with seed. Ein Feld mit Hafer —, to sow a field with oats. II. *v. r.* ſich —, 1) to form seed, to run to seed. 2) to be propagated by seed.

Beſan, *f.* [*pl.* -e] [in D. the aftermost sail is called *bezaan*] [a sea term] the mizzen. Die — durchkaien, to change the mizzen; die — auftoppen, to peek the mizzen; die — losmachen, to set the mizzen; die — auf das Gat ſetzen or dicht hohlen, to haul the mizzen-sheets close aft.

Beſan[s]=brohk, *m.* throat-brail of the mizzen. Die —brohktalje, the whip of the mizzen throat-brail, —**mars**, *m.* the mizzen-top. —**maſt**, *m.* mizzen-mast. —**raa**, *f.* the mizzen-yard. —**ſegel**, *n.* mizzen-sail. —**wand**, *f.* mizzen-shroud.

Beſanden, I. *v. tr.* to strew with sand; *it.* to fill with sand. Das Eiſen —, [in forges] to cover the iron with sand. II. *v. r.* ſich —, to be filled with sand. V. Verſanden.

Beſänftigen, *v. tr.* to soften. *Fig.* to soften, to appease, to calm, to still, to pacify. Durch Liebkoſungen oder Schmeicheleien —, to soften by caresses or flattery; einen Zornigen —, to pacify a man when angry; ſeinen Zorn, ſeine Wuth —, to pacify his wrath, his rage; ſich —, to be appeased,

Beſänftigung, *f.* the act of appeasing or pacifying [wrath &c.], appeasement, pacification.

Beſänftigungsmittel, *n.* 1) a means to appease or pacify. 2) a palliative, lenitive.

Beſatz, *m.* [-es, *pl.* -ſätze] border, trimming, garniture.

Beſatzteich, *m.* [-es, *pl.* -e] a fish-pond.

Beſatzung, *f.* 1) [a body of troops stationed in a fort or fortified town] garrison. — haben, to be garrisoned. 2) [among locksmiths] ward.

†**Beſauen**, *v. tr.* to dirty.

†**Beſaufen**, *ir. v. r.* ſich —, to get drunk. Beſoffen ſeyn, to be intoxicated, fuddled, drunk; er iſt beſtändig beſoffen, he is a regular drunkard. *Fig.* to speak or to act like a drunken person. Ein Beſoffener, a drunken person.

†**Beſäufen**, [unusual] *v. tr.* to make drunk.

Beſäumen, *v. tr.* 1) to hem, to seam [a pocket-handkerchief &c.]. 2) to panel [a wainscot].

Beſäumung, *f.* 1) the act of hemming, panelling. 2) [the border of a garment doubled and sewed to strengthen it and prevent the ravelling of the threads] hem.

Beſchaben, I. *v. tr.* 1) to shave, to scrape, to grate. Holz mit Glas —, to scrape wood with glass; Käſe —, to pare cheese. 2) to sprinkle by rubbing. II. *v. r.* ſich —, to wear out by rubbing. Beſchabt ſeyn, to be worn out.

Beſchachteln, *v. tr.* to rub with shave-grass.

Beſchädigen, I. *v. tr.* to hurt or harm, to impair, to damage. Korn oder Heu kann durch den Regen beſchädigt werden, rain may damage corn or hay; ein Sturm kann ein Schiff —, a storm may damage a ship; Häuſer werden oft durch Feuer beſchädigt, houses are often damaged by fire; ſtarker Regen beſchädigt die Landſtraßen, great rains damage or injure the roads. II. *v. r.* ſich —, to hurt one's self.

Beſchädiger, *m.* [-s, *pl.* -] hurter.

Beſchädigung, *f.* 1) the act of damaging. 2) damage, hurt, harm, injury.

‡**Beſchaffen**, *v. tr.* 1) to create, to produce. 2) [instead of beiſchaffen and verſchaffen] to procure [in this sense less obsolete].

Beſchaffen, [past part. of the obsolete verb beſchaffen] *adj.* having a certain state or qualities. Die Sache iſt ſo —, the matter is thus, this is the nature of the matter; ſchlecht —, ill conditioned; es iſt ſchlecht mit ihm —, he is in low circumstances; wie iſt Ihre Geſundheit —? how is [it with] your health?

Beſchaffenheit, *f.* state, a particular mode of being [applied to external circumstances, to the body, to the mind, and to things], condition. Die — der Luft, the constitution of the air or atmosphere; die Leibes—, constitution; die — einer Flüſſigkeit, the nature of a fluid; die — des Gemüths, the condition of the mind; die — einer Handlung in Beziehung auf Recht oder Unrecht, the quality of an action, in regard to right or wrong; nach — der Umſtände, according to circumstances.

Beſchaffenheitswort, *n.* [in grammar] adverb.

Beſchäften, *v. tr.* to furnish with a shaft, stock or leg. Ein Gewehr —, to stock a gun; Stiefel —, to furnish boots with legs.

||**Beſchäftig**, *adj.* and *adv.* V. Geſchäftig.

Beſchäftigen, *v. tr.* to employ, to occupy, to use. Wir — unſere Hände bei der Arbeit, we employ our hands in labour; dieſer Beamte beſchäftigt ſechs Schreiber, this public functionary has employment for six clerks; dieſer Fabrikant beſchäftigt 200 Arbeiter, this manufacturer gives employment to 200 workmen; die Aufmerkſamkeit iſt beſchäftigt, wenn, &c., the attention is engaged, when &c.; ſich —, to bus[y] or employ one's self; jedermann ſollte ſich mi[t] einer nützlichen Arbeit —, every man should b[e] occupied, or should occupy himself with som[e] useful labour; beſchäftigt ſeyn, to be busied, occupied, engaged; mit etwas beſchäftigt ſeyn, to be about any thing; ſeine Gedanken ſind [zu] ſehr beſchäftigt, his thoughts are too much en[-]gaged.

Beſchäftigung, *f.* business, occupation. employment. Leute, deren einzige — darin beſteh[t] Andere zu beluſtigen, werden mit Recht gerin[g] geachtet, men, whose sole employment is to mak[e] amusement for others, are justly despised; [die] Zeit, welche ihm ſeine andern —en geſtatten, t[he] time that his other occupations will permit; nü[tz]liche —en, useful occupations.

Beſchalen, *v. tr.* to furnish with a shell [or] cover. Meſſer —, to put handles to, to ha[ft] knives; die Decken der Zimmer —, to lath t[he] ceiling of rooms.

1. **Beſchälen**, [from Schale = shell, husk] [*v.*] *tr.* to strip of bark, to peel, to husk, to decort[i]cate. Einen Baum —, to bark a tree; Aepf[el] —, to peel apples.

2. **Beſchälen**, *v. tr.* [probably from the A. S[ax.] *scelmelan* = ſpringen] to cover, to horse [a mare]. Das —, covering, horsing.

Beſchaler, *m.* [-s, *pl.* -] a workman th[at] puts handles to knives.

1. **Beſchäler**, *m.* [-s, *pl.* -] one that stri[ps] of bark &c.

2. **Beſchäler**, *m.* [-s, *pl.* -] 1) stallion, ston[e] horse. 2) [also Beſchälknecht] [in studs] the groo[m] attending the stallion.

Beſchäl=geld, *n.* money paid to the own[er] of a stallion for the covering of mares. —**knecht**, *m.* V. 2. Beſchäler 2). —**zeit**, *f.* the time wh[en] mares are covered, horsing time.

Beſchalung, *f.* 1) the act of furnishi[ng] with a shell or cover. 2) that, which is employ[ed] for covering. Die — der Wände eines Zimmer[s], the laths or boards used for lining the walls of [a] room.

1. **Beſchälung**, *f.* the act of husking, pe[el]ing &c.

2. **Beſchälung**, *f.* the covering of a mare.

Beſchämen, *v. tr.* to make ashamed, to co[n]fuse or confound, to abash, to shame. Sie h[ör]ten und waren beſchämt, they heard and [were] abashed; Einen durch Güte —, to confound a[ny] one by kindness.

Beſchämung, *f.* 1) shaming, confoundi[ng,] abashing 2) abashment, shame, confusion.

Beſcharren, *v. tr.* to cover scraping.

Beſchatten, *v. tr.* to shade. Dieſer Ba[um] beſchattet einen großen Raum, this tree shad[es] a great space. [In Scripture] V. Ueberſchatten.

Beſchattung, *f.* that which shades.

Beſchätzen, *v. tr.* to charge with taxes, [to] lay under contribution. Jeden Bürger nach [ſeinen] gehörigen Verhältniſſe —, to assess each ci[tizen] in due proportion.

Beſchätzung, *f.* a tax or specific sum charg[ed] on the person or property, assessment.

Beſchaubar, *adj.* and *adv.* visible, perc[ep]tible, evident.

Beſchauen, *v. tr.* 1) to look on or at, [to] view. Ein Gemählde —, to look on a pictu[re;] ſich im Spiegel —, to gaze or look at on[e's] self in the glass. 2) to look into, to view a[nd] examine for the purpose of ascertaining the q[ua]lity or condition of any thing, to inspect. G[ü]ter, das Mehl &c. —, to inspect goods, the fl[our] &c. *Fig.* a) to examine and judge critically. E[i]...

litterarische Arbeit —, to criticise a literary work. *b*) to view or consider with continued attention, to study, to meditate on, to contemplate. Die Werke der Schöpfung —, to contemplate the works of creation; ein —des or beschauliches Leben, a contemplative life; sich —, to look into one's self.

Beschauens-werth, —würdig, *adj.* and *adv.* worthy of being looked at.

Beschauer, [-s, *pl.* -] 1) viewer, looker on, examiner [frequently used in compositions, as:] Der Güter—, Fleisch—, Mehl—, public inspector of goods, meat, flour &c. *Fig.* Ein Buch—, a critic. 2) custom-house officer [seldom used].

Beschaufeln, *v. tr.* to shovel [earth] upon.

Beschaulich, *adj.* 1) visible, perceptible. 2) contemplative. Das —e Leben, contemplative life.

Beschaulichkeit, *f.* contemplation.

Beschäumen, *v. tr.* to cover with foam, scum. Die Wellen — das Ufer, the waves foam on the shore.

Beschauung, *f.* 1) the act of looking, viewing, examining, contemplating. 2) meditation, study, contemplation.

Bescheeren, V. Bescheren.

Bescheid, *m.* [-es, *pl.* -e] 1) an answer. Einem — geben, to give any one an answer; Einem — sagen lassen, to send any one word, to let any one know; er gab mir einen lügenhaften —, he gave me false information; Einem einen schnöden — geben, to give a person a blunt answer. 2) judicial answer, decision. Ein obergerichtlicher —, a decree of a high court of law; bis auf weitern —, till further orders, provisionally. 3) [in drinking] a pledge. Einem — thun, to pledge any one; Einer, der dem Andern — thut, pledger. 4) [joined with wissen] acquaintance with a thing. Um etwas — wissen, to know, to be acquainted, familiar or conversant with a thing; von or über etwas — geben, to give information of something; ich weiß keinen — hier, I am a stranger here.

Bescheiden, *ir.* I. *v. tr.* 1) to grant as a share, to give, to assign, to allot [chiefly used in the past part. beschieden]. Ein jeder sei mit dem zufrieden, was ihm die Vorsehung beschieden hat, let every man be contented with that which providence has allotted to him; seinen beschiedenen Theil erhalten, to receive one's portion; ihm war das Glück nicht beschieden, he was not fortunate. 2) to order [any one] to any place. Er ist zu seinem Regimente beschieden worden, he has been ordered to join his regiment; Einen zu sich —, to send for any one; er ist an den Hof beschieden worden, he has been called to court. 3) to inform. Ich lasse mich —, I am open to conviction; eines Bessern —, to set to right. II. *v. r.* sich —, to concede any thing. Wir — uns gern, daß &c, we concede willingly, that &c.

Bescheiden, [past participle of bescheiden] *adj.* and *adv.* modest. Ein —er Jüngling, ein —es Mädchen, a modest youth, a modest girl; er ist sehr —, he is very modest; eine —e Bitte, a modest request; —e Wünsche, moderate wishes; sich — betragen, to behave modestly.

Bescheidenheit, *f.* modesty [as opposed to arrogance, presumption or impudence]. Er sagt mit — seine Meinung, he expresses his opinions modestly.

Bescheider, *m.* [-s, *pl.* -] [in mills] a miller's man, foreman.

Bescheinen, [from Schein = shine] *ir. v. tr.* to shine upon.

Bescheinen, Bescheinigen, [from Schein = certificate] *v. tr.* 1) to attest, to certify. Ich will Ihnen den Empfang —, I will give you a receipt for it. 2) to prove, to verify, to certify, to attest.

Bescheinigung, *f.* 1) certification. 2) certificate, written attestation. Die — über eine empfangene Zahlung, acquittance.

† **Bescheißen,** *ir. v. tr.* to beshit, to shite upon. *Fig.* Jemanden —, to cheat any one.

Beschellen, *v. tr.* to hang or attach bells to horses, cows &c.

Beschenken, *v. tr.* to favour any one with a gift, to make a present to any one. Ich beschenkte ihn mit Schillers Werken, I presented him with a copy of Schiller's works; er ist reich beschenkt worden, he has received handsome presents, *fig.* he is richly endowed [by nature].

1. **Bescheren,** [from scheren = to shave] *ir. v. tr.* to shave [the head &c.]. Ein Mann mit beschorenem Kopfe, a shaveling.

2. **Bescheren,** [Sw. *beskaera*; Eng. *share* = theilen] *v. tr.* to give, to confer, to impart, to bestow [unexpectedly]. Einem etwas —, to bestow something on any one; Einem etwas zu Weihnachten —, to give any one a christmas-box.

1. **Bescherung,** *f.* the act of shaving.

2. **Bescherung,** *f.* 1) the act of conferring, bestowing &c., [especially] of giving a christmas-box. 2) gift, present, [especially] a christmas-box. *Fig.* [in familiar language] Eine schöne —! a fine business this! da haben wir die —! there we've got it!

Beschicken, *v. tr.* 1) to send to a place. 2) to put in good order, to put in the condition desired, to prepare. Die Erze —, [in metallurgy] to melt the ore with fluxes or fluxstones; das Gold oder Silber —, to alloy gold or silver [by mixing it with a portion of a metal less valuable]; den Acker —, to manure, to till or sow the field. 3) to put in order, to arrange. Die Tafel —, to lay the table. 4) to take care of, to tend. Ein Kind —, to nurse, to foster a child; das Vieh —, to take care of cattle. 5) [with hunters] to impregnate [said of stags].

Beschickung, *f.* 1) the act of preparing &c.; [in metallurgy] alloyage. 2) [in metallurgy] a rule concerning the alloying of metals.

Beschickungsregel, *f.* [in arithmetic] alligation.

Beschielen, *v. tr.* to squint at.

Beschienen, *v. tr.* to furnish or cover with bands of iron. Eine Achse —, to clout an axle-tree.

Beschießen, *ir.* I. *v. tr.* 1) to fire [on a town &c.]. Einen Wall —, to batter a rampart; eine Festung —, to batter a fortress with cannon, to cannonade a fortress; mit Bomben —, to bombard. 2) Einen Flintenlauf —, to prove a gun-barrel. II. *v. intr.* [u. w. seyn] to be covered on the surface. Die Wand ist mit Salpeter beschossen, the wall is covered with saltpetre.

Beschiffbar, *adj.* and *adv.* navigable.

Beschiffen, *v. tr.* to pass over in ships, to sail on. Das atlantische Meer —, to navigate the Atlantic.

Beschilden, *v. tr.* to furnish with a shield.

Beschilfen, I. *v. tr.* to cover with reeds. Beschilft, reeded. II. *v. intr.* [u. w. seyn] to be overgrown with reeds. Das beschilfte Ufer, the reedy shore.

Beschimmeln, *v. intr.* [u. w. seyn] to contract mould, to become mouldy, to be covered with mould. Beschimmeltes Brod, mouldy bread.

Beschimmern, *v. tr.* to make glittering, to give a lustre to. Die Morgensonne beschimmert die Spitzen der Kirchthürme, the morning-sun makes the spires glitter.

Beschimpfen, *v. tr.* to treat with gross abuse or insolence by words or actions, to insult, to dishonour. Sich —, to prostitute one's self; eine —de Rede, a defamatory speech; eine Sache —, to injure a thing.

Beschimpfer, *m.* [-s, *pl.* -] an insulter, abuser.

Beschimpfung, *f.* any gross abuse offered to another either by words or actions, insult. Beschimpfungen geduldig ertragen, to bear injuries, to pocket affronts, *prov.* to carry coals.

Beschindeln, *v. tr.* to cover with shingles. Ein Haus —, to shingle a house.

Beschinden, *ir.* I. *v. tr.* to strip off the cover or bark. Einen Baum —, to bark a tree. II. *v. r.* sich —, to knock off one's skin.

Beschirmen, *v. tr.* 1) [to cover from external injury] to shelter, to protect, to screen. Unsere Häuser — uns vor der rauhen Witterung, our houses protect us from the inclemencies of the weather; er beschirmte ihn mit seinem Schilde, he shielded him; die Wälle — die Festung, the ramparts protect the fortress; das Lager wird vom Flusse beschirmt, the camp is defended by the river. *Fig.* Die Gesetze — unsere Personen und unser Eigenthum, the laws protect our persons and property. 2) V. Verwahren.

Beschirmer, *m.* [-s, *pl.* -] a defender, protector.

‖ **Beschlabbern,** *v. tr.* to beslubber.

Beschlafen, *ir. v. tr.* 1) [in familiar language] Eine Sache —, to advise with one's pillow. — Sie die Sache, take counsel of your pillow, consider it for a night, sleep upon it. 2) Ein Frauenzimmer —, to lie with a woman, to get a woman with child.

Beschlag, *m.* [-es, *pl.* -schläge] 1) sequestration, seizure. In — nehmen, to take forcible possession of by law, to seize; Schulden halber in — nehmen, to seize for debt, to distrain; man hat seine Leibrente mit — belegt, um seine Gläubiger zu bezahlen, his annuity is sequestered to pay his creditors; der — auf das Eigenthum eines Fremden, foreign attachment; Schiffe in — nehmen, to lay an embargo on ships. 2) any metal appendage either for the purpose of fastening or ornamenting. Der — einer Thür, the iron-work of a door; der — einer Flinte, the mounting of a gun; der — am untern Ende eines Stockes, the cap of a cane, ferrule; der — eines Pferdes, shoeing; der eiserne — eines Blocks, the iron-work of a block. 3) [in seamen's language] the serving. 4) [in chimistry] lute, luting. 5) mouldiness, mustiness, mould. 6) [in mines] efflorescence.

Beschlag-bindsel, *n.* —**bendsel,** *n.* —**leine,** *f.* furling lines, seizings, stops. —**leger,** *m.* [in law] seizer. —**legung,** *f.* sequestration. —**nehmer,** *m.* V. —leger. —**nehmung,** *f.* embargo, sequestration. —**seising,** *f.* [a sea term] a gasket. —**tasche,** *f.* a farrier's pouch. —**verwalter,** *m.* a sequestrator. —**verwaltung,** *f.* sequestration. Ein Gut unter —verwaltung legen, to sequester an estate. —**zange,** *f.* farrier's tongs. —**zeug,** *n.* farrier's tools.

Beschläge, *n.* [-s, *pl.* -] any article [particularly of metal] fastened to a thing with the hammer, for the purpose of strength or ornament, mounting. Das — eines Wagens, the iron-work of a carriage; das — eines Raperts, [in seamen's lang.] transom plate; das — der Achse eines Rades, clout; das — eines Buches, clasps of a book.

Beschlagen, *ir.* I. *v. tr.* 1) to beat repeatedly, to hammer. Die Thaler —, [in mints] to round the dollars. 2) to nail any appendage [particularly of metal] to a thing for the purpose of strength or ornament. Eine Thür, ein Fenster —, to bind a door, a window with iron-work; ein Pferd —, to shoe a horse; ein Rad —, to put the tire on a wheel; einen Stab mit Silber —, to tip a rod with silver; mit Silber —, mounted with silver; mit Eisen —, to clout; mit Nägeln oder Buckeln —, to adorn with studs or shining knobs, to stud; mit goldenen Nägeln —, nailed with gold; einen Koffer mit Leder —, to cover a trunk with leather. *Fig.* [in familiar language] In einer Sache gut or wohl beschlagen seyn, to be well versed in a thing. 3) [with carpenters, joiners, stone-masons] to square. Einen Baum —, to square a tree. 4) to mark, to stamp. Die Tücher —, [in cloth-manufactories] to append stamped lead to the cloths. 5) [in chymistry] to lute [a retort &c.]. 6) [in seamen's language] Die Segel —, to furl the sails. 7) [in husbandry] Einen Hof mit Vieh —, to store a farm with cattle. 8) [with hunters] to impregnate [said of stags and some other animals]. Der Hirsch beschlägt das Thier, the stag lines the hind; ein —es Thier, a hind heavy with young. 9) *Fig.* to seize, to sequester, to lay an embargo on. [in Beschlag nehmen, Beschlag auf etwas legen is more used] V. Beschlag 1.

II. *v. intr.* [u. w. seyn] to contract moisture or mould on the surface. Der Spiegel beschlägt, the looking glass tarnishes; das Brod beschlägt, the bread grows mouldy.

Beschlämmen, V. Beschlemmen.

Beschlängeln, *v. tr.* to surround with serpentine lines.

Beschleíchen, *ir. v. tr.* to approach sneaking, to fall upon unexpectedly. Einen —, to surprise any one; *fig.* to deceive, cheat any one.

Beschleiern or **Beschleiern**, *v. tr.* to veil. Sich —, to cover one's self with a veil.

1. **Beschleifen**, [from schleifen = to whet] *ir. v. tr.* to whet a little here and there.

2. **Beschleifen**, [from schleifen = to glide] *ir. v. tr.* to glide or slip upon. Er beschliff die zugefrorene Oberfläche des Teiches, he slid across the frozen surface of the pond.

3. **Beschleifen**, [from Schleife = knot] *v. tr.* to furnish or adorn with knots of ribbands.

Beschleímen, *v. tr.* to cover with slime.

Beschlèmmen, *v. tr.* to cover with mud.

Beschleúnigen, *v. tr.* to haste or hasten, to accelerate. Die schweren Körper — im Fallen ihre Bewegung, heavy bodies accelerate their motion in falling down; er beschleunigte seine Abreise, he hastened his departure; Jemands Tod —, to hasten a man's death; den Verfall einer Regierung —, to accelerate the ruin of a government; den Marsch —, to force a march; das Wachsthum der Pflanzen, Blumen, Früchte —, to accelerate the growth of plants, flowers, fruits.

Beschließen, *ir. v. tr.* to lock, to lock up. Waaren, Vorräthe —, to lock up goods, stores; [in seamen's language] Eine beschlossene Rhede, a road protected from the reigning winds and the swell of the sea, a snug, sheltered roadstead. *Fig. a*) to bring to a conclusion, to end, to finish, to conclude, to close. Das Jahr, die Woche —, to close or to end the year, the week; das Leben —, to terminate this life, to die; eine Rede —, to conclude a discourse. *b*) [to end or settle a point in the mind] to determine. Paulus hatte beschlossen, vor Epheso überzuschiffen, [in Scripture] Paul had determined to sail by Ephesus; eine Sache —, to resolve on a matter; was Gott über uns beschlossen hat, what God has decreed concerning us; es wurde im Rathe beschlossen, it was decreed by the council; sie überlegen immer und — nichts, they are constantly deliberating, and conclude nothing; mit Einem etwas —, to agree with any one on a thing.

Beschließer, *m.* [-s, *pl.* -] locker-up, house-keeper, caterer, steward.

Beschließerinn, *f.* house-keeper, cateress.

Beschlíngen, *ir. v. tr.* 1) to twine, to twist round, to entwine, to enclose in a net. 2) *Fig.* [unusual] to captivate.

Beschlößen, *v. intr.* [u. w. seyn] to be covered with hail.

‖**Beschlöten**, *v. tr.* to furnish with dikes, drains.

‖**Beschlúmpern**, *v. tr.* to bedaggle [one's clothes]. Sich —, to bespatter one's clothes.

Beschlúß, *m.* [-sses, *pl.* -schlüsse] the act of locking, shutting, and the state of being shut or locked. Unter dem —sse, under lock and key; etwas in oder unter seinem —sse haben, to have a thing in one's keeping, custody or charge. *Fig. a*) the close or conclusion [applied to time or things]. Wir kommen zum —, we arrive at the end; zum — des Jahres, at the close of the year; zum —, in the end or conclusion, to conclude, to sum up all, in fine. *b*) determination, final decision. Nach einer langen Debatte faßte das Unterhaus diesen —, after a long debate, the house of commons came to this conclusion; diesem —sse gemäß, conformable to this resolution. *c*) decree, order.

Beschmaúchen, *v. tr.* [rather vulgar] to foul with smoke, to smoke. *Fig.* Beschmauchte Gemählde, smoky pictures.

Beschmaúsen, [in familiar language] I. *v. tr.* Einen —, to feast at the expense of another; er beschmaust uns öfters, he spunges often upon us. II. *v. r.* sich —, to feast to excess.

†**Beschmeißen**, *ir. v. tr.* 1) [= bewerfen] to throw at. Er beschmiß ihn mit Steinen, he pelted him with stones. 2) to pelt with dirt, to soil, to foul; [of flies] to blow. Wie ein von Fliegen beschmissener Unschlittkuchen, like a fly-blown cake of tallow.

Beschmíeren, *v. tr.* [to overspread with any soft substance that adheres] to besmear. Mit Oel, Fett, Butter, Theer, Pech —, to oil, to grease, to butter, to tar, to pitch; ein mit Butter beschmiertes Stück Brod, a slice of bread and butter. *Fig.* Viel Papier — [= versudeln], to scribble over, to soil a deal of paper.

Beschmitzen, *v. tr.* 1) to soil, to foul. *Fig.* Eines guten Namen —, to tarnish any one's reputation, to injure his reputation, to defame or slander him. ‖2) Eine Peitsche —, to provide a whip with a lash; ich bemerkte, daß eure Peitsche nicht beschmitzt war, I observed that your whip wanted a lash to it.

Beschmúnzeln, *v. tr.* to smile at.

Beschmútzen, *v. tr.* to soil, to dirty. Beschmutzte Kleider, foul clothes.

Beschnárchen, *v. tr.* 1) to snore or snort at. 2) *Fig.* to blame with harshness.

Beschnaúben, **Beschnaufen**, *v. tr.* to snuff at, to smell at.

‖**Beschnaúfeln**, *v. tr.* V. Beschnüffeln.

Beschneíden, *ir. v. tr.* 1) [to shorten by cutting off the extremities, to cut off with shears or scissors] to clip. Dem Vogel die Flügel —, to clip a bird's wings; einen Baum —, to lop a tree; eine Hecke —, to poll a hedge; einen Weinstock —, to prune or dress a vine; ein Buch —, to cut a book; Geldstücke —, to clip money; [with the Jews] einen Knaben —, to circumcise a boy; der Beschnittene, a circumcised person. *Fig.* [in familiar language] Einem die Flügel —, to clip any one's wings; einem die Gelegenheit —, to cut any one off the opportunity; Einem seine Besoldung —, to reduce, to curtail a man's salary or wages.

Beschneidesbank, *f.* [among letter-founders] dressing-bench. —**brett**, *n.* [with bookbinders] riglet —**eisen**, *n.* [among tawers] edge-tool. —**hobel**, *m.* [among bookbinders] plough-knife. —**messer**, *n.* V. —eisen. —**presse**, *f.* [among bookbinders] cutting-press.

Beschneíder, *m.* [-s, *pl.* -] clipper, [with Jews] circumciser.

Beschneídung, *f.* the act of clipping &c.; *it.* [among the Jews] circumcision.

Beschneíen, *v. intr.* [u. w. seyn] to be covered with snow. Beschneite Felder, snowy fields.

Beschneíteln, [*dimin.* of beschneiden] *v. tr.* to lop, to prune [trees].

Beschníppeln, **Beschnippen**, *v. tr.* [to cut off the edges or ends of a thing] to clip, to snip. Die Wolle —, [among clothiers] to take off the points of wool.

Beschnítzeln, **Beschnitzen**, *v. tr.* to carve, to cut figures or devices on hard materials.

‖**Beschnóppern**, **Beschnúppern**, V. Beschnüffeln.

†**Beschnüffeln**, *v. tr.* to snuffle at, to smell at. *Fig.* Er beschnüffelt Alles [= hat seine Nase in Allem, or steckt seine Nase in Alles], he smells out every thing, he thrusts his nose in every-where.

Beschnüren, *v. tr.* to bind with cords, to cord. Eine Rackete —, [in pyrotechnics] to choke a rocket or squib.

Beschȫnen, [more usual] **Beschȫnigen**, *v. tr.* to set in a fair light, to colour, to excuse. Fehler, Laster —, to palliate faults, vices. Syn. V. Bemänteln.

Beschȫnung, [more usual] **Beschȫnigung**, *f.* colouring, palliation.

Beschößen, *v. tr.* to furnish with points [used only in the past part. beschoßt]. Ein kurz beschoßter, ein lang beschoßter Rock, a short or long skirted coat.

Beschränken, I. *v. tr.* to confine, to limit, to set a limit to, to circumscribe. Die Aussicht —, to confine the prospect; den Gesichtskreis —, to limit or bound the horizon; jener Berg beschränkt unsere Aussicht, yonder hill confines our prospect. *Fig.* Die Gewalt eines Menschen —, to set bounds to a man's power; wir — es auf jene Pflichten allein, welche &c., we restrain it to those only duties, which &c.; unser Wissen —, to narrow our knowledge; unsere Wünsche —, to bound our wishes; seine Wünsche auf Kleinigkeiten —, to reduce one's wishes to trifles; beschränkend, restrictive; auf eine beschränkte Weise, limitedly. V. Beschränkt. II. *v. r.* sich —, to content one's self [with any thing]. Sich auf etwas —, to restrict one's self to a thing. Syn. Beschränken, Begrenzen. Beschränken adds to the idea of limiting or bounding, which is common to both these words, also that of restraining within certain limits, of preventing further encrease or extension. Begrenzen, on the contrary, signifies merely to fix the furthest point of extension of an object, natural or moral. Our view is beschränkt [confined] by a building which prevents our having a more extensive view; a line is begrenzt [terminated] by its points, which determine its extent.

Beschränker, *m.* [-s, *pl.* -] he that confines, limits, restrains.

Beschränkt, [past part. of beschränken] *adj.*

and *adv.* bounded, confined, limited, narrow, circumscribed. Eine —e Aussicht, a confined view; in ihrer Nahrung —, scanted in their nourishment; ich war etwas in meiner Zeit —, I was something scanted in time; —e Gewerbe, limited professions; ein —er Monarch, a limited monarch; das Universum ist hier auf unsere Erde —, the universum is here limited to our earth; der größte Verstand ist —, the greatest understanding is narrow; ein —er Kopf, [a person rather deficient in understanding] a shallow-brained, a narrow-minded person.

Beschränktheit, *f.* state of being bounded or confined, limitedness. Die — menschlicher Talente, the limitedness of human capacities; die — neuerer Sprachen, the narrowness of modern tongues; die — unseres heroischen Verses, the scantiness of our heroic verse; die — deines Vermögens, the scantiness or narrowness of thy fortune; die — ihres Geistes und Verstandes, the narrowness or shallowness of their minds and understanding; seine —, his shallow-mindedness.

Beschränkung, *f.* 1) the act of bounding or circumscribing, limitation, circumscription. 2) limitation = restriction, restraint. Die Regierung sichert die bürgerliche Freiheit durch — der natürlichen Rechte, government by the limitation of natural rights secures civil liberty; es ist zwecklos, den Menschen —en aufzulegen, it is to no purpose to lay restraints on men.

Beschreiben, *ir. v. tr.* 1) to write upon, to fill with writing. Einen ganzen Bogen —, to fill a whole sheet with writing. 2) to delineate or mark the form or figure, to describe. Einen Kreis mit dem Zirkel —, to describe a circle with compasses; ein Dreieck —, to describe a triangle. *Fig. a)* [to make or exhibit a figure by motion] to describe. Ein Stern beschreibt am Himmel einen Kreis oder eine Ellipse, a star describes a circle or an ellipsis in the heavens. *b)* [to show or represent to others in writing or words, to communicate the resemblance of a thing, by naming its nature, form or properties] to describe. Sie beschrieb mir ihn, she described him to me; eine —de Erzählung, a descriptive narration; er beschrieb ausführlich alle Verhandlungen, he gave a detail of all the transactions; der Dichter beschreibt das trojanische Pferd, the poet describes the Trojan horse; der Geschichtschreiber beschreibt die Schlacht von Pharsalus, the historian describes the battle of Pharsalia; der Geograph beschreibt Länder und Städte, the geographer describes countries and cities; es ist nicht zu —, wie viel er gelitten hat, his sufferings are not to be described or expressed. || 3) to take or give an inventory of furniture, goods, property &c.

Beschreiber, *m.* [-s, *pl.* -] describer [particularly in compound words, as: Erdbeschreiber &c.].

Beschreiblich, *adj.* and *adv.* describable.

Beschreibung, *f.* 1) the act of describing, [illegible], description. 2) [a representation of [illegible] nature or properties, that gives to another a [illegible] thing] description. Homer ist reich an [illegible] —en, Homer abounds in beautiful de[illegible]. 3) description, inventory. Die voll[illegible] Guts — ist in der Allgemeinen Zeitung [illegible], the detailed description of the pre[illegible] to be found in the „Allgemeine Zei[illegible]".

Beschreien, *ir. v. tr.* 1) to cry at. 2) to talk ill of, to decry. [chiefly used in the past part.] Beschrieen, notorious, famous, decried. Er ist seiner Spielsucht wegen beschrieen, he is notorious for his gaming. 3) [with superstitious persons] to enchant, to charm by words, particularly by great praise. Ein Kind —, to bewitch a child; Jemands Glück —, to exalt a man's fortune.

Beschreikraut, *n.* [-es] the blue flowered flea-bane.

Beschreiten, *v. tr.* to stride or to step over, to bestride. Kaum hatte er die Schwelle des Zimmers beschritten, als &c., he had scarcely crossed the threshold, when &c; ein Pferd —, [seldom used] to bestride a horse.

Beschrieen, [past part. of beschreien] V. Beschreien.

Beschröten, *v. tr.* 1) to cut off the ends or sides of a thing, with a large instrument, as a saw &c. Die Bleitafeln —, [among plumbers] to edge the lead-sheets; eine Schüssel —, [with goldsmiths] to edge a dish off; ein Metall —, to beard off a metal. *Fig.* Er beschrotet ihre Pfründen, he curtails their livings. 2) to gnaw, to nibble.

Beschrümpeln, Beschrümpfen, *v. intr.* [u. w. seyn] to shrink, to shrivel.

Beschründen, *v. intr.* [u. w. seyn] to open in chinks.

Beschuhen, *v. tr.* 1) [generally to cover] Einen Pfahl —, to shoe a pale with iron. 2) [to fit the foot with a shoe] to shoe. Sich —, to put on one's shoes, or to provide one's self with shoes.

Beschuhung, *f.* 1) shoeing. 2) shoes.

Beschulden, *v. tr.* 1) [unusual] to burden with debts. Beschuldet, V. Verschuldet. 2) V. [the more usual verb] Beschuldigen.

Beschuldigen, *v. tr.* 1) to charge any one with a fault, to accuse. Sie — Einer den Andern, they accuse one another. 2) to charge with or to impute to. Einen des Diebstahls —, to charge any one with theft; Einen eines Verbrechens —, to accuse any one of a crime; der [die] Beschuldigte, the person accused, the defendant. Syn. V. Anklagen.

Beschuldiger, *m.* [-s, *pl.* -] —inn, *f.* accuser, accusant, plaintiff.

Beschuldigung, *f.* 1) the act of charging with a crime or offence, the act of accusing of any wrong or injustice, accusation. 2) the charge of an offence or crime, accusation. Die ungegründeten —en unserer Feinde, the groundless imputations of our enemies.

|| and † **Beschummeln**, *v. tr.* to cheat. Einen —, to take any one in.

Beschuppen, *v. tr.* 1) to strip of scales, to scale [a fish]. *Fig.* † Einen —, to take any one in, to cheat or blind any one. 2) to cover with scales. Alle Fische sind beschuppt, all fishes are scaly; ein beschuppter Panzer, scale or plate armour.

Beschüppen, *v. tr.* to throw upon with a shovel.

Beschürfen, *v. tr.* [in mining] Einen Gang —, to find a load.

Beschürzen, *v. tr.* to provide with an apron. Beschürzt, aproned.

Beschütten, *v. tr.* to throw or cast on; *it.* to pour on. Die Wurzeln eines Baumes mit Erde —, to cover the roots of a tree with earth; Einen mit Wasser —, to dash water on any one, to splash any one; er hat sich sein ganzes Kleid mit der Suppe beschüttet, he spilt the soup over his whole dress.

Beschützen, *v. tr.* to cover or shield from danger or injury, to protect, to skreen. Einen Acker oder Garten —, to hedge or fence a field or garden; eine Stadt —, to protect, to defend a city; Waffen — uns vor feindlichen Anfällen, arms protect us from assaults; ich will dich vor dieser Gefahr —, I will secure thee from that danger; vor dem Regen beschützt, sheltered from the rain.

Beschützer, *m.* [-s, *pl.* -] a defender, protector.

Beschützerinn, *f.* protectress, defendress.

Beschützung, *f.* 1) the act of protecting &c. 2) protection, defence, shelter.

Beschwägern, *v. tr.* to become the brother-in-law of a person by marrying.

Beschwämmen, V. Beschwemmen.

† **Beschwängern**, *v. tr.* to get with child. V. [the more usual] Schwängern.

Beschwänzen, *v. tr.* to furnish with a tail. V. Schwänzen. Beschwänzte Noten, [in music] V. Geschwänzte Noten.

Beschwärzen, *v. tr.* 1) to make black, to blacken. 2) to soil, to bedaub.

Beschwätzen, *v. tr.* 1) to talk over, to persuade, to palaver, to wheedle, to cajole. Lassen Sie sich nicht —, don't let yourself be gulled. 2) to speak ill of a person, to slander.

Beschwefeln, *v. tr.* 1) to cover with sulphur. 2) V. Schwefeln.

Beschweifen, *v. tr.* to furnish with a tail or train. Beschweifte Kometen, Comets with a train.

Beschweißen, *v. tr.* to moisten with sweat, to soil with sweat. Beschweißt, [with hunters] bloody.

Beschwemmen, *v. tr.* to flood, to inundate.

|| and ‡ **Beschwer**, *f* [*pl.* -en] V. Beschwerde.

Beschwerde, *f.* [*pl.* -n] 1) that which is borne with labour or difficulty, that which is grievous, wearisome or oppressive, burden. Bürgerliche —n, civil charges [as rents, taxes, impositions on land or estate &c.]. 2) that which burdens, oppresses or injures, whatever oppresses the body. Die —n des Lebens, the hardships of life; zu —n abgehärtet, inured to hardships; die —n des Krieges, the fatigues of war; körperliche —n, bodily complaints; Brust—n, a complaint on the chest; Glieder—n, pain in the joints or limbs; Kopf—n, head-ache; die —n des Alters, the infirmities of old age. 3) molestation, disturbance, annoyance, uneasiness. Einem — verursachen, to give any one trouble or uneasiness; —n abhelfen, to redress grievances. 4) expression of grief, pain, complaint. Er hat keine Ursache zu —n, he has no cause of complaint; eine — gegen Einen [vor Gericht / in court, in a court of law] vorbringen or erheben, to prefer a complaint against any one; über etwas — führen, to complain of a thing; die Juden brachten viele —n gegen Paulum vor, [in Scripture] the Jews laid many complaints against Paul.

Beschwerde=führer, *m.* —führerinn, *f.* [in law] complainant. —voll, *adj.* and *adv.* full of pain or hardships, painful, laborious, toilsome.

Beschweren, I. *v. tr.* to lay on a heavy load, to incumber with weight, to load, to burden. Das Papier —, [with printers] to load the paper. *Fig. a)* [to oppress or burden the body] Diese Speise beschwert den Magen, this food lies heavy upon the stomach. *b)* to charge, to load, to burden. Das Volk mit Steuern und Abgaben —, to burden the nation with taxes and duties. c) to give trouble to, to give inconvenience to, to annoy. Es ist mir leid, daß ich Sie damit beschwere, I am sorry to put you to that trouble; Einen mit seinen Besuchen — or [more usual] belästigen, to be troublesome to, to bore any one by one's visits; mit Bitten —, to annoy with petitions. II. *v. r.* sich —, to complain.

Sich über eine Sache —, to complain of a thing; ich habe alle Ursache, mich über Sie zu —, I have good reason to complain of you; ich habe keinen Grund, mich zu —, I have no cause of complaint; sie beschwerten sich bei dem Könige über ihren Heerführer, they laid complaints before the king against their commander.

Beschwerlich, *adj.* and *adv.* grievous to be borne, causing uneasiness or fatigue, burdensome, troublesome, toilsome. Ein —er Weg, a difficult road; der Dienst in diesem Hause ist —, the service is hard in this house; Einem — fallen, to molest, to trouble any one, to weary any one by importunity, to fatigue, to bore him; einem Heere durch eine anhaltende Kanonade — fallen, to annoy an army by a continued cannonade; Besuche von Fremden zu ungelegenen Stunden fallen einer Familie —, visits of strangers at unseasonable hours incommode a family; ein modischer Anzug fällt uns oft —, we are often incommoded by a fashionable dress; das Gehen fällt or ist ihm —, he can only walk with great difficulty; die allzugroße Helle ist or fällt den Augen —, too great a quantity of light is painful to the eyes; —e Gebräuche, inconvenient customs; sein hohes Alter fällt ihm nicht —, his old age is no trouble to him; Sie fallen mir —, you are a trouble to me.

Beschwerlichkeit, *f.* 1) troublesomeness. 2) trouble, hardship, labour, toil, fatigue. Die —en des Lebens, the hardships of life; die —en des Alters, the inconveniencies of old age; die —en des Krieges, the fatigues of war; Regen und schlechte Wege sind große —en für den Reisenden, rain and bad roads are great inconveniencies to the traveller; es ist mit vielen —en verbunden, it is connected with many inconveniencies.

Beschwerung, *f.* 1) the act of burdening &c. 2) load, burden; *fig.* trouble.

Beschwichtigen, *v. tr.* to still [a crying child], to appease. *Fig.* Sein freundlicher Zuspruch hat oft meinen heftigen Schmerz beschwichtiget, his friendly and consolatory words have often soothed my inordinate grief; er suchte ihn zu —, allein der Erzürnte hörte nicht auf ihn, he tried to appease him, but the angry man would not listen to him; der den Sturm und die tobenden Wellen beschwichtiget, he who lulls the storm and stills the raging waves; sein Gewissen —, to silence one's conscience.

Beschwichtiger, *m.* [-s, *pl.* -] he that stills or silences.

Beschwingen, *v. tr.* 1) to furnish with wings, to wing. *Poet.* Seinen Lauf — or [more usual] beflügeln, to accelerate one's course; sich —, to hasten. 2) to fit with feathers, to feather.

Beschwingung, *f.* 1) the act of winging or feathering. 2) wings.

Beschwitzen, V. Beschweißen.

Beschwören, *ir. v. tr.* 1) to take one's oath upon, to swear to, to confirm by an oath. Die Zeugen haben die Wahrheit ihrer Aussage beschworen, the witnesses have sworn to the truth of their statement. 2) to call on or summon by a sacred name or in a solemn manner, to implore with solemnity, to conjure. Den Teufel oder böse Geister —, to exorcise a demon or evil spirits; ich beschwöre dich, dies zu thun, I conjure thee to do it; ich beschwöre Sie bei Allem, was Ihnen heilig ist, thun Sie es nicht, I conjure you by all that's sacred, not to do it; ich beschwöre dich bei dem lebendigen Gotte, [in Scripture] I conjure thee by the living God; sie beschworen sie, eine so günstige Gelegenheit nicht vorübergehen zu lassen, they adjured them not to let so favourable an opportunity pass.

Beschwörer, *m.* [-s, *pl.* -] conjurer, exorciser.

Beschwörung, *f.* 1) the act of conjuring, exorcising, conjuration, exorcism. 2) [certain words used in conjuring] adjuration.

Beschwörungsformel, *f.* adjuration.

Beseelen, *v. tr.* 1) to endue with a soul, to inspirit, to animate. Beseelt, animate; beseelte Geschöpfe, animate beings. *Fig.* Die Vaterlandsliebe beseelte ihn, the love of country animated him; ein beseeltes Auge, an animated or bright eye; beseelte Züge, an animated countenance, lively and intelligent features.

Beseeler, *m.* [-s, *pl.* -] he that endues with a soul. *Fig.* he that animates.

Besegeln, *v. tr.* 1) to sail, to pass over in ships, to sail on. Das Meer —, to navigate the sea. 2) to furnish with sails. Wohl besegelt, well fitted out in sails. 3) [in seamen's language] Ein Schiff —, to join a ship at sea.

Besehen, *ir.* I. *v. tr.* [to look on by way of examination] to look on or at, to view [a house, a garden &c.] Etwas sorgfältig —, to inspect a thing carefully, to examine it; die Bilder —, to look at the pictures. *Fig.* Wenn man es beim Lichte besieht, if one examines it closely or narrowly; beim Lichte —, ist der ganze Plunder meine Mühe nicht werth, on narrower inspection I find, the whole thing is not worth the trouble I took; einander or sich —, to look at each other; sie — sich or einander, one looks on the other. II. *v. r.* Sich im Spiegel —, to view one's self, to look at one's self in the glass or mirror; sich in einer Stadt —, to take a view of the town, to ramble about the town. SYN. Besehen, Besichtigen, Betrachten. Besehen signifies to look at, to inspect in order to gain a more intimate knowledge of a thing. Besichtigen conveys the idea of a more particular attention to the thing which is the object of sight than Besehen, and that the inspection is made for the purpose of examining, or discovering the real state of a thing. Betrachten differs from Besehen and Besichtigen in expressing a higher degree of attention of the mind, a more careful contemplation of the object.

Besehens-werth, **—würdig**, *adj.* and *adv.* worthy or deserving of being seen, worth seeing.

Besehnen, *v. tr.* to string [a bow]. *Fig.* Besehnte Glieder, sinewy limbs.

† **Beseichen**, V. Bepissen.

Beseifen, V. Einseifen.

Beseilen, *v. tr.* to furnish with ropes.

Beseiten, *v. tr.* to furnish with sides; [in heraldry] to furnish with ornaments on the sides; [in fortification] to flank.

Beseitigen, *v. tr.* to set aside, to put away, to put at a distance, to remove. *Fig.* Streitigkeiten —, to accommodate differences; Vorurtheile —, to do away prejudices.

Beseligen, *v. tr.* [to make happy] to bless.

Beseliger, *m.* [-s, *pl.* -] [one who bestows a blessing] blesser.

Besen, *m.* [-s, *pl.* -] [allied either to Busch, Mid. Lat. *boessonus*, or more probably from binden] [a brush, generally of twigs, for sweeping] besom, broom. Ein — zum Fegen der Teppiche, turk's-head broom; ein Spanischer —, [in seamen's language] a large brush, to scrub the ship's bottom under water; der kleine —, a whisk. *Prov.* Neue — kehren gut, a new broom sweeps clean.

Besen-binder, *m.* broom-maker, broom-man. **—binderinn**, *f.* broom-woman. **—flachs**, *m.* flax-leaved goose-foot, belvidere, or summer-cypress. **—förmig**, *adj.* and *adv.* having the form of a broom. ‖**—frau**, *f.* V. —binderinn. **—heide**, *f.* small green-flowered heath. **—kraut**, *n.* 1) flix-weed. 2) V. —flachs. 3) field southernwood. 4) common broom. 5) narrow-leaved dittander. 6) common southernwood. **—mädchen**, *n.* broom-girl. **—malve**, *f.* small yellow-flowered upright mallow. **—markt**, *m.* a market where brooms are exposed to sale. **—moos**, *n.* a species of bryony. **—pfrieme**, V. —kraut. **—reis**, *n.* birchen twig. **—stiel**, *m.* broom-staff, broom-stick. **—trespe**, *m.* ryebroomgrass.

Besenden, *ir.* and *r.* V. [the more usual verb] Beschicken.

Besengen, *v. tr.* to singe here and there.

Besessen, [past part. of besitzen] *adj.* and *adv.* affected by some power. —, [in Scripture, affected by demons] possessed; †er schreit wie —, wie ein —er, he screams as if the very devil was in him; von Geiz, von Neid — seyn, to be possessed with avarice, envy. Der Besessene, die Besessene, a human being possessed by a demon, a demoniac, one possessed.

Besetze, *n.* [-s, *pl.* -] V. Besatz.

Besetzen, *v. tr.* 1) to place on a thing or along the side of a thing. Den Tisch mit Schüsseln —, den Tisch mit Speisen —, to put or set dishes on the table, to serve the table; ein unbewohntes Land mit Einwohnern —, to people, to colonize an uninhabited country; eine Stadt —, or mit Truppen —, to furnish a town with soldiers, to garrison a town; Festungswerke mit Soldaten —, to line works with soldiers; einen Zaun mit Scharfschützen —, to line a hedge with riflemen; der Feind hatte die Anhöhen besetzt, the enemy had occupied the heights; ein Schiff mit Mannschaft —, to man a ship; einen Teich mit Fischen —, to store a pond with fish; einen Park mit Rothwild —, to stock a park with deer; einen Pachthof mit dem erforderlichen Vieh —, to stock a farm with the necessary cattle; mit Kanonen besetzt, mounted with cannon; einen Garten mit Bäumen —, to plant a garden with trees; ein Blumenbeet mit Buchs —, to edge a flowerbed with box; einen Rock mit Silber oder mit Seidenzeug —, to lace a coat with silver or to face a coat with silk; ein Halstuch mit Spitzen —, to lace a cravat; mit Juwelen reich besetzt, with jewels richly set; [in seamen's language] ein Bindsel —, to fasten or to belay the end of a lashing or seizing. *Fig.* Ein Zimmer, einen Platz — [= einnehmen or in Beschlag nehmen], to occupy a room, a place; die Zimmer sind schon besetzt, the chambers are preoccupied, engaged, let; ein Amt oder eine ledige Stelle —, to fill an office or vacancy; [at cards] ich habe den König doppelt besetzt, I have my king doubly guarded; eine Karte —, to lay, to set down, to stake money upon a card. 2) to pave. 3) [in seamen's language] besetzt seyn, to be embayed.

Besetz-schlägel, **—stößel**, *m.* [among pavers] a paver's rammer.

Besetzer, *m.* [-s, *pl.* -] he that laces c… &c. with silver &c.

Besetzung, *f.* trimming, lacing &c. *Fig.* — von Aemtern, appointment or nomination to offices; die — der sämmtlichen leer gebliebenen Aemter or Stellen ist jetzt vollendet, the different vacancies in office have all been filled up; — einer Pfründe, collation.

Besetzungsrecht, *n.* [the right of presentation to a church or ecclesiastical benefice] patronage.

Beseufzen, *v. tr.* to sigh over, to mourn for, to bemoan. Der Eine belachte Thorheiten, der Andere beseufzte Verbrechen, one laughed at follies, one lamented crimes.

Besichtigen, *v. tr* to view for the purpose of examination, to examine, to inspect, to survey. Gewehre —, to inspect arms; die Gre…

eines Feldes —, to visit the borders of a field; einen Todtgefundenen (Erschlagenen &c.) —, to hold an inquest on or over a dead body [a slain person &c.]. Syn. V. Besehen.

Besichtiger, *m.* [-s, *pl.* -] [one who inspects, views or oversees] inspector, surveyor. Der Leichen—, [in England] a coroner, [in some German states called also Leichenbeschauer] one appointed by the authorities, whose duty it is, closely to inspect the body of any person recently deceased before its interment, to prevent the possibility of burying any one alive.

Besichtigung, *f.* inspection, official view. Die — eines Todtgefundenen, Erschlagenen &c., official examination of a dead body, a coroner's inquest on the body of a slain person.

Besieben, *v. tr.* to bestrew or besprinkle through a sieve.

Besiegbar, *adj.* and *adv.* conquerable, vanquishable.

Besiegeln, *v. tr.* to seal [a writing, a deed &c.]. Ein unterschriebener und besiegelter Vertrag, a contract signed and sealed. *Fig.* Meine Hand besiegelt die Liebe unserer treuen Herzen, with my hand I seal our true hearts' love.

Besiegen, *v. tr.* to overcome, to vanquish, to conquer. Die Feinde in der Schlacht —, to overcome enemies in battle; die Römer besiegten Carthago, the Romans conquered Carthage; die Besiegten, the vanquished. *Fig.* Schwierigkeiten, Hindernisse —, to overcome difficulties, to surmount obstacles; er besiegte alle Hindernisse, he triumphed over all obstacles; die Leidenschaften —, to conquer, to subdue the passions; Widerwillen —, to conquer reluctance.

Besieger, *m.* [-s, *pl.* -] conqueror, vanquisher.

Besieglich, V. Besiegbar.

Besilbern, *v. tr.* [to cover superficially with silver] to silver.

Besingen, *ir. v. tr.* to celebrate in song, to sing. Kleist hat den Frühling besungen, Kleist sung the spring; Petrarcha besang Laura's Schönheit, Petrarch celebrated in song his Laura's beauty; Homer hat die Thaten des Achilles und die Irrfahrten des Ulysses besungen, Homer sung the deeds of Achilles and the wanderings of Ulysses.

Besinnen, *ir. v. r.* sich —, 1) [to recover or recall the knowledge of, to bring back to the mind or memory] to recollect. Ich konnte mich auf seinen Namen nicht —, I could not recollect his name; ich kann mich nicht —, was gesagt wurde, I cannot recollect what was said; sich der vorigen Zeiten — or [more usual] erinnern, to remember former times. 2) to weigh in the mind, to deliberate. Ich muß mich erst —, I must first think on it; er ist schnell besonnen, his resolution is quickly taken. V. Besonnen. Syn. V. Anstehen. [to decree within one's self] to resolve. Sich eines Andern —, to change or alter one's mind; sich eines Bessern —, to bethink one's self better. [to recover] one's recollection or one's senses. Er kann sich noch gar nicht —, he has not yet recovered his senses.

Besinnung, *f.* 1) recollection. Zur — kommen, to collect one's self, to come to one's senses. 2) consciousness. Er ist bis an seinen Tod bei — geblieben, he retained his consciousness till the moment of his death; die — verlieren, to lose one's senses, to become insensible.

Besinnungs-kraft, *f.* [the power of recalling ideas to the mind] recollection. —los, *adj.* and *adv.* having lost one's senses, insensible, senseless. —voll, *adj.* and *adv.* full of recollection.

Besitz, *m.* [-es, *pl.* -e] 1) [the having, holding or detention of property in one's power or command] possession. Rechtmäßiger —, legitimate possession; eine Sache in — nehmen, to take possession of a thing; — ergreifen, to take possession, to occupy; wir nahmen das Königreich Neapel in —, we possessed ourselves of the kingdom of Naples; in — setzen, to possess of or with, to give possession; Einen aus dem —e setzen oder treiben, to dispossess any one; im —e einer Sache seyn, to be possessed of a thing; im —e aller seiner Kräfte, in possession of all his strength; im langen —e von Fortunens Gunst, of Fortune's favour long possessed; der fürsorgliche —, [in law] possession in trust or feoffment. 2) [the thing possessed] possession.

Besitz-ergreifer, *m.* occupant, occupier. —ergreifung, *f.* [the act of taking possession] occupancy, occupation. —fähig, *adj.* and *adv.* able to possess. Der Erbe ist —fähig, the heir is of age. —nahme, *f.* V. —ergreifung. Widerrechtliche —nahme, usurpation. —nehmer, *m.* V. —ergreifer. —stand, *m.* [chiefly in law] state of possessing, possession. Im —stande seyn, to possess or be in possession of.

Besitzen, *ir. v. tr.* 1) to sit on. Der Vogel besitzt die Eier, the bird incubates or sits on eggs [for the purpose of hatching young]. 2) *Fig.* to be possessed of, to have, to possess. Einen Meierhof —, to possess a farm; Fähigkeiten —, to be possessed of talents; wenn sie ein ehrliches Gemüth —, if they are possessed with honourable minds; sie besitzt Schönheit, she is endowed with beauty; er besitzt Witz, he is witty.

Besitzer, *m.* [-s, *pl.* -] —inn, *f.* [a person that has possession] possessor. Der — eines Gartens, the owner or proprietor of a garden; der — eines bedeutenden Vermögens, the possessor of, or possessed of, a large fortune.

Besitzthum, *n.* [-es, *pl.* -thümer] [the thing possessed, lands, estates or goods owned] possession.

Besitzung, *f.* 1) [the state of possessing] possession. 2) [the state of being under the power of demons or invisible beings] possession. 3) [the thing possessed] possession. Auswärtige —en, foreign possessions; er hatte große —en, he had great possessions.

Besocken, *v. tr.* to furnish with socks. [in gardening] Bäume am Fuße —, to open trees at the root.

Besohlen, *v. tr.* to furnish with soles. Ein Paar Schuhe —, to sole a pair of shoes.

Besolden, *v. tr.* 1) to give pay to. Dazu bin ich nicht besoldet, for that I am not paid. 2) to have in pay, to stipend. Viele Truppen —, to keep a great army.

Besoldung, *f.* 1) the act of giving pay to or having in pay. 2) pay, salary or wages for service. Die —en der Minister in diesem Lande sind sehr hoch, the salaries of the ministers in this country are very high; dieser Beamte suchte um eine Erhöhung seiner — an, this functionary applied for an increase of salary; eine feste —, a fixed salary.

Besömmern, *v. tr.* [in husbandry] to sow or plant with summer-vegetables.

Besondere, der, die, das, *adj.* [pertaining to a single person or thing, not general] particular. Jede Sache hat ihren besondern Platz, every thing has its distinct place; diese Bemerkung hat eine — Anwendung, this remark has a particular application; er spielt auf eine — Person an, he alludes to a particular person; die meisten Menschen haben einen besondern Zug des Charakters, most persons have a particular trait of character; die — Vorsehung Gottes, the especial providence of God; mein Schicksal ist Juno's — Sorge, my fate is Juno's peculiar care; eine — Schreibart, a peculiar style; er hat eine — Wohnung, he has a separate lodging; durch — or aus —r Gnade, by special favour; die besondern Umstände anführen, to cite the particulars; das ist meine — Meinung, that is my individual opinion; das —, [in logic] concrete. *Fig.* *a)* [more than ordinary] particular. Ein —r Fall, an uncommon or extraordinary instance; ein —s Verlangen nach &c., an uncommon longing after &c.; — Talente, distinguished talents. *b)* particular = odd, singular. Ein —s Benehmen, a strange behaviour.

Besonderheit, *f.* 1) particularity, individuality. Die — seiner Schreibart, the peculiarity of his style. 2) [distinct notice, a distinct, separate or minute part] particularity. Ich kenne alle —en dieses Vorfalls, I know all the particulars of this occurrence. 3) [something peculiar or singular] a particularity, curiosity.

Besonders, *adv.* [in a state of separation as to place] separately, apart. Es steht —, it stands by itself; legt es —, put it asunder. *Fig.* *a)* apart, separately, individually, distinctly. Erwäge die zwei Vorschläge —, consider the two propositions apart. *b)* [in an especial manner] particularly. Er hat mir seine beiden Kinder, — das älteste, empfohlen, he has recommended to my care his two children, more especially the eldest; ich finde nichts — schön or Schönes daran, I find nothing extraordinarily beautiful about it. *c)* much, in a high degree.

Besonnen, [past participle of Besinnen] *adj.* and *adv.* 1) circumspect, cautious, prudent, discreet, wary, not rash. 2) having the power of recollecting, recollective.

Besonnen, *v. tr.* to shine upon a thing [said of the sun]. Besonnte Wege, sunny roads.

Besonnenheit, *f.* 1) circumspection, discretion, prudence. 2) thought, reflection. 3) presence of mind.

Besorgen, I. *v. tr.* to take care of, to direct the concerns of. Ein Geschäft —, to conduct, to carry on a business; die Geschäfte einer Familie —, to manage the affairs of a family; alles Nöthige —, to provide for all things necessary; er hat den Auftrag besorgt, he has acquitted himself of his commission, he has done the errand; die Kinder —, to nurse, to take care of the children. V. Besorgt 1). II. *v. intr.* to be in apprehension of evil, to fear. Claudius war um sein eigenes Leben nicht wenig besorgt, Claudius was in no small apprehension for his own life. V. Besorgt 2).

Besorger, [-s, *pl.* -] he that takes care of a thing, manager, commissioner, agent.

Besorglich, *adj.* and *adv.* 1) apprehensive, fearful. 2) careful, provident.

Besorglichkeit, *f.* 1) apprehensiveness, fearfulness. 2) apprehension, fear. 3) [seldom used] the apprehended evil.

Besorgniß, *f.* [*pl.* -sse] 1) care, superintendence, management. Er hat die — or [more usual] Besorgung meiner häuslichen Angelegenheiten, he manages all my domestic concerns. 2) apprehension, fear. Eine wundervolle — für den Ruf ihrer Freunde, a wonderful solicitude for the reputation of their friends.

Besorgniß-voll, *adj.* and *adv.* 1) fearful, apprehensive, in expectation of evil. 2) causing apprehension or fear.

Besorgsam, *adj.* and *adv.* inclined, disposed to take care of any thing.

Besorgt, [past participle of Besorgen] *adj.* and *adv.* 1) taking care of. Für etwas — seyn, to take care of any thing; wollt Ihr für mein Pferd or für die Unterbringung meines Pferdes

— seyn? will you look to my horse? 2) regarding with care, solicitous, anxious. Wir sind um das Schicksal unserer Flotte —, we are concerned for the fate of our fleet; Sie waren um meinen Ruf —, you have been in solicitude for my reputation; ich bin um den Ausgang der Schlacht —, I am anxious for the issue of the battle; ich bin um meines Sohnes Schicksal äußerst —, I am extremely anxious about the fate of my son.

Besórgung, *f.* the act of taking care of any thing.

Besorgungsgebühren, *pl.* charges for agency or commission, provision.

Bespánnen, *v. tr.* to put [horses, oxen, and the like] to a carriage &c. Den Pflug mit Ochsen —, to yoke oxen to the plough; dieser Frachtwagen ist mit zehn Pferden bespannt, this waggon has ten horses to it; ein mit Eseln bespannter Karren, a cart drawn by asses; die Lappländer fahren auf mit Hunden bespannten Schlitten, the Laplanders drive in sledges drawn by dogs. 2) to strain or stretch a thing over another. Eine Geige mit Saiten —, to string a violin. 3) [to measure by the hand extended] to span.

Bespeíen, *ir. v. tr.* to daub or soil with spittle, to bespit.

Bespeilern, *v. tr.* V. Speilern.

Bespícken, *v. tr.* to lard [veal &c.] *Fig.* [in familiar language] Den Beutel —, to furnish the purse with money; sich —, to enrich one's self.

Bespíegeln, I. *v. tr.* to furnish with looking-glasses. *Fig.* Der von den Strahlen der Sonne bespiegelte Strom, the river enlightened by the rays of the sun. II. *v. r.* sich —, to view one's self, to gaze at one's self in a mirror. Sich bespiegelnd, glass-gazing.

Bespíkern, *v. tr.* [a sea term] to nail [the sheathing] with filling nails.

Bespínnen, *ir. v. tr.* 1) to make of an equal surface by spinning. 2) to cover with webs. Die Raupen — die Zweige, the caterpillars cover the twigs with webs. 3) V. Ueberspinnen.

Bespließen, *v. tr.* to shingle [a roof].

Bespórnen, *v. tr.* and *v. r.* sich —, to put on spurs. Gestiefelt und bespornt, booted and spurred.

Bespötteln, *v. tr.* to ridicule, to banter, to jeer, to scoff, to joke, to jest.

Bespótten, *v. tr.* to mock, to rally.

Besprèchen, *ir.* I. *v. tr.* 1) to converse. Mit Einem etwas —, to converse with any one on something. 2) to bespeak [a seat in a public coach &c.]. 3) [with superstitious people] to affect, in some manner, by magic words or arts, to conjure. Das Feuer —, to stop the fire by magic words. ||4) to defame. II. *v. r.* sich — mit Jemand, to discourse, to hold a parley, to confer, to deliberate with any one; ich besprach mich mit ihnen, I conferred with them; er besprach sich mit ihr eine Zeitlang, he parleyed with her a while; wir besprachen uns eifrig über diese Materie, we discussed this matter eagerly; wir besprachen uns über unsere gegenseitigen Angelegenheiten, we discoursed together on our mutual concerns.

Besprècher, *m.* [-s, *pl.* -] [with superstitious people, he that conjures] a conjurer.

Besprèchung, *f.* 1) mutual discourse or conversation, conference. 2) bespeaking. 3) conjuring, incantation.

Bespreiten, **Bespreizen**, *v. tr.* to cover [the table &c.].

Besprèngen, *v. tr.* to sprinkle over, to besprinkle. Einen mit Wasser —, to sprinkle water upon any one; Fleisch mit Salz —, to sprinkle meat with salt; einen Bienenschwarm mit Sand —, to besprinkle a swarm of bees with sand; Schwerter mit Blut besprengt, swords drenched in blood.

Besprènkeln, *v. tr.* to speckle, to bespeckle.

Bespríngen, *ir. v. tr.* 1) to leap, to cover [said of stallions &c.]. Das —, supersaliency. 2) [chiefly with hunters] to come suddenly upon by a leap.

Bespritzen, *v. tr.* to besprinkle, to squirt at. Einen mit Wasser —, to spatter any one with water; mit Koth —, to splash.

Besprúdeln, *v. tr.* to wet sputtering.

Bespúcken, *v. tr.* to soil with spittle, to bespit.

Bespülen, *v. tr.* [to moisten in flowing] to wash. Die See bespült viele Inseln, the sea washes many islands.

Bespúnden, **Bespünden**, *v. tr.* to bung [a cask].

Bésser, [*compar.* of gut] [allied to the provincial batten = nutzen, and also to Buße] *adj.* and *adv.* better. [having good qualities in a greater degree than another] Ein —er Boden, a better soil; ein —es Haus, a better house; ein —er Mensch, a better man; ein —er Doktor, a better physician; — arbeiten, to perform work better; — bebautes Land, land better cultivated; — schreiben oder sprechen als ein Anderer, to write or speak better than another; einen Gegenstand — verstehen, als ein Anderer, to understand a subject better than another; es — haben, als ein Anderer, to be better off than another; es — machen, — werden, to ameliorate, to amend; dieser Wein wird im Keller — werden, this wine will improve in the cellar; wäre es nicht — für uns, nach Egypten zurückzukehren? [in Scripture] were it not better for us to return to Egypt? Gehorsam ist —, denn Opfer, [in Script.] to obey is better than sacrifice; je mehr, desto —, the more the better; je eher je —, the earlier the better; es kommt selten etwas —es nach, seldom comes a better; desto —, so much the better. *Prov.* Gut ist gut, doch — ist —, though good be good, yet better is better or better carries it; ich fahre weit — dabei, wenn ich den ganzen Vorrath auf einmal verkaufe, I come better off in selling the whole stock at once; nehmen Sie diese Uhr, Sie fahren bestimmt — damit, take this watch, you will be better satisfied with it; Sie werden mit ihm — fahren or — daran seyn, als mit jedem andern Dienstboten, you will be better served by him, than by any other servant. [in a more limited sense] *a*) [improved in health] Der Kranke ist —, the patient is better; sich — befinden, to be, to find one's self better; — werden, to grow better, to recover from illness. *b*) [in fam. lang.] = more. Er kann — essen als ich, he eats more than I; er nimmt sich jetzt — in Acht, he is more cautious now; — hinauf, a little more upwards; du mußt — schreien, you must speak louder.

Bésserlich, *adj.* and *adv.* susceptible of amelioration or amendment, improvable.

Béssern, I. *v. tr.* 1) to better, to improve, to meliorate. Dünger bessert das Land, manure betters land; die Wege — or ausbessern, to repair the roads; ||einen Acker —, to manure a field; Einen — [in seinen Sitten], to mend, to correct [a person's manners]. 2) to amend [our conduct &c.]. II. *v. r.* sich —, *a*) to grow better, to mend, to improve, to meliorate. Ein Kranker bessert sich, a sick man mends or is convalescent; es bessert sich mit ihm, he is getting better, he is in a fair way of recovery; seine schwache Leibesbeschaffenheit bessert sich täglich, his feeble constitution mends daily; was bin ich dadurch gebessert? what am I the better for it? *b*) [to advance in goodness, knowledge or other excellence] to improve. Er bessert sich täglich, he improves daily. *c*) [to grow or become better by reformation, or rectifying something wrong in manners or morals] to amend. Er bessert sich, he amends; wirst du dich jemahls —? will you ever leave off your old tricks? er ist nicht mehr zu —, he is incorrigible.

Bésserung, *f.* 1) a making better, amelioration, melioration. Die — or Verbesserung der Straßen, the improvement of roads. 2) advance or progress from any state to a better, an alteration or change for the better. Die — [eines Kranken], convalescence, recovery; es läßt sich mit dem Kranken zur — an, the patient is improving in health, he is getting better, he is convalescent; die — [in morals], reformation of life by quitting vices, amendment; sein jetziges Betragen verspricht —, his present conduct promises improvement; Satire geißelt das Laster zur —, satire lashes vice into reformation. 3) a valuable addition, excellence added. Eine neue Ausgabe mit verschiedenen —en und Zusätzen, a new edition with several improvements and additions.

Besserungs-fähig, *adj.* and *adv.* [that may be reformed] corrigible. **—haus**, *n.* house of correction. **—mittel**, *n.* [that which has the power of correcting] corrective. Strafen sind —mittel für eine unmoralische Aufführung, penalties are correctives of immoral conduct.

Bestácheln, *v. tr.* to furnish with a prick.

Bestáhlen, *v. tr.* to steel [the point of a lance &c.].

Bestállen, *v. tr.* to appoint to an office, to invest with an employment, to install.

Bestállung, *f.* 1) appointment to an office, instalment, installation. 2) public office, employ and the salary annexed to it. 3) a writing conferring some employ, a commission. Er erwartet seine — täglich, he expects his commission every day.

Bestallungs-brief, *m.* **—urkunde**, *f.* a writing conferring an employ, a commission, letters-patent.

Bestámmen, *v. tr.* to furnish with a stem.

Bestánd, *m.* [-es, *pl.* -stände] 1) a state of lasting, duration, continuance. Von —e seyn, to be lasting, to be durable, to endure, to be permanent; dein Reich wird nicht von —e seyn, thy kingdom shall not continue; das Glück hat keinen —, fortune is inconstant, mutable, changeable, variable; [in law] mit — Rechtens, according to law, legally, lawfully. 2) [that of which a thing consists] Der — des Waldes ist von tausend Aeckern or Morgen, the forest comprehends, comprises a thousand acres; Form und Materie gehören zum —e &c., form and matter constitute &c.; der — der Waare, [in commerce] remainder; der — der Kasse [Kassen—], clear amount, balance of cash. 3) [the sum that is left after any deduction] remainder. 4) rent, hire. Der Pächter hat das Gut auf ein Jahr in —, the tenant rents his estate for a year; ein Gut in — nehmen, to farm an estate.

Bestands-buch, *n.* inventory. **—geld**, *n.* rent. **—gut**, *n.* property which is farmed or let, leasehold. **—herr**, *m.* the owner of a property which is let. **—los**, *adj.* and *adv.* inconsistent. **—mann**, *m.* tenant. **—müller**, *m.* he that rents a mill. **—rolle**, *f.* V. —buch. **—stück**, *n.* **—theil**, *m.* an essential or constituent part, an element, ingredient. Der Sauerstoff und Wasserstoff sind die —theile des Wassers, oxygen and hydrogen are the constituent or component parts of water; die —theile einer Arzenei, the ingredients of a medicine. **—vertrag**, *m.* V. Pachtvertrag. **—zeit**, *f.* V. Pachtzeit.

Beständer, *m.* [-s, *pl.* -] renter, farmer, tenant. Der — eines Meierhofes, the tenant of a farm; der — einer Wirthschaft or eines Wirthshauses, the tenant of a public house.

Beständheit, *f.* consistency.

Beständig, I. *adj.* [not intermitting, unceasing, used in reference to time &c.] continual, constant in the same state, unalterable, unchangeable; invariable. Ein —er [anhaltender] Regen, a steady rain; ein —er Zank, a continual dispute; ein —er Lärm, a continual noise; —e Klagen, perpetual complaints; es ist nichts —es unter der Sonne, there is nothing stable here below; [in law] ein zu Recht —er [rechtsbeständiger] Vertrag, a legal contract; —es Wetter, settled weather; ein —er Freund, Liebhaber, a constant or firm friend, a constant lover; ein —es Glück, durable happiness; eine —e [dauerhafte] Farbe, a lasting colour; —es [dauerhaftes] Tuch, durable cloth; —e Größen, [in mathematics] constant quantities [such as remain the same, while others decrease or increase]; —e or — wehende Winde, steady or constant winds, trade-winds, monsoons. II. *adv.* 1) [without pause or cessation] continually. Der Ozean rollt — seine Wellen an das Ufer, the ocean is continually rolling its waves on the shore; er bleibt für — hier, he remains for always, he is settled here; wir müssen in der —en Erwartung leben, daß &c., we must live in hourly expectation that &c.; die himmlischen Körper sind — in Bewegung, the heavenly bodies are perpetually in motion. 2) [without alteration or change] invariably. Der Wind wehete — aus Westen, the wind settled in the west; wir verfolgen — den Weg der Pflicht, we invariably pursue the path of duty; — seyn, to be constant.

Beständigkeit, *f.* 1) continuance, duration, a permanent state, constancy. 2) [persevering resolution, steadiness in attachments, stability in love or friendship] constancy.

†**Beständiglich**, *adv.* V. Beständig II.

Beständeln, *v. tr.* to furnish with poles or sticks for support, to stake.

Bestärken, I. *v. tr.* to make more firm, to strengthen, to make persevering in the execution of a purpose &c., to make more certain, to confirm. Jemanden in seinem Entschlusse —, to fortify any one's resolution; es bestärkte sie sehr in ihren Wünschen, it greatly confirmed her in her wishes; die Unterthanen in ihrer Pflicht —, to confirm the subjects in their duty; sein Zeugniß wird durch &c. bestärkt, his testimony is corroborated by &c.; im Glauben —, to strengthen in the faith. II. *v. r.* Sich in seiner Meinung &c. —, to become firm or steady in one's opinions &c.; sich in seinem Glauben —, to fortify one's faith.

‖**Bestäten**, V. Bestätigen.

Bestätigen, I. *v. tr.* 1) to approve and sanction, to make valid. Einen Vertrag —, to ratify or confirm a treaty; der oberste Gerichtshof bestätigte das Urtheil, the supreme court affirmed the judgment. 2) to confirm, to establish. Ich bestätige dich im Priesteramte, I confirm thee in the priesthood; Jemanden in seinen Besitzungen und Vorrechten —, to establish a person in possessions and privileges. 3) [to make firm or certain, to give new assurance of truth and certainty] to confirm [a news &c.]. Es wird durch neuere Nachrichten bestätiget, it is corroborated by recent advices; das göttliche Gesetz bestätiget die Wahrheit, the divine law ascertains the truth. 4) [with hunters] Einen Hirsch —, to ascertain the place, where a stag is harboured. ‖ 5) V. Ausstatten. II. *v. r.* sich —, to be made firm or certain, to be confirmed. Diese Nachricht bestätiget sich, that news is confirmed, gains strength.

Bestätigung, *f.* 1) [the act of confirming or establishing, a making more certain and firm, the act of ratifying, the act of giving new evidence] confirmation. Die — eines Vertrages, the ratification of a covenant; die — eines Gerüchtes, the confirmation of a report. 2) [that which confirms] confirmation. Diese Thatsache oder dieser Beweis ist eine — des vorher Angeführten, this fact or this argument is a corroboration of what was before alledged.

Bestätigungsurtheil, *n.* a confirmatory judgment.

Bestatten, *v. tr.* ‖ 1) V. Ausstatten. 2) to convey to a place. Zur Erde —, to convey to the place of interment, to bury, to inter, to entomb. ‖ 3) to cultivate [the ground].

Bestätter, *m.* [-s, *pl.* -] [in trading-places] conveyer. V. Güterbestätter.

Bestauben, *v. intr.* [u. w. seyn] to contract dust, to get covered with dust.

Bestäuben, *v. tr.* 1) to sprinkle, soil or cover with dust, to dust, to bedust. Ein Kleid —, to soil a garment with dust; bestäubte Stiefel, dusted boots; bestäubte Bücher, dusty books; sich —, to get covered with dust; Insekten mit bestäubten Flügeln, [in nat. hist.] lepidopters. 2) to sprinkle as with dust. Das Haar mit Puder —, to powder the hair; mit Zucker —, to powder over with sugar.

Bestauden, *v. r.* sich —, to form a stalk,

· **Bestaunen**, *v. tr.* to gaze or stare at, to be astonished at.

Beste, [der, die, das; *superl.* of gut] [V. Besser] *adj.* best; am besten, *adv.* best. [most pleasant to the senses, most good, having good qualities in the highest degree] Der —e Geschmack, the best taste; die —e Ansicht einer Landschaft, the best view of a landscape; es klingt am —en, wenn &c., it sounds best, when &c.; am —en gefallen, to please best; der — Mensch, the best man; er ist der — Mensch von der Welt, [in fam. lang.] he is the best man alive; der — Weg, the best road; das — Tuch, the best cloth; die —n Früchte, the finest fruits; die Menschen sind alle Sünder, die —n von ihnen &c., men are all sinners, the best of them &c.; in den —n Jahren, in the prime of life, in the flower of age; der erste [der] —, the first the best; welches Werkzeug können Sie am —n brauchen? what instrument can you best use? ein Jeder hält das Seinige für das —, every one likes his own things best; Geld wird am —n [vortheilhaftesten] in Fabriken angelegt, money is best employed in manufactories; diese Arzenei wird im gegenwärtigen Falle am —n helfen, this medicine will answer best in the present case; eine Sache am —n auslegen or auf das — deuten, to put the best construction upon a thing; ich halte es für das —, I think it best; zu Ihrem —n, to your advantage, in your behalf; wie thue ich am —n? what had I best do? what course had I best take? auf das — mit etwas umgehen, es aufs — benutzen, to make the best of a thing; nach meinem —n Wissen, to the best of my knowledge; ich will mein —s thun, I'll do my best; zum —n, for the best; reden Sie zu meinem —n, intercede for me; zum —n rathen, to advise for the best; das — des Landes, the good of the country; gib ihm stets vom —n, give him always of the prime; *prov.* das — kauft man immer noch wohlfeil, the best is cheap; er weiß es am —n, it is best known to himself; aufs —, zum —n, best; von der —n [schönsten] Seite betrachtet, at [the] best; die Lehre von der —n Welt, optimism; mein —r, meine —, [in fam. language] dear sir, dear madam; etwas zum —n geben, to give for the enjoyment of others, to treat, to regale; geben Sie uns ein Lied zum —n, give us a song; zum —n der Armen, for the benefit of the poor; etwas zum —n haben, to be possessed of something, to be worth something; nicht viel zum —n haben, to have not much to spend, to be poor; Jemanden zum —n haben, to mock, to deride a person, to laugh at, to make sport of any one.

Bestechen, *ir. v. tr.* to prick repeatedly; [in sewing] to border a thing with small stitches. Die Bandstreifen der Bücher —, [among bookbinders] to headband a book; das Leder —, [with shoemakers] to quilt the leather. *Fig.* to bribe, to corrupt. *a*) [to give or promise a reward or consideration, with a view to pervert the judgment or corrupt the conduct, to hire for bad purposes] Einen Richter, Zeugen —, to bribe a judge, a witness. *b*) [to gain by a bribe].

Bestech=bar, *adj.* and *adv.* capable of being bribed, corruptible. V. Bestechlich. **—draht**, *m.* [with shoemakers] stitching thread. **—naht**, *f.* [with shoemakers] a flat seam. **—ort**, *m.* [with shoemakers] a sort of awl. **—presse**, *f.* [with bookbinders] a press used in headbanding a book.

Bestechlich, *adj.* and *adv.* capable of being bribed, corruptible.

Bestechlichkeit, *f.* susceptibility of being bribed, corruptibleness.

Bestechung, *f.* 1) bribery. 2) bribe.

Besteck, *n.* [-es, *pl.* -e] 1) a case of instruments. Ein — für Messer, a case for knives; das chirurgische —, a case of surgical instruments. 2) a set [of knives &c.]. Silberne [Tisch-] —e, silver knives and forks. 3) [in seamen's lang.] *a*) day's work or the ship's place as pricked on the nautical chart. Ein — machen, to prick a chart [to trace a ship's course on a chart]; mit dem — voraus seyn, to be a-stern of one's reckoning; mit dem — zurück seyn, to run a-head of one's reckoning. *b*) scheme which contains the general dimensions of a ship, from which the shipwright is to form a draught for constructing her.

Besteckmacher, *m.* a manufacturer of instrument-cases.

Bestecken, *v. tr.* 1) to stick. Ein Stück Rostbraten mit Rosmarin —, to stick a piece of roast-beaf with rosemary; ein Beet mit Kartoffeln —, to plant a bed with potatoes; sich mit Blumen —, to adorn one's self with flowers; die zu bezeichnenden Stellen mit Nadeln —, [in military and nautical science] to prick places [on a chart or map]. 2) to furnish with poles for support. Bohnen —, to pole beans.

Bestecker, *m.* [-s, *pl.* -] [a sea term] the person who bargains with a shipwright to build a ship, called the contractor or ship's husband.

Bestehen, *ir.* I. *v. intr.* [u. w. seyn and haben] 1) to stand, to be immovable. *Fig. a*) [u. w. seyn] *α*) not to yield, not to give way, to resist. Ziehet an den Harnisch Gottes, daß ihr — könnet gegen die Anläufe des Teufels, [in Script.] put on the whole armour of God, that ye may be able to stand against the wiles of the devil. *β*) to be found good by experience or trial. Troilus ist in der Probe bestanden, Troilus stood the trial. *γ*) [in a general sense = to prove or to show] Er ist dabei mit Schanden bestanden, it was a disgrace to him. *b*) [u. w. seyn and haben] *α*) to retain the present state or condition, to continue, to subsist. Möge es so lange — als &c., may it last as long as &c; sein Reich wird nicht —, his kingdom shall not continue. *β*) to have means of living, to exist; er kann bei seinem Gehalte nicht —, he cannot live with, cannot subsist on his pay. *γ*) to exist, to be, to subsist. Diese zwei Sachen können nicht neben einander —, these two things cannot exist together, are incompatible; er ist vor Allem und es bestehet Alles in ihm, [in Script.] he was before all things, and by him all things consist. *δ*) to be composed, to consist. Es bestehet aus &c., it consists of &c.; unser Leben bestehet aus der Verbindung des Leides mit der Seele, our life consists in the union between the body and the soul; was nur aus Speise und Trank bestand, [in Script.] which stood only in meats and drink. c) [u. w. haben] to have existence by means of something else, to subsist. d) [u. w. seyn] to insist on. Auf augenblicklicher Bezahlung einer Schuld —, to insist on immediate payment of a debt; und dann noch auf Sicherheit —, and then stand upon security; er besteht auf seiner Meinung, he persists in his opinion. 2) [u. w. seyn] [to turn from a fluid to a solid state] to congeal, to coagulate, to curdle. Das Wasser besteht, water congeals; Milch und Blut —, milk curdles, blood coagulates, thickens. 3) [u. w. seyn] to stand long enough.

II. *v. tr.* 1) to get the better. Er bestand den Angriff, he stood the shock; Gefahren —, to go through dangers; er bestand es, he overcame it; ich will des Würfels Ungefähr —, I will stand the hazard of the die; er wird die Probe nicht —, he won't stand the test. ‖2) to rent, to farm.

Bestéhlen, *ir. v. tr.* to steal from, to rob. Eine öffentliche Kasse —, to peculate.

Besteifen, V. Bestärken [but in a worse sense than Bestärken].

Besteigen, *ir. v. tr.* to get upon an elevated place. Ein Pferd —, to mount or to back a horse; einen Berg, einen Baum —, to ascend a hill, a tree; ein Schiff —, to get on board a ship; die Kanzel —, to mount the pulpit; einen Thron —, to mount a throne.

Besteinen, *v. tr.* to set out with stones, particularly with precious stones.

Bestéllen, *v. tr.* 1) to cover any thing by placing or putting other things on it. Der Tisch war mit Büchern bestellt, the table was covered with books; der Hofraum war ganz mit Kutschen bestellt, the yard was filled up with coaches. 2) to order any one to a place. Wir sind auf den Mittag bestellt, we are ordered to come at noon; bestelle den Wagen an das Thor, order the carriage to the gate; Einen zu einem Amte —, to appoint any one to a place; wer hat ihn zum Richter bestellt? who constituted him judge? 3) to order or engage to a future time. Ich habe meinen Platz [im Postwagen] bestellt, I have secured my place [in the stage-coach]; einen Platz in der Briefpostkutsche —, to bespeak a place in the mailcoach; tausend Exemplare sind bestellt, a thousand copies are bespoken; eine Kutsche —, to send for, to order a coach; haben Sie die Pferde bestellt? have you sent for the horses? 4) to perform any business. Einen Brief —, to deliver a letter; einen Auftrag —, to deliver a message; haben Sie nichts an Ihren Bruder zu —? have you no commission to your brother, nothing I can execute for you? 5) to put in suitable order. Den Acker —, to prepare the field for crops, to cultivate the field. *Fig.* Sein Haus —, to make one's will, to prepare for death. 6) [among dyers] Den Kessel oder die Küpe —, to fill the boiler or the vat with water.

Bestellzeit, *f.* [in husbandry] the time of working or cultivating the ground.

Bestéller, *m.* [-s, *pl.* -] 1) he that orders, bespeaks any thing, one who delivers messages &c.; [in commerce] committer. 2) one who prepares land for crops, cultivator.

Bestéllung, *f.* 1) the act of appointing, ordering, bespeaking, delivering, cultivating. Auf —, at command. 2) something ordered or bespoken, order, message, commission, rendezvous. Sie gab ihm eine — auf acht Uhr an diesen Ort, she gave him an appointment for eight o'clock at this place.

Bestellungsbuch, *n.* [in commerce] a book in which are registered all things bespoken, order-book.

Bestémpeln, *v. tr.* to stamp [cards &c.]. Papier —, to stamp paper.

Bestèngelt, *adj.* [in heraldry] tige.

Béstens, *adv.* in the best manner. Ich werde es — besorgen, I will execute it to the best of my ability.

Bestèppen, *v. tr.* to sew in the manner of a quilt, to quilt, to stitch.

Bestèrnen, *v. tr.* 1) to set or furnish with stars. Der besternte Himmel, the starry sky. 2) to distinguish by stars. Ein besternter Herr, a gentleman decorated with a star, the badge of an order.

Besteúern, *v. tr.* to load with imposts, to tax. Ein Volk —, to impose duties on a nation; der Besteuerte, one that pays taxes.

Besteúerung, *f.* taxation.

Besteuerungsrecht, *n.* the right to tax.

Béstgelegen, *adj.* and *adv.* best situated.

Béstgut, *n.* [-es, *pl.* -güter] [in commerce] the best sort of American tobacco-leaves.

Bésthaupt, *n.* [-es, *pl.* -häupter] [in law] V. Hauptfall.

* **Bestialisch**, *adj.* and *adv.* [having the qualities of a beast] bestial.

* **Bestialität**, *f.* [*pl.* -en] bestiality.

Bestich, *m.* [-es, *pl.* -e] [with shoemakers] bar.

Besticken, *v. tr.* to adorn with embroidery, to embroider.

* **Bèstie**, *f.* [*pl.* -n] beast, brute.

Bestieben, I. *v. intr.* [u. w. seyn] to be sprinkled with dust. II. *v. tr.* to sprinkle with dust, to dust.

Bestiefeln, *v. tr.* to furnish with boots, or to put on boots, to boot. Bestiefelt und bespornt, booted and spurred; sich —, to put on one's boots.

Bestielen, *v. tr.* to furnish with a helve or handle. Eine Axt —, to helve an ax. [in botany] Bestielte Blätter, petiolate or petioled leaves.

Bestieren, *v. tr.* to stare or gaze on.

Bestimmbar, *adj.* and *adv.* determinable, definable. Die Zeit oder Periode ist nicht —, the time or period is not definable.

Bestimmen, I. *v. tr.* 1) to mark accurately. Eine Zeit, eine Stunde, einen Tag —, to fix a time, an hour, a day; sie bestimmten Zeit und Ort zur Zusammenkunft, they appointed a time and place for the meeting; wir können die rechte Zeit dazu nicht —, we cannot determine the proper season for it; einen Begriff —, to define a notion or an idea; eine bestimmte Person, a designated person. 2) [to give a direction to, to influence the choice] to determine. Dieser Umstand bestimmte ihn, die Rechte zu studieren, this circumstance determined him to the study of law. 3) to determine = to decide. Es ist noch nicht bestimmt, was &c., it is not yet decided, what &c. 4) to appoint to a use, purpose &c., to destine. Es war mir vom Schicksal bestimmt, I was doomed to it by fate; er ist es, den die Götter zu unserm Herrscher bestimmten, 'tis he whom the gods have destined to reign over us; wir sind Alle dazu bestimmt, we are all destined to it; ich bin zum Leiden bestimmt, I am doomed to suffer; er hat dieses Geld für die Armen bestimmt, he designed or intended this money for the poor; vorher —, to predestine. II. *v. r.* sich —, to determine, to resolve. Ich habe mich nunmehr dazu bestimmt, I am now resolved upon it.

Bestimmer, *m.* [-s, *pl.* -] he who determines, definer.

Bestímmt, [past part. of Bestimmen] *adj.* and *adv.* 1) fixed, determinate. Am —en Tage, on the appointed day; zur —en Zeit, at the stated time; das Weltall wird durch —e Gesetze regiert, the universe is governed by fixed laws; eine —e Zeit oder Periode, a definite time or period; ein —es Maß, a definite measure; eine —e Regel, a determinate rule; ein —er Ausdruck, a definite term or expression; ich habe keinen —en Wohnsitz, I have no certain abode; zur —en Stunde, at the hour appointed; — [= ausdrücklich], decidedly. 2) certain, sure. —e Nachrichten, certain news; eine —e Erklärung, a positive declaration; dies ist — Ihre Handschrift, this is positively your hand-writing; er wird — kommen, he will certainly come. 3) appointed to a use, destined. — zu, destined for, to; die —e Stunde des Todes, the destined hour of death; —, für unsere Sünden und Irrthümer zu leiden, doomed to suffer for our sins and errors; vorher —, predestinate. 4) [of ships] bound. Das Schiff ist nach Jamaika bestimmt, the ship is bound for Jamaica.

Bestímmtheit, *f.* state of being determinate, certain or precise, determinateness, definiteness. Die — der Wörter und Ausdrücke, the preciseness of words and expressions; sich mit — ausdrücken, to express one's self with accuracy or precision.

Bestímmung, *f.* 1) the act of fixing, determining, determination. 2) the thing determined or defined, definite. 3) definition. 4) [the purpose for which any thing is intended or appointed] destination. Seiner — folgen, to follow one's destiny; sich an den Ort seiner — begeben, to repair to the place of one's destination.

Bestimmungs-begriff, *m.* a defining notion. —**grund**, *m.* [that which determines the choice or moves the will] motive. —**ort**, *m.* [the place to which a thing is appointed] destination. Der —ort eines Schiffes, the place of destination of a ship, the place, where a ship is bound to. —**wort**, *n.* adverb, modifier.

Bèstmöglich, I. *adj.* best possible. II. *adv.* as well as possible.

‖ **Bestöbern**, I. *v. intr.* [u. w. seyn] to be dusty. II. *v. tr.* to sprinkle with dust, to dust.

Bestócken, I. *v. intr.* [u. w. seyn] to get a stalk. II. *v. r.* sich —, to get a stalk or halms.

Bestöpseln, *v. tr.* to cork [a bottle &c.].

Bestößen, *ir.* I. *v. tr.* 1) to press against with force, to push repeatedly; [with combmakers and workers in metal] to rub and smooth with a rough-file; [with joiners and other workers in wood] to work with a jack-plane. Das Bestoßen der Buchstaben, [am. letter-founders] the dressing of letters. 2) to hurt, to injure, to impair by pushing repeatedly. Der Deckel dieses Buches ist sehr —, the cover of this book is much worn out. II. *v. r.* sich —, to be injured or impaired by repeated pushes.

Bestoß-feile, *f.* [with combmakers &c.] rough-file. —**hobel** [= Schrupphobel], [among joiners] jack-plane. —**zeug**, *n.* [with letter-founders] dressing-bench.

Bestráfen, *v. tr.* to punish [an offender, or crime &c.]. Ein Vater bestraft sein Kind wegen Ungehorsam, a father chastises his child for disobedience.

Bestráfer, *m.* [-s, *pl.* -] punisher.

Bestráfung, *f.* punishing, punishment.

Bestráhlen, *v. tr.* 1) to shed light or lightness on, to irradiate. 2) *Fig.* to irradiate = to illuminate.

Bestráhlung, *f.* irradiation.

Bestránden, V. Beschiffen.

‖ **Bestréb**, *m.* [-es] V. Bestreben *n.*

Bestrében, *v. r.* sich —, [to exert physical strength or intellectual power, for the accomplishment of an object] to endeavour. Bei einem Wettrennen bestrebt sich ein Jeder, seinen Gegner hinter sich zu lassen, in a race, each man endeavours to outstrip his antagonist; er bestrebte sich &c., he exerted himself &c., he strove; er bestrebte sich eines schönen Vortrages, he endeavoured after a handsome elocution.

Bestreben, *n.* [-s, *pl.* -] an effort, an exertion of physical strength or the intellectual powers, towards the attainment of an object, endeavour. Sein ganzes — ist darauf gerichtet, all his efforts or endeavours tend towards it; mein stetes — wird seyn, Ihre Zufriedenheit zu verdienen, my constant endeavour shall be, to merit your approbation.

Bestrebsam, *adj.* and *adv.* endeavouring, exerting one's self.

Bestreicheln, *v. tr.* to stroke in a caressing manner.

Bestreichen, *ir. v. tr.* 1) to overspread with a soft or liquid substance Leinwand mit Pflaster —, to spread plaster on linen; eine Wand mit Röthel —, to besmear or bedaub a wall with red chalk; mit Oel —, to anoint with oil, to rub over with oil, to oil; mit Eierweiß —, to smear with the white of an egg, to glair; mit Fett —, to smear with grease or fat, to grease; mit einem Magnete —, to rub or touch with a loadstone. 2) to touch in passing, to brush the surface of a thing in passing. Der Wind bestreicht den Berg, the wind brushes the hill; eine Stadt mit Stücken —, to cannonade a town; bestrichene Winkel —, [in fortification] flanked angles. *Fig.* Jene Anhöhe bestreicht die Stadt, yonder height commands the town.

Bestreifen, *v. tr.* 1) to streak, to stripe. 2) to touch lightly in passing, to brush, to graze.

Bestreitbar, *adj.* and *adv.* contestable, disputable, controvertible.

Bestreiten, *ir. v. tr.* to attack, to fall upon with force. *Fig. a*) to oppose by force, to combat, to contend against. Einen Gegner —, to combat an antagonist; Gründe oder Meinungen —, to combat arguments or opinions; diese Wahrheit kann nicht bestritten werden, this truth is incontestable; der Advokat bestritt jeden Punkt, the advocate contested every point; eine Behauptung —, to dispute an assertion; die Gültigkeit eines Anspruchs —, to dispute the validity of a claim; die Gültigkeit der Lose wird von Einigen bestritten, von Andern vertheidigt, the lawfulness of lots is impugned by some, and defended by others; eine Lehre —, to raise objections to a doctrine. *b*) to effect, to accomplish by the necessary or required physical strength or intellectual powers. Wir können das Unternehmen nicht —, we are not equal to the undertaking; er kann seine Geschäfte nicht —, he is unable to manage his business; die Kosten sind zu groß, er kann sie nicht —, the expenses are too great, he is not able to bear, to defray them, he cannot afford them; mit dieser Summe kann man nicht alle Bedürfnisse —, that sum cannot answer all the occasions; Jemands Bedürfnisse —, to supply a person's wants; er bestritt die Kosten, he bore the charges, he defrayed the expenses.

Bestreiter, *m.* [-s, *pl.* -] 1) one that combats or contests, an opposer, opponent. 2) defrayer.

Bestreitung, *f.* 1) the act of opposing, contesting, disputing &c. V. Bestreiten. *Fig.* Die — der Kosten, the bearing of the charges. 2) argument urged in opposition to any thing.

Bestreuen, *v. tr.* to scatter over, to bestrew. Ein Papier mit Sand —, to besprinkle a paper with sand; etwas Geschriebenes mit Sand —, to strew sand on a writing; der Weg war mit Blumen bestreut, the road was strewed with flowers; mit Zucker bestreut, sprinkled over with sugar.

Bestricheln, *v. tr.* to mark with small strokes.

Bestricken, *v. tr.* 1) to furnish with cords. 2) to surround with knitwork. *Fig.* Die schmeichlerische Zunge ist geschickt, den arglosen Jüngling zu —, the flattering tongue is apt to insnare the artless youth; sie hat sein Herz bestrickt, she captivated his heart.

Bestricker, *m.* [-s, *pl.* -] insnarer.

Bestriemen, *v. tr.* to stream, to stripe.

Beströhen, *v. tr.* to cover [a roof &c.] with straw, to thatch.

Beströmen, *v. tr.* to touch in streaming. Der Fluß beströmt den Fuß des Berges, the river washes the foot of the hill. *Fig* Thränen beströmen seine Wangen, tears run down his cheeks.

Beströmung, *f.* 1) the act of touching in streaming or washing. 2) a stream.

Bestücken, *v. tr.* to furnish [a ship &c.] with cannon. Ein mit 60 Kanonen bestücktes Schiff, a ship mounting 60 guns.

Bestückung, *f.* Die — eines Schiffs, the complement of cannons with which a ship is furnished.

Bestufen, *v. tr.* to furnish with steps.

Bestülpen, *v. tr.* to top [boots].

Bestürmen, *v. tr.* to touch in storming. Wind und Wellen — das entmastete Schiff, winds and waves assault the dismasted ship; eine Stadt —, to storm a town. *Fig.* Einen mit Bitten —, to assail, to importune, to besiege any one with solicitations; Eifersucht und Rachsucht bestürmten sein Herz, jealousy and the thirst of revenge seized his heart, his heart is a prey to jealousy and the thirst of revenge.

Bestürmer, *m.* [-s, *pl.* -] he that storms a town &c., an assaulter.

Bestürmung, *f.* storming, storm, assault.

Bestürzen, I. *v. tr.* 1) to furnish with a cover. Einen Topf —, to cover a pot. 2) to clap on a cover. 3) *Fig.* to perplex with terror, to terrify, to confound, to dismay, to astonish, to throw into consternation, to stupify with amazement [used chiefly in the past part. bestürzt]. II. *v. intr.* [u. w. seyn] to be confounded or perplexed, to be thrown into consternation.

Bestürzt, [past part. of Bestürzen] *adj.* and *adv.* confounded, perplexed, astonished, thrown into consternation, disconcerted. Einen — machen, to confound any one; vor &c. — seyn, to be stupified with &c.

Bestürzung, *f.* astonishment, surprise, consternation. — zeigte sich auf jedem Gesichte, confusion dwelt in every face.

Besuch, *m.* [-es, *pl.* -e] 1) the act of visiting, visit, resort. Einen — machen, ablegen or abstatten, to pay a visit, to make a call; ich mache nicht gern —e, I hate visiting; er macht dort oft —e, he often visits there; der Tag, wo man —e abzustatten or anzunehmen pflegt, visiting-day. 2) the act of frequenting or resorting to often or habitually, frequenting. Der — der Messen, the frequentation of fairs; auf den — gehen, [with hunters] to go in quest of game. 3) visiter, visitor. Ich würde schwerlich einen — finden, I should hardly find a visitor.

Besuch-ameise, *f.* a species of ant [formica migratoria]. **—karte** [Visitenkarte], visiting-card or ticket. **—knecht**, *m.* [with hunters] a huntsman going in quest of game.

Besuchen, *v. tr.* 1) to visit, to call upon [a friend &c.]. Dieser Arzt besucht seine Kranken nie, ohne ihnen etwas zu verschreiben, this physician never visits his patients without prescribing something for them. *Fig.* Die Nahten —, [in seamen's language] to survey or examine the seams. 2) to visit often, to resort to often or habitually, to frequent, to haunt. Die Bierhäuser —, to visit ale-houses; ein Ort, der häufig besucht wird, a place of resort; N. ist ein stark besuchter Vergnügungsort unfern der Hauptstadt, N., in the vicinity of the capital, is a much frequented place of amusement; ein sehr besuchtes Bad, a watering-place greatly resorted to. 3) [with hunters] to go in quest of [game]. 4) [in Script.] to salute with a present. Simson besuchte sein Weib mit einem Ziegenböcklein, [in Script.] Simson visited his wife with a kid. Syn. Besuchen, Aufwarten. Besuchen signifies to visit in a friendly manner, to keep up the interchange of civilities and salutations; Aufwarten, to pay a visit of respect or ceremony.

Besudeln, *v. tr.* to make filthy, to defile, to soil, to foul. Die Kleider —, to dirty one's clothes. *Fig.* Seine Hände mit Blut —, to stain one's hands with blood.

Betadeln, *v. tr.* to blame, to censure, to find fault with. Ein Buch —, to criticize a book; Jemands Ausgaben —, to criticize a man's expenses.

Betäfeln, *v. tr.* to wainscot.

Betagen, I. *v. tr.* 1) to appoint a day. Sich mit Jemand —, to agree upon a certain day with a person; Einen —, to cite or summon any one to appear in court on a certain day. 2) to date [a letter, a deed &c.]. II. *v. intr.* [u. w. seyn] 1) to advance in years [used only in the past part. betagt]. Ein betagter Mann, an aged man; betagt seyn, to be advanced in years. 2) to be due. Die Schuld ist betagt, the debt is due.

Betagung, *f.* 1) the appointing of a day for meeting &c. 2) [the addition to a writing which specifies the year, month and day when it was given or executed] date.

Betakeln, *v. tr.* [in seamen's language] 1) to fit with tackling, to rig. Ein Schiff —, to rig a ship [to fit the shrouds, stays, braces &c. to their respective masts and yards]. 2) Das Ende eines Taues —, to whip the end of a rope.

Betakelung, *f.* [in seamen's language] 1) [the act of fitting with tackling] rigging. 2) [the ropes which support the masts, extend and contract the sails &c. of a ship] rigging. V. Takelwerk.

Betalgen, *v. tr.* to smear with tallow.

‖**Betalpen, Betappen**, *v. tr.* to touch or feel clumsily or indecently, to grope, to fumble, to paw.

Betasten, *v. tr.* to feel, to touch, to handle frequently. Geld —, to finger money. Das Betasten, frequent handling, attrectation. Syn. V. Berühren.

Betäuben, *v. tr.* 1) to stun with noise, to din. Vom Geschrei oder Lärm betäubt, deafened with clamour or tumult; ein zu starker Lärm betäubt die Ohren, too strong a noise stuns the ears. 2) to make senseless, to deprive of sensation, to benumb. Dieser Schlag betäubte ihn, that blow stunned him; ein —des Mittel, [a medicine which stupifies the senses and renders insensible to pain] a narcotic; dieser Wein ist mir zu stark, er betäubt mich, this wine is too strong for me, it makes my feel quite muzzy; der Tabaksqualm in diesem Zimmer betäubt mich, the tobacco-smoke in this room quite stupifies me; diese Ausdünstungen sind höchst betäubend, these exhalations are very narcotic. *Fig.* Die Sinne —, to benumb, to stupify the senses; sein Gewissen —, to overcome the scruples of one's conscience, to silence one's conscience.

Betäubung, *f.* 1) the act of stunning with noise or of causing stupor. 2) [suspension or diminution of sensibility] stupor.

Betäubungsmittel, *n.* a narcotic.

Betaumeln, *v. tr.* to make dizzy or reeling, to giddy. *Fig.* Hochmuth betaumelt ihn, haughtiness intoxicates him.

Betaxen, *v. tr.* to tax [a people], to lay taxes on. In diesem Lande ist Alles betaxt, in this country every thing is taxed.

1. **Bete**, V. Beete.

2. **Bete**, *f.* [*pl.* -n] (from bitten] ‖ 1) V. Bitte. 2) a kind of voluntary donations or services due to any landlord from his tenant.

3. ***Bete**, *f.* [*pl.* -n] [Fr. *la bête*] a term of loss in certain games at cards. — werden, to be beasted or looed.

1. **Betel**, *m.* [-s] [a species of pepper] betel.

2. **Betel**, *m.* [-s] [a sea term] chisel.

Beten, I. *v. intr.* [allied to bitten, perhaps to the L. *petere*] [to address the Supreme Being with solemnity and reverence] to pray. Vor oder nach Tische —, to say grace. *Prov.* Wer nicht — kann, werde ein Schiffmann, he that will learn to pray, let him but go to sea. II. *v. tr.* 1) to recite, to rehearse in prayer. Das Vaterunser —, to rehearse the Lord's prayer; sein Gebet —, to say one's prayers. 2) to ask with prayers.

Bet-bruder, *m.* a person who pretends to be constantly praying, a bigot, a methodist, a devotee. —buch, *n.* V. Gebetbuch. —fahrer, *m.* a pilgrim. —fahrt, *f.* [in the Romish church] pilgrimage. —gemach, *n.* [a close apartment for private devotions] an oratory. —glocke, *f.* the prayer-bell. —halle, *f.* a chapel. —haus, *n.* a place for public worship, an oratory, a chapel. —kammer, *f.* V. —gemach. —saal, *m.* [a room in which divine service is performed] an oratory. —schemel, *m.* a footstool to kneel upon in praying, hassock. —schwester, *f.* a person who pretends to be constantly praying, a devote or devotee, a bigot, a hypocrite. ‖ —sonntag, *m.* rogation-sunday. —stube, *f.* V. —gemach. —stuhl, *m.* [a seat inclosed in a church] a pew. —stunde, *f.* 1) the hour for prayers. 2) prayers in church. —stunde halten, to read prayers. —stundenbuch, *n.* [a book containing the daily services of the Romish church] a breviary. —tag, *m.* fast-day. ‖ —woche, *f.* rogation-week. —zimmer, *n.* V. —gemach.

Beter, *m.* [-s, *pl.* -] one who prays.

Beth, V. Bienenharz and Vorstoß.

Bethwachs, *n.* hive-dross, bee-glue.

Bethätigen, *v. tr.* 1) to set at work. 2) to prove by one's actions. Seine Freundschaft —, to prove one's self an active friend.

Bethauen, *v. tr.* to bedew. Die bethauten Pflanzen, the dewy plants. *Poet.* Ihr Antlitz ist von Thränen bethauet, tears bedew her face.

Betheilen, *v. tr.* Einen —, to give any one his share.

Betheiligen, *v. tr.* to let share or have part. Bei etwas betheiligt seyn, to have a share; wir sind nicht alle bei &c. betheiligt, we are not all interested in &c.; ich bin dabei betheiligt, I have a concern in it; der Betheiligte, one who has a share in common with others, a partaker, a person concerned or interested in any thing.

‡**Bethen**, V. Beten.

Betheeren, *v. tr.* to tar.

Betheuern, *v. tr.* to affirm or aver positively, or with solemnity, to assever, to asseverate. Ich betheuere Ihnen, daß ich keine Kenntniß von der Verhandlung habe, I protest to you, I have no knowledge of the transaction. Die Betheuerung, asseveration, protestation.

Bethören, *v. tr.* to fool, to befool, to infatuate. Die Liebe zu sinnlichen Freuden bethört oft die Menschen, men are often infatuated by a love to sensual pleasure.

Bethränen, *v. tr.* 1) to moisten with tears. Das bethränte Auge, the eye bedewed with tears; er hörte der Erzählung mit bethränten Augen zu, he listened to the story with tears in his eyes. 2) to weep for, to bewail.

Bethun, *ir. v. r.* sich —, 1) to bestir one's self. 2) to soil one's self.

Bethürmen, *v. tr.* to furnish with a tower or with towers.

Beting, V. Bäting.

Betiteln, *v. tr.* 1) to give a title to, to give or prefix a name or appellation. Ein Buch —, to entitle a book. 2) [to dignify by a title or honourable appellation] to title.

Betitelung, *f.* 1) entitling. 2) title.

Betölpeln, *v. tr.* V. Uebertölpeln.

Betonen, *v. tr.* [to utter with a particular stress or modulation of the voice] to accent. Eine Silbe —, to accent a syllable; er betonte die letzten Worte seiner Rede ganz besonders, he gave particular emphasis to, or laid particular stress on the last words of his speech.

***Betonie**, *f.* [*pl.* -n] [a plant] betony.

Betracht, *m.* [-es] the act of considering. In — ziehen, to take into consideration; in diesem —, in this respect; in — seiner langen Dienste, in consideration of his long services; in — der Wohlthaten, welche &c., in respect to the benefits, which &c.; in — des Nachtheils, den die Kirche durch &c. erlitt, in regard of the injury the church received by &c.; in jedem —, on all accounts, in every respect, in all respects.

Betrachten, *v. tr.* to view, to look on or at. Ein Gemählde —, to look on a picture; was betrachten Sie so aufmerksam, what are you looking at with such attention? den Himmel —, to contemplate the heavens. *Fig.* *a*) to fix the mind on, with a view to a careful examination, to consider. SYN. V. Besehen. *b*) [to study, to meditate on] to contemplate. Ein —des [beschauliches] Leben, a contemplative life. *c*) to consider = to view, to think, to look on. Ich betrachte ihn als einen Menschen, der &c., I look on him as a man who &c. *d*) to take into consideration, to consider. Bei jeder Handlung betrachte or bedenke das Ende, in every action reflect upon the end.

Betrachtens-werth, —würdig, *adj.* and *adv.* worthy of consideration, worthy of regard or attention.

Betrachter, *m.* [-s, *pl.* -] considerer, contemplator.

Beträchtlich, I. *adj.* 1) worthy of consideration, worthy of regard or attention, considerable. 2) considerable = important, valuable. Eine —e Summe Geldes, a considerable sum of money. II. *adv.* considerably. Europa gewinnt dabei —, Europe gains considerably by it.

Beträchtlichkeit, *f.* considerableness.

Betrachtsam, *adj.* and *adv.* [given to contemplation] contemplative.

Betrachtung, *f.* the act of viewing or looking on, view. *Fig.* *a*) [= Ueberlegung] Etwas in — ziehen, to take any thing into consideration, to consider it. SYN. V. Ansehung. *b*) [meditation, study, continued attention of the mind to a particular subject] contemplation. *c*) meditation, reflection. —en über etwas anstellen, to meditate on a thing; schwermüthige —en, melancholy reflections; Hiob's —en über &c., Job's reflections on &c. *d*) [holy meditation] contemplation.

Betrachtungs-buch, *n.* book of meditation. —satz, *m.* a theme as an object of meditation. —stelle, *f.* a text.

Betrag, *m.* [-s] the amount [of an account &c.]. Der — dieser Summe beläuft sich auf &c., the total of this sum amounts to &c.

Betragen, *ir.* I. *v. tr.* to cover or spread over the surface. Das Silber —, [am. goldsmiths] to overlay the silver with gold in amalgam with quicksilver. II. *v. r.* sich —, to conduct one's self, to behave, to comport. Sich schlecht —, to behave one's self ill, to misbehave; er betrug sich auf eine ungebührliche Weise, he comported himself insolently. III. *v. tr.* and *intr.* [to rise to, to reach by an accumulation of particulars, into an aggregate whole, to compose in the whole] to amount. Es beträgt fünfzig Thaler, it amounts to fifty dollars; wie viel beträgt es? what is the amount of it?

Betragen, *n.* [-s] behaviour, carriage, deportment, demeanour, personal manners. Ein lobenswerthes —, a laudable conduct; ein freundliches, liebreiches —, affability. V. Anstand.

Betrampeln, *v. tr.* to trample frequently or repeatedly.

‡**Betrauen**, *v. tr.* V. Vertrauen [used only in the past part.] Betraut.

Betrauern, *v. tr.* to mourn for, to bemoan, to deplore. Den Verlust eines Kindes —, to bewail the loss of a child; Einen — or [more usual] um or für Einen trauern, to wear mourning for, to mourn a person.

Beträufeln, *v. tr.* to sprinkle with small drops.

Beträufen, *v. tr.* to bedrop. Fleisch mit Butter oder Fett —, to drip butter or fat upon meat [as it turns upon the spit, in roasting], to baste meat.

Betraut, [past part. of Betrauen] *adj.* and *adv.* trusty. Ein —er Mann, a trustworthy man; ein —er Posten, an office of trust; ein —er Botschafter, an accredited envoy.

Betreff, *m.* [-es] respect, relation, regard, reference, concern, circumstance [mostly joined with in, in the form of an adverb]. In — seiner Ehrlichkeit, with respect to his honesty; in — dieser Angelegenheit, touching this affair.

Betreffen, *ir.* I. *v. tr.* to take unawares, to surprise. Einen auf einer Lüge —, to catch any one in a lie. Betroffen, [past part.] embarrassed, perplexed, confounded. II. *v. intr.* 1) to relate or belong to, to concern. Diese Sache betrifft mich allein, that affair touches me alone; was mich betrifft, concerning me, as to me, as for me; es betrifft sein Leben, his life is concerned. V. Angehen I. *b*). SYN. V. Anlangen. 2) to happen to, to occur to. Das Schlimmste, was mich — kann, the worst that can befall me; es hat ihn ein großes Unglück betroffen, he has met with a great misfortune. Betreffend, relating to, concerning, touching. Diese Sache betreffend, concerning this affair, or as to this affair.

Betreiben, *ir. v. tr.* 1) to drive upon. Die Felder mit den Schafen —, to drive the sheep upon the fields. 2) to drive = to carry on, to prosecute. Einen Handel —, to drive a trade; ein Geschäft —, to carry on a business; Jemandes Angelegenheiten —, to manage any one's affairs; die Art, wie Sie Ihre Studien —, ist durchaus fehlerhaft und tadelnswürdig, the manner in which you conduct your studies is quite faulty and blamable; einen Rechtshandel —, to carry on a suit of law; eifrig —, to urge; wenn Sie die Sache nicht besser —, so wird sie nie ein Ende nehmen, if you don't get better forward this affair, it will never come to an end. 3) [unusual, V. Treiben] to do, to commit [in an ill sense]

Betreibung, *f.* 1) the act of driving upon. 2) *Fig.* pursuit, management.

Betreibungslehre, *f.* V. Lehrart.

Betreten, *ir. v. tr.* 1) to set the foot on, to step upon. Hätte ich doch nimmer diesen Boden Englands —! would I had never trod this English earth! ein Haus —, to enter a house; ein —er Weg, a trodden path; diese Wege, die nie ein Fuß betrat, these ways, where never foot did tread. 2) [to love as the male bird the female] to tread. Der Hahn betritt [tritt] die Henne, the cock treads the hen. 3) to catch, to surprise. Einen auf frischer That or bei der That —, to catch any one in the act. 4) *Fig.* [in the past part.] Betreten, perplexed, embarrassed, puzzled. Ich war über diese Frage zuerst so —, the question at first so staggered me; Sie waren etwas —, you were a little confused.

Betrieb, *m.* [-es] 1) the act of driving cattle upon a place. 2) *Fig.* *a*) the act of driving or carrying on a business &c. Der — der Angelegenheiten einer Familie, the management of the affairs of a family; der — des Buchhandels, [the occupation of selling books] hook-trade. *b*) [influence on the mind] impulse. Auf Jupiters —, by Jove's impulse. || 3) V. Vertrieb.

Betriebskapital, *n.* a fund or capital employed in carrying on any work, business or financial operation.

Betriebsam, *adj.* and *adv.* industrious, active, diligent. Ein —es Volk, an industrious nation.

Betriebsamkeit, *f.* activity, industry.

Betriefen, V. Beträufen.

Betriegen, V. Betrügen.

Betrinken, *ir. v. r.* sich —, to get drunk.

Betröcknen, *v. intr.* [u. w. seyn] to become somewhat dry.

Betroddeln, *v. tr.* to furnish or hang with tassels.

Betroffen, V. Betreffen.

Betroffenheit, *f.* perplexity.

Betröpfeln, *v. tr.* to sprinkle with small drops.

Betropfen, *v. tr.* to bedrop. V. Beträufen.

Betrüben, I. *v. tr.* to make muddy, to trouble [seldom used in this proper sense]. *Fig.* to afflict, to grieve. Sein Tod betrübt mich, his death grieves me; betrübt euch dies nicht? do you not grieve at this? nicht darüber, daß ihr seid betrübt worden, sondern daß ihr seid betrübt worden zur Reue, [in Script.] not that ye were made sorry, but that ye sorrowed to repentance; betrübend, afflictive, distressing. II. *v. r.* sich —, to grieve, to sorrow. Sich über einen Verlust —, to grieve at a loss.

Betrübniß, *f.* [*pl.* -sse], || *n.* [-sses, *pl.* -sse] 1) [the state of being afflicted, a state of pain, distress or grief] affliction. 2) [the cause of continued pain of mind] affliction, calamity, adversity, misfortune, distress.

Betrübnißvoll, *adj.* and *adv.* sorrowful.

Betrübt, [past part. of Betrüben] *adj.* and *adv.* 1) afflicted, grieved. Eine —e Miene, a rueful countenance; die —e Wittwe, the afflicted widow; Hanna sprach, ich bin ein —es Weib, [in Scripture] Hannah said, I am a woman of a sorrowful spirit; — seyn über den Tod eines Kindes, to be afflicted at the death of a child; — über ihren Verlust, grieved at their loss. 2) [expressing grief, having the external appearance of sorrow] sad, downcast, gloomy. Ein —es Gesicht, a sad or gloomy countenance; — aussehen, to look sad or grieved. 3) gloomy, melancholy. —e Gedanken, sad thoughts. 4) [causing grief or sorrow] afflictive, sad, calamitous. —e Nachrichten, melancholy news, sad tidings; ein —es Ereigniß, a distressing event; —e Zeiten, calamitous times.

Betrug, *m.* [-es] cheat, deceit, fraud, deception, imposture. Ein Mensch voller —, a deceitful man; einen — begehen, to practise fraud or deception; Einem einen — spielen, to practise a deceit upon any one, to play a trick upon any one; durch —, by fraud, by deceit, fraudulently; ein frommer —, a pious fraud [practised under the pretence of religion]; ein — der Sinne, delusion.

Betrügen, *ir.* I. *v. tr.* to cheat, to deceive. Jemand in einem Handel —, to deceive or defraud any one in a bargain; Einen im Kartenspiel —, to cheat a person at cards; er hat mich um zehn Thaler betrogen, he has defrauded me of ten dollars; Einen um sein Recht —, to defraud a man of his right. *Prov.* Es ist kein Schalk so verlogen, er wird zuweilen auch betrogen, he that deceives another, is often deceived himself, biters are often bit. *Fig.* to deceive = to delude, to beguile. Die Schlange betrog mich also, daß ich aß, [in Script.] the serpent beguiled me, and I did eat; es betrog seine Hoffnungen, his hopes were deceived; oft betrügt uns ein falscher Schein, we are often deluded by false appearances. II. *v. r.* sich —, to be defeated in one's expectation, hope, desire or intention. Ich fand mich in meinen Erwartungen betrogen, I found myself disappointed in my expectations; ich fand mich in ihm betrogen, I was deceived in him.

Betrüger, *m.* [-s, *pl.* -] -inn, *f.* a person who cheats, a cheat, a cozener, a defrauder, a deceiver, an impostor, a sharper. Ein — im Handel, a cheater.

Betrügerei, *f.* 1) deceitfulness, fraudulence, fraudulency. 2) a cheat, fraud.

Betrügerisch, I. *adj.* [tending to deceive] deceptive, deceptious, deceitful, deceptory. II. *adv.* deceitfully, fraudulently.

Betrüglich, I. *adj.* 1) containing fraud, founded on fraud. Ein —er Handel, ein —er Bankerott, a fraudulent bargain, a fraudulent bankruptcy. 2) tending to deceive, deceptive, deceiving expectations, deceitful, false. Ein —es Versprechen, a deceitful promise; ein —er Schein, a delusive or fallacious appearance; —e Hoffnungen, fallacious or illusory hopes. II. *adv.* deceitfully, fraudulently. — handeln, to practise fraud or deception, to baffle.

Betrüglichkeit, *f.* deceitfulness, fraudulence, fraudulency.

Betrunken, [past part. of Betrinken] *adj.* and *adv.* drunk, drunken, intoxicated, inebriated, tipsy. Ein —er Mensch, a drunken person.

Bett [e], *n.* [-es, *pl.* -en] [seems to be allied to bauen, Bude, wohnen] 1) any place of repose; [with hunters] the lodge of deer. Der Hirsch, der Damhirsch ist im —, the stag is harboured, the buck is lodged. 2) [an article of furniture to sleep and take rest on] a bed. In's —, zu — gehen, sich zu — legen, to go to bed, || to turn in; im —e liegen, to lie a-bed; das — hüten, to keep one's bed; das — machen, to make the bed; am —e, bed-side, at the bed-side; sie kam nie von seinem —, she never quitted his bed-side. *Fig.* Das — der Ehre, the bed of honour; auf dem — der Ehre sterben, to die on the field of battle; [in law] von Tisch und — scheiden, to separate or divorce from bed and board. [in a narrower sense] *a*) the bed = bedstead. *b*) [the furniture of a bed, the materials of a bed] bedding. Das Kopfende des —es, bed-head; das Fußende des —es, foot of the bed; ein — aufschlagen, to put up a bed; ein — mit Vorhängen [Himmelbett], canopy-bed; das königliche —, the royal couch. 3) [the channel of a river, or the part in which the water usually flows] bed; [in mills] leat. 4) [= Stückbett] any raised place on which cannon are planted, a battery.

Bett-bank, *f.* a press-bed, settle-bed. —behänge, *n.* bed-hangings, bed-curtains. —bezug, *m.* V. —überzug. —boden, *m.* the bottom of a bedstead. —decke, *f.* a cover for a bed, a coverlet, counterpane. Eine wollene —decke, a blanket; eine durchnähte or gesteppte —decke, a quilt or counterpoint; eine rauhe —decke, a rug. —drell, *m.* clothing-diaper. —feder, *f.* bed-feather. —flasche, *f.* warming-pan. —franse, *f.* valance. —frau, *f.* bed-maker. —fuß, *m.* [a plant] wild basil. —gardine, *f.* [= —vorhang] bed-curtain. —genoß, *m.* bed-fellow, bed-mate. —geräth, *n.* the furniture of a bed, bedding. —gestell, *n* bedstead. —gras, *n.* many-spiked cotton-grass. —gurt, *m.* bed-girth. —himmel, *m.* [the top-covering of a bed] tester, canopy. —käfer, *m.* V. —wanze. —kammer, *f.* bed-room, bed-chamber. —kasten, *m.* press-bed. —lade, *f.* V. —kasten and —gestell. —lägerig, *adj.* and *adv.* confined to bed by age, infirmity or sickness, bedrid, bedridden. —lägerig seyn, to be sick a-bed, to keep one's bed. —lägerigkeit, *f.* the state of being bedrid. —laken, || —leintuch, *n.* sheet. —leiste, *f.* bedstaff. —linnen, *n.* sheeting-linen, sheeting. —macherinn, *f.* V. —frau. —pfanne, *f.* V. —flasche. —pfoste, *f.* bedpost. —pissen, *n.* pissing in bed. —pisser, *m.* a person that pisses in bed. —rolle, *f.* bedcaster. —sack, *m.* a leather sack used for packing beds in. —säule, *f.* V. —pfoste. —schere, *f.* bedstaff. —schirm, *m.* bed-screen. —schnur, *f.* bed-lace. —schragen, *m.* truckle-bed. —schrank, *m.* wardrobe-bedstead, bed-closet, turn-up bed. †—seicher, *m.* 1) V. —pisser. ||2) *Fig.* V. Kellerassel. —sponde, —statt, —stätte, —stelle, *f.* V. —gestell. —stollen, *m.* bedpost. —stroh, *n.* bedstraw. Unserer lieben Frauen —stroh, [a plant] our Lady's bedstraw. V. also Wegekraut. —stuhl, *m.* bed-chair [for sick persons]. —tisch, *m.* table-bed, bureau-bed. —tische [für Kranke], *pl.* bed tables [for sick persons]. —troddel, *f.* bed-tassel. —tuch, *n.* sheet. —überzug, *m.* the cover for the bedding, pillow-case. —umhang, *m.* bed-hangings, bed-curtains. —vorhang, *m.* bed-curtain. —wanze, *f.* bed-bug, house-bug, wall-louse. —wärmer, *m.* —wärmflasche, *f.* V. —flasche. —wäsche, *f.* bed-linen. —zeug, *n.* the furniture of a bed, bedding, bed-clothes. —zieche, —züge, *f.* bed-tick, pillow-case.

Bettel, *m.* [-s] 1) the practice of asking alms, begging. Er lebt vom —, he lives by begging. 2) any thing worthless, trash, trumpery.

Bettel-arm, *adj.* and *adv.* beggarly, wholly destitute. —brief, *m.* a begging-letter. Durch —briefe sich ernähren, †to live upon the kedge. —brod, *n.* the bread of mendicity. Das —brod essen, to live by begging, to eat the bread of charity. —bruder, *m.* V. —mönch. —bube, *m.* a beggar-boy. —frau, *f.* a beggar-woman. *Fig.* —fürst, *m.* a beggarly prince. —geld, *n.* V. —lohn. —haft, *adj* and *adv.* beggarly. —handwerk, *n.* the business of begging alms. —herberge, *f.* a beggar's inn or haunt, beggar's bush; †kedger's coffee-house. *Fig.* —hochzeit, *f.* a beggarly wedding. *Fig.* —hoffahrt, *f.* beggarly pride. —jude, *m.* a poor jew. —junge, *m.* a beggar-boy. *Fig.* —könig, *m.* a poor king. —läuse, *pl.* 1) hedge parsley. 2) marsh ladies' bed-straw. 3) lesser burdock. 4) common meadow-saffron. —leben, *n* the life of a beggar, mendicity. —leute, *pl.* beggars, mendicants. *Fig.* —lohn, *m.* a miserable payment, a niggardly reward. —mädchen, *n.* a beggar-girl. —mann, *m.* a beggar-man, beggar. —mönch, *m.* a mendicant friar, begging friar. —nonne, *f.* beguin. —orden, *m.* order of mendicant friars. —pack, *n.* beggarly crew. *Fig.*—prinz, *m.* V.—fürst. —sack, *m.* a beggar's bag. *Prov.* —sack wird nimmer voll, a beggar's purse is always empty. —sammet, *m.* plush. —schenke, *f.* beggar's bush. *Fig.* —staat, *m.* contemptible or beggarly finery. —stab, *m.* the condition of a beggar, mendicity, beggary. *Fig.* An den —stab kommen, to be reduced to beggary, to be brought to a morsel of bread; Einen an den —stab bringen, to reduce a man to poverty, to beggar any one. —stand, *m.* mendicity. *Fig.*—stolz, *m.* beggarly pride. *Fig.*—tanz, *m.* dispute, scuffle. —trotz, *m.* a beggar's obstinacy or impertinence, *fig.* low beggarly pride. —vogt, *m.* a low officer employed in watching the beggars, constable, beadle. —volk, *n.* beggarly crew [in a proper and in a fig. sense]. *Fig.* Hochmüthiges —volk, arrogant beggars. —weib, *n.* a beggar-woman. —wirth, *m.* the landlord of a beggar's haunt.

Betteléi, *f.* 1) mendicity, beggary. 2) importunate or abject petition.

Bétteln, [from bitten] *v. intr.* and *v. tr.* 1) to ask or supplicate in charity, to beg or practise begging, to live by asking alms. Sein Brod —, to beg one's bread; — gehen, to go a-begging; sich vom — ernähren, to live by begging; ich schäme mich, zu —, I am ashamed to beg. *Fig.* Die Kunst geht —, arts or sciences yield no great profits. 2) to beg much and frequently, to beg, to crave. Um ein Amt —, to beg for an employ.

Bétten, I. *v. tr.* 1) to make the bed. *Prov.* Wie man sich bettet, so schläft man, you shall have as good, as you bring; do well and have well. 2) to place in a bed, to bed. II. *v. r.* sich —, to get a bed for one's self. Sich zusammen —, to bed together; sich von einander —, to bed asunder.

Béttler, *m.* [-s, *pl.* -] beggar, mendicant. Die —inn, a female beggar, beggar-woman. *Prov.* Einem — ist es leid, wenn er Andere betteln sieht, it's beggar's woe, to see another by the door go; es ist keine Klinge, die schärfer schnitt', als wenn ein — zum Herren wird, set a beggar on horseback and he'll ride a gallop; — mehren, Reiche nähren, beggars breed and rich feed.

Bettler-herberge, *f.* beggar's bush. V. also Bettelherberge. —kraut, *n.* sweet-scented virgin's bower. —läuse, *pl.* V. Klebkraut. —läusekraut, *n.* lesser burdock. —mantel, *m.* 1) the cloak of a beggar. 2) *Fig.* the thorny oyster. —pack, *n.* V. Bettelvolk. —sprache, *f.* beggar's cant.

Béttlerisch, *adj.* and *adv.* beggarly.

Béttung, *f.* 1) the act of making the bed or of bedding. 2) the furniture of beds, bedding. 3) [in fortification and gunnery, any raised place covered with planks on which cannon are planted] platform. 4) [in hydrostatics] a frame of ground-timber. 5) [in seamen's lang.] Die —en, worauf das Schiff ablauft, [pieces of timber which support a ship in running from the stocks] bulgeways.

Betúchen, *v. tr.* to cover with cloth.

Betünchen, *v. tr.* to parget.

Betüpfeln, *v. tr.* to mark with small dots or spots.

Betúpfen, *v. tr.* to mark with dots, to dot.

Betüpfen, *v. tr.* to tip.

Betúschen, *v. tr.* to paint with Indian-ink.

Bétze, *f.* [probably from the Slavon. *bisn*, to run] 1) bitch. 2) V. Metze.

‖ **Beúche**, *f.* [*pl.* -n] [allied to weichen] 1) [the act of soaking cloth in lie for bleaching] bucking. 2) [the cloth or clothes soaked or washed in lie] buck.

‖ **Beúchen**, *v. tr.* to buck [linen &c.].

Beuch-faß, *n.* —‖stunze, *f.* —zuber, *m.* bucking tub.

Beúge, *f.* [*pl.* -n] 1) a bend, a curve, an incurvation. Die Knie—, hock. 2) an instrument of coopers for bending hoops, a bender.

Beúgen, [Goth. and Sw. *buga*, A. S. *bugan*, Dan. böve, allied to the Lat. *pago, pango*] I. *v. tr.* 1) to inflect, to bend. Niederwärts —, to bend downward; die Planken —, [in seamen's language] to bend or supple the planks as by heat or moisture; den Arm —, to bend the arm; das Knie —, to bend the knee; den Kopf —, to bow the head; den Körper —, to incline the body [in acts of reverence or civility], to bow. 2) *Fig. a)* to cast down, to depress, to humble, to mortify. Jemands Hochmuth —, to bring down, to humble any one's pride; dieses Unglück hat ihn gebeugt, this misfortune dejected him; dieser Sieg beugte Roms Stolz, this victory humbled the pride of Rome. *b)* [in grammar] to inflect, to decline. *Fig.* Das Recht —, to warp justice. II. *v. r.* sich —, to bend, to incline. Sich vor Einem or vor Etwas —, to bow down to or before any one or any thing. *Fig. a)* to bend, to bow, or be submissive. Er beugte sich vor dem Willen des Volkes, he was flexible to the will of the people. *b)* to humble one's self. Syn. Beugen, Biegen. Biegen signifies to bend, to incline from a straight line in any direction. Beugen denotes to bend from an erect or perpendicular line, to incline downwards, to become lower.

Beugzange, *f.* [in seamen's lang.] a wooden engine formed like a pair of pincers, and employed to confine the planks of a ship in their places, till they can be nailed or bolted to the timbers.

Beúger, *m.* [-s, *pl.* -] [in anatomy] flexor.

Beúglich, *adj.* and *adv.* [that may be bent] flexible, pliable.

Beúgsam, *adj.* and *adv.* flexible, flexile, pliable, limber. Die Weide ist eine —e Pflanze, the willow is a pliable plant; ein —er Faden, a pliant thread. *Fig. a)* flexible in disposition, pliable, pliant. Das —e Gemüth der Jugend, the flexible mind of youth. *b)* [in grammar] declinable.

Beúgsamkeit, *f.* flexibility, pliableness, pliability, pliancy.

Beúgung, *f.* bend, flexure, incurvation. Die — der Lichtstrahlen, [in optics, a property of light by which its rays, when they approach a body, are bent towards it or from it] inflection. *Fig.* Die — der Stimme, inflection of the voice; — der Kniee [Kniebeugung], genuflection; die — der Nennwörter &c., [in grammar] inflection.

Beúle, *f.* [*pl.* -n] [perhaps from biegen] 1) a swelling occasioned by a contusion, any thing swelled or pushed beyond the surrounding or adjacent surface, a prominence, a protuberance, a bunch, a bump, a lump. Die Kugel machte eine — in seinem Küraſſe, the bullet made a dint in his cuirass; die venerische —, bubo; die — in einem Gefäße, a dint in a vessel. 2) [in architecture] bossage. 3) [in anatomy] process.

Beulenmelone, *f.* V. Warzenmelone.

Beúlig, *adj.* and *adv.* full of protuberances, lumps or dints.

Beúling, *m.* [a sea term] the trough or sausage filled with powder, which communicates the flame from the train to the fire-trunks or powder-barrels in a fire-ship.

Be-úmständen, *v. tr.* to circumstantiate, to detail.

Be-únruhigen, *v. tr.* to disquiet, to disturb. Es beunruhigte die Einwohner dieser Stadt, it disquieted the inhabitants of this town; Parteiungen — den Staat, plots disturb the state; die Annäherung des Feindes beunruhiget uns, we are alarmed at the approach of the enemy; den Feind —, to harass the enemy; das Gemüth —, to disturb the mind; diese Nachricht beunruhiget mich sehr, that news agitates me very much; dies beunruhiget mein Gewissen, this troubles my conscience; ich will Sie nicht —, I'll not disturb you, I'll not put you to any inconvenience.

Be-úrbaren, *v. tr.* [to plow ground the first time] to break up.

Be-úrkunden, *v. tr.* 1) to prove and support with documents. 2) to give the evidence of authenticity, to authenticate, to verify. Die Beurkundung, the act of authenticating, verification.

Beurkundeamt, *n.* notarial office.

Be-úrkunder, *m.* [-s, *pl.* -] a public notary.

Be-úrlauben, I. *v. tr.* 1) to grant leave of absence to. Einen Offizier —, einen Soldaten —, to give leave of absence to an officer, to give furlow to a soldier; ein beurlaubter Soldat, a soldier on furlow. 2) to give leave of departure to. Einen —, to give any one leave to go; der König beurlaubte die Versammlung, the king dismissed the assembly. II. *v. r.* sich —, [in familiar lang.] to take leave, to withdraw. Er beurlaubte sich in aller Stille, (= er stahl sich, schlich sich davon) he took French leave.

Be-úrlaubung, *f.* the act of granting leave of absence. Die — eines Soldaten, the furlowing of a soldier.

Be-úrtheilen, *v. tr.* to form a judgment of, to give one's judgment upon. Eine That nach dem Erfolge —, to judge of an action by the event; kritisch —, to judge critically; eine literarische Arbeit —, to criticise a literary work; Andere nach sich —, to judge others by one's self.

Be-úrtheiler, *m.* [-s, *pl.* -] he that forms a judgment of any thing, especially a person who judges of the merit of a literary performance, a judge, a critic.

Be-úrtheilung, *f.* 1) the act of judging. Die — einer literarischen Arbeit, criticising. 2) judgment, critical examination, critique, critic.

Beurtheilungskraft, *f.* the judicative faculty, judgment, discernment. Ein Mann von gesunder —, a man of sound judgment.

1. **Beúte**, *f.* [either allied to the prov. batten = nutzen, or more probably to the Low Sax. büten = theilen] spoil taken from an enemy in war, booty, prey, spoil, plunder. Auf — ausgehen, to go a-plundering. *Fig.* Er wurde seinen Feinden zur —, he became the prey of his enemies; die Welt ihr Schlachtfeld und das Menschengeschlecht ihre —, the world their field and the human kind their prey; mit — beladen, laden with spoil; [in seamen's language] dieses Schiff hat mehrere —n (Prisen) gemacht, this ship has taken or made several prizes.

2. **Beúte**, *f.* [*pl.* -n] [allied to Butte, Bütte, Gr. πίδος] 1) [with bakers] a large kneading trough. 2) a wooden bee-hive.

1. **Beútel**, *m.* [-s, *pl.* -] [allied perhaps to Butte and 2. Beute] 1) [in mills] a bolter. 2) a pouch or false belly in which some animals carry their young. 3) a small bag or pouch, used to preserve or hold any thing, especially a small

bag in which money is contained or carried in the pocket, a purse. *Fig.* Seinen — spicken, to fill, to line one's purse; aus seinem eigenen — zehren, to live at one's own expense; ein Kluger richtet sich nach seinem —, a prudent man limits his expenses by his income. *Prov.* Nach dem — richte den Schnabel, let your purse be your master. *Fig.* *a*) ‡ the public coffers, the treasury, purse. *b*) [in Turkey, a sum of money, about 50 l. sterling or 600 florins rhenish] a purse.

Beutel-arm, *m.* [in mills] a piece of wood shaking the bolter, the arm of the bolter. —faß, *n.* a cask [used by the gunners on board a ship] with a leather covering, that draws together like a purse. ‡—faul, *adj.* and *adv.* unwilling to part with money. —förmig, *adj.* and *adv.* purse-shaped. —gans, *f.* pelican. —garn, *n.* [in fishing] purse-net. —kammer, *f.* [in mills] bolting-house. —kasten, *m.* [in mills] the box containing the bolter. —krabbe, *f.* V. —krebs. ‡—krank, *adj.* and *adv.* having an empty purse. —krebs, *m.* purse-crab. —meise, *f.* penduline titmouse, mountain-titmouse. —netz, *n.* V. —garn. —perrücke, *f.* a bag-wig. —ratte, —ratze, *f.* the opossum. —schneider, *m.* a cutpurse, purse-cutter, pick-pocket. —schneiderei, *f.* picking pockets, cheating, pilfering, cheat. —schneiderkraut, *n.* [a plant] shepherd's purse. —schnur, *f.* purse-string. —sieb, *n.* [in mills] the bolting-sieve, bolter. —stecken, *m.* V. —arm. —stolz, *m.* pursepride. —stolz, *adj.* and *adv.* purse-proud. —thier, *n.* V. —ratte. —tuch, *n.* bolting-cloth. —werk, *n.* bolting-mill.

2. Beutel, *m.* [-s, *pl.* -] [probably from the old batten = schlagen] [in husbandry] a piece of wood for beating flax, a beater.

3. Beutel, *m.* [-s, *pl.* -] [probably from the Low Sax. biten = beißen] [with joiners and carpenters] dipping-chisel, former.

Beutelig, *adj.* and *adv.* bag-like. Dieser Rock ist —, this coat puckers.

1. Beuteln, *v. tr.* [allied to the old batten = schlagen] 1) [in mills, to sift or separate bran from flour] to bolt. || and † 2) to shake. Er hat ihn tüchtig gebeutelt, he shook him violently or soundly.

2. Beuteln, [from 1. Beutel] *v. r.* and *v. intr.* to pucker, to wrinkle. Dieser Aermel beutelt sich, this sleeve puckers.

1. Beuten, *v. tr.* to make booty. V. 1. Beute.

2. Beuten, *v. tr.* to fill a hive with bees. V. 2. Beute.

Beuten-honig, *m.* the honey of wild bees, wild-honey. —kitt, *m.* bee-glue.

Beutheie, *f.* [Beut is allied to batten = schlagen] V. Pochheie.

Beutler, *m.* [-s, *pl.* -] purse-maker, glover, breeches maker. V. also || Säckler.

[illegible], *m.* [-s, *pl.* -] V. Zeidler.

[illegible], *v. tr.* 1) to provide with a curator [illegible] unden. 2) to provide with a su[illegible] or bailiff.

[illegible], [more usual] Bevölkern, I. *v. tr.* [illegible] with inhabitants, to people, to popu[illegible] vereinigten Staaten [von Nordamerika] [illegible] Auswanderer von Europa bevölkert [illegible] emigrants from Europe have peopled [illegible] d States. *Fig.* Ein Kaninchengehege [illegible] ck a rabbit-warren. II. *v. r.* sich —, to [illegible]

[illegible] kerung, *f.* 1) [the act or operation of [illegible]] population. 2) [the whole number of people [illegible] a country] population. Man schätzt [illegible] ngland auf zehn Millionen Seelen, [illegible] on of England is estimated at ten millions of souls.

Bevölkerungs-liste, *f.* an account of the population of a country. Die —liste aufnehmen [= eine Volkszählung vornehmen], to take the census. —stand, *m.* [the state of a country with regard to its number of inhabitants] population.

Bevollmächtigen, *v. tr.* to give authority, warrant or legal power to, to give a right to act, to empower, to authorize. Ein bevollmächtigter Gesandter, a plenipotentiary; der Bevollmächtigte, a person invested with full power to transact any business, a plenipotentiary commissioner; an attorney, a proxy; durch einen Bevollmächtigten handeln, to act by proxy.

Bevollmächtiger, *m.* [-s, *pl.* -] he that empowers or authorizes, constituent, warranter.

Bevollmächtigung, *f.* 1) the act of authorizing, authorization. 2) warrant, authority.

Bevor, *conj.* [previous to] before.

Bevormunden, *v. tr.* to provide [a minor &c.] with a guardian. Der Bevormundete, a ward.

Bevorrechten, Bevorrechtigen, *v. tr.* to invest with a particular right or immunity, to privilege. Einen —, to grant a prerogative to any one; der Bevorrechtete, a privileged person, a patentee; bevorrechtigte Waaren, patented goods.

Bevorrechtigung, *f.* privileging, privilege.

Bevorrechtigungs-brief, *m.* —schreiben, *n.* a patent.

Bevorreden, *v. tr.* to preface [a book or discourse].

Bevorstehen, *ir. v. intr.* and *v. imp.* to be near, to be approaching [in a figurative sense]. Die Gefahren, welche dem Lande —, the dangers that hang over the country; ein —des Uebel, an impendent evil; eine —de [nahe = drohende] Gefahr, an imminent danger; die —de Woche, next week; die —den Feiertage, the approaching festival.

Bevortheilen, *v. tr.* to overreach, to cheat, to defraud. Er hat ihn bei diesem Handel arg bevortheilt, in this bargain he took great advantage of him.

Bevorthun, V. Zuvorthun.

Bevorworten, *v. tr.* to prologue.

Bevorzugen, *v. tr.* 1) to furnish with the necessary qualities, to qualify. Die Natur bevorzugte ihn hierzu, nature qualified him for it. 2) to give preference to, to prefer, to regard more.

Bewachen, *v. tr.* to watch [a prisoner &c.]. Das Gepäck eines Heeres —, to guard the baggage of an army. *Fig.* Jemands Handlungen oder Bewegungen —, to watch any one's actions or motions.

Bewachsen, *ir. v. intr.* [n. w. seyn] to be overgrown [with herbage, hair &c.]. Mit Gras —, overgrown with grass, grass-grown; mit Moos —, moss-grown, mossy, mossed.

Bewaffnen, *v. tr.* 1) [to cover with whatever will add strength, force or security] to arm. Einen Polstein or Magneten —, to arm a loadstone; Glastafeln —, to overspread tables of glass [with a thin coat of tin]. 2) [in a narrower sense] to arm [the militia &c.]. Vom Kopfe bis zu den Füßen bewaffnet, armed cap-a-pie; die Völker — sich, the nations arm themselves; mit bewaffneter Hand angreifen, to attack with open force. *Fig.* Bewaffne dein Herz gegen Versuchungen, guard thy heart against temptations.

Bewahren, *v. tr.* 1) to save from injury or decay. Den Körper vor Kälte —, to protect the body from cold; ein Haus vor den Flammen —, to save a house from the flames; man bedient sich des Salzes, um das Fleisch vor Fäulniß zu —, salt is used to preserve meat from putrefaction; Jemanden vor einem Verluste —, to preserve any one from a loss; bewahre mich, Herr! vor den Gottlosen, [in Scripture] keep me, o Lord! from the hands of the wicked; die Jugend vor dem Laster —, to preserve youth from vice; bewahre dein Herz vor Versuchungen, guard thy heart against temptations; es bewahret das Gemüth vor Täuschung, it preserves the mind from being imposed on; bewahre deine Lippen vor der Lüge, keep thy lips from telling lies; hiedurch können sie dieselben vor kleinen Fehlern —, by this they may keep them from little faults; sich vor Schaden —, to preserve one's self from injury; Gott bewahre! God forbid! by no means! not at all! 2) to keep. Ein Geheimniß —, to keep a secret; ich werde Ihnen stets dieselben freundschaftlichen Gesinnungen —, I shall always preserve for you the same friendly feelings. Syn. Bewahren, Aufbewahren, Verwahren, Aufheben. Aufheben signifies merely to put a thing into a place where it may not easily be lost or suffer injury. Ich habe einen Brief sorgfältig aufgehoben, means, that I have laid it in a place where I can easily find it again. Bewahren and Aufbewahren imply also an employment of the means necessary to preserve a thing from injury or destruction. One may bewahren [preserve] meat from becoming putrid by salting it, and for this purpose it is usual es aufzubewahren [to keep it] in a cool cellar. Verwahren means, to preserve by putting the thing intended to be kept into such a place of safety, that nothing which might be injurious to it can get at it.

Bewähren, *v. tr.* 1) to evince, establish or ascertain as truth, to prove true, to verify. Die Richtigkeit einer Erklärung —, to prove the truth of a declaration. 2) to ascertain by trial or experience. Eine Pflanze, die sich als heilsam gegen das Fieber bewährt, a plant that proves salutary against fever; das Gerücht hat sich nicht bewährt, the report has not been confirmed; bewährte Zeugnisse, authentic testimonies; bewährte Urkunden, authentical documents; bewährt seyn, to stand proof or the test; ein Mann von bewährter Treue, a man of approved fidelity; ein bewährter Freund, a tried friend. 3) to ascertain the value of [coins &c.]. Das Bewähren, verification, confirmation, proof, test. Syn. V. Erproben.

Bewahrer, *m.* [-s, *pl.* -] 1) one who has the care, custody or superintendence of any thing, especially in compound words, as: Siegel—, keeper of the seal; der Kleider— des Königs [von England], the clerk of king's wardrobe. 2) a preserver, conservator.

Bewährer, *m.* [-s, *pl.* -] one that ascertains as truth, prover.

Bewahrheiten, *v. tr.* to prove true. Eine Sache —, to verify a thing.

Bewährlich, *adj.* and *adv.* provable.

Bewährt, [past part. of bewähren] *adj.* and *adv.* V. Bewähren.

Bewährtheit, *f.* the state of being proved or verified. Die — von Urkunden, the authenticity of documents.

‡ Bewälden, *v. tr.* to convert ground into forest. Ländereien —, to afforest land.

Bewäldet, [past part. of the unusual Bewalden = to cover with wood] *adj.* covered with woods, woody, wooded. —e Berge, woody mountains; ein —er Abhang, a wooded bank.

|| Bewäldrechten, *v. tr.* to roughhew, to square [timber].

1. Bewällen, [from Wall = Erhöhung, Aufwurf, *bank*, *dam*] *v. tr.* [to raise earth about plants] to hill [hops &c.].

2. **Bewállen**, [from wallen = *to walk*] [unusual] *v. tr.* to go visiting.

Bewältigen, V. Ueberwältigen.

Bewálzen, *v. tr.* to press or level with a roller. Ein Feld —, to roll a field.

Bewándern, *v. tr.* to visit wandering. *Fig.* V. Bewandert.

Bewândern, *v. tr.* V. Drapiren.

Bewándert, [past part. of bewandern, fig.] *adj.* and *adv.* acquainted by familiar use or study. Er ist in den besten klassischen Schriftstellern —, he is conversant with the best classical writers; in einer Kunst —, learned in an art; in Sprachen —, versed in languages; er war sowohl in der Baukunst als in der Perspective sehr —, he was well skilled both in architecture and in perspective.

Bewânderung, *f.* V. Drapirung and Draperie.

Bewándniß or **Bewandtniß**, *f.* [*pl.* -sse] and || *n.* [-sses, *pl.* -sse] condition, state, the quality or nature of circumstances [n. with haben, but only in the third person singular]. Es hat damit eine ganz andere —, als Sie glauben, the thing is quite different from what you think; damit hat es eine besondere —, thereby hangs a tale.

Bewándt, [past part. of bewenden] having a certain state or quality, circumstanced. So ist die Sache —, such is the state of the affair; bei so —en Umständen, this being the case.

‡ **Bewáppnen**, V. Bewaffnen.

Bewássern, *v. tr.* to water, to irrigate, to inundate. Eine Wiese —, to water a meadow; Einen Garten —, to irrigate a garden; der Nil bewässert alljährlich die Felder Aegyptens, the Nile every year inundates the fields of Egypt; die Bewässerung, irrigation.

Bewédeln, *v. tr.* 1) to cool and refresh by moving the air with a fan, to fan. 2) to wag at [of dogs].

Bewégbar, I. *adj.* [that may be moved] movable. II. *adv.* movably.

Bewégen, *reg.* and *ir.* I. *v. tr.* to move, to impel. Der Wind bewegte das Schiff oder das Meer, the wind moved the ship or agitated the sea; ich kann die Hand nicht —, I cannot move my hand; von der Stelle —, to stir from the place. *Fig. a)* to move = to persuade, to prevail on, to draw or incline the will to a determination by presenting motives to the mind. Ich wäre froh, wenn ich ihn — könnte, eine Kritik über &c. zu schreiben, I would be glad, if I could persuade him to write a critic on &c.; sie bewogen den Kaiser, den Vertrag zu bestätigen, they prevailed on the emperor to ratify the treaty; sie konnten den König nicht —, den Verbrecher zu begnadigen, they could not prevail with the king to pardon the offender; man konnte ihn nicht —, Theil an dem Streite zu nehmen, he could not be induced to take part in the contest; ich finde mich bewogen, zu verordnen, daß &c., I find myself called upon to order, that &c.; aus —den Gründen, for moving reasons; [in this sense the verb is generally ir.]. *b)* to move = to excite tenderness, pity or grief in the heart, to affect, to touch pathetically, to excite feeling in. Bis zu Thränen bewegt, moved to tears. V. Rühren. *c)* to move = to excite tumult or commotion. Das Volk —, to rouse up the people. II. *v. r.* sich —, 1) [to change place or posture] to move. Die Erde bewegt sich um ihre Achse, the earth moves on its axis; die Vögel — sich in der Luft, birds move in the air; es bewegte sich kein Lüftchen, there was not a breeze stirring. 2) to use action or exercise. Er bewegt sich nicht [more usual: er macht sich keine Bewegung], he takes no exercise.

Bewegemuskel, *m.* [in anatomy] motatory muscle. **Beweggrund**, *m.* [that which moves the will] motive. Starke oder schwache —gründe, strong or weak motives; aus welchem —grunde hat er es gethan? what inducement made him do it? —**kraft**, *f.* motive power or force.

Bewéger, *m.* [-s, *pl.* -] 1) [he that moves] mover. 2) [in anatomy] a muscle.

Bewéglich, I. *adj.* 1) [that which moves] movable. —e Feste, movable feasts [as Easter and all festivals depending thereon]; —e Zeichen, [in astrology] movable signs [Aries, Cancer, Libra and Capricorn]; er hat eine recht —e Zunge, he has a very voluble, glib tongue; er ist ein gar —es Männchen, he is a bustling active little fellow. *Fig.* moving, touching, pathetic, affecting. Eine —e Rede, a moving discourse; ein —er Blick, a moving look. 2) [that which may be moved] movable. —e Güter, movables; eine —e Brücke, a flying bridge. II. *adv.* 1) movably. 2) *Fig.* movingly, pathetically. Seine Stimme, seine Blicke sprechen alle so — für ihn, his voice, his looks all speak so movingly in his behalf.

Bewéglichkeit, *f.* movableness, mobility, volubility. *Fig.* patheticalness.

|| **Bewégniß**, *n.* [-sses, *pl.* -sse] V. Antrieb.

Bewégsam, *adj.* and *adv.* [that may be moved] movable.

Bewégsamkeit, *f.* movableness, mobility.

Bewégung, *f.* movement, motion. Die — eines Rades oder einer Maschine, the movement of a wheel or a machine; in stürmischer — [of the sea], in agitation; einige Maschinen werden durch Federn oder Gewichte in — gesetzt, some machines are moved by springs or weights; eine Mühle in — setzen, to set a mill a-going; die schulrechte [schulgerechte] — eines Pferdes, [in manege] cadence; die —en eines Heeres, the movements of an army; das Heer setzte sich in — und nahm eine Stellung hinter einem Walde, the army moved and took a position behind a wood; die Säfte in — bringen, to stir the humours; er ist immer in —, he is always stirring; sich — machen, to take exercise. *Fig. a)* motion. Eine Sache in — bringen, to put a thing in motion, to set a thing on foot. *b)* a moving of the mind or soul, any agitation of mind or excitement of sensibility. Die — in meinem Innern, the motion in my breast; ihre zitternde Stimme verräth ihre innere —, her trembling voice betrays her emotion. *c)* commotion, disturbance, disorder. Er veranlaßte diese aufrührerischen —en, he occasioned these stirs or riots. *d)* motive, impulse. Er hat es aus eigener — gethan, he did it of his own impulse.

Bewegungs-gesetz, *n.* the laws of motion. —**grund**, *m.* V. Beweggrund. —**kraft**, *f.* the motive power or force. —**kreis**, *m.* [in astronomy] deferent circle or deferent. —**kunst**, *f.* [a mathematical science which shows the effects of powers or moving forces] mechanics. —**lehre**, *f.* that science which treats of the doctrine of motion, mechanics. —**lehrig**, I. *adj.* [pertaining to the principles of mechanics] mechanic, mechanical. II. *adv.* mechanically. —**los**, *adj.* and *adv.* motionless. —**punkt**, *m.* the point of movement. —**trieb**, *m.* momentum. —**ursache** [Beweg-ursache] *f.* motive.

Bewéhen, *v. tr.* to throw or drive a current of air upon.

Bewéhren, *v. tr.* 1) to provide with weapons, to arm. Bewehrt, [in heraldry] armed. *Fig.* Bewehrt seyn, [in seamen's language] to be wind or weather bound. 2) to furnish with a mill-dam, to dam.

Bewéhrung, *f.* 1) arming &c. 2) [in heraldry] the teeth, horns and claws of animals.

Beweíben, *v tr.* to match to a wife, to wive. Sich —, to marry a woman; beweibt, married.

Beweíden, *v. tr.* to feed on, to graze. Das Vieh beweidet die Wiesen, the cattle grazes the meadows.

Beweínen, *v. tr.* to weep, to lament with tears, to bewail. Den Tod eines Vaters —, to bemoan the loss of a father.

Beweinens-werth, —**würdig**, *adj.* and *adv.* deserving sorrow, lamentable, deplorable.

Beweís, *m.* [-ses, *pl.* -se] 1) the act of proving. Den — eines Problems in der Erdmeßkunst führen, to demonstrate a problem in geometry; den — liefern, to furnish evidence. 2) [that degree of evidence, which convinces the mind of the certainty of truth or fact] proof. Ein überzeugender or schlagender —, a convincing proof; ein deutlicher —, ein mathematischer —, a clear proof, a mathematical demonstration; Beweise für die Wahrheit einer Erklärung beibringen, to prove the truth of a declaration; ich erbiete mich, den — zu führen, daß &c., I am ready, to prove, that &c.; ein schriftlicher —, a written proof, evidence; der — durch Zeugen [Zeugenbeweis], proof by witnesses; ein direkter or unmittelbarer —, a direct evidence; ein indirekter or mittelbarer —, ein künstlicher — [Beweis durch Umstände, Anzeigenbeweis, in law], circumstantial evidence; Beweise für eine Sache zusammengenommen, [in law] evidence; er hat uns Beweise seines Muthes gegeben, he showed himself a man of courage, he gave us proofs of his courage; ein — der Freundschaft, a token of friendship.

Beweis-artikel, *m.* 1) [in law] a point concerning which a witness' evidence is taken. 2) V. —punkt. —**führer**, *m.* the person who produces proofs and argues upon them, arguer, demonstrator. —**führung**, *f.* arguing, demonstration. —**grund**, *m.* a reason offered in proof, to convince the mind, argument. —**kraft**, *f.* the power of demonstrating. Diese Urkunde ermangelt aller —kraft, [in law] this document is wholly void of authenticity; der Zeuge hat hier keine —kraft, [in law] this witness' evidence cannot prove the fact. —**mittel**, *n.* a means to prove any thing. —**punkt**, *m.* [in logic] argument. —**schrift**, *f.* any official or authoritative paper containing proof for information, and the establishment of facts, a document. —**stelle**, *f.* a quotation adduced for the sake of authority. —**stück**, *n.* any thing, circumstance, document, writing &c. which contains proof, evidence. —**zeuge**, *m.* [in law] a witness who proves a fact.

Beweísbar, *adj.* and *adv.* provable, demonstrable.

Beweísen, *ir.* I. *v. tr.* 1) to prove = to show, to manifest. Dieser Tag wird es —, this day will prove it; nichts beweist vollkommener die Verdorbenheit der Menschen, als &c. nothing evinces the depravity of men more fully, than &c.; es beweist, wie irrig die gewöhnliche [illegible] nung ist, it proves how erroneous is the common opinion; Sie haben mir viel Gutes bewiesen, you have shown me much goodness; Einem [illegible] —, to show mercy to any one. 2) to prove = to evince; to establish or ascertain as truth, reality or fact, by testimony or other evidence; *it.* to show or prove to be certain, to demonstrate. Der [illegible] ger muß die Wahrheit seiner Aussage —, the plaintiff must prove or establish the truth of his declaration; einen Satz aus der Sittenlehre —, to demonstrate a proposition in ethics; eine Aufgabe in der Erdmeßkunst —, to demonstrate a problem in geometry. II. *v. r.* sich —, to act in a certain manner. Sich sehr gütig gegen Einen —, to show any one a great deal of kindness; er hat sich als Mann von Muth bewiesen, he has shown himself a man of courage.

Beweíslich, *adj.* and *adv.* provable, demonstrable.

Beweísthum, *n.* [-es, *pl.* -thümer] proof, argument.

Beweißen, *v. tr.* V. Weißen.

Bewénden, *ir. v. intr.* [used only in the infinitive joined with lassen, and as past part.] Es dabei — lassen, to leave a thing at rest, to leave it as it is, to be satisfied, to acquiesce; gut denn, ich lasse es bei Ihrem Urtheile —, well, I leave it to your decision. Das Bewenden, the leaving of a thing at rest; dabei hat es sein —, there the matter rests. V. Bewandt.

‖**Bewèrb**, *m.* [-es, *pl.* -e] endeavour to attain or acquire a thing, business.

Bewèrben, *v. r.* sich —, to use efforts to obtain. Sich um ein Frauenzimmer —, to woo, to court a lady; sich um ein Amt —, to sue for an office, to canvass for an office; Hunderte — sich um dieses Amt, hundreds court this place; sich um einen Freund —, to canvass for a friend; er hat sich um ihre Stimmen für seinen Freund beworben, he canvassed their votes for his friend.

Bewèrber, *m.* [-s, *pl.* -] candidate, suitor, wooer. Ein — um das Amt eines Scheriffs, a candidate for the office of a sheriff.

Bewèrbung, *f.* suing for, courting. Die — um ein Amt, the suing for an office.

Bewèrfen, *ir. v. tr.* to strike or cover with something thrown. Einen mit Steinen, mit Koth —, to pelt any one with stones, with dirt; eine Mauer mit Kalk —, to plaster a wall.

Bewèrkstelligen, *v. tr.* to effect, to effectuate, to bring to pass, to bring about, to accomplish. Die Bewerkstelligung, effecting, execution, performance.

Bewíckeln, *v. tr.* to envelop, to enwrap, to cover by wrapping. Bäume mit Stroh —, to wind straw about trees.

Bewílligen, *v. tr.* to grant, give or yield, to concede. Eine Pension —, to allow a pension; er bewilligte die nöthigen Summen, he granted the necessary sums; Gott bewilligte sein Verlangen, God granted him his request; die bewilligte Sache, grant.

Bewílligung, *f.* 1) the act of granting, a bestowing, grant, concession. 2) allowance, license or liberty granted, permission.

Bewíllkommen, *v. tr.* to welcome, to receive kindly. Die Bewillkommung, welcome, kind reception of a new comer.

Bewímmern, *v. tr.* Etwas —, to whine over a thing.

Bewímpeln, *v. tr.* to furnish with pendants.

Bewínden, *ir. v. tr.* to cover by winding, to wind round.

Bewindhaber, *m.* [in seamen's lang.] director of a trading company, administrator, manager, master.

Bewínseln, *v. tr.* to whimper [at a thing].

Bewírkbar, *adj.* and *adv.* effectible, practicable, feasible.

Bewírken, *v. tr.* to produce as a cause or agent, to effect. Bewirkt durch &c., caused, occasioned by &c.

Bewírklichen, *v. tr.* to realize [a scheme or project]. V. Verwirklichen.

Bewírthen, *v. tr.* to entertain, to treat at table, to treat. Er hat uns für unser Geld sehr gut bewirthet, he treated us very well for the money; man könnte Sie wohl besser, aber nicht herzlicher —, better cheer you may have, but not with better heart; der Gastfreie macht sich ein Vergnügen daraus, seine Freunde zu —, the hospitable man delights in the entertainment of his friends. Die Bewirthung, [the receiving and accommodating of guests, either with or without remuneration] entertainment.

Bewírther, *m.* [-s, *pl.* -] [he who receives company out of hospitality or for remuneration] entertainer.

Bewírthschaften, *v. tr.* to conduct the affairs of a place. Eine Meierei —, to manage a farm.

Bewírthschafter, *m.* [-s, *pl.* -] [one who has the management of a farm &c.] manager.

Bewítthum, *n.* [-es, *pl.* -thümer] V. Witthum.

Bewítthumen, *v. tr.* to provide with a jointure.

Bewítzeln, *v. tr.* to treat with light wit. Er bewitzelt Alles [in contempt], he sneers at every thing.

Bewóhnbar, *adj* and *adv.* habitable. —e Welten, habitable worlds.

Bewóhnbarkeit, *f.* habitableness.

Bewóhnen, *v. tr.* to live or dwell in, to inhabit. Die Bewohnung, [act of inhabiting] habitation.

Bewóhner, *m.* [-s, *pl.* -] -inn, *f.* inhabitant. Der — eines Hauses, the inhabitant of a house; die — eines Landes, einer Stadt, eines Dorfes, the inhabitants of a country, a town or a village.

Bewólben, *v. tr.* to vault.

Bewólken, *v. tr.* to overspread with a cloud or clouds. Der Himmel ist bewölkt, the sky is clouded. *Fig.* Gram bewölkte sein Auge, sorrow clouded or dimmed his eyes.

Bewóllen, *v. tr.* to cover with wool.

Bewórfeln, *v. tr.* to cover by shoveling.

Bewúnderer, *m.* [-s, *pl.* -] admirer.

Bewúndern, *v. tr.* to admire [any one's skill, beauty, talents &c.].

Bewunderns-werth, —würdig, *adj.* and *adv.* admirable.

Bewúnderung, *f.* admiration. Mit — erfüllt, or von — ergriffen, struck with admiration.

Bewunderungs-werth, —würdig, *adj.* and *adv.* admirable. Der —würdige Bau des Körpers, the admirable structure of the body. —würdigkeit, *f.* admirableness.

Bewúrden, *v. tr.* [unusual] to dignify, to promote. Eine bewürdete Person, a graduate.

Bewúrf, *m.* [-es] a covering of plaster, plastering.

Bewúrzeln, *v. intr.* [u. w. seyn] to strike root, to root.

Bewúrzelt, [from the unusual *v. tr.* Bewurzeln = to furnish with roots] *adj.* having roots. Ein stark —er Baum, a tree with many or strong roots.

‖**Bewúßt**, *m.* [-es] V. Wissen.

Bewúßt, *adj.* and *adv.* 1) known. Es ist Jedermann —, every one knows it; die —e Sache, the matter in question. 2) [knowing from memory, knowing by conscience, or internal perception or persuasion] conscious. Mir ist die Sache nicht —, I am not conscious of the fact; es ist mir nicht —, daß ich ein Aergerniß gegeben hätte, I am not conscious of having given an offence; ich bin mir keiner Schuld, keines Verbrechens —, I am unconscious of any fault or crime; ich bin mir meiner nicht —, I am not conscious to myself; sich einer Sache — seyn, to recollect a thing.

Bewußt-los, *adj.* and *adv.* having no mental perception, unconscious, senseless. —losigkeit, *f.* the state of being unconscious, unconsciousness, senselessness. —seyn, *n.* 1) [the knowledge of sensations and mental operations, or of what passes in one's own mind] consciousness. Er hat alles —seyn verloren, he has quite lost his senses; er ist ohne —seyn, he has lost all consciousness, he has fallen into complete senselessness. 2) [internal sense or knowledge of guilt or innocence] consciousness. Ich werde mich im —seyn meiner Tugend stets glücklich fühlen, I shall ever be happy in the consciousness of my virtue.

* **Bey** *m.* [-'s, *pl.* -s] [in the Turkish dominions, a governor of a town or particular district of country] Bey.

Bey, *prep.* and *adv.*, and compound words beginning with Bey-, V. the more usual Bei, Bei-.

Bezácken, *v. tr.* to indent, to notch, to jagg. Den Rand des Papiers —, to indent the edge of paper.

Bezáhlbar, *adj.* and *adv.* [that may or ought to be paid] payable.

Bezáhlen, *v. tr.* to pay [one's creditors, the army &c.]. —, was man kauft, to pay for what one buys; bar —, to pay ready money; Einem eine Waare mit barem Gelde —, to pay any one in cash for a commodity; eine Zeche —, to pay a reckoning; eine Schuld —, to discharge a debt; einen Wechsel —, to answer a bill of exchange; er kann [seine Gläubiger] nicht —, he is insolvent; er hat seine Gläubiger bezahlt, he discharged his creditors; ich bin noch nicht für meine Arbeit bezahlt worden, I am not yet paid for my labour; sich bezahlt machen, to get paid. *Fig.* Ich habe ihn mit gleicher Münze bezahlt, I paid him in his own or in the same coin; das ist nicht mit Geld zu —, [in fam. lang.] it is beyond all price; die Schuld der Natur —, to pay the debt of nature, to die; Güte mit Vernachlässigung —, to repay kindness with neglect; die Menschen — oft ihre Versehen mit dem Leben, men often pay for their mistakes with their lives; ich will euch — ! I'll pay you! Syn. V. Abtragen.

Bezáhler, *m.* [-s, *pl.* -] [one that pays] payer. Ein guter oder schlechter —, a good or bad paymaster.

Bezáhlung, *f.* 1) [the act of paying] payment. Bare —, prompt payment. 2) pay. Der Kaufmann erhält seine — für verkaufte Waaren, the merchant receives pay for goods sold.

Bezáhmbar, *adj.* and *adv.* tameable, tractable, manageable. *Fig.* governable.

Bezáhmen, I. *v. tr.* to tame [a lion &c.]. *Fig.* to restrain, to guide, to govern, to keep in due subjection. Seine Leidenschaften —, to bridle one's passions; — Sie Ihre ungestümen Wünsche, moderate your violent desires; bezähmet euren Zorn, restrain your anger. II. *v. r.* sich —, to be master of one's self, to have the command or control of one's own passions, to govern one's self.

Bezáhmer, *m.* [-s, *pl.* -] tamer, subduer.

Bezáhnen, *v. tr.* V. Zahnen.

Bezánken, *v. tr.* to quarrel about a thing, to contest, to dispute.

Bezaúbern, *v. tr.* to charm, to enchant. Ein bezauberter Wald, an enchanted forest. *Fig.* to delight to the highest degree, to charm, to ravish with pleasure. Ihre Schönheit bezaubert mich, her beauty enchants me; weibliche Schöne bezaubert den unvorsichtigen Jüngling, female beauty fascinates the unguarded youth; er ist ganz von ihr bezaubert, he is quite bewitched with her; wir sind von der Musik bezaubert worden, we were enchanted with the music; die Unterhaltung bezauberte uns, we were charmed with the conversation; der Reiz der Dichtkunst bezaubert unsere Seelen, the charms of poetry bewitch our souls; eine —de Stimme, an enchanting voice; die Dame singt auf eine —de Weise, the lady sings enchantingly; diese Gegend ist —d schön, this landscape is enchantingly beautiful. Die Bezauberung, [the act of enchanting, the state of being enchanted] enchantment.

Bezäumen, *v. tr.* to bridle [a horse].

Bezäunen, *v. tr.* to inclose with a hedge. Ein Feld oder einen Garten —, to hedge or fence a field or a garden.

Bezéchen, I. *v. tr.* to make drunk, to fuddle. II. *v. r.* sich —, to get drunk or tipsy.

Bezeichnen, *v. tr.* 1) to mark [a horse, a hat &c.]. Einen Selbstlauter mit einem Accente —, to accent or accentuate a vowel; irrig oder falsch —, to mark erroneously. *Fig.* Ich habe Sie zur Ausführung dieses Unternehmens bezeichnet, you are the person I designated for the execution of this enterprise. 2) to fill with drawings [a paper]. 3) to show by the finger or by other means, to point out, to indicate. *Fig.* to indicate, to denote, to signify, to express. Diese einzige That bezeichnet seinen Charakter, this single act shows his character; dieses Benehmen bezeichnet deutlich seine innere Schlechtigkeit, this conduct indicates clearly his inward wickedness; die allgemeine Ruhe in diesem Lande bezeichnet eine kräftige Regierung, the general tranquillity in this country is a proof of a strong government; dieses Wort bezeichnet ein &c., this word signifies a &c.; ein —des Wort, an expressive word; du sollst ihnen den Weg — auf den &c., thou shalt show them the way in which &c.; genau —, to give exact direction.

Bezeichnung, *f.* the act of marking, designation, mark, sign. Die — der Selbstlauter mit Accenten, accentuation; die — eines Landstreichers, the description of a vagabond.

Bezeichnungszettel, *m.* [a little piece of paper, or a title, affixed to a bag or bottle, expressing its contents] a label.

Bezeigen, I. *v. tr.* to prove by deed, to show. V. Erzeigen. Seine Freude —, to express one's satisfaction, to demonstrate one's joy; Einem Liebe —, to express love to any one; seine Dankbarkeit —, to testify one's gratitude. II. *v. r.* sich —, to act, to behave. Er hat sich sehr gütig gegen mich bezeigt, he showed me a great deal of kindness.

Bezeihen, *ir. v. tr.* to accuse of. Einen des Hochverraths —, to charge any one with high treason. V. also Bezichten or Bezichtigen.

Bezétteln, *v. tr.* to affix a label to. Waaren —, to label goods.

Bezeugen, *v. tr.* 1) to bear witness, to testify, to attest. Die Wahrheit einer Thatsache —, to attest the truth of a fact. *Fig.* Die Ruinen von Palmyra bezeugen seine ehemalige Pracht, the ruins of Palmyra attest its ancient magnificence. 2) to attest = to call to witness.

Bezeúgung, *f.* attestation, testimony, witness.

Bezeugungseid, *m.* [in law] an oath, by which any thing is attested.

|| **Bezícht**, *m.* [-es, *pl.* -e] V. Bezichtigung.

Bezíchten, Bezíchtigen, *v. tr.* to accuse of. Jemanden eines Diebstahls —, to charge a man with theft; Einen der Unwahrheit —, to impute a falsehood to any one.

Bezíchtigung, *f.* the act of accusing, imputation. Ich weiß nicht, was Sie zu dieser Bezichtigung berechtigt, I don't know what grounds you have for thus accusing one.

Beziehen, *ir.* I. *v. tr.* 1) to draw one thing upon or over another. Ein Tonwerkzeug —, to string an instrument of music; ein Bett —, to furnish a bed with clean linen; ein Kopfkissen — [überziehen], to case a pillow; Schamröthe bezog [more usual überzog] ihr Antlitz, a blush suffused or mantled her cheeks. *Fig.* Ein Volk mit Krieg — [überziehen], to make war upon a nation; etwas auf sich —, to take a thing for one's self. 2) to resort to a place. Die Jahrmärkte —, to frequent the fairs; eine Wohnung —, to enter a lodging; das Beziehen [die Beziehung] einer Wohnung, the entering of a lodging; ein Lager —, to encamp; einen Posten —, to occupy a post. 3) to get, to gain possession of. Er bezieht einen großen Gehalt, he receives a high salary; Geld —, to draw money; er bezieht monatlich eine Guinee, he has a guinea a month; diese Schriften sind bei &c. zu —, these writings are to be had at &c.; er bezieht diese Waaren aus England, he procures these commodities from England; einen Wechsel —, to get the payment of a bill of exchange; der Bezogene, [in commerce, the person on whom an order or bill of exchange is drawn] drawee. II. *v. r.* sich —, 1) to be covered. Der Himmel bezieht [überzieht] sich, the sky clouds over. 2) to refer to, to make an appeal to. Er bezieht sich auf mich, he makes an appeal to me. 3) to allude to, to have reference to by intimation without naming. Ich beziehe mich auf eine wohlbekannte Thatsache, I refer to a well-known fact. 4) to respect, to have relation. Viele Stellen der Schrift — sich auf die besondern Gebräuche der Morgenländer, many passages of Scripture refer to the peculiar customs of the Orientals; aber sie — sich nicht auf den Gegenstand, but they are not relevant to the subject.

Bezieher, *m.* [-s, *pl.* -] [in commerce, he who draws a bill of exchange] drawer.

Beziehlich, I. *adj.* having relation, respecting, relative. Ein —es [beziehendes] Fürwort, [in grammar] a pronoun relative; ein —er Begriff, [in logic] a relative notion. II. *adv.* relatively.

Beziehung, *f.* 1) the act of covering, stringing &c. V. Beziehen. 2) *Fig.* *a*) relation = reference, respect, regard. In — auf &c., in relation to. *b*) [connection between things, mutual respect, or what one thing is with regard to another] relation. Unsere —en zu einer Familie, our relations to a family; dieser Herr und diese Dame stehen in sehr vertrauten —en zu or mit einander, this gentleman and this lady stand in very close connection with one another; unsere —en zu fremden Staaten or zum Auslande, our foreign relations.

Beziehungsbegriff, *m.* a relative notion.

Bezielen, *v. tr.* to aim at.

Beziffern, *v. tr.* to mark with ciphers. *Fig.* Der bezifferte Baß, [in music, that bass which, while a certain chord or harmony is continued by the parts above, moves in notes of the same harmony] the figured bass.

Bezimmern, *v. tr.* [to shape by cutting or hewing] to hew [timber].

Bezirk, *m.* [-es, *pl.* -e] [zirk is allied to the Lat. *circus*, and to the Gr. γῦρος &c.] 1) [the limit or boundary of a space] compass. 2) circuit, district. Städte und Länder werden in —e eingetheilt, cities and countries are divided in districts.

Bezirksamt, *n.* the jurisdiction of a certain district. —**gericht**, *n.* an inferior court of justice, a court, the jurisdiction of which is limited to a certain district of no great extent.

Bezirken, V. Begrenzen.

* **Bézoar**, *m.* [-s, *pl.* -e] [Arab. *bedzahar* signifies any antidote or counter-poison] bezoar, bezoar-stone. Der gegrabene —, fossil-bezoar; der mineralische oder künstliche —, bezoar mineral; mit — versetzte Arzneien, bezoardics.

Bezoarsäure, *f.* [in chymistry] bezoardic acid.

Bezoárdisch, *adj.* bezoardic.

Bezóllen, *v. tr.* to impose a toll or duty on.

Bezüchtigen, *v. tr.* V. Bezichtigen.

Bezúckern, *v. tr.* to sugar [a cake &c.].

Bezug, *m.* [-es, *pl.* -züge] 1) that which is drawn upon something. Der — einer Geige, the strings of a violin; ein — Saiten, a set of strings. 2) relation, reference. In — auf &c., in relation to; — auf etwas nehmen, to refer to a thing; dies hat — darauf, this is in relation to it.

Bezugnahme, *f.* V. Beziehung 2. *a*). Mit — nahme auf &c., with reference to &c.

Bezüglich, *adj.* and *adv.* relative.

Bezwácken, *v. tr.* to pinch off. [in a figurative sense] †Jemands Nahrung —, to pinch any one of his meat.

1\. **Bezwécken**, *v. tr.* [from Zweck, *m.* or Zwecke, *f.* = peg, pin] to beset with small nails, pegs or tacks, to peg.

2\. **Bezwécken**, *v. tr.* [from Zweck, *m.* = aim, end] to aim at, to have in view. Ich bezweckte dabei nichts anderes, als &c., I had no other object in view than &c.; das kann nichts —, that can lead to no result.

Bezweifelbar, *adj.* and *adv.* questionable.

Bezweifeln, *v. tr.* to doubt of, to question. Ich bezweifle die Wahrheit dieser Nachricht, I doubt of the truth of this news, I hold it questionable; das ist nicht zu —, there can be no doubt about it, no doubt of it.

Bezwingbar, *adj.* conquerable.

Bezwingen, *ir. v. tr.* to overcome, to subdue, to vanquish. Er hat den Feind bezwungen, he overcame the enemy; Länder —, to conquer countries. *Fig.* Er bezwang seine Leidenschaften, he conquered his passions; ihre Schönheit bezwingt jedes Herz, her beauty overcomes every heart; sich —, to be master of one's self, to have the command or control of one's passions. Die Bezwingung, subduing, conquering.

Bezwinger, *m.* [-s, *pl.* -] overcomer, vanquisher, subduer.

Bezwinglich, *adj.* conquerable, superable.

Bezwisten, *v. tr.* [unusual] to bring into dispute or litigation, to dispute.

Bibel, *f.* [*pl.* -n] [from the Gr. βίβλια, Mid. Lat. *biblia, ae, f.*] the Bible, Scripture, the Book.

Bibelsabschnitt, *m.* a section of a chapter of the Bible. —**ausdruck**, *m.* a scriptural expression. —**ausgabe**, *f.* an edition of the Bible. —**ausleger**, *m.* an interpreter or explainer of the Bible. —**auslegung**, *f.* exegesis. Die —auslegung betreffend, exegetical. —**erklärer**, *m.* V. —ausleger. —**feind**, *m.* an opponent of the Bible. —**fest**, *adj.* and *adv.* Scripture-proof. Der —feste, Scripturist. —**freund**, *m.* an assiduous reader of the Bible, a true and ardent admirer of the Bible. † or ‡ —**husar**, *m.* V. —reiter. —**kenntniß**, *f.* biblical knowledge. —**lehre**, *f.* scriptural doctrine. —**mäßig**, *adj.* and *adv.* scriptural. Ein —mäßiges Wort, a scriptural word. † or ‡ —**reiter**, *m.* [a] nickname of a preacher, whose sermons are stuffed with passages of the Bible. —**sprache**, *f.* scriptural language. —**spruch**, *m.* a scriptural sentence. —**stelle**, *f.* a passage of the Bible. —**verehrer**, *m.* V. —freund. —**werk**, *n.* a bi[ble] with explanatory notes and commentations o[f] work containing the Bible in several languages, a polyglot Bible. —wort, *n.* a scriptural word. —wortweiser, *m.* [a dictionary in which the principal words used in the Scripture are arranged alphabetically] concordance.

Biber, *m.* [-s, *pl.* -] [Ice. *bifr*, Lat. *fiber*, Slav. *bobr*, seems to be allied to Weber, *faber* &c. In Allemanic bobbern signifies hämmern = to hammer or beat hammering] [an amphibious quadruped of the genus castor] the beaver.

Biber=bau, *m.* the lodge or habitation of a beaver. —baum, *m.* [a tree] swamp magnolia. —ente, *f.* the dun-diver. —falle, *f.* beaver-trap. —fang, *m.* the catching of beavers. —fänger, *m.* one who catches beavers. —fell, *n.* the fur of the beaver, beaver. —geil, *n.* castor. —haar, *n.* the hair of the beaver. —hund, *m.* V. Otternhund. —hut, *m.* a beaver. —jagd, *f.* beaver hunting. —klee, *m.* marsh-trefoil, bog-bean. —kraut, *n.* V. Fieberkraut. —ratte, —ratze, *f.* V. Bisamratte. —schwanz, *m.* 1) the tail of the beaver. 2) *Fig.* a flat tile. —schwarz, *n.* [with dyers] a particular black. —taucher, —vogel, *m.* V. —ente. —wamme, *f.* beaver's womb. —wurz, *f.* V. Fieberwurz.

***Bibliognosie**, *f.* [*pl.* -en] bibliognosy. V. Bücherkenntniß.

***Bibliograph**, *m.* [-en, *pl.* -en] [one skilled in literary history] bibliographer. V. Bücherkenner.

***Bibliographie**, *f.* [*pl.* -en] bibliography. V. Bücherkunde.

***Bibliographisch**, *adj.* and *adv.* bibliographic, bibliographical.

***Bibliomane**, *m.* [-n, *pl.* -n] [one extremely fond of books] bibliomaniac. V. Büchernarr.

***Bibliomanie**, *f.* bibliomania. V. Büchersucht, Bücherwuth.

***Bibliothek**, *f.* [*pl.* -en] library. V. Büchersammlung.

***Bibliothekar**, *m.* [-s, *pl.* -e] librarian. V. Bücheraufseher.

Biblisch, *adj.* biblical, scriptural. —e Geschichten, Scripture-histories.

***Biblist**, *m.* [-en, *pl.* -en] scripturist, biblist.

Bickbeere, *f.* V. Heidelbeere.

Bicke, V. Picke.

Bickelhäring, V. Pickelhäring and Pöckelhäring.

Bicken, V. Picken.

Bicksand, *m.* [-es] scouring sand.

Bieder, *adj.* [old G. biderb, from bei and derb] 1) ‡ useful. 2) virtuous, honest, upright, generous.

Bieder=herz, *n.* an honest, upright heart; *fig.* an honest, upright man. —herzig, *adj.* and *adv.* upright, honest. —mann, *m.* an upright, honest man. —männisch, —sinnig, *adj.* and *adv.* honest, virtuous, noble-minded. —sinnig handeln, to deal fairly and honestly. —sinn, *m.* an honest, upright, generous disposition. —wesen, *n.* an honest, upright, virtuous character.

Biederkeit, *f.* —sinn, *m.* [-es] honesty, uprightness, probity.

Biegbar, *adj.* supple, flexible, pliant.

Biege, *f.* [*pl.* -n] V. Beuge.

Biegefall, *m.* [in grammar] case.

Biegeln, V. Bügeln.

Biegen, [allied to fügen, pochen] *ir.* I. *v. tr.* to bend, to curve, to inflect. Den Arm —, to bend the arm; eine Klinge —, to bend the blade of a sword; einen Draht krumm —, to crook a wire; eine gebogene Linie, a curved line, a curve; einwärts gebogen, [in seamen's lang.] out of winding; ein einwärts gebogenes Blatt, [in botany] an inflected leaf; ein gebogener Lichtstrahl, [in optics] an inflected ray. V. Beugen. II. *v. intr.* [u. w. seyn] to bend, to inflect. *Prov.* Besser ist — als brechen, better to bow than break. III. *v. r.* sich —, 1) to bend, to crook, to be curving. Der Baum biegt sich unter seiner Last, the tree bends under the load. *Fig.* Sich schmiegen und —, to creep and crouch, to cringe. 2) to bend = to incline, to lean or turn. Der Weg biegt sich gegen Westen, the road bends to the west.

Biegzange, *f.* [with workers in metals] wire-pliers.

Biegsam, *adj.* easy to be bent, supple, flexible, ductile. Ein —er Faden, a pliant thread; die Weide ist eine —e Pflanze, the willow is a pliable plant; der —e Rüssel des Elephanten, the elephant's lithe proboscis. *Fig.* Eine —e Sprache, a pliant or flexible tongue; ein —es Gemüth, a flexible mind, *it.* a manageable character; ein —es Wesen, pliant manners. V. Beugsam.

Biegsamkeit, *f.* pliability, flexibility, pliableness. *Fig.* Die — des Charakters, flexibility, pliancy of temper.

Biegung, *f.* 1) the act of bending. 2) a bend, curve, flexion, crook [of a road or river &c.]. 3) [in grammar] V. Umendung.

Biene, *f.* [*pl.* -n] [Sw. *bi*, Engl. *bee*, A. S. *beo*; is said to come from the A. S. *byan* = bauen; more probably it may belong to the root of wehen = sich bewegen] 1) a bee. Die männliche —, a drone; die —n in den Stock thun, die —n einfassen, to hive bees. *Prov.* Wer sich an —n, Fluß und Dornen nicht will wagen, wird weder Honig, Fisch, noch Rosen davon tragen, or wer Honig lecken will, muß den Stachel der —n nicht scheuen, the honey is sweet, but the bee stings. 2) [in astronomy, a southern constellation] the fly.

‖ **Bienen=baum**, *m.* V. Maserle or Weißerle. —beute, *f.* V. —stock. —brod, *n.* 1) [the pollen of flowers collected by bees, as food for their young] bee-bread. 2) V. —harz. —brut, *f.* the young bees, skaddons. —erz, *n.* [in mining] alveolar ore. —falk, *m.* honey-buzzard. —falter, *m.* the phalæna, tin-melonella. —fänger, —fraß, —fresser, *m.* [a bird that feeds on bees] bee-eater. —fasser, *m.* a sack or vessel to take bees in. —feind, *m.* V. —fänger. —flug, *m.* the quantity of bees kept at any place. —garten, *m.* bee-garden. —halter, *m.* one who keeps bees, bee-master. —harz, *n.* bee-glue, propolis, hive-dross. —haube, *f.* V. —kappe. —haus, *n.* bee-house, a stand for bee-hives, an apiary. —heide, *f.* marsh-ledum. —hütte, *f.* V. —stand 1). —käfer, *m.* [in entomology, a division of the genus Attelabus] clerus. —kappe, *f.* a cap worn by those who have the management of bees. —kasten, *m.* a box which serves as a habitation for bees. —kitt, *m.* V. —harz. —klee, *m.* the creeping white trefoil, dutch clover. —könig, *m.* —königinn, *f.* queen-bee. V. Weiser. —korb, *m.* bee-hive. —kraut, *n.* V. Honigblume. —lager, *n.* a number of bee-hives. —laus, *f.* a species of louse [pediculus apis]. —mann, —meister, *m.* bee-master, hiver. —meise, *f.* blue titmouse, nun. —milbe, *f.* a species of tick [acarus gymnopterorum]. —mutter, *f.* queen-bee. V. Weiser. —pflege, *f.* the care and cultivation of bees. —pfleger, *m.* V. —vater. —reich, *adj.* and *adv.* rich in bees. —salbe, *f.* V. —schminke. —saug, *n.* V. Kuhpolei. —schauer, *m.* V. —stand 1). —schminke, *f.* a salve, with which the inside of bee-hives is smeared. —schwalbe, *f.* V. —fänger. —schwarm, *m.* a swarm of bees. —specht, *m.* V. —fänger. —stand, *m.* 1) a stand or shed for bees, an apiary. 2) a stock of bees. —stock, *m.* bee-hive. —vater, *m.* bee-master, hiver. V. ‖ Zeidler. —volk, *n.* the bees. —wabe, *f.* V. Honigwabe. —wachs, *n.* bee's wax. —wärter, *m.* V. —vater. —wirth, *m.* one who keeps bees. —wolf, *m.* V. —fänger. —zelle, *f.* a cell in a bee-hive, alveol, alveolus. —zucht, *f.* the rearing and management of bees.

Biener, *m.* [-s, *pl.* -] V. [the more usual] Bienenvater.

‖ **Biensaug**, *m.* [-es] V. [stinkender] Waldandorn.

Bier, *n.* [-es, *pl.* -e] [A. S. *bear* [Meth], Fr. *bière*, is said to be allied to βρύζειν, brate, braue] beer. — brauen, to brew beer; — schenken, to sell beer, to keep an ale-house; ‖ zum [‖ zu] —e gehen, to go to the ale-house; braunes —, brown ale; dünnes —, small-beer. V. Halbbier, ‖ Kofent; ungehopftes oder starkes, süßes —, Weizenbier, ale; weißes —, pale ale; starkes —, strong beer, † stout; starkes, bitteres —, porter; das dicke —, muddy beer, † tap-lash.

Bier=ähnlich, —artig, *adj.* and *adv.* like beer. —bank, *f.* 1) ale-bench. 2) V. —haus. —bann, V. —zwang. —bottich, *m.* beer-vat, ale-vat. —brauen, *n.* the brewing of beer. —brauer, *m.* a brewer [of beer], porter-brewer. —brauerei, *f.* a brewery. —bruder, *m.* 1) a drinker of beer. 2) *Fig.* ale-knight. —esel, *m.* 1) a spectre haunting ale-houses. 2) [a bird] the golden oriole. 3) a drunken fellow. —essig, *m.* vinegar made of beer. —faß, *n.* a beer-barrel. —fiedler, *m.* [in a proper and in a figurative sense] an alehouse-fiddler, a scraper. —flasche, *f.* beer-bottle, ale- or porter-bottle. —gast, *m.* a customer in a beer-house. —gefäß, *n.* a beer-barrel. —geld, *n.* 1) a duty paid by the sellers of beer. 2) beer-money, drinking-money. —glas, *n.* a beer-glass. —hahn, *m.* V. —krahn. —haus, *n.* ale-house, beer-house. —hefe, *f.* barm. ‡—held, *m.* one who drinks beer to excess. —hold, —holer, *m.* V. Goldamsel. —kanne, *f.* pitcher for beer, ale-pot. —karre, *f.* a dray-cart. —kegel, *m.* V. —wisch. —keller, *m.* 1) beer-cellar, ale-cellar. 2) [in some parts of Germany] a tavern [especially connected with a large beer-cellar] where beer is retailed. †—kneipe, *f.* pot-house. —koster, *m.* ale-taster. —krahn, *m.* a beer-cock. —kranz, *m.* V. —schild. —krug, *m.* 1) a beer-jug. ‖ 2) *Fig.* an ale-house. —kuffe, *f.* beer-back. V. —bottich. ‖ and †—lümmel, beerswiller. —maß, *n.* a measure for ale. —meile, *f.* V. —zwang. —molken, *f.* posset. —pfahl, *m.* V. —zeichen. —pfennig, *m.* a duty on beer or ale. —probe, *f.* ale-tasting. —prober, *m.* ale-taster. —rausch, *m.* the state of being inebriated with beer. —rechnung, *f.* ale-shot. —reisig, *n.* V. —wisch. —schank, *m.* the right of retailing beer, retail of beer. —schenk, *m.* ale-house-keeper. —schenke, *f.* a beer-shop, a beer-house, an ale-house. —schild, *n.* an alehouse-sign. —schröter, *m.* a beer-porter. —steuer, *f.* a tax on beer. V. also Tranksteuer. —stube, *f.* ale-room, tap-room. —suppe, *f.* beer-soup, ale-berry. —tonne, *f.* beer-barrel. —trinker, *m.* a drinker of beer or ale. —verkauf, *m.* selling of beer. —wirth, *m.* alehouse-keeper. —wirthinn, *f.* ale-wife. —wisch, *m.* a bush [as a sign of an ale-house]. —würze, *f.* wort. —zapfer, *m.* the tapster. —zeche, *f.* ale-shot. —zeichen, *n.* the sign of an ale-house, ale-stake, ale-post. —zins, *m.* —zinse, *f.* V. —steuer. —zwang, *m.* the monopoly of selling beer within a certain district.

Biest, **Beest**, *n.* [-es, *pl.* -e] [Lat. *bestia*] a beast.

Biest=butter, *f.* [Biest allied to the Gr. πῦος,

from φύω] butter prepared from beestings.

Biester, *m.* [-s] [among painters, a sort of brown colour] bister.

‖ **Biestern**, *v. intr.* to wander about, to stray about.

Biestlauch, *m.* [-es] [Biest allied probably to Bin(e)] cut-leek.

Biestmilch, *f.* [in husbandry] the beestings.

Bieswurm, *m.* [-es, *pl.* -würmer] V. Bremse.

‖ **Biet**, *n.* [-es, *pl.* -e] [from Bauen] [in carpentry] any scaffolding.

Bieten, [allied to the Lat. *petere*, and *vitare* and *in-vitare*; in Low-Sax. beden signifies gebieten and darbieten] *ir. v. tr.* [to present for acceptance or rejection] to offer. Einem die Hand, den Arm —, to offer one's hand, one's arm to a person; Einem einen Trunk —, to tender or to offer a draught or drink to any one; Einem die Hände —, to offer one's aid, protection or assistance to any one; Einem hülfreiche Hand —, to offer to lend any one a helping hand; Einem Schläge —, to threaten any one with blows; Einem den Rücken —, to turn one's back upon any one; Einem die Spitze —, to make head against any one; Trotz —, to bid defiance; der Vorsehung Trotz —, to dare, to brave providence; Schach —, [at chess] to give check; ein Unglück bietet dem andern die Hand, misfortune succeeds to misfortune; das dürfte mir Niemand — [= zumuthen], I would not suffer that from any one; einen guten Morgen —, to bid good morrow; Einem so und so viel — [als Bezahlung, Preis], to offer = to bid, as a price; ich bot zehn Thaler für einen Ring, I offered ten dollars for a ring; auf etwas —, to bid for; Waaren feil —, to offer or expose goods for sale.

Bieter, *m.* [-s, *pl.* -] bidder.

‖ **Biez**, *m.* [-es, *pl.* -e] [from the same root as Butz] a teat, a dug, the nipple.

‖ **Biezen**, *v. intr.* to draw the breast, to suck.

* **Bigamie**, *f.* bigamy.

* **Bigótt**, *adj.* and *adv.* bigot, bigotted.

* **Bigotterie**, *f.* bigotry.

* **Bijou**, *n.* a jewel, toy, trinket.

* **Bijouterie**, *f.* [*pl.* -en] toys, trinkets, jewelry, jewellery.

Bijouterie-handel, *m.* the jeweller's or toyman's trade. —laden, *m.* jeweller's shop, toy-shop. —waaren, *pl.* jewellery, toys and trinkets.

* **Bijoutier**, *m.* [-s, *pl.* -s] a jeweller.

* **Bilánze**, *f.* [*pl.* -n] **Bilánz**, *f.* [*pl.* -en] [in commerce] balance. Die — ziehen, to draw balance.

‖ **Bilchmaus**, *f.* V. Haselmaus.

Bild, *n.* [-es, *pl.* -er] [A. S. *bilith*, Dan. Billede, Sw. *belaetie*, old G. *bilide*; probably from bei and the obsolete Leit = Gesicht, Gestalt, V. Antlitz] 1) [a representation or similitude of any person or thing, formed of a material substance] *a*) image. Ein aus Stein, Holz oder Wachs geformtes —, an image wrought out of stone, wood or wax; ein in Stein ausgehauenes —, ein steinernes Stand—, Stein—, a statue; ein bronzenes or ehernes [Stand-] —, a bronze-statue; das hölzerne — eines Heiligen, the wooden image of some saint; das — eines Mannes in Gyps, the figure of a man in plaster; das zweite Gebot verbietet den Bilderdienst, the second commandment forbids the worship of images. *b*) [the likeness of any thing on canvass] a picture, a resemblance painted, an image. Ein wohlgetroffenes —, a picture that is like; das — ist dem Originale sehr ähnlich, the picture is very like the original; dieß ist sein — [= Bildniß], this is his portrait; Einen im —e hängen oder verbrennen, to hang or burn any one in effigy; die —er in einem Kartenspiele, the coat-cards. *c*) [in manufactures, a design or representation wrought on damask, velvet and other stuffs] a figure. Das — angeben, [with weavers] to tell the pattern. *d*) [any copy, representation or likeness] image. Das Kind ist das — seiner Mutter, the child is the image of his mother; dieser Knabe ist das leibhafte — [Eben—] seines Vaters, this boy is the very picture of his father. *Fig. a*) the shape or external appearance of a thing, form. Die Gestalt der Dinge zeigt sich unter einem schrecklichen —e, the face of things a frightful image bears. *b*) [an idea, a representation of any thing to the mind, a picture drawn by fancy] image. *c*) [= Beschreibung] Der Dichter hat ein vortreffliches — von dem Kummer entworfen, the poet has drawn an exquisite picture of grief. *d*) [in dancing, the several steps which the dancer makes in order and cadence, considered as they form certain figures on the floor] figure. *e*) [in rhetoric, a mode more beautiful and emphatical than the ordinary way of expressing the sense] a figure of speech, metaphor. In —ern sprechen, to speak figuratively; voll —er, full of metaphors. *f*) [in music] a running or variation. *g*) = emblem, symbol, type. Der Hund ist das — [Sinnbild] der Treue, the dog is the emblem of fidelity. 2) [in famil. lang. or poet., especially in compound words, as: Manns—, Frauen— &c.] a person or thing. Ein häßliches —, an ugly person.

Bild-anbeter, V. Bilderanbeter. —anbetung, V. Bilderanbetung. —former, *m.* one that gives form or fashion to a mass of matter, image-maker. —formerkunst, *f.* plastic art —gestell, *n.* pedestal. —gießer, *m.* a founder of statues. —gießerei, *f.* the art of founding statues. —graber, *m.* a graver of figures or images. —hauer, *m.* a sculptor, statuary. —hauerarbeit, *f.* statuary. —hauereisen, *n.* a sculptor's chisel or graver. —hauerkitt, *m.* badigeon. —hauerkunst, *f.* statuary, sculpture. —hauerschule, *f.* an academy of sculpture. —los, *adj.* and *adv.* without figures or images. —säule, *f.* 1) statue. V. also Standbild. Eine —säule zu Pferde, zu Fuß, an equestrian statue, a pedestrian statue. 2) [in architecture] supporter. —schnitzer, *m.* carver. —schnitzerkunst, *f.* carving, sculpture. *Fig.* [in fam. lang.] —schön, *adj.* and *adv.* very beautiful. Ein —schönes Mädchen, ein —schönes Kind, ein —schöner Mensch, a very beautiful girl, child, youth. —seite, *f.* the obverse or face of a coin. —stecher, *m.* engraver. —stecherkunst, *f.* engraving. —stein, *m.* figurate stone. —werk, *n.* 1) imagery. 2) the work of sculpture, carving and the like, figures. —wirker, *m.* V. Damastweber. —wirkerei, *f.* V. Damastarbeit.

Bildbar, *adj.* and *adv.* that may be easily formed or moulded to a different shape. *Fig.* V. Bildsam.

Bildchen, *n.* [-s, *pl.* -] a small image or picture.

Bilden, *v. tr.* to give form or fashion to a mass of matter, to shape, to mould or fashion into a particular shape or state, to figure. Früchte aus Wachs —, to form fruits of wax; ein wohlgebildeter Mensch, a well-shaped man; die —den Künste, plastic arts; die —de Hand des Schöpfers, the plastic hand of the Creator. *Fig. a*) to imagine, to fancy. *b*) to mould by instruction and discipline, to mould, to form. Einen Jüngling —, to form a youth; gute Offiziere —, to make good officers; er hat sich nach großen Mustern gebildet, he has formed himself upon great models; den Verstand —, to cultivate the mind; gebildet, instructed in arts, learning and civil manners, civilized; ein sehr gebildeter junger Mann, an accomplished young man; ein sehr gebildetes Frauenzimmer, an accomplished lady; das Herz —, to improve the heart; sich —, to improve or cultivate one's mind. *c*) [in grammar, to make by derivation or by affixes and prefixes] to form [a verb &c.]. Das Bilden, V. Bildung.

Bildes-kraft, *f.* plastic virtue. —kunst, *f.* plastic art.

Bilder, *pl.* of Bild.

Bilder-achat, *m.* figurate agate. —anbeter, *m.* [one who worships images] iconolater [a name given to the Romanists]. —anbetung, *f.* image-worship, iconolatry. —aufseher, *m.* the overseer, inspector or superintendent of a picture-gallery. —beschreibend, *adj.* iconographic. —beschreiber, *m.* iconographer. —beschreibung, *f.* iconography. —bibel, *f.* a bible with figures or prints. —blende, *f.* a niche for a statue. —bogen, *m.* a sheet of paper filled with figures or prints [for children]. —buch, *n.* a book with prints, picture-book. —cabinet, *n.* a collection of pictures and prints. —deutung, *f.* iconology. —diener, *m.* iconolater. V. —anbeter. —dienst, *m.* iconolatry. V. —anbetung. —feind, *m.* one who rejects the use of images in religious worship. —fibel, *f.* an abecedary with figures or prints. —form, *f.* [with potters] pattern. —fuß, *m.* pedestal. —gallerie, *f.* —gang, *m.* picture-gallery. —gemach, *n.* V. —cabinet. —gerüst, —gestell, *n.* [the frame on which painters place their canvass] easel. —halle, *f.* V. —gallerie. —handel, *m.* trade in pictures or prints. —händler, *m.* a dealer in pictures or prints. —kammer, *f.* V. —cabinet. —kenner, *m.* a connoisseur in pictures or prints. —krämer, *m.* 1) a dealer in figures or prints of little value. 2) [in contempt] a dealer in old pictures and prints. —krieg, *m.* a dispute between the Greek and Romish church about the worshipping of images. —kunde, *f.* V. —lehre 1). —laden, *m.* the shop of a dealer in pictures and prints. —leer, *adj.* and *adv.* void of figures. —lehre, *f.* 1) iconology. 2) the art of representing moral truths by allegories. —liebhaber, *m.* an amateur of pictures or paintings. —los, *adj.* and *adv.* containing no figures or pictures. —mann, *m.* V. —händler. —marmor, *m.* figurate marble. —rahmen, *m.* the frame of a picture. —reich, *adj.* and *adv.* rich in images or imagery. *Fig.* Eine sehr —reiche Beschreibung, a description highly figurative. —saal, *m.* V. —gallerie. —sammlung, *f.* a collection of pictures or paintings. —schatz, *m.* a rich collection of pictures or paintings. —schrift, *f.* hieroglyphics. —sprache, *f.* metaphorical expressions, figurative style. —stein, *m.* formed stone. —stuhl, *m.* pedestal. —stürmend, *adj.* inconoclastic. —stürmer, *m.* iconoclast. —stürmerei, *f.* the act of breaking images. —verehrer, *m.* a worshipper of images, iconolater. —verehrung, *f.* iconolatry. —voll, *adj.* and *adv.* full of images.

Bildern, *v. intr.* 1) to look at the pictures or prints in a book. 2) [rather unusual] to speak figuratively.

Bildhauerei, *f.* [*pl.* -en] sculpture.

Bildlich, I. *adj.* 1) [representing by resemblance] figurative, metaphorical. Ein —er Ausdruck, a figurative expression. 2) typical. II. *adv.* 1) figuratively. 2) typically, symbolically, metaphorically. — vorstellen, to typify.

Bildner, *m.* [-s, *pl.* -] —inn, *f.* a that forms or shapes, an image-maker, a artist, sculptor, statuary. *Fig.* one who cul or improves. Der — unserer Sitten, he th lishes our manners.

Bildnerkunst, Bildnerei, *f.* plastic art, sculpture.

Bildniß, *n.* [-sses, *pl.* -sse] 1) [the picture or representation of a person, and especially of a face, drawn from life] an image, portrait, likeness. Ein geschmeicheltes —, a flattered likeness; ein nach dem Leben gezeichnetes —, a portrait drawn from life; du sollst dir kein — machen, [in Script.] thou shalt not make to thyself any graven image; ihr schiefmäuliges —, her wry-mouthed portraiture; Einen im Bildnisse hängen, to hang any one in effigy. 2) [rather unusual] the work of a sculptor or founder of statues.

Bildniß-mahler, *m.* portrait-painter. —**mahlerei**, *f.* a portrait-painting.

Bildsam, *adj.* and *adv.* that may be easily formed or moulded to a different shape. —es Wachs, pliant wax. *Fig.* Ein —es Gemüth, a pliant or ductile mind.

Bildsamkeit, *f.* [in a fig. sense] pliantness.

Bildschnitzerei, *f.* V. Bildschnitzerkunst.

Bildstecherei, *f.* V. Bildstecherkunst.

Bildung, *f.* 1) the act of forming, formation. *Fig.* Die — des Verstandes, der Sitten, the cultivation or culture of the mind, the polishing of manners. 2) *Fig.* *a*) form, structure, organization. *b*) the form of the head or the human body, shape. Ein Frauenzimmer von zierlicher —, a lady of an elegant figure; ein Mensch von guter —, a man of a good figure. *c*) formation of manners, instruction, education. — habend, instructed in arts, learning and civil manners; eine feine —, a polite education; gelehrte —, classic learning; ein Mann, ein Frauenzimmer von vollendeter —, an accomplished man, an accomplished female.

Bildungs-anstalt, *f.* [a place of education] a school. —**fähig**, *adj.* and *adv.* capable of being instructed, educated or civilized. —**kraft**, *f.* the plastic virtue [of nature]. —**lehre**, *f.* the doctrine of the physical laws, zoonomy. —**los**, *adj.* and *adv.* V. Ungebildet. —**mangel**, *m.* want of instruction, education or civilization. —**trieb**, *m.* [in physic] the forming principle or forming impulse in generation [a law of nature assumed by Blumenbach]; *fig.* this principle applied to that power of the mind which gives birth to new images.

Billespiel, *n.* V. Beilkespiel.

Billketafel, *f.* V. Beilketafel.

Bill, *f.* [allied to Wille, Gr. βούλομαι, L. *velle*] 1) law. 2) [a form or draft of a law, presented to a legislature, but not enacted] a bill.

***Billard**, *n.* [*pron.* Billjarr] [allied to Ball] 1) billiards. 2) billiard-table. V. Ball and Balltafel.

Billard-kugel, *f.* billiard-ball. —**spiel**, *n.* V. Billard 1). —**spieler**, *m.* billiard-player. —**stock**, *m.* cue.

1. **Bille**, *f.* [*pl.* -n] [allied to Pfeil, Bolze] [a pin on which a ruddle turns] pivot. 2) [in mills] a pick-axe for sharpening mill-stones.

2. **Bille**, *f.* [*pl.* -n] [allied to Pfahl] [in seaman's language] Die —n des Schiffes, buttocks.

Billen, *v. tr.* [in mills] to sharpen [millstones].

***Billet**, *n.* [pron. Billjétt] [-s, *pl.* -e] a small paper or note in writing, a short letter addressed to some person, a note, billet.

Billig, [from Bill = Gesetz] *adj.* and *adv.* just, equitable, fair. Eine —e Vertheilung des Besitzthumes, an equitable distribution of the estate; eine —e Foderung, a reasonable claim; eine —e [gerechte] Entscheidung, an equitable decision; der Held wird — belohnt, the hero is justly rewarded; — [gerecht] richten, to judge right; es ist nicht mehr als —, 'tis but just; diese Maßregel muß alle —e Leute befriedigen, this measure must satisfy all fair men; ein —er Vorschlag, a fair proposal; sein Anerbieten ist —, his offer is fair; —er Weise, justly, fairly, of right; wir müssen seine Foderung —er Weise bewilligen, we must, in equity, allow his claim; zu einem —en [= mäßigen] Preise, at a reasonable rate; ein —er Ueberschlag, a moderate computation.

Billigen, *v. tr.* 1) to find just and fair. 2) [to admit the propriety of] to approve. Wir — die Maßregeln der Regierung, we approve the measures of the administration; ihr billiget die Thaten eurer Väter, you allow the deeds of your fathers; die Eltern billigten die Heirath, the parents gave their consent to the marriage. Die Billigung, approbation, approval.

Billigkeit, *f.* 1) equity, equitableness, justice, right. Die — einer Entscheidung, the equitableness of a decision; die — eines Vertrags, the fairness of a contract. 2) justice, a just regard to right or claim, equity. Der — gemäß, in equity. 3) reasonableness, moderation. Die — einer Foderung, the reasonableness of a demand.

Billigkeitsgericht, *n.* [in England] court of equity.

Billing, *m.* [-es, *pl.* -e] 1) [a fish] a species of cyprin [cyprinus aspius]. 2) [a plant] a species of melochia.

Billion, *f.* [*pl.* -en] [from the Lat. *bis*, zweimahl] [a million of millions] billion.

Bilse, *f.* [*pl.* -n] [Bohem. *blje*, Dan. *bulme*] black or common henbane.

Bilsen-kraut, *n.* V. Bilse. —**öl**, *n.* an oil expressed from the seed of the henbane. —**pflaster**, *n.* a plaster composed of the juice of the henbane. —**salbe**, *f.* a salve composed of the juice of the henbane.

Bilz, *m.* V. Pilz.

‖**Bimmel**, *f.* [*pl.* -n] a small sounding bell.

‖**Bimmeln, Bimbeln**, *v. intr.* 1) to ring small bells. 2) to sound [said of small bells].

Bimsen, *v. tr.* to rub with pumice.

Bimsstein, *m.* [-es, *pl.* -e] [A. S. *pumigstan*, probably from the Lat. *pumex*, which is allied to *spuma* = Schaum] pumice, pumice-stone.

Binde, *f.* [*pl.* -n] 1) a band, fillet, ligature; [in surgery] a fillet, roller, swath, [used in dressing or binding up wounds] a bandage, ligature, fascia. Den Arm in der — tragen, to wear one's arm in a sling. 2) a piece of cloth worn round the head &c. Eine Hals—, a cravat, stock; eine Kopf—, a band for the head, bandeau; eine Leib—, a sash. 3) something resembling a bandage. *a*) [in heraldry, a band or girdle] fesse. *b*) [in architecture] band, fascia, face or plinth. 4) [that which unites two things] [in anatomy] the name of some ligaments.

Binde-balken, *m.* V. Bindbalken. —**baum**, *m.* V. Heubaum. —**kalk**, *m.* mortar prepared of gypsum, Roman cement. —**los**, *adj.* and *adv.* having no band or bandage, without a ligature. —**messer**, *n.* V. Bandmesser. —**mittel**, *n.* 1) [any substance capable of uniting bodies in close cohesion] cement; [in medicine] agglutinants. 2) [in building, a stronger kind of mortar] cement. —**scheide**, *f.* the sheath for the addice of the coopers. —**sohle**, *f.* a sandal. —**sparren**, *m.* [in carpentry] V. Binder. —**stein**, *m.* V. Binder. —**strich**, *m.* ligature. —**werk**, *n.* V. Bindwerk. —**wort**, *n.* [in grammar] conjunction. —**zeichen**, *n.* the hyphen. —**zeug**, *n.* 1) implements for binding up something. 2) a surgeon's case. —**ziegel**, *m.* [in architecture] pilaster-brick.

Binden, [allied to winden, wenden, Lat. *vincio*, Gr. σφίγγειν] *ir.* I. *v. tr.* 1) to tie, to bind, to fasten with a knot. Grobe Leinwand um die Lenden —, to gird the loins with sack-cloth. 2) to tie together, to fasten, as with a band, cord or any thing that is flexible. Reben an kleine Pfähle gebunden, vines bound to small stakes. *Fig.* to bind = to oblige by a promise or any moral tie, to engage; *it.* to tie, to oblige, to constrain. Die Ehre bindet ihn, honour ties him; durch einen Eid gebunden, bound by an oath; wir sind durch die Gesetze der Natur gebunden, we are bound by the laws of nature; die —de Kraft eines Befehles, the binding force of a command; wir sind an gewisse Regeln gebunden, we are tied to certain rules; an eine Frau gebunden, bound to a wife; Ehre und Gutmüthigkeit können ihm die Hände —, honour and good nature may tie up his hands; ich, im Geist gebunden, fahre hin gegen Jerusalem, [in Scripture] I go bound in the spirit to Jerusalem; *Einem etwas auf die Nase —, to put a sham upon any one; *einen Verlust ans Bein —, to bear a loss. 3) to secure by a band, to restrain. Ein Faß —, to hoop a barrel; ein Buch —, to bind a book; bindet ihm Hände und Füße, bind him hand and foot. *Fig.* Einem die Zunge —, to tie up any one's tongue; es bindet mir die Zunge, it restrains my tongue; die gebundene Rede, a metrical composition, verses [as distinguished from prose]; gebundene Noten, [in music] notes tied together [which are marked thus ⌒]; Alles, was du auf Erden — wirst, soll auch im Himmel gebunden seyn, [in Script.] whatsoever thou shalt bind on earth, shall be bound in heaven. 4) to unite by binding. Garben —, to bind sheaves, to sheaf corn; bindet sie in Bündel, bind them in bundles; Besen —, to make brooms; einen Strauß —, to make a nosegay; Heu —, to bundle hay. 5) to unite [bodies] in close cohesion, to agglutinate. Bindend, tending to cause adhesion, agglutinant, agglutinative; der Leim bindet gut, the glue cements well.

II. *v. r.* sich —, 1) to unite and cohere, to cement. Der Sand bindet sich, the sand unites and coheres. 2) to tie one's self. Sie binden sich so genau an die Einheit des Ortes, they tie themselves so strictly to unity of place; sich durch ein Gelübde —, to tie one's self up by a vow; sich durch ein Versprechen —, to bind one's self by a promise.

Bind-ahl, *m.* —**ahle**, *f.* [with saddlers, strap-cutters, harness-makers] a sort of awl. —**axt**, *f.* carpenter's axe. —**balken**, —**e-balken**, *m.* [in architecture] the principal beam, girder, architrave. —**eisen**, *n.* [in glass-manufactories] a sort of bunting-iron. —**faden**, *m.* packthread, twine. —**holz**, *n.* [in carpentry] any rail. —**loch**, *n.* [with sempstresses] a bound eyelet or eyelet-hole. —**e-lohn**, *m.* money paid for binding books or other things. —**messer**, *n.* V. Bandmesser. —**riegel**, *m.* [in carpentry] rail. —**riemen**, *m.* a strap, latchet. —**rolle**, *f.* a roller for packthread. —**scheibe**, *f.* V. —e-scheibe. —**stock**, *m.* V. Knebel. —**weide**, *f.* V. Bandweide. —**werk**, *n.* [in architecture] lattice-work. —**wurm**, —**el-wurm**, *m.* the gourd-worm or fluke. —**zeug**, *n.* V. —e-zeug.

Binden, *n.* [-s] V. Binden. *Fig.* Das — der Klinge, [in fencing, a method of securing or crossing the adversary's sword with a pressure, accompanied with a spring of the wrist] binding.

Binder, *m.* [-s, *pl.* -] 1) a person who binds, [in husbandry] one who binds sheaves, a binder; chiefly used in compound words, as Buch—, bookbinder; Faß—, cooper &c. 2) any thing that binds or holds together, a binder. —, *a*) [=

Bindsteine, in masonry] stretchers [as distinguished from headers]. *b*) [= Bindesparren, in carpentry] tie-beam.

Bindling, *m.* [-es, *pl.* -e] V. Zaunwinde.

Bindsel, *n.* [-s, *pl.* -] 1) any thing that binds as a fillet, cord, rope or band. 2) [in seamen's language] lashing.

Bindung, *f.* 1) the act of fastening with a band or obliging, binding. 2) *Fig.* [in music] ligature, tie [marked thus ⁀].

Bindungsmittel, *n.* V. Bindemittel.

‖**Binetsch**, *m.* [-es] V. Spinat.

Binge, *f.* [*pl.* -n] V. Pinge.

Bingelkraut, *n.* [-es] dog's mercury.

‖**Binnbaum**, *m.* [-es, *pl.* -bäume] V. Maßholder.

Binnen, *adv.* [from be and innen] [especially used in law] [in the compass of, not beyond] within. — acht Tagen, within a sennight; — Jahr und Tag, within the space of a year; — heut und morgen, between this and to-morrow.

Binnen-deich, *m.* inner dam [digue]. —gewässer, *n.* waters of the continent, inland-water. —hafen, *m.* the basin of a port, a harbour's port shut by a boom. —handel, *m.* the traffic or commerce with the interior or the inland-provinces. —land, *n.* [*pl.* -länder] an inland country or province. —länder, *m.* 1) an inhabitant of inland-countries. 2) [a small vessel] bilander. —laufen, *v. intr.* [in seamen's lang.] to sail into a harbour or river. —lehn, *n.* inland feoff. —lichter, *m.* [a small vessel] lighter. —schoot, *n.* [in seamen's language] the tack of a studding-sail. —see, *m.* an inland-lake. —steven, —vorsteven, *m.* [in seamen's lang.] the apron. —steven hinten, —hintersteven, *m.* the inner post [which is seldom seen in English built vessels]. —wasser, *n.* 1) V. —gewässer. 2) water of a pond. —zeit, *f.* V. [the more usual] Zwischenzeit.

Binomisch, *adj.* [in algebra] binomial.

Binse, *f.* [*pl.* -n] [from binden, as *juncus* from *jungo*, *σχοῖνος* from *ἴσχω*] [a plant] rush. Die wohlriechende —, sweet rush.

Binsen-blume, *f.* flowering rush, or water-gladiole. —busch, *m.* rush-bed. —geflecht, *n.* a twist of rushes. —gras, *n.* 1) marsh creeping clubrush. 2) the jointed rush. —korb, *m.* a basket made of rushes. —licht, *n.* a rush-candle, a rush-light. —matte, *f.* rush-mat. —reuse, *f.* a weel made of rushes. —seide, *f.* [a plant] many-spiked cotton-grass. —stuhl, *m.* rush chair.

Binsicht, *adj.* and *adv.* rush-like.

Binsig, *adj.* and *adv.* aboundigg with rushes, rushy.

***Biograph**, *m.* [-en, *pl.* -en] biographer. V. Lebensbeschreiber.

***Biographie**, *f.* [*pl.* -en] biography. V. Lebensbeschreibung.

***Biographisch**, *adj.* and *adv.* biographic, biographical.

***Biquadrat**, *n.* [-es, *pl.* -e] [in mathematics, the fourth power, arising from the multiplication of a square number or quantity by itself] biquadrate.

***Biquadratisch**, *adj.* [in mathematics] biquadratic. Eine —e Gleichung, Parabel, a biquadratic equation, parabola.

Birke, *f.* [*pl.* -n] [perhaps from bären, to produce] [a genus of trees] birch, birch-tree. Die Canadische —, the Canadian birch.

Birken, *adj.* and *adv.* birch, birchen.

Birken-baum, *m.* V. Birke. —besen, *m.* birchen broom. —busch, *m.* a ground planted with young birch-trees. —häher, *m.* [a bird] common roller. —holz, *n.* the wood of the birch-tree, birch-wood. —kork, *n.* the cork boletus. —land, *n.* land planted with birches. ‡—meier, *m.* a birchen goblet. —messer, *m.* V. —spanner. —öl, *n.* birch-oil. —pilz, V. —schwamm. —reis, *n.* birchen rod. —reizker, *m.* a species of agaric [agaricus tormentosus]. —rinde, *f.* the bark of the birch-tree, birch bark. —ruthe, *f.* birch, birchen rod. —saft, *m.* birch-wine. —schwamm, *m.* birch-agaric. —spanner, *m.* the birch-moth. —spinne, *f.* a species of spider [aranea betulæ]. —theer, *n.* V. —öl. —vogel, *m.* V. —spanner. —wald, *m.* V. Birkwald. —wanze, *f.* a species of bug [cimex betulæ]. —wasser, *n.* V. —saft. —wein, *m.* V. —saft.

Birk-falk, *m.* V. Bergfalke. —fuchs, *m.* the fox having a bushy tail, white at the tip. —häher, *m.* V. Birkenhäher. —hahn, *m.* gorcock, moorcock. V. —huhn. —henne, *f.* the female of the gorcock, gorhen, moorhen. V. —huhn. —holz, *n.* V. Birkenbusch, Birkwald. —huhn, *n.* red-grouse or red-game. —wald, *m.* birch-wood, birch-grove. —wildbrät, *n.* red-grouse, red-game. —wurzel, *f.* 1) [a plant] common fennel giant. 2) V. Tormentille.

Birmane, *m.* [-n, *pl.* -n] Burmese.

Birmanisch, *adj.* and *adv.* Burmese.

Birn, **Birne**, *f.* [*pl.* -n] [Lat. *pirum*; seems to come from bären, to produce; in old G. *piric* signifies fruitful] pear.

Birn-apfel, *m.* pear-main. —baum, *m.* pear-tree. —baumen, *adj.* and *adv.* made of pear-tree. —baumholz, *n.* V. —holz. —brei, *m.* V. —muß. —förmig, *adj.* and *adv.* having the form of a pear, pyriform. Der —förmige Muskel, [in anatomy, a muscle of the thigh] pyriformis. —holz, *n.* wood of the pear-tree. —kürbiß, *m.* a species of gourd. —most, *m.* perry. —motte, *f.* the codling moth. —mundstück, *n.* [in manege] pear-bit. —muß, *n.* a confection of pears boiled with sugar, a marmalade. —pflaume, *f.* pear-plum. —quitte, *f.* pear-quince. —quittenbaum, *m.* pear-quince-tree [pyrus cydonia oblonga]. —saft, *m.* 1) the juice of the pear. 2) the inspissated juice of pears ‖—schnitz, *f.* a piece of a pear cut and dried. —sirop, *m.* V. —saft 2. —stamm, *m.* the trunk of a pear-tree. —stiel, *m.* the stalk of a pear. —wein, *m.* V. —most. —zitrone, *f.* a sort of lemon.

Biröle, **Birolf**, **Birolt**, V. Goldamsel.

Birschen, V. Bürschen.

Bis, I. *adv.* [either from bei zu or from bei das] [noting the place] — nach Mannheim, as far as Mannheim; von London — Paris, from London to Paris; — an den Hals im Wasser, up to the chin in water; — über den Kopf ins Wasser gehen, to go beyond one's depth; er wird roth — an die Ohren, he blushes up to his ears; — zur Höhe von vier Zoll, to the height of four inches; von Kopf — zu Fuß, from top to toe; ich sehe — auf den Grund, I see to the bottom; ein Haus — auf den Grund niederreißen, to make a house even with the ground; — auf die Haut naß werden, to get wet to the skin. *Fig. a*) [noting the time] Vom Anfang — zu Ende, from beginning to end; vom Morgen — Abend, from morning till night; — zwei Uhr, till two o'clock; — zu dem heutigen Tage, till this day. *b*) [noting the degree] — zum Uebermaße trinken, to drink to excess; — an den Hals in Schulden stecken, to be deeply indebted, to be over head and ears in debt; seine Güte erstreckt sich — auf ihre Kindeskinder, his kindness extends to their children's children; — auf die Letzt, to the last. *c*) [noting amount] — zum Belauf eines Schillings auf den Tag, to the value of a shilling a day.

II. *conj.* [to the time when] till. — die Gesandten zurückkamen, till the ambassadors were come back.

Bisam, *m.* [-s] [in Hebrew Basam signifies Aroma] musk. Nach — riechend, musky; *it.* musked.

Bisam-affe, *m.* musk-ape. —apfel, *m.* musk-apple. V. also Muskatellerapfel. —artig, *adj* and *adv.* musky. —birn, *f.* musk-pear. V. also Muskatellerbirn. —blume, *f.* yellow sweet sultan. —bock, *m.* 1) the male of the musk. 2) V. —käfer. —büchse, *f.* a box with musk. —duft, *m.* muskiness. —duftend, *adj.* musky, musked. Ein —duftendes Herrchen, a perfumed dandy. —ente, *f.* Guinea duck, Muscovy duck. —farbig, *adj.* and *adv.* having the colour of musk. —fell, *n.* the skin of the musk. —geruch, *m.* the smell of musk. —hirsch, *m.* V. —thier. —käfer, *m.* a species of insects [silpha vespillo]. —katze, *f.* musk-cat, civet-cat. V. also Zibethkatze; —kirsche, *f.* musk-cherry. V. also Muskatellerkirsche. —knopf, *m.* 1) musk-ball. 2) the button of the yellow sweet sultan. —knospe, *f.* V. —kraut. —kohl, *m.* musk-cabbage. —korn, *n.* —körner, *pl.* musk-seed, abel-musk. —kraut, *n.* musk-crowfoot, moschatel. —küchlein, —kügelchen, *n.* musk-paste pellet. —kugel, *f.* V. —knopf 1. —lauch, *m.* musk-smelling garlick. —malve, *f.* musk-mallow. —melone, *f.* musk-melon. —narzisse, *f.* musk-narcissus. —nieren, *pl.* [Beutelbisam *m.*] musk in bags or cods. —pappel, *f.* V. —kraut. —ratte, —ratze, *f.* musk-beaver, musk-rat, musquash [Muscusbiber]. —rose, *f.* musk-rose. V. also Moschusrose. —samen, *m.* V. —korn. —schwein, *n.* a species of wild swine in America. —thier, *n.* the musk. —ziege, *f.* V. —thier.

Bischen, *n.* V. Bißchen.

Bischof, *m.* [-es, *pl.* -schöfe] [from the Gr. *ἐπίσκοπος*] 1) [in the Greek, Latin, and some Protestant churches, a prelate, or person consecrated for the spiritual government and direction of a diocese] bishop. 2) [the name of a mixture of wine, oranges and sugar] bishop.

Bischofs-hut, *m.* V. —mütze. —mantel, *m.* the cloak of a bishop. —mütze, *f.* 1) mitre. 2) *Fig. a*) [a shrub] arnotta or anata. *b*) [a plant] alpine barrenwort. *c*) [a plant] mitella. *d*) a species of shell [voluta mitra episcopalis], the brown Amboina trumpet. —stab, *m.* crosier.

Bischöflich, *adj.* and *adv.* episcopal. *Fig.* bishoply, bishop-like. Die —e Gerichtsbarkeit, episcopal jurisdiction; die —e Kirche, the episcopal church; die —e Würde, the office or dignity of a bishop, episcopate; nach der —en Würde streben, to aspire to a bishopric; der —Gesinnte, an episcopalian, a church-man.

***Biscuit**, *m.* [-s, *pl.* -e] 1) [a kind of bread] biscuit. 2) [a cake] sponge-cake.

Bisher and **Bisher**, *adv.* hitherto, till now.

Bisherig and **Bisherig**, *adj.* what has hitherto been done or happened. Das —e Wetter, the weather we have had till now; die —en Nachrichten, the news we have received up to the present time.

Bismuth, V. Wismuth.

Bison, *m.* [-s, *pl.* -s] [Lat. *bison*, Old G. Wisant = der Weisende] the bison.

Biß, *m.* [-sses, *pl.* -sse] 1) [the act of biting] the bite. Der — eines Hundes, the bite of a dog. *Fig.* Gewissensbisse, pricks of conscience. 2) the wound made by the teeth, bite. 3) [with hunters] V. Gebiß.

Bißchen, ‖**Bißlein**, *n.* [-s] [the diminutive of Biß] a little bit. Ein — Brod, a bit of bread, some bread. *Fig.* Ein — Gelehrsamkeit, a little learning; wartet ein —, stay a moment; ein —, a little, somewhat, rather; ich habe nicht ein — geschlafen, I have not had a wink of sleep; das ist ein — früh, that's rather early.

Bissen, *m.* [-s, *pl.* -] a small piece, a mouthful or morsel, bit, a bite, a small piece of food. Ein — Brod or Brodes, a bit of bread; ein — Fleisch, a morsel of meat; keinen —, not a bit. *Fig.* [ein wenig] einen — essen, to eat a little.

Bissenweise, *adv.* by bits.

Bissig, *adj.* and *adv.* V. Beißig.

‖**Bisten**, *v. tr.* V. Pischten.

Bisthum, [-es, *pl.* -thümer] 1) the see of a bishop, diocese, bishopric. 2) the office and dignity of a bishop, episcopate.

* **Bisturi**, *n.* [-s] [in surgery] bistoury. V. also Einschnittmesser.

Bisweilen, *adv.* sometimes, now and then, from time to time, occasionally.

Bitte, *f.* [*pl.* -n] 1) the act of entreating, or petitioning, begging, entreaty, petition, prayer. Auf Ihre —, at your request; bei Einem eine — einlegen, to make a request to any one; die demüthige —, supplication; eine dringende —, an instant or earnest sollicitation; eine trotzige —, a petulant demand. 2) the thing asked for or requested, request. Ich will eure —n gewähren, I will grant your requests; soll ich seine — gewähren? shall I comply with his request? er aber gab ihnen ihre —, [in Script.] he gave them their request; ich habe noch eine — an Sie zu thun, I have one more favour to beg of you; taub für deine —, deaf to thy entreaties; die sieben —n des Vaterunsers, the seven petitions of the Lord's prayer.

Bitten, [allied to beten and probably to the Lat. *petere*] *ir. v. tr.* 1) to ask, as for a favour, to request, to petition. Bittet, so wird euch gegeben, [in Script.] ask, and it shall be given you; er bat um Brod, he asked for bread; Joseph bat um den Leib Jesu, [in Script.] Joseph begged the body of Jesus. Isaak bat den Herrn für sein Weib, [in Script.] Isaac entreated Jehovah for his wife; für Jemand —, to intercede for any one, to pray in church for any one; ich bitte Sie um Geduld, I beseech your patience; ich bitte um Gnade, I crave for mercy; Herr, ich bitte Euch, verzeihet mir, I beseech you, Sir! pardon me; ich bitte Sie um Verzeihung, I beg your pardon; ich bitte Sie tausend Mahl um Verzeihung, I ask you a thousand pardons; man bat den König, Frieden zu machen, the peace was begged of the king; darf ich Sie um Ihren Namen —? may I crave your name? er ist im — unermüdlich, he is never weary of craving; durch vieles —, by dint of prayer and supplication; zu Gott —, to pray to God; ich bitte dich um Gottes willen, I beseech you for God's sake. 2) to ask, to invite. Gäste zu einer Hochzeit —, to ask or invite guests to a wedding, to bid to a wedding; Einen zum Mittagessen oder Abendbrode —, to invite any one to dinner or supper; bitte meinen Freund, hereinzutreten, ask my friend to step into the house; er war nicht gebeten, he was unasked, uninvited.

Bitt-brief, *m.* a petitionary letter. —gang, *m.* an extraordinary procession of clergy and people in the Romish church [in calamitous times or for turning away a dreaded or actual calamity]. —gesang, *m.* [in the Romish church] litany, rogation. —schreiben, *n.* a petitionary letter. —schreiber, *m.* petitioner, supplicant. —schrift, *f.* a written supplication from an inferior to a superior, a petition. Habt Ihr Eure —schrift Sr. Majestät überreicht? have you presented to his Majesty your humble petition? —steller, *m.* petitioner, supplicant. —weise, *adv.* in the form of a request or petition.

Bitter, *m.* [-s, *pl.* -] one who asks, a petitioner [chiefly used in compound words as Hochzeit—, Leichen— &c.].

Bitter, [from beißen, Low Sax. biten] *adj.* and *adv.* bitter, sharp or biting to the taste. Der Wermuth hat einen —n Geschmack, wormwood is bitter; die —e Sohle or Mutter, [in salt-works] V. —sohle; — wie Galle, as bitter as gall. *Fig.* —er Haß, bitter enmity; —e Worte, bitter or sharp words; —e Vorwürfe, bitter reproaches; in —er Laune, in an acid humour; es machte mir das —ste Herzeleid, I was pained to my very heart; —er Ernst, sad earnest; es ist — kalt, 'tis bitter cold; — tadeln, to censure bitterly; —e Thränen weinen, to weep bitterly; —e Klagen, grievous complaints; mit —er Verachtung, with acrimonious contempt; [in Script.] daß nicht etwa eine —e Wurzel aufwachse und Unfrieden anrichte, lest any root of bitterness springing up, trouble you.

Bitter-apfel, *m.* bitter-apple, bitter-gourd, coloquintida. —baum, *m.* V. —holzbaum. —bier, *n.* porter. —böse, *adj.* and *adv.* [in fam. lang.] 1) very wicked. 2) very angry. —distel, *f.* blessed thistle. —erde, *f.* V. Talkerde. —feind, *adv.* very hostile. —gurke, *f.* V. —apfel. —holz, *n.* 1) quassia. 2) Jamaica bitter-wood. —holzbaum, *m.* the quassia-tree. —hydrat, *n.* native magnesia, hydrate of magnesia. —kalk, *m.* 1) lime made of limestones. 2) [in mineralogy] magnesian limestone. —klee, *m.* common buck-bean, or march-trefoil. —kraut, *n.* a species of picris. —kresse, *f.* 1) bitter cress. 2) scurvy grass. —salz, *n.* bitter-salt, Epsom salts, sulphate of magnesia. —salzerde, *f.* V. Talkerde. —sohle, *f.* [in salt-works, the brine remaining after the salt is concreted] the bittern. —spath, *m.* bitter-spar, cristallized muricalcite, compound spar, dolomite spar, rhombe-spar. —stein, *m.* jade, hemanite. —süß, I. *n.* [a plant] bitter-sweet [solanum dulcamara, L.]. II. *Fig. adj.* and *adv.* bitter-sweet. Er bewilligte ihre Bitte mit einem —süßen Lächeln, he complied with her request with a forced smile. —tropfen, *pl.* bitters. —wasser, *n.* bitter mineral waters. —weide, *f.* Baumwollenweide. —wein, *m.* wormwood-wine. —wurz, *f.* bitterwort [Genziana lutea, L.].

Bitterkeit, *f.* 1) [a taste] bitterness. Die — des Wermuths, the bitter taste of wormwood. 2) *Fig.* *a*) bitterness = keenness of reproach, sharpness, pungency. Die — eines Ausdruckes, the acrimony of an expression; die — eines Vorwurfes, the bitterness of a reproach; —en, bitter words, *it.* = adversities, annoyances &c. bitters [opposed to sweets]; die — des Todes, the sharpness of death. *b*) bitterness = extreme enmity, grudge, hatred. Die — des Zornes, [in Script.] the bitterness of anger.

Bitterlich, I. *adj.* somewhat bitter, bitterish. II. *adv.* [in a manner expressing poignant grief] bitterly. Er, sie weinte —, he, she wept or cried bitterly.

Bitterlichkeit, *f.* bitterishness.

Bitterling, *m.* [-es, *pl.* -e] 1) [a plant] pale-flowered persicaria. 2) the pepper-agaric.

Bittern, *v. tr.* [unusual] to make bitter.

Bittlich, *adj.* and *adv.* 1) by means of petition, petitioning, resting upon a request or petition. Einen — um etwas angehen, to ask something from any one; bei &c. — um etwas einkommen, to pray something of &c. 2) [in law, held by doubtful tenure] precarious. — besitzen, to hold precariously.

* **Bituminös**, *adj.* bituminous. Bituminöses Holz, bituminous or carbonated wood, fibrous brown coal; erdiges bituminöses Holz, earthy brown-coal, earth-coal; bituminöser Mergelschiefer, bituminous marle-slate.

‖**Bitzeln**, [from beißen] *v. intr.* to be pricking. Auf der Zunge —, to be stimulating to the tongue.

Bitzling, *m.* [-es, *pl.* -e] [a fish] smaris.

Bitzweizen, *m.* V. Fuchsschwanz.

Bitzwurz, *f.* V. Küchenschelle.

* **Bivouac**, *m.* [-s, *pl.* -s] [an encampment without tents] bivouac.

* **Bivouaquiren**, [pronounce: Biwuakiren] *v. intr.* [to encamp without tents, as a whole army] to bivouac.

* **Bizárr**, I. *adj.* odd, strange. Ein —er Mensch, an odd fellow, an oddity; ein —es Wesen, a strange behaviour, whimsical actions; er ist ein höchst —er Charakter, he is a very eccentric character. II. *adv.* oddly, strangely [dressed &c.].

* **Bizarrerie**, *f.* [*pl.* -en] oddity, strangeness.

Blách, [seldom used, except in certain compound words] *adj.* and *adv.* [has affinity with flach] flat, plain, level [said of fields or a ground].

Blach-feld, *n.* a plain, level field or land, champaign. —frost [more correctly: Blackfrost], *m.* black-frost. —mahl, *n.* [in chimistry] the slag which rises at the top of melted silver.

Blacker, V. Placker.

Blackfisch, *m.* [-es, *pl.* -e] 1) V. Tintenfisch. ‖ 2) V. Bleihe.

‖**Blackthier**, *n.* V. Tintenthier.

‖**Blaffen**, V. Bellen.

Blaffer, *m.* [-s, *pl.* -] a barking dog.

‖**Blaffert**, *m.* [-s, *pl.* -e] a sort of coin.

Blähe, *f.* V. Plache and Plane.

Blähen, [allied to the Lat. *flare*, Gr. φλάω] I. *v. tr.* 1) to distend by injecting air, to blow up, to inflate. Der Wind blähet die Segel, the wind swells the sails. *Fig.* Stolz oder Eitelkeit blähet ihn (auf), he is puffed up with pride or vanity. 2) to generate wind in the stomach. Erbsen sind ein —des Gemüse, pease are a flatulent vegetable, —de Hülsenfrüchte, windy pulse; die Senespflanze verliert durch das Abkochen etwas von ihrer —den Eigenschaft, senna loses somewhat of its windiness by decocting. II. *v. r.* sich —, to be inflated, to swell; *fig.* to be puffed up with pride or conceit, to be ostentatious.

Blähsucht, *f.* windiness in the stomach, flatulence, flatulency.

Blähung, *f.* 1) the act of generating wind in the stomach. 2) flatulence, flatulency, flatus. —en, windiness in the stomach; —en haben, to be troubled with wind; sich der —en entledigen, to break wind; —en vertreibend, carminative.

Blähungsmittel, *n.* a carminative.

‖**Bläker**, *m.* [-s, *pl.* -] a flat candlestick, a sconce.

* **Blamiren**, *v. tr.* 1) to slander, to defame. 2) to expose to ridicule, to disgrace.

Blánk, [*compar.* —er, *superl.* —ste] *adj.* and *adv.* [allied to blinken, bleich, blicken] 1) blank, white. —er [weißer] Wein, white wine. 2) smooth and shining, bright, lustrous. —es Zinn, nitid tin; —es Küchengeräth, well-scoured, bright kitchen-utensils; das Leder — stoßen, [with tawers] to gloss a skin with a glass-sleeker. 3) uncovered, naked. Mit —en Füßen, barefoot, barefooted; — ziehen, [to unsheath one's sword] to draw; ein —er Degen, a drawn or naked sword; —e Karte, [a piece of paper at the bottom of which a person has signed his name, the rest being void, commonly entrusted to arbiters, friends &c. for the settlement of a dispute &c.] a blank, [or a blank paper, signed at the bottom with a person's name, and sometimes sealed with his seal, given to another person with permission to superscribe what conditions he pleases] carte blanche.

Blank=frost, *m.* V. Blachfrost. —**haken**, *m.* [with slaters] an S hook. —**leder**, *n.* sleek-leather. —**macher**, *m.* a glosser, a polisher. —**stoßbock**, *m.* V. Satzbock. —**stoßkugel**, *f.* a glass-sleeker.

‖ **Blänke**, *f.* [*pl.* -n] a board or shelf for kitchen-utensils.

‖ **Blänke**, *f.* [*pl.* -n] an open place in a forest, a glade

Blänken, *v. tr.* to polish, to gloss. Waffen —, to furbish arms.

‖ **Blänkern**, *v. intr.* 1) [u. w. seyn] to be bright, to shine. 2) [in military affairs] to fire in a scattered manner as riflemen.

* **Blánko**, *adv.* In — trassiren, [in commerce] to draw in blank.

Blánkscheit, *n.* [-s, *pl.* -e] husk.

* **Blanquét**, *n.* [-s, *pl.* -s or -e] carte blanche. V. Blank 3.

Bläschen, Bläslein, *n.* [-s, *pl.* -] [diminut. of Blase] a little bladder or vesicle.

Bläschenkraut, *n.* V. Blasenkraut.

Blase, *f.* [*pl.* -n] 1) any vesicle, blister or pustule, especially if filled with air, or a thin watery liquor, a bladder. Die — auf dem Wasser, bubble; — werfen, to bubble; eine — aufblasen, to blow a bladder; eine — auf der Haut, a pimple or wheal, a pustule; —n ziehen, to raise a blister [by a plaster of flies or a vesicatory]; —n unter den Füßen bekommen, to get blisters on one's feet. [in a less comprehensive sense] *a*) [a thin membraneous bag in animals which serves as the receptacle of some secreted fluid] a bladder. Die Harn—, the urinary bladder, [by way of eminence] the bladder; die Gallen—, the gall-bladder. *b*) [in botany, a distended membranaceous pericarp] bladder. —n an der Wurzel, bladders [= bags at the root]. 2) a large copper vessel used in distilling ardent spirits, a still, alembic.

Blasen=ampfer, *m.* bladder-dock. —**artig**, *adj.* and *adv.* [in anatomy] folliculous. —**ball**, *m.* balloon. —**baum**, *m.* [a tree] bladder-senna. —**bruch**, *m.* [in surgery] cystocele. —**entzündung**, *f.* an inflammation of the urinary bladder, cystitis, cystiphlogia. —**erbse**, *f.* smooth-leaved heart-pea, or heart-seed. —**erdrauch**, *m.* [a plant] bladdered fumitory. —**fieber**, *n.* [in medicine] a sort of putrid fever. —**fuß**, *m.* —**fußfliege**, *f.* thrips. —**gang**, *m.* [in anatomy] the cystic duct. —**gries**, *m.* gravel. —**grün**, *n.* sap green. —**grund**, *m.* [in anatomy] the bottom of the bladder. —**hals**, *m.* [in anatomy] the neck of the bladder. —**helm**, —**hut**, *m.* the head of an alembic, helm. —**käfer**, *m.* Spanish fly. —**kirsche**, *f.* V. Judenkirsche. —**klee**, *m.* strawberry-trefoil —**kohl**, *m.* Spanish rocket [brassica vesicaria]. —**kopf**, *m.* V. —hut. —**krampf**, *m.* a spasm in the bladder. —**kraut**, *n.* common bladderwort, or hooded milfoil. —**lebergang**, *m.* [in anatomy] cysthepatic duct. —**nuß**, *f.* five-leaved bladder-nut. —**öffnung**, *f.* 1) [in anatomy] the lower orifice of the ureter. 2) [in surgery] the operation of cutting, or piercing the bladder, cystotomia. —**perle**, *f.* pearl-bubble. —**pflaster**, *n.* a plaster of flies, or other matter, applied to raise a vesicle, a vesicatory, a blister, blistering-plaster. —**räumer**, *m.* [an instrument of surgery] a scoop. —**schlagader**, *f.* [in anatomy] cystic artery. —**schnitt**, *m.* V. —öffnung, 2). —**schnur**, *f.* [in anatomy, the ligamentary chord that arises from the urinary bladder, along which it runs, and terminates in the umbilical chord] urachus. —**senna**, *f.* V. —baum. —**stahl**, *m.* common steel. —**stein**, *m.* a stone in the bladder. —**steinsauer**, *adj.* [in chimistry] —steinsaures Salz, lithiate. —**steinsäure**, *f.* [in chimistry] the lithic acid. —**stich**, *m.* V. —schnitt. —**strauch**, *m.* V. —baum. —**vorfall**, *m.* [in surgery] a prolapsus of the inner membrane of the bladder, exocystus. —**wurm**, *m.* hydatid. —**ziehend**, *adj.* and *adv.* blistering. Ein —ziehendes Mittel, V. —pflaster. —**zins**, *m.* a duty upon distillery.

Blasen, [allied to blähen, the Lat. *flare* and the Gr. φλύειν] *ir.* I. *v. intr.* 1) [to move as air] to blow. Der Wind bläset, the wind blows. 2) to breathe upon. In das Feuer —, to blow the fire. *Prov.* †In die Büchse — müssen, to be fined, or to be under a penalty. 3) to blow [on an instrument]. Die Reiter — gut, the trumpets of these cavalry are well blown; er bläst falsch, zu stark, he blows out of tune, too strong. *Fig.* *Mit Jemand in ein Horn —, to act in concert with any one, to have an understanding with any one. 4) [to betoken or direct by a sound] to sound. Zum Angriffe —, to sound the charge; zum Rückzuge —, to sound the retreat; zum Aufsitzen —, to sound to horse; Lärm —, to sound an alarm. II. *v. tr.* 1) to effect, to produce by breathing upon or by blowing. Die Speisen kalt —, to cool meat by blowing upon it; [in glass-works] Glas —, to blow glass; [in metallurgy] das Eisen —, to smelt the iron in a blast-furnace; [at draughts] einen Stein —, to huff a man. *Fig.* [in famil. lang.] Das läßt sich nicht —, it is not easily done; was dich nicht brennt, das blase nicht, don't meddle with what does not concern you. 2) [to sound a wind instrument] to blow. Die Trompete —, to blow or sound the trumpet; die Flöte —, to play on the flute, to flute; blase das gellende Horn, wind the shrill horn. 3) [= einblasen] Einem in die Ohren —, to whisper in any one's ear.

Blase=balg, *m.* bellows, a pair of bellows. —**balgsröhre**, *f.* the nozle of a pair of bellows. —**backen**, *pl.* [in seamen's language] wash-boards under the cheeks or doubling of the cut-water, or the planks nailed on the outside of it, underneath the cheeks of the head. —**baß**, *m.* [seldom used] [in music] a bassoon, fagot. —**geräth**, *n.* a musical wind-instrument. —**horn**, *n.* 1) the horn of a nightwatch or a herdsman. 2) [a species of the whelk] the shell inflated. —**laute**, *m.* [in grammar] a hissing labial. —**loch**, *n.* the mouth piece or embouchure [of a musical wind-instrument]. —**rohr**, *n.* 1) [an iron instrument used in making glass] a blow-pipe. 2) a blow-pipe [to fuse or vitrify metals]. V. Löthrohr. 3) [in popular lang.] a trunk or shooting-trunk. —**werk**, *n.* [in metallurgy] blast-furnace. —**werkzeug**, *n.* a musical wind-instrument.

Bläser, *m.* [-s, *pl.* -] 1) [one who blows] a blower. 2) the hare globe-fish.

Bläser, *m.* [-s, *pl.* -] 1) [one who blows, especially who sounds a wind-instrument] a blower. Der Flöten—, a performer on the flute, flutist. *Fig.* Ohren—, a tell-tale, tale-bearer. 2) a magnet that repulses the iron. 3) [in mineralogy] shorl, tourmaline.

Blasicht, *adj.* and *adv.* resembling a bladder.

Blasig, *adj.* and *adv.* full of bladders or blisters.

Blasius, *m.* [a name of men] Blase.

Bläsleinsenne, V. Blasenbaum.

* **Blasoniren**, *v. tr.* [in heraldry] to blazon.

* **Blasphemie**, *f.* [*pl.* -n] blasphemy.

* **Blasphemiren**, *v. tr.* and *v. intr.* to blaspheme.

* **Blasphémisch**, *adj.* and *adv.* blasphemous.

Blaß, [compar. blasser or blässer, superl. blasseste or blässeste] *adj.* and *adv* [allied to bleich, blinken, blicken] [white or whitish, wan, deficient in colour, not ruddy or of fresh colour, not bright] pale. Ein blasses Gesicht, a pale face; — aussehend, pale-faced; blasse Wangen, pale cheeks; — wie der Tod, pale as death; der blasse Tod, *poet.* white death; das blasse Licht des Mondes, the pale light of the moon; — werden, — seyn, to grow or turn pale or wan, to be pale, to change colour; es sieht blässer aus, it looks paler Das Blaß, paleness. SYN. Blaß, Bleich. That is said to be blaß, which has suffered only a partial loss or diminution of its natural colour, so that the original colour is still distinguishable. Blaß is therefore used in composition to denote a somewhat paler shade of any colour, as: Blaßroth, Blaßgelb &c. Bleich on the contrary, is said of that which has completely lost its primitive colour, which has become entirely colourless.

Blaß=äugig, *adj.* and *adv.* having pale blue or pale grey eyes, light-coloured eyes. —**blau**, *adj.* and *adv.* pale blue. Eine —blaue Farbe, a faint blue. —**braun**, *adj.* and *adv.* light brown. —**gelb**, *adj.* and *adv.* pale yellow. —**grau**, *adj.* and *adv.* pale grey —**grün**, *adj.* and *adv.* pale green. Eine —grüne Farbe a palish green colour. —**roth**, *adj.* and *adv.* pale red, pink. Ins —rothe spielend, white lightly blushed with red.

Bläßchen, *n.* [-s, *pl.* -] V. Bläßhuhn.

Blässe, *f.* [*pl.* -n] 1) paleness, wanness. 2) [a white spot on the forehead or face of a horse &c.] blaze. 3) *m.* or *f.* a horse or horn-cattle with a blaze.

Blässen, *v. intr.* [u. w. seyn] to grow pale. V. Erblassen.

Bläßente, *f.* 1) the common wild duck. 2) V. Bläßhuhn.

Bläßhuhn, *n.* [-es, *pl.* -hühner] [a water-fowl] coot, moor-hen.

Blatt, *n.* [-es, *pl.* Blätter] [probably allied to the A. S. *blaed*, *bled* = Gewächs, Fr. blé, Getreide, others suppose it to be the same as platt, Gr. πλατυς, breit] 1) [in botany] leaf. Die Blätter eines Baumes, the leaves of a tree; Blätter bekommen, to leaf; voll Blätter, leafy; Weinblätter, vine-leaves. *Fig.* *Das — hat sich gewendet, the tables are turned; kein — vor das Maul nehmen, to speak freely; [with hunt.] der Rehbock läuft auf das —, the buck comes near at the call [at the noise made by blowing on a leaf and imitating his voice]. 2) [the name of several broad and flat things] *a*) Die Blätter einer spanischen Wand, the leaves of a screen; das — [Schulter—] [especially with hunters] the blade of the shoulder, shoulder-blade, blade-bone; das — eines Tisches [Tisch—], the board of a table; zu Blättern schlagen, [metal] to foliate; das — einer Säge, the blade of a saw; das — einer Scheere, the cutting blade of scissors; das — des Weidmessers, [with hunters] the blade of a hanger; das — eines Riemens [Ruders], the blade or wash of an oar; das — des Ankers, V. Ankerflügel; das — bei den Webern, reed; das — [= die Bahn] eines Zeuges, [with tailors sempstresses] breadth; das — von diesem Zeuge ist schmal, the breadth of this stuff is small; das — or Karten—, a card; die Blätter eines Buches, the leaves of a book; ein Stück vom — weg spielen, [in music] to play at sight, diese Blätter enthalten eine Antwort für meinen Gegner, these sheets contain an answer to my opponent; ein fliegendes —, a pamphlet; öffentliche Blätter, news-papers. 3) [in natural history] Das gehörnte —, a species of hornwort; das wandelnde —, a species of cricket [mantis]; das fliegende —, a species of butterfly; das gelbe —, a species of tethys [tellina folinea].

Blatt=ähnlich, *adj.* and *adv.* resembling a leaf. —**ansatz**, *m* [in botany] stipule. —**auge**, *n.* V. —knospe. —**beil**, *n.* V. Breitbeil. —**bezeichnung**, *f.* [with printers] signature. V. also Signatur. —**blei**, *n.* sheet-lead. —**eisen**, *n.* sheet-iron. —**erbse**, *f.* V. Platterbse. —**federchen**, *n.* [in botany] plume, plumule. —**floh**, *m.* chermes. —**förmig**, *adj.* and *adv* having the form of a leaf. —**gerste**, *f.* a sort of common barley [hordeum frutescens]. —**gold**, *n.* leaf-gold, foliated gold. —**halter**, *m.* [with printers] retinaculum. —**häutchen**, *n.* [in botany] sheath, strap. —**hüter**, *m.* [with printers] the catch-word. —**käfer**, *m.* [a genus of insects] chrysomela. —**kissen**, *n.* [in gilding] cushion. —**knospe**, *f.* [in botany] leaf-bud. —**kohl**, *m.* a sort of cabbage. —**kupfer**, *n.* sheet-copper. —**lahm**, *adj.* and *adv.* [with hunters] strained in the shoulder [said of dogs]. —**laus**, *f.* plant-louse. —**lausfresser**, *m.* an insect that preys with avidity on plant-lice [hemerobius perla]. —**lauskäfer**, *m.* [a species of insects that feed on plant-lice] coccinella. —**lauslöwe**, *m.* V. —lausfresser. —**los**, *adj.* and *adv.* leafless. —**lose**, *f.* [the name of plants] 1) smooth rupturewort. 2) biting stone-crop. —**macher**, *m.* [am. weavers] reed-maker. —**metall**, *n.* sheet-metal. —**raupe**, *f.* a caterpillar feeding on leaves. —**reich**, *adj.* and *adv.* full of leaves, leafy. —**roller**, *m.* [an insect] a species of curculio. —**sauger**, *m* [a genus of insects] chermes. —**scheide**, *f.* [in botany] sheath. —**seite**, *f.* a page. —**setzer**, *m.* V. —macher. —**silber**, *n.* leaf-silver. —**ständig**, *adj.* and *adv.* [in botany] Eine —ständige Ranke, a tendril-bearing leaf. —**stiel**, *m.* [in botany] a leaf-stalk, petiol. —**stielständig**, *adj.* and *adv.* [in botany] petiolar, petiolary. Eine —stielständige Ranke, a petiolar tendril. —**stück**, *n.* [in carpentry] raising or wall-plate. —**vergoldung**, *f.* [with sword-cutlers] the gilding with leaf-gold. —**versilberung**, *f.* [with sword-cutlers] the silvering with leaf-silver. —**weise**, *adv.* leaf by leaf, in leaves. —**weiser**, *m.* an index. —**wender**, *m.* a tassel of a book. —**wespe**, *f.* saw-fly. —**wickler**, *m.* V. Wickelraupe. —**winkel**, *m.* [in botany] the angle formed by the leaf and stalk. —**zeichen**, *n.* V. —bezeichnung. —**zinn**, *n.* 1) leaf-tin. 2) tin-foil.

Blättchen, [diminut. of Blatt] *n.* [-s, *pl.* -] 1) a leaflet, [in botany] a foliole. 2) [in anatomy] fontanella [fons pulsatilis]. 3) a leaf or thin plate of metal used in gilding, foil.

Blättchengold, *n.* V. Blattgold.

Blättelschere, *f.* [*pl.* -n] [with cardmakers] stock-shears.

Blatten, *v. tr.* to strip of the superfluous leaves by plucking. Den Taback —, to leaf tobacco.

Blatten, *v. tr.* [with hunters] to lure by whistling on a leaf.

Blatter, *f.* [*pl.* -n] 1) a pimple or wheal, a pustule. 2) [a pustule raised on the surface of the body in the variolous and vaccine diseases] a pock. Die —n [natürliche —n], the small pox; die —n haben, to have the small pox; die —n einimpfen, to inoculate. 3) a disease in horn-cattle, sheep and swine.

Blatter=grube, *f.* V. —narbe. —**grubig**, *adj.* and *adv.* V. —narbig. —**holz**, *n.* pock-wood, guaiacum. —**krank**, —**nkrank**, *adj.* and *adv.* diseased with the small pox. —**krankheit**, *f.* the state of being diseased with the small pox. —**kraut**, *n.* noble liverwort. —**mal**, *n.* V. —narbe. —**malig**, *adj.* and *adv.* V. —narbig. —**narbe**, *f.* pock-hole. —**narbig**, *adj.* and *adv.* pitted or marked with the small pox. —**stein**, *m.* variolite. ‖ —**steppig**, *adj.* and *adv.* V. —narbig. —**zug**, *m.* V. —kraut.

Blätter, *pl.* of Blatt leaf, leaves.

Blätter=anhang, —**ansatz**, *m.* [in botany] V. Blattansatz. —**blende**, *f.* [in mineralogy] a sort of sulphuret of zinc. —**blume**, *f.* a species of phyllanthus. —**erde**, *f.* [in chimistry] a salt formed by the union of acetic acid with tartaric acid. —**erz**, *n.* [in mining] black tellurium ore. —**fall**, *m.* [= Spätjahr, Herbst] the fall of the leaf. —**flechte**, *f.* a species of lichen [lichen pustulatus]. —**gelb**, *n* a yellowish green, [in painting] folio-mort. —**gold**, *n.* V. Blattgold. —**knospe**, *f.* V. Blattknospe. —**kohl**, *m.* V. Blattkohl. —**kohle**, *f* slate coal, foliated coal, black coal, common coal. —**los**, *adj.* and *adv.* leafless, [in botany] aphyllous. —**magen**, *m.* the third stomach of ruminating animals, the tripe. —**reich**, *adj.* and *adv.* full of leaves, leafy. —**schwamm**, *m.* agaric. —**spath**, *m.* foliaceous spar. —**stein**, *m.* any foliated or lamellar stone. —**taback**, *m.* tobacco in leaves, leaf-tobacco. —**teig**, *m.* puff-paste —**tellur**, *m.* V. —erz. —**thon**, *m.* a sort of adhesive slate. —**torf**, *m.* V. Papiertorf. —**tragend**, *adj.* and *adv* foliferous. —**voll**, *adj.* and *adv.* leafy. —**weise**, *adv.* as leaves or thin lamins, lamellar. —**werk**, *n.* [in architecture and landscape-painting] foliage. —**wuchs**, *m.* foliation. —**wurz**, *f.* V. Tormentill. —**zahn**, *m.* an exfoliating tooth. —**zeolith**, *m.* [in mineralogy] foliated or radiated zeolite.

Blätterig, *adj.* and *adv.* 1) furnished with leaves, leafy, leaved [especially in compound words, as Viel—, many-leaved]. 2) [consisting of leaves or thin lamins] Ein —er Bruch, [in mineralogy] a foliated fracture; ein —er Stein, a foliated stone; —er Teig, puff-paste; die —e Wurzel, [in botany] an imbricated root.

Blättern, *v. intr.* to have the small pox.

Blättern, I. *v. intr.* to turn over the leaves [of a book]. In einem Buche —, to run over a book, to skim a book. II. *v. tr.* to deprive of leaves. Den Taback —, to leaf tobacco. III. *v. r.* sich —, 1) to shed the leaves. Die Rose blättert sich, the rose sheds its leaves. 2) to separate or come off in thin lamins or scales. Der Stein blättert sich, the stone scales, exfoliates; der Knochen blättert sich, the bone exfoliates; die alten Schalen des Hummers — sich, the old shells of the lobster scale off. Die Blätterung, foliation, foliature.

Blättlein, *n.* V. Blättchen.

Blau, [*compar.* —er, *superl.* —este] [Fr. *bleu*; probably allied to bleich &c.] I. *adj.* and *adv.* blue; [in heraldry] azure; *poet.* azure, cerulean. Das —e Meer, the cerulean ocean; der —e Himmel, the azure sky; ein —es Band, a blue ribbon; — machen, färben, to make blue, to dye of a blue colour, to blue; den Stahl — anlaufen lassen, to blue steel; der —e Hof um die Augen, a black circle round one's eyes. *Fig* Einen braun und — schlagen, [in fam. lang.] to beat any one black and blue; mit einem —en Auge davon kommen, [in famil. lang.] to get off cheaply; Einem einen —en Dunst vormachen, [in famil. lang.] to cast a mist before any one's eye; † and ‡ Einen — anlaufen lassen, 1) to cheat, to deceive any one, 2) to puzzle any one; der —e Montag, Crispin's holiday. II. *s.* 1) [das Blau or das Blaue or etwas Blaues] blue colour. Ein schönes —, a fine blue. 2) as a colour used for dying. Berliner —, Prussian blue; das holländische Lasur—, Dutch blue; Indigo—, indigo blue &c.

Blau=äderig, *adj.* and *adv.* blue-veined. —**auge**, *n.* [in fam. lang.] a blue eye. Du kleines —auge, you little blue-eyed creature! —**äugig**, *adj.* and *adv.* blue-eyed. Die —äugige Göttin [Minerva], the blue-eyed goddess [Minerva]. —**bart**, *m.* a blue or bluish beard. Ritter —bart, [in the well-known nursery-tale], Blue-beard. —**bärtig**, *adj.* and *adv.* having a bluish beard. —**beere**, *f.* bilberry. —**bleierz**, *n.* blue lead-ore. —**eisenerde**, *f.* blue iron-ore. Kristallisirte —eisenerde, foliated blue iron-ore. —**farbe**, *f.* 1) blue colour. 2) blue-glass. V. Schmalte. —**farbenbereitung**, *f.* the preparation of blue colours. —**farbenglas**, *n.* enamel. —**farbenhafen**, *m.* a pot or crucible in which saffre is melted. —**farbenkobalt**, *m.* cobalt [used for preparing a blue colour]. —**farbenwerk**, *n.* a manufactory of blue colour. —**färber**, *m.* a dyer in blue, dyer. —**felchen**, *m.* [a fish] blue-cap V. Balche. —**fisch**, *m.* blue-fish. —**fleckig**, *adj* blue-spotted. —**flieder**, *m.* lilac. —**flügel**, *m.* pine-creeper. —**fuß**, *m.* hen-harrier, blue hawk. —**geblümt**, *adj.* and *adv.* embellished with blue flowers, blue-flowered. —**gesäuert**, *adj.* and *adv.* [in chimistry] —gesäuertes Salz, prussiate. —**glas**, *n.* V. —farbenglas. —**grau**, *adj.* and *adv.* grey and blue, blue-grey. —**grün**, *adj.* and *adv.* sea-green. —**haarig**, *adj.* blue-haired. —**holz**, *n.* logwood, campeachy-wood. —**kehlchen**, *n.* 1) blue-bird 2) the blue-throated warbler. —**kohl**, *m.* red cabbage. —**kopf**, *m* 1) a species of teal [anas americana]. 2) the squirrel fish. 3) a species of carabus [carabus cyanocephalus]. —**krähe**, *f.* V. —racke. —**küpe**, *f.* [with dyers] blue-vat. —**lockig**, *adj.* and *adv.* blue-haired. —**meise**, *f.* titmouse. —**mütze**, *f.* [a plant] blue-bonnet. —**racke**, *m.* [a bird] common roller. —**rock**, *m* 1) a person wearing a blue coat.* ‖ and ‡2) a soldier. —**sauer**, *adj.* and *adv.* [in chimistry] composed of cyanogen, prussic gas and hydrogen. —**säure**, *f.* prussic acid. —**schecke**, *f.* a flea-bitten gray horse. —**schimmel**, *m.* a dapple-gray horse. —**spath**, *m.* azure-spar. —**specht**, *m.* [a bird] nut-hatch. —**stein**, *m.* azure stone, azure spar. —**strumpf**, *m.* a nickname for a beadle or bailiff, also for an informer; *it.* for a female pedant or learned lady, a blue-stocking. —**taube**, *f.* stock-pigeon. —**vogel**, *m.* V. —kehlchen. —**ziemer**, *m.* [a bird] the field-fare.

Bläue, *f.* 1) blue colour, blueness. *Poet.* Des Himmels —, the azure skies. 2) blue starch.

Bläueln, *v. tr.* to beat [the linen, flax &c.].

Blauen, I. *v. intr.* [u. w. seyn] to grow blue, to be blue. *Poet.* So weit der Himmel blauet, far as the firmament extends. II. *v. tr.* V. Bläuen.

Bläuen, I. *v. tr.* 1) to make blue, to dye of a blue colour, to blue. †2) [more usual durchbläuen] to beat black and blue. II. *v. r.* sich —, to grow blue. Der Himmel bläuet sich, the sky clears up.

Blauer, *m.* [-s, *pl.* -] a dyer of cloth and silk [especially in bright colours].

Bläuer, *m.* [-s, *pl.* -] [an instrument for beating or pounding] a beater.

Bläulich, *adj.* and *adv.* bluish. Das —e, bluishness.

Bläulichweiß, *adj.* and *adv.* bluish white.

Bläuling, *m.* [-es, *pl.* -e] [a fish] blue-cap.

Blech, *n.* [-es, *pl.* -e] [allied to flach and to the Fr. *plaque*, Gr. πλάξ] 1) a thin plate of metal, thin plate Zu — schlagen, to beat into thin flat pieces or lamens, to plate; Eisen—, iron-plate; Weiß—, tin. *Fig.* †money, cash. 2) [in gunnery] Das — auf dem Zündloche einer Kanone, apron.

Blech=abschnitt, *m.* a cutting of iron-plate. —**ausschuß**, *m.* [in commerce] waster. —**gefäß**, *n.* a vessel of iron-plate. —**hammer**, *m.* 1) iron-works or a forge where wrought-iron is converted into plates. 2) a great hammer used for beating wrought-iron into plates. —**haube**, *f.* a casque or helmet made of iron-plate to defend the head, a morion. —**hütte**, *f.* a forge where metal is plated and tinned. —**kappe**, *f.* V. —haube. —**maß**, *n.* 1) [with goldsmiths] an iron-plate with incisions, to measure the thickness of gold and silver plates. 2) [with wire-drawers] a brass-plate with holes of different sizes, in order to determine whether the draw-hole has its proper size and wideness [= das Zängelmaß]. —münze, *f.* anciently a thin sort of coin, bracteate. —mütze, *f.* a cap of iron-plate. —pfennig, *m.* V. —münze. —schere, *f.* plate-shears. —schläger, *m.* a tin-man. —schmied, *m.* tinker. V. also Pfannenschmied, Kesselflicker. —schneider, *m.* [in iron-works] a clipper of iron-plate. —verzinnung, *f.* the tinning of iron-plate. —waare, *f.* tin-ware. —zinn, *n.* V. Blattzinn.

†**Blechen**, *v. tr.* and *intr.* to pay. Ich habe bereits eine tüchtige Summe geblecht, I have already forked out a handsome sum; er muß artig —, he must come down handsomely.

Blechen, **Blechern**, *adj* and *adv.* made of tin or iron-plate. Ein —er Leuchter, a tin-candlestick.

Blechig, *adj.* and *adv.* [with tawers] hard, compact.

‖**Blechner**, *m.* [-s, *pl.* -] tin-man. V. Blechschläger, ‖ Flaschner, Klempner.

Blecken, [allied to blicken] I. *v. intr.* [unusual] to be visible, to appear. II. *v. tr.* to lay open, to show. Die Zähne —, to show the teeth.

‖**Bleckern**, *v. intr.* to come in sight, to appear often.

Bleckzahn, *m.* [-es, *pl.* -zähne] a prominent tooth.

1. **Blei**, *m.* [a fish] V. Bleihe.

2. **Blei**, *n.* [-es] [allied to the Gr. *μόλυβδος*, Slav. *molowo*, *olowo*, Lat. *plumbum*. A. S. *bloma* signifies metal in general] 1) [a metal] lead. [in alchimy and chimistry] saturn. Mit — ausgießen, auslegen, füttern, überziehen, to lead; von —, leaden; wie —, plumbeous, plumbean; phosphorsaures — [bunt —erz], phosphate of lead, green and brown lead-ore; arseniksaures —, arseniate of lead; chromsaures —, chromate of lead, red lead-spar, red lead-ore; kohlensaures —, V. —spath; kupferhaltiges schwefelkohlensaures —, green carbonate of copper, cupreous sulphato-carbonate of lead; molybdänsaures —, yellow lead-ore, molybdate of lead; rhomboedrisches schwefelkohlensaures —, sulphato-tri-carbonate of lead; prismatisches schwefelkohlensaures —, sulphato-carbonate of lead; salzsaures —, corneous lead-ore, muriate of lead, murio-carbonate of lead; scheelsaures —, tungstate of lead; — mit Schwefel und Arsenik versetzt [Roth—erz], chromate of lead, red lead-spar, red lead-ore; Wasser—, black-lead; — in Blöcken, pig-lead; gerolltes —, sheet-lead. *Fig.* [in familiar lang., denoting a heaviness or weariness] Es liegt mir wie — in den Gliedern, I feel a weight in my limbs. 2) several things made of lead. *a)* [with hunters] shot. Pulver und —, powder and shot. *b)* [in seamen's lang., a plummet or mass of lead, used in sounding at sea] lead. *c)* [with mechanics &c.] a mass of lead attached to a line, and used to ascertain the perpendicular position of any thing, a plummet. *d)* a stamp of lead. ‖ *e)* V. —stift.

Bleiader, *f.* [in mines] a lode of lead. —anschuß, *m.* [in chimistry] the shooting of lead in crystals. —arbeit, *f.* [works in lead] plumbery. —arbeiter, *m.* a plumber. —artig, *adj.* and *adv.* plumbean, plumbeous. —arzenei, *f.* a medicine prepared with lead. —asche, *f.* lead-ashes, plumbagin. —auflösung, *f.* [in chim.] the solution of litharge in vinegar. —balsam, *m.* [in chimistry] a solution of acetate of lead or oxyde of lead in oil of turpentine. —baryt, *m.* Axotomer —baryt, V. rhomboedrisches schwefelkohlensaures —; diprismatischer —baryt, V. kohlensaures —; hemiprismatischer —baryt, V. chromsaures —; peritomer —baryt, new ore of lead, lead-spar from Mendip; prismatischer —baryt, V. —vitriol; pyramidaler —baryt, V. molybdänsaures —; rhomboedrischer —baryt, V. phosphorsaures —. —baum, *m.* [in chimistry] arbor saturni. —blatt, *n.* a sheet of lead. —blech, *n.* lead-plate. —blick, *m.* [in metallurgy] the shine of lead. —blumen, *pl.* flowers of lead. —blüthe, *f.* V. arseniksaures —. —butter, *f.* [in chimistry] sublimated muriate of lead. —dach, *n.* [a flat roof covered with lead] leads. —darmgicht, *f.* dry-gripes. —decker, *m.* one who covers roofs with lead, a plumber. —drüse, *f.* lead-crystal. —erde, *f.* earthy carbonate of lead, indurated and friable earthy lead-ore. —erz, *n.* lead-ore, plumbagin. —erz von Mendip, V. peritomer —baryt; mulmiges —erz, [in mining] belland. —erzstufe, *f.* pee. —essig, *m.* vinegar of saturn. —fahlerz, *n.* a sort of antimonial sulphuret lead-ore. —falk, *m.* the ring-tail. —farbe, *f.* lead-colour. —farben, —farbig, *adj.* and *adv.* leady-coloured. —farbiges Blau, lead-coloured blue. *Fig.* livid. Sein Gesicht, seine Lippen wurden ganz —farbig, his countenance, his lips became quite livid. —feder, *f.* lead-pencil. —fluß, *m.* crystallized lead. —frischofen, *m.* [in metallurgy] a finery. —funken, *f.* [in mining] knits. —füßig, *adj.* and *adv.* leaden-heeled. —gang, *m.* V. —ader. —gänge, bowse. —geist, *m.* spirit of saturn. —gelb, *n.* yellow oxyde of lead, massicot, masticot [sometimes used by painters]. —gemisch, *n.* the amalgam of mercury with lead. —gewerk, *n.* [manufactory of lead] a plumbery. —gewicht, *n.* 1) weight of lead, plummet. 2) *Fig.* a heavy load. Es hing mir wie ein —gewicht an den Füßen, it impeded my feet like a leaden weight. —gießer, *m.* a plumber. —gießerei, *f.* 1) [the art of casting lead] plumbery. 2) the shop of a plumber. —glanz, *m.* 1) lead-glance, sulphuret of lead. Klein und feinspeisiger —glanz, granular galena; streifiger —glanz, stripmalm. 2) V. —schweif. —glas, *n.* 1) lead-glass. 2) [in mineralogy] a sort of white lead-ore, sparry white lead-ore, or carbonate of lead. —glätte, *f.* litharge. —grau, I. *n.* lead-coloured blue. II. *adj.* and *adv.* leady. —grube, *f.* lead-mine. —haft, *adj.* and *adv.* resembling lead, plumbean, plumbeous. —haltig, *adj.* and *adv.* containing lead. —hammer, *m.* a plumber's hammer. —herd, *m.* [in metallurgy] V. Treibherd. —holz, *n.* marsh leather wood. —hornerz, *n.* V. salzsaures —. —hütte, *f.* lead-work. —hütte mit Gebläse, smelting house, blast-house. —kalk, *m.* oxyd of lead, white-lead. —kamm, *m.* a leaden comb. —karbonat, *n.* rhomboedrisches —karbonat, V. rhomboedrisches schwefelkohlensaures —. —kehlchen, *n.* [a bird] blue-throathed warbler. —kessel, *m.* lead-bucket. —klumpen, *m.* a lump of lead. —knecht, *m.* [with glaziers] V. Flintmesser. —könig, *m.* [in chimistry] regulus of lead. —kraut, *n.* V. —wurz. —kugel, *f.* a ball of lead. —loth, *n.* a plummet, lead, plumb-line. Mit dem —loth ergründen or austiefen, to sound; mit dem —loth abmessen or lothrecht machen, to plumb. —löthung, *f.* the sodering with lead. —maß, *n.* a plummet, lead. —milch, *f.* [in chimistry] solution of lead with vinegar. —mulde, *f.* pig-lead. —mulm, *m.* black lead-ore. —nagel, *m.* lead-nail. —niederschlag, *m.* [in chim.] magistery of lead. —ocher, *m.* ocher of lead. —öl, *n.* V. —balsam. —oxyd, *n.* gelbes —oxyd, V. —glätte; natürliches rothes —oxyd, V. Mennig; wolframsaures —oxyd, V. scheelsaures —. —platte, *f.* a sheet of lead. —pulver, *n.* powdered lead. —quick, *n.* V. —gemisch. —rab, *n.* V. —zug. —rahm, *m.* [in chimistry] citrate of lead. —rauch, *m.* [in lead-works] flight. —recht, I. *adj.* plumb, perpendicular. II *adv.* plumb, in a perpendicular direction. Die Mauer steht —recht, the wall stands plumb. —rohr, *n.* a pencil-case, porte-crayon. —röhre, *f.* a pipe of lead, leaden pipe. —roth, *n.* V. Mennig. —safran, *m.* V. Mennig. —salbe, *f.* a salve prepared with lead. —salpeter, *m.* [in chimistry] nitrate of lead. —salz, *n.* [in chimistry] acetate of lead. —sand, *m.* sand of lead. —schaum, *m.* V. —asche. —scheit, *n.* V. —wage. —schicht, *f.* [in metallurgy] the quantity of lead fused in 24 hours. —schiefer, *m.* plumbiferous slate. —schlacke, *f.* slag of lead. —schlich, *m.* [in metallurgy] schlich of lead. —schnur, *f.* plumb-line, plumb-rule. —schwärze, *f.* black lead-ore. —schweif, *m.* [in mineralogy] compact galena or lead-glance. —schwer, *adj.* and *adv.* heavy as lead. [in a proper and in a figur. sense] Der Schlaf liegt —schwer auf mir, the leaden hand of sleep is upon me. —siegel, *n* a leaden seal [appendant to cloth, goods &c.]. —sinter, *m.* a sort of ocher of lead. —spath, *m.* white lead-ore, sparry white lead-ore, carbonate of lead. —spiegel, *m.* [in mineralogy] specular galena. —stange, *f.* a rope-dancer's pole, a poy. —stein, *m.* plumbago. —stift, *m.* ‖ *n.* lead-pencil. Ein schwarzer —stift, a black lead pencil; ein rother —stift, a red lead pencil. —stiftmacher, *m.* a manufacturer of pencils. —stufe, *f.* lead-mine. —sulphatokarbonat, *m.* V. prismatisches schwefelkohlensaures —. —superoxyd, *n.* red-lead V. Mennig. —tafel, *f.* a sheet of lead. —vitriol, *m.* [in chimistry] sulphate of lead. —wage, *f.* 1) [an instrument used by carpenters, masons &c.] a plummet, level [—scheit]. 2) [a long piece of lead attached to a line used in sounding the depth of water] a plummet, lead [—loth]. —weiß, *n.* 1) V. —spath. 2) ceruse, white-lead, Spanish-paint. 3) plumbago. —weißauflösung, *f.* a solution of ceruse in vinegar. —weißfarbe, *f.* white paint. —weißschneider, *m.* V. —stiftmacher. —winde, *f.* V. —zug. —wurf, *m.* 1) a plummet, lead. 2) sounding with a plummet. —wurz, *f.* 1) European leatherwort. 2) Ceylon leadwort. —zieher, *m.* one who draws lead for glaziers. —zucker, *m.* V. —salz. —zug, *m.* [with glaziers] vice. —zugmacher, *m.* V. —zieher.

Bleiben, [A. S. *be-lafan*, Old G. *bi-liban*, Go. *λιλα-εαν*. The Sw. *lifwa*, the Ice. *lifa* and the Engl. *leave* are = hinterlassen] *ir. v. intr.* [u. w. seyn] 1) to continue, to rest or abide in a place for an indefinite time, to remain. Sie blieben einen Monat in Rom, they remained a month in Rome; ich werde zwei Tage hier —, I shall tarry here two days; wir — in einem Wirthshause die Nacht, we remain at an inn for a night; — Sie hier, stay here; bleibe bei mir, abide with me; bleibe zu Jerusalem, in diesem Lande, [in Script.] abide at Jerusalem, in this land; zu Hause —, to stay at home; zurück —, to stay behind; hier ist meines —s nicht, here is no abiding for me. *Fig.* *Bleibe mit deinem Witze zu Hause, spare your wit; bleib' mir vom Leibe, stand off, keep off; wo ist mein Freund geblieben? what has become of my friend? [where is he? what is his condition?]; es muß unter uns —, we must keep it a secret or to ourselves. 2) to delay one's coming. Wo — Sie so lange? where did you stay or tarry so long? er bleibt sehr lange, he stays away a long while, he is very long in coming; die Post bleibt sehr lange, the post is very long in coming. 3) to continue unchanged, or in a particular state, to remain. Stehen —, sitzen —, to continue standing, to stand still, to stop, to continue sitting; die Uhr ist stehen geblieben, the watch has stopped; gesund —, to continue or remain in health; es wird nicht dabei —, the affair will not rest thus; bleibend, [in botany, continuing without withering] persistent, persisting [opposed to marcescent]; gelassen —, to keep one's temper; Noah allein blieb leben, Noah only remained in life er blieb seinem Entschlusse nicht treu, he did not keep his resolution; er blieb dabei, he persevered in it; dumm —, to remain stupid; die beiden nordischen Mächte blieben neutral, the two Northern powers remained neuter; neutral —, to stand neuter; kinderlos bist du, kinderlos bleibe, childless thou art, childless remain; es bleibt dabei, agreed! done! bei der Wahrheit —, to adhere to, to observe the truth; bei dem Buchstaben —, to adhere strictly to the letter; der Meinung —, to abide by an opinion; ich bleibe der Meinung, I stand to the opinion; des festen Vorsatzes —, to stand to one's firm resolution. 4) to last, to be durable. Ein —der Eindruck, a lasting impression; ein —des [dauerhaftes] Hochroth, a standing crimson; seine Gerechtigkeit bleibet ewiglich, [in Script.] his righteousness endureth for ever; denn er wird ewiglich —, [in Scripture] surely, he shall not be moved for ever; er hat keine —de Stätte, he never stays in any place, he is never quiet, he has no fixed place of rest. 5) to be left, to remain. Es bleibt ihm nichts als die Hoffnung, he has nothing left but hope; der Name ist ihm geblieben, he was ever after called by that name; ihm bleibt kein Mittel, he has no resource left; es wird mehr als die Hälfte übrig —, there will be more than the half left. 6) to be left undone. Wo sind wir letzthin [stehen] geblieben? where did we leave off or stop the other day? 7) [u. w. lassen] to leave off, to abstain from, to omit, to avoid doing. Er läßt es dennoch nicht —, he does not leave off or forbear doing it, he still does it; laß das Schwatzen —, forbear prattling; soll ich es — lassen? shall I forbear? wenn du nicht willst, so lasse es —, if you don't choose it, let it alone. 8) to perish, to be killed [in battle or in a duel]. Er blieb in der Schlacht von Wagram, he lost his life, he died at the battle of Wagram. *Fig.* [in seamen's language] Das Schiff ist geblieben, the ship has been lost.

Bleich, [allied to blicken] *adj.* and *adv.* 1) bleak, pale, wan. — seyn or aussehen, to look pale; —e Wangen, pale or pallid cheeks; — von Gesicht, pale-faced; vor Entsetzen — werden, to grow pale with horror. *Fig.* Die —e Furcht, pale-faced fear. 2) not bright or vivid. Eine —e Farbe, a faint colour; ein —es Roth, a faint red; — werden, to fade [said of colours]. Syn. V. Blaß.

Bleich-blau, *adj.* and *adv.* pale blue. —**farbig**, *adj.* and *adv.* having a faint colour, faded. —**gelb**, *adj.* and *adv.* Eine —gelbe Farbe, a palish yellow colour. —**gesicht**, *n.* [in pity or contempt] a sallow-faced fellow. —**grün**, *adj.* and *adv.* Eine —grüne Farbe, a palish green colour. —**sucht**, *f.* 1) [in medicine] the green sickness, chlorosis. Die —sucht habend, chlorotic. 2) [an affection of plants, which causes the loss of their green colour] chlorosis; *it.* [a disease in oysters] white sickness. —**süchtig**, *adj.* diseased with the green sickness, chlorotic. —**wassersucht**, *f.* [in medicine] leucophlegmacy.

Bleiche, *f.* [*pl.* -n] 1) a sickly whiteness of look, paleness, wanness. Die — der Farben, the faintness of colours. 2) [the act or art of whitening, especially cloth] bleaching. 3) [a place for bleaching] bleaching-place, bleachery. Eine Wachs—, a wax bleachery.

Bleichen, I. *v. intr.* [u. w. seyn] to grow white, to bleach. Siehe, wie mein Haar vor Kummer gebleicht ist, behold, how my hair has been bleached by grief. II. *v. tr.* to whiten, to make white or whiter, to bleach [applied to many things, but particularly to cloth and thread]. Wachs —, to bleach wax; gebleichter Zwirn, bleached thread, sister's thread; Endivie oder Lattich —, [in gardening] to blanch endive or lettuce; Krankheit hat seine Wangen gebleicht, sickness has blanched his cheeks. *Prov.* Einen Mohren — or weißwaschen, to wash an Æthiop white. Das Bleichen, the act of bleaching, dealbation.

Bleich-plan, —**platz**, *m.* bleaching-place, bleachery. —**salz**, *n.* oxymuriatic acid. —**stätte**, *f.* V. —platz. —**wand**, *f.* a clay-wall. —**werk**, *n.* V. —wand. —**wiese**, *f.* a meadow for bleaching.

Bleicher, *m.* [-s, *pl.* -] —**inn**, *f.* 1) a bleacher. 2) [seldom used] a wine of a clear pale red colour, claret.

Bleicher-korb, *m.* hamper. —**lohn**, *m.* money paid for bleaching cloth &c.

Bleicherei, *f.* [in contempt] bleaching.

Bleien, *v. tr.* 1) to fit with lead, to lead. 2) to mark with a leaden seal, to append a leaden seal to. 3) to adjust by a plumb-line, to plumb [a building or a wall]. 4) [among glaziers] to draw lead with a vice.

Bleier, *m.* [-s, *pl.* -] V. Bleigießer.

Bleiern, *adj.* and *adv.* [consisting of lead] leaden, plumbean, plumbeous. Eine —e Kugel, a leaden ball. *Fig.* *a*) [heavy] Der Schlaf lag — auf ihnen, they were heavy with sleep. *b*) leaden, heavy, indisposed to action.

Bleihe, *m.* [-s, *pl.* -n] [probably from bleich] [a fish] the bleak, white-bait, blay.

Bleiicht, *adj.* and *adv.* resembling lead, plumbean, plumbeous.

Bleiig, *adj.* and *adv.* containing lead.

Bleken, V. Blecken.

Blende, *f.* [*pl.* -n] 1) something to hinder the sight, a blind. *a*) a screen, a cover, a blind. Eine — für Pferde [das Blendleder, Scheuleder], a blind or blinker for a horse; die —n vor den Cajütenfenstern, [in seamen's lang.] dead lights. *b*) a folding-screen. *c*) [in the milit. art] blinds. Einen Laufgraben mit —n decken, to cover a trench with blinds. 2) [with miners] a dark-lantern. 3) [in mineralogy] mock-lead, blend, sulphuret of zinc, black-jack. Schwarze, braune, rothe, gelbe und grüne —, verglaste — [Rubin—, Zink—], black, brown, red, yellow and green blend; dichte — [Schaalen—], fibrous blend. 4) [in architecture] *a*) a blind or mock-door or -window. *b*) [Mauerblende] a niche. In dieser — steht ein Heiligenbild, there stands the image of a saint in this niche.

Blenden, [allied to blind] *v. tr.* 1) to make blind, to deprive of sight, to blind. Dieser morgenländische Fürst ließ alle seine Brüder —, this Eastern prince caused all his brothers' eyes to be put out; ein Pferd —, [ihm Blenden vor die Augen machen] to blindfold a horse. *Fig.* Seine bescheidene Miene kann mich nicht —, his air of modesty can not impose upon me. 2) to overpower with light, to dazzle. Der Glanz der Sonne blendet die Augen, the brightness of the sun dazzles the eyes; blendend, striking with splendour, dazzling; ein —der Glanz, a dazzling lustre; —d weiß, dazzling white. *Fig.* Von einem glänzenden Ruhme geblendet werden, to be dazzled by a resplendent glory; weibliche Schöne blendet den arglosen Jüngling, female beauty fascinates the unguarded youth; eine —de Schönheit, a brilliant beauty; —d schön, surpassingly beautiful; den Verstand —, to darken the understanding; das Gemüth —, to blind the mind. 3) [with hunters] Etwas —, to cover with blinks; [with furriers] die Felle —, to dye the furs; die Zeuge —, [with dyers] to dip the stuffs for the first time in the dye; [in fortific.] Einen Laufgraben —, to blind a trench. 4) Gold —, to dim or tarnish gold.

Blend-fenster, *n.* [with engravers] a blind for a window, made of oiled paper or gauze. —**hell**, *adj.* and *adv.* overpowering by a strong light, dazzling. —**kugel**, *f.* [in military art] smoke-ball. —**lampe**, *f.* V. Spiegellampe. —**laterne**, —**leuchte**, *f.* a dark-lantern. —**leder**, *n.* a blind for a horse. —**rahmen**, *m.* [with painters] a blind frame. —**stein**, *m.* ridge-tile, gutter-tile, pantile. —**werk**, *n.* 1) something that misleads the eye. V. Blendung, 2). 2) *Fig.* *a*) something that misleads or blinds the understanding. Einem ein —werk vormachen, to delude any one. *b*) deception, delusion, illusion. Es ist nichts als —werk, it is all a deception.

Blendig, *adj.* and *adv.* [in mineral.] blendous.

Blendling, *m.* [-s, *pl.* -e] 1) [with men] a bastard [seldom used]. 2) [an animal of a mixed breed] a mongrel.

Blendung, *f.* 1) the act of blinding. *Fig.* Der Schnee verursacht eine — der Augen, snow dazzles the eyes. 2) any thing that misleads the eye, a blind; [in the military art] blinds [Blendwerk]; —en für die Schanzgräber, [in fortification] mantelet, mantlet; [in optics] diaphragm, partition. *Fig.* delusion, illusion.

||**Blesse**, *f.* [*pl.* -n] V. Blässe 2.

***Blessiren**, *v. tr.* to wound. V. Verwunden.

***Blessur**, *f.* [*pl.* -en] a wound. V. Wunde.

Bletz, *m.* [-es, *pl.* -e] [Sw. *plös*, allied to the Gr. πλήσσω, schlagen] [in mining] an iron wedge.

Blick, *m.* [-es, *pl.* -e] 1) [a sudden shoot of light or splendour] glance, gleam. Der Sonnen—, a sudden burst of light in the clouds or atmosphere, coruscation; Sonnen—e, glances of the sun; das Silber thut einen —, [in metallurgy] the silver appears shining [when purified by cupellation or testing]. 2) any body that appears shining in testing. —e, [with painters and engravers] touches of light. 3) a shoot or darting of sight, a rapid or momentary view or cast, a snatch of sight, a glance of the eye. Einen — auf etwas thun or werfen, to look at a thing with a sudden, rapid cast of the eye, to cast a glance on a thing, to glance at a thing; sie schien nie einen — auf mich zu werfen, she never seemed to cast a glance on me; sie wirft —e [äugelt], she glances; ein — von ihr, a twinkling of her eye; sie sprach mit mir durch —e, she spoke with me by her looks, ihre Augen schießen gefährliche —e, her eyes dart malignant glances; er warf einen wüthenden — auf die Menge, he cast a furious look on the crowd; jeder — erfüllte ihn mit tödtlicher Angst, every look filled him with anguish; verliebte or zärtliche —e, amorous glances, sheep's eyes; ein niedergeschlagener — verräth Sittsamkeit, a downcast look indicates modesty; der — seitwärts [Seitenblick], a sidelong glance; auf den ersten —, at the first glance, at first sight; mit einem —e, with one look, at one view. *Fig* Seine —e [Augen] auf etwas heften, to fix one's eyes upon something; richten wir unsere —e auf Gott, let us look up to God; einen — des Mitleids auf seinen Verlust werfend, glancing an eye of pity on his loss.

Blick-feuer, *n.* 1) [in seamen's language] beacon, signal-light. 2) false-fire. —**gold**, *n.* [in metallurgy] gold that contains a little silver after cupellation. —**silber**, *n.* refined silver. —**weise**, *adv.* by single looks. —**ziel**, *n.* point of view.

Blicke, *f.* [*pl.* -n] [a fish] a species of the bleak [cyprinus nasus].

Blicken, [in Sw. *bliga* signifies ansehen; probably instead of belicken and licken, allied to the provinc. lugen, Gr. λεύσσω, schauen] I. *v. intr.* 1) to shoot or dart a ray of light or splendour, to glance. Die Sonne blickt durch die Wolken, the sun breaks through the clouds; das Silber blickt [auf dem Treibherde], silver appears shining. *Fig.* Er darf sich nicht — lassen, he dares not show his face; der Geiz blickt ihm aus jeder Miene, every feature of him shows his avarice. 2) to look with a sudden rapid cast of the eye, to snatch a momentary or hasty view, to glance. Auf Einen, nach Jemand —, to cast a glance on any one; seitwärts —, to look sideways. II. *v. tr.* rather *poet.* to express by the look. Er blickt Zorn und Verachtung, his looks express anger and contempt.

‖ **Blickling**, *m.* [-es, *pl.* -e] V. Weißfisch.

Blimbing, *m.* [-es, *pl.* -e] [a shrub, native of India] Bilimbi.

Blink, *n.* [-es, *pl.* -e] [in ship-building] a wooden machine to drive the wedges under a ship's bottom, when she is to be launched.

Blind, [allied to blenden] *adj.* and *adv.* 1) [lustre-less] dull, tarnished. Der Spiegel ist —, the mirror is dull; dieß Silbergeschirr sieht ganz — aus, this plate looks quite tarnished. 2) [destitute of the sense of seeing] blind. — an einem Auge, blind of an eye; ein —er Mann, ein —er, a blind man. *Prov.* Ein —er Mann, ein armer Mann, a blind man is a poor man; er urtheilt davon wie der —e von der Farbe, blind men can judge no colours; ein —er findet wohl manchmahl ein Hufeisen, a blind man may perchance hit the mark; führt ein —er Mann den andern, werden Beide nicht weit wandern, if the blind lead the blind, both fall into the ditch; —e Kuh spielen, to play at blindman's buff. *Fig. a)* [destitute of the necessary or usual openings] —e Fenster, —e Thüren, [in architecture] blind or mock windows or doors; [with tailors] —e Taschen, blind pockets; —e Knopflöcher, blind buttonholes; die —e Mauer, blind wall; der —e Darm, V. —darm. *b)* [not having the faculty of discernment, destitute of intellectual light] blind. Schriftsteller sind — für ihre eignen Fehler, authors are blind to their own defects; —er Tadel, blind reprobation; — zufahren, to go blindly to work; —er Gehorsam, passive obedience; Einem —es Vertrauen schenken, to give implicit confidence to any one; eine —e Liebe, a fond love or passion; —e Wuth, eyeless rage; das —e Glück, blindfolded fortune. *Prov.* Die Liebe ist —, love is blind, Cupid is blindfolded. *c)* imitating reality, but not real. Ein —er Lärm, a false alarm; der —e Angriff, a feigned attack, false attack; — laden, to load without shot, to charge with blank cartridge; — schießen, to shoot in the air, without a bullet; to shoot at random; ein —er Soldat, [in military affairs] a pass-volant; ein —er Postreisender, a passenger in the stage-coach that got a place without paying the fare or being booked; [in seamen's language] die Vorsegel liegen —, the after-sails becalm the fore-sails. *d)* [at a wrong, an unseasonable time &c.] — kommen or — ankommen, to meet with a bad reception, to meet a repulse. 3 [where one cannot see] blind, dark, obscure. In —er Nacht, in a dark night. 4) [that which is not seen] —e Klippen, [in seamen's lang.] breakers; ein —es Schloß, a dead-lock; ein —er Afterblutfluß, blind piles.

Blind-aal, *m.* a fish in the Mediterranean, resembling the eel. **—boden**, *m.* [in breweries] false bottom. **—darm**, *m.* [in anatomy] the blind gut, cæcum. **—fenster**, *n.* V. Blendfenster. **—fisch**, *m.* the little needlefish. **—geboren**, *adj.* and *adv.* born blind. **—gewölbe**, *n.* [in fortification] casemate. **—glaube**, *m.* [in theology] orthodoxy. **—gläubig**, *adj.* and *adv.* [in theology] orthodox. **—holz**, *n.* [with joiners] wood which is to be veneered, or covered with finer wood. **—maus**, *f.* the blind rat. **—rahmen**, *m.* V. Blendrahmen. **—schleiche**, *f.* blindworm, slow-worm.

1. **Blinde**, *m.* [-n, *pl.* -n] V. Blind [blinder Mann]. Die —, a blind woman.

2. **Blinde**, *f.* [*pl.* -n] [in seamen's language] sprit-sail. Die Augen der —, the eyes or waterholes of the sprit-sail of a ship.

Blindekuh, *f.* [a play] blindman's buff. Wollen wir — spielen? shall we play at blindman's buff?

‖ **Blinden**, V. Blenden.

Blindheit, *f.* blindness, ablepsy. *Fig.* Unsere eigene — und Unwissenheit, our own blindness and ignorance; er ist mit — geschlagen, he is struck with blindness.

Blindlings, *adv.* [without sight] blindly. *Fig.* Sich von einem Andern — leiten lassen, to be blindly led by another; ich glaube Ihrem Worte —, I implicitly believe your word; der Weg ist mir so bekannt, daß ich ihn — finden könnte, I know the way so well, that I could find it blindfolded.

Blink, I. *adj.* and *adv.* gleaming. II. *m.* [-s, *pl.* -e] [in seamen's lang.] a clear spot in a cloudy sky.

Blinken, [from the root of blicken] *v. intr.* 1) to sparkle with light, to gleam, to glitter. Ein blinkendes Schwert, a gleaming sword; überall blinkte Gold und kostbares Geschmeide, gold and jewels sparkled all around; seine Augen blinken vor Freude, his eyes sparkle with joy; der Wein blinkt im Glase, the wine sparkles, shines in the glass. *Fig.* Ich sah es nur —, I got only a glimpse of it. 2) to blink, to twinkle. Mit den Augen —, to twinkle with the eye.

‖ **Blinkern**, *v. intr.* to glitter, to glisten.

‖ **Blinzelmaus**, V. Blindekuh.

Blinzeln, **Blinzen**, [from blind] *v. intr.* 1) [to open and shut the eyes by turns] to blink, to twinkle, to wink. Der Blinzelnde, winker. 2) [to see obscurely] to blink. Ein Auge blinzelte und lahm war das eine Bein, one eye was blinking and one leg was lame.

Blinzer, *m.* [-s, *pl.* -] [one who blinks or has bad eyes] blinkard.

Blinzhaut, *f.* V. Nickhaut.

Blinzler, *m.* [-s, *pl.* -] 1) one who blinks, blinkard, winker. 2) [a fish] a species of the wrasse or gold finny.

Blitz, *m.* [-es, *pl.* -e] [probably from blicken] 1) a sudden shoot of light or splendour, a flash of light, a glimpse. Der — seines Auges, the flash of his eye; die —e seines Schwertes, the glitter of his sword; der — eines Feuergewehres, the flash of a gun. 2) lightning. Das Leuchten des —es, flashes of lightning; Donner und —, thunder and lightning; der — hat in den Kirchthurm geschlagen, a thunderbolt has fallen upon the steeple of the church; vom —e getroffen or gerührt, thunder-struck; so schnell wie der —, as quick as lightning.

Blitz-ableiter, *m.* a conductor of lightning [to secure buildings from the effects of lightning]. **—artig**, *adj.* and *adv.* like lightning. †**—blau**, *adj.* and *adv.* black and blue. Er würgte ihn, bis er —blau im Gesicht wurde, he choked him till he grew black in the face. **—eile**, **—eseile**, *f.* 1) the swiftness of lightning. 2) *Fig.* the greatest haste. **—feuer**, *n.* electricity. **—feuerhaltig**, *adj.* and *adv.* electric, electrical. **—funken**, *m.* electric spark or flash. **—röhre**, *f.* V. —sinter. **—schlag**, *m.* thunderclap. **—schnelle**, **—esschnelle**, *f.* the rapidity of lightning. **—schwanger**, *adj.* and *adv.* electric [said of clouds]. **—sinter**, *m.* [in mineralogy] vitreous tubes. **—stoff**, *m.* electric substance, electricity. **—strahl**, *m.* flash of lightning.

Blitzen, I. *v. intr.* and *imp.* 1) to glance, to glitter. Ein —des Schwert, a glittering sword; —de Augen, sparkling eyes. 2) to flash, to burst forth or dart, as lightning, to lighten. Es blitzt, it lightens. *Fig.* V. Aufblitzen. II. *v. tr.* [rather poetical] Sein Auge blitzte Wuth und Rache, his eyes glared forth wrath and vengeance.

Blöchtaube, *f.* V. Blocktaube.

Block, *m.* [-es, *pl.* Blöcke] [allied to Pflock, probably allied to legen. But in the sense of Gefängniß it is contracted from Be-lock; Old G. *piloh*, from luken = schließen] 1) a heavy piece of timber or wood, a mass of wood, iron or other metal, a block. Ein — Marmor [Marmor—], a block of marble; ein — Zinn oder Blei, a pig of tin or lead. 2) a mass of wood or metal, with at least one plain surface, such as artificers use, a block. Der — zum Zuhauen der Faßdauben, a cooper's block; der Henker—, the executioner's block; den Kopf auf dem —e verlieren, to come to the block. 3) with engravers and lapidaries, a small block of lead, with one plain surface, on which they set their work. 4) [at cards] a piece of money used for marking up. 5) [in seamen's language] a block. Ein einscheibiger —, a single block; ein zweischeibiger —, a block with two sheaves, a double block; der — am Ende der großen Raa für die Marssegelschoten und großen Topenants, top-sail sheet-block; ein laufender —, a running block; einen — stroppen, to strop a block; ein gestroppter —, a stropped block; — an —, block and block; der — läuft auf dem Heerde, the sheave runs foul. 6) a prison. Einen in den — legen, to confine any one in a prison or jail.

Block-blei, *n.* pig-lead. **—dreher**, *m.* [in ship-building] blockmaker. **—haus**, *n.* 1) [in military art] block-house. 2) [in the North-American settlements] log-house, log-hut. **—holz**, *n.* log-wood. **—hütte**, *f.* V. —haus 2. **—karren**, *m.* V. —wagen. **—kasten**, *m.* [in military affairs] block-box, a box filled with stones and rubbish, for the purpose of blocking up a passage. **—keller**, *m.* V. Balkenkeller. **—kopf**, *m.* [a stupid person] blockhead, loggerhead. **—köpfig**, *adj.* block-headed, logger-headed. **—köpfigkeit**, *f.* blockishness. **—meißel**, *m.* a chisel fastened in a block, such as blacksmiths and nailmakers use. **—mörser**, *m.* a mortar for bombs, fastened in a block. **—nagel**, *m.* a strong peg used on rafts or floats. **—pfeife**, *f.* a fife made out of one piece or block. **—rad**, *m.* 1) a wheel formed out of one block. 2) a strong wheel made of wood alone, a truck. **—rolle**, *f.* 1) a block = a pulley. 2) [in seamen's language] the sheave. **—säge**, *f.* pit-saw. **—schiff**, *n.* a float or raft. **—seife**, *f.* soap in squares. **—stück**, *n.* [a mass of tin or lead] a pig. **—taube**, *f.* ring-dove. **—wagen**, *m.* 1) a waggon made of wood alone. 2) a truck. **—werk**, *n.* Das —werk eines Schiffes, the blocks of a ship. **—zinn**, *n.* block-tin.

***Blockade**, [*pl.* -n] **Blockirung**, *f.* blocking up, blockade.

Blocken, [allied to legen] I. *v. intr.* [in falconry, to light on a tree] to perch. II. *v. tr.* [with shoemakers] Einen Stiefel —, to stretch a boot over the tree.

Blöcken, [V. Block 6] *v. tr.* [rather vulgar] Einen stöcken und —, to put any one in stocks and blocks, to imprison any one.

***Blockiren**, *v. tr.* to blockade, to block up [a town &c.].

†**Blocksberg**, *m.* [-es] V. Brocken. *Fig.* Jemand auf den — wünschen, to wish a person far off, to wish any one at Jericho.

Blödauge, *n.* [-s, *pl.* -n] 1) a dim-sighted or weak-eyed person. 2) [a fish] a species of cod.

Blöde, [Ice. *blaudur*, furchtsam; in Old G. *blugo* signifies schwach and *ploden* sich fürchten] *adj.* and *adv.* 1) weak, feeble [said of the eyes]. — Augen haben, to be weak sighted or dim-sighted. *Fig. a)* [of the understanding] Ein —r Verstand, a weak understanding. *b)* reserved, modest, timid, bashful, abashed, coy. Was macht Euch so —, mein guter Freund? what makes you so shy, my good friend? ein —r Jüngling, a bashful youth. ‖ 2) worn, thin. Mein Rock ist ziemlich —, my coat is rather worn out; mein Leinenzeug ist so oft schon gewaschen, daß es viele —Stellen hat, my linen has been so frequently washed that it has many thin places.

Blöd-sichtig, *adj.* and *adv.* weak-sighted, dim-sighted, purblind. —**sichtigkeit**, *f.* dimness of vision, purblindness. —**sinn**, *m.* weakness of understanding, imbecility, simplicity, harmless folly, silliness. —**sinnig**, *adj.* and *adv.* weak in intellect, imbecile, simple, silly. Ein Blödsinniger, a fool. —**sinnigkeit**, *f.* V. Blödsinn.

Blödigkeit, *f.* weakness [of sight]. *Fig. a)* weakness [of understanding], imbecility. *b)* timidity, bashfulness, reserve, shyness.

Blödling, [unusual] *m.* [-es, *pl.* -e] an imbecile person.

Blöhm, *m.* [-es, *pl.* -e] **Blöhme**, *f.* [*pl.* -n] [seems to be corrupted from Plan] [with sportsmen] the rutting-place of stags.

Blöken, [seems to come from the old leuen = schreien, see Löwe] *v. intr.* 1) to cry as a sheep or as a calf, to bleat, to baa. 2) [in contempt] to brawl.

Blond, [A. S. *blondon* signifies gefärbt and also gelb] *adj.* and *adv.* having light-coloured hair, free from a dark hue, fair. —e Haare, light-coloured hair; eine —e Perrücke, a flaxen wig; der —e, a youth of light-coloured hair; die —e [—ine], a female of light-coloured hair and fair complexion.

Blond-gelockt, *adj.* and *adv.* having light-coloured curly hair, fair-haired. —**haarig**, *adj.* and *adv.* having light-coloured hair, fair-haired. *—**kopf**, *m.* 1) a man with light-coloured hair. 2) = die Blonde. V. Blond. —**köpfig**, V. —haarig. —**lockig**, V. —gelockt.

Blondchen, *n.* [-s, *pl.* -] [in famil. lang.] a fair-haired little girl.

Blonde, *f.* [*pl.* -n] blond-lace.

Blondheit, *f.* the state of having light-coloured hair, fair-hairedness.

Bloß, [Low S. *bloot*, Dan. *blot*, Sw. *blott*, allied to the provinc. blutt = unbedeckt] *adj.* and *adv.* [without covering] bare. Mit —en Füßen [barfüßig], with the feet bare, barefooted; mit —em Haupte [bloßköpfig], with uncovered head, bareheaded; die Arme waren —, the arms were naked; mit —er Brust, with an open breast; nackt und —, naked and bare; *fig.* [= entblößt, arm &c.] poor, indigent; ein —es [entblößtes] Schwert, a naked or drawn sword; das —e Auge, the naked eye [not assisted by glasses]; auf der —en Erde liegen, to lie on the bare ground; er kam mit —en Händen, he came bare of money, empty-handed; unter dem —en Himmel, under the canopy of heaven. *Fig. a)* exposed [= not protected &c.]. Im —en seyn, im —en stehen, to be deprived of the necessaries of life; seine Unwissenheit — geben, to betray or expose one's ignorance; sich — geben, [in fencing] to lay one's self open; die Reiterei war sehr — gestellt, the horse was very much exposed; den König &c. — stellen, [at chess] to unguard the king; [in backgammon] der —e Stein, a blot; einen —en Stein schlagen, to hit a blot; Einen — stellen, to expose any one to inconveniences, to disgrace or insult any one; die Ehre und Sicherheit eines Volkes — stellen, to compromise the honour and safety of a nation. *b)* [this or that only] mere. Es ist ein —er Argwohn, it is a mere suspicion; — als Vermuthungen, only as conjectures; der —e Glaube, the naked belief; —e Worte, bare words; er nannte — die Straße, he barely named the street; ein Fürst — dem Titel nach, a prince barely in title; — um Ihre Freunde zu verbinden, merely to oblige your friends.

Blöße, *f.* [*pl.* -n] 1) bareness, nakedness, nudity. *Fig.* Seinem Gegner eine — geben, [in fencing] to lay one's self open; eines Menschen — aufdecken, to expose the faults of a person, to lay them open, to make them public. 2) a naked or uncovered place. *a)* [in a wood or forest] a glade. *b)* [upon a skin of fur, where the hair is come off] a bare place.

‖**Blößen**, *v. tr.* [to strip off the covering, to make naked] to bare. Die Brust —, to bare the breast. V. Entblößen.

Blößling, *m.* [unusual] [-es, *pl.* -e] 1) a skin of fur, where the hair has come off. 2) a very poor or indigent person.

‖**Blötz**, *m.* V. Plötz.

‖**Blubbern**, V. Flubbern.

Blühen, [allied to the Lat. *flos*, the Gr. φλόος, Bast, as well as to βλα-στάνω, sprossen, and φλέω, φλύω, fließen, and signifies originally sich bewegen. According to others, however, it is allied to blicken, glühen &c.] *v. intr.* 1) to bloom, to flower, to blossom, to blow. Die Pfirsichbäume — gewöhnlich im April und die Aepfelbäume im Mai, peachtrees usually flower in April and appletrees in May; das — der Pflanzen, blossoming; —de Rosen, blowing roses; —de Felder, flowery fields. *Fig.* Eine —de Gesichtsfarbe, a florid complexion; die Wüste wird — wie die Rose, [in Script.] the desert shall blossom as the rose; —de Schönen, bloomy beauties; meine —de Jugend, my flowering youth; —de Reize, blooming charms or graces; das —de Alter, the flower of age, the prime or spring of life; eine *—de Einbildungskraft, a florid fancy; eine —de Schreibart, a flowery style; der Ackerbau, Handel blühet, agriculture, commerce flourishes; eine —de Stadt, a flourishing town; damahls blühten Künste und Wissenschaften, arts and sciences flourished then; jetzt blühet sein Glück, *jetzt blühet sein Waizen, now fortune smiles upon him. 2) Das Kupfer blühet, [in metallurgy] fused copper throws up vesicles in cooling, effloresces; das Wasser blühet, [stagnant] water gathers a green film on its surface.

Blühe-stand, *m.* V. Blütestand. —**zeit**, *f.* V. Blütezeit.

Blümchen, *n.* [-s, *pl.* -] 1) a floret, floweret. 2) *Fig.* V. Blume *fig.*

Blume, *f.* [*pl.* -n] [V. Blühen] 1) [in general something starting, or looking, or coming forth] *a)* [with hunters] the tip of a fox's tail. Der Fuchs mit einer weißen —, V. Birkfuchs; der Fuchs mit einer schwarzen — [Brandfuchs], the brant fox. *b)* [with hunters, the tail of deer] the single, [and of hares] the scut. *c)* Die — an einem Geschwür, the white of an ulcer. *d)* [with dyers] the blue froth of the indigo when boiling up in the vat. *e)* [with some authors, menstrual discharges] flowers. 2) [in the general signification] flower. *a)* [in botany, that part of a plant which contains the organs of fructification, with their coverings] = blossom. — haben, to flower; —n hervorbringend, floriferous. *b)* [such plants, as are pleasant to the eye or to the smell &c. and are chiefly cultivated for ornament, as roses, lilies &c.]. —n pflücken, brechen, to crop, pluck flowers; —n sammeln, to gather flowers; den Weg mit —n bestreuen, to strew the way with flowers. *c)* [an imitated or artificial flower]. Ein Zeug mit —n, a flowered stuff; mit —n verziert, flower-inwoven. *Fig. a)* ornament. Rede—n, flowers of rhetoric; die Wahrheit bedarf der —n der Rede nicht, truth needs no flowers of speech; *durch die — sprechen, to speak in metaphors. *b)* the best and finest part of a thing. Die — vom Mehle, flour; die — der Ritterschaft, the crown of knighthood; [in chimistry] Schwefel—n, flowers of sulphur; Zink—n, flowers of zinc; dieser Wein hat eine vorzügliche —, this wine has an excellent bouquet or flavour.

‖**Blumen-asch**, *m.* V. —topf. —**bau**, *m.* V. —zucht. —**becher**, *m.* V. —kelch. —**beet**, *n.* flower-bed. —**bette**, *n.* V. Fruchtboden, Fruchtlager. —**binse**, *f.* flowering rush, or water gladiole. —**blatt**, *n.* floral leaf, [in botany] petal. —**blattlos**, *adj.* and *adv.* [in botany] apetalous. —**bremse**, *f.* humble-bee. —**brett**, *n.* a board or shelf for holding flower-pots. —**büschel**, *m.* a cluster of flowers, [in botany] corymbe. —büschel tragend, corymbiferous. —**decke**, *f.* [in botany] perianth. —**erde**, *f.* garden-mould. —**farbig**, *adj.* and *adv.* having the colour of flowers, variegated. —**feld**, *n.* 1) a field covered with flowers, a flowery field. 2) a piece of ground destined for flowers. —**flor**, *m.* 1) the blow of flowers. 2) a quantity of flowers in blossom. Sie haben hier einen recht schönen —flor, you have a fine collection of [blossoming] flowers. —**flur**, *f.* a flowery field. —**garten**, *m.* a flower-garden. —**gärtner**, *m.* flower-gardener, a cultivator of flowers, florist. —**gefilde**, *n.* a flowery field. —**gehänge**, *n.* 1) a garland, a wreath or a chain of flowers. Mit —gehängen geschmückt, verziert, flower-kirtled. 2) [in architecture] festoon. —**geschirr**, *n.* V. —topf. —**geschmückt**, *adj.* and *adv.* decked out with flowers. —**gestell**, *n.* a stand for flowers, flower-stage. —**gewächs**, *n.* any flowering plant. —**gewand**, *n.* a garment adorned with flowers. —**gewinde**, *n.* V. —gehänge. —**göttinn**, *f.* the goddess of flowers, Flora. —**grapp**, *m.* the female plant of the dyer's madder. —**gras**, *n.* 1) umbelled holosteum. 2) greater stitchwort. —**griffel**, *m.* [in botany] the style. —**haar**, *n.* 1) hair adorned or decked out with flowers. 2) [a plant] common dodder. —**holz**, *n.* flower-wood [from Ceram]. —**käfer**, *m.* [a genus of insects] 1) mordella. 2) anthrenus. —**kaiser**, *m.* [in botany] a doubly proliferous flower. —**kelch**, *m.* [in botany] empalement or flower cup. —**kenner**, *m.* [one skilled in flowers] a florist. —**kette**, *f.* —gehänge. —**kohl**, *m.* cauliflower. —**könig**, *m.* V. —kaiser. —**kranz**, *m.* a wreath or garland of flowers. —**krapp**, V. —grapp. —**krone**, *f.* 1) [in botany, the inner cover of a flower] corol, corolla. 2) V. —kranz. —**kugel**, *f.* [a plant] sphæranthus. —**kunst**, *f.* the art of cultivating and improving flowers. —**leben**, *n.* the life of flowers. —**lese**, *f.* 1) the act of gathering flowers. 2) *Fig.* [a collection of beautiful passages from authors] anthology. —**liebhaber**, *m.* a florist. —**los**, *adj.* flowerless. —**mahler**, *m.* a painter of flowers, flower-painter. —**mahlerei**, *f.* painting of flowers. —**mehl**, *n.* [in botany] pollen. —**monat**, *m.* flower-month. —**nelke**, *f.* pink, carnation. —**orden**, *m.* the name of a society of poets [founded at Nuremberg about 1644]. —**reich**, *adj.* and *adv.* bloomy, flowery. Ein —reicher Garten, a flowery garden. *Fig.* Eine —reiche Schreibart, a flowery or florid style; eine —reiche Rede, a flowery discourse. Das Blumenreiche, floridness. —**ring**, *m.* V. —kranz. —**rohr**, *n.* Indian cane. —**saft**, *m.* the sweet juice collected by bees from the flowers of plants. —**same**, *m.* flower-seed.

—scheibe, *f.* [in botany] spathe. —scherbe, *f.* a flower-pot. —schnur, *f.* V. —gehänge. —seite, *f.* [with leather-dressers] the hair-side [of a skin]. —specht, *m.* the humming bird. —spiele, *pl.* the celebrated Jeux floraux [at Toulouse]. —sprache, *f.* [with Orientals] the language of flowers. —staub, *m.* V. —mehl. —stengel, *m.* the stalk of a flower. —stiel, *m.* [in botany] the peduncle, flower-stalk. —stielchen, *n.* pedicel, pedicle. —stielständig, *adj.* and *adv.* peduuculate. —stock, *m.* 1) a flowerstick. 2) a plant or flower in a pot. Ueberall standen —stöcke vor den Fenstern, everywhere there were flower-pots in the windows. —strauß, *m.* a bunch of flowers, a nosegay, a posy. —stück, *n* 1) a flower-plot in a garden, a parterre. 2) [in painting] a flower-piece. —thal, *n* a flowery valley. —thee, *m.* the imperial or bloom-tea. —topf, *m.* a flower-pot. —uhr, *f.* a horologe consisting of flowers. *Poet.* —umgürtet, *adj.* flower-kirtled. —voll, *adj.* and *adv* abounding in flowers, bloomy, flowery. —werk, *n.* 1) flower-work, artificial flowers. 2) the collective mass of flowers. —zapfen, *m.* [in botany] catkin. —zeit, *f.* [the season when plants blossom] flowering, florescence, florification. —zieher, *m.* [a cultivator of flowers] a florist. —zucht, *f.* the cultivation of flowers. —zwiebel, *f.* [in botany] bulb.

Blümeln, I. *v. intr.* 1) to visit the flowers [said of bees]. 2) *Fig.* [to use florid language] to flourish. Die blümelnde Schreibart, a flowery or florid style [used only in a contemptous sense]. II. *v. tr.* [to adorn with artificial flowers] to flower. Ein geblümelter Zeug, a flowered stuff.

Blümen, *v tr.* [to adorn with artificial flowers] to flower [a ribbon &c.]. Geblümt [beblümt] flowered; ein geblümter Schlafrock, a flowered dressing gown.

Blümicht, *adj.* and *adv.* resembling flowers.

Blümig, *adj.* and *adv.* 1) bloomy, flowery. 2) [adorned with artificial flowers] flowery. Ein —er Zeug, a flowered stuff. *Fig.* Das Blümige, floridness, floweriness.

Blüminn, [unusual] *f.* the goddess of flowers, Flora.

Blumist, *m.* [-en, *pl.* -en] V. Blumenkenner and Blumenzieher.

Blüse, *f.* [*pl.* -n] [in seamen's language] V. Backe, 1).

Blüt, *n.* [-es] [appears to be allied to the Gr. βλύειν, hervorquellen; 1) [in poetry, the juice of some fruits, especially of red ones] blood. Das — der Reben, the blood of grapes. 2) [the fluid which circulates through the arteries and veins of the human body and of other animals; which fluid is generally red] blood. Dickes —, thick blood; geronnenes —, clotted blood, gore; — auswerfen, to spit blood; — lassen, to let blood, to blood, to bleed; das — stillen, to stop or stanch the blood; mit — bespritzt, blood-bespotted, blood-stained; sein — ist in Wallung, his blood is up; das — stieg ihm ins Gesicht, he blushed; sie sieht aus wie Milch und —, she looks all roses and lilies; — vergießen, to shed blood, to wound or kill a person; das ist mein — des neuen Testamentes, welches vergossen wird für Viele, zur Vergebung der Sünden, [in Scripture] this is my blood of the New Testament, which is shed for the remission of sins; im —e schwimmen, to deluge in blood. *Fig.* *a*) Bis aufs —, to the quick. *b*) [= Mord] Seine Hände mit — beflecken, to commit murder; sich in —e baden, to bathe in blood; nach — dürsten, to be desirous to shed blood, to be blood-thirsty; die Stimme deines Bruders —es schreiet zu mir von der Erde, [in Scripture] the voice of thy brother's blood crieth to me from the ground. *c*) = life or death. Sollte ich sein — nicht fordern von euern Händen? [in Scripture] shall I not require his blood at your hands? nachdem wir durch sein — [= durch seinen Tod] gerecht geworden sind, [in Script.] being now justified by his blood. *d*) [guilt and punishment]. Euer — sei über euer Haupt, [in Scripture] your blood be upon your own heads. *e*) [fleshy nature, the carnal part of men]. *f*) [the price of blood]. Wehe dem, der die Stadt mit — bauet, wo to him that buildeth a town with blood. *g*) *[= Mensch] Ein junges —, a young person, a young creature, a youth; ein liederliches —, an extravagant youngster, a debauched fellow, a rake. *h*) [kindred, consanguinity; hence the word is used for a child, a family, kindred, descent, lineage, progeny, descendants]. Du bist mein Fleisch, mein —, meine Tochter, thou art my flesh, my blood, my daughter; aus edlem —e entsprossen, of a noble lineage; die Bande des —es, the ties of blood; das steckt im —e, it runs in the blood. *Prov.* Das — verläugnet sich nicht, true blood will always show itself. *i*) [temper of mind] Mit kaltem —e eine That begehen, to commit an act in cold blood. *k*) [in vulgar or in fam. lang.] Schweiß und —, hard work, and that which is got by it. *l*) Fleisch und —, man, or human wisdom or reason; denn Fleisch und — hat dir das nicht geoffenbaret, sondern mein Vater im Himmel, [in Scripture] flesh and blood hath not revealed it to thee, but my father who is in heaven. *m*) In familiar language, in composition with adjectives it sometimes expresses extremity or a high degree, as: —arm, —jung, —schlecht &c.

Blut=achat, *m.* a blood coloured agate, hæmachates. —ader, *f.* [in anatomy] a vein. —apfel, *m.* [a sort of apple] red calville. *—arm, *adj.* and *adv.* extremely poor. —auge, *n.* a bloodshot eye. —ausleerung, *f.* V. —verlust. —auswurf, *m.* expectoration of blood. —bad, *n.* slaughter, massacre, carnage. —bann, *m.* [in the law of the middle ages] penal judicature. —baum, *m.* V. —holz. —befleckt, *adj.* and *adv.* blood-bespotted, blood-stained. —begier, *f.* V. —gier. —begierig, *adj.* and *adv.* V. —gierig. —behälter, *n.* V. —gefäß. —bereitung, *f.* V. —erzeugung. —bespritzt, —besudelt, *adj.* V. —befleckt. —birn, *f.* [a sort of pear] the sanguinole. —blume, *f.* [a genus of plants] blood-flower, [Hæmanthus L.]. —brechen, *n.* a vomiting of blood, [in medicine] hæmatemesis. —bruch, *m.* [in medicine] hæmatocele. —buche, *f.* purple-beech. —bühne, *f.* V. —gerüst. —durst, *m.* thirst after blood, bloodiness. —dürstend, —durstig, —dürstig, *adj.* and *adv.* blood-thirsty, eager to shed blood, sanguinary. —egel, *m.* [commonly —igel] 1) a leech, the blood-sucker [Hirudo medicinalis]. 2) *Fig.* a cruel, rapacious man, a blood-sucker. —erz, *n.* [= Rothgültigerz] red silver, ruby silver, antimoniated sulphuret of silver. —erzeugung, *f.* [in animal economy, the production of blood, the conversion of chyle into blood] sanguification. —farbe, *f.* blood-colour. —farben, —farbig, *adj.* and *adv.* having the colour of blood, red, sanguine. —feige, *f.* V. Feigendistel. —fink, *m.* bull-finch, the rubicilla. —flagge, *f.* [in seamen's language] flag of defiance, blood-red flag. —flosser, *m.* [a fish] V. Bitling. —fluß, *m.* a flow or flux of blood, a hæmorrhage. —flußstillend, stopping hæmorrhages. —flüssig, *adj.* and *adv.* affected with a flux of blood. *—fremd, *adj.* and *adv.* quite strange, quite a stranger. —gang, *m.* 1) ‡ consanguinity. 2) a flow of blood, especially monthly courses. Mit dem —gang behaftet, bloody-fluxed. —gefärbt, *adj.* and *adv.* stained with blood, bloody. —gefäß, *n.* [in anatomy] blood-vessel [an artery or a vein]: Die —gefäße, the sanguiferous vessels. —gefäßlehre, *f.* [in medicine] angiology. —gefeuchtet, *adj.* and *adv.* moistened with blood. —geld, *n.* [in ancient law, a fine or amercement, paid as a composition for the shedding of blood] blood-wite [commonly das Wehrgeld, weregeld], the price of blood. —gericht, *n.* criminal court. —gerüst, *n.* [a stage or elevated platform for the execution of a criminal] a scaffold. —geschwulst, *f.* phlegmon. —geschwür, *n.* a boil or sore filled with blood; [in veterinary art] ambury or anbury. —gier, *f.* disposition to shed blood, bloodiness. —gierig, *adj.* and *adv.* desirous to shed blood, bloody-minded, sanguinary. —gras, *n.* V. —hirse. —hänfling, *m.* [a bird] the red-pole, or lesser red-pole. —harnen, *n* the voiding of blood with urine, [in medicine] hæmaturia; [a disease among cattle] red-murrain. —hirse, *f.* slender spiked cock's-foot panic-grass. —hochzeit, *f.* the massacre of the Huguenots on St. Bartholomew's night [1572]. —holz, *n.* [a name given to log wood, from its colour] blood-wood. —hund, *m.* 1) [a species of dog] a blood-hound. V. Schweißhund. 2) *Fig.* a blood-shedder, a cruel or blood-thirsty man; *it.* a tyrant. —husten, *m.* a discharge of blood by coughing. —igel, *m.* V. —egel. *—jung, *adj.* and *adv.* very young. —kohl, *m.* a species of dioscorea [dioscorea sativa]. —koralle, *f.* the best sort of red coral. —krankheit, *f.* V. —harnen. —kraut, *n.* [a name given to several plants] 1) sanguinary. 2) bloody-veined dock, bloodwort. 3) great burnet. 4) the lesser or upland burnet. 5) bloody crane's-bill. 6) common or great celandine. 7) common knot-grass. 8) scleranthus alchimella or saxifraga. 9) common shepherd's purse. 10) willow-herb. 11) blood-flower [Pumex sanguineus L.]. —krautwurz, *f.* [a plant] meadow-sweet. —kügelchen, *n.* [in anatomy] a globule of blood. —lassen, *n.* blood-letting, bleeding. —lauf, *m.* 1) the circulation of the blood in the body. 2) bloody-flux, the dysentery. —lauge, *f.* [in chimistry] lixivium of blood. —laugensalz, *n.* V. —lauge. —lechzend, *adj.* and *adv.* desirous of shedding blood, blood-thirsty. —leer, *adj.* and *adv.* bloodless. —leiter, *m.* [in anatomy] the sinuses of the dura mater. —lilie, *f.* a sort of bulb-bearing, or orange lily. —los, *adj.* and *adv.* bloodless, destitute of blood. —lose Thiere [in natural history] exsanguineous animals [such as are destitute of red blood]. —masse, *f.* the whole mass of blood in the body. —milchen, *n.* [a] disease in cattle. —nabelbruch, *m.* [in medicine] hæmatomphalocele. —nuß, *f.* red filbert. —pfirsich, *f.* the peach, or nectarine tree. —pfropf, *m.* V. Adergeschwulst. —pudding, *m.* blood-pudding. —rache, *f.* [among the Arabs &c.] the avengement of the blood of a slain relation or kinsman on the slayer, bloody vengeance, *it.* deadly [family-] feud. —rächer, *m.* he that revenges the blood of a relation or kinsman. —regen, *m.* blood-raining. —reich, *adj.* sanguine, sanguineous, plethoric. —reinigend, *adj.* and *adv.* that which purifies the blood. —reinigung, *f.* 1) the purification of the blood. 2) a remedy for purifying the blood. ‖ —richter, *m.* criminal justice. —roth, *adj.* and *adv.* blood-red [rather provinc.]. —rünstig, *adj.* and *adv.* bleeding, bloody. Eine —rünstige Wunde, a bleeding wound; Einen —rünstig schlagen, to beat any one till blood is drawn. *—sauer, *adj.* and *adv.* very toilsome, very hard. Es sich —sauer werden lassen, to toil and moil, to work hard. —sauger, *m.* ‖ 1) V. —egel. 2) [a species of rhombshell] the smooth [illegible] 3) [an animal of the bat species] vampire. 4) *Fig.* blood-sucker, a cruel, rapacious man. —schande, *f.* incest. —schande treiben, begehen, to commit incest. —schänder, *m.* an incestuous person. —schänderisch, *adj.* and *adv.* incestuous. *—schlecht, *adj.* and *adv.* extremely [illegible] Es gefällt mir hier —schlecht, I am dev[illegible] badly pleased with this place. —schuld[illegible] blood-guiltiness. —schwamm, *m.* trimmed agaric. —schwären, *m.* a boil filled with blood, [a distemper in horses] V. —geschwür. —schweiß, *m.* bloody-sweat. —schwell, *m.* —schwelle, *f.* [a distemper in horses] blood-spavin. —sfreund, *m.* —sfreundinn, *f.* a person related by blood, a blood relation; [in general] some near relation. —sfreundlich, *adj.* and *adv.* consanguineous. —sfreundschaft, *f.* the relation of persons by blood, consanguinity. —spath, *m.* V. —schwell. —speien, *n.* the spitting of blood. —stallen, *n.* V. —harnen [said of horses and cattle]. —stätte, *f.* the place where a person has been put to death. —stein, *m.* bloodstone, red hematite, fibrous red iron ore. Ockeriger —stein, red ochre, ochry red ironstone. —stillend, *adj.* and *adv.* styptic. —stillende Mittel, styptics. —stockung, *f.* a stagnation of blood. —strieme, *f.* a blood-shot stripe. —strom, *m.* a stream of blood. —stropfen, *m.* drop of blood. —sturz, *m.* a vomiting of blood, [in medicine] hæmatemesis. —sverwandt, *adj.* and *adv.* consanguineous. Der, die —sverwandte, a person related by blood, a near relation. —sverwandtschaft, *f.* consanguinity, near relationship. —taufe, *f.* martyrdom. —that, *f.* a bloody act or deed. —theilchen, *pl.* sanguineous particles. —triefend, *adj.* and *adv.* sanguifluous, overflowing with blood. —umlauf, *m.* the circulation of the blood in the body. —unterlaufung, *f.* the state of being blood shot. —urtheil, *n.* sentence of death —vergießen, *n.* the shedding of blood. blood-shedding. —vergießer, *m.* he that sheds blood; [in a general sense] a murderer. —verlust, *m.* a loss of blood. —verwandlung, —wandlung, *f.* V. —erzeugung. —voll, *adj.* and *adv.* stained with blood, bloody. —warm, *adj.* and *adv.* blood-warm, luke-warm. —wärme, *f.* the natural warmth of the blood. —warze, *f.* Die schwammige —warze, [a distemper in horses] V. —geschwür. —wasser, *n.* [in anatomy] lymph, ichor. Die —wassergefäße, lymphatics. —wässerig, *adj.* and *adv.* lymphatic, ichorous. *—wenig, *adj.* and *adv.* extremely little. —wolle, *f.* fell-wool. —wurst, *f.* a sausage, blood-pudding, black-pudding. —wurz, *f.* [the name of plants] bloodwort. *a*) bloody crane's bill. *b*) tormentil, septfoil. —zehente, *m.* the tithe paid of live-stock. —zeuge, *m.* [one who, by his violent death, bears witness to the truth of the gospel] martyr. —zwang, *m.* [in medicine] dysenteric tenesmus.

Blütblatt, *n.* [-es, *pl.* -blätter] [in botany] V. Nebenblatt, Deckblatt.

1. Blüte, Blüthe, *f.* [*pl.* -n] 1) [the opening of flowers in general, the state of blossoming] bloom, growth. Die Bäume stehen jetzt in der —, trees are now in blossom, the trees are clothed with bloom. *Fig.* [rather poetical] a blooming girl. Diese holde —, this charming blooming creature. 2) the time when plants blossom; [in botany] florescence. In der Kirschen—, in the blowing-time of cherry-trees. *Fig.* Die — der Jugend, the bloom of youth; in der — des Lebens, in the flower of life; in der — seiner Jahre, in the prime of his age; sie steht in ihrer schönsten —, she is in the blossom of her youth. 3) [the flower of a plant, an expanded bud] blossom, bloom; [in botany, that part of a plant which contains the organs of fructification with their coverings] flower. Männliche —n, male flowers [having no pistil]; weibliche —n, female flowers [having no stamina]; Zwitter—n, hermaphrodite flowers, hermaphrodites [that contain both the anther and the stigma or the supposed male and female organs of generation]. [sometimes for: menstrual discharges] the flowers, flower.

Blütenauge, *n.* [in botany] a bud, gem. —baum, *m.* a blowing tree. —blatt, *n.* flower-leaf. —busch, *m.* a flowering shrub. —decke, *f.* [in botany] perianth. —doldig, *adj.* and *adv.* [in botany] umbellated. —gehänge, *n* V. Blumengehänge. —gesträuch, *n.* a flowery shrub. —kelch, *m.* V. Blumenkelch. —reich, *adj.* and *adv.* full of bloom, flowery, blossomy, bloomy. —stand, *m.* [in botany] inflorescence. —ständig, *adj.* and *adv.* [in botany, immediately attending the flower] floral. Ein —ständiges Blatt, a floral leaf. —strauch, *m.* V. —busch. —theile, *pl.* [in botany, the generative parts of plants] attire. —zeit and Blütezeit, *f.* 1) florescence, florification. *Fig.* In der —zeit Athens, when Athens flourished. 2) *Fig.* youth.

2. ‖ Blüte, *f.* V. Uckelei.

Bluten, *v. intr.* 1) [originally = Flüssigkeit von sich geben, to throw out or exude some liquid] Die Weinrebe blutet, the vine bleeds. 2) [usually] to lose blood, to bleed. Die Wunde blutet, the wound bleeds; die Nase blutet ihm or er blutet aus der Nase, he bleeds at the nose; er hat stark geblutet, he lost a great deal of blood. *Poet.* = to die a violent death. Er hat für sein Vaterland geblutet, he bled for his country. *Fig.* Das Herz blutet mir, my heart bleeds; er soll mir dafür schon — [= er soll es büßen] he shall suffer for it, he shall atone for it.

Blüthe, *f.* V. 1. Blüte.

Blütig, *adj.* and *adv.* 1) furnished with blood [in compound words blütig, as: vollblütig &c., plethoric &c.]. 2) stained with blood, bloody. Ein —er Finger, a bloody finger; — machen, to bloody; die —e Hand, [anciently] *a*) a blood-shedder, murderer, *b*) V. Blutbann. *Fig.* *Keinen —en Heller haben, to be pennyless. 3) [attended with bloodshed] bloody. Eine —e Schlacht, a bloody battle; ein —er Krieg, a sanguinary war; — or auf eine —e Weise enden, to end bloodily.

Bö, *f.* [*pl.* -en] [a sea term] a sudden squall of wind. Eine schwere —, a heavy gust, or squall of wind; eine Regen—, a squall of wind accompanied with rain; eine Hagel—, a squall of wind accompanied with hail.

Bóbartsgras, *n.* [-es] [a plant] bobarthia [Morea spathacea].

Bóberelle, *f.* [*pl.* -n] V. Judenkirsche.

1. Bóck, *m.* [-es, *pl.* Böcke] [according to some from pochen, that is stoßen; but probably it is allied to the Lat. *bos*, to the Fr. *vache* &c., the Swed. *baegga*, sheep, and to Vieh, as also to the Lat. *feo*, Gr. *φύω*] 1) the male of several quadrupeds. Der Reh—, roe-buck; [especially the male of goats] der Ziegen—, Gais—, buck, he-goat. *Fig.* †Geil wie ein —, lecherous as a goat. *Prov.* Den — zum Gärtner setzen, ‖ den — auf die Haferkiste setzen, to set the fox to keep one's geese, to give a wolf the wether to keep. †*Fig.* *a*) a lustful man, a lecher, a goat. Der geile —, satyr. *b*) [in derision] a tailor. *c*) [a play] Einem den — stehen, to play at leapfrog. 2) [what is made of buck-skin] a bag-pipe. 3) [in antiquity] a battering-ram.

Bocksbeinig, *adj.* and *adv.* V. —füßig. —fell, *n.* 1) buckskin, goatskin. 2) †*Fig.* a vile female. —flöte, *f.* V. —pfeife. —(s)fuß, *m.* 1) the foot of a goat. 2) a foot resembling that of a goat. —(s)füßig, *adj.* and *adv.* footed like a goat. —geruch, *m.* a goatish or rank smell. —haut, *f.* V. —fell, 1). —hirsch, *m.* the Indostan antelope. —käfer, *m.* V. Holz—. —kalb, *n.* a buck of the first year. —kohle, *f.* caking-coal. —lamm, *n.* [in husbandry] a male lamb of the first year. —leder, *n.* buckskin. —ledern, *adj.* and *adv.* made of buckskin. —lederne Beinkleider, buckskin breeches; —lederne Handschuhe, kid- or kid-skin-gloves. —melkerei, *f.* *Fig.* useless labour, useless contention, an expression made use of by the great philosopher Kant, to mark the fruitless discussions of logomachy. —pfeife, *f.* 1) a sort of pipe or flute. 2) a bag-pipe. —pfeifer, *m.* bag-piper. —pimpinelle, *f.* goat's parsley. —sauge, *n.* [a genus of animals] *a*) the sea-ear. *b*) the limpet. —sbart, *m.* 1) a goat's beard. 2) a beard like a goat's. 3) *Fig.* [the name of several plants] *a*) goat's beard. *b*) the grey hair grass. *c*) sheep's-fescue grass. *d*) small yellow fox-glove. 4) the root of the purple goat's-beard, salsafy. —sbeere, *f.* 1) dewberry bramble. 2) common black currant. 3) red bilberry, whortleberry, or cowberry. —sbeutel, *m.* a sort of tobacco pouch, used in Hungary, made of the scrotum of a buck. *Fig.* *1) old usage, old prejudice. Einem den —sbeutel anhängen, to ridicule a person. ‖ 2) the bottle for a sort of wine called Steinwein, growing in the neighbourhood of the town of Wurzburg in Bavarian Franconia. *—sbeutelei, *f.* old pedantic sayings or doings, obsolete customs, inveterate prejudice. —sbohne, *f.* common buck-bean, or marsh trefoil. —sdorn, *m.* goat's thorn. —seife, *f.* [Bergseife] mountain soap. —sgeile, *f.* [a plant] the greater goat's stones, satyrium. —shorn, *n.* 1) a buck's horn. *Fig.* *In das —shorn blasen, to sound alarm; Einen in das —shorn jagen, to bully or intimidate any one. 2) *Fig.* *a*) [the name of plants] *α*) fenugreek. *β*) licorice vetch. *b*) —shörner or —sohren, [in seamen's language] bolts with a ring and a hook. —skraut, *n.* 1) stinking goose-foot. 2) common lungwort. 3) woolly-leaved anemone. 4) a species of hypericum [hypericum hircinum]. *Fig.* *—ssprung, *m.* a goat-leap, a caper, a leap, a skip, gambol, as in dancing or mirth, or in the frolick of a goat or lamb; [in manege] a capriole. —ssprünge machen, to caper, to prance, to spring, to gambol, to romp. *—sstreich, *m.* a silly or foolish act.

2. Bóck, *m.* [-es, *pl.* Böcke] [allied either to biegen, Buckel, or to the Lat. *bajulus*, Lastträger, and to the Gr. *βαστάζω* &c.] 1) a machine by which any thing is supported, a stand or support for scaffolding, a wooden frame with legs, a trestle, a contrivance for bearing or propping any thing. Der Säge—, Holz—, a sawyer's frame or trestle, a horse, a jack; der Holz—, Brand—, Feuer—, an andiron, a dog; der — einer Kutsche [Kutsch—], coach-box; die Böcke, Eisböcke [an Brucken], the starlings of a bridge. 2) [in husbandry] a cradle. 3) a machine for lifting or raising heavy weights, a gin. [in seamen's language] Die Spieren des —s, the sheers.

Bocksdecke, *f.* the cover of a coach-box, hammer-cloth. —holz, *n.* 1) [in colloquial lang.] log-wood. 2) [with coachmakers] standard. —kissen, *n.* V. —polster. —mühle, *f.* 1) a wind-mill. 2) a stamping-mill. —polster, *n.* the cushion on a coach-box. —schemel, *m.* the foot-board of a coach-box. —stütze, *f.* standard. —verstellung, *f.* [in architecture] a scaffolding.

3. Bóck, *m.* [-es, *pl.* Böcke] [probably allied to pochen, V. 1. Bock] 1) anciently any beam or block, now a beam or block for beating or thrusting. 2) the heavy block of a rammer.

4. Bóck, *m.* [-es, *pl.* Böcke] [allied to Bug, Buckel, biegen] 1) an incurvated or elevated surface. 2) a wooden engine to confine the arms and legs of offenders, the stocks. Einen Gefangenen in den — spannen, to put a prisoner in the stocks. 3) [in anatomy, the small anterior protuberance below the anterior extremity of the helix] the tragus. 4) [the thickest part of the nave of a wheel in which the spokes are inserted] the stock.

5. Bóck, *m.* [es, Böcke] [of uncertain derivation, generally supposed to be a figurative sense of 1. Bock] a gross mistake, a blunder. Einen —

machen or schießen, to make or commit a blunder.

Böckchen, n. [-s, pl. -] a kid.

Böckelhaube, f. V. Pickelhaube.

1. Böckeln, v. intr. to smell somewhat like a goat, to have a goatish or rank smell.

2. Böckeln, V. [the correct word] Pöckeln.

1. Böcken, [from 1. Bock] v. intr. 1) to desire the male, to lust as she-goats. Die Geis bocket, [with hunters] the she-goat goes to rut. 2) to smell of the goat. 3) Fig. [in seamen's language] to pitch, to heave up and down. 4) [rather vulgar] [of a horse] to bend down the neck and fling out behind [for the purpose of throwing the rider].

2. Böcken, v. tr. [= pochen] Den Flachs —, to stamp flax in the stamping-mill.

Böcken, Böcken, adj. and adv. Bockenes or böckenes Fleisch, the flesh of a goat, goat's flesh.]

Böckicht, adj. and adv. resembling a goat in any quality, of a rank smell, goatish.

Böckig, adj. and adv. lustful as she-goats.

Böcklein, n. [-s, pl. -] a kid.

Boden, m. [-s, pl. Böden and Boden] [appears to be allied to the Gr. πέδον, with pes, Fuß, fußen &c.] 1) the surface of the earth, or a floor or pavement. Auf dem — liegen, to lie upon the ground; auf dem bloßen — schlafen, to sleep on the bare ground; den — berühren, to touch the ground; er fiel zu —, he fell to the ground; warum willst du, daß ich dich zu — schlage? [in Script.] wherefore should I smite thee to the ground? unter dem —, under ground. Fig.*[= Grab] Deine schlechte Aufführung bringt mich noch unter den — or unter die Erde, your bad conduct will bring me to my grave; er ist schon lange unter dem —, he has long been under the sod. 2) ground, earth considered with relation to its vegetative qualities, soil. Fruchtbarer oder unfruchtbarer —, fruitful or barren soil; schwerer —, a strong soil; ein sandiger —, a sandy soil. Fig. Diese Ermahnungen fielen bei ihm auf guten —, he will profit by these admonitions. Prov. Handwerk hat einen goldenen —, trade is the mother of money. 3) [land, estate, possession] ground. Mein Grund und —, my soil and ground. 4) [region, territory] ground. Britischer —, British ground. 5) the lowest part of any thing. Der — eines Fasses, the head of a cask; der — einer Kufe, the bottom of a vat; der — einer Flasche, the bottom of a bottle; der — eines Tintenfasses, the bottom of an inkhorn; einen — einsetzen, to put a bottom; einen — legen, to lay a floor; der bretterne — einer Bettstelle, the boarded bottom of a bedstead; der — eines Schiffes, the bottom of a ship; ein Fahrzeug mit plattem —, a flat-bottomed vessel; mit schmalem —, narrow-bottomed; der — (Käse) einer Artischocke, the bottom of an artichoke; der — des Meeres, the bottom of the sea. Fig. Dieses schlägt unsere Hoffnungen zu —, this annihilates or disappoints all our hopes; dieser Verlust hat ihn gänzlich zu — gedrückt, this loss has completely overwhelmed him. 6) [in metallurgy] the lower part of the blast-furnace. 7) [with violinmakers and lute-makers] the bottom-piece of a violin, the lower part of the body or belly of a lute; [with weavers &c.] Stoff mit einem atlassenen, mit einem gelben —, stuff with a satin, a yellow ground. 8) [the highest floor, immediately under the roof] loft. V. also Speicher, Bühne. Der Korn—, corn-loft; der Heu—, hay-loft.

Boden-blatt, n. [in tobacco plantations] the leaves growing next to the ground and which are of little value. [in metallurgy] the flat bottom of the muffle. —blech, n. [in saltworks] tin-plate bottoms. —bohne, f. dwarf kidney-bean. —eisen, [in ship-building] calking-iron. —eule, f. barn-owl. —feld, n. V. —stück. —fenster, n. dormar-window. —fries, m. the breech-mouldings [of a cannon]. —geschoß, n. [more usual: Erdgeschoß] ground-floor. —hefen, pl. the bottom of beer, the grounds, dregs or lees. —holz, n. [timber for the head of casks] heading. —kammer, f. a chamber in the loft, a garret. —kupfer, n. copper-bottoms. —loch, n. luthern. —los, adj. and adv. bottomless, fathomless. Fig. Ein —loses Gerücht, an unfounded report. —luke, f. V. —loch. —matte, f. floor-mat. —planke, f. Die —planken eines Schiffes, the exterior and interior planks of the ship's bottom. —pumpe, f. [in seamen's lang.] bilge-pump. —rad, n. [in horology] great-wheel. —säge, f. [with coopers] a cooper's saw. —satz, m. grounds, dregs, lees, sediment. —schicht, f. the lowest layer [of sand, clay &c.]. —schnur, f. [with weavers] coat. —schraube, f. V. —zieher 2. or Zangzieher. —schwelle, f. [in mills] the sills of the leat. —stein, m. [in mills] the nether-stone, bed of a mill; [in oil-mills] bedder, bedetter. —stück, n. 1) [with coopers = —holz] heading. 2) the breech [of a cannon]. 3) [in horology] the bottom of a watch-case. —tafel, f. V. —blech. —talg, m. [with chandlers] drug. —teig, m. the bottom-piece, under-crust of any pastry-work. —thür, f. loft-door, garret-door. —treppe, f. loft-stairs. —zieher, m. 1) [in surgery] V. Schädelbohrer. 2) [with coopers] a turrel. —zins, m. 1) [unusual] a rent paid for a loft. 2) ground-rent. V. also Grundzins.

Bödmen, Bödmen, v. tr. 1) to furnish with a bottom. Ein Zimmer —, to floor a room; ein Faß —, to head a cask. 2) [in maritime commerce] to borrow money and pledge the keel or bottom of a ship, that is, the ship itself, as security for the repayment of the money.

Bodmerei, f. [in maritime commerce] bottomry. Geld auf — aufnehmen, to take money upon a ship's bottom.

Bodmerei-brief, m. letter or bill of bottomry. —geber, m. the advancer of bottomry-money. —geld, n. money of bottomry. —nehmer, m. a collector of bottomry-money.

Böfist, m. [-es, pl. -e] [a fungus] puck-ball, puck-fist.

Bögen, m. [-s, pl. Bogen and Bögen] 1) in general any curvature or bending. Der Fluß macht einen —, the river makes a turn. 2) any part of the circumference of a circle or curved line, lying from one point to another, [in geometry] an arc, a segment. Der — des Himmels, des Friedens [= Regenbogen], a rainbow; [in geom.] gleiche, ähnliche, concentrische —, equal, similar, concentric arcs. Fig. In Bausch und —, in the lump [good and bad together]; etwas in Bausch und — kaufen, to buy something in the lump. 3) [in architecture, a concave or hollow structure of stone or brick, supported by its own curve] an arch. Ein voller —, a perfect arch; ein gedrückter —, an elliptical arch; ein flacher —, a flat arch; gothische —, pointed or Gothic arches. 4) an instrument, a tool, in the form of an arch. a) [anciently an instrument of war and hunting] bow. Einen — spannen, to draw a bow; die den — spannende Hand, bow-hand. Prov. Spanne den — nicht zu strenge, soll er halten in die Länge, a bow long bent at last grows weak. b) [Fiedelbogen] bow of a violin, fiddle-stick. Dieser Violinspieler führt seinen — äußerst zart, this violin-player manages his bow very delicately. c) [with hatters = Fachbogen] bow. d) [= Sattelbogen] bows of a saddle. 5) a sheet [of paper]. Ein Buch Papier hat vier und zwanzig —, a quire of paper consists of twenty four sheets. 6) [in anatomy] the fornix.

Bogen-bezeichnung, f. [with printers] signature. —bohrer, m. 1) a drill. 2) V. Richtspindel. —decke, f. a vaulted ceiling. —brille, f. V. —bohrer. —fahrt, f. purchase in the lump. —feile, f. [with several workmen in metal] a sort of small file. —fenster, n. bow-window, bay-window. —fisch, m. the arc-fish. —fläche, f. convexity. —form, f. the form of a sheet of paper once doubled. Ein Buch in —form, a folio. —förmig, adj. and adv. having the form of a bow, [in botany] arcuate. —führend, adj. and adv. bearing or using a bow. —gang, 1) a long or continued arch, a walk arched above, especially an arched avenue of trees in gardens. 2) [in architecture] arcade. 3) [in anat.] Die drei —gänge des Irrganges im Ohre, the three semi-circular canals placed in the posterior part of the labyrinth in each ear. —gerüst, n. [with masons] the centering. —gewölbe, n. an arched vault. —größe, f. a size, formed by once doubling a sheet of paper. Ein Buch in —größe, a folio. —halle, f. a covered walk, an arcade. —laube, f. V. —gang 1. —lehne, f. V. —gerüst. —linie, f. a circular line. —macher, m. V. Bogener. —rolle, f. [in architecture] the lintel of the door-post. —rund, adj. and adv. bent like a bow, arcuate. —rüstung, f. V. —gerüst. —säge, f. bow-saw. —schlagen, n. [in architecture] arching. —schluß, m. 1) the closing of an arch or vault. 2) the key-stone [of an arch]. —schreiber, m. hackney-writer. —schuß, m. 1) bow-shot, flight-shot. 2) [a shot with the muzzle of the gun elevated above a horizontal line] random-shot. —schütze, m. a bow-man, an archer. —sehne, f. 1) [in geometry] chord. 2) bow-string. —spanner, m. 1) a rack for a cross-bow. 2) a person skilful in using the bow. —sprung, m. [in manege, a particular leap of a horse] pannade. —stellung, f. 1) [in architecture] a range of arches, an arcade. 2) [in dancing] an arcade. —strich, m. a drawing of the bow over the strings of a violin. Er hat einen trefflichen —strich, he draws a good bow. —thür, f. an arched door. —tragend, adj. and adv. bearing or using a bow. —weise, adv. in sheets, by sheets, by the sheet. —wölbung, f. arching. —zahl, f. 1) the number of sheets in a book. 2) [with printers] signature. —zeichen, n. [with printers] signature. —zirkel, m. [a small sort of compasses] bow-compasses.

Bögen, Bögen, v. tr. [in husbandry] to bend, to inflect. Sich —, to bend.

Bögener, Bögner, m. [-s, pl. -] one who makes bows, a bowyer.

Bögig, adj. bent, curved, scalloped. —e Blätter, [in botany] sinuous leaves.

Bögspriet, V. Bugspriet.

|| Böhl, n. [-es, pl. -e] a hide of land.

Böhle, f. [pl. -n] [appears to be allied to Pfahl, Balken] a thick strong board, a plank.

Bohlen-geld, n. [rent paid for a stall] stallage. —säge, f. pit-saw.

Böhlen, v. tr. to cover or lay with planks, to plank, to board.

Böhme, m. [-n, pl. -n] -inn, f. a native of Bohemia, a Bohemian.

Böhmen, n. [-s] Bohemia.

Böhmer, m. [-s, pl. -] the Bohemian chatterer [a bird] V. Haubendrossel.

Böhmisch, adj. Bohemian. —e Brüder, Bohemian brethren, Moravians [a religious sect]. —e Leinwand, Bohemian linen. Fig. *Das sind ihm —e Dörfer, that is Greek to him.

Böhnchen, Böhnlein, n. [-s, pl. -] [diminutive of Bohne] a little bean.

Böhne, f. [pl. -n] [Bohem. bob, Lithuan. pu[illegible] Lat. faba] a bean. Weiße —n, white beans; grüne —n, French beans, [opposed to dried or pickled beans] fresh beans; die welsche —, kidney bean; Gartenbohnen, the common garden-bean; Feldbohnen, the horse-bean; —n legen, stecken, to plant beans; —n einmachen, to pickle beans; —n dörren, to dry beans. *Fig.* [in manege, a little black spot in the cavity of the corner-teeth of a horse about seven or eight years old] the marks.

Bohnen-baum, *m.* 1) bean-tree of America. 2) bind-bean-tree. 3) three-horned acacia. 4) bean-trefoil. 5) bean-trefoil-tree. —egel, —igel, *m.* [a sort of maggot] mida. —erz, *n.* pea-iron-ore, pisiform clay-ironstone. —hülse, [—schelfe] *f.* the husk of beans. —kaper, *f.* [a tree] bean-caper. —keim, *m.* V. Bohne *fig.* —könig, *m.* the king on twelfth day. —kraut, *n.* summer savory. —kuchen, *m.* the twelfth-night-cake. —mehl, *n.* bean-flour. —schuß, *m.* V. Bohne *fig.* —stange, *f.* a bean-stick. —stroh, *n.* bean-straw. *Prov.* † Er ist grob wie —stroh, he is a very coarse fellow.

Bohnen, *v. tr.* [appears to come from the root of bahnen] to rub [floors, tables and the like] with wax, to wax.

Bohn-axt, *f.* [with carpenters] a hatchet or smoothing-axe. —bürste, *f.* a rubbing-brush. —erz, *n.* V. Bohnenerz. —lappen, *m.* a rubbing-clout. —zeug, *n.* tools used for rubbing and polishing with wax.

Bohnern, *v. tr.* = Bohnen.

Böhnhase, *m.* [-n, *pl.* -n] 1) a clumsy awkward workman, a bungler, a botcher, [especially of tailors]. 2) a petty-broker.

Böhnlein, V. Böhnchen.

Böhren, [Lat. *foro*] I. *v. tr.* 1) to bore [a hole &c.]. Eine Kanone —, to bore or drill a cannon; ein Loch durch ein Stück Metall —, to drill a hole through a piece of metal; einen Schlüssel —, to drill a key. *Fig.* Einen Esel —, to bite the thumb at, to laugh at any one. 2) [bohrend versenken] Ein Schiff in den Grund —, to sink a ship. II. *v. intr.* to pierce the earth with scooping-irons, to bore. III. *v. r.* sich —, to pierce or enter by boring. Der Wurm hat sich durch das Buch gebohrt, the worm has bored through the book.

Bohr-ahl, *m.* —ahle, *f.* a joiner's awl. —bank, *f.* 1) [with gun-smiths] a sort of bench used in boring the barrel of a gun. 2) [with cartwrights] a frame used in boring naves. —block, *m.* [in seamen's lang.] clave. —blume, *f.* [a plant] glycine. —eisen, *n.* [the point of an auger] the bit, bite. —fäustel, *m.* [in mining] a hammer to drive the borer. —führer, *m.* [in horology] a guide. —käfer, *m.* death-watch. —klippe, *f.* [in mining] pinchers for drawing the pieces of a broken borer from the bore. —krätzer, *m.* [in mining, an instrument by which the bore-dust is taken out of the hole] a scoop. —lade, *f.* [in cannon-founderies] a boring-frame. —loch, *n.* [the hole made by boring] bore, auger-hole. —löffel, *m.* scooping-iron. —mehl, *n.* bore-dust. —mühle, *f.* a machine moved by water for boring tubes, barrels &c. —muschel, *f.* 1) pholas. 2) the terebratula. —pfriem, *m.* 1) [in seamen's language] a wimble to clear the vent of a cannon. 2) priming-iron, priming-wire. —schmied, *m.* V. Zeugschmied. —schnecke, *f.* V. Schraubhorn. —späne, *pl.* bore-chips. —spitze, *f.* the point of an auger or other borer, the bit, bite. —stange, *f.* rod. —wurm, *m.* V. Schiffwurm. —zeug, *n.* [with locksmiths] boring-tools.

Böhrer, *m.* [-s, *pl.* -] 1) [one who bores] borer. 2) [an instrument to make holes with by turning] drill. Ein kleiner —, ein Nagel—, a gimblet; ein großer —, [in carpentry, with shipwrights &c.] an auger.

Boi, *m.* [-es] [D. *baey*, Dan. Bai, French *bay*, also *baie*, Eng. *baize*] [a coarse woolen stuff] baize.

Boien, *adj.* and *adv.* made of baize.

Bojär, *m.* [-en, *pl.* -en] [in the Russian empire, a nobleman, a lord] a boiar or boyar.

Bóje, **Búje**, *f.* [*pl.* -n] [in Sw. *boja* signifies also a chain; from biegen, here probably = befestigen] [in seamen's lang.] buoy. Die — auswerfen, to stream the buoy.

Bójer, **Bújer**, *m.* [-s, *pl.* -] a vessel or boat employed for laying the buoys.

Boj-leine, *f.* [in seamen's language] buoy-rope. —salz, *n.* bay-salt.

Bokäl, V. Pokal.

Bökel, V. Pöckel.

Bökeln, V. Pöckeln.

Böl, *m.* [-es, *pl.* -e] [from the Lat. *bolus?*] [in mineralogy, a kind of fine clay] bole. V. Bolus.

Böld, [from the old *baldo*, *balde* = kühn, bold] an obsolete word, used only in compound words, as Trunken—, Rauf— &c.

Böleine, *f.* [*pl.* -n] [in seamen's language] bowline. Die großen —n, the main bowlines; die großen Marsboleinen, the main-top bowlines; die großen Bramboleinen, the main-top-gallant bowlines; die großen Oberbramboleinen, the main-top-gallant royal bowlines; die —n anholen, to hawl taught the bowlines.

Böll, *m.* V. Pohl.

‖ **Böll**, *adj.* and *adv.* hard, stiff.

Böllchen, *n.* [-s, *pl.* -] V. Dengelstock.

Bölle, *f.* [allied to the D. *bol* = Kopf] [*pl.* -n] a round body, [in botany] bulb. Das —ngewächs, a bulbous plant.

‖ **Böller**, *m.* [-s, *pl.* -] [from bellen = tönen] a small mortar for throwing shells.

‖ 1. **Böllig**, *adj.* and *adv.* hard, stiff.

‖ 2. **Böllig**, [V. Bolle] *adj.* and *adv.* round, roundish, bulbous. —e Gewächse, bulbous plants.

Böllwerk, *n.* [-es, *pl.* -e] [probably for Wallwerk] [in fortification] a bastion, rampart, [anciently] a bulwark.

Bollwerks-ohr, *n.* [in fortification] orillon. —wehr, *f.* [in fortification] counter-guard. —winkel, *m.* [in fortification, angle of the bastion] the flanked angle.

‖ **Böllwurz**, *f.* V. Tollkirsche.

Bolognéserspath, —stein, *m.* radiated heavy-spar, Bolognese-spar, Bolognian-stone.

Bölus, *m.* [from the Lat. *bolus?*] 1) [in mineralogy] [a sort of fine clay often highly coloured by iron] bole. Der armenische —, Armenian bole. 2) [medicine made up in the form of a pill] a bolus. Der — für Pferde zur Herstellung der Freßlust, [with sportsmen] chew-ball.

‖ **Bölze**, *m.* V. Kater.

Bölzen, *m.* [-s, *pl.* -] [appears to be allied to Pfeil] 1) a bolt, an arrow, a pointed shaft. *Fig.* *Einem alles zu — drehen, to misinterpret all any one says; die — verschießen, die ein Anderer gedreht hat, to be another's instrument to do mischief. 2) the heater [put into a box-iron for ironing and smoothing clothes]. 3) [a strong cylindrical pin, of iron or other metal, used to fasten something] a round bolt. 4) [in ships, bolts are used in the sides and decks, and have different names, as Tack—, rag-bolts, Aug—, eye-bolts &c.]. Viereckige —, square-bolts; — mit diamantenen Knöpfen, square-headed bolts. 5) [in mining] *a*) a prop. *b*) an iron-wedge. 6) [with shoemakers] a wedge.

Bolzen-ausheber, *m.* [in ship-building] bolt-drawer. —bohrer, *m.* [in ship-building] bolt-auger. —schloß, *n.* a cylindrical padlock. —treiber, *m.* bolt-driver. —zange, *f.* a sort of pinchers for drawing out bolts.

* **Bombárde**, *f.* [*pl.* -n] 1) a warlike machine formerly used for throwing large stones, afterwards a great gun [now out of use], a bombard. 2) full-organ.

* **Bombárdement**, *n.* [-s, *pl.* -s] bombardment.

* **Bombardier**, *m.* [-s, *pl.* -e] [one whose business is to attend the loading and firing of mortars] bombardier.

Bombardier-galiote, *f.* bomb-ketch, bomb-vessel. —käfer, *m.* a species of carabus [carabus crepitans].

* **Bombardiren**, *v. tr.* to bombard [a town &c.]. † *Fig.* Einen mit Fragen, mit Bitten — &c. —, to storm a person with questions, petitions &c.

* **Bómbasett**, *m.* [-s] [in commerce] bombazett.

* **Bómbasin**, *m.* [-s] bombasine.

1 **Bómbast** and **Bombást**, *m.* [-es] [is allied to Bombe] [high sounding words, swelling words without much meaning] bombast.

2. **Bómbast**, *m.* [-es] [from *bombace* = *cotton-tree*] [a sort of fustian] bombast, bumbast.

Bómbe, *f.* [*pl.* -n] bomb, shell. —n werfen, to throw bombs; mit —n beschießen, to bombard.

Bomben-fest, *adj.* and *adv.* bomb-proof. —kessel, *m.* mortar. —kiste, *f.* bomb-chest. —schießer, *m.* bombardier. —schiff, *n.* bomb-ketch, bomb-boat. —werfen, *n.* bombardment. —werfer, *m.* bombardier.

‖ **Bómmel**, *f.* V. Bammel.

Bonifacius, *m.* [a name of men] Boniface.

* **Bonificiren**, *v. tr.* [in commerce] to make good, to make an allowance. V. Vergüten.

Bonítfisch, *m.* [-es, *pl.* -e] [a fish of the tunny kind] bonito.

* **Bónnet**, *n.* [-s, *pl.* -s] 1) [a covering for the head, worn by females] bonnet. 2) [in fortification, a small work with two faces, having only a parapet] bonnet. 3) or Bonnette, *f.* [in seamen's language, an addition to a sail or an additional part laced to the foot of a sail] bonnet. Das unterste —, drabbler; Sturm—, the first bonnet laced on the sail; ein — losmachen, to unlace the bonnet, to shake off the bonnet.

Bónze, *m.* [-n, *pl.* -n] [an Indian priest] a bonze.

Boot, [-es, *pl.* -e, with some authors Böte] [allied to Bütte, Fr. *bateau* &c.] 1) [a small open vessel, also a small vessel carrying a mast and sails] boat. Das große — eines Schiffes, the long boat; das kleine —, skiff; das — eines Seeoffiziers, a barge; das Packet—, a packet-boat; ein Dampf—, a steam-boat. ‖ 2) a measure of capacity for liquids [= a hogshead or 120 gallons].

Boots-anker, *m.* a grappling or grapnel. —gesell, *m.* V. —knecht. —haken, *m.* 1) [in seamen's language] boat-hook. 2) *Fig.* [a genus of animals] the devil's claw. —knecht, *m.* boatman, boatsman, seaman, sailor. —krabber, *pl.* [in seamen's language] gripes. —leute, *pl.* V. —mann, 1). —mann, *m.* 1) [an officer on board of ships] boatswain [Hochbootsmann]. 2) *Fig.* [a fish] the pilot-fish —pfeife, *f.* boatswain's call. —ringe, *pl.* the boat-rings. —seil, —tau, *n.* boat's-painter.

Bórar, *m.* [-es] [a salt formed by the combination of boracic acid with the marine alcali of soda] borax, subborate of soda. Roher —, V. in —sauer.

Borar-blei, *n.* borate of lead. —eisen, *n.* borate of iron. —salze, *pl.* [in chimistry] borates. —sauer, *adj.* and *adv.* [in chimistry] —saure Bittererde or Bitterspath, borácite, borate of magnesia; —saures Natron [roher —, prismatisches —salz], borate of soda. —säure, *f.* native boracic acid.

Borazit, *m.* [-es] borate of magnesia, boracite, boracited calx.

Bord, *m.* and *n.* [-es, *pl.* -e] [probably allied to por in empor and the verb bären = heben, tragen] 1) the outer edge of any thing. Der — or Rand eines Gefäßes, the rim or brim of a vessel; der — or Saum eines Kleides, the border or edge of a garment. 2) the land adjacent to the border of the sea or of a lake; but more commonly the side of a ship, board. Das Back—, lar-board; das Steuer—, starboard; das hohe — eines Schiffes, the weather-side; ein Schiff von hohem —e, V. Kriegsschiff; ein Schiff von niedrigem —e, a trading-vessel; über — fallen, to fall over board; vom — herunterglitschen, to slip by the board; der Mast fiel über —, the mast went by the board; — an —, board and board; über — werfen, to throw over board; ein Schiff an — treiben, to fall aboard of a ship. *Fig.* [the deck of a ship, the interior part of a ship] board. An — gehen, to go on board; am — seyn, to be on board [*a-board]; an — legen [entern], to board, to lay aboard; am — verkaufen, [in commerce] to sell free on board; am — notirt, [in commerce] quoted on board. 3) *m.* [in coins] outer rim.

Bord-anker, *m.* [in seamen's language] V. Haupt- or Nachtanker.

Borde, *f.* V. Borte.

‖**Börde**, *f.* [*pl.* -n] [from Bord] a fruitful plain, a corn-country.

***Bordell**, *n.* [-s, *pl.* -e] [properly a little house; in Swed. and A. S. *bord* signifies a house] brothel, brothel-house.

Borden, *v. tr.* 1) [to make a border, to adorn with a border of ornaments] to border [a garment &c.]. 2) V. Entern.

Bordenhame, *m.* [-n, *pl.* -n] a shrub of Ethiopia.

***Bordiren**, V. Borden 1.

1. **Borg**, *m.* [-es, *pl.* -e] [perhaps from the old word bargen = schneiden] a male hog castrated, a barrow.

2. **Borg**, *m.* [-es] [V. Borgen] borrowing or lending. Einem etwas auf — geben, to give or sell something to any one on trust, on credit, ‡on tick; etwas auf — nehmen, to take or buy something on credit, to borrow something.

Borg-mann, *m.* [one who borrows] a borrower. —[s]weise, *adv.* in the way of loan, on credit.

3. **Borg**, *m.* [-es] [from the root of bergen] [in seamen's lang.] preventer. — in der Wand, stopper for the rigging made use of in time of action, when the shrouds or other ropes are cut by the enemy's shot; — von Ketten an der Raa, chains in which the yards are hung in time of action; — an der Ruthe or Gaffel, preventer.

Borg-bindsel, *n.* —bindsel des Bonnets, the preventer of a bonnet. —brassen, *pl.* preventer-braces. —raa, *f.* spare-yard. —stag, *n.* preventer-stay. —stenge, *f.* spare-top-mast. —tau, *n.* Das —tau zum Aufsetzen der Stenge, a rope serving to take hold of the heel of the top-mast, to help the top-rope, while the mast is hoisting up. —wandtau, *n.* swifter.

Borgen, [allied to bergen] I. *v. tr.* 1) to borrow [a book, a sum of money &c.]. *Prov.* — macht Sorgen, he that goes a borrowing, goes a sorrowing; he that borrows must pay again with shame or loss. 2) to take or buy [goods] on credit. 3) to lend, to give on credit, to give or sell upon trust. *Prov.* Lange geborgt ist nicht geschenkt, forbearance is no acquittance. Syn. V. Erborgen. II. *v. intr.* V. Warten, Harren.

Borger, *m.* [-s, *pl.* -] [one who borrows] borrower.

Borke, *f.* [*pl.* -n] [perhaps from bergen] 1) the rind of a tree, the bark, the outer bark. Syn. V. Bast. 2) a scab, a crust.

Borkenkäfer, *m.* the leather-eater [dermestes typographus].

Born, *m.* [-es, *pl.* -e] [for Bronn, Brunn, Brunnen] 1) water, a fountain of water, an issue of water from the earth, a spring. *Fig.* Der Born der Freuden, the spring of joy. 2) [in salt-works] salt-pit.

Born-distel, *f.* V. Mariendistel. —kresse, *f.* V. Brunnenkresse. —wurz, *f.* blessed thistle.

‖**Bornen**, **Börnen**, *v. tr.* to water [a horse &c.].

Borretsch, *m.* [-es] [a plant] borage.

Bors, *m.* [-ses, *pl.* -se] [a fish] the perch.

Borsdorfer, *m.* [-s, *pl.* -] [= Borsdorfer Apfel] a borsdorf apple.

***Börse**, *f.* [*pl.* -n] [Fr. *bourse*] 1) a purse. Eine leere —, an empty purse. 2) [the place, where the merchants, bankers and brokers of a city meet to transact business, at certain hours; *it.* the whole of these merchants &c. assembled at this place] the exchange. Die Londoner — ist ein stattliches Gebäude, the exchange of London is a noble edifice; die — war, in Folge dieser Nachrichten, heftig bewegt, in consequence of this news, there was a great stir on 'change; das Gerücht ging auf der —, daß &c., there was a rumour on 'change, that &c.

‖**Börsen-alte**, *pl.*, —spiel, *n.* stock-jobbing. —tag, *m.* the day when the merchants, bankers and brokers meet at the exchange.

‖**Borst**, *m.* [-es, *pl.* -e] **Borste**, *f.* [*pl.* -n] [V. Bersten] a cleft, a crack, a chink.

Borste, *f.* [*pl.* -n] [perhaps from bären = heben. *Barr* signifies in Scandinavian the pointed leaves of the pine] 1) [the stiff glossy hair of swine; similar hair on other animals] bristle. Mit —n versehen, to bristle [a shoemaker's thread &c.]. *Fig.* [in contempt] the stiff hair of men. Seine Haare stehen wie —n in die Höhe, his hair stands on end like bristles. 2) [in botany, a species of pubescence on plants] bristle.

Borst[en]-besen, *m.* hair-broom. —[en]pinsel, *m.* a painting-brush made of bristles. —same, *m.* V. Mönchpfeffer. —wisch, *m.* hair-broom.

Borsten-artig, *adj.* and *adv.* [like bristles] bristly. —artige Haare, hair like bristles, bristly hair. —bart, *m.* a bristly beard. —binse, *f.* moss-rush, or goose corn. —blatt, *n.* [in botany] a bristle-shaped leaf. —floße, *f.* —flosser, *m.* [a fish] a species of clupea [clupea thrissa]. —förmig, *adj.* bristle-shaped. —gras, *n.* common mat-grass. —voll, *adj.* and *adv.* [thickly set with bristles] bristly. —zahnfisch, *m.* V. Klippfisch.

Borsten, *v. r.* sich —, 1) [to rise and stand erect] to bristle. Sein Haar borstet sich, his hair bristles. 2) to bristle the hair. Die Katze borstet sich, the cat erects its hair.

Borstig, *adj.* and *adv.* bristly or bristle-shaped, [in botany] setaceous. Der —e Eber, the bristly boar; ein —es Blatt, a setaceous leaf. †and‡*Fig.* Borstig werden, to fly into a passion.

Bort, V. Bord.

Borte, *f.* [*pl.* -n] [from the root of Bord] 1) the outer edge of any thing, especially the edge or border of ornaments of a garment, galloon. Goldene, silberne —n, gold-lace, silver-lace; ein Hut mit goldenen —n besetzt, a gold-laced hat; mit —n besetzen, to lace [a cloth &c.]. 2) [in architecture] V. Fries.

Borten-arbeit, *f.* lace-maker's work. —macher, *m.* lace-maker. —werk, *n.* V. —arbeit. —wirker, *m.* V. —macher.

Börteln, *v. tr.* [unusual] to border.

Borten, *v. tr.* to lace [a garment &c.].

Bösartig, *adj.* and *adv.* 1) malignant = malicious. Ein —es Herz, a malignant heart; ein —er Mensch, an ill-natured man. 2) malignant = virulent, dangerous to life. Ein —es Geschwür, a malign ulcer; ein —es Fieber, a malignant fever.

Bösartigkeit, *f.* 1) malignancy [of heart &c.]. 2) malignancy = virulence or tendency to a fatal issue. Die — eines Geschwürs oder eines Fiebers, the malignancy of an ulcer or of a fever.

Böschen, *v. tr.* [seems to be the same as the Fr. *baisser*] to form with a slope, to slope. Den Boden in einem Garten —, to slope the ground in a garden; einen Wall —, to escarp a rampart.

Böschung, *f.* 1) the act of sloping. 2) [in architecture and in fortification] a slope, talus. Die — einer Bastion, the talus of a bastion.

‖**Böse**, V. Pose.

Böse, [D. *boos*, Goth. *baud*, Engl. *bad*; Fr. *bas* signifies niedrig, gemein] *adj.* and *adv.* [contrary to good, physical and moral] bad, ill, evil. — Wege, bad roads; *fig.* wicked ways; — Luft, bad air; ein —s Klima, an ill climate; — Wetter, bad weather; — Augen, sore eyes; —e Zeiten, hard times; ein —r Nachbar, a bad neighbour; ein —r Mensch, a wicked man; ein —s Herz, a bad or malignant heart; er wandelt auf —n Wegen, his ways are ill; meide das — und thue Gutes, eschew evil, and do good; — Gedanken, evil thoughts; zu derselben Stunde aber machte er Viele gesund von —n Geistern, [in Script.] that hour he cured many of evil spirits; der — Feind, the devil, fiend; er hat ein —s Gewissen, his conscience is not clear. [in a less extensive signification] *a*) easily irritated or provoked to contest; easily moved to anger. Ein —s Weib, a peevish, prating, turbulent, vexatious woman, a shrew, a termagant; ein —r Hund, a biting, surly, snarling dog or cur; Einen — machen, to make any one angry, to provoke any one; auf Jemanden — seyn or Einem — seyn, to be angry with any one; — aussehen, to look angry, grim or cross; sich — stellen, to feign anger; es ist nicht — gemeint, it is not meant ill, there is no harm intended. *b*) bad = noxious, hurtful. Einem —s thun, to hurt any one; Gutes mit —m vergelten, to return evil for good; habe ich übel geredet, so beweise es, daß es — sei, [in Script.] if I have spoken evil, bear witness of the evil; — Beispiele, noxious examples; er gibt ein —s Beispiel, he sets an ill example; —e Gesellschaften, bad company; eine böse Zunge, —s Maul, a mischievous, malicious tongue; ein —s Ende, an ill end; das — Wesen, [rather obsolete or provinc.] epilepsy. *Prov.* — kommt geritten, geht aber weg mit Schritten, mischiefs come by the pound, and go away by the ounce; —s muß man mit —m vertreiben, desperate cuts must have desperate cures; —e Beispiele verderben gute Sitten, evil examples corrupt good manners. *c*) shameful, disgraceful. Ein —r Name, a bad name; sie sagt allen Leuten etwas —s nach, she speaks ill of every one; die — Krankheit, a bad = venereal disease.

Bösewicht, *m.* [-es, *pl.* -er] 1) a wicked wretch, a profligate man or wretch, a villain, a reprobate, a miscreant, a ruffian.

Boshaft, I. *adj.* 1) [harbouring ill will or enmity without provocation, malevolent in the extreme, malignant in heart; *it.* inclined to do harm, disposed to mischief or sin] malicious. Ein —es Gemüth, a malignant mind; ein —er Kerl, a spiteful fellow; ein —er Junge, a mischievous boy; der Affe ist ein —es Thier, a monkey is a mischievous animal. II. *adv.* maliciously, mischievously.

Bosheit, *f.* [*pl.* -en] 1) [the quality of being

licious, extreme enmity or disposition to injure others without cause, from mere personal gratification or from a spirit of revenge] malignity, maliciousness, malice. *Prov.* — ist ihr eigener Henker, malice hurts itself the most. 2) [disposition to do harm, or to vex or annoy] mischievousness. Das Kind weint nur aus —, the child cries only from spite. 3) done by design, mischief.

Bosheits-sünde, *f.* [in theology] sin of malice.

Bösherzig, *adj.* and *adv.* having a malignant heart, bad-hearted, ill-natured.

Böslich, *adj.* and *adv.* malicious. Seine Freunde verließen ihn — or —er Weise, his friends forsook him maliciously; —e Verlassung, [in law] desertion [said of married persons].

‖**Bössel, Boßel, Boßkugel**, *f.* [from the old Boß = rund] the bowl used in playing at nine-pins.

Bossel-bahn, *f.* —**platz**, —**schub**, *m.* V. Kegelbahn.

Bósseln, Bóssern, [V. Bossel] ‖ I. *v. intr.* to play at nine-pins. II. *v. tr.* [Bossiren] to emboss [in wax &c.].

Bössinnig, *adj.* and *adv.* evil-minded.

***Bossirer**, [Bosseler] *m.* [-s, *pl.* -] one who embosses.

Böswillig, *adj.* and *adv.* malevolent.

Böswilligkeit, *f.* malevolence.

‡**Bot**, *n.* [-es, *pl.* -e] V. Gebot.

***Botanik**, *f.* botany.

***Botániker**, *m.* [-s, *pl.* -] botanist.

***Botánisch**, *adj.* and *adv.* botanic, botanical. Ein —er Garten, a botanic garden.

***Botanisiren**, *v. intr.* [to seek for plants, to study plants] to botanize.

***Botárgo**, *f.* [a relishing sort of food, made of the roes of the mullet] botargo.

Böte, V. Bothe.

***Botelier**, *m.* [-s, *pl.* -e] [in seamen's language] Der — eines Schiffes, steward.

Boteliers-maat, *m.* steward's mate.

Bothe, Böte, *m.* [-n, *pl.* -n] [from bieten; the Eng. to bid] 1) a person deputed to execute some important business, as in Scripture, angels and apostles. 2) [more commonly one who bears a message or an errand] a messenger, runner. [Bote is also frequently used in compound words, as:] Der Eigen—, a messenger sent express, an express; ‖ a private messenger; der Fuß—, foot-post; der Eil— or reitende —, estafet, estafette; der Liebes—, a love-messenger; ein Trauer—, a messenger of bad news &c. Er sandte einen —n an seinen Gesandten in Frankreich ab, he dispatched a messenger to his envoy in France. *Fig.* Der hinkende —, long Tom the carrier; unpleasant news. 3) [he who regularly carries letters and goods from one town or village to another] a postman, a carrier, waggoner.

Bothen-amt, *n.* the office or business of a messenger or carrier. —**gang**, *m.* 1) the walk or gait of a messenger. *Fig.* a slow and awkward gait. 2) the distance a messenger goes and his fee. 3) [any special business to be transacted by a messenger] errand. —**laufen**, *n.* the going of a messenger on a business, the business of a messenger or carrier. —**laufer**, *m.* a messenger, runner, foot-post. —**lohn**, *m.* messenger's pay, wages or fee. —**meister**, *m.* an officer superintending the public messengers. —**schild**, *n.* a round plate on which a coat of arms is represented, worn by public messengers on the arm or on the breast.

Bothschaft, *f.* 1) message, errand, news, intelligence. Er richtete seine — aus, he told his errand, he delivered his message; er brachte gute —, he brought good news, tidings. 2) embassy [a most common sense in the Bible].

Bothschafts-rath, *m.* a counsellor to an ambassador. —**secretär**, *m.* a secretary to an ambassador.

Böthschafter, *m.* [-s, *pl.* -] ambassador. Groß—, minister, plenipotentiary.

Böthschaftlich, *adv.* by a messenger, in the form of a message.

Botlereí, *f.* [in seamen's language] steward's room.

Bötmäßig, *adj.* and *adv.* obedient, subordinate.

Bötmäßigkeit, *f.* [right of governing] dominion, government. Unter der — eines Andern stehen, to be under the dominion of another.

Bótte, V. Butte.

Bóttich, *m.* [-es, *pl.* -e] [from Botte, Bütte &c.] a coop, vat.

Bottich-hefen, *pl.* [in breweries] the bottom of beer. —**macher**, *m.* V. Bötticher.

Bötticher, Böttcher, *m.* [-s, *pl.* -] cooper.

Bötticher-arbeit, *f.* cooper's work. —**bohrer**, *m.* 1) a cooper's borer. 2) [in natural history] *a*) a species of whelk [buccinum glabratum]. *b*) the commander [conus dux]. —**holz**, wood employed by coopers. —**lohn**, *m.* cooperage. —**schlägel**, *m.* a cooper's mallet. —**zirkel**, *m.* a cooper's compass.

Böttichereí, *f.* 1) cooper's trade. 2) a cooper's shop.

***Bouillon**, *m.* broth. V. Fleischbrühe.

***Bouquét**, [pronounce: Bukét] *n.* [-es, *pl.* -e] 1) a nosegay, posy. V. Blumenstrauß. 2) [the flavour of wine, die Blume] bouquet.

***Boússole**, *f.* [*pl.* -n] a box-compass.

***Bouteille**, *f.* [*pl.* -n] a bottle. V. Flasche.

Bouteillen-bier, *n.* bottle-beer. —**glas**, *n.* bottle-glass. —**korb**, *m.* a hamper. —**kühler**, *m.* cooler.

***Boutike**, *f.* [*pl.* -n] a shop. V. Bude.

Bóxen, V. Baxen.

Boý, V. Boi.

Brabánt, *n.* [-s] [a name of a province in the Netherlands] Brabant.

Brabánter, *m.* [-s, *pl.* -] 1) an inhabitant of Brabant. ‖ 2) a Brabant-dollar.

Brabántisch, *adj.* from or belonging to Brabant. —e Leinwand, brabantes.

Brách, *adj.* [= mangelhaft, from Brechen] [in husbandry, unsown, not tilled, left to rest after a year or more of tillage] fallow. Einen Acker — liegen lassen, to let a field lie fallow. *Fig.* — liegen lassen, to forbear to use or to employ, to neglect [talents &c.].

Brach-acker, *m.* fallow ground, fallow field, fallow. —**distel**, *f.* the common eryngo. —**fahre**, *f.* fallowing. —**feld**, *n.* fallow field, fallow. —**flur**, *f.* a tract of fallow ground. —**gras**, *n.* grass gathered on fallows. —**huhn**, *n.* the golden plover. —**hut**, —**hütung**, *f.* the right and act of tending sheep or cattle on fallows. —**käfer**, *m.* the hoary beetle. —**land**, *n.* V. —acker. —**lerche**, *f.* the meadow lark. —**männchen**, **männlein**, *n.* the common mushroom or champignon. —**monat**, *m.* the month of June. —**schein**, *m.* the new moon in June. —**schlag**, *m.* 1) V. —flur. 2) V. —hut. —**schnepfe**, *f.* the common curlew. —**vogel**, *m.* [the name of several birds] 1) V. —schnepfe. 2) the little bustard. 3) the grey sand-piper. 4) the missel-thrush, 5) the spotted plover. —**wiese**, *f.* fallow-meadow. —**zeit**, *f.* the time of fallowing.

Bráche, *f.* 1) [a fallow state] fallowness. 2) fallow ground, fallow. 3) fallowing. 4) V. Brachzeit.

Bráchen, [from brechen] *v. tr.* 1) to fallow [cold, strong, clayey land &c.] ‖ 2) *a*) Einen Teich —, to plow and seed a drawn pond. *b*) Den Flachs —, to rake the flax. *c*) to leave to rest after a year or more of tillage.

Brácher, *m.* V. Brachvogel.

Bráchse, *f.* [*pl.* -n] V. Brassen, *m.*

Bráchsenkraut, *n.* [-es, *pl.* -kräuter] quillwort.

1. **Bráck**, *m.* [-en, *pl.* -en] [Bracke] [Fr. *brac*, Ital. *bracco*, D. *braak*; Swed. *racka* signifies a bitch] a setting dog [used only in heraldry].

Brackenhaupt, *n.* [in heraldry] the head of a dog with pendulous ears.

2. **Bráck**, *n.* [from brechen] 1) [that which is rejected as useless, waste matter] refuse. 2) V. Wrack.

Brack-gut, *n.* [in commerce] refuse of merchandise.

Bráck, *adj.* [of sea-water] a little saltish, brackish. Das Bracke, the brack, brackishness.

Brackwasser, *n.* brackish water.

Brácken, *v. tr.* to reject and cast out what is bad.

Brackendistel, *f.* V. Brachdistel.

Brácker, *m.* [-s, *pl.* -] [in commerce] sorter.

***Bracteáten**, *pl.* V. Blechmünze.

Bräden, V. Brassen.

Brägen, *v. tr.* [perhaps to recken] [with tawers] to scrape [the skins] on the flesh-side.

Brägen, V. Gehirn.

Brägenwurst, *f.* a sausage made of the brain of pigs.

Brähme, Bráhne, V. 1. Brame.

Brähmen, Brähnen, *v. intr.* [a hunting term] to go to brim.

1. ‖**Bräke**, *f.* [*pl.* -n] V. Reisholz.

2. **Bräke**, *f.* [in seamen's language] brake.

1. **Bräm**, *m.* [-es] **Brámen**, *m.* [-s] V. Ginster or Pfriemenkraut.

2. ‖**Bräm**, *m.* [-es, *pl.* -e] the brim, border.

3. **Bräm**, *m.* V. Prahm.

Bräm, [in seamen's lang., probably = 2. Brame; only used in compound words]

Bram-brassen, *pl.* [in seamen's language] Die großen —brassen, or großen —segelbrassen, the main-top-gallant braces. —**fall**, *m.* [in seamen's lang.] top-gallant-halliards. —**segel**, top-gallant-sail. Ein fliegendes —segel, a flying top-gallant-sail; das große —segel, the main-top-gallant-sail. —**segelbrassen**, V. —brassen. —**segelkühlte**, *f.* [in seamen's lang.] top-gallant-mast-breeze. —**stenge**, *f.* [in seamen's lang.] top-gallant-mast. Die große —stenge, main-top-gallant-mast; die —stenge mit einem langen Topp, top-gallant mast with a long pole-head, eine —stenge mit einem stumpfen Topp, top-gallant-mast with a stump head. —**stengenstag**, *n.* [in seamen's lang.] breast-back-stay. —**stengenwand**, *f.* [in seamen's lang.] the top-gallant-shrouds.

***Bräma**, [-s or des Brama] [the chief deity of the Hindu nations] Brahma, Brama, Bruma.

Bramapriester, *m.* bramin, brahmin. Die Frau eines —priesters, braminess, braminee.

***Bramárbas**, *m.* a puffing, boasting fellow, a braggart, a swaggerer, a bully, a blusterer.

***Bramarbasiren**, *v. intr.* to puff, to swagger, to bully, to bluster.

Brámbeere, *f.* V. Brombeere.

1. Brāme, Brāme, *f.* [*pl.* -n] Brām, *m.* [-es, *pl.* -e] [allied to Braue] 1) brim, border [used only in some compound words]. 2) [in forests] purlieu.

2. Brāme, *f.* [*pl.* -n] [allied to Pfriem] something long and pointed.

Brāme, *f.* [*pl.* -n] V. Brunst.

Brāmen, V. 1. Bram.

Bramīne, *m.* [-n, *pl.* -n] V Bramapriester.

Brāmling, *m.* [-es, *pl.* -e] [a bird] a sort of yellow bunting.

1. Bránd, *m.* [-es, *pl.* Brände] 1) a burning, combustion. In — kommen, to begin to burn with flame, to kindle, to catch fire; das Schiff gerieth in —, the ship took fire; in — bringen, to cause to burn; in —, a-fire, on fire. 2) [the burning of a house or town] a conflagration. Constantinopel hat sehr viel durch — gelitten, Constantinople has suffered great losses by fire; der große — zu Boston in Jahre 1771, the great fire in Boston in 1771; der trojanische —, the burning of Troy; in — stecken, to set on fire, to set fire to; einen — löschen, to quench a fire. 3) *Fig. a)* a fatal inflammation in any part of the animal body. Der kalte —, mortification, gangrene, sphacelus. *b)* [a disease incident to plants] blight, blast; [a foul black substance which forms on corn] smut; [a morbid excrescence in grain] ergot. *c)* the heat or raging of passion, burning. 4) [a burning piece of wood, or a stick or piece of wood partly burnt whether burning or after the fire is extinct] a brand. Ein Feuer—, a firebrand. 5) [in pyrotechnics] a match. 6) [the operation of burning, as in brickmaking] burn. 7) any quantity of a thing burnt or baked at one time. Ein — Ziegel, a batch of tiles; ein — thönerner Pfeifen, a baking of clay tobacco-pipes. 8) the place where there has been a fire, or a hurt or injury caused by the action of fire, a burn, scald. 9) [a mark made by burning with a hot iron] a brand, as upon sheep &c. 10) the dirt or soil left in a gun by the powder. Auf den — laden, to charge a gun without cleansing it before. 11) *Fig.* [vulgar and student's cant] Er hat einen tüchtigen —, he is regularly intoxicated. 12) [in some compound words = röthlich] V. —fuchs, —hirsch.

Brand-ader, *f.* 1) [in anatomy] *a)* the crural artery, or crural vein. V. Schenkelader. *b)* V. Krummdarmader. 2) [in husbandry] a barren place on a cornfield. —apfel, *m.* a sort of apples of a red colour. —asche, *f.* the ashes of burnt houses. —assecuranz, *f.* V. —versicherung. —begnadigung, *f.* a favour granted by government to those who have suffered by fire. —bettler, *m.* a person who begs under plea of having been a sufferer from fire. —blase, —blatter, *f.* a pustule, a thin bladder on the skin occasioned by a burn, a blister. —blut, *n.* a fatal disease among swine. —bock, *m.* fire-dog, creeper. —böcke, *pl.* andirons. —brassen, *m.* [a fish] a sort of bream. —brief, *m.* 1) a written attestation of loss by fire. 2) an incendiary letter. *Fig.* [rather vulgar] any impudent or threatening letter. —eisen, *n.* 1) branding-iron. 2) andirons, fire-dog, creeper. —ente, *f.* the shield-drake or borough-duck. —entschädigung, *f.* indemnification for loss sustained by fire. —erz, *n.* bituminous marle slate, bituminous marlite. —faß, *n.* [in seamen's language] fire-barrel. —fest, *adj.* and *adv.* fire-proof. —fieber, *n.* a fever attending upon a burn, or accompanying gangrene or mortification. —fleck, *m.* V. —ader, 2). —flecken, *m.* a mark of burning, a burn or scald. —fleckig, *adj.* and *adv.* having marks of burning. —fuchs, *m.* 1) brant-fox. 2) sorrel-horse. —gasse, *f.* a space or alley between houses to prevent the communication of fire. —gerste, *f.* V. —getreide. —getreide, *n.* blighted or blasted corn. —glocke, *f.* firebell, a bell to give the alarm of fire. —haken, *m.* 1) fire-hook. 2) [a sea term] fireboom [Branderhaken]. —hemd, *n.* [sea term] curtains. —hirsch, *m.* the horse-stag. —holzbaum, *m.* [a shrub] a species of protea [protea conifera]. —horn, *n.* the endive-shell. —kasse, *f.* fire-insurance-office. —kitt, *m.* a sort of cement to prevent the communication of fire. —korb, *m.* fire-guard. —korn, *n.* blighted corn. —kugel, *f.* [a ball filled with powder or other combustibles] fireball, carcass. —lattich, *m.* V. Huflattich. —leiter, *f.* fire-ladder. —mahl, *n.* 1) [a mark made by burning with a hot iron as upon a criminal, or a cask] a brand. *Fig.* Das —mahl des Brudermords zeichnete seine Stirn, the brand of fratricide marked his fore-head; das —mahl der Schande und des Lasters war ihm sichtbar aufgedrückt, the brand of infamy and vice was visibly imprinted on him; die —mahl in ihrem Gewissen haben, [in Scripture] having their conscience seared with a hot iron. 2) a scar occasioned by a burn. —mahlen, —marken, *v. tr.* 1) to brand [a criminal]. 2) *Fig.* to stigmatize [a vice with infamy &c.] —mauer, *f.* a strong brick- or stone-wall between houses to prevent any communication of fire. —meise, *f.* coal-titmouse. —meister, *m.* fireward, firewarden. —messer, *m.* pyrometer. —mittel, *n.* a remedy for burns. —opfer, *n.* [anciently among the Jews] burnt-offering, burnt-sacrifice. —opferaltar, *m.* an altar for burnt-offerings. —ordnung, *f.* the laws and regulations in case of fire. —otter, *f.* V. —schlange. —pfahl, *m.* the stake at which criminals are burnt. —pfeil, *m.* [in military affairs] fire-arrow. —pflaster, *n.* a plaster for a burn. —probe, *f.* [in mints] assay by fire. —raketen, *pl.* war-rockets, Congreve-rockets. —regen, *m.* a blighting rain. —roggen, *m.* V. —korn. —röhre, *f.* 1) [in seamen's lang.] fire-trunk. 2) Die —röhre einer Bombe oder Granate, the fusee or fuse of a bomb or grenade. —rose, *f.* [in medicine] gangrenous erysipelas. —ruthe, *f.* V. —bock. —salbe, *f.* an ointment for burns. —schade[n], *m.* loss occasioned by fire. —schiefer, *m.* bituminous slate. —schiff, *n.* fire-ship. V. Brander. —schlag, *m.* [in pyrotechnics] a small pipe filled with combustible matter by which fire is communicated to fire-works. —schlange, *f.* garden or yellowish grey boa. —schutt, *m.* the rubbish of burnt houses. —silber, *n.* [in metallurgy] refined silver. —spritze, *f.* fire-engine. —statt, *f.* V. —stätte. —stätte, *f.* 1) a place where there has been a fire. 2) a fire-place, a hearth. —stein, *m.* brick. —stelle, *f.* V. —stätte 1). —steuer, *f.* a tax or rate imposed to relieve those who have suffered by fire. —stifter, *m.* [any person who sets fire to a building] an incendiary. —stiftung, *f.* the malicious burning of a dwelling-house or any other building; [in law] arson. —thür, *f.* a door which is fire-proof. —versichert, *adj.* and *adv.* insured against loss by fire. —versicherung, *f.* insurance against loss by fire. —versicherungsanstalt, *f.* fire-office. —vogel, *m.* [a bird] the scare-crow, black gull. —wache, *f.* fire-watch. —weizen, *m.* V. —getreide. —zeichen, *n.* 1) a mark made by burning with a hot iron, a brand [in a proper as well as in a figurative sense]. 2) a sign or signal of fire. —zeug, *n.* [in pyrotechnics] quick-match. Das —zeug an einer Hülse, an einer Rackete, mit einem Papierdeckel verwahren, to cap a case, a rocket. ||—ziemer, *m.* the black bird, ouzel.

2. Bránd, *m.* [-es, *pl.* Brände] [perhaps allied to Rand] the lowest part of any thing, as in coal-pits, the bed of coals.

Bránden, [perhaps allied to the old Goth. *brana*, schäumen] *v. intr.* [in seamen's lang.] to break. Die See brandet, the sea breaks.

Bránder, *m.* [-s, *pl.* -] 1) [in seamen's lang.] fire-ship. —haken, V. Brandhaken, 2). 2) [in pyrotechnics] the fusee of rockets &c.

Brándicht, *adj.* and *adv.* smelling, tasting, or looking as if burnt. Dieses Fleisch riecht —, this meat smells of burning.

Brándig, *adj.* and *adv.* blasted, blighted, smutted [said principally of plants].

||Brändlein, *n.* [-s, *pl.* -] [a bird] a sort of wren.

Brándschatzen, *v. tr.* Ein Land &c. —, to levy contributions upon a country &c. in the power of an enemy; *it.* [in a more general sense] to impose heavy taxes on. **Fig.* to importune any one [especially in pecuniary matters].

Brándschatzer, *m.* [-s, *pl.* -] one who levies contributions upon a country &c. in the power of an enemy &c.

Brándschatzung, *f.* the act of levying contributions upon a country &c. in the power of an enemy &c.

Brándsohle, *f.* [*pl.* -n] [Brand seems to be allied to Rand] the inner sole of a shoe.

Brándung, *f.* [the waves which break against a rock] breakers, surf.

Bránge, *f.* [*pl.* -n] [probably allied to Reckes and to the Lat. *brachium*] the crank for moving the saw in a saw-mill.

Bránke, Bránte, *f.* [*pl.* -n] [among hun… the paw of a bear.

Brán[n]twein, *m.* [-es, *pl.* -e] [an ardent s… distilled from the lees of wine, from fruits and p… brandy, brandy-wine. Der Korn—, a s… distilled from grain, whisky; der Wachho… —, geneva, gin; der Franz—, cognac.

Bran[n]twein-blase, *f.* the still for b…dy. —brenner, *m.* a distiller of brandy, …dy-distiller. —brennerei, *f.* a distillery … brandy. —flasche, *f.* brandy-bottle. —geist, *m.* spirit of wine, or pure or highly rect… spirit, alcohol. —haus, *n.* brandy-shop, … shop. —schenke, *f.* V. —haus. —spülich, *n.* the refuse matters of a brandy-distillery, … wash. —trank, *m.* V. —spülicht.

Brasiliāner, *m.* V. Brasilier.

Brasiliānisch, *adj.* V. Brasilisch.

Brasilien, *n.* [-s] Brazil.

Brasilien-holz, *n.* Brazil, Brazil- [Fernambuk], Braziletto [Jamaikaholz]. —ta… *m.* Brasilian-tobacco.

Brasilier, *m.* [-s, *pl.* -] —inn, *f.* a… of Brazil, a Brazilian.

Brasilisch, *adj.* and *adv.* Brazilian.

||Bráß, *m.* [-sses] trash.

Brásse, *f.* [*pl.* -n] [Fr. *bras*] [in seamen's… brace. Die großen —n, main braces; die… anholen, to haul on the braces; die —n a… len, to brace the yards in or haul in the wea… braces.

Braßschenkel, *pl.* [in seamen's languag… brace-pendants of the yard-arms.

Brássen, [V. Brasse] *v. tr.* [a sea term] to … Verkehrt —, to brace the sails aback; luv —, to brace up the yards, to brace them to wind; ins Kreuz or Vierkant —, to square yards; auf den Wind —, to bring to; scharf dem Winde —, or auf den Rand —, to trim sharp; voll —, to brace the sails full; die Se… in den Wind —, to brace the sails in the wi…

Bräſſen, *m.* [-s, *pl.* -] [a fresh-water-fish] the bream.

Bräſſenfarn, *m.* [-s] V. Brachſenkraut.

Brätchen, Brätlein, *n.* [-s, *pl.* -] *dimin.* of Braten.

Bräteln, *v. intr.* to roast a little.

Bräten, [with some authors *ir.*] [allied to rösten, to the Fr. *rôtir*, to brauen, A. S. *braedan*; *brastlian*, brennen] I. *v. intr.* to be roasted, to be prepared for food by exposure to heat. *Fig.* to be parched or scorched. Beſſer wäre es für uns, in Afrika's brennender Sonne zu —, we had rather be scorched by the burning sun of Africa. II. *v. tr.* 1) to roast [meat, apples, potatoes &c.]. Am Spieße —, to roast on a spit; in der Pfanne —, to fry; Fleiſch auf dem Roſte —, to broil meat on a grid-iron; Fleiſch im Ofen —, to bake meat in an oven; dieſes Fleiſch iſt gut, zu wenig, zu viel gebraten, this meat is well done, underdone, overdone. Das Braten, roasting. *Prov.* Nach dem der Mann iſt, bratet man ihm die Wurſt, we must adapt ourselves to the taste and understanding of those we have to deal with. || 2) [in metallurgy] to roast.

Brat-apfel, *m.* 1) baking-apple. 2) a roasted apple. —birn, *f.* 1) baking-pear. 2) a roasted pear. —bock, *m.* the rack. —fiſch, *m.* 1) fish whose relish is improved by frying. 2) a fried fish. —koch, *m.* a cook who prepares roast-meat. —ofen, *m.* [in kitchens] an oven for baking meat. —pfanne, *f.* frying-pan. —röhre, *f.* frying-tube. —roſt, *m.* a roaster, grid-iron. —ſpieß, *m.* 1) a spit, a broach. 2) *Fig.* [in joke, a sword] a toaster. —ſpille, *f.* [in seamen's lang.] windlass. —trommel, *f.* a cradle-spit. —wurſt, *f.* a sausage.

Braten, *m.* [-s, *pl.* -] roast meat; any piece of meat fit for roasting. Ein Rinds- [or Roſt-] —, roast-beef; Kalbs—, roast veal; Hammels—, roast mutton; Schweins—, roast pork; Gänſe—, roast goose; Wild—, roast venison; den — anſtecken, to spit a piece of meat; den — umwenden, to turn the spit; den — begießen, to baste meat. *Prov.* Den — riechen or merken, to smell a rat; um den — hergehen, to beat about the bush.

Braten-brühe, *f.* a sauce [to be eaten with roast-meat for improving its relish]. —fett, *n.* dripping. ‡*Fig.* —kleid, *n.* a festive garment. —meiſter, *m.* [in the kitchens of princes] the overseer of the roast-meat. —rock, *m.* V. —kleid. —ſchüſſel, *f.* a dish for serving up roast-meat. —ſpicker, *m.* a larder. —wender, *m.* 1) a turn-broach, a turn-spit. 2) a kitchen-jack, a smoke-jack.

Bräter, *m.* [unusual] [-s, *pl.* -] turn-broach, turn-spit.

Braterei, *f.* [*pl.* -en] a place where meat is roasted and sold.

Brätlein, V. Brätchen.

Brätling, *m.* [-es, *pl.* -e] 1) [a fish] the sprat. 2) a species of boletus [boletus lactifluus].

Bratſche, *f.* [*pl.* -n] viol.

Bratſchen-ſpieler, *m.* a performer on the viol, violist. —ſtimme, *f.* the part of the viol in any composition.

Bräzel, *f.* [*pl.* -n] V. Brezel.

Brau, *n.* [-es, *pl.* -e] V. Gebräue.

Brau-berechtigt, *adj.* and *adv.* having the privilege of brewing beer. Der —berechtigte, licensed brewer. —bottich, *m.* a vat. —geräth, the apparatus for brewing. —gerechtigkeit, the privilege of brewing beer. —haus, *n.* a brew-house, a brewery. —herr, *m.* the master of a brewery. —hof, *m.* V. —haus. —innung, *f.* V. Brauergilde. —keſſel, *m.* a copper or large boiler used in breweries. —knecht, *m.* a brewer's man. —krücke, *f.* V. Malzkrücke. —kufe, *f.* V. —bottich. —meiſter, *m.* the brewer. —ofen, *m.* an oven used in breweries. —ordnung, *f.* 1) [in some countries] the succession in which the brewers exercise the right of brewing. 2) regulation for brewing. —pfanne, *f.* the brewing-copper. —recht, *n.* V. —gerechtigkeit. —reihe, *f.* V. —ordnung 1). —ſchenke, *f.* a beerhouse. —weſen, *n.* the trade and occupation of brewing. —wirth, *m.* the keeper of a beer-house.

Brauch, *m.* [-es, *pl.* Bräuche] 1) [the act of employing any thing to any purpose] use. 2) [practice long continued] usage, custom. Nach altem —, according to ancient custom. V. Gebrauch.

Brauchbar, *adj.* and *adv.* fit for use, of use. Ein ſehr —es Wort, a very useful word; ein recht —er Menſch, a very useful or serviceable fellow; ein —es Pferd, a serviceable horse.

Brauchbarkeit, *f.* fitness for use, usefulness, serviceableness, utility.

Brauchen, [Goth. *brukon*, A. S. *brukan*, perhaps the same as the Gr. *βρύκω*, the Lat. *fruor*, eſſen, genießen] I. *v. tr.* 1) to want, to lack, to need. Ich brauche keinen Arzt, I do not need a physician; Geld —, to want money; man braucht ſo viel Tuch zu einem Rocke, it takes so much cloth to make a coat; ich brauche Bücher, I have occasion for books; denſelben Grundſatz kann man —, the same principle may be admitted; man braucht ſich nicht zu wundern, it is not to be wondered at; das braucht Niemand zu wiſſen, there is no necessity for any one's knowing that; er braucht ſich nur gut aufzuführen, he needs but conduct himself well; Sie — es nur zu ſagen, you need only say the word. 2) V. Gebrauchen. II. *v. imp.* it is required, it needs. Es brauchte viele or vieler Mühe, it required much trouble. Syn. Brauchen, Gebrauchen. The two words are frequently used synonymously, this distinction is, however, to be observed, that brauchen signifies rather, to want, to require; gebrauchen, to use, to apply. There is a great difference between Arznei brauchen, and Arznei gebrauchen. A person who only imagines himself ill gebraucht Arznei [uses medicine], although er keine braucht [he does not require any], and many who think themselves well brauchen [want] medicine, and gebrauchen keine [do not make use of any].

Bräuchig, Bräuchlich, *adj.* and *adv.* V. Gebräuchlich.

Braue, *f.* [*pl.* -n] V. Augenbraue.

Brauen, [allied to brennen, braten] *v. tr.* 1) to brew [beer]. 2) **Fig.* *a*) to brew, to mingle. Was — Sie da für ein Gemiſch zuſammen? what sort of a mess are you compounding there? *b*) to prepare. Einen Punſch —, to make punch. *c*) to contrive, to plot. Ich merke, daß ſie etwas mit einander —, I see they are plotting something together.

Brauer, *m.* [-s, *pl.* -] brewer.

Brauergilde, *f.* brewers' company.

Brauerei, *f.* 1) the art or trade of brewing beer. 2) brew-house, brewery.

Braun, [allied to brennen, Brand] *adj.* and *adv.* 1) brown. Einen — und blau ſchlagen, to beat any one black and blue; —e Butter, fried butter; — machen, to imbrown; das —, the brown colour or a brown colour; ein dunkeles —, a dark brown; ein —es Frauenzimmer [*eine Brünette], a brunette. *Fig.* Das —e Mädchen, [a plant] common adonis or bird's eye. 2) [in poetry] dark, dusky.

Braun-äugig, *adj.* and *adv.* brown-eyed. —beere, *f.* 1) black currant [ſchwarze Johannisbeere]. 2) V. Brombeere. —bier, *n.* brown beer. —bleierz, *n.* Grün und —bleierz [phosphorſaures Blei], phosphate of lead, green and brown lead-ore, [partly] arsenicate of lead. —eiſenocker, *m.* brown iron-ocher, ochry brown iron-ore. —eiſenſtein, *m.* Faſeriger —eiſenſtein, brown hematite, fibrous brown iron-ore; dichter —eiſenſtein, compact brown iron-ore; ockeriger —eiſenſtein, V. —eiſenocker. —erz, *n.* a sort of black-jock. —fiſch, *m.* the porpoise. —fuchs, *m.* a fox with a white spot at the tip of his brush. ||—geier, *m.* V. Fiſchaar. —gelb, *adj.* and *adv.* having the colour of a faded leaf. Das —gelbe, feuillemort. —grün, *adj.* and *adv.* brownish green. —haarig, *adj.* and *adv.* having brown hair. Ein —haariges Mädchen, a brown-haired girl. —häutling, *m.* [a bird] the greater red-pole. —heil, *n.* [the name of several plants] *a*) a species of protea [protea vulgaris]. *b*) common privet. *c*) common self-heal. —heilig, *n.* [a plant] the curled mint. —holz, *n.* V. Braſilienholz. —huhn, *n.* a species of sand-piper. —kalk, *m.* brown or pearl spar. —kehlchen, *n.* [a bird] whin-chat. —kohl, *m.* curled garden-cole. —kohle, *f.* peat. Gemeine or muſchelige —kohle, brown coal; holzige or faſerige —kohle, bituminous wood, fibrous brown-coal; erdige —kohle, earth-coal, earthy brown-coal; trapezoidale or Moor—kohle, moor or trapezoidal coal. —kopf, *m.* [a bird] brown-head. —lippe, *f.* [a shell] the smooth-edged truncated venus. —lockig, *adj.* and *adv.* having brown curly hair. —menackerz, *n.* Gelb und —menackerz, titanitic siliceous ore. —narbig, *adj.* and *adv.* having a brown grain [said of Russian leather]. —roth, I. *adj.* and *adv.* brownish red, bay. II. *n.* [a species of ocher] Indian red. —ſchecke, *f.* a piebald horse. —ſchwarz, *adj.* and *adv.* brownish black. —ſilge, *f.* [a plant] common sweet basil. —ſpath, *m.* V. —kalk. —ſtein, *m.* manganese. Glänzender —ſtein, compact brown iron-ore; piemonteſiſcher —ſtein, cummingtonite, withamite, manganesian epidote; rother —ſtein, rhomboidal red manganese, carbonate of manganese; ſchwarzer —ſtein, foliated black manganese-ore. —ſteinblende, *f.* sulphuret of manganese. —ſteinerz, *n.* Granatförmiges —ſteinerz, precious or oriental manganesian garnet; blätteriges or verhärtetes Schwarz—ſteinerz, V. ſchwarzer —ſtein. —ſteinglas, *n.* V. glänzender —ſtein. —ſteinkies, *m.* V. —ſteinblende. —ſteinkönig, *m.* [in chimistry] regulus of manganese. —ſteinmetall, *n.* V. —ſteinkönig. —ſchaum, *m.* scaly brown iron-ore or brown iron-froth. —ſtengel, *m.* V. Wundkraut. —wurz, *f.* [the name of several plants] *a*) [a species of scrophularia, the vernalis or yellow figwort, with brown stalks] brown-wort. *b*) the black mullein. *c*) pilewort or lesser celandine. *d*) brown-wort = prunella.

Bräunchen, *n.* [-s, *pl.* -] [in joke] a female with a brown or dark complexion, a brunet, brunette.

Braune, *m.* and *f.* [-n, *pl.* -n] 1) a person with a brown or dark complexion. 2) a brown or bay horse.

Bräune, *f.* 1) brown colour. Die — der Kaſtanien, the brownness of chestnuts. 2) [an inflammation of the throat, a species of angina] quinsy; die häutige —, [cynanche trachealis] croup; [in farriery] anticor.

Bräunewurzel, *f.* squinancy-wort.

Braunelle, *f.* [*pl.* -n] 1) [commonly] Braunellchen, *n.* [a bird] hedge-sparrow, or hedge-warbler. 2) [a plant] brown-wort, prunella.

Bräunen, I. *v. intr.* to become brown. II. *v. tr.* to make brown, to brown. Die Sonne hat ſeine Haut gebräunt, the sun has tanned his skin;

von der Sonne gebräunt, bronzed by the sun.

Bräunlich, *adj.* and *adv.* brownish.

Braunschweig, [-s] [the name of a duchy and town in Germany] Brunswick.

Braunschweiger, *m.* [-s, *pl.* -] -inn, *f.* a native of Brunswick, an inhabitant of the duchy or town of Brunswick.

Braunschweiger, Braunschweigisch, *adj.* and *adv.* from or belonging to Brunswick.

Braus, *m.* [-ses] [allied to prasseln, the Fr. *bruire*] bustle, tumult [used only in the phrase] *In Saus und — leben, to revel and riot, to play the good fellow.

Braushahn, *m.* [a bird of the genus tringa] ruff. Die Braushenne, *f.* reeve. V. Streithahn and Streithuhn.

||**Brausche**, *f.* [*pl.* -n] [perhaps allied to brechen, Sw. *brytta*, Ice. *briota*, the Engl. *bruise*] a bruise or bump [occasioned by a fall].

1. **Brause**, *f.* fermentation. Das Bier ist in der —, the beer is fermenting or working; [of boiling water] ebullition.

Brausebeutel, *m.* 1) a distemper among pigs. 2) V. Windbeutel. —erde, *f.* bituminous red clay. —kopf, *m.* a hot-headed person, a noisy, tumultuous or boisterous fellow. —köpfig, *adj.* and *adv.* boisterous. —thon, *m.* V. —erde. —wind, *m.* an effervescent, a boisterous youth.

2. **Brause**, *f.* [*pl.* -n] [probably allied to Rose = something raised, to kraus &c.] 1) the rose of a watering pot. 2) a watering pot [used by gardeners]. 3) a pot or pitcher.

Brausen, [allied to the Fr. *bruire*, rauschen &c.] *v. intr.* 1) to roar, to be tumultous, to be boisterous. Der Wind brauset, the wind blusters; die —den Winde, the roaring winds; die See brauset, the sea roars; die Ohren — mir, my ears tinkle, or I have a tinkling in my ears. 2) to bubble and hiss [as fermenting liquors, or any fluid, when some part escapes in an elastic form], to effervesce. Der neue Apfelwein brauset, new cider effervesces or ferments; neuer Wein brauset, new wine works; der Champagner brauset im Glase, champagne sparkles in the glass. *Fig.* Er brauset vor Zorn, he is furious with anger, he is in a violent rage; brausend, boisterous; die Jugend brauset, youth gives a loose to the passions. 3) to snort [as high spirited horses].

Brauser, *m* [-s, *pl.* -] any thing that effervesces or ferments.

1. **Braut**, *f.* [*pl.* Bräute] [A. S. *brid*, = Braut and Gattin; old Ice. *brudur*, jede Frau; allied to the A. S. *bridde*, das Junge] 1) a female betrothed but not yet married, an intended bride, [also a name applied to a woman at the marriage festival, before she is married, as well as after the ceremony] bride. Sie ist —, she is betrothed. *Prov.* Wer das Glück hat, führt die — heim, fortune gains the bride, the luckiest gains the day; einer glücklichen — fällt der Regen in den Schooß, happy is the bride the sun shines on, and the corpse the rain runs on. 2) [a bird] the summer duck. 3) Die — in Haaren, small fennel-flower.

Braut-altar, *m.* hymeneal altar. V. Trau-altar. —bett, *n.* the bridal-bed, marriage-bed. —diener, *m.* V. —führer. —fest, *n.* bridal. V. Hochzeitfest. —führer, *m.* bride-man, bride's man, bridegroom's man. —führerinn, *f.* bride-maid, bride's maid. —gelag, *n.* V. Hochzeitschmaus. —gemach, *n.* bridal-chamber. —geräth, *n.* paraphernalia, bride's apparel &c. —geschenk, *n.* a present which persons betrothed make to each other; a present made on the wedding day by others to the new married couple, nuptial present. —gewand, *n.* wedding dress. —haus, *n.* the habitation of the intended bride. —hemde, *n.* wedding shirt or shift. —jungfer, *f.* bride-maid, bride's maid. —kammer, *f.* wedding chamber, bridal chamber. —kleid, *n.* wedding-gown, wedding dress, nuptial garment. —kranz, *m.* a wreath of flowers worn by virgins on their wedding day, bridal garland. —kuß, *m.* nuptial kiss. —leute, *pl.* V. —paar. —lied, *n.* a nuptial song or poem [in praise of the bride and bridegroom], epithalamium, epithalamy. —lösung, *f.* a license to marry. —mahl, *n.* wedding-dinner. —maie, *f.* maypole, bride-stake. —messe, *f.* music performed before the wedding ceremony. —mutter, *f.* 1) the mother of the bride. || 2) a woman who prepares the bridal-bed. —nacht, *f.* wedding-night. —paar, *n.* the betrothed couple. —ring, *m.* wedding-ring. —schatz, *m.* 1) dower, dowery, portion. 2) the presents which a man and woman make to each other on the day of their being betrothed. —schmuck, *m.* ornaments worn by the bride at her wedding. —staat, *m.* bridal dress, bridal attire. —stand, *m.* the state of being betrothed. —suppe, *f.* a feast before the wedding; cakes &c. sent to the guests after the marriage day. —tag, *m.* the day of affiance, the wedding day. —wagen, *m.* the bridal carriage which conveys the intended couple to church. —werber, *m.* one who asks a woman in marriage for another.

2. **Braut**, *f.* [from Brausen] 1) [with tanners] a sort of putrefactive fermentation of the chamois leather. 2) something that roars or blusters, in the compound words Wasser—, Winds—.

Bräutigam, *m.* [-s, *pl.* -e] a man betrothed to a woman, or a man about to be married, bridegroom.

Bräutigamsabend, *m.* bridegroom's evening.

Bräutlich, *adj.* and *adv.* [belonging to a bride, or to a wedding] bridal, nuptial. Der —e Schmuck, bridal ornaments; der —e Morgen, the morning of the wedding-day.

Brav, [allied to the Lat. *prob*-us] *adj.* and *adv.* 1) beautiful, excellent, good. [with hunters] Ein —es Gehörn, fine horns; er singt sehr —, he sings very well; — [Bravo]! sehr — [Bravissimo]! well done! 2) upright, honest. Ein —er Mann, an honest man; — handeln, to deal fairly and honestly. 3) brave, courageous, intrepid, fearless of danger. Ein —er Soldat, a brave warrior; ein —er Offizier, a gallant officer; sich — halten, to conduct one's self bravely, or to fight gallantly; der —e, a brave man or warrior. 4) [rather vulgar, sometimes for] much. — Geld gewinnen, to win a rare sum of money; Einen — prügeln, to beat any one handsomely.

* **Bravade**, *f.* [*pl.* -n] bravado, boast.

Bravheit, *f.* 1) an honest mind or behaviour. 2) bravery, courage, heroism, intrepidity, gallantry.

* **Bravissimo**, *interj.* V. Brav 1).

* **Bravo**, I. *interj.* V. Brav 1). II. *m.* [-s, *pl.* -s] an Italian bandit.

* **Bravour**, *f.* bravery, intrepidity, gallantry.

Bravourarie, *f.* bravura.

Brechbar, *adj.* and *adv.* 1) easily broken, frangible, fragile, brittle. 2) [in optics] capable of being refracted [as rays of light], refrangible.

Brechbarkeit, *f.* 1) [rather unusual] fragility, brittleness. 2) [in optics] refrangibility.

Breche, *f.* [*pl.* -n] 1) [an instrument or machine to break flax or hemp] a brake. 2) [in a smith's shop] a screen, to intercept the heat of the fire.

Brechen, [allied to the Gr. *ῥήγνυμι*, the Lat. *frag-o*, *frango*] *ir.* I. *v. intr.* [u. w. seyn] 1) [to part, to separate, to divide in two] to break. Der Balken brach, the beam broke; das Eis bricht, the ice breaks. *Prov.* Es muß biegen oder —, it must bend or break; dicke Zeuge brechen eher als &c., strong stuffs rub out sooner in the folds than &c. *Fig.* *a*) to break = to fail in trade, to become bankrupt. *b*) to break = to decline in strength. Die Augen brachen ihm, his eyes grew dim [said of a dying person]; mit gebrochener Stimme, with a broken voice. *c*) to afflict grievously, to cause great sorrow or grief. Das Herz möchte mir vor Kummer —, my heart is ready to break with sorrow. Ein gebrochenes Herz, a broken heart. *d*) to break = to suffer an interruption of friendship, to fall out. Brich mit Verräthern, break with traitors. 2) [in mining] to be found. Das Gold bricht nie in Flötzen, gold is never found in layers or strata. 3) [with hunters] *a*) [to turn up the earth with the snout, as swine] to root. *b*) to hide in the snow [said of partridges]. 4) [to break through] to break = to make way with violence or suddenness. Ein Dieb brach in das Haus, a robber broke into the house; aus dem Gefängnisse —, to break out of prison; sie brachen durch die feindlichen Reihen, they broke through the ranks of the enemy; die Sonne bricht durch die Wolken, the sun breaks through the clouds. V. Hereinbrechen.

II. *v. tr.* 1) [to part or divide by force and violence, to rend apart] to break. Einen Stock —, to break a stick; eine Lanze mit Jemanden —, to break a lance with any one, *fig.* to enter the lists with any one; Flachs oder Hanf —, to break flax or hemp [*reg.* in that signif. ich brechte, gebrecht]; Getreide oder Malz —, to bruise corn or malt in a mill; Einem den Hals —, to break a person's neck; sich den Hals —, to break one's neck; einer Flasche den Hals —, to crack a bottle; Brod —, to break bread; den Stab über Einen — [in criminal courts] to pronounce sentence of death upon a convicted felon; *it.* *Fig.* *to decide unfavourably upon a person or a person's reputation, as for instance: die ganze Gesellschaft brach über sein Benehmen den Stab, the whole company censured his conduct severely. *Fig.* *a*) to lessen. [with painters] Die Farben —, to blend the colours; Kalke — die Säure, chalks oppose or remove acidity, chalks are antiacid; Feigen — sehr die Schärfe, figs are great subduers of acrimony; ein Bund Heu brach den Fall, a bundle of hay broke the fall; Einem seinen Eigensinn —, to subdue any one's obstinacy. *b*) to finish. *Eine Sache über das Knie — or ab—, to precipitate a business; das hat ihm den Hals gebrochen, that was his ruin; das bricht mir das Herz, it breaks my heart. *c*) to break = to separate continuous parts. Eine gebrochene Zahl, [in arithm.] a broken number, a fraction; gebrochene Zahlen, fractional numbers; gebrochenes Deutsch sprechen, to speak broken German; die gebrochene Schreibart, an aphoristic style; gebrochene Töne, notes performed in a distinct or detached manner, staccato notes. *d*) to break = to violate. Ein Gesetz —, to infringe a law; einen Vertrag —, to break or infringe a contract; sein Wort, sein Versprechen —, to break one's word, one's promise; seinen Eid —, to violate one's oath. *e*) to break = to interrupt, to cause to cease. Das Stillschweigen —, to break silence; die Freundschaft —, to break friendship; den Frieden —, to break peace; die Ehe —, to violate the marriage-bed, to commit adultery. 2) [to sever, to divide] to break [illegible] Blumen —, to break flowers; Erbsen —, to pick peas; Obst —, to pluck fruit. *Fig.* *Einen Streit vom Zaune —, to seek a pretext for a quarrel, to pick a quarrel. 3) to separate by breaking. Marmor —, to quarry marble; ein gebrochener Stein, a stone out of the quarry; Erz —, to dig out ore; dieses Pferd bricht die Zähne, that horse breaks its teeth; das Schloß von der Thür —, to break off the lock from the door. 4) to force fro[illegible] the original or straight direction, to cause to deviate from a direct course. **Servietten —**, to plait napkins; **einen Bogen Papier —**, to double a sheet of paper; **einen Brief —**, to fold a letter; **ein gebrochenes Dach**, a curved roof; **die Lichtstrahlen —**, [in optics] to refract the rays of light; **die gebrochene Schrift**, German-text; **eine gebrochene Treppe**, resting-stairs, landing-stairs; [in tapestry-making and in architecture] **der gebrochene Stab**, a broken batoon; **der gebrochene Sparren**, [in heraldry] chevron rompu [broke]. 5) *Fig.* to break through. **Die Bahn —**, to beat or tread a path. V. **Bahn**, 1).

III. *v. r.* **sich —**, 1) to break = to burst, by dashing against something. **Die Wellen — sich an den Klippen**, the waves break upon the rocks; **die Wolken — sich**, clouds break away. *Fig.* to break = to change. **Das Wetter bricht sich**, the weather breaks; **die Kälte hat sich gebrochen**, the weather has grown mild, the air has softened; **die Krankheit bricht sich**, the disease comes to a favourable crisis. 2) to deviate from a direct course. **Die Lichtstrahlen — sich im Wasser**, water refracts the rays of light. 3) to eject from the stomach, to vomit. V. **Sich Erbrechen**.

Brech-arzenei, *f.* V. **—mittel**. **—bank**, *f.* 1) a baker's bench, a sort of brake. 2) V. **Brake**. **—betel**, *m.* a crooked chisel. **—bohne**, *f.* common kidney-bean. **—beißel**, *f.* [in seamen's lang.] a heavy adz. **—distel**, *f.* [a plant] common eryngo. **—eisen**, *n.* a crow-bar; *it.* a crooked chisel. **—fieber**, *n.* a fever attended with vomiting. **—hammer**, *m.* a heavy hammer used by masons and in coppermills. **—kamm**, *m.* [among cloth-makers] scribbling-card. **—meißel**, *m.* a locksmith's crooked chisel. **—mittel**, *n.* [in medicine] an emetic, a vomit, a puke. **—mühle**, *f.* a sort of stamping-mill. **—nuß**, *f.* 1) the emetic-nut, vomiting-nut. 2) [a shrub] the angular leaved physic-nut, Barbadoes nut. **—pille**, *f.* a vomitory pill. **—pulver**, *n.* an emetic powder. **—punkt**, *m.* [in optics] point of refraction. **—stange**, *f.* an iron crow, a handspike. **—tanne**, *f.* V. **Lerchenbaum**. **—trank**, *m.* a vomitory potion. **—vitriol**, *m.* vitriol vomitory. **—weide**, *f.* the crack-willow. **—weinstein**, *m.* tartar emetic. **—winde**, *f.* [a plant] fly honeysuckle. **—wurz**, *f.* ipecacuanha [the root of the Viscaea ipecacuanha]. **—zeug**, *m.* instruments for breaking open doors or locks.

Brecher, *m.* [-s, *pl.* -] 1) [the person who breaks any thing, also an instrument used to break something] breaker [used only in compositions as **Mauer—**, **Eis—**, **Zahn—**]. 2) [in seamen's lang.] a rock which breaks the waves.

Brecherlich, *adj.* and *adv.* inclined to vomit, affected with nausea, sick.

Brechlich, [unusual] *adj.* and *adv.* V. **Zerbrechlich**.

Brechung, *f.* 1) [in optics &c.] refraction. **Die — der Lichtstrahlen**, refraction of rays of light. **Die — der Farben**, [in painting] degradation.

Brechungs-ebene, *f.* [in physics] plane of refraction. **—stütze**, *f.* [in physics] sine of refraction. **—verhältniß**, *n.* [in physics] the ratio of the sine of the angle of inclination to the sine of the refracted angle. **—winkel**, *m.* [in physics] angle of refraction. **—zeichen**, *n.* [in grammar] hyphen.

Brefgang, *m.* [-es] [in seamen's language] the planks between the channel-wale and gunnel.

Bregen, *m.* V. **Brägen**.

Brehme, *f.* V. **Bräme** and **Brombeere**.

Brei, *m.* [-es] [allied to **Brühe**] 1) a kind of food made by boiling bread, flour &c. in water or milk to the consistence of pulp, such as pap, frumenty, panada and the like. *Prov.* **Viele Köche verfalzen den —**, too many cooks spoil the broth; **er geht d'rum herum wie die Katze um den heißen —**, he goes about the bush. 2) *trifling and tedious talk.

Brei-artig, *adj.* and *adv.* like pap, pappy. **—geschwulst**, *f.* [in surgery] atheroma, atherome. **—löffel**, *m.* pap-spoon. **—maul**, *n.* a jabberer. **—pfännchen**, *n.* a small pan for boiling pap. **—umschlag**, *m.* a poultice, a cataplasm. **—weich**, *adj.* and *adv.* soft as pap, pappy. †*Fig.* **Einen —weich schlagen**, to beat any one into a jelly.

Breihahn, V. **Breyhan**.

Breiicht, *adj.* and *adv.* like pap, pappy.

Breiig, *adj.* and *adv.* soft as pap, pappy.

Breisgau, *n.* [-es] Brisgow [formerly a district or **Gau** of the southwest Suabia, now part of the Grand-Duchy of Baden].

Breisgauer, [-s, *pl.* -] **-inn**, *f.* a native or inhabitant of the Brisgow.

Breisgauisch, *adj.* and *adv.* from or belonging to the Brisgow.

Breislakit, *m.* [-es, *pl.* -en] [a newly discovered Vesuvian mineral] Breislakit.

Breisling, **Beisling**, *m.* [-es, *pl.* -e] a sort of small herring.

Breit, [probably from **bären** = **tragen**, **bareit**, as it were, thus = **auseinandergetragen**] *adj.* and *adv.* broad [as distinguished from long, thick and high]. **Ein —er Tisch**, a broad table; **eine —e Straße**, a broad street; **drei Zoll —**, three inches wide; **sechs Fuß lang und vier Fuß —**, six feet by four; **ein —er Fluß**, a broad river; **ein —es Band**, a wide ribbon; **ein —es Gesicht**, a broad face; **mit —em Rande**, broad-brimmed; **die Nadeln zu den Oehren — schlagen**, [with pinmakers] to flatten the needles at one end; **es ist so — als lang**, 'tis as broad as 'tis long, **fig.* it is all one, there is no difference; **weit und —**, far and wide. *Fig.* **Ein —er Wind**, [in seamen's language] quarter wind or quartering wind, a free wind; **nicht eines Fingers [einen Finger] — von seiner Meinung abweichen**, not to budge an inch from one's opinion, to be wedded to one's opinion; ***sich — machen**, to walk with an affected dignity, to strut, to be puffed up with pride or vanity; ***sich mit etwas — machen**, to boast of a thing; ***ein Langes und ein —es von einer Sache schwatzen**, to enlarge upon a topic; **eine —e Aussprache**, a broad pronunciation; †**Einen — schlagen**, to mislead any one by imposing on his credulity, to dupe any one.

Breit-art, *f.* V. **—beil**. **—beil**, *n.* [in carpentry] broad-axe. **—blatt**, *n.* V. **—laub**. **—blätterig**, *adj.* and *adv.* broad-leaved, broad-leafed. **—brüstig**, *adj.* and *adv.* broad-chested. **—eisen**, *n.* a carver's chisel. **—fisch**, *m.* any broad fish. **—füßig**, *adj.* and *adv.* broad-footed. **—gefiedert**, *adj.* and *adv.* broad-winged. **—geschultert**, *adj.* and *adv.* broad-shouldered. **—geschwänzt**, *adj.* and *adv.* broad-tailed. **—gestirnt**, *adj.* and *adv.* broad-fronted. **—gewölbt**, *adj.* and *adv.* broad-vaulted. **—gold**, *n.* [with gold-beaters] a sort of leaf-gold. **—hammer**, *m.* [in iron-works] flatting-hammer. **—hüftig**, *adj.* and *adv.* having broad hips. **—kopf**, *m.* 1) a broad head. 2) V. **Kaulquappe**. **—köpfig**, *adj.* and *adv.* broad-fronted, large-headed. **—laub**, *n.* [a tree] the Norway maple. **—lippe**, *f.* the great broad-lipped whelk. **—muschel**, *f.* [a genus of animals, class vermes] a species of tellina [tellina cornea]. **—nasig**, *adj.* and *adv.* flat-nosed. **—randig**, *adj.* and *adv.* broad-brimmed. **—schnabel**, *m.* [the name of two sorts of ducks] *a*) the shoveler. *b*) the grey-headed duck, the morillon. **—schnäbler**, *m.* any bird having a broad bill. **—schulterig**, *adj.* and *adv.* broad-shouldered. **—schwanz**, *m.* 1) any broad-tailed animal. 2) the broad-tailed snake. **—schwert**, *n.* broad-sword. **—stahl**, *m.* a turner's paring-chisel. **—stirnig**, *adj.* and *adv.* broad-fronted. **—wegerich**, *m.* V. **Wegebreit**. **—zackig**, *adj.* and *adv.* having broad notches. **—zange**, *f.* V. **Richtzange**. **—ziegel**, *m.* a tile.

Breite, *f.* [*pl.* -n] 1) breadth. **Die — eines Weges**, the broadness of a road; **die — eines Flusses**, the width or breadth of a river; **die größte —e eines Schiffes**, [in seamen's language] the main-breadth of a ship. *Fig.* [in geography] latitude. **Dieser Ort liegt 43 Grade nördlicher —**, that place is situated under the forty-third degree of north latitude; [in astronomy] **die — der Gestirne**, the latitude of the stars; **die heliocentrische —**, [the latitude of a planet as it would appear from the sun] heliocentric latitude; **die geocentrische —**, [the latitude of a planet as seen from the earth] geocentric latitude. 2) a broad body, a large plain, an expanse, also the extent of a stuff from side to side. **In diesem Unterrocke sind drei —n**, are three breadths in this petticoat. 3) [in husbandry] the state of being spread on the ground for the sake of drying. **Der Flachs liegt auf der —**, the flax is spread for drying.

Breiten-grad, *m.* degree of latitude. **—kreis**, *m.* 1) [in astronomy] circle of latitude [a great circle of the sphere passing through the poles of ecliptic, and consequently perpendicular to it]. 2) *pl.* [in geography, small circles of the sphere parallel to the equator] the parallels of latitude. **—messung**, *f.* [in geography and astronomy] the measuring of the distance from the equator and from the ecliptic. **—zirkel**, *m.* V. **—kreis**.

Breiten, I. *v. tr.* 1) to extend in breadth, to spread. **Ein Tuch über den Tisch —**, to spread a cloth upon the table; **einen Teppich auf** or **über den Boden —**, to spread a carpet on the floor; **den Flachs, den Mist auf dem Felde —**, to spread flax, to spread manure on the ground; [in seamen's language] **die Segel —**, to square the sails. 2) [with dyers] to pour chalk into the blue-vat. II. *v. r.* **sich —**, to extend itself in breadth, to spread.

Breitlich, *adj.* and *adv.* broadish.

Breitling, *m.* [-es, *pl.* -e] [a fish] the sprat.

Breme, *f.* V. **Bram**, **Bräme** and **Bremse**.

Bremen, [a Hanseatic town in Germany] Bremen.

Bremer, *m.* [-s, *pl.* -] **—inn**, *f.* an inhabitant of Bremen.

||**Bremmeln**, V. **Brummen**.

Bremmer, *m.* [-s, *pl.* -] [in mining] a shamble.

Bremmerschacht, *m.* [in mining] a shaft with shambles.

Bremmern, *v. tr.* [in mining] to throw [the ore] from one shamble to the other and thus to raise it to the top.

Brems, *m.* [-ses, *pl.* -se] V. **Bremse**.

Brems-berg, *m.* [in mining] self acting plane. **—haspel**, *m.* [in mining] **Der —haspel mit stehender Welle**, rope barrel; **der —haspel mit liegender Welle**, rope sheave.

Bremse, *f.* [*pl.* -n] 1) [either from the Greec βρέμω, that is **brummen**, or allied to the Lat. *premere* and to the D. *praamen*, **drücken**] the breese or gadfly. 2) [allied to the Lat. *premere*, D. *praamen*] [the name of several tools] *a*) [a tool used by farriers to hold unruly horses by the nostrils] horse-twitchers, barnacles, twitch. *b*) [in seamen's lang.] tails of a top-staff. *c*) [in mining] a brake.

Bremsen, *v. tr.* 1) to apply the twitch or barnacles to [a horse]. ||2) to squeeze, to press. 3) [in mining] to stop [a wheel].

Brennbar, *adj.* and *adv.* that may be burnt, combustible. **—e Stoffe**, combustibles; **das —e**, [the principle of inflammability] phlogiston.

Brennbarkeit, *f.* combustibleness, combustibility.

Brennen, commonly *ir.* I. *v. intr.* 1) to emit light and heat, to burn. Das Feuer brennt, the fire is burning. *Fig.* Eine brennend rothe Farbe, a glowing red colour; in seinen Augen brannte heftiger Zorn, his eyes glowed with violent anger. 2) to be on fire, to burn. Das Holz brennt, the wood burns; das Licht brennt, the candle burns; das Haus, die Stadt brennt, the house, the town is burning, is on fire, is in flames; die Kohlen —, the coals glow. *Fig.* Vor Liebe —, to burn with love; vor Verlangen —, to be inflamed with desire; —der Eifer, ardent or glowing zeal; —de Scham, burning shame; er brennt (vor Begierde) ihn zu sehen, he longs to see him. 3) to take or catch fire. Der Schwamm will nicht —, the tinder will not catch fire; Stroh brennt leicht, straw easily catches fire; Steine — nicht, stone will not ignite. *Fig.* *Es brennt ihm auf der Seele, he has no rest. Das Brennen, the act of burning. 4) to communicate heat. Die Sonne brennt heute sehr, the sun has a great effect to day; —der Sand, burning sand; das kochende Wasser brennt, boiling water scalds; —de Lippen, burning lips; —de Wangen, glowing cheeks; sein Gesicht brennt, his face burns. *Fig.* Ihm brennt die Stelle unter den Füßen, he is impatient, hasty, he cannot endure delay. 5) to make a burning or smarting impression. Die Nessel brennt, the nettle stings; der Pfeffer brennt auf der Zunge, pepper applied to the tongue, makes it smart, or pepper has a pungent taste; ein —der Durst, a burning thirst; —de Schmerzen, pungent pains.

II. *v. tr.* 1) [to injure by fire, to affect the flesh by fire] to burn. Einem mit dem Lichte die Finger —, to burn any one's fingers with a candle; sich an or mit etwas —, to burn one's self with a thing; von der —den Sonne gebrannt, scorched by the burning sun. *Prov.* Gebrannte Kinder fürchten das Feuer, a burnt child dreads the fire, a scalded cat fears cold water. *Prov.* Was dich nicht brennt, das blase (lösche) nicht, scald not your lips with other folks broth. 2) to subject to the action of fire, to burn. Schweine —, to singe pigs; eine Wunde —, [in surgery] to cauterize a wound; das — einer Wunde, [in surgery] cauterization; Planken —, [in seamen's language] to bend planks or to make them pliant by heating them; ein Schiff —, [in seamen's lang.] to bream a ship. 3) to consume with fire, to burn. Sengen und —, to destroy by fire; Oel —, to burn oil; er brennt Steinkohlen, he burns sea-coals. 4) to make or prepare by fire. Holz zu Kohlen und Asche —, to reduce wood to coals and ashes by the action of fire, to burn up wood; Kohlen —, to burn wood into coal, to char wood; Steine zu Kalk —, to burn stones to lime; Theer —, to burn tar; Branntwein —, to distil brandy [from wine, potatoes &c.]; Ziegel —, to burn or bake bricks; Pfeifen —, to bake tobacco-pipes. *Fig.* *Sich rein or sich weiß —, to want to clear one's self, to exculpate, to white-wash one's self. 5) to roast. Kaffee, Mehl —, to roast coffee, meal; gebrannte Mandeln, crisp almonds. 6) to purify by fire. Das Silber fein —, to refine silver. 7) to burn or impress a mark with a hot iron, to brand. Ein Faß, ein Pferd —, to brand a cask, a horse. 8) to cause a burning or smarting sensation. Die Nessel hat mich gebrannt, the nettle stung me; die Augen — mich, my eyes smart; der Sod brennt mich, I have the heart-burn.

Brenn-arbeit, *f.* [in metallurgy] the refining of silver. —**blase**, *f.* [a chimical vessel used in distillation] an alembic. —**bock**, *m.* [in ship-building] V. Feuerbock. —**bündel**, *n.* [a bundle of brush-wood used in fireships] fire-basin. —**eisen**, *n.* an iron for burning. *a)* [an instrument for curling the hair] curling-iron, curling-tongs. *b)* [in surgery] a searing-iron [to burn a sore with], a cauter. *c)* [in veterinary art] cauting-iron. *d)* a marking-iron. *e)* [in seamen's lang.] V. Feuerbock. —**geld**, *n.* the money paid for burning or branding any thing. —**glas**, *n.* burning-glass. —**haus**, *n.* 1) an oven; a bake-house; a distillery. 2) [in metallurgy] a finery. —**helm**, *m.* V. Blasenhelm. —**herd**, *m.* 1) the hearth. 2) *Fig.* V. —punkt. —**hitze**, *f.* the heat of a furnace &c. —**holz**, *n.* wood for fuel, firewood. —**kasten**, *m.* a coffin [used in baking tobacco-pipes]. —**kolben**, *m.* the still, alembic, cucurbite. —**kraut**, *n.* [the name of plants] *a)* bulbous crowfoot. *b)* the sweet-scented virgin's bower. —**linie**, *f.* 1) [in mathematics] V. Parabel. 2) [in geometry, a curve formed by a coincidence of rays of light reflected from another curve] caustic curve. —**luft**, *f.* inflammable air. —*****material**, *n.* V. —stoff 2). —**messer**, *n.* [in veterinary art] cauting-iron. —**mittel**, *n.* [in medicine] a caustic. —**nessel**, *f.* [a plant] the common nettle. —**ofen**, *m.* a kiln, furnace, oven. —**öl**, *n.* lamp-oil. —**palme**, *f.* a species of the caryota [caryota urens]. —**pfanne**, *f.* a melting-pot, crucible [used in glass-works]. —**punkt**, *m.* 1) [in optics, a point in which any number of rays of light meet, after being reflected or refracted] focus. Der —punkt einer Linse, the focus of a lens. 2) [in geometry and conic sections, a certain point in the parabola, ellipsis and hyperbola, where rays reflected from all parts of these curves concur or meet] focus. —**punktsabstand**, *m.* [in optics] focal distance. —**raum**, *m.* [in physics] focal space. —**silber**, *n.* an amalgama used in the silvering of copper or brass. —**spiegel**, *m.* a burning-glass. —**stoff**, *m.* [in physics and chimistry, the matter of fire in composition with other bodies] 1) phlogiston. Mit —stoff geschwängert or angefüllt, phlogistic. 2) any combustible body, fuel [as wood, coals &c.]. —**stoffleer**, *adj.* and *adv.* dephlogisticated. —stoffleere Luft, dephlogisticated air, oxygen. —**stofflehre**, *f.* a system of the phlogiston. —**stofflich**, *adj.* and *adv.* phlogistic. —**weite**, *f.* [in optics] focal distance. —**wind**, *m.* [a pernicious wind that blows from the south-east in Italy] the Syrian wind, sirocco. —**wurz**, *f.* 1) V. —kraut. 2) spurge laurel. —**zeug**, *n.* all the utensils belonging to a distillery.

1. **Brenner**, *m.* [-s, *pl.* -] [from brennen = to burn] 1) a person who burns or prepares any thing by fire, much used in composition, as Branntwein—, distiller of spirits; Kohlen—, charcoal-burner; Ziegel—, tile-maker, brick-maker; Mord—, incendiary. 2) [a disease of plants] blight, blast.

Brennererde, *f.* combustible earth, as dry-turf &c.

2. **Brenner**, *m.* [-s] a well-known mountain in the Tyrol.

Brennerei, *f.* a place, a house &c. where any thing is burnt or prepared by fire, as eine Ziegel—, a brick-kiln; eine Branntwein—, a distillery of brandy &c.

Brennlich, *adj.* and *adv.* combustible, that may be burnt. Das —e Wesen, [in metallurgy] V. Brennstoff.

Brente, *f.* [*pl.* -n] **Brenten**, *m.* [-s, *pl.* -] [in Italian *brenta* signifies a low-built skiff] a sort of wooden vessel.

Brentgans, *f.* [-gänse] V. Baumgans.

Brenzeln, [from brennen] *v. intr.* to smell or taste of burning.

Brenzlich, *adj.* and *adv.* having the smell or taste of burning, [in chimistry] empyreumatic, empyreumatical. —e Oele, empyreumatic oils; der —e Geruch, empyreuma.

***Bresche**, *f.* [*pl.* -n] [originally from brechen] a breach. V. Sturmlücke. — schießen, to batter a breach.

Breschbatterie, *f.* a battering train.

‡**Bresthaft**, [from bresten, that is bersten] *adj.* and *adv.* invalid, broken.

Brett, **Bret**, *n.* [-es, *pl.* -er] [Engl. *board*, D. *berd*, *bord*; A. S. *braede* and *börd* is a table; allied to breit] 1) a board, plank. Ein eichenes —, an oaken plank; —er sägen, schneiden, to saw boards; mit —ern gedeckt, boarded. 2) a table or frame for a game, board, as Spiel—, draught-board; Schach—, chess-board &c.; im —e spielen, to play at draughts or backgammon. *Prov.* Bei Jemand einen Stein im —e haben, to be in great favour with any one. 3) [in familiar language] a board = a table. *Fig.* Hoch am —e sitzen, to be in high favour; hoch bei Einem am —e seyn oder stehen, to be in great favour with any one; hoch an's — kommen, to get an exalted rank or place, to be raised to great honours; †er muß vor's —, he is called before the justice.

Brett-baum, *m.* a tree, intended to be cut into boards, or a tree fit for boards. —**block**, *m.* V. —klotz. —**bohle**, *f.* a sawed plank. —**eiche**, *f.* an oak fit for board. —**er-dach**, *n.* a board-roof. —**er-kasten**, *m.* a trunk made of boards. —**er-wand**, *f.* a partition of boards in a building. —**er-werk**, *n.* something made of boards. —**er-zaun**, *m.* a fence made of boards. —**fiedel**, —**geige**, *f.* a small pocket-fiddle, a kit. —**klotz**, *m.* a log of wood which is to be cut into boards. —**mühle**, *f.* a saw-mill. —**nagel**, *m.* a board-nail. —**säge**, *f.* a pit-saw. —**schneider**, *m.* a sawyer. —**spicker**, *m.* a sort of nails with broad heads, spike-nails. —**spiel**, *n.* 1) [a game, played by two persons upon a table] draughts, [with box and dice] backgammon. 2) a board used for draughts, backgammon, draught-board or tables. —**spielblume**, *f.* common fritillary or chequered lily. —**spieler**, *m.* a person playing at draughts or backgammon. —**stamm**, *m.* V. —baum. —**stein**, *m.* a man at draughts or backgammon. —**wand**, *f.* V. Bretterwand.

Brettchen, **Brettlein**, *n.* [-s, *pl.* -] [*diminutive* of Brett] a small, thin or little board or plank.

Brettern, *adj.* and *adv.* made of boards. Eine —e Wand, a partition of boards in a building; einen —en Boden in ein(em) Zimmer legen, to board a room. ‡*Fig.* Ein —er Busen, a flat breast; eine —ne Stirne, a front as hard as a board.

Brettern, *v. tr.* to board [a room &c.]. Einen Boden —, to plank or board a floor.

Bretticht, *adj.* and *adv.* like a board, stiff as a board.

***Breve**, *n.* [*pl.* -s] 1) [in general] a short written order [the old German Brief], a writ. 2) [more especially, a letter which the pope dispatches to a prince &c.] an apostolical brief. 3) [in music] Alla Breve, alla-breve.

***Breviarium**, *n.* [-s, *pl.* -rien] **Brevier**, *n.* [-s, *pl.* -e] [a book containing the daily service of the Romish church] a breviary.

Brewsterit, *m.* [-s] [a mineral] brewsterite, radiated zeolite, foliated zeolite.

Breyhahn, *m.* [-s] a sort of pale ale [thus called after its inventor Cord Breyhahn, who first brewed it in Hanover in the year 1526].

Brezel, **Prezel**, *f.* [*pl.* -n] [probably allied to the provincial Braß = Strick; others derive it from the Lat. *brachium*] a cracknel.

1. **Bricke**, **Pricke**, *f.* [*pl.* -n] [from the Low Sax. brick = fleischig?] a fried lamprey preserved in vinegar.

2. ‖ **Bricke**, *f.* [*pl.* -n] [appears to be allied to ecken, ragen] a small board.

Brickenkäse, *m.* a sort of square cheese ried on small boards.

'**Bricöll[e]**, *f.* the rebound of a tennis-ball or billiard-ball after a side-stroke, bricolle or ricoil.

Brief, *m.* [-es, *pl.* -e] [allied to the Lat. *brevis*, ad the G. brechen] 1) a folded paper. Ein — Nadeln or Stecknadeln, a paper of pins. 2) any fficial or authoritative paper, a document. Der Freiheits—, charter, letters patent or overt; der roße Freiheits— [der Engländer], Magna Chara; der Kaper—, letter of marque; der Aufschub—, letter of respite; der Fracht—, bill of ading &c.; [in commerce] Wechsel—e, bills of xchange, draughts; langsichtige —e, [in commerce] bills at long date. 3) a written or printed nessage, an epistle, a letter. Einen — schreiben, iegeln, überschreiben, to write, to seal, to direct letter; der Bettel—, a begging letter; die —e es Plinius oder Cicero, the epistles of Pliny r of Cicero. 4) a piece of paper inclosing somehing, as: Ein — Taback, a packet of tobacco, in — Stecknadeln, a paper of pins.

Brief-adel, *m.* nobility obtained by leters patent, not by inheritance. —**aufschrift**, direction of a letter, address. —**beschwerer**, , letter-presser. —**beutel**, *m.* a bag for the onveyance of letters, mail-bag. —**bothe**, *m.* tter-carrier, postman. —**buch**, *n.* 1) V. —steller.) letter copy-book. —**form**, *f.* 1) epistolary tyle. 2) any writing in letters. Eine Erzählung —form, an epistolary narration. 3) any thing aving the form of a letter. —**gedicht**, *n.* [ei 'Epistel], an epistolary poem, an epistle [in rse]. —**geld**, *n.* postage. —**gewölbe**, *n.* rchives. —**gut**, *n.* letter land or goods. —**ahler**, *m.* V. Kartenmahler. —**nadel**, *f.* per-pin, sheet-pin. —**papier**, *n.* letter-pa. —**porto**, *n.* postage. —**post**, *f.* 1) postice. 2) mail-coach. —**scheide**, *f.* the cover of etter. —**schreibekunst**, *f.* epistolography. **teller**, *m.* 1) a writer of letters or epistles. a book to teach letter-writing, a letter-writer. [in commerce, sometimes for] a drawer of a bill exchange. —**streicher**, *m.* letter-folder, lding-stick, paper-knife. V. also Falzbein. —**back**, *m.* tobacco in packets. —**tasche**, *f.* 1) tter-case. 2) pocket-book. —**taube**, *f.* the rier-pigeon. —**träger**, *m.* letter-bearer, letr-carrier, postman. —**umschlag**, *m.* the cover a letter. —**wechsel**, *m.* [intercourse between sons at a distance by means of letters sent and anrs received; also the letters which pass between correspondents] correspondence. Der vertraute —echsel, close correspondence. —**wechseln**, *v.* tr. to correspond. —**wechsler**, [more usual respondent] *m.* correspondent. —**zettel**, *m.* billet, note.

Briefchen, **Brieflein**, *n.* [-s, *pl.* -] [*dimin.* Brief] a small letter, a note; frequently used compound words, as Liebes—, billet-doux &c.

Brieflich, *adj.* and *adv.* 1) written, in wring. 2) epistolary. —e Unterhaltungen, epistory correspondence.

Briefschaften, *pl.* letters, papers.

Brigade, *f.* [*pl.* -n] [in military affairs] bride. In eine — formiren, to form into a bride or into brigades, to brigade.

Brigadier, [pronounce Brigàdje] *m.* [-s] 1) a general officer who commands a brigade, igadier. ‖ 2) a non-commissioned officer in mmand of a detachment.

Brigantine, *f.* [*pl.* -n] [a sort of two-masted ssel] a brigantine. V. Brigg.

Brigg, *f.* [*pl.* -en] [a vessel with two masts, square-rigged, or rigged nearly like a ship's mainmast and foremast] a brig.

* **Brillant**, [pronounce brilljánt] I. *adj.* brilliant, glittering, sparkling with lustre. II. *m.* [*pl.* -en] [a diamond of the finest water] a brilliant.

* **Brillantiren**, [pronounce brilljantiren] *v. tr.* to cut a diamond into angles.

Brille, *f.* [*pl.* -n] [is said to come from Beryll] 1) [glasses to assist the sight] spectacles, eye-glass. —n mit einfachen Stangen, single-jointed spectacles; —n mit doppelten Stangen or Gelenken, double-jointed spectacles; —n für diejenigen, die noch keine gebraucht haben, first-sight spectacles; eine — gegen Staub, Kälte, [Reise—n], goggles; mit einer — versehen, spectacled; eine — aufsetzen, to put on spectacles. **Fig.* Etwas durch die — ansehen, to look at things with a magnifier; Alles durch die schwarze — sehen, to see every thing with a jaundiced eye; er sieht Alles durch eine rosenfarbene —, he sees every thing on the sunny side; Einem eine — aufsetzen, to deceive or trick any one. 2) something in the shape of spectacles. *a*) the seat in the necessary. Die — eines Nachtstuhls, the seat of a close-stool. *b*) [in fortification, an enveloped counterguard, or elevation of earth made beyond the second ditch, opposite to the places of arms] lunette, lunet.

Brillen-fledermaus, *f.* a species of bat. —**futter**, —**futteral**, *n.* a case for spectacles, spectacle-case. —**glas**, *n.* one of the glasses of the spectacles. —**kraut**, *n.* V. Bauernsenf. —**macher**, *m.* a spectacle-maker, an optician. —**nase**, *f.* [a bird] Jamaica goat-sucker. —**rohr**, *n.* a perspective, telescope. —**schlange**, *f.* the spectacle-snake, cobra de cabelo. —**schleifer**, *m.* a grinder of eye-glasses. —**senf**, *m.* [a genus of plants] buckler-mustard. —**zirkel**, *m.* càliber-compasses [for measuring the diameter of guns].

Brill-ente, *f.* the great black duck from Hudson's bay. —**gatt**, *n.* [in seamen's lang.] the hole of the privy. —**ofen**, *m.* [in metallurgy] a sort of furnace.

* **Brilliren**, [pronounce brilljiren] *v. intr.* to sparkle with lustre, to glitter.

Bringen, [probably for baringen, old *baringan*, from the old baren, bären, tragen] *ir. v. tr.* Eigentlich tragen. *a*) to bear = to produce. Früchte —, to bear fruits. *Fig.* Unglück —, to bring ill luck; nichts bringt Einem mehr Ehre, als &c., nothing brings a man more honour, than &c *Prov.* Die Zeit bringt Rosen, time bears roses. *b*) to bear, to convey from one place to another, or from a distant to a nearer place, to bring. Bringe mir einen Bissen Brod, bring me a morsel of bread; Steine wohin —, to carry stones to a place; Güter von England nach Frankreich —, to convey goods from England to France; unter Dach —, to inn; Einen zu Bette —, to place any one in a bed, to bed any one; einen Missethäter ins Gefängniß —, to carry a criminal to gaol; Jemanden nach Hause —, to bring or conduct any one home; ich will Sie nach Hause —, I will see you home; ein Pferd auf die Reitbahn —, *fig.* to commence a horse; bringt mir eine Kutsche, bring me a coach; bringe mir ein Wildpret, und mache mir ein Essen, [in Scripture] bring me venison, and make me savoury meat; — Sie ihn mit, bring him with you; Einen auf den rechten Weg —, to put any one in the right way [also in a figurative sense]; zwischen zwei Feuer —, [in tactics] to inclose between two fires, to double upon; — Sie es mit, bring it along with you; in Sicherheit —, to render safe; seine Gedanken zu Papiere —, to set down one's thoughts; in ein Verzeichniß —, to make a list, or catalogue of, to inventory; ein Kind zur Welt —, to bring a child into the world, to bring forth a child. *Prov.* Wer was bringt, ist überall willkommen, no man is esteemed so well, as he that comes full-handed. *c*) = to get or to effect something by a certain motion of the body. Den Stiefel nicht vom Fuße —, not to be able to get a boot off; Tintenflecke sind schwer aus der Wäsche zu —, it is difficult to take out ink blots from linen; Schmutz an sich —, to make one's self filthy, to foul one's self. *Fig.* *α*) = to bring. Nachricht —, to bring or convey news; Einem Nachricht —, to bring word to any one; — Sie Ihrem Vater meine Grüße, my compliments to your father; was — Sie Neues? what's the best news? was — Sie? what's your desire? *β*) = to place in a certain condition. Nachdenken bringt Einen zur Besinnung, reflection brings a man to his senses; Einen zur Vernunft —, to bring any one to reason; ich werde ihn nie dazu — [vermögen], I shall never bring him to do it; Einen außer sich selbst —, to put any one beside himself; Einen zur Verzweiflung —, to reduce any one to despair; Einen wieder zu sich selbst —, to bring any one to his senses again; eine Batterie zum Schweigen —, [in tactics] to silence a battery; Jemanden an den Bettelstab —, to reduce any one to poverty; dieß wird ihn an den Galgen —, that will bring him to the gallows; Einen in Schulden —, to bring any one into debt; Einen in Ansehen —, to bring any one upon the stage; Jemanden auf seine Seite —, to bring a person over to one's side; ein Mädchen zu Falle —, to debauch, to deflower a young woman; zum Gehorsame —, to bring in, to reduce to obedience, to bring under; etwas in Ordnung —, to set a thing in order; in Gang —, to bring up; ein Pferd in Galopp — [setzen], to put a horse to gallop; zwei Narren an einander —, to set two fools together; zwei Zänker aus einander —, to part, to separate two wranglers; etwas unter seine Gewalt oder Herrschaft —, to bring something under one's power or dominion; Alexander brachte einen großen Theil der civilisirten Welt unter seine Herrschaft, Alexander subjected a great part of the civilized world to his dominion; ein Gerücht unter die Leute —, to spread a report; Neuigkeiten in Umlauf —, to spread news abroad; einen Verbrecher vom Leben zum Tode —, to put a criminal to death, to execute a criminal; einen ums Leben —, to take any one's life away, to deprive any one of life, to kill any one; Einen um seinen guten Namen —, to blast a man's reputation; er ist um Alles gebracht worden, he has lost all; Einen um seinen Verstand —, to deprive any one of reason; Einem etwas ins Gedächtniß —, to remind any one of something; etwas aus Einem heraus —, to bring or pump something out of any one; man kann es ihm nicht aus den Gedanken —, it will not out of his head; seine Töchter an den Mann —, to supply one's daughters with husbands, to get them married; eine Waare an den Mann —, to dispose of a commodity, to get rid of it; in Rechnung —, to pass to account; etwas an den Tag —, to bring a thing to light, to bring it out; ein Verbrechen an den Tag —, to bring out a crime; eine Sache auf die Seite —, to conceal, to hide something, eine Sache auf die Bahn —, to bring a thing into question; ein Heer auf die Beine —, to raise an army; etwas auf Einen —, to lay to one's charge; man konnte nichts auf ihn —, nothing could be proved against him; er hat sein Leben auf vierzig Jahre gebracht, he attained the age of forty; etwas über das Herz —, to make up one's mind to a thing; zu Wege, zu Stande —, to bring about, to effect, to accomplish, to bring to the desired issue; es an Einen —, to provoke any one; er wird es noch weit, noch hoch —, he will make great progress or attain great success yet; er hat es endlich dahin gebracht, daß &c., he has brought things to such a pass, that &c.; er hat es weit gebracht, he has raised himself very high, he has attained a great proficiency in knowledge &c.; es bis zu einem ungewöhnlichen Grade von Vollkommenheit —, to arrive at an unusual degree of excellence or perfection; er bringt es zu nichts, he does not get on in life, he will never be rich; ich habe nichts vor mich gebracht, I could save nothing. γ) = to effect or produce a certain state. Unglück —, to bring ill luck; Unglück über Jemand —, to make any one miserable, to distress any one.; nichts bringt Einem mehr Ehre, als &c.; nothing brings a man more honour, than &c.; die Umstände — es so mit sich, circumstances require it; sein Amt bringt diese Strenge mit sich, his office requires that rigour, renders it necessary.

Bringer, *m.* [-s, *pl.* -] one who brings or conveys to, bringer, bearer, carrier.

||**Brink**, [probably the same word with the Engl. *brink*, Rand] *m.* [-es, *pl.* -e] 1) a hillock overgrown with grass, a grassy hillock. 2) a green sward. 3) a ridge.

Britannien, [-s] Britain. V. Großbritannien.

Brite, *m.* **Britinn**, *f.* V. Britte, Brittinn.

Britisch, *adj.* and *adv.* V. Brittisch.

Britsche, **Pritsche**, *f.* [*pl.* -n] [appears to be allied to Brett] 1) a piece of wood with one end broader than the other, a bat. Die — des Hanswursts, Harlequin's wooden sabre; Einem die — geben, to breech any one with a bat. 2) [in iron-works] a wooden hammer, a mallet [used for flattening the sheets of copper]. 3) the back-seat of a sledge. 4) a common English saddle. 5) a bed of boards in guard-rooms, bakeries &c. 6) [in fortification] a raised platform used in firing en barbe. 7) [in air-guns] a square piece of steel which supplies the spring in common guns or rifles.

Britschenmeister, *m.* a buffoon dressed in party-coloured clothes, who plays tricks, to divert the populace, a harlequin.

Britschen, **Pritschen**, *v. tr.* to beat with a bat, to breech with a wooden sabre.

Brithinsalz, *n.* [-s] Prismatisches —, V. Glauberit.

Britte, *m.* [-n, *pl.* -n] **Brittinn**, *f.* [a native of Britain] Briton [mostly used as an appellation in a higher style; in general:] Englishman, English-woman.

Brittisch, *adj.* and *adv.* British, English.

***Brocad** or **Brocat**, *m.* [-s] brocade, brocado [a silken stuff with gold or silver].

***Broccoli**, *m.* [a sort of Italian cabbage] broccoli.

* **Brochiren**, **Broschiren**, *v. tr.* 1) [with bookbinders] to sew or to stitch [sheets, a book &c.]. 2) to weave flowers &c. into silken or woolen stuffs.

* **Brochüre**, **Broschüre**, *f.* [*pl.* -n] a stitched book, a pamphlet.

Bröckchen, **Bröcklein**, *n.* [-s, *pl.* -] [*dimin.* of Brocken]

Bröcke, *f.* [*pl.* -n] [from brechen] a small piece of bread broken off, crumb.

Bröckeln, [from brechen] I *v. tr.* to break into small fragments, to crum, to crumble. II. *v. intr.* to fall into small pieces, to crumble. Diese Mauer fängt an zu —, this wall begins to crumble. III. *v. r.* sich —, to break or part into small fragments, to crumble. Der Stein bröckelt sich, the stone crumbles.

1. **Brocken**, *m.* [-s, *pl.* -] [from brechen] a small fragment or piece; usually, a small piece of bread or other food, broken or cut off, a crumb, a morsel. Die — in den Steingruben, ragged stones; — Fleisch, scraps of meat. *Fig.* [in contempt] a bit, scrap. Lateinische —, scraps of Latin.

Brocken-perle, *f.* a ragged pearl. —**stahl**, *m.* one of the best sorts of steel. —**weise**, *adv.* by crumbs, like crumbs.

2. **Brocken**, *m.* [-s] [allied to Berg] [one of the highest mountains in Germany] the Brocken. [famous in the popular traditions of Germany as the great rendez-vous of all evil spirits, witches &c. in the night of the first of May, and as such commonly called Blocksberg; hence the vulgar expression] Jemanden auf den — [Blocksberg] wünschen, to wish a person far off or to wish a person at the devil.

Brockenbirke, *f.* a variety of the common birch-tree.

Brocken, [from the root of brechen] *v. tr.* to break into small pieces. Brod in die Milch —, to crum bread in milk. *Prov.* Er hat nichts zu beißen und zu —, he has not a morsel of any thing to put in his mouth.

Brockkohle, *f.* a sort of pit-coal.

Bröck[e]lig, *adj.* and *adv.* easily crumbled, friable.. —er Mörtel, shivery mortar.

Bröcklein, V. Bröckchen.

Brod, **Brot**, *n.* [-es, *pl.* -e] [some derive it from braten, others suppose it to be allied to the Gr. *βι-βρώ-σκω*, essen, to the Hebr. *beroth*, Speise] 1) food in general. Bienen—, bee-bread; ||Gottes —, alms; *it.* a meal, as in Mittags—, dinner, Abend—, the evening meal, supper. *Fig.* bread. *a*) [food in general]. Unser tägliches — gib uns heute, [Lord's prayer] give us this day our daily bread. *b*) [support of life in general, maintenance]. Sein — haben, to enjoy a competency; Einen um sein — bringen, to deprive any one of his livelihood; sein — verdienen, to get one's bread or livelihood; er stehet in meinem Lohne und —e, he is in my service; sein eignes — essen, to be one's own master. 2) [= Laib] Ein — Zucker, [in sugar-houses] a loaf of sugar. 3) [food made of ground corn] bread. Ein Laib —, a loaf of bread; frisches —, new bread; grobes —, cribble bread; schwarzes — [Schwarz—], brown bread; weißes — [Weiß—], white bread; hausbackenes —, household bread; — backen, to bake bread; gesäuertes —, leavened bread; ungesäuertes —, unleavened bread, das — brechen, to break bread, [in Scripture] to eat; er hat nichts als Wasser und —, he lives upon bread and water; das geweihete —, consecrated bread, the consecrated wafer.

Brod-backen, *n.* the baking of bread. —**bäcker**, *m.* a common baker. —**bank**, *f.* a table or stall for selling bread. —**baum**, *m.* the bread-fruit-tree, bread-tree. —**brei**, *m.* panada, panado. —**dieb**, *m.* 1) a person who steals bread. 2) *a person who supplants another in his livelihood. —**erwerb**, *m.* the getting of one's livelihood. —**fach**, *n.* profession. Die drei gelehrten —fächer, the three professions [divinity, law and physic]. —**frucht**, *f.* 1) the bread-fruit. 2) yam. —**fruchtbaum**, *m.* V. —baum. —**gelehrsamkeit**, *f.* professional learning. —**gelehrte**, *m.* a learned man by profession. —**gewicht**, *n.* V. —taxe. —**gewinner**, *m.* [in seamen's language] driver. —**hange**, *f.* shelves to lay bread on. —**herr**, *m.* the master of a family [in relation to his servants]. —**herrschaft**, *f.* the master of a family and his wife as maintaining servants. —**käfer**, *m.* a species of leather-eater [dermestes pellis]. —**kammer**, *f.* [in ships] bread-room. —**korb**, *m* bread-basket. †*Fig.* Einem den —korb höher hängen, to narrow any one's means of subsistence, to keep any one on short commons. —**korn**, *n.* bread-corn. —**krume**, *f.* a small piece of bread broken off, a crumb. —**kruste**, *f.* the crust of bread. —**kuchen**, *m.* bread in the form of cake. ||—**kümmel**, *m.* [a plant] common caraway. —**mangel**, *m.* a scarcity of bread, or of bread-corn. —**markt**, *m.* bread-market. —**messer**, *n.* 1) a table-knife. 2) a whittle. *—**neid**, *m.* envy excited by the sight of another's success in the same trade. —**pflaster**, *n.* V. —rindenpflaster. —**raspel**, *f.* bread-rasp. —**reibe**, *f.* bread-grater. —**rinde**, *f.* crust of bread. —**rindenpflaster**, *n.* a cataplasm made of the crust of bread. —**röster**, *m.* bread-toaster. || —**satz**, *m.* V. —taxe. || —**scharren**, *m.* V. —bank. —**schätzer**, *m.* a magistrate, who regulates the price of bread. —**schau**, *f.* the inspection of bread. —**schauer**, *m.* a magistrate that inspects bread. —**scheibe**, *f.* 1) a slice of bread. 2) [in husbandry] honeycomb. 3) V. —schieber. —**schieber**, *m.* a baker's peel. —**schneider**, *m.* bread-chipper. —**schnitte**, *f.* a slice of bread. —**schragen**, *m.* V. —bank. —**schrank**, *m.* a cupboard in which bread is kept. —**schwamm**, *m.* V. Brödling 2). —**spende**, *f.* distribution of bread. —**suppe**, *f.* b[read] broth or soup. —**taxe**, *f.* assize of bread. —**teig**, *m.* bread-dough. —**teller**, *m.* b[read] plate. —**torte**, *f.* bread-tart. —**verwandlung** or —**wandlung**, *f.* [in the Romish [church]] transsubstantiation. —**wabe**, *f.* V. —sche[ibe]. —**wagen**, *m.* [with armies] a close or co[vered] waggon to convey provisions in. —**wasser** bread-water, toast and water. —**winner**, [V.] —gewinner. —**wissenschaft**, *f.* learned [pro]fession. Die —wissenschaften, the learned [pro]fessions, such as the law, divinity &c. —**wurzel**, *f.* yam.

Brödchen, **Brödlein**, *n.* [-s, *pl.* -] [di[min.] of Brod] a small or little loaf, a roll, fr[equently] used in compound words, as: Milchbrödch[en].

Brodel, *m.* [-s] V. Broden and Prud[el].

Brodeln, [allied to braten] *v. intr.* [to [rise in] bubbles] to bubble.

Broden, **Brodem**, *m.* [-s] vapour, steam; [in mining] exhalation.

Brodenritze, *f.* an orifice at the to[p of a] bee-hive. —**röhre**, *f.* ventilators.

***Broderie**, *f.* [*pl.* -n] embroidery. V. [Stic]kerei.

***Brodiren**, *v. tr.* to embroider. V. Sti[cken].

Brödling, *m.* [-es, *pl.* -e] 1) [unusual] [ser]vant, domestic. 2) St. George's agaric.

Brodlos, *adj.* and *adv.* 1) [without brea[d, des]titute of food] breadless. — seyn, to want [a live]lihood. 2) useless, unprofitable. —se Kün[ste], unprofitable tricks.

||**Brodung**, *f.* baking.

Bröhl, *m.* [in seamen's language] 1) a [...] Der —, um ein Schiff aufzuholen, a large [...] used in dock-yards to haul a ship up. 2) — einer Kanone, the breeching of a ca[nnon]. 3) a coat. Der — im Hennegat, the [...] coat; — in der Ausfütterung der Stückp[forten], a canvas hose in the half-ports.

Brohltalje, *f.* the whip of the brail.

Broihahn, *m.* V. Breyhahn.

Brombeere, *f.* [*pl.* -n] [either from t[he] word Bramen = Stachel or from Rahm = [...]] black-berry, bramble.

Brombeer-hecke, *f.* a hedge of bram[bles]. —**staude**, *f.* —**strauch**, *m.* bramble, [black]berry-bush, rasp-berry-bush.

Bromhahn, *m.* **Bromhenne**, *f.* [...] huhn, *n.* V. Birkhahn and Birkhenne.

||**Brommer**, V. Brombeere.

***Bronze**, *f.* [pronounce: Brongs] bronze [...] zu Statuen, statue-metal.

***Bronziren,** [pronounce: Bronßiren] *v. tr.* to imitate bronze, to bronze.

Brösame, *f.* [-n, *pl.* -n] [from the old word brosen = brechen] a crumb of bread.

Brösschen, *n.* [-s, *pl.* -] [perhaps allied to Brosame] the sweet-bread especially of calves and lambs.

Broschiren, *v. tr.* V. Brochiren.

Broschüre, *f.* [*pl.* -n] V. Brochüre.

‖**Brösel,** *n.* [-s, *pl.* -] a crumb.

‖**Bröseln, Brösen,** I. *v. tr.* to crum, to crumble. II. *v. intr.* to crumble.

‖**Brösling,** *m.* [-es, *pl.* -e] white straw-berry.

Brösse, *f.* [*pl.* -n] [allied to Sprosse] V. Pappelknospe.

Brot, *n.* V. Brod.

Brötzen, V. Protzen.

Bruch, *m.* [-es, *pl.* Brüche] 1) a breach in ny body, especially a breach caused by vio-lence, a rupture of a solid body, a fracture. Der — eines Beines, Armes, the fracture of a leg, of an arm; die Grube gehet zu —e, or kommt zu —e, [in mining] the pit falls in; das Pferd hat seine Brüche gethan, [in farriery] the horse has shed his milk-teeth. *Fig.* Der — der Ehe [Ehe-—], the violation of the marriage-bed, adulte-ry; der — des Friedens [Friedens—], a breach of peace. 2) a breach, a crack [in a wall], a rent [in a garment]; [with hunters, the place where wild swine rooted] the rooting; [with charcoal-burners] the opening in a charcoal-pile. 3) [any place or pit, from which stones, metals &c. are taken, especially in composition, as:] Stein—, stone-pit, quarry; Marmor—, marble-quarry; Schiefer—, slate-quarry; Kalk—, chalk-pit &c.; ‖[Neu—] [in husbandry] break. 4) [in surgery] a burst, a rup-ture, hernia. Einen — haben, to be afflicted with hernia; der Hoden—, scrotocele; der Netz-—, epiplocele &c. 5) [the manner in which a mineral breaks, and by which its texture is displayed] fracture. Ein faseriger —, a fibrous fracture. 6) [in gunnery] ranforce. 7) that which is broken off, a broken part of an integral or integer, a fragment. *a*) *pl.* [with hunters] blinks. *b*) [in arithmetic and algebra] fraction. Der Nenner eines —es, the denominator; der Zähler eines —es, the numerator. *c*) *pl.* [in mining] ragged stones, rocks. Zu —e gehen, to choak, or to run. *Fig.* In die Brüche fallen, to come to nought; in die Brüche kommen, to lose.

Bruch-artig, *adj.* and *adv.* like a fracture. —arzt, *m.* a surgeon who cures ruptures. —band, *n.* a hernia-truss, a truss. —bandmacher, *m.* truss-maker. —dach, *n.* a curved roof. —fällig, *adj.* and *adv.* ‖ 1) friable. 2) decaying, ruinous. —kraut, *n.* [the name of several plants] 1) rupturewort. 2) willow-leaved inula. 3) the orpine or live-long. 4) common sanicle. 5) common agrimony. —mandel, *f.* V. Krachmandel. —ort, *m.* a breach. —pflaster, *n.* hernia-plaster. —satz, *m.* a detached sentence, aphorism. —satzartig, *adj.* and *adv.* aphoristic, aphoristical. —schiene, *f.* [in surgery] splint. —schlange, *f.* 1) V. Blindschleiche. 2) V. Haselwurm. —schneider, *m.* V. —arzt. —silber, *n.* broken-plate. —stein, *m.* 1) a stone out of a quarry. 2) [a plant] V. Beinbrech, 1). —stück, *n.* fragment. *Fig.* —stücke der alten Schriftsteller, fragments of ancient writers. —stückweise, *adv.* in fragments. —wurz, *f.* [the name of several plants] 1) V. —kraut 5). 2) a species of hemp-agrimony. 3) V. —kraut. 4) common thorough-wax. 5) common birth-wort. 6) perfoliate pond-weed.

Bruch, *m.* and *n.* [-es, *pl.* Brüche or Brücher] [Low Sax. brook, D. *Broeck* is generally derived from brechen; but more probably it is allied to the A. S. *broca*, Fluß] boggy land, a morass, moor, or marsh, a fen, a swamp, a bog.

Bruch-artig, *adj.* and *adv.* boggy, marshy, fenny, swampy. —beere, *f.* [a plant] great or marsh bilberry, whortleberry, or cowberry. —dorf, *n.* a village situated on a moor. —drossel, *f.* the greater reed-sparrow. —holz, *n.* wood which grows in marshes or moors. —schnepfe, *f.* the common snipe. —wasser, *n.* water from bogs. —weide, *f.* the crack-willow.

‖**Brüche, Brüchte,** *f.* [*pl.* -n] [in law] an offence, and the fine paid by way of penalty for it, a mulct.

‖**Brüchen-geld, Brüchten-geld,** *n.* a fine, a mulct. ‖—gericht, *n.* an inferior court of law.

‖**Brüchen, Brüchten,** *v. tr.* [in law] to fine.

Brüchig, *adj.* and *adv.* 1) what is already or becoming broken. Das Tuch wird —, the cloth is wearing out, is getting holes in it. 2) easily breaking or easily broken, fragile, brittle. —e Steine, brittle stones.

Brückchen, Brücklein, *n.* [-s, *pl.* -] [*dimin.* of Brücke] a small or little bridge.

Brücke, *f.* [*pl.* -n] [Sw. and Dan. *bro* and *broe*; seems to be allied to por in empor; Wendish *breh*, *broh* signifies the bank, to which the Hungar. *berw*, pl. *berwi*, is also allied] 1) [any structure of wood, stone, brick or iron, raised over a river &c., for the passage of men, cattle, carriages &c.] bridge. Eine steinerne —, a stone bridge; eine — bauen, schlagen, to build, to erect a bridge; eine — über einen Fluß schlagen, to throw a bridge over a river; eine — abwerfen, to pull down a bridge; eine fliegende —, a flying bridge; eine hängende — [Hängebrücke], a supension bridge; eine Ketten—, a chain bridge. *Fig.* Der Tod ist die — zum Leben, death is the transition into life. 2) [in printing] till, shelves.

Brücken-balken, *m.* a horizontal beam that supports the floor of a wooden bridge. —bau, *m.* 1) the building of a bridge. 2) the art of building bridges. —baum, *m.* V. —balken. —bogen, *m.* the arch of a bridge. —boot, *n.* a pontoon. —geld, *m.* a toll paid for passing over a bridge, bridge-toll, pontage. —haupt, *n.* V. —kopf. —joch, *n.* a wooden structure to support the timbers of a bridge, the props or supports of a bridge. —knecht, *m.* a pontage-gatherer. —kopf, *m.* [in fortification] a tête-de-pont. —lehne, *f.* parapet, balustrade. —meister, *m.* a person that superintends the bridges in a district. —pfeiler, *m.* pier. —pfennig, *m.* V. —geld. —ruthe, *f.* V. —balken. —schanze, *f.* V. —kopf. —schiff, *n.* a pontoon. —schreiber, *m.* the receiver of the bridge-toll. —steg, *m.* [in heraldry] V. Turnierkragen. —zoll, *m.* V. —geld.

Brücken, *v. tr.* to build a bridge or bridges over, to bridge.

Brücklein, V. Brückchen.

Brückung, *f.* the slope floor in the stall of a horse.

Brudel, V. Prudel.

Bruder, *m.* [-s, *pl.* Brüder] [from the verb bären (gebären) V. Braut] brother. 1) [a human male born of the same father and mother] Meine Brüder, my brothers; ein leiblicher or rechter —, a full brother; der Halb—, Stief—, halfbrother; — von der mütterlichen Seite, brother by the mother's side; meines —s Frau, my sister-in-law; wie Brüder, brotherly. 2) a name applied to a kinsman by blood more remote than a son of the same parents; and in a more general sense —, brother, or Brüder, brethren, is used for men in general, all men being children of the same primitive ancestors, and forming one race of beings. 3) *Fig.* *a*) one that resembles another in manner. Wer laß ist in seiner Arbeit, der ist ein — deß, der das Seine umbringt, [in Script.] he that is slothful in his work, is brother to him, that is a great waster. *b*) any one closely united, an associate, as *Duz—, a very familiar friend who is addressed by *thou* [Du] instead of *you* [Sie]. *c*) persons of the same profession call each other —, as judges, clergymen, professors, members of societies united in a common cause, monks and the like. V. Amts—. Waffenbrüder, brothers in arms; lustige Brüder, good or jovial companions; die barmherzigen Brüder, charity friars; die grauen Brüder, cistercians; die mährischen —, the Moravian brethren. *Prov.* Gleiche Brüder, gleiche Kappen, tell me with whom thou goest, and I'll tell thee what thou doest. Kings give to each other the title of —; clergymen address their congregations by the title of Brüder, brethren; meine lieben Brüder, my beloved brethren.

Bruder-band, *n.* a connection between brothers or friends. —kind, *n.* the child of a brother, nephew or niece. Sie sind —kinder, they are cousin-germans or cousins. —kuß, *m.* a fraternal kiss. —liebe, *f.* brother-love, brotherly love. —los, *adj.* and *adv.* brotherless. —mord, *m.* fratricide. —mörder, *m.* —mörderinn, *f.* fratricide. —s-sohn, *m.* the brother's son, nephew. —s-tochter, *f.* the brother's daughter, niece. —volk, *n.* an allied nation.

Brüder-gemeinde, *f.* the society or communion of the united brethren, the communion of the Moravians [Herrnhuther—]. —kirche, *f.* the community of the united brethren, of the Moravians. —los, V. Bruderlos.

Brüderchen, Brüderlein, *n.* [-s, *pl.* -] [*dimin.* of Bruder] little brother.

Brüderlich, I. *adj.* brotherly, fraternal. Die —e Liebe, brotherly or fraternal love or affection; eine —e Umarmung, a fraternal embrace. II. *adv.* in a brotherly manner, fraternally.

Brüderlichkeit, *f.* a fraternal behaviour, fraternity.

Brüdern, [rather unusual] I. *v. intr.* to live together as brothers, to associate or hold fellowship as brothers, to fraternize. II. *v. r.* sich —, to fraternize.

Brüderschaft, *f.* 1) [the connection between brothers or friends] brotherhood, fraternity. *Mit Einem — machen, to fraternize with any one. 2) [in the Romish church, a number of persons united for the purpose of public worship] brotherhood, fraternity. Die — des Rosenkranzes, the confraternity of the rosary.

Brühahn, V. Breyhahn.

Brühe, *f.* [*pl.* -n] [from brauen] any liquid or liquor drawn from a substance. *a*) [with dyers] a colouring liquor, dye. *b*) [in tobacco-manufactories] a solution for macerating tobacco-leaves. *c*) [with other mechanics] lye &c. Der Wolle die — geben, [with dyers] to scour the wool. *d*) [in cookery] liquor in which flesh, fish &c. is boiled and macerated, as Fleisch—, broth; Braten—, a sauce obtained from roast-meat; — zu Fischen, fish-sauce. *e*) any sauce or condiment. Eine — an etwas machen, to sauce a thing. †*Fig.* Eine lange — über etwas machen, to enlarge on a topic.

Brühen, *v. tr.* to expose to a boiling or violent heat in water, to scald [chickens &c.]. Ich habe mich gebrüht or verbrüht, I scalded myself.

Brüh-erz, *n.* a sort of yellow copper-ore.

—faß, *n.* scalding-tub. —futter, *n.* scalded fodder. *—heiß, *adj.* and *adv.* scalding hot, boiling hot. —käse, *m.* a sort of cheese. —näpfchen, *n.* sauce-boat, sauce tureen. —trog, *m.* a scalding-trough. *—warm, *adj.* and *adv.* scalding hot. —wasser, *n.* boiling water used for scalding.

‡Brühl, *m.* [-es, *pl.* -e] [from Bruch a marshy place, especially when grown with bushes.

Brühne, *f.* [*pl.* -n] [a sea term] the lowest side-plank of a flat-bottomed boat.

‖Brüll, *m.* [-es, *pl.* -e] a hollow loud noise, bellow, roar.

‖Brüllochs, *m.* a bull. †*Fig.* a clamorous fellow, a brawler.

Brüllen, [allied to the Fr. *brâiller*] *v. intr.* 1) to cause a loud continued sound. Die Winde —, the winds roar; —der Donner, bellowing thunder. 2) to make a hollow loud noise, to bellow, to roar. Ein —der Ochse, Löwe, a bellowing bull, a roaring lion; die —de Herde, the lowing herd; das Brüllen, bellowing, roaring. 3) [in contempt] to bellow, to vociferate or clamour; to brawl.

Brüllending, *m.* [with butchers] a bull one year old.

Brumft, *f.* V. Brunft.

Brumm, *m.* [-es, *pl.* -e] hum.

Brumm-bär, *m.* the bear. **Fig.* V. —bart. *—bart, *m.* a growler, grumbler, snarler. *—baß, *m.* 1) full-organ. 2) V. Baßgeige. —eisen, *n.* jews-harp, jews-trump. —fliege, *f.* drone, dung-fly. —kreisel, *m.* the humming-top. *—ochs, *m.* the bull. —ton, *m.* a humming sound. —vogel, *m.* humming-bird, colibri.

‖Brummel, *m.* [-s, *pl.* -] the bull.

‖Brummeln, *v. intr.* to bellow, to roar a little; *fig.* to grumble, to murmur.

Brummen, [Lat. *fremo*, Gr. *βρεμω*] I. *v. intr.* 1) to make a dull, heavy noise, to hum. Der Brummkreisel brummt, the humming-top hums; ein —der Ton, a droning sound. 2) to bellow, to roar, to low as an ox or cow. 3) [in a proper as well as in a figurative sense] to growl, to grumble, to murmur with discontent. II. *v. tr.* 1) to sing in a low voice. Ein Liedchen —, to hum a tune. 2) to express by growling, to growl. *Etwas in den Bart —, to grumble, or murmur something to one's self.

Brummer, *m.* [-s, *pl.* -] 1) a growler, grumbler. 2) the bull. 3) [a fish] miller's thumb or river-bullhead.

Brummig, Brummisch, I. *adj.* peevish, querulous. II. *adj.* peevishly, with discontent and murmuring.

1. Brunelle, *f.* [*pl.* -n] V. Braunwurz.

*2. Brunelle, *f.* [*pl.* -n] prunello.

*Brunet, *adj.* and *adv.* of dark hair, of a brown or dark complexion. Die Brünette, a brunet or brunette.

Brunft, *f.* [from the root of Brunst] [with hunters, the copulation of deer] rut, [the copulation of boars] brimming. Der Hirsch tritt in or auf die —, the stag goes to rut, bellows; aus der — treten, to cease to rut; in der —, ruttish.

Brunft-bürsche, *f.* rut-hunting. —hirsch, *m.* a stag which is rutting. —stand, *m.* the place, where stags rut. —wildbret, *n.* the hind, when she goes to tourn. —zeit, Brunstzeit, *f.* rutting-time.

Brunften, *v. intr.* [with hunters] [to lust as deer] to rut, [to lust as boars] to brim. Das Thier und die Rehgeis brunften, the hind and roe go to tourn, they rut; die Damhirschkuh brunftet, the doe goes to rut or is rutting. Brunftend, ruttish.

*Bruniren, *v. tr.* to burnish, to polish, to brighten.

Bruniereisen, *n.* a burnishing-stick, a burnisher.

Brunnäscher, *m.* [-s, *pl.* -] [with parchment-makers] lime-pit.

Brunnen, *m.* [-s, *pl.* -] [another form of Born] 1) fountain, well. Einen — graben, to dig a well. [Often used in compositions, as:] Zieh—, Pump— &c. *Fig.* Klugheit ist ein lebendiger —, [in Script.] understanding is a well spring of life. *Prov.* Kleine — sind leicht erschöpft, a little good is soon spent; den — zudecken, wenn das Kind hineingefallen ist, when the steed is stol'n the stable-door is shut; Wasser in den — tragen, to throw water into the Thames; to carry coals to Newcastle. 2) water of a well or spring, springwater, opposed to river-water, especially water of medicinal springs. Den — trinken, to use the waters; sie trinkt den —, she is at the wells; er geht nach Karlsbad, um den — zu trinken, he repairs to Karlsbad for the benefit of the waters; der Pyrmonter —, the waters of Pirmont; der Gesund—, Heil—, a spring of mineral water, spaw, spa; a watering-place, the wells; der Stahl—, der Sauer—, chalybeate water or spring, acidulæ. 3) V. Pumpe. 4) [in seamen's language] V. Pumpensood. 5) [in fortification, holes in the form of a well, serving as entrances to galleries, or giving vent to the enemy's mines] cascans.

Brunnen-ader, *f.* the vein or source of a well. —anstalt, *f.* watering-place. —arzt, *m.* the physician of a watering-place. —becken, *n.* basin. —bohrer, *m.* a bore used by well-diggers. —cur, *f.* mineral waters used as a remedy. Er geht alle Jahre nach Töplitz, um die —cur zu gebrauchen, he visits Toeplitz every year, to use the mineral waters. —dach, *n.* well-house, well-roof. —decke, *f.* —deckel, *m.* the cover put upon a well. —eimer, *m.* a bucket. —feger, *m.* well-cleanser. —gast, *m.* a visitor at a watering-place. —gebrauch, *m.* V. —cur. —göttinn, *f.* V. —nymphe. —gräber, *m.* a well-digger. —haken, *m.* V. —stange. —kasten, *m.* the wooden railing or lining of a well. —kette, *f.* the chain on a wheel by which the bucket is drawn up. —kranz, *m.* V. —kasten. —kraut, *n.* oyster-green. —kresse, *f.* V. Brunnkresse. —kur, V. —cur. —läufer, *m.* [a bird] the creeper. —leberkraut, *n.* water-liverwort. —loch, *n.* well-hole, well-pit. —meister, *m.* 1) the inspector of wells, fountains and waterworks. 2) the maker of wells and pumps. —moos, *n.* water-moss. —nymphe or —nimfe, *f.* a water nymph, a naid, naiad. —ort, *m.* a watering-place. —rad, *n.* a wheel by which the water is drawn up. —räumer, *m.* V. —feger. —röhre, *f.* 1) the pipe or tube of a pump. 2) conduit-pipe. —salz, *n.* salt prepared from brine-springs. —säule, *f.* [in draw-wells] a fulcrum or post. —schrank, *m.* the case or covering of a well. —schwengel, *m.* swipe, sweep. —seil, *n.* a long cord for drawing water from a well. —stange, *f.* the pole of a draw-well. —stube, *f.* 1) a building raised over wells or waterworks. 2) a reservoir. —wasser, *n.* spring-water, well-water, pump-water. —zeit, *f.* the time or season for drinking or using the waters. —ziegel, *m.* well-brick.

Brunnen, *v. tr.* [with parchment-makers] to soak in lime-water.

Brunnkresse, *f.* [a plant] water-cresses.

Brunnquell, *m.* [-es], Brunnquelle, *f.* [*pl.* -n] 1) the spring of a well, well-spring, well-head. 2) *Fig.* spring, source, origin. Er ist der Brunnquell alles Lebens, he is the source of all life.

Brunst, *f.* [from Brennen] the state of being consumed by fire; ‖ [*pl.* Brünste] conflagration, fire; ‖ *fig.* heat. *Fig.* *a*) *inclination in beasts to the sexual congress, [with hunters Brunft] rut. *b*) ardent passion, lust, concupiscence, carnal appetite.

Brunstzeit, *f.* V. Brunftzeit.

Brünstig, *adj* and *adv.* ‖ hot. *Fig.* *a*) having lust or eager desire of carnal gratification, libidinous, lustful. *b*) ardent, fervent. V. Inbrünstig.

Brünstigkeit, *f.* ardour, ardency, warmth, passion, love.

†Brunzen, V. Pissen.

Brüsch, *m.* [-es, *pl.* -en] [Lat. *ruscum*, appears to be allied to the old brisen = brechen] [the name of plants] *a*) prickly butcher's broom. *b*) common heath.

Brüssel, *n.* [-s] Brussels. —er Spitzen, Brussels lace.

Brust, *f.* [*pl.* Brüste] [Low Sax. Borst: perhaps allied to bären = heben] 1) [originally something prominent or projecting] *a*) [in metallurgy] the partition in the furnace over the fire-place. *b*) the part between the handle and the guard of a sword. 2) [the forepart of the thorax] breast. Die — eines menschlichen Wesens, the breast of a human being, the bosom, the chest; mit starker —, broad-chested; die — eines Thieres, the breast of an animal, brisket; dieses Pferd hat eine schöne —, that horse has a fine brisket; eine breite —, a broad chest; Einen an die — drücken, to press any one to one's bosom; eine schmale — habend, narrow-chested. **Fig.* Ei[...] in die — werfen, to thrust the chin into the neck, to behave proudly. 3) the breast = the cavity of the chest with the heart and lungs. Es beklemmt mir die —, it oppresses my breast; er hat eine starke —, he has got good lungs; er schrie aus voller —, he screamed with all [...] might; er leidet auf der —, his lungs are [...]fected. 4) [the soft protuberant body, adhering to the thorax, which in females furnishes milk for infants] breast. Eine böse — haben, to have a sore breast; an der — saugen, to draw the breast; eine[m] Kinde die — geben or reichen, to give suck to a child, to suckle a child; ein Kind von der — ent[...]wöhnen, to wean a child from the breast, [...] wean a child. 5) *Fig.* the breast = the bo[...] the seat of the affections and passions. Er [...]wahrt sein Geheimniß in seiner —, he keeps [...] secret in his breast. 6) V. Schnürbrust.

Brust-ader, *f.* [in anatomy] thoracic v[...] —arzenei, *f.* pectoral medicine, pectoral. —band, *n.* stay-lace, stay-string. —baum, [...] the beam of a cloth-weaver's loom. —b[...]baum, *m.* [a shrub] common jujube. —be[...] *f.* jujub, jujube. —bein, *n.* breast-bone, sternum. —beklemmung, *f.* [a sense of [...]ness or weight in the breast] oppression of the c[...] —beschwerde, *f.* a complaint of the c[...] —bild, *n.* 1) a bust. 2) a half-length pic[...] it. * [in general] a portrait. —binde, *f.* [in sur]gery] a bandage for the breast. —blatt, [...] strap that runs across a horse's breast] breast-[...] —blutader, *f.* [in anatomy] mammary ve[...] bohrer, *m.* a sort of bore, driven by the br[...] breast-bore. —brett, *n.* [with some mech[...] breast-board. —daube, *f.* V. —brett. —dr[...] *f.* 1) [in anatomy] thymus gland. 2) the s[weet]bread of the calf. —drüsenschlagader [...] [in anatomy] thymus artery. —eisen, *n.* a[...] busk. —ende, *n.* [in anatomy] the end of the [cla]vicle. —entzündung, *f.* inflammation of [the] chest. —essenz, *f.* pectoral essence. —f[...] *n.* V. Zwerchfell. —fieber, *n.* asthmatic f[...] —finne, *f.* pectoral fin [with fishes]. —fl[...]

m. 1) a breast-cloth, a stomacher. 2) an apron. 3) [in fencing] plastron. —flosse, f. V. —finne. —gang, m. [in anatomy] the thoracic duct. —gefäß, n. [in anatomy] mammary vessel. —geschwür, n. [a collection of pus, or matter, in the cavity of the chest] empyema. —glas, n. breast-glass, breast-fountain, breast-pipe. V. Milchsauger or Milchpumpe. —gurt, m. breast-plate. —harnisch, m. breast-plate, cuirass, poitrel. —haut, f. [in anatomy] the pleura. —hautsack, m. [in anatomy] a bag in the cavity of the breast. —höhle, f. cavity of the breast. —holz, n. 1) [with shoemakers] breast-board. 2) breast-beam of a ribbon-weaver's loom. 3) [in seamen's lang.] cut-water. —honig, m. pectoral honey. —kern, m. a piece of meat from the breast. —kette, f. breast-chain. —knochen, m. V. —bein. —knorpel, m. [in anatomy] xiphoides. —knoten, m. [in anatomy] thoracic ganglion. —krankheit, f. a complaint in the breast, chest or lungs, asthma. —krause, f. frill. —kuchen, m. —küchelchen, n. pectoral lozenge. —latz, m. a breast-cloth, a stomacher. —leber, n. V. —fleck 2. —lehne, f. 1) breast-work, parapet. 2) railing on a bridge &c., breast-height. —mauer, f. V. —lehne, 1). —milch, n. pectoral emulsion. —mittel, n. pectoral medicine, pectoral. —muskel, m. [in anat.] pectoral muscle. —nadel, f. a golden pin worn on the frill, breast-pin. —nerve, m. [in anat.] thoracic nerve. —pflaster, n. a plaster for the chest. —pille, f. pectoral pill. —platte, f. breast-plate. —pulver, n. pectoral powder. —pumpe, f. V. —glas. —reinigend, adj. and adv. expectorant. —reinigung, f. expectoration. —riegel, m. [the piece into which balusters are inserted] rail. —riemen, m. V. —blatt. —ring, m. a ring of iron fixed to the breast-plate. —saft, m. pectoral sirup [in medicine], lohoc or lohoch. —schild, n. 1) a plate worn on the chest for ornament. 2) [in Jewish antiquity] breast-plate. 3) the scutel or escutcheon [of insects]. —schlagader, f. [in anatomy] thoracic artery. —schleier, m. a stomacher worn by nuns. —schleife, f. a knot of ribands worn on the breast, a breast-knot. —schlitz, m. the bosom of a shirt. —schmerz, m. a pain in the chest. —stimme, f. [in singing] the natural voice as opposed to falsetto. —streif, m. frill [of a shirt]. —stück, m. 1) V. —kern. 2) [in entomology] the scutel or escutcheon. 3) [armour for the breast] breast-plate. 4) [in fencing] plastron. 5) [in sculpture] a bust, [in painting] a half-length picture 6) [in heraldry] a knight armed at all points. —syrop, V. —saft. —thee, m. a decoction of herbs for the chest. —trank, m. a decoction for the chest, pectoral potion. —tropfen, pl. pectoral drops. —tuch, n. a waistcoat; it. handkerchief for the neck [worn by females]. —wamms, n. doublet. —warze, f. the pap of a woman, the nipple, the teat or tit, the pap or nipple of a cow or other beasts, the dug, the teat or tit. —wasser, n. 1) water collected in the chest. 2) a sort of brandy, pectoral liquor. —wassersucht, f. dropsy in the chest, hydrothorax. —weh, n. V. —schmerz. —wehre, f. [in fortification] breast-work, parapet, rampart. ||—wenzel, m. [a bird] robin red-breast. —werk, n. 1) the front of an organ. †2) full breast or bosom. Sie hat ein tüchtiges —werk, she has a full bosom. —wirbel, pl. [in anatomy] the true vertebres. —wurz, —wurzel, f. [the name of plants] a) angelica. b) common alexanders. —zucker, m. V. Gerstenzucker. —zungenbeinmuskel, m. [in anatomy, a muscle attached to the sternum] the sterno-hyoides.

Brüstchen, Brüstlein, n. [-s, pl. -] dimin. of Brust.

Brüsten, v. r. sich —, to strut, to perk. Fig. to be proud [of any thing], to pride one's self upon. Sich mit seinen Fähigkeiten —, to be proud of one's talents; sich mit seinem Vaterlande —, to be proud of one's country; er brüstet sich mit seiner Geschicklichkeit, he plumes himself on his skill.

Brüstig, adj. and adv. breasted. Used only in compound words, as eng—, narrow-chested; breit—, broad-chested &c.

Brüstlein, V. Brüstchen.

||Brüstling, m. [-es, pl. -e] [a bird] V. Bluthänfling.

Brüstung, f. 1) parapet. 2) [in seamen's lang.] the diminishing of a vessel at the stem and stern.

Brut, f. [pl. —en] [from bären, gebären] 1) the act of covering the eggs, or of brooding, incubation. Die Hühner sind in der —, the hens are brooding. 2) a brood, a hatch. Die — Hühner, a brood of chickens; eine — Vögel, a covey; eine — [Hecke] Kanarienvögel, a brood of canary-birds; die — der Bienen oder anderer Insekten, eggs of bees or other insects; die — der Seidenwürmer, the seed of the silk-worms; die — der Fische, the fry. 3) [often in composition, as] Bruthühner, brooding-hens; Brutvögel, brooding-birds &c. 4) [in contempt] set, [especially of children] brats.

Brut-biene, f. the drone. —ei, n. an egg fit for hatching, brood-egg. —haus, f. hatching-house. —mast, f. [in husbandry] worms and grubs in the ground, considered as food for pigs. —ofen, m. hatching-oven. —scheibe, f. the honey-comb which contains the young brood. —zeit, f. brooding-time. —zelle, f. the cell of a honey-comb, which contains the young brood. —zwiebel, f. a small flower-bulb.

*Brutal, adj. and adv. brutal, savage. Ein —es Wesen, brutal manners; ein —er Mensch, a brutal person, a brute.

*Brutalität, f. [pl. -en] brutality, savageness, churlishness, brutal behaviour, brutal insult.

Brüten, v. intr. and tr. to sit on eggs for hatching, to brood. Der Vogel brütet, the bird broods; die Hühner —, the hens are sitting. Fig. Ueber etwas —, to brood over any thing, to have the mind uninterruptedly dwell a long time on a subject; Böses —, to hatch mischief.

Bruthenne, f. brood-hen.

Brütig, adj. and adv. broody.

*Brutto, adv. [in commerce] gross. Die —einnahme, gross receipt; das —gewicht, gross-weight.

Bst! Pst! interject. 1) [a word commanding silence] bist! hush! 2) a word used in calling to attract any one's attention.

Bubbeln, v. intr. to bubble.

Bübchen, Büblein, n. [-s, pl. -] dimin. of Bube.

Bube, m. [-n, pl. -n] [Lat. pu-er, pu-pus, Gr. παῖς, allied to φύω, erzeugen] 1) a boy, a lad; it. [in contempt] a bad boy, an ill-mannered boy. 2) a knave = a rogue, villain. 3) [a card with a soldier painted on it] the knave.

Buben-distel, f. teazle, fuller's thistle. —kraut, n. V. Mangold. —streich, m. —stück, n. a knavish trick, or action, roguery.

||Bübelei, f. dimin. of Büberei.

Buben, v. intr. [rather obsolete or unusual] to act as a knave or rogue. Huren und —, to whore and revel.

Büberei, f. a knavish action, knavery, roguery, villany.

Bübinn, f. a bad female.

Bübisch, adj. and adv. knavish, roguish, mischievous, malicious. Eine —e Handlung, a knavery.

Büblein, V. Bübchen.

*Bucentaur, m. [-en, pl. -en] [formerly the state barge of Venice] the bucentaur.

*Bucephalus, m. [sometimes pl. -sse] [in ancient history, the horse of Alexander the great] bucephalus.

Buch, n. [-es, pl. Bücher] [probably from biegen] 1) book. a) [any number of sheets when bound or sewed together; a volume of blank paper, intended for any species of writing, as for memorandums, for accounts or receipt; especially a printed composition] Ein in Pappe or Pappendeckel gebundenes [ein cartonirtes] —, a book in boards; ein ungebundenes or rohes —, a book in sheets; ein weißes [leeres or unbeschriebenes] —, a blank book; ein gutes —, a good book; ein — schreiben, to write or compose a book; ein — drucken, to print a book; ein — binden, to bind a book; ein — von Neuem auflegen, to reprint a book; *immer über den Büchern liegen, to be given to reading, to be fond of study, to be bookish. b) [in commerce, a volume or collection of sheets in which accounts are kept; a register of debts and credits, receipts and expenditures &c.]. — halten, to keep the books; etwas zu —e bringen or tragen, to enter in the books, to book something. 2) [a part of any written or printed composition; a particular part of a literary composition; a division of a subject in the same volume] book. Im zweiten —e [Theile] seines Werkes, in the second part or book of his work; ein episches Gedicht in vier und zwanzig Büchern, an epic poem in twenty four books. 3) [a collection of paper consisting of twenty four sheets, each having a single fold] a quire. 4) V. Blättermagen.

Buch-adel, m. parchment-nobility. —binder, m. bookbinder. —binderahle, f. a bookbinder's awl. —binderbericht, m. a notice for the bookbinder. —binderei, f. 1) book-binding. 2) a bookbinder's shop. —bindergeselle, m. journeyman bookbinder. —bindergold, n. beaten gold leaves, gold-leaf. —binderhandwerk, n. the trade of a bookbinder. —binderhobel, m. [= Beschneidehobel] plough-knife. —binderkleister, m. bookbinder's paste. —binderkreuz, n. a peel. —binderleder, n binding-leather. —binderleim, m. bookbinder's glue. —bindermesser, n. bookbinder's knife. —binderpresse, f. bookbinder's press —bindersäge, f. bookbinder's saw. —bindersilber, n. silver-leaf. —binderspähne, pl. scale boards. —binderwasser, n. V. Leimwasser. —drucker, m. 1) printer, typographer. 2) the pressman. —druckerballen, m. ball. —druckerei, f. 1) the art of printing, printing, typography. 2) printing-office. —druckerfarbe, f. V. —druckerschwärze. —druckergesell, m. journeyman printer. —druckerherr, m. the master of a printing-office. —druckerjunge, m. printer's apprentice. —druckerkreuz, n. a peel. —druckerkunst, f the art of printing, printing, typography. Zur —druckerkunst gehörig, typographical. —druckerleiste, f. V. —druckerstock. —druckerpresse, f. printing-press. —druckerschrift, f. V. —stabe, 2). —druckerschwärze, f. printer's ink. —druckerstock, m. printer's flower, vinnet, tailpiece. —führer, m. 1) [unusual] a person that hawks about and retails books. 2) bookkeeper. —futteral, n. book-case. —gelehrsamkeit, f. book-learning, letter-learning. V. Stubengelehrsamkeit and Belesenheit. —gelehrt, adj. and adv. book-learned, letter-learned. V. Stubengelehrt and Belesen. —gläubiger, m. [in commerce] book-creditor. —halten, n. bookkeeping. —halter, m. 1) bookkeeper. 2) V. Schrifthalter.

—halterei, *f.* 1) bookkeeping. 2) a book-keeper and his clerks. 3) bookkeeper's office. —haltung, *f.* [in commerce] book-keeping. Die einfache —haltung, bookkeeping by single entry; die doppelte —haltung, double entry; die Bücher nach der italienischen oder doppelten —haltung führen, to keep books after the Italian method or by double entry. —handel, *m.* book-trade, book-selling business, the business of a bookseller. —händler, *m.* bookseller. Often used in compound words, as: Verlags—händler, Sortiments—händler &c. —handlung, *f.* 1) book-trade. 2) a shop where books are sold, book-store, bookseller's shop. —laden, *m.* bookseller's shop, [in America] book-store. —leinwand, *f.* [a sort of Saxon linen folded in book form] book-linen. —macherei, *f.* [in contempt of mercenary authors] book-making. —schuld, *f.* [in law] book-debt. —schuldner, *m.* [in law] book-debtor. —titel, *m.* the title of a book.

Buche, Büche, *f.* [*pl.* -n] [Gr. φηγός, Lat. *fagus*, probably allied to φύω] the beech, beech-tree.

Buch-ampfer, *m.* [a plant] the wood-sorrel. —äsche, *f.* V. Weißbuche. —baum, *m.* V. Buche. —eichel, *f.* beech-nut. —engang, *m.* a walk planted with beech-trees, an avenue of beech-trees. —enhecke, *f.* a hedge of beeches. —enholz, *n.* beech-wood, beech. —enland, *n.* a tract of land where beeches grow. —enraupe, *f.* a sort of moth. —enwald, *m.* beech-grove. —esche, *f.* V. Weißbuche. —fink, *m.* the chaffinch. —klee, *m.* V. —ampfer. —marder, *m.* the pine-martin. —mast, *f.* beech-mast. —maus, *f.* V. Haselmaus. —nuß, *f.* V. —eichel. —öl, *n.* beech-oil. —schwamm, *m.* a species of boletus [boletus ramosissimus]. —weizen, *m.* [a plant and a species of grain] buckwheat. —weizengrütze, *f.* grit of buckwheat. —winde, *f.* black buckwheat or bindweed.

Büchelchen, Büchlein, *n.* [-s, *pl.* -] *dimin.* of Buch.

Buchen, *v. tr.* [in commerce, to enter, write or register in a book] to book. Gleichförmig —, to note in conformity.

Büchen, *adj.* and *adv.* beechen. Ein —es Gefäß, a beechen vessel.

Bücher, *pl.* of Buch.

Bücher-aufseher, *m.* a bibliothecary, a librarian. —brett, *n.* a shelf, or set of shelves, for books, book-stand. —censor, V. Censor. —censur, V. Censur. —dieb, *m.* 1) one who steals books. 2) one who steals from books, a plagiary. —diebstahl, *m.* 1) the stealing of books. 2) the stealing from books, plagiarism. —fertiger, *m.* a petty author, a scribbler. —fertigung, *f.* scribbling. —freund, *m.* a lover of books, bibliophile. —gestell, *n.* V. —brett. —halle, *f.* [an edifice, or an apartment for holding a collection of books] a library. —handel, *m.* the selling of second-hand books. —händler, *m.* a seller of second-hand books. —kenner, *m.* [one skilled in literary history] a bibliographer. —kenntniß, *f.* bibliography, bibliognosy. Die —kenntniß betreffend, bibliographical. —kram, *m.* V. —handel. —krämer, *m.* a seller of second-hand books. —kunde, *f.* V. —kenntniß. —kundige, *m.* V. —kenner. —laus, *f.* a species of tick [acarus eruditus]. —leiste, *f.* V. Buchdruckerstock. —machen, *n.* [in contempt] book-making. —macher, *m.* a scribbler. —markt, *m.* a market where books are sold. —messe, *f.* fair for the sale of books and for transacting business relative to books. —narr, *m.* bibliomaniac. —register, *n.* V. —verzeichniß. —saal, *m.* book-room. —sammlung, *f.* [a collection of books] a library. —schau, *f.* censure [more usual: Censur]. —schauamt, *n.* censorship [more usual: Censorschaft, Censoramt]. —schauer, *m.* a censor [more usual: Censor]. —schrank, *m.* book-case. —schreiber, *m.* [in contempt] a writer, author. —skorpion, *m.* the scorpion-tick. —sprache, *f.* book-language, refined language. —sucht, *f.* bibliomania. —titel, *m.* V. Buchtitel. —trödel, *m.* petty trade in old books. —trödler, *m.* a dealer in old books. —verleiher, *m.* one who keeps a circulating library. —verzeichniß, *n.* a catalogue of books. —wesen, *n.* literature. —wurm, *m.* 1) [an insect] book-worm. 2) *Fig.* [a student too closely attached to books] book-worm. —wuth, *f.* V. —sucht. —zimmer, *n.* book-room.

Büchlein, V. Büchelchen.

Buchsbaum, Buxbaum, *m.* [-es, *pl.* -bäume] [Lat. *buxus*, Gr. πύξος, probably from φύω, erzeugen, V. Buche] [a tree or shrub, used for bordering flower-beds] box. Dem — ähnlich, boxen.

Buchsbäumen, *adj.* and *adv.* box, box-wood, boxen.

Büchschen, Büchslein, *n.* [-s, *pl.* -] *dimin.* of Büchse.

Buchsdorn, *m.* [-s] box-thorn.

Büchse, *f.* [*pl.* -n] [appears to be allied to biegen, Bug, Fr. *boite*, *boussole* &c.] 1) [a hollow case or chest, especially of a cylindric form, either of wood or metal &c., for holding different things] a box. [Frequently used in compositions, as: Nadel—, Sand—&c.] 2) a rifle gun, a rifle. 3) [also Buchse; a cylindrical hollow iron used in wheels, in which the axle-tree runs; also a hollow tube in a conduit] box, bushel or bush. 4) the bose [of a printing-press]. 5) [in seamen's language] a pipe. Die metallene — für die Pinne des Gangspills, the iron socket or saucer of the capstern; bleierne —n in den Speigaten, lead scuppers; Scheiben von Pockholz mit metallenen —n, sheaves of lignum vitæ with brass coaks. 6) [in botany] theca.

Büchsen-bohrer, *m.* gun-borer. —förmig, *adj.* and *adv.* having the form of a box, resembling a box. —futter, *n.* a gun-case [made of cloth or leather]. —geld, *n.* money collected in an alms-box. —kugel, *f.* bullet for a rifle-barrel. —lauf, *m.* rifle-barrel. —macher, *m.* gun-smith. —meißel, *m.* a sort of chisel used by gun-smiths. —meister, *m.* gunner, master gunner. —pulver, *n.* gun-powder. —rohr, *n.* V. —lauf. —sack, *m.* 1) gun-case. 2) sportsman's pouch. —schaft, *m.* gun-stock. —schäfter, *m.* gunstock-maker. —schloß, *n.* the lock of a gun. —schmied, *m.* 1) V. —macher. 2) armourer of a vessel of war. —schuß, *m.* a gun-shot. Einen —schuß weit, within the reach of a gun-shot, as far as a rifle carries. —schütze, *m.* 1) [formerly] a soldier armed with an arquebuse, an arquebusier. 2) [now] a rifleman. Die Tyroler sind gute —schützen, the Tyrolese are good riflemen. —spanner, *m.* a person whose business is to charge and prepare the gun for his master. —wärter, *m.* the keeper of the armoury.

1. **Büchsen**, [seldom used] *v. tr.* to furnish with boxes. Ein Rad —, to box a wheel.

2. **Büchsen**, [unusual] *v. intr.* to shoot with a gun.

Büchslein, V. Büchschen.

Buchstabe, *m.* [-n, *pl.* -n] 1) a character, written, printed, engraved or painted, a letter. Ein großer —, a capital letter; ein stummer —, [in grammar] a mute; —n versetzen, to transpose the letters of a word; die —n eines Namens versetzen, to anagrammatize. *Fig.* Der — des Gesetzes, the letter [the verbal expression, the literal meaning] of the law; denn der — tödtet, aber der Geist macht lebendig, [in Script.] for the letter killeth, but the spirit gives life. 2) [a character formed of metal or wood, used in printing books] a letter, a type. Ueberhängende —n, kerned letters; die —n in falsche Fächer legen, [in printing] to distribute the letters into wrong boxes; ein verwechselter —, a wrong letter; mit —n drucken or zeichnen, to letter [the Titel of a book, with bookbinders].

Buchstaben-ansatz, *m.* [in grammar] paragoge [as the Lat. verb *dicier* for *dici*]. —arche, *f.* a species of ark-shell [arca scripta]. —folge, *f.* [the series of letters which form the elements of speech] alphabet. Nach der —folge, alphabetically. —krämer, *m.* [in contempt] literalist. —muschel, *f.* 1) the lettered venus. 2) fine letter tellen. —note, *f.* [in music] a note expressed by a letter. —ordnung, *f.* V. —folge. —porzellane, *f.* the nutmeg cowry. —räthsel, *n.* a logogriphe. —rech[n]enkunst, *f.* logistic, algebra. —rechner, *m.* algebraist, logist. —rechnung, *f.* 1) algebra. 2) an algebraic operation or calculation. —schnecke, *f.* V. —tute. —schrift, *f.* writing in letters [as opposed to writing in picture]. —spielerei, *f.* a transposition of letters, of names &c. —tute, *f.* the tiger stamper. —versetzung, *f.* 1) [in grammar] metathesis [as *pistris* for *pristis*]. 2) [in poetry] an anagram. —wechsel, *m.* V. —versetzung. —zahl, *f.* 1) [in algebra] algebraic number. 2) [in printing] alphabet.

Buchstäbeln, Buchstaben, *v. intr.* 1) to pick out the verbal sense of a word or sentence. 2) V. Buchstabiren.

Buchstabiren, *v. tr.* to spell. Falsch —, to misspell.

Buchstäbler, *m.* [-s, *pl.* -] 1) [one that spells] speller. 2) one that sticks to the literal sense.

Buchstäblich, *adj.* and *adv.* [following the letter, or exact words] literal, verbal. Die —e Bedeutung, literal meaning.

Bucht, *f.* [*pl.* -en] [from biegen] 1) an inlet, creek, a bay of the sea, a cove. Voll kleiner —en, creeky. 2) [in botany] a break in the margin of a leaf.

Buchtenfarn, *m.* [a species of fern] lonchitis.

Buchtig, *adj.* and *adv.* 1) consisting of inlets or creeks, creeky. 2) [in botany] Ein —es Blatt, a sinuate leaf.

1. **Buckel**, *m.* [-s, *pl.* Buckel] [from biegen] 1) † the back. 2) a crooked back, crook-back, hump-back, hump. Der — auf dem Rücken eines Kameels, eines Büffels, the hump or bunch on a camel's or a buffalo's back.

Buckel-käfer, *m.* the bruchus. —ochs, *m.* the bison. —thier, *n.* any animal with a hump, as a camel &c.

2. **Buckel**, *f.* [*pl.* -n] [from biegen] an ornamental knob, a stud, a boss [used on bridles, harness &c.].

Buckel-eisen, *n.* [with hair-dressers] curling-iron, curling-tongs.

Bückelasche, *f.* buck-ashes.

Buckelicht, *adj.* and *adv.* resembling a hump.

Buckelig, *adj.* and *adv.* hump-backed, bunch-backed, crook-backed, hunch-backed. Der, die —e, a hump-backed person, a hunchback. † *Fig.* Sich — lachen, to split one's sides with laughing.

1. **Buckeln**, [unusual] I. *v. tr.* to carry on the back. II. *v. intr.* to make a crooked back.

2. **Buckeln**, *v. tr.* to adorn with shining studs or knobs, to stud.

Bücken, *v. r.* [from biegen] sich —, to bend, to curve, to bow. Diese Thüre ist so niedrig, daß man sich im Durchgehen — muß, this door so low, that one must stoop to go through it; *it.* [in token of deference, respect or civility]. Sich vor Einem —, to bow to any one. *Fig.* Sich vor Gott —, to humble one's self before God; dieß ist der Götze, vor dem die Welt sich bückt, this is the idol before whom the world bows.

Bücklicht, V. Buckelicht.

Bücklig, V. Buckelig.

1. **Bückling**, *m.* [-es, *pl.* -e] [an inclination of the head, or a bending of the body in token of reverence, respect or civility] a bow. Einen tiefen — machen, to make a profound reverence.

2 **Bückling**, *m.* [-es, *pl.* -e] [probably from backen = dörren] a red herring.

Bude, *f.* [*pl.* -n] [from bauen] 1) a small house, a mean lodge or dwelling, a hut. 2) a booth, stall, shop. Die — eines Schuhflickers, a cobbler's stall; die —n auf Jahrmärkten, Messen, the stalls in fairs.

Buden-tisch, *m.* shop-table. —zins, *m.* [rent paid for a stall] stallage.

Budel, *m.* V. Pudel.

***Búdget**, *n.* [pronounce as in the French] [-s, *pl.* -s] [from the Engl. *budget*, Beutel] [the papers respecting the finances of a country] the budget; *it.* [in general] the estimate of the income and the expenses of a state.

Budget-mäßig, *adj.* and *adv.* conformable to the stipulations of a budget. —satz, *m.* a sum fixed in a budget for a certain object.

Büffel, *m.* [-s, *pl.* -] [Gr. βούβαλος, Lat. *bubalus*, Fr. *boeuf*, der Ochse] 1) the buffalo, buffle. 2) buff-jacket. † and ‡ 3) *Fig.* a person of coarse manners, a rude fellow.

Büffel-artig, *adj.* and *adv.* like a buffle. —haft, *adj.* and *adv.* *fig.* [in contempt] of coarse manners, rude, rough. —haut, *f.* 1) the skin of a buffalo. 2) *Fig.* [in contempt of men] a thick or coarse skin. —käfer, *m.* a species of beetle [scarabæus bison]. —kopf, *m.* 1) the head of a buffalo. 2) *Fig.* *a*) † and ‡ a buffle-head, a blunder-headed person. *b*) [a bird] buffle's head-duck, buffel. —leder, *n.* buffskin, buff. —ochs, *m.* V. Büffel 1. —schlange, *f.* the great boa.

† **Büffelei**, *f.* [*pl.* -en] a rude or rough behaviour.

Büffelicht, *adj.* and *adv.* V. Büffelhaft.

† and ‡ **Büffeln**, *v. intr.* to drudge, to plot, to toil.

***Büffet**, *n.* 1) sideboard. 2) sideboard-table.

Bug, *m.* [-es, *pl.* Büge] [from biegen] 1) any bended surface and the place where any body bends, a flexure, bow, bend. 2) [the joint by which the foreleg of a quadruped is connected with the body] the shoulder. 3) [the joint between the knee and the fetlock] hock. 4) bow of a ship. Ein scharfer or schmaler —, a lean bow; ein voller —, a bluff bow; ein springender or vornüberhangender —, a flaring bow; mit dem — gegen einander laufen, to run foul of each other's stem on. auf einen andern — wenden, to tack or veer.

Bug-ader, *f.* [in anatomy] the plat vein of a horse. —anker, *m.* bow-anchor, bower. —band, *n.* [in seamen's language] breast-hook, fore-hook. —holz, *n.* [in seamen's language] hawse-piece. —lahm, *adj.* and *adv.* strained in the shoulder, as a horse, shoulder-shotten. Ein Pferd —lahm machen, to splay a horse. —lähme, *f.* the state of being strained in the shoulder, as a horse. —spriet, *n.* [in seamen's language] bowsprit. —sprietband, *n.* [in seamen's lang.] breast-hook of the bowsprit. —spriet-stange, —stange, *f.* [in seamen's language] fore-mast. —stück, *n* 1) [in shipbuilding] V. —holz. Die —stücke, durch welche die Klüsen gebohrt sind [Klüshölzer], the knight-heads or bollard-timbers, the hawse-pieces which are nearest the stem. 2) [in seamen's language] bow-chase. 3) [with butchers] the shoulder-piece of an animal.

Bügel, *m* [-s, *pl.* -] [from biegen] 1) any piece of wood or metal in form of a curve Der — an einem Degen, the bow of a sword's hilt; der — am Schießgewehr, the guard of a gun; der — an einem Schlüssel, bow of a key; der — an einer Wiege, the hoop of a cradle; der — an einem Korbe, the ear or handle of a basket; der Steig— am Reitzeuge, stirrup; der — eines Bogens, [part of a circle] curve; [in seamen's language] der — des Klüvers, jib-iron; die — des Kompasses und Nachthauses, gimbals of the seacompass and of the lamp; die — des Ankerstocks, the hoops of the anchor-stock; die — der Leesegelspieren, the studding-sail-boom irons; eiserne — über den Luken, hatch-bars; — in den Fischen des Gangspills, an iron hoop that lines the hole of the deck, within which the capstern turns upon its spindle; die — um die Masten, mast-hoops. 2) [in architecture] a flat iron hoop 3) [with butchers] an iron ring used for stuffing sausages.

Bügel-brett, *n.* [with tailors &c.] sleeve-board. —dohne, *f.* [with hunters] a gin or springe made of willow. —eisen, *n.* 1) a smoothing-iron, a flat-iron, [with tailors] goose. 2) a sort of horse-shoe. —fest, *adj.* and *adv.* steady in the stirrups. *Fig.* sitting steadily in riding, firm on horseback. —garn, *n.* [with fowlers] bow-net. —los, *adj.* and *adv.* without stirrups. Er wurde —los, he lost his stirrups. —messer, *m.* [a hair-dresser's] smoothing-iron. —netz, *n.* V. —garn. —riemen, *m.* stirrup-leather. —ring, *m.* an iron ring for receiving the stirrup-leather. ‡—rock, *m.* V. Reifrock. —stahl, *m.* V. —eisen. ‡—tasche, *f.* a purse. —tuch, *n.* a blanket used in ironing linen &c.

Bügeln, *v. tr.* to smooth with an instrument of iron, to iron.

***Bugsiren**, *v. tr.* [in seamen's language] to tow.

Bugsirtau, *n.* [in seamen's language] tow-rope.

Bugt, *f.* [*pl.* -en] [from biegen] [in seamen's lang.] rounding or convexity. Die — der Balken, the rounding or convexity of the beams; Auf—, the round or rounding up; Aus—, rounding out; Ein—, rounding in; Nieder—, rounding down; Es—, a crooked piece of the figure of an S; — eines aufgeschossenen Taues, the coil; die —en fangen sich, the fakes catch each other, there are catch-fakes in the cable; —en des auf's Deck geholten Ankertaues, wenn der Anker fallen soll, ranges; den Anker mit zwei oder drei —en fallen lassen, to let go the anchor with two or three ranges.

Bugtig, *adj.* and *adv.* [in seamen's language] crooked. — Holz, a crooked piece of timber.

‖**Bühel**, *m.* [-s] [allied to Bug] a word of frequent occurrence in old German appellations of hilly places, as: the Jetten—, Jutta's hill [near the town of Heidelberg] &c. V. Hügel.

Buhle, 1) *m.* [-n, *pl.* -n] lover, paramour, [in contempt] an adulterous lover, the favoured lover of a married woman. 2) *f.* [*pl.* -n] [also die Buhlinn] paramour, mistress, [in contempt] an unchaste female.

Buhlen, *v. intr.* [seems to be allied to the Gr. φιλεῖν, lieben] 1) to make love, to woo, to court. *Fig.* Um Beifall —, to court applause. 2) to have an improper intercourse with a person of a different sex; to caress a woman for lewd purposes.

Buhl-dirne, *f.* a wanton girl, a prostitute, a whore, a strumpet. —kraut, *n.* [a plant] stinking goose-foot. —lied, *n.* an amorous tune, [or in a bad sense] a wanton song. —schwester, *f.* V. Buhlerinn.

Buhler, *m.* [-s, *pl.* -] lover, paramour, [in a bad sense] a gallant. Used also in compound words, as: Neben— &c.

Buhlerei, *f.* 1) attempts to attract love from vanity, affectation of amorous advances, trifling in love, coquetry. 2) illicit commerce between the sexes, gallantry, lewdness, debauchery.

Buhlerinn, *f.* an unchaste female, a lewd woman, a kept woman, mistress.

Buhlerisch, *adj.* and *adv.* 1) coquetish. 2) [in a bad sense] wanton, lewd, lascivious. Ein —er Blick, a wanton look; —e Geberden, lascivious gestures. *Poet.* Die —en Weste, the wanton west-winds.

Buhlinn, *f.* V. Buhle 2).

Buhlschaft, *f.* [rather obsolete] 1) a love affair, an intrigue, an amorous intercourse. 2) a paramour, beloved object.

Buhne, *f.* V. Bühne *e*) and *g*).

Bühne, *f.* [*pl.* -n] [allied to the Gr. βουνός, Hügel] any thing made of boards, planks or poles; hence *a*) ‖ loft. *b*) scaffold, scaffolding. Often used in compositions, as: Schau—, Blut—, &c. *c*) [the theater, the place of scenic entertainments; theatrical representations] the stage. Auf der — auftreten, to tread the stage; to enter on the stage; dieser Schauspieler ist vollkommen heimisch auf der —, this actor is quite at home on the boards; von der — abtreten, to go off the stage; also, *fig.* to die; die — ist nicht immer eine Schule der Moral, the stage is not always a school of morality. *Fig.* Die — des Lebens, the stage of life. *d*) [in mining] shambles; scaffold, or channel. *e*) [in sea-towns] a wharf or quay. *f*) a pen, a crawl. *g*) well of a fishing-vessel.

Bühnen-bekleidung, *f.* scene, scenery. —darstellung, *f.* stage-representation. —dichter, *m.* a dramatic author, dramatist, [seldom used] a stage-writer. V. also Schauspieldichter. —gott, *m.* a god introduced into a play to save difficulty, or perform some exploit, which exceeds human power [deus ex machina]. —held, *m.* —heldinn, *f.* 1) the principal personage in a play, the hero, the heroine. 2) an experienced player, an old stager. —mahler, *m.* scene-painter, decoration-painter. —mahlerei, *f.* 1) scene-painting. 2) [the paintings representing the scenery of a play] scenery. —mäßig, I. *adj.* resembling the manner of dramatic performers, theatrical. Ein —mäßiger Anzug, theatrical dress. II. *adv.* in a manner suiting the stage, theatrically. —meister, *m.* [in sea-towns] quay-master. —schmücker, *m.* [unusual] V. —mahler. —spiel, *n.* a play. —spieler, *m.* 1) V. Schauspieler. 2) a performer in the orchestre. Die —spieler, the orchestre, orchestra. —stiefel, *m.* the buskin. —streich, *m.* a striking event, theatrical stroke [coup de théâtre]. —stück, *n.* a drama. —tanz, *m.* a ballet. —verzierung, *f.* V. —bekleidung. —vorstellung, *f.* theatrical performance. —wand, *f.* [Coulisse] side-scene. Die —wände, the scenes [which are changed as occasion requires], decoration. —werk, *n.* the machinery of a theatre. —werkmeister, *m.* machinist.

Bühnen, *v. tr.* to cover with boards, to board. Einen Schacht —, to line a shaft.

Bühnloch, *n.* [-es, *pl.* -löcher] [in mining] a hollow in shafts to receive the stemples.

Búise, *f.* [*pl.* -n] [in seamen's lang.] buss [a small fishing-craft].

Búje, V. Boje.

Bújen, *v. tr.* [in seamen's language] Mit Planken — [auf—], to plank a ship.

Bujer, V. Bojer.

*Bukolisch, *adj.* and *adv.* bucolic. Die —en Gedichte [Hirtengedichte] Virgils, the bucolics of Virgil.

Bulge, *f.* [*pl.* -n] a leathern waterpail.

Buline, *f.* V. Boleine.

1. ǂBulle, *m.* [-n, *pl.* -n] [from the old bullen = brummen] a bull.

Bullen-beißer, *m.* a bull-dog. —hatz, *f.* bull-baiting. —kalb, Bullkalb, *n.* a bull-calf, male-calf. —kraut, *n.* purple, spurge. Bullochs, *m.* a bull. Bullwurz, *f.* [a plant] shrubby Atropa.

2. Bulle, *f.* [*pl.* -n] [from the L. *bulla*, allied to the old or provinc. Ger. boll = rund] [a seal of wax or lead appended to the edicts and briefs of the pope and to imperial edicts; also the edict itself] bull. Eine — ausgehen lassen, schleudern, to fulminate a bull; die goldene —, [so called from its golden seal, is an edict or imperial constitution, made by the emperor Charles IV, containing the fundamental law of the German empire] the golden bull.

Bullenbuch, *n.* bullary.

3. Bulle, *f.* [*pl.* -n] [from Bole] [in seamen's language] a hulk, or pontoon for careening ships.

Bullen-stall, *m* [in seamen's language] the manger. —tau, *n.* [in seamen's language] Das — tau des Ankers, V. Porteurlien; das —tau vom Fockhals, loof-hook-rope; das —tau eines Jacht- oder Schlupsegels, the guy of a boom.

4. ‖Bulle, *f.* [*pl.* -n] V. Flasche.

‖Bullerig, *adj.* and *adv.* blustrous, boisterous.

‖Bullern, *v. intr.* 1) to be tumultuous, to bluster, to roar. Die —den Winde, the boisterous winds. 2) V. Poltern. 3) * to chide with boisterous clamour, to scold.

*Bulletin, *n.* [pronounce as in the French] [-s, *pl.* -s] bulletin.

‖Bulow, *m.* V. Kirschvogel.

Bultsäcke, *pl.* [in seamen's lang.] straw-beds.

Bumm, [allied to the Gr. βόμβος, der Schall] a word imitating the dull tone of bells.

‖Bummeln, *v. imp.* [V. Bumm] to ring [said of small bells].

‖Bummeln, *v. intr.* V. Bammeln.

‖Bummen, [V. Bumm] *v. intr.* to make a dull noise [said of great bells], to bum.

†Bums, *interj.* [V. Bumm] bounce!

1. Bund, *m.* [-es, *pl.* Bünde] [from binden] 1) in general eine Verbindung: *a*) [a contract between two or more persons, bodies of men or states, combined in support of each other, in some act or enterprise] a league or covenant, a confederacy. Der Deutsche —, German confederacy; Graubündten or die Graubünde, the country of the Grisons; in — treten, to unite in a league, to confederate; Rußland und Oestreich schlossen einen —, um sich dem Ehrgeize Napoleons zu widersetzen, Russia and Austria leagued to oppose the ambition of Napoleon; mit Jemand im —e stehen, to be leagued with any one; der — der Ehe, the matrimonial tie; sie schlossen einen — auf Leben und Tod, they pledged their faith for life and death. *b*) [in theology] Der alte —, the Mosaic dispensation; der neue —, the Gospel dispensation; die Schriften des alten —es, des neuen —es, the Old Testament, the New Testament. 2) any thing that binds, any ligament by which a number of things are confined together. *a*) [with locksmiths] a band of iron. *b*) *pl.* [with bookbinders] bands. *c*) [in fire-works] the cover of rockets &c. *d*) [with tailors and sempstresses] band. Der — an den Hosen [Hosen—], waistband. *e*) [with glaziers] the lead in which the panes are set. 3) several things confined together. Der türkische —, *α*) a turban; *β*) a sort of pastry; *γ*) pompian lily; *δ*) pompion, or pumpkin gourd.

Bund-brüchig, *adj.* and *adv.* breaking the covenant, faithless to the terms of agreement. —esacte, *f.* an instrument containing the conditions &c. of a confederacy; the act of the German confederacy. —esangelegenheit, *f.* an affair concerning a confederacy, federal affair. —esarchiv, *n.* the archives of a confederacy. —esausträgalgericht, *n.* —esausträgalinstanz, *f.* V. Austrägalgericht. —esbeschluß, *m.* decision, decree of a confederacy. —escontingent, *n.* the troops which any state forming part of a confederacy is bound to furnish. —eseinrichtung, *f.* any regulation concerning a confederacy. —esfeldherr, *m.* the commander in chief of the army of a confederacy. —esfestung, *f.* a fortress belonging to a confederacy. —esflüchtig, *adj.* and *adv.* V. —brüchig. —esfreund, *m.* an ally, a confederate. —esfürst, *m.* a prince who is a member of a confederacy. —esgebiet, *n.* the territory of all the members of a confederacy. —esgemäß, *adj.* and *adv.* V. —esmäßig. —esgenoß, *m.* an ally, a confederate. —esgenossenschaft, *f.* [the persons or parties allied] alliance. —esgesetz, *n.* a law obligatory to all the members of a confederacy. —esgesetzgebung, *f.* the legislation of a confederacy. —esgesetzlich, —esgesetzmäßig, *adj.* and *adv.* according to the laws of a confederacy. —esgewalt, *f.* the power and authority belonging to a confederacy. —esglied, *n* a member of a league or confederacy. —esgrenze, *f.* the frontier of a confederacy's territory. —esgrenzfluß, *m.* a river which forms such a frontier. —esheer, *n.* the army of a confederacy. —eshülfe, *f.* mutual support afforded by the members of a confederacy to each other. —eskanzlei, *f.* an office for transacting the affairs of a confederacy. —eskasse, *f.* the treasury of a confederacy. —eskrieg, *m.* a war in which the whole confederacy takes part. —eslade, *f.* [in Jewish antiquity] the ark of the covenant. —eslande, *pl.* countries belonging to a confederacy. —esleistung, *f.* supplies furnished by the individual members for the good of the confederacy, as: money, troops &c. —esmäßig, *adj.* and *adv.* conformable to the league or confederacy. —esmatrikel, *f.* the fixed number of the population in the different states of a confederacy, according to which money and troops to be furnished are levied. —esmatrikularausschlag, *m.* the stipulation of what each member has to furnish according to the —esmatrikel. —esmatrikularmäßig, *adj.* and *adv.* conformable to the —esmatrikel. —esmilitärcommission, *f.* a committee of officers to whom the military affairs of a confederacy are referred. —esmitglied, *n.* V. —esglied. —espflicht, *f.* a duty incumbent upon every member of a confederacy. —espflichtmäßig, *adj.* and *adv.* conformable to such duty. —espräsidialgesandte, *m.* the president of the German diet [which is always the deputy of Austria]. —espräsidialgesandtschaft, *f.* the embassy of that member of the German confederacy (Austria), to whom the presidency of the diet is conferred. —espräsidium, *n.* presidentship of the diet. —esrecht, *n.* the federal laws. —esregierung, *f.* the government of a confederacy, or of a state which is a member of a confederacy. —esschiedsgericht, *n.* V. Austrägalgericht. —esstaat, *m.* a state which is a member of a confederacy. —esstadt, *f.* [formerly] a hanse town, [now] a town forming part of the Deutsche Bund or German confederate states; also, the town where the Deutsche Bundesversammlung or the German diet is sitting. —estag, *m.* 1) the day on which confederates meet. 2) the meeting of confederates. Der Deutsche —estag, the German diet [at Frankfort O. M.]. —estagsausschuß, *m.* a committee of the deputies who represent the German diet. —estagsbeschluß, *m.* V. —esbeschluß. —estagscommission, *f.* V. —estagsausschuß. —estagsferien, *pl.* the vacations of the German diet. —estagsgesandte, *m.* one of the 17 deputies who represent the members of the German confederacy at the diet. —estagsgesandtschaft, *f.* one of the 17 embassies forming the German diet. —estagsordnung, *f.* the rules for the transaction of business at the German diet. —estagsprotocoll, *n.* record of the sessions of the German diet. —estagssitzung, *f.* the session or sitting of the German diet. —estruppen, *pl.* the troops of a confederacy, federal troops. —esverein, *m.* a league. —esverfassung, *f.* the constitution of a confederacy. —esverfassungsmäßig, *adj.* and *adv* conformable to such a constitution. —esverhandlungen, *pl.* the transactions of a diet. —esversammlung, *f.* V. —estag. —esvertrag, *m.* federal pact. —esverwandt, *adj.* and *adv.* [engaged in a confederacy] allied, confederate. Der —esverwandte, an ally, a confederate; die —esverwandten, the confederates. —esverwandtschaft, *f.* confederacy. —eszweck, *m.* the object of a confederacy. —frei, *adj.* and *adv.* having two strings for each hammer [said of a piano-forte]. —haube, *f.* a sort of head-dress for females. ‡—schuh, *m.* a sort of high shoe. —ständer, *m.* [in carpentry] a scantling in a partition. —stege, *pl.* [with printers] gutter-sticks.

2. Bund, *n.* [-es, *pl.* -e] [from the same root as 1. Bund] 1) [a number of things tied together] a bunch. Ein — Schlüssel [Schlüssel—], a bunch of keys; ein — Stroh, a truss of straw; vier — Stroh, four bundles of straw; ein — Heu, a bundle of hay, a bottle; ein — Pfeile, a sheaf of arrows. 2) a fixed number of things tied together. Ein — Fensterglas, six panes of glass; ein — Garn, 18000 threads; ein — Hüsing, [in seamen's language] a skein of housing, or houseline; ein — Messingdraht, a bundle of brass wire; ein — Stockfische, a couple of salt-fish.

Bund-axt, *f.* [with carpenters] a sort of axe or a strong iron in the form of a joint hook. —blume, *f.* [a plant] bellium. —futter, *n.* straw as fodder for cattle in winter. —holz, *n.* fagots. —seide, *f.* silk in hanks. —weise, *adv.* by bunches or bundles.

Bündchen, *n.* [-s, *pl.* -] [diminut. of Bund] a small bunch or bundle, a small pack.

Bündel, *n.* and *m.* [-s, *pl.* -] 1) a little bundle or parcel, a fardel, a small pack. Ein — Heu, a bundle of hay; ein — Stroh, a wisp of straw; ein Reise—, a traveller's bundle. 2) a fixed quantity of things of the same kind. Ein — Felle, [with tawers] the number of twelve skins; ein — gerauften Flachses, a handful of pulled flax. 3) the intestines of a fish, especially of a carp.

Bündel-stahl, *m.* [in commerce] fagot-steel. —weise, *adv.* in or by little bundles or parcels.

Bündeln, [unusual] *v. tr.* to make up in bundles, to fardel. Kleider —, to bundle up clothes.

‖Bündig, *adj.* and *adv.* 1) [in carpentry] jointed [said of two pieces of wood, when they form a straight line]. 2) *Fig.* *a*) binding, valid. Ein —er Beweis, a convincing proof; ein —er Schluß, a conclusive argument. *b*) comprehensive, comprehending much in few words, concise. Eine —e Schreibart, a concise style; eine —e Rede, a concise speech; eine —e Kürze, solidity and conciseness.

Bündigkeit, *f.* 1) validity, solidity. 2) conciseness.

Bündner, *m.* [-s, *pl.* -] 1) V. Bundesgenoß. 2) [an inhabitant of the Eastern Swiss Alps] a Grison.

Bündniß, *n.* [-sses, *pl.*-sse] [the treaty, league, or compact, which is the instrument of confederacy] alliance.

‖**Bünge**, *f.* [*pl.* -n] [probably allied to the Sw. *bunga*, *to beat*] 1) a drum, or kettle-drum. 2) a basket for catching fish, [local] a kipe. 3) a bundle or bunch.

Bünge, *f.* [in mining] V. Pinge.

Búngel, *m.* [-s] [in seamen's lang.] goose-wing. Einen — von der Fock machen, to make a goose-wing of the fore-sail [in order to send before the wind].

‖**Búngeln**, *v. tr.* V. Bungen.

‖**Búngen**, [V. Bunge] I. *v. tr.* to drum. II. *v. intr.* to hold to by cleaving to the surface, to stick, to adhere.

Búngenblut, *n.* [-es] a distemper in cattle.

Búngensucht, *f.* **Búngenwasser**, *n.* V. Wassersucht.

Búnkenstahl, *m.* [-es] Swedish steel in tubs.

Búnt, *adj.* and *adv.* [the derivation is uncertain; it is supposed very improbably to come from *mus ponticus*; many suppose it to be allied to the L. *punctus*] 1) [having divers colours] party-coloured, gay. —e Federn, party-coloured plumes; eine —e Blume, a party-coloured flower; —er Marmor, variegated marble; die —e Jacke, pied-coat; die —e Karte, [at cards] a court-card, coat-card; —er Druck, coloured impression. *Fig.* *a*) consisting of various kinds or different things, mixed. Eine —e Reihe, a checkered line. *b*) confused, blended, extravagant. Er macht es ein wenig —, he goes a little too far, he is rather an extravagant person; hier ging es — zu, there was a great bustle and uproar; in diesem Hause geht es — über Eck, every thing is at sixes and sevens in this house. 2) [with dyers as well as in familiar language] every colour besides white and black. Ein —es Kleid anhaben, to have a coloured dress on [as opposed to a white or black one]. 3) [among weavers] flowered; [with some other mechanics] concave br convex.

Bunt-aal, *m.* the sea-serpent. —**bleierz**, *n.* phosphate of lead, green and brown lead-ore. —**druck**, *m.* [with printers] decorative printing. —**farbig**, *adj.* and *adv.* party-coloured, variegated, coloured. —**flügel**, *m.* [a bird] sea-loom. —**fleckig**, —**gefleckt**, *adj.* and *adv.* spotted, pied. —**fuß**, *m.* a species of spider [aranea lævipes]. —**gesprenkelt**, *adj.* and *adv.* speckled. —**gras**, *n.* a sort of reed, canary-grass. —**kupfererz**, *n.* variegated copper-ore, purple copper. —**schekig**, *adj.* and *adv.* piebald. *Fig.* *promiscuous. Die Gesellschaft war ziemlich —scheckig, the company was rather mixed. —**schwänzel**, *m.* the fishing-hawk. —**specht**, *m.* great spotted woodpecker. —**streifig**, *adj.* and *adv.* having stripes of different colours, striped. —**wenzel**, *m.* a species of robin red-breast in America.

‖**Búnt**, *n.* [-es] [V. Bunt, *adj.*] V. Rauchwerk.

Bunt-futterer, —**macher**, —**werker**, *m.* a furrier. —**werk**, *n.* V. Rauchwerk.

Búnzelhammer, *m.* [-s, *pl.* -hämmer] [Bunzel is allied to the Fr. *poinçon*, and to the Ital. *punzello*] [with some workers in metal] a sort of hammer used in forming bosses or protuberances.

Búnzeln, *v. tr.* [allied to the Fr. *poinçon*, and to the Ital. *punzello*] to form bosses or protuberances on tin-plate or iron-plate by means of a puncheon.

Búnzen, **Búnzel**, *m.* [-s, *pl.* -] [V. Bunzeln] [with some workers in metal] a puncheon.

Búnzenbüchse, *f.* [*pl.* -n] [with some workers in metal] a case for puncheons.

Búnzzeug, *n.* [-es] [with some workers in metal] the tools employed in forming bosses or protuberances on tin-plate or iron-plate.

***Burat**, *m.* [-s] a kind of woollen stuff.

Bürde, *f.* [*pl.* -n] [from bären, baren = *to bear*, or *carry*] 1) a burden, a load [in a proper as well as in a figurative sense]. Eine — Holz, a load of wood; eine schwere —, a heavy load; dieses Volk erliegt fast unter Abgaben und andern —n, this people is almost oppressed with taxes and other charges; Einem eine schwere — auflegen, to lay on any one a heavy load, to burden any one with a load; des Lebens —n mit Geduld tragen, to bear the burdens of life with patience; eine — erleichtern, to alleviate a burden. *Prov.* Würden sind —n, honours are chargeable. 2) [sometimes for a birth] burden. ‖3) V. Bündel.
Syn. Bürde, Last. Eine Bürde is a burden borne by some living power. Therefore, only that is so called, which is borne by animals, but more especially by men. Any heavy weight, by whatever body it may be borne or supported is called eine Last. We should not say, that a wagon breaks down under its Bürde, but under its Last. Thus, therefore, as Bürde signifies properly only a load borne by men, so in a moral sense it signifies a burden which is voluntarily undertaken.

Bürdestahl, *m.* a sort of steel in bars.

Bürden, *v. tr.* to load, to lay on or impose as a burden, to charge any thing upon a person. *Fig.* Einem etwas auf den Hals —, to burden any one with any thing oppressive; bürde dir nicht mehr auf, als du tragen kannst, burden not thyself above thy power.

***Búreau**, [pronounce: Büro] *n.* [-s, *pl.* -s, or, with some, -x] 1) a chest of drawers for keeping papers, a bureau. 2) an office. Das — eines Advokaten, a lawyer's office; often used in compositions, as: Post —, post-office &c.

Búrg, *f.* [*pl.* -en] [Gr. *πύργος*, from bergen] 1) a fortified place, a strong-hold, as in Wagen—, a fortification or bulwark, formed by the waggons and carriages of an army; die — des Biebers, [with hunters] the lodge of a beaver. 2) anciently a town; in the middle ages, a burg, borough; [also the house or mansion of a prince or nobleman, fortified for defence against an enemy, situated on a hill] a castle. *Fig.* a place of security, or a thing which gives security. Herr, mein Fels, meine —, [in Script.] the Lord is my rock, and my fortress. 3) now sometimes for the house of a nobleman or prince. Die kaiserliche — in Wien, the Castle of the Emperor at Vienna.

Burg-bann, *m.* 1) the precincts of a castle. 2) the jurisdiction belonging to a castle. —**bewohner**, *m.* the inhabitant of a castle. —**dienst**, *m* services rendered by the vassals in defending, or by the subjects in fortifying, a castle. —**ding**, *n.* [in the middle-ages] castle-court. —**flecken**, *m.* burg, borough. —**frau**, *f.* the lady of the castle. —**freiheit**, *f.* the jurisdiction of the castle. —**friede**, *m.* 1) a sort of fence or fortification. 2) a castle intended for the peace and security of the neighbourhood. 3) sometimes the jurisdiction of a castle. 4) a compact between the owners of castles. 5) the public and established security enjoyed by royal and princely castles. 6) the peace or public tranquillity which is guarantied by the laws. —**gerechtigkeit**, *f.* the right of owning a castle. —**gericht**, *n.* a castle-court. —**gesessen**, *adj.* and *adv.* owning a castle. —**graben**, *m.* the ditch, that rounds a castle, a moat. —**graf**, *m.* 1) a governour or constable of a castle, a castellan. 2) a burgrave. 3) a sort of magistrate. —**gräflich**, *adj.* and *adv.* belonging or relating to a castellan or burgrave. —**grafschaft**, *f.* 1) castellany. 2) the dignity of a castellan or burgrave. —**grafthum**, *n.* castellany. —**haken**, *m.* [in seamen's lang.] dovetails. —**halde**, *f.* a hill or declivity, on which formerly stood a castle. —**hauptmann**, *m.* the captain of a castle, a castellan. —**herr**, *m.* the lord or owner of a castle. —**lehen**, *n.* 1) a castle and the extent of its land and jurisdiction held of a prince or nobleman. 2) a castle in trust, granted by a prince or lord, to be held by the grantee on condition of defending the castle. —**mann**, *m.* 1) the owner of a castle. 2) a castellan or burgrave. 3) a vassal of the castle or a soldier belonging to the castle. —**mannschaft**, *f.* castellany. —**meister**, *m.* V. —mann. —**pfaff**, *m.* the chaplain to the castle. —**richter**, *m.* the judge of the castle. —**saal**, *m.* the hall of a castle. —**saß**, *m.* one subject to the jurisdiction of the castle. —**sitz**, *m.* 1) the residence in a castle as a castellan. 2) the castle itself, which is the residence of a lord. —**stall**, *m.* V. —halde. —**thor**, *n.* castle-gate. —**thurm**, *m.* keep. —**trümmer**, *pl.* the ruins of a castle. —**verließ**, *n.* an underground gaol of a castle, a dungeon, keep. —**vogt**, *m.* 1) anciently = a castellan. 2) the steward or bailiff of a castle. —**vogtei**, *f.* 1) castellany. 2) the dignity, office, or jurisdiction of a —vogt. —**wache**, *f.* the guard of the castle. —**warte**, *f.* a watch-tower.

Bürge, *m.* [-n, *pl.* -n] [probably from borgen] a surety, a bondsman, a bail. Wer für einen Andern — wird, der wird Schaden haben, [in Script.] he that is surety for a stranger, shall smart for it; einen —n stellen, to give security; ich bin Ihnen — dafür, I am your guarantee for it.

Bürgelkraut, *n.* V. Burzelkraut.

Búrgemeister, *m.* [-s, *pl.* -] V. Bürgermeister.

Bürgen, *v. intr.* [V. Bürge] to become surety, to be surety, to guaranty. Er bürgt mir dafür, he answers me for it; ich bürge dafür, daß es gut ist, I warrant it good; ich getraue mir, dafür zu —, I'll dare to guaranty for it; ich kann dafür nicht —, I cannot answer for it; das Parlament bürgte dem Könige hinlänglich dafür, daß &c., the parliament gave the king sufficient guarantee, that &c.

Bürger, *m.* [-s, *pl.* -] [from Burg] 1) an inhabitant of a borough, town or city, who enjoys the freedom and privileges of the borough, town or city in which he resides, a burgher, a burgess, a citizen. Die — von London, the citizens of London; der — einer Stadt, the freeman of a town; — werden, to get the freedom of a city; zum — aufnehmen, to make a citizen, to citizenize. 2) a dweller in any city or town [as opposed to country people]. 3) one of the commons or third state; one under the degree of nobility, a commoner; any member of civil society [der Staats—]. *Fig.* every member of human society, man, as an inhabitant of the earth or world. Ein Welt—, a citizen of the world, a cosmopolite.

Bürger-adel, *m.* [anciently] 1) the dignity of the patricians of an imperial city. 2) the nobility or the patricians of an imperial city. —**ausschuß**, *m.* common-council. —**buch**, *n.* a book or roll in which the names of the citizens are entered. —**eid**, *m.* citizen's oath. —**fest**, *n.* a city feast. —**frau**, —**sfrau**, *f.* the wife of a citizen or burgher, a city woman. —**freund**, *m.* a friend of citizens, [in general] a friend of the people. —**freund-**

lich, *adj.* and *adv.* friendly to the people. —gasse, *f.* —gabholz, *n.* a sufficiency of wood for fuel, house-bote, fire-bote. —gehorsam, *m.* a prison for citizens. —geld, *n.* money paid for the freedom of a city. —gemeinde, —gemeine, *f.* community, commonwealth. —gerechtsame, *f.* the rights and privileges of citizens. —glocke, *f.* a bell used to notify the time of meeting of an assembly of citizens. —hauptmann, *m.* a captain of the city-militia-men, a trainband-captain. —haus, *n.* 1) the house of a citizen or mechanic. 2) *Fig.* the family of a citizen. —kranz, *m.* V. —krone. —krieg, *m.* civil war. —krone, *f.* [with the ancient Romans] the civic crown. —leben, *n.* civil life. —lehen, *n.* a fee held by a commoner, burgage. —mädchen, —smädchen, *n.* the daughter of a citizen or burgher, city-girl. —meister, *m.* the burgomaster; mayor. Der —meister von London, the lord mayor of London. —meisteramt, *n.* —meisterstelle, *f.* the office of a burgomaster; mayoralty. —meisterei, *f.* the house or mansion of a burgomaster or mayor. —meisterlich, *adj.* and *adv.* belonging or relating to a burgomaster. —meisterwürde, *f.* the dignity of a burgomaster; mayoralty. —pflicht, *f.* the duty of a citizen. —recht, *n.* 1) the freedom of a city, citizenship, burghership. Das —recht erlangen, erhalten, to get the freedom of a city; Einem das —recht verleihen, to citizenize any one; das —recht besitzend, citied. 2) the rights and privileges of a citizen. —reich, *adj.* and *adv.* rich in citizens. —reich, *n.* government by the people, democracy, popular government, commonwealth. —rolle, *f.* V. —buch. —schule, *f.* city-school. —sfrau, *f.* V. —frau. —sinn, *m.* civism. —sitte, *f.* the citizens' custom. —smädchen, *n.* V. —mädchen. —smann, *m.* a townsman, a tradesman, a citizen. —soldat, *m.* a city militia-man, a soldier of the national guard. —stand, *m.* 1) citizenship. 2) the collective body of citizens, the city, or the citizens and subjects of a state, the commons. —stochter, *f.* the daughter of a citizen. —stolz, *m.* citizen pride. —stube, *f.* the room in which the citizens assemble, common-hall. —tugend, *f.* the civil virtue, civism. —versammlung, *f.* a meeting of the citizens. —volk, *n.* 1) the population of a town. 2) the collective body of commoners [opposed to nobility], commonalty. 3) [in contempt] the lower classes, the plebeians. —wache, *f.* the city militia, train-bands, national guard.

Bürgerhaft, *adj.* and *adv.* becoming or suitable to a citizen.

Bürgerinn, *f.* a city woman.

Bürgerlich, *adj.* and *adv.* 1) relating to a citizen or commoner, or to the citizens and subjects of a state. Einer, der —e Nahrung treibt, tradesman; —e Rechte, Freiheiten, civil rights, civil privileges; das —e Recht, civil law; der —e Krieg, civil war, intestine war; der —e Beamte, civil officer; ein —es Amt, civil office; die —e Gesellschaft, civil society; der —e Stand, commonalty; der —e, a commoner. *Fig.* — leben, to live citizenlike; —e Sitten, simple manners; der —e Tod, [in law] civil death [as distinguished from natural death]. 2) civil = common, ordinary. Das —e Leben, civil life; der —e Tag, the civil day [in reference to civil transactions], the natural day [in distinction from the artificial day]; das —e Jahr, civil year [as distinguished from the natural year]; die —e Baukunst, civil architecture [in contradistinction to military and naval architecture].

Bürgerschaft, *f.* 1) the collective body of citizens, the freemen or burgesses, community. 2) the inhabitants of a city, the city.

Bürgschaft, *f.* 1) the state of being surety, the obligation of a person to answer for another, suretiship. Unter seiner —, under his guaranty. 2) the security given for another, also the person or persons giving bail, a bail, a surety, a bondsman. Er leistete — für ihn, he became surety for him; eine unsichere —, a floating security.

Bürgschafts-fähig, *adj.* bailable. —sicherheit, *f.* the security afforded by a bail. —schein, *m.* a bond, bail-bond.

Burgúnd, *n.* [-s] Bourgogne, Burgundy [in France].

Burgúnder, *m.* [-s, *pl.* -] 1) a native of Burgundy; Burgundian. 2) [wine of the province of Burgundy] Burgundy. 3) a sort of vine [Burgunderrebe].

Burgunder-harz, —pech, *n.* Burgundy pitch. —rebe, *f.* V. — 3). —wein, *m.* V. — 2).

Burgúndisch, *adj.* and *adv.* Burgundian.

***Burlésk**, *adj.* and *adv.* burlesque, jocular. Eine —e Darstellung, a ludicrous representation.

Búrsche, *m.* [-n, *pl.* -n] [probably from bären [ge-bären] = erzeugen, and allied to the Lat. *puer, por,* Gr. παῖς, Lacedæm. ποῖρ] 1) [a companion, an associate] fellow; [especially in students' cant] a student at the university. Ein Jung—, a student in the second year of his university-life; ein Alt—, a student in the third year of his university-life; ein alter or ‡bemooster —, an old or veteran student, a student of a long standing. 2) a boy, lad or youth, especially a youth bound to a master for the purpose of instruction in the knowledge of a trade or business [Lehr—], an apprentice. 3) * = [man-] servant. 4) [an appellation in praise or contempt] fellow. Ein braver, gewandter —, a clever fellow; ein unverschämter —, a saucy fellow.

Burschen-leben, *n.* a student's life [especially used to express the jovial life of young men at universities]. —sitte, *f.* [—comment as it is called in students' cant], any custom and self-exacted regulations of the students of a university.

Bürschchen, *n.* [-s, *pl.* -] *dimin.* of Bursch 2 and 4.

Bürsche, Bürsch, *f.* [*pl.* -n] [probably from the Old Scandinav. *beria*, bohren stechen] 1) the act of shooting [chiefly out of a rifle-barrel]. Auf die — gehen, [with hunters] to go a-shooting with a rifle-gun. ‖ 2) shooting. 3) the right of shooting. 4) [from the Mid. Lat. *bersa* = Park] the precincts of a chase or of a district where every one may go a-shooting.

Bürsch-bezirk, *m.* a district where every one may go a-shooting. —büchse, *f.* V. —rohr. —geld, *n.* money paid to a game-keeper for shooting a head of game. ‖—gerechtigkeit, *f.* the right of shooting. —hund, *m.* V. Schweißhund. —pulver, *n.* the finest sort of gun-powder. —rohr, *n.* [in sportsmanship] a rifle-gun, a rifle for the chase. —zeit, *f.* the time of shooting with rifle-guns.

Bürschen, *v. tr.* 1) to shoot [a hare, a partridge &c.]. 2) to shoot with a rifle.

Búrschenschaft, *f.* a certain [now forbidden] [political] association of students at some universities in Germany.

Bürste, *f.* [*pl.* -n] [from the root of Borste] 1) [an instrument for cleaning any thing of dust or dirt] a brush. Often used in compositions, as: Kleider— &c. 2) a tuft of coloured bristles, which coach-horses wear on the head as an ornament. 3) [a genus of plants] perdicium.

Bürsten-binder, *m.* a brush-maker. —gras, *n.* V. Borstengras. —käfer, *m.* [a genus of insects] anthribos. —macher, *m.* V. —binder. —pflanze, *f.* [a genus of plants] carthamus, wild or bastard saffron. —rad, *n.* a wheel set with bristles. —wurm, *m.* V. Bauchwanze.

Bürsten, *v. tr.* to brush [a hat &c.]. †*Fig* Einen —, Einem den Kopf —, to give any one a severe reprimand.

‖**Bürstling**, *m.* [-es, *pl.* -e] V. Flußbarsch.

Bürtig, *adj.* and *adv.* [unusual] for gebürtig. Used in some compound words, as: eben—, edel— &c.

Bürzel, Pürzel, *m.* [-s, *pl.* -] [from bor, the same as empor, from the verb bären = heben] 1) the short tail of some animals; [with hunters] *a*) [the tail of a fox] the brush; *b*) [the tail of a stag] the single; *c*) [the tail of a wild boar] the wreath. ‖ 2) the rump of a fowl, the croup or croop, the vent-let. 3) the rump or buttocks. 4) a short piece.

‖**Búrzelich, Purzelich**, [rather Burzelig] *adj.* and *adv.* 1) little. 2) like a tumbler.

‖**Búrzeln, Púrzeln**, *v. intr.* [u. w. (sein)] to tumble head over heels.

Burzel-baum, Purzelbaum, *m.* a summerset, somersault, somerset. Einen —baum machen, schießen, schlagen, to make a summerset. —dorn, *m.* [a genus of plants] tribulus. —kraut, *n.* garden purslain. —mann, *m.* 1) a little tumbling puppet. 2) *Fig.* ‡ a little man.

Búsch, *m.* [-es, *pl.* Büsche] [Mid. Lat. *boscus, buscus*, Fr. *bos-quet, bocage*, is probably to be derived from φύω = entstehen] 1) a wood of sm[all] growth, or consisting of underwood or brus[h]wood, a copse or coppice. *Fig.* *Lange um — gehen, to hesitate, to balance long; bei [Ei]nem auf den — klopfen, to feel any one's pul[se], to sound a person. *Prov.* Einer schlägt auf [den] —, der Andere kriegt [bekommt] den Vog[el], one beats the bush, and another catches [the] bird. *Botany.* Der brennende —, [a plant] e[ver]green thorn or mespilus. 2) a shrub, bush. [3)] a number of twigs or plants tied together, [a] tuft. Ein — Blumen, a bunch of flowers. 4) a collection of small things in a knot or [bunch]. Ein — Haare, a tuft of hair; ein — F[edern], a tuft of feathers, a plume of feathers. [Often] used in compound words, as: Feder—, [...] — &c.

Busch-affe, *m.* orang-outang. —am[eise], *f.* wood-ant. —ampfer, *m.* the wood [sor]rel, the three-leaved sorrel. —baum, *m.* [in gar]dening] a shrubby dwarf-tree. —bohne, *f.* d[warf] bean. —dorn, *m.* V. Buchsdorn. —elster, [*f.*] the great shrike. —eule, *f.* the aluco owl. [—]holz, *n.* 1) bushwood, underwood. 2) a sh[...] —hummel, *f.* a species of bee. —klaft[er], *f.* a stack of underwood. —klepper, [*m.* a] roving thief, a foot-pad, a bush-ranger. —k[ohl], *m.* V. Büschelkohl. —laube, *f.* arbour. —ma[nn], *m.* [a name which the Dutch give to the wild and [fero]cious inhabitants of Africa near the Cape of Good [Hope]] a bush-man. —maus, *f.* the rock cavy. [—]schnepfe, *f.* V. Waldschnepfe. —spinne, [*f.* the] bird-catching spider. —weide, *f.* 1) rose [wil]low. 2) V. Palmweide. —werk, *n.* a clust[er of] bushes.

Büschchen, *n.* [-s, *pl.* -] *dimin.* of Bus[ch].

Büschel, *n.* [-s, *pl.* -] [*dimin.* of Busch] [a] bunch [of hair &c.] Ein — Federn, a tuft of [feath]ers; ein — Binsen, a tuft of rushes; ei[n —] Stroh, a wisp of straw; ein — Seide, a t[uft of] silk. Often used in compound words, as: [...] — &c. 2) [in botany] fascicle.

Büschel-artig, *adj.* and *adv.* 1) li[ke a] bunch or tuft. 2) [in botany] fascicular. Eine [—]artige Wurzel, [a root of the tuberous kind with knobs collected in bundles] a fascicular root. [—]erbse, *f.* a sort of common pea. —föhre, [*f.*] the common three-leaved Virginian pine.

förmig, *adj.* and *adv.* 1) resembling a bunch or tuft. 2) [in botany] fascicular. —kirsche, *f.* V. Traubenkirsche. —kohl, *m.* the bore-cole. —weise, *adv.* in bundles or bunches. [in botany] —weise stehende Blätter, fasciculate, fasciculated or fascicled leaves.

Büschen, *v. r.* sich —, to become tufty or bushy.

Büschicht, *adj.* and *adv.* thick and spreading like a bush, bushy; arbuscular. Eine —e Ebene, a shrubby plain; ein —er Bart, a bushy beard.

Büschig, *adj.* and *adv.* full of bushes, overgrown with shrubs, bushy, arbustive. Der —e Theil eines Baumes, tuft; —e Bäume, tufty trees.

Büscht, *m.* [-es, *pl.* -e] [probably allied to Busch] [in papermills] a pack of 180 sheets inserted between felt.

Buschtfilz, *m.* felt used in papermills.

‖**Büse**, *f.* [*pl.* -n] 1) the soft hair of cats. 2) the down [on some plants].

‖**Buse-katze**, *f.* —kätzchen, *n.* a little cat, puss.

Büse, *f.* [*pl.* -n] [D. *buise*, Mid. Lat. *bussa*, *busa* &c.] buss, herring-buss.

Busen, *m.* [-s, *pl.* -] [allied to Bug &c.] 1) any crook or bend [used only in] Meer—, bay, gulf. 2) a fold, a plait. Einem Garne — geben, [in sportsmanship] to furnish a net with folds. 3) [the folds and covering of clothes about the breast] bosom. Stecke deine Hand in deinen —, [in Script.] put thy hand in thy bosom. *Fig.* Er wird die Lämmer in seinem — tragen, [in Script.] he will carry the lambs in his bosom; in seinen — greifen, to dive into one's heart; seine Geheimnisse in den — eines Freundes niederlegen, to deposit one's secrets in the bosom of a friend. 4) the bosom, breast [especially of women]. Ein voller —, a full breast; sie hat einen schönen —, she has a fine breast.

Busen-band, *n.* a riband worn on the breast. —flor, *m.* a gauze worn on the breast. —freund, *m.* bosom friend. —geschmeide, *n.* trinkets worn on the breast. —gewand, *n.* the covering or clothes about the breast. —kind, *n.* the child of one's bosom, a darling child. —krause, *f.* a ruffle, frill. —nadel, *f.* a pin commonly of gold, worn on the breast, a breast-pin or brooch. —schleier, *m.* a veil worn on the breast. —schleife, *f.* breastknot. —strauß, *m.* a nose-gay worn on the breast. —streif, *m.* 1) [a small piece of linen that shades the breast of women] tucker. 2) a ruffle, frill. —sünde, *f.* [in theology] bosom sin. —tuch, *n.* handkerchief for the neck. —wurm, *m. fig.* [rather unusual] sorrow or grief which preys on the heart.

Buslappen, *m.* [-s, *pl.* -] [in seamen's lang.] a second lining of the bow, to preserve a ship from being damaged by pieces of floating ice.

Bussaar, *m.* [-en, *pl.* -en] [probably from pusten, busen, Gr. φυσάω, blasen] the buzzard.

Buße, *f.* [*pl.* -n] [allied to baß, besser &c.] [satisfaction or reparation made by giving an equivalent for an injury, or by doing or suffering that which is received in satisfaction for an offence or injury] atonement, expiation. [in a more limited sense] *a*) [the suffering in person or property which is annexed by law or judicial decision to the commission of a crime, offence or trespass, as a punishment] penalty. Die Geld—, pecuniary penalty, a fine, an amercement. *b*) punishment of any kind. Die Kirchen—, [an ecclesiastical punishment inflicted by the church] penance; [also in compound words: Ein—, Zu—]. *c*) [in theology] the expiation of sin by penitence and amendment of life. — thun, to do penance; die Leute von Ninive thaten — nach der Predigt Jonas, [in Scripture] Ninive repented at the preaching of Jonas. *Prov.* Nicht mehr thun ist die beste —, by-gones be by-gones, and fair play for the time to come. *d*) V. Bußstück.

Buß-buch, *n.* [among the Romanists] penitential. —fällig, *adj.* and *adv.* V. Straffällig. —fertig, I. *adj.* penitent, contrite, repentant. Der —fertige, the penitent, penitentiary. II. *adv.* penitently, with repentance, or contrition for sin. —fertigkeit, *f.* penitence, penitency, contrition. —gebet, *n.* 1) the prayer of a penitent sinner. 2) fast-day's prayer. —hemd, *n.* a shirt or shift made of hair cloth. —lied, *n.* a hymn of repentance. —prediger, *m.* one who preaches repentance. —predigt, *f.* 1) a sermon which inculcates repentance, an exhortation to repent. 2) a sermon delivered on a day of prayer and repentance. —priester, *m.* penitentiary. —psalm, *m.* penitential psalm. Die sieben —psalmen, the seven penitential psalms. —richter, *m.* [seldom used] V. —priester. —seite, *f.* [with hatters] the left side of a hat. —stück, *n.* [with hatters] the remainder of a capade. —tag, *m.* a solemn day of prayer and repentance. —tagspredigt, *f.* a sermon delivered on a solemn day of prayer and repentance. —text, *m.* a text for a sermon on a day of prayer and repentance. —thräne, *f.* penitential or repentant tear. —übung, *f.* —werk, *n.* the exercise of penitence, penance.

Büßen, I. *v. tr.* 1) [formerly for] to mend, to repair [used only with hatters]. *Prov.* Die Lücken — müssen, to be one that is made use of in case of necessity. 2) to answer or make reparation or satisfaction for an offence or crime, to atone. Seine Verbrechen —, to atone for one's crimes; oder Jeder büße seine strafbare Liebe mit seinem Leben, or each atone his guilty love with life; ein Unrecht —, to expiate an injury; sie — oft für ihre Versehen mit dem Kopfe, they often pay for their mistakes with their heads; einen Schaden —, to restore a damage; der Büßende, penitent. *Prov.* Mancher muß —, was Andere verbrochen haben, one does the harm and another bears the blame. 3) [obsolete] to inflict a penalty on, to punish. 4) Seine Lust —, to satisfy one's desire. II. *v. intr.* to suffer punishment. Er hat sich den Ausschweifungen überlassen, jetzt büßet er dafür, he indulged himself in extravagances, and he now suffers for it. Die Büßung, *f.* expiation.

Büßer, *m.* [-s, *pl.* -] -inn, *f.* a person that does penance, a penitent, penitentiary. Used also in compound words, as Lücken— &c.

Büßer-kleid, *n.* the garment of a penitent. —thräne, *f.* penitential or repentant tear.

Bußhard, V. Bussaar.

Bußschießer, *pl.* [in seamen's lang.] sailors in a man of war whose duty is to coil the cable, to make cartridges and to serve the guns.

***Büste**, *f.* [*pl.* -n] [in sculpture] a bust.

‖**Buten**, *adv.* [in seamen's lang.] out.

Butluf, *m.* [-s, *pl.* -s] [in seamen's lang.] bumkin. —s-Schenkel, shrouds for the bumkins [not used in English ships].

Butskopf, V. Butzkopf.

‖**Butt**, *adj.* and *adv.* short and thick, stubby. *Fig.* weak in intellect, silly.

Butt, *m.* [-es, *pl.* -e] [a fish] V. Butte, 3).

1. **Butte**, *f.* [*pl.* -e] [allied to Butz] 1) a stubby thing, as in the word Hagebutte. 2) a little dumpy person or animal. 3) [Butte] a genus of fishes that are commonly known by the name of flat-fish; the principal species are the flounder, the plaice, the holibut, the pearl, the turbot &c.

2. **Butte, Bütte**, *f.* [*pl.* -n] [allied to the Fr. *bout-eille*, the Gr. πίθος, Faß, βυθός, Tiefe] a wooden vessel of divers sizes and various uses, as a dosser, ‖a tub, or a sort of small cask [as in the word Theerbutte].

Butten-korb, *m.* [in saltworks] a sort of basket. —ruß, *m.* soot in casks. —träger, *m.* 1) a pedlar. 2) [in vintage] one who carries away the grapes after they are gathered in a dosser, basket or wooden vessel on his back.

Buttel, *f.* [*pl.* -n] [vulgar and provinc.] a bottle.

Buttel-bier, *n.* bottle-beer, bottled beer. —rose, *f.* V. Hagebutte.

Büttel, *m.* [-s, *pl.* -] [perhaps from Bote] beadle, jailer, jackketch.

Büttelei, *f.* jail, goal.

Buttelnase, *f.* [from Butt = stumpf] [a bird] the puffin or coulterneb.

Butten, *m.* [-s] [with cloth-shearers] a sort of blunt shears.

Butter, *f.* [provinc. *m.*] [Gr. βούτυρον, Lat. *butyrum*; appears to be allied to battern = schlagen] 1) [an oily substance obtained from cream or milk by churning] butter. Frische —, fresh or new butter; gesalzene —, salt butter; Schmier—, grease butter; mit — schmieren, bestreichen, to smear with butter, to butter. *Prov.* — verdirbt keine Kost, soft fire makes sweet malt. *Fig.* *Er bestehet wie — an der Sonne, he is utterly confounded, greatly ashamed. 2) [something resembling butter] *a*) in chimistry, a name applied to various preparations, as: Spießglas—, butter of antimony, now called the sublimated muriate of antimony &c. *b*) — in den Augen, gum.

Butter-ähnlich, *adj.* and *adv.* buttery, like butter. —ampfer, *m.* V. Buchampfer. —artig, *adj.* and *adv.* resembling butter, buttery. —bämme, *f.* a slice of bread and butter, bread spread with butter. Eine geröstete —bämme, a toast and butter. —baum, *m.* shea-tree. —birne, *f.* butter-pear. Die weiße —birne, the dean's pear. —blume, *f.* [a name applied to several plants] butter-flower. 1) wood crowfoot, or goldy-locks. 2) marsh marigold. 3) garden marigold. 4) common butterwort. 5) alternate-leaved golden saxifrage. —bohrer, *m.* a sort of bore for piercing a butter-cask and taking out some butter for trial. —brezel, —prezel, *f.* butter-cracknel. —brod, *n.* 1) bread and butter. ‖2) supper. —brühe, *f.* butter-sauce. —büchse, —dose, *f.* butter-box —faß, —fäßchen, *n.* 1) butter-vat, butter-tub. 2) [butter-] churn. —fisch, *m.* the spotted blenny. —fladen, *m.* butter-cake. —fliege, *f.* butterfly. —form, *f.* butter-print, butter-stamp. —frau, *f.* butter-woman, butter-wife. —gebackne, *n.* pastry. —guß, *m.* butter-boat. —handel, *m.* the sale of butter. —händler, *m.* butterman. —hose, *f.* a butter-firkin. —kraut, *n.* 1) V. —blume 4). 2) cultivated gold of pleasure. —kringel, *f.* V. —brezel. —laden, *m.* a shop in which butter is sold by retail. —mann, *m.* butterman. —markt, *m.* a market where butter is exposed to sale. —milch, *f.* buttermilk. —milcherz, *n.* buttermilk silver, earthy corneous silver. —öl, *n.* oil of butter. —prezel, V. —brezel. —schminke, *f.* cheese-colouring. —schnitte, *f.* V. —bämme. —sieb, *n.* butter-forcer. —span, *m.* butter-trowel. —ständer, *m.* butter-tub. —stecher, *m.* butter-trowel. —stempel, *m.* churn-staff. —stolle, *f.* 1) V. —bämme. 2) a sort of pastry. —stößel, *m.* V. —stempel. —striezel, *f.* a fritter. —stulle, *f.* V. —stolle. —teig, *m.* puff-paste. —theilchen, *pl.* butter-parts. —topf, *m.* butter-pot, butter-jar, butter-crock. —tute, *f.* [a shell] butter-tub. —vogel, *m.* V. —fliege. —weck, *m.* a sort of bunn made with butter. —weich, *adj.* and *adv.* soft as butter. —wurz, *f.* [a plant] butterwort. —zopf, *m.* V. —stolle.

Butterricht, *adj.* and *adv.* buttery.

Buttern, *v. intr.* 1) to stir or agitate cream for making butter. Das —, churning. 2) to turn to butter.

Buttfisch, *m.* [-es, *pl.* -e] V. Butte, 3).

||**Buttheit**, **Buttigkeit**, *f.* 1) silliness, simplicity. 2) ill-breeding.

Buttner, *m.* [-s, *pl.* -] V. [the more usual] Böttcher.

Buttsohle, *f.* [*pl.* -n] [a fish] the sole.

Butz, *m.* [-es, *pl.* -e] **Butzen**, *m.* [-s] [from butten, butzen, putzen = schneiden, Lat. *putare*] 1) something pointed or prominent, the top, tip. Der — am Lichte, snuff. 2) [the central part of fruit] core. Der — in einem Apfel, the core of an apple; der — in einem Geschwüre, [the inner part of an ulcer or boil] core. 3) [with printers] a blot.

Butzholz, *n.* [with masons] a short piece of wood used for cleansing the trowel.

Butzig, *adj.* and *adv.* little.

Butzkopf, *m.* [-s] the sword grampus.

Bux, *m.* [-es] V. Buchs.

***Buxiren**, V. Bugsiren.

***Byssolith**, *m.* V. Strahlstein.

***Byssus**, *m.* the asbestus, byssus.

C.

C, **c**, [a consonant] c [this consonant being, in many instances, exactly the same in power as K, the orthography fluctuates in the use of the two letters, some persons writing a K where others write a C, of which the student must be aware, that he may look under K, if he does not find a word under C, and vice versa. C has also the soft pronunciation of Z before the vowels e and i or y as well as before the diphthong ä and [partly] ö, and in such cases, if the word is not found under this letter, it must be looked for under Z]. 1) *n.* C. 2) [in music, the first note of the natural major key] c, do.

C-schlüssel, *m.* [in music] C cliff, the tenor cliff, the key of C.

***Cabale**, *f.* [*pl.* -n] cabal, intrigue, secret artifices of a few men united in a close design. —n machen, schmieden, to cabal, to intrigue; der —nmacher, caballer.

***Cabane**, *f.* [*pl.* -n] 1) cabin [in a ship]. 2) hut, cabin [of the North American Indians].

***Cabbala**, *f.* [tradition, or a mysterious kind of science among Jewish rabbins, pretended to have been delivered to the ancient Jews by revelation, and transmitted by oral tradition] cabal, cabala.

***Cabbalist**, *m.* [-en, *pl.* -en] cabalist.

***Cabbalistisch**, *adj.* and *adv.* cabalistic, cabalistical.

***Cabinet**, *n.* [-es or -tes, *pl.* -e or -te] 1) cabinet. *a*) = a closet, a small room, or retired apartment. *b*) a private room, in which consultations are held. *c*) the select or secret council of a prince, cabinet-council. Das — von St. James, the cabinet of St. James; *it.* = Regierung. Das österreichische —, the Austrian Government. 2) a collection of works of art, natural productions, or curiosities.

Cabinets-befehl, *m.* an order of government. —minister, *m.* cabinet-minister, privy-minister. —prediger, *m.* a private chaplain to the sovereign. —rath, *m.* 1) a cabinet-council. 2) a privy-counsellor. —secretär, *m.* private secretary. —siegel, *n.* privy-seal. —stück, *n.* a cabinet-piece, some object of nature or art, deserving a place in a collection of curiosities &c.

***Cabotage**, *f.* [pron. as in the French] coasting-trade, cabotage.

***Cabotiren**, *v. intr.* [in seamen's lang.] to carry a coasting trade.

***Cabriole**, *f.* [*pl.* -n] V. Luftsprung.

***Cabriolet**, *n.* [-s, *pl.* -e] a cabriolet, gig.

***Cacadu**, *m.* [-'s, *pl.* -e] [a sort of parrot] the cockatoo.

***Cacao**, *m.* [-'s] [a tree] cacao, or cocoa.

Cacao-bohne, *f.* cacao-nut, or cocoa-nut, chocolate-nut. —butter, *f.* cocoa-butter. —schale, *f.* cocoa-shell. —teig, *m.* cocoa-paste.

***Cachectisch**, *adj.* and *adv.* [in medicine] cachectic, cachectical.

***Cacherie**, *f.* cachexy.

***Cacholong**, *m.* [-es] quarz-agathe cacholong.

Cäcilia, **Cäcilie**, V. Cecilia, Cecilie.

***Cacochymie**, *f.* cacochymy.

***Cacodämon**, [-s] *m.* an evil spirit, cacodemon.

***Cacophonie**, *f.* [*pl.* -en] [in music, a combination of discordant sounds] cacophony.

***Cadaver**, *m.* [-s, *pl.* -] a corpse, cadaver. V. Leichnam.

***Cadaverös**, *adj.* and *adv.* cadaverous.

***Cadenz**, *f.* [*pl.* -en] [in music, the manner of closing a song, embellishment at the close] cadence.

***Cadet**, *m.* [-(t)en, *pl.* -(t)en] 1) a younger son. 2) a military cadet.

Cadettenhaus, *n.* a military school.

***Caducität**, *f.* V. Hinfälligkeit.

***Caduk**, *adj.* V. Hinfällig.

***Caffee**, V. Kaffee &c.

***Caffetier**, [pronounce Caffetieh] *m.* [-s, *pl.* -s] the keeper of a coffee-house.

***Caftan**, *m.* [-es, *pl.* -e] caftan.

***Cajüte**, *f.* V. Kajüte.

***Calabasse**, *f.* [*pl.* -n] calabash.

Calabassebaum, *m.* calabash-tree.

***Calabrese**, *m.* [-n, *pl.* -n] **Calabrier**, *m.* [-s, *pl.* -] Calabresinn, Calabrierinn, *f.* an inhabitant of Calabria, Calabrian, Calabrese.

***Calabresisch**, **Calabrisch**, *adj.* and *adv.* belonging to or coming from Calabria, Calabrese.

***Calabrien**, *n.* [-s, *pl.* -] Calabria [a province of South-Italy].

***Calamank**, *m.* [-s] [a woolen stuff, of a fine gloss, and checkered in the warp] calamanco or calimanco.

***Calamität**, *f.* [*pl.* -en] calamity, distress.

***Calcant**, [-en, *pl.* -en] the bellows-blower.

***Calciniren**, *v. tr.* [in chimistry] to calcine, to calcinate.

Calcinir-ofen, *m.* [in glass-works] calcar. —tiegel, *m.* calcinatory.

***Calculiren**, *v. tr.* to calculate.

***Calculator**, *m.* [-s, *pl.* -en] a calculator, a controller.

***Calecut**, [in the East-Indies] Calicut, Calcutta. Der — or —ische Hahn, turkey, turkey-cock; die —ische Henne, turkey-hen.

***Caledonien**, *n.* [-s] Caledonia [the ancient name of Scotland].

***Caledonier**, *m.* [-s, *pl.* -] -inn, *f.* inhabitant of Caledonia, Caledonian.

***Caledonisch**, *adj.* and *adv.* belonging to or coming from Caledonia, Caledonian.

***Calendä** or **Calenden**, *pl.* [among the ancient Romans, the first of every month] calends. *Fig.* and *Prov.* Einen auf die griechischen — verweisen, to refer a person at the Greek calends.

***Calesche**, *f.* [*pl.* -n] a light chariot or carriage, calash.

***Calfatern**, *v. tr.* V. Kalfatern.

***Caliber**, *m.* [with others *n.*] [-s, *pl.* -] 1) [in gunnery, the bore of a gun, or the diameter of its bore] caliber. Ein Geschützstück von schwerem —, a piece of ordnance of large caliber. 2) [of goods, and * and ‡ of men] sort, kind, calibre.

***Calico**, *m.* [-'s, *pl.* -s or -e] calico [a sort of cotton stuff].

***Calligraph**, *m.* [-en, *pl.* -en] [one that writes a good or fine, elegant hand] penman.

***Calligraphie**, *f.* caligraphy, or calligraphy, penmanship.

***Calligraphisch**, *adj.* and *adv.* caligraphic.

***Callös**, *adj.* and *adv.* callous, hard, indurated.

***Callus**, *m.* callus.

***Calmank**, V. Calamank.

***Calmiren**, *v. tr.* [in medicine] to calm, to still, to quiet.

***Calmuck**, *m.* [-s] a sort of hair-cloth.

***Calomel**, *n.* [-s] [a preparation of mercury, much used in medicine] calomel.

***Calotte**, *f.* [*pl.* -n] [a little cap, especially worn by priests] calotte. [in modern language often in contempt for] priest or priesthood.

***Calumnie**, *f.* [*pl.* -en or Calumnien] [in law] calumny.

***Calumniös**, *adj.* and *adv.* [in law] calumnious, calumniatory.

***Calumniren**, *v. tr.* and *intr.* [in law] to calumniate.

***Calvinismus**, *m.* [-s] the theological tenets or doctrines of Calvin, calvinism.

***Calvinist**, *m.* [-en, *pl.* -en] a follower of Calvin, calvinist.

***Calvinistisch**, *adj.* and *adv.* calvinistic, calvinistical.

***Camaschen**, V. Gamaschen.

***Cambial-Recht**, *n.* V. Wechselrecht.

***Cambio**, *m.* [-'s] V. Wechsel.

***Cambiren**, *v. intr.* to deal in notes, or bills of exchange.

***Cambist**, *m.* [-en, *pl.* -en] a banker, cambist.

***Cambodjanuß**, *f.* [*pl.* -nüsse] Cambodia-nut.

***Cambrai**, **Cambrik**, *m.* [-s, *pl.* -s] [a species of fine white linen] cambric.

***Camee**, *f.* [*pl.* -n] cameo.

***Camelie**, *f.* [*pl.* -n] camelia [a plant, Camellia Japonica].

***Camelot**, *m.* [-s, *pl.* -s or e] [a stuff originally made of camel's hair] camlet.

***Camera obscura**, *f.* [= dunkle Kammer] [in optics] camera obscura, dark-tent, dark-chamber.

***Camerad**, *m.* [-ed, *pl.* -en] comrade, a mate, fellow or companion, an associate in occupation.

***Cameradschaft**, *f.* partnership, fellowship, society.

***Cameral**, *adj.* financial, or relating to poli

tical economy.

Cameral-sache, *f.* a business relating to finances. ||—verwalter, *m.* steward or superintendent of a domain. —wesen, *n.* finances. —wissenschaft, *f.* the science of finances.

*Cameralist, *m.* [-en, *pl.* -en] 1) a financier. 2) a student of finances.

*Camill, [a name of men] [-s] Camillus.

*Camilla, [a name of women] [-'s or Camillens] Camilla.

*Camille, *f.* V. Kamille.

*Camin, *n.* V. Kamin.

*Camisol, *n.* V. Kamisol.

*Campágne, [pronounce: Campannje] *f.* [*pl.* -n] campaign [mostly in fam. lang. amongst military men] V. also Feldzug.

*Campèscheholz, *n.* [-es, -hölzer] logwood.

*Cámpher, *m.* [-s] camphor, camphire. Mit — anmachen, mit — waschen, to camphire.

Campher-baum, *m.* camphor tree [laurus camphora L.]. —kraut, *n.* camphorata monspeliensis, stinking ground-pine. —spiritus, *f.* camphorate spirits of wine or brandy.

*Campiren, *v. intr.* to encamp. Das —, camping.

*Canaille, [pron. Canailje] *f.* [*pl.* -n] [vulgar or in contempt or outbreak of indignation] 1) rabble, mob. 2) rascalion.

*Canal, *m.* [-es, *pl.* -näle] a water course, canal. Der brittische —, the British channel.

*Cánapee, *n.* [-'s, *pl.* -s] a seat of repose, a couch, a sofa.

*Canariensekt, *m.* [-es] canary.

*Canariengras, *n.* canary-grass [phalaris canariensis L.].

*Canariensame, *m.* [-ns] canary-seed [phalaris canariensis L.].

*Canarienvogel, *m.* [-s, *pl.* -vögel] canary-bird.

*Canarisch, *adj.* and *adv.* Die —en Inseln, the Canary Islands.

*Canáster, *m.* V. Knaster.

*Candeláber, *m.* [-s, *pl.* -] a chandelier.

*Cándia, Cándien, *n.* [-s] Candia [a Greek island, the ancient Creta].

*Candidat, *m.* [-en, *pl.* -en] candidate. Ein — der Theologie, young divine.

*Cándier, *m.* [-s, *pl.* -] Candiót, *m.* [-en, *pl.* -en] Candierinn, Candiotinn, *f.* an inhabitant of Candia, Candiot.

*Candiren, *v. tr.* to candy.

*Cándiszucker, *m.* [-s] sugar-candy.

*Candít, *m.* [-s] [a mineral] pleonaste.

*Canéel, *m.* [-s] cinnamon.

*Cánnefas or Cánnavaß, *m.* [-sses] [a coarse cloth made of hemp] canvas.

*Cannelíren, *v. tr.* V. Auskehlen.

*Cannèlkohle, *f.* [*pl.* -n] cannel-, candle- or parrot-coal.

*Cannibal[e], *m.* 1) a cannibal, a man-eater, an anthropophagite. 2) [in general and fig.] a savage.

*Cannibalisch, I. *adj.* cruel, sanguinary. II. *adv.* 1) cannibally. 2) cruelly.

*Canoë, *n.* [*pl.* -n or -s] a canoe.

*Cănon, *m.* [-s, *pl.* -e or Canones] 1) [in ecclesiastical affairs, a law, or rule of doctrine or discipline] canon. 2) [in music, a composition, in which the parts follow each other] canon, a catch. 3) [with printers, a large sort of printing letter] canon. Die grobe —, great canon; die kleine —, lean canon.

*Canōne, *f.* V. Kanone.

*Canonicalien, *pl.* canonicals.

*Canonicat, *n.* [-es, *pl.* -e] canonry, canonship.

*Canōnicus, *m.* [*pl.* Canonici or Canonicusse] canon, prebendary.

*Canonie, *f.* [*pl.* -n] V. Canonicat.

*Canonisation, *f.* canonization.

*Canōnisch, *adj.* and *adv.* canonical. Die —en Bücher der heiligen Schrift, canonical books or canonical scriptures; das —e Recht, canon law; die —en Strafen, canonical punishments; das —e Leben, canonical life.

*Canonisiren, *v. tr.* to canonize.

*Canonissin, *f.* canoness.

*Canonist, *m.* [-en, *pl.* -en] one versed in or a professor of canon law, canonist.

*Canonistisch, *adj.* and *adv.* canonistic.

*Cantate, *f.* [*pl.* -n] a poem set to music, cantata.

*Cantharide, *f.* [*pl.* -n] Spanish fly. —n, *pl.* Spanish flies, cantharides.

*Cantille, [pron. Cantilje] *f.* purl.

*Cántor, *m.* [-s, *pl.* -en] the chief singer, chanter; in some parts of Germany a title given to a village-schoolmaster, who as a parish-clerk leads the singing in church.

*Canzōne, *f.* [*pl.* -n] canzonet.

*Cáp, *n.* [-s] a head-land, cape, promontory. Das — Horn, Cape Horn; das — der guten Hoffnung, or das —, the Cape of Good Hope.

Cap-stadt, *f.* Cape Town. —wein, *m.* Constantia wine, Cape wine.

*Capellan, *m.* [-es, *pl.* -e] chaplain.

*Capellanei, *f.* 1) the office or business of a chaplain, chaplainship. 2) the house of a chaplain.

1. *Capèlle, *f.* [*pl.* -n] [allied to Kufe, Lat. *cupa*] [a small cup or vessel used in refining metals] a cupel.

2. *Capèlle, *f.* [*pl.* -n] [a house for public worship] chapel. Die Haus—, domestic chapel. *Fig.* *a*) the choir of singers or musicians belonging to a chapel. *b*) a band of musicians appointed for the service of a great personage.

Capellmeister, *m.* the leader of a musical band, especially in the service of a prince or great personage.

1. *Caper, *f.* V. Kaper *f.*

2. *Caper, *m.* [-s, *pl.* -] 1) the commander of a privateer. 2) a privateer.

Caper-brief, *m.* letter of marque. —gasten, *f.* the crew of a privateer. —schiff, *n.* a privateer.

*Capereí, *f.* the occupation of privateering.

*Capern, *v. tr.* 1) to capture [a ship]. *Fig.* * and ‡ 2) to seize suddenly and cunningly.

*Capital, *n.* [-es, *pl.* -e or -ien] [from the Lat. *caput*, Haupt] a sum of money put to interest, a stock in trade, in manufactories &c., capital. — und Interessen, the principal and interest; das große imaginäre —, [in commerce] the floating capital [consisting in open credit with one's mercantile friends]; das ursprüngliche Grund—, capital stock.

*Capital, [from the Lat. *caput*, Haupt, adj. *capitalis*] I. *adj.* 1) capital, chief, principal, first in importance. 2) large, of great size. —buchstaben, capital letters. 3) punishable by loss of the head or of life. Das —verbrechen, a capital crime. II. *adv.* capitally.

*Capitäl, *n.* [-s, *pl.* -er] [the uppermost of a column, pillar or pilaster] capital, chaptrel.

*Capitälchen, *n.* [-s, *pl.* -] 1) *dimin.* of Capital. 2) *dimin.* of Capitäl.

Capitälchenschrift, *f.* [with print.] small capitals.

*Capitalist, *m.* [-en, *pl.* -en] a man of large property, a man who has a capital or stock in trade, a capitalist; [in the most extensive sense] a man living on his own private fortune.

*Capitan, *m.* [-s, *pl.* -s or -e] captain. Der — eines Kauffahrers, the master of a merchantman. V. Hauptmann.

*Capitel, *n.* [-s, *pl.* -] chapter. *a*) [a division of a book, or treatise]. Die Genesis enthält fünfzig —, Genesis contains fifty chapters. *Fig.* * Einem das — lesen, to chapter or lecture any one. *b*) [in ecclesiastical polity, a society or community of clergymen, belonging to a cathedral or collegiate church]. — halten, to hold a chapter, to assemble the canons; im — or —weise, *adj.* and *adv.* chapterly; zu einem — gehörig, in Form eines —s, capitular[ly].

Capitel-fest, *adj.* and *adv.* *fig.* —fest seyn, to be well read in the scriptures. —haus, *n.* chapter-house. —herr, *m.* [the member of a chapter] capitulary. —schluß, *m.* an act passed in a chapter. —stube, *f.* chapter-room.

*Capitōl or Capitōlium, *n.* [-s] 1) [the temple of Jupiter in Rome and a fort or castle, on the Mons capitolinus] the capitol. Zum — gehörig, capitoline. *2) [in joking] the understanding, brain.

*Capitolinisch, *adj.* capitoline. Der —e Jupiter, Jupiter capitoline.

*Capitulär, *m.* 1) [-s, *pl.* -e] a capitulary, a prebendary. 2) or Capitulare [-s, *pl.* -larien] capitular [of the ancient Frank kings].

*Capitulation, *f.* 1) capitulation. *a*) the act of capitulating or surrendering to an enemy upon stipulated terms or conditions. *b*) the treaty or instrument containing the conditions of surrender. *c*) [Wahl—] formerly in German polity, a contract which the emperor made with the electors, before he was raised to the imperial dignity. 2) a contract or agreement, a pact. Meine — ist auf sechs Jahre, [in military affairs] I am bound to six years service.

Capitulations-mäßig, *adj.* and *adv.* by capitulation or treaty, conformable to a capitulation or treaty. —widrig, *adj.* and *adv.* V. Vertragswidrig.

*Capituliren, *v. tr.* [to surrender to an enemy by treaty] to capitulate. Der Feind verlangt zu —, the enemy requests a parley.

*Capláken, *pl.* [in seamen's lang.] primage.

*Caplan, *m.* V. Capellan.

*Caplanei, *f.* V. Capellanei.

1. *Capót, *m.* [-(t)es, *pl.* -(t)e] a great coat or cloak.

2. *Capót, [pron. Capoh] *m.* [at the game of piquet] capot. *adj.* — machen, to capot. V. Matsch.

*Capriccio, *n.* [in music, a loose irregular species of composition] a capriccio.

*Caprice, [pronounce: Caprihse] *f.* [*pl.* -n] a whim, freak, or particular fancy, caprice.

*Capriciōs, *adj.* and *adv.* capricious.

*Caprification, *f.* [a method of ripening figs] caprification.

*Capriōle, *f.* [*pl.* -n] [in manege] capriole. V. Luftsprung.

*Capút, *adj.* lost, spent, undone, ruined.

*Caput Mórtuum, *n.* [in chimistry] caput mortuum.

*Capúze, *f.* [*pl.* -n] a capouchin, capuccio,

capuch, a stuff-cap or cowl. Mit einer — bekleiden, to capuch; in eine — gehüllt, capuched.

*Capuziner, *m.* [-s, *pl.* -] [monk of the order of St. Francis] a capuchin-monk. Die —, capuchins.

Capuziner-bruder or —mönch, *m.* a capuchin friar or monk. —kloſter, *n.* a capuchin convent or monastery. —predigt, *f.* a capuchin's sermon. *Fig.* ‡ a ridiculous or humorous sort of sermon.

*Carabiner, *m* [-s, *pl.* -] carabine, carbine.

*Carabinier, [pron. Carabinjeh] *m.* [-s, *pl.* -s] a carabineer.

*Carácke, *f.* [*pl.* -n] [a Portuguese vessel of burden] carack.

*Caracōle, *f.* [-n] caracole.

*Caracolīren, *v. intr.* to caracole.

*Caráffe, *f.* V. Caraffine.

Caraffenbricke, *f.* decanter-stand.

*Caraffine, *f.* [*pl.* -n] [a glass vessel or bottle used for holding wine or other liquors, for filling the drinking glasses] a decanter.

*Carambolāge, [pron. Carambolahſche] *f.* [*pl.* -n] [at billiards] the act of touching the two balls, cannon.

*Carambolīren, *v. intr.* [at billiards] to touch the two balls, to cannon.

*Carāt, *n.* V. Karat.

*Caravāne, *f.* V. Karawane.

*Caravèle, Caravèlle, *f.* [*pl.* -n] [a sort of light round small sailing vessels] a caravel, carvel.

*Carbonāde, *f.* [*pl.* -n] a small piece of meat for cooking, a cutlet, steak.

*Carbúnkel, *m.* [-s, *pl.* -] a carbuncle, anthrax.

*Cárcaſſe, *f.* 1) [the frame or main parts of a thing] carcass. 2) [the decaying remains of a bulky thing, as of a boat or ship] carcass. 3) [in gunnery] carcass.

*Cárcer, *n.* [-s, *pl.* -] the prison or place of confinement in schools and universities.

*Cardamōme, *f.* [*pl.* -n] [a plant of the genus Amomum] cardomomum.

*Cardināl, *adj.* cardinal, chief, principal. Die — Tugenden, the cardinal virtues; die — Zahlen, the cardinal numbers; die — Winde, cardinal winds.

*Cardināl, *m.* [-s, *pl.* -näle] 1) [an ecclesiastical prince in the Romish church] cardinal. 2) *Fig.* a sort of drink or beverage [compounded of white wine, oranges, sugar and spices].

Cardinal-fink, *m.* the cardinal [a bird]. —s-blume, *f.* cardinal-flower. —s-hut, *m.* a cardinal's hat. —s-würde, *f.* cardinalate, cardinalship.

*Cardinalāt, *n.* [-s, *pl.* -e] cardinalate, cardinalship, the purple.

*Cardobenedíctenkraut, *n.* [-s] [a plant] holy thistle, carlina.

*Cardūskoker, *m.* [-s] [a sea term] cartridge-box.

*Carèſſe, *f.* [*pl.* -n] [vulgar] an act of endearment, caress.

*Careſſīren, *v. tr* [vulgar] 1) to caress, to fondle, to embrace with tender affection. 2) to make love, to court [also used as an *intr.*].

*Carfiōl, *m.* [-s] cauliflower. V. Blumenkohl.

*Cargadōr, *m.* [-s, *pl.* -e] [in commerce] supercargo.

*Caricatūr, *f.* [*pl.* -en] a caricature.

*Caricaturíſt, *m.* [-en, *pl.* -en] a caricaturist.

*Cariōle, *f.* V. Carriole.

*Cariōs, *adj.* and *adv.* ulcerated as a bone, carious.

*Cárl, [-s] [name of men] Charles.

*Carlīn, V. Carolin.

*Carmelíter, *m.* [-s, *pl.* -] a carmelite.

Carmeliter-birne, *f.* carmelite. —bruder or —mönch, *m.* a carmelite friar or monk. —nonne, *f.* carmelite-nun. —waſſer, *n.* carmelite-water.

*Cármen, *n.* [-s, *pl.* Carmina] a poem, song.

*Carmeſīn, V. Carmoiſin.

*Carmīn, *m.* [-s] [a powder or pigment, used by painters in miniature, das Carminroth] carmine.

*Carminatīv, *n.* [-s, *pl.* -e] [a medicine, which tends to expel wind, or to remedy colic and flatulencies] a carminative.

*Carmoiſīn, [pron. Carmoaſihn] *n.* [-s] and *adj.* and *adv.* crimson.

*Carnatiōn, *f.* [flesh colour] carnation.

*Cárnaval, Carneval, [-s] *n.* [the feast or season of rejoicing, before Lent] carnaval, carnival.

*Carneōl, Carniōl, *m.* [-s, *pl.* -e] [a siliceous stone, a variety of chalcedony] carnelian, carneol.

*Carnieß, V. Karnieß.

*Carōbe, *f.* 1) [with goldsmiths, the 24th part of a grain] carobe. 2) V. Johannisbrod.

*Carolīn, *m.* [-s, *pl.* -en] [a gold coin, nearly equal in value to a pound sterling] carolin.

1. *Carolīna, *f.* [the criminal codex of the Emperor Charles V.] Carolina.

2. *Carolīna, [-'s or -nens] or Cároline, [-ns] [a name of women] Carolina or Caroline.

3. *Carolīna, *n.* [*pl.* -'s] [the name of two states of the North-American Union] Carolina.

*Carolīnen, *pl.* [name of certain islands of Polynesia or in the South Sea] Carolinas.

*Caróſſe, *f.* [*pl.* -n] state-coach.

*Carótte, *f.* [*pl.* -n] 1) red beet. 2) [an esculent root] carrot. 3) carrot-tobacco.

*Carouſſèl, [pron. Caruſell] *n.* [-s, *pl.* -s] an equestrian game, tilting, carousal or carrousel.

*Carrē, *n.* [-'s, *pl.* -s] V. Viereck.

*Cárreau, [pron. Caro] *n.* [-'s] [a suit of cards] diamonds. V. Eckſtein.

*Carrète, *f.* [*pl.* -n] [formerly] a sort of vehicle or carriage [now mostly used in contempt or jocosely, of an old unwieldy crazy vehicle].

*Carrière, *f.* 1) V. Laufbahn. 2) V. Schnelllauf.

*Carriōle, *f.* [*pl.* -n] Carriol, *n.* [-s, *pl.* -e] a gig, whisky.

*Carronāde, *f.* [*pl.* -n] [a sort of short field-pieces] carronade.

*Cartèl, *n.* [-s] cartel. *a*) [a writing or agreement between states, for the exchange of prisoners, or the mutual delivering up of deserters]. *b*) [a letter of defiance or challenge to single combat].

*Carthauſe, *f.* [*pl.* -n] carthusian monastery.

*Carthäuſer, *m.* [-s, *pl.* -] a carthusian, a carthusian friar. Die — betreffend, carthusian. *Fig.* *Er lebt or er führt ein Leben, wie ein —, he leads a life like a carthusian [a very secluded life].

Carthäuſer-nelke, *f.* carthusian-pink. —pulver, *n.* carthusian powder [an antimonial preparation].

*Cárton, [pron. Cartong] *m.* [-s, *pl.* -s] 1) a sheet of paste-board, or large strong paper. 2) [in painting] a cartoon. 3) [also a design coloured for working in mosaic, tapestry &c.] a cartoon. 4) a portfolio for prints and drawings.

*Cártouche, [pron. Cartuſche] *f.* 1) an edge or border for ornament. 2) [in gunnery] a small cartridge-box, cartouch.

*Caryatiden, *pl.* [in architecture] caryatides, caryates.

*Cascāde, *f.* [*pl.* -n] a waterfall, a cascade.

*Cascarílle, *f.* [*pl.* -n] [a shrub] cascarille.

*Caſel, *f.* [*pl.* -n] 1) a hood, surplice. 2) [unusual] a frock.

*Caſemátte, *f.* [*pl.* -n] [in fortification] casemate.

*Caſèrne, *f.* [*pl.* -n] barrack.

1. *Caſimīr, [-s, if used in the *pl.* -e] [a name of men] Casimir.

2. *Caſimir, *m.* [-s, *pl.* -e] [a thin twilled woolen cloth] cassimer.

*Caſino, *n.* [-'s, *pl.* -s] 1) a house of entertainment, where guests are supplied with refreshments and where men meet for conversation. 2) [a game at cards] cassino.

*Cáspiſch, *adj.* and *adv.* Caspian. Das —e Meer, Caspian sea.

*Casquét, [pron. Caskett] *n.* [-s, *pl.* -s or -e] a cask, a head-piece, a helmet.

*Cáſſa, Caſſe, *f.* [*pl.* -n] 1) chest, chiefly for holding money, money-box. 2) cash, ready money. Bei — ſeyn, to be in cash.

Caſſen-beamte, *m.* an officer of the revenue. —dieb, *m.* peculator. —diebſtahl, peculation.

*Caſſándra, [-'s or -drens] [a name of women] Cassandra, Cass.

*Caſſatiōn, *f.* cassation. Der —shof, the court of cassation [in France and in some other countries with French legal institutions]. 2) cashiering.

*Caſſāva, *f.* [*pl.* -ven] [a plant] cassavi, cassada [Jatropha L.].

*Cáſſe, V. Caſſa.

*Caſſerōle, *f.* [*pl.* -n] stew-pan.

*Cáſſia, *f.* [*pl.* -ien] [a genus of plants] cassia.

Caſſia-rinde, *f.* cassia bark. —röhre, *f.* cassia stick.

*Caſſier, [-s, *pl.* -e] Caſſirer, [-s, *pl.* -] *m.* cashier, treasurer.

*Caſſinenſtaude, *f.* [*pl.* -n] cassians, cassine, cassena.

*Caſſino, V. Caſino.

*Caſſīren, *v. tr.* 1) to cashier. 2) to annul, to vacate, to make void. Die Caſſirung, cassation.

*Caſtagnètte, [pron. Caſtanjette] *f.* [*pl.* -n] [an instrument of music, used by Spaniards, Moors and Bohemians] castanet.

*Caſtānie, V. Kaſtanie.

*Caſteien, V. Kaſteien.

*Caſtèll, *n.* [-s, *pl.* -e] 1) castle. 2) the castle of a ship. Das Vorder—, fore-castle; das große —, poop.

*Caſtellān, *m.* [-s, *pl.* -e] castellan.

*Caſtellaneí *f.* castellany.

*Caſtilianer, *m.* [-s, *pl.* -] -inn, *f.* a native or inhabitant of Castilia, Castilian.

*Caſtilianiſch, *adj.* and *adv.* Castilian.

*Caſtilien, *n.* [-s, *pl.* -] [kingdom in ancient Spain] Castilia. Die beiden — [Alt- und Neu-] the two Castiles [the provinces Old and New Castile in modern Spain]. Caſtilier, *m.* Caſtilierinn, *f.* Caſtiliſch *adj.* and *adv.* V. Caſtilianer &c.

1. *Caſtōr, *m.* [-s, *pl.* -e] castor, beaver.

Caſtorhut, *m.* a castor-hat, beaver.

2. *Cáſtor und Póllux, 1) [in astronomy a] moiety of the constellation Gemini, called also Ap[...] Castor and Pollux. 2) [in meteorology and ...]

[..stamen] Castor and Pollux, corposant.

*Castōreum, *n.* [-s] [a medicine made of the liquor contained in little bags near the beaver's groin] castoreum or castor.

*Castrāt, *m.* [-en, *pl.* -en] [a male person emasculated for the purpose of improving his voice for a singer] castrato.

*Castratiōn, *f.* castration.

*Castrīren, *v. tr.* to castrate [a man, a hog], to geld [a horse], to emasculate [a man].

*Casuālien, *pl.* casualties.

*Casualitāt, *f.* [*pl.* -en] casualty.

*Cásuar, *m.* [-s, *pl.* -e] [a fowl of the genus struthio] cassowary.

*Casuíst, *m.* [-en, *pl.* -en] casuist.

*Casuístik, *f.* casuistry.

*Casuístisch, *adj.* and *adv.* casuistical.

*Cäsūr, *f.* [-en] [a pause in verse] cæsura, cesure.

*Causalitāt, *f.* [*pl.* -en] [in philosophy] causality.

*Caustérium, Cautérium, *n.* [-s, *pl.* -rien] a cautery, cauter.

*Caústica, *pl.* [in medicine] caustics.

*Causticitāt, *f.* [*pl.* -en] causticity.

*Caústisch, *adj.* and *adv.* caustic, caustical. *Fig.* caustic. Er besitzt einen —en Witz, he has a caustic or sarcastic wit.

*Cautél, *f.* [-en] caution, provisional condition.

*Cautérium, V. Causterium.

*Cautiōn, *f.* 1) surety, security, bail. — stellen, to give bail. 2) V. Haftgeld.

*Cavalcade, [pron. Cawalcade] *f.* [*pl.* -n] a procession of persons on horseback, cavalcade.

*Cavallerie and Cávallerie, *f.* [pron. Cawallerie] cavalry, horse.

*Cavallerist and Cávallerist, [pron. Cawallerist] *m.* [-en, *pl.* -en] a horseman, cavalier, a soldier serving on horse-back, a horse-soldier, a trooper.

*Cavalier, [pron. Cawalier] *m.* [-s, *pl.* -e] 1) a knight, cavalier. 2) a man of noble birth or noble rank. *Auf —sparole, upon a gentleman's honour.

Cavaliermäßig, *adj.* cavalierlike.

*Cavalièrement, *adv.* [pron. as in the French] [in fam. lang.] 1) cavalierly, haughtily. 2) superficially, slightly.

*Cavatine, [pron. Cawatine] *f.* [*pl.* -n] [in music, a short air] cavatina.

*Cavént, *m.* [-en, *pl.* -en] [in law] a bail or surety.

*Cáviar, [pron. Kawiahr] *m.* [-s] [the roes of certain large fish, prepared and salted] caviar.

*Cavīren, *v. intr.* to warrant.

*Cayénnepfeffer, *m.* [-s] Cayenne pepper.

*Cecilia, [-'s] Cecilie, [-ns] [a name of women] *f.* Cæcilia, Cecily.

*Cedént, *m.* [-en, *pl.* -en] [in law] ceder, assigner.

*Ceder, *f.* [*pl.* -n] cedar [der Cederbaum].

Cedern-gleich, *adj.* and *adv.* cedar-like. —harz, *n.* cedria, cedrium. —holz, *n.* cedar wood. —öl, *n.* cedar oil.

*Cedern, *adj.* cedarn, cedrine.

*Cedille, [pron. Sedilje] *f.* [*pl.* -n] [in grammar, a mark which is put under a c to give it the sound of s] cedilla, cerilla.

*Cedīren, *v. tr.* to relinquish and grant, to cede [all claims to a disputed right &c.]. Bonis —, [in law] to surrender all one's property to one's creditors.

1. Celle, [a town in the kingdom of Hanover] Celle.

2. *Celle, *f.* V. Zelle.

*Cellist, [pron. either Zellist or Tschellist] *m.* [-en, *pl.* -en] violoncellist. V. Violoncellist.

*Cello, [pron. either Zello or Tschello] *n.* [*pl.* Celli] V. Violoncello.

*Celte, *m.* [-n, *pl.* -n] [one of the primitive inhabitants of the South of Europe] a Celt.

*Celtisch, *adj.* and *adv.* Celtic. Das —e, the language of the Celts, Celtic; die —e Narde, Celtic spikenard.

*Cemént, *m.* [-es, *pl.* -e] [any glutinous or other substances capable of uniting bodies in close cohesion, as mortar, glue &c.] cement.

Cementwasser, *n.* cementwater.

*Cementīren, *v. tr.* to cement. Die Cementirung, cementation.

*Cementīrer, *m.* [-s, *pl.* -] cementer.

*Cenchrit, *m.* [-en, *pl.* -en] roestone.

*Cenotáphium, *n.* [-s, *pl.* -ien] [an empty tomb erected in honour of some deceased person] a cenotaph.

*Censīren, *v. tr.* 1) to examine, to review, to censure [a man's writings]. 2) to examine all manuscripts and books before they are committed to the press, and to see that they contain nothing against the interests of the state and of morality.

*Cénsor, *m.* [-s, *pl.* -en] 1) a censor. 2) one that critically examines a new publication, and communicates his opinion upon its merits, a reviewer.

*Censūr, *f.* [*pl.* -en] 1) the act of examining all manuscripts and books before they are committed to the press, and to see that they are consistent with, or at least not hurtful to, the interests of the state and of morality. 2) [in literature, a critical examination of a new publication with remarks] review. 3) the court judging of the contents of a book. 4) license to print a book.

*Cént, *n.* [-es, *pl.* -e] a hundred. Pro — [sometimes Per —], per cent [by the hundred]; zehn Pro — [Per —], ten per cent.

*Centaúr, *m.* [-s, *pl.* -en] [in mythology, a fabulous being, supposed to be half man and half horse] a centaur.

*Centifōlie, *f.* [-n] centifolious rose.

*Céntner, *m.* [-s, *pl.* -] a hundred pounds in weight, a hundred-weight, quintal. *Fig.* —schwer, *adj.* and *adv.* excessively heavy.

*Centrāl, *adj.* and *adv.* central. —bewegung, central motion; die —kräfte, central forces; das —feuer, central fire or the [supposed] fire in the centre of the terrestrial globe; der —punkt, the centre.

*Centralisatiōn, *f.* concentration, simplification.

*Centralisīren, *v. tr.* to concentrate, to simplify.

*Centralitāt, *f.* centrality.

*Centrifugāl, *adj.* and *adv.* [tending to recede from the centre] centrifugal. Die —kraft eines Körpers, the centrifugal force of a body.

*Centripetāl, *adj.* and *adv.* [tending towards the centre] centripetal. Die —kraft, centripetal force.

*Centrīren, *v. tr.* to centre.

Centrirmaschine, *f.* [in optics] centre-lathe.

*Céntrum, *n.* [-s, *pl.* -Centra or Centren] the centre.

Centrumbohrer, *m.* centre-bit.

*Centuplīren, *v. tr.* to multiply a hundred fold, to centuple.

*Centūrie, *f.* [*pl.* -n] a hundred. *a*) century, an ancient division of the Roman citizens. *b*) a century, a company of a hundred men, the captain of which was called centurio. *c*) [a period of a hundred years] century.

*Ceraunianſinter, *m.* [-s] [a fossil] vitreous tubes.

*Ceraunít, V. Meteorstein.

*Ceremonial, *n.* [-s, *pl.* -ien] V. Ceremoniell.

*Ceremoniāl, *adj.* and *adv.* ceremonial.

*Ceremōnie, *f.* [*pl.* -n] ceremony. Der —nmeister, master of the ceremonies.

*Ceremoniéll, *n.* [-s, *pl.* -e] [external rite, or established forms or rites, including all the forms prescribed] ceremonial.

*Ceremoniōs, I. *adj.* [formal, according to the rules of civility; too observant of forms] ceremonious. II. *adv.* ceremoniously, formally.

*Cerér, *n.* [-s] Basisch flußsaures —, [in mineralogy] fluate of cerium with excess of base; neutrales flußsaures —, fluate of cerium.

*Cererít, *m.* [-s] cerium-ore, cerit.

*Céres, *f.* [in mythology, the goddess of agriculture, and the daughter of Saturn and Cybele] Ceres.

*Cerimōnie, *f.* V. Ceremonie.

*Cerin, *n.* [-s] [a fossil] cerium allanite.

Cerinstein, *m.* V. Cerit.

*Cerít, V. Cererit.

*Cérium, *n.* [-s] Oxydirtes, kieselhaltiges —, V. Cererit.

*Cèrtapartei, *f.* [in commerce, an agreement respecting the hire of a vessel and the freight] charter-party.

*Certificāt, *n.* [-es, *pl.* -e] [a declaration in writing intended to verify a fact] a certificate.

*Certificatiōn, *f.* certification.

*Certificīren, *v. tr.* to certify.

*Certīren, *v. intr.* V. Wetteifern and Streiten.

*Cervelātwurst, [pron. Serwelat—] *f.* [*pl.* -würste] brain-sausage, a sausage made of the brain of pigs.

*Cès, [in music] C flat.

*Cessiōn, *f.* [in law] assignement; [in case of bankruptcy] a voluntary surrender of a person's effects to his creditors, cession.

*Cessionār, *m.* [-s, *pl.* -e] [in law] assignee; [in case of bankruptcy] cessionary or cessionary-bankrupt.

*Cessīren, *v. intr.* [chiefly in law] to cease.

*Chabasie, *f.* Chabasin, *m.* [-s] [a fossil] chabasite.

*Chabráque, [pron. Schabrake] *f.* [*pl.* -n] V. Satteldecke.

*Chagrín, [pron. Schagrin] *m.* [-s] shagreen.

*Chaine, [pron. Schähn] *f.* [*pl.* -n] a chain [in dancing].

*Chaise, [pron. Schähse] *f.* [*pl.* -n] a carriage.

*Chaldäa, [pron. Ch as K] *n.* [-'s] [an ancient region of Asia] Chaldea.

*Chaldäer, [pron. Ch as K] *m.* [-s, *pl.* -] the Chaldean.

*Chaldäisch, [pron. Ch as K] *adj.* and *adv.* Chaldaic. Die —e Sprache, the Chaldaic tongue, the Chaldee.

*Chalkográph, [pron. Ch as K] *m.* [-en, *pl.* -en] chalcographer.

*Chalkographie, [pron. Ch as K] *f.* chalcography.

*Chalkográphisch, [pron. Ch as K] *adj.* and *adv.* relating to chalcography.

*Chalkolíth, [pron. Ch as K] *m.* [-es, *pl.* -en] [a mineral] uranmica, phosphate of uranium, micaceous uranite.

*Chálon, [pron. as in the French] *m.* [-s] [a slight woolen stuff] shalloon, shaloons.

*Chaloúpe, [pron. Schaluppe] *f.* [*pl.* -n] a sloop, shallop.

*Chalzedōn, [pron. Ch as K] *m.* [-s, *pl.* -e] [a mineral] calcedonius, common calcedony.

*Chamáde, [pron. Sch] *f.* [in war] chamade. — schlagen or blasen, to sound a parley.

*Chamäleon, [pron. Ka] *n.* [-s, *pl.* -s] [an animal of the genus lacerta or lizard] chameleon.

*Chamarríren, [pron. Scha] *v. tr.* to daub or lace over.

*Champágner, [pron. Schampannjer] *m.* [-s] [a kind of wine] champagne, champaign. Eine —bouteille [or —flasche], a champagne-bottle; ein —glas, a champagne-glass.

*Champignon, [pron. as in the French] *m.* [-s, *pl.* -s] a kind of mush-room, champinion, champignon.

Champignonsame, *m.* mushroom-spawn.

*Chān, [pron. Kahn] *m.* [-s, *pl.* -e] khan.

*Chāos, [pron. Kaos] *n.* [*gen.* — or -sses] chaos.

*Chápeau, [pron. as in the French] *m.* [-'s, *pl.* -s or -x] a male attendant, a partner.

*Charāde, [pron. Scharade] *f.* [*pl.* -n] a charade.

*Charákter, [pron. Ch as K] *m.* [-s, *pl.* -e] 1) character. *a*) = a letter, a mark or figure used to form words and communicate ideas. *b*) = a mark or figure made by stamping or impression, as on coins. *c*) the peculiar qualities, impressed by nature or habit on a person, which distinguish him from others, character. 2) title, dignity.

Charaktergold, *n.* [a mineral] graphic-tellurium, graphic-ore.

*Charakterisíren, [pron. Ch as K] *v. tr.* 1) to characterise. 2) to title, to give an honorary title.

*Charakterístisch, [pron. Ch as K] *adj.* and *adv.* characteristic, characteristical. Das Charakteristische, characteristicalness.

*Charfreitag, [pron. Ch as K] *m.* [-es, *pl.* -e] Good Friday.

*Chárge, [pron. as in the French] *f.* [*pl.* -n] 1) a burden, a load, a charge. 2) the charge of a gun. 3) [in military affairs, a signal to attack] charge. — blasen, to sound the charge. 4) an office, employ.

Charge-d'affaires, *m.* V. Geschäftsträger.

*Chargíren, [pron. Schargiren] *v. tr.* 1) to load or burden, to charge. 2) to charge, to load [a musket or a cannon]. 3) to rush on, to charge [also used *intr.*] 4) to put or lay on [implying superfluity], to charge.

*Chargírung, [pron. Schargirung] *f.* 1) entrusting. 2) charging or loading.

*Chárité, [pron.: Scharitéh] *f.* [*pl.* -en] a charitable institution, an infirmary, a hospital [a well known institution of this sort is, for instance, die Charité at Berlin].

*Charivāri, [pron. Schariwari] *n.* [-'s, *pl.* -s] mock-music.

*Chárlatan, [pron. Scharlatan] *m.* [-s, *pl.* -e] a charlatan, a quack, a mountebank, an empiric.

*Charlataneríe, [pron. Sch—] *f.* [*pl.* -en] charlatanry, quackery, wheedling, deception by fair words.

*Charlótte, [pron. Scharlotte] [-ns] [a name of women] Charlotte.

*Charmánt, [pron. Scharmant] I. *adj.* charming, pleasing in the highest degree. II. *adv.* charmingly.

*Charmíren, [pron. Scharmiren] *v. tr.* 1) to charm, to delight. 2) to ogle.

*Charníer, [pron. Scharnihr] *n.* [-s, *pl.* -e] hinge.

*Charpíe, [pron. as in the French] *f.* [linen scraped into a soft substance, and used for dressing wounds and sores] lint.

*Chárte, [pron. Karte] *f.* V. Karte.

*Chartéke, [pron. Scharteke] *f.* [*pl.* -n] a mean publication. Eine alte —, an old worm-eaten book.

*Chārwoche, [pron. Karwoche] *f.* [*pl.* -n] the week before easter, passion-week.

*Chasseúr, [pron. as in the French] *m.* [-s, *pl.* -e or -s] a kind of light armed soldier, chasseur.

*Chatúlle, [pron. Schatullje or *Schatulle] *f.* [*pl.* -n] a small box, a casket.

*Chausséé, [pron. Schosseh] *f.* [*pl.* -n] causeway, high-road, turnpike-road. V. Kunststraße.

*Chemíe, *f.* V. Chymie.

*Chémisch, I. *adj.* chimical. *a*) [pertaining to chimistry]. Eine —e Verrichtung, a chimical operation. *b*) [resulting from the operation of the principles of bodies by decomposition, combination &c.] —e Veränderungen, chimical changes. *c*) [according to the principles of chimistry] Eine —e Mischung, a chimical combination. II. *adv.* chimically.

*Chérub, *m.* [-s] [in the celestial hierarchy, spirits next in order to seraphs] cherub.

*Chérubim, *pl.* [the Hebrew plural of Cherub] cherubim.

*Chevaúx legers, [pron. as in the French] *pl.* light horse.

*Chiastolíth, *m.* [-en, *pl.* -en] [a fossil] chiastolit, macla or hollow spar.

*Chicāne, [pron. Schikahne] *f.* [*pl.* -n] chicane, shift, turn, trick, cavil.

*Chicaneúr, [pron. as in the French] *m.* [-s, *pl.* -s] a chicaner, a caviller, a sophister, an unfair disputant.

*Chicaníren, [pron. Schikaniren] *v. tr.* and *intr.* to chicane. Das Chicaniren, chicanery.

*Chiffer, Chiffre, [pron. Schiffer] *f.* [*pl.* -n] 1) [an arithmetical character] cipher. 2) [a secret or disguished manner of writing] cipher.

Chiffreschrift, *f.* cryptography.

*Chiffreúr, [pron. as in the French] *m.* [-s, *pl.* -s] cryptographer.

*Chiffríren, [pron. Schiffriren] *v. tr.* and *intr.* to cipher.

*Childrenít, *m.* [-en, *pl.* -en] [a mineral] childrenit.

*Chimǟre, *f.* [*pl.* -n] 1) [in fabulous history, a monster with three heads, that of a lion, of a goat and of a dragon, vomiting flames] chimera. 2) [in modern usage] a vain or idle fancy, chimera.

*Chimǟrisch, *adj.* and *adv.* chimerical, merely imaginary, fanciful, fantastic.

1. *China, *n.* [-s] [a great empire in Asia] China.

China-apfel, *m.* V. Apfelsine. —wurz, *f.* China-root, Chinese smilax.

2. *China [-rinde], *f.* bark, Peruvian bark, Jesuit's bark.

*Chinése, *m.* [-n, *pl.* -n] -sinn, *f.* a native of China, Chinese.

*Chinésisch, *adj.* Chinese. Das —e, the language of China, Chinese.

*Chīragra, *n.* [-s] the gout in the hand, chiragra.

*Chirománt, *m.* [-en, *pl.* -en] chiromancer.

*Chiromantíe, *f.* [divination by the hand] chiromancy.

*Chiromántisch, *adj.* chiromantic.

*Chirúrg[us], *m.* [-en, *pl.* -en] surgeon.

*Chirurgíe, *f.* surgery.

*Chirúrgisch, *adj.* surgical.

*Chíts, *m.* [a sort of cotton cloth] calico.

*Chlōr, *m.* [-s] [in chimistry] chlorin, chlorine.

Chlor-gas, *n.* chloric gas [oxymuriatic gas]. —kalk, *m.* [in chimistry] chloride of lime. —kupfer, *n.* [in mineralogy] muriate of copper. —opal, *m.* [a newly observed mineral] chloropal. —ophan, *m.* [a variety of fluor spar from Siberia] chlorophane. —säure, *f.* [in chimistry] chloric acid. —silber, *n.* muriate of silver, horn ore, corneous silver-ore, horn-silver.

*Chlorít, *m.* [-en, *pl.* -en] [a mineral of a grass green colour] chlorite. Gemeiner —, common chlorite; erdiger —, chlorite earth; blätteriger —, foliated chlorite.

Chloritschiefer, *m.* chlorite slate.

*Chlorophacít, *m.* [-en, *pl.* -en] [a rare mineral found in small nodules] chlorophite.

*Chlorōsis, *f.* [the green sickness] chlorosis.

*Chocoláte, [pron. Schokolate] *f.* chocolate.

*Cholérieus, [*pl.* -ci] Choleriker, [-s, *pl.* -] *m.* a choleric man.

*Cholérisch, *adj.* choleric, irascible, inclined to anger.

*Chondrodít, *m.* [-en, *pl.* -en] [a mineral called also brucite] chondrodite.

*Chōr, [pron., as all the words belonging to Chor, always Kohr] *m.* [-es, *pl.* Chöre] 1) [a number of singers, a company of persons singing in concert] chorus, choir, quire. 2) [the persons who are supposed to behold what passes in the acts of an opera or a tragedy] chorus [among the Greeks a chorus consisted of a number of singers and dancers]. 3) verses of a song in which the company join the singer, chorus. 4) [that part of a church appropriated for the singers, separated from the chancel and the nave] choir, quire.

Chor-altar, *m.* high or great altar. —amt, *n.* cathedral service. —dienst, *m.* choir-service. —frau, *f.* canoness. —hemd, *n.* a surplice, a clergyman's gown, an alb. —herr, *m.* canon, prebendary. —knabe, *m.* a ministrant boy. —pult, *n.* reading-desk. —regent, *m.* the leader of a quire, particularly in divine service, the precentor. —rock, *m.* cope, a sacerdotal vestment. —schüler, *m.* [a singing boy in a choir] a chorister. —stunde, *f.* canonical hour. —ton, *m.* choral tune.

*Chorāl, *m.* [-es, *pl.* Choräle] choral song, the plain, unvaried chant of churches, plain song.

Choralbuch, choral-book.

*Choralíst, *m.* [-en, *pl.* -en] choral-singer, chorister.

*Choréus, [pron. Ch as K] *m.* [in poetry, a foot of two syllables, - υ] the choreus or trochee.

*Choriámb, [pron. Ch as K] *m.* [-en, *pl.* -en] [in poetry, a foot consisting of four syllables, - υ υ -] the choriamb, choriambus.

*Choríst, [pron. Ch as K] *m.* [-en, *pl.* -en] [Chorschüler, Chorsänger] chorist, chorister.

*Chorográph, [pron. Ch as K] *m.* [-en, *pl.* -en] chorographer.

*Chorographíe, [pron. Ch as K] *f.* [the art or practice of making a map of a particular region, country or province] chorography.

*Chorographisch, [pron. Ch as K] adj. and adv. chorographical.

*Chrestomathie, [pron. Krestomathie] f. [pl. -en] a collection of passages from authors.

*Chrisam, n. [-s] [in the Romish and Greek churches, oil consecrated by the bishop, and used in the administration of baptism, confirmation, ordination, and extreme unction] chrism.

*Christ, [pron., as all the other words coming from Christ: Krist] 1) the Saviour of the world, Christ, the Anointed. Der heilige —, the holy Christ, the child Christ. 2) m. [-en, pl. -en] -inn, f. a christian. Zum —en machen, to christianize. *3) [or der heilige Christ] a present given [especially to children] on Christmas-day, a Christmas-box.

Christ-abend, m. Christmas-eve. —dorn, m. 1) Christ's-thorn. 2) smooth fruited gooseberry. 3) great American hawthorn. 4) holly. —ens-gemeinde, f. the communion of Christians. —fest, n. Christmas. —geschenk, n. Christmas-box. —kindlein, n. 1) the infant Jesus Christ. *2) Fig. a christmas-box. —messe, —mette, f. [in the Romish church, early service in the morning of Christmas] Christmas-matins. —monat, m. December. —nacht, f. the night preceding Christmas-day, Christmas-night. —orden, m. the order of Christ [in Portugal]. —tag, m. Christmas-day, Christmas. —wurz, —wurzel, f. 1) Christmas-flower, hellebore. 2) perennial or spring adonis. 3) tuberous bitter vetch. 3) the common herb christopher.

*Christel, [pron. Ch as K] [in fam. lang. abbr. for Christian and Christiana] [m. -s, f. -] Chris.

*Christenheit, [pron. Ch as K] f. christendom, christianism.

*Christenthum, [pron. Ch as K] n. [-s] the Christian religion, christianity, christianism.

*Christian, [pron. Ch as K] [-s] [a name of men] Christian.

*Christiana, [-s] Christiane, Christine, [-es] [pron. Ch as K] [a name of women] Christiana, Christian.

*Christianit, [pron. Ch as K] m. [-en, pl. -en] [a newly discovered Vesuvian mineral] christianite.

*Christlich, [pron. Ch as K] I. adj. christian, christianly. a) [pertaining to Christ, taught by him] Die —e Religion, the Christian religion, Christianism; die —en Lehren, the Christian doctrines. b) professing the Christian religion. c) [belonging to the religion of Christ] Das —e Glaubensbekenntniß, the Christian profession. II. adv. christianly, in a christian manner.

*Christoph, [pron. Ch as K] [-s] [a name of men] Christopher.

Christophs-hut, m. the common herb christopher. —kraut, n. 1) V. —hut. 2) common vetch or tare.

*Christus, [pron. Ch as K] [- or -sti] Christ.

Christuslanze, f. [a plant] water horehound.

*Chrom, [pron. Ch as K] n. [-s] [a metal] chrome. —blei, chromate of lead, red lead-spar, red lead-ore; —eisenstein, oxidulated iron; —oxid, oxide of chrome; oktaedrisches —erz, chromate of iron.

Chrom-sauer, adj. —saures Eisen = —eisenstein. —säure, f. [in chimistry] chromic acid.

*Chromatisch, [pron. Cromatisch] I. adj. 1) relating to colour, chromatic. 2) [noting a particular species of music, that proceeds by several consecutive semitones, or semitonic intervals] chromatic. Die —e Tonleiter, chromatic or semitonic scale. II. adv. chromatically.

*Chronica, [now more usual] Chronik, [pron. Ch as K] f. [pl. -en] [a historical account of facts and events disposed in the order of time] chronicle. Das erste und zweite Buch der Chronica, [two books of the Old Testament] chronicles.

Chronikschreiber, Chronist, m. a chronicler, an annalist, a historian.

*Chronisch, [pron. Ch as K] adj. chronic, chronical. —e Krankheiten, chronic diseases.

*Chronogramm, [pron. Ch as K] n. [-es, pl. -e] [an inscription in which a certain date or epoch is expressed by numeral letters] chronogram.

*Chronogrammatisch, [pron. Ch as K] adj. and adv. chronogrammatic, chronogrammatical.

*Chronogrammenschreiber, [pron. Ch as K] m. [-s, pl. -] chronogrammatist.

*Chronograph, [pron. Ch as K] m. [-en, pl. -en] chronographer. V. Chronolog.

*Chronographie, [pron. Ch as K] f. [pl. -en] chronography. V. Chronologie.

*Chronographisch, [pron. Ch as K] adj. and adv. chronographical. V. Chronologisch.

*Chronolog, [pron. Ch as K] m. [-en, pl. -en] chronologer, chronologist.

*Chronologie, [pron. Ch as K] f. [pl. -en] [the science of time] chronology.

*Chronologisch, [pron. Ch as K] adj. and adv. chronological.

*Chronometer, [pron. Ch as K] m. [-s, pl. -] [any instrument that measures or that divides time into equal portions] chronometer.

*Chronosticon, [pron. Ch as K] n. [-s, pl. -ca] V. Chronogramm.

*Chrysalis, [pron. Ch as K] f. chrysalis, aurelia. V. Puppe.

*Chrysoberyll, [pron. Ch as K] m. [-s, pl. -e] [a siliceous gem, of a dilute yellowish green colour] chrysoberyl.

*Chrysolith, [pron. Ch as K] m. [-en, pl. -en] [also vulkanischer, basaltischer or prismatischer —, a mineral, called by Haüy and Brongniart peridote, and by Jameson prismatic chrysolite] chrysolite. Orientalischer —, V. Chrysoberyll; Sächsischer —, Brazilian, or topaz.

*Chrysopal, [pron. Ch as K] m. [-s, pl. -e] V. Chrysoberyll. Unreifer —, common opal.

*Chrysopras, [pron. Ch as K] m. [-ses, pl. -se] [a mineral, a subspecies of quarz] chrysoprase.

*Churfürst, [pron. Ch as K] V. Kurfürst.

*Chymicus, [pl. -ci] [now more usual] Chymiker, [-s, pl. -] m. chimist.

*Chymie, f. chimistry.

*Chymisch, V. Chemisch.

*Chymus, m. V. Magenbrei.

*Cibebe, f. [pl. -n] Damask raisin, Cyprus raisin.

*Cicade, f. [pl. -n] balm-cricket or locust.

*Cichorie, f. [pl. -n] succory.

Cichorien-artig, adj cichoraceous. —fabrik, f. a manufactory where succory-roots are roasted and ground to powder, which in some countries is mixed with coffee. —kaffee, m. succory thus prepared and used for coffee.

*Cicero, f. [in print.] pica. Kleine —, small pica.

*Cicisbeo, m. cicisbeo.

*Cider, m. [-s] cider.

Cider-apfel, m. eleot. —brauer, m. ciderist. —essig, m. cider-vinegar.

*Cigare, [pron. Sigarre] f. [pl. -n] a cigar or segar.

Cigaren-büchse, f. cigar-box. —mundstück, n. cigar-tip, cigar-tube.

*Cimolit, m. [-en, pl. -en] [a species of clay] cimolite.

*Cinnament, Cinnamon, m. [-s] [the inner bark of a tree in the island of Ceylon] cinnamon.

*Circular, I. adj. circular. II. or —schreiben, n. circular letter or paper, a circular.

*Circulation, f. circulation. Die — des Blutes im Körper, the circulation of the blood in the body. Fig. Die — des Geldes, the circulation of money.

*Circuliren, v. intr. [to move in a circle] to circulate. Das Blut circulirt im Körper, the blood circulates in the body. Fig. Geld circulirt im Lande, money circulates in the country; eine Geschichte circulirt in der Stadt, a story circulates in town.

*Circumcisionsmesser, n. [-s, pl. -] [in surgery] phimosis-knife.

*Circumflex, m. [-es, pl -e] [in grammar, an accent serving to note or distinguish a syllable of an intermediate sound between acute and grave] circumflex.

*Circumvallationslinie, f. [pl. -n] [in fortification] line of circumvallation.

*Cirkel, V. Zirkel.

*Cis, n. [in music] C sharp.

*Cisalien, pl. clippings, clipped money.

*Cise, f. [pl. -n] minting-mill.

*Cissoide, f. [pl. -n] [in mathematics, a curve of the second order] cissoid.

*Cistenröschen, n. [-s, pl. -] the rock-rose, cistus.

*Cistercienser, m. [-s, pl. -] cistercian-monk.

*Cisterne, f. [pl. -n] cistern.

*Cistrose, V. Cistenröschen.

*Citadelle, f. [pl. -n] [a fortress or castle in or near a city] citadel.

*Citat, n. [-es, pl. -e] citation, quotation.

*Citation, f. 1) citation, quotation. 2) [in law] citation, a summons. Schriftliche —en, letters citatory.

Citationszeichen, n. sign of quotation, the inverted commas.

*Cither, V. Zither.

*Citiren, v. tr. 1) to cite, to summon. 2) to call up, to conjure up [a ghost]. 3) to cite, to quote. Eine Stelle aus der Schrift —, to cite a passage from Scripture.

*Citronat, m. or n. [-es] candied lemon-peel.

*Citrone, f. [pl. -n] citron, lemon.

Citronen-baum, m. lemon-tree, citron-tree. —brod, n. lemon-biscuit. —farbig, —gelb, adj. lemon-coloured, citrine. Der —gelbe Krystall, citrine. —holz, n. candle-wood, light-wood. —kraut, n. [a plant] balm. —muß, n. lemon-froth. —presse, f. lemon-squeezers. —ritzer, m. lemon-racer. —saft, m. lemon-juice. —schale, f. lemon-peel. —sieb, n. lemon-strainer. —stecher, m. lemon-scoop. —wasser, n. citron-water. —wein, m. wine with lemon and sugar.

*Citrulle, f. [pl. -n] water-melon, citrul.

*Civil, adj. and adv. V. Bürgerlich.

Civil-liste, f. [in modern lang., a certain sum from the public treasury appropriated to the private use of the sovereign of a country and for the maintenance of his court] civil list. —obrigkeit, f. a civil magistrate. —prozeß, m. a civil suit. —recht, n. civil-law.

*Civilisation, f. civilization.

*Civilisiren, v. tr. to civilise.

*Civilisirt, adj. civilized.

*Civilist, m. [-en, pl. -en] civilian.

*Clairét, [pron. Clärett] Clairétwein, [-s] m. claret.

*Clarin, n. [-s, pl. -en] clarion.

*Clarinétt, n. [-s, pl. -e] Clarinétte, f. [pl. -n] [a wind instrument of music] clarinet.

*Clarinettíst, m. [-en, pl. -en] a performer on the clarinet, a clarinet-player.

*Clariren, v. tr. [in commerce] to clear outward at the custom-house [a ship].

*Cláſſe, f. [pl. -n] 1) [an order or rank of persons; a number of students in a college or school, of the same standing, or pursuing the same studies] class. 2) [a scientific division or arrangement]. In —n ordnen, to class or classify.

*Classification, f. classification.

*Classificiren, v. tr. to classify [diseases, plants, animals &c.].

*Clássiker, m. [-s, pl. -] 1) [an author of the first rank] a classic, a classic author, a classic writer. Zu den römischen Classikern rechnet man Cicero, Livius u. s. w., among the Roman classics are reckoned Cicero, Livy &c. 2) [a book written by an author of the first class] classic. Ich habe in meiner Bibliothek eine vollständige Sammlung der deutschen —, I have got in my library a complete collection of the German classics.

*Clássisch, adj. and adv. classic, classical. a) [relating to ancient Greek and Roman authors of the first rank or estimation, which, in modern times, have been and still are studied as the best models of fine writing] Cicero, Virgil sind —e Schriftsteller, Cicero, Virgil are classic authors. b) [pertaining to writers of the first rank among the moderns; being of the first order] Die —e Literatur, classic learning; —e Werke, classics.

*Claúdia, [-'s] Claúdie, [-iens] [a name of women] Claudia.

*Claúdius, [a name of men] Claudius.

*Claús, [-sens] [a name of men] Nicholas, Nick.

*Claúsel, f. [pl. -n] [an article in a contract or other writing; a distinct part of a contract, will, agreement &c.; a distinct stipulation, condition, proviso &c.] a clause.

*Clausūr, f. [pl. -en] 1) claustral confinement, clausure. 2) clasps to a book. 3) a leaf doubled down in a book, a dog's ear.

*Clāves, pl. [in an organ or harpsichord] the keys or finger keys or stops.

*Claviatūr, f. [pl. -en] [in an organ or harpsichord] the keys.

*Clavicymbel, f. [pl. -n] a sort of harpsichord.

*Clavier, n. [-s, pl. -e] a clavichord, a square pianoforte.

Clavier-draht, m. music-wire. —lehrer, m. a teacher of playing on the pianoforte, pianoforte-master. —schule, f. book of instruction for playing the pianoforte, consisting of progressive exercises. —spiel, n. playing on the pianoforte. —spieler, m. pianoforte-player. —stimmer, m. pianoforte-tuner. —stunden, pl. —unterricht, m. lessons or instruction of playing on the pianoforte.

*Clāvis, f. [pl. Claves] 1) a key. 2) [in music] a key or stop of a clavichord, organ or harpsichord.

*Cleriker, m. [-s, pl. -] a clergyman [especially used of Roman catholic divines], a priest.

*Clerisei, f. the clergy.

*Cliént, m. [-en, pl. -en] -inn, f. client.

*Cliéntschaft, f. clientship.

*Cloák, f. [pl. -en] a sewer, sink, drain.

*Clúb, m. [-s, pl. -s] [a collection or assembly of men; any small private meeting of persons] club.

*Clubíst, m. [-en, pl. -en] a member of a [political] club [only used in a bad sense].

*Clystier, V. Klistier.

*Coadjūtor, m. [-s, pl. -en] a joint or coadjutant bishop, a cobishop.

*Cocárde, f. [pl. -n] a cockade.

*Cochenille, [pron. Coschenillje] f. [an insect] cochineal.

*Cócon, [pron. as in the French] m. [-s, pl. -s] [an oblong ball or case in which the silkworm involves itself, formed by threads which compose silk] cocoon.

*Cócosbaum, m. [-es, pl. -bäume] cocoa.

*Cócosnuß, f. [pl. -nüsse] cocoa, cocoa-nut.

Cocosnuß-öl, n. cocoa-nut-oil. —palme, f. cocoa-nut-tree. —seife, f. cocoa-nut-soap.

*Cōdex, m. [pl. Codices] 1) [any collection or digest of laws] code. 2) an old manuscript.

*Codicill, n. [-s, pl. -e] [a writing by way of supplement to a will] codicil.

*Codille, [pron. Codillje] n. [a term at ombre, when the game is won] codille.

*Coefficiént, m. [-en, pl. -en] [in algebra, a number or known quantity put before letters, or quantities known or unknown, and into which it is supposed to be multiplied] coefficient.

*Coeūr, [pron. as in the French] n. [one of the suits of cards] hearts.

*Cóexistenz, f. coexistence.

||Cōfent, m. [-es] light beer.

*Cóffer, V. Koffer.

*Cógnac, [pron. as in the French] m. [-s] Cognac brandy.

*Cognāten, [pron. Congnaten] pl. any male relations through the mother, cognates.

*Cognitiōn, [pron. Congnition] f. [in law] cognition.

*Cohärént, adj. and adv. coherent, cohesive.

*Cohärénz, Cohäsiōn, f. coherence, coherency, cohesion.

Cohäsionskraft, f. the power of cohesion.

*Cohibīren, v. tr. [in law] to restrain.

*Cohobīren, v. tr. [among chimists] to cohobate.

*Cōitus, m. coition, copulation.

1. *Cölestin, m. [in mineralogy, native sulphate of strontian] celestin, celestine.

2. *Cölestin, [-s] [a name of men] Celestin.

*Cölestina or Cölestine, [-s or -ns] [a name of women] Celestine.

*Cölestiner, m. [-s, pl. -] celestine. —inn, f. celestine nun.

Cölestiner-mönch, m. V. Cölestiner. —nonne, f. V. Cölestinerinn.

*Cölibāt, m. or [with some authors] n. [-es] celibacy of Catholic priests.

*Cölibri, m. [-s, pl. -s] the humming bird.

*Cōlik, V. Kolik.

*Collaborātor, m. [-s, pl. -en] V. Mitarbeiter.

*Collaterāl-Verwandte, pl. collateral relations or kinsmen, collaterals.

*Collatiōn, f. 1) [in law] the act of bestowing or conferring an estate, collation. 2) [a comparison of one copy or thing of a like kind with another] collation. 3) [a repast between full meals] collation. Eine kalte —, a cold collation.

*Collationīren, I. v. tr. to collate [a book, or manuscript]. Die Bogen —, [in printing] to collate the sheets [which is the examining of every sheet by its signature for the purpose of seeing, if they follow in order]. II. v. intr. to take a collation.

*Collationīrung, f. [in printing] the act of collating the sheets.

*Collātor, m. [-s, pl. -en] [one who collates to a benefice] collator.

*Collatūr, f. [pl. -en] [the presentation of a clergyman to a benefice] collation.

*Collé, adv. [at billiards] close. Der —ball, a close ball; der —stoß, the act of giving a close ball.

*Collectānea or Collectāneen, pl. collectaneous notes.

*Collectāneenbuch, n. [-es, pl. -bücher] a book compiled from other books, a compilation, a collection, a commonplace book.

*Collècte, f. [pl. -n] 1) a collection, or gathering of money [mostly for charitable purposes]. 2) a short comprehensive prayer, collect.

*Collecteūr, [pron. as in the French] m. [-s, pl. -e] [an officer appointed and commissioned to collect and receive customs, duties &c.] collector.

*Collectiōn, f. collection.

*Collectīren, I. v. tr. to collect, to obtain from contribution. II. v. intr. to make a short comprehensive prayer at the altar.

*Cóllectiv or Cóllectīvum, n. [-s, pl. -e or -va] [in grammar] a collective noun or name.

*Cóllectivisch, adj. and adv. collective.

*Collége, m. [-n, pl. -n] colleague, fellow, companion, partner.

*Collégia, pl. V. Collegium.

*Collegiāl, adj. collegial, collegiate. —e or Collegiatkirche, a collegiate church.

*Collegiālisch, adj. collegial.

*Collegiāt, m. [-s, pl. -e] the member of a college, a collegian, collegiate.

Collégium, [Colleg] n. [-s, pl. Collegien, or Collegia] 1) college. a) [a collection or assemblage of men, invested with certain powers, performing certain duties of a public nature]. Das Kriegs—, the college of war; das Justiz—, the college of justice; das Handels—, the college of commerce, the board of trade. b) [an edifice appropriated to the use of students, who are acquiring the languages and sciences]. 2) [in universities, a formal or methodical discourse, intended for instruction] a public lecture [on morals, on theology &c.]. Der Professor liest [ein] — über Erdmeßkunst, the professor lectures on geometry.

*Collétt, n. [-es, pl. -e] 1) the cape of a coat, a collar. Fig. Einem auf's — steigen, to have a rub at any one. 2) a riding jacket.

*Collidīren, v. intr. to collide.

*Cóllier, [pron. Colljeh] n. [-s, pl. -s] [something worn round the neck] a collar.

*Collisiōn, f. 1) a striking together of two hard bodies, collision. 2) Fig. collision = opposition, interference. Eine — der Privatvortheile, a collision of private interests; eine — der Pflichten, a collision of [opposite] duties.

*Collocatiōn, f. the collocation of the creditors in a bankrupt.

*Colludīren, v. intr. [in law] to collude, to act in concert.

*Collusiōn, f. [in law, a secret understanding between two parties] collusion.

*Collusōrisch, adj. and adv. [in law] collusive, collusory.

*Cōlon, V. Kolon.

*Coloniāl, adj. Das —system, colonial-system; —waaren, pl. colonial produce.

*Colonie, *f.* [*pl.* -en] colony.

*Coloniſt, *m.* [-en, *pl.* -en] colonist, planter.

*Colonnade, *f.* [*pl.* -n] colonnade.

*Colónne, *f.* [*pl.* -n] column. *a*) [a division of a page]. [with printers] Die gerade —, even page; die ungerade —, odd page; die —n in die Form bringen, to impose a form. *b*) [a large body of troops drawn up in order].

Colonnen-maß, *n.* scale, rule. —ſchnur, *f.* page-cord. —titel, *m.* running-title. —träger, *m.* bearer. —weiſe, *adv.* in columns.

*Colophónium, *n.* [-s] colophony [used for the bows of fiddles &c.].

*Coloquínte, *f.* [*pl.* -n] coloquintida, colocynth, or bitter-apple.

*Coloratúren, *pl.* [in music, all manner of variations, shakes &c. intended to adorn or make a song agreeable] colloratures.

*Coloriren, *v. tr.* [in painting] to colour, to illuminate.

*Coloriſt, *m.* [-en, *pl.* -en] colourist, illuminator.

*Colorít, *n.* [-s] [in painting] colouring.

*Colúmne, *f.* V. Colonne *a*).

*Colúr, *m.* [*pl.* -en] [in astronomy and geography, two great circles supposed to intersect each other at right angles in the poles of the world] colure.

*Combinatión, *f.* combination.

*Combiniren, *v. tr.* to combine.

*Comét, *m.* [-en, *pl.* -en] V. Komet.

*Cómiker, V. Komiker.

*Commandánt, *m.* [-en, *pl.* -en] a commander, the governour of a town or fortress.

*Commandántinn, *f.* commandress.

*Commandeúr, [pron. Commandöhr] *m.* [-s, *pl.* -s] 1) the commander of a regiment or any other body of troops; commanding officer. 2) V. Commenthur.

*Commandiren, *v. tr.* to command. Mit der Signalpfeife —, [in seamen's lang.] to wind a call.

*Commanditär, *m.* [-s, *pl.* -e] [in commerce] sleeping-partner.

*Commandíte, *f.* [*pl.* -n] [in commerce] partnership, wherein one lays out his money without performing any functions.

*Commándo, *n.* [-s, *pl.* - or -s] 1) [supreme power] command. Ein Offizier, der eine Brigade unter ſeinem — hat, an officer, who has a brigade under his command; die —worte, the words of command. 2) a detachment [of soldiers].

Commando-pfeife, *f.* Die —pfeife des Hochbootsmannes, [in seamen's lang.] boatswain's call or whistle. —ſtab, *m.* the staff of command.

*Comménde, *f.* [*pl.* -n] [a kind of benefice or fixed revenue, belonging to a military order, conferred on knights of merit] a commandery, or commandry.

*Cómment, [pron. like the French word *comment*] *m.* [-s] [students' cant] V. Burſchenſitte.

Commentár, *m.* [-s, *pl.* -e] [illustration of difficult and obscure passages in an author] a comment, a commentary.

*Commentátor, *m.* [-s, *pl.* -en] [one who comments] a commentator, an expositor, an annotator.

*Commenthúr, *m.* [-s, *pl.* -e] a commander of an order of knigthood.

*Commentiren, *v. tr.* V. Auslegen, Erklären.

*Commèrce [pron. Commerrß], Commèrz, [-es] *m.* 1) commerce, trade, traffick. 2) [student's cant] a convivial drinking-party.

Commerceſpiele, *pl.* games depending on skill, as whist &c. [as opposed to games that depend on hazard].

*Commèrcienrath, *m.* [-es, *pl.* -räthe] [a title] a counsellor of commerce.

*Commilitónen, *pl.* fellow-students.

*Cómmis, *m.* [-, *pl.* -] merchant's clerk.

*Commíß, used in composition denotes a furnishing by contract, as: [with soldiers] —brod, *n.* ammunition-bread. —hemden, —ſchuhe, —ſtrümpfe, *pl.* shirts, shoes, stockings furnished by contract.

*Commiſſär, *m.* [-s, *pl.* -e] a commissary.

*Commiſſariát, *n.* [-es, *pl.* -e] 1) commissariship. 2) commissariate.

*Commiſſión, *f.* 1) commission, charge, order, mandate, authority given. Waaren, Bücher &c. in — haben, to have in commission merchandises, books &c. 2) a number of persons joined in an office or trust, a commission, committee.

Commiſſions-büreau, *n.* commission-office. —gebühr, *f.* commission. —geſchäft, *n.* —handel, *m.* commission-business. —haus, *n.* —handlung, *f.* commission-house, commission-trade.

*Commiſſionär, *m.* [-s, *pl.* -e] a commissioner.

*Committént, *m.* [-en, *pl.* -en] committent.

*Commóde, *f.* [*pl.* -n] a chest of drawers.

*Cómmodor, *m.* [-s, *pl.* -e] [the officer who commands a squadron or detachment of ships, destined on a particular enterprise; also a title given by courtesy to the senior captain] commodore.

*Commúne, *f.* [*pl.* -n] V. Gemeinde.

*Communicánt, *m.* [-en, *pl.* -en] [one who communes at the Lord's table] communicant, receiver.

*Communicát, *n.* [-s, *pl.* -e] something communicated or imparted.

*Communiciren, I. *v. tr.* to communicate, to impart. II. *v. intr.* to partake of the Lord's supper, to commune, to communicate.

*Communión, *f.* the celebration of the Lord's supper, communion. Er macht heute ſeine erſte —, or geht heute zum erſten Male zur —, he is going to receive the sacrament for the first time to-day.

*Comödie, *f.* V. Komödie.

*Compáct, *adj.* and *adv.* compact, firm, close, solid, dense.

*Compagnie, [pron. Companie] *f.* [*pl.* -en] 1) any assemblage of persons, company. 2) [the soldiers united under the command of a captain] company. 3) partnership. Sie ſind in —, they are partners.

Compagniechef, *m.* captain.

*Cómpagnon, [pron. Companjohn] *m.* [-s, *pl.* -s] partner, associate.

*Cómparativ[us], *m.* [-s, *pl.* -e] [in grammar] the comparative degree of an adjective, as: heller [brighter or more bright], kleiner [smaller], feiner [finer] &c.

*Comparént, *m.* [-en, *pl.* -en] [in law] one who is present in court, appearer.

*Compariren, *v. intr.* [in law] to make one's appearance in court.

*Comparitión, *f.* [in law] a being present in court, appearance.

*Cómpaß, *m.* [-ſſes, *pl.* -ſſe] [an instrument for directing or ascertaining the course of ships at sea] compass. Der See—, mariner's compass; die —punkte vergleichen, [in seamen's lang.] to box the compass.

Compaß-häuschen, *n.* compass-box. —roſe, the card of the compass. —ſtrich, *m.* the rhumb, or point of the compass.

*Compendiáriſch, Compendiös, *adj.* and *adv.* short, contracted, compendious.

*Compéndium, *n.* [-s, *pl.* -dien] [in literature, a brief compilation or composition, containing the principal heads, or general principles of a larger work or system] compend, compendium.

*Compenſatión, *f.* compensation.

*Compenſiren, *v. tr.* to compensate.

*Competént, I. *adj.* and *adv.* qualified, fit, competent. Er iſt hierin ein —er Richter, he is a competent judge in this matter. II. *m.* competitor.

*Competénz, *f.* [*pl.* -en] legal capacity or qualifications, competence, competency.

*Compilatión, *f.* [a collection of certain parts of a book or books, into a separate book or pamphlet] a compilation.

*Compilátor, *m.* [-s, *pl.* -en] compiler, compilator.

*Compiliren, *v. tr.* to collect parts of different authors, to compile.

*Complét, *adj.* and *adv.* complete, perfect.

*Completiren, *v. tr.* V. Ergänzen.

*Complexión, *f.* [the temperament, habitude, or natural disposition of the body] complexion.

*Complicatión, *f.* complication.

*Compliciren, *adj.* and *adv.* complicated, intricate.

*Complicität, *f.* 1) complication. 2) [in law] participation in guilt.

*Complimént, *n.* [-s, *pl.* -e] 1) inclination of the head, or a bending of the body, in token of reverence, a bow. 2) an expression of civility, respect or regard, compliment. Machen Sie ihm mein —, give or present my compliments to him; mein — zu Hauſe! remember me to all at home! keine or ohne —e! no ceremony! —e machen, to stand upon ceremonies.

*Complimentiren, I. *v. tr.* to compliment, to congratulate, to wish joy. II. *v. intr.* to use ceremony or ceremonious language, to pass compliments, to compliment.

*Complót, *n.* [-tes, *pl.* -te] 1) a plot. 2) conspiracy.

*Complottiren, *v. intr.* to plot, to hatch treason, to conspire.

*Componiren, *v. tr.* 1) to form a compound, to compose. 2) [in music, to form a tune or piece of music with notes, arranging them on the stave in such a manner as, when sung or performed, to produce harmony] to compose.

*Componíſt, *m.* [-en, *pl.* -en] [one who forms tunes] a composer.

*Compoſitión, *f.* 1) [in a general sense, the act of composing, or that which is composed] composition. 2) [in literature, the act of inventing or combining ideas, clothing them with words, arranging them in order] composition. 3) [in painting, the arrangement of various figures in a picture] composition. 4) [in music, the act or art of forming tunes; or a tune, song, anthem, air, or other musical piece] composition. 5) a composition or mixture of metals.

*Cómpote, [pronounce: Compott] *f.* stewed fruit.

*Compréß, *adj.* and *adv.* close, dense, compact.

*Compréſſe, *f.* [*pl.* -n] [in surgery, a bolster of

soft linen cloth, with several folds, used to cover a plaster or dressing] a compress.

*Compressiōn, *f.* compression.

Compressionsmaschine, *f.* condensing engine.

*Comprimīren, *v. tr.* to compress [air &c.].

*Compromíß, *m.* [-sses, *pl.* -sse] [in law, a mutual promise or contract of two parties in controversy, to refer their differences to the decision of arbitrators] compromise.

Compromiß=gericht, *n.* V. Schiedsgericht. —richter, *m.* V. Schiedsrichter.

*Compromissārisch, *adj.* and *adv.* compromissorial.

*Compromittīren, I. *v. tr.* 1) to choose as an arbitrator. 2) to compromit [the honour or the safety of a person, a nation &c.]. II. *v. r.* sich —, to compromit one's self.

*Comptánt, *adv.* V. Contant.

*Cōmptoir [Comptoīr] [pron. either as in the French or Komptoahr or Kontoahr] or Kontōr, *n.* [-s, *pl.* -s or -e] 1) counting-house, counting-room. 2) merchant's or banker's office.

Comptoir=bock, *m.* counting-house stool. —buch, *n.* ledger. —diener, *m.* a merchant's or banker's clerk. —stelle, *f.* a place in a counting-house, clerkship.

*Comptonít, *m.* [a newly discovered mineral] comptonite.

*Comptoríst, *m.* [-en, *pl.* -en] [in commerce] book-keeper, clerk in a counting house.

*Comthūr, V. Commenthur.

*Concāv, *adj.* and *adv.* concave [opposed to convex]. Ein —es Glas, a concave glass.

*Concavitǟt, *f.* concavity.

*Concentratiōn, Concentrīrung, *f.* concentration.

*Concentricitǟt, *f.* the state of being concentric.

*Concentrīren, *v. tr.* 1) to concentrate [the troops in an army, rays of light into a focus &c.]. 2) to bring to a closer union.

*Concéntrisch, *adj.* and *adv.* 1) concentric. 2) concentrated.

*Concèpt, *n.* [-es, *pl.* -e] the first sketch of a subject taken in writing. *Fig.* Aus dem —e kommen, to be puzzled; Einem das — verrücken, to put any one out of his bias, to puzzle any one.

Conceptpapier, *n.* ordinary [copy] paper.

*Conceptiōn, *f.* [the act of conceiving] conception.

*Concèrt, *n.* [-es, *pl.* -e] 1) [the music of a company of singers or musicians] concert. 2) [a piece of music for a concert] concerto.

Concert=geber, *m.* one that undertakes a musical entertainment. —meistèr, *m.* 1) a manager or conductor of a musical entertainment. 2) an honorary title given by German Princes to distinguished musicians. —saal, *m.* concert-room, music-room.

*Concertánte, *n.* [in music, those parts of a piece that play throughout the whole, to distinguish them from those that play only in some parts] concertante.

*Concertīren, I. *v. intr.* [in music] to contend or emulate with the voices or instruments in the parts of refined music, so that each instrument or voice has in its turn the principal part. II. *v. tr.* to concert [measures &c.].

*Concessiōn, *f.* [the act of granting, or yielding; the thing yielded] concession.

*Conchoīde, *f.* [*pl.* -n] [the name of a curve] conchoid.

*Conchȳlien, *pl.* shells and shell-fish.

Conchyliensammlung, *f.* a collection of shells and shell-fish.

*Conchyliolōg, *m.* [-en, *pl.* -en] conchologist.

*Conchyliologīe, *f.* conchology.

*Concílium, *n.* [-s, *pl.* -lien] [an assembly of men summoned or convened for consultation, deliberation and advice, especially (in the Roman catholic church) an assembly of prelates and doctors, convened for regulating matters of doctrine and discipline in the church] council.

*Concipiént, *m.* [-en, *pl.* -en] V. Concipist.

*Concipīren, *v. tr.* to compose or draw up a rough sketch of any thing on paper, to pen.

*Concipíst, *m.* [-en, *pl.* -en] composer, penman.

*Concīs, *adj.* and *adv.* brief, short, concise [applied to language or style].

*Concisiōn, *f.* brevity in writing or speaking, conciseness.

*Conclāve, *n.* [the room in which the Cardinals of the Romish church meet in privacy, for the election of a Pope; also the assembly or meeting of the Cardinals, shut up for the election of a Pope] conclave.

*Concludīren, *v. tr.* [chiefly in law] to judge.

*Conclusiōn, *f.* conclusion.

*Conclūsum, *n.* [*pl.* -clusa] conclusion, inference.

*Concoctiōn, *f.* digestion or solution in the stomach, concoction.

*Concordánz, *f.* [*pl.* -en] 1) accordance, agreement. 2) [a dictionary, in which the principal words used in the Scriptures, are arranged alphabetically, and the book, chapter and verse in which each word occurs are noted] concordance.

*Concordāt, *n.* [-es, *pl.* -e] [in canon law, an agreement made by a Sovereign with the Pope, relative to the collation of benefices &c.] concordate.

*Concórdia, *f.* 1) [the Goddess of concord] Concordia. 2) concord, agreement between persons.

*Concretiōn, *f.* concretion.

*Concubināt, *n.* [-es] concubinage.

*Concubīne, *f.* [*pl.* -n] concubine.

*Concurrént, *m.* [-en, *pl.* -en] competitor.

*Concurrénz, *f.* [*pl.* -en] competition.

*Concurrīren, *v. intr.* 1) to concur. 2) to seek or strive for the same thing as another, to compete.

*Concúrs, *m.* [-ses, *pl.* -se] 1) [in law] a meeting or concourse of creditors, a commission in a case of bankruptcy. 2) [in law] bankruptcy. — machen, to become a bankrupt. 3) competition.

Concursmasse, *f.* the bankrupt's estate.

*Condensatiōn, *f.* condensation. Die — des Dampfes, the condensation of vapour.

*Condensātor, *m.* [-s, *pl.* -en] [a pneumatic engine, in which air may be compressed] condenser.

*Condensīren, *v. tr.* to condensate.

*Condiscípel, *m.* [-s, *pl.* -n] a school-fellow, a condisciple.

*Conditiōn, *f.* 1) condition, stipulation. 2) = Dienst. Dieser Handlungsdiener steht bei Herrn N. N. in —, that clerk is in Mr. N. N.'s service.

*Conditionèll, *adj.* and *adv.* conditional.

*Conditionīren, *v. intr.* to be in service [as a clerk in a mercantile house or a journeyman with a tradesman].

*Conditionīrt, *adj.* in a certain state or condition. Gut—e Waaren, well-conditioned goods.

*Conditor, *m.* [-s, *pl.* -s] confectionary, confectioner.

Conditorwaaren, *pl.* confectionary, sweet-meats in general.

*Conditoreí, *f.* [a place where sweet-meats and similar things are made or sold] confectionary, confectioner's shop.

*Condolénz, *f.* [*pl.* -en] condolence. Ein —brief or —schreiben, a letter of condolence.

*Condolīren, *v. intr.* to condole.

*Condonatiōn, *f.* [in law] donation.

*Cóndor, *m.* [-s, *pl.* -s] [the largest species of fowl hitherto discovered, a native of South-America] condor.

*Conducteūr, [pron. Konduktöhr] *m.* 1) a leader, a guide. 2) the conductor or guard of a diligence or stage-coach.

*Condúctor, *m.* [-s, *pl.* -en] [in electrical experiments, any body that receives and communicates electricity] conductor.

*Condúite, *f.* personal behaviour, deportment, conduct. Die —nliste, [in military affairs] a book kept in every regiment in which the conduct of the respective officers is registered.

*Confèct, *n.* [-es, *pl.* -e] sweet-meats, confectionary. —devisen, little devices in sugar.

*Conferénz, *f.* [*pl.* -en] [consultation, a meeting for consultation] conference.

*Conferīren, I. *v. intr.* [to consult together] to confer. II. *v. tr.* to confer [a title or an honour].

*Confessiōn, *f.* [a formulary in which the articles of faith are comprised] confession. Die Augsburgische —, the Augustan confession.

*Confirmánd, *m.* [-en, *pl.* -en] -inn, *f.* the person who communes for the first time at Lord's table.

*Confirmatiōn, *f.* [an ecclesiastical rite] confirmation.

*Confirmīren, *v. tr.* [to admit to the full privileges of a Christian] to confirm.

*Confiscatiōn, *f.* [in law] confiscation.

*Confiscīren, *v. tr.* [in law] to confiscate.

*Confiscīrt, *adj.* and *adv.* confiscate.

*Confitǖre, *f.* [*pl.* -n] confiture, a sweet-meat, confection, comfit.

*Conflíct, *m.* [-es, *pl.* -e] [a striking or against each other] conflict [in a proper as well as a fig. sense]. Der — der Elemente, the conflict, strife, contest of the elements.

*Conföderatiōn, *f.* confederacy.

*Conföderīrt, *adj.* and *adv.* confederate. Die Conföderirten, confederates, allies.

*Confórm, *adj.* and *adv.* conform, conformable.

*Conformatiōn, *f.* conformation.

*Conformīren, *v. r.* sich —, [to comply with, yield] to conform.

*Conformíst, *m.* [-en, *pl.* -en] [one who complies with the worship of the church of England or established church] a conformist.

*Conformitǟt, *f.* [*pl.* -en] conformity.

*Confrāter, *m.* [-s, *pl.* -] [a member of a society] brother.

*Confraternitǟt, *f.* confraternity.

*Confrontatiōn, *f.* [in law] confrontation.

*Confrontīren, *v. tr.* [to bring in the presence, as an accused person and a witness, in court, for examination and discovery of the truth] to confront. Die Zeugen mit dem Angeklagten —, to confront the witnesses with the accused.

*Confus, *adj.* and *adv.* confused, disconcerted.

*Confusion, *f.* confusion, agitation, perturbation.

*Congestion, *f.* [an accumulation of blood in a part] congestion.

*Congregation, *f.* [an assembly of persons, and more especially, an assembly of persons met for the worship of God, and for religious instruction] congregation.

*Congreß, *m.* [-sses, *pl.* -sse] a meeting of individuals, a congress. Der Wiener —, the congress of Vienna; der — in den or der Vereinigten Staaten, the congress of the United States.

*Congruént, *adj.* and *adv.* congruent, agreeing, correspondent. [in geometry] —e Linien, congruent lines [which when laid over one another, exactly correspond].

*Congruiren, *v. intr.* to be in congruity.

*Conisch, V. Konisch.

*Conjectūr, *f.* [*pl.* -en] conjecture.

*Conjugatiōn, *f.* [in grammar] conjugation.

*Conjugīren, *v. tr.* [in grammar] to conjugate.

*Conjunctiōn, *f.* 1) [in astronomy, the meeting of two or more stars or planets in the same degree of the zodiac] conjunction. 2) [in grammar] conjunction.

*Conjunctūr, *f.* [*pl.* -en] [combination of many circumstances and causes] conjuncture.

*Conjuratiōn, *f.* V. Verschwörung.

*Connivénz, *f.* [*pl.* -en] connivance.

*Connossemént, *n.* [-s, *pl.* -e] [in commerce] bill of lading.

*Cónrad, Conradin, [-s] [a name of men] Conrad.

*Cónrector, *m.* [-s, *pl.* -en] the codirector of a Latin school.

*Conscribīren, *v. tr.* to enrol. Der Conscribirte, an enrolled soldier, a conscript. Die Conscription, *f.* conscription.

*Consecratiōn, *f.* consecration.

*Consecrīren, *v. tr.* to consecrate.

*Cōnseil, [pron. as in the French] *n.* [-s, *pl.* -s] council.

*Conservationsbrille, *f.* [*pl.* -n] spectacles for the conservation of the sight.

*Consérve, *f.* [*pl.* -n] [a sweet-meat made of the inspissated juice of fruit, boiled with sugar] conserve.

*Conservīren, *v. tr.* to conserve, to preserve from loss, waste, decay.

*Consignatiōn, *f.* [in commerce, the thing consigned] consignment.

*Consignīren, *v. tr.* to consign.

*Consilīren, *v. tr.* [at the German universities] to dismiss from the university, for disorderly conduct or offences against the rules and regulations of the college, to rusticate.

*Consilium, *n.* [-s, *pl.* -lia or -lien] 1) council. 2) consultation, deliberation. 3) [at the German universities] Das — abeundi, the dismission [of a student]. V. Consiliiren. Einem das — abeundi ertheilen or geben, V. Consiliiren.

*Consistént, *adj.* and *adv.* consistent, compatible, congruous.

*Consisténz, *f.* consistence, consistency.

*Consistoriālrath, *m.* [-es, *pl.* -räthe] a counsellor of the consistory.

*Consistōrium, *m.* [-s, *pl.* -rien] [an assembly or council of clerical ministers] consistory.

*Cónsole, *f.* 1) V. Kragstein or Tragstein, 2) a table standing between windows, pier-table.

*Consonánt, *m.* [-en, *pl.* -en] [in grammar] a consonant.

*Consonánz, *f.* [in music, an accord of sounds which produces an agreeable sensation in the ear] consonance.

*Consonīren, *v. intr.* [in music] to be consonant.

*Consórten, *pl.* [in law] associates, accomplices.

*Cónstabler, *m.* [-s, *pl.* -] [in seamen's lang.] gunner. ||[in general] an artilleryman, a gunner.

Constablerkammer, *f.* [in ships] gun-room.

*Constellatiōn, *f.* [in astrology] constellation.

*Constituīren, *v. tr.* 1) to constitute = to set, to fix. 2) to constitute = to appoint. Die constituirten Autoritäten, the constituted authorities.

*Constitutiōn, *f.* constitution. *a*) [the state of being]. Eine starke oder schwache —, a robust or feeble constitution. *b*) [the established form of government in a state, kingdom or country].

*Constitutionéll, *adj.* and *adv.* constitutional, legal.

*Constructiōn, *f.* construction. *a*) [the form of building, the manner of putting together the parts of a building]. *b*) [in grammar, syntax or the arrangement and connection of words in a sentence, according to established usages, or the practise of good writers and speakers]. *c*) [the manner of describing a figure or problem in geometry].

*Construīren, *v. tr.* 1) to build. 2) to construe.

*Consubstantialitāt, *f.* [*pl.* -en] [the existence of more than one in the same substance] consubstantiality.

*Consubstantiatiōn, *f.* [the union of the body of our blessed Saviour with the sacramental elements] consubstantiation.

*Consubstantiéll, *adj.* and *adv.* consubstantial.

*Cónsul, *m.* [-s, *pl.* -n] consul. *a*) [the chief magistrate of the ancient Roman Republic]. *b*) [in modern usage, a name given to a person commissioned by a king &c. to reside in a foreign country as an agent, or representative, to protect the rights, commerce, merchants and seamen of the state].

*Consulārisch, *adj.* and *adv.* consular.

*Consulāt, *n.* [-es, *pl.* -e] consulate, consulship [applicable to modern consuls, as well as to the ancient Roman].

*Consulént, *m.* [-en, *pl.* -en] counsel, advocate.

*Consultatiōn, *f.* consultation. Eine ärztliche — über einen Patienten halten, to hold a medical consultation on a patient.

*Consultīren, *v. tr.* to consult.

*Consumīren, *v. tr.* to consume, to spend.

*Consūmo, *m.* [-'s] Consumtion, *f.* consumption. V. also Verbrauch.

Consumtionssteuer, *f.* a tax imposed on articles of consumption.

*Contagiōs, *adj.* and *adv.* contagious. Eine —se Krankheit, a contagious disease.

*Contāgium, *n.* [-s, *pl.* -ien] [a pestilential disease, venomous exhalations] contagion.

*Contánt, I. *adj.* [in commerce] ready. II. *adv.* in ready money, cash in hand.

*Contemplatīv, *adj.* and *adv.* contemplative.

*Cónterfei, *n.* [-es, *pl.* -e] likeness, picture, portrait.

*Continént, *n.* [-es, *pl.* -e] [in geography] continent.

*Continentāl, *adj.* and *adv.* continental. Die —mächte von Europa, the continental powers of Europe; —sperre, the continental system of Napoleon, which was to debar England from all commerce or intercourse with the continent of Europe.

*Cónto, *n.* [with others] *m.* [-'s, *pl.* -s or Conti] [in commerce] account, count. — nehmen, to take credit; — geben, to give credit, a (à) —, on account.

Conto-buch, *n.* account-book. —courant, *m.* account-current. —finto, *m.* pro-forma or simulated account. —saldo, *m.* balance account.

*Contōr, *n.* V. Comptoir.

*Contorist, *m.* V. Comptorist.

*Cóntrabande, V. Contrebande.

*Cóntrabaß, *m.* V. Contrebaß.

*Contráct, *adj.* and *adv.* lame, paralytic.

*Contráct, *m.* [-es, *pl.* -e] a contract, a bargain, a compact.

Contractmäßig, *adj.* and *adv.* agreed upon, stipulated.

*Contrahént, *m.* [-en, *pl.* -en] contractor.

*Contrahīren, I. *v. intr.* 1) to contract, to make a mutual agreement. 2) V. Zusammenziehen. II. *v. tr.* [chiefly in law] Schulden —, to contract debts; eine Verbindlichkeit —, to contract, to incur an obligation.

*Cóntrapunct, *m.* [in music] counterpoint.

*Contrasignīren, *v. tr.* to countersign.

*Contrást, *m.* [-es, *pl.* -e] [opposition or dissimilitude of figures, by which one contributes to the visibility or effect of the other; also opposition of things or qualities] contrast. Welcher — zwischen der Sittsamkeit und der Unverschämtheit! what a contrast between modesty and impudence!

*Contrastīren, *v. intr.* to be set in opposition with.

*Contraventiōn, *f.* [in law] contravention.

*Cōntre, [pron. as in the French] *adv.* counter, chiefly in composition, as —admiral, rear admiral; —approchen, [in fortification] counter-approaches.

*Cōntrebande, [pron. Konterbande] *f.* [prohibited goods] contraband, contraband goods.

*Contrebandier, [pron. either as in the French or Konterbandjeh] *m.* [-s, *pl.* -s] contrabandist, smuggler.

*Contrebandīren, [pron. Konterbandihren] *v. intr.* to traffick illegally or with prohibited goods, to smuggle.

*Cōntrebaß, *m.* [-sses, *pl.* -bässe] base-viol.

*Contremarque, [pron. as in the French] *f.* [-n] countermark.

*Cōntremarsch, [pron. Kontermarsch] *m.* [-es, *pl.* -märsche] [in military affairs] countermarch.

*Cōntremine, [pron. Kontermine] *f.* [*pl.* -n] [in fortification] countermine.

*Cōntreordre, [pron. as in the French] *f.* [*pl.* -s or -n] a contrary order, countermand.

*Cōntrepartie, [pron. Konterpartih] *f.* 1) [in commerce] V. Gegenbuch. 2) [in music, the part to be applied to another] counterpart.

*Cōntrerevolution, [pron. Konterrevoluzjohn] *f.* counter-revolution.

*Cōntrerevolutionär, [pron. Konterrevoluzjonähr] I. *adj* and *adv.* counterrevolutionary. II. *m.* [-s, *pl.* -e] a person engaged in effecting a counterrevolution.

*Cōntrescarpe, [pron. as in the French] *f.* [*pl.* -n] [in fortification, the exterior talus or slope of the ditch, or the talus that supports the earth of the covered way] counterscarp.

*Contresignal, [pron. Konterſinjahl] n. [-es, pl. -e] [a naval term] countersignal.

*Contretanz, [pron. Kontertanz] m. [-es, pl. -tänze] contra-dance or counter-dance, country-dance.

*Contretranchee, [pron. as in the French] f. [pl. -n] [in fortification] countertrench.

*Contribuiren, v. tr. to contribute.

*Contribution, f. [in a military sense, impositions upon a country in the power of an enemy] contribution. Ein Land in — setzen, to put a country under contribution. Fig. * and ‡ Einen in — setzen, to make a person contribute his share, to lay under contribution.

*Contrólle, f. [pl. -n] control.

*Controlleur, [pron. Kontrolöhr] m. [-s, pl. -e] controller.

*Controlliren, v. tr. to control.

*Controverspredigt, f. [pl. -en] a controversial sermon.

*Contumaz, f. 1) [in law] a willful contempt and disobedience to any lawful summons or order of court, contumacy. 2) quarantine, quarantain.

*Contusche, f. [pl -n] a short gown or rather a loose jacket.

*Contusion, f. [in surgery] a bruise, contusion.

*Convalescent, m. [-en, pl. -en] convalescent.

*Convalescenz, f. convalescence, convalescency.

*Convenienz, f. [pl. -en] suitableness, fitness, propriety, convenience, conveniency.

Convenienzheirath, f. a match of convenience.

*Convent, m. [-s, pl. -e] 1) an assembly, convention. Der National—, the national convention [in France]. 2) [a body of monks or nuns] convent. 3) [a religious house] convent.

*Conventikel, m. [-s, pl. -] conventicle.

*Convention, f. convention, agreement.

Conventions-geld, n. —münze, f. convention-money [coined according to the Vienna standard, in consequence of a convention or agreement between several states of the German Empire]. —thaler, m. convention-dollar [= to 4 shillings English].

*Conventionell, adj. and adv. 1) conventional. 2) according to the rules of propriety.

*Conventual, m. [-s or -en, pl. -en] —inn, f. [a monk or nun] conventual.

*Convergent, adj. and adv. convergent. —e Linien, Strahlen, converging lines, rays.

*Convergenz, f. convergence, convergency.

*Convergiren, v. intr. [to tend to one point] to converge. Convergirend, adj. converging.

*Convex, adj. and adv. convex [opposed to concave].

*Convictorium, n. [-s, pl. -rien] a refectory, dining-room.

*Convoi, [pron. either Konwoi or as in the French] f. convoy.

*Convoiren, [pron. konwoihren] v. tr. to convoy.

*Convolut, n. [-s, pl. -e] something rolled together or convoluted, a bundle. Fig. something huddled together. Sein Buch ist ein — von Unsinn und Verstand, Kenntnissen und Unwissenheit, his book is a heterogeneous mixture of sense and nonsense, knowledge and ignorance.

*Convulsion, f. [a preternatural, violent motion, more especially an involuntary contraction of the muscular parts of an animal body] convulsion.

*Copahubalsam, m. [-s] copayva [a gum from a tree of Brazil].

*Copie, f. [pl. -en] a likeness or ressemblance of any kind, copy.

Copiewechsel, pl. [in commerce] bills in sets.

*Copiren, v. tr. to form a like work or composition by writing, printing or engraving, to transcribe, to copy.

Copir-buch, n. copybook. —maschine, f. copying machine.

*Copist, m. [-en, pl. -en] copier, copyist.

*Copula, f. [pl. -läs] [in logic, the word which unites the subject and predicate of a proposition] copula.

*Copulation, f. V. Trauung.

*Copuliren, v. tr. to unite by the marriage ceremony, to marry.

*Coquelicot, [pron. as in the French] adj. and adv. having the colour of wild poppy, coquelicot, coquelico.

*Coquet, [pron. kokett] adj. and adv. coquettish.

*Coquette, [pron. Kokette] f. [pl. -n] coquet, coquette.

*Coquetterie, [pron. Koketterie] f. coquetry.

*Coquettiren, [pron. kokettihren] v. intr. to coquet.

*Coram, before [only used in law or in the following phrase:] †Fig. — nehmen, to take to task, to haul over the coals.

*Cordierit, m. [a mineral] cordierite, iolite, dichroite.

*Cordilleren, pl. the Andes.

*Cordon, [pron. as in the French] m. [-s, pl. -s or -e] a line of troops.

*Corduan, m. [-es] [goat-skin tanned and dressed] Spanish leather, cordwain, cordovan.

Corduanmacher, m. a worker in cordwain, cordwainer.

*Coriander, m. [-s, pl. -] [a plant] coriander.

*Corinth, [-s] [a city of Greece] Corinth.

*Corinthen, pl. [small dried grapes] currants.

*Corinthisch, adj. and adv. Corinthian. Die —e Säulenordnung, [in architecture] the Corinthian order.

*Cornet, m. [-(t)es, pl. -(t)e] [an officer of cavalry] a cornet.

*Cornette, f. [pl. -n] [a head-dress] cornet.

*Corollarium, n. [-s, pl. -rien] [in logic] a corollary.

*Corporal, m. [-s, pl. -räle] [the lowest non-commissioned officer of a company of infantry, next below a sergeant] corporal.

*Corporation, f. V. Körperschaft.

*Corpus, m. 1) body. Fig. ‡ belly. Der Herr hier hat einen artigen —, this gentleman has got a famous paunch. Fig. n. [pl. - or Corpora] — Juris, a body of Roman laws [the book itself as well as the contents of it]. 2) [in printing, = Garmond] the long primer.

*Correct, adj. and adv. correct, right, conformable to truth, not faulty, free from error.

*Correctheit, f. correctness.

*Corrector, m. [-s, pl. -en] a corrector [of the press &c.], reader.

*Correctur, f. [pl. -en] 1) the act of correcting, the correction of a book, or of the press. 2) the correction in the margin of a proof-sheet &c. 3) the sheets for correction. Die erste, zweite &c. —, the first, second &c. revise; die letzte —, reading for press.

Correctur-bogen, m. proof. Die —bogen, proofs; der —bogen für die zweite —, revise. —zange, f. [with printers] pincers. —zeichen, n. [with printers] sign of correction.

*Correlativ, adj. and adv. correlative. Vater und Sohn, Mann und Frau sind —e Ausdrücke, father and son, husband and wife, are correlative terms.

*Correspondent, m. [-en, pl. -en] correspondent.

*Correspondenz, f. [pl. -en] correspondence, correspondency. Sie führten eine — über &c., they had a correspondence on &c.

*Correspondiren, v. intr. to correspond.

*Corrigiren, v. tr. to correct [a copy for the press &c., the task of a school-boy &c.].

*Corrosiv, [-s, pl. -e], or Corrosivum, [-s, pl. -va or -ven] n. a corrosive.

*Corrosiv, adj. and adv. corrosive.

*Corsar, m. [-en, pl. -en] a corsair, a pirate.

*Corse, m. [pl. -n] Corsinn, f. Corsican.

*Corset, n. [-s, pl. -e] bodice, stays, quilted with whalebone or steel, worn by women.

*Corsica, n. [-s] Corsica.

*Corsicaner, m. [-s, pl. -] —inn, f. V. Corse, Corsinn.

*Corsisch, adj. and adv. Corsican.

*Cortine, f. [pl. -n] 1) [in fortification, the wall or distance between the flanks of two bastions] curtain. 2) [in theatricals] curtain.

*Corunna, [-s] [a Spanish town] the Groyn, Corunna.

*Corvette, [pron. Korwette] f. [pl. -n] a corvett, a sloop of war, an advice-boat.

*Corybantisch, adj. and adv. [inflamed like the Corybantes] corybantic.

*Coryphäus, m. [- or -phäen, pl. -phäen] [the chief of a chorus] corypheus. Fig. the first, the leader. Als die Coryphäen der deutschen Literatur betrachtet man Schiller, Goethe, Lessing, Wieland &c., Schiller, Goethe, Lessing, Wieland &c. are considered as the leading or standard writers in the German literature.

*Cosinus, m. [in geometry, the sine of an arc which is the complement of another to ninety degrees] cosine.

*Cosmisch, adj. and adv. [in astronomy] cosmical.

*Cotelette, [pron. Kottlett(e)] f. [pl. -s or -n] V. Carbonade.

*Cottonerz, n. [-es] [in mineralogy] yellow tellurium.

*Coulisse, [pron. Kulisse] f. [pl. -n] moveable scene, side-scene.

Coulissenmaler, m. scene-painter.

*Coupiren, [pron. Kupihren] I. v. tr. to cut. Ein Pferd — (englisiren), to dock [the tail of] a horse. II. v. intr. to divide a pack of cards, to cut. Wer coupirt? whose cut is it?

*Coupon, [pron. as in the French] m. [-s, pl. -s] [a corresponding indenture] a check.

*Cour, [pron. Kuhr] f. 1) levee, drawing-room. Bei Hofe ist heute große —, there is a great drawing-room held at court to-day. 2) address to gain favour, civility, flattery, court. *Die — machen, to make court; einem Frauenzimmer die — machen, to pay one's addresses to, to court a lady.

*Courage, [pron. Kurahsche] f. courage, heart, spirit.

*Courant, [pron. Kurannt] I. adj. [in commerce]

current. II. *n.* or —geld, current money, currency.

*Courbette, [pron. Kurbette] *f.* [*pl.*-n] [in manege, a particular leap of a horse] a curvet.

*Courbettiren, [pron. Kurbettihren] *v. intr.* [in the manege] to curvet.

*Courier, [pron. Kurihr] *m.* [-s, *pl.* -e] courier. — reiten, to ride post.

Courier=peitsche, *f.* messenger's whip. —stiefel, *m.* jack-boot.

*Cours, [pron. Kurß] *m.* [-ses, *pl.*-se] 1) course, circulation. 2) exchange, course of exchange. 3) [a naval term; a passage or motion on water] course. Seinen — nach England richten, to stand on the course to England.

Cours=zettel, *m.* bill of the course of exchange.

*Coursiren, [pron. Kursihren] *v. intr.* to be current.

*Courtage, [pron. Kurrtahsche] *f.* [in commerce] brokerage.

*Courtier, [pron. as in the French] *m.* [-s, *pl.* -s] a broker.

*Courtine, V. Cortine.

*Cousin, [pron. either as in the French or Kusihn] *m.* [-s, *pl.* -s] V. Vetter.

*Cousine, [pron. Kusihne] [*pl.* -n] V. Base, Muhme.

*Couvert, [pron. Kuwerrt] *n.* [-s, *pl.* -e] 1) the cover of a letter, envelop. 2) a cover at table consisting of plate, knife and fork, spoon, napkin &c.

*Couvertiren, [pron. Kuwerrtihren] *v. tr.* to cover, to envelop.

*Couverture, [pron. either as in the French or Kuwerrtuhre] *f.* [*pl.*-n] 1) a coverlet. 2) an envelop [of a letter].

*Couzeranit, *m.* [a fossil] couzeranite.

*Covent, V. Cofent.

*Cravate, [pron. Krawatte] *f.* [*pl.* -n] a cravat, neck-cloth, stock.

*Crayon, [pron. as in the French] *m.* [-s, *pl.* -s] crayon.

Crayonpapier, *n.* chalk-paper.

*Crayonniren, [pron. Kräjonnihren] *v. tr.* to hatch with a crayon, to crayon.

*Creas, *f.* [a kind of coarse linen cloth] dowlas.

*Creatur, V. Kreatur.

*Credenzen, *v. tr.* to taste [meat or] drink before it is presented. Sie credenzte ihm voll Anmuth den Becher, she graciously presented him the bowl.

Credenz=teller, *m.* a salver. —tisch, *m.* cup-board, buffet.

*Credenzschreiben, [-s, *pl.* -] Creditiv, [-s, *pl.* -e] *n.* credentials. V. Beglaubigungsschreiben.

*Credit, *m.* [-es, *pl.* -e] credit. *a*) = honour, estimation, reputation. *b*) [in commerce] = trust. Auf — kaufen, to buy on credit; einen — bei Jemanden eröffnen, to open a credit with any one.

Credit=brief, *m.* a letter of credit.

Creditiren, *v. tr.* 1) to credit [goods or money]. 2) and *v. intr.* to give or to sell on credit.

Creditor, *m.* [-s, *pl.* -en] creditor. V. Gläubiger.

Cremor=tartari, *m.* [in chimistry] cream of tartar.

Crepe, [pron. Krepp] *m.* [-s] [a thin transparent stuff] crape.

Crepon, [pron. as in the French] *m.* [-s] thickcrape.

*Cretin, [pron. either as in the French or Kretihn] *m.* [-s, *pl.* -s or -en] [a name given to certain deformed and helpless idiots in the Alps] a cretin.

*Crichtonit, *m.* [a mineral so called from Dr. Crichton, physician to the emperor of Russia] crichtonite.

*Criminal, I *adj.* [in law] criminal [opposed to civil]. Ein —verbrechen, a capital crime, a criminal offence. II. *adv.* criminally.

Criminal=amt, *n.* V. —gericht. —coder, *m.* a criminal code. —gericht, *n.* a criminal court. —proceß, *m.* criminal procedure, trial of criminal cases. —recht, *n.* 1) criminal law. 2) science of the criminal law. —richter, *m.* criminal judge. —sache, *f.* a criminal case.

*Crimm, *f.* the Crimea.

*Crispit, *m.* [an oxyd of titanium] rutil, rutile, sphene.

*Critisch, V. Kritisch.

*Crocodill, V. Krokodill.

*Cronstedtit, *m.* [a fossil] cronstedtite.

*Croupaden, [pron. Krupahden] *pl.* [in manege] croupade, croopade.

*Crousade, [pron. Krusahde] *f.* [*pl.*-n] [a Portuguese coin] crusade.

*Crucifix, *n.* [-es, *pl.* -e] [a cross on which the body of Christ is fastened in effigy] a crucifix.

*Cubebe, *f.* [*pl.* -n] [the small spicy berry of the Piper cubeba] cubeb.

*Cubik, [in mathematics] cubic [only used in compositions]. Der —fuß, cubic foot; ein —fuß Wasser, a cubic foot of water; der —inhalt, the cubic content; die —wurzel, cube-root; 3 ist die —wurzel von 27, 3 is the cube-root of 27; die —zahl, cubic number; die Cubo=—zahl, cubocube.

*Cubisch, *adj.* and *adv.* cubic, cubical. Das —e, cubicalness.

*Cubus, *m.* [in geometry and arithmetic] cube.

*‖Cucumer, *f.* [*pl.*-n] V. Gurke.

*Culmination, *f.* culmination [in a proper as well as in a fig. sense].

*Culminiren, *v. intr.* [in astronomy, to come or be in the meridian, to be in the highest point of altitude, as a planet] to culminate.

*Cultiviren, *v. tr.* to cultivate, to culture [land]. *Fig.* Den Geist —, to cultivate the mind.

*Cultur, *f.* [*pl.* -en] culture, cultivation. *Fig.* Die Geistes—, the culture of the mind; das Fortschreiten der —, the march of intellect.

*Cultus, [-, *pl.* -e] Cult, [-es, *pl.* -e] *m.* worship, divine service.

*Cur, *f.* [*pl.* -en] [a healing] cure. Die Bade—, use of the baths, die Brunnen—, use of the waters.

*Curaß, V. Küraß.

*Curatel, *f.* [*pl.* -en] [in law] guardianship, trusteeship.

*Curator, *m.* [-s, *pl.* -en] a guardian appointed by law, curator.

*Curcuma, Curcumei, *f.* [a plant] turmeric.

*Curd, [-s] [for Conrad] Conrad.

*Curialstyl, *m.* [-es] law-style, official style.

*Curiren, *v. tr.* to cure.

*Currendaner, Currendschüler, *m.* [-s, *pl.* -] one of those singing school-boys.

*Currende, *f.* a set of school-boys who walk through the streets, and sing for alms.

*Current, *adj.* [in compositions] current.

Current=geld, *n.* current money. —gläubiger, *m.* a creditor in account current. —schrift, *f.* current hand-writing, common hand-writing. —schuld, *f.* debt incurred by small or gradual expenses [opposed to bond-debt].

*Curschmid, *m.* V. Kurschmied.

*Cursivschrift, *f.* [with printers] Italics or Italic letters or characters.

*Cursus, *m.* [*pl.* Cursus or Curse] course. V. Lehrgang.

*Custos, *m.* [*pl.* Custoden] 1) a keeper, especially the keeper of a public library. 2) [in printing] catch-word, direction-word.

*Cutter, *m.* [-s, *pl.* -] [a vessel with one mast and a straight running bowsprit] a cutter.

*Cyane, *f.* [*pl.* -n] [a plant] the blue bottle.

*Cykloidal, *adj.* and *adv.* cycloidal.

*Cykloide, *f.* [*pl.* -n] [a geometrical curve on which depends the doctrine of pendulums] a cycloid.

*Cyklometrie, *f.* [the art of measuring cycles or circles] cyclometry.

*Cyklope, *m.* [*pl.* -n] [in fabulous history, the sons of Neptune and Amphitrite] Cyclop.

*Cyklus, *m.* [*pl.* Cykeln] cycle.

*Cylinder, *m* [-s, *pl.* -] cylinder.

Cylinderuhr, *f.* horizontal watch.

*Cylindrisch, *adj.* and *adv.* cylindric, cylindrical.

*Cymbel, *f.* [*pl.*-n] [a musical instrument used by the ancients] a cymbal.

*Cyniker, *m.* [-s, *pl.* -] a cynic.

*Cynisch, *adj.* and *adv.* cynic, cynical.

*Cynism[us], *m.* [-s] cynicalness.

*Cyper, 1) *m.* [-s] [a thin transparent black stuff] cyprus. V. also Trauerflor. 2) *f.* [*pl.* -n] Cyprus-plum. 3) *f.* [*pl.*-n] or —katze, Cyprian cat, cyparet.

Cyper=wein, *m.* V. Cyperwein. —wurz, *f.* galangal, zedoary, a species of Kæmpferia.

*Cypern, *n.* [-s] or Die Insel —, Cyprus.

Cypern=holz, *n.* prince-wood. —wein or [more usual] Cyperwein, *m.* Cyprus wine.

*Cypresse, *f.* [*pl.* -n] cypress.

Cypressen=baum, *m.* cypress-tree. —nüsse, *pl.* cypress-cones. —späne, *pl.* [with joiners] cypress-shingles [for wainscoting].

*Cyprin, *m.* [-s] [a mineral, the vesuvian of Werner] idocrase.

*Cytisus, *m.* [a shrub or tree] cytisus.

*Czar, *m.* [-s, *pl.* -e] [a title of the emperor of Russia] czar.

*Czarinn, *f.* [a title of the empress of Russia] czarina, czaress.

*Czarisch, *adj.* and *adv.* czarish.

D.

D, d, [a consonant] D, d. 1) *n.* d. 2) [in music] *a*) [the nominal of the second note in the natural diatonic scale] d, re. *b*) the stop or key d of an organ or harpsichord. *c*) [the second string of the violin] d.

Da, [old Engl. *tho*, Swed. *da*, old G. do] I. *adv.* 1) [at any place] Wo —? where? wo denn —? where then? 2) [in this place, in the place where the speaker is present, opposed to there] Sieh', — bin ich, behold, here I am; baue — sieben Altäre, build here seven altars; — und dort, here and there. 3) [opposed to here and denoting a more distant place] Hier stand ich, du standst —, here I stood, you there. 4) [denoting presence] Wer ist —? who is there? das Kind ist —, the child is come; wo Witz ist, — ist auch Verstand, where wit is, there is understanding. 5) [denoting any relation] *a*) [to a place] Ich lebe an einem Orte, — [better wo] mich Niemand kennt, I live in a place where I am known to nobody; von — begab er sich nach England, from that place, thence he went to England. *b*) [to time] Was werde ich erst — empfinden, wenn ich &c, what shall I feel then, when I &c.; zu einer Zeit, — &c., at a time when &c.; es vergeht kein Tag, — &c, not a day passes that &c.; wenn ich — noch lebe, if I am then alive. *c*) [to persons and things] Das ist nicht wahr, was Sie — sagten, it is not true, what you said there. 6) [sometimes it is used as an expletive for rounding periods, or for expressing a slight discontent] — haben Sie etwas Schönes angerichtet, there you have made a pretty business.

II. *conj.* 1) [noting a particular time] — ich ihn sah, war ich glücklich, when I saw him, I was happy; der König kam vorbei, — sie sich stritten, the king came by, as [when or while] they were disputing. 2) [noting a cause] — Sie doch hier sind, since you are here; — es so steht, kann ich Ihnen nicht helfen, since it is so, I cannot help you; — nun zum Sehen Licht erforderlich ist, whereas seeing requires light; — nun Kriege im Allgemeinen Armuth verursachen, whereas wars are generally causes of poverty. 3) [when on the contrary] Du lachst, — du doch Thränen vergießen solltest, you laugh, where you should shed tears; — doch der wahre Eifer immer mit der wahren Kenntniß beginnen sollte, whereas true zeal should always begin with true knowledge.

III. It is combined with prepositions and represents demonstrative pronouns, as davon, thereof, of that; damit, therewith, with that &c.

Daal, *n.* [-s] [in seamen's language] V. Pumpendaal.

Dabei; 1) Dābei, thereby, by that. — blieb es, there the matter rested; — mag es bleiben, let it be so. 2) Dabei, *a*) near that, near, by. — bleiben, to remain at a certain point; er saß —, he sat by; nahe —, hard by; — seyn, to be there, to be or make one of the party or company, to put in for one; wir waren nicht —, we were not there, we did not partake. *Fig.* — bleiben, to be settled, to remain as it was or as it is; to persist in. *b*) [= außerdem] besides, moreover. Er hat tausend Gulden Besoldung und — freie Wohnung, he has a salary of a thousand florins and free lodging besides; — hat er noch viel Unheil angestiftet, he has done much mischief besides.

***Da cāpo**, from the beginning [in music signifies that the piece of music at the end of which it stands, shall be repeated from the commencement]; *it.* [an expression made use of by the audience if they wish the repetition of a song &c.] da capo, encore. — rufen, to encore.

Dách, *n.* [-es, *pl.* Dächer] [from decken] 1) the cover of a thing, but especially the cover or upper part of a house or other building, roof. Ein — von Schindeln oder Ziegeln, a roof covered with shingles or tiles; ein einhängiges —, a pent-roof, shed-roof, lean-to; ein zweihängiges —, a roof consisting of two sloping sides; ein holländisches —, a hip-roof or hipped roof; ein französisches or gebrochenes —, curved roof; ein italienisches or flaches [plattes] —, a flat roof, a terrace; das — aufsetzen, [with carpenters] to bring up the carcass roofing; ein Gebäude unter das — or unter — bringen, to roof a building; mit einem —e, roofy; ohne —, roofless; das — decken, to cover a roof [with straw, shingles, tiles &c.]; ein Gebäude in — und Fach erhalten, to keep a building in repair; einer Sache — und Fach geben, to bring a thing under shelter, to roof a thing. *Prov.* Wer ein gläsernes — hat, soll Andere nicht mit Steinen werfen, who has glass-windows of his own, must take heed how he throws stones at his neighbour's house; ein Sperling in der Hand ist besser, als eine Taube auf dem —e, a bird in the hand is worth two in the bush, an egg is better to-day than a pullet to-morrow. **Fig.* Einem auf dem —e seyn or sitzen, to keep strict eye upon any one; Einem etwas auf das — geben, to cuff any one; da ist bei ihm gleich Feuer im —e, he takes fire presently. 2) a house or dwelling. *Fig.* *Einem — und Fach geben, to give shelter to any one, to harbour, to lodge a person; er hat weder — noch Fach, he has ne toft ne croft. 3) [in mining] upper stratum. 4) [also das Chinesische —, a shell] a species of the wreath [turbo tectum persicum].

Dach-balken, *m.* beam to the roof or girder to the garret-floor. —**decker**, *m.* one who roofs a house or other building, a slater, tiler. —**ente**, *f.* little grebe, didapper, dipper, dobchick, small ducker, loon, arse-foot. —**fahne**, *f.* vane, weathercock. —**fenster**, *n.* a window in the roof of a house, dormar-window. Das runde — fenster, V. Ochsenauge —**fette**, *f.* [in carpentry] purlin. —**flechte**, *f.* goldwiry lichen. —**firste**, *f.* —**forst**, *m.* —**förste**, *f.* [the top of the roof of a building] the ridge. —**geschoß**, *n.* the garret-floor. —**gesims**, *n.* [in architect.] the cornice of a roof. —**gesperre**, *n.* the timber-work of a roof. —**haken**, *m.* a roof-hook. —**hammer**, *m.* slater's hammer. —**hauslaub**, *n.* common house-leek. —**käfer**, *m.* a species of carabus [carabus fastigiatus]. —**kammer**, *f.* V. — stube. —**kasten**, *m.* V. — mulde. —**kohle**, *f.* V. Schieferkohle. —**latte**, *f.* [a thin, narrow board or slip of wood nailed to the rafters of a building to support the tiles or covering] a lath for the roof. —**luke**, *f.* a luthern. —**marder**, *m.* the martin. ‖ *Fig.* † Er schreit wie ein — marder, he screams horribly. —**moos**, *n.* V. — flechte. —**mulde**, *f.* slater's tray. —**muschel**, *f.* [in conchology] pinna. —**pfanne**, *f.* roof-tile. —**rahm**, *m.* [in carpentry] V. — fette. —**reiter**, *m.* a small tower erected on a roof. —**rinne**, *f.* a gutter. —**röhre**, *f.* the spout of a gutter. —**schale**, *f.* [in mining] upper stratum of a slate quarry. —**schiefer**, *m.* slate [used for covering buildings]. —**schindel**, *f.* shingle. —**schwelle**, *f.* [in carpentry] V. — balken. —**span**, *m.* a splinter or shide of wood put under tiles in roofing. —**sparren**, *m.* [in carpentry, a roof-timber] a principal rafter. —**spitze**, *f.* 1) the pitch of the roof. 2) [in carpentry] king-piece. —**spließe**, *f.* 1) V. — span. 2) a large sort of shingle. —**stein**, *m.* 1) a slate or tile. 2) [in mining] any sort of stone forming the upper stratum. —**stroh**, *n.* thatch. —**stube**, *f.* garret. —**stuhl**, *m.* 1) [in carpentry] the props and supports of a roof. 2) the seat without a back, or stool on which the slater or tiler sits. —**stuhlfette**, *f.* V. — fette. —**stuhlsäule**, *f.* [in carpentry] principal rafter. —**stuhlschwelle**, *f.* V. — schwelle. —**stütze**, *f.* V. — spitze 2. —**traufe**, *f.* 1) the dropping of the roof. 2) V. — rinne. 3) [the edge or lower border of the roof of a building, which overhangs the walls, and casts off the water that falls on the roof] eaves. —**traufenziegel**, *m.* eaves-tile. —**wand**, *f.* V. — schale. —**werk**, *n.* roofing. —**ziegel**, *m.* a tile. —**ziegelartig**, *adj.* and *adv.* lying one on another like tiles. —**ziegelförmig**, *adj.* and *adv.* shaped like a tile; [in botany] tiled [said of leaves].

Dächlein, ‖**Dächelchen**, *n.* [-s, *pl.* -] *dimin.* of Dach.

Dáchs, *m.* [-ses, *pl.* -se] [allied to stechen] 1) the badger. Das Junge eines Dachses, a pig. 2) [a sort of small dogs] a badger dog, terrier.

Dachs-bau, *m.* the burrow or earth of a badger. —**beinig**, *adj.* and *adv.* badger-legged. —**falle**, *f.* a trap for catching badgers. —**fänger**, *m.* V. Dachs 2. —**fell**, *n.* badger's skin. —**fett**, *n.* the fat of the badger. —**finder**, *m.* V. Dachs 2. —**graben**, *n.* the digging up of a badger's burrow or cover, unearthing a badger. —**grau**, *adj.* and *adv.* grey like a badger. —**haube**, *f.* a net for catching badgers. —**hund**, *m.* V. Dachs 2. —**jagd**, *f.* badger hunting. —**kriecher**, *m.* V. Dachs 2. —**röhre**, *f.* badger's hole. —**schmalz**, *n.* V. — fett. —**schwarte**, *f.* [with hunters] V. — fell.

Dächseln, *v. intr.* [with hunt.] to hunt a badger.

Dächsinn, *f.* the female of a badger; [with hunters] the sow.

‖**Dácht**, *m.* V. Docht.

‖**Dáchtel**, *f.* [*pl.* -n] [perhaps from denken! as if it were = Denkzettel] a box on the ear.

‖**Dáchteln**, *v. tr.* to box any one's ears.

Dáchung, *f.* 1) roofing. 2) roof.

Dachungsverbindung, *f.* [in carpentry] the timbers of a roof fitted and joined in the form proposed, the frame of a roof.

***Dädālisch**, *adj.* and *adv.* [mostly used in a higher style of writing] dedalian, intricate, complex.

Dadurch, 1) Dādurch, through it, through that place. Gehe nicht hierdurch, sondern —, do not go through this, but through that place. *Fig.* thereby, by that, by that means. — wirst du nichts erlangen, you will get nothing by it. 2) Dadúrch, by that, by it. Man hat — viel Gutes bewirkt, much good was done by it.

Dafern, *conj.* if, in case that.

Dafür, 1) Dāfür, *a*) for this, concerning or relative to this. — mag er selbst sorgen, he may look to that himself. *b*) instead of that, instead of it, in return or recompense for th[...] or that. Er sollte arbeiten, aber er spielt —, [...] should work, but on the contrary he plays; [...] ist er desto witziger, he makes amends by his w[...] was wird uns — ? [in Script.] what shall we ha[...] therefore? — gäbe ich keinen Heller, I wo[...] not give a farthing for it. 2) Dafür, for th[...] for it. Meine Arzenei ist gut —, my physic [...] good for it; ich bin dir gut —, I warrant you [...] answer for it; ich kann nicht —, it is not [...] fault, I cannot help it; was wird mir — ? w[...] am I to earn by it? — halten, V. Halten.

Dafürhalten, *n.* [the judgment which [...] mind forms of any proposition, event &c.] op[...] Meines — haltens wird es morgen regne[...] am of opinion that it will rain to morrow.

Dág, *n.* [-s, *pl.* -en] **Dágge**, *f.* [*pl.* -[...] seamen's language] a rope's end [used for puni[...] offenders]. Durch die —en laufen, to run [...] gantlet or gantlope.

Dagegen, 1) Dāgegen. — läßt sich nicht [...]gen, einwenden, there is nothing to be said ag[...] that. 2) Dagegen, *a*) against that, against i[...] er die Thür verschlossen fand, schlug er mit G[...] —, finding the door locked, he knocked [...] violence against it. *Fig.* Ich habe nichts — zuwenden, I have no objection to it; — ein[...]den, to object to; ich bin —, I am against i[...] hilft nichts, there is no remedy for it. *b*) [com[...] to it] Sein Verdienst ist groß, das deinig[...] nichts —, his merit is great, yours is nothi[...] it; — halten, to compare; die Abschrift is[...]tig, ich habe die Urschrift — gehalten, the [...] is correct, I have compared it with the ori[...] *c*) in exchange of it, in return for it. D[...] mir Geld, ich gebe dir Waaren —, you gi[...] money, I give you goods in exchange; wa[...]ben Sie mir — ? what do you give me in [...] er gab mir ein Buch, ich gab ihm einen Rin[...] he gave me a book, it is true, but I, on the [...] hand gave him a ring.

Dágge, *f.* V. Dag.

Dahangen, *ir. v. intr.* to hang at a place.

Daheim, *adv.* at home. Er fand sie nicht [...] he found her not at home.

Daher, 1) Dāher. *a*) from this place, hence. Ich komme —, er kommt dorther, I come from here, he comes from yonder; bis —, to here, thus far. *Fig.* — kommt es, daß &c., hence it comes, that &c. *b*) at this place. Stelle es —, put it there. *Fig.* Bis — bin ich immer gesund gewesen, as yet I have always been well. 2) Dahēr. *a*) [with verbs] = einher. V. —fließen &c. *b*) *Fig.* [deßwegen] for that or this reason, therefore.

Dahēr-fahren, *ir. v. intr.* [u. w. seyn] to come driving, to drive along. —**fliegen**, *ir. v. intr.* [u. w. seyn] to come flying, to fly along. —**fließen**, *ir. v. intr.* [u. w. seyn] to come flowing, to flow along. —**gehen**, *ir. v. intr.* [u. w. seyn] to walk along, to go on. *Fig.* Er geht or kommt daher, wie ein Bettler, he makes a beggarly appearance, he walks about like a beggar. —**glänzen**, *v. intr.* to shine or to appear shining from a place. —**gleiten**, *ir. v. intr.* [u. w. seyn] to approach sliding, to slide along. —**hinken**, *v. intr.* [u. w. seyn] to come hobbling, to hobble along. —**kommen**, *ir. v. intr.* [u. w. seyn] 1) to come from another place. 2) *Fig.* to draw near in time, to approach. —**laufen**, *ir. v. intr.* [u. w. seyn] to run along. —**prangen**, *v. intr.* to prance on or along. —**rauschen**, *v. intr.* [u. w. seyn] to rush on or along. —**rennen**, *ir. v. intr.* [u. w. seyn] to come running, to come hastily. — —**schleichen**, *ir. v. intr.* [u. w. seyn] to approach sneaking, to sneak along. —**schwanken**, *v. intr.* [u. w. seyn] to totter along, to come tottering. —**ziehen**, *ir. v. intr.* [u. w. seyn] to draw near, to draw along, to come near in a formal march, or moving with ceremonious solemnity or in solemn procession.

Dahier, *adv.* here.

Dahin, *adv.* 1) Dāhin, *a*) to that place, thither. — könnt ihr nicht kommen, thither ye cannot come; führt dieser Weg —? does this road lead to it? wir gehen —, we go thither; nimm dies — mit, take this along with you. *Fig.* — habe ich es nie bringen können, I could never bring it to that, I could never succeed so far; er spricht von Dingen, die gar nicht — gehören, he speaks of things that have nothing to do in this place, that don't belong to it. *b*) *Fig.* in a direction to. Alle seine Sorgen sind — gerichtet, all his care is bent that way; meine Meinung geht —, that's my opinion. 2) Dahin: Die glücklichen Tage sind —, the happy days are gone; diese Zeiten sind —, these times are gone by; alle meine Hoffnungen sind —, all my hopes have flown.

Dāhinaus, *adv.* out of that place, out of there. **Dahin-blühen**, *v. intr.* [u. w. seyn] to fade, to wither. *Fig.* Ihre Schönheit blühte —, her beauty faded away. —**bringen**, *ir. v. tr.* to carry to a place. *Fig* to persuade, to induce. Ich habe ihn nicht —bringen können, I could not prevail on him; sie konnten den König nicht —bringen, den Verbrecher zu begnadigen, they could not prevail with the king to pardon the offender. —**eilen**, *v. intr.* [u. w. seyn] to haste away. —**ein**, *adv.* into that place, into there. —**fahren**, *ir. v. intr.* [u. w. seyn] to drive along. *Fig.* Er fuhr —, he died [chiefly in a bad sense]. Er fuhr in seinen Sünden —, he died in his wickedness. —**fallen**, *ir. v. intr.* [u. w. seyn] 1) to fall down. 2) *Fig.* to fade, to droop, to vanish. —**fliegen**, *ir. v. intr.* [u. w. seyn] to pass rapidly. —**fliehen**, *ir. v. intr.* [u. w. seyn] 1) to fly, to flee, to run away. 2) *Fig.* to fly, to pass rapidly, as time. —**fließen**, *ir. v. intr.* [u. w. seyn] to flow along. *Fig.* Schnell fließen die fliehenden Stunden dahin, swiftly fly the fleeting hours. —**geben**, *ir. v. tr.* 1) to give up, to resign, to abandon to, to indulge in. Sich Einem ganz —geben, to give one's self wholly up to a person. 2) to offer up, to sacrifice. —**gehen**, *ir. v. intr.* [u. w. seyn] to go or walk to a place; *fig.* to pass or pass away, to vanish; *it.* to die, to depart this life. —**gleiten**, *ir. v. intr.* [u. w. seyn] to flow, to glide along smoothly, to pass away. —**haben**, *v. tr.* to have got. Er hat seinen Lohn —, he has got his reward. —**kommen**, *ir. v intr.* [u. w. seyn] to come so far. Wir werden heute nicht mehr — kommen, we shall not reach that place to-day; es ist mit ihm — gekommen, daß &c., it has come so far with him that &c. —**laufen**, *ir. v. intr.* [u. w. seyn] to fly, to run away. —**raffen**, *v. tr.* to carry off, to destroy. Das Fieber hat ihn —gerafft, the fever carried him off. —**reißen**, *ir. v. tr.* to carry away or along. *Fig. a*) to bear away with joy or delight, to ravish, to transport. *b*) to hurry or carry away by violence of passion, to transport. —**schlüpfen**, *v. intr.* [u. w. seyn] to slip away, to depart or withdraw secretly, to slink off. —**schmachten**, *v. intr.* [u. w. seyn] to pine or sink under sorrow or any continued passion, to languish. —**schwinden**, *ir. v. intr.* [u. w. seyn] to faint, to vanish, to die. —**seyn**, *ir. v. intr.* to be gone, to be lost. Alle meine Hoffnungen sind —, all my hopes have vanished; unsere Freuden sind —, our joys are over; diese glücklichen Tage sind —, these happy days are gone; diese Zeiten sind —, these times are gone by. —**sinken**, *ir. v. intr.* [u. w. seyn] to sink down. *Fig.* to sink, to drop, to decay, to vanish, to die. —**stehen**, *ir. v. imp.* to be doubtful or uncertain. Es steht —, it may be questioned; es steht —, ob Galenus &c., it is questionable, whether Galen &c. —**stellen**, *v. tr.* to put in or on a place. *Fig.* Etwas — gestellt seyn lassen, to leave something undecided. —**sterben**, *ir. v. intr.* [u. w. seyn] to die, to drop. Wir sehen einen Freund um den andern um uns herum —sterben, we see one friend after another dropping round us. —**streifen**, *v. intr.* [u. w. seyn] to touch a thing slightly in passing, to graze a thing. —**taumeln**, *v. intr.* [u. w. seyn] to stagger away. —**wandeln**, *v. intr.* [u. w. seyn] to walk on. *Fig.* to pass away.

Dahinten, *adv.* [remaining after departure of] behind. — bleiben, to stay behind; weit —, far behind.

Dahinter, *adv.* 1) Dāhinter. — muß es stekken, it is behind that that it must be. *Fig.* — muß ich noch kommen, that I have yet to find out. 2) Dahinter, behind that, behind this, behind it. Er stellte sich —, he placed himself behind it. *Prov.* Man sucht Niemanden hinter der Thür, wenn man nicht selbst — gewesen ist, the old woman would never have looked for her daughter in the oven, had she not been there herself; one judges of others by one's self. *Fig.* Es steckt etwas —, there is some secret in it; es steckt nichts —, there is nothing in it; ich werde gewiß — kommen, I shall certainly come to the knowledge of it, I shall certainly find it out; ich will mich — [her] machen, I will set about it, set to work at it.

Dahinwärts, *adv.* towards that place, towards yonder.

Dahlbord, *m.* and *n.* [-es, *pl.* -e] [from the Low Saxon daal = niedrig] [in ship-building] border, edging, side planks all round the deck.

||**Dahlen**, [perhaps allied to the A. S. *dwelian, dwolian* = albern seyn] *v. intr.* to dally, to trifle, to toy, to dandle, to amuse one's self with idle play.

***Daktylioglyphik**, *f.* V. Steinschneidekunst.

***Daktyliothek**, *f.* [*pl.* -en] [a collection of rings] dactyliotheca.

***Daktylisch**, *adj.* dactylic.

***Dáktylus**, *m.* [*pl.* Daktylen] [a poetical foot consisting of three syllables - υ υ] dactyl. Daktylen, dactylic verses, dactyls.

Dāliegen, *ir. v. intr.* to lie in a certain place.

Dalmātien, *n.* [-s] Dalmatia.

Dalmātier, [-s, *pl.* -] -inn, *f.* a native of Dalmatia, a Dalmatian.

Dalmātisch or **Dalmāzisch**, *adj.* coming from or belonging to Dalmatia.

Dāmahlig, *adj.* then being, at that time happening, at that time done. Die —e Mode, the fashion of those times; der —e König, the then reigning king.

Dāmahls, *adv.* then, at that time. Dich, — ein Knabe, thee, then a boy.

Damáscus or **Damásk**, *n.* [-s] Damask [a town in Syria]. Von —, damascene.

***Damást**, *m.* [-es, *pl.* -e] 1) damaskeening. 2) damask. *a*) [a silk stuff, originally from Damascus]. Der seidene —, damask-silk; der halbseidene —, caffart-damask. *b*) [a kind of wrought linen, in imitation of damask-silks]. Der leinene —, damask-linen.

Damast-artig, *adj.* and *adv* like damask. —**flor**, *m.* damaskeened gauze. —**leinwand**, *f.* V. Damast, 2) *b*). —**macher**, *m.* V. —weber. —**muster**, *n.* a pattern for damaskeening. —**stuhl**, *m.* the loom of a damask-weaver. —**weber**, *m.* damask-weaver.

***Damásten**, *adj.* and *adv.* wrought like damask. —es Tisch- or Tafelzeug, damask tabling.

***Damaszéner**, *m.* [-s, *pl.* -] [a sabre, so called from the manufacture of Damascus] Damaskin.

Damaszener-arbeit, *f.* damaskeening. —**klinge**, *f.* [a sword-blade manufactured at Damask] Damascus blade. —**pflaume**, *f.* Damask-plum, Damask-plume, damson, damsin, Damascene, damasine. —**rose**, *f.* Damask-rose. —**säbel**, *m.* V. Damaszener. —**stahl**, *m.* Damascus steel. —**traube**, *f.* grapes from Damascus, Damask-grape.

***Damaszīren**, *v. tr.* 1) [to form flowers on stuff] to damask. 2) [to make incisions in iron, steel &c., and to fill them with gold or silver wire, for ornament] to damask, to damasken or damaskeen. Das —, damaskeening.

Dámbock; *m.* [-es, *pl.* -böcke] V. Damhirsch.

Dambrett, **Dāmenbrett**, *n.* [-es, *pl.* -er] a board used for draughts, draught board.

Damenbrett-blume, *f.* common fritillary, chequered lily. —**tute**, *f.* V. Tigertute.

Dāme, *f.* [*pl* -n] [Fr. *dame*, from the Lat. *domina, domna*] 1) [a woman of distinction or any woman of genteel education] a lady. 2) a dignified piece in some games, [at cards, at chess] queen; [at draughts] king. Einen Stein zur — machen, [at draughts] to crown or to king a man. 3) [a kind of game resembling chess] draughts. — spielen or die — ziehen, to play at draughts. 4) the last line of squares or houses on a draught-board. In die — kommen, [at draughts] to get a crown.

Damen-brett, *n.* draught-board. V. Dambrett. —**papier**, *n.* the smallest and finest sort of paper. —**sattel**, *m.* a saddle for a woman, a lady's saddle, a side-saddle. —**spiel**, *n.* V. Dame, 3). —**spieler**, *m.* a player at draughts. —**stein**, *m.* [a movable piece at draughts] man.

Dámgeiß, *f.* [*pl.* -en] [the female of the fallow deer] a she-deer, doe.

Dámhirsch, *m.* [-es, *pl.* -e] [Lat. *dama*; it is also called Tannhirsch, perhaps from Tanne?] [the male of the fallow deer] buck.

||**Dāmisch**, *adj.* and *adv.* silly, foolish.

Damit, I. *adv.* 1) Dāmit, with that or this. — hat er seine Feinde überwunden, therewith he has conquered his foes; der ganze Streit endigte sich —, daß &c., all the debate came to this &c.; was wollen Sie — sagen? what do you mean by it? — ist es noch nicht vorbei, that is not yet the end of the matter; unsere Sitten stimmen sehr — überein, our manners have a great conformity therewith; es ist aus —, there is an end to it; so sprach er, und — ging er fort, he spoke thus, and then went away. 2) Damit. Er nahm meinen Hut und ging — fort, he took my hat and walked off with it; nur heraus —! speak out, out with it! er thut zu groß —, he boasts or brags too much of it. II. *conj.* Damit [denoting purpose or rather introducing the clause expressing purpose] that. — wir den Gegenstand vollkommen verstehen, that we may fully understand the subject; — nicht, that not, for fear that, lest; — Sie nichts verlieren, lest you should loose any thing; — es nicht gestohlen werde, for fear it might be stolen.

‖**Dämlich**, V. [the more usual] Dämisch.

Dámm, *m.* [-es, *pl.* Dämme] [allied to the Gr. δέμω, bauen] 1) a mole, bank, or mound of earth or stones especially any wall raised to obstruct a current of water, or intended to prevent low lands from being inundated by the sea or a river, a dam, dike, [in mining] stopping, stoppage. Dämme schützen die Niederungen Hollands, the low countries of Holland are defended by dikes; einen — machen, aufwerfen, to make a dam, to throw up a dike; einen — durchstechen, to open a dike. *Fig.* Dem Laster einen — entgegensetzen, to restrain vice. 2) [a way, raised above the natural level of the ground, by stones, earth, timber, fascines &c. serving as a dry passage over wet or marshy grounds] causey. 3) [in organs, boards, whereon the stock of the pipes rests] traverse. 4) [in anatomy, a ligament between the scrotum and the anus] perinæum.

Damm-bau, *m.* damming, diking. —**bruch**, *m.* 1) the rupture of a dike. 2) a breach in a dike. —**erde**, *f.* 1) earth for making a dam or dike. 2) [in mining] upper-earth, meat. 3) black-mould or mold. —**gegend**, *f.* [in anatomy] V. Damm 4. —**grube**, *f.* [with bell-founders] a pit. —**holz**, *n.* V. Satzkolben. —**läufer**, *m.* a vessel navigated in the canals of Holland. —**meister**, *m.* dike-reeve, dike-grave. —**muskel**, *m.* [in anatomy] a muscle of the perinæum. —**schlagader**, *f.* [in anatomy] the artery of the perinæum. —**setzer**, *m.* V. Steinsetzer. —**weg**, *m.* V. Damm 2.

‖**Dámmeln**, *v. intr.* to dally, to toy, to dandle.

1. **Dámmen**, *v. tr.* [to make a dam or dike] to dam. Einen Fluß —, to dam up a river. *Fig.* Seine Begierden —, to check one's desires.

2. **Dämmen**, [seems to be allied to dämpfen] *v. intr.* to riot, to revel.

Dämmerglück, *n.* [-es] dawning happiness [only used in a high style of writing].

Dämmerhell, *adj.* and *adv.* crepuscular, crepusculous.

Dämmerig, *adj.* and *adv.* crepuscular, crepusculous, dusky. Es wird schon —, it begins to grow dusky; —es Wetter, cloudy or misty weather.

Dämmerlich, *adj.* and *adv.* duskish.

Dämmerlicht, *n.* [-es] a dusky or dim light.

Dämmern, [Swed. *dimmer*, Ice. *dimmur*, Swiss dimber, allied to the Lat. *tenebrae*; probably allied to τύπτω, stampfen, that is stoßen, drücken, thus it denotes a state in which the light is suppressed; some consider it to be allied to Dampf] I. *v. imp.* to grow twilight, to grow light or dusky [before sunrise and after sunset]. Der Tag, der Morgen dämmert, the day dawns, the morning dawns; der Abend dämmert, night is coming on. *Fig.* Eine —de Hoffnung, a faint hope. II. *v. tr.* to make dusky. Der —de Hain, the twilight grove.

Dämmerung, *f.* 1) twilight, crepuscule, crepuscle. Die Morgen—, morning-twilight, dawn; die Abend—, evening-twilight. 2) *Fig.* darkness. Wir wandeln auf Erden in —, we walk this earth in darkness.

Dämmerungs-falter, *m.* [in entomology] the hawk-moth, sphinx. —**kreis**, *m.* [in physics] crepuscular circle. —**licht**, *n.* twilight, crepuscule. —**zeit**, *f.* the time of the crepuscule.

***Dämon**, *m.* [-s, *pl.* -en] an evil spirit or genius, a demon.

Dämonisch, *adj.* and *adv.* [influenced by demons or like a demon] demoniac, demonical, demonian.

Dámpf, *m.* [-es, *pl.* Dämpfe] [Engl. and D. *damp*; Sw. *dimma, dimpa* signifies Nebel; V. Dämmern] 1) that which rises in the form of vapour, fume or steam, exhalation, reek; vapour from combustion, smoke, fume; the vapour of water, steam. Der — des brennenden Holzes, the fume of burning wood; der Tabaks—, the fume of tobacco; der — von Holzkohlen, the smoke of charcoal; der — von kochendem Wasser, the vapour of boiling water, steam; Kartoffeln im —e kochen, to steam potatoes; Dämpfe, die aus der Erde emporsteigen, exhalations issuing from the earth; Dämpfe an etwas gehen lassen, to apply smoke to something, to medicate something by smoke, to smoke or fumigate it: ich muß jeden Tag Dämpfe an die leidenden Theile meines Körpers gehen lassen, um sie von dem rheumatischen Stoffe zu befreien, I am obliged, to have artificial vapours applied to the suffering parts of my body, in order to free them from the rheumatic matter. †*Fig.* Er thut mir allen — an, he vexes me to the utmost; *er ist ein Hans —, he is a giddy, giddy-headed, or heedless fellow; *it. Fig.* er hat einen —, he is a little flustered. 2) [perhaps from dämmen, that is drengen] a shortness of breath. Der — bei Pferden, broken wind; das Pferd hat den —, the horse is broken-winded.

Dampf-auflösung, *f.* [in chimistry] a solution by vapour. —**bad**, *n.* 1) [in medicine] *a*) fomentation. *b*) steam-bath. 2) [in chimistry] vapour-bath. —**balg**, *m.* fumigating bellows. —**boot**, *n.* a steam-boat, steamer. —**erzeuger**, *m.* [a vessel in which steam is generated] generator. —**flinte**, *f.* steam-gun. —**getriebe**, *n.* V. [the more usual word] —maschine. —**gitter**, *n.* [an open cover for the hatches of ships of war] grating, gratings. —**heizung**, *f.* a heating by steam. —**kessel**, *m.* steam-boiler, boiler. —**kochen**, *n.* a cooking by steam. —**küche**, *f.* steamer, steam-kitchen [a sort of stove for dressing meat by steam]. —**kugel**, *f.* 1) [a hollow ball of metal, with a pipe or slender neck, used in hydraulic experiments] eolipile. 2) [in military affairs] smoke-ball. —**loch**, *n.* steam-hole [in steam-engines]. —**maschine**, *f.* [an engine worked by steam] steam-engine. —**messer**, *m.* [in physics] elaterometer. —**mittel**, *n.* [in medicine] a palliative. —**mühle**, *f.* steam-mill. ‖—**nudeln**, *pl.* [in cookery] a sort of small dumplings. —**packetboot**, *n.* steam-packet. —**presse**, *f.* [a newly invented printing-press] steam-press. —**pumpe**, *f.* steam-pump. —**qualm**, *m.* a thick smoke. —**röhre**, *f.* [in steam-engines] steam-pipe. —**schiff**, *n.* steam-boat, steam-vessel, steamer. —**topf**, *m.* pea-boiler. —**ventil**, *n.* steam-valve. —**wagen**, *m.* [a carriage propelled by steam] steam-carriage. —**werk**, *n.* steam-work.

Dámpfen, I. *v. intr.* 1) to throw off volatile matter in the form of vapour or exhalation, to emit smoke, to smoke, to fume, to steam. Die Kohlen —, the coals smoke; man sieht die Wiesen —, one sees the exhalations rising from the meadows. 2) * to cause a smoke, as in smoking. Er dampft den ganzen Tag, he smokes [his pipe] all day long. II. *v. tr.* * to cause to smoke, as a pipe or cigar. Er dampft immerfort seine Pfeife, he is constantly smoking his pipe.

1. **Dämpfen**, *v. tr.* [with hunters and fowlers] to confine [a decoy-bird] in a dark place.

2. **Dämpfen**, *v. tr.* 1) to damp, to weaken, to dull. Den Ton —, to deaden the sound, eine Geige —, to apply a sordino or mute to a violin [to render the sound fainter]; eine Trommel —, to muffle a drum; gedämpft, [in music, is sometimes placed over a passage, to imply that the movement or passage is to be performed moderately loud] sotto-voce; mit gedämpfter Stimme, [in speaking or reciting] with a voice moderately loud; [in painting] gedämpfte Farben, retiring colours. 2) to extinguish, to deaden, to quench, to suffocate, to destroy. Ein Feuer —, to stifle a fire [by ashes &c.]; den Staub —, to lay the dust. *Fig.* Einen Aufruhr —, to suppress, to quell a mutiny or riot; eine Leidenschaft —, to quench a passion; den Muth —, to depress courage. 3) [to boil slowly in a moderate manner, or with a simmering heat] to stew [meat, apples &c.]. Syn. Dämpfen, Stillen. Dämpfen signifies to abate, to lessen in degree any motion or agitation; stillen, to cause it to cease altogether. In dämpfen force is used and resistance supposed, das Stillen may be effected also by soothing means. Man dämpft einen Aufruhr [one puts down a tumult] by menaces, the advance of an armed force &c.; man stillt ihn [one appeases it] by exhortation, promises &c. Man dämpft eine Begierde [one suppresses a desire] by resisting it, so as gradually to extirpate it; man stillt sie [one appeases it] by gratification.

Dämpf-horn, *n.* V. Dämpfer, 1). —**pfanne**, *f.* stew-pan.

Dämpfer, *m.* [-s, *pl.* -] 1) [a hollow conical utensil, to be put on a candle to extinguish it] extinguisher. 2) [a small instrument of wood or brass applied to the bridge of a violin or violoncello to render the sound fainter] a sordino or mute. 3) [a part of the mechanism of a pianoforte, by which the sound is deadened] damper. *Fig.* a damper, moderat[…] Er hat den Leidenschaften, den Begierden die[…]ses Menschen einen Dämpfer aufzusetzen gew[…] he contrived to damp the passions, the desires [of] this violent person.

Dämpfig, *adj.* and *adv.* having short or thi[ck] breath. Ein —es Pferd, a brokenwinded hors[e].

Dämspiel, V. Damenspiel.

Dámthier, *n.* V. —geiß.

‖**Dámtiegel**, *m.* V. Brummkreisel.

Dámwild, **Damwildbrett**, *n.* [-es] [fal]low deer.

Danach, 1) Dānach [in the beginning of [a] sentence] [with some authors darnach], *a*) [after] that, after it. — strebt er, he aspires after it; — sieh, look to it. *b*) by that, by it[…] richte dich, go by that. 2) Danách, *a*) after [that,] after it. Es war Bisam in dieser Büchse[…] riecht noch —, there was musk in this bo[x,] still smells of it; wer fragt —? who asks after [it,] who cares for it? er fragt nichts —, he does [not] mind it; ihm wässert der Mund —, his m[outh] waters at it. *b*) by that, by it. Dies sind [gute] Regeln, um — zu leben, these are good r[ules] to live by. *c*) thereafter, accordingly. Er [wird] auch — belohnt werden, he will be rewarded [ac]cordingly; — handeln, to act accordingly[…] es fällt, as it happens; es läßt sich nicht — [an,] there is no appearance of it; — die Umstände[…] according to circumstances. *d*) noting time[…]ne Stunde —, an hour after; gleich —, im[me]diately after.

Däne, *m.* [-n, *pl.* -n] 1) [a native of Denm[ark]

Dane. 2) a Danish horse.

Daneben, *adv.* 1) by the side of that place, near it, by it. Gleich —, hard by; ich wohne gleich —, I live close by; er schoß —, he missed the mark. 2) moreover, besides.

Dänebrogsorden, *m.* [-s] [a Danish order] the order of Danebrog.

Dänemark, [-s] [kingdom] Denmark.

‖**Dängeln**, V. Dengeln.

‡**Danieden**, *adv.* below, down.

Danieder, *adv.* on the ground, down [especially in composition].

Danieder-beugen, *v. tr.* 1) to bend down or downward. 2) *Fig.* to depress, to deject. Den Geist —beugen, to depress the mind. —**brechen**, *ir. v. tr.* to break down; *fig.* [also] to destroy. —**fallen**, *ir. v. intr.* [u. w. seyn] to fall down. —**kommen**, V. [the more usual word] Niederkommen. —**kunft**, *f.* V. [the more usual word] Niederkunft. —**liegen**, *ir. v. intr.* to lie on the ground. *Fig.* Krank —liegen, to lie sick in bed, to be affected disease of any kind; er lag krank am Podagra —, he was laid up with the gout. —**schlagen**, *ir. v. tr.* to beat down, to knock to crush. *Fig.* Dieser Verlust schlug ihn that loss dispirited, discouraged, or discouraged him; —geschlagen, *adj.* despondent, as Niedergeschlagen; die Hoffnung —schlagen, to destroy hope. —**sinken**, *ir. v. intr.* [u. w. seyn] to sink down; *fig.* [also] to perish. —**stoßen**, *ir. v. tr.* to throw down; *fig.* to discourage, to dishearten.

Däninn, *f.* a Danish woman.

Dänisch, *adj.* and *adv.* Danish. —es Haar, Danish dog's hair; das —e, the language of the Danes, Danish.

Dank, *m.* [-es] [from Denken, as if it were Gedenken] 1) approbation, satisfaction. Einem etwas zu —e machen, to do something to one's liking; es ist mir zu — bezahlt worden, it is paid to my satisfaction; zu —e annehmen, to receive with pleasure. 2) something given or done in return of a favour, acknowledgment. Eine Gunst mit — erkennen, to acknowledge a favour with thanks. § and † Des Teufels — von etwas [geleisteten Diensten &c.] haben, to be finely recompensed for a thing [for services performed &c.]. 3) the owning of a benefit received, accompanied with gratitude, acknowledgment. Gott aber sei —, der uns den Sieg gegeben hat, [in Script.] thanks be to God, which giveth us the victory; — sagen, to give thanks; Einem — sagen, to thank any one; Einem etwas — sagen, abstatten, to make acknowledgments for something, to return thanks for something; das Geschenk wurde mit — angenommen, the gift was gratefully received; Einem etwas — wissen, to be grateful to a person for something, to be obliged to any one for something; — den eifrigen Bemühungen seines Arztes wurde er bald wieder hergestellt, thanks to the assiduities of his physician, he soon recovered; Gott sei —! thank God! God be thanked! 4) [formerly the reward gained in tournaments or tilting matches] prize.

Dank-adresse, *f.* an address of thanks. —**altar**, *m.* an altar for thanksoffering. —**beflissen**, *adj.* and *adv.* studious to be grateful. —**begier**, —**begierde**, *f.* desire of being grateful. —**begierig**, *adj.* and *adv.* desirous to be thankful, grateful. —**fest**, *n.* [a day set apart for religious services, especially to acknowledge the goodness of God] thanksgiving. Ein —fest feiern, to celebrate a thanksgiving. —**gebet**, *n.* a prayer of thanks, thanksgiving. —**gefühl**, *n.* a lively sense of good received, thankfulness, gratitude. —**lied**, *n.* a hymn of thanksgiving. —**los**, *adj.* and *adv.* V. Undankbar. —**opfer**, *n.* 1) [in Jewish antiquity] thank-offering. 2) any prayer or hymn of thanksgiving. —**predigt**, *f.* a sermon of thanksgiving. —**rede**, *f.* a speech of thanksgiving, a speach of thanks. Er hielt eine lange —rede an die Versammlung, he thanked the assembly in a long speech. —**sagen**, *v. intr.* to return thanks. —**schrift**, *f.* V. —adresse. —**vergessen**, *adj.* and *adv.* thankless, ungrateful. Ein —vergessener Mensch, an unthankful person. —**verpflichtet**, *adj.* and *adv.* bound in gratitude. —**würdig**, *adj.* and *adv.* deserving thanks, thankworthy.

Dánkbar, I. *adj.* and *adv.* thankful, grateful. Ein —es Herz, a grateful heart; seid ihm —, be thankful to him. II. *adv.* thankfully, with a grateful sense of favour or kindness received. Das Geschenk wurde — angenommen, the gift was gratefully received.

Dánkbarkeit, *f.* thankfulness, gratitude.

‡**Dánkbarlich**, V. Dankbar II.

Dánken, 1) *v. intr.* to thank, to express gratitude for a favour, to make acknowledgments [to any one] for kindness bestowed. Gott —, to thank God; für eine Wöchnerinn —, to announce the happy delivery of a woman, and to return thanks to God for it; darf ich Ihnen von diesem Gericht anbieten? - Ich danke Ihnen, ich bin schon versehen, may I offer you some of this dish? - No, I thank you, I am already served; § ich danke dafür, I am much obliged to you; [ich] danke schön, [ich] werde es bleiben lassen, thank you, I'll take care how I do it. 2) *v. tr.* [to be obliged to ascribe to] to owe. Wir — Gott das Leben, we are indebted to God for life; ihm danke ich Alles, was ich besitze, I owe to him all I possess; wir haben eurer Liebe wenig zu —, little are we beholden to your love; das hat er sich selbst zu — [= das ist seine eigene Schuld], he may thank himself for it, that is his own fault. 3) *v. intr.* to make return for any thing given, done or suffered. Dank' dir's Gott, God reward it; ich grüßte ihn, aber er dankte mir nicht, I greeted him, but he did not return it.

Dankenswerth, *adj.* and *adv.* deserving thanks, thankworthy.

Dánksagung, *f.* 1) [the act of rendering thanks or expressing gratitude for favours or services] thanksgiving. 2) [in churches] a prayer of thanksgiving.

Danksagungs-gesundheit, *f.* grace-cup. —**schreiben**, *n.* a letter of thanks or grateful acknowledgment.

Dánn, *adv.* 1) [appears to be allied to dehnen] [noting time] then. — und wann, now and then. 2) [afterward, in consequence, or to strenghten a phrase] then. Erst versöhne dich mit deinem Bruder, — komme und opfere deine Gabe, [in Script.] first be reconciled to thy brother, then come and offer thy gift; wenn sich dieses Alles so verhält, — besitzt der Mensch eine natürliche Freiheit, if all this be so, then man has a natural freedom; selbst —, wenn es wahr wäre, even if it were true.

Dánnen, [perhaps instead of d a a n] *adv.* [rather obsolete] [noting a place; it is always preceded by the preposition von] Von —, thence, from thence; stehet auf und laßt uns von — gehen, [in Script.] arise, let us go hence; er ritt von —, he rode away.

‡**Dánnenhero**, *adv.* V. Daher.

***Dánno**, *m.* [-s] [in commerce] damage, loss.

Dánzig, [a town in Prussia] Dantzic. —er Wasser, [a sort of brandy distilled at Dantzic, also called —er Goldwasser] Dantzic brandy or gold-cordial.

***Daourít**, *m.* [in mineralogy] red tourmalin, rubellite.

Dār, for da in composition.

Daran, *adv.* 1) Dāran, [in the beginning of the sentence or with a particular stress of the voice] on that, on it. — mag ich gar nicht denken, I don't like to think on it; — sehe ich nun aber nichts Kluges, therein I see no great wisdom. 2) Darān [contracted drān] *a)* on that or this, thereon. Ich kann nicht ohne Wehmuth — denken, I cannot think about it without sorrow. *b)* near that, near it. Nahe —, hard by, close to. *c)* to that, to it. Thue Salz —, salt it; gieß' Wasser —, pour water to it. *d)* in that or this thing. Er fand Gefallen —, he took pleasure in it; ich zweifle nicht —, I have no doubt of it. *e)* at that, at it. Er will nicht gern —, he does not like this business, does not set about it willingly; ich habe lange genug daran gearbeitet, I have been working long enough at it. *f)* by that, by it. Ich kannte ihn —, I knew him by it or thereby.

Darān-gehen, *ir. v. intr.* [u. w. seyn] to go near. *Fig.* to set one's self about a business. Ich werde —gehen, I shall go about it. *Prov.* Er geht —, wie der Dieb zum Galgen, he goes to it, like a bear to the stake. —**kommen**, *ir. v. intr.* [u. w. seyn] 1) to come to a thing. 2) to come to one's turn. Nun komme ich —, now is my turn; wenn Sie —kommen, when it comes to your turn. —**liegen**, *ir. v. imp.* and *intr.* [used with seyn and ‖with haben] 1) to lie near any thing. 2) *Fig.* to import, to be of moment or consequence to. Es liegt nichts —, this matters not; was liegt —? what matters it? was liegt dir —? what imports it you? es liegt mir gar nichts —, I do not care a straw for it. —**machen**, I. *v. tr.* to attach, tie, bind or fasten to a thing. II. *v. r.* sich —machen, to set one's self to a business. Ich habe mich —gemacht, I went about it; er wird sich bald —machen, he will soon set about it. —**mögen**, *ir. v. intr.* to be disposed or inclined, to have a wish, to have a liking to a thing. —**müssen**, *ir. v. intr.* to be obliged to take one's turn, to be obliged to do something. † Er muß —, he must die. —**setzen**, *v. tr.* to set near any thing. *Fig.* to expose to chance, to venture, to risk. Sein Leben —setzen, um einen Freund zu retten, to hazard one's life to save a friend; ein Fürst, der so viel —setzte, a prince, who had so much at stake. —**seyn**, *ir. v. intr.* to be at or on a thing. *Fig.* *a)* to be in a certain state or condition. Ich weiß nicht, wie ich — bin, I know not what to think of it; *it.* I don't know on what to depend; er ist übel —, he is badly off; ich bin übel —, I am in a disagreeable situation; bei Einem gut —seyn, to be in favour with any one; wenn ich anders recht — bin, if I am not mistaken, if I am not wrong; er war sehr nahe —, gefangen zu werden, he was very near being taken; es ist nichts —, there is no truth in it; *it.* it is good for nothing. *b)* to be at a thing, to be occupied with a thing. Er ist eifrig —, he is hard at it. —**sollen**, *v. intr.* to be obliged to come to one's turn. —**wagen**, *v. tr.* to hazard, to venture. —**wollen**, *ir. v. intr.* to be inclined or disposed to do something. Er will nicht —, he declines or refuses to do it.

Darauf, *adv.* 1) Dārauf, [in the beginning of the sentence or with a particular stress of voice] on that, on it, upon that, upon it. — sitzt er, he sits on it. *Fig.* — müßt Ihr denken, you must think on it; — können Sie sich verlassen, you may depend on it; — lasse ich mich nicht ein, I do not enter into it, I do not meddle with it; — geht er eben aus, that is what he aims at; — fingen seine Thränen an zu fließen, thereupon his tears began to flow; — antwortete ich, on that, I answer. 2) Daraúf [contracted draúf] on that, on it, upon that, upon it. Hier iſt eine Geige, ſpiele —, there is a violin, play on it; gerade — zu, directly towards it. *Fig.* Sie können ſich — verlaſſen, you may rely upon it; er bringt —, he insists upon it; ich ſchwöre —, I take my oath upon it; zählen Sie beſtimmt —, depend on or upon it; ſieh' —, look to it; eiferſüchtig —, jealous on it; er ſetzte einen zu hohen Werth —, he set too high a value upon it, he overprized it; er beſtand —, he insisted on it; er baut —, he reckons upon that; er wagt es —, he ventures it; es ſtehet der Tod —, it is forbidden or prohibited under pain of death; es ſteht der Kopf —, it is a hanging-matter. *b*) [to point out an immediate consequence] *α*) thereupon. Und — gab er mir ſeine Tochter, and thereupon he gave me his daughter. *β*) after that, thereafter. — ging er zu Bette, thereafter he went to bed; wir aßen zu Mittag, und — gingen wir ſpazieren, we dined, and afterwards took a walk; drei Stunden —, three hours after; den Tag —, the day after; einige Zeit —, some while after; bald —, soon after.

Daraúf⸗geben, *ir. v. tr.* 1) to give an earnest. 2) to confide in the truth of a thing. Er gibt nichts —, he gives no credit to it. —**gehen**, *ir. v. intr.* [u. w. ſeyn] 1) to be spent or consumed. Er läßt viel —gehen, he spends high or a great deal; aller Wein iſt —gegangen, the wine is all drunk up. 2) to perish, to die. —**geld**, *n.* earnest, earnest-money. —**kommen**, *ir. v. intr.* [u. w. ſeyn] to call a thing to mind, to recollect it.

Daraus, *adv.* 1) Dāraus, [in the beginning of a sentence or with a particular stress of voice] out of that, out of it. — folgt, thence follows; — ſehe ich, thence I see; — iſt ein Sprichwort geworden, it has become proverbial; — entſpringen alle Laſter, thence arise all vices; — ſchließe ich, thence I conclude. 2) Daraús, [contracted draús] out of that place, thereout. *Fig.* Es iſt nichts — geworden, it has all come to nothing, was wird endlich — werden? what will at last become of it? ich mache mir nichts —, I do not mind it, I do not care about it; ich kann — nichts machen, I can make nothing of that; du machſt eine Gewohnheit —, you make a custom of it; er machte einen Rock —, he made a coat out of it.

Dárben, [Sw. *tarfwa* and A. S. *thearfan* signifies Mangel leiden, and nöthig haben; [be-]dürfen is allied to it] *v. intr.* to suffer extreme hunger or want, to be very indigent, to starve, to famish. Das —, want, indigence.

Dārbieten, *ir.* I. *v. tr.* to offer gratuitously for reception, to present for acceptance, to tender. Ein Geſchenk —, to proffer a gift; Einem ein Geſchenk —, to present a gift to any one. *Fig.* Das Schloß bietet eine der ſchönſten Ausſichten in Deutſchland dar, the castle presents one of the finest prospects in Germany; Freuden —, to afford pleasures. II. *v. r.* ſich —, 1) to present itself, to be at hand. Die Gelegenheit bietet ſich dar, the occasion offers; der erſte Gegenſtand, der ſich meinen Augen darbot, the first object which presented itself to my sight. 2) [to declare a willingness] to offer.

Dārbringen, *ir. v. intr.* literally, to bring to or before, hence to present for acceptance, to offer. Bringe Gott deine Gebete dar, offer up to God thy prayers. Das —, offering.

• ***Dardanéllen**, *pl.* the Dardanelles.

Darein, *adv.* 1) Dārein, into that place, therein. — geht dieſer Wein nicht, das Faß iſt zu klein, this wine won't all go in, the cask is too small. *Fig.* — werde ich nie willigen, that I shall never consent to. 2) Darein, [in colloquial lang.] into that place, in it, therein, thereinto. Thue andere Zuthaten —, put other ingredients to it. *Prov.* Wer Andern eine Grube gräbt, fällt endlich ſelbſt —, one is often caught in the snare one lays for another. *Fig.* Miſche dich nicht —, meddle not in or with it; gib dich geduldig —, submit patiently to it; — kann ich mich nicht finden, I can't comprehend this thing, I can't make it out, I can't accustom myself to it.

Darein⸗geben, *ir. v. tr.* to give [something] into the bargain, or over and above. —**gehen**, *ir. v. intr.* [u. w. ſeyn] to go into the bargain. —**legen**, *v. r.* ſich —, to interfere in a thing, to act indifferently between contending parties with a view to reconciliation. Er legte ſich —, he mediated. —**reden**, *v. intr.* to interrupt by speaking. Rede mir nicht —, do not interrupt me. —**ſchlagen**, *ir. v. intr.* to strike at random. —**ſehen**, *ir. v. intr.* 1) to look into. 2) to remark upon by way of censure, to animadvert.

Dārgeben, *ir. v. tr.* to offer up. V. Hingeben.

‖**Dārhalten**, *v. tr.* V. Hinhalten.

Darin, *adv.* 1) Dārin, [in the beginning of a sentence or with a particular stress of voice] in that place, in it, therein, thereinto. *Fig.* — halte ich es mit ihnen, there I hold with them; — irren Sie ſich, there you are mistaken; — ſtimmen unſere Briefe nicht mit einander überein, therein our letters do not agree; — ſehe ich nichts, therein I see nothing. 2) Darin [contracted drin], in that place, in it, therein, thereinto. Wer iſt —? who is within? Es iſt nichts —, there is nothing in it; mit — begriffen, included; er hat ein Haus, aber er wohnt nicht —, he has a house, but he does not live in it. *Fig.* Er betrügt ſich —, he is mistaken in &c.

Dārkommen, *ir. v. intr.* V. Daherkommen.

Dārlage, *f.* [*pl.* -n] 1) something laid down, money laid down. 2) [in law] law-expenses. 3) ‖ [incorrectly for] Darlegung *f.*

Dārlangen, *v. tr.* V. Darreichen.

Dārlegen, *v. tr.* literally: to lay before, to put before, hence: Eine Sache —, to explain, to expound a thing; mit Gründen etwas —, to prove something; er legte die Umſtände dar, he stated the circumstances. Die Darlegung, statement.

Dārlehn, Dārlehen, [-s, *pl.* -] [money lent] a loan. Einem ein — geben, to lend any one a sum of money.

Dārleihe, *f.* [*pl.* -n] V. Darlehn.

Dārleihen, *v. tr.* to lend, to loan. Einem eine Summe Geldes —, to lend any one a sum of money.

Dárm, *m.* [-es, *pl.* Därme] [A.S. *thearm*, Ice. *tharm*] [the intestinal canal of an animal] gut. Die Därme, intestines, bowels; die dünnen Därme beſtehen aus drei Theilen, nämlich dem Zwölffinger—, dem Leer— und dem Krumm—, small intestines consist of three portions, namely the duodenum, the jejunum and the ileum; die dicken Därme beſtehen ebenfalls aus drei Theilen, nämlich dem blinden — [Blind—], dem Grimm— und dem Maſt—, large intestines consist also of three portions, namely the cæcum, the colon and the rectum.

Darm⸗bad, *n.* a clyster. —**bandwurm**, *m.* intestinal tape-worm. ‖—**beere**, *f.* the fruit of the wild service, sorb or mapple-leaved service. —**bein**, *n.* [in anatomy] the haunch-bone. —**beinhöcker**, *m.* [in anatomy] the crest [crista] of the haunch-bone. —**beinkrümmung**, *f.* [in anatomy] the sigmoid flexure. —**beinmuskel**, *m.* [in anatomy] iliac muscle. —**beinſchlagader**, *f.* [in anat.] iliac artery. —**bewegung**, *f.* [in anatomy] peristaltic motion. —**bruch**, *m.* [in surgery, intestinal hernia, a rupture of the intestines] enterocele. —**drüſe**, *f.* [in anat.] intestinal gland. —**entzündung**, *f.* an inflammation of the intestines, enteritis. —**fell**, *n.* [in anatomy] the peritoneum. —**fiſtel**, *f.* [in surgery] intestinal fistula. —**gicht**, *f.* [in medicine] the iliac passion, miserere, twisting of the guts. —**gichtig**, *adj.* and *adv.* affected with the iliac passion. —**gichtiſch**, *adj.* and *adv.* having a tendency to produce the iliac passion. —**gichtkraut**, *n.* pale-flowered vetch. —**grimmen**, *n.* the colic, dry-belly-ache. —**haſpel**, *m.* catgut-spinner's reel. —**haut**, *f.* V. —fell. —**jammer**, *m.* V. —gicht. —**kaſten**, *m.* catgut-spinner's dosser. —**knochen**, *m.* V. —bein. —**krampf**, *m.* V. —gicht. —**lehre**, *f.* [in medicine] enterology. —**naht**, *f.* [in anatomy] enteroraphe. —**röhre**, *f.* [a genus of animals, class vermes] teredo. —**ruhr**, *f.* [in medicine] lientery. —**ſaft**, *m.* [in anatomy] intestinal juice or humour. —**ſaite**, *f.* cat-gut, gut-string. Kleine —ſaiten, catlings. —**ſaitenmacher**, *m.* catgut-spinner, gut-spinner. —**ſaitenrahm**, *m.* [with catgut-spinners] tender. —**ſaugader**, *f.* [in anatomy] V. Milchgefäß. —**ſchleim**, *m.* [in anatomy] mucus [which covers the lining membrane of the intestinal canal]. —**ſchnitt**, *m.* [in surgery] enterotomy. —**ſchwanz**, *m.* [in anatomy] a worm-formed appendage to the blindgut. —**ſpritze**, *f.* clyster-pipe. *Fig.* † —**ſtreicher**, *m.* a gut-scraper, an awkward fiddler, a scraper. —**ſtrenge**, *f.* V. —gicht. —**verſchließung**, *f.* V. —gicht. —**waſſerbruch**, *m.* [in surgery] hydro-enterocele. —**weh**, *n.* V. —gicht. —**wurm**, *m.* an intestinal worm, ascaris. —**zwang**, *m.* V. —gicht.

Darnach, Darnieder, V. Danach, Danieder.

‡**Darób**, [contracted into drob] at that, on that account. Sie erröthet —, she blusheth thereat.

Dárre, Dörre, *f.* [*pl.* -n] 1) the act of roasting or drying in kilns. 2) a kiln for drying grain, flax &c. Die Malz—, malt-floor, malt-kiln; die Hopfen—, hop kiln, hop-oast. 3) [a disease] *a*) [in plants] consumption, tabes. *b*) [in animals] consumption. *c*) [with men] V. Schwindſucht. *d*) [in birds] roup.

Darr⸗balken, Dörrbalken, *m.* a beam or iron bar on which the grate of a kiln rests. —**blech**, *n.* a grate used in kilns for drying grain. —**brett**, *n.* a board with holes used instead of a grate in kilns for drying grain. —**fieber**, *n.* hectic fever. —**gekrätz**, *n.* [in metallurgy] washings-slag. —**gras**, *n.* meadow soft-grass. —**haus**, *n.* [a house with a kiln] a drying-house, a kiln. —**horde**, —**hürde**, *f.* a hurdle or crate used for drying malt &c. —**krätze**, V. —gekrätz. —**kupfer**, *n.* [in metallurgy] copper left behind after liquation. —**malz**, kiln-dried malt. —**ofen**, *m.* 1) a drying-stove, a kiln. 2) [in metallurgy] a furnace for reducing copper by liquation. —**ſtaub**, *m.* malt-dust. —**ſtube**, *f.* a room with a kiln. —**ſucht**, *f.* [a disease] consumption, phthisis. —**ſüchtig**, *adj.* and *adv.* phthisical. —**wand**, *f.* V. —blech.

Dārreichen, *v. tr.* [to deliver with the hand extending the arm] to reach, to hand. Er reichte mir eine Pomeranze dar, he reached me an orange.

Dárren, [from the root of dörren] *v. tr.* to kiln-dry, to dry. Malz —, to kiln-dry malt; Hopfen —, to dry hops. *Fig.* [in metallurgy] Kupfer —, to reduce copper by liquation.

Dárrling, *m.* V. Darrkupfer.

Dārſchießen, *ir. v. tr.* to advance [money].

Dārſtellbar, *adj.* and *adv.* that may be exhibited or represented, presentable.

Dárstellen, I. *v. tr.* to set, place or introduce into the presence or before the face of a person. Einen —, to present any one; sich Einem —, to present one's self before any one; [in painting] to represent. Der Maler hat sie schöner dargestellt, als sie ist, the painter has represented her as more beautiful than she is. *Fig.* a) [zeigen] Einen in seiner Blöße —, to expose any one's faults. *b*) to exhibit, to show by action, represent. Die zugetheilte Rolle gut —, to the part assigned. *c*) to make evident, ...ibit to the mind in words, to describe, ...resent. Er hat das Laster mit allen seinen ...eln dargestellt, he has painted vice with horrors. II. *v. r.* sich —, to represent itself. ...Sache stellt sich ganz anders dar, als wir er...ten, the thing has a very different appea... from what we expected.

...ärsteller, *m.* [-s, *pl.* -] one who shows, ex...s or describes, exhibitor, representer. Der ...f der Bühne, he that represents a character ...lay, a stage player, an actor.

...ärstellig, *adj.* and *adv.* representing.

...ärstellung, *f.* presentation, exhibition, re...tation. Die — einer Schlacht, the repre...ion of a battle; die — einer Rolle auf der ..., the representation of a part or character ... stage; es war die erste — dieser Schau...inn, it was the first exhibition of this ...; eine — der Welt, a representation of ...orld; die lebhafte — eines Geschichtschrei..., the lively representation of an historian.

...rstellungs=art, *f.* the manner of re...ting a thing. —gabe, *f.* the gift of repre...ion. —kunst, *f.* the art of representing. ...mögen, *n.* the power or faculty of repre...ion.

...rstrecken, *v. tr.* 1) V. [the more usual] Hin... 2) *Fig.* to advance [money]. V. also Vor...

...thun, *ir. v. tr.* to prove, to evidence, to ... the guilt of an offender &c.], to show, to ...

...tragen, V. Auftragen, Vorsetzen.

...über, 1) darüber, over that place, over ...er it. — geht der Weg nach Albany, over ... the road to Albany. *Fig.* — ist er hin... ...e is above it, that does not move him; ... ich mich nicht beklagt, I have not com... of that; — geht nichts, there is noth...e it, nothing is superior to this. 2) ... over that, over it. Er fiel —, he tumbled ... man muß es — schreiben, one must write ... *Fig.* Ich werde mit ihm — sprechen, ...peak with him about that; es gibt — ...e Meinungen, there are divers opin... ...t it; ich will — nachdenken, I will re...t; haben Sie — nachgedacht? did you ...it or of it? er ist in Sorgen —, he ... himself about it; sie erröthet —, she ...n it; *es geht alles drunter und drüber, ... topsy-turvy; der Verfasser starb —, the ...ied during it; — vergeht die Zeit, time ...er it, thus time will pass away; zwei ...b —, two years and above; fünf Thaler ... five dollars and more; es ist schon ein ... —, it is already a quarter past.

..., I. [= um dieses] 1) dárum. *a*) for that, — gebe ich keinen Heller, for that I give not ...ing; — seid unbesorgt, do not trouble ...f about it; —, weil, because; *er hat für ...darum zehn — bei der Hand, for one why he ...m because at hand. *b*) of that, of it. — hat ... mich gebracht, they have deprived me of it. ...es ist mir bloß — zu thun, daß &c., all that ...ire is, I am only anxious, that &c. 2) darúm [contracted drum] *a*) for that, for it. Zehn tausend Thaler wollte ich — geben, ten thousand dollars I would give for it; ich bekümmere mich nicht —, I do not care for it; ich lobe Sie —, I commend you for it; sich — bekümmern, to be concerned for; ich bitte Sie inständig —, I earnestly intreat this of you; es sei —! let it be so, may be. *b*) of that, of it. Sie weiß —, she is privy to it, she is in the secret; ich bin — gekommen, I have lost it. *c*) [in colloquial lang.] around that, around it. Ich habe einen Acker gekauft und beabsichtige, eine Hecke — [um denselben] zu pflanzen, I have bought a field, and intend to plant a hedge round it. II. *conj.* dárum [= deßwegen], for that or this reason. — wird ein Mann Vater und Mutter verlassen und an seinem Weibe hangen, [in Script.] therefore [for this cause] a man shall leave father and mother and cleave to his wife.

Darumherum, [contracted into drumherum] *adv.* around that or this place.

Darúnten, *adv.* down, below.

Darunter, 1) dárunter, under that, under it. — muß Feuer gemacht werden, thereunder the fire must be kindled. *Fig.* — leidet seine Eigenliebe, thereby suffers his self-love; — kann ich es nicht lassen, for less I cannot give it. 2) darúnter [contracted into drunter] *a*) under that, under it. Sie suchten ihn im Bette und er stak —, they looked for him in the bed, and he was under it; was verstehen Sie —, what do you understand by this? was sucht er —? what is his view in it? *Fig. a*) *Es geht Alles drunter und drüber, all goes topsy-turvy; die Kinder von zwei Jahren und —, the children of two years of age and below. *b*) [conjoined or mingled with, or making part of a number] among. — seyn, to be of the number; mit — begriffen, included, comprehended; dies ist das beste —, this is the best among them; mische Wasser —, mix water with it; es ist kein Unterschied —, there is no difference between them.

Dárwägen, *ir. v. tr.* to weigh before the face of a person.

Dárweisen, *ir. v. tr.* to exhibit or present to the view of others, to show, to display. Einem etwas —, to show something to any one. V. also Darthun.

Dárwerfen, *ir. v. tr.* to throw before the face of a person. V. also Hinwerfen and Vorwerfen.

Dárzählen, *v. tr.* to count down, to pay down.

Dárzeigen, *v. tr.* V. Darweisen.

‖**Darzu**, V. Dazu.

‡**Darzwischen**, V. Dazwischen.

Das, V. Der.

‖**Dase**, *f.* V. Bremse.

Daselbst, *adv.* in that place, there. — wirst du wohnen, there thou shalt abide; — sollst du mich finden, you will find me there; ich habe ihn — nicht gesehen, I did not see him there.

‖**Daselbstig**, V. Dasig.

Dáseyn, *ir. v. intr.* [u. w. seyn] 1) to be present in a certain place. Er ist dagewesen, he has been here. 2) to be, to exist. Als wenn er nie dagewesen wäre, as if he had never existed.

Dáseyn, *n.* [-s] 1) the existence of a person or thing in a certain place, presence. Es ist während meines —s geschehen, that happened when I was present, whilst I was there. 2) being, existence. Das — Gottes läugnen, to deny the existence of a God; die, denen wir das — zu verdanken haben, those to whom we owe our existence, our lives.

Dásjenige, V. Derjenige.

‡**Dásig**, *adj.* being at that place. Um meine —en Freunde zu sehen, to see my friends there.

Dásitzen, *ir. v. intr.* to sit at a certain place.

Dásmahl, *adv.* this time, this once.

Dáß, [originally = das] *conj.* that. *a*) [it denotes the object of the verb going before; sometimes it is the representative of the part of the sentence which follows]. Ich habe gehört, — die Griechen die Türken geschlagen haben, I have heard that the Greeks have defeated the Turks; ich sehe, — er kommt, I see he comes; ich befürchte, — es nur zu wahr ist, I fear it is too true; ich zweifle nicht, — er kommen werde, I do not doubt but he will come; jede Uebertretung des Gesetzes verdient, — sie bestraft werde, every violation of the law merits punishment. *b*) [noting a reason] Ich wundere mich, — Sie hier sind, I wonder at your being here; ich freue mich, — Sie kommen, I am glad that you come; es verdrießt ihn, — man ihn nicht holen ließ, he is vexed that he was not sent for. *c*) [noting a consequence, or introducing an explanation of something going before] Es fing an zu regnen, so — wir nicht abreisten, it began to rain, so we did not depart; ich war zu betrübt, als — ich hätte sprechen sollen, I was too much grieved to be able to speak; in einem solchen Grade, —, in such a degree as. *d*) [noting an object] Kommen Sie, — ich Ihnen meinen Garten zeige, come that I may show you my garden; [sometimes it is preceded by auf] Du sollst deinen Vater und deine Mutter ehren, auf — du lange lebest im Lande &c., [in Script.] honour thy father and mother: that thy days may be long in the land &c. *e*) [noting a condition] Es sei, nur — Sie damit fürlieb nehmen, I consent to it, provided you put up with it; vorausgesetzt, — &c., provided that &c. *f*) [noting time] Es ist noch keine Stunde, — ich ihn gesehen habe, it is not an hour since I saw him; warte, bis — ich komme, wait till I come. *g*) [expressing a wish, utter detestation, consternation, a command &c.] Wollte Gott, — ihr es gethan hättet, I wish to God you had done it; — du verdammt wärest! be damned! — dich der Teufel hole! the devil take you! ach, — Gott erbarme! Lord have mercy upon us! — man uns nur nicht aufhält, if the people only don't stop us; — ich ein Narr wäre, as if I were a fool.

Dasselbe, V. Derselbe.

Dástehen, *ir. v. intr.* to stand in a certain place. Er stand ganz verdutzt da, he stood there quite confounded; er stand wie ein armer Sünder da, he looked or stood there like a culprit.

***Dasymèter**, *m.* [with some] *n.* [-s, *pl.* -] [an instrument for measuring the density of the air] dasimetre.

***Dáta**, *pl.* data, facts.

***Dataria**, *f.* [the chancery of Rome where the datum Romæ is affixed to the pope's bulls] datary.

***Dáten**, *pl.* V. Data.

***Datiren**, *v. tr.* to date [a letter, a bond, a deed &c.]. Der Brief ist vom zehnten August datirt, the letter is dated the tenth of August; von wann ist der Brief hier datirt? what date does this letter bear? zurück —, to antidate.

***Dátiv[us]**, [-s, *pl.* -ive] *m.* [in grammar] dative.

***Dáto**, *adv.* of the date. Bis —, till now, hitherto.

***Datolíth**, *m.* [-en, *pl.* -en] [in mineralogy] borate of lime.

Dáttel, *f.* [*pl.* -n] [from the Gr. δάκτυλος] [the fruit of the great palmtree or date-tree] date, palm-fruit, palm-berry.

Dattel=baum, *m.* the great palm-tree, date-tree. —bohne, *f.* a species of kidney-bean [phaseolus humilis]. —kern, *m.* the kernel of a date. —muschel, *f.* a species of the pierce-stone. —öl, *n.* V. Palmöl. —palme, *f.* V. —baum. —pflaume, *f.* date-plum. —schnecke, *f.* the olive shell. —sperling, *m.* the Capsa sparrow, the Capsa finch. —wald, *m.* a grove of date-trees, date-grove.

*Datum, *m.* [-s] date. Ohne —, dateless; das spätere —, post-date; welches — hat der Brief hier? what date does this letter bear?

Daúbe, *f.* [*pl.* -n] [Fr. *douve*, provinc. Dauge, D. *Duige*] [with coopers, a thin narrow piece of timber of which casks are made] staff, stave, clap-board. Ein Faß in —n schlagen, to stave a cask.

Daubenholz, *n.* staff-wood.

Däúchten, [allied to denken] I. *v. imp.* to judge, to conclude, to think Mir däucht, it seems to me, it appears to me, meseems, methinks; mir däucht, es wird morgen regnen, I think it will rain to-morrow; mich däuchte, it seemed to me, I thought, methought, meseemed; mich däuchte, ich hätte sie gesehen, methought I had seen her. II. *v. r.* sich —, to figure one's self, to fancy, to entertain a flattering opinion of one's self. Er däuchte sich ein Gelehrter zu seyn, he was conceited of his learning.

1. Daüen, V. [the usual word] Verdauen.

2. Daüen, [perhaps allied to the Gr. δεύειν] *v. tr.* [with some tanners] to dye in red, black &c.

Daúer, *f.* duration. *a*) [power of continuance] Dieser Zeug ist von guter —, this stuff wears well; mit verschiedenen Graden der —, with several degrees of lasting; die — des Cedern- oder Eichenholzes, the durability of cedar or oak timber; die — des Thier- und Pflanzenlebens ist sehr beschränkt, the durability of animal and vegetable life is very limited. *b*) [continuance in time] Die — des Lebens, the duration of life; ewige —, everlasting duration; auf die — kann dieß nicht so bleiben, this cannot be of long continuance.

Dauer-gewächs, *n* 1) a perennial plant, perennial. 2) any fruit that keeps long. —pflanze, *f.* a perennial.

Daúerbar, *adj.* and *adv.* V. Dauerhaft.

Daúerhaft, *adj.* and *adv.* [having the quality of lasting] durable [timber, cloth &c.]. Eine —e Farbe, a lasting colour; ein —es Werk, a permanent work. *Fig.* Ein —es Glück, durable happiness; eine —e Gesundheit, a strong health; eine —e Freundschaft, a lasting friendship.

Daúerhaftig, *adj.* and *adv.* V. [the more usual] Dauerhaft.

Daúerhaftigkeit, *f.* durability, durableness, lastingness, permanence, endurance.

Daúerlos, *adj.* and *adv.* not lasting, not permanent, existing or continuing for a short time only, ephemeral.

1. Daúern, [probably allied to the Lat. *durus*, hart, Slavon. *twrde*] *v. intr.* 1) to continue unimpaired, not to decay or perish, to last. Eisen und Steine — lange, iron and stones last long; diese Obstart dauert nicht, this sort of fruit will not keep. 2) to remain in a place, to continue. Er kann nicht in der Kälte —, he cannot stand the cold. 3) to hold on in time or to last, to continue, to endure. Eine Predigt sollte nie zu lange —, a sermon should never be too long; es dauerte nicht lange, so sah ich ihn kommen, it was not long before I saw him come. Syn. Dauern, Währen. Dauern signifies, to remain in existence, to continue in the same state without perishing, not to decay, and contains the cause of a thing's endurance. Währen refers only to the time and to the state, the length of which is marked by the changes of what passes. One may say: die ägyptischen Pyramiden haben bis auf den heutigen Tag gedauert, but not gewährt [the Egyptian pyramids have endured to the present day] being constructed of most durable materials; der Wechsel der Jahreszeiten währet und dauert noch immer fort, the change of the seasons endures continually.

2. Daúern, [Old G. turen] *v. tr.* and *imp.* 1) to grieve at, to be sorry for any thing. Mich dauert der Verlust an Zeit, I regret the loss of time; sein Verlust dauert mich sehr, I grieve much at his loss. 2) to feel pain, sorrow or regret for something done or spoken, to repent. Es dauert mich, I repent of it. 3) to feel pain or grief for any one in distress. Du dauerst mich von ganzem Herzen, I pity you heartily; er hat mich sehr gedauert, I was much concerned for him, I pitied him greatly. Syn. Dauern, Verdrießen, Gereuen. Es gereuet mich differs from es dauert and es verdrießt mich, in referring merely to something which is past, and for which we feel ourselves to blame. Es dauert mich, may be said of something that has happened accidentally. Thus we may say: die Zeit dauert mich [I grieve for the time] which I have been obliged to spend in any business, and mich gereut [reut] die Zeit [I regret the time] which I have foolishly or carelessly thrown away. Verdrießen denotes a higher degree of sorrow or vexation.

‡Daülich, V. Verdaulich.

Daúm, *m.* [-es, *pl.* Däume] V. Daumen.

Daum-kraft, *f.* [in seamen's lang.] hand-screw, jack. —leder, *n.* V. Daumenleder. —ring, *m.* V Daumenring.

Däúmchen, *n.* [-s, *pl.* -] *dimin.* of Daum.

‖Däúmeln, *v. tr.* to put any one's thumb into a thumb-screw. V. Daumenschraube.

Daúmen, *m.* [-s, *pl.* -] [A. S. *thuma*; Ice. *thuma* signifies die Hand; perhaps it is allied to Stamm, Stumpf] 1) the thumb. **Fig.* Gegen Einen den — beißen, [as a gesture of contempt or provocation] to bite the thumb at a person; Einem den — auf's Auge setzen, to keep a tight hand over any one; Einem den — drehen, to flatter any one; Einem den — halten, to support, favour or patronize any one. 2) a measure equal to the breadth of a thumb. Eines —s breit, an inch. 3) [in mills &c.] lift.

Daumen-beuger, *m.* [in anatomy] the flexor of the thumb, flexor. —[s]dick, *adj.* and *adv.* as thick as one's thumb. Das —sdicke Band, thumb-band. *Fig.* —dreher, *m.* a flatterer. —drücker, *m.* [in locks] the handle of the latch. Die Thürklinke mit einem —drücker, thumb-latch. —eisen, *n.* 1) [with wiredrawers] thumb-iron. 2) sometimes for —schraube. 3) [with goldsmiths] a kind of anvil. —klapper, *f.* castanet; *pl.* castanets, snappers. —klopfer, *m.* [in anatomy, an abducent muscle of the thumb] thenar [flexor brevis pollicis manus]. —leder, *n.* [with shoemakers] a ring or sheath of leather to put on the thumb, thumb-stall. —ring, *m.* 1) ‡ thumb-ring [a ring which people of quality formerly wore on the thumb]. 2) or Dummring, V. —leder. —schraube, *f.* an engine of torture applied to the thumb, thumb-screw; *pl.* thummikins. —stock, *m.* V. —schraube. —strecker, *m.* [in anatomy, muscles which serve to extend the thumb] extensor of the thumb. —welle, *f.* [in mills] a rundle on which the lifts are fixed.

Däúmerling, V. Däumling.

Däúmling, *m.* [-es, *pl.* -e] 1) that part of a glove which covers the thumb; a sheath of leather to put on the thumb, thumb-stall. 2) a workman's thimble. 3) a little man, mannikin, †hop o' my thumb [der Knirps, †Drei-Käse-Hoch]. Klein—, [in nursery-tales] litte Tom thumb. 4) *pl.* [in seamen's language] palm.

Daúne, Düne, *f.* [*pl.* -n] [probably from dehnen] [the fine soft feathers of fowls, particularly of the duck kind and especially of the eider-duck] down.

Daúnicht, *adj.* and *adv* [resembling down] downy.

Daúnig, *adj.* [of down] downy.

Daús, *n.* [-ses, *pl.* Däuser] [from the Fr. *deux*] 1) [in German cards, a card with two spots, and also a die with two spots] deuce. 2) [in French cards, a card with one spot; also a die with one spot] ace. **Fig.* Wie ein —, neatly; geputzt wie ein — or Däuschen, neatly dressed; er versteht sich darauf wie ein —, he understands it very well.

‡Dausmann, *m.* a man of distinction, a personage.

*Daúphin, [pron. as in the French] *m.* [-s, *pl.* -s, or, when pronounced Doffin, -e] [the eldest son of the king of France] dauphin.

Daüungssaft, *m.* V. Verdauungssaft.

David, [-s] [a name of men] David, Davy.

Davids-gerste, *f.* V. —korn. —harfe, *f.* [a species of whelk] the harp. Die große —harfe, the musical harp; die edle —harfe, the fair wing; die kleine länglichte —harfe, the small harp stamper. —korn, *n.* a variety of the spring barley.

Davon, 1) Dävon, of that, of it. — weiß ich nichts, I know nothing of it; — ist nicht die Rede, that is not the question; — ist noch Niemand gesund geworden, thereby nobody has yet been restored. 2) Davón. *a*) noting separation or distance. Daß ihr nicht — weichet, weder zur Rechten, noch zur Linken, [in Script.] that ye turn not aside therefrom to the right hand or to the left; ich wohne nicht weit —, I live not far from here. *b*) of or from this thing. Denn welches Tages du — issest, wirst du des Todes sterben, [in Script.] in the day thou eatest thereof, thou shalt surely die; Sie werden keinen Gewinn — haben, you shall not profit by it; was habe ich —? what do I get by it? *c*) concerning, relating to. Haben Sie — gehört? did you hear of it? ... weiß ein Lied — zu singen, I could tell a tale of it. *d*) of the number. Die Meisten — liefen zu den Waffen, die Andern ergriffen die Flucht, most part of them ran to arms, the rest took to their heels; ein Theil — wurde erschlagen, part of these was slain; geben Sie mir die Hälfte —, give me half of it.

Davón-bleiben, *ir. v. intr.* [u. w. ...] to forbear, to hold one's self from moving, or interfering in an affair. —bringen, *ir. v. tr.* ... save, to preserve. —eilen, *v. intr.* [u. w. ...] to haste or hasten away. Er eilte mit Flügelschnelle —, he flew away as on bird's wings. —fahren, *ir. v. intr.* [u. w. seyn] to drive away. —flattern, *v. intr.* to flutter off, or away. —fliegen, *ir. v. intr.* [u. w. seyn] to fly off, ... away. Der Vogel flog —, the bird has flown. —fliehen, *ir. v. intr.* [u. w. seyn] to flee, to ... off, to escape. —führen, *v. tr.* to carry ... —gehen, *ir. v. intr.* [u. w. seyn] to go off, ... depart, to desert. —helfen, *ir. v. intr.* ... help out, to aid in delivering from diffi... Einem —helfen, to help any one out. 2) ... of. Er besaß Geld, aber sie halfen ihm — ... had money, but they rid him of it, they ... him to spend it. —hüpfen, *v. intr.* [u. w. ...] to leap off, or away. —huschen, *v. intr.* [u. w. seyn] to slip off, to flutter away. —jagen, I. ... to chase away, to scare away, to turn off, to ... out of doors. II. *v. intr.* [u. w. seyn] to run or ... off or away in haste or with utmost speed. —kommen, *ir. v. intr.* [u. w. seyn] to come off, to ... to make one's escape, to escape, to get free. ... sie glücklich —kommen, so nenne ihre Befreiung ein Wunder, if they come off safe, call ... deliverance a wonder. **Fig.* Mit einem bl... Auge —kommen, to come off with a little ...

er ist noch gut —gekommen, he came out well at last; ohne Schaden, or ungeschlagen —kommen, to come off clear; glauben Sie so —zukommen? do you think to come off so? er soll nicht so leichten Kaufs —kommen, he shall not get off with impunity. —können, *ir. v. intr.* to be able to get off. Er kann nicht —, he cannot get off —kriechen, *ir. v. intr.* [u. w. seyn] to sneak off. †—kriegen, *v. intr.* V. 1. Abkriegen, 1. —laufen, *ir. v. intr.* [u. w. seyn] to run away, to quit a service without permission. Euer Kind läuft vor einem Frosche —, your child runs away at sight of a frog; bei der Annäherung des Feindes lief das ganze Regiment —, on the approach of the enemy the whole of the regiment ran off or betook themselves to flight; er lief seinem Herrn —, he left his master abruptly; er diente fünf Jahre in Indien, und lief dann —, he served five years in India and deserted afterwards. **Fig.* Es ist zum —laufen, it is insupportable. —machen, *v. r.* sich —machen, to withdraw, or absent one's self in a private manner, to abscond. Er hat sich —gemacht, he departed suddenly, he took French leave; eines Nachts machte sie sich heimlich —, one night she stole away. —müssen, *v. intr.* 1) to be obliged to give up, to leave, to quit or to relinquish something. †and *2) to go off, to die, to decease. —reisen, *v. intr.* [u. w. seyn] to take or go a journey, to depart, to withdraw for safety, to retire. —reiten, *ir. v. intr.* [u. w. seyn] to go away on horseback, to flee on horseback. —rennen, *ir. v. intr.* [u. w. seyn] to run off. —schleichen, *ir. v. intr.* and *r.* to depart or withdraw secretly, to slip away, to sneak or slink off. Er schlich sich —, he stole away. —schwimmen, *ir. v. intr.* [u. w. seyn] 1) to swim away. 2) to be carried away by a current of water, to float away. —sprengen, *v. intr.* [u. w. seyn] to ride away at full speed, at full gallop. —springen, *ir. v. intr.* [u. w. seyn] to leap forth and away, to run off, to get out, to escape. —traben, *v. intr.* [u. w. seyn] to ride away trotting, to trot off. —tragen, *ir. v. tr.* 1) to carry away, particularly to take and carry away [illegible]ly. 2) *Fig.* to get, to obtain. Den Sieg —tragen, to gain the victory, to get the day, to win; durch gute Aufführung Lob —tragen, to get praise by good conduct; Ehre oder Schande —tragen, to come off with honour or disgrace; den Preis —tragen, to gain a prize; Ehren oder Lorbeern —tragen, to earn honours or laurels; Undank —tragen, to be badly thanked for [a] thing; er hat den Schnupfen —getragen, he [has caught] a cold. —trippeln, *v. intr.* [u. w. seyn] to trip off. —ziehen, *ir. v. intr.* [u. w. seyn] to draw off, to retire, to retreat.

Davor, noting presence or motion in the front of any object. 1) Dávor. —mache ich einen Riegel, I shall bolt it. *Fig.* — fürchte ich mich nicht, I am not afraid of it; — hüte dich, take heed of it; — behüte uns Gott! God forbid! 2) Davör. Er steht ja —, he stands before it; ich werde ein Schloß —legen, I shall put a lock on it; es hängt ein Schloß —, it is padlocked. *Fig.* Ich habe einen Abscheu —, I have a horror of it; er machte so viel Lärm, daß man — kein einziges Wort hören konnte, he made so much noise that we could not hear one word.

Dawider, 1) Däwider, noting opposition, contrariety. — habe ich nichts, I do not oppose [it]; — setzte er sich, aber ohne Erfolg, he opposed [it], but without success. 2) Dawider, [bearing upon] against that, against it. Er lehnte sich —, he leaned against it. *Fig.* noting opposition, contrariety. Er mag thun, was er will, ich habe nichts —, he may do what he likes, I have no objection; dafür und — streiten, to dispute pro and con.

Dazu, ||**Darzu**, 1) Däzu, noting motion towards, to that, to it. — thue das fünfte Theil, [in Script.] add the fifth part thereto. *Fig.* — ist es gekommen? is it come to this? — kommt noch dies, thereto comes this; ich rathe Ihnen —, I recommend it to you, I advise you to it; — habe ich keine Lust, I have no mind to it; — ist es bestimmt, it is destined for it; — ist er da, it is for that purpose that he is there, that is his business; — gehört Geld, that requires money. 2) Dazü, noting motion towards. Lege es —, put it thereto; es ist alles gut verwahrt, es kann Niemand —, it is well taken care of, nobody can get at it. *Fig.* Er gehört mit —, he has a hand in it, he is a sharer in the business; wer gibt das Geld —? who will find the money for it? er hat ein großes Vermögen, aber Niemand weiß, wie er — gekommen ist, he has a large fortune, but nobody knows how he came by it; der Schneider muß das Futter und die Knöpfe — geben, the tailor must find the lining and the buttons; er hat nichts — gegeben, he has not contributed to it; sie werden mich nie — zwingen, they shall never compel me to it; er gab ihm noch Schläge —, he beat him to boot; um uns — zu bewegen, to persuade us thereto; ich habe nicht den Muth —, I have no heart for it; er spricht auch —, he puts in his word; was sagen Sie —? what do you say to it? er lachte —, he laughed at it; er war ihm behülflich —, he helped him to it; thun Sie —, make haste, set about it.

Däzumahl, *adv.* at that time, then.

Dazwischen, 1) Däzwischen, noting situation or motion between two or more things. — soll es gehängt werden, there between them it shall be hung. 2) Dazwischen, noting situation or motion between two or more things. Der Raum — ist zu enge, the intermediate space, the intermedium is too narrow; das atlantische Meer liegt —, the Atlantic intervenes between them. *Fig.* — kommen, to come between, to happen in a way to disturb, cross or interrupt, to intervene; Ereignisse können — kommen &c., events may intervene &c.; es ist mir etwas — gekommen, my expectation, hope, desire or design was defeated, I was disappointed; rede mir nicht —, do not interrupt me; sich — legen or — schlagen, to interpose one's authority.

Dazwischenkunft, *f.* interposition, intervention. *Fig.* Ohne die — einer fremden Macht, without the intervention of a foreign power; durch die — einer dritten Person, by the intervention, interference, mediation of a third person.

***Debátte**, *f.* [*pl.* -n] [contention in words or arguments] debate. Die —n im Parlamente, the debates in parliament; die —n, [the published report of arguments for or against a measure] debates.

***Debattiren**, *v. tr.* and *intr.* to debate. Eine Frage —, to debate a question; über einen Punkt —, to discuss a point.

***Débet**, *n.* [-s] [in mercantile language = debt] debit. Sie stehen im —, you are on the debtor-side or debit-side; Einen in das — eintragen, to debit a person.

***Debít**, *m.* [-s] [in commerce] sale. Den — dieses Artikels besorgen die Herren N. & Comp., Messrs. N & Comp. are commissioned with the sale of this article.

***Debitiren**, *v. tr.* [in mercantile lang.] 1) to debit. 2) to sell [merchandise &c]. *Fig.* * and ‡ to deal, to distribute. Er debitirte einen artigen Vorrath von Anzüglichkeiten, he dealt, he distributed a sufficient quantity of invectives.

***Débitor**, *m.* [-s, *pl.* -en] debitor, debtor.

***Débitum**, *n.* [-s, *pl.* -ta] debt.

***Deblokiren**, *v. tr.* [in military affairs] to raise the siege of a town or port.

Debōra, [a name of women] [-'s or -borens] Deborah Debby.

***Debüt**, *n.* [-s, *pl.* -s] [first entrance on any business] outset, particularly the first appearance on the stage, debut. Sein — in der Welt als Redner, his first appearance in the world as an orator.

***Debütiren**, *v. intr.* to set out [in life or the world &c.] Sie debütirt heute Abend, to-night she makes her first appearance on the stage; er debütirte im Parlament mit einem heftigen Angriff gegen &c., he made his maiden-speech in parliament with a violent invective against &c.

***Decade**, *f.* [*pl.* -n] [in the almanac of the French Republic, a number of ten days] decade.

***Decān**, [-s, *pl.* -e] **Decanus**, *m.* [*pl.* -canen] dean. *a*) [an ecclesiastical dignitary in cathedral and collegiate churches; the head of a chapter; the second dignitary of a diocese]. *b*) [in universities, the president of a faculty]. Der — der medizinischen Facultät, the dean of the faculty of medicine.

Decanusstab, *m.* verge.

***Decanāt**, *n.* [-es, *pl.* -e] [the office of a dean] deanery, deanship.

***Decatiren**, **Decatisiren**, *v. tr.* [in commerce and with tailors] to spunge cloth, and gloss it afterwards by a press.

***Decèmber**, *m.* V. Dezember.

***Decèmvir**, *m.* [-s, *pl.* -n] [one of the ten magistrates, who had absolute authority in ancient Rome] decemvir.

***Decemvirāt**, *n.* [-es, *pl.* -e] decemvirate.

***Decénnium**, *n.* [-s, *pl.* -cennien] [a period of ten years] decennary.

***Decént**, *adj.* and *adv.* decent.

***Decénz**, *f.* decency, propriety, modesty.

***Dechánt**, **Déchent**, *m.* [-en, *pl.* -en] V. Decan.

***Dechaneí**, **Decheneí**, *f.* [the house of a dean] deanery.

Décher, *m.* [-s, *pl.* -] [Mid. Lat. *dicra*; allied to the Gr. *δέκα*, zehn] [among dealers in leather, the number of ten hides or skins] dicker.

***Dechiffreūr**, *m.* [-s, *pl.* -s or -e] [pron. Deschiffröhr] decipherer.

***Dechiffrīren**, [pron. Deschiffrihren] *v. tr.* to decipher [a letter written in ciphers].

***Decimāl**, *adj.* [in compositions] increasing or diminishing by ten, decimal.

Decimal-bruch, *m.* decimal fraction. —rechnung, *f.* decimal arithmetic. —system, *n.* decimal system. —zahl, *f.* decimal number.

***Decimīren**, *v. tr.* [to take the tenth part, to select every tenth man] to decimate, to tithe.

Déck, *n.* [-es, *pl.* -e] [in seamen's language] V. Verdeck.

Deck-planke, *f.* deck plank. —schwabber, *m.* main stay-sail. —stützen, *pl.* V. Stützen. worpen, —wrangen, *pl.* the deck-transoms.

Décke, *f.* [*pl.* -n] 1) any thing which is laid, set or spread over another thing, a cover, as die Bett—, the covering of a bed, a quilt, a coverlet, a counterpane; Pferde—n, horse-cloths; Sattel—n, saddle-cloths; die Tisch—, table-cloth; die — eines Kutschenbocks, hammer-cloth *Fig.* *Mit Jemanden unter einer — stecken or liegen, to act in concert with any one, to collude with any one; sie stecken unter einer —, † they piss through one quill; unter der — der Nacht, under cover of night; *poet.* die Nacht breitete ihre dunkle — auf or über die Fluren, night spread her dusky mantle over the fields; der Winter breitete seine weiße — über das Land, winter spread his mantle of snow over the country. *Prov.* Jeder strecke sich nach der —, stretch your arm no further, than your sleeve will reach; stretch your legs according to your coverlet; cut your cloak according to your cloth. 2) [with bookbinders] paper, parchment &c. for the cover of a book; *it* the cover or binding itself 3) [with hunters] the skin of wolves, bears, badgers &c. 4) [in botany; in ferns, a tender membrane (indusium)] the cover which surrounds the seeds. 5) the snow and any thing which protects plants and herbs from cold in winter. 6) [with tanners] Eine — von ausgebeizter Lohe machen, to top the pit. 7) the covering which overlays the inner roof of a building, or the timbers which form the top of a room, ceiling. 8) any thing which veils or conceals, a screen, disguise, cover.

Decken=flechter, *m.* mat-maker. —gemählde, *n.* ceiling-piece. —macher, *m.* V. —flechter. —stück, *n.* V. —gemählde.

Deckel, *m.* [-s, *pl.* -] 1) [that which shuts the opening of a vessel or box] a cover, a lid. Ein kleiner —, a covercle; der — eines Kastens oder Koffers, the lid of a chest or trunk; der — eines Topfes, a pot-lid; der — eines Glases, the cover of a glass; der — einer Kanne, the lid of a tankard. 2) [in architecture, the uppermost member of the entablature of a column] cornice. 3) [in botany, a lid or cover to a capsule, in conchs, the plate or door with which some species of testàceous animals close the aperture of their shells] operculum. Mit einem — versehen, operculate, operculated. 4) [in gunnery, a piece of thin or sheet lead that covers the vent of a cannon] apron. 5) [with bookbinders] the cover of a book, binding. || 6) a piece of tinned iron plate to cover the linch-pin. 7) [in printing] tympan. Der große —, the outer tympan; den — überziehen, to put on the tympans, to cover the tympans. 8) [in metallurgy] the uppermost board of the bellows. † and ‡ 9) a hat.

Deckel=band, *n.* a joint, a hinge. —feder, *f* [with gunsmiths] hammer-spring. —glas, *n.* a glass with a cover. —kanne, *f.* a pitcher with a cover, a tankard. —korb, *m.* a basket with a cover. —schnecke, *f.* the name of operculate snails. —sieb, *n.* a sieve with a double bottom [the lowest of which is made of leather]. —stuhl, *m.* [in printing] gallows.

Decken, I. *v. tr.* to overspread the surface of a thing with another substance, to lay or set over, to deck. Ein Tischtuch auf den Tisch —, to cover the table with a cloth; den Tisch —, to lay the cloth, to spread the table; es ist gedeckt, the cloth is laid; ein Dach —, to cover a roof with tiles &c.; ein Haus —, to cover the roof of a house, to nail a house; den Wein —, to earth vines [to protect them from cold]. [in mathematics] to coincide exactly when laid over one another. Zwei Figuren, Linien, die sich —, figures, lines, that are in congruity; gedeckte Pfeifen, [in organs] pipes with a cover. *Fig. a)* to cover, to conceal by some intervening object. Die Anhöhe deckt das Haus, the house is covered from our sight by the hill. *b)* [among free-masons] die Loge —, to be no longer a freemason. *c)* to cover, to shelter, to protect, to defend. Eine Schwadron Reiter deckte die Truppen auf dem Rückzuge, a squadron of horse covered the troops on the retreat. *d)* [in a more figurative sense] to cover, [in commerce] to reimburse. Ich bin hinlänglich gedeckt, I have sufficient security; die Einnahmen — die Schulden nicht, the receipts do not cover the expenses. II. *v. r.* sich —, to be covered, [in mathematics] to be in congruity.

Deck=bank, *f.* Die —bank in einem Steinbruche, the top of a quarry. —bett, *n.* a feather-bed which serves as a quilt, upper-bed. —blatt, *n.* [in botany] a leaf which covers another leaf. —farbe, *f.* [in painting] an opaque colour. —feder, *f.* [in nat. history] Die —federn der Vögel, the coverts of birds. —fisch, *m.* [a fish] stromateus. —formen, *pl.* ground-blocks for calico-printers. —gang, *m.* 1) a covered walk or alley. 2) [in fortification] covert-way. —garn, *n.* V. —netz. —hammer, *m.* nail-drawer. —korb, *m.* voider. —lehm, *m.* V. Zierlehm. —lehne, *f.* V. Deckel 6. —mantel, *m.* a cover, a disguise a pretext, a cloak, a fair pretence. Der —mantel einer Schlechtigkeit, cover-shame; unter dem —mantel der Religion, under the mask of religion. —messer, *n.* [with charcoal-burners] a knife with a crooked point. —netz, *n.* [with hunters, fowlers] sweep-net. —platte, *f.* [in building] a flagstone. Die —platte eines Brunnens, the brim of a well, the verge. —rasen, *m.* sod, turf for lining parapets. —reisig, *n.* —reiser, *pl.* brush-wood used for covering charcoal-piles. —stein, *m.* V. —platte. —werk, *n.* [in fortification] blinds.

1. Decker, *m.* [s, *pl.* -] [from Decken] he that covers or decks, [used chiefly in composition]. Der Tafel—, table-decker; Dach—, one who roofs a house or other building, a tiler, slater &c.

2. Decker, *m.* [-s, *pl.* -] [from Deck] only used in compositions: as ein Zwei—, a two-decked ship, a two-decker; ein Drei—, a three-decked ship, a three-decker.

Deckung, *f.* 1) the act of covering. 2) *Fig. a)* cover, shelter, defence. *b)* [in commerce] reimbursement 3) that which covers, covering, cover.

*Declamatiōn, *f.* 1) [speaking or reading rhetorically; often it is used for a noisy harangue, without solid sense or argument] declamation. —en, [public speeches of students, practised as exercises in oratory] declamations. 2) [the art or manner of uttering a discourse publicly with propriety and gracefulness] delivery.

*Declamātor, *m.* [-s, *pl.* -en] declaimer, declaimant.

*Declamatōrik, *f.* [the art of uttering a discourse publicly with propriety and gracefulness] delivery.

*Declamatōrisch, *adj.* and *adv.* declamatory.

*Declamatōrium, *n.* [-s, *pl.* -ria or -rien] a public entertainment at which poems, passages from plays &c. are recited.

*Declamiren, *v. tr.* and *intr.* 1) to declaim, to recite, to deliver. 2) to speak loudly or earnestly, to declaim, [in contempt] to declaim.

*Declinābel, *adj.* and *adv.* [in grammar] declinable.

*Declinatiōn, *f.* 1) [in grammar] declension, inflection [of nouns, adjectives and pronouns]. 2) [in astronomy] declination.

*Declinatōrisch, *adj.* and *adv.* declining.

*Declinatōrium, *n.* [-s, *pl.* -ria or -rien] [an instrument in dialing] declinator, declinatory.

*Decliniren, I. *v. tr* [in grammar] 1) to decline, to inflect [a noun &c.]. 2) to shun or avoid, to refuse, not to engage in, to decline. II. *v. intr.* [to turn aside] to deviate.

*Decóct, *n.* [-es, *pl.* -e] decocture, decoction. Ein schwaches — von China, a weak decoction of Peruvian bark.

*Decoctiōn, *f.* decoction [the act of boiling a substance in water, for extracting its virtues; a substance drawn by decoction].

*Decontenanciren, [pron. Dekongtenangsihren] *v. tr.* to put out of countenance, to disconcert, to intimidate, to brow-beat.

*Decorateūr, [pron. Dekoratöhr] *m.* [-s, *pl.* -s] V. Bühnenmahler.

*Decoratiōn, *f.* 1) V. Bühnenmahlerei. 2) [in theatres, the scenes, which are changed, as occasion requires] decoration. 3) decoration, ornament [of an order of knighthood &c].

*Decoriren, *v. tr.* 1) to decorate, to embellish, to adorn. Ein Zimmer —, to furnish a room with pictures, curtains &c. 2) to decorate, to distinguish any one with a riband or star.

*Decōrum, *n.* [-s] decorum, decency. Um das — zu beobachten, for decency's sake.

*Decouragiren, [pron. Dekuraschihren] *v. tr.* to discourage, to dishearten, to dispirit.

*Decrescéndo, *adv.* [in music] decrescendo.

*Decrét, *n.* [-es, *pl.* -e] [judicial decision, an order, edict or law] decree.

*Decretālen, *pl.* [a collection of the popes' decrees] decretals.

*Decretiren, *v. tr.* [to determine judicially: to fix or appoint] to decree.

*Dedicánt, *m.* [-en, *pl.* -en] dedicator.

*Dedicatiōn, *f.* dedication.

*Dediciren, *v. tr.* to dedicate [a book &c.].

*Deduciren, *v. tr.* 1) to deduce [unknown truths from principles already known &c.]. 2) to evince, to prove.

*Deductiōn, *f.* 1) [consequence drawn] deduction. 2) proof, evidence.

*Defect, I. *adj.* and *adv* defective; [especially used amongst printers] imperfect. II. *m.* [-es, *pl.* -e] any want, defect, deficiency, deficience; [in printing] imperfection.

Defect=bogen, *m.* [in printing] imperfect sheet. —kasten, *m.* [in printing] case of imperfections. —regal, *n.* [in printing] the frame for the cases of imperfections. —zettel, *m.* [with printers] the bill of the imperfect fount.

*Defectiva and Defectiva, *pl.* [in gra[mmar]] defective verbs [which want some of the tenses

*Defensiōn, *f.* defence [chiefly in law].

*Defensiv and Defensiv, *adj.* and *adv.* [de]fensive [especially in military affairs]. Sich — [auf] der —e [ver]halten, to stand upon the defen[sive]. Die —e, defensive; die —e ergriffen haben, [to] be on the defensive, to stand on the def[ensive]

*Defensor, *m.* [-s, *pl.* Defensōren] [in ...] pleader, advocate.

*Deficit, *n.* [-s, *pl* -s or -e] deficiency, de[ficit]. Ein — [or Ausfall] bei den Steuern, a defi[ciency in] the taxes.

*Defilée, *n.* [-s, *pl.* -n] [in milit. affairs] d[efile], defilee.

*Defiliren, *v. intr.* 1) to march off in a [line] or file by file, to defile, to file. 2) [to go ab[out in a] military procession] to parade. Vor dem Feld[herrn] vorbei —, to march past the general.

*Definiren, *v. tr.* 1) to define [the words, v[ir]tue &c.]. 2) to describe, to define [a line or angle &c.].

*Definitiōn, *f.* [in logic] definition.

*Definitiv, *adj.* and *adv.* definitive, deter[]mining, final.

Definitiv=beschluß, *m.* final decision. —friede, *m.* final peace. —sentenz, *f.* definitive sentence. —tractat, —vertrag, *m.* definite treaty. —urtheil, *n* final judgment

*Definitum, *n.* [-s] [thing defined] definite.

*Defraudánt, *m.* [-en, *pl.* -en] a defrauder, a cheat, a smuggler.

*Defraudatiōn, *f.* cheat, smuggling.

*Defraudiren, I. *v. tr.* to defraud, to commit a fraud on, to cheat. Den Zoll, die Ac[cise] —, to defraud the customs, the excise, to [com]mit a fraud on the revenue. II. *v. intr.* to sm[ug]gle.

Degen, *m.* [-s, *pl.* -] 1) [allied to the S

daggert, Ital. *daga*, Fr. *dague*, Dolch, to the Eng. *to dig*. bohren] [an offensive weapon] sword. Ein Galanterie—, ein Hof—, a dress-sword, a court-sword; einen — tragen, to wear a sword; den — ziehen, to draw the sword; sich auf den — schlagen, to fight with swords. 2) [A. S. and Sw. *thaegn*; perhaps from taugen] *Fig.* a swords-man, warrior, soldier; *it.* a good fellow, an honest blade. 3) V. Laufstock.

Degen=band, *n.* sword-knot. **—fisch**, *m.* V. Schwertfisch. **—fläche**, *f.* the flat side of the sword-blade. **—förmig**, *adj.* and *adv.* having the shape of a sword, sword-shaped, ensiform. **—förmige Blätter**, ensiform leaves. **—futter**, *n.* V. —scheide 1. **—gefäß**, *n.* sword-hilt. **—gehenk**, *n.* sword-belt, sword-girdle. **—griff**, *m.* the haft of a sword, sword-hilt. **—gürtel**, *m.* sword-girdle. **—haken**, *m.* sword-hook. **—heft**, *n.* V. —griff. *Fig.* **—held**, *m.* [in contempt] sworder. **—klinge**, *f.* sword-blade. **—knopf**, *m.* pommel. *Fig.* Ein alter deutscher —knopf, an honest blade, a good old fellow, a blunt honest fellow. **—koppel**, *f.* V. —gehenk. **—kraut**, *n.* the great burr-reed. **—öl**, *n.* V. —schwarz. **—quast**, *m.* **—quaste**, *f.* sword-knot [Portepee]. **—schärfe**, *f.* 1) the sharpness of a sword. 2) the cutting part of the sword-blade. **—scheide**, *f.* 1) the sheath of a sword, scabbard. 2) *Fig.* [in conch.] a species of nautilus [nautilus legumen]. **—schmied**, *m.* sword-cutler. V. also Schwertfeger. **—schwarz**, *n.* a thick oil used in distempers of horses. **—spitze**, *f.* the point of a sword. **—stich**, **—stoß**, *m.* the thrust or stab of a sword. **—stock**, *m.* sword-stick, sword-cane, tuck-stick.

***Degeneratiōn**, *f.* degeneracy, degenerateness.

***Degeneriren**, *v. intr.* [to become worse] to degenerate. Pflanzen, Thiere —, plants, animals degenerate.

***Degradiren**, *v. tr.* to degrade [an officer &c.].

Dehnbar, *adj.* and *adv.* [capable of extension; easy to be drawn] extensible, ductile.

Dehnbarkeit, *f.* extensibility, ductility, ductileness. Die — des Goldes oder Eisens, the ductility of gold or iron.

Dehnen, [allied to the Gr. τείνω (τένω τάω) and the Lat. *tendo* and *teneo*] I. *v. tr.* to stretch in any direction, to extend. Das Gold läßt sich am meisten —, gold is the most ductile of metals. *Fig.* a) to draw out in pronunciation, to utter in a slow lengthened tone. Die Wörter —, to drawl one's words; ein gedehnter Ton, a lengthened sound; eine gedehnte [schleppende] Sprache, drawl; eine gedehnte Silbe, a lengthened syllable [as vōr, nāch]. *b*) to extend, to lengthen [a discourse &c.]. II. *v. r.* sich —, 1) to be extended, to stretch. Lederne Handschuhe — sich, leather gloves stretch or widen. *Fig.* Die Nacht dehnt sich lang, the night lasts long; der Weg dehnt sich sehr, the way is very long. 2) to stretch one's self.

Dehn=ton, *m.* [in grammar] lengthened tone. **—zeichen**, *n.* V. Dehnungszeichen.

Dehnung, *f.* extending, stretching. *Fig.* Die — einer Silbe, the lengthening of a syllable.

Dehnungszeichen, *n.* [an accent serving to note or distinguish a syllable of an intermediate sound between acute and grave] circumflex.

Deich, *m.* [-es, *pl.* -e] [probably from the A. S. *dician*, graben, Eng. *to dig*] 1) [a mound of earth, of stones, or other materials, intended to prevent low lands from being inundated by the sea or a river] dike, dam, causey, causeway. Einen — aufführen, to make a dam; einen — einlegen, zurücklegen, einziehen or eine Einlage machen, to form a dammed dike on a shorter line; einen — durchstechen, to pierce a dike; zu —e fahren, to betake one's self to a dike in order to repair it; die —e belaufen, to visit, to inspect the dikes; den — aus der Last bringen, to repair a breach in a dike. 2) a pile, rick or stack of dry turf.

‖**Deich=amt**, *n.* dike-office, dike-court. **—anker**, *m.* the ground or foundation upon which a dike is raised. **—arbeit**, *f.* the work done at dikes, the raising of dikes. **—arbeiter**, *m.* a workman employed at dikes. **—aufseher**, *m.* the overseer of the dikes. **—bau**, *m.* 1) the act of raising or building a dike. 2) the art of raising or building dikes. **—baumeister**, *m.* a builder of dikes. **—beamte**, *m.* an officer employed at dikes. **—beschauer**, *m.* V. —gräfe. **—besteck**, **—bestick**, *n.* the profile of a dike. **—bruch**, *m.* a breach, a break in a dike. **—damm**, *m.* a small dike. **—eidige**, *m.* a sworn overseer of the dikes. **—erde**, *f.* earth fit for constructing a dike. **—frei**, *adj.* and *adv.* free from the charge of keeping a dike in repair. **—fuß**, *m.* V. —anker. **—geschworne**, *m.* V. —eidige. **—gräber**, *m.* dike-digger. **—gräfe**, *m.* dike-grave, dike-reeve. **—gräfenamt**, *n.* the office of a dike-reeve. ‖**—hauptmann**, *m.* V. —gräfe. **—herr**, *m.* the owner of a part of a dike, which he must keep in repair. **—kamm**, *m.* the ridge of a dike. **—kolbe**, *f.* [a plant] great cat's tail, or reed-mace. **—kosten**, *pl.* the expenses of constructing dikes and keeping them in repair. **—land**, *n.* diked land. **—lücke**, *f.* a hole in a dike made by water. **—meister**, *m.* dike-master. **—nachbar**, *m.* dike-neighbour. **—pflicht**, *f.* the charge of keeping a dike in repair. **—pflichtig**, *adj.* and *adv.* obliged to keep a dike in repair. **—rath**, *m.* a counsellor of the dike-court. **—recht**, *n.* dike-laws. **—richter**, *m.* dike-judge. **—schatz**, *m.* dike-contribution. **—schau**, *f.* the visitation of the dikes. **—schleuse**, *f.* the sluice, or watergate of a dike. **—schoß**, *m.* dike-contribution. **—schulze**, *m.* a surveyor of dikes. **—sohle**, *f.* the sods which cover the sides of a dike. **—ufer**, *n* dike-bank. **—verlag**, *m.* an advance of money &c. made for keeping dikes in repair. **—weg**, *m.* dike-way, dike-path. **—wesen**, *n* all that belongs to the constructing of dikes. **—zwang**, *m.* dike-judicature.

Deichen, *v. intr.* to raise or build a dike, also to repair a dike.

Deicher, *m.* [-s, *pl.* -] a workman employed at dikes, a ditcher.

Deicherlohn, *m.* the wages of a workman employed at dikes.

1. **Deichsel**, *f.* [*pl.* -n] [allied to Deich] [an iron instrument used for chipping a horizontal surface of timber] an adz.

2. **Deichsel**, *f.* [*pl.* -n] [allied either to Stock, Stecken, (Slavon. *Tyc* signifies Pfahl) or to ziehen, Low-Sax. tehen] the pole of a carriage, the beam, shaft, thill, the tongue or neap.

Deichsel=arm, *m.* shaft-bar. **—blech**, *n.* pole-plate, beam-plate. **—eisen**, *n.* a long narrow piece of iron fastened to the right side of a carter's saddle, that supports the stirrup. **—gabel**, *f.* the shafts. **—haken**, *m.* pole-hook. **—kette**, *f.* V. Halskette. **—nagel**, *m.* the pin on which the pole is fixed, thill-pin. **—pferd**, *n.* shaft-horse, wheel-horse, thill-horse, thiller, wheeler. **—ring**, *m.* thill-ring. **—steg**, *m.* [with cartwrights] the foot-board of a carriage.

1. **Dein**, *pron. possessive* representing the second person [Goth. *theins*, Ice. *thinn*, Engl. *thine* &c.] 1) [belonging to thee, relating to thee] thy. — Kopf, thy head; — Freund, thy friend; —e Mutter, thy mother; —e Eltern, thy parents; — großes Haus, thy great house; [joined with Halben, Wegen, Willen; the final n is changed in t] deinethalben, deinetwegen, deinetwillen, for thy [your] sake, in thy [your] behalf, on thy [your] account; — ist das Reich und die Kraft und die Herrlichkeit, thine is the kingdom, and the power, and the glory; ich will nichts von dem nehmen, was — ist, I will not take any thing that is thine; diese Bücher sind nicht —, these books are not thine; über das Dein und Mein streiten, to contend for one's property. 2) [for der, die, das Deinige; when the nom. and accus. case is changed in deiner, deines (deins) and deiner, deine, deines (deins)] thine. Dies ist nicht mein Buch, sondern deines, that book is not mine, but yours; er schickte es nicht meinem Bruder, sondern deinem, he sent it not to my brother, but to yours.

2 **Dein**, [the second case of the pron. du, contracted for deiner]. Ich erbarme mich —, I pity you.

Deine, [der, die, das] [the abstract form of the pronoun possessive dein V. Dein 1.] thine, yours. Ich bin der —, I am yours; grüße die —n, my compliments to your family.

1. **Deiner, Deine, Deines**, [deins] *pron. possessive* [that represents the second person, V. Dein 1.] thine, yours.

2. **Deiner**, [genitive case of the pron. possessive du] of thee, of you. Man lachet —, they laugh at you; wir haben — gewartet, we have waited for you.

Deinethalben, —wegen, —willen, V. Dein 1.

Deinige, [der, die, das] [the abstract form of the pron. possessive dein] thine, yours. Mein Führer ist hier, wo ist der —? here is my guide, where is yours? [also as a noun] nimm das — in Acht, take care of your property, thue das —, do what is thine, do your duty; grüße die —n, my compliments to your family.

Deining, *f.* [*pl.* -en] [in seamen's lang., the waves or fluctuation of the sea after a storm] swell.

Deinsen, *v. intr.* [in seamen's lang., to remain behind] to go or fall astern, to make sternway.

***Deismus**, *m.* [the doctrine or creed of a deist] deism.

Deissel, *m.* [-s, *pl.* -n] [among ship-carpenters] adz.

Deisseln, *v. tr.* [among ship-carpenters] to dub.

***Deist**, *m.* [-en, *pl.* -en] [one who believes in the existence of a God, but denies revealed religion] deist.

***Deistisch**, *adj.* and *adv.* deistic, deistical. Ein —es Buch, a deistical book.

***Del Crédere**, [in commerce] warrantee. — stehen, to stand surety, to stand or warrant del credere.

***Delegat**, *m.* [-en, *pl.* -en] a delegate, a deputy, a vicar.

***Delegiren**, *v. tr.* to delegate, to send away, to send on embassy.

***Delegirter**, *m.* [-ten, *pl.* -ten] V. Delegat.

***Delicāt**, *adj.* and *adv.* 1) delicate = fine, soft. 2) delicate = nice, pleasing to the taste. Eine —e Schüssel or ein —es Gericht, a delicate dish. 3) delicate = that must be touched with care. Ein —er Punkt, a delicate point; eine —e Frage, a delicate question.

***Delicatèsse**, *f.* [nice susceptibility of impression] delicacy.

***Delicatèssen**, *pl.* delicacies, dainties.

***Delictum**, *n.* [-s, *pl.* -e] [a law term] a crime.

***Delinquént**, *m.* [-en, *pl.* -en] [in law] a delinquent, an offender.

***Delinquéntinn**, *f.* [a female that offends] a female delinquent.

***Delirium**, *n.* [-s] [a roving or wandering of the mind, disorder of the intellect; an alienation of mind connected with fever] delirium.

*Delphin, *m.* [-s, *pl.* -e] 1) [a genus of cetaceous fish] dolphin. 2) *pl. Fig.* [two handles placed on the second reinforce-ring of brass cannons] dolphins.

*Delphinit, *m.* [-s] [in mineralogy] V. Epidot.

*Delta, *n.* [-s] [the Greek name of the letter *d*, Δ] *Fig.* Das — [in Aegypten], a part of Egypt, thus called from its triangular form, the Delta.

Delta=förmig, *adj* and *adv.* [resembling the Greek Δ] deltoid, triangular; [in botany] ein —es Blatt, a deltoid leaf. —muskel [or deltaförmige Muskel], *m.* [in anatomy, a muscle of the shoulder] the deltoid muscle.

Dem, [the dative case of the singular number of the article and relative pron. der and das] to the, to whom, to which. V. Der, Das.

*Demagog, *m.* [-en, *pl.* -en] [a leader of the people, any leader of the populace] a demagogue.

*Demagogisch, *adj.* and *adv.* demagogical. —e Umtriebe, [in modern language] demagogical stratagems.

Demant, [Diamant] *m.* [-s or -en, *pl.* -e or -en] [from the Gr. ἀδάμας] 1) [a mineral, gem or precious stone, of the most valuable kind] diamond. Ein roher or ungeschliffener —, a rough diamond; ein roher —, [among jewellers] brait; ein eckig geschliffener —, brilliant; künstliche oder nachgemachte —en, factitious diamonds or paste. 2) *Fig.* *a*) [an instrument among glaziers for cutting glass] diamond, diamond-pencil, quarrel. *b*) [a very small printing letter] diamond.

Demant [Diamant(en)]=band, *n.* a diamond necklace or bracelet. —bort, *n.* diamond-dust or powder. —büschel, *m.* and *n.* a tuft of diamonds. —druse, *f.* V. Quarzdruse. —förmig, *adj.* and *adv.* diamonded. —gewicht, *n.* [the weight of four grains used by jewellers in weighing precious stones and pearls] carat. —glanzblättchen, [among jewellers] a foil [placed under diamonds]. —grube, *f.* diamond-mine. —handel, *m.* jeweller's trade. —händler, *m.* jeweller. —kette, *f.* a diamond chain. —knopf, *m.* a diamond button. —kreuz, *n.* a diamond cross. —mörser, *m.* a mortar in which diamonds are pounded or bruised with a pestle. —mutter, *f.* diamond-ore. —nadel, *f.* a diamond pin. —pulver, *n.* V. —bort. —ring, *m.* a diamond ring. —schale, *f.* [with jewellers] a small cup in which diamond-dust is kept. —schleifen, *n.* the grinding or cutting of diamonds. —schleifer, *m.* diamond-cutter. —schmuck, *m.* jewels or a set of diamonds. —schneiden, *n.* the cutting of diamonds. —schneider, *m.* diamond-cutter. —spath, *m.* the corindon-harmophane [of Haüy], corindon adamantin [of Brogniart], the korund [of Werner], the adamantin spar [of Kirwan], corundum[-stone]. —spatherde, *f.* a sort of earth found in the corundum. —staub, *m.* V. —bort. —strauß, *m.* V. —büschel. —tinte, *f.* [with jewellers] the colour for foils. —uhr, *f.* a watch set with diamonds, a diamond watch. —werk, *n.* a mine where diamonds are found in strata.

Demanten, [Diamanten] *adj.* and *adv.* 1) [consisting of diamonds, or set with diamonds] diamond. Eine demantne Kette, a diamond chain. 2) *Fig.* [resembling a diamond] diamond.

*Demarkation, *f.* [the act of marking, or of ascertaining and settling a limit] demarcation.

Demarkationslinie, *f.* line of demarcation.

‖Demat, Diemat, *n.* [-es, *pl.* -e] a measure of length for surveying ground.

Demnach, *conj.* in consequence of something. Wenn es — eine göttliche Vorsehung gibt, if then there be a divine providence; er erröthet, — ist er schuldig, he blushes, therefore he is guilty; — sollte man glauben, daß &c., according to that, one would think, that &c.

Demnächst, *adv.* 1) shortly, in a little time, as soon as possible. 2) thereon, thereupon.

Demohngeachtet, Demohnerachtet, Demungeachtet, V. Ungeachtet.

*Demoiselle, [usually pronounced, when put before the christian or the proper name Demoasell (pl. -s), but when speaking of unmarried ladies or misses in general, Demoaselle (pl. -n)] *f.* 1) a maiden lady. 2) a miss.

*Demokrat, *m.* [-en, *pl.* -en] democrat.

*Demokratie, *f.* [*pl.* -en] democracy.

*Demokratisch, I. *adj.* democratic, democratical. II. *adv.* democratically.

*Demoliren, *v. tr.* to demolish, to raze, to destroy. Eine Festung —, to demolish a fortification.

*Demolirung, *f.* demolition. Die — von Befestigungswerken, the demolition of military works.

*Demonstration, *f.* 1) [certain proof exhibited] demonstration. 2) [in military affairs] threatening operation.

*Demonstriren, *v. tr.* to demonstrate [a problem in geometry &c.] V. Beweisen, Darthun, Erklären.

*Demontiren, *v. tr.* [in military affairs] 1) to dismount, to unhorse. Der Soldat demontirte seinen Gegner, the soldier unhorsed his adversary. 2) [to break the carriages or wheels of guns, and render them useless] to dismount [a cannon].

*Demoralisiren, *v. tr.* to dishearten, to dispirit [troops]; [in a more general sense] to demoralize [a people].

Demungeachtet, V. Ungeachtet.

1. ‖Demuth, *m.* [-es] V. Thymian.

Demuth=pflanze, *f.* V. Sinnkraut.

2. Demuth, *f.* [De appears to be allied to the Ice. *thy*, der Knecht, *thia*, demüthigen, as well as to dienen] [humbleness of mind, a modest estimate of one's own worth] humility. Dem Herrn dienend mit aller —, [in Script.] serving the Lord with all humility of mind; wandelt mit aller — und Sanftmuth, [in Script.] walk with all lowliness and meekness. *Prov.* —, Zucht und Höflichkeit ziert mehr als ein goldnes Kleid, an ounce of discretion is worth a pound of wit.

Demuthsvoll, *adj.* and *adv.* humble, lowly, submissive.

Demüthig, I. *adj.* humble, lowly, meek, submissive. —e Bitten, humble prayers; — seyn, to be submissive. Der Demüthige, the humble. II. *adv.* with humility, humbly, meekly, submissively.

Demüthigen, I. *v. tr.* 1) to humble, to humiliate, to abase, to reduce arrogance and self-dependence. Und wer stolz ist, den kann er —, [in Script.] those that walk in pride he is able to abase; ich werde seinen Stolz —, I shall bring down his pride; dieser Sieg demüthigte Roms Stolz, this victory humbled the pride of Rome; stolze Blicke —, to bring down high looks; wie oft wird der Ehrgeizige durch das Lob gedemüthigt, welches man ihm ertheilt, wenn &c., how often is the ambitious man mortified by the very praises, he receives, if &c. 2) to humble, to break, to subdue. Seine Feinde —, to humble one's enemies. II. *v. r.* sich —, 1) [to have a low opinion of one's self, and a deep sense of unworthiness in the sight of God] to humble one's self. Hiskia demüthigte sich, daß sein Herz sich erhoben hatte, [in Script.] Hezekiah humbled himself for the pride of his heart. 2) to humble one's self, to submit. So demüthigt euch nun unter die gewaltige Hand Gottes, daß er euch erhöhe zu seiner Zeit, [in Script.] humble yourselves under the mighty hand of God, that he may exalt you.

‡Demüthiglich, *adv.* humbly.

Demüthigung, *f.* 1) [the act of humbling] humiliation. 2) humiliation, mortification.

1. Den, the accusative case of the singular number of the article and the relative pronoun der.

2. Den, the dative case of the plural number of the article der.

*Dendrit, *m.* [-en, *pl.* -en] [an arborescent mineral] dendrite.

Denen, the dative case of the plural number of the relative pronoun der.

‖Dengel, *m.* [-s, *pl.* -] the border of bedaggled clothes.

‖Dengeln, [allied to the Sw. *daenga*, schlagen] *v. tr.* [in husbandry] to sharpen scythes or sickles by beating them with a hammer.

Dengel=hammer, *m.* [in husbandry] a hammer used for sharpening scythes or sickles. —stock, *m.* [in husbandry] a small anvil on which scythes or sickles are sharpened with a hammer. —zeug, *n.* [in husbandry] the hammer and anvil used for sharpening scythes or sickles.

Denkbar, *adj.* and *adv.* that may be imagined or conceived, imaginable. Es ist nicht —, daß &c., it is not conceivable, that &c.; Denkbare, any thing that may be imagined or thought.

Denkbarkeit, *f.* conceivableness.

Denken, [appears to be allied to the Lat. tang… berühren, the Gr. θιγγάνω, δέχ-ομαι, δοκ-εῖν] *v. intr.* and *tr.* 1) [to have the mind occupied … some subject, to have ideas] to think. Denn … ich bin, weiß ich, weil ich denke, for that I am … know, because I think; der Mensch ist ein —… Wesen, man is a thinking being. 2) to dwell … any thing in thought. Viel —, to philosoph… much; ein —der Kopf, a thinking man; … nünftig —, to think reasonably; hin und … —, to revolve thoughts in the mind; bei sich … to think with one's self; über etwas [bei sich] … und her —, to ruminate over a thing; er … niemals, was er denkt, he never speaks … thoughts; auf etwas —, to think on or upon … thing; auf Beweise —, to devise arguments; … Mittel —, welche &c., to contrive the means … which &c.; auf etwas Böses —, to plot, to … chinate; er denkt auf Ihr Verderben, he con… trives your ruin; nur auf or an sich —, to re… one's own interest solely; und als Petrus … dachte, hob er an zu weinen, [in Scripture] … when Peter thought thereon, he wept; er … nicht an die Zukunft, he is thoughtless of … future; ich denke dies und jenes, I think of … and that; Gutes oder Uebles von Einem —, … think well or ill of any one; er dachte der … seligkeit, die &c., he thought of the happi… which &c.; ich kann [es] mir nicht —, wie … I cannot imagine how &c.; [in familiar or … lang.] — Sie, was mir begegnet ist! im… what has happened to me! 3) to think … judge, to conclude, to hold as a settled opi… Ihr denkt, Ihr seid sicher, you think, you … safe; ich — es, I think so; ich denke, es … morgen regnen, I think it will rain to-morr… er denkt, wie ich, he is of my way of think… *[in scorn] er denkt Wunder, was es wäre, … makes a wonder of it. 4) to think = to imag… to suppose, to fancy. Sie können leicht —, … &c., you may easily imagine, that &c. 5) to … in mind, to remember. Die Sache denkt … nicht mehr, the fact is out of my mind; — … zuweilen an mich, remember me sometimes wird mir lange —, I shall long remember it; ... muß immer daran —, it will not out of my ...ind; denkt an mich, think upon me; denke der ...rgangenen Tage, remember the past. 6) to ...ink = to presume. Denkt nur nicht, daß Ihr ...i euch wollt sagen, wir haben Abraham zum ...ater, [in Script.] think not to say within your...lves, we have Abraham to our father. 7) to ...ink = to intend, to purpose. Was denken Sie ... thun? what do you intend to do? er denkt ...gzubleiben, he has a mind to stay away; *wo — Sie hin? what do you think? *er denkt hoch ...naus, he has great designs; *gedacht, gethan, ... be quickly resolved, to undertake a thing no ...ooner said than done. *Prov.* Der Mensch denkt, ...ott lenkt, man proposes, and God disposes. 8) ... have a certain disposition of mind. Er denkt ...el, he is of a noble, of a generous mind; er ...kt niedrig or gemein, he is a low-minded ...llow; edel —d, noble-minded; schlecht —d, ...minded. Das Denken, thinking, cogitation.

Denk-art, *f.* 1) the peculiar and habitual ...de of thinking. Er ist ein Mann von edler ...art, he is a noble-minded man. 2) improperly ...d for Denkungsart. —bild, *n.* 1) form, image, ...del of any thing in the mind, idea. 2) a device. ...latt, *n.* a sheet of paper, or symbolical print ... some written lines serving as a token of re...mbrance. —brod, *n.* V. Schaubrod. —buch, ... 1) a book of record. 2) note-book, remem...nce-book, memorandum-book. —fähig, ... and *adv.* capable of thinking. —fähig...it, *f.* the faculty of thinking. —fest, *n.* a ...t celebrated in memory of some event, a com...moration-festival. —form, *f.* form of think...g. —freiheit, *f.* freedom of thought, [in a ...e extensive or figur. sense] liberty of the press. ...egel, *m.* V. Obelisk. —kraft, *f.* the faculty ...thinking, the intellect. —lehre, *f.* 1) [the art ...thinking and reasoning justly] logic. 2) a trea...e on logic. —lehrer, *m.* a logician. —leh...g, *adj.* and *adv.* [pertaining to logic, according to ... rules of logic] logical. Ein —lehriger Beweis, ...gical argument; —lehrig schließen, to argue ...ically. —los, *adj.* and *adv.* incapable of ...nking. —mahl, *n.* [-es, *pl.* -mahle or -mähler] ...y thing by which the memory of a person or event ...reserved or perpetuated] monument. Einem ein ...mahl errichten, stiften, to erect a monument ...any one; die —mähler griechischer Kunst, the ...numents of Greek art; —mähler des Frie...s, memorials of peace; von allen Gesetzen ...es Königreiches sind schriftliche —mähler vor...den, all the laws of this kingdom have some ...morials thereof in writing. —münze, *f.* a ...dal. Ein Kenner von —münzen, a medallist. ...echt, V. —richtig. —richtig, *adj.* and *adv.* ...ording to the rules of logic] logical. —richtig ...ßen, to argue logically. —ring, *m.* a ring ...ving as a token of remembrance. —säule, *f.* ...numental column, a monument. —schrift, ...) inscription. 2) memoir. —schriften über ...französische Staatsumwälzung, memoirs on ...rench revolution. 3) memorial. —sonder...keit, *f.* 1) paradoxicalness. 2) [the tenet ...roposition contrary to received opinion, or seem...y absurd, yet true in fact] a paradox. —spitz...le, *f.* V. Obelisk. —. —spruch, *m.* 1) [a ...arkable saying] an apophthegm, apothegm, ...otto. Ein Sammler von —sprüchen, apo...gmatist; —sprüche sagen, to apothegmatize; —spruch auf einem Ringe, a posy. 2) a maxim, ...xiom, a sentence. —sprüchlich, *adj.* and ... apophthegmatic, apothegmatical, sen...al. —stein, *m.* a monumental stone. — ...f, *m.* the object of thinking, matter for ...king or thought. —tempel, *m.* mauso...m. —übung, *f.* exercise in thinking. — ...fähig, *adj.* and *adv.* incapable of think...ing. —vermögen, *n.* V. —kraft. —vers, *m.* 1) a remarkable verse. 2) a verse in remembrance of something, commemoratory verse. —versuch, *m.* an exertion of the mind for thinking. —weise, *f.* V. —art. Das ist so seine —weise, it is his way of thinking. —wissenschaft, *f.* V. —lehre. —wort, *n.* a sentence, a maxim. —würdig, I. *adj.* 1) worthy of being revolved in the mind. 2) worthy of being remembered. —würdige Thaten, memorable deeds. II. *adv.* memorably. —würdigkeit, *f.* 1) worthiness of being remembered. 2) a memorable occurrence, or event, or narration &c. Die —würdigkeiten aus der englischen Geschichte, the memoirs of the English history. —zeichen, *n.* a token of remembrance. —zeit, *f.* [in chronology] epoch. Die merkwürdigen —zeiten in der Geschichte der Juden, the remarkable epochs in the history of the Jews. —zettel, *m.* 1) [a note to help the memory] a memorandum. 2) [among the Jews, a slip of parchment, on which was written the decalogue] phylactery. 3) [in law] a note or bill, specifying the court-day. 4) *Fig.* [jocosely or threateningly] any sensible token of remembrance, as a box on the ear, a blow &c.

Dénker, *m.* [-s, *pl.* -] [one who thinks, but chiefly one who thinks in a particular manner] thinker. Ein tiefer —, a deep thinker; ein seichter —, a shallow thinker or head; die — [more usual die Denkenden] the thinking ones.

Denkereí, *f.* superficial thinking.

Dénkler, *m.* [-s, *pl.* -] [in contempt or scorn] a superficial thinker.

Dénkungsart, *f.* [*pl.* -en] [natural constitution or temper of the mind] disposition. V. Denkart 2.

Dénmark, *n.* [-s] V. Baldrian.

Dénn, [allied to dann] *conj.* 1) [a word by which a reason is introduced of something before advanced] for. Geben Sie sich nicht mit ihm ab, — er ist ein ausgemachter Schelm, have nothing to do with him, for he is a confirmed rascal. 2) [in consequence, in that case] then. So wollen wir — fort, let us then set out. 3) noting a condition. Es sei —, daß, unless, if, provided; er bezahle mich —, unless he pays what he owes me. 4) [expressing comparison between what precedes and what follows, but now rather obsolete in this sense] than. Wer ist reicher — [als] er? who is richer than he? So sagte Elijah, ich bin nicht besser — meine Väter, thus Elijah said, I am not better than my fathers. 5) [a particle by which the meaning of the foregoing sentence is bounded or restrained] but. Nichts — [als] Gold, nothing but gold. 6) used sometimes to give roundness or force to a period. Hast du — auch davon gehört? did you hear of it yet? Wo ist er —? where is he?

Dénngras, *n.* [-ses, *pl.* -gräser] common knot-grass.

Dénnoch, *conj.* nothwithstanding, nevertheless, however, yet. Sie ist häßlich, und — liebt er sie, she is ugly and yet he loves her.

***Dentíst**, *m.* [-en, *pl.* -en] V. Zahnarzt.

***Denunciánt**, *m.* [-en, *pl.* -en] [chiefly in law] an accuser, informer, denunciator.

***Denunciát**, *m.* [-en, *pl.* -en] [chiefly in law] the accused or denounced person.

***Denunciatión**, *f.* [chiefly in law] an information, a charge or accusation exhibited to a magistrate or court, denunciation.

***Denunciíren**, *v. tr.* [chiefly in law] to inform against, to communicate facts by way of accusation, to denounce. A hat den B denuncirt, A has informed against B.

***Depártement**, *n.* [-s, *pl.* -e, or when the word is pronounced as in the French, -s] 1) [a division of territory] department. 2) [a separate allotment or part of business] department. Das — der innern Angelegenheiten, home department; das Kriegs-—, the war department.

***Dependént**, *adj.* and *adv.* dependant.

***Dependénz**, *f.* V. Abhängigkeit, 2).

***Depésche**, *f.* [*pl.* -n] dispatch.

***Dephlogístisch**, *adj.* and *adv.* uninflammable.

***Dephlogistisíren**, *v. tr.* [in chimistry] to dephlogisticate. Dephlogistisirte Luft, dephlogisticated air, oxygen, oxygen gas, or vital air.

***Deponént**, *m.* [-en, *pl.* -en] 1) [in law, one who deposes or gives a deposition under oath] a deponent, a witness, an evidence. — gab an, daß &c., witness stated, that &c. 2) one who deposits or commits something to the care of another, deponent.

***Deponíren**, *v. tr.* 1) to deposite, to lay in the hands of a person for safe-keeping or other purpose. 2) to depose, to give testimony on oath.

***Deportatión**, *f.* deportation, transportation.

***Deportíren**, *v. tr.* to deport, to transport.

***Depositär**, *m.* [-s, *pl.* -e] depository, trustee.

***Depósitor**, *m.* [-s, *pl.* -en] V. Deponent.

***Depósitum**, *n.* [-s, *pl.* -siten] a deposit. In Deposito, in deposit.

***Dépot**, [pron. as in the French] *n.* [-s, *pl.* -s] [in military affairs, a place of reception for recruits, or to detached parties belonging to different regiments] depot.

***Deputát**, *n.* [-s, *pl.* -e] an allowance of fuel, provisions or other articles, made to certain persons at the public expense; sometimes an equivalent in money for such allowance.

Deputatholz, *n.* fire-bote.

***Deputatión**, *f.* deputation. *a*) [the act of appointing and sending a deputy or substitute to transact business for another, as his agent]. *b*) [the person or persons deputed]. Eine — abschicken, to send a deputation.

***Deputíren**, *v. tr.* to depute.

***Deputírte**, *m.* [-n, *pl.* -n] a deputy. Die Kammer der —n or die —nkammer, the chamber of deputies [corresponding to the British House of Commons].

Dér, Díe, Dás, I. *article* used for nouns to express the distinction of sex and to limit their signification to one or more specific things of the kind, discriminated from others of the same kind. Der Vater, the father; der Mond, the moon. When a noun or name is used in an unlimited sense or in an indefinite sense, the article may be omitted, as Hunde sind gefräßige Thiere, dogs are voracious animals; with some nouns only in the plural number, Menschen sind vernünftige Wesen, man is a rational being. It is also omitted before names whose signification is general, and requires no limitation, as Zorn ruht im Herzen eines Narren, [in Script.] anger resteth in the bosom of fools. When the sense of words is sufficiently certain by the construction, the article may be omitted, as Nachsicht gereicht vielen Kindern zum Verderben, many children are ruined by indulgence. The article is often combined with the preposition, as im for in dem; am for an dem; also with the adjective, as die Geschichte alter und neuer Zeit, the history of ancient and modern time. II. *pron.* 1) [= dieser] this, that. Der Mann hier, this man here; das Kind dort, that child there; er ist den Augenblick gekommen, he has arrived this moment; nicht der Reiche, denn der kann nie Unrecht haben, not the rich man, for he can never be in the wrong; sind das die Männer? are those the men? was wissen die nicht, what do they not know; im Laufe der Unterhaltung wurde dessen [deß] erwähnt, in the course of conversation, that was mentioned; dem sei, wie ihm wolle, be that as it may; der Narr, der! fool that he is! zu dem wissen Sie, besides you know; zu dem macht Religionseifer sie strenge; moreover zeal for religion makes them rigid; es ist an dem, it is so; es war an dem, daß er gefangen wurde, he was near being taken; es ist an dem zwölf Uhr, it is near twelve o'clock; mit alle dem, or bei alle dem, notwithstanding; [das is often used as a substitute for words of any of the three genders in the singular number and the plural] das sind eure Bücher, those are your books; das sind Leute von unerschrockenem Muthe, these are men of undaunted courage; das ist ihr Wille, it is her will; du behauptest, der Mann sei unschuldig, das ist er nicht, you alledge the man is innocent, that he is not. 2) [= derjenige] Hier ist das Buch, welches wir suchten, here is the book, we have been seeking; hier geht der Mann, von dem wir gesprochen haben, here goes the man we were talking of; ich gab es dem Bothen, den Sie darnach geschickt haben, I gave it to that [the] messenger, you sent for it; der Wille dessen or deß, der mich gesandt hat, the will of him, who has sent me. 3) [= welcher] Das sind die Bücher, die Sie mir versprochen haben, these are the books which you promised me; die Person, die du liebst, the person [whom] you love; wer ist die Person, die ein Recht hat &c.? who is the person who has a right &c.? die Frage, deren Auflösung ich verlange, the question whose solution I require; Sprachen, deren viele &c., languages, many of which &c.; drei Indianer, deren einer &c., three Indians, one of whom; der, der spricht, he that speaks; unser Vater, der du bist im Himmel, [in the Lord's prayer] our father which art in heaven. The genitive case as well of the demonstrative as of the relative *pron.* dessen, deren, is often joined to the words halben, wegen, willen, and by adding a t to render these compounds agreeable to the ear. The words thus formed, as: dessenthalben [deshalb], derenthalben, dessentwegen [deswegen], derentwegen, dessentwillen [deswillen] and derentwillen, on their account, on whose account, on that account, are chiefly used in familiar language.

*Derangiren, [pron. Derangschihren] *v. tr.* to put out of order, to derange. Derangirt, deranged, involved in debt.

Derb, [is very nearly allied to the Gr. τέρπ-ω, originally = dick machen, to τρέφω, which has the same signification to the Lat. *trab-s*, Balken, originally something thick, as also to the Slav. *derewo*, Baum &c.] *adj.* and *adv.* [closely and firmly united, as the particles of solid bodies] compact, firm, close, solid, dense. —es Fleisch, firm flesh; —e Nahrung, solid food; —es Tuch, a cloth of firm texture, substantial cloth; ein —er Mann, a stout man; sein Gliederbau, eher — als zärtlich, his limbs rather sturdy than dainty; eine —e Leibesbeschaffenheit, a solid constitution of body, a sound or strong constitution; —es Erz, V. Derberz. *Fig.* in colloquial language, it is used to express a high degree in the action or verbs or in the quality of things, as: Einen — durchprügeln, to beat any one soundly; ein —er Streich, a sound or sturdy stroke; ein —er Hieb, a smart lash; — zuschlagen, to strike stoutly; ein —er Kuß, a smacking kiss; er erhielt einen —en Verweis, he was severely reprimanded; er gab ihm eine —e Lection [or er gab ihm die Sache handgreiflich zu verstehen] he gave him a rough lesson; er gab ihm eine —e Antwort, or er antwortete ihm —, he gave him a smart answer; Einem — die Wahrheit sagen, to reproach any one roundly with his faults; eine —e Lüge, a plump lie, a round lie. Syn. Derb, Dicht. Dicht refers only to the closeness or compactness of the individual parts of a substance; derb, when applied to animal or vegetable bodies, includes also the idea of the strength and elasticity which a firm body possesses in a higher degree than one less compact. Derbes Fleisch is such as is not only dicht [close, compact], but also the reverse of flabby, firm.

Derberz, *n.* [in mining] rich ore.

Derbheit, *f.* [*pl.* -en] 1) compactness, firmness, solidity, stoutness, sturdiness; *it.* a compact or firm thing. 2) = insolence, rough manners, roughness in behaviour; *it.* an insolent speech, rough word. Einem —en sagen, to give any one hard words.

Dereinst, *adv.* at a future time, in future.

Dereinstig, I. *adj.* future. II. *adv.* in future.

Derenthalben, Derentwegen, Derentwillen, V. Der, *pron.*

Dergestalt, *adv.* 1) in such a manner, in such a degree, so. — daß, so that. 2) on that manner, on condition that.

Dergleichen, Deßgleichen, an indeclinable *pronoun*; of that kind, of the like kind. — habe ich nie gesehen, I never saw the like; — wird sich nicht mehr ereignen, the like will never happen again; — habe ich nicht mehr, I have no more of that sort; und — [mostly written or printed u d. or u. dergl.], and such like.

Derhalben, Derohalben, *conj.* therefore.

*Derivata, *pl.* derived words, derivatives.

*Derivation, *f.* [in grammar] derivation.

*Derivatum, *n.* [-s, *pl.* -vata] [in grammar] a derivative.

*Deriviren, *v. tr.* to derive [a word from a root &c.].

Derjenige, Diejenige, Dasjenige, *pron.* he, she, that. Derjenige, der viel begehrt, he, that much desires; diejenigen, die arm sind, such as are poor; diejenigen, die mich ohne Ursache hassen, sind mehr als &c., they that hate me without a cause, are more than &c.; diejenigen meiner Nachbarn, die &c, those of my neighbours, that &c.; derjenige, der mit Weisen umgeht, der wird weise, he that walketh with wise men, shall be wise.

‡Derlei, V. Dergleichen.

Derlen- or Derlitzenbaum, *m.* V. Derlitzen- or Kornelkirschenbaum.

‡Dermahleinst, *adv.* V. Dereinst.

Dermahlen, *adv.* at present, actually.

Dermahlig, *adj.* present, actual.

Dermaßen, *adv.* in such a manner, in such a degree, so much.

‡Dero, the genitive case of the pronoun relative der, used in ceremonious language for Ihr or Ihre, your, in the singular and plural number. Ich werde — Befehle befolgen, I shall comply with your commands.

Dero-halben, —wegen, V. Deshalb, Deswegen.

Derselbe, Dieselbe, Dasselbe, [or Derselbe &c.] *pron.* 1) pointing at a certain person or thing, that is named in the foregoing or subsequent part of the sentence. Dies ist derselbe Mann, der &c, this is the same man, who &c; ein Schiff legt nicht dieselbe Entfernung wie ein anderes in derselben Zeit und mit demselben Winde zurück, one ship will not run the same distance as another in the same time, and with the same wind; wir sehen bei den Menschen in allen Ländern dieselben Leidenschaften und dieselben Laster, we se in men in all countries, the same passions and the same vices; ungefähr dasselbe sagen, to speak much to the same purpose; er ist ganz derselbe, der er sonst war, he is the very same, he was formerly; das ist eins und dasselbe, that is one and the same thing, 'tis all one. 2) as a relative it refers to a preceding noun or sentence. Ein schöner Garten, aber wer ist der Besitzer desselben? a fine garden, but who is the possessor of it er steckt tief in Schulden, und er weiß nun nicht wie er dieselben bezahlen soll, he is over head and ears in debt and is now at a loss how to pay them off. 3) in ceremonious language, it is often used for the pronoun personal Sie. Was befehlen Dieselben? speak your pleasure; in Erwiederung auf das, was Dieselben die Güte hatten mir zu schreiben, in answer to what you have been pleased to write me; [also in the dative case by adding en] wie es Den[en]selben beliebt, as you please; [the same words are used as epithets of rank & distinction by adding Hoch, Höchst, Allerhöchst, a Hochdieselben, Höchstdieselben, Allerhöchstdieselben]

Derweile, *adv.* in the mean time, in the mean while.

*Derwisch, *m.* [-es, *pl.* -e] [a Turkish priest & monk] dervis.

1. Des, the genitive case of the article and the pronoun der and das.

2. Des, [in music] d flat [= C sharp].

*Descendent, *m.* [-en, *pl.* -en] descendant [especially in law]. In Ermangelung von —en [er]ben die Seitenverwandten, failing descendants the collateral relations inherit; die —en dieses Prinzen, the progeny of this prince.

*Descendenz, *f.* [*pl.* -en] [chiefly in law] offspring, progeny, issue, descendants. Seine eh[e]liche — bestand aus &c., his legitimate progeny or offspring consisted of &c.

*Descendiren, *v. intr.* [chiefly in law] to proceed as progeny, to issue.

*Descension, *f.* [in astronomy] descension.

‖Dese, *f.* [*pl.* -n] [V. Döse, Dose] a sm[all] wooden box.

‖Desem, *m.* [-s, *pl.* -e] a small steel-yard.

*Desert, V. Dessert.

*Deserteur, [pron. Desertöhr] *m.* [-s, *pl.* -e] [a soldier or seaman who quits the service without permission, and in violation of his engagement] a deserter, runaway.

*Desertion, *f.* desertion.

*Desertiren, *v. intr.* to desert, to run aw[ay]. Er desertirte vom Heere, he deserted [from] the army.

Desfalls, [deßfalls] *adv.* 1) for this reason, on that account. 2) nevertheless.

Desfallsig, *adj.* [rather stiff] referring to a certain purpose, point, case or matter. [Seine] —en Absichten sind mir unbekannt, his intentions regarding this point are unknown to me.

Desgleichen and Desgleichen, [deßgleichen] I. an indeclinable *adj.* of that kind, of the like kind. Er war ein Mann, — ich nie wieder sehen werde, he was a man, I shall not look on his like again; ein Sturm, — ich noch nie gesehen, I never saw such a storm; gute Freunde und —, good friends, and such like. II. *adv.* in [like] manner, likewise. Sowohl er als sie, — sein Vater, he as well as she, as also his father.

Deshalb, Deshalben, [deßhalb, deßhalben] *adv.* [for that, for this reason, referring to a thing previously stated] therefore. Ich habe ein Weib genommen, — kann ich nicht kommen [in Scripture] I have married a woman, ther[efore] cannot come.

*Designiren, *v. tr.* to appoint, to designate. Einen Offizier zum Befehlshaber eines Postens —, to designate an officer for the command of a station; dieser Offizier war für diesen Posten designirt, this officer was designated to that station.

||Desmann, *m.* [-s, *pl.* -e] V. Bisamratte.

*Desperation, *f.* V. Verzweiflung.

*Despot, *m.* [-en, *pl.* -en] 1) [an emperor, king or prince invested with absolute power] despot. 2) [in a bad sense] a despot = a tyrant.

*Despotie, *f.* [*pl.* -en] 1) the power of a despot [V. Despot, 1.]. 2) [or Despotismus] despotism.

*Despotisch, I. *adj.* despotic, despotical. Ein —er Fürst, a despotic prince; —e Gewalt, despotic authority or power. II. *adv.* despotically.

*Despotisiren, *v. tr.* and *intr.* to rule in a despotic manner, to exercise power despotically.

*Despotismus, *m.* V. Despotie 2.

Deß, [des] for dessen, V. Dessen.

*Dessein, [pron. like the Fr. *dessin*] *n.* [-s, *pl.* -s] 1) pattern, figure, design. 2) [the idea or scheme intended to be expressed by an artist] design.

Dessen, the genitive case of the pronoun Der.

Dessenthalben, Dessentwegen, Dessentwillen, V. Der, *pron.*

Dessenungeachtet, Deßungeachtet, V. Ungeachtet.

*Dessert, *n.* [-s, *pl.* -s] [a service of fruits and sweetmeats, at the close of an entertainment, the last course at the table, after the meat is removed] dessert.

Dessert-messer, *n.* dessert-knife. —service, *n.* dessert-set. —teller, *m.* dessert-plate.

Deßfalls, V. Desfalls.

Deßfallsig, V. Desfallsig.

Deßgleichen, V. Dergleichen and Desgleichen.

Deßhalb, Deßhalben, V. Deshalb, Deshalben.

Deßungeachtet, V. Dessenungeachtet.

Deßwegen, V. Deswegen.

Deßwillen, V. Deswillen.

Destillateur, [pron. Destillatöhr] [-s, *pl.* -s or Destillirer, *m.* [-s, *pl.* -] a distiller.

Destillation, *f.* distillation. Die nochmalige —, [in chimistry] cohobation.

Destilliren, *v. tr.* to distil [brandy from wine &c.]. Destillirt, distilled; nochmals —, [in chimistry] to cohobate; zu —, distillable; zum —, distillatory.

Destillir-blase, *f.* alembic. —helm, *m.* the head of a still. —kolben, *m.* retort, cucurbit, alembic. —kunst, *f.* the art of distilling, distillery. —ofen, *m.* a furnace for distilling. —stube, *f.* laboratory, still.

Desto, *adv.* [Dan. and Old G. *thes*] [it is used before adjectives in the comparative degree] the. — schwerer ist es, sich zu bessern, the more difficult it is to reform; je mehr, — besser, the more, the better; — besser, so much the better; — schlimmer, so much the worse.

Deswegen, [deßwegen] *adv.* for that or this reason, for this cause, therefore. Ich achte ihn [darum] nicht weniger, I don't respect him the less, on that account; eben —, for that very reason.

Deswillen, [deßwillen] *adv.* [generally preceded by um] for that reason, on that account.

*Detachement, [pron. as in the French] *n.* [-s, *pl.* -s] [a body of troops, selected or taken from the main army, and employed on some special service or expedition] a detachment.

*Detail, *m.* [-s, *pl.* -s] 1) [a narration of particulars; a minute and particular account] detail. Er erzählte die Geschichte im —, he related the story in detail. 2) [the sale of commodities in small quantities or parcels, or at second hand] retail. Im — verkaufen, to retail [groceries &c.].

Detailhändler, *m.* retailer.

*Detailliren, [pron. Detailjihren] *v. tr.* 1) to detail [all the facts in due order &c.]. 2) to retail [commodities].

*Deterioriren, *v. tr.* to deteriorate, to make worse.

*Determiniren, *v. tr.* to determine [a cause &c.]. Ein determinirter Mann, a resolute, determined man [having a form or fixed purpose].

Deuchten, V. Däuchten.

Deul, *n.* [-s, *pl.* -e] [allied to Theil] [in iron-works] bloom.

Deut, *m.* [-es, *pl.* -e] [D. *dugt*] [a small piece of money] a doit. **Fig.* Er ist keinen — werth, he is not worth a straw; ich gebe keinen — dafür, I wouldn't give a farthing for it.

Deutel, *m.* [-s, *pl.* -] [with ship-carpenters] a wedge which is driven into the end of a tree-nail, to swell it.

Deuteleisen, *n.* a kind of iron wedge, used for opening the head of a tree-nail in order to put in small wooden wedges.

Deutelei, *f.* 1) [in contempt] interpretation [of dreams, visions &c.]. 2) a childish and absurd interpretation, misconstruction.

Deuteln, *v. tr.* 1) [in contempt] to interpret. 2) to explain or interpret in a childish or trifling manner, to put a wrong construction on.

Deuten, [perhaps allied to the Low. Sax. stöten, that is stoßen or to zeihen, zeigen, Ice. *tia*] I. *v. tr.* a) to direct towards an object or place. Mit dem Finger auf Einen —, to point the finger at any one; man deutete mit Fingern auf ihn, they pointed the finger of scorn at him. *b*) to make a sign to. Mit den Augen —, to hint or direct by the motion of the eyelids, to wink. *Fig.* α) [obsolete] to indicate, to point out, to show, to discover. β) to interpret, to explain. Einen Schrifttext —, to expound a text of Scripture; Träume —, to show, to interpret dreams; sage deinen Knechten den Traum, so wollen wir ihn —, [in Scripture] tell thy servants the dream, and we will shew the interpretation; die Zeichen am Himmel —, to astrologize; Blicke oder Zeichen —, to interpret looks or signs; unrecht —, to misinterpret; etwas zum Aergsten —, to misinterpret a thing. *Prov.* Dem sei Leid, der's übel deut', evil be to him, that evil thinks. Syn. V. Auslegen. II. *v. intr.* to have a particular direction. Der Schweif des Kometen deutet gegen Osten, the train of the comet is directed towards the east; der Wetterhahn deutet nach Norden, the weathercock looks towards the north. *Fig.* to be a sign of, to be the omen of. Eine besondere Art Wolken deutet auf Regen, a particular kind of cloud indicates the approach of rain; ein klarer Himmel bei Sonnenuntergang deutet auf einen schönen Tag, a clear sky at sunset prognosticates or presages a fair day; diese Märsche des Heeres — auf einen Krieg, those marches of the army are signs of a war; meine Träume — auf ein nahes Glück, my dreams presage some joyful news at hand; das deutet auf nichts Gutes, this presages or augurs nothing good.

Deuter, *m.* [-s, *pl.* -] one that explains, expounds or interprets, an expositor, an expounder, chiefly used in composition, as: Traum—, an interpreter of dreams; ein Stern—, an astrologer &c. ||*Fig.* an admonition.

Deuterei, *f.* [in contempt] 1) [the act of interpreting] interpretation, chiefly used in composition, as Stern—, astrology &c. 2) interpretation, exposition.

Deuterwort, *n.* [with some authors] the article.

Deutig, *adj.* and *adv.* susceptible of a signification, used in composition, as Zwei—, equivocal, ambiguous; gleich—, synonymous &c.

Deutler, *m.* [-s, *pl.* -] one that interprets in a childish or trifling manner, a misconstruer.

Deutlich, *adj.* and *adv.* easily discovered, distinguished, seen or understood. Eine —e Stimme, a clear voice; ein —er Ton, a clear sound; ein —er Anblick, a clear view, a distinct view; — aussprechen, to utter articulately; einen Gegenstand — sehen, to view an object distinctly; — sprechen, to speak intelligibly; — schreiben, to write intelligibly or plainly; in —en Ausdrücken, in plain terms; er drückt sich — aus, he conveys his meaning in plain words; er hat die Sache — erklärt, he explained it plainly; ein —er Beweis, an evident proof; eine —e Ursache, an obvious reason; das ist — im Vertrage angeführt, that is explicitly stated in the contract; —e Begriffe, clear ideas; der Sinn ist —, wenn &c., the sense is perspicuous, when &c.; ich will es durch ein Beispiel — machen, I'll make it obvious by an example. Syn. Deutlich, Begreiflich, Verständlich. A thing is deutlich, which is evident to the understanding, clear to the mental eye, not obscure or difficult to be seen or understood, distinct. That is begreiflich, which is capable of being comprehended, conceivable by the mind. Verständlich that which can be understood.

Deutlichkeit, *f.* distinctness, clearness, plainness, obviousness. Die — der Stimme, the clearness of the voice; die — eines Ausdrucks, the intelligibility or intelligibleness of an expression; — im Schreiben und Sprechen, perspicuity in writing and speaking; die — der Ansichten, Beweise, Erklärungen, the clearness of views, arguments, explanations.

Deutsch, [instead of deutisch, from Deut, ancient Diot = Volk, probably allied to the A. S. *theodan, thyddan* = zusammenfügen; it might be also allied to the Goth. *thiuts*, gut, of the same root] *adj.* and *adv.* German. Die —e Sprache [das Deutsche], the German language, the German; —e Kunst und Sitte[n], German art and manners; eine —e Meile, a German mile [of which 15 make a degree of the equator]; er spricht —, he speaks German; die —e Bibel, the German bible; —e Bücher, German books; ein —es Wörterbuch, a dictionary of the German language; die —en Ritter or Herren, the knights of the Teutonic order; [in trades, arts &c.] ein —er Schlüssel, [with locksmiths] a pipe-key; ein —er Riegel or eine —e Falle, [with locksmiths] a bolt of iron in a German lock; ein —es Schloß, [with locksmiths] a German lock; —es Silbergewicht, [in commerce] Cologne mark weight; die —e Ordnung, [in architecture] the German order; ein —es Dach, [in architecture] a sort of hip-roof; das Deutsche, the German language; *it.* German life and manners, German opinions and doctrines &c. *Fig.* *— heraus, in plain terms; *— zu sagen, die Zeitungen lügen, to speak frankly, the papers lie; —e Treue, an inviolable fidelity; ein —es Herz, an honest heart; ein —es Versprechen, a promise to be depended upon; —er Muth, great courage; —er Fleiß, persevering application.

Deutsch-herrig, —herrisch, —herrlich, *adj.* and *adv.* belonging to the Teutonic order.

Deútsche, *m.* and *f.* [-n, *pl.* -n] a native of Germany, a German. Die alten —n, the ancient Germans, the Teutons. *Fig.* Er ist ein alter —r, he is a good honest man.

‡**Deútschen**, *v. tr.* to translate into German.

Deútscher, *m.* (ein) V. Deutsche.

Deútschheit, *f.* 1) the quality of being German, a German fashion. 2) a Germanism.

Deútschland, [-s] Germany. Das alte —, ancient Germany; das neue —, modern Germany.

Deútschmeister, *m.* [-s] (also called des Deutschen Ordens or Deutschordens-Großmeister or Hochmeister] the grand-master of the Teutonic order.

Deútschthum, *n.* [-s] V. Deutschheit 1.

Deútschthümler, *m.* [-s, *pl.* -] a teutomane.

Deutschthümelei, *f.* teutomania.

Deútung, *f.* 1) [the act of interpreting] interpretation, explanation. 2) [the sense given by an interpreter] interpretation, exposition. Man findet zuweilen verschiedene —en einer und derselben Stelle in der Schrift, we sometimes find various interpretations of the same passage of Scripture; einer Sache eine üble — geben, to put a bad construction upon a thing, to misconstrue a thing.

Deutungs-art, *f.* manner of interpreting. —**buch**, *n.* V. Wörterbuch. —**voll**, *adj.* and *adv.* 1) susceptible of many interpretations. 2) ominous. Sein —volles [bedeutungsvolles] Schweigen weissagte ihm nichts Gutes, his ominous silence boded him no good.

***Déventer**, *n.* [-s] [the name of a town in Holland] Daintry.

***Devise**, *f.* [*pl.* -n] 1) a device or motto. 2) [in commerce = Wechsel] a bill of exchange.

***Devonít**, *m.* V. Wevellit.

***Dezémber**, *m.* [-s] [the last month in the year] december.

***Diadém**, *n.* [-s, *pl.* -e] 1) [the mark or badge of royalty, worn on the head] a diadem, a crown. 2) [an ornament resembling a coronet, worn on the head by women] a diadem.

***Diagnöse**, *f.* [*pl.* -n] [in medicine, the sign or symptom by which a disease is known or distinguished from others] diagnostic.

***Diagnóstisch**, *adj.* and *adv.* diagnostic.

***Diagonál**, *adj.* and *adv.* [in mathematics] diagonal. Die —linie [Diagonale], a diagonal line.

***Diakón**, *m.* [-s, *pl.* -e or -en] 1) V. Dekan, Dechant. 2) [in the Greek Hierarchy, one of the lower clergy] a diaconos. 3) [more usual Diakonus] [in the Protestant church] a curate.

***Diakonát**, *n.* [-s, *pl.* -e] 1) diaconry. 2) the office of a diacon.

***Diakonissinn**, *f.* deaconess.

***Diakústik**, *f.* diacoustics.

***Dialékt**, *m.* [-es, *pl.* -e] dialect.

***Dialéktik**, *f.* [that branch of logic which teaches the rules and modes of reasoning] dialectics.

***Dialéktiker**, *m.* [-s, *pl.* -] a dialectician, a logician.

***Dialóg**, *m.* [-es, *m.* -e] [a conversation or conference between two or more persons; also a written conversation] dialogue. Einen — halten, to dialogize; der — des Cicero de Oratore, the dialogue of Cicero de Oratore.

***Dialógisch**, *adj.* and *adv.* dialogistic.

***Diamánt**, *m.* [-s or -en, *pl.* -en] V. Demant.

***Diamánten**, V. Demanten.

***Diámeter**, *m.* [-s, *pl.* -] diameter.

***Diamétrisch**, *adj.* and *adv.* diametrical. *Fig.* — entgegengesetzt, diametrically opposed.

***Diána**, [-'s or -nens] [in mythology] Diana.

***Diaphrágma**, *n.* [-s, *pl.* -ta, -s or -men] V. Zwerchfell.

***Diarrhöe**, V. Durchfall.

***Diät**, *f.* 1) diet, regimen. 2) daily allowance of money. —en, —engelder, *pl.* allowance, charges.

***Diät**, *adv.* — leben, [to eat according to rules prescribed] to diet.

***Diätétisch**, *adj.* dietary, dietetic, dietetical.

***Diatónisch**, *adj.* and *adv.* [in music, ascending or descending, as in sound, or from sound to sound] diatonic.

***Diatribe**, *f.* [*pl.* -n] diatribe.

***Dicastérium**, *n.* [-s, *pl.* -sterien] a court or high local authority, a board.

Dich, [Goth. *thuk*, Swed. and Dan. *dig*] the accusative case of the singular number of the personal pronoun du.

Dicht, [allied to Dick V.] I. *adj.* and *adv.* 1) dense, close, compact. Ein —er Körper, a dense body; ein —es Stück Tuch, a close piece of cloth; ein —es Gewebe, a close texture; ein —es Schiff, [in seamen's lang.] a tight ship; — und fest, [in seamen's language] tight and strong; ein —es Faß, a tight cask; Platina ist das —este Metall, platina is the densest of metals; ein —es Blatt, [in botany] a compact leaf; eine —e Wolke, a dense cloud; ein —er Nebel, a thick fog; eine —e Laube, a close arbour or bower; ein —er Laubenweg, a close walk; aus —em Silber gemacht, made of massy silver. Syn. V. Derb. 2) having parts close to each other. Ein —er Wald, a thick forest or wood; —es Gras oder Korn, thick grass or corn; die Kugeln flogen — wie Hagel, the balls flew thick as hail; das Volk stand in —en Haufen, the people were gathered thick together. II. *adv.* with little space intervening, close, closely. Ein — anschließendes Wamms, a close jacket; der — an die Bande gelegte [collirte] Ball, a close ball [at billiards]. — auf den Fersen, closely to the heels; — am Boden hin, close to the ground; — dabei, close by; — vor meinen Augen, close to my eyes; [in seamen's lang.] — beim Winde, near the wind; — an der Küste hinsegeln, to hug the land; — beim Windesegeln, to hug the wind; halt ganz — beim Winde! keep her as near she will lie. *Fig.* Ein Ereigniß folgte — auf das andere, one event followed closely upon another; — hinter ihr folgte der Tod Schritt für Schritt, behind her Death close followed, pace for pace.

Dicht-buschig, *adj.* and *adv.* bushy, tufty. *Fig.* bushy, woolly. —**eisen**, *n.* V. Kalfateisen. —**hammer**, *m.* V. Kalfathammer. —**nähtig**, *adj.* and *adv.* close-seamed.

Dichtart, *f.* [*pl.* -en] 1) the manner of composing in verse. 2) the various kinds of poems.

Dichte, *f.* 1) density, denseness, closeness of constituent parts, compactness, thickness. Die — des Nebels, the thickness or density of fog; die — der Schatten, the thickness of shades. 2) V. Dickicht.

Dichtenmesser, *m.* an instrument to measure the density of fluids.

Dichtelei, *f.* [in contempt] 1) versifying. 2) mean poetry.

1. **Dichten**, *v. tr.* [allied to the Gr. τεύχω, root τυχ-] to make close, to cause the parts of a body to approach, or to unite more closely, by mechanical force. Ein Faß —, to drive the staves of a cask close together; die Nahten —, [in seamen's lang.] to calk the seams.

2. **Dichten**, [allied to the Gr. τεύχω, V. 1. Dichten; allied to denken &c.] *v. intr.* and *v. tr.* 1) [rather obsolete or unusual] to think on, to muse on, to meditate on. Er dichtet auf etwas Böses, he devises or imagines mischief; das — [Dichten] und Trachten des menschlichen Herzens, the conceits and endeavours of the human heart. 2) to frame by the imagination, to invent [the machinery of a poem &c.]. Eine Erzählung —, to compose a story. 3) to compose metrically, to make poetry, to poetize. Ein Lied —, to compose a song. 4) [for erdichten] to contrive falsely, to forge. Lügen —, to invent falsehoods. Syn. Dichten, Erdichten. Dichten signifies, to produce by the creative powers of the mind and imagination, something that did not before exist. Erdichten joins to this the idea of inventing fiction, or something by which another is to be deceived.

Dichter, *m.* [-s, *pl.* -] [the author of a poem; one skilled in making poetry] poet. Ein berühmter —, a renowned poet; in der Sprache der —, in poetic language.

Dichter-ader, *f. Fig.* poetic vein. Er hat keine —ader, he has no poetic talent. —**anlage**, *f.* a particular genius for metrical composition, poetic talent. —**beruf**, *m.* the calling of a poet. —**born**, *m.* [in mythology] the Pierian spring, Hippocrene. —**feuer**, *n.* poetical fire. Mit —feuer, with a poet's fire. —**flug**, *m.* a flight of poetry, flight of imagination. —**freiheit**, *f.* poetic license [licentia poetica]. —**gabe**, *f.* —**geist**, *m.* V. —anlage. —**glut**, *f.* the inspiration, the fire of a poet. —**gott**, *m.* [the God of poetry] Apollo [with the Greeks and Romans], Braga [with the ancient northern nations]. —**kopf**, *m.* V. —anlage. —**pferd**, *n.* V. —roß. —**quell**, *m.* V. —born. —**roß**, *n.* [in mythology, a winged horse belonging to Apollo and the Muses] Pegasus. —**schönheit**, *f.* beauty of poetry. —**schwarm**, *m.* a crowd of poets. —**sprache**, *f.* poetical language. —**traum**, *m.* the dream of a poet [= the poetical composition of a poet]. —**volk**, *n.* the poets [in contempt]. —**werk**, *n.* the work or composition of a poet. —**wort**, *n.* 1) a poet's word or saying, a poet's word. 2) the decision of a poet, poet's authority.

Dichterei, *f.* pitiful poetry.

Dichterinn, *f.* a female poet, poetess, po[etr]ess.

Dichterisch, I. *adj.* poetic, poetical. [Ein] —er Geist, a poetic genius; —es Talent, poetic talent; —e Schönheiten, beauties of poetry; ein —er Ausdruck, a poetical expression. *F[ig.]* —e Hoffnungen, chimerical hopes. II. *adv.* po[et]ically.

Dichterischschön, *adj.* and *adv.* roma[n]tically beautiful.

Dichterling, *m.* [-s, *pl.* -e] a petty poet, pitiful rhymer or writer of verses, a poetaster.

Dichterschaft, *f.* 1) the quality of a p[oet]. 2) the poets in general.

Dichtheit, **Dichtigkeit**, *f.* V. Dichte.

Dichtigkeitsmesser, *m.* V. Dichtenm[esser].

Dichtkraft, *f.* 1) imagination. 2) the po[wer] of composing in verse.

Dichtkunde, *f.* poetics.

Dichtkunst, *f.* 1) [the art of composing in ve[rse]] poetry, poesy. 2) poetics.

Dichtlehre, *f.* [*pl.* -n] V. Dichtkunst, 2.

Dichtung, *f.* 1) [the art or skill of compo[sing] poems] poetry, poesy. 2) poetical compo[sition,] poetry, poesy, a poem. Ich lese gerne —en, [I am] fond of reading poetry. 3) fiction. Er hält [Ho]mer und den ganzen Trojanischen Krieg für [eine] schöne —, he thinks Homer and the whole [war] of Troy only a beautiful fiction; kennen Sie the's „Wahrheit und —"? do you know Goethe's „Truth and Fiction"?

Dichtungs-art, *f.* V. Dichtart. —**gabe**, *f.* V. Dichtergabe. —**kraft**, *f.* V. Dichtkraft. —**lehre**, *f.* V. Dichtkunst, 2). —**vermögen**, *n.* V. Dichtvermögen. —**wesen**, *n.* poesy.

Dichtvermögen, *n.* [-s] V. Dichtkraft.

Dick, [allied to Dicht, to the Goth. *theikan*, and to the Germ. gedeihen] I. *adj.* and *adv.* thick. *a*) [having more depth or extent from one surface to its opposite than usual, opposed to thin] Eine —e Planke, a thick plank; —es Tuch, Papier, thick cloth, thick paper; ein —er Bauch, a big belly; ein —es Buch, a large book; Karl der —e, Charles the Fat; ein —es Kind, a corpulent child; der —e Darm [—darm], large intestines; †eine Frau mit einem —en Bauche, a bigbellied woman, a woman big with child; die —e Lippe, blubberlip; das —e Ende, butt-end; — werden, to grow in flesh; [also for inflated, tumefied] ein —es Bein, a swelled leg; eine —e Backe, a swollen cheek. *Fig.* †Ein —es Fell haben, to be insensible; *—er Witz, heavy wit; *— thun, to brag, to boast; *er thut damit —, he brags of it; ‡—e Freunde, thick or intimate friends. *b*) [noting the diameter of a body] Sieben Zoll —, seven inches thick; mein kleiner Finger soll —er seyn, denn meines Vaters Lenden, [in Scripture] my little finger shall be thicker than my father's loins. *c*) = close, dense. Ein —er Wald, a thick wood or forest; — stehendes Getreide, thick corn; eine —e Wolke, a thick cloud; —e Dünste, thick or dense vapours; ein —er Nebel, a thick fog; ein sehr —er Nebel, [in seamen's lang.] a mist; —e Finsterniß, thick darkness; eine —e Luft, a thick air. *d*) = inspissated, thickened as a liquor. —e Tinte, ink that is too thick; —e Milch, curd; *durch — und dünn, through thick and thin; *sie folgte ihm durch — und dünn, through thick and thin she followed him; —e Farben [—farben], thick colours; das —e der Milch, the thick part of the milk; das —e der Molken, the cheesy parts of whey; das —e des Kaffees, the sediment of coffee. II. *adv.* thick, thickly. — besäet, thick-sown; — mit Dung belegt, covered thick with manure.

Dick-armig, *adj.* and *adv.* having thick arms. —**backig**, *adj.* and *adv.* blobcheeked. —**balken**, *m.* [in shipbuilding] a great thick beam. —**bauch**, *m.* 1) a great belly. 2) † and ‡ a bigbellied man. 3) *Fig.* [a species of whelk] the small ice casket. —**bäuchig**, *adj.* and *adv.* bigbellied, ...rbellied. —**bein**, *n.* thigh. —**beinig**, *adj.* and *adv.* having thick legs. —**blatt**, *n.* [a plant] ...assula. —**blütig**, *adj.* and *adv.* having a thick blood. —**darm**, *m.* great-gut. —**farbe**, *f.* a thick colour. —**farbig**, *adj.* and *adv.* having thick colours. —**fellig**, *adj.* and *adv.* having a thick skin. —**fisch**, *m.* the fin-scale or rud. —**fuß**, *m.* [a bird] the thick-kneed plover. —**füßig**, *adj.* and *adv.* having thick feet. ‡—**glaubig**, *adj.* and *adv.* hyper-orthodox. —**hals**, *m.* 1) a thick neck. 2) a thick-necked man. 3) *Fig.* [a species of the blenny] the gattorugin blenny. —**hälsig**, *adj.* and *adv.* thick-necked. —**härig**, *adj.* and *adv.* having thick hair. —**häutig**, *adj.* and *adv.* thick-skinned, thick-coated. **Fig.* Ein —häutiger Mensch, an insensible man, fellow. —**hülsig**, *adj.* and *adv.* having thick husks or shells. —**kopf**, *m.* 1) a man with a thick head. *Fig.* a thick-head, a block-head. 2) [in natural history] *a*) [a fish] the chub. *b*) the buffle-headed duck. *c*) the loggerheaded turtle. —**köpfig**, *adj.* and *adv.* having a thick head. *Fig.* thick headed, thick-skulled, dull, stupid. —**köpfigkeit**, *f.* thick-headedness, dullness, stupidity. —**laubig**, *adj.* and *adv.* having thick leaves, thick-leaved. —**leibig**, *adj.* and *adv.* big-bellied, corpulent. **Fig.* Ein —leibiges Buch, a voluminous book. —**leibigkeit**, *f.* corpulency. —**lippe**, *f.* 1) a thick lip, blobberlip. 2) a thick or blobber lipped person. 3) *Fig.* *a*) the great broad lipped wheck. *b*) the thick lipped top. —**lippig**, *adj.* and *adv.* having thick lips, blobber-lipped. —**maß**, *n.* [with hunters = Gesege] rub. —**maul**, *n.* 1) a thick mouth. 2) a blobber-lipped man or woman. —**maulig**, *adj.* and *adv.* blobber-lipped. —**milch**, *f.* curd. —**nasig**, *adj.* and *adv.* thick-nosed. —**nudel**, *f.* macaroni. —**öhrig**, *adj.* and *adv.* 1) being thick of hearing. 2) **Fig.* not listening, not regarding, not moved, persuaded or convinced, deaf. —**quetsche**, —**quetschform**, *f.* [among goldbeaters] a sort of mould. —**rindig**, *adj.* and *adv.* thick-rinded. —**rübe**, *f.* [Runkelrübe] root of scarcity. —**saft**, *m.* an inspissated juice. —**säulig**, *adj.* and *adv.* [in architect.] said of a row of columns, which stand four times their thickness apart. —**schälig**, —**schalig**, *adj.* and *adv.* thick-shelled. —**schnabel**, —**schnäbler**, *m.* the haw-finch. —**schnäbelig**, *adj.* and *adv.* having a thick bill, thick-billed. —**stämmig**, *adj.* and *adv.* having a thick trunk. —**taffet**, *m.* taffeta of Tours. —**tau**, *n.* V. Kabeltau. —**thaler**, *m.* a sort of Spanish silver-coin. *—**thuer**, *m.* boaster, bragger, braggart. *—**thuerei**, *f.* vaunting, boasting, bragging. *—**thuerisch**, *adj.* and *adv.* vaunting, boasting, boastful. —**tuch**, *n.* swanskin. —**waldig**, *adj.* and *adv.* thickly grown with wood. —**walke**, *f.* [with fullers] a certain manner of fulling. —**wanst**, *m.* V. —bauch. —**wanstig**, V. —bäuchig. —**wurzel**, *f.* V. —rübe. —**zirkel**, *m.* calliper-compasses.

Dicke, *f.* thickness. *a*) [size] largeness, bigness. Die — eines Buches, the largeness of a book. *b*) [the extent of a body from side to side, or from surface to surface] Die — eines Baumes, eines Brettes, the thickness of a tree, of a board; die — einer Erdschichte, the thickness of a layer of earth; die übermäßige —e eines Menschen, obesity. *c*) [closeness of the parts, the state of being crowded or near] denseness, density. Die — eines Waldes, the thickness of a wood. *d*) [the state of being concrete or inspissated] Die — der Schminke, des Mörtels, the thickness of paint, of mortar; die — des Honigs, the thickness of honey; dieser Syrup muß mehr — haben, this sirup must have more consistence, more body; die — des Blutes, the thickness of the blood; die — des geronnenen Blutes, the spissitude of coagulated blood.

Dickheit, *f.* [the state of being thick] thickness.

Dickicht, *n.* [-es, *pl.* -e] a thicket.

Dickigkeit, *f.* 1) thickness. *a*) [as opposed to length and breadth]. *b*) [the state of being thick, close, dense]. 2) an inspissated body [as opposed to a liquid].

Dicklich, *adj.* and *adv.* somewhat thick, thickish.

Dickung, *f.* V. Dickicht.

***Dictāt**, *n.* [-es, *pl.* -e] 1) [in logic] dictate = rule. 2) [chiefly in *pl.*] dictates = inspiration. 3) dictate = something dictated.

***Dictātor**, *m.* [-s, *pl.* -en] a dictator.

***Dictatōrisch**, *adj.* and *adv.* *Fig.* dictatorial, dictatory, imperious, dogmatical. Ein —er Ton, a dictatorial tone.

***Dictatūr**, *f.* [*pl.* -en] dictature, dictatorship.

***Dictiōn**, *f.* [expression of ideas by words] diction, style, manner of expression.

***Dictionnār**, *m.* or *n.* [-s, *pl.* -e or -s] a dictionary.

***Dictīren**, *v. tr.* to dictate [a letter &c.]. Herr B. dictirte seine Predigten, Mr. B. indited his sermons.

***Didāktik**, *f.* the art of teaching or instructing.

***Didāktisch**, *adj.* and *adv.* didactic, didactical. Die —e Poesie, V. Lehrgedicht.

Die, V. Der.

Dieb, *m.* [-es, *pl.* -e] [allied to the Polish *dybie*, schleichen, lauern] 1) thief. *Prov.* Gelegenheit macht —e, opportunity makes a thief; einem —e ist nicht gut stehlen, he that will deceive the fox, must rise betimes; die kleinen —e fängt man, die großen läßt man laufen; nicht alle —e werden gehängt, there are more thieves than the law exposes to a turn at Tyburn. Often used in composition, as Taschen—, pickpocket; Molken—, [an insect] butterfly &c. 2) [an excrescence or waster in the snuff of a candle] a thief.

Diebkäfer, *m.* V. Kräuterdieb.

Dieb(e)s-auge, *n.* a thievish eye. —**bande**, *f.* a gang of thieves. —**daum**, *m.* the thumb of a hanged thief. **Fig.* Er trägt einen —daumen bei sich, he has good luck in every thing. —**fänger**, *m.* thief-catcher, thief-taker. —**finger**, *m.* **Fig.* —finger haben, to have a dexterous hand for thieving, to have sleight fingers. —**genoß**, *m.* a thief's accomplice. —**geschichte**, *f.* a story of thieves. —**gesell**, *m.* V. —genoß. **Fig.* —**gesicht**, *n.* a hanging-face. —**gesindel**, *n.* a brood of thieves. **Fig.* —**glück**, *n.* unmerited fortune, undeserved luck. —**handwerk**, *n.* the trade of a thief. —**hehler**, *m.* the concealer of a thief, [in law] a receiver. —**hehlerei**, *f.* the concealment of a thief and the receiving of stolen goods. —**herberge**, *f.* an inn where lodging is furnished to thieves. —**höhle**, *f.* a den of thieves or robbers. —**inseln**, *pl.* the Ladrone Islands. —**kniff**, *m.* a thievish trick. *Fig.* —**laterne**, *f.* a dark lantern. —**leiter**, *f.* the ladder by which thieves may ascend a building. **Fig.* Die —leiter halten, to be an accomplice in a theft. —**leuchte**, *f.* V. —laterne. —**loch**, *n.* V. —höhle. —**nest**, *n.* a nest of thieves or robbers. —**pack**, *n.* V. —gesindel. *Fig.* —**pfeife**, *f.* dog-whistle. —**pfiff**, *m.* V. —kniff. —**rotte**, *f.* a gang of thieves or robbers. —**schlüssel**, *m.* picklock. —**sprache**, *f.* the cant or slang of thieves. —**streich**, *m.* a thievish trick. —**volk**, *n.* V. —gesindel. —**werkzeug**, *n.* tools which serve to thieves. —**wirth**, *m.* the landlord of an inn where lodging is furnished to thieves. —**zeichen**, *n.* a sign which thieves give to each other.

Dieberei, *f.* theft, thievery.

Diebinn, *f.* a female thief. *Fig.* Often in compositions, as Herzens— &c.

Diebisch, *adj.* and *adv.* thievish; thievishly, by theft. *a*) [partaking of the nature of theft] Etwas —er Weise entwenden, to take something by theft or thievishly. *b*) [addicted to the practice of theft] Ein —er Knabe, a thievish boy.

Diebstahl, *m.* [-es, *pl.* -stähle] 1) [the act or practice of stealing] theft, thievery. 2) [a single act of stealing] theft, larceny. Einen — begehen, to commit a theft; der — mit Einbruch, burglary. *Fig.* Der gelehrte —, plagiarism.

1. **Diele**, *f.* [*pl.* -n] [A. S. *dael*, Swed. *tilja*, allied to Theil, to the Fr. *tailler*, to the Lat. *talea*] a deal, board, or plank.

Dielen-handel, *m.* deal-trade. —**händler**, *m.* a trader in deals. —**kopf**, *m.* [in architecture] a cortel or bracket, mutule. —**säger**, *m.* V. Brettschneider. —**wand**, *f.* a wall built of deals or boards. —**werk**, *n.* any work made of deals.

2. **Diele**, *f.* [*pl.* -n] [appears to be allied to the Low. Sax. Daal = niedrig, if it does not belong to

1. Diele] ||1) a clay floor. 2) V. Hausflur. ||3) the ceiling of a room. ||4) a court, where small matters are heard and decided.

Dielen, *v. tr.* to board [a room &c.]. Ein Haus mit tannenen Borden —, to floor a house with pine-boards; einen Fußboden —, to plank a floor; das —, planching.

Dienen, [A. Sax. *theovian*; Goth. *thius* signifies a Diener] *v. intr.* 1) [to be a servant or slave; to be employed in labour for another] to serve. Also diente Jakob um Rahel sieben Jahre, [in Script.] and Jacob served seven years for Rachel. 2) to serve = to perform domestic offices to another, to wait, to attend. Bei Jemanden —, to be in any one's service; Einem —, to serve any one; er dient bei mir als Kammerdiener, he lives with me as a valet de chambre; in der Küche —, to be employed in the kitchen; bei Tische, or zu Tische —, to wait at table; Messe —, to serve at mass; Niemand kann zween Herren —, [in Script.] no man can serve two masters. 3) to transact or manage business for another. Er dient mir in dieser Sache als Anwalt, he is my attorney in that affair. 4) to serve = to perform duties, as in the army, navy, or in any office. Unter der Reiterei —, to serve in the cavalry; er diente dem Könige in drei Feldzügen, he served the king in three campaigns; er hat fünf Jahre in Indien gedient, he served five years in India; unter Einem —, to serve under any one; ein —der, one that serves. V. Bedient, 2). *Fig.* Gott —, to serve God; Götzen oder falschen Göttern —, to serve idols or false gods; der Sünde —, to serve sin. 5) to serve = to help by good offices. Seinem Vaterlande —, to serve one's country; wenn ich Ihnen womit — kann, if I can be serviceable to you in any thing; wenn Ihnen damit gedient ist, if this be of any service to you; Ihnen zu —, at your service. 6) to serve = to conduce, to be of use. Unser Sieg diente nur dazu &c., our victory only served &c.; damit ist mir nicht gedient, this will not do for me; es diente ihm auf eine oder die andere Weise, he made it subservient in one way or other; es dient unsern Absichten, it furthers our purposes; wozu dient dies alles? what is all this for? das dient zu nichts, this is of no use, this is to no purpose. 7) to serve, to be in the place of any thing to a person. Ein Sopha dient den Türken zum Sitzen und zum Bette, a sopha serves the Turks for a seat and a couch; es dient ihm zur Entschuldigung, it serves him for an excuse; das soll mir zur Warnung —, this shall be a warning to me; dies diene zur Antwort, this may serve in return. 8) V. Passen. Syn. Dienen, Aufwarten. Aufwarten, signifies, to attend or wait on, to be present in order to receive and execute the commands of another. Dienen to execute the commands, to perform services for another.

Diener, *m.* [-s, *pl.* -] 1) a person who serves another or acts as his minister. Ein — des Staates [ein Staatsdiener], a person who serves the state, a public functionary; ein — der Gerechtigkeit, a judge; ein — der Kirche, a minister; ein — des Wortes Gottes, a minister of the Gospel. *Fig.* Ein — Gottes, a servant of God; ein Götzen—, an idolater; — seines Zornes, vassals to his anger, ministers to his wrath. 2) [in a more limited sense, a person, that attends another for the purpose of performing menial offices to him, and is subject to his command] servant [the word is correlative to master]. Meine —, my servants, domestics. V. also Bedient, 2). 3) one who helps by good offices. Er war immer ein treuer — Ihres Hauses, he always served your family faithfully. *Fig.* [a word of civility] servant. Ihr gehorsamer —, your obedient servant; [in an ironical sense] gehorsamer —, ich werde es bleiben lassen, I shall not do it forsooth.

Diener-haus, *n.* V. Gesindehaus. —kleid, *n.* —kleidung, *f.* servant's dress, livery. —tracht, *f.* V. —kleid.

Dienerinn, *f.* a female servant. *Fig.* Ihre —, [a word of civility] your servant; Ihre —, [ironically] thank ye!

Dienerschaft, *f.* servants, domestics [collectively].

Dienlich, *adj.* and *adv.* serviceable, useful, beneficial, advantageous. Jedes —e Mittel anwenden, to employ every expedient; der Gesundheit —, wholesome; Betriebsamkeit ist dem Körper —, industry is beneficial to the body; Nahrung, die mir — ist, food convenient for me; zum Kriege —, fit for war; wenn Sie es für — erachten, if you think fit or proper; *wenn ich Ihnen in etwas — seyn kann, if I can be of service to you in any thing; wozu ist das —? of what use is that?

Dienlichkeit, *f.* subservience, subserviency.

Diensam, *adj.* and *adv.* 1) V. Dienlich. 2) obliging, officious.

Dienst, *m.* [-es, *pl.* -e] 1) service. *a*) [in a general sense, labour of body or of body and mind, performed at the command of a superior, or in pursuance of duty, or for the benefit of another]. Freiwilliger oder gezwungener —, voluntary or involuntary service; persönliche —e, personal services [which a tenant owes to his lord for his fee]; Frohn—e, socage. *Fig.* Der — Gottes, the worship of God; der Götzen—, idolatry; der Gottes—, divine service; sich dem —e Gottes weihen, to devote one's self to the service of God. *b*) [the business of a servant; attendance to a superior] employment, business. Zum —e verbunden seyn, to be obliged to serve; —e bei Jemanden nehmen, to enter any one's service; in —en bei Jemanden stehen or seyn, to be in any one's service; denn Keiner wollte in — treten, for none would go to service; als Richter —e leisten, to perform the services of a judge; den — haben, [at court] to be in waiting; der öffentliche — [Staats—], public service; der Kriegs- oder See—, military or naval service; er steht in —en der Regierung, he is in the employment of government; er trat im achtzehnten Jahre in Kriegs—e, he entered the service at eighteen years of age; in französischen [Kriegs-] —en seyn or stehen, to serve in the French army; die Compagnie ist im —e, the company is on duty; Lieutenant N. hat heute [den] —, Lieutenant N. is on duty to-day. *c*) = useful office, advantage conferred, that which promotes interest or happiness. Einen — leisten, to do or render a service; er kam, um ihm seine —e anzubieten, he came to offer him his services; sie thun der Religion keinen besondern —, they do not much service to religion; Einem einen schlechten — erweisen, to do any one a bad office. *Prov.* Ein ungebetener — ist selten angenehm, proffer'd service stinks; ein — ist des andern werth, one good turn deserves another. *Fig.* [a word of civility] Was stehet Ihnen zu —e? what are your commands? ich stehe zu Ihren —en, I wait on you or on your pleasure; ich bin ganz zu Ihren —en, I am wholly at your service; Liebes—e, offices of love, charitable services, charities. *d*) [place of a servant; place, office] Außer — seyn, to be out of service; den — aufsagen, to give warning; einen — suchen, to look out for a place; er hat diesen — erhalten, he has obtained that service: ein mühsamer —, a laborious employment; er bekleidet einen öffentlichen —, he fills a public office, he has a place under the government; ein Kirchen—, ecclesiastical office. *Fig.* *Einem auf den — warten, lauern or passen, to endeavour to supplant any one, to have a watchful eye upon any one. 2) persons in waiting at court.

Dienst-adel, *m.* nobility, which a man derives from an office conferred. —alter, *n.* priority in office, seniority. —anerbieten, *n.* an offer of service. —angelegenheit, *f.* V. —sache. —anweisung, *f.* instruction, direction, order. —arbeit, *f.* any labour required by one's service or office. —bar, *adj.* and *adv.* 1) bound to service without wages; subjected to the authority of another. Einem —bar seyn, to be any one's bondsman. 2) serviceable, officious. *Fig.* —bare Geister, administering spirits. —barkeit, *f.* 1) servitude, bondage, slavery. In —barkeit gerathen seyn, to be reduced to bondage, to be enslaved. 2) [in law] a common, or right of common. —beflissen, *adj.* and *adv.* obliging, ready to do service, officious, devoted to any one's service. —beflissenheit, *f.* officiousness, serviceableness, readiness to do service. —bothe, *m.* [a person male or female, that attends another for the purpose of performing menial offices for him] servant, serving-man, serving-maid. Die —bothen, domestics, servants. —brief, *m.* appointment, patent. —bruder, *m.* fellow servant, comrade. —brüderschaft, *f.* fellowship, companionship in service. —eid, *m.* oath of office. —eifer, *m.* eagerness to serve, officiousness, zeal of office. —eifrig, *adj.* and *adv.* eager to serve, zealous in service. —entshebung, *f.* 1) relief from service. 2) dismission or suspension from service. —entsetzung, *f.* dismission from service. —erbietig, *adj.* and *adv.* V. —willig. —erbietung, *f.* proffer of service. —ergeben, *adj.* and *adv.* devoted, addicted to any one's service. —fach, *n.* offices, employments. Das bürgerliche —fach, civil offices. —fähig, *adj.* and *adv.* fit for service. [Kriegs-] —fähige Leute, men fit for military service. —fähigkeit, *f.* fitness for service. —fehler, *m.* a neglect of service, a fault committed in service. —fertig, *adj.* and *adv.* 1) officious. 2) ready to serve others. —fertigkeit, *f.* eagerness to serve, officiousness. —fleiß, *m.* application to service. —frau, *f.* serving-woman, a menial. —frei, *adj.* and *adv.* 1) exempt or free from certain services. Ein —freies Gut, a freehold property, a land held by fee simple. 2) exempted from military service or duty. 3) exempt from any service, not invested with public office or employment. Das —freie Leben, private life. —freundlich, *adj.* and *adv.* officious, kind. ||—freundschaft, *f.* [in official style] collegial or official friendship. ||—freundschaftlich, *adj.* and *adv.* V. —freundschaft. —führung, *f.* the act of officiating. —gefällig, V. —fertig. —geflissen, V. —beflissen. —gehalt, *m.* salary. ||—geld, *n.* money paid in lieu of service. —genoß, *m.* [a partner or associate in the same office, employment or commission] colleague. —genossenschaft, *f.* partnership in office, colleagueship. —gerechtigkeit, *f.* V. —recht. —geschäft, *n.* V. Amtsgeschäft. ||—haft, V. —pflichtig. —herr, *m.* 1) [the proprietor of a manor] a lord [for whom certain services are to be performed]. 2) [one who has servants] master. —jahr, *n.* a year spent in service. Er hat dreißig —jahre, he has served [illegible] years. —kamerad, *m.* [in military colloq. [illegible]] brother officer. —kleid, *n.* —kleidung, *f.* livery, uniform. —knecht, *m.* serving-man, [illegible] servant. —leistung, *f.* 1) [voluntary or [illegible]tary] service. Es waren keine besondere —leistungen für die Krone vorbehalten, there were no services reserved to the crown. 2) [any thing done by way of duty, or voluntarily] service. —leute, *pl.* V. —mann. —lohn, *m.* [the reward, [illegible] recompense paid for personal service] hire, wages. —los, *adj.* and *adv.* out of service. —mädchen, *n.* serving-maid. —magd, *f.* maid-servant, serving-maid, a menial. —mann, *m.* a person bound to certain services, a vassal, bondman, socman, [in old English law] a villain. *it.* formerly, a tenant or vassal who held his lands by service which was due to the lord within his manor [Hausleute, Hausgenossen]. ||—**pfennig**, *m.* V. Miethpfennig. —**pferd**, *n.* 1) a horse used to perform services for another. 2) [in military affairs] a charger with which the government provides every officer of cavalry. —**pflicht**, *f.* 1) the obligation to perform certain services. 2) that which a person is bound, by his office or employment, to do or perform. Aus—pflicht, by virtue of one's office [ex officio]. ||3) oath of allegiance. —**pflichtig**, *adj* and *adv.* liable to certain services. Der—pflichtige, an attendant; ein —pflichtiger Bauer, a socman. —**recht**, *n.* a right to the service of another. —**rock**, *m.* V. —kleid. —**sache**, *f.* an affair, matter relating to public service. —**schuldig**, *adj.* and *adv.* V. —pflichtig. —**tauglich**, *adj.* and *adv.* able to perform service. —taugliche Soldaten, soldiers able to perform military service. —**thuend**, *adj.* and *adv.* performing service, or actual service. Die —thuenden Leute in einem Heere, the effective men in an army. —**treue**, *f.* faithfulness, fidelity, constancy in the performance of duties or services. —**tüchtig**, *adj.* and *adv.* able to perform [especially military] service. —**unfähig**, *adj.* and *adv.* disabled to perform active service, especially military service, invalid. —**unfähigkeit**, *f.* inability to perform active service. —**untauglich**, —**untüchtig**, *adj.* and *adv.* disabled from performing active service. —**verhältniß**, *n.* relations, respecting one's service, office or employment. —**verkauf**, *m.* vendition of offices. —**verlust**, *m.* loss of or removal from office or employment, dismission. —**verwandt**, *adj.* and *adv.* liable to perform certain services. —**verweisung**, *f.* V. —verlust. —**volk**, *n.* V. Gesinde. —**willig**, *adj.* and *adv.* ready to serve others, officious. —**zeit**, *f.* 1) the time which a person is bound to serve. 2) time spent in service. —**zwang**, *m.* the right of exacting certain services.

Dienstag, *m.* V. Dinstag.

Diensten, *v. intr.* [unusual] to be in waiting.

Dienstlich, *adj.* and *adv.* 1) serviceable, useful. 2) kind, officious.

Dienstling, *m.* [-es, *pl.* -e] [in contempt] one who renders a service.

||**Dientel[baum]**, *m.* [-s, *pl.* -] cornel-tree.

Dientisch, *m.* [-es, *pl.* -e] dumb-waiter. V. also ||Kammerdiener 2.

Dies, V. Dieser.

Diese, *f.* [*pl.* -n] [in forges] tewel.

Diesemnach, *conj.* consequently, in consequence of this.

Dieser, Diese, Dieses, [A. S. *thes, theos, this*, D. *dez, deze, dit*, allied to der] *pron.* this. *a*) [denoting something that is near in place, or time, or something just mentioned]. Dieses Buch, this book; dieses Buch ist besser als jenes, this book is better than that; diese Bäume, these trees; diese Insel ist sehr fruchtbar, this island is very fertile; dieses Haus gehört dem Verräther, this is the traitor's house; dieses Ihr Haus gefällt mir, this house of yours pleases me; dieser Garten des Herrn Thomas ist schön, this garden of Mr. Thomas is fine; zu dieser Zeit, at this time; in diesen Tagen, or dieser Tage werde ich Sie besuchen, I'll come to see you one of these days. [when dieser and jener refer to different things before expressed, dieser refers to the thing last mentioned, and jener to the thing first mentioned] Die Sparsamkeit und die Verschwendung sind zwei entgegengesetzte Dinge; jene macht die Menschen reich, diese macht sie arm, frugality and extravagance are opposite things; the former makes men rich, the latter makes them poor; jene geben ihren ganzen Wohlstand zum gemeinschaftlichen Gebrauch her, und diese behaupten ihre abgesonderten Zellen und ihr Eigenthum, those bestow all their wealth in common, and these maintain their separate cells and properties. *b*) often it represents a word, or sentence. Dieser ist es, von dem ich sprach, this is the man I spoke of; dies gehört Ihnen, this is yours; dies ist ganz dasselbe, this is quite the same thing; den zwölften dieses [Monats], on the twelfth instant; Ueberbringer dieses [Schreibens &c.], the bearer of this; vor diesem, before now. *c*) sometimes it is a substitute for what has preceded. Da sie aber dieses hörten, ging's ihnen durch's Herz, [in Script.] when they heard this, they were pricked to the heart.

||**Dieserhalben, Dieserwegen**, V. Deshalb, Deswegen.

Dieserlei, *adj.* and *adv.* of this kind.

Diesfalls, *adv.* in this case.

Diesfallsig, *adj.* relating to this case.

Diesjährig, *adj.* and *adv.* of this year. —er Wein, wine of this year, this year's wine.

Diesmahl, *adv.* [for dieses Mahl] this time, for the present.

Diesmahlig, *adj.* present, now existing.

Diesseitig, *adj.* being on this side. Auf dem —en Rheinufer, on this side of the Rhine. *Fig.* on our side, on our part. Die —en Kriegsrüstungen, our preparations of war.

Diesseits, *adv.* on this side. —des Rheines, der Alpen, this side the Rhine, the Alps.

Dieß, [in colloq. lang., contracted for dieses (hier, da, dort) this. — sind meine Brüder, these are my brothers; sind — nicht gute Leute? are not these good people? — beweist, daß &c., this proves that &c., the proof of it is, that &c.

Diete, *f.* V. Düte.

1. **Dietrich**, [-s] [a name of men] Derrick.

2. **Dietrich**, *m.* [-s, *pl.* -e] [appears to be allied to the Swed. *dirck, dyrck*] a false key, a pick-lock.

‡**Dieweil**, I. *conj.* because. II. *adv.* during the time that, while.

***Diffamation**, *f.* defamation [especially used in law].

***Diffamator**, *m.* [-s, *pl.* -en] a defamer, a slanderer, a detractor, a calumniator.

***Diffamiren**, *v. tr.* to defame, to calumniate.

***Differential**, *adj.* [in mathematics, an epithet applied to an infinitely small quantity, so small as to be less than any assignable quantity] differential. Die —größe, a differential quantity; die —rechnung, differential calculus, or analysis of infinitesimals.

***Differenz**, *f.* [*pl.* -en] difference.

***Differenziren**, *v. tr.* [in mathematics] to difference [quantities = to find a differential which, taken an infinite number of times, is equal to a given quantity].

***Differiren**, *v. intr.* to differ.

***Digeriren**, *v. tr.* [in chimistry, to soften and prepare by heat] to digest. Digerirend, digestive. Die Digerirung, [in chimistry] digestion.

Digerir-ofen, *m.* [in chimistry, a digesting furnace] athanor. —**topf**, *m.* Der Papinianische —topf, a digester.

***Digestion**, *f.* digestion. V. Verdauung.

***Digestiv**, *n.* [-s, *pl.* -e] V. Verdauungsmittel.

***Dilemma**, *n.* [-s] 1) [in logic] dilemma. 2) dilemma, = perplexity, embarrassment, awkward position. Er wußte nicht, wie er sich in diesem — benehmen, wie er sich aus diesem — ziehen sollte, he did not know how to get out of this scrape.

***Dilettant**, *m.* [-en, *pl.* -en] an amateur, a dilettante.

***Dilettantinn**, *f.* a female amateur or dilettante.

***Dilettantism[us]**, *m.* amateurship.

***Diligence**, *f.* [pron. as in the French] [*pl.* -n] stage-coach.

Dill, *m.* [-s] **Dille**, *f.* [a plant] [appears to be allied to the Dutch tillen = aufheben] dill.

Dill-fenchel, *m.* —**kraut**, *n.* a species of dill. —**öl**, *n.* a volatile oil drawn from the seed of dill.

1. ||**Dille**, *f.* [*pl.* -n] [appears to be allied to Dohle, Fr. *douille*] nozle, nozzle. Die — an einem Leuchter, socket.

2. **Dille**, *f.* [*pl.* -n] [with locksmiths] [perhaps allied to Theil, Diele] a flat piece of iron which covers the ward.

***Diminutiv[um]**, *n.* [-s, *pl.* -a or -e] [in grammar] a diminutive.

***Diminutiv**, *adj.* and *adv.* diminutive, nice, little.

***Dimission**, *f.* [removal from office or employment; discharge, either with honour or disgrace] dismission. Unzufrieden mit dem Gange der Regierung, gab er seine — ein, dissatisfied with the proceedings of the government, he tendered his dismission.

1. **Ding**, *n.* [-s, *pl.* -e] [appears to be allied to the Lat. *tango* (*tingo*), to the Gr. *δείκ-ω* and to the Germ. zeigen] thing. *a*) matter, not a person; sometimes an affair, business. *b*) [*pl.* -er] = a substance unknown, indeterminate or not specified. Was ist das für ein —? what is this? wie heißt das —? how do you call that thing? das ist ein schönes —, that is a fine thing. *Fig.* Das böse —, [in surgery] whitlow; das heilige —, [in medicine] erysipelas, [in popular lang.] St. Anthony's fire. ||**c*) used of persons. Das arme — seufzte, the poor thing sighed; er hat schon ein halbes Dutzend arme junge —er verführt, he has already seduced half a dozen of poor young things [girls]; [in contempt] was will das — da? what does the urchin want? *d*) any substance, that which is created [used only in the plural]. Gott ist der Schöpfer aller —e, God has created every thing. *e*) whatever is, that which happens or falls out, or that which is done, told or proposed. Vor allen —en, before all, first of all, above all, first and foremost, principally; er geht mit großen —en schwanger, he forms great schemes; ich habe große —e vor, I have a great game to play; laß das — bleiben, let it alone! *Prov.* Geschehene —e sind nicht zu ändern, it is too late to consult to-day about what was done yesterday. *Guter —e seyn, to make good cheer, to be merry; bewandten —en nach, according to circumstances; neuer —en or neuerdings, newly, lately. Syn. Ding, Sache. Whatever exists, when spoken of with reference merely to its existence, is called ein Ding. Sache is that which is not a person, thing.

‡2. **Ding**, *n.* [-es, *pl.* -e] [probably allied to the former word] 1) the judges assembled for hearing and deciding causes, a court. Das — hegen, to sit in judgment; ||das — und Recht, a court where civil causes are heard and decided. 2) *a*) a conversation, or familiar discourse. *b*) a meeting. *c*) a disputation, or rather a judicial contest. *d*) a law-suit.

||**Ding-bank**, *f.* the seat of justice, bench. —**flüchtig**, *adj.* and *adv.* escaped the court. —**gericht**, *n.* a court of law. ||—**hof**, *m.* 1) the place where a court of justice is held by the lord of a manor. 2) a farm. ||—**hofsherr**, —

hofsmann, —hörer, *m.* an assessor in the court called —hof. —kauf, *m.* a court held extraordinarily at the expenses of the demandant. ||—mann, *m.* V. —hofsmann. —pflichtig, *adj.* and *adv.* subject to a court. —stätte, *f.* the seat of justice.

Dingel, *m.* [-s] [a plant] a species of the orchis.

Dingelchen, *n.* [-s, *pl.* -] *dimin.* of 1. Ding, *b*), a little thing.

Dingen, *ir.* I. *v. intr.* to treat about a purchase, to bargain, to chaffer. II. *v. tr.* 1) to engage in service for a stipulated reward, to hire. Einen Bedienten auf ein Jahr —, to hire a servant for a year; Arbeiter —, to hire labourers. 2) to engage in immoral or illegal service for a reward, to hire, to bribe. Ein gedungener Zeuge, a hireling witness; ein gedungener Mörder, a hireling murderer; ein gedungener Lobredner, a hireling praiser. ‡3) *a*) to speak. *b*) to summon. *c*) to vow, to promise. *d*) to dispute in law, to litigate. *e*) to pass sentence. *f*) to appeal.

Dinge-brief, *m.* a written agreement with a tradesman for work to be done by him. —herr, *m.* [in metallurgy] one that roasts the ores. —pfennig, *m.* earnest, earnest money.

Dingerchen, *pl. diminut.* of Dinger. V. 1. Ding *b*), little things.

1. **Dinglich**, *adj.* and *adv.* [in law, pertaining to things fixed, permanent or immovable, as to lands and tenements] real. Das —e Recht, real right.

‡2. **Dinglich**, *adj.* and *adv.* judicial.

Dinkel, *m.* [-s] [probably allied to the root of stechen (V. Dachs, Degen) thus = gespaltenes Korn, Spelt] spelt, German corn.

Dinkel-gerste, *f.* great barley. —mehl, *n.* spelt-flour. —spelze, *f.* perennial darnel, or ray-grass.

Dinstag, *m.* [-es, *pl.* -tage] tuesday.

Dinstägig, *adj.* and *adv.* being or done on tuesday.

Dinte, *f.* V. Tinte.

*__Diöces__, __Diöcese__, *f.* [*pl.* -n] diocese.

*__Diöcesan__, *m.* [-es, *pl.* -e] diocesan.

*__Dionysius__, __Dionys__, *m.* [-ses, *pl.* -se] [a name of men] Denis, Dennis or Dionysius.

*__Diopterlineal__, *n.* [the label index or ruler, movable about the centre of an astrolabe] alidade, alhidade.

*__Dioptrik__, *f.* [in optics] dioptrics.

*__Dioptrisch__, *adj.* and *adv.* dioptric, dioptrical.

*__Diorit__, *m.* [-s, *pl.* -e] V. Grünstein.

*__Diphthong__, *m.* [-s, *pl.* -e, -en] V. Doppellaut.

*__Diplom__, *n.* [-s, *pl.* -e] [a letter or writing conferring some power, authority, privilege, or honour] diploma.

*__Diplomat__, *m.* [-en, *pl.* -en] diplomatic.

*__Diplomatie__, *f.* 1) diplomacy. 2) a diplomatic body.

*__Diplomatik__, *f.* [the science of diplomas, or of ancient writings, literary and public documents, letters, decrees, charters &c., which has for its object to decipher old writings, to ascertain their authenticity, their date &c.] diplomatics.

*__Diplomatisch__, *adj.* and *adv.* diplomatic. Das —e Corps, [the whole body of ministers at a foreign court] the diplomatic body, diplomacy.

Diptam, *m.* [-s] [a plant] dittany.

Dir, the dative case of the singular number of the personal pronoun du.

*__Direct__, *adj.* and *adv.* direct.

*__Direction__, *f.* direction, administration, management, guidance, superintendence. Often used in compositions, as Landes—, Bergwerks—, Theater— &c.

*__Director__, *m.* [-s, *pl.* -en] director, superintendent, manager. Der — einer Bank, der Indischen Handelsgesellschaft, the director of a bank, or of the India company; der — eines Collegiums, the director of a college or board; der — eines Theaters [Theater—], the manager of a theatre.

*__Directorium__, *n.* [-s, *pl.* -rien] directory.

*__Directrice__, *f.* [pron. Directriße] [*pl.* -n] directress.

*__Dirigiren__, *v. tr.* to direct, to manage, to conduct, to carry on.

Dirk, *m.* [in seamen's language] Der — der Besahnruthe, derrick; der — des Besahnsegels, peek-halliards of the mizen; der — eines Gaffelsegels, peek-halliards of a gaff.

Dirne, *f.* [*pl.* -n] [in Swed. *taerna* signifies a maid] 1) formerly, a maid, maiden, a virgin, now almost only used in this sense for a young unmarried female of the lower orders. 2) a maid, maiden, or female servant. 3) a young woman of ill fame, a wench, a hussy, a female of the town.

Dirnenhaus, *n.* a brothel.

Dis, V. Dieser.

*__Dis__, *n.* [in music] d sharp.

*__Discant__, *m.* [-es] [in music] treble. Der — durch die Fistel, faint-treble.

Discant-bratsche, *f.* treble-viol. —hoboe, *f.* treble-hoboe. —saite, *f.* treble-string. —sänger, *m.* treble-singer. —stimme, *f.* treble-voice.

*__Disciplin__, *f.* [*pl.* -en] 1) [subjection to laws, rules, order, precepts, or regulations] discipline. 2) V. Kirchenzucht.

*__Discipliniren__, *v. tr.* to discipline [troops &c.].

*__Discontiren__, *v. tr.* [in commerce] to discount [five or six per cent &c. for prompt or for advanced payment].

*__Disconto__, *m.* [in commerce, the sum deducted or refunded] discount. Der — stand auf fünf Procent, the discount was at five percent.

*__Discretionstage__, *pl.* [in commerce] days of grace.

*__Discur[r]iren__, *v. intr.* to discourse, to converse.

*__Discurs__, *m.* [-ses, *pl.* -se] discourse, conversation.

*__Discus__, *m.* disk, quoit.

*__Discussion__, *f.* discussion, debate.

*__Discutiren__, *v. tr.* to discuss, to debate, argue.

*__Disharmonie__, *f.* [*pl.* -n] disharmony, discord.

*__Disharmonisch__, *adj.* and *adv.* unharmonious.

*__Dispache__, *m.* [pron. Dispasche] [in commerce] average.

*__Dispacheur__, [pron. Dispaschöhr] *m.* [in seamen's lang.] a judge appointed to decide upon matters of average.

*__Dispens__, *m.* [-ses, *pl.* -se] __Dispense__, *f.* [*pl.* -n] dispensation.

*__Dispensatorium__, *n.* [-s, *pl.* -rien] [in medicine] dispensatory.

*__Disponibel__, *adj.* and *adv.* disposable.

*__Disponiren__, I. *v. intr.* to dispose, to regulate. Er hat über sein Haus disponirt, he has disposed of his house. **Fig.* Ueber Einen —, to dispose of a person; — Sie ganz über mich, or ich stehe ganz zu Ihrer Disposition, I am entirely at your disposition. II. *v. tr.* to dispose, to incline. *Einen zu einer Sache —, to dispose any one to a thing; *gut disponirt, cheerful, in good humour.

*__Disposition__, *f.* 1) disposition, order, method. Die — einer Predigt, the arrangement of a sermon. 2) disposition. Sein Aussehen zeigt eine — zur Auszehrung, his appearance shows a disposition to consumption.

*__Disputant__, *m.* [-en, *pl.* -en] a disputant, a controvertist.

*__Disputation__, *f.* disputation, controversy in words.

*__Disputatorium__, *n.* [-s, *pl.* -rien] [an exercise in colleges] disputation.

*__Disputiren__, *v. intr.* to dispute.

*__Dissenter__, *m.* [-s, *pl.* -] [in England] a dissenter.

*__Dissertation__, *f.* [a written essay, treatise, or disquisition] dissertation.

*__Dissident__, *m.* [-en, *pl.* -en] [one who separates from the established religion; a word applied to the members of the Lutheran, Calvinistic, and Greek churches in Poland] a dissident, non-conformist.

*__Dissonanz__, *f.* [*pl.* -en] dissonance, discord [in the proper as well as the fig. sense].

*__Dissoniren__, *v. intr.* to discord. —de Töne, dissonant notes [in a proper as well as in a fig. sense].

*__Distanz__, *f.* [*pl.* -en] distance. Eine große oder kleine —, a great or small distance.

Distel, *f.* [*pl.* -n] [probably allied to the A. S. *thydan*, stechen] [the common name of numerous prickly plants of the class syngenesia; the name is also given to other prickly plants not of that class] thistle. Mit —n bewachsen, voller —n, overgrown with thistles, thistly. *Fig.* Unser Lebenspfad führt häufig durch —n und Dornen, the path of our life often leads through thistles and thorns; die gelbe oder weiche —, V. Kratzkraut; die englische —, melancholy-thistle; die krause —, curled thistle; die knollige —, tuberous thistle; die Frauen- or Marien—, milk or ladies' thistle; die Karden—, fuller's thistle.

Distel-blume, *f.* the flower of thistles. —falter, *m.* [an insect] painted-lady. —fink, *m.* thistle-finch, gold-finch. —hacke, *f.* sharp-hoe. —hörnchen, *n.* V. —schnecke. —kohl, *m.* pale-flowered cnicus, or water-thistle. —kopf, *m.* the head of a thistle. —laus, *f.* the thistle aphis. —orden, *m.* [an English order] the Order of the Thistle. —pfad, *m.* a path overgrown with thistles [used also in a figurative sense]. —schnecke, *f.* prickle-whelk. —sichel, *f.* V. —hacke. —staude, *f.* shrubby thistle. —vogel, *m.* V. —fink. —wolle, *f.* thistle-down.

Distelicht, *adj.* and *adv.* like a thistle.

Distelig, *adj.* and *adv.* overgrown with thistles, thistly.

*__Disthen__, *m.* [-s] [a mineral] disthene.

*__Distichon__, *n.* [-s, *pl.* Disticha or Distichen] [in poetry] a distich.

*__Distilliren__, V. Destilliren.

*__Distrikt__, *m.* [-es, *pl.* -e] district. V. Bezirk.

*__Dithyramb[us]__, *m.* [-es, *pl.* -n] [in ancient poetry] dithyramb, dithyrambus.

*__Dithyrambisch__, *adj.* and *adv.* dithyrambic, wild, enthusiastic.

*__Divan__, *m.* [-s] 1) [among the Turks and other Orientals, a court of justice, or a council] divan. 2) a sofa.

*__Divergenz__, *f.* [*pl.* -en] divergence. Die — zweier Linien, the divergence of two lines.

*__Divergiren__, V. Abweichen.

*__Diversion__, *f.* [in war] diversion.

*Divertiménto, *n.* [-s] [in music, a light composition, written in a familiar style] divertimento.

*Divertiren, V. Belustigen.

*Dividénd[us], *m.* [-es, *pl.* -en] [in arithmetic, the number to be divided into equal parts] dividend.

*Dividénde, *f.* [*pl.* -n] [a part or share, particularly, the share of the interest or profit of stock employed in trade or otherwise, which belongs to each proprietor according to his proportion of the stock or capital] dividend.

*Dividiren, *v. intr.* and *tr.* [in arithmetic] to divide.

*Division, *f.* 1) [the act of dividing; in arithmetic, the dividing of a number or quantity into any parts assigned] division. 2) [a part of an army, a body consisting of a number of brigades, usually two, and commanded by a major-general; but the term is often applied to other bodies or portions of an army, as to a brigade, a squadron, or a platoon] division.

*Divisor, *m.* [-s, *pl.* -en] [in arithmetic] divisor.

‖Dóbbe, *f.* [in hydraulics] a slimy ground.

‖Dóbber, *m.* [-s, *pl.* -s] [a sea term] buoy.

‖1. Döbel, *m.* [-s, *pl.* -] [a fish] the chub.

‖2. Döbel, *m.* [-s, *pl.* -] [appears to be allied to the Gr. τύπ-τω and the Germ. dupfen, stopfen] 1) a pin, a peg. 2) [with stone-cutters] a kind of wedge. 3) [in mining] V. Frosch.

Döbelboden, *m.* the double floor between two stories. —bohrer, *m.* [with coopers] a wimble.

‖Döbeln, *v. tr.* [V. 2. Döbel] to pin. Den Boden eines Fasses —, [with coopers] to pin the bottom-pieces of a tub.

Doch, *conj.* 1) [noting an addition to supply what is wanting to elucidate, or modify the sense of the preceding part of a sentence or of a discourse, or to continue a discourse, or to exhibit a contrast] *a*) yet, nevertheless, notwithstanding, however. Ich werde mich Ihrem Vorhaben nicht widersetzen, — kann ich es nicht billigen, I shall not oppose your design, I cannot however approve of it; sie ist häßlich, — liebt er sie, she is ugly, yet he loves her; ob er gleich geschickt ist, so hat er — einen großen Fehler begangen, clever as he is, he has nevertheless committed a great blunder. *b*) but. Es gefällt mir, — nur eine Zeit lang, it pleases me, but only for a time; er hatte versprochen zu kommen, — er kam nicht, he had promised to come, but he came not. 2) sometimes it is used to fill up or strengthen an expression. Es ist — wohl nichts Böses? 'tis nothing ill, I hope? o könnten Sie — kommen! O that you could come! werfen Sie mir — das nicht vor, pray, do not upbraid me with that; machen Sie mir — dieses Vergnügen, do give me this pleasure; ja —! yes! nein — ! no, no! nicht — ! by no means! höre — ! pray, do hear me!

Docht, *m.* [-es, *pl.* -e] [from ziehen, Low Sax. tehen] wick [of a candle, lamp &c.]. *Fig.* Der — des Lebens ist abgebrannt, the lamp of his life is extinguished.

Dochtbank, *f.* [with tallow-chandlers] cutting-board. —garn, *n.* wick-yarn. —messer, *n.* [with tallow-chandlers] chopping-knife. —nadel, a wire used by tallow-chandlers. —schneider, *m.* [with wax-chandlers] cutting-board. —spieß, *m.* V. Lichtspieß.

Dociren, I. *v. intr.* to instruct, to teach. II. *v. tr.* to lecture on. Er docirt das Römische Recht, he lectures on the Roman law.

Döckchen, *n.* [-s] *dimin.* of 3. Docke 3).

1. Dócke, *f.* [*pl.* -n] [allied to Dachs V.] a large dog, a mastiff.

2. Dócke, *f.* [*pl.* -n] [allied to Deich and to the A. S. *dican, to dig*] [a broad deep trench on the side of a harbour, or bank of a river, into which ships are brought for the more convenient taking in or discharging their cargoes, or for repairing, calking &c.] dock; [ein Schiff] in die — schaffen, to dock.

Dockenbank, *f.* a bank in a dock.

3. Dócke, *f.* [*pl.* -n] [allied to Stock and to the Gr. δοκός, Balken] 1) a short thick column, [with several mechanics] a short square or turned pillar, an upright post. *a*) [with joiners] mandrel. Die —n [of a lathe], puppets. ‖*b*) [with cartwrights] *pl.* standards. *c*) [in architect.] a baluster. 2) any thing round and long, a roll, a bundle. Die — Seide, sleave-silk; eine — Garn, a skein of yarn. 3) a puppet or baby for a child, a doll. *Fig.* *Sie ist geputzt wie eine — or ein Döckchen, she is dressed like a doll. 4) a sort of head-dress for females. 5) [in certain instruments] jack, sautereau.

Dockengeländer, *n.* [in architecture] balustrade. —krämer, *m.* a dealer in dolls or puppets. —macher, *m.* a maker of puppets. —spiel, *n.* puppet-show. —spieler, *m.* puppet-player. —stock, *m.* [with joiners] the wooden base of a mandrel. —werk, *n.* V. —geländer.

1. Dócken, [unusual] I. *v. tr.* to form into a roll or bundle. II. *v. intr.* to play with a doll.

2. Dócken, *v. tr.* [in seamen's lang.] to dock [a ship].

Döckenblätter, *pl.* [a plant] the sharp-pointed dock.

‖*Dóctern, *v. intr.* [in contempt or joke] to make use of remedies, to pretend the art of medicine, to quack.

*Dóctor, *m.* [-s, *pl.* -en] 1) doctor. *a*) a learned man, a man of erudition. Wie ein —, doctorly. *b*) [a person who has received the highest degree in a faculty] Ein — der Rechte, a doctor in or of laws; ein — der Theologie, a doctor in or of divinity; ein — der Medicin, a doctor of medicine; — werden, to commence doctor. 2) = physician.

Doctordiplom, *n.* diploma or patent for a doctor's degree. —hut, *m.* the doctor's cap. —mantel, *m.* the doctoral gown. —mäßig, *adj.* and *adv.* doctoral. —würde, *f.* doctorship, a doctor's degree. Die —würde ertheilen, to doctorate; die —würde erhalten, to get one's degree as doctor.

*Doctorát, *n.* [-es, *pl.* -e] doctorship, doctorate.

*Doctorinn, *f.* a female doctor, doctress, doctoress, a female physician.

*Doctrinär, *m.* [-s, *pl.* -s or -e] 1) [a member of a congregation called the christian doctrine] doctrinary. 2) [a system-maker] doctrinist.

*Doctrine, *f.* [*pl.* -n] doctrine, learning, tenets, maxims. Die — des Plato, the doctrine of Plato.

*Document, *n.* [-es, *pl.* -e] [any official or authorative paper containing instructions or proof, for information and the establishment of facts] document.

*Documentiren, *v. tr.* to prove by a document or documents.

*Documentirt, *adj.* documental.

Dógboot, *n.* V. Dogger.

Dógge, *m.* and *f.* [*pl.* -n] a bull-dog. V. 1. Docke.

Dógger, *m.* [-s, *pl.* -] [a Dutch fishing-vessel used in the German Ocean] a dogger.

Dóggern, *v. intr.* to fish in a dogger.

*Dógma, *n.* [-'s, *pl.* -men] [a principle, maxim or tenet] dogma.

*Dogmátik, *f.* the positive divinity.

*Dogmátiker, *m.* [-s, *pl.* -] dogmatist.

*Dogmátisch, I. *adj.* dogmatic, dogmatical. II. *adv.* dogmatically.

*Dogmatisiren, *v. intr.* to dogmatize.

1. Dóhle, *f.* [*pl.* -n] [a bird] the jack-daw, chough.

2. Dóhle, *f.* [*pl.* -n] [allied to Thal; in Swed. *Tull* and in Pol. *Dol* signifies a ditch or channel] a drain, a watercourse.

Dóhne, *f.* [*pl.* -n] [probably from dehnen] a springe, a gin, a noose [for catching birds]. In —n fangen, to springe.

Dohnenfang, *m.* 1) the catching of birds in springes. 2) the privilege of catching birds in springes. —steig, —strich, *m.* the line in which the springes are set in a wood.

Dolch, *m.* [-es, *pl.* -e] [formerly dalgen signified stoßen] a dagger, a poniard, a dirk. *Fig.* Ihre Worte sind —e, und jedes Wort verwundet tödtlich, she speaks poniards and every word stabs.

Dolchbewehrt, *adj.* and *adv.* armed with a poniard. —förmig, *adj.* and *adv.* like a dagger or poniard. —stab, —stock, *m.* a dart-stick, dart-cane, tuck-stick, Jacob's staff. —stich, —stoß, *m.* a stab with a dagger.

Dölbchen, *n.* [-s] *dimin.* of Dolde. a little umbel, umbellet, umbellicle.

Dólde, *f.* [*pl.* -n] [from the old dolen = tragen, heben] 1) the top of any thing, especially of trees. 2) [in botany, a particular mode of inflorescence or flowering] umbel. Die einfache oder zusammengesetzte —, the simple or compound umbel; [in general] cluster. Der Baum war über und über mit Blumen[Blüten]—n bedeckt, the tree was entirely covered with clusters of flowers.

Doldenartig, *adj.* and *adv.* [in botany, having an umbel] umbellar. —blume, *f.* an umbellate flower. —blütig, *adj.* and *adv.* umbelliferous. —erbse, *f.* the rose or crown pea. —isop, *m.* a species of hyssop. —pflanze, *f.* umbelliferous plant. —traube, *f.* [in botany] corymb.

Dóldig, *adj.* and *adv.* umbellate, umbellated.

Dóldocke, *f.* [*pl.* -n] [a plant] isophyrum.

Doll, V. Toll.

‖Dölle, *f.* [*pl.* -n] [a pit or hollow place] dell.

*Dolman, *m.* [-s, *pl.* -s or -e] [a short Turkish cloak] doliman; [also a name given to the jacket worn by Hussars] pelisse.

Dólmetsch, *m.* [-en, *pl.* -en] V. Dolmetscher.

Dólmetschen, [probably allied to the Pol. *tlumatze* = to explain in the vulgar tongue] *v. tr.* to interpret [the German to an Englishman &c.].

Dólmetscher, *m.* [-s, *pl.* -] an interpreter, a translator; [in the Levant and other parts of the East] a dragoman, drogman. *Fig.* Er ist der — meiner Absichten, he interprets my designs.

Dólmetschung, *f.* 1) [the act of interpreting] interpretation. 2) [the sense given by an interpreter] interpretation, exposition.

*Dolomít, *m.* [-en, *pl.* -en] [a variety of magnesian carbonate of lime] dolomite. Kristallisirter und stängeliger —, cristallized muricalcite, compound spar, dolomite-spar, rhomb-spar, or bitterspar.

*Dōm, *m.* [-es, *pl.* -e] [from the Gr. δῶμα, Lat. *domus*] 1) [a spherical roof raised over the middle of a building] a dome, a cupola. 2) *Fig.* *a*) a church adorned by a cupola. *b*) [the see or seat of a bishop, the principal church of a diocese] a cathedral, a cathedral church. *c*) a collegiate church. *d*) [in poetry] any high or lofty building, resembling a dome or cupola. Der blaue — des Himmels [Himmels—] wölbte sich über ihm, the blue dome of the heavens spread above his head.

Dom=capitel, *n.* 1) the chapter of a cathedral. 2) chapter-house. —**dechant**, *m.* the dean [of a cathedral or collegiate church]. ||—**frau**, *f.* V. Stiftsfrau. —**herr**, *m.* a prebendary, a canon. —**herrlich**, *adj.* and *adv.* prebendal, capitular. —**kirche**, *f.* 1) a church having a cupola. 2) a cathedral church. —**küster**, *m.* 1) the sexton of a cathedral. 2) a title given to a laic canon. —**pfaff**, *m.* 1) a canon. *Fig.* [frequently in contempt or joke] Er ist so fett wie ein —pfaff, he is as sleek as a priest. 2) [a bird] the bullfinch. —**pfarrer**, —**prediger**, *m.* the pastor of a cathedral or collegiate church. —**probst**, *m.* the provost of a cathedral. —**probstei**, *f.* the office or dignity of a provost of a cathedral. —**pröbstlich**, *adj.* and *adv.* belonging to or vested in provosts of cathedrals. —**schnepfe**, *f.* the whimbrel. —**stift**, *n.* 1) a cathedral. 2) chapter.

***Domäne**, *f.* [*pl.* -n] domain, demain, demesne. Die Königlichen —n, the king's domains; die Staats—, state-domains.

Domänen=gut, *f.* domain, demesne. —**kammer**, *f.* the office of domains. —**rath**, *m.* an officer, counsellor appointed for the domains. —**verwalter**, *m.* an administrator, manager of domains.

***Domestik**, *m.* [-en, *pl.* -en] a domestic, servant.

***Domicellär**, *m.* [-s or -en, *pl.* -e or -en] a young canon.

***Dominánte**, *f.* the dominant [in music, of the three notes essential to the tone, the dominant is that which is a fifth from the tonic].

***Dominicáner**, *m.* [-s, *pl.* -] a dominican friar, a dominican, a jacobine.

Dominicaner=kloster, *n.* a monastery of dominican friars. —**mönch**, *m.* V. Dominicaner. —**nonne**, *f.* V. Dominicanerinn. —**orden**, *m.* the order of dominicans [founded about the year 1216].

***Dominicánerinn**, *f.* a dominican nun.

***Dominiren**, *v. tr.* and *intr.* to domineer, to lord it [in a proper as well as in a fig. sense].

***Dómino**, *n.* [-'s, *pl.* -s] 1) a masquerade-dress, a domino. 2) [a game] domino.

1. ***Dón**, *m.* [-s] [a river in Russia] the Don.

2. ***Dón**, *m.* [*pl.* -s] [from the Lat. *dominus*] [a title of courtesy in Spain and Portugal, put before Christian names of men] don.

***Donát**, *m.* [-s, *pl.* -e] a Latin grammar, composed by Donatus, formerly much in use in the grammar schools of Germany.

Fig. ***Donatschnitzer**, *m.* a grammatical blunder.

***Donatár**, *m.* [-s, *pl.* -e] [in law] donee.

***Donatión**, *f.* [that which is given or bestowed] donation.

***Donátor**, *m.* [-s, *pl.* -en] [in law] donor.

Dónau, *f.* [allied to Dón, Düna] [a river] Danube.

Donau=fahrt, *f.* a voyage on the Danube. —**strudel**, *pl.* the whirlpools or eddies in the Danube.

Dóne, *f.* V. Dohne.

Dónfach, *n.* [-es, *pl.* -fächer] [Don is allied to the Engl. *down*] [in mining] the distance between two traverses in a hading-shaft.

Dónholz, *n.* [-es, *pl.* -hölzer] [in mining] a traverse in a hading-shaft.

***Dónisch**, *adj.* from the river Don. Die —en Kosacken, the Don Cossacks.

Dónlage, *f.* [*pl.* -n] [in mining] hade.

Dónlegig, *adj.* and *adv.* [in mining] hading. Donlege or —e Schächte, hading-shafts.

***Dónna**, [the feminine of don, V. 2. Don] donna.

Dónner, *m.* [-s, *pl.* -] [from tönen] 1) [the sound which follows an explosion of lightning] thunder. *Fig.* [used for lightning or thunderbolt] Vom — gerührt werden, to be struck by lightning; [in a more figurative sense] ich war wie vom — gerührt, I remained as a man thunderstruck [amazed, astonished]; [in vulgar lang., an oath or a term of execration] daß dich der —! damn you! 2) [any loud noise] thunder. Der — der Brandung, der Wogen, eines Wasserfalls, the roaring of the surf, of the billows, the thunder of a cataract; der — des Geschützes, the thunder of cannon; der — der Stimme, thundering voice.

Donner=axt, *f.* V. —keil. ||—**bart**, *m.* common houseleek. —**bohne**, *f.* orpine, lesser houseleek, or live-long. ‡—**büchse**, *f.* a large short piece of artillery. —**flamme**, *f.* lightning. —**flug**, *m.* [a plant] bulbous fumitory. —**gekrach**, *n.* the clattering or rattling sound of thunder. —**geroll**, *n.* the rumbling of thunder. —**geschoß**, *n.* lightning. —**gewölk**, *n.* thunder-clouds. —**gott**, *m.* Jupiter, Jove, [among the ancient Germans] Thor. —**haus**, *n.* [an instrument for illustrating the manner in which buildings receive damage by lightning] thunder-house. —**keil**, *m.* 1) a shaft of lightning, thunderbolt. 2) [a genus of fossile shells, common in chalk and limestone] arrow-head, or finger-stone, vulgarly called thunderbolt, or thunder-stone. —**kraut**, *n.* 1) common houseleek. 2) V. —bohne. —**kröte**, *f.* father-lasher. —**nelke**, *f.* sweet-william. —**nessel**, *f.* the great nettle. ||—**rebe**, *f.* ground-ivy. —**regen**, *m.* thunder-shower. —**schlag**, *m.* a burst of thunder, thunder-clap. —**schläge**, peals of thunder. —**stein**, *m.* thunder-stone, otherwise called brontia. —**stimme**, *f.* a thundering voice. —**strahl**, *m.* a flash of lightning. —**sturm**, *m.* thunder-storm. —**wagen**, *m.* a thundering-chariot. —**wetter**, *n.* thunder and lightning, thunder-weather. *Fig.* [in vulgar lang.] —wetter! zounds! damnation! —**wolke**, *f.* thunder-cloud. —**wort**, *n.* a terrifying word, a dreadful sentence.

Dónnerer, *m.* [-s, *pl.* -] [an epithet for Jupiter] the thunderer.

Dónnern, I. *v. imp.* to thunder. Es donnert, it thunders. II. *v. intr.* 1) to produce a loud noise. An die Thür —, to thunder against the door; und rolle den —den Wagen über die Erde, and roll the thundering chariot over the ground; die Kanone donnert, the cannon thunders; mit —der Stimme, with a thundering voice. 2) to thunder. Kannst du mit gleicher Stimme —, wie er thut? [in Script.] canst thou thunder with a voice like him?

Dónnerstag, *m.* [-es] [from Thor or Donner = Donnergott] Thursday. Der grüne —, Maundy-thursday, holy-thursday.

Dónsbaum, *m.* [-es, *pl.* -bäume] V. Wollsamenstaude.

Doodshoftblock, *m.* [a sea term] dead block.

Doodsmannsauge, *n.* [a sea term] dead-eye.

Dóp, *m.* [-s, *pl.* -e] [a sea term] dobb.

Dóppel or **Dúppel**, *m.* a copper coin in the south of Germany, worth half a Kreutzer.

Dóppel = Doppelt in composition, denotes two ways, or twice the number or quantity.

Doppel=adler, *m.* 1) the spread-eagle. 2) *Fig.* *a*) the late German [or better Roman] empire; *b*) [in commerce] a name given to the second sort of bombasin. —**artig**, *adj.* and *adv.* of a double kind. —**atlas**, *m.* double-atlas. *Fig.* —**äugig**, *adj.* [= trügerisch] double-eyed. —**band**, *n.* 1) double-ribbon [which is right on both sides]. 2) [with coopers] a large iron hoop. —**becher**, *m.* dice-box. —**bier**, *n.* double-beer, double strong beer. —**blasebaß**, *m.* counter-bassoon. —**blatt**, *n.* 1) a double leaf. 2) [with card-makers] doublets. 3) V. Bohnenkaper. —**blume**, *f.* [a plant] atragene. —**bogen**, *m.* a double sheet. —**büchse**, *f.* V. —haken. —**dach**, *n.* a roof with two rows of tiles. —**deutig**, *adj.* and *adv.* ambiguous, equivocal. —**draht**, *m.* [with shoemakers] double thread. —**drähtig**, *adj.* and *adv.* double-threaded. —**dukaten**, *m.* a double ducat. —**ehe**, *f.* bigamy. —**fagott**, *n.* V. —blasebaß. —**fenster**, *n.* a double window. —**fleck**, *m.* [a fish] a species of wrasse or gold-finny. —**flinte**, *f.* a double-barreled gun. —**flor**, *m.* craped gauze. —**flöte**, *f.* 1) [with the ancients] a double flute. 2) [in organs] a stop, where the pipes are covered, and furnished with two lips. —**flügel**, *m.* a harpsichord having two fore-parts. —**fuge**, *f.* [in music] the double fugue [which contains two subjects]. —**furche**, *f.* a twice ploughed furrow. —**gänger**, *m.* fetch. —**geige**, *f.* [in music] viol d'amour. —**gesang**, *m.* a song in two parts, a duo. —**gespann**, *n.* a team of four horses. —**gestirn**, *n.* the constellation Castor and Pollux. —**glas**, *n.* a large drinking cup. —**gold**, *n.* [with goldbeaters] a sort of [illegible] gold-leaves used for gilding. —**goldstück**, [illegible] a doubloon. —**haken**, *m.* a large firelock [now out of use], matchlock. —**harfe**, *f.* a harp with 43 strings. —**haue**, *f.* [in mining] mandril. —**häuptig**, *adj.* and *adv.* double-headed [as Janus]. —**heirath**, *f.* double marriage. Es ist heute eine —heirath or —hochzeit in der Familie, there were two weddings in this family to-day. —**herzig**, *adj.* and *adv.* double-hearted, deceitful, treacherous. —**horn**, *n.* a rising anvil. —**hügel**, *m.* 1) two neighbouring hills. 2) *Fig.* [as a poetical or jocose term] the [illegible] of a woman. —**kamm**, *m.* V. Kartätsche. —**kartaune**, *f.* [in gunnery] bastard cannon, or carthoun. —**kinn**, *n.* a double chin. —**lauf**, *m.* the double barrel of a gun. —**läufig**, [illegible] and *adv.* double-barreled. —**laut**, *m.* [in grammar] diphthong. —**lauter**, *m.* a letter or sign [illegible]ing a diphthong. —**leben**, *n.* amphibio[illegible] —**leber**, *m.* V. Amphibium. —**lebig**, *adj.* [and] *adv.* [= beidlebig; having the power of living [in] two elements] amphibious. —**lerche**, *f.* the [illegible] lark. —**mord**, *m.* a double murder. —[illegible]**zisse**, *f.* double daffodil. —**nase**, *f.* a double nose. —**ort**, *m.* [with shoemakers] a great [illegible] —**pforte**, *f.* a folding door. —**punkt**, [illegible] [in grammar] colon (:). —**register**, *n.* [in organs] principal. —**reif**, *m.* a double hoop. —**reihe**, *f.* a double row [of trees &c.]. —[illegible] *adj.* and *adv.* 1) forming a double row. 2) [in botany] double [said of the envelope]. —[illegible] *m.* hand-in-hand ring. —**salz**, *n.* [in [illegible]] sulphate of tartar. —**sammet**, *m.* double velvet. —**saß**, *m.* [in printing] double. —[illegible]**tig**, *adj.* and *adv.* [in geography] Die —[illegible]gen Völker, amphiscii, or amphiscians. —[illegible] *f.* a double layer. —**schild**, *m.* 1) a double shield. 2) [in botany, a genus of plants] [illegible] mustard. —**schlag**, *m.* 1) [in music] the [illegible]tition of a note [marked thus: ˜]. 2) [a poetical [illegible] consisting of three syllables, - ∪ ∪] a dactyl. —**schleicher**, *m.* [a genus of serpents] amphis[illegible] amphisbena. —**schlitz**, *m.* [in architecture, an ornament on friezes] digliph. —**schlitzig**, *adj.* [and] *adv.* ornamented with a digliph. —**schl**[illegible] [in logic] a dilemma. —**schnabel**, *m.* 1) a double bill. 2) a species of dipper. —**schnepfe**, [illegible] the common curlew. —**schritt**, *m.* [= Dup[illegible] schritt; in military affairs] quick march. —schüppe, f. [a fish] a species of sciæna [sciæna cappa]. —schuß, m. [with cloth-weavers] a certain defect in weaving. —seitig, adj. and adv. having two sides, double-sided. —sichtig, adj. and adv. seeing an object double. —sichtigkeit, f. [a disease in the eye in which the person sees an object double] diplopia. —sinn, m. double meaning of a word or expression, double entendre, doublets. —sinnig, adj. and adv. having two meanings, double-meaning, ambiguous, equivocal. —sinnigkeit, f. ambiguousness, ambiguity. —spath, m. calcareous spar, calc-spar, Iceland spar, double refracting spar. —spiel, n. 1) dice and cards. 2) a duet, duetto. —spieler, m. a player at dice or at cards. —steiger, m. [a foot in verse, consisting of four syllables, or two iambics, - v - v] a diambic. —stein, m. 1) [at draughts] a king. 2) [with jewellers] V. —spath. —stich, m. a double stitch. —stück, n. 1) duplicate, doublet. 2) a duet or duetto, or a piece of music played on a harpsichord by four hands. —stuhl, m. [in carpentry] the high trusses of a curved roof which admit two lofts. —sünde, f. a double sin. —taffet, m. double taffety. —thür, f. double doors. —treppe, f. a double flight of steps. —vers, m. a couple of verses or poetic lines, a distich. —waffe, f. a sword or sabre whose hilt is a pistol. —züngig, adj. and adv. double-tongued, deceitful. —züngigkeit, f. double-dealing, deceitfulness. —züngler, m. double-dealer. —zweigig, adj. and adv. having double twigs. —zwirn, m. double linen thread.

Doppeler, Doppler, m. [-s, pl. -] 1) one who plays at dice or cards; hence Fig. a cheat. 2) [with card-makers] a doubling-iron.

Doppelheit, f. doubleness, duplicity. Fig. doubleness of heart or speech, duplicity.

1. Doppeln, v. tr. 1) to double [a sum of money] V. Verdoppeln. 2) [with shoemakers] to sew double. 3) || Die Schuhe —, to sole shoes; ein Stück an einem Kleide —, [with tailors] to line part of a garment with linen; eine Wand —, [with masons] to loam a wall twice; ein Schiff —, [in seamen's lang.] to sheathe a ship.

2. Doppeln, [perhaps allied to the Swed. taefla Brettspielen, to the Wallis. taflu, to throw] v. intr. 1) to play at backgammon. 2) to practice cheating, hence Fig. to cheat a person at cards.

Doppelt, [L. duplus, Gr. διπλόος = zwiefach] adj. and adv. double. Ein —er Antheil, a double portion; — zusammenlegen, to fold double; ein —er Knoten, a double knot; eine —e Reihe Knöpfe habend, with two rows of buttons; eine —e Thür, a double door; — verschließen [eine Thüre], to double-lock [a door]; ein —er Bätingsschlag, [in seamen's lang.] a bit of the cable; — vergolden, to double-gild; eine — ausgefertigte Schrift, a writing in duplicate; — bezahlen, to pay double; — sehen, to see double; mit —em Verluste, with double the loss; den —en Werth or das —e bezahlen, to pay double the value; ein —er Dukaten, a double ducat; drei—, threefold; ein —es Gebläse, [in forges] two contiguous bellows in motion; [in botany] eine —e Blütendecke, a double calyx; —e Staubbeutel, twin anthers [swelled into two protuberances]; ein —er Adler, the double-eagle; eine —e Flinte, a double-barreled gun; ich war — so alt wie sie, I was double their age. Fig. [= noch mehr] Er hat — Unrecht, he is twice in the wrong, doubly wrong; — gut, doubly good; daß Sie kommen, ist mir — angenehm, your coming is doubly pleasing to me. In composition, V. Doppel.

Doppelt-hochrund, adj. and adv. convex on both sides, double-convex. —hohlrund, adj. and adv. concave on both sides, double-concave. —liegend, adj. and adv. [in botany] conduplicate leafing, is said of a bud when the two sides of a leaf are doubled over each other at the mid-rib. —sehen, n. V. Doppelsichtigkeit.

Doppelung, f. [in seamen's language] V. Spikerhaut.

Doppen, v. tr. [in seamen's lang.] to make a mortise to receive the ring to clinch a bolt.

Doppen, pl. [a sea term] round and hollow cleats.

*Doppio, adv. [in music, double] doppio.

Doppler, V. Doppeler.

Dorchen, [-s] [a name of women] Doll, Dolly.

Dorf, n. [-es, pl. Dörfer] [allied to the Germ. Truppe, the Lat. turba, the Welsh Torf] 1) village. Fig. the country opposed to the town. Auf dem —e wohnen, to live in the country. Prov. Das sind ihm böhmische Dörfer, these are strange things to him, 'tis all Greek to him. 2) the inhabitants of a village. Das ganze — versammelte sich, the whole village assembled.

Dorf-bäcker, m. a baker in a village. †—bengel, m. a country-clown, country-bumpkin. —bewohner, m. a villager. —bull, m. the bull of a village. —fleischer, m. a butcher of a village. —flur, f. the country or district around and belonging to a village. —geistliche, m. V. —pfarrer. —herrschaft, f. the lord of a village. —hirt, m. the herdsman in a village. —hochzeit, f. V. Bauernhochzeit. —jugend, f. the young villagers, village-children. —junker, m. [mostly in contempt or in joke] a country squire. —kirche, f. a country church. —leben, n. a country life. —leute, pl. the inhabitants of a village, the villagers, rustics. ‡—lieger, m. a villager. —mädchen, n. a country lass, a country girl. —mann, m. [pl. -leute] V. Bauer. —mark, f. V. —flur. —mäßig, adj. and adv. country-like, rustic. —pfarre, —pfarrei, f. V. Landpfarre. —pfarrer, m. a country clergyman, village-parson. —recht, m. the privileges of a village. —richter, m. country judge. —schäfer, m. the shepherd in a village. —schenke, f. country inn, village public-house. —schmied, m. the village-smith. —schmiede, f. the forge in a village, village-smithy. —schneider, m. a country tailor. —schöne, f. a country-girl, a village-belle. —schule, f. a country-school. —schulmeister, m. a village schoolmaster. —schulze, m. village-magistrate. —schuster, m. the village-shoemaker. —sprache, f. rustic language. —stier, m. V. —bull. —weihrauch, m. V. Bauernweihrauch.

Dörfchen, Dörflein, n. [-s] dimin. of Dorf. a small village, a hamlet.

1. Dörfer, pl. of Dorf.

2. Dörfer, m. [-s, pl. -] —inn, f. 1) a villager, [in this sense also] Dörfler, m. and Dörflerinn, f. 2) in composition, a person or thing belonging to a village, as der Bors—, a) an inhabitant of Borsdorf, b) a sort of apple, originally from the village of Borsdorf.

Dörfisch, adj. villatic.

Dörflich, adj. and adv. pertaining to a village, rural, rustic.

Dörfner, m. [-s, pl. -] —inn, f. V. 2. Dörfer 1).

Dörfschaft, f. 1) village, villagery. 2) the body of villagers, the villagers.

Dorisch, adj. and adv. Dorian, Doric. Die —e Säulenordnung, [in architect.] the Doric order of columns; die —e Mundart, the Doric dialect; —e Spracheigenheit, a dorism, a doricism.

Dorisschnecke, f. [pl. -n] sea lemon.

Dörlenbaum, m. [-es, pl. -bäume] V. Kornelle.

Dörlstrauch, m. [-es, pl. -sträucher] Virginian itea.

1. Dorn, m. [-es, pl. -en and, in some instances, Dörner] [allied to Thor and durch, as also to the A. S. taeran, to tear; thus: = etwas Bohrendes &c.] 1) [generally the name of certain pointed pricking things] a) formerly a pin. b) the tongue of a buckle. c) [with workers in metal] a punch. d) [with locksmiths] the stem of a lock; a flat piece of metal that covers the hole of a padlock; the bolt of a hinge. e) [with gunsmiths] a long round bar of iron used in welding. f) [with workers in steel] a small piece of iron used as an anvil. g) [in pyrotechnics] a spike. h) [in saltworks] pl. briars which surround the bunches of thorns used for the graduating brine. 2) any slender pointed substance, especially a sharp process of the woody part of a plant, a thorn, a spine, a prickle. Der — an einer Rose, the thorn or prickle of a rose. Prov. Was zum —e werden will, spitzt sich bei Zeiten, it early pricks, that will be a thorn. Fig. any thing troublesome; great difficulties and impediments. Auf —en gehen, to walk upon thorns; das ist ihm ein — im Auge, that annoys him; ich will deinen Weg mit —en vermachen, [in Script.] I will hedge up thy way with thorns. 3) [any tree or shrub armed with spines or sharp ligneous shoots] thorn. Der Schwarz—, the black thorn; der Weiß—, the white thorn &c.

Dorn-apfel, m. thorn-apple. —baum, m. 1) three-horned acacia. 2) white-thorn. —besäet, adj. and adv. thorny. Fig. Der —besäete Weg des Lasters, the thorny path of vice. —brassen, —karpfen, m. [a fish] the bream. —busch, m. thorn-bush, bramble, brake. —butte, f. V. Stachelbutte. —dreher, m. the butcher-bird or wood-chat. —en-bahn, f. fig. a thorny path. —en-bündel, m. a bunch of thorns. —en-gebüsch, n. a small wood or place where briars and thorns grow. —en-hecke, f. thorn-hedge. —en-krone, f. a thorny crown [in a proper as well as in a fig. sense]. —en-los, adj. and adv. thornless; [also in a fig. sense]. —en-pfad, m. V. —enbahn. —en-steg, m. a thorny footpath. Fig. the thorny path of life. —en-stengel, m. a thorny stem. —en-stock, m. brier-stick. —en-voll, adj. and adv. full of thorns or spines, thorny. —en-weg, m. Fig. V. —enbahn. —fisch, m. the fifteen-spined stickle-back. —fortsatz, m. [in anatomy] spinal process. —genist, n. V. —enhecke. —grundel, f. the thorny loach. —hai, m. prickly dog-fish. —hecke, f. thorn-hedge. —heher, m. V. —dreher. —hund, m. V. —hai. —käfer, m. [a genus of insects] hispa. —karpfen, m. V. —brassen. —knopf, m. [a genus of plants] neudra [neudra procumbens]. —könig, m. V. Zaunkönig. —koralle, f. a species of madrepore [madrepora muricata]. —kratzer, m. V. —dreher. —myrte, f. V. Mäusedorn. —muschel, f. [a genus of testaceous animals] a species of donax. —muskel, m. [in anatomy] spinal muscle. Der —muskel des Nackens, spinal muscle of the neck [spinalis cervicis]. —nadel, f. a species of whelk [buccinum murinum]. —reich, m. the name of several birds, that build in thorn-hedges, as the titmouse &c. —roche, m. shagreen-ray. —rose, f. V. Weinrose. —rücken, m. V. Nagelroche. —schwamm, m. the little champignon or fairy agaric. —schwein, n. V. Stachelschwein. —stock, m. V. —enstock. —strauch, m. brier. —treter, m. V. —dreher. —wand, f. [in saltworks] a wall overlaid with bundles of briers in houses for graduation.

2. Dorn, *m.* [-s] [probably from dörren] [in metallurgy] the slag of copper.

Dornen, *adj.* and *adv.* made of thorns, rough with thorns.

Dornicht, *adj.* and *adv.* resembling thorns. *Fig.* —es Zinn, tin mixed with many particles of iron.

Dornig, *adj.* and *adv.* thorny, spinous, prickled, prickly. Ein —er Strauch, a thorn-bush; ein —er Baum, a spiny tree; [in botany] ein —er Stengel, a prickly stalk; ein —es Blatt, a spiny leaf; eine —e Blumendecke, a thorny perianth; die —e Pimpernelle, [a plant] thorny burnet. *Fig.* [troublesome, vexatious, perplexing] thorny. Die —e Bahn des Lebens, the thorny path of life.

Dörnlein, *n.* [-s] V. 2. Dorn.

‖Dörnling, *m.* [-es, *pl.* -e] V. Dornschwamm.

Dorothëa, [-'s] Dörothee, [-ns] [a name of women] Dorothea, Dorothy.

Dorren, *v. intr.* [Lat. *torreo*, Gr. θέρω] [u. w. seyn] to dry, to wither.

Dörren, [V. Dorren] *v. tr.* to dry, to torrefy. Malz —, to dry malt.

Dörr-balken, *m.* V. Darrbalken. —kraut, *n.* V. Dürrwurz. —made, *f.* dracunculus. —sucht, *f.* V. Darrsucht, Dürrsucht. —warze, *f.* a wart in the mouth of horses.

Dörrer, *m.* [-s, *pl.* -] he that dries, drier. [in husbandry] a workman that dries madder.

Dorsch, *m.* [-es, *pl.* -e] [a fish] the torsk.

Dorschlein, *m.* [-s] a sort of flax.

*Dorsettin, *m.* [-s] dorsetteen.

Dort, [Old G. *thorot, doret*, appears to be allied to da] *adv.* [opposed to here, denoting a place where the speaker is not present] there, yonder. Er war erst hier, jetzt ist er —, he was here first, now he is there; werden Sie — seyn? shall you be there? hier und —, here and there; — schelten zwei Aepfelweiber, yonder are two apple-women scolding. *Fig.* denoting life to come. — werden wir uns wiedersehen, in the next world we shall meet again.

Dort-her, *adv.* from that place, from yonder, thence. Von —her, from thence; —heraus, out of that place; —herein, therein; —herum, thereabout. —hin, *adv.* to that place, thither. Gehe —hin, go thither; hierher und —hin, hither and thither; bis —hin, up to there, up to that time or place, thitherto; nach —hin, thitherward; —hindurch, through that place; —hinauf, up there; —hinaus, out there; —hinunter, down there. —seitig, *adj.* V. Jenseitig. —selbst, *adv.* for Dort. —wärts, *adv.* thitherward.

Dortig, *adj.* being there, being in that place. Ich will nach Paris reisen, um meine —en Freunde zu besuchen, I will go to Paris and see my friends there.

Dösch, *m.* V. Dorsch.

Döschen, *n.* [-s] *dimin.* of Dose. 1) a very small box, a little snuff-box. 2) [in nat. history] a species of ostrea [ostrea pusio].

1. Dose, *f.* [*pl.* -n] [appears to be the same as 2. Dose or Döse V.] 1) a small box. Eine Tabaks—, a tobacco-box; eine Schnupftabaks—, a snuff-box. 2) [in nat. hist., a sort of oysters, a division of the genus ostrea, which have their valves furnished with ears] scallop.

Dosen-baum, *m.* 1) V. Alpenkiefer and Fichte. 2) [with potters] a stand or frame for supporting newly made earthen vessels. —deckel, *m.* the lid of a small box. —form, *f.* [with turners] a mould to shape small boxes of tortoise-shell. —stück, *n.* a picture upon the lid of a snuff-box.

‖2. Döse, Döse, *f.* [*pl.* -n] [in Bohem. *dize* signifies a milk-pail, a small basket, Engl. *dish*] a round wooden vessel, a tub.

3. Döse, *f.* [*pl.* -n] V. Dosis.

‖Döseln, Döseln, *v. intr.* to doze.

‖Döserei, *f.* doze, doziness, dozing.

‖Dösig, *adj.* and *adv.* dozy.

*Dosis, *f.* [*pl.* Dosen] [the quantity of medicine given or prescribed to be taken at one time] dose; [in a more general sense] a dose, any small portion of certain things or substances.

*Dossiren, *v. tr.* [in fortification] V. Böschen.

Dost, *m.* [-es, *pl.* -en] Dosten, *m.* [-s, *pl.* -] [a plant] 1) common marjoram. 2) [in common lang.] wild basil.

Dostenkraut, *n.* common eupatorium, or hemp agrimony, the Dutch agrimony.

*Dotation, *f.* dotation, endowment.

*Dotiren, *v. tr.* to endow [a church, a college &c.].

‖1. Dotter, *m.* [-s, *pl.* -] [corrupted from *Datura* = der Stechapfel] the dodder, thorn-apple.

2. Dotter, *m.* [-s, *pl.* -] [allied to the Dutch *touteren* = zittern] V. Flachsseide.

3. Dotter, *m.* [-s, *pl.* -] [A. S. *tudor* = das Junge] the yolk of an egg.

Dotter-blume, *f.* a name given to several yellow plants, as common dandelion; garden marigold; field marigold; the globe-flower; cultivated gold of pleasure. —brod, *n.* yolk sweetmeat. —gelb, *adj.* and *adv.* yellow like the yolk of an egg. —kraut, *n.* cultivated gold of pleasure. —porzellane, *f.* saltspeckled cowry. —schnecke, *f.* the yolk nerite. —weide, *f.* the yellow willow.

Dotterricht, *adj.* and *adv.* like yolk, resembling yolk.

Dotterig, *adj.* and *adv.* containing yolks.

*Douane, *f.* [pron. Duahne] [*pl.* -n] custom-house.

*Douanier, [pron. as in the French] *m.* [-s, *pl.* -s] an officer of the customs, a custom-house officer.

*Doublette, *f.* [*pl.* -n] a double piece, a double copy of a book.

*Doublirschritt, V. Doppelschritt.

‖1. Drache, *m.* [-n, *pl.* -n] [the male of the duck kind] the drake.

2. Drache, *m.* [-n, *pl.* -n] 1) dragon. *a*) [a genus of animals] the draco. *b*) [a kind of winged serpent, often named in the Greek mythology, and also much clebrated in the romances of the middle age; also a fiery, shooting meteor, or imaginary serpent]. *c*) [in Scripture it seems sometimes to signify a large marine fish or serpent, Is. XXVII; where the leviathan is also mentioned; also Ps. LXXIV; sometimes it seems to signify a venomous land serpent, Ps. XCI; it is often used for the devil, who is called the old serpent, Rev. XX. 2]. *Fig.* [a fierce, violent person, male or female] dragon. Dieses Weib ist ein —; this woman is a perfect termagant. 2) *a*) [also der fliegende Drache; a fat heterogeneous meteor in the shape of a flying dragon] flying dragon. *b*) [an old piece of artillery which was a forty pounder] dragon. *c*) [a light frame of wood and paper constructed for flying in the air for the amusement of boys] kite. Einen —n fliegen lassen, to fly a kite. 3) V. Drachenfisch. 4) [a constellation of the northern hemisphere] draco, dragon.

Drachen-anker, *m.* V. Dreg. —auge, *n.* 1) the eye of a dragon. 2) *Fig.* an ugly terrific eye. —baum, *m.* 1) dragon-tree. 2) a species of the Adam's needle [yucca draconis]. 3) the common bird-cherry tree. —blut, *n.* [a gum or resin drawn from the dragon-tree, and other trees of a similar nature] dragon's blood. —blut-baum, *m.* V. —baum. —blutfruchtbaum *m.* a species of the pterocarpus. —fänger, [a plant] barleria. —fisch, *m.* dragon-fish. fliege, *f.* [a genus of insects] dragon-fly. —haarig, *adj.* and *adv.* set with hair of a dragon. haupt, *n.* —kopf, *m.* 1) the head of a dra on. 2) *Fig. a*) eaves having the shape of a dra on's head. *b*) [in astronomy] dragon's head. —schwanz. *c*) [in botany, a genus of plants] dra on's head. *d*) [—köpfchen] the dragon cowr the beetle porcellane. —kraut, *n.* V. Oberm nig. —nest, *n.* the nest of a dragon. —pflanze, *f.* a common name of plants from whi dragon's blood is drawn. —schlange, *f.* [heraldry] a winged dragon. —schwanz, *m.* [in astronomy] dragon's tail [dragons head and t are the nodes of the planets, or the two points in wh the orbits of the planets intersect the ecliptic]. 2) plant] dragon's water. —stein, *m.* [a shell] serpent-stone, ammonite. —wagen, a chariot drawn by dragons. —wurz, *f.* 1) genus of plants] dragons. 2) dragon's-wort. zahn, *m.* 1) a tooth of the fabled dragon, drag on's tooth. 2) a name given to some fossils.

3. Drache, *m.* [-n] V. Dreg.

*Drachme, *f.* [*pl.* -n] drachma. *a*) [the part of an ounce] dram. *b*) [a Grecian coin, value of seven pence, three farthings sterling].

Dräbel, *m.* [-s, *pl.* -] [with rope-makers entangling of the strands in rope-making

*Dragoman, *m.* [-s, *pl.* -e] [an interpreter Eastern countries] dragoman. V. also Dolmetscher

*Dragonade, *f.* [*pl.* -n] dragoonade.

*Dragoner, *m.* [-s, *pl.* -] dragoon.

Dragoner-fisch, *m.* [a fish] sordid onet. —mütze, *f.* 1) the cap of a dragoon. *Fig.* dragon-shell.

*Dragonit, *m.* [-s, *pl.* -e] V. Bergkristall.

*Dragun, *m.* [-es, *pl.* -e] [a plant]

Dragunessig, *m.* tarragon-vineg

Draht, *m.* [-es, *pl* -e, in common Drähte] [from drehen] 1) [a very small tw wool, cotton, silk] thread. Pech—, a thread. 2) [a thread of metal, any metallic drawn to an even thread] wire. Eisen—, durch die dritte Ziehbank gezogener—, wire; Gold—, gold-wire; — ziehen, to d metal into wire, to wire-draw. 3) a twisted of straw, of which bee-hives and the like made.

Draht-ader, *f.* a single winding of a ring. —arbeit, *f.* something made of wire, work. —arbeiter, *m.* a worker in wire. —b *f.* a wire-drawing machine. —bauer, *m.* made of wire. —blume, *f.* V. Dotterblume. boden, *m.* [with sieve makers] the wiry of a sieve. —bohrer, *m.* wire-bore. —b *f.* wire brush, scratcher. —deckel, *m.* lid. —eisen, *n.* a plate of steel with for wire-drawing. —fenster, *n.* a window ered with a wire grate. —formen, moulds. —gitter, *n.* wire-grate, w hammer, *m.* wire-drawing mill. —ke chain made of wire. —klinke, *f.* V —kugel, *f.* [in gunnery] cross-bar-shot. ter, *m.* a wire candle-stick. —maß pinmakers] wire-gage, iron-gage. —m wire-drawing mill. —natter, *f.* a viper [coluber Minervæ]. —plätten, *n.* the ting of gold or silver-wire. —puppe, *f.* *Fig.* [in contempt or in joke] Er hält sich wie eine —puppe, he holds himself as a puppet. —rädchen, *n.* a small wooden on which wire is wound. —ring, *m.* 1) ring. 2) a quantity of rolled wire. —rolle, 1) a wooden roll on which wire is wound. rolled wire. —saite, *f.* wire-string. —scher wire-shears. —schleife, —schlinge, *f.* a wire-match to a hook, eye. —schmielen, *pl.* the heath hair-grass. —schnecke, *f.* the thread pirted whelk. —schneider, *m.* [among pinmakers] wire-cutter. —sieb, *n.* wire-sieve. —silber, *n.* [in mining] massy silver shaped like wire. —spindel, *f.* bead-wire. —spinnen, *n.* wire-drawing. —stäbe, *pl.* wires. *Fig.* —steif, *adj.* wiry. —stift, *m.* wire-tack. —stülpe, *f.* wire-fender. —werk, *n.* wire-work. —winde, *f.* wire-reel. —wurm, *m.* wire-worm, hair-worm, water hair-worm. —zange, *f.* round-nosed pliers, wire-pliers. —zieheisen, *n.* a small plate of steel with holes used for wire-drawing. —zieher, *m.* wire-drawer. —zieherei, *f.* —zug, *m.* 1) wire-drawing. 2) wire-drawing mill. 3) the workshop of wire-drawers.

Drähtern, *adj.* and *adv.* made of wire, wiry. Ein —es Gitter, a wire-grate. *Fig.* wiry.

Drähtig, *adj.* and *adv.* [used in composition only] denoting one of the threads of which a rope is composed.

Dräll, *m.* [-es, *pl.* -e] **Drälle**, *f.* [*pl.* -n] [allied to drehen, drillen] [with gun-makers] the rifle of a gun-barrel.

‖**Dräll**, [allied to drehen, drillen] *adj.* and *adv.* compact, well put together, well-made, active, lively. Ein —es Mädchen, a sprightly girl.

***Dräma**, *n.* [-'s, *pl.* -s] the drama. *Fig.* Das — seines Lebens ist ausgespielt, the drama of his life has been played out.

***Dramátisch**, *adj.* and *adv.* dramatic, dramatical, theatrical. Der —e Dichter, a dramatist, a writer of plays.

***Dramatisíren**, *v. tr.* to dramatize [the history of the Old Testament &c.].

***Dramatúrg**, *m.* [-en, *pl.* -en] a teacher of the scenic art.

***Dramaturgíe**, *f.* scenic science.

***Dramatúrgisch**, *adj.* and *adv.* relating or belonging to the scenic art.

Drän, V. Daran.

Dráng, *m.* [-es] 1) a crowd, throng. V. Gedränge. 2) pressure. *Fig.* Der — der Geschäfte, the pressure of business; im —e von Geschäften, in the hurry of business; im —e der Noth, in the extreme necessity; er empfand einen — zu Pharao zu gehen, [in Script.] he found an impulse upon his mind to go to Pharao; er folgte dem —e seiner Leidenschaft, he followed the impulse of his passion.

‖**Dränge**, *adj.* and *adv.* close, crowded, joined, in contact.

Drängeln, [*dimin.* of Drängen] *v. tr.* to press or crowd.

Drängen, [allied to drehen, drücken] I. *v. tr.* to throng, to press. Es folgte ihm viel Volks nach und sie drängeten ihn, [in Scripture] much people followed him, and thronged him; —de Haufen — euch im Vorübergehen, thronging crowds press on you as you pass; Einen an den Baum —, to push any one against the tree; im Schauspielhause war es gedrängt voll, the theatre was crowded; ein gedrängtes Blatt, [in botany] an aggregate leaf. V. Gedrängt. *Fig.* Seine Schuldner —, to vex one's debtors; von Gläubigern gedrängt, dunned by creditors. II. *v. intr.* to push on, to urge. *Er drängt und treibt immerfort, he keeps constantly pushing and urging forwards. III. *v. r.* sich —, to urge forward with force, to urge one's way, to pass by pressing, to squeeze. Sich durch das Volk —, to squeeze through the crowd; der Bach drängt sich hier durch die Spalte des Felsens, the river forces itself through the cleft of the rock. *Fig.* Er drängt sich zwischen mich und meine Hoffnung, he thrusts himself in between me and my hopes; noch dränge dich nicht zu nah an den Thron, nor press too near the throne; er drängt sich überall hinzu, he thrusts himself in every where.

Dränger, *m.* [-s, *pl.* -] oppressor.

Drángsal, *n.* [-s, *pl.* -e] oppression, vexation. —e leiden, to suffer vexations; die —e des Krieges, the miseries of war.

Drangsalvoll, *adj.* and *adv.* full of trouble, vexatious.

Drängwasser, *n.* [-s] V. Grundwasser.

***Draperíe**, *f.* [*pl.* -en] [in sculpture and painting, the representation of the clothing or dress of human figures; also tapestry, hangings, curtains &c.] drapery.

***Drapíren**, *v. tr.* to furnish with drapery. Die Drapirung, V. Draperie.

Dräsekammer, *f.* V. Tresekammer.

***Drástisch**, *adj.* [in medicine, powerful, acting with strength or violence, efficacious] drastic.

Dräth, V. Draht.

Dräuen, *v. tr.* and *intr.* [in poetry for drohen] to threaten, to lower.

Dräuer, *m.* [-s, *pl.* -] threatener.

Draúf, V. Darauf.

Draúfbohrer, *m.* V. Trauchbohrer.

Draúfgeld, *n.* V. Aufgeld.

Draús, V. Daraus.

‖**Dräuschen**, [allied to dreschen] *v. intr.* 1) to patter. Es regnet, daß es dräuscht, it rains as fast as it can pour, it pours down. 2) to chatter.

Draußen, [instead of dar (i. e. da) außen] *adv.* [not within; on the outside of a place; out of doors, out of the walls of a house] without, abroad. Er ist —, he is without; es ist heute sehr kalt —, it is very cold out of doors to-day.

Drechseler, *m.* V. Drechsler.

Drechseln, [from drehen] *v. tr.* to form on a lathe, to make round, to turn. Eine Kugel —, to turn a ball; in Elfenbein —, to turn ivory; sein ganzer Körper ist wie gedrechselt, his whole person is finely turned. *Fig.* V. Künsteln.

Drechsel-bank, *f.* a turner's lathe. —mühle, *f.* a turner's mill.

Drechsler, *m.* [-s, *pl.* -] [one whose occupation it is to form things with a lathe, especially one who turns wood] turner.

Drechsler-arbeit, *f.* [things made by a turner or on the lathe] turnery. —bude, *f.* a turner's shop. —gesell, *m.* a turner's journeyman. —handwerk, *n.* the trade of a turner. —kunst, *f.* [the art of forming into a cylindrical shape by the lathe] turnery. —waare, *f.* turnery-ware. —werkstatt, *f.* a turner's shop.

Dreck, *m.* [-es, *pl.* -e and -er] [D. *dryt*, *torde*, Engl. *dirt*, *turd*; allied to the Engl. *dregs*, Hefen, Schlamm, appears to be allied to the Lat. s-*terc*-us] 1) any foul or filthy substance, excrement, mud, mire, dust, whatever adhering to any thing, renders it foul or unclean, filth, dirt. *Fig.* [*pl.* -er] [in contempt] something mean, muck. 2) [in husbandry] the recrement of pressed honey-combs. 3) [in metallurgy] the dross of copper.

Dreck-baum, *m.* [a genus of plants] sterculia. —haufen, *m.* a heap of dirt. —käfer, *m.* the dung-beetle. —kante, *f.* the border of a garment, which is suffered, in walking, to reach the dirt. —karren, *m.* a dung-cart, a tumbrel. —lilie, *f.* V. Affodilllilie. —loch, *n.* a place of deep mud or mire, a hole full of mire, a slough. —saum, *m.* draggle tail. †—seele, *f.* a dirty, mean or base fellow. —stein, *m.* V. Stückstein. —vogel, *m.* 1) mud-sucker. 2) carrion-crow. —winkel, *m.* a dirty corner or place.

Dreckig, *adj.* and *adv.* 1) foul, nasty, filthy, not clean, dirty. —e Hände, dirty hands. 2) foul, rainy. —es Wetter, foul weather.

Dreg, *m.* [-es, *pl.* -e] [a sea term] a grapling or grapnel.

Dreg-haken, *m.* [in seamen's lang.] creeper. —tau, *n.* Das —tau des Bootes or der Schluppe, the mooring-rope of a boat; das —tau, den Anker zu fischen, drag-rope.

Dreggen, *v. tr.* [in seamen's language] to drag or sweep the bottom.

Drehen, [appears to be allied to the Lat. *torqueo*, and to the Gr. τρέπειν] I. *v. tr.* 1) [to cause to move in a circular course] to turn [a wheel, a spindle &c.]. Den Bratspieß [den Braten] —, to turn the spit; drehe es herum, give it a turn; den Kopf —, to turn one's head; ihr dreht uns den Rücken zu, you turn your back to us; [in botany] ein gedrehtes Blatt, a vertical leaf. *Fig.* to alter, or change in any manner. Eine Sache nach Gefallen —, to turn a thing at one's pleasure; das Recht —, to wrest or distort the sense of law; drehet einmahl das Recht nach euerm Ansehen, wrest once the law to your authority. 2) [to form by convolution, or winding separate things round each other] to twist [a rope &c.]. [in seamen's lang.] Die Duchten eines Taues —, to twist the strands of a rope; ein Tau gegen die Runde —, to twist a rope the wrong way; die Taue zur vollen Härte —, to give a full twisting to a rope; [in botany] eine gedrehte Granne, a twisted or tortile awn [an awn coiled like a rope]. 3) to wrest [a sword from another's hand &c.]. 4) to form on a lathe, to turn. In Elfenbein —, to turn ivory; Kugeln —, to throw balls in a lathe. *Fig.* *Einem eine Nase —, to put a sham upon any one.

II. *v. intr.* [seldom used] to move round, to turn, as in dancing. *Fig.* Drehend, turning round, giddy.

III. *v. r.* sich —, 1) to turn, to change direction. Die Magnetnadel dreht sich nach dem Pole, the needle turns to the pole; sie — sich sofort vom Tanz zum süßen Mahle, forthwith from dance to sweet repast they turn; der Wind hat sich gedreht, the wind has shifted or veered; wo oft der Wind sich drehet, where wind veers oft. *Fig.* Er dreht sich nach jedem Winde, wie ein Wetterhahn, he shifts like a weathercock with every wind; er weiß nicht, wie er sich — und wenden soll, he does not know which way to turn himself, he is in the greatest embarrassment; er weiß sich zu — und zu wenden, [he is an active, clever man] he is never at a loss for a shift; sein Glück hat sich gedrehet, fortune has turned the back on him. 2) to have a circular motion, to turn. Das Rad dreht sich um seine Achse, the wheel turns on its axis; die Erde drehet sich um die Sonne, the earth revolves round the sun; ein Mann dreht sich auf seinen Fersen, a man turns on his heels. *Fig.* Die Frage drehet sich um einen einzelnen Punkt, the question turns on a single point.

Dreh-bahn, *f.* a rope-walk. —bank, *f.* a turner's lathe, turning-lathe, [with some mechanics] a turn-bench. —basse, *f.* [a sea term] pederero, swivel-gun. —baum, *m.* 1) a bar or beam which turns, serving to stop a passage, turn-pike. 2) [in seamen's language] a handspike to twist a rope. —bogen, *m.* drill-bow. —brücke, *f.* turn-bridge. —eisen, *n.* any iron tool used in turning, a turner's chisel. —gelenk, *n.* [in anatomy] turning-joint. —hals, *m.* V. Wendehals. ‖—handel, *m.* chicane. —käfer, *m.* the whirling-dun, the water-flea. —krahn, *m.* [in seamen's language] a crane. —krank, *adj.* and *adv.* affected with vertigo [said of sheep]. —krankheit, *f.* [a distemper in sheep] vertigo. —kraut, *n.* officinal hart-wort. —kreuz, *n.* [a turnpike in a foot path] turnstile. —lade, *f.* [with pewterers] turnbench. —orgel, *f.* a barrel-organ, a hand-organ. —pfähle, *pl.* [in seamen's language] laying pole. —**pforte**, *f.* turning door. —**pult**, *m.* turning desk. —**punkt**, *m.* 1) centre of motion. 2) [in geography] pole. —**rad**, *n.* 1) turning wheel. 2) [with button-makers &c.] twisting wheel. —**reep**, *n.* [in seamen's language] tye. —**scheibe**, *f.* 1) [with diamond-cutters, button-makers &c.] turning wheel. 2) potter's wheel. 3) [with wire-drawers] a round board turning on a pivot, on which the wire is wound. 4) turner's bow. —**spiegel**, *m.* a swing-glass. —**sprung**, *m.* the turning upon one leg, the other up. —**stahl**, *m.* [with turners, workers in metal] a chisel or other tool used in turning. —**stift**, *m.* [with clock-makers] arbor. —stiftstühle, arbor-stands. —**stock**, *m.* [with potters] turning-staff. —**stuhl**, *m.* 1) turning-chair; music-stool. 2) [with workers in metal, clock-makers] turn-bench. —**tanz**, *m.* a name given to several dances, as the waltz &c. —**tisch**, *m.* 1) [with belt-makers] turn-bench. 2) any table turning on a pivot. —**würfel**, *m.* a whirl-bone, totum. —**zange**, *f.* 1) pincers used in glasshouses. 2) [with button-makers] a small turn-bench.

Drehen, *n.* [-s] 1) turning. 2) V. Drehkrankheit.

Dreher, *m.* [-s, *pl.* -] 1) he that turns something; one who turns, a turner [also in composition, as Bein—, Bernstein—]. *Fig.* Ein Rechts—, one who wrests the sense of the law, a chicaner. 2) a name given to several instruments that turn about, or with which something is turned, as one of the timbers that turns with the gate of a court, garden or other inclosed ground; the winch of a weaver's loom; [in seamen's language] a winch; [with rope-makers] laying books; [in tackling] a fid; [in anatomy, the second vertebra of the neck] axis. 3) a certain dance, a sort of slow waltz. Der deutsche —, allemande. 4) a sheep affected with vertigo.

Drehermuskel, *m.* [in anatomy] turning muscle.

Dreherei, *f.* [in contempt] forming on the lathe, turning. *Fig.* chicane.

Drehling, *m.* [-es, *pl.* -e] 1) an instrument with which to turn something forcibly, as a winch to turn a wheel. 2) a sheep affected with vertigo.

Drei, [Gr. τρεῖς, Lat. *tres*, A. S. *thri*, *threo*] I. *adj.* and *adv.* 1) [two and one] three. Den — Brüdern, to the three brothers; — Kreuzer, three kreutzers; vor — Jahren, three years ago; um — Uhr, at three o'clock; ich fand es [auf] Seite —, I found it at page three; [it is inflected thus, gen. dreier, dat. dreien, when the article is omitted, or when it is used like other adjectives, without the noun to which it refers] Vater —er Söhne, father of three sons; es gehört —en Schwestern, it belongs to three sisters; es gehört uns —en, it belongs to us three; wir waren unserer —, there were three. *Prov.* Aller guten Dinge sind —, number three is always fortunate; was — wissen, erfahren bald dreißig, three may keep counsel, if two be away. II. 1) *n.* [-es] three united. 2) *f.* *a*) the number three. *b*) three at cards, the trey.

Drei-achtel, [the accent on ách] *adj.* three eighth. Der —achtelstakt, [in music] the time of three quavers in a bar [marked thus, 3/8]. —**armig**, *adj.* and *adv.* having three arms. —**arten**, —**ärten**, *v. tr.* to trifallow. —**ästig**, *adj.* and *adv.* having three branches. Eine —ästige Ranke, [in botany] a tripartite tendril. —**band**, *n.* 1) [in manufactures of steel] the best sort of steel. 2) three-band flax. —**bätzner**, [-bätz-] *m.* a silver coin of the value of three batzs [= 4 pence English]. —**bein**, *n.* a three-legged thing. —**beinig**, *adj.* and *adv.* three-legged. Ein —beiniger Stuhl, a three-legged stool, a trevet; ein —beiniger Tisch, a table with three legs, a trevet-table. —**bekreuzt**, *adj.* and *adv.* marked with three crosses. —**blatt**, *n.* 1) [a name of plants] *a*) trefoil. *b*) common buck-bean, marsh trefoil. 2) a game of cards played with three cards. —**blätterig**, *adj.* and *adv.* trifoliate, three-leaved, tripetalous. [in botany] Ein —blätteriger Kelch, a three-leaved calyx; eine —blätterige Hülle, a triphyllous involucre; eine —blätterige Blütendecke, a triphyllous perianth; —blätteriges Gras, [Klee] three-leaved grass. —**blumig**, *adj.* and *adv.* three-flowered. [in botany] Ein —blumiger Blütenstiel, a triflorous peduncle; eine —blumige Blumenscheibe, a triflorous spathe. —**bohrig**, *adj.* and *adv.* three-bored. —bohrige Röhren, pipes of 3½ inches in diameter. —**brachen**, *v. tr.* V. Dreiarten. —**buchstäbig**, *adj.* and *adv.* consisting of three letters. Ein —buchstäbiges Wort, a triliteral word, a triliteral; eine —buchstäbige Wurzel, a triliteral root. —**bund**, *m.* a triple alliance. —**decker**, *m.* a ship with three decks, a three-decker. ||—**ding**, *n.* a low court of law. —**doppelt**, *adj.* and *adv.* triple, threefold, trigeminous. —**draht**, *m.* [cloth for bed-ticks, or cases for beds] ticken. —**drähtig**, *adj.* and *adv.* consisting of three threads, made of three twisted threads. —**eck**, *n.* 1) triangle, [in astronomy and astrology] trigon, a trine. Ein gleichseitiges —eck, an equilateral triangle; ein gleichschenkliges —eck, an isosceles or equicrural triangle; ein ungleichseitiges —eck, a scalene triangle; ein rechtwinkeliges —eck, a right-angled or rectangular triangle. 2) [in natural history] *a*) [a genus of fishes] ostracion. *b*) [a genus of testaceous animals] donax. —**eckig**, *adj.* and *adv.* having three angles or corners, triangular, trigonal, trigonous, three-cornered. Ein —eckiger Hut, a three-cornered hat; die —eckige Naht der Hirnschale, the lamdoidal suture. —**eckmuschel**, *f.* V. —eck, 2) *b*). —**eckslehre**, *f.* [the science of determining the sides and angles of triangles, by means of certain parts which are given] trigonometry. Die ebene or sphärische —eckslehre, plane or spherical trigonometry. —**eckslehrig**, *adj.* and *adv.* trigonometrical. —**ecksmeßkunst**, *f.* V. —eckslehre. —**eine**, [-eine] *m.* V. —einige. —**einheit**, [-einheit] *f.* 1) trinal unity, triunity. 2) V. —einigkeit. —**einig**, [-einig &c.] *adj.* and *adv.* triune. Der —einige Gott, the triune God. —**einigkeit**, *f.* [in theology] the Trinity. —**einigkeitsbekenner**, *m.* trinitarian. —**einigkeitsfest**, *n.* the feast of Trinity. —**einigkeitsgegner**, *m.* antitrinitarian. —**einigkeitsglaube**, *m.* belief in the doctrine of the Trinity. —**einigkeitsgläubige**, *m.* V. —einigkeitsbekenner. —**einigkeitsläugner**, *m.* V. —einigkeitsgegner. —**einigkeitssonntag**, *m.* Trinity-Sunday. —**fach**, *adj.* and *adv.* threefold, trinal, triple, trigenimous, triplicate. Ein —faches Seil, a threefold rope; ein —facher Knoten, a triple knot; ein hoher Thurm, mit —fachen Mauern umgeben, a lofty tower with treble walls; die —fache Krone des Papstes, the pope's triple crown, tiar, tiara; [in botany] —fache Blätter, tern leaves; ein —fach geripptes Blatt, a three-nerved or trinerved leaf; ein —fach gefiedertes Blatt, a tripennated leaf; eine —fache Strafe, a triple punition; eine gute That —fach belohnt, a good deed trebly recompensed; das —fache, three times as much. —**fächerig**, *adj.* and *adv.* three-celled. [in botany] Eine —fächerige Kapsel, a trilocular capsule. —**fachheit**, *f.* triplicity. —**fädig**, *adj.* and *adv.* V. —drähtig. —**faltig**, —**fältig**, *adj.* and *adv.* threefold. Eine —faltige Schnur, a threefold cord; eine —fältige Frucht, a triple fruit. *Fig.* [-fältig] triune. Der —faltige Gott, the triune God. —**faltigkeit**, [-falt- &c.] *f.* the Trinity. —**faltigkeitsblume**, *f.* the pansy violet, or heart's ease. ||—**faltigkeitsglöckchen**, *n.* the marsh violet. —**farbig**, *adj.* and *adv.* three-coloured. —**felderwirthschaft**, *f.* manner of cultivation in which the land underwent three different processes during the year, now fallen into disuse. —**feldig**, *adj.* and *adv.* [in heraldry] tierce. —**fingerig**, *adj.* three-fingered. —**firner**, *m.* wine three years old. —**flach**, *n.* a prism. —**flügel**, *m.* [a genus of plants] triopteris. —**flügelig**, *adj.* and *adv.* having three wings. [in botany] Ein —flügeliger Same, three-winged seed. —**förmig**, *adj.* and *adv.* triform. —**fuß**, *m.* any thing provided with three feet, a trevet, [in mythology] a tripod. —**füßig**, *adj.* and *adv.* having three feet, three-footed, tripedal. —**futtermaß**, *n.* [-fútter-] [a fixed allowance of forage] a ration. —**gehäusig**, *adj.* and *adv.* three-capsuled, tricapsular. —**gekürzt**, *adj.* Der —gekürzte Versfuß, tribrach. —**gesang**, *m.* a concert of three parts, a trio. —**gespräch**, *n.* trialogue. —**gestaltet**, *adj.* and *adv.* triform. —**gestrichen**, *adj.* and *adv.* [in music] Die —gestrichene Note, demi semiquaver. —**getheilt**, *adj.* and *adv.* three-parted, tripartite. —**gliederig**, *adj.* and *adv.* consisting of three parts. Eine —gliederige Größe, [in mathematics] a trinome. —**götterei**, *f.* tritheism. —götterei betreffend, tritheistic. —**götterer**, *m.* tritheist, tritheite. —**göttisch**, *adj.* and *adv.* tritheistic. —**granne**, *f.* [a genus of a grass] aristida. —**haarig**, —**härig**, *adj.* and *adv.* cunning. —**hauig**, *adj.* and *adv.* [in
that may be mowed thrice. —**haupti**
and *adv.* having three heads. —**heit**, *f.*
—**herr**, *m.* triumvir. —**herrig**, *adj.* a
having three masters. —**herrlich**, and
adv. belonging to triumvirs. —**herrsch**
triumvirate, triumviri. —**herrschaftli**
and *adv.* V. —herrlich. —**herrscher**, *m.*
vir. —**horn**, *n.* [a genus of fishes] ostraci
hörnig, *adj.* and *adv.* having three ho
hundert, [-húndert] *adj.* three hundred.
dertel, *n.* the three hundredth part of
—**hundertste**, *adj.* [the ordinal of three
three hundredth. —**jahr**, *n.* a period
years. —**jährig**, *adj.* and *adv.* 1)
three years old. 2) [continuing three yea
nial. —**jährlich**, *adj.* and *adv.* [happe
three years] triennial. —jährliche Wahl
nial elections. —**kantig**, *adj.* and *a*
cornered. [in botany] Ein —kantiger
three-cornered stem. —**klang**, *m.*
the common chord or harmony] triad. 2
klangsgedicht, *n.* [in poetry] a poe
verses. —**klappig**, *adj.* and *adv.* th
Eine —klappige Kapsel, [in botany] a
capsule. —**klöber**, *m.* [with coopers]
tool. —**klöbig**, *adj.* and *adv.* V. —
knöpfig, *adj.* and *adv.* [in botany]
valvular capsules. —**kohl**, *m.* comm
bean, or marsh trefoil. —**königsfe**
n. epiphany. —**königstag**, *m.* the
of January, twelfth-day. —**köpfig**,
adv. having three heads, three-headed
omy] Der —köpfige Armmuskel, a mus
arm having three heads or beginnings
—**kreuzerstück**, [-kreú-] *n.* a silve
the value of three kreutzers [= a penny].
f. the pope's triple crown, tiar, tiara
pig, *adj.* and *adv.* three-lobed. [in bota
lappiges Blatt, a three-lobed leaf. —
m. [in grammar] triphthong. —**laut**
mark of character used in writing to
triphthong. —**leibig**, *adj.* and *adv.*
ral. —**mähdig**, *adj.* and *adv.* V.
mahl, *adv.* 1) thrice, three times.
viel, thrice as many; das —mahlheili
in which the word *holy* is repeated three ti
gion. 2) often. —**mahlig**, *adj.* and
three times, repeated three times. Ein

ger Versuch, an experiment thrice repeated. —mann, m. triumvir. Fig. || and ‡ —männer=Wein, a very strong wine; it. a very sour and bad wine. —männerig, adj. and adv. [in botany, having three stamens] triandrion. Die —männerige Pflanze, triander. —master, m. a ship with three masts, a three-master. —mastig, adj. and adv. having three masts, three-masted. —mäulig, adj. three-mouthed. Der —mäulige Cerberus, three-mouthed Cerberus. —monatig, adj. and adv. lasting three months, three months old. —monatlich, adj. and adv. happening every three months, quarterly. —namig, adj. having or bearing three names, trinominal. —nerbig, adj. and adv. [in botany] trifid [said of the style]. —ocker, m. [a plant] narrow leaved salomon's seal. —paarig, adj. and adv. [in botany] —paarig gefiedert, trijugous. —personig, adj. and adv. consisting of three persons. —pfeifig, adj. trifistulary. —pfennigstück, [-pfén-] n. V. Dreier 2). —pfünder, m. a three-pounder. —pfündig, adj. weighing three pounds. Eine —pfündige Kanone, V. —pfünder. —reifig, adj. three-hooped. —reihig, adj. and adv. having three ranks or rows. —reim, m. triplet or tripled rhymes. —rippig, adj. and adv. three-nerved. [in botany] Ein —rippiges Blatt, a trinerve or trinerved leaf. —röhrig, adj. and adv. three-fistulary. —ruderer, m. a ship with three ranks of oars on a side, a trireme. —ruderig, adj. and adv. provided with three benches or ranks of oars on a side. Die —ruderige Galeere, a trireme. —sang, n. V. —gesang. —satz, m. [in arithmetic] the rule of three, rule of proportion. —sätzig, adj. and adv. [in arithmetic] Die —sätzige Regel, V. —satz. —schäftig, adj. and adv. [with rope-makers] composed of three strands. —schichtig, adj. and adv. consisting of three layers. —schlag, m. 1) [peculiar pace of a horse] amble. 2) [in husbandry] combination of three strokes in thrashing. 3) [in music] triple time. 4) V. Drillich. —schlitz, [in architecture] triglyph. —schlitzig, adj. and adv. [in architect.] consisting of three glyphs. —schneidig, adj. and adv. three-edged [said of a sword or similar weapons]. —schnitt, m. [in geometry] trisection. —schürig, adj. and adv. Eine —schürige Wiese, a meadow that may be mowed three times. —seitig, adj. and adv. having three sides, three-sided, trilateral. [in botany] Ein —seitiger Stengel, a three-sided stem; ein —seitiges Blatt, a three-sided leaf. —silber, m. trisyllable. —silbig, adj. and adv. trisyllabic, trisyllabical. —sitzig, adj. and adv. having three seats. —spaltig, adj. and adv. three-cleft, trifid. [in botany] Eine —spaltige Blütendecke, a trifid perianth. —spänner, m. a carriage with a team of three horses. —spännig, adj. and adv. with a team of three horses. —spelzig, adj. and adv. [in botany] Ein —spelziger Balg, trivalvular glume. —spiel, n. [in music] a trio. —spitz, m. V. —zack. —spitzig, adj. and adv. three-pointed, tricuspidate. —stäbig, adj. and adv. [in grammar] triliteral. —stachel, m. an instrument with three prongs, as a hay-fork &c. —stachelig, adj. and adv. having three prongs, three-pronged. —stimmig, adj. and adv. [in music] in three parts, or composed for three voices. Ein —stimmiges Tonstück, ein —stimmiger Gesang, a trio. —stöckig, adj. and adv. having three stories, three-storied. —strahlig, adj. and adv. consisting of three rays. —strängig, adj. and adv. consisting of three threads. —stüber, m. three-pence. —stündig, adj. and adv. lasting three hours. —stündlich, adj. and adv. happening every three hours. —tägig, adj. and adv. every three days, triduan, lasting three days; three days old. —täglich, adj. and adv. occurring every third day. Ein —tägliches [better —tägiges] Fieber, a tertian fever. —tausend, [-taú-] adj. three thousand. —tausendste, adj. [the ordinal of three thousand] three-thousandth. —theilig, adj. and adv. tripartite, trichotomous. [in botany] Eine —theilige Blütendecke, a tripartite perianth; ein —theiliger Griffel, a trifid style; ein —theiliges Blatt, a three-parted leaf; ein —theiliger Stengel, a trichotomous stem; [in mathematics] Eine —theilige Größe, a trinome. —theiligkeit, f. trichotomy. —theilung, f. tripartition, trichotomy. Der —theilungszirkel, a trisecting compass. —treffer, m. [in lottery] three winning numbers. —verein, m. triple-alliance. —viertelkartaune, [-vier-] f. [in gunnery] a 16-pounder. —viertelstakt, m. [in music] time of three crotchets in a bar. —weg, m. a place where three roads meet. —weibig, adj. and adv. having three wives at the same time; [in botany] trigynian. —winkel, m. a triangle. —winkelig, adj. and adv. triangular. —wöchentlich, adj. and adv. occurring or repeated every third week. —wöchig, adj. and adv. lasting three weeks; three weeks old. —zack, m. 1) an instrument with three pricks or prongs, [in mythology] trident. 2) V. Salzbinse. —zackig, adj. and adv. having three prongs, trident, tridented. —zackstab, m. V. —zack, 1). —zählig, adj. and adv. consisting of three pieces or parts. [in botany] Ein —zähliges Blatt, a trifoliate leaf. —zähnig, adj. and adv. trident, tridented, tridentate. [in botany] Ein —zähniges Blatt, a tridentate leaf; eine —zähnige Blütendecke, a tridentate perianth. —zehe, f. an animal with three toes. —zehig, adj. and adv. having three toes. —zehn, thirteen. Die —zehn, the number 13. —zehner, m. a member of a council or commission of thirteen. —zehnerlei, adj. of thirteen different kinds. —zehnte, adj. [the ordinal of thirteen] thirteenth. Der —zehnte April, the thirteenth of April. —zehntel, n. the thirteenth part of any thing. —zehntens, adv. in the thirteenth place. —zeilig, adj. and adv. consisting of three lines. Ein —zeiliger Vers, a triplet. —zinkig, adj. and adv. having three prongs, three-pronged. Eine —zinkige Gabel, a fork with three prongs. —zöllig, adj. and adv. containing three inches. Eine —zöllige Planke, a three-inch plank. —züngig, adj. and adv. Fig. containing three languages. Eine —züngige Bibel, a bible containing three languages, polyglot. —zweiteltakt, m. [in music] triple time of three minims.

Dreier, m. [-s, pl. -] 1) a number of three. 2) a small copper coin, half-penny. Fig. Er hat keinen — im Vermögen, he is pennyless; es ist keinen — werth, it is of no value. 3) a council, commission or board of three.

Dreier=brod, n. a half-penny roll or loaf. —herr, m. a commissioner of the three.

Dreierlei, adj. and adv. of three kinds.

Dreiling, m. [-es, pl. -e] 1) a thing equal to three others. 2) a small coin, a half-penny. 3) a half-penny loaf. 4) the third part of a whole. 5) [in mills] V. 1. Drilling. 6) [a tree of America] triplaris.

Dreisch, m. [-es, pl. -e] a fallow meadow.

Dreißig, [ßig from the old Germ. zig = the number ten] adj. thirty. Der Monat Juni hat — Tage, the month of June consists of thirty days; Joseph war — Jahre alt, Joseph was thirty years old; [it is inflected when used alone] er ist Einer von den —en, he is one of the council, commission or board of thirty; die —Seelenmessen, [in the Roman church] trentals; er war nahe an den —en, his age bordered upon thirty.

Dreißigjährig, adj. of thirty years. Der —jährige Krieg, the thirty years' war; —jährige, treu geleistete Dienste berechtigten ihn zu diesem bedeutenden Ruhegehalte, thirty years service made his claim good for, or entitled him to, this considerable pension.

Dreißiger, m. [-s, pl. -] 1) one belonging to the council or commission of 30. 2) a person 30 years old. 3) a thing consisting of thirty parts. 4) something produced in the last year 30, as wine &c. Der — war nicht so gut als der Elfer, the wine of [eighteen hundred and] thirty was not so good as that of eleven.

Dreißigerinn, f. a female 30 years old. Deborah ist eine angehende —, Deborah is on the merrier side of thirty.

Dreißigerlei, adj. of thirty different kinds.

Dreißigste, adj. [the ordinal of thirty] thirtieth.

Dreißigstel, n. [-s, pl. -] the thirtieth part of any thing.

Dreißigstens, adv. in the thirtieth place.

Dreist, [appears to be allied to the Gr. θρασύς] adj. and adv. 1) bold, courageous, fearless, confident, not timorous. — machen, to embolden, to encourage. 2) [sometimes in an ill sense] bold, forward, impudent. Syn. Dreist, Kühn. Both words express that quality of mind which enables men to encounter danger and difficulty with firmness, or without fear. Kühn, however, implies a greater degree of boldness, and is opposed to fearful or cowardly; dreist conveys the idea merely of assurance or confidence, and is opposed to bashful or timid.

Dreistigkeit, f. [pl. -en] I. [without a plur.] 1) boldness, courage, bravery. 2) freedom from timidity, boldness, liberty. Eine edle —, a noble boldness, a manly assurance. 3) excess of freedom, bordering on impudence, boldness, effrontery. Seine — ist unerträglich, his assurance is insupportable. II. [with a plur.] a bold or impudent action.

1. Drell, m. V. Drall.

Drellbohrer, m. V. Drillbohrer.

2. Drell, m. [-es] V. Drillich.

Drellen, adj. and adv. made of ticken.

Drempel, Trempel, m. [-s, pl. -] 1) [in hydraulics] the sill of a floodgate. 2) [in seamen's language] V. Pfortsdrempel.

Dreschen, [probably allied to treten, and to the Lat. trit-us, zerrieben] ir. v. tr. 1) to beat soundly with a stick or whip, to drub, to thrash. 2) to thrash [wheat, oats &c.]. Prov. Leeres Stroh —, to wash an Æthiop white. Fig. to chatter, to prate, to tattle. 3) to tread out [grain &c. with cattle]. Du sollst dem Ochsen, der da drischet, nicht das Maul verbinden, [in Script.] thou shalt not muzzle the ox, when he treadeth out the corn.

Dresch=bank, f. a thrashing-machine. —flegel, m. flail. —flur, f. V. —tenne. —maschine, f. thrashing-machine. —mühle, f. thrashing-mill. —tenne, f. thrashing-floor. —wagen, m. a heavy waggon formerly used to force the grain out of the ears. —walze, f. a roller used to force the grain out of the ears. —werk, n. V. —bank. —zehnte, m. tithe paid in grain, which has been thrashed out. —zeit, f. the usual time of thrashing.

Drescher, m. [-s, pl. -] 1) thrasher. 2, the name of a fish.

Drescher=haus, n. the house of a thrasher. —lohn, m. wages paid for thrashing, thrasher's hire. —staub, m. the dust from thrashing, chaff.

Dresden, n. [-s] [the capital of the kingdom of Saxony] Dresden.

Dresd[e]ner, m. I. [-s, pl. -] -inn, f. an inhabitant or native of Dresden. II. adj. Die — Gemähldegallerie, the collection of pictures at Dresden, the Dresden gallery.

Dresd[e]nerisch, adj. and adv. of or from Dresden, in the Dresden manner or fashion.

Dreſekammer, *f.* V. Treſekammer.

Dreſſe, V. Treſſe.

*Dreſſiren, *v. tr.* 1) to teach and form by practice, to train. Hunde —, to train or break dogs; ein Pferd —, to break a horse. 2) [with periwig-makers] to curl, to crisp.

*Dreſſür, *f.* training, breaking.

Dreuſchen, V. Dräuſchen.

Driebrachen, *v. tr.* [in husbandry] V. Dreiarten.

‖Driesch, *adj.* and *adv.* fallow. — liegen laſſen, to leave untilled.

‖Drieschen, *v. tr.* to fallow [clayey &c. land].

‖Drieſel, *m.* [-s, *pl.* -] [in Swed. *trissa* signifies a movable disk] 1) a roll, block, pulley. 2) a top.

Drieſeln, [V. Drieſel] I. *v. tr.* to twist. II. *v. intr.* to be unwoven, to ravel.

Driet, *n.* [-es, *pl.* -e] [probably from treten] [with velvet-weavers] V. Schlitzeiſen.

1. Drift, *m.* [-es, *pl.* -e] [with dyers] an iron hoop covered with a net of cords used in dying.

2. Drift, *m.* [-es, *pl.* -e] [in seamen's lang., any thing that floats upon the water] drift.

Drillen, *v. tr.* 1) to cause to move in a circular course. 2) [to pierce with a drill] to drill [a hole through a piece of metal &c.]. ‖3) [in a military sense, to teach and train raw soldiers to their duty, by frequent exercise] to drill. 4) [in seamen's lang.] Mit dem Ruder —, to work at the steering wheel; mit der Drillſäge —, to cut off iron with a hack-saw. 5) [a sea term] to track or tow a ship by a rope with a single block. 6) to vex with importunity or impertinence, to harass, annoy, disturb, or irritate by petty requests, to tease, to bore.

Drill-bohrer, *m.* [a kind of bore] a drill. —fiſch, *m.* electrical eel. ‖—haus, *n.* a house or place where soldiers are drilled. ‡—häuschen, *n.* a sort of pillory. ‖—meiſter, *m.* an officer that drills raw soldiers, drill-sergeant. —ſäge, *f.* [in seamen's lang.] hack-saw. —ſtange, *f.* drillstock.

Driller, *m.* [-s, *pl.* -] a teaser, a bore.

Drillich, *m.* [-es, *pl.* -e] [cloth for bed-ticks or cases for beds] ticken.

Drillichen, *adj.* and *adv.* made of ticken.

1. Drilling, *m.* [-es, *pl.* -e] [from drillen = drehen] [in mills] pin-wheel.

Drillings-ſcheibe, *f.* rundle. —ſtock, *m.* pin. —rolle, *f.* arbor.

2. Drilling, *m.* [-es, *pl.* -e] [instead of Dreiling] a three-twin-child.

Drillings-geburt, *f.* —kind, *n.* V. 2. Drilling.

Dringen, [allied to drücken, drängen] *ir.* I. *v. intr.* [u. w. ſeyn] to urge forward with force, to press, to make way, to penetrate. Er drang durch die Menge, he urged his way through the multitude, he squeezed through the crowd; das Volk drang haufenweiſe in das Zimmer, the people crowded into the room; in ein Land —, to penetrate a country; der Feind iſt in die Stadt gedrungen, the enemy forced the town; der Regen dringt nicht durch dieſen Zeug, this stuff is water-proof; Licht dringt durch Glas, light permeates glass; Waſſer und Oel dringen durch Tuch, Leder, Holz, cloth, leather and wood are permeable to water and oil; die Sonne dringt durch die Wolken, the sun breaks through the clouds; die Luft dringt durch jede Ritze in das Zimmer, the air enters the room at every crevice; die Kälte dringt durch Mark und Bein, the cold is very keen. *Fig.* Bis ins Herz —, to pierce the heart, to wound the feelings; es dringt bis aufs Leben, it cuts to the quick, it affects deeply; in ein Geheimniß —, to pierce a secret, to dive or penetrate into a secret; in den Geiſt eines Schriftſtellers —, to enter into the spirit of an author; in Jemanden —, to urge a person importunately, to run a person hard; er drang in ſeinen Sohn, ſich zu entfernen, he urged his son to withdraw; er drang in mich, ſein Anerbieten anzunehmen, he pressed me to accept his offer; auf etwas —, to press or urge for any thing; auf augenblickliche Zahlung einer Schuld —, to insist on the immediate payment of a debt.

II. *v. tr.* [V. Drängen] *Fig. v. tr.* and *intr.* to urge with vehemence or importunity, to press. Die Noth dringt [better drängt] ihn dazu, necessity compels or drives him to it; eine —de Urſache, an urgent or cogent reason; ſie baten ihn dringend, they besought him instantly; eine —de Gefahr, an imminent danger; —de Geſchäfte, urgent affairs; es drang Paulum der Geiſt zu bezeugen den Juden Jeſum, daß er Chriſt ſei, [in Script.] Paul was pressed in spirit, and testified to the Jews that Jesus was Christ.

Dringlich, *adj.* and *adv.* urging, urgent, pressing, driving, impelling.

Dringlichkeit, *f.* urgency. Die — der Geſchäfte, the pressure of business.

‖Driſchel, *m.* [-s, *pl.* -] V. Dreſchflegel.

Driſchel-kürbiß, —kürbs, *m.* long gourd.

Drittarten, V. Dreiarten, Driebrachen.

Dritte, I. *adj.* [the ordinal of three] third. Die — Stunde, the third hour; am —n Auguſt, on the third of August; zum —n Mahle, for the third time; Georg der —, Georg the third; [often it denotes a person or thing distinct from two other persons or things] an einem —n Orte zuſammenkommen, to meet in any place; durch die Dazwiſchenkunft eines —n, by the intervention of a third person; ich habe es aus der —n Hand erfahren, I heard it of a person unconcerned in it, having no interest in it; der — Mann or der —, arbitrator; die — Hand, [a sea term] sea yoke. II. *f.* [in music] a third; a tierce. V. Terzie.

Drittehalb, Dritthalb, *adj.* two and half.

Drittel, *n.* [-s, *pl.* -] 1) [the third part of any thing] third. Das — einer Pipe, [forty two gallons] a tierce; zwei —, two thirds. 2) the third part of a dollar.

Drittelſtück, *n.* V. Drittel 2.

Dritteln, *v. tr.* to divide in three parts.

Drittens, *adv.* thirdly.

Dritthalb, V. Drittehalb.

Drittheil, *n.* V. Drittel 1).

Drittletzt, *adj.* and *adv.* pertaining to the last but two. Die —e Silbe, antipenult.

Drittperſönlich, *adj.* and *adv.* impersonal. —e Zeitwörter, [in grammar] impersonal verbs.

Drittſchein, *m.* [-es] full moon.

Dröb, V. Darob.

Dröben, [instead of da oben] *adv.* there above.

*Droguerien, [pron. Drogerien] *pl.* [from the G. trocken, D. *droogh*] drugs, grocery-wares.

*Droguétt, [pron. Drogett] *m.* [-s, *pl.* -e] [a sort of stuff] drugget.

*Droguiſt, [pron. Drogiſt] *m.* [-en, *pl.* -en] druggist, grocer.

Drohen, [allied to drücken, Swed. *truga*] *v. intr.* [and *tr.*] to threaten, to menace, [in poetry] to threat. Eure Augen — mir, your eyes menace me; —de Blicke, threatening looks; —de Briefe, threatening letters; der Feind droht der Stadt mit einer Belagerung, the enemy menaces the town with a siege; das Haus droht den Einſturz, the house menaces ruin; ſeine Blicke — Tod und Verderben, his looks threat death and destruction. *Prov.* Vom — ſtirbt Niemand, threat'ned folks live long.

Droh-brief, *m.* a letter containing menaces, a threatening letter. —wort, *n.* a threatening expression, menace.

Dröhm, *n.* V. Trumm.

Dröhne, *f.* [*pl.* -n] [probably from dröhnen = tönen] [the male of the honey-bee] a drone.

Drohnen-brut, *f.* the eggs from which drones are produced. —fänger, *m.* V. Hummelfänger. —ſcheibe, *f.* [in husbandry] a honeycomb serving as a repository for the eggs which produce drones. —weiſel, *m.* [in husbandry] the queen-bee of the drones. —würgung, *f.* the killing of the drones. —zäpflein, *n.* a great cell in a honeycomb serving as a repository for the eggs from which drones are produced.

Dröhnen, V. Drönen.

Dröhung, *f.* 1) [the act of menacing] threatening, [in law] assault. 2) a menace, threatening, threat.

Dróllbohrer, *m.* V. Drillbohrer.

Dróllig, [Fr. *drôle*, perhaps from trollen = rollen, ſich bewegen] *adj.* and *adv.* droll [*adv.* drollingly], merry, facetious, comical. Ein —er Menſch, a droll fellow, a droll; —e Einfälle, odd fancies, etwas —, drollish.

Dróllígkeit, *f.* 1) the state of being droll. 2) a drollery.

*Dromedär, *n.* [-s, *pl.* -e] [a species of dromedary.

Drömling, *m.* [-es, *pl.* -e] [among wea V. Trumm.

Drómmeln, V. Trommeln.

Drommète, *f.* [*pl.* -n] [V. Trompete] [a instrument of music] trumpet.

Drommetenſchall, *m.* the sound trumpet.

Drommèten, I. *v. intr.* to sound a II. *v. tr.* 1) to perform on the trumpet. 2 to trumpet.

Drommèter, *m.* [-s, *pl.* -] a trumpet, peter.

Drönen, [Ital. *tronare*, D. *dreunen*] 1) to give a low, heavy, dull sound. Des bodens —der Ton, the cymbal's droning 2) to cause a local pain by a shaking soun blow. 3) to be shaken with a heavy sound.

Drónte, *m.* [-n, *pl.* -n] [a bird] the dod didus.

Drös, *n.* [-ſſes] [a sea term] dregs of bad

‖Dröſchel, *m.* [-s, *pl.* -] V. Dreſchflegel.

Dröske, [commonly but incorrectly Droſchke or Troſchke] *f.* [*pl.* -n] [a Russia a drosk.

Dröſſe, *f.* [*pl.* -n] [in seamen's lang.] ling of the mizzen-mast.

1. Dröſſel, *f.* [*pl.* -n] [in common lang.] 1) the prominent part of the Adam's apple. 2) the throttle, windpi rynx.

2. Dröſſel, *f.* [*pl.* -n] [with some the collar bone.

Droſſel-ader, *f.* the jugular lar. —bein, *n.* [with some anatomists] bone.

3. Dröſſel, *f.* [*pl.* -n] [a bird] the

Droſſelbeere, *f.* the berry of the elder. —beerſtrauch, *m.* the water-eld

‖Dröſt, *m.* [-en, *pl.* -e] [in Scandinav. dro nifies Herr and Volk] an officer or magistrat district.

Drüben, [instead of da üben] *adv.* on the

side [of a street, of a river &c.]. Er ist —, he is in the other room.

Drüber, V. Darüber.

Drúck, *m.* [-es, *pl.* -e] 1) from drucken. *a*) the act of pressing, especially the act of impressing, printing. In den — geben, to put in print. *b*) [the state of being printed and published] Im — erscheinen, to appear in print; der erste —, the first impression or edition; während des —s, while printing. *c*) [the impressions of types in general, as to form, size &c.] print. Ein kleiner —, a small print; ein schöner —, a fine print. *d*) [the representation of any thing made by impression] print. Alte deutsche —e, old German prints; Kupfer—, copperplate printing; das ist Stein—, it is a lithography; einen — abziehen, [in printing] to take off a proof. 2) from drücken, the act of pressing, or of pressing into a narrower compass, pressure, compressure. Ein — mit der Hand, a squeeze with the hand; der — der Luft, the pressure of the air; der — der Gewichte, the pressure of weights; der — der Schwere, gravitation; der Grad des —es steht im Verhältnisse zu dem Gewichte des drückenden Körpers, the degree of pressure is in proportion to the weight of the pressing body. *Fig.* pressure, oppression. Der — der Abgaben, the pressure of taxes.

Druck-baum, *m.* a long piece of wood used in pressing. —**berichtiger**, *m.* a corrector of the press. —**berichtigung**, *f.* correction of the press. —**besorger**, *m.* the editor of a printed work, a publisher. —**besorgung**, *f.* the publication of any book or writing, edition. —**bewilligung**, *f.* the licence granted to publish a work. —**buchstabe**, *m.* letter, type. —**farbe**, *f.* V. Druckerfarbe. —**fehler**, *m.* an error or mistake in printing, a misprint, erratum. —**fertig**, *adj.* and *adv.* ready or prepared for publication. —**firniß**, *m.* 1) amber-varnish. 2) V. Druckerschwärze. —**form**, *f.* print form. —**formen**, *pl.* printing-blocks. —**freiheit**, *f.* 1) the liberty of the press. ‖2) V. —bewilligung. —**genehmigung**, *f.* V. —bewilligung. —**hebel**, *m.* a lever which acts downwards or by pressure. —**jahr**, *n.* the year in which a book is printed. —**kosten**, *pl.* expenses of printing. —**kraft**, *f.* the power of pressure. —**kugel**, *f.* [in pyrotechnics] globe of compression. —**nagel**, *m.* the trigger of a cross-bow. —**ort**, *m.* the place at which a book is printed. —**papier**, *n.* printing-paper. —**probe**, *f.* [in printing] proof. —**pumpe**, *f.* [in mining] forcing-pump. —**richtig**, *adj.* and *adv.* correct in the printing. —**richtigkeit**, *f.* correctness. —**schau**, *f.* V. —berichtigung. —**schauer**, *m.* V. —berichtiger. —**schleier**, *m.* Silesia lawn for printing. —**schönheit**, *f.* typographical beauty. —**schrift**, *f.* print, book. —**schriften**, *pl.* *a*) prints, books. *b*) printing-types. —**schwarz**, *n.* German or Frankfort black. —**schwärze**, *f.* ink for the rolling-press. —**spiel**, *n.* V. Beilkespiel. —**stempel**, *m.* the embolus of a pump, forcer. —**tafel**, *f.* 1) V. Billiertafel. 2) a kind of billiard-table. —**tisch**, *m.* [with cotton-printers] a long table used in printing cotton. —**verbesserer**, *m.* V. —berichtiger. —**verbesserung**, *f.* V. —berichtigung. —**verbot**, *n.* a prohibition to publish a book. —**werk**, *n.* 1) any piece of mechanism, which acts by pressure, a forcing pump. 2) any printed work. —**zange**, *f.* [in metallurgy] pincers.

Drúckbar, 1) *adj.* and *adv.* that may be printed. 2) that may be pressed.

Drückel, *m.* [-s, *pl.* -] [in mining] a lever which acts by pressure.

Drúcken, *v. tr.* to impress, to print [figures on cloth &c., a book &c.]. Gedruckte Leinwand, printed linen; Noten —, to print music; — lassen, to put in print, to print. *Prov.* Er lügt wie gedruckt, he is a very great liar.

Drücken, I. *v. tr.* 1) to press closely, to squeeze. Einem die Hand —, to squeeze any one's hand; Einen an die Brust —, to press any one to one's bosom, to embrace any one; Leucothea drückte Palämon fester in ihre Arme, Leucothoe pressed Palemon closer in her arms; Einen an die Wand —, to press any one against the wall; [in architecture] ein gedrückter Bogen, a scheme-arch. *Fig.* Einen —, to treat any one with unjust severity or rigour; er drückt seine Unterthanen, he oppresses his subjects; die Schulden —, die Noth drückt ihn, he is pressed with debts, with want; —de Auflagen, oppressive taxes. 2) to pain by pressure or compression. Die Schuhe — mich, the shoes pinch me; es drückt mich im Magen, I have pains in my stomach; ich habe ein — auf der Brust, I have an oppression at my breast; der Alp hat ihn gedrückt, he had the nightmare; vom Alp gedrückt werden, to be oppressed by the nightmare. *Prov.* Jeder weiß am besten, wo der Schuh ihn drückt, the wearer best knows, where the shoe wrings him. 3) to put upon by pressure. Das Siegel auf eine Urkunde —, to set the seal upon a document, to seal a document. 4) *Fig.* [in painting] to deepen the shades, to paint in obscurer colours. II. *v. intr.* to bear upon, to act on as weight or force. Die Gewichte —, the weights draw; die Uhrfeder drückt, the spring of a watch acts by pressure; diese Bildsäule drückt schwer auf ihr Fußgestell, that statue bears heavily on its base; [in astronomy] die Planeten — gegen die Sonne hin, the planets gravitate towards the sun or centre of the solar-system. *Fig.* Die Luft ist —d, the air is sultry or oppressive. III. *v. r.* sich —, 1) to be hurt by pressure. Er hat sich beim Reiten gedrückt, he was galled by riding; ein gedrücktes Pferd, a galled horse. 2) † to withdraw or steal away privately. Er hat sich aus der Gesellschaft gedrückt, he sneaked away from the company. 3) [with hunters] to crouch, to squat. Die Feldhühner haben sich gedrückt, the partridges lie close.

Drück-läppchen, —**polster**, *n.* [in surgery] a compress, a pledget.

Drúcker, *m.* [-s, *pl.* -] 1) [one that prints books or cloth with figures] a printer. Der Kupfer—, a copper-plate printer; der Stein—, a lithographer. 2) [in printing-offices] the pressman. 3) *Fig.* [in painting] a strong stroke.

Drucker-arbeit, *f.* press-work. —**ballen**, *m.* printing-ball. —**farbe**, *f.* printing-ink. —**kunst**, *f.* V. Druckerei 1. —**lohn**, *m.* 1) printer's wages. 2) money paid for printing. —**presse**, *f.* printing-press. —**schrift**, *f.* V. Druckschrift, *pl.* *b*). —**schwärze**, *f.* 1) printing-ink. 2) ink for the rolling press. —**zimmer**, *n.* [in printing-offices] press-room.

Drücker, *m.* [-s, *pl.* -] 1) an instrument for pressing, especially the thumb of the latch of a door. Der — an einem Schießgewehr, the trigger of a gun. 2) [in mints] an instrument used for cutting the blanks. 3) [in some watches, in repeaters] the knob which moves the spring. 4) [in seamen's lang.] Der — unter dem Krahnbalken, the supporter of the cat-head; die — in den Rusten, the knees on the chain-wales; die — unter den Rusten, the knees or supporters under the chain-wales.

Druckereí, *f.* 1) the art of printing, typography. 2) a printer's work-house, chapel. 3) [in contempt] print.

‖**Drúcksen**, [from drücken] *v. intr.* to tarry, to hesitate.

Drūd, *m.* [-en, *pl.* -en] **Drūde**, *f.* [*pl.* -n] [allied to the Swed. *tryta*, to weary] 1) an enchanter, a wizard, a sorcerer, a witch, a magician. 2) a hobgoblin, a fairy. 3) nightmare. Das —endrücken, the nightmare.

Druden-baum, *m.* fairy-tree. —**fuß**, *m.* V. Bärlapp. —**stück**, *n.* [with butchers] a certain piece of the shoulder of beef.

‖**Drúffel**, *f.* [*pl.* -n] a bunch, cluster [of raisins, apples &c.]. Eine — von Bäumen, a cluster or group of trees, a clump.

‖**Drúffeln**, *v. tr.* to group.

Druide, *m.* [-n, *pl.* -n] [perhaps from the old Drot, Druth, Herr] 1) a god. 2) [a priest among the ancient Celtic nations in Gaul, Britain and Germany] Druid. Der Ober—, arch-druid. 3) V. Drud 1.

Drüll, *m.* [-es, *pl.* -e] [a sea term] a driver.

Drúm, V. Darum.

‖**Drúmpelbeere**, *f.* V. Heidelbeere.

Drúnten, [instead of da unten] *adv.* there below; below.

Drūsbeutel, V. Drüsenblume.

Drūschling, *m.* [-es, *pl.* -e] V. Herrenpilz.

1. **Drūse**, *f.* [*pl.* -n] [in Swed. *Druse* signifies a heap] a stone with a drusy surface, a druse.

2. **Drūse**, *f.* [*pl.* -n] [perhaps allied to the Bohem. *drazowity*, full of holes] [in mining] ore decayed by the weather. Große —, opens.

Drusen-kobalt, *m.* [in mining] drusy cobalt.

3. **Drūse**, *f.* [*pl.* -n] [a distemper in horses] V. Drüse 3.

4. **Drūse**, *m.* [*pl.* -n] -**sinn**, *f.* one of the Druses [a well known people in Syria]. Die —n, the Druses.

Drūse, *f.* [*pl.* -n] [allied to dreben; thus = something round] 1) [in anatomy] gland. Die Speichel—n, salivary glands; die Thränen—n, lachrymal glands; geschwollene —n, [a disease] the mumps. 2) [in botany, an excretory or secretory duct in plants] a gland, glandule. 3) [a distemper in horses] the glanders. Von der — befallen, glandered.

Drüsen-beschreibung, *f.* [in anatomy] adenography. —**blume**, *f.* [a genus of plants] adenanthera. —**geschwulst**, *f.* the mumps. —**körnchen**, *pl.* [in anatomy] muscous follicles. —**krankheit**, *f.* a disease of the glands. —**lehre**, *f.* [in anatomy] adenology. —**los**, *adj.* and *adv.* having no glands. —**pulver**, *n.* [in farriery] a powder for the glanders. —**zergliederung**, *f.* [in anatomy] adenotomy.

‖**Drūsen**, *pl.* 1) lees, dregs. 2) the husks or skins of grapes after they have been once pressed.

Drusen-asche, *f.* V. Weinhefenasche. —**schwarz**, *n.* German or Frankfort black.

Drūsicht, *adj.* and *adv.* [in mineralogy] resembling druses.

Drūsicht, *adj.* and *adv.* resembling a gland, glandulous, glandiform.

Drūsig, *adj.* and *adv.* 1) [in mineralogy] having its surface coated with small crystals, drusy. 2) [in mining] filled with ore decayed by the weather.

Drūsig, *adj.* and *adv.* 1) glandulous, glandular. [in botany] Ein —er Blattstiel, a glandulous petiole or leaf-stalk. 2) [in farriery] glandered.

Drūswurz, *f.* 1) bulbous crow-foot. 2) water-drop-wort.

***Dryāden**, *pl.* [in mythology] dryads.

Dū, [Lat. *tu*, Gr. *σύ*, Doric *τύ*] *pron.* thou. [Auf] — und — mit Jemanden seyn, to thou any one, to treat any one with familiarity; bist du's? is it thou? [Du is used only in very familiar language or in the solemn style].

*Duális, m. [-es, pl. -e] [in grammar] the dual number [in Greek &c.].

*Dualísmus, m. duality.

Dúbhammer, [Dub allied to tief] m. [-s, pl. -] [in copper-works] a sort of great hammer moved by water.

*Dublétten, V. Doubletten.

*Dublín, n. [-s] [the capital of Ireland] Dublin.

Dublíner, I. m. [-s, pl. -] -inn, f. an inhabitant or native of Dublin. II. adj. of or from Dublin.

*Dublóne, f. [pl. -n] [a Spanish coin] a doubloon.

*Ducáten, V. Dukaten.

Dúcht, f. [pl. -en] [in seamen's language] 1) a strand. Eine ungeschorne —, a strand which is not twisted. 2) a thwart. Die —en eines Flußkahnes, thwarts; die —en in dem Boot, in der Schlupe, thwarts or seats of rowers in a boat; die Mast—, Segel—, the main-thwart or middle-thwart; Krumpel—, Krüppel—, stern-thwart.

Dúckdalben, pl. [in seamen's language] poles in a harbour.

Dúcken, [allied to tauchen] v. r. sich —, 1) to duck, to bow, to stoop. †2) Fig. to be submissive.

Duck-fenster, n. a small window. —mäuser, m. 1) a sly hypocritical fellow. 2) a sullen dull person. —mäuserig, adj. and adv. sly, hypocritical. —taube, f. the black guillemot.

Dúckstein, [probably from the old Dock = Röhre] m. [-es, pl. -e] 1) (Tuffkalk, Kalktuff) tufaceous limestone, calk-tuff. 2) a sort of beer at Kœnigslutter in the Dutchy of Brunswic.

Dudeldeí, n. [-es] [from dudeln] 1) trifling talk, prattle. 2) a trifle.

Dudeleí, f. [pl. -en] 1) the act of piping or singing badly. 2) something badly played or piped, or sung.

Dúdeler, Dúdler, m. [-s, pl. -] one that plays or sings badly; a poor poet, a rhymester.

Dúdeln, I. v. intr. 1) to play on the bagpipe. 2) to play or sing badly or imperfectly. II. v. tr. 1) to play or sing badly. 2) to make poor verses.

Dudel-sack, m. a bagpipe. —sackpfeifer, m. bagpiper.

Dúdu, m. [-'s, -s] V. Dronte.

*Duéll, n. [-s, pl. -e] a single combat, duel.

*Duellánt, m. [-en, pl. -en] a dueller, duellist.

*Duellíren, v. r. sich —, to fight in single combat, to duel. Das Duelliren, duelling.

*Duétt, n. [-es, pl. -e] [in music] duet, duetto.

‖Dúff, V. Dumpf.

Düffel, m. [-s] [a kind of coarse woolen cloth] coating-duffel.

‖Dúffig, V. Dumpfig.

1. Dúft, m. [-es, pl. Düfte] [allied to Dunst, dehnen] 1) [all substances which impair the transparency of the atmosphere, as smoke, mist, fog &c.] vapour. 2) scent, smell, odour. Der angenehme — der Rosen, the pleasing scent, the fragrancy of roses.

Duft-bruch, m. [among foresters, looseness of the heart in a tree] coltiness. —gebüsch, n. a fragrant bush. —gewölk, n. haze. —strauch, m. [a genus of plants] diosma. —wolke, f. a thin, hazy cloud.

2. Dúft, V. Ducht, 2).

Düftchen, n. [-s, pl. -] dimin. of Duft.

Dúften, [V. Duft] I. v. intr. 1) to perspire gently; it. to emit moisture as walls. 2) to rise or spread in the shape of vapour, to diffuse odours. Es duftet ein lieblicher Geruch aus den Blumen, plants exhale a fragrant odour. 3) to exhale, to emit an odour or particular scent. Die Rose duftet angenehm, the rose exhales a fragrant odour. II. v. tr. [used only in a high or poetical style] to exhale fragrance, to emit an odorous scent. Ihr Athem duftet Rosen und Veilchen, her breath exhales fragrance sweet as roses and violets. V. [the more correct] Düften.

Düften, v. tr. to exhale, to send out. Die Rose düftet einen süßen Geruch, the rose exhales a fragrant odour.

Düftetopf, m. a jar filled with the leaves of all sorts of flowers, to perfume a room.

Dúftig, adj. and adv. 1) vaporous, hazy. 2) emitting or exhaling an odour or particular scent, fragrant.

Düftling, m. [-s, pl. -e] [a genus of plants] osmites.

Dukáten, m. [-s, pl. -] [from the lat. ducatus; a Duke of Ferrara caused the first to be struck] [in Germany, Holland &c. a gold coin, in its actual value worth about nine shillings English; in Italy and Spain a silver coin in value of from three shillings to four shillings English] a ducat.

Dukaten-gold, n. the purest gold. —röschen, n. [a plant] mouse-ear.

Düking, f. [a sea term] the dip of the horizon.

Dúldbar, adj. and adv. tolerable, supportable.

Dúldbarkeit, f. tolerableness.

Dúlden, [A. S. tholian, Allem. tolen, Lat. tul-i, tol-ero, Gr. ταλάω] v. tr. and intr. 1) to suffer without resistance, or without yielding, to endure, [in poetry] to bear. Der Mensch ist zum — geboren, man is born to bear; Schmach und Pein —, to suffer pain and disgrace; Liebe duldet alles, charity is patient. V. Erdulden. 2) not to forbid or hinder, to allow or permit negatively, by not preventing. Wollen Sie es —, daß man Sie mißhandle? will you suffer yourself to be insulted? man sollte das Schreien der Kinder nicht —, crying should not be tolerated in children; die protestantische Religion ist in Italien geduldet, the Protestant religion is tolerated in Italy. Das —, die Duldung, toleration, tolerance, sufferance. Syn. Dulden, Leiden. Leiden denotes merely, to permit, to suffer, not to resist, without specifying whether the thing tolerated is an evil or not. Dulden always supposes that the thing borne or suffered, voluntarily or involuntarily, is an evil or misfortune, and is felt as such. Dulden is said only of men and beasts; Leiden also of inanimate objects. One may say: Die Präposition Ohne leidet nur den Accusativ nach sich [the preposition ohne admits only the accusative case after it], but not duldet.

Dúlder, m. [-s, pl. -] -inn, f. one who bears with patience what is inconvenient, endurer, sufferer.

Dúldsam, adj. and adv. 1) supporting with patience, or without yielding, patient in affliction. 2) indulgent, tolerant.

Dúldsamkeit, Dúldung, f. toleration, tolerance.

Dúllbaum, m. [-es, pl. -bäume] [in seamen's language] the string under the gunnel, into which the tholes are driven.

Dúllbord, V. Schandeck.

Dúllen, pl. [a sea term] tholes or thole-pins.

‖Dúlt, m. [-es, pl. -e] [probably instead of Indult = Indulgenz] a fair or market. Der berühmte Münchener —, the celebrated fair at Munich.

Dúmm, [allied to dumpf, stumm, stumpf and taub, and to verbs as the Gr. τύπ-τω, the Ger. stupfen, i. e. stoßen, as the Gr. κωφός from κόπτω, thus = gedrückt] Fig. adj. and adv. 1) slow of understanding, dull, stupid, doltish, blockish. Ein —er Mensch, a blockhead, a dolt. 2) proceeding from want of understanding or common judgment. —es Geschwätz, foolish prate; —es Zeug, silly words, nonsense; —e Streiche, silly tricks, foolish conduct; ein —es Benehmen, a sottish behaviour. 3) clumsy, awkward. Er stellt sich zu Allem — an, he does every thing awkwardly. 4) tasteless, insipid [said of salt &c.]. 5) [in staining of a blue colour] dull, clouded, tarnished

Dumm-bart, m. a blockhead, a dolt, a dunce, a dullard, a dull-head, a thickskull. —bärtig, adj. and adv. doltish, blockish. —dreist, adj. and adv. stupidly bold, forward, saucy, impudent. —dreistigkeit, f. 1) a silly forwardness or assurance, impudence. 2) an action, proceeding from a silly forwardness. —fromm, I. adj. bigot, bigoted. II. adv. bigotedly. —frömmelei, f. bigotry. —kopf, m. [a word of reproach] blockhead, dolt, dunce. —köpfig, adj. and adv. doltish, blockish. —kühn, adj. and adv. foolishly bold, fool-hardy. —trotzig, adj. and adv. stupidly impertinent.

Dúmmen, V. Verdummen.

Dúmmerjan, [contracted from dummer Jahn or Johann = Jack ass] m. [-es, pl. -e] a stupid fellow, a sot, a simpleton.

Dúmmerlich, adj. and adv. somewhat stupid, simple.

Dúmmheit, f. 1) [without a plural] dulness, stupidity, blockishness. 2) [with a plural] a silly action, a foolish behaviour, a folly.

Dúmmlich, adj. and adv. dull, stupid, simple.

Dümmling, m. [-es, pl. -e] a simpleton, a noodle.

Dúmmrian, m. [-s, pl. -e] 1) V. Dummerjan. 2) [a plant] meadow inula, or middle fleabane.

Dúmpeln, v. intr. [in seamen's lang.] to heave and set.

Dúmpf, [allied to dumm, thus = gedrückt] adj. and adv. 1) hollow, deep, low, dull. Ein —er Ton, a hollow or dead sound; ein —es Geräusch, a hollow noise; ein —es Gemurmel, a dull murmur; es macht mir den Kopf ganz —, it quite stupefies my brain; ein —es Schweigen, a gloomy silence. 2) not much sensible or perceptible. Ein —er Schmerz, a dull, inward pain.

Dúmpf, m. V. Dumpfen.

Dümpfel, m. [-s, pl. -] [allied to the D. dompelen, to dive] a deeper place in a river or lake; also a pool, puddle.

Dúmpfen, m. [-s] [in common language] shortness of breath, pursiness.

Dümpfer, m. [-s, pl. -] one of the cylinders in a chime.

Dúmpfheit, f. dulness, insensibility, torpor

Dúmpfig, adj. and adv. 1) damp, moist, humid. Eine —e Luft, a damp air; ein —es Gewölbe, a damp vault; ein —es Zimmer, a musty room. 2) musty, fusty. Ein —er Geruch, fustiness; das Mehl riecht —, the flour has a musty smell.

Dúmpflachter, f. [in mining] a measure of four ells.

Dúmpfsinn, m. [-es] a stupid or senseless state, stupefaction.

Düne, f. [pl. -n] V. Daune.

Dunenbett, n. a bed of downs, down-bed

Düne, *f.* [*pl.* -n] [A. S. *dun* signifies a hill, Gr. θὶν the bank] [a bank or elevation of sand, thrown up by the sea; a large open plain] down.

Dünen=gras, *n.* cotton-grass. —**halm**, *n.* sea reed-grass. —**rose**, *f.* Scotch rose.

||**Dung**, *m.* [-es] V. Dünger.

Dung=gabel, *f.* dung-fork. —**käfer**, *m.* kister. —**lage**, *f.* dung-hill.

Düngen, *v. tr.* to manure with dung, to dung. Das Feld —, to dung or manure land; gedüngt, dunged. Das —, manuring with dung, stercoration; die Düngung, *a*) manuring with dung, *b*) manure, dung.

Dünger, *m.* [-s] [Engl. *dung*, Swed. *dynga*; seems to be allied to stinken, the A. S. *dyngan* = sich entleeren] [any matter which fertilizes land, as the contents of stables, marl, ashes, salt, and every kind of animal and vegetable substance applied to land, or capable of furnishing nutriment to plants] manure. Der Pferde—, horse-dung.

Dünger=art, *f.* sort of manure. —**erde**, *f.* [among gardeners] garden-mould, rotten dung. —**haufen**, *m.* dung-hill.

Dunkel, [A.S. *doc*; Swed. *tökk* signifies Dampf, Isl. *dokha*, schwarz werden] *adj.* and *adv.* 1) [wholly or partially black] dark. Eine dunkle Farbe, a dark colour; dunkle Augen, dark eyes; ein dunkles Braun, a dusky brown; ein dunkler Zeug, a dark-coloured stuff; — halten, [in painting] to give a darker hue, to deepen. 2) [destitute of light; i.e. not luminous, partially dark] dark, obscure. Ein dunkles Zimmer, a dark room; eine dunkle Höhle, an obscure cavern; ein dunkles Haus, a darksome house; eine dunkle Nacht, a dark night; ein dunkler Körper, a dark or opaque body; ein dunkles Thal, a dusky valley; dunkle Wolken, dark clouds; schwach und — brennen, to burn faint and dim; dunkle Schatten, dim shades; es wird schon —, it is already growing dusky; im —n, in the dark; dunkles Wetter, dull weather; ein dunkler Tag, a cloudy day; es wird mir ganz — vor den Augen, my head swims. *Fig.* *a*) [not noted, unknown, unnoticed, humble] obscure. Ein Mensch von dunkler Herkunft, a person of obscure birth; im —n leben, to live in obscurity. *b*) [not certainly known] dark, obscure. Die dunkle Zukunft, dark futurity; eine dunkle Rückerinnerung, a faint, indistinct recollection; wir schweben Alle im —n, we are all in the dark; sie erfahren nur, was mündliche Ueberlieferung — ihnen zugeführt hat, they learn only what tradition has darkly conveyed to them; oft sind die Wege der Vorsehung für den menschlichen Verstand —, the ways of providence are often dark to human reason; die dunklen Wege Gottes, the mysterious ways of God. *c*) [not easily understood or explained] obscure, dark, abstruse. Eine dunkle Stelle in einem Schriftsteller, a dark passage in an author; dunkle Begriffe, obscure notions. Syn. Dunkel, Undeutlich. As in the literal sense dunkel implies a total absence of light, and undeutlich only partial obscurity or indistinctness, so in a figurative sense, that is said to be dunkel which is so obscure as to be perfectly incomprehensible, undeutlich that which is not perfectly clear, not obviously intelligible.

Dunkel=äugig, *adj.* and *adv.* having dark eyes. —**blau**, *adj.* and *adv.* dark-blue. —**braun**, *adj.* and *adv.* dark-brown. —**farbig**, *adj.* and *adv.* dark-coloured. —**fuchs**, *m.* a dark chestnut or sorrel horse. —**gelb**, *adj.* and *adv.* dark-yellow, tawny. —**grau**, *adj.* and *adv.* dark-grey. —**grün**, *adj.* and *adv.* dark-green. —**haarig**, *adj.* and *adv.* dark-haired. Die —haarige, a brunet, brunette. —**klar**, *adj.* and *adv.* dark and clear at the same time. Das —klare, [in painting] clare-obscure. —**licht**, *n.* twilight, crepuscule. —**roth**, *adj.* and *adv.* dark-red, murrey. —**schwarz**, *adj.* and *adv.* very black.

Dunkel, *n.* [-s] darkness, obscurity [also in a figurative sense].

1. **Dünkel**, *m.* V. Dinkel.

2. **Dünkel**, *m.* [-s] [from dünken] favourable or self-flattering opinion, a lofty and vain conception of one's own person or accomplishments, conceit, conceitedness, presumption, arrogance.

Dünkelvoll, *adj.* and *adv.* conceited, arrogant.

Dünkelhaft, *adj.* and *adv.* conceited, presumptuous, arrogant.

Dunkelheit, *f.* 1) [without a plural] [absence of light] darkness, obscurity, obscureness. Die — der Nacht, the darkness of the night. *Fig.* Diese Geschichten sind in undurchdringliche — gehüllt, these stories are wrapt in impenetrable obscurity; die — einer Stelle in einem Schriftsteller, the obscurity of a passage in an author; er lebt in größter —, he lives in utter obscurity. 2) [with a plural] an obscure thing. Seine Rede ist voll —en, his discourse is very obscure.

Dunkeln, I. *v. intr.* to grow dark or darker, to darken. Es fängt an zu —, it begins to grow dusky. II. *v. tr.* to make dark, to deprive of light, to darken. III. *v. r.* sich —, to grow dark or dusky.

Dünkeln, *v. intr.* [unusual] to think, to fancy erroneously.

Dünken, [Swed. *tycka*, Gr. δοκεῖν, from the root of denken] I. *v. intr.* and *imp.* to seem, to appear. Er thut Alles, was ihm gut dünkt, he does all that suits his fancy; es wird dir lächerlich —, it will appear ridiculous to you; mir [mich] dünkt, meseems, it seems to me; mich dünkte, ich sah &c., methought I saw &c.; wie mich dünkt, as I presume. II. *v. r.* sich —, to figure to one's self, to fancy, to believe or suppose without proof. Er dünkt sich recht geschickt zu seyn, he thinks himself a very clever fellow; *er dünkt sich Wunder was [zu seyn], he fancies himself a very great personage.

Dünkirchen, *n.* [-s] [a town in France] Dunkirk.

Dünkling, *m.* [-es, *pl.* -e] a conceited, or self-sufficient person.

Dünn, [allied to dehnen, as the Lat. *tenuis* to *ten*-do] *adj.* and *adv.* 1) [having little thickness or extent from one surface to the opposite] thin. Ein —es Papier, Brett, a thin paper, board; eine —e Decke, a thin covering; ein —er Schleier, a thin veil; ein —er Stengel, a slender stem; ein —es Gewebe, a nice texture; ein —er Faden, a fine or delicate thread. *Fig.* *—e Ohren haben, to have a good or quick ear. 2) [not close or compact] thin. Das Getreide oder Gras steht —, the corn or grass is thin; ein —er Wald, a thin forest; — gesäeter Samen, seed sown thin; —es Haupthaar, thin hair; der Feind hat unsre Reihen — gemacht, the enemy has thinned our ranks. *Fig* Das Geld ist —, money is scarce. 3) [rare, not dense, applied to fluids] thin. —es Blut, thin blood; —e Milch, thin milk; eine —e [schwache] Fleischbrühe, a thin broth; —es Bier, small beer; —e Luft, thin, or subtil air; *durch Dick und —, through thick and thin.

Dünn=bärtig, *adj.* and *adv.* thin-bearded. —**bauch**, *m.* 1) a thin belly. 2) [a fish] a species of carp [cyprinus cultratus]. —**bäuchig**, *adj.* and *adv.* having a thin belly. —**bier**, *n.* small beer, thin drink. —**blätterig**, *adj.* and *adv.* thin-leaved. —**eisen**, *n.* a sort of thin iron, good for tinning. —**eiterig**, *adj.* and *adv.* sanious. —**füßig**, *adj.* and *adv.* thin-legged. —**gras**, *n.* V. Wollgras. —**haarig**, *adj.* and *adv.* having thin hair. —**halsig**, *adj.* and *adv.* having a slender neck. —**häutig**, *adj.* and *adv.* thin-skinned [said of a pear &c.]. —**hülsig**, *adj.* and *adv.* having thin husks. —**lech**, *n.* [in mining] V. Spurstein. —**leibig**, *adj.* and *adv.* thin-bodied. —**lippig**, *adj.* and *adv.* thin-lipped. —**öhrig**, *adj.* and *adv.* *fig.* having a quick ear. —**öl**, *n.* [with printers of copper-plates] thin nut-oil for thinning the ink for the rolling-press. —**quetsche**, *f.* [with goldbeaters] the third sort of vellum-mould. —**rippe**, *f.* [a sort of shell] the old wife, the old woman. —**schale**, *f.* 1) a species of cowry [cypræa fragilis]. 2) double-wedge shell. —**schälig**, *adj.* and *adv.* having thin shells, thin-coated. —**scheibe**, *f.* hod. —**schenkelig**, *adj.* and *adv.* thin-legged. —**schlagform**, *f.* [with goldbeaters] the last vellum mould. —**schwanz**, *m.* 1) an animal with a thin tail. 2) [a genus of fishes] trichiurus. —**stein**, *m.* a light diamond. —**tuch**, *n.* lawn.

Dünne, *f.* [*pl.* -n] **Dünnheit**, 1) [without a plural] [the state of being thin] thinness. Die — des Eises, the thinness of the ice; die — der Luft, the subtility of air. ||2) [something thin] [with a plural] *a*) V. Weichen. *b*) temples.

Dünnen, *v. tr.* to make thin, to thin. Den Leim —, to thin glue; einen Wald —, to thin the trees of a forest.

Dünnung, *f.* V. Dünne 1).

Duns, *m.* [-ses, *pl.* -se] [V. Dunsen] a dunce, a dullard, a dolt, a thickskull.

Dunsen, [allied to dehnen] *ir. v. intr.* [u. w. seyn] to dilate, to swell [used only in the past participle]. Ein gedunsenes Gesicht, a bloated face.

Dunst, *m.* [-es, *pl.* Dünste] [probably from Dehnen] 1) [in a general sense, an invisible elastic fluid, rendered aeriform by heat, and capable of being condensed, or brought back to the liquid or solid state, by cold, a visible fluid floating in the atmosphere] vapour. Der — des kochenden Wassers, steam; aus der Erde steigen Dünste auf, the earth exhales vapours; aus warmen Speisen steigt ein — auf, hot meats send forth vapour; schädliche Dünste, noxious exhalations, mephitis, mephitism; die Dünste des Weines, the fumes of wine; in — verfliegen, sich in — auflösen, to evaporate. Der feurige — auf dem Mast, [in seamen's language] Helena [when one is seen alone], Castor and Pollux [two appearing at once]. **Fig.* Einem einen blauen — vormachen, to cast a mist before any one's eyes. 2) *Fig.* *a*) [with sportsmen] small shot, dust-shot. ||*b*) the finest flour. *c*) [in gunnery] Eine Bombe aus dem —e werfen, to throw a bomb by one firing.

Dunst=bad, *n.* vapour-bath. —**bild**, *n.* [mental fume, unreal fancy] vapour. —**bläschen**, *pl.* vesicular vapours. —**flinte**, *f.* fowling-piece. —**frei**, *adj.* and *adv.* destitute of vapour. —**gebilde**, *n.* idle conceit, vain imagination, fume. —**grübchen**, *n.* pore. Die —grübchen der Pflanzen, the pores of plants. —**kreis**, *m.* atmosphere. —**kreisig**, *adj.* and *adv.* atmospheric, atmospherical. —**kugel**, *f.* 1) V. —kreis. 2) V. Dampfkugel. —**luft**, *f.* [in chimistry] gas. —**raum**, *m.* V. —kreis.

Dunsten, *v. intr.* 1) to rise in the shape of vapour. 2) to emit fumes, to vapour. Fließendes Wasser dunstet nicht so stark als stehendes Wasser, running waters vapour not so much as standing water; der Kranke dunstet mäßig, the sick perspires gently.

Dünsten, *v. tr.* to stew [meat &c.].

Dunstig, *adj.* and *adv.* [full of vapours or exhalations] vaporous, vaporish. Die —e Luft der Thäler, the vaporous air of valleys.

***Duodecimalmaß**, *n.* [-es, *pl.* -e] duodecimal measure, in which the unit is divided in

12 equal parts.

*Duodecimālrechnung, *f.* the calculating in the above manner.

*Duodecimālsystem, *n.* [-es, *pl.* -e] the system of dividing the unit into 12 equal parts.

*Duodecime, *f.* [*pl.* -n] [in music] an interval of 12 diatonic intervals.

*Duodĕz, *n.* [-es, *pl.* -e] [a book in which a sheet is folded into twelve leaves] duodecimo. Ein Buch in —, a book of duodecimo form or size.

Duodez-band, *m.* a duodecimo volume. *Fig.* —fürst, *m.* a petty prince. †—männchen, *n.* hop-o'-my thumb.

*Duodrāma, *n.* [-'s, *pl.* -men] V. Zweipersonenspiel.

Dúpeisen, *n.* [-s, *pl.* -] [a sea term] nail-driver.

Dúpfen, [tupfen is allied to the Gr. τύπ-τω] *v. tr.* 1) [to strike gently with some soft or moist substance] to dab. Ein Geschwür mit Charpie —, to dab a sore with lint. 2) [with engravers] to tap with the ball of the thumb, or with a small ball made of new taffety filled with cotton, the backside of a copper-plate.

Dupf-bällchen, *n.* [with engravers] a small ball made of new taffety and filled with cotton. —wasser, *n.* V. Aetzwasser.

*Duplicität, *f.* duplicity.

*Duplík, *f.* [*pl.* -en] [in law pleadings] V. Erwiederungsschrift.

*Duplikāt, *n.* [-es, *pl.* -e] duplicate.

*Dupliren, *v. tr.* to double [a sum of money].

*Dúplum, *n.* [-s, *pl.* Dupla or Duplen] double.

Dur, *adj.* [in music] sharp, major.

Dúrch, [Old Engl. *thorough*, modern Engl. *through*, Old G. and provinc. *durah*, *durih*, allied to the Gr. τείρω, Lat. *terere* = bohren] I. *adv.* 1) consumed or rendered useless by wearing. Die Schuhe sind —, the shoes are worn out. 2) [from one end or side to the other] through. Ich bin — und — naß, I am wet through and through; es sticht ihn — und —, it pierces him through and through. *Fig.* Es wurde — und — ausgebessert, it underwent a thorough repair. 3) [when — comes at the end = hinüber] Er schwamm den Fluß —, he swam across the river. *Fig.* Den Tag — hält er sich versteckt, in the day time he keeps himself concealed; die ganze Nacht —, throughout the whole night; die Nacht — arbeiten, to sit up at work. V. —seyn.

II *prep.* 1) [from end to end, or from side to side, from one surface or limit to the opposite; noting passage in the midst of or among] through. Das Licht bricht — die Wolken, the light breaks through the clouds; der Schuß ging — die Hirnschale, the ball passed through his skull; — ein Dickicht laufen, to run through a thicket; — die Nase reden, to speak through the nose; — die Brille sehen, to see through the spectacles; — ein Gitter sehen, to look through a grate; — die Stadt gehen, to go through the town; — ein Thor gehen, to pass through a gate; — das Wasser schwimmen, to swim through the water; — ganz Irland, throughout Ireland; es ging — seine Hände, [*fig.*] it passed through his hands; es geht mir —s Herz, [*fig.*] it pierces my heart; Einem — die Finger sehen, [*fig.*] to overlook any one's faults, to pass by any one's faults indulgently. *Fig. a)* [= während] Der Kalender enthält die bestimmten Festtage — das ganze Jahr, the almanac contains the stated festivals for the whole year. *b)* [by means of, by the agency of, noting instrumentality] through. — Bücher, — Lektüre, through books; — die Sinne, through the senses; er starb — den Degen, he died by the sword; — die Post, by the post; — Geburt, by birth; Einige werden reicher — Geben, als Andere — Empfangen, some grow richer by giving than others by receiving; — Ihren Beistand, with your assistance; — Zufall, by chance; — gerechte Gesetze, by just laws; — ihn bin ich glücklich, through him I am happy. 2) [in some phrases for unter] Alles — einander mengen, to mix all confusely.

III. Durch as a prefix or inseparable particle in the composition of verbs, is sometimes separated from the verb or placed after it. When durch is not separated from the verb, the accent falls on the latter, and the particle ge is omitted in the past tense, as er hat viele Länder durchreiset [not durchgereiset]; ich wünschte Italien zu durchreisen [not durchzureisen] &c. The accent falls on durch when it is separated from the verb or placed after it; the particle ge in the past tense and zu in the infinitive mode is retained, but zu is placed between durch and the verb, as Er ist heute durchgereiset; ich bin gesonnen nur durchzureisen &c.

Durchächzen, *v. tr.* [ich durchächze, durchächzt, zu durchächzen] to pass groaning. Die Nacht —, to spend the night in groaning.

Durchackern, *v. tr.* 1) dúrchackern [ich ackere durch, durchgeackert, durchzuackern] *a)* to plow through. *b)* to plow deep enough. 2) durchackern. [ich durchackere, durchackert, zu durchackern] *a)* to plow thoroughly. *b)* *Fig.* *α)* to work through. *β)* to efface, to erase. *γ)* to correct, to amend.

Dúrchängsten, *v. tr.* and *r.* sich —, [ich durchängste, durchängstet, zu durchängsten] to put to extreme anguish, to torment. Sich —, to torture one's self.

Durcharbeiten, *v. tr.* and *r.* sich —, 1) dúrcharbeiten [ich arbeite durch, durchgearbeitet, durchzuarbeiten] *a)* to work thoroughly. Den Teig —, to knead or work the dough thoroughly. *Fig.* Einen —, to beat any one soundly. *b)* to make sore by working. *c)* Sich —, to pass through by pressing and urging forward, to squeeze through; sich durch das Gedränge mühsam —, to squeeze hard to get through the crowd; durch Winde und Wellen arbeitet er sich durch, through winds and waves he works his way; sich durch Schwierigkeiten —, to get through difficulties; sich durch Mühseligkeiten —, to go through hardships. 2) durchárbeiten [ich durcharbeite, durcharbeitet, zu durcharbeiten] to work through or with labour, to improve by successive operations, to finish with great diligence.

Durchāthmen, *v. tr.* [ich durchathme, durchathmet, zu durchathmen] 1) to fill with one's breath. Der Hauch Gottes durchathmet die Welt, the breath of God pervades the world; ein wohlwollender Sinn durchathmet das ganze Werk or athmet or weht aus dem ganzen Werke, a spirit of benevolence breathes through the whole work. 2) to diffuse, to spread, as emanations or effluvia. Der Pflanzen Gedüfte durchathmet würzig die Luft, odoriferous plants spread their fragrance.

Dúrchätzen, *v. tr.* [ich ätze durch, durchgeätzt, durchzuätzen] to corrode thoroughly.

Durchaus, [sometimes dúrchaus] *adv.* 1) in every part, from one extremity to the other, throughout. Der Boden besteht — aus Sand, the ground consists entirely of sand. 2) positively, absolutely. Weil Sie es — wollen, since you insist upon it; sie kann ihn — nicht leiden, she has a fixed aversion to him; — nicht, not in the least, by no means.

Dúrchbacken, *ir. v. intr.* [u. w. seyn] [ich backe durch, durchgebacken, durchzubacken] to bake thoroughly.

Durchbähen, *v. tr.* [ich bähe durch, ich durchbähe; durchgebähet, durchbähet; durchzubähen, zu durchbähen] 1) to foment thoroughly. 2) to toast [bread] thoroughly.

†Dúrchbalgen, *v. tr.* and *r.* [ich balge durch, durchgebalget, durchzubalgen] to beat soundly. Einen —, to beat any one soundly. Sich —, to fight one's way through.

Durchbálsamen, *v. tr.* [ich durchbalsame, durchbalsamet, zu durchbalsamen] to perfume thoroughly [a garden, a garment &c.].

Dúrchbauschen, *v. tr.* [ich bausche durch, durchgebauscht, durchzubauschen] 1) [in mining] V. Durchschlagen. 2) [in painting] to prick a design and rub it over with coal-dust.

Durchbēben, *v. tr.* [ich durchbebe, durchbebt, zu durchbeben] to shake, to agitate throughout.

Durchbeißen, *ir. v. tr.* and *r.* 1) dúrchbeißen [ich beiße durch, durchgebissen, durchzubeißen] to bite through. Der Hund hat mir den Finger durchgebissen, the dog has bit through my finger; das Aetzwasser wird es bald —, aqua fortis [nitrite acid] will soon eat through it; sich —, to force a way through any place by biting, to pass through. *Fig.* Sie beißt sich überall durch, she gets out everywhere with biting words. 2) durchbeißen [ich durchbeiße, durchbissen, zu durchbeißen] *a)* to bite through. Das Brod ist nicht zu durchbeißen, one cannot bite this bread through. *b)* to eat through and through.

Durchbeizen, *v. intr.* and *tr.* 1) dúrchbeizen [ich beize durch, durchgebeizt, durchzubeizen] *a)* to penetrate with a sharp or corroding substan[ce]. Das Scheidewasser hat schon durchgebeizt, a[qua] fortis has already eaten through. *b)* to steep most to solution, to macerate it. Eine Haut Lohe —, to tan a hide. 2) durchbeizen [u. w. ...] [ich durchbeize, durchbeizt, zu durchbeizen] to u[nder]go the action of a sharp and caustic substa[nce]. Das Leder ist noch nicht gehörig durchbeizt, leather is not yet tanned enough.

Durchbèllen, *v. tr.* [ich durchbelle, durchb[ellt], zu durchbellen] to fill with barking.

Durchbeten, *v. tr.* 1) dúrchbeten [ich [bete] durch, durchgebetet, durchzubeten] to pray from [be]ginning to end, to go through in praying. [Den] Rosenkranz —, to rehearse the rosary. 2) du[rch]bēten [ich durchbete, durchbetet, zu durchbete[n]] [to] spend in prayers. Er hat die ganze Nacht d[urch]betet, he spent the whole night in prayer.

Durchbetteln, I. *v. r.* sich dúrchbet[teln] [ich bettle mich durch, durchgebettelt, sich du[rchzubet]teln] to get one's livelihood by begging, t[...] II. *v. tr.* durchbétteln [ich durchbettele, [durch]bettelt, zu durchbetteln] to wander over as a [men]dicant. Er durchbettelt die ganze Gege[nd, he] begs over the whole country.

Dúrchbeuteln, *v. tr.* [ich beutele durch, gebeutelt, durchzubeuteln] [in mills] to bolt [...]

Dúrchbewegen, *v. tr.* and *r.* sich beweg[e ...] durchbewegt, durchzubewegen] 1) to move [...] a place. 2) to move through and throu[gh].

Dúrchbildern, *v. tr.* [ich bildere durch, bildere; durchgebildert, durchbildert; [...]bern, zu durchbildern] to turn over all the [...] or pictures [in a book].

Durchblasen, *ir. v. tr.* 1) dúrchbl[asen] [ich blase durch, durchgeblasen, durchzublasen] [*a)* to] blow through an opening. *b)* to blow fro[m be]ginning to end. Ein Stück —, to blow a [...] through; sich ein Stück —, to exercise one' [...] in blowing a tune. *c)* to blow through, to [...] flate. 2) durchblāsen [ich durchblase, [...]sen, zu durchblasen] to blow through, to [...] Das Durchblasen, perflation.

Durchblättern, *v. tr.* 1) dúrchblät[tern] [ich blättere durch, durchgeblättert, durchzublä[ttern] ...

to turn over every leaf of a book. Bücher —, to turn over books. *Fig.* Ich habe das Buch durchgeblättert, I ran over the book. 2) durchblättern [ich durchblättere, durchblättert, zu durchblättern] to pass the eye over [a book] hastily.

Durchbläuen, *v. tr.* 1) †dúrchbläuen [ich bläue durch, durchgebläuet, durchzubläuen] to beat soundly. 2) durchbläuen [ich durchbläue, durchbläuet, zu durchbläuen] to blue thoroughly.

Dúrchblick, *m.* [-es, *pl.* -e] a look through any thing. Ein — durch einen Wald &c., a vista through a wood. *Fig.* penetration.

Durchblicken, I. *v. intr.* dúrchblicken [ich blicke durch, durchgeblickt, durchzublicken] to look through an opening, to peep through. Die Sonne blickt zuweilen durch, sometimes the sun breaks through the clouds. *Fig.* In seinem Betragen blickt Haß und Neid durch, his behaviour betrays hatred and envy; überall blickt des Verfassers Absicht durch, seinen Gegner herunterzusetzen, we see everywhere the author's aim of slandering his adversary. II. *v. tr.* durchblicken [ich durchblicke, durchblickt, zu durchblicken] to look through. *Fig.* Einen —, to look through any one; er durchblickt seine verrätherischen Plane, he penetrates his treacherous designs.

Durchblinken, I. *v. intr.* dúrchblinken [ich blinke durch, durchgeblinkt, durchzublinken] to gleam or shine through. II. *v. tr.* durchblinken [ich durchblinke, durchblinkt, zu durchblinken] to penetrate or fill with gleam or brightness.

Durchblitzen, I. *v. intr.* dúrchblitzen [ich blitze durch, durchgeblitzt, durchzublitzen] to lighten or flash through. Ihre funkelnden Augen blitzen durch den Schleier durch, her piercing eyes gleam through the vail. II. *v. tr.* durchblitzen [ich durchblitze, durchblitzt, zu durchblitzen] to cross lightning or flashing. Es durchblitzt die schwarzen Wolken, it flashes through the black clouds.

Durchbohren, *v. tr.* and *r.* 1) dúrchbohren [ich bohre durch, durchgebohrt, durchzubohren] to bore through, to perforate. Ein Brett —, to bore a board through; sich —, to bore through, as a worm. 2) durchbóhren [ich durchbohre, durchbohrt, zu durchbohren] to pierce with a pointed instrument; *it.* to force a way into, to pierce. Den Boden eines Gefäßes —, to perforate the bottom of a vessel; Einen mit dem Degen —, to pierce any one with a sword; Einem die Hirnschale —, to trepan any one; das Durchbohren, perforation; ein Schiff —, to sink a vessel; ein Schuß durchbohrte das Schiff, a shot pierced the ship. *Fig.* Einen mit Blicken —, to pierce any one with a look, to look any one through; es durchbohrt mir das Herz, that pierces my heart.

Durchbraten, *ir.* I. *v. intr.* [u. w. seyn] dúrchbraten [ich brate durch, durchgebraten, durchzubraten] to be roasted thoroughly. II. *v. tr.* durchbráten [ich durchbrate, durchbraten, zu durchbraten] to roast. Von der brennenden Sonne —, scorched with the burning sun.

Durchbrausen, I. *v. intr.* dúrchbrausen [ich brause durch, durchgebrauset, durchzubrausen] to pass through roaring. Der Wind brauset zwischen den Bergen durch, the wind roars through the hills. II. *v. tr.* durchbraúsen [ich durchbrause, durchbrauset, zu durchbrausen] to penetrate roaring.

Durchbrechen, *ir.* I. *v. tr.* 1) dúrchbrechen [ich breche durch, durchgebrochen, durchzubrechen] *a)* to rend apart, to break. Einen Stock —, to break a stick. *b)* to open [a passage] by breaking. Eine Mauer —, to make a breach in a wall; eine Thür — lassen, to get a door made in a wall; die Zähne fangen bei diesem Kinde an durchzubrechen, this child begins to cut its teeth. 2) durchbréchen [ich durchbreche, durchbrochen, zu durchbrechen] *a)* to work in eyelet-holes, to pierce with small holes. Durchbrochene Arbeit, pinking; durchbrochene Drahtfaden-Arbeit, filigree, filigrane. *b)* to make way with violence or suddenness. Der Fluß durchbrach die Dämme, the river forced its way through the dikes. II. *v. intr.* [u. w. seyn] to make way with violence or suddenness, to break through. Sie versuchten, auf dem rechten Flügel des Feindes durchzubrechen, they made an effort to break through the right wing of the enemy; das Wasser brach durch den Damm, the water forced its way or burst through the dike; der Gefangene brach durch, the prisoner broke out; das Wild ist durchgebrochen, the game broke through; die Knospen brechen durch, the buds open. III. *v. r.* sich —, to break loose. Die Gefangenen haben sich in vergangener Nacht durchgebrochen, the prisoners escaped last night by breaking through the wall.

Durchbrennen, *ir.* I. *v. intr.* dúrchbrennen [ich brenne durch, durchgebrannt, durchzubrennen] to burn through and through. II. *v. tr.* durchbrénnen [ich durchbrenne, durchbrannt, zu durchbrennen] 1) to burn through. 2) to fill with fire. *Fig.* Eine heftige Liebe durchbrannte sein Herz, a vehement love consumed his heart.

Durchbringen, *ir.* I. dúrchbringen [ich bringe durch, durchgebracht, durchzubringen] 1) *v. tr.* *a)* to bring, to carry, to convey, to lead through a place. Man hat heute Gefangene hier durchgebracht, to-day prisoners were transported through this place. *b)* to get through with difficulty. Verbotene Waaren —, to run prohibited goods; er konnte den Arm nicht — [in familiar or common language, durchbekommen, durchkriegen] he could not get his arm through [a hole]. *Fig.* Pflanzen —, to winter plants; das Vieh bringt man mit gutem Futter gut durch, cattle winter well on good fodder. *c)* *Fig.* to spend lavishly or profusely, to squander. Sein Vermögen —, to dissipate one's fortune; ein Besitzthum —, to run through or to sink an estate. 2) *v. r.* sich —, to get the means of living. Die Frau bringt sich mit Spinnen durch, the woman gets her livelihood by spinning; sich ehrlich —, to get an honest living, to get honestly through the world. II. durchbringen [ich durchbringe, durchbracht, zu durchbringen] *v. tr.* Weinend durchbrachte sie die Nächte, she passed the nights in tears.

Dúrchbringer, *m.* [-s, *pl.* -] a prodigal, a spendthrift.

Dúrchbröckeln, *v. intr.* [u. w. seyn] [ich bröckele durch, durchgebröckelt, durchzubröckeln] to crumble through.

Dúrchbruch, *m.* [-es, *pl.* -brüche] 1) the act of breaking through, or state of being broken through. Wenn die Zähne am — e sind, when the teeth are ready to cut; der — der Blattern, the eruption of small pox; der — der Glieder des Feindes, the breaking through the ranks of the enemy; der — eines Flusses, the overflowing of a river. [with certain bigots] the beginning of one's conversion. *[in joke] Es ist bei ihm zum — gekommen, he has begun to reform. 2) [with sempstresses] pinking. 3) [in familiar or common language] diarrhoea. 4) [a plant] V. Durchwachs.

Durchbruchs-meisel, *m.* [with braziers and tinmen] a chisel used for piercing with small holes. —nadel, *f.* [with sempstresses] pinking-pin. —stich, *m.* [with sempstresses] a sort of stitch used in pinking.

Dúrchbrühen, *v. tr.* [ich brühe durch, durchgebrüht, durchzubrühen] to scald through.

Durchbrüllen, *v. tr.* 1) dúrchbrüllen [ich brülle durch, durchgebrüllt, durchzubrüllen] to sing through in a roaring manner. 2) durchbrǘllen [ich durchbrülle, durchbrüllt, zu durchbrüllen] to fill with roaring.

Durchbrummen, *v. tr.* 1) dúrchbrummen [ich brumme durch, durchgebrummt, durchzubrummen] to hum through. Ein Stückchen —, to hum a tune through. 2) durchbrúmmen [ich durchbrumme, durchbrummt, zu durchbrummen] to fill with roaring.

Durchbrüten, *v. tr.* 1) dúrchbrüten [ich brüte durch, durchgebrütet, durchzubrüten] to brood through or thoroughly. Die Henne hat die Eier noch nicht völlig durchgebrütet, the hen has not yet hatched the eggs. 2) durchbrǘten [ich durchbrüte, durchbrütet, zu durchbrüten] *Fig.* to spend in brooding. Er durchbrütet die Nächte, he spends the nights in brooding.

Dúrchbuchstabiren, *v. tr.* to spell through.

Dúrchbürsten, *v. tr.* [ich bürste durch, durchgebürstet, durchzubürsten] 1) to brush thoroughly, to clean by brushing. 2) to make sore by brushing. *Fig.* †Einen —, to reprimand any one severely.

Durchdácht, *past part.* of Durchdenken.

Durchdämmern, I. *v. intr.* [u. w. seyn] dúrchdämmern [ich dämmere durch, durchgedämmert, durchzudämmern] to dawn through. II. *v. tr.* durchdä́mmern [ich durchdämmere, durchdämmert, zu durchdämmern] to illuminate by a dawning light. *Fig.* [student's cant] to saunter through. Jeden Abend kannst du sie die Straßen — sehen, every evening you may see them lounging through the streets.

Durchdampfen, I. *v. intr.* dúrchdampfen [ich dampfe durch, durchgedampft, durchzudampfen] to smoke through. Das ist die Oeffnung, wo es durchdampft, that is the aperture through which the smoke pervades. II. *v. tr.* durchdámpfen [ich durchdampfe, durchdampft, zu durchdampfen] to pervade as smoke, to fill with smoke.

Dúrchdauern, *v. intr.* to last. Den Winter —, to winter.

Durchdenken, *ir. v. tr.* 1) dúrchdenken [ich denke durch, durchgedacht, durchzudenken] to muse on, to meditate over and over again. Sie — die Gefahr des Morgens, they ruminate the morning's danger. 2) durchdénken [ich durchdenke, durchdacht, zu durchdenken] to think on or upon, to revolve in the mind, to ponder. Seinen Stoff —, to digest one's matter well; ein wohl durchdachter Plan, a well meditated scheme; durchdenke wohl diese Begriffe, turn these ideas about in your mind.

Dúrchdienen, *v. tr.* [ich diene durch, durchgedient, durchzudienen] to perform services successively from beginning to end. Er hat alle Grade durchgedient, he has served through every grade.

Durchdólchen, *v. tr.* [ich durchdolche, durchdolcht, zu durchdolchen] to stab with a dagger. Er wurde durchdolcht, he was stabbed by a dagger.

Durchdónnern, *v. tr.* [ich durchdonnere, durchdonnert, zu durchdonnern] 1) to fill with a thundering noise. Das Geschütz durchdonnerte Wald und Flur, the artillery thundered through woods and plains. *Fig.* Diese Nachricht durchdonnerte ihn, this news struck him with alarm. 2) to pass thundering or to open thundering.

Dúrchdörren, *v. tr.* [ich dörre durch or ich durchdörre, durchgedörrt, durchzudörren] to dry thoroughly.

Dúrchdrängen, *v. tr.* and *r.* [ich dränge durch, durchgedrängt, durchzudrängen] to pass through by pressing and urging forward. Sich —, to bore through the crowd; er drängte sich durch, he squeezed through.

Durchdreschen, *ir.* I. *v. intr.* dúrchdreschen [ich dresche durch, durchgedroschen, durchzudreschen] to thrash successively or from beginning to end. II. *v. tr.* 1) to break by thrashing.

Fig. †Einen —, to beat any one soundly. 2) durchdréschen [ich durchdresche, durchdroschen, zu durchdreschen] to thrash thoroughly.

Durchdringen, *ir.* I. *v. intr.* [u. w. seyn] dúrchdringen [ich dringe durch, durchgedrungen, durchzudringen] to pass by pressing, to urge one's way; *it.* to force a way into a thing. Er konnte durch die Menschenmenge kaum —, he could hardly get through the crowd; der Regen ist durch meinen Rock durchgedrungen, the rain has soaked through my coat; ein Regen, der durchdringt, a soaking rain; seine Stimme kann nicht —, his voice is not piercing enough, he cannot make his voice heard; *die Schläge werden bei ihm schon —, he shall feel the blows yet. *Fig.* Er drang mit seinem Plane durch, he brought his design about, he brought it to the desired issue; er dringt bestimmt noch durch, he will certainly succeed or gain his object. II. *v. tr.* durchdríngen [ich durchdringe, durchdrungen, zu durchdringen] to urge one's way through. Eine Truppencolonne durchdrang das Hauptcorps des Feindes, a column of troops pierced the main body of the enemy; ein —der Ton, a piercing sound; eine —de Stimme, a piercing or shrill voice; eine —de Kälte, a sharp, biting, nipping or pinching cold. *Fig.* Ihre Thränen werden ein Marmorherz —, her tears will pierce a marble-heart; deine Worte — mein Herz, thy words shoot through my heart; dein Aechzen durchdrang des nie gezähmten Bären Brust, thy groans did penetrate the breast of ever angry bears; dessen Geheimnisse kein Auge — kann, whose secrets are pervious to no eye; eine —de Rede, a penetrating speech; *it.* a searching discourse; ein —der Schmerz, a keen, severe, pungent or sharp pain; ein —der Verstand, an acute, discerning or penetrating mind; ein —der Geist, a penetrant spirit.

Dúrchdringlich, *adj.* and *adv.* [that may be penetrated, entered or pierced by another body] penetrable. Glas ist — für das Licht, glass is permeable or pervious to light.

Dúrchdringlichkeit, *f.* penetrability, permeability, perviousness.

Dúrchdrücken, *v. tr.* and *r.* [ich drücke durch, durchgedrückt, durchzudrücken] 1) to press through. Den Saft —, to press or squeeze the juice through. *Fig.* †Sich —, to resort to expedients for a livelihood. 2) to break or hurt by pressing. Der Sattel hat das Pferd durchgedrückt, the saddle has galled the back of the horse.

Durchduften, I. *v. intr.* dúrchduften [ich dufte durch, durchgeduftet, durchzuduften] to smell through. II. *v. tr.* durchdúften [ich durchdufte, durchduftet, zu durchduften] to fill with odour, to scent. Diese Blumen — die ganze Stube, these flowers perfume the whole room.

Durchdüften, *v. tr.* [ich durchdüfte, durchdüftet, zu durchdüften] [to fill or impregnate with a grateful odour] to perfume. Ein Kleid —, to perfume a garment.

Dúrchdunsten, *v. tr.* [ich dunste durch, durchgedunstet, durchzudunsten] to be exhaled or emitted as vapour.

Durchdünsten, *v. tr.* [ich durchdünste, durchdünstet, zu durchdünsten] to fill with odour or vapour. Die Blumen — das Zimmer, the flowers scent the room.

Dúrchdürfen, *v. intr.* [ich darf durch, durchgedurft, durchzudürfen] to be permitted to pass.

Durcheilen, I. *v. intr.* [u. w. seyn] dúrcheilen [ich eile durch, durchgeeilt, durchzueilen] to hasten through, to hurry through. II. *v. tr.* durcheílen [ich durcheile, durcheilt, zu durcheilen] to hasten through a place. *Fig.* Ein Buch —, to run over, to skim, to hurry through a book.

Dúrcheimern, *v. intr.* [u. w. seyn] [ich eimere durch, durchgeeimert, durchzueimern] [with charcoal-burners] to burn through.

Dúrcheinander, **Durcheinánder**, *adv.* in confusion, pell-mell.

Durcheitern, *v. intr.* 1) dúrcheitern [ich eitere durch, durchgeeitert, durchzueitern] to fester or suppurate through and through. 2) durcheítern [ich durcheitere, durcheitert, durchzueitern] to fester or suppurate through.

Durchfahren, *ir.* I. dúrchfahren [ich fahre durch, durchgefahren, durchzufahren] 1) *v. intr.* [u. w. seyn] *a*) to pass or move quickly and violently through. Ein Blitz fuhr durch und tödtete ihn, a flash of lightning passed through and killed him; schnell unter einer Brücke —, to shoot a bridge. *b*) to pass in a carriage or to drive through. *Fig.* *Er will überall mit dem Kopfe —, he wishes to carry any thing by main force. 2) *v. tr.* to wear through by driving. Einen Weg —, to cut up a road, by driving much upon it. II. durchfáhren [ich durchfahre, durchfahren, zu durchfahren] *v. tr.* to move quickly through a place. *Fig.* Schauer durchfuhr ihm den Körper, a shivering fit seized his body.

Dúrchfahrt, *f.* [*pl.* -en] 1) the act of driving through a place. Ich sah ihn auf seiner —, I saw him on his passage. 2) a place where men may pass in a carriage, passage, gate-way, thoroughfare. Die — in einem Hause, the gate of a house; die Dienstbarkeit der —, [in law] an obligation to let others pass through one's gate or court-yard.

Durchfahrtszoll, *m.* transit-duty.

Dúrchfall, *m.* [-es, *pl.* -fälle] [a disease in men and animals] flux from the bowels, a looseness, lax, diarrhoea. Den — haben, to purge.

Dúrchfallen, *ir.* [ich falle durch, durchgefallen, durchzufallen] I. *v. intr.* [u. w. seyn] to fall through an aperture. *Fig.* Der Bewerber wird in [bei] der Wahl —, the candidate will not run [he will not be supported by votes]; er ist bei der Wahl durchgefallen, the choice went against him, he was not successful in his canvass; beim Ballotiren —, to be blackballed; in der Lotterie —, to get a blank in a lottery; das Stück fiel durch, the piece was damned. II. *v. r.* sich —, to hurt one's self by falling.

Durchfálten, *v. tr.* [ich durchfalte, durchfaltet, zu durchfalten] to fold throughout.

Dúrchfäule, *f.* [in farriery] a sorrance at the pastern of horses.

Dúrchfaulen, [ich faule durch, durchgefaulet, durchzufaulen] *v. intr* [u. w. seyn] to rot through. Der Huf des Pferdes ist durchgefaulet, the hoof of the horse is rotten through.

Dúrchfechten, *ir.* [ich fechte durch, durchgefochten, durchzufechten] I. *v. tr.* to defend, to vindicate by words or arguments. Seine Meinung —, to maintain one's opinion. II. *v. r.* sich —, to fight one's way through; *fig.* to shift; [journeymens' cant] to get through by begging, to beg one's way through. Er hat sich durch ganz Frankreich durchgefochten, he begged his way through all France.

Durchfegen, *v. tr.* I. dúrchfegen [ich fege durch, durchgefegt, durchzufegen] 1) to sweep through an aperture. 2) to sweep thoroughly. 3) *Fig.* *a*) to check by reproof, to rebuke. *b*) to cudgel. II. durchfégen [ich durchfege, durchfegt, zu durchfegen] to sweep over and over.

Durchfeilen, *v. tr.* 1) dúrchfeilen [ich feile durch, durchgefeilet, durchzufeilen] to file through. Einen Draht —, to file a wire through. 2) durchfeilen [ich durchfeile, durchfeilt, zu durchfeilen] to file thoroughly.

Durchfeuchten, I. *v. intr.* dúrchfeuchten [ich feuchte durch, durchgefeuchtet, durchzufeuchten] to moisten through. II. *v. tr.* durchfeúchten [ich durchfeuchte, durchfeuchtet, zu durchfeuchten] to wet thoroughly, to drench, to soak.

Durchfeuern, *v. tr.* 1) dúrchfeuern [ich feuere durch, durchgefeuert, durchzufeuern] *a*) to heat thoroughly. *b*) to fire or shoot through. 2) durchfeúern [ich durchfeuere, durchfeuert, zu durchfeuern] to set on fire through and through, to fire thoroughly.

†**Durchfiedeln**, *v. tr.* 1) Dúrchfiedeln [ich fiedele durch, durchgefiedelt, durchzufiedeln] to scrape [a tune] through. 2) durchfiedeln [ich durchfiedele, durchfiedelt, zu durchfiedeln] *a*) to go through fiddling. *b*) to spend [the night &c.] in fiddling.

Durchfingern, *v. tr.* [ich durchfingere, durchfingert, zu durchfingern] to finger through.

Durchfischen, *v. tr.* [ich durchfische, durchfischt, zu durchfischen] to fish thoroughly.

Durchflammen, I. *v. intr.* dúrchflammen [ich flamme durch, durchgeflammt, durchzuflammen] to flame through an aperture. II. *v. tr.* durchflámmen [ich durchflamme, durchflammt, zu durchflammen] *Fig.* to fire, to animate.

Durchflattern, I. *v. intr.* [u. w. seyn] dúrchflattern [ich flattere durch, durchgeflattert, durchzuflattern] to flutter through a place or aperture. II. *v. tr.* durchflättern [ich durchflattere, durchflattert, zu durchflattern] to pass fluttering.

Durchflechten, *ir. v. tr.* [ich durchflecht, durchflochten, zu durchflechten] to plait through, to interweave, to entwine. Haare mit Blumen durchflochten, hair and flowers interwoven. *Fig.* Unser Leben ist mit Rosen und Dornen durchflochten, our life is interwoven with roses as well as thorns, is mixed up with good and bad.

Durchfliegen, *ir.* I. *v. intr.* [u. w. seyn] dúrchfliegen [ich fliege durch, durchgeflogen, durchzufliegen] to fly through. Da ist der Vogel durchgeflogen, there the bird flew through. *Fi*[...] Er reiset so schnell, daß er durch die Länder [...] durchfliegt, he travels so fast, that he only [...] through countries. II. *v. tr.* durchfliegen [...] durchfliege, durchflogen, zu durchfliegen] to [...] with velocity or celerity by the aid of [...] through a place or space. Der Adler durchflie[...] die Luft, the eagle flies through the air. *F*[...] Er durchfliegt das Buch, he runs over, he [...] the book.

Durchfliehen, *ir.* I. *v. intr.* [u. w. [...] dúrchfliehen [ich fliehe durch, durchgeflo[...] durchzufliehen] to flee or fly or run through. [...] *v. tr.* durchfliehen [ich durchfliehe, [...] hen, zu durchfliehen] to hasten through fleeing.

Durchfließen, *ir.* I. *v. intr.* [u. w. seyn] dúr[...] fließen [ich fließe durch, durchgeflossen, [...] fließen] to flow through. Hier fließt das [...] ser durch, there the water flows through. II. [...] *tr.* durchfließen, [ich durchfließe, [...] zu durchfließen] to flow through. Der Bach [...] fließt das Thal, the brook flows through [...] valley.

Durchflimmern, I. *v. intr.* dúrchfli[...] mern [ich flimmere durch, durchgeflimmert, [...] zuflimmern] to glitter through. II. *v. tr.* dur[...] flimmern [ich durchflimmere, durchflimmert, [...] durchflimmern] to fill with feeble scattered [...] of light, with a glimmering light.

Dúrchflößen, *v. tr.* [ich flöße durch, dur[...] flößet, durchzuflößen] to float through. Das [...] unter der Brücke —, to float the wood throu[...] the arches of a bridge.

Dúrchflucht, *f.* the flight through a pla[...] or country.

Dúrchflüchten, *v. intr.* [u. w. seyn] [ich flüchte durch, durchgeflüchtet, durchzuflüchten] to run or flee through. Das —, running or fleeing through a place or country.

Dúrchflug, *m.* [-es] a passing through a place or country by the help of wings, a flying through. *Fig.* a speedy journey, a short visit on a journey.

Dúrchfluß, *m.* [-sses, *pl.* -flüsse] a flowing through.

Durchflüstern, *v. tr.* [ich durchflüstere, durchflüstert, zu durchflüstern] to fill with whispering.

Durchfluten, I. *v. intr.* dúrchfluten [ich flute durch, durchgeflutet, durchzufluten] to flow through. II. *v. tr.* durchflúten [ich durchflute, durchflutet, zu durchfluten] to flow rapidly through, to fill with a flood.

Durchforschen, *v. tr.* 1) dúrchforschen [ich forsche durch, durchgeforscht, durchzuforschen] to search through. 2) durchfórschen [ich durchforsche, durchforscht, zu durchforschen] to examine thoroughly, to inquire into with care and accuracy. Die Ursachen der Naturereignisse —, to investigate the causes of natural phenomena.

Durchfragen, *v. tr.* 1) dúrchfragen [ich frage durch, durchgefragt, durchzufragen] to interrogate successively. Er fragte sie Alle durch, he interrogated them all one after the other. 2) durchfrágen [ich durchfrage, durchfragt, zu durchfragen] to wander over asking or interrogating, to ask every where.

Durchfressen, *ir.* I. dúrchfressen [ich fresse durch, durchgefressen, durchzufressen] 1) *v. tr.* and *intr.* to bite, eat or gnaw through. Die Mäuse haben das Leder durchgefressen, the mice have gnawed the leather through; Bretter, welche die Würmer durchgefressen haben, worm-eaten boards; das Scheidewasser hat an mehreren Stellen durchgefressen, the aqua fortis has eaten through in several places. 2) *v. r.* sich —, to live by spunging upon others. II. durchfréssen [ich durchfresse, durchfressen, zu durchfressen] *v. tr.* to eat through. Würmer — die Gedärme, worms perforate the guts; ein Geschwür frißt ihm das Bein durch, an ulcer eats through his leg; Aetzwasser durchfrißt Kupfer, nitric acid corrodes copper.

Durchfrieren, *ir. v. intr.* dúrchfrieren [ich friere durch, durchgefroren, durchzufrieren] to be penetrated by frost, to freeze throughout. 2. durchfríeren [ich durchfriere, durchfroren, zu durchfrieren] to be penetrated by frost, to freeze throughout, to freeze over and over. Ich bin ganz durchfroren, or ich bin ganz durchgefroren, I am chilled all over, I shiver with cold; meine Füße sind ganz durchgefroren, my feet are benumbed by cold.

Durchfröhnen, *v. tr.* [ich durchfröhne, durchfröhnt, zu durchfröhnen] to spend [a day, a week &c.] in performing services due to the lord of the manor.

Dúrchfuchteln, *v. tr.* [ich fuchtele durch, durchgefuchtelt, durchzufuchteln] 1) to cudgel, to belabour. 2) to cudgel all successively or one after the other.

Durchfühlen, I. dúrchfühlen [ich fühle durch, durchgefühlet, durchzufühlen] 1) *v. tr.* to feel through. 2) *v. r.* sich —, *a*) to feel one's way through a thing. *b*) to get out by feeling. II. durchfǘhlen [ich durchfühle, durchfühlt, zu durchfühlen] *v. tr.* to discern, to discriminate by feeling.

Dúrchfuhre, *f.* [*pl.* -n] the conveyance or transport of goods &c. through a place or country, transit.

Durchfuhr-handel, *m.* V. Durchgangshandel. —zoll, *m.* transit-duty.

Dúrchführen, *v. tr.* [ich führe durch, durchgeführt, durchzuführen] to convey, carry, bear or transport through. Durchgeführt, said of iron-plates drawn through melted tin. *Fig.* Er hatte seine Plane sehr gut durchgeführt, he had carried his designs very well through; ein Unternehmen —, to go through an undertaking.

Durchfunkeln, I. *v. intr.* dúrchfunkeln [ich funkele durch, durchgefunkelt, durchzufunkeln] to shine through. II. *v. tr.* durchfúnkeln [ich durchfunkele, durchfunkelt, zu durchfunkeln] Der Stern durchfunkelt die dichte Finsterniß, the star glimmers through the dense obscurity.

Durchfúrchen, *v. tr.* [ich durchfurche, durchfurcht, zu durchfurchen] to furnish or mark with furrows. *Poet.* to furrow, to intrench. Seine durchfurchte Stirn, his furrowed brow.

Durchfúttern, *v. tr.* [ich durchfuttere, durchfuttert, zu durchfuttern] to line throughout. Ein Kleid mit Seide —, to line a garment throughout with silk.

Dúrchfüttern, *v. tr.* [ich füttere durch, durchgefüttert, durchzufüttern] 1) to feed during the winter. Vieh —, to winter cattle. 2) to feed all successively or one after another. 3) to feed thoroughly, to feed sufficiently.

Durchgaffen, *v. intr.* 1) dúrchgaffen [ich gaffe durch, durchgegafft, durchzugaffen] to gape through. 2) durchgáffen [ich durchgaffe, durchgafft, zu durchgaffen] Die ganze Stadt —, to walk gaping and staring over the whole town.

Durchgähnen, *v. tr.* [ich durchgähne, durchgähnt, zu durchgähnen] to pass or spend yawning. Er durchgähnte or gähnte durch das ganze Stück, he yawned through the whole play.

Dúrchgähren, *ir. v. intr.* [u. w. seyn] [ich gähre durch, durchgegohren, durchzugähren] 1) to ferment thoroughly. 2) V. Durcheimern.

Durchgällen, *v. tr.* [ich durchgälle, durchgällt, zu durchgällen] to fill with gall, to embitter.

Dúrchgang, *m.* [-es, *pl.* -gänge] 1) [a passing over or through] passage. Der — von Waaren durch ein Land, the transit of goods through a country; gestattet für dieses Unternehmen ungestörten — durch eure Besitzungen, give quiet pass through your dominions for this enterprize; der — der Venus durch die Sonne, the transit of Venus over the sun's disk. 2) [a place where men or things may pass, a way through] passage, thorough-fare. Ein enger —, a narrow passage, an alley; ein — unter einem Berge, a passage or an excavation under a mountain; Brunel's großartiges Werk, der — unter der Themse in London, Mr. Brunel's grand work, the Thames-tunnel in London; die Durchgänge auf der Simplonstraße, the galleries on the Simplon-road; dieses Haus hat einen —, this house is a thorough-fare.

Durchgangs-gerechtigkeit, *f.* the right a person has to pass through another's house or grounds. —gut, *n.* goods that pass through a country, transit-goods. —handel, *m.* the trade with transit-goods. —instrument, *n.* [in astronomy] transit-instrument. —waare, *f.* V. —gut. —zoll, *m.* transit-duty.

Dúrchgangbar, *adj.* and *adv.* passable.

Dúrchgänger, *m.* [-s, *pl.* -] V. Ausreißer 2.

Dúrchgängig, I. *adj.* 1) having a way through. Ein —es Haus, [rather unusual] a house that is a thorough-fare. 2) general, universal. Die —e Meinung ist, daß &c., the universal opinion is, that &c. II. *adv.* universally, generally. Es ist — Sitte, it is prevailing custom; es herrscht — die Meinung, 'tis the general opinion; eine — herrschende Krankheit, a popular disease, an epidemic sickness, an epidemic.

Dúrchgänglich, *adj.* and *adv.* yielding a passage, passable, permeable.

Dúrchgäten, *v. tr.* [ich gäte durch, durchgegätet, durchzugäten] to weed throughout.

Dúrchgebrauchen, *v. tr.* [ich gebrauche durch, durchgebraucht, durchzugebrauchen] to make use of all successively or to use something throughout, to the end, to finish the use of any thing.

Durchgehen, *ir.* I. dúrchgehen [ich gehe durch, durchgegangen, durchzugehen] 1) *v. intr.* [u. w. seyn] *a*) to go through, to walk through. Das Wasser ist dort so seicht, daß man — kann, the water is there so shallow, that one may wade through; der Schuß ging durch das Schiff durch, the shot pierced the ship; die Waaren gehen hier durch, the goods pass here; wo eine Kugel nicht — würde, where a bullet would not pierce. *Fig.* α) to pass. Ist der Gesetzvorschlag durchgegangen? is the bill past? β) to run away. Er ist mit dem Gelde durchgegangen, he ran away with the money; dieses Pferd wird mit Ihnen —, that horse will run away with you. 2) *v. tr.* to go from one side to the other, to go through. Einen Wald —, to walk over a wood. *Fig.* α) to go over, to read, to peruse. Ein Buch flüchtig —, to pass the eye over a book hastily, to run over it. β) to view or review, to examine. Eine Rechnung —, to go over an account; ein Bücherverzeichniß —, to look over a catalogue of books; die Probebogen eines Buches —, to inspect the proof-sheets of a book. γ) to wear out by walking. Sich die Füße —, to walk one's feet sore; sich die Schuhe —, to wear out one's shoes. II. durchgéhen [ich durchgehe, durchgangen, zu durchgehen] *v. tr.* to go or walk through. Er durchgeht die Stadt, he walks over the town. *Fig.* to go over, to think over, to proceed or pass in mental operation. Durchgehe die gegenwärtigen und die vergangenen Zeiten, look over the present and the former times.

Dúrchgehends, *adv.* generally, universally. V. Durchgängig, II.

Durchgeigen, I. *v. tr.* 1) dúrchgeigen [ich geige durch, durchgegeigt, durchzugeigen] *a*) to perform on the fiddle from beginning to end. Ein Stück —, to fiddle a tune through. *b*) to exercise on the fiddle. *Fig.* †Einen —, to reprimand any one severely. 2) durchgéigen [ich durchgeige, durchgeigt, zu durchgeigen] *a*) to fiddle through. *b*) to spend fiddling. *c*) to walk over fiddling. II. *v. r.* sich —, to sustain one's self by fiddling, to get through by fiddling.

Dúrchgeißeln, *v. tr.* [ich geißele durch, durchgegeißelt, durchzugeißeln] to scourge thoroughly.

Dúrchgeleiten, *v. tr.* [ich geleite durch, durchgeleitet, durchzugeleiten] to accompany, or to escort through.

Dúrchgerben, *v. tr.* [ich gerbe durch, durchgegerbt, durchzugerben] to tan thoroughly. *Fig.* †Einen —, to beat any one soundly, to tan any one's hide.

Dúrchgießen, *ir. v. tr.* [ich gieße durch, durchgegossen, durchzugießen] to pour through. Bier oder Wein —, to pour beer, or wine through; Wasser durch einen Seiher —, to filter water.

Durchglänzen, I. *v. intr.* dúrchglänzen [ich glänze durch, durchgeglänzt, durchzuglänzen] to glisten or shine through. Hie und da glänzte ein Sternlein durch, here and there a little star glistened through. II. *v. tr.* durchglä́nzen [ich durchglänze, durchglänzt, zu durchglänzen] to fill with glitter.

Durchgleiten, *ir.* and *reg.* I. *v. intr.* [u. w. seyn] dúrchgleiten [ich gleite durch, durchgeglitten, durchzugleiten] to glide through. II. *v. tr.* durchgleiten [ich durchgleite, durchglitten, zu durchgleiten] to pass gliding, to glide through.

Dúrchglimmen, *ir. v. intr.* [ich glimme durch, durchgeglommen, durchzuglimmen] to glimmer through.

Dúrchglitschen, *v. intr.* [u. w. seyn] [ich glitsche durch, durchgeglitscht, durchzuglitschen] to slide through.

†**Dúrchglotzen**, *v. tr.* [ich glotze durch, durchgeglotzt, durchzuglotzen] to stare, to gloat through.

Durchglühen, I. dúrchglühen [ich glühe durch, durchgeglüht, durchzuglühen] 1) *v. intr.* to glow through. 2) *v. tr.* to heat so as to shine, to glow. Durchgeglühtes Eisen, red-hot iron. II. durchglühen [ich durchglühe, durchglüht, zu durchglühen] *v. tr.* to heat so as to shine, to heat through. *Fig.* to inflame. Von Zorn durchglüht, inflamed with anger.

Durchgraben, *ir.* I. dúrchgraben [ich grabe durch, durchgegraben, durchzugraben] 1) *v. tr.* *a*) [to open a passage through] to dig through. *b*) [to make an opening from one side to the other] to dig through. 2) *v. r.* sich —, to get a passage, to get free by digging. II. durchgráben [ich durchgrabe, durchgraben, zu durchgraben] to dig through. *Fig.* Das Herz —, to pierce the heart.

Durchgrämeln, *v. tr.* [ich durchgrämele, durchgrämelt, zu durchgrämeln] to pass or spend peevishly [the night &c.].

Durchgrämen, *v. tr.* [ich durchgräme, durchgrämt, zu durchgrämen] to pass or spend sorrowfully. Sein Leben —, to spend one's life sorrowfully.

Durchgrasen, *v. tr.* [ich durchgrase, durchgraset, zu durchgrasen] to walk over grazing.

Dúrchgreifen, *ir.* [ich greife durch, durchgegriffen, durchzugreifen] I. *v. intr.* to put the hand through an opening [in order to seize something]. *Fig.* to proceed without ceremony, to act decidedly, to use authority. Hier muß die Obrigkeit —, it requires energy in the magistrate. [Often used in the present part. durchgreifend]—de Maßregeln, effectual, or energetic measures. II. *v. tr.* to wear out by handling. Ein durchgegriffener Hut, a worn-out hat.

Dúrchgriff, *m.* [-es, *pl.* -e] a griping or grasping by putting the hand through an opening.

Durchgrübeln, *v. tr.* [ich durchgrübele, durchgrübelt, zu durchgrübeln] to meditate on earnestly or minutely, to muse on. Eine Sache —, to rake into a matter; die Natur der Dinge —, to dive into the nature of things. V. Ergrübeln.

Durchgründen, *v. tr.* [ich durchgründe, durchgründet, zu durchgründen] V. Ergründen.

Durchgucken, I. *v. intr.* dúrchgucken [ich gucke durch, durchgeguckt, durchzugucken] [in familiar or common lang. for Durchsehen, or Durchschauen] to look through, to peep through. II. *v. tr.* durchgúcken [ich durchgucke, durchguckt, zu durchgucken] to view thoroughly. Wir durchguckten alle Zimmer und Winkel, we inspected every room and corner.

Dúrchguß, *m.* [-sses, *pl.* -güsse] 1) a pouring through. 2) the place where any thing is poured through, a gutter, a drain. 3) a colander, a strainer.

Dúrchhaben, *ir. v. tr.* [ich habe durch, durchgehabt, durchzuhaben] to have done with. Ich habe das Buch durch, I have perused the book.

Dúrchhacken, *v. tr.* [ich hacke durch, durchgehackt, durchzuhacken] to hew through. Ein Stück Holz —, to hew a piece of wood through.

Dúrchhageln, *v. imp.* [es hagelt durch, durchgehagelt, durchzuhageln] to penetrate as hail. Es hat durch das Dach durchgehagelt, the hail has come through the roof.

Dúrchhaken, *v. tr.* [ich hake durch, durchgehakt, durchzuhaken] to hook through.

Dúrchhalftern, *v. r.* sich —, [ich halftere durch, durchgehalftert, durchzuhalftern] Sich mühsam —, to get through with labour and difficulty, to struggle through difficulties.

Durchhallen, I. *v. intr.* dúrchhallen [ich halle durch, durchgehallt, durchzuhallen] to penetrate as sound. II. *v. tr.* durchhállen [ich durchhalle, durchhallt, zu durchhallen] to fill with sound. Der Donner durchhallt Berg und Thal, thunder resounds through hill and valley.

Dúrchhämmern, *v. tr.* [ich hämmere durch, durchgehämmert, durchzuhämmern] 1) to get through an aperture by hammering. 2) to wear out by hammering.

Durchharken, *v. tr.* 1) dúrchharken [ich harke durch, durchgeharkt, durchzuharken] *a*) to rake through. *b*) to rake thoroughly. Ein Gartenbeet gut —, to rake well a bed in a garden. *c*) to rake successively or from beginning to end. 2) durchhárken [ich durchharke, durchharkt, zu durchharken] to rake thoroughly.

Durchhärmen, *v. tr.* to spend or pass grieving [used only in the past part. durchhärmt]. Eine durchhärmte Nacht, a night spent in grieving.

Durchharren, *v. tr.* [ich durchharre, durchharrt, zu durchharren] to spend or pass waiting.

Durchhärten, *v. tr.* dúrchhärten [ich härte durch, durchgehärtet, durchzuhärten]; *it.* durchhärten [ich durchhärte, durchhärtet, zu durchhärten] to harden thoroughly. Ein wohl durchhärteter or durchgehärteter Stahl, well hardened steel. *Fig.* to render callous.

Durchhauchen, I. *v. intr.* dúrchhauchen [ich hauche durch, durchgehaucht, durchzuhauchen] to breathe through. II. *v. tr.* durchhaúchen [ich durchhauche, durchhaucht, zu durchhauchen] to fill with one's breath. *Fig.* Von Freude durchhaucht, animated with joy, exulting.

Durchhauen, *ir.* I. *v. tr.* 1) dúrchhauen [ich haue durch, durchgehauen, durchzuhauen] to hew through, to cut through and through. 2) [to beat soundly] Einen —, to whip or lash any one soundly. 3) durchhaúen [ich durchhaue, durchhauen, zu durchhauen] to hew or cut through. II. *v. r.* sich —, to force one's self through by cutting or fighting. Sich durch die Feinde —, to cut one's way through the enemy.

Dúrchhaus, *n.* [-ses, -häuser] a house that is a thorough-fare.

Dúrchhecheln, *v. tr.* [ich hechele durch, durchgehechelt, durchzuhecheln] to hatchel [flax] thoroughly. *Fig.* *Einen —, to censure a man, to blame or censure his manners or his conduct; er war niederträchtig genug, mich in einer Schmähschrift durchzuhecheln, he had the baseness, to traduce me in a libel.

Dúrchheizen, *v. tr.* [ich heize durch, durchgeheizt, durchzuheizen] to heat thoroughly.

Dúrchhelfen, *ir. v. tr.* [ich helfe durch, durchgeholfen, durchzuhelfen] to help through. *Fig.* Einem —, to help any one out, to help any one over a difficulty; Geld wird Ihnen —, money will do your business; sich —, to get out hardly, to free one's self from embarrassment with great labour or difficulty; sich mühsam —, to work hard for a living; sie hilft sich mit Spinnen durch, she gets her livelihood by spinning.

Durchhellen, *v. tr.* [ich durchhelle, durchhellt, zu durchhellen] to fill or spread over with light. Ein Wetterstrahl durchhellt die Nacht, a flash of lightning lights the night.

Durchherrschen, *v. tr.* [ich durchherrsche, durchherrscht, zu durchherrschen] to govern throughout. *Fig.* Durchherrschend, universal, prevalent; ein —des Uebel, a universal ill; eine —de Unsitte, a prevalent abuse.

Durchheulen, I. dúrchheulen [ich heule durch, durchgeheult, durchzuheulen] 1) *v. intr.* to howl or roar through. 2) *v. tr.* to sing through in a howling manner. II. durchheúlen [ich durchheule, durchheult, durchzuheulen] *v. tr.* 1) to fill with howling, to run over howling. Der Wind durchheult den Wald, the wind roars throughout the wood. 2) to surpass in howling.

Dúrchhieb, *m.* [-es, *pl.* -e] 1) [with hunters] a way cut in a wood, a riding. 2) [in mining] cross-board, stenting.

‖**Durchhin**, *adv.* throughout.

Durchhinken, I. *v. intr.* dúrchhinken [ich hinke durch, durchgehinkt, durchzuhinken] to limp or halt through. II. *v. tr.* durchhínken [ich durchhinke, durchhinkt, zu durchhinken] to go or walk through halting.

Durchhitzen, *v. tr.* dúrchhitzen [ich hitze durch, durchgehitzt, durchzuhitzen]; *it.* durchhítzen [ich durchhitze, durchhitzt, zu durchhitzen] to heat thoroughly. Er kam ganz durchhitzt an, he arrived very much heated.

Durchhöhlen, *v. tr.* dúrchhöhlen [ich höhle durch, durchgehöhlt, durchzuhöhlen]; *it.* durchhöhlen [ich durchhöhle, durchhöhlt, zu durchhöhlen] to hollow throughout, to bore through, to excavate. V. Aushöhlen.

Dúrchhöhnen, *v. tr.* [ich höhne durch, durchgehöhnet, durchzuhöhnen] to treat with derision or scorn, to ridicule. Jemands Betragen —, to scoff at any one's conduct.

‖ and †**Dúrchholen**, *v. tr.* [ich hole durch, durchgeholt, durchzuholen] Einen —, to censure any one, to hawl any one over the coals.

Durchhorchen, *v. tr.* [ich durchhorche, durchhorcht, zu durchhorchen] to walk over hearkening or listening, to listen, to overbear. Er durchhorcht alle Winkel, he listens in every corner.

Dúrchhören, *v. tr.* [ich höre durch, durchgehört, durchzuhören] to hear through.

Durchhüpfen, I. *v. intr.* [u. w. seyn] dúrchhüpfen [ich hüpfe durch, durchgehüpft, durchzuhüpfen] to leap, to jump, to hop through. II. *v. tr.* durchhǘpfen [ich durchhüpfe, durchhüpft, zu durchhüpfen] to leap, or jump over [a garden &c.].

Dúrchhuschen, [ich husche durch, durchgehuscht, durchzuhuschen] I. *v. intr.* to pass quickly through, to flit through, to pop through. †II. *v. tr.* to slap on the face soundly.

Durchirren, *v. tr.* [ich durchirre, durchirrt, durchzuirren] to err, to wander, or to ramble through. *Fig.* Mit den Augen —, to pass the eye over hastily, to consider cursorily.

Durchjagen, I. dúrchjagen [ich jage durch, durchgejagt, durchzujagen] 1) *v. tr.* *a*) to drive, or chase through, to hurry through. *b*) to chase, to hunt through. 2) *v. intr.* to pass through with velocity, to ride through, to gallop through. II. durchjágen [ich durchjage, durchjagt, zu durchjagen] *v. tr.* 1) to pass through with velocity. Er durchjagte Thal und Wald, he rode through valleys and woods; wenn das flüchtige Roß die Ebene durchjagt, when the fleet horse scours the plain; ein heftiger Nordwind durchjagte das Land, a violent north-wind hurried over the country. 2) to chase or hunt throughout. Er durchjagte die Felder, he hunted throughout the fields.

Durchjámmern, *v. tr.* [ich durchjammere, durchjammert, zu durchjammern] to pass or spend moaning.

Durchjauchzen, *v. tr.* [ich durchjauchze, durchjauchzt, zu durchjauchzen] to pass or spend joy fally, to shout through.

Durchjúbeln, *v. tr.* [ich durchjubele, durchjubelt, zu durchjubeln] to pass reveling or rioting. Wir durchjubelten einige Tage mit ihm, we reveled or caroused some days with him; die Nacht —, to pass the night in revelry.

Dúrchkaien, *v. tr.* [ich kaie durch, durchgekaiet, durchzukaien] [in seamen's language] Den Besahnmast —, to shift or change the mizzen.

Durchkälten, *v. tr.* [ich durchkälte, durchkältet, zu durchkälten] to chill through and through. Ganz durchkältet, benumbed with cold.

Dúrchkämmen, *v. tr.* [ich kämme durch, durchgekämmt, durchzukämmen] to comb [hair]. Sich —, to comb one's hair.

Durchkämpfen, *v. tr.* 1) dúrchkämpfen [ich kämpfe durch, durchgekämpft, durchzukämpfen] *a*) to support or maintain against denial, censure, or objections. Seine Meinungen —, to vindicate one's opinions. *b*) to fight to the end. *c*) Sich —, to cut one's way through. *Fig.* Ich habe mich durch alle Schwierigkeiten durchgekämpft, I have surmounted every obstacle. 2) durchkämpfen [ich durchkämpfe, durchkämpft, zu durchkämpfen] to pass or spend fighting, or *fig.* struggling with adversity.

Durchkauen, *v. tr.* dúrchkauen [ich kaue durch, durchgekauet, durchzukauen] *it.* durchkáuen [ich durchkaue, durchkauet, zu durchkauen] to chew sufficiently, to masticate thoroughly.

Durchkäuen, V. Durchkauen.

Dúrchkehren, *v. tr.* [ich kehre durch, durchgekehrt, durchzukehren] to sweep through an aperture.

Dúrchkeltern, *v. tr.* [ich keltere durch, durchgekeltert, durchzukeltern] to press throughout [grapes or apples].

Durchkénnen, *ir. v. tr.* [ich durchkenne, durchkannt, zu durchkennen] to know thoroughly.

Durchkeuchen, I. *v. intr.* [u. w. seyn] dúrchkeuchen [ich keuche durch, durchgekeucht, durchzukeuchen] to go or walk through panting. II. *v. tr.* durchkeúchen [ich durchkeuche, durchkeucht, zu durchkeuchen] to go or walk through panting.

Durchklären, *v. tr.* [ich kläre durch, durchgeklärt, durchzuklären] to filter, to percolate. Wein —, to pass wine through a filter.

Durchklimmen, *ir.* I. *v. intr.* [u. w. seyn] dúrchklimmen [ich klimme durch, durchgeklommen, durchzuklimmen] to climb through. II. *v. tr.* durchklímmen [ich durchklimme, durchklommen, zu durchklimmen] to climb all over.

Durchklopfen, *v. tr.* 1) dúrchklopfen [ich klopfe durch, durchgeklopft, durchzuklopfen] *a*) to beat through. *b*) to beat thoroughly. *c*) to make sore by beating. *d*) to beat, to drub. 2) durchklópfen [ich durchklopfe, durchklopft, zu durchklopfen] to beat all over.

Durchkneten, *v. tr.* 1) dúrchkneten [ich knete durch, durchgeknetet, durchzukneten] to knead through. 2) durchknéten [ich durchknete, durchknetet, zu durchkneten] *a*) to knead thoroughly. *b*) to stir and mix, to work by kneading.

Durchkochen, I. dúrchkochen [ich koche durch, durchgekocht, durchzukochen] 1) *v. intr.* *a*) to boil thoroughly. *b*) to penetrate boiling. 2) *v. tr.* to boil or cook one by one, to boil or cook thoroughly. II. durchkóchen [ich durchkoche, durchkocht, zu durchkochen] *v. tr.* to boil thoroughly. *Fig.* Das Blut durchkocht mir die Adern, my blood runs boiling through my veins.

Dúrchkollern, *v. intr.* [u. w. seyn] [ich kollere durch, durchgekollert, durchzukollern] to roll through.

Dúrchkommen, *ir. v. intr.* [u. w. seyn] [ich komme durch, durchgekommen, durchzukommen] 1) to come through, to pass. Ich kam hier mehrmahls durch, I passed here several times. 2) to get through. Die Wege sind sehr schlecht, es ist schwer durchzukommen, the roads are very bad, it is difficult to proceed; dieses Holz ist zu hart, ich kann mit dem Bohrer nicht —, this wood is too hard, I can't get the gimlet through. 3) to go through with. *Fig.* to come off, to get off, to get clear. Er ist glücklich durchgekommen, he came off safe; er kam zuletzt noch gut durch, he has come out well at last; mit dieser Entschuldigung kommen Sie nicht durch, that excuse will not do.

Dúrchkönnen, *ir. v. intr.* [ich kann durch, durchgekonnt, durchzukönnen] to be able to pass or get through. Ich kann nicht durch, I cannot proceed, or get through [the crowd]; das Thor ist so weit, daß ein Wagen durchkann, the gate is wide enough to admit a carriage.

Durchkosten, *v. tr.* dúrchkosten [ich koste durch, durchgekostet, durchzukosten]; *it.* durchkósten [ich durchkoste, durchkostet, zu durchkosten] to taste a whole set of things, one after the other, to taste sufficiently.

Durchkrämpeln, *v. tr.* dúrchkrämpeln [ich krämpele durch, durchgekrämpelt, durchzukrämpeln] *it.* durchkrämpeln [ich durchkrämpele, durchkrämpelt, zu durchkrämpeln] to card thoroughly.

Dúrchkratzen, *v. tr.* [ich kratze durch, durchgekratzt, durchzukratzen] 1) to make sore by scratching. 2) to scratch through, to get out by scratching or scraping.

Durchkräuseln, *v. tr.* dúrchkräuseln [ich kräusele durch, durchgekräuselt, durchzukräuseln] *it.* durchkräúseln [ich durchkräusele, durchkräuselt, zu durchkräuseln] 1) to curl throughout, to curl thoroughly. 2) to move curling over.

Durchkreisen, *v. tr.* [ich durchkreise, durchkreiset, zu durchkreisen] to run through in a circle.

Durchkreuzen, *v. tr.* and *r.* [ich durchkreuze, durchkreuzt, zu durchkreuzen] to pass or move over, to cross in all directions. Blitze — die Luft, lightnings cross the air; schnell wie die Sternschnuppe im Herbst die Nacht durchkreuzt, swift as a shooting star in autumn thwarts the night; welche Meere Ihr durchkreuzt, what seas you travers'd; sich —, [to lie or be athwart] to cross; diese beiden Linien — sich, these two lines cut each other; sich —de Wege, cross-ways. *Fig.* Unsere Meinungen — sich, our opinions thwart each other; einen Plan —, to cross a design; warum durchkreuzt Ihr alle unsere Pläne? why do you traverse all our designs?

Durchkreúzung, *f.* 1) the act of crossing or thwarting. 2) [with velvet-makers] crossing.

Durchkriechen, *ir.* I. *v. intr.* [u. w. seyn] dúrchkriechen [ich krieche durch, durchgekrochen, durchzukriechen] to creep through. Hier ist der Gefangene durchgekrochen, here the prisoner crept through; ein Loch zum —, a hole, to creep out at. II. *v. tr.* durchkriechen [ich durchkrieche, durchkrochen, zu durchkriechen] to creep all over. Alle Winkel —, to get into every hole.

Dúrchkriegen, *v. tr.* [ich kriege durch, durchgekriegt, durchzukriegen] to get through, to pass through. Ich kann den Faden nicht —, I cannot get the thread through [the eye of the needle].

Dúrchkugeln, *v. tr.* [ich kugele durch, durchgekugelt, durchzukugeln] to bowl through.

Durchlachen, I. *v. intr.* dúrchlachen [ich lache durch, durchgelacht, durchzulachen] to see through laughing. II. *v. tr.* durchláchen [ich durchlache, durchlacht, zu durchlachen] 1) to pass laughing. Die Nächte —, to spend the nights laughing. 2) to fill with laughter.

Dúrchlangen, [ich lange durch, durchgelangt, durchzulangen] I. *v. intr.* to be extended, to reach through. II. *v. tr.* to reach through.

Dúrchlängen, *v. tr.* [ich länge durch, durchgelängt, durchzulängen] [among miners] to dig out a load in its length.

Durchlärmen, *v. tr.* [ich durchlärme, durchlärmet, zu durchlärmen] to fill with noise, to disturb with noise, to run through with noise.

Dúrchlaß, *m.* [-sses, *pl.* -lässe] 1) the act of letting a person or thing pass through. 2) an instrument for letting things pass or run through, as a sieve, or a skreen for gravel and sand. 3) [in metallurgy] the washing-trough. 4) [in mints] flatting-mill.

Dúrchlassen, *ir. v. tr.* [ich lasse durch, durchgelassen, durchzulassen] to let through, to allow or to cause to pass through. Es wurde Niemand durchgelassen, nobody was allowed to pass; einen Absud —, to percolate a decoction; trüben Wein —, to filter turbid wine; [in mints] die Silberzaine —, to flatten the ingots of silver; [in metallurgy] Erze —, to fuse ores; dieses Tuch läßt das Wasser nicht durch, this cloth is waterproof, is impervious to water.

Dúrchlaucht, *f.* [*pl.* -en] [a title given to several princes] Serene Highness. Se. kurfürstliche —, his Serene Highness the Elector; Ihre — die Fürstinn, her Serene Highness the princess; Ihre —en die Herzoge von Sachsen, their Serene Highnesses the dukes of Saxony.

Dúrchlauchtig, [-ste] *adj.* 1) [formerly] renowned, illustrious. 2) [a title given to several princes] Serene. Der —ste Fürst, his most Serene Highness the prince.

Durchlauern, *v. tr.* [ich durchlauere, durchlauert, zu durchlauern] to pass lurking.

Dúrchlauf, *m.* [-s, *pl.* -läufe] 1) a running through an aperture or space, passage. 2) [a disease] a purging, flux, diarrhea.

Durchlaufen, *ir.* I. dúrchlaufen [ich laufe durch, durchgelaufen, durchzulaufen] 1) *v. intr.* [u. w. seyn] *a*) to run through. *b*) to be pervious or permeable. Durch einen porösen Stein lauft das Wasser durch, a porous stone is pervious to water; — lassen, [in metallurgy] to size. 2) *v. tr.* *a*) to run through [a thicket &c.]. *b*) to wear out by running. Durchgelaufene Schuhe, wornout shoes. II. durchlaúfen [ich durchlaufe, durchlaufen, zu durchlaufen] *v. tr.* to run all over. Den ganzen Garten —, to run all over the garden; die Planeten — in bestimmten Zeiten ihre Bahn, the planets run their periodical courses. *Fig.* *a*) to spread rapidly. Das Gerücht durchlief die ganze Stadt, the report circulated in the whole town. *b*) to pass the eye over hastily, to run over. Ich durchlief die Rechnung, I glanced over the bill; einen Brief —, to run over a letter; einen Band Geschichte —, to dip into a volume of history; er durchlief mit aufmerksamen Blicken die ganze Landschaft, he took an attentive survey of the whole landscape.

Durchläutern, *v. tr.* 1) dúrchläutern [ich läutere durch, durchgeläutert, durchzuläutern] to strain through. 2) durchläútern [ich durchläutere, durchläutert, zu durchläutern] to purify thoroughly.

Durchleben, *v. tr.* 1) dúrchleben [ich lebe durch, durchgelebt, durchzuleben] to live through a space of time. 2) durchlében [ich durchlebe, durchlebt, zu durchleben] to pass through while living. Er hat harte Zeiten durchlebt, he has passed through hard times.

Dúrchleiten, *v. tr.* [ich leite durch, durchgeleitet, durchzuleiten] to conduct or lead through.

Dúrchlernen, *v. tr.* [ich lerne durch, durchgelernt, durchzulernen] to learn to the end, to learn thoroughly.

Durchlesen, *ir. v. tr.* 1) dúrchlesen [ich lese durch, durchgelesen, durchzulesen]; durchlésen [ich durchlese, durchlesen, durchzulesen] to read through, to peruse. Einen Brief —, to read a letter through.

Durchleuchten, I. dúrchleuchten [ich leuchte durch, durchgeleuchtet, durchzuleuchten] 1) *v. intr.* to shine through. *Fig.* Ueberall leuchtet seine Eitelkeit durch, every where his vanity shines through. 2) *v. tr.* to light through. Einen —, to light one through [any place]. II. durchleúchten [ich durchleuchte, durchleuchtet, zu durchleuchten] *v. tr.* *a*) to light throughout. *b*) to spread over with light. Alle Winkel —, to light through every hole.

Durchlichten, *v. tr.* [ich durchlichte, durchlichtet, zu durchlichten] to lighten, to fill with light, to illuminate.

Dúrchliegen, *ir. v. r.* sich —, [ich liege mich durch, durchgelegen, sich durchzuliegen] to make sore a part of one's body by lying too long upon it.

Dúrchlochen, *v. tr.* [ich loche durch, durchgelocht, durchzulochen] [with workers in iron or other metal] to punch [a hole in a plate of metal].

Durchlöchern, *v. tr.* [ich durchlöchere, durchlöchert, zu durchlöchern] to make a hole or holes through any thing. Den Boden eines Gefäßes —, to perforate the bottom of a vessel; deine Strümpfe sind ganz durchlöchert, your stockings are full of holes.

Durchlöchung, *f.* 1) the act of punching. 2) perforation.

Durchlodern, I. *v. intr.* dúrchlodern [ich lodere durch, durchgelodert, durchzulodern] to blaze through. II. *v. tr.* durchlódern [ich durchlodere, durchlodert, zu durchlodern] to fill with blaze or flames.

Durchlüften, *v. tr.* dúrchlüften [ich lüfte durch, durchgelüftet, durchzulüften] *it.* durchlúften [ich durchlüfte, durchlüftet, zu durchlüften] to give access to the open air, to cause the air to pass through, to ventilate. Ein Zimmer —, to air a room. V. Auslüften.

Dúrchlügen, *ir. v. r.* sich —, [ich lüge mich durch, durchgelogen, sich durchzulügen] to help one's self on by lying. Er hat sich glücklich durchgelogen, he has managed to get out of the scrape by lying.

Dúrchmachen, [ich mache durch, durchgemacht, durchzumachen] I. *v. tr.* 1) to pass something through. 2) to perform thoroughly, to go through, to finish. 3) to go through, to suffer, to undergo, to sustain to the end. Er hat viele Mühseligkeiten durchgemacht, he has gone through many hardships. II. *v. r.* sich —, to run away.

Dúrchmarsch, *m.* [-es, *pl.* -märsche] the march through a place or country.

Dúrchmarschiren, *v. tr.* [ich marschire durch, durchmarschirt, durchzumarschiren] to march through.

Durchmauern, *v. tr.* [ich durchmauere, durchmauert, zu durchmauern] to wall all over.

Dúrchmeißeln, *v. tr.* [ich meißele durch, durchgemeißelt, durchzumeißeln] to hole with a chisel, to chisel through.

Dúrchmeistern, *v. tr.* [ich meistere durch, durchgemeistert, durchzumeistern] to criticise thoroughly, to master strongly.

Durchmengen, *v. tr.* 1) dúrchmengen [ich menge durch, durchgemengt, durchzumengen] to mingle or mix thorougly. 2) durchméngen [ich durchmenge, durchmengt, zu durchmengen] to blend by mingling. *Fig.* Unsere Freuden sind mit Leiden durchmengt, our pleasures are mixed with grief.

Durchmessen, *ir. v. tr.* 1) dúrchmessen [ich messe durch, durchgemessen, durchzumessen] to measure to the end. *Fig.* to measure to the bottom. 2) durchméssen [ich durchmesse, durchmessen, zu durchmessen] *a*) to measure throughout. *b*) [to pass through or over] Einen weiten Weg —, to measure a long way.

Dúrchmesser, *m.* [-s, *pl.* -] 1) a person that measures through. 2) [in mathematics] diameter. Der — eines Baumes, the diameter of a tree.

Durchmischen, *v. tr.* 1) dúrchmischen [ich mische durch, durchgemischt, durchzumischen] to blend, to mix, to mingle thoroughly. 2) durchmíschen [ich durchmische, durchmischt, zu durchmischen] to blend by mixing. *Fig.* Sein Lob mit Tadel —, to mix one's praise with blame.

Durchmisten, *v. tr.* 1) dúrchmisten [ich miste durch, durchgemistet, durchzumisten] to manure all successively. 2) durchmísten [ich durchmiste, durchmistet, zu durchmisten] to manure thoroughly.

Dúrchmühen, *v. r.* sich —, [ich mühe mich durch, durchgemühet, sich durchzumühen] to help one's self on with labour or difficulty, to strive on hardly.

Durchmurmeln, I. *v. intr.* dúrchmurmeln [ich murmele durch, durchgemurmelt, durchzumurmeln] 1) to murmur through an aperture. 2) to speak through murmuring. II. *v. tr.* durchmúrmeln [ich durchmurmele, durchmurmelt, zu durchmurmeln] to run or flow through murmuring. Ein Bach durchmurmelt das Thal, a brook runs murmuring through the valley.

Dúrchmüssen, *ir. v. intr.* [ich muß durch, durchgemußt, durchzumüssen] to be obliged to pass through or get through.

Durchmustern, *v. tr.* dúrchmustern [ich mustere durch, durchgemustert, durchzumustern] *it.* durchmústern [ich durchmustere, durchmustert, zu durchmustern] to view all one by one, to examine with critical care, to scrutinize throughout. Jemands Handlungen —, to scan any one's actions; er musterte mich von allen Seiten durch, he surveyed me round.

Durchnächten, [ich durchnachte, durchnachtet, zu durchnachten] I. *v. tr.* to involve in darkness, to shroud with the shades of night. Die Wolken durchnachten den Himmel, the clouds benight the sky. II. *v. intr.* to pass the night.

Durchnageln, *v. tr.* 1) dúrchnageln [ich nagele durch, durchgenagelt, durchzunageln] to nail through. Ein Brett —, to nail a board through. 2) durchnágeln [ich nagele durch, durchnagelt, zu durchnageln] to nail throughout or all over.

Durchnagen, *v. tr.* 1) dúrchnagen [ich nage durch, durchgenagt, durchzunagen] to gnaw through. Die Mäuse haben das Leder durchgenagt, the mice have gnawed the leather through. 2) durchnágen [ich durchnage, durchnagt, zu durchnagen] to gnaw through and through. *Fig.* Kummer durchnagt sein Herz, sorrow preys on his heart, gnaws at his heart.

Durchnähen, *v. tr.* 1) dúrchnähen [ich nähe durch, durchgenäht, durchzunähen] to make sore by much sewing. Sich die Finger —, to make one's fingers sore by much sewing. 2) durchnähen [ich durchnähe, durchnähet, zu durchnähen] to sew through and through. Eine Bettdecke —, to quilt a bed-cover; [with shoemakers] die Absätze weiß —, to sew the heels with white thread.

Durchnarben, *v. tr.* [ich durchnarbe, durchnarbt, zu durchnarben] to cover all over with scars. Ein durchnarbtes Gesicht, a face full of scars.

Durchnässen, I. *v. intr.* dúrchnässen [ich nässe durch, durchgenäßt, durchzunässen] to penetrate, as water or wetness. II. *v. tr.* durchnä́ssen [ich durchnässe, durchnäßt, zu durchnässen] to wet thoroughly, to soak. Meine Kleider sind ganz durchnäßt, my clothes are all wet; die Erde ist von heftigen Regen ganz durchnäßt, the earth is soaked with heavy rains.

Dúrchnehmen, *ir. v. tr.* [ich nehme durch, durchgenommen, durchzunehmen] to set about a thing. Er hat mit ihm den ganzen Cornelius Nepos durchgenommen, he has gone through the whole of Cornelius Nepos with him. *Fig.* Einen —, to censure any one, to take any one to task.

Durchnetzen, V. Durchnässen.

Durchölen, *v. tr.* [ich durchöle, durchölt, zu durchölen] to oil thoroughly.

Durchörtern, *v. tr.* [ich durchörtere, durchörtert, zu durchörtern] [in mining] to cut, to hole.

Dúrchpaß, *m.* [-sses, *pl.* -pässe] [a narrow passage or way] a defile. V. Engpaß.

Dúrchpassiren, *v. intr.* [ich passire durch, durchpassirt, durchzupassiren] to pass through.

†**Dúrchpatschen**, [ich patsche durch, durchgepatscht, durchzupatschen] I. *v. intr.* [u. w. seyn] and *v. tr.* to splash through [a pool of water]. II. *v. tr.* to slap well Ein Kind —, to slap a child.

Dúrchpeitschen, *v. tr.* [ich peitsche durch, durchgepeitscht, durchzupeitschen] 1) to whip through a place or aperture. 2) to whip soundly.

Durchpfeffern, *v. tr.* [ich durchpfeffere, durchpfeffert, zu durchpfeffern] to pepper thoroughly. *Fig.* Mit beißenden Sarkasmen durchpfeffert, seasoned with biting sarcasms.

Durchpfeifen, *ir. v. tr.* 1) dúrchpfeifen [ich pfeife durch, durchgepfiffen, durchzupfeifen] to whistle [a tune] through. 2) durchpfeifen [ich durchpfeife, durchpfiffen, zu durchpfeifen] to fill with whistling, to whistle through. Der Wind durchpfeift die Luft, the wind whistles through the air.

Durchpflanzen, *v. tr.* [ich durchpflanze, durchpflanzt, zu durchpflanzen] to plant all over.

Durchpflastern, *v. tr.* [ich durchpflastere, durchpflastert, zu durchpflastern] to pave all over. Einen Hof —, to pave a court all over.

Durchpflügen, *v. tr.* 1) dúrchpflügen [ich pflüge durch, durchgepflügt, durchzupflügen] to plough through. 2) durchpflǘgen [ich durchpflüge, durchpflügt, zu durchpflügen] to plough thoroughly or all over.

Durchpichen, *v. tr.* [ich durchpiche, durchpicht, zu durchpichen] to pitch all over, to cover with pitch.

Dúrchpicken, *v. tr.* [ich picke durch, durchgepickt, durchzupicken] 1) to peck through an aperture. 2) to peck through or make sore by pecking.

Durchpilgern, I. *v. intr.* dúrchpilgern [ich pilgere durch, durchgepilgert, durchzupilgern] to wander through as a pilgrim. II. *v. tr.* durchpílgern [ich durchpilgere, durchpilgert, zu durchpilgern] to wander over as a pilgrim. Die Welt —, to wander over the world as a pilgrim.

Durchpissen, I. *v. intr.* dúrchpissen [ich pisse durch, durchgepißt, durchzupissen] to piss through. II. *v. tr.* durchpíssen [ich durch durchpißt, zu durchpissen] to bepiss all over.

†**Dúrchplacken**, V. Durchplagen.

Dúrchplagen, *v. r.* sich —, [ich plage mich durch, durchgeplagt, sich durchzuplagen] to toil and drudge for getting one's livelihood.

Durchplappern, *v. tr.* dúrchplappern [ich plappere durch, durchgeplappert, durchzuplappern] *it.* durchpláppern [ich durchplappere, durchplappert, zu durchplappern] to pass or spend pratling or babbling.

Durchplaudern, *v. tr.* dúrchplaudern [ich plaudere durch, durchgeplaudert, durchzuplaudern] *it.* durchplaúdern [ich durchplaudere, durchplaudert, zu durchplaudern] to Pass or spend prating or tattling.

Durchplündern, *v. tr.* 1) dúrchplündern [ich plündere durch, durchgeplündert, durchzuplündern] to pillage, to plunder, to ransack all successively. 2) durchplǘndern [ich durchplündere, durchplündert, zu durchplündern] *a)* to plunder or pillage throughout. *b)* to go or march through plundering or pillaging.

Dúrchpochen, *v. tr.* [ich poche durch, durchgepocht, durchzupochen] [in metallurgy] to wash [the ore] in the washing-trough. †*Fig.* Einen —, to drub any one soundly.

Durchprasseln, I. *v. intr.* dúrchprasseln [ich prassele durch, durchgeprasselt, durchzuprasseln] to pass through rattling. II. *v. tr.* durchpráſseln [ich durchprassele, durchprasselt, zu durchprasseln] to fill with rattling sounds.

Durchprassen, *v. tr.* dúrchprassen [ich prasse durch, durchgepraßt, durchzuprassen] *it.* durchprássen [ich durchprasse, durchpraßt, zu durchprassen] 1) to spend lavishly and profusely, to waste. Sein Vermögen —, to squander one's estate. 2) to pass or spend in revelry. Durchpraßte Nächte, nights spent in revelry.

Dúrchpressen, *v. tr.* [ich presse durch, durchgepreßt, durchzupressen] 1) to force between two bodies, to squeeze through. Den Arm durch ein Gitter —, to squeeze one's arm through a grate. 2) to compel or cause to pass. Wasser durch einen Filz —, to squeeze water through a felt. 3) to injure, to make worse, to wear out by pressing.

Durchproben, *v tr.* 1) dúrchproben [ich probe durch, durchgeprobt, durchzuproben] to taste or try all in succession. 2) durchpróben [ich durchprobe, durchprobt, zu durchproben] to taste or try thoroughly.

Dúrchprügeln, *v. tr.* [ich prügele durch, durchgeprügelt, durchzuprügeln] to thrash, to drub, to belabour, to lick, to pepper.

Durchpudern, *v. tr.* dúrchpudern [ich pudere durch, durchgepudert, durchzupudern] *it.* durchpúdern [ich durchpudere, durchpudert, zu durchpudern] to powder all over.

Durchqualmen, I. *v. intr.* dúrchqualmen [ich qualme durch, durchgequalmt, durchzuqualmen] to steam or smoke through. II. *v. tr.* durchquálmen [ich durchqualme, durchqualmt, zu durchqualmen] to fill with smoke or steam. Ein durchqualmtes Haus, a house filled with smoke, a smoky house.

Dúrchquetschen, *v. tr.* [ich quetsche durch, durchgequetscht, durchzuquetschen] 1) to squeeze through. 2) [= zerquetschen] Sich die Finger —, to make one's fingers sore by squeezing.

1. **Dúrchrädern**, *v. tr.* [ich rädere durch, durchgerädert, durchzurädern] to run through a standing sieve [gravel &c.].

2. **Durchrädern**, *v. tr.* dúrchrädern [ich rädere durch, durchgerädert, durchzurädern] *it.* durchrǟdern [ich durchrädere, durchrädert, zu durchrädern] to crush by a wheel. Ich bin wie durchrädert [von langem Fahren], I am harassed with fatigue [from having been so long jolted about].

Dúrchragen, *v. intr.* [ich rage durch, durchgeragt, durchzuragen] to jut through an aperture.

Durchranken, I. *v. intr.* dúrchranken [ich ranke durch, durchgerankt, durchzuranken] to ramp through. II. *v. tr.* durchránken [ich durchranke, durchrankt, zu durchranken] to entwine ramping.

Durchrasen, I. *v. intr.* dúrchrasen [ich rase durch, durchgerast, durchzurasen] to hasten through furiously. II. *v. tr.* durchrāſen [ich durchrase, durchrast, zu durchrasen] to run over furiously; *it.* to pass or spend in fury. Die Stadt —, to run furiously over the town. *Fig.* Der Sturm durchrast den Wald, the storm rages through the forest.

Dúrchraspeln, *v. tr.* [ich raspele durch, durchgeraspelt, durchzuraspeln] 1) to rasp throughout. 2) to break by rasping.

Durchrasseln, I. *v. intr.* [u. w. seyn] dúrchrasseln [ich rassele durch, durchgerasselt, durchzurasseln] to pass through rattling. II. *v. tr.* durchrásseln [ich durchrassele, durchrasselt, zu durchrasseln] to rattle through. Die Wagen — die Straßen, the carriages rattle through the streets.

Durchrauchen, I. *v. intr.* dúrchrauchen [ich rauche durch, durchgeraucht, durchzurauchen] to fume or smoke through. Es raucht durch, it smokes through. II. *v. tr.* durchraúchen [ich durchrauche, durchraucht, zu durchrauchen] to fill with fume or smoke. Durchrauchte Zimmer, smoky rooms.

Durchräuchern, *v. tr.* 1) dúrchräuchern [ich räuchere durch, durchgeräuchert, durchzuräuchern] to impregnate with smoke, to smoke through and through. Die Schinken sind noch nicht durchgeräuchert, the hams are not smoked enough yet. 2) durchräúchern [ich durchräuchere, durchräuchert, zu durchräuchern] to smoke thoroughly. Briefe, Kleider &c. —, to fumigate letters, clothes &c.

Durchrauschen, I. *v. intr.* [u. w. seyn] dúrchrauschen [ich rausche durch, durchgerauscht, durchzurauschen] to rush through. II. *v. tr.* durchraúschen [ich durchrausche, durchrauscht, zu durchrauschen] to rush through, to fill with noise; *it.* to pass through rushing. Die Winde — den Wald, winds rush through the forest; das Rothwild durchrauscht das verschlungene Brombeergesträuch, the deer rustles through the twining brake.

Durchrechen, *v. tr.* 1) dúrchrechen [ich reche durch, durchgerecht, durchzurechen] to rake throughout. 2) durchréchen [ich durchreche, durchrecht, zu durchrechen] to rake thoroughly.

Durchrechnen, *v. tr.* 1) dúrchrechnen [ich rechne durch, durchgerechnet, durchzurechnen] to go through reckoning. 2) durchréchnen [ich durchrechne, durchrechnet, zu durchrechnen] *a)* to count over, to reckon over. *b)* to pass or spend counting or reckoning. Ganze Tage —, to spend whole days in reckoning.

Durchregnen, I. *v. intr.* and *imp.* 1) dúrchregnen [es regnet durch, durchgeregnet, durchzuregnen] to rain through. Hier regnet es durch, here it rains through. II. *v. tr.* durchrégnen [ich durchregne, durchregnet, zu durchregnen] to wet or soak all over with or by rain, to rain through. Ich bin ganz durchregnet, I am wet through by rain; das Feld ist ganz durchregnet, the field is quite soaked by heavy rain.

Dúrchreiben, *ir. v. tr.* [ich reibe durch, durchgerieben, durchzureiben] 1) to rub through. 2) to make sore by rubbing. 3) to separate by rubbing.

Dúrchreichen, [ich reiche durch, durchgereicht, durchzureichen] I. *v. tr.* to reach through. Er reichte mir eine Orange durch das Gitter durch, he reached me an orange through the grate. II. *v. intr.* to reach through. *Fig.* Sie werden damit nicht —, you will not succeed in that, this will not help you through; er wird wohl mit seinem Gelde nicht —, he will probably fall short of his money.

Dúrchreise, *f.* [*pl.* -n] a travelling through a place or country. Bei seiner —, on his passage.

Durchreisen, I. *v. intr.* [u. w. seyn] dúrchreisen [ich reise durch, durchgereiset, durchzureisen] to travel through a place or country, to pass through. II. *v. tr.* durchreisen [ich durchreise, durchreiset, zu durchreisen] to travel, to journey over. Er hat das ganze Königreich England durchreiset, he travelled the whole kingdom of England.

Durchreißen, *ir.* I. dúrchreißen [ich reiße durch, durchgerissen, durchzureißen] 1) *v. tr.* to tear asunder, to rend. Ein Papier —, to rend a paper; der Blitz durchreißt eine Eiche, lightning rends an oak. 2) *v. intr.* [u. w. seyn] to be torn asunder. II. durchreißen [ich durchreiße, durchrissen, zu durchreißen] *v. tr.* to rend through.

Durchreiten, *ir.* I. [u. w. seyn] dúrchreiten [ich reite durch, durchgeritten, durchzureiten] 1) *v. intr.* to pass through on horseback, to ride through. 2) *v. tr.* to gall by riding. Ein Pferd —, to gall the back of a horse by riding; sich —, to wound one's self by riding. II. durchreiten [ich durchreite, durchritten, zu durchreiten] *v. tr.* to ride over. Das Feld —, to ride over the field.

Durchrennen, *ir.* I. dúrchrennen [ich renne durch, durchgerannt, or durchgerennet, durchzurennen] 1) *v. intr.* [u. w. seyn] to run through with great velocity. 2) *v. tr.* to run through, to pierce. Einen [mit dem Schwerte] —, to run a sword through any one's body, to pierce any one. II. durchrénnen [ich durchrenne, durchrannt or durchrennet, zu durchrennen] *v. tr.* 1) to run over. Vier feurige Pferde durchrannten die Ebene, four fiery horses scoured through the plain. 2) to pierce in running.

Dúrchriechen, *ir. v. intr.* [ich rieche durch, durchgerochen, durchzuriechen] to smell through.

Durchrieseln, I. *v. intr.* [u. w. seyn] dúrchrieseln [ich riesele durch, durchgerieselt, durchzurieseln] to rill through. II. *v. tr.* durchrieseln [ich durchriesele, durchrieselt, zu durchrieseln] to run, to glide through purling. Der Bach durchrieselt die Wiesen, the brook glides purling over the meadows. *Fig.* Ein Schauer durchrieselte seine Glieder, a shudder crept over his limbs.

† and ‖ **Dúrchriffeln**, *v. tr.* [ich riffele durch, durchgeriffelt, durchzuriffeln] to censure or blame severely.

Durchrinnen, *ir.* I. *v. intr.* dúrchrinnen [ich rinne durch, durchgeronnen, durchzurinnen] to run or flow through. II. *v. tr.* durchrinnen [ich durchrinne, durchronnen, zu durchrinnen] to run or flow through.

Dúrchriß, *m.* [-es, *pl.* -sse] a fissure, a breach made by force, a rent.

Dúrchritt, *m.* [-es, *pl.* -e] a riding through, a passing through on horseback.

Durchritzen, *v. tr.* 1) dúrchritzen [ich ritze durch, durchgeritzt, durchzuritzen] to scratch through, to make sore by scratching. 2) durchrítzen [ich durchritze, durchritzt, zu durchritzen] to scratch all over.

Durchrollen, I. dúrchrollen [ich rolle durch, durchgerollt, durchzurollen] 1) *v. intr.* [u. w.

seyn] to roll through. 2) *v. tr. a)* to roll through. Die Kugel —, to roll the bowl through. *b)* to mangle all [the linen] in succession, to roll thoroughly. II. durchróllen [ich durchrolle, durchrollt, zu durchrollen] *v. tr.* to move rumbling through. Der Donner durchrollt die Lüfte, thunder rumbles through the air.

Dúrchröschen, *v. tr.* [ich rösche durch, durchgeröscht, durchzuröschen] [in mining] to provide with conduits or stream-works made across the rock.

Durchrosten, *v. intr.* [u. w. seyn] 1) búrchrosten [ich roste durch, durchgerostet, durchzurosten] to be rusted through. 2) durchrósten [ich durchroste, durchrostet, zu durchrosten] to rust all over. Durchrostete Degen, rusted swords.

Dúrchrösten, *v. tr.* [ich röste durch, durchgeröstet, durchzurösten] to toast thoroughly. Brod —, to toast bread thoroughly.

Dúrchrücken, [ich rücke durch, durchgerückt, durchzurücken] I. *v. intr.* [used with seyn] to move through in a military manner, to march through. II. *v. tr.* to move through a place or aperture by a short impulse.

Durchrudern, I. *v. intr.* [u. w. seyn] búrchrudern [ich rudere durch, durchgerudert, durchzurudern] to row through. II. *v. tr.* durchrúdern [ich durchrudere, durchrudert, zu durchrudern] to row through or over. Unbekannte Meere —, to row over unknown seas.

Durchruhen, *v. tr.* [ich durchruhe, durchruhet, zu durchruhen] to pass or spend resting or reposing.

Dúrchrühmen, *v. tr.* [ich rühme durch, durchgerühmt, durchzurühmen] to praise all in succession or in every thing.

Dúrchrühren, *v. tr.* [ich rühre durch, durchgerührt, durchzurühren] 1) to mix thoroughly by stirring. 2) to strain by stirring.

Dúrchrutschen, *v. intr.* [u. w. seyn] [ich rutsche durch, durchgerutscht, durchzurutschen] to slip or slide through.

Durchrütteln, *v. tr.* búrchrütteln [ich rüttele durch, durchgerüttelt, durchzurütteln]; *it.* durchrútteln [ich durchrüttele, durchrüttelt, zu durchrütteln] to shake thoroughly.

Dúrchsäbeln, *v. tr.* [ich säbele durch, durchgesäbelt, durchzusäbeln] to cut through with a sabre.

Durchsäen, *v. tr.* [ich durchsäe, durchsäet, zu durchsäen] to sow all over.

Durchsägen, *v. tr.* búrchsägen [ich säge durch, durchgesägt, durchzusägen]; *it.* durchsä́gen [ich durchsäge, durchsägt, zu durchsägen] to saw through. Ein Brett —, to saw a board through; durchsägte Bäume, sawed trees.

Durchsalben, *v. tr.* búrchsalben [ich salbe durch, durchgesalbt, durchzusalben]; *it.* durchsálben [ich durchsalbe, durchsalbt, zu durchsalben] to oint or anoint all over.

Durchsalzen, *v. tr.* búrchsalzen [ich salze durch, durchgesalzen, durchzusalzen], *it.* durchsálzen [ich durchsalze, durchsalzt, zu durchsalzen] to salt throughout. Durchgesalzenes or durchsalztes Fleisch, well-salted meat.

Durchsäuern, I. búrchsäuern [ich säuere durch, durchgesäuert, durchzusäuern] 1) *v. tr.* to leaven thoroughly. Der Teig ist wohl durchgesäuert, the dough is well leavened. 2) *v. intr.* [u. w. seyn] to be leavened thoroughly. II. durchsä́uern [ich durchsäuere, durchsäuert, zu durchsäuern] *v. tr.* to leaven entirely.

Durchsäuseln, I. *v. intr.* búrchsäuseln [ich säusele durch, durchgesäuselt, durchzusäuseln] to blow gently through an aperture or space, to breeze through. II. *v. tr.* durchsä́useln [ich durchsäusele, durchsäuselt, zu durchsäuseln] to penetrate as a breeze or gentle gale. Der West durchsäuselt die Zweige, the west-wind breezes through the boughs.

Durchsausen, I. *v. intr.* búrchsausen [ich sause durch, durchgesauset, durchzusausen] to bluster, to roar through. II. *v. tr.* durchsáusen [ich durchsause, durchsauset, zu durchsausen] to penetrate blustering or roaring. Der Sturm durchsauset den Wald, the storm roars through the forest.

Durchschaben, *v. tr.* búrchschaben [ich schabe durch, durchgeschabet, durchzuschaben] *it.* durchschä́ben [ich durchschabe, durchschabt, zu durchschaben] to scrape through.

Dúrchschaffen, *v. tr.* [ich schaffe durch, durchgeschafft, durchzuschaffen] to bring or get through.

Durchschäkern, *v. tr.* [ich durchschäkere, durchschäkert, zu durchschäkern] to pass or spend toying, playing, jesting.

Durchschallen, *reg.* and *ir.* I. *v. intr.* búrchschallen [ich schalle durch, durchgeschallt, durchzuschallen] to penetrate as sounds. II. *v. tr.* durchschállen [ich durchschalle, durchschallt, zu durchschallen] to fill with sound. Lauter Beifall durchschallte die Halle, the hall resounded, rang with acclamations.

Durchscharren, *v. tr.* 1) búrchscharren [ich scharre durch, durchgescharret, durchzuscharren] *a)* to scrape or scratch through. *b)* to penetrate scraping. 2) durchschárren [ich durchscharre, durchscharrt, zu durchscharren] to scrape through, to separate by scraping.

Durchschaudern, *v. tr.* [ich durchschaudere, durchschaudert, zu durchschaudern] 1) to fill with horror. 2) to pervade with a shivering or shuddering sensation. Grauen durchschauderte ihn, he shivered with horror.

Durchschauen, I. búrchschauen [ich schaue durch, durchgeschauet, durchzuschauen] 1) *v. intr.* to penetrate with the eye, to look through; *fig.* to penetrate with the understanding, to look through. Es ist nicht schwer, seinen Plan durchzuschauen, it is not difficult to see through his plan. 2) *v. tr.* to view all successively. *Fig.* V. Durchschaüen. II. durchschaüen [ich durchschaue, durchschauet, zu durchschauen] *v. tr.* to view one by one. Die ganze Gegend —, to survey the whole country, to take a survey of the whole country. *Fig.* to look through, to penetrate, to discern, to understand. Jemands Absichten —, to penetrate any one's designs; eines Andern Politik —, to see through the policy of another; ich kann ihn nicht —, I don't know his intention, I don't know what to make of him.

Durchschauern, *v. tr.* [ich durchschauere, durchschauert, zu durchschauern] to pervade with a shivering or shuddering sensation, to thrill. Kaltes Grauen durchschauert mich, I shiver with cold horror.

Durchschaufeln, *v. tr.* 1) búrchschaufeln [ich schaufele durch, durchgeschaufelt, durchzuschaufeln] *a)* to shovel through. *b)* to shovel open, to penetrate with a shovel. *c)* to shovel all one by one. 2) durchschaúfeln [ich durchschaufele, durchschaufelt, zu durchschaufeln] to shovel thoroughly.

Dúrchscheinbar, *adj.* and *adv.* transparent, pervious to light.

Dúrchscheinbarkeit, *f.* [without a plural] translucency, pellucidity, pellucidness, transparency, diaphaneity.

Durchscheinen, *ir.* I. *v. intr.* búrchscheinen [ich scheine durch, durchgeschienen, durchzuscheinen] to shine through. Die Sonne kann nicht —, the sun cannot shine through [the clouds]; durchscheinend, pervious to light, transparent, diaphanous, pellucid [as glass, water, air &c.]. II. *v. tr.* durchschéinen [ich durchscheine, durchschienen, zu durchscheinen] to supply with light. Viele Lampen — den Saal, many lamps illuminate the hall.

Dúrchschelten, *ir. v. tr.* [ich schelte durch, durchgescholten, durchzuschelten] to scold, to rail at clamorously. Einen —, to taunt any one; Bediente tüchtig —, to rattle off servants sharply.

Durchschèrzen, *v. tr.* [ich durchscherze, durchscherzt, zu durchscherzen] to pass or spend jesting, joking, bantering. Manchen Tag —, to spend many a day joking.

Dúrchscheuchen, *v. tr.* [ich scheuche durch, durchgescheucht, durchzuscheuchen] to scare, frighten or drive through.

Dúrchscheuern, *v. tr.* [ich scheuere durch, durchgescheuert, durchzuscheuern] 1) to scour all successively. 2) to scour or scrub thoroughly or completely. *Fig.* †Einen —, to reprimand any one severely. 3) to wear off or out by scouring or scrubbing [used also fig.]. 4) to make sore by scouring or scrubbing. Sich die Hände —, to make one's hands sore by scouring or scrubbing.

Durchschicken, *v. tr.* 1) búrchschicken [ich schicke durch, durchgeschickt, durchzuschicken] to send through. 2) durchschícken [ich durchschicke, durchschickt, zu durchschicken] to send for in every part. Die ganze Stadt —, to send for throughout the town.

Dúrchschieben, *ir. v. tr.* and *intr.* [ich schiebe durch, durchgeschoben, durchzuschieben] 1) to shove through. 2) to wear out by bowling.

Dúrchschielen, *v. intr.* [ich schiele durch, durchgeschielt, durchzuschielen] to squint through.

Durchschießen, *ir.* I. búrchschießen [ich schieße durch, durchgeschossen, durchzuschießen] 1) *v. intr.* [u. w. haben] to shoot or fire through; [u. w. seyn] to run or flow rapidly through. 2) *v. tr.* *a)* to shoot through. Ein Brett —, to shoot through a board. *b)* to count over by throws. II. durchschießen [ich durchschieße, durchschossen, zu durchschießen] *v. tr.* 1) to shoot through. Sein Fuß ist durchschossen, his foot is shot through. 2) to pass through with swiftness, to shoot. 3) to interleave [a book]. Ein durchschossenes Buch, a book interleaved. 4) [in printing] to interline, to lead.

Durchschießlinie, *f.* [in printing] space rule, lead.

Durchschiffen, I. búrchschiffen [ich schiffe durch, durchgeschifft, durchzuschiffen] 1) *v. intr.* [u. w. seyn] to pass through in a ship, to sail through. 2) *v. tr.* to transport in ship. Es werden viele Waaren hier durchgeschifft, a great quantity of merchandise is shipped through this place. V. Durchschiffen. II. durchschíffen [ich durchschiffe, durchschifft, zu durchschiffen] *v. tr.* to pass over in ships. Das atlantische Meer —, to navigate the Atlantic; welche Meere er durchschifft, what seas he traverses.

Durchschimmern, I. *v. intr.* búrchschimmern [ich schimmere durch, durchgeschimmert, durchzuschimmern] to glitter or glimmer through. II. *v. tr.* durchschímmern [ich durchschimmere, durchschimmert, zu durchschimmern] to fill with glimmer or glitter. *Fig.* Freude durchschimmert die Augen der Frauen, the ladies' eyes glisten with pleasure.

Durchschlafen, *v. tr.* [ich durchschlafe, durchschlafen, zu durchschlafen] to pass or spend sleeping. Er durchschläft den Tag, he passes the day in sleep.

Dúrchschlag, *m.* [-es, *pl.* -schläge] 1) the act of making a hole to get through [especially in mining]. 2) an opening, aperture or passage. 3) an instrument used in several arts for p[illegible] forating holes in plates of metal &c., a punch. *a*) [in carpentry] mortise-chisel. *b*) [with smiths and locksmiths] a pointed hammer to make holes with in iron. *c*) [in cookery] a strainer, a colander, a sile-dish. *d*) [in metallurgy] a wire-grate to run the washed ore through. *e*) [in hydraulics] a dike made across standing water.

Durchschlag=hammer, *m.* [with braziers and tinmen] a strong hammer or mallet to make holes with. —**meißel**, *m.* [with braziers and tinmen] a chisel to make holes with. —**scheere**, *f.* cardmaker's shears. —**tuch**, *n.* V. Seihetuch.

Durchschlagen, *ir.* I. **dúrchschlagen** [ich schlage durch, durchgeschlagen, durchzuschlagen] 1) *v. tr. a*) to make a breach or opening. Eine Wand —, to make a breach into a wall. *b*) [in cookery] to strain [pease &c.]. Reis, in Molken gekocht und durchgeschlagen, rice boiled in whey and strained. *c*) Einen —, to beat or drub any one soundly, to beat any one sore. 2) *v. r.* sich —, to force one's way through, to cut one's way through; to break through the enemy; [with hunters] to get out, to break cover. 3) *v. intr. a*) to penetrate, to make way. Der Regen schlägt durch, the rain wets thoroughly; das Wasser schlägt durch, the water penetrates, soaks through; die Tinte schlägt durch, the ink soaks into the paper; die Arzenei hat durchgeschlagen, the medicine has worked. *b*) to sink, to blot [said of paper]. Das Papier schlägt durch, the paper sinks; Papier, das nicht durchschlägt, paper that bears ink. II. **durchschlágen** [ich durchschlage, durchschlagen, zu durchschlagen] *v. tr.* to partition [a room &c.].

Durchschlängeln, I. *v. r.* **dúrchschlängeln** [ich schlängele mich durch, durchgeschlängelt, sich durchzuschlängeln] sich —, to wind through. Ein Fußpfad schlängelt sich durch, a footpath winds or meanders through [the valley &c.]. II. *v. tr.* **durchschlängeln** [ich durchschlängele, durchschlängelt, zu durchschlängeln] to wind, to meander, to serpentize through. Der Weg durchschlängelt ein hohes Lustgebüsch, the road serpentizes through a tall shrubbery; Blitze — die Luft, lightnings serpentize through the air.

Durchschleichen, *ir.* I. **dúrchschleichen** [ich schleiche durch, durchgeschlichen, durchzuschleichen] 1) *v. intr.* [used with seyn] to sneak or slink through. 2) *v. r.* sich —, to sneak through, to go through unperceived. II. **durchschleichen** [ich durchschleiche, durchschlichen, zu durchschleichen] *v. tr.* to sneak through, to glide stealthily through [a room &c.].

1. **Dúrchschleifen**, [from schleifen] *v. tr.* [ich schleife durch, durchgeschleift, durchzuschleifen] to carry through on a sled, to drag or to trail through.

2. **Dúrchschleifen**, [from schleifen] *ir. v. tr.* [ich schleife durch, durchgeschliffen, durchzuschleifen] to wear by grinding. Sich —, to be worn by grinding.

Durchschlendern, I. *v. intr.* [used with seyn] **dúrchschlendern** [ich schlendere durch, durchgeschlendert, durchzuschlendern] to saunter or stroll lazily through. II. *v. tr.* **durchschléndern** [ich durchschlendere, durchschlendert, zu durchschlendern] to saunter through. Er durchschlenderte die Stadt, he strolled over the town.

Dúrchschleppen, *v. tr.* [ich schleppe durch, durchgeschleppt, durchzuschleppen] to trail or drag through. **Fig.* Einen —, to help any one out.

Dúrchschleudern, *v. tr.* [ich schleudere durch, durchgeschleudert, durchzuschleudern] to fling through. Steine —, to fling stones through [the window &c.].

Durchschliefen, V. Durchschlüpfen.

Durchschlingen, *ir. v. tr.* 1) **dúrchschlingen** [ich schlinge durch, durchgeschlungen, durchzuschlingen] *a*) to twine through. *b*) to tie in a noose, to noose. *c*) to swallow. 2) **durchschlíngen** [ich durchschlinge, durchschlungen, zu durchschlingen] to interlace, to entwine.

Durchschlitzen, *v. tr. & intr.* 1) **dúrchschlitzen** [ich schlitze durch, durchgeschlitzt, durchzuschlitzen] to slit through. Die Haut —, to slit the skin through. 2) **durchschlitzen** [ich durchschlitze, durchschlitzt, zu durchschlitzen] to slit through and through. Durchschlitzte Nasen und Ohren, slitted noses and ears.

Durchschlúmmern, *v. tr.* [ich durchschlummere, durchschlummert, zu durchschlummern] to pass or spend [an hour &c.] slumbering, dozing. Er durchschlummert einige Stunden des Tages, he passes some hours of the day in slumber.

Durchschlüpfen, I. *v. intr.* [u. w. seyn] **dúrchschlüpfen** [ich schlüpfe durch, durchgeschlüpft, durchzuschlüpfen] to slip, sneak or slink through. *Fig.* Er ist noch gut durchgeschlüpft, he had a narrow escape. II. *v. tr.* **durchschlüpfen** [ich durchschlüpfe, durchschlüpft, zu durchschlüpfen] to visit or to pass through slipping. Er durchschlüpft jeden Winkel, he searches every corner.

Durchschmáchten, *v. tr.* [ich schmachte durch, durchgeschmachtet, durchzuschmachten] to pass or spend languishing.

Dúrchschmarotzen, [ich schmarotze durch, durchschmarotzt, durchzuschmarotzen] I. *v. tr.* to pass or spend [time] spunging or living upon others. Er hat die ganze Woche durchschmarotzt, he has been living on others the whole week through. II. *v. r.* sich —, to get one's livelihood by spunging on others.

Durchschmauchen, I. **dúrchschmauchen** [ich schmauche durch, durchgeschmaucht, durchzuschmauchen] 1) *v. intr. a*) to smoke through. *b*) to be smoked thoroughly. 2) *v. tr.* to smoke through. II. **durchschmauchen** [ich durchschmauche, durchschmaucht, zu durchschmauchen] *v. tr. a*) to apply smoke to. Angesteckte Kleider —, to fumigate infected clothes. *b*) to pass or spend smoking. Den ganzen Abend —, to pass the whole evening in smoking.

†**Durchschmeißen**, *ir. v. tr.* V. Durchwerfen.

Dúrchschmelzen, *ir. v. tr.* [ich schmelze durch, durchgeschmolzen, durchzuschmelzen] to melt down, to melt thoroughly.

Durchschmettern, I. **dúrchschmettern** [ich schmettere durch, durchgeschmettert, durchzuschmettern] 1) *v. intr.* [u. w. seyn] to penetrate crashing. 2) *v. tr.* to throw through with a crash. II. **durchschmettern** [ich durchschmettere, durchschmettert, zu durchschmettern] *v. tr.* to penetrate with a crash. *Fig.* Nachtigallen — den Hain, nightingales quaver throughout the grove.

Durchschmieden, *v. tr.* 1) **dúrchschmieden** [ich schmiede durch, durchgeschmiedet, durchzuschmieden] *a*) to break by forging. *b*) to forge all or the whole successively. 2) **durchschmieden** [ich durchschmiede, durchschmiedet, zu durchschmieden] to forge thoroughly. Wohl durchschmiedetes Eisen, well-forged iron.

Durchschmieren, *v. tr.* 1) **dúrchschmieren** [ich schmiere durch, durchgeschmiert, durchzuschmieren] *a*) to smear all one by one; † to drub, to beat. *b*) to smear through. 2) **durchschmieren** [ich durchschmiere, durchschmiert, zu durchschmieren] to smear thoroughly.

Durchschnauben, *v. tr.* [ich durchschnaube, durchschnaubt, zu durchschnauben] to run through snorting. Das Roß durchschnaubte die Ebene, the horse ran snorting through the plain.

Durchschneiden, *ir.* I. **dúrchschneiden** [ich schneide durch, durchgeschnitten, durchzuschneiden] 1) *v. tr.* to cut through, to cut in two. Papier —, to cut paper through. 2) *v. intr.* to pass by a shorter course, to cut across. II **durchschnéiden** [ich durchschneide, durchschnitten, zu durchschneiden] *v. tr.* to cut, to cut asunder. Das Land —, to trench and turn up land with a plough, to plough land. Eine durchschnittene Gegend, a country intersected with rivers, canals &c.; die Linie or den Gleicher —, [in seamen's lang.] to cross or pass the line; ein Schiff durchschneidet die salzige Tiefe, a ship ploughs the briny deep; die Luft —, to cut the air; [in mathematics] eine Linie durchschneidet eine andere in rechten Winkeln, a line cuts another in right angles; die Ekliptik durchschneidet den Gleicher, the ecliptic cuts the equator; ein Weg, der einen andern durchschneidet, a road that crosses another, a cross-road; [also as a *v. r.*] zwei Linien durchschneiden sich, two lines intersect each other; [in heraldry] ein durchschnittener Schild, a field party per bend. *Fig.* Dies durchschnitt mir das Herz, this pierced my very heart.

Dúrchschneien, *v. imp.* [es schneiet durch, es hat durchgeschneiet, durchzuschneien] to snow through.

Dúrchschnellen, [ich schnelle durch, durchgeschnellt, durchzuschnellen] I. *v. intr.* [u. w. seyn] to jerk through, to spring through with an elastic impulse. II. *v. tr.* 1) to jerk through. 2) to fillip through.

Dúrchschnitt, *m.* [-es, *pl.* -e] 1) the act of cutting through or separating by cutting, section. *Fig.* Den — finden, im —e berechnen, to find the mean of unequal sums or quantities, to reduce to a medium, to average; im —, upon an average. 2) the thing cut through, the opening made, a channel made by cutting or digging, the cut; der Rhein— bei N., the cut of the Rhine near N. 3) [in architecture, the draught of a building, representing it as if cut down perpendicularly from the roof to the foundation] the profile or section of a building, sciagraphy. 4) a machine for cutting, as in mints, a machine for cutting the blanks or planchets.

Durchschnitts=ansicht, *f.* the view of a building &c. in profile. —**preis**, *m.* the average-price. —**punkt**, *m.* the point where two lines intersect, intersection. —**riß**, *m.* the profile [of a pyramid &c.] —**senne**, *f.* [in trigonometry] the secant. —**summe**, *f.* a medial sum or quantity, average. —**zahl**, *f.* average-number.

Durchschnüffeln, *v. tr.* **dúrchschnüffeln** [ich schnüffele durch, durchgeschnüffelt, durchzuschnüffeln] *it.* **durchschnüffeln** [ich durchschnüffele, durchschnüffelt, zu durchschnüffeln] to snuff one by one; *fig.* † to examine one by one.

Dúrchschrammen, *v. tr.* [ich schramme durch, durchgeschrammt, durchzuschrammen] to make sore by scratching. Sich —, to wound one's self by scratching.

Durchschreien, *ir.* I. *v. intr.* **dúrchschreien** [ich schreie durch, durchgeschrieen, durchzuschreien] 1) to cry through. 2) to penetrate with cries or clamour. II. *v. tr.* **durchschreien** [ich durchschreie, durchschrieen, zu durchschreien] to fill with cries or clamour. Das ganze Haus —, to clamour throughout the house.

Durchschreiten, *ir.* I. *v. intr.* **dúrchschreiten** [ich schreite durch, durchgeschritten, durchzuschreiten] to walk through with long steps, to stride through, to stalk through. II. *v. tr.* **durchschreiten** [ich durchschreite, durchschritten, zu durchschreiten] to walk over striding. Er durchschritt das Feld, he strode or stalked over the field.

Dúrchschüppen, *v. tr.* [ich schüppe durch, durchgeschüppt, durchzuschüppen] 1) to shovel through. 2) to make way by shoveling.

Dúrchschuß, *m.* [-sses, *pl.* -schüsse] 1) the act of shooting through, of interleaving or interlining. 2) [with carpet-makers] the woof, the weft. 3) [in printing] leads, space-lines, interline.

Durchschütteln, *v. tr.* 1) dúrchschütteln [ich schüttele durch, durchgeschüttelt, durchzuschütteln] *a*) to shake through. *b*) to shake up [beds &c.]. 2) durchschǘtteln [ich durchschüttele, durchschüttelt, zu durchschütteln] to shake thoroughly, to mix well by shaking.

Dúrchschütten, *v. tr.* [ich schütte durch, durchgeschüttet, durchzuschütten] to pour through.

Dúrchschüttern, *v. tr.* [ich schüttere durch, durchgeschüttert, durchzuschüttern] to shake vehemently. V. Erschüttern.

Durchschwärmen, I. *v. intr.* [u. w. seyn] dúrchschwärmen [ich schwärme durch, durchgeschwärmt, durchzuschwärmen] to swarm through. Die Bienen sind durchgeschwärmt, the bees swarmed through. II. *v. tr.* durchschwǻrmen [ich schwärme durch, durchschwärmt, zu durchschwärmen] 1) to wander over, to rove. Die Stadt —, to rove over, through or about the town, to ramble about the town. 2) to pass revelling. Die Nacht —, to spend the night in revelry.

Durchschwätzen, *v. tr.* [ich durchschwatze, durchschwatzt, zu durchschwatzen] to pass or spend prating.

Durchschweben, I. *v. intr.* [u. w. seyn] dúrchschweben [ich schwebe durch, durchgeschwebt, durchzuschweben] to hover through. Durch das Zimmer —, to hover through the room. II. *v. tr.* durchschwében [ich durchschwebe, durchschwebt, zu durchschweben] to hover. Die Luft —, to hover through the air.

Durchschwefeln, *v. tr.* dúrchschwefeln [ich schwefele durch, durchgeschwefelt, durchzuschwefeln] *it.* durchschwéfeln [ich durchschwefele, durchschwefelt, zu durchschwefeln] to impregnate with sulphur thoroughly.

Durchschweifen, *v. tr.* [ich durchschweife, durchschweift, zu durchschweifen] to wander over, to rove over, through or about. Das Land —, to ramble over the country. *Fig.* Seine Blicke — das Thal, his looks run óver the valley.

Dúrchschweißen, [ich schweiße durch, durchgeschweißt, durchzuschweißen] I. *v. tr.* to hammer iron, to forge it throughout. II. *v. intr.* to percolate, to ooze out.

Durchschwelgen, *v. tr.* dúrchschwelgen [ich schwelge durch, durchgeschwelgt, durchzuschwelgen] *it.* durchschwélgen [ich durchschwelge, durchschwelgt, zu durchschwelgen] to pass or spend in banqueting or in revelry. Die Nächte —, to spend nights carousing; ein Besitzthum —, to run through an estate.

Durchschwimmen, *ir.* I. *v. intr.* [u. w. seyn] dúrchschwimmen [ich schwimme durch, durchgeschwommen, durchzuschwimmen] 1) to swim through. 2) to swim or float through. II. *v. tr.* durchschwimmen [ich durchschwimme, durchschwommen, zu durchschwimmen] to swim through. Flüsse —, to swim rivers.

Dúrchschwingen, *ir.* [ich schwinge durch, durchgeschwungen, zu durchschwingen] I. *v. tr.* 1) to swing [a lance &c.] through. 2) to winnow, to van throughout [corn]. 3) to swingle thoroughly [the flax]. II. *v. r.* sich —, to swing through. Er schwang sich durch eine Oeffnung, he swang through an opening.

Durchschwitzen, I. dúrchschwitzen [ich schwitze durch, durchgeschwitzt, durchzuschwitzen] *v. tr.* and *intr.* 1) to sweat through and through. †*Fig.* to forget entirely. Er hat all sein Latein schon lange durchgeschwitzt, his Latin has long ago oozed away from him. 2) to be penetrated with sweat. Er ist ganz durchgeschwitzt, he drops with sweat. II. durchschwítzen [ich durchschwitze, durchschwitzt, zu durchschwitzen] *v. tr.* to penetrate with sweat.

Durchsegeln, I. *v. intr.* dúrchsegeln [ich segele durch, durchgesegelt, durchzusegeln] to sail through. II. *v. tr.* durchségeln [ich durchsegele, durchsegelt, zu durchsegeln] to sail through or over, to sail. Das Meer —, to sail the sea. *Fig.* Die Lüfte —, to sail the air.

Dúrchsehbar, *adj.* and *adv.* capable of being seen through, reviewed or examined.

Durchsehen, *ir.* I. dúrchsehen [ich sehe durch, durchgesehen, durchzusehen] 1) *v. intr.* to see through, to look through. 2) *v. tr. a*) to penetrate with the eye, to look through. *b*) to look over, to go over, to examine all one by one. Rechnungen —, to look over accounts; Probebogen —, to revise proof-sheets, to look over proof-sheets; flüchtig —, to glance the eye hastily over. II. durchséhen [ich durchsehe, durchsehen, zu durchsehen] *v. tr. a*) to see thoroughly. *b*) to view, to penetrate with a scrutinizing eye. Die Durchsehung, review, revision.

Dúrchseher, *m.* [unusual] [-s, *pl.* -] reviewer.

Durchseifen, *v. tr.* dúrchseifen [ich seife durch, durchgeseift, durchzuseifen] *it.* durchseífen [ich durchseife, durchseift, zu durchseifen] to soap one by one, to soap all over, to soap throughout.

Dúrchseihen, *v. tr.* [ich seihe durch, durchgeseiht, durchzuseihen] to pass through a filter, to filter, to filtrate. Milch —, to percolate milk.

Dúrchseiher, *m.* [-s, *pl.* -] 1) a person that filters. 2) a filter, a strainer, a colander.

Durchsenden, *v. tr.* 1) dúrchsenden [ich sende durch, durchgesendet, durchzusenden] to send through. 2) durchsénden [ich durchsende, durchsendet, zu durchsenden] to send throughout.

Dúrchsengen, *v. tr.* [ich senge durch, durchgesengt, durchzusengen] to singe one by one, to singe throughout.

Durchsetzen, I. dúrchsetzen [ich setze durch, durchgesetzt, durchzusetzen] 1) *v. intr.* [u. w. seyn] to pass over at a step, to pass through leaping. Die Reiterei setzte muthig durch, the horse made boldly through. 2) *v. tr. a*) to carry through. Ein Project —, to carry a project through. *b*) [in metallurgy] *α*) to run through a wire-sieve. Gepochtes Erz —, to size washed ore. *β*) to run = to fuse, to melt. *c*) [with printers] to compose [a book] throughout. II. durchsétzen [ich durchsetze, durchsetzt, zu durchsetzen] *v. tr.* [in mining] Eine durchsetzte Steinart, any species of stone penetrated with another fossil or with metallic particles.

Durchseufzen, *v. tr.* [ich durchseufze, durchseufzt, zu durchseufzen] to pass or spend sighing. Sein Leben —, to pass one's life sighing.

Dúrchseyn, *ir. v. intr.* [ich bin durch, durchgewesen, durchzuseyn] 1) to be through. Er ist schon durch, he is already through [a window &c.], *it.* he has already passed through [a town &c.]. *Fig.* Er ist glücklich durch, he came off safe; ich bin damit durch, I have done with it. 2) to be worn through. Die Schuhe sind ganz durch, the shoes are quite worn through.

Dúrchsicht, *f.* [*pl.* -en] 1) the act of looking or seeing through. 2) review, inspection. Die — eines Probebogens, the revision of a proof-sheet. 3) a vista. Eine — durch einen Wald [Wald—], a vista through a wood.

Durchsichts-bild, *n.* a transparent picture, a transparency. —lehre, *f.* [a part of optics] dioptrics. —lehrig, *adj.* and *adv.* [pertaining to optics] dioptric, dioptrical.

Dúrchsichtig, *adj.* and *adv.* pervious to light, transparent, diaphanous, pellucid. Ein —es Glas, a transparent glass.

Dúrchsichtigkeit, *f.* transparency, transparentness, translucency, pellucidness, diaphaneity. Die — der Luft, the pellucidity of the air.

Dúrchsickern, *v. intr.* [u. w. seyn] [ich sickere durch, durchgesickert, durchzusickern] to percolate, as a liquid through the pores of a substance or through small openings, to ooze. Der Regen ist durchgesickert, the rain dripped or trickled through.

Dúrchsieben, *v. tr.* [ich siebe durch, durchgesiebt, durchzusieben] to sift, to garble. Mehl —, to sift or bolt meal.

Durchsieden, *ir.* I. dúrchsieden [ich siede durch, durchgesotten, durchzusieden] V. Durchkochen I. II. durchsíeden [ich durchsiede, durchsotten, zu durchsieden] V. Durchkochen II.

Durchsingen, *ir. v. tr.* 1) dúrchsingen [ich singe durch, durchgesungen, durchzusingen] to sing one by one or to the end, to sing repeatedly. 2) durchsíngen [ich durchsinge, durchsungen, zu durchsingen] *a*) to fill with songs. Die Vögel — den Wald, the birds sing throughout the wood. *b*) to pass or spend singing.

Durchsinken, *ir.* I. *v. intr.* [u. w. seyn] dúrchsinken [ich sinke durch, durchgesunken, durchzusinken] to sink through. II. *v. tr.* durchsínken [ich durchsinke, durchsunken, zu durchsinken] [in mining, to make by digging or delving] to sink [a pit].

Dúrchsinnen, *ir. v. tr.* [ich sinne durch, durchgesonnen, durchzusinnen] to spend musing or meditating.

Dúrchsintern, *v. intr.* [u. w. seyn] V. Durchsickern.

Durchsitzen, *ir. v. tr.* 1) dúrchsitzen [ich sitze durch, durchgesessen, durchzusitzen] to wear [illegible] by sitting upon. 2) durchsítzen [ich durch[illegible] durchsessen, zu durchsitzen] to pass sitting. [illegible] Nacht beim Spiele —, to sit up the whole [illegible] at play.

Dúrchsollen, *v. intr.* [ich soll durch, durch[illegible] sollt, durchzusollen] to be under the necessity [illegible] passing through.

Durchsonnen, *v. tr.* dúrchsonnen [ich [illegible] durch, durchgesonnt, durchzusonnen] *it.* dur[illegible] sónnen [ich durchsonne, durchsonnt, zu durch[illegible] nen] to insolate, to sun. Durchsonne dich in fr[illegible] Luft, sun thyself in open air.

Durchsórgen, *v. tr.* [ich durchsorge, [illegible] sorgt, zu durchsorgen] to spend sorrowing. [illegible] Nächte —, to spend one's nights in sorrow.

Durchspähen, I. *v. intr.* dúrchspähen [illegible] spähe durch, durchgespäht, durchzuspähen] to [illegible] through spying. II. *v. tr.* durchspä́hen [illegible] durchspähe, durchspäht, zu durchspähen] to exa[illegible] with a prying eye. *Fig.* Ich kann seine [illegible] nicht —, I cannot fathom his design; Einen — to explore a person.

Durchspalten, I. dúrchspalten [ich [illegible] durch, durchgespalten, durchzuspalten] 1) *v.* [illegible] [u. w. seyn] to split, to part asunder. Das [illegible] ist ganz durchgespalten, the board is quite [illegible] through. 2) *v. tr.* to split, to cleave. II. dur[illegible] spálten [ich durchspalte, durchspalten, zu [illegible] spalten] 1) *v. intr.* [u. w. seyn] to be full of c[illegible] 2) *v. tr.* to split or cleave throughout. Die [illegible] spaltene Eiche, the riven oak.

Dúrchspeien, *ir. v. tr.* [ich speie durch, [illegible] gespieen, durchzuspeien] to spit through.

Durchspicken, *v. tr.* 1) dúrchspicken [illegible] spicke durch, durchgespickt, durchzuspicken] to [illegible] one by one, to lard all over. 2) durchspic[illegible] [ich durchspicke, durchspickt, zu durchspicken] to [illegible] all over. Einen Hasen —, to lard a hare. *F*[illegible] Er durchspickte mit trockenem Witze seine [illegible] gerige Prosa, he larded with dry wit his h[illegible] ry prose; durchspickt mit &c., interlarded by &c.

Durchspielen, *v. tr.* 1) dúrchspielen [ich spiele durch, durchgespielt, durchzuspielen] *a*) to play all or the whole in succession, to play to the end. Sie spielten alle Spiele durch, they played at all games; mehrere Tonstücke —, to play several tunes. *Fig.* Seine Rolle auf der Lebensbühne gut —, to play one's part well on the stage of life. *b*) to exercise one's self by playing a tune. *c*) to make sore, to hurt [one's fingers] by playing too long on a musical instrument. 2) durchspielen [ich durchspiele, durchspielt, zu durchspielen] *a*) to penetrate playing, wantoning. Der Wind durchspielt das wogende Schilf, the breeze plays through the waving sedges; der Wind durchspielt ihre goldenen Locken, her golden tresses wanton in the wind. *b*) to pass or spend playing. Die Nacht —, to sit up all night at play.

Durchspießen, *v. tr.* dúrchspießen [ich spieße durch, durchgespießt, durchzuspießen] *it.* durchspießen [ich durchspieße, durchspießt, zu durchspießen] to pierce with a spear.

Dúrchspornen, *v. tr.* [ich sporne durch, durchgespornt, durchzuspornen] to urge, push or drive through by spurring, to spur through.

Dúrchspotten, *v. tr.* [ich spotte durch, durchgespottet, durchzuspotten] to treat with derision or scorn, to deride one by one.

Dúrchsprechen, *ir. v. tr.* [ich spreche durch, durchgesprochen, durchzusprechen] 1) to speak through an aperture or any instrument. 2) to reason, to discuss, to discuss sufficiently.

Durchsprengen, I. dúrchsprengen [ich sprenge durch, durchgesprengt, durchzusprengen] 1) *v. intr.* [u. w. seyn] to pass through at full speed, to gallop through. 2) *v. tr. a*) to cause to pass through leaping. *b*) to separate wholly by blowing up. II. durchsprèngen [ich durchsprenge, durchsprengt, zu durchsprengen] *v. tr. a*) to pass over, to gallop over. Er durchsprengte die Stadt, he galloped over the town. *b*) to sprinkle throughout.

Durchspringen, *ir.* I. *v. intr.* [u. w. seyn] dúrchspringen [ich springe durch, durchgesprungen, durchzuspringen] 1) to leap or jump through. 2) to crack, to burst through. II. *v. tr.* durchspríngen [ich durchspringe, durchsprungen, zu durchspringen] to run over. Die Stadt —, to run over the town.

Durchspritzen, I. dúrchspritzen [ich spritze durch, durchgespritzt, durchzuspritzen] 1) *v. tr.* to squirt or spout through. 2) *v. intr.* [u. w. seyn] to spout or spirt through. II. durchsprítzen [ich durchspritze, durchspritzt, zu durchspritzen] *v. tr.* to sprinkle throughout.

Durchsprossen, *v. intr.* [u. w. seyn] [ich sprosse durch, durchgesproßt, durchzusprossen] to sprout through.

Durchsprudeln, I. dúrchsprudeln [ich sprudele durch, durchgesprudelt, durchzusprudeln] 1) *v. intr.* [u. w. seyn] to pass through bubbling with a gurgling noise. 2) *v. tr.* to send forth bubbling. II. durchsprúdeln [ich durchsprudele, durchsprudelt, zu durchsprudeln] *v. tr.* to run or flow through gurgling. Bäche — die Ebene, brooks gurgle over the plain.

Dúrchsprühen, *v. intr.* [ich sprühe durch, durchgesprüht, durchzusprühen] to spark or sparkle through. *Fig.* Ihre Feueraugen, sprühend durch stählerne Visiere, their eyes of fire sparkling through sights of steel.

Durchspüren, *v. tr.* 1) dúrchspüren [ich spüre durch, durchgespürt, durchzuspüren] to hunt through or over, to pry or examine into. 2) durchspǘren [ich durchspüre, durchspürt, zu durchspüren] [among hunters] to beat the wood or plain for game.

Durchstacheln, *v. tr.* 1) dúrchstacheln [ich stachele durch, durchgestachelt, durchzustacheln] *a*) to goad through. *b*) to make sore, to wound by a goad. 2) durchstácheln [ich durchstachele, durchstachelt, zu durchstacheln] to prick thoroughly.

Durchstählen, *v. tr.* [ich durchstähle, durchstählt, zu durchstählen] to steel throughout [also in a fig. sense].

Durchstampfen, *v. tr.* 1) dúrchstampfen [ich stampfe durch, durchgestampft, durchzustampfen] *a*) to strike or beat forcibly through with the bottom of the foot, to stamp through. *b*) to stamp all one by one. *c*) to penetrate stamping. 2) durchstámpfen [ich durchstampfe, durchstampft, zu durchstampfen] *a*) to stamp throughout. *b*) to mix by stamping.

Durchstänkern, *v. tr.* 1) dúrchstänkern [ich stänkere durch, durchgestänkert, durchzustänkern] to rummage with scrutinizing curiosity, impertinently. 2) durchstä́nkern [ich durchstänkere, durchstänkert, zu durchstänkern] to fill with a stink.

Durchstauben, *v. intr.* 1) dúrchstauben [ich staube durch, durchgestaubt, durchzustauben] to penetrate as dust, to pass through as dust. 2) [u. w. seyn] durchstaûben [ich durchstaube, durchstaubt, zu durchstauben] to be dusted throughout.

Durchstäuben, *v. tr.* 1) dúrchstäuben [ich stäube durch, durchgestäubt, durchzustäuben] *a*) to drive through as dust. Kohlenstaub durch ein durchstochenes Papier —, to dust a pricked paper. *b*) to dust throughout. Das Haar wohl —, to powder well one's hair. 2) durchstä́uben [ich durchstäube, durchstäubt, zu durchstäuben] *a*) to dust all over. *b*) to hurry through, making a dust.

‖**Durchstaubern**, V. Durchstöbern.

Dúrchstäupen, *v. tr.* [ich stäupe durch, durchgestäupt, durchzustäupen] 1) to whip any one, to beat any one with rods. 2) to carry or drive through flogging or whipping.

Durchstechen, *ir.* I. dúrchstechen [ich steche durch, durchgestochen, durchzustechen] 1) *v. intr.* to thrust through with a pointed instrument. Das Leder ist so dick, daß man nicht — kann, the leather is so thick, that one cannot pierce it through. 2) *v. tr.* Einen Damm —, to open a dike, to cut through a dike, to open a passage through a dike; das Getreide —, to stir corn. *Fig.* *Mit Einem etwas —, to plot something with any one. II. durchstèchen [ich durchsteche, durchstochen, zu durchstechen] *v. tr.* to pierce through, to transpierce. Einen mit dem Degen —, to pierce any one with a sword, to run a sword through any one's body; er durchstach ihn mit einem Speere, he transfixed him with a spear; durchstochenes Papier, pricked paper; ein durchstochenes Blatt, [in botany] a perfoliate or perforated leaf.

Dúrchstecher, *m.* [-s, *pl.* -] [with cartwrights] a piercer.

Durchstecherei, *f.* [in colloquial language] joint contrivance, an intrigue, a plot.

Durchstecken, *v. tr.* 1) dúrchstecken [ich stecke durch, durchgesteckt, durchzustecken] to put through. Einen Faden durch ein Nadelöhr —, to pass a thread through the eye of a needle, to thread a needle. 2) durchstécken [ich durchstecke, durchsteckt, zu durchstecken] to stick all over.

Dúrchstehlen, *ir.* I. *v. tr.* [ich stehle durch, durchgestohlen, durchzustehlen] to steal one by one or thoroughly or to the end. II. *v. r.* sich —, [ich stehle mich durch, durchgestohlen, sich durchzustehlen] to steal through, to slip through unperceived.

Durchsteigen, *ir.* I. *v. intr.* [u. w. seyn] dúrchsteigen [ich steige durch, durchgestiegen, durchzusteigen] to climb, mount or ascend through, to swerve through. II. *v. tr.* durchsteígen [ich durchsteige, durchstiegen, zu durchsteigen] to climb, mount or ascend throughout.

Dúrchstellen, *v. tr.* [ich stelle durch, durchgestellt, durchzustellen] [with hunters] to encompass with toils.

Durchstèppen, *v. tr.* [ich durchsteppe, durchsteppt, zu durchsteppen] to quilt all over.

Durchsteuern, I. *v. intr.* [u. w. seyn] and *v. tr.* dúrchsteuern [ich steuere durch, durchgesteuert, durchzusteuern] to steer through [used also in a figurative sense]. II. *v. tr.* durchsteúern [ich durchsteuere, durchsteuert, zu durchsteuern] to steer through. Er durchsteuerte die Wogen, he steered through the waves.

Dúrchstich, *m.* [-es, *pl.* -e] 1) the act of piercing through, transpiercing, cutting through. 2) the place where a cut is made through a dike, cut, breach.

Durchstícheln, *v. tr.* [ich durchstichele, durchstichelt, zu durchsticheln] to prick [a paper &c.] all over.

Durchsticken, *v. tr.* 1) dúrchsticken [ich sticke durch, durchgestickt, durchzusticken] to embroider through, to embroider to the end or thoroughly. 2) durchstícken [ich durchsticke, durchstickt, zu durchsticken] to embroider all over.

Durchstieben, V. Durchstauben.

Dúrchstimmen, *v. tr.* [ich stimme durch, durchgestimmt, durchzustimmen] 1) to tune thoroughly. Eine Geige —, to tune a violin thoroughly. 2) to tune all successively, to tune to the end.

Durchstinken, *ir.* I. *v. intr.* dúrchstinken [ich stinke durch, durchgestunken, durchzustinken] to stink through. II. *v. tr.* durchstínken [ich durchstinke, durchstunken, zu durchstinken] to fill with a stink.

Durchstöbern, *v. tr.* dúrchstöbern [ich stöbere durch, durchgestöbert, durchzustöbern] *it.* durchstö̈bern [ich durchstöbere, durchgestöbert, zu durchstöbern] to rake, to rummage, to stir about. Alle Winkel eines Ortes —, to search with eagerness all corners of a place.

Durchstochern, *v. tr.* dúrchstochern [ich stochere durch, durchgestochert, durchzustochern] *it.* durchstóchern [ich durchstochere, durchstochert, zu durchstochern] to pick or poke through. Sich die Zähne —, to pick one's teeth. *Fig.* †to search impertinently, to rummage through.

Durchstöhnen, *v. tr.* [ich durchstöhne, durchstöhnt, zu durchstöhnen] to pass or spend groaning.

Dúrchstopfen, *v. tr.* [ich stopfe durch, durchgestopft, durchzustopfen] to stuff or thrust through an aperture.

Durchstören, V. Durchstöbern.

Durchstoßen, *ir. v. tr.* 1) dúrchstoßen [ich stoße durch, durchgestoßen, durchzustoßen] *a*) to thrust or push through an aperture. *b*) [with some artificers] to thrust or drive in. Eine Klinge —, to mount a sword. *c*) to penetrate or break by thrusting. *d*) [in glassworks] to clean by thrusting or pushing. 2) durchstö̀ßen [ich durchstoße, durchstoßen, zu durchstoßen] *a*) to thrust through, to pierce. Einen mit einem Degen —, to run any one through with a sword; ein durchstoßenes Blatt, [in botany] a pertuse or pertused leaf. *b*) [to shake with sudden jerks, as a carriage on rough ground] to jolt.

Durchstottern, *v. tr.* dúrchstottern [ich stottere durch, durchgestottert, durchzustottern] *it.* durchstóttern [ich durchstottere, durchstottert, zu durchstottern] to read through stuttering, to stammer through.

Durchstrahlen, I. *v. intr.* dúrchstrahlen

[ich strahle durch, durchgestrahlt, durchzustrahlen] to radiate through. II. *v. tr.* durchstrählen [ich durchstrahle, durchstrahlt, zu durchstrahlen] to penetrate with rays of light, to illuminate, to irradiate. Die Sonne durchstrahlt die Erde, the sun enlightens the earth.

Dúrchstrecken, *v. tr.* [ich strecke durch, durchgestreckt, durchzustrecken] to reach through.

Durchstreichen, *ir.* I. dúrchstreichen [ich streiche durch, durchgestrichen, durchzustreichen] 1) *v. tr. a)* to strike out, to erase, to efface, to blot out. *b)* to wander over, to rove. Die ganze Gegend —, to rove [over, through or about] the whole country, to ramble over the whole country. ||c) to strain. Erbsen —, to strain pease. 2) *v. intr.* [used with seyn] *a)* to pass through with velocity. Der Wind streicht hier durch, there is a current of air here; die Luft durch ein Zimmer — lassen, to open and expose a room to the free passage of air, to ventilate a room. *b)* to stretch or to be extended through. II. durchstreichen [ich durchstreiche, durchstrichen, zu durchstreichen] *v. tr. a)* to strike out, to erase, to efface. Zeilen in einer Schrift —, to cancel the lines of a writing, to cross and deface them. Das —, cancelling. *b)* to wander over, to rove. Ich durchstrich die Stadt, I rambled about the town.

Durchstreifen, *v. tr.* 1) dúrchstreifen [ich streife durch, durchgestreift, durchzustreifen] *a)* to go over or move about from place to place. Der Feind streift das ganze Land durch, the enemy ranges through the whole country. *b)* to strip through. 2) durchstreifen [ich durchstreife, durchstreift, zu durchstreifen] *a)* to walk over, to rove. Der Wolf und der Wilde — den Wald, the wolf and the savage roam the forest; das Gehölz jagend —, to beat the wood for game. *b)* to variegate with stripes throughout, to stripe or streak all over.

Durchstreiten, *ir. v. tr.* 1) dúrchstreiten [ich streite durch, durchgestritten, durchzustreiten] Eine Sache —, to carry a matter through; sich —, to force or cut one's way through [also in a figurative sense]. 2) durchstreiten [ich durchstreite, durchstritten, zu durchstreiten] *a)* to carry through. *b)* to pass or spend in contention.

Durchstreuen, *v. tr.* 1) dúrchstreuen [ich streue durch, durchgestreut, durchzustreuen] to strew or scatter through. 2) durchstreuen [ich durchstreue, durchstreuet, zu durchstreuen] to strew or scatter all over.

Dúrchstrich, *m.* [-es, *pl.* -e] 1) a stroke made through a line in writing &c., a dash. 2) passage of birds.

Dúrchstriegeln, *v. tr.* [ich striegele durch, durchgestriegelt, durchzustriegeln] to curry [a horse] thoroughly. *Fig.* †Einen —, to chide any one for a fault.

Durchströmen, I. *v. intr.* dúrchströmen [ich ströme durch, durchgeströmt, durchzuströmen] to stream or flow through. II. *v. tr.* durchströmen [ich durchströme, durchströmt, zu durchströmen] to stream, run or flow through, to flow through in streams. Der Fluß durchströmt die Stadt, the river flows through the town. *Fig.* Von einer angenehmen Empfindung durchströmt, pervaded by an agreeable sensation.

Dúrchstudiren, *v. tr.* [ich studire durch, durchstudirt, durchzustudiren] 1) to study through [a doctrine]; to read [a book] with attention. 2) to pass or spend in study. Die Nacht —, to lucubrate.

Durchstürmen, I. *v. intr.* dúrchstürmen [ich stürme durch, durchgestürmt, durchzustürmen] 1) to blow with violence or to storm through. 2) to rush through. II. *v. tr.* durchstürmen [ich durchstürme, durchstürmt, zu durchstürmen] to pervade with impetuosity, violence and tumultuous rapidity. Der Nordwind durchstürmt den Wald, the north-wind rushes through the forest. *Fig.* Ich wurde von den heftigsten Empfindungen durchstürmt, I was penetrated with the most violent emotions, I was agitated by the strongest sensations.

Durchstürzen, I. dúrchstürzen [ich stürze durch, durchgestürzt, durchzustürzen] *v. intr.* [u. w. seyn] to fall through suddenly and with violence, to precipitate through. 2) *v. tr.* to throw through headlong, to precipitate through. II. durchstürzen [ich durchstürze, durchstürzt, zu durchstürzen] *v. tr.* to move through with tumultuous rapidity, to rush through.

Durchsuchen, *v. tr.* 1) dúrchsuchen [ich suche durch, durchgesucht, durchzusuchen] to search thoroughly, to ransack [files of papers &c.]. Ich habe die verschiedenen Höhlen durchgesucht, I ransacked the several caverns. 2) durchsúchen [ich durchsuche, durchsucht, zu durchsuchen] to search thoroughly. Unsere Leute durchsuchten jeden Schlupfwinkel, our men rummaged every hole; Einen —, to search, to examine any one; sie durchsuchten alle Winkel des Waldes, they searched every corner of the forest; ich durchsuchte jedes Eckchen in der Gegend, I explored all corners of the country.

Durchsucher, *m.* [-s, *pl.* -] one who searches, especially one whose office it is to search, searcher.

Durchsuchung, *f.* the act of searching thoroughly.

Durchsummen, I. *v. intr.* dúrchsummen [ich summe durch, durchgesummt, durchzusummen] to move through buzzing or humming. II. *v. tr.* durchsúmmen [ich summe durch, durchsummt, durchzusummen] 1) to fly through buzzing or humming. 2) to fill with hum or buzz.

Durchsumsen, V. Durchsummen.

Durchsüßen, *v. tr.* [ich durchsüße, durchsüßt, zu durchsüßen] to sweeten thoroughly, to edulcorate.

Durchtändeln, *v. tr.* [ich durchtändele, durchtändelt, zu durchtändeln] to pass or spend dallying amorously, trifling, playing. Seine Zeit —, to spend one's time in toying.

Durchtanzen, *v. tr.* 1) dúrchtanzen [ich tanze durch, durchgetanzt, durchzutanzen] *a)* to dance through. *b)* to dance from beginning to end. *c)* to wear through with dancing. 2) durchtánzen [ich durchtanze, durchtanzt, zu durchtanzen] *a)* to dance all over. *b)* to pass dancing. Die Nächte —, to spend the nights in dancing.

Durchtappen, I. dúrchtappen [ich tappe durch, durchgetappt, durchzutappen] 1) *v. intr.* to grope through an aperture. 2) *v. r.* sich —, to grope one's way. II. durchtáppen [ich durchtappe, durchtappt, zu durchtappen] *v. tr.* to grope throughout.

Durchtasten, I. dúrchtasten [ich taste durch, durchgetastet, durchzutasten] 1) *v. intr.* to feel through. 2) *v. tr.* to handle and feel all over. II. durchtásten [ich durchtaste, durchtastet, zu durchtasten] *v. tr. a)* to handle and feel throughout, all over. *b)* to search by handling and feeling.

Durchtaumeln, I. *v. intr.* dúrchtaumeln [ich taumele durch, durchgetaumelt, durchzutaumeln] to reel through, to stagger through. II. *v. tr.* durchtaúmeln [ich durchtaumele, durchtaumelt, zu durchtaumeln] to walk over reeling or staggering.

Durchthauen, I. *v. imp.* dúrchthauen [es thauet durch, es hat durchgethauet, durchzuthauen] to thaw thoroughly. II. *v. tr.* durchthaûen [ich durchthaue, durchthauet, zu durchthauen] to cover or moisten thoroughly or all over with dew, to bedew completely.

Durchtoben, I. *v. intr.* dúrchtoben [ich tobe durch, durchgetobt, durchzutoben] to move through with impetuousity, or boisterously. II. *v. tr.* durchtöben [ich durchtobe, durchtobt, zu durchtoben] to move over with impetuousity, or boisterously, to pass or spend boisterously or tumultuously. Der Sturm durchtobt den Wald, the storm rages through the forest.

Durchtönen, I. *v. intr.* dúrchtönen [ich töne durch, durchgetönt, durchzutönen] to penetrate as a sound. Seine Stimme tönet durch, he has a piercing voice. II. *v. tr.* durchtönen [ich durchtöne, durchtönt, zu durchtönen] to fill with sounds. Geschrei durchtönte das ganze Haus, the whole house resounded, echoed with cries.

Durchtosen, V. Durchtoben.

Durchtraben, I. *v. intr.* [u. w. seyn] dúrchtraben [ich trabe durch, durchgetrabt, durchzutraben] to trot through. II. *v. tr.* durchträben [ich durchtrabe, durchtrabt, zu durchtraben] to trot over.

Dúrchtragen, *ir. v. tr.* [ich trage durch, durchgetragen, durchzutragen] 1) to bear or carry through. Einen durch das Wasser —, to carry any one through the water. 2) to waste, to impair, to hole by wearing. Seine Kleider sind ganz durchgetragen, his clothes are worn full of holes.

Durchträllern, *v. tr.* 1) dúrchträllern [ich trällere durch, durchgeträllert, durchzuträllern] to hum [a tune] from beginning to end. 2) durchträllern [ich durchträllere, durchträllert, zu durchträllern] to wander over humming a tune.

Durchtrampeln, *v. tr.* dúrchtrampeln [ich trampele durch, durchgetrampelt, durchzutrampeln] *it.* durchtrámpeln [ich durchtrampele, durchtrampelt, zu durchtrampeln] *a)* to trample thoroughly. *b)* to hole by trampling.

Durchtrauern, *v. tr.* [ich durchtrauere, durchtrauert, zu durchtrauern] to pass mourning. Sein Leben —, to spend one's life in sadness.

Durchträufeln, I. *v. intr.* dúrchträufeln [ich träufele durch, durchgeträufelt, durchzuträufeln] to drop or drip through. II. *v. tr.* durchträufeln [ich durchträufele, durchträufelt, zu durchträufeln] to drip [meat &c.] thoroughly or all over.

Dúrchtraufen, [ich traufe durch, durchgetrauft, durchzutraufen] *v. tr.* and *intr.* to drip or drop through.

Durchträumen, *v. tr.* 1) dúrchträumen [ich träume durch, durchgeträumt, durchzuträumen] to pass dreaming. Die ganze Nacht —, to spend the whole night in dreams. 2) durchträumen [ich durchträume, durchträumt, zu durchträumen] to pass dreaming. Sein Leben —, to dream away one's life.

Dúrchtreffen, *ir. v. intr.* [ich treffe durch, durchgetroffen, durchzutreffen] to hit through.

Durchtreiben, *ir.* I. dúrchtreiben [ich treibe durch, durchgetrieben, durchzutreiben] 1) *v. tr.* to drive through. Das Vieh durch das Dorf —, to drive the cattle through the village; Erbsen —, to strain pease. *Fig.* *Eine Sache —, to carry a thing through. 2) *v. intr.* [a term in mining] to cut a passage through an old shaft filled up. II. durchtreiben [ich durchtreibe, durchtrieben, zu durchtreiben] *v. tr.* to drive over. Eine Wiese mit der Viehherde —, to drive a herd of cattle all over a meadow. *Fig.* ||Durchtrieben, V. Durchtrieben.

Durchtreten, *ir.* I. dúrchtreten [ich trete durch, durchgetreten, durchzutreten] 1) *v. intr.* [u. w. seyn] *a)* to tread through, to wear through with treading. *b)* to break through, as water through a dike. 2) *v. tr. a)* to wear out by treading

ing. *b*) to tread through, to force through by treading. *c*) to tread thoroughly. II. durchtrḗten [ich durchtrete, durchtreten, zu durchtreten] *v. tr. a*) to tread throughout. *b*) to work [to stir and mix] by treading. Die Ziegelerde —, to work brick-earth by treading.

Dúrchtrichtern, *v. tr.* [ich trichtere durch, durchgetrichtert, durchzutrichtern] to pour [wine &c.] through a tunnel.

Dúrchtrieb, *m.* [-es, *pl.* -e] the act of driving [cattle] over another's grounds and the right of doing so.

Durchtrieben, [*part.* of Durchtreiben] *adj.* and *adv.* cunning, artful, shrewd, sly, crafty, astute, designing. Ein —er Schalk, Vogel, Gast, a cunning fellow, a sly chap.

Durchtriebenheit, *f.* cunningness, cunning, craft, slyness.

Dúrchtriefen, *ir. v. intr.* [u. w. seyn] [ich triefe durch, durchgetrieft, durchzutriefen] to drip, drop or trickle through. Das Fett trieft durch die Pfanne durch, the fat drips through the pan.

Durchtrillern, *v. tr.* 1) dúrchtrillern [ich trillere durch, durchgetrillert, durchzutrillern] to trill or quaver [a tune] from beginning to the end. 2) durchtríllern [ich durchtrillere, durchtrillert, zu durchtrillern] to go or walk through quavering.

Durchtrinken, *ir.* I. *v. intr.* dúrchtrinken [ich trinke durch, durchgetrunken, durchzutrinken] to drink one by one, to drink successively, to drink to the end. II. *v. tr.* durchtrínken [ich durchtrinke, durchtrunken, zu durchtrinken] to pass drinking. Die Nächte —, to spend the nights in drinking.

Durchtrippeln, *v. intr.* and *tr.* dúrchtrippeln [ich trippele durch, durchgetrippelt, durchzutrippeln] *it.* durchtríppeln [ich durchtrippele, durchtrippelt, zu durchtrippeln] to walk through with a light step, to trip through.

Durchtrocknen, dúrchtrocknen [ich trockne durch, durchgetrocknet, durchzutrocknen] *it.* durchtrócknen [ich durchtrockne, durchtrocknet, zu durchtrocknen] I. *v. intr.* [u. w. seyn] to deprive wholly of water or moisture. Heu ist in zwei Tagen durchgetrocknet, hay will dry sufficiently in two days; durchgetrocknetes Bauholz, seasoned timber; der Fluß ist ganz durchgetrocknet, the river is quite dried up. II. *v. tr.* to dry thoroughly. Der Wind durchtrocknet die Erde, wind dries the earth.

Dúrchtröpfeln, [ich tröpfele durch, durchgetröpfelt, durchzutröpfeln] I. *v. intr.* [u. w. seyn] to drip, drop or trickle through. Der Wein tröpfelt durch, the wine oozes through. II. *v. tr.* to drip or drop through.

Dúrchtropfen, *v. intr.* [u. w. seyn] ich tropfe durch, durchgetropft, durchzutropfen] to drop through.

Dúrchüben, *v. tr.* [ich übe durch, durchgeübt, durchzuüben] to exercise from beginning to end.

Durchwachen, I. *v. intr.* and *tr.* dúrchwachen [ich wache durch, durchgewacht, durchzuwachen] to pass waking. Durchgewachte [also durchwáchte] Nächte, pernoctations. II. *v. tr.* durchwáchen [ich durchwache, durchwacht, zu durchwachen] = dúrchwachen. Die Nacht beim Spielen —, to sit up all night at play; ich habe drei Nächte mit euch durchwacht, I have watched two nights with you.

Dúrchwachs, *n.* [-ses] [the name of several plants] 1) common thorough-wax. 2) Italian honeysuckle. 3) V. Singrün. 4) V. Zweiblatt.

Durchwachsen, *ir.* I. *v. intr.* [u. w. seyn] dúrchwachsen [ich wachse durch, durchgewachsen, durchzuwachsen] to grow through a thing. II. *v. intr.* and *tr.* durchwáchsen [ich durchwachse, durchwachsen, zu durchwachsen] to grow through or among. —es Fleisch, meat marbled, interlarded or mixed with fat and lean; [in botany] ein —es Blatt, a perfoliate or perforated leaf [one that has the base entirely surrounding the stem transversely].

Dúrchwagen, *v. r.* sich —, [ich wage mich durch, durchgewagt, sich durchzuwagen] to venture to go, pass or travel through any place.

Durchwägen, *v. tr.* dúrchwägen [ich wäge durch, durchgewägt, durchzuwägen] *it.* durchwä́gen [ich durchwäge, durchwägt, zu durchwägen] to weigh one by one or from beginning to end.

Dúrchwalken, *v. tr.* [ich walke durch, durchgewalkt, durchzuwalken] to full or mill throughout or thoroughly. †*Fig.* Einen —, to thrash or drub any one.

Durchwallen, I. *v. intr.* [u. w. seyn] dúrchwallen [ich walle durch, durchgewallet, durchzuwallen] to wander through. II. *v. tr.* durchwállen [ich durchwalle, durchwallet, zu durchwallen] 1) to wander or walk over. Den Garten, das Thal —, to walk over the garden, the valley [mostly used in a poetical style]. 2) [from wallen, to boil up] *Fig.* Zorn durchwallet sein Blut, his blood boils with anger.

Durchwallfahrten, I. *v. intr.* [u. w. seyn] dúrchwallfahrten [ich wallfahrte durch, durchgewallfahrtet, durchzuwallfahrten] to wander through as a pilgrim. II. *v. tr.* durchwállfahrten [ich durchwallfahrte, durchwallfahrtet, zu durchwallfahrten] to wander over as a pilgrim. Das Land —, to wander over the country as a pilgrim.

Durchwálten, *v. tr.* [ich durchwalte, durchwaltet, zu durchwalten] 1) to govern throughout. *Fig.* to reign through, to prevail. Ein Geist des Wohlwollens durchwaltet sein ganzes Buch, the spirit of benevolence pervades his whole book. 2) to walk or pass through.

1. **Dúrchwalzen**, [from walzen = to roll] *v. tr.* to roll thoroughly.

2. **Durchwalzen**, [from walzen = to waltz] I. dúrchwalzen [ich walze durch, durchgewalzt, durchzuwalzen] 1) *v. intr. a*) to waltz through a space. *b*) to waltz to the end. 2) *v. tr.* to wear out by waltzing. II. durchwálzen [ich durchwalze, durchwalzt, zu durchwalzen] *v. tr. a*) to waltz through. *b*) to pass waltzing. Eine ganze Stunde —, to spend a whole hour in waltzing.

Dúrchwälzen, *v. tr.* [ich wälze durch, durchgewälzt, durchzuwälzen] to roll through an aperture or space.

‖and †**Dúrchwamsen**, *v. tr.* [ich wamse durch, durchgewamset, durchzuwamsen] [literally: to beat one's jacket on one's back soundly, to dust any one's jacket] to thrash or drub.

Durchwandeln, I. dúrchwandeln [ich wandele durch, durchgewandelt, durchzuwandeln] 1) *v. intr.* [u. w. seyn] to wander through a place or space. 2) *v. tr.* [u. w. seyn and with haben] to walk through or over. Ich habe [ich bin] den Garten durchgewandelt, I walked all over the garden. II. durchwándeln [ich durchwandele, durchwandelt, zu durchwandeln] *v. tr.* to walk through or over. Die Stadt —, to wander about the town. *Fig.* Seine Blicke durchwandelten die ganze Landschaft, he took a survey of the whole landscape.

Durchwandern, I. dúrchwandern [ich wandere durch, durchgewandert, durchzuwandern] 1) *v. intr.* [u. w. seyn] to walk through or over a place or country; to go or pass on foot. 2) *v. tr.* to wander over, to journey over. Ganz Frankreich —, to travel the whole kingdom of France. II. durchwándern [ich durchwandere, durchwandert, zu durchwandern] *v. tr.* to walk through or over. Die Stadt —, to wander about the town; das Feld —, to wander over the fields; das Dorf durchwandernd, roving [over, through or about] the village; ein Land nach dem andern —, to peregrinate; das — verschiedener Orte, peregrination, pererration.

Durchwanken, I. *v. intr.* [u. w. seyn] dúrchwanken [ich wanke durch, durchgewankt, durchzuwanken] to stagger or reel through a place. II. *v. tr.* durchwánken [ich durchwanke, durchwankt, zu durchwanken] to reel or stagger through or over.

Durchwärmen, *v. tr.* dúrchwärmen [ich wärme durch, durchgewärmet, durchzuwärmen]; *it.* durchwä́rmen [ich durchwärme, durchwärmt, zu durchwärmen] to warm through or thoroughly. Die Sonne durchwärmet die Erde, the sun warms the earth.

Durchwaschen, *v. tr.* 1) dúrchwaschen [ich wasche durch, durchgewaschen, durchzuwaschen] *a*) to wash all in succession. *b*) to wear out by washing. Dieser Zeug wascht sich bald durch, this stuff will soon wear out in washing. 2) durchwáschen [ich durchwasche, durchwaschen, zu durchwaschen] to wash through, to wear out by constant washing [as a river does a dike &c.].

Durchwässern, *v. tr.* dúrchwässern [ich wässere durch, durchgewässert, durchzuwässern]; *it.* durchwä́ssern [ich durchwässere, durchwässert, zu durchwässern] to water or soak thoroughly. Ländereien —, to irrigate land.

Durchwaten, I. *v. intr.* [u. w. seyn] dúrchwaten [ich wate durch, durchgewatet, durchzuwaten] to wade through water. II. *v. tr.* durchwáten [ich durchwate, durchwatet, zu durchwaten] to wade through. Einen Fluß —, to wade through a river.

Durchweben, *v. tr.* [ich durchwebe, durchwebt, zu durchweben] to interweave. Mit Seide und Silber durchwebt, interwoven with silk and silver. *Fig.* Ueberall mit Gespräch durchwebt, everywhere interlaced with dialogue.

Dúrchweg, *m.* [-es, *pl.* -e] a road or passage through, an entrance or avenue.

Dúrchweg, *adv.* always, every time; absolutely.

Dúrchwegsam, *adj.* and *adv.* that may be converted into a road or passage.

Durchwehen, I. dúrchwehen [ich wehe durch, durchgewehet, durchzuwehen] 1) *v. intr.* to blow through any aperture or space. 2) *v. tr.* to blow through, to perflate, to penetrate blowing. II. durchwéhen [ich durchwehe, durchwehet, zu durchwehen] *v. tr.* to penetrate blowing, to blow through. Vom Winde wohl durchwehete Städte, well-ventilated cities. *Fig.* to breathe. Alle seine Schriften durchwehet ein Geist des Wohlwollens, through all his writings there breathes a spirit of benevolence.

Durchweichen, [from weichen] I. dúrchweichen [ich weiche durch, durchgeweicht, durchzuweichen] 1) *v. intr.* [u. w. seyn] to soak thoroughly, to become soft. 2) *v. tr.* to soak, to wet thoroughly. Der starke Regen hat den Boden durchgeweicht, the earth is soaked with heavy rains. II durchwéichen [ich durchweiche, durchweicht, zu durchweichen] *v. tr.* to soak thoroughly; to macerate in water or other fluid.

Durchweiden, *v. tr.* dúrchweiden [ich weide durch, durchgeweidet, durchzuweiden]; *it.* durchwéiden [ich durchweide, durchweidet, zu durchweiden] to pasture all over.

Durchweinen, *v. tr.* dúrchweinen [ich weine durch, durchgeweint, durchzuweinen]; *it.* durchweinen [ich durchweine, durchweint, zu durchweinen] to pass weeping. Die Nächte —, to spend the nights in tears.

Dúrchweisen, *ir. v. tr.* [ich weise durch, durchgewiesen, zu durchweisen] 1) Einen —, to show any one the way through any unknown place. 2) Einem den Weg —, to show any one the way through.

Dúrchwerfen, *ir. v. tr.* [ich werfe durch, durchgeworfen, durchzuwerfen] 1) to cast or throw through. 2) to run through a sieve, to sift.

Durchwetzen, *v. tr.* dúrchwetzen [ich wetze durch, durchgewetzt, durchzuwetzen]; *it.* durchwétzen [ich durchwetze, durchwetzt, zu durchwetzen] to wear through by whetting or grinding.

Dúrchwichsen, *v. tr.* [ich wichse durch, durchgewichst, durchzuwichsen] to wax throughout. †*Fig.* Einen —, to thrash or drub any one.

Durchwímmeln, *v. tr.* [ich durchwimmele, durchwimmelt, zu durchwimmeln] to crowd or swarm through.

Durchwímmern, *v. tr.* [ich durchwimmere, durchwimmert, zu durchwimmern] to pass or spend lamenting, whimpering.

Durchwinden, *ir. v. tr.* 1) dúrchwinden [ich winde durch, durchgewunden, durchzuwinden] to wind through. Sich —, to wind one's self through a narrow place; *fig.* to resort to expedients for a livelihood, or for accomplishing a purpose, to shift, to get through difficulties. 2) durchwínden [ich durchwinde, durchwunden, zu durchwinden] to intwine. Ein mit Blumen durchwundener Kranz, a wreath of flowers intwined.

Durchwínseln, *v. tr.* [ich durchwinsele, durchwinselt, zu durchwinseln] to pass moaning or whining.

Dúrchwintern, *v. tr.* [ich wintere durch, durchgewintert, durchzuwintern] to winter [flowers, fruit &c.].

Durchwirbeln, I. *v. intr.* [used with seyn] dúrchwirbeln [ich wirbele durch, durchgewirbelt, durchzuwirbeln] to whirl through. II. *v. tr.* durchwírbeln [ich durchwirbele, durchwirbelt, zu durchwirbeln] 1) to move through whirling or in whirls. 2) to penetrate warbling. Die Lerche durchwirbelt die Lüfte, the lark soars warbling through the skies or air.

Durchwirken, *v. tr.* 1) dúrchwirken [ich wirke durch, durchgewirkt, durchzuwirken] to work or knead [the dough] thoroughly. 2) durchwírken [ich durchwirke, durchwirkt, zu durchwirken] to interweave. Mit Seide und Silber durchwirkt, interwoven with silk and silver.

Dúrchwischen, [ich wische durch, durchgewischt, durchzuwischen] I. *v. tr.* to wipe, to rub, to scour thoroughly. II. *v. intr.* [u. w. seyn] to depart or withdraw secretly, to slip away, to get off, to escape. *Fig.* to escape punishment.

Durchwíttern, *v. tr.* [ich durchwittere, durchwittert, zu durchwittern] 1) to mix with substances which have been dissolved by the action of air. 2) to stand out the wheather. *Fig.* Ein durchwittertes Gesicht, a weather-beaten countenance.

Durchwölben, *v. tr.* [ich durchwölbe, durchwölbt, zu durchwölben] to vault, to arch throughout.

Dúrchwollen, *ir. v. intr.* [ich will durch, durchgewollt, durchzuwollen] to purpose, intend, wish, or attempt to go or pass through.

Durchwühlen, *v. tr.* 1) dúrchwühlen [ich wühle durch, durchgewuhlt, durchzuwühlen] *a*) to mix or mingle by turning over. *b*) Sich —, to work or dig through any thing. 2) durchwǘhlen [ich durchwühle, durchwühlt, zu durchwühlen] *a*) to root throughout. Die Schweine — den Wald, swine root all over the forest. *b*) to rummage. Jemands Papiere —, to ransack any one's papers, to rummage through any one's papers.

Dúrchwünschen, *v. tr.* [ich wünsche durch, durchgewünscht, durchzuwünschen] to wish to get through any place or to be freed from danger.

Dúrchwurf, *m.* [-es, *pl.* -würfe] 1) the act of casting or throwing through. 2) [in mining] V. Durchlaß.

Durchwürgen, *v. tr.* 1) dúrchwürgen [ich würge durch, durchgewürget, durchzuwürgen] to swallow down with difficulty. 2) durchwǘrgen [ich durchwürge, durchwürget, zu durchwürgen] to slay or destroy thoroughly.

Durchwúrzeln, *v. tr.* [ich durchwurzele, durchwurzelt, zu durchwurzeln] to penetrate with roots, to root throughout.

Durchwürzen, *v. tr.* [ich durchwürze, durchwürzt, zu durchwürzen] to season throughout. Aromatische Pflanzen — die Luft, aromatic plants scent the air. *Fig.* Seine Gespräche mit witzigen Bemerkungen —, to season one's conversation with witty remarks.

Durchwüthen, *v. tr.* [ich durchwüthe, durchwüthet, zu durchwüthen] to go or pass raging through. *Fig.* Zorn durchwüthet seine Brust, anger rages in his bosom.

Durchzählen, *v. tr.* dúrchzählen [ich zähle durch, durchgezählt, durchzuzählen]; *it.* durchzǟhlen [ich durchzähle, durchzählt, zu durchzählen] to count all one by one, to count all over.

Durchzánken, *v. tr.* [ich durchzanke, durchzankt, zu durchzanken] to pass quarreling. Den ganzen Tag —, to spend the whole day in quarreling.

Durchzausen, *v. tr.* 1) dúrchzausen [ich zause durch, durchgezauset, durchzuzausen] to touse through. 2) durchzaúsen [ich durchzause, durchzauset, zu durchzausen] to touse thoroughly.

Durchzèchen, *v. tr.* [ich durchzeche, durchzecht, zu durchzechen] to pass drinking or carousing.

Dúrchzeichnen, *v. tr.* [ich zeichne durch, durchgezeichnet, durchzuzeichnen] 1) to draw [a figure] through transparent paper, to trace. Papier zum —, tracing-paper. 2) to draw or delineate all one by one.

Dúrchzeigen, V. Durchweisen.

Dúrchzerren, *v. tr.* [ich zerre durch, durchgezerret, durchzuzerren] to drag through, to pull through.

Durchziehen, *ir.* I. dúrchziehen [ich ziehe durch, durchgezogen, durchzuziehen] 1) *v. tr.* to draw through. Einen Faden —, to pass a thread through the eye, to reeve, to thread a needle; einen Balken —, [in carpentry] to lay a summer. * *Fig.* Einen —, to censure, or to blame any one; *it.* to jeer any one. 2) *v. intr.* to draw, to move, or march through or over, to journey over with a train or accompanied by others. Die Truppen, welche gestern durch die Stadt durchgezogen sind, the troops which marched through the town yesterday; ein Truppencorps kann nicht durch diesen Wald —, this wood is not pervious to a body of troops. II. durchziehen [ich durchziehe, durchzogen, zu durchziehen] *v. tr.* to go or walk over, to travel over or through. Das Land —, to ramble over the country; die Flüssigkeit durchzieht das Papier, the liquid penetrates the paper.

Dúrchzielen, *v. intr.* [ich ziele durch, durchgezielt, durchzuzielen] to aim through an aperture.

Durchzischen, I. *v. intr.* dúrchzischen [ich zische durch, durchgezischt, durchzuzischen] to pass through whizzing or with a hissing sound. II. *v. tr.* durchzischen [ich durchzische, durchzischt, zu durchzischen] to penetrate whizzing. Die Kugel durchzischte die Luft, the ball flew whizzing through the air.

Durchzittern, I. *v. intr.* [u. w. seyn] dúrchzittern [ich zittere durch, durchgezittert, durchzuzittern] to pass through trembling. II. *v. tr.* durchzíttern [ich durchzittere, durchzittert, zu durchzittern] to go over trembling, to thrill. *Fig.* Fieberschauer durchzittert seinen Körper, his body shivers with ague.

Dúrchzoll, *m.* V. Durchgangszoll.

Durchzúcken, *v. tr.* [ich durchzucke, durchzuckt, zu durchzucken] to give a sudden shock to. Ein elektrischer Schlag durchzuckte uns, we were electrified; der Gedanke durchzuckte ihn, daß &c., the thought suddenly crossed his brain, that &c.

Durchzúckern, *v. tr.* [ich durchzuckere, durchzuckert, zu durchzuckern] to sweeten thoroughly.

Dúrchzug, *m.* [-es, *pl.* -züge] 1) the act of drawing, going, passing, or marching through. 2) the passage or march of many persons through a place or country. Der — eines Truppenkorps, the passage of a body of troops. *Fig.* Dem — der Luft verschlossen, impervious to the air; dem französischen Heere wurde der — gestattet, the French army was allowed to pass. 3) something drawn through, as in carpentry, the summer. 4) that through which any thing is drawn, as with goldsmiths a liquid through which gilded things are drawn.

Dúrchzupfen, *v. tr.* [ich zupfe durch, durchgezupft, durchzuzupfen] to pull or pluck through.

Dúrchzwängen, *v. tr.* [ich zwänge durch, durchgezwängt, durchzuzwängen] to force through. *Fig.* Sich —, to wedge one's way.

Dúrchzwicken, *v. tr.* [ich zwicke durch, durchgezwickt, durchzuzwicken] to make sore by pinching.

Dúrchzwingen, *ir. v. tr.* [ich zwinge durch, durchgezwungen, durchzuzwingen] to force through, to force to go through.

Dürfen, [formerly taren, barren, allied to the Welsh *dewr*, bold, and to the Ice. *thör*, bold] *ir. v. intr.* 1) [rather obsolete in this sense] [to have courage for any purpose, to be bold enough, to venture] to dare. Ich darf Alles thun, was einem Manne geziemen mag, I dare do all that may become a man; thue es, wenn du darfst, do it if you dare; ich darf es schon darauf ankommen lassen, I may dare to run the hazard of it, I dare abide by the consequences. 2) to have permission, to be permitted, to be allowed to do any thing. Er darf thun, was nicht gegen die Sittsamkeit anstößt, he may do what is not against decency; darf sie kommen? is she permitted to come? darf ich fragen? may I ask? wenn ich so frei seyn darf, if I may take the liberty; wenn ich so sagen darf, if I may say so. 3) to need, to want, to have need. Die Gesunden — [more usual: bedürfen] des Arztes nicht, the whole need not a physician; du darfst es nur fordern, you need only ask for it; er darf nur reden, he needs only to speak. 4) to have a reason, motive for doing any thing. Er darf sich nicht darüber beklagen, he has no reason to complain of it; Sie — nicht glauben, daß &c., you must not believe that &c. 5) it sometimes denotes what is possible, implying ignorance of the fact in the speaker, as: Es dürfte ein Leichtes seyn, it might be an easy matter; es dürften zu diesem Zwecke Befehle gegeben [se] orders might have been given for the purpose; es dürfte wohl or leicht geschehen, it might easily happen.

Dürftig, [V. Dürfen 3] I. *adj.* and *adv.* needy, necessitous, indigent, very poor. Die —en unterstützen, to relieve the needy; —e Umstände, necessitous circumstances; — seyn, to be in need; —e Kleidung, poor clothes. Syn. V. Bedürftig. *Fig.* —e Begriffe von Gott und seinen Vollkommenheiten, inadequate ideas of God and of his perfections; —e Nachrichten, defective or unimportant news; eine —e Erklärung, an imperfect or defective definition or explanation; eine —e Beschreibung, an inadequate [incomplete or defective] description; ein —er Aufsatz, a meager composition; eine —e Ausflucht, a poor excuse; ein —es Auskunftsmittel, an insufficient means. II. *adv.* needily, in want or poverty.

Dürftigkeit, *f.* neediness, want, poverty, indigence. Der — preisgegeben, exposed to penury.

Dürr, [Swed. *torr*, trocken, D. *dor*, *dorre*, *torka*, to dry, Gr. θέρω, Lat. *torreo*, dörren] *adj.* and *adv.* 1) destitute of moisture; free from juice or sap, dry. —es Holz, dry wood; ein —er Zweig, a dead bough; —e Blätter, dry leaves; —e Früchte, dried fruits. 2) free from rain, not rainy. Ein —er Sommer, a dry summer. 3) adapted to exhaust moisture. Ein —er Wind, a drying wind. 4) *Fig.* *a*) not producing plants, not fertile, steril. —es Land, dry or arid land; eine —e Einöde, a barren waste. *b*) lean, meager, not fat. Eine lange, dürre Gestalt, a tall, meager figure; ein —er Ochs, a poor ox. *c*) —e Erze, [in metallurgy] silver-ores that contain no lead. *d*) plain, unembellished, dry. *Einem etwas mit —en Worten sagen, to speak to any one in plain terms, to be plain with any one; *etwas — heraussagen, to speak one's mind freely, bluntly [without delicacy or the usual forms of civility]. Syn. Dürr, Trocken. Dürr differs from trocken in being applied to bodies which are destitute of the moisture which forms the fluid part of animal substances. Eine trockene Hand, is one, which is not wet or damp, eine dürre, one which no longer contains the juices indispensable to life. Trockener Sand is merely such as is not wet, dürrer Sand such as possesses no nutritive moisture for plants, on which nothing can vegetate.

Dürr-beinig, *adj.* and *adv.* having lean legs, lean-legged. —**feder**, *f.* [with watchmakers] a small sort of spring in a watch. —**kraut**, V. Dürrwurz. —**leibig**, *adj.* and *adv.* lean, meager. —**maden**, *pl.* V. Mitesser. —**ofen**, V. Darrofen. —**wurz**, *f.* [the name of several plants] *a*) trailing inula, or flea-bane. *b*) ploughman's spikenard. *c*) Canadian erigeron.

Dürre, *f.* [*pl.* -n] 1) [destitution of moisture] dryness, siccity. Die — eines Bodens, the dryness, aridity of a soil. 2) [want of rain] dryness, drought. 3) *Fig.* [want of strength] feebleness.

Dürrsucht, *f.* atrophy. V. also Darrsucht.

Dürrsüchtig, *adj.* and *adv.* affected with atrophy. V. also Darrsüchtig.

‡1. **Durst**, *f.* [Gr. θάρσος, Eng. *to dare*, I &c. durst, wagen, ich &c. wagte] boldness, rashness.

2. **Durst**, *m.* [-es] [allied to Dürr V.] [a painful sensation of the throat or fauces, occasioned by the want of drink; also a vehement desire of drink] thirst. — haben, empfinden, to be thirsty, or dry; seinen — löschen, stillen, to quench one's thirst; ein brennender —, a burning or ardent thirst. *Prov.* Je mehr man trinkt, um so mehr —, ever drunk, ever dry. *Fig.* Der — nach weltlichen Ehren, a thirst for worldly honours; der — nach Wahrheit, a thirst for truth; der — nach Rache, the thirst for vengeance.

Durst-drang, *m.* a vehement desire of drink. —**natter**, —**schlange**, *f.* [a sort of serpent] dipsas.

Dursten, **Dürsten**, *v. intr.* and *imp.* to thirst. Ich durste, mich durstet, I am dry, or thirsty; der Boden dürstet nach Regen, the ground thirsts after rain. *Fig.* Er dürstet nach Ehre, he thirsts for honour; nach Blut —, to thirst after blood; seine Seele dürstete nach Wissenschaft, he had a soul athirst for knowledge; meine Seele dürstet nach dem lebendigen Gott, [in Script.] my soul thirsteth for the living God; [also without nach, as a *v. tr.*] sie dürsteten sein Blut, they thirsted for his blood.

Durstig, *adj.* and *adv.* [feeling a painful sensation of the throat or fauces for want of drink] thirsty, athirst. — seyn, to be thirsty, to be dry; *ein —er Bruder, a fuddlecap, a tippler. *Fig.* [feeling a vehement desire of any thing] thirsty. Nach Blut — [more usual blutdürstig], blood-thirsty; seine Seele ist nach Wahrheit —, his soul thirsts after truth; — nach &c., athirst for &c.

Durstigkeit, *f.* thirstiness.

‡1. **Durstiglich**, *adj.* and *adv.* bold. V. ‡1. Durst.

2. **Durstiglich**, *adj.* and *adv.* [rather obsolete] thirsty, eager, desirous. — nach, athirst for.

1. **Dusel**, *f.* [*pl.* -n] [with sportsmen] the female of small birds.

2. ‖**Dusel**, **Düssel**, *m.* [-s] [allied to the A. S. *disi*, *dysi*, and perhaps to tosen] 1) a whirling in the head, dizziness, giddiness, vertigo. Er ist immerfort in einem —, he is constantly fuddled. 2) doziness. 3) headlessness, thoughtlessness.

Düsse, *f.* [a sea term] untarred oakum.

‖**Düsselig**, **Duselig**, [V. 2. Dusel] *adj.* and *adv.* 1) dizzy, giddy. Es wird mir —, my head turns. 2) dozy. 3) thoughtless, headless.

‖**Düsseln**, **Düsseln**, **Duseln**, *v. intr.* 1) to be dizzy or giddy. Das —, giddiness, dizziness. 2) to doze.

‖**Dussig**, *adj.* and *adv.* giddy, dizzy.

Düster, [allied to Dunst?] *adj.* and *adv.* dark, gloomy. Die —n Zellen eines Klosters, the gloomy cells of a convent; ein —es Thal, a dusky valley; ein —er Himmel, a cloudy, overcast sky; ein —er Schatten, a dismal shade; die —n Schatten der Nacht, the gloomy shades of night; düstere Farben, dull colours. *Fig.* Eine —e Miene, a sad countenance; ein —es Schweigen, a sullen silence; —e Gedanken, sad or melancholy thoughts; eine —e Gemüthsstimmung, a gloomy state of mind; —e Blicke, cloudy looks; — verließ ich das Fest, sullen I forsook the feast; Einen — machen or stimmen, to make a person gloomy or melancholy; sein Unglück hat ihn sehr — gemacht, the calamity that befell him saddened his heart greatly.

Düster-blau, *adj.* and *adv.* being of a dull blue. —**klar**, *adj.* and *adv.* [in painting] clare-obscure. —**roth**, *adj.* and *adv.* murrey.

Düsterheit, **Düsterkeit**, *f.* gloominess, darkness, dismalness. Die — der Nacht, the obscurity of the night; die — eines Waldes, the gloom of a forest. *Fig.* Das Gemüth in — hüllen, to involve the mind in gloominess; sein Gemüth ist in — versunken, his mind is sunk into gloom.

Düsterling, *m.* [-es, *pl.* -e] V. Finsterling.

Düstern, I. *v. intr.* to grow dark or gloomy. Es düstert, it darkens. II. *v. tr.* 1) to make dark, to fill with gloom, to gloom, to darken. 2) *Fig.* [rather unusual] to make gloomy or melancholy, to make sad or sorrowful, to sadden. 3) ‖*Fig.* *v. tr.* and *intr.* to appease a person. Sie suchten an ihm or ihn zu —, so gut sie konnten, they tried to pacify him as well as they could. III. *v. r.* sich —, to grow dark or gloomy, to cloud. Der Himmel düstert sich, the sky clouds over.

1. **Dütchen**, *n.* [-s, *pl.* -] [from Deut, D. *duyt*, probably from the Fr. *tête*] the name of several small coins.

2. **Dütchen**, *n.* [-s, *pl.* -] *dimin.* of Düte, a small cornet.

Dütchen-dreher, —**krämer**, *m* [in contempt] a retailer.

Dütchenweise, *adv.* in small cornets, by small quantities.

Düte, *f.* [*pl.* -n] V. Kegelschnecke.

Düte, *f.* [*pl.* -n] [allied to the Slav. *duty*, hollow] [a little cap of paper, or a paper-case in which grocers and retailers inclose small wares] a cornet or coffin. Eine —e machen, drehen, to make a cornet or coffin.

Düten-dreher, *m.* [fig. and in contempt] a paltry grocer, a petty shop-keeper. —**förmig**, *adj.* and *adv.* having the form of a cornet or coffin, conic, conical.

Düteln, *v. tr.* to plait with a conical smoothing-iron.

Düteleisen, *n.* a conical smoothing-iron.

Düten, V. Tuten.

Dütenbaum, *m.* [-es, *pl.* -bäume] [a tree] American mammea.

Dütenschnecke, *f.* V. Kegelschnecke.

Dutzend, *n.* [-s, *pl.* -e] [allied to the Lat. *duodecim*] [the number twelve of things of the same kind] a dozen. Ein — Eier, a dozen of eggs; zwölf — Handschuhe, twelve dozen of gloves; zwölf —, a gross.

Dutzendweise, *adv.* by the dozen, by dozens.

***Duumvir**, *m.* [-s, *pl.* -e] [one of two Roman officers or magistrates united in the same public functions] duumvir.

***Duumvirät**, *n.* [-es, *pl.* -e] duumvirate.

Düven, *v. tr.* [in seamen's language] Die Ruderpinne luvwärts —, to put the helm a-weather; das Schiff durch den Wind —, to put the helm a-lee.

‖**Duwak**, *m.* [-es] V. Kannenkraut.

Duzen, *v. tr.* to address by the familiar term *thou*, to treat with familiarity, to thou.

Duzbruder, *m.* a very familiar friend, who is addressed by thou [instead of you]; a brother by the cup.

Dwäll, *m.* [-es] [a sea term] a mop.

Dwällen, *v. tr.* [in seamen's lang.] to mop.

Dwärreln, [V. Dwars] *v. intr.* [a sea term] Der Wind dwarrelt hin und her, the wind is variable.

Dwars, [probably allied to quer] *adv.* [a sea term] athwart. Der Wind wehet — über das Revier, the wind comes athwart; — durch die Seen segeln, to sail against the setting of the sea; — Sees liegen, to stand athwart the waves or with fids parallel.

Dwarsbalken, *m.* cross-beam, cross-piece.

Dweil, **Dweilen**; V. Dwall, Dwallen.

***Dynämik**, *f.* [that branch of dynamical mechanical philosophy, which treats of the force of moving bodies] dynamics.

***Dynämisch**, *adj.* and *adv.* dynamical.

***Dynást**, *m.* [-en, *pl.* -en] dynast.

***Dynastie**, *f.* [*pl.* -en] dynasty.

***Dysenterie**, *f.* [*pl.* -en] dysentery.

***Dysodil**, *m.* [-s] [a species of coal] dysodile.

***Dystömspath**, *m.* [-es, *pl.* -e] Prismatischer —, V. Datolith.

E.

E, e, [a vowel] e. 1) *n.* e. 2) [in music] *a*) [the name of the third note in the gamut] E mi = moll, E flat. *b*) [the name of a string or key] E. Das — auf der Geige, [the highest or most acute of the four strings of a violin tuned to E above the treble cliff note] the chanterelle.

Ebbe, *f.* [*pl.*-n] [allied to ab, Abend] [the reflux of the tide, the return of tide-water towards the sea] ebb. Die niedrige —, low tide, neap-tide; — und Fluth, ebb and flood; — und Fluth tritt zwei Mahl in vier und zwanzig Stunden ein, the tide ebbs and flows twice in twenty four hours; [in seamen's language] die erste — [Vor—], the beginning of the ebb; die halbe —, half-ebb; die letzte — [Hinter—], the end of the ebb-tide. *Fig.* Die — des Glückes, the ebb of prosperity; *in seiner Kasse ist eine ziemliche — eingetreten, his finances are at low-water mark.

Ebb-anker, *m.* [in seamen's lang.] the ebb-anchor.

Ebben, *v. intr.* and *imp.* to ebb. Das Meer ebbet, es ebbet, the tide ebbs or falls.

Eben, I. *adj.* and *adv.* [èben or ében] even, level, smooth, of an equal surface, flat. Ein ebener or ebner Strich Landes, an even tract of land; ein —er Boden, a plain ground; eine —e Oberfläche, an even or level surface, a plane. *Fig.* *Er ist ein recht —er Mann, he is very exact, nice; er ist in allen Sachen sehr —, he is very particular in all his dealings. II. *adv.* [èben] 1) [noting a like manner or degree] even, accurately, precisely, exactly. — so soll es Andern ergehen, even so shall it be done to others; *es ist mir — eins, it is the same with me; *es geschieht dir — recht, it serves you right; — dich, even thee; — deswegen, for that very reason; — so viel, just as much; es ist — so viel, it is all one. 2) near or nearly in time, just. — jetzt, just now; — damahls, just then; ich wollte — gehen, I was just going; das wollte ich — sagen, I was just going to say that. 3) sometimes it serves to denote a restriction or to soften a refusal, to grant. Das will ich nun — nicht sagen, I do not mean to say that exactly; das nun — nicht, not precisely that; es braucht nicht — jetzt zu seyn, it needs not to be just now.

Eben-bild, *n.* likeness, resemblance. Das Kind ist das —bild seiner Mutter, the child is the image of its mother. **—bürtig,** *adj.* and *adv.* [chiefly in law] of equal birth. **—bürtigkeit,** *f.* [chiefly in law] equality of birth. **—daselbst,** *adv.* at the same place. **—derselbe, —dieselbe, —dasselbe,** *pron.* the very same. **—drähtig,** *adj.* and *adv.* even-threaded [said of linen]. **—falls,** *adv.* also, too, likewise. **—gewicht,** *n.* V. Gleichgewicht. **—maß,** *n.* 1) [an agreement of things in dimensions] equality. 2) [a due proportion of the several parts of a body to each other] [in architecture, painting and sculpture] symmetry; [in rhetoric] eurythmy. Das —maß seines Gliederbaues, the symmetry of his limbs; das —maß eines Gebäudes, the symmetry of a building. **—mäßig,** I. *adj.* and *adv.* 1) equal. Zwei Männer von —mäßigem Range, two men of equal rank. 2) symmetrical. II. *adv.* 1) equally. 2) likewise. 3) symmetrically. **—nächte,** *pl.* [in astronomy] equinoctial nights. **—nächtlich,** *adj.* and *adv.* equinoctial. **—sölig,** *adj.* and *adv.* [in mining] horizontal. **—weit, —weitig,** *adj.* and *adv.* parallel. —weite Linien, parallel lines, parallels. **—wesenheit,** *f.* identity, sameness. **—zeitig,** *adj.* and *adv.* contemporary.

Eben, *m.* [-s, *pl.* -] [is generally derived from the Hebr. *aeben*, Stein; but it is probably allied to the Lat. *abies*, to the Germ. Eibe, and to the G. verb beben] [a tree] ebony-tree [only used in compositions, except in poetry].

Eben-baum, *m.* ebony-tree. Der falsche —baum, laburnum, formerly called bean-trefoil-tree. **—holz,** *n.* ebony. Von, aus —holz gemacht, schwarz wie —holz, ebon, ebony; die Farbe des —holzes geben, to ebonize. **—holzen** or **—hölzern,** *adj.* and *adv.* ebon, ebony. Eine —holzene Büchse, an ebony box. **—tischler,** *m.* V. Ebenist.

Ebene, *f.* [*pl.* -n] [level land, or a surface little varied by inequalities] plain. Die — des Jordans, the plain of Jordan.

Ebenen, Ebnen, I. *v. tr.* to make even or level, to even, to level, to plain. Einen Weg —, to level a road; er ebnet die Berge, he levels mountains; er ebnete die Wasser der Tiefe, he smoothed the waters of the deep. *Fig.* Ebene meinen Weg zu den Reichen des Lichts, smooth my passage to the realms of day. II. *v. r.* sich —, to grow even or plain.

Ebener, *m.* [-s, *pl.* -] an evener, a leveler.

Ebenheit, *f.* accuracy, exactness, precision.

Ebenist, *m.* [-en, *pl.* -en] cabinet-maker.

‡**Ebenteuer,** V. Abenteuer.

||1. **Eber,** [-s, *pl.* -] [also Näber, allied to the Fr. *navrer*, to pierce] [in common language] a bore or gimlet.

||2. **Eber,** *m.* [-s, *pl.* -] [in familiar lang. Ewer] a sort of boat or barge.

3. **Eber,** *m.* [-s, *pl.* -] [probably allied to Bär = Thier] [the male of swine] a boar, wild-boar. Der junge —, a boar-pig. *Fig.* formerly a 12-pounder.

Eber-hirsch, *m.* the Indian hog or babyroussa. **—schwein,** *n.* [the male of swine not castrated] a boar.

Eber-esche, *f.* [Eber = after, aber] [a tree] mountain-service, mountain-ash, quicken tree, roan tree. **—reis,** *n.* V. Aberraute. **—wurz, —wurzel,** *f.* 1) V. Aberraute or Stabwurz. 2) corymbed carthemus.

Eberhard, [a name of men] [-s, *pl.* -e] Everard.

Eberhardine, [a name of women] [-ns] Everardina.

Ebnen, V. Ebenen.

Ebräer, *m.* V. Hebräer.

Ebrisch, *m.* V. Stabwurz.

***Eccentrisch,** V. Excentrisch.

***Echinit,** *m.* [-s] [a fossil found in chalk-pits] echinite.

***Echo,** 1) *n.* [-'s, *pl.* -s] [a sound reflected or reverberated from a solid body] echo. Das — entfernter Berge, the echo of distant hills. [also used in a fig. sense] Seine Worte fanden ein — in ihrer Brust, his words found an echo in their breasts. 2) *f.* [*gen.* der Echo, or Echo's] [in fabulous history, a nymph, the daughter of the air and Tellus] Echo.

Echt, [from Ehe *f.* V.] *adj.* and *adv.* 1) lawfully begotten or born. —e Kinder, legitimate children. 2) genuine, natural, true. —er Balsam, true balsam; —e Vaterlandsliebe, true patriotism. 3) durable, of long continuance. Eine —e Farbe, a lasting colour.

Echtmaß, *n.* V. Eichmaß.

Echtheit, *f.* genuineness. Die — einer Urkunde, the authenticity of a document.

Echtigen, *v. tr.* [unusual] to legitimate [illegitimate children].

Eck, for Ecke, frequently to be found in composition with proper names, and denoting some projecting part of a cliff or mountain or of a ridge of hills, on which mostly a castle, tower &c. used to be built, as Rolands-Eck, Fürsten-Eck, Rhein-Eck &c.

Eckbert, V. Egbert.

Eckchen, *n.* [-s] *dimin.* of Ecke, V. Ecke.

Ecke, *f.* [*pl.* -n] [allied to Egge, to bewegen, to the Gr. *ἀγνυμι*, brechen] 1) the extreme border or point of any thing. Die — eines Tisches, the edge or corner of a table; die —n des Karrens, [in printing] corners; die — des Brodes, the crust of bread. **Fig.* Bunt über Eck gehen, to be at sixes and sevens [in disorder]. 2) a corner, an angle. Die — zweier Straßen, the corner of two streets; die — eines Waldes [Wald-—], the [outside] corner of a wood or forest; ich sah ihn an der — des Waldes dort stehen, I saw him standing at yonder corner of the wood; die — eines Felsens [Felsen-—], the projecting angle of a rock. *Fig.* [in familiar or common language, an inclosed place, a secret or retired place, or indefinitely any part, a part] corner, nook. Sie suchten ihn in allen —n, they searched for him in every corner; von allen —n her, from all parts. 3) a small space, a short distance. Es ist nur eine kleine — or ein Eckchen bis dahin, it is not far off. [in botany] the interstice of the incisure of a leaf. Syn. Ecke, Winkel. The exterior point where two converging lines or surfaces meet is called Ecke; the interior point, or internal angle Winkel. When I call a hat dreieckig [three-cornered], I consider it with regard to its external surface; and when I say, that the Winkel [angles] of a triangle are equal to two right angles, I refer to the space comprised within the sides of a triangle, the internal angles. In common language, however, ein Winkel is often called eine Ecke, but eine Ecke never ein Winkel. One frequently says: the stick is standing in der Ecke, instead of, in dem Winkel; but never: I hurt myself an einem Winkel, but an einer Ecke.

Eck-apfel, *m.* [a sort of apple] calville. **—band,** *n.* an iron-band about the edge or corner of a thing. **—beere,** *f.* 1) Indian mulberry. 2) Indian mulberry-tree. **—beschläge,** *n.* corner-clips. **—brett,** *n.* corner-board. **—ens-halm,** *m.* V. Kugelbinse. **—enschanze,** *f.* [in fortification] a cornered entrenchment. **—ensteher,** *m.* 1) a person that waits at the corners of streets to look after commissions, to run errands or perform menial services &c. [peculiar to Berlin]. 2) [in contempt] an idle fellow. **—enzierde,** *f.* V. Eckzierde. **—feile,** *f.* angular file. **—fenster,** *n.* corner-window. **—forst,** *m.* [in architecture] one of the four corners of a hipped roof. **—haus,** *n.* corner-house. **—kammer,** *f.* a small room at the corner of a house. **—laden,** *m.* a shop at the corner of a street, a corner shop. **—loch,** *n.* a hole at the corner of any thing, especially the hazard at the corner of a billiard-table. **—pfeiler,** *m.* a pillar at a corner. **—pfosten,** *m.* corner-post. **—platz,** *n.* a place at the corner of any thing. **—rasen,** *m.* [in fortification] gazon or pieces of turf to line the corners of the talus of bastions. **—saal,** *m.* the saloon at the corner of a building. **—säule,** *f.* 1) a column at the corner of an edifice. 2) *Fig.* [in mathematics] a prism. **—säulicht,** *adj.* and *adv.* prismatic, prismatical. **—schaft,** *m.* [in architecture] corner-wall. **—schanze,** *f.* an entrenchment at a corner of fortifications. **—schrank,** *m.* corner-cup-board. **—schuh,** *m.* V. —band. **—sparren,** *m.* V. Gradsparren or Lehnsparren. **—ständer,** *m.* corner-post, corner-pillar. **—steher,** *m.* V. Eckensteher. **—stein,** *m.* 1) corner-stone, curb-stone. *Fig.* Da Jesus Christus der —stein ist, [in Script.] Christ himself being the chief corner-stone; der Stein, den die Bauleute verworfen haben, der ist zum —stein geworden, [in Script.] the stone which the builders rejected is become the head of the corner. 2) stone-stud. 3) [in architecture] V. Untersatz. 4) mere-stone. 5) [one of the four suits at cards] diamond. —stiel, *m.* V. —ständer. —stube, *f.* a room at the corner of a house. —stütze, *f.* V. Strebepfeiler. —thor, *n.* 1) corner-gate. 2) anciently one of the gates of Jerusalem. —tisch, *m.* a table in the corner of a room. —zahn, *m.* corner-tooth. Die —zähne eines Pferdes, the corner-teeth of a horse. —ziegel, *m.* header. —zierde, —zierath, *f.* [in architecture] corners; *it.* crosettes. —zimmer, *n.* a room at the corner of a house.

Ecken, *v. tr.* to edge, to border.

Ecker, *f.* [*pl.* -n] V. Eichel.

Eckig, *adj.* and *adv.* having corners or angles, cornered, angular. Eine —e Figur, an angular figure; ein —er Hut, a cocked hat; [in botany] ein —er Stengel, an angular stem; ein —er Staubbeutel, an angular anther; eine —e Narbe, an angular stigma. **Fig.* Ein —er Mensch, an awkward person; ein —es Wesen, an awkward manner; —e Bewegungen, awkward motions or gestures.

***Eclipse**, V. Ellipse.

***Ecossäse**, *f.* [*pl.* -n] a Scotch dance.

Edam, *n.* [-s] [a town in Holland] Edam. —er Käse, Edam cheese.

Edel, [allied to Adel] *adj.* and *adv.* 1) [of the best kind, choice, excellent, principal, capital] noble. Eine edle Rebe, a noble vine; ein edler Wein, a generous wine; ein edles Gebäude, a noble edifice; die edlen Theile des Körpers, the noble parts of the body; ein edles Pferd, a generous steed; ein edler Gang, [in mining] a rich vein; edles Erz, rich ore; edle Metalle, precious metals [gold, platina, silver]; edle Steine [Edelsteine], precious stones; [in ancient botany, some plants are called edel, as] das edle Leberkraut, noble liverwort; [with hunters] ein edler Hirsch [Edelhirsch], a full-grown stag. 2) [exalted in excellence, or distinguished by station] noble. Die —n der Kinder Israels, the noble of the children of Israel; von edler Geburt, nobly born or descended. 3) an epithet [rather obsolete] of distinction for commoners, to which Hoch and Wohl are added, as, der hochedle or wohledle Herr Bürgermeister, his worship the burgomaster; ein Hochedler or Wohledler Stadtrath hat beschlossen, it has been decreed by the worshipful town-council. [in addressing] Ew. or Euer Hoch- or Wohledlen! your honour! formerly a title of honour for princes, counts &c. 4) [great, elevated, dignified; generous, liberal; exalted, sublime] noble. Ein edles Gemüth, a noble mind; ein edler Mann, an honourable man; ein edler Muth, a noble courage; edle Thaten, noble deeds; eine edle Dreistigkeit, a generous boldness; ein edles Herz, a noble heart; ein edles Gemüth, a noble mind, a generous disposition; eine edle Schreibart, a noble style; eine edle Bauart, nobleness of structure.

Edel-bürger, *m.* a patrician. —bürtig, *adj.* and *adv.* nobly born or descended. —dame, *f.* a noble lady, noblewoman. —denkend, *adj.* and *adv.* noble-minded. —dirne, *f.* V. —fräulein. —entsprossen, *adj.* and *adv.* nobly born or descended. —erz, *n.* a rich ore. —falke, *m.* the gentle falcon. —frau, *f.* a noblewoman. —fräulein, *n.* an unmarried lady of noble rank, noble-maid. —geboren, *adj.* and *adv.* an epithet of distinction for commoners, to which Hoch is added, as Hochedelgeborner Herr [much honoured Sir]. —gestein, *n.* precious stones. —herrscher, *m.* V. Adelherrscher. —herzig, *adj.* and *adv.* having a noble heart, noble-minded. —hof, *m.* a nobleman's mansion in the country, a nobleman's seat, manor-house. —knabe, *m.* a page. —knecht, *m.* formerly an attendant on a knight, an esquire. —leberkraut, *n.* V. Leberklee. —mann, *m.* [*pl.* -leute] a nobleman. Die —leute, noblemen, nobles. —männisch, *adj.* and *adv.* belonging to a nobleman, becoming a nobleman, nobleman-like. —marder, *m.* pine-martin. —muth, *m.* greatness of mind, magnanimity. —müthig, *adj.* and *adv.* elevated in soul or sentiment, exhibiting nobleness of soul, magnanimous. Ein —müthiger Feind, a generous foe; eine —müthige That, a generous action. —sinn, *m.* a noble mind, elevation of mind, nobleness of mind, magnanimity, generosity. —sinnig, *adj.* and *adv.* noble-minded, magnanimous. —stein, *m.* a precious stone, a jewel. —steinhandel, *m.* the trade of a jeweler. —steinhändler, *m.* a jeweler. —steinschleifer, *m.* —steinschneider, *m.* lapidary. —stoff, *m.* brocade. —tanne, *f.* V. Fichte. —that, *f.* a noble or generous deed.

Edeling, *m.* [-es, *pl.* -e] [rather unusual] a nobleman [in contempt], an aristocrat.

Edeln, *v. tr.* to ennoble, to dignify, to exalt.

***Eden**, *n.* [-s] Eden. *Fig.* a paradisiacal country, place or residence.

***Edikt**, *n.* [-es, *pl.* -e] a proclamation of command or prohibition, an edict. Die —e der Römischen Kaiser, the edicts of the Roman emperors.

Edinburg, *n.* [-s] [the capital of Scotland] Edinburgh.

Edinburger, *m.* [-s, *pl.* -] -inn, *f.* an inhabitant, citizen or native of Edinburgh.

Edinburger, *adj.* coming from or belonging to Edinburgh, at Edinburgh.

***Edingtonit**, *m.* [-en, *pl.* -en] [a mineral] edingtonit.

***Ediren**, *v. tr.* 1) to edit. 2) to publish [a book].

***Edition**, *f.* V. Ausgabe 3.

***Editor**, *m.* [-s, *pl.* -en] 1) editor. V. also Herausgeber. 2) publisher. V. also Verleger.

Edle, *m.* [-n, *pl.* -n] instead of Edele. V. Edel.

Edmund, [-s, *pl.* -e] [a name of men] Edmund.

Eduard, [-s, *pl.* -e] [a name of men] Edward.

Eduardchen, *n.* [-s] *dimin.* of Eduard. Ned.

***Education**, *f.* V. Erziehung.

||**Efer**, *adj.* and *adv.* [also in metallurgy] briny, salinous.

***Effect**, *m.* [-es, *pl.* -e] V. Erfolg or Wirkung.

***Effecten**, *pl.* effects, goods and chattels, movables.

***Egal**, V. Gleich. †Das ist mir ganz —, it is all one to me.

Egbert, [-s, *pl.* -e] [a name of men] Egbert.

Ege, **Egge**, *f.* [*pl.* -n] [Lat. *occa*, Old G. *egida*, allied to the Lat. *acuo*] 1) [an instrument of agriculture] harrow. ||2) the edge of cloth, selvedge.

Ege[Egge]-balken, *pl.* pieces of timber in the harrow crossing each other, and set with iron-teeth. —haken, *m.* a stick with a hook to lift the harrow. —pflug, *m.* a sort of great harrow. —schlitten, *m.* harrow-sledge. —zahn, —zinken, *m.* an iron or wooden tooth, with which the pieces of timber in a harrow are set.

Egel, *m.* [-s, *pl.* -] and *f.* [*pl.* -n] [appears to be allied to Aal] 1) [Blutegel, commonly Blutigel] a leech. 2) V. Egelschnecke.

Egelbaum, *m.* V. Elsebeerbaum. —kraut, *n.* 1) creeping loose-strife, or money-wort. 2) the lesser spearwort. 3) great water-plantain. —schnecke, *f.* the gourd-worm or fluke.

Egen, **Eggen**, *v. tr.* to harrow [land or ground].

1. **Eger**, *m.* [-s, *pl.* -] one who harrows, harrower.

2. **Eger**, *n.* [-s] [a town in Bohemia] Egra. *f.* [*gen.* der Eger] [a river in Bohemia] the Egra.

Eger-brunnen, *m.* the mineral waters of Egra. —salz, *n.* salt of Egra. —wasser, *n.* V. Egerbrunnen.

***Egeran**, *m.* [-s] [a subspecies of pyramidal garnet] egeran.

||**Egert**, **Eggert**, *n.* [-s, *pl.* -e or -en] a shrubby plain.

Egge, **Eggen**, V. Ege and Egen.

||**Egle**, *m.* [-n, *pl.* -n] V. Börs.

***Egoismus**, *m.* egotism, selfishness.

***Egoist**, *m.* [-en, *pl.* -en] an egotist, a selfish man.

***Egoistisch**, *adj.* and *adv.* egoistic, egoistical, selfish. — seyn, to egotize.

Ehe, *poet.* and ***Eh**, [am ehesten, aufs eheste] *adv.* [allied to the Goth. *air* = frühe] 1) [preceding in time] sooner than, ere, before. Komme herab, — mein Sohn stirbt, [in Scripture] come down ere my child dies; — er kam, before he came; [in common lang. and in Script. it is often joined with als or the ‡denn instead of als] — als ich aufhöre zu lieben, ere I cease to love; eher, [comp. degree] sooner; je eher, je lieber, the sooner the better; ehest [superl. degree] soonest, speediest, first; am ehesten, soonest; mit dem ehesten, with the next; ehester Tage, one of these days, with the next; aufs eheste, with the first opportunity. *Fig.* Ich wollte eher sterben, als &c., I would rather die, than &c. 2) [= leichter, besser, schneller &c.] Er kann es eher [= leichter] thun als ich, he can do it easier than I. 3) [= vorher, früher] before this time, ere-now, formerly. Ich habe das eher gesehen, I saw it before.

Ehe-dem, *adv.* [ehedessen, ehevor] before now, heretofore, formerly. —gestern, *adv.* the day before yesterday, two days ago. —gestrig, *adj.* on the day before yesterday. ||—hin, V. —mahls. —mahlig, *adj.* old, former. —mahls, *adv.* in former times, formerly. ||—vor, V. Zuvor.

Ehe, *f.* [*pl.* -n] [Low-Sax. and D. Echt, A. S. *ev*; allied to the A. S. *ae*, Gesetz] [the legal union of man and woman for life] marriage, matrimony, wedlock. Der Stand der —, the married state; in den Stand der — treten, to enter into the conjugal state, to enter upon wedlock, to marry; die — brechen, to commit adultery; eine Person zur — haben, to be married to a person; er gab ihm seine Tochter zur —, he gave his daughter to him in marriage; zu einer neuen — schreiten, to marry again; die — vollziehen, to consummate marriage; außer der —, out of wedlock, unmarried; außer der — leben, to lead a single life; ein außer der — erzeugtes Kind, an illegitimate child, a spurious child; eine — stiften, schließen, to strike a match; das Ehestiften, match-making [often in contempt or joke]; zur — gehörig, matrimonial. *Prov.* —n werden im Himmel geschlossen, marriages are made in heaven. *Fig.* [in botany] Eine heimliche or verborgene —, cryptogamy; vielfache —n, polygamy.

Ehe-band, *n.* the nuptial knot. Die —bande, the bonds of Hymen. —beredung, *f.* [in law] marriage-articles. —bett, *n.* the marriage-bed. *Fig.* Das —bett beflecken, to defile the nuptial bed. —brechen, *v. intr.* to commit adultery. —brecher, *m.* adulterer. —breeherei, *f.* V. —bruch. —brecherinn, *f.* adulteress. —brecherisch, *adj.* and *adv.* [guilty of adultery, pertaining to adultery] adulterous. —bruch, *m.* 1) [violation of the marriage-bed] adultery. —bruch begehen, to commit adultery. Das im —bruch erzeugte Kind, a child issuing from an adulterous connection, adulterine. 2) the crime of adultery, [in law] criminal conversation. —brüchig, *adj.* adulterous, adulterate. —bund, *m.* —bündniß, *n.* matrimonial union, conjugal union. V. —band. —fähig, *adj.* and *adv.* fit to be married, marriageable, nubile. —feind, *m.* a hater of marriage, misogamist. —fest, *n.* V. Hochzeitsfest. —frau, *f.* a lawful wife, spouse, consort, mate. —freude, *f.* connubial joys, connubial bliss. —friede, *m.* matrimonial unanimity. —gatte, *m.* a person joined with another in matrimony, a wife or husband, consort; but chiefly the husband. Die —gatten, man and wife, husband and wife. —gattinn, *f.* V. —frau. —gedanke, *m.* V. Heirathsgedanke. —||geld, *n.* V. Heirathsgut. —gelübde, *n.* marriage vow. —gemach, *n.* the bed-chamber of married people. ‡—gemächt, *n.* V. —gatte. —gemahl, *m.* —gemahlinn, *f.* consort. V. Gemahl and Gemahlinn. —genoß, *m.* —genossinn, *f.* consort, mate. —genuß, *m.* the enjoyment of nuptial joys. —gericht, *n.* the spiritual court., consistory. —glück, *n.* connubial happiness. —gott, *m.* the god of marriage, Hymen. ||—gürtel, *m.* V. Blätterschwamm. —haft, *f.* 1) [in some parts of Germany] freehold estate, land which is the absolute property of the owner, allodium. 2) [in the old Saxon law] a lawful hinderance. ‡—haft, *adj.* and *adv.* lawful. —hälfte, *f.* [frequently used in joke] consort, mate. Meine —hälfte, my spouse or wife, my better half. ‡ and ||—halt, *m.* [-en, *pl.* -en] a menial servant. —haß, *m.* misogamy. —hasser, *m.* V. —feind. —herr, *m.* V. —gatte. Ihr —herr, her lord and husband. —herrlich, *adj.* and *adv.* becoming a husband, marital. —joch, *n.* the yoke of marriage. —kette, *f.* conjugal ties. —kind, *n.* a legitimate child. —kreuz, *n.* pains or sufferings, vexations in marriage. *Fig.* ‡Mein —kreuz, my wife, my dear spouse [ironically]. —krüppel, *m.* [mostly in joke] an impotent husband. —leiblich, *adj.* and *adv.* lawful, legitimate. Sein —leiblicher Sohn, his lawful begotten son. —leute, *pl.* married people. —liebste, *m.* and *f.* consort, mate. —los, *adj.* and *adv.* single, unmarried. Ein —loses Leben, a single life, celibacy. Das —lose Leben der römisch-katholischen Geistlichkeit, celibate. —losigkeit, *f.* single life, celibacy, [in the Romish church] celibate. —lustig, *adj.* and *adv.* inclined to marry. —mann, *m.* a husband, spouse, mate. —männlich, *adj.* and *adv.* becoming a husband, marital. —ordnung, *f.* decrees, ordinances relating to matrimony. —paar, *n.* a married couple. —pacten, *pl.* marriage-articles. —pfänder, *pl.* children. —pflicht, *f.* the conjugal duty. —procurator, *m.* matrimonial agent. —recht, *n.* 1) matrimonial right. 2) laws concerning matrimony and married people. —sache, *f.* a marriage-cause, a marriage-affair. —schatz, *m.* ‡ or ‡ 1) consort, spouse, mate. ||2) the dower, dowry. —scheidung, *f.* divorce. —scheu, *f.* an aversion to matrimony. —scheue, *m.* a misogamist. —segen, *m.* 1) the blessing spoken at the marriage ceremony. 2) conjugal blessing, children [often in joke]. Ein starker —segen, plenty of children. —spiel, *n.* a game at cards. —stand, *m.* the married or nuptial state, marriage, matrimony, wedlock. In den —stand treten, to marry. —standsfesseln, *pl.* nuptial ties, matrimonial bonds. —steuer, *f.* the dower, dowry. —stifter, *m.* —stifterinn, *f.* a person that brings about a marriage, match-maker. —stiftung, *f.* 1) match-making. 2) marriage-articles. —streit, *m.* contention among married people. —teufel, *m.* Asmodi [then, in general] any person that creates discord between man and wife. —trennung, *f.* V. —scheidung. —unlustig, *adj.* and *adv.* not inclined to marry, averse to marriage. —verbindung, *f.* V. Heirath. —vergleich, *m.* V. —vertrag. —verlöbniß, *n.* V. Verlöbniß. —versprechen, *n.* a promise of marriage. —vertrag, *m.* marriage-articles. —weib, *n.* wife, spouse, mate. —werber, *m.* [one who solicits a marriage] a courter, suitor, wooer. ||—zarter, —zärter, *m.* a contract on which a marriage is founded. —zwist, *m.* a discord, disunion or dissension among married people, matrimonial differences.

Ehelein, *m.* [-s, *pl.* -] V. Elsebeerbaum.

Ehelich, *adj.* and *adv.* 1) [pertaining to marriage] matrimonial, connubial, nuptial, hymeneal. Die —e Liebe, conjugal affection, connubial love; die —en Bande, conjugal ties; die —en Pflichten, matrimonial duties; die —e Treue, the fidelity of a husband or wife. 2) [derived from marriage] matrimonial. Die —e Gewalt, matrimonial power. 3) proceeding from or born in marriage. —e Kinder, children born in wedlock, legitimate children.

Ehelichen, I. *v. tr.* [to take for husband or wife] to marry. Er ehelichte ihre Tochter, he married her daughter. II. *v. r.* sich —, to enter into the conjugal state, to take a husband or wife, to marry, to wive.

Eher, V. Ehe *adv.*

Ehern, [A. S. *aren*, Lat. *aereus*, allied to the Engl. *iron*] *adj.* and *adv.* [made of brass] brazen. Ein —er Helm, a brazen helmet. *Fig.* Das —e Zeitalter, brazen age; eine —e Stirne haben, to have a brazen face, to be brazen-faced, impudent.

Ehernhufig, *adj.* and *adv.* brazen-hoofed.

Eheste, V. Ehe *adv.*

Ehestens, *adv.* very soon, as soon as possible.

Ehr, Ehrn, an inferior title, now nearly obsolete, applied in the law-style to ecclesiastics in particular, as the English *Reverend*, but not always so respectful; sometimes used in joke, like master.

Ehrbar, *adj.* and *adv.* 1) consistent with honour or decency. Ein —es Betragen, decent conduct; ein —er Anzug, a decent or decorous dress; —e Absichten, honest views; Aesop's Jungfrau saß —unten am Tische, Esop's damsel sat demurely at the board's end; Weiber können lustig und dabei doch —seyn, wives may be merry and yet honest [chaste] too. 2) [worthy of respect, entitled to honour] honourable [often a title given to a commoner or citizen].

Ehrbarkeit, *f.* [that which is fit, suitable or becoming in words or behaviour] decency, propriety of conduct.

‡**Ehrbarlich**, V. Ehrbar.

1\. **Ehre**, *f.* [*pl.* -n] [Ice. *aera*, A.S. *are*, is perhaps allied to *ar*, *hehr* = hoch] 1) [the preference given to a person above or before another] honour. Er macht or rechnet sich's zur —, he is proud of it; ich mache mir eine — daraus, Ihnen zu dienen, I am ambitious to serve you; Einem — machen, to be an honour to any one. *Prov.* — dem — gebührt, respect must be paid to every one according to his rank; — sei Gott in der Höhe, [in Scripture] glory to God in the highest; [also as an expression of civility] ich habe die — zu seyn Ihr &c., I have the honour to be, your &c. 2) honour, dignity, distinction, exalted rank or place. Ich habe dir Reichthum und — gegeben, [in Script.] I have given thee riches and honour; zu großer — erhoben werden, to be raised to great honours. *Prov.* Große —n können den Sinn verkehren, honours change manners; je größer die —, je größer die Beschwerde, honour and ease are seldom bedfellows. 3) [testimony of esteem, any expression of respect or high estimation by words or actions] honour. Etwas in —[n] halten, to honour something; Einem eine — anthun, to treat any one with respect; Eines in allen —n gedenken, to mention any one honourably, to make honourable mention of any one; Einem — erweisen, to do any one honour; Einem die ihm gebührende — erweisen, to pay or give any one the honour due to him; die —n (Honneurs) des Hauses machen, to do the honours of a house; kriegerische —n, military honours; Einem die letzte — erweisen, to do the funeral honours to any one; sie erwiesen ihm göttliche —[n], they paid divine honours to him. 4) [the esteem paid to worth, high estimation] honour. In großer — leben, to be in great esteem; *Ihr Wort in —n, with your leave. *Prov.* Eitle — überlebt den dritten Tag nicht, vain glory is a tree which all deceives, yielding no fruit, but fruitless leaves. 5) honour, reputation, good name. Seine — ist unbefleckt, his honour is unsullied; Eines — kränken, to injure any one's reputation; *Einem die — abschneiden, to calumniate, to slander any one; bei — bleiben, to preserve one's honour or reputation; *mit —n loskommen, to come off with credit; bei meiner —, on or upon my honour [words accompanying a declaration which pledge one's honour or reputation for the truth of it]. *Prov.* — verloren, Alles verloren, that has an ill name is half hanged; take aw[ay] my good name, and take away my life; die [—] einer Jungfrau ist eine weiße Schürze, the fai[rest] silk is soonest stained. *Fig.* Auf dem Bette [der —] sterben, to die on the bed of honour. 6) h[on]our, decorum, decency. Die Gesetze der —, l[aws] of honour; aber in allen —n, but honestly [in] Zucht und —n, in all honour and decency; [ein] Kuß in —n, an honest kiss; —n halber [etwas] thun, to be bound in honour to do somet[hing]; *mit —n zu melden, with or saving your [rever]ence or honour. 7) [true nobleness of mind] [hon]our. Er ist ein Mann von —, he is an honou[rable] man, or a man of honour. 8) [a person or thin[g that] honours] honour. Die Frau ist des Manne[s —], the wife is an honour to her husband.

Ehre, Ruhm. Ruhm is a higher degree of [honour]. One who is distinguished in his native to[wn] among his fellow citizens for his unsullied good [name] has Ehre, but not Ruhm. Der Ruhm require[s that] the worth of a man should be more generally k[nown, and] that his exalted reputation be derived from the praise of great or remarkable exploits or [achieve]ments.

Ehr-abschneider, *m.* a calumniato[r, slan]derer. —abschneiderei, *f.* calumny, s[lander]. —amt, *n.* V. Ehrenamt. —angreife[nd, *adj.*] and *adv.* injurious. —begabt, *adj.* a[nd *adv.*] honoured. —begierde, *f.* [a desire of [honour]] ambition. —begierig, *adj.* and *adv.* [desirous of honour] ambitious. —beraubung, *f.* [calum]ny, slander. —(e)bringend, *adj.* and [*adv.*] honorific. —drang, *m.* ambitiousness, [am]bition. —durst, *m.* a vehement desire of [hon]our, a thirst for honours. —dürstig, *adj.* [and] *adv.* vehemently desirous of honour. —e[...] *m.* an anxious desire to preserve one's hono[ur, so]licitude for one's honour, sense of honour, [...] of honour. —erbietig, I. *adj.* [marked or cha[r]acterized by respect] respectful. Eine —erbieti[ge] Haltung, a respectful deportment; ein —erbietiges Betragen, reverent behaviour; eine —e bietige Dankbarkeit, a reverential gratitude; eine —erbietige Scheu, a reverential awe. II. *adv.* respectfully, with respect, regardfully, reverently, reverentially. Einen —erbietig behandeln, to treat a person with respect. ‖—**erbietsam**, *adj.* and *adv.* V. —erbietig. —**erbietung**, *f.* reverence, respect, regard, deference. Jemandem seine —erbietung bezeugen, to pay respect to any one by outward action, to give reverence to any one. Syn. Ehrerbietung, Ehrfurcht. Ehrfurcht is a feeling of admiration or reverence mingled with awe, and inspired by the consciousness of our own insignificancy and littleness. Ehrerbietung is not an internal emotion, but merely an act of respect or obeisance. —**furcht**, *f.* reverence, veneration, reverential fear, awe. —furcht gegen seine Eltern hegen, to feel reverence for one's parents; —furcht gegen Gott hegen, to reverence God; —furcht gebietend, to be reverenced, awful, fearful; die —furcht gebietende Majestät Jehova's, the awful majesty of Jehovah; Einem —furcht einflößen, to strike any one with awe or reverence. *Fig.* Eine —furcht gebietende Stellung einnehmen, to take or hold an imposing position. Syn. V. —erbietung. —**furchtbebend**, *adj.* and *adv.* shaking with awe. —**fürchten**, *v. tr.* [seldom used] to reverence, to respect. Eltern —fürchten, to venerate parents. —**fürchtig**, V. —furchtsvoll. —**furchtsvoll**, *adj.* respectful. —**furchtswerth**, —**furchtswürdig**, *adj.* and *adv.* worthy of veneration and reverence, venerable. —**gefühl**, *n.* sense of honour; ambition. Er hat ein feines —gefühl, he has a nice sense of honour; sein —gefühl ist ziemlich stumpf or abgestumpft, his sense of honour is pretty well blunted. —**geiz**, *m.* [an inordinate desire of preferment or of honour] ambition. Syn. Ehrgeiz, Ruhmbegierde, V. Ehre, Ruhm. —**geizen**, *v. intr.* to seek after ambitiously. —**geizig**, *adj.* [desirous of honour, superiority, or excellence, aspiring] ambitious. —**gier**, *f.* an inordinate desire of honour. —**gierig**, *adj.* and *adv.* coveting honour. —**liebe**, *f.* a moderate desire of honour, a moderate ambition. —**liebend**, *adj.* and *adv.* moderately desirous of honour. Ein —liebender Mann, a man of honour, careful of his honour. —**los**, *adj.* and *adv.* 1) [destitute of honour] dishonourable, without honesty, honourless. Ein —loser Mensch, a dishonourable man. 2) [staining the character, and lessening the reputation] dishonourable. Eine —lose Handlung, a disgraceful action; Einen —los erklären, to brand any one with infamy; ein —loser Mensch kann nicht als Zeuge dienen, an infamous person cannot be a witness. Syn. Ehrlos, Unehrlich. The man is unehrlich, who is undeserving of any respect or esteem; he is ehrlos, who is publicly branded with infamy, or who is destitute of all feeling of honour. The swindler is unehrlich in as much as he acts dishonestly, but not necessarily ehrlos, until his dishonest actions are publicly known. —**losigkeit**, *f.* dishonour, total loss of reputation, public disgrace, infamy. —**punkt**, *m.* V. Ehrenpunkt. —**schatz**, *m.* [in feudal law, a fine paid to the lord by every one who came to an inheritance of land held in capite] relief. —**schätzig**, *adj.* and *adv.* [in feudal law] obliged to pay a relief. —**sucht**, *f.* an inordinate desire of honour or of preferment, ambition. —**süchtig**, *adj.* and *adv.* coveting honour, eager for fame, ambitious. —**trieb**, *m.* an inborn desire of honour, or of preferment, a laudable ambition. —**vergessen**, *adj.* and *adv.* unmindful of honour, mean, despicable, vile. —**verletzung**, *f.* V. Ehrenverletzung. —**voll**, *adj.* and *adv.* V. Ehrenvoll. —**widrig**, *adj.* and *adv.* dishonourable, disreputable. Ein —widriges Betragen, a disgraceful conduct. —**würde[n]**, [a title of respect given to ecclesiastics] reverend. Ew. —würden, your reverence. —**würdig**, *adj.* and *adv.* 1) [worthy of veneration or reverence] venerable. Ein —würdiger Greis, a venerable old man; eine —würdige Dame, a respectable lady; —würdig groß, venerably great. 2) [an epithet of respect given to ecclesiastics] reverend. —würdiger Herr, reverend sir. —**würdigkeit**, *f.* venerableness, respectableness, respectability.

‖2. **Ehre**, *f.* [*pl.* -n] V. Ahorn.

Ehren, *pl.* of Ehre, honours.

Ehren-abschneider, *m.* V. Ehrabschneider. —**amt**, *n.* 1) [an office or function to which no salary or reward is attached and which is conferred or filled, as it were, merely for honour's sake] an honorary place. 2) a place conferring honour, a post of honour. —**bahn**, *f.* course or career of honour. —**beiwort**, *n.* an honourable predicate. —**belohnung**, *f.* honorary reward. —**benennung**, *f.* an appellation of dignity given to persons, a title. —**besuch**, *m.* an honorary visit. —**bett**, *n.* state-bed. —**bezeigung**, *f.* expression of esteem, mark of honour. Er wurde mit allen gebührenden —bezeigungen empfangen, he was received with all due honours. —**bild**, *n.* 1) V. —stück. ‖2) a statue. —**bogen**, *m.* a triumphal arch. —**bothe**, *m.* an ambassador. —**bürger**, *m.* an honorary citizen. —**bürgerrecht**, *n.* the honorary freedom of a corporate town &c. —**dame**, *f.* [at courts] lady of honour. Eine —dame der Königinn, a lady of honour to the queen. —**degen**, *m.* V. —schwert. —**denkmahl**, *n.* V. —mahl, 1). —**dieb**, *m.* a slanderer, a calumniator, a defamer. —**dienst**, *m.* civilities paid. Den —dienst verrichten, to do the honours. —**erklärung**, *f.* reparation of honour, apology. —**erleuchtung**, *f.* illumination. —**fall**, *m.* 1) a case where one's honour is at stake. 2) an occasion on which a display of show and splendour is to be made, for the purpose of honouring a person. ‡—**fest**, *adj.* and *adv.* honourable. —**frau**, *f.* a matron. —**fräulein**, *n.* [at courts] maid of honour. —**gedächtniß**, *n.* a memorial of honour, a monument. —**gedicht**, *n.* a poem of honour. —**gehalt**, *m.* a pension. —**geld**, *n.* honorary. —**gepränge**, *n.* ceremony or pomp for honouring any one. —**gericht**, *n.* court of honour, a court of chivalry. —**geschenk**, *n.* a present or gift of honour. —**grab**, *n.* a cenotaph. —**grad**, *m.* an honorary degree. —**gruß**, *m.* a salute of honour. —**haft**, *adj.* and *adv.* honourable. —**halber**, *adv.* for honour's sake. —**halle**, *f.* pantheon. —**handel**, *m.* an affair of honour. —**hold**, *m.* V. Herold. —**kette**, *f.* a chain given or worn as an honorary distinction. —**klage**, *f.* an action for an injury to a person, an action for libel. —**kleid**, *n.* a festive dress, a robe of honour, [among the Turks] caftan. —**kränkung**, *f.* an injury to reputation. —**kranz**, *m.* an honorary wreath. —**krone**, *f.* 1) an honorary crown. 2) *Fig.* the felicity of heaven prepared for the children of God, celestial bliss, glory. —**kuß**, *m.* a kiss of civility. —**leer**, *adj.* and *adv.* destitute of honour, honourless. —**legion**, *f.* [in France] the order of the legion of honour. —**lehen**, *n.* [in law] a tenure in capite, honour. —**leute**, *pl.* persons of respectability. —**lohn**, *m.* honorary. —**lüge**, *f.* an officious lie. —**mahl**, *n.* 1) a monument in honour of a person, honorary monument. 2) an entertainment, a feast in honour of a person. —**mann**, *m.* a man of honour, an honourable man, a gentleman in the true sense of the word, a perfect gentleman. —**mitglied**, *n.* an honorary member [of a society]. —**münze**, *f.* a medal in honour of some remarkable performance, a medallion. —**mutter**, *f.* a matron. —**name**, *m.* a name of honour, a title. —**pfad**, the path of honour. ‡—**pfennig**, *m.* a coin struck in honour of a person. —**pforte**, *f.* a triumphal arch. —**platz**, *m.* place of honour. Einem den —platz bei Tische einräumen, to assign a person the uppermost place at table. —**preis**, *m.* [a genus of plants] speedwell. —**punkt**, *m.* the point of honour. —**raub**, *m.* slander, calumny. —**räuber**, *m.* a slanderer, a calumniator, a defamer. —**rede**, *f.* a panegyric. —**reich**, *adj.* and *adv.* rich in honour, honourable. —**reich**, *m.* [a name of men] Erick. V. also Erich. —**reihe**, *f.* [in heraldry] the chief. —**retter**, *m.* a vindicator. —**rettung**, *f.* the defence of one's honour, vindication. —**rock**, *m.* V. —kleid. —**ruf**, *m.* call of honour. —**rührig**, *adj.* and *adv.* defamatory, calumnious, slanderous. —rührige Worte, defamatory words. —**sache**, *f.* an affair of honour. —**säule**, *f.* a statue erected in honour of a person, a monument. —**schänder**, *m.* 1) a defamer, calumniator, slanderer, libeller. 2) a deflourer. —**schänderisch**, *adj.* and *adv.* slanderous, calumnious, defamatory. —**schild**, *m.* [in heraldry] a scutcheon of honour. ‡—**schilling**, *m.* money saved with a view to some occasion where honour is concerned. —**schmuck**, *m.* an ornament for distinguishing any one. —**schuld**, *f.* debt of honour. —**schuß**, *m.* a shot in honour of a person. —**schwert**, *n.* 1) a sword given or worn as an honorary distinction. 2) [a genus of plants] China ixia. —**sitz**, *m.* seat of honour. —**sold**, *m.* honorary, salary. —**spiegel**, *m.* a description of the virtues and merits of others. —**staffel**, *f.* V. Ehrenstufe. —**stelle**, *f.* 1) honour, dignity, exalted rank or place. 2) [in heraldry] honour-point. —**strafe**, *f.* a punishment which affects one's civil honour or involves the loss of one's civil honour. —**streit**, *m.* a dispute on honour. —**stück**, *n.* [in heraldry] honourable ordinary. —**stufe**, *f.* the degree of honour. ‡ and ‖ —**tafel**, *f.* a court of chivalry, court of honour. —**tag**, *m.* day of honour [such as a wedding-day &c.]. —**tanz**, *m.* dance of honour. —**tempel**, *m.* pantheon. —**titel**, *m.* title of honour. —**tod**, *m.* an honourable death. —**trunk**, *m.* a health drunk in honour of any one, a toast. —**verletzung**, *f.* an injury to reputation. [in law] Die thätliche —verletzung, [Realinjurie] an injury done to a man's person by acts; die wörtliche —verletzung, [Verbalinjurie] a verbal injury; eine schriftliche —verletzung, an injury done by libel. —**voll**, *adj.* and *adv.* [conferring honour] honourable. —volle Wunden, honourable wounds; bei Hofe —voll aufgenommen, honourably received at court. Das —volle, honourableness. —**wache**, *f.* a guard of honour. —**wein**, *m.* wine of honour. —**werth**, *adj.* 1) worthy of esteem and honour, respectable, honourable. 2) [a title of baronets and knights and of members of Parliament in England] honourable. Der —werthe Sir Eduard N., the honourable Sir Edward N.; das —werthe Mitglied, the honourable member. Eine —werthe Gesellschaft, a respectable company; ein —werther Mann, a respectable man. Das —werthe, honourableness. —**wort**, *n.* word of honour. Er gab mir sein —wort, daß er mich bezahlen würde, he gave me his word he would pay me, he pledged me his honour that he would pay me. —**zeichen**, *n.* [a mark, sign, token or thing, by which a person is distinguished] badge, as titles, orders &c.

Ehren, *v. tr.* 1) to honour, to revere, to respect. Du sollst Vater und Mutter —, [in Script.] honour thy father and thy mother; die Götter —, to worship the gods; auf daß sie Alle den Sohn —, wie sie den Vater —, [in Script.] that all men should honour the son, even as they honour the father. Der —de, he that honours, honourer. 2) [honoriren] [in commerce, to accept and pay when due] to honour [a bill of exchange]. 3) to dignify, to elevate in rank or station, to honour, to exalt. *Fig.* Ich ehre mir deinen Vater, er war ein guter Mann, I praise your father for his goodness.

Ehrer, *m.* [-s, *pl.* -] honourer.

Ehrlich, *adj.* and *adv.* 1) honourable. **Fig.* Das hat mich etwas —es gekostet, it cost me handsomely. 2) being in good repute, held in esteem, or accompanied with testimonies of esteem. Von —en Eltern geboren seyn, to be born of reputable parents; ein —es Begräbniß, an honourable burial. 3) honest, fair. Ein —er Mann, an honest man; — handeln, to deal honestly, fairly; —e Absichten, honest views, honourable intentions; ein —es Gewerbe treiben, to pursue a creditable occupation; er scheint —e Zwecke zu haben, his intentions appear to be honourable; sein —es Auskommen haben, to live honestly or like a man of honour. *Prov.* — währt am längsten, knavery may serve for a turn, but honesty is best in the long run, honesty is the best policy. 4) honest, chaste, faithful. Ein —es Weib, an honest wife.

Ehrlichkeit, *f.* [moral rectitude of heart, a disposition to conform to justice and correct moral principles, in all social transactions] honesty, probity. Die — eines Kaufmanns, the fair dealing of a merchant.

Ehrsam, *adj.* and *adv.* honoured, honourable, respectable. Ein —er Mann, an honourable man; ein —es Gewerbe, a creditable occupation.

‖**Ehs, Ehse**, *adj.* and *adv.* [= eßbar] [with bakers] eatable.

Ei, a suffix of many nouns, as Bettelei, beggary; Heuchelei, hypocrisy; Abgötterei, idolatry; Gerberei, tannery; Brauerei, brewery &c. &c.

Ei, *interj.* [an exclamation, expressive of surprise or wonder, joy, dislike, contempt &c., according to the manner of utterance] ah. — wie schön! hey! heyday! eigh! how pretty! —! Sie rühmen sich dessen, why! you boast of it; —! —! Sie müssen davon nicht sprechen, why! you must not speak of it; — wirklich! zweifeln Sie daran? why! do you question it? —, daran dachte ich nicht, indeed! I did not mind it.

Ei, *n.* [-es, *pl.* -er] [A. S. *aeg*, Engl. and Sw. *egg*, Gr. *ὠόν*, Lat. *ovum*, appears to be allied to the Lat. *ago*, to the Germ. be-weg-en] 1) [something round] *a*) [in architect.] ovolo, called also the quarter round. *b*) *pl.* the testicles. *c*) [in natural history] the name of several snails. 2) an egg. Die —er der Vögel, Fische und anderer Thiere, the eggs of fowls, fish and other animals; —er legen, to lay eggs; frische —er, fresh or new laid eggs; alte —er, stale eggs; faule —er, rotten eggs; Setzeier, poached eggs; gebackene —er, fried eggs; weichgesottene —er, soft boiled eggs; gerührte —er, buttered eggs. *Prov.* Ein faules — verdirbt den ganzen Brei, one ill weed mars a whole pot of pottage; das — will klüger seyn als die Henne, Jack Sprat would teach his grandam to grope hens; besser ein halbes —, als eine leere Schale, better half an egg, than an empty shell; better one small fish, than an empty dish; half a loaf is better than no bread; something has some savour; gebratene —er geben keine Küchlein, you can't eat your cake, and have your cake; haben wir nicht —er, so braten wir das Nest, if you have not a capon, feed an onion; sie gleichen einander, wie ein — dem andern, they are as like as two drops of water; er ist kaum aus dem — gekrochen, he is but just out of the shell; sich um ungelegte —er bekümmern, to fight with the sword, that is yet at the cutler's.

Ei-form, *f.* the shape of an egg. —**förmig**, *adj.* and *adv.* oval, oblong. Ein —förmiger Körper, an oval; ein —es Blatt, [in botany] an ovate [ovated] leaf. —**gestalt**, *f.* V. —form. —**lienicht**, *adj.* and *adv.* elliptic, elliptical. —**linie**, *f.* [in geometry] ellipsis. —**linig**, *adj.* and *adv.* oval. —**rund**, I. *adj.* and *adv.* oval, ovate, ovated. II. *n.* an oval. —**ründe**, *f.* the figure or shape of an egg. —**weiß**, *n.* the white of an egg, glair. Mit —weiß bestreichen, to glair, to varnish. —**weißstoff**, *m.* [in botany, the substance of the lobes of seeds corresponding to the white of an egg] albumen.

Eia, *interj.* [an exclamation, expressing joy, but often used in an ironical sense] hey!

Eibe, *f.* [*pl.* -n] [A. S. *iv*, Fr. *if*; allied to the Lat. *abies*, and to the Germ. heben, *cf.* Eiche] [a tree] yew, yew-tree. Von dem Holze der — verfertigt, yewen.

Eibenbaum, *m.* = Eibe.

Eiben, *adj.* yewen.

Eibisch, *m.* [-es] [Gr. *ἰβισκος*, allied to Eibe] [the name of several plants] *a*) althea, marsh-mallow. *b*) hibiscus. *c*) tree Lavatera or mallow.

Eibischbaum, *m.* V. Eberesche. —**kraut**, *n.* V. Eibisch *a.* —**saft**, *m.* the juice of althea. —**salbe**, *f.* dialthæa. —**wurz**, *f.* V. Eibisch *a.*

1. **Eiche**, *f.* [*pl.* -n] [A. S. *aec*, Old G. *eih*, Swed. *ek*, Ice. *akarn*, allied to the Goth. *aukan*, A. S. *eakan*, Lat. *augeo*] [a tree] oak. Eine junge —, an oakling. *Prov.* Durch öftere Streiche fällt endlich die —, little strokes fell great oaks. Often used in compositions, as: Stein—, Hag— &c.

Eich-apfel, *m.* V. Gallapfel. —**baum**, *m.* V. 1. Eiche —**farn**, *m.* oak-farn, oak-fern. —**grund**, *m.* a low tract of land overgrown with oaks. —**hase**, *m.* a sort of fungus [boletus ramosissimus]. —**holz**, *n.* V. —enholz. —**horn**, —**hörnchen**, *n.* squirrel. Das fliegende —horn, the flying squirrel. —**hornaffe**, *m.* [a small monkey of South America] tamarin. —**land**, *n.* land suitable to the production of oaks, or planted with oaks. —**mast**, *f.* V. Eichelmast. —**pilz**, —**schwamm**, *m.* oak-leather. —**thal**, *n.* a valley overgrown with oaks. —**traube**, *f.* agaric [boletus igniarius]. —**wald**, *m.* —**waldung**, *f.* oak-forest, wood of oaks. —**wäldchen**, *n.* oak-grove.

Eichen-blatt, *n.* oak-leaf. —**blattlaus**, *f.* oak-puceron. —**bohrer**, *m.* a species of gall-fly. —**farn**, *m.* V. Eichfarn. —**gehölz**, *n.* —**hain**, *m.* oak-grove. —**gruppe**, *f.* a clump of oaks. —**holz**, *n.* 1) oak-grove. 2) oak-wood, oaken timber. —**kranz**, *m.* an oaken garland. —**kraut**, *n.* V. Vergißmeinnicht. —**laub**, *n.* the oak-leaves. —**lunge**, *f.* V. Steinflechte. —**mistel**, *f.* a sort of misseltoe growing on oaks. —**moos**, *n.* moss growing on oaks. —**motte**, *f.* a species of moth. —**rinde**, *f.* oak-bark. —**rippe**, *f.* [in seamen's lang.] an oaken rib. —**rose**, *f.* an excrescence on oak-leaves. —**schwamm**, *m.* the oak agaric. —**stamm**, *m.* the stem of an oak. —**stock**, *m.* an oaken stick, †oaken towel. —**streicher**, *m.* the great egger-moth. —**wurm**, *m.* the gall-fly.

2. **Eiche**, *f.* [*pl.* -n] [appears to be allied to the Lat. *aequus*, the Gr. *εικός*] 1) [without a pl.] the act of gauging or gaging. 2) the gauge, standard. V. Eichmaß. 3) [in mills] the water-gauge.

Eich-elle, *f.* standard-yard. —**faß**, *n.* gauging-cask. —**gebühr**, *f.* gauger's fee. —**maß**, *n.* the gauge, standard. —**meister**, *m.* V. Eicher. —**pfahl**, *m.* [in mills] the water-gauge. —**stab**, *m.* gauging-rod.

Eichel, *f.* [*pl.* -n] [appears to be allied to the Lat. *aescul*-us, and to the Gr. *ἄκυλος*] 1) [the seed or fruit of an oak] acorn. Die Schweine in die —n treiben or schlagen, to place swine to feed on acorns; —n tragend, glandiferous. 2) *Fig.* *a*) [in anatomy] the nut of the penis, glans. *b*) the name of one of the suits of German cards, so named from its figure [club in French cards].

Eichel-drüse, *f.* [in anatomy] a gland of the nut of the penis. —**förmig**, *adj.* and *adv.* having the form of an acorn. —**garten**, *m.* nursery of oaks. —**hafer**, *m.* a species of oats [avena strigosa]. —**häher**, *m.* V. Nußhäher. —**kaffee**, *m.* a surrogate of coffee, made of roasted and pulverised acorns. ‖—**kamp**, V. —garten. —**kelch**, *m.* V. —näpfchen. —**kost**, *f.* food of acorns. —**kranz**, *m.* a wreath of oak-leaves, an oaken garland. —**mast**, *f.* the fruit of the oak, acorns, mast. —**muschel**, *f.* chama [chama calyculata]. —**näpfchen**, *n.* acorn-cup. —**öl**, *n.* oil of acorns. —**rand**, *m.* [in anatomy] the corona of the nut of the penis. —**schwein**, *n.* a pig fed on acorns. —**spitze**, *f.* the point of the acorn. —**waldung**, *f.* a forest of oaks.

Eichen, *adj.* and *adv.* oaken. —es Holz, oak-wood; —e Bretter, oaken planks.

Eichen, [V. 2. Eiche] *v. tr.* to gage, to gauge [a cask, or vessel &c.]; to adjust to a standard [weights, ells].

Eicher, Eichner, *m.* [-s, *pl.* -] [an officer appointed for the purpose of inspecting and marking weights and measures] a gauger.

Eichicht, *n.* [-es, *pl.* -e] a collection of oaks closely set, a thicket of oaks.

Eichner, V. Eicher.

Eid, *m.* [-es, *pl.* -e] [Goth. *aiths*, Swed. ed, D. *eed*, perhaps allied to the Ice. *eiga*, haben. The holding, bounding] 1) oath. Einen — ablegen, schwören, to take oath; einen — auf etwas ablegen [etwas beschwören], to take an oath of a thing, to swear to a thing; Einem den — abnehmen, to take another man's oath; Jemanden den — zuschieben, to put any one to his oath, to tender any one the oath; einen — schwören lassen, to administer an oath; ein gezwungener —, an oath extorted by violence; der —, den man auf die Bibel schwört, bible-oath; ein körperlicher or feierlicher —, a corporeal oath, a solemn oath; ein falscher — heißt Meineid, a false oath is called perjury; einen falschen — schwören, to perjure one's self. 2) the form of an oath.

Eid-bruch, Eides-bruch, *m.* oath-breaking, perjury. —**brüchig**, *adj.* and *adv.* guilty of perjury, perjured. —**bruder**, *m.* one associated with another by an oath. —**bürge**, *m.* a surety, a bondsman, a bail upon oath. —**es-ablehnung**, *f.* a refusal to take an oath. —**es-erbietung**, *f.* an offer to take an oath. —**es-formel**, *f.* the form of an oath. —**es-kräftig**, *adj.* and *adv.* being upon oath, by oath. —**es-leistung**, *f.* the act of taking an oath. —**es-pflicht**, *f.* the homage. Einem —espflicht leisten, to do homage to any one. —**es-verweigerung**, *f.* V. —esablehnung. —**es-zuschiebung**, *f.* the act of putting any one to his oath. —**genoß**, *m.* 1) one associated with another by an oath. 2) Die —genossen, the Helvetic confederacy, Helvetic states. —**genossisch**, ‖—**genössisch**, *adj.* and *adv.* associated by an oath, leagued together; *it.* referring to the Helvetic confederacy.. —**genossenschaft**, *f.* 1) league, confederacy. 2) the Helvetic confederacy, Helvetic states. —**haft**, —**haftig**, *adj.* and *adv.* V. Eidlich. —**schwur**, *m.* the act of taking an oath, the oath. —**vergessen**, *adj.* and *adv.* V. —brüchig.

Eidam, *m.* [-es, *pl.* -e] [allied either to Eid or to eigen] son-in-law.

Eidechse, *f.* [*pl.* -n] [A. S. *athexe*, D. *ahtisse*, Ice. *ethla*, allied to the Gr. *αἴθω*, Old G. eiten = brennen?] 1) lizard. Eine kleine —, an eft, a newt. 2) *Fig.* [in astronomy, a constellation in the northern hemisphere] lacerta.

Eidechsenschwanz, *m.* [a plant] lizard-tail.

Eidechsfisch, *m.* a genus of fishes.

1. **Eider**, *f.* [a river in Holstein] the Eyder. **Eider-fluß**, —**strom**, *m.* V. 1. Eider.

2. **Eider**, *m.* [-s, *pl.* -] [probably from the Old eiten = brennen, glänzen] V. Eidergans.

Eider-dunen, *pl.* eider-down. —**gans**, *f.* the eider-duck. —**vogel**, *m.* V. —gans.

Eidlich, *adj.* and *adv.* done by means of an oath, or being upon oath, by oath, with an oath. Eine —e Erklärung, an affidavit; — aussagen, to declare upon oath; — erhärten, to make affidavit; — abläugnen, to deny by oath; sich — verpflichtet haben, to be under an oath.

Eier, *pl.* of Ei, eggs.

Eier-apfel, *m.* the fruit of the large-fruited nightshade, or egg-plant. —**baum**, *m.* V. —staude. —**becher**, *m.* egg-cup. —**blätter-schwamm**, *m.* V. —schwamm. —**blume**, *f.* V. Löwenzahn. —**bohne**, *f.* V. Erbsbohne. —**brod**, *n.* [with bakers] a sort of bread made with eggs and milk. —**brühe**, *f.* egg-sauce. —**dotter**, *m.* 1) the yellow part of an egg, the yelk or yolk, the vitellus. 2) [in natural history] the yelk nerita. —**gerste**, *f.* [in cookery] a sort of soup, made with the yolks of eggs. —**grütze**, *f.* the finest sort of buckwheat-groats. —**händler**, *m.* an eggler, cadger, huckster. —**igel**, *m.* a species of sea-urchin. —**käse**, *m.* [in cookery] custard. —**kelle**, *f.* egg-slice. —**kirsche**, *f.* a sort of cherry. —**klar**, *n.* V. Eiweiß. —**krebs**, *m.* the female of the crawfish. —**kuchen**, *m.* 1) [a kind of pancake] an omelet. 2) *Fig.* [in conchology] the omelet-stamper. —**kugel**, *f.* [in entomology] a genus of worms [volvox beroe]. —**leiste**, *f.* [in architect. and sculpt.] a carving on the edges of buildings. —**linie**, *f.* V. Eilinie. —**lingsbaum**, *m.* V. Elsebeerbaum. —**löffel**, *m.* egg-spoon. —**näpfchen**, *n.* V. —becher. —**öl**, *n.* eggs-oil. —**pfanne**, *f.* a pan for baking omelets. —**pflanze**, *f.* egg-plant. —**pflaume**, *f.* an egg-plum, magnum bonum. —**platz**, *m.* V. —kuchen. —**salat**, *m.* 1) a sort of cabbage lettuce. 2) a salad dressed with the yolks of hard-boiled eggs. —**schale**, *f.* 1) egg-shell. 2) [in conchology] V. Warzendotter. —**schaufel**, *f.* V. —kelle. —**schwamm**, *m.* the yellow agaric. —**staude**, *f.* large-fruited nightshade, egg-plant. —**stock**, *m.* ovary, racemation of eggs. —**stockband**, *n.* [in anatomy] the ligament of the ovary. —**suppe**, *f.* egg-soup. —**tanz**, *m.* [a popular amusement in many parts of Germany] a sort of dance through several ranges of eggs, with covered eyes. —**wein**, *m.* mulled wine.

Eifer, *m.* [-s] [allied to the Ice. *aefr*, brennend, …, zornig] 1) [passionate ardour in the pursuit of any thing] zeal. Der — für Freiheit, a zeal for liberty; er studirt mit vielem —, he pursues study with great ardour; die Menschen streben mit — nach Ehre, men pursue honour with eagerness; mit frommem — beten, to pray with fervency; alle Parteien nahmen sich mit — der Sache der Griechen an, the cause of the Greeks has been espoused with warmth by all parties. 2) anger, indignation. In — gerathen, to fall into a passion; ich sprach in meinem —, alle Menschen sind Lügner, I said in my haste, all men are liars; er hat ihn zum — gereizt or er hat ihn in — gebracht, he exasperated him, he excited him to anger; der Prediger zog mit vielem — gegen die Laster des Zeitalters los, the preacher declaimed with great warmth against the vices of the age.

Eifer-geist, *m.* 1) V. —sucht. 2) spirit of rivalry. —**gesetz**, *n.* [in Script.] a law respecting jealousy. —**hitze**, *f.* violent jealousy. —**opfer**, *n.* V. Rügeopfer.

Eiferer, *m.* [-s, *pl.* -] 1) one who declaims with warmth against any thing. 2) one who engages warmly in any cause; a zealot. Er ist ein blinder — in seinem Glauben, he is a blind zealot in his faith.

Eiferig, **Eifrig**, *adj.* and *adv.* 1) feeling anger, resentment, showing anger, angry, passionate. Ein —er Streit, a warm contest. 2) warmly engaged or ardent in the pursuit of an object, zealous. Sich einer Person — annehmen, to wed any one's cause, to espouse any one's cause with warmth; — werden, to become warm, ardent or animated.

Eifern, I. *v. intr.* 1) to speak warmly against. — ist gut, wenn's immerdar geschieht um das Gute, [in Script.] it is good to be zealously affected always in a good thing; denn ich eifere über euch mit göttlichem Eifer, [in Script.] I am jealous over you with a godly jealousy; sie — um euch nicht fein, sondern sie wollen euch von mir abfällig machen, daß ihr um sie sollt —, [in Script.] they zealously affect you, but not well; yea, they would exclude you, that ye might affect them; ich habe geeifert um den Herrn, den Gott Zebaoth, [in Script.] I have been very jealous for the Lord, God of hosts; er eiferte heftig gegen den Sklavenhandel, he declaimed with great warmth against the slave-trade; er eiferte gewaltig gegen dieses Unwesen, he was strenuous in his opposition against this abuse. 2) to be angry, to show anger. Ueber die Gottlosen —, to be angry with the wicked; ‡des Anblicks —, to be angry at the view. 3) to show zeal or ardour in the pursuit of an object. 4) to strive to excel, to strive for mastery, to emulate, to rival.

‡II. *v. tr.* to repeat, to do again.

Eifersucht, *f.* jealousy. — ist mit dem Neide nahe verwandt, jealousy is nearly allied to envy; — zeigen, blicken lassen, to manifest a jealousy [of others]; — erwecken, erregen, to excite jealousy.

Eifersuchts-frei, —**los**, *adj.* and *adv.* free from jealousy.

Eifersüchtelei, *f.* mean jealousy, petty jealousy. —en, small jealousies.

Eifersüchteln, *v. intr.* to indulge in petty jealousy.

Eifersüchtig, *adj.* and *adv.* jealous, suspicious, apprehensive of rivalship. Ein junger Mann ist — auf die Frau, die er liebt, a young man is jealous of the woman he loves; er ist — auf seinen Nebenbuhler, he is jealous of his rival; sei nicht — auf das Glück Anderer, be not envious of the prosperity of others; dieses Volk ist höchst — auf seine Rechte, this people is very jealous of its rights; er hält — auf seinen Rang, he is jealous of his rank or station.

Eifersüchtler, *m.* [-s, *pl.* -] —**inn**, *f.* a person that indulges in petty jealousy.

Eifrig, V. Eiferig.

Eige, *m.* [-n, *pl.* -n] formerly for Eigner, owner.

Eigen, [from the old Ger. verb *eigan*, Gr. ἔχειν, haben] *adj.* and *adv.* 1) [belonging to, possessed] own. Er hat ein —es Haus, he has a house of his own; nichts —es besitzen, to have nothing of one's own; das Buch ist nicht mein —, the book is not my own; unser —er Sohn, our proper son; sein —er Herr seyn, to be one's own master, to be self-dependent; —e Leute [Leibeigene], bondmen, serfs, servants; er hat seine —en Leute [keine fremde Bedienung] bei sich, he has his own servants or domestics with him. *Prov.* —er Herd ist Goldes werth, the smoke of a man's own house, is better than the fire of another's. *Fig.* *a*) [naturally or essentially belonging to a person or thing] peculiar, proper. Das ist ihm —, that is peculiar to him; dem Blute — [**fig.* es steckt im Blute], inherent in the blood; es ist einem alten Sünder — &c., it is the property of an old sinner &c.; diese Krankheit ist dem Menschen —, this disorder is incident to humanity; jedes Thier hat seine —en Gewohnheiten, every animal has its proper habits; jede Kunst hat ihre —en Regeln, every art has its proper rules; jede Gegend hat ihre eigenen Reize, every country has its peculiar charms; sich etwas [zu] — machen, to make a thing one's own; mache dir die Schrift zu —, be familiar with the Scriptures; er ist ein ganz —er Mensch, he is an odd kind of man; auf eine ganz —e Art, peculiarly; ich war darin ganz — glücklich, I was very peculiarly favoured by fortune in that. *b*) intended for a particular purpose. Einen —en Bothen schicken, to send a messenger express. *c*) accurate, exact, precise. Ich konnte die sonderbare Erscheinung ganz — beobachten, I could observe the singular phenomenon accurately, exactly, perfectly. *d*) particular, singular. Er ist sehr — in seiner Kleidung, he is very nice in his dress; er war sehr — im Betreff seiner Zähne und Wäsche, he was very particular about his teeth and linen; der Mann hat etwas —es in seiner Haltung, the man has something peculiar in his deportment; es ist doch —, it is strange. 2) [belonging to, peculiar, usually expressing property with emphasis, or in express exclusion of others] own. Mit —en Augen sehen, to see with one's own eyes; er schrieb es mit seiner —en Hand, he wrote it with his own hand; lernt es durch —en Schaden, learn it at your proper cost; —e Wechsel, [in commerce] bills of exchange drawn upon one's self. *3) [that must be touched with care] delicate, nice. Es ist so eine —e Sache, sich in Familienangelegenheiten zu mischen, it is a nice point to meddle with the affairs of a family.

Eigen-ansicht, *f.* 1) ocular view, personal observation, autopsy. 2) view or opinion of one's own. —**artig**, *adj.* and *adv.* being of a particular kind. ‖—**behörig**, *adj.* and *adv.* V. Leibeigen. —**bothe**, *m.* an express. —**dünkel**, *m.* [an overweening opinion of one's own person or accomplishments] self-conceit. —dünkel besitzend, self-conceited. —**dünkelig**, *adj.* and *adv.* self-conceited. —**dünkler**, *m.* a self-conceited person. —**gehörig**, *adj.* and *adv.* belonging to, own. —**gewalt**, *f.* self-assumed power or authority. —**gier**, *f.* egotism. —**gierig**, *adj.* and *adv.* egotistic. —**gut**, *n.* freehold estate, allodium. —**gutserbe**, *m.* the heir of allodial land. —**händig**, *adj.* and *adv.* done or written with one's own hand, autographic, autographical. Die —händige Schrift, autograph, autography. —**hirt**, *m.* a herdman who tends his own cattle. —**hörig**, *adj.* and *adv.* V. —behörig and Leibeigen. —**leibig**, *adj.* and *adv.* [peculiar to some part of the body] idiopathic. Eine —leibige Krankheit, idiopathy. —**liebe**, *f.* 1) self-complacency. 2) selfness, self-love. —**liebig**, —**liebisch**, *adj.* and *adv.* 1) self-complacent. 2) loving but one's own [dear] self. —**lob**, *n.* the praise of one's self, self-praise, self-applause. *Prov.* —s lob stinkt, neither praise nor dispraise thyself, thine actions serve the turn. —**löhner**, *m.* [among miners] a private person that undertakes the working of mines at his own expense. —**macht**, *f.* self-assumed power, arbitrary power; despotism. —**mächtig**, *adj.* and *adv.* arbitrary; despotical. —mächtige Veränderungen, arbitrary changes; eine —mächtige Entscheidung, an arbitrary decision; er verfuhr nicht gesetzmäßig, sondern sehr —mächtig, he acted not lawfully, but very arbitrarily; sich —mächtig Recht verschaffen, to take the law into one's own hand. —**mittel**, *n.* [a remedy that certainly cures a particular disease] a specific. —mündig, *adj.* and *adv.* by word of mouth, oral —name, *m.* proper name. —nutz, *m.* self-interest, self-ends, selfishness. —nützig, *adj.* and *adv.* regarding one's own interest chiefly or solely, selfish, interested. —nützigkeit, *f.* self-interestedness. —nutzlos, *adj.* and *adv.* free from self-interest, disinterested. —post, *f.* post, post-horses. Mit —post reisen, to travel post. —rache, *f.* V. Selbstrache. —richterlich, *adj.* and *adv.* judging in one's own cause. —ruhm, *m.* self-glorifying —schrift, *f.* autograph, autography. —sinn, *m.* 1) one's own will, self-will, obstinacy, wilfulness. *2) a self-willed person *Sie ist ein kleiner —sinn, she is a wayward little person. —sinnig, *adj.* and *adv.* governed by one's own will, self-willed, obstinate, capricious, whimsical, wayward. Ein —sinniger Mensch, a wilful man. —sucht, *f.* egotism. —süchtig, *adj.* and *adv.* egotistic. —thätig, —thätlich, *adj.* and *adv.* V. —mächtig. —wille, *m.* self-will. —willig, *adj.* and *adv.* self-willed.

Eigends, V. Eigens.

Eigenen, Eignen, I. *v. tr.* V. Zueignen. II. *v. intr.* 1) to be one's own. 2) to be proper or becoming, to fit. Sie sind dazu nicht geeignet, you are not qualified for it; dieser Gegenstand ist nicht für die Schaubühne geeignet, this subject is not adapted, not calculated for the stage. III. *v. r.* sich —, to suit. Uebertrage mir kein Amt, das sich so schlecht für mich eignet, give me not an office, that suits with me so ill; diese Rolle eignet sich nicht für ihn, or er ist nicht für diese Rolle geeignet, this part is not suited to him.

Eigener, Eigner, *m.* [-s, *pl.* -] —inn, *f.* owner, proprietor, possessor.

Eigenheit, *f.* [something peculiar to a person or thing] peculiarity. Die —en eines Menschen, the singularities of a person; die —en des Alters, the oddities of old age; die —en der Sprache [Sprach—en], idiotisms; körperliche —en, idiosyncrasy.

Eigenheitswort, *n.* [in grammar] adjective.

Eigenheitlich, *adj.* and *adv.* [that marks the peculiar, distinctive qualities of a person or thing] characteristic, characteristical. Das —e, the characteristic.

Eigens, *adv.* particularly, expressly, on purpose. Durch einen — abgeschickten Bothen, by a messenger sent express.

Eigenschaft, *f.* 1) property, quality. Natürliche und zufällige —en, natural or accidental qualities; Weichheit ist eine natürliche — der Wolle und des Pelzwerkes, softness is a natural quality of wool and fur; die Flüssigkeit der Metalle ist eine zufällige —, the fluidity of metals is an accidental quality; die zufällige —, [in logic] accident; die wesentliche — eines Dings, an essential quality of a thing, property; [with logicians] an essential mode; Farbe ist eine — des Lichtes, colour is a property of light; Ausdehnung und Gestalt sind —en der Körper, extension and form are properties or affections of bodies; die —en der Größe, [in mathematics] the affections of quantity; die — einer Flüssigkeit, the nature of a fluid; die —en der Pflanzen, the qualities of plants; gute oder schlechte —en, good or bad qualities; eine — Gottes, a divine attribute; Macht und Weisheit sind —en des höchsten Wesens, power and wisdom are properties of the Supreme Being. 2) [an acquired or artificial quality; that which is given by art or bestowed by man] property. Dieses Gedicht besitzt die —en, welche &c., the poem has the properties, which &c. 3) quality, character. In der — von Augenzeugen, in the quality of lookers-on; in seiner — als Oberscheriff, in his character of high-sheriff.

Eigenschafts-wort, *n.* a noun adjective, an attributive or attribute. Als —wort gebraucht werden, to be used adjectively. —zeichen, *n.* an attribute. Der Anker ist das —zeichen der Hoffnung, the anchor is an attribute of Hope.

Eigenschaften, *v. intr.* [seldom used except in the past part.] [u. w. seyn] to have properties or qualities. Er ist dazu nicht geeigenschaftet, he is not qualified for it.

Eigenschaftlich, *adj.* and *adv.* expressing a quality.

Eigenthum, *n.* [-es, *pl.* -thümer] 1) [the exclusive right of possessing, enjoying and disposing of a thing] property, ownership. 2) [the thing owned] property. Ein — haben, besitzen, to own something; das unbewegliche — [Grundeigenthum], real property; bewegliches —, movables; sich des —s einer Person bemächtigen, to invade a man's property.

Eigenthums-herr, *m.* V. Eigenthümer. —recht, *n.* property, ownership. Das —recht zu [an] einer Sache haben, to have the ownership of a thing

Eigenthümer, *m.* [-s, *pl.* -] owner, proprietor, possessor.

Eigenthümerinn, *f.* proprietress.

Eigenthümlich, *adj.* and *adv.* 1) possessed as property. Etwas — besitzen, to have the ownership or property of a thing; das Haus gehört ihm —, he possesses that house; ein Gut — an sich bringen, to acquire the property of an estate. 2) proper, peculiar. Fast jeder Schriftsteller hat eine ihm —e Schreibart, almost every writer has a peculiar style; —e Namen, proper names; die —e Schwere des Goldes, the specific gravity of gold; das —e, [that which distinguishes a person or thing from another] the characteristic, natural disposition.

Eigenthümlichkeit, *f.* peculiarity. Die — der Schreibart, Kleidung, the peculiarity of style, in dress.

Eigentlich, *adj.* and *adv.* 1) proper, not figurative. Die —e Bedeutung eines Wortes, the proper signification of a word. 2) in a strict sense, just, exact. Das Elend des Lebens kann man — dem &c. nicht zuschreiben, the miseries of life are not properly ascribable to &c. 3) [in exact conformity to truth] accurate, exact. Man weiß die —en Umstände noch nicht, the particulars are not known yet; ich weiß es so — nicht zu sagen, I cannot tell it so precisely; — zu reden, properly speaking; was soll dies — bedeuten? what is the meaning of this?

Eignen, Eigner, V. Eigenen, Eigener.

Eiland, *n.* [-es, *pl.* -e or —länder] [Ice. *ey* signifies Insel] an island [chiefly used in poetry, or to denote a smaller sort of island = kleine Insel].

Eilandsmeer, *n.* a sea interspersed with many isles, Archipelago.

Eiländer, *m.* [-s, *pl.* -] —inn, *f.* an inhabitant of an island, an islander.

Eiländisch, *adj.* and *adv.* belonging to an island.

Eile, *f.* haste, speed, swiftness, despatch [applied only to voluntary beings and never to other bodies]. In größter —, in the greatest hurry; er reiste in größter —, he travelled post-haste; wir haben —, we are in a hurry; ich habe große —, I am in great haste; es hat keine —, the business requires no haste; unser Geschäft treibt uns zur — an, our business hurries us. Syn. Eile, Hast. Eile differs from Hast, in proceeding merely from external causes, Hast, on the contrary, arises from internal. That person is eilig, who has not much time to accomplish a thing in; he is hastig, who from an inward restless ardour does every thing in a hurry.

Eilen, [allied to the Gr. *ελλέω*, bewegen?] I. *v. intr.* [u. w. seyn and w. haben] 1) [to move with celerity] to haste, to hasten. Einem zu Hülfe —, to run to the assistance of a person; Sie haben zu sehr geeilt, you were in to great a hurry: was [warum] — Sie so? what is your hurry? er eilte fort, he hasted away. 2) [u. w. haben] *Fig.* *a*) to hurry, to proceed with celerity or precipitation. Die Sache ist dringend, laßt uns —, the business is urgent, let us hurry; mit einer Sache —, to hurry a thing. *Prov.* — thut kein gut, the more haste, the worse speed; eile mit Weile, fair and softly goes far in a day; wer zu sehr eilet, wird langsam fertig, most haste, worst speed, Eile sehr brach den Hals, haste makes waste, and waste makes want, and want makes strife between the good man and his wife. *b*) to pass quickly, as time. II. *v. r.* sich —, to make haste, to speed. Gehe, aber eile dich, go, but make despatch.

Eil-bothe, *m.* a messenger, who travels with speed, a courier express. —bothschaftlich, *adj.* and *adv.* by a messenger travelling post-haste, by a courier express. —fertig, I. *adj.* and *adv.* hasty, hurrying. —fertig seyn, to haste, to hasten; das Geschäft wurde —fertig verrichtet, the business was done with despatch. Syn. V. Eilig. II. *adv.* with speed, haste, expedition, or despatch, speedily. —fertigkeit, *f.* haste, speediness, quickness, despatch. —flug, *m.* a speedy flight. *Fig.* a passing quickly away, as time. —gewohnt, *adj.* and *adv.* accustomed to haste. In seiner —gewohnten Art, in his usual hurried manner. —marsch, *m.* forced march. —pos[t] *f.* 1) a mail-coach. 2) news speedily arrive[d] —postreiter, *m.* an estafet. —wagen, *m.* flying-coach, stage-coach. —weilen, *v. intr.* [unusual] [u. w. seyn] not to make too much haste to proceed not hastily or rashly. —zug, *m.* forced march.

Eilend, [*pres. part.* of eilen] Eilends, *adv.* hastily, in haste, with speed or quickness, speedily. — ging er davon, he hasted away

Eilf, Eilfeck, V. Elf, Elfeck.

Eilig, *adj.* and *adv.* 1) hasty, speedy. I[ch] bin sehr —, I am in great haste; —st, in the greatest haste. 2) requiring haste. Ich habe ei[-] nen —en Gang zu machen, I am in a hurry to go out. Syn. Eilig, Eilfertig, Hastig. Each of these words implies an eagerness to dispatch some thing in a short time. But he is eilig, who has no much time left, and has therefore the motive for performing much in a short space of time. Der Eilfertig[e] actually does dispatch much in a short time, is quick in performance, not as der Hastige whose motions are accelerated by an inward restless impulse, but because the circumstances are urgent. Eilfertig can be said of persons only, eilig also of things. One may ask a person who is writing a letter: Warum sind Sie so eilfertig? and the answer may be: der Brief ist eilig, i. e. it must be speedily at the place of its destination.

Eimer, *m.* [-s, *pl.* -] [old Ger. *eimpar*, from ein and baren = tragen?] 1) a pail. Der — a[n] einem Ziehbrunnen, a bucket; der —voll, a pailful; der — voll kostet zehn Gulden, it costs ten florins a pailful. 2) a German liquid measure containing [in the different states] from 8 to [..] and 36 gallons.

Eimer-kette, *f.* bucket-chain. —kol-ben, *m.* V. Taschenkolben. —kunst, *f.* [hydraulics] a sort of waterwork with buckets. —weise, *adv.* in pails, by pails, or by a certain liquid measure called Eimer. *Fig.* * by pailfuls.

Eimerig, *adj.* and *adv.* containing an Eimer.

Ein, [L. *unus*, old Gr. *οἶνος*] is used as a numeral, an adjective, an article and a pronoun. I. as a numeral. 1) [single in number] one. — Gott, — Glaube, one Lord, one faith; — Mann, —e Flasche, one man, one bottle; es ist nur — Gott, there is but one God; es gibt nur —e Sonne in unserm Planetensysteme, there is one sun only in our planetary system; es ist nur — Einziger gekommen, there came one only; —er der Zeugen, one of the witnesses; meiner Freunde —er war zugegen, a friend of mine was present; mein —es Haus habe ich verkauft, I sold one of my houses; [in numbering we say eins, as] hundert und —s, a hundred and one; es schlägt —s, it strikes one o'clock. 2) [single by union] one. —es Wesens, consubstantial, coessential; die Orthodoxen glauben, daß der Sohn —es Wesens mit dem Vater sey, the orthodox believe the son to be consubstantial with the father. 3) [not different or other] the same. Sie wohnen in —em Hause, hey live in one and the same house; sie sind von —er Größe, they are of the same size. As a numeral it is used in composition, as —äugig, —ylbig &c.

II. *adj.* [different, diverse] one. Das —e Haus t neu, das andere alt, one house is new and he other is old; es ist — Ding, richtig zu denken, und — anderes, sich deutlich auszudrücken, is one thing to think right and another to tpress one's self clearly; von —em Ende der Rabt [bis] zum andern, from one extremity of he town to the other; frage von dem —en Ende es Himmels zum andern, [in Script.] ask from one de of heaven to the other; [—, like many other djectives, is used without a noun, and is to be conidered as a substitute for some noun understood] wir rnen —er von dem Andern, we learn of one nother; —er betrügt den Andern, one cheats he other; [in this use — may be plural] die —en nd reich, die Andern arm, some are rich, and thers poor; die —en sprechen von Dingen, die e nicht verstehen, die Andern &c., some talk of bjects they do not understand, others &c.

III. *art.* [noting an individual or thing indefinitely; s opposed to der, die, das, which are used as definitives] one, an, a. An —em Tage, —es Tages, ne day; es war einmahl — Mann, there was nce a man; — Haufen Steine, a heap of stones; —e Menge Käufer, a great many buyers; gib ir —e Blume, da ist —e, give me a flower, here is one; welch' —e Freude! what joy! [in familiar or common language, we use solch' —, solch' s, so — &c., as] solch' — Mann, such a man; —e Ehre, such an honour; an so —em Orte, such a place; [sometimes — is placed before proper names, it expresses discrimination of person with rticular emphasis] selbst — Cicero würde &c., en a Cicero [an orator like Cicero] would &c.; is placed also before corporate bodies by way of distinction, and then written with a large initial letter] — hochedler Stadtrath hat beschlossen, the rshipful corporation of aldermen has decreed; familiar language it precedes a word of number uantity, with the sense of *about* or *near*] — zwanMeilen davon entfernt, some twenty miles tant; [in vulgar language the syllable er is suffixed he noun] — Tager drei her, three days ago.

IV. as a *pron.* Ein is used indefinitely for any son; as, was —er sieht, what one sees; wie es —er machen? how shall one do it; unser r, one like me.

Ein, [from the root of in] a word which is perly to be considered as a substitute for the position in and is sometimes preceded by the n; as, Jahr aus, Jahr —, year by year; quer b —, across the fields; it is much used in the composition, as, Einwohner, Eingeweide, Einbrechen, Einschlagen &c.; when joined with verbs to a compound, it is separable from them, as, die Diebe brachen bei ihm —, the thieves broke and entered his house.

Einackern, *v. tr.* [in husbandry, to cover by plowing] to plow in [wheat &c.].

Einander, *pron.* one another. Liebet —, love one another; es ist unsere Pflicht, — beizustehen, it is our duty to assist each other; sie fressen —, they eat one another; an —, together, to one another, upon one another; zwei Dinge an — nähen, to sew two things together; auf [über] —, upon one another; auf [nach, hinter] —, in succession; aus — reißen, to tear asunder; bei — in einem Hause leben, to live together in one house; bei — liegen, to lie together; durch —, confusedly, promiscuously, higgledy-piggledy; allerhand durch —, miscellaneous matters; gegen —, against each other; zwei Personen [Zeugen &c.] gegen — stellen, to confront two persons [witnesses &c.]; wir ergingen uns mit — in dem Walde, we walked together in the wood; Dinge mit — vermischen, to mix things together; sie hadern mit —, they contend with one another; neben —, by each other, at the side of each other; über —, over one another; von — or aus — bringen, von — or aus — gehen, to separate.

Einängstigen, *v. tr.* 1) to intimidate, to put in anguish, to make anxious. *Er hat ihn arg eingeängstigt, he has frightened him sadly. 2) to persuade by anguishing or earnest entreaties to do a thing. Einem einen Löffel Arzenei —, to persuade any one by earnest entreaties to take a spoonful of medicine.

Einantworten, *v. tr.* to hand over, to deliver.

Einarbeiten, I. *v. tr.* to make up for by labour. II. *v. r.* sich —, 1) to exert one's self to get in a place. 2) to make one's self thoroughly acquainted with any thing by constant exertion. Wenn man sich einmal in das Geschäft eingearbeitet hat, geht es viel leichter, when one has once familiarised one's self with the business, it is much easier.

Einarmig, *adj.* and *adv.* one-armed.

Einarten, I. *v. intr.* [u. w. seyn] not to degenerate. II. *v. tr.* to inhere naturally to. Eingeartet seyn, to be implanted, imnate, to be inherent to.

Einartig, *adj.* and *adv.* 1) being of one kind. 2) being of the same kind.

Einäschern, *v. tr.* 1) [in chimistry] *a*) to incinerate. Das —, cinefaction. *b*) [to reduce to a metallic calx] to calcine. 2) to reduce to ashes by combustion, to burn to ashes, to lay in ashes. Eingeäscherte Städte, cities reduced to ashes. 3) to steep in ashes. 4) [in the Romish church] to sprinkle ashes on [the heads of penitents]. Sich —, to besprinkle one's self with ashes.

Einathmen, *v. tr.* 1) to inhale, to inspire [air &c.]. Man athmet hier die reine Bergluft ein, one breathes or inhales here the pure air of the mountains. 2) to infuse by breathing, to inspire.

Einätzen, *v. tr.* 1) to etch in. 2) V. Einbeizen I. 2.

Einäugeln, *v. tr.* 1) to inoculate, to bud [apples, pears &c.]. 2) to inoculate [a person with the matter of cow-pox or small pox].

Einäugen, V. Einäugeln, 1).

Einäugig, *adj.* and *adv.* one-eyed, monocular, monoculous.

||**Einback**, *m.* [-es, *pl.* -e] a sort of pastry.

||**Einbacken**, *adj.* and *adv.* once baked.

Einbacken, *v. tr.* to inclose by baking, to put in baking.

Einballen or [in fam. lang.] **Einballiren**, *v. tr.* to form into a bale or pack. Waaren —, to pack goods. Die Einballung, Einballirung, wrapper.

Einbalsamen or [in fam. lang.] **Einbalsamiren**, *v. tr.* 1) to embalm [a dead body &c.]. 2) to fill with sweet scent. Sich —, to perfume one's clothes &c.

Einband, *m.* [-es, *pl.* -bände] 1) the act of binding a book. 2) [the cover of a book] the binding.

Einbansen, *v. tr.* [in husbandry] to lay up in the barn [the sheaves].

Einbau, *m.* [-es, *pl.* -e] 1) a pilework or fence made on the bank of a river, to prevent the water from washing away the shore. ||2) a recess in a building.

Einbauen, I. *v. intr.* to build in a place, to form a settlement in a place. II. *v. tr.* 1) to build a thing within another, to fix within by building. 2) to spend, to consume by building one thing within another.

Einbedingen, *ir. v. tr.* to stipulate [some articles in a contract].

Einbeere, *f.* [*pl.* -n] [a plant] one-berry, true-love.

*Einbeeren, *v. tr.* [with fowlers] to furnish the springes with berries of the service-tree.

Einbegreifen, *ir. v. tr.* to comprise, to comprehend, to contain. Einen Theil der Geschichte Frankreichs mit einbegriffen, a part of the history of France included.

Einbehalten, *ir. v. tr.* to keep back, to detain, to withhold. Man behielt ihm seinen Lohn zur Bezahlung seiner Schulden ein, his wages were withheld for the payment of his debts.

Einbehaltungsrecht, *n.* [-es] [in law] the right of detainer.

Einbeißen, *ir.* I. *v. intr.* 1) to bite into. 2) to penetrate biting, as acids and salts. 3) *Fig.* to cause a painful biting sensation. II. *v. r.* sich —, 1) to get into by biting. 2) *Fig.* V. I. 3).

Einbeizen, I. *v. tr.* 1) to macerate, to soak in a liquid. Fleisch —, to steep meat in vinegar. 2) Buchstaben, Figuren &c. in die Haut —, to mark the skin with letters, figures &c. by eating or corroding substances, to tattow. II. *v. r.* sich —, to penetrate eating.

Einbekennen, *ir. v. tr.* to confess, to own [the truth &c.].

Einbekommen, *ir. v. intr.* to get possession of. Geld —, to get in money.

Einberichten, *v. tr.* to report, to make report. Er hat die Sache seiner Regierung einberichtet, he has sent in a statement of the case to his government.

Einbeten, *v. tr.* to lull asleep by praying.

Einbetteln, I. *v. tr.* to collect by begging. II. *v. r.* sich —, to get admission to by begging. *Fig.* Er wußte sich in seine Gunst schlau einzubetteln, he insinuated himself with him by cringing supplications.

Einbetten, I. *v. tr.* to put up a bed in a place. II. *v. r.* sich —, to put up one's bed in a place or in any one's house, or room. *So bette ich mich bei Ihnen ein, so, then, I shall take up my night's-lodging with you.

Einbeuchen, *v. tr.* to put into lye, to buck [linen &c.].

Einbeugen, *v. tr.* to bend in, to bend inwards or downwards. Die Kniee — [more usual beugen], to bend the knees.

Einbeuteln, *v. tr.* to put in a purse. Geld —, to purse or pocket money.

Einbiegen, *ir.* I. *v. tr.* to bend in, to bend inwards, or downwards, to incurve, to incurvate. Den Draht —, to bend the wire inwards; eingebogen, incurvate. II. *v. intr.* to bend one's steps or course again to the common or right way. III. *v. r.* sich —, to bend, to crook or be crooking. Die Einbiegung, 1) the act of bending any thing inward. 2) a bending inward, incurvity.

Einbilden, *v. tr.* 1) to incorporate the image of any thing with another thing. 2) to imagine, to fancy. Sich —, to figure to one's self, to imagine, to fancy. Ich bildete mir ein, daß sie mich liebte, I fancied that she loved me; das bildete ich mir wohl ein, I thought as much; ein eingebildetes Glück, an imaginary happiness; eingebildete Uebel, imaginary ills; die Athener bildeten sich viel auf ihre Wissenschaft und feinen Sitten ein, the Athenians were conceited or vain of their own science and politeness; er bildet sich zu viel ein, he thinks too much of himself; er bildet sich etwas auf seine Talente ein, he presumes upon his parts; ein eingebildeter Mensch, a conceited coxcomb; wenn Sie mich für zu eingebildet halten, if you think me too conceited.

Einbilder, *m.* [-s, *pl.* -] [unusual] a fanciful or fantastic person.

Einbilderisch, **Einbildisch**, *adj.* and *adv.* entertaining a flattering opinion of one's self, having a vain or too high conception of one's own person or accomplishments, conceited.

Einbildling, *m.* [-es, *pl.* -e] [not much used] a conceited or presuming person, a coxcomb.

Einbildung, *f.* 1) the act of forming ideas in the mind, imagining. 2) [the power or faculty by which the mind forms images or representations of things at pleasure] imagination, fancy. 3) an unsolid or fanciful opinion, fancy, imagination, conceit. Eine bloße —, a mere fancy, or conceit, chimera. 4) favourable or self-flattering opinion, a lofty or vain conception of one's own person or accomplishments, conceit. Voller — seyn, to be very conceited.

Einbildungs-kraft, *f.* imagination, fancy. V. Einbildung. **—krank**, *adj.* and *adv.* sick in conceit. **—krankheit**, *f.* imaginary sickness.

Einbinden, *ir. v. tr.* 1) to bind one thing into another, to inwrap, or involve. Junge Bäume in Stroh —, to bind up young trees in straw; ein Buch —, to bind a book; ein Buch in Leder —, to bind a book with leather; die Segel —, [in seamen's language] to furl the sails; die Jungfern —, [in seamen's language] to bend the dead eyes to the shrouds; ein Reff —, to take in a reef; die Garne —, [with hunters] to fix the toils to hoops or sticks. 2) *Fig.* *a*) Einem Pathen etwas —, to make a present to a god-child at the time of its christening. *b*) to impress by frequent admonitions, to urge on the mind, to inculcate. Er band ihm die Beobachtung dieser Pflichten aufs Schärfste ein, he strictly enjoined him the observation of these duties.

Einbinde-geld, *n.* a present made to a god-child at the christening. **—nadel**, *f.* [with shoemakers] an awl.

Einbitten, *ir.* I. *v. tr.* to gather by begging. II. *v. r.* sich —, to get admission to by begging.

Einbittern, [unusual] *v. tr.* to make bitter by steeping in a bitter substance.

Einblasen, *ir. v. tr.* 1) to breathe into, to inject by breathing. Luft in eine Blase —, to blow a bladder; und er blies ihm ein den lebendigen Odem in seine Nase, [in Scripture] and he breathed into his nostrils the breath of life. 2) *Fig.* *a*) to whisper in any one's ear, or to suggest something forgotten. Einem Schauspieler etwas —, to prompt an actor. *b*) to instil, to infuse gently, to introduce artfully, to insinuate. *c*) to persuade or induce. 3) to blow down. 4) [rather unusual] to breathe or blow asleep.

Einbläser, *m.* [-s, *pl.* -] a prompter, whisperer.

Einblatt, *n.* [-es, *pl.* -blätter] [a name of several plants] 1) one-blade or least Solomon's seal. 2) common marsh-parnassia or grass of Parnassus.

Einblätterig, *adj.* and *adv.* 1) having one leaf only, one-leaved, monophyllous. Die —e Blütendecke, [in botany] a monophyllous perianth; eine —e Blumenkrone, [in botany] a monopetalous corol. 2) consisting of one sheet of paper.

Einblauen, *v. tr.* [with dyers] to dress the blue vat.

Einbläuen, *v. tr.* 1) to blue [linen &c.]. †2) to inculcate by beating. *Fig.* Einem Lebensart —, to beat any one into good manners; Einem die Grammatik —, to flog the grammar into a person.

Einblenden, *v. tr.* V. Einblinden.

Einblicken, *v. intr.* to glance the eye into. In einen Brief —, to cast a look into a letter.

Einblinden, *v. tr.* [in architecture] to place into a nich or niche; to furnish with a recess.

Einblocken, *v. tr.* to put into the stocks.

Einblumig, *adj.* and *adv.* bearing one flower only, uniflorous. Ein —er Blumenstiel, a uniflorous peduncle.

Einbluten, *v. tr.* to wet all over with one's blood.

Einböckeln, V. Einpökeln.

Einbohren, I. *v. intr.* and *tr.* to perforate or penetrate by boring. Löcher —, to bore holes. *Fig.* to thrust or push into. II. *v. r.* sich —, to pierce or enter by boring.

Einbohrig, *adj.* and *adv.* having but one bore, that is, being of a limited width or aperture [said of tubes, pipes].

Einborden, *v. tr.* [unusual] to put on board a ship.

Einbraten, *ir.* I. *v. intr.* [u. w. seyn] to shrink by roasting. II. *v. tr.* to roast beforehand.

Einbrauen, *v. tr.* 1) to put in brewing. 2) to brew beforehand.

Einbrechen, *ir.* I. *v. intr.* [u. w. seyn] 1) to break and fall inward. Das Eis brach unter der Last ein, the ice broke beneath the load; der Boden brach ein, the floor gave way; [in husbandry] die Gerste, der Hafer bricht ein, the over-riped ears of barley, oats break off. 2) *Fig.* *a*) to come on, to approach suddenly. Die Nacht bricht ein, the night draws on, night is coming; die Kälte bricht ein, the cold sets in. *b*) *Fig.* to gain ground, to become prevalent. Sittenverderbniß bricht überall ein, corruptness is breaking in everywhere, corruption gains ground on all parts. 3) to break and enter a place. Die Diebe sind durch das Fenster, die Mauer &c. eingebrochen, the thieves broke in through the window, the wall &c. *Fig.* Die Reiterei brach in den Feind ein, the horse broke in upon the enemy; in ein Land feindlich —, to make an incursion, an inroad into a country. II. *v. tr.* 1) to break down, to pull down. Ein Haus —, to pull down a house. 2) [in seamen's lang.] Die Segel —, to flat in.

Einbrennen, *ir.* I. *v. intr.* 1) to penetrate burning. Eine eingebrannte Stelle, a mark made by burning. ‖2) V. Einfeuern. II. *v. tr.* 1) to impress by burning or with a hot iron. Ein Zeichen auf ein Faß —, to brand a cask. 2) to expose to a boiling heat over a fire, either in water or other liquid; to scald. 3) [in cookery] to roast meal with melted butter. Eine eingebrannte Suppe, a potage made of roasted meal. 4) to purify a thing by burning a match in it. Ein Faß —, [with coopers] to match a cask. III. *v. r.* sich —, to shrink by burning, or roasting.

Einbringen, *ir. v. tr.* to bring in, to import. Das Getreide —, to get in the corn; fremde Waaren —, to introduce foreign goods; [in mining] frische Wetter —, to introduce fresh air into a shaft. *Fig.* *a*) to bring on an action. Einen Gesetzesvorschlag [eine Bill] —, to bring in a bill. *b*) to recover, to restore. Die verlorne Zeit wieder —, to retrieve the time lost; einen Verlust wieder —, to make good, to make up, to repair a loss. *c*) to bring to one's husband in marriage. Sie hat ihm 100,000 Gulden in die Ehe eingebracht, she brought him 100,000 florins in marriage. Das Eingebrachte, the portion given with a wife, the dowry. *d*) to bring in, to bring profit. Seine Arbeit bringt ihm viel ein, his labour yields much to him; seine Stelle bringt ihm nicht viel ein, his place does not bring him in much. *e*) [with printers] to keep in.

Einbrocke, *f.* [*pl.* -n] a crum [in milk, in a potage &c.].

Einbrocken, *v. tr.* to crum [bread into milk &c. †*Fig.* Er hat etwas einzubrocken [er hat etwas in die Milch zu brocken], he has got wherewith to make the pot boil, he got enough to live upon; er hat viel bei dieser Unternehmung eingebr[ockt], he has been a great loser in this enterpri[se]; sich etwas —, to commit a fault, to do am[iss]. *Prov.* Was man eingebrockt hat, muß man a[uch] ausessen, as you have brewed, so you must dri[nk], every bird must hatch her own egg.

Einbruch, *m.* [-es, *pl.* -brüche] 1) a bre[ak]ing in. Der — des Eises, the breaking of [the] ice. *Fig.* Der — der Nacht, the coming on [of] night, night-fall. 2) the act of breaking in. [Der] — eines Diebes, [by daylight] house-breaki[ng], [by night] burglary. *Fig.* Der — des Feindes, sudden invasion or incursion, the irruption [of] the enemy; Einem in seine Rechte — thun, [to] invade, to violate any one's rights. 3) a [hole] committed by house-breaking or burglary. [4)] [in mining] a pit made in layers of earth or st[one].

Einbrüderig, *adj.* and *adv.* [in botany] adelphian. Die —en Pflanzen, the monadel[phia].

Einbrüdern, I *v. tr.* to receive, to admit to an order or fraternity. II. *v. r.* sich —, to [en]ter into fraternity.

Einbrühen, *v. tr.* to steep or soak in boil[ing] water, to scald.

Einbucken, *v. tr.* [with tailors] to turn in [the] edge of cloth &c.].

Einbugen, *v. tr.* [in seamen's language] to [put] or enter into a harbour.

Einbündeln, *v. tr.* to bundle, to bundl[e up] [clothes &c.]. Die Borsten —, [with brush[makers]] to bind the bristles in a bundle.

Einbürgern, I. *v. tr.* to make a citizen, t[o ad]mit to the rights and privileges of a citizen[, to] citizenize; to naturalize. *Fig.* Fremde W[örter] —, to naturalize foreign words. II. *v. r.* sich [—,] to settle as a citizen in any place. Die Ein[bür]gerung, citizenizing; naturalisation.

Einbürsten, *v. tr.* to cause to enter by bru[sh]ing. Statt ihn wegzubringen, hat er den Sch[mutz] noch mehr in den Rock eingebürstet, instead [of] getting the dirt away, he has only brushed it much the more in.

Einbuße, *f.* [*pl.* -n] any loss of property sustained, damage.

Einbüßen, *v. tr.* 1) to suffer loss or damage, to lose. Er hat viel dabei eingebüßt, he suffered great damage by it. 2) to lose, to be deprived of. Sein Leben oder seine Ehre —, to lose one's life or honour.

***Eincassiren**, *v. tr.* to require, to exact, to call in, to ask, to collect money for interest, contribution &c.

Eindammen, [rather unusual] *v. tr.* to use or spend in raising dams or dikes. Die Eindammung, any thing used or spent in raising dams or dikes.

Eindämmen, *v. tr.* to confine by dikes, to dike, to embank. Den Strom —, to dam in, to dam up the stream of water. *Fig.* Leidenschaften durch das Gesetz —, to restrain passions by laws. Die Eindämmung, 1) damming in or up, embankment. 2) [inclosure by a bank] embankment.

Eindämmer, *m.* [-s, *pl.* -] one who dams in or up.

Eindampfen, I. *v. intr.* to penetrate as smoke, steam or vapour. II. *v. tr.* to envelop in vapour or smoke.

Eindämpfen, *v. tr.* [with fowlers] Einen Vogel —, to confine a bird in a dark place or cage.

Eindecken, *v. tr.* Ein Dach —, [with tilers] to join the tiles of a roof with lime; [in husbandry] die Weinstöcke —, to earth the vines.

Eindeichen, *v. tr.* to dike. V. Eindämmen [in the proper sense].

Eindeutig, *adj.* and *adv.* having one meaning only. Ein —es Wort, a univocal word.

Eindicken, *v. tr.* 1) to thicken as fluids. [in chemistry] Das —, inspissation. 2) to bring to greater consistence by evaporating the thinner parts, to inspissate.

Eindingen, *ir. v. tr.* to include in the bargain. Das habe ich bei dem Vertrage mit eingedungen or einbedungen, I stipulated that in the contract.

Eindorren, *v. intr.* [u. w. seyn] to shrink in, to shrivel up by drying, to dry up, to grow dry, to wither, to parch.

Eindörren, *v. tr.* 1) to lessen by drying. 2) to dry beforehand.

Eindrang, *m.* [-es, *pl.* -dränge] 1) the act of penetrating, penetration. 2) penetration, immission. 3) V. Zudrang.

Eindrängen, *v. tr.* to squeeze or force in. Der Mann drängte sich in das Zimmer ein, the man crowded into the room. *Fig.* to thrust one's self in, to force one's self in, to intrude. Dränge dich niemahls da ein, wo man dich nicht gerne sieht, never intrude where your company is not desired.

Eindrehen, *v. tr.* to introduce by turning or winding. Den Zapfen in das Zapfenloch —, to wind the tenon into the mortise.

Eindreschen, *v. tr.* to break with a flail, or by thrashing. *Fig.* †Einem etwas —, to thrash any thing into a person.

Eindrillen, *v. tr.* [with metallists] to drill or bore into.

Eindringen, *ir. v. intr.* [u. w. seyn] to force a way into another body, to penetrate. Der Feind drang in die Stadt ein, the enemy forced its way into the town, the enemy forced the town; der Feind drang auf uns ein, the enemy rushed upon us or fell on us; Oel dringt in Holz ein, oil penetrates wood; das Wasser dringt in die Erde ein, water soaks into the earth; das Wasser dringt in das Schiff ein, water enters the ship; der Regen dringt in die Ritzen der Felsen ein, the rain insinuates itself into the crevices of rocks. *Fig.* In die Geheimnisse der Natur —, to penetrate into the secrets of nature; in die Natur der Dinge —, to dive into the nature of things; dieser Schauspieler dringt in den Geist seiner Rolle ein, that player enters into the spirit of his part; sie mochte in seine Gesinnung nicht —, she would not pierce into his meaning; sie sind in alle Umstände eingedrungen, they searched into all the particulars.

Eindringlich, *adj.* and *adv.* penetrative, piercing. Eine —e Beredtsamkeit, a piercing eloquence; eine —e Rede, an impressive discourse; er sprach sehr —, he spoke very affectingly.

Eindruck, *m.* [-es, *pl.* -drücke] 1) the act of impressing, as one body on another, impression. 2) mark, stamp made by pressure, impression. Der — eines Petschafts auf [or in] dem Wachse, the impression of a seal on wax. *Fig.* Die Wahrheiten der Bibel machen einen tiefen und dauernden — auf das Gemüth, the truths of the Gospel make a deep and lasting impression on the mind; welchen — die Gegenstände auf die Organe eines Andern machen, what impresses the objects make upon the organs of another; dieser Vorfall machte keinen — auf ihn, that event made no impression on him; sein Schauspiel machte keinen — auf die Zuschauer, his play did not affect the auditory. 3) a hollow, depression.

Eindrucken, *v. tr.* 1) to imprint on a place or among other things. 2) to make a mark or figure on any thing by pressure, to imprint, to impress. Figuren auf Kattun —, to print figures on calico.

Eindrücken, *v. tr.* 1) to press in. Butter in die Büchse —, to press butter into the box. *Fig.* Sein Bild ist meinem Herzen auf immer eingedrückt, his image is for ever imprinted on my heart; dem Gedächtnisse —, to impress on the memory. 2) to crush by pressing inward, to bruise by pressure. Ein Ei —, to crush an egg; [in botany] ein eingedrücktes Blatt, a retuse leaf.

Eindrücklich, *adj.* and *adv.* marking or tending to make an impression, having the power of affecting, or of exciting attention and feeling, impressive. Eine —e Rede, an impressive discourse; eine —e Ermahnung, an impressive admonition.

Eindudeln, *v. tr.* to toot asleep.

Einduften, *v. tr.* to scent, to perfume.

Eindunsten, *v. intr.* [u. w. seyn] to penetrate as vapour.

Eindünsten, *v. tr.* 1) to let vapour pass through. 2) to envelop in vapours.

Eindupfen, V. Eintüpfen.

Einebenen, *v. tr.* to lay flat, to level. Berge —, to level hills. *Fig.* to suit, to proportion, to level.

Eineg[g]en, *v. tr.* to harrow in.

Einen, I. *v. tr.* to unite closely. *Fig.* Herzen in Liebe —, to unite hearts in love. II. *v. r.* sich —, to unite.

Einengen, *v. tr.* to force into a narrower compass, to bring within narrow limits or space. Einen Platz —, to straiten a place; zwischen Felsen eingeengt, by rocks confined; eingeengte Gewässer &c., waters when straitened &c. *Fig.* *a*) to confine, to limit. *b*) to press, to pinch. Als wenn es ihr das Herz einengte, as if it pressed her heart. *c*) to concentrate. Die Einengung &c., angustation.

Einenger, *m.* [-s, *pl.* -] 1) one that forces something into a narrower compass. 2) [in physics] condenser.

Einer, I. the numeral **ein**, when it is used without a noun or an article. V. Ein. II. *m.* [-s, *pl.* -] [in arithmetic] a unit.

Einerlei, *adj.* 1) one and the same. 2) of the same kind, of the same description. — Leidenschaften und — Laster, the same passions and the same vices; es ist fast —, it is much the same; es ist mir Alles —, it is all one, all the same to me; er ist immer — (ein und derselbe), he is always the same; [sometimes it is used as a noun] ein ewiges —, an eternal dull repetition of the same thing, a never-broken monotony, a dull and perpetual uniformity.

Einerleiheit, *f.* 1) sameness, identity. 2) [in mathematics] congruity.

Einerleiseyn, *n.* [-s] V. Einerleiheit.

Einernten, *v. tr.* to reap or cut and bring into barns, to get in harvest, to gather, to harvest. Korn —, to harvest corn; der Arbeiter Lohn, die euer Land eingeerntet haben, [in Script.] the hire of the labourers, which have reaped down your fields; wir haben schon eingeerntet, we have yet reaped. *Fig.* Ehren, Lorbeeren —, to reap honours, laurels; Ruhm —, to earn fame; Lob —, to gain praise.

***Einexerciren**, I. *v. tr.* to exercise well, to drill well or thoroughly [recruits]. Trefflich einexercirte Leute, well-drilled men. II. *v. r.* sich —, to exercise one's self.

Einfach, *adj.* and *adv.* [consisting of one thing, not double, uncompounded] simple, single. Ein —es Dach, a roof with single tiles; ein —er Dukaten, a single ducat; ein —er Adler, [in heraldry] an eagle with a single head [as opposed to the spread eagle]; eine —e Flinte, a single barreled gun; —e Scheren, [in fortification] single tenaille; [in botany] —e Wurzeln, Aehren, simple roots, spikes; ein —er Stengel, a simple stem; eine —e Traube, a simple raceme; eine —e Dolde, a simple umbel; eine —e Rispe, a simple panicle; —e Blumen, single flowers [as opposed to double flowers]; eine —e Zahl, a unit; —e Zahlen, [in arithmetic] prime numbers; eine —e Gleichung, [in algebra] a simple equation; eine —e Größe, [in mathematics] a simple quantity; die —e Zahl, [in grammar] the singular number; ein —es Wort, a simple word [as Haus &c.]; —e Begriffe, single ideas. *Fig.* *a*) containing little of the principal quality, or little strength, weak. —es Bier, small beer; —er Taffet, plain taffeta. *b*) simple, plain. Ein —er Landmann, a simple [artless, sincere, harmless] husbandman; er ist sehr — in seinem Betragen, he is very plain in his manner; —e Sitten, simple [unaffected, unconstrained, *it.* not luxurious] manners; ein —er Anzug, a simple or plain dress. *c*) [not much varied by modulations] plain. Ein —es Lied, a simple air or tune. *d*) [not luxurious] plain. Eine —e Kost, a plain diet, simple fare. *e*) simple, not complex or complicated. Eine Maschine von —er Bauart, a machine of simple construction; eine —e Handlung, a simple action; dieses Stück hat eine sehr —e Handlung, this piece has a very simple action; ein —er Schluß, [in logic] an incomplex syllogism.

Einfache, *n.* [-n] 1) singleness [the opposite of doubleness or multiplicity]. Das Doppelte gegen das — wetten, to bet two to one. 2) V. Einfach [when used as a substantive] das Einfache.

Einfächerig, *adj.* and *adv.* having one cell only, unilocular. Ein —er Staubbeutel, [in botany] a unilocular anther.

Einfachheit, *f.* simplicity [of a machine, of a dress, of style, of manners, of Scriptural doctrines or truth &c.].

Einfädeln, *v. tr.* to pass a thread through the eye. Eine Nadel —, to thread a needle.

*Fig. Eine Sache fein —, to contrive, to devise, or plan a thing artfully or dexterously.

Einfahren, *ir.* I. *v. tr.* 1) to carry in [by means of a vehicle]. Das Getreide —, to carry home the corn, to get in corn. 2) to break, tame and accustom to draw. Ein Paar gut eingefahrene[r] Pferde, a pair of well-broken carriage-horses. *Fig.* Sich —, to exercise one's self in driving. 3) to break down a thing by driving over it. II. *v. intr.* [u. w. seyn] 1) to enter a place with a carriage or ship. In den Hafen —, to enter the port. 2) [in mining] to go under ground.

Einfahrer, *m.* [-s, *pl.* -] [in mines] an officer who superintends several mines.

Einfahrt, *f.* [*pl.* -en] 1) the act of driving in, of entering. Die — eines Schiffes in den Hafen, the entrance of a ship into the port; die — eines Bergmannes, the descent of a miner into a pit. 2) the gate, passage or avenue, by which a place may be entered, entrance. Die — eines Hafens, the entrance of a port; die — eines Hauses, gate-way; die — eines Schachtes, adit.

Einfall, *m.* [-es, *pl.* -fälle] 1) the act of falling in or into. Der — der Klinke, the falling and catching of the latch. *Fig.* Die Engländer machten Einfälle in Schottland und die Schotten in England, the English made inroads into Scotland, and the Scots into England; die Gothen und Vandalen machten ehemals Einfälle in den Süden von Europa, the South of Europe was formerly overrun by the Goths and Vandals; der — des Lichtes, the entry of day-light [into a room]. 2) downfall, ruin, destruction. Der — eines Hauses, the ruin of a house; er wurde bei dem — des Hauses erschlagen, he was killed by the falling in of the house; dieses Haus droht den —, this house threatens ruin. 3) a thing that falls in or down. *Fig.* *a*) a spring or darting of intellect, fancy or imagination, a sudden thought, a sudden idea. Ein witziger —, a flash of wit; witzige Einfälle, sallies of wit; ein lustiger —, a jest, or joke; er gerieth auf den —, das ganze Königreich England zu Fuße zu durchreisen, he took it into his head to travel over the whole kingdom of England on foot; ein seltsamer —, a whimsical purpose, a vagary; † and ‡ er hat Einfälle wie ein [altes] Haus, he has pitiful fancies in his head. *b*) [in music] beat. 4) the place where something falls into or enters. 5) an aperture. *a*) [with hunters] the mouth of the earths of badgers, foxes &c. *b*) [with organ-builders] Der — des Windes, an opening in the sound-board of an organ, by which a pipe is filled with wind.

Einfall-haken, *m.* [in musical clocks] detent. **—linie**, *f.* [in mechanics, physics] line of incidence; [in catoptrics] cathete of incidence. **—schnalle**, *f.* [in repeaters] detent. **—s-loth**, *n.* [in physics] axis of incidence. **—s-punkt**, *m.* [in physics] point of incidence. **—s-stütze**, *f.* [in physics] sine of incidence. **—s-winkel**, *m.* [in physics] *a*) angle of incidence. *b*) angle of inclination.

Einfallen, *ir. v. intr.* [u. w. seyn] 1) to fall in or into any place. Das —de Licht, the light entering any dark room; der —de Strahl, [in optics] the incident ray; einfallend, [in mining] downcast; die Klinke fällt nicht ein, the latch does not catch. *Fig.* Beim Gesange —, to join in a song; mit dem Chore —, to sing in chorus, to quire; er fiel ein [er fiel dem Sprechenden in die Rede], he interrupted the speaker; er ließ einige Worte —, he put in some words [while others were discoursing]; es fällt Kälte ein, cold sets in; Thauwetter fällt ein, it begins to thaw; er redet, wie es ihm einfällt, he speaks at random, what comes uppermost; es ist mir ein gutes Mittel eingefallen, a good remedy occurred to me; das ist mir niemahls eingefallen, that came never into my mind; das hätte ich mir nie [or *im Schlafe nicht] — lassen, I should never have dreamed of that; was fällt dir wieder ein? what whim has got possession of you now? es will mir nicht —, it does not occur to my recollection. 2) to fall into ruins, to ruin. Das Haus fiel ein, the house fell to ruins; das Gerüste ist eingefallen, the scaffolding gave way. *Fig.* Eingefallene Augen, hollow or sunken eyes; eingefallene Backen or Wangen, hollow cheeks; ein eingefallenes Gesicht, a hollow countenance. 3) to appear suddenly and unexpectedly, usually with hostile intentions. Die französischen Armeen fielen in Holland ein, the French armies invaded Holland. [with fowlers] Die Vögel fallen ein, the birds alight on the fowling-floor; das Federwildpret fällt ein, [with hunters] the feathered game stoops.

Einfallen, *n.* [-s] [in seamen's language] Das — der Inhölzer oder der Seiten des Schiffs, tumbling home of the top-timbers or housing in.

Einfaller, *m.* [-s, *pl.* -] [with slaters] a small piece of slate used in slating a roof.

‖**Einfällig**, *adj.* and *adv.* ruinous, tottering.

1. **Einfalt**, *f.* [the state of being not complex or of consisting of few parts] simplicity. *Fig.* *a*) [freedom of artificial ornament] simplicity, plainness. Die — der Schreibart, the simplicity of style. *b*) [in ethics] simplicity, artlessness. Die — der Sitten, simplicity of manners. *c*) [freedom of subtility or abstruseness] simplicity, plainness. Die — der biblischen Lehren, the simplicity of Scriptural doctrines. *d*) [formerly, freedom from duplicity, freedom from a propensity to cunning or stratagem] simplicity. In seines Herzens —, in the singleness of his heart. *e*) [weakness of intellect, silliness] simplicity. Göttliche —, [in Script.] godly simplicity.

Einfaltspinsel, *m.* [a person of weak intellect] a simpleton, a ninny, a dunce, a booby.

‖2. **Einfalt**, *m.* [-s, *pl.* -e] and *f.* V. Einfaltspinsel.

Einfälteln, *v. intr.* [to double in narrow streaks] to fold, to plait [a gown, a sleeve &c.].

Einfalten, *v. tr.* to lap or lay in plaits, to fold [a piece of cloth].

Einfaltig, *adj.* & *adv.* consisting of one fold.

Einfältig, *adj.* and *adv.* [consisting of one thing] simple, single. *Fig.* *a*) simple, plain, artless, sincere, harmless. Die ba —en Herzens sind, the single in heart. *b*) simple, silly. Ein —er Mensch, a simpleton; er sieht sehr einfältig aus, he looks very silly. *c*) [proceeding from want of understanding or common judgment] silly. Ein —es Betragen, a silly behaviour; —es Zeug, silly words.

Einfältigen, *v. tr.* [unusual] to make simple, to simplify.

Einfältigkeit, *f.* 1) simplicity, silliness. 2) [in Scripture] simplicity, sincerity, artlessness.

Einfalzen, *v. tr.* 1) to furnish with a rabbet, to rabbet, to fold [paper &c. with the folding-knife]. Die Dauben —, [with coopers] to rabbet the staves. 2) to lap or unite the edge of boards &c., to rabbet.

Einfangen, *ir. v. tr.* 1) to seize, to catch and shut up. Diebe, Landstreicher —, to take up thieves, vagabonds; eingefangen seyn, [with hunters] to be seized [said of a prey]. 2) to take in, to inclose. Einen Garten mit einem Zaune —, to fence a garden with a hedge. 3) to take up with a shovel.

Einfangsschaufel, *f.* [in metallurgy] a wooden shovel.

Einfarbig, Einfärbig, *adj.* and *adv.* being of one colour, one-coloured. Ein —er Zeug, a plain stuff; das —e Gemählde, a brooch, monochrama.

Einfassen, *v. tr.* 1) to confine within, to include. Getreide —, to sack corn; Bier —, to put beer into casks, to tun beer; einen Bienenschwarm —, [in husbandry] to hive a swarm of bees. V. also Fassen. 2) to infix or inclose in another body so as to be held fast, but not concealed. Das Bild in einen Rahmen —, to put the picture in a frame; Blumenbeete mit Buchsbaum —, to border or to edge flower-beds with box; ein Frauenkleid mit Spitzen —, to trim, to edge a gown with lace; einen Teppich —, to bind a carpet; einen Brunnen —, to curb a well; einen Garten mit einem lebendigen Zaune —, to fence a garden with a hedge, to enclose a garden with a quick-set fence; einen Demant in Gold —, to set a diamond in gold; Schalen mit Edelsteinen eingefaßt, bowls with gems enchased.

Einfaß-band, *n.* a ribbond used for bordering a garment. **—tresse**, *f.* [with lace-makers] trimming gold or silver lace.

Einfassung, *f.* 1) the act of confining within, of inclosing, bordering, enchasing, trimming, edging. 2) that with which any thing is bound or bordered, that which is added on the border; [with printers] framing. Die — eines Bildes, the frame of a picture; die — eines Blumenbeetes, the border of a flower-bed; die — eines Kleides, the edging, trimming, welt [of] a garment; die — eines Ringes, the collet, — [more usual Fassung] eines Edelsteines, the setting of a stone; die — eines Brunnens, the cu[rb]; die — einer Brille, the frame of a pair of [spec]tacles; die —en an Thüren und Fenstern, frames of doors and windows.

‖**Einfätschen**, V. Einwindeln.

Einfaulen, *v. intr.* [u. w. seyn] to rot in

‖**Einfedern**, V. Befedern.

Einfehmen, *v. tr.* [in husbandry] to p[ut] [pigs] to feed in the woods, to put to mast.

Einfeilen, *v. tr.* 1) to file into, to perfo[rate] with a file. 2) to form by filing [characters

Einfesseln, *v. tr.* to confine by fetters, [to] fetter, to shackle.

Einfetten, *v. tr.* to smear or anoint [with] grease or fat. Leder —, to grease leather.

Einfeuchten, *v. tr.* to wet, to moisten. [Pa]pier —, [with printers] to wet the paper.

Einfeuern, *v. intr.* to make fire in a

Einfiedeln, *v. tr.* 1) to fiddle asleep. [2) to] learn by fiddling repeatedly.

Einfinden, *ir. v. r.* sich —, to come, to ap[pear]. Sie fanden sich an dem bestimmten Orte ein, [they] met at the appointed place; er hatte sich eingefunden, he was present there; ich werde dort —, I will be there; ich werde mich um [die] bestimmte Stunde dort —, I shall repair thi[ther] at the appointed hour. *Fig.* Der Schlaf fi[ndet] [stellt] sich bei mir ein, I am inclined to sl[eep], I am sleepy or drowsy.

Einfitzen, *v. tr.* [with needle-makers] to [per]forate with a file. Das Oehr in eine Nähn[adel] —, to perforate a needle with a file.

Einflechten, *ir.* I. *v. tr.* 1) to plait, to bra[id]. Die Haare —, to plait the hair. 2) to twist, [to] intertwine, to interweave, to interlace. Perlen [in] das Haar —, to inweave the hair with pea[rls]. *Fig.* Eine Fabel —, to insert a fable; eine e[in]geflochtene Dichtung, Erzählung, Handlung, episode; etwas —, to mention a thing by [the] way. II. *v. r.* sich —, to meddle officiously, to [in]terpose or interfere improperly, to interm[eddle].

Einfleischen, *v. tr.* to clothe with flesh, [to] embody in flesh [used only in a figurative sense

Ein eingefleischter Teufel, a devil incarnate.

Einflicken, *v. tr.* to insert a patch or patches. *Fig.* Ein überflüssiges Wort —, to insert a superfluous word; sich —, to insinuate one's self.

Einfliegen, *ir. v. intr.* [u. w. seyn] to fly into a place or aperture.

Einfließen, *ir. v. intr.* [u. w. seyn] to flow in, to enter. Der Ort, wo der Main in den Rhein einfließt, the place where the Main enters the Rhine, the confluence of the Main and the Rhine; das —de Wasser auspumpen, to pump out the entering water. *Fig. a*) to mention slightly, to touch on or upon, to insert indirectly, incidentally or by way of digression. Etwas in eine Schrift oder Rede — lassen, to throw in something in a writing or discourse; ein Wort — lassen, to slide in a word; ein belehrendes Wort in einen Brief — lassen, to drop a word of instruction in a letter. *b*) to act on and affect. Der Eigennutz fließt fast auf alle menschliche Handlungen ein, almost all human actions are influenced by self-interest.

Einflößen, *v. tr.* 1) to instil, to infuse by drops. *Fig.* Einem gute Grundsätze —, to instil good principles into any one's mind; flöße jungen Gemüthern einen edlen Eifer ein, infuse into young minds a noble ardour; Einem Muth —, to inspire any one with courage. 2) to throw wood &c. into water, in order to float it.

Einflöten, *v. tr.* 1) to lull asleep by fluting. 2) to learn by fluting repeatedly.

Einflug, *m.* [-es, *pl.* -flüge] 1) the act of flying into any place or aperture. 2) the aperture through which doves enter a dove-cot &c.

Einflugloch, *n.* V. Einflug 2.

Einflügelig, *adj.* and *adv.* 1) having but one fold or wing. 2) [in botany] having one wing only, as a seed or seed-vessel.

Einfluß, *m.* [-sses, *pl.* -flüsse] the act of flowing in, influx. Der — des Mains in den Rhein, the entering of the Main into the Rhine. *Fig.* Beweise hatten keinen — auf die Geschwornen, arguments had no influence on the jury; der — der Planeten auf die Schicksale der Menschen, the influence of the planets on the fortunes of men; die Obrigkeit hat keinen — auf das Volk, the magistrate has no influence with the people; er hat einen großen — auf den Fürsten, he has a great credit with the prince; diese Gründe sollten auf alle Menschen — haben, these reasons should prevail with all men; er hat seinen — auf ihn geltend gemacht, he used his credit with him; ein Mann von großem — bei Hofe, a man who has a great credit with the court, one who has great interest at court; das Vergnügen hat — auf die Menschen, men are influenced by pleasure.

Einflußreich, *adj.* and *adv.* having great influence, credit or interest. Ein —reicher Mann, an influential person.

Einflüstern, *v. tr.* to whisper to. Einem —, to whisper any one in the ear. *Fig.* Einem etwas —, to insinuate something to any one; welcher Geist hat dir diese Einbildung eingeflüstert? what spirit suggested to you this imagination?

Einflüsterung, *f.* 1) the act of whispering. 2) *Fig.* a suggestion, secret notification or incitement, insinuation. Heimliche —en, secret suggestions.

Einfodern, Einfordern, *v. tr.* to demand and receive, to collect, to call in [debts or money]. Eine Schuld —, to make a demand of a debt, to call on.

Einform, *f.* [*pl.* -en] 1) the same form. 2) *V.* Uniform.

Einförmig, I. *adj.* having always the same form and manner, uniform; without variety or diversity. Diese Landschaft ist zu —, the landscape has too much sameness; ein —es Leben führen, to lead a uniform life; eine —e Rede, a discourse that wants variety. II. *adv.* without diversity of one from another, uniformly.

Einförmigkeit, *f.* 1) continued or unvaried sameness, uniformity, monotony. 2) a thing that wants variety.

Einfreien, *v. r.* sich —, 1) to enter a family by marriage. 2) to enter a corporation.

Einfressen, *ir.* I. *v. tr.* to swallow eating. †Seinen Aerger — [in sich fressen], to devour one's vexation. II. *v. r.* sich —, to eat in or into. III. *v. intr.* to eat in or into, to make way by corrosion. Die Salpetersäure frißt in Kupfer ein, nitric acid corrodes copper.

Einfrieden, Einfriedigen, *v. tr.* [to inclose with a hedge, wall, to secure by an inclosure] to fence [a garden &c.].

Einfrieren, *ir. v. intr.* [u. w. seyn] to freeze in, to become totally surrounded with ice, so as to be incapable of advancing, to be frozen up. Ein eingefrornes Schiff, an ice-bound vessel.

Einfrömmeln, *v. r.* sich —, to insinuate one's self by affected piety.

Einfugen, *v. tr.* 1) to joint [wood]. 2) *Fig.* to insert [a passage in a composition &c.].

Einfügen, *v. tr.* 1) [to set or bring one thing in contiguity with another] to join [commonly in a fig. sense]. Sich —, to accommodate one's self to a thing. 2) V. Einfugen, 2).

Einfuhr, [*pl.* -en] ||**Einfuhre**, [*pl.* -n] *f.* 1) the act of bringing, carrying or conveying a thing into a place. Die — des Getreides in die Scheuer, the getting in of corn; die — von ausländischen Waaren, the importation of foreign commodities; die — verbotener Waaren, contraband, smuggling. 2) import, importation.

Einfuhr=artikel, *m.* V. —waare. —**handel**, *m.* import-trade. —**verbot**, *n.* the prohibition of introducing foreign goods. —**waare**, *f.* [the wares or commodities imported] importation, import. —**zoll**, *m.* customs or duty paid on imported goods.

Einführbar, *adj.* and *adv.* that may be imported, importable; that may be introduced.

Einführbarkeit, *f.* the quality of being importable, or of being introduced.

Einführen, I. *v. tr.* to carry, to convey or to transport into a place or country. Getreide —, to get in corn; ausländische Waaren —, to import, to introduce foreign goods; Großbrittanien führt Baumwolle aus Amerika und Indien ein, Great Britain imports cotton from America and India. *Fig.* Einen Fremden bei Jemanden —, to introduce a stranger to a person; Einen in ein Amt oder eine Pfründe —, to induct any one to an office or benefice; den Präsidenten eines Collegiums —, to inaugurate the president of a college; Einen in eine geschlossene Gesellschaft —, to initiate any one to a club; einen Prediger —, to install a minister of the Gospel; sich bei dem Publicum —, to introduce one's self to the public; er wurde durch seinen Oheim in die Welt eingeführt, he was ushered into the world by his uncle; einen Gesellen —, [with mechanics] to help a journeyman to work; Einen redend —, to cite any one's words; eine neue Mode —, to introduce a new fashion; ein längst eingeführter Gebrauch, a custom long received; der eingeführte Glaube, the established faith; die eingeführte Kirche, the established church. II. *v. r.* sich —, 1) to introduce one's self. Er hat sich [selbst] ohne Umstände bei ihm eingeführt, he introduced himself to him without any ceremony. 2) to come into vogue. Solche Meinungen führen sich jetzt ein, such opinions are now getting in vogue.

Einführer, *m.* [-s, *pl.* -] introducer. Er war mein — in der Gesellschaft, he introduced me to the society.

Einfuhrt, *f.* [*pl.* -n] the place of ingress, entrance. Buchten und —en, bays and inlets.

Einführung, *f.* introduction. Die — von Waaren, the importation or introduction of commodities. *Fig.* Die — eines Fremden bei Hofe, the introduction of a stranger to a court; die — eines Beamten, Geistlichen, installation; die — in ein geistliches Amt, induction; die — neuer Gesetze, the establishing of new laws; die — neuer Kleidermoden, the introduction of new fashions of dress.

Einfüllen, *v. tr.* to put into a vessel &c. Bier [in Fässer] —, to tun beer; Bier [in Flaschen] —, to bottle beer.

Einfurchen, *v. tr.* to make furrows in, to furrow. *Fig.* Der Gram hat seine Stirne eingefurcht, sorrow furrowed his brow.

Einfüßig, *adj.* and *adv.* having but one foot. Ein —er Tisch, a table with one foot, a monopodium.

Einfüttern, *v. tr.* to inwrap, to enclose, to cover, to envelop [something with a sheath]. Mit Stroh —, to cover with straw.

Eingabe, *f.* [*pl.* -n] [any thing given in in writing to some public office, to the government &c., especially a written supplication from an inferior to a superior] petition. V. Eingeben, 2).

Eingang, *m.* [-es, *pl.* -gänge] 1) [the act of entering into a place] entrance. Der — einer Person in ein Haus oder Zimmer, the entrance or entry of a person into a house or an apartment. *Fig.* Einem den — gestatten, to give entrance to any one; er fand mit seinen Bitten keinen —, his prayers were not regarded or heard. 2) the act of entering or importing goods, importation. 3) the customs or duty paid on imports. 4) the door, gate, passage or avenue, by which a place may be entered, entrance. Das Haus hat zwei Eingänge, the house has two entries or doors. 5) [with hunters] the morning-view or slot of a stag or deer, repairing to the woods. 6) something introductory. Der — eines Buches, the introduction, a preface or preliminary discourse; der — eines Schauspiels, the prologue; der — eines Singspiels, the overture; der — eines Tonstücks, the prelude; der — der Messe, [in the Romish church] the entry of the mass. [in rhetoric, the first part of an oration or discourse] introduction, exordium.

Eingangs=fährte, *f.* [with hunters] the view or slot of a stag at the entrance of a wood. —**geld**, *n.* [with mechanics] entry-money, entrance. —**pforte**, *f.* entrance. —**preis**, *m.* money paid for the admission to the play-house or to other exhibition, entrance-money —**thor**, *n.* —**thür**, *f.* a gate or door by which a house may be entered, entrance. —**zoll**, *m.* customs paid on imports, duty of entry.

||**Eingangs**, *adv.* in the beginning. Die — erwähnten Umstände, the particulars mentioned before.

Eingebäude, *n.* [-s] V. Einbau.

Eingeben, *ir. v. tr.* 1) to give [medicine to a sick person &c.]. *Fig.* to put into any one's mind, to suggest. Sprecht, was euer Herz euch eingiebt, speak what your heart prompts you to; Ihr habt diesen heiligen Entschluß meinem Herzen eingegeben, you have inspired into my heart this holy resolution; alle Schrift ist von Gott eingegeben, [in Script.] all Scripture is given by inspiration of God. 2) to exhibit, to present. Eine Bittschrift —, to present a petition; eine Klage —, to bring on, to enter an action. 3) [unusual] to give up to. Ich gab ihm mein Haus zur Wohnung ein, I left him the use of my house.

Eingebildet, *past part.* of Einbilden. *adj.* and *adv.* 1) imaginary, chimerical. 2) presumptuous, self-conceited. Ein —er Mensch, an arrogant person.

Eingebinde, *n.* [*pl.* -] present given to a godchild at its christening, [hence, in general] a present or token given in celebration of a certain peculiar day, as Geburtstags—, Namenstags—.

Eingebogen, *past part.* of Einbiegen. *adj.* and *adv.* inflected, incurvated. Mit —er Nase, flat-nosed.

1. **Eingeboren**, *adj.* only-begotten [used only in Scripture]. Der eingeborne Sohn Gottes, the only-begotten son of God.

2. **Eingeboren**, *adj.* and *adv.* 1) born in a country, native, indigenous. Der Eingeborne, a native or indigene. 2) V. Angeboren.

Eingebrachte, *n.* [-n] dowry, parapherna, paraphernalia.

Eingebung, *f.* 1) the act of giving, presenting, suggesting or leaving to any one's use. 2) the infusion of ideas into the mind. Die —en der Phantasie, the suggestions of fancy; folge nur den —en deines wohlwollenden Herzens, do but follow the suggestions of they kindly heart; durch göttliche —, by divine inspiration.

Eingebungs-schwärmer, *m.* a mystic. —schwärmerei, *f.* mysticism.

Eingeburt, *f.* [*pl.*-n] [rather unusual] the state of being born in a country, of being an indigene.

Eingeburtsrecht, *n.* right possessed by a native.

Eingedenk, *adj.* and *adv.* [bearing in mind, keeping in mind] mindful. Einer Sache — seyn, to be mindful of any thing; seines Versprechens — seyn, to remember one's promise.

‡**Eingedenksam**, *adj.* and *adv.* remembering well.

Eingefleischt, V. Einfleischen.

Eingehen, *ir.* I. *v. intr.* 1) [u. w. seyn] to go in, to walk in, to enter. Zur Thüre —, to enter the door; bei Jemanden aus- und —, to frequent any one's house; bei Jemanden frei aus- und —, to have free access to a person. *Fig.* *a*) In das ewige Leben —, to depart [from] this life, to leave this world, to die; in den Sinn eines Schriftstellers —, to enter into, to understand an author's meaning; ein Schauspieler geht recht in den Charakter seiner Rolle ein, wenn &c., an actor humours well his part, if &c.; ohne auf die einzelnen Umstände einzugehen, without entering into the particular parts. *b*) = begriffen werden, to enter into the understanding, to be understood or conceived. Es geht mir nicht ein, wodurch &c., I cannot conceive by what means &c.; einige Dinge, die schwer —, some things hard to be understood; es geht ihm schwer ein, he learns it with difficulty, he thinks that very hard; dies will mir nicht —, this will not down with me. 2) to come or pass into, to enter. —de Waaren, imported goods, imports; die heute eingegangenen Briefe, the letters which have come in to-day. *Fig.* Seine Pachtgelder gehen regelmäßig ein, his rents come in regularly; das Geld ging ihm auf den Tag ein, wo es fällig war, he received the money on the day it was due; es gingen Nachrichten von Konstantinopel bei uns ein, we had news from Constantinople; es geht gerade die Nachricht ein, news has just arrived. 3) to enter in return, to re-enter. Ein —der Winkel, [in geometry] a re-entering angle. 4) to contract spontaneously, to shrink. Wollenes Tuch geht im heißen Wasser ein, woolen cloth shrinks in hot water; beim Walken —, to shrink in fulling; ein hänfenes Seil geht ein, wenn es feucht wird, a hempen cord contracts by moisture. 5) *Fig.* to cease gradually. Er will seinen Handel — lassen, he will leave off his trade; eingeführte Gebräuche — lassen, to abrogate, to abolish established customs, to allow established customs fall into disuse. 6) to be gradually impaired. Bäume gehen ein, trees decay; alle seine Rosen sind eingegangen, all his roses perished. 7) [in metallurgy] to melt, to run. II. *v. tr.* to consent, to agree to. Eine Wette —, to accept [of] a wager, to hold a wager; eine eheliche Verbindung —, to marry; diese Bedingungen werde ich nie —, I shall never yield to these terms; das wird er niemals —, he will never consent to that.

Eingeigen, *v. tr.* 1) to learn by fiddling repeatedly. 2) to lull asleep by fiddling. 3) to teach by fiddling.

Eingeisten, **Eingeistern**, V. Begeistern.

Eingelegt, *past part.* of Einlegen. V. Einlegen. —e Arbeit, marquetry, mosaic.

Eingemacht, V. Einmachen.

Eingenommen, [past part. of Einnehmen, V.] *adj.* and *adv.* 1) inclined previously to favour. — seyn von einer Person oder Sache, to be prepossessed with a person or thing; er ist sehr von ihr —, he is much infatuated with her; von sich —, conceited. 2) prejudiced, prejudicial. Er ist sehr gegen diesen jungen Menschen —, he is greatly prejudiced against this young man; da er einmal in dieser Sache von Vorurtheilen — ist, since he is prejudiced in this matter.

Eingenommenheit, *f.* 1) prepossession [in one's favour]. 2) prejudice.

†**Eingerben**, V. Einprügeln.

Eingerichte, *n.* [-s] [with locksmiths] ward.

Eingerückte, *n.* [-n] [the thing inserted] insertion.

Eingeschlossenheit, *f.* 1) [state of being inclosed, shut up] inclosure. 2) confinement, imprisonment.

||**Eingeschneitel**, *n.* [-s, *pl.* -] estate settled on a widow, jointure.

Eingeschnittene, *n.* [-n] [in cookery] a fricassee.

||**Eingeschnitz**, *n.* [-es, *pl.* -e] V. Eingeschnittene.

Eingeschränkt, [past part. of Einschränken] *adj.* and *adv.* restrained, confined, limited. Er muß sehr — leben, he is obliged to live very economically, sparingly; ein —er Kopf, a shallow-brained person.

Eingeschränktheit, *f.* limitedeness. Die — des Raumes, the narrowness of space. *Fig.* Die — der Einsicht, narrowness of knowledge.

Eingesessen, [past part. of Einsitzen] *adj.* and *adv.* settled in a place as an inhabitant. Der —e, inhabitant.

Eingeständniß, *n.* [-sses, *pl.* -sse] confession, avowal.

Eingestehen, *ir. v. tr.* 1) to confess, to own, acknowledge or avow, as a crime or fault. 2) to admit as true, just or proper, to concede, to grant. Eingestandener Maßen, declaredly.

†**Eingeteufelt**, *adj.* and *adv.* devilish.

Eingewebe, *n.* [-s, *pl.* -] 1) something interwoven or inwoven. 2) *Fig.* an episode.

Eingeweide, *n.* [-s, *pl.* -] [the internal parts of animal bodies] the bowels, guts or intestines, the entrails, inwards, garbage, viscera. Das — des Federviehes, trail; zu den —n gehörig, visceral.

Eingeweide-lehre, *f.* splanchnology, enterology. —nerv, *m.* [in anatomy] splanchnic nerve. —schlagader, *f.* [in anatomy] celiac artery. —wurm, *m.* tape-worm.

Eingeweihte, *m.* [-n, *pl.* -n] 1) one who is initiated. Ein —r in die Mysterien der Ceres, an initiate into the mysteries of Ceres. 2) an adept.

Eingewohnen, *v. intr.* [u. w. seyn] to get accustomed to a place [used only in the past participle].

Eingewöhnen, *v. tr.* 1) to accustom to a place. 2) to make familiar by frequent use or practice. Den Kindern Gehorsam —, to habituate children to obedience; sich —, to habituate one's self.

Eingezogen, [past part. of Einziehen] *adj* and *adv.* secluded from much society or from public notice. Ein —es Leben führen, to live a retired life, to live in seclusion; ein —er Mensch, a domestic man; —e Sitten, sober manners. ein —es Wesen, a retired, modest behaviour.

Eingezogenheit, *f.* 1) retirement, reclusion retreat. 2) retiredness, modesty, simpleness.

Eingießen, *ir. v. tr.* 1) to pour in, to infuse Wein in eine Tafelflasche —, to pour wine into a decanter, to decant wine; *Verstand kann man Einem nicht —, wit cannot be infused into any one. *Fig.* Und er, der ihm die Seele, so in ihm wirket, eingegossen, [in Script.] and he that inspired into him an active soul. 2) to fix a piece of wood or iron in a wall &c. with melted lead to seal.

Eingittern, *v. tr.* to grate [a window &c.]

Eingleiten, *ir. v. intr.* [u. w. seyn] to slid in, to glide in.

Eingötterl[er], *m.* [-s, *pl.* -] unitarian.

Eingötterei, *f.* the creed of the unitarian

Eingottslehre, *f.* the doctrines of the u tarians, unitarianism.

Eingraben, *ir. v. tr.* 1) to deposit and co in the earth, to hide in the earth, to earth. nen Leichnam —, to inter, to bury a corp sich —, to get into a place by digging, to one's self; *fig.* to intrench one's self. Sich seine Bücher —, to confine one's self to o studies. 2) [to cut figures, letters, devices, on or metal] to engrave, to grave. Und sollst zwei Steine — die Namen der Kinder Israel Script.] thou shalt engrave the two stones the names of the children of Israel. 3) to di cut a trench around a place, to surround a ditch. Einen Acker —, to ditch a field.

Eingreifen, *ir. v. intr.* to take or lay h Der Anker greift ein, the anchor bites; die ne dieses Rades greifen gut ein, the teeth of wheel catch well the cogs of another whee greifen in einander ein, they lock into each o der Hirsch greift ein, [with hunters] the stag strongly his view or slot; der Leithund greift the limer noses the ground closely. *Fig.* In Sache —, to seize on or upon a thing; in sein Amt —, to encroach on the office o other; in eines Andern Gewalt —, to press another's power; —de Maßregeln, energ measures.

Eingreifig, *adj.* and *adv.* [in husbandry] —er Baum, a tree that may be spanned.

Eingrenzen, *v. tr.* to bound, to limit. Feld —, to inclose a field.

Eingriff, *m.* [-es, *pl.* -e] the act of king hold, of catching, catch. *Fig.* encroa ment, invasion. Der — in Anderer Gerechtsa the encroachment on the prerogatives of oth der König that —e in die Rechte des Adels, king intrenched on the rights of the nobles that —e in die Rechte des Volkes, he invaded the rights of the people.

Eingürteln, Eingurten, *v. tr.* to gird [a man]; to girth [a horse].

Einguß, *m.* [-sses, *pl*, -güsse] 1) the act of pouring in, infusion. 2) the liquid poured in, as a mixture for a horse, a drench. 3) [in mints and in forges] the iron-moulds in which the bars of silver are cast and receive their form, the iron-mould in which the glaziers cast their lead. 4) [with workers in metal &c.] the aperture through which the melted metal is poured into the mould, the jet.

Eingußthierchen, *n.* [in entomology] a worm of the infusory order of worms.

Einhacken, I. *v. intr.* to hew or cut into a thing. II. *v. tr.* to add by hacking.

Einhäfteln, *v. tr.* V. Einhäkeln.

Einhageln, *v. imp.* 1) to hail through an aperture. 2) to break by hail.

Einhägen, Einhegen, *v. tr.* to hedge, to fence [a field or garden]. Einen Park —, to inclose a park.

Einhäkeln, *v. tr.* to catch by a small hook, to hook in, to fix by a small hook.

Einhaken, *v. tr.* to catch by a hook, to hitch. [in seamen's language] Ein Segel —, to shift [to change] a sail; der Anker hakt in den Meeresgrund ein, the anchor catches or holds.

Einhallig, Einhällig, [most usual] **Einhellig**, *adj.* and *adv.* unisonous. *Fig.* Es wurde — beschlossen, it was agreed by common consent, unanimously determined; — handeln, to act in concert; mit —er Stimme, with one voice.

Einhälligkeit, Einhelligkeit, *f.* unanimity.

Einhalt, *m.* [-es] 1) [the act of stopping] stop. *Fig.* Einer Sache — thun, to put a stop to any thing; der Bettelei — thun, to put down begging; dem Laster — thun, to arrest the progress of vice, to restrain vice; den Mißbräuchen — thun, to suppress abuses; dem Aufruhr — thun, to repress sedition; er mußte dem Ungestüm seiner Leute — thun, he was obliged to restrain the impetuosity of his men. 2) [in music] a pause. 3) [in law] inhibition.

Einhalten, *ir.* I. *v. tr.* 1) [to put an end to any motion or action] to stop, to hold in. Einen Verbrecher auf seiner Flucht —, to stop a criminal. *Fig.* Seine Begierden —, to restrain, to keep in, to keep under one's appetites; *sich —, to keep in the house, to keep within doors; seine schwache Gesundheit nöthigt ihn, sich einzuhalten, his feeble health obliges him to observe a strict diet. 2) [with tailors and sempstresses] to pucker, to pucker up. 3) to follow, to observe. Ich werde bei dieser Gelegenheit folgendes Verfahren —, I shall observe in this affair the following mode of acting; den Termin —, [in law] to keep the term. II. *v. intr.* 1) to cease from any course of action; [in music, to cease to sing or play for a time] to pause. Haltet ein! stay there! desist! mit der Bezahlung —, to stop payment, or to put it off; mit der Arbeit —, to cease from work; im Lesen —, to cease to read for a time, to pause in reading. V. also Innehalten. 2) to be steadfast in any course. Mit den Zahlungen —, to be punctual in payments, not to be behindhand in paying money when due.

Einhämmern, *v. tr.* 1) to hammer or beat into. 2) to break by hammering.

Einhandeln, *v. tr.* 1) to buy, to purchase, to truck, to barter [goods &c.]. Etwas mit —, to include something in a bargain. 2) to impoverish by trade. Sein ganzes Vermögen —, to lose one's entire fortune by trading.

Einhändig, *adj.* and *adv.* one-handed, single-handed.

Einhändigen, *v. tr.* to put into another's hand. Einem etwas —, to hand something to any one; er händigte mir einen Brief ein, he delivered a letter to me; Einem zur Verwahrung —, to place in another's hands.

Einhändigung, *f.* delivery.

Einhändigungsschein, *m.* a bill of delivery, a receit or receipt.

Einhängen, *v. tr.* to hang or suspend. Eine Thür —, to hang a door on hinges; die Ohrringe —, to fasten the ear-rings to the ears; die Hemmkette —, to put the skid to a wheel, to lock a wheel; das Dach —, [in roofing] to hang the tiles on the laths.

Einhängezirkel, *m.* watch-maker's compasses.

Einhängig, *adj.* and *adv.* [in architecture] having but one sloping side. Ein —es Dach, a shed-roof, pent-roof or lean-to.

Einhaschen, *v. tr.* to snatch, to seize.

Einhauchen, *v. tr.* 1) to inject by breathing, to breathe or blow into [chiefly used in a fig. sense]. Neues Leben —, to inspire with new life; Einem tugendhafte Gesinnungen —, to inspire any one with sentiments of virtue. 2) to inspire, to inhale [also in a fig. sense]. Irrthümer —, to imbibe errors.

Einhauen, *ir.* I. *v. tr.* 1) to hew in, to cut in, to cut into. Ein Zeichen —, to cut in a mark. 2) to hew open [a door &c.]. 3) to mince, to chop and put up [meat &c.]. *Fig.* † Einen or Jemanden in's Salz —, to cut any one into pieces, *it.* to traduce or backbite any one. II. *v. intr.* to hew or cut into something, to enter sabring. Die Reiterei hieb in den Feind ein, the horse charged the enemy.

Einhäufen, *v. tr.* to heap in.

Einhauig, Einhäuig, *adj.* and *adv.* [in husbandry] what is cut or may be cut but once. —e Wiesen, meadows that are mowed but once.

Einhausen, [unusual] *v. tr.* to station for lodging.

Einhäusler, *m.* [-s, *pl.* -] [in botany] a monecian plant.

Einheben, *ir. v. tr.* to put into by lifting or heaving. Eine Thür —, to heave a door into the hinges; eine Form —, [with printers] to put a form into the press.

Einheften, *v. tr.* 1) to sew in, to stitch in or among. Ein eingehefteter Bogen, a sheet sewed in. 2) to sew together. Ein Buch —, to sew a book; Gerichtspapiere —, to file judicial papers.

Einhegen, V. Einhägen.

Einheilen, I. *v. intr.* [u. w. seyn] to remain in after the wound is healed up. Die Kugel ist in die Wunde eingeheilt, the wound healed, but the bullet remained in. II. *v. tr.* to heal up a wound and leave something in it.

Einheimen, [unusual] I. *v. tr.* to bring in one's own country, to naturalize. II. *v. intr.* [u. w. seyn] to be received as a native.

Einheimisch, *adj.* and *adv.* home-born, home-bred, domestic, not foreign, not exotic. —e Thiere, native animals; —e Pflanzen, indigenous plants, not exotics; —e Fabriken, domestic manufactories; —e Waaren, home-made or home-spun goods; — seyn, to be born in a place or country, to be a native, *it. fig.* to be familiar with, to be well-versed in; der Aussatz war in Juda —, leprosy was endemic in Judea; ||—e Fleischer, butchers settled in a town or city [as opposed to butchers settled in the country]; —e Kriege, intestine wars, civil wars. *Fig.* Der Fremdling war in ihrem Herzen — geworden, the stranger was no more a stranger to her heart.

||**Einheimsen**, *v. tr.* to house, to inn [corn &c.].

Einheirathen, *v. intr.* to get into [a family] by marriage. Sich —, to marry into a family.

Einheit, *f.* 1) [the state of being one] oneness, unity. Die — Gottes, the oneness of God. 2) such a combination of things as to constitute one single being. Die — Gottes, the unity of God; die — des Sohnes mit dem Vater, [in theology] the consubstantiality of the Son with the Father. 3) the state of being indivisible or of admitting no division. Die — der Sonnenstäubchen, the indivisibility of atoms. 4) [in mathematics, the abstract expression for any unit whatsoever] unity. 5) [the principle by which a uniform tenor of story and propriety of representation is preserved] unity. In dem Drama giebt es drei —en, die — der Handlung, die — der Zeit, die — des Orts, in the drama there are three unities, the unity of action, the unity of time and that of place. 6) [in arithmetic] unity, unit. Die Drei besteht aus drei —en, the number three consists of three units. 7) [in grammar] the singular number. 8) [an indivisible thing] a monade.

Einheits-begriff, *m.* the idea of unity. —**lehre**, *f.* the doctrine of the monades. —**voll**, *adj.* and *adv.* showing throughout unity or concord.

Einheizen, I. *v. intr.* to heat a stove. *Fig.* † Man hat ihm brav eingeheizt, he has been grievously frighted. II. *v. tr.* to cause to be warmed, to heat [a stove]. Ein Zimmer —, to make a fire in a room. Das —, calefaction.

Einheizloch, *n.* V. Ofenloch.

Einheizer, *m.* [-s, *pl.* -] -**inn**, *f.* the person that heats, calefactor.

Einhelfen, *ir. v. intr.* 1) V. Hineinhelfen. 2) *Fig.* to help out, to assist a speaker when at a loss, by pronouncing the words forgotten or next in order. Einem Schauspieler —, to prompt an actor; Einem —, to set any one in.

Einhelfer, *m.* [-s, *pl.* -] prompter.

Einhellig, V. Einhällig.

Einhelligkeit, V. Einhälligkeit.

Einhemmen, *v. tr.* 1) to put the skid to a wheel. Das Rad —, to lock or hem the wheel. 2) to inclose. *Fig.* Von Schwierigkeiten überall eingehemmt, hemmed in by difficulties everywhere, on all parts.

Einhenkelig, *adj.* and *adv.* having one handle or ear.

Einhenken, *v. tr.* to hook in. Thüren —, to hang doors on the hinges.

Einhèr, *adv.* forth, on, along, used only in a figurative sense and in composition with verbs.

Einher-fahren, *ir. v. intr.* [u. w. seyn] to pass along in a carriage, to drive along with a ceremonious solemnity. *Fig.* *Hoch—fahren, to ride the high horse, to show pride. —**fliegen**, *ir. v. intr.* [u. w. seyn] to fly along. —**gehen**, *ir. v. intr.* [u. w. seyn] to walk along, also to walk in a stately manner. *Fig.* *Erbärmlich —gehen, to go miserably clothed, to go ragged. —**gleiten**, *ir. v. intr.* [u. w. seyn] to glide along. —**prangen**, —**prunken**, *v. intr.* to prance along. —**rollen**, *v. intr.* [u. w. seyn] to roll along. —**schreiten**, *ir. v. intr.* [u. w. seyn] to walk gravely along, to stride or stalk along. —**segeln**, *v. intr.* [u. w. seyn] to sail along. —**stolzen**, —**stolziren**, *v. intr.* [u. w. seyn] to prance along, to strut along. ||—**strotzen**, *v. intr.* [u. w. seyn] to strut along. —**treten**, *ir. v. intr.* [u. w. seyn] to step along, to walk along. —**wanken**, *v. intr.* to totter along. —**ziehen**, *ir. v. intr.* [u. w. seyn] to move on.

Einherbsten, *v. tr.* to get in harvest, to harvest, to gather. Den Wein —, to gather the vintage.

Einhetzen, *v. tr.* to exercise in baiting, to train [hounds]. Ein auf wilde Schweine eingehetzter Hund, a dog trained to hunt the wild boar, a limer. *Fig.* †Er ist in dieses Geschäft tüchtig eingehetzt, he is well trained to this business.

Einheucheln, *v. r.* sich —, to insinuate one's self by hypocrisy.

||**Einheuern**, *v. tr.* to take a lodging for some body.

Einheurathen, V. Einheirathen.

Einhode, *m.* [-n, *pl.* -n] one, that has but one testicle.

Einhodig, *adj.* and *adv.* having but one testicle.

Einholen, *v. tr.* 1) = hereinholen. [in seamen's language] to haul home [any rope &c.]. Die Segel —, V. Bergen. 2) to go to meet and conduct into a place with ceremonious solemnity. 3) to come up with in a course, or in pursuit, to overtake. Einen Ausreißer —, to overtake a deserter; ein Schiff —, to come up with a ship. 4) *Fig. a*) to match, to equal. Einen in Kenntnissen —, to match any one in knowledge. *b*) to request and obtain from another place. Die Stimmen —, to collect the votes; Nachricht —, to get intelligence; Jemands Einwilligung —, to obtain any one's consent. *c*) [in husbandry] Einen Wald —, to measure a forest.

Einholtalje, *f.* [a sea term] a rope used to hold a ship whilst careened.

Einholer, *m.* [-s, *pl.* -] Der — des Klüvers, [in seamen's language] inhaler or inhauler.

Einhölzer, *pl.* V. Innhölzer.

Einhorn, *n.* [-s, *pl.* -hörner] 1) the unicorn, the monoceros; [in heraldry] the unicorn. 2) [a fish of the whale-kind] the sea-unicorn, narwal. 3) a species of beetle [scarabæus hercules, gideon &c.]. 4) *Fig. a*) formerly a sort of small cannon. *b*) a small anvil.

Einhorn-fisch, *m.* V. Einhorn, 2). —**käfer**, *m.* V. Einhorn, 3).

Einhörnig, *adj.* and *adv.* unicornous.

||**Einhotzeln**, **Einhutzeln**, *v. intr.* [u. w. seyn] to shrink up, to dry up.

Einhufig, *adj.* and *adv.* solidungulous. Das Pferd ist ein —es Thier, the horse is a solidungulous animal.

Einhüllen, *v. tr.* 1) to cover by winding something round, to involve, to wrap up. Sich —, to inwrap one's self [in a cloak, in a blanket &c.]; die Truppen waren in Staub eingehüllt, the troops were enveloped in dust. 2) to inclose, to contain.

Einig, *adj.* and *adv.* 1) only, sole. Es gibt nur einen —en Gott, there is only one God; Gott ist der —e Schöpfer und Herr der Welt, God is the sole creator and sovereign of the world; — im Wesen, [in theology] consubstantial, co-essential. 2) agreeing, assenting. Sie sind darüber mit einander —, they agree in it; die Meinungen sind hierüber noch nicht —, they differ in opinion yet; die Schriftsteller sind hierüber nicht —, authors differ about it; ich bin darüber mit mir selbst noch nicht —, I am not, as yet, determined with myself on that score; er ist mit sich selbst noch nicht —, he is not at one with himself; im Handel — werden, to agree to the price. 3) = friedlich. — mit einander leben, to agree well together, to live on friendly terms; mit Jemanden — werden, to reconcile to any one.

Einigen, *v. tr.* to make to agree, to unite. Sich —, to unite; sich mit Jemand —, to agree with a person.

Einiger, **Einige**, **Einiges**, *adj.* and *indef. pron.* [in the sing. it is only used with collective nouns] Einiger Rauch, some smoke; einige Beute, some prey; einiges Wasser, some water; er hat noch einiges Geld, he has some money yet; ohne einigen Schaden, without any loss; wenn noch einige Hoffnung vorhanden ist, if there be yet any hope left. [in the plur. it is used either alone, or with numerals or with nouns] Es waren einige Personen dabei, als sich die Sache zutrug, several persons were present when the event took place; einige Mahlle, sometimes; in einigen Punkten, in some points; [it sometimes precedes a word of number or quantity, with the sense of about or near] ein Dorf von einigen achtzig Häusern, a village of some eighty houses; ich war einige zwanzig Meilen weit davon, I was some twenty miles off. [Einige is often opposed to Andere] Einige glauben dies, Andere das, some men believe one thing, others another. Syn. **Einige**, **Etliche**, **Manche**. Manche denotes an indeterminate number of persons or things; not all, but many: einige and etliche convey an idea of a smaller number; more than two, but not many.

Einigermaßen, *adv.* in some degree, in some measure.

Einigkeit, *f.* 1) [the state of being one] unity, oneness. Die — Gottes, the oneness of God. 2) the existence of more than one in the same substance. Die — Gottes, the union of three persons in one Godhead. 3) [chiefly for] concord, agreement and conjunction of mind, will, affections or interest, union. Es herrscht eine vollkommene — unter ihnen, a perfect union subsists between them; sie leben in —, they live in harmony. *Prov.* Wo — ist, da wohnt Gott, where there is peace, God is there.

Einigung, *f.* 1) the act of uniting. 2) agreement, compact, contract, stipulation.

Einigungs-buch, *n.* [in theology] book of concord. —**formel**, *f.* [in ecclesiastical history] form of concord. —**punkt**, *m.* point of union.

Einimpfen, *v. tr.* to inoculate. Einem Kinde die Kuhpocken —, to inoculate a child with the cow-pox, to vaccinate a child; der Eingeimpfte, a vaccinated person. *Fig.* Jungen Gemüthern muß man bei Zeiten gute Gesinnungen —, good sentiments must be early instilled into the minds of youth.

Einjagen, I. *v. tr.* 1) to drive into, to chase into. *Fig.* Einem Furcht —, to fright or frighten any one, to strike or impress any one with fear; Einem Schrecken —, to strike any one with terror. 2) to break in [a dog] for the chase. II. *v. intr.* [u. w. seyn] 1) to drive, or ride into a place with great celerity. 2) to encounter with great celerity or rapidity.

Einjährig, *adj.* and *adv.* being one year old. Ein —es Kind, a child one year old; —e Pflanzen, [in botany] annuals.

Einjochen, *v. tr.* to put a yoke on. Ochsen or ein Paar Ochsen —, to yoke oxen or a pair of oxen.

||**Einkacheln**, V. Einheizen.

||**Einkaken**, V. Kaken.

Einkalken, *v. tr.* to smear, dress or prepare with lime. Die Felle —, [with tawers] to dress the skins with lime; ein Dach —, to join the tiles with lime.

Einkamm, *m.* [-es, *pl.* -kämme] [in carpentry] a flat tenon.

Einkämmen, *v. tr.* 1) to join by combing 2) [in carpentry] to join by a tenon.

Einkammern, *v. tr.* 1) to inclose, to confine into a small room, or closet. 2) [einkammriren] [in the Romish church] to unite lands, revenues, or other rights to the pope's domain. Das —, incameration.

Einkappen, *v. tr.* V. Verkappen.

Einkarren, *v. tr.* to cart into a place

Einkassen, [more usual] **Einkassiren**, *v. tr.* to call in money which is due. V. Eintreiben.

Einkästeln, *v. tr.* to inclose in a box or chest, to box, to enshrine.

Einkauen, *v. tr.* 1) to take in, to swallow chewing. 2) to feed with something previously chewed. *Fig.* †Einem etwas —, to explain something to any one repeatedly.

Einkauf, *m.* [-es, *pl.* -käufe] 1) the act of buying or purchasing, purchase. Sie versteht den —, she understands marketing. 2) [the thing purchased] purchase.

Einkauf-buch, *n.* [in commerce] purchase-book. —**s-preis**, *m.* first-cost, prime-cost.

Einkaufen, *v. tr.* 1) to buy, to purchase [goods, victuals &c.]. Vorräthe —, to buy or procure provisions, to cater. 2) to enter a society by purchase. Einen in das Spital —, to get a place for a person in a hospital by purchase. sich in die Sterbekasse —, to insure one's life.

Einkäufer, *m.* [-s, *pl.* -] —**inn**, *f.* a person that buys or provides provisions, purchaser, caterer, cateress.

Einkeep, V. Keep.

Einkeepen, *v. tr.* [in seamen's language] to score.

Einkehle, *f.* [*pl.* -n] 1) a gutter between two buildings, or a corner on a roof. 2) [with fishermen] the funnel-shaped opening of a sack-net. 3) [with hunters] a small netting used for catching partridges.

Einkehlen, *v. tr.* to provide with a gutter or a channel. Ein Dach —, to provide a roof with a gutter; eine Säule — [kannelliren], to channel, to chamfer or to flute a column.

Einkehlstein, *m.* a gutter-tile, pan-tile

Einkehr, *f.* [*pl.* -en] 1) the act of stopping at an inn, of putting up at an inn. Seine — bei Jemanden nehmen, to put up at any one's house; das Wirthshaus hat viele —, the inn is much frequented. *Fig.* [with religious enthusiasts] Die — des Gemüthes, abstraction. 2) house for the lodging and entertainment of travellers, an inn, public-house. Bierhäuser sind die —en für Müßiggänger, alehouses are the resort for the idle.

Einkehren, *v. intr.* [u. w. seyn] 1) [to visit] Bei Einem —, to visit a person; werden Sie im Vorbeigehen ein wenig bei mir —? will you call upon me in your way, for a short while? 2) to take lodgings. Wir kehrten in dem goldenen Adler ein, we put up at the Golden Eagle; er war im Kreuze eingekehrt, he inned at the Cross; und sie kehrten bei ihm ein, [in Script.] and they turned in unto him.

Einkeilen, *v. tr.* to fasten with a wedge, or wedges. Den Stiel in die Axt —, to wedge in the helve of an ax; einen Mühlstein —, to wedge in a mill-stone; die Form —, [in printing] to quoin [in] the form.

Einkellern, *v. tr.* to put or place in a cellar. Wie viele Fuder Wein haben Sie letzten Herbst eingekellert? how many tuns of wine did you lay in last autumn?

Einkerben, *v. tr.* 1) to cut in small hollow

zu jag. Einen Stock —, to notch a stick; eine Schachtel —, to make notches on a box; den Schweif eines Pferdes —, to nick a horse's tail [to make him carry it higher]. 2) to mark with notches or scores. Eine Schuld —, to mark a debt by cutting notches on a tally.

Einkerkern, *v. tr.* to incarcerate, to imprison, to confine in a jail. Die Einkerkerung, incarceration, imprisonment, confinement.

Einkernig, *adj.* and *adv.* [in botany] monopyrenous.

Einketteln, *v. tr.* V. Einketten.

Einketten, *v. tr.* to hang the chain in and confine by it.

Einkeulen, *v. tr.* to beat in with a club. *Fig.* †Einem Gehorsam —, to beat any one into obedience.

Einkind, *n.* [-es, *pl.* -er] V. Einkindschaft.

Einkinden, V. Ankinden.

Einkindschaft, *f.* 1) a regulation by which children of different beds receive equal portions. 2) adoption.

Einkitten, *v. tr.* to fix a piece of wood &c. in any thing with cement.

Einklagen, *v. tr.* to seek for in law. Eine Schuld —, to sue any one for debt.

Einklammern, *v. tr.* 1) to join or to fix something with cramp-irons. 2) *Fig.* to include [a word &c.] in hooks, curved lines or brackets, [in printing] to inclose. Eingeklammert, in a parenthesis.

Einklang, *m.* [-es, *pl.* -klänge] 1) accordance of sounds, unisonance; [in music] consonance. Der süße — der Töne, the sweet harmony of sounds. *Fig.* agreement, harmony. Im —e, in unison, in harmony; in — bringen, to accord; diese Regel steht im —e mit der Schrift und Vernunft, this rule is consonant to Scripture and reason; diese beiden Eheleute leben im musterhaftesten —e, this couple live in the most exemplary harmony. 2) [in music] unison. Im —e seyn, to be unisonous.

Einklängig, *adj.* and *adv.* unisonous, unisonant, harmonious.

Einklappen, I. *v. intr.* [u. w. seyn] to thrust or drive together, to clap together. *Fig.* || and * [u. w. haben] to tally. Es will nicht —, it won't tally. II. *v. tr.* to shut, to fold. Ein Taschenmesser —, to fold a pocket-knife into the handle; ein Messer zum —, a clasp-knife.

Einklappig, *adj.* and *adv.* [in botany] univalve, univalvular. Eine —e Blumenscheide, a univalve spathe.

Einklassen, *v. tr.* [seldom used] to arrange in a class or classes, to class.

Einklauig, *adj.* and *adv.* 1) having but one claw. 2) V. Einhufig.

Einkleben, *v. tr.* to fasten into with paste, to paste in.

Einkleiden, *v. tr.* 1) to put garments on, to clothe, to invest. *Fig.* Eine Sache gut —, to give a gracious turn to a thing; seine Gedanken gut —, to express one's thoughts with elegance or beauty, to clothe one's thoughts in beautiful language; er wußte seine Worte geschickt einzukleiden, he knew how to give a dexterous turn to his words. 2) to invest with a particular dress. Einen Mönch, eine Nonne —, to vest a friar or a nun with religious garments, to receive them into a monastic order; einen Geistlichen —, [in the Romish church] to induct a clergyman [to put him in actual possession of an ecclesiastical living, with the customary forms and ceremonies].

Einkleidung, *f.* 1) the act of putting garments on, or of investing with a particular dress, investment. Körperliche —, [in law] corporal investiture. 2) that with which any thing is clothed, [in a figurative sense] manner of arranging words in a sentence. Einer Sache eine gute — geben, to give an elegant turn to a thing, to recite a thing well.

Einkleistern, *v. tr.* 1) to fasten into with paste, to paste in. 2) to smear with paste or an unctuous substance. Die Haare —, to oint the hair.

Einklemmen, *v. tr.* to press between two bodies, to squeeze.

Einklettern, *v. intr.* [u. w. seyn] to climb into.

Einklingen, *ir. v. intr.* [u. w. seyn and haben] 1) to sound in, to penetrate with a sound. 2) to be unisonant, to accord.

Einklinken, I. *v. intr.* [u. w. seyn and haben] to catch the latch [said of a door]. Die Thür klinkt nicht recht ein, the latch of that door does not shut well. II. *v. tr.* to put in the latch, to latch.

Einklopfen, *v. tr.* 1) to knock in, to drive in. Einen Nagel mit dem Hammer —, to drive a nail into [wood &c.] with a hammer. *Fig.* †to instil by beating or knocking. 2) to break by beating, knocking.

Einknebeln, *v. tr.* 1) to insert a short stick or a gag in an opening. 2) to fasten by a short stick or gag; [in seamen's language] to put a rope in the beckets or fasten it by means of a wooden roller.

Einkneten, *v. tr.* to mix with the dough by kneading, to knead in.

Einknicken, *v. tr.* to bend so as to cause a break, to break partially, to crack.

Einknieen, *v. tr.* 1) to make hollow by kneeling. Die Stufen des Altars sind ganz eingekniet, the steps of the altar are worn by kneeling. 2) to break or crush with one's knees.

Einknöpfen, *v. tr.* to fasten in by buttoning.

Einknüpfen, *v. tr.* to fasten in by means of a knot. Geld in ein Taschentuch —, to tie money in a handkerchief. *Fig.* †Einem etwas —, to enjoin something on any one, to lay a command on any one.

||**Einknütten**, *v. tr.* V. Einstricken.

||**Einkobern**, *v. tr.* to basket.

Einkochen, I. *v. intr.* [u. w. seyn] 1) to diminish by boiling. Das Wasser ist zur Hälfte eingekocht, the water has half boiled up or away. 2) to thicken, to be inspissated by boiling. II. *v. tr.* 1) to inspissate or thicken by boiling. 2) to boil [water &c.] down. 3) to boil for future use.

Einkoffern, *v. tr.* [unusual] 1) to put in a trunk. 2) *Fig.* ‡to confine in a jail, to incarcerate.

Einkommen, *ir. v. intr.* [u. w. seyn] 1) to come in, to get in, to arrive. Die erforderlichen Urkunden sind heute eingekommen, the necessary documents have arrived or have been sent in today. 2) to apply to a person, court &c. for any thing. Er kam bei dem Fürsten um ein Amt ein, he applied to the prince for an office; um eine Stelle —, to put in for a place; mit einer Bittschrift —, to present a petition; mit einer Klage —, to prefer a complaint, [in law] to institute an action; bei einem Gerichtshofe —, to make application to a court; bei dem Gerichte um Schadenersatz —, to sue for damages; um die Begnadigung eines Verbrechers —, to sue out a pardon for a criminal; um die Abschaffung einer Verordnung —, to petition the abolishment of a decree; gegen etwas —, to protest against something; ||zu Rathhause —, [at Hamburgh &c.] to become a bankrupt. 3) to come in as profit, or revenue. Seine Pachtgelder kommen regelmäßig ein, his rents come in regularly; es kommt hier sehr wenig ein, the income is very small here. *4) to enter the thoughts, to have ideas come into the mind. Laß dir das nicht —, do not think of it.

Einkommen, *n.* [-s] 1) V. Einkunft, 1. 2) the act of applying to a person, court &c. for any thing. 3) income, revenue. Das — von Privatleuten, das — eines Staates, the income of private persons, the revenue of a state; euer — ist gering, your means are slender; von seinem — leben, to live on one's income.

Einkömmling, *m.* [unusual] [-es, *pl.* -e] 1) V. Ankömmling. 2) V. Häusling.

Einkömmlingsschein, *m.* [in almanacs] embolism.

Einkoppeln, *v. tr.* [in husbandry] to fence [a field].

Einkörben, *v. tr.* to basket. Einen Bienenschwarm —, to hive a swarm of bees.

Einkorn, *n.* [-es, *pl.* -körner] 1) the one-grained wheat. 2) [a genus of plants] phryma.

Einkörpern, *v. tr.* to include in a body, to incorporate.

Einkrachen, *v. intr.* [u. w. seyn] to crash, to break in, fall in or tumble down crashing or with a crash.

Einkrallen, *v. intr.* to strike in with the claws.

Einkramen, *v. tr.* 1) to put up, or pack up goods that were laid out for sale. *Fig.* *a*) to gather and put up. *b*) to cease trading or selling, and to fail. ||2) to buy in.

Einkratzen, *v. tr.* to excavate by scratching. Ein Loch —, to scratch a hole; seinen Namen in eine Wand —, to scratch one's name on a wall.

Einkreisen, *v. tr.* to encircle, to encompass. Wild —, [with hunters] to go round a thicket where game is lodged.

Einkriechen, *ir. v. intr.* [u. w. seyn] 1) to creep into. 2) [to contract spontaneously] to shrink. Wollenes Tuch kriecht im heißen Wasser ein, woolen cloth shrinks in hot water.

†**Einkriegen**, 1) V. Einbekommen. 2) V. Einnehmen. 3) V. Einholen.

Einkrimpen, *v. intr.* [in seamen's language] to slacken. Der Wind krimpt ein, the wind slackens.

Einkritzeln, *v. tr.* 1) to write in awkwardly. Seinen Namen in ein Buch —, to scrawl one's name into a book. 2) sometimes for Einkratzen.

Einkrümeln, *v. tr.* to crum into. Brod in Milch —, to crum bread into milk.

Einkrümmen, *v. tr.* and *r.* sich —, to bend inward.

Einkugeln, I. *v. tr.* to break by bowling. II. *v. r.* sich —, to roll one's self into a round form. Der Igel kugelt sich ein, wenn man ihn angreift, the hedge-hog, when attacked, rolls himself into a round form.

Einkunft, *f.* 1) [without a plural] the coming in. Nach — der erforderlichen Papiere, after the arrival of the requisite papers. 2) [*pl.* -künfte; chiefly used in the *pl.*] income, revenue. Er hat geringe Einkünfte, his means are slender; von seinen Einkünften leben, to live on one's income; die Einkünfte des Königs, the revenue of the king; die Einkünfte eines Staats [Staatseinkünfte], the revenues of a state or country.

Einkürzen, *v. tr.* 1) to make shorter, to shorten; [in seamen's language] to warp. 2) [in painting, to shorten figures for the sake of showing those behind] to fore-shorten.

Einkürzung, *f.* 1) shortening; [in seamen's language] warping. 2) [in painting] fore-shortening.

Einkürzungsleine, *f.* [in seamen's lang.] warp.

Einkutten, *v. tr.* [seldom used] to cowl.

Einkütten, V. Einkitten.

1. **Einladen**, [from laden = to load] *ir. v. tr.* to put in as a freight, to lade in. Waaren in ein Schiff —, to lade a ship with goods; einen Bienenschwarm —, [in husbandry] to hive a swarm of bees.

2. **Einladen**, [from laden = to bid] *ir. v. tr.* to invite, to ask, to bid. Gäste zu einer Hochzeit —, to ask guests to a wedding; Einen zum Mittagsessen —, to invite any one to dinner; Gesellschaft zu einem Gastmahle —, to invite company to an entertainment. *Fig.* Dieses Wetter ladet uns zu einem Spaziergange ein, this weather invites us to walk abroad; einladend, inviting, alluring, tempting.

1. **Einlader**, *m.* [-s, *pl.* -] loader.

2. **Einlader**, *m.* [-s, *pl.* -] inviter.

1. **Einladung**, *f.* the act of lading.

2. **Einladung**, *f.* 1) the act of inviting, invitation. 2) [the requesting of a person's company to visit &c.] invitation.

Einladungs-schreiben, *n.* a letter of invitation. —**schrift**, *f.* a program, or programma.

Einlage, *f.* [*pl.* -n] 1) the act of laying in, also the act of putting up or packing up goods that were laid out for sale [as at fairs &c.]. 2) that which is inclosed, inclosure. Die — [Inlage] in einem Briefe, the paper, note inclosed in a letter. 3) *the inner part of a folded stuff. 4) money deposited or contributed. Die — in or beim Spiel, stake V. also Einsatz.

Einlager, *n.* [-s, *pl.* -] [rather obsolete] 1) the state of being quartered or lodged in a place. 2) the right of taking lodgings at a person's house, or formerly in law, a kind of detention of a debtor at an inn [which he could not leave, till he had satisfied his creditor]. 3) the cantoning of troops in winter. — halten, or im — stehen, to be cantoned. 4) [the place of lodging or temporary residence of officers and soldiers] quarter, [or more usually] quarters.

Einlagergeld, *n.* quarter-money.

Einlagern, *v. tr.* [rather obsolete] to billet, to quarter [troops in the city or among the inhabitants, or on the inhabitants]. Sich —, to quarter; er lagerte sich im goldenen Hirsche ein, he took up his quarters at the Golden Stag.

Einlallen, I. *v. intr.* to fall in with a faltering tongue. II. *v. tr.* to lull asleep.

Einländer, V. Inländer.

Einländisch, V. Inländisch.

Einlangen, I. *v. tr.* to deliver with the hand, to deliver in. Eine Bittschrift — [more usual: einreichen], to present a petition. II. *v. intr.* [u. w. seyn] *a*) to arrive. Die Post langt um 7 Uhr ein, the post arrives at 7 o'clock; der Brief ist noch zeitig eingelangt, the letter arrived betimes or in due time. *b*) [of things] to be received. Es sind Klagen gegen ihn eingelangt, complaints were laid against him.

Einlappen, *v. intr.* [u. w. seyn] [with clockmakers] to be caught in the pallets [said of the ends of the verge].

Einlappig, *adj.* and *adv.* [in botany] monocotyle, monocotyledonous.

Einlaß, *m.* [-sses, *pl.* -lässe] 1) the act of letting in; *fig.* admission. Der — in die Stadt findet bis nach Mitternacht statt, the gate of the town is open till after midnight. 2) [in some towns] a small gate, a wicket. 3) [with goldbeaters] a thin iron bar with a hole, fastened to the rollers of the wire-drawing machine.

Einlaßgeld, *n.* money paid for admission, entrance-money. —**karte**, *f.* a ticket for the play-house or for other exhibition. —**klappe**, *f.* [in machines] a valve. —**ofen**, *m.* [in metallurgy] V. Kupferofen. —**preis**, *m.* V. —geld. —**zettel**, *m.* V. —karte.

Einlassen, *ir.* I. *v. tr.* 1) to permit or suffer to enter, to admit, to let in. Laßt meinen Freund ein, let in my friend. 2) to let flow or run. 3) to sink in, to fasten in, [in carpentry] to trim in. Nägel —, to drive nails entirely into the wood; in Blei eingelassene Nägel, nails mortised with lead; einen Zapfen —, [with ship-carpenters] to fill up a mortise with its tenon; die Scheerstöcke der Decke sind in die Deckbalken eingelassen, the ceilings are scored into the beams. II. *v. r.* sich —. Sich in etwas or auf etwas —, to have to do with a thing, to enter into a thing; sich mit Jemanden in ein Gespräch —, to join in conversation with any one; sich in Parteistreitigkeiten —, to engage in party disputes; sich in ein Bündniß —, to enter into a league; der junge Mann ließ sich unbesonnener Weise in Spekulationen ein, the young man embarked rashly in speculations; ich lasse mich darauf nicht ein, I do not meddle with it; ich kann mich auf Ihren Vorschlag nicht —, I cannot enter into your proposal; sich mit Jemanden —, to have to do with a person; *sich mit einem Frauenzimmer —, to have an intrigue or familiarity with a woman; sich mit Jemanden tief —, to go a great length with any one; sich auf eine Klage —, to answer to an action or charge.

Einlauben, *v. tr.* [seldom used] to furnish with leaves, to cover with leaves.

Einlauf, *m.* [-es, *pl.* -läufe] 1) the act of entering into a place. Der — [more usual das Einlaufen] des Schiffes in den Hafen, the sailing of a ship into the harbour. 2) [in studs] liberty granted to a stallion, to walk freely among the mares.

Einlaufen, *ir. v. intr.* 1) to enter into, to run in, to run into, to step in with celerity. Aus- und —, to run out and in; das Wasser läuft ein [in den Kahn], the water enters the boat; eine Kugel — lassen, to drop a bullet into the barrel; der Hengst läuft ein, [in studs] the stallion walks freely among the mares; —, [of ships] to sail into a port, to touch or call at any port; in einen Hafen —, to enter a harbour; wir liefen in Calais ein, we put in at Calais, we ran in to Calais. 2) [of things] to come in, to arrive. Die heute eingelaufenen Briefe, the letters which have come in to-day; es liefen Nachrichten aus London ein, we had news from London; es lief gerade die Nachricht ein, news has just arrived; es sind viele Klagen über or gegen ihn eingelaufen, many complaints have gone in against him. 3) to contract spontaneously, to shrink; [in printing] to get in. Wollenes Tuch läuft im heißen Wasser ein, woolen cloth shrinks in hot water; beim Walken —, to shrink in fulling.

Einlaugen, *v. tr.* to soak or steep in lye, to wash in lye. Leinwand —, to buck linen-cloth.

Einlaut, [unusual] *adj.* and *adv.* uniform.

Einläuten, *v. tr.* to announce [a feast &c.] by the ringing of bells.

Einlegen, *v. tr.* 1) to lay in, to put in. Holz —, to put wood into the stove; einen Brief —, to inclose a letter; das Papier in den Deckel —, [in printing] to put in the blank sheets; Reben —, to provine; Nelken —, to lay carnations; Aurikeln —, to earth auriculas; die Häute —, [with tanners] to put the hides in the pit; die Häute in's Treibfaß —, [with leather-dressers] to soak the hides; Häringe —, to water herrings; Wäsche —, to steep linen in water. 2) to lay or put in the fixed place. Die Lanze —, to fix the spear in the rest [in the posture of attack], to couch the spear; mit geschlossenen Visiren, mit eingelegten Lanzen, their vizors closed, their lances in the rest; eingelegte Arbeit, work inlaid with variegations of fine wood, shells, ivory and the like, inlaid work, marquetry; in Elfenbein —, to inlay with ivory; eingelegt, inlaid, ornamented with marquetry; mit Gold, mit Silber eingelegte Stahlarbeit, damaskeened steel-work. *Fig.* Soldaten zur Besatzung —, to garrison a fort or town; den Einwohnern Soldaten —, to quarter or billet troops among the inhabitants or on the inhabitants; ||Einem den Presser [Exequenten, Steuerbüttel] —, to quarter the bumbailiff in any one's house; ein gutes Wort für Jemanden —, to put in a word for any one, to plead in favour of any one, to intercede for any one; Lob, Schande mit etwas —, to get praise or disgrace by a thing; Ehre mit etwas —, to get, to gain honour by a thing; eine Berufung —, [in law] to appeal. 3) to lay up, to lay in a place for preservation, to reposit for preservation or for future use. Bier, Wein —, to deposit beer or wine in a cellar, to lay in beer, wine; Vorräthe —, to lay in, to store up provisions; Aepfel für den Winter —, to put up apples for winter; Gurken —, to pickle cucumbers; Fleisch —, to put up meat; Waaren bei Jemanden —, to deposit goods in the hands of a person. 4) to lay inward, to fold. Ein Messer zum —, a knife which folds into the handle, a clasp-knife; ein Stück Zeug —, to fold, to turn in a piece of stuff.

Einlege-deckel, *m.* [in printing] the inner-tympan. —**gabel**, *f.* a clasp-fork. —**geld**, *n.* entrance-money. V. also Legegeld. —**holz**, *n.* [with cabinet-makers] veneer. —**löffel**, *m.* a clasp-spoon. —**messer**, *n.* a clasp-knife. —**schaufel**, *f.* [in glassworks] a sort of shovel. —**stuhl**, *m.* a folding-chair.

Einleger, *m.* [-s, *pl.* -] 1) he that lays in or puts in; he that inlays. 2) the layer of a vine. ||3) a clasp-knife.

Einlehren, *v. tr.* to teach, to instruct.

‡ **Einleiben**, V. Einverleiben.

Einleimen, *v. tr.* to glue in.

Einleiten, *v. tr.* to lead or bring in, to conduct into a place, to introduce. In die Stadt —, to conduct into the town. *Fig.* Eine Sache —, to give a direction to an affair, to manage it; Kennen Sie D.'s neueste Schrift, eingeleitet von Göthe? do you know D.'s latest work, introduced by [or with a preface of] Goethe? einleitend, serving as the means of bringing something forward, introductive; einleitende Bemerkungen, introductory remarks; den Frieden —, to plan, to lay the preliminaries to the peace; eine Untersuchung —, to institute an inquiry. eine Rechtssache —, to institute a suit.

Einleiter, *m.* [-s, *pl.* -] he that conducts a person into a place, or that gives a direction to an affair, or manages it.

Einleitung, *f.* 1) the act of managing, of setting in operation, of instituting. Die — einer Rechtssache, the instituting of a suit; die —en zum Frieden, the preliminaries to the peace; die nöthigen —en zu etwas treffen, to arrange the necessary preparatives to something. 2) [the pr of a discourse &c. which precedes the main work] introduction. Die — eines Buches, something written as introductory to a book, the preface; die — einer Rede, preamble, exordium; Bemerkungen, welche als — dienen, introductory remarks; die — zu einem Singspiele, overture, prelude. 3) an introduction to any science. — zur Rechtswissenschaft, an introduction to jurisprudence.

Einleitungs-punkt, *m.* preliminary article. Die —punkte des Friedens, the preliminaries to the peace. —**spiel**, *n.* prelude, overture.

Einlenken, I. *v. intr.* to turn back to the right direction. In den Weg —, to turn back to the right way. *Fig. a*) to return from a digression, to resume a discourse; to give a turn to a thing. *Er war nahe daran, mir Grobheiten zu sagen, lenkte aber klüglich wieder ein, he was in the point of using insulting language towards me, but prudently changed his tone; aber lassen Sie uns wieder —, but let us return! but to return! *b*) to return to virtue, to mend, to reform. II. *v. tr.* to lead or conduct into the right way.

Einlernen, *v. tr.* to learn, or get by heart, to commit to memory, to study. Seine Predigt —, to learn one's sermon by heart; eine Rede —, to con a speech.

Einlesen, *ir. v. tr.* 1) [in weaving] to sley. ||2) to gather in, to glean. 3) Sich —, *a*) to make one's self acquainted with by reading or perusing. Haben Sie sich schon in diese Akten, Papiere &c. eingelesen? have you already gone over these records, papers &c.? *b*) [rather unusual] to read asleep.

Einleser, *m.* [-s, *pl.* -] gatherer, gleaner.

Einleuchten, *v. intr.* to penetrate as a light. *Fig.* Der Grund ist einleuchtend, the reason is clear; Dinge, welche Gelehrten —, things, obvious to scholars; ein —der Beweis, a plain argument; es leuchtet ein &c., it is evident &c.

Einlieben, [unusual] *v. r.* sich —, to insinuate one's self into favour, to make one's self beloved.

Einliefern, *v. tr.* to put into another's hand or power. Waaren —, to deliver goods; Einem Geld —, to deliver money to any one; gestohlene Dinge —, to deliver up stolen things; einen Verbrecher —, to commit a criminal; einen Ausreißer —, to bring back a runaway. Die Einlieferung, the act of putting into another's hand or power, delivery, deliverance.

Einliegen, *ir. v. intr.* [u. w. seyn] to lie in a place, to be lodged or quartered in a place.

Einlieger, *m.* [-s, *pl.* -] 1) lodger. 2) V. Häusler.

Einling, *m.* [unusual] [-es, *pl.* -e] a single thing.

Einlippig, *adj.* and *adv.* having but one lip, [in botany] unilabiate, as a corol.

Einlispeln, *v. tr.* to whisper in. *Fig.* to insinuate, to suggest.

Einlochen, *v. tr.* [in carpentry] to hole [a post for the insertion of rails &c.].

Einlöffeln, *v. tr.* 1) to take [a potion] by spoons. 2) to give or administer with a spoon.

***Einlogiren**, [pronounce: einlogiren] *v. tr.* to lodge, to house, to quarter. Sich —, to take a lodging or apartment, to take up one's quarters.

Einlösen, *v. tr.* to purchase back, to regain possession of a thing alienated or pawned, by repaying the value of it to the possessor, or pawnee. Ein Pfand —, to redeem a pledge; sein Versprechen —, to redeem one's promise, to make good one's word; einen Wechsel —, to answer or draw in a bill.

Einlöthen, *v. tr.* to solder in.

Einludeln, *v. tr.* [in gunnery] to prime [a cannon].

Einlullen, *v. tr.* to lull asleep. *Fig.* to lull, to calm, to soothe.

Einmachen, *v. tr.* 1) to cover by wrapping, to inwrap. In einen Pack —, to pack; in eine Schachtel —, to put up in a box. 2) to condite, to candy, to preserve. In Zucker —, to candy; eingemachte Quitten, preserved quinces; eingemachte Kirschen, candied cherries; Champignons —, to condite mush-rooms; in Töpfe eingemachtes Geflügel, potted fowl; Gurken —, to pickle cucumbers; Fleisch —, to put up meat; Fische —, to marinate fish; Eingemachtes, something preserved, preserve, confection. 3) to mix with water. Den Teig —, to moisten and knead the dough; Kalk —, to dilute lime. 4) [*frikassiren] [in cookery] to mince and dress with a sauce. Eingemachtes [*frikassirtes] Kalbfleisch, minced veal dressed with a sauce.

Einmähdig, *adj.* and *adv.* [in husbandry] capable of being mown only once a year.

Einmahl, *adv.* I. Einmahl. 1) one time, once. Nur — in zwei Jahren, but once in two years; — des Jahres, once a year; ich war noch — so alt wie sie, I was double their age; noch mehr als — so lang, more than as long again; er ist noch — so dick, he is as big again; lesen Sie die Stelle noch —, read this passage again; wenn ich Sie noch — mit Ihren Streichen ertappe, if I discover you at your tricks again; erzählen Sie es noch —, tell it over again; — über das andere, again and again; — eins ist eins, one multiplied by one produces the number one; das Einmahleins, the multiplication-table; das große Einmahleins, the great multiplication-table. *Fig.* *Ein so unwissender Mensch, der es noch nicht bis zum Einmahleins in dieser Wissenschaft gebracht hat, a fellow so ignorant that has not got through the very first rudiments of this science. *Prov.* Wer — stiehlt, ist immer ein Dieb, once a knave, and never an honest man; — ist keinmahl, once is no custom. 2) at the same point of time, not gradually; unexpectedly, suddenly. Auf —, on a sudden, all at once; auf — erheben sich die Winde, die Donner rollen, at once the winds arise, the thunders roll. 3) often it is used as an expletive, or emphatically. Da wir nun — vom Kriege sprechen, now that we are speaking of war; ich sage es — für allemahl, es kann nicht seyn, I tell you that, once for all, it cannot be! 4) it is often opposed to another time. — reden sie so, das andere Mahl so, or anders, at one time they say so, at another so; — will er es haben, das andere Mahl wieder nicht, one time he will have it, another time he will not.

II. Einmähl. 1) noting a former time, a time to come, the present time, or an indefinite time. Es war — ein Mann, there was once a man. 2) in familiar or common language it is used emphatically, as, kommen Sie doch — her, pray, do come here; stellen Sie sich — vor, well, imagine, only think; kommst du endlich —? do you come at last? 3) sometimes it is joined to a negation, as, ich habe es nicht — gehört, I did not so much as hear it; er hat mir nicht — geantwortet, he did not so much as answer me; er besann sich nicht —, he did not even hesitate. 4) V. Einmahl 1. 5) V. Einmahl 2.

Einmahleins, *n.* V. Einmahl 1.

‡**Einmahlen**, *adv.* V. Einmahl.

1. **Einmahlen**, [from mahlen = to grind] *v. tr.* 1) to lessen or diminish by grinding. 2) to grind [corn to meal] for future use.

2. **Einmahlen**, [from mahlen = to paint] *v. tr.* to paint in. Sie sollten hier noch ein Schlaglicht einmahlen, you should paint in a stroke of light there.

Einmahlig, *adj.* done but once, happening but once.

Einmahnen, *v. tr.* to get in by urging for payment.

Einmaischen, V. Einmeischen.

Einmännerig, *adj.* and *adv.* having but one man. *Fig.* [in botany] monandrian. —e Pflanzen, monanders.

Einmännig, *adj.* and *adv.* adapted for one man.

Einmännisch, *adj.* and *adv.* adapted for one man. Ein —es Bett, a single bed.

|| and †**Einmanschen**, *v. tr.* to dabble in water, to plash.

Einmarken, *v. tr.* to border with mere-stones.

||**Einmarkten**, *v. tr.* to market, to buy.

Einmarsch, *m.* [-es, *pl.* -märsche] the marching in.

Einmarschiren, *v tr.* to march in. Die Truppen sind in die Stadt einmarschirt, the troops entered the town.

Einmaß, *n.* [-es] [in husbandry] a loss of corn by mice &c. when heaped up.

Einmaster, *m.* [-s, *pl.* -] a vessel with a single mast, as a sloop or cutter.

Einmastig, *adj.* and *adv.* having a single mast, one-masted.

Einmauern, *v. tr.* 1) to fix [a bullet &c.] in a wall with brick or stone, and mortar. Das eine Ende [eines Balkens &c.] —, [in carpentry] to tail in. 2) to surround with walls, to inclose within walls. Einen Sarg —, to immure a coffin; einen Mönch, eine Nonne —, [formerly, in convents, for punishment] to immure a monk, a nun; Verbrecher —, to immure criminals in prison, to confine criminals in a jail.

Einmehlen, [seldom used] *v. tr.* to sprinkle with flour. Sich —, to besprinkle one's self with flour.

Einmeischen, *v. tr.* Malz —, to soak malt with boiling water.

Einmeißeln, *v. tr.* 1) to work in with the chisel. Ein Loch in den Stein —, to hole the stone by chiseling. 2) to hole, to open with a chisel.

Einmengen, *v. tr.* to mix in, to mix up. *Fig.* Sich —, to meddle officiously, to interpose or interfere improperly, to intermeddle. Einer, der sich in Alles einmengt, a meddler, an officious person, a busy-body.

Einmengsel, *n.* [s, *pl.* -] [in contempt] something intermingled, a superfluous ingredient; *it.* medley, hodge-podge.

Einmessen, *ir.* I. *v. tr.* to measure into. Korn —, to measure corn and to pour it into sacks; Wein —, to measure wine and to pour it into a vessel. II. *v. r.* sich —, to be lessened in measuring, to diminish by being measured.

||**Einmiethe**, *f.* [*pl.* -n] a duty paid for permission to gather fire-wood in a forest.

Einmiethen, *v. tr.* to take a lodging for somebody. Sich —, to take a lodging; er hatte sich in dieses Haus auf ein Jahr eingemiethet, he took this house for a year; ||sich in einen Wald —, to get permission to gather fire-wood in a forest, by paying a certain duty.

Einmischen, I. *v. tr.* to put some things with others, to intermix. Fremde Wörter in eine Rede —, to interlace a discourse with foreign words; sie mischten einige Irrthümer ein, they interlaced some errors; Unwahrheiten in eine Erzählung —, to interlace a narration with falsehoods. II. *v. r.* sich —, to meddle officiously, to intermeddle.

Einmummeln, Einmummen, *v. tr.* to cover close, particularly the neck and face, to muffle, to muffle up. Sich —, to muffle one's self up.

Einmünden, *v. intr.* 1) to disembogue, to fall into. Die Elbe mündet in die Nordsee ein, the Elbe falls into the Northern Ocean; der Neckar mündet in den Rhein ein, the Neckar discharges its waters into the Rhine; unzählige Flüsse münden in das Weltmeer ein, innumerable rivers disembogue into the ocean. 2) [in anatomy] to inosculate. Eine Blutader mündet in eine Schlagader ein, a vein inosculates with an artery.

Einmündung, *f.* 1) disemboguement. 2) [in anatomy] anastomosy, anastomosis.

Einmündungswinkel, *m.* the angle of disemboguement.

Einmünzen, *v. tr.* 1) to coin, to mint. 2) to coin, or mint anew.

Einmustern, *v. tr.* to enroll, to enter in the muster-roll.

Einmuth, *m.* [also *f.*] [unusual] concord or agreement in sentiments, harmony.

Einmuthen, *v. tr.* to sollicit admission into a society or corporation.

Einmüthig, I *adj.* agreeing, living in peace and friendship, harmonious, unanimous. Eine —e Familie, Gesellschaft, a harmonious family, society. II. *adv.* in peace and friendship, harmoniously. Sie leben sehr — zusammen, they live in great harmony.

Einmüthigkeit, *f.* harmony, peace and friendship, unanimity, unanimousness.

‡**Einmüthiglich**, *adj.* and *adv.* V. Einmüthig.

Einnageln, *v. tr.* to fasten with nails in the inside of a thing.

Einnagen, *v. r.* sich —, to enter by gnawing. Es muß sich eine Maus in diesen Käse eingenagt haben, a mouse must have gnawed a hole in this cheese. *Fig.* Der Kummer nagt sich in mein Herz ein, sorrow preys upon my heart.

Einnähen, *v. tr.* 1) to fasten into by sewing. Einen Aermel in das Hembe —, to sew a sleeve to the shirt; sein Geld war in seine Kleider eingenäht, his money was sewed up in his clothes. 2) to work with the needle figures or ornaments upon a thing. 3) to take in by sewing.

Einnahme, *f.* [*pl.* -n] 1) the act of gaining possession of a thing. Die — einer Stadt, the taking of a town [by force or capitulation]; die — eines Schiffes, the capture of a ship; die — des Geldes, the receipt of the money. 2) the thing received, that gain which proceeds from labour, business or property of any kind, the proceeds of professional business, the profit of commerce or of occupation. Die jährliche —, the annual receipts; eine geringe or schmale —, a small income; ein kluger Mann regelt seine Ausgaben nach seiner —, a prudent man limits his expenses by his income; die —n des Staates, the revenues of the state; die — an der Kasse betrug am heutigen Theaterabend 200 Gulden, the receipts at the theatre last night were 200 florins. 3) the place where money is received, the receiver's office. Die Zoll—, the receipt of custom.

Einnahmebuch, *n.* receipt-book.

Einnässen, *v. tr.* to wet thoroughly.

Einnebeln, *v. tr.* [rather unusual] to cover with fog. *Fig.* Die Wahrheit —, to cloud the truth.

Einnehmen, *ir. v. tr.* 1) to take in, to take. Die Segel —, to take in, to shorten, to brail or furl the sails. 2) to take, as meat or drink, as medicine &c. Das Frühstück —, to breakfast; das Abendbrot [Abendessen] —, to sup; das Mittagsmahl —, to dine; Pillen —, to take pills; Arzenei —, to take physic; einen Trank —, to take down a potion; [as a *v. intr.*] ich habe heute eingenommen, I have taken physic to-day. 3) to take in, to admit, to receive. Einen —, to receive any one into one's house; Besatzung —, to receive a garrison; das Schiff lief in den Hafen ein, um Wasser und Holz einzunehmen, the ship put into port, to take in water or to water and to wood. *Fig.* *Vorwürfe —, to take reproaches; Beleidigungen —, to put up injuries; Beschimpfungen —, to bear indignities; ‖eine Klage —, to hear a suit. 4) to gain possession of, to take. Eine Festung —, to take a fort; eine Stadt, to conquer a city; nach tapferem Widerstande von Seiten des Feindes nahmen wir endlich das Dorf ein, after a gallant resistance on the part of the enemy we possessed ourselves at length of the village; ein Schiff —, to take or capture a ship; einen Posten —, to take a post; einen Wald —, to occupy a forest. *Fig.* Dieser Wein nimmt den Kopf ein, this wine affects the head, intoxicates; der Champagner nimmt den Kopf ein, Champagne is a heady wine; Jemanden mit etwas —, to persuade any one to something; von Vorurtheilen eingenommen seyn, to be prepossessed with prejudices; das Herz —, to win on the heart; er war von dieser Sache so eingenommen, he was so taken with this thing; eingenommen von Jemanden seyn, to be captivated with a person; gegen Jemanden —, to prejudice against any one; Jemanden durch sein Betragen für sich —, to win any one by one's conduct; eine —de Gesichtsbildung, a pleasing countenance; —de Manieren, engaging manners; eine —de Schönheit, a captivating or fascinating beauty; von sich selbst eingenommen seyn, to have a vain or too high conception of one's person or accomplishments, to be conceited. 5) to fill a space or place. Eines Andern Stelle —, to take a place which another has left, *fig.* to succeed any one; eine feste Stellung —, [in military affairs] to take up a strong position; ein ganzes Haus —, to occupy a whole house; einen großen Raum —, to take up a great deal of room. 6) to receive that gain which proceeds from labour, business or property of any kind. Geld —, to receive money; viel, wenig —, to have a great or small income; öffentliche Gelder —, to receive public money; Steuern —, to collect or gather taxes. Syn. V. Erobern.

Einnehmer, *m.* [-s, *pl.* -] an officer appointed to receive public money. Ein Steuer—, a collector of taxes, tax-gatherer.

Einnehmerei, *f.* 1) the office or function of a collector of taxes. 2) the house or office of a collector.

Einnetzen, *v. tr.* to wet thoroughly. Wäsche —, to sprinkle linen with water; Tuch —, to spunge cloth.

Einnicken, *v. intr.* [u. w. seyn] to fall asleep nodding.

Einnieten, *v. tr.* to fasten by riveting in the inside of a thing.

Einnisteln, *v. r.* sich —, to nest. *Fig.* *Sich in einem Orte —, to nestle one's self in a place, to settle there clandestinely.

Einnisten, I. *v. intr.* to nestle, to n[illegible]t. Die Schwalben nisten hier ein, the swallows build here. II. *v. r.* sich —, to nestle. *Fig.* *Sich —, to nestle one's self in a place, to gain footing in a place.

Einnöthigen, *v. tr.* Einem Essen oder Trinken —, to urge or press a person to take meat or drink.

Einöde, I. *adj.* and *adv.* desert, waste. II *f.* [*pl.* -n] a solitude, a wilderness, a desert. *Fig.* Dieses Haus ist eine wahre —, this house is quite a solitude. Syn. Einöde, Wüste, Wildniß. Einöde is a place uninhabited by human beings, but not necessarily uninhabitable. Wildniß is a place that is uncultivated and uninhabitated, but may by industry and art be rendered habitable. Wüste is a tract of land not only not cultivated or inhabitated, but from the sterility of the soil or other cause incapable of becoming so.

Einöhrig, *adj.* and *adv.* having one ear only

Einölen, *v. tr.* to smear the inside of a thing with oil, to oil. Ein Schloß —, to oil the inside of a lock; Leder —, to smear leather over with oil; die alten Ringkämpfer pflegten sich vor dem Beginn des Kampfes wohl einzuölen, ancient gladiators used to anoint themselves before a combat.

Einpacken, I. *v. tr.* to put in a trunk, box &c. to pack, to pack up. Kleider zu einer Reise — to put up clothes for a journey; Waaren —, pack up goods. II. *v. intr.* to pack up. Ich ka[nn] Sie nicht begleiten, ich muß erst —, I can't a[c]company you, I must first pack up. *Fig.* † [er] mußte —, he was disappointed of his intentio[n]; sie hat arg eingepackt, she has sadly fallen [from her former beauty].

Einpalmen, *v. tr.* [in seamen's language] haul in [a rope].

Einpapieren, *v. tr.* [rather unusual] to [en]velop with paper. Die Zuckerhüte —, to enve[lop] the sugar-loaves with paper; [with clothiers] Tuch —, to put pressing-cards in the folds o[f a] lapped piece of cloth.

Einpappen, *v. tr.* to paste in. Papier in e[ine] Kiste —, to line a box with paper.

‖**Einpaschen**, *v. tr.* to import clandestin[ely] and contrary to law, to smuggle in.

Einpassen, I. *v. intr.* to fit in, to be adapt[ed]. II. *v. tr.* 1) to fit one thing into another. Ein Fenster —, to fit in a window. 2) [in carpentry] trim in [as a piece of timber into other work].

Einpassiren, *v. intr.* to pass in, to enter

†**Einpauken**, I. *v. tr.* 1) to break by kn[ock]ing. 2) *Fig.* V. Einbläuen. II. *v. r.* sich —, [stu]dent's cant] 1) to exercise one's self in figh[ting]. 2) *Fig.* to become skilled in, or acquainted [with] a thing by much exercise or study.

Einpeitschen, *v. tr.* 1) to cause to ente[r by] whipping. 2) *Fig.* to teach, to instil by [repe]tition of blows.

Einpelzen, *v. tr.* 1) [in gardening] to i[nsert] by inserting the cion into the bark. 2) to [wrap] up in fur.

Einpersönig, [rather unusual] *adj.* and [*adv.*] consisting of one person only.

Einpersönlich, [rather unusual] *adj.* and [*adv.*] one person only being present.

Einpfählen, *v. tr.* to inclose, to fence [with] pales, stakes or palisades, to pale. Einen [Garten einpfäh]len, to fence a garden with pales.

Einpfarren, *v. tr.* to unite with a [parish.] Eingepfarrte Dörfer, villages belongi[ng to a] parish; die Eingepfarrten, the inhabit[ants of] such villages, the parishioners.

Einpfeffern, *v. tr.* 1) to sprinkle [pepper] copiously, to season with much pepper. [2) to] preserve in pepper.

Einpfeifen, I. *v. intr.* to penetrate whist[ling]. Der Wind pfeift hier ein, the wind wh[istles] through here. II. *v. tr.* [in gardening] to inoc[ulate] [French, enter en flûte].

Einpferchen, *v tr.* to pen, to fold [sheep]. *Fig.* *Wir saßen bei Tische wie eingepfercht, we were much crowded at table.

Einpflanzen, *v. tr.* 1) to plant [trees &c.]. 2) *Fig.* to implant. Ein eingepflanzter Haß, an inveterate hatred or enmity.

Einpflastern, *v. tr.* 1) to surround [a place, a way &c.] with pavement. 2) to put stones into a place to be paved.

Einpflöcken, *v. tr.* to fasten a thing into another with pegs, to peg in.

Einpflücken, *v. tr.* to gather and throw into a basket &c.

Einpflügen, *v. tr.* 1) to plough in, to cover by ploughing. Den Mist oder Dünger —, to plough in dung. 2) to do away by the plough.

Einpfropfen, *v. tr.* 1) to ingraft by inserting the cion into the bark. *Fig.* to stuff, to cram. Eingepfropfte Meinungen, ingrafted opinions. 2) to cork in. 3) *Fig.* † to cram. Man pfropfte uns in den engsten Sitz ein, we were squeezed or crammed into the narrowest seat.

Einpfünder, *m.* [-s, *pl.* -] one-pounder [said of small cannon].

Einpfündig, *adj.* and *adv.* of one pound.

Einpfützen, *v. tr.* [in mining] to scoop in [water].

Einpichen, *v. tr.* 1) to fix a thing in another with pitch. 2) to smear or pay over with pitch. Ein Seil —, to pitch a rope.

Einpilgern, *v. intr.* [u. w. seyn] to enter a place as a pilgrim.

Einplacken, *v. tr.* [in seamen's lang.] Haar und Papier hinter die Spikerhaut —, to apply the sheathing-hair to a ship's bottom.

Einplaudern, *v. tr.* 1) to lull asleep by talking. 2) to talk something into a person.

Einplumpen, I. *v. intr.* [u. w. seyn] to plump into water. II. *v. tr.* † to plump in.

Einpochen, *v. tr.* to break by knocking, to knock in.

Einpökeln, *v. tr.* to pickle [beef &c.].

Einprägen, I. *v. tr.* to impress, to imprint, to stamp. Auf Wachs —, to imprint on wax. *Fig.* Einem etwas —, to inculcate something on any one. SYN. V. Einschärfen. II. *v. r.* sich —, to be fixed on the mind. Seines Vaters Ermahnungen haben sich seinem Gemüthe eingeprägt, his father's admonitions are imprinted on his mind.

Einpredigen, I. *v. tr.* 1) to teach or to instil by preaching. 2) to inculcate any thing with earnestness. Ich habe ihnen oft Bekehrung eingepredigt, I often preached to them conversion. II. *v. r.* sich —, to exercise one's self in preaching.

Einpressen, *v. tr.* to press, to squeeze. Die Schnürbrust preßt den Unterleib zu sehr ein, the stays press too much the belly; Bücher —, to put books into the press, to press books. *Fig.* Sich —, to squeeze into a narrow space; eingepreßt seyn, to be pressed by want of sufficient room.

Einproben, **Einprobiren**, *v. tr.* 1) to try to put a thing into another thing. 2) to repeat in private for experiment and improvement. Eine theatralische Aufführung —, to rehearse a theatrical representation; seine Rolle —, to rehearse one's part.

Einprügeln, *v. tr.* to teach or instil by blows.

Einpudern, *v. tr.* to powder thoroughly, to powder. Das Haar —, to powder the hair; sich —, or sich das Haar —, to powder one's hair.

Einpumpen, *v. tr.* to pump in.

Einpünktig, *adj.* and *adv.* 1) having one point only. 2) having a common centre, concentric.

Einpuppen, *v. r.* sich —, [in entomology] to change to a chrysalis.

Einpusten, *v. tr.* to breathe or blow down.

***Einquartiren**, *v. tr.* to quarter [soldiers]. Soldaten in Privathäuser —, to billet soldiers in private houses.

Einquellen, I. *v. tr.* to soak [seeds, pease &c.]. II. *v. intr.* 1) to penetrate [as water]. 2) V. Aufquellen.

Einquerlen, *v. tr.* to mill or beat in.

Einquetschen, *v. tr.* to squeeze between something.

Einraffen, *v. tr.* 1) to snatch or huddle together. 2) [in seamen's language] V. Einreffen.

Einrahmen, *v. tr.* to put in a frame. Ein Bild —, to frame a picture.

Einrammeln, **Einrammen**, *v. tr.* to ram into the earth. Pfähle —, to ram piles into the earth.

***Einrangiren**, [pron. einrangiren] *v. tr.* to place in a series or row, to arrange in a continued line, [of soldiers] to enroll.

Einrathen, *ir. v. tr.* to persuade [a person to do something]. Man hat ihm eingerathen, vorsichtig zu seyn, he was advised to be cautious.

Einrauchen, *v. intr.* [seldom used] to penetrate as smoke. Es raucht ein, smoke enters the room.

Einräuchern, *v. tr.* 1) to apply smoke to, to smoke. Kleider, ein Zimmer —, to fumigate clothes, a room; sie pflegten die Bildsäule des Gottes einzuräuchern, they used to incense the statue of the god. 2) to smoke [meat &c.] for future use.

Einräumen, *v. tr.* 1) to move [goods &c.] into any place. 2) to give room to. Einem seinen Platz —, to yield one's place to a person; Einem ein Zimmer —, to accommodate any one with an apartment. 3) *Fig.* *a*) to admit as true, to allow, to grant. Die Wahrheit eines Satzes —, to allow the truth of a proposition; dies kann ich nicht —, I cannot admit that; wir räumen ein, daß ihre Bürger &c., we concede that their citizens &c. *b*) to allow, to permit. Er räumt seinen Knaben zu viele Freiheiten ein, he allows his boys too many liberties.

Einraunen, *v. tr.* Einem ein Wort —, to whisper a word in any one's ear; *fig.* to suggest something to any one.

Einrechen, *v. tr.* to rake into a place.

Einrechnen, *v. tr.* to reckon in, to include in the account. Die Auslagen or Vorschüsse —, to comprise the disbursements in the account.

Einrede, *f.* [*pl.* -n] 1) contradiction, opposition, objection, remonstrance. Er kann keine — vertragen, he cannot bear any contradiction. 2) [in law] *a*) exception, plea. Eine — vorbringen, to put in a plea. *b*) a forbidding of the bans. — thun, to forbid the bans.

Einreden, I. *v. tr.* to persuade by talking. Einem etwas —, to persuade any one to do or believe something; Einem Muth —, to encourage any one; er läßt sich nichts —, he is deaf to advices. II. *v. intr.* 1) to interrupt any one that speaks. Rede ihm nicht ein, do not interrupt him. 2) to contradict any one, to oppose any one by words. Er läßt sich nicht —, he does not bear opposition.

Einreffen, *v. tr.* [in seamen's lang.] to reef [the sails].

***Einregistriren**, *v. tr.* to enregister, to register, to record, to enrol.

Einregnen, *v. imp.* to penetrate as rain. Es regnet hier ein, the rain enters here.

Einreiben, *ir. v. tr.* 1) to cause to enter by rubbing, to rub in. Eine Salbe —, to rub in a salve; mit Spiritus —, to embrocate with spirit; Fleisch mit Salz —, to rub meat with salt. 2) to add to by rubbing. Brod in die Milch —, to rasp bread into milk. 3) to rub with something on the inside. Die Form —, [in casting busts and statues] to rub the inside of the mould with oil; Farben —, [with painters] to rub colours.

Einreibeholz, *n.* a small piece of wood with notches used by bookbinders.

Einreiber, *m.* [-s, *pl.* -] he that rubs something in.

Einreibung, *f.* 1) the act of rubbing in. 2) [in medicine and surgery] embrocation. Die — von Mercurialmitteln, mercurial unction.

Einreichen, I. *v. tr.* to transmit from one's self to another, to present. Eine Bittschrift —, to present a petition; seine Beschwerden schriftlich —, to exhibit a written statement of one's grievances. II. *v. intr.* *Fig.* Dieses Pferd reichet ein, [in manege] this horse overreaches.

Einreichung, *f.* presentation.

Einreichungs-frist, *f.* term for presentation. **—zeit**, *f.* the date of presentation.

Einreihen, *v. tr.* 1) to place in series, to arrange into a continued line, to range, to rank. 2) to enrol, to enlist [a soldier]. 3) [with tailors and sempstresses] to gather and baste. 4) [with weavers] Die Fäden —, to separate the threads of the warp. 5) to thread, to string [pearls &c.].

Einreiher, *m.* [-s, *pl.* -] 1) he that places persons or things in a series &c. 2) something gathered and basted in sewing, as a ruff.

Einreihig, *adj.* and *adv.* consisting of one row. [in botany] Eine —e Traube, a unilateral raceme.

Einreißen, *ir.* I. *v. intr.* [u. w. seyn] 1) to be torn inward. Dieser Zeug reißt leicht ein, this stuff rends easily; das Holz reißt ein, the wood splits. 2) *Fig.* *a*) to spread. Gefährliche Krankheiten sind in diesem Jahre eingerissen, dangerous diseases prevail this year; üble Gewohnheiten reißen ein, bad habits gain ground; das Uebel reißt immer mehr ein, the evil continues to spread. *b*) *Es reißt in's Geld or in den Beutel ein, it costs a great deal of money. II. *v. tr.* 1) to tear, to rend. Ein Stück Zeug —, to rend a piece of stuff. 2) to pull down, to pull to pieces. Eine Mauer, einen Zaun —, to throw down a wall, a fence; ein Haus, ein Gerüst —, to take down a house, a scaffolding.

Einreiten, *ir.* I. *v. intr.* [u. w. seyn] to pass into a place on horseback, to ride in. Er ritt in die Stadt ein, he made his entry into the city on horseback, he entered the town on horseback. II. *v. tr.* to overturn [a stall &c.] by riding over, to break [a door, a window &c.] by riding violently against it.

Einrenken, *v. tr.* to set [a dislocated joint].

Einrennen, *ir.* I. *v. intr.* [u. w. seyn] 1) to enter a place running, to run in. 2) *Fig* to run or flow in [said of liquids]. 3) Aufeinander —, to run one against another. II. *v. tr.* to break or force upon by running against. Er hat die Thüre eingerannt, he ran against the door and broke it in; eine Mauer mit dem Sturmbock —, to batter a wall with a battering ram.

Einrichten, *v. tr.* 1) [to return to its proper place and state, to replace] to set [a bone or a leg]. 2) to put right. Ein Hufeisen —, [with farriers] to flatten a horse-shoe. *Fig.* *a*) to set in order, to arrange. Sein Hauswesen ist gut eingerichtet, his household affairs are well regulated; er ist recht hübsch eingerichtet, he has fitted up his lodgings very prettily; ein Haus zum Empfange eines Gastes —, to fit up a house for a guest; er ist noch nicht eingerichtet, he has not furnished his house yet; einen Laden —, to set up a shop; ||seine Tochter —, to supply one's daughter with household furniture; eine Gesellschaft —, to organize a club; ein gut eingerichteter Staat, a commonwealth well ordered; ein gut eingerichtetes Hauswesen, a well ordered house. *b*) to make suitable, to fit or suit, to adapt or accommodate. Seine Handlungen nach dem Gesetze —, to square one's actions by the law; unser Leben nach den Vorschriften der heiligen Schrift —, to frame our lives according to the rules of the Gospel; unser sittliches Betragen nach den Gesetzen der Gesellschaft —, to regulate our moral conduct by the laws of society; unsere Ausgaben nach unserm Einkommen —, to proportion our expenditures to our income; richtet den Unterricht nach der Fassungskraft der Jugend ein, let instruction be adapted to the capacities of youth; richte die Geberden nach der Leidenschaft ein, die ausgedruckt [or ausgedrückt] werden soll, suit the gestures to the passion to be expressed; Sie müssen die Sachen darnach —, you must dispose matters accordingly; er richtete die Sache so ein, daß er mit ihr allein blieb, he ordered the matter so, as to be alone with her; [in arithmetic] gemischte Brüche —, to reduce mixed fractions or numbers into imperfect fractions. 3) [with hunters] [= einschließen] Das Wild —, to inclose the game with toils.

Einrichter, *m.* [-s, *pl.* -] a disposer, a regulator, an arranger.

Einrichtung, *f.* 1) the act of putting in proper order, arrangement. Die — eines Knochens, reduction; die — einer Schule, the setting up of a school; die — einer Manufactur, the setting up of a manufactory. 2) manner in which things are arranged. Die — der verschiedenen Theile eines Gebäudes, the disposition of the several parts of an edifice; die — der Theile einer Rede, the disposition of the parts of a discourse; die — einer Maschine, the mechanism of an engine. 3) previous disposition, arrangement, preparation. —en zu etwas treffen, to make arrangements for something; er traf verschiedene gute —en, he made several good regulations. 4) * clothes, furniture, goods, vessels, necessary or convenient for house-keeping, utensils necessary or convenient for any trade. 5) establishment, household-establishment. 6) *pl.* [with locksmiths] wards. 7) *pl.* the shelves of a cup-board.

Einriegeln, *v. tr.* 1) to shut a bolt. 2) to confine [any one in a room] by bolting the door. Sich —, to shut one's self in by bolting the door.

Einriffen, V. Einreffen.

Einringeln, I. *v. tr.* 1) to curl [the hair]. 2) to fit with a small ring. Einen Knaben —, to pass a ring through the prepuce of a boy, to practice infibulation on a boy. II. *v. r.* sich —, 1) to curl &c. 2) to coil in.

Einringen, [rather unusual] *v. tr.* to encircle, to surround with something resembling or having the form of a ring.

Einrinnen, *ir. v. intr.* [u. w. seyn] to leak into a space or opening.

Einriß, *m.* [-sses, *pl.* -sse] a rent, tear, fissure, a slit.

Einritt, *m.* [-es, *pl.* -e] entrance on horseback.

Einritzen, *v. tr.* 1) to make a scratch in a thing. Einen Stamm —, [in gardening] to slit a stem for the insertion of a cion. 2) to scratch into. Seinen Namen in eine Fensterscheibe —, to scratch one's name on a pane of glass.

Einröhrig, *adj.* and *adv.* consisting of one tube.

Einrollen, I. *v. tr.* 1) to roll inwards. Eine eingerollte Knospe, [in botany] an involuted bud. 2) to roll, to roll up in. Geld —, to roll up money in paper. 3) [rather unusual] to write in a roll or register, to enrol. Der Eingerollte, a man enrolled for service. II. *v. intr.* [u. w. seyn] to roll inwards, to roll into.

Einrollung, *f.* 1) the act of rolling inwards, the act of enrolling, enrolment. 2) something rolled up, a roll.

Einrosten, *v. intr.* [u. w. seyn] 1) to stick to any thing by rust. Der Degen ist in die Scheide eingerostet, the sword has rusted into the scabbard. 2) to contract rust, to rust.

Einrücken, I. *v. intr.* [u. w. seyn] to enter a place in a military manner, to march into. Ins Lager —, to march into the camp, to encamp. 2) to succeed or come in the place of another. II. *v. tr.* 1) to move inwards. [chiefly used] *Fig.* to insert. Ich werde seine eigenen Worte —, I shall insert his own words; eine Klausel —, to put in a clause; eine Bekanntmachung in ein öffentliches Blatt —, to insert an advertisement in a public paper; das Eingerückte, the thing inserted, insertion. 2) Eine Zeile —, [in writing or printing] to draw in a line.

Einrückegebühr, *f.* money paid for the insertion of an advertisement or a notice in a public paper. Die —gebühren, *pl.* costs of advertisement.

Einrücksel, *n.* [-s, *pl.* -] V. [the more usual word] Inserat.

Einrückung, *f.* 1) the act of marching into a place. 2) *Fig.* insertion.

Einrückungsgebühr, *f.* V. Einrückegebühr.

Einrudern, *v. intr.* [u. w. seyn] to enter a place by rowing. In den Hafen —, to row into the harbour.

Einrufen, *ir. v. tr.* to call in.

Einrühren, *v. tr.* 1) to mix by beating. Ein Ei in die Fleischbrühe —, to beat up an egg with the broth. 2) to stir up together with another thing. Ein Pulver mit Wasser —, to mix a powder with water; eingerührte Eier, buttered eggs. 3) to stir, to mingle for future use.

Einrunzeln, *v. intr.* [u. w. seyn] to wrinkle, to shrink.

Einrußen, *v. tr.* to cover or foul with soot, to soot. Eingerußt, soiled with soot, sooted.

Einrütteln, *v. tr.* 1) to cause to enter shaking. 2) to shake up well.

Eins, *contr.* of Eines, V. Ein. I. as a *subst.* and as a *pron. indef.* Die —, eine —, the number one; —, zwei, drei, one, two, three. *Fig.* In Einem fort, continually, unceasingly; — ist Noth, one thing is necessary; — und das Andere, this and that; — für das Andere, one thing for another; *es ist mir Alles —, it is all one to me; *es kömmt auf — heraus, it is all one, it comes to the same thing; †er hat ihm — angehängt, he has fastened something, some joke upon him. II. *adv.* 1) of one mind, in a state of concord, of friendship or of agreement. Ich bin nicht mit ihm —, we differ in opinion; über eine Sache — werden, to agree on a thing; er ist mit mir über den Preis — geworden, he agreed with me for the price. ||2) V. Einmahl. Mit —, at once, on a sudden.

Einsaat, *f.* [in husbandry] the seed-corn.

Einsäckeln, *v. tr.* 1) to pocket. 2) *Fig.* receive.

Einsacken, *v. tr.* to put in a sack. Getr[i] —, to sack corn, to confine corn in a sack. *F[i]* †to pocket [used also *intr.*] †Er hat tüchtig gesackt, he has pocketed handsomely.

Einsäen, *v. tr.* to scatter seed over for gro[...] Einen Acker —, to sow a field.

|| and ‡**Einsage**, *f.* [*pl.* -n] V. Einrede.

Einsagen, *v. tr.* to direct or dictate wha[t] to be uttered or written, to indite. Einem Sch[...] spieler etwas —, to prompt an actor; Ein[...] etwas —, to dictate something to any one.

Einsägen, *v. tr.* to cut into with a saw.

Einsaitig, *adj.* and *adv.* having one st[...] only. Ein —es Tonwerkzeug, a monochord.

Einsalben, *v. tr.* 1) to anoint, to smear wi[...] an unctuous substance. Den Kopf —, to ano[...] the head. 2) [in the Romish church] to confirm [...] anointing. ||3) to embalm.

Einsalzen, *v. tr.* to sprinkle with salt, [...] preserve and season with salt, to salt, to p[...] Rindfleisch —, to corn beef.

Einsam, *adj.* and *adv.* 1) not having [...] pany, lonely, solitary. Ein —es Leben —, [...] litary life; er führt ein —es Leben, he l[...] retired life; die — in dem Walde wohnen[...] dwell solitarily in the wood; der —e [...] the lonely traveller; —e Thiere, solitar[y] gregarious animals [which never or seldom are in flocks or herds]. 2) *Fig. a*) retired, not frequented, solitary. Ein —er Ort, a so[...] place; in einem —en Thale, in a secluded [...] questered valley; —e Landsitze, lonesome [...] in —en Wäldern, in lone woods; seine —e [...] his lonely cell. *b*) noting a time, when w[...] alone, and not disturbed by noise. In der [...] Stunde der Mitternacht, in the solitary or [...] hour of midnight. *c*) enjoyed in solitude [...] parated from company or observation. Ein [...] Vergnügen, a pleasure enjoyed in solitude [...] —es Gebet, a private prayer; eine —e Be[...] tung, a private meditation. ||*d*) lone; singl[...] married, childless. Syn. Einsam, Allei[n] [Al]lein expresses merely the state of being alone, [...]ing company, without any reference to the d[...] this state. Einsam is applied to one who usua[...] in solitude, or who is remote from all society. [...] therefore, always implies a greater seclusion [...]ciety.

Einsa[a]mig, *adj.* and *adv.* having o[...] only, [in botany] monospermous.

Einsamkeit, *f.* 1) [a state of being alon[e] [...]liness, solitude. In —, in solitude or p[...] retiredly; in — leben, to live a retired [...] *Fig. a*) loneliness, solitude [applied to plac[es] — eines Waldes oder Thales, the soli[...] solitariness of a wood or valley; die — [...] Klosters, the retiredness of a cloister. 3) [...]ly place, a solitude. In diesen —en, i[...] solitudes.

||**Einsamlich**, *adj.* and *adv.* V. Einsa[m].

Einsammeln, *v. tr.* to gather, to [...] Früchte —, to gather or collect fruits; [...] —, to collect flowers; Wein —, to ga[ther the] crop of grapes; die Stimmen —, to ga[ther,] collect the votes; Steuern —, to collec[t ...] Beiträge —, to collect contribution[s ...] Kenntnisse —, to acquire knowledge or [...] any branch of science or literature. Das [Ein]sammeln or die Einsammlung, a gathering [...]lecting.

Einsammler, *m.* [-s, *pl.* -] collector, [...]eror.

Einsang, [unusual] *m.* [-es, *pl.* -sänge [...] music] a solo.

Einsargen, *v. tr.* to coffin [a dead human body].

1. **Einsasse**, *m.* [-n, *pl.* -n] V. Insaß[e].

2. **Einsasse**, *m.* [-n, *pl.* -n] [in carpentry] a mortise.

Einsatz, *m.* [-es, *pl.* -sätze] 1) the act of putting in, of laying, or staking. Den — thun, to stake, to lay. 2) that which is set, thrown down, or laid, stake. Der — beträgt zehn Thaler, the stakes are ten dollars; der — beim Würfeln, set; die Einsätze bei gewissen Kartenspielen &c., pool, poule 3) a thing set upon another, pile; as Dukaten im — wägen, to weigh ducats by piles. 4) a set of things of which one fits into the other or a number of things inserted in each other. Ein — Schachteln, a nest of boxes; ein — Schüsseln, a nest or set of dishes; ein — Gewichte, a pile of weights, cup-weight. ||5) a pledge or pawn. 6) [rather unusual] something inserted in a public paper, insertion, notice, advertisment. 7) a reservoir, a small fish-pond. 8) [with goldsmiths] a hold-fast.

Einsatz-becher, *m.* a cup which fits into another cup. —**eisen**, *n.* V. Einsatz 8. —**gewicht**, *n.* cup-weight. —**schachtel**, *f.* a box which fits into another. —**teich**, *m.* a small fish-pond.

†**Einsauen**, *v. tr.* to befoul, to soil [a book, one's clothes &c.].

Einsäuern, *v. tr.* 1) to mix with leaven. Den Teig —, to leaven the dough. ||2) *a)* to pickle [cucumbers &c.]. *b)* to marinate [fish].

Einsaufen, *ir. v. tr.* to drink in, to take down, to swallow.

Einsaugen, *ir.* I. *v. tr.* to draw into the mouth, to drink in, to suck in, to suck up. Böse Milch —, to suck in bad milk; der Schwamm saugt das Wasser ein, the spunge imbibes or absorbs water. *Fig.* Einsaugende Gefäße, [in anatomy, in botany] lymphatic vessels; Irrthümer, schlechte Grundsätze —, to imbibe errors, bad principles. II. *v. r.* sich —, 1) to penetrate sucking. 2) *Fig.* to adhere closely, to hang to.

Einsauge-ader, *f.* V. Saugader. —**gefäß**, *n.* 1) [in anatomy] V. Saugader. 2) [in botany] lymphatic vessel. —**mittel**, *n.* [in medicine] an absorbent. —**röhre**, *f.* a lymphatic vessel.

Einsäugen, *v. tr.* to instil as by sucking the breast.

Einsäumen, *v. tr.* [to fold and sew down the edge of cloth to strengthen it] to hem.

Einsäuseln, I. *v. intr.* [n. w. seyn] to enter blowing gently, to penetrate with a low, rustling sound. II. *v. tr.* to cause to sleep by a low amusing sound, or by blowing gently, to lull asleep by gentle breezes, by the sounds of an Aeolian harp &c.

Einsausen, *v. intr.* [n. w. seyn] to enter blustering, roaring, like a hurricane.

Einschaben, *v. tr.* 1) to add a thing to another by scraping. 2) to scratch into.

Einschachern, *v. tr.* to purchase by chaffering or haggling.

Einschachteln, *v. tr.* 1) to inclose or shut up in a box. 2) to put one box into another, to insert a box in another. *Fig.* Eine Stelle in die andere —, to insert one passage in another.

Einschaffen, I. *v. tr.* 1) to bring in, to import. 2) to buy. Lebensmittel —, to buy or procure provisions, to cater. ||II. *v. r.* *Er hat sich diese Materie tüchtig eingeschafft, he made himself thoroughly acquainted with this concern.

Einschalig, *adj.* and *adv.* univalve, as a shell. —e Muscheln, univalves.

Einschalten, *v. tr.* to insert. Einen Tag —, to intercalate a day; der eingeschaltete Tag [Schalttag], the intercalary day; die eingeschalteten Monate, [in chron.] the embolismal months; das eingeschaltete Jahr, the embolismic year; ein Wort in eine Schrift —, to insert a word in a writing; eine Stelle —, to put in a passage; eine eingeschaltete Erzählung, an episode.

Einschaltung, *f.* 1) the act of inserting, insertion. Die — eines Schalttages im Kalender, intercalation; [in astronomy] embolism. 2) something inserted, [in grammar, the insertion of a letter or syllable in the middle of a word] epenthesis, epenthesy. 3) [in the polite arts and sciences] an episode.

Einschaltungszeichen, *n.* [in grammar] caret.

Einschanzen, *v. tr.* to fortify [a city, town or harbour]. Das Heer schanzte das Lager ein, the army entrenched the camp. *Fig.* Einen Ort —, to ensconce, to secure a place. V. Verschanzen.

Einschärfen, *v. tr.* 1) to sharpen, to whet. V. Schärfen. 2) *Fig.* to inculcate with earnestness. Einem etwas —, to impress a thing on any one; ein Vater schärft seinen Kindern die Pflicht des Gehorsams ein, a parent enjoins on his children the duty of obedience. Syn. Einschärfen, Einprägen. Einprägen signifies merely to impress something on the mind in order that it may be retained in the memory; einschärfen implies, to enforce, to urge something on the mind, so as to move it to action, and incite it to the fulfillment of duties. We endeavour einzuprägen [to impress] upon on the memory of a child the words of a language which it is required to learn, but we einschärfen [enforce] on its mind rules for its conduct, obedience to its parents.

Einscharren, *v. tr.* 1) to cover with earth, to bury. 2) [in contempt] to bury, to inter [hastily, slovenly or without any religious ceremonies]. Sie haben ihn draußen an der Kirchhofsecke eingescharrt, they buried him at the corner of the churchyard. 3) Geld —, to sweep in money.

Einschatten, *v. tr.* to shade, to obscure.

Einschattig, *adj.* and *adv.* having the shadow fall one way only, heteroscian. [in geography] Die —en Völker, heteroscians.

Einschauern, [unusual] *v. tr.* to bring under a shed, to bring into shelter.

Einschaufeln, *v. tr.* to shovel in.

Einschaukeln, *v. tr.* to cause to sleep by swinging, to rock asleep. *Fig.* Von den Meereswellen eingeschaukelt, rocked asleep by the billows.

Einscheiden, [rather unusual] *v. tr.* 1) to sheath [a sword in a scabbard]. 2) *Fig.* to inclose as in a sheath.

Einschenken, *v. tr.* 1) to pour in. Wein oder Bier —, to pour wine or beer into a glass; Kaffee —, to pour coffee into a cup; erlauben Sie mir, Ihnen ein Glas einzuschenken, give me leave to pour you out a glass; einem Gaste ein Glas —, to fill a glass for a guest; soll ich Ihnen ein Glas Wein —? shall I help you to a glass of wine? *Fig.* *Einem klaren Wein —, to tell any one the plain truth; † Einem eins —, to play any one a trick. 2) [at tennis] to send [the ball which is to be driven by a racket] with the hand.

Einscherig, V. Einschürig.

Einscheuern, *v. tr.* 1) to bring into the barn. Das Getreide —, to get in corn. 2) *Fig.* [rather vulgar] to gather, to secure.

Einschichten, *v. tr.* to lay into a stratum, to couch.

Einschichtig, *adj.* and *adv.* having but one layer, stratum or couch.

Einschicken, *v. tr.* to send in. Berichte —, to transmit dispatches; eine Bittschrift —, to address a petition to somebody.

Einschieben, *ir. v. tr.* 1) to shove in. Brod in den Ofen —, to shove bread into the oven; eine Leiste —, [with joiners] to shove a clamp into the groove; Geld —, to pocket money. 2) to shove among others, to put in. [chiefly] Ein Wort —, eine Stelle —, [to foist in, to insert a spurious word or passage in a manuscript or book] to interpolate a word, a passage; eine eingeschobene Stelle, *a)* a surreptitious passage [in a manuscript or book], an interpolation. *b)* a parenthesis; *Einen —, to put any one in the place or office of another without just right; sich —, to intrude on the place or office of another, to supplant an other. 3) to break or rend a part in playing at nine-pins. 4) *Fig.* Sich —, to exercise one's self in playing at nine-pins on a certain bowling-ground.

Einschiebe-essen, *pl.* [small plates set between the principal dishes at table] entremets, side-dishes. —**leiste**, *f.* [with joiners] a clamp. Einen Tisch mit einer —leiste versehen, to clamp a table to prevent its casting, warping]. —**zeichen**, *n.* parenthesis [()].

Einschiebsel, *n.* [-s, *pl.* -] [frequently in contempt] something put in, inserted or interpolated, a parenthesis.

Einschießen, *ir.* I. *v. tr.* 1) to destroy by shooting, that is, by fire-arms or artillery. Eine Mauer mit Kanonen —, to batter down a wall with cannon. 2) to prepare for shooting, to fit for shooting. Ein Gewehr —, to try a gun by repeated shooting; ein Pferd —, to use a horse to stand fire. 3) to shove in, to put in. Das Brod —, [with bakers] to shove the bread into the oven. 4) to throw among other things, to throw in, [among weavers] to cross the weft or woof by means of the shuttle. II. *v. r.* sich —, 1) to exercise one's self in shooting. 2) *Fig.* *to exercise one's self, to make one's self well acquainted by exercise or study. Gut eingeschossen in &c., well versed or skilled in &c.

Einschiffen, I. *v. intr.* to sail into. In den Hafen —, to sail into port, to put in. II. *v. tr.* to put on board of a ship, to ship. Waaren —, to ship goods; Truppen —, to embark troops; sich —, to go on board of a ship, to go aboard, to embark.

Einschildern, *v. tr.* Farben —, [with cotton-printers] to paint calico [as opposed to print].

Einschirren, *v. tr.* to harness [the horses].

Einschlachten, *v. tr.* to butcher for future use, to kill [swine, geese &c.] for the use of the house.

Einschlafen, *ir. v. intr.* [n. w. seyn] 1) to fall asleep, to get asleep. Ein Kind durch Wiegen, Singen &c. — machen, to rock, to sing &c. a child asleep. *Fig.* Der Fuß ist mir eingeschlafen, my foot is asleep. 2) *Fig.* *a)* to fall asleep, to die. Er ist sanft eingeschlafen, he died an easy death. *b)* to slacken, to abate, to cease. Sein Eifer schläft ein, his zeal abates; die Sache schlief ein, the affair dropt. *c)* [in seamen's language] to lose way.

Einschläfen, V. Einschläfern.

Einschläferig, *adj.* and *adv.* single [said of a bed].

Einschläfern, *v. tr.* to cause to sleep, to dispose to sleep. Ein Kind durch Wiegen, mit or durch Singen —, to rock, to sing or lull a child to sleep; einschläfernd, inducing sleep, causing sleep, narcotic, narcotical, soporific, soporiferous, somniferous; ein —des Mittel, a soporific, a narcotic; —des Geschwätz, drowsy prate. *Fig.* Einen durch leere Versprechungen —, to lull any one into security by idle promises.

Einschläferung, *f.* 1) the act of causing sleep. 2) something causing or inducing sleep, or disposing to sleep, drowsy words or prate.

Einschläferungsmittel, *n.* a soporific, a narcotic.

Einschlag, *m.* [-es, *pl.* -schläge] 1) the act of striking into, of putting into, as the act of giving a person one's hand or of shaking hands with any one [in sign of an agreement being concluded]. 2) that which is put in or between, as with weavers, the threads that cross the warp in weaving, the woof or weft, the filling. 3) that which is inclosed in another thing. Der — eines Briefes, a note, paper or letter, inclosed in a letter. 4) [with tailors and sempstresses] that part of a garment, shirt &c. which is folded, doubled, or turned in, fold, doubling. 5) [with farriers] V. Umschlag. 6) [something put or hung into a cask to relish wine or to give it a higher colour] pearl. 7) [with hunters] that which sticks to the claws of a stag in walking. 8) [in commerce] coopering.

Einschlagseide, *f.* shoot-silk.

Einschlagen, *ir.* I *v. tr.* 1) to drive into by striking or beating, to beat into. Einen Nagel in das Holz —, to drive a nail into wood with a hammer; Pfähle in die Erde —, to ram piles into the earth; den Eintrag —, [with weavers] to weave the weft across the warp; Eier —, [in cookery] to break eggs and put them into something [as into broth &c.]; eingeschlagene Eier, poached eggs. *Fig.* to teach, to inculcate, to instil by blows 2) to cause to enter, to put in as by beating or striking. Getreide —, to measure corn and sack it; Salz —, to put salt in baskets, to basket salt; Holz —, to pile wood; den Wein —, to put pearl into wine 3) to wrap up, to cover by putting something round; [in printing] to wrap in. Waaren —, to wrap up goods in paper &c., to pack goods; der Kaufmann schlägt Waaren in Packtuch ein, the merchant envelops goods with canvass; einen Brief —, to envelop a letter in paper, or to inclose a letter in another; Bäume —, to earth the roots of transplanted trees; Rüben, Möhren in Sand —, to cover turnips and carrots with sand for preservation. *Fig.* [with hunters] Jagdhunde bei Jemanden —, to charge a person to nourish one's hounds; Schweine —, [in husbandry] to place hogs to feed in the woods, to turn out hogs to mast, to put hogs to mast; einen Bienenschwarm —, to hive a swarm of bees. 4) to part by force or violence, to beat to pieces, to break. Thüren —, to break doors open; sie schlugen ihm die Fenster ein, they broke his windows; dem Fasse den Boden —, to stave in the head of a cask; Einem die Zähne —, to beat out any one's teeth. 5) [with tailors and sempstresses] to turn in [the edge of cloth]. 6) [in a more figurative sense] Einen Weg —, to take a road; schlagen Sie diesen Weg ein, take this way. *Fig.* Den Weg der Güte —, to use fair means; einen Vergleich —, to come to an arrangement.

II. *v. intr.* 1) [u. w. haben] *a*) to give a person one's hand or to shake hands with any one [in sign of an agreement being concluded]. Schlag ein! give me your hand upon it! *b*) to dig in, to break ground. Nach einem Dachse —, [with hunters] to dig a badger; der Töpfer und Ziegelbrenner schlägt ein, the potter and the brickmaker digs for clay; der Bergmann schlägt ein, the miner digs for ore. *c*) to fall [as lightning]. Der Blitz schlug an mehreren Orten ein, the lightning fell into different places; der Blitz hat in die Kirche eingeschlagen, or es hat in die Kirche eingeschlagen, the church was struck or injured by lightning. *d*) *Fig.* to have reference or relation to. Dieser Satz schlägt in die Naturlehre ein, this proposition belongs to physics; *das schlägt in mein Fach ein, that's my province. 2) [u. w. seyn] *a*) to recede from the surface, to strike in. Die Farbe schlägt ein, [with painters] the colour soaks in; die Blattern schlagen ein, the small-pox strikes in, disappears. *b*) to proceed, to thrive. Seine Kinder sind alle gut eingeschlagen, all his children are successfully educated; wenn das Getreide dies Jahr gut einschlägt, if the corn turns out well this year; diese Pflanzen schlagen gut ein, these plants come on, thrive well; unser Handel und unsre Manufakturen schlagen gut ein, our commerce and manufactures prosper; dieser Plan schlug nicht ein, that design did not succeed; das Spiel schlägt mir nicht ein, the play does not favour me; endlich schlug ihm das Spiel ein und er gewann, at last he got a run of luck and he won.

Einschlagemesser, *n.* V. Einlegemesser.

Einschläger, *m.* [-s, *pl.* -] he that drives in &c., especially a miner that digs for ore.

Einschlägig, *adj.* and *adv.* belonging to. Die —en Behörden, Gerichtshöfe, the competent authorities, courts.

Einschleichen, *ir. v. intr.* [u. w. seyn] and *v. r.* Sich in einen Ort —, to creep, sneak or steal into a place; es hat sich ein Dieb eingeschlichen, a thief entered the house secretly. *Fig.* Er schlich sich in die Gunst des Hofes ein, he insinuated himself into the good graces of the court; es haben sich einige Irrthümer in die Abschrift dieser Geschichte eingeschlichen, some errors have crept into the copy of that history; es haben sich allerhand Mißbräuche in die Verwaltung eingeschlichen, sundry abuses have crept into the administration.

Einschleiern, *v. tr.* 1) to cover with a veil, to veil. 2) to give [a novice] the veil.

1. **Einschleifen**, [from schleifen = to grind] *ir. v. tr.* to mark by grinding. Dem Glase einen Namenszug —, to form, to cut a monogram on a glass.

2. **Einschleifen**, [from schleifen = to drag] *v. tr.* 1) to drag in, to bring in upon a sledge or a drag. 2) *Fig.* V. Einschleppen.

Einschleppen, *v. tr.* 1) to drag in [wood &c.]. Ein Schiff —, to tow a ship into port. 2) to import secretly. Waaren —, to import goods which are forbidden by the gouvernment to be imported, to run goods; verbotene Bücher —, to bring in stealthily forbidden books; eine Seuche aus einem Orte or Lande in einen andern Ort or ein anderes Land —, to introduce a pestilential disease from one place or country into another, in some clandestine manner.

Einschleudern, *v. tr.* to break by something thrown with a sling.

Einschließen, *ir.* I. *v. intr.* to catch [said of a lock]. II *v. tr.* 1) to cause to catch [said of a lock]. Das Schloß —, to lock. 2) to confine within, to include, to shut in, to inclose, to surround, to take in. Eine Perle ist in einer Muschel eingeschlossen, a pearl is inclosed in a shell; einen Brief —, to inclose a letter, or to inclose a letter in another; der Brief war in den meinigen eingeschlossen, the letter was inclosed in mine; einen Vogel in einen Käfig —, to encage, or to coop a bird; ein Feld mit einem Zaune —, to inclose a field with a fence, to fence a field; eine Stadt mit Wällen oder Mauern —, to inclose a town with walls, to wall a town; von Bergen eingeschlossen, shut in, environed with mountains; von Truppen eingeschlossen, surrounded with troops; eine Festung —, to inclose a fort with troops; eine Stadt —, to invest, to begird, to blockade a town; eine Besatzung in einer Stadt —, to confine a garrison in a town; ein Belagerungsheer schloß die Stadt Jerusalem ein, a besieging army encompassed the city of Jerusalem; eine Stelle —, to include a passage in brackets, to put it in parenthesis; eingeschlossen, in a parenthesis. *Fig.* to include, to comprehend, to comprize. Die Geschichte von England schließt einen Theil der Geschichte Frankreichs nothwendig in sich ein, the history of England necessarily includes a portion of that of France; der or den König von Schweden mit eingeschlossen, the king of Sweden included; schließen Sie mich in Ihr Gebet ein, remember me in your prayers. 3) to shut up, or confine, as with a lock, to lock up. Schließen Sie Ihr Geld ein, lock up your money; Schmucksachen in einem or in ein Kästchen —, to inclose trinkets in a box; in eine Kiste —, to lock up in a chest; Einen —, to lock any one up; er schloß mich in ein dunkles Zimmer ein, he shut me up in a dark room; in ein Gefängniß —, to shut up in prison, to lock in a prison; er hat sich eingeschlossen, um nicht von lästigen Besuchern gestört zu werden, he shut himself up, not to be troubled by tiresome visitors; sich in seine Bibliothek —, to shut one's self up in one's library; der Studirende schließt sich freiwillig in Mauern ein, a student immures himself voluntarily; sich in ein Kloster —, to cloister one's self.

Einschließzeichen, *n.* V. Einschließungszeichen.

Einschließlich, *adj.* and *adv.* including, comprehended in the number or sum, inclusive. Vom Montag bis zum Sonnabend —, from Monday to Saturday inclusive.

Einschließung, *f.* the act of locking in or up, of shutting up, of including or inclosing, inclusion, or the state of being included, inclosure. Die — einer Stadt, investment of a town.

Einschließungszeichen, *n.* a bracket, hook. Mit —zeichen versehen, to put in parenthesis.

1. **Einschlingen**, [from schlingen = to swallow] *ir. v. tr.* to swallow, to englut. Gierig —, to swallow eagerly, to gulp, to regorge. *Fig.* *to swallow, to receive implicitly.

2. **Einschlingen**, [from schlingen = to twine] *ir. v. tr.* 1) to put in a loop. 2) to furnish with a loop.

Einschlitzen, *v. tr.* to slit [the ear or tongue &c.].

Einschlucken, *v. tr.* to swallow, to take. Pillen —, to take pills; einen Trank —, to take down a potion; Staub —, to gather dust. *Fig.* †Vorwürfe —, to pocket reproaches.

Einschlummern, I. *v. intr.* [u. w. seyn] to fall into a slumber, to begin to slumber, to nod. *Fig.* Gewisse Leidenschaften schlummern bei den Menschen nie ein, certain passions in men never decrease; die Sache ist eingeschlummert, the affair dropt; er ist sanft eingeschlummert, he died an easy death. II. *v. tr.* [unusual] to cause to slumber, to dispose to sleep.

Einschlüpfen, *v. intr.* [u. w. seyn] to slip into.

Einschlürfen, *v. tr.* to sip, to sup [wine, tea &c.]. Ein Ei —, to sup up an egg.

Einschluß, *m.* [-sses, *pl.* -schlüsse] 1) the act of including, of inclosing, inclusion, inclosure. *Fig.* Mit — der öffentlichen Gebäude, the public buildings included; mit — der Kinder, including the children; durch — or d. E., words usually written on the envelop of an inclosed letter. 2) that which is inclosed or contained in an envelop, inclosure. Aus dem — werden Sie ersehen, by the inclosed [letter, note &c.] you will observe.

Einschlußweise, *adv.* as an inclosure.

Einſchmalzen, *v. tr.* to rub with grease or fat. Die Wolle —, [with clothiers] to oil wool.

Einſchmalztrog, *m.* [with clothiers] oiling-trough.

†**Einſchmauchen**, *v. tr.* to apply smoke to, to expose to smoke, to smoke. Meine Kleider ſind in dieſem Bierhauſe ganz eingeſchmaucht worden, my clothes have been quite impregnated with smoke in this alehouse.

Einſchmeicheln, I. *v. r* ſich —, to ingratiate one's self, to work one's self into favour. Sich bei Einem —, to steal into any one's favour; Demagogen ſchmeicheln ſich bei dem gemeinen Volke ein, Demagogues ingratiate themselves with the populace; er ſchmeichelte ſich bei dem Herzoge ein, he insinuated himself into the good favour of the duke; ſein —des Betragen, his insinuating behaviour or manners. II. *v. tr.* to persuade to by flattery. Die Einſchmeichelung, ingratiating, insinuation.

Einſchmeichlich, [rather unusual] *adj.* and *adv.* ingratiating, insinuative.

†**Einſchmeißen**, *ir. v. tr.* to break by something thrown [especially with the hand].

Einſchmelzen, *ir.* and *reg. v. tr.* to melt down, to melt, to fuse. Geld —, to melt down coin. Die Einſchmelzung, a melting down [of bells &c.]

Einſchmettern, I. *v. intr.* [u. w. ſeyn] to break crashing. II. *v. tr.* to crash, to break, to bruise.

Einſchmieden, *v. tr.* Einen —, to put any one into irons.

Einſchmiegen, *v. r.* ſich —, to get in by winding or bending.

Einſchmieren, *v. tr.* 1) to smear into a place or opening. †Einem Kinde den Brei —, to put the pap into the child's mouth; †etwas in ein Buch —, to scrawl something into a book. *Fig.*† Einem etwas —, to beat something into a person, to explain something to any one in the plainest and simplest manner. 2) to smear, anoint with grease or fat, to grease. Den Kopf mit Salbe —, to anoint one's head; die Häute mit Talg —, [with tanners] to grease the hides; ein Schloß —, to oil a lock; die Räder —, to grease the wheels.

Einſchmuzen, *v. tr.* to foul, to soil, to dirt [linen &c.].

Einſchnallen, *v. tr.* 1) to put the chape into the back strap. 2) to buckle.

Einſchnappen, I. *v. intr.* [u. w. ſeyn] to lock in clapping. II. *v. tr.* Luft —, to gasp or catch for breath, to take in breath by gasping.

Einſchnarchen, *v. intr.* [u. w. ſeyn] to fall asleep and snore.

Einſchnauben, *v. tr.* to breathe snorting, to respire with difficulty. *Fig.* Er ſchnaubt nur Zorn ein, he breathes nothing but anger.

Einſchneide, *f.* [*pl.* -n] [with turners] a sort of chisel in the shape of the hook.

Einſchneiden, *ir.* I. *v. intr.* 1) to enter and divide the parts, to cut in; [in printing] to grease. 2) to make a cut in any thing. Der Wundarzt ſchneidet in das Fleiſch ein, the surgeon makes an incision in the flesh. II. *v. tr.* 1) to cut into a substance. Eine Schachtel —, to notch a box; ein eingeſchnittenes Bollwerk, [in fortification] cut bastion; [in botany] ein eingeſchnittenes Blatt, a gashed leaf. 2) to cut on hard materials. Seinen Namen in Holz —, to cut one's name on wood; den Boden —, [with coopers] to cut out the head of a cask; [ein Buch] auf dem Rücken —, [with bookbinders] to sink the bands into the back; die Sohle —, [with shoemakers] to cut out the sole and sew it on or to; Schießſcharten —, [in fortification] to make embrasures in a wall or walls. 3) to add to by cutting into small pieces. Brod —, to slice bread into the soup; Kraut —, to slice or cut up cabbage; Eingeſchnittenes, a fricassee. 4) to gather by cutting down. III. *v. r.* ſich —, to diminish by being cut.

Einſchneideſäge, *f.* a bookbinder's hand-saw.

Einſchneider, *m.* [-s, *pl.* -] he that cuts into a substance &c. 2) a sort of cutting bore.

Einſchneidig, *adj.* and *adv.* having but one sharp edge. Ein —es Schwert, a backsword.

Einſchneien, I. *v. tr.* to cover snowing or with snow. Eingeſchneiet, covered or surrounded with snow; die Bewohner dieſer Länder ſind im Winter ganz eingeſchneiet, the inhabitants of these countries are snowed up during the winter. II. *v. intr.* and *imp.* to snow into a place or through an aperture. Es ſchneiet hier ein, snow enters here.

Einſchnitt, *m.* [-es, *pl.* -e] 1) a cutting, a cut, incision. Der Wundarzt macht mit ſeinem Meſſer einen — in das Fleiſch, und der Gärtner in einen Baum, the surgeon with his knife makes an incision in the flesh, and the gardener in a tree; zehn gleiche —e auf einem Stocke, ten equal notches on a stick; die —e in den Trieben der Uhren, leaves; der — an den Blättern, a jagg; der — in einer Mauer, Bruſtwehr, an opening in a wall or parapet, through which cannon are pointed and discharged, an embrasure *Fig.* *a*) [in poetry, a pause in verse, so introduced as to aid the recital, and render the versification more melodious] cesura, cesure, rest. *b*) [in music] a pause, rest. 2) the place, where a cut is made into a thing. ‖3) that which is cut or reaped. Der — vom vorigen Jahre war nicht ſehr ergiebig, the harvest of the last year was not very abundant.

Einſchnittthier, *n.* [in zoology] an insect.

Einſchnitzeln, *v. tr.* V. Einſchnitzen.

Einſchnitzen, *v. tr.* 1) to cut figures, devices &c. on hard materials, to carve 2) [in husbandry] to slice pears or apples for drying and preserving them for future use.

Einſchnupfen, *v. tr.* to take [snuff] into the nose, to snuff up.

Einſchnüren, *v. tr* 1) to put together and bind fast. to pack any thing with cords, to cord. Ein Frauenzimmer —, to lace a woman's stays; ſich —, to put on one's stays. ‖2) to string, to file Perlen —, to string pearls.

Einſchnurren, *v. intr.* [u. w. ſeyn] to contract spontaneously, to shrink.

Einſchöpfen, *v. tr.* to throw in, as a fluid, with a ladle or dipper, to lade [water] into [a tub].

Einſchrammen, *v. tr.* to scratch into.

Einſchränken, *v. tr.* to inclose with rails or bars. Einen Platz —, to inrail a place. *Fig.* to confine within certain bounds, to limit, to restrain, to restrict. Die Freiheit eines Menſchen —, to restrain any one of his liberty; man hat unſere Privilegien eingeſchränkt, we are curtailed of our privileges; ſeine Wünſche —, to moderate one's desires; ſchränken Sie ſich auf die nothwendigſten Bedürfniſſe ein, stint yourself to necessaries; ſchränken Sie Ihre Wünſche auf das Mögliche ein, confine your wishes within the bounds of possibility; ſehr eingeſchränkt leben müſſen, to be reduced to a small pittance; ſeine Ausgaben —, to retrench one's expenses; ſich —, to live at less expense, to retrench; eine eingeſchränkte Gewalt, a limited power; eingeſchränkte Kenntniſſe, small acquirements or attainments; ein eingeſchränkter Verſtand, a shallow mind, a limited understanding; einſchränkend, restrictive.

Einſchränkung, *f.* 1) confinement within bounds, limitation, restriction. Er hat große —en in ſeinem Hausweſen vorgenommen, he has made great retrenchments in his household. 2) [something restraining or restricting] restriction. Mit der —, daß &c., with this restriction, that &c.

Einſchrauben, *v. tr.* 1) to screw in. Den Fuß —, to screw in a leg [of a table &c.]. 2) to fasten by screws. Ein Stück Eiſen —, to fasten a piece of iron in a vice; einem Miſſethäter die Daumen —, to put the thumb-screws on a criminal.

Einſchrecken, *v. tr.* 1) to force upon by fright. 2) to fright into, to scare into a place. 3) to put in fear, to intimidate.

Einſchreiben, *ir. v. tr.* to enter or write in a list, catalogue or book. Die Namen ſämmtlicher Steuerpflichtigen ſind hier eingeſchrieben, the names of all the contribuables are registered here; in das Taufbuch or Taufregiſter —, to enter into the register of baptisms; Ausgaben und Einnahmen —, to book expenses and receipts; ſchreibt es in ein Buch ein, [In Script.] note it in a book; Einen in die Soldatenliſte or in die Rolle —, to enrol any one for service; der Eingeſchriebene, a person enrolled for service; in die Matrikel —, to matriculate; den Namen eines Pferdes —, [in horse-racing] to enter a horse; ſich —, to enter one's name in [any book]. Die Einſchreibung, registering, entering, registration, enrolment.

Einſchreibegeld, *n.* —**gebühr**, *f.* money or fee paid for enrolling, registering or booking.

Einſchreiber, *m.* [-s, *pl.* -] he that registers or enrolls, enroller; registrar.

Einſchreien, *v. tr.* to cry into any one's ears.

Einſchreiten, *ir. v. intr.* [u. w. ſeyn] 1) to walk into a place, to step in or into, to stride in. 2) *Fig.* to step in between parties at variance, to interpose [one's authority &c.] in an affair, to interfere. Der Tumult wuchs ſo ſehr, daß die bewaffnete Macht — mußte, the tumult increased to such a height that the armed force was called in; er mußte mit ſeinem ganzen Anſehen —, he was obliged to interpose all his authority.

Einſchreitung, *f.* 1) interposition, intervenient agency. ‡2) encroachment.

Einſchroten, *v. tr.* Ein Faß Wein, Bier &c. —, to roll or let down a cask of wine, beer &c. into the cellar.

Einſchrumpeln, **Einſchrumpfen**, *v. intr.* [u. w. ſeyn] to contract, to shrink, to shrivel, to be drawn into wrinkles. Die Haut ſchrumpft durch Alter ein, the skin shrivels with age; viele Stoffe ſchrumpfen durch Trocknen ein, many substances shrink by drying; ein Seil ſchrumpft ein, wenn es naß [gemacht] wird, a cord shortens by being wet. * and ‡ *Fig.* Sein Beutel iſt eingeſchrumpft, his purse is very low.

Einſchub, *m.* [-es, *pl.* -ſchübe] 1) the act of putting between. *Fig.* Der — einer Perſon in eine eröffnete Stelle, the act of thrusting a person in a vacant place without just right or claim; der — [better das Einſchieben or Einſchalten] eines Tages im Kalender, intercalation. 2) something shoved in.

Einſchüchtern, *v. tr.* to put in fear, to intimidate. Er läßt ſich leicht —, he is soon intimidated, he is easily to be put in fear.

Einſchulen, *v. tr.* to train, as a horse. Ein Pferd —, to manage a horse.

Einſchüppen, *v. tr.* to shovel in.

Einschüren, *v. tr.* to put in by stirring.

Einschürig, **Einscherig**, *adj.* and *adv.* 1) only once shorn in a year [said of sheep]. —e Wolle, the wool of sheep shorn but once in a year. 2) once cut, once mowed in a year [said of meadows].

Einschürzen, *v. tr.* [with saddlers] to thread [a needle].

Einschuß, *m.* [-sses, *pl.* -schüsse] [with millwrights] the water-course directed on the mill-wheels.

Einschüsseln, *v. tr.* to put in a dish, to dish.

Einschütteln, *v. tr.* to cause to enter by shaking.

1. **Einschütten**, *v. tr.* to pour in. Mehl —, to pour flour into a vessel; dem Vieh Futter —, to lay fodder for cattle in the manger; Getreide —, to sack corn.

2. ||**Einschütten**, *v. tr.* to confine in a public pound. Vieh —, to pound cattle.

Einschwärmen, *v. intr.* [u. w. seyn] to enter swarming [as bees].

1. **Einschwärzen**, *v. tr.* to blacken all over, to cover with black. Die Kupferplatte —, to black the copperplate with ink for the rolling-press. Die Wäsche —, to soil linen.

2 **Einschwärzen**, *v. tr.* to import clandestinely or contrary to law. Waaren —, to smuggle or run goods. *Fig.* Sich —, [mostly in a jocose sense] to smuggle one's self in.

Einschwatzen, *v. tr.* to persuade by talking. Ich lasse mir das nicht —, they shall never persuade me of it; er hat ihm eingeschwatzt, daß &c., he talked him into believing that &c.; sich bei Jemanden —, to ingratiate one's self with a person by talking.

Einschwefeln, *v. tr.* to impregnate with brimstone. Ein Faß —, to match a cask.

Einschwellen, I. *v. tr.* to swell the water by a sluice &c. II. *ir. v. intr.* [u. w. seyn] 1) to enter swelling. 2) to swell, to be swollen. Das Auge ist eingeschwollen, the eye is swelled up.

Einschwemmen, *v. tr.* to cause to float in.

Einschwenken, *v. intr.* [in military affairs] to wheel inward. Die Truppen schwenkten rechts ein, troops wheeled inward to the right.

Einschwimmen, *ir. v. intr.* [u. w. seyn] to swim in.

Einschwinden, *ir. v. intr.* [u. w. seyn] V. Einschrumpfen.

Einschwingen, *ir. v. tr.* 1) to swing into. 2) to swing asleep.

†**Einseckeln**, V. Einsäckeln.

Einsegeln, *v. intr.* [u. w. seyn] to sail into [a port &c.] In einen Hafen —, to run into a harbour.

Einsegnen, *v. tr.* to consecrate by prayer, to invoke a blessing upon, to bless. Ein Paar Verlobte —, to marry a couple; eine Sechswöchnerinn —, to church a woman; Kinder —, to confirm children; einen Sterbenden —, to administer the communion to a dying person; einen Prediger —, to ordain a minister of the Gospel; Brot und Wein —, to consecrate the bread and wine in the Eucharist.

Einsegnung, *f.* benediction, consecration. Die — der Verlobten, the nuptial benediction; die — eines Geistlichen, ordination.

Einsehen, *ir.* I. *v. intr.* to see into. In das Buch eines Andern —, to look into another's book. II. *v. tr* 1) [in law] to look over, to read over, to examine. 2) *Fig.* to see, to comprehend, to understand, to be aware of. Ich sehe den Nutzen davon nicht ein, I do not see the utility of it; sehr oft sehen wir die Absichten Gottes nicht ein, very often we do not comprehend the designs of God; sie sehen es nunmehr ein, daß es besser gewesen wäre, einzuwilligen, als &c., they are now sensible it would have been better to comply, than &c.; *ein — †kriegen, bekommen, to get an insight; *er sollte doch ein — haben, he should have some consideration; *die Polizei sollte darin ein — haben, the police should animadvert upon it

Einseifen, *v. tr.* to spread over with the lather of soap, or to rub or wash over with soap. Den Bart —, to lather the beard; Wäsche —, to soap linen.

Einseitig, *adj.* and *adv.* 1) having but one side, one-sided. Ein —es Dach, a pent-roof, a lean-to; [in botany] eine —e Aehre, a unilateral spike; eine —e Traube, an one-sided or unilateral raceme; eine —e Rispe, a one-sided panicle. 2) ||leaning to one side. Er ist — or — gewachsen, he is crooked or of a crooked stature. 3) *Fig.* done to favour one thing, more than the other. Ein —er Vertrag, an agreement, in which but one party binds himself to do or forbear some act; eine Sache — darstellen, to represent a thing under one point of view only; eine sehr —e Ansicht der Sache, a very biassed view of the subject, *it.* a very confined view of the matter; — urtheilen, to judge partially; eine Sache — behandeln, to treat of a thing with partiality; —e Kenntniß, a defective knowledge.

Einseitigkeit, *f.* 1) an undue bias of mind towards one party or side, which is apt to warp the judgment, partiality. 2) a defective state of erudition or manners; *it.* partial judgment, partiality.

Einsenden, *ir. v. tr.* to send into a place, to transmit to a person. Berichte —, to transmit reports; Waaren —, to remit goods; Nachrichten —, to communicate news; die an die Regierung eingesandten Nachrichten, the news transmitted to government. Die Einsendung, transmission, remittance.

Einsender, *m.* [-s, *pl.* -] he that sends in, remits or transmits, transmitter.

Einsengen, *v. tr.* 1) to produce something on the inside of a thing by singing. 2) to singe, to singe sufficiently.

Einsenken, *v. tr.* to let in or down, to sink in, to insert, to permit to sink or fall. Den Sarg —, to lower the coffin in the earth or in a vault; Zweige —, to place boughs in the earth for growth; Pflanzen, Reben —, to lay plants, vines; einen Schraubenkopf —, to sink the head of a screw below the surface. *Fig.* to sink into, to implant.

Einser, *m.* [-s, *pl.* -] 1) the number one. 2) [*pl.*] the numbers from one to ten, units.

Einsetzen, I. *v. tr.* to set, put, place or fix in any place. Einen Dieb —, to put a thief into a prison, to imprison a thief; Gänse —, to coop up geese for fattening; Zähne —, to put in artificial teeth; eingesetzte Zähne, artificial teeth; Masten —, [in seamen's language] to ship masts; das Boot or die Schlupe —, [in seamen's language] to hoist and take the boat on board; einen Flicken or Flicklappen —, to sew on a patch; eine Scheibe —, to put in a pane into the window-frame; Pflanzen oder Bäume —, to place plants or trees in the earth for growth; Brod —, [with bakers] to put the bread into the oven; Leder —, [with tanners] to lay leather in a tan-pit; Geld —, to stake money; in die Lotterie —, to put into the lottery; die Klauen —, to fasten the claws in the flesh. *Fig. a*) to give or deposit in pledge. Etwas zum Pfande —, to pawn something. *b*) to give possession, to put in possession of. Einen in ein Amt —, to invest a person with an office, to install any one in an office; Pharao wird dich wieder in dein Amt —, [in Scripture] Pharaoh shall restore thee to thy place; einen König wieder —, to reinstate a king in the possession of his kingdom; den Gläubiger in des Schuldners Güter —, to put the creditor in possession of the debtor's estate. *c*) to appoint, to constitute. Er hat mich zum Erben eingesetzt, he made me his heir; er hat ihn zu seinem Testamentsvollstrecker eingesetzt, he appointed him his executor; das Abendmahl ist von Christus eingesetzt worden, Christ instituted the Eucharist; einen Feiertag —, to appoint a feast. II. *v. r.* sich —, to seat one's self in a coach &c. *Fig.* to take root, to become planted or fixed [said of customs &c.].

Einsetzeisen, *n.* V. Einsatz 8. —löffel, *m.* V. Eintragelöffel 2.

Einsetzer, *m.* [-s, *pl.* -] the person who establishes, installs, institutes &c.

Einsetzling, *m.* [-s, *pl.* -e] a set, a twig, a slip.

Einsetzung, *f.* the act of setting, putting, placing or fixing in any place. *Fig. a*) pawning, pledging. *b*) the act of putting in possession; investiture, installment, installation. *c*) constituting, appointing, institution. Die — des heiligen Abendmahles, the institution of the sacrament of the Lord's supper.

Einsetzungsworte, *pl.* words pronounced by Jesus at the institution of the Eucharist.

Einsicht, *f.* [*pl.* -n] sight or view of the interior of any thing, insight. *Fig. a*) a looking into, inspection, examination by the eye. Sie nahmen — davon, they took a view of it. *b*) || animadversion, reproof, blame, punishment. *c*) understanding, knowledge, exact comprehension. Meiner — nach, as I see it; meine — reicht nicht so weit, it is not within my comprehension, it is not within the range of my understanding; ich hätte Ihnen mehr — zugetraut, I should have expected from you more prudence; aus Mangel an —, from the want of discernment; dieser Mann spricht mit vieler — über &c., this man converses very sensibly on &c.; ein Mann von großen —en, a man of great or nice penetration; er hat eine tiefe — in or von dieser Sache, he has a deep insight into this matter; beschränkte —en, a small understanding, confined view.

Einsichtsvoll, *adj.* and *adv.* intelligent, discerning, judicious, sharp-sighted, penetrating, acute. Ein —voller Mann, a sensible man.

Einsichtig, *adj.* and *adv.* V. Einsichtsvoll.

Einsichtlich, *adj.* and *adv.* that may be understood or comprehended, comprehensible.

Einsickern, *v. intr.* [u. w. seyn] to penetrate by oozing.

Einsiedelei, *f.* 1) a solitary abode, a recluse place. 2) [the habitation of a hermit] a hermitage. 3) solitude, a lonely life.

Einsiedeln, *v. intr.* [unusual] to live in solitude.

Einsieden, *ir.* I. *v. intr.* [u. w. seyn] 1) to be lessened by boiling. 2) to be inspissated by boiling. II. *v. tr.* 1) to lessen by boiling, to boil down. 2) to inspissate by boiling. 3) to b[...] for future use.

Einsiedler, *m.* [-s, *pl.* -] 1) a person who dwells solitarily in a secluded or unfrequented place, in a wood &c.; [more especially] a person who lives in solitude for the purpose of religious contemplation and devotion, a hermit, an anchoret, or anchorite. 2) [the name of birds] *a*) the hermit-crow, the wood-crow. *b*) the solitary sparrow. *c*) the dodo. 3) [a genus of crabs] wron[...] bair.

Einſiedlerkrebs, *m.* V. Einſiedler 3.

Einſiedlerei, *f.* V. Einſiedelei.

Einſiedleriſch, *adj.* and *adv.* hermitical. *Fig.* Ein —es Leben führen, to live in solitude, to lead a hermit's life.

Einſiegeln, *v. tr.* to seal up in a thing.

Einſilber, *m.* [-s, *pl.* -] a monosyllable.

Einſilbig, *adj.* and *adv.* monosyllabic. Ein —es Wort, a monosyllabic word, a monosyllable. *Fig.* *Ein —er Menſch, a person sparing of words, giving short answers; er iſt ziemlich —, he is rather taciturn or of taciturn habits.

Einſilbigkeit, *f.* the state of being monosyllabic. *Fig.* *Die — eines Menſchen, the taciturnity of a person.

Einſingen, *ir. v. tr.* 1) to sing asleep. 2) to get or gain by singing. II. *v. r.* ſich —, to exercise one's self in singing.

Einſinken, *ir. v. intr.* [u. w. ſeyn] 1) to sink in, to fall within the surface of any thing. Der Boden ſinkt ein, the floor sinks; das Eis ſank ein und die Pferde ertranken, the ice gave way and the horses were drowned 2) sometimes for to sink. Ein Pferd oder Wagen iſt in den Koth eingeſunken, a horse or a carriage is mired. *Fig.* Sie ſank ein, she fell away.

Einſintern, *v. intr.* [u. w. ſeyn] to penetrate by drops or dripping.

Einſitzen, *ir. v. intr.* 1) [unusual] to sit in my place. 2) to dwell in any place. Ein Eingeſeſſener, a dweller. 3) ||to be in prison. 4) to take a seat in any place. Wir waren im Begriff einzuſitzen, we were about to step into the coach.

Einſitzig, *adj.* and *adv.* furnished with one seat. Ein —er Wagen, a carriage with one seat.

Einsmahls, **Einſtmahls**, *adv.* at some past or future time, once, one day.

Einſohlig, *adj.* and *adv.* single-soled.

Einſommern, *v. intr.* [u. w. ſeyn] [unusual] to ...re to heat in summer.

Einſpänen, *v. tr.* [among clothiers] to furnish with pressing-cards.

Einſpannen, *v. tr.* 1) to stretch [cloth &c.] in a frame. 2) to put horses &c. to a carriage. 3) *Fig.* Einen Fluß —, to dam up a river.

Einſpannenadel, *f.* [with clothiers] a sort of needle used for stretching cloth.

1. **Einſpänner**, *m.* [-s, *pl.* -] 1) he that stretches cloth in a frame &c., he that puts horses &c. to a carriage. ||2) a person employed in lading goods. ‡3) a servant employed in charging the gun for his master. V. Büchſenſpanner.

2. **Einſpänner**, *m.* [-s, *pl.* -] a vehicle with one horse, a one-horse-chaise, a one-horse-cart.

Einſpännig, *adj.* and *adv.* 1) drawn by one horse or ox only. — fahren, to drive with one horse. ||2) *Fig.* calculated for a single person. Ein —es Bett, a single bed.

Einſpeichern, *v. tr.* V. Aufſpeichern.

Einſpelzig, *adj.* and *adv.* [in botany] univalve. Ein —er Balg, a univalve glume.

||1. **Einſperren**, *v. tr.* to wedge in.

2. **Einſperren**, *v. tr.* 1) to shut up, to confine, to lock or fasten in. Einen Gefangenen —, to shut up a prisoner; Einen auf Zeitlebens —, to imprison any one for life; in ein Kloſter —, to shut up or confine in a cloister, to cloister; eingeſperrt, incarcerated. *Fig.* Eingeſperrt, sequestered, recluse; *Einen eingeſperrt halten, to restrain any one. 2) to inclose, to surround, to block up. Eine Stadt —, to invest a town.

1. **Einſpielen**, I. *v. tr.* to lull asleep by playing on an instrument. II. *v. r.* ſich —, to exercise one's self in playing frequently on an instrument or in playing at certain games, as ninepins &c.

2. **Einſpielen**, *v. tr.* to fasten in with slips of wood.

Einſpinnen, *ir. v. tr.* 1) to insert by spinning. 2) to surround with a web. Sich —, to envelop one's self with a sort of web; der Seidenwurm hat ſich eingeſponnen, the silkworm has involved itself in a cocoon.

Einſprache, *f.* [*pl.* -n] objection, protest, [in law] exception. — thun, to protest. V. Einſpruch.

Einſprechen, *ir.* I. *v. tr.* to speak to, to communicate. Einem Muth —, to inspire any one with courage, spirit or strength of mind, to encourage any one; Einem Troſt —, to comfort any one. II. *v. intr.* 1) to oppose by words, to contradict; [in law-pleadings] to deny what the opposite party has alledged, to traverse, to make an exception or exceptions. 2) to make a short visit to, to make a call. Bei Einem —, to call on any one, to give any one a call.

Einſprecher, *m.* [-s, *pl.* -] [in law] he that traverses, exceptor.

Einſprengen, I. *v. tr.* 1) to besprinkle [linen &c.]. Das Fleiſch mit Salz —, to sprinkle meat with salt, to salt meat; den Schnitt [eines Buches] —, [with bookbinders] to marble a book's edge. 2) to scatter in small particles. Eingeſprengt, [in mineralogy] disseminated. 3) to burst open, to force open. II. *v. intr.* to ride with full speed into a place.

Einſpringen, *ir.* I. *v. intr.* [u. w. ſeyn] 1) to leap into any place or aperture. 2) *Fig.* to enter in return: Ein —der Winkel, a reentering angle. 3) to catch with the spring [said of a lock]. II. *v. tr.* to break or burst open by leaping against.

Einſpritzen, *v. tr.* 1) to inject by means of a syringe, to wash and cleanse by injections from a syringe, to syringe. Den Hals —, to syringe the throat. 2) to injure by squirting or syringing.

Einſpruch, *m.* [-es, *pl.* -ſprüche] protestation against any proceeding, prohibition of any proceeding. Gegen eine Heirath — thun, to forbid the bans.

Einſprudeln, I. *v. intr.* to enter or penetrate bubbling or in bubbles. II. *v. tr.* to wet bubbling.

Einſprung, *m.* [-es, *pl.* -ſprünge] a leap into a place or the place where one leaps in.

Einſprüßelich, **Einſprüßig**, *adj.* and *adv.* [with huntsmen] having but one antler [said of stags].

Einſpünden, *v. tr.* to inclose by bunging.

Einſt, [from Ein] *adv.* 1) ||at one time, once. 2) at a former time or at a future time, at one day. — war ich glücklich, once I was happy; mein Herz empfand — eine thörichte Liebe für dich, my heart had once a foolish fondness for you; du wirſt — deine Thorheit bereuen, you will one day repent of your folly.

Einſtäben, *v. tr.* [with tanners] to dress with hot water.

Einſtallen, *v. tr.* to put into a stable. Vieh —, to stable cattle.

Einſtämmig, *adj.* and *adv.* having but one stem, made out of one stem.

Einſtampfen, *v. tr.* 1) to thrust or thrive in with violence, to ram. Die Erde —, to stamp in the earth. 2) to break by ramming or stamping.

Einſtand, *m.* [-es, *pl.* -ſtände] 1) entrance into an office. *Fig.* money paid at the entrance into an office. Einen — geben, to entertain, to feast certain persons at one's entrance into an office. 2) entrance into the rights of a purchaser. 3) [in law] preemption. V. also Vorkaufsrecht.

Einſtands-geld, *n.* 1) money paid at the entrance into an office, entrance-money, entrance. 2) *a*) money paid to one's substitute in military service. *b*) the money or sum, such a substitute receives. **—gerechtigkeit**, *f.* **—recht**, *n.* V. Einſtand, 2) and 3).

Einſtänkern, *v. tr.* to fill with a stink.

Einſtauben, *v. intr.* [u. w. ſeyn] to penetrat as dust.

Einſtäuben, *v. tr.* to dust all over. Ein Kleid —, to soil a garment with dust. *Fig.* Das Haar —, to powder the hair.

Einſtauen, *v. tr.* to stow in [goods &c.].

Einſtechen, *ir.* I. *v. tr.* 1) to make by pricking or piercing. Löcher in die Erde —, to cut holes in the earth; Löcher in ein Papier —, to prick a paper; kleine Löcher in die Haut —, to puncture the skin, to tattoo. 2) [in printing] to prick. 3) [with shoemakers] Die Brandſohle —, to sew the overleather to the second sole. II. *v. intr.* 1) [in seamen's language] Seewärts —, to stand out to sea. 2) *Fig.* [at cards] Mit einer Farbe —, to take with a trumpcard, to trump.

Einſtech-bogen, *m.* [in printing] tympan-sheet. **—ort**, *m.* [with shoemakers] an awl.

Einſtecher, *m.* [-s, *pl.* -] [in seamen's lang.] a piece of timber employed to replace a removed futtock.

Einſtecken, *v. tr.* 1) to put into, to fasten in. Den Degen in die Scheide —, to sheathe a sword; einen Dieb —, to shut up a thief; den Zipfel eines Dinges —, to tuck in the skirt of any thing. 2) to put or conceal in the pocket; *it.* to take clandestinely, to pocket. Geld —, to pocket money. *Fig.* *Eine Beſchimpfung —, to pocket an insult or affront, or to put up with an insult or affront.

Einſteckſchwert, *n.* [with bookbinders] a sword-shaped piece of wood.

Einſtehen, *ir. v. intr.* [u. w. ſeyn] 1) ||[rather unusual] to enter into office or service; *it.* to enter into military service as a substitute. 2) to answer for, to become surety. Ich kann dafür nicht —, I cannot answer for it; für die Folgen —, to be responsible for the consequences. 3) to enter into the rights of a purchaser. In einen Handel mit —, to partake of a purchase.

Einſteher, *m.* [-s, *pl.* -] one that enters office, one that becomes surety &c.; [especially] one that enters military service for another, a substitute.

Einſtehlen, *ir. v. r.* ſich —, to steal in, to enter privily, to insinuate or introduce one's self stealthily. *Fig.* Sich in ein Amt —, to enter into an office by secret, artful or illicit means; er ſtahl ſich in ihr Herz ein, he stole her heart.

Einſteigen, *ir. v. intr.* [u. w. ſeyn] to mount into, to get in. Sie ſind ſchon eingeſtiegen, they have already got into the coach, they have already taken ship or embarked; der Dieb iſt auf einer Leiter eingeſtiegen, the thief entered the house by means of a ladder.

Einſteinen, *v. tr.* to wall or face with stones. Einen Brunnen —, to stone a well.

Einſtellen, I. *v. tr.* 1) to put into a place. Waaren —, to deposit or reposit goods that were put up to sale; ein Pferd —, to stable a horse; Rindvieh —, to place cattle out [to feed]; Gänſe —, to coop geese for fattening. *Fig.* *a*) ||to constitute, to appoint. Er hat ihn zum Erben eingeſtellt, he made him his heir. *b*) to leave off, to put a stop to, to cause to cease. Eine Reiſe —, to put off a journey; eine Arbeit —, to discontinue a work; die Zahlungen —, to stop payment;

die Feindseligkeiten —, to forbear hostilities; Mißbräuche —, to reform abuses. *c)* ‖ Einen Mann —, to substitute another [for military service]. 2) [with huntsmen] to surround with toils. II. *v. r.* sich —, to be present, to come, to come in. Ich werde mich —, I will be there. *Fig.* Der November stellte sich mit scharfen Frösten ein, November set in with keen frosts; sein Schmerz hat sich wieder eingestellt, his pain is renewed.

Einsteller, *m.* [-s, *pl.* -] one that puts into a place &c.; ‖[especially] one who gives a substitute [for military service].

Einstemmen, *v. tr.* to work with an ax or chisel on the inside of any thing.

‡**Einsten**, **Einstens**, V. Einst.

Einsticken, *v. tr.* to embroider in or upon a thing.

Einstieben, *v. intr.* V. Einstauben.

Einstig, *adj.* [that is to be or come hereafter] future. Zu —em Gebrauche, for future use.

Einstimmen, *v. intr.* 1) to agree in pitch and tone, to accord. 2) to join in. Ich stimmte in das Freudengeschrei der Menge ein, I joined in the acclamations of the multitude; mit — im Singen, to sing in concert. 3) to give one's voice or vote in concert with others, to coincide in opinion, to harmonize in opinion, to agree. Ich stimme mit ein, I consent to it; die Mitglieder des Rathes stimmten alle ein, the members of the council were unanimous.

Einstimmig, I. *adj.* concordant, consonant, harmonious. *Fig.* unanimous. II. *adv.* 1) harmoniously. 2) unanimously. — seyn, to be of one mind, to be unanimous; alle Partheien sind darin —, all the parties agree in it. 3) sung by a single voice, played by a single instrument. Ein —er Gesang, a solo.

Einstimmigkeit, *f.* 1) consonancy, concord. 2) unanimity.

Einstmahls, V. Einsmahls.

Einstöbern, I. *v. intr.* 1) [u. w. seyn] V. Einstauben. 2) [u. w. haben] to enter in small flakes, as snow. II. *v. tr.* V. Einstäuben.

Einstockig, ‖**Einstöckig**, *adj.* and *adv.* having but one story or floor, one-storied.

Einstopfen, *v. tr.* to stuff in. Tabak in die Pfeife —, to fill a pipe with tobacco; etwas in einen Korb —, to cram any thing into a basket; den Zipfel eines Dinges —, to tuck in the skirt of any thing. *Fig.* †Er hat wacker eingestopft, he stuffed or crammed.

Einstoßen, *ir. v. tr.* 1) to thrust in, to push or drive in, to drive down or together. Pfähle in die Erde —, to ram piles into the earth; eine Patrone —, to ram down a cartridge; sich einen Splitter in die Hand —, to run a splinter into one's hand; die Erde —, to ram the earth; die Farbe —, [with dyers in blue] to pack up the colour; die Butter —, to press down butter in a barrel &c; das Leder —, [with tanners] to pack leather in vats. 2) to break by knocking. Eine Thür —, to break open, to thrust open a door; einem Fasse den Boden —, to stave in the head of a cask; sich die Hirnschale —, to knock out one's brains.

Einstrahlen, *v. intr.* to beam into a place or aperture

Einstreichen, *ir.* I. *v. tr.* to put in by a stroking motion. Mörtel in die Fugen —, to fill up the joints with mortar; Farben irgendwo —, to paint within; einem Kinde den Brei —, to put the pap into a child's mouth; Geld —, to take money by a promiscuous sweep and pocket it; Alles —, to sweep stakes; [with locksmiths] to make with a file, to file in; Einschnitte —, to make cuts with a file; [with sportsmen] Lerchen —, to take larks with a sweep-net. *Fig.* †Ich will es ihm schon —, I'll make him pay for it. II. *v. intr.* [with huntsmen] to light on fields [said of partridges &c.].

Einstreichfeile, *f.* a cutting-file.

Einstreiten, *v. tr.* to persuade by disputing or contending.

Einstreuen, I. *v. tr.* to strew or scatter into. Ein Pulver in die Wunde —, to strew a powder over a wound; den Pferden —, to litter horses. *Fig.* Verse in eine Rede —, to intersperse a discourse with verse; in das Gedicht waren überall Gespräche eingestreuet, the poem was every where interlarded with dialogue. II. *v. intr.* [= streuen] to litter. Dem Vieh, den Pferden —, to litter the cattle, the horses.

Einstreuung, *f.* 1) the act of strewing or scattering into, *fig.* interspersion. 2) *Fig.* something interspersed, remarks interspersed. Boshafte —en, malicious insinuations.

Einstrich, *m.* [-es, *pl.* -e] 1) the act of putting in by a stroking motion, and the thing taken by a promiscuous sweep. 2) [with locksmiths] ward. Die —e eines Schlosses, oder in dem Barte eines Schlüssels, the wards of a lock, or in the key-bit.

Einstricken, *v. tr.* 1) to knit in, to adorn with knitted letters, figures &c. 2) to fasten with cords, to confine or restrain, as with a cord.

Einströmen, *v. intr.* [u. w. seyn] to flow in, to run in in a continuous current, to stream in. Die Menge strömte durch das Thor ein, the multitude crowded through the gate.

Einstückeln, *v. tr.* to mend by sewing on a piece or pieces. Etwas in den Rock —, to piece a coat.

Einstücken, *v. tr.* 1) [with tailors and sempstresses] to sew on a piece or pieces, to piece. 2) to divide in parts.

***Einstudiren**, *v. tr.* to make one's self master of, to fix in the mind, to con. Eine Rede —, to study a speech; er hatte seine Rolle gut einstudirt, he got his part well.

Einstürmen, I. *v. intr.* to rush in with violence. *Fig.* Sie stürmten auf mich ein, they all fell on me. II. *v. tr.* [rather unusual] to destroy by storming. Der Wind hat das Haus eingestürmt, the wind blew down the house.

Einsturz, *m.* [-es, *pl.* -stürze] a falling in or down, a falling into ruins. Der — eines Hauses, the falling in of a house; eine Mauer, die den — droht, a wall that menaces to fall; ein den — drohender Thurm, a tower threatening fall and ruin.

Einstürzen, I. *v. intr.* [u. w. seyn] to fall in or down, to fall into ruins, to ruin. Das Gerüst stürzte ein, the scaffolding gave way. *Fig.* to fall on, to assault, to assail. Sie stürzten von allen Seiten auf ihn ein, they assailed him from all sides. II. *v. tr.* to cause to ruin, to ruin, to demolish [a wall &c.].

Einstutzen, *v. tr.* 1) to cut short. Einen Baum —, [in gardening] to lop, prune or crop a tree. 2) to push and break something with the horns [said of horned cattle].

Einstweilen, *adv.* in the mean-while, or mean-time; in the interim.

Einstweilig, *adj.* provisional, temporary.

Einsümpfen, *v. tr.* [with tile-makers] Die Lehmerde —, to wet the clay thoroughly.

Einsüßen, *v. tr.* to sweeten thoroughly.

Eintägig, *adj.* and *adv.* beginning and ending in a day, continuing or existing one day only, ephemeral, ephemeric. Ein —es Fieber, [a fever of one day's continuance only] ephemera; ein —es Ziefer or Insekt, an ephemera; eine —e Pflanze, an ephemeral plant.

Eintagsfliege, *f.* [*pl.* -n] the day-fly, ephemera.

Eintagsgeschöpf, **Eintagsthier**, [-es, *pl.* -e] **Eintagswesen**, [-s, *pl.* -] *n.* an ephemeral creature, or animal.

Eintagswurm, *m.* [-es, *pl.* -würmer] ephemeron-worm.

Eintanz, *m.* [-es, *pl.* -tänze] [unusual] a dance performed by one person only, a solo-dance.

Eintanzen, I. *v. tr.* to break by pushing against in dancing. II. *v. intr.* V. Hereintanzen. III. *v. r.* sich —, to exercise one's self in dancing. Eingetanzt seyn, to be well skilled in dancing or in a certain sort of dance[s].

Eintaschen, *v. tr.* [with silk-dyers] to bag [raw silk].

Eintauchen, I. *v. tr.* to put into a fluid and withdraw, to dip, to immerse. Ein Stück Zwieback in Wein —, to dip a piece of biscuit into wine; einen Körper in Wasser —, to plunge a body in water; er hat den Finger in das Blut eingetaucht, he has dipped his finger in the blood; die Dochte in den Talg —, [with tallow-chandlers] to dip the wicks. II. *v. intr.* [u. w. seyn and haben] to duck, to dive or plunge in.

Eintauchkessel, *m.* [in paper-mills] a large vessel of copper used for sizing paper.

Eintaucher, *m.* [-s, *pl.* -] 1) one that dips, dipper; *it.* one that plunges or dives, a diver. 2) [in paper-mills] V. Schöpfer.

Eintauschen, *v. tr.* to give in exchange, to exchange, to barter, to truck. Messer für Goldstaub —, to truck knives for gold dust.

‖**Einte**, der, die, das, a numeral word expressing sometimes, the one, sometimes, the first.

Einteichen, V. Eindeichen.

Einteigen, *v. tr.* [unusual] 1) to make a dough of [flour]. 2) to knead dough with leaven.

Eintheilen, *v. tr.* 1) to divide a whole so as to suffice. Die Vorräthe —, to divide provisions adequately to wants; seine Zeit —, to portion one's time. 2) to distribute in distinct portions. Seine Rede war in drei Theile eingetheilt, his speech was divided in three parts; in Klassen —, to arrange in classes, to classify, to class; Pflanzen —, to distribute plants into classes, orders, kinds or species; einen Thermometer in Grade —, to graduate a thermometer; Länder, Städte sind in Bezirke eingetheilt, countries, cities are divided into districts.

Eintheilig, *adj.* and *adv.* 1) to be divided into one part or portion only. 2) consisting of one part or portion.

Eintheilung, *f.* division, distribution, regulation, arrangement. Er hat eine gute — in seinen Vorräthen getroffen, he divided his provisions adequately to his wants; die — in Klassen, classification; die — in Bezirke, a division into districts.

Einthe[e]ren, *v. tr.* to tar [ropes &c.].

Einthun, *ir. v. tr.* 1) to put in a place, to confine, to shut up. 2) to lay in, to provide previously. Getreide —, to lay up corn; Äpfel für den Winter —, to put up apples for winter.

Einthüren, *v. tr.* Die Flügel —, to shift the sweeps of a windmill.

‖**Einthürmen**, *v. tr.* to confine in a prison or jail, to imprison.

Eintönen, *v. intr.* 1) to be unisonous. 2) to join in, to fall in with tone.

Eintönig, *adj.* and *adv.* continued in the same tone without inflection or cadence, monotonous. *Fig.* uniform.

Eintönigkeit, *f.* uniformity of tone or sound, want of inflection of voice in speaking, want of cadence or modulation, monotony. *Fig.* uniformity, sameness.

Eintonnen, *v. tr.* to put into casks, to tun beer &c.). Häringe —, to barrel herrings.

Eintraben, *v. intr.* [u. w. seyn] to enter a place trotting.

||1. **Eintracht**, *f.* [unusual] V. 2. Eintrag.

2. **Eintracht**, *f.* peace, harmony, concord, union in opinions, sentiments, views &c., agreement and conjunction of mind, will, affections or interest, concord. In — leben, to live in harmony or concord, to be at peace; glücklich ist die Familie, unter deren sämmtlichen Mitgliedern — herrscht, happy is the family where perfect union subsists between all its members.

Eintrachtskirche, *f.* a church appropriated to the religious worship and alternate use of Catholics and Protestants.

Einträchtig, *adj.* and *adv.* agreeing, harmonious, agreeing in opinion or determination, unanimous. Eine —e Familie, a harmonious family; — leben, to live in peace and friendship; sie leben höchst —, they live in perfect concord.

Einträchtigkeit, *f.* agreement, accordance, unanimousness.

1. **Eintrag**, *m.* [-es, *pl.* -träge] 1) the act of writing in a book &c., registering. V. Eintragen, *fig. a.* 2) the thing or subject entered or registered, entrance. 3) [with weavers] the woof or weft.

2. **Eintrag**, *m.* prejudice, damage, injury. Einem — thun, to prejudice any one; sie thun dem Ansehen des Landesherrn —, they are a prejudice to the authority of the sovereign; es thut der Ehre eines Fürsten keinen —, ein demüthiger Christ zu seyn, to be a humble Christian is no disparagement to a prince.

Eintragsfaden, *m.* [with tapestry-makers] thread of the woof.

Eintragen, *ir. v. tr.* to bear in, to carry in. Wasser —, to carry water into the house; die Bienen tragen [Honig] ein, the bees convey the honey to the cells; —, [with weavers] to weave the woof across the warp. *Fig. a)* to write in a book, to enter, to register, to book, to record. Einen Schuldposten —, to enter a debt in the journal; ich trug eine Bemerkung in mein Taschenbuch ein, I entered a memorandum in my pocket-book. *b)* to yield, to produce, to bring in. Ländereien tragen nicht mehr als drei Procent ein, lands yield not more than three per cent; sein Amt trägt jährlich tausend Thaler ein, his office yields one thousand dollars a year; ein Geschäft, der wenig einträgt, an unprofitable employment.

Eintrage-gabel, *f.* a fork used by glass-makers. —**kolben**, —**löffel**, *m.* 1) [with glass-makers] strokal. 2) a small copper-spoon used by silversmiths.

Einträger, *m.* [-s, *pl.* -] [rather unusual] he that bears or carries in; he that books or registers, a bookkeeper; *it.* a registrar.

Einträglich, *adj.* and *adv.* yielding or bringing profit or gain, profitable. Ein —er Handel, a profitable trade; ein —es Geschäft oder Amt, a lucrative business or office.

Eintränken, *v. tr.* to soak in a liquid, to steep, to imbue. Metalle —, [in metallurgy] to soak metals in fused lead; eine Fläche mit Leimwasser —, [with painters] to size a surface. *Fig.* †Ich werde es ihm —, I'll make him pay for it.

Einträufeln, I. *v. tr.* to drip or drop in, to infuse by drops, to instil. Einem Oel in die Wunde —, to drip oil in any one's wound. II. *v. intr.* [u. w. seyn] to penetrate dripping or dropping.

Eintreffen, *ir. v. intr.* [u. w. seyn] 1) [to come to or reach] to arrive. Die Post trifft um sieben Uhr ein, the post arrives at seven o'clock; er traf am Sonntag in der Hauptstadt ein, he reached the capital on sunday. Syn. V. Ankommen. 2) *Fig. a)* to be effected, to be accomplished, to be fulfilled, as a prophecy or prediction. Seine Hoffnungen oder Erwartungen treffen nicht ein, he is disappointed of his hopes or expectations, or his hopes or expectations are disappointed. *b)* to coincide, to agree, not to differ in the least. Die Rechnung trifft ein, the account is right.

Eintreiben, *ir. v. tr.* to drive in or into. Das Vieh in den Stall —, to drive cattle into the stable; Pfähle in die Erde —, to ram piles into the earth; einen Keil in das Holz —, to drive a wedge into wood; das Leder —, [with tanners] to soak the leather. *Fig.* Geld, Schulden —, to call in money, debts.

Eintreiber, *m.* [-s, *pl.* -] he that drives in. *Fig.* Der — der gerichtlichen Gebühren, a collector of fees.

Eintreiblich, *adj.* and *adv.* that may be obtained from a debtor. Die Schuld ist —, the debt is recoverable.

Eintreten, *ir.* I. *v. intr.* [u. w. seyn] to enter, to go in, to step in. Nachdem ich eingetreten war, after I had gone in. *Fig.* Die Fluth tritt ein, the tide makes; in ein Amt —, to enter upon an office; in ein Geschäft —, to enter into a business; es ist Neulicht [Neumond] eingetreten, it is new-moon; die Nacht tritt ein, night is coming on; der Winter tritt ein, winter sets in; wenn der Fall — sollte, in the event or contingency, if it should so fall out or happen, in case. II. *v. tr.* 1) to tread in or down, to beat or press with the feet, to make fast by treading. Die Wurzeln eines Baumes —, to fix the roots of a tree in the earth by treading them down; sich einen Nagel —, to run a nail into one's foot. 2) to break by treading. Eine Thür —, to kick a door open; den Boden eines Fasses —, to stave in the head of a cask; die Schuhe —, to tread one's shoes down at the heels.

Eintrichtern, *v. tr.* to pour in by means of a funnel. Bier in Flaschen —, to bottle beer by means of a funnel. *Fig.** to infuse, to inculcate. Gelehrsamkeit läßt sich nicht —, learning is not acquired without difficulty.

Eintrinken, *v. tr.* to drink [especially with some avidity]; *fig.* to drink in, to imbibe.

Eintritt, *m.* [-es, *pl.* -e] [the act of entering into a place] entrance, entry. Der — in ein Haus oder Zimmer, the entrance into a house or apartment. [in astronomy] ingress. Der — der Sonne in das Zeichen des Widders, the ingress of the sun into the sign of the ram; der — des Mondes in den Schatten der Erde, the ingress of the moon into the shadow of the earth [in eclipses]. *Fig.* entrance, [of things also] commencement, beginning. Der — in das Amt, the entrance into office; er hat freien — im or beim Theater, he has free admission to the theatre; der — des Frühlings, the beginning of the spring.

Eintritts-billet, *n.* ticket of admission. —**fähig**, *adj.* and *adv.* capable of entering [a society &c.], admissible. —**geld**, *n.* entrance-money, entrance. —**karte**, *f.* —**schein**, *m.* ticket of admission. —**zettel**, *m.* 1) V. —billet. 2) V. Antheilschein. —**zimmer**, *n.* an antechamber.

Eintrocknen, *v. intr.* [u. w. seyn] 1) to dry, to dry up. 2) to shrink by drying.

Eintröpfeln, I. *v. tr.* to drip or drop in. II. *v. intr.* [u. w. seyn] to enter or penetrate dripping or dropping. V. Einträufeln.

||**Eintropfen**, *v. tr.* to infuse by drops, to instil.

Eintunken, *v. tr.* to dip in. Das Fleisch in die Brühe —, to dip the meat in the sauce; die Feder —, to dip the pen in ink; Brod in Wein, Kaffee &c. —, to sop bread in wine, coffee &c.; eingetunktes Brod, a sop.

Eintüpfen, *v. intr.* to touch with a point, to tip in. Der Leithund tüpft ein, [with hunters] the leading-hound touches the ground with his nose in hunting.

Einüben, *v. tr.* to use for improvement in skill, to exercise. Rekruten —, to drill recruits; ein wohl eingeübtes Heer, a well disciplined army; ein Pferd —, to train a horse; sich —, to exercise one's self.

Einung, *f.* 1) [the act of uniting or of joining two or more things into one] union. 2) the thing agreed on.

Einverleiben, *v. tr.* to incorporate, to unite. Eroberte Länder einem Königreiche —, to incorporate conquered countries into a kingdom; sie sind Alle einer Gesellschaft einverleibt, they are all incorporated into one company; einem Vertrage noch einen Punkt —, to insert one article more in a treaty.

Einverleibung, *f.* incorporation. Die — der eroberten Länder mit dem römischen Freistaate, the incorporation of the conquered countries into the Roman republic.

Einvernehmen, *n.* [-s] good understanding, harmony, agreement. Sie stehen im besten — [mit einander], they agree thoroughly, they are on the best terms [with one another].

||**Einverstand**, *m.* [-es, *pl.* -stände] V. Einverständniß.

Einverständigen, *v. tr.* to make to agree, to unite.

Einverständniß, *n.* [-sses, *pl.* -sse] intelligence between two or more persons, agreement of minds, union of sentiments. Es herrscht ein gutes — zwischen dem Könige und seinem Volke, there is a good understanding or a good intelligence between the king and his people.

Einverstehen, *ir. v. r.* Sich mit Jemanden — or mit Jemanden einverstanden seyn, to agree with any one; ich bin vollkommen mit Ihnen einverstanden, I am perfectly of your opinion, of your way of thinking; sie sind mit einander einverstanden, there is a good intelligence between them, they understand one another; einverstanden! agreed!

Einverwachsen, *ir. v. intr.* [u. w. seyn] to grow together, to coalesce.

Einvettern, *v. r.* [unusual] sich —, to get related with any one.

Einvieren, *v. tr.* [rather unusual] to reduce to a square, to square.

Einvierung, *f.* [rather unusual] the reducing of a figure to a square. Die — des Zirkels, the quadrature of the circle.

Einwachsen, *ir. v. intr.* [u. w. seyn] 1) to grow in. Der Nagel ist mir eingewachsen, my nail has grown into the flesh. 2) *Fig.* V. Einwurzeln.

Einwage, *f.* [*pl.* -n] that which is lost by weighing out. Ein Pfund — auf den Centner rechnen, to reckon one pound loss in the hundred.

Einwägen, [with some authors *ir.*] I. *v. tr.* to weigh and put in, to put something that is weighed into a vessel. II. *v. r.* sich —, to be lessened, to diminish or lose by weighing.]

Einwalken, *v. tr.* 1) to work in by fulling. Den Thran —, [with leather-dressers] to work in the train-oil by fulling. 2) to make compact, to full [cloth].

Einwalzen, *v. tr.* to press in by rolling.

Einwälzen, *v. tr.* 1) to roll into a place. 2) to break by rolling against.

Einwand, *m.* [-es, *pl.* -wände] adverse reason or argument, objection. V. Einwendung 3. Ein leerer —, a frivolous objection.

Einwanderer, *m.* he that wanders into a place, an immigrant.

Einwandern, *v. intr.* [u. w. seyn] 1) to wander into another country and settle there, to immigrate. 2) [with mechanics] to put up at an inn.

Einwärts, *adv.* [toward the inside, toward the interiour] inward, inwards. Etwas — biegen, to bend a thing inward.

Einwärts-kehrung, —wendung, *f.* Die —kehrung der Augenliederhaare, [a disease in the eye-lashes, in which they are turned in towards the bulb of the eye] trichiasis. **—zieher**, *m.* [in anatomy] adductor oculi [a muscle which draws the eye to the nose].

Einwässern, *v. tr.* to soak in water, to steep in water. Häringe —, to water herrings.

Einweben, [commonly *ir.*] *v. tr.* to weave in. Seide in Baumwolle —, to interweave silk and cotton; Blumen, Bilder —, to weave flowers, figures into a stuff. *Fig.* Eine eingewebte Dichtung, Erzählung, an episode.

Einwechseln, *v. tr.* to change. Dukaten —, to buy ducats; neue Balken —, [in carpentry] to replace old beams with new ones.

Einwehen, I. *v. intr.* to blow in. Der Wind wehet hier zu jeder Ritze ein, the wind enters here at every crevice. II. *v. tr.* to prostrate by wind, to blow down.

Einweibig, *adj.* and *adv.* [in botany] monogynian. Eine —e Pflanze, a monogyn.

Einweichen, *v. tr.* to soak in a liquid, to steep. Brod —, to soak bread; Leinwand beim Bleichen in Lauge —, to steep linen in lye in bleaching; Häute —, to macerate hides; trokkene Blätter in warmes Wasser —, to infuse dried leaves in warm water.

Einweihen, *v. tr.* 1) to appropriate to sacred uses, to devote to the service and worship of God; *it.* [in general] to introduce or establish with solemnity, to inaugurate. Eine Kirche —, to consecrate a church; [in the Romish church] einen Geistlichen —, to ordain a priest; eine Nonne —, to bless a nun. *Fig.* *to use any thing the first time; *it.* to celebrate the first use of a thing [the using any thing the first time]. Einen Rock —, to handsel a coat. 2) to instruct, to acquaint with, to initiate. Einen in die höhern Zweige der Größenlehre —, to initiate any one in the higher branches of mathematics; Einen in die Geheimnisse der Ceres —, to initiate a person into the mysteries of Ceres; ein Eingeweihter, an initiate; an adept.

Einweihung, *f.* 1) consecration; *it.* inauguration. 2) initiation.

Einweihungs-feier, *f.* 1) a religious ceremony, by which any one is initiated; inaugural ceremony; initiatory rites. 2) baptism. **—fest**, *n.* inaugural feast or solemnity. **—lied**, *n.* an inauguratory song. **—predigt, —rede**, *f.* an inaugural sermon or speech. **—schrift**, *f.* [in universities] an inaugural dissertation. **—tag**, *m.* the day of consecration or inauguration.

Einweisen, *ir. v. tr.* to show into a place, to conduct into a place. *Fig.* Jemand in ein Amt —, to place or instate any one in an office, to install any one; Einen in des Andern Güter —, to put any one in possession of another's estate.

Einwelken, *v. intr.* [u. w. seyn] 1) V. Verblühen. 2) to diminish by drying up.

Einwenden, *reg.* and *ir. v. tr.* 1) to turn into. V. Einbiegen, Einlenken. 2) to present or offer in opposition as a reason adverse to something supposed to be erroneous or wrong, to object. Einem etwas —, to object something to or against any one; dagegen ist gar nichts einzuwenden, there is no objection.

Einwendung, *f.* 1) the act of turning. 2) the act of objecting, objection. 3) adverse reason or argument, objection. Der Rath machte —en gegen die Zulassung der Zeugen, the council objected to the admission of the witnesses; er machte einige —en gegen den Beweis, he made some exceptions to the argument.

Einwerfen, *ir. v. tr.* 1) to cast in, to throw in. Bomben —, to bombard a fort. ||*Fig.* Einem einen Zweifel —, to make an objection to any one; er warf Verschiedenes dagegen ein, he made several exceptions to it. 2) [with tailors and sempstresses] to baste in [a sleeve &c.]. 3) to break by throwing.

Einwerfer, *m.* [-s, *pl.* -] 1) he that breaks by throwing &c. 2) *Fig.* objector.

Einwichsen, *v. tr.* 1) to smear or rub with wax, to wax. Die Stiefel oder Schuhe —, to blacken boots or shoes [with shoe-blacking]. †Sich —, to wax one's hair or beard. *Fig.* † —, to teach or instil by blows.

Einwickeln, *v. tr.* 1) to involve, to infold, to inwrap, to envelop. In einen Mantel —, to inwrap in a cloak; etwas in Stroh —, to wrap up something in straw; Waaren in Packtuch —, to envelop goods with canvas; ein Kind —, to swathe or swaddle a child; sich —, to wrap one's self up in a cloak. 2) V. Zusammenwickeln.

1. **Einwiegen**, *ir. v. tr.* V. Einwägen.

2. **Einwiegen**, *v. tr.* to rock [a child] asleep. *Fig.* to lull, to quiet. Er wiegte ihn in eine solche Sicherheit ein, daß &c., he lulled him into such security, that &c.

Einwilligen, *v. intr.* to agree in mind and will, to consent. In etwas —, to consent to a thing; er wollte nicht —, he refused to give his consent to it.

Einwilligung, *f.* [a yielding of the mind or will to that which is proposed] consent. Ein Vater gibt seine — zur Heirath seiner Tochter, a father consents or gives his consent [assent] to the marriage of his daughter.

Einwindeln, [rather unusual] *v. tr.* to swathe, to swaddle [a child].

Einwinden, *ir. v. tr.* 1) to wrap up, to inwrap, to twine. Blumen in einen Eichenkranz —, to entwine flowers in a garland of oakleaves. 2) to put in a place by means of a windlass. [in seamen's language] Das Ankertau mit der Kabelaring —, to heave upon the cable with the voyol; das Ankertau mit der Bratspill —, to heave up the cable with the windlass; das Ankertau mit dem Gangspill —, to weigh the anchor with the ship's capstern.

Einwintern, I. *v. tr.* to preserve till the winter. II *v. intr.* [u. w. seyn] to be inured to the winter. III. *v. r.* [unusual] sich —, to inure one's self to the winter.

1. **Einwirken**, *v. tr.* to weave into, to work in or among other things. Blumen —, to weave flowers into a stuff; Bänder mit eingewirktem Silber, ribbons interwoven with silver. Das Einwirken or die Einwirkung, the act of weaving into or interweaving.

2. **Einwirken**, *v. intr.* to operate on. Der Schrecken wirkte so auf seinen Verstand ein, daß &c., terror had such an effect upon his mind, that &c.; ein Redner kann auf das Volk —, an orator may influence the people; die göttliche Gnade wirkte auf sein Gemüth ein, his mind was wrought upon by divine grace.

Einwirkung, *f.* influence. Die vermeintliche — der Planeten auf das Schicksal der Menschen, the supposed influence of the planets on the fortunes of men.

Einwirren, *v. tr.* to entangle [thread &c.]. *Fig.* to bring into confusion, to entangle.

Einwischen, I. *v. tr.* to soil with rubbing or scouring. II. *v. intr.* [u. w. seyn] to slip into a place.

Einwittern, *v. intr.* [u. w. seyn] [in mini to be brought into by subterraneous vapours

Einwöchig, *adj.* and *adv.* 1) lasting week. 2) in the space of one week.

Einwohnen, I. *v. intr.* to live or dwell i place. *Fig.* Die dem Magnete —den Eigensch ten, the inherent qualities of the magnet. Inwohnen. II *v. r.* sich —, to habituate one's to a dwelling, to accustom one's self to a pl by residing there for a shorter or longer ti

Einwohner, *m.* [-s, *pl.* -] —inn, *f.* inh tant. Die — einer Stadt, the inhabitants a town.

Einwohnerschaft, *f.* all the inhabitants a town or place.

Einwölben, *v. tr.* to vault in.

Einwölken, *v. tr.* to envelop in a cloud.

Einwollen, *v. intr.* [in common language] intend, to strive or to endeavour, to enter place. *Fig.* *Das will mir nicht ein, it won't down with me; *it.* I can't comprehend that.

Einwüchsig, *adj.* and *adv.* being of joint [said of plants]. Ein —es Rohr, a can one joint.

Einwühlen, I. *v. tr.* to dig into. Die Sch ne haben große Löcher eingewühlt, the made great holes into the ground by II. *v. r.* sich —, to penetrate by rooting.

Einwurf, *m.* [-es; *pl.* -würfe] advers son or argument, objection. Einen — m to make, to start, or to raise an objection machte ihm verschiedene Einwürfe, he made eral objections to him.

Einwürgen, *v. tr.* to swallow greedily gorge, to glut [meat].

Einwurzeln, *v. intr.* [u. w. seyn] 1) to root, to strike root. Eingewurzelte Bä rooted trees; er stand wie eingewurzelt he stood as if rooted to the place 2) *Fig.* to tablished, to take root, to root. Eing Vorurtheile, rooted prejudices; eingewu Uebel, inveterate ills; eingewurzelter Ha veterate enmity.

Einzacken, *v. tr.* to indent, to jagg. eingezacktes Blatt, a jagged leaf.

Einzahl, *f.* [in grammar] the singular nu

Einzählen, *v. tr.* 1) to count and pu vessel or place. Zählen Sie die Eier in Korb ein, count the eggs into this basket. include in the number, to comprehend in number or sum. Die Weiber mit eingezähl women included.

Einzahnen, *v. tr.* 1) to impress the teet 2) to fasten by means of the teeth. 3) to fa or to fasten on tooth-like things, to inden

Einzangeln, *v. tr.* to take with pin

Einzapfen, *v. tr.* 1) to draw a liquid vessel by tapping. 2) [in carpentry, to jo tenon and mortise] to mortise [a beam into a joist into a girder].

Einzaubern, *v. tr.* to instil by witchcraft.

Einzäunen, *v. tr.* to inclose with a hedge or fence; to take in. Einen Garten —, to hedge a garden; ein Feld —, to fence a field; ein eingezäunter Platz, an inclosure.

Einzehig, *adj.* and *adv.* having one toe only, monodactylous

Einzehren, I. *v. intr* to be diminished by slow dissipation, consumption or evaporation, to waste. Der Wein zehret ein, wine kept in wood loses in quantity. II. *v. r.* sich —, to be diminished by slow consumption or evaporation, to waste.

Einzeichnen, *v. tr.* 1) [= einschreiben] Etwas —, to note something in a book; einen Namen auf or in ein Taschentuch —, to mark a handkerchief; sich —, to enter one's name in a book, list &c. 2) to draw [a picture or figure] in or upon any thing.

Einzelding, *n.* [-es, *pl.* -e] an individual thing.

Einzelglied, *n.* [-es, *pl.* -er] a single member.

Einzelheit, *f.* 1) a state of oneness, individuality. 2) a single being, an individual. 3) distinct, separate or minute part. Er erzählte mir alle —en der Geschichte, he told me all the particulars of the story, he related the story with all the minutiæ, he gave me all the details of the story; sich über —en verbreiten, to enter into particulars.

Einzelleben, *n.* [-s] private life.

Einzelleidend, *adj.* and *adv.* idiopathic.

Einzelleidenheit, *f.* [an original disease in a particular part of the body] idiopathy.

Einzeln, [from ein, eins] *adj.* and *adv.* 1) single, individual. Gott ist ein —es Wesen, God is an individual being; ein —es Ding, a single thing or being; ein —es menschliches Wesen, an individual or single or solitary human being. 2) alone, single. Ein —er Baum, a single tree; ein —es Beispiel, a solitary example; ein —es Haus, a lone house, an isolated house, a detached house; ein —er Handschuh, an unmatched glove; ein —er Band, an odd volume; —es or kleines Geld, small money; sie kamen alle —, they came all one by one; — verkaufen, to sell separately; *it.* to sell by retail; ein —er Mensch, a man that lives alone, or a man that lives by himself [without company]; [in botany] simple, as a bulbous root; ein —es Afterblatt, a solitary stipule. *Fig.* Die —en Umstände der Geschichte, the particulars of the story; er erzählte die Geschichte mit den —en Umständen, he related the story in detail; ich kann mich aufs —e nicht einlassen, I cannot enter into particulars. 3) ‡ lonely, solitary. 4) laying in single parts. Dieser Zeug liegt —, this stuff is one-fold.

Einzelnheit, *f.* singleness.

Einzelstimme, *f.* [*pl.* -n] [in music] a single voice, solo-part.

Einzelverkauf, *m.* [-es, *pl.* -verkäufe] the selling by retail.

Einzelverkäufer, *m.* [-s, *pl.* -] -inn, *f.* retailer.

Einzelwesen, *n.* [-s, *pl.* -] an individual being, an individual.

Einzelwesenheit, *f.* individuality.

Einziehen, *ir.* I. *v. tr.* 1) to draw in or into. Einen Balken —, to put in a new beam or sill; einen Faden —, to run a thread through a stuff; den Faden in die Nadel —, to thread a needle. *Fig.* *a*) Schulden —, to collect debts; Geld —, to call in money; der König zog das Lehen ein, the king granted no more the escheated fief; die Steuern —, to collect taxes; eine Stelle —, to confer no more a vacant office; Jemands Besoldung —, to deprive any one of his salary; Jemands Güter —, to confiscate any one's estate; einen Verbrecher —, to arrest a criminal; Nachricht —, to get intelligence. *b*) † or ‖ Einen —, to entice, to inveigle any one. 2) to draw in, to pull to a smaller compass, to pull back. Die Segel —, to brail or furl the sails, to take in sail; die Schnecke ziehet die Hörner ein, the snail draws in the horns; die Schultern —, to keep in the shoulders. *Fig.* †Die Pfeife —, to speak in a lower strain, to lower one's tone, to submit. 3) to draw into a less compass, to contract, to narrow. Einen Damm, einen Graben —, to narrow a dike, a ditch; Handkrausen —, to contract cuffs [by running a thread through them]; eine Mauer —, to taper a wall. 4) to drink in, to suck up, to imbibe. Der Schwamm zieht das Wasser ein, the spunge absorbs water; das Löschpapier zieht die Tinte ein, blotting paper imbibes ink; die Luft —, to draw air, to inhale air.

II. *v. intr.* [u. w. seyn] to enter. *a*) to enter in a procession, to march in. Die Truppen ziehen heute ein, the troops will march in to-day. *b*) to enter a house as lodger, to enter into a new lodging. Er zog bei ihm ein, he took lodgings at his house; sind Sie heute eingezogen? have you got into your new lodging to-day? *c*) to enter into pores or interstices. Der Regen ziehet in die Erde ein, rain soaks into the earth.

III. *v. r.* sich —, 1) to contract, to shrink. Das Tuch ziehet (sich) ein, cloth shrinks [by moisture]. 2) [used in the past participle as an *adv.*: eingezogen] Er lebt sehr eingezogen, he retrenches much his expenses; *it.* he leads a very secluded life.

Einziehung, *f.* 1) the act of drawing in &c., pulling back &c. *Fig.* Die — der Steuern, the collection of taxes; die — der Güter, confiscation. 2) *Fig.* *a*) [in architecture] the contraction of the upper part of a wall, a tapering of a wall. *b*) [the contraction of the upper part of a column] diminution. 3) [a semicircular cavity between the tores in the bases of columns] scotia, trochil, trochilus, [and with workmen] the casement.

Einzig, [from ein] *adj.* 1) alone in its kind, this above all others. Dieser —e Mann war der Krone werth, this man alone was worth or worthy the crown. 2) one alone, single, only. Johann war der —e Mensch, der zugegen war, John was the only man present; dessen —e Freude es war &c., whose only joy was &c.; ein —es Kind, an only child; —er Sohn, [in Script.] only-begotten son; der —e Erbe, sole heir; nicht ein —es Wort, not a single word; dies ist — in seiner Art, this is most extraordinary; unparalleled; unprecedented. II. *adv.* [with allein] alone, only, without another. — und allein, only and solely; sich — und allein auf seine eigene Stärke verlassen, to rely solely on one's own strength.

Einzigkeit, *f.* the quality of being one, oneness.

Einzingeln, V. Umzingeln.

Einzischeln, *v. tr.* to whisper in the ear. Er hat ihm etwas eingezischelt, he whispered something in his ear.

Einzögling, [rather unusual] *m.* [-es, *pl.* -e] 1) he that settles in any country or place, settler. 2) a native.

Einzöglingsrecht, *n.* V. Eingeburtsrecht.

Einzöllig, *adj.* and *adv.* containing one inch.

Einzuckern, *v. tr.* to cover with sugar, to sugar.

Einzug, *m.* [-es, *pl.* -züge] 1) entry, entrance with ceremonious solemnity. Der König hielt seinen feierlichen —, the king made his solemn entrance [into the town]; die Truppen hielten heute ihren —, the troops marched in to-day; der — in ein Haus, the entry into a house as lodger. 2) a thing drawn in, put in; [with carpenters] a new beam or sill put in.

Einzwängen, I. *v. tr.* 1) to force between close bodies, to squeeze in. Die Hand —, to wedge in one's hand. 2) to press forcibly together. Ein geleimtes Brett —, to put a glued board in the press; wie zwängt den schlanken Leib die enge Schnürbrust ein, how the strait stays the slender waist constrain. II. *v. r.* sich —, 1) to squeeze one's self into or between. 2) *Fig.* *to put on strait clothes.

Einzweigen, *v. tr.* to ingraft a twig of one tree on another.

Einzwingen, *ir. v. tr.* to force in, to force into. Einem Trinken —, to press any one to drink; Jemandem Arzenei —, to force a person to take or swallow physic.

Eis, *n.* [-ses] [allied to Eisen, from the old aiten = leuchten] 1) [water or fluid congealed] ice. Es frieret —, it freezes; der Wein ist zu — gefroren, the wine is frozen; das — gehet auf, the ice breaks up; [in seamen's lang.] das — fängt an zu gehen, the ice begins to break up; ein vom Eise besetztes Schiff, an ice-bound ship; festes —, body of the ice; fahrbares —, open ice; — in großen zusammenhängenden Massen, packed ice; schwimmende —massen, a vast body of floating ice, ice-isles; des Hauptes —, [in poetry] a hoary head. *Fig.* Das — brechen, to break the ice [to make the first opening to any attempt, to remove the first obstructions or difficulties, to open the way]; die Liebe hat nie das — seines Herzens aufgethauet, his icy or unfeeling heart was never softened to love; vor Schrecken gerann mein Blut zu —, terror curdled my blood into ice. 2) [with confectioners, Gefrornes] ice [for eating].

Eis-achat, *m.* uncoloured agate. —**alaun**, *m.* rhomboidal alumstone. —**apfel**, *m.* V. Glasapfel. —**bad**, *n.* a bath prepared with ice. —**bahn**, *f.* a slide. —**balken**, *m.* [in hydraulics] one of the beams of an ice-breaker. —**bank**, *f.* ice-isle. —**bär**, *m.* 1) the polar or white bear. 2) **Fig.* a peevish or ill-humoured person. —**baum**, *m.* V. —bock. —**becher**, *m.* ice-cup. —**bedeckt**, *adj.* and *adv.* covered with ice, frozen. —**beere**, *f.* snow-berry. —**beifuß**, *m.* the silky wormwood. —**bein**, *n.* [in anatomy] hip-bone. —**berg**, *m.* 1) iceberg. 2) a glacier. —**bier**, *n.* V. Pfingstbier. —**birn**, *f.* [a species of pear] the virgoule or virgoleuse. —**blick**, *m.* [in the Arctic regions] iceblink. —**blume**, *f.* [chiefly used in *pl.* -n] crystallisations [on the windows formed by the frost]. —**bock**. —**brecher**, *m.* an ice breaker, breaker. —**bruch**, *m.* the breaking of the ice. —**büchse**, *f.* [with confectioners] a cylindrical box for preserving ice. —**dorn**, *m.* the common star-fish. —**eimer**, *m.* ice-pail. V. also Kühlgefäß. —**ente**, *f.* the long-tailed duck. —**entlein**, *n.* the smeath or smee, white nun. —**essig**, *m* concentrated vinegar. —**fahrt**, *f.* 1) skating. 2) V. —gang 2. —**feigenkraut**, *n.* V. —kraut. —**feld**, *n.* a field of ice, ice-field, a large body of floating ice. —**fisch**, *m.* the ice-whale. —**frei**, *adj.* and *adv.* free from ice. —**gang**, *m.* 1) the breaking up of the ice. 2) a walk on the ice. —**gebirge**, *n.* a chain of glaciers. —**gefilde**, *n.* fields of ice, a plain of ice. —**gefüllt**, *adj.* and *adv.* 1) icy. 2) *Fig.* cold, frigid, destitute of affection or passion, icy. —**grau**, *adj.* and *adv.* frosty, hoary. —graue Haare, hoary hair; ein —grauer Kopf, a hoary head; —graue Locken, snowy locks. —griff, *m.* [a sharp pointed piece of iron on a shoe for a horse, used to prevent the animal from slipping] a calkin, calker, ||calk. —grube, *f.* ice-house. —hauer, *m.* a person who cuts the ice. —haupt, *n.* a frosty or hoary head. —kalt, *adj.* and *adv.* cold as ice. Eine —kalte Nacht, a frosty night. *Fig.* Ein —kaltes Herz, an icy or frosty heart. —kälte, *f.* iceness, icy coldness [used also in a fig. sense]. —keller, *m.* ice-house, ice-cellar. —kessel, *m.* an elegant copper-vessel for cooling liquor in ice. —kibitz, *m.* the small cloven-footed gull. —kluft, *f.* [a long cleft in trees &c., proceeding from frost] fissure. —klüftig, *adj.* and *adv.* having fissures [said of trees]. —knochen, *m.* V. —bein. —kraut, *n.* diamond figmarigold, or ice-plant. —kruste, *f.* the crust of ice. *Fig.* Die —kruste [better —rinde] ihres Herzens, the icy cover of her heart. —lauf, *m.* skating. —leben, *n.* [a plant] bladder campion, or spatling poppy. —lockig, *adj.* and *adv.* 1) having icy curls. 2) *Fig.* having hoary or snowy locks. —luft, *f.* a frosty air. —mann, *m.* 1) the figure of a man in ice. 2) *Fig.* a frosty person. —mauer, *f.* a wall of ice. —meer, *n.* the polar sea, the frozen Ocean. —meve, *f.* the fulmar petrel. —nagel, *m.* frost-nail. Mit —nägeln versehen, rough-shod. —nebel, *m.* rime. —netz, *n.* a great net used for fishing in winter. —pfahl, *m.* a pale or post to break the floating ice. —pfeiler, *m.* a pillar placed in a river, to break the floating ice, and prevent it from injuring a bridge below. —pflanze, *f.* a plant covered with icy pimples as the iceplant. —pflug, *m.* an instrument for cutting the ice, ice-plough. —pol, *m.* the North pole, Arctic pole. —punkt, *m.* [Gefrierpunkt] the freesing point on a thermometer. —rinde, *f.* V. —kruste. —säge, *f.* a machine resembling a saw for cutting the ice. —schemel, *m.* a layer of ice [in Switzerland]. —schimmer, *m.* V. —blick. —scholle, *f.* a flake of ice. —schuh, *m.* V. Schlittschuh. —spath, *m.* [a variety of feldspar] icespar. —spiegel, *m.* [or Zuckereis, with confectioners, concreted sugar] ice. —spitze, *f.* 1) icicle. 2) V. —griff. —sporn, *m.* 1) an iron point fixed under shoes, to enable a person to walk on the ice, creeper. ||2) [*pl.* -sporen] V. —pfeiler. —stein, *m.* [a fluate of soda and alumin, found in Greenland] cryolite. —topf, *m.* [a vessel for making ice in] ice-pail. —vogel, *m.* 1) the king's-fisher, halcyon. 2) the frigate-bird. 3) the puffin or coulterneb. 4) a species of day-butterfly [papilio populi]. —wermuth, *m.* the silky wormwood. —wind, *m.* a frosty wind, a chilly breeze. —zacken, —zapfen, *m.* icicle. —zucker, *m.* white sugar-candy.

1. **Eisen**, [from Eis = ice] I. *v. tr.* 1) to cut the ice [more used in compos. as aufeisen, auseisen, loseisen &c.]. 2) to convert into ice, to ice. 3) *Fig.* to chill, to freeze, to ice. II. *v. intr.* [u. w. seyn] to congeal into ice.

2. **Eisen**, [from Eisen = iron] *v. tr.* to shoe [a horse &c].

Eisen, *n.* [-s] [probably from the old eisen = brennen, leuchten; Goth. *ais* signifies Erz] 1) [a metal] iron, [in the old chimistry] mars. Gediegenes —, native iron; rohes — [Roheisen], pig-iron; sprödes —, brittle iron; geschmeidiges —, soft or pure iron, malleable iron; rothbrüchiges —, red-short iron; kaltbrüchiges —, cold-short iron; geschnittenes —, slit-iron; [in mineralogy] arseniksaures —, cube-ore, arseniate of iron; chromsaures —, chromate of iron, chromiferous oxydulated iron; kohlensaures —, carbonate of iron; oktaedrisches — [Meteoreisen], meteoric native iron; oxalsaures —, humboldit; phosphorsaures —, blue iron-ore, phosphate of iron; [in general] altes —, old-broken iron, scrap-iron, bushel-iron. *Fig.* † and || [said of antiquated and useless things, and also of women, whose beauty or prime of life is past] Sie gehört jetzt unter das alte —, she has grown rather rusty. *Prov.* Das — schmieden, weil es warm ist, to strike the iron while it is hot; Noth bricht —, necessity has no law. 2) an instrument or utensil made of iron, an iron, as ein Plätt—, ein Bügel—, &c. 3) [in common language] a horse-shoe. Einem Pferde die — aufschlagen, to shoe a horse; in die — hauen, to hit the legs together in going, to cut. 4) *pl* irons, fetters. Einen in die — legen or schmieden, to fetter any one.

Eisen-ader, *f.* a vein of iron-ore. —arbeit, *f.* 1) the working in iron. 2) [any thing made of iron] ironwork. —arbeiter, *m.* a worker in iron. —arsenik, *m.* arseniate of iron. —artig, *adj.* and *adv.* partaking of iron, irony, ferruginous, [in chimistry] martial, ferric. —arzenei, *f.* a medicinal preparation of iron. —auflösung, *f.* a solution of iron in acids. —bahn, *f.* iron rail-road, rail-way. ||—bart, *m.* V. Eisvogel. —baum, *m.* 1) [in ironworks] a wooden pole tipped with iron. 2) [in ship-building] a crow. 3) [in nat. history] *a*) ironwood, sideroxylon. *b*) purple dracæna. —beerbaum, *m.* 1) V. Rainweide. 2) V. Hartriegel. —beize, *f.* [in ironworks] iron-liquor. —bergwerk, *n.* iron-mine. —beschlag, *m.* 1) V. Eisenblüthe. 2) any iron covering or garnishment. —bitterspath, *m.* iron-bitterspar. —blau, *n.* blue iron-ore, phosphate of iron. Blätteriges —blau, V. —blauspath; erdiges —blau, V. —blauerde; späthiges —blau, V. —blauspath. —blauerde, *f.* blue martial earth, blue iron-earth, native Prussian blue. —blauspath, *m.* foliated blue iron-ore. —blech, *n.* 1) iron-plate. Verzinntes —blech, white iron. 2) sheet-iron or iron in sheets. —blumen, *pl.* —blüthe, *f.* flower of iron [flos ferri], a variety of arragonite, coralloidal arragonite. —bohrer, *m.* a bore used for boring iron. —brand, *m.* the magnet or loadstone. —branderz, *n.* oxidated argito-bituminiferous iron. —braunkalk, —braunspath, *m.* brown- or pearl-spar. —brech, *n.* the moon-wort. —bruch, *m.* iron-mine. —chrom, *m.* chromate of iron, chromiferous oxydulated iron. —draht, *m.* iron-wire. —druse, *f.* crystallized iron-ore. —erde, *f.* martial earth. Blaue —erde, V. —blauerde, —erz, *n.* iron-ore. Dodekaedrisches —erz, V. Franklinit; diprismatisches —erz, V. Lievrit; oktaedrisches —erz, magnetic iron-stone, oxydulated iron; prismatisches —erz, brown iron-ore; rhomboedrisches —erz, V. —oxyd. —farbe, *f.* iron-gray colour, ferruginous colour. —farbig, *adj.* and *adv.* iron-gray. —feil, —feilicht, *n.* iron-filings. —fest, *adj.* and *adv.* hard as iron, irony. *Fig.* Er hat einen —festen Körper, he has got an iron constitution; er besitzt einen —festen Willen, his will is firm as iron. —firniß, *m.* iron-varnish. —fleck, —flecken, *m.* iron-mould. —fleckig, *adj.* iron-moulded. —fluß, *m.* V. —blüthe *Fig.* † and * —fresser, *m.* a noisy, blustering, overbearing fellow, a bully, a hector. Ein wahrer —fresser, a brave. —funke, *m.* a spark or sparkle of iron. —gang, *m.* a lode or vein of iron-ore. —gans, *f.* a pig or sow of melted iron. —gehalt, *m.* the ferruginous parts of any body. —gemisch, *n.* [in chimistry] amalgam of iron. —geräth, *n.* an iron utensil. —gießer, *m.* iron-founder. —gießerei, *f.* iron-foundery. —gitter, *n.* an iron-grate. Die —gitter an Fenstern, iron-bars, stanchions. —glanz, *m.* 1) iron-glance, specular iron. Späthiger —glanz, or muschliger and gemeiner —glanz, common iron-glance; schuppiger —glanz, micaceous iron-glance, iron mica. —glas, *n.* brittle iron-ore. —glimmer, *m.* V. —glanz. Prismatischer —glimmer, blue iron-ore, phosphate of iron. —grau, *adj.* and *adv.* iron-gray. —graupe, *f.* [with miners, Wolfram] an ore of tungsten, wolfram. —griff, *m.* 1) an iron handle. 2) an iron or firm grasp. —grube, *f.* iron-mine, ironpit. —gußwaare, *f.* cast-iron ware. —haltig, *adj.* and *adv.* [containing particles of iron] ferruginous. —haltige Erde, martial earth; —haltiges Wasser, ferruginous water. —hammer, *m.* 1) [in iron-mills] a large hammer. 2) an iron-mill, iron-works. —hand, *f.* 1) iron-hand, an artificial hand made of iron. 2) *Fig.* iron-hand. —handel, *m.* iron-trade, hardware-trade. —händler, *m.* iron-monger, hardware-man. —hart, *adj.* and *adv.* as hard as iron, irony. *Fig.* Ein —hartes Herz habend, iron-hearted. —härte, *f.* 1) the hardness of iron. 2) *Fig.* firmness, fixedness; *it.* great hardness. —helm, *m.* 1) an iron helmet. 2) the wooden helve or handle of an iron utensil. —holz, *n.* —holzbaum, *m.* V. —baum 3. —hütchen, —hütlein, *n.* 1) a small iron hat or helmet, [in heraldry] vair. 2) [a plant] common monk's hood, or wolf's bane. —hütte, *f.* iron-mill, iron-works. —joch, *n.* [*fig.*] fetters. —kalk, *m.* 1) calcined iron. 2) Schuppiger und dichter —kalk, sparry ironstone, spathose iron. —kies, *m.* martial or iron-pyrites, sulphuret of iron. Hexaedrischer —kies, = —kies; prismatischer —kies, white iron-pyrites, coxcomb; hepatic and cellular pyrites. —kiesel, *m.* iron-flint, ferruginous quartz. —kitt, *m.* iron glue. —klump[en] *m.* sow-iron. —knecht, *m.* [in iron-mills] a small piece of iron on the anvil. —kram, *m.* hardware-trade or -shop, iron-mongery. —krämer, *m.* V. —händler. —kraut, *n.* 1) iron-wort, vervain. 2) smooth crepis, or yellow succory. 3) the white annual stachys. —krystalle, *pl.* [in chimistry] crystals formed by dissolving iron in acids. —kuchen, *m.* wafer. V. Waffel. —kütt, *m.* V. —kitt. —lack, *m.* iron-varnish. —lahn, *m.* flattened iron-wire. —letten, *m.* iron-clay. —loth, *n.* a cement for soldering broken iron. —luppen, *pl.* iron lumps. —mahl, V. —[illegible] —mann, *m.* V. —glimmer. —marmor, *m.* V. Basalt. —miner, *m.* V. —erz. —mo[illegible] *m.* earthy magnetic iron-stone, earthy oxydulated iron. —mulm, *m.* V. —mohr. —niere, *f.* kidney-shaped or veniform clay-iron-stone. —ocker, *m.* red ochre. —ofen, *m.* [in iron-works] a finery. —öl, *n.* [in chimistry] a solution of iron in muriatic acid. —opal, *m.* ferruginous opal, jasper opal. —oxyd, *n.* [a crystallized oxide of iron] oligist iron. Schwefelsaures —oxyd, V. —vitriol. —oxyd-hydrat, *n.* = prismatisches —erz. —oxydul, *n.* = [illegible] saures —. —pecherz, *n.* V. —sinter. —platte, *f.* iron-plate. Dünne —platten, sheets of iron. —probe, *f.* 1) iron-test, the trial of metals on iron. 2) [an ancient form of trial to determine guilt or innocence by touching a red-hot iron bar &c.] fire-ordeal. —rahm, *m.* brown hematite, fibrous brown iron-ore, iron-glimmer. Brauner —rahm, scaly brown iron-ore, bronze iron-froth. —rahmig, *adj.* and *adv.* hematitic. —rost, *m.* rust on iron. Der aufgelöste —rost, iron-liquor. —röst, *m.* an iron grate. —safran, *m.* a solution of iron. —salmiakblumen, *pl.* [in chimistry] a mixture of sal ammoniac and muriate of iron. —salz, [in chimistry] sulphate of iron. —sammet[erz], *n.* scaly brown iron-ore, or brown iron-froth. —sand, *m.* iron-sand, arenaceous magnetic ironstone. —sau, *f.* 1) [in mining] sow of iron. 2) [in metallurgy] scorious iron. —schaum, *m.* scaly red iron-ore, red iron-froth. —scheel, V. Wolfram. —scheibe, *f.* a miner's compass. —schimmel, *m.* an iron-gray horse. —schlacke, *f.* slag of iron, iron-dross. —schl[ag], *m.* 1) sparks of iron. V. also Hammerschlag.

the privilege or monopoly of dealing in iron-wares. —schlich, *m.* muddy iron-ore. —schmied, *m.* iron-smith, black-smith. —schmiede, *f.* iron-forge, smithy. —schneider, *m.* V. Stempelschneider. —schrot, *n.* small shot. —schuß, *m.* V. —glimmer and —erz. —schüssig, *adj.* and *adv.* ferruginous. —schwärze, *f.* [in mining] 1) V. —glimmer. 2) a sort of blacking prepared from iron. —schweif, *m.* [in mining] granular iron-glance. —schweifig, *adj.* and *adv.* [in mining] 1) containing or resembling granular iron-glance. 2) V. —schüssig. —sinter, *m.* pitchy iron-ore. —sirup, *m.* an inspissated tincture of iron, iron-sirup. —späne, *pl.* V. —feil. —spath, *m.* sparry ironstone, spathose iron. —spiegel, *m.* specular ironstone. —stab, *m.* —stange, *f.* an iron bar. —staub, *m.* iron-dust. —stein, *m.* ironstone, an ore of iron. —steinig, *adj.* and *adv.* containing ironstone. —stufe, *f.* an ore of iron. —theilchen, *n.* an irony particle. —thon, *m.* iron-clay, toadstone. —thor, *n.* an iron gate. —thür, *f.* an iron door. —tinctur, *f.* [in medicine] tincture of iron. —titan, *m.* ferruginous titanium. —vitriol, *m.* 1) green vitriol, sulphate or vitriol of iron. 2) = —salz; [in chimistry] sulphate of iron. —waare, *f.* iron-ware. —wasser, *n* chalybeate water. —weinstein, *m.* tartrate of iron. —werk, *n.* 1) [any thing made of iron] ironwork. 2) ironworks. —wurz, *f.* [a plant] scabious centaury, or great knap-weed. —zeit, *f.* iron times. —zeug, *n.* iron tools.

Eiserich, *m.* [-s] V. Eisenkraut.

Eisern, *adj.* and *adv.* 1) [made of iron, consisting of iron] iron. Ein —es Thor, an iron gate; Götz von Berlichingen, mit der —en Hand, Goetz of Berlichingen with the iron hand. *Fig.* *a*) firm, robust, iron. Eine —e Natur, an iron constitution. *b*) steady, persevering. Eine —e Treue, an unshaken fidelity; —e Beharrlichkeit, unwearied or indefatigable perseverance; mit —em Fleiß, with an indefatigable application. *c*) harsh, severe, unfeeling. Ein —es Herz habend, ironhearted, hardhearted. *d*) harsh, rude, miserable, iron. Das —e Zeitalter, the iron age of the world. ||*e*) that cannot be legally separated from a thing, belonging to a thing for ever. —es Vieh, —e Pferde, unalienable cattle, horses. ||*f*) Ein —er Brief, [in law] a letter of respit. 2) relating to iron instruments or tools. Ein —es Geprassel, a rattling caused by iron weapons; das —e Feld der Schlacht, the field of battle; ein —er Regen, a shower of balls.

Eiserpäthen, V. Sandriedgras.

Eisewig, *m.* [-s] [a plant] common hyssop.

Eisig, *adj.* and *adv.* 1) [covered with ice] icy. 2) chilling, chilly, icy.

Eissprußel, *m.* [-s] [with huntsmen] the brow-antler.

1. **Eitel**, [perhaps from the old eiten, brennen, glänzen, that is nicht dunkel, thence lauter, pur &c.] *adj.* that and that only, mere, pure. —es Brod essen, to eat nothing but bread, to eat dry bread; er that dies aus —em Mitleiden, he did that from pure compassion; — Bosheit, pure malice.

2. **Eitel**, [eitler, eitelste] [does not appear to be allied to 1. Eitel, but to belong to öde] *adj.* 1) empty, void, idle, trifling, vain. —es Geschwätz, idle talk; —e Hoffnungen, vain hopes; noch hege die —e Hoffnung, nor vainly hope; eine —e Chimäre, a vain chimera; —le Gedanken, foolish thoughts; —e Ehre, vain glory; —e Schönheit, perishable beauty; wie — sind die Freuden dieses Lebens! how transient are the pleasures of this life! es ist Alles ganz —, es ist Alles ganz —, [in Script.] vanity of vanities, all is vanity; —e Künste, unprofitable tricks. 2) idle, ineffectual, fruitless, vain. Alle Versuche, alle Anstrengungen waren —, all attempts, all efforts were vain. 3) [proud of petty things, or of trifling attainments, conceited] vain. Ein —er Mensch, a vain person; — auf ihre Kunst, vain of their art; er ist — auf seine Person, seine Talente, he is conceited of his person, of his talents; — im Anzuge, foppish; [also of things] ein —er Anzug, an ostentatious dress.

‡**Eitelmuth**, *m.* empty pride, vanity, vainness.

Eitelkeit, *f.* [*pl* -en] 1) the state of being vain, the idleness. Die — dieses Lebens, the vanity of [this] life; die — seiner Hoffnungen, the vanity of his hopes; die — ihrer Wünsche, the vanity of their desires; die — seiner Bemühungen, the vanity of his efforts. 2) [empty pride, inspired by an overweening conceit of one's personal attainments or decorations] vanity, vainness. — ist die Hoffnung der Narren, vanity is the food of fools; er besitzt eine große —, he is very vain. 3) idleness, [empty pleasure, idle show, unsubstantial enjoyment] vanity. 4) [vain or perishable things collectively, the things of this world, as opposed to eternity] idleness. So lange wir in dieser — leben, as long as we live in this world.

Eiter, *m.* [-s, *pl.* -] [from the old eiten = brennen; A. S. *Aeter* and *Ater* signifies Gift] [the white or yellowish matter generated in ulcers and wounds in the process of healing &c.] matter, pus, suppuration. — absetzen, to suppurate.

Eiter-auge, *n* [in surgery, a disease in the eye] hypopion. —befördernd, *adj.* and *adv.* promoting suppuration, suppurative. Das —befördernde Mittel, a suppurative, maturant. —beule, *f.* a boil, an abscess, imposthume, impostumation. —blase, *f.* a bladder or vesicle filled with pus. —blatter, *f.* a purulent pustule, pimple or wheal. —bruch, *m.* [in medicine] empyomphalocele. —brust, *f.* [in medic.] empyema. —butzen, *m.* V. —stock. —fluß, *m.* 1) the discharge of pus. 2) a running sore. —fraß, *m.* 1) corrosion caused by an ulcer. 2) a part of the body affected with a corrosive ulcer. —geschwulst, *f.* V. —beule. —machend, *adj.* and *adv.* V. —befördernd. —milch, *f.* purulent milk. —nessel, *f.* the small nettle. —stock, *m.* [the inner part of an ulcer or boil] the core. —weiß, *adj.* and *adv.* white like pus. —ziehend, *adj.* and *adv.* promoting suppuration, suppurative.

Eiterícht, *adj.* and *adv.* resembling pus.

Eiterig, *adj.* and *adv.* purulent, mattery. Ein —es Geschwür, a purulent ulcer.

Eitern, *v. intr.* to generate pus, to suppurate. Die Wunde eitert, the wound festers.

Eiterung, *f.* [the process of generating purulent matter] suppuration. In — übergehen, to suppurate.

Eiterungsmittel, *n.* a suppurative.

***Ejiciren**, *v. tr.* [in law] to disseize [a tenant of his freehold &c.].

||**Eke**, *f.* [*pl.* -n] 1) V. Eiche. 2) a sort of boat.

***Ekebergit**, *m.* [-es, *pl.* -en] [a mineral, supposed to be a variety of scapolite] ekebergite.

Ekel, [Ekel and Eckel] *m.* [-s] [probably allied to the A. S. *ace*, Schmerz] 1) [an unpleasant sensation excited in the organs of taste by something disagreeable, and when extreme, producing loathing or nausea] disgust, disrelish, distaste. — verursachen, to disgust; einen — bekommen, to nauseate; er bekam einen — davor, he was disgusted at it. 2) nausea, qualm, loathing, squeamishness of the stomach. Einen — vor Arzeneien haben, to loathe medicines, to distaste drugs; der Kranke hat einen — vor gesunden Speisen, the patient nauseates wholesome food; der — vor gewissen Speisen, distaste for a particular kind of food. 3) dislike, aversion, disgust. Ein grobes, bäurisches Betragen erregt —, clownishness in behaviour excites disgust; es wird Einem zum — &c., it sickens one. 4) a thing that disgusts. Das Leben wurde ihm zum —, he took a disgust at life; das Landleben ist ihm zum —, he is sick of a country-life.

Ekel, [ekeler, ekelste] *adj.* and *adv.* 1) feeling disgust. 2) nice, squeamish, fastidious, queasy. Er ist sehr — im Essen, he is very nice in his diet; sein —er Magen, his queasy stomach; er ist sehr — in der Wahl seiner Freunde, he is very particular in the choice of his friends. 3) delicate, nice, fine. Eine —e Farbe, a delicate colour. 4) disgusting, disgustful, loathsome, nauseous, regarded with abhorrence. Ein —er Anblick, an offensive sight.

Ekelname, *m.* [opprobrious appellation] nickname.

Ekelhaft, [ekelhafter, ekelhafteste] *adj.* and *adv.* 1) disgusting, disgustful, loathsome, nauseous. Eine —e Arzenei, a nauseous drug or medicine; ein —er Geruch, an offensive smell; eine —e Krankheit, a loathsome disease; auf eine —e Weise [—], nauseously, disgustingly; ein —er Mensch, a disgusting person. *Fig.* Ein — knechtisches Wesen, a disgusting servility. 2) [used incorrectly for ekel] having a stomach that is easily turned or that readily nauseates any thing, squeamish. — seyn, to have a stomach that is easily turned.

Ekelhaftigkeit, *f.* loathsomeness, nauseousness.

Ekelig, [ekeliger, ekeligste] *adj.* and *adv.* 1) experiencing disgust at, squeamish. 2) V. Ekelhaft 1.

Ekeln, I. *v. intr.* to excite disgust. Essen und Trinken ekelt mir [erregt mir Ekel, ist mir ekelhaft], I loathe food and drink. II. *v. imp* Es ekelt mich, I feel disgust; es ekelt mich jede Speise or mir ekelt vor jeder Speise, I loathe every meat. *Fig.* Es — mich gemeine Sitten, I am disgusted with vulgar manners; mich — gemeine Scherze, I disrelish vulgar jests; mich ekelt deine Thorheit, I am disgusted at your folly. III. *v. r.* sich —, to feel disgust, to nauseate, to loathe Ich ekele mich davor, I feel disgust at it, I loathe it.

***Eklektiker**, *m.* [-s, *pl.* -] [a philosopher, who selected from the various systems such opinions and principles as he judged to be sound and rational] an eclectic.

***Eklektisch**, *adj.* and *adv.* eclectic.

***Eklipse**, *f.* [*pl.* -n] [in astronomy] an eclipse [of the moon &c.].

***Eklipsiren**, *v. tr.* to eclipse [the sun or a star]. *Fig.* Den Ruhm eines Helden — [better verdunkeln], to eclipse the glory of a hero.

***Ekliptik**, *f.* [in astronomy] the ecliptic.

***Ekliptisch**, *adj.* and *adv.* [in astron.] ecliptic.

***Ekloge**, *f.* [*pl.* -n] eclogue. Virgils —n, the eclogues of Virgil.

Ekstase, **Ekstase**, *f.* [*pl.* -n] ecstacy, rapture, transport. Freude kann zur — werden, joy may rise to ecstacy.

El, a suffix to a great many nouns, is sometimes used for lein in diminutives, as in Brösel, Bündel &c.; it denotes also an agent, as in Wärtel, Stöpsel &c.; but in general it denotes an instrument or tool, as in Angel, Deichsel &c.

***Elasticität**, *f.* elasticity.

***Elastisch**, I. *adj.* elastic, elastical. Die Luft ist —, the air is elastic; die Dämpfe sind —, the vapours are elastic; dieser Ball ist sehr —, this ball is very elastic. II. elastically.

*Elaterít, *m.* [-s, *pl.* -en] elastic bitumen, mineral caoutchouc, elastic mineral pitch.

||Èlbbutte, *f.* [*pl.* -n] [a fish, Glattbutte] the pearl.

Èlbe, *f.* [in Swed. *elf* signifies river] [a river] the Elbe.

Elb-kahn, *m.* —schiff, *n.* a sort of flat-bottomed lighter employed on the Elbe. —schifffahrt, *f.* the navigation on the Elbe.

||Èlbele, *m.* [*pl.* -n] V. Elbling.

||Èlbkatze, *f.* [*pl.* -n] V. Iltis.

Èlbling, *m.* [-es, *pl.* -e] Èlblinger, *m.* [-s, *pl.* -] [a sort of grape] the sweet water.

Élbogen, Ellenbogen, *m.* [-s, *pl.* -] [V. Elle] 1) elbow. Sich auf den — stützen, to lean on one's elbow; mein Rock ist am — zerrissen, or der — guckt zum Rocke heraus, my coat is out at the elbow; Einen mit dem — stoßen, to elbow any one. 2) [in horses] the cubit.

Elbogen-bein, *n.* [in anatomy] the ulna, cubit, or greater focil. Das kleinere —bein, the lesser focil, the radius or fibula. —blutader, *f.* [in anatomy] ulnar vein. —knorren, *m.* [in anatomy] olecranon. —muskel, *m.* [in anatomy] cubital muscle. —nerve, *m.* [in anatomy] the cubital or ulnar nerve —röhre, *f.* [in anatomy] the lesser focil, the radius or fibula. —schlag-ader, *f.* [in anatomy] cubital artery.

||Èlbricht, *m.* [-es, *pl.* -e] V. Elbling.

||Èlbthier, *n.* [-es, *pl.* -e] V. Iltis.

Èlder, *f.* [*pl.* -n] V. Erle.

Èlderitz, *f.* [*pl.* -en] V. Elritze.

*Eleaolít, *m.* [-s, *pl.* -en] V. Nephalin.

*Elegánt, I. *adj.* elegant. —e Wagen und Pferde, an elegant equipage; ein —er [zierlicher, feiner, geschmackvoller, anmuthiger] Styl [Schreibart] an elegant style. II. *adv.* elegantly. — gekleidet, elegantly dressed; ein — eingerichtetes Zimmer, a room elegantly furnished.

*Élegant, [pron. as in the Fr.] *m.* [-s, *pl.* -s] a man of dress, a fine, gay man, a beau.

*Elegánz, *f.* elegance, elegancy, show, splendour. Die — im Anzuge, the fineness of dress.

*Elegíe, *f.* [*pl.* -n] [a mournful or plaintive poem, or a funeral song] elegy.

Elegiendichter, *m.* elegiast, elegist.

*Elègisch, *adj.* and *adv.* elegiac, plaintive.

*Elektív, *adj.* and *adv.* elective, by option.

*Elektricität, *f.* [in physics] electricity.

*Elèktrisch, I. *adj.* electric, electrical. Ein —er Stoff, an electric substance [such as amber, glass &c.]; das —e Fluidum, electric fluid; der —e Stoß, electric shock; die —e Flasche, electrical jar; eine —e Batterie, electrical battery; das —e Licht in den Masten und Raen, corposant. II. *adv.* electrically. — anziehen, to electrize.

*Elektrisíren, *v. tr.* to charge with electricity, to affect by electricity, to give an electric shock to, to electrify. *Fig.* Die ganze Versammlung war elektrisirt, the whole assembly was electrified. Das Elektrisiren, electrification.

Elektrisirmaschine, *f.* electrical machine.

*Elektrométer, *n.* [-s, *pl.* -] [an instrument for measuring the quantity or intensity of electricity, or its quality] electrometer.

*Elektrophór, *m.* [-s, *pl.* -e] [an instrument for preserving electricity a long time] electrophor, electrophorus.

*Elèktrum, *n.* [-s] argentiferous gold.

*Elemént, *n.* [-es, *pl.* -e] 1) [the first or constituent principle or minutest part of any thing] element, rudiment. 2) *pl.* [the first rules or principles of an art or science] elements, rudiments. Die —e der Erdmeßkunst, the elements of geometry. 3) [fire, air, earth and water] element. Die vier —e, the four elements. 4) *Fig.* [the proper state or sphere of any thing] element. Parteiung ist das — eines Demagogen, faction is the element of a demagogue.

Elementstein, *m.* asteria.

*Elementár, is only used in compositions, as —buch, *n.* a book that contains the rudiments or first principles of an art or science. —feuer, *n.* the elementary fire. —geist, *m.* a spirit supposed to exist in one of the four elements, or a personification of the element itself. —regeln, *pl.* the first rules of a language or science. —schule, *f.* elementary school. —unterricht, *m.* the first instruction in the elements of an art or science.

*Elementārisch, *adj.* and *adv.* 1) elementary, primary, uncombined. 2) [treating of elements, digesting or explaining principles] elementary.

Elémiharz, *n.* [-es] [Gummi Elemi] the gum elemi, elemi.

Elémistrauch, *m.* [-es, *pl.* -sträucher] gum elemi-tree.

1. Élend, Élendthier, *n.* [-es, *pl.* -e] [appears to be allied to Elephant; in Slav. *jelen* signifies a stag] the elk, ||moose-deer.

Elend-hirsch, *m.* the moose-deer. —s-haut, *f.* elk-skin, moose-skin. —s-klaue, *f.* elk-hoof. —s-leder, *n.* elk-leather.

2. Élend, *n.* [-es] [from the old *el* = fremd, allied to the Lat. *al*-ius, Gr. ἄλ-λος, to the Goth. *aljath* = anderswohin] exile. Einen ins — verweisen, to exile or to banish a person.

3. Élend, *n.* [-es] [allied either to the former, or to the Engl. *ill* = schlecht] 1) great unhappiness, extreme pain of body or mind, misery. Im —e schmachten, to live in misery; Einer, der im tiefsten —e schmachtet, a miserable person, a wretch; das — seiner Lage, the wretchedness of his condition. 2) affliction, calamity, distress. 3) extreme poverty. 4) the miseries of life.

Élend, [V. 3. Elend] [elender, elendeste] *adj.* and *adv.* 1) very poor or bad, miserable. Eine —e Hütte, a miserable hut; die Gefangenen hatten eine —e Wohnung, the prisoners were wretchedly lodged; ein —er Boden, a poor soil; —e Kleidung, miserable clothing; ein —es Pferd, a wretched horse; eine —e Entschuldigung, a sorry excuse; ein —es Gedicht, a wretched poem; ein —er Schriftsteller, a paltry author. 2) despicable, wretched. Ein —er Mensch, a miserable person, a wretch. 3) very miserable, sunk into deep affliction or distress, wretched. 4) miserable, very afflicting. In —en Umständen seyn, to be in indigent circumstances, to be in distress; — leben, to live miserably; der —e Zustand der Sklaven in Afrika, the wretched condition of slaves in Africa; ein —er Anblick, a pitiful sight; —e Zeiten, calamitous times. 5) very sick or indisposed, diseased, disordered. Er sieht sehr — aus, he looks very ill.

Elend-voll, *adj.* and *adv.* very miserable, distressful. —wurzel, *f.* V. Mannstreu.

‡Élèndig, *adj.* and *adv.* V. Elend.

‡Élèndiglich, *adv.* miserably.

Eleonōra, [-'s] Eleonōre, [-ns] [a name of women] Eleanor.

Elephánt, *m.* [-en, *pl.* -en] [Gr. and Lat. *elephas*; Goth. *albandus* signifies Kameel] 1) [a quadruped] the elephant. Vom —en kommend, zum —en gehörig, wie ein —, elephantine. *Prov.* Aus einer Mücke einen —en machen, to make a mountain of a mole-hill. 2) *Fig.* *a*) [at chess] rook or castle. *b*) [in natural history] elephant-beetle.

Elephanten-auge, *n.* a sort of disease in the eye. —aussatz, *m.* [a species of leprosy] elephantiasis. —führer, *m.* elephant-driver, [in the East-Indies] mahout. —fuß, *m.* [a plant] the elephantopus, elephant's-foot. —kopf, *m.* [a plant] a species of cock'scomb [rhinantus elephas]. —laus, *f.* 1) a species of tick [acarus elephantinus]. 2) the cashew-nut. —lausbaum, *m.* the cashew —nase, *f.* [a fish] Brasilian pike. —orden, *m.* [an order of knighthood in Denmark] Order of the Elephant. —papier, *n.* very large and stout white paper, elephant-paper. —rüssel, *m.* 1) the snout or trunk of an elephant, the proboscis. 2) *Fig.* *a*) [a fish] the bearded eel. *b*) the thick-lipped cake-shell. *c*) [a plant] long-flowered martyngia. —schwein, *n.* tapir. —zahn, *m.* 1) the tusk of the elephant. 2) *Fig.* [a shell] the elephant's tooth.

*Elève, *m.* [-n, *pl.* -n] V. Zögling.

||Elère, *f.* [*pl.* -n] common bird-cherry-tree.

Èlf, [eilf comes from eins lief, d. h. blieb, one left after ten, i. e. ten and one] I. [a cardinal number] eleven. — Söhne, eleven sons; es ist — Uhr, it is eleven o'clock; eine Flöte mit — Klappen, an eleven-keyed flute; die —en [sc. Männer, Gr. οἱ ἕνδεκα], the eleven men. II. *f.* [*pl.* -en] the numeral character 11.

Elf-eck, *n.* [in geometry] hendecagon. —eckig, *adj.* and *adv.* having eleven angles. —füßig, *adj.* and *adv.* 1) having eleven feet. 2) [in measuring] having eleven feet in length. —jährig, *adj.* and *adv.* eleven years old. —mahl, *adv.* eleven times. —mahlig, *adj.* occurring or being done eleven times. —pfündig, *adj.* and *adv.* weighing eleven pounds. —silber, *m.* hendecasyllable. —silbig, *adj.* and *adv.* having eleven syllables.

1. Èlfe, *m.* [-n, *pl.* -n] [V. 2. Else] [a fish] the shad.

2. Èlfe, *m.* [-n, *pl.* -n] and *f.* [*pl.* -n] [probably allied to the Sw. *elf* = Fluß, to Elbe &c.] an elf, a fairy, a hobgoblin. Zu den —n gehörig, elvish.

Elfen-könig, *m.* the king of the elves or fairies. —königinn, *f.* the queen of the elves, fairy-queen. —kreise, *pl.* fairy-circles. —reich, *n.* fairy-land. —ringe, *pl.* fairy-rings.

Èlfenhaft, *adj.* and *adv.* elfish, like fairies.

Èlfenbein, *n.* [-es] [Elf = Elephant] the tusk of the elephant, ivory, elephant. Das gebrannte —, bone-black; geraspeltes —, ivory shavings; eine Dose von —, an ivory box; Spielmarken von —, ivory counters. *Fig.* and in poetry. something resembling ivory.

Elfenbein-drechsler, *m.* ivory-turner. —schwarz, *n.* ivory black, velvet-black. —tute, *f.* the ivory stamper. —weiß, *adj.* and *adv.* white like ivory.

Èlfenbeinen, or Èlfenbeinern, *adj.* and *adv.* consisting of ivory, ivory. Ein —er Kamm, an ivory comb.

Èlfer, *m.* [-s, *pl.* -] 1) eleven units considered as a whole, or a whole containing eleven units. 2) a member of a society composed of eleven persons. Der Rath der —, the council of the eleven. 3) the renowned [Rhenish] wine of the year 1811.

Èlferlei, *adj.* and *adv.* of eleven sorts.

Èlffach, *adj.* and *adv.* eleven-fold.

Èlfte, [the ordinal of eleven] *adj.* eleventh. Das — Kapitel, the eleventh chapter.

||Èlfte, *f.* [*pl.* -n] [a fish] the shad.

Èlftehalb, *adj.* ten and a half.

Elftel, *n.* [-s, *pl.* -] the eleventh part.

Elftens, *adv.* for the eleventh, in the eleventh place, eleventhly.

Elias, [a name of men] [*pl.* Eliasse] Elias.

Elisa, Elise, [a name of women] [-'s, -ens, *pl.* -sen] Eliza.

Elisabeth[a], [-s, -ens, *pl.* -e] [a name of women] Elizabeth.

*__Elisäisch__, V. Eliseisch.

*__Eliseisch, Elysisch__, *adj.* and *adv.* elysian. Die —en Gefilde, elysian fields, elysium; die elisäischen Felder, the Elysian Fields [in Paris].

*__Elision__, *f.* [in grammar] elision.

*__Elisium, Elysium__, *n.* [-s] [in ancient mythology] elysium.

*__Elixir__, *n.* [-s, *pl.* -e] [in medicine] elixir.

Elldritz, *f.* [*pl.* -en] V. Elritze.

Elle, *f.* [*pl.* -n] [Lat. *ulna*, Gr. *ὠλένη*. Is probably allied to Ahle = something long] [a measure] 1) ell; yard. Das Messen mit der —, alnage; nach der — verkaufen, to sell by the ell. Ich brauche vier —n [Tuch &c.] zu einem Rocke, I want four ells [of cloth &c.] for a coat. 2) a quantity of cloth &c. measured by the ell. Zwanzig —ntuch, cloth that measures twenty ells.

Ellen-breit, *adj.* and *adv.* 1) having one ell in breadth. *2) *Fig.* very broad. —handel, *m.* the sale of commodities by the ell. —lang, *adj.* and *adv.* 1) having one ell in length. 2) *Fig.* very long. —maß, *n.* 1) a measure of an ell. 2) the length of an ell. —waare, *f.* ware or wares sold by the ell. —waarenhandel, *m.* V. —handel. —waarenhändler, *m.* dry-good merchant. —waarenhandlung, *f.* a shop where commodities are sold by the yard, [in America] a dry-good store. —weise, *adv.* by the ell. Waaren —weise verkaufen, to sell goods by the ell.

Ellenbogen, V. Elbogen.

Ellent, *n.* [-es] [a plant] common eryngo, holly.

Eller, *f.* [*pl.* -n] the alder. V. Erle.

Elleritze, *f.* [*pl.* -n] **Ellerling**, *m.* [-es, *pl.* -e] V. Elritze.

Ellipse, *f.* [*pl.* -n] 1) [in grammar, a figure of syntax] ellipsis. 2) [in geometry, an oval figure] ellipsis.

Ellipsoide, *f.* [*pl.* -n] [in conics] ellipsoid.

Elliptisch, I. *adj.* 1) [defective] elliptic, elliptical. Ein —er Satz, an elliptical phrase. 2) [in geometry] elliptic, elliptical. II *adv.* 1) [defectively] elliptically. 2) [in geometry] elliptically.

Elmsfeuer, *n.* [-s, *pl.* -] [in meteorology] n. St. Elm's fire, corposant, corpusance.

Eln, a contraction of eleu, and a suffix of many verbs formed by derivation, as in lächeln, from lachen; sometimes it is used in a contemptuous sense, as in liebeln, klügeln; it denotes also an iteration of the same act, as klingeln, schütteln.

Elpel, *f.* [*pl.* -n] common bird-cherry-tree.

Elritze, *f.* [*pl.* -n] [in Norway *Elveritze* from Elve = stream] 1) [a fish] the minnow. 2) [a tree] wild service, sorb, or maple-leaved service.

Elsaß, *n.* [-sses] [a province of France] Alsatia. Alsace. Elsässer, *m.* -inn, *f.* a native or inhabitant of Alsatia, Alsatian. Elsässer, Elsassisch, *adj.* and *adv.* Alsatian, belonging to or coming from Alsatia.

1\. **Else**, *f.* [*pl.* -n] V. Alose.

2 **Else**, *f.* [*pl.* -n] V. Erle.

Else-baum, —beerbaum, *m.* V. —beere. —beere, *f.* the fruit of the alder buckthorn, or berrybearing alder, of the common bird cherry-tree, and of the wild service, sorb, or maple-leaved service.

3\. **Else**, [a name of women] [-ns] Alice.

Elster, *f.* [*pl.* -n] [better written Aister, Old Germ. Agalastra, from galan, gällen = tönen] the mag-pie.

Elster-auge, *n.* V. Hühnerauge. —baum, *m.* V. Erle.

Elte, *m.* [*pl.* -n] [a fish] V. Alant.

Elterlich, *adj.* parental. Das —e Haus, the parental house; die —e Zärtlichkeit, parental tenderness.

Eltermutter, *f.* [*pl.* -mütter] great-grandmother.

Eltern, [for Aeltern from alt] *pl.* parents.

Eltern-los, *adj.* and *adv.* parentless, orphan. Ein —loses Kind, an orphan. —mord, *m.* parricide. —mörder, *m.* —mörderinn, *f.* a parricide. —mutter, *f.* V. Eltermutter. —vater, *m.* V. Eltervater.

Eltervater, *m.* [-s, *pl.* -väter] great-grandfather.

*__Elysisch, Elysium__, V. Eliseisch and Elisium.

*__Email__, *m.* [-s] [a substance imperfectly vitrified; that which is enameled] enamel.

Emailmahler, *m.* a painter in enamel.

*__Emailleur__, [pron. as in the French] *m.* [-s, *pl.* -s or -e] enameler.

*__Emailliren__, [pron. Emalljihren] *v. tr.* to enamel. Das —, enameling.

*__Emancipation__, *f.* emancipation. Die — eines Sklaven, Sohnes, Volks, the emancipation of a slave, of a son, of a people.

*__Emancipiren__, *v. tr.* to emancipate [a slave &c.]. Sich —, to emancipate one's self.

*__Emballage__, [pron. as in the French] *f.* [*pl.* -n] package.

*__Emballiren__, [pron. amballihren] *v. tr.* to pack, to embale [goods]. Die Emballirung, embaling.

*__Embárgo__, *n.* [- or -'s, *pl.* -s] [in commerce] embargo.

Embergans, *f.* [*pl.* -gänse] [Ember is perhaps allied to Ammer] ember-goose.

Emberitz, *m.* [*pl.* -e] V. Goldammer.

*__Emblém__, *n.* [*pl.* -e] emblem.

*__Emblemátisch__, I. *adj.* emblematical, emblematic. II. *adv.* emblematically.

*__Embryo__, *m.* [-s, *pl.* -nen] [in physiology] embryo, embryon.

Emeu, [*pl.* -e] [a bird] emeu, cassiowary.

*__Emigránt__, *m.* [-en, *pl.* -en] —inn, *f.* an emigrant.

*__Emigration__, *f.* emigration.

*__Emigriren__, *v. intr.* [u. w. seyn] to emigrate [to America &c.].

Emilia, Emilie and **Emilie**, [-'s and -ens, *pl.* -lien] [a name of women] Emily.

*__Eminénz__, *f.* [*pl.* -en] 1) V. Vorzug, Vortrefflichkeit, Hoheit. 2) [a title of honour given to Cardinals] eminence.

*__Emir__, *m.* [-s, *pl.* -e] [a title of dignity among the Turks, denoting a prince] Emir.

||**Emmel**, *f.* [*pl.* -n] V. Baumlaus.

1\. **Emmerling**, *m.* [-es, *pl.* -e] [a bird] the yellow hammer. V. Goldammer.

2\. **Emmerling**, *m.* [-es, *pl.* -e] [probably allied to the A. S. *Haemil* = Kornwurm] the grub of the cock-chafer.

3\. **Emmerling**, *m.* [-es, *pl.* -e] [instead of Amarelle] the Morello cherry.

||**Emmern**, *pl.* [Dan. *emmer*; probably allied to Am-sel, Am-bra &c.] embers, cinders.

*__Emolumént__, *n.* [-es, *pl.* -e] V. Vortheil, Nutzen.

‡**Empfähen**, *ir. v. intr.* V. Empfangen.

Empfáng, *m.* [-es] [the act of receiving, the state of being received] reception. Eine Sache in — nehmen, to receive a thing; den — einer Summe Geldes bescheinigen, to give a receipt for a sum of money; der — eines Briefes, the receipt or reception of a letter; die Gäste waren mit dem — sehr zufrieden, the guests were well pleased with their reception; ein freundlicher —, a kind reception; ein feierlicher — wurde ihm zu Theil, he met with a solemn reception; der — eines Gesandten an einem fremden Hofe, the reception of an envoy by a foreign court.

Empfang-nehmung, *f.* receipt, reception. —schein, *m.* receipt.

Empfángen, *ir.* I. *v. tr.* 1) to receive [a letter, money &c.]. Das Abendmahl —, to partake of the Lord's supper, to communicate. *Fig.* Befehle —, to receive orders; Vergebung der Sünden —, to get the remission of sins; das Gemüth empfängt Eindrücke von äußern Gegenständen, the mind receives impressions from external objects. 2) to welcome, to lodge and entertain, to receive, as a guest Er wurde freundlich empfangen, he met with a kind reception. II. *v. intr.* to conceive, to become pregnant. Meine Mutter hat mich in Sünden —, [in Script.] in sin did my mother conceive me.

Empfänger, *m.* [-s, *pl.* -] -inn, *f.* a person that receives. Der — einer Geldsumme, eines Briefs, the receiver of a sum of money, of a letter.

Empfänglich, *adj.* and *adv.* susceptible. Ein der or für Liebe —es Herz, a heart susceptible of love; — seyn für Freude und Schmerz, to be sensible of pleasure and pain; jedes Ohr muß dafür — seyn, every ear must be sensible of it; die Gemüther der Kinder sind —er, als die älterer Personen, the minds of children are more susceptible than those of persons more advanced in life.

Empfänglichkeit, *f.* susceptibility. Die — für Liebe, Eindrücke &c., the susceptibility of love, of impressions &c.

Empfängniß, *f.* [the act of conceiving] conception. Die — der Jungfrau Maria, the conception of the Virgin Mary.

||**Empféhl**, *m.* [-es, *pl.* -e] [an expression of civility, respect or regard] compliment. Mache ihm meinen —, present him my compliments.

Empfehlbrief, *m.* V. Empfehlungsbrief.

Empféhlbar, *adj.* and *adv.* recommendable.

Empféhlen, [for anbefehlen] *ir.* I. *v. tr.* 1) [to represent as worthy of notice, regard or kindness, to speak in favour of, to commit, to intrust or give in charge] to commend. Ich empfehle Ihnen meine Schwester, I commend to you my sister; Mäcenas empfahl den Horaz und Virgil dem August, Maecenas recommended Horace and Virgil to Augustus; Vater, in deine Hände empfehle ich meinen Geist, [in Script.] father, into thy hands I commend my spirit. 2) [to make acceptable] to commend, to recommend. Eine anständige Dreistigkeit empfiehlt selbst den Fremden, a decent boldness e'en a stranger recommends; ein Buch, das sich durch sich selbst empfiehlt, a book that recommends itself; eine —de Miene, a prepossessing countenance; [as an expression of civility] — Sie mich Ihrer Frau Gemahlinn, my compliments to your lady; ich empfehle mich Ihrem gütigen Andenken, I beg to be remembered kindly by you. SYN. V. Anpreisen. II. *v. r.* sich —, to take one's leave. Er empfahl sich, he took his leave, he took leave; ich empfehle mich Ihnen! I have the honour to wish you good morning, good afternoon &c.

Empfehlens-werth, —würdig, *adj.* and *adv.* recommendable.

Empfehler, *m.* [-s, *pl.* -] he that recommends, recommender.

Empfehlung, *f.* 1) [the act of commending or recommending] recommendation. Was gut ist, bedarf keiner —, *prov.* that which is good does never need a sign. 2) [that which procures a kind or favourable reception] recommendation, commendation. Wo Mißgeschick eine mächtige — war, where misfortune was a powerful recommendation 3) [an expression of civility, respect or regard] compliment. Machen Sie ihm meine —, present my compliments to him, remember me to him.

Empfehlungs-brief, *m.* —schreiben, *n.* letter of introduction; letter of recommendation. —werth, —würdig, *adj.* and *adv.* V. Empfehlenswerth.

Empfindbar, *adj.* and *adv.* perceptible to the senses or by the mind, sensible. Ein —er Grad von Hitze, a perceptible degree of heat; —e Gegenstände, sensitive objects; — or auf eine —e [merkliche] Weise zunehmen, to grow or increase sensibly.

Empfindbarkeit, *f.* sensibleness.

Empfindelei, *f.* affectation of exquisite sensibility, sentimentality.

Empfindeln, *v. intr.* to affect sensibility.

Empfinden, *ir. v. tr.* [instead of in (viz. sich) finden] [to have the sense of, to be affected by, to perceive mentally] to feel. Schmerz oder Freude —, to feel pain or pleasure; das Licht —, to perceive light; Wärme oder Kälte —, to be sensible of heat or cold; Hunger oder Durst —, to be hungry or thirsty, to hunger or thirst; Kummer —, to feel grief. *Fig.* Dieses Land wird die Verwüstungen, die der Krieg darin angerichtet hat, lange empfinden, this country will long feel the effects of the ravages caused in it by the war; sie weiß nicht, was ich für sie empfinde, she knows not what I feel for her; ich empfinde lebhaft Ihre Großmuth, I am penetrated with a lively sense of your generosity; übel oder *hoch —, to take ill or to resent.

Empfinden, *n.* [-s] 1) feeling, sensation. Das — des Schmerzes, the sensation of pain. 2) that which one feels.

Empfindler, *m.* [-s, *pl.* -] [one that affects sentiment or exquisite sensibility] sentimentalist.

Empfindlerinn, *f.* a female that affects sentiment or exquisite sensibility, sentimentalist, an oversensitive lady.

Empfindlich, *adj.* and *adv.* 1) [quick of perception] sensible, sensitive. Das Auge ist ein sehr —er Theil des Körpers, the eye is a very sensitive part of the body; das ist seine —ste Seite, that's his most sensible part. *Fig.* *a)* [movable by a very small weight or impulse] sensible. Eine —e Wage, a sensible balance. *b)* [affected by a slight degree of heat or cold] sensible. Ein —er Wärmemesser, a sensible thermometer. 2) easily provoked or irritated, quick to feel an injury or affront, sensitive, resentive. Ein —er Mensch, a susceptible person, a touchy person; er war so — über &c., he was so resentful of &c.; er war sehr — über die Beleidigung, he felt the offence deeply; zuletzt ward er darüber —, at last he took it ill, at last he resented it. 3) [that affects the senses or the mind] sensible. Ein —er Schmerz, an acute pain; eine —e Kälte, a pinching cold; der Schimpf war —er als der Schmerz, the disgrace was more sensible than the pain.

Empfindlichkeit, *f.* 1) actual perception by the mind or body. Die — für Freude und Schmerz, sensibility to pleasure or pain. 2) susceptibility of slight impressions. Die — des Auges, the sensibleness of the eye. *Fig.* Die — einer Wage oder eines Wärmemessers, the sensibility or sensibleness of a balance or of a thermometer. 3) [the quality of being easily irritated] irritability, touchiness.

Empfindling, *m.* [-es, *pl.* -e] a sentimentalist, a sentimental fool.

Empfindniß, *n.* [-sses, *pl.* -sse] moral perception, capacity of being affected by moral good or evil.

Empfindsam, *adj.* and *adv.* 1) possessing great sensibility. Ein —er Mensch, a feeling man; ein —es Herz, a feeling heart; [frequently used in a bad sense and denoting an affectation of sentiment or feeling] sentimental. Ein —es Dämchen, an affectedly sentimental lady. 2) affecting, moving, sentimental Yorick's —e Reise, Yorick's sentimental journey.

Empfindsamkeit, *f.* 1) nice sensibility, feeling; [frequently used in a bad sense V. Empfindsam] false sentimentality, sentimentalism. 2) sentimentality.

Empfindselig, [rather unusual] *adj.* and *adv.* full of sensibility, strongly affected.

Empfindung, *f.* 1) sensation. Die — des Schmerzes, the sensation of pain; schmerzliche oder angenehme —en, painful or pleasurable sensations. 2) susceptibility of impressions, sensibility. 3) sensibility, feeling, sentiment. Ein Gedicht voller —, a poem full of sentiment. 4) [the faculty of perceiving] perception, sensitive faculty. V. Gefühl.

Empfindungs-eigenheit, *f.* idiosyncrasy. —gedicht, *n.* a lyric poem. —kraft, *f.* power of perception, power of sensation. —laut, *m.* [in grammar] an interjection, exclamation. —leer, *adj.* and *adv.* wanting sensibility, unfeeling, senseless. —los, *adj.* and *adv.* 1) wanting the faculty of perception, insensible, senseless. 2) unfeeling, wanting sympathy, insensible, senseless. —losigkeit, *f.* insensibility. —schauer, *m.* a shivering caused by particular sensations. —tödtend, *adj.* and *adv.* destroying feeling or sentiment. —vermögen, *n.* sensitive faculty, perception. —voll, *adj.* and *adv.* 1) very feeling or sensible. 2) expressing sensibility. 3) affecting, moving, sentimental. —wort, *n.* V. —laut.

***Emphase, Emphasis**, *f.* [in rhetoric] emphasis.

***Emphatisch**, I. *adj.* emphatic, emphatical. II. *adv.* emphatically.

***Empirie**, *f.* [*pl.* -en] empiricism.

***Empiriker**, *m.* [-s, *pl.* -] an empiric.

***Empirisch**, I. *adj.* empiric, empirical. II. *adv.* empirically.

Empor, [for entbor, from bören = to lift up] *adv.* upwards, on high, up. [this adverb is used chiefly in composition, and joined to verbs forms numerous compounds].

Empor-arbeiten, *v. tr.* to work up. Bis wir uns zu diesem Grade von &c. —gearbeitet haben, till we have wrought ourselves to &c. —blasen, *ir. v. tr.* to blow up. —blicken, *v. intr.* to look up, to cast one's eyes upwards. —blühen, *v. intr.* [u. w. seyn] to grow up blooming. —brausen, *v. intr.* [u. w. seyn and haben] V. Aufbrausen. —bringen, *ir. v. tr.* to raise. *Fig.* to exalt, to elevate, to raise. —dampfen, *v. intr.* [u. w. seyn and haben] to rise in vapours. —drängen, *v. intr.* and *r.* to force one's way upwards. —dringen, *ir. v. intr.* [u. w. seyn] to penetrate upwards. *Fig.* Seufzer drangen sich aus ihrer Brust empor, she heaved deep sighs. —dunsten, *v. intr.* to steam. —eilen, *v. intr.* to hasten upwards. —flammen, *v. intr.* [u. w. seyn] to mount on high [said of flames], to blaze up. —flattern, *v. intr.* [u. w. seyn] to flutter upward. —fliegen, *ir. v. intr.* [u. w. seyn] to fly upward. Wie die Funken —fliegen, as the sparks fly upward. —heben, *ir.* I. *v. tr.* to lift up. Den Kopf —heben, to lift the head. *Fig.* *a)* Jemands Gemüth —heben [erheben], to raise the feelings of a person; er fühlt seine Seele durch das Lesen der Werke dieses Dichters immer —gehoben [erhoben], by reading the works of this poet he feels his mind always exalted. *b)* Die Stimme —heben [more usual erheben], to raise the voice. II. *v. r.* sich —heben, to arise, to rise, to raise one's self, to ascend. *Fig.* *a)* to appear in sight, to rise. *b)* to be revived in the memory. —helfen, *ir. v. tr.* to help up. *Fig.* Einem Freunde —helfen, to support a friend; den Betrübten —helfen, to relieve the afflicted. —kirche, *f.* [in churches] gallery. —klettern, *v. intr.* [u. w. seyn] to clamber up. —klimmen, *ir. v. intr.* [u. w. seyn] to climb up. —kommen, *ir. v. intr.* [u. w. seyn] to gain elevation in rank, fortune or public estimation, to rise, to thrive. —kömmling, *m.* an upstart. —kriechen, *ir. v. intr.* [u. w. seyn] to creep upward. —laube, *f.* a balcony. —läutern, *v. tr.* [in chimistry] to sublimate. *Fig.* to refine and exalt, to heighten, to sublimate. —lodern, *v. intr.* to rise blazing. *Fig.* to grow hot, or angry. —lüpfen, —lupfen, *v. tr.* to lift, to lift up, to raise [a weight &c.]. —quellen, *ir. v. intr.* [u. w. seyn] to spring [said of water]. —raffen, *v. r.* sich —raffen, V. Aufraffen, *v. r.* —ragen, *v. intr.* [u. w. seyn] to rise up, to be above other things, to tower. —ranken, *v. intr.* and *r.* to climb up by the help of tendrils. —richten, *v. tr.* to lift, to take up, to heave. Sich im Bette —richten, to raise the body in bed. V. Aufrichten. —schauen, *v. intr.* to look up. —schäumen, *v. intr.* to rise frothing, or foaming. —scheune, *f.* the loft of a barn. —schießen, *ir. v. intr.* [u. w. seyn] to shoot up, to sprout up. —schleudern, *v. tr.* to fling upward. —schweben, *v. intr.* [u. w. seyn] to rise hovering, to soar aloft. —schwellen, I. *ir. v. intr.* [u. w. seyn] to swell [said of a river]. *Fig.* to increase rapidly. II. *reg. v. tr.* to swell. *Fig.* to raise to arrogance, to swell. —schwingen, *ir.* I. *v. tr.* to swing upward, to brandish aloft. II. *v. r.* sich —schwingen, to rise aloft, to soar. Der Adler schwingt sich —, the eagle soars aloft. *Fig.* Sich durch Verdienst —schwingen, to rise by merit. —sehen, *ir. v. intr.* 1) to look up. 2) *Fig.* to be directed upward, to be erect. —sprießen, V. —sprossen. —springen, V. Aufspringen. —sprossen, *v. intr.* [u. w. seyn] to sprout up. —sprudeln, I. *v. intr.* [u. w. seyn] to bubble up. II. *v. tr.* to cause to bubble up. —sprühen, *v. intr.* to mount up [as sparks]. —starren, *v. intr.* to stare upwards. —stehen, *ir. v. intr.* [u. w. seyn] 1) to stand upright or erected; to be high or tall. 2) to become erect. Vor Entsetzen standen mir die Haare —, my hair with horror stood; sein Haar steht —, his hair stands an end. —steigen, *ir. v. intr.* [u. w. seyn] 1) to rise, to ascend, to mount. Ein Nebel steigt aus einem Flusse —, a fog rises from a river; ein Luftballon steigt über die Wolken —, a balloon rises above the clouds; Dünste steigen aus feuchten Orten —, vapours arise from humid places. 2) *Fig.* *a)* to gain elevation in rank, to be promoted, to rise. *b)* to become audible, to arise, as sounds. *c)* to rise, to grow, to spring up, as a plant. *d)* to spring, to ri

—streben, *v. intr.* 1) to strive to rise. 2) [chiefly] *Fig.* to be animated with an ardent desire of power, importance, or excellence. Ein —strebender Geist, an aspiring genius. —thürmen, I. *v. tr.* V. Aufthürmen. II. *v. r.* sich —thürmen, to tower, to rise aloft, to soar. —treiben, *ir. v. tr.* 1) to drive, to urge upwards. 2) *Fig.* [in chimistry] to sublimate [camphor, sulphur &c.]. Das —getriebene, [the production of a sublimation] sublimate. Das —treiben, sublimation. —treibung, *f.* 1) the act of driving, urging upwards. 2) [in chimistry] sublimation. —treibungsort, *m.* [a place, where sublimation is performed] sublimatorium. —treten, V. Auftreten I. 2. —wachsen, *ir. v. intr.* [u. w. seyn] to rise, to grow, to spring up, as a plant. —winden, *ir.* I. *v. tr.* V. Aufwinden I. 2. II. *v. r.* sich —winden, to wind upwards. —wirbeln, *v. intr.* [u. w. seyn] to whirl upward. —ziehen, *ir.* I. *v. intr.* [u. w. seyn] to march upward. II. *v. tr.* to draw up, to lift. III. *v. r.* sich —ziehen, to rise, to ascend, to move upwards in a line or file.

‖Empōre, *f.* [*pl.* -n] V. Emporkirche.

Empōren, [V. Empor] I. *v. tr.* to stir violently, to stir up. Der Sturm empört die Wellen, the storm raises or tosses the waves. *Fig.* to excite. Der Anblick so vielen Elends empörte mich, I was shocked at the sight of so much misery; das Gemüth, das Gefühl —, to revolt the mind, the feelings; den Goliath empörte die Herausforderung Davids, Goliath was indignant at the challenge of David; eine —de That, a revolting act; ein Volk —, to stir up a people to rebellion. II. *v. r.* sich —, [to renounce allegiance and subjection to one's prince or state] to revolt, to rebel. Die Soldaten empörten sich gegen ihre Offiziere, the soldiers rose upon their officers, mutinied against their officers. *Fig.* Dawider empört sich die Vernunft, it is highly revolting to reason.

Empōrer, *m.* [-s, *pl.* -] 1) a stirrer up to rebellion. 2) a revolter, rebel, mutineer.

Empōrerisch, *adj.* and *adv.* rebellious, mutinous. Ein —es Betragen, a seditious behaviour.

Empōrung, *f.* 1) the act of revolting, revolt, rebellion. 2) [open resistance to lawful authority] rebellion, revolt, [in the army or navy] mutiny.

Empōrungsgeist, *m.* seditiousness.

Emsig, [Ice. *amr* signifies work] *adj.* and *adv.* [constant in application] assiduous. Ein —er Mann, a diligent or industrious person; — in seinem Geschäfte seyn, to be assiduous in one's occupation; ein im Dienste —er Offizier, an active officer; die —e Biene, the busy bee; er studirt —, he studies assiduously, or diligently; — nachforschen, to make diligent search or researches.

Emsigkeit, *f.* [constant or diligent application] assiduousness, assiduity, diligence. Die — der Biene, the industry of the bee.

Emsiglich, *adv.* V. Emsig.

En, a suffix to many words especially to verbs, also a plural termination of nouns.

Enállage, *f.* [*pl.* -n] [a figure in grammar] enallage [as, *exercitus victor* for *victoriosus*].

Encyklopädie, *f.* [*pl.* -en] encyclopædia, encyclopedia, encyclopedy.

Encyklopädisch, *adj.* and *adv.* encyclopedian.

Encyklopädist, *m.* [-en, *pl.* -en] encyclopedist.

Endchen, *n.* [-s, *pl.* -] *dimin.* of Ende.

Ende, *n.* [-s, *pl.* -n] [Old G. *enti* signifies Stirne. The Epirotic dialect *Vend* signifies both Stirne and Gegend. Perhaps allied to wenden] the extreme or last part in general, the end. 1) [applied to space; the extreme point of any thing that has more length than breadth] end. Das — eines Tisches, the end of a table; das — eines Seiles, the end of a rope; das äußerste —, extremity; das — [with huntsmen] α) [the tail of a stag] the single. β) [a start or a branch of the horns of the stag] antler. Die obersten kleinen —n am Hirschgeweih, trochings; ein Hirsch von zehn —n, a stag of ten branches; den Hirsch nach seinen —n ansprechen, to ascertain the age of a stag by its horns. Ein — or Endchen Licht, a candle's end; von einem — bis zum andern, from one end to the other; er wohnt am — der Welt, *fig.* he dwells far off; etwas beim rechten — angreifen, *fig.* to go the right way to work, to set about a thing properly; der am — Unterschriebene [*Endesunterschriebene], the undersigned; an allen Ecken und —n, everywhere; von allen —n, from all sides, from all quarters; das — eines Kapitels, the end of a chapter; das Buch hat kein —, the book has no end. *Fig.* [utmost point, furthest degree] extreme. 2) [applied to number] Denn es sind der Schätze kein —, [in Script.] there is no end of the store. 3) [applied to time] the end; *it.* close of a particular state of things. Das — des Jahres, the end of the year; das — des Tages, der Nacht, the close of the day or night; des Lebens —, the close of life; das — einer Rede, the end of a discourse; [the closing part of a discourse] epilogue; das — eines Schauspiels, the conclusion of a play; alles Fleisches — ist vor mich gekommen, [in Scripture] the end of all flesh is come; der Streit ist zu —, the quarrel is done or over; eine Sache zu — bringen, to finish, to close, to conclude, to terminate a thing, an affair &c.; einen Krieg zu — bringen, to end a war; ein — nehmen, to end, to terminate, to close, to conclude; der Winter geht im März zu —, winter ends in March; es will kein — nehmen, it will not end; *fig.* das — vom Liede war &c., the conclusion was &c.; am —, after all; das — der Unternehmung, the end of the enterprise. *Prov.* — gut, Alles gut, all is well that ends well, the end crowns all; das — bewährt alle Dinge, good to begin well, better to end well. 4) [in a more limited sense] *a*) close of life, death, decease. Seinem — nahe seyn, to draw towards one's end. *b*) the ultimate point or thing at which one aims or directs his views, purpose intended. Zu dem —, to the end, for the purpose.

End-absicht, *f.* final design. —art, *f.* a particular manner to inflect or decline. —bescheid, *m.* a final or definitive sentence. —beschluß, *m.* a definitive decree. —brett, *n.* the board at the end. V. Schwarte. —buchstabe, *m.* the last letter of a word or a line. —eslos, V. —los. —fall, *m.* [in grammar] case. —kürzung, *f.* [the cutting off, or omission of the last letter or syllable of a word] apocope, apocopy. —los, *adj.* and *adv.* endless, boundless. Eine —lose Linie, an endless or indefinite line; eine —lose Dauer, an endless or infinite duration. —losigkeit, *f.* endlessness; endless duration. —punkt, *m.* 1) the extreme point of any thing. 2) *Fig.* the point beyond which no progression can be made, end. —rede, *f.* epilogue. —reim, *m.* *a*) rhyme at the end of a verse. *b*) *pl.* bouts-rimes. —silbe, *f.* the final syllable. —spitze, *f.* 1) the utmost point of any thing, extremity. 2) *Fig.* extreme. —spruch, *m.* 1) final sentence or judgment. 2) the last sentence or period of a discourse. —stück, *n.* a piece at the end of any thing. —tag, *m.* 1) the last day of a series of days or of a certain period. 2) the day of the final judgment, doom'sday. —ursache, *f.* the final cause. —urtheil, *n.* a final judgment. —verkürzung, *f.* V. —kürzung. —wort, *n.* the last word of a line or period. —zeile, *f.* the last line of a page. —ziel, *n.* the ultimate end [of our actions &c.]. —zweck, *m.* purpose intended, end, aim, design, scope, drift. Seinen —zweck erreichen, to compass one's designs, to succeed in one's purposes. Syn. V. Absicht.

‡Endelich, *adj.* and *adv.* active, hasty, speedy.

*Endēmisch, *adj.* and *adv* [peculiar to a people or nation] endemic, endemical, endemial. Eine —e Krankheit, an endemic disease.

Énden, I. *v. intr.* to end, to cease, to come to a close. Ein gutes Leben endet in Frieden, a good life ends in peace; hiermit endigte er, herewith he ceased to speak; der Engel endete, the angel ended; er hat geendet, he has closed his earthly career, he has breathed his last. II. *v. r.* sich —, to end, to terminate, to close, to conclude. Die Rede endete sich mit eindrücklichen Worten, the discourse ended with impressive words. III. *v. tr.* 1) to end, to finish, to close, to conclude, to terminate. Einen Krieg —, to end a war; sein Leben —, to cease to live, to die. 2) to finish entirely, to complete, to accomplish. 3) [rather unusual] to furnish with a point or end.

Énder, *m.* [-s, *pl.* -] [with huntsmen] a stag whose horns are furnished with antlers [used chiefly in compositions, as Sechs—, Acht— &c.].

Énderling, *m.* V. Engerling.

Éndig, *adj.* and *adv.* having an end [used chiefly in compositions]. Zwei—, having two ends.

Éndigen, I. *v. intr.* to end, to cease, to come to a close. II. *v. r.* sich —, to end, to terminate. Eine Linie endiget sich am Gleicher, a line terminates at the equator. *Fig.* Die Debatte endigte sich um sechs Uhr, the debate closed at six o'clock; oft beginnt Liebe in Freuden und endiget sich in Leiden, love often begins in joy, and concludes in sorrow. III. *v. tr.* 1) to end, to put an end to, to terminate [a controversy &c.]. Sein Leben —, to cease to live, to die; er hat sein Leben selbst geendigt, he put an end to his existence, he committed suicide. 2) to finish entirely, to complete, to accomplish.

Éndigung, *f.* 1) ending, termination, conclusion. 2) [in grammar] ending.

Endivie, *f.* [*pl.* -n] [a plant, used as a salad] endive.

Éndlich, I. *adj.* 1) having a limit, bounded, finite. —e Größen, finite numbers [as opposed to infinite numbers]; ein —es Wesen, a finite being; ein —es Daseyn, a finite existence; das —e [= Zeitliche], the transient things of this world. 2) final, last, ultimate. Der —e Bescheid [Endbescheid], final or definitive sentence. 3) happening or taking place at last, final. Die —e Eroberung Irlands, the final conquest of Ireland. II. *adv.* 1) in the end, at the conclusion, finally, ultimately, at length, after all. Aber die Römer siegten —, but the Romans finally conquered. 2) in the end or conclusion, to conclude, to sum up all, in fine, finally, lastly. 3) at last, at length. Er kam — zurück, he returned at last; [in familiar or common language, it is sometimes used by way of exclamation] da bin ich —! here am I at last!

Éndliche, *m.* [-n, *pl.* -n] a being subject to death, a mortal. Das Endliche, V. Endlich I. 1.

Éndlichkeit, *f.* 1) finiteness. 2) a finite being. 3) limited existence; this world [as opposed to eternity].

Éndling, *m.* [-es, *pl.* -e] V. [the more usual word] Endsilbe.

Éndschaft, *f.* [the close or conclusion applied to time] end. Seine — erreichen, to come to a close; die Sache hat ihre — erreicht, the thing came to an end.

Éndung, *f.* ending, termination. Die — eines Worts, the termination of a word.

*Energie, *f.* [internal or inherent power; power exerted; strength of expression] energy.

***Enèrgisch**, I. *adj.* and *adv.* energetic, energetical. —e Maßregeln, energetic measures. II. *adv.* energetically.

Eng, V. Enge, *adj.* and *adv.*

***Engagiren**, [pron. anggagihren] [mostly in fam. or vulgar language] I. *v. tr.* to engage, to prevail upon, to win, to persuade. Einen Soldaten —, to enlist a soldier. II. *v. r.* sich —, to engage one's self, to promise, to offer. Ich engagire mich, Ihnen in dieser Angelegenheit zu dienen, I engage myself to serve you in this affair.

Enge, [allied to the Lat. *ango*, Gr. ἄγχω] *adj.* and *adv.* [having little distance from side to side] narrow. Eine — Straße, a narrow street; ein —r Paß, Weg, a narrow passage or way, a defile; ein —r Gang, a close alley; ein —s Zimmer, a small, confined room; — sitzen, to sit close; — schreiben, to write close; ein —r Rock, a tight or strait coat; — Schuhe, tight shoes; ein —r Kamm, a small tooth-comb; ein Gefangener in —r Haft, a prisoner closely confined; eine Stadt — einschließen, to invest a town closely; eine — Umarmung, a close embrace. *Fig.* Die Pforte ist —, und der Weg ist schmal, der zum Leben führt, [in Script.] strait is the gate, and narrow is the way that leadeth to life; ein —es Bündniß, a strict alliance; in Freundschaft — verbunden, closely connected in friendship; ein —es Gewissen, a strict or delicate conscience; es wird mir so — ums Herz, my heart is oppressed with grief; der —ste Sinn eines Wortes, the strictest sense of a word; im —sten Sinne des Wortes, strictly taken; Patriotismus im —sten Sinne des Wortes, patriotism strictly so called; der —re Ausschuß, select committee; — Harmonie, [in music] strait, contracted harmony [the intervals being nigh to each other].

Eng=bäuchig, *adj.* and *adv.* narrow-bellied. —beinig, *adj.* and *adv.* Ein —beiniges Pferd, a horse, whose houghs are too close together, a jarretier. —brüstig, *adj.* and *adv.* 1) narrow-breasted or chested. 2) asthmatic. 3) *Fig.* V. —herzig. —brüstigkeit, *f.* asthma. —halsig, *adj.* and *adv.* small or narrow-necked [said of a bottle &c.]. —herzig, *adj.* and *adv.* narrow-hearted, narrow-minded, narrow-souled. Ein —er Mensch, a man of a contracted soul or mind. —herzigkeit, *f.* narrowness of mind, contractedness, illiberality. —paß, *m.* defile, strait; narrows. —sichtig, *adj.* and *adv.* V. Kurzsichtig.

Enge, *f.* [*pl.* -n] 1) [smallness of distance from side to side] narrowness. Die — einer Straße, eines Weges, the narrowness of a street, or highway; die — des Hauses, the narrowness of the house; die — eines Zimmers, the narrowness of an apartment; die — eines Ganges, the straitness of a passage; die — eines Platzes, the straitness of a place. 2) a narrow place or passage. Die —n besetzen, to line the straits with soldiers. *Fig.* Einen in die — bringen or treiben, to drive any one to straits, to put any one to difficulties; in die — gerathen or kommen, to be put to difficulties; in der — seyn, to be in straits. *Prov.* Durch die — zum Gepränge, the way to bliss lies not on beds of down; the way to heaven is by wearing the cross.

Engel, *m.* [-s, *pl.* -] [from the Gr. ἄγγελος] [in Scripture, a messenger of God; but appropriately a spirit, or a spiritual intelligent being employed by God to communicate his will to men] an angel. Sie hat ein Gesicht wie ein —, she has an angelical face; sie singt wie ein —, she sings beautifully; die — des Abgrundes, [in a bad sense] the angels of the bottomless pit. *Fig.* *a*) [in the style of love, a very beautiful person] an angel. So wahr ich lebe, Herr, sie ist ein wahrer —, Sir, as I have a soul, she is an angel! *b*) [in natural history] *α*) [a species of shark] the monk- or angel-fish. *β*) [a species of ray] the scate. *c*) the 128th part of the penny-weight.

Engel=art, *f.* a class of angels. —bett, *n.* [an open bed without bedposts] angel-bed. —blume, *f.* [a name of several plants] *a*) mouse-ear, scorpion-grass. *b*) flowering cudweed. *c*) the globe-flower. —brod, *n.* [in Scripture] angel's food, manna. —fisch, *m.* V. —, *fig.* *b.* *α* and *β*. —gestalt, *f.* an angelical figure or shape. —gleich, I. *adj.* resembling angels, angel-like, angelic, angelical. II. *adv.* angelically. —kraut, *n.* the mountain arnica. —lehre, *f.* angelology. —rai, *m.* —s=rai, *m.* V. —roche. —rein, *adj.* and *adv.* as pure or innocent as an angel. —reine, —reinheit, *f.* the purity or innocence of an angel. —roche, *m.* [a species of ray] scate. —schaar, *f.* a host of angels. —schön, *adj.* and *adv.* beautiful as an angel, angelically beautiful, surpassingly beautiful. —schwinge, *f.* the wing of an angel. —s=gestalt, *f.* V. —gestalt. —sgruß, *m.* [in the Romish church] ave Maria. —skopf, *m.* 1) an angel's head. *Fig.* a beautiful head. 2) [in architecture] the head of a child furnished with wings. —sköpfchen, *n.* 1. V. —skopf 1. 2) [a plant] common or small maple. —slächeln, *n.* an angelical smile. —smark, *f.* penny-weight. —s=miene, *f.* angelical mien. —seele, *f.* a pure or virtuous soul or mind. —speise, *f.* [in Scripture] angel's food, manna. —stimme, *f.* a beautiful voice. Mit einer —stimme, angel-like voiced. —s=trankwurzel, *f.* [a plant] common motherwort. —süß, *n.* [a species of fern] polypody. Das gemeine — süß, wallfern. —thaler, *m.* 1) V. Engelot. 2) an ancient Saxon coin, bearing the figure of an angel. —trank, *m.* V. —strankwurzel. —wurz, —wurzel, *f.* [a plant] angelica. —wurzöl, *n.* a volatile oil drawn from the angelica.

Engelchen, *n.* [-s, *pl.* -] *dimin.* of Engel. [in natural history] *a*) [a plant] poetic or white narcissus. *b*) [a bird] the siskin.

Engelinn, *f.* [unusual] a female resembling an angel.

‡Engelland, V. England.

***Engelót**, *m.* [-es, *pl.* -e] **Engelótte**, *f.* [*pl.* -n] [an ancient English coin struck at Paris while under the dominion of England] angelot.

Engen, [V. Enge] I. *v. tr.* to narrow, to straiten. Die Schuhe — [*drücken] mich, my shoes pinch me. *Fig.* to contract, to abridge, to narrow, to shorten, to lessen. II. *v. intr.* to narrow, to become narrower, to contract. *Fig.* to contract, to shrink.

Engerling, *m.* [-es, *pl.* -e] [perhaps from Anger, field] 1) [a maggot that infects the back of deer and cattle] wornil. 2) the grub of the cock-chafer. 3) the gourdworm. 4) the mole-cricket, fen-cricket.

Engern, [unusual] *v. tr.* [a frequentative verb, from Engen] to narrow; *fig.* to shorten, to lessen.

England, *n.* [-s] England.

Engländer, *m.* [-s, *pl.* -] 1) an Englishman. 2) an English horse. 3) a horse, which has its tail docked.

Engländersucht, *f.* anglomania.

Engländerei, *f.* 1) Anglomania. 2) an English idiom, anglicism.

Engländerinn, *f.* an English woman.

Engländern, *v. tr.* V. [the more usual word] Englisiren.

Engländisch, [more usual] **Englisch**, *adj.* & *adv.* English. Die —e Sprache, the English language, English; die —e Kirche, anglican church; —e Sitten, English manners; der —e Tanz, the English country-dance; V. also Anglaise; —es Zinn, pewter; —es Salz, Epsom salt; —es Blau, queen's blue; —es Braunroth, Indian red; —es Pflaster, court plaister; die —e Haut, gold-beater's skin; —es Leder, satinet; die —e Krankheit, [a disease which affects children] rickets; mit der —n Krankheit behaftet, rickety.

Englisch, [from Engel] I. *adj.* angelic, angelical. Der —e Gruß [das Angelus], V. Engelsgruß. *Fig.* Eine —e Stimme, an angel-like voice. II. *adv.* angelically.

Englisiren, *v. tr.* Ein Pferd —, to dock the tail of a horse.

***Enharmonisch**, *adj.* [in music] enharmonic, as an interval.

‖Enke, *m.* [-n, *pl.* -n] [allied to the Lat. *ancilla* and to the following Enkel, originally = a young man] a servant, hind.

1\. **Enkel**, *m.* [-s, *pl.* -] [V. Enke] 1) grand-child, grand-son. 2) a descendant.

2\. **‖Enkel**, *m.* [-s, *pl.* -] [from engen, i. e. biegen, to bend] [the joint which connects the foot with the leg] ancle.

‖Enkel, *adj.* and *adv.* simple [as opposed to double].

Enkelinn, *f.* 1) grand-daughter. 2) a female descendant.

***Ensemble**, *n.* [*pl.* -s] [pron. as in the French] [in music] ensemble.

Ent, a prefix or inseparable proposition, denotes a moving from, separation, as in entfernen, entfliehen, entführen &c.: hence *fig.* it often expresses a negative, as in entfärben, enterben, enthüllen &c. Sometimes it augments the sense; it denotes also origin, beginning, as in entbrennen, entspinnen, entstehen &c.

Entáchten, **Entächten**, [unusual] *v. tr.* to [...] claim a person's outlawry.

Entádeln, *v. tr.* to deprive of nobility. Einen Edelmann —, to degrade a nobleman. *Fig.* Das Laster entadelt den Menschen, vice degrades a man.

Entádern, *v. tr.* to deprive of sinews, to take out the sinews [of butchered cattle].

Entámten, [rather unusual] *v. tr.* to remove from office, service or employment, to discard, to dismiss.

Entámtung, [rather unusual] *f.* removal from office or employment, dismission. Die einstweilige or vorläufige —, suspension.

Entánkern, [rather unusual] *v. tr.* to [...] from its anchors, to disanchor [a ship].

Entárten, I. *v. intr.* [n. w. seyn] to degenerate, as plants, animals &c. II. *v. tr.* to cause to degenerate.

Entártung, *f.* degeneracy, degeneration. *Fig.* Die — der Menschen in neuerer Zeit, the degeneracy of men in modern times.

Entásten, **‖Entästen**, *v. tr.* to deprive of branches, to disbranch.

Entáthmen, [rather unusual] *v. tr.* 1) to deprive of breath; *fig.* to deprive of life, to [...] 2) to emit with one's breath.

Entäußern, I. *v. tr.* to free, to rid. Einen von einer Sorge —, to rid any one of his care. II. *v. r.* sich —. Sich einer Sache —, to part with a thing, to dispose of it, to give it up, to resign it.

Entbállen, [rather unusual] *v. tr.* to unpack goods.

Entbánnen, [unusual] *v. tr.* 1) V. Verbannen. 2) V. Abschaffen.

Entbéhren, [from the old bären, i. e. tragen, eben] *v. tr.* [sometimes governs the genit., sometimes he accus.] 1) to want, not to have, to be deficient in. Er entbehrt die Annehmlichkeiten des ebens, he wants the comforts of life; er entehrte zuweilen der Nahrung, he was sometimes destitute of food; das Land entbehrte der Mittel, den Krieg fortzuführen, the country as deficient in the means of carrying on war. Das —, the state of not having, want, privation.) to do without. Ich kann es nicht —, I cannot o without it; können Sie dieses Buch einige eit —? can you spare this book a while? wir ätten seiner Gesellschaft — können, we could ave dispensed with his company; ich kann Ihen Dienste nicht —, I cannot dispense with your rvices.

Entbéhrlich, *adj.* and *adv.* not wanted, not quisite, easily spared. Geld ist für ihn eine —e ache, he can do without money; er ist uns hr —, we can do very well without him. Die ntbehrung, the state of not having, want, ivation.

Entbéhrlichkeit, *f.* the capability of being spensed with, dispensableness.

Entbíeten, [somewhat obsolete] *ir. v. tr.* 1) to d, to command, to order, to direct. Er wurde seinem Regimente entboten, he was ordered oin his regiment; Einen zu sich — [lassen], end for any one. 2) to give notice, to make own, to announce. Der König Alexander entt seinem Bruder seinen Gruß, king Alexan- greets [sends kind wishes to] his brother.

Entbínden, *ir. v. tr.* to remove a band n, to unbind, to untie, to unfasten, to loose losen, to set free from shackles. *Fig. a)* [in mistry,] Der Wärmestoff muß während dem mischen] Processe entbunden werden, caloric n be disengaged during the process; bei der hrung entbindet sich Gas, fermentation is acmpanied by an extrication of gas. *b)* to deliver a child, to put to bed. Eine Frau —, to der a woman; von einem Knaben entbunden den, to be brought to bed of, to be delivered son. *c)* to disengage from, to free from. Ei seines Versprechens —, to release any one n a promise; Einen von einer Verbindlich- —, to liberate any one from an obligation; m einer Pflicht —, to clear a man from ty; der Sorge entbunden, freed from care.

Entbíndung, *f.* 1) the act of unbinding, cating &c. 2) disengagement, liberation or se from an obligation. 3) the delivery of a an with child, childbirth. Die — von ei Sohne, the act of being brought to bed son.

ntbindungs-anstalt, *f.* lying-in house spital. V. also Klinik. —**kunst**, *f.* midwi-, the obstetric art, obstetrics. —**stuhl**, *m.* bstetric chair. —**werkzeug**, *n.* obstetric uments. —**zange**, *f.* obstetric pincers.

ntbläsen, [rather unusual] *ir. v. tr.* to de- of by blowing.

ntblättern, *v. tr.* to deprive of leaves. Ei ose —, to strip a rose of its leaves. Das [in botany] defoliation. *Fig.* Die Blume aschuld —, to deflower, to deprive of maiod.

tblöden, *v. r.* sich —, to be shameless or dent enough to do or to say something, to ld-faced enough, to dare. Er entblödet sich Dinge zu behaupten, die er nicht weiß, he res to assert things which he does not .

Entblößen, *v. tr.* 1) to strip off the covering, to uncover. Einen Gang —, [in mining] to uncover a lode [by removing the upper earth]; den Degen —, to draw the sword. 2) to deprive of clothes, to make naked, to denude, to denudate. Die Brust —, to bare the breast; das Haupt —, to uncover the head, to take off the hat or cap; sich —, to divest one's self of clothes, or to uncover one's breast or any part of one's body. *Fig.* Eine Festung —, to degarnish or disgarnish a fort [to deprive it of a garrison or troops necessary for defence]; von Geld entblößt, bare or destitute of money; aller Güter entblößt, deprived of all goods, destitute.

Entblößung, *f.* 1) baring, denudation. 2) *Fig.* deprivation, destitution.

Entblühen, *v. intr.* [u. w. seyn] 1) to spring up, to rise flowering or blossoming. 2) V. [the more usual word] Verblühen. 3) *Fig.* [unusual] to die.

Entblüten, [rather unusual] *v. tr.* to deprive of blossoms or flowers.

Entbórgen, V. Entlehnen.

Entbréchen, *ir.* I. *v. intr.* [u. w. seyn] [unusual] to separate violently. II. [rather stiff] *v. r.* sich —. Sich einer Sache —, to abstain from a thing, to forbear. Ich kann mich nicht —, es zu thun, I cannot forbear doing it. V. [the more usual word] Enthalten.

Entbrénnbaren, [rather unusual] *v. tr.* [in chemistry] to deprive of phlogiston, to dephlogisticate.

Entbrénnen, *ir.* I. *v. intr.* [u. w. seyn] to take fire, to be inflamed. *Fig.* Er entbrannte vor Liebe, vor Zorn, he burned with love, with anger; er entbrannte in Liebe für sie, he fell violently in love with her. II. *v. tr.* to cause to burn with flame, to kindle.

Entbrénnstoffen, [rather unusual] *v. tr.* [in chemistry] to deprive of phlogiston, to dephlogisticate.

Entbürden, *v. tr.* to disburden, to unload, to discharge. *Fig.* Sich seiner Sorgen —, to disburden one's self of one's cares, to cast away one's sorrows.

Éntchen, *n.* [-s, *pl.* -] [diminut. of Ente] a duckling.

Entdáchen, [rather unusual] *v. tr.* to uncover [a building], to unroof.

Entdámpfen, *v. intr.* [u. w. seyn] to rise in vapours.

Entdâmpfen, *v. tr.* to free from vapours, to cause to evaporate.

Entdârmen, [rather unusual] *v. tr.* to disbowel [a bird &c.].

Entdéckeln, [rather unusual] *v. tr.* to divest of the lid.

Entdécken, I. *v. tr.* [to remove a covering] to uncover, to discover. ||Ein Haus —, to unroof a house. *Fig.* Die Seeleute entdeckten Land, the seamen descried land; Columbus entdeckte die Abweichung der Magnetnadel, Columbus discovered the variation of the magnetic needle; Einem ein Geheimniß —, to reveal a secret to any one; Einem sein Herz —, to open one's heart to a person; ich habe ihm den Zustand meiner Angelegenheiten entdeckt, I opened him the state of my concerns; wenn ich Ihnen meine Leidenschaft entdecke, if I disclose my passion to you; einen Dieb —, to detect or find out a thief; als der Dieb sah, daß er entdeckt war, versuchte er zu entfliehen, the thief, finding himself discovered, attempted to escape; einen Diebstahl —, to find out a theft; entdeckt werden, to come to light; die Verschwörung ist entdeckt, the plot is out; wir entdeckten den Kunstgriff, we discovered the artifice; ich will mich Ihnen —, I will unclose to you my mind; er entdeckte sich ihm, he discovered himself to him. II. *v. r.* sich —, to begin to appear, to open. Der Hafen entdeckte sich unsern Blicken, the harbour opened to our view. *it.* to become evident. Als man ihn näher untersuchte, da entdeckte sich, daß &c., when he was more closely searched, it was found out, that &c. SYN. V. Erfinden.

Entdécker, *m.* [-s, *pl.* -] a discoverer, a detector, a descrier. Columbus ist der — Amerika's, Columbus discovered America.

Entdéckung, *f.* 1) the act of disclosing to view, or bringing to light. Die — eines Diebes, the detection of a thief; die — eines Komplotts, the detection or discovery of a plot; die — des Magnetismus, the discovery of magnetism; die — Amerika's durch Columbus, the discovery of America by Columbus. 2) [that which is discovered, found out or revealed] discovery. Die Eigenschaften des Magnets waren eine wichtige —, the properties of the magnet were an important discovery.

Entdeckungs-reise, *f.* a voyage of discovery.

Entdréhen, *v. tr.* to wring from. Seinen Händen die Waffen —, to wring the arms from his hands.

Entdríngen, V. [the more usual word] Hervordringen.

Entdúnsten, *v. intr.* [u. w. seyn] to evaporate.

Entdünsten, *v. tr.* to clear of vapours. Ein Gewitter entdünstet die Luft, a thunder-storm purifies the air.

Énte, *f.* [*pl.* -n] [Lat. *Anas*, gen. *anat*-is] [a waterfowl] a duck. Eine junge —, a duckling. Die wilde — [Wildente], wild-duck, the mallard.

Enten-adler, *m.* the bald buzzard, the sea-eagle, the ospray. —**beize**, *f.* the practice of taking wild ducks by means of hawks, brook-hawking. —**brut**, *f.* 1) the brood of ducks. 2) *Fig.* V. —muschel. —**büchse**, *f.* duck-gun. —**dunst**, *m.* [with huntsmen] duck-shot. —**ei**, *n.* a duck's egg. —**fang**, *m.* 1) duck-hunting. 2) [a place for catching wild ducks] decoy, decoy-pond. —**fänger**, *m.* decoy-man. —**flott**, *n.* V. —grün. —**flug**, *m.* 1) the flight of wild ducks. 2) [a flock of wild ducks flying in company] a flight of wild ducks. —**fuß**, *m.* [the name of plants] *a)* duck's-foot, may-apple. *b)* cut-leaved navel-wort. —**gras**, *n.* the floating fescue-grass, manna-grass. —**gries**, *m.* —**grün**, *n.* —**grütze**, *f.* [a plant] duck-meat, duck's meat, duck-weed. —**habicht**, *m.* V. —adler. —**hagel**, *m.* V. —dunst. —**haus**, *n.* a decoy. —**hund**, *m.* a dog used in, or trained for catching ducks. —**hütte**, *f.* V. —haus. —**jagd**, *f.* duck-shooting. —**muschel**, *f.* the barnacle, or goose-shell. —**pfuhl**, *m.* a duck-pool, duck-pond. —**ruf**, *m.* [among hunters. a pipe to call ducks by imitating their voice] a call. —**schlag**, *m.* duck-shooting. —**schnabel**, *m.* [in conchology] *a)* the duck-muscle. *b)* the white snouted peg. *c)* the sand-gaper. —**stößer**, *m.* a name given to all birds of prey feeding on ducks, but chiefly to the ospray.

Entéhren, *v. tr.* 1) to deprive of honour. Einen Offizier — [more usual degradiren], to degrade an officer; eine Jungfrau —, to dishonour, to debauch, to deflour a virgin; die Entehrte, a deflowered maid. 2) to dishonour, to disgrace. Eine —de Handlung, a dishonourable or disgraceful action; die Menschen rühmen sich oft —der Thaten, men often boast of actions, which disgrace them; es entehrt seinen Namen, it disgraces his name; den Namen Gottes —, to profane the name of God; die Heiden entehrten das Heiligthum des Herrn, the pagans defiled the sanctuary of the Lord; sich —, to dishonour one's self.

Entehrer, *m.* [-s, *pl.* -] a dishonourer, [especially] a deflourer.

Entehrung, *f.* dishonouring, disgracing. Die — eines Offiziers, the degradation of an officer; die — einer Jungfrau, defloration.

Entehrungsurtheil, *n.* [in law] a sentence, by which a person is branded with infamy.

Enteignen, *v. tr.* [rather unusual] to deprive of property. Sich einer Sache —, to give up a property.

Enteilen, *v. intr.* [u. w. seyn] to hasten away, to hurry away. Er enteilte dem Blutbade, he hastened away from the massacre; *it.* he escaped the massacre *Fig.* Die Zeit enteilt, time passes rapidly; schnell — die flüchtigen Stunden, swiftly fly the fleeting hours.

Enteinen, [unusual] I. *v. tr.* V. Entzweien. II. *v. r.* sich —, to break friendship, to divide.

Enteisen, [rather unusual] *v. tr.* to free from ice. Des Frühlings Wärme enteiset die Flüsse, the warmth of spring opens the icebound rivers.

Enterben, *v. tr.* to disinherit, [in law] to exheredate. Seinen Sohn —, to disinherit one's son.

Enterbung, *f.* a disinheriting, [in law] exheredation.

Enterbungsrecht, *n.* [in law] the right of exheredation.

Enterden, [rather unusual] *v. tr.* to clear of earth.

Enterich, *m.* [-s, *pl.* -e] [the male of the duck kind] the drake. Der wilde —, mallard.

Entern, [perhaps from the Fr. *entrer*] *v. tr.* [in seamen's language] to grapple, to board [a ship]. Der Feind enterte das Schiff, the enemy boarded the ship. Die Enterung, grappling, boarding.

Enterbeil, *n.* [in seamen's language] a pole-axe, boarding-axe. —**haken**, *m.* [in seamen's language] a grappling-iron, a grapnel, grappling, or grapple. — an den Nocken der Raaen eines Branders, sheerhooks. —**luke**, *f.* [in seamen's lang.] a scuttle in the quarter-deck or on the forecastle.

Entfächern, [unusual] *v. tr.* to deprive of compartments.

Entfädeln, *v. tr.* to unthread [a needle].

Entfahren, *ir. v. intr.* [u. w. seyn] to fly out of place. Das Ruder entfuhr seinen Händen, the oar slipped out of his hands. *Fig.* Unbedacht entfuhr mir dieses Wort, that word slipp'd out, before I was aware; ein unbedachtsames Wort entfuhr seinen Lippen, an unguarded expression fell from his lips; ein unwillkührlicher Seufzer entfuhr ihm, an involuntary sigh escaped him.

Entfallen, *ir. v. intr.* [u. w. seyn] to fall out of. Das Schwert entfiel seiner Hand, the sword dropped from his hand. *Fig.* Es ist ihm ein unbedachtsames Wort —, an unguarded expression fell from him; es entfielen ihm einige Bemerkungen, he threw out some observations; es ist mir —, it slipped out of my memory; sein Name ist mir —, his name is out of my memory; sein Name ist mir ganz —, I have quite forgotten his name.

Entfalten, I. *v. tr.* to unfold, to expand. Einen Fächer —, to open a fan; eine Blume entfaltet ihre Blätter, a flower expands its leaves; der Nordwind entfaltete seine Flügel, [poetically] the northern wind his wings did display; entfalte die drohende unfreundliche Stirne, unknit that threatening unkind brow. *Fig.* to display, to show, to exhibit to the eyes or to the mind. Er entfaltete mir sein Herz, he opened his heart to me; er entfaltete ihm das ganze Ränkegewebe, he unravelled, unfolded or developed to him the whole intrigue. II. *v. r.* sich —, to become free from folds or wrinkles; *it.* to open, to spread, to expand. Seine krause Stirne entfaltete sich, he smoothed his frowning brow, his frowning brow cleared up; die Blumen — sich im Frühling, flowers expand in spring. *Fig.* Ihre Schönheit entfaltet sich täglich mehr, her beauty expands daily; ihr Herz entfaltete sich mir, she opened her heart to me.

Entfaltung, *f.* 1) the act of unfolding, display. 2) [in the dramatic art] development.

Entfärben, *v. tr.* and *v. r.* 1) to change the colour of, to alter the natural hue of, to alter the complexion, to discolour, to fade. 2) to take away the colour. Die Angst entfärbte ihn, he grew pale with fear; er entfärbte sich, he grew pale, he changed colour. Die Entfärbung, discoloration.

Entfasern, *v. tr.* to deprive of fibers or strings. Bohnen —, to string beans.

Entfernen, I. *v. tr.* to cause to change place, to put from its place, to move to a distance, to remove. Der Herr ist entfernt vom Hause, the master is away from home; der Saturn ist ungefähr neun hundert Millionen Meilen von der Sonne entfernt, Saturn is nearly nine hundred million miles distant from the sun; an einem so entfernten Orte, in so removed or distant a place; ein entferntes Land, a remote country; ein entfernter Gegenstand, a distant object; entfernte Blätter, [in botany] remote leaves; böse Menschen aus der Gesellschaft —, to drive, expel or banish bad men from society; das Schicksal entfernte mich von meinen Freunden, I was separated by fate from my friends. *Fig.* Wir müssen ihn vom Hofe —, we must remove him from court; Einen von seinem Amte —, to remove any one from his employment; eine entfernte Aehnlichkeit in Gestalt oder Farbe, a remote or distant resemblance in form or colour; die entfernte Aehnlichkeit, remoteness of resemblance; eine entfernte Hoffnung, a distant hope; sie sind entfernt verwandt mit &c., they are remotely or distantly allied to &c.; entfernte Verwandte, remote kinsmen; die entfernten Ursachen einer Krankheit, the remote [distant, primary] causes of a disease; etwas auf eine entfernte Art zu verstehen geben, to give one a distant or slight hint, to intimate slightly. II. *v. r.* sich —, to quit a place or company, to retire, to retreat. Er entfernte sich aus der Gesellschaft um zehn Uhr, he withdrew from the society at ten o'clock; ich entfernte mich auf einen Tag von Hause, I left home for a day; sich heimlich —, to abscond; sich entfernt halten, to keep at a distance; haltet euch entfernt! stand off! sich nach und nach von der Küste oder dem früheren Curse —, [in seamen's lang.] to edge away. *Fig.* Sich vom Wege der Pflicht —, to stray from the path of duty, to deviate; sich von der Tugend —, to deviate from virtue.

Entfernung, *f.* 1) the act of removing, removal, remove. Die — jener Personen von ihren Aemtern, the removal of those persons from their posts. *Fig.* Seine lange —, his long absence. 2) [an interval or space between two objects] distance. Eine kleine oder große —, a small or great distance, a small or great remove; die — eines Sternes, the remoteness of a star; sich in der gehörigen — halten, to keep one's distacne [used also in a fig. sense].

Entfernungskraft, *f.* [in physics] the centrifugal force.

Entfesseler, *m.* [-s, *pl.* -] he that unfett &c. V. Befreier.

Entfesseln, *v. tr.* to unfetter, to un Die Hände —, to unshackle the hands. Den Geist —, to unfetter, to unshackl mind, to free it from prejudices; alle Le schaften —, to unchain all passions, to free scope to all passions; Aeolus entfesselt Winde, Aeolus let lose the winds.

Entfestigen, [rather unusual] *v. tr.* to d of fortifications. Eine Stadt —, to dem the fortifications of a town.

Entfetten, *v. tr.* to remove the fat or g of.

Entfiedern, *v. tr.* to strip of feathe plumes, to unplume.

Entflammen, I. *v. intr.* [u. w. seyn] to b out, as a flame. *Fig.* Es entflammte sein Z he grew angry; von Rache entflammt, fired revenge II. *v. tr.* to inflame [chiefly in a sense]. Ihre Augen — jedes Herz, her ey flame every heart; ein edler Wetteifer entf deine Brust, a noble emulation heats your b Die Entflammung, the act of inflaming, flammation.

Entflammer, *m.* [-s, *pl.* -] the person inflames, inflamer.

Entflattern, *v. intr.* [u. w. seyn] to flit or ter away.

Entflechten, *ir. v. tr.* 1) to unbraid [the Ein Seil — [aufflechten], to untwist a rop to loosen, to separate or disconnect things w are interwoven, to disentangle.

Entflecken, [rather unusual] *v. tr.* to tak a stain or stains [from cloth &c.].

Entfleischen, *v. tr.* to deprive of flesh. fleischt, fleshless.

Entfliegen, *ir. v. intr.* [u. w. seyn] 1) to away rapidly. Der Stein entflog seiner the stone flew from his hand. *Fig.* Die Ze fliegt, time passes rapidly, flies. 2) to fl [by the aid of wings]. Der Vogel ist entflog bird is flown [used also in a fig. sense, fro soner that has escaped his prison]; ein en Vogel, a bird that has flown away.

Entfliehen, *ir. v. intr.* [u. w. seyn] to flee, to run away, to evade, to escape dem Gefängnisse —, to make one's escap prison; der Feind entfloh bei dem ersten the enemy fled at the first fire; er entfle Egypten, he fled into Egypt; entfliehe Gebirge, escape to the mountains; es möglich zu —, it was impossible to get Gefahr —, to hasten from danger; *it.* to a danger; den Gefahren —, to evade pe entflieht ihm, she escapes him. *Fig.* Sc die flüchtigen Stunden, swiftly fly the hours; die Gelegenheit war entflohen, portunity was lost.

Entfließen, *ir. v. intr.* [u. w. seyn] from, to run from. Thränen entflossen ih gen, tears flowed from her eyes, or h streamed with tears. *Fig.* Kein Wort seinen Lippen, not a word issued from h die Zeit entfließt, time passes away.

Entflüchten, [unusual] *v. intr.* [u. w. evade, to escape.

Entflügeln, *v. tr.* to deprive of wing flügelt, wingless.

Entfrachten, *v. tr.* to discharge of to unload, to disburden.

Entfremden, *v. tr.* 1) to estrange, to Er ist seinem Lande ganz entfremdet [w

...e has become or grown quite a stranger to his own country; Einen seinen Jugendfreunden —, to alienate a man from the friends of his youth; ich weiß bis zu dieser Stunde nicht, was ihn von mir entfremdet hat, I do not know, to this hour, what it is that has estranged him from me. 2) [chiefly in law] V. Entwenden. Die Entfremdung, withdrawing or estrangement, alienation.

Entführen, *v. tr.* 1) to lead off, to carry away, [especially] to carry away by violence. Ein Mädchen —, to run away with a girl; er hat sie ihrem Manne entführt, he ravished her from her husband; sie hat sich von ihm — lassen, she eloped with him. 2) to take from, to take away.

Entführer, *m.* [-s, *pl.* -] —inn, *f.* a ravisher.

Entführung, *f.* the act of carrying away, [especially] a seizing or carrying away by force, &c. Die — einer Frau, the ravishment of a woman from her husband; die — eines Kindes, the ravishment of a child from his parents.

Entfüllen, V. 1. Ausfüllen.

Entfurchen, *v. tr.* to unknit, to smooth [the brow].

Entfürsten, [unusual] *v. tr.* to strip of princedom.

Entgegen, *adv.* and *prep.* moving in an opposite direction. Auf! ihm —! let us meet him! **Entgegen-arbeiten**, *v. tr.* to defeat or frustrate by contrary agency, to counteract, to counterwork. —**bellen**, *v. intr.* to bark at, to approach barking, as a dog. —**blasen**, *ir. v. intr.* to come blowing to meet any one; *it.* to blow in an opposite or contrary direction. Von allen Seiten blasen die Winde sich or einander —, winds from all quarters oppositely blow. —**bringen**, *ir. v. tr.* to bring to a person that is coming. Sie brachten ihm Blumen und Früchte —, they met him with flowers and fruits. —**eilen**, *v. intr.* [u. w. seyn] to hasten to meet any one. Sie eilten ihm —, they hastened to meet him. Fig. Sieh doch, wie ihre dankbaren Herzen dir — eilen, see, they encounter thee with their hearts' thanks; seinem Unglück —eilen, to run to one's ruin. —**fahren**, *ir.* I. *v. intr.* [u. w. seyn] 1) to go in a coach to meet any one. Sie fuhren ihm —, they came in a coach, they drove to meet him. 2) to sail against. Dem Winde —fahren, to sail against the wind, to beat to windward. II. *v. tr.* to carry or convey something on a waggon, &c., towards a person that is coming. —**fliegen**, *ir. v. intr.* [u. w. seyn] to fly toward a person or thing drawing near. Die Kugeln flogen ihm —, the balls flew toward him. *Fig.* Sie flog ihm freudig —, joyfully she flew to meet him. —**führen**, *v. tr.* to lead towards a person that is coming. Dem Vater die Kinder —führen, to lead the children to meet their father; er führte das Heer dem Feinde —, he led the army to meet or against the enemy. —**gehen**, *ir. v. intr.* [u. w. seyn] Einem —gehen, to go to meet any one. *Fig.* Der Gefahr, dem Tode —gehen, to face danger, death. —**halten**, *ir. v. tr.* to hold something towards a person drawing near. *Fig.* *a*) to set against, to put in opposition, to oppose, to contrast. *b*) to compare [reasons and arguments &c.]. Der Freude den Schmerz —halten, to compare pleasure with pain. —**handeln**, *v. intr.* to act in opposition or contrary to [the will of one's father &c.]. Einem Gesetze —handeln, to infringe a law; den Tugendlehren —handeln, to run counter to the rules of virtue. —**jauchzen**, —**jubeln**, *v. intr.* Einem —jauchzen, to receive, to welcome any one shouting. —**kommen**, *ir. v. intr.* [u. w. seyn] to come to meet any one. *Fig.* Einem —kommen, to show great kindness or courtesy to any one; *it.* to make the first steps. —**laufen**, *ir. v. intr.* [u. w. seyn] Einem —laufen, to run to meet any one. *Fig.* *Es lauft seinem eigenen Vortheile —, it is contrary to his own interest. —**leben**, *v. intr.* Eines Befehlen —leben, to infringe any one's commands; er lebt mir in Allem absichtlich —, he crosses me purposely in every thing. —**nehmen**, *ir. v. tr.* to take or receive what is offered, to accept. Der Monarch geruhte das Beglaubigungsschreiben des Gesandten —zunehmen, the monarch pleased to receive the credentials of the ambassador. —**reisen**, *v. intr.* [u. w. seyn] to travel to meet any one. —**reiten**, *ir. v. intr.* [u. w. seyn] to go on horseback to meet any one. Sie ritten ihm —, they went on horseback to meet him. —**rennen**, *ir. v. intr.* [u. w. seyn] to run to meet any one. —**richten**, *v. tr.* to direct towards. —**rücken**, I. *v. tr.* to push, to pull towards. II. *v. intr.* [u. w. seyn] to march toward. Wir rückten dem Feinde —, we marched to meet the enemy. —**rudern**, *v. intr.* [u. w. seyn] 1) to row towards a person or thing drawing near. 2) to row against. —**schicken**, *v. tr.* to send toward something that is coming or whose coming is expected. —**schiffen**, *v. intr.* [u. w. seyn] 1) to sail toward something that is coming. 2) to sail or ride against. Dem Winde — schiffen, to ride against the wind. —**schwimmen**, *ir. v. intr.* [u. w. seyn] 1) to swim towards a person or thing that is coming. 2) to swim against. Dem Strome — schwimmen, to swim against the stream [used also in a fig. sense]. —**segeln**, *v. intr.* [u. w. seyn] to sail towards something that approaches. Wir segelten dem Feinde —, we sailed to meet the enemy. —**sehen**, *ir. v. intr.* to look towards a person that is coming. *Fig.* Ich sehe Nachrichten mit der Post —, I look for news by the arrival of the post; wir sehen einem versprochenen Besuche —, we expect a visit that has been promised; dem Tode getrost —sehen, to look on death confidently. —**senden**, *ir. v. tr.* 1) to send to meet any one. 2) to send something towards a person that is coming or expected to come. —**setzen**, *v. tr.* to set against, to oppose. Dem Wasser einen Damm —setzen, to restrain water by a dike; sich —setzen, [also in a fig. sense] to oppose; ich werde mich seinen Wünschen nicht — setzen, I will not make opposition to his wishes; —gesetzter Meinung seyn, to differ; —gesetzte Meinungen, contrary opinions; gerade —gesetzt, diametrically opposite; —gesetzte Bedeutungen, opposite significations. Die Entgegensetzung &c., [in rhetoric] antithesis. —**seufzen**, *v. intr.* to sigh after or for any thing. —**seyn**, *ir. v. intr.* [u. w. seyn] to be against. Der Wind ist uns —, [in seamen's language] the wind heads us; man hat es darauf abgesehen, uns in Allem — zu seyn, people make a point of crossing us in all things; es ist unsern Wünschen —, it is contrary to our wishes; er ist allen meinen Plänen —, he thwarts or he opposes all my designs; er ist dieser Maßregel —, he makes opposition to this measure. —**stehen**, *ir. v. intr.* [u. w. seyn and haben] to stand opposite to, to face. *Fig.* Alle Hindernisse, die meinem Willen — standen, all impediments that opposed my will. —**stellen**, *v. tr.* to set against, to oppose. Die Zeugen einander —stellen, to confront the witnesses with one another; sich dem Feinde auf dem Schlachtfelde —stellen, to face the enemy in the field of battle. *Fig.* Vielerlei stellt sich der Erfüllung meiner Wünsche —, much stands in the way of my wishes. Die Entgegenstellung, V. Entgegensetzung. —**strömen**, *v. intr.* [u. w. seyn] to stream in an opposite direction. *Fig.* Das Volk strömte ihm —, a flood of people came to meet him. —**wirken**, *v. intr.* to act in opposition to, to counteract, to countercheck, to check, to hinder, defeat, or frustrate by contrary agency. Böse Beispiele wirken oft den guten Lehren —, good precepts are often counteracted by bad examples. Die Entgegenwirkung, antiperistasis. —**ziehen**, *ir.* I. *v. tr.* 1) to draw or advance something towards or against a certain point. 2) to draw in contrary direction. II. *v. intr.* [u. w. seyn] to draw or advance towards a person or thing that is coming.

Entgegenen, [more usual] **Entgegnen**, *v. tr.* to return an answer, to answer, to reply..

Entgehen, *ir. v. intr.* [u. w. seyn] [used only in a fig. sense] Er entging dem Streiche, der seinem Kopfe galt, he evaded the blow aimed at his head; der Dieb entging seinen Verfolgern, the thief escaped his pursuers; einem Feinde —, to elude an enemy; die Kräfte — mir, my strength begins to fail me; der Athem entgeht ihm, he loses his breath; der Gefahr —, to escape or avoid danger; dem Tode kann man nicht —, *prov.* there is no dying by proxy; wie vielem Verdruß wäre er entgangen, how much trouble had he escaped; viele Dinge können ihnen —, many things may escape them [may pass unobserved by them]; es ist mir kein einziges Wort entgangen, not a single word escaped my notice; das muß mir entgangen seyn, that I must have overlooked, overheard &c.

Entgeilen, [unusual] *v. tr.* to geld, to castrate [a horse &c.].

Entgeisten, [rather unusual] *v. tr.* to deprive of life.

Entgeistern, *v. tr.* to deprive of life. *Fig.* *a*) to deprive of spirit, fire, courage or energy, to make dull. *b*) to deprive of one's senses.

Entgelt, *n.* [-es, *pl.* -e] occurring only in the phrase: ohne —, gratis, without recompense, for nothing; ohne — dienen, to perform service gratis.

Entgelten, *ir. v. intr.* to make amends [joined with the verbs lassen, müssen, sollen]. Ich werde es ihm — lassen or er soll es mir —, I will make him pay for it; er mußte es —, he atoned or suffered for it.

Entgießen, *ir. v. tr.* V. [the more usual word] Ausgießen.

Entgleiten, *ir.* [with some authors *reg.*] *v. intr.* [u. w. seyn] 1) to slip out of. 2) to slip along, to glide along.

Entgliedern, [rather unusual] *v. tr.* to deprive of members or limbs. *Fig.* Einen Staatskörper —, to disorganize a body politic. Die Entgliederung eines Staatskörpers, the disorganisation of a body politic.

Entglimmen, *ir. v. intr.* [u. w. seyn] to begin to glow or to begin to burn with flame, to kindle. *Fig.* Sein Zorn entglomm, he grew angry.

Entglitschen, *v. intr.* V. Entgleiten.

Entglühen, *v. intr.* [u. w. seyn] to begin to shine with intense heat, to begin to glow. *Fig.* Er entglühte für sie, he burned with love for her.

Entgöttern, *v. tr.* to divest of divinity, to ungod. Die Entgötterung, the act of ungodding.

Entgräten, *v. tr.* V. Ausgräten.

Entgrünen, *v. intr.* [u. w. seyn] to spring up verdant.

Entgültigen, [rather unusual] *v. tr.* to invalidate [an agreement, a contract &c.].

Entgürteln, *v. tr.* to ungird. *Fig.* Eine Jungfrau —, to deflour a virgin.

Entgürten, *v. tr.* to ungird, to ungirth. Sich —, to take off one's girdle.

Enthaaren, *v. tr.* to strip of hair, to depilate. Sich —, to loose one's hair.

Enthalftern, *v. tr.* [rather unusual] to unhalter. Sich —, to unhalter one's self. Dieses Pferd hat sich enthalftert, this horse has slipped its halter.

Enthallen, *v. intr.* V. Ertönen.

‖**Enthalt**, *m.* [-es] V. Aufenthalt and Inhalt.

Enthalten, *ir.* I. *v. tr.* 1) to hold, to contain, as a vessel. Das Faß enthält eine Ohm, the cask contains one awme. 2) to contain, to comprehend, to include. Die Geschichte des Livius enthält hundert und vierzig Bücher, the history of Livy contains a hundred and forty books; die Rechnung enthält diesen Artikel nicht, this article is not contained in the account. II. *v. r.* sich —, to abstain from, to forbear or refrain from. Sich des Essens und Trinkens —, to abstain from eating and drinking; daß ihr euch enthaltet vom Götzenopfer, [in Scripture] abstain from meats offered to idols; ich konnte mich des Lachens nicht —, I could not forbear laughing; ich kann mich des Weinens nicht —, I cannot help weeping. Die Enthaltung &c, abstinence, forbearance.

Enthaltsam, *adj.* and *adv.* abstemious, abstinent, continent. — im Essen und Trinken, temperate or moderate in eating and drinking. Der Enthaltsame, the abstemious.

Enthaltsamkeit, *f.* abstemiousness, abstinence, continence, continency.

Enthärten, *v. tr.* [rather unusual] to free from hardness, rigour or asperity, to mollify, to soften; to deprive of temper [as iron or steel].

Entharzen, *v. tr.* to deprive of resin.

Enthaupten, *v. tr.* to behead, to decapitate, to decollate [a criminal &c.]. Einen mit dem Fallbeile —, to guillotine a person. Die Enthauptung, decapitation. Die — des h. Johannes des Täufers, the decollation of St. John the Baptist.

Enthäuten, *v. tr.* to skin Einen Ochsen —, to flay an ox. Die Enthäutung, excoriation.

Entheben, *ir. v. tr.* to heave away. *Fig.* to exempt, to free. Einen irgend einer Schuldigkeit —, to exempt any one from any obligation; der Verantwortung —, to discharge of responsibility, to exonerate from responsibility; aller Sorgen enthoben, freed from all care; der Förmlichkeiten und Ceremonien —, to dispense with forms and ceremonies Der Enthobene, exempt.

Entheiligen, *v. tr.* to desecrate, to unhallow, to profane. Den Namen Gottes —, to profane the name of God; den Sabbath —, to profane the sabbath; einen Tempel —, to profane or defile a temple. Die Entheiligung, profanation. Die — des Namens Gottes durch Fluchen, the profanation of the name of God by swearing.

Entheiliger, *m.* [-s, *pl.* -] profaner.

Enthelmen, [rather unusual] *v. tr.* to take off one's helmet.

Enthinken, [rather unusual] *v. intr.* [u. w. seyn] to limp away.

Entholzen, *v. tr.* to deprive of wood.

Enthonigen, [rather unusual] *v. tr.* [in husbandry] to clear [wax] of honey.

Enthufen, [rather unusual] *v. tr.* to unsole a horse, to take off the sole of its foot.

Enthüllen, *v. tr.* to divest of a cover, to discover, to uncover. Den Busen —, to unveil the breast; sich —, to uncover one's self. *Fig.* Ein Geheimniß —, to reveal a secret; die Plane des Ministeriums sind durch die Begebenheiten enthüllt worden, events have disclosed the designs of the ministry; das Laster —, to unmask vice; alle zukünftige Ereignisse — sich dem allsehenden Auge, all futurities are naked before the all-seeing eye; wisse, daß ich gesandt bin, dir zu —, was die Zukunft bringt, know, I am sent, to show thee what shall come in future days. Die Enthüllung, [the act of disclosing to view, or bringing to light] discovery, disclosure. *Fig.* Die — eines Complots, the discovery of a plot; die — eines Geheimnisses, the revealing of a secret.

Enthülsen, *v. tr.* to husk [pease &c.].

Enthumpeln, [rather unusual] *v. intr.* [u. w. seyn] to limp or halt away.

Enthüpfen, *v. intr.* [u. w. seyn] 1) to jump away. 2) to escape.

***Enthusiasmiren**, *v. tr.* to fill with rapture or enthusiasm, to ecstasy.

***Enthusiasmus**, *m.* enthusiasm, heat of imagination. Sein — für die Sache dieses unglücklichen Volkes, his zeal for the cause of this unfortunate people.

***Enthusiast**, *m.* [-en, *pl.* -en] enthusiast. Der — für Dichtkunst oder Musik, an enthusiast for poetry or music.

***Enthusiastisch**, I. *adj.* enthusiastic, enthusiastical. Ein —er Bewunderer des Homer, an enthusiastic admirer of Homer. II. *adv.* enthusiastically.

Entian, *m.* V. Enzian.

Entjochen, [rather unusual] *v. tr.* to unyoke [oxen]. *Fig.* to free from thraldom, to deliver from a yoke.

Entjuden, [unusual] *v. tr.* to free from Hebrew manners.

Entjungfern, *v. tr.* to deprive of virginity, to deflour.

Entkeimen, *v. intr.* [u. w. seyn] to vegetate and rise out of the ground, to spring up, to sprout, to bud up. *Fig* Sie fanden, daß neue Hoffnung der Verzweiflung entkeimt, they found new hope to spring out of despair.

Entkerkern, *v. tr.* to liberate from prison, to release.

Entkernen, *v. tr.* V. [the more usual word] Auskernen 1.

Entketten, [rather unusual] *v. tr.* to free from chains, to unchain, to unfetter [used also in a fig. sense].

Entkleiden, *v. tr.* to strip or divest of clothes, to undress, to unclothe. Sich —, to put off one's clothes. *Fig* Die Wahrheit von allem Schmucke —, to divest truth of all ornaments. Syn. V. Auskleiden.

Entkleistern, [rather unusual] *v. tr.* [with card-makers] to free from superfluous paste.

Entklettern, *v. intr.* to escape clambering.

Entklimmen, [with some authors *ir.*] *v. intr.* [u. w. seyn] to escape climbing.

Entknöpfen, *v. tr.* V. [the more usual word] Aufknöpfen.

Entknoten, [rather unusual] *v. tr.* to unravel [threads &c.].

Entkommen, *ir. v. intr.* [u. w. seyn] 1) to get off, to come off, to escape, to get free. Dem Gefängnisse or aus dem Gefängnisse —, to get out of prison; die Galeeren entkamen, the galleys got off; mit genauer Noth —, to make a narrow escape. 2) [rather provincial] to be lost. Der Hund ist mir —, I have lost the dog.

Entkönigen, [unusual] *v. tr.* to deprive of royalty, to unking.

Entkoppeln, *v. tr.* Hunde —, to loose dogs from their couples, to uncouple dogs.

Entkörpern, *v. tr.* to divest of body, to disembody. Die entkörperte Seele, the disembodied soul. Die Entkörperung, the act of disembodying.

Entkräften, *v. tr.* to deprive of strength, to debilitate, to enfeeble. Den Körper —, to weaken, to enervate or enerve the body; durch große und zu lange Anstrengung den Körper — to exhaust the strength of the body by severe and long exertion, to fatigue the body; eine entkräftende Arbeit, an exhausting labour; sich —, to waste one's strength. *Fig.* Lange Kriege — einen Staat, long wars enfeeble a state; einen Einwurf oder Beweis —, to weaken the force of an objection or argument. Syn. Entkräften, Schwächen. A thing may be reduced in strength or force as well by depriving it of its natural inherent properties of strength, as by reducing the degree of power which it has till now been able to exert. In the first instance a thing is said to be entkräftet, in the second geschwächt. Schwächen is therefore said only of the strength or force, entkräften of the thing possessing it. When the force of a stream of water is weakened by some intervening obstacle, it is said to be geschwächt, as the water loses a certain degree of its former impetus, but not entkräftet, for the inherent qualities of the water remain the same

Entkräftung, *f.* 1) the act of enfeebling, enfeeblement, debilitation. 2) the state of being weakened, or enfeebled, infirmity. Er starb an völliger —, he died of a total loss of strength or of debility.

Entkräftungsgrund, *m.* a reason by which the force of any objection or argument is weakened.

Entkränzen, [unusual] *v. tr.* to strip of a wreath or garland.

Entkräuseln, [unusual] *v. tr.* to uncurl.

Entkriechen, *ir. v. intr.* [u. w. seyn] V. [the more usual word] Wegkriechen.

Entkrönen, [rather unusual] *v. tr.* to uncrown, to dethrone [a king &c.].

Entkuppeln, *v. tr.* to uncouple [dogs].

Entküssen, [rather unusual] *v. tr.* to kiss off.

Entladen, *ir.* I. *v. tr.* to discharge of a load or cargo, to unload, to disburden. Einen Karren, ein Schiff —, to unload a cart, to unload or discharge a ship; eine Flasche —, [in physics] to discharge an electric jar. *Fig.* Sein Gewissen —, to ease one's conscience; Einen der Furcht or von der Furcht —, to free any one from fear. II. *v. r.* sich —, to ease one's self of a load or burden Die Gewitterwolke hat sich —, the thundercloud discharged itself, burst. *Fig.* Sich der Verantwortlichkeit —, to exonerate one's self from responsibility.

Entladung, 1) the act of unloading &c., exoneration, discharge. 2) [that which is thrown out] discharge.

Entlang, *adv.* [by the length, in a line with the length] along. Den Weg or des Weges —, along the way; die Truppen marschirten das or des Flußufer —, the troops marched along the bank of the river.

Entlarven, *v. tr.* to unmask, to dismask. *Fig.* Einen —, to unmask any one; einen Betrüger —, to detect a cheat.

Entlarvung, *f.* the act of unmasking or dismasking. *Fig.* Die — eines Bösewichts, the unmasking of a villain.

Entlassen, *ir. v. tr.* 1) to dismiss. Die Truppen —, to dismiss the soldiers [after a mustering]; *it.* to disband soldiers; er entließ die Versammlung, he dismissed the assembly. *Fig.* to set free or release from some obligation, to set free by dissolving an engagement. Einen Sklaven —, to liberate, to free or to manumit slave; die Kinder der väterlichen Gewalt —, [among the ancient Romans] to emancipate one's children; einen des Amtes, des Dienstes —, to remove any one from office, employment or service, to dismiss any one from employment or service; der König entläßt seine Minister ihres Amtes, the king dismisses his ministers; einen alten Diener —, to discard, to turn away or out, or to discharge an old servant; Einen seines Eides —, to absolve a person from an oath; einen Gefangenen —, to discharge a prisoner; [in law] vom Gerichte völlig —, dismissed without a day; seines Verhaftes — werden, to be set free, to have a writ of ease. 2) [= weichen lassen] Den Stahl —, [in ironworks] to anneal steel. SYN. V. Abdanken.

Entlassung, *f.* release from obligation, removal from office or employment, dismission. Der Offizier erhält seine —, the officer is dismissed or obtains a discharge; die — aus väterlicher Gewalt, [among the ancient Romans] emancipation from paternal authority; die — eines Gefangenen, a delivery or discharge of a prisoner.

Entlassungsschreiben, *n.* [in diplomatics] recredentials.

Entlasten, Entlastigen, *v. tr.* to disburden, to unload, to discharge. Einen einer Bürde —, to ease any one of a load or burden. *Fig.* Eines Geschäftes entlastet, discharged of a business; der Gläubiger entlastet seinen Schuldner, the creditor discharges his debtor; das Gemüth seiner Sorgen und Bekümmernisse —, to disencumber the mind of its cares and griefs; sein Gewissen —, to unload one's conscience; seiner Schuld entlastet, freed from one's guilt.

Entlauben, *v. tr.* to deprive of leaves. Ein entlaubter Baum, a leafless tree. Die Entlaubung, the act of depriving or leaves.

Entlauber, *m.* [-s, *pl.* -] he that deprives of leaves. *Fig.* [in poetry] Der rauhe Winter, der — unserer Wälder, rude winter that strips the forest-foliage.

Entlaufen, *ir. v. intr.* [u. w. seyn] to run away, to elope. Seinem Vormunde —, to run away from one's ward; aus dem Dienste —, to forsake the service in which one is engaged; er entlief vom Heere, he deserted the army or from the army; er entlief von seinem Regimente, he deserted his colours. *Fig.* [in common language] to evade, to escape perils. Er ist ein Thunichtgut, er entläuft dem Galgen sicherlich nicht, he is a good-for-nothing, he'll come to the gallows.

Entledigen, *v. tr.* to remove from a thing any incumbrance, or obstruction, to disengage from. Einen der Fesseln —, to unfetter any one; entledige sie von ihren Lasten, ease them of their burdens; sein Herz —, to disclose the secret thoughts of one's heart; *it.* to speak one's mind freely; sich der Sorgen —, to ease one's self of cares; sich seiner Pflicht —, to perform or to discharge one's duty, to acquit one's self of one's duty; sich seines gegebenen Wortes —, to keep, fulfill or make good one's word. Die Entledigung, the act of removing from a thing any incumbrance or obstruction, disencumbrance, riddance.

Entleeren, I. *v. tr.* to deprive of the contents. Ein Gefäß —, to empty a vessel. II. *v. r.* sich —, to become empty, to empty. *Fig.* † to ease one's belly.

||**Entlegen**, [obsolete and stiff] *v. r.* sich —, to avoid, to help, to forbear.

Entlegen, [past part. of the unusual verb Entliegen] *adj.* and *adv.* remote in place, distant. Dieses Dorf ist beinahe zwei deutsche Meilen von der Stadt —, that village is nearly two German miles distant from the town; ein —er Ort, a remote place; sie verweilten in einem sehr —en Walde, they tarried in a wood that was far off.

Entlegenheit, *f.* removedness, distance from any place, farness.

Entlehnen, *v. tr.* 1) to borrow [a book, a sum of money &c.]. *Fig.* Eine Stelle aus einem gedruckten Buche —, to borrow a passage from a printed book; eine Stelle aus dem Homer entlehnend, sagte er, &c., quoting a passage from Homer, he said: &c.; *sich mit entlehnten Federn schmücken, to dress one's self in borrowed plumes. SYN. V. Erborgen. ||2) V. Auslehnen.

Entlehner, *m.* [-s, *pl.* -] -inn, *f.* a borrower.

Entleiben, *v. tr.* to deprive of life. Einen —, to kill or murder any one; er entleibte ihn mit einem Schwerte, he slew him with a sword; sich selbst —, to commit suicide.

Entleiden, I. *v. tr.* to make disagreeable. II. *v. intr.* [u. w. seyn] to become or to be disagreeable, to have no relish for any thing, to grow weary for any thing.

Entleihen, *ir. v. tr.* 1) to borrow [a book &c.]. Etwas von Jemand —, to borrow something from any one. ||2) V. Ausleihen.

Entleiten, *v. tr.* to lead astray.

Entlichtstoffen, [unusual] *v. tr.* [in chimistry] to deprive of phlogiston, to dephlogisticate.

Entlocken, *v. tr.* 1) to draw from or away by enticement or by something flattering or acceptable, to entice away. 2) to draw from, to force out. Seine Beredtsamkeit entlockte den Zuhörern Thränen, his eloquence drew tears from the audience; die bezaubernden Töne, welche sie der Harfe entlockte, the charming sounds she drew from her harp; Einem sein Geheimniß —, to draw out a secret from any one; †to pump any one.

Entlodern, *v. intr.* [u. w. seyn] to blaze up, to burn up [chiefly in a fig. sense].

Entlosen, *v. tr.* V. [the more usual word] Befreien.

Entmähen, *v. tr.* V. [the more usual word] Wegmähen.

Entmannen, *v. tr.* to deprive of virility, to emasculate, to unman, to castrate, to eunuchate. Entmannt, emasculated, emasculate; der Entmannte, an eunuch. *Fig.* to deprive of masculine strength or vigour, to vitiate by unmanly softness, to render effeminate, to emasculate, to unman, to effeminate.

Entmannung, *f.* emasculation, castration. *Fig.* emasculation, unmanly weakness.

Entmarken, *v. tr.* to enervate. Müßiggang und Wollust — den Körper, idleness and voluptuous indulgences enervate the body.

Entmartern, *v. tr.* to extort by torture or by the rack. Einem Geständnisse —, to extort confessions from any one by torture.

Entmasken, *v. tr.* to unmask, to dismask. Sich —, to unmask.

Entmasten, *v. tr.* to deprive of a mast or masts. Der Sturm entmastete das Schiff, the storm dismasted the ship.

Entmenschen, *v. tr.* to deprive of human shape, to deprive of the constitutional qualities of a human being, to unman, to deprive of humanity [in a proper as well as in a fig. sense]. Lange Kriege — selbst civilisirte Völker, by long wars even civilised nations will fall back into a state of barbarity. Entmenscht, inhuman, savage, cruel, unfeeling; ein entmenschtes Volk, a barbarous people.

Entmenschung, *f.* 1) the act of depriving of humanity. 2) inhumanity. V. Unmenschlichkeit.

Entmüden, [unusual] *v. tr.* to free from tiredness or weariness.

Entmummen, *v. tr.* to strip of any disguise, to unmask.

Entmünzen, *v. tr.* to cry down or call in coin.

Entmurmeln, *v. intr.* [u. w. seyn] to flow murmuring out or from.

Entmuthen, Entmuthigen, *v. tr.* to discourage, to dishearten, to disanimate. Ein entmuthigtes Heer, a disheartened army.

Entnägeln, *v. tr.* to open by drawing the nail or nails.

Entnasen, [unusual] *v. tr.* to deprive of the nose.

Entnaturen, [unusual] *v. tr.* to unnaturalize.

Entnebeln, [rather unusual] *v. tr.* to free from mist, to make bright. Den Himmel —, to clear the sky.

Entnehmen, *ir. v. tr.* 1) to take away, to remove. *Fig.* to free from any thing. Sie entnahmen sie der Gerichtsbarkeit ihrer Bischöfe, they exempted them from the jurisdiction of their bishops. 2) to deprive of, to bereave. 3) to borrow. Geld von einem Andern —, to borrow money from another; eine Stelle aus einem Buche —, to borrow a passage from a book; [in commerce] eine Summe auf Einen —, to draw on any one. 4) *Fig.* to deduce by inference, to collect or learn by reasoning. Aus dem, was ich höre, entnehme ich, daß er anwesend war, from what I hear, I gather, that he was present; wir haben daraus entnommen, hence we concluded.

Entnehmer, *m.* [-s, *pl.* -] he that takes away &c.; [in commerce, he who draws a bill of exchange] the drawer.

Entneigt, V. [the usual word] Abgeneigt.

Entnerven, *v. tr.* to enerve, to enervate. Den Arm —, to unnerve the arm; Ausschweifungen — den Körper, debauchery enervates the body; entnervt, enervated.

***Entomolog**, *m.* [-en, *pl.* -en] entomologist.

***Entomologie**, *f.* [-n] [that part of zoology which treats of insects; the science or history and description of insects] entomology.

***Entomologisch**, *adj.* and *adv.* entomological.

Entpaaren, [unusual] *v. tr.* to separate a pair or couple, to dispair.

Entpanzern, *v. tr.* to deprive of a coat of mail. Sich —, to take off one's coat of mail.

Entpechen, [unusual] *v. tr.* to free from pitch.

Entpflichten, [rather unusual] *v. tr.* to exempt from a duty or obligation. Ich entpflichte Sie davon, I acquit you from it.

Entpflücken, *v. tr.* V. [the more usual word] Wegpflücken.

Entpfropfen, *v. tr.* to uncork [a bottle].

Entpressen, *v. tr.* to force out by pressure, to squeeze out. *Fig.* to extort.

Entprügeln, [rather unusual] *v. tr.* to extort by blows.

Entpuppen, *v. r.* sich —, [in entomology] to divest one's self of the pupa.

Entpurpern, [rather unusual] *v. tr.* to strip of the purple, to dethrone.

Entqualmen, *v. intr.* [u. w. seyn] to rise in vapours, to issue as smoke.

Entquellen, *ir. v. intr.* [u. w. seyn] to spring, to issue. Wasser — den Bergen, waters spring from hills; Thränen entquollen seinen Augen, tears flowed or started from his eyes. *Fig.* Weisheit entquoll seinem Munde, wisdom issued or flowed from his mouth.

Entraffen, *v. tr.* to snatch away. *Fig.* Sich —, to disengage one's self from any thing; der Tod entraffte uns die tapfersten Jünglinge, death took from us our bravest youth.

Enträgen, *v. intr.* V. [the usual word] Hervorragen.

Entrasen, [rather unusual] *v. tr.* to strip of the turf or grass.

Entrasseln, *v. intr.* [u. w. seyn] 1) to issue, to come forth rattling. 2) to fall from rattling. 3) to remove, to withdraw rattling.

Entrathen, *ir. v. intr.* to be without, [used only in the following phrase] Er kann sich dieser Sache nicht —, he cannot be without it.

Enträthseln, *v. tr.* to unriddle [an enigma or mystery]. *Fig.* to decipher [an ambiguous speech &c.].

Entraufen, V. [the more usual word] Ausraufen.

Entraümen, V. [the more usual word] Wegräumen.

***Entrechat**, [pron. as in the French] *m.* [-s, *pl.* -s] a cross-caper. Einen — schlagen, to cut a caper.

***Entree**, [pron. as in the French] *n.* [-s, *pl.* -s or -en] 1) entry. 2) entrance-money.

Entreebillet, *n.* a ticket of admission.

Entregeln, [rather unusual] *v. tr.* to make irregular, to disorder.

Entreiben, V. [the more usual word] Austreiben.

Entreißen, *ir.* ||I. *v. intr.* [u. w. seyn] to run away. *Fig.* Meine Geduld ist entrissen, my patience has gone. II. *v. tr.* to take away by force, to tear from. Er entriß das Schwert seinen Händen, he wrested the sword from his hands. *Fig.* Der Feind entriß unsern Händen den Sieg, the enemy wrested the victory from our hands; Einen dem Tode —, to save any one's life; Einen der Gefahr —, to rescue or free any one from danger; Einem ein Geheimniß —, to wring a secret from any one; des Schicksals Hand hat dich mir entrissen, the hand of fate has torn thee from me; das Schicksal hat mir das Geständniß entrissen, fate has wrested the confession from me; sich —, to get loose or free, to get off, to disengage one's self; er entriß sich ihren umschlingenden Armen, he tore himself from her embrace.

Entreiten, [rather unusual] *ir. v. intr.* [u. w. seyn] to ride away, to make one's escape on horseback.

Entrennen, *ir. v. intr.* [u. w. seyn] to run away, to escape by running [away].

***Entrepreneür**, [pron. as in the French] *m.* [-s, *pl.* -s or -e] V. Unternehmer.

***Entreprise** or **Entreprise**, [pron. Angtenpris(e)] *f.* [*pl.* -n] V. Unternehmung.

Entrich, V. Enterich.

Entrichten, *v. tr.* to discharge what is due. Steuern —, to pay taxes; die Schuld der Dankbarkeit —, to pay the debt of gratitude; die Entrichtung einer Schuld, discharge, payment of a debt.

Entriegeln, I. *v. tr.* to unbolt [a door, a gate]. II. *v. r.* sich —, to open. Diese Thüre entriegelt sich leicht, this door opens easily, is easily unbolted.

Entrieseln, [rather unusual] *v. intr.* [u. w. seyn] to purl along.

Entrinden, [rather unusual] *v. tr.* to strip of bark, to bark.

Entringeln, [rather unusual] *v. tr.* to unring.

1. **Entringen**, [rather unusual] *v. tr.* to unring.

2. **Entringen**, *ir.* I. *v. tr.* to twist or extort from by violence, to pull or force from by violent wringing or twisting, to wrest. Ich entrang seiner Hand das Schwert, I wrenched the sword from his hands. *Fig.* Der Feind entrang uns den Sieg, the enemy wrested the victory from our hands. II. *v. r.* sich —, to get loose or free by wrestling, striving or struggling.

Entrinnen, *ir. v. intr.* [u. w. seyn] 1) to run or flow down. *Fig.* Die Zeit entrinnt, time runs. 2) to flee, to run away, to escape. Aus der Schlacht —, to fly from the battle; Benhadad, der König der Syrier, entrann auf einem Rosse, [in Script.] Benhadad escaped on a horse; der Gefahr —, to escape or avoid danger; welche aber dem Schwerte —, die werden wieder kommen mit geringen Haufen, [in Script.] a small number that escape the sword shall return.

Entrollen, I. *v. intr.* [u. w. seyn] to roll away, to roll from. Ihrem Auge entrollten Thränen, tears trickled from her eye. *Fig.* Die Zeit entrollt, time rolls on. II. *v. tr.* 1) to roll down. 2) [to open what is rolled or convolved] to unroll [cloth &c.]. *Fig.* to unroll, to display. III. *v. r.* sich —, to unfold itself, to come unfolded. *Fig.* to display. Der Nebel verzog sich, und die reizendste Landschaft entrollte sich seinen bewundernden Blicken, the mist cleared off and a charming landscape unfolded itself to his view.

Entronnen, *past part.* of Entrinnen.

Entrücken, *v. tr.* 1) to seize and bear away, to snatch or hurry away. Entrückt in einem mit feurigen Rossen bespannten Wagen, rapt in a chariot drawn by fiery steeds; den Augen entrückt werden, to vanish from the sight. *Fig.* Er fühlte sich in das Paradies entrückt, he felt himself transported into paradise; der Tod entrückte ihn, er starb, death carried him off, he died. ||2) to take away, to remove clandestinely, to steal.

Entrückung, *f.* a seizing and bearing away. *Fig.* rapture, transport, ecstasy.

Entrudern, [rather unusual] *v. intr.* to row away.

Entrunzeln, *v. tr.* to unwrinkle. Die Stirn —, to smooth the brow.

Entrupfen, *v. tr.* to pull out, to pluck out. Einem Huhn die Federn —, to pluck the feathers from a fowl, to pluck a fowl.

Entrüsten, I. *v. tr.* to make angry, to anger, to put in a passion, to provoke to anger. Einen —, to exasperate a person. II. *v. r.* sich —, to grow angry, to get into a passion, to be filled with indignation. Sich über eine Sache —, to become angry at any thing, to become indignant at a thing. Die Entrüstung, indignation, anger, passion, wrath.

Entsäften, [rather unusual] *v. tr.* to deprive of juice.

Entsagen, I. *v. intr.* to desist from any thing, to give it up, to renounce it, to abandon it. Einem Rechte oder Anspruche —, to relinquish, to waive a right or claim; einer Erbschaft —, to give up an inheritance; Ehren oder Würden —, to quit honours; der Krone —, to resign the crown; der Welt —, to renounce the world; der Hoffnung ganz —, to give up all hope; er entsagte der Fuchsjagd, he left fox-hunting; der Unmäßigkeit —, to relinquish the practice of intemperance; dem Laster —, to turn from vice, to abandon one's vicious life. ||II. *v. tr.* 1) to renounce by a vow. 2) to forbid, to prohibit. Einem etwas —, to prohibit a person to do a thing. Die Entsagung, renunciation, denial.

Entsälzen, *v. tr.* to free from salt.

Entsätteln, *v. tr.* 1) to take the saddle from, to unsaddle [a horse]. 2) to unhorse, to dismount [an adversary].

Entsätz, *m.* [-es] 1) the raising of a siege. Er eilte zum —e der Stadt herbei, he hastened to succour the besieged town. 2) the troops which bring relief to a besieged town or fort, succour.

Entsäuern, *v. tr.* [in chimistry] to disoxydate. Die Entsäuerung, [in chimistry] disoxydation.

Entsaugen, V. Aussaugen I. 1.

Entsäulen, [rather unusual] *v. tr.* to deprive of columns.

Entschädigen, *v. tr.* to make good, to reimburse to any one what he has lost, to indemnify, to compensate. *Fig.* Dieses Wiedersehen entschädigt mich für alle vergangene Leiden, this meeting makes up for all my past sorrows.

Entschädigung, *f.* 1) [reimbursement of loss, damage or penalty] indemnification. 2) [that which is given for services, want, loss or suffering] compensation, amends, remuneration, recompense, indemnity.

Entschädigungs-forderung, *f.* claim for damages, claim of indemnity. **—geld**, *n.* a sum of money paid by way of indemnity. **—sicherheit**, *f.* [in law] indemnity. **—summe**, *f.* a sum of recompense, a sum for making good.

Entschälen, *v. tr.* 1) to shell [nuts &c.]. 2) [with silk dyers] Die Seide —, to scour silk.

Entscharren, V. Ausscharren I. 1.

Entschatten, [rather unusual] *v. tr.* to deprive of shadow.

Entschäumen, I. *v. intr.* [u. w. seyn] to issue, to come forth foaming. II. *v. tr.* V. [the more usual word] Abschäumen.

||**Entscheid**, *m.* [-es, *pl.* -e] V. Entscheidun

Entscheidbar, *adj.* and *adv.* decidable, terminable.

Entscheiden, *ir.* I. *v. tr.* 1) to decide, determine. Der Gerichtshof entschied die zu Gunsten des Klägers, the court decided cause in favour of the plaintiff; das Gericht schied zu Gunsten des Beklagten, the court cided in favour of the defendant; er erwog Umstände des Falles und entschied folgen maßen, he considered all circumstances of case and came to the following decision; —de Antwort, a decisive or final answer; ein des Urtheil, a determinate judgment; ein — Spruch, a definitive sentence; ein —der weis, a peremptory or decisive argument; —de Stimme, the casting vote or casting vo das Schicksal der Reformbill ist entschieden, fate of the reform-bill is decided; dieses niß entschied mein Schicksal, this event mined my fate; ein Reservekorps entschi Kampf, a body of reserve decided the c der Sieg der Verbündeten war —d, the of the allies was decisive. ||2) *a*) to d to discern. Das Böse von dem Guten —, criminate good from bad. *b*) to separate. I sich —, 1) to make known explicitly some mination. Er entschied sich für die Verbünd he declared for the allies. 2) to be decide come to a determination. Sich über etwa to resolve upon something; es wird sich n it will be decided now.

Entscheide-stimme, *f.* the casting or casting vote. **—wort**, *n.* final proposi or any final condition, ultimatum.

Entscheider, *m.* [-s, *pl.* -] decider, determinator.

Entscheidung, *f.* 1) [the act of deciding or determining] determination. 2) decision, determination, final judgment or opinion. Die — des obersten Gerichtshofes, the decision of the supreme court; eine gerichtliche —, a judicial decision, decree.

Entscheidungs-augenblick, *m.* [the point of time, when an affair is arrived to its height, and must soon terminate or suffer a material change] the decisive moment, crisis. —**grund**, *m.* 1) a decisive reason. 2) the motive of decision. 3) a motive which leads to a decision. —**punkt**, *m.* V. —augenblick. —**stimme**, *f.* V. Entscheidestimme. —**tag**, *m.* 1) critical day. 2) decretory day. —**voll**, *adj.* and *adv.* wholly decisive. —**zeichen**, *n.* a critical sign, token, [in medicine] a critical symptom. —**zustand**, *m.* the decisive state of things; [in medicine] the change of a disease which indicates its event, crisis.

Entscheuchen, *v. tr.* V. [the more usual word] Verscheuchen.

Entschieden, [past part. of Entscheiden] *adj.* and *adv.* decided, decidedly.

Entschiedenheit, *f.* 1) [exemption from doubt] certainty. 2) [firmness] decision, resolution.

Entschiffen, I. *v. intr.* [u. w. seyn] V. Wegschiffen. II [unusual] *v. tr.* to ship off [convicts &c.].

Entschirren, *v. tr.* to loosen from harness or gear, to unharness.

Entschlafen, *ir. v. intr.* [u. w. seyn] to fall asleep. *Fig.* to expire, to die. Er entschlief sanft in den Armen seiner Freunde, he gently breathed his last in the arms of his friends; so sind auch die, die in Christo — sind, verloren, [in Script.] then they also which are fallen asleep in Christ are perished; sie, die in Jesus — sind, them that sleep in Jesus.

Entschlagen, *ir. v. tr.* to remove by beating, to get out by beating. *Fig.* Sich einer Sache —, to part with a thing; er entschlug sich ihrer Freundschaft, he declined their friendship; sich der Sorgen —, to unbend the mind of care; sich aller Sorgen —, to put away, to banish all cares.

Entschleichen, [rather unusual] *ir. v. intr.* [u. w. seyn] to slip away unperceived, to steal away.

Entschleiern, *v. tr.* to remove a veil from. Sie entschleierte ihr Gesicht, she unveiled her face; sich —, to unveil one's self. *Fig.* Die Wahrheit —, to unveil truth, to make it known; die Zukunft —, to disclose futurity.

Entschleimen, *v. tr.* to free from slime.

Entschleudern, *v. tr.* to fling away.

Entschlichten, *v. tr.* [with linen-weavers] to free from starch.

Entschließen, *ir.* I. *v. tr.* [rather unusual] to open. Eine Thüre —, to unlock a door. II. *v. r.* sich —, 1) to unclose itself, to open [said of blossoms]. 2) [to fix in opinion or purpose, to determine in mind] to resolve, to make up one's mind, to determine. Er entschloß sich, es zu thun, he resolved to do it; ich habe mich dazu entschlossen, I resolved upon it.

Entschließung, *f.* 1) [fixed purpose or determination of mind] resolution. 2) [decision of a question in the mind] determination, resolution. V. Entschluß.

Entschlingen, *ir. v. tr.* to take out of a noose.

Entschlossen, [past part. of Entschließen] *adj.* and *adv.* 1) [determined in purpose] resolved. —, zu sterben, resolved to die. 2) determined, resolute. Ein —er Mann, a determined man, a resolute man; eine —e Haltung, a determined countenance.

Entschlossenheit, *f.* decision, firmness, constancy in execution, implying courage, resolution, resoluteness. Mit —, resolvedly, resolutely.

Entschlummern, *v. intr.* [u. w. seyn] to begin to slumber, to fall asleep. *Fig.* Er ist [sanft] entschlummert, he gently expired, died an easy death.

Entschlüpfen, *v. intr.* [u. w. seyn] to slip from, to slip away, to escape. Der Aal entschlüpfte meinen Händen, the eel slipped out of my hands; der Arrestant entschlüpfte, the prisoner made his escape. *Fig.* Lasse die Gelegenheit nicht —, let not the occasion slip; unversehens entschlüpfte mir dies Wort, that word slipped out, before I was aware; dies wird meinem Gedächtnisse —, that will slip out of my memory.

Entschluß, *m.* [-sses, *pl.* -schlüsse] [fixed purpose or determination of mind] resolution, resolve. Einen — fassen, to take a resolution, to fix upon a resolution, to come to a resolution, to form a firm purpose; er faßte den —, seinen Lebenswandel zu ändern, he resolved to abandon his course of life; er hatte den — gefaßt, zu reisen, he had determined upon travelling; ich habe den — gefaßt, daß &c., I am purposed that &c.; er änderte seinen —, he changed his purpose.

Entschlußlos, *adj.* and *adv.* V. Unschlüssig.

Entschmeicheln, [rather unusual] *v. tr.* to obtain or to get by flattery.

Entschmücken, [unusual] *v. tr.* to strip of ornament or ornaments.

Entschnüren, *v. tr.* V. [the more usual word] Aufschnüren 1. and Losschnüren.

Entschöpfen, *v. tr.* V. [the more usual word] Herausschöpfen.

Entschröpfen, *v. tr.* V. [the more usual word] Ausschröpfen.

Entschuhen, *v. tr.* to strip of shoes. Sich —, to take off one's shoes, to slip one's shoes. Entschuhet, unshod.

Entschuldbar, *adj.* and *adv.* admitting of excuse or justification, excusable.

Entschulden, V. [the usual word] Entschuldigen.

Entschuldigen, *v. tr.* 1) to free from guilt, blame, to exculpate, to excuse [a person]. Eva suchte sich zu —, daß sie die verbotene Frucht gegessen, Eve endeavoured to exculpate herself for eating the forbidden fruit; es entschuldiget den Verfasser nicht, it does not disculpate the author. 2) to pardon, to admit an apology for. Entschuldige einige Fehler, excuse some faults; es läßt sich nicht —, it admits of no excuse; zu —, excusable. 3) to throw off an imputation by apology, to excuse. Sich —, to excuse one's self; er entschuldigt sich wegen &c., he makes excuses for &c.; ich kam, um mich bei Ihnen zu —, I came to make my excuse to you; mein Correspondent entschuldigte sich, daß er einen meiner Briefe nicht beantwortet hatte, my correspondent apologized for not having answered one of my letters; sich wegen etwas —, to make an apology for something; — Sie sich nicht, make no apologies. 4) to free from an obligation or duty, to excuse. Ich bitte dich, entschuldige mich, [in Script.] I pray thee have me excused.

Entschuldigung, *f.* 1) [the act of excusing or apologizing] excuse. 2) excuse, apology. —en vorbringen, to offer excuses, to make excuses; ich nehme diese — an, I admit of this excuse; seine Narrheit muß ihm zu einer — dienen, his folly must be his excuse, must plead his apology. Syn. V. Ausrede.

Entschuppen, *v. tr.* to deprive of scales, to scale [a fish].

1. **Entschürzen**, *v. tr.* V. Aufschürzen.

2. **Entschürzen**, [rather unusual] *v. tr.* to strip of an apron.

Entschütteln, *v. tr.* to remove by shaking.

Entschütten, [unusual] *v. tr.* to shed, to pour out, to effuse. *Fig.* [provincial, but rather unusual] Einen der Sorgen —, to free any one from cares; sich einer Bürde —, to ease one's self of a burden; ich kann mich nicht —, I cannot avoid, help or forbear.

Entschwärmen, *v. intr.* [u. w. seyn] to fly off swarming.

Entschwefeln, *v. tr.* to desulphate. Das —, desulphuration.

Entschwellen, *ir.* [with some authors *reg.*] *v. intr.* [u. w. seyn] 1) to swell from, to rise from. 2) to swell and overflow.

Entschwimmen, *ir. v. intr.* [u. w. seyn] 1) to swim off. 2) to swim or float away.

Entschwinden, *ir. v. intr.* [u. w. seyn] to vanish, to disappear. Das Schiff entschwand den Blicken der Zuschauer am Lande, the ship vanished from the sight of the spectators on land; die Farbe entschwindet ihren Wangen, the colour forsakes her cheeks. *Fig.* Die Zeit entschwindet, time passes away swiftly.

Entschwingen, *ir.* I. *v. tr.* 1) to fling away, to throw from the hand. 2) to deprive of wings. II. *v. r.* sich —, to soar away from.

Entseelen, *v. tr.* 1) to deprive of the soul or of life [used only in the past participle]. Der entseelte Leichnam, the dead, lifeless or exanimated corpse. 2) to deprive of one's senses.

Entsegeln, [rather unusual] *v. intr.* [u. w. seyn] to sail away, to sail off, to escape sailing.

‡**Entsehen**, *ir. v. r.* sich —, to be ashamed, to be afraid. Sich nicht —, to have the effrontery, the hardihood.

Entsenden, *ir.* [with some authors *reg.*] *v. tr.* 1) to send, to send off. *Fig.* Den Wurfspieß —, to send [to throw or cast] a javelin; Töne —, to send forth, pour forth tones or sounds. 2) to send away, to dismiss.

Entsetzbar, *adj.* and *adv.* 1) that may be removed from a post or office, removable [said of public functionaries &c.]. 2) capable of being succoured or relieved [said of a blockaded fortress &c.].

Entsetzen, I. *v. tr.* 1) to put out of possession, to deprive of the actual occupancy of a thing. Einen seiner Stelle or seines Amtes —, to displace any one from an office, to remove any one from an office or employment; einen König seines Thrones —, to dethrone a king, to depose a king. 2) to relieve [a place that is besieged]. Eine belagerte Stadt —, to raise the siege of a town. II. *v. r.* sich —, to be suddenly moved or shocked by an impression of fear, terror or surprise, to be struck with sudden terror. Sich vor einer or über eine Sache —, to be startled at any thing; er entsetzte sich vor dem Tode, he startled at death; er entsetzte sich vor dem schrecklichen Anblick, he was affrighted at the terrific sight, the terrific sight filled him with horror.

Entsetzen, *n.* [-s] affright, fright, terror, horror. Von — ergriffen, struck with horror, horror-struck; tiefes — ergreift jede menschliche Brust, a deep horror seizes every human breast; die Erzählung einer blutigen That füllt uns mit —, the recital of a bloody deed fills us with horror.

Entsetzen[s]voll, *adj.* and *adv.* frightful, dreadful, terrific.

Entsetzlich, I. *adj.* 1) causing terror, terrific, horrific, terrible, dreadful, frightful, shocking. Ein —er Anblick, a terrific or horrid sight; eine —e Geschichte, a horrible story; eine —e That, ein —es Verbrechen, an atrocious deed, a heinous crime; ein —er Mensch, an atrocious man or fellow. II. *adv.* [in colloquial language =

very, very greatly] terribly. — kalt, terribly cold; der arme Mann schrie —, the poor man squalled most terribly; — erschrocken, horribly afraid; — hoch, enormously high; — reich, immensely rich.

Entsetzlichkeit, *f.* terribleness, dreadfulness, horridness, atrocity, enormity. Die — eines Anblicks, the terribleness of a sight.

Entsetzung, *f.* 1) the act of deplacing from an office or employment, removal. Die — eines Bischofs oder anderer Geistlichen, deposition, deprivation. 2) the act of relieving a place that is besieged, or of raising a siege.

Entsiegeln, *v. tr.* to unseal [a letter]. *Fig.* to open; [poet.] to thaw. Der Lenz entsiegelt die eisgebundenen Bäche, spring thaws the ice-bound brooks.

Entsinken, *ir. v. intr.* [u. w. seyn] to sink or fall from. Das Messer entsank meiner Hand, the knife dropped from my hand. *Fig.* to pass away, to be lost, to vanish. Es entsinkt mir der Muth, my heart or courage fails me; bei kühnen Unternehmungen sollte dem Helden nie der Muth —, in bold enterprises, courage should never fail the hero.

Entsinnen, I. *v. tr.* [unusual] to deprive of sensation, to render senseless. II. *v. r.* sich —, 1) *ir.* to bring a thing back to the mind or memory, to recall to mind. Aber ich konnte mich seines Namens nicht —, but I could not recollect his name. 2) [unusual] *reg.* to become bereft of one's reason.

Entsinnlichen, *v. tr.* to rid of sensual or material qualities, to purify from the feculences of the world, to spiritualize. Ein Wort —, [rather unusual] to use a word figuratively.

Entsittlichen, *v. tr.* to corrupt or undermine the morals of, to demoralize, to deprave; *it.* to throw back into barbarity, to uncivilize. Die Entsittlichung, demoralization.

Entsöhnen, *v. tr.* V. [the more usual word] Aussöhnen.

Entsonnen, [unusual] *v. tr.* to deprive of sunshine.

Entspannen, [unusual] *v. tr.* 1) V. Losspannen. 2) to unbend [a bow].

Entsperren, [unusual] *v. tr.* to relieve [a place that is besieged].

Entspinnen, *ir.* I. *v. tr.* to produce spinning. *Fig.* Einen Krieg —, to plan, to devise or to plot a war. II. *v. r.* sich —, to be occasioned, to be excited, to give birth to. Daraus entspann sich ein Prozeß, thence a lawsuit arose; es entspann sich ein heftiger Streit, a violent contest sprung up, ensued, resulted; es entspann sich ein blutiger Hader zwischen den Fröschen und Mäusen, there fell out a bloody quarrel betwixt the frogs and the mice.

Entsprechen, *ir.* I. *v. intr.* to be adequate to, to answer. Der Erfolg entspricht unserer Erwartung nicht, the success does not answer our expectation, fell short of our expectation; alles entspricht unsern Wünschen, every thing falls out or succeeds according to our wishes; der Sohn entspricht den Hoffnungen des Vaters, the son answers the hopes of his father; Handlungen sollten den Worten —, actions should correspond with words; eine —de Belohnung, a corresponding reward; eine —de Antwort, a suitable answer. ||II. *v. tr.* to deny.

Entsprießen, *ir. v. intr.* [u. w. seyn] to come up, to spring, to shoot or rise above the earth [as a plant]. *Fig.* Aus königlichem Blute entsprossen, issued from royal blood; ein Held, königlichem Blute entsprossen, a hero, sprung from a race of kings; aus einer religiösen Erziehung — viele Tugenden, from a religious education will proceed many virtues; daraus kann nichts Gutes —, nothing good can come from this.

Entspringen, *ir. v. intr.* [u. w. seyn] 1) to run away, to escape. Aus dem Gefängnisse —, to make one's escape from jail or prison, to get out. 2) to spring, to proceed or issue, as from a fountain or source. Der Fluß entspringt auf jenem Berge, the river rises from that hill; der Rhein entspringt auf den Alpen, the Rhine has its source on the Alps; den Quellen — Bäche, from springs proceed rivulets. *Fig.* Aus einem edlen Geschlechte entsprungen, sprung from a noble race; aus Priams königlichem Geschlechte war meine Mutter entsprungen, of Priam's royal race my mother came; aus kleinen Unklugheiten — zuweilen große Uebel, great evils sometimes rise from small imprudences.

Entspritzen, I. *v. intr.* [u. w. seyn] V. Hervorspritzen. II. *v. tr.* to spirt or spurt.

Entsprossen, *v. intr.* [u. w. seyn] V. Entsprießen.

Entsprudeln, *v. intr.* [u. w. seyn] to come forth bubbling or purling, to purl along.

Entsprühen, *v. intr.* [u. w. seyn] to fly out in small particles. Dem glühenden Eisen — Funken, red-hot iron sparkles. *Fig.* Seinen Augen entsprühet Feuer, his eyes sparkle.

Entspülen, *v. tr.* V. [the more usual word] Wegspülen.

Entstalten, [unusual] *v. tr.* to deform, to disfigure. Entstaltet, deformed, disfigured, distorted, ugly.

Entstammen, *v. intr.* V. Abstammen.

Entstängeln, *v. tr.* to deprive of the stalk. Entstängelter Taback, stemmed tobacco.

Entstäuben, *v. tr.* V. Abstäuben.

Entstehen, *ir. v. intr.* 1) [u. w. seyn] to originate, to take rise, to arise, to spring, to begin to exist. Meteore — in dem Dunstkreise, meteors are engendered in the atmosphere; der Regen entsteht aus den Wolken, clouds produce rain; ein Wurm, der im Holz entsteht, a worm that breeds in the wood; und Stürme — dort, and storms engender there; es entstand ein Feuer, a fire broke out; es entstand ein Streit, a quarrel arose; aus der Unmäßigkeit — viele Krankheiten, intemperance is the source of many diseases, or engenders many diseases; jede Sünde entsteht im Herzen, all sin has its rise in the heart; aus kleinen Ursachen — zuweilen große Wirkungen, small causes sometimes produce great effects; jedes Ding, das ist, entstand aus des Nichts fruchtbarem Leibe, every thing that is, out of the fruitful womb of nothing rose; daraus entsteht all unser Unglück, thence spring all our misfortunes. 2) [rather stiff] [u. w. haben] to be wanting. Das wird mir nie —, it will never fail me; ein Amt wird ihm nie —, he will never want an employment.

Entstehlen, [rather unusual] *ir. v. tr.* to take and carry away feloniously, to steal. *Fig.* Er entstahl sich der Gesellschaft, he stole away from company.

Entstehung, *f.* 1) the first beginning or existence of any thing, rise, source. Die — Roms, the origin of Rome; die — des Weltalls, the origination of the universe; alle Ereignisse auf ihre — zurückführen, to trace all events to their origin; die — vieler unserer Gebräuche, the origin of many of our customs. 2) [rather stiff for Ermangelung] In — dessen, for want of which.

Entstehungs-art, —weise, *f.* the manner in which any thing originates or took its rise, mode of existence.

Entsteigen, *ir. v. intr.* [u. w. seyn] to arise out of. Dem Bette —, to rise from bed; Dünste — feuchten Oertern or Orten, vapours arise from humid places; die Sonne entsteigt dem Meere, the sun emerges from the sea; ein tiefer Seufzer entstieg ihrer Brust, she heaved a deep sigh, she sighed deeply.

Entsteinen, *v. tr.* to free from stones, to stone.

Entstellen, *v. tr.* to disfigure, to deform, to deface, to distort. Der Gram hat ihn ganz entstellt, grief has quite disfigured him.

Entstellung, *f.* 1) the act of deforming, disfiguring. 2) the state of being deformed.

Entsterben, *ir. v. intr.* V. [the more usual word] Absterben 1.

Entstieben, *ir. v. intr.* [u. w. seyn] 1) to fall off as dust. 2) to rise as dust.

Entstiefeln, [rather unusual] *v. tr.* to strip of boots. Einen —, to pull off any one's boots; entstiefelt, [usual] unbooted.

Entstielen, *v. tr.* to deprive of stalk or of stalks.

||**Entstöbern**, *v. tr.* to free from dust, to dust.

Entstrahlen, *v. intr.* [u. w. seyn] to issue as rays or beams of light.

Entstricken, [rather unusual] *v. tr.* to unbind, to untie, to unfasten. Die Arme eines Gefangenen —, to unbind a prisoner's arms. *Fig.* Sich —, to disengage one's self. Er entstrickte sich ihren Armen, he disengaged, tore himself from her arms.

Entströmen, I. *v. intr.* [u. w. seyn] 1) to stream. Blut entströmt einer Ader, blood streams or gushes from a vein; Thränen entströmten seinen Augen, tears gushed from his eyes, or his eyes streamed with tears; Worte des Zorns entströmten seinem Munde, angry words issued from his mouth; Licht entströmt der Sonne, [in poetry] light flows from the sun. II. *v. tr.* to cause to stream, to pour out or forth.

Entstürmen, I. *v. intr.* [u. w. seyn] to [illegible] away, or withdraw with a tumultuous rapidity, to rush away, off or out. II. [unusual] *v. tr.* to [illegible] away with violence or tumultuous rapidity.

Entstürzen, I. *v. intr.* [u. w. seyn] to rush down, or to gush out. Die Wasser entstürzten dem Felsen, the waters gushed out of the rock; eine Thränenflut entstürzte ihren Augen, a flood of tears gushed from her eyes; er entstürzte der Versammlung, he rushed out of the assembly. II. [rather unusual] *v. tr.* to cause to rush down.

Entsühnen, V. Entsöhnen and Aussöhnen.

Entsündigen, *v. tr.* to free from guilt or from the defilement of sin, or to free from pollution solemnly or ceremoniously. Einen —, to purify any one from sin, to remit any one's sins; [illegible] Herz —, to purify the heart; einen Altar —, to purify an altar; sich —, to purify one's [illegible] *Fig.* Die Zukunft muß die Vergangenheit —, futurity must atone [make compensation or [illegible]] for the past. Die Entsündigung, a cleansing from guilt or the pollution of sin, purification.

Enttäfeln, *v. tr.* 1) to strip of the wainscot. 2) [with clothiers] to strip of the pressing-[illegible]

Enttauchen, *v. intr.* [u. w. seyn] to emerge from the water.

Enttäuschen, *v. tr.* to undeceive, to disengage from fallacy or deception. Einen —, to disabuse any one.

Entthronen, *v. tr.* to dethrone. Einen König —, to depose a king. Die Entthronung, dethronement, dethroning. Die — eines Kaisers, deposition of an emperor. Der Entthroner, dethroner.

Entträufeln, *v. intr.* [u. w. seyn] to drip from

Enttröpfeln, I. *v. intr.* [u. w. seyn] to issue trickling, to trickle from, to trickle down. Wasser enttröpfelt der Dachrinne, water trickles from the eaves. II. *v. tr.* to drop down, to distil.

Enttröpfen, *v. intr.* [u. w. seyn] to issue dropping, to drop from, to drop down. Wasser enttropft den Wolken, water drops from the clouds.

Entübrigen, [rather stiff] *v. tr.* 1) V. Erübrigen. 2) to excuse from, to dispense with. Ich kann diese Sache nicht —, I cannot dispense with this thing; dieser Mühe können Sie entübrigt seyn, you may be spared this trouble.

Entvölkern, *v. tr.* to depopulate, to dispeople [a country &c.]. Die Entvölkerung, depopulation.

Entwachen, [unusual] *v. intr.* [u. w. seyn] to awake out of sleep.

Entwachsen, *ir. v. intr.* [u. w. seyn] to grow too great or too old for any thing. Diese Kinder sind ihren Kleidern —, these children have outgrown their garments. *Fig.* Der Ruthe — seyn, to be passed the age of correction.

Entwaffnen, *v. tr.* to disarm [one's foes &c.]. *Fig.* Den Zorn —, to disarm anger or passion. Die Entwaffnung, disarming.

Entwähren, *v. tr.* 1) [in law] to dispossess by a judicial process, or course of legal proceedings. Einen —, to evict any one. 2) = außer Werth setzen, [coin] to depreciate in value, to put out of currency.

Entwährschaft, *f.* [dispossession by judicial sentence] eviction.

Entwälden, *v. tr.* to deprive of woods.

1. **Entwallen**, [rather unusual] *v. intr.* [u. w. seyn] to deprive of walls or mounds. Entwallt, unwalled, dismantled.

2. **Entwallen**, *v. intr.* [u. w. seyn] 1) to boil over. 2) to move gently, or to wander out of a place, to wander from, to glide or pass away.

Entwandern, *v. intr.* [u. w. seyn] to wander from.

Entwaschen, V. [the more usual word] Abwaschen.

Entwässern, *v. tr.* 1) to free from water, to dry, to drain. Eine Wiese —, to drain a meadow. 2) to deprive of superabundant water, as by evaporation or distillation, [in medicine] to dephlegmate.

Entwässerung, *f.* dephlegmation, also concentration [particularly when acids are the subject].

Entwässerungsmittel, *n.* [in medicine] a medicine having the property of expelling phlegm.

Entweben, *ir. v. tr.* to untwist, to untwine.

Entwecken, [unusual] *v. tr.* to awaken. *Fig.* V. Hervorlocken.

Entweder, *conj.* [for ein weder, V. Weder] [a distributive, preceding the first of two or more alternatives, and is answered by oder before the second or succeeding alternatives] either. Sie können — nach London oder nach Windsor fahren, you may either ride to London or to Windsor; — dies oder das, either this or that; [it is sometimes omitted] Sie können die Rechte oder Medizin studiren, you may study law or medicine; Leibes- oder Geistesübungen, exercises either of body or of mind.

Entwehen, I. *v. intr.* [u. w. seyn] to pass as air, to breathe. II. *v. tr.* to blow off. Der Wind hat den Bäumen das Laub entweht, the wind has blown off the leaves from trees.

Entwehren, I. *v. tr.* ‖ 1) to disarm. 2) [in law] to seize property which has been unlawfully sold. II. *v. r.* sich —, to get rid of. Ich kann mich seiner nicht —, I cannot get rid of him.

Entweiben, [rather unusual] *v. tr.* 1) to unwoman. 2) to rid from effeminacy.

Entweichen, *ir. v. intr.* [u. w. seyn] 1) to give way, to fail, to yield to force. V. 2. Ausweichen. 2) to slip out of a place. 3) to withdraw, to retire. *Fig.* Der Nebel entweicht nach und nach, the fog dissipates gradually; die Wolken —, the clouds break away; die Finsterniß entweicht vor der aufgehenden Sonne, darkness vanishes before the rising sun. 4) to depart or withdraw secretly, to slip away. Die Gefangenen sind entwichen, the prisoners have made their escape. *Fig.* Der Gefahr —, to get out of the way of, to escape danger.

Entweihen, *v. tr.* 1) [rather unusual] to divest of a sacred character or office. Einen Priester —, to desecrate a priest. 2) to profane, to defile, to pollute. Die Heiligkeit einer Kirche —, to violate the sanctity of a church.

Entweiher, *m.* [-s, *pl.* -] a violator [of sacred things].

Entweihung, *f.* 1) desecration. 2) profanation.

Entweilen, [unusual] *v. tr.* to free from ennui, to recreate, to divert.

Entwelken, *v. intr.* [u. w. seyn] to fade or wither and fall off.

Entwenden, *reg.* and *ir. v. tr.* to take away, to deprive of, to bereave; [commonly for] to purloin, to pilfer, to make away with, to steal.

Entwender, *m.* [-s, *pl.* -] he that takes away, a purloiner, a pilferer, a thief.

Entwerden, [unusual] *ir. v. intr.* [u. w. seyn] 1) to cease to exist, to perish. 2) to become senseless, to faint. 3) to be freed from, to lose. 4) to slip away, to evade [one's pursuers &c.].

Entwerfen, *ir. v. tr.* 1) [unusual] to cast off. 2) to form a draught or representation of any intended work, to plan. Ein Gemählde —, to sketch a picture; den Riß eines Gebäudes —, to design the plan of a building; den Umriß einer Sache —, to trace the outline of any thing; eine Rede —, to sketch a discourse; einen Brief —, to sketch a letter; ein Testament —, to draw a will; einen Plan —, to chalk out a plan; den Plan eines Vertrags —, to draw up the plan of a treaty; einen Plan zur Abtragung der Staatsschulden —, to project a plan for paying off the national or public debt; Pläne —, to lay down plans; Friedensartikel —, to draw up articles of peace; der Redner entwarf ein schreckliches Gemählde des menschlichen Elends, the orator drew a terrific picture of human misery. 3) to set down a short sketch or note of any subject in writing, to minute. Seine Gedanken —, to minute down one's thoughts.

Entwerfer, *m.* [-s, *pl.* -] one who sketches any thing or who forms a plan, a designer, a planner or projector.

Entwerthen, *v. tr.* to depreciate, to undervalue, to slight, to misprize.

Entwettert, *adj.* and *adv.* freed from storms or thunderstorms.

Entwickeln, I. *v. tr.* to unfold, to unroll [cloth &c.]; *it.* to unfold, to evolve, to lay open, to spread. Die Rose entwickelt ihre Blätter, the rose expands its leaves. *Fig.* Eine Sache —, to develop any thing; der Heerführer fing an, den Plan seiner Unternehmungen zu —, the general began to develop the plan of his operations; die Grundsätze einer Wissenschaft —, to unfold the principles of a science; seine Gedanken —, to unfold one's thoughts, to be explicit; die Anlagen des Geistes —, to develop the faculties of the mind; die Intrigue eines Schauspiels —, to unravel, to develop the plot or intrigue of a play. II. *v. r.* sich —, to develop itself. Die Knospe entwickelt sich, the bud develops itself, expands; ihre Brust fängt an sich zu —, her breast begins to swell; die Puppe hat sich zum Schmetterlinge entwickelt, the pupa has been transformed into a butterfly. *Fig.* Sein Geist entwickelt sich täglich mehr, his mind improves every day; der Verstand eines Kindes entwickelt sich schnell, wenn &c.; the mind of a child will quickly develop itself, if &c.; es muß sich bald —, it will ere long be cleared up.

Entwickelung, Entwicklung, *f.* 1) the act of unfolding, development. *Fig.* Die geistige —, the culture of the mind. 2) the state of being developed, development, evolution. Die — des Hühnchens im Eie, the formation of the chicken in the egg; die — des Kindes im Mutterleibe, the formation of the child in the womb. *Fig.* the unraveling of a plot &c., denouement. Die — der Begebenheit, the development of the event; die — des Stücks, the development of the plot in a play, unravelment, the catastrophe.

Entwickelungslehre, *f.* the doctrine of evolution [in the theory of generation].

Entwilden, [rather unusual] *v. tr.* to reclaim from a savage state, to civilize.

Entwildern, [rather unusual] I. *v. tr.* V. Entwilden. II. *v. r.* sich —, to become civilized.

Entwimpeln, [rather unusual] *v. tr.* to strip of the pennon or pennons.

Entwindeln, [rather unusual] *v. tr.* to unswathe [a child &c.].

Entwinden, *ir. v. tr.* to wind from, to wrest, to twist or force from by violence. Einem den Degen —, to wrench a sword from another's hand; er entwand sich ihrer Umarmung, he broke from her arms. *Fig.* Sich den Sorgen des Lebens —, to disentangle one's self from the cares of life; er entwand ihm den Sieg, he wrested the victory from his hands.

Entwinken, [unusual] *v. tr.* to wave or beckon away.

Entwipfeln, *v. tr.* to top [a tree].

Entwirbeln, I. *v. tr.* [rather unusual] to whirl off or away. II. *v. intr.* [u. w. seyn] to rise twirling.

Entwirren, I. *v. tr.* to unravel, to disentangle, to untwist, to loosen [threads that are knit &c.]. Einen Strang Garn —, to disentangle a skein of yarn. *Fig.* Ein Geschäft —, to unravel a business, to clear it from complication or difficulty. II. *v. intr.* [u. w. seyn] to unravel, to be disentangled.

Entwischen, I. *v. intr.* [u. w. seyn] to slip away, to escape. Der Gefangene entwischte seinen Verfolgern, the prisoner evaded his pursuers, he escaped his pursuers. *Fig.* Laße die Gelegenheit nicht —, let not slip the occasion; es ist ihm das Wort entwischt, that word fell from him. II. *v. tr.* V. [the more usual word] Abwischen.

Entwohnen, *v. intr.* [u. w. seyn] to lose the habit of any thing, to get out of practice. Einer Sache entwohnt seyn, to have lost the practice of any thing; der Mühseligkeiten entwohnt, disused to toils.

Entwöhnen, *v. tr.* to accustom to a want or deprivation of any thing. Ein Kind —, to wean a child; sich des Weines —, to disuse wine. Syn. Entwöhnen, Abgewöhnen. Entwöhnen applies to the inward, abgewöhnen to the outward actions. Ich habe mich des Tabakrauchens ent-

wöhnt, signifies, that I no longer find any pleasure in smoking tobacco, I have accustomed myself to the want of it, it is no longer an object of desire to me; ich habe mir das Tabakrauchen **abgewöhnt**, I have broken myself of the practice of smoking.

Entwöhnung, *f.* the act of accustoming to a want or deprivation of any thing. Die — eines Kindes, weaning.

Entwölken, I. *v. tr.* to uncloud. Ein entwölkter Himmel, an unclouded sky. *Fig.* Die Stirn —, to unknit the brows. II. *v. r.* sich —, to become free from clouds, to clear, to clear up. Der Himmel entwölkt sich wieder, the sky clears [up] again.

Entwürden, [rather unusual] *v. tr.* to strip of honours, to degrade [a nobleman &c.].

Entwürdigen, *v. tr.* to dishonour, to disgrace. Das Laster entwürdigt den Menschen in den Augen Anderer, vice degrades a man in the eyes of others; sich —, to dishonour or to disgrace one's self.

Entwúrf, *m.* [-es, *pl.* -würfe] 1) an outline or general delineation of any thing, a first rough or incomplete draught of a plan or any design. Der — eines Gebäudes or zu einem Gebäude, the sketch of a building; der — eines schriftlichen Vertrages, the sketch of a writing. 2) a scheme devised, a project. Der — eines Vertrags, the plan of a treaty; eitle Entwürfe, idle schemes or projects; den — von or zu etwas machen, to project or to chalk a plan for any thing.

Entwurfmacher, *m.* a projector, a schemer, a speculator.

Entwúrzeln, *v. tr.* to pluck up by the roots, to tear up by the roots, to extirpate, to eradicate. Eine Eiche —, to unroot an oak. Die Entwurzelung, eradication.

Entwürzen, [rather unusual] *v. tr.* to deprive of savour or relish [also in a fig. sense].

Entzápfen, *v. tr.* to draw from a vessel.

Entzaubern, *v. tr.* to free from enchantment, to deliver from the power of charms or spells, to disenchant, to uncharm.

Entzäumen, [rather unusual] *v. tr.* to unbridle [a horse].

Entzéptern, [rather unusual] *v. tr.* to deprive of the scepter, to divest of royal dignity or sovereignty, to dethrone.

Entzíehen, *ir.* I. *v. tr.* 1) to draw away or off, to take away. *Fig.* Einem etwas —, to deprive any one of something, to bereave any one of something possessed or enjoyed; Einem seinen Beistand oder seine Hülfe —, to withdraw one's aid or assistance from any one; Einem seine Gerechtsame —, to abridge any one of his rights; man entzog den Soldaten einen Theil ihrer Löhnung, the soldiers were cut short of their pay; das Entziehen eines Vermächtnisses, einer Schenkung, [in law] ademption. II. *v. r.* sich —, to withdraw. *Fig.* Sich einer Sache —, to avoid something; sich schlechter Gesellschaft —, to shun evil company; sich dem Arme der Gerechtigkeit —, to fly from justice; sich den Geschäften —, to withdraw from business; sich der väterlichen Gewalt —, to forsake one's duty to a father; sich dem Joche der Tyrannei —, to shake off the yoke of tyranny, to set one's self free from it.

Entzífferbar, *adj.* and *adv.* that may be deciphered.

Entzífferer, *m.* [-s, *pl.* -] a decipherer.

Entzíffern, *v. tr.* 1) to decipher [a letter &c. written in ciphers &c.]. 2) to unfold, to unravel, to explain what is obscure or difficult to be understood, to decipher. Eine alte Inschrift —, to decipher an ancient inscription. Die Entzifferung, deciphering. Die Entzifferungskunst, the art of deciphering.

Entzücken, *v. tr.* [originally = wegziehen] *Fig.* to bear away with joy or delight, to delight, to ecstasy, to transport, to ravish, to enravish, to enrapture, to entrance. Ihr Gesang entzückt mich, her singing enchants me; die Musik entzückte uns, we were enchanted or charmed with the music; dieses Schauspiel entzückte uns sehr, this spectacle charmed us greatly; *it.* it was a very charming sight for us; diese Gegend entzückte uns, this country pleased us highly.

Entzücken, *n.* [-s, *pl.* -] 1) extreme joy or pleasure, transport, ecstasy, rapture. Zum — schön, ravishingly handsome. 2) a ravishing thing. V. Entzückung.

Entzückung, *f.* trance, transport, overjoy.

Entzückungsvoll, *adj.* and *adv.* highly ravished, transported, ecstasied, overjoyed.

Entzügeln, [rather unusual in the proper sense] *v. tr.* to unbridle [a horse]. *Fig.* Entzügelte Leidenschaften, unbridled [licentious, unrestrained, let loose] passions.

Entzündbar, *adj.* and *adv.* inflammable [as oils, spirits].

Entzündbarkeit, *f.* inflammableness, inflammability.

Entzünden, I. *v. tr.* to set on fire, to kindle, to cause to burn, to inflame. *Fig.* Sie hat mein Herz entzündet, she kindled the flame of love in my heart; sie wurden gegen sie entzündet mit böser Lust, [in Script.] their lust was inflamed towards her. II. *v. r.* sich —, to take fire, to kindle. Feuchtes Heu &c. entzündet sich leicht von selbst, damp hay &c. is apt to take fire. *Fig.* Ein verwundeter Theil des Körpers entzündet sich, a wounded part of the body inflames; entzündete Augen, sore eyes; ein entzündetes Geschwür, an angry sore; der Krieg entzündete sich von neuem, war broke out anew.

Entzündlich, *adj.* and *adv.* that may be set on fire, inflammable.

Entzündung, *f.* 1) the act of setting on fire or inflaming, inflammation; *it.* the act of taking or catching fire. 2) [in medicine and surgery] the state of being inflamed, inflammation. Die — der Augen, an inflammation of the eyes; die — des Gehirns, phrenitis.

Entzündungs-fieber, *n.* an inflammatory fever. **—krankheit**, *f.* an inflammatory disease.

Entzúpfen, *v. tr.* V. [the more usual word] Wegzupfen.

Entzwei, [for in zwei] *adv.* in two, asunder. Das Tau riß —, the cable parted; das Fenster ist —, the window is broken; das Kleid ist —, the garment is torn; — brechen, to break in two; — fallen, to fall into pieces; die Schuhe — gehen, to wear out one's shoes; — schneiden, to cut asunder.

Entzweien, I. *v. tr.* to disunite, to set at variance. Freunde —, to disunite friends. II. *v. intr.* [used only in the past part. with seyn] to be at variance with, to live in discord with. III. *v. r.* sich —, to fall out, to quarrel. Sich mit einem —, to fall out with any one; Brüder — sich, brothers divide.

Énzian, *m.* [-s] [Lat. *gentiana*] [a plant] gentian. Der kleine —, the cross-wort gentian; der bittere —, felwort; der weiße —, V. Hundekoth.

***Epákten**, *pl.* [in astronomy] epact.

***Epaulette**, [pron. as in the French] *f.* [*pl.* -n] [† das Epolett, *pl.* -en] an epaulet, a shoulder-knot.

||**Epeler**, *m.* [-s] [a plant] common or small maple.

***Ephemére**, *f.* [*pl.* -n] the day-fly, ephemera. *Fig.* any thing slight and transient. Pamphlete, Parteischriften und dergleichen —n, pamphlets, party-writings and such ephemeral productions.

***Ephemeriden**, *pl.* [a journal or account of daily transactions] ephemerides; *it.* [in general] newspapers.

***Ephemérisch**, *adj.* and *adv.* [beginning and ending in a day] ephemeral, ephemeric, diurnal. *Fig.* [existing or continuing for a short time only] ephemeral.

Épheu, *m.* [-s] [allied to Eibe and Eppich] ivy. Der Baum —, tree-ivy; der Erd—, ground-ivy; mit — überwachsen, umrankt or um- or übersponnen, vom — umschlungen, ivied, ivy-mantled, ivy-clad; — hervorbringend, hederaceous, hederiferous; aus — bestehend, hederal.

Epheu-artig, *adj.* and *adv.* resembling ivy. —artige Pflanzen, [in botany] hederaceous plants. **—geranke**, *n.* clasps of ivy, clasping ivy. **—harz**, *n.* ivy-resin. **—kranz**, *m.* ivy-wreath. **—ranke**, *f.* clasper of ivy. **—same**, *m.* ivy-berry.

***Ephorát**, *n.* [-es, *pl.* -e] ephoralty.

***Ephorus**, *m.* [*pl.* Ephōren] ephor.

***Epicycloide**, *f.* [*pl.* -n] [in geometry, a curve] epicycloid.

***Epidemíe**, *f.* [*pl.* -n] [a popular disease, a disease generally prevailing] an epidemic disease, epidemic.

***Epidémisch**, *adj.* and *adv.* epidemic, epidemical [it is used in distinction from endemic or local]. Eine —e Krankheit, an epidemical disease.

***Epidérmis**, *f.* [in anatomy] the cuticle or scarf-skin of the body, epidermis.

***Epidót**, *m.* [-en, *pl.* -en] [a mineral] epidote. Erdiger —, granular epidote.

***Epigrámm**, *n.* [-s, *pl.* -e] epigram.

***Epigrammátisch**, I. *adj.* epigrammatic, epigrammatical. Die —e Schreibart, epigrammatic style. II. *adv.* epigrammatically.

***Epigrammatíst**, *m.* [-en, *pl.* -en] an epigrammatic poet. Martial war ein berühmter —, Martial was a noted epigrammatist.

***Epikuréer** [**Epikuräer**], *m.* [-s, *pl.* -] a follower of Epicurus, an epicurean, epicure. *Fig.* a man devoted to sensual enjoyments, an epicure, a sensualist.

***Epikuréisch**, **Epikúrisch**, *adj.* and *adv.* epicurean. Die —e Philosophie, the epicurean philosophy. *Fig.* epicurean, luxurious. Ein —es Leben führen, to epicurize, to riot, to feast.

***Epikureísmus** and **Epikurísmus**, *m.* epicurism, luxury, voluptuousness.

***Epilepsíe**, *f.* [*pl.* -n] [in medicine] the falling sickness, epilepsy.

***Epiléptisch**, I. *adj.* epileptic, epileptical. Der —e, epileptic. II. *adv.* epileptically.

***Epilóg**, [-es, *pl.* -e] **Epílogus**, *m.* [in oratory and in the drama] epilogue. Einen — halten, to epiloguize.

***Epiphánia**, *f.* [-iä] [a Christian festival celebrated on the sixth day of January] epiphany.

***Epíphora**, *f.* [*pl.* -oren] [a figure of speech] epiphora.

***Épisch**, *adj.* and *adv.* epic. Ein —es Gedicht, an epic poem, a heroic poem.

***Episkopálen**, *pl.* episcopalians.

***Episkopát**, *n.* [-es, *pl.* -e] 1) [governme-

of the church by bishops] episcopacy. 2) episcopate.

*Episōde, *f.* [*pl.* -n] an episode.

*Episōdisch, I. *adj.* episodic, episodical. II. *adv.* episodically.

*Epístel, *f.* [*pl.* -n] an epistle. Die —n des Paulus, des Plinius, oder Cicero, the epistles of Paul, of Pliny, or of Cicero. *Einem die — lesen, to reprimand any one severely, to chapter any one.

*Epistilbít, *m.* [-es] [a mineral] epistilbite.

*Epistolárisch, *adj.* and *adv.* epistolary. Die —e Schreibart, the epistolary style.

*Epitāph, [-s, *pl.* -e] Epitāphium, *n.* [-s, *pl.* -phien] an inscription on a monument, epitaph.

*Epithēt, [-s, *pl.* -e] Epítheton, *n.* [-s, *pl.* -ta] an epithet [as a „verdant" lane &c.].

*Epitrít, *m.* [-s, *pl.* -e] [in prosody] epitrite [the 1st ∪---, the 2d -∪--, the 3d --∪-, and the 4th ---∪].

*Epizeúxis, *f.* [a figure of speech] epizeuxis, anadiplosis [as in Cicero's orations, „dic, dic plasius"].

*Epóche, *f.* [*pl.* -n] [in chronology] epoch. Merkwürdige —n in der Geschichte Englands, remarkable epochs in the history of England. *Fig.* — machen, to make a noise, to be in vogue; R.'s Schriften haben zu ihrer Zeit — gemacht, N.'s writings had their day.

*Epopēe, *f.* [*pl.* -n] V. Epos.

*Épos, *n.* an epic or a heroic poem, epopee, epos.

Éppich, *m.* [-s] [allied to Epheu, Eibe] [name of several plants] *a*) parsley. *b*) smallage. *c*) common ivy. *d*) broad-leaved water-parsnep. *e*) marsh elinum. *f*) pilewort, or lesser celandine.

*Equilibrist, *m.* V. Aequilibrist.

*Equipāge, *f.* [pron. Ekipahsche] [*pl.* -n] 1) baggage, travelling-baggage. 2) a carriage and horses, equipage. 3) [in seamen's lang.] the crew. 4) [the furniture of an army] equipage.

Equipagenmeister, *m.* [in seamen's lang.] master.

*Equipīren, [pron. Ekipihren and Ekwipihren] *v. tr.* 1) to equip, to dress, to habit [especially used among military men]. 2) to man, to equip [a ship].

*Equipīrung, [pron. Ekipihrung and Ekwipihrung] *f.* equipment. Die — eines Offiziers, equipage; die — eines Schiffes, the equipment of a ship.

Équivoque, [pron. as in the French] I. *adj.* and *adv.* equivocal. II. [pron. Ekiwoke] *n.* and *f.* an ambiguous term, an equivoke.

Er, [allied to the Lat. *vir*, Goth. *vair*, Ice. *ver*] *m.* a male, a he-animal [used chiefly of birds]. Ein — oder eine Sie, a male or a female [bird]. *pron.* [a substitute for the third person, masculine gender, representing the man or male person or the thing named before] he. Wo ist dein Bruder? — ist zu Hause, where is your brother? he is at home; — hat den Hals gebrochen, he has broken his neck; — selbst, he himself; — und Niemand anders, he and nobody else; ein schöner Garten, aber — ist zu abgelegen, a fine garden, but it is too much out of the way; [it sometimes has reference to a person that is named in the subsequent part of the sentence] — ist der Mann, he is the man; [er is also commonly used in addressing inferiors] wie heißt Er? what's your name?

Er, a termination of a great many nouns; a prefix to many verbs.

Eráchten, *v. tr.* to think, to believe, to consider, to esteem. Noch erachte Anderer Hülfe für überflüssig, nor think superfluous others' aid; es ist leicht zu —, one may easily conceive; meines —s, according to my judgment, in my opinion.

Erächzen, [rather unusual] *v. tr.* to get or gain by groaning.

Eráckern, *v. tr.* to get or gain by agriculture or husbandry.

Erángeln, *v. tr.* to take with the angle. *Fig.* †Etwas —, to get something by assiduity.

Eránkern, *v. tr.* to reach with the anchor. †*Fig.* Etwas —, to get something by fraud or deceit.

Erárbeiten, *v. tr.* to earn by labour, to obtain by labour.

Eräugeln, *v. tr.* 1) to get or obtain by ogling. 2) to see by ogling repeatedly.

Erbāden, [unusual] *v. tr.* to get or gain by bathing.

Erbángen, *v. intr.* [u. w. seyn] to be afraid, to feel anxiety on account of some expected evil, to fear.

Erbármedich, I. [as an interjection or exclamation] have mercy on me! II. *n.* the miserere [a title given to a latin song].

Erbármen, I. *v. tr.* to move to pity. Sein Unglück erbarmet mich, I compassionate his unhappiness. II. *v. r.* sich —, to feel pity, to manifest compassion towards a person in distress. Er erbarmte sich seiner, he showed mercy on him; mich erbarmet dieses Armen, I commiserate that poor man; wer sich des Armen erbarmet, der leihet dem Herrn, [in Scripture] he that hath pity upon the poor, lendeth to the Lord; daß sich Gott erbarme! God have mercy; erbarme dich mein, have mercy upon me; es will sich Niemand meiner —, nobody will have compassion on me; wie ein Vater sich über seine Kinder erbarmet, so erbarmet sich der Herr über die, so ihn fürchten, [in Scripture] like as a father pitieth his children, so the Lord pitieth them that fear him.

Erbármen, *n.* [-s] compassion manifested towards a person in distress, commiseration, pity, mercy. — haben, to take pity; er sieht *zum — aus, he looks pitifully; *es ist zum —, it is to be pitied.

Erbarmenswerth, *adj.* and *adv.* deserving pity, worthy of compassion, pitiable.

Erbármer, *m.* [-s, *pl.* -] one who pities, commiserator. O, All—, oh all-merciful God!

Erbármlich, *adj.* and *adv.* 1) moving compassion, deserving pity, pitiable. Ein höchst —er Anblick, a sight most pitiful; der Fünfte wurde auf eine —e Weise erstochen, the fifth was miserably stabbed to death; sie seufzten so —, they sighed so pitifully. 2) pitiful, miserable, paltry, contemptible, despicable, worthless. Ein —er Kerl, a pitiful fellow; ein —er Wicht, a wretch; ein —es Gedicht, a wretched poem; sie spielte —, she played miserably; eine —e Arbeit, a sorry work; eine —e Belohnung, a paltry reward.

Erbärmlichkeit, *f.* 1) miserableness; pitifulness, contemptibleness. 2) a miserable, pitiful or worthless thing.

Erbármung, *f.* pity, commiseration, mercy.

Erbarmungs-los, *adj.* and *adv.* pitiless, merciless. —werth, —würdig, *adj.* and *adv.* V. Erbarmenswerth.

Erbaúen, *v. tr.* 1) to build, to construct, to raise. Eine Kirche —, to build a church; einen Tempel —, to erect a temple. *Fig.* Die Predigt hat mich erbauet, I was edified by the sermon; sich —, to improve in moral or religious knowledge; sein Betragen erbauet mich nicht, I am not pleased with his behaviour. 2) to cause to grow, to raise, to cultivate. Weizen —, to grow wheat. V. Bauen. 3) to get or obtain by building.

Erbaúer, *m.* [-s, *pl.* -] one who builds or erects, a builder, an erector. Der — einer Stadt, the founder of a city.

Erbaúerinn, *f.* a female builder, a foundress.

Erbaúlich, *adj.* and *adv.* 1) [unusual] what may easily be built &c. 2) building up in Christian knowledge, edifying. Eine —e Predigt, an edifying or edificatory sermon; er predigte sehr —, he preached very edifyingly.

Erbaúung, *f.* 1) a building up, construction, erection. Nach der — Roms, after the foundation of Rome. 2) *Fig.* a building up, in a moral and religious sense, edification.

Erbauungs-buch, *n.* —schrift, *f.* an edifying book, a religious tract or writing, book of devotion. —stunde, *f.* the hour for edifying the mind or for religious exercises. —vortrag, *m.* an edificatory discourse.

1. Érbe, *m.* [-n, *pl.* -n] [A. S. *aerfwa* signifies erwerben (V. Werben); appears allied to the Gr. αἴρω, i. e. bekommen] 1) [the man who is to inherit after the death of another] heir, inheritor. Eines Mannes —n sind seine Kinder, a man's heirs are his children; Einen zum —n einsetzen, to constitute a person one's heir; *fig.* *lachende —n, remote kinsmen, who are to inherit after the death of a relative; der muthmaßliche —, heir-presumptive; der unstreitige —, heir-apparent. *Fig.* Er ist der — der Tugenden seines Vaters, he inherited the virtues of his father. 2) [one who is to inherit after the death of his parents] heir, inheritor. Ohne —n, heirless; er hat keine —n, he has no children; er starb ohne —n, he died without leaving children behind him.

2. Érbe, *n.* [-s, without a *pl.*] [probably the same as the Lat. *arv*-um, the Swed. and Ice. *arf* = Erbe, Besitzthum; Ice. *urfa* signifies to plough] 1) an estate, a property. 2) an estate derived from an ancestor to an heir by succession or in course of law, inheritance. 3) an estate given or possessed by inheritance, donation, or divine appropriation. Diesen sollst du das Land austheilen zum — nach der Zahl der Namen, [in Script.] unto these the land shall be divided for an inheritance according to the number of the names. 4) the estate or possession which descends to an heir, that which is inherited, heritage. Das väterliche —, patrimony; da antworteten Rahel und Lea, und sprachen zu ihm, wir haben doch kein Theil noch — mehr in unsers Vaters Hause, [in Scripture] and Rahel and Lea answered and said, is there yet any portion or inheritance for us in our father's house? heische von mir, so will ich dir die Heiden zum — geben, [in Scripture] ask of me, and I will give thee the heathen for thine inheritance.

Erb-acker, *m.* an inherited piece of ground —adel, *m.* 1) inherited nobility. 2) persons that are noble by inheritance, hereditary nobility. —amt, *n.* a hereditary office. —antheil, *m.* the lawful part of an estate by inheritance. —art, *f.* an inherited or natural condition. —bannerherr, *m.* [formerly] a banneret by inheritance. —beamte, *m.* an officer who fills a hereditary office. —bedienung, *f.* V. —amt. —begierde, *f.* the desire to inherit. —begierig, *adj.* and *adv.* desirous to inherit. —begräbniß, *n.* hereditary sepulchre [common to all the descendants of a family], family-vault. —besitz, *m.* hereditary possession. —bestand, *m.* V. —pacht. —beständer, *m.*

V. —pächter. —bestandsgeld, —standsgeld, n. V. —pachtgeld. —bestandsgut, n. V. —pachtgut. —buch, n. V. Grundbuch. —eslos, V. —los. —eshandlohn, m. V. Handlohn. —eigen, *adj.* and *adv.* possessed by inheritance. Ein —eignes Gut, an hereditary estate. —eigener, —eigenthümer, m. one who possesses a hereditary estate. —einigung, f. [in German law] a covenant, or a treaty between several families of the same lineage, for the sake of mutual friendship, assistance and succession. —enslos, V. —los. —erschleicher, m. V. —schleicher. —fähig, *adj.* and *adv.* capable of inheriting [an estate &c.], inheritable. —fall, m. 1) inheriting, inheritance, heritage. 2) [in law] the right of inheriting something of a vassal or subject. —fällig, *adj.* and *adv.* 1) descending to an heir, hereditary. 2) subject to a lord's right of inheritance. —fehler, m. a natural or hereditary defect or deformity. —feind, m. hereditary enemy, a sworn enemy. —feindschaft, f. hereditary enmity. —folge, f. the succession of heirs to the estates of their ancestors, hereditary succession; *it.* entail. Die gesetzliche —folge, succession by course of law; die —folge durch Vertrag, succession by treaty; die —folge bei einer Grundherrschaft bestimmen, to entail a manor to any person. —folgegesetz, n. rule of descent settled for an estate, the law of entail, entail. —folgekrieg, m. a war undertaken for succession. Der Spanische —krieg, the Spanish war of succession. —folger, m. the heir of an estate entailed. —folgsordnung, f. the mode of descent, entailment. —folgsrecht, n. V. —folgsordnung. —frau, f. the lady of the manor. —fürst, m. —fürstinn, f. a prince or a princess that possesses a principality by the title of succession. —fürstenthum, n. hereditary principality. ||—gang, m. V. —folge. ||—gangsrecht, n. V. —folgsrecht. —geld, n. money got by inheritance. —genoß, m. V. Miterbe. —genossenschaft, f. a participation of a share of an inheritance. —genossinn, f. V. Miterbinn. —gerechtigkeit, f. V. —recht. —gericht, n. 1) hereditary jurisdiction. 2) a court-baron. —gerichtsbarkeit, f. 1) hereditary jurisdiction. 2) low jurisdiction. —gerichtsherr, m. a lord, proprietor of a manor which has a court-baron. ||—gesessen, *adj.* and *adv.* propertied. —gierig, *adj.* and *adv.* desirous to inherit. —graf, m. the heir [eldest son] of a German count. —gräfinn, f. the heiress [eldest daughter] of a German count. —grind, m. scaldhead. —gruft, f. the family-vault. —grund, m. landed property possessed by inheritance. —grundherr, m. lord of the manor. —gut, n. 1) inherited property. 2) freehold estate, allodium. 3) an absolute fee or fee-simple. —herr, m. lord of the manor. —herrlich, *adj.* and *adv.* manorial. —herrschaft, f. 1) hereditary possession of a manor. 2) the lord of the manor and his wife. —hof, m. hereditary farm. —huldigung, f. oath of fealty; homage. —jagd, f. the right of hunting, acquired by inheritance. —kaiser, m. a hereditary emperor. —kaiserthum, n. hereditary empire. —kämmerer, m. a hereditary officer [chamberlain] in many countries and ecclesiastical establishments. —kauf, m. an irrevocable bargain. —könig, m. a hereditary king. —königreich, n. hereditary kingdom. —koth, m. V. Kindspech. —krankheit, f. hereditary disease. —land, n. hereditary land. Die kaiserlichen —lande, the emperor's patrimonial dominions. —landamt, n. hereditary office. —ländisch, *adj.* and *adv.* belonging to hereditary land or to patrimonial dominions. —lasser, m. testator, devisor. —lasserinn, f. testatrix. —lassungsrecht, n. the right of bequeathing one's property by will. —lehen, n. an absolute fee or fee-simple. —lehnbar, *adj.* and *adv.* that may be granted in fee-simple. —lehngut, n. V. —lehen. —lehnmann, m. the grantee. —lehnsherr, m. the lord or donor, the landlord. —lehnwaare, f. money paid to the donor at the death of the grantee. —los, *adj.* and *adv.* 1) disinherited. Einen —los machen, to disinherit or [in law] to exheredate a person. 2) destitute of an heir, or of heirs, heirless. Ein —loses Gut, [in law] an estate in abeyance. —losung, f. V. Näherrecht. —lust, f. 1) the desire of inheriting. 2) an original lust or passion, inherent in any one's nature. —maier, m. V. —pächter. —mangel, m. 1) a natural defect or deformity. 2) *Fig.* [in farriery] a certain infirmity, as the glanders, the grease &c. ||—mann, m. a proprietor of landed property. —mannslehen, n. V. Stammlehen. —marschall, m. hereditary marshal. —nehmer, m. an heir, inheritor. Erben und —nehmer, [in law] heirs at law and descendants. —pacht, m. and f. 1) a lease, that may be transmitted by the lessee to his heirs by course of law, an inheritable lease; also the rent paid for such lease. —pachter, —pächter, m. the person to whom an inheritable lease is given. —pachtgeld, n. the rent paid for an inheritable lease. —pachtherr, m. the person who gives an inheritable lease. —pflicht, f. homage; oath of fealty. —postmeister, m. [formerly an office in the German empire] hereditary postmaster general. —postmeisteramt, n. the office of hereditary postmaster general. —postmeisterwürde, f. the dignity of hereditary postmaster general. —prinz, m. the eldest son of a reigning prince, hereditary prince. —prinzessinn, f. the consort of the eldest son of a reigning prince, hereditary princess. —prinzlich, *adj.* and *adv.* belonging to the eldest son of a reigning prince. —receß, m. V. —vergleich. —recht, n. 1) right of inheriting, heirship, hereditary right. 2) an inheritable right. —reich, n. hereditary realm or kingdom. —richter, m. 1) hereditary judge. 2) an arbitrator chosen to determine in causes concerning an inheritance. ||3) lord of the manor. ||4) a public officer. —ritter, m. 1) an hereditary knight. 2) a baronet. —saß, m. the owner of an estate. —schacht, m. [in mining] the deepest pit in a mine. —schaden, m. 1) hereditary defect, or infirmity. 2) *Fig.* hereditary blemish or fault. 3) an injury done to property, by which the heirs suffer. —schatzmeister, m. hereditary treasurer. —schätzung, f. valuation of inherited estates. —schicht, —schichtung, f. [in law] the division of an inheritance among the heirs. —schichter, m. V. —richter 2. —schleicher, m. —schleicherinn, f. a person who flatters and courts for legacies, a legacy-hunter. —schleicherei, f. legacy-hunting. —schoß, m. a rent paid for landed property. —schuld, f. a debt descending to the heir together with the inherited property. —setzer, m. testator. —sohn, m. a son who is an heir. Sein —, his son and sole heir. —stand, m. V. —bestand. —statthalter, m. hereditary governor [formerly in the Netherlands]. —stück, n. a piece of property inherited, heir-loom. —sünde, f. [in theology] original sin. —theil, n. 1) [the part of an estate given to a child or heir, or descending to him by law, and distributed to him in the settlement of the estate] portion. 2) any landed property. —theilung, f. V. —schicht. —tochter, f. a daughter who is an heiress. Seine —tochter, his daughter and only heiress. —übel, n. 1) hereditary evil. 2) V. —sünde. —verbrüdern, *v. tr.* used only in the past participle —verbrüdert. —verbrüderte Häuser, families engaged in a compact of inheritance. Die —verbrüderung, a compact of inheritance by which the survivor succeeds to the property of the rest. —vergleich, m. 1) an agreement respecting claims of inheritance. 2) an agreement respecting a manor &c., between a sovereign and his agnates or relatives. —vermacher, m. testator. —vermacherinn, f. testatrix. —vermächtniß, n. legacy, bequest. —vertrag, m. V. —vergleich. —zins, m. rent of assize or quit-rent. —zinsgut, n. hereditary fee-farm. —zinsgüter, hereditary emphyteutic lands. —zinsmann, m. the lessee of hereditary emphyteutic lands. —zinsregister, n. a terrar or register of lands.

Erbeben, *v. intr.* [u. w. seyn] to shake, as a house in a tempest. Sinai's grauer Scheitel wird —, Sinai's gray top shall tremble.

Erbeißen, *ir. v. tr.* 1) to bite to death. *Fig.* [with miners] Das Gestein hat ihn erbissen, he leaved off working the mine. 2) [more usual aufbeißen] to open by biting. Nüsse —, to crack nuts with the teeth. 3) to bite through.

Erbellen, [unusual] *ir.* and *reg. v. intr.* to begin to bark.

Erben, I. *v. tr.* 1) to inherit, to heir [the estate of one's father &c.]. *Fig.* Oft erbt der Sohn die Krankheit seines Vaters, the son is often the heir of his father's disease; die Kinder — oft die Gebrechen ihrer Eltern, the children often inherit the infirmities of their parents; die Tochter erbt die Gemüthsstimmung von ihrer Mutter, the daughter inherits the temper of her mother. ||2) to transfer as inheritance. V. Vererben. ||3) for beerben. Einen —, to be a person's heir, to succeed to any one's estate; du sollst mich —, you shall be my heir. II. *v. intr.* 1) [u. w. seyn] to descend or devolve by inheritance. Das Gut erbt auf ihn, he is the heir to the estate; die Krone erbt auf ihn, the crown devolves on him. 2) to take or have possession or property, to inherit. Du sollst nicht — in unsers Vaters Hause, [in Scripture] thou shalt not inherit in our father's house.

Erbeten, *v. tr.* to obtain by prayer.

Erbetteln, *v. tr.* to get or obtain by asking in charity, or by begging. Sein Brod —, to beg one's bread, to live by begging. *Fig.* to obtain by asking earnestly or submissively. Lob —, to beg for praise.

Erbeuten, *v. tr.* to gain as booty. Viel —, to get a great booty.

Erbieten, *ir. v. tr.* to offer, to present. Sich —, to present verbally, to declare a willingness; sich zu etwas —, to offer one's self, to tender one's services in any thing; er erbot sich, seinen Bruder zu begleiten, he offered to accompany his brother; er erbot sich, seine Befehlshaberstelle bei dem Heere niederzulegen, he made a proffer to lay down his commission of command in the army.

Erbieten, n. **Erbietung**, f. V. Anerbieten.

Erbietig, *adj.* and *adv.* declaring a willingness or offering to do something. Er war — &c., he made a proffer, he expressed a readiness or willingness to &c. V. Erbötig.

Erbinn, f. heiress, inheritress, inheritrix.

Erbitten, *ir. v. tr.* 1) to persuade or move by entreaty or prayer. Er läßt sich nicht —, he is inexorable. 2) to obtain by dint of entreaty or prayer, to impetrate. 3) [rather unusual for losbitten] Einen Verbrecher —, to sue out a pardon for a criminal.

Erbittern, I. *v. tr.* to make bitter, to embitter. *Fig.* to anger, to exasperate, to incense, to irritate to a high degree. Einen —, to exasperate a person; auf Einen sehr erbittert seyn, to be very angry with any one. II. *v. r.* sich —, to grow angry, to feel resentment.

Erbitterung, *f.* 1) [the act of exciting to anger] exasperation, irritation. 2) [the state of being angry] extreme degree of anger, violent passion, exasperation.

Erbittlich, *adj.* and *adv.* 1) that may be moved or persuaded by entreaty, exorable, flexible. 2) that may be obtained by entreaty or prayer.

Erblasen, *v. tr.* to gain by blowing a wind-instrument. Er hat seinen Unterhalt —, he got his livelihood by sounding a wind-instrument.

Erblassen, *v. intr.* [u. w. seyn] to grow pale. Er erblaßt vor Zorn, he turns pale with anger. *Fig.* Der erblaßte Körper, the exanimated or dead body.

Erbleichen, *ir. v. intr.* [u. w. seyn] to grow pale. Seine Lippen —, the colour forsakes his lips. *Fig.* Er erblich, he died.

Erblich, *adj.* and *adv.* hereditary, inheritable. Ein —es Gut, an inheritable estate; die Krone von England ist —, the crown of England is hereditary; es gehört ihm —, it belongs hereditarily to him. *Fig.* Eine —e Krankheit, hereditary disease; —e Eigenschaften, Gebrechen, inheritable qualities, infirmities.

Erblichkeit, *f.* the quality of being hereditary or inheritable. Die — eines Gutes oder der Krone, the descendibility of an estate or of a crown.

Erblicken, *v. tr.* to see, to view, to perceive, to behold. Die Seeleute erblickten das Land, the seamen descried land. *Fig.* Das Licht der Welt —, to be born.

Erblinden, I. *v. intr.* [u. w. seyn] to grow blind; *it.* to be overpowered by light, to dazzle. *Fig.* to be deprived of the faculty of discernment, to become unable to understand or judge. [rather unusual] *v. tr.* to make blind, to deprive of sight, to blind.

Erblöden, I. [rather unusual] *v. tr.* to make bashful or ashamed. II. *v. r.* sich —, to be ashamed, abashed, to be afraid. Erblödest du dich nicht, das zu thun? are you not ashamed to do that? Er erblödete sich nicht, he had the impudence. V. also Entblöden.

Erblühen, *v. intr.* [u. w. seyn] to bloom, to blossom [in a proper as well as in a fig. sense]. Ein neues Glück erblüht mir hier, new fortune opens to me here.

Erborgen, *v. tr.* to borrow. Eine Summe Geldes —, to borrow a sum of money. *Fig.* Seine Schreibart ist von einem Andern erborgt, he borrowed his style of writing of another; ein erborgter Name, a false name; erborgtes Wissen, second-hand knowledge. V. Borgen, Leihen, Lehnen, Abborgen.

Erborger, *m.* [-s, *pl.* -] borrower.

Erboßen, I. *v. tr.* to exasperate, to provoke. Einen —, to irritate a person. II. *v. intr.* [u. w. seyn] to grow angry. III. *v. r.* sich —, to fret, to be chafed or irritated. Erboßt, *adj.* and *adv.* angry.

Erbot, *n.* [-es, *pl.* -e] the act of declaring willingness to do something, an offer.

Erbötig, *adj.* and *adv.* declaring a willingness to do something, ready. — seyn, to be willing or ready; er ist dazu —, he offers to do it.

Erbrechbar, *adj.* and *adv.* that may be broken open.

Erbrechen, *ir.* I. *v. tr.* 1) to open by force, to break open. Eine Thür —, to break open a door; ein Schloß —, to force a lock; einen Brief —, to open or to unseal a letter. ‖2) V. Gebrechen or Fehlen. II. *v. r.* sich —, to vomit, to puke.

Erbrechen, *n.* [-s] 1) the act of breaking open. 2) vomiting, vomition. —erregend, vomitory, vomitive, emetic; das schwarze —, the yellow fever, [vulgarly called] black vomit.

Erbrennen, *ir. v. intr.* [u. w. seyn] to begin to burn, to kindle. *Fig.* In Liebe — [more usual entbrennen], to burn with love.

Erbrüllen, *v. tr.* to obtain by bellowing.

Erbrüten, *v. tr.* V. [the more usual word] Ausbrüten.

Erbschaft, *f.* 1) heritage, inheritance. Eine — thun, to inherit property, to come into some property by inheritance. 2) the estate or property possessed by inheritance, inheritance. Eine — antreten, to take possession of an inheritance.

Erbschafts-masse, *f.* the mass of property, to be divided among the heirs. —sache, *f.* a thing or cause concerning an inheritance. —verfüger, *m.* testator. —vermögen, *n.* V. —masse.

Erbse, *f.* [*pl.* -n] [allied to the Lat. *ervum*, Gr. ὄροβος] pea. Grüne —n, green-pease; zwei oder drei —n, two or three peas; ein Scheffel —n, a bushel of pease; durchgeschlagene —n, pease-pudding, *it.* pease-soop, porridge.

Erbsbohne, *f.* dwarf kidney-bean.

Erbsen-bau, *m.* the cultivation of pease. —baum, *m.* acacia. —beet, *n.* a bed of pease. —bein, *n.* [in anatomy] [the fourth bone of the first row of the carpus] pisiform os. —blüte, *f.* pease-blossom. —brei, *m.* pease-pudding. —brod, *n.* bread made of pease. —brühe, *f.* V. —suppe. —farbig, *adj.* and *adv.* having the colour of pease, orobine. —förmig, *adj.* and *adv.* pisiform. —käfer, *m.* a kind of caterpillar found among pease [bruchus pisi]. —kette, *f.* a small golden chain. —mehl, *n.* pease-meal. —schale, *f.* pease-cod, pea's shell. —schote, *f.* 1) V. —schale. 2) [in conch.] *a*) a species of razor-sheath [solen ensis]. *b*) a species of nautilus or sail-shell [nautilus legumen]. —stein, *m.* [a carbonate of lime slightly coloured by the oxyd of iron] peastone, pisolite. —strauch, *m.* a species of acacia [robinia frutescens]. —stroh, *n.* pease-bolt, pease-haulm. —suppe, *f.* pease-soup. —wicke, *f.* a species of common vetch or tare. —zähler, *m.* [in contempt, of an over-nice person] a cotquean.

Erbselbeere, *f.* [*pl.* -n] common barberry.

Erbsigdorn, *m.* [-es, *pl.* -e] V. Berberisbaum.

Erbuhlen, *v. tr.* to gain by coquetry. *Fig.* to gain by much wooing, caressing or coaxing. Er erbuhlte damit ihren Beifall, he won their applause by it.

Erbürsten, *v. tr.* to gain by brushing.

Erdämmern, *v. intr.* [u. w. seyn] to begin to grow light in the morning, to dawn.

Erdämpfen, *v. intr.* [u. w. seyn] to vapor vehemently.

Erdarben, *v. tr.* to get or obtain by suffering want or privation.

Erde and **Erde**, *f.* [it has in some instances a *pl.* -n] [probably allied to Aehre (= freier Platz); Lat. *area*] 1) the ground, the surface of the earth. Er fiel auf die —, he fell to the earth or to the ground; in die — scharren oder verbergen, to earth. *Fig.* * Einen unter die — bringen, to shorten any one's life. 2) country, region, earth. [in Script. it is used as a part of the world] Du sollst deinen Vater und deine Mutter ehren, auf daß du lange lebest auf —n, [in Script.] honour thy father and mother, that thy days may be long upon the earth. 3) the terraqueous globe which we inhabit, the earth. Die Oberfläche der —, the surface of the earth; die — bewegt sich um ihre Achse und um die Sonne, the earth revolves on its axis and about the sun; herrschet über alles Thier, das auf —n kriecht, [in Script.] have dominion over every living thing, that moves upon earth; [in Scripture, dry land, as opposed to sea] Und Gott nennete das Trockene —, God called the dry land earth. 4) [the particles which form the fine mold on the surface of the globe] earth. Die Pflanzen—, vegetable earth, soil; einen Graben mit — ausfüllen, to fill a ditch with earth; Erden, [in chimistry, such substances as have neither taste nor smell, compounds of oxygen with bases of metallic oxyds] earths; köllnische —, earth-coal, earthy brown-coal; lemnische —, bole. 5) [in astronomy, sometimes] any planet. 6) *Fig.* that which is earthly and perishable. Denn du bist — und sollst zu — werden, [in Script.] dust thou art, and to dust shalt thou return.

Erd-abriß, *m.* V. Landkarte. —achse, *f.* the axis of the earth. —altar, *m.* an altar made of earth. —apfel, *m.* [the name of several plants] *a*) the common potato. *b*) tuberous-rooted sunflower or Jerusalem artichoke. *c*) common cyclamen. *d*) mandrake. ‖*e*) the gourd. *f*) the truffle. —arbeit, *f.* [in fortification] clearing away the superfluous earth. —art, *f.* [or Erde, *pl.* Erden] a species of earth, as clay &c, earth. —artig, *adj.* and *adv.* 1) resembling earth, earthy. 2) partaking of earth, terrene. —artischocke, *f.* V. —apfel *b.* —aufwühlend, *adj.* and *adv.* turning up the earth. Die —aufwühlenden Schweine, the rooting swine. —back, *n.* V. Thonback. —bahn, *f.* [in astronomy] the orbit of the earth. —ball, *m.* the terrestrial globe. *Fig.* Er beherrscht den —ball, he rules the world. —balsam, *m.* [an inflammable mineral substance of the bituminous kind] naphta. —bank, *f.* 1) [in fortification, a little raised way or footbank, running along the inside of the parapet] banquette or banquet. 2) [in military affairs] —bänke, earthbags forming an elevation for covering soldiers from an enemy's shot. —bathengel, *m.* [a plant] Alpine speedwell. —bau, *m.* the subterraneous part of a building, an underground building, a subterrane, souterrain. —bauend, *adj.* and *adv.* cultivating the ground. —beben, *n.* earthquake. —bebenmesser, *m.* [in physics] sismometer. —beerapfel, *m.* [a sort of apple] the calville. —beerbaum, *m.* the strawberry-tree, arbute. —beere, *f.* [a plant and its fruits of the genus fragaria] strawberry. —beerklee, *m.* the strawberry-trefoil. —beerkraut, *n.* esculent strawberry. —beermeier, *m.* [a plant] the berry-headed strawberry blite. —beerspinat, *m.* strawberry spinach, blite. —beschreibend, I. *adj.* geographic, geographical. II. *adv.* geographically. —beschreiber, *m.* geographer. —beschreibung, *f.* 1) [a description of the earth or terrestrial globe] geography. Die messende —beschreibung, mathematical geography; die natürliche —beschreibung, physical geography; die bürgerliche —beschreibung, political geography. 2) [a book containing the description of the earth] geography. —biber, *m.* common beaver. —biene, *f.* the humble bee. —bildung, *f.* the formation of the earth. —bildungslehre, *f.* geogony. —birn, *f.* 1) V. —apfel, *it.* V. Kartoffel. —blume, *f.* 1) V. Himmelsblume. 2) V. Lenzblume. —boden, *m.* 1) the upper part of the earth, the ground, soil. Ein fruchtbarer —boden, a fruitful soil; ein thoniger —boden, a clayey soil; der —boden war trocken, [in Scripture] the earth was dried. *Fig.* Dem —boden gleich machen, to break down, to demolish [a town, a house &c.]. 2) the globe. —bogen, *m.* [in architecture] an arch in the wall forming the foundation of a building. —bohrer, *m.* [an instrument which is used to find out the quality of any ground] trepan, a scooping-iron. —

brand, *m.* subterraneous fire. —**brod**, *n.* V. Erdapfel b. —**buch**, *n.* V. Grundbuch. —**bülle**, *m.* V. Rohrdommel. —**bürger**, *m.* inhabitant of the earth, human being, man. —**damm**, *m.* earth-bank. —**decke**, *f.* a covering of earth. —**dunst**, *m.* vapours rising from the earth. —**durchmesser**, *m.* the diameter of the earth. —**eichel**, *f.* V. —nuß. —**eichhorn**, *n.* the ground-squirrel. —**eidechse**, *f.* the common lizard. —**enge**, *f.* a neck or narrow slip of land by which two continents are connected, or by which a peninsula is united to the main land, an isthmus. Die —enge von Darien, the isthmus of Darien. —**engerling**, *m.* V. —grille. —**entstehungslehre**, *f.* geogony. —**epheu**, *m.* 1) ground-ivy, called also alehoof and gill. 2) common ivy. 3) English cistus. —**erschütternd**, *adj.* earth-shaking. —**erschütterung**, *f.* earth-quake. —**eule**, *f.* a species of owl [strix cunicularia]. —**fahl**, *adj.* and *adv.* earth-coloured, gray, ashy. —**fall**, *m.* a sinking of the ground. —**farbe**, *f.* 1) earth-colour. 2) a colour prepared from an earthy substance. —**farben**, *adj.* and *adv.* V. —fahl. —**farbig**, *adj.* and *adv.* earthy-coloured. —**faß**, *n.* [in pyrotechnical exhibitions] fire-pot. —**feige**, *f.* V. —nuß. —**ferne**, *f.* [in astronomy, that point in the orbit of the sun or moon, which is at the greatest distance from the earth] apogee. —**fernrohr**, *n.* a terrestrial telescope. —**fest**, *adj.* and *adv.* permanent in place. —feste Güter, immovable estate, [in law] real estate. —**fett**, *n.* V. —harz. —**feuer**, *n.* 1) subterraneous fire. 2) pyrotechnical exhibitions on land. —**finsterniß**, *f.* V. Sonnenfinsterniß. —**fläche**, *f.* 1) a plain. 2) surface of the earth. —**flachs**, *m.* V. Bergflachs. —**fliege**, *f.* V. —schnake. —**floh**, *m.* ground-flea, spring-tail. —**flötz**, *n.* V. —lage. —**fruchtklee**, *m.* subterraneous trefoil. —**furche**, *f.* V. Furche. —**galle**, *f.* ||1) [a plant] the lesser centaury. 2) a moist spot in the ground, also a disease of vines arising from such spots. —**gans**, *f.* the shield-drake, or borough-duck. —**geboren**, *adj.* earthborn. Die —gebornen Riesen, the earthborn giants; der —geborne, a mortal. —**geflügel**, *n.* land-fowl. —**gegend**, *f.* V. —strich. —**geier**, *m.* V. Aasgeier. —**geist**, *m.* a gnome. —**gelb**, I. *n.* V. Ocker. II. *adj.* and *adv.* having an ochorous colour. —**geruch**, *m.* an earthy smell. —**geschmack**, *m.* an earthy taste. —**geschöpf**, *n.* an earthly creature. —**geschoß**, *n.* the ground-floor. —**gestalt**, *f.* the figure of the earth. —**gestirn**, *n* the earth. —**gewächs**, *n.* a plant that grows on land [as opposed to a marine plant]. —**gott**, *m.* V. Erdengott. —**grab**, *n.* a grave, a tomb [simply dug in the earth, as opposed to a vault]. —**grau**, *adj.* and *adv.* V. —fahl. —**grille**, *f.* the mole-cricket, fen-cricket. —**grübling**, *m.* a truffle. —**grün**, *n.* [a species of green earth, used by painters] terre-verte. —**grund**, *m.* [in painting] front of a landscape, fore-ground. —**gürtel**, *m.* [in geography, a division of the earth with respect to the temperature of different latitudes] zone Die gemäßigten, die heißen, die kalten —gürtel, the temperate or variable zones, the torrid, the frigid zones. —**gut**, *n.* [in commerce] the middle sort of Dutch leaf-tobacco. —**hähnchen**, *n.* V. Hausotter. —**halbmesser**, *m.* the semi-diameter of the earth. —**haltig**, *adj.* and *adv.* containing earth. —**harz**, *n.* [this name is used to denote various inflammable substances, of a strong smell, and of different consistencies, which are found in the earth, as amber &c.] bitumen. Gelbes —harz, amber. —**hase**, *m.* V. Springer. —**haue**, *f.* [in mining] a pitcher. —**haufen**, *m.* a heap of earth. —**höhle**, *f.* a deep hollow place in the earth, a cavern. —**hopfen**, *m.* [a plant] St. John's wort. —**hügel**, *m.* a little elevation of land, a hill of earth, a knoll. —**hummel**, *f.* V. Erdbiene. —**hütte**, *f.* a hut in the earth or made of earth. —**käfer**, *m.* V. Laufkäfer. —**karte**, *f.* Landkarte. —**kastanie**, *f.* 1) V. —nuß. 2) V. Rübenkerbel. —**keim**, *m.* [in botany] a germ with lobes beneath the surface of earth. —**kiefer**, *f.* 1) ground-pine. 2) [a plant] Montpelier coris. —**kloß**, *m.* a hard lump of earth, a mass of earth cohering, clod. Die —klöße auf dem Felde klein schlagen, to break the clods in a field. *Fig.* [the body of man compared to his soul] clod. —**kluft**, *f.* a crevice in the earth. —**knollen**, *m.* 1) an esculent tuberous plant. 2) V. —nuß. —**kobalt**, *m.* terreous cobalt. Brauner or gelber —kobalt, brown and yellow cobalt-ochre; erdiger rother —kobalt, cobalt crust, earthy red cobalt-ochre; grüner —kobalt, nickel-ochre, arseniate of nickel; strahliger rother —kobalt, cobalt-bloom, radiated red cobalt-ochre; verhärteter und zerreiblicher schwarzer —kobalt, black cobalt-ochre, earthy cobalt. —**kohle**, *f.* earth-coal, earthy brown-coal. —**körper**, *m.* 1) V. —ball. 2) a terrestrial body. —**kraut**, *n.* V. —rauch. —**krebs**, *m.* V. —grille. —**kreis**, *m.* the earth, the whole surface of the earth. —**krokodill**, *n.* [an animal of the lizard tribe] the scink or skink. —**krone**, *f.* V. Huflattig. —**kröte**, *f.* V. Feldkröte. —**kugel**, *f.* 1) the earth, the terraqueous ball, the globe. 2) [an artificial sphere, on whose convex surface is drawn a map or representation of the earth] a terrestrial globe. 3) planisphere. 4) [in pyrotechnics] a ball. —**kugelkarte**, *f.* V. —kugel 3. —**kunde**, *f.* geology. Die allgemeine —kunde betreffend, geological. —**kundig**, I. *adj.* geological, geognostic. Der Erdkundige, geologist. II. *adv.* geologically. —**lage**, *f.* —**lager**, *n.* a layer or stratum of earth. —**leberkraut**, *n.* the ash-coloured ground-liverwort. —**lehre**, *f.* geology. —**lehrig**, *adj.* and *adv.* geological. —**linie**, *f.* [in painting and drawing] the ground-line. —**loch**, *n.* a hole or cavity in the earth. —**los**, *adj.* and *adv.* without earth; *fig.* incorporeal. —**made**, *f.* V. Regenwurm. —**mandel**, *f.* tuberous lathyrus. —**männchen**, ||—**männlein**, *n.* [an imaginary being] a gnome. —**masse**, *f.* a mass of earth. —**mast**, *f.* V. Brutmast. —**maus**, *f.* 1) the short-tailed field-mouse. 2) *Fig.* V. —nuß. —**mehl**, *n.* fossil-dust. —**mensch**, *m.* an earthling, a mortal. —**messer**, *m.* a geometer or geometrician. —**meßkunst**, *f.* geometry. —**messung**, *f.* 1) the measuring of the earth. 2) mathematical geography. —**meve**, *f.* [a bird] the shearwater petrel. —**milbe**, *f.* the tant or taint, the scarlet spider. —**mistel**, *f.* a species of mistletoe [viscum terrestre]. —**mittelpunktig**, *adj.* and *adv.* geocentric. —**moos**, *n.* the common club-moss. —**morchel**, *f* V. Trüffel. —**nähe**, *f.* perigee, perigeum [opposed to apogee]. —**naturbeschreibung**, *f.* physical geography. —**nebel**, *m.* a fog in the atmosphere near the earth. —**nuß**, *f.* 1) the ground-nut, earth-nut. 2) the pig-nut, earth-nut or bunium. 3) the common star of Bethlehem. —**oberfläche**, *f.* the surface of the earth. —**ochse**, *m.* [an insect] the grub of the dung-beetle. —**öl**, *n.* rock-oil, petrol or petroleum. —**pech**, *n.* mineral pitch, as jew's pitch &c. Elastisches —pech (Federharz), V. Elaterit; erdiges oder thonartiges —pech, earthy or cohesive mineral pitch, semi-compact mineral pitch, earthy bitumen; zähes —pech, pissasphalt, mineral or Barbadoes-tar, cohesive mineral pitch. —**pfau**, *m.* V. Kirschlorb. —**pfriem**, *m.* V. Ginster. —**platz**, *m.* [in a play-house] the pit. —**pol**, *m.* [the extremity of the earth's axis] the pole of the earth. —**punkt**, *m.* a point or stand on the earth. —**ralle**, *f.* [a bird] the crake or land-rail. —**ratte**, *f.* the Norway rat, or the common rat. —**rauch**, *m.* [a plant] common fumitory. —**räumer**, *m.* a miner's shovel. —**raute**, *f.* [a plant] common fumitory. —**reich**, *n.* 1) the whole surface of the earth. 2) [sometimes for] the terraqueous globe. 3) a distinct place of the globe, country, region. 4) the superficial part of the earth in respect to its nature or quality, ground, land, soil. Fruchtbares —reich, good land; schlechtes —reich, poor land. —**rohr**, *n.* V. —fernrohr. —**rose**, *f.* 1) the Scotch rose. 2) rose-flowered lychnis, or wild red champion. —**rübe**, *f.* 1) the turnip-rooted cabbage, the cabbage-turnip. 2) cyclamen, or sow-bread. —**rücken**, *m.* a long elevation of land, a ridge of hills. Ein hoher —rücken, a high ridge. —**rund**, *n.* V. Erdenrund. —**sack**, *m.* earthbag [used for defence in war]. —**saft**, *m.* any mineral juice, as petroleum and asphaltum. —**salz**, *n.* saltpetre. —**sand**, *m.* sand found on land [opposed to sea-sand, river-sand]. —**säure**, *f.* terreous acid. —**schabe**, *f.* V. Stinkschabe. —**schaber**, *m.* a miner's scraper. —**schaf**, *n.* [a small species of camel] the lama. —**scheibe**, *f.* the disk of the earth [as it would appear if seen from the moon]. —**schicht**, *f.* V. —lage. —**schildkröte**, *f.* the land tortoise. —**schlacke**, *f.* [in mineralogy] earth slag. —**schmeer**, *m.* [a genus of fungi] stinking morel. —**schmied**, *m.* V. Holzwurm. —**schnake**, *f.* the pathfly. —**schnecke**, *f.* 1) V. Landschnecke. 2) the snail or slug. —**schocke**, *f.* V. Artischocke. —**scholle**, *f.* a large lump of earth, a clod. —**schwalbe**, *f.* the sand martin. —**schwamm**, *m.* 1) a mushroom that grows in moist ground [as opposed to a mushroom that grows on a tree]. 2) *Fig.* a simpleton. —**schwarz**, *n.* [a kind of coal which is pounded and used in fresco] earthblack. —**schwefel**, *m.* V. Bärlapp. —**schwein**, *n.* [in zoology] great ant-eater. —**seife**, *f.* V. Bergseife. —**sperling**, *m.* V. Wiesenlerche. —**spinne**, *f.* the field-spider. —**spinnenkraut**, *n.* 1) branching anthericum. 2) grass-leaved anthericum. 3) the spiderwort. —**spitze**, *f.* [a long narrow tract of land projecting from the main body] a neck of land. —**stein**, *m.* an eagle-stone, filled with an earthy matter, geode. —**stern**, *m.* 1) [a plant] V. [illegible]kraut. 2) the earth as a star. —**stoß**, *m.* a concussion, a shock of the earth. —**strich**, *m.* [a division of the earth, with respect to the temperature of different latitudes] zone. Der heiße —strich, the torrid zone; die gemäßigten —striche, the temperate or variable zones; die kalten —striche, the frigid zones. *Fig.* Ein kalter —strich, a cold climate. —**stufe**, *f.* a terrace. —**talg**, *n.* talk [a mineral stone composed of plates generally parallel, flexible, elastic and transparent]. —**thier**, *n.* an animal that lives on land. —**toffel**, *f.* potato. —**torf**, *m.* a species of turf, peat. —**umschiffer**, *m.* he that circumnavigates the globe, circumnavigator. —**umschiffung**, *f.* circumnavigation of the globe. —**umsegler**, *m.* V. —umschiffer. —**umseglung**, *f.* V. —umschiffung. —**vielfuß**, *m.* [a genus of multiped insects] julus. —**wahrsager**, *m.* geomancer. —**wahrsagerei**, *f.* geomancy. —**wand**, *f.* earthen wall, earth-bank. —**wärts**, *adv.* towards the earth. —**wasserball**, *m.* the terraqueous globe. —**weichsel**, *f.* a sort of [illegible] [prunus fruticosa]. —**weide**, *f.* the dwarf [illegible]ing willow. —**weihrauch**, *m.* ground-[illegible]. —**weizen**, *m.* purple cow-wheat. —**werk**, *n.* [in fortification] an earth-work. —**winde**, *f.* [illegible] sharp-pointed toad-flax or fluellin. 2) small field bindweed. —**winkel**, *m.* a secret or retired place, a corner of the earth. —**wolf**, *m.* 1) the water-rat. 2) V. Maulwurfsgrille. —**wurm**, *m.* earthworm. *Fig.* a mean sordid wretch, earthworm. —**zeislein**, *n.* the variegated marmot. —**zirkel**, *m.* a circle of the sphere [as the meridians, the ecliptic, the equator &c.]. —**zunge**, *f.* a neck of land.

Erdebegraben, *adj.* buried. —**bewohnend**, *adj.* inhabiting the earth, earthly, [illegible] restrial. —bewohner, *m.* an inhabitant of the earth, earthling. —bürger, *m.* V. Erdenbürger. —geboren, *adj.* V. Erdgeboren. —gefährte, *m.* V. Erdengefährte. —gefäß, *n.* 1) an earthen vessel. 2) *Fig.* the human body. —geschöpf, *n* a human being, a frail creature. —hütte, *f.* V. Erdhütte. —kriechend, *adj.* creeping. —leben, *n.* V. Erdenleben. —natur, *f.* the earthly nature of men. —sohn, *m.* V. Erdensohn. —träger, *m.* a bearer of the globe. —wendung, *f.* the [diurnal] revolution of the earth, and the time in which it is performed.

Erden=ab, *adj.* away from the earth. —ball, *m.* V. Erdball. —bürger, *m.* an earthling, a mortal. —freude, *f.* a transient pleasure. Die —freuden, the transient pleasures of this life, earthly pleasures. —gefährte, *m.* a fellow-man, fellow-mortal. ||—geld, *n.* V. Erdzins, Grundzins. —glück, *n.* earthly happiness. —gott, *m.* an earthly god. *Fig.* [frequently ‡] prince or king. —gottheit, *f.* 1) an earthly god. 2) *Fig.* terrestrial things, as money &c. —herr, *m.* man [often ‡, as opposed to inferior animals]. —kind, *n.* an earthling, a mortal. —kloß, *m.* [a mass of earth cohering] clod. *Fig.* [the body of man compared to his soul] clod. —kugel, *f.* V. Erdkugel. —leben, *n.* life on earth, earthly life. —leiden, *n.* earthly pain. —mann, *m.* human being, a mortal. —nähe, *f.* V. Erdnähe. —rund, *n.* the terrestrial globe. [often used ‡.] Auf dem weiten —runde, all the world over. —schlamm, *m.* [*fig.*] sensual lust. —schoß, *m.* the interior of the earth; [*fig.*] the grave. —sohn, *m.* 1) a fabled earthborn giant [often called also Erdensohn]. V. also Titan. 2) a son of the earth, a mortal, earthling. —staub, *m.* earthly dust, things on the earth. —tand, *m.* terrestrial trifles. —thon, *m.* common clay. —wallen, mortal pilgrimage. —waller, *m.* a wanderer on this earth, man. —wärts, *adv.* towards the earth. —wurm, *m.* ground-worm. *Fig.* man. V. also Erdwurm.

Erden, *adj.* and *adv.* made of earth, earthen. [irdene] Gefäße, earthen vessels.

Erdenhaft, Erdhaft, *adj.* and *adv.* resembling earth, earthy.

Erdénkbar, *adj.* and *adv.* imaginable.

Erdénken, *ir. v. tr.* 1) to strike out by thinking, to excogitate, to contrive, to invent, to imagine. Die Mittel —, welche &c., to contrive means, which &c.; einen Vertheidigungsplan —, to devise a plan of defence; Unwahrheiten, Lügen —, to fabricate lies. ||2) to recollect [a fact].

Erdénklich, *adj.* and *adv.* imaginable. Dieser Punkt ist mit aller —en Klarheit bewiesen, this point is proved with all imaginable clearness.

Erdénkung, *f.* 1) the act of devising in the thoughts, invention, contrivance, excogitation. 2) scheme formed in the mind, plan, contrivance, device, imagination.

Erdeútbar, *adj.* and *adv.* interpretable.

Erdeúten, *v. tr.* to interpret [books, signs &c.].

Erdhaft, V. Erdenhaft.

Erdicht, *adj.* and *adv.* resembling earth, earthy. Ein —er Stoff, an earthy matter; ein —er Geschmack, an earthy taste; ein —er Bruch, [in mineralogy] earthy fracture. V. Erdig.

Erdíchten, *v. tr.* 1) to invent and form. Unwahrheiten —, to invent falsehoods; eine Lüge, eine Geschichte —, to fabricate a lie or story; Neuigkeiten —, to forge news; die Geschichte ist erdichtet, the story is a fiction; eine erdichtete Nachricht, a false report; ein erdichteter Name, a feigned name; erdichtete Personen, fictitious persons; die erdichtete Darstellung, fictitiousness. 2) to obtain by poetry or by publishing a poetical composition. Sich Ruhm und Geld —, to get fame and money by one's poetical compositions. Syn. V. 2. Dichten.

Erdíchter, *m.* [-s, *pl.* -] one who invents, forges or fabricates something, as news, reports &c., one who invents fictitious stories, a romancer.

Erdíchtung, *f.* 1) the act of inventing, feigning or forging, fiction. 2) that which is feigned, invented or imagined, fiction. Diese Geschichte ist eine —, this story is a fiction; die rechtliche —, [in law] fiction of law [fictio juris].

Erdíenen, [rather unusual] *v. tr.* to get or gain by serving a master. Er hat sich ein kleines Vermögen erdient, he has saved up a little fortune in service.

Erdig, *adj.* and *adv.* consisting of earth, partaking of earth, earthy. Ein —er Stoff, terrene substance; —e Theilchen, terreous particles; das Erdige, earthiness.

Erdólchen, *v. tr.* to pierce with a dagger or poniard. Einen —, to poniard any one; erdolcht werden, to be stabbed by a dagger.

Erdónnern, *v. intr.* to begin to thunder. *Fig.* to make any loud noise.

Erdórren, [unusual] *v. intr.* [u. w. seyn] to dry, to wither.

Erdräuen, [rather unusual] *v. tr.* to get or obtain by threats or menaces.

Erdreísten, *v. r.* sich —, to dare, to venture. Er erdreistet sich, Dinge zu behaupten, die er nicht weiß, he ventures to assert things which he does not know; wie mag er sich — &c., how can he have the effrontery, the hardihood, to &c.; darf ich mich —, may I presume? darf ich mich —, Sie zu fragen, ob &c., may I be so bold as to ask you, if &c.?

Erdréschen, *ir. v. tr.* to gain by thrashing.

Erdrohen, *v. tr.* to extort by threats.

Erdröhnen, *v. intr.* to give a low, heavy, dull sound.

Erdrósseln, *v. tr.* to destroy life by stopping respiration, to strangle, to choke, to suffocate. Sich [selbst] —, to strangle one's self.

Erdrúcken, *v. tr.* 1) to overwhelm by pressure, to beat or force down by an incumbent weight, with breaking and bruising, to kill by pressure, to crush to death. Der fallende Baum erdrückte ihn, he was crushed by the falling tree; trete auf diese Spinne und erdrücke sie, tread on that spider and kill it. ||2) V. Eindrücken.

Erdúlden, *v. tr.* to suffer, to undergo, to endure. Trübsal —, to bear calamity; Hunger —, to endure hunger; Kälte —, to suffer with cold; Sie werden noch mehr Kränkungen — müssen, you will have to sustain more new disgraces.

Erdúnkeln, [rather unusual] *v. intr.* [u. w. seyn] to grow dark or darker, to darken.

Erdúrsten, [unusual] *v. intr.* [u. w. seyn] 1) to become thirsty, to thirst. 2) to perish by thirst, to die of thirst.

*Érebus, *m.* [in mythology, the region of the dead] Erebus.

Ereífern, I. *v. intr.* [u. w. seyn] [rather unusual] to grow angry. Er ereiferte über den Knaben, he grew angry with the boy. II. *v. r.* sich —, to fall into a passion, to become angry.

Ereígnen, [for eräugnen = dem Auge darstellen] *v. r.* sich —, to come to pass, to chance, to happen, to fall out. Sag' uns, was sich heute ereignet hat, tell us, what has chanced to-day; wenn der Fall sich ereignet, daß &c., in case that &c.; dabei ereigneten sich lächerliche Dinge, it was attended with some ridiculous circumstances.

Ereígniß, *n.* [-sses, *pl.* -sse] [that which comes, arrives or happens, that which falls out, any incident good or bad] event. Die gewöhnlichen Ereignisse des Lebens, the ordinary occurrences of life; ein zufälliges —, an accident.

Ereílen, *v. tr.* to come up with in a course, pursuit, progress or motion, to catch, to overtake. Der Hirsch ereilet die Vorderfährte, [with huntsmen] the stag puts the hind-foot in the track of the fore-foot. *Fig.* Die Nacht ereilte uns, we were overtaken by the night, or we were benighted; Rache wird den Gottlosen —, vengeance shall overtake the wicked.

*Eremít, *m.* [-en, *pl.* -en] a hermit.

*Eremitäge, [pron. Eremitabsche] *f.* [*pl.* -n] the habitation of a hermit, hermitage.

Ererben, *v. tr.* to inherit. Er hat das Gut ererbt, he received the estate by inheritance. *Fig.* Das ewige Leben —, to inherit everlasting life.

Erfábeln, *v. tr.* to fable.

Erfáchen, V. [the more usual word] Anfachen.

Erfáhren, *ir. v. tr.* 1) to kill by driving over. V. [the usual word] Ueberfahren. 2) [rather unusual] to gain by driving or conducting a team. Er erfuhr ein kleines Vermögen, he got a small fortune by driving a carriage. 3) [properly durchfahren] *Fig.* to prove, to try, to examine. Erforsche mich, Gott, und erfahre mein Herz, [in Script.] search me, o God, and know my heart. 4) [properly einholen] *Fig.* *a*) to perceive [the cold of ice &c.]. *b*) to experience [sorrow and pleasure &c.]. *c*) to know, to learn. Noah ließ eine Taube ausfliegen, daß er erführe, ob das Wasser gefallen wäre auf Erden, [in Script.] Noah sent forth a dove from him, to see if the waters were abated from off the face of the ground. *d*) to learn, to be informed. Ich erfahre, daß der Gesetzesvorschlag im Congreß durchgegangen ist, I understand that congress have passed the bill; wie hat er es —? how came he to hear of it?

Erfáhren, [past part. of Erfahren] *adj.* and *adv.* [taught by practice or by repeated observations] experienced, skilful. Ein —er Künstler, an experienced artist; ein —er Operateur, an expert operator in surgery; ein —er Arzt, a skillful physician; — in den Künsten des Krieges, versed in the art of war; der Rechte or in den Rechten — seyn, to be expert in law; Moses war in allen Künsten Aegyptens —, Moses in all the Egyptian arts was skilled.

Erfáhrenheit, *f.* skill derived from practice, expertness, skillfulness. Die — im Seewesen, expertness in seamanship.

||Erfáhrniß, *f.* V. Erfahrenheit.

Erfáhrung, *f.* 1) [the use of the senses] experience. Wir kennen die Wirkung des Lichtes, des Geruches aus —, we know the effect of light, of smell by experience; den Alter und lange — weise gemacht haben, whom age and long experience made wise; aus der — geschöpft, experimental; die durch — erlangten Erkenntnisse, [in philosophy, knowledge acquired by the senses] experiences. *Prov.* — ist die beste Lehrmeisterinn, the wind in a man's face makes him wise. 2) knowledge acquired by hearing. Etwas in — bringen, to learn something; ich habe in — gebracht, daß &c., I understand that &c. 3) [knowledge derived by use, practice, or from a series of observations] experience. Unangenehme —en machen, to experience disagreeable things; ein Mann von —, an experienced man.

Erfahrungs=arzt, *m.* an empiric. —begriff, *m.* an idea derived from experience. —

beweis, *m.* an argument derived from experience. —kreis, *m.* sphere of experience. —kunde, *f.* knowledge depending merely on experience, empiricism. —los, *adj.* and *adv.* unexperienced. —mäßig, I. *adj.* empiric, empirical. II. *adv.* empirically. —reich, *adj.* and *adv.* having made many experiences. —satz, *m.* a position founded upon experience, a principle derived from experience, an empirical position. —seelenkunde, —seelenlehre, *f.* empiric psychology. —weise, *m.* an empiric philosopher. —wesen, *n.* [in contempt] empiricism.

Erfállen, [unusual] *ir.* I. *v. tr.* to kill by falling upon. II. *v. r.* sich —, to kill one's self by a fall.

Erfássen, *v. tr.* to lay hold on. Er erfaßte seine Hand, he took him by the hand, he seized his hand; einen Dieb —, [rather unusual] to seize a thief. *Fig. a)* to take hold of, to come upon suddenly. Ein Fieber erfaßte den Kranken, a fever seized the patient; Hoffnung und Zweifel — wechselsweise ihre Seele, hope and doubt alternate seize her soul *b)* to take in the mind, to understand, to conceive. Einen Begriff —, to take in an idea.

Erféchtbar, *adj.* and *adv.* that may be got by fighting.

Erféchten, *ir. v. tr.* 1) to obtain by fighting. Den Sieg —, to gain the victory, to carry the day, to win; Cäsar erfocht einen Sieg bei Pharsalus, Cæsar was victor at Pharsalia. † 2) [in journeymens' lang.] to get or gain by begging.

Erféchter, *m.* [-s, *pl.* -] one who gains something by fighting, he that gains the victory, victor.

†**Erfiedeln**, *v. tr.* to get or gain by playing awkwardly on a violin. Sich sein Brod —, to get one's bread by scraping.

Erfíndbar, *adj.* and *adv.* that may be invented, contrivable, devisable.

Erfínden, *ir. v. tr.* 1) [rather unusual] to find, to meet with, to light on. V. Finden, Ausfinden, Auffinden, Antreffen. 2) to discover or know by trial or experience. Einen als treu —, to find any one faithful; eine als heilsam erfundene Pflanze, a plant that proves salutary. 3) to find out, to invent. Ein neues Tonwerkzeug —, to invent a new instrument of music; das Schießpulver —, to invent gunpowder; eine neue Schreibart —, to devise a new mode of writing; eine Geschichte —, to fabricate a story; die Mittel —, welche &c., to contrive or to devise the means which &c. Syn. Erfinden, Entdecken. Entdecken signifies, to find out or come to the knowledge of something which before existed, though to us unknown; erfinden, to devise something new, to contrive and produce something that did not before exist. As soon as the telescope was erfunden [invented], Galileo entdeckte [discovered] the satellites of Jupiter.

Erfínder, *m.* [-s, *pl.* -] inventor. Die — nützlicher Künste, the inventors of useful arts.

Erfinderreich, *adj.* and *adv.* rich in persons who find out something new, rich or abundant in inventive minds.

Erfínderinn, *f.* inventress.

Erfínderisch, *adj.* and *adv.* inventive, ingenious. Ein —er Kopf, an inventive head.

Erfíndsam, *adj.* and *adv.* V. Erfinderisch.

Erfíndsamkeit, *f.* faculty of inventing or devising, device, ingenuity, genius.

Erfíndung, *f.* 1) the action or operation of finding out something new, invention. Die — der Buchdruckerkunst, the invention of the art of printing; die — der Logarithmen, the invention of the logarithms; die — neuer Wahrheiten, the discovery of new truths. 2) [that which is invented] invention. Das Dampfschiff ist die — Fultons, the steam-boat is the invention of Fulton; eine schöne —, a pretty contrivance. 3) [unusual] inventive faculty.

Erfindungs-fähig, *adj.* and *adv.* able to invent, inventive, ingenious. —gabe, *f.* faculty, talent of inventing. —geist, *m.* ableness to invent, faculty of inventing, genius, device. —kunst, *f.* the art of inventing. —reich, *adj.* and *adv.* inventive, fertile in inventions, quick at contrivance, ready at expedients. —voll, *adj.* and *adv.* inventive, ingenious, deviceful.

Erfíschen, *v. tr.* V. Auffischen. **Fig.* Etwas —, to obtain something by artifice.

Erflámmen, [rather unusual] *v. intr.* [u. w. seyn] to break out as a flame [chiefly in a figurative sense].

Erfláttern, *v. tr.* to arrive at, to reach fluttering.

Erfléhen, *v. tr.* 1) to entreat for, to seek by earnest prayer, to supplicate, to implore. Segen über die christlichen Bemühungen zur Verbreitung der Bibel —, to supplicate blessings on the Christian efforts to spread the Gospel. 2) to obtain by entreaty. 3) to win, soften or move [a person] by earnest prayer or supplication. Er ließ sich nicht —, he was inexorable.

Erflícken, [rather unusual] *v. tr.* to get or gain by mending or repairing shoes &c.

Erflíegen, *ir. v. intr.* to fly up to [also in a figurative sense].

Erflíehen, [rather unusual] *ir. v. tr.* to arrive at or reach fleeing.

Érfling, *m.* [-es, *pl.* -e] V. Kühling.

† and ‖**Erflúnkern**, *v. tr.* V. Erlügen.

Erfóderlich and **Erfórderlich**, *adj.* and *adv.* requisite, necessary. Die Luft ist zur Erhaltung des thierischen Lebens —, air is necessary to support animal life; die Hitze ist zum Wachsthume der Pflanzen —, heat is requisite to vegetation; Zufriedenheit ist zu einem glücklichen Leben —, contentment is a requisite to a happy life; so viel Tuch ist zu einem Rocke —, it takes so much cloth to make a coat; —en Falles, in case of exigency, if need be.

Erfódern and **Erfórdern**, *v. tr.* ‖1) to send for, to call for. 2) to make necessary, to require. Die Umstände — es, the circumstances render it necessary; die Ausführung dieses Werkes erfodert große Betriebsamkeit und Sorgfalt, the execution of this work demands great industry and care; des Königs Geschäft erfoderte Eile, the king's business required haste.

Erfódernis and **Erfórderniß**, *n.* [-sses, *pl.* -sse] 1) requisiteness, necessity. 2) that which is necessary, a requisite. Zufriedenheit ist ein — zu einem glücklichen Leben, contentment is a requisite to a happy life.

Erfólg, *m.* [-es, *pl.* -e] 1) result, consequence, or effect. 2) end or ultimate result, consequence, issue. Der — entsprach unsrer Erwartung nicht, the issue did not answer our expectation. Syn. V. Ausgang.

Erfolgs-reich, *adj.* and *adv.* rich in favourable results, successful. —s-voll, *adj.* and *adv.* successful.

Erfólgen, *v. intr.* [u. w. seyn] to ensue, to follow, to succeed, to come after, to result. Er sprach, und es erfolgte Stillschweigen, he spoke and silence ensued; daraus kann leicht ein Unglück —, a misfortune may easily be the consequence; auf den Fluch erfolgten diese zerstörenden Wirkungen, those destructive effects succeeded the curse; aus diesem Uebel erfolgte wenigstens einiges Gute, out of this evil some good at least resulted.

Erfórderlich, V. Erfoderlich.

Erfórdern, V. Erfodern.

Erfórderniß, V. Erfoderniß.

Erfórschen, *v. tr.* 1) to inquire and examine into with care and accuracy, to investigate, to search into, to scrutinize. Die Kräfte der Natur —, to investigate the powers of nature; er erforschte die innersten Tiefen der Wissenschaft, he penetrated into the depths of science; die Ursachen der natürlichen Lufterscheinungen —, to investigate the causes of natural phenomena; die Wahrheit —, to search out truth; er erforschte mehrere Theile des Innern von Afrika, he explored several parts of the interior of Africa. 2) [= prüfen] to search, to try, to examine. Gott erforscht die Herzen, God is the searcher of hearts.

Erfórscher, *m.* [-s, *pl.* -] 1) investigator explorator. 2) an examiner, a trier. Gott ist d — der Herzen, God is the searcher of hearts

Erfórschlich, *adj.* and *adv.* that may be i quired or investigated.

Erfórschung, *f.* investigation, inquir searching, exploration.

Erforschungsstunde, *f.* V. Prüfu stunde.

Erfrágen, *v. tr.* to find out by asking seek by request. Ich konnte ihn nicht —, I not find him out.

Erfréchen, *v. r.* sich —, to have the b ness, the assurance, the effrontery, the im dence to do any thing. Und Sie — sich, das selbst zu sagen, and you have the im dence to tell me so.

Erfréien, *v. tr.* to obtain [an estate &c. marriage.

Erfréuen, I. *v. tr.* to make glad, to ch to exhilarate; *it.* to give or afford high faction or joy, to gratify. Der Wein erf des Menschen Herz, wine glads the heart of die Friedensnachrichten — unsre Herzen, news of peace gladdens our hearts; eine Nachricht erfreuet unser Herz, good news c the heart; wer Weisheit liebet, erfreuet s Vater, [in Scripture] whoso loveth wisdo joiceth his father; das Auge oder das Oh to regale the eye or the ear; eine schöne l schaft erfreuet das Auge, a beautiful lan delights the eye; erfreut über unsern Sieg ous of our conquest; da sie den Stern s wurden sie hoch erfreut, [in Scripture] when saw the star, they rejoiced with exceeding joy; [as expressions of civility] ich bin sehr erf Sie zu sehen, I am very glad to see you; i sehr erfreut, Sie wiederzusehen, I am quite joyed to see you again; — Sie uns mit I Besuche, pray, favour us with a visit.

II. *v. r.* sich —, 1) to become glad, to re Das Vaterland wird [illegible] eurer or an euern ten stets —, your country will always j your deeds. 2) [in a more fig. sense] to have, sess and use with satisfaction. Wir — uns freien Verfassung und unschätzbarer Vorrecht Freirechte, we enjoy a free constitution and estimable privileges.

Erfréulich, *adj.* and *adv.* highly pleasi delightful. —e Nachrichten, gratifying, joy or agreeable news; es ist mir —, I delight i ein —es Schauspiel, eine —e Erscheinung pleasant spectacle or sight.

Erfríeren, *ir. v. intr.* [u. w. seyn] 1) to by means of cold, to freeze to death. Ein erfriert, a man freezes to death; alle Nußb sind erfroren, all nut-trees are blasted with

2) to be deprived of sensation by cold. Sich die Hände, Füße —, to freeze one's hands, feet; *it.* to lose the use of one's hands, feet by frost; erfrorne Glieder, frozen limbs. 3) to be chilled, to shiver with cold, to freeze. Ich bin ganz erfroren, I am quite benumbed with cold; *sie ist sehr erfroren, she is very sensible to cold.

Erfrischen, *v. tr.* to refresh, to cool, to freshen. Ein Thau nach der Hitze erfrischet Alles wieder, [in Scripture] a dew coming after a heat refresheth; erfrischend, refreshing, cooling, refrigerant; ein —des Getränk, a cooling drink; den Körper —, to refresh the body; die Pferde —, to refresh the horses; die Mannschaft sich — lassen, to let the troops refresh themselves; der Regen erfrischt die Pflanzen, rain refreshes the plants; sich —, to refresh one's self; die Seide —, [with silkdyers] to rinse the silk.

Erfrischung, *f.* 1) [act of refreshing] refreshment, collation.. 2) [that which gives fresh strength ad vigor] refreshment.

‡**Erfrischungseinlager**, *n.* [in military fairs] quarter of refreshment. —**mahl**, *n.* collation.

Erfroren, *past part.* of Erfrieren.

Erfüllen, I. *v.tr.* to fill, to fill up. Seid fruchtar und mehret euch, und erfüllet das Wasser im Meere, [in Scripture] be fruitful and multiply, ad fill the waters in the seas; ein Zimmer mit Wohlgeruch —, to perfume a room; würzige Pflanzen — die Luft mit Wohlgeruch, aromatic lants scent the air. *Fig.* Diese glückliche Begenheit erfüllt dein ganzes Herz, that happy rent fills up all thy heart; mein Herz ist von e erfüllt, I am taken with her; einen Jeden it Bewunderung —, to fill every body with dmiration; und zu bitten, daß ihr erfüllet wert mit Erkenntniß seines Willens, [in Scripture] ad to desire, that ye might be filled with the nowledge of his will; du thust deine Hand auf, d erfüllest Alles, was lebet, mit Wohlgelen, [in Scripture] thou openest thine hand, ad satisfiest the desire of every living thing; ß ich hinfort nicht mehr davon essen werde, bis s erfüllet werde im Reich Gottes, [in Script.] I l not eat any more thereof, until it be fulfilled the kingdom of God; dieselbige meine Freu ist nun erfüllet, [in Script.] this my joy therere is fulfilled; eine Prophezeiung —, to acmplish a prophecy; Daniel's Prophezeiung erfüllet, the prophecy of Daniel is completed; e Weissagung —, to fulfil a prediction; ein sprechen —, to fulfil a promise; sein Verechen —, to keep one's promise; sein Gebe —, to perform or to accomplish a vow; Gesetz —, to answer a law by obedience, to l a law; seine Pflicht —, to perform one's ty; Jemandes Wünsche —, to do any one's shes; die Erwartung des Publikums —, to isfy the expectation of the public; Hoffnun —, to complete hopes.

I. *v. r.* [rather unusual] sich —, to fill, to feed the full.

Erfüllung, *f.* the act of filling, or filling up. . fulfilling, fulfilment, execution, performe, entire completion, accomplishment. Die nsrer Wünsche oder Zwecke, the accomplisht of our wishes or ends; die — eines Verchens, the fulfilment of a promise; die — r Prophezeihung, the fulfilment or accomhment of a prophecy.

rfüllungseid, *m.* [in law] a suppletory .

rfünkeln, *v. intr.* [u. w. seyn] to begin to kle, to appear sparkling.

rgänzen, *v. tr.* to fill up, as any deficiency pens, to add or afford what is wanted, to supply what is wanting [also in a figurative sense]. Ein Heer —, to recruit an army; das Fehlende —, to make up for a deficiency; ein Buch, einen Schriftsteller —, to fill up the gaps in a book, in an author; eine Stelle in einem Buche —, to restore a passage in a book; eine Sammlung —, to complete a collection; ein Winkel von 30 Grad ergänzt einen Winkel von 60 Grad zu einem rechten, [in geometry] an angle of 30 degrees is the complement of what an angle of 60 degrees wants of a right angle.

Ergänzend, adj. and *adv.* supplying, supplementary, suppletory.

Ergänzer, *m.* [-s, *pl.* -] repairer, restorer.

Ergänzung, *f.* 1) the act of supplying what is wanting. 2) an addition to any thing by which its defects are supplied, supplement. [in geometry] Die — eines Winkels, complement of an angle [viz. what an acute angle wants to a right angle]; [in astronomy] die — der Höhe eines Sternes, the complement of a star [its distance from the zenith]; [in music] die — eines Intervalls, complement [that quantity which is wanting to any interval to fill up the octave]; [in mathematics] die arithmetische — eines Logarithmen, arithmetical complement of a logarithm [viz. what the logarithm wants to 10,000,000]; die — des Logarithmus einer Tangente, eines Sinus oder einer Secante, the complement of the logarithm of any tangent, sine or secant to 90 degrees, antilogarithm.

Ergänzungs-band, *m.* a supplementary volume. —**bogen**, *m.* [in printing] V. Defectbogen. —**eid**, *m.* V. Erfüllungseid —**gesetz**, *n.* a supplementary law. —**mannschaft**, *f.* [in military affairs] a depot of soldiers. —**pferd**, *n.* [in milit. affairs] a new horse to remount a trooper. Die —pferde für ein Regiment &c., remounting. —**richter**, *m.* a suppletory judge. —**stück**, *n.* complement. —**tag**, *m.* [formerly in the French Almanac] a complemental day. —**vorrath**, *m.* a depot of military stores. —**wörterbuch**, *n* a supplement to a dictionary.

Ergarnen, *v. tr.* 1) to catch in a net, to get into one's power by nets. * or † 2) *Fig.* to insnare, to seduce by artifice, to take by wiles, stratagem or deceit, to lure.

‖**Ergattern**, *v. tr.* [in colloquial or vulgar lang.] to get into one's power by lurking, to take [in] by wiles or artifice.

Ergeben, *ir.* I. *v. tr.* 1) to put into another's power, to commit to the discretion of, to deliver over. Welch Volk seinen Hals ergibt unter das Joch des Königs zu Babel, [in Scripture] but the nations that bring their neck under the yoke of the king of Babylon; sich —, to give up one's self into the power of another, to surrender; der Feind ergab sich nach der ersten Auffoderung, the enemy surrendered at the first summons; die Stadt ergab sich dem Feinde, the town surrendered to the enemy; sich auf Gnade und Ungnade —, to surrender at discretion; der Feind ergab sich, the enemy submitted; sich in den göttlichen Willen —, to resign ourselves to the will of God; sich Einem —, to devote one's self to any one; sich den Wissenschaften —, to devote one's self to science; ergib dich ihnen ganz, give thyself wholly to them; er ist dem Trunke —, he is addicted to drinking; das Volk ergibt sich der Wollust und dem Vergnügen, the people are given to luxury and pleasure; er ergab sich der Unmäßigkeit, he gave himself up to intemperance; er ergibt sich schlechten Gewohnheiten, he indulges in bad habits; als die Babylonier sich aller Art von Lastern — hatten, when the Babylonians had given themselves over to all manner of vice. 2) to show, to prove. Das ergibt die Erfahrung, experience proves it.

II. *v. r.* sich —, 1) [of men] V. Ergeben I. 1. [of things] to come to pass, to happen, to arrive. Es hat sich eine bedeutende Veränderung —, a considerable change took place. 2) to follow, to result from. Es ergibt sich aus diesen Thatsachen, daß der Angeklagte schuldig ist, it follows from these facts that the accused is guilty; hieraus ergibt sich, hence it follows.

Ergeben, [past part. of Ergeben] *adj.* and *adv.* devoted, addicted, given to. Einer Person — seyn, to be devoted to a person; den Wissenschaften — seyn, to be devoted to science; dem Trunke —, given to drink; der Unmäßigkeit —, addicted to intemperance; [also an expression of civility] ich bin Ihr —er Diener, I am your humble or obedient servant; ich bitte ganz —st, I most humbly beg; ich danke Ihnen —st, I am much obliged to you.

Ergebenheit, *f.* devotedness, addictedness. Seine — für den König, his devotion to the king; seine — für eine Parthei, his attachment to a party.

Ergebniß, *n.* [-sses, *pl.* -sse] 1) consequence or effect, result. 2) [in arithmetic, the amount of two or more numbers multiplied] product.

Ergebung, *f.* 1) surrender. 2) submission, resignation. Die — in den göttlichen Willen, submission to the will of God.

Ergebungs-marsch, *m.* [in war] chamade. —**zeichen**, *n.* a signal of surrender.

Ergegnen, *v. intr.* [chiefly in law] to reply.

Ergehen, *ir.* I. *v. tr.* 1) to go or walk to the end of. 2) to get or obtain by going. II. *v. r.* sich —, to walk for air or exercise. Hunderte von Studenten — sich täglich auf der Terrasse, hundreds of students daily walk on the terrace. III. *v. intr.* [u. w. seyn] to go out [not used]. *Fig.* *a*) to be published. Es erging ein Gesetz, a law was promulgated; Befehle — lassen, to promulgate or issue orders; ein Urtheil — lassen, to pass sentence or judgment. *b*) to come to pass, to happen. *c*) to happen to, to occur to [it always denotes something ill or unpleasant]. Laßt mich das Schlimmste wissen, was über mich — kann, let me know the worst, that can befall me; es ist über ihn großes Unglück ergangen, he has met with a great misfortune; etwas über sich — lassen, to submit to a thing, to bear or suffer it. IV. *v. imp.* to be attended with any circumstances or train of events, fortunate or unfortunate, to be subjected to a certain train of incidents. Es erging ihm sehr schlecht, he fared very ill; so erging es dem Hirsche unter den wüthenden Hunden, so fared the stag among th'enraged hounds; wir wollen sehen, wie es ihm — wird, we will see how it will fare with him; wie wird es den Wenigen —? what will betide the few?

Ergehung, [unusual] *f.* a walk for amusement or exercise; promenade.

Ergehungsplatz, *m.* [a place for walking] promenade.

Ergeigen, *v. tr.* to gain by playing on the fiddle. Sich Geld —, to get money by fiddling.

Ergeizen, *v. tr.* 1) to acquire, to save by sordid parsimony or avarice. 2) [rather unusual] to covet ambitiously.

Ergelben, ‖**Ergilben**, *v. intr.* [u. w. seyn] to become yellow.

Ergetzbar, *adj.* and *adv.* susceptible of amusement.

Ergetzen, [getzen is allied to the Gr. *γηθέω*, to the Lat. *gaudeo*, old Swed. *gädas*, sich freuen] I. *v. tr.* to excite agreeable sensations or emotions in, to affect with great pleasure. Einen —, to amuse any one; das Ohr, das Auge —, to regale the ear, the eye; es ergetzt das Auge, it pleases the eye; eine schöne Landschaft ergetzt das Auge, a beautiful landscape delights the eye; dieser Anblick ergetzet mich, I am delighted with this view; Spiele — die Kinder, the children are diverted with sports; die Vögel des Waldes — uns mit ihrem Gesange, the birds of the forests regale us with their song; Lappereien or Tändeldinge — uns, we are amused with trifles; ja ihr sollt an Jerusalem ergetzet werden, [in Scripture] and ye shall be comforted in Jerusalem. II. *v. r.* sich —, to have or take great pleasure, to be greatly pleased or rejoiced, to delight. Sich an einer Sache —, to delight in any thing; wir — uns an Lappereien, we are amused with trifles; sie — sich an den Possen des Harlekins, they are diverted with harlequin's tricks; ihr sollt dafür saugen, und euch — von der Fülle ihrer Herrlichkeit, [in Scripture] that ye may milk out, and be delighted with the abundance of her glory.

Ergétzer, *m.* [-s, *pl.* -] he that amuses, amuser, diverter.

Ergétzlich, *adj.* and *adv.* amusing, amusive, entertaining, divertive. Eine —e Unterhaltung, a pleasant conversation; ein —er Auftritt, a diverting scene.

Ergétzlichkeit, *f.* 1) the quality of being amusing or of affording great pleasure. 2) that which amuses, that which furnishes a pleasurable occupation of the senses, as dancing, sports &c., amusement.

Ergétzung, *f.* 1) the act of amusing, entertaining, or diverting. 2) that which affords amusement, or great pleasure and satisfaction, diversion.

Ergiebig, *adj.* and *adv.* 1) productive. Ein —er Boden, a rich soil; dieser Acker ist sehr —, that piece of ground yields a plentiful crop; ein —es Bergwerk, a rich mine. *Fig.* Dein Name wird or soll der —e Stoff meines Liedes seyn, thy name shall be the copious matter of my song. ||2) [sometimes for] considerable.

Ergiebigkeit, *f.* productiveness, richness.

Ergießen, *ir.* I. *v. tr.* to pour out. Der Fluß ergießt sein[e] Gewässer ins Meer, the river discharges its waters into the sea, the river disembogues into the sea. *Fig.* Er ergießt seine Wuth über mich, he pours out his fury on me. II. *v. r.* sich —, 1) to disembogue. Unzählige Flüsse — sich in den Ozean, innumerable rivers disembogue into the ocean. *Fig.* Gefühle oder Empfindungen, die sich in sanften Thränen —, sensations, that issue forth in soft tears; die Andacht des Herzens ergießt sich in demüthigen Bitten und Gebeten, the devotion of the heart pours itself forth in supplications and prayers. 2) to spread abundantly. Der Strom ergießt sich über das niedere Land, the stream overflows or inundates the low lands; der Fluß schwoll an und ergoß sich über die nahe liegende Ebene, the river rose and diffused its waters over the adjacent plain; die Galle ergießt sich, the gall overflows; das — der Galle, the overflowing of the gall or the suffusion of the bile. *Fig.* Er ergoß sich in einen Strom von Worten, he poured out a stream of words; sich in Lobeserhebungen [über &c.] —, to run out in praise [of &c.].

||**Ergilben**, V. Ergelben.

Ergirren, *v. tr.* to obtain by cooing.

Erglänzen, I. *v. intr.* to shine, to radiate. *Fig.* Die Flur erglänzt, the field glows; der Fluß erglänzt in den Stralen der Frühsonne, the river shines in the beams of the morning-sun; die thauige Flur erglänzt im Morgenlichte, the dewy fields sparkle in the morning-sun; ihr Auge erglänzte, her eye brightened. II. [unusual] *v. tr.* to fill with brightness, to brighten.

Erglimmen, *ir. v. intr.* 1) to begin to glimmer. 2) to begin to catch fire, to begin to glow.

Erglitzern, *v. intr.* to begin to glimmer or glisten, to begin to twinkle.

Erglühen, I. *v. intr.* [u. w. seyn] 1) to glow. Das Eisen erglühet, the iron glows or shines with a white heat. *Fig.* [to feel the heat of passion, to be animated] to glow. Sie erglühte in Liebe, she glowed with love. 2) to exhibit a strong bright colour, to be red, to glow. Die Spitzen der Alpen erglühten in der untergehenden Sonne, the summits of the Alps glowed in the setting sun. II. *v. tr.* to heat so as to shine, to glow.

Ergötzen, V. Ergetzen.

Ergraben, *ir. v. tr.* to get, gain or obtain by digging. Sich seinen Lebensunterhalt —, to get one's livelihood by digging.

Ergrämen, [unusual] *v. tr.* to get by grieving.

1. **Ergrauen**, [from grau = grey, hoary] *v. intr.* [u. w. seyn] 1) to become gray or hoary. Er ist im Dienste des Staates ergrauet, he has grown grey in the public service; ein vom Alter ergrautes Haupt, a head frosted by age. 2) to begin to grow light, to begin to dawn.

2. **Ergrauen**, [from Grauen = horror] *v. intr.* [u. w. seyn] to be afraid. Er ergraute vor dem Tode, he was afraid of death.

Ergrausen, I. *v. intr.* [u. w. seyn] to be inspired with fear or horror. II. *v. tr.* to inspire with fear or horror.

Ergreifen, *ir. v. tr.* to seize or lay hold on [especially suddenly or violently], to gripe or grasp [suddenly]. Einen bei der Hand —, to seize any one by the hand; einen Dolch —, to clutch a dagger; sie ergriff einen Zweig, she caught hold of a bough; einen Dieb —, to take up or to apprehend a thief; die Waffen —, to take up arms, to take arms, [*fig.*] to begin war; sie ergriffen die Waffen, they betook themselves to arms; das Feuer ergriff das Haus, the fire caught the house; damit das Feuer die Hecken nicht ergreife, that the fire may not take the hedges. *Fig.* Er wurde auf frischer That ergriffen, he was taken in the very act; Angst hat mich ergriffen, fear seized me; die Geschichte eures Lebens, die wunderbar das Ohr — muß, the history of your life, which must take the ear strangely; er ergriff die Gelegenheit, um eine Gunst zu erzeigen, he embraced the opportunity of doing a favour; ein Mittel —, to have recourse to an expedient; einen Vorschlag —, to adopt or to assume a proposition; sie ergriffen unser altes Gewerbe, they took up our old trade; den Weg Rechtens —, to go to law; Parthei —, to take interest in one party, to take side; Eines Partei —, to side with any one; er ergriff die Partei der Minister, he sided with the ministerial party; die Flucht —, to take to flight, to flee, to take to the heels; ich ergreife [more usual begreife] Sie nicht, I take not your meaning. V. Begreifen. Die Ergreifung, seizure, apprehension.

Ergrimmen, I. *v. intr.* [u. w. seyn] to fall into violent anger, to rage, to chafe, to fret. Und ergrimmete mit Zorn wider David, [in Scripture] and his anger was kindled against David. II. [rather unusual] *v. tr.* to irritate, to exasperate, to provoke.

Ergrößern, [rather unusual] I. *v. intr.* [u. w. seyn] to grow larger. II. *v. r.* sich —, to grow larger, to extend, to dilate, to expand. Die Schatten jener hohen Berge — sich, the shadows of you high hills grow longer.

Ergrübeln, *v. tr.* to strike out by thinking, to find out by close meditation, examination or scrutinizing, to find out by careful disquisition.

Ergründen, *v. tr.* [to try the depth] to fathom, to sound. *Fig.* to find the bottom or extent, to fathom, to penetrate. Ich vermag seine Absicht nicht zu —, I cannot fathom his design; er hatte die Plane des Fürsten nicht ergründet, he had not penetrated into the designs of the prince; ein Geheimniß —, to find out a secret; die Tiefen der Wissenschaft —, to explore the depths of science; das Wesen der Dinge —, to dive into the nature of things.

Ergründer, *m.* [-s, *pl.* -] one who fathoms or explores, an explorator, a profound thinker, a profound enquirer.

Ergründlich, *adj.* and *adv.* that may be fathomed or sounded, [*fig.*] penetrated or comprehended, or that is capable of being thoroughly explored.

Ergründlichkeit, *f.* capability of being fathomed, penetrated or comprehended.

Ergründung, *f.* fathoming, sounding.

Ergrünen, *v. intr.* [u. w. seyn] to grow green. Die ergrünten Felder, verdant fields.

||**Ergucken**, *v. tr.* to see, to descry, to espy.

Erguß, *m.* [-sses, *pl.* -güsse] a flowing or issuing out, discharge. *Fig.* Ergüsse der Gnade, effusions of grace; Ergüsse des Herzens, emanations of the heart. V. Ausfluß.

Erhaben, *adj.* and *adv.* raised aloft, elevated, elevate. —e [erhobene] Arbeit, embossed work, relief, relievo. *Fig.* Er ist über alle Falschheit —, he is above all falsehood; über sein Schicksal —, superior to one's fate; —e Gesinnungen, elevate sentiments; —e Gedanken, elevated or sublime thoughts; ein —er Gedanke, a grand conception; ein —er Gesang, a noble song; —e Lieder, lofty strains; die —e Schreibart, a grand and lofty style, a style that expresses lofty conceptions, the sublime; sich — ausdrücken, to express one's self sublimely.

Erhabenheit, *f.* 1) elevation in place or position, loftiness, height, altitude, sublimity. Die — eines Berges, the loftiness of a mountain. *Fig.* Die — einer Berglandschaft, the grandeur of mountain scenery; die — der Gesinnungen, elevation of sentiments; die — seiner Gedanken, the sublimity of his thoughts; die — der Schreibart, the loftiness or grandeur of style, sublimeness; die — der Tugend, the sublimity of virtue. 2) a part rising or projecting beyond the surface. —en der Haut, prominences or protuberances on the skin; die —en auf einer glatten Fläche, eminences on a smooth surface; —en auf der Erdoberfläche, protuberances on the surface of the earth. *Fig.* [a title of honour given to cardinals and other priests elevated in rank] eminence. Eure —en, [more usual Eure Eminenz] your Eminences.

Erhacken, *v. tr.* 1) to get or gain by hoeing, hewing or splitting. 2) to hew through, to hew roughly or to pieces. Ich kann dieses Stück Holz nicht —, I cannot manage to split this piece of wood.

Erhadern, *v. tr.* to get or obtain by contention.

Erhallen, [rather unusual] *v. intr.* [u. w. seyn] to resound.

Erhaltbar, *adj.* and *adv.* 1) that may be preserved, preservable. 2) that may be obtained, obtainable.

Erhalten, *ir.* I. *v. tr.* to hold from action, to keep or restrain from proceeding. Die [illegible] de ließen sich nicht —, the horses could not be held in. *Fig.* a) to retain in one's possession, to hold. Sein Besitzthum —, to keep one's property. b) to conserve. In gutem Stande —, to keep in a safe or sound state; erhalte Alles in gutem Zustande, keep all things in repair; gut —e Gemählde, well-preserved paintings; Einen bei Ehren —, to maintain any one's honour; den Frieden der Gesellschaft —, to conserve the peace of society; in Ordnung —, to keep in order; Einen in der Ungewißheit — or lassen, to keep any one in suspense; das Leben —, to preserve life; sich das Leben —, to save one's life; Einen beim Leben —, to save any one's life; seinen Glauben [Credit] —, to keep up one's credit; Gott erhält die Welt, God preserves the world; eine Familie —, to sustain or support a family; eine Familie durch Arbeit —, to maintain a family by labour; wohlfeil — werden, to be kept at a moderate price. c) to obtain. Antworten auf Briefe —, to obtain answers to letters; einen Brief —, to receive a letter; etwas durch Bitten —, to obtain something by entreaty, to impetrate something; Lob oder Tadel —, to get praise or blame; den gebührenden Lohn für seine Arbeit —, to get a due reward for one's labour; er erhielt volle Entschädigung, he received ample compensation; ein Amt —, to get an office or appointment; den Sieg —, to gain the victory; er erhielt den Sieg, he won the day. d) to prove, to evince. Eidlich —, to give evidence on oath; einen Bericht eidlich —, to swear to the truth of a statement. II. *v. r.* sich —, to preserve one's self from falling by taking hold of any thing; *it.* to remain in any state. Sich mit den Beinen or Füßen —, to keep upright, to keep on one's legs. *Fig.* a) [of things] to keep, to last, not to perish or be impaired. Sich gesund —, to remain in a good state of health; suche für den Winter Aepfel aus, die sich —, seek for winter's use apples that will keep. b) [of persons] to maintain one's self. Er erhält sich von Kräutern, he subsists on herbs.

Erhaltens-werth, —würdig, *adj.* and *adv.* deserving to be kept, worthy of being conserved or preserved.

Erhälter, *m.* [-s, *pl.* -] **-inn,** *f.* the person or thing that preserves or conserves, maintainer. O du — der Menschen! O thou preserver of men!

Erhaltung, *f.* the act of preserving &c., the keeping of a thing in a safe or entire state. Die — des Lebens, der Gesundheit, the preservation of life, of health; es trägt zur — der Gesundheit bei, it contributes to the support of health; die — einer Familie, the support of a family; die — des Friedens, the conservation of peace; die — der guten Ordnung, the maintenance of good order; diese Summe reicht zur — [Unterhaltung] so vieler Armen nicht hin, this sum is not sufficient for the subsistence of so many poor people.

Erhaltungs-brille, *f.* conservers of the sight. **—werth, —würdig,** *adj.* and *adv.* V. Erhaltenswerth.

Erhämmern, *v. tr.* 1) to shape with a hammer. 2) to get or acquire by hammering.

Erhandeln, *v. tr.* 1) to obtain by purchase. Ein Haus —, to buy a house. 2) to obtain by bargaining, chaffering or haggling. 3) [rather unusual] to get or gain by trade. Er hat ein großes Vermögen erhandelt, he made a large fortune in trade.

Erhängen, *v. tr.* [only used in the last phrase sich —] to hang up, to suspend. Einen Dieb —, to hang a thief; sich —, to hang one's self.

Erharren, *v. tr.* to stay for, to wait. Erharre der or die Zeit, wait for the time.

Erhärten, *v. intr.* [u. w. seyn] to become hard or more hard, to harden. Der Mörtel erhärtet, wenn er trocken wird, mortar hardens by drying.

Erhärten, *v. tr.* to make hard or more hard, to harden. *Fig.* to prove, to confirm. Mit Gründen —, to support by arguments; eidlich —, to declare upon oath; [in law] to make an affidavit. Die Erhärtung, proving, confirmation.

Erhäschen, *v. tr.* to seize hastily or abruptly, to snatch. Einen Vogel —, to catch a bird; einen Kuß —, to snatch a kiss. *Fig.* Einen Vortheil —, to catch hold of an advantage; die Gelegenheit beim Schopf —, to seize opportunity by the fore-lock.

Erhauen, *ir. v. tr.* 1) to hoe, to hew or cut through. Er kann es nicht —, his strength fails him for cutting &c. it through. 2) to bring to the ground by cutting. Bäume —, to fell trees. 3) to kill by striking. 4) to get or obtain by hoeing &c. or striking.

Erheben, *ir.* I. *v. tr.* 1) to heave, to lift, to take up, to raise. Ich kann eine so große Last nicht —, I cannot lift so great a load. 2) to lift, to lift up, to heave, to elevate. Die Füße —, to lift the feet; das Haupt —, to raise one's head; die Hände gen Himmel —, to lift up one's hands to heaven; der Wind erhebt den Staub, the wind raises the dust; und einen Sturmwind erregte, der die Wellen erhob, [in Script.] and raiseth the stormy wind, which lifteth up the waves thereof; das Jagdzeug —, [with huntsmen] to lift the toils; die Augen —, to lift up the eyes. *Fig.* Seine Stimme —, to raise one's voice; to lift up the voice; ein Geschrei —, to raise, to set up a cry; ein Lamento —, to take up a lamentation; Klagen wider Jemand —, to complain of any one; sein Herz oder seine Gedanken zu Gott —, to lift up one's heart or thoughts to God; es erhebt das Gemüth, it rears, elevates, exalts the mind; Einen zu hohen Würden —, to raise any one to high dignities; Einen zu hohen Aemtern —, to exalt any one to offices of distinction; in den Adelstand —, to raise to nobility, to ennoble; [in arithmetic] eine Zahl in's Quadrat —, to square a number; Einen [mit Worten] —, to raise any one in words or eulogy; Jemands Tugenden bis in den Himmel —, to extol any one's virtues to the very skies; er ist meines Vaters Gott, ich will ihn —, [in Script.] he is my father's God, I will exalt him; [in painting] etwas —, to set off a part in a picture; die Schatten auf einem Gemählde — den Glanz der Farben, the shadows in a picture set off the brightness of the colours. 3) [as it were hebend wegnehmen] *Fig.* a) to raise, to levy [toll, tribute, contributions]. Steuern —, to raise or levy taxes; die Zölle —, to collect the customs. b) [in law &c.] to inquire into. Die Umstände einer Begebenheit —, to inquire into the particulars of any event; einen Protest beim Notar —, to enter a protest.

II *v. r.* sich —, 1) to rise, to ascend. Es erhob sich ein Staub, a dust arose, there arose a dust. *Fig.* to begin to exist, to rise. Der Wind erhob sich um 12 Uhr, the wind rose or sprung up at 12 o'clock; es erhob sich ein großes Geschrei, there arose a great cry; und da das Volk hinaus kam aufs Feld, Israel entgegen, erhob sich der Streit im Walde Ephraim, [in Script.] so the people went out into the field against Israel, and the battle was in the wood of Ephraim. 2) to rise from a bed or seat, to get up. Sie erhoben sich von ihren Stühlen, they rose from their chairs; er erhob sich von seinem Sitze, he stood up; das Wild erhebt sich, [with huntsmen] the game starts up; der Hof hat sich in die Kirche erhoben, the court betook itself to the church. *Fig.* a) to rise, to break forth into public commotions. Dieses Volk hat sich gegen seine Unterdrücker erhoben, this nation has risen against their oppressors; sie erhoben sich gegen ihre Offiziere, they arose or rose upon their officers. b) to be distinguished above others, to be prominent. Er erhebt sich durch seine Verdienste über seine Mitbewerber, he surpasses his competitors in merits; [sometimes in a bad sense] sich über Andere —, to elevate one's self above others; und wird sich in seinem Herzen —, [in Script.] he shall magnify himself in his heart; sich seiner Talente — or überheben, to presume upon one's parts. 3) [= hoch seyn] to rise, to ascend, to be elevated above the level or surface. Die Cordilleren — sich mehr als 20,000 Fuß über die Fläche des Ozeans, the Andes rise more than 20,000 feet above the level of the ocean. 4) to rise, to be more elevated; *fig.* to appear more elevated. Das Land erhebt sich, wenn man einer Küste zusegelt, in sailing towards a shore, the land rises. SYN. **Erheben, Erhöhen.** Erheben signifies to raise from a low place to a higher; erhöhen to give additional height to. One says: Die Hände gen Himmel **erheben** [to lift one's hands towards heaven]; das Haus ist um ein Stockwerk **erhöhet** worden [the house has been raised a story]. The same distinction is observed in the figurative sense of these words. Thus one says: Der König hat ihn in den Adelstand **erhoben** [the king has elevated him to the rank of nobility]; der König hat ihm seine Besoldung **erhöhet** [the king has increased his salary].

Erheber, *m.* [-s, *pl.* -] he that raises, collects or levies, raiser. Der — der Steuern, the collector of taxes; der — des Geldes, the raiser of money.

Erheblich, *adj.* and *adv.* what may be raised, levied &c. [used only in a fig. sense] important, weighty, momentous. —e Gründe, weighty reasons; —e Schwierigkeiten, considerable difficulties; wenig —, of little consequence, of little importance.

Erheblichkeit, *f.* importance, weightiness. Es ist von keiner —, it is of no consequence; das Zeugniß ist bei der Sache von keiner —, the testimony is not relevant to the case.

Erhebniß, *n.* [-sses, *pl.* -sse] [in mining] old slags [used in melting tin].

Erhebung, *f.* the act of raising, elevation. *Fig.* Die — einer Person auf einen Thron, the elevation of a man to a throne; er verdankt seine — seiner Frau, he is indebted to his wife for his exaltation in rank or honour, for his promotion; die — der Stimme, the elevation of the voice; die — in den Adelstand, ennoblement; die — der Steuern, the raising of taxes; die — der Zehnten, the collecting of tithes; die — seines Gemüthes, the raising of one's mind, *it.* [incorrectly for Erhabenheit] the exaltation, grandeur or sublimity of one's mind.

Erheirathen, *v. tr.* to obtain or to acquire by marriage.

Erheischen, *v. tr.* to require, to demand. Des Königs Geschäft erheischt Eile, the king's business requires haste.

Erheitern, I. *v. tr.* to clear, to clear up, to make bright. *Fig* Das Gesicht —, to clear the brow; die Musik erheitert das Herz, music cheers the heart; der Wein erheitert ihn, wine enlivens him; sie — den Traurigen, they enliven the gloomy; seine Seele zu —, to serene his soul; die erheiternden Strahlen der Sonne, the cheering rays of the sun. II. *v. r.* sich —, to clear, to clear up [off, away]. Der Himmel erheitert sich, the sky clears, it clears away, it clears off. *Fig.* Unsere Aussichten — sich, our prospects brighten!

Erheiterung, *f.* 1) the act of clearing up

&c. 2) recreation.

Erhéizbar, *adj.* and *adv.* that may be heated thoroughly.

Erhéizen, *v. tr.* to heat sufficiently, to heat thoroughly.

Erhéllen, I. *v. tr.* to fill with light, to illuminate, to enlighten. Ein Zimmer —, to light a room; den Zucker —, to clarify sugar. *Fig.* Etwas —, to discover or publish any thing. II. *v. intr.* to grow bright, to brighten. *Fig.* to become bright, clear, evident, apparent. Aus diesem Briefe erhellt, daß &c., by this letter appears that &c.

Erhellkessel, *m.* a pan used in clarifying sugar.

Erhéllung, *f.* lighting, enlightening. *Fig.* discovering, manifesting.

Erhellungskessel, *m.* V. Erhellkessel.

Erhénken, *v. tr.* to hang up [a thief &c.]. Sich —, to hang one's self. V. Erhängen.

Erhérben, [unusual] I. *v. intr.* [u. w. seyn] to become sour, to sour. II. *v. tr.* to make sour, acid and austere or astringent. III. *v. r.* sich —, [*fig.*] to grow angry.

Erhéucheln, *v. tr.* to obtain by hypocrisy.

Erhéulen, *v. tr.* to get or obtain by howling. † *Fig.* to get or obtain by loud lamentations.

Erhéxen, *v. tr.* to obtain, to procure by witchcraft.

Erhítzen, I. *v. tr.* to heat, to make hot. Das Eisen —, to heat iron; die Sonne erhitzt die Erde, the sun warms the earth; der Wein erhitzt mich, wine heats me; vom Weine erhitzt, inflamed with wine; den Körper —, to inflame the body; das Blut —, to heat the blood; —de Mittel, medicines of an inflammatory nature. *Fig.* Ein edler Wetteifer erhitzt eure Brust, a noble emulation heats your breast; auf etwas erhitzt seyn, to be hot in the pursuit of any thing; eine erhitzte Einbildungskraft, a heated imagination. II. *v. r.* sich —, 1) to grow warm or hot. Laufen Sie nicht so schnell, Sie werden sich —, do not run so fast, you will overheat yourself; er hat sich beim Gehen erhitzt, he got warm by walking. 2) to grow hot or angry, to inflame.

Erhöben, V. Erhaben and Erheben.

Erhóffen, *v. tr.* 1) to hope for. 2) [rather unusual] to obtain by hoping.

Erhöhen, *v. tr.* 1) to set upright, to erect [a cross &c.]. 2) to raise higher, as a wall, a dike. *Fig.* *a*) to raise, to exalt, to elevate in condition, to magnify one's self. Wer sich selbst erhöhet, der soll erniedrigt werden, [in Script.] he that exalteth himself shall be abased. *b*) to raise, to increase, to enhance. Den Werth des Geldes —, to raise the value of money; den Preis der Waaren —, to raise or to advance the price of goods; Jemands Lohn —, to add to any one's wages; um das Doppelte oder Dreifache —, to double, to treble; das Vergnügen wird durch &c. erhöht, pleasure is enhanced by &c. *c*) to heighten, to increase. Den Muth der Soldaten zu —, to heighten the soldiers' courage; unser Wohlgefallen an geistigem Vergnügen —, to heighten our relish for intellectual pleasure; seine Tugenden — den Glanz seiner Würde, his virtues heighten the glory of his dignity; eine Farbe —, to brighten a colour, to increase its luster. *d*) to raise in words or eulogy, to extol, to exalt in commendation, to praise. Den Namen Gottes —, to magnify the name of God. SYN. V. Erheben.

Erhöhung, *f.* 1) the act of erecting or raising higher. *Fig.* elevation, exaltation, increase, augmentation. Die — des Werthes, Preises, Genusses, Vergnügens, the enhancement of value, price, enjoyment, pleasure. 2) [only in the proper sense] V. Erhabenheit.

Erhöhungswinkel, *m.* [in gunnery, the angle which the chace of a cannon or mortar, or the axis of the hollow cylinder, makes with the plane of the horizon] elevation.

Erhölen, I *v. tr.* || 1) to overtake. || and ‡ 2) to mention. II. *v. r.* sich —, 1) to recover one's breath, strength or health, to recreate. Sich nach einer Krankheit —, to regain or recover health or strength after sickness; sich von einer Ohnmacht wieder —, to recover from a swoon, to come to one's self again. *Fig.* Er erholt sich mit der Pflege der Künste, he recreates himself with the culture of arts; ich kann mich von meinem Erstaunen nicht —, I cannot recover from my astonishment. 2) to indemnify one's self, to make one's self amends [for a loss]. Sich an einer Person oder Sache —, to be reimbursed by a person or thing; sich von seinem Verluste wieder —, to recover from one's loss; || sich seines Schadens —, to retrieve or repair a loss; *Sie müssen sich am Braten —, you must have recourse to the roast meat. 3) Sich bei Jemandem Raths —, to apply for advice to a person, to ask advice of any one; erhole dich Raths bei Gott, ask counsel of God.

Erhölung, *f.* 1) the act of recovering, of repairing a loss &c, recovery. 2) refreshment of the strength and spirits after toil, recreation, diversion, amusement. Laßt Musik — gewähren, let music be recreative.

Erholungs-mahl, *n.* [in monasteries] refection. **—saal**, *m.* [in monasteries] refectory. **—stunde**, *f.* hour of recreation.

Erhórchen, *v. tr.* to learn by hearkening or listening, to overhear.

Erhören, *v. tr.* 1) to hear, to learn. Das ist nicht erhört, never was such a thing heard of, that is unheard of. 2) to perceive by the ear, to hear. Ich konnte ihn nicht —, I could not hear him; sie konnten es nicht —, they were out of hearing. 3) *Fig.* to grant an answer to prayer, to hear [favorably]. Gott hat die Bitten seines Volkes erhört, God has heard the prayers of his people; der Fürst erhörte ihre Bitte und schenkte ihrem Gatten das Leben, the prince heard her prayer and pardoned her husband.

Erhörlich, *adj.* and *adv.* that may be heard or granted.

Erhörung, *f.* 1) hearing. 2) granting, grant. Sein Gebet hat — gefunden, his prayer has been heard.

Erhúngern, [rather unusual] I. *v. intr.* [u. w. seyn] 1) to become hungry. 2) to get or acquire by hunger. 3) to die of hunger, to famish. V. Verhungern. II. *v. r.* sich —, to famish one's self.

Erhúpfen, *v. tr.* 1) to come to, arrive at, or reach jumping. 2) [mostly in a jocose sense] to get by jumping. *Fig.* Vestris hat sich ein artiges Vermögen erhüpft, Vestris has acquired a handsome fortune by his dancing, Vestris has danced to some purpose.

†**Erhúren**, *v. tr.* to get by prostitution.

Erínnerer, *m.* [-s, *pl.* -] one who reminds any one of a thing, remembrancer, monitor.

Erínnerlich, *adj.* and *adv.* what is remembered, present to recollection. Mir ist noch Alles wohl —, I remember all well; so viel mir — ist, as far as I remember.

Erínnern, I. *v. tr.* 1) to put in mind, to bring to the remembrance of, to remind. Jemanden an sein Versprechen —, to remind a person of his promise; Einen an seine Pflicht —, to remind or admonish any one of his duty; einen Schuldner —, to demand a debt of a debtor; ich erinnerte sie an die glücklichen Stunden, I recalled to her memory the happy hours, die Gebrechlichkeiten des Alters — uns an unsre Sterblichkeit, the infirmities of old age remind us of our mortality; — Sie mich daran, put me in mind of it. 2) to mention. Etwas —, to observe, to mention something; ich habe dabei nichts zu —, I have nothing to remark on it; ich habe nichts dagegen zu —, I have nothing to object to it. II. *v. r.* sich —, to recover or call back ideas to the memory, to bring back to the mind or memory. — Sie sich dieses Mannes? do you remember this man? ich kann mich nicht —, was gesprochen wurde, I cannot recollect what was said; ich konnte mich seines Namens nicht —, I could not recollect his name; ich erinnere mich Ihrer nicht, I do not recollect you, Sir; so viel ich mich erinnere, as much as I remember or recollect.

|| or ‡**Erínnersam**, *adj.* and *adv.* V. Erinnerlich.

Erínnerung, *f.* 1) the act of reminding, or putting in mind, suggestion. 2) remembrance, recollection, reminiscence. Etwas in — bringen, to call something to remembrance, to revive something in memory; was vergessen worden, in — bringen, to recall to mind what has been forgotten; angenehme —en, agreeable recollections. 3) remembrance, admonishing of any duty, admonition. 4) remembrance, memorial, a token by which any thing is kept in the memory. Zur —, in memory of.

Erinnerungs-buch, *n.* memorandum-book. **—kraft**, *f.* **—vermögen**, *n.* power of remembering, remembrance, reminiscence, memory. **—los**, *adj.* and *adv.* not recollecting or reminding; *it.* without a memorial. **—mahl**, *n.* 1) memorial, monument. 2) a meal designed to commemorate any person or event, as the Lord's supper. **—schreiben**, *n.* a monitory letter. **—tafel**, *f.* memorial-tablet. **—vermögen**, *n.* V. —kraft. **—zeichen**, *n.* remembrance, memorial, token, keepsake.

Erjägen, *v. tr.* 1) to come up with in a course, to overtake. Einer erjagte den Andern, they overtook one another. *Fig.* Einen Vortheil —, to get an advantage by great exertion; Ehre, Lob zu — suchen, to hunt for honour or praise. 2) to get in hunting. Einen Hasen —, to catch a hare in hunting; sich seinen Unterhalt —, to get one's livelihood by hunting.

Erkálten, *v. intr.* [u. w. seyn] 1) to become less hot, to lose heat, to cool. Laſſe den Kaffee, Thee —, let the coffee or tea cool. *Fig.* Sein Eifer, seine Liebe erkaltet, his zeal, his love abates. 2) *Fig.* to die.

Erkälten, I. *v. tr.* to make cold. *Fig.* to cool. II. *v. r.* sich —, to catch cold. Ich habe mich erkältet, I have caught cold.

Erkältung, *f.* a cold caught. Sich eine — zuziehen, to catch cold.

Erkältungs-fieber, *n.* a rheumatic fever. **—übel**, *n.* a rheumatism.

Erkämpfen, *v. tr.* to obtain by fighting. Den Sieg —, to gain the victory, to carry the day; sich Ruhm —, to get fame by war.

Erkánnt, *past part.* of Erkennen.

Erkárgen, *v. tr.* to acquire by niggardliness.

Erkáufen, *v. tr.* to purchase, to buy. *Fig.* *a*) [= loskaufen] Christus hat uns erkauft mit seinem Blute, Christ redeemed us by his blood. *b*) to hire for bad purposes, to bribe, to hire. Einen Richter —, to corrupt a judge; erkaufte Dienste, mercenary services; eine erkaufte Stimme, a venal vote.

Erkäuflich, *adj.* and *adv.* venal, mercenary

Ein —er Richter, a mercenary judge.

Erkécken, *v. r.* sich —, to dare, to be bold enough.

Erkénnbar, *adj.* and *adv.* that may be, or is easy to be, recognised or perceived, perceptible, discernible, distinguishable.

Erkénnbarkeit, *f.* quality of being recognisable, perceptibility.

Erkénnen, *ir. v. intr.* and *tr.* to perceive, to know. Mit den Sinnen, mit den Augen —, to perceive by the senses, to distinguish by the eye; ich kann es nicht —, I cannot discern or see it; etwas durch den Verstand —, to perceive something by our understanding; deutlich —, to know clearly; man hat mir zu — gegeben, I have been given to understand; man hat ihm zu — gegeben, it was intimated to him; als ich Ihnen meine Liebe zu — gab, when I did impart my love to you. [in a more limited sense] *a*) to perceive with certainty, to know. Den Baum an seinen Früchten —, to know a tree by the fruit; eine erkannte Wahrheit, an acknowledged truth; das Gute vom Bösen —, to discern good from ill; [sometimes for kennen, as] sich —, to know one's self. *b*) to recognise by recollection, remembrance, representation or description, to know. Eine Person in der Ferne —, to recognise a person at a distance; wir — sie von Weitem, we ken them from afar; Jemands Züge, seine Stimme —, to recognise any one's features, his voice; Jemanden an seinem Bildniß —, to know a man from having seen his portrait; Einen an der Beschreibung seiner Person —, to know any one by having heard him described; er gab sich uns zu —, he made himself known to us. *c*) to know by experience, or trial. Einen Freund erkennet man in der Noth, *prov.* a friend in need is a friend indeed. *d*) to acknowledge, to own. Erkennet mich für euren Sohn, own me for your son; eine Unterschrift für die seinige —, to own one's sign manual; ich erkenne ihn für einen großen Redner, I acknowledge him to be a great orator; etwas für wahr —, to admit a thing to be true; welche keiner von den Obersten dieser Welt erkannt hat, denn wo sie die erkannt hätten, hätten sie den Herrn der Herrlichkeit nicht gekreuziget, [in Script.] which none of the princes of this world knew, for had they known it, they would not have crucified the Lord of Glory; er erkennt nun sein Unrecht, he is now sensible of his wrong; ich erkenne es mit Dank, I am gratefully sensible of it; ich erkenne sehr Ihre Güte, I am very sensible of your kindness; etwas dankbar —, to acknowledge something gratefully. *e*) to judge, to form a judgment of. Ich erkenne es für recht, in my judgment it is right; er erkannte es für unbillig, he judged it unjust or unreasonable; [in law] dieser Gerichtshof erkennt in bürgerlichen und peinlichen Sachen, this court takes cognizance of civil and criminal causes; das Parlament hat darüber zu —, this falls under the cognizance of the parliament; der Gerichtshof erkannte auf die Ehescheidung, the court passed judgment of divorce [of the parties]. *f*) to have sexual commerce with, to know. Adam erkannte sein Weib Eva und sie ward schwanger, [in Scripture] Adam knew his wife, and she conceived. *g*) [in commerce] Einen für eine Summe —, to credit any one with a sum.

Erkénner, *m.* [-s, *pl.* -] he that recognises, decides; [in law] decider.

Erkénntlich, *adj.* and *adv.* 1) V. Erkennbar. —e Züge, features that may be recognised. 2) willing to acknowledge and repay benefits, grateful, thankful. Ein —er Mensch, a grateful man; ein —es Gemüth, a grateful mind; für eine Gunstbezeigung — seyn, to acknowledge a favour.

Erkénntlichkeit, *f.* 1) acknowledgment, gratefulness, gratitude, thankfulness. 2) [something given in return for a favour] an acknowledgment, a gratuity.

Erkénntniß, *f.* [*pl.* -sse] and *n.* [-sses, *pl.* -sse] 1) the act of perceiving or recognising, perception, cognizance. 2) knowledge, perception, cognition; *it.* certain knowledge, science. Eine klare —, a clear perception; eine anschauliche —, intuitive knowledge; die — der Wahrheit, the comprehension of truth by the mind; eine tiefe —, a deep science; die — Gottes, the science of God; der Baum des —sses Gutes und Böses, [in Script.] the tree of knowledge of good and evil. 3) the act of owning, acknowledgment, confession. Die — seiner Fehler, the acknowledgment of one's faults. 4) [das Erkenntniß] the judicial decision, determination, the ending of a suit by the judgment of a court. Zum —sse in einer Sache schreiten, to come to a decision, to determine a cause.

Erkenntniß-grund, *m.* 1) principle of knowledge. 2) a motive of, or a reason for, a [judicial] decision. **—kraft**, *f.* V. —vermögen. **—kreis**, *m.* the sphere of one's knowledge. **—quelle**, *f.* the source of knowledge. **—vermögen**, *n.* the faculty of knowing. Das vernünftige —vermögen, the understanding, the intellect, the intellectual faculty.

Erkénnung, *f.* the act of recognising. V. Erkennen.

Erkennungs-wort, *n.* a watchword, a military watchword, the countersign. **—zeichen**, *n.* a sign or signal by which a person or thing is or makes himself [or itself] known from another person or thing.

Érker, *m.* [-s, *pl.* -] [med. Lat. *arcora*, probably allied to the Lat. *arcus*] a projecting part of a house, a projection, a jutty.

Erker-fenster, *n.* a bow-window, bay-window, jut-window. **—stube**, *f.* a room with a projection.

Erkíesen, [rather obsolete] *v. tr.* to select, to choose. Einen zu etwas —, to select any one for any thing. V. Erwählen.

Erkláftern, *v. tr.* to measure or to encompass by the arms extended, to fathom.

Erklámmern, *v. tr.* V. Umklammern.

Erklärbar, *adj.* and *adv.* explicable, explainable. Manche Schwierigkeiten in alten Schriftstellern sind nicht —, many difficulties in old authors are not explicable; sein Benehmen ist mir nicht —, his conduct is inexplicable, unaccountable to me.

Erklären, I. *v. tr.* 1) to explain [the Scriptures &c.]. Der letzte Vers ist noch nicht hinlänglich erklärt, the last verse is not yet sufficiently explicated; ein Gesetz —, to expound a law; einen Traum —, to show a dream; einen Schriftsteller —, to interpret an author; eine Stelle in einem Schriftsteller durch eine Anmerkung —, to illustrate a passage of an author by a comment; das Wort Tugend —, to define the word *virtue*; —de Noten, explanatory, expository, or exegetical notes; ich kann mir das nicht —, I cannot account for it. 2) to make known, to tell explicitly, to declare. Seine Liebe —, to declare one's love; sie haben den Angeklagten für schuldig erklärt, they found the accused guilty; Einen in die Acht —, to outlaw, or to proscribe any one; ein erklärter Feind Ihres Geschlechtes, a professed foe to your sex; den Krieg —, to denounce war. II. *v. r.* sich —, [to show openly what one thinks, or which side one espouses] to declare one's self. Die verbündeten Mächte erklärten sich wider Frankreich, the allied powers declared against France; der Fürst erklärte sich für die Verbündeten, the prince declared for the allies; der Sieg hatte sich für uns erklärt, victory had declared for us; — Sie sich deutlicher, speak more plainly; — Sie sich frei heraus, speak your mind freely, speak out; sie haben sich gegen einander erklärt, the parties came to an explanation. Syn. V. Auslegen.

Erklärensbedürftig, *adj.* and *adv.* that wants to be explained.

Erklärer, *m.* [-s, *pl.* -] an explainer, or expositor, a commentator, an interpreter. Der — eines Schriftstellers, a scholiast.

Erklärung, *f.* 1) the act of explaining, expounding, or interpreting, explanation, exposition, illustration, interpretation. Die — einer Schriftstelle, the explanation of a passage in a writing; die — der Parabeln unsers Heilandes, the explication of the parables of our Saviour; die — eines Wortes, the definition of a word; diese Stelle bedarf keiner —, this passage needs no explanation. 2) [in logic, in lexicography] definition. 3) an open expression of facts or opinions, verbal utterance, declaration. Die — seiner Meinung, the declaration of his opinion; die — eines Gesandten, [a diplomatic communication in writing] a note; die letzte —, [in diplomacy] ultimatum; die — des Krieges [Kriegs—], a denunciation of war; die — seiner Liebe [Liebes—], the declaration of his love; mit einem zur — kommen, to come to an explanation with any one.

Erklärungs-art, *f.* the manner of explaining any thing. **—kunst**, *f.* the art of explaining, or illustrating a subject, chiefly the art of finding the meaning of an author's words, hermeneutics, or the art of expounding the Scriptures, hermeneutic theology. **—schrift**, *f.* comments or commentaries. **—urtheil**, *n.* an explanatory judgment or decree. **—wissenschaft**, *f.* hermeneutics.

Erklécken, [rather provinc.] *v. intr.* 1) to be of use. 2) to be enough or sufficient, to suffice.

Erklécklich, *adj.* and *adv.* 1) enough, sufficient, adequate to wants, competent. 2) [rather provinc.] considerable.

Erklètterbar, *adj.* and *adv.* V. Erklimmbar.

Erklèttern, *v. tr.* to clamber, to climb. Einen Baum —, to climb a tree; ein Dach —, to clamber up a roof.

Erklímmbar, *adj.* and *adv.* climbable.

Erklímmen, *ir.* [with some authors *reg.*] *v. tr.* to climb, to ascend with effort or difficulty. Einen Berg —, to climb up a mountain; einen Baum —, to climb up into a tree.

Erklíngeln, [rather unusual] I. *v. intr.* to begin to ring as a bell. II. *v. tr.* to awake or arouse by ringing the bell.

Erklíngen, *v. intr.* [u. w. seyn] 1) to ring, to sound. Laßt die Gläser —, let's touch glasses. 2) to resound, to ring. Das Haus erklang von ihrem Jubel, the house resounded with their merriment.

Erklírren, *v. intr.* [u. w. seyn] to ring or jingle, to clink.

Erklópfen, *v. tr.* 1) to beat through. 2) to break by knocking, to break in pieces. 3) to give notice by knocking. 4) to awake by knocking, to knock up.

Erklügeln, *v. tr.* to find out by subtile investigation or drawing subtile conclusions. V. Ausklügeln.

Erknácken, [rather unusual] *v. tr.* to break open by cracking, to crack [a nut].

Erknállen, *v. intr.* to give a report. Die Peitsche erknallt, the whip cracks.

Erknárren, *v. intr.* 1) to begin to creak. 2)

to creak. Die Angel einer Thür erknarrt beim Herumdrehen, the hinge of a door creaks in turning.

Erknaüsern, *v. tr.* [chiefly in fam. lang.] to get or to acquire by niggardliness.

Erknickern, *v. tr.* V. Erknausern.

Erknürren, *v. tr.* to obtain by snarling.

||**Erköbern**, *v. intr.* [in husbandry] to get stocked with bees.

Erködern, *v. tr.* to take by means of a bait [fish &c.] [used also familiarly in a fig. sense].

|| or ‡**Erkören**, *v. tr.* to select, to choose [chiefly used in the past participle] Erkoren, chosen. Die Erkorenen, the elect.

Erkösen, I. *v. tr.* to obtain by caressing or coaxing. Sie erkosete es von ihm, she coaxed or wheedled him out of it. II. [unusual] *v. r.* sich mit Jemand —, to amuse one's self by caressing a person.

Erkrächen, *v. intr.* to crash.

Erkrächzen, *v. intr.* to croak.

Erkrällen, *v. tr.* to seize with the claws.

Erkränkeln, *v. intr.* [u. w. seyn] to become sickly.

Erkränken, *v. intr.* [u. w. seyn] to fall sick.

Erkrätzen, *v. tr.* to get by scratching. †*Fig.* to obtain by niggardliness.

Erkriechen, *ir. v. tr.* to reach creeping. *Fig.* to obtain by cringing.

1. **Erkriegen**, [from the somewhat vulgar verb kriegen = to get] *v. tr.* V. [the more usual words] Bekommen, Ergreifen.

2. **Erkriegen**, [from Krieg = war] *v. tr.* to wage war, or to gain by war. Länder —, to conquer, to win countries; Ehre —, to get renown by waging war.

Erkritzeln, [in fam. lang.] *v. tr.* to get by writing unskilfully and inelegantly, to acquire by scribbling.

Erkrümmen, [rather unusual] *v. intr.* [u. w. seyn] to become crooked.

Erkrümmen, [rather unusual] *v. tr.* to crook [a wire].

Erkühlen, I. *v. intr.* [u. w. seyn] to become cool, to cool. II. *v. tr.* to cool, to refresh, to refrigerate.

Erkühnen, *v. r.* sich —, to dare, to venture. Er erkühnt sich, Dinge zu behaupten, die er nicht weiß, he ventures to assert things which he does not know; er erkühnte sich, den König anzureden, he was bold enough to address the king.

Erkümmern, *v. tr.* to save by living poorly.

Erkünden, I. *v. tr.* to explore. Moses sandte Kundschafter aus, um das Land von Canaan zu —, Moses sent spies to explore the land of Canaan; das feindliche Lager —, to reconnoitre the enemy's camp. II. *v. r.* sich —, V. [the more usual word] Erkundigen, sich.

Erkündigen, I. *v. tr.* V. Erkunden. II. *v. r.* sich —, to inquire. Erkundige dich nach Saul von Tarsus, inquire for Saul of Tarsus; erkundige dich nach dem rechten Wege, inquire for the right road, inquire after the right way; sie hatten sich nach Simons Hause erkundigt, they had made inquiry for Simon's house; haben Sie sich wegen dieser Angelegenheit erkundiget? have you made inquiries concerning or about that affair? erkundige dich bei ihm, inquire of him; sich — lassen, to cause inquiry to be made; ich will mich nach seinem Befinden — lassen, I will send to enquire, send to know how he finds himself. Die Erkundigung, inquiry, information. Erkundigung einziehen, to make inquiry.

Erkündschaften, *v. tr.* to find out, to detect. V. Auskundschaften.

Erkünsteln, *v. tr.* 1) [rather unusual] to effect by nice elaboration, to bring about by artificial means. 2) *Fig.* to study the appearance of what is not natural, or real, to affect. Ernst —, to affect to be grave; sie erkünstelt Liebe, she feigns love; erkünstelte Freundschaft, affected friendship; erkünstelte Thränen, artificial tears. Die Erkünstelung, affectation.

Erküppeln, *v. tr.* to acquire or to obtain by panderism.

Erläben, *v. tr.* to refresh. Sich —, to refresh one's self. *Fig.* V. Ergetzen.

Erlächen, [rather unusual] *v. tr.* to obtain by a laugh.

Erlähmen, *v. intr.* [u. w. seyn] to grow lame.

Erlängen, *v. tr.* to touch by extending the arm, to reach. *Fig. a)* to attain, to reach, to gain possession of by almost any means. Man erlangt Aemter durch Gunst, offices are procured by favour; eine Erbschaft —, to obtain an inheritance; viel Vermögen —, to get a large fortune; seinen Zweck —, to attain one's end; die Freiheit —, to get free; seine Freiheit wieder —, to recover one's liberty; Jemands Freundschaft —, to win any one's friendship; Verzeihung —, to obtain one's pardon; durch Bitten —, to obtain by request or entreaty, to impetrate; den Sieg —, to gain the victory, to carry the day; Fertigkeit —, to acquire skill; Ruf —, to gain reputation; Ruhm —, to gain fame; Einfluß —, to gain influence, to win upon. *b)* to persuade, to induce. Ich konnte es nicht von ihm — &c., I could not prevail with, on or upon him &c. Die Erlangung, the act of attaining or obtaining, attainment.

Erlängen, *v. tr.* to extend in length, to lengthen, to prolong, to prolongate.

Erlängern, *v. tr.* V. Erlängen.

||**Erlänglich**, *adj.* and *adv.* attainable, obtainable.

Erläß, *m.* [-sses, *pl.* -sse] 1) remission [of a tax, or duty &c.]. 2) an order, decree, edict.

Erlaß-brief, *m.* a letter, writing or deed dispensing with an obligation or duty, dispensation, dispense. —**geld**, *n.* money paid for dispensation. —**jahr**, *n.* [among the Jews] *a)* every fiftieth year, jubilee. *b)* a release. Ueber sieben Jahre sollst du ein —jahr halten, [in Script.] at the end of every seven years thou shalt make a release. —**recht**, *n.* V. Erlassungsrecht. —**schein**, *m.* V. Erlassungsschein. —**sünde**, *f.* V. Erlassungssünde.

Erlässen, *ir. v. tr.* 1) [= fortlassen] Einen der Haft —, to release any one from confinement, to set any one free. *Fig.* to free from obligation or penalty. Einen seines Versprechens or Einem sein Versprechen —, to release any one from a promise; Einen des Eides or Einem den Eid —, to dispense any one with an oath; ich kann Ihnen die Ausführung dieses Auftrags nicht —, I cannot dispense you from the execution of this commission; Einem eine Schuld —, to release any one from a debt; wenn Einer seinem Nächsten etwas geliehen hat, der soll's ihm —, [in Scripture] every creditor that lendeth ought unto his neighbour shall release it; man hat ihm diesen Frohndienst —, he is exempted from that piece of vassalage; die Strafe —, to remit punishment; Einem die Strafe —, to pardon any one; welchen ihr die Sünden erlasset, denen sind sie —, [in Script.] whose soever sins ye remit, they are remitted to them. 2) to transmit from one's self to another by writing. Ein Schreiben an Einen —, to write a letter to any one; einen Befehl —, to issue an order; eine Vorschrift —, to issue a precept.

Erläßlich, *adj.* and *adv.* dispensable, remissible. —e Sünden, venial sins [in opposed to mortal sins].

Erläßlichkeit, *f.* dispensableness.

Erlässung, *f.* release, remission, dispensation, dispense. Die — der Sünden, the remission of sins, absolution.

Erlassungs-recht, *n.* the right of dispensation, or remission. —**schein**, *m.* a writing, a note by which any thing is remitted. —**sünde**, *f.* a venial sin.

Erlaüben, *v. tr.* to allow, to permit, to grant license to. Die Gesetze — das zu thun, was nicht ausdrücklich verboten ist, the laws permit us to do what is not expressly forbid; ich erlaube dir zu kommen, I give you leave to come; — Sie mir &c., give me your permission &c.; ein erlaubtes Vergnügen, an innocent pleasure; ein erlaubter Handel, a legal or an innocent trade; gesetzlich erlaubt, permitted by law; man erlaube mir, I beg leave; es ist ihm erlaubt, he is permitted; seine Dürftigkeit erlaubt ihm nicht &c., his indigence does not permit him &c.

Erlaübniß, *f.* [*pl.* -sse] allowance, license or liberty granted, permission, permittance. — geben, to grant permission; die — haben, to be permitted; die obrigkeitliche — bekommen, einen Gasthof zu halten, to be licensed to keep an inn; um — bitten, to beg leave; [as a word of civility] mit Ihrer —, with your permission, under your favour.

Erlaubnißbrief, *m.* license, letters patent.

Erlaübtheit, *f.* the quality of being permitted.

Erlaücht, *adj.* & *adv.* 1) [formerly] renowned, illustrious, eminent. 2) [a title of honour] illustrious. Der —e Graf, the noble count; Eure — your highness; eine —e Gesellschaft, a noble company.

Erlaüen, [unusual] I. *v. intr.* [u. w. seyn] to become lukewarm or tepid. 2) to cool. II. *v. tr.* to make lukewarm, to warm.

Erlaüern, *v. tr.* 1) to obtain by lurking. to lay wait for. Einen —, to waylay any o *Fig.* Die Gelegenheit —, to watch for an opportunity.

Erlaüfen, *ir. v. tr.* 1) to overtake in runni *Prov.* Einen reifen Dieb erläuft ein hink Scherge, punishment will overtake a thief for the gallows. 2) to obtain by running af Sich Hunger —, to get hungry by running; ein Amt —, to obtain a place by dint of runn after it.

Erlaüschen, *v. tr.* to obtain or to learn listening. Ein Geheimniß —, to discover a cret by listening, to overhear a secret. *Fig.* Gelegenheit —, to watch for an opportun einen Vortheil —, to be on the watch for so gain or profit.

Erläütern, *v. tr.* to make clear, to clea fine. *Fig.* to make clear, intelligible or obv Eine Frage —, to clear a question; ein Be wird den Gegenstand —, an example will elu date the subject; eine Stelle der Schrift — illustrate a passage of Scripture; einen Sch steller —, to gloss an author; ein — des Urth an analytical judgment.

Erläüterung, *f.* 1) the act of elucidati illustrating, elucidation, illustration, expla tion. 2) [words or things intended to elucidate a su ject] elucidation, illustration, explanation. E Beispiel mag zur — des Gegenstandes dien an example may serve for an elucidation of t subject; ein Beweis oder Gleichniß, welches

— eines Gegenstandes dient, an argument or simile illustrative of the subject; kurze —en, short remarks intended to illustrate a subject, short glosses or comments.

Erläuterungszeichen, *n.* [in grammar] a colon [:].

Erle, *f.* [*pl.* -n] [also Elder, Lat. *alnus*; either from the old *al* = Wasser, or more probably allied to the Lat. *alo* = wachsen machen] 1) alder. ||2) V. Faulbaum.

Erlen-baum, *m.* alder, alder-tree. —bruch, *m.* a marshy place overgrown with alders, alder-plot. —busch, *m.* a grove of alder-trees. —fink, *m.* [a bird] the siskin or aberdavine. —gang, *m.* a walk or an avenue set with alders. —holz, *n.* alder-wood. Von —holz, aldern. —könig, *m.* V. Erlkönig. —laub, *n.* the leaves of an alder. —rinde, *f.* the bark of an alder. —strauch, *m.* a shrubby alder. —wald, *m.* alder-bed.

Erleben, *v. tr.* 1) to come at, to reach as with one's life. Sein achtzigstes Jahr —, to attain one's eightieth year of age; er hat es nicht erlebt, he did not live to see it; er wird die Nacht nicht —, he will die before night comes on; ich werde nie den Tag —, I shall never see the day. 2) to try by use, by suffering or by enjoyment. Kummer oder Freude —, to experience sorrow or pleasure; er hat viel Unglück erlebt, he has experienced many misfortunes; ein solches Schauspiel erlebte ich noch nie, such a spectacle I never witnessed.

Erledigen, *v. tr.* to ease, to relieve, to exempt. Die Schulter von einer Last —, to ease the shoulder of a load; das Erz von dem Gebirge —, [in metallurgy] to wash the ore. *Fig.* ||*a*) to release from confinement. Einen Gefangenen —, to set a prisoner at liberty, to discharge a prisoner; der Gefangene ist der Haft erlediget, the prisoner is freed from arrest. *b*) to free, to disengage from. Einen einer Verbindlichkeit, Pflicht oder Schuld —, to release any one from an obligation, a duty or debt; Einen der Sorgen or von den Sorgen —, to free any one from cares. *c*) to finish, to settle. Die Sache ist erlediget, the cause is decided; einen Zweifel —, to remove a doubt. *d*) to make vacant, to vacate. Ein erledigter Thron, a vacant throne; die erledigte Stelle, a vacancy.

Erledigung, *f.* 1) release. 2) [the state of being destitute of an incumbent] vacancy. Die — einer Pfründe, avoidance.

Erledigungsschein, *m.* a note of acquittance, a receipt.

Erlegen, *v. tr.* 1) to slay, to kill. Einen Gegner —, to slay one's adversary; einen Hirsch —, to bring down, to shoot a stag. 2) to pay down. Steuern —, to pay taxes; eine Geldstrafe —, to pay a fine.

Erlehren, *v. tr.* 1) to gain or to acquire by teaching. 2) to effect by teaching.

Erleichtern, I. *v. tr.* 1) to make lighter. Ein Schiff —, to lighten a ship [by unloading]. *Fig.* Sorgen —, to alleviate or to slacken cares; meinen Kummer zu —, to assuage my grief; Pioniere können den Marsch eines Heeres —, pioneers may facilitate the march of an army; ein Amt —, to facilitate the discharge of an office; erleichtere du die Knechtschaft deines Vaters, ease thou the servitude of thy father; sie fühlt sich sehr erleichtert, she finds herself very much eased; sein Gewissen —, to clear one's conscience. 2) to ease, to relieve. Er erleichtert mein Herz des Grames or vom Grame, he relieves my heart from sorrow. II. *v. r.* sich —, 1) to ease one's self of any burden. 2) to ease one's self = to ease the belly.

Erleichterung, *f.* 1) the act of lightening &c. 2) alleviation, relief. Die Theilnahme der Freunde dient dem Bedrängten or Bekümmerten zu einiger —, the sympathy of friends affords some relief to the distressed.

Erleichterungsmittel, *n.* an alleviation [of grief &c.].

Erleiden, *ir. v. tr.* to suffer, to bear, to undergo, to sustain. Einen Verlust —, to sustain a loss.

Erleiern, *v. tr.* to get or to acquire by playing on the hurdy-gurdy.

Erlen, *adj.* and *adv.* aldern.

Erlernbar, *adj.* & *adv.* that may be learned.

Erlernen, *v. tr.* to learn [the principles of a science &c.]. Eine Sprache —, to learn a language.

Erlesen, *ir. v. tr.* 1) to choose or take from a number, to select, to pick out, to cull. Erlesene Truppen, select troops; eine erlesene Gesellschaft, a select company or society. 2) to acquire, to get by lecturing [on any art or science]. Er hat sich ein großes Vermögen —, he got a large fortune by his lectures.

‡**Erletzen**, V. Erlaben.

Erleuchten, *v. tr.* to light, to illume, to illumine, to illuminate. Die Sonne erleuchtet die Erde, the sun enlightens the earth; die Straßen einer Stadt —, to light the streets of a town; seine Blitze — die Welt, his lightnings enlighten the world; ein Haus — [with lamps &c.], to illuminate a house; einen Theil eines Gemähldes —, to illuminate a part of a picture. *Fig.* to illuminate, to enlighten, to illume, to illumine. Den Verstand —, to enlighten the mind or understanding; ein erleuchteter Verstand, a clear understanding; ein erleuchteter Mann, a well-instructed or informed man; denn es ist unmöglich, daß die, so einmahl erleuchtet sind, und geschmeckt haben die himmlische Gabe &c., [in Scripture] for it is impossible for those who were once enlightened, and have tasted of the heavenly gift &c.; gedenket aber an die vorigen Tage, in welchen ihr, erleuchtet, erduldet habt einen großen Kampf des Leidens, [in Scripture] but call to remembrance the former days, in which, after ye were illuminated, ye endured a great fight of afflictions.

Erleuchtung, *f.* 1) the act of illuminating or rendering luminous, illumination. 2) [festal lamps or lights hung out as a token of joy] illumination. 3) the state of being illuminated. *Fig.* *a*) [infusion of intellectual light] illumination. *b*) [the special communication of knowledge to the mind by the Supreme Being] illumination.

Erliegen, *ir. v. intr.* [u. w. haben and seyn] 1) [unusual] to lie. 2) to be overwhelmed or depressed, to sink. Einer Last or unter einer Last —, to sink under a burden. *Fig.* Unser Vaterland erliegt dem Joche, our country sinks beneath the yoke; Trübsalen —, to succumb under calamities.

Erlindern, [unusual] *v. tr.* to make or cause to be more mild, to soften, to mitigate.

Erlisten, *v. tr.* to obtain by art or cunning.

Erlkönig, **Erlenkönig**, *m.* [-s, *pl.* -e] a fabulous being in the ancient German mythology and popular superstitions, the erl-king.

Erlogen, [past part. of Erlügen] *adj.* and *adv.* not true, not conformable to fact, false. Eine —e Nachricht, false news; die Geschichte ist —, the story is untrue.

Erlös, *m.* [-ses, *pl.* -se] [the sum of goods sold or converted into money] the proceeds.

Erlöschen, I. *ir. v. intr.* [u. w. seyn] to become extinct, to go out. Ein Licht erlischt, a candle goes out; das Licht ist erloschen, the light is extinct, or out; das Feuer erlischt, the fire goes out. *Fig.* *a*) to diminish in light, to lose light, to become invisible or indistinct. Der Tag erlischt, the day declines; das Leben erlischt, life goes out; die Töne sind erloschen, the sounds died away; die Schrift ist erloschen, the writing is obliterated [by the slow operation of time or natural causes]. *b*) to cease to exist. Eine Familie oder ein Geschlecht ist erloschen, a family or race is extinct; seine Liebe ist erloschen, his love is gone. II. *v. tr.* to put out, to extinguish [fire &c.].

Erlöschung, *f.* extinction.

Erlosen, *v. tr.* to obtain by drawing lots.

Erlösen, *v. tr.* 1) to redeem, to ransom. Ein Pfand —, to redeem a pledge; einen Gefangenen —, to ransom a prisoner. *Fig.* [= erretten or befreien] Einen aus der Gefangenschaft —, to rescue or to deliver any one from captivity; [= befreien] er ist nun von seinen Leiden erlöset, i. e. er ist gestorben, he is now delivered from his sufferings; [in Script.] to redeem; sondern erlöse uns von dem Uebel, [the Lord's prayer] but deliver us from evil; Gott, erlöse Israel aus aller seiner Noth, redeem Israel, o God, out of all his troubles; Christus aber hat uns erlöset von dem Fluche des Gesetzes, Christ has redeemed us from the curse of the law; ich will sie — aus der Hölle, und vom Tode erretten, I will ransom them from the grave and redeem them from death; die Erlöseten des Herrn werden wiederkommen, the ransomed of the Lord shall return. Syn. V. Befreien. 2) to get by selling goods or converting them into money. Das erlösete Geld, the proceeds.

Erlöser, *m.* [-s, *pl.* -] 1) one who redeems or ransoms, redeemer. 2) the saviour of the world, the redeemer, Jesus Christ.

Erlösung, *f.* redemption, ransom, release. *Fig.* Die — aus der Gefangenschaft, release from captivity, deliverance; die — von allem Uebel, the releasement of all evils; [in Scripture] redemption; an welchem wir haben die — durch sein Blut, in whom we have redemption through his blood; des Menschen Sohn ist gekommen &c., daß er gäbe sein Leben zu einer — für Viele, the Son of man came &c., to give his life a ransom for many.

Erlösungs-stunde, *f.* the hour of deliverance or redemption. —werk, *n.* the work of redemption.

|| and †**Erluchsen**, *v. tr.* V. Erlisten.

Erlügen, *ir. v. tr.* 1) to contrive falsely, to forge, to fabricate, to invent. V. Erlogen. 2) to assume a false appearance, to make a show of, to pretend, to counterfeit, to feign, to affect. Seine Gelassenheit ist erlogen, his calmness is feigned.

|| and ‡**Erlungern**, *v. tr.* to obtain by covetousness or greediness.

Erlusten, [more usual] **Erlustigen**, *v. tr.* to divert, to amuse. Sich —, to amuse one's self; *er erlustigt sich eben an einer gebratenen Hammelskeule, he is enjoying himself on a roasted leg of mutton; sich über Einen —, to make sport of any one.

Erlustigung, *f.* diversion, sport, play, pastime. Die —en der Jugend, the diversions of youth.

Ermächtigen, I. *v. tr.* to authorize, to empower. Einen zu etwas —, to empower any one to do any thing. II. *v. r.* sich —, to seize and hold in possession by force or without right. V. [the more usual word] Bemächtigen.

Ermächtigung, *f.* 1) authorization. 2) usurpation.

Ermagern, [unusual] *v. intr.* [u. w. seyn] to

become lean, to lose flesh, to fall away.

1. **Ermahlen**, [from mahlen = to grind] *v. tr.* 1) to get through grinding or milling, to grind or mill to the end. 2) to get or acquire by grinding or milling.

2. **Ermahlen**, [from mahlen = to paint] *v. tr.* 1) to get through painting. 2) to get or acquire by painting.

Ermahnen, *v. tr.* 1) to incite by words or advice, to exhort. Einen Schuldner — [= mahnen], to endeavour to obtain by reminding any one of a debt, to dun a debtor, und nun ermahne ich euch, daß ihr unverzagt seid, [in Scripture] and now I exhort you to be of good cheer. 2) to warn or notify of a fault, to reprove with mildness. Sondern ermahnet ihn als einen Bruder, [in Script.] but admonish him as a brother. ||3) to remind [any one of a thing]. Einen seines Versprechens —, to remind any one of his promise.

Ermahner, *m.* [-s, *pl.* -] an exhorter, admonitor or admonisher, a monitor.

Ermahnung, *f.* 1) [the act of exhorting or admonishing] exhortation, hortation. 2) [words, arguments used to incite to good deeds] exhortation. *it.* [gentle reproof] admonition.

Ermahnungs-rede, *f.* a hortatory speech. —**schreiben**, *n.* a hortatory letter.

Ermangeln, *v. intr.* and *imp.* 1) to be wanting or deficient. Die Kraft ermangelt ihm, his strength fails, ich kann nicht schreiben, denn mir ermangelt die Zeit, I cannot write for want of time; ich will es an meinem Fleiße nicht — lassen, my application shall not be wanting; es ermangelt ihm nicht an gutem Willen, he wants no good will. 2) to fail, to omit, not to perform. Ich werde nicht —, zu kommen, I shall not fail to come.

Ermangelung, *f.* defect, want, failure. In — von &c., in fault of, in default of &c.

Ermannen, I. *v. intr.* [u. w. seyn] to show one's self a man. II *v. r.* sich —, to resume courage, to pluck up the heart. III. *v. tr.* to strengthen, to fortify [the mind &c.].

Ermartern, *v. tr.* to extort.

Ermäßigen, *v. tr.* 1) to lessen, to diminish, to abate, to moderate. 2) [in law &c.] to consider, to judge.

Ermatten, I. *v. intr.* [u. w. seyn] to become feeble, to decline or fail in strength and vigour, to faint. Die Kraft ermattet, the strength flags. *Fig.* Farben — und schwinden, colours fade and vanish. II. *v. tr.* to deprive of strength, to enfeeble, to weaken; *it.* to tire, to weary, to fatigue. Große Hitze ermattet, a great heat weakens; der lange und beschwerliche Weg ermattete uns ziemlich, the long and difficult way fatigued us considerably. Die Ermattung, lassitude, weakness, weariness.

Ermeißeln, *v. tr.* 1) to chisel through [a stone &c.]. 2) to get or acquire by chiseling.

Ermel, V. Ärmel.

|| and ‡**Ermelden**, *v. tr.* to quote, to mention. Obermeldeter Bescheid, the above-mentioned decree.

Ermessen, *ir. v. tr.* [rather unusual in the proper sense] to measure. Die Tiefe des Meeres —, to sound the sea. *Fig* *a*) to judge, to value. Andere nach sich —, to judge of others by one's self. *b*) to ponder in the mind, to consider or examine, to weigh, to judge, to think, to esteem. Nach meinem —, to my judgment. *c*) to deduce. Daraus mögen Sie das Uebrige —, thence you may infer the rest. *d*) to conceive, to understand, to comprehend. Ich kann nicht —, wie &c., I cannot conceive how &c.

Ermeßlich, *adj.* and *adv.* susceptible of measuration, measurable.

Ermetzeln, *v. tr.* 1) [rather unusual] to slaughter, to butcher, to kill, to slay. 2) to get through slaughtering &c., to slaughter to the end.

Ermeucheln, *v. tr.* to assassinate.

Ermildern, *v. tr.* to moderate.

Ermorden, *v. tr.* to kill with premeditated malice, to murder, to slay. Der Ermordete, a murdered or slain person. Die Ermordung, murder.

Ermüden, I. *v. intr.* [u. w. seyn] to become weary, to be fatigued, to tire. Ein schwacher Körper ermüdet bald bei schwerer Arbeit, a feeble body soon tires with hard labour; einer Sache —, to become weary, to weary of a thing. II. *v. tr.* to weary, to tire, to fatigue. Eine ermüdende Arbeit, a fatiguing labour; eine ermüdende Reise, a tiresome journey; ein ermüdendes Tagewerk, a wearisome day's work; sich —, to weary one's self *Fig.* Einen durch Zudringlichkeit —, to weary any one by importunity, to fatigue him.

Ermüdlich, *adj.* and *adv.* that may be wearied, fatigable.

Ermühen, *v. tr.* to get or obtain by trouble or pains.

Ermuntern, *v. tr.* to wake from sleep or repose, to rouse. Sich —, to cease to sleep, to waken. *Fig. a*) to make cheerful, gay or joyous, to enliven. Guter Wein ermuntert das Gemüth, good wine exhilarates the mind, sie — die Düstergestimmten, they enliven the gloomy. *b*) to excite, rouse or animate to action or more vigorous exertion by some pungent motive or by persuasion, to incite, to stimulate, to encourage, to animate. Einen durch die Aussicht auf Ruhm —, to stimulate any one by the prospect of glory; Einen durch Belohnungen zu größerm Fleiße —, to excite any one to greater application by recompenses.

Ermunterung, *f.* 1) the act of rousing; *fig.* incitement to action or to practice. Eine — zur Tugend, an encouragement to virtue. 2) [that which serves to incite or encourage] encouragement. Die Künste bedürfen der —, arts want encouragement.

Ermürben, [unusual] I. *v. intr.* [u. w. seyn] to become tender, as flesh. II. *v. tr.* to make tender.

Ermuthen, **Ermuthigen**, *v. tr.* to give courage to, to give or increase confidence of success, to encourage, to embolden, to animate, to incite, to inspirit. Sich —, to resume courage, to pluck up the heart. Die Ermuthigung, the act of giving courage to, of encouraging.

Ern, a termination to many verbs and adjectives. Annexed to verbs it denotes bringing into any state or condition, an imitation, an iteration of the same act, or a desire to be present in any state; annexed to adjectives it denotes the stuff or matter of which any thing is formed, as, beinern, gläsern &c, excepting such adjectives which are used only in a moral sense, as albern, lüstern, nüchtern, schüchtern &c.

Ernähen, *v. tr.* to gain by sewing. Sich seinen Unterhalt —, to get one's livelihood by needle-work.

Ernähren, I. *v. tr.* to nourish, to support, to maintain by feeding. Seine Familie —, to support one's family; es hält schwer, in diesem Lande ein Heer zu —, it is difficult to subsist an army in this country; sich von Jemanden — lassen, to depend upon somebody for one's maintenance. *Prov.* Friede ernährt, Unfriede verzehrt, by wisdom peace, by peace plenty. II. *v. r.* sich —, to maintain one's self [by trade or labour &c.]. Er ernährt sich von Almosen, he subsists on charity; die Vögel — sich von Saamen und Ziefern, fowls live or feed on seeds and insects.

Ernährer, *m.* [-s, *pl.* -] nourisher, supporter.

Ernährerinn, *f.* a female, that nourishes or supports.

Ernährung, *f.* sustenance, maintenance, sustentation. Die — einer Familie, the maintenance of a family.

Ernährungs-art, *f.* the kind, method or means of maintenance, nourishing or nourishment. —**geschäft**, *n.* nutrition. —**kunde**, *f.* [in medicine] dietetics.

Erndte, **Erndten**, V. Ernte, Ernten.

Ernennen, *ir. v. tr.* to name or designate by name for an office or place, to nominate, to appoint. Zu einer Stelle —, to appoint to an office; Einen zu einem geistlichen Amte —, to collate any one to an ecclesiastical benefice; Einen zum Richter —, to create any one a judge; Einen zum Erben —, to nominate any one as heir.

Ernenner, *m.* [-s, *pl.* -] he that appoints to a place, nominator.

Ernennung, *f.* the act of naming or appointing to office, designation to office, appointment, nomination Die — zu einem geistlichen Amte durch den Bischof, collation; die — von Pairs in England, the creation of peers in England.

Ernennungs-brief, *m.* a diploma, commission. —**recht**, *n.* the power of nominating or appointing to office, nomination. —**urkunde**, *f.* V. —brief.

Erneuen, **Erneuern**, I. *v. tr.* 1) to restore to a former state, or to a good state after decay or depravation, to renew, to renovate. Ein Haus —, to rebuild or repair a house; ein Gemählde —, to refresh a picture; ein Kleid —, to mend a garment; einen Weinberg —, to renew a vineyard, und erneuete den Altar des Herrn, [in Scripture] and renewed the altar of the Lord. [in a more limited sense] *a*) to put a competent substitute in the place of another displaced or of something old or decayed. Die Beamten —, to appoint new officers. *b*) to begin again. Den Krieg —, to renew a war; einen Streit —, to recommence a contest; wenn die Sonne ihren Lauf erneuert, when the sun shall renew his course. *c*) to renew, to revive. Das Andenken großer Männer — [erneuern], to revive the memory of great men. *d*) to renew, to reestablish, to confirm. Laßt uns gen Gilgal gehen, und das Königreich daselbst —, [in Script.] let us go to Gilgal and renew the kingdom there. *e*) to renew, to repeat. Ein Versprechen —, to renew a promise; einen Versuch —, to renew an attempt; Freundschaftsversicherungen —, to renew expressions of friendship. *f*) to make again, to renew. Einen Vertrag —, to renew a treaty; ein Pacht, der nach Belieben erneuert werden kann, a renewable lease. *g*) [in theology] to make new, to renovate, to transform, to renew. Erneuert euch aber im Geist eures Gemüths, [in Script.] and be renewed in the spirit of your mind. II. *v. r.* sich —, to begin anew. Mein Schmerz erneuert sich, my pain begins anew; das Jahr erneuert sich, the year returns.

Erneuer, **Erneuerer**, *m.* [-s, *pl.* -] renewer.

Erneuern, V. Erneuen.

Erneuung, **Erneuerung**, *f.* 1) the act of renewing, renewal, renovation. Die — eines Vertrags, the renewal of a treaty. 2) [a state of being renewed] renovation, renewal, renewedness.

Erniedern, *v. tr.* to make low, to lower. *Fig.* Einen redlichen Mann —, to debase an honest man; Einen —, to degrade any one; sich —, to humble one's self. Die Erniederung lowering; *fig.* debasing.

Erniedrigen, *v. tr.* to reduce in altitude or magnitude, to lower. *Fig. a)* to reduce low, to humble, to humiliate, to degrade. Wer sich selbst erhöhet, der wird erniedriget werden, [in Script.] whosoever exalteth himself shall be abased; Völlerei und Wollust — den Menschen unter das Thier, intemperance and debauchery debase men almost to a level with beasts; das Laster erniedrigt uns in den Augen Anderer, vice degrades a man in the view of others. *b)* to let down. Sich —, to humble one's self; Christus hat sich selbst erniedriget, Christ humbled himself. c) to stoop or descend, to sink into debasement, to condescend. Mein Gemüth wird sich nimmer dazu —, my mind will never condescend to it.

Erniedriger, *m.* [-s, *pl.* -] debaser.

Erniedrigung, *f.* the act of reducing in altitude, lowering, degradation. *Fig. a)* abasement, debasement, degradation. Die — des Adels, the depression of the nobility. *b)* [descent from an elevated state or rank to one that is low and humble] humiliation Christus im Stande der —, Christ in the state of humiliation.

Ernst, [a name of men] [-s, *pl.* -e] Ernest.

Ernst, *m.* [-es, without a *pl.*] [appears to be allied to the Sw. *arna* = to work] 1) ardour and zeal in the pursuit of any thing. Eine Arbeit mit — unternehmen, to engage in a work with earnestness; er studirt mit — die allgemeine Erdkunde, he is intently employed in the study of geology. 2) earnest, seriousness. In vollem —e, in good earnest; ist es Ihr —, oder machen or treiben Sie Scherz? are you in earnest or in jest? gieb Acht, daß aus diesem Scherze nicht dereinst — wird, take heed that this jest do not one day turn to earnest; bis sie in allem —e starb, till she came to die for good and all; in reinem —e, in sober sadness. 3) gravity of manner or of mind, seriousness, sobriety. Er sprach mit vielem —e, he spoke with great seriousness, or with an air of seriousness; der — dieses Schauspiels, the solemnity of this spectacle. 4) sternness, severity. — brauchen, to use severity; mit — Einen zurechtweisen, to reprimand any one severely; Einen alles —es bedeuten, to enjoin on any one sternly.

Ernst-feuer, *n.* a firing with grenades, fire-balls &c. **—voll**, *adj.* and *adv.* serious, grave, with great se iousness.

Ernst, [V. Ernst *m.*] *adj.* and *adv.* 1) being in earnest, serious, not jesting or making a false pretence. Sein —es Benehmen, his serious carriage, his grave demeanour or conduct; ein —er Blick, ein —es Aussehen, a grave look, a grave appearance; ein —es Wort, a serious word; eine —e Stille, a solemn silence; die —en Thorheiten der Weisen und Großen, the sober follies of the wise and great. 2) [sometimes for] stern, severe, austere. Ein —er Blick, a stern look; — sprach er &c. aus, sternly he pronounced &c.

Ernsten, [unusual] *v. intr.* to speak seriously or in earnest [as opposed to jest].

Ernsthaft, *adj.* and *adv.* grave in manner or disposition, serious. Ein —er Mann, a serious man; ein —es Gesicht, a serious or grave countenance; mit einer —en Miene, with an air of seriousness; er sprach sehr —, he spoke with great seriousness; ein —es Benehmen, a grave deportment; — lächelt die Königinn, the queen gravely smiles; ein —es Gespräch, a serious conversation; was scheidet das muntere Frankreich von dem —en Spanien? what parts gay France from sober Spain? *Fig.* serious, important. Ein —es Gefecht, a serious fight; eine —e Wunde, a serious wound.

Ernsthaftigkeit, *f.* seriousness, graveness, gravity, sobriety, soberness.

Ernstlich, *adj.* and *adv.* really intending what is said, being in earnest. Ein —er Befehl, an express order; —e Worte, forcible words; —? in earnest? ganz —, in sober sadness; sagt mir —, wen Ihr liebt, tell me in earnest who she is you love; er sprach so —, he spoke with so much earnestness; denke — über das nach, was gesprochen wurde, think seriously of what has been spoken; es ist mein —er Wille, den Uebertreter gerichtlich zu belangen, it is my express will to prosecute the trespasser; er beschäftigt sich — damit, he is intently employed in it; er gab ihm einen —en Verweis, he gave him a grave reprimand.

Ernte, *f.* [*pl.* -n] [ären and arnen signified formerly erwerben in general; in Sw. *arna* is = arbeiten] 1) originally = the getting in of the crops, the crops themselves. *a)* [the ripe corn or grain collected and secured in barns or stacks] harvest. Die — fällt dieses Jahr reichlich aus, the harvest this year is abundant; eine gesegnete —, a plenteous crop. *b)* any fruits or produce collected or gathered. Die Wein—, vintage; die Seiden—, the gathering of cocoons. *Fig.* any gain or profit, fruit. Sie werden eine gute — dabei halten, they will derive great fruits from it. 2) [the season of reaping and gathering in corn and other crops] harvest, reaping-time. Die Weizen—, the wheat-harvest; die Heu—, the hay-harvest; die — nahet heran, the harvest is approaching. *Fig. a)* [the proper season for business]. *Prov.* Wer in der — schläft, wird zu Schanden, he that sleepeth in harvest, is a son that causes shame. *b)* [a seasonable time for instructing men in the Gospel] Darum bittet den Herrn der —, daß er Arbeiter in seine — sende, pray ye therefore the Lord of the harvest, that he will send forth labourers into his harvest; lasset beides mit einander wachsen bis zur —; die — ist das Ende der Welt, let grow both together until the harvest; the harvest is the end of the world. 3) the fruits of the earth, which are gathered, crop Die — steht schön, the crops promise well; Gefilde, mit goldenen —n bedeckt, fields covered with golden crops. *Fig.* [a people whose sins have ripened them for judgment] Schlage die Sichel an, denn die — ist reif, [in Script.] put ye in the sickle, for the harvest is ripe.

Ernte-arbeit, *f.* labour in harvest. **—bier**, *n.* harvest-beer. **—dienst**, *m.* service to be rendered to the lord of the manor at harvest-time. **—ferien**, *pl.* the holydays at harvest-time. **—fest**, *n.* the feast made at the gathering of corn, harvest-home. **—frohne**, *f.* V. —dienst. **—geräthschaft**, *f.* implements used in reaping, as reaping-hooks, sickles, scythes. **—göttinn**, *f.* the goddess of corn, Ceres. **—kranz**, *m.* harvest-wreath, harvest-garland. **—lied**, *n.* the song sung by the reapers at the harvest-home, harvest-song. **—mahl**, *n.* the repast at harvest-home. **—monat**, *m.* harvest-month, August. **—predigt**, *f.* a sermon for the harvest, a solemn thanksgiving for the favourable termination of the harvest. **—reif**, *adj* and *adv.* ripe. —reifes Korn, ripe corn. **—schmaus**, *m.* V. —mahl. **—seuche**, *f.* V. Marschkrankheit. **—tag**, *m.* 1) the day when corn or other crops are reaped, the season of reaping and gathering corn, harvest. 2) a day that favours harvesting. **—wagen**, *m.* a cart used for gathering corn or other crops; *it.* a gaily decorated waggon laden with the first produce of the harvest. **—wetter**, *n.* dry weather, good harvest-weather. **—zeit**, *f.* harvest-time, harvest.

Ernten, I. *v. tr.* to reap or gather ripe corn and other fruits, to harvest. Weizen —, to reap wheat; Heu —, to make hay. Das Ernten, inning. *Fig.* Die Früchte seiner Bemühungen —, to reap the fruits of one's exertions; Freuden —, to reap joy; wer auf sein Fleisch säet, der wird von dem Fleisch das Verderben —, [in Scripture] he that soweth to the flesh, shall of the flesh reap corruption; darum säet euch Gerechtigkeit, und erntet Liebe, [in Script.] sow to yourselves righteousness, reap in mercy. II. *v. intr.* to reap. Im Juli —, to reap in July. *Prov.* Wie man säet, so wird man —, as they sow, so let them reap. *Fig.* Die mit Thränen säen, werden mit Freuden —, [in Scripture] they that sow in tears, shall reap in joy.

Ernter, *m.* [-s, *pl.* -] a labourer in gathering grain, a reaper, harvester.

Ernüchtern, [rather unusual] I. *v. intr.* [u. w. seyn] to become sober, to recover from intoxication. II. *v. r.* sich —, to cease to sleep, to waken.

Eröberer, *m.* [-s, *pl.* -] conqueror.

Erobern, *v. tr.* 1) to save, to spare, to lay by, to gain, to win. V. [the usual word] Erübrigen. *Es ist dabei nichts zu —, there is nothing to be got by it. 2) to take possession by violent means, to gain by force. Alexander eroberte Asien, Alexander conquered Asia; ein Heer erobert ein Land oder eine Stadt, an army conquers a country or a city; er eroberte viele Inseln, he won many islands; eine Festung mit Sturm —, to take a fort by assault; ein Schiff —, to capture a ship. *Fig.* Herzen —, to win hearts; ihre Tugend und Schönheit erobert jedes Herz, her virtue and beauty overcomes every heart; den Frieden —, to conquer peace; Einen —, to win a man's love. SYN. Erobern, Einnehmen. Einnehmen signifies in general, to take possession of a thing; erobern implies a forcible taking possession by a sovereign or in his name of what belongs to an enemy. A stranger nimmt ein [occupies] as many rooms in an inn as he has need of and are assigned to him by the landlord; a general erobert [conquers] a country or city, which in the name of his sovereign he takes from the enemy by forcible means.

Eroberung, *f.* 1) [the act of conquering] conquest Die — einer Stadt, the conquest of a city. *Fig.* Die — der Herzen, the conquest of hearts. 2) [that which is conquered] conquest. Es war eine kostbare — für England, it was a valuable conquest for England. *Fig.* *Sie hat eine — an ihm gemacht, she made a conquest of him.

Eroberungs-begierde, *f.* a thirst for conquests. **—gierig**, V. —süchtig. **—krieg**, *m.* a war undertaken in order to conquer countries. **—liebe**, *f.* the love of conquest. **—sucht**, *f.* a thirst of conquest. *Fig.* coquetry. **—süchtig**, *adj.* and *adv.* having a vehement desire of conquering countries. *Fig* Ein —süchtiges Mädchen, a coquet or coquette, a jilt.

Eröffnen, I. *v. tr.* 1) to open [a door &c]. Fremden das Haus —, to give entrance into a house to strangers; einen Brief —, to open or to unclose a letter. *Fig. a)* [in medicine] to open. Ein —des Mittel, an aperient, or an aperitive medicine; die Gefäße, Gänge —d, anastomatic. *b)* [= erlauben] to grant. Die Weide —, to grant leave to graze cattle; den Wald —, to grant leave to enter a wood [which has been in defense]. *c)* [= beginnen] Den Ball —, to open the ball, to lead off the dance; den Feldzug —, to open the campaign; eine Sitzung —, to open a session; die Versammlung wurde gestern eröffnet, the assembly opened yesterday. *d)* [= bekannt machen, mittheilen &c.] Er wird seine Missethat —, he shall discover his misdeed; seine Gedanken —, to break one's mind; Einem etwas —, to make known something to any one; die verbündeten Fürsten haben dem spanischen Hofe ihre Absicht eröffnet, the allied sovereigns have notified to the Spanish court their purpose; Einem seine Meinung —, to tell or declare one's mind to any one; ein Urtheil —, to publish a sentence. *e*) Ein Lehen wird eröffnet, a fee becomes vacant [by the death of a feoffee]. 2) [=anfangen, etwas grabend &c. zu machen] Die Laufgräben —, to open the trenches [in military affairs, to begin to dig, or to form the lines of approach]; einen Durchgang —, to open a passage. II. *v. r.* sich —, to open, to unclose itself. *Fig.* Sich einem Freunde —, to open one's heart to a friend.

Eröffnung, *f.* 1) the opening [of a house, garden &c.]. *Fig. a*) [das Beginnen] Die — des Balles, the opening of the ball; die — einer neuen Schenke, the opening of a new inn. *b*) [something communicated] notification, communication. Die — eines Geheimnisses, the disclosure of a secret; die — eines Testaments, the opening of a will.

Eröffnungs-rede, *f.* 1) an opening speech. 2) prologue. —stück, *n.* the overture [in theatrical entertainments].

Eröftern, [unusual] *v. tr.* to mention often.

Erörtern, *v. tr.* to agitate by argument, to debate, to discuss. Eine Frage —, to discuss or to agitate a question; die Sache war gut erörtert, the cause was well argued; Streitigkeiten —, to decide controversies.

Erörterung, *f.* the agitation of a point or subject with a view to elicit truth, discussion, debate, disquisition.

***Eros**, *m.* [the God of love among the ancient Greeks] Eros.

***Erotisch**, *adj.* and *adv.* erotic, erotical. Ein —es Gedicht, an amorous poem, an erotic.

Erpachten, *v. tr.* to take at a certain rent or rate, to farm. Ein Gut auf ein Jahr —, to rent an estate for a year.

Erpacken, *v. tr.* to take hold of, to seize.

Erpassen, *v. tr.* to wait for. Eine Gelegenheit —, Einen zu beschimpfen, to watch for an opportunity of abusing or insulting any one.

||**Erpel**, *m.* [-s, *pl.* -] V. Enterich.

Erpfeifen, *ir. v. tr.* 1) to call by whistling. 2) to gain by whistling. *Fig.* †to gain by playing on wind-instruments. N. hat sich ein schönes Vermögen mit seiner Flöte erpfiffen, Mr. N. has made a handsome fortune by his flute-blowing.

Erpflügen, *v. tr.* 1) to get over or through plowing. 2) to gain by plowing.

Erpicht, [probably allied to the Sw. *pigg* = Stachel, to the Lat. *pug* in pupngi] [chiefly used in fam. lang.] *adj.* and *adv.* ardently wishing or longing. Der Liebhaber ist — auf den Besitz des Gegenstandes seiner Zuneigung, the lover is eager to possess the object of his affections; — auf das Spiel, given to gaming; — auf ihre Götzen, mad after their idols; auf seine Meinung — seyn, to be headstrong.

Erplündern, *v. tr.* to get by plundering, by pillage.

Erpochen, *v. tr.* 1) to comminute and pulverize by beating, to pound. 2) to rouse by knocking. 3) to get or obtain by knocking.

||**Erprachern**, *v. tr.* to obtain by importunate intreaties.

Erprasseln, *v. intr.* [u. w. seyn] to begin to crackle.

Erpredigen, *v. tr.* to effectuate by preaching; *it.* to earn [glory &c.] by preaching.

Erpressen, *v. tr.* 1) to gain by violence or oppression, to extort. Eroberer — Kriegssteuern von eroberten Ländern, conquerors extort or exact contributions from conquered countries. 2) to extort, to force out, to squeeze out. Er hat mir Thränen erpreßt, he drew tears from me.

Erproben, *v. tr.* 1) to try, to make experiment of, to test. 2) to try, to find by experience. Er ist ein Mann von erprobter Treue, he is a man of proved, tested fidelity; erprobte Eigenschaften, tried qualities; erprobt seyn, to stand the touch. Syn. Erproben, Bewähren. Bewähren signifies simply, to come to the knowledge of the worth and perfection of a thing. Erproben includes also the idea of having obtained this knowledge by actual trial of a thing, by having put it to the test. Ein bewährter Freund, [a known friend] is one, whose friendship by long experience we have become acquainted with; ein erprobter, [a tried friend] one, of whose friendship by repeated proofs we are convinced.

Erprüfen, *v. tr.* 1) to discover by trying. 2) to find by experience. Eine erprüfte Tugend, a tried virtue.

Erprügeln, *v. tr.* to effectuate by cudgeling.

Erquälen, *v. tr.* to obtain by tormenting or teasing.

Erquicken, [from quicken = bewegen, V. Quecksilber] *v. tr.* 1) to give new strength to, to refresh. Einen Durstigen —, to refresh a thirsty person; Nahrung und Ruhe erquickt Menschen und Vieh, man and beast is refreshed by food and rest; ein —der Schlaf, a refreshing sleep; der Regen erquickt die Pflanzen, rain refreshes the plants; die freie Luft erquickt die Lunge ungemein, the open air exceedingly recreates the lungs; sich —, to refresh one's self; und deiner Magd Sohn und Fremdling sich —, [in Scripture] and the son of thy handmaid, and the stranger may be refreshed. 2) to revive, reanimate, to comfort, to quicken, to refresh with joy or hope. Willst du uns denn nicht wieder —? [in Scripture] wilt thou not revive us again? Wenn ich mitten in der Angst wandle, so erquickest du mich, [in Scripture] though I walk in the midst of trouble, thou wilt revive me.

Erquicklich, *adj.* and *adv.* refreshing, recreative.

Erquickung, *f.* 1) the act of refreshing, refreshment. 2) that which gives new strength or vigour, refreshment. Zur — dienend, recreative.

Erquickungs-mahl, *n.* a refreshing meal or repast, a collation.

Erraffen, *v. tr.* to seize hastily or abruptly, to snatch. *Fig.* Die Gelegenheit —, to catch at the opportunity.

Erranken, *v. tr.* to reach by the help of tendrils.

Errasseln, [unusual] *v. intr.* [u. w. seyn] to make a rattling sound.

***Errata**, *pl.* errors or mistakes in writing or printing, errata.

Errathbar, *adj.* and *adv.* that may be guessed, divined or anticipated.

Errathen, *ir. v. tr.* to guess [another's meaning &c.] Könntest du —, was Verliebte dulden, could you divine or conjecture what lovers bear; ein Räthsel —, to find out the meaning of an enigma, to solve, explain or unriddle it; Eines Gedanken —, to guess any one's thoughts, or at any one's thoughts; Sie haben es richtig —, you hit it right; ich errieth die Folgen, I anticipated the consequences; etwas ganz genau —, *prov.* to hit the nail on the head. Die Errathung, guessing.

Errauben, *v. tr.* to get by robbery.

Erraufen, *v. tr.* 1) V. Ausraufen. 2) to get by pulling or plucking.

Errechnen, *v. tr.* 1) to get or obtain by computation. 2) V. Ausrechnen.

Errechten, [rather unusual] *v. tr.* to obtain by lawsuits.

Erreden, *v. tr.* to obtain by speaking or eloquence.

Erregbar, *adj.* and *adv.* easily moved, excitable, irritable.

Erregbarkeit, *f.* excitability, irritability.

Erregen, *v. tr.* 1) to put in action or motion, to raise. Der Wind erreget den Staub, the wind raises the dust; er erregete einen Sturmwind, [in Script.] he raiseth the stormy wind. *Fig. a*) [in medicine] —d, excitatory; ein —des Mittel, an exciter, a stimulant. *b*) to stir up, to raise. Das Volk —, to stir up the people; Aufruhr —, to excite or to stir up an insurrection; Streit —, to stir up strife; Lärm —, to raise tumult; Jemands Zorn —, to raise any one's passion; dieses Verbrechen erregt Gottes Zorn, this crime stirs up God's anger; Verwirrung —, to create confusion; einen Streit —, to blow up a contention; Unzufriedenheit —, to cause discontent; Aerger —, to excite anger, to provoke anger; Schrecken —, to move terror, to alarm; welche die öffentliche Aufmerksamkeit erregt haben, which have excited the public attention; Freude —, to cause joy. 2) [in mining] Ein Bergwerk —, to discover a mine.

Erreger, *m.* [-s, *pl.* -] he that excites, exciter. *Fig.* that which excites, exciter, excitement, stimulant.

Erregung, *f.* excitation, incitation, incitement.

Erregungs-lehre, *f.* [in medicine] the doctrine of stimulants. V. Reizlehre. —mittel, *n.* [in medicine] a stimulant.

Erreiben, *ir. v. tr.* 1) to get over or through rubbing. 2) to waste or impair by rubbing, [to] wear.

||**Erreich**, *m.* [-es] 1) the act of reaching. [2)] [the power of extending to] reach.

Erreichbar, *adj.* and *adv.* that may [be] reached by efforts of the body or mind, th[at] may be attained, attainable. Vollkommenheit [ist] in diesem Leben nicht —, perfection is not [at]tainable in this life.

Erreichen, *v. tr.* 1) to extend to, to tou[ch] by extending, either the arm alone, or with [an] instrument in the hand, to reach. Er konnte [den] Zweig nicht —, he could not reach the bou[gh]; ich kann den Gegenstand mit meinem St[ock] nicht —, I cannot reach the object with [my] cane; ich kann das Buch nicht —, the book [is] out of my reach. 2) [in general hingelangen zu [ei]nem, zu etwas] Das Schiff erreichte wohlbe[hal]ten den Hafen, the ship reached her port in sa[fety]; den Hafen —, [in seamen's lang.] to make a po[rt or] harbour; die Spitze eines Berges —, to [gain] the top of a mountain; er erreicht nun Ka[naan], Canaan he now attains; wir erreichten Roche[ster] am 10. Juli, we reached or arrived at Roche[ster] July 10; die Kanonen der Festung konnten [den] Feind nicht —, the cannons of the fort could [not] reach the enemy; die Kugel erreichte ihn, [the] bullet reached him. *Fig.* Die Rache wird [die] Gottlosen —, vengeance will overtake the wick[ed]; das Ziel —, to reach the aim; seine Endschaft —, to come to close, to end; seinen Zweck —, to a[ttain]

tain one's end, to reach or come to the end; seinen Zweck nicht —, to miss one's aim; die höchste Vollkommenheit —, to reach the highest point of excellence; einen ungewöhnlichen Grad von Vollkommenheit —, to arrive at an unusual degree of excellence; ich kann sie nicht —, they are out of my reach; ein hohes Alter —, to have reached an advanced age; sie hatte ein hohes Alter erreicht, she was far advanced in years; das Mannesalter —, to arrive at manhood, to grow up; das männliche Alter —, to come to man's estate; die Rathschläge Gottes —, to reach or to penetrate into the designs of God; die Ursache der Lufterscheinungen kann oft der menschliche Verstand nicht —, the causes of phenomena are often beyond the reach of human intellect.

Erreichung, *f.* the act of attaining to, of reaching or arriving at &c. Die — der Vollkommenheit, the attainment of perfection.

Erreisen, *v. tr.* to get or obtain by travelling. Er hat sich große Erfahrung erreiset, he got great experience by his travels.

Erreißen, *ir. v. tr.* V. [the usual word] Zerreißen.

Erreiten, *ir. v. tr.* 1) to overtake in riding on horseback. 2) to get or obtain [a prize &c.] by riding on horseback. Er erritt sich bei dem Wettrennen den ersten Preis, he carried off the first price in the race. 3) [rather unusual] to kill by riding on horseback. 4) to ride over on horseback. Die Ebene war so ausgedehnt, daß ich sie beinahe nicht — konnte, the extent of the plain was such, that I was almost unable to ride across it.

Erreizen, [rather unusual] *v. tr.* to provoke, to make angry.

Errennen, *ir. v. intr.* 1) to overtake in running. 2) to get by running. Sich die Schwindsucht —, to fall into a consumption by running. 3) [rather unusual] to run down.

Errettbar, *adj.* and *adv.* capable of being saved, savable.

Erretten, *v. tr.* to save [a man from drowning &c.]. Einen aus der Gefahr —, to rescue any one from danger; Einen vom Tode —, to save, to rescue any one from death; und hast meine Seele errettet aus der tiefen Hölle, [in Script.] and thou hast delivered my soul from the lowest hell; errette mich durch deine Gerechtigkeit, [in Script.] deliver me in thy righteousness.

Erretter, *m.* [-s, *pl.* -] one that saves or preserves, one who releases or rescues, deliverer, preserver. Er ist der — meines Lebens, he is the saver of my life; jaget nach und ergreifet ihn, denn da ist kein —, [in Script.] persecute and take him, for there is none to deliver him.

Erretterinn, *f.* a female that rescues or delivers. Meine —, my saver!

Errichten, *v. tr.* to erect, to set up, to build. Einen Tempel —, to erect a temple; ein Denkmahl —, to raise a monument; [with coopers] ein Faß —, to put together the staves of a cask. *Fig.* Eine Schule —, to set up a school; Universitäten —, to institute or found universities; eine Fabrik —, to set up a manufactory; ein Bündniß —, to make or to establish a covenant; Freundschaft mit Einem —, to form or contract a friendship with any one. Syn. V. Anlegen.

Errichtung, *f.* 1) erection. Die — eines Denkmahls, the erection of a monument. 2) *Fig.* erection, institution, establishment.

Erringbar, *adj.* and *adv.* that may be gained or obtained by exertions.

Erringen, *ir. v. tr.* to get or gain by wrestling. Sich den Preis —, to win or carry the prize in wrestling. *Fig.* to gain possession of a thing by exertion or great efforts. Sich einen Vortheil —, to obtain an advantage; sich Ruhm —, to gain renown; sich Gunst —, to gain favour; den Sieg —, to gain the victory, to win the day.

Erröthen, I. *v. intr.* to grow or become red, to redden. *Fig.* to redden, to blush, to colour. Appius erröthet über jedes deiner Worte, Appius reddens at each word you speak; erröthe über deine Laster, blush at your vices; erröthe über dein erniedrigtes Vaterland, blush for your degraded country; — machen, to cause to blush, to shame, to put to the blush; ich erröthe nicht, es zu sagen, I am not ashamed of saying it; Einen über etwas — machen, to shame any one of a thing; erröthe vor dir selbst, blush for yourself. Das Erröthen, blushing, blush. II. *v. tr.* [rather unusual] to make red, to redden.

Errudern, *v. tr.* 1) to reach by rowing. 2) to gain by rowing.

Errufen, *ir. v. tr.* to reach by the voice. Man kann ihn —, he is within call; ich kann ihn nicht —, he is out of my calling.

||Erringenschaft, *f.* [in law &c.] acquired property [as opposed to inherited property, feuds &c].

Ersagen, [rather stiff or obsolete] *v. tr.* to mention. Die ersagten Bedingungen, the said conditions.

Ersägen, *v. tr.* 1) to saw through. 2) to gain by sawing.

Ersättigen, *v. tr.* to satisfy appetite or desire, to feed to the full, or to furnish enjoyment to the extent of desire, to satiate. Er ist nicht zu —, he is quite insatiable; sich —, to eat to the fill; wer kann seine Begierden —? who can satisfy his desires? [rather stiff] sich einer Sache —, to be tired with a thing; des Beifalls ersättigt, satiate of applause.

Ersättlich, *adj.* and *adv.* capable of being satiated or satisfied [as opposed to insatiable].

Ersatz, *m.* [-es] 1) reimbursement of loss or damage, indemnification. Einem — geben, to reimburse any one's loss, to indemnify any one, to reimburse to any one what he has lost. 2) that which is given or received as an equivalent for loss or damage, compensation, amends. — leisten, to make amends. 3) a surrogate, substitute.

Ersatz-mann, *m.* he that succeeds into the place of another, a substitute, deputy. — **mittel**, *n.* substitute, succedaneum.

Ersäuern, *v. intr.* [u. w. seyn] to become acid, to sour.

Ersaufen, *ir. v. intr.* [u. w. seyn] to perish in water, to drown [of men one says less vulgarly ertrinken]. Beim Uebergang über diesen Fluß ersoffen viele Pferde, many horses were drowned in passing that river; [in husbandry] der Same oder das Getreide ersäuft, the seed or corn is overwhelmed in water, is drowned; ersoffene Aecker, Wiesen, drowned fields, meadows. *Fig.* In Wollüsten ersoffen seyn, to drown one's self in sensual pleasure.

Ersäufen, *v. tr.* to drown. In der Türkei pflegt man die ungetreuen Weiber zu — [less vulgarly ertränken], in Turkey it is the custom to drown faithless women; ersäufe diese Brut junger Katzen, drown this litter of kitten; sich —, to drown one's self; [with masons] den Kalk —, to dilute lime too much.

Ersäuseln, *v. intr.* [u. w. seyn] to begin to breathe, as air. *Fig.* Das Laub ersäuselt, the foliage begins to rustle.

Ersausen, *v. intr.* [u. w. seyn] to begin to roar or to bluster, as wind.

Erschaben, *v. tr.* 1) to wear by scraping. *2) to get by scraping. *Fig.* to scrape together [said of a miser].

Erschachern, *v. tr.* to gain by chaffering.

Erschaffen, *ir. v. tr.* 1) to cause to exist, to bring into being from nothing, to create. Gott erschuf die Welt, God created the world; jene Schmerzen, die wir uns selbst —, those pains that we ourselves procure. Der Erschaffene, creature, man. Die Erschaffung, creation. Die — der Welt, the creation of the world. ||*reg.* 2) to get through some work or business, to work to the end. Ich habe alle Hände voll zu thun, ich kann es nicht —, I have my hands full of work, I cannot get through it.

Erschaffer, *m.* [-s, *pl.* -] creator.

Erschäkern, *v. tr.* to get by joking or toying.

Erschallen, *ir.* and *reg.* I. *v. intr.* [u. w. seyn] 1) to sound. Er ließ seine Stimme —, he made his voice resound, he called loudly, he shouted. *Fig.* Es erscholl ein Gerücht, a report spread; was ist der gewöhnliche Ruf, der aus allen Welttheilen erschallt, als &c., what is common fame, which sounds from all quarters of the world or globe, but &c.; was erschallt in Fabeln oder Romanen von Uther's Söhnen, what resounds in fable or romance of Uther's sons. 2) to sound, to resound, to ring. Der Saal erschallt von lautem Gelächter, with loud laughs the saloon rings; daß das ganze Ufer davon erschallte, that all the shore rang of it. *Fig.* Die ganze Stadt erschallt von seinem Ruhme, the whole town rings with his fame. II. [rather unusual] *v. tr.* to make resound. Das Lob Gottes —, to sound or resound God's praise.

Erscharren, *v. tr.* to get by scraping, to scrape together. *Fig.* * to gather by close industry or small gains or savings. Ein hübsches Besitzthum —, to scrape together a good estate.

Erschärten, *v. tr.* [in mining] to explore by digging.

* **Erschaudern**, *v. intr.* [u. w. seyn] to shudder, to shiver. Ich erschaudere vor einer solchen That, I shudder at such a deed.

Erschauen, *v. tr.* 1) to perceive by the eye, to see. 2) to perceive, to see, to understand. Ich erschaue seine Beweggründe, I see his motives.

Erschauern, *v. intr.* [u. w. seyn] to shudder, to shiver.

Erscheinen, *ir. v. intr.* [u. w. seyn] to become visible. *a*) to come in sight, to appear, [in poetry] to peer. Der Mond, die Sonne erscheint, the moon, the sun appears; ein Geist erschien ihm im Traume, a spectre appeared to him in a dream; da erschien der Herr dem Abraham und sprach, [in Script.] the Lord appeared to Abram and said; und der Engel des Herrn erschien ihm in einer feurigen Flamme aus dem Busche, [in Script.] and the angel of the Lord appeared to him in a flame of fire out of the midst of the bush. *b*) to make one's appearance, to appear. Er erschien zum ersten Male bei Hofe, he made his first appearance at court; gerade so erscheint sie vor einem sich erhebenden Sturme, just such she shows before a rising storm; der Beklagte erschien nicht [vor Gericht], the defendant did not appear; vor Gericht —, to appear in court; der Erschienene, he that appears in court; der glückliche Tag ist erschienen, the happy day has come; das Buch erscheint in Quarto, the work comes out in quarto; der erste Band von N.'s Wörterbuch ist heute erschienen, the first volume of N.'s dictionary has been published to-day; heute iſt erſchienen und durch alle Buchhandlungen zu erhalten: „Lehrbuch der engliſchen Sprache von N. &c.“, published this day and to be had of all booksellers „Grammar of the English language by N. &c.“; ein Verzeichniß ſämmtlicher in der Leipziger Herbſtmeſſe erſchienenen neuen Werke, a list of all the works newly come out at the Leipsic autumn-fair. *Fig.* to be obvious, to be clear or made clear by evidence, to appear, to appear to the mind. Mir erſcheint die Sache nicht ſo, the thing does not appear to me to be so; und iſt noch nicht erſchienen, was wir ſeyn werden, [in Scripture] it doth not yet appear what we shall be; darum habe ich dich erwecket, daß meine Kraft an dir erſcheine, [in Script.] I raised thee up, to show in thee my power; aber die Sünde, auf daß ſie erſchiene, wie ſie Sünde iſt, [in Script.] but sin, that it might appear sin. Das Erſcheinen, appearance.

Erſcheinung, *f.* 1) [the act of coming into sight] appearance. Die — eines Kometen, the appearing of a comet; die — Chriſti, the appearance of Christ; das Feſt der — Chriſti, epiphany or twelfth-tide; die — vor Gericht, a being present in court, appearance; ſeine — or ſein Erſcheinen beſänftigte die Wuth des aufgeregten Volkes, when he appeared, the fury of the excited people abated. 2) the thing appearing, a visible object. *a*) a visible spirit, an apparition, an appearance, a spectre, a ghost. *Fig.* Sie iſt eine liebliche —, she is a lovely creature; keine Träume, aber ſeltſame —en, no dreams, but visions strange; eine ſehr ſeltſame —, a very strange sight or spectacle. *b*) a remarkable or unusual appearance, a phenomenon, [in nat. hist.] an appearance, a phenomenon. Eine — am Himmel, an appearance in the sky; Luft—en, the phenomena of the atmosphere [as a storm of wind, rain, rainbow &c.]; eine feurige oder wäſſerige Luft—, a meteor. Syn. Erſcheinung, Geſicht. In the language of the Bible ein Geſicht is an image of the fancy, which a person in his sleep or in a trance imagines to be real and existing distinct from himself, a vision; eine Erſcheinung, on the contrary, is the image impressed on the senses whilst the person is awake, and not under the influence of a trance, an apparition.

Erſcheinungs=lehre, *f.* [in modern philosophy] transcendental idealism. —**lehrer**, *m.* [in modern philosophy] one who adheres to and explains the doctrines of transcendental idealism. —**ſüchtig**, *adj.* and *adv.* visionary, affected by phantoms. —**zauberei**, *f.* effects produced by natural magic, or by optics, catoptrics, phantasmagoria.

Erſcherzen, *v. tr.* to get or obtain by jesting.

1. **Erſchießen**, *ir. v. tr.* to kill by a ball, arrow, or other thing shot, to shoot to death, to shoot. Einen Haſen —, to shoot a hare; einen Ausreißer —, to shoot a deserter; ſich —, to shoot one's self, to blow out one's brains.

2. **Erſchießen**, *ir. v. intr.* [u. w. ſeyn] 1) to shoot, to sprout. ||2) [unusual] *Fig.* to take effect.

Erſchiffen, *v. tr.* 1) to get or gain by navigation. 2) to reach navigating.

Erſchimmern, *v. intr.* [u. w. ſeyn] to glisten, to sparkle with light. Die Augen — vor Freude, the eyes sparkle with joy.

Erſchimpfen, *v. tr.* to get or obtain by abuse.

†**Erſchinden**, *ir. v. tr.* to get or obtain by low and oppressive avarice, or by usury.

Erſchlaffen, I. *v. intr.* [u. w. ſeyn] to decrease in tension, to slack, to slacken. *Fig.* Seine Kräfte —, his strength fails or flags; die Lebensgeiſter —, the spirits flag. II. *v. tr.* to lessen tension, to slack, to slacken, to relax. *Fig.* Die Wollüſte — den Körper, voluptuous indulgences enervate the body; weder erſchlaffe Lob, noch erſchrecke Schwierigkeit, nor praise relax, nor difficulty fright.

Erſchlaffer, *m.* [-s, *pl.* -] [in anatomy] the lax membrane.

Erſchlaffung, *f.* relaxation. *Fig.* Die — der Lebensgeiſter, a relaxation of the spirits.

Erſchlagen, *ir. v. tr.* 1) to get through beating, to beat sufficiently. 2) to slay; *it.* to kill by a blow or stroke. Einen —, to strike any one dead; und der Herr machte ein Zeichen an Kain, daß ihn Niemand erſchlüge, wer ihn fände, [in Script.] and the Lord set a mark upon Cain, lest any finding him should kill him; es iſt ihm ein Ziegel auf den Kopf gefallen und hat ihn —, a tile fell on his head and killed him; vom Blitze —, struck dead by lightning. 3) [in mining] Ein Grubengebäude —, to make an adit.

||**Erſchlappen**, *v. intr.* and *tr.* V. Erſchlaffen.

Erſchleichen, *ir. v. tr.* 1) to catch by surprise, to surprise. Einen Dieb —, to seize a thief unawares. *Fig.* Das Alter, der Tod erſchleicht uns, old age, death surprises us. 2) to obtain by surprise or surreptitiously. Sich Eines Gunſt —, to insinuate one's self into a person's favour; vielleicht es für erſchlichen haltend, perhaps supposing it surreptitious or obreptitious; du haſt es erſchlichen, thou hast got it surreptitiously. Die Erſchleichung, surreption, obreption.

1. **Erſchleifen**, [from ſchleifen = to grind] *ir. v. tr.* 1) to get through grinding. 2) to get by grinding. 3) to wear by grinding.

2. **Erſchleifen**, [from ſchleifen = to drag] *v. tr.* 1) to drag to the end, to get through dragging. ||2) V. Erſchleppen.

Erſchleppen, *v. tr.* to move or draw with labour. Er kann ſich kaum —, he can hardly drag himself along.

Erſchleudern, *v. tr.* 1) to reach by slinging. 2) [rather unusual] to kill with a sling and a stone.

Erſchließbar, *adj.* and *adv.* that may be unlocked, opened or disclosed.

Erſchließen, *ir.* I. *v. tr.* to unlock [a door]. *Fig.* Eine Wahrheit —, to gather or deduce a truth from premises. II. *v. r.* ſich —, to unclose itself, to open. Die Erde erſchloß ſich und &c., the earth opened and &c.

Erſchmecken, *v. tr.* to learn by the taste or by tasting.

Erſchmeicheln, *v. tr.* to obtain by flattery, by coaxing or wheedling. Jemands Gunſt —, to win any one's favour by blandishments, praise or enticements.

†**Erſchmeißen**, *ir. v. tr.* 1) to reach throwing [a stone]. 2) [rather unusual] to kill with a stone.

Erſchmollen, *v. tr.* to obtain by pouting.

Erſchnappen, *v. tr.* to catch with open mouth, to snap. †*Fig.* Einen Kuß —, to snatch a kiss; ein Amt —, to snatch an office; ein Wort —, to catch up a word.

Erſchnüffeln, *v. tr.* to find out by smell; †*fig.* to find out by sagacity, to smell out.

Erſchöpfbar, *adj.* and *adv.* that may be scooped or drained off, exhaustible [also in a fig. sense].

Erſchöpfen, *v. tr.* to empty by lading or scooping. Einen Brunnen —, to scoop a well; dieſer Brunnen iſt nicht zu —, this well is inexhaustible. *Fig.* Seine Kräfte ſind erſchöpft, his strength is exhausted; Kummer erſchöpft die Kräfte, sorrows waste the strength; die Schätze des Fürſten ſind erſchöpft, the treasures of the prince are exhausted; ſeine Hülfsquellen waren erſchöpft, his resources were exhausted; Kriege — ein Land an baarem Gelde, wars drain a country of specie; die Mundvorräthe waren erſchöpft, the provisions were spent; ein Vorrath, der nicht zu — iſt, an exhaustless store; Jemands Geduld —, to exhaust any one's patience; einen Gegenſtand —, to exhaust a subject; ſich —, to say all one knows. Die Erſchöpfung, the state of being deprived of strength, exhaustion.

Erſchöpflich, *adj.* and *adv.* exhaustible.

Erſchöpftheit, *f.* the state of being exhausted, the state of being deprived of strength or spirits, exhaustion.

Erſchrecken, I. *ir. v. intr.* [u. w. ſeyn] to be frightened. Ich erſchrak bei dem Anblicke, I was struck with fear by the sight; über eine ſchlimme Nachricht —, to be alarmed at evil news; vor einem Schuſſe —, to startle at a shot; erſchrocken über das Feuergeſchrei, affrighted at the cry of fire; und ſie erſchraken und ſchlugen ihre Angeſichter nieder zu der Erde, [in Script.] and as they were afraid, and bowed down their faces to the earth; in den Tod erſchrocken, frighted to death. II. Erſchrecken. *reg. v. tr.* to impress with sudden fear, to affright, to fright, to frighten, to terrify or alarm. Ich erſchreckte ihn, I frighted him; das Geräuſch wird die Heerde —, the noise will scare the herd.

Erſchrecklich and **Erſchrecklich**, *adj.* and *adv.* exciting alarm, impressing terror, frightful, terrible, dreadful. Ein —er Schrei, a dismal scream; ein —er Anblick, a dreadful, horrible or terrific sight; ein —er Sturm, a dreadful storm; ein —es Ungewitter, a frightful tempest; ein —er Menſch, a terrible man; eine —e Nachricht, alarming news; ſie ſieht heute — aus, she looks frightfully to-day. *Fig. adv.* [in common or familiar language for very] terribly. — kalt, terribly cold; der arme Mann ſchrie —, the poor man squalled terribly; — häßlich, frightfully ugly.

Erſchrecklichkeit, *f.* frightfulness, terribleness, dreadfulness. Die — eines Anblicks, the terribleness of a sight.

||**Erſchreckniß**, *n* [-ſſes, *pl.* -ſſe] 1) fright, terror. 2) [that which may excite fear or dread] terror. Jene ungeheuern Erſchreckniſſe des Nils, those enormous terrors of the Nile.

Erſchreiben, *ir. v. tr.* 1) to get through writing. Sie haben mir ſo viel zu copiren or abzuſchreiben gegeben, ich kann es beinahe nicht —, you gave me so much to copy, I can scarcely get through it. 2) to acquire, gain or obtain by writing. Dieſer Schriftſteller hat ſich ein artiges Vermögen erſchrieben, this author has gained a handsome fortune by his pen.

Erſchreien, *ir. v. tr.* 1) to attain or reach by crying. 2) to get or obtain by crying.

Erſchreiten, *ir. v. tr.* to attain striding. *Fig.* Die höchſte Ehrenſtufe —, to attain the highest degree of honour.

Erſchrocken, [past part. of Erſchrecken] *adj.* and *adv.* 1) frighted, affrighted, terrified. 2) timorous, timid.

Erſchrockenheit, *f.* 1) fright, terror. 2) fear, timidity.

Erſchroten, *v. tr.* 1) to roll to the end, to get through rolling. 2) Eine Grube —, [in mining] to find water in digging.

Erſchürfen, *v. tr.* Eine Grube, einen Gang —, [in mining] to open a pit, to discover a vein in digging.

Erſchütteln, *v. tr.* 1) to shake thoroughly. 2) to effect by shaking.

Erſchütten, [rather unusual] *v. tr.* to pour out.

Erſchüttern, I. *v. tr.* 1) to cause to move with quick vibrations, to shake. Ein Erdbeben e ſchüttert die Berge oder die Erde, an earthquake shakes the hills or the earth; die raſchen Räder — des Himmels Grundfeſte, the rapid wheels shake heaven's basis; [rather fig.] das Zwerchfell —, to cause loud laughter. *Fig.* Die Gothen erſchütterten das römiſche Reich, the Goths threatened to overthrow the Roman empire; nichts ſollte unſern Glauben an das Daſeyn Gottes —, nothing should shake our belief in the being of God; es iſt hinreichend, um die Treue ſeines Volkes zu —, it is enough to stagger his people in their allegiance; ſein Anſehen iſt dadurch ſehr erſchüttert worden, his authority has been very much lessened by it; Todesfurcht erſchüttert auch den Standhafteſten, the fear of death shakes the stoutest man alive; er war ganz erſchüttert bei dem Anblicke, he was highly moved at the sight; dieſer unerwartete Schickſalsſchlag erſchütterte ihn tief or heftig, this unexpected calamity struck him deeply or violently. II. *v. intr.* to be agitated with a waving or vibratory motion. Das Haus erſchütterte bei einem Ungewitter, the house shook in a tempest. III. *v. r.* ſich —, to shake, to tremble, to shiver, to quake.

Erſchütterer, *m.* [-s, *pl.* -] a person that shakes. Der — der Erde, the shaker of the earth.

Erſchütterung, *f.* 1) the act of shaking or agitating, shaking. Durch die — der Luft, from the concussion of the air. 2) shaking, concussion, a shock. Die — des Gehirns durch einen Schlag, the concussion of the brain by a stroke; —en der Erde, concussions of the earth; eine elektriſche —, an electrical commotion.

Erſchwächen, *v. intr.* [u. w. ſeyn] [unusual] to grow weak, to be deprived of strength.

Erſchwärmen, *v. tr.* 1) to get by enthusiasm, to attain in visions 2) to get, obtain or acquire by revery.

Erſchwätzen, *v. tr.* to get or obtain by prattling.

Erſchwellen, *ir. v. intr.* [u. w. ſeyn] V. Aufſchwellen. *Fig.* Sein Muth erſchwillt, his courage increases.

Erſchweren, *v. tr.* to make heavy, to aggravate. *Fig.* Eine Arbeit —, to render a labour more difficult; die Ausführung von Plänen —, to render the execution of designs laborious; er erſchwerte ihm den Vollzug ſeines Auftrags auf alle Weiſe, he threw all sorts of obstacles in the way of his errand; Einem das Leben —, to render any one's life more burdensome or troublesome. Die Erſchwerung, aggravation.

Erſchwerniß, *n.* [-ſſes, *pl.* -ſſe] whatever renders progress or execution of designs laborious, difficulty.

Erſchwimmen, *ir. v. tr.* to reach swimming.

1. **Erſchwingen**, [from ſchwingen = to swing] *ir. v. tr.* 1) [rather unusual] to swing. 2) to attain swinging. *Fig.* Das Ziel der Vollkommenheit —, to reach the point of excellence; ſich —, to soar; wie hohen Flugs ſein Entſchluß ſich erſchwingt, how high a pitch his resolution soars.

2. **Erſchwingen**, *ir. v. tr.* [probably allied to the Sw. and A. S. *winna*, to the Engl. *win*, arbeiten, erarbeiten] 1) to gain or win. 2) to supply the means of paying with difficulty. Ich kann das Geld dazu nicht —, I am not able to bear the expenses of it, I cannot afford it; ich kann die Unkoſten nicht —, I cannot afford the charges; ich vermag es nicht zu —, I cannot afford it.

Erſchwinglich, *adj.* and *adv.* that may be gained or afforded.

Erſchwitzen, I. *v. tr.* to obtain by sweating, to attain sweating. II. *v. intr.* [rather unusual] [u. w. ſeyn] to perspire.

Erſehen, *ir.* I. *v. tr.* 1) to perceive by the eye, to see, to behold. Die Seeleute erſahen [das] Land, the seamen descried land. *Fig.* Man kann daraus —, wie die Sache zuging, you may see by it how the thing came to pass; ich erſehe aus Ihrem Briefe, daß &c., I learn by your letter that &c.; hieraus iſt zu —, by this appears. 2) to reach with the eye Ich kann die Farben in einer ſolchen Entfernung nicht —, I cannot discern the colours at such a distance. *Fig* Zeit und Gelegenheit —, to watch for the proper time. 3) *Fig.* [= auserſehen] to make choice of, to choose, to select. Sich das ſchönſte Mädchen zur Gattinn —, to select the handsomest girl for one's wife. II. *v. r.* ſich —, 1) [rather unusual] to amuse, or occupy one's self with looking at a thing, to amuse one's self by looking about. || 2) V. Verſehen, ſich.

Erſehlich, *adj.* and *adv.* that may be seen or reached with the eye.

Erſehnen, *v. tr.* to desire eagerly or ardently, to long for, to hanker after. Erſehnt, wished for.

Erſetzbar, *adj.* and *adv.* that may be retrieved or made good, reparable, as a loss. [of persons] Er iſt in dieſer Stelle leicht —, he is easy to be replaced in this office or place, his place is easy to be filled up.

Erſetzen, *v. tr.* to put a competent substitute in the place of another displaced or of something lost. Das Papier iſt verloren gegangen und kann nicht wieder erſetzt werden, the paper is lost and cannot be replaced; einen Verluſt —, to make up a loss; die Koſten —, to reimburse the expenses; wenn Sie verlieren, ſo will ich Ihren Verluſt —, if you suffer loss, I will make it good to you; einen Schaden —, to repair a damage; jemanden einen Schaden —, to reimburse to any one what he has lost, to indemnify any one; der Verluſt iſt zu —, the loss is reparable; haben Sie einen Vorrath von Freunden, um die zu —, welche geſtorben ſind? have you a supply of friends to make up for those who are gone? das erſetzt Ihnen die ausgeſtandene Angſt reichlich, this will richly compensate for the anxiety you suffered; nichts kann den Verluſt des guten Namens —, nothing can compensate for the loss of reputation; eine Entſchädigung in Geld kann den Verluſt eines Gliedes nicht —, damages in money cannot be an equivalent for the loss of a limb; Tugend kann körperliche Mängel —, virtue can atone for bodily defects. Syn. Erſetzen, Erſtatten. Erſtatten implies as well, the restoring or returning of a thing in its original state, as the indemnifying by means of an equivalent; the signification of Erſetzen is limited to the latter sense, and the compensation given as an equivalent is der Erſatz. A thief who has stolen a horse, if it is found with him uninjured, muß es wieder erſtatten, [must restore it] by returning it to its owner; if he has injured it so as to be no longer serviceable, muß er den Schaden erſtatten, [he must make good the damage] either dadurch, daß er ihn erſetzt, [by supplying one of equal value], or by paying the worth of the horse.

Erſetzlich, *adj.* and *adv.* that may be retrieved or made good, reparable.

Erſeufzen, I. *v. intr.* to sigh aloud. II. *v. tr.* 1) to wish for sighing, to sigh after. 2) to attain sighing, to get or obtain by sighing.

Erſichtlich, *adj.* and *adv.* perceivable by the eye, that can be seen, visible. *Fig.* Ein —er Vortheil, an evident advantage; hieraus iſt —, by this appears.

Erſichtlichkeit, *f.* visibleness, visibility; *fig.* evidence.

Erſiechen, [rather unusual] *v. intr.* [u. w. ſeyn] to sicken, to fall into disease.

Erſiegen, *v. tr.* to obtain by victory. Ein verlornes Land —, to reconquer a country.

Erſingen, *ir. v. tr.* to get by singing. Sich Geld —, to get money by singing; die Catalani hat ſich ein fürſtliches Vermögen erſungen, the Catalani got a princely fortune by her singing.

Erſinken, *ir.* I. *v. intr.* to sink, to subside. Das Schiff erſank, the ship sunk [rather unusual in the proper sense]. *Fig.* Er erſank unter der Laſt der Jahre, he sunk under the weight of years. II. *v. tr.* [in mining] to obtain by sinking a pit or mine.

Erſinnen, *ir. v. tr.* to strike out by thought, to excogitate. Einen Vertheidigungsplan —, to devise a plan of defence; eine Maſchine —, to devise or invent a machine; die Mittel —, welche ihn zu ſeinem Zwecke führen, to contrive the means which conduct him to his end; neue Moden —, to invent new fashions; Böſes —, to imagine mischief.

Erſinner, *m.* [-s, *pl.* -] a deviser, a contriver.

Erſinnlich, *adj.* and *adv.* that can be invented, or imagined. Mit aller —en Klarheit, with all imaginable clearness; mit aller —en Höflichkeit, with all imaginable politeness.

Erſitzen, *ir.* I. [unusual] *v. intr.* [u. w. ſeyn] to sit. Die Sache blieb —, the affair dropped; auf etwas erſeſſen ſeyn, V. Erpicht, Verſeſſen. II. *v. tr.* to get by sitting. *Fig.* [in law] to acquire by uninterrupted possession, to acquire by prescription.

Erſorgen, *v. tr.* to get by cares.

Erſpähen, *v. tr.* to espy, to descry. Von dem Maſttop eines Schiffes Land —, to spy land from the mast-head of a ship.

Erſpannen, *v. tr.* 1) to span [a space or distance]. 2) to be able to draw or stretch. Ich kann den Bogen nicht —, I cannot draw the bow.

Erſparen, *v. tr.* ||1) to spare, to withhold from any particular use or occupation. 2) to spare, to save. Eine Kleinigkeit —, to save a groat; die Koſten —, to save the expenses; wir hätten uns dieſe Mühe und Ausgabe — können, we might have spared ourselves this toil and expense; Ordnung in allen Sachen erſpart Zeit, order in all affairs saves time; willſt du nicht reden, um einer Dame das Erröthen zu —? will you not speak to save a lady's blush? — Sie ihr dieſe Schande, save her that shame; erſpare dir die Thränen, forbear weeping; er hätte mir den Aerger — können, he might have spared me that mortification. Die Erſparung, sparing, saving.

Erſparniß, *f.* [-ſſes, *pl.* -ſſe] 1) saving. Eine — machen, to make a saving; er hat allerlei zweckmäßige Erſparniſſe in ſeiner Haushaltung eingeführt, he made several useful savings in his household. 2) [what is saved] savings. Er hat ſeine Erſparniſſe in der Erſparniß- or Sparkaſſe niedergelegt, he has put his savings into the savings-bank.

Erſpielen, *v. tr.* to get by playing, or gaming. Sich große Summen —, to win great sums by gaming; dieſer Schauſpieler hat ſich viel Geld erſpielt, this actor got much money by playing.

Erſpießen, *v. tr.* V, [the usual word] Aufſpießen.

Erſpinnen, *ir. v. tr.* to get by spinning. Sich ſeinen Lebensunterhalt —, to live by spinning, to spin for one's livelihood.

Erſpötteln, Erſpotten, *v. tr.* to obtain by sportive insult or by sneering jests.

Ersprengen, *v. tr.* V. [the usual word] Aufsprengen.

Ersprießen, *ir. v. intr.* [u. w. seyn] to shoot up. *Fig.* [rather stiff or obsolete] to be of use or advantage, to bring good to, to profit. Das wird ihm sehr — [more usual ersprießlich seyn], it will do him much good.

Ersprießlich, *adj.* and *adv.* profitable, useful, advantageous. Was dem Reiche so — war, what was so profitable to the empire; eine für das Beste unseres Vaterlandes —e Handlung, an action conducive to the good of our country; eine —e Wirkung, a salutary effect; — für den Körper, beneficial to the body; — seyn, to be of use or advantage, to avail.

Ersprießlichkeit, *f.* use, advantage.

Erspringen, *ir. v. tr.* 1) to attain by leaping. 2) to overtake by running.

Erspüren, *v. tr.* to trace up.

Erst, *adv.* properly the superlative degree of ehe. 1) [before any thing else in the order of time] first. Ich bekomme es —, I receive it first; — wollen wir die Vernehmung der Zeugen anhören, first let us attend to the examination of the witnesses; man muß sich — an ihn wenden, he must be previously applied to. **Fig.* wenn er nur — hier wäre! if he were only here! was wird — Ihr Vater sagen! what will your father say! 2) at the beginning or origin, at first, at the first. — war es nicht meine Absicht, nach Paris zu reisen, at first it was not my intention to proceed to Paris. 3) before, at first. Thue das —, do that first or before. 4) [= früher] — erwähnt, — gedacht, — gemeldet, afore-said, before-mentioned. 5) *Fig.* no more than, no farther than. — sechszehn Jahre alt, but sixteen years old; — jetzt, jetzt —, but now, just now; not longer ago than.

Erstámpfen, *v. tr.* 1) to stamp much. 2) to break by stamping.

Erstárken, *v. intr.* [u. w. seyn] to grow strong, to gather strength of body or of mind.

Erstärken, [rather unusual] *v. tr.* to give new strength or vigour, to invigorate.

Erstárren, I. *v. intr.* [u. w. seyn] to become torpid. Vor Kälte —, to be benumbed by cold; meine Hände — mir, my hands become torpid; mit erstarrten Augen, with eyes aghast; mein Blut erstarrt, wenn ich nur daran denke, it chills my blood but to think on it. II. *v. tr.* to render torpid, to numb, to benumb. —de Kälte, numbing cold. Die Erstarrung, torpidity, numbness.

Erstátten, *v. tr.* 1) to reimburse in kind or something equivalent. Einem die Unkosten —, to repay to a person his expenses, to reimburse him; eines Kaufmanns Verluste —, to compensate a merchant for his losses; einem das Verlorne —, to restore something lost to the owner; der soll von dem Besten auf seinem Acker und Weinberge wieder —, [in Script.] of the best of his own field, and of the best of his own vineyard, shall he make restitution. 2) Bericht —, to render an account, usually an official account to a superior, to hand in a statement; Offiziere — Bericht über die Anzahl der Kranken oder Dienstfähigen, officers return the number of men sick or capable of duty. Syn. v. Ersetzen.

Erstáttlich, *adj.* and *adv.* that may be reimbursed, retrievable, reparable.

Erstáttung, *f.* compensation, restitution.

Erstaúnen, I. *v. intr.* [u. w. seyn] to be confounded with fear, sudden surprise or wonder, to be astonished, to be amazed. Daniel erstaunte über das Gesichte, Daniel was astonished at the vision; man erstaunt über tollkühne Thaten des Heldenmuthes oder über die Erzählung wunderbarer Ereignisse, we are surprised at desperate acts of heroism, or at the narration of wonderful events; ich bin darüber erstaunt, I am amazed at it. II. *v. imp.* Es erstaunt mich, I am astonished at it.

Erstaúnen, *n.* [-s] astonishment, amazement, amazedness. In — setzen, to amaze, to astonish. Dieser Anblick setzte mich in —, I was surprised at this view; nichts kam seinem — gleich &c., nothing could equal his surprise; das ist zum —, that is astonishing.

Erstaunens=voll, *adj.* and *adv.* much amazed or astonished. —werth, —würdig, *adj.* and *adv.* astonishing, very wonderful.

Erstaúnlich, *adj.* and *adv.* astonishing, amazing, surprising. Eine —e Geduld, surprising patience; eine —e Höhe, a stupendous altitude; —e Ereignisse, wonderful events; eine —e Menge Wassers, a prodigious quantity of water; — groß, prodigiously great; — verändert, marvellously changed; er gab sich eine —e Mühe, das Leben seines Gefährten zu retten, he exerted himself surprisingly to save the life of his companion; [in common or familiar language] es würde Sie — freuen &c., it would amazingly delight you; er war — erfreut, he was prodigiously pleased; es gefällt mir —, I like it prodigiously.

Erstaúnung, *f.* V. [the usual word] Erstaunen, *n.*

Erstaunungsvoll, *adj.* and *adv.* much amazed or surprised.

Erste, [der, die, das] [properly the superlative degree of eher] first. *a*) preceding all others in the order of time; foremost in place. Der — Tag der Woche, the first day of the week; der — Tag im Jenner, the first day of January; Adam war der — Mensch, Adam was the first man; Cain war der — Mörder, Cain was the first murderer; die —n Bewohner eines Landes, aboriginals, aborigines; der — der beste, the first the best; die — Kirche, the primitive church; die —n Früchte, first-fruits, first-fruit; der — Mann bei einer marschirenden Truppe ist &c., the first man of a marching troop is &c; für das —, or für's —, for the first, in the first place. *Prov.* Der — kriegt die beste Beute, the foremost dog catches the hare. *b*) preceding all others in numbers or a progressive series. Eins ist die — Zahl, one is the first number; der — unter den Brüdern, the eldest brother; der — im Spiele seyn, to be the eldest hand at play. *c*) preceding all others in rank, dignity or excellence. Demosthenes war der — Redner Griechenlands, Demosthenes was the first orator of Greece; der — Minister, the first minister of state, the prime minister, the premier; einer unserer —n Schriftsteller, one of our first-rate authors; die —n Leute der Stadt, the principal men of the town; er ist der — Mann der Stadt, he is the chief man in town; Tuch von der —n Qualität, cloth of a prime quality; [in music] die — Stimme, the first part; die — Geige spielen, to perform the first violin; die — Classe, [in a school or college] the first class.

Erstéchen, *ir. v. tr.* 1) to perforate, to lance. V. [the usual word] Aufstechen. 2) to kill by the thrust of a pointed instrument, to stab. Einen mit dem Dolche —, to poniard any one; er erstach sich, he stabbed himself; er erstach ihn im Zweikampfe, he ran him through in a duel.

Erstéhen, *ir.* I. *v. intr.* [u. w. seyn] 1) to get up, to rise. 2) to arise, to spring up. *Fig.* to revive, to rise, to arise. Christus ist von den Todten erstanden, Christ is risen from the dead. II. *v. tr.* 1) to buy at an auction. 2) to go through. Seine Lehrjahre —, to serve out one's apprenticeship; eine Strafe —, to suffer a punishment.

Erstéhlen, *ir. v. tr.* to get or acquire by stealing. Seinen Unterhalt —, to steal one's livelihood.

Ersteigen, *ir. v. tr.* to ascend by steps, to climb, to mount, to scale. Einen Berg —, to ascend a hill; einen Baum —, to climb a tree; eine Mauer —, to escalade a wall; [and applied to the walls of a fortified place] eine Festung —, to scale a fort, to mount it in assault or storm. *Fig.* Die Höhen des Ruhmes —, to climb the ascents or heights of fame. Die Ersteigung, scaling. Die — eines Walles, [in the military art] escalade, scalade, scalado.

Ersteiglich, *adj.* and *adv.* scalable.

Ersteinen, *v. intr.* [u. w. seyn] [rather unusual] to become stone, to petrify.

Erstens, *adv.* in the first place, firstly.

Erstérben, *ir. v. intr.* [u. w. seyn] 1) [= absterben] Das Glied ist erstorben, the limb is deprived of sensation, is benumbed; der Baum erstirbt, the tree perishes; die Worte scheinen auf seinen Lippen zu —, the words seem to die on his lips. *Fig.* [= aufhören] to die, to expire. Ein Geschlecht erstirbt, a family becomes extinct; das Wort erstarb mir auf der Zunge, I could not utter one word; die Töne erstarben, the sounds died away; der Glanz der Sterne wird —, the stars shall fade away; as a closing of a letter, dedication, petition &c. [rather obsolete or stiff] ich ersterbe Ihr unterthänigster Diener, your very humble servant till death. 2) to fall to a person by the death of another.

Ersteúern, *v. tr.* to reach by steering.

Erstgeboren, *adj.* first born, primigenial, primogenial. Der —e Sohn, the first-born son, the eldest son; das —e Kind, the first-born; welcher ist das Ebenbild des unsichtbaren Gottes, der Erstgeborne vor allen Creaturen, [in Script.] who is the image of the invisible God, the first born of every creature.

Erstgeburt, *f.* [*pl.* -n] 1) the state of being first born. Das Recht der —, the right of primogeniture, primogenitureship. 2) the first-born child or animal. Alle —, die unter deinen Rindern und Schafen geboren wird, das ein Männlein ist, [in Scripture] all the firstling males that come of thy herd and of thy flock; die — des Viehes, the firstlings of cattle. 3) the right of primogeniture, primogenitureship. Meine — hat er dahin, [in Script.] he took away my birthright; Esau verkaufte seine —, Esau sold his birth-right.

Erstgeburtsrecht, *n.* primogeniture, primogenitureship.

Ersticken, I. *v. intr.* [u. w. seyn] 1) to be suffocated or choked, to smother. Im Rauche oder in Stickluft —, to be suffocated in smoke or in carbonic acid gas; in einem engen Zimmer —, to be stifled in a close room; *zum — heiß, suffocatingly hot; in seinem Blute —, to be suffocated by one's blood; das Vieh erstickt leicht, wenn es Kartoffeln ißt, cattle are apt to choke when eating potatoes. *Fig.* Ich ersticke vor Wuth, I choke with rage; vor Lachen —, to burst with laughter. 2) [of plants &c., to be impeded in growth] Der Same erstickt im Wasser, seeds are choked in water; das junge Holz erstickt im Dickicht, young trees are choked in thickets. II. *v. tr.* 1) to choke, to suffocate. Ein Kind unter Betten —, to smother a child in bed; die —den Kohlendämpfe, the stifling vapours of coals; von Küssen erstickt, stirbt er eines süßen Todes, stifled with kisses, a sweet death he dies; einen Bürgerkrieg im Entstehen —, to stifle a civil war in its birth, die Sorge dieser Welt und Betrug des Reichthums erstickt das Wort, und bringet nicht Frucht, [in Script.] the care of this world, and the deceitfulness of riches, choke the word, and becomes unfruitful. 2) [to impede in growth] Die Dornen wuchsen auf und erstickten es, [in Script.] the thorns sprung up and choked them. Die Erstickung, suffocation.

Erstigkeit, [rather unusual] *f.* 1) [the state of being antecedent in time] priority. 2) [in law] priority [of debts = a superior claim to payment, or to payment before others]. 3) the first produce, firstling, first-fruit or first-fruits.

Erstigkeitsurtheil, *n.* a judgment of priority of debts.

Erstillen, I. *v. tr.* to succeed in stopping or stilling. Ich kann das Blut nicht —, I cannot staunch the blood. II. *v. intr.* [u. w. seyn] [unusual] to become still, calm or quiet.

Erstinken, [unusual] *ir. v. intr.* [u. w. seyn] to become stinking. *Fig.* †Das ist erstunken und erlogen, that is a monstrous or impudent lie.

Erstlich, *adv.* 1) first, at first. 2) in the first place, firstly.

Erstling, *m.* [-es, *pl.* -e] the first, earliest in its kind. Die —e seiner Dichtkunst, the first fruits of his poetry, his first poems; die —e des Viehes, the firstlings of cattle; und Habel brachte auch von den —en seiner Heerde, und von ihren Fetten, [in Script.] and Abel, he also brought of the firstlings of his flock and of the fat thereof.

Erstlings-blume, *f.* an early flower. —**flaum**, *m.* the first down of the chin. —**kuß**, *m.* the first kiss. —**lamm**, *n.* the firstling of a sheep. —**sohn**, *m.* the first-born, the eldest son. —**tochter**, *f.* the eldest daughter. —**versuch**, *m.* the first specimen, a first trial or experiment.

Erstmahls, *adv.* for the first time.

Erstmann, *m.* [-es, *pl.* -männer] the chief workman in saltworks.

Erstoppeln, *v. tr.* to gather by gleaning. Erstoppeltes Korn, corn gleaned in the field, gleanings. *Fig.* *Das ganze Werk ist erstoppelt, the whole work is gleaned from different authors.

Erstorben, [past part. of Ersterben]. *Fig.* —e Gefühle, deadened feelings.

Erstoßen, *ir. v. tr.* 1) to reach thrusting. 2) [rather unusual] to push out of its place. 3) [rather unusual] to break or kill by repeated thrusts.

Erstreben, *v. tr.* to obtain by great exertion or by endeavours. Das Lob der Kenner —, to endeavour to gain the praise of skilful or knowing persons.

Erstrecken, I. *v. tr.* to extend, to stretch. *Fig.* Er erstreckte seine milden Gaben auch auf die Heiden, his charities extended also to the heathen. II. *v. r.* sich —, 1) to extend, to stretch, to reach. Deutschland erstreckt sich von der Ostsee bis zum Adriatischen Meere, Germany extends from the Baltic to the Adriatic sea; seine Ländereien — sich bis an das Ufer des Hudson, his land goes to the banks of the Hudson. *Fig.* So weit erstreckt sich meine Gewalt nicht, my power does not extend so far, it is not within the reach of my power; die Macht der Großen erstreckt sich weit, *prov.* great men have reaching or long hands. 2) [in fishing] to grow [said of young carps].

Erstreiten, *ir. v. tr.* 1) to get or obtain by fighting, contention or litigation, to obtain by dispute. Die Griechen erstritten ihre Freiheit, the Greeks victoriously combated for their liberty. 2) to obtain by great exertions.

Erstricken, *v. tr.* to get by knitting. Sich seinen or den Unterhalt —, to gain one's livelihood by knitting.

Erstummen, [unusual] *v. intr.* [u. w. seyn] to be struck dumb.

Erstumpfen, *v. intr.* [u. w. seyn] to grow blunt. *Fig.* Der Geist erstumpft unter solchen Arbeiten, such labours dull the mind.

Erstürmen, *v. tr.* to take [a fortified town &c.] by storm, to storm.

Ersuchen, *v. tr.* ||1) V. [the usual word] Aussuchen. 2) to find out by searching, to get through searching. 3) *Fig.* to express desire to, to ask, to request. Einen um etwas —, to ask or beg something of any one; wir ersuchten einen Freund, uns zu begleiten, we requested a friend to accompany us.

Ersuchen, *n.* [-s, *pl.* -] ||**Ersuch**, *n.* [-s, *pl.* -e] an asking, a petition, a request. Auf sein —, at his request; er erhielt es auf wiederholtes dringendes —, he obtained it by repeated solicitations.

Ersudeln, *v. tr.* to get or acquire by dirty work. *Fig.* [in contempt] Er hat sich mit seinen Schriften ein hübsches Vermögen ersudelt, he gained a handsome fortune by his miserable scribbling.

Ertagen, [rather unusual] *v. intr.* [u. w. seyn] to dawn.

Ertändeln, *v. tr.* to obtain by toying.

Ertanzen, *v. tr.* to get or obtain by dancing. Sich seinen Unterhalt —, to gain one's livelihood by dancing.

Ertappen, *v. tr.* 1) to get by groping. 2) to seize, to catch. Einen Dieb —, to catch or surprise a thief; er wurde auf frischer That ertappt, he was taken in the very act. *Fig.* Einen auf einem Fehler —, to overtake any one in a fault; Einen auf einer Lüge —, to find any one in a lie.

Ertasten, *v. tr.* to search by feeling. Wir ertasteten unsern Weg um Mitternacht, we groped our way at midnight.

Ertauben, [unusual] *v. intr.* [u. w. seyn] to become deaf.

Ertauschen, *v. tr.* to obtain by exchange.

Erthätigen, [rather stiff] *v. tr.* to prove by the fact.

Ertheilen, *v. tr.* to give, to confer, to bestow. Einem einen Titel —, to confer a title on any one; die Krönung ertheilt dem Könige keine königliche Gewalt, coronation confers on the king no royal authority; Würden ertheile Andern, honours to others impart; Rath —, to give counsel or advice; Nachricht —, to give notice or intelligence, to inform, to send word; Lob —, to praise; Einem Lob —, to bestow praise on any one; Einem wegen einer Sache Lob —, to praise any one for a thing; er bat mich um Erlaubniß, und ich ertheilte sie ihm, he asked my leave and I granted it him; Befehle —, to give or to issue orders; Unterricht —, to give instruction, to teach; Unterricht in Sprachen —, to teach languages; er ertheilt Unterricht im Italienischen, he gives lessons in Italian; er ertheilt ihnen Unterricht in der Religion, he instructs them in religion.

Erthürmen, *v. tr.* V. [the more usual word] Aufthürmen.

Ertoben, I. *v. intr.* [unusual] [u. w. seyn] to begin to rage. II. *v. tr.* to get or obtain by raging.

Ertödten, *v. tr.* [used to inforce the meaning of tödten, but now obsolete in the proper sense] to kill wholly. *Fig.* to root out, to eradicate, to destroy wholly. Ertödte deine sündigen Lüste, mortify thy sinful lusts; das Fleisch —, to mortify the flesh [corporeal appetites, or inordinate passions]. Die Ertödtung, mortification [of our lusts &c.].

Ertönen, I. *v. intr.* [u. w. seyn] 1) to sound in a manner so as to be heard. Seine Stimme — lassen, to speak aloud. 2) to sound, to resound, to ring. Der Hain ertönte vom Gesange der Vögel, the woods rung with the song of birds. *Fig.* Die ganze Stadt ertönt von seinem Ruhme, the whole town rings with his fame. II. *v. tr.* to sound, to celebrate or honour by sounds. Jemands Lob —, to sound any one's praise.

Ertraben, *v. tr.* 1) to get through trotting. 2) to overtake trotting.

Ertrag, *m.* [-es] 1) produce, product, revenue. Der — einer Meierei, the produce of a farm; der — einer Fabrik, the produce of a manufactory; der — eines Bergwerkes, the produce of a mine; der — eines Gutes, the proceeds of an estate; Ländereien von großem —e, lands which yield large products; der jährliche — der Steuern, the annual produce of taxes, the revenue from taxes. 2) gain beyond all expenses or charges, profit. Der rohe or Brutto— ist 20, der reine or Netto— ist 15 Procent, the gross profit is 20 per cent, the net profit 15 per cent; der reine — von dem Verkauf seiner Waaren betrug 10 Prozent, he cleared ten per cent by the sale of his goods.

Ertragen, *ir. v. tr.* to bear, to sustain, to uphold. *Fig.* to support, to endure, to bear, to suffer, to tolerate. Etwas mit Geduld —, to bear something with patience; Kälte, Hitze, Hunger, Durst —, to endure cold, heat, hunger, thirst; sie kann das Reisen nicht —, she cannot stand the fatigue of travelling; ich kann die Kälte nicht —, I cannot stand the cold; eine Hitze, die nicht zu — ist, insupportable heat; Unglücksfälle —, to support misfortunes; Mühseligkeiten —, to bear or undergo hardships; das Auge kann das Licht der Sonnenscheibe nicht —, the eye will not support the light of the sun's disk; ich kann seine Unverschämtheit nicht —, I cannot tolerate or suffer his impertinence; solche Beleidigungen kann man nicht —, such insults are not supportable, or tolerable; ich kann es nicht —, I cannot abide it. Die Ertragung, a bearing or suffering with patience, sufferance. Die — von Schmerz, endurance of pain. Syn. **Ertragen, Tragen, Vertragen.** Tragen signifies merely, not to loathe or abhor, not to have any aversion to a thing. Ertragen, to overcome or suppress one's aversion. Tragen, therefore, is said of lesser ills, ertragen of greater. Vertragen signifies, to be insensible to that which to others is burdensome or annoying. An unsusceptible person verträgt Beleidigungen [bears offences], from insensibility; a meek person erträgt sie [tolerates them], from the mildness of his temper. The former verträgt, the latter erträgt. One says of a wine-drinker, er kann viel vertragen, [he can stand a great deal], when a great quantity of wine does not affect him, or cause him any inconvenience.

Erträglich, *adj.* and *adv.* 1) supportable, endurable. Die Kälte in Canada ist streng, aber —, the cold in Canada is severe, but tolerable; — warm, tolerably warm; er ist ein recht —er Mensch, he is a person to our liking. 2) moderately good or agreeable, tolerable. Eine —e Bewirthung, a tolerable entertainment; — singen, to sing tolerably; er spricht das Französische ziemlich —, he speaks French tolerably well.

Erträglichkeit, *f.* supportableness, tolerableness.

Erträgsam, *adj.* and *adv.* yielding large products, productive.

Erträllern, *v. tr.* to get by singing or quavering.

Ertränken, *v. tr.* to drown. Sich —, to drown one's self. *Fig.* Sich in Wollüsten —, to wallow in sensualities.

Erträumen, *v. tr.* 1) to produce in a dream. **Erträumte Uebel**, imaginary ills; **ein erträumtes Glück**, an imaginary happiness; **ein erträumter Glücksfall**, a piece of good fortune one could never have dreamed of; **erträumte Dinge**, reveries, chimeras. 2) to get by dreaming. **Joseph erträumte sich den Haß seiner Brüder**, the brethren of Joseph hated him for his dreams.

Ertreten, [rather unusual] *ir. v. tr.* to crush under the foot, to kill by treading on.

Ertrillern, *v. tr.* to get or obtain by singing with tremulous modulations of voice or by quavering.

Ertrinken, *ir.* I. *v. intr.* [u. w. seyn] to be drowned, to drown. **Er ist ertrunken**, he was drowned; **die Saat ertrinkt**, the seeds are overwhelmed in water, drown. II. *v. tr.* to get by drinking. **Er hat sich die Wassersucht ertrunken**, he has drunk himself into a dropsy.

Ertrödeln, *v. tr.* 1) to get or procure from fripperers. 2) to gain by frippery or by the traffick in old clothes.

Ertrommeln, [rather unusual] *v. tr.* 1) to awake by drumming. 2) to gain by drumming. **Sich seinen Unterhalt** —, to gain one's livelihood by drumming.

Ertrotzen, *v. tr.* to obtain by importunity, obstinacy, or insolence, by bidding defiance.

Erüben, [rather unusual] *v. tr.* to obtain or acquire by exercise.

Erübrigen, *v. tr.* to save from being spent. **Alle Zeit, die er — konnte**, all the time he could spare; **Geld** —, to save or lay by money.

***Erudition**, *f.* erudition, learning. **Die Scaligers waren Leute von sehr großer** —, the Scaligers were men of deep erudition. V. **Gelehrsamkeit.**

Erve, *f.* [*pl.* -en] [Gr. ἔροβος] [a plant] spring bitter vetch.

Ervenwürger, *m.* [a plant] broom-rape.

Erwachen, *v. intr.* [u. w. seyn] to cease to sleep, to awake, to wake. **Er erwacht bei dem kleinsten Geräusche**, he wakes at the slightest noise; **Jakob erwachte aus dem Schlafe**, Jacob awaked out of sleep; **Turnus, —d mit dem anbrechenden Tage**, Turnus, wakening with the light; **aus tiefem Schlafe** —, to disentrance; **der Erwachende**, waker. *Fig.* **Vom Tode** —, to rise from the dead, to awake; **sanfte Lüfte, die so eben erwachte Erde zu fächeln**, gentle airs to fan the earth now wak'd; **der —de Tag**, the springing day; **meine —den Hoffnungen**, my springing hopes; **die Liebe erwachte in seinem Busen**, love rose in his breast; **wenn das Gewissen erwacht**, when the conscience is awakened.

Erwachsen, *ir. v. intr.* [u. w. seyn] to grow. *a*) to grow up, to grow tall. *b*) to be produced by vegetation, to grow. **Reis erwächst nur in warmen Erdstrichen**, rice grows only in warm climates. *Fig.* *α*) to increase, to grow. **Der Wind erwuchs zum Sturme**, the wind grew to a tempest. *β*) to proceed as from a cause, to grow. **Neue Hoffnung erwuchs aus der Verzweiflung**, new hope sprung out of despair; **sie — aus euren Lüsten**, they come of your lusts; **daraus wird viel Böses** —, much evil will spring from it; **der Regierung erwächst ein Gewinn beim Münzen des Kupfers**, a profit accrues to government from the coinage of copper. *γ*) [in law &c.] to come to hand, to be delivered. *c*) to arrive at full size or stature. **Ein —er Mensch**, a grown person, an adult person; **der —e**, an adult.

Erwägen, *reg.* and [more frequently] *ir. v. tr.* to weigh through, to weigh to the end. *Fig.* to weigh in the mind, to ponder. **Er sollte die Sache reiflich** —, he ought maturely to consider it; **alles wohl erwogen**, every thing well weighed. Syn. V. **Bedenken.**

Erwägung, *f.* weighing intellectually, pondering. **Etwas in — ziehen**, to take a thing into consideration, to ponder a thing; **in** —, in consideration, in respect, in regard of; **nach reifer** —, after mature deliberation.

Erwählen, *v. tr.* to choose from among a number. **Einen Präsidenten** —, to elect a president; **einen Deputirten** or **Abgeordneten ins Parlament &c.** —, to elect or return a member to parliament &c.; **einen zu einem Amte** —, to elect any one to an office; **zum Könige erwählt**, raised to the throne by election; **einen zu seinem Freunde** —, to select any one for one's friend, to make choice of a person for one's friend; **welchen der Herr erwählet, der sei heilig**, [in Script.] the man the Lord doth choose shall be holy. **Die Erwählung**, election. **Die — eines Königs**, the election of a king.

Erwähler, *m.* [-s, *pl.* -] a chooser, an elector.

Erwähnen, *v. tr.* to mention. **Im Laufe der Unterhaltung wurde dieses Umstandes erwähnt**, in the course of conversation, that circumstance was mentioned; **erwähne andrer Götter nicht**, make no mention of other gods; **er erwähnte seiner nicht**, he did not name him; **namentlich** —, to mention by name; **das oben Erwähnte**, the above-mentioned; **die in dem Vertrage erwähnten Punkte**, the points specified in the contract. **Die Erwähnung**, mention. **Einer Sache Erwähnung thun**, to make mention of a thing, to mention a thing.

Erwähren, *v. r.* **sich** —, to become true. **Das Sprichwort erwährt sich**, the proverb proves to be true.

1. **Erwallen**, [from **wallen** = to boil] *v. intr.* [u. w. seyn] to boil up.

2. **Erwallen**, [from **wallen** = to wander] *v. tr.* to reach, to attain by wandering [about] as a pilgrim.

Erwandern, *v. tr.* 1) to reach by wandering, or by travelling on foot. 2) to gain or acquire by wandering or by travelling on foot.

Erwarmen, *v. intr.* [u. w. seyn] to grow warm, to warm. **Die Erde erwarmt bald an einem hellen Sommertage**, the earth soon warms in a clear day in summer; **das Wasser erwarmt langsam**, the water heats slowly. *Fig.* **Sein Herz erwarmte bei solchem Anblick**, his heart warmed at such a sight.

Erwärmen, *v. tr.* to make warm, to warm [a liquor &c.]. **Die Sonne erwärmt im Sommer die Erde**, the sun in summer warms the earth; **sich** —, to warm one's self. *Fig.* to make warm or bring to a glow.

Erwarten, *v. tr.* 1) to rest or remain stationary in expectation of the arrival of, to stay for, to wait. **Und — mit sehnsüchtigen Augen den verheißenen Führer**, and wait with longing eyes their promised guide; **ich will nach dem Gasthofe gehen und Sie dort** —, I will go to the inn, and there wait till you come; **ich versprach, drei Tage mein Schicksal zu** —, three days I promised to attend my doom; **die Stunde** —, to wait for the arrival of the hour. *Fig.* **Ein rühmlicher Lohn erwartet die Guten**, a glorious reward awaits the good; **Glück oder Elend erwartet uns nach dem Tode**, happiness or misery attends us after death. 2) to have a previous apprehension of something future, whether good or evil, to look for, to expect. **Wir — einen Besuch**, we expect a visit; **Nachrichten** —, to look for news; **das läßt sich nicht** —, it is not a thing to be expected; **das erwartete ich mir**, that I anticipated; **ich erwartete mir, daß es so kommen würde**, I was prepared for this happening. 3) to desire with expectation of good, or a belief that it may be obtained, to hope. **Zu** —, to be hoped for; **wir — eine günstige Antwort auf unsre Bitten**, we hope for favourable answers to our demands.

Erwartlich, *adj.* and *adv.* expectable.

Erwartung, *f.* 1) [the state of expecting] expectation, expectance, expectancy. **In — eines Bessern**, till something better happens. 2) [something expected] expectation, expectance, expectancy. **Thörichte —en hegen**, to indulge [in] absurd expectations; **ich bin in meinen —en getäuscht worden**, I have been disappointed in my expectations, or my expectations have been disappointed; **in — der kommenden Uebel**, in anticipation of the approaching evils.

Erwartungsvoll, *adj.* and *adv.* full of expectation.

Erwaten, *v. tr.* to reach by wading.

Erweckbar, *adj.* and *adv.* that may be wakened or excited.

Erwecken, *v. tr.* 1) to excite or rouse from sleep, to waken. **Einen aus dem Schlafe** —, to awaken any one out of sleep; **die Todten** —, to awake the dead. 2) *Fig.* **Heiliget einen Streit, erwecket die Starken**, [in Script.] prepare war, wake up the mighty men; **das Herz zur Tugend** —, to excite the heart to virtue; **den Muth** —, to excite the spirits or courage; **die schlummernden Geistesfähigkeiten** —, to rouse the dormant faculties; **Tyrtäus kriegerische Muse erweckte die Welt**, Tyrtæus' martial muse waken'd the world; **das Gemüth** —, to edify the mind; **Empfindungen wieder zu** —, **welche das Gemüth einmal gehabt hat**, to revive perceptions, which the mind has once had; **gesalzenes Fleisch erweckt Durst**, salt meat produces thirst; **Verdienst erweckt Neid**, merit calls up envy.

Erweckmittel, *n.* incentive.

Erwecklich, *adj.* and *adv.* 1) V. **Erweckbar.** 2) *Fig.* edifying. **Eine —e Predigt**, an edifying sermon.

Erwehren, I. *v. tr.* ||V. **Verwehren.** II. *v. r.* **sich** —, to hinder from approaching us, to defend one's self from. **Eines Feindes sich** —, to keep off an enemy; **ich konnte mich der Mücken nicht** —, I could not keep off the flies; **ich konnte mich der Bettler nicht** —, I could not get rid of the beggars; **ich kann mich des Schlafes nicht** —, I cannot forbear sleeping, I cannot resist slumbering.

Erweichbar, *adj.* and *adv.* that may be softened, mollifiable.

Erweichen, I. *v. intr.* [u. w. seyn] to become less hard, to soften. **Das Wachs erweicht in der Hitze**, wax softens in heat. II. *v. tr.* and *intr.* to make soft or tender, to soften, to mollify, to intenerate. **Leder im Wasser** —, to soften leather by steeping it in water, to macerate leather; **Gerste erweicht**, barley is emollient; **—de Mittel**, [in medicine] emollients. *Fig.* **Er wurde erweicht**, he was moved; **vielleicht wird er durch den Anblick des Kindes erweicht**, he may soften at the sight of the child; **sie war bis zu Thränen erweicht**, she was moved to tears; **ich will Herzen von Stein** —, I will soften stony hearts.

Erweichlich, *adj.* and *adv.* that may be softened, mollifiable.

Erweichung, *f.* mollification, emollition.

Erweichungsmittel, *n.* [in medicine] an emollient.

Erweinen, I. *v. intr.* [unusual] to utter a loud voice in weeping, to cry. II. *v. tr.* to obtain by weeping.

Erweis, *m.* [-es, *pl.* -e] proof, evidence.

Erweisen, *ir.* I. *v. tr.* 1) to show, to bestow. Einem eine Gunst —, to bestow a favour on any one; erweise ihm weder Gutes noch Schlimmes, do him neither good nor evil; Ehre —, to do honour; einem die ihm gebührende Ehrfurcht —, to pay due respect to any one; einem die letzte Ehre —, to pay the funeral honours to the dead. 2) to evidence, to prove. Das Zeugniß zweier Zeugen ist gewöhnlich hinreichend, um die Schuld eines Verbrechers zu erweisen, the testimony of two witnesses is usually sufficient to evidence the guilt of an offender; die Wahrheit einer Aussage —, to prove the truth of a declaration; die Unrichtigkeit einer Voraussetzung —, to evince the falsity of a supposition; die Sache ist erwiesen, the fact is established by evidence; eine erwiesene Sache, a thing evinced or proved; sein Recht —, to evince one's right or authority. II. *v. r.* sich —, to prove, to make one's self known. Sich heilsam —, to prove salutary; sie hat sich sehr gütig gegen mich erwiesen, she has shown me a great deal of kindness; sich gnädig gegen einen —, to show mercy on a person [an offender &c]; *it.* to prove gracious to any one; er erwies sich immer als meinen Freund, he has always proved himself my friend.

Erweislich, *adj.* and *adv.* capable of proof, provable, evincible. Ein —er Satz, a demonstrable proposition; eine —e Thatsache, verifiable fact; auf eine —e Art, in a manner to preclude doubt, demonstrably, evincibly.

Erweislichkeit, *f.* demonstrableness.

Erweitern, I *v. tr.* to make greater in dimensions. Eine Bresche —, to widen a breach; eine Wunde —, [in surgery] to dilate a wound; der —de Nasenmuskel, [in anatomy] dilator; seine Besitzungen —, to enlarge one's possessions; die Grenzen —, to extend the boundaries. *Fig.* Den Handel —, to extend commerce; einen Vertrag —, to extend the terms of a treaty; erweiterte Begriffe, enlarged ideas; die —de Bulle Clemens IX, the ampliating brief of Clement IX; der Sinn davon ist erweitert, aber nicht verändert, its meaning is amplified, but not altered; einen Satz —, to extend a proposition; das Herz —, to expand the heart. II. *v. r.* sich —, *a*) to grow wider, to widen. Schuhe — sich im Tragen, shoes widen by wearing; die Bögen — sich, arches widen. *b*) to enlarge, to extend, to dilate, to expand. Eine Ebene erweitert sich, a plain extends; der See erweitert sich, the lake expands. *Fig.* Mein Blick erweitert sich, my view is more extended; mein Herz, mein Geist erweitert sich, my heart dilates, or is enlarged, my mind is enlarged; sein Wirkungskreis hat sich erweitert, his sphere of action is extended. III. *v. intr.* [u. w. seyn] to grow wider, to widen.

Erweiterung, *f.* 1) the act of widening, extending, &c. *Fig.* Die — eines Satzes, the amplification of a proposition. 2) [the state of being widened, extended, &c.] enlargement, dilatation, expansion. Die — des Herzens, der Herzöhrlein und Arterien, [in medical science] a dilation of the heart, auricles and arteries, systole or diastoly.

Erweiterungsurtheil, *n.* a synthetic reasoning.

Erwerb, *m.* [-es, *pl.* -e] 1) the act of acquiring, acquisition. Von seinem —e leben, to gain one's living by manual labour; die Art des —es, manner of acquest [of property]. 2) that which is gained by labour, services or performance, earnings. Der reine —, clear profits. 3). Geistige —e, mental acquirements.

Erwerbsfähig, *adj.* and *adv.* capable of acquiring or earning. Er ist ein —fähiger Mensch, he is old enough to earn his bread. —fleißig, *adj.* and *adv.* V. —lustig. —los, *adj.* and *adv.* wanting capacity to acquire or deprived of the means to acquire. —lose Zeiten, hard times. —lustig, *adj.* and *adv.* industrious. —schule, *f.* a school of industry. —sfleiß, *m.* industry. —smittel, *n.* means to acquire or gain something. —squelle, *f.* a source of gain. Der Seedienst ist eine gute —squelle für viele Engländer, many Englishmen get a good living by sea-service. —sstand, *m.* the productive class of the people. —szweig, *m.* any business which a person carries on for procuring a subsistence or for profit, trade, occupation, profession.

Erwèrben, *ir. v. tr.* [V. Werben] to gain by labour, to acquire, to earn. Sein Brod —, to get one's bread; seinen Unterhalt durch Händearbeit —, to obtain one's living by handicraft; Vermögen —, to gain property; sich Reichthum durch Sparsamkeit —, to get wealth by economy; täglich einen Thaler —, to earn a dollar a day; die Art Eigenthum zu —, the manner of acquiring property; sich Kenntnisse, Geschicklichkeit —, to acquire learning, skill; sich Gunst —, to gain favour; sich Eines Gunst —, to get into any one's favour; sich Ruf —, to gain reputation; sich Lob —, to get praise; sich Ehren oder Lorbeeren —, to earn honours or laurels; sich ein Recht auf etwas —, to acquire a right or title to any thing; sich Ansprüche —, to procure titles [to a thing]; sich Jemands Liebe —, to win any one's love; durch Bescheidenheit erwirbt man sich Liebe und Achtung, modesty procures love and respect; sich Freunde —, to acquire friends; natürliche oder erworbene Eigenschaften, abilities, natural or acquired; erworbene Talente, Fähigkeiten or Fertigkeiten, acquirements.

Erwèrber, *m.* [-s, *pl.* -] acquirer.

Erwèrbniß, *n.* [-ßes, *pl.* -ße] [the thing acquired or gained] acquisition. Geistige —ße, acquirements.

Erwèrbsam, *adj.* and *adv.* industrious.

Erwèrbsamkeit, *f.* industry.

Erwèrfen, *ir. v. tr.* 1) to reach by throwing. 2) [unusual] to kill by throwing.

Erwètten, *v. tr.* to gain by laying bets, by wagering.

Erwidern, [less correct erwiedern] 1) [in general] to return, to render Einen Gruß —, to return a salutation; eine Wohlthat —, to repay a benefit; Eines Liebe —, to make a return to any one's love; Gleiches mit Gleichem —, to return like for like, to retaliate. 2) to return an answer, to answer, to reply. Er erwiderte nichts, he gave no answer. SYN. V. Antworten.

Erwiderung, *f.* 1) return for any office good or bad, requital. 2) answer, reply.

Erwiderungsschrift, *f.* [in law-pleadings, the reply of the plaintiff to the defendant's rejoinder] surrejoinder.

||**Erwiedern**, [unusual] *v. tr.* to repeat, to iterate.

Erwilden, [unusual] *v. intr.* [u. w. seyn] to grow wild.

Erwimmern, *v. tr.* to obtain by whimpering or low lamentations.

1. **Erwinden**, [unusual] *ir. v. tr.* to raise by a windlass.

2. **Erwinden**, [probably allied to winnen in gewinnen] I. [unusual] *ir. v. tr. Fig. a*) to get or acquire by effort or labour, to earn. || *b*) to effect II. [rather stiff and unusual] *v. r.* sich —, to dare, to be bold enough.

3 ||**Erwinden**, [unusual] *ir. v. intr.* [allied to schwinden] [in law &c.] to be wanting.

Erwinken, *v. tr.* 1) to reach beckoning, to nod, to wink sufficiently. 2) to give a hint to approach.

Erwirken, *v. tr.* V. Auswirken, I. 2.

Erwischen, [somewhat vulgar] *v. tr.* to seize hastily or by artifice. Einen —, to surprise any one, auf frischer That erwischt, caught in the act; er lief davon, aber sie erwischten ihn endlich doch, he ran off, but they overtook him at length; ein Amt —, to get an office.

Erwittern, *v. tr* V. Auswittern, II. 2. *Fig.* [rather vulgar] to find out.

Erwuchern, *v. tr.* to get by usury.

Erwünschen, *v. tr.* 1) to wish for. Eine erwünschte Gelegenheit, an opportunity to be wished for; ein erwünschtes Talent, a desirable accomplishment; erwünschter bist du mir niemals gekommen, your presence was never more agreeable to me. 2) to obtain by wishing.

Erwürfeln, *v. tr.* to win at dice.

Erwürgen, I *v. intr.* [u. w. seyn] to be suffocated or stifled. II. *v. tr.* 1) to destroy life by stopping respiration, to choke, to suffocate, to strangle. Die Wölfe — die Schafe, wolves worry the sheep; sich —, to strangle one's self. Das —, suffocation, strangulation. 2) to kill by cutting the throat. *Fig.* to put to death, to slay, to massacre.

Erwürger, *m.* [-s, *pl.* -] strangler.

Èrz and **Érz**, *n.* [-es, *pl.* -e] [Sw. and A. S. *aer*, Lat. *aes*, gen. *aer-is*; allied to the Engl. *iron*, Eisen, thus originally perhaps = das Glänzende. Others deduce it from the Heb. *arez* = Erde] 1) [a metal or semi-metal in a mineral state] ore. Silber —, silver-ore; Zinn —, tin-ore, oxide of tin; Blei —, lead-ore; [in mining] das — aufbreiten, to clean the ore; das — abschlacken, to scum the ore in melting. 2) [in mining] any mineral or fossil substance, as Alaun —, alum-ore or alum-stone. 3) brass. Korinthisches —, Corinthian brass. 4) [in common life, a compound of copper and tin] bronze. 5) [chiefly in poetry] *a*) any thing made of metal, as arms, trumpets &c. *b*) any thing resembling in colour, sound, substance &c. metal, brass or bronze. Eine Stimme von —, a stentorian voice; eine Brust von —, a chest of iron

Erz-abgabe, *f.* [in mining] due or lot. —ader, *f.* a metallic vein, a lode. —arbeit, *f.* a work made of metal. —arbeiter, *m* a worker in metal, a metallist. —art, *f.* 1) any species of ore. 2) [in mining] V. Gangart. —asche, *f.* flowers of zinc. —auge, —äuglein, *n.* a grain of metal. —bild, *n.* a statue or bust cast of bronze, a bronze. —blinkend, *adj.* and *adv.* having a shining lustre like metal —blume, *f.* [in mineralogy] spar, marcasite. —bruch, *m.* a mine. —dieb, *m.* one that steals ores. —druse, *f.* an ore coated with small crystals, a drusy ore. —fall, *m.* [in mining] bunny. Reicher —, a gulph of ore. —farben, *adj.* and *adv.* having the colour of brass, brassy. —faß, *n.* and [dimin.] —fäßlein, *n.* [in mining] a tub, used for carrying the ore to the furnace. —gang, *m.* a metallic vein, a lode. —gebirge, *n.* 1) mountains containing mines. 2) the Erzgebirge, a chain of mountains which extend between Bohemia and Saxony, and a district in the latter kingdom so called. —gebirger,

m. —gebirgerinn, *f.* a person that is a native of, or inhabits, the Erzgebirge. —gebirgisch, *adj.* and *adv.* belonging to the Erzgebirge. —gepanzert, *adj.* and *adv.* furnished with a brassy coat of mail, mailed in brass. —gießer, *m.* a founder or caster of brass or bronze. —gräber, *m.* a miner. —grube, *f.* a mine. —haftig, *adj.* and *adv.* 1) resembling ore. 2) [in mining] V. —haltig. —halde, *f.* [in mining] a heap of ores. —haltig, *adj.* and *adv.* containing ore. —haltige Bergarten, rocks containing ore. —haltigkeit, *f.* the quality of containing ore. —haufe, *m.* [in mining] parcel, pile of ore. —höhle, *f.* a cart used in mines. —hütte, *f.* V. Schmelzhütte. —kunde, *f.* the docimastic art, or metallurgy; mineralogy. —kundige, *m.* a mineralogist. —kupe, *f.* [in mining] farm. —kutter, V. —scheider. —maß, *n.* [in mining] bing. —masse, *f.* 1) a mass of ore. 2) a great piece of founded metal. —messer, *m.* [in mining] barmaster. —mittel, *n.* [in mining] moor of ore. —mutter, *f.* 1) the gangue or matrix of the ore. 2) spar, marcasite. —nest, *n.* pipe. —ofen, *m.* a furnace. —platz, *m.* [in mining] bing-place, ore-plot. —pocher, *m.* [in metallurgy] one who stamps ore. —probe, *f.* the test of ore, assay. —reich, *adj.* and *adv.* rich in ores, abounding with metals. —schaum, *m.* the scoria of metals, the scum. —scheidekunst, *f.* the docimastic art, docimacy, metallurgy. —scheiden, *n.* the sorting of ores. —scheider, *m.* a person that performs the sorting of ores. —schicht, *f.* 1) [in mining] a shift. 2) the quantity of ore melted in one shift. —schlich, *m.* [the ore of a metal when pounded and prepared for working] slich. —schürfer, *m.* [in mining] searcher. —schwer, *adj.* and *adv.* heavy like ore. —staub, *m.* the dust of ores —stufe, *f.* a small piece [a fragment] of ore. —trog, *m.* [in metallurgy] the washing-trough. —tropfen, *m.* [in mining] sulphuret of silver, silver-glance or vitreous silver which occurs in the form of red drops. —truhe, *f.* V. —höhle. —trum, *n.* [in mining] rib, sticking, string Flaches —trum, floor. —waage, *f.* [in metallurgy] a balance used for weighing the ores in assaying. —wand, *f.* any great mass of ore. —werk, *n.* a work made of brass or metal.

Érz, [a word used only in composition, originating from the ancient *ari*, now erst, Gr. ἄριστος, in Greek compositions ἀρχι-; it denotes the principal or most eminent in any quality good or bad] arch, chief, principal; very.

Erz-amt, *n.* the principal office; formerly a high [the highest] office of the German empire. —banneramt, *n.* the office of a chief-banneret. —betrieger, *m.* a arch-deceiver. —bettler, *m.* a chief beggar. —bischof, *m.* archbishop, metropolitan. —bischöflich, *adj.* and *adv.* archiepiscopal. Der —bischöfliche Stuhl, an archiepiscopal see. —bisthum, *n.* archbishopric. —bösewicht, *m.* an arrant rogue, an arch-villain. —dieb, *m.* an arrant thief, a notorious thief or robber. —dumm, *adj.* and *adv.* extremely stupid. —dummkopf, *m.* an archdolt. —engel, *m.* an angel of the highest order, archangel. —engelwurz, *f.* [a plant] the garden angelica. —faul, *adj.* and *adv.* very lazy. —feind, *m.* arch-enemy, arch-fiend, arch-foe. Er ist mein —feind, he is my bitterest enemy; Satan, der —feind, Satan, the arch-fiend; Satan, der —feind der Menschen, Satan, the arch-enemy of mankind. —feldherr, *m.* V. Oberfeldherr. —flegel, *m.* an arch-churl. —gauner, *m.* an arrant rogue, an arch-villain. —graf, *m.* an archcount. —grob, *adj.* and *adv.* very churlish. —grobian, *m.* V. Erzflegel. —gut, *adj.* and *adv.* extremely good. —haus, *n.* the arch-ducal house of Austria. —herzog, *m.* arch-duke. —inn, *f.* archduchess. —herzoglich, *adj.* and *adv.* archducal. —herzogthum, *n.* archduchy, archdukedom. —heuchler, *m.* arch-hypocrite. —hirt, *m.* arch-pastor [an epithet given to Christ]. †—hure, *f.* an arch-whore. —jude, *m.* an arch-usurer. —kämmerer, *m.* [formerly an officer of the German empire] archchamberlain. —kanzler, *m.* [formerly an officer of the German empire] archchancellor. —kanzlerwürde, *f.* the dignity of an archchancellor. —ketzer, *m.* an arch-heretic. —ketzerei, *f.* arch-heresy. —knauser, *m.* an arch-niggard. —kritiker, *m.* arch-critic. —liederlich, *adj.* and *adv.* extremely loose, wanton or dissolute, very debauched. —lügner, *m.* arch-lier. —marschall, *m.* [formerly an officer of the German empire] arch-marshal. —marschallamt, *n.* the office of an archmarshal. —marschallswürde, *f.* the dignity of an archmarshal. —narr, *m.* an arch-fool. —pfalz, *f.* V. Kurpfalz. —pfuscher, *m.* arch-botcher. —priester, *m.* archpriest, archpresbyter. —priesterlich, *adj.* and *adv.* pertaining to an archpriest. —priesterthum, *n.* the office or dignity of an archpriest, archpresbytery. —schatzmeister, *m.* [formerly an officer of the German empire] archtreasurer. —schatzmeisteramt, *n.* arch-treasurership. —schelm, *m.* an arrant knave, a rank rogue. —schenke, *m.* 1) [formerly an officer of the German empire] archbutler. 2) [in Scripture] the chief butler or archbutler of kings. —schmeichler, *m.* arch-flatterer. —schwer, *adj.* and *adv.* 1) very heavy. 2) extremely difficult. —spieler, *m.* a professed gamester. —staatskanzler, *m.* the chief chancellor of the state. —stift, *n.* an archiepiscopal church and chapter. —truchseß, *m.* [formerly an officer of the German empire] arch-dapifer. —vater, *m.* patriarch. —väterlich, *adj.* and *adv.* patriarchal. —würde, *f.* the highest dignity, the office of a dignitary of the first class. —zauberer, *m.* arch-magician.

Erzagen, [rather unusual] *v. intr.* [u. w. seyn] to grow faint-hearted, to be disheartened.

Erzählbar, *adj.* and *adv.* that may be related, told or narrated.

Erzählbarkeit, *f.* the quality of a story that may be narrated.

Erzählen, *v. tr.* to express in words, to tell, to narrate, to rehearse, to recite, to recount. Eine Geschichte —, to tell a story; er erzählte die näheren Umstände, he stated the particulars; die Abenteuer des Don Quixote —, to relate the adventures of Don Quixote; man erzählt, it is reported; die —de Schreibart, the narrative style.

Erzählenswerth, *adj.* and *adv.* that deserves to be narrated.

Erzähler, *m.* [-s, *pl.* -] teller, relater, narrator. *Fig.* a writer of tales, an author in the line of tale-writing. Zu den besten neueren —n der Deutschen rechnet man Tieck, Hoffmann, Hauff u. s. w. Tieck, Hoffmann, Hauff &c. are ranked amongst the best modern tale-writers.

Erzählung, *f.* 1) [the act of narrating] narration, rehearsal, recital. 2) narration, relation, statement, story, history. Meine — gefiel Cynthio sehr, Cynthio was much taken with my narrative; die —en von Tieck or Tieck's —en, Tieck's tales or tales by Tieck.

Erzählungs-lied, *n.* epode. —weise, *adv.* narratively.

Erzähmen, [rather unusual] *v. tr.* to make gentle and familiar, to tame [a wild beast]. Die wilden Waldbewohner —, to tame [to civilize] the ferocious inhabitants of the forest.

Erzänken, *v. tr.* to get or obtain by wrangling.

Erzaubern, *v. tr.* 1) to procure or to effect by witchcraft. 2) *Fig.* to effect by fascination.

Erzechen, *v. tr.* to get by drinking hard, or by carousing.

Erzeigen, *v. tr.* to exhibit or present to the view of others, to show. Sich —, to show one's self. *Fig.* Er erzeigte sich stets als meinen Feind, he has always proved himself my enemy; sich gütig gegen Einen —, to show favour on any one, to extend one's kindness to any one; Einem eine Gefälligkeit —, to do a favour to any one. — Sie uns die Güte, bei uns zu Mittag zu speisen, oblige us with your company at dinner; Einem viel Gutes —, to do any one much good; Einem Wohlthaten —, to confer benefits on any one; Gnade —, to impart favour; Einem wichtige Dienste —, to render important services to any one.

Èrzen or Érzen, *adj.* and *adv.* V. Ehern.

1. Érzen, [from Erz = ore, brass &c.] *v. tr.* cover with brass.

2 ||Érzen, [from er] *v. tr.* to address with pronoun er [which is sometimes used by superi in addressing inferiors instead of Du, Ihr or Si

Erzeugbar, *adj.* and *adv.* that may be duced, producible.

Erzeugbarkeit, *f.* the capability of produced, producibleness.

Erzeugen, *v. tr.* to beget, to generat produce, to engender, to procreate, to Kinder —, to beget children; Korn —, to duce corn; Früchte —, to produce fruits; zen —, to grow wheat; selbst erzeugte W wool of one's own sheep; die Meere — F in Menge, the seas produce fish in abund *Fig.* Zornige Worte — Streit, angry w engender strife; das Laster erzeugt Elend, produces misery; Unmäßigkeit erzeugt töd Krankheiten, intemperance engenders fatal adies; Wollust erzeugt Gebrechlichkeiten, breeds infirmities; Ehrgeiz erzeugt Part gen, ambition breeds factions; Kummer to cause sorrow.

Erzeuger, *m.* [-s, *pl.* -] 1) one that creates, procreator, engenderer, begetter, erator, genitor, a sire, a father. 2) *pl.* pa 3) [Producent] producer.

Erzeugerland, [unusual] *n.* the land of one's father or ancestors, fatherla

Erzeugerinn, *f.* a female that procr a female parent, a mother. Die Erde, aller Dinge, the earth, the parent of all t

Erzeugniß, *n.* [-sses, *pl.* -sse] produ product, produce. Die —sse der Erde, the ductions of the earth; Naturerzeugnisse, na productions; die Kunsterzeugnisse, the ductions of art; vulkanische —sse, volcanic ductions; die —sse des Verstandes, the ductions of intellect.

Erzeugte, *m.* [-n, *pl.* -n] Erzeugte [-n, *pl.* -n] the immediate progeny of a child, a son or daughter.

Erzeugung, *f.* 1) the act of be breeding, procreation, generation. 2) t produced, production.

Erzeugungsfähigkeit, *f.* pr ity.

Erziehen, *ir. v. tr.* ||1) to draw away breed, to bring up, to nurse and foster zahlreiche Nachkommenschaft —, to rear a numerous offspring. 3) to breed, to educate, to instruct, to form by education. Es ist die erste Pflicht der Eltern, ihre Kinder gut zu —, to educate children well is the first duty of parents; einn ihn zur Tugend zu —, to rear him up to virtue; sie wurde auf Kosten meines Vaters erzogen, she was educated at my father's charge; wohl erzogen, well-bred, polite; schlecht erzogen, ill-bred, unpolite. SYN. Erziehen, Auferziehen, Aufziehen. Aufziehen differs from Erziehen and Auferziehen in referring to the mere physical perfection, which consists in the preservation and care of the body; Erziehen and Auferziehen include that formation or improvement of the mind, which enables a man one day to provide for himself. Thus one says of animals and even of plants, daß man sie aufgezogen habe, [that one has reared them], but not erzogen or auferzogen.

Erzieher, *m.* [-s, *pl.* -] 1) the person, who brings up, or educates, educator; instructor, breeder, tutor or governor. 2) a teacher of children, a pedagogue.

Erzieheramt, *n.* pedagogism.

Erzieherinn, *f.* a female tutor, a tutoress, an instructress, a governess.

Erziehung, *f.* 1) the rearing or bringing up, as of a child, pedagogy. 2) breeding, nurture, education, instruction, formation of manners. Eine gute —, a good education; eine christliche —, a religious education; ein Mensch von guter —, a wellbred man; ein Mann von Stand und —, a gentleman.

Erziehungs-anstalt, *f.* a place of education, a seminary, any school, academy. Er hat seinen Sohn und seine Tochter in eine —anstalt gegeben, he has sent his son and daughter to a boarding-school. —**art**, *f.* the method of breeding, educating or instructing, system of education. —**buch**, *n.* a book on education. —**fach**, *n.* that branch of science, which relates to education. —**fähigkeit**, *f.* the ability to instruct or educate others. —**geschäft**, *n.* the business of educating young children. —**grundsatz**, *m.* a principle respecting the education of young children, educational maxim. —**haus**, *n.* a boarding-school. —**kunde**, *f.* the science of education. —**kunst**, *f.* the art of educating young children, pedagogy. —**lehre**, *f.* 1) a theory or system of education. Zur —lehre gehörig, pedagogical. 2) a writing or essay on education. —**lehrer**, *m.* a pedagogue. —**los**, *adj.* and *adv.* without education. —**regel**, *f.* a rule of education. —**schreiber**, *m.* an author that writes on education, a pedagogical author or writer. —**schrift**, *f.* a writing, a book on education. —**schule**, *f.* a boarding-school. —**wissenschaft**, *f.* pedagogy.

Erzielen, *v. tr.* 1) [from zielen i. e. ziehen] to procreate, to generate. Getreide —, to grow corn; Kinder —, to beget children; erzielte Früchte, fruits produced. 2) to aim at. Einen Vogel im Fluge —, to aim at and hit a bird flying. *Fig.* Ein Bündniß —, to aim at an alliance; er hat es erzielt, he has attained it.

Erzischen, *v. intr.* to begin to hiss, to hiss aloud.

Erzittern, *v. intr.* 1) to tremble vehemently, to shake, to quake, to quiver, to shiver, to shudder. 2) to be afraid, to fear.

Erzürnen, I. *v. intr.* [u. w. seyn] to grow angry. Ueber Einen —, to get angry with any one. II. *v. tr.* to make angry, to irritate, to provoke to anger. III. *v. r.* sich —, 1) to grow angry. Ueber etwas sich —, to grow angry at something. 2) to quarrel. Mit Einem sich —, to quarrel with any one.

Erzwacken, *v. tr.* to obtain by pinching or pressing.

Erzwecken, *v. tr.* 1) V. Beabsichtigen. 2) to attain one's end.

Erzwingen, *ir. v. tr.* to obtain or gain by force. Jemands Einwilligung —, to enforce any one's consent; vergieb mir, Portia, dies erzwungene Unrecht, Portia, forgive me this enforced wrong; ein durch Waffengewalt erzwungener Friede, a peace obtained by the force of arms; ein erzwungenes Versprechen, an extorted promise; ein erzwungenes Lächeln, a forced smile. *Fig.* Einen Sinn —, to wrest the sense of a word, passage &c.

Es, Es, *pron.* [A. S. *hit*, *hyt*, Eng. *it*, Dan. *det*, Sw. *thet*, allied to das] it. || *a*) for du, ihr, er, sie in addressing a person, as kommt — oder kommt's her, come here! *b*) a substitute or pronoun demonstrative [dieses] of the neuter gender standing for any thing, as, — ist sein erster Versuch, it is his first essay; — ist mein Vater, it is my father; — ist das erste Mahl, it is for the first time. *c*) it is much used as the nominative case or word to verbs called impersonal, as, — schneiet, — regnet, it snows, it rains. *d*) also to other verbs, as, — ist, it is; — gibt Leute, there are people; [*it*. used to introduce a sentence] — klopft jemand, somebody knocks; — spiele, wer da will, let play who will; — lebe der König! long live the king! God bless or save the king! *Prov.* — ist nicht alles Gold, was glänzt, all is not gold that glitters. *e*) sometimes es may be referred to *matter*, *affair* or some other word, as, ist — dazu gekommen, has *it* come to this? *f*) as a pronoun demonstrative for dasselbe, it refers sometimes to a word of the neuter gender, [in the oblique cases we use seiner, ihr, es] as, ich gebe — [viz. das Buch] dir, I give it to you; ich fand es [viz. das Mädchen] nicht zu Hause, I found her [the girl] not at home; wecke das Kind nicht auf, — liegt in tiefem Schlafe, don't waken the child, it is fast asleep; sometimes it refers to words of any of the three genders in the singular and in the plural number, as, wer ist da? — ist ein Mann, eine Frau, ein Kind, who is there? it is a man, a woman, a child; Kinder sind —, they are children; — sind nur Männer, they are but men; sometimes it refers to an adverb or a whole sentence but indefinitely, as, er behauptet — mit einer solchen Kühnheit, daß wir — glauben, he asserts it with such a boldness, that we believe it; sehen Sie zu, ob — Ihnen ansteht, see whether that will serve your turn; sometimes there is no determinate thing to which it can be referred, as, — läuft auf Eins hinaus, it comes to the same thing; ihr gedachtet — böse mit mir zu machen, aber Gott gedachte — gut zu machen, [in Script.] ye thought evil against me, but God meant it for good. *g*) for derjenige &c. Wer war —, der Christus verrieth? who was it, that betrayed Christ? In writing and in common or familiar language, the vowel e is often dropped, as, nimm's, take it; ist's dazu gekommen? has it come to this?

Es, [in music] E flat [the minor third of E]. Das Stück geht aus —, the piece is in the key of E flat.

***Escadre**, [pron. as in the French] *f.* [*pl.* -n] [a division of a fleet] a squadron.

***Escadron**, *f.* [*pl.* -s or -en] [a body of cavalry] a squadron.

Escadronschef, *m.* a captain of cavalry.

***Escarpe**, *f.* [*pl.* -n] [in fortification, the interior talus or slope of the ditch next the place, at the foot of the rampart] the scarp.

Esch, *m.* [-es, *pl.* -e] V. ||Esche.

Eschblau, *n.* [-es] [in painting] a sort of fine blue colour.

1. **Esche**, *f.* [*pl.* -n] [a fish] V. Äscher.

2. **Esche**, *f.* [*pl.* -n] **Eschenbaum**, *m.* [also Aesche, old German Ask, allied to Eiche and the Lat. *aesc-ulus*] 1) [a tree] the ash, or ash-tree. Die dornige —, V. Bertrambaum. 2) *Fig.* [with poets] a lance or spear made of ash.

Eschen-blatt, *n.* the leaf of the ash-tree. —**holz**, *n.* the wood of the ash-tree, ash. —**rinde**, *f.* the bark of the ash-tree. —**wald**, *m.* a wood of ash-trees.

Eschel, cobalt-blue.

Eschen, *adj.* and *adv.* ash, ashen.

Escheritz, *f.* [*pl.* -en] the fruit of the wild service.

Eschern, V. Äschern.

Escherwurz, *f.* V. Aschwurz.

Eschlauch, V. Aschlauch.

Eschrose, *f.* [*pl.* -n] **Eschrösel**, *n.* 1) sorbus tree, service or sorb. 2) wild service, sorb or mapple leaved service.

||**Eschweihe**, *m.* [-n, *pl.* -n] a name given by manufacturers of serge to clumsy workmen.

Eschwurz, V. Aschwurz.

***Escorte**, *f.* [*pl.* -n] a guard, escort.

***Escortiren**, *v. tr.* to escort [a general, a prisoner, a train of artillery &c.].

1. **Esel**, *m.* [-s, *pl.* -] [Bohem. *osel*, Lat. *asin-us*, Engl. *ass*, allied to Ochs, originally = Thier] 1) the ass. Der männliche —, the jack-ass; wie ein — schreien, to bray. *Prov.* Den — will Jedermann reiten, all lay load on the willing horse; vom Pferde auf den — kommen, to thrive backward, to fall out of the frying pan into the fire; den — zum Doktor machen, to make a dunce an able man, den — suchen und darauf reiten, the butcher look'd for his knife when he had it in his mouth; wo sich der — einmal stößt, da nimmt er sich in Acht, hang a dog on a crab-tree, and he'll never love verjuice; ein — heißt den andern Langohr, the kettle calls the pot black arse; ein schwer belasteter — geht sicher, the ox when weariest treads surest. *Fig.* [in contempt] a dull, heavy, stupid fellow, an ass, a dolt. 2) [that which resembles an ass in form or shape.] *a*) [a wooden machine on which petty offenders ride by way of punishment] a horse, a timber-mare. *b*) a machine by which something is supported, a wooden frame with legs, a horse, a stand. *c*) [in paper-mills] a dropping-board. *d*) [in fam. lang.] Einem einen — bohren, to make sport of any one, ‡to bite one's thumb at a person. 3) a species of cowry, the whasp.

Esel-falb, *adj.* and *adv.* grey like an ass. —**fisch**, *m.* a species of cod-fish. —**füllen**, *n.* an ass's foal. —**grau**, *adj.* and *adv.* grey like an ass. —**mann**, *m.* V. —treiber. †—**s-arbeit**, *f.* hard labour, toilsome work, hard work in servile occupations, drudgery. —**s-bohne**, *f.* the bean [vicia faba]. —**s-brücke**, *f.* [in contempt] a book or other help, which renders things too easy and favours stupidity or laziness, ass's bridge. —**s-distel**, *f.* musk thistle. —**s-farn**, *m.* 1) true maidenhair, lady's hair. 2) common maidenhair. †—**s-fieber**, *n.* V. Ochsenfieber. —**s-geschrei**, *n.* the braying of an ass. —**s-gurke**, *f.* the squirting momordica or wild cucumber. Der —gurkensaft, [in medicine] elaterium. —**s-haupt**, *n.* 1) the head of an ass. 2) [in seamen's language] cap. Das große —haupt, cap of the main mast; das —haupt des Bugspriets, cap of the bowsprit; das —haupt des Flaggenstocks, cap of the flag-staff, the truck. —s-haut, *f.* 1) the skin of an ass. 2) a sort of parchment. 3) dark-spotted cowry. —s-heu, *n.* V. —s-wicke. —s-huf, *m.* 1) the hoof of an ass. 2) *Fig.* *a*) a defective high hoof in horses. *b*) [a shell] the thorny oyster. *c*) [a plant] colt's foot. —s-kopf, *m.* the head of an ass. † *Fig.* a dolt, a blockhead, an ass. —s-kraut, *n.* creeping hairy spurge. —s-kuh, *f.* V. Elephantenschwein. —s-kürbiß, *m.* V. —sgurke. —s-lattig, *m.* V. Huflattig. —s-milch, *f.* 1) ass's milk. 2) *Fig.* [a plant] creeping hairy spurge. —s-möhre, *f.* [a plant] wild carrot, or bird's nest. —s-ohr, *n.* 1) the ear of an ass. *Prov.* Er kann die —ohren nicht verstecken, or die —ohren gucken hervor, he cannot hide his stupidity or blockishness. 2) *Fig.* *a*) [in contempt] *pl.* long ears *b*) [the corner of a leaf in a book turned down] a dog's ear. *c*) [a species of snail] horned broad-lip. *d*) *pl.* [in seamen's language] strops under the cap of top-masts. —s-rücken, *m.* the back of an ass. *Fig.* *a*) two flat surfaces meeting and forming an obtuse angle. Mit einem —rücken, shelving on both sides. *b*) [in architecture] a Gothic arch. *c*) [in seamen's language] an opening or hole in the deck for the whip-staff. —s-tracht, *f.* [an ass's load; three bushels of corn, eighty pots of wine] ance or asnee. —s-wicke, *f.* oval-leaved hedysarum. —s-wurz, *f.* V. —smilch 2. —treiber, *m.* ass-driver.

2. Esel, *m.* [-s, *pl.* -] V. Assel.

Eselchen, *n.* [-s, *pl.* -] [*dimin.* of Esel] a small ass.

†Eselei, *f.* 1) stupidity, blockishness, doltishness. 2) a gross blunder or mistake.

Eselein, *n.* [-s, *pl.* -] [*dimin.* of Esel] a small ass.

Eselhaft, *adj.* and *adv.* ass-like, doltish, stupid, blockish.

Eselinn, *f.* a she-ass.

†Eseln, I. *v. intr.* 1) to commit gross oversights, to blunder. 2) to work hard, to work in mean offices, to labour with toil and fatigue, to drudge. II. *v. tr.* to call [a person] an ass.

Eshammer, *m.* [-s, *pl.* -hämmer] [with blacksmiths and armourers] a sort of hammer with a head shaped like an S.

*Esmarkit, *m.* [-es, *pl.* -e] V. Datolith.

*Esoteriker, *m.* [-s, *pl.* -] an initiate.

*Esoterisch, *adj.* and *adv.* esoteric, private.

*Esparsette, *f.* [*pl.* -n] a kind of sainfoin, esparcet.

Espe, *f.* [*pl.* -n] the aspen, the trembling poplar.

Espen-baum, *m.* [Eng., Dan. and Sw. *asp*, perhaps allied to the Gr. ἀσπ-αίρω, zappeln] the asp, aspen or trembling poplar-tree. —blatt, *n.* aspen leaf. *Er zittert wie ein —blatt, he quakes like an aspen leaf. —holz, *n.* aspen wood. —laub, *n.* V. —blatt. —motte, *f.* the asp-moth. —wald, *m.* a wood of aspen. —wanze, *f.* a species of bug.

Espen, *adj.* and *adv.* aspen, made of aspen wood.

‖Esping, *m.* [-es, *pl.* -e] a sort of ship of burden in the Baltic.

*Esplanade, *f.* [*pl.* -n] 1) a grass-plot, esplanade. 2) [in fortification, the glacis of the counterscarp, or the sloping of the parapet of the covered way towards the country; or the void space between the glacis of a citadel and the first houses of the town] esplanade.

Eß, Eßchen, V. Aß.

Eßbar, *adj.* and *adv.* eatable, esculent. —e Pflanzen, Fische, esculent plants, fish; einiges Fleisch ist nicht —, some flesh is not edible; —e Dinge, eatables, esculents.

‖Eßping, V. Esping.

Esse, *f.* [*pl.* -n] [allied to heiß and Hitze, to the Heb. *aesch*, Feuer] 1) a blacksmith's forge. 2) a chimney.

‖Esse-geld, *n.* money paid for a customary public meal. —n-kehrer, *m.* chimney-sweeper.

Essel, *m.* [-s, *pl.* -] [with printers] a shaving tub.

Essen, [Lat. *edo*, Gr. anciently ἔδω, later ἐσθίω] *ir.* I. *v. tr.* and *intr.* to eat. *a*) to bite or chew and swallow, to eat. Brod —, to eat bread; er ißt wenig, he is a little eater; er aß beständig an des Königs Tische, he continually eat at the king's table; warum isset euer Meister mit den Zöllnern und Sündern? [in Script.] why eateth your master with publicans and sinners? Nebukadnezar aß mit den Thieren, Nebuchadnezzar tabled with the beasts; geh', und schaffe mir etwas zu —, go, and get me some repast. *Prov.* Iß, was gahr ist, trink, was klar ist, sprich, was wahr ist, speak the truth and shame the devil; wer gut kauft, ißt gut, as you brew, so you must drink. *Fig.* Eines Brod —, to be maintained in food by a person; [hence the proverb] weß Brod ich esse, deß Lied ich singe, I stand for the person that feeds me; er ißt meines Brodes, von meinem Brode, he is at my service. *b*) to take food or to take meals at a usual time. Zu Mittag —, to dine; zu Abend —, to sup; wir — drei Mahl des Tages, we eat three meals in a day; Leute, die spät zu Mittag —, — nicht zu Abend, people who dine late, eat no supper; zusammen or an demselben Tische —, to intercommon; wir — alle vier zusammen, we are four at a mess; wo die Offiziere eines Regiments an einem gemeinschaftlichen Tische aßen, where the officers of a regiment were messing; an einer Wirthstafel im Gasthofe —, to dine at an ordinary; es ist Zeit, zu —, it is dinner-time, or supper-time. *c*) [in Script.] to eat, to feast. Lasset uns — und trinken, wir sterben doch morgen, let us eat and drink, for to-morrow we shall die. II. *v. r.* Sich satt —, to eat to the fill; sich rund, dick —, to grow corpulent or fleshy by eating much.

Eß-gelage, *n.* a feast, banquet, entertainment. —gemach, *n.* dining-room. —gier, *f.* a strong desire of food, [in contempt] gluttony. —gierig, *adj.* and *adv.* having a strong desire of food, [in contempt] gluttonous. Ein —gieriger Mensch, a glutton. —kastanie, *f.* chesnut. —kastanienbaum, *m.* chesnut-tree. —korb, *m.* a basket with meats, a basket of fruits. —laube, *f.* 1) an arbour for dining in. 2) [in Scripture] a parlour. —löffel, *m.* a table-spoon. —lust, *f.* a desire of food and drink, appetite, stomach. —lustig, *adj.* and *adv.* having a desire of food and drink, with great appetite. —saal, *m.* dining-room. —stube, *f.* dining-parlour. —stunde, *f.* dinner-time, supper-time. —tafel, *f.* —tisch, *m.* dining-table. —waare, *f.* food, victuals, eatables. —werk, *n.* = Eßwaare. —wurzel, *f.* [a name of plants] *a*) common loose-strife. *b*) broad-leaved tree-primrose. —zeit, *f.* V. Essenszeit. —zimmer, *n.* V. —stube.

Essen, *n.* [-s] 1) the act of eating with respect to the usual time of eating meals. Nach dem —, after dinner or supper. *Prov.* Wie man sich zum — stellt, so stellt man sich zur [Ar]beit, quick at meat, quick at work; nach — soll man stehen, oder tausend Schritte g[ehen], after dinner sit a while, after supper wa[lk a] mile. 2) provisions for the table, food, or [vic]tuals prepared or dressed. Das — zurichten, [to] dress meat; das — anrichten, to serve up mea[t on] the table, das — ist aufgetragen, dinner is se[rved] or on the table; das — abtragen, to clear the ta[ble]. 3) the meat or provisions served in a dish, h[ence] any particular kind of food, a dish. 4) [a] repast; also a rich entertainment of meat [and] drink, an entertainment, a feast, banquet. [Das] Mittag—, dinner; das Abend—, supper; [ein] — ausrichten, to make [to provide] a dinner; [sei]nen Freunden ein — geben, to entertain ou[r] friends at table; der Lord Mayor von Lond[on] gibt beim Antritt seines Amtes ein großes [—], the Lord Mayor of London gives at his i[n]auguration a great feast.

Essens-zeit, *f.* the usual time for eat[ing] a meal, dinner-time, supper-time.

*Essenz, *f.* [*pl.* -en] essence. Pfefferm[ünz]—, the essence of mint; wohlriechende [—n], perfumes, odours, essences.

Esser, *m.* [-s, *pl.* -], -inn, *f.* 1) a [person] that eats, eater. Viele — haben, to maint[ain] many persons; er ist ein starker —, he i[s a] great eater; ein schwacher —, a little ea[ter]. 2) used in composition, as, Mit—, *fig.* a sort [of] cutaneous worms which breed in the flesh [of] children, crimones, comedones.

‖Esserlich, *adj.* and *adv.* having a desire [of] food. Mir ist nicht —, I have no appetite.

Essig, *m.* [-es, *pl.* -e] [allied to äzen = [...] [vegetable acid] vinegar. — machen, bra[uen], sieden, to make vinegar; Wein—, Bier—, [wine] or beer vinegar; Obst—, verjuice; abgezog[ener] —, acetous acid. *Prov.* Sauer wie —, as [sour] as verjuice.

Essig-aal, *m.* —älchen, *n.* vinegar [eel]. —baum, *m.* elm-leaved sumach. —bec[her], *m.* [a mushroom] the cup peziza. —braten [...] [Sauerbraten] roast-meat seasoned with vi[negar], boeuf-à-la mode. —brauer, *m.* V. —[sieder]. —brauerei, *f.* V. —siederei. —dorn, [*m.*] Berberis. —faß, *n.* a cask of vinegar. —[fla]sche, *f.* vinegar-bottle, a cruet. —gähr[ung], *f.* the acid or acetous fermentation. —g[eist], *m.* spirit of vinegar. Versüßter —geist, [dul]cified spirit of vinegar. —glas, *n.* V. [...] —gurke, *f.* 1) common cucumber 2) [a] pickled cucumber, a gherkin. —han[del, *m.*] vinegar-trade. —händler, *m.* vinegar-[merchant]. —hefen, *pl.* the lees of vinegar. —ho[nig, *m.*] [a syrup] oxymel. —krämer, *m.* V. —[händler]. —meth, *m.* V. —honig. —mücke, *f.* [vinegar] worm-fly. —mutter, *f.* mother of [vinegar] [by which the acid or acetous fermentation [is pro]duced]. —rose, *f.* the red rose. —[...] *n.* acetite of potash. —sauer, *adj.* [and] *adv.* 1) sour, sharp or biting to the [taste, as] acid. *Fig.* Er machte ein —saures Gesi[cht bei] dieser Nachricht, he looked as sour as vine[gar at] this news. 2) [in chimistry] formed by the [union] of acetic acid or radical vinegar with any [sali]fiable base. —saures Blei, acetate of lea[d]; [—]saures Kupfer, acetate of copper. —sä[uer]lich, *adj.* and *adv.* [in chimistry] aceto[us]. —säure, *f.* 1) the acidity of vinegar. 2) [in chim]istry] radical vinegar, acetic acid. —sie[der], *m.* one that makes and sells vinegar, [vinegar-]brewer. —siederei, *f.* the house wh[ere vin]egar is made. —tunke, *f.* a sauce [made] with vinegar. —wasser, *n.* water mixed [with] vinegar, oxycrate. —zucker, *m.* a mixture [of] vinegar and sugar, oxysaccharum.

*Estaffette, *f.* [*pl.* -n] an estafet.

Esther, [-s] [a name of women] Esther, Hester.

***Estrade,** *f.* [*pl.* -n] estrade.

Estrich, *m.* [-es, *pl.* -e] [medio-Lat. *astracum*; origin uncertain] 1) any paved way. 2) a floor, or covering, a pavement [of bricks, of marble &c.]. 3) a plaster-floor. 4) a plaster-ceiling. 5) [a cone] the Italian pavement.

***Etabliren,** *v. tr.* 1) to establish, to found. 2) to establish, to settle. Sich —, to settle.

***Etablissement,** *n.* [-s, *pl* -s] [pron. as in the French] 1) establishment. 2) settlement.

***Etage,** *f.* [*pl.* -n] [pron. Etahsche] V. Geschoß or Stockwerk.

***Etamin,** *m.* [-s, *pl.*-s or -e] [a woolen stuff] taminy, or tammy.

***Etappe,** *f.* [*pl.*-n] a resting-place for troops on their march, etappe.

***Etat,** [pron. as in the French] *m.* [-s, *pl.*-s] an account, a list.

***Ethik,** *f.* [the doctrines of morality or social manners] ethics.

***Ethiker,** *m.* [-s, *pl.*-] ethologist.

***Ethnograph,** *m.* [-en, *pl.* -en] ethnologist, ethnographer, a writer on ethnography.

***Ethnographie,** *f.* [*pl.* -en] a treatise on nations, ethnology.

***Ethnographisch,** *adj.* and *adv.* ethnological.

***Etiquette,** [pron. Etikette] *f.* 1) [seldom used in the *pl.*, -n] [forms of ceremony or decorum] etiquet, etiquette. 2) [*pl.* -n] a label [affixed to a bottle, to the vessels of an apothecary &c.].

Etlicher, Etliche, Etliches, *adj.* and *indef. pron.* [et seems to be allied to es, Low. Sax. et, id] [in the sing. it is only used with collective nouns; in the plur. it is used either alone, or with numerals or with nouns] 1) it denotes a small indeterminate quantity or number; some, any, several. Etlicher Rauch, some smoke; etliches Salz, some salt; und indem er säete, fiel etliches an den Weg, [in Script.] and when he sowed, some seeds fell by the way side; etliches fiel in das Steinigte, [in Script.] some fell upon stony places; etliche gute Freunde, some good friends; etliche Feinde, sundry foes; vor etlichen Jahren, some years ago; im Beisein etlicher Offiziere, in the presence of some officers; etliche meiner Bücher, some books of mine; es waren ihrer etliche da, there were several of them; etliche Worte, a few words; etliche Mahl[e], several times; zu etlichen Mahlen, at several times, repeatedly. 2) it sometimes precedes a word of number or quantity with the sense of *about* or *near.* Ein Dorf von etlichen und zwanzig Häusern, a village of some twenty houses; etliche achtzig Mann, some eighty men. 3) it is used also in composition, [but rather stiffly] as, etlichjährig, some years old, lasting some years. Syn. V. Einiger.

Etmahl, *n.* [-s] [in seamen's lang.] day-work.

Etrurisch, *adj.* and *adv.* Etruscan.

Etsch, *f.* [a river in Italy] Adige.

Etter, *m.* [-s, *pl.* -] 1) [appears to be allied to the Lat. *atr-ium*; A. S. *heder* is = Zaun] the boundaries of a place, or the fields of a village. 2) for Eiter.

***Etui,** [pron. as in the French] *n.* [-'s, *pl.* -s] a sort of box or case fitted to the form of the thing intended to be preserved in it, a case, a box, a sheath. Ein chirurgisches —, a case of surgical instruments.

Etwa, ‡Etwan, *adv.* [V. Etlicher] [signified originally] *a*) some where, any where. *b*) at some time or other. ‖*c*) now and then. [now more usually] *Fig.* *α*) perhaps, by chance. Wenn sie Ihnen — nicht gefallen, should they not happen to please you. *β*) about, nearly. Es waren — drei hundert Stück Vieh, there were about three-hundred head of cattle. *γ*) something or other, in some manner or other.

Etwaig, ‡Etwanig, *adj.* that which is done in some manner or other.

Etwas, *pron.* [et-was, V. Etlicher] 1) noting a thing unknown, indeterminate or not specified. Er hat — zu thun, he has something to do; — wünschen, to wish for something; haben Sie mir — zu sagen? have you any thing to say to me? — Neues, some news; eine Maschine steht still, weil — ihre Bewegung hindert, a machine stops, because something obstructs its motion; [in common or familiar life this word is frequently abbreviated into was]; ich habe was vor, I am about something; sometimes it is used as a substantive, as: Sie hat ein gewisses — in ihrem Benehmen, there is a something in her behaviour; das namenlose —, nameless something. 2) noting a part, a portion more or less. Von seinem Wenigen konnte er doch noch — erübrigen, from his little he could something spare; — Geld, some money; trinken Sie — Wein, drink some wine. *Prov.* Besser — als gar nichts, better something than nothing at all. 3) noting a little. Der Mann bat mich um einen Thaler, ich gab ihm aber — mehr, the man asked me a dollar, but I gave him something more; diese Salze schmecken — nach Salpeter, these salts have somewhat of a nitrous taste; der Wein ist — sauer, the wine is a little sour; er ist — anmaßend, he is somewhat arrogant; er ist — weitschweifig, he is rather prolix; er befindet sich — besser, he is a little better; wollen Sie — weiter gehen? will you go any further? 4) = etwas Bedeutendes. Einer, der — [*was] gelernt hat, a person well instructed, a person furnished with erudition, or versed in letters; noting a certain degree of a thing, as, er gilt — bei ihm, he is in favour with him.

‖ and ‡ **Etwelcher,** [or etwélcher &c.] **Etwelche, Etwelches,** *pron.* for einiger, etlicher, etwas. Etwelcher Maßen, somewhat.

‖ and ‡ **Etwelcherlei,** *adv.* some.

***Etymolog,** *m.* [-en, *pl.* -en] an etymologist.

***Etymologie,** *f.* [*pl.* -en] 1) [that part of philology which explains the origin and derivation of words; also the deduction of words from their originals; the analysis of compound words into their primitives] etymology. 2) [in grammar, comprehends the various inflections and modifications of words, and shows how they are formed from their simple roots] etymology.

***Etymologisch,** *adj.* and *adv.* etymological.

***Etymologisiren,** *v. intr.* to search into the origin of words, to deduce words from their simple roots, to etymologise.

Etzen, V. Aetzen.

Eu, a diphthong peculiar to the upper German.

Euch, [Sax. iu, io, juk, Eng. *you*] the dative and accusative case of the plural of the personal pronoun du; you. Wer — verachtet, der verachtet mich, [in Script.] he that despiseth you, despiseth me; ich gebe es —, I give it you; mit —, with you; mehrere von —, several of you.

***Euchysiderit,** *m.* [-s, *pl.*-e] [a mineral, considered as a variety of augite] euchysiderite.

***Eudialyt,** *m.* [-s, *pl.* -e] [a mineral of a brownish red colour] eudialyte.

1. **Euer,** [V. 2. Euer] the genitive case of the plural of the pronoun personal du or the genitive case of the personal pronoun ihr; you. Ich kann — nicht vergessen, I can never forget you; it is often used in composition with the words Halbe, Weg, Wille, as, Eurethalben or Euerthalben, Eurenthalben, Euretwegen, Euertwegen, Eurentwegen, and Euretwillen, Euertwillen, Eurentwillen, for your sake, on your account, or in your behalf; this contraction may be avoided by putting the word selbst between, as, es geschieht um — selbst willen, it is for your sake.

2. **Euer,** [A. S. *eover*, D. *uwe*, Isl. *idar*] *pron.* [it is used with a noun, but also as a substitute for a noun]. — Vater, your father; Eure Mutter, your mother; — Kind, your child; Eure Unterthanen, your subjects; dies ist — Buch, this book is yours; it is used as a word of civility in addressing letters to people of all ranks, as, Eure [Ew.] Königliche Hoheit, your Royal Highness; Eure [Ew.] Excellenz, your Excellency; it refers often to a preceding noun, as, ist der Garten —? is the garden yours? dies ist nicht mein Buch, sondern eures, this is not my book, but yours; ich habe keine Feder, gebt mir eure, I have no pen, give me yours.

Euererseits, Eurerseits, *adv.* from your side.

Euerthalben, Euertwegen, Euertwillen, V. 1. Euer.

Eugen, [-s, *pl.* -e] Eugenius [name of men]; Eugenie [name of women] Eugene.

***Eukairit,** *m.* [-s, *pl.* -e] cupreous seleniuret of silver, eukairite.

***Euklas,** *m.* [a species of emerald] euclase.

Eulchen, *n.* [-s, *pl.* -] diminut. of Eule, a little owl, owlet.

Eule, *f.* [*pl.* -n] [Lat. *ul-ŭla*, from heulen] 1) an owl, owlet. Die weiße —, the snowy-owl; die graue —, ivy-owl. *Prov.* Wie die — unter den Krähen, a butt of sport, a laughing-stock; er war da wie die — unter den Krähen, they made an owl of him; die — hält ihre Kinder für die schönsten, the crow thinks her own bird fairest; a man thinks his own geese swans; —n nach Athen tragen, to carry coals to Newcastle. 2) [denomination of several other things] *a*) a species of butterfly. *b*) [in seamen's lang.] Eine — fangen, to broach to, *it.* to bring by the lee.

Eulen-artig, *adj.* and *adv.* owl-like. **—flucht,** *f.* the dusk of the evening, owl-light. **—flug,** *m.* the flight of owls. **—flügel,** *m.* an owl's wing. **—gesicht,** *n.* an ugly face. **—winkel,** *m.* a dark place, where owls build their nests.

Eulenspiegel, *m.* [-s, *pl.* -] the name of a renowned adventurer, who lived in the 14th century and died at Moelln, Owlglass. *Fig.* a fool, buffoon.

Eulenspiegelstreich, *m.* a merry trick.

***Eunuch,** *m.* [-en, *pl.*-en] [a male of the human species castrated] a eunuch.

***Euphemism[us],** *m.* [-s, *pl.* -en] [a figure in rhetoric by which a delicate word or expression is substituted for one which is offensive to good manners or to delicate ears] euphemism.

***Euphonie,** *f.* [*pl.*-en] [an easy, smooth enunciation of sounds] euphony.

***Euphonisch,** *adj.* and *adv.* euphonic, euphonical.

***Euphorbie,** *f.* [*pl.* -en] [in botany] spurge, or bastard spurge, euphorbia.

Euphorbienharz, *n.* a gummi-resinous substance, euphorbium.

Euphrat, [-s] **Euphrates,** [abbr. Phrat] *m.* [a river] Euphrates.

***Euphuismus,** *m.* [-s, *pl.*-en] euphuism.

Eure, [der, die, das] V. 2. Euer.

Eurer, Eurenthalben, Eurethalben, V. 1. Euer.

Eurerseits, V. Euererseits.

Eurige, [der, die, das] *adj.* [V. 2. Euer] yours. Dies Buch ist das —, this book is yours; mein Schwert und das — sind mit einander verwandt, my sword and yours are kin; [sometimes it is used as a noun] behaltet das — (Eure), keep what belongs to you; grüßet die —n, my compliments to your family.

Europa, *n.* [-'s or Europens] a proper name, Europe.

Europäer, *m.* [-s, *pl.* -] a European.

Europäerinn, *f.* [*pl.* -en] a European.

Europäisch, *adj.* and *adv.* European.

***Eurus,** *m.* the east wind, Eurus.

***Eurythmie,** *f.* [in architecture, painting, and sculpture, ease, majesty and elegance of the parts of a body] eurythmy.

Euter, *n.* [-s, *pl.* -] [allied to the Gr. οὖθαρ, Lat. *uber* Dan. Yver, probably allied to über, hob &c. = etwas Gehobenes, Rundes] the udder [of a female beast]. Das — der Kühe, the bag of cows; mit vollen —n, big-uddered.

Eutern, *v. intr.* [u. w. haben] to get big-uddered.

Eva, [-'s or Evens] [a name of women] Eve.

***Evangelisch,** I. *adj.* 1) [relating to the Gospels, according to the rules of the Gospel] evangelic, evangelical. —e Frömmigkeit, evangelical piety; eine —e Lehre, an evangelical doctrine. 2) protestant, Lutheran. Die —e Kirche, the Lutheran church. 3) Lutheran and Calvinistic as opposed to Catholic. II. *adv.* evangelically.

***Evangelist,** *m.* [-en, *pl.*-en] 1) a preacher or publisher of the Gospel of Jesus Christ. 2) [a writer of the history of our blessed saviour Jesus Christ] an evangelist. Die vier —en Matthäus, Markus, Lukas und Johannes, the four evangelists, Matthew, Mark, Luke and John.

***Evangelium,** *n.* [Evangelii and Evangeliums, *pl.* Evangelia or Evangelien] 1) [originally] good tidings. 2) the Gospel. Das — predigen, to gospel, to instruct in the Gospel; er predigte den Heiden das —, he preached the Gospel to the heathens, he evangelized the heathens; den Wilden das — predigen, to gospelize the savages. 3) the Gospel according to the evangelists Matthew, Mark, Luke and John; Einer, der das — am Altar vorliest, a gospeller. 4) evangelistary.

Evenskind, *n.* **Evenssohn,** *m.* a child or son of Eve, the descendants of our common mother.

Evenstochter, *f.* a female devoted to this world and its enjoyments; *it.* [mostly in a jocose sense] one inheriting the faults of our common mother, a daughter of Eve.

||**Ever,** *m.* V. 2. Eber.

***Evidenz,** *f.* evidence, clearness, manifestness, perspicuity.

***Evocation,** *f.* [in law, a calling from one tribunal to another] evocation.

***Evocatorium,** *n.* [Evocatorii or -s, *pl.* Evocatoria or Evocatorien] [in law] V. Vorladungsschreiben.

***Evolution,** *f.* [in military tactics] evolution.

Ewig, [allied to the Lat. *aevum*, Gr. αἰών, to the Sw. *aefwe*, die Lebenszeit; the primitive sense is that of extension] *adj.* and *adv.* 1) [in mining] Eine —e Teufe, a great and unknown depth. 2) *Fig.* *a*) [without end of existence or duration; *it.* existing at all times without change] eternal, everlasting, endless. —er Ruhm, eternal glory, immortal fame; —e Liebe und Freundschaft, perpetual love and amity; die —e Dauer der Gesetze, the perpetuity of laws; —e Dauer, endless duration; ich werde ihn — hassen, I'll hate him everlastingly; auf —e Zeiten, for perpetuity; der —e Jude, the wandering Jew. *b*) eternal. Eine —e Wahrheit, an eternal truth; was moralisch gut ist, muß es — und unveränderlich seyn, that which is morally good, must be eternally and unchangeably so; was soll ich Gutes thun, daß ich das —e Leben möge haben? [in Script.] what shall I do, that I may have eternal life? 3) [without beginning or end of existence] eternal. Der —e Gott, the eternal God, the everlasting God; der —e, [an appellation of God] the Eternal. 4) eternal, perpetual, incessant, continual, endless. Ein —es Geschrei, endless clamour; —e Streitigkeiten, everlasting disputes; wo westliche Lüfte — herrschen or wehen, where western gales eternally prevail. *Fig.* [it is used in common and familiar language for the sake of emphasis] Es ist doch — Schade, it is a great pity.

Ewigen, [rather unusual] *v. tr.* to eternize. Ein Gesetz —, to eternize a law; einen Namen — (verewigen), to perpetuate a name.

Ewiggrün, *n.* [-s] [a genus of plants] periwinkle.

Ewigkeit, *f.* [in poetry *pl.* -en] 1) time or duration, whose beginning is not remembered, or cannot be traced and ascertained. Von — her, from time immemorial or from time out of mind. *Fig.* *a*) something of which there will be no end, a perpetuity. *b*) [in common and familiar language] In — nicht, never; es ist schon eine —, daß er mir nicht geschrieben hat, it is an age since he wrote to me; ich werde es in alle — nicht zugeben, I will never consent to it. 2) endless duration, continuance to eternity, perpetuity. In alle —, to all eternity. 3) [duration or continuance without beginning or end] eternity. Die — Gottes, the eternity of God; von — zu —, world without end; Gott ist von — zu —, God is from all eternity; Gott, der du bist von — zu —, [in Script.] from everlasting to everlasting, thou art God. 4) [the state or time which begins at death] eternity. In die — gehen, to depart this life, to leave this world; er ist in die — gegangen, he departed this life.

||**Ewiglich,** *adv.* eternally, for ever and ever. Das ist mein Name —, [in Script.] this is my name for ever.

||**Ewischbaum,** *m.* [-es, *pl.* -bäume] V. Eberesche.

***Examen,** *n.* [-s, *pl.* - or Examina] examination.

***Examinand[us],** *m.* [-en, *pl.*-en] the person to be examined, examinant.

***Examinant,** *m.* [-en, *pl.*-en] V. Examinator.

***Examinationscommission,** *f.* an examining committee.

***Examinator,** *m.* [-s, *pl.* -en] examinator, examiner.

***Examiniren,** *v. tr.* to examine [the classes in college &c.].

***Exanimiren,** *v. tr.* to exanimate, to dishearten, to discourage.

***Exaudi,** the name of the Sunday before Whitsuntide.

***Excellent,** *adj.* and *adv.* excellent.

***Excellenz,** *f.* excellence, excellency; also a title of honour. [*pl.* -en] Eure —, your excellency.

***Excentricität,** *f.* [*pl.* -en] eccentricity, extravagancy. Die — der Erdenbahn, [in astronomy] the eccentricity of the earth's orbit.

***Excentrisch,** *adj.* and *adv.* [deviating or departing from the centre] eccentric, eccentrical. *Fig.* [departing from the usual course] eccentric, eccentrical. Ein —es Betragen, eccentric or extravagant conduct; ein —er Kopf, an eccentric genius, an extravagant mind.

***Exception,** *f.* [in law] exception, defence.

***Excerpt,** *n.* [-es, *pl.* -e] an extract from writings, books or authors.

***Exceß,** *m.* [-sses, *pl.* -sse] [in morals] excess.

***Excipiren,** *v. intr.* [in law] to except. Gegen einen Zeugen —, to except to a witness.

***Excludiren,** *v. tr.* to exclude.

***Exclusion,** *f.* exclusion.

***Exclusive,** *adv.* exclusively.

***Excommunication,** *f.* [the act of ejecting from a church] excommunication.

***Excommuniciren,** *v. tr.* to expel from communion, to eject from the communion of the church, to excommunicate.

***Excremente,** *pl.* excrements, alvine discharges.

***Excretion,** *f.* excretion.

***Execution,** *f.* 1) execution. V. Ausführung [of a work, musical performance &c.]; Vollstreckung [of a testament &c.]. 2) execution. V. Hinrichtung [of a sentenced criminal].

***Executiv,** *adj.* and *adv.* executive. Die — Gewalt, executive power or authority.

***Executor,** *m.* 1) executor, executioner. 2) — Testamenti or Testaments —, the person appointed by a testator to execute his will, or [illegible] see it carried into effect, executor.

***Exegese,** *f.* [*pl.*-n] exposition, explanation, chiefly an interpretation of the Scriptures, exegesis.

***Exeget,** *m.* [-en, *pl.*-en] an explainer, interpreter; chiefly an interpreter of the Scriptures.

***Exegetik,** *f.* the art of explaining or interpreting.

***Exegetisch,** I. *adj.* explanatory, exegetical. II. *adv.* exegetically.

***Exempel,** *n.* [-s, *pl.* -] example, instance. Ich könnte Ihnen mehrere — davon anführen, I could give you several instances of it; — [illegible] etwas nehmen, to take example by any thing; ein — statuiren, to set forth for an example; zum —, for example, for instance. *Prov.* [illegible] —, halbe Predigt, a good Jack makes a good Jill.

***Exemplar,** *n.* [-es, *pl.* -e] 1) a copy [of a] book &c.]. 2) a single piece in a collection [of] mineral substances, animals, plants &c., [a] sample, a specimen.

***Exemplarisch,** I. *adj.* exemplary. Eine —e Strafe, an exemplary punishment; ein —es Leben führen, to be exemplary in one's life, [to] lead an exemplary life. II. *adv.* exemplarily. [illegible] bestrafen, to punish exemplarily.

***Exem[p]t,** *m.* [-en, *pl.* -en] a person [who] is exempted, free from, an exempt.

||***Exequent,** *m.* [-en, *pl.* -en] bailiff.

***Exequien,** *pl.* funeral rites and solemnities, obsequies, masses for the deceased.

***Exequiren,** *v. tr.* to execute.

*Exerciren, I. *v. intr.* to exercise arms. II. *v. tr.* to drill [recruits].

Exercir-kunst, *f.* tactics. —meister, *m.* drill-sergeant. —platz, *m.* exercise ground, parade.

*Exercitium, *n.* [-s, *pl.* Exercitien] 1) the drilling of recruits, the exercising. 2) a short dissertation composed by a student, a theme, an exercise.

Exercitienmeister, *m.* a master of exercises.

*Exhibiren, *v. tr.* [in law] to exhibit, to present.

*Exhibition, *f.* [in law] exhibition.

*Exhibitum, *n.* [Exhibiti or -s, *pl.* Exhibita] the writing exhibited.

*Exil, *n.* [-s, *pl.* -e] exile, banishment.

*Exiliren, *v. tr.* to exile, to banish. Ein Exilirter, an exile.

*Existenz, *f.* 1) [the state of being or having essence] existence. 2) support of life, livelihood. *Fig.* Seine unbesonnenen Reden können ihm leicht seine *— gefährden, his inconsiderate speeches may easily endanger his livelihood.

*Existiren, *v. intr.* 1) to exist, to have being, to live. 2) to live, to feed, to subsist.

*Exmission, *f.* [in law] judicial dispossession.

*Exmittiren, *v. tr.* [in law] to dispossess judicially.

*Exorcism [us], [-s, *pl.* -en] *m.* exorcism.

*Exorcist, *m.* [-en, *pl.* -en] exorcist.

*Exordium, *n.* [Exordii or -s, *pl.* Exordia or Exordien] [in oratory, the beginning] exordium.

*Exoteriker (or Exoteriker), *m.* [-s, *pl.* -] a uninitiated person.

*Exoterisch, *adj.* and *adv.* exoteric, uninitiated.

*Exotisch, *adj.* exotic. Eine —e Pflanze, an exotic or exotical plant.

*Expansion, *f.* expansion.

Expansiv, *adj.* and *adv.* expansive.

Expectoriren, *v. tr.* to expectorate. * *Fig.* sich —, to unbosom one's heart.

Expediens, *n.* an expedient.

Expedient, *m.* [-en, *pl.* -en] a copist.

Expediren, *v. tr.* to dispatch, to expedite. ig. † or * to dispatch. — Sie mich doch, ich ste schon so lange, pray, dispatch my busis, I have been waiting so long; sie haben ihn ell expedirt, they finished him quickly. V. b Abfertigen.

Expedition, *f.* 1) dispatching, sending y. 2) dispatching, performing, speedy cution. 3) a newspaper or postoffice. 4) march of an army or the voyage of a fleet; o any enterprise, undertaking or attempt by umber of persons, expedition. Die — der nzosen nach Egypten, the expedition of the nch to Egypt; die Regierung sandte eine nach dem stillen Meere, the government t an expedition to the Pacific.

Experiment, *n.* [-es, *pl.* -e] an experiment, rial. Chemische —e, experiments in chitry; —e machen, to experiment.

Experimental, *adj.* experimental. —s Che- oder Physik, experimental chimistry or sics.

Experimentiren, *v. intr.* to experiment, to e trial.

Explosion, *f.* a bursting with noise, exion.

Exponent, *m.* [-en, *pl.* -en] 1) [in algebra, the number or figure which, placed above a root at the right hand, denotes how often that root is repeated] the exponent [as, a^2 &c.]. 2) [the quotient arising when the antecedent number is divided by the consequent] the exponent [thus 6 is the exponent of the ratio of 30 to 5].

*Exponiren, *v. tr.* 1) [obsolescent] to construe. Die Schüler exponirten das 3te Kapitel des Livius, the scholars construed the IIId chapter of Livy. 2) [mostly in fam. lang.] to expose. Sich —, to expose one's self to dangers.

*Exportation, *f.* exportation.

*Exporten, *pl.* exported goods, exports.

*Exportiren, *v. tr.* to export [goods &c.].

*Expreß, *adv.* expressly; * and † purposely. Er hat es — gethan, he did it purposely, or on purpose.

*Expresser, Expresse, *m.* [-n', *pl.* -n] a messenger sent on a particular errand or occasion, an express.

*Exspectant, *m.* [-en, *pl.* -en] an expectant, an aspirant.

*Exspectanz, *f.* [*pl.* -en] survivorship, expectancy.

*Extase, *f.* ecstasy.

*Extemporiren, *v. intr.* to speak extempore, to extemporize.

Extra, *adv.* a latin proposition, denoting beyond or excess, extra.

Extra-ausgabe, *f.* 1) particular or extraordinary expenses. 2) an uncommon, singular edition or publication of a work &c. —blatt, *n.* a gazette or newspaper, public paper extraordinary. —fein, *adj.* and *adv.* superfine. —ordinär, *adj.* extraordinary. —post, *f.* travelling expeditiously by the use of fresh horses taken at certain stations. —post reisen, to travel post. —vagant, *adj.* extravagant. —vaganz, *f.* extravagance, extravagancy. —vagiren, *v. intr.* V. Faseln.

*Extrakt, *m.* [-es, *pl.* -e] an extract [of books, of substances].

*Extrem, *n.* [-s, *pl.* -e] extreme. Vermeide —e, avoid extremes.

*Extremität, *f.* [*pl.* -en] 1) the utmost point or side, extremity. 2) extreme or utmost distress, extremity. 3) *pl.* the utmost parts, extremities. Die —en des Körpers in der Malerei und Bildhauerkunst sind der Kopf, die Hände und Füße, the extremities of the body, in painting and sculpture, are the head, hands and feet.

*Exulant, *m.* [-en, *pl.* -en] an exile.

Ey, V. Ei.

F.

F, f, [a consonant] f. 1) *n.* f. 2) [in music] *a)* [the fourth note in the natural diatonic scale] F, or fa. — dur, the key sharp or mode major of F natural; — moll, the key flat or mode minor of F natural. *b)* [it denotes also one of the Greek keys in music, destined for the base] F. Der —schlüssel, the cliff of the bass. *c)* the key or finger-key F in an organ or harpsichord.

Fabel, *f.* [*pl.* -n] [from the Lat. *fabula*] [a feigned story or tale; also a fictitious narration intended to enforce some useful truth or precept] a fable. Die —n Aesops, Esop's fables. *Prov.* Er ist der Wolf in der —, talk of the devil and his imps appear.

Fabel-buch, *n.* a book containing fables. —dichter, *m.* a fabler, fabulist. —geschichte, *f.* 1) a fabulous story. 2) the history of the fables of the ancient pagans, but chiefly of the Greeks and Romans. *—hans, *m.* a dealer in feigned stories, a fabler; *it.* ‖ [for Faselhans] a doter, raving fellow. —held, *m.* a fabulous hero. —land, *n.* 1) the country of fables. 2) a fabulous country. —lehre, *f.* mythology. —lehrig, *adj.* and *adv.* mythological. —lese, *f.* a collection of choice fables. —name, *m.* 1) a fabulous name. 2) a feigned or fictitious name. —reich, *adj.* and *adv.* 1) described in fables, fabulous. Das —reiche Morgenland, the fabulous East. 2) or —n-reich, rich in fables or fabled stories. —reich, *n.* V. —land. —schmied, [mostly in contempt] *m.* the inventor of fabulous stories, a romancer. —volk, *n.* a fabulous or fabled people. —weisheit, *f.* wisdom in fables. —welt, *f.* the early age of a country, the accounts of which are mostly fabulous. Die —welt Griechenlands und Roms, the fabulous age of Greece and Rome. —werk, *n.* 1) fabulous stories. 2) a book containing fables. —zeit, *f.* the fabulous age.

Fabelei, *f.* [*pl.* -en], 1) [in contempt] a fabulous invention, a feigned story or tale. ‖2) doting, raving.

Fabelhaft, I. *adj.* fabulous, mythic. Eine —e Geschichte, a fabulous story; —e Helden, fabulous heroes; das —e einer Geschichte, the fabulousness of a story. II. *adv* fabulously.

Fabeln, *v. intr.* 1) to invent fables, to fable, to romance. ‖2) to talk irrationally, to rave.

*Fabriciren, *v. tr.* to form by art and labour, to manufacture, to fabricate [woolens &c.].

*Fabrik, *f.* manufactory.

Fabrik-arbeit, *f.* manufacture, salework. —arbeiter, *m.* a workman in a manufactory, manufactory-man, mechanic, operative. —herr, *m.* proprietor of a manufactory. —meister, *m.* superintendant or overseer in a manufactory. —stadt, *f.* manufacturing-town.

*Fabrikant, *m.* [-en, *pl.* -en] manufacturer. Ein Uhren—, a maker of watches; ein Tuch—, a cloth-manufacturer, a clothier.

*Fabrikat, *n.* [-s, *pl.* -e] a manufacture [as, cloth, cabinet work &c.]. Ein ausgezeichnetes —, an exquisite piece of workmanship.

*Fabrikation, *f.* Fabrikatur, *f.* fabrication.

*Fabulant, *m.* [-en, *pl.* -en] [chiefly in contempt] a fabler or romancer, a fabulist.

*Fabulist, *m.* [-en, *pl.* -en] [a writer of fables] a fabulist.

*Façade, *f.* [pron. Fassahde] [*pl.* -n] [in archit.] the principal face or side, facade, front.

*Facette, *f.* [pron. Fassette] [*pl.* -n] 1) a small surface, facet. Die —n eines Demants, the facets of a diamond. 2) a diamond cut with facets.

Fach, [allied to the following adj. or adv.] in composition denotes the same quantity added, as zwei—, twofold, double; vier—, fourfold, quadruple; zehn—, tenfold, decuple; viel—, many-fold; &c.

Fach, *n.* [-es, *pl.* Fächer, -e] [from fahen = fassen, einfassen] originally any enclosed space, z. B. ‖Das — zwischen Sparren, bay; ‖ die Fächer in den Scheuern [die Bansen], bays in a barn; die Fächer eines Schrankes, shelves; das — in einem Bienenstocke, a cell in a bee-hive; die Fächer in einem Schriftkasten, Schreibtische, pigeon-holes; das — in einem Schriftkasten, [with printers] a box; Fächer zum Herausziehen, drawers; die Fächer in einer Wand, the bays in a wall; alle Fächer durchsuchen, to rummage

every shelf, every pigeon-hole. [in a more limited sense] *a*) a space enclosed, as, with fishermen, a fishery. *b*) the interval between columns, beams &c. space; hence the phrases, unter Dach und — bringen, to house; ein Haus in Dach und — erhalten, to keep a house in repair; [fam.] *Einem Dach und — geben, to lodge any one. *c*) Die Fächer [with hatters, pieces of fur or wool, of which hats are made], capade. *d*) [with weavers = der Sprung, das Geleise] the space between the threads of the weft when lifted in the loom. *Fig.* α) a class to which any thing belongs. In Fächer bringen, to classify. β) any part of human knowledge, a science, an art, a department or course of business. Man spricht von Leuten von demselben —e, we speak of men in the same line of business; im Handels—e, in the line of trade; die gelehrten Fächer, the learned professions; er hat sich dem Rechtsfache gewidmet, he follows the profession of law; er ist im —e der Erdmeßkunst gut bewandert, he is versed in geometry. γ) the proper office or business of a person. Es schlägt in das — des Richters, it is the province of the judge &c.; bleibe bei deinem —e, keep to your profession; dies schlägt nicht in mein —, that is out of my way or out of my line.

Fach=baum, *m.* 1) [in watermills and wears] a tree to stop and raise the water. 2) [with clothiers and hatters] V. —bogen. —**bogen**, *m.* [with clothiers or hatters, an instrument for breaking fur and wool] a bow. —**gerte**, *f.* split timbers or sticks wattled into the stakes of a loam-wall. —**holz**, *n.* the stakes for filling up the bays of a loam-wall. —**ordnung**, *f.* classification. —**reuse**, *f.* a kind of twiggen trap for fish. —**schule**, *f.* a school or institution in which some particular branch of science is taught. —**sieb**, *n* a hatter's sieve. —**stake**, —**stange**, V. —holz. —**tisch**, *m.* a table on which hatters and clothiers break fur and wool. —**weise**, *adj.* and *adv.* divided into classes. —**werk**, *n.* the act of building in bays, and these bays with the wood and loam which belong to them. *Fig.* that in which different things are placed as in compartments. Das —werk menschlicher [Wissens=] Begriffe, the classification of human notions.

Fäche, *f.* [with hatters and clothiers] 1) the act of breaking fur and wool with the bow. 2) [*pl.* -n] the broken fur and wool.

||**Fächel**, *m.* [-s, *pl.* -] V. Fächer.

Fächeln, I. *v. tr.* to cool and refresh, by moving the air with a fan, to fan. *Fig.* Sanfte Lüfte fächelten ihre Wangen, soft breezes fanned her cheeks. II. *v. r.* sich —, to fan one's self. Er fächelte sich mit einem großen Baumblatte, he fanned himself with a large leaf.

1. **Fächen**, [from Fach] *v. tr.* 1) to furnish with divisions or compartments. 2) to distribute into classes, to classify.

2. **Fächen**, [appears to be the same as the following] *v. tr.* [with hatters and clothiers] to break [fur and wool] with the bow.

3. **Fächen**, [allied to wehen, wackeln] *v. tr.* V. Anfachen.

Fächer, *m.* [-s, *pl.* -] [with hatters] the workman that breaks the fur.

Fächer, *m.* [-s, *pl.* -] 1) [something by which the air is moved, a wing, a fan, particularly an instrument used by ladies to agitate the air and cool the face in warm weather] a fan. 2) *pl.* [in botany, a hollow place in a pericarp, particularly in a capsule, in which seeds are lodged] cells.

Fächer=alve, *f.* the fan-alves. —**baum**, *m.* a tree cut in the form of a woman's fan. —**falter**, *m.* [a species of butterfly] pterophore. —**fisch**, *m.* coriphene. —**förmig**, *adj.* and *adv.* fan-shaped. Karlsruhe ist —förmig or in Gestalt eines Fächers gebaut, the town of Carlsruhe is built like a fan, i. e. the streets radiate from a central point like the sticks of an expanded fan. [in botany] Ein —förmiges Blatt, a fan-shaped leaf. —**macher**, *m.* a maker of fans. —**palme**, *f.* the fan-palm, or wine-palm. —**schwamm**, *m.* fan-shaped mushroom. —**spiel**, *n.* playing or dallying with a fan. —**stab**, *m* fan-stick.

Fächerchen, *n.* ||**Fächerlein**, *n.* [-s, *pl.* -] diminut. of Fächer, a little fan.

Fächerig, *adj.* and *adv.* containing partitions or cells, [in botany] cellular.

Fächern, *v. tr.* to fan or to play with a fan. Sich —, to fan one's self.

***Fachine**, pronounce and V. Faschine.

Fächlein, *n.* [-s, *pl.* -] diminut. of Fach, a small partition or compartment.

||**Fächsen**, *v. tr.* 1) to cultivate, to grow. 2) to gather, to reap.

Fächser, *m.* [-s, *pl.* -] [allied either to fassen or to wachsen] [in Scripture often Fäser or Feser] a shoot or twig of a plant, laid under ground for growth or propagation, a layer, particularly a stock or branch of a vine laid in the ground for propagation.

***Facit**, *n.* [-s, *pl.* - or -s] the sum total of two or more particular sums or quantities, the amount.

Facke, *f.* [the interval left between a ship's timbers] room and space.

Fackel, *f.* [*pl.* -n] [allied to the Lat. *fax*, *facula*, to the D. *fak* = Feuer] 1) a flambeau, a torch. Often used in compositions, as die Pech—, a link; die Kien—, a resin torch; die Hochzeits— [in the proper as well as in a fig. sense], the nuptial torch. [poet.] Die — des Mondes, the light of the moon. *Fig.* Die — des Krieges, the flames of war; er schleuderte die — der Zwietracht unter sie, he fomented discord between them; die — des Lebens auslöschen, to extinguish the flame of life. 2) [in astronomy, a name given to certain bright spots in the sun] facula.

Fackel=baum, *m.* the water-elder. —**beere**, *f.* the berry of the water-elder. —**blume**, *f.* great mullein. —**distel**, *f.* [a plant of the genus cactus] torch-thistle. —**feuer**, *n.* 1) the fire of a burning flambeau or torch. 2) a flaring fire. —**fliege**, *f.* lantern-fly. —**föhre**, *f.* wild pine-tree. —**holz**, *n.* 1) the wood of the water-elder. 2) the resinous wood of which a torch is made. —**jagd**, *f* 1) a mode of catching hares &c. by holding a torch. 2) bat-fowling. —**kohle**, *f.* cannel-, candle-, or parrot-coal. —**kraut**, *n.* [a plant] torch-wort. —**licht**, *n.* V. —schein. —**mann**, *m.* 1) torch-bearer, linkman, link-boy. 2) *Fig.* an enlightener. —**schein**, *m.* torch-light. —**ständchen**, *n.* a serenade by torch-light. —**stuhl**, *m.* an instrument or utensil to hold a flambeau or torch. —**tanz**, *m.* [in courts] formerly, a procession by torch-light, usual in Germany at the nuptials of princes, when the new married couple were accompanied to their chamber by the courtiers bearing torches or flambeaus. —**träger**, *m.* torch-bearer. —**zug**, *m.* a procession with flambeaus.

Fackeln, *v. intr.* [= wackeln, i. e. to move to and fro] to flare, to flutter, to waver. Das Licht fackelt, the candle flares. **Fig.* to act without seriousness, to trifle, to sport. Ich werde mit ihnen nicht —, I shall not sport with them.

***Façon**, *f.* [pron. Fassohn] [*pl.* -en] [the word is chiefly used in familiar lang.] 1) fashion, form, mode. 2) [rather unusual] way, manner, look. Ein Mensch von guter —, a well-looking man. 3) ceremony, compliment, formality.

***Facsimile**, *n.* an exact copy or likeness, as of handwriting, facsimile.

***Faction**, *f.* a party, a faction. Rom wurde fast immer von —en beunruhigt, Rome was almost always disturbed by factions.

***Factisch**, *adj.* and *adv.* founded on facts.

***Factor**, *m.* 1) [-s, *pl* -e] Factor, [an agent employed by merchants] a factor. [in printing offices] the foreman. 2) [-s or -en, *pl.* -en] Factor, [in arithmetic] the multiplier and multiplicand, from the multiplication of which proceeds the product, factor.

***Factorei**, *f.* [the house and business of a factor] factory; factorship.

***Factotum**, *n.* [-s] factotum.

***Factum**, *n.* [-s, *pl.* Facta] a fact.

***Factur**, *f.* [*pl.* -en] [in commerce] invoice.

Facturbuch, *n.* [in commerce] invoice-book.

***Facultät**, *f.* 1) faculty, ability. 2) [one of the members or departments of a university] faculty. Auf den meisten Universitäten gibt es vier —en, in most universities there are four faculties.

***Facultist**, *m.* [-en, *pl.* -en] a member of a faculty.

***Fade**, [Fr. *fade*, perhaps allied to the Lat. *fat-uus*, Fr. *fat*] *adj.* and *adv.* flat, insipid, tasteless. *Fig.* Ein —s Gesicht, an unmeaning face; eine — Unterhaltung, a dull conversation.

Fadelkraut, *n.* [-es] common meadow saffron.

Fädeln, I. *v. tr.* to thread [a needle]. II. *v. r.* sich —, to ravel, to be unwoven.

Faden, *m.* [-s, *pl.* -, also Fäden; dimin. das Fädchen or Fädlein] [usually derived from fa-ben = fassen, binden] 1) thread. Ein zwirner or leinener —, a linen thread; ein seidener —, a silken thread; aus Fäden bestehend, thread... zu — schlagen, den — schlagen, [with tailors, to sew with long stitches] to baste; der —, in commerce, a thread of a certain length, commonly four ells. *Fig.* Er hat nicht einen trockenen — am Leibe, he is wet to the skin; der — des Gespräches, the thread of discourse; den — des Gespräches wieder anknüpfen, wieder aufnehmen, to resume a discourse; den — abbrechen, abreißen, to break off, to discontinue, to interrupt; der — einer Erzählung, the thread of a narrative; [in poetry] der — des Lebens [Lebensfaden], vital thread; sein Leben hängt nur an einem *—, his life hangs upon a thread. Etwas —ähnliches, something resembling a thread. *a*) [with huntsmen = das Fädlein] a little stripe in the slot of a stag. *b*) [in botany] α) [a long body at the bottom of the flower] the thread. β) [the tough substance that unites the two parts of the pericarp of leguminous plants] string. Die — der Bohnen, the strings of beans. γ) V. Staubfaden. 3) [a measure of length containing six feet, the space to which a man may extend his arms] Ein — [Klafter] Holz, a cord of wood; Holz — setzen, or zu — schlagen, to cord wood; [used chiefly at sea for measuring distances and the depth of the sea] fathom.

Faden=bruch, *m.* slipping, gliding, running threads. —**dreieck**, *n.* [in astronomy] reticule. —**flechte**, *f.* a species of lichen [usnea]. —**fliege**, *f.* a species of lantern-fly. —**förmig**, *adj.* and *adv.* thread-like, filiform, thread-shaped. [in botany] Eine —förmige Wurzel, a filamentous root; ein —förmiger Staubfaden, a filiform filament; ein —förmiger Griffel, a thread-like style. —**führer**, *m.* —leiter. —**garn**, *n.* linen-thread. —**gerade**, *adj.* and *adv.* according to the thread. Ein Ge...

Leinwand —gerade schneiden, to cut a piece of linen by a thread. *Fig.* ‖ *Der Weg läuft — gerade fort, the road is as straight as an arrow; —gerade, straightway. —gold, *n.* gold-thread. —gras, *n.* [a genus of plants] manisurus. —halter, *m.* a bent wire on silk-reels. —hebel, *m.* V. Lize. —holz, *n.* V. Klafterholz. —käfer, *m.* [an insect] alurnus. —keim, *m.* [in botany] the filiform germ of mosses. —klee, *m.* the least trefoil. —kraut, *n.* cudweed. —kreuz, *n.* 1) [with weavers] the threads of the woof crossing one another. 2) [in astronomy] a cross in a telescope formed by two threads crossing one another in right angles. —leiter, *m.* the guide on silk-reels. * and † —nackend, *adj.* and *adv.* stark naked. —nudel, *f.* [in cookery] vermicelli. —recht, *adj.* and *adv.* after the thread. —recht zerschneiden, to cut by a thread. —saum, *m.* a fringe. —scheid, *m.* [with goldspinners] the third or lightest sort of gold or silver-thread. —scheinig, *adj.* and *adv.* threadbare. —scheiniges Tuch, threadbare cloth; ein —scheiniger Rock, a threadbare coat. —schlag, *m.* [with tailors] basting. —sichtig, *adj.* and *adv.* V. —scheinig. —silber, *n.* 1) silver-thread. 2) silver from burnt silver-lace. —weise, *adv.* 1) by threads, in single threads. 2) by fathom; by cords. Das Holz —weise aufsetzen, to cord wood. —wurm, *m.* the muscular hair-worm. —yucca, *f.* [a shrub] Virginian Adam's needle.

Fädenig, *adj.* and *adv.* [in common or familiar language, fädenicht, fädemig, fädemicht] 1) having threads, threaden, filaceous; [in composition] threaded. Zwei—, two-threaded. 2) thready.

Fädig, V. Fädenig.

Fädlein, *n.* [-s, *pl.* -] V. Faden. 2. *a.*

Fädmen, to string [beans &c.].

***Fagótt**, *n.* [-es, *pl.* -e] a fagot or bassoon.

***Fagottíst**, *m.* [-en, *pl.* -en] a performer on the bassoon, a bassoonist.

Fähe, *f.* [*pl.* -n] [from the old *föda*, Lat. *feo*] [with huntsmen] the female of a dog, and of other carnivorous quadrupeds.

Fahen, [Sw. *fa*, old German for fangen] [it is used only in Scripture and in solemn style] *ir.* I. *v. tr.* to take, to catch, to seize. II. *v. intr.* to have the intended effect, to take. Meine Rede fähet nicht unter euch, [in Script.] my word has no place in you.

Fähig, [from fahen = fassen] *adj.* and *adv.* *Fig.* 1) endued with power competent to the object. Zu einem Amte —, able to perform an office; er ist zu allem —, he is fit for any thing; — zu urtheilen, capable of judging; es ist einer langen Dauer —, it is capable of long duration; ein Herz, der Liebe —, a heart susceptible of love; Stärke macht den Menschen zur Arbeit —, by strength a man is enabled to work; ein Bösewicht, der zu allem — ist, a daring villain, who is capable of any thing; sich zu etwas — machen, to qualify one's self for any thing; —zu erben, able to take by inheritance; — machen, to enable; einen — machen, [in law] to furnish any one with legal power or capacity, to qualify any one [for any thing]. 2) possessing mental powers. Ein —er Richter, a capable judge; ein —er Kopf, an able man, of a clever mind.

Fähigen, [rather unusual] *v. tr.* to make able, to enable. Einen zu einem Amte —, to capacitate any one for an office; sich —, to qualify one's self. V. Befähigen.

Fähigkeit, *f.* 1) physical power, whether bodily or mental, natural or acquired, ability. Der Unterricht sey den —en der Jugend angemessen, let instruction be adapted to the capacities of youth; —en, faculties of the mind or acquired qualifications; ein Mensch von großen —en, a man of great talents, or parts. 2) [in a legal sense] legal power or right, ability, capacity. Die — zu testiren, the capacity to give or leave by will.

Fahl, [Fr. *pâle*, Lat. *pall*-idus, *ful*-vus, *flav*-us, in German blaß, that is blaw, blab, and allied to *βλέπ-ω*, sehen = scheinen] *adj.* and *adv.* 1) of a yellowish dark colour, pale yellow, fallow. Ein —es Pferd, a pale dun-coloured horse; der —e Löwe, the tawny lion; eine —e Farbe, a pale colour. *Prov.* Einen auf dem —en Pferde ertappen, to take any one in a lie. 2) become less vivid, as colour, faded.

Fahl-erz, *n.* gray copper. Lichtes —erz, arsenical gray copper; dunkles —erz, antimonial gray copper, black copper-ore. —gelb, *adj.* and *adv.* of a yellowish dark colour. —kupfererz, *n.* V. —erz. —leder, *n.* a sort of leather which is intended to form the upper part of shoes and boots. —roth, *adj.* and *adv.* pale red, fallow. —stein, *m.* gray slate.

Fahlheit, *f.* the quality of being fallow.

Fahlunít, *m.* [-s, *pl.* -en] [a subspecies of octahedral corundum] fahlunite, automalite. Harter —, cordierite, iolite or dichroite.

‖**Fähm**, **Fähmen**, V. Fehm and Fehmen.

Fahnden, [from fahen] [rather provincial] *v. intr.* 1) to inform against. 2) Auf einen Verbrecher, eine gestohlene Sache &c. —, to endeavour to catch or seize a criminal, or to regain some thing stolen &c.

Fähndrich, *m.* V. Fähnrich.

Fähnchen, *n.* V. Fähnlein.

Fahne, *f.* [*pl.* -n] [Lat. *pann*-us, Gr. *πῆνος*; in Sw. *fana* signifies cloth; it appears, however, to have signified originally something moving or extending in breadth] 1) the vane of a weathercock. 2) the beard of a quill. 3) [in botany, the upper petal of a papilionaceous flower] the standard or banner, vexil. 4) [with huntsmen, the tail of a squirrel] the brush. 5) [in printing] a reference or mark referring the reader to a note in the margin, an obelisk. 6) [with fullers] a list of fulled cloth. 7) = das Fähnchen, a small net on a staff for catching larks. 8) the reckoning at an ale-house. 9) a piece of a texture, a cloth, hence in contempt or ironically, a light and poor garment [Fähnchen, Fähnlein]. 10) [with clothiers] that part of cloth which has been teased and which hangs down the teasing-table. 11) a cloth on which are usually painted or wrought certain figures, and borne on a staff, particularly at a procession of the clergy and people or certain congregations in the Romish church, a flag. Die — schwingen, to flourish or to wave a flag or banner; die weiße — ausstecken, to hang out the white flag; also the flag or banner of a military band, a banner, a standard, an ensign; mit fliegenden —n, with streaming colours; zur — schwören, to swear to one's colours; die — verlassen, to desert one's colours. *Fig.* a company of soldiers, a troop. Sechs —n or Fähnlein Reiter, six squadrons of cavalry, six troops.

Fahn-flüchtig, *adj.* deserting one's colours. Ein —flüchtiger, a deserter. —junker, *m.* ensign-bearer. —lehen, *n.* V. Fahnenlehen. —schmied, *m.* V. Fahnenschmied.

Fahnen-futter, *n.* the case or cover for the colours. —hafer, *m.* a sort of cultivated oats. —junker, *m.* V. Fahnjunker. —lehen, *n.* [in German law] a sort of high fee, which was granted in presenting a banner. —marsch, *m.* the tune or march which is struck up, when the colours are lodged. —schmied, *m.* a farrier of a squadron of cavalry. —schuh, *m.* colour-sheath, soc. —schwenker, —schwinger, *m.* one who in processions waves the standard or banner. —stange, *f.* ensign-staff. —stock, *m.* 1) ensign-staff. 2) colour-stand. —träger, *m.* colour-bearer, ensign-bearer. —wache, *f.* standard-guard. —weise, *adv.* by companies or squadrons.

Fähnlein, *n.* [-s, *pl.* -] [*dimin.* of Fahne] 1) a small flag. Das — an einer Lanze, a banner. 2) *Fig.* a company of soldiers, a troop.

Fähnrich, *m.* [-s or -es, *pl.* -e] [an officer in a company of foot, holding a rank between the commissioned and non-commissioned officers] ensign.

Fähnrichs-stelle, *f.* an ensigncy.

Fahr, *f.* [*pl.* -en] [V. Gefahr] [‡ and in Scripture] danger, peril.

Fahrbar, *adj.* and *adv.* 1) that which may be carried away in a vehicle. —e Güter, movables, [in law] chattels personal. 2) that may be passed or travelled over, [in seamen's lang.] navigable. Ein —er Weg, a practicable road.

‡**Fährden**, [V. Gefährden] *v. tr.* to put in hazard, to endanger.

Fähre, *f.* [*pl.* -n] 1) a furrow. ‖2) a ferry-boat.

Fähre, *f.* [*pl.* -n] 1) a ferry, ferry-boat, passage-boat. In einer — übersetzen, to ferry over. 2) [the place or passage where boats pass over water to convey passengers] ferry.

Fähr-beständer, *m.* one who holds by lease the possession of a ferry. —geld, *n.* the fare for crossing a river, ferriage, the passage or passage-money. —gerechtigkeit, *f.* the right of transporting passengers over a river, ferry. —herr, *m.* ferry-owner, ferry-man. —kahn, *m.* ferry-boat. —knecht, *m.* a ferryman's mate. —leute, *pl.* ferrymen. —lohn, *m.* the fare for crossing a river, ferriage. —mann, *m.* [*pl.* —leute] ferryman. —meister, *m.* V. —mann. ‖—mutter, *f.* the female of the hogkind or of swine, the sow. —pacht, *f.* the rent paid for the possession of a ferry. —pächter, *m.* the lessee of a ferry. —schiff, *n.* a ferry-boat with mast and sails. —tafel, *f.* a board posted near a ferry, on which the price or fare, to be paid at the ferry, is written. —zoll, *m.* a tax or toll paid at a ferry.

1. **Fahren**, [allied to the Lat. *fero*, to the Gr. *φέρω*, *πορ-εύομαι* &c.] *ir.* I. *v. intr.* [u. w. seyn] 1) to move. Mit der Hand hin und her —, to move one's hand to and fro, to wave one's hand; der Blitz fuhr in den Baum, lightning fell on the tree; der Schuß fuhr in die Mauer, the shot pierced the wall; der Stein fuhr in seine Stirn, [in Script.] the stone sunk into his forehead; das Tauwerk fährt, [in seamen's lang.] the cordage runs through the blocks; es fuhr mir aus der Hand, it slipt out of my hand; mit der Hand in die Tasche —, to thrust the hand into the pocket; aus dem Bette —, to start up from one's bed; †einen [Wind] — lassen, to break wind; —de Habe, movables, [in law] chattels personal; der Schmerz [or *es] ist mir bis in den kleinen Finger gefahren, the pain tingles down to my little finger; der Schreck ist mir in alle Glieder gefahren, the panic seized all my limbs; gen Himmel —, to ascend to heaven; und als sie ihm nachsahen gen Himmel —d, [in Script.] and while they looked stedfastly toward heaven as he went up; zur Hölle —, to go or to descend to hell; auf daß nicht, wo du schweigest, ich gleich werde denen, die in die Hölle —, [in Script.] lest, if thou be silent to me, I

become like them that go down into the pit; du hast mich lebendig behalten, da die in die Hölle fuhren, [in Script.] thou hast kept me alive, that I should not go down to the pit; in die Grube —, to descend to the grave, to drop into the grave, to die; *man möchte aus der Haut —, 'tis enough to drive one mad. *Fig.* *a*) [= schwinden] Den Kummer, die Sorge — lassen, to banish grief, or sorrow; alle Hoffnung — lassen, to abandon all hope, to give up all hope; seine Ansprüche — lassen, to relinquish one's pretensions; Vorurtheile — lassen, to disabuse one's self of prejudices; lassen Sie die Gelegenheit nicht —, let not the occasion slip; es ist ein böser Geist in ihn gefahren, he is possessed by an evil spirit, or devil; einem über das Maul —, to browbeat any one, also, to give any one a smart reply, to snap any one up short; einem durch den Sinn —, to subdue any one's obstinacy, not to comply with any one's will or mind. *b*) [to put in a certain state or condition] Schlecht bei einer Sache —, to speed ill; sie werden nicht schlimmer — als ihre Nachbarn, they shall fare no worse than their neighbours; dabei fährt er am besten, he has the best of the bargain; wir werden sehen, wie er dabei fährt, we shall see how it will fare with him. 2) to move from one place to another, to travel, also to walk, to march or go on foot. Fahret nicht hoch her, [in Script.] neither be ye of doubtful mind; fahre wohl! farewell or fare you well [I wish you a happy departure, may you be well in your absence]; [in contempt] ein —der Bettler, a vagrant beggar; —de Ritter, knights errant; der Hase fährt, [with huntsmen] the hare runs fast; Schrittschuhe or Schlittschuhe —, to skate. 3) to move from one place to another in a vehicle or in a vessel. Und er fuhr auf dem Cherub und flog daher, [in Script.] he rode on a cherub, and did fly; in einer Kutsche —, to ride or drive in a coach, to go in a carriage; in einem Kahne oder Schiffe —, to go in a boat or ship; auf dem Schlitten —, to ride in a sleigh; er fuhr nach London, he drove to London; er fuhr in seinem Wagen nach London, he drove in his carriage to London; zu jemanden —, to drive to a person's house; spazieren —, to take an airing [in a coach &c.], to drive out; Extrapost —, to travel post; fahre zu, Kutscher! drive on, coachman! wir fuhren von London nach Canton, we sailed from London to Canton; über einen Fluß —, to cross a river, to pass over a river; ich fuhr über die See auf einem Dampfschiffe, I crossed the sea in a steam-boat; zur See —, to navigate; gegen den Wind —, [in seamen's lang.] to sail against the wind; zu Wasser —, to go by water; ans Land —, to land; auf den Grund —, to run aground, to ground [said of a ship]; die —de Post, the stage-coach, or the stage [opposed to the reitende Post].

II. *v. refl.* Sich irre —, to ride astray; sich müde —, to be tired with riding.

III. *v. tr.* to convey or transport in a vehicle or in any kind of water-craft, to carry. Holz in die Stadt or zur Stadt —, to carry wood to the town; einen Herrn über den Fluß —, to ferry a gentleman over the river; Truppen über einen Fluß —, to transport troops over a river; einen in einer Kutsche —, to drive any one in a coach; Steine, Mist &c. —, to cart stones, dung &c.; ich fahre mich selbst, I drive my carriage.

IV. *v. imp.* and *refl.* Es fährt sich sehr gut in diesem Wagen, this carriage is very commodious; dieser Wagen fährt sich leicht, this carriage is easily moved or drawn.

Fahr=bahn, *f.* [in rivers, the deeper part or hollow in which the principal current flows] channel. —bogen, *m.* [in mining] an official account rendered by a sworn officer respecting the mines he has visited. —buch, *n.* [in mining] the journal. —damm, *m.* a dike, that may be passed in a vehicle. —gebühr, *f.* —geld, *n.* 1) the fare for conveyance in a coach or waggon, fare, carriage, waggonage. 2) the fare for crossing a river, ferriage. ||3) V. Brückengeld. ||4) a sort of ground-rent. —geleise, *n.* V. —leise. —genosse, *m.* a fellow traveller in a coach, fellow passenger on board a vessel. —gut, *n.* movables, [in law] chattels personal. —kappe, *f.* a miner's cap. —kummet, *n.* horse-collar. —kuttel, *f.* [a genus of shellfish] argonauta. —lässig, *adj.* and *adv.* inattentive to business or duty, careless, heedless, regardless, negligent, indolent, supine. —lässigkeit, *f.* inattention, carelessness, heedlessness, disregard, negligence. —leder, *n.* the leather apron used by miners. —leise, *f.* the track of a carriage. —maus, *f.* V. Reitmaus. —nagel, *m.* V. Deichselnagel. —post, *f.* stage-coach, stage. —schacht, *m.* [in mining] footway-shaft. —seil, *n.* 1) rein. 2) ferry-rope. —sessel, *m.* 1) a wheel-chair. 2) [in mines] a chair in which a person is drawn up. —stuhl, *m.* 1) V. —sessel. 2) a slater's seat or chair. —wasser, *n.* [in seamen's language] fair way. —weg, *m.* carriage-road, cart-way. —wetter, *n.* [in seamen's language] fair weather for navigation. —wind, *m.* [in seamen's language] a fair wind. —zeug, *n.* a vessel, boat, ship, a craft of any description.

2. ‡Fähren, [Sw. *fara*, Lat. *ver-eri*] *ir. v. intr.* to fear.

3. ‡Fähren, [appears to be allied to wahren, gewahren] *ir. v. intr.* to perceive.

Fährenkraut, *n.* V. Farnkraut.

Fährer, *m.* [-s, *pl.* -] he that drives, sails &c.; it is used particularly in composition, as, See—, a seafarer, a mariner, *fig.* [in contempt] Land—, vagabond &c.

Fährig, *adj.* and *adv.* 1) [in husbandry] Ein —er Wald, —es Holz, young trees whose tops are not within the reach of cattle. 2) *in comp.* with will, V. Willfährig.

Fährlich, *adj.* and *adv.* [‡ and in Scripture] dangerous, perilous.

Fährlichkeit, *f.* 1) dangerousness, perilousness. 2) peril, danger, hazard.

Fährlos, *adj.* and *adv.* 1) free from danger, undangerous, dangerless. ‡2) inattentive to business or duty.

Fährlosigkeit, *f.* the quality of being undangerous.

Fährniß, *f.* [*pl.* -nisse] ||1) [especially in law] movables, chattels personal [as opposed to Liegende Güter, immovables]. 2) household furniture.

Fährt, *f.* [*pl.* -en] 1) the act of moving from one place to another, a walk, a journey, a ride, a drive; [in mining] the act of entering or of leaving a mine; more commonly in the compound words Abfahrt, Auffahrt, Hinfahrt, Rückfahrt, Schifffahrt, Wallfahrt, which see. Auf der — seyn, *a*) to be absent on a drive, to be travelling, *b*) *Fig.* *to be upon the point, to be about. 2) the course. Eine — zu Wasser, zu Schiffe machen, to sail or pass by water, to voyage; [in seamen's lang.] die — eines Schiffes, the way of a ship; dem Schiffe — geben, um zu wenden, to give the ship way, that she may stay; die — verfehlen, to lose way. 3) it is used sometimes for any enterprise, undertaking by a number of persons, an expedition. ||4) plowing. 5) ground appropriated for travel, an open way or public passage, a road. 6) [in mining] a ladder. 7) a road under the surface of the ground formed by moles or foxes. 8) track or trace. 9) as much as is usually carried at once on a vehicle or in a ship. Eine — Heu, a cart-load of hay. ||10) the time, when one changes his place, his lodgings, or leaves his service.

Fahrt=maß, *n.* —messer, *m.* [in navigation, a machine for measuring the rate of a ship's velocity through the water] the log. —schenkel, *m.* one of the two side-pieces of a miner's ladder. —sprosse, *f.* the round of a miner's ladder. —stange, *f.* V. —schenkel.

||Fährt, *adv.* last year.

Fährte, *f.* [*pl.* -n] 1) [in mining, it is used sometimes for Fahrt] a miner's ladder. 2) a beaten path, a road, track. 3) [among hunters] *a*) footprint, track, trace. Die — eines Löwen, Bären, the track of a lion, bear; die — des Rothwildes, the view or slot; die — eines Rehbocks, the fusee; die — des Fuchses, the ball; die — der Otter, the seal; die — des Hasen, the prick of a hare; die — eines Feldhuhns, Haselhuhns, einer Wachtel, eines Wachtelkönigs, the rode; die — einer Schnepfe, Waldschnepfe, the creeps; die — eines Stück Rothwildes im Schnee verfolgen, to track a deer in the snow; die — aufnehmen, to draw the scent; die Hunde haben die — verloren, the dogs are at fault. *b*) also the track of clawed beasts [das Gefährt].

Fährtenlaut, Fährtlaut, *adv.* [with hunters] babbling.

Fährtgerecht, *adj.* and *adv.* [in hunting] Ein —er Jäger, a hunter that is well acquainted with the tracks of game.

||Fährtig, *adj.* and *adv.* being of the last year.

Fährung, *f.* [in mining] foot-way.

*Faïence, *n.* [pron. Fajahngs] delft-ware, delf.

||Faim, Faimen, V. Fehm, Fehmen.

Faisch, Faischhund, Faischschnur, [with hunters] *f.* V. Schweiß &c.

||Faland, *m.* [-s] [from bal = böse] the devil

Falb, [allied to the Lat. *flavus*, *fulv-us*, ... fahl] *adj.* and *adv.* pale yellow, fallow. Ein —es Pferd, a dun horse. V. Falbe.

Falbe, *m.* [-n, *pl.* -n] Falbe, *f.* [*pl.* -n] 1) a flea-bitten grey horse. 2) the white willow

*Falbala, *f.* [*pl.* Falbalen] V. Falbel.

Falbel, *f.* [*pl.* -n] [Fr. falbala] a flounce or furbelow. Einen Unterrock mit —n besetzen, to flounce a petticoat, to furbelow a petticoat.

Fälbel, *m.* V. Felbel.

Falben, *v. intr.* [u. w. seyn] to become yellow, to fade.

Fälben, *v. tr.* to cause to wither, to fade

Falbenrock, *m.* [-s] [a plant] corn horse-tail

||Fälber, *f.* [*pl.* -n] [from falb] the white willow.

||Fälbersaft, *m.* [a sort of resinous gum] liquid amber.

Falbicht, *adj.* and *adv.* somewhat fallow

Falbig, *adj.* and *adv.* pale-yellow, fallow

Falche, *f.* [*pl.* -n] V. Walche.

Falgen, [D. felghen = umbrechen] *v. tr.* ... twifallow, or to trifallow.

*Falkade, *f.* [*pl.* -n] [in manege] a falcade.

*Falkaune, *f.* [*pl.* -n] [a sort of cannon] falcon.

Falke, *m.* [-n, *pl.* -n] [seems to be allied to the Lat. *falx*, Sichel] 1) [a genus of fowls] falcon, or hawk, [in falconry] a hawk trained to sport. Der männliche —, tercel; ein junger

—, an eyas, a nias; ein einjähriger —, a sore; ein zweijähriger —, a hawk of the first coat; ein edler — [Edel—], a falcon genteel; ein frischer oder junger —, a yearling falcon; ein alter —, a haggard-falcon; einen —en abrichten, to man a hawk; den —n steigen oder fliegen lassen, to cast a hawk. *Prov.* Augen wie ein — haben, to be hawkeyed. 2) [a sort of cannon] falcon.

Falkenauge, *n.* falcon's eye, hawk's eye. *Fig.* Sie hat —augen, she is hawkeyed. —**beize**, *f.* hawking, falconry. —**blick**, *m.* *Fig.* an acute sight. —**eule**, *f.* hawk-owl. —**feder**, *f.* a feather from the gyrfalcon. —**geschuhe**, *n.* [in falconry] jesses. —**haube**, *f.* V. —kappe. —**hof**, *m.* a place where hawks are trained for sport. —**jagd**, *f.* hawking, falconry, fowling. —**jäger**, *m.* a falconer, hawker. —**junge**, *m.* the apprentice of a falconer. —**kappe**, *f.* [in falconry] a hood, rufter-hood. —**meister**, *m.* chief falconer. —**mist**, *m.* muting. —**nest**, *n.* [among sportsmen] an airy. —**pille**, *f.* a cure. —**riemen**, *m.* the lune of a hawk. —**schelle**, *f.* a hawk's bell. —**schlag**, *m.* [in falconry] the descent of the hawk. —**schuh**, *m.* a jess. — —**sperling**, *m.* hedge-sparrow, or hedge-warbler. —**spiel**, *n.* a kind of net for catching hawks. —**stange**, *f.* the perch. —**stoß**, *m.* V. —spiel. —**wärter**, *m.* a person that attends and feeds the hawks. —**weg**, *m.* the flight of a hawk.

Falkener, Falkenier, Falkner, *m.* [-s, *pl.* - and Falkeniere] V. Falkenjäger.

Falkeniertasche, *f.* a hawking-bag or pouch. **Falknerkunst**, *f.* V. Falknerei 1.

Falknerei, *f.* 1) [the art of training hawks to the exercise of hawking] falconry. 2) falconers. 3) the place where falcons are kept and where falconers reside.

***Falkonett**, *n.* [-s] [a sort of cannon] saker.

Fall, *m.* [-es, *pl.* Fälle] 1) [properly a state of motion]. *Fig.* *a*) any accident, incident, that which falls out. Ein trauriger —, a melancholy accident, a sad incident; auf alle Fälle gefaßt seyn, to be prepared for all events; ich komme auf jeden —, I will come at all events; der Sachwalter trug den — vor, the lawyer stated the case; im —e, in case [in the event or contingency, or if it should so fall out or happen]; das Schlimmste, was mir in diesem —e begegnen kann, the worse that can befall me in this case; in einem solchen —e, in such a case; ich setze den —, I put the case, I suppose; setzen Sie den —, daß es so wäre, put the case, it be so; das ist ein anderer —, it is another case; wenn der — eintritt, in case that; im — der Noth [nöthigen or erforderlichen —s], in case of necessity, if need be. Often used in compositions, as Glücksfall, Zufall, Unfall &c. *b*) [in grammar, the inflection of nouns] case. Der erste —, the nominative case, the nominative; der zweite —, the genitive case; der dritte —, the dative case; der vierte —, the accusative or objective case. *c*) Das Gut steht auf dem —e, [in feudal law] that estate will soon fall to the lord of the manor by escheat. 2) fall. Der — des Wassers, the descent of water; der — des Quecksilbers in der Röhre, the falling of the mercury in the glass-tube. *Fig.* der — der Staatspapiere, the fall of the funds; die Spanischen Staatsschuldverschreibungen haben einen bedeutenden — erlitten, the Spanish bonds have experienced a heavy fall; der — dieses Ministers, Günstlings &c., the fall of this minister, this favourite &c.; ein jeder bedauert Ihren — [Sturz], every one is grieved at your fall; der — dieses Reichs, Herrschers &c., the fall or downfall of this empire, monarch &c. *Prov.* Hochmuth kommt vor dem —, pride goes before, and shame follows after; der — eines Handlungshauses, a breaking or becoming insolvent, failure of a mercantile house; der — der Engel, the fall of angels; der — Adams, [in theology] the fall of Adam, the fall; ein Mädchen zu —e bringen, to ruin a girl; er hat sie zu —e gebracht, he has debauched her, he got her with child; seine Tochter ist zu —e gekommen, his daughter has been ruined, or got with child; beklage seinen —, wail his fall [death]. 3) [the act of falling] fall, tumble. Einen schweren — thun, to have a great fall; der — von einem Pferde, a fall from a horse; zu —e kommen, to fall, to have a fall. *Fig.* *Knall und —, suddenly; Einen Knall und — verabschieden, to discard a person very abruptly. 4) extent of descent, the distance which any falls, fall. Das Wasser eines Teiches hat fünf Fuß —, the water of a pond has a fall of five feet. 5) a fall of the water of a river or stream down a steep place. Der Rhein—, the fall of the Rhine; der Wasser—, waterfall, a cascade, a cataract; die Fälle des St. Lorenzstroms, the falls of the St. Lawrence. 6) that which falls. Fälle, [in mining] fissures. 7) [with hunters, a beast that has died by sickness or mischance] morkin. 8) [with blacksmiths] the inclination of the pipe of a bellows to the fire-place of the forge. 9) [in seamen's lang.] halliard. 10) *Fig.* that part of a tenant's movables which falls to the lord of the manor by his death.

Fallbaum, *m.* 1) [in fortification] portcullis, orgues. 2) [with fowlers] a perch near the fowling-floor for birds to light on. —**beil**, *n.* a guillotine. Einen durch das [or mit dem] —beil hinrichten, to guillotine any one. —**block**, *m.* 1) [in archit.] a rammer. 2) [in seamen's lang.] top-sail halliard-block. —**blume**, *f.* corn or red poppy. —**brett**, *n.* a shutter, or slider. —**brücke**, *f.* 1) [an engine for catching men] a trap. 2) a draw-bridge. —**eisen**, *n.* 1) a piece of iron in a trap or pitfall. 2) V. Fangeisen *a*). —**endung**, *f.* [in grammar] termination in a case of declension. —**fenster**, *n.* a sash-window. ||—**fertig**, *adj.* and *adv.* like to fall, about to fall. —**gatter**, *n.* [in fortif. a portcullis in the form of a harrow and beset with iron spikes] a herse, a sarrasine or cataract. —**granate**, *f.* [in the art of war] a sort of grenade used in storming. —**grube**, *f.* a pitfall. —**gut**, *n.* V. Schupflehen. ||—**haus**, *n.* the house of a flayer, where he keeps the skins of morkins. —**holz**, *n.* windfallen wood. —**hut**, *m.* a pudding, guard [worn by children]. —**käfer**, *m.* [in entom.] cryptocephalus. —**klappe**, *f.* trap-board. —**klinke**, *f.* a falling latch. —**klotz**, *m.* V. —block. —**knecht**, *m.* V. Schinderknecht. —**kraut**, *n.* 1) the mountain arnica. 2) the meadow inula. —**laden**, *m.* the shutter of a sky-light. —**lehen**, *n.* V. Schupflehen. —**meister**, *m.* V. Abdecker. —**mütze**, *f.* V. —hut. —**netz**, *n.* V. Schlagnetz. —**pfahl**, *m.* V. —baum. —**reep**, *n.* [in seamen's language] V. —tau. Das Volk auf das —reep fallen lassen, to man the side. —**reepstreppe**, *f.* [in seamen's lang.] an accommodation-ladder. —**reif**, *m.* V. —tau. —**riegel**, *m.* V. —klinke. —**schirm**, *m.* a parachute. —**schloß**, *n.* a trunk-lock. —**stein**, *m.* a stumbling-stone, stumbling-block. —**strick**, *m.* a snare, a gin. *Fig.* a trap, trapan, an ambush. —stricke legen, to lay snares. —**sucht**, *f.* the falling sickness, epilepsy. —**süchtig**, *adj.* and *adv.* affected with epilepsy, epileptic. Der —süchtige, an epileptic. —**suchtmittel**, *n.* an antiepileptic remedy. —**tau**, *n.* [in seamen's lang.] entering-rope. —**thor**, *n.* V. —gatter. —**thür**, *f.* a trap-door. Die —thüren vor den Luken, [in seamen's language] hatches. —**thürlein**, *n.* V. Falle 3. —**tisch**, *m.* V. Klapptisch. —**ton**, *m.* a fall of the voice in reading or speaking, cadence. —**trank**, *m.* Swiss tea. —**treppe**, *f.* trap-stairs. —**übel**, *n.* V. —sucht. —**wildbret**, *n.* [with hunters] morkin. —**wind**, *m.* [in seamen's lang.] eddy-wind.

Fällbar, *adj.* and *adv.* —e Bäume, trees that may be felled.

Falle, *f.* [*pl.* -n] 1) an engine that shuts suddenly in certain cases, particularly an inclosure with a trap-door for confining ferocious beasts. 2) a trap for catching mice and other beasts. Die Mäuse—, a mouse-trap; Füchse in der — fangen, to trap foxes; Biebern eine — stellen, to trap for beaver; eine — stellen, to set a trap. *Fig.* In die — gehen, to insnare one's self; er ist in die — gerathen, he fell into the snare; Einem eine — stellen, legen or bauen, to lay, to set a snare for any one. 3) [in anatomy] valve. 4) Die schließende —, [with locksmiths] a book in a lock which supports the spring. 5) [in mills, the frame which shuts or stops the passage of water through a dam into a flume] a gate.

Fallenohr, *n.* [in locks] latch.

Fallen, *ir.* I. *v. intr.* [allied to the Ger. wallen, the Gr. σφάλλειν, the Lat. *fallere*] to fall. 1) To move from a higher to a lower place, to fall. Das Licht fällt durch jede Ritze in das Zimmer, light enters the room by every crevice; es wird auch nicht auf sie — die Sonne oder irgend eine Hitze, [in Script.] neither shall the sun light on them, nor any heat; das stärkere Licht muß auf jene Stellen des Gemäldes fallen, wo &c., the greater light must strike on those places of the picture where &c. Die Rhone fällt in das mittelländische Meer, the Rhone falls into the Mediterranean sea; die Donau fällt in das schwarze Meer, the Danube falls into the Euxine; falle in's Boot! [in seamen's language] man the boat! [in mining] to extend or lead downwards. Ein Gang, der seiger fällt, a hade; ein Gang, der donlege fällt, a hading shaft; —de Gänge, inclining shafts; [in seamen's language] in Lee —, to fall to leeward; das Schiff fällt verkehrt, the ship casts the wrong way. *Fig.* *a*) to pass into a certain state. Der Brief fiel in die Hände seines Nebenbuhlers, the letter fell into the hands of his rival; unter die Mörder —, to get among murderers; in die Augen, in die Sinne —, to strike the eyes, the senses; gut oder angenehm in die Augen —, to look well or pleasant; das fällt in die Augen, that catches the eye, it attracts attention; Einem in die Hände —, to fall into any one's hands; sich hüten, in Jemands Klauen zu —, to keep out of any one's clutches; den Gerichten in die Hände —, to fall into the hands of justice; dem Arzte in die Hände —, to have occasion for, or to want a physician; in eine Krankheit —, to fall sick; in Ohnmacht —, to faint, to swoon; in Schlaf —, to fall asleep; in Anfechtung —, to fall into temptation; bei Einem in Ungnade —, to incur any one's disfavour, to fall under any one's displeasure; in Mißcredit —, to sink into disrepute; aus der Gunst —, to lose favour; in Strafe —, to incur a penalty. *b*) to hit upon, to come upon in one's thoughts. Keiner von ihnen fiel auf diese Kunst, none of them fell on or hit upon this art; warum — Sie auf mich? why do you suppose that it is I? er ist gerade auf ein Auskunftsmittel gefallen, welches &c., he has just thought on an expedient, that &c.; wie sind Sie darauf gefallen? how came it into your head? darauf bin ich nicht gefallen, it never came into my mind. *c*) to fall to any one's share. Das Gut fiel an seinen Bruder, the estate fell to his brother; das Commando fiel an den nächsten Offizier im Range, the command devolved on the next officer in rank;

die Wahl fiel auf ihn, the choice fell on him. *d*) to happen, to take place. Die Frühlingsnachtgleiche fällt jetzt um zehn Tage früher, the vernal equinox falls now about ten days sooner; wie es fällt, according as it shall happen. *e*) to touch properly, to hit. Der Verdacht fiel auf Jemand, der unschuldig an dem Verbrechen war, they suspected a person who was innocent of the crime; die Schuld fällt nicht auf mich, 'tis not my fault. *f*) to have the likeness of. Diese Farbe fällt mehr ins Grüne, this colour inclines more to green; dieser Zeug fällt ins Röthliche, this stuff inclines to red; seine Scherze — in's Pöbelhafte, his jests are rather vulgar; es fällt in's Possenhafte, it is buffoon-like; in den Possenreißer —, to play the buffoon. *g*) = to be. Schwer —, to be difficult; beschwerlich —, to be troublesome; es fällt mir unmöglich, zu kommen, it is impossible for me to come; in warmen Erdstrichen — Ziefern [Insekten] sehr beschwerlich, in warm climates, insects are very troublesome; ich wünsche nicht als Gast lästig zu —, I wish not to be troublesome as a guest; meine Mutter wird mir nie lästig —, my mother will never be burdensome to me; es fiel ein Schuß, a shot was heard; es fielen ein oder zwei Schüsse, one or two shots have been fired. *h*) fallen lassen = äußern. Er ließ einige Ausdrücke —, some expressions fell from him; er ließ kein Wort über diesen Gegenstand —, not a word fell from him on the subject; er ließ ein Wort zu seines Freundes Gunsten —, he dropped a word in favour of his friend; Bemerkungen — lassen, to throw out observations. 2) to sink, to be lowered, to fall. Das Wasser eines Flusses steigt und fällt, the water of a river rises and falls; die Flüsse — im Sommer, the rivers lower in summer; der Nebel fällt, the fog falls; es ist gestern ein tiefer Schnee gefallen, a deep snow fell yesterday; es fällt ein starker Regen, it rains very fast; das Messer fiel mir aus der Hand, the knife dropped from my hand; — lassen, to let fall, to drop; ich habe meine Uhr — lassen, I dropt my watch; den Anker — lassen, [in seamen's lang.] to drop or let go the anchor; reifes Obst fällt von dem Baume, ripe fruit falls or drops from the tree; das Laub fällt von den Bäumen, the leaves fall from the tree. *Prov.* Der Apfel fällt nicht weit vom Stamme, like sire, like son, or such a father, such a son; *die Hoffnung ist mir in den Brunnen gefallen, [fig.] my hopes were deceived, my hopes are disappointed or I am disappointed in my hopes; *seine Worte sind nicht auf die Erde gefallen, *his words did not fall to the ground. *Fig. a*) to decline, to sink, to fall. Die Stimme — lassen, to sink or let fall the voice; sie ließ ihre Stimme —, she depressed or lowered her voice. *b*) to decrease, to be diminished in weight, value or quality, to fall. Der Preis der Waaren fällt und steigt, the price of goods falls and rises; der Werth der Ländereien fällt in Friedenszeiten, the price of lands sinks in time of peace; das — und Steigen der öffentlichen Fonds, the fluctuation of the funds; sein Ansehen ist sehr gefallen, his reputation is much fallen; ich lasse nicht alle Hoffnung — [sinken], I give not up all hope; das Gespräch — lassen, to drop a conversation; eine Motion — lassen, to wave a motion. 3) to drop from an erect posture, or from a seat, to fall. Er fiel vom Pferde, he fell from his horse; von einem Gerüste —, to tumble from a scaffold; er fiel von der Leiter, he fell from the ladder; er fiel zu Boden, he tumbled down; rücklings —, to fall backward; über einen Stein —, to tumble over a stone; ein Ochse fiel in eine Grube, an ox fell into a pit; die —de Sucht, the falling sickness, epilepsy; die —de Wuth, [in dogs] tumbling madness; *er ist nicht auf den Kopf gefallen, [fig.] he does not want sense; *mit der Thür ins Haus —, [fig.] to act or talk inconsiderately. *Fig. a*) to die, particularly by violence, to fall. Ob Tausende — zu deiner Seite, [in Script.] a thousand shall fall at thy side; sie fielen durch das Schwert, they died by the sword; viele Edelleute fielen in dieser blutigen Schlacht, many nobleman were killed in that bloody battle. *b*) to die [used only in Script.]. Durch Pestilenz —, to die by pestilence; [more commonly of large animals] ihm sind seine Pferde an dieser Seuche gefallen, his horses died by that infectious disease; gefallenes Wild, [with hunters] morkin; || gefallenes Leder, the skins of beasts that have died by sickness. *c*) to be brought forth, to fall. Es sind ihm von der Stute zwei Füllen gefallen, his mare dropped two colts. *d*) to decline in power, wealth or glory, to be overthrown or ruined, to fall. Wenn Rom — muß, if Rome must fall; das Handelshaus ist gefallen, the commercial house failed, broke, or became insolvent or bankrupt; der Gottlose wird — durch sein gottloses Wesen, [in Script.] the wicked shall fall by his own wickedness. *Prov.* Wer da fällt, über den läuft alle Welt, if a man once fall, all will tread on him. *e*) = to fail. Denn ein Gerechter fällt siebenmahl und stehet wieder auf, [in Script.] for a just man falleth [sins] seven times and riseth up again; [in theology] Adam fiel, da er von der verbotenen Frucht aß, Adam fell by eating the forbidden fruit; die gefallenen Engel, the fallen angels; sie ist gefallen, [said of a female] she has been ruined; eine gefallene Jungfrau, eine Gefallene, a deflowred virgin. *f*) to be lost, to perish, to fall. Mit ihm fiel unsre Hoffnung, our hope was gone with him. 4) to do something with a hasty or sudden motion; [with hunters] to run, to fly, to leap [said of beasts]. Die Sau fällt in den Zeug, the sow runs into the toils; die Vögel — auf das Aas, the birds fall on carrion; die Vögel — auf einen Baum, the birds light on a tree; die Falken — auf ein fremdes Land, the hawks fly astray; das Wildbret fällt über den Graben, the game leaps the ditch. Einem zu Füßen —, to fall down at any one's feet; und ich fiel ihm zu seinen Füßen, [in Script.] I fell at his feet to worship him; auf die Kniee —, to fall on the knees, to kneel; mit Begierde auf etwas —, to fall on any thing eagerly; dem Pferde in die Zügel —, to seize the bridle of a person's horse; ein Kerl fiel seinem Pferde in die Zügel, a fellow clapt hold of his bridle; da nahm Saul das Schwert und fiel darein, [in Script.] therefore Saul took a sword, and fell upon it; dem Feinde in's Land —, to invade the enemy's country; der rechte Flügel fiel dem Feinde in den Rücken, the right wing fell upon the enemy's rear; sie fielen einander in die Haare, they fell together by the ears, they went together by the ears. *Fig.* In eines Andern Gerechtsame —, to encroach on the jurisdiction of another; Einem Andern in den Kauf —, to interfere with another's bargain.

II. *v. tr.* it is used sometimes as an transitive verb or as a verb reciprocal, as: Einen todt —, to kill any one by falling upon him; sich wund —, to get a bruise or a wound by a fall; sich zu Tode —, to fall to death, to be killed by a fall; sich den Arm aus dem Gelenke —, to dislocate one's arm by a fall.

Fällen, *v. tr.* 1) to cause to fall, or move downwards. Den Anker —, [in seamen's language] to let go an anchor, to cast anchor, to anchor; einen Schacht —, [in mining] to sink a shaft; einen festen Körper —, [in chimistry] to precipitate [metals by alkaline salts &c.]; eine senkrechte Linie —, [in geometry] to draw a perpendicular line. 2) to cause something to fall or become lower. Das Wasser —, to diminish the water; die Fock —, [in seamen's lang.] to tally or haul the sheets of the fore-sail fla[t] aft. 3) to cause something to fall or fall over; to fell, to fall, to cut down. Einen Baum —, to fall a tree; eine Wand &c. —, [with masons] to pull down a wall &c.; er fällte den Riesen, he felled the giant; ein Thier —, [with hunters] to kill by a ball or other thing shot, to shoot, to bring down; sie spannen ihren Bogen, daß sie fällen den Elenden und Armen, [in Script.] they have bent their bow, to cast down the poor and needy. *Fig.* ‡ to ruin. Sein Anschlag wird ihn —, [in Scripture] his own counsel shall cast him down. 4) to let fall. || Die Zähne —, to cast teeth. *Fig.* to pass [sentence or judgment]. Sie konnten kein Urtheil in der Sache —, they could not judge in the case; ein Urtheil über das Verdienst einer Person —, to judge of the merit of a person.

Fäll-silber, *n.* [in chimistry] precipitated silver. —**wasser**, *n.* [in chimistry] precipitant.

Fällig, *adj.* and *adv.* 1) *Fig.* [that ought to be paid] due, owed. Die Zinsen sind —, the interest is due; ein —er Wechsel, a bill of exchange due. 2) frequently used in compositions, as Augen—, bei—, hin— &c.

***Falliment, Fallissement**, *n.* [-es, *pl.* -s or -e] a breaking or becoming insolvent, failure, failure in trade, bankruptcy.

***Falliren**, *v. intr.* [= fallit seyn], to become insolvent or bankrupt, to fail, to break.

***Fallit**, *m.* [-en, *pl.* -en] an insolvent trader, a bankrupt.

Falls, *adv.* in case. — Sie ihn sehen sollten, in case you should see him.

***Falsarius**, *m.* [*pl.* Falsarien] [in law] a falsifier, a forger of counterfeit deeds, bonds &c.

Falsch, [Lat. *fals*-us, seems to be allied to fallen, fehlen] *adj.* and *adv.* *a*) counterfeit, not genuine or real, false. —es Gold, false gold; ein —er Diamant, a false diamond; —e Zähne, false teeth. *b*) [= erheuchelt] —e Thränen, false tears; eine —e Bescheidenheit, a counterfeit or false modesty; eine —e Freundschaft, false friendship. *c*) [heuchlerisch] ein —er Freund, a counterfeit friend; ein Falscher, a hypocrite. *Prov.* Vor den Augen gut, — hinterrück [= von hinten], das ist anjetzt das Meisterstück, flattery now-a-days gets friends. *d*) counterfeit for the purpose of deception. —e Münze, false coin; —es Geld, base money; ein —es Siegel, a false seal; ein —er Schlüssel, a false key; ein —er Boden, a false bottom; ein —er Schein, a false note; eine —e Obligation, a counterfeit bond; —e Wechsel, forged or counterfeit bills of exchange; eine —e Quittung a forged receipt; —e Urkunden, counterfeit deeds; ein —er Eid, a false oath; einen —en Eid schwören, to swear falsely; ein —es Zeugniß ablegen, to testify falsely. *e*) [= darauf ausgehend, Andere zu vervortheilen] Ein —er Spieler, a sharper; ein —er Münzer, a maker of base money, a coiner, a forger; ein —er Zeuge, a false witness; ein —er Mensch, a double-dealer; — seyn, to be guilty of duplicity; [in Scripture] corrupted in principles or conduct, vicious, corrupt, depraved. *f*) [unrichtig] wrong, not true, not conformable to fact, false. Ein —er Weg, a wrong way; eine —e Nachricht, a false report; eine —e Anklage, a false accusation; eine —e Behauptung, a false assertion; ein —er Bericht, a wrong or incorrect statement; eine —e Voraussetzung, an erroneous supposition; —e Maßregeln, false measures; eine —e Politik, a faulty policy; ein —er Schluß, false conclusion; wo er aber — befunden wird, so wird sie ihn verlassen, daß er verderben muß, [in Script.] if he go wrong, she will give him over to his own ruin; eine —e Hoffnung, vain hope.

g) not agreeable to rule and propriety, false. Eine —e Aussprache, a wrong pronunciation, a mispronunciation; ein Wort oder einen Namen — aussprechen, to mispronounce a word, a name; ein —es Wort, an improper word; — schreiben, to miswrite; [in music] ein —er Ton, a discordant sound; — singen, to sing out of tune; [in fencing] ein —er Stoß, a feigned pass; [in painting] ein —es Licht, a false light. *Fig.* Jemands Handlungen in ein —es Licht setzen, to misrepresent any one's actions; der Sachwalter setzte den Gegenstand in ein —es Licht, the advocate gave the subject a false colouring; Vorurtheil setzt die Gegenstände in ein —es Licht, prejudice puts a false colour upon objects. *h*) not true, not according to the lawful standard, false. —es Gewicht oder Maß, false weight or measure; —e Waaren, adulterated goods; —e Farben, false colours [which either lose their colour or change to some other, or corrode stuffs]. and † *i*) apt to take fire, irritable, irascible. Einen — machen, to irritate or exasperate any one; über etwas — werden, to be vexed or to fret at any thing; — auf Einen seyn, to fret against any one.

Falsch-gläubig, *adj.* and *adv.* 1) heterodox. 2) heretical. Der —gläubige, *a*) a heterodox person, *b*) a heretic. —gläubigkeit, *f.* 1) heterodoxy. 2) heresy. —gründig, *adj.* and *adv.* resting on a false foundation. —herzig, *adj.* and *adv.* false-hearted. —münzer, *m.* a maker of false money, a coiner, a forger. —münzerei, *f.* 1) the act of counterfeiting the legal coin. 2) the forgery of coin. —nagel, *m.* [with metalists] a false rivet. —namig, *adj.* and *adv.* having a false or feigned name, pseudonymous. —paarig, *adj.* and *adv.* [in botany] —paarige Blätter, dissimilar opposite leaves. —spieler, *m.* a sharper.

Fälsch, *n.* [-es] ‖1) defect, fault, imperfection. 2) want of veracity, falsehood, falseness, deceit. Ohne —, guileless.

Fälschen, *v. tr.* 1) to falsify, to make impure by an admixture of baser materials. Wein —, to adulterate wine. 2) to give a false appearance. [with butchers] Kalbfleisch —, to swell, to inflate or to blow veal. 3) to make a likeness or resemblance of any thing, with a view to defraud, to counterfeit [a deed or other thing in writing &c.].

Fälscher, *m.* [-s, *pl.* -] a counterfeiter, a forger, a falsifier.

Fälschheit, *f.* 1) doubleness of heart or speech falseness, duplicity, double-dealing. 2) contrariety or inconformity to fact or truth, falsehood, falsity. Die — einer Nachricht, the falsehood of a report. 3) an untrue assertion, falsehood, an untruth, a lie.

Fälschlich, *adj.* and *adv.* 1) not true, false. Einen — anklagen, to accuse any one falsely. 2) treacherous, deceitful, false. — handeln, to practise deceit; — mit Einem umgehen, to deal falsely with any one.

Falsétt, *n.* [-es, *pl.* -e] [a sound of the voice beyond the natural pitch] falsetto.

Fälsum, *n.* [Falsi or -s, *pl.* -sa] [in law, the crime of counterfeiting] forgery.

Fält, V. Fältig, in composition.

Fältchen, *n.* [-s, *pl.* -] [*dimin.* of Falte] a small fold or plait.

Falte, *f.* [*pl.* -n] [from fallen?] a doubling, a fold, a plait, a rumple; [in botany] the plaited part of a corolla. In —n legen, to lap or lay in plaits, to fold [a piece of cloth &c.]; in kleine —n legen, to pucker; eine falsche —, an irregular fold, a crease; die falschen —n aus einem Tuche ausstreichen, to take the creases out of a cloth; die —n in der Haut, wrinkles in the skin; —n im Gesicht habend, furrow-faced; die Stirn in —n legen, *fig.* to knit the brows, to frown. *Fig.* Die geheimsten or verborgensten —n unserer Seele, the most secret recesses of our soul.

Falten-blume, *f.* [a plant] bindweed. —bund, *m.* top-shell, button-shell, [in conch.] trochus [t. tuber]. —fisch, *m.* pike-headed whale, or mysticete. —flechte, *f.* a species of liverwort [lichen plicatus]. —kammer, *f.* [in sugar-houses] a room where the sugar-loaves are enveloped with paper. —klappe, *f.* [in conch.] spondylus [plicatus]. —kleid, *n.* a plaited gown. —kniff, *m.* 1) a doubling or folding. 2) the manner of plaiting. —los, *adj.* and *adv.* having no folds. *Fig.* Eine —lose Stirne, a serene or cheerful look, an open look; ein —loses Leben, an open life. —magen, *m.* [the third stomach of ruminating beasts] the manyplies, the tripe V. also Blättermagen. —morchel, *f.* a genus of fungi, hevella [h. mitra]. —rand, *m.* the plaited border of a petticoat or gown, furbelow. —reich, *adj.* and *adv.* having many folds or plaits. —rock, *m.* a plaited gown. —saum, *m.* V. —rand. —schlag, *m.* [in sculpture and painting] drapery. —schwamm, *m.* an agaric with a cap striate and plaited. —träger, *m.* the plaited lizard. —tuch, *n.* a texture of cotton consisting of many small folds. —voll, *adj.* and *adv.* full of folds or plaits; *it.* rumpled. —walze, *f.* [in conch.] the small Indian musicshell or furrow-spire. —weise, *adv.* in folds. —wurf, *m.* V. —schlag.

Fälteln, *v. tr.* to gather into small folds, to plait, to pucker. Halskrausen —, to pucker ruffs.

Fälten, *v. tr.* 1) to double, to lap or lay in plaits, to fold. Ein Stück Tuch —, to fold a piece of cloth; einen Aermel —, to plait a sleeve; einen Brief —, to fold a letter, to make up a letter; die Stirn —, to wrinkle the brow, *fig.* to knit the brows, to frown; gefaltete Blätter, [in botany] plaited leaves. 2) to double or lay together, to fold. Mit gefalteten or gefaltenen Händen beten, to pray with one's hands joined; sie faltete die or ihre Hände, she clasped her hands together.

Falt-stock, *m.* a folding-stick, a folder. —stuhl, *m.* a folding-chair. —tisch, *m.* a folding-table.

Fälter, *m.* [-s, *pl.* -] a butterfly.

Fältig, *adj.* and *adv.* having folds, laid in plaits, folded; *it.* rumpled. Ein —es Kleid, a plaited gown; eine —e Stirn, wrinkled brows; mein Rock ist ganz — geworden, my coat has become quite rumpled.

Fältig, Fältig, in composition, the same quantity added, fold, as einfältig, one fold; vielfältig, manifold; mannigfaltig, manifold, various &c.; hundertfältig, a hundredfold, centuple.

1. Fälz, *f.* V. Balz.

2. Fälz, *m.* [-es, *pl.* -e or Fälze, *dimin.* das Fälzchen or ‖ Fälzlein] [= Falte] 1) [with bookbinders] a fold, [also] a guard; [with tanners and strapcutters] the bended part of a shaver or shaving-knife; [with coppersmiths] the bended edge of parts that are to be sodered. 2) a furrow, channel or long hollow cut by a tool, [among joiners] a channel in the edge of a moulding, style or rail, a groove. Eine Säule mit —en, a channelled or fluted column; der (die) — an einem Büchsenschafte, the gutter of a gun-stock. 3) a hollow cut or channel for guiding any thing. Der — in dem Ständer einer Schleuse, the reigle of a side-post for a flood-gate. 4) a cut on the side of a board &c. to fit it to another by lapping, a rabbet. Der — in den Faßdauben, a croe or crow.

Falz-amboß, *m.* a coppersmith's anvil. —bank, *f.* [with carpenters and joiners] lapping-board. —bein, *n.* [an instrument used in folding paper] a folder. —blume, *f.* [a plant] micropus. —bock, *m.* a wooden leg whereupon a tanner scrapes hides. —brett, *n.* [with bookbinders] folding-board. —eisen, *n.* [with tanners] a shaver, or shaving-knife. —haken, *m.* a tanner's hook. —hammer, *m.* [with coppersmiths] a sodering-hammer. —hobel, *m.* [a joiner's instrument for grooving] a plow. —messer, *n.* V. —eisen. —zange, *f.* 1) [with braziers and tinmakers] tongs used in sodering. 2) a shoemaker's pincers. —ziegel, *m.* a gutter-tile.

1. Fälzen, *v. tr.* 1) to bend and lay over or on, to fold. Die Bogen eines Buches —, to fold the sheets of a book; einen Brief —, to fold a letter. 2) to bend and lay the edges over or on Einen Kessel —, [with coppersmiths] to soder a caldron. 3) to groove, to furrow, to rabbet. Eine Säule —, to flute a column. 4) [with leather-dressers] to shave [hides].

2. Fälzen, *v. intr.* V. Balzen.

Fälzer, *m.* [-s, *pl.* -] -inn, *f.* a person that folds, a folder.

Fälzicht, *adj.* and *adv.* resembling a fold or groove.

Fälzig, *adj.* and *adv.* having folds, folded, grooved.

*Fāma, *f.* [der Fama or -'s] [the goddess of report] Fame. *Fig* public report or rumor, fame.

*Familiār, *m.* [-s or -en, *pl.* -en] an affiliate of the Spanish Inquisition, a familiar.

*Familiār, *adj.* and *adv.* familiar, intimate.

*Familiarisiren, *v. tr.* to familiarize. Sich mit etwas —, to familiarize one's self with a thing.

*Familiarität, *f.* [*pl.* -en] familiarity, intimate and frequent converse, or association in company.

*Familie, *f.* [*pl.* -n] 1) a household, including parents and children, family. — haben, to have children; eine große — haben, to have a large family; —n-angelegenheiten, domestic concerns, family affairs. 2) those who descend from one common progenitor or stock, a tribe or race, kindred, lineage, family. Von guter — seyn, to be of good family, to be a man of family; aus einer alten — seyn, to be born of a noble or respectable family, to be well-born; die königliche —, the royal family. *Fig.* [in botany] an order, class or genus of plants. Eine Pflanzen—, a family of plants. 3) [rather unusual] number of men, united by occupation, as die — der Schmiede, the body of smiths.

Familien-austrag, *m.* family court. —begräbniß, *n.* family vault. ‖—brod, *n.* home-made bread. —fehler, *m.* hereditary failing, family-failing. —geist, *m.* 1) family spirit. 2) a sense of domestic life. —gemälde, *n.* family picture. *Fig.* a description of a family and a relation of its fate, a representation of family-incidents. Die —gemälde eines Lafontaine, Starke &c., the domestic novels of a Lafontaine, Starke &c.; Iffland's —gemälde, the family-dramas of Iffland. —geräth, *n.* inalienable family-furniture, heir-loom. —glück, *n.* domestic happiness. —gruft, *f.* V. —begräbniß. —gut, *n.* an estate or fee entailed, entail. —haupt, *n.* the chief or head of a family. —krankheit, *f.* hereditary disease. —kreis, *m.* domestic circle. —leben, *n.* domestic life. —los, *adj.* and *adv.* having no household, or destitute of children or offspring, childless. —losigkeit, *f.* the state of having no household or of being childless. —rath,

m. family council. —stolz, m. family pride. —stück, n. 1) a piece of a family's furniture or any thing kept in a family as a memorial. 2) family picture. —tafel, f. [at courts] a table for the members of the reigning prince's family. —verbindung, f. a connection between families, a family connection. —vermächtniß, n. an entailed legacy. —vertrag, m. family compact. —zirkel, m. V. —kreis.

*Fămulus, m. [- or Famuli, pl. -sse or Famuli] an amanuensis.

*Fanătiker, m. [-s, pl. -] a fanatic.

*Fanătisch, I. adj. fanatic, fanatical. II. adv. fanatically.

*Fanatĭsmus, m. fanaticism, fanaticalness.

*Fănfaron, m. [pron. as in the French] a bully, a hector, a swaggerer, a vain pretender, a fanfaron.

*Fanfaronāden, pl. fanfaronades, vain boasting.

Făng, m. [-es, pl. Fănge] 1) the act of catching, taking or seizing, catch, capture. Auf den — ausgehen, to be or lie upon the catch; einen guten — thun, to make a good catch; [it is often used in composition, as, Fisch—, fishing; Vogel—, bird-catching &c.]. 2) the place where any thing is caught by force, surprise or stratagem, and an instrument for catching wild beasts, as, pitfalls, traps, snares; also a fishery, nets, wears and other instruments for catching fish, as, Aal—, eel-fishery; Lachs—, salmon-fishery. 3) a claw or talon, fang. Die Fänge eines Adlers, the fangs or talons of an eagle. 4) = Fangzahn. fang, tusk. Die Fänge eines wilden Schweins, the fangs or tusks of a boar. 5) [with hunters] a) a thrust with a hanger or cutlass. Einem Hirsche den — geben, to stab a stag. b) the bite of a dog.

Fang-ball, m. a ball for play. —baum, m. [am Kunstgestänge, in mining] catch. —brief, or —es-brief, m. a warrant of arrest. —bühne, f. wharf or quay. —damm, m. a dike. —gebühr, f. —es-geld, —geld, n. 1) money paid for arresting a person. 2) money paid for catching noxious animals. —eisen, n. [with hunters] a) an iron trap. † Fig. a wedding-ring. b) a boar-spear or a huntman's pole. —es-messer, n. a small hanger or cutlass. —es-reuse, f. V. Legereuse. —es-stock, —stock, m. a bailiff's pole, with which they catch runaways. —es-strick, —strick, m. 1) a gin, snare or noose. 2) [with huntsmen] a leash. ‖—es-vogel, —vogel, m. a goshawk. —es-zahn, —zahn, m. a tusk, fang. —gier, f. coquetry, flirtation. —gierig, adj. and adv. coquetish. —heuschrecke, f. praying-cricket. —leine, f. [in seamen's lang.] tow-line. Die — leine des Boots, painter. —lust, f. V. —gier. —lustig, V. —gierig. —messer, V. —es-messer. —stahl, m. V. Hirschfänger. —taue, pl. [in seamen's language] short pieces of rope or ratline. —tuch, n. [in seamen's language] tinder. —werkzeug, n. [in boring-instruments, in mining] beche.

Făngen, [allied to fahen and fassen] ir. I. v. tr. [and sometimes intr.] 1) to seize, in a general sense, to catch; it. to catch or seize with the fangs or claws [as birds of prey], or with the teeth [as dogs]. Einen Ball —, to catch a ball; einen Floh —, to catch a flea; Fliegen —, to catch flies; [with hunters] der Hund fängt in den Fangstrick, the dog bites the leash. Prov. Mit gefangen mit gehangen, bad company puts a bad end. Fig. Grillen —, V. Grille. 2) to seize in pursuit, to catch. Einen —, to catch or overtake any one, or to take any one prisoner. 3) to seize as in a snare or trap, to get into one's power by engines or nets. Füchse in Fallen —, to take foxes with traps; Biber —, to trap beavers; Fische —, to catch fish; Vögel —, to catch birds, to bird; Mäuse —, to catch mice, to mouse; [with hunters] einen Hirsch —, to stab a stag; ein wildes Schwein —, to spear a boar. Fig. Und sie sandten zu ihm etliche von den Pharisäern und Herodis Dienern, daß sie ihn fingen in Worten, [in Script.] they sent certain of the Pharisees and of the Herodians, to catch him in his words; er läßt sich nicht —, he is not to be bubbled; wir werden zuweilen mit unsern eigenen Worten gefangen, we are sometimes entrapped in our own words; *er hat die Schöne gefangen, he caught the fair; *sie hat ihn durch ihre Schönheit gefangen, he is captivated by her beauty. 4) to fix or confine. [With hunters] die Leine —, to fasten the line of a net to a tree &c.; den Rauch —, to confine smoke; [in seamen's language] den Anker —, to fish the anchor, to get the anchor up along the bow [in order to clear the cables]; die Ankerboie —, to hitch the buoy; die Raaen mit Ketten —, to secure the yards by chains [in time of action]. 5) to take hold, to catch. Feuer —, to catch fire; der Schwamm fängt gut, the spunk takes fire readily. Fig. *Er fängt leicht Feuer, he is very irascible; he is easily captivated.

II. v. r. sich —, 1) to be caught or trapped. Der Fuchs hat sich gefangen, the fox got into the trap. Fig. Er hat sich in seinen eignen Worten —, he has entrapped or caught himself in his own words. 2) to be fixed, or confined. Der Wind fängt sich in dem Schornstein, a current of wind got into the chimney, the wind blows down in the chimney; [in seamen's language] die Bugten — sich, the fakes catch each other, there are catch-fakes in the cable.

Fănger, m. [-s, pl. -] Făngerinn, f. a person that catches, catcher, taker. Fig. [rather unusual] coquet, coquette.

Făngereí, f. catching, taking. Fig. [rather unusual] coquetry, flirtation.

Făngerisch, [rather unusual] adj. and adv. coquetish.

Fănt, m. [-es, pl. -e; diminut. das Fäntchen] [in Sw. fant signifies Diener, fänta eine junge Magd; many suppose, though improbably, that it is derived from the Lat. infans] [in slight contempt] a lad, youth, youngster; it. a coxcomb.

*Fantasíe, [more commonly Phantasie] f. 1) fancy, imagination. 2) [pl. -en] a vain or idle fancy, chimera; it. whim. Er ist so reich, daß er seine ausschweifendsten —en befriedigen kann, he is so rich, that he can indulge his most extravagant whims; Fieber—en, fever-fancies, delirium. 3) [in music, a piece played by a musician extemporarily, according to his fancy] a voluntary.

*Fantasīren, v. intr. 1) to have vain or idle fancies, to be affected by phantoms, to be visionary. 2) to rave, to dote. Nervenfieberkranke pflegen oft zu —, nervous fevers often cause delirium. 3) to play a voluntary, to flourish.

*Fantăst, m. [-en, pl. -en] a fantastic or fantastical person, a fancy-monger; it. an extravagant person; it. a coxcomb. Er ist ein echter —, he is a regular coxcomb.

*Fantăstisch, I. adj. 1) fantastic, fantastical, fanciful, imaginary, chimerical. 2) fantastic, fantastical, fanciful, whimsical, capricious, indulging the vagaries of imagination, extravagant, odd. II. adv. 1) in a fantastic manner, fantastically. 2) fantastically, whimsically.

*Fantōm, n. [-s, pl. -e] a phantom, a spectre, fantasm.

‖Fănze, f. [pl. -n] V. Firlefanz.

Fărb, adj. and adv. V. Farben.

Fărbe, f. [pl. -n] [perhaps from fahren, = bringen, tragen] 1) [in physics, a property
herent in light, which, by a difference in the
and the laws of refraction, or some other cause,
to bodies particular appearances to the eye] co
Die vornehmsten —n sind roth, orange,
grün, blau, indigoblau und violet, the pri
colours are red, orange, yellow, green, bl
digo and violet; weiß ist eigentlich kei
white is not properly a colour; schwarz is
deutliche oder bestimmte —, black is no d
colour. 2) colour, hue, dye. Die — [fahren]
to lose colour, to fade; Blumen von alle
flowers of all hue; ein Zeug hält or beh
—, a stuff retains its colour; Seewasser be
dem Silber die —, silver is discoloured b
water; echte oder falsche —n, true or fal
lours. Prov. Wie der Blinde von der —
len, blind men can judge no colours. Fi
— halten, to be fixed or firm in mind
tion, to be constant; die — nicht halten
inconstant, fickle. 3) a certain colour.
tawers] yellow. b) [with bakers] the y
brown colour of bread. c) [a red colo
freshness or appearance of blood in the face] c
Er verändert die —, his colour chang
[that which is used for colouring, a col
substance] colour, paint. Die weiße —,
paint; mineralische —n, mineral colours
farben, oil-colours; Wasserfarben, water-c
trockene —n, dry colours; — reiben, to
colours; die —n mischen, to mix colours;
auftragen, to apply colours; die Art
aufzutragen, [among painters] colouring;
ler, der die —n gut aufzutragen weiß, a c
5) [in a more limited sense] a) printing-i
ink for the rolling-press. Die — auftr
printing] to distribute the ink. b) [= F
manner of applying colours, colouring.
—n, a lively colouring. Fig. Einen mi
digen —n abmalen, to set any one o
proper colours; Homer beschreibt die Th
ner Helden mit glühenden —n, Homer
the achievements of his heroes in glo
lours; *einer Sache eine gute — geben,
[glänzende] — anstreichen, to set a th
fair light, to give it a specious a
6) a coloured body. a) [with sportsm
blood. b) [at cards] a suit of cards
verleugnen, not to follow suit, to
to revoke; sometimes the suit of car
takes any of the other suits. c) a form
by which noblemen and gentlemen di
their servants, livery. Er trägt die —
ses Doria, he wears the livery of the
Doria.

Farbe-ballen, m. [in printing]
—geben, n. 1) the act of dyeing,
2) [with painters] the manner of applyi
colouring. —los, adj. and adv. d
colour. —loses Wasser, colourless wa
Fernröhren, achromatic telescopes.
m. the furnace of a dyer. —stein,
ing] ink-block. —voll, adj. and
or highly coloured. Ein —volles
florid face or complexion. —wechs
and adv. changeable [silk &c.].

Fărben, adj. and adv. coloured [
composition]. Asch—, ash-coloured; fe
coloured; rosen—, rosy &c.

Fărben, pl. of Farbe.

Farben-arbeiter, m. a w
dye-house. —auftrag, m. the act
ing colours. —bild, n. 1) a coloured i
[in optics] a coloured spectrum, iris.
m. a dazzling colour. —blume, f. 1) a
flower. 2) a two-coloured carnation. —
m. a coloured bow; the rainbow, iris.
chung, f. [with painters] the mixture
—brett, n. [among painters] a palette. —

f. Färbebrühe. —dreieck, *n.* [in optics]. chro-hatic triangle. —eisen, *n.* [in printing] slice. —erde, *f.* Farberde, earth coloured by a mix-ure of metal. —faß, *n.* [with tanners] colour-ub. —fell, *n.* a dyed-hide. —flechte, *f.* V. Färbemoos. —flecken, *m.* a coloured pot. —gebung, *f.* [among painters] colouring. —glanz, *m.* brightness or strength of colour, riency. —holz, V. Färbeholz. —kasten, *m.* [diminut. das Farbenkästchen] a box of colours. —essel, *m.* V. Färbekessel. —klavier, *n.* *Fig.* cular harpsichord. —klecker, *m.* a coarse ainter, a dauber. —kobalt, *m.* a cobalt of a reyish-white colour. —körper, *m.* a colouring ody. —kundige, *m.* a colourist. —lehre, science of colours. —leiter, *f.* a scale of olours. —los, V. Farbelos. —messer, *n.* [among painters] horn. —mischung, *f.* [among inters] the mixture of colours; colouring. —ühle, *f.* colour-mill. —muschel, *f.* colour-ell. —piramide, V. —dreieck. —pulver, a pulverized colour. —rand, *m.* [in optics] is. —reiber, *m.* a colour-grinder. —reich, *dj.* and *adv.* many-coloured. —setzung, *f.* V. gebung. —spatel, *f.* a spatula used by colour-inders. —spiel, *n.* 1) iridescence, as in a acock's tail. 2) V. —klavier. —stein, *m.* 1) inding-stone. 2) [in printing] ink-block. —ift, *m.* [among painters] 1) a crayon used in signing or painting in pastel. 2) a red or black ayon. —strahl, *m.* [in optics] a coloured y of light. —stufe, *f.* degree or gradation colours, shade. —stufung, *f.* gradation colours, shading. —tafel, *f.* [diminut. das täfelchen] a cake of paint. Eine rothe —fel, a cake of red. —tuch, *n.* coloured cloth. —verbreitung, *f.* V. —zerstreuung. —waare, *f.* 1) [in commerce] colours. Er handelt —waaren, he deals in colours. 2) V. Färbe-ug. —wechsel, *m.* variation of colours. —echsler, *m.* [an animal of the genus lacerta] ameleon. —zerstreuung, *f.* [in optics] the rergency of the rays of light, dispersion. —ug, *m.* a coloured stuff. —zeug, *n.* V. Färbe-ug.

Färben, I. *v. tr.* to colour, to dye, to tinge, to in. Grün —, to dye green; leicht —, to tint; ch —, to colour cloth; Leder, Hüte —, to dye ther, hats; in der Wolle gefärbt, dyed in the in, ingrained; gefärbtes Holz, stained wood; Schnitt der Bücher —, [in bookbinding] to ge the edge of books; sich die Augenbrauen warz —, to black one's eye-brows; Ruß färbt Hände schwarz, soot soils the hands; mit t gefärbt, stained with blood; die Gelbsucht bt die Augen gelb, the jaundice tinges the eyes h yellow; die Sonne färbt die Früchte, the sun ours the fruits; gefärbt, [in botany] coloured epithet for a leaf that is of any other colour than en]. II. *v. r.* sich —, to get a colour. Die Trau— sich, the grapes begin to turn; der Pelz isser Thiere färbt sich im Winter, the fur of ain animals turns in winter; das Wildbret bt sich, game moults.

Färbe-brühe, *f.* a colouring-liquor, dye. —istel, *f.* officinal bastard-saffron. —flechs *f.* the large yellow-saucered dyer's lichen. —eräth, *n.* a dyer's utensils. —haus, *n.* ye-house. —holz, *n.* 1) dyeing-wood, as, wood, Campeachy wood. 2) [with bakers] ece of green wood soaked in water used in ing bread. —kessel, *m.* dyeing-copper. —ner, *pl.* 1) [with dyers] a sort of yellow co- fabricated at Avignon. 2) [a plant] the ging buckthorn. —kraut, *n.* V. Grapp. —ufe, *f.* a dyeing vat. —kunst, *f.* the art of uring cloth, hats &c., colouring, dyeing. —pchen, *n.* Spanish clout, French turnsole l in painting the face or in dying sweetmeats. —moos, *n.* dyer's lichen. —scharte, *f.* V. Färberscharte. —stoff, *m.* [a preparation used by painters, dyers &c., to impart colour to bodies] paint, pigment. —waare, *f.* V. Farbenwaare. —zeit, *f.* moulting. —zeug, *n.* the implements of a dyer.

Färber, *m.* [-s, *pl.* -] Färberinn, *f.* a person whose occupation is to dye cloth and the like, dyer.

Färber-kraut, *n.* anchusa tinctoria. —kunst, *f.* V. Färbekunst. —röthe, *f.* V. Grapp. —scharte, *f.* serratula tinctoria. —wald-meister, *m.* wild madder, asperula tinctoria. —wurzel, *f.* V. Grapp.

Färberei, *f.* 1) the art of colouring cloth, hats &c., dyeing. 2) the trade of a dyer, and a dyer's shop or dye-house.

Färbig, *adj.* and *adv.* 1) coloured. —es Papier —, stained paper; —e Leute, coloured people, black people. 2) [in a more limited sense] coloured, as opposed to black and white, which are not properly colours. 3) it is often used in composition, as, asch—, ash-coloured; viel—, many-coloured &c.

Färbung, *f.* 1) coloration. 2) the quality of a colour.

Färbwerk, *n.* [-s, *pl.* -e] V. Blaufarben-werk.

*Farce, [pron. Farße] *f.* [*pl.* -n] 1) [a kind of dramatic composition] farce. 2) [in the culinary art] V. Füllsel.

*Farciren, [pron. Farßihren] *v. tr.* [in the culinary art] to stuff. Farcirt, stuffed.

||Fardel, *n.* [-s, *pl.* -] [in Ital. is *fardello* = ein Pack] a measure used for measuring cloth [it is 1080 ells].

*Farin, Farinzucker, *m.* [-s] cask-sugar, cassonade.

Farken, *m.* [-s, *pl.* -] [in seamen's language] hog.

Farkentreiber, *m.* [in contempt] a slow or bad sailor.

Farn, *m.* [-s] Farnkraut, *n.* [-es, *pl.* -kräuter] [seems to be allied to Faser; according to others from fahren] fern.

Farn-krautmännlein, *n.* male polypody or fern. —krautweiblein, *n.* female polypody. —samen, *m.* [a plant] bulbous fumitory.

Farre, *m.* [-n, *pl.* -n] [originally = Thier; allied to Bär, Eber] a young bull or ox.

Farren-äugig, *adj.* and *adv.* *fig.* having large eyes. —schwanz, *m.* a bull's pizzle.

Farrenkraut, *n.* [-es, *pl.* -kräuter] V. Farn.

Färse, Farse, *f.* [*pl.* -n] [allied either to Farr or belonging to bären = tragen, as πόρτις to φέρω] a young cow, heifer, || why.

Färsenkalb, *n.* a female calf, ||why-calf.

*Fasan, *m.* [-en, *pl.* -en] pheasant. Der —hahn, pheasant-cock; die —henne oder das —huhn, a hen-pheasant; der junge —, pheasant-powt; der böhmische —, the Bohemian pheasant; der weiße —, the white pheasant.

Fasanen-auge, *n.* [a plant] pheasant's eye or bird's eye. —beize, *f.* hawking at pheasants. —beller, *m.* a dog used in pheasant-shooting, a springing spaniel or cocker. —braten, *m.* a roasted pheasant. —ente, *f.* the sea-pheasant, cracker, or pintail. —garten, *m.* —gehege, *n.* pheasant-walk, pheasant-preserve. —hahn, *m.* —henne, *f.* —huhn, *n.* V. Fasan. —haus, *n.* a house in a pheasant-walk where pheasants brood, pheasant-house. —hof, *m.* V. Fasanerie. —hund, *m.* V. —beller. —jagd, *f.* pheasant-shooting. —jäger, *m.* [at courts] a huntsman whose business is pheasant-shooting. —kraut, *n.* 1) common milfoil. 2) spring bitter vetch. —meister, *m.* [at courts] the keeper of pheasants. —stand, *m.* V. Kirrung. —wärter, —wirth, *m.* V. —meister. —zucht, *f.* breeding of pheasants.

Fasanvogel, *m.* V. Fasan.

Fasanerie, *f.* [*pl.* -en] 1) the art of keeping and breeding pheasants. 2) pheasant-walk or pheasant-preserve.

*Fasces, *pl.* [in Roman antiquity] fasces.

1. Fasch, *m.* [-es, *pl.* -e] [perhaps allied to the Ital. *fascia*] [with curriers and leather-dressers] a piece of leather for soles one ell long and two ells broad.

2. ||Fasch, *m.* [-es, *pl.* -e] [probably allied to the Sw. *fösa*, bewegen, = Ausschlag] [ulcers in the mouth and fauces of suckling children] thrush.

3. Fasch, Fetsch, *s.* [-es, *pl.* -e] [with hunters] V. Blut or Schweiß.

Fasche, Fäsche, *f.* [*pl.* -n] [V. 1. Fasch] [in common language] a sort of stays, or bodice.

Faschen, *v. intr.* [with hunters] to run with blood, to bleed.

*Faschine, *f.* [*pl.* -n] [in fortif.] a fagot, fascine.

Faschinen-bank, *f.* a frame whereupon fascines are bound up. —blendung, *f.* chandeleers. —haken, *m.* a mattock used for pulling down a work made with fascines. —messer, *n.* hedging-bill. —werk, *n.* a work made with fascines.

Fasching, *m.* [-es, *pl.* -e] [corrupted from Fasten] carnaval or carnival. V. also Fastnacht 3).

*Fascikel, *n.* a bundle of writings or scriptures. Ein — Akten or Akten—, a bundle or file of public papers, acts, &c.

1 Fase, *f.* [*pl.* -n] V. Fasen *m.*

2. Fase, *f.* [*pl.* -n] [from fahen, fassen] [in carpentry] a mortise.

Fasebrett, *n.* [among joiners and carpenters] a triangular piece of timber or a lath for lattice-work.

||Fasel, *m.* [-s, *pl.* -] also die Fasel [from fahen = sich vermehren, Lat. *feo*, Gr. φύω, allied to Vieh, *pec-us*] 1) the brood of fishes or of birds &c. 2) propagation [used of beasts]. 3) breed. Ein Schwein von guter —, a hog of a good breed. ||4) [the male of the bovine genus of quadrupeds] a bull.

||Fasel-gebühr, *f.* —geld, *n.* stallionage. ||—hammel, *m.* the male of the sheep or ovine genus, the ram. ||—hengst, *m.* a stallion. ||—ochs, *m.* a bull. ||—schwein, boar or sow. —vieh, *n.* 1) beasts for breeding. 2) lean cattle.

Fasele, Faseole, *f.* [*pl.* -n] a sort of kidney-bean, phasel, phaseolus. V. Schminkbohne.

Faselei, *f.* 1) a silly manner of thinking and acting. Die — des hohen Alters, dotage. 2) a silly or foolish action.

Faseler, *m.* [-s, *pl.* -] 1) a nonsensical talker. 2) a silly fellow. Ein alter —, dotard, doter.

Faselhaft, *adj.* and *adv.* silly, foolish, fickle.

Faselhaftigkeit, *f.* 1) silliness, foolishness, 2) fickleness.

Faselig, *adj.* and *adv.* 1) dotish. 2) fickle. Ein —er Liebhaber, a fickle lover.

1. Faseln, [V. Fasel] *v. intr.* 1) to bring forth young, [used chiefly of swine] to farrow. 2) to increase in number. Die Biene faselt, the hive multiplies. *Prov.* Unrecht faselt nicht, goods ill gotten never prosper.

2. Faseln, [allied to the Sw. *fösa* = bewegen] *v. intr.* 1) to talk irrationally, to rave. 2) to think or act in a silly or trifling manner, to be silly, to dote, to trifle. Das —, doting, dotage.

Fasel⸗gørge, —hans, *m.* a trifler, nonsensical talker.

3. Faseln, [V. Faden] I. *v. tr.* to ravel out. II. *v. r.* sich —, to be unwoven, to ravel.

†Faselnackt, *adj.* and *adv.* stark naked.

Fasen, *m.* [-s, *pl.* -] ‖ Fase, *f.* [*pl.* -n] [= Faden], [diminut. das Fäschen, Fäslein.] a thread. Nicht einen trocknen — an sich haben, not to have a dry thread on, to be wet to the skin.

†Fasennackt, V. Faselnackt.

1. Fasen, [V. Faden] I. *v. tr.* to ravel out. II. *v. r.* sich —, to be unwoven, to ravel.

2. ‖Fasen, [allied to the Sw. *fösa* = bewegen] I. *v. tr.* to seek. II. *v. intr. Fig.* to talk irrationally, to rave.

Faseöle, *f.* V. Fasele.

Faser, *f.* [*pl.* -n] [allied to Faden] 1) a thread, filament. 2) a thread, a fine, slender body which constitutes a part of the frame of animals, a filament or slender thread in plants or minerals, the small slender root of a plant, fiber or fibre, string.

Faser⸗apatit, *m.* [a subspecies of apatite] phosphorite. —arragon, *m.* fibrous arragonite. —baryt, *m.* fibrous heavy spar. —blende, *f.* fibrous blende. —bündel, *m.* a bunch of fibres. —datolith, *m.* fibrous datolithe or datholite. —gewächs, *n.* 1) a fibrous plant. 2) liverwort. —gyps, *m.* fibrous or striated gypsum. —kalk, *m.* fibrous limestone, satin-spar, stalactitic carbonate of lime. —kiesel, *m.* radiated quarz. —malachit, *m.* fibrous malachite, fibrous green carbonated copper. —olivenit, *m.* wood-copper. —schwefel, *m.* fibrous sulphur. —stoff, *m.* [a peculiar organic compound substance found in animals and vegetables] fibrin. —zeolith, *m.* sulphosphate of alumine, hydrargillite. —zinnober, *m.* fibrous cinnabar.

Faser, *m.* V. Fächser.

Faserchen, *n.* [-s, *pl.* -] [diminut. of Faser] fibril.

Faſericht, *adj.* and *adv.* thread-like, filamentous.

Faserig, *adj.* and *adv.* 1) thready, filaceous. 2) composed or consisting of fibres, fibrous, filamentous. —es Fleisch, stringy meat; [in botany] eine —e Wurzel, a stringy or fibrous root; ein —er Stengel, a filamentous stalk or stem; —e Steinfrüchte, fibrous stone-fruits; [in mineralogy] ein —er Bruch, a fibrous fracture.

Fasern, I. *v. tr.* V. Fasen or Faseln. II. *v. r.* sich —, to ravel out.

Fasig, *adj.* and *adv.* 1) easily parting with threads, feazy, thready. 2) stringy. — werden, to grow stringy; —es Fleisch, stringy meat.

Faß, *n.* [-sses, *pl.* Fässer] [Lat. *vas*; from fassen = in sich aufnehmen] 1) any utensil for holding liquors and other things, used only in composition, as, Butter—, a churn; Tinte—, an inkstand; Salz—, a salt-box; Wasch—, a washing-tub &c. 2) a close vessel for containing liquors, a cask, a hogshead, a barrel, a tun, a coop. Ein Bier—, a beer-barrel; ein Wein—, wine-cask; ein — binden, to hoop a barrel. *Fig.* Es ist noch nicht in dem —, darin es gähren soll, the thing is not yet ripe for execution. *Prov.* Schlechtes — nicht leicht zerbricht, naught is never in danger; leeres — macht nicht naß, when good cheer is lacking, our friends will be backing; leere Fässer klingen hohl, empty vessels make the greatest sound. 3) a certain measure for liquids, a barrel; *it.* also a measure for other commodities, but chiefly for corn, a barrel. 4) [in nat. hist.] the Ceilan rib'd partridge shell, the spotted tun.

Faß⸗därme, *f.* V. —hefen. —baum, *m.* a tree which may serve for making casks. —bier, *n.* beer drawn from the cask [as opposed to bottled beer]. —binder, *m.* a cooper, a hooper. —boden, *m.* the head of a cask. —bohrer, *m.* piercer. —brücke, *f.* a bridge formed of empty and floating casks. —butter, *f.* butter preserved in casks, firkin butter. —daube, *f.* a thin narrow piece of timber, of which casks are made, a stave. —faul, *adj.* and *adv.* tasting of the cask. —feige, *f.* a fig from Cyprus. —hefen, *pl.* the lees of beer in casks. —holz, *n.* wood for staves, heading &c. —meßkunst, *f.* gauging. —pech, *n.* cooper's pitch. —reif, *m.* a hoop, —waare, *f.* commodities preserved in casks. —weise, *adv.* by casks, in casks. —werk, *n.* several casks for the same use.

Fäßchen, Fäßlein, ‖Fässel, *n.* [-s, *pl.* -] 1) a small cask, a cag or keg. Ein — Häringe, a cade of herrings [the quantity of five hundred]. 2) [in nat. hist.] a species of wreath [turbomuscorum].

Fäßchenstahl, *m.* steel in tubs.

Fassait, *m.* [-s, *pl.* -e] [a mineral, a variety of angite] fassaite.

Fassen, [allied to fahen] I. *v. tr.* 1) to seize, to take hold of, to catch. Mit den Händen —, to take hold with the hands; Einen bei der Hand —, to take any one by the hand, to seize any one's hand; sich an den Händen —, to take hold of each others' hands [as in a circular dance]; den Topf beim Henkel —, to take a pot by the handle; etwas mit den Zähnen —, to take hold with the teeth; Einen bei den Haaren —, to seize any one by the hair. *Fig. a*) to take hold of, to seize. Es faßte ihn ein plötzlicher Schauder, a sudden horror seized him; es faßte sie eine plötzliche Furcht, a sudden fear came upon them; Einen bei seinem Worte —, to take any one at his word; Einen an seiner schwachen Seite —, to take any one on his weak side; sie wußten ihn schon zu —, they knew how to catch him; etwas kurz —, to abridge a thing; Muth —, ein Herz —, to take heart; neuen Muth —, to resume courage, to pluck up heart; einen Entschluß —, to take a resolution; eine große Zuneigung zu Einem —, to take a great affection to any one; ein Vorurtheil wider Einen —, to take a prejudice against any one; er hatte einen großen Widerwillen gegen ihn gefaßt, he had conceived a great aversion to him; fasse die Zucht, laß nicht davon, [in Script.] take fast hold of instruction, let her not go; etwas in die Augen —, to fix one's eyes on something; einen Hasen —, to aim a gun at a hare; etwas zu Herzen —, to take something to heart. *b*) to take, hold or contain in the mind. Er hat mich nicht gefaßt, he took not my meaning, he did not comprehend me; ich faßte den Prediger, I understood the preacher; Dinge klar und deutlich —, to conceive things clearly and distinctly; — Sie dies? can you understand the meaning of it? eine Rede —, to understand a discourse. 2) to put into a vessel, to put in a barrel or cask, in a sack &c. Bier —, to tun beer; Korn —, to sack corn; Bienen —, to hive bees; [in military affairs] Brod —, to draw bread; die Mannschaft hat heute 100 Paar Kamaschen gefaßt, the men have received 100 pairs of gaitres from the stores, to-day. 3) to infix or inclose in another body, so as to hold fast, to enchase. Einen Demant in Gold —, to set a diamond in gold; gefaßte Steine, enchased stones; ein Gemälde in einen Rahmen —, to fra[me] a picture; einen Stollen —, [in mining] t[o] line a shaft. 4) to contain, or to have capa[city] to receive and contain, to hold. Die Kirche fa[ßt] zwei tausend Menschen, the church holds tw[o] thousand people; dieses leere Faß faßt dreiß[ig] Gallonen, this empty cask holds thirty gallons.

II. *v. r.* sich —, to take hold with the hand[s]. Der Knabe faßte sich an einem Ast, the boy caught hold of a bough. *Fig. a*) to recover from a deconcerted state, to recover resolution or composure of mind, to collect one's self. Um's Himmelswillen, — Sie sich, for heaven's sake compose yourself; der Mann antwortete sehr gefaßt, ich bin es, the man very composedly answered, it is I; sich gefaßt machen, to make one's sel[f] ready, to prepare; er ist auf Alles gefaßt, he i[s] ready for every thing; ich bin auf das Schlimmst[e] gefaßt, I am prepared for the worst. *b*) Sich kurz —, to be short [in speaking or writing].

Fasser, *m.* [-s, *pl.* -] 1) [unusual] one that seizes, takes hold of &c. 2) [in husbandry] a small hive for hiving a swarm of bees.

*Fassette, *f.* V. Facette.

*Fassion, [from the Lat. *fiteor*, *fassus* sum] *f.* [in law] a judicial declaration of one's property or income for paying one's dues according to it.

Faßlich, I. *adj.* conceivable by the mind, comprehensible, intelligible II. *adv.* in a conceivable or intelligible manner, conceivably. — schreiben, to write intelligibly.

Faßlichkeit, *f.* capability of being understood, comprehensibleness.

Fassung, *f.* 1) [properly the act of taking, seizing &c. something] *Fig.* Die — ein[es] Entschlusses, the act of taking a resoluti[on]. 2) the act of inclosing &c. Die — ei[nes] Steines, the setting of a stone; die — ei[nes] Stollens, [in mining] the lining of a sha[ft]; die — des Bieres, the tunning of beer. 3) [the state of being gefaßt] *Fig.* — behalten, to re[tain] one's self-possession, to be collected; aus [der] — bringen, to put out of countenance, to u[n]settle the mind, to disconcert, to discompo[se]; aus der —, out of countenance, disconce[rted]. 4) inclosure, setting [of stones].

Fassungs⸗gabe, —kraft, *f.* capa[city] of the mind to understand, power of the und[er]standing to receive and contain ideas, capa[city] of knowing, comprehension. Schnelle —kr[aft], a quick apprehension. —los, *adj.* and *adv.* [1)] not being inclosed &c. 2) *Fig.* out of coun[te]nance, disconcerted, discomposed. —vermögen, *n.* V. —kraft.

Fast, [perhaps allied to the Sw. *fösa* = beweg[en], thus properly = hinbewegt] *adv.* almost, nea[rly], well nigh, for the greatest part. — alle Gegenwärtigen, almost all who are present; es ist — Nacht, it is almost night; das Factum ist — erwiesen, the fact is nearly demonstrated; wir spe[isen] — immer um zwei Uhr, we almost always di[ne at] two o'clock; er wußte — niemals seine Aufg[abe], he hardly ever knew his lesson; es ist — [zwölf] Uhr, it is near twelve o'clock; er war — to[dt], he was nigh dead.

‖Fastbäcker, *m.* [-s, *pl.* -] a baker who bak[es] rye bread, or brown bread.

‖Fastbäckerbrot, *n.* a sort of brown bre[ad].

‖1. Faste, *f.* [*pl.* -n] V. Fasten.

2. Faste, *f.* [*pl.* -n] V. 2. Fase.

‖Fastelabend, *m.* [-s, *pl.* -e] V. Fastenabe[nd].

‖Fasteltag, *m.* [-es, *pl.* -e] V. Fasttag.

Fasten, 1) [-s, without a *pl.*] the act [of] fasting, the state of abstaining, voluntarily involuntarily, from food [in this sense *n.*]; especially [-, *pl.*-] a voluntary abstinence from food or from particular kinds of food for a certain time, as also the time of fasting, fast, fasting [in this sense *f.* or properly the *pl.* of Fasten]. Die — beobachten, to observe fasting; die — war schon vorüber, [in Script.] the fast was now already past. 2) [the quadragesimal fast, or fast of forty days, observed by a part of the Christian church before Easter] Lent, quadragesima. Mitten in der —, at mid-lent.

Fasten-abend, *m.* [the day immediately preceding the first of Lent] Shrove-tide, Shrove-Tuesday, confession Tuesday. —**blume**, *f.* common cowslip. —**gebet**, *n.* Lent-prayer. —**prediger**, *m.* a preacher who preaches during Lent. —**predigt**, *f.* Lent-sermon. —**prezel**, *f.* a sort of cracknel baked [formerly] for Lent. —**schlier**, *m.* [a bird] the common curlew. —**sonntag**, *m.* a Sunday in Lent —**speise**, *f.* Lenten food, Lent-provision. —**suppe**, *f.* a Lenten porridge. —**zeit**, *f.* the time of fasting, Lent.

Fásten, [properly = beobachten sc. das Gesetz; allied to fest] *v. intr.* 1) [to abstain from food either voluntarily or involuntarily; especially, to abstain from food voluntarily] to fast. Um das Kind fastetest und weintest du, [in Script.] thou didst fast and weep for the child; das Fasten, fasting, fast. *Prov* Langes — spart kein Brod, ever spare, ever bare. 2) [to abstain from food partially or from particular kinds of food] to fast. Die Katholiken — während der Fasten, the Catholics fast in Lent; ein —der, one who fasts.

Fáster, [rather unusual] *m.* [-s, *pl.*-] one who fasts, faster.

Fástnacht, *f.* 1) Ash-Wednesday eve. 2) Shrove-tide, Shrove-Tuesday. 3) [the feast or season of rejoicing before Lent, observed in Catholic countries, with great solemnity, by feasts, balls, operas, concerts &c.] carnival, carnaval. Die große — or kalte —, Shrove-Sunday; die Herren— or Pfaffen—, the third or [with others] the first Sunday before Lent.

Fastnachts-bruder, *m.* one who joins the festivities of Shrove-tide. —**heer**, *n.* V. wüthende] Heer. —**huhn**, *n.* [in feudal law] a fowl which is due on Shrove-tide to the lord of the manor. —**lust**, *f.* shroving. —**lustbarkeit**, *f.* the festivities on Shrove-tide, shroving. —lustbarkeiten, the amusements of the carnival. —**narr**, *m.* one that plays the fool at a masquerade on Shrove-tide, a masker, a zany. *Fig.* a coxcomb. —**schmaus**, *m.* a meal given on Shrove-tide. —**spiel**, *n.* a carnival play, farce. —**spuk**, *m.* carnival tricks. —**woche**, the week preceding Shrove-Sunday.

Fásttag, *m.* [-es, *pl* -e] [the day on which fasting is observed] fast-day. —e, days of abstinence.

Fāta, *pl* fates. *Fig.* [mostly in a jocose sense] fortunes. Münchhausens — und Abenteuer, the fortunes and adventures of Munchhausen.

Fatál, *adj.* and *adv.* 1) fatal, calamitous. [in fam. lang.] disagreeable, shocking, odious.

Fatalísmus, *m.* [the doctrine that all things are subject to fate] fatalism.

Fatalíst, *m.* [-en, *pl.* -en] fatalist.

Fatalístisch, *adj.* and *adv.* fatalistic, fatalistical. —e Ansichten, fatalistical opinions.

Fatalität, *f.* [*pl.* -en] mischance, ill-luck, misfortune.

Fatigánt, *adj.* and *adv.* [in familiar lang.] fatiguing.

Fatiguen, [pron. Fatihgen] [in colloquial lang.] fatigues. Die — des Krieges, the fatigues of

***Fātum**, *n.* [-s, *pl.* Fata] destiny depending on a superior and uncontrollable cause, fate.

Fätze, *f.* [*pl.* -n] [in seamen's language] a small sail under the foot of a top-sail.

Faul, *adj.* and *adv* [origin uncertain; the primitive signification was probably that of Zerbrechen &c.] 1) putrid, corrupt, rotten. —es Fleisch, putrid flesh; ein —es Ei, an addle egg; ein —er Apfel, a rotten apple; ein —er Zahn, a carious or decayed tooth; —es Holz, rotten wood; — im Leibe used of a beast whose stomach and bowels are inflamed; ein —es Fieber (—fieber), a putrid fever; —e Fische, [fig. in fam lang.] suspicious acts; shifts, subterfuges. *Fig* *a*) disinclined to action or exertion, naturally or habitually slothful, sluggish, lazy. *Sich auf die —e Seite legen, to indulge in sloth; — verträumt er seine Zeit, lazily [sluggishly, slothfully, idly] he dreams away his time; nicht *—, lief er fort, suddenly he ran away; der Faule, a drone, a sluggard, an idle fellow. *Prov.* —, arm und dennoch zehren, geschieht nicht lang mit Ehren, he who spends more than he should, shall not have to spend when he would; —e Hände müssen ein Mißjahr haben, idle folks lack no excuses; an ill workman quarrels with his tools; der Faule stirbt über seinen Wünschen, he is full of good meanings and wishes. *b*) [in common and familiar language] sleepy, dull, heavy; [in compos.] disinclined to any exertion, as maul-—, averse to speaking; beutel—, disinclined to expend money, unwilling to part with money; [in seamen's language] eine —e See, a calm; —es Geschwätz, idle talk. 2) proceeding from putrefaction or pertaining to it, putrid. Ein —er Geruch, a putrid scent, a putrescent smell; —riechend, putredinous. 3) [among iron-workers] —es Eisen, brittle iron. 4) || foul, dirty, filthy [not much used]. —e Wäsche, foul linen. 5) [formerly] ugly, deformed.

Faul-baum, *m.* 1) alder-buckthorn or berry-bearing alder. 2) the water elder. 3) common bird cherry-tree. 4) common privet. —**beere**, *f.* the fruit of the common bird cherry-tree. —**bett**, *n.* a seat of repose, a couch. —**brut**, *f.* the rotten brood of bees. —**butte**, *f.* [in paper-mills] fermenting trough —**fieber**, *n.* putrid fever. —**fleck**, —**flecken**, *m.* a putrid spot. —**fleckig**, *adj.* and *adv.* having putrid spots. —**fuß**, *m.* the unau or two-toed sloth. —**gebirge**, *n.* V. Fäule 4. —**krankheit**, *f.* 1) a putrid disease. 2) a certain laziness in affairs. —**matte**, *f.* a door-mat. —**pfründe**, *f.* a sinecure. —**pfründner**, *m.* a person who holds a sinecure, sinecurist. —**thier**, *n.* the ai or three-toed sloth. —**thieraffe**, *m.* [a genus of quadrupeds] lemur. —**weide**, *f.* the sweet willow.

Faúlbar, *adj.* and *adv.* putrescible.

Fäule, *f.* 1) rottenness, putridness, putridity. Die trockene —, [in seamen's language] dry rot. 2) [a fatal distemper incident to sheep] the rot. ||3) a sort of blight on corn. 4) [in mining] brittle stones.

Faulen, *v. intr.* 1) to rot, to putrefy. 2) to moulder.

Fäulen, *v. tr.* to cause to dissolve, to cause to rot, to putrefy, to rot.

Faúlenzen, *v. intr.* to smell putrid or to have a putrid taste. *Fig.* to be lazy, to indulge in idleness, to lounge. Die Zeit mit — zubringen, to idle away time.

Faúlenzer, *m.* [-s, *pl.* -] a lazy fellow, a sluggard, a drone, an idler, a lounger.

Faulenzereí, *f.* laziness, slothfulness, sluggishness.

Faúlheit, *f.* rottenness, putridness, putridity. *Fig.* sloth, sluggishness, laziness, idleness. *Prov.* — lohnt mit Armuth, poverty is the reward of idleness.

Faúlicht, *adj.* and *adv.* 1) putrescent. 2) [indicating a state of dissolution] putrid. —e Krankheiten, putrid diseases.

Fäulig, *adj.* and *adv.* rotten, putrid. —es Obst, rotten fruit.

Fäuling, [unusual] *m.* [-es, *pl.*-e] a sluggard, a drone.

Fäulniß, *f.* putridness, putridity, putrefaction, rottenness.

Fäulniß-befördernd, *adj.* and *adv.* septic, septical. —**hindernd**, *adj.* and *adv.* antiseptic.

||**Faúm**, V. Schaum.

Faum-kelle, *f.* Schaumkelle. —**löffel**, *m.* V. Schaumlöffel.

||**Fäumen**, V. Schäumen.

***Faún**, *m.* [-es or -en, *pl.* -e or -en] [among the Romans, a kind of demi-god or rural deity] a faun, called also sylvan, and differing little from a satyr [used also in a fig. sense of a lascivious person, of an old debauchee].

Faunen-blick, *m.* a lascivious look. —**miene**, *f.* an ugly face. —**nase**, *f.* a large and ugly nose —**tanz**, *m.* a lascivious dance.

Faúnenhaft, *adj.* and *adv.* resembling a faun, ugly.

Faúst, *f* [*pl.* Fäuste] [allied either to fangen or fügen, in like manner as *pugnus* to *pango*, πυγμη to πήγ-νυμι] 1) [the hand clenched] fist. Eine — machen, to clench the hand; sich mit den Fäusten schlagen, to fight with the fist, to box. 2) [the extremity of the arm] hand. Mit dem Degen in der —, with sword in hand; ein Pferd aus dem Schritte gleich von der — ansprengen lassen, [in manege] to fall into a gallop. *Fig.* †Das paßt wie die — auf's Auge, *prov.* there is neither rhyme nor reason; in die — or in das Fäustchen lachen, *prov.* to laugh in one's sleeve. 3) [also a measure of four inches] V. Hand.

Faust-amboß, *m* [with coppersmiths] hand-anvil. —**birn**, *f.* V. Pfundbirn. —**büchse**, *f.* [rather unusual] a small fire-arm, a pistol. ||—**degen**, *m.* a dagger. —**dick**, *adj.* and *adv.* as thick as a fist. *Fig.* †Er hat es —dick hinter den Ohren, he is an arrant wag. —**dicke**, *f.* the bigness of a fist. —**fechter**, *m.* a boxer, a pugilist. —**gefecht**, *n.* V. —kampf. —**gehörn**, *n.* [among hunters] the horns of a stag with a palmated top. —**gerecht**, *adj.* and *adv.* 1) as much as the fist will contain, a handful. 2) *Fig.* expert in the use of the fist or hand, dextrous. —**gewehr**, *n.* V. —degen. —**hammer**, *m.* 1) a small hammer. 2) a hammer used by coppersmiths for beating out. 3) formerly a sort of battle-ax. —**handschuh**, *m.* a mitten. —**hobel**, *m.* a small plane without any handle, used by joiners, as a smoothing-plane. —**kampf**, *m.* a combat with the fist, a boxing-match, fisticuff. —**kämpfen**, *n.* boxing, pugilism. —**kämpfer**, *m.* a boxer, pugilist. —**kolben**, *m.* V. Streitkolben. —**kraft**, *f.* the strength of the fists. —**pinsel**, *m.* [with masons] a small paint-brush. —**recht**, *n.* the law of armed force, the right of private warfare, the swordlaw, clublaw, the right of might. —**rohr**, *n.* V. Fäustling 2. —**säge**, *f.* a large handsaw. —**schlag**, *m.* a blow with the fist, a cuff. —schläge, fisticuffs. —**spinne**, *f.* bird-catching spider. —**stange**, *f.* [in Script.] hand-staff. —**stoß**, *m.* a thrust with the fist. —**streich**, *m.* V. —schlag.

Fäústchen, Fäústlein, *n.* [-s] [*dimin.* of Faust] a small fist.

Fäústel, *m.* [-s, *pl.* -] [in mining] a hammer.

||Fäusten, *v. tr.* 1) to strike with the fist, to fist. 2) [with hatters] to stretch or extend with the fist.

Fäusterling, *m.* V. Feisterling.

Fäustling, *m.* [-es, *pl.* -e] ||1) a stick. 2) a pocket-pistol. 3) [in mining] a stone that may be grasped with the fingers. 4) a mitten.

*Favorisiren, *v. tr.* to favour, to support.

*Favorit, *m.* [-en, *pl.* -en] -inn, *f.* a favourite.

||Fäxen, [from fegen = to move to and fro] *pl.* fooleries, buffooneries, tricks.

Faxenmacher, *m.* a buffoon, a droll.

Feberkraut, *n.* [-es] yellow-flowered scull-cap.

*Februär, *m.* [-s, *pl.* -e] V. Hornung.

Fechdistel, *f.* [*pl.* -n] V. Frauendistel.

Fechsen, V. Fächsen.

Fechser, *m.* V. Fächser.

Fechten, [probably from fegen = to move to and fro] *ir.* I. *v. intr.* 1) to move swiftly to and fro. Mit den Händen —, to gesticulate. *Fig.* to practise begging [used of journeymen when on their travels]. —gehen, to go about begging. 2) [to practise the art of fencing] to fence. Gut — können, to fence well. *Fig.* Mit Worten —, to contend by words; mit einem Schatten —, to fight against a chimera. 3) to fight and defend by giving and avoiding blows or thrusts, to fence, to fight. Sie fochten mit großer Tapferkeit, they fought with great bravery. *Fig.* to defend and preserve, to strive, to contend. Er ficht für die Freiheit, he fights the cause of liberty. 4) it is also used in composition, as, anfechten, ausfechten, verfechten. II *v. tr.* to fight [battles &c.].

Fecht-boden, *m.* fencing-room, fencing-school. —degen, *m.* a sword used in fencing. —eisen, *n.* a foil. —hähnchen, *n.* V. Fechter, 3. —handschuh, *m.* a fencing-glove. —haus, *n.* a fencing-school. —kunst, *f.* fencing, fence. —meister, *m.* fencing-master, a fencer. —platz, *m.* 1) fencing-room. 2) V. Kampfplatz. —schuldegen, *m.* a foil. —schule, *f.* fencing-school. —schüler, *m.* a scholar in a fencing-school. —stunde, *f.* fencing-lesson. —übung, *f.* fencing-exercise.

Fechter, *m.* [-s, *pl.* -] 1) *Fig.* a beggar. 2) [one who practises the art of fencing] a fencer. *Fig.* he that defends well his cause [it is used chiefly in the compound words Feder—, Klopf— &c.]. 3) [in conch.] a species of strombus [strombus pugilis].

Fechter-gang, *m.* V. —kampf. —handwerk, *n.* [in contempt] fencing. —kampf, *m.* a fight between fencers or gladiators. —kunst, *f.* fencing. —spiel, *n.* the combats of fencers or gladiators. —sprung, *m.* a fencer's leap. —streich, *m.* [in fencing] a feint.

Fede, V. Fehde.

1. Feder, *f.* [*pl.* -n] [seems to come from the root of wegen, bewegen; many compare it to the Gr. πτέρον, properly πέτερον, from πέτ-ομαι, allied to the Lat. *peto*, to the Gr. βαδ-ίζω, to the Germ. waden. The idea of motion is common to all.] 1) certain things moving. *a*) [in fishes] Die Floß—n, fins. *b*) Die —n, [with hunters] the bristles of a wild boar, and the prickles or quills of a hedgehog. *c*) [in botany] V. Federchen. *d*) [with hunters] α) [the tail of a deer] the single. β) [the tail of a hare] the scut. *e*) Die —n, [in forges] the flames seen on the chimney of a furnace. *f*) [a body which, when bent or forced from its natural state, has the power of recovering it] a spring. Die — in einer Uhr, in einem Schloß, the spring of a watch or clock, of a lock; die stählernen —n an einem Wagen, the steel springs of a carriage; der Wagen hängt in —n, the carriage is hung in springs. *g*) [in organs = Klappenfeder] a spring. 2) [a general name of the covering of fowls] a feather, a plume. Mit —n, plumigerous; einem Vogel die —n ausrupfen, to plume a bird; so leicht wie eine —, as light as a feather; —n schleißen, to strip quills. *Prov.* An den —n erkennt man den Vogel, the tree is known by its fruit; schöne —n, schöne Vögel, fine feathers make fine birds. *Fig.* Mit fremden —n fliegen, to perform something by the aid of others; sich mit fremden —n schmücken, to deck one's self with borrowed plumes; man muß nicht fliegen wollen, ehe einem die —n gewachsen sind, no flying without wings, or he would fain fly, but he wants feathers. 3) several sorts of feathers, as a feather worn as an ornament, a plume; but especially an instrument of writing usually made of the quills of some large fowl, a pen. Eine — schneiden, to make a pen; *it.* to mend a pen; die — spitzen, to sharpen a pen; eine — voll Tinte, a penful of ink. *Fig.* Das ist aus seiner — geflossen or das ist von seiner —, that is from his pen, of his composition; ein passender Gegenstand für seine —, the proper subject for his quill; er hat or führt eine gute —, he carries a good quill [he writes well]; eine spitzige oder beißende — haben, to write mordaciously or sarcastically; sich mit der — seinen Unterhalt erwerben, to gain one's livelihood by writing; ich will es der — nicht anvertrauen, I will not commit it to paper, or pen it; ein Werk unter der — haben, to be about to write a book; Einem etwas in die — sagen, to indite something to any one; Neid und Haß haben ihm die — geführt, he wrote it out of envy and hatred. Ein Mann von der —, *a*) a penman. Er ist ein Mann von der —, nicht vom Degen, he is a penman and no swordsman. *b*) an author, a writer. Die Leute von der — sind ein empfindliches Geschlecht, authors are a sensitive race. 4) a thing filled with feathers, a feather-bed, a bed. In den —n liegen, to lie a bed; Einen aus den — jagen, to turn out of bed.

Feder-ähnlich, *adj.* and *adv.* feathery. —alaun, *m.* 1) natural alum. 2) [a kind of asbestus] plume-alum. 3) fibrous or striated gypsum. —anschuß, *m.* [in mining] a mineral which occurs in plumous concretions. —artig, *adj.* and *adv.* 1) resembling feathers, feathery, plumous, plumose. 2) [in botany] cubescent [used of a stigma]. —auge, *n.* [in organs] the eye of a pipe. —ball, *m.* 1) a ball stuffed with feathers. 2) a shuttle-cock. 3) [a plant] spiked water-milfoil. —besen, *m.* feather-broom, feather-brush, feather-duster. —bett, *n.* feather-bed. —binse, *f.* [a plant] many-spiked cotton-grass. —blatt, *n.* [with locksmiths] the spring plate of a lock. —bleiche, *f.* 1) the bleaching of feathers. 2) the washing of foul plumes. —blume, *f.* 1) feather-flower. 2) a feathery flower. —brett, *n.* [in organs] spring board. —büchse, *f.* a pen-case. —bügel, *m.* spring-chape. —bürste, *f.* feather-brush. V. —besen. —busch, *m.* 1) a tuft of feathers on the head of some fowls, a crest. 2) a plume of feathers, plume, plumage. 3) Der Afrikanische —busch, [a plant] the narrow-leaved phlomis or lion's tail. 4) [a genus of insects] the plumous tipula. —buschträger, *m.* V. —busch 4. —dose, *f.* spring-box. —eisen, *n.* a small rising anvil. —erz, *n.* plumous sulphuret of antimony. —farbe, *f.* a colour for dyeing feathers. —fechter, *m.* 1) a sort of pugilist. 2) [in contempt] a quarrelsome and scribbling author. —feilkloben, *m.* pin-vice. —förmig, *adj.* and *adv.* penniform. —fuß, *m.* 1) a feathered foot. 2) [a fowl that has feathers on its feet] a plumiped. 3) V. Lachtaube. —füßig, *adj.* and *adv.* plumiped. —gehäuse, *n.* V. —haus. —gips, *m.* fibrous or striated gypsum. —gras, *n.* feather-grass. —haken, *m.* 1) the trigger [of a gun]. 2) spring vice. —handel, *m.* trade in feathers. —händler, *m.* feather-seller. —hart, I. *adj.* 1) as hard as a steel spring. 2) elastic, elastical. II. *adv.* elastically. —härte, *f.* the degree of hardness or temper of a steel spring. —harz, *n.* elastic gum or gum elastic, Indian rubber. Elastisches —harz, elastic bitumen, mineral caouchouc, elastic mineral pitch. —harzbaum, *m.* the syringe tree of Cayenne. —haspel, *m.* a sort of reel used by hunters. —haus, *n.* [in horology] the barrel. —hausrad, *n.* [in horology] barrel-wheel. —held, *m.* [in contempt] a hero of the quill, a boasting scribbler. —hiazinthe, *f.* V. Korallenhiazinthe. —hut, *m.* 1) a hat or bonnet with feathers. 2) a cocked hat. —kampf, *m.* a contention or strife in writing, a controversy. —kämpfer, *m.* one engaged in a strife in writing. —kappe, *f.* 1) a cap made of feathers; *it.* a cap with feathers. 2) [a species of ducks in China] mandarin-duck. —kasten, *m.* a box for holding feathers. —kiel, *m.* a quill. —kissen, *n.* feather-cushion. —knopf, *m.* [a plant] the Cagoecia. —kohl, *m.* V. Krauskohl. —kork, *m.* [in conch.] the finger-shaped sea-pen. —kraft, *f.* elasticity [in a proper as well as in a fig. sense]. Die —kraft seines Geistes, the elasticity of his spirit. —kräftig, *adj.* and *adv.* elastic, elastical. —kraut, *n.* golden-rod. —krieg, *m.* contest or strife in writing, controversy. —lappen, *pl.* [with hunters] a bunch of feathers tied to a net, to frighten game. —lecker, *m.* [in contempt, a bad writer] a scribbler. —leicht, *adj.* and *adv.* as light as a feather, feathery. —leinwand, *f.* a sort of fustian. —lesen, *n.* the picking of feathers. *Fig.* *Nicht viel —lesens machen, not to insist upon formalities, not to be ceremonious; sie machten nicht viel —lesens mit ihm, they handled him rather roughly. —leser, *m.* —leserinn, *f.* 1) a feather driver. 2) [rather unusual] a loiterer [in contempt]. —los, *adj.* and *adv.* destitute of feathers, featherless, plumeless. —mann, *m.* [in contempt] a scribbler. Ein armer —mann, a poor author. —meißel, *m.* [in surgery] a pledget. —messer, *n.* pen-knife. Das —messer mit einem Falzbein, a folding pen-knife. —muff, *m.* feather-muff. —mütze, *f.* a feathered cap. —nelke, *f.* feathered pink, sop-in-wine. —pfühl, *n.* a bolster filled with feathers. —riegel, *m.* spring-bolt. —rohr, *n.* V. —büchse. —salz, *n.* V. —alaun. —schachtel, *f.* a box in which feathers are kept. —schleißen, *n.* the picking of feathers. —schleißer, *m.* —schleißerinn, *f.* a person who picks feathers. —schmücker, *m.* —schmückerinn, *f.* a person who makes ornamental feathers, a feather-maker, plumassier. —schraube, *f.* [with gun makers] spring-vice. —schrift, *f.* written letters [as opposed to printed ones or types]. —schütz, *m.* one who hunts feathered game well, a hunter who shoots feathered game well on the wing. —spanner, *m.* [in horology] spring-tool. —spiel, *n.* 1) V. —lappen. 2) [in falconry] *a*) lure. V. Vorlaß. *b*) hawking. 3) feathered game. 4) a sort of play, spillekins. —spule, *f.* a writing quill. —staar, *m.* [in medicine] elastic cataract. —stahl, *m.* spring-steel. —staub, *m.* down. —stauber, *m.* 1) feather-broom, feather-duster. 2) a feather-seller, feather-driver. —stein, *m.* [in conch.] the ligament or cartillage by which the valves of the pearl-gaper are connected. —stift, *m.* [in horology] arbor. —strauß, *m.* a tuft of feathers, a plume of feathers. —

ſtreit, *m.* a contest or strife in writing, a controversy. —ſtrich, *m.* a touch of the pen, a stroke of the pen. —ſtutz, *m.* [a feather worn as an ornament or hunting-trophy] a plume. —thaler, *m.* [in Switzerland] a French dollar. —träger, *m.* [a genus of plants] pteronia. —uhr, *f.* a watch or time-piece that is moved by a spring. —vieh, *n.* poultry, dunghill fowls, barn-door fowls. —wage, *f.* spring steel-yard. —weiß, *n.* 1) [in mineralogy] fibrous or striated gypsum. ||2) white lead. —wild, —wildbret, *n.* feathered game. —winder, *m.* V. —ſpanner. —wiſch, *m.* V. —beſen. —wismuth, *m.* sulphuret of bismuth. —zange, *f.* [with organmakers] spring-pliers. —zeichnung, *f.* a drawing made with pen and ink. —zeug, *n.* V. —büchſe. —zins, *m.* a rent paid in poultry. —zirkel, *m.* spring dividers. —zug, *m.* a touch of the pen, a stroke of the pen, also a fanciful stroke of the pen. Die —züge um einen großen Buchſtaben, the flourishes about a great letter; kecke —züge machen, to flourish with the pen.

2. Feder, *f.* [*pl.* -n] [probably from faßen = befeſtigen] 1) [in hydraulics] an iron clamp or hook. 2) [in mining] a sort of wedge. 3) Die —n [Wind—n], the bordering boards of a roof of thatch. 4) [with hunters = Schweins—] a boar-spear. 5) the pole of a turner's bow.

Federchen, Federlein, *n.* [-s, *pl.* -] [diminut. of Feder] a little feather. 2) [in botany, calyx consisting of hair] the down or pappus.

Federicht, *adj.* and *adv.* [resembling feathers] feathery, plumose, plumous. [in botany] Eine —e Granne, a feathered awn; das —e Haar, plumose hair; [in mining] —es Spießglaserz, plumose sulphuret of antimony.

Federig, *adj.* and *adv.* feathered, feathery. Er hat ſich ganz — gemacht, his clothes are covered with feathers or down.

Federn, I. *v. intr.* to lose the feathers [used of birds]. II. *v. r.* ſich —, 1) to shed, cast or mew the feathers, to moult. 2) [rather unusual] to be elastic.

Fee, [*pl.* -n] [Sp. and Ital. *fata* and *fada*] a fairy, or fay.

Feen-gunſt, *f.* fairy favour. —könig, *m.* king of fairies. —königinn, *f.* queen of fairies. —mährchen, *n.* fairy tale. —palaſt, *m.* V. Feenſchloß. —reich, *n.* fairy land. *Fig.* dream-land. —ſchloß, *n.* fairy palace. *Fig.* a magnificent palace. —ſtreich, *m.* fairy-trick. —tanz, *m.* fairy dance. —welt, *f.* fairy land. *Fig.* dream-land.

Feenhaft, *adj.* and *adv.* fairylike. *Fig.* wonderful, astonishing.

Feerei, *f.* fairyism.

Fege, *f.* [*pl.* -n] 1) the act of cleaning, sweeping or cleansing by brushing, sweep. 2) an instrument for cleansing or sweeping. V. Kornfege, Staubfege.

Fege-feuer, *n.* [among Catholics] purgatory. —geld, *n.* money paid for sweeping a chimney &c., sweeping-money. —hader, *m.* a mop. Mit einem —hader abwiſchen, to mop. —hammer, *m.* [in saltworks] a saltstone or saltboiler's hammer. —kraut, *n.* V. Kannenkraut. —mühle, *f.* sweeping-mill. —opfer, Wir ſind ſtets als ein Fluch der Welt und ein Fegopfer aller Leute, [in Script.] we are made as the filth of the earth, and are the offscouring of all things unto this day. —rolle, *f.* a sort of riddle. —ſalpeter, *m.* saltpetre on walls. —ſchober, *m.* [in saltworks] scum-pan. —zeit, 1) the time of sweeping. 2) [in husbandry] the proper time of taking part of the honey away from the hives [in March].

Fegen, [allied to fächeln, fackeln, bewegen] I. *v. tr.* 1) to clean, to cleanse. Ein Schwert —, to furbish a sword; den Schornſtein —, to sweep a chimney; einen Graben, einen Brunnen —, to cleanse a ditch, a well; das Getreide —, to riddle corn; ein Zimmer —, to sweep a room. *Fig.* †Einem den Beutel —, to drain any one's purse; †ich will ihn —, I shall rebuke him, I will give him a rubbing. 2) to clean by brushing, to rub over with a brush, broom or besom. Die Stube —, to sweep the floor of a room; den Hut —, to brush a hat; [in husbandry] die Bienen —, to take part of the honey away from the hives. II. *v. intr.* [in fam. lang.] to move nimbly in dancing, to waltz.

Feger, *m.* [-s, *pl.* -] Fegerinn, *f.* 1) a person that cleans, or sweeps, a cleanser, a sweeper, chiefly used in composition, as, Schwert—, swordcutler, Schornſtein—, chimney-sweeper. 2) a clumsy or awkward person or animal.

Fegſel, *n.* [-s, *pl.* -] sweepings, rubbish.

1. Fehde, *f.* [*pl.* -n] [seems to be allied to fechten] private warfare, a feud. Einem — bieten, to challenge any one.

Fehde-brief, *m.* a letter of defiance or challenge, a cartel. —gut, *n.* a feud, fief or fee. —handſchuh, *m.* Den —handſchuh hinwerfen, to throw the glove [with our ancestors, was to challenge to single combat]. —los, *adj.* and *adv.* without a feud, peaceable. —recht, *n.* feudal law.

2. ||Fehde, *f.* [*pl.* -n] [is said to come from *fides*] a security, caution, bail.

Fehden, [unusual] *v. intr.* to be engaged in a feud, to wage war.

Fehder, *m.* [-s, *pl.* -] one that challenges or throws the glove.

Fehdlich, *adj.* and *adv.* feudal.

Fehe, *f.* [*pl.* -n] [allied to Vieh, Lat. *pecus*] [a kind of fur procured from the back (ſchwarze —) or from the belly (weiße —) of the Siberian squirrel] meniver.

Feh-rücken, *m.* [= ſchwarze Fehe] V. Fehe. —wamme, *f.* [= weiße Fehe] V. Fehe.

Fehl, *adv.* used in composition with some verbs, to express, to no purpose, in vain; in a wrong manner, in a wrong direction; contrary to the end proposed; erroneously, wrong; in many instances it answers to the English particle *mis*.

Fehl, *m.* [obsolescent] [-es, *pl.* -e] fault, defect, blemish.

Fehlbar, *adj.* and *adv.* liable to fail or mistake, fallible. Alle Menſchen ſind —, all men are fallible; ||der Fehlbare, an offender, delinquent.

Fehlbarkeit, *f.* fallibility.

Fehlen, [is probably allied to fallen] *v. intr.* 1) to fail of reaching the object, to fail to hit, to miss. Er fehlte beim Schießen, he missed in shooting; der Jäger fehlte den Haſen, the huntsman missed the hare; er fehlt ſeines Weges ſelten, seldom he misses his way. 2) to do wrong from ignorance or inattention, to commit error, to err, to mistake. In der Ausſprache —, to pronounce incorrectly, to mispronounce; in der Schreibung —, to miswrite; in der Rechtſchreibung —, to misspell; du fehlſt in der Beurtheilung meiner Beweggründe, you judge wrongly of my motives, you have misjudged my motives; weit gefehlt, far from it; wer kann wiſſen, wie oft er fehle, who knows, how often he errs; wir — alle mannichfaltig, [in Script.] in many things we offend all. *Prov.* Klugheit fehlt auch, the best horse stumbles. 3) to be absent or deficient, to want. Einer von den Zwölfen fehlt, one of the twelve is wanting; wir haben die Mittel, aber die Anwendung fehlt, we have the means, but the application is wanting; den Unglücklichen fehlt es nie an Feinden, the unhappy never want enemies; es fehlt ihm nicht an gutem Willen, he does not want the will; an der Summe fehlt ein Thaler, the sum wants a dollar; an mir ſoll es nicht —, I shall not be wanting on my part; es hat ihm nie etwas or an etwas gefehlt, he never failed in his designs; ich glaubte, es könne ihm nicht —, I thought he could not fail of success; [rather unusual] einer Sache —, to omit a thing. 4) [as an impersonal verb] to be distant in time, or in the course of events. Es fehlte nicht viel, ſo wäre er ertrunken, he had like to have been drowned; es fehlte nicht viel, ſo wäre der linke Flügel geſchlagen worden, the left wing was near being routed; es fehlte nicht viel, ſo hätte er ſeine Stelle verloren, he had like to have lost his place; es fehlte wenig, ſo wäre er getödtet worden, he was very near being killed; weit gefehlt, ſie zu lieben, haſſe ich ſie vielmehr, I am so far from being in love with her, that I hate her; es konnte nicht —, it must happen; es konnte nicht —, daß es ihm ſchadete, it must hurt him. 5) to affect with uneasiness of body or mind. Was fehlt dir? what ails you? what is the matter with you? es fehlt ihm oft etwas, he is often indisposed.

Fehl-bitte, *f.* a useless prayer, useless entreaty, unsuccessful application. Eine —bitte thun, to meet with a refusal. —bitten, *ir. v. intr.* [u. w. haben] to beg in vain. —blatt, *n.* a sheet which is wanting, but especially a card which is wanting in a suit. V. —karte. —blick, *m.* an error, an oversight. —bogen, *m.* V. Defect-bogen. —bohren, *v. tr.* to bore in a wrong direction. —druck, *m.* [with printers] foul impression. —drucken, *v. tr.* to print wrong, to misprint. —fahren, *ir. v. intr.* [u. w. ſeyn] to drive astray. —farbe, *f.* [in cards] renounce. —führen, *v. tr.* to lead into a wrong way or path, to mislead. *Fig.* to guide into error, to mislead. —gang, *m.* 1) a walk on a wrong way or path. 2) a useless walk. —gebären, *ir. v. intr.* to suffer abortion, to miscarry. —geburt, *f.* [the fetus brought forth before it is perfectly formed] abortion. —gehen, *ir. v. intr.* [u. w. ſeyn] 1) to go astray, to miss the way. 2) *Fig.* to fail of the intended effect, to miscarry. —gewinn, *m.* a gain or profit that has miscarried. —gießen, *ir. v. intr.* to miss in pouring, to pour on one side. —greifen, *ir. v. intr.* 1) to lay the hand upon a wrong object. Er hat fehlgegriffen, [with printers] he got into the wrong box. 2) *Fig.* to mistake. —griff, *m.* the act of laying the hand upon a wrong object. *Fig.* a mistake, a fault. —hauen, *ir. v. intr.* to make a false cut. —hieb, *m.* a false cut. —jagen, *v. intr.* to be disappointed in the chase. —jahr, *n.* a sterile year, a year in which the crops fail wholly or partially. —karte, *f.* [in cards] a card that is wanting in a suit. —kauf, *m.* a bad bargain. —kaufen, *v. intr.* to make a bad bargain. —lage, *f.* [in printing] a defective gathering. —laufen, *ir. v. intr.* [u. w. ſeyn] 1) to run astray. 2) to run in vain. —leiten, *v. tr.* to mislead, to misguide. —los, *adj.* and *adv* 1) V. Fehlerlos. 2) infallible, certain. —reiten, *ir. v. intr* [u. w. ſeyn] 1) to ride the wrong way. 2) to ride in vain. —rennen, *ir. v. intr.* [u. w. ſeyn] 1) to run the wrong way. 2) to miss the mark in running. —richten, *v. tr.* to point the wrong way. —rippe, *f.* the lower rib of a young ox. —ritt, *m.* 1) a ride on a wrong way. 2) a ride made in vain. —ſägen, *v. intr.* 1) to saw the wrong way. 2) to miss in sawing. —schicken, v. tr. 1) to send the wrong way, or to a wrong place. 2) to send in vain. —schießen, ir. v intr. to miss one's mark in shooting. *Fig.* Er schoß fehl, his conjectures were unfounded. —schlag, m. a blow that is missed, a false blow, a miss. *Fig.* failure. —schlagen, ir. v. intr. 1) [u. w. haben] to miss one's blow 2) [u. w. seyn] to miscarry, to fail, to miss. Seine Erwartungen schlugen fehl, he was disappointed in his expectations, or his expectations were disappointed; oft schlagen unsre theuersten Hoffnungen fehl, our dearest hopes are often defeated; ein fehlgeschlagener Plan, an abortive scheme. —schleudern, v. intr. 1) to fling or hurl the wrong way. 2) to miss in flinging or hurling. —schließen, ir. v. intr. to draw a wrong conclusion, to conclude erroneously, to misinfer. —schluß, m. [in logic] a fallacious argument or false reasoning, a paralogism. —schmeißen, ir. v. intr. 1) to throw the wrong way. 2) to miss one's blow. —schneiden, ir. v. intr. 1) to cut wrong. 2) to miss in cutting. —schnitt, m. a wrong cut. —schreiben, ir. v. intr. 1) to make a mistake in writing, to miswrite. 2) to write in vain. —schuß, m. a shot which has missed its aim. —sehen, ir. v. intr. to see wrong. *Fig.* to make a mistake or oversight. —setzen, v. tr. to put in a wrong place, to misplace. Sich —setzen, to miss the seat or chair in sitting down. —springen, ir. v. intr. [u. w. seyn] to miss in leaping. —sprung, m. a wrong leap. —stechen, ir. v. intr. to miss in stabbing. —stecken, v. tr. to misplace. —stich, m. a wrong stab. —stoß, m. a false thrust, a wrong thrust. —stoßen, ir. v. intr. to thrust amiss, to miss in thrusting. —streich, m. a false stroke; *fig.* failure. —summe, f. a deficit [in the taxes or revenue &c.]. —treten, ir. v. intr. 1) to trip in walking. 2) to miss in stepping. —tritt, m. a trip in walking, a false step. Das Pferd that einen —tritt, the horse stumbled. *Fig.* an error or fault, a slip, a lapse. —werfen, ir. v. intr. 1) to throw wrong. 2) to miss the mark in throwing. —wort, n. 1) a word that is wanting. 2) a wrong word. —wurf, m. an unsuccessful throw. *Fig.* an undertaking or enterprise that has miscarried. —zeichnen, v. intr. 1) to mismark. 2) to draw badly. —ziehen, ir. v. intr. to pull in a wrong direction. —zielen, v. intr. 1) to take false aim. Fehlgezielt, misaimed. 2) to miss the aim. —zug, m. 1) a wrong pull. 2) a wrong move. 3) [a lot by which nothing is gained] a blank.

Fehler, m. [-s, pl. -] 1) any want or imperfection, defect. Ein — an den Sehorganen, a defect in the organs of sight; organische —, defects in the organs; ein — an einem Gliede, a defect in a limb; der — in der Rechnung, a mistake in the account; ein — an einem Tonwerkzeuge, a defect in a musical instrument; diese Zeichnung hat viele —, there are many faults in this drawing; ein — im Sprechen oder Schreiben, a fault in the language, fault of grammar or a mistake made in writing, an error, a slip of the pen; ein — in der Schreibart, a lapse in style. 2) any deviation from propriety, a neglect of duty or propriety, a slight offence, fault. Einen — begehen, to commit a fault; seine — bereuen und verbessern, to repent and mend one's faults; nachsichtig gegen —, to failings mild; ein — aus Uebereilung, a blunder; ein verzeihlicher —, a pardonable fault; er hat viele — an sich, he is very liable to fail; sein — ist, daß er zu streng ist, he injures himself in being too rigid; jeder hat seine —, niemand ist ohne —, *Prov.* every bear hath its black.

Fehler=frei, *adj.* and *adv.* without fault, ree from incorrectness, perfect, faultless. Ein —freies Gedicht oder Gemälde, a faultless poem or picture; ein —freies Pferd, a sound horse; ein —freier Ausdruck, a correct expression. —los, *adj.* and *adv.* = —frei. —voll, *adj.* and *adv.* full of faults or failings.

Fehlerhaft, *adj.* and *adv.* 1) [containing faults] faulty, defect, imperfect. Ein —hafter Aufsatz, a faulty composition; eine —hafte Rechnung, a miscast; ein —haftes Gemälde, a faulty picture; ein —hafter Plan, a faulty plan or design; ein —es Pferd, a faulty horse. 2) [guilty of a fault or faults] Ein —er Mensch, a faulty man.

1. **Fehm**, *f.* [*pl.* -en] [probably allied to fahen, therefore from the same verb, as 2 Fehm.] 1) an old Saxon name for a court of criminal law. 2) formerly a secret court of criminal justice in Westphalia.

Fehm=ding, *n.* V. — 2. —gericht, *n.* V. — 2. —recht, *n.* rights and customs of the secret court of criminal justice in Westphalia. —richter, *m.* a judge of the secret court. —schöppe, *m.* an assessor of the secret court.

2. ‖**Fehm**, *f.* [from fahen = einschließen] 1) [the food of swine in the woods, as: beech, nuts, acorns &c.] pannage, pawns Die Schweine in die — treiben, to feed swine upon mast. 2) the licence of having pannage.

Fehm=geld, *n.* [the money paid for the licence of having pannage] pannage. —mahl, *n.* a mark put upon swine feeding upon mast. —sache, *f.* any thing concerning pannage. —schwein, *n.* a sow upon pannage. —verzeichniß, *n.* a list of swine feeding upon mast.

3. **Fehm**, *m.* [-es, *pl.* -e] **Fehmen**, *m.* [-s, *pl.* -] [probably also from fahen = zusammenfassen] a pile, a stack, a rick. Ein — Holz, a pile of wood; ein — Heu, a stack of hay; ein — Getreide, a rick of corn.

1. ‡**Fehmen**, *v. tr.* to cite into a court of criminal law, to punish.

2. **Fehmen**, *v. intr.* to put swine upon acorn-pastuse or beech-mast.

Fehmer, *m.* [-s, *pl.* -] V. Fehmrichter.

‖**Fehn**, *n.* [-es, *pl.* -e] V. Eimer.

Fehrücken, *m.* [-s, *pl.* -] **Fehwamme**, *f.* [*pl.* -n] V. Fehe.

Feie, [*pl.* -n] V. Fee.

Feier, *f.* [Lat. *feriae*, origin uncertain] 1) intermission of business, freedom from employment. Die — der Gerichte, vacation, non-term. 2) a distinguishing by ceremonies, or by marks of joy or respect, celebration, solemnization. Die — eines Geburtstages, the celebration of a birthday; die — eines Festtages, the celebration of a religious festival; die — der Sonn- und Festtage, the observing of Sundays and holidays. 3) a holiday suit of clothes. 4) a feast, festival, holiday.

Feier=abend, *m.* 1) the evening time, when work ceases. Um 6 Uhr —abend machen, to leave off work at six o'clock. 2) *Fig.* the conclusion of a business, the cessation of any thing. 3) time of rest, evening. Einen zum —abende besuchen, to pay an evening visit to any one. 4) formerly, the evening before a holiday, eve. —abendsarbeit, *f.* extra-work [done in the hours of rest]. —abendsgesell, *m.* a journeyman who is hired by tailors to work a fortnight before a holiday. —abendstunde, *f.* the hour when work is left off. —blume, *f.* a flower worn on a festival. —brauch, *m.* ceremony. —brauchsordnung, *f.* ritual. —eiche, *f.* a species of oak. —gang, *m.* a procession [of clergy and people in the Romish church &c.]. —gebrauch, *m.* V. —brauch. —gesang, *m.* a hymn. —gewand, *n.* a holiday garment. —jahr, *n.* [in the Jewish economy, every seventh year, in which the Israelites were commanded to suffer their fields and vineyards to rest or lie without tillage] sabbatical year. —klang, *m.* 1) a festival song, festive tune. 2) [for feierlicher Klang] a solemn tone. Der Glocken —klang, the solemn peal of bells. —kleid, *n.* 1) a holiday garment. —kleider, a holiday suit of clothes. 2) a gay dress. *Fig.* Die Natur im —kleide, nature clothed with verdure. —lied, *n.* V. —klang 1. —mahl, *n.* a festival entertainment, a feast. —morgen, *m.* a festive morning. —stunde, *f.* 1) hour of rest [particularly in the evening]. 2) a solemn hour, an awful hour. —tag, *m.* 1) a day of exemption from labour, a day of amusement, a holiday. 2) [an anniversary festival, devoted to religious solemnities] a holiday. Die Weihnachtsfeiertage, Christmas holidays; ein strenger —tag, a close holiday. —täglich, *adj.* and *adv.* pertaining to a festival. Ein —täglicher Anzug, a holiday suit of clothes. —tanz, *m.* a festive dance. —tisch, *m.* an altar. —zug, *m.* a procession.

Feierer [Feiernder], *m.* [-s, *pl.* -] 1) one that rests, or is free, from labour. 2) one that celebrates &c., a celebrator, solemnizer.

Feierlich, I. *adj.* 1) [affecting with seriousness] sober, serious. Eine —e Stille, a solemn silence; *poet.* die Natur in des Herbstes —em Kleide, nature clad in autumn's solemn dress. 2) [religiously grave, attended with religious rites, marked with solemnities] solemn. Einen Tag — begehen, to celebrate a day; Christi Geburt — begehen, to solemnize the birth of Christ; ein —er Tag, a solemn day. 3) grave, serious, or affectedly grave, solemn. Ein —es Gesicht, a solemn face. 4) sacred, solemn. Ein —es Versprechen, a solemn promise. II. *adv.* solemnly. Ich erkläre — daß ich unschuldig bin, I solemnly declare myself innocent.

Feierlichkeit, *f.* 1) the quality of striking something with awe, solemnity, awfulness. Die — eines Tages, the solemnity of a day; die — einer Rede, the solemnity of a discourse. 2) a ceremony, solemnity. Die gestrigen —en, the solemnities of yesterday. 3) gravity, steady seriousness, solemnity. Die — der Spanischen Sprache, the solemnity of the Spanish language. 4) the practice of too much ceremony. Er liebt die —en, he is a friend of ceremoniousness.

Feiern, [V. Feier] I. *v. intr.* 1) to cease from labour, work or performance, to rest. Nach der Arbeit —, von der Arbeit —, to rest from work. *Fig.* Die Freude der Pauken feiert, [in Script.] the mirth of tabrets ceaseth; der Acker feiert, the field rests or lies without tillage. 2) to be at leisure, to be unoccupied, to be idle for want of work. Die Bäcker —, the bakers bake not. *Fig.* —des Geld, unemployed money. 3) = nachhangen [rather unusual]. Seinen Grillen —, to indulge whims, fancies. 4) to tarry, to delay, to defer. 5) to observe silence. II. *v. tr.* 1) [to distinguish by solemn rites, to honour or distinguish by ceremonies and marks of joy and respect] to celebrate. Einen Festtag —, to celebrate a holiday; ein Fest —, to hold a feast; und sollt diesen Tag haben zum Gedächtniß, und sollt ihn — dem Herrn zum Fest, [in Script.] and this day shall be unto you for a memorial, and ye shall keep it a feast to the Lord; einen Geburtstag —, to celebrate a birth-day; Christi Geburt —, to solemnize the birth of Christ; den Aufgang der Sonne —, to celebrate the rising of the sun; [in poetry] den Frühling —, to celebrate spring. 2) to praise, to extol, to commend, to celebrate. Den Namen des Allerhöchsten —, to celebrate the name of the Most High; ein gefeierter Schriftsteller, a celebrated author; ein hochgefeierter Name, a highly celebrated name, an illustrious name. 3) to make or declare to be holy or sacred, to consecrate. Der gefeierte Tempel, the consecrated temple.

Feifel, *m.* [-s, *pl.* -] and *f.* [*pl.* -n] [perhaps allied to the Lat. *faba*, Wabe] [a disease of horses] the fives or vives.

Feifelader, *f.* [in horses] a sublingual vein.

||**Feigblatter**, *f.* [*pl.* -n] [allied to weich] 1) a tubercle or tumor near the anus and pudenda. 2) *Fig.* [a plant] marsh or celery-leaved crow-foot.

Feigbohne, *f.* [*pl.* n] [Feige allied to Wicke] [a plant] lupine.

Feige, [allied to weich, to the Gr. φεύγ-ω, to the Lat. *fug-io*] *adj.* and *adv.* 1) [in mining] brittle. 2) [wanting courage to face danger] cowardly, timorous, fearful, pusillanimous. Ein —r Mensch, a coward wretch; ein —r, eine — Memme, a coward, a poltroon; — seyn, to be a poltroon. 3) [proceeding from fear of danger] cowardly. Ein —s Betragen, a cowardly behaviour. ‡4) sad, dejected.

1. **Feige**, *f.* [*pl.* -n] V. Ohrfeige.

2. **Feige**, *f.* [*pl.* -n] [Lat. *fic-us*; perhaps allied to weich] 1) [the fruit of the fig-tree] a fig. *Fig.* Einem die —(n) weisen, to insult any one with ficoes or contemptuous motions of the fingers, to give one the fico, to fig any one. 2) the figtree, fig. 3) [the name of several plants] die Indische —, common Indian fig, or prickly pear; die Afrikanische —, the fig-marigold. 4) *Fig.* *a*) [a genus of testaceous animals] a species of dipper [bulla ficus], the fig-shell. *b*) [in medicine] a herpetic eruption on the eye-lids.

Feigen-apfel, *m.* [a species of apple] fig-apple. —**baum**, *m.* the fig or fig-tree. Der gemeine Indische —baum, Indian fig-tree, poplar-leaved fig-tree; der Bengalische —baum, Bengal fig-tree; der Egyptische —baum, Egyptian fig or sycomore; daß Juda und Israel sicher wohnten, ein jeglicher unter seinem Weinstocke, und unter seinem —baum, [in Script.] and Judah and Israel dwelt safely, every man under his vine, and under his fig-tree. —**baumlack**, *m.* gum lac. —**birn**, *f.* fig-pear. —**blatt**, *n.* fig-leaf. *Fig.* *a*) [a thin covering] a fig-leaf [chiefly in a jocose sense]. *b*) [with hunters] the parts of generation of does and hinds. —**bohrer**, *m.* [an insect of the ... kind] fig-gnat. —**distel**, *f.* Indian fig. —**drossel**, *f.* [a bird] fig-pecker, becafico. —**förmig**, *adj.* and *adv.* resembling a fig, caricous. —**fresser**, *m.* V. —drossel. —**garten**, *m.* a plantation of fig-trees. —**geschwulst**, *f.* a caricous tumor [such as occur often in the ...]. —**holz**, *n.* the wood of the fig-tree. —**käse**, *m.* fig-cheese. —**korb**, *m.* a frail. —**körner**, *pl.* the seed of the fig-tree. —**lack**, *m.* V. —baumlack. —**moos**, *n.* the articulated coralline of Jamaica. —**picker**, *m.* V. —drossel. —**schnecke**, *f.* the fig-shell. —**schnepfe**, *f.* V. —drossel. —**wald**, *m.* fig-grove.

Feigheit, *f.* cowardice, pusillanimity, cowardliness, faintheartedness.

Feigherzig, *adj.* and *adv.* cowardly, faint-hearted, timorous, dejected.

Feigherzigkeit, *f.* faintheartedness, cowardice.

Feigling, *m.* [-es, *pl.* -e] a coward, poltroon.

Feigsinn, *m.* [-es] a cowardly mind.

Feigsinnig, *adj.* and *adv.* cowardly, timorous, fainthearted.

Feigwarze, *f.* [*pl.* -n] a tumor in the anus or pudenda, caricous tumor.

Feigwarzen-kraut, *n.* fig-wort. —**wurz**, *f.* V. Feigwarzenkraut. **Feigwurz**, *f.* the septfoil, tormentil.

Feil, [Dan. and Sw. *ful*, Isl. *falur*; origin uncertain] *adj.* and *adv.* that is to be sold, that may be sold, set to sale. — haben, to set or expose to sale; ist diese Waare —? is this commodity to be sold? etwas — bieten, to offer or to expose to sale; der Garten ist ihm nicht —, he sells not his garden; *fig.* † Maulaffen — haben, to stand gaping. *Fig.* Eine —e Muse, a venal muse; ein —er Richter, a merceuary judge; eine —e Dirne, a prostitute, a strumpet.

||**Feil-bäcker**, *m.* a baker who exposes his bread for sale. —**bieten**, *n.* —**bietung**, *f.* offering for sale. —**dirne**, *f.* a prostitute, a strumpet. —**träger**, *m.* a hawker, a pedlar.

Feilbar, *adj.* and *adv.* that may be filed.

Feilbogen, *m.* [-s, *pl.* -] a locksmith's bow.

Feile, *f.* [*pl.* -n] [in Bohem. *pilo* signifies eine Säge; V. feilen] a file. Die stumme oder stille —, soft file; die flache —, flat file; —n feilen, to cut files; Messerschärfe —n, [with locksmiths] triangular or saw-files. *Fig.* Ein Werk unter die — nehmen, einem Werk die letzte — geben, die letzte — an ein Werk legen, to give the last polish to a work.

Feilen-halter, *m.* [with file-cutters] a file-holder or fastener. —**hauer**, *m.* a file-cutter. —**stiel**, *m.* file-handle.

1. **Feilen**, [rather unusual] [V. Feil] *v. tr.* 1) to set to sale, to expose to sale; *fig.* to make show of. 2) V. Feilschen.

2. **Feilen**, [perhaps allied to the Lat. *polio*] *v. tr.* to rub and smooth with a file, to file, to polish. *Fig.* An einem Werke —, to give the last polish to a work; gut gefeilte Zeilen, well-filed lines.

Feilheit, *f.* the state of being set to sale; *fig.* venality, mercenariness.

Feilicht, *n.* [-es] filings, scobs.

Feilkloben, *m.* [-s, *pl.* -] [with metallists] tail-vice.

Feilkolben, *m.* [-s, *pl.* -] [with goldsmiths] hand-vice.

Feilnagel, *m.* [-s, *pl.* -nägel] [with tin-founders] filing-board.

Feilschaft, *f.* [rather provincial] goods to be sold, merchandise, commodities.

Feilschen, [V. Feilen] *v. tr.* 1) to sell or to expose to sale, to offer for sale. 2) to treat about a purchase, to bargain, to haggle. Eine Waare —, to cheapen a commodity; um etwas —, to chaffer for something.

Feilscher, *m.* [-s, *pl.* -] a chafferer, a cheapener, a bargainer, a buyer.

Feilsel, *n.* [-s] V. Feilicht.

Feilspänbad, *n.* [-es, *pl.* -bäder] [in chimistry] a medicated bath saturated with filings.

Feilspäne, *pl.* V. Feilicht.

Feilstaub, *m.* [-es] file-dust, filings.

Feilstock, *m.* [-es, *pl.* -stöcke] hand-vice.

Feilstrich, *m.* [-es, *pl.* -e] a stroke with the file.

Feiltuch, *n.* [-es, *pl.* -tücher] barras, Dutch barras.

1. ||**Feim**, *m.* [-es] V. Schaum.

2. **Feim**, *f.* V. Fehm.

Feimen, V. Fäumen or Fehmen

Fein, [appears to be allied to the Gr. φαί-νω, φα-ω = scheinen] *adj.* and *adv.* 1) fine = pleasing to the eye, fair. Ein —er Garten, a fine garden; ein —es Haus, a handsome house; ein —es Gesicht, a fine face; eine —e Haut, a fine skin; ein —es Mädchen, a fair girl; ein —es Liebchen, (Feinsliebchen) a fair sweet-heart. *Fig.* *a*) fine = elegant. Sich* — machen, to dress one's self finely; — gekleidet, elegantly dressed; — gekleidet gehen, to be elegantly clothed, to be genteelly dressed. *b*) ample, large. Ein —es Vermögen, a handsome fortune. *c*) nice in forms, regulated by minute observance of propriety. Ein —es Betragen, a delicate behaviour; —e Sitten, delicate, genteel or polite manners; eine —e Lebensart, a genteel address; —e Leute, gentlefolks; die —e Welt, the polite world; [in a contemptuous or jocose sense] ein —es Dämchen, ein —er(es) Herr(chen), a fine lady, a fine gentleman. *d*) [in fam. language] as an adverb it is used emphatically. Kommt — bald wieder, come back soon, I pray; seyd — lustig! now, be merry! 2) fine, thin, slender, minute. Ein —er Faden, a fine or delicate thread; —e Seide, fine silk; ein —es Haar, a fine hair; —es Papier, fine or thin paper; ein —er Dunst, a subtil vapour; —er Sand, fine sand; — gepülvert, finely pulverized; der Stein sollte nicht zu — gepülvert seyn, the stone should not be too finely powdered; —e Leinwand, fine linen; ein —es Gewebe, a nice or delicate texture; — gewirkt, finely wrought; ein —er Kamm, a small tooth-comb; eine —e Feder, a fine-pointed pen. *Fig.* *a*) fine = clear, pure, free from feculence or foreign matter. —es Gold oder Silber, fine gold or silver. *b*) nice, elegant. —e Arbeit, nice workmanship; —e Waaren, elegant commodities, [in common popular language] costly goods. *c*) fine = nice, delicate. Ein —er Geschmack, a fine taste; der Hund hat eine —ere Nase als sein Herr, the dog has a better nose than his master; ein —er Geruch, a delicate flavour; ein —es Gefühl, a fine sense; eine —e Beurtheilungskraft, eine —e Fassungsgabe, a nice discernment, a fine perception; ein —er Kopf, a man of fine genius, *it.* *a sly, artful or cunning person; *ein —er Fuchs, a subtle fellow, a cunning blade; ein — angelegter Plan, a scheme subtly contrived; ein —er, a hypocrite; die —e, a hypocritic female; die —en, a sect of hypocrites in Holland. *d*) delicate, fine, ingenious. Ein —es Lob, a delicate panegyric; eine —e Antwort, an ingenious reply; auf eine —e Art, delicately, with nice regard to propriety and the feelings of others, in a delicate manner; einen —en Unterschied machen, to make a nice distinction, to discern nicely; eine —e Anspielung, a delicate allusion.

Fein-brenner, *m.* [in metallurgy] refiner. —**empfinder**, *m.* —**empfinderinn**, *f.* a person of delicate feeling, a person of fine perception. —**fädig**, *adj.* and *adv.* having fine threads, fine-threaded. —**flöte**, *f.* V. Vogelpfeife. —**fühlend**, *adj.* and *adv.* delicate —**gefühl**, *n.* delicacy of feeling. —**gehalt**, *m.* fineness of texture, delicacy. —**gespitzt**, *adj.* and *adv.* having a fine point, sharp-pointed. —**körnig**, *adj.* and *adv.* fine-grained. —körniges Pulver, priming-powder. —**kupfer**, *n.* [in metallurgy] rosette copper. —**machen**, *n.* 1) [in papermills] second stamping. 2) [in metallurgy] refining. —**maler**, *m.* a miniature-painter. —**malerei**, *f.* miniature. —**maschig**, *adj.* and *adv.* having fine meshes. —**raspel**, *f.* a fine rasp; *it.* a planchet-file used in mints. —**säulig**, *adj.* and *adv.* [in archit.] Ein —säuliges Gebäude, a diastyle. —**sichtig**, *adj.* and *adv.* clear-sighted. —**sinn**, *m.* a fine sense. —**sinnig**, *adj.* and *adv.* 1) delicate. 2) ingenious. —**sinnlich**, *adj.* and *adv.* sensual in a delicate manner. —**sittlich**, *adj.* and *adv.* having delicate manners. —**s-liebs-**

chen, *n.* a fair sweet-heart. —spitzer, *m.* [with needlers] the pointer. —wollig, *adj.* and *adv.* having fine wool. —zucker, *m.* refined sugar.

Feind, *adj.* and *adv.* 1) feeling hatred. Einem — werden, to entertain a great aversion for a person; ihm ist jeder —, every one hates him. 2) hostile. Er ist jedem Fortschritt — (ein Feind jedes Fortschritts) he is hostile to every progress. It is also used in the compound words *spinnefeind, todfeind &c.

Feind, *m.* [-es, *pl.* -e] [from the old *fian* = hassen, which seems to be figuratively formed from the A. S. *vigian* = fechten] an enemy in war, a foe. Die —e in der Schlacht besiegen, to overcome the enemies in battle; der — rückte vor, the enemy advanced; in —es Land, in the enemy's country, in a hostile country. *Prov.* Dem fliehenden —e soll man eine goldne Brücke bauen, do not pursue a flying enemy too eagerly. *Fig.* an enemy, a foe, an adversary. Ich aber sage euch, liebet eure —e, [in Script.] I say to you, love your enemies; und des Menschen —e werden seine eigenen Hausgenossen seyn, [in Script.] a man's foes shall be they of his own household; ein abgesagter or geschworner —, a mortal or inveterate foe; ein erklärter —, a professed foe; er ist ein — der Complimente or von Complimenten, he hates ceremony; er ist ein — des Spieles or vom Spielen, he has an aversion to gaming; er ist ein — vom Trinken, he dislikes drinking; ein — des schönen Geschlechtes, a woman-hater; der Menschen—, a man-hater, misanthrope. *Prov.* Jeder ist sein ärgster —, no man hath a worse friend than he brings from home; besser ein offenbarer —, als ein verstellter Freund, or Gott bewahre mich vor meinen Freunden, mit meinen —en will ich schon fertig werden, God keep me from my friends, I'll keep myself from my enemies; ein — Gottes, an enemy to God; ein — der Wahrheit, an enemy to truth; ein — der Tugend, a foe to virtue; der böse —, the Enemy, the archfiend, the devil, [in Scripture] the adversary.

‖**Feinden**, *v. tr.* to hate [it is used only in the compound words anfeinden, verfeinden].

Feindinn, *f.* a female enemy or foe. Die Leidenschaften sind —en der Gesundheit, passions destroy health.

Feindlich, *adj.* and *adv.* possessed by a public enemy, hostile. Ein —es Land, a hostile country. *Fig.* inimical, hostile, unfriendly. —e Absichten, hostile intentions; — gegen Einen gesinnt seyn, to hate a person; das —e Schicksal, adverse fate; —e Farben, [with painters] repugnant colours.

Feindlichkeit, *f.* enmity, ill-will, hatred.

Feindschaft, *f.* enmity, ill-will, hatred. Eine eingewurzelte oder unversöhnliche —, inveterate enmity, implacable enmity; eine persönliche — wider Jemand haben, hegen or nähren, to bear a personal rancour towards a person, to entertain a personal aversion for a person; — stiften, to create hatred.

Feindschaftlich, *adj.* and *adv.* inimical, hostile.

Feindselig, *adj.* and *adv.* 1) inimical, hostile, unfriendly. —e Absichten, hostile intentions; Einen — behandeln, to treat any one in a hostile manner or hostilely. ‖2) hateful, odious.

Feindseligkeit, *f.* 1) [attacks of an enemy] hostility. Diese verborgene Feindschaft brach in —en aus, this secret enmity broke out in hostilities. 2) private enmity.

1. **Feine**, *m.* and *f.* V. Fein, *fig.* a.

2. **Feine**, *f.* V. Feinheit.

Feineln, [rather unusual] I. *v. tr.* to make somewhat less coarse. II. *v. intr.* to play the cunning man.

Feinen, [rather unusual] *v. tr.* to fine, to refine, to purify. Zucker —, to refine sugar.

Feinern, [unusual] *v. tr.* to refine.

Feinheit, *f.* 1) fineness, thinness, smallness, minuteness, delicacy. Die — eines Fadens, the fineness or delicacy of a thread; die — des Sandes, the fineness of sand; die — der Leinwand, the fineness of linen; die — der Haut, the delicacy of the skin. *Fig.* *a*) fineness = freedom from foreign matter, purity. Die — des Goldes, the fineness of gold. *b*) fineness = niceness, delicacy. Die — der Arbeit, the niceness of work; die — des Geschmacks, the fineness or niceness of taste. *c*) fineness = subtility, artfulness, ingenuity. Die — des Verstandes, the fineness of wit. *d*) delicacy, softness of manners. Die — des Betragens, delicacy of behaviour. *e*) nice susceptibility of impression, tenderness. Die — des Gefühls, delicacy of feeling. 2) something fine or beautiful. Die —en einer Sprache, the delicacies or niceties of a language; dieses Gedicht enthält viele —en, there are many delicate thoughts in this poem.

Feirer, *m.* V. Feierer.

Feist, [appears to be allied to the Gr. πί-ων, to the Lat. *fi-mus* and perhaps to fein, thus originally = glänzend] I. *adj.* and *adv.* fat, fleshy [used of animals]. —e Schaafe, fat sheep; ein —es Thier, a fatling; [sometimes also of men] ein —er Pfaffe, a sleek priest or monk. *Fig.* Der —e Donnerstag, [in the Romish church] Shrove Thursday; [in a jocose or contemptuous sense] eine —e Seele, a cold, reserved or stupid soul. II. *n.* [-es] [with hunters] the fat or suet of deer.

Feist-ader, *f.* V. Fettader. —zeit, *f.* [with hunters] the time when stags are fat.

Feiste, *f.* [*pl.* -n] 1) [the quality of being fat] fatness, greasiness. 2) a fat thing, a fat body.

Feisten, *v. tr.* to make fat, to make fleshy or plump with fat, to fatten. Die Zeit des —s, the time when swine are put upon acorn pasture or beech-mast.

Feisterling, *m.* [-es, *pl.* -e] 1) [for Fäusterling] a sort of apple. 2) a species of mushroom.

Feistigkeit, *f.* fatness, greasiness.

Felbe, *f.* V. Fälber.

Felbel, *m.* [-s] [appears to be allied to Fell] [a kind of cloth made in imitation of velvet] velveteen.

Felber, *f.* V. Fälber.

Felch, *m.* **Felche**, *f.* V. Balche.

Feld, *n.* [-es, *pl.* -er] [seems to be allied to the Sw. *fala* = Ebene, perhaps also to the Lat. *villa*, the Fr. *ville*] 1) *a*) [in architecture] a square piece of board, or other piece somewhat similar inserted between other pieces, as, the panel of a door, tympan, the interval between columns, beams &c., space. V. Fach. *b*) [with coopers] the interval between the hoops. *c*) [in heraldry, the whole surface of the shield or the continent] field. Er führt einen schwarzen Adler im goldnen —e, he bears or an eagle sable. *d*) [in organs] the middle of an organ. *e*) [with comb-makers] the bridge or middle of a comb. *f*) one of the sixty-four houses or squares on a chess-board. 2) an open field, a tract of ground without hills, a campaign, campain, champain, champaign. Die Elysä[i]schen —er, [in mythology] the Elysian fields, Elysium. 3) land between cities and villages. Im freien —e, in the open field; über — gehen, fahren, to take a trip across the fields. *Fig.* Die Sache steht noch im *weiten —e, the matter is far from bei[ng] settled; hier haben wir ein weites — vor [uns], here we have a large field to expatiate in; die[ser] Gegenstand öffnet der Betrachtung ein wei[]tes —, this subject opens a wide field for con[]templation. 4) properly land not covered wi[th] wood, tillage land, field. Der Hausherr ist b[ei] seinen Arbeitern auf dem —e, the master of the house is in the field with his labourers; er [ist] im —e und macht Heu, he is in the field making hay; das — bauen, to till the ground; die — düngen, to manure the fields; der Hirsch [] or geht Nachts zu —e, [with hunters] the [hart] goes a-feeding in the night-time; fruchtba[re] —er, fruitful fields or land; —er, die bra[ch] liegen, fallow fields, fallows. *Fig.* the proper office or business of a person. Das gehört nicht in mein —, that is not within my province. V. Fach, *fig.* 5) [in common or popular lang.] tillage. 6) [in mining] the proper ground, where miners dig ore. 7) an open field where an army lives in tents or is in a state of active operations. Zu —e gehen, ziehen, to go into or to take the field; zu —e liegen, to keep the field; ein Heer ins — stellen, to take the field with an army; die[se] Veteranen sind herrliche Soldaten im —e, the[se] veterans are excellent soldiers in the field. 8) the field of battle, the field. Das — behaupten, behalten, to remain master of the field; [der] Feind mußte das — räumen, the enemy w[as] obliged to retire. Syn. V. Acker.

Feld-altar, *m.* the altar of an army [that] keeps the field. —ameise, *f.* the little [] ant. —ampfer, *m.* [a plant] sheep's sorrel. —anger, *m.* [a strip of ground thrown up by a [] or left between furrows] a ridge. —apothe[ke], *f.* the medicine-chest of an army. —apot[he]ker, *m.* field-apothecary. —arbeit, *f.* till[age]. —arbeiter, *m.* a tiller, cultivator or hus[band]man, a labourer. —art, *f.* the division of arable land in three classes. —arzneikas[ten], *m.* V. —apotheke. —arzt, *m.* army-physic[ian]. —bach, *m.* V. Regenbach. —bachstelze, *f.* [] lark. —backen, *n.* the baking of bread for [an] army, also for the villages. —bäcker, *m.* army-baker. —bäckerei, *f.* 1) the establish[]ment of army-bakers. 2) the baking of [bread] for an army. —backofen, *m.* an oven, where bread for an army is baked. —banner, —[pa]nier, —panner, *n.* field-banner. —ba[u], 1) agriculture, husbandry. Sich auf den — legen, den —bau treiben, to till the ground. [] arable land. —bauer, *m.* 1) an agricultur[ist], husbandman, a tiller. 2) a peasant living [in a] plain. —baum, *m.* a single tree standing [in a] field. —beifuß, *m.* field southern-wood. —bett, *n.* [diminut. das —bettchen, —bettlein] camp-bed, folding-bed, field-bed. —bew[oh]ner, *m.* a husbandman, tiller. —biene, *f.* [] bee. —binde, *f.* [a belt worn for ornament] sash. —binse, *f.* hairy field-rush. —birn[e] the fruit of the crab or wilding. —birnbau[m], *m.* the crab or wilding. —blume, *f.* sil[ver] cinquefoil, silver-weed or wild tansey. —boh[ne], *f.* the bean cultivated in fields, as the great b[ean] the horse-bean &c. —breite, *f.* [in husban[dry]] the breadth of a cultivated field. —brücke, [*f.*] a bridge over a ditch or over a rivulet. 2) stil[e]. —brustwehre, *f.* [in fortif. that mass of earth w[hich] serves as a parapet to the covered way] the glacis. —busch, *m.* a clump of bushes or trees in a fi[eld]. —darm, *m.* V. Hühnerdarm. —decke, [*f.*] frieze-blanket used by soldiers in the field. —degen, *m.* a sword worn in the field, a sold[ier's] sword. —demuth, V. Quendel. —dieb, *m.* a thief that robs the fields. ‖2) *Fig.* the ho[use] sparrow. —dieberei, *f.* the practice of [rob]bing the fields. —dienst, *m.* 1) husbandry [ser]vice. 2) [in milit. affairs] military service in [the] field, active service. —dienstbarkeit, *f.*

law] common. —distel, *f.* corn sawwort, or way-thistle. —ebereis, *n.* V. Stabwurzel. —eisenkraut, *n.* red dead nettle or nettle-hemp. —ente, *f.* [a species of bustard] field-duck. —enzian, *m.* [a plant] field-gentian. —erbse, *f.* the wild pea. —erzeugniß, *n.* any produce of the fields. —esel, *m.* V. Waldesel. —fernlicht, *f.* perspective plane. —flagge, *f* [in milit. affairs] field-colours, bandrol. —flasche, *f.* a soldier's flask, canteen. —flöte, *f.* V. —pfeife. ‖—flucht, *f.* desertion. ‖—fluchter, *m.* a dove feeding in the fields. ‖—flüchtig, *adj.* and *adv.* deserting. —flüchtig werden, to desert from the army; der —flüchtige, a deserter. —frevel, *m.* mischief done to fields or to the produce of the field. —frucht, *f.* produce of the fields. —gang, *m.* a walk over the fields. —garten, *m.* a field cultivated as a garden. —geflügel, *n* birds that harbour in the fields, such as partridges, quails &c. —gehege, *n.* a piece of ground appropriated to the breeding and preservation of hares, partridges &c., a preserve. —geist, *m.* a spirit that haunts the fields. —geistliche, *m.* V. —pater, —prediger or —priester. —geistlichkeit, *f.* the clergy of an army. —gepäck, *n.* [the tents, clothing, utensils, and other necessaries of an army] the baggage. —geräth, *n.* 1) the implements of husbandry. 2) V. —gepäck. —geräthschaft, *f.* V. —geräth. —gerecht, *adj.* and *adv.* Ein —gerechter Jäger, [with hunters] a hunter well skilled in the art or practice of hunting game that breeds in fields, as hares, partridges &c. —gericht, *n.* 1) court of the manor. 2) V. Kriegsgericht. —gesang, *m.* a rural song, a song in the fields. —geschirr, *n.* 1) V. —geräth. 2) the harness of a farmhorse. —geschleppe, *n.* V. —gestänge. —geschrei, *n.* 1) [a particular cry of troops when they rush to the attack] war-cry, whoop, war-whoop. 2) the watchword. —gestänge, *n.* [in mining] flats or flat rods or poles, sweep. —gewächs, *n.* a plant. ‡—gewaltiger, *m.* the provost marshal of an army. —glocke, *f.* [slang] the gallows. Ein Klöppel in der großen —glocke werden, to be executed by the halter, to swing. —gott, *m.* a rustic god. —gottesdienst, *m.* divine service performed in the field or in camps. —gottheit, *f.* a rustic godship. —göttinn, *f.* a rustic goddess. —graben, *m.* a ditch in the fields. —gras, *n.* grass growing in the fields. —grenze, *f.* the borders of a field. —grille, *f.* the field-cricket. —gut, *n.* a farm. —hahn, *m.* V. —huhn. —hase, *m.* field-hare. —hauptmann, *m.* [especially in Script.] a general or commander. —henne, *f.* V. —huhn. —herd, *m.* a fowling-floor in the fields. —herr, *m.* a commander in chief. Napoleon war ein großer —herr, Napoleon was a great captain. —herrngabe, *f.* generalship. —herrnstab, *m.* the staff of a commander in chief. —herrnwürde, *f.* the dignity of a commander in chief. —heu, *n.* hay made on fields. —hirte, *m.* V. —hüter. —holder, —holunder, *m.* the dwarf-elder. —holz, *n.* a bush in the fields. —hopfen, *m.* V. Johannskraut. —huhn, *n.* the partridge Das Männchen or der —hahn, the cock partridge; das Weibchen or die —henne, the hen partridge; das graue —huhn, the grey partridge; das rothe —huhn, the redlegged partridge; die —hühnerjagd, partridge shooting. —hühnerdarm, *m.* a species of chickweed [alsine segetalis]. 1. —hut, *m.* a hat worn by labourers in the fields, a straw-hat. 2. —hut[h], *f.* the guarding of the fields from depredation. —hüter, *m.* a man set to guard the fields from depredation —hütte, *f.* 1) a cabin or a hut for the person set to guard the fields from depredation. 2) a soldier's hut, barrack. —jäger, *m.* 1) a gamekeeper for the smaller game, such as hares, partridges &c. 2) an officer in armies employed to bear a message, or an order, to serve as courier. —jaspis, *m.* jasper found near the surface of the earth. —kanzlei, *f.* army-office. —kasse, *f.* 1) the cash of an army. 2) the cash-keepers of an army. —katze, *f.* —kätzchen, ‖—kätzlein, *n.* V. Mäuseöhrchen. —keller, *m.* 1) a cellar dug in the field. 2) a canteen. —kerze, *f.* V. Königskerze. —kessel, *m.* a camp kettle. —kirche, *f.* a church standing alone in the fields, an isolated church. —klee, *m.* the procumbent trefoil. —klette, *f.* V. Klettenkerbel. —knoblauch, *m.* V. Ackerknoblauch or Hundsknoblauch. —knotenmoos, *n.* threadmoss —koch, *m.* a army-cook. —kohl, *m.* 1) the field cabbage. 2) wild raddish. —kommissär, *m.* commissary of the army. —kopf, *m.* V. —busch. —krämer, *m.* —krämerinn, *f.* a person who follows an army and sells to the troops provisions and liquors, a sutler. —krankenhaus, *n.* an army hospital. —krankheit, *f.* a disease which affects soldiers in the field. —kraut, *n.* an herb growing in the fields. —kresse, *f.* common lady's smock, or cuckow-flower. —kriegskanzlei, *f.* V. —kanzlei. —kriegskasse, *f.* V. —kasse. —kröte, *f.* a species of toad. —küche, *f.* 1) a sutler's kitchen. 2) [rather unusual] *Fig.* V. Schindanger. —kümmel, *m.* 1) common caraway. 2) the mother of thyme. —kunst, *f.* [in mining] any machine for removing waters from the pits. —kunstpfeifer, *m.* [unusual] a military musician. —lager, *n.* a camp, and the place where an army is encamped. —lattig, *m.* 1) prickly lettuce. 2) the corn valerian or lamb's lettuce, corn salad. —lauch, *m.* V. —knoblauch. —läufer, *m.* 1) field- or land-bird, as opposed to water-fowl. 2) V. Flurschütz. —lehre, *f.* agricultural science, agriculture. —lerche, *f.* the sky-lark. —lilie, *f.* pompian lily. —linse, *f.* the small lentil. —luft, *f.* open air. —lust, *f.* V. Landlust. —mann, *m.* V. 2. Bauer. —mannstreu, *f.* the common eryngo or holly. —marder, *m.* V. Baummarder. —mark, *f.* 1) the borders of a field, landmark. 2) the fields belonging to a manor or village. —marschall, *m.* field-marshal. —masholder, *m.* V. Masholder. —maß, *n.* V. Ackermaß. —maus, *f.* field-mouse. —meier, *m.* [a plant] common or narrow-leaved mouse-ear. ‖—meister, *m.* V. Schinder. —messen, *n.* 1) the measuring of land, a survey of land. 2) surveying. —messer, *m.* a surveyor of land, a land-surveyor. —meßkunst, *f.* surveying. —messung, *f.* V. —messen, 1. —mohn, *m.* corn or red poppy. —münze, *f.* corn mint. —nachbar, *m.* the owner of a field that joins that of another man. Sie sind —nachbarn, their fields are contingent. —nägelein, *n.* V. —nelke. —narde, *f.* [a plant] a species of spikenard. —nelke, *f.* field-pink, Carthusian pink. ‡—oberste, *m.* a name given to a commander of the cavalry. —obst, *n.* fruit from fruit-trees standing in the fields —ochs, *m.* a farm-ox. —ofen, *m.* 1) V. —backofen. 2) a kiln for baking tiles. —ortstrecke, *f.* [in mining] level. —panier, —panner, *n.* V. —banner. —pappel, *f.* the round-leaved mallow. —pater, *m.* catholic chaplain of a regiment. —pfau, *m.* V. Kibitz. —pfeife, *f.* 1) a rural pipe. 2) [in organs] *a*) a pipe sounding like a flute. *b*) the flute stop. —polei, *m* V. Quendel. —post, *f.* army-post. —postamt, *n.* military post-office. —posten, *m.* the out-post of an army. —postmeister, *m.* field-postmaster. —prediger, *m.* protestant chaplain of a regiment. —priester, *m.* V. —pater. —probst, *m.* protestant chaplain general. —quartiermeister, *m.* the quartermaster of an army in the field. —quendel, *m.* common thyme. —rapunzel, *f.* 1) rampion-like bell-flower. 2) the corn-valerian or lamb's lettuce. —rauch, *m.* V. Erdrauch. —recht, *n.* 1) rights or privileges attached to fields. 2) rural law. —regiment, *n.* a regiment of the line. —reich, *adj.* and *adv.* rich in fields. —richter, *m.* 1) a judge of a manorial court. 2) the judge of a regiment or army. —ringelblume, *f.* field marigold. —rittersporn, *m.* branching larkspur. —rohr, *n.* a rural pipe. —rose, *f.* 1) any wild rose, as, the wild briar, the eglantine rose &c. 2) the wood anemone. —rüstung, *f.* V. Kriegsrüstung. —ruthe, *f.* a surveyor's rod. —salat, *m.* V. —lattig. —schaden, *m.* damage done to the fields. —schanze, *f.* field-redoubt, field-work. —schar, *f.* [obsolescent] a regiment of the line. —scharte, *f.* V. Haferdistel. ‖—scheide, *f.* V. —scheidung. —scheider, *m.* V. —messer. —scheidung, *f.* land-mark. —scherer, *m.* 1) an army-surgeon. 2) a surgeon. —scheuche, *f* a scarecrow. ‖—schieber, *m.* V. —messer. —schlacht, *f.* action in the field, a battle. —schlange, *f.* 1) a serpent that breeds in dry places. 2) *Fig.* a sort of cannon. Die ganze —schlange or Rothschlange, culverin; die halbe —schlange demy-culverin; die Viertelfeldschlange or Falkaune, falcon; die halbe Viertelfeldschlange or kleine Falkaune, aspic. —schmiede, *f.* travelling forge of an army. —schnecke, *f.* slug. —schnepfe, *f.* the common snipe [as opposed to Waldschnepfe = wood-cock]. ‖—schön, *adj.* and *adv.* handsome at a distance. —schoten, *pl.* V. —erbsen. —schreiber, *m.* the clerk of a regiment. ‖ or ‡—schultheiß, *m.* V. —richter. —schuppen, *m.* a shed in the fields. —schütz, *m.* 1) V. —hüter. 2) formerly a gunner. —schwamm, *m.* [a kind of mushroom] champignon. —schwarzkümmel, *m.* wild nigella. —see, *m.* a lake surrounded by fields. —senf, *m.* V. Ackersenf. —siech, *adj.* and *adv.* leprous. —soldat, *m.* a soldier serving in the field, a soldier of the line. —spath, *m.* [a mineral widely distributed and usually of a foliated structure] feldspath, felspath, feldspar, felspar. Gemeiner —spath, common felspar; dichter —spath, compact felspar; edler or dichter —spath, labrador or opalescent felspar, labradorstone; dichter blauer —spath, azure-spar; glasiger —spath, glassy felspar; krummblätteriger —spath, siliceous spar or felspar, or albite, cleavelandite; muscheliger —spath, Brasilian topaz; opalisirender —spath, moon-stone, adularia; prismatischer —spath, V. —spath; pyramidaler —spath, wernerite; rhomboedrischer —spath, nephelin, nepheline; zum —spath gehörig oder daraus bestehend, feldspathic. —sperling, *m.* the hedge-sparrow. —spinat, *m.* angular-leaved goosefoot, English mercury, or all-good, good Henry, good king Harry, or wild spinach. —spinne, *f.* the crab-spider. —stein, *m.* 1) a stone found on fields. 2) land-mark. 3) compact felspar, rock flint, rock stone, petrosilex. —stück, *n.* 1) [a cannon which is carried along with armies, and used in the field of battle] a field-piece. 2) a picture of country-scenery, a landscape. —stuhl, *m.* a camp-chair or folding-chair. ‡—sucht, *f.* leprosy. —taube, *f.* stock-pigeon or a pigeon that feeds in the fields. —teich, *m.* a pond in the fields. —teufel, *m.* a demon that haunts the fields, a faun. —theilung, *f.* the surveying of land. —theilungskunst, *f* surveying. —thier, *n.* a wild beast. —tisch; *m.* a folding-table. —ton, *m.* the tone of a trumpet or any other military wind-instrument [E flat]. —trompete, *f.* a trumpet. —trompeter, *m.* a trumpet, a trumpeter. —ulme, *f.* the common elm. —verpflegung, *f.* purveyance of an army. —

verpflegungsamt, *n.* military purveyance-office. —**vogel**, *m.* 1) field-bird. 2) land-bird. —**vogt**, *m.* 1) V. —**hüter**. ||2) the steward of a manor. —**wache**, —**wacht**, *f.* [a post or station without the limits of a camp, or at a distance from the main body of an army, and the troops placed at such a station] outpost, piquet. —**wächter**, *m.* V. —**hüter**. —**wage**, *f.* V. Ackerwage. —**waid**, *m.* V. Sommerwaid. —**wake**, *f.* wacke or wacky that occurs in fields. —**wanze**, *f.* a species of the bug [cimex campestris]. —**wärts**, *adv.* towards the field. —**webel**, *m.* [a non-commissioned officer] sergeant. —**weg**, *m.* a way or path that crosses the fields, field-way. —**weges**, *n.* formerly a certain measure of distance, a furlong. —**wehre**, *f.* V. Landwehre. —**weide**, *f.* the trailing willow. —**werk**, *n.* [in milit. affairs] field-works. —**wicke**, *f.* 1) common vetch or tare. 2) smooth tare. —**wiese**, *f.* a meadow among fields. —**winde**, *f* small or field bindweed. —**wirthschaft**, *f.* 1) husbandry, agriculture, economics. 2) a farm. —**wundarzt**, *m.* an army surgeon. —**wurm**, *m.* V. Regenwurm. —**zaun**, *m.* a hedge [round a field to fence it]. —**zehnte**, *m.* predial tithe. —**zeichen**, *n.* a military sign, military emblem. —**zeugmeister**, *m.* master of the ordnance. —**ziegelofen**, *m.* V. —ofen, 2. —**zikorie**, *f.* V. Hindläufte. —**zipresse**, *f.* V. Erdkiefer. —**zug**, *m.* [the time that an army keeps the field, without entering into winter-quarters] a campaign or campain. Der Winter—zug, a winter campaign; einen —zug antreten, to open or begin a winter-campaign. —**zwiebel**, *f.* [a name of several plants] *a*) yellow star of Bethlehem. *b*) lily-rooted squill.

Feldchen, ||**Feldlein**, *n.* [-s, *pl.* -] [diminut. of Feld] a small field.

Feldein, *adv.* fieldwards, towards the fields, off the highroad. Quer —, across the fields.

Felderbau, *m.* [-es] [in coal-mines] pannel-work.

Felderdecke, *f.* [*pl.* -n] [in archit.] soffit.

Feldig, *adj.* and *adv.* composed of fields, in the compound words drei—, vier—.

Feldung, *f.* panel [of a door &c.].

Felge, *f.* [*pl.* -n] [allied to the Lat. *valgus*, to the Germ. wölben &c.] ||1) the state of ground, when it is just broken up, or lightly ploughed, after its crop. 2) the felly [of a wheel]. [in seamen's language] Die —n des Steuerrades, the fellies, felloes or jaunts of the rudder.

Felgen-bank, *f.* [with wheel-wrights] felly-board. —**hauer**, *m.* a wheel-wright.

Felgen, [V. Felge] *v. tr.* ||1) to break up, to plough lightly after the crop. 2) Ein Rad —, to provide a wheel with fellies.

Fell, *n.* [-es, *pl.* -e] [allied to the Lat. *pell-is*, *vell-us*, and belonging to *vel-o*, old Germ. felen = decken or to fillen = abziehen] in general something covering, something resembling a skin or pellicle, a membrane, as, das Zwerch—, the diaphragm, or midriff; das — im Auge, a film on the eye. 1) [the natural covering of animal bodies] the skin. † Einem das — gerben, to thrash or drub any one; Einem das — über die Ohren ziehen, to flay any one; *fig.* to strip any one of money, to fleece any one. *Fig.* Ein dickes — haben, to be void of feeling, to be insensible, to want sensibility. 2) [the skin of smaller animals separated from the body whether green, dry or tanned] a skin, hide, pelt, or felt. Ein Kalb—, the hide or skin of a calf, or leather made of that skin, a calf-skin; ein Ziegen—, a goat's-skin; das Hunds—, the skin of a dog; das Reh—, [with hunters] the skin of a roe. 3) [in vulgar lang.] a person. Er ist ein gutes —, he is a good-natured fellow; sie ist ein altes —, ein liederliches —, she is an old puss, a strumpet. 4) something made of a skin, something made of skins, a knapsack. Syn. V. Balg.

Fell-bereiter, *m.* a skin-dresser. —**eisen**, *n.* 1) a portmanteau, wallet, a cloak-bag. 2) a bag for the conveyance of letters, a mail. —**eisenmacher**, *m.* a portmanteau-maker. —**gar**, *adj.* and *adv.* [with furriers] dressed. —**händler**, *m.* fellmonger, skinner, peltmonger. —**riß**, *n.* [a name of several plants] *a*) the vervain mallow. *b*) common holly-hock. *c*) common dandelion. *d*) hypecoum. —**schmitze**, *m.* a dyer of skins. —**werk**, *n.* peltry.

***Felonie**, *f.* [*pl.* -n] V. Lehnsuntreue.

Fels, *m.* [-ses or -sen, *pl.* -sen] [is allied to spalten, Eng. *spelt*, A. S. spellern, in the same manner as the Lat. *rupes* from *rumpo*] 1) V. Felsen. 2) *Fig.* [in Scripture, a defence, means of safety, protection, strength, asylum] rock. Der Herr ist mein — und meine Burg, the Lord is my rock and my fortress.

Fels-ab, *adv.* down the rock. —**abhang**, *m.* the slope of a rock, rocky steep, precipice. —**achat**, *m.* rock-agate. —**adler**, *m.* an eagle that builds on rocks. —**alaun**, *m.* rock- or roche-alum. —**arten**, *pl.* [in geognosy] rocks. —**bucht**, *f.* a bay surrounded by rocks. —**geboren**, *adj.* and *adv.* born on rocks. —**geklüft**, *n.* V. Felsengeklüft. —**grath**, *m.* the ridge of a rock. —**hang**, *m.* the slope of a rock, a rocky steep, precipice. —**haupt**, *n.* V. Felsenhaupt. —**kies**, —**kiesel**, *m.* rock-agate. —**klippe**, *f.* a high and steep rock, a cliff. —**kluft**, *f.* a chasm, cleft or precipice in a rock. —**ritze**, *f.* a cleft in a rock. —**stein**, *m.* 1) the stony matter of which rocks are composed. 2) a detached piece of a rock. —**stück**, *n.* a detached piece of a rock, a fragment of a rock. ||—**trumm**, *m.* fragments of rocks. —**wand**, *f.* V. Felsenwand.

Felsen, *m.* [-s, *pl.* -] [V. Fels] 1) [a large mass of stony matter, usually compounded of two or more simple materials, either bedded in the earth or resting on its surface] a rock. Den vergleiche ich einem klugen Manne, der sein Haus auf einen — bauete, [in Script.] I will liken him unto a wise man, which built his house upon a rock. 2) *Fig.* *a*) Er erhöhet mich auf einem —, [in Script.] he shall set me upon rock; du bist Petrus, und auf diesen — will ich bauen meine Gemeine, [in Script.] thou art Peter, and upon this rock I will build my church. *b*) [in compos.] stoniness, hardness of heart, insensibility.

Felsen-ader, *f.* 1) a vein of rocks. 2) [formerly] axillar vein. —**adergang**, *m.* V. —blutleiter. —**alaun**, *m.* roche- or rock-alum. —**altar**, *m.* a rock used as an altar. —**an**, *adv.* up the rock. —**artig**, *adj.* and *adv.* resembling a rock, very hard, rocky. —**becken**, *n.* rock-basin. —**beifuß**, *m.* creeping wormwood. —**bein**, *n.* [in anatomy] petrous bone. —**berg**, *m.* a rock-mountain, a rocky mountain. —**bette**, *n.* the rocky bed of a river. —**block**, *m.* a detached block of a rock. —**blutleiter**, *m.* [in anatomy] vein of the petrous bone —**bock**, *m.* a name given to the wild goat, the chamois goat &c. —**bogen**, *m.* a rocky arch. —**brombeere**, *f.* the fruit of the stone bramble. —**brombeerstrauch**, *m.* stone-bramble. —**brust**, *f.* *Fig.* a rocky breast. —**bucht**, *f.* V. Felsbucht. —**damm**, *m.* a dike of rocks. —**durchgang**, *m.* a passage made through rocks, gallery, tunnel. —**fall**, *m.* the steep declivity of a rock. —**fest**, *adj.* and *adv.* fast as a rock, unshaken. —**feste**, *f.* a fort on a rock, rock-fortress. —**fisch**, *m.* [a genus of fishes] teuthis [teuthis java]. —**föhre**, *f.* V. Alpenkiefer. —**fortsatz**, *m.* [in anatomy] the apophysis of the petrous bone. —**gang**, *m.* gallery cut in a rock. —**gebirge**, *n.* a chain of rocky mountains. —**geklüft**, *n.* chasms or clefts in rocks. —**gestade**, *n.* a rocky shore. —**gestalt**, *f.* 1) the form of a rock. 2) a petrified figure. —**gewinde**, *n.* the windings in the rocks. —**gewölbe**, *n.* a rocky vault, a grotto. —**grab**, *n.* a tomb formed by rocks. —**gruft**, *f.* a cavity in the rocks, a tomb or grave excavated in rocks. —**grund**, *m.* a rocky bottom, stony ground. —**hang**, *m.* a high and steep rock, a cliff. —**hart**, *adj.* and *adv.* very hard, rocky. *Fig.* Eine —harte Brust, a stony bosom. —**härte**, *f.* the hardness of a rock. —**haupt**, *n.* the top of a rock. —**haus**, *n.* 1) a house of rocks. 2) a cavern in rocks. —**herz**, *n.* *Fig.* a stony or flinty heart. —**himbeere**, *f.* V. —brombeere. —**höhe**, *f.* the height of a rock. —**höhle**, *f.* a cavern in a rock, a grotto. —**hügel**, *m.* a rocky hill. —**kehle**, *f.* a cavity in a rock. —**keller**, *m.* a cellar cut in rocks. —**kette**, *f.* a chain of rocks. —**klippe**, *f.* a high and steep rock, a cliff. —**kluft**, *f.* Felskluft. —**klumpen**, *m.* a heap of rocks. —**kräutchen**, *n.* V. Felsenmoos. —**kriecher**, *m.* a species of the wrasse or goldfinny [labrus rupestris]. —**krone**, *f.* the rocky crown of a mountain. —**labkraut**, *n.* a species of lady's-bed-straw growing on rocks. —**leer**, *adj.* and *adv.* rockless. —**leib**, *m.* *Fig.* a rocky body. —**masse**, *f.* a mass of rocks. —**muschel**, *f.* [in conch.] the furbelowed cha[m] —**nessel**, *f.* [in entom.] a species of [...] nettle. —**nest**, *n.* a nest built on a rock. *Fig.* a place or mansion on a rock, but especially an old castle perched on a rock. —**pfad**, *m.* a rocky, stony, rugged path. —**pforte**, *f.* 1) a gate made of rocks. 2) *Fig.* a small passage; a channel between rocks. —**quelle**, *f.* a well issuing from a rock. —**riedgras**, *n.* a species of sedge [carex saxatilis]. —**riff**, *n.* a reef. —**riß**, *m.* the cleft of a rock. —**ritze**, *f.* a crevice in a rock. —**rose**, *f.* rock-rose. —**rücken**, *m.* the ridge of a rock. —**salz**, *n.* a s[alt] found on walls sheltered from rain, as, salt-petre. —**schacht**, *m.* 1) a shaft sunk in a rock. 2) a deep cavern in rocks. —**schwalbe**, *f.* the rock-swallow. —**schwer**, *adj.* and *adv.* very heavy. —**spitze**, *f.* the top or point of a rock. —**stadt**, *f.* a town built on rocks. —**stein**, *m.* V. Felsstein. —**stirn**, *f.* 1) a front like a rock, a brazen face. 2) the brow of a rock. —**strauch**, *m.* the white-berried heath, and the black-berried heath. —**stück**, *n.* V. Felsstück. —**sturz**, *m.* a steep rock, a cliff, a precipice. —**tasche**, *f.* [a plant] the rock bastard-cress. —**taube**, *f.* rock-pigeon. —**thal**, *n.* a rocky vale. —**theil**, *m.* [in anatomy] V. —bein. —**wand**, *f.* a natural wall of rock, rock-work. —**werk**, *n.* [in mining] V. [...]mehl. —**ziege**, *f.* the wild she-goat. —**zw**[...], *m.* [in anatomy] the nervus communicans [...] or the portio dura of the moderns.

Felsern, [rather unusual] *adj.* and *adv.* composed of rocks [also in a fig. sense].

Felsicht, *adj.* and *adv.* resembling a rock. Ein —es Gebirge, a chain of rocky mountains. *Fig.* courageous, bold, daring.

Felsig, *adj.* and *adv.* full of rocks, rocky, stony, rugged. Ein —es Gestade, a rocky shore.

Felsit, *m.* [-en, *pl.* -en] V. Feldstein 3).

***Felucke**, *f.* [*pl.* -n] [a boat or vessel used in the Mediterranean] felucca.

||**Femel**, **Femmel**, *n.* [-s] V. Fimmel.

Fench, *m.* [-es] [allied to the Lat. *panic*[um]] Italian panic grass.

Fenchel, *m.* [-s] [allied to the Lat. *foeni*[cu]*lum*] [a plant] fennel or finckle.

Fenchel-apfel, *m.* V. Anisapfel. —**bl**[...]

me, *f.* fennel-flower. —gurke, *f.* pickled cucumber. —hirse, *f.* V. Fenchel. —holz, *n.* sassafras-tree. —öl, *n.* fennel-oil. —wasser, *n.* fennel-water.

Fenchgras, *n.* [-ses] V. Fench.

‖**Fenn**, *n.* [-es, *pl.* -en] **Fenne**, *f.* [*pl.* -n] [the Goth. *Fani*, as also the Ice. and A. S. *Fenn* signify a swamp] a fen, boggy land, a moor or marsh.

Fennbeere, *f.* European cranberry.

Fenster, *n.* [-s, *pl.* -] [Lat. *fenestra*, origin uncertain] 1) in general an opening. *a*) [in Script.] Und thaten sich auf die — des Himmels, and the windows of heaven were opened; *fig.* und finster werden die Gesichte durch die —, and those that look out of the windows [viz. eyes] be darkened. *b*) [in glassworks] an opening in the furnace. *c*) [in anatomy, a name for two holes in the barrel of the ear, next the drum, one of which is called ovalis, and the other rotunda] fenestra. *d*) [in common or familiar lang.] space unfilled in a writing, a blank. 2) an opening in the wall of a building for the admission of light, and of air when necessary, window. Zum — hinaussehen, to look out at the window; zu einem — gehörig, fenestral. *Fig.* *Aus hohen —n sehen, to carry it high; *das Geld zum — hinauswerfen, to expend money extravagantly or without necessity, to be prodigal of one's money. 3) [the sashes or frames with which windows are shut] window. Das — öffnen, to open the window; das — zumachen, to shut the window; ein kleines — in einem großen, a casement; das — auf Mistbeeten in Gärten, a garden-frame; mit —n versehen, to window.

Fenster-artig, *adj.* and *adv.* windowy. —austritt, *m.* a balcony. —band, *n.* the part of a hinge which is fixed on the casement. —bank, *f.* 1) window-sill, sill. 2) a frame of boards, a step or stair before a window. —bekleidung, *f.* the case of a window. —beschlag, *m.* —beschläge, *n.* iron-work of a window. —blei, *n.* glazier's lead [in which panes of glass are set for windows]. —bogen, *m.* the arched head-piece of a window-frame. —brett, *n.* 1) a board used by masons in making the lintel of a window-frame. 2) the breast-board of a window-frame. 3) a board to which curtains are attached. 4) a flowerstand fixed before the window. —brüstung, *f.* the lowest part of the sill. —einfassung, *f.* V. —bekleidung. —fach, —feld, *n.* a light or pane of glass. —flügel, *m.* a sash. Die —flügel, sashes, casements. —förmig, *adj.* and *adv.* [in entom.] fenestrate. —futter, *n.* case of a window. —geld, *n.* window-tax. —gewände, *n.* the side-pieces of a window. —giebel, *m.* [in archit., a member which serves as an ornament over windows] fronton, frontal. —gitter, *n.* the iron lattice of a window. —glas, *n.* window-glass. —haken, *m.* a hook at the munnions. —haspe, *f.* that part of a hinge which is fixed or inverted in the window-frame, a hook. —kette, *f.* a clasp fixed in a sash. —kissen, *n.* a window cushion. —kitt, *m.* [a kind of paste or cement, used in fastening glass in sashes] putty. —korb, *m.* the wooden lattice of a window. —kreuz, *n.* the munnions or mullions. —laden, *m.* a window-shutter. —lehne, *f.* V. —brüstung. ‖—lied, *n.* V. —laden. —los, *adj.* and *adv.* having no windows, without windows. Eine —lose Mauer, a dead wall. —nagel, *m.* a pin-nail used for fastening the curtains to a board. —öffnung, *f.* a bay for a window. —pfeiler, *m.* [a part of the wall of a house between windows] pier. —pfoste, *f.* V. —säule. —polster, *n.* V. —kissen. —rahm, —rahmen, *m.* window-frame. —rahmenband, *n.* the iron-work of a window-frame. —raute, *f.* a square of glass, a pane, [in commerce] a quarrel of glass. —reiber, *m.* the hasp of a casement, snacket, snecket. —riegel, *m.* sash-bolt. —säule, *f.* 1) prick-post or window-post. 2) pier. —scheibe, *f.* a pane of glass. Ein Fenster mit zwölf —scheiben, a window with twelve lights. —schirm, *m.* 1) window-blind. 2) Venetian window-blind. 3) V. —korb. —schmiege, *f.* [in architecture, the enlargement of the aperture of a window, on the inside of the wall for admitting more light] embrasure. —schwalbe, *f.* V. Hausschwalbe. —schweiß, *m.* the dew or moisture on windows. —seite, *f.* 1) the side-piece of a window. 2) the principal face of a building, the front of a house. —spiegel, *m.* 1) pier-glass. 2) a small looking-glass at the outside of a window. —spinne, *f.* V. Hausspinne. —sprosse, *f.* cross-bar of a window. —steuer, *f.* window-tax. —stock, *m.* V. —säule. —sturz, *m.* the head-piece of a window-frame, lintel. —thür, *f.* a glass-door. —vertiefung, *f.* V. —schmiege. —vorhang, *m.* [a cloth hanging at a window, intended for ornament, or for use] window-curtain. —wand, *f.* 1) the wall of a house or room which is furnished with windows. 2) V. —pfeiler. —wandspiegel, *m.* V. —spiegel 1. —wirbel, *m.* V. —reiber. —zarge, *f.* V. —futter. —zwickel, *m.* a triangular piece of glass between round panes of glass.

Fensterchen, ‖**Fensterlein**, *n.* [-s, *pl* -] a small window.

Fenstern, I. *v. tr.* to furnish with windows of glass, to window. Ein Haus —, to glaze a house. *Fig.* †Einen — [ausfenstern], to snub any one. II. *v. intr.* — gehen, to go and look in at the windows for one's sweet-heart.

‡**Fent**, *m.* [-es, *pl.* -e] [V. Fant] a man-servant, a man.

1\. **Ferch**, *m.* [-es, *pl.* -e] [from fahren?] [in mining] noxious exhalations issuing from mines or coal-pits, damps.

2\. **Ferch**, *m.* [-es, *pl.* -e] [V. Pferch] the excrement of animals, dung.

‖**Ferchen**, *v. tr.* to make ready, to expedite.

Ferdinand, [a name of men] [-s, *pl.* -e]. Ferdinand[o].

Ferding, *m.* [-es, *pl.* -e] [from vier, niederf. veer] the fourth part of a mark, a farthing.

‖**Ferge**, *m.* [-n, *pl.* -n] V. Fährmann.

*__Fergusonit__, *m.* [-en, *pl.* -en] [a mineral] fergusonite.

*__Ferien__, *pl.* days of exemption from labour, holidays, vacancies. Schul—, vacations.

Ferkel, **Ferklein**, [allied to Farr, Bär, to the Lat. *porcus*] *n.* [-s, *pl.* -] a young pig, ‖far.

Ferkel-kaninchen, *n.* agouty, long-nosed cavy. —kraut, Ferkleinskraut, *n.* 1) common knot-grass. 2) least hyoseris. 3) the hypocheris.

Ferkeln, *v. intr.* 1) [originally] to farrow, to pig. 2) † *Fig.* *a*) to behave filthily, nastily or dirtily. *b*) to act or to speak obscenely.

*__Ferm__, *adj.* and *adv.* [mostly in common or vulgar lang.] 1) firm, constant, steady. ‖2) ready, dexterous, skilful, expert.

*__Fermate__, *f.* [*pl.* -n] [in music] a general stop or pause.

*__Ferment__, *n.* [-es] ferment.

*__Fermentation__, *f.* fermentation [in a proper as well as in a fig. sense].

*__Fermentiren__, *v. intr.* to ferment, to work, to effervesce [in a proper as well as in a fig. sense].

Fern, [**Ferne**] [allied to vor, to the Lat. *porro*, Gr. πόῤῥω] *adj.* and *adv.* [separated by a wide space from the place where one is] far, distant. Ein —es Land, a far, remote or distant country; die Völker nah und —, the nations near and far; — von der Stadt, far from the town, at a great distance from town; — von Hause, far from home; fort! und halt' dich —, hence! and stand aloof! sich — halten, to keep aloof; sich — halten von Spielern, to avoid the company of gamesters; [in poetry] — dem Vaterlande, far from one's country; von —, from far, from afar. *Fig.* Jeder ist geneigt zu glauben, daß die Zeit seines Todes noch — sey, every man is apt to think the time of his dissolution remote; in —er Zeit, at a distant period; — sey es von mir, Grausamkeiten zu rechtfertigen, far be it from me to justify cruelties. As an *adv.* it is joined to in, so, wo, wie, so—, in so—, and then used as a conjunction, as, ich werde Ihnen helfen in so— ich es kann, I shall help you as far as I can; sometimes so— is used instead of wenn, as, so— es dir gefällt, if you are pleased with it; so— Johann kömmt, so &c., if John shall arrive &c.; wie— or in wie— is used in interrogatories, as, ich weiß nicht in wie— das wahr ist, I don't know how far it is true; it is also used in the compound words, dafern, sofern, wiefern, if.

Fern-ansicht, *f.* a view of objects from a distance, perspective. —berühmt, *adj.* and *adv.* far-famed. —darstellung, *f.* 1) [the act of drawing on a plane surface true resemblances or pictures of objects, as the objects appear to the eye from any distance or situation, real and imaginary] perspective. Die Regeln der —darstellung, the rules of perspective. 2) [a representation of objects in perspective] perspective. —getön, *n.* sounds from a distance. —glas, *n.* 1) a perspective, a spyglass, a telescope. 2) an eye-glass. —her, *adv.* from afar. —hin, *adv.* to a distance. —hintreffer, *m.* the farshooting-god [Apollo]. —ländisch, *adj.* and *adv.* belonging to a distant country, coming from a distant country, foreign. —meßkunde, *f.* perspective, the science of perspective. —rohr, *n.* V. —glas 1). —saulig, *adj.* and *adv.* [in architecture]. Ein —sauliges Gebäude, an areostyle. —schaulich, *adj.* and *adv.* perspectively. —schein, *m.* the appearance of objects in perspective. —scheinig, *adj.* and *adv.* perspective. —scheinlehre, *f.* [in painting] [the art of representing objects in perspective] perspective. —scheinlehrig, *adj.* and *adv.* perspective —schön, *adj.* and *adv.* handsome at a distance. —schreibekunst, *f.* telegraphic art. —schreiber, *m.* a person that practices the telegraphic art. —schrift, *f.* signals for communicating intelligence from a distance, telegraphic signals. —sicht, *f.* V. —ansicht. Man genießt von diesem Berge einer reizenden —sicht, one can enjoy a fine prospect from this mountain. —sichtig, *adj.* and *adv.* able to see far, long-sighted. —sichtigkeit, *f.* presbyopia. —spiegel, *m.* a telescope. —treffend, *adj.* and *adv.* far-shooting. —treffer, *m.* the far-shooting god [Apollo]. —zeichnung, *f.* V. —darstellung.

Fernambuck, *m.* [-es] brazil, brazil-wood, or braziletto.

Fernambucks-auszug, *m.* a tincture of brazil. —holz, *n.* V. Fernambuck. —papier, *n.* paper dyed red with brazil.

‖**Fernd**, *adv.* last year.

‖**Ferndig**, *adj.* of or from the last year. —er Wein, wine of the last year; der —e Schnee, last year's snow.

Ferne, *f.* [*pl.* -n] 1) farness, distance, remoteness. *Fig.* *a distant time. Das ist noch weit in der — or in weiter —, that is yet very remote; [hence] very uncertain. 2) distant places or objects. Die —n, [with painters] remotenesses.

Fernen, I. *v. tr.* [rather unusual] to remove to a distance. Sich —, to remove. II. *v. intr.* 1) [rather unusual] [u. w. seyn] to be removed. 2) [u. w. haben] to appear fair or handsome at a distance. Sie fernet, she looks beautiful or handsome only at a distance.

Ferner, *m.* V. Firner.

Ferner, *adj.* and *adv.* [comparative of fern] farther, further. Ein —er Grund für diese Meinung, a further reason for this opinion; welche Maßregeln — ergriffen werden, ist ungewiß, what ulterior measures will be adopted is uncertain; was — verhandelt wurde, weiß ich nicht, what was subsequently transacted, I don't know; bekümmern Sie sich nicht — darum, take no further care of it; und so —, and so on, and so forth, or et cetera; [sometimes it is used as a conjunction] — sollten die Gesetze verständig seyn, furthermore the laws should be judicious; er sagte — zu mir, he said further to me.

Ferner=hin, *adv.* for the future, henceforward. ||—**weit**, *adj.* and *adv.* V. Ferner.

||**Fernig**, *adj.* and *adv.* V. Fernd and Ferndig.

Fernung, *f.* 1) the act of removing to a distance. 2) state of being distant in space, remoteness.

||**Ferresbeere**, *f.* V. Berberisbeere.

1. **Ferse**, *f.* V. Färse.

2. **Ferse** and **Ferse**, *f.* [*pl.* -n] [appears to be allied to Fährte from fahren = gehen] 1) [the hind part of the foot] heel. Einem auf den —n nachfolgen, to be at any one's heels; *die —n geben or —geld geben, to show the heels, to take to the heels. * *Fig.* Er reicht ihm in der Gelehrsamkeit nicht an die —n, he is far from equalling him in learning. 2) [that part of a stocking intended for the heel] heel.

Fersegeflügelt, *adj.* and *adv.* winged at the heels. Der —geflügelte Merkur, winged-heeled Mercury.

Fersen=befiederung, *f.* wings at the heels. —**bein**, *n.* [in anatomy] the heel-bone. —**flechse**, *f.* [in anatomy] tendon-Achilles. —**geld**, *n.* [in common lang.] —geld geben, to show the heels, to take to the heels, to betake to flight. —**höcker**, *m.* [in anatomy] a protuberance or knob on the heel-bone. —**leder**, *n* the hind part of a shoe, heel, [with shoemakers] quarter, quarter-piece of a shoe. —**punkt**, *m.* V. Fußpunkt.

Fertig, *adj.* and *adv.* [from fahren = sich bewegen &c.] ready, prepared. — machen, to make ready, to prepare, to provide and put in order; sich zur Abreise — machen, to prepare for one's departure; sich — halten, to be ready; ich bin —, I am ready; also in the compound words, marsch—, ready for marching; reise—, ready for the journey; segel—, ready to sail, ready for sea, &c. *Fig. a*) quick in action or execution, ready. Sehr —, Befehle zu ertheilen, very prompt in giving orders; ein —er Schreiber, a ready writer; eine —e Hand, a dexterous hand; — lesen, reden, to read, to speak fluently; eine —e Zunge, a fluent tongue; ein —er Spieler [on a musical instrument], one who plays with execution; sie singt —, she sings with great facility. *b*) willing, disposed, ready. — zum Wohlthun, ready to do others good; also in composition, as, buß—, penitent; dienst—, kind, obliging; fried—, peaceable, peaceful, &c *c*) finished. Eine —e Arbeit, a finished piece of workmanship. *d*) = come or coming to an end. Ich kann damit nicht — werden, I cannot finish it; *ich getraue mir, bald mit ihm — zu werden, I hope to finish with him speedily, or I hope to bring him to reason; er ist mit seinem Vermögen —, he has spent all his fortune; *er ist —, he is ruined, *it.* he is past recovery; nun bin ich —, now I have done; ich würde nicht — werden, wenn ich klagen wollte, I would never have done complaining.

Fertig=machen, *n.* 1) the act of making things ready or of preparing one's self. 2) [with letter founders] the adjusting of letters or types. —**macher**, *m.* 1) a finisher. 2) [in glassworks] the first workman

Fertigen, I. *v. tr.* 1) to form by art and labour, to make, to fabricate. Ein Werk —, to make a work; ein Bild —, to paint a resemblance. V. Verfertigen. 2) to execute, to discharge, to do. V. Ausrichten 3) V. Abfertigen 4) to dispatch, to expedite. V. Ausfertigen. ||5) = unterzeichnen. Der Gefertigte, the undersigned. II. *v. r.* sich —, to prepare one's self, to get ready; *it.* to hasten to a place.

Fertiger, *m.* [-s, *pl.* -] 1) maker. ||2) V. [the more usual word] Spediteur.

Fertigkeit, *f.* 1) readiness, quickness, promptness, promptitude, facility. — im Reden, readiness of speech. 2) readiness proceeding from skill or use, ease of performance, habitual facility of performance, dexterity. Unser Schriftsteller macht mit großer — Anmerkungen, our author has a great knack at remarks; dies ist ihm schon zur — geworden, that has become quite familiar to him; — [im Spielen], execution [in playing on musical instruments]; sich nützliche —en erwerben, to acquire dexterity in many things.

Fertigung, *f.* 1) the act of making or performing. V. Verfertigung. 2) security.

Fertigungs=brief, *m.* 1) a bond. 2) a deed concerning the land-marks. —**gebühr**, *f.* [in law] clerk's fees for drawing up the deed of feoffment.

Feser, *m.* V. Fächser.

Fessel, *f.* [*pl.* n] [from fassen] 1) a slender strip of leather or other like substance, used for fastening or tying things. V. Hornfessel, Wurffessel. 2) formerly that part of the belt in which a sword was hung. 3) [more commonly] fetter, chain [chiefly used in the plural]. Einem —n anlegen, Einen in —n schlagen, legen, to put any one in fetters, to fetter, to chain, or to shackle any one; in —n, enchained. *Fig.* Die —n der Liebe tragend, fettered in amorous chains; den Leidenschaften —n anlegen, to bind passions in fetters; der sein Vaterland in —n schlug, who chained his country; dem gesunden Menschenverstande —n anlegen, to put shackles upon good sense; selbst sein Wille scheint in Banden und —n zu liegen, his very will seems to be in bonds and shackles. 4) [in horses] the pastern.

Fessel=ader, *f.* a name given to the veins in the pastern. —**beladen**, *adj.* and *adv.* bound by fetters, fettered. —**frei**, *adj.* and *adv.* free from fetters or restraint, fetterless. —**gelenk**, *n.* pastern joint. —**geschwür**, *n.* V. Durchfäule. —**haare**, *pl.* fetlock. —**los**, *adj.* and *adv.* free from fetters or restraint, fetterless. —**wund**, *adj.* and *adv.* 1) wounded or hurt by fetters. 2) galled in the pastern.

Fesseln, *v. tr.* to bind in fetters, to confine the feet with a chain, to fetter, to chain, to shackle. Einen Verbrecher —, to shackle a criminal; gefesselt, enchained; ein Pferd —, to fetter a horse. *Fig.* Sie hat ihn gefesselt, she has enchained or captivated him, she engaged his affections; ich weiß nicht, was mich an sie fesselt, I don't know, what attaches me to her; er wußte ihn sehr an sich zu —, he contrived to attach him greatly to his person; er hat den Sieg an seinem[n] Wagen gefesselt, he has chained victory to his car; die Tugend fesselt alle Herzen, virtue attaches all hearts; die Unterhaltung fesselte uns, we were charmed with the conversation; die Aufmerksamkeit —, to engage or attract the attention; sein Wille scheint gefesselt zu seyn, his will seems to be in shackles.

Fest, [allied to fassen; also in Persian besten signifies befestigen] *adj.* and *adv.* 1) firm, solid [as opposed to fluid or liquid]. —e Körper, solid bodies; das —e Land, firm land, [in geography] a continent. *Fig. a*) not easily subdued or taken. Ein —es Schloß, eine —e Stadt, a strong castle, a strong town; die Feinde zogen sich in ihre —en Plätze zurück, the enemy retired to his fastnesses. *b*) of long continuance, lasting. Ein —er Körper, a solid constitution of body, a sound or strong constitution; eine —e Gesundheit, sound health; eine —e Freundschaft, firm friendship. *c*) close, as sleep, deep, sound. Ein —er Schlaf, a fast sleep, sound sleep; — schlafen, to be fast asleep. *d*) incapable of receiving injury, invulnerable. Sich — machen, to make one's self invulnerable by spell. *e*) strong, valiant [used only as a title of honour] Fester, Lieber und Getreuer, most valiant, well-beloved and feal! 2) closely compressed, compact. —es Holz, hard wood; eine —e Mauer, a solid wall; ein —er Pfeiler, a solid pier; die Theile eines Pfeilers — untereinander verbunden, the parts of a pier solidly united; — zusammenhängende Theilchen eines Stoffes, particles of matter firmly adhering; —er Boden, a solid ground; —es Fleisch, firm or hard flesh; ein —es Gewebe, a firm texture; [in botany] eine —e Zwiebel, a solid bulb; ein —er Stengel, a solid stem; ein —er Strunk, a solid stalk. 3) firmly fixed, closely adhering, fast. Der die Berge — setzet in seiner Kraft, [in Script.] who, by his strength, setteth fast the mountains; der Leim hält —, glue sticks close; der Rock sitzt —, the coat sits close to the body; Einen — binden, to bind any one fast; ein Seil — machen, to make fast a rope; einen Strick an einem Haken — machen, to fix a cord to a hook; ein Segel — machen, [to wrap or roll a sail close to the yard, stay or mast, and fasten it with gaskets] to hand or furl a sail; ein Tau — machen, to belay a rope [to fasten it by winding it round a cleat, kevil or belaying-pin]; Schiffe in einem Hafen — machen, to make a ship fast; die Kanonen — machen [in seamen's lang.] to house the guns; halte —, take fast hold; die Thür — zumachen, to shut fast the door; sich die Ohren — zuhalten, to stop one's ears; in or im Koth — stecken, to stick fast in mire; einen Wagen im Kothe — fahren, to stall a carriage; —er machen, to tighten, to draw tighter, to make more close in any manner; eine —e Hand, a steady hand [in popular language] a set price; einen Dieb — machen, — nehmen, to put a thief into a prison, to imprison a thief. *Fig.* Sich — essen or trinken, to be detained in custody in an inn for want of money to pay one's reckoning; eine —e Besoldung, a settled salary; eine —e Regel, an established rule; eine Sprache auf —e Regeln zurückführen, to settle a language; ein Mann von —en Grundsätzen, a man of stable principles; ein —er Charakter, a stable character; es ist unser —er Vorsatz, 'tis our firm intent; eine —e Ueberzeugung, a firm persuasion; er glaubt — an den göttlichen Ursprung der heil. Schrift, he believes firmly in the divine origin of the Scriptures; glaubet — daß &c., steadfastly believe that &c.; sein Entschluß steht —, his resolution is firmly fixed; ein —es Vorhaben, a settled purpose; er hält — an seiner Partei, he firmly adheres to his party; eine — gegründete Regierung, a government stably settled; dem widerstehet — im Glauben, [in Script.] him resist stedfast in the faith; etwas steif und — behaupten, to maintain a thing stiffly; steif und — bei seiner Meinung beharren, to be firmly or unduly adhering to one's own opinion; sich an einem Orte — setzen, to settle in any place; die Belgier setzten sich auf der südlichen Küste Britanniens —, the Belgians settled on the southern coast of Britain; ohne einen —en Wohnsitz, without a settled abode; sich in einer Kunst — setzen, to acquire skill in any art; er sucht sich in der Musik — zusetzen, he exercises himself in music.

Fest-drücken, *v. tr.* to squeeze hard, to press fast. —**halten**, *v. tr.* to arrest, to take or lay hold fast. —**land**, *n.* continent. Es reisen immer viele Engländer auf dem europäischen —lande, there are always many Englishmen travelling on the European continent. —**setzen**, I. *v. tr.* 1) to settle, to appoint. Eine Zeit — setzen, to appoint a time; zur — gesetzten Stunde erscheinen, to appear at the set hour, fixed hour; — gesetzte Arbeitsstunden, stated hours of business. 2) to fix or establish by grant, gift or any legal act. Der — gesetzte Gehalt, a stated salary. 3) to settle, to fix, to establish. Die Thronfolge — setzen, to settle the succession to a throne II. *v. r.* sich —, to adhere closely, to stick. V. Ansetzen. *Fig.* Der Gedanke an Rache hat sich in seiner Seele — gesetzt, he harbours a thought of revenge. —**setzer**, *m.* appointer. —**stehen**, *n.* steadfastness, fixedness in place. —**stellen**, *v. tr.* to place firmly, to fix.

Fést, *n.* [-es, *pl.* -e] [Lat. *festum*] 1) a feast or festival. Das Pfingst—, the feast of Pentecost; bewegliche —e, movable feasts [as Easter &c.]; unbewegliche —e, immovable feasts [as Christmas-day &c.]; ein Freuden—, an anniversary day of joy; das Hochzeits—, wedding-feast; das Namens—, fête-day; das Geburts- or Wiegen—, birthday; die Morgen-Trompeten verkündeten das —, the morning trumpets the festival proclaimed; ein — feiern, to hold a feast. 2) [a sumptuous entertainment, particularly a rich or splendid public entertainment] a feast. 3) [social joy or exhilaration of spirits at an entertainment] festivity. *Ein — or sein — mit jemand haben, to make sport of any one.

Fest-abend, *m.* the eve or evening before any feast, vigil. —**abschnitt**, *m.* V. —tagsabschnitt. —**altar**, *m.* an altar adorned on a holiday. —**einzug**, *m.* a festival entry. —**geläute**, *n.* a ringing of bells on a holiday. —**gesang**, *m.* a festive song. —**gewand**, *n.* a holiday garment. —**kleid**, *n.* V. —gewand. —**lied**, *n.* a festive song. —**mahl**, *n.* a festival entertainment. —**opfer**, *n.* a sacrifice or offering on a festival, oblation. —**ordnung**, *f.* feast-rite. —**prediger**, *m.* a priest who preaches on holidays. —**predigt**, *f.* a sermon on holidays. —**rechnung**, *f.* the computation of feasts —**schmaus**, *m.* a festival entertainment, a banquet. —**schmuck**, *m.* a holiday attire. —**stille**, *f.* the stillness of a holiday. —**tag**, *m.* 1) a holiday or festival. 2) a feastful day. —**täglich**, *adj.* and *adv.* festival. Eine — tägliche Kleidung, a holiday suit of clothes. —**tagsabschnitt**, *m.* a passage from the Gospel, as a lesson in divine service. —**tagskleid**, *n.* V. —kleid. —**tagsprediger**, *m.* V. —prediger. —**tagspredigt**, *f.* V. —predigt.

Féste, *f.* [*pl.* -n] 1) [the state of being fast and firm] fastness, firmness, solidity. 2) a firm, hard or solid thing, as, in mining, a huge and strong rock. 3) a strong-hold, a fortress or fort, a place fortified, a castle, a fastness. 4) *Fig.* Die — des Himmels, [in Scripture] the firmament.

Fésten, Féstigen, *v. tr* 1) to make more close or compact. Einen Körper —, to condense a body. *Fig. a*) to make certain, to put beyond hazard or doubt, to make firm, to confirm, to settle. Einen Wechsel —, [in commerce] to cause a bill of exchange to be accepted by the drawee. ‖ *b*) to accept as a feud. 2) to arrest and to banish.

Féstigen, V. Festen.

Féstigkeit, *f.* [the state of being fast and firm] fastness, firmness, solidness, solidity, compactness. Die — des Holzes, eines Steines, the firmness of wood, the compactness of a stone; die — einer Mauer, the solidity of a wall. *Fig.* Die — der Gesundheit, the soundness of health; die — seiner Leibesbeschaffenheit, the strength of his constitution; die — eines Entschlusses, the firmness of a resolution; die — eines Mannes, oder seines Muthes, the firmness of a man, or of his courage; die — des Gemüths, firmness of mind; die — der Grundsätze, the solidness or solidity of principles.

‡**Féstiglich**, *adv.* V. Fest.

***Féstin**, [pron. as in the French] *n.* [- or -s, *pl.* -s] V. Fest 2, Festmahl, Gastmahl.

***Festivität**, *f.* festivity.

Féstlich, *adj.* and *adv* 1) festive, festival. Ein —es Kleid, a holiday garment; ein —es Mahl, a festival entertainment, banquet. 2) marked with pomp or solemnities, solemn Ein —er Tag, a solemn day; ein —er Aufzug, a solemn procession.

Féstlichkeit, *f.* 1) the quality of being festive or solemn. Die — des Tages, the awfulness of the day. 2) a feast, or festival 3) [a ceremony adapted to impress awe] solemnity. V. Feierlichkeit.

***Festón**, [by some pronounced as in the French] *m.* [- or -s, *pl.* -s] a garland or wreath, [in architecture] an ornament of carved work in the form of a wreath of flowers, fruits and leaves intermixed or twisted together, festoon.

Féstung, *f.* 1) [in this sense more usual Festigung] the act of fortifying. 2) any fortified place, a fort, a stronghold, a fortress. Eine starke —, a strong fortress; eine kleine —, [fort] a fortlet; eine — anlegen, to fortify a place; eine — belagern, stürmen, to besiege, to storm a fortress; eine — schleifen, to raze a fortress. 3) a fortress or castle, in or near a city, intended for its defence, a citadel. 4) [in conchol.] a species of limpet [patella granatina].

Festungs-achat, *m.* a sort of agate variegated with veins that form the figure of a fortified place. —**arrest**, *m.* arrest in a fortress. —**bau**, *m.* 1) the act of fortifying, fortification. 2) the working at fortifications [as, er wurde zum —bau verurtheilt, he was condemned to (hard) labour (work) at the fortifications, a punishment]. —**bauamt**, *n* the office intrusted with the fortification of places. —**baukunst**, *f.* [the art or science of fortifying places] fortification, military architecture. —**gefangene**, *m.* a criminal condemned to work at fortifications —**pfahl**, *m.* V. Schanzpfahl. —**strafe**, *f.* confinement in a fortress, as punishment. —**wall**, *m.* wall[s] of a fortress. —**werk**, *n.* a work erected to defend a place against attack. Die —werke von Dünkirchen, the fortifications of Dunkirk.

Fétisch, *m.* [-es, *pl.* -e] [an African idol] a fetich.

Fetisch-anbeter, *m.* a worshipper of fetichs. —**dienst**, *m.* fetichism, feticism.

Fétt, [is generally supposed to come from fòden = nähren, but the original signification seems to have been glänzend] *adj.* and *adv.* ‖ 1) smeared or defiled with grease, greasy. —e Kleider, greasy clothes. 2) defiled, foul, dirty, soiled. —e Wäsche, foul linen; —e Hände, dirty hands. 3) [abounding with an oily concrete substance] fat, greasy, oily, unctuous Eine —e Brühe, a fat sauce; —e Speisen, fat meats; ein —er Teig, rich pastry; —e Milch, creamy milk; —e Butter, fat butter; —er Käse, fat cheese; sich — machen, to soil one's self with grease, to make one's self greasy; juicy, succulent [used of plants]; die —e Henne, [a plant] orpine. *Fig.* like grease or oil, greasy. Ein Miner, — anzufühlen, a fossil that has a greasy feel. 4) [the contrary to lean] fat. Ein —er Ochse, a fat ox; ein junges —es Thier, a fatling; eine —e Gans, a fat goose; er hat einen —en Bauch, he has a fat belly; —e Bienen, bees whose combs are filled with honey; [jocosely, of men] ein —er [wohlbeleibter] Herr, a fat gentleman. *Prov.* Das Auge des Herrn macht das Pferd —, the master's eye makes the horse fat. *Fig. a*) fat = rich, fertile. Ein —er Boden, a fat soil. *b*) fat = rich, nourishing. Eine —e Weide, fat or rich pasture. *c*) fat = rich, producing a large income. Eine —e Pfründe, a fat benefice. *d*) rich in provisions, abounding with a variety of food. Eine —e Küche, good cheer. *e*) fat = rich, wealthy. *f*) [with painters and engravers] thick, large. — malen, to lay on colours amply; —e Züge, large strokes.

Fétt, *n.* [-es] fat, [animal fat in a soft state] grease. — ansetzen, to grow fat or corpulent; **fig.* er legt sich — an, he fattens; Schweine—, hog's lard; Gänse—, goose-grease; Nieren—, suet; das von einem Braten abtropfende —, dripping; einen Braten mit — begießen, to baste meat in roasting; das — abschöpfen, to skim fat; *Fig.* † & *Prov.* Einen mit seinem eignen —e begießen, to pay any one in his own coin.

Fett-ader, *f.* [in anatomy] the adipose or adipous vein. —**ammer**, *f.* the ortolan. —**auge**, *n.* 1) [in medicine, a protuberance of the eye out of its natural position] exophthalmia. 2) a globule of fat on broth or any other liquor. —**bauch**, *m.* a fat belly. *Fig.* [especially in contempt] a corpulent person. —**bäuchig**, *adj.* and *adv.* having a fat belly. —**bruch**, *m.* [in medicine, a swelling of the scrotum, containing fat] steatocele. —**darm**, *m.* V. Afterdarm. —**feder**, *f.* [in birds, especially in geese] one of the feathers which cover the rump. —**fell**, *n.* [in medicine, a disease of the eye] albugo, leucoma. —**finne**, *f.* 1) [in fishes] fleshy dorsal fin. 2) a pustule or spot in the flesh of animals, especially of swine. —**flecken**, *m.* a spot of grease. —flecken in die Kleider machen, to grease one's clothes. —**gang**, *m.* [in anatomy] adipose duct. —**gans**, *f.* penguin or great auk. —**gar**, *adj.* and *adv.* [with leather-dressers] dressed with oil. —gares Leder, V. Sämischleder. —**gesäuert**, *adj.* and *adv.* [in chimistry] V. —säure. —**glanz**, *m.* a faint or dull lustre. —**haut**, *f.* Die —haut auf der Milch, the fat or oily part of the milk, the cream part of the milk; [in anatomy] the adipose membrane. —**käfer**, *m.* V. Speckkäfer. —**klumpen**, *m.* a lump of fat. *Fig.* [mostly in contempt] a very corpulent man. —**kohle**, *f.* V. Glanzkohle. —**kram**, *m.* a dealing in fat or greasy goods [as oil, tallow, butter &c.]. —**krämer**, *m.* a dealer in fat or greasy goods. —**krankheit**, *f.* a kind of disease in silkworms, swelling. —**kraut**, *n.* butterwort. —**loch**, *n.* a sort of sack or bag in badgers. —**magen**, *m.* [the fourth stomach of a ruminating beast] the maw. ‡—**männchen**, *n.* a small coin in value three farthings. —**markt**, *m.* a market where butter, lard, oil &c. are exposed to sale. —**masse**, *f.* a mass of fat. *Fig.* a fat man. —**noppen**, *n.* [with clothiers] a viewing or examining of cloth after burling. —**nopper**, *m.* [with clothiers] a person that views or inspects cloth after burling. —**pfründe**, *f.* a fat benefice. —**pfründner**, *m.* one who holds a fat benefice. —**rahmig**, *adj.* and *adv.* containing fat cream. —**sauer**, *adj.* and *adv.* [in chimistry] sebacic. —saures Kali, sebate of potash; —saures Quecksilber, sebate of mercury; —saure Salze, sebates. —**säure**, *f.* [in chimistry] the sebacic acid. —**schmelzen**, *n.* [a distemper in horses] molten-grease.—**schwanz**, *m.* the fat tail of a species of sheep in Asia and in Africa. —**speiser**, *m.* V. —krämer. —**stein**, *m.* [a mineral] nephelin, nepheline. —**thon**, *m.* fuller's earth. —**waare**, *f.* fat, greasy or oily goods, as, oil, butter, lard, suet &c. —**wanst**, [in joke or contempt] *m.* fat guts. —**wanstig**, *adj.* and *adv.* big-bellied. —**wasser**, *n.* water in which wool has been scoured. —**weide**, *f.* fat pasture. —**wolle**, *f.* [in husbandry] wool in the yolk. —**wurm**, *m.* V. Speckwurm. —**zelle**, *f.* [diminut. das —zellchen]. Die —zellen, [in anatomy] adipous cells.

1. **Fette**, *f.* 1) fatness, greasiness, oiliness, unctuosity, unctuousness. Die — des Leibes, fatness of body. 2) a fat substance, fat.

2. **Fette**, *f.* [*pl.* -n] [perhaps allied to fassen, Isl. *fitjan*] [in architecture, = Dach—, Dachstuhl—, Stuhl—] purlin.

Fetten, *v. tr.* 1) to make fat, to fatten [an ox &c.] Den Fraß der Hunde —, [with hunters] to put grease into the food of dogs. 2) to smear with grease or fat, to grease. Die Haare —, to pomatum the hair; die Wolle —, [with clothiers] to oil wool.

Fetticht, *adj.* & *adv.* like grease or oil, greasy, smooth. Ein —er Stoff, a fatty substance; der Thon fühlt sich — an, clay has a greasy feel; eine —e Oberfläche, a smooth surface.

Fettig, *adj.* and *adv.* fat, greasy, oily, unctuous. Sich — machen, to besmear one's self with grease or fat; —e Hände, greasy hands.

Fettigkeit, *f.* 1) [the quality of being fat] fatness. Die — eines Ochsen, the fatness of an ox. *Fig.* Die — des Bodens, the fatness or richness of the soil. 2) a fat substance, a fat or oily matter. Die — des Oelbaumes, [in Scripture] the olive-oil.

Fettlich, *adj.* and *adv.* fattish.

Fettung, *f.* 1) the act of fattening. 2) a fat, oily, or unctuous substance, a globule of fat on any liquor, the fat or oily part on milk.

Fetzchen, ||**Fetzlein**, *n.* [-s, *pl.* -] [diminut. of Fetzen].

Fetzen, *m.* [-s, *pl.* -] [allied to fitzen = hauen, and perhaps to the Lat. findo, *fiss*-um] a long and narrow piece cut off, or a part torn and hanging to the thing. Die —, shreds, shreddings, tatters; in — reißen, schneiden, hauen, to rend or tear into rags, to shred, to cut into pieces, to chop; ein Kleid in —, a tattered garment; ein — Brod, Fleisch, a cut of bread, a small piece of meat, scrap.

Fetzen, *v. tr.* to rend or tear into rags, to shred. In den Zeug —, to slash a stuff, to shred it; mit dem Degen —, to scratch the surface of any thing with the edge of a sword; || and †*fig.* einem Kinde den Hintern — [|| fitzen], to breech a child.

Fetzer, *m.* [-s, *pl.* -] 1) [unusual] a person that rends or tears into rags, that shreds. 2) [rather unusual] an instrument for cutting or shredding. || and † Ein —, a sword. 3) a whipping on the breech. Einem Kinde einen — geben, to breech a child. || and † 4) the lower part of the body behind, the breech. Einem den — voll hauen, to breech any one soundly.

Fetzig, *adj.* and *adv.* hanging in rags, ragged, tattered.

||**Fetzlein**, V. Fetzchen.

Feucht, [allied to the old Scandinav. *fuki*, Dunst] *adj.* and *adv.* humid, moist, damp, wettish. Diese Betttücher sind noch —, these sheets are still damp; ein —es Zimmer, a damp room; —es Stroh, muggy straw; die —e Luft, a humid or moist air; —e Dünste, humid vapours; —es Wetter, wet weather; seine Augen sind von Thränen —, his eyes are wet with tears; —er Natur, phlegmatic; etwas —es, a moist or damp body.

Feucht-arsch, *m.* [in popular lang.] [a bird] the cormorant. —**brett**, *n* [in printing] paper-board. —**glied**, *n.* [with hunters] the pizzle. —**kalt**, *adj.* and *adv.* cold and damp. —**mulde**, *f.* [in printing] wetting-tray.

Feuchte, *f.* V. Feuchtigkeit.

Feuchte-messer, *m.* hygrometer. —**zeiger**, *m.* hygroscope, hygrometer [the latter is now chiefly used].

Feuchten, I. *v. tr.* to wet in a small degree, to moisten, to damp. Das Papier —, [in printing] to wet the paper. II. *v. intr.* 1) to emit moisture; to grow damp or moist. 2) [with hunters] to make water, to stale.

Feuchtheit, *f.* moistness, moisture.

Feuchtigkeit, *f.* 1) humidity, moistness, moisture, dampness. Die — der Luft, des Bodens, eines Tischtuches, the dampness of the air, of the ground, of a table-cloth. 2) moisture, humour. Die natürliche — eines Körpers, the radical moisture of a body; die —en im menschlichen Körper, the humours; die wässerichte — des Auges, aqueous humour of the eye.

Feuchtlich, *adj.* and *adv.* somewhat moist or wettish.

Feuchtniß, *f.* V. Feuchtigkeit 1).

***Feudal**, *adj.* and *adv.* feudal.

Feudal-recht, *n.* feudal-law. V. also Lehenrecht] —**succession**, *f.* V. Lehensfolge. —**system**, *n.* the feudal system, feudalism. V. also Lehenswesen.

***Feudalist**, *m.* [-en, *pl.* -en] feudist.

1. **Feuer**, *n.* [-s, *pl.* -] [allied to the Gr. πῦρ, to the Lat. *buro*, to the Ger. bern-en or brennen, and probably also to feucht, weben &c. V. 2 Feuer] 1) fire, [in chimistry] caloric [in the popular acception of the word, fire is the effect of combustion]. 2) [the burning of fuel on a hearth, or in any other place] fire. Das — brennt, the fire burns, blazes; — schlagen, to strike fire; — anzünden, machen, anmachen, to light, to kindle a fire; das — unterhalten, to maintain fire, to nourish the fire; das — schüren, to stir the fire; *fig.* das — der Zwietracht schüren, to fan the flame of discord; — fangen, to take fire, to ignite; — anlegen, to set on or to fire, to fire; die Stadt stehet in —, the town is all in flames; — fangen, to catch fire, to ignite, to fire. V. also *Fig. c*); das Haus stehet in —, the house is on fire; das Haus ist in — aufgegangen, the house has been destroyed by fire; das — geht aus, the fire goes out; das — löschen, auslöschen, to extinguish, to quench fire; in — setzen, [in chimistry] to ignite; im — arbeiten, [with blacksmith, chimists &c.] to work by fire; den Schiffsboden mit — unterfahren, [in seamen's language] to burn the filth of a ship's bottom; einen Verbrecher zum — verurtheilen, to sentence a criminal to fire; ein flammendes —, a blazing fire; unterirdisches —, subterraneous fire; der Berg speiet —, the mountain vomits fire; das — Gottes, [in Scripture] lightning; das höllische —, hell; Griechisches —, [an artificial or factitious fire which burns even under water] wild fire, Greek fire; V. —werk 2). [in farriery] einem Pferde das Englische — geben, to fire a horse; Oel in's — gießen, to cast oil in the fire; *fig.* to add fewel to the fire; für Einen durch's — laufen, [*fig.*] to go through fire and water to serve or do any one good. *Fig. a*) the quality of a substance that excites a sensation of heat. Dieser Wein hat viel —, this wine is very fiery. *b*) spirit, constitutional ardour, briskness, liveliness, sprightliness. Das — der Jugend, the mettle of youth; ein Pferd, das viel — hat, a mettlesome horse; ein Jagdhund, der zu vieles — hat, a hound that has too much mettle; mit aller Kraft, mit allem — der Beredsamkeit, with all the strength and heat of eloquence; er sprach mit vielem —, he spoke with great animation. *c*) ardour of temper, violence of passion, fire. — fangen, [chiefly in fam. lang.] to take fire, to fall into a passion; *it.* to fall in love; *Einen in — und Flammen setzen, to exasperate a person; *— und Flamme sprudeln, to fret and fume; das — der Einbildungskraft, heat or glow of imagination; das — der Liebe, the fire of love; der —eifer, the fire of zeal; mit —eifer, with a burning zeal, with glowing ardour. *d*) violence, rage. Das — des Krieges, the flames of war. *e*) [in Scripture] trouble, affliction. So du ins — gehest, sollst du nicht brennen, [in Script.] when thou walkest through the fire, thou shalt not burn. 3) [in a more limited sense] any burning substance or body, as, the discharge of fire-arms, fire. — geben, to fire; —! [a military term] fire! — an Backbord, an Steuerbord! [in seamen's lang.] fire to larboard, to starboard! ein lebhaftes —, a brisk fire; in's — gehen, to go into fire; diese Truppen gehen sehr kaltblütig in's —, these troops are very steady under fire; dem feindlichen — sehr ausgesetzt seyn, to be very much exposed to the enemy's fire; unter dem feindlichen —, in face of the enemy; das erste — aushalten, to abide the first charge; zwischen zwei — bringen, to inclose between two fires, to double upon [in familiar lang. sometimes used in a fig. sense]; eine Flotte zwischen zwei — bringen, to double a fleet. 4) [in seamen's language] *a*) a lighthouse, a beacon, light or lantern. Das — von Helgoland, the lighthouse on Heligoland. *b*) light, lantern. Das Schiff führt drei —, the ship carries three lights; — aufstecken, to show lights. 5) fire, light, lustre, splendour. Der Himmel war lauter —, the sky was all on fire; das — der Edelsteine, the brilliancy of precious stones; das — ihrer Augen, the fire of her eyes; seine Augen sprühten —, his eyes flashed. 6) redness of the face, heat, flush. Das — stieg ihm ins Gesicht, his face flushed; er war lauter — im Gesicht, his face burned, or was in a glow. *Fig.* an eruption of a fiery acrid humor, on some part of the body. Das heilige, das St. Anton's—, St. Anthony's fire, the erysipelas; das wilde —, [in swine] anticor; das heilige —, [a disease of sheep] wild-fire; das — or die —krankheit des Rindviehes, an inflammation of the blood in black cattle; das — der Pferde [die Darre], consumption.

Feuer-ader, *f.* a vein below the tail of black cattle. —**amt**, *n.* the office of one who superintends the firemen. —**anbeter**, *m.* a worshiper of fire, a fire-worshiper. —**anbetung**, *f.* the worship of fire, pyrolatry. —**anstalt**, *f.* an institution to prevent, or extinguish fire in towns, fire-office. —**anzeiger**, *m.* pyro-telegraph. —**arbeit**, *f.* any work performed by fire. —**arbeiter**, *m.* a workman who applies fire in his operations, as a locksmith, blacksmith &c. —**artig**, *adj.* and *adv.* renbling fire, igneous. —assekuranz (= ...ſhalt), *f.* V. —versicherung. —auge, *n.* fiery eye. —augig, *adj.* and *adv.* having ...ery eyes. —bach, *m.* a stream of fire. —...ahn, *f* a broad way in a forest intended to ...event the communication or the spreading ...f fire. —bake, *f* [in seamen's lang.] a beacon, light-house, light or lantern. —ball, —ballen, *m.* 1) V. —kugel. 2) the sun. —band, *m.* [with coopers] a hoop driven by ...ire. —baum, *m.* the juniper-tree. —becken, ..., a firepan. —beckenrichteisen, *n.* [with ...etallists] a kind of anvil. —berg, *m.* burn...g mountain, volcano. ||—beschau, *f* V. —schau. —beständig, *adj.* and *adv.* 1) fire-...roof. 2) [in natural philosophy, bearing a high ...at without evaporation or volatilization] fixed. —beständige Körper, fixed bodies. —beständigkeit, *f.* [in natural philosophy] fixedness. ...ie —beständigkeit des Goldes, the fixedness ...f gold. —bewaffnet, —bewappnet, ...j. and *adv.* armed with fire —bild, *n.* a ...ry image; *fig.* a glowing image. —blase, *f.* V. Brandblase. —blattern, *pl.* [in ...edicine] epinyctides [sores, so called because ...ey are particularly painful in the night]. —...lick, *m.* a fiery look. Der —blick der Sonne, ...e glow of the sun. —blume, *f.* corn or red ...ppy. —bock, *m.* an andiron, a dog. —...bohne, *f.* upright kidney-bean. —brand, ... 1) [a piece of wood kindled or on fire] fire-...and, firestick. *Fig.* Den —brand der Zwie...acht unter or zwischen sie werfen, to sow ...e seeds of dissension amongst them. 2) a ...nflagration or fire. —braun, *adj.* and *adv.* ...rnt or bronzed by the sun. —büchse, *f.* ... a tinder-box. 2) V. Büchse 2. or —rohr. —...bühne, *f.* [in mining] a pile of burning wood. —butzen, *m.* [in pyrotechnics] a small fireball. —diener, *m.* V. —anbeter. —dienst, *m.* ...rolatry. —dorn, *m.* [a plant] V. Mahlfuß...m. —drache, *m.* fire-drake. —dreieck, [with some astronomers] fiery triplicity [a triangle ...med in the heavens by the ram, the lion, and the ...gittary]. —ecke, *f.* rough edge, wire-edge [in ...new knives &c.]. —eifer, *m.* 1) glowing ardour, ...rning zeal. 2) [in Script.] burning wrath. —eimer, *m.* firebucket. ||—eisen, *n.* V. —stahl. —...essenamt, *n.* formerly a title or office in the ...rman empire, the office of the chief fireward ... firewarden. —esse, *f.* 1) a chimney. 2) a ...rge. —fach, *n.* that part of a cottage which ...ntains the hearth. —fächer, *m.* a fan [to ...e the fire]. —fahne, *f* an ensign used as a ...nal that a fire has broken out. —farb, —...rben, *adj.* and *adv.* flame-coloured. Ein —...färber, a flamecoloured horse. —farbe, *f.* ...me-colour, coquelicot, coquelico. —faß, *n.* ...e-tub. —fest, *adj.* and *adv.* 1) fire-proof. ... [in physics] —feste Körper, apyrous bodies. —flamme, *f.* 1) the flame of fire. 2) *Fig.* V. ...flöhchen. —flammen, *v. intr.* [u. w. haben] ...flame, to blaze. —flasche, *f.* a flask filled ...h powder and other combustibles, intended ...be thrown among enemies, and to injure by ...losion, [in seamen's language] powder-flask. —fließend, *adj.* and *adv.* ignifluous. —...ß, *m.* a stream of fire or a flood of lava. —flußstein, *m.* lava [when cool and hardened]. —fluth, *f.* a flood of fire. —folge, *f.* the ...y of citizens to aid firemen in extinguishing ... —fuchs, *m.* a sorrel-horse. —funken, ... a spark or sparkle. *Fig.* Seine Augen sprühen —funken, his eyes were sparkling. —gabel, ...refork, fruggin. —garbe, *f.* [in pyrotechnics] ...hinese tree. —gatter, *n.* a small rectan...ar grate in stoves formed of Dutch tiles. —...bend, *adj.* and *adv.* ignescent. —gebende ...teine, ignescent stones. —gebirge, *n.* ...ning mountains, volcanoes. —geist, *m.*

1) a fiery spirit. *Fig.* spirit [used of stimulating liquors]. Dieser Wein hat einen wahren —geist, this wine is very spirituous. 2) [in demonology] a spirit or demon inhabiting fire, a salamander. —geld, *n.* V. Herdgeld. —geräth, *n.* —geräthschaft, *f.* implements and engines used for extinguishing fire in towns; *it* [commonly] fire-tools. —geschoß, *n.* V. —gewehr. —geschrei, *n.* the cry of fire. —gewehr, *n.* a firelock. —gewehre, fire-arms. —gitter, *n.* fire-guard. —glanz, *m.* 1) the brightness of fire. 2) a bright dazzling light, a glare. —glast, *m* glare. —glocke, *f.* fire-bell, alarm-bell. —glut, *f.* the glow of fire. *Fig.* an intense glow. —gott, *m.* [the god of subterraneous fires] Vulcan. —grube, *f.* a hollow place in the earth encavated for holding fire. —haken, *m.* fire-hook. —hell, *adj.* and *adv.* bright, glaring, fiery. *Fig.* passionate, fiery. —hemde, *n.* 1) [in seamen's lang.] curtains [sailcloth overspread with combustibles to set ships on fire]. 2) a shirt or covering of the body made of asbestos, which prevents the wearer from being injured by the fire. —herd, *m.* a hearth or fireplace. —herr, *m.* ||1) an officer who has authority to direct others in the extinguishing of fires, fireward, firewarden. 2) [formerly a hereditary office of the German empire] chief fireward, or firewarden. —himmel, *m.* 1) the sky or firmament red or glaring like fire. *Fig.* [rather poet.] a fiery or very hot climate. Unter dem —himmel Afrika's, Ostindien's &c., under the burning skies of Africa, India &c. 2) the empyrean or empyreum. —holz, *n.* wood or fuel, firewood, firing. —hund, *m.* 1) a dog trained to fire 2) V. —bock. —hüter, *m.* [in mining] fire-watch. —käfer, *m.* V. Hirschkäfer. —kasse, *f.* fire-office. —katze, *f.* formerly a sort of cannon, a pederero. —kessel, *m.* [in mining] fire-kettle. —keule, *f.* [in pyrotechnics] fire-club. —kieke, *f.* foot-stove. —kiste, *f.* [in seamen's lang.] fire-trunk. ||—kluft, *f.* fire-tongs. —knäuel, *m.* [in milit. affairs] fire-clew. ||—knecht, *m.* a man servant whose charge is to extinguish fires in towns. —kopf, *m.* a fiery head, a fiery nature. —körper, *m.* an igneous body, as, the sun. —krankheit, *f.* a distemper in black cattle. V. — 6. *Fig.* —kranz, *m.* a fiery or burning garland. —kraut, *n.* the scarlet-tipp'd cup-lichen. —kreuz, *n.* [in ancient Scotland, as a sign of war] fire-cross. —krone, *f.* a bright or glaring crown. —kröte, *f.* the laughing toad. —krücke, *f.* fire-rake. —krug, *m.* V. —topf. —kübel, *m.* —kufe, *f.* V. —faß. —kugel, *f.* 1) fire-ball. 2) [a meteor which passes rapidly through the air and explodes] a fireball. 3) a ball filled with powder and other combustibles, as, grenades, fireballs &c. —kunst, *f.* pyrotechny. —künstler, *m.* pyrotechnist. —kuß, *m.* [rather poet.] a fiery kiss. —land, *n.* [in geography] Terra del Fuego. —länder, *m.* —länderinn, *f.* an inhabitant of the Terra del Fuego —ländisch, *adj.* and *adv.* belonging to the Terra del Fuego. —lanze, *f.* fire-arrow. —lärm, *m.* the cry of fire, an alarm of fire. —lärm machen, schlagen, [with soldiers] to sound or beat the alarm at the cry of fire. —läufer, *m.* a person in the country whose business is, to give notice in the neighbouring villages when a fire breaks out. —läuterung, *f.* purification by fire. —lehre, *f.* pyrology. —leiter, *f.* fire-ladder, fire-escape, [in popular lang. often used for] any long ladder. —liebe, *f.* [rather poet.] a fiery love. —lilie, *f.* bulb-bearing or orange lily. —loch, *n.* the mouth of a stove, oven &c. by which the fire is received. —los, *adj.* and *adv.* without fire or ardour. —löschungsanstalt, *f.* V. —anstalt. —luft, *f.* [in chimistry] oxygen or oxygen gas. —luke, *f.* [in seamen's lang.] fire-scuttle. —mahl, *n.*

1) a hurt or injury of the flesh caused by the action of fire, burn. 2) a brown spot or mark on the human body, a mole. —mahlerei, *f.* painting on glass or porcelain. —männchen, *n.* [in popular lang.] jack with a lantern, Jack o'lantern, Will o'the whisp, an ignis fatuus. —marter, *f.* fiery torture. —masse, *f.* a mass of fire. —mauer, *f.* 1) the shaft of a chimney, a funnel. chimney. 2) a party-wall. —mauerkehrer, *m.* chimney-sweeper. —meer, *n.* a flood of fire, a sea of fire. —messer, *m.* 1) pyrometer. 2) pyroscope. —meßkunst, *f.* pyrometry. —messung, *f.* the measuring of the intensity of heat radiating from a fire. —mörser, *m.* [a short piece of ordnance] a mortar. —nadelbüchse, *f.* [in pyrotechnics] a sort of Chinese tree. —napf, *m.* [in pyrotechnics] fireworks representing a fountain —ofen, *m.* a stove; *it.* an oven. —opal, *m.* [a mineral] fire-opal. —ordnung, *f.* fire-regulation. —pein, *f* pain produced by fire. —pfanne, *f.* 1) firepan; a brasier. 2) a vessel for holding pitch-rings used as a light. —pfeil, *m.* fire-arrow. —pfeiler, *m.* a column of fire. —pfuhl, *m.* 1) purgatory. 2) hell. —pinsel, *m.* a pyrotechnical exhibition resembling a painter's brush. —platte, *f.* the back of a chimney. —probe, *f.* 1) a trial by fire. 2) [an ancient form of trial to determine guilt or innocence] fire-ordeal; *fig.* a fiery trial. —punkt, *m.* [in mining] a hearth. —rachen, *m.* ignivomous jaws. —rad, *n.* 1) [a small solid wheel formerly fixed to the pans of firelocks for firing them off] rouet. 2) [in pyrotechnics] fire-wheel, St. Catharine's wheel. —regen, *m.* [in pyrotechnics] a fiery rain. —reich, *adj.* and *adv.* spirituous, ardent. Ein —reicher Wein, a spirituous wine. —reich, *n.* the infernal regions. —religion, *f.* the worship of fire, pyrolatry. —rohr, *n.* a gun or rifle-barrel. —röhre, *f.* [in pyrotechnics] a hollow cylinder filled with gunpowder, sulphur and other inflammable materials. —rose, *f.* —röschen, ||—röslein, *n.* [a plant] pheasant's eye, bird's eye. —rost, *m.* fire-grate. —roth, *adj.* and *adv.* as red as fire, flame-coloured. —sammler, *m.* [in physics] an engine used in collecting fire or heat. —säule, *f.* 1) [in Jewish antiquity] a column of fire. 2) fire-spout. V. also —strahl 2. 3) [with some authors] V. Pyramide or Spitzsäule. —sbrunst, *f.* a conflagration, a fire, [rather emphatically] a burning love. —schaden, *m.* damage caused by fire. —schau, *f.* official view or inspection of buildings to guard against fire. —schaufel, *f.* fire-shovel. —schein, *m.* 1) the brightness of fire. 2) [with wax-chandlers] having the brown colour of melted wax. —scheu, I. *adj.* and *adv.* afraid of fire. II. *f.* fear of fire. —schiff, *n.* a fireship. V. also Brander. —schirm, *m.* a screen used to intercept the heat of fire, fire-skreen. —schlange, *f.* garden or yellowish-grey boa. ||—schlippe, *f.* V. Brandgasse. —schloß, *n.* 1) the lock of a gun. 2) formerly a lock with a rouet. —schlund, *m.* an ignivomous throat. —schlünde, cannons. —schnaubend, *adj.* and *adv.* fiery, vehement, impetuous. —schrift, *f.* fiery letters. —schröter, *m.* V. Hirschkäfer. —schwaden, *m.* [in mining] fire-damp. —schwamm, *m.* touch-wood, spunk. —schweif, *m.* a fiery tail, a train of light, as in comets. —schwert, *n.* [in pyrotechnics] a sort of wooden sword filled with gun-powder, sulphur and other inflammable materials. —schwinge, *f.* fiery wing; *it.* the velocity of fire or light. —seele, *f.* a fiery spirit; *it.* a person gifted with a fiery spirit or glowing mind. —segen, *m.* [in the popular belief] conjuration of the fire by certain words. —setzen, *n.* [in mining] the firing of piles of wood

in pits. —**s=gefahr**, *f.* 1) danger of fire. 2) [in fam. language] a conflagration. —**s=glut**, *f.* V. —glut. —**sicher**, *adj.* and *adv.* fire-proof. —**s=noth**, *f.* [in common language] distress of fire, a conflagration. —**sonne**, *f.* a pyrotechnical exhibition of a burning sun. ‖—**sorge**, *f.* V. —liefe. —**spanner**, *m.* formerly the key by which the rouet was cocked. —**speiend**, *adj.* and *adv.* ignivomous. Ein —speiender Berg, an ignivomous mountain, a volcano or burning mountain. —**speier**, *m.* 1) a person vomiting fire. 2) [rather unusual] an ignivomous mountain, a volcano. —**spiegel**, *m.* V. Brennspiegel. —**spieß**, *m.* V. —lanze. —**spitz=säule**, *f.* a pyrotechnical exhibition of a pyramid. —**spritze**, *f.* fire-engine. —**spur**, *f.* the trace of a fire. —**stahl**, *m.* a steel [used in striking fire]. —**stätte**, *f.* 1) burning place. 2) a fireplace, a hearth; *it. fig.* a dwelling-house. —**stein**, *m.* 1) [a stone used in firearms &c. to strike fire] a flint. 2) [in natural history, a subspecies of quarz] flint. —**stoff**, *m.* the nature of fire. —**strafe**, *f.* torture by burning with fire. —**strahl**, *m.* 1) a flash of fire. 2) fire-spout. —**strom**, *m.* a stream of fire. *Fig.* heat, life, vivacity. ‖—**stube**, *f.* —**stübchen**, *n.* V. —kieke. —**stülpe**, *f.* fender. —**taufe**, *f.* Der wird euch mit dem heiligen Geist und mit der —taufe taufen, [in Script.] he shall baptise you with the Holy Ghost and with fire. —**theil**, *m.* an igneous particle. —**thurm**, *m.* V. —bake. —**tod**, *m.* capital punishment by fire. —**tonne**, *f.* V. —faß. Die —tonnen eines Branders, fire-barrels. —**topf**, *m.* 1) a pot filled with burning coals. 2) a firepot [used in military operations]. —**tropfen**, *m.* a fiery drop. —**vergoldung**, *f.* [Blattvergoldung] hot-gilding. —**verheert**, *adj.* and *adv.* consumed by fire. —**versicherung**, *f.* insurance against fire. —**versicherungsanstalt**, *f.* an office for making insurance against fire, fire-insurance-office. —**versicherungsgesellschaft**, *f.* insurance-company whose business is to insure against fire. —**versicherungskasse**, *f.* V. Brandkasse. —**versilberung**, *f.* [Blattversilberung] hot-silvering. —**voll**, *adj.* and *adv.* full of fire, vehement, ardent, fiery. —**wache**, *f.* fire-watch. —**wächter**, *m.* a man set for a guard to give an alarm of fire. —**wagen**, *m.* a fiery wagon. *Fig.* [in poetry] thunder and lightning. —**wahrsager**, *m.* —**wahrsagerinn**, *f.* a person who pretends to divine by fire, pyromantic. —**wahrsagerei**, *f.* pyromancy. —**wange**, *f.* [rather poet.] a glowing cheek. —**warte**, *f.* V. —bake. —**wedel**, *m.* V. —fächer. —**weiser**, *m.* V. —anzeiger. —**werk**, *n.* 1) a workshop in which fire is applied, as blacksmiths' shops &c. 2) firework, fireworks. 3) firing, fuel, firewood or coal. —**werker**, *m.* 1) fireworker. 2) artillery-man. —**werkerei**, *f.* 1) V. —werkskunst. 2) [a place where fireworks are prepared] laboratory. —**werkerkunst**, —**werkskunst**, *f.* pyrotechnics. —**werks=künstig**, *adj.* and *adv.* pyrotechnic, pyrotechnical. —**werksnadelbüchse**, *f.* V. —nadelbüchse. —**wolf**, *m.* a blast of fire, that sometimes shoots out of a furnace. —**wurm**, *m.* V. Hirschkäfer. —**zange**, *f.* fire-tongs. —**zeichen**, *n.* 1) V. —mahl. 2) V. —kugel, 2. 3) a signal by a lighted fire. —**zeiger**, *m.* V. —anzeiger. —**zeit**, *f.* [in mining] time fixed for firing or burning. —**zeug**, *n.* tinder-box, also flint, steel and tinder. —**ziegel**, *m.* fire-brick [Windsor brick]. —**zunder**, *m.* tinder, spunk, touch-wood.

2. **Feuer**, *n.* [-s, *pl.* -] [has affinity to feucht, V. 1. Feuer] [in seamen's language] Holz, welches das — hat, druxy timber.

Feuerchen, *n.* ‖**Feuerlein**, *n.* [-s, *pl.* -] [diminut. of Feuer] a little fire.

Feuerig, V. Feurig.

Feuern, I. *v. tr.* 1) to use as fuel, or as an aliment to fire. Holz —, to burn wood. 2) Den Wein —, to sulphurate wine. II. *v. intr.* 1) [u. w. seyn] to discharge artillery or fire-arms, to fire. Sie feuerten auf die Stadt, they fired on the town. 2) [u. w. haben] *a)* to feed with combustible matter; to store with fuel or firing, to fuel. Mit Torf —, to burn peat. *b)* to emit sparks of fire. *c)* to be heated, to be in a glow. Das Gesicht feuert ihm, his face burns. *c)* to shine, to sparkle, to burn.

Feuerung, *f.* 1) the act of feeding or alimenting fire. 2) fire maintained to any purpose. 3) firing, fuel, firewood, coal, or peat.

Feuerungsmittel, *n.* V. Feuerung, 3.

Feurig, *adj.* and *adv.* 1) containing fire, full of fire, igneous. Eine —e Kohle, a live coal; ein —er Ofen, a glowing stove or oven. *Fig. a)* full of spirit, strong. Ein —er Wein, a brisk or generous wine. *b)* vehement, ardent, passionate. Ein —er junger Mensch or Mann, a brisk young man, a fiery youth; ein —es Roß, a fiery or brisk steed, a mettlesome horse; ein —er Liebhaber, a fervent lover; ein —er Kuß, a fiery kiss; —e Liebe, ardent love; das —e Temperament, fieriness of temper; mein —ster Dank, my warmest thanks; ein —es Auge, a fiery eye, a flashing eye; eine —e Einbildungs=kraft, a glowing imagination. 2) resembling fire. —e Wolken, fiery clouds; eine —e Erscheinung, a fiery or an igneous appearance; — aussehen, to be red with heat, to glow; —e Augen, sparkling eyes.

Feyer, *f.* V. Feier.

***Fiaker**, *m.* [-s, *pl.* -] 1) hackney-coach. 2) hackney-coachman; Jarvie.

Fibel, *f.* [*pl.* -n] [coming from *biblia*] a child's horn-book, battle-door, primer, spelling-book, A B C book.

Fiber, *f.* [*pl.* -n] [Lat. *fibra*] fiber, fibre. V. Fleischfaser. Die kleine —, febril.

Fibrolit, *m.* [-s, *pl.* -e] [a mineral] fibrolite.

‖**Ficheln**, *v. intr.* 1) to touch lightly. 2) to feign.

‖**Fichler**, *m.* [-s, *pl.* -] a dissembler or hypocrite.

Fichte, *f.* [*pl.* -n] [probably = die Pechichte] pine, pine-tree. Die wilde —, pineaster; die italienische —, pine [of Italy]. *Fig.* † Jemand um die —, or hinter die — führen, to mislead any one by a trick or false pretence, to impose on any one.

Fichten=apfel, *m.* the cone of the pine-tree. —**baum**, *m.* V. Fichte. —**hacker**, *m.* V. Kirschfink. —**hain**, *m.* pine grove. —**harz**, *n.* common resin or turpentine. —**holz**, *n.* pine-wood. —**käfer**, *m.* pine-weevil [curculio pini]. —**kernbeißer**, *m.* [a bird] the pine cross-beak or cross-bill. —**läufer**, *m.* [a bird] pine-creeper. —**laus**, *f.* the pine-aphis. ‖—**lehde**, *f.* uncultivated land where pines grow. —**marder**, *m.* [Baummarder] the pine-martin. —**motte**, *f.* the pine lappit-moth. —**nuß**, *f.* V. Zirbelnuß. —**öl**, *n.* essence of turpentine. —**puder**, *m.* V. Ziperpulver. —**raupe**, *f.* pine-caterpillar. —**rinde**, *f.* the bark of the pine-tree. —**same**, *m.* the seed of pine-trees. —**sauger**, *m.* [in entom.] a species of chrysomela [chrysomela pini]. —**spargel**, *m.* [a plant] yellow bird's nest. —**wald**, *m.* pine-forest. —**wäldchen**, *n.* pine-grove, a clump of pines. —**wanderer**, *m.* V. —motte. —**wanze**, *f.* pine-bug. —**wurm**, *m.* 1) V. —raupe. 2) a species of leather-eater [dermestes piniperda]. —**zapfen**, *m.* the cone of the pine-tree.

Fichten, *adj* and *adv.* made of pine or consisting of pine. —e Bretter, planks of pine, —e Dielen, pine-boards, deal-boards.

† and ‖**Fick**, *m.* [-s] coition.

‖**Ficke**, *f.* [*pl.* -n] pocket, fob.

‖ and †**Ficken**, *v. tr.* [allied to fegen] 1) to rub backwards and forwards, hence, † to fuck. 2) to punish with the whip, to whip. Einen Schulknaben —, to flog a schoolboy.

‖ and †**Fickenfaul**, *adj.* and *adv.* close-fisted, covetous, niggardly.

‖ and †**Fickfacken**, *v. intr.* 1) to be moving hastily from place to place, to bustle about, to flirt. 2) to intrigue, to be cunning.

‖ and †**Fickfacker**, *m.* [-s, *pl.* -] a cunning fellow, an intriguer.

‖ and †**Fickfackerei**, *f.* secret machinations, intrigue.

‖**Fickmühle**, *f.* V. Zwickmühle.

***Fide(i)commiß**, *n.* [-sses, *pl.* -sse] [an estate or fee entailed, or limited in descent to a particular heir or heirs] entail.

***Fidel**, *adj.* and *adv.* [in vulgar lang., especially students' cant] merry, jolly. Ein —er Kerl, a jolly dog; es ging dort recht — her, we had great fun there.

***Fidibus**, *m.* [*pl.* -usse] a narrow piece of paper folded up to light something with, a lighter.

***Fiduciarius**, *m.* [-arii or -, *pl.* -arii or -arien] [in law] a fiduciary, a trustee.

Fieber, *n.* [-s, *pl.* -] [Lat. *febris*, Dan. feber, probably allied to weben i. e. bewegen] [a disease] fever. Ein auszehrendes —, hectic fever; ein nach lassendes, überspringendes or ein Wechsel—, intermittent fever; ein anhaltendes [chronisches] — continued or continual fever, a chronic fever; ein hitziges —, a burning ague; das hitzige — or Entzündungs—, inflammatory fever; das faule — [Faul—], putrid fever; das gelbe —, the yellow fever [vomito negro]; ein bösartiges —, a malignant fever; das tägliche or alltägliche —, quotidian fever; das dreitägige —, tertian fever; das viertägige —, quartan fever; das [eis]kalte —, the cold ague; ein leichtes —, feveret; ein —, welches nach einer [...] entsteht, a secondary fever; — haben, to be in a fever; der Kranke hat ein wenig —, the patient is feverish; das [kalte] — habend, aguish; mit dem — behaftet or vom — befallen, ague-struck; er hat das — verloren, he got rid of his fever. It is often used in composition, [...] Wund— &c., *fig.* Liebes—.

Fieber=anfall, *m.* ague-fit, the paroxysm of a fever. —**angst**, *f.* anxiety, uneasiness caused by a fever. *Fig.* a state of anxiety [...] uneasiness resembling that caused by a fever. —**anstoß**, *m.* V. —anfall. —**artig**, *adj.* and *adv.* feverous. Eine —artige Krankheit, a feverish disease. —**arzenei**, *f.* a febrifuge. —**auge**, *n.* the eye of a feverish person. —**bild**, *n.* picture drawn, or image formed [...] a feverish fancy. —**blässe**, *f.* a febrile paleness. —**brand**, *m.* febrile heat. —**erzeugend**, *adj.* and *adv.* febrific, feverish. —**farbe**, *f.* a febrile paleness. —**fest**, *adj.* and *adv.* ague or fever proof. —**frei**, *adj.* and *adv.* free from fever or ague. Bei einem dreitägigen Fieber ist immer ein Tag um den andern der —frei, a tertian fever intermits every other day. —**frost**, *m.* [in a proper as well as fig. sense] the cold fit of a fever, chill, rigour. —**frostig** —**fröstelnd**, *adj.* and *adv.* 1) shuddering in the cold fit of an ague. 2) causing a feverish shivering. —**glühend**, *adj.* and *adv.* glowing with febrile heat. —**haft**, *adj.* and *adv.* [...]

erish, agued. —haftigkeit, *f.* feverishness, guishness. —hitze, *f.* febrile heat. Die —itze kühlend, fever-cooling. —kalt, *adj.* and *adv.* old as in an ague. —kälte, *f.* chill, rigour. -klee, *m.* common buck-bean or marsh treoil. —krank, *adj.* and *adv.* fever-sick. Der -kranke, a person sick of a fever. *Fig.* Eine -kranke Einbildungskraft, an unsound or disrdered imagination, a fevered imagination. -krankheit, *f.* V. Fieber. —kraut, *n.* [a name given to several plants] *a*) [kleines Tausendgüldenkraut] the lesser centaury or fenrfew. *b*) [Mutterkraut] common feverfew. [stinkende Mannstreu] fever-weed. *d*) [Schildkraut] skull-cap. *e*) [Färberkraut] trifid water-hemp, agrimony, or burr-marygold. —ichen, *m.* [a hard tumour on the left side of the lly, lower than the false ribs, supposed to be the ffect of intermitting fevers] ague-cake. —latwerge, *f.* a febrifuge or antifebrile electuary. —lehre, *f.* the doctrine of fevers, pyretology. -los, *adj.* and *adv.* having no fever, rid of one's fever. —materie, *f.* V. —stoff. —mittel, *n.* V. —arzenei. —öl, *n.* [in chimistry] ippel's animal oil. —pulver, *n.* ague-powder. —rinde, *f.* the Peruvian or Jesuit's rk, bark. —rindenbaum, *m* officinal chinona. —salz, *n.* a febrifuge salt. —schauer, 1) a paroxysm of cold or shivering, chilliss, rigours, as in an ague, ague-fit. 2) a shivering th cold. —schlummer, *m.* slumber of a fer-sick person. *Fig.* uneasy slumber, broken umber. —stoff, *m.* febrific matter. —sturz, a violent ague-fit. —tag, *m.* the day on ich the paroxysm of a fever comes on. —aum, *m.* a dream of a fever-sick person. *Fig.* träume, disordered fancies, chimeras. —ahn, *m.* delirium produced by a fever. *Fig.* usion of a fevered imagination. —wechsel, intermission. *Fig.* any sudden alteration. wurz, —wurzel, *f.* 1) [a plant of the genus -teum] fever-root. 2) common ocrum. —ttel, *m.* [in popular superstition, called also ssettel] ague-spell.

Fieberisch, Fiebrisch, *adj.* and *adv.* 1) nish, feverous, aguish. — sprechen, to talk tionally, to rave 2) [indicating fever or ded from it] febrile. —e Krankheitszeichen, fee symptoms.

Fiebern, *v. intr.* to be affected with fever gue. *Fig.* to talk irrationally, to rave.

Fiedel, *f.* [*pl.* -n] [from fiedeln = wedeln, is to move or wave to and fro; Isl. *fitla*, signie touch gently] [in contempt or joke, or provinr] a fiddle or violin. V. Geige.

iedel-bogen, *m.* fiddle-stick. *Prov.* r die Wahrheit geigt, dem schlägt man mit —bogen auf den Kopf, all truth must not old at all times; he that follows truth too the heels, will have dirt thrown in his ; truth finds foes where it makes none. —rer, *m.* a drill. —brett, *n.* 1) a stringed rd. 2) a bad fiddle.

Fiedel, *m.* [-s, *pl.* -n] [a fish] a species almon [salmo maroenula].

iedeler, *m.* V. Fiedler.

iedeln, *v. intr.* & *tr.* 1) to rub lightly kwards and forwards [in contempt or joke, or ncially]. 2) to play on a fiddle or violin, to le. Ein Stückchen —, to play a tune on fiddle, to fiddle a tune. 3) to play awkwardly violin, to scrape.

iedermesser, *n.* [-s, *pl.* -] [probably allied e Icel. *fidra*, *fitla* = to touch gently] [more nonly das Fügeeisen; with glaziers] grossing

iedern, *v. tr.* 1) to fit with feathers, to r with feathers, to feather. Gefiedert, fledged, fledge [used of birds]; ein gefiederter Pfeil, a feathered arrow; ein gefiedertes Thier, a feathered animal; a fowl or bird; die Anschläger eines Fortepiano —, to pen the sautercaux or jacks of a piano-forte; ||die Betten —, to fill or stuff beds with feathers; [in botany] ein gefiederter Moosstengel, a pinnated shoot; ein zusammengesetztes Blatt heißt gefiedert, a compound leaf is said to be pinnate; halb gefiedert, pinnatified; abgebrochen gefiedert, abruptly pinnate; ungepaart gefiedert, imparo-pinnate; gegenüberstehend gefiedert, oppositely pinnate; abwechselnd gefiedert, alternately pinnate; ungleich gefiedert, interruptedly pinnate; gelenkweise gefiedert, articulately pinnate; abnehmend gefiedert, decursively pinnate; verbunden gefiedert, conjugate pinnate; doppelt gefiedert, bipinnate, bipinnated; dreifach gefiedert, trijugous; doppelt halb gefiedert, bipinnatified, bipennatified; das Laub der Farnkräuter heißt gefiedert, the frond of the ferns is called pinnated; das Federchen an einer Blume heißt gefiedert, the pappus or down of a flower is said to be hair-like. 2) [in mining] to furnish with iron wedges.

Fiedern, *v. tr.* [with glaziers] in the compound word abfiedern. V. Abfiedern.

Fiederung, *f.* 1) the act of feathering or penning. 2) feathers.

Fiedler, *m.* [-s, *pl.* -] [formerly] a fiddler, a violin-player; [now only used for] an awkward fiddler, a scraper [in contempt], a fiddler [in jest].

||Fiek, *m.* [-es, *pl.* -e] [perhaps from ficken = stechen] 1) [a genus of worms, which infests the intestines of the haddock and other sea-fishes] the strap worm. 2) [in surgery] the whitlow, [a distemper in black cattle and horses] the whitlow.

Fiekbohne, *f.* V. Feigbohne.

||Fiemen, *m.* V. Fehmen, Schober.

Fierding, Fierke, V. Vierding.

Fierkraut, *n.* [-s] common maiden-hair.

*Figūr, *f.* [*pl.*-en] [shape, form; appearance of any kind; in rhetoric; in painting; in dancing] figure. Er spielt eine glänzende, eine schlechte —, he cuts a great figure, a poor figure.

*Figuren-karte, *f.* figured card. —schneider, *m.* V. Formenschneider.

*Figuralgesang, *m.* [-es] a prick-song, a variegated song [in distinction from a plain song].

*Figurānt, *m.* [-en, *pl.* -en] an actor or dancer who only figures in a play or dance, a figurant.

*Figuratiōn, *f.* the act of figuring.

*Figurirbank, *f.* V. Drechselbank.

*Figuriren, I. *v. tr.* to figure, to represent. II. *v. intr.* to make a figure, to be distinguished. Der Gesandte figurirte am Hofe von St. Cloud, the envoy figured at the court of St. Cloud.

*Figurist, *m.* [-en, *pl.* -en] V. [the usual word] Bildner or Bildhauer.

*Figūrlich, *adj.* and *adv.* figurative. Ein —er Ausdruck, a figurative expression; das —e, figurativeness Wörter werden — gebraucht, wenn &c., words are used figuratively, when &c.

*Filēt, *n.* [-es, *pl.* -e] a piece of net-work, netting.

*Fileten, *pl.* [with book-binders] backtools.

*Filiāl, *n.* [-s, *pl.* -e] 1) chapel of ease. ||2) a hamlet or a complex of single houses whose inhabitants have to make use of a chapel of ease, also called Filialort.

Filial-kirche, *f.* V. Tochterkirche. —loge, *f.* V. Tochterloge.

*Filiatiōn, *f.* 1) filiation. 2) [unusual] filial duty.

*Filigrānarbeit, *f.* [*pl.* -en] filigrane.

||Fillen, *v. tr.* [allied to the Lat. *pilare*, *vello*, to the Fr. *peler*] 1) to flay. 2) to cut awkwardly. 3) to flay, to whip.

Filpen, *v. intr.* [with organ-builders] to utter or produce a shrill piercing sound: Die Pfeife filpet, the pipe shrills.

*Filtratiōn, Filtrīrung, *f.* filtration.

*Filtrīren, *v. tr.* to filter [a liquor].

Filtrir-papier, *n.* filtering paper, sinking paper. —sack, *m.* filtering bag. —stein, *m.* a porous stone used as a filter, a filtering stone, a drip stone. —tuch, *n.* V. Seihtuch or Durchschlag.

1. Filz, *m.* [-es, *pl.* -e] [appears to be allied to fillen = schlagen, walken] 1) [a cloth or stuff made of wool, or wool and hair] felt. — machen, to felt. 2) any thing made of felt, as, a hat made of felt, a felt. Er zog seinen — [joc.], he touched his beaver; dem — die Form geben, [with hatters] to put the felt upon the block. 3) [in paper-mills] a piece of thick woolen cloth put between the newly fabricated sheets, felt. 4) [in Hungarian mines] the softest slime. 5) *Fig.* [in contempt] a miser. Ein karger —, a sordid wretch.

Filz-arbeit, *f.* [with hatters] felting. —bällchen, *n.* [with engravers] a ball of rags used in cleansing a copper-plate. —baum, *m.* V. Wollbaum. —blech, *n.* V. —eisen. —decke, *f.* a coverlet made of felt. —eisen, *n.* a hatter's basin. —fleck, *m.* a piece of felt for making a hat. —geige, *f.* [—holz] a piece of wood covered with felt or cloth used by combmakers in polishing combs, a combmaker's polishing blade. —herd, *m.* V. Schlammherd. —holz, *n.* V. —geige. —hut, *m.* a felt-hat, a felt. —kappe, *f.* a cap of felt. —kegel, —kern, *m.* [with hatters] parting paper. —kleid, *n.* a garment of felt. —kraut, *n.* [a name given to several plants] *a*) common dodder. *b*) common cudweed. *c*) marsh marigold. *d*) heart-leaved uvularia. —lappen, *m.* 1) a small piece of felt used in cleansing the frames of pictures. 2) [with hatters] felt-cloth. —laus, *f.* [a species of louse which infects the axilla and pudenda] crab-louse. —macher, *m.* feltmaker. —mantel, *m.* a felt-cloak, a coarse frock, a gabardine. —mütze, *f.* felt-cap. —perrücke, *f.* a periwig made of wool. —platte, *f.* V. —tafel. —schuh, *m.* felt-shoe, felt-slipper. —socke, *f.* a sock of felt. —stiefel, *m.* a boot of felt. —stoß, *m.* a heap of felts. —tafel, *f.* [with hatters] felting board. —tuch, *n.* V. —lappen. —werk, *n.* felted things. —wolle, *f.* 1) wool for felts. 2) felted wool.

†2. Filz, *m.* [-es, *pl.* -e] [probably from fillen = schlagen, rupfen] 1) a chiding, rebuke. Einem einen derben — geben, to rebuke any one sharply. ||2) a quarrel, a contest.

1. Filzen, I. *v. tr.* 1) to work into a felt. Die Wolle, die Haare —, to felt wool, hair. 2) [with hatters] to make to clot or mat together in a basin. II. *v. intr.* to clot together like felt, to felter.

†2. Filzen, *v. tr.* to rebuke.

1. Filzer, *m.* [-s, *pl.* -] he that felts.

†2. Filzer, *m.* [-s, *pl.* -] a sharp rebuke.

Filzicht, *adj.* and *adv.* resembling felt, [in botany] downy, nappy.

Filzig, *adj.* and *adv.* 1) feltering. —e Locken, feltering locks. 2) *Fig.* very covetous, sordid, miserly, niggardly. Ein —er Mensch, a miser.

Filzigkeit, *f.* 1) the quality of feltering.

2) *Fig.* mean covetousness, niggardliness.

1. **Fimmel**, *m.* [-s, *pl.* -] [allied to Finne, Lat. *pinna*, to the Lat. verb. *findo*] 1) [in mining] a strong iron wedge. ‖2) a strong hammer.

2. **Fimmel**, *m.* [-s, *pl.* -] [from the Lat. *femella?*] female-hemp, fimble-hemp.

Fimmelhopfen, *m.* [-s] V. Hopfen.

Fimmeln, *v. tr.* to pull fimble-hemp.

***Finale**, *n.* [the last note or end of a piece of music, or that which closes a concert] finale.

***Financier**, [pron. as in the French] *m.* [-s, *pl.* -s] [one who is skilled in the principles or system of public revenue] a financier.

Finanz, *f.* [*pl.* -en] [from the Medio-Lat. *financia*; the verb. *finare* signified in Med. Lat. = to collect taxes] 1) formerly, artifice, stratagem, subtlety of contrivance to gain a point, also fraud, usury. 2) *pl.* public resources of money, revenue, finances; *it.* budget. Die —en der Regierung standen schlecht, the finances of the government were in a low condition; die —en waren erschöpft, the finances were exhausted; die —en verwalten, to manage the public revenue; er legte den Abgeordneten eine Uebersicht der —en vor, he laid the budget before the deputies. *Fig.* * [in a jocose sense] meine —en stehen schlecht, my finances are at a low ebb.

Finanz-kammer, *f.* a board of financiers, which manages the public revenue, [in England] the exchequer. —**kollegium**, *n.* V. —rath. —**kunst**, *f.* art or skill in financial operations. —**rath**, *m.* 1) a board of financiers which superintends and manages the public revenue. 2) a counsellor of the finances. —**sache**, *f.* any thing relating to finances or public revenue. —**wesen**, *n.* financial concerns and operations. —**wissenschaft**, *f.* the principles or system of public revenue.

‡**Finanzen**, *v. tr.* to cheat.

‡**Finanzer**, *m.* [-s, *pl.* -] a cheat.

Finanzerei, *f.* V. Finanzkunst.

Findebuch, *n.* [-s, *pl.* -bücher] 1) a catalogue or account of particular things, inventory. 2) a repertory.

Findeeisen, *n.* [-s, *pl.* -] [also das Sucheisen, in surgery] a probe.

Findegeld, *n.* [-es, *pl.* -er] V. Findelgeld.

Findegröße, *f.* [*pl.* -n] V. Findezahl.

Findel, *f.* [*pl.* -n] V. Findelhaus.

Findel-geld, *n.* a sum of money or reward paid for the recovery of any thing lost. —**haus**, *n.* a foundling hospital. —**kind**, *n.* [an exposed infant] a foundling. —**lohn**, *m.* V. —geld. —**mutter**, *f.* a woman that takes care of a foundling; [especially] a woman entrusted with the care of foundlings in a foundling hospital. —**pfleger**, *m.* a person entrusted with the care of foundlings; *it.* the superintendent of a foundling hospital. —**vater**, *m.* a man who takes care of a foundling; [especially] a man entrusted with the care of foundlings in a foundling hospital.

Findelohn, *m.* [-es] V. Findellohn.

Finden, [provinc. **finnen**, old Fr. *finer*, probably allied to the Lat. *fendo* (in of-*fendo*) and to the Germ. wenden, as also to the Lat. *ven*-ire, in *invenire*] *ir.* I. *v. tr.* to come to, to light on, to meet with, to find. Wir sondirten und fanden Grund, we sounded and found bottom; man findet überall angenehme Spaziergänge, one finds pleasant walks everywhere; man findet immer Gesellschaft, you always meet with company; man findet dich in Hainen und in Wäldern, in woods and forests thou art found; ich werde gefunden von denen, die mich nicht suchten, [in Script.] I am found of them that sought me not; ich fand ihn schlafend or schlafen, I found him sleeping; der Hund findet, [with hunters] the dog finds [game]; einen Beutel —, to find a purse; der gefundene Schatz, [in law] treasure trove; das verlorene Geld ist noch nicht wieder gefunden, the lost money has not yet been found again. *Fig. a)* to discover something not before seen or known, to meet, to find. Er spricht zu ihm, wir haben den Messiam gefunden, [in Script.] he saith to him, we have found the Messiah; und der Weg ist schmal, der zum Leben führet, und wenige sind ihrer, die ihn —, [in Script.] and narrow is the way, which leadeth to life, and few there be that find it; den Stein der Weisen —, to find the philosopher's stone; er hat Mittel gefunden, seine Absicht zu erreichen, he found means to attain his end; keine Worte —, to want words; den Sinn einer Parabel —, to find out the meaning of a parable; aus zwei Zahlen die dritte —, to find a third number by two given numbers; [hence] das Gefundene, [in arithmetic] the amount; [in Script.] to find, to select, to choose. Ich habe gefunden meinen Knecht David, [in Script.] I have found David my servant. *b)* to find, to get, to obtain. Bittet, so wird euch gegeben, suchet, so werdet ihr —, [in Script.] ask, and it shall be given you, seek, and ye shall find; ich begab mich zu dem Minister, konnte aber kein Gehör —, I waited on the minister, but could not obtain a hearing; Sie hätten leicht eine gute Stelle bei einem Kaufmann in London gefunden, you could easily have found a good place in London at a merchant's; ich finde nichts Tröstlicheres in meinem Unglück, I find nothing more comfortable in my troubles; so werdet ihr Ruhe — für eure Seelen, [in Script.] and ye shall find rest to your souls; Muße —, einen Besuch zu machen, to find leisure for a visit; statt—, to take place; dies kann nicht statt—, that cannot be admitted or conceded; diese Nachricht findet keinen Glauben, no credit is given to this news. *c)* [= bemerken] to find, to meet with. Wir fanden manche bemerkenswerthe Dinge, we met with many things worthy of observation; ich fand eine Stelle, die mir sehr gefiel, I met with a passage, which pleased me much; der große Cäsar fand an unsern Vätern keine zu verachtende Feinde, great Caesar found our fathers no mean foes; was kann ein Frauenzimmer an ihm —? what can a woman see engaging about him? ich finde bei Allen Schönheit oder Verstand, beauty or wit in all I find; haben Sie etwas nach Ihrem Geschmack gefunden? have you seen any thing to your liking? *d)* to find, to have the sense of. Wie — Sie das? how do you find it? — Sie es nach Ihrem Geschmacke? is it to your taste? wie — Sie diesen Wein? what do you think of this wine? how do you like this wine? und wie — Sie die Musik? and how do you like the music? ich finde es sehr kalt, I think, it is extremely cold; ich finde, daß er sehr gut aussieht, methinks he looks very well. *e)* [= fühlen] to find, to have, to experience. Vergnügen —, to find pleasure; ich fand große Erleichterung in seiner Gesellschaft, I found great relief in his company; ich finde keinen Geschmack daran, I do not like it; er fand so vieles Wohlgefallen an dieser Aussicht, he was so taken with this prospect. *f)* to discover or know by experience, to find. Man findet nunmehr, daß der heiße Erdstrich bewohnbar ist, the torrid zone is now ascertained to be habitable; ich fand, daß er gelogen [hatte], I found him in a lie; man fand, daß es wahr war, that was found true, it proved to be true; ich fand, daß seine Meinungen mit den meinigen übereinstimmen, I found his opinions to accord with my own; [formerly] ein Urtheil —, to pronounce a judgment or sentence, to find a verdict; ich finde es überflüssig, I think it superfluous; ich finde es klug, zu schweigen, I deem it prudent to be silent; sich beleidigt —, to feel hurt; er findet sich dadurch sehr geehrt, he feels much honoured by it; er läßt sich zu allem willig —, he complies with any thing. *g)* to search for and find, in order to punish. Ich werde ihn schon zu — wissen, I'll make him pay for it; Gott wird ihn schon —, God will not suffer him to pass without punishment; man wird ihn schon zu — wissen, he shall meet with the punishment he deserves. V. Antreffen.

II. *v. r.* sich —, to be found, to be recovered by searching for it or by accident. Meine Uhr hat sich wieder gefunden, my watch has been found again. *Fig. a)* [= sich vorfinden] to be present in any place. Es findet sich, there is; es — sich Liebhaber dazu, there are persons who like it; zur Zeit der Noth fand sich für uns eine schnelle Hülfe, in time of distress we met with a prompt assistance. *b)* [= sich wo befinden] to come together or to approach near, or into company with, to meet. Wir fanden uns auf dem Wege, we met on the road; sie fanden sich in einem fremden Lande, they met in a foreign country. *c)* to be found out, to be discovered. Beim Zählen fand sich, daß einer von den Zwölfen fehlte, in counting, it appeared that one of the twelve was wanting; die Wahrheit wird sich —, truth will come to light. *d)* to come to pass, to happen. Es wird sich —, it will come of course; we shall see. *e)* Sich in etwas —, to have just and adequate ideas of a thing, to understand it; also, to submit one's self to any thing; man findet sich in Gebräuche und Moden, we yield to customs and fashions; sich in Zeit und Umstände zu — wissen, to serve the time, to accommodate one's self to circumstances; er findet sich in die unvermeidlichen Trübsale des Lebens, he submits patiently to the inevitable evils of life; sich in jemands Laune —, to comply with a man's humour; sich zurecht —, to find out one's way or to find out the right way.

Findenswerth, *adj.* and *adv.* that deserves to be found.

Findeort, *m.* [-es, *pl.* -örter] the place where any thing is found.

Finder, *m.* [-s, *pl.* -] 1) a person who meets or falls on any thing, finder. 2) [or Saufinder, with hunters] a dog used in hunting the wild boar, a limer.

Finderinn, *f.* a female who meets or falls on any thing, finder.

Findezahl, *f.* [*pl.* -en] [in arithmetic] one of the numbers which are given to find another, as in the rule of three, the three numbers by which a fourth number or fourth proportional is found.

Findig, *adj.* and *adv.* used only with machen, or in compound words. — machen, [in mining] to find, to discover; aus— machen, to find out, to discover; spitz—, subtle.

Findlich, *adj.* and *adv.* that may be found.

Findling, *m.* [-s, *pl.* -e] 1) foundling. 2) [in husbandry] a swarm of bees found in a wood or any other place.

Findung, *f.* 1) finding, discovery. ‖2) *a)* sentence, finding [of a jury]. *b)* decision.

Findungsrecht, *n.* the right of property in the finder to a thing found.

***Finesse**, *f.* [*pl.* -n] finesse, artifice, stratagem [used only in fam. or common lang.]

Finger, *m.* [-s, *pl.* -] [allied to fangen: greifen] 1) one of the extreme parts of the hand or foot, fit to be an instrument of catching, seizing and holding. Die — eines Falken, [with hunters] the talons. 2) [in a more limited sense, one of the extreme parts of the hand] finger. Die — haben Gelenke, the fingers are jointed; die fünf —, the five fingers; [in a fig. as well as in proper sense] mit den —n auf jemand zeigen, to point the finger at any one, to point the finger of scorn at any one; man weiset mit —n auf ihn, they point at him [in a fig. as well as in proper sense]; eines —s breit, a finger's breadth, digit; mit den —n essen, to eat with one's fingers. *Fig.* Etwas auf den —n or an den —n ausrechnen, herrechnen, vorrechnen, to recount something with great accuracy; er weiß es an den —n herzuzählen, er kann es an den —n hersagen, he has it at his finger's end; er ist jetzt so geschmeidig, daß man ihn um den — wickeln könnte, he is now so pliant, that you may turn him round your little finger; einem [einen is more correct] auf die — sehen, to watch the proceedings of a person, especially of a thievish person; to have an eye upon any one; lange — machen, or die — kleben lassen, to be light-fingered, to steal [at a time favourable for the purpose]; er läßt die — kleben, his fingers are lime-twigs; einem [einen is more correct] auf die — klopfen, to give any one a rap on the knuckles; to punish any one; eine Nachricht aus den —n saugen, to invent a news; mein kleiner — hat es mir gesagt, a little bird told me so; einem durch die — sehen, not to punish or censure any one, to wink at any one's faults; den — auf den Mund legen, to be silent; sich die — verbrennen, to burn one's fingers, to suffer from imprudence; er hat mehr Verstand in seinem kleinen —, als du in deinem ganzen Körper, he hath more wit in his little finger, than thou in thy whole body. *Prov.* Wenn man ihm einen — gibt, will er gleich die ganze Hand haben, give him an inch, and he'll take an ell. 3) *Fig.* [in Scripture] power, strength or operation. Der — Gottes, the finger of God; da sprachen die Zauberer zu Pharao, das ist Gottes —, [in Script.] the magicians said to Pharaoh, this is the finger of God. 4) the finger of a glove. Handschuhe mit —n, gloves with fingers; Handschuhe ohne —, mittens. 5) [a cartilaginous slender appendage sometimes observable in fishes between the pectoral and ventral fins] finger.

Finger=arbeit, *f.* delicate work made with the fingers, fingering. —becken, *n.* finger-glass. —bein, *n.* [in anatomy] a small bone of the finger. Die —beine, phalanx. —beuger, *m.* [in anatomy] the extensor of a finger. —blutader, *f.* [in anatomy] digital vein. —blutadernetz, *n.* [in anatomy] a small net or congeries of the digital veins. —breit, V. —sbreit. —brett, *n.* [diminut. das —brettchen] 1) V. Griffbrett. 2) [in an organ or harpsichord] the key or finger-key. —ende, *n.* 1) V. —spitze. 2) [in anatomy] the nether part of the metacarpus. —farn, *m.* finger-fern. —fisch, *m.* the finger-fish. —fläche, *f.* [in anatomy] surface of the bones of the hand. —fuß, *m.* [in poetry] a dactyle [- ∪ ∪]. —gang, *m.* [the manner of touching an instrument of music] fingering. —gelenk, *n.* the joint of a finger. —geschwür, *n.* [in surgery] a whitlow or felon. —glied, *n.* the joint of a finger. —gras, *n.* slender-spiked cock's foot, panic grass. —gucker, *m.* 1) a person that looks on the fingers of another. 2) *pl.* [at gaming-tables] the assistants of the banker [Croupiers]. —handschuh, *m.* a glove with fingers. —hut, *m.* 1) [a kind of cap or cover of the finger usually made of metal, used by tailors and seamstresses] thimble. *Fig.* Ein —hut voll Wein, a little wine. 2) [in natural history] *a)* [a plant] small yellow fox-glove. *b)* a species of whelk [buccinum glabratum]. —hüter, *m.* thimble-maker. —kork, *m.* [an animal in the form of a plant] dead man's head. —kraut, *n.* creeping cinque-foil. —kuppe, *f.* V. —spitze. —leiter, *pl.* [in music] finger-guides, cheiroplast [invented by Logier]. —muschel, *f.* [in conchology] finger-shell. —muskel, *m.* V. —beuger. —nagel, *m.* [the horny substance growing at the end of the human fingers] nail. —nerve, *m.* [in anatomy] a nerve on the back of a finger. —rechnen, *n.* counting on the fingers. —rech[n]enkunst, *f.* the art of numbering on the fingers, dactylonomy. —rechnung, *f.* 1) V. —rechnen. 2) an account made by numbering on the fingers. —reif, —ring, *m.* a ring [worn on the fingers]. —rücken, *m.* [in anatomy] the back of a finger. —satz, *m.* [in music] *a)* [disposing of the fingers in a convenient, natural, and apt manner in playing on an instrument, but more especially on the organ and piano-forte] fingering. *b)* [a term applied to piano-forte exercises] the act of placing figures over or under the notes to signify the finger with which each corresponding key is to be struck. Stücke, die mit dem —satze versehen sind, fingered tunes. —s=breit, *adj.* and *adv.* as broad as a finger. ‖*n.* and —s=breite, *f.* a finger's breath. —schlag, *m.* 1) a blow given with the finger. 2) [in poetry] V. —fuß. —schlagader, *f.* [in anatomy] digital artery. —schnecke, *f.* [a cetaceous animal] nacre. —s=dick, *adj.* and *adv.* as thick as a finger. —setzen, *n.* —setzung, *f.* V. —satz *a.* —s=hoch, *adj.* and *adv.* as long or as thick as a finger. —s=lang, *adj.* and *adv.* as long as a finger. —spiel, *n.* 1) a playing with the fingers. 2) [an Italian play] the morra. —spitze, *f.* the end of a finger. —sprache, *f.* [the act or art of communicating ideas or thoughts by the fingers] dactylogy. —stein, *m.* [a fossil resembling an arrow] finger-stone, belemnite, arrow-head, commonly called thunderbolt, or thunder-stone. —stock, *m.* [with glovers] glove-stretcher. —strecker, *m.* [in anatomy] the muscle which extends all the joints of the fingers [extensor digitorum communis]. —stück, *n.* [with glovers] forset. —tuch, *n.* a towel or napkin. —vers, *m.* a dactylic verse. —werk, *n.* [in Scripture] Denn ich werde sehen die Himmel, dein —werk, [in Script.] when I consider thy heavens, the work of thy fingers. —wurm, *m.* V. Wurm [im —]. —zahl, *f.* [in arithmetic, any integer under ten, so called from counting on the fingers] digit. —zeig, *m.* the pointing with the finger. *Fig.* hint. —zeigend, *adj.* and *adv.* pointing with the finger. —zweig, *m.* [in anatomy] one of the branches of nerves which ramify and extend to the fingers.

Fingerchen, *n.* [-s, *pl.* -] 1) a little finger. 2) V. Fingerschnecke.

Fingerig, *adj.* and *adv.* having fingers, fingered, in the compound words, vier—, having four fingers, four-fingered; sechs—, having six fingers; lang—, having long fingers, long-fingered [in a proper as well as fig. sense].

‖Fingerlein, *n.* [-s, *pl.* -] 1) a little finger. ‡2) a ring worn on the finger.

Fingerling, *m.* [-s, *pl.* -e] 1) [formerly] a ring worn on the finger. 2) finger-stall. 3) [in seamen's language] *a)* thumb-stall. *b)* *pl.* [clamps of iron bolted on the stern-post of a ship, whereon to hang the rudder] googings, or goodings. ‖4) a sort of mushroom.

Fingern, I. *v. intr.* to touch often with the fingers. *Prov.* Er kann wohl geigen aber nicht —, he has but a superficial knowledge of it. II. *v. tr.* 1) to play with the fingers, to play on an instrument, to finger. 2) to furnish with fingers. Gefingerte Handschuhe, gloves with fingers. *Fig.* [in botany] Eine gefingerte Wurzel, a fingered or digitate root; ein zusammengesetztes Blatt ist or heißt gefingert, a compound leaf is said fingered or digitate.

*Fingiren, *v. tr.* 1) to invent, to contrive. 2) to feign, to pretend.

*Fingirt, *adj.* invented, feigned.

Fink, *m.* [-es, *pl.* -e or -en] [perhaps allied to funkeln] [a bird] finch [used also in composition, as, der Blut—, bullfinch; der Distel—, goldfinch]. *Fig.* a thoughtless and debauched young man.

Finken=bauer, *m.* a small cage for finches. —falk, *m.* the sparrow-hawk. —fang, *m.* the catching of finches. —garn, *n.* a net used in catching finches. —habicht, *m.* V. Sperber. —herd, *m.* a fowling-floor where finches are caught. —meise, *f.* the great titmouse. —netz, *n.* 1) V. —garn. 2) [in seamen's language] quarter netting. —same, *m.* the seed of the cultivated gold of pleasure and that plant itself. —schlag, *m.* the song of finches.

Finkchen, ‖Finklein, *n.* [-s, *pl.* -] a small finch.

Finkeler, Finkler, *m.* [-s, *pl.* -] a sportsman who takes finches or wild fowls, a bird-catcher, a fowler. Heinrich der —, a surname of the Emperor Henry I., Henry the Fowler.

Finkeln, *v. intr.* to catch finches.

Finnaal, *m.* [-es, *pl.* -e] [a genus of fishes] the gymnotus.

‖Finne, *f.* [*pl.* -n] [allied to the Gr. πίν-ος, Schmutz, to the Fr. *fange* and probably to the Lat. *fons*] a march or tract of low watery ground, fen, moorland.

1. Finne, *f.* [*pl.* -n] [Lat. *pinna*, perhaps allied to *findo*, spalten] 1) a pointed thing, hence, a mountain, a hill. 2) the top of a thing, hence, the top of a mountain. 3) the thin end of a hammer. 4) a tack or stud. 5) [with joiners] the clock [which confines the work in a turner's lathe].

2. Finne, *f.* [*pl.* -n] [perhaps allied to the Lat. *panus*, Geschwür] 1) a small inflammatory tumour, pimple, a pustule, a whelk or beal. 2) *pl.* [a disease in swine] the measles.

Finnenblasenbandwurm, *m.* a species of tape-worm which infects the flesh of swine.

3. Finne, *f.* [*pl.* -n] [allied to *pinna*, *penna*] the fin [of a fish].

Finne, *m.* [-n, *pl.* -n] a Finn or Fin. V. Finnländer.

Finnen, *v. intr.* to work with the thin end of the hammer.

Finnfisch, *m.* [-es, *pl.* -e] fin-fish, or fin-backed mysticete.

Finnhammer, [V. 1. Finne 3)] *m.* [-s, *pl.* -hämmer] a hammer with one thin end, a goldsmith's hammer.

Finnig, *adj.* and *adv.* 1) having red pustules on the skin, pimpled. 2) measled, measly [said of swine].

Finnisch, *adj.* and *adv.* V. Finnländisch.

Finnland, *n.* [-es] [a province of Russia] Finland.

Finnländer, *m.* [-s, *pl.* -] —inn, *f.* a native of Finland, a Finn or Fin.

Finnländisch, *adj.* and *adv.* of or from Finland; in the manner of the Fins.

Finster, [origin uncertain, perhaps from the Low. Sax. bister] *adj.* and *adv.* destitute of light, dark, obscure, tenebrous. Eine —e Nacht, a dark night; im —n, in the dark; im —n tappen, to search or attempt to find in the dark, to feel one's way in the dark, to grope; und es war — auf der Tiefe, [in Scripture] and darkness was on the face of the deep; ein —er Ort, a dark place; ein —es Haus, a darksome house; —e Wolken, darksome clouds; —es Wetter, dull weather; ein —er Tag, a gloomy day; die —n Zellen eines Klosters, the gloomy cells of a convent; die —n Schatten der Nacht, the gloomy shades of the night; das —e Zeug, [with hunters] thick toils [as opposed to nets]; —e Hölzer, [in forestry] firs, pines &c.; den Ofen — führen, [in metallurgy] to heat the furnace moderately; [in painting] [having the quality opposite to white] dark. —e Farben, dark colours Fig. a) not enlightened with knowledge, destitute of learning and science, ignorant, dark. Ein —es Zeitalter, a dark age; in seinem Kopfe sieht es noch sehr — aus, he is yet intellectually clouded; im —n tappen, [to seek blindly in intellectual darkness without a certain guide or means of knowledge] to grope; wir tappen alle im —n, we are all in the dark. b) gloomily angry and silent, cross, sour, affected with ill humour. Ein —es Gesicht, a sullen face; eine —e Miene, a sour countenance; —e Blicke, stern looks; — aussehen, to look peevish; wie — er aussieht! how gloomy he looks! einen — ansehen, to look black upon any one; eine —e Gemüthsstimmung, a gloomy or sullen temper; eine —e Verschlossenheit, a morose taciturnity. c) dark, gloomy, dismal. —e Gedanken, gloomy thoughts; ein —es Geschick, a dark or dismal fate. d) dark, obscure, concealed. — wie euer Geschick, dark as your fortune; Dinge im —n vollbracht, things done in the dark; im —n wirkend, dark-working. e) dark, unclean, foul. Sein Auge erblickte die —n Abgöttereien Juda's, his eye survey'd the dark idolatries of Judah.

Finster-gelockt, *adj.* and *adv.* [rather poet.] having dark locks. —kasten, *m.* [in optics, an apparatus representing an artificial eye, in which the images of external objects, received through a double convex glass, are exhibited distinctly, and in their native colours, on a white matter, placed within the machine, in the focus of the glass] camera obscura, or dark chamber. —sehen, *n.* a sour countenance.

||Finstere, *f.* dark, darkness. Die — des Waldes, the gloom of the forest.

Finsterling, *m.* [-es, *pl.* -e] 1) an ignorant person, an ignoramus. 2) a promoter or partisan of intellectual darkness or ignorance.

Finsterniß, *f.* [-sse] 1) absence of light, darkness, obscurity, tenebrosity, gloominess. Eine dicke —, deep darkness; die — der Mitternacht, the gloom of midnight; [in astronomy] eine — [an interception or obscuration of the light of the sun, moon or other luminous body] an eclipse. Eine Sonnen—, an eclipse of the sun; eine Mond(s)—, an eclipse of the moon. *Fig.* a) want of clearness or perspicuity, darkness, obscurity. So wird dein Licht in — aufgehen, und dein Dunkel wird seyn wie der Mittag, [in Scripture] then shall thy light rise in obscurity, and thy darkness be as the noon-day; die Zukunft ist in — gehüllt, futurity lies hid in night; die Menschen liebten die — mehr, denn das Licht, [in Scripture] men loved darkness rather than light; — bedecket das Erdreich, und Dunkel die Völker, [in Script.] the darkness shall cover the earth, and gross darkness the people; [great trouble and distress]; Sie werden nichts finden, denn Trübsal und —, [in Scripture] they shall behold trouble and darkness; was ich euch sage in —, das redet in Licht, [in Script.] what I tell you in darkness [= secrecy], that speak ye in light. b) infernal gloom, hell. Werfet ihn in die äußerste — hinaus, da wird seyn Heulen und Zähnklappern, [in Script.] cast him in utter darkness, there shall be weeping and gnashing of teeth. c) empire of Satan. Welcher uns errettet hat von der Obrigkeit der —, [in Script.] who hath delivered us from the power of darkness. d) Das Land der —, [in Script.] the land of darkness, the grave.

Finte, *f.* [*pl.* -n] [from the Fr. *feinte*?] 1) an artful or ingenious device, artifice, stratagem; an assumed or false appearance, a feint. 2) [in fencing] a feint.

Fiorit, *m.* [-s, *pl.* -e] [a mineral] siliceous or pearl sinter.

||Fippern, *v. intr.* [allied to weben, webern] to be moving hastily from place to place, to flirt.

||Fipps, *m.* [-es, *pl.* -e] a fillip upon the nose.

||Fippsen, *v. tr. prov.* 1) to fillip. 2) to rub to and fro, hence † to unite in sexual embrace.

Firke, *m.* [-n, *pl.* -n] V. Vierding.

Firlefanz, *m.* [-es] trifles, childish tricks, fiddle-faddle, nonsense.

Firlefanzer, *m.* [-s, *pl.* -] a person who talks at random or nonsensically, a trifler.

Firlefanzerei, *f.* childish talk or tricks, employment about things of no importance, trifling.

*Firma, *f.* [*pl.* Firmen] [in commerce, the name or title under which a person or a company transacts business] firm. Die — von Frege & Co., the firm of Frege & Co.

*Firmament, *n.* [-es] the sky or heavens, the firmament.

*Firmeln, Firmen, *v. tr.* and *intr.* [in the Romish and Greek churches] to confirm, to bishop.

Firmelung, *f.* [in the Romish and Greek churches] confirmation.

||Firn, [appears to be allied to vorn, vorig] *adj.* and *adv.* belonging to the preceding year, of the preceding year. —er Wein or —ewein, wine of the last year; im —en Jahre, last year.

||Firner, *m.* [-s, *pl.* -] [allied to Firste] a glacier.

Firnewein, *m.* [-es, *pl.* -e] 1) wine of the last year. 2) old wine.

Firniß, *m.* [-sses, *pl.* -sse] [Fr. *vernis*; appears to be allied to brennen, bernen] 1) [a thick, viscid, glossy liquid, laid on work by painters and others, to give it a smooth hard surface and a beautiful gloss] varnish. Der Bernstein—, amber varnish; der Lack—, black varnish; dicker, starker, zur Druckerschwärze tauglicher —, [with printers] thick varnish. 2) Trockner —, [a resin in white tears, obtained from the juniper-tree] varnish or sandarach, sandarac. 3) a species of amber found in large pieces.

Firniß-baum, *m.* varnish-tree, poison ash, or poison oak. —blase, *f.* boiling pot. —farbe, *f.* any colour mixed with varnish. —sumach, *n.* V. —baum.

Firnissen, *v. tr.* and *intr.* to lay varnish on, to varnish. Einen Tisch —, to varnish a table.

Firstbalken, *m.* [-s, *pl.* -] [in architecture] a beam in the ridge of a roof.

Firste, *f.* [*pl.* -n] [allied to vor, vorz; in Engl. *first* signifies der erste] 1) the top of any thing, the summit, hence || the top or summit of a mountain; also a name given to the Vosges. 2) [in mining] roof. Die — verzimmern, to line a roof with boards. 3) the top of the roof of a building, the ridge. ||4) a house.

Firsten-bau, *m.* [in mining] the working in the roof. —erz, *n.* ore found in the roof. —nagel, *n.* a pin for fastening ridge-tiles. —stein, *m.* slate used for covering the ridge of a roof. —ziegel, *m.* ridge-tile.

Firstenweise, *adv.* [in mining] towards the surface. Das Erz bricht —, ore is found in the roof.

Fis, [as a subst. *n.*] [in music] F sharp.

*Fiscal, *m.* [-s, *pl.* -e] attorney general.

Fiscalisch, *adj.* and *adv.* fiscal.

*Fiscus, *m* [- or Fisci] the fisc.

1. Fisch, *m.* [-es, *pl.* -e] [Lat. *piscis*, Gr. ἰχθύς, Welsh *pysg*; perhaps allied to the Welsh *isch* Wasser] 1) [in general any aquatic animal] aquatic animal, such as lobsters, shell-fish &c.; *fig.* in the Romish church, this term has been extended to animals which feed on fish. 2) a fish. Der männliche —, [Milcher], a milter; der weibliche — [Rogener], a spawner; —e fangen, to catch fish; Fluß—e, river-fishes; See—e, sea-fishes; ein Gericht —e, a dish of fish; versteinerte —e, fishstones, ichthyolites; *gesund wie ein —, as sound as a trout; *stumm wie ein —, as mute as a fish; *Prov.* —e wollen schwimmen, fish must swim thrice; frische —e, gute —e, fresh fish and new-come guests smell, by that they are three days old; große —e sind nicht immer die besten, the greatest crabs are not always the best meat. *Fig.* *Faule —e, foul play; *it.* frivolous excuses or pretexts. 3) [the flesh of fish used as food] fish. 4) *pl.* [in astronomy, the twelfth sign or constellation in the zodiac] the fishes or pisces.

Fisch-aar, —adler, *m.* 1) the osprey. 2) the bald eagle or fishing-hawk. —am... —we, *f.* V. Seeschwalbe. —adler, *m.* V. — —amber, *m.* black amber. —angel, *f.* hook for catching fish, fish-hook, an angle. —augenstein, *m.* [a mineral] apophyllite. —bank, *f.* V. —markt. —bär, *m.* the ... bear feeding on fish. ||—bärn, *m.* V. — —beerbaum, *m.* V. Mehlbeerbaum. —bee... *f.* V. Mehlbeere. —behälter, *m.* V. — —bein, *n.* 1) (weißes —bein) cuttle-bone. (schwarzes —bein) whale-bone. Ungerissenes —bein, whale-fins. —beinern, *adj.* and *adv.* made of whale-bone. —beinform, *f.* [with goldsmiths] a mould made of cuttle-bone. —beinreißen, —beinsieden, *n.* the splitting of whale-fins. —beinreißer, —beinsieder, *m.* [in sea-towns] a splitter of whale-fins. —beinrock, *m.* hoop-petticoat. —beschreibung, *f.* a description of fishes, ichthyology. —bewohnt, *adj.* and *adv.* inhabited by fish, fishy. —blase, *f.* the air-bladder of a fish, sound. —blütig, *adj.* and *adv.* V. Kaltblütig [also * in a figurative sense]. —bret, *n.* a board used in cookery for dressing fish. —brühe, *f.* [in cookery] fish-sauce. —brut, *f.* fry of fishes. —butte, *f.* fish-tun. —darm, *m.* 1) the gut of a fish. 2) [in conchology] the twined serpola. —dieb, *m.* one who steals fishes. —egel, *m.* a species of leech. — *n.* V. —rogen. —essend, *adj.* and *adv.* ichthyophagous. —esser, *m.* fish-eater, ichthyophagus. —fang, *m.* 1) the act of catching fish, fishing. 2) a fishery, fishing or fishing-place. —fänger, *m.* 1) a fisher or fisherman. 2) Jamaica dog-wood tree. —faß, *n.* fish-tub. —feder, *f.* V. —floße. —flosse, *f.* V. Floßfeder. —fressend, *adj.* and *adv.* piscivorous, as many species of aquatic fowls. —frosch, *m.* fish-frosh, toad-fish. —gabel, *f.* fish-gig, fish-spear. —galle, *f.* the gall of a fish. —gallerte, *f.* fish-jelly. —garn, *n.* V. —garn. —gebackene, *n.* V. —pastete. —geie...

m. V. —aar. —geräthe, n. —geräthschaften, pl. V. Fischergeräth and Fischergerathschaften. —gräte, f. fish-bone. —grube, f. a pit in a pond for catching fish. —gurren, m. a species of loche [cobitis fossilis]. —häher, m. V. —reiher. —haken, m. landing-hook. —hälter, m. a chest with holes at the top to keep fish alive in the water, a cauf; also a well. —hamen, m. landing-net. —handel, m. the trade of a fishmonger. —händler, m. fishmonger. —händlerinn, f. fish-woman. —haus, n. a fish-house. —haut, f. the skin of a fish, especially that kind of grained leather prepared of the skin of a fish, a species of squalus, shagreen. —herr, m. an officer who superintends fisheries. —holz, n. brushwood. —käfer, m. V. Wasserkäfer. —kasten, m. a chest with holes at the top to keep fish alive in the water, a cauf; also, a well. —kelle, f. fish-trowel. —kessel, m. fish-kettle. —kiefer, m. —kieme, f. V. —ohr. —koch, m. a cook whose occupation is to prepare fish for the table. —köder, m. bait for fish. —korb, m. fish-basket. —körner, pl. the seed of the jagged moon-seed. —kram, m. V. —handel. —krämer, m. V. —händler. —krämerinn, f. V. —händlerinn. —kraut, n. V. Braunwurz. —kümmel, m. common caraway. —kunde, f. ichthyology. —kundige, m. ichthyologist. —lager, n. a place where fish are bedded. —lake, f. fish-brine. —leer, adj. and adv not stored with fish. —lehre, f. V. —kunde. —leich, m. spawn. —leim, m. fish-glue, isinglass, ichthyocol, ichthyocolla. V. Hausenblase. —loch, n. V. —grube. —löffel, m. V. —kelle. —markt, m. fishmarket. —maul, n. 1) [a genus of univalve or univalviter shells] nerite. Ein versteinertes —maul, neritite. Fig. 2) a lover of fish. —meister, m. an officer who superintends fisheries. ||—menger, m. fishmonger. —mewe, f. V. Fischer 2). —milch, f. milt. —mondsame, m. jagged moon-seed. —netz, n. V. —ergarn. Ein —netz um etwas Verlornes aufzusuchen, [in seamen's language] a sweep. —ohr, n. gill. Die Fische holen Athem im Wasser durch die —ohren, fish perform respiration under water by the gills. —öl, n. V. —thran. —ordnung, f. the fishing-laws. —otter, f. the common otter. —otterhund, m. a dog used for hunting otters, otter-hound. —pfanne, f. fish-pan. —pforte, f. a sort of fish-warren. —pinsel, m. a pencil made of otters' hair. —raffel, f. a sweep-net. —recht, n. [in law] piscary. —reich, adj. and adv. abounding with fish. Ein —reicher Teich, a fishful pond, a pond well-stocked with fish. —reiher, m. the heronshaw and common heron. —reuse, f. a kind of basket-work for catching fish, a wear. —rogen, m. V. Rogen. —satz, m. fry. —schiefer, m. bituminous marl-slate. —schuppe, f. the small shell or crust which composes a part of the covering of a fish, scale. —schwanz, m. the tail of a fish. —seuche, f. a contagious disease in fishes. —speise, f. a meal of fish, fish-diet, fish-meal. —stechen, n. the spearing of fish, harpooning. —stein, m. V. —schiefer. —tag, m. 1) a day of fishing. 2) fish-day, meagre-day. —tau, n. [in seamen's lang.] the mooring-rope of a boat. —teich, m. fish-pond. —thran, m. train-oil, fish-oil. —tiegel, m. a fish-pan with feet. —topf, m. fish-tub. ||—trampe, f. a pole for stirring up water. —trog, m. a trough for keeping fish alive in water. —tunke, f. V. —brühe. —verkäuferinn, f. fish-woman, fish-wife. —waare, f. V. —werk. —wage, f. scales for weighing fish. —wanne, f. a tub in which fish are kept. —wasser, n. a stream or piece of water containing fish. —wate, f. a large net for catching fish, a sein. —wehr, n. fish garth. —weib, n. fish-wife. Fig. a woman of coarse manners. —weiberhaube, f. a species of limpet [patella equestris]. —weide, f. a fishful place in a pond. —weihe, f. V. —erfalk. —weiher, m. V. —teich. —werk, n. all sort of fish used as food, or fish in general as an article of merchandise. —wimmelnd, adj. and adv. swarming with fish. —wirthschaft, f. the management of fisheries, fish-ponds. —wurm, m. [in ichthyology] the hay. —wurzel, f. V. Feigwarzenkraut. —zahn, m. a stone formed by the petrification of a fish-tooth. —zaun, m. [among fishermen] a kind of fence on the sea-coast intended to catch fish at the flood. —zehnte, m. the tithe of fish. —zeug, n. fishing tackle. —zoll, m. a toll paid for vending fish in a fair, market, or the like. —zug, m. a draught of fishes [in Script.].

2. Fisch, m. [-es, pl. -e] V. Fische 1).

Fischband, n. [with locksmiths] a particular sort of hinges whose ends are fixed or inserted into the wood.

Fischchen, n. [-s, pl. -] [diminut. of Fisch] 1) also ||Fischlein, a little fish. Fig. 2) [in fam. lang. as an expression of endearment] Mein —, my chick or chicken! [a vulgar exclamation] Potz —, odds fish! 3) [markers at different games] fishes. 4) [in entomology] a genus of insects, lepisma.

Fische, f. [pl. -n] 1) [with locksmiths] the end of a hinge inserted into wood. 2) pl. [in seamen's lang.] partners. Die — des großen Mastes, partners of the main mast.

Fischeinen, V. [the more usual word] Fischeln.

Fischel, m. and n. [-es, pl. -e] a sort of penny stamped with the figure of a fish.

Fischeln, v. intr. to have a fishy taste or smell, to smell of fish.

Fischen, I. v. tr. 1) to catch from out of the water. Perlen —, to dive for pearls; Bernstein —, to fish up amber; den Anker —, [in seamen's lang.] to fish the anchor, to sweep for the anchor, to hook the anchor. 2) [to attempt to catch fish, by angling or drawing nets] to fish. Prov. Im Trüben ist gut —, it's good fishing in troubled waters. Fig † to attempt or seek to obtain by artifice or indirectly, to seek to draw forth, to fish. Hier giebt es nichts zu —, there is nothing to be fished for! II. v. intr. [in seamen's lang.] Das Steuer fischt, the rudder makes foul water; das Boiseil des Ankers fischt, is said of the buoy-rope, when it runs foul of the rudder.

Fischenzen, v. intr. V. [the usual word] Fischeln.

Fischer, m. [-s, pl. -] 1) fisher, fisherman. 2) [a genus of birds] the lesser gannet.

Fischer-amt, n. V. —innung. —barke, f. a fisher-boat. —baum, m. [a tree of the genus nyssa] tupelo. —boot, n. V. —barke. —dorf, n. a village inhabited by fishermen. —falk, m. fish-hawk. —garn, n. fishing-net. —gedicht, n. a piscatory eclogue. —geräth, n. —geräthschaften, pl. fishing-tackle, fishing-apparatus, fishing-gear. —hütte, f. a fisherman's hut. —innung, f. company of fishermen. —kahn, m. a fisher-boat, a fishing-boat. —karpen, m. a carp given in payment to fishermen for sewing a pond. —lein, n. V. Fischer 2). —netz, n. V. —garn. —ring, m. fisherman's ring [annulus piscatoris, a papal seal]. —schiff, n. fishing-vessel or ship. —stadt, f. fishertown. —stechen, n. a kind of joust or mock fight of fishermen on rivers. —weide, f. the osier. —zunft, f. V. —innung.

Fischerei, f. 1) the act or practice of catching fish, the business of catching fish, fishing, fishery, piscation. Von der — leben, to live by fishing. V. Perlen— &c. 2) [— Recht], the right or privilege of fishing in certain waters, piscary. 3) a fishery or fishing-place.

Fischicht, adj. and adv. fishlike, fishy. Ein —er Geruch, a fishy smell.

||Fischlein, n. [-s, pl. -] [diminut. of Fisch] a little fish.

Fischler, m. [rather unusual] [-s, pl. -] a dealer in fish, a fishmonger.

Fischungen, pl. V. Fische 2.

Fispern, v. tr. and intr. V. Flüstern.

||Fisse, f. [pl. -n] V. Fitze.

||Fissen, v. tr. V. Zerknittern.

Fistel, f. [pl. -n] [from the Lat. fistula] 1) [in music] a feigned treble, a feigned voice, falsetto. 2) [in medicine, a deep, narrow and callous ulcer] fistula. Das Aufschneiden einer —, syringotomy. 3) V. Fustel.

Fistel-artig, adj. and adv. 1) as with a feigned voice. —artig singen, to sing with a feigned voice, to sing falsetto. 2) [in medicine] fistulous. Ein —artiges Geschwür, a fistulous ulcer. —kassie, f. Alexandria purging-cassia, cassia-stick tree, or pudding pipe-tree. —kraut, n. common lousewort. —messer, n. [in surgery, an instrument for cutting fistulas] syringotome. —sänger, m. one who sings a faint treble or falsetto. —schneider, m. 1) a surgeon that cuts fistulas. 2) a surgical instrument. V. —messer. —stimme, f. a disagreeable sharp and acute voice

Fisteln, v. intr. to sing falsetto.

Fistulös, adj. and adv. fistulous. Ein —es Geschwür, a fistulous ulcer.

||Fitscheln, v. intr. to rub to and fro.

Fittig and Fittich, m. [-s, pl. -e] [the syllable Fitt is allied to the syllable Fed in Feder] 1) originally something which moves. a) [in common language and in contempt] the arm. Nimm ihn am — und führe ihn hinaus, seize him by the arm and take him out! ||b) a part of a garment or dress that hangs loose, lappet. 2) a wing, or pinion. Fig. [in poetry] Die —e des Ruhmes, the wings of fame; auf den —en des Windes, on the wings of the wind. Fig. [in Scripture, protection, generally in the plural] wing.

Fittig-lahm, adj. and adv. lame in the wing. ||—stein, m. a tile.

Fittigen, v. tr. to furnish with wings, to wing.

Fitzband, n. [-es, pl. -bänder] V. Fitze 1.

Fitze, f. [pl. -n] [seems to be allied to Faden] 1) a piece of thread for tying the yarn when it is reeled. 2) [a knot of yarn] a skein. Eine — Zwirn, a skain of twine. 3) a crease, fold or wrinkle.

Fitzeln, V. Fitzen.

1. Fitzen, [from Fitze] v. tr. 1) to tie in a skein, to form skeins. 2) to fold, to wrinkle. Die Stirne —, to knit the brows. 3) to feaze, to unravel, to disentangle.

2. Fitzen, [allied to fiedeln = to move to and fro, to rub] v. tr. 1) to rub rapidly, to move to and fro rapidly. 2) [in vulgar language] Ein Kind —, to beat a child with a rod.

Fitzfaden, m. [-s, pl. -] V. Fitze 1.

Fitzfeile, f. [pl. -n] [with needle-makers] a file for perforating needles.

Fitzhaken, m. [-s, pl. -] a sieve-maker's hook.

Fitzruthe, *f.* [*pl.* -n] [with weavers] temple.

Fitzstock, *m.* [-es, *pl.* -stöcke] a sieve-maker's stick.

Fitzzange, *f.* [*pl.* -n] a pin-maker's pincers.

Fix, *adj.* and *adv.* [allied to weich-en, bewegen, to the Lat. *fug*-io, to the Gr. φυγ- in φεύγ-ω] [in fam. lang.] light and quick in motion, nimble, lively, swift.

Fix-fingerig, *adj.* and *adv.* nimble-fingered.

***Fixiren**, I. *v. tr.* 1) to fix, to establish, to settle. 2) Einen —, to fix one's eyes on a person. II. *v. r.* *sich an einem Orte —, to take one's permanent residence, to establish one's self at a place.

***Fixirung**, *f.* determining, settling.

***Fixstern**, *m.* [-s, *pl.* -e] [in astronomy] a fixed star.

***Fixum**, *n.* [-s, *pl.* Fixa] a stated salary or pay.

†**Flabbe**, *f.* [*pl.* -n] 1) loose hanging lips. Eine — habend, flap-mouthed. 2) [in contempt] the mouth.

Flach, [seems to be allied to Lage, legen] I. *adj.* and *adv.* 1) [without elevations or depressions] flat, plain. —er Boden, plain or level ground; —es Land, flat land; ein —er Landstrich, an even tract of land; das —e Feld, an open field; die —e Hand, the palm; [in heraldry] [die —e ausgestreckte Hand] apaume; ein —er Zug, [in mining] flat lodes, lode plots; das —e Licht, [in painting] a broad light. 2) [having little depth] flat. Eine —e Schüssel, a flat dish; das Schiff ist nur — zwischen Decks, the ship is not high between the decks; ‖ ein —er Winkel, a obtuse angle; das Wasser ist sehr —, the water is very shallow or shoal; —e See, smooth sea. 3) [having little height] flat. Ein —es Dach, a flat roof; ein —er Hügel, a sloping hill; ein —er Gang, ein —er Stollen, [in mining] a flat lode, a flat stulm; Münz oder —, [a popular play with money] cross and pile. 4) [in botany] Eine —e Dolde, a flat umbel; ein —es fleischiges Blatt, a plain or flat fleshy leaf; mit —en Blättern, flat-leaved, planipetalous; eine Blume mit —en Blättern, a planifolious flower; der —e Hut eines Pilzes, the flat cap of a fungus or mushroom; eine —e Blumendecke, a flat [common] perianth. *Fig.* Ein —er Kopf, a shallow-brained person, shallow-brain, shallow-pate; ein —es Urtheil, superficial judgment; ein —es Geschwätz, a shallow, an insipid talk. II. *adv.* 1) flatly. *Fig.* Sehr — [geistlos], very flatly. 2) [in seamen's language] — vor dem Winde segeln, or den Wind — vor dem Laken haben, to sail right afore the wind or the wind right aft; — in den Wind, dead to windward, or right in the wind's eye.

Flach-bohrer, *m.* a pulley-maker's auger. —**deichsel**, *f.* [in carpentry] a flat beam. —**drath**, *m.* [with goldsmiths] a flat wire. —**eisen**, *n.* 1) [with goldsmiths] a small anvil. 2) [in forges] a flat piece of iron, plate. —**feld**, *n.* V. Blachfeld. ‖—**fisch**, *m.* a species of cod. —**flöte**, *f.* [in organs] a flat-lipped organ-pipe. —**fuß**, *m.* a flat-foot. —**füßig**, *adj.* and *adv.* flat-footed. —**gangen**, *pl.* [in seamen's lang.] planks of the bottom or floor. —**garn**, *n.* [with hunters] V. Steckgarn. —**gelehrt**, *adj.* and *adv.* reaching or comprehending only what is obvious or apparent, superficial, shallow. —**hohleisen**, *n.* a sculptor's gouge. —**kettig**, *adj.* and *adv.* [with carpet-manufacturers] having a plain or flat warp. —**kopf**, *m.* a shallow-brained person, shallow-brain, shallow-pate. —**köpfig**, *adj.* and *adv.* shallow-brained. —**land**, *n.* V. Blachfeld. —**mahler**, *m.* V. Anstreicher. —**meißel**, *m.* a flat chisel [as opposed to a gouge]. —**nase**, *f.* a flat nose. —**näsig**, *adj.* and *adv.* flat-nosed. —**ruthe**, *f.* [with velvet-makers] a flat wire or a long pin. —**scheibe**, *f.* a flat round plate. —**seitig**, *adj.* and *adv.* flat-sided. —**spiegel**, *m.* a plain mirror. —**stahl**, *m.* a turner's flat chisel. —**stange**, *f.* a small anvil used by belt-makers in stamping buttons. —**stichel**, *m.* a flat style. —**teller**, *m.* 1) a flat plate. 2) a plate on which any thing is presented, a salver. —**tellerförmig**, *adj.* and *adv.* salver-shaped. [in botany] Eine —tellerförmige Blumenkrone, a hypocrateriform corol. —**vertieft**, *adj.* and *adv.* concave. Ein —vertieftes Glas, a concave glass. —**werk**, *n.* 1) shallow or superficial work. 2) [in architecture] flat roofing. —**zeiger**, *m.* [with engravers of coats of arms] a graver with a small round plate. —**ziegel**, *m.* flat tile.

Fläche, *f.* [*pl.* -n] 1) a surface without relief or prominences. Die — eines Degens, the flat of a sword; die — eines Buchstabens, [in printing] the face of a letter. 2) evenness of surface, flatness, plainness, levelness. Die — eines Tellers, the flatness of a plate. 3) [something level or flat] *a*) a level part of the earth, a level or extended plain, a flat. Eine unermeßliche —e, an immeasurable plain. *b*) [in geometry, an even or level surface] plane. Die abhängige oder geneigte —, [in mechanics] inclined plane. *c*) [in surveying mines] the hypotenuse. *d*) [with masons] pick-axe.

Flächelmeisel, *m.* [-s, *pl.* -] a sort of graver used by braziers and tinmen.

Flächeln, *v. tr.* [with braziers and tinmen] to cut with a graver.

Flächen, *v. tr.* to flat or flatten, to level. Einen Gang —, to level a walk.

Flächen-fuß, *m.* V. —maß. —**größe**, *f.* —**inhalt**, *m.* the superficial content of any figure, area. Der —inhalt eines Vierecks, Dreiecks, the area of a square of a triangle. —**maß**, *n.* 1) an instrument for measuring plain surfaces. 2) [in geometry] square-measure. —**meile**, *f.* a square mile. —**meßkunst**, *f.* planimetry. Die —meßkunst betreffend or dazu gehörig, planimetric, planimetrical. —**messung**, *f.* the measurement of plain surfaces. —**raum**, *m.* superficies, superficial extent [of a country &c.]. —**ruthe**, *f.* square rod. —**schuh**, *m.* square foot. —**zahl**, *f.* a square or square number [thus 64 is the square of 8]. Die doppelte —zahl, the cube [thus 64 is the cube of 4]. —**zoll**, *m.* square inch.

Flachheit, *f.* 1) evenness of surface, flatness, levelness. *Fig.* Die — seiner Urtheile, the shallowness of his reasonings. 2) *Fig.* a flat, dull or insipid thing. Er sagte nichts wie —en, he talked most stupidly.

Flächlich, [unusual] *adj.* and *adv.* superficial.

Flächling, [unusual] *m.* [-es, *pl.* -e] a superficial scholar.

Flachs, *m.* [-es] [appears to be allied to flechten, Flocke, Locke] [a plant of the genus linum; also the skin or fibrous part of the plant when broken and cleaned by hatcheling or combing] flax. — raufen, to pull flax; — brechen, to break flax; — dörren, rösten, to dry, to raite flax; — zubereiten, to dress flax [to break and clean it]; — spinnen, to spin flax.

Flachs-acker, *m.* V. Leinacker. —**ader**, *f.* V. Flechse. —**arbeit**, *f.* any work done in dressing flax. —**artig**, *adj.* and *adv.* flaxen, flaxy, like the down of the chin. —**bart**, *m.* 1) a thin flaxy beard. 2) a person with a flaxy beard. —**bärtig**, *adj.* and *adv.* having a flaxy beard. —**bau**, *m.* the culture of flax. —**baum**, *m.* [a shrub, native of the East Indies] antidesma. —**bereitung**, *f.* the dressing of flax. —**blatt**, *n.* a leaf of flax. —**bläuel**, *m.* a mallet for beating flax. —**blüte**, *f.* the flower of flax. —**blüthfarbe**, *f.* gridelin. ‖—**bose**, *f.* V. —[illegible] —**breche**, *f.* a machine to break flax, brake. —**brechen**, *n.* the breaking of flax. —**brecher**, *m.* —**brecherinn**, *f.* a person that breaks flax, flaxdresser. —**bündel**, *m.* a bundle of flax. —**darre**, *f.* a kiln for drying flax. —**dotter**, *m.* V. Leindotter. —**farbe**, *f.* the colour of flax. —**farben**, —**farbig**, *adj.* and *adv.* of the colour of flax, flaxen. —**feld**, *n.* V. Leinfeld. —**fink**, *m.* V. Hänfling. —**gelb**, *adj.* and *adv.* being of a light colour, flaxy. —gelbes Haar, flaxen hair. —**gras**, *n.* many-spiked cotton-grass. —**haar**, *n.* 1) flaxen hair. 2) a flaxen-haird boy or girl. —**handel**, *m.* dealing in flax. —**händler**, *m.* a dealer in flax. —**hechel**, *f.* flax-comb, ‖ hatchel. —**knoppe**, *f.* —**knoten**, *m.* V. Leinknoten. —**kopf**, *m.* [diminut. das —köpfchen.] 1) flaxen hair. 2) a person with flaxen hair. Sahen Sie den nieblichen —kopf or das niebliche —köpfchen, did you see the pretty flaxen-haired girl? —**köpfig**, *adj.* and *adv.* having flaxen hair. —**kraut**, *n.* [a name of plants] *a*) common dodder, lady's laces. *b*) toad-flax, snap-dragon, or calves' snout. *c*) bastard toad-flax. ‖*d*) V. Quendel. —**land**, *n.* 1) land grown with flax. 2) land fit for growing flax. —**markt**, *m.* a market where flax is exposed to sale. —**raufe**, *f.* 1) the pulling of flax. 2) [an instrument for cleaning flax] a ripple. —**röste**, *f.* 1) the raiting or rating of flax. 2) the time of raiting or rating flax. 3) rating-pool. —**schwinge**, *f.* a swingle or swingling-knife. —**seide**, *f.* V. —kraut, *a.* —**spinnen**, *n.* the spinning of flax. —**werg**, *n.* tow of flax.

Flächsen, *adj.* and *adv.* made of flax, flaxen.

Flächsicht, *adj.* and *adv.* resembling flax, flaxen, flaxy.

Flack, *n.* [-es, *pl.* -e] [= flach] [in seamen's lang.] flat bottom or floor.

Flacken, [allied to fliegen &c.] I. *v. intr.* to waver, to flutter, to flare, to burn with an unsteady light. II. *v. tr.* 1) to render less dense [illegible] compact, to loosen by beating. Die Wolle — [with clothiers] to beat wool with sticks. 2) [in [illegible] fishery] to split and dry on flakes [said of [illegible] fish].

Flacker, *m.* [-s, *pl.* -] a workman that beats wool.

Flacker-binse, *f.* common soft rush. —**feuer**, *n.* flaring fire. *Fig.* a blazing [illegible] transient fire. Seine Liebe ist nur —feuer, [illegible] love is only a short-lived glow.

Flackerig, *adj.* and *adv.* flaring.

Flackern, [from flacken] *v. intr.* 1) to play [illegible] move quickly to and fro. Das Licht flackert, the candle flares [that is, the light wanders from [illegible] natural course]; ein —des Licht, a flickering light. 2) [u. w. seyn] to flirt, to flutter.

Flackfisch, *m.* [-es, *pl.* -e] the best sort [illegible] cod-fish dried on flakes.

***Flacon**, [pron. as in the Fr.] *m.* [-s, -s] a phial, smelling-bottle. V. also Riechfläschchen.

Fladdern, V. Flattern.

Fladen, *m.* [-s, *pl.* -] [allied to platt] 1) something in the form of a cake rather flat than high, but roundish, a flat cake or bread. Butter—, a slice of bread and butter. 2) V. [illegible]—.

Fladenbrod, *n.* unleavened bread.

‖**Flader**, *f.* [*pl.* -n] [perhaps from flattern] 1) a streak or vein in wood or stone. 2) V. Maßholderbaum. 3) the hole of a bee-hive.

Flader-gitter, *n.* the lattice of the hole of a bee-hive. —**gras**, *n.* common millet-gras. Das straussichte —gras, clustered millet-grass. —holz, n. veiny wood. —loch, n. V. —, 3.

Fläderig, *adj.* and *adv.* veiny. —es Holz, veiny wood; [in mining] —es or fladerichtes Gestein, flawy rocks.

||**Fläge,** *f.* [*pl.* -n] 1) [allied to flach] low marshy ground. 2) [in seamen's lang.] [allied to fliegen] flaw. Eine Regen—, flaw of rain; eine Wind—, flaw of wind. 3) [allied to Fleck] [in mining] feeder of a vein.

***Flageolét,** *n.* [pron. Flascholett] [-s, *pl.* -s or -e] a little flute, flagelet, flageolet.

Flággast, *m.* [-es, *pl.* -en] [in seamen's lang.] a sailor, seaman, mariner.

Flágge, *f.* [*pl.* -n] [from fliegen] [in seamen's lang.] 1) flag. Die — am Bugspriet, a jack; die — aufstecken, to hoist the flag; die — fliegen lassen, to display the flag or colours; die — streichen, to strike or lower the flag; die — im Schau wehen lassen, to hoist the ensign with a waft. 2) the flag by which a commodore is distinguished from other ships of his squadron.

Flagge-fahrt, *f.* signal displayed for sailing, blue-peter. —n-bild, *n.* the ornamental figure on a flag. —n-führer, *m.* flag-officer. —n-schiff, *n.* flag-ship. —stange, *f.* —stock, *m.* flag-staff. —tuch, *n.* bunting or buntine.

Flággen, I. *v. tr.* to dress a ship. II. *v. intr.* to make a signal by flags or pendants.

Fláke, *f.* [*pl.* -n] [from flechten?] a large fishing-net, trammel.

Fláken, *v. tr.* to catch fish with trammels.

Flakeréi, *f.* fishing with trammels.

Flámänder, *m.* [-s, *pl.* -] **Flámänderinn,** a native of Flanders, Fleming.

***Fláme,** *f.* [*pl.* -n] [in farriery] a fleam.

Fláming, *n.* [-es, *pl.* -e] Flanders or the low countries of Europe.

Fláminger, *m.* [-s, *pl.* -] **Flámingerinn,** a native of Flanders, Fleming.

Flamíngo, *m.* [-s, *pl.* -s or -e] [a fowl] the flamingo.

1. **Flämisch,** *adj.* and *adv.* Flemish. —es Tuch, Dutch sail-duck, sheeting linen; —e Leinwand, Flanders; das —e Recht, Flemish law; ein Pfennig —, three pence. *Fig.* † in a high degree, much. — trinken, to drink much.

2. **Flämisch,** *adj.* and *adv.* [perhaps from flennen] affected with ill humour, cross, sour, sullen.

Flämmchen, ||**Flämmlein,** *n.* [-s, *pl.* -] [diminut. of Flamme] a little flame.

Flámme, *f.* [*pl.* -n] [Lat. *flamma*, appears to be allied to flimmern, flackern = sich schnell hin und her bewegen] 1) blaze, flame. Das Feuer brennt mit einer —, the fire blazes; mit einer hellen — brennen, to burn with a bright flame; in —n ausbrechen, to burst out in a flame; in —n setzen, to inflame; in —n stehen, to be in flames; etwas den —n opfern, to throw something into the fire; die — verzehrt Alles, flames consume every thing. *Fig.* *a*) the passion of love, ardent love. Mein Herz steht in —n, my heart's on flame. *d*) heat of passion, combustion, flame, violent contention. Ein eifersüchtiges Weib kann ein ganzes Dorf in —n setzen, a jealous wife will set a whole village in a flame; die —[n] des Krieges [Kriegs—], the flames of war. 2) [something resembling a flame] *a*) a meteor or light which appears in the night, sometimes adhering to a part of a ship [Castor and Pollux], or over marshy grounds [ignis fatuus, vulgarly called Will with the whisp or Jack with a lantern]. *b*) [with sportsmen] a naked spot or red membrane over and near the eyes of the cock of the wood and grouse. *c*) light, luster, fire. Die — in ihren Augen, the fire in her eyes. 3) [in mining] Ein Flämmchen Erz, a slight indication of metal in a lode.

Flammen-auge, *n.* an eye like a flame. Mit —augen, flame-eyed; das —auge des Tages, [in poetry] the blaze of day. —bart, *f.* the blazing beard [of a blazing-star or comet]. —beschweift, *adj.* and *adv.* having a coma or train of light [as a blazing-star]. —blume, *f.* lychnidea. —farbe, *f.* flamecolour. —farben, *adj.* and *adv.* flamecoloured. —gezeug, *n.* tools used by joiners for working wood in the shape of a flame. —gleich, *adj.* and *adv.* like flame, flameous. —glut, *f.* the glow of flames. —haar, *n.* blazing hair [that is the coma or train of light of a blazing-star]. —haß, *m.* violent hatred. —hauch, *m.* flamy breath. —heer, *n.* a fiery host. —kranz, *m.* a flamy garland. —kuß, *m.* a fiery kiss. —licht, *n.* a blazing light. —meer, *n.* 1) a fiery sea. 2) *Fig.* *a*) a burning heat; burning pain. *b*) a sea of brightness. Die Stadt war glänzend erleuchtet, sie glich einem —meere, the town was brilliantly illuminated, it resembled a sea of flame. —naht, *f.* [with seamstresses] pyramidical seam. —reich, *adj.* and *adv.* rich in flames, fiery. —reiher, *m.* V. Flamingo. —ruthe, Flammruthe, *f.* 1) [in Scripture] fiery rod. 2) [with joiners] a wavy pattern or model. —säule, *f.* 1) a fiery column. 2) a blazing fire. —schild, *n.* a fiery shield. —schütz, *m.* a surname of Cupid. —schwert, *n.* a fiery sword. —stich, *m.* [with seamstresses] 1) pyramidical stitch. 2) V. —naht. —stock, Flammstock, *m.* 1) [with joiners] the handle with a notching-iron. 2) a bar used by locksmiths for forming grates. —strom, *m.* a stream of flames, a fiery stream. —tod, *m.* the perishing by flames. —vogel, *m.* V. —reiher. —wagen, *m.* [chiefly in sacred poetry] a fiery waggon, lightning. —wirbel, *m.* a volume of flames. —wort, *n.* a flaming word. —zug, *m.* a fiery stroke or touch of the pen. Mit or in —zügen schilderte er ihnen die Schmach der Unterdrückung, with [in] fiery words he described to them the disgrace of servitude.

Flámmeisen, *n.* [-s, *pl.* -] [with joiners] notching-iron.

Flámmen, I. *v. intr.* 1) to burn in vapour or in a current, to flame, to blaze. Das Feuer flammt, the fire blazes. 2) to shine with excess of heat, to burn. 3) to shine like burning gas, to flame. Ein —der Stern, a blazing star; ein —des Gelb, a flaming yellow; warum flammt dein Auge? wherefore burn your eyes? sein Auge flammte vor Zorn, his eyes flashed with anger; sein Auge flammte vor Freude, his eyes sparkled with joy; ein —des Schwert, a flaming sword. 4) to be on fire, to flame, to burn. Die Stadt flammt, the town is in flames. *Fig.* to be inflamed with passion or desire. II. *v. tr.* 1) to burn the surface of a thing, to singe. Eine gerupfte Gans —, to singe a plucked goose; die Häute —, [with curriers] to expose the skins to the heat of burning coals. 2) to work in the shape of a flame, to give a wavy appearance to. Seide —, to water or tabby silk; geflammtes Seidenzeug, watered, waved or tabbied silk; geflammtes Zeug, watered stuff; geflammtes Holz, grained wood; geflammte Säulen, striated columns; eine Leiste —, [with joiners] to notch, or to jag a ledge. 3) to display, to exhibit conspicuously, to blazon.

Flámmern, [rather unusual] *v. intr.* to burn in flame.

Flámmicht, *adj.* and *adv.* 1) flamy. 2) watered, tabbied.

Flámmruthe, *f.* [*pl.* -n] V. Flammenruthe.

Flámmstock, *m.* [-es, *pl.* -stöcke] V. Flammenstock.

Flánderer, *m.* [-s, *pl.* -] V. Flamänder.

Flándern, *n.* [-s, *pl.* -] [a proper name] Flanders. Die beiden —, East- and West-Flanders.

Flándrisch, *adj.* and *adv.* Flemish.

Flanéll, *m.* [-es, *pl.* -e] [a soft nappy woolen cloth] flannel. Geköperter —, swanskin.

Flanellmacher, *m.* flannel-maker.

Flánke, *f.* [*pl.* -n] [allied to lenken, legen] 1) [the fleshy or muscular part of the side of an animal between the ribs and the hip] flank. 2) [the side of an army, or of any division of the army, as of a brigade, regiment or battalion] flank. Dem Feinde in die — fallen, to attack the enemy in flank, to flank the enemy. 3) [in fortification, that part of a bastion which reaches from the curtain to the face, and defends the opposite face, the flank and the curtain, or a line drawn from the extremity of the face towards the inside of the work] flank. Mit —n decken, to flanker. 4) [in heraldry] flanch.

||**Flánken,** *m.* [-s, *pl.* -] a cantle of bread or meat.

***Flanqueúr,** [pron. Flangköhr] *m.* [-s, *pl.* -s] [in military affairs] a light infantery-man, a rifleman, a flanker.

***Flanquíren,** [pron. Flangkihren] I. *v. intr.* 1) [to secure or guard on the side] to flank. 2) [to attack sideways] to flanker. ||3) † to wave or move violently. Er flanquirte heftig mit dem Messer, he brandished his knife. II. *v. tr.* to rove about, to range.

Fläschchen, ||**Fläschlein,** *n.* [-s, *pl.* -] [diminut. of Flasche] 1) phial. 2) [a distemper in sheep] wen [at the throat].

Fläsche, *f.* [*pl.* -n] [A. S. *flaxa*, Fr. *flasque*, *flacon*, Engl. *flasket* signifies a basket. It seems to be allied to Logel, Lägel, the Lat. *lag-ena* &c.] 1) in general something hollow. *a*) a cylinder [instead of a ball] in air-guns. *b*) the shell of a block. *c*) [with some metallists, a kind of ledge, inclosing a board which, being filled with wet sand, serves as a mold for castings] frame. 2) a kind of bottle, flagon, flask. Eine — Wein, a flask of wine; Wein, Bier auf —n füllen, to bottle wine, beer; *fig.* über or bei der [Wein-] — sitzen, to sit over one's wine; er liebt die —, he is fond of his bottle; Oel in —n, flask-oil; [in physics] die Leidener — or Kleistische —, the Leyden phial [a glass vessel partly coated with tinfoil, to be used in electrical experiments]. 3) V. Kugelfisch.

Flaschen-baum, *m.* 1) custard apple. 2) V. —kürbis. —bier, *n.* bottled beer, bottle-ale. —birn, *f.* the Colmar pear, the manna pear. —büchse, *f.* an air-gun with a cylinder. —bürste, *f.* a bottle-brush. —eisen, *n.* [with lapidaries] an iron tool on which the stone is fastened. —futter, *n.* a bottle case. Das —futter in einer Kutsche, well. *—held, *m.* 1) a hard drinker. 2) a bottle-swaggerer. —keller, *m.* 1) a partition in a cellar where bottled liquors are kept. 2) V. —futter. —korb, *m.* bottle-basket. —kürbis, *m.* calabash, bottle-gourd, or long gourd. —rahm, —rahmen, *m.* [among founders, a kind of ledge, inclosing a board filled with wet sand] frame. —rick [—Repositorium], *m.* bottle-rack. —sack, *m.* a rushy sack for conveying bottles. —schanze, *f.* [in physics] an electrical battery. —schraube, *f.* cork-screw. —teller [—Untersetzer], *m.* decanter-stand. —träger, *m.* bottle-carrier [for upright bottles]; bottle-tray [for lying bottles]. —zug, *m.* [a machine consisting of many pulleys] polyspast.

||**Fläschel,** *n.* [-s, *pl.* -] [diminut. of Flasche]

1) a little bottle, a phial. 2) V. Fläschchen, 2.

*Flaschinétt, *n.* [-es, *pl.* -e] 1) flageolet. 2) [in organs] flageolet-register.

Fläschner, *m.* [-s, *pl.* -] tin-man.

1. Flāser, *f.* [*pl.* -n] 1) a streak or vein in wood or stone. V. also Flader 1. 2) [with bookbinders] a coloured picture on horn-books.

2. Fläser, *m.* [-s, *pl.* -n] and *f.* [*pl.* -n] V. Masholder.

Fläserig, V. Fladerig.

‡Fläth, *m.* [-es] cleanness, in the compound word Unflath.

Fläts, *m.* [-es, *pl.* -e] V. Fläz.

Flätsche, *f.* [*pl.* -n] [allied to Fladen] 1) something in the form of a large cake rather flat than high but roundish, especially a roundish heap of hay on a meadow, a hay-cock. 2) any swelling, a tumour.||and †3) a large mouth.

Flätschen, V. Fletschen.

Flätterer, *m.* [-s, *pl.* -] 1) [rather unusual] one that flutters [as a bird, a butterfly &c.]. 2) a fickle or inconstant person, a rover.

Flätterhaarig, *adj.* and *adv.* soft [said of wool].

Flätterhaft, *adj.* and *adv.* of a changeable mind, not firm in opinion or purpose, wavering, unstable, irresolute, inconstant, fickle. Ein —er Mensch, a fickle or inconstant person, a rover; ein —er Liebhaber, a fickle lover.

Flätterhaftigkeit, *f.* a wavering, wavering disposition, inconstancy, instability, unsteadiness in opinion or purpose. Die — der Liebhaber, the fickleness of lovers; die — der Jugend, the volatility of youth; eine Anlage zur —, a flitting disposition.

*Flatterie, *f.* [*pl.* -en] [in common lang.] flattery.

Flätterig, *adj.* and *adv.* V. Flatterhaft.

Flätterig, Flättrig, *m.* [-es] [a tree] plectronia [plectronia ventosa].

Flätterling, *m.* [-s, *pl.* -e] a fickle person.

Flättern, *v. intr.* [allied to the Engl. *to flit* = sich schnell wegbewegen] 1) to move with quick vibrations or undulations, to flutter. Ein —des Segel, a fluttering sail; —de Fahnen, flowing colours; im Winde —d, waving in the wind, playing in the wind; ihre goldnen Locken — im Winde, her golden tresses wanton in the wind. *Fig.* Muntere Scherze — um deine Lippen, merry jests play on your lips; —de Gedanken, fluttering thoughts; sein Herz flattert stets von einer Schönen zur andern, his mind is ever roving from one beauty to another. 2) to move about briskly, without consequence, to flutter, to rove carelessly or irregularly. Von einem Orte zum andern —, to ramble; die Mädchen — durch die Straße, the girls flirt about the street. 3) to beat the wing, to flutter, to flicker, to flit, to flitter. Der Vogel flattert, the bird flutters; —d auf ihrem Neste, flickering on her nest.

Flatter-aspe, *f.* V. Espe. —geist, *m.* 1) fickleness. 2) a fickle person. —kohl, *m.* —kraut, *n.* curled cole-wort. —mine, *f.* [in fortification, a little mine in the form of a well, 8 or 10 feet wide, and 10 or 12 deep, dug under some work] fougade. —ruß, *m.* the finest soot. —schönheit, *f.* beauty speedily vanishing, transitory beauty. —sinn, *m.* fickleness, inconstancy, changeableness, flirtation. Der —sinn der Jugend, the levity of youth.

Flaú, *adj.* and *adv.* [allied to lau] 1) [in seamen's language] Der Wind wird —er, the wind lulls. 2) weak, feeble. Der Wein wird —, wine becomes stale; [in painting] die —e, a soft bluish tint of distant objects. *Fig.* Es wird ihm —, [in common language] he faints; *die Liebe wird —, love abates. 3) heavy of sale, dull. Die Gerste war auch —, barley was also dull.

Flaúen, *v. tr.* [allied to fließen, Dutch *vloyen*] 1) to cleanse with a second or repeated application of water, after washing. Die Wäsche —, to rinse linen. 2) [to separate extraneous matter from] to wash. Die Erze —, [in mining] to buddle ore.

Flaúfaß, *n.* [-sses, *pl.* -fässer] [in mining] buddle.

Flaúigkeit, *f.* weakness, feebleness.

Flaúm, *m.* [-es, *pl.* -e] [allied to the Lat. *pluma*, and probably to *fla*-re, blasen = wehen, sich bewegen] 1) soft down, flue. Isländischer —, Iceland down. 2) a bed of down, down-bed. 3) the first fine feathers of fowls, down. 4) the down of the chin.

Flaum-bart, *m.* a downy beard. *Fig.* * a stripling, a youth. —bärtig, *adj.* and *adv.* having a downy beard. —[en]lager, *n.* a down-bed. —feder, *f.* [the fine soft feathers of fowls] down.

Flaúmen, *pl.* [in common language] the suet of swine, also the raw fat of geese, fowls and fish.

Flaúmig, *adj.* and *adv.* downy.

Flaús, Flaúsch, *m.* [-es, *pl.* -e] [allied to Flies] 1) a tuft of hair or wool. 2) a great coat made of a sort of coarse cloth, a Flushing coat.

Flaus-rock, *m.* V. Flaus 2.

Flaúse, *f.* [*pl.* -n] [in fam. lang.] trick, artifice, evasion, shuffling. —n machen, to practice shifts.

Flausen-macher, *m.* a shuffler. —macherei, *f.* shuffling.

*Flaúto, *n.* [-s, *pl.* -s or Flauti] a small wind-instrument, a flute.

Flaútrog, *m.* [-es, *pl.* -tröge] [in metallurgy] washing-trough.

Fläz, *m.* [-es, *pl.* -e] a coarse fellow, a boor.

Flèchse, *f.* [*pl.* -n] [allied to Flachs-haar] [in anatomy, that which unites a muscle to a bone] a tendon, a sinew.

Flechsen-artig, *adj.* and *adv.* partaking of the nature of a tendon or sinew, tendinous. —haube, *f.* [in anatomy, the aponeurotic expansion which covers the head like a cap] coif. —haut, *f.* [in anatomy] aponeurosis, aponeurosy.

Flèchsicht, *adj.* and *adv.* [partaking of the nature of a tendon] tendinous.

Flèchsig, *adj.* and *adv.* tendinous, sinewy.

Flèchtchen, ||Flèchtlein, *n.* [-s, *pl.* -n] diminut. of Flechte.

Flèchte, *f.* [*pl.* -n] 1) the connection of slender bodies interwoven, but chiefly a braid of hair, a tress, a plait. Die —n auflösen, to unbraid hair. 2) [in husbandry] a texture of twigs or osiers, but chiefly a kind of basket or hamper of wicker-work for a cart or waggon. Die Käse—, a hurdle or crate on which cheeses are dried. 3) [a genus of diseases] herpes, tetter. Die einfache Flechte, the miliary tetter; die lebendige or um sich fressende —, the corroding tetter. 4) the itch-mite. 5) [a genus of plants] lichen. 6) [in conchology] serpula [serpula filigrana].

Flechten-artig, *adj.* and *adv.* 1) herpetic. 2) partaking of the nature of lichens. —beschreibung, *f.* 1) a description of the herpes. 2) lichenography.

Flèchten, *ir.* I. *v. tr.* [allied to the Gr. πλέκ-ω, to legen &c., for flechten is = zusammenlegen] 1) to interweave, to braid, to plait. Die Haare —, to plait the hair; Bänder, Blumen in die Haare —, to twist hair with ribbons, or flowers; Weidenruthen zu einem Korbe —, to make a basket of osiers interwoven; einen Missethäter auf das Rad —, to fasten a criminal on the wheel. *Fig.* [obsolete] to implicate, to involve. V. Ver—. *it.* To diversify by mixture, to interlard. V. Durch—, Ein—. 2) to form by texture. Einen Kranz —, to wreath[e] a garland; sie flochten eine Dornenkrone und setzten sie auf sein Haupt, [in Script.] when they had plaited a crown of thorns, they put it on his head; einen Zaun —, to plash a hedge; eine geflochtene Decke, a mat; ein geflochtener Stuhl, a wicker chair. II *v. r.* sich —, to turn around something. Die Rebe flicht sich um die Ulme, the vine winds around the elm; Rauchsäulen, um die sich Flammenkränze —, pillars of smoke twisted about with wreaths of flame.

Flecht-korb, *m.* a wicker-basket. —weide, *f.* a willow used in making baskets, osier. —werk, *n.* plaited work, basket-work. —zaun, *m.* a plashed hedge, a hurdle.

Flèchting, *n.* [-s] [in seamen's lang.] shrouds and other rigging at the mast-head.

Flèck, *m.* [-es, *pl.* -e] I. [probably allied flach, Fläche, legen &c.] 1) a small extent space, a spot. Ein — Land, a spot of ground, patch; in or auf diesem — der Erde or Erd—, this corner of the globe; es ist der schönste — der Erde, it is the finest spot on earth; — Gras, [Gras—] a spot of grass; 'es noch ein ziemlicher — bishin, 't is a l stretch from here to that place. 2) a place, particular place, a spot. Er ging nicht vom he did not stir; fest auf einem —e, fixed to spot; den rechten —, or auf den rechten —fen, to hit the point. 3) a speck, a spot. — auf dem Papier, a spot or stain on pa blot; ein — im Kleide, a speck on a II. [probably allied to the Sw. *fläcka* = th a small piece of any thing. 1) a piece of sewed on a garment to repair it, a patch. auf einen Rock setzen, to patch a coat; — die Schuhe setzen, to piece shoes. 2) [with makers, a piece of leather on the heel of a shoe] piece. 3) a shred or piece of cloth. Ein — einer Haube, a piece of cloth for a cap. [4) apron. 5) [in cookery and with butchers] [the stomach of ruminating animals, prepared for tripe. Eine Pastete von —en, a pie of tripe.

Fleck-fieber, *n.* 1) a purple fever. petechial fever. —kehlchen, *n.* a species wind-thrush. —kugel, *f.* a ball of soap or preparation to take out stains. —leder sole-leather for boots. ||—sieder, *m.* a that boils tripes.

Flèckchen, ||Flècklein, *n.* [-s, *pl.* -] di of Fleck. Dieses — der Erde lacht mir vor andern, this corner of the earth smiles t before all others.

||Flèckel, *n.* [-s, *pl.* -] diminut. of Fleck Flecken.

Flècken, *m.* [-s, *pl.* -] [= Fleck I.] 1) a country-town, a borough, a market-town place of a different colour from the g spot. Ein weißes Pferd mit braunen — horse with brown spots; hochrothe —, stains; rothe — auf der Haut, red spots skin; — in der Sonne, spots in the sun Auge, specks in the eye; ||die —, the m discoloration from foreign matter, a spot speck. Ein — im Kleide, oder im Tuch, a a speck on a garment or cloth; Sie — in Ihr Taschentuch machen, you wil your handkerchief; einen — aus einem herausmachen, to take out a stain or spot a garment; ein Tinten—, a blot; ein Fett—, a spot of grease. *Fig.* a stain on character or reputation, disgrace, reproach, fault, blemish, a blur, a spot, a taint. Dem guten Namen eines Andern — anhängen, to stain or to blur any one's reputation; sein Betragen ist ohne —, his behaviour is free from taint.

Flecken-kraut, *n.* 1) [Schildkraut] skull-cap. 2) [Sauerklee] wood-sorrel. —**los**, *adj.* and *adv.* spotless, stainless, taintless. Ein —loses Gemüth, a spotless mind.

Flecken, [V. Fleck I. and II.] I. *v. tr.* 1) to discolour, to stain, to spot [a garment, paper]. 2) to speckle. Eine gefleckte Schlange, a speckled serpent. 3) [in coining] to shear [the small money]; [with pinmakers] den Draht —, to flatten a wire; [with shoemakers] die Schuhe —, to patch shoes; Absätze —, to mend the heels of shoes [by the addition of new heel-pieces]. ||4) to mend [a garment, stockings]. II. *v. intr.* 1) to alter the colour of a thing, to spot. Oel, Fett fleckt, oil, grease spots. 2) to get spotted or stained. Das Weiße fleckt leicht, white is a colour that soils easily. 3) to get on, to proceed, to advance. *Fig.* † and * Es will nicht —, it goes on tardily. ||4) to be ill of the measles.

Flecket, *adj.* and *adv.* V. Fleckig.

Fleckicht, *adj.* and *adv.* resembling a spot.

Fleckig, *adj.* and *adv.* 1) spotty. —es Vieh, spotted cattle; — im Gesichte seyn, to have a spotty face; —e Kleider, stained clothes; —e Hände, dirty hands. 2) [in mining] —es Zinn, hard tin.

Fleckling, *m.* [-es, *pl.* -e] V. Kakarlak.

Fledermaus, *f.* [Fleder allied to Feder] [*pl.* -mäuse] 1) a bat, a flittermouse, rear-mouse. 2) *Fig.* formerly a small coin of Silesia of the value of three pence.

Fledermaus-blume, *f.* the chalcedonian iris. —**flügel**, *m.* [in anatomy] the thick round portion of the broad ligament of the uterus by which the ovarium is connected with the uterus.

Flederratte, Flederratze, *f.* [*pl.* -n] V. Fledermaus.

Flederwisch, *m.* [-es, *pl.* -e] 1) a goose-wing used for kindling fire or for cleaning any thing of dust. *Fig.* * and † Sie hat —e feil, she is prudish [said of a virgin]. 2) [in contempt] a sword. Heraus mit eurem —! out with your arm!

Flegel, *m.* [-s, *pl.* -] the bat of a flail; flail. *Fig.* a clown, boor or churl, a rude or insolent fellow.

Flegel-jahr, *n.* or *pl.* die —jahre, youthful age. —**kappe**, *f.* the strap of a flail.

Flegelei, *f.* rustic manners or behaviour; any act of rudeness or ill-breeding, incivility.

Flegeler, Flegler, *m.* [-s, *pl.* -] [in the German history of the 15th century] a man armed with a flail. V. Flegelkrieg.

Flegelhaft, *adj.* and *adv.* clownish, boorish, rustic. Ein —er Mensch, a clownish fellow, a churl, a clown, a boor; ein —es Betragen, a rude behaviour; sich — betragen, to behave rudely, churlishly.

Flegeln, I *v. intr.* to behave uncivilly, rudely or unmannerly. II. *v. tr.* to call [any one] churl or clown.

Flegler, *m.* [-s, *pl.* -] V. Flegeler.

Flegler-krieg, *m.* [in German history] a war carried on in the 15th century by peasants armed with flails.

Flehen, [allied to fliegen, flechten, drehen, drehen; only used fig. as in Lat. *supplicare*] I. *v. intr.* to crave [for mercy]. Um Hülfe —, to implore any one's help; zum Gnadenthrone —, to supplicate the throne of grace; vor dem Herrn, zu dem Herrn or dem Herrn —, to pray God; inständig zu einem —, to beseech any one instantly. II. *v. tr.* to ask with submission or humility, to implore. Er flehete ihn, daß er ihn begnadige, he craved his pardon; er flehete Gott um die Vergebung seiner Sünden, he supplicated God to pardon his sins; er flehete ihn darum, he entreated him for it; das —, urgent prayer, entreaty, supplication.

Flehentlich, *adj.* and *adv.* suppliant. Einen — bitten, to beseech any one instantly.

Fleher, *m.* [-s, *pl.* -] a humble petitioner, a supplicant.

Flehgesang, *m.* [a solemn form of supplication, used in public worship] a litany.

Fleisch, *n.* [-es] [perhaps allied to Leiche = Körper] = the soft substance of which bodies usually consist. 1) the soft pulpy substance of fruit and plants. Das — einer Orange, the pulp of an orange. 2) flesh [as distinguished from the bones and the fluids]. Unter der allgemeinen Benennung —, begreift man die Muskeln, das Fett, die Drüsen &c., welche die Knochen umgeben und die Haut bedecken; zuweilen ist diese Benennung nur auf die Muskeltheile des thierischen Körpers beschränkt, under the general appellation of flesh, we include the muscles, fat, glands &c., which invest the bones and are covered with the skin; it is sometimes restricted to the musculous parts of the animal body; wildes — in einer Wunde, proud flesh in a wound; das rohe — in einer Wunde, raw flesh of a wound; vom —e kommen or fallen, to lose flesh gradually, to become lean or meagre; durch Nahrung kommt man wieder zu —e, food recruits the flesh; hartes —, hard flesh; weiches —, soft flesh; derbes —, brawn; das lebendige oder gesunde —, the quick; in's gesunde — schneiden, to cut to the quick. 3) [the body of beasts and fowls, used as food, distinct from fish; animal food] flesh. In der Fastenzeit enthalten sich die Katholiken des —es, in Lent the Catholics abstain from flesh; das — der kräuterfressenden Thiere ist im allgemeinen schmackhaft, the meat of herbivorous animals is generally palatable; — und Gemüse, meat and vegetables; geschlachtetes —, butcher's meat; gekochtes —, boiled meat; gebratenes —, roast meat; — auf dem Roste gebraten, broiled meat; geschmortes —, stewed meat; geräuchertes —, smoked meat; eingesalzenes —, pickled meat. *Prov.* Wo — ist, da sind auch Knochen, he that buys flesh, buys many bones; he that buys land, buys many stones. 4) it is used sometimes for any sort of butcher's meat, as sausage. 5) the colour of flesh, seen through the skin, [in painting] the natural colour of flesh, carnation. 6) [in Scripture] flesh. = *a*) animal nature, animals of all kinds. Alles —es Ende ist vor mich kommen, [in Script.] the end of all flesh is come before me. *Prov.* Den Weg alles —es gehen, to go the way of all flesh, to die. *b*) human nature. Und das Wort ward — und wohnete unter uns, [in Script.] the word was made flesh, and dwelt among us. *Fig.* α) = fleshly i. e. earthly-minded; *it.* men in general, mankind. Die Menschen wollen sich meinen Geist nicht mehr strafen lassen, denn sie sind —, [in Script.] my spirit shall not always strive with man, for that he is also flesh. β) a carnal state, a state of unrenewed nature. Die nicht nach dem —e wandeln, sondern nach dem Geist, [in Script.] who walk not after the flesh, but after the spirit. γ) carnality, corporeal appetites, flesh. Durch fasten kreuziget man das —, fasting serves to mortify the flesh. δ) — und Blut, = the corruptible body of man, or corrupt nature. — und Blut können das Reich Gottes nicht ererben, [in Script.] flesh and blood cannot inherit the kingdom of God. ε) the present life, the state of existence in this world. Aber es ist nöthiger im — bleiben um euretwillen, [in Script.] to abide in the flesh is more needful for you. ζ) legal righteousness, and ceremonial services. Was sagen wir denn von unserm Vater Abraham, daß er gefunden habe nach dem —, [in Script.] what shall we then say that Abraham, our father, as pertaining to the flesh hath found. η) kindred, stock, family. Er ist unser Bruder, unser — und Blut, [in Script.] he is our brother, and our flesh; sie werden seyn ein —, [in Script.] they shall be one flesh. ϑ) outward appearances. Ihr richtet nach dem —, [in Script.] ye judge after the flesh.

Fleisch-ader, *f.* [in anatomy] a branch of the subclavian vein. —**bank**, *f.* 1) the place where butcher's meat is sold, a flesh-market, shambles. 2) *Fig.* † [in contempt] a large naked breast of a female. —**baum**, *m.* a pole whereon meat, sausage &c. are hung in smoke. —**beil**, *n.* a butcher's ax. —**blättchen**, *n.* one of the soft parts in the frush of a horse. —**blume**, *f.* red-flowered meadow-lychnis. —**bohne**, *f.* upright kidney-bean, tree kidney-bean. —**bruch**, *m.* [in surgery] sarcocele. —**brühe**, *f.* fleshbroth. Eine kräftige —brühe, strong broth, soup. —**brühsuppe**, *f.* broth. —**brühtafel**, *f.* [*Bouillon] portable soup. —**bündel**, *m.* a bundle of muscular fibres. —**darstellung**, *f.* [in painting, the parts of a picture which are naked] carnation. —**eisen**, *n.* [with leather-dressers, tanners, furriers] a fleshing-knife. —**erzeugend**, *adj.* and *adv.* anaplerotic. —**esser**, *m.* a flesh-eater. —**farbe**, *f.* 1) flesh-colour. 2) the natural colour of flesh, carnation. —**farben**, —**farbig**, *adj.* and *adv.* flesh-coloured. —**faser**, *f.* fibre, fiber. —**faß**, *n.* powdering-tub. —**fell**, *n.* V. —haut. —**fliege**, *f.* flesh-fly. —**fressend**, *adj.* and *adv.* carnivorous, sarcophagous. —fressende Thiere, carnivorous animals [as the lion, tiger, dog, wolf &c.]. —**gabel**, *f.* flesh-hook. —**gebackene**, *n.* V. —pastete. —**geschwulst**, *f.* 1) V. —bruch. 2) any fleshy excrescence on an animal body, sarcoma. —**gewicht**, *n.* V. —ergewicht. —**hacker**, *m.* —**hackerinn**, *f.* V. —er and —erinn. —**hafen**, *m.* V. —topf. —**haken**, *m.* a hook for suspending meat. —**halle**, *f.* V. —bank. —**haltung**, *f.* [in painting] the manner of painting the parts of a picture which are naked, carnation. —**hauer**, *m.* —**hauerinn**, *f.* V. —er and —erinn. —**haut**, *f.* [in anatomy] a fibrous membrane which covers some parts of the body, as the coat which immediately covers the testes, the dartos. —**horn**, *n.* 1) a fleshy excrescence. 2) [in conchology] the buff cowry. —**kammer**, *f.* a room where meat is kept, larder. —**kloß**, *m.* [diminut. das —klößchen] 1) a kind of small pudding of minced meat, meat-ball. 2) [in contempt] a plump female. —**klumpen**, *m.* 1) a mass of flesh. 2) [in contempt] a plump person. —**koch**, *m.* [at court] a cook whose occupation is to prepare flesh or meat for the table. —**korb**, *m.* meat-basket. —**kork**, *m.* [in conchology] the fleshy alcyonium. —**kost**, *f.* flesh-diet. —**krone**, *f.* the cornet or coronet of a horse. —**kuchen**, *m.* V. —pastete. —**lake**, *f.* a pickle for meat. —**lappen**, *m.* [in anatomy] a name given to muscles. —**lauch**, *m.* Welsh onion, or ciboul. —**lehre**, *f.* sarcology. —**leim**, *m.* sarcocol, sarcocolla. —**linse**, *f.* [in conchology] the wedge muscle. —**los**, *adj.* and *adv.* fleshless, lean. —**machend**, *adj.* and *adv.* V. —erzeugend. —**made**, *f.* a species of ascaris infesting the flesh. —**mahler**, *m.* a painter, who represents well the flesh to the life. —mahlerei, *f.* that part of painting which relates to carnation. —mangel, *m.* a want of meat. —markt, *m.* a flesh-market, shambles. —masse, *f.* 1) mass of flesh. 2) [in contempt or joke] a plump person. —maul, *n.* [in common language] a person that has a passion for meat. ‖—menger, *m.* V. —er. —messer, *n.* a cook's great knife. —milbe, *f.* a species of mite that breeds in flesh. —pastete, *f.* meat-pie. —pfennig, *m.* V. —steuer. —roth, *adj.* and *adv.* flesh-coloured. —scharren, *m.* V —bank 1). —schäßer, *m.* a public officer whose duty is to examine the quality of meat offered for sale and to regulate the prize of meat. —schäßung, *f.* the assize of meat sold in shambles. —schau, *f.* official view or inspection of shambles. —schauer, *m.* V. —schäßer. —schnecke, *f.* [in conchology] a species of strombus [strombus pugilis]. —schnitt, *m.* 1) a cut to the quick. 2) a small piece of meat for cooking, a steak, a cutlet. —schranne, *f.* V. —bank 1). —seite, *f.* V. Aasseite. —sohle, *f.* the flesh in a horse's foot encompassed by the sole. —speise, *f.* flesh-meat. —ständer, *m.* a powdering-tub. —steuer, *f.* a tax on flesh or meat. —suppe, *f.* soup made of meat, flesh-broth. —tag, *m.* a day on which Catholics are permitted to eat meat, flesh-day. —taxe, *f.* the assize of bread. —topf, *m.* 1) flesh-pot. 2) [in Scripture] plenty of provisions. Wollte Gott wir wären in Egypten gestorben, durch des Herrn Hand, da wir bei den —töpfen saßen, [in Script.] would to God, we had died by the hand of the Lord in the land of Egypt, when we sat by the flesh-pots. —torte, *f.* a tart of meat. —waare, *f.* butcher's meat considered as a commodity, meat. —wage, *f.* meat-scales. —warze, *f.* [diminut. das —wärzchen, ‖—wärzlein] carbuncle. —werk, *n.* meat, flesh-meat. —wuchs, *m.* the recruiting of flesh. —wunde, *f.* flesh-wound. —wurm, *m.* V. —made. —wurst, *f.* sausage. —zapfen, *m.* 1) [in surgery] papillary muscle. 2) [a sort of gall] carneous follicle [folliculus carneous, found on the leaves of the black poplar]. —zehnte, *m.* tithe paid of animals killed for meat. —zeit, *f.* flesh-days [as distinguished from fast-days].

Fleischen, *v. tr.* 1) to flesh [a hide]. V. Ab—. 2) [rather unusual] to clothe with flesh, to embody in flesh, to incarnate, in the compound word ein—.

Fleischen, *adj.* and *adv.* V. Fleischern.

Fleischer, *m.* [-s, *pl.* -] one who slaughters animals for market, a butcher.

Fleischer-bursch, *m.* a butcher's journeyman. —gang, *m.* *Fig.* *labour in vain, wild goose chase [the pursuit of something as unlikely to be caught as the wild goose]. —gesell, —knecht, *m.* V. —bursch. —gewerk, *n.* V. —handwerk. —gewicht, *n.* butcher's weight. —handwerk, *n.* the trade of a butcher. —hund, *m.* a butcher's dog, mastiff.

Fleischern, *adj.* and *adv.* made of flesh, having the quality of flesh, fleshy, carneous. *Fig.* carnal, fleshly.

Fleischeslust, *f.* and [*pl.*] -lüste, carnal appetites, fleshly lusts.

Fleischicht, *adj.* and *adv*, resembling flesh, fleshy, carneous.

Fleischig, *adj.* and *adv.* 1) full of pulp, fleshy, pulpous. —e Früchte, fleshy, pulpy fruits. [in botany] Eine —e Wurzel, a fleshy root; ein —er Stengel, Strunk, a fleshy stalk or stipe; ein —es Blatt, a fleshy leaf; ein —er Kürbiß, a pulpy pumpion; eine —e Hülse, a fleshy legume. 2) full of flesh, fleshy. Ein —er Fuß, a fleshy foot. 3) fleshy, gross, corpulent. 4) [in astrology] die —en Zeichen, the signs of the zodiac, Virgo, Libra and Aquarius [the virgin, the balance and the waterbearer].

Fleischlich, *adj.* and *adv.* 1) fleshly, corporeal, carnal. Die —e Erkenntniß, carnal knowledge [sexual intercourse]; eine Person — erkennen, sich — mit ihr vermischen, mit ihr —en Umgang haben, ihr — beiwohnen, [chiefly in law] to have carnal knowledge of a female, to lie with her. 2) fleshy, sensual, carnal [as opposed to spiritual]. —e Lüste, carnal appetites; enthaltet euch von —en Lüsten, [in Script.] abstain from fleshly lusts.

Fleischlichkeit, *f.* fleshliness, carnal passions and appetites.

Fleiß, *m.* [-es] [allied to the Sw. *flyta*, Engl. to *flit*, = eilen, to the German fließen] 1) [obsolete] diligence, speed, dispatch. Thue —, daß du vor dem Winter kommest, [in Script.] do thy diligence to come before winter. 2) steady application in business of any kind, due attention, industry, assiduity, diligence. — anwenden, to give diligence; so wendet allen euren — daran, und reichet dar in eurem Glauben Tugend, [in Script.] and besides this giving all diligence, add to your faith virtue; — zeigen, to show one's self assiduous; zum — aufmuntern, to exhort to be assiduous; vielen — auf etwas wenden, to be constant in effort or exertion, to accomplish what is undertaken, to prosecute something with constant effort; mit — betrachten, to contemplate attentively. *Prov.* Hans ohne —, wird nimmer weis', of idleness comes no goodness. 3) diligence, care, heed, heedfulness. Behüte dein Herz mit allem —, [in Script.] keep thy heart with all diligence. 4) purpose, design, intention. Mit —, on purpose, of purpose; er that es mit —, he did it designedly, purposely or intentionally.

Fleißbelohnung, *f.* the reward of industry.

‡**Fleißen**, *ir. v. r.* Sich einer Sache —, to apply one's self to any thing. V. the more usual Befleißen.

Fleißig, *adj.* and *adv.* 1) instant, earnest, urgent. Einen — bitten, to beseech any one instantly; — beten, to pray incessantly; einen — besuchen, to visit a person often; er besucht — die Schenken, he frequents public-houses; sich — Bewegung machen, to take exercise frequently. 2) diligent, assiduous, attentive, industrious. Ein —er Arbeiter, an active workman; ein —er Knabe, a diligent lad; ein Mann — in seinem Geschäfte, a person diligent in his business, or assiduous in his occupation; — seyn, to be steady in application to business. 3) careful, regular in attendance. Ein —er Zuhörer, an assiduous hearer; suche — nach, make diligent search. 4) performed with constant diligence or attention, assiduous. Eine —e Arbeit, an assiduous labour.

‡**Fleißigen**, *v. r.* Sich — einer Sache, to apply one's self to any thing. V. the more usual word Befleißigen.

‡**Fleißiglich**, *adv.* diligently, assiduously.

‖**Flennen**, [allied to the Sw. *flina* = den Mund (lächelnd) öffnen] *v. intr.* to weep with a wry face; or [seldom used] to laugh with a wry face.

1. ‖**Flensen**, *v. intr.* the frequentative verb of flennen.

2. ‖**Flensen**, [appears to be allied to the Sw. *fla* = schinden] *v. tr.* [in whale-fishery] to cut the blubber in pieces.

***Flesche**, *f.* [*pl.* -n] [in fortification, a work of two faces, often constructed before the glacis] fleche.

‖**Fleth**, *n.* [-s, *pl.* -e] **Flethe**, *f.* [*pl.* -n] a fleet, or canal.

Flethe, *f.* [*pl.* -n] [allied to Fladen, fletschen &c.] [with clothiers] *a*) the quantity of wool combed at one time. *b*) carded wool. *c*) a flock or lock of wool cleaving to a card.

Flethenlocke, *f.* [with spinners] a flock or lock of wool.

Fletschen, [allied to platt, Fladen &c.] *v. tr.* 1) to beat flat or to extend in breadth. Metall mit dem Hammer —, to flatten a metal by hammering. 2) to show the teeth as in scorn, to grin. Das Maul —, to make faces.

Fletschzahn, *m.* a prominent tooth.

Fletz, *n.* [-es, *pl.* -e] V. Flötz.

Fleuen, V. Flauen.

Fleute, *f.* [*pl.* -n] **Fleutschiff**, *n.* [-es, *pl.* -e] V. Flüte, Flütschiff.

Fleuthe, *f.* [*pl.* -n] V. Fleth.

***Flexion**, *f.* [in grammar] inflection.

Flick, V. Flügge.

Flicken, [from Fleck] *v. tr.* to mend with a patch or patches, to repair with pieces fasten on, to patch. Ein Kleid —, to patch or to p a garment; Schuhe —, to cobble shoes; ei Kessel —, to mend a kettle, to tinker a k geflickte Kleider, patched clothes; schlecht ungeschickt —, to botch, to bungle; Strümp to darn stockings; das Dach eines Hauses patch the roof of a house; einen Zaun repair or to mend a hedge. *Fig.* Minis am Staate, Ministers botch the state; i sprach mir nie viel von Ihrem geflickten I had never much hopes of your vampe of your patched up piece. ‖To tear in to rend, to lacerate.

Flick-arbeit, *f.* 1) the act of patch patchwork. ‖—gans, *f.* half a smoked —häring, *m.* red-herring. —lappe piece of cloth sewed on a garment to re a patch. —werk, *n.* 1) patching. 2) pa patch-work. *Fig.* Seine Schrift ist ein his work is a bad compilation. —wör expletive. Die Griechische Sprache ist —wörtern (Füllwörtern), the Greek abounds with expletives.

Flicker, *m.* [-s, *pl.* -] -inn, *f.* a perso patches or botches, a patcher, botcher the compound words, Schuh—, a co Kessel—, a tinker &c. *Fig.* † or ? [in jok Arzt ist unsers Herrn Gottes [Herrgotts] physician mends whatever the Lord send

Flickerlohn, *m.* the money paid fo ding.

Flickerei, *f.* 1) patching, botching. 2) work, patchery.

Flieboot, *n.* [-es, *pl.* -böte] [from hen = sich schnell bewegen] [a large Dutch vessel] fly-boat, flute.

Fliede, *f.* [*pl.* -n] V. Flethe.

Flieder, *m.* [-s] [probably from fladd flattern] common elder. V. Holunder. Spanische —, the common lilac.

Flieder-baum, *m.* V. Flieder. —be *f.* elder-berry. —blau, *adj.* and *adv.* bei the colour of the lilac. —blüte, *f.* the bl of the elder. —essig, *m.* vinegar of eld holz, *n.* V. Holunderholz. —muß, *n.* lundermuß. —schwamm, *m.* [a species gus] Jew's-ear. —thee, *m.* V. Holunderth

Fliege, *f.* [*pl.* -n] 1) [a winged insect of species] the fly, [in common language] the fly. —n fangen, to catch flies; —n to kill flies with a fly-flap; mit —n an to fly-fish; die Spanische —, Spanish fly, tharide [when bruised, used as a vesicatory]

blistering plaster], *es ärgert ihn die — an der Wand, he frets at nothing, he is very touchy. *Prov.* Zwei —n mit einem Schlage treffen or mit einer Klappe schlagen, to kill two birds with one stone; to catch two pigeons with one bean. *Fig.* *Eine liederliche or wüste —, a thoughtless and wanton youth. 2) [in astronomy, a southern constellation] the fly. 3) [in seamen's lang.] V. Anker—. 4) [perhaps from fegen] aim of a gun. Die — einer Vogelflinte, the sight of a fowling-piece.

Fliegen-baum, *m.* the common elm. —blume, *f.* 1) the fly-ophrys. 2) butterfly orchis. —dreck, *m.* 1) fly-blow. 2) [in ornithology] the sand-stamper. —ente, *f.* the shoveler. —falle, *f.* 1) [an instrument for catching flies] fly-catcher 2) [a plant] Venus' fly-trap. —fänger, *m.* [a genus of birds] the muscicapa, the fly-catcher. —fittig, *m.* a marly slate-stone mixed with copper, with impressions representing the wings of a fly.. —fürst, *m.* [in theological speculations] Beelzebub, Satan, the prince of this world. —garn, *n.* V. —netz. —gift, poison for flies, fly-bane. —glas, *n.* a glass filled with honey used for catching flies. —käfer, *m.* [an insect] the necydalis. —klappe, *f.* 1) a wooden instrument for catching flies. 2) fly flap. 3) [in seamen's lang.] top-gallant-sail of a Dutch smack. —klatsche, *f.* fly-flap. —kopf, *m* 1) [a small tumour in the uvea... of the eye] myocephalon. 2) [in printing] turned letter. Die —köpfe berichtigen, to rectify the turned letters. —kraut, *n.* V. Stechapfel. —meister, *m.* V. —fürst. —netz, *n.* net for covering horses against flies, fly-net —pflaster, *n.* a vesicatory made of cantharides. —pilz, *m.* V. —schwamm. —pulver, *n.* a powder used as a poison for flies. —schimmel, *m.* a flea-bitten grey horse. —schnäpper, *m.* 1) [genus of birds] the muscicapa or fly-catcher; the pied fly-catcher. 2) [a plant] Venus' fly-trap. —schrank, *m.* a meat-safe, meat-screen. —schwamm, *m.* the bug agaric or red agaric. —schwarm, *m.* a swarm of flies. —spießer, —stecher, *m.* V. —schnäpper, 1. —stein, *m.* native arsenic. —vogel, *m.* 1) V. —schnäpper, 1. 2) the humming-bird. —wanze, *f.* the fly-bug. —wasser, *n.* V. —gift. —wedel, *m.* something to drive away flies, a fly-flap.

Fliegen, *ir.* I. *v. intr.* [u. w. seyn] 1) to fly, to flutter, to vibrate or play, as a flag in the wind. Die Fahnen — lassen, to display the colours; mit —den Fahnen, with flying colours; —de Haare, loose or flowing hair, dishevelled hair; [in seamen's lang., to let go suddenly] die Schoten — lassen, to let fly the sheets. 2) [to pass or move in air by the force of wind or other impulse] to fly. Der —de Fisch, [a small fish which flies by means of its pectoral fins] the flying-fish; die Feder fliegt, the feather flies, or floats in the air; die Knaben ließen einen Drachen —, the boys flew a kite; ein —des Blatt, a leaf floating in the air; die Funken — aufwärts, the sparks fly upward; ein —des Feuer, a fiery body or appearance flying or floating in the atmosphere, a meteor; eine Kugel fliegt aus der Kanone, a ball flies from a cannon; eine Mine fliegt in die Luft, a mine is blown up; das Schiff flog in die Luft, the ship was blown up. 3) [to move through the air by the aid of wings] to fly, to be on the wing. Vögel —, birds fly; hoch —, to soar, to tower, [in a fig. sense] to soar, *it.* [ironically in contempt or rebuke] to take too high a flight; Adler fliegen hoch, the flight of eagles is high, eagles soar; Schwalben — schnell, the flight of swallows is rapid; fort—, to take wing; [u. w. kommen] ein Vogel kam [gegen uns or auf uns zu] geflogen, a bird flew towards us. *Fig.* — ehe die Federn gewachsen sind, no flying without wings, or, he would fain fly, but he wants feathers; Keiner sollte zu hoch —, every one ought to live according to his condition, or, make not thy tail broader than thy wings. 4) to move or pass rapidly, to fly *a*) [of men] Er flog seinem bedrängten Freund zu Hülfe, he flew to the relief of his distressed friend; er flog in ihre Arme, he threw himself into her arms. *b*) [of things, conditions] to pass rapidly, to fly. Eine —de Hitze, an intermittent heat; ein —des Gerücht, a flying rumour or report; ein —des Blatt, a pamphlet; —de Worte, words uttered, spoken rapidly; *ein Wort — lassen, to drop a word 5) to move rapidly from place to place, to fly. Ein —des Lager, a flying camp; ein —des Krankenhaus, [in military affairs] a flying hospital; ein —des Hoflager, an ambulatory court; die —de Brücke, flying-bridge; ein —des Corps, [in military affairs] flying-party.

II. *v. tr.* to do or perform something with rapidity. Sie flogen [the stress is laid on flogen] den fröhlichen Tanz, they flew through the merry dance.

Flieger, *m.* [-s, *pl.* -] [in seamen's language] middle stay-sail.

Fliegfisch, *m.* [-es, *pl.* -e] flying-fish.

Fliegsam, *adj.* and *adv.* disposed to fly or to soar.

Fliehen, [allied to fliegen] *ir.* I. *v. intr.* [v. w. seyn] to run with rapidity, to flee. Die Thränen flohen schamhaft von ihren Wangen, [in poetry] bashful tears escaped from her cheeks; zu Einem —, or in Eines Arm —, to flee to a person for safety, or to take refuge with any one; in ein fremdes Land —, to flee to a foreign country for refuge; der Feind floh bei dem ersten Feuer, the enemy fled at the first fire; er floh nach Egypten, he flew into Egypt; vor der Gefahr —, to flee, or to hasten from danger; vor dem Laster —, to shun vice; fliehet vor dem Götzendienste, [in Script.] flee from idolatry; widerstehet dem Teufel, so fliehet er von euch, [in Script.] resist the devil, and he will flee from you. *Fig.* Der Mensch fleucht wie ein Schatten und bleibet nicht, [in Script.] he fleeth also as a shadow, and continueth not. II. *v. tr.* to flee, to shun, to avoid, to decline. Den Anblick eines uns verhaßten Menschen —, to fly the sight of one we hate; er fliehet sie, he flees from her; das Böse —, to fly from evil.

Fliehkraft, *f.* [in physics] the centrifugal force [of a body].

Flieschen, Flieslein, *n.* [-s, *pl.* -] diminut. of Fliese.

Fliese, *f.* [*pl.* -n] [Sw. *flis* and Low. Sax. Fliese signify a piece or fragment of stone, in Ital. *losa* signifies a square stone] 1) a small square of stone or earthen-ware for covering walls or floors, a flat stone, or flag. Schwedische —n or —nsteine, marble slabs of little value; Holländische —n, Dutch bricks; mit —n belegen, to flag; ein mit —n belegter Boden, a pavement. ||2) allied to the Sw. *flisast* = spalten] piece of wood inlaid in floors for ornament.

Fliesen-brett, *n.* [with potters] a mould for moulding floor-bricks. —stein, *m.* V. Fliese.

Fliessingen, *n.* [-s] [a town in the Netherlands] Flushing.

1. **Fließ**, *n.* [-es, *pl.* -e] [perhaps allied to flechten, Flocke] 1) a lock of wool or hair, a flock. 2) [the coat of wool shorn from a sheep at one time] fleece. Das goldne —, the golden fleece [brought away from Colchis by Jason]; der Orden vom goldnen —e, the order of the golden fleece [instituted by Philip the good, duke of Burgundy, in 1429].

Fließritter, *m.* a knight of the golden fleece.

2 **Fließ**, *m.* [-es, *pl.* -e] [V. Fließen] [rather provincial] a streamlet, a rivulet, a brook.

Fließ-blattern, *pl.* [in medical science] the confluent small-pox. —garn, *n.* a large fishing-net. —gold, *n.* gold found in running water. —harz, *n.* turpentine. —loch, *n.* [in metallurgy] the door of the furnace. —papier, *n.* blotting-paper. —pocken, *pl.* V. —blattern. ||—stein, *m.* V. Flußstein. —wasser, *n.* 1) running water. 2) [in anatomy, water or a coloured fluid in animal bodies separated from the blood and contained in certain vessels called lymphatics] lymph. —wassergang, *m.* —wassergefäß, *n.* [in anatomy] lymphatic.

Fließen, [allied to fliehen, to the Lat. *fluo*, the Gr. φλύω] *ir. v. intr.* 1) [u. w. seyn] *a*) to hang loose and waving, to flow. Ein —der Mantel, —de Haare, a flowing mantle, flowing locks. *b*) [to move along an inclined plane, or on descending ground, as a fluid] to flow. Flüsse — dem Ocean zu, rivers run to the ocean; der Main fließt in den Rhein, the Main disembogues into the Rhine; Thränen flossen ihm über die Wangen, tears ran down his cheeks; Thränen flossen aus ihren Augen, tears flowed from her eyes; das Harz fließt aus den Bäumen, resin flows from trees; —des Wasser, running water [as opposed to standing water, pump-water or, also, to sea water]; [in botany] ein —der Moosstengel, a floating shoot. *Fig.* α) to pass as time, to run. So schnell als unsre Zeit dahin fließt as fast as our time runs; schnell — die flüchtigen Stunden dahin, swiftly fly the fleeting hours. β) to glide along smoothly, to be smooth, as composition or utterance, to flow. Das —de, [in sculpture] smoothness; die Umrisse müssen —d seyn, the outlines must be smooth; eine —de Periode, a flowing period; die Worte — ihm sehr gut, he speaks fluently, he is a fluent speaker; —d sprechen, to speak fluently, to have a flowing tongue; ein Redner der außerordentlich —d spricht, a speaker of remarkable fluency; eine —de Rede, a fluent speech; die Hexameter des Virgil sind —d, Virgil is flowing in his hexameters; [in poetry] badend in Strömen —der [sanfter] Melodie, bathing in streams of liquid melody; ein —der Vers, a verse that runs well, a smooth verse; diese Zeilen sind sehr —d, these lines run smoothly; —d schreiben, to write fluently; eine —de Schreibart, a fluent style; eine —de Hand, a running hand, cursive hand. γ) to proceed, to issue, to flow. Dies floß nicht aus seiner Feder, it came not out of his pen, he has not written it; dies fließt natürlich aus dem Gesagten, it follows naturally from the premises; aus diesen Thatsachen fließt die Schuld des Angeklagten, it follows from these facts, that the accused is guilty; aus dem Zeugnisse fließt &c., it results from testimony &c. *c*) to be liquid or fluid, to run. Das Wachs fließet, wax dissolves, melts; —des Pech, pitch in fusion. 2) [u. w. haben] *a*) to emit moisture, to run. Die Quelle fließt nicht mehr, the fountain runs no more; ein —des Geschwür, a running sore; —de Augen, running eyes; *it.* blear eyes. *b*) to melt, to flow, to fuse. Das Licht fließt, the candle gutters; die —de Hitze, [Schweißhitze; in iron-works] welding-heat. *c*) to draw moisture. Das Papier fließt, the paper runs; —der Sand, drifting sand.

1. **Fliete**, *f.* [*pl.* -n] [with carpet-manufacturers, a sort of spool] a flute.

Flietenkasten, *m.* [with carpet manufacturers] a case for flutes.

2. **Fliete**, *f.* [*pl.* -n] [allied to the Gr. πλήσσω, to the Fr. *blesser*] [in surgery, an instrument used for letting blood] fleam.

3. **Fliete**, *f.* [*pl.* -n] V. Flöte.

Flimme, *f.* [*pl.* -n] V. Floßfeder.

Flimmen, [allied to Flamme, glimmen &c.] *v. intr.* to gleam, to glitter, to glimmer.

Flimmer, *m.* [-s, *pl.* -n] 1) something glittering, any thing sparkling, a spangle. 2) tinsel. 3) [in mining] glimmer, mica. 4) gold sand.

Flimmern, [from flimmen] *v. intr.* to shine with a tremulous intermitted light, or with a broken quivering light, to twinkle. —de Sterne, glistening or sparkling stars; die Augen flimmerten ihm wie ein Paar Sterne, his eyes sparkled like a pair of stars; ||es flimmert mir vor den Augen, V. Flirren.

Flinder, *m.* [-s, *pl.* -] [from flimmern] 1) [a small plate or boss of shining metal, something brilliant used like an ornament] a spangle, tinsel. V. Flitter. 2) [formerly] a small coin of the value of 16 pence. 3) [from flattern] *pl.* [with hunters] scare-toils.

Flinder-gold, *n.* V. Flittergold. —schläger, *m.* a maker of spangles.

Flink, [allied to lenken = bewegen] *adj.* and *adv.* 1) quick, active, brisk, nimble, prompt. Ein —es Mädchen, an active girl. ||2) shining, pretty.

||**Flinke**, *f.* [*pl.* -n] a species of bleak. V. also Blicke *f.*

Flinken, *v. intr.* to shine with a tremulous intermitted light, to twinkle.

Flinkenerz, *n.* [in mining] ore which appears on rocks in thin, flexible, elastic lamins which exhibit a high polish and strong lustre.

Flinker, *m.* [-s, *pl.* -] [= Flimmer] something glittering, especially in mining. V. Flinkenerz.

Flinkerchen, ||**Flinkerlein**, *n.* [-s, *pl.* -] V. Flitter or Flitterchen.

Flinkern, [the frequentative verb of flinken] *v. intr.* to twinkle.

Flinkheit, *f.* quickness, activity, briskness, nimbleness, promptness.

Flinkmesser, *n.* [-s, *pl.* -] [Bleiknecht; with glaziers] latherkin.

‡**Flinrich**, *m.* [-es, *pl.* -e] V. Flinder, 2.

||**Flins**, *m.* [-ses, *pl.* -se] V. Feuerstein, Hornstein.

Flinse, *f.* [*pl.* -n] V. Fliese.

Flinte, *f.* [*pl.* -n] [is usually derived from the Old German Flins, A. S. Flint = Feuerstein; more probably, perhaps, allied to the Ice. *flein* = Pfeil] 1) a musket, or other gun, with a lock, which is discharged by striking fire with flint and steel, a firelock. 2) a light musket or firelock, a gun, a fowling-piece.

Flinten-dolch, *m.* bayonet. —kolben, *m.* the butt-end of a gun or musket. —krätzer, *m.* gun-worm. —kugel, *f.* a musket-ball, a bullet. —lauf, *m.* gun-barrel. —riemen, *m.* gun-sling. —schaft, *m.* gun-stock. —schloß, *n.* gun-lock, lock. —schloßblech, *n.* the lock-plate. —schuh, *n.* a carabine-case. —schuß, *m.* 1) discharge of a gun or musket, shot. 2) a musket-shot. —schütz, *m.* a fusileer. —spieß, *m.* bayonet. —stein, *m.* 1) a flint [for a gun]. 2) [a sub-species of quarz] flint. — —träger, *m.* [mostly in contempt] a soldier, musket-bearer.

||**Flinten**, *pl.* pebbles.

Flinter, *m.* [-s, *pl.* -] V. Flinder, Flinkerz.

Flinterstaat, *m.* [-es] V. Flitterstaat.

Flintglas, *n.* [-ses, *pl.* -gläser] flint-glass.

Flintsche, *f.* [*pl.* -n] V. Flitsche.

Flinz, *m.* [-es] [a mineral] sparry iron-stone, spathose iron.

||**Flirren**, [allied to flattern] *v. intr.* to shine with a tremulous intermitted light, to twinkle. Es flirrt mir vor den Augen, I cannot discern one thing from another.

||**Flirtchen**, *n.* [-s, *pl.* -] a lazy and thoughtless female; *it.* a flirt.

Flispern, **Flistern**, V. Flüstern.

Flitschbogen, *m.* [-s, *pl.* -] V. Flitzbogen.

Flitsche, *f.* [*pl.* -n] [probably allied to Bletz, Sw. *Plös*, *Platt* = Stück] [in mineralogy] a thin, flexible and elastic lamin, which exhibits a high polish and strong lustre.

Flitschenerz, *n.* V. Flinkenerz.

Flitschgold, *n.* [-es] gold found in grains.

Flitschhobel, *m.* [-s, *pl.* -] [with carpenters and joiners] moving fillister.

Flitschpfeil, *m.* [-es, *pl.* -e] V. Flitzpfeil.

Flitschrose, *f.* [*pl.* -n] V. Feldmohn.

Flitter, *m.* [-s, *pl.* -] **Flitter**, *f.* [*pl.* -n] [allied to flattern] 1) a small plate or boss of shining metal, a spangle, tinsel. 2) V. Flitterwerk. 3) [a plant] annual honesty.

Flitter-amboß, *m.* a small anvil used by makers of spangles. —erz, *n.* V. Flinkenerz. —gedanke, *m.* a specious conception. —gelehrsamkeit, *f.* tinsel- or superficial learning. —glanz, *m.* 1) the lustre of spangles. 2) a false lustre. —gold, *n.* 1) tinsel-brass. 2) *Fig.* tinsel-ornaments; *it.* tinsel-accomplishments. —golden, *adj.* and *adv.* 1) made of tinsel-brass; adorned with tinsel-brass. 2) *Fig.* having tinsel-ornaments; *it.* having tinsel-accomplishments. —goldschläger, *m.* one whose occupation is to beat or foliate tinsel-brass. —gras, *n.* middle or common quaking grass. —haube, *f.* a spangled cap or head-dress for women. —jahr, *n.* the first year after marriage. —kram, *m.* tinsel-finery. —monat, *m.* the first month after marriage, honey-moon, honey-month. —pappel, *f.* V. Zitterespe. —prunk, *m.* tinsel-ornament, tinsel-appearance. Das ist bloßer —prunk, that is mere show. —sand, *m.* glimmer-sand. —schein, *m.* 1) the lustre of spangles. 2) a false lustre, tinsel-lustre. —schimmer, *m.* tinsel-lustre. —schläger, *m.* a maker of spangles. —schuh, *m.* a spangled shoe. —silber, *n.* silver beaten into thin flat pieces or lamins, silver leaf. —staat, *m.* 1) tinsel finery, tawdriness. 2) tinsel-appearance, gaudiness. —stempel, *m.* a stamp for beating spangles. —werk, *n.* a showy trifle, trinket gewgaw. —witz, *m.* tinsel wit. —woche, *f.* Die —wochen, [the first month after marriage] honey-moon.

Flitterchen, ||**Flitterlein**, *n.* [-s, *pl.* -] *dimin.* of Flitter, a little spangle or tinsel.

Flittich, *m.* [-es, *pl.* -e] 1) the wing of barn-door-fowl. 2) *Fig.* *a*) the arm. *b*) the flap of a garment.

Flitzbogen, *m.* [-s, *pl.* -] a small cross-bow.

Flitzpfeil, *m.* [-es, *pl.* -e] a dart or arrow to be shot with a small cross-bow.

Flockasche, *f.* flowers of ashes.

Flockblume, *f.* [*pl.* -n] V. Flockenblume.

1. **Flocke**, *f.* [*pl.* -n] [a sort of net] V. Flake.

2. **Flocke**, *f.* [*pl.* -n] **Flocken**, *m.* [-s, *pl.* -] *dimin.* das Flöckchen, ||Flöcklein, [from fliegen] 1) a flock or lock. Eine Schnee—, a flake, or flock of snow; es schneit große —n, it in great flakes. 2) [with clothiers] waste wool [in mining] flaky stone. 4) [in fulling] a crease.

Flocken-bett, *n.* a flock-bed. —blu *f.* 1) scabious centaury, or great knapweed silver-knapweed. —erz, *n.* arseniate of l —gekräusch, *n.* curled flocks, wool. —g wölke, *n.* flaky clouds. —kraut, *n.* V. blume, 2. —salpeter, *m.* efflorescent sa petre. —seide, *f.* V. Flockseide. —teppi *m.* V. Flockteppich. —tuch, *n.* coarse cloth.

Flocken, I. *v. tr.* to form into flakes, flake. II. *v. intr.* 1) to fall [from the clouds from the air] in flakes. Es flocket, it snows. to separate in flakes, to flake. Das Garn flockt the yarn flakes.

Flock-feder, *f.* V. Flaumfeder. —feuer *n.* a quick and perishable flame. —gestäub —gestiebe, —gestöbe, *n.* [in metallurgy nill. —gras, *n.* V. Bartgras. —seide, floss-silk, silk-flock, ferret-silk. —seiden band, *n.* ferret-ribbon. —tapeten, *pl.* flock paper hangings. —wolle, *f.* [with cloth-shearings.

Flöcker, *m.* [-s, *pl.* -] **Flöckerinn**, *f.* [clothiers] a person that flakes washed wool hurdles.

Flöckicht, *adj.* and *adv.* resembling flakes flocks.

Flöckig, *adj.* and *adv.* flocky. Das — flocculence.

Floh, *m.* [-es, *pl.* Flöhe] [from fliehen sich schnell bewegen] a flea. *Fig.* †Er hört Flöhe husten, he lays claim to infallibility einem einen — ins Ohr setzen, to send a one away with a flea in his ear; Flöhe hüt to keep fleas, to undertake a very useless th

Floh-biß, —stich, *m.* 1) [the bite of a or the red spot caused by the bite] flea-bite, biting. 2) [a trifling wound or pain, like that bite of a flea] flea-bite, flea-biting. —braun and *adv.* V. —farben. —falle, *f.* flea-trap farbe, *f.* a dark brown colour, puce-colou farben, —farbig, *adj.* and *adv.* of a brown colour, puce. —heuschrecke, *f.* flea locust. —jagd, *f.* [in jest] flea-hunting käfer, *m.* [an insect] the mordella. —kre *m.* V. Wasserfloh. —pfeffer, *m.* water or ing persicaria or common arse-smart. —pfl ze, *f.* flea-bane. —riedgras, *n.* flea-sedge flea-grass. —same, *m.* the shrubby plantai

Flöhen, *v. tr.* to flea. Sich —, to rid on self of fleas.

Flöh-alant, *m.* V. Flöhkraut. 1. kraut, *n.* [a name given to several plants] trailing inula, or flea-bane. 2) pale-flo persicaria. 3) flea-bane. V. Flohpfeffer. 4 wort. V. Flohsamen. 5) V. Flohpflanze. 6) the penny royal mint.

Flöhig, *adj.* and *adv.* having fleas, abound ing with fleas.

1. **Flor**, *m.* [-es, *pl.* Flöre] [probably allied to the Lat. *flos*, the Germ. blü-hen, to signify something light, waving or fluttering] 1) gauze, or a thin transparent stuff, much used in mourning, black crape. Der glatte — [Milchflor] plain crape; der krause — [Krepp], double crape. *Fig.* *Einem den — von den Augen ziehen, to open any one's eyes, to undeceive one. 2) [with velvet-makers] the shag or nap of velvet.

Flor-band, *n.* gauze-ribbon. —binde, *f.* a band of black crape [for the arm, or hat in mourning]. —fliege, *f.* a species of fly. —gewand, *n.* a garment of crape. —haube, *f.* a gauze-cap. —hut, *m.* 1) a gauze bonnet. 2) a hat or bonnet with a band of black crape. —**Kappe**, *f.* V. —**Haube**. —**Kleid**, *n.* a gauze gown. —**Leinwand**, *f.* linen-gauze. —**Messer**, *n.* V. Sammetmesser. —**Saffran**, *m.* V. Färbedistel. —**Schleier**, *m.* a gauze or crape veil. —**Schürze**, *f.* a gauze apron. —**Seide**, *f.* [with silk-weavers] a sort of organzine twisted into three or four threads. —**Stuhl**, *m.* gauze-loom. —**Tuch**, *n.* 1) a gauze handkerchief. 2) gauze. —**verhüllt**, *adj.* and *adv.* veiled, shrouded in crape. —**Weber**, *m.* gauze-maker. —**Zeug**, *n.* gauze.

2. **Flor**, *m.* [-es, *pl.* -e] and *f.* [*pl.* -en] (Lat. *flos*, allied to blühen, Flur] 1) the blowing or flowering of plants, blossoming, bloom. Im — stehen, to blow, to bloom, to blossom, to flower; die Tulpen stehen jetzt in ihrem —e or im —, tulips are now in their blowth. *Fig.* Der — des Landes, the flourishing or prosperous state of the country; *it.* [the youth or young people] the flower of a land; Künste und Wissenschaften sind im —, arts and sciences flourish. 2) the time when flowers of the same kind blossom, florescence, florification; especially in the compound words, Nelkenflor, Tulpenflor &c. 3) a collection of blooming flowers of the same kind. Sie haben hier einen schönen Tulpenflor, you have here a fine bed of tulips. 4) [in botany] flora.

3. **Flor**, *m.* [-es, *pl.* Flöre] V. [the usual word] Flur.

4. **Flor**, *m.* [-es] [with dyers] an orange-coloured flower of the officinal bastard-saffron.

***Flora**, 1) [-s or Florens] [in antiquity, the goddess of flowers] flora. 2) [*gen.* -] *f.* [a catalogue or account of flowers or plants] flora.

1. **Floren**, *adj.* and *adv.* made of gauze or crape.

‡2. **Floren**, *m.* [-s, *pl* -e] [a coin originally made at Florence] florin.

***Florence**, [pron. as in the French] *m.* [a kind of silk cloth] florentine.

Florentia, [-s or -iens] [a name of women] Florentia or Florence.

Florentiner, [-s, *pl.* -] *m.* **Florentinerinn**, *f.* a native of Florence, Florentine.

Florentinisch, *adj.* and *adv.* Florentine.

Florentius, [a name of men] Florence.

Florenz, *n.* [a town in Italy] Florence.

Floretband, *n.* [-es, *pl.* -bänder] ferret-ribbon.

Floretseide, *f.* ferret-silk. V. Flockseide.

Florett, *n.* [-es, *pl.* -e] a foil.

***Floriren**, *v. intr.* to flourish. *Fig.* Der Handel florirt, commerce flourishes.

***Florist**, *m.* [-en, *pl.* -en] florist.

***Floskel**, *f.* [*pl.* -n] [generally in contempt] flourish. —n anbringen, to use florid language, to flourish; das sind bloße —n, these are mere phrases.

Floß, *n.* [-es, *pl.* Flöße] [from fließen] ‖1) a stream of water, a current, a flow. 2) a float, a raft. 3) [seldom used] a vessel or ship. 4) a floating fishing-net. ‖5) [in mining] V. Flötz. 6) [in iron-works] a loop of $2^1/_2$ cwt.

Floß-band, *n.* a rafter athwart for fastening together pieces of timber in a raft. —**beamte**, *m.* the inspector of a float or raft. —**bett**, *n.* [in hydraulics] a scaffolding in water to receive a rammer. —**brücke**, *f.* floating-bridge. —**eisen**, *n.* V. Flußeisen. —**feder**, *f.* V. Flosse, 1. —**fittig**, *m.* V. Floßfeder. —**führer**, *m.* the steersman of a raft. —**füßig**, *adj.* and *adv.* web-footed, fin-footed, pinnatifid. —**galle**, *f.* V. Flußgalle. —**garn**, *n.* V. Fliesgarn. —**gerechtigkeit**, *f.* the right of floating wood. —**handel**, *m.* trade with floated wood. —**herr**, *m.* the owner of a float or raft. —**holz**, *n.* floated wood. —**knecht**, *m.* a journey-man on a raft ‖—**loch**, *n.* the runner of a furnace. —**mann**, *m.* V. Floßführer. —**meister**, *m.* a person that superintends floats or rafts. —**ofen**, *m.* V. Flußofen. —**ordnung**, *f.* regulations for the floating of wood. —**platz**, *m.* a place where floated wood is piled for sale. —**rechen**, *m.* a structure or frame of cross-barred wood for stopping floating wood. —**recht**, *n.* V. Floßgerechtigkeit. —**rücken**, *m.* [a fish] a species of gymnotus. —**scheit**, *n.* a shide of floated wood. —**teich**, *m.* a pond where wood for floating is collected. —**wasser**, *n.* water on which wood is conveyed by floating. —**wehr**, *n.* a dam for stopping floating wood. —**winde**, *f.* the twig of an osier used for fastening together the boards or planks of a raft.

Flöß, V. Flötz.

Flöß-amt, *n.* float-office. —**bach**, *m.* a brook or rivulet on which wood is floated. —**bauholz**, *n.* floated timber. —**baum**, *m.* a floated tree. —**butter**, *f.* V. Schmelzbutter.

Flosse, *f.* [*pl.* -n] [from fließen] 1) the fin of a fish. Ohne —n, finless; mit —n, furnished with fins, finny; ein —nähnliches Ruder, a finlike oar. 2) the buoys on a fishing-net.

Flöße, *f.* [*pl.* -n] [from fließen] 1) a place on a river where the floating of wood is carried on; *it.* the right of floating wood from one place to another. 2) the act or employment of floating wood. 3) timber, boards or planks, fastened together and conveyed down a stream. ‖4) V. Trifft. 5) V. Blockschiff. 6) a small float on rivers for washer-women &c. 7) [in mining] a trough in the ground in which tin-ore is washed. 8) [in metallurgy] a stonevessel used in refining tin.

Flößen, I. *v. tr.* 1) to infuse by drops, to instil. Einem Kinde Milch in den Mund —, to infuse milk into a child's mouth. 2) to cause to be conveyed on water, to float [fire-wood, timber &c.] 3) to skim [milk]. ‖4) to cleanse with a second or repeated application of water, after washing, to rinse [clothes &c.]. 5) to fish with a buoying fishing-net. ‖6) to liquify, to melt. II. *v. intr.* [u. w. seyn] to float, to swim.

Flossenreif, *m.* [-es, *pl.* -e] the corked border of a fishing-net.

Flößer, *m.* [-s, *pl.* -] 1) a person, who has the superintendence of the journeymen employed on a raft. 2) the proprietor, in whole or in part, of a raft. ‖3) V. Floßknecht.

Flötchen, ‖**Flötlein**, *n.* [-s, *pl.* -] a little flute, a flageolet.

1. **Flöte**, *f.* [*pl.* -n] [perhaps allied to blasen, Lat. *flare*] [a small wind-instrument] a flute. Die — spielen, to play the flute; auf der — blasen, spielen, to flute.

Flöten-bläser, *m.* a performer on the flute, flutist. —**bohrer**, *m.* a bore for boring flutes. —**futter**, *n.* a flute-case. —**gesang**, *m.* a soft song. —**macher**, *m.* flute-maker. —**pfeife**, *f.* [in organs] an open pipe. —**röhre**, *f.* a flute-pipe. —**spiel**, *n.* 1) the playing on the flute. 2) a tune intended for the flute. 3) any harmonious wind-instrument of music, consisting of pipes, which are filled with wind, and which is blown by a bellows. —**spieler**, *m.* a performer on the flute, a flutist. —**sprache**, *f.* a soft and tender language. —**stimme**, *f.* 1) a soft, sweet or fluty voice. 2) the part of the flute in a piece of music arranged for several instruments. —**stück**, *n.* 1) a tune intended for the flute. 2) one of the pieces of a flute. —**tafel**, *f.* a table serving to show by signs the manner of playing the flute. —**ton**, *m.* 1) the sound of a flute. 2) a soft sweet voice. —**uhr**, *f.* flute-clock. —**werk**, *n.* an instrument of music with a flute-stop. —**zug**, *m.* [in organs] flute-stop.

2. **Flote** or **Fliete**, *f.* [*pl.* -n] [probably allied to the Sw. *plit* = Degen, V. Fliete] [with linen-weavers] a spool, a flute.

3. **Flote**, *f.* [*pl.* -n] [also Flethe; appears to be allied to platt, Fladen] a flock or lock of wool cleaving to a card.

4. **Flote**, V. Flüte.

5. ‖**Flöte**, *f* [*pl.* -n] [fig. perhaps from Flöte 1.?] a kind of drinking-glass.

1. **Flöten**, *v. intr.* and *tr.* 1) to play on the flute, to flute. Einen in den Schlaf —, to lull any one asleep by fluting; [in poetry] die Nachtigall flötet, the nightingale utters sweet or melodious sounds. 2) to sound sweetly or melodiously.

2. ‖**Floten**, *v. intr.* [allied to fließen, Low. Sax. fleten] to fleet, to skim, or to cream [milk].

3. **Flöten**, [the Sw. *flyta* signifies, to hasten] *v. intr.* ‖ and † [u. w. gehen] — gehen, to fleet away; *it.* to go down, to fail, to come to nothing.

1. **Flott**, [allied to fließen, V. Flöten] *adj.* and *adv.* floating, swimming, borne on the water. Das Schiff ist —, the ship is afloat, the ship fleets; ein Schiff — machen, to set a ship afloat; ein gescheitertes Schiff wieder — machen, to get a stranded ship afloat or off from the ground into deep water. *Fig.* *Die gestrandete Unterhaltung wieder — machen, to resume a conversation; * — leben, to live luxuriously, or in abundance, to live in clover, to live gaily; *da ging's — zu, every thing was there in abundance.

Flott-gras, *n.* the floating fox-tail grass. —**seide**, *f.* a skein of silk. —**stahl**, *m.* a sort of steel easily rendered fluid.

2. ‖**Flott**, *n.* [-es] [from fließen, Low. Sax. fleten] [the oily part of milk] cream.

Flotte, *f.* [*pl.* -n] [from fließen, Low. Sax. fleten] 1) a navy or squadron of ships, a fleet. Eine Kauffartei—, a fleet of merchantmen; die Kriegs—, a fleet of men-of-war, a fleet; die Silber—, flota; eine — ausrüsten, to fit out a fleet; eine kleine —, a flotilla. 2) [with dyers] the dye in the blue-stone vat.

Flottenführer, *m.* the commander of a fleet, admiral, commodore.

***Flottille**, [pron. Flotillje] *f.* [*pl.* -n] a little fleet, a flotilla.

Flötz, *n.* [-es, *pl.* -e] [allied to platt = breit] ‖1) *a)* formerly, level land. *b)* V. Flur. 2) [in mining] layer, stratum. Ein stehendes —, course; Kohlen—e, strata or stratums of coal; Steinkohlen—, a seam of coals.

Flötz-bau, *m.* [in mining] the working of a layer, seam or stratum. —**berg**, *m.* secondary mountain. —**dolomit**, *m.* [in mineralogy] red land-limestone, dolomite. —**erz**, *n.* ore that occurs in mountains formed in horizontal strata. —**gebirge**, *n.* secondary rocks. —**granit**, *m.* [in mineralogy] secondary granite. —**grauwacke**, *f.* [in mineralogy] new red conglomerate. —**gyps**, *m.* älterer —, granulary gypsum; jüngerer —, secondary gypsum. — —**kalk**, *m.* fester —, mountain limestone. —

kluft, *f.* [in mining] fissure in a stratum. —**lage**, *f.* V. —schicht. ‖ and † —**maul**, (Fletschmaul) *n.* a large mouth. —**muschel-kalkstein**, *m.* forest-marble, lias —**quarz-gestein**, *n.* quarz rock, granular quarz rock. —**riffel**, *m.* [in mining] a lode that contains no metal. —**sandstein**, *m.* new red sandstone, red marl, red ford, variegated sandstone. —**schicht**, *f.* [in mining] horizontal stratum. —**schwarte**, *f.* V. Dachschale. —**treppe**, *f.* stairs with broad steps. —**weise**, *adv.* [in mining] in layers, beds or strata. **Man findet den Thon oder Lehm —weise**, clay is often found stratified.

‖**Flübbern**, *v. tr.* [= plappern] to utter or tell in a thoughtless manner, to blab.

Fluch, *m.* [es, *pl.* Flüche] [V. Fluchen] 1) [in Scripture] denunciation of evil. **Also soll der Priester diese Flüche auf einen Zettel schreiben**, [in Script.] the priest shall write all these curses in a book. 2) curse, malediction, execration, imprecation, swearing. *Fig.* *a*) affliction, torment, great vexation. **Ich will diese Stadt zum — aller Heiden auf Erden machen**, [in Script.] I will make this city a curse to all nations. *b*) condemnation, sentence of divine vengeance on sinners **Christus hat uns erlöset von dem — des Gesetzes**, [in Script.] Christ has redeemed us from the curse of the law.

Fluch-abwender, *m.* one that averts a curse. —**befreit**, *adj.* and *adv.* delivered from a curse. —**beladen**, *adj.* and *adv* blasted by a curse. —**eid**, *m.* an oath uttered with an imprecation. —**entlastet**, *adj.* and *adv.* redeemed from a curse. —**maul**, *n.* [in common lang.] a profane person, a curser, a swearer. —**volk**, *n.* a cursed people. —**wasser**, *n.* [in Script.] cursed water. —**würdig**, *adj.* and *adv.* deserving to be cursed, execrable.

Fluchen, [perhaps originally signified: **sagen, sprechen**, as also **schwören**] I. *v. intr.* 1) to swear, to be profane. **Er flucht wie ein Landsknecht**, he swears like a trooper; **das —**, swearing, profaneness 2) to utter a wish of evil against any one. **Er fluchte mir**, he cursed me; **auf Einen —**, to imprecate evil upon any one, to execrate any one; **den Göttern sollst du nicht —**, [in Script.] thou shalt not revile the gods; **segnet, und fluchet nicht**, [in Script.] bless, and curse not. II. *v. tr.* to call for mischief or injury to fall upon, to imprecate evil on. **Einem eine Krankheit an den Hals —**, to call for a disease to fall upon a person to invoke a disease on any one; **er fluchte ihm Böses an den Hals**, he invoked evil on him.

Fluchenswerth, *adj.* and *adv.* deserving to be cursed, execrable.

Flucher, *m.* [-s, *pl.* -] 1) one who curses or utters a curse, curser. 2) [in Script.] blasphemer.

Flucht, *f.* 1) the act of fleeing, the act of running away, to escape danger or expected evil, flight. **Die — nehmen, ergreifen**, to betake to flight, to take to the heels, to flee, [in seamen's language] to bear away; **sich durch die — retten**, to save one's self by flight; **die — Muhameds von Mekka nach Medina**, Hegira; **den Feind in die — schlagen**, to put the enemy to flight, to turn the enemy to flight; **in der —**, in flight. 2) [= Eile] **Er ist sehr in der —**, he is in a great hurry; **ich habe ihn nur in der — gesehen**, I have seen him only in passing; *fig.* * **er ist vor ihm sehr in der —**, he fears him much. 3) place of refuge. **— und Schweiß haben**, [with hunters] to track game by the blood it has lost and to know where it is harboured. 4) [in architecture] the space requisite to the motion, or movement of any thing. **Die Thüre hat zu viel —**, the door has too much play. 5) things in a line, a range, row or rank. **Sechs Fenster in einer —**, six windows in a row. 6) V. Flug.

Flucht-bau, *m.* [with hunters] V. Rothbau. —**röhre**, *f.* a small hole or earth where hunted foxes creep in.

Flüchten, I. *v. intr.* [u. w. seyn] to run with rapidity, as from danger, to hasten from danger or expected evil, to flee. **Bei der Annäherung des Feindes —**, to flee or to fly at the approach of the enemy; **sie flüchteten sich unter einen Felsen**, they took shelter under a rock; **sich in ein fremdes Land —**, to flee to a foreign country for safety; **einer der sich flüchtet**, a refugee. II. *v. tr.* 1) to save by flying. **Er flüchtete seine besten Sachen in eine Festung**, he [hastily] removed his most valuable goods into a fortress for safety. *Fig.* **Den Blick —**, to turn one's head or eyes; **wohin ich meinen Blick flüchte, seh' ich nur Jammer und Noth**, wherever I turn my eyes I see but misery. 2) to put to flight, to turn to flight. III. *v. r.* **sich —**, to take or seek refuge. **Flüchte Dich an mein Herz, in meine Arme**, flee to my bosom, seek shelter in my arms; **er flüchtete sich zu dem Herrn**, he sought refuge with the Lord; **er flüchtete sich hinter leere Vorwände**, he sheltered himself behind empty pretexts.

Flüchtig, *adj.* and *adv.* 1) hanging loose and waving. **Ein —es Gewand**, [in painting] flowing drapery. 2) moving or able to move with rapidity. **Ein —es Pferd**, a fleet horse; [in poetry] **die —e Welle**, the gliding wave; **einen —en Pinsel haben**, [in painting] to paint with easiness or lightness. *Fig.* running, hasty, slight, superficial. **Eine —e Skizze**, a hasty sketch; **eine —e Uebersicht**, a cursory view; **nach einer —en Ansicht dieser Landschaft**, after a transient view of this landscape; **eine —e Erinnerung**, a faint recollection; **ich las das Papier — durch**, I read the paper cursorily; **ein Buch — durchsehen**, to run over a book; **ich berühre hier nur — einige wenige Regeln**, I touch here but transitorily on some few rules &c. 3) wandering, vagabond, fugitive. **Unstät und — sollst du seyn auf Erden**, [in Script.] a fugitive and a vagabond shalt thou be in the earth. *Fig.* [in law, obsolescent] **—e Ländereien**, alienable land. 4) fleeing, running from danger or pursuit, fugitive, fugacious. **Ein —es Heer**, a flying army. *Fig.* readily escaping, fugitive. **Die —en Stunden**, the fleeting hours; **ein —er Gedanke**, a fugitive idea; **— wie ein Ton, schnell wie ein Schatten, kurz wie ein Traum**, momentary as a sound, swift as a shadow, short as a dream; **—e Freuden**, transient or fugacious pleasures. 5) = flying asunder. *a*) fugacious, volatile, exhalable. **Die —en Theile**, the fugitive parts; **ein —es Salz**, a volatile salt. *b*) [in mining] brittle. **—es Gestein**, brittle rock. *c*) [with woolen-weavers and silk-weavers] **—e Zeuge**, slight stuffs.

Flüchtigkeit, *f.* 1) swiftness, rapidity, velocity, celerity, speed. **Die — eines Pferdes oder Hirsches**, the fleetness of a horse, or stag. *Fig.* **Die — des Pinsels**, [in painting] lightness; **mit — arbeiten**, to do one's work in a running or hasty manner, cursorily. 2) a passing with short continuance, transitoriness. **Die — der Zeit**, the fleetness of time; **die — aller irdischen Glückseligkeit**, transitoriness of all sublunary happiness. 3) [in chymistry] volatileness, volatility. **Die — der Geistwasser**, the fugacity of spirits.

Flüchtling, *m.* [s, *pl.* -e] 1) *Fig.* a fickle or inconstant person. 2) one who flees from danger, a fugitive. **Ein — (aus seinem Vaterlande)**, a refugee [from one's country]. 3) one that deserts his colours, a deserter, a fugitive.

Flück, V. Flügge.

Flüder, *m.* [-s] [allied to Fluth] [in mining and in hydraulics] a channel that conveys water, a trough.

Flüderholz, *n.* wood floated out of a channel into a river.

Flüdern, *v. tr.* to float [wood] on a channel into a river.

Flug, *m.* [-es, *pl.* Flüge] 1) the act of flying, a passing through the air by the help of wings, volation, flight. **Der — der Vögel und Ziefer** or **Insekten**, the flight of birds and insects; **im —e schießen**, to shoot flying *Fig.* any rapid or rapidly transient motion. *it.* a mounting, a soaring, lofty elevation and excursion, flight. **Der — der Zeit**, the flight of time; *it.* **der — der Einbildungskraft**, the flight of imagination or fancy. 2) a flock of birds or insects flying in company. **Ein — Tauben**, a flight of pigeons; **ein — Bienen**, a swarm of bees; [with hunters] **ein — Wachteln**, a bevy of quails; **ein — wilder Enten** [Wildenten], a flock or team of wild ducks, a flush; **ein — wilder Gänse**, a flock or gaggle of wild geese; **ein — Turteltauben**, a dule of turtles; **ein — Zaunkönige**, a herd of wrens. 3) a term in blazon for the wings of a bird. **Ein ausgebreiteter —**, vol; **ein halber — oder Halb—**, demi-vol [is said when only a single wing is borne in a coat of arms]. 4) the place from which any thing flies, as, the chase of a mortar. 5) a periodical flying of birds in flocks, flight **Der Enten— im Frühling**, the spring flight of ducks. 6) = fleetness, rapidity. **Der — der Zeit**, the fleetness of time; * **etwas im —e thun**, to do a thing in a hurry.

Flug-achse, *f.* V. Räderachse. —**besuch**, *m.* a flying visit. —**bett**, *n.* [in mills] a separate partition under the ceiling where mill-dust settles. —**biene**, *f.* a working-bee or neuter. —**blatt**, *n.* a fugitive composition, a pamphlet. —**brand**, *m.* a kind of blight incident to wheat, oats and barley. —**fertig**, *adj.* and *adv.* ready to fly. —**gestiebe**, *n.* V. Flockgestiebe. —**hafer**, *m.* V. Windhafer. —**haut**, *f.* 1) a membrane in the flying-squirrel &c. which serves as a wing. 2) the limb of an insect by which it flies, wing. —**heer**, *n.* a flying party, a flying camp. —**lager**, *n.* V. —heer. —**loch**, *n.* the entrance of a bee-hive or the pigeon-hole in a dove-cot or pigeon-house. —**mehl**, *n.* mill-dust. —**sand**, *m.* quicksand. —**schiene**, *f.* a small piece of wood over the opening of a bee-hive. —**schießen**, *n.* the act of shooting flying. —**schiff**, *n.* a small fast-sailing vessel, a cutter. —**schrecken**, *m.* panic fear. —**schrift**, *f.* fugitive composition, a pamphlet. —**schütze**, *m.* a sportsman that shoots flying. —**taube**, *f.* V. Feldtaube. —**wildpret**, *n.* feathered game. —**wisch**, *m.* [in contempt] a pamphlet.

Fluge, V. 2. Flocke.

Flügel, *m.* [-s, *pl.* -] 1) any thing turned by the wind, as, **die — einer Windmühle**, the sweeps of a windmill. 2) something floating or waving, hence a piece of bunting placed at the top of a mast, a vane. 3) commonly the limb of a fowl or insect by which it flies, wing. **Die — ausbreiten**, to spread, to display, to stretch the wings; **mit ausgebreiteten —n**, [in heraldry] with wings expanded; **mit den —n schlagen**, to beat the wing, to clap or flap the wings; **der Falke schlägt die —**, the hawk baits; **sich mittelst der — erheben**, to mount upon the wing, to soar; **die — schwingen**, to flap the wings; **die — binden** or **lähmen**, to bind or confine the wings; **einem Vogel die — lähmen**

to pinion a bird; die — hangen lassen, to hang the wings, [fig.*] to be dejected, dispirited or crest-fallen, to despond; [in cookery, the wing of a fowl stript of feathers, and dressed] soll ich Ihnen einen — von diesem Rebhuhn vorlegen? can I help you to a wing of that partridge? die — des Schiffes, [in poetry] the sails of a ship. Fig. *Einem die — beschneiden, to clip any one's wings; die Angst gab ihm —, fear added wings to his flight; *die — sind ihm schon gewachsen, he is now qualified or fit for something; *sich die — verbrennen, to burn one's fingers; unter dem Schatten deiner — rühme ich dich, [in Script.] under the shadow of thy wings will I rejoice; deine Zuversicht wird seyn unter seinen —n, [in script.] under his wings shalt thou trust; auf den —n des Windes, on the wings of the wind [with the utmost velocity]; die — der Liebe, des Ruhmes, the wings of love, of fame. 4) something resembling a wing. a) [in famil. language] the arm, wing. Einen beim — nehmen, to take one by the arm. b) the flank or extreme body or part of an army or of a fleet. Der linke — wurde in die Flucht geschlagen, the left wing was put to flight; die — einer Flotte, the wings of a fleet. c) [with hunters] the right and left side of a chase, hence die —, roads cut in a wood, ridings. d) [in architecture, a side-building, less than the main-edifice] wing; die — eines Chors, einer Kirche, the wings of a choir, the aisles, the wings or aisles of a church. e) [in fortification, the longer sides of horn-works, crown-works &c.] wing. f) [in mining] wing. g) [in hydraulics] a massive-work of masonry laid in a river to defend the shore from the impulse of the waves or to change the channel of a river. h) [in anatomy] Die — der Nase, the sides of the nostrils; die — der Ohren, the superior parts of the ears. i) Die — einer Thür, the valves, the leaves of a folding-door; die — eines Fensters, French sashes, or casements. k) Die — an einem Rocke [Rockflügel], the skirts of a coat. l) [with joiners] rest. m) [in botany] α) Die —, [the two side-petals of a papilionaceous flower] the wings. β) [a cartilaginous membrane on the seed and the pericarp] the wing. n) pl. [in anatomy] the two apophyses of the sphenoid bone o) a grand pianoforte.

Flügel-band, n. [in anatomy] the dowling of the capsular ligament. —**bauer**, m. a maker of grand-pianofortes. —**decke**, f. [in entomology] wing-shell, wing-sheath. Mit —decken versehen, sharded; Ziefer mit halben —decken, hemipters. —**erbse**, f. winged pea. —**farn**, m. female fern, brake [whose fructification is in lines under the margin of the leaf or adj. —**feder**, f. a feather of a fowl's wing. Die — auf dem zweiten Gelenk des Flügels, secondary. —**förmig**, adj. and adv. wing-shaped, wing-like, [in anatomy] aliform. —**fortsatz**, m. [in anatomy] one of the wing-like processes of the sphenoid bone. —**frucht**, f. 1) [in botany] winged fruit. 2) [a tree] pterocarpus —**fuß**, m. winged foot. —**futter**, n. [with shoemakers] leather for lining the straps of a shoe. —**gott**, m. the winged god [Cupid or Mercury]. V. Flügelkind. —**haube**, f. [a head-dress] cornet. —**heck**, n. [in seamen's lang.] vane-cock. —**herd**, m. [in metallurgy] a frame in stamping-mills where stamped gold ores are refined. —**horn**, n. 1) a bugle or hunting-horn. 2) [in conchology] the screw. —**hut**, m. [in mythology] the winged cap [of Mercury or Perseus]. —**kasten**, m. 1) the body of a grand-pianoforte. 2) a case for a grand-pianoforte. —**kind**, n. [in the polite arts] an imaginary being represented by a boy with wings on his back. —Kinder, [often called Amoretten or kleine Liebesgötter] amori or little Cupids. —**kleid**, n. 1) a child's garment with two broad pendants on the back; hence fig. [denoting the state of boyhood or girlhood] Als ich noch im —kleide ging, when I was yet in the days of my infancy 2) a light garment. —**knabe**, m. V —kind. —**kölbchen**, n. [in entomology] Die —kölbchen, [two small round bodies under the wings of dipterous insects] poisers. —**lahm**, adj. and adv. having lost the use of a wing, pinioned. —**lauf**, m. winged course. —**los**, adj. and adv wingless. —**macher**, m. V. —bauer. —**mann**, m. the leader of a file, [in some armies] the leader of a file, flugelman. —**mantel**, m. a cloak with hanging open sleeves. —**muskel**, m. [in birds, and in anatomy] aliform muscle. —**mütze**, f. V. —haube. —**nerve**, m. [in anatomy] pterygoid nerve. —**ort**, m. [in mining] level. —**paar**, n. a pair of wings. —**pfeil**, m. a swift-flying arrow. —**pferd**, n. a flying horse, [in mythology] the winged horse, Pegasus. Fig Das —pferd besteigen, reiten, to mount Pegasus, to make poetry. —**rinne**, f. [in anatomy] pterygoid foss. —**roß**, n. V. —pferd. —**samen**, m. [a plant] scarlet-flowered pentapetes. —**schlag**, m. 1) the clapping of wings. 2) Fig. a) speedy passage, transientness [said of time] Der —schlag der Zeit, the winged flight of time. b) soaring Der —schlag des Dichtergeistes, der Einbildungskraft, the soaring of genius, of imagination. —**schlag-ader**, f. [in anatomy] pterygoid artery. —**schnecke**, f. V. —horn, 2. —**schnell**, adj and adv. with winged speed. —**schnelle**, f. winged speed. —**schraube**, f. [with metallists] winged screw. —**schritt**, m. swift or rapid pace. —**sohle**, f. the winged heel of Mercury. —**spill**, n. [in seamen's lang.] spindle of a vane. Der Knopf an dem —spill, acorn. —**thier**, n. [especially in mythology &c.] a winged animal. —**thor**, n. a folding-gate. —**thür**, f. a folding-door. —**tuch**, n. the sails of a wind-mill —**welle**, f. the arbour of a wind-mill. —**werk**, n. 1) fowls, poultry. 2) a dish of wing-bones. —**wurm**, m. [in conchology] the clio.

Flügelchen, ||**Flügelein**, n. [-s, pl. -] [diminut. of Flügel] a small wing.

Flügelig, adj. and adv. having wings, winged [in botany]. V. Ein—, zwei—, drei— &c.

Flügeln, I. v. tr. to furnish with wings, to wing. Geflügelt, winged, aliferous, aligerous; geflügelte Schlangen, winged snakes; ein geflügeltes Pferd, [in mythology] a winged horse; [in botany] ein geflügelter Stengel, a winged stalk or stem; ein geflügelter Blattstiel, winged petiole; eine geflügelte Steinfrucht, winged drupe. Fig. [in poetry] Wer flügelt die Stürme? who wings the storms? geflügelt, swift, rapid, winged; mit geflügelter Eile, with winged haste. 2) [among sportsmen, to wound in the wing] to wing. Einen Vogel —, to wing a bird. II. v. intr. [u. w. seyn and kommen] to approach, to come near with winged haste.

Flügge, adj. and adv. fledge, fledged. Nicht —, unfledged.

Flugs, adv. [now, mostly used in fam. lang. or in jocose style] quickly, speedily, instantly, directly, immediately.

Fluhbirn[e], f. [pl. -en] Alpine mespilus.

Fluhblume, f. [pl. -n] auricula or bear's ear.

||**Fluhe**, f. [pl. -n] [Sw. flo = eine Schicht] 1) a stratum, layer, or bed. Eine Sand—, a stratum of sand. 2) a natural wall of rock, rock-work.

***Fluidum**, n. [-s or Fluidi, pl. Fluida] a fluid or liquid. Wasser, Blut sind Fluida, water, blood are fluids.

Flúnder, **Flünder**, m. [-s] [a fish] the flounder, fluke or flowk

Flünder-affe, m. [a genus of fishes] tetragonoptere.

||**Flúnk**, m. [-es, pl. -e] **Flunke**, f. [pl. -n] a wing, especially the fluke [of an anchor]

||**Flúnkern**, v. intr. to glitter. Fig. *to brag, to gasconade.

Flur, f. [pl. -en] [Ice. flaar Engl. floor, A. S. fleer signify a paved floor; it appears to be allied to Flube] 1) flat land. 2) the extent of land that belongs to the inhabitants of a town, village, or manor Die Dorf—, the fields of a village; die — begehen, beziehen, to perambulate the borders or bounds of a township, or the fields of a village or manor. 3) some contiguous fields. 4) in some counties the three divisions of a field, as, Sommer—, Winter—, Brach—. 5) the porch or entrance into a house, or a large open space before the entrance of the ordinary apartments. a vestibule. 6) [in seamen's language, the bottom of a ship] floor.

Flur-begang, m. —**beziehung**, f. V. —gang. —**buch**, n. 1) [a book or roll in which the lands of private persons or corporations are described by their site, boundaries, number of acres &c.] terrar, terrier 2) V. Steuerbuch. —**en-behüter**, m. V. —schütze. —**en-gott**, m. V. —gott. —**en-umringt**, adj and adv. surrounded by fields. —**fenster**, n. a window over the entrance-door of a house or in the vestibule. —**gang**, m 1) annual survey of the borders or bounds of a parish or township, perambulation. 2) a long gallery leading to several chambers, corridor. —**gott**, m. a rustic god, the god of gardens, Priapus. —**göttinn**, f. a rustic goddess. —**graben**, m. a ditch bordering a parish or township. —**grenze**, f. the borders or boundaries of a parish or township. —**recht**, n. 1) the jurisdiction over the fields belonging to a village or town. 2) any particular right or immunity or the privileges belonging to the fields of a village or town. —**register**, n. V. —buch. —**scheide**, —**scheidung**, f. the borders or bounds of the fields of a village or town. —**schütze**, m. field-guard. —**stein**, m. 1) mere-stone, landmark. 2) a square tile. Mit —steinen belegen, to pave with square tiles. —**umringt**, adj. and adv. V. —enumringt. —**zaun**, m. a hedge by which the limits of the fields of a village or town may be known and preserved.

Flúren, **Flüren**, v. tr. and intr. 1) to designate with landmarks the boundaries of a township or of the fields belonging to a village or manor. 2) to perambulate the boundaries of a township or of the fields belonging to a village or manor.

Flürer, m. [-s, pl. -] V. [the more usual word] Flurschütze.

Flúß, m. [-sses, pl. Flüsse] 1) the act of running or moving as a fluid, flowing, flux. Der — eines Stromes, the flowing of a stream. Fig. Der — einer Rede, flow, fluency of speech, volubility; das Gespräch or die Unterhaltung kommt in —, the conversation begins to flow; der — der Beredtsamkeit, the flow of eloquence; der — der Töne, melodious flow of sounds, harmony. 2) any flow or issue of matter, [in medicine] an extraordinary issue or evacuation from the bowels or other part, flux. Der Blut—, a flux of blood; der weiße —, der Mutter—, [in common or familiar language das Weiße] the whites; der weibliche —, menstrual flux, the monthly courses, flowers. 3) [in medicine and in common or familiar language] a disease or pain proceeding from a stagnation of the sharp humours in any part of the human body, fluxion; *it.* a painful disease affecting muscles and joints of the human body, chiefly the larger joints, [der scharfe —] rheumatism. Mit Flüssen behaftet seyn, to be affected with rheumatisms; der — auf der Brust, der schleimige —, [formerly der kalte —], a catarrh, cold. 4) [in metallurgy] the fusion of metals. Ein Metall in — bringen, to fuse a metal; Eisen oder Gold im Flusse, iron or gold in fusion. 5) a current, a river, stream. Ein schiffbarer —, a navigable river; ein fischreicher —, a river abounding in fish; über einen — setzen, to pass a river, or to cross a river; ein künstlicher —, a canal; ein kleiner —, a rivulet or streamlet, a brook, a rill. 6) [in metallurgy] a metal in fusion, chiefly iron in a state of fusion. Den — durch den Stich auf den Vorherd lassen, to let the smelted iron out of the dam of the furnace by the sow. 7) a run of cards of the same suit, a flush. 8) [in metallurgy and chimistry] any substance or mixture used to promote the fusion of metals or minerals, as alkalies, borax, tartar and other saline matter, or in large operations, limestone or fluor, flux. Der weiße —, the white flux; der —spath, fluor spar or the foliated fluate of lime, is named Fluß from its use as a flux for certain ores. 9) [in mineralogy] *a*) Dichter —, V. —stein. Erdiger —, V. —erde. *b*) any coloured, translucent or opake and vitreous species of spar, crystallized, as, Smaragd—, smaragdine fluor; Amethyst—, amethystine fluor &c. 10) [with jewellers] an artificial mixture in imitation of precious stones or gems, paste.

Fluß-adler, *m.* V. Meeradler. —**anwohnend**, *adj.* and *adv.* living on the banks of a river. —**artig**, *adj.* and *adv.* [in medicine] rheumatic. —artige Anfälle, rheumatic affections. —**bad**, *n.* a river bath. —**barsch**, *m.* V. —börs. —**bartfisch**, *m.* V. Barbe. —**bett**, *n.* 1) [the place where a river flows, including the whole breadth of the river] the bed of a river. 2) [in a more limited sense] the channel of a river. V. —rinne. —**blume**, *f.* V. Mottenkraut. —**börs**, *m.* [a river-fish] the perch. —**brassen**, *m.* the bream, that inhabits rivers. —**bricke**, *f.* river-lamprey. —**büchse**, *f.* a wooden box, for keeping tartar, saltpetre and granulated lead used in assaying or as fluxes. —**dorn**, *m.* the river thorny shell. —**eisen**, *n.* [in metallurgy] a mass of iron in fusion. —**erde**, *f.* earthy fluor. —**fahrzeug**, *n.* a vessel, ship or boat used on rivers. —**falk**, *m.* a common falcon, that inhabits the banks of rivers. —**fall**, *m.* the water-fall in a river; *it.* the fall of a river. —**fieber**, *n.* a catarrhal or rheumatic fever. —**fisch**, *m.* a river-fish, fresh-water fish. —**galle**, *f.* [a soft swelling on a horse's leg] a wind-gall, vessicon, vessigon. —**geist**, *m.* 1) a water-spirit, ‖ hobgoblin, elf. V. also —nimfe 1) *b*). 2) [in mineralogy] V. —spathgeist. —**gestirn**, *n.* [in astronomy, a southern constellation] Eridanus. —**gold**, *n.* grains of native gold found in rivers. —**gott**, *m.* [in mythology] river-god. —**göttinn**, *f.* V. —nimfe. —**granate**, *f.* garnet occurring in rivers. —**haloid**, *n.* Oktaedrisches —haloid, fluate of lime, fluor; rhomboedrisches —haloid, phosphate of lime. —**kahn**, *m.* river-boat. —**kannenkraut**, *n.* [a plant] river horse-tail. —**karpfen**, *m.* river-carp. —**kiesel**, *m.* a water-worn pebble, pebble-stone. —**krebs**, *m.* fresh-water- or river-crawfish. —**messer**, *n.* a tawer's fleshing-knife. —**mittel**, *n.* 1) an anticatarrhal remedy, an anticatarrhal. 2) [in metallurgy] a flux or fluxstone. —**moos**, *n.* the water-moss. —**muschel**, *f.* a shell-fish that inhabits rivers. —**nadel**, *f.* [in conchology] the screw that inhabits rivers. —**nimfe** [—nymphe], *f.* 1) *a*) [in the Greek and Roman mythology] a water-nymph, naid or naiad. *b*) [in German poetical mythology] Undine. V. Wassergeist. 2) a species of dragon-fly that inhabits the banks of rivers and brooks. —**nixe**, *f.* V. —nimfe 1) *b*). —**ochs**, *m.* V. —pferd. —**ofen**, *m.* [in metallurgy] blast-furnace. —**otter**, *f.* the common otter. —**pferd**, *n.* the hippopotamus, or river-horse. —**pflaster**, *n.* an anticatarrhal plaister. —**pricke**, *f.* V. —bricke. —**pulver**, *n.* 1) rheumatic powder. 2) [in metallurgy] a powder serving as a flux. —**rauch**, *m.* V. —pulver, 1. —**rinne**, *f.* —**rinnsal**, *n.* [with some authors *m.*] the channel of a river. —**sand**, *m.* river-sand. —**sauer**, *adj.* and *adv.* V. —spathsauer. —**säure**, *f.* V. —spathsäure. —**schiff**, *n.* a river-ship, a boat. —**schifffahrt**, *f.* navigation on rivers, inland-navigation. —**schildkröte**, *f.* river-turtle. —**schnecke**, *f.* the lake-snail. —**schwamm**, *m.* the common sponge that inhabits rivers. —**schwimmschnecke**, *f.* a nerite that inhabits rivers. —**seite**, *f.* the river-side [of a town &c.]. —**spath**, *m.* 1) fluor spar, sparry fluor. 2) V. —stein. —**spathdunst**, *m.* fluoric gas. —**spatherde**, *f.* earthy fluor. —**spathgeist**, *m.* [in chimistry] fluorated aether. —**spathsauer**, *adj.* and *adv.* [in chimistry] fluorated. —spathsaure Salze, fluates; —spathsaures Blei, fluate of lead; —spathsaurer Kalk, fluor, fluate of lime; —spathsaures Natron, fluate of soda; neutrales —saures Cerer, fluate of cerium &c. —**spathsäure**, *f.* fluoric acid or fluor-acid. —**spindel**, *f.* [in conchology] a species of the spindle-shell. —**stein**, *m.* 1) any stone found in rivers. 2) a fluxstone. 3) compact fluor. 4) lava. —**stoff**, *m.* [in medicine] rheumatic matter. —**taback**, *m.* a sort of tobacco good against catarrhs, rheumatisms or colds. —**teufel**, *m.* [a bird] the greater coot. —**thier**, *n.* any animal that inhabits rivers. —**ufer**, *n.* the side of a river, bank [as distinguished from shore, the coast or land adjacent to the ocean or sea]. —**wage**, *f.* [in hydrostatics] a level with a double square in the form of a T. —**wasser**, *n.* river-water [as distinguished from rain-water, sea-water or pump-water]. —**wate**, *f.* [in fishery] a sort of fishing-net used at the mouth of rivers or in stagnant water. —**zinn**, *n.* stream-tin, granular tin.

Flüßchen, ‖**Flüßlein**, *n.* [-s, *pl.* -] a small river or stream, a streamlet, a rivulet, a brook.

Flüßig, *adj.* and *adv.* 1) fluid, liquid. —e Körper, liquids, fluids [as opposed to solids]. Wasser, Blut, Luft sind —e Körper, water, blood, air are fluids; alle Körper können durch Hitze oder Wärmestoff — gemacht werden, all bodies may be rendered fluid by heat or caloric; das Blut des h. Januarius wurde —, the blood of St. Januarius liquified; —es Wachs, melted wax. *Fig.* [in grammar, pronounced without any jar, smooth] liquid. Ein —er Buchstabe, a liquid letter; L, M, N und R sind —e Buchstaben, L, M, N and R are liquids. 2) subject to catarrhs, colds or rheumatisms; also in composition, as, Blut—, affected with a bloody flux; Bauch—, affected with a flux of the bowels &c.

Flüßigkeit, *f.* 1) [the quality of being fluid or liquid] liquidity, liquidness, fluidity, fluidness. — ist eine Wirkung der Hitze, fluidity is the effect of heat; die — der Luft, the fluidity of air; die — des Wassers, oder des Feuers, the fluidness of water, the fluidity of fire. 2) a fluid body, a fluid, or liquid, a liquor. Geistige —en, liquors, ardent spirits. 3) a disposition of the human body to catarrhs, colds, rheumatisms.

Flüstern, [Dutch *luysteren*, allied to wispern] I. *v. intr.* to whisper. Das —de Lüftchen, the whispering breeze. II. *v. intr.* and *tr.* to whisper. Es ist unschicklich in Anderer Gegenwart zu —, it is ill-bred to whisper in company; einem etwas ins Ohr —, to whisper in any one's ear; er flüsterte mir ein Wort ins Ohr, he whispered a word in my ear; sie — unaufhörlich, they do nothing but whisper; sie schütteln die Köpfe und — sich ins Ohr, they shake their heads and whisper one another in the ear.

Flut, **Fluth**, *f.* [*pl.* -en] [from fließen, Low Saxon fleeten] 1) [sometimes] water in general. Die —en, [= ein Fluß, das Meer &c.] floods, waves, billows; er fand seinen Tod in den —en, he perished in the waves. 2) a body of moving water, a body of water rising or swelling, a flood. 3) a great body of any fluid substance, a flood. Eine — von Thränen, a flood of tears; [in mining] water falling from a stamping-mill, and a pond wherein it falls. *Fig.* *a*) a great quantity, a flood. Eine — von Assignaten, a flood of assignats. *b*) abundance, copiousness. Eine — von Worten, a stream of words. 4) the swell or rise of water, a moving swell or volume of water, hence, the flowing of the tide, the flood. Ebbe und —, ebb and flood, tide, [in hydrography] flux and reflux; [in seamen's language] die Vor—, a young flood; die halbe —, half flood; das Letzte der — [die Hinter—], high-tide, high-water; die hohe — [Spring—], spring-tide; eine —, [the time that the water continues rising] flood-tide; mit der — fahren, to tide; das Schiff lief mit der — in den Hafen ein, the ship entered the harbour on the flood. 5) a body of water overflowing land, not usually covered with water, a flood, or inundation. Die Noachische —, die Sünd—, Noah's flood, the flood, the deluge. 6) [in the saltworks at Halle in Prussia] the state of the salt-well when it is completely filled.

Fluth-anker, *m.* [in seamen's language] stream-anchor. —**bett**, *n.* 1) V. Flußbett. 2) [in mills and in hydrostatics, the channel that conveys water] trough. 3) [in mills] a bank of earth or any work in a river that stops water in a pond. 4) [in mining] a conduit. —**gang**, *m.* V. —bett. —**graben**, *m.* [in mills and in mining] a trench to conduct water from a mill, or from a mine, a leat. —**tag**, *m.* [in the saltworks at Halle in Prussia] the day when the salt-well is filled with brine. —**werk**, *n.* 1) V. Gerinnwerk. 2) [in metallurgy] ore found in water falling from a stamping-mill. —**zeichen**, *n.* high water-mark. —**zeit**, *f.* flood-tide, flood.

Flüte, *f.* [*pl.* -n] [from fließen, Low Saxon fleeten, fließen, V. Fliet(schiff)] a large flat-bottomed Dutch vessel, a fly-boat.

Flut[h]en, I. *v. intr.* to rise, as the tide, to flow. Das Meer ebbet und flutet, the sea ebbs and flows; es flutet, the tide flows; die Menge flutete durch die Thore in den Palast, the multitude crowded through the gates into the palace; geflutet, [in heraldry] wavy. II. *v. tr.* to carry away as by a flood, to float away.

Flutschiff, *n.* [-es, *pl.* -e] V. Flüte.

1. **Focke**, *f.* [*pl.* -n] [perhaps allied to fegen, Dutch *focke*] [in seamen's lang.] the fore-sail [Focksegel].

Fock-mars, *m.* [in seamen's lang., the platform erected at the head of the foremast] fore-top. —**mast**, *m.* [in seamen's lang.] fore-mast. —**raa**, —**rahe**, *f.* [in seamen's lang.] fore-yard. —**reep**, *n.* [in seamen's lang.] fore-tye. —**schmiete**, —**schote**, *f.* [in seamen's lang.] fore-sail sheet. —**segel**, *n.* [in seamen's lang.; Focke] fore-sail. —**stag**, *m.* [in seamen's lang.] fore-stay. —**stagsegel**, *n.* fore-stay-sail. —**stange**, —**stenge**, *f.* [in seamen's lang.] fore-top-mast. —**wand**, *f.* [in seamen's lang.] fore-shrouds.

2. **Focke**, *f.* [*pl.* -n] [seems to be allied to fegen

=bewegen] [a genus of birds] the night heron. *Fig.* * and † Ein loser —n, a thoughtless or frivolous youth.

Fockfeder, *f.* one of the three long white feathers on the head of the night-heron.

Föcker, *m.* [-s, *pl.* -] [a genus of birds] V. Focke 2.

*Föcus, *m.* [in optics, the point in which any number of rays of light meet, after being reflected or refracted] focus.

Föder, *n.* [-s] a sort of tin-plate.

*Föderation, *f.* federation, confederacy.

*Föderirte, *pl.* confederates.

Födern, better Fördern, [this is probably not allied to the Lat. *peto*, the Gr. ποθέω, but comes from vor, vorder, and is allied to fördern] *v. tr.* 1) to request to meet or come, to invite or summon to come or be present. Einen vor Gericht —, [to give notice to a person to appear in court and defend] to summon any one, to cite any one; Einen vor die Klinge — or *Einen —, to call a person out, to challenge any one. 2) to speak for, to ask, to request, to call for. Zu essen —, to call for a dinner; er foderte Brod, he asked for bread. To demand, to ask, to claim. Seinen Lohn —, to claim one's wages; wie viel — Sie? what price do you ask, or demand? der Gläubiger fodert sein Capital mit den Interessen, the creditor demands principal and interest of his debt; Gehorsam —, to claim obedience; wir — von Einem, daß er etwas thue, we require a person to do a thing; fodert nur getrost von mir Morgengabe, [in Scripture] ask me never so much dowry; Rechenschaft von Einem —, to call any one to account; das höchste Wesen fodert von uns Verehrung und Huldigung, the Supreme Being challenges our reverence and homage. *Fig.* To require, to make necessary, to need, to demand. Die Ausführung dieses Werkes fodert große Sorgfalt, the execution of this work demands great care; die Umstände — es, the circumstances require it; Krankheit foderte seine Entfernung vom Hofe, sickness necessitated his removal from court.

Födern, V. [the usual word] Fördern.

Föderung and Förderung, *f.* 1) an asking, a calling on another for something due, or supposed to be due, demand, claim. Die — des Gläubigers war billig, the demand of the creditor was reasonable. 2) the asking or requiring a price for goods offered for sale, demand. that which is or may be claimed as due, claim, demand. Eine Schuld—, a claim of a debt.

Föderungssatz, *m.* [a position or supposition, which is considered as self-evident, or too plain to require illustration] postulate, postulatum.

1. ||Föhlen, *n.* [-s, *pl.* -] [Lat. *pullus*, Gr. πῶλος, allied to the old Lat. *feo*, Gr. φύω, Lat. *fio*] foal, a colt.

2. ||Föhlen, *v. intr.* to foal.

Föhn, *f.* [-s] [allied to wehen] V. Südwind.

1. Föhre, *f.* [*pl.* -n] V. Forelle.

Föhrenbach, *m.* V. Forellenbach.

2. Föhre, Föhre, *f.* [*pl.* -n] [perhaps allied to Farbe] 1) wild pine-tree. 2) [with some botanists, the name of several species of the genus pinus] fir.

Föhren-holz, *n.* fir-wood. —kloß, *m.* block. —wald, *m.* a forest of fir-trees.

Föhren, *adj.* and *adv.* pertaining to fir-trees, made of fir. —e Dielen, planks of fir, deals.

1. Fölge, *f.* [*pl.* -n] (V. Folgen) 1) series of things following one another, either in time or place, succession. Eine — von traurigen Begebenheiten or Unfällen, a succession, a series of calamitous events; eine — von Wörtern und Sätzen, a succession of words and sentences; eine — von Farben, a succession of colours; eine — von Tönen, a succession of sounds; eine — der Ideen, a train of ideas; in der — der Zeiten, in the process or course of time; in einer —, in one row, or line; die — in der Herrschaft, im Amte, succession to dominion, to an office. 2) continuance, continuation. Die — der Geschichte, the continuation of the story; haben Sie die — seiner Abentheuer gelesen? have you read the sequel of his adventures? 3) a number or collection of things of the same kind following one another and forming a whole, a set, suit. Eine — von Münzen der Römischen Kaiser, a set of medals of the Roman Emperors; eine vollständige — der Griechischen Classiker, a complete collection of Greek classics. 4) succeeding time, time to come. Die — wird es lehren, time will try; in der —, when time shall be, in time to come, hereafter; was in der — verhandelt wurde, weiß ich nicht, what was subsequently transacted, I do not know; Sie werden in der — Ihre Gesundheit wieder erlangen, you will in time recover your health. 5) that which proceeds naturally or logically from facts, premises or the state of things, inference, consequence, conclusion, a consequent. Daraus läßt sich die — ziehen, from that we may infer; die — davon ist, daß Sie Unrecht haben, from thence it follows that you are in the wrong. 6) a complying with the commands of another, or with the requirements of law or duty. Einem — leisten, to obey any one; Diener, leistet euren Herren in allen Dingen —, servants obey in all things your masters; den Gesetzen des Staates — leisten, to observe the laws of the state; einem Befehle — leisten, to comply with an order or command; in — or zu — [chiefly written zufolge, infolge] deines Befehles, according to your command; zu — eines Befehles des Heerführers, in pursuance of an order of the general; seinem Versprechen zu —, in conformity to his promise; Nachrichten aus Lissabon zu— hat die Königinn &c., by news from Lisboa we learn that the queen &c. V. Zufolge. 7) the obligation under which a person is to assist, when summoned, a superior in executing any thing [it is chiefly used in the compound words, Amts—, Gerichts—, Heeres— &c., which see]; also the power or a right to require the same of others. Die — in eines andern Jagdbezirk haben, to have a right to pursue wounded game on the manor of another. 8) that which follows from any act, cause, or series of actions, hence, an event or effect produced by some preceding act or cause, sequel, consequence. Armuth und Krankheit sind die natürlichen —n der Ausschweifung, poverty and disease are the natural effects of dissipation; von wichtigen —n, of great consequence; die —n der Unmäßigkeit, the consequences of intemperance; eine — des schlechten Bezahlens, a consequent of ill-payment; die — davon würde unser Verderben seyn, the sequel would be our ruin; das ist eine — Ihrer schlechten Aufführung, this is a consequence of your ill conduct; seine Armuth war eine — seiner Laster, his poverty was consequent on his vices; unbekümmert um die —n, inconsiderate of consequences; in — [chiefly written infolge] seiner Befehle, in consequence of his orders; in — seiner unerhörten Verschwendung, in consequence of his unheard of extravagance. 9) *pl.* certain instruments, as, the prongs of a fire-hook. 10) [in hydraulics] the height of the water in the tubes or pipes of a pump.

Folge-alter, *n.* succeeding age, time to come, futurity. —diener, *m.* [rather unusual] a follower, an attendant, servant, a footboy or footman, a lackey. —geschlecht, *n.* succeeding generation, descendants, posterity. —jahr, *n.* a subsequent year. —leistung, *f.* compliance, obedience. —magd, *f.* [rather unusual] an attendant maid-servant, a female slave. —n-los, *adj.* and *adv.* not of consequence, inconsequential. —n-macher, *m.* a person that draws consequences from trifles or unimportant facts. —n-reich, *adj.* and *adv.* followed by many and great effects, of great consequence. —n-reihe, *f.* a series of consequences. —n-zieher, *m.* V. —macher. —recht, *adj.* and *adv.* 1) regularly consequential, conclusive. 2) consistent, uniform. Ein —rechtes Benehmen, consistency of behaviour; seine —rechte Handlungsweise, his consistent conduct; —recht handeln, to act consistently —reihe, *f.* succession of things, sequence, series. Eine —reihe von Königen, a series of kings. —richtig, *adj.* and *adv.* V. —recht. —richtigkeit, *f.* a just deduction of consequences, consequence justly connected with the premises. —richtigkeit im Handeln, consistency. —satz, *m.* 1) inference. 2) a corollary. Ein unrichtiger —satz, a sophism. —schluß, *m.* consequence, conclusion, result. —stern, *m.* a secondary planet or moon, satellite. Die Erde hat einen —, den Mond, the earth has one satellite, the moon. —trumpf, *m.* a principal trump, a matadore. —vers, *m.* the subsequent verse. —welt, *f.* V. Nachwelt. —widrig, *adj.* and *adv.* 1) not following from the premises, inconsequent, inconsequential. 2) not uniform, being contrary at different times. Ein —widriges Betragen, an inconsistent behaviour. —widrigkeit, *f.* 1) inconsequence. 2) [want of agreement or uniformity] inconsistency. —zeiger, *m.* V. Blatthüter. —zeit, *f.* time to come, futurity, following ages, posterity.

2. ||Fölge, *f.* V. Gelte.

Fölgen, [seems to be allied to wallen, to the Gr. πολ-έω, πωλ-έομαι] *v. intr.* [u. w. seyn] to go after or behind, to walk, ride or move behind, to follow. Der Diener folgt seinem Herrn, a servant follows his master; Peter folgte von Weitem, in der Ferne, Peter followed afar off; Einem auf dem Fuße —, to be at any one's heels, to follow any one closely; der Leiche —, to attend the burial of the dead; Eines Beispiel —, to imitate the example of any one; ein folgsames Kind folgt dem Beispiel seiner Eltern, an obedient child copies his parents; folge seinen Fußstapfen, follow his footsteps; einem guten Rathe —, to follow a good advice; guten Lehren —, to follow good precepts; wehe den tollen Propheten, die ihrem eignen Geiste —, [in script.] wo to the foolish prophets, who follow their own spirit; er folgt in Allem seinem Kopfe, he does every thing out of his own head; der Stimme der Menschlichkeit —, to listen to the calls of humanity; er will mir nicht —, he won't do as I would have him. *Fig.* *a*) to come after another, to follow. Der zweite folgt auf den ersten, the second follows the first. *b*) to succeed in order of time, to follow. Auf Regen folgt Sonnenschein, rain is followed by sunshine; auf den Tag folgt die Nacht, night succeeds to day; Einem im Amte —, to succeed any one in office; er folgte ihm auf dem Throne, he succeeded in his throne; am —den Tage, the following day, next day; die —den Jahre, the subsequent years; die —den Worte, the subsequent words; die auf einander —den Jahrhunderte, the successive ages; fünfzig auf einander —de Jahre, fifty consecutive years; —der Gestalt, —der Maßen, as follows; die Sache verhielt sich —der Maßen, the circumstances were as follows, or were such as follow; er äußerte sich —der Maßen or —der Gestalt, he spoke to this intent or purport, seine Worte waren —de, his words were as follows. c) to be consequential, to result from, as effect from a cause, to follow. Aus Völlerei folgt oft Krankheit und Armuth, intemperance is often followed by, or attended with, disease or poverty. d) to result from, as an inference or deduction, to follow. Aus diesen Thatsachen folgt, daß der Angeklagte schuldig ist, it follows from these facts that the accused is guilty. e) to act in conformity to, to follow.

||**Fólgends**, *adv.* 1) in the sequel, afterwards. 2) for the future, henceforth. 3) further, moreover. 4) consequently.

Fólger, *m.* [-s, *pl.* -] follower; especially in composition, as, Nach—, Ver— &c.

Folgeréi, *f.* 1) inference from false premises. 2) a disposition to draw false and frivolous inferences from the discourse or acts of others.

Fólgern, *v. tr.* to deduce, to draw or derive as a fact or consequence, to infer. Was — Sie daraus? what do you conclude from thence? der gefolgerte Satz, the inferred proposition.

Fólgerung, *f.* [*pl.* -en] 1) that which is collected or drawn from premises, consequence inferred, inference, conclusion. Eine — machen, to draw an inference; die Welt wird die — ziehen, daß ich ein schuldiges Gewissen habe, the world will conclude I have a guilty conscience. 2) [in logic] corollary.

Folgerungssatz, *m.* V. Folgesatz.

Fólglich, I. *adj.* and *adv.* || that is to be or come hereafter, future, subsequent. II. *conj.* by consequence, consequently. Er erröthet, — ist er schuldig, he blushes, therefore he is guilty.

Fólgsam, *adj.* and *adv.* submissive to authority, yielding compliance with commands, orders, or injunctions, obedient. Ein —es Kind, an obedient child; —e Kinder, tractable children; ein —es Betragen, an obsequious behaviour or conduct; ein —es Thier, a docile animal; — seinen Befehlen, obsequious to his orders; sie erheben sich und begeben sich — hinweg, they rise and obsequiously withdraw. sich gegen jemand — zeigen, to behave obediently towards a person.

Fólgsamkeit, *f.* ready obedience, prompt compliance with the orders of a superior, obsequiousness, tractableness.

***Foliánt**, *m.* [-en, *pl.* -en] a book of the largest size, a book in folio, a folio.

***Fólie**, *f.* [*pl.* -n] [a thin leaf of metal placed under precious stones] foil.

***Fólio**, *n.* [- or -s] 1) [form of a book] folio. Ein Buch in —, a book in folio. 2) [among merchants, a page, or rather both the right and left hand pages of an account-book, expressed by the same figure] folio.

||**Fólkbeere**, *f.* [*pl.* -n] Alpine currant.

Fólter, *f.* [*pl.* -n] [is said to come from the Old-Franconian *puledrus*, Ital. *poledro*, Fr. *poultre* = Füllen, on account of its form] an engine for torture, the rack; *it.* a stretching on the rack, racking, torture. Einen auf die — bringen, spannen, to put to the rack, to put to the question; auf der — seyn, liegen, to be on the rack; einem Angeklagten ein Geständniß durch die — auspressen, to extort a confession from an accused person by torture. *Fig.* extreme pain, anguish of body or mind, pang, agony, torment, torture, rack. Er spannte mich mit seinen Reden auf die —, his discourse put me to the rack; es gibt keine ärgere —, als ein schuldiges Gemüth, there's no fiercer torment than a guilty mind.

Folter=bank, *f.* a rack [in the shape of a bench]. —**bein**, *n.* a certain instrument of torture. —**geräth**, *n.* implements of torture. —**kammer**, *f.* torture-chamber. —**pein**, *f.* extreme pain, anguish. —**qual**, *f.* torture, anguish of body or mind, pang. —**seil**, *n.* a cord for stretching or straining the members of a person on the rack. —**stube**, *f.* V. —kammer. —**zeug**, *n.* V. —geräth.

***Fomént**, *n.* [-s, *pl.* -e] [the lotion applied, or to be applied, to a diseased part of the body] fomentation.

***Fomentíren**, *v. tr.* and *intr.* to apply warm lotions to, to foment.

***Fónd[s]**, [by many pronounced like the Fr. *fond* and *fonds*] *m.* [-s, *pl.* -s] 1) [chiefly in fam. lang.] fundament. Er hat in den Sprachen einen guten — gelegt, he laid a good basis in his study of the languages. 2) [money lent to government] fund. Die öffentlichen —s, the funds or public funds. *Fig.* *Ein — von Gelehrsamkeit, a store of learning.

Fönich, *m.* [-s, *pl.* -e] V. Fench.

***Fontäne**, *f.* [*pl.* -n] a jet, or fountain.

***Fontanéll**, *n.* [-es, *pl.* -e] [in surgery] an issue, a fontanel. Ein — setzen, to apply a fontanel.

Fontanell=erbse, *f.* orange-pea. —**papier**, *n.* issue-paper. —**pflaster**, *n.* issue-plaster.

Föppen, [seems to be allied to the Engl. *to fib*] *v. tr.* 1) to make a joke of, to mock, to make game of, to jeer, to deride, to scoff. *Prov.* Wer foppt, wird wieder gefoppt, mocking is catching. 2) to disconcert, to abash, to embarrass.

Föpper, *m.* [-s, *pl.* -] a mocker, a jeerer, a scoffer, a railer. ||*f.* —inn, a female scoffer &c.

Fopperéi, *f.* [*pl.* -en] 1) making a joke of, mocking, making game of, jeering, derision. 2) mockery, jeer.

||**Fórche**, *f.* V. Fohre, Föhre.

Fórchel, *f.* V. Forkel.

||**Förchling**, *m.* [-es, *pl.* -e] [allied to Föhre, Forche] the orange agaric.

Fórder, *n.* V. Foder.

Forderblech, *n.* V. Foder.

||**Förder**, *adv.* [obsolete] farther, moreover.

Förder=fahrt, *f.* [in mining] hurrying-way. —**gefäß**, *n.* [in mining] a basket. —**junge**, *m.* [in mining] foal. —**mann**, *m.* [in mining] putter, trammer. —**schacht**, *m.* [in mining] a by-pit. —**volk**, *n.* [in mining] putters, trammers. —**wagen**, *m.* [in mining] tram.

Förderer, *m.* [-s, *pl.* -] one who helps to advance, a furtherer, a promoter.

Förderlich, *adj.* and *adv.* 1) inclined to be useful to any one. Einem — seyn, to be serviceable to any one. 2) forwarding, helping, promoting. Der Tugend und Religion — seyn, to promote virtue and religion; er war meinem Plane —, he furthered or promoted my design; Thätigkeit ist der Gesundheit —, industry is beneficial to health; dem Wohl des Landes —, conducive to the good of the country; wo es zu einem andern Zwecke — seyn kann, where it can serve another end; auf das Förderlichste, in the speediest manner.

Fórdern, V. Fodern.

Förbern, [allied to vor, vorder] I. *v. tr.* 1) to bring forward, to advance. [in mining] Das Erz, die Steine in den Gruben —, to draw the ore, the stones from the pits. *Fig.* [...] Buch zu Tage —, to send a book into [...] world, to publish a book. [often in joke [...] contempt] 2) *Fig.* a) to accelerate motio[n] [...] progress. Er förderte seine Schritte, he [...] his steps; seine Arbeit —, to execute a [...] speedily; sein Geschäft —, to dispatch [...] business; seine Kunden —, to speed [...] customers; künstliche Hitze fördert das [...]thum der Pflanzen, artificial heat expe[dites,] forwards or advances the growth of plant[s] [...] to help forward, to further. Das Int[eresse] des Handels oder der Landwirthschaft — [...] promote the interest of commerce or of [agri]culture; ein gutes Vorhaben —, to fo[rward] a good design; der Himmel fördre dieses [Un]ternehmen, may heaven speed this und[ertaking]; ein Bergwerk —, to advance the w[ork]ing of a mine; einen Gesellen —, [with [me]chanics] to help a journey-man to work. II. sich —, to make haste, to speed. Fördert [euch,] make haste. III. *v. imp.* Es fördert, it sp[eeds,] it has a good success; es fördert ihm die [Ar]beit, his business goes on well.

Förderniß, *n.* [-sses, *pl.* -sse] ||1) fur[ther]ing, furtherance. 2) [in mining] the rem[oval] of ores and stones. 3) that which furth[ers,] forwards, promotes or advances any th[ing.] Ein — der Mildthätigkeit, a promoter [of] charity.

Fördersam, *adj.* and *adv.* [rather stiff] 1) inclined to promote the interests of others, ser[]viceable. 2) expeditious, quick, speedy. — Folge leisten, to obey readily, promptly. [...] *adv.* before-hand, previously.

Förderung, *f.* V. Foderung.

Förderung, *f.* 1) a helping forward, fur[]therance, promotion, advancement. 2) [with some mechanics] a) work that is bespoken. [...] the place where any work is carried on.

Forélle, *f.* [*pl.* -n] [= Fohre, seems to [be] allied to Farbe] the trout.

Forellen=bach, *m.* trout-stream. —**fang**, *m.* trout-fishing. —**kirschbaum**, *m.* tree bearing the agriot. —**kirsche**, *f.* agrio[t.] —**radieschen**, *n.* trout-coloured garde[n] radish. —**salat**, *m.* the trout-coloured gar[]den-lettuce. —**teich**, *m.* trout-pond.

||**Fórke**, *f.* [*pl.* -n] [Lat. *furca*, Ital. *for[ca,]* allied to bohren] [in husbandry] a pitchfork or dungfork.

Fórkel, [Lat. *furca*] *f.* [*pl.* -n] [with hunter[s]] forked sticks used to support the nets upon.

Fórkeln, *v. tr.* to raise or pitch with a for[k.] Heu —, to fork hay; der Hirsch forkelt [die] Hunde, [with hunters] the stag gores the hound[s.]

Fórm, *f.* [*pl.* -en] [from the Lat. *forma*] [...] shape or external appearance of a body, form. [...] — eines Hutes, eines Tellers, the shape of a h[at,] of a plate. *Fig.* a) [manner of arrangement, dispos[ition] of component parts] shape, form. Die — ei[ner] Sache ändern, to change the shape of a thing; die — eines Buches, the size of a book. [...] — der Arche, the fashion of the ark; ein B[uch] in Bogen—, a book in folio, a folio; ein B[uch] in Viertel—, in quarto, a quarto; ein B[uch] in Achtel—, a book in octavo, an octavo, an octavo volume; in der — einer Bittschr[ift,] in the shape of a petition; in der — Recht[ens,] in form of the law; die — der Begri[ffe,] the form of ideas; die — eines Vernunftschlus[]ses, the form of a syllogism; in bester [—,] in the best form; die vorgeschriebene —, [...] form; in gehöriger or gebührender —, in d[ue] form; die —en beobachten, to observe [...] forms; einer der sich streng an die —en b[indet,] a formalist; die steifste or strengste — [...]

n diesem Hofe, the strictest etiquette prevails t this court; es ist nur eine Sache der —, it s a mere matter of form; *it.* eine — des Got=tesdienstes, a mode of worship; eine andere Regierungs—, another form of government; ie gerichtlichen —en, the forms of judicial roceedings. *b*) in grammar, the variation of verb to express manner of action or being. Die thätige —, active or transitive verb; die eidende —, passive verb; die unbestimmte —, the infinitive mode. 2) something in-nded to give shape, or on which things re fashioned, a form, a model, or mould. Die — zu Kugeln, a mould for casting balls r bullets; eine — zu Backsteinen, a mould or forming bricks, hence; [among sculptors] ie verlorene —, cast; [in paper-mills] a mould; with goldbeaters] a mould; V. Quetsch—, Haut=—; [with chandlers] a mould; [with printers] the hase, [when it is empty, but when it is filled with pe or letter] the form; die kleine —, a small-hase [without a short cross]; die ausgedruckte —, e form worked off; die — zurichten, to make ady the form. *Fig.* Eine Sache in eine an=ere — gießen, to change the shape of a thing.) that which is formed or moulded, as, the wel [an iron pipe in a forge to receive the pipe of bellows] also the stone on which it rests.

Form=band, *n.* a hatter's pack-thread. -bank, *f.* a sort of lathe in founderies. —bolzen, *m.* [in founderies] a bolt used in cast-g pipes. —brett, *n.* [with founders] the ould.—eisen, *n.* [in cannon-founderies] a punch. -en=krämer, *m.* V. —krämer. —en=machen, the making of forms or moulds. —en=acher, *m.* one that makes forms or moulds. en=schneiden, *n.* the cutting of forms. en=schneider, *m.* form-cutter. —en=og, *m.* [in sugar-houses] a trough over which e forms are filled. —en=wesen, *n.* V. —ten. —erde, *f.* any species of earth used material for moulds, particularly clay. —asche, *f.* V. Flasche, 2. *Fig. c.* —futter, [with gold-beaters] the cover of the mould. —iffel, *m.* a style used by modelers in wax. haken, *m.* [in forges] a hook used for clean-g tewels. —hammer, *m.* a gold-beater's mmer. —holz, *n.* V. —brett. —kappe, [with tin-founders] case. —kleidung, *f.* ith founders] the coat. —kopf, *m.* [with r-dressers] a wooden head for periwigs. krämer, *m.* a formalist. —kugel, *f.* ith founders] form-ball. —lade, *f.* [with nders] moulding-table. —los, *adj.* and *adv.* formless, shapeless. 2) ill-formed, defor-d, misshapen, misshaped. —losigkeit, shapelessness. —nath, *f.* [with founders] rd. —presse, *f.* a gold-beater's press. —hmen, *m.* [in printing] chase. —sand, *m.* ulding-sand. —scheibe, *f.* 1) top of a pot-'s wheel. 2) [with glaziers] the smallest pane, chneider, *m.* V. —enschneider. —spath, a mixture used by founders instead of moul-g sand. —spindel, *f.* [in cannon-founderies] ender piece of pine-wood. —steg, *m.* [with ters] Die —stege, furniture. —stein, *m.* forges] a stone on which the tewel rests. empel, *m.* [with bookbinders] a flourishing l. —stock, *m.* a glover's forming stick. —ßer, *m.* [in forges] an iron used for clean-; the tewel. —stück, *n.* V. —stein. —tisch, mould-frame. —trog, *m.* V. Formentrog. aare, *f.* fashioned goods —wesen, *n.* a t observing of forms or etiquette; *it.* mere as. —zacken, *m.* [in forges] an iron plate which the tewel rests. —zeug, *n.* moulding-s, moulds.

ormalien, Formalitäten, *pl.* formalities, mere forms, ceremonies.

Formalienkrämer, *m.* V. Formkrämer.

*Formalisiren, I. *v. intr.* to observe forms, to formalize. II. *v. r.* sich — über etwas, [in fam. lang.] to find fault or to be displeased with a thing.

*Format, *n.* [-es, *pl.* -e] the size of a book.

Format=leim, *m.* English glue. —schla=gen, *n.* [with bookbinders] the last beating of the folded sheets.

*Formation, *f.* 1) [the act of forming or making, or, the manner in which a thing is formed] formation. 2) [in geology, a single mass of one kind of rock more or less extensive, or a collection of mineral substances, formed by the same agent, under the same or similar circumstances, or conveying the idea, that certain masses or collections of minerals were formed not only by the same agent but also at the same time] formation.

Formbar, *adj.* and *adv.* that may be formed or moulded, mouldable.

Formel, *f.* [*pl.* -n] [Lat. *formula*] a prescribed form of words, form, formule, formula. Eine Gebet—, a form of prayer.

Formel=buch, *n.* [a book containing stated and prescribed forms] formulary. —wesen, *n.* [in contempt] forms, formules.

Formeln, *v. tr.* and *intr.* 1) [in contempt] to form, to shape. Hier formelt der laute Hammer weiblichen Tand, here the loud hammer fashions female toys. 2) Den Filz —, [with hatters] to put the felt upon the block.

Formen, *v. tr.* to mould or fashion into a particular shape or state, to form, to shape. Ein Bild von Stein oder Thon —, to form an image of stone or clay.

Former, *m.* [-s, *pl.* -] 1) he that forms, a former, a moulder, particularly a moulder of tobacco-pipes. 2) V. Formenmacher.

Formig, *adj.* and *adv.* having a certain form or shape; used only in composition, as, ein—, uniform; kegel—, conical &c.

*Formiren, *v. tr.* 1) to form, to shape, to mould, to frame. 2) to combine in a particular manner, to form, to arrange. [in military affairs] Ein Quarré —, to form a square of troops; sich —, to form the ranks.

Formlich, *adj.* and *adv.* 1) having a regular form or shape. 2) done in due form, or with solemnity, formal. Er gab seine —e Einwilligung zu dem Vertrage, he gave his formal consent to the treaty; der Vertrag wurde von beiden Theilen — bestätiget, the treaty was ratified formally by both parties. ||3) full of, or addicted to, formalities or ceremonies, formal. Er ist ein sehr —er Mensch, he is an over-ceremonious or very punctilious person.

Formlichkeit, *f.* [*pl.* -en] 1) the quality of being formal 2) established order, form, formality. Gesetzliche —en, formalities of law; der Mangel an —, informality; alle —en beobachten; to observe forms; die Beobachtung der —en, formality.

*Formular, *n.* [-es, *pl.* -e or ‡-ien] prescribed form, formulary.

Forschbegier, Forschbegierde, *f.* the disposition to obtain information, by researches into facts, causes or principles, inquisitiveness.

Forschbegierig, *adj.* and *adv.* inclined to seek information by researches into facts, causes or principles, inquisitive.

Forschblick, *m.* [-es] a scrutinizing look.

Forscheisen, *n.* [-s, *pl.* -] V. Sucheisen or Sonde.

Forscheln, ||Forscheln, *v. intr.* [mostly in contempt] to attempt to discover something with scrutinizing curiosity. Nach Familien=Geheimnissen —, to pry into family secrets.

Forschen, [perhaps allied to fragen, or to the Low Sax. fargen, Dutch vergen] *v. intr.* and *tr.* to seek, to try to find. Einen [more usual nach Einem] —, to search for any one. *Fig. a*) to make enquiry, to inquire. Nach Wahrheit —, to seek for truth; das — nach Wahrheit, search after truth; und forschte oft nach den Winden und nach der Ebbe und Flut, and oft of winds inquired, and of the tide; von Einem etwas —, to enquire something of any one. *b*) to seek for truth by artful interrogatories. Er hat bei ihm darnach geforscht, he pumped him for it. *c*) to seek for truth by argument or the discussion of questions, or by investigation, to inquire. Der —de Verstand, an inquiring mind; er forscht täglich in der Schrift, the Scriptures are his daily study; vernunftmäßig —, to philosophize.

Forscher, *m.* [-s, *pl.* -] one who seeks for truth or information, a seeker, an inquirer, a searcher, investigator, philosopher.

Forschgeist, *m.* [-es] an inquisitive mind.

Forschgier, *f.* V. Forschbegier.

Forschgierig, *adj.* and *adv.* inquisitive.

Forschkraft, *f.* [*pl.* Forschkräfte] sagacity, penetration.

Forschsucht, *f.* [*p.* -en] a scrutinizing curiosity to learn what is not known.

Forschsüchtig, *adj.* and *adv.* impertinently curious to learn what is not known.

Forschung, *f.* 1) the act of inquiring, a seeking, search, a careful inquiry to find out what is unknown, investigation. Er brachte sein Leben mit der — nach Wahrheit hin, he spent his life in search of truth. 2) [subject of search or of attention] study.

Forschungsgeist, *m.* V. Forschgeist.

1. Forst, *m.* [-es, *pl* -e and die Förste] [Fr. *forêt*, is said to have origin from the Med. Lat. *forestum*, and this from the ancient *voralbah* Föhre] 1) a certain territory of woody grounds governed and regulated by forest laws, and privileged to hold a superior's game, a forest; or in general a forest managed scientifically. 2) the compass of ground in a forest belonging to the office of a forest-officer, or regarder, or verderer, regard.

Forst=amt, *n.* 1) a board, or court for managing forest-concerns. 2) an employment or office in the forest. —anschlag, *m.* a valuation of a forest. —aufseher, *m.* an officer who has the charge to preserve the vert and venison, a verderer or verderor. —baum, *m.* a forest-tree, forester. —baumzucht, *f.* the propagation and nursing of forest-trees. —beamte, *m.* a forest-officer, a regarder of the forest, a verderer or verderor. —bediente, *m.* any forest-officer who has the charge to preserve the vert and venison. —besitzer, *m.* the owner of a forest. —bewohner, *m.* an inhabitant of a forest, a forester. —bezirk, *m.* the compass of ground in a forest, under the inspection of a forester, forest-district ||—brüche, *f.* a mulct or fine paid for transgressing any forest law. —buch, *n.* 1) a book containing the forest laws and regulations for the management of woods, and every thing belonging to them. 2) a book concerning woods and forests and their management. —diebstahl, *m.* the stealth of wood committed in a forest. —dienst, *m.* 1) an office in the forest. 2) the service in a forest which a tenant owes to his lord. ‡—ding, *n.* forest court. —frevel, *m.*

any offence or trespass within a forest committed against vert; assart. —frevler, *m.* a person that commits any offence or trespass in a forest against vert. —frohne, *f.* the service in a forest which a tenant owes to his lord. ||—garbe, *f.* forest-tithe. —gebühr, *f.* dues paid to the forester. —gefälle, *pl.* profits or revenue arising from a forest. —geräume, *n.* a piece of land cleared, or an assart granted to a forester, or verderer. —gerecht, *adj.* and *adv.* experienced in the concerns of a forest, or in preserving the vert and venison. —gerechtigkeit, *f.* the ownership of a forest. —gericht, *n.* forest court, [in England] court of regard, court of Swainmote, court of attachment, court of justice seat. —gesetz, *n.* forest law. —gewächs, *n* vert. ‡—graf, *m.* V. Holzgraf, Waldgraf. —grenze, *f.* 1) the boundaries of a forest. 2) the boundaries of a regard. —hammer, *m.* an axe used for marking trees that are to be cut. —haus, *n.* the forester's house. —herr, *m.* —herrschaft, *f.* the owner or proprietor of a forest. —hut, *f.* the view of the forest, the preserving of the vert and venison. —hüter, *m.* a game-keeper, a warder of the vert and venison —inspector, *m.* an officer whose business is to view the forest, and inspect the offices, a regarder. —karte, *f.* a map of a forest. —knecht, *m.* V. —läufer. —kunde, *f.* the science of the management of woods or forests —kundig, *adj.* and *adv.* skilled in the management of woods or forests. —läufer, *m.* V. —hüter. —lehen, *n.* a forest held of a superior. —lehranstalt, *f.* an academy for teaching the management of forests. —mann, *m.* a person skilled in the management of forests. —mäßig, *adj.* and *adv.* according to the rules established for the management of woods or forests. —meister, *m.* a higher officer appointed to watch a forest, to preserve the vert and venison, and institute suits for trespasses, a ranger of a forest. —miethe, *f.* V. —zins. —nützung, *f.* the produce and profits of a forest. —ordnung, *f.* an edict concerning the management of forests. —rath, *m.* a councillor of the forest board. —rechnung, *f.* an account of the expense and produce of a forest —recht, *n.* 1) the right of manor, or properly, over a forest, or the vert and venison. 2) the right of property over the wood or vert exclusive of the venison. 3) a right which a person has to cut wood in the forest of the lord of the manor, to pasture his cattle or the like. 3) body of the forest laws. 4) fees paid to a forester. —rechtlich, *adj.* and *adv.* founded on the right of manor over a forest. —regal, *n.* the sovereign right over a forest. —regel, *f.* a rule in the management of forests. —revier, *n* the compass of ground belonging to the office of a forester or regarder. —richter, *m.* justice of the forest. —rüge, *f.* the instituting of suits for trespasses within a forest committed against [venison and] vert. —sache, *f.* forest concern. —säule, *f.* a pillar or stone for marking the limits of a forest. —schreiber, *m.* forest-clerk. —schule, *f.* V. —lehranstalt. —sekretair, *m.* V. —schreiber. —stein, *m.* a landmark by which the limits of a forest may be known and preserved. —stock, *m.* the stub of a forest-tree. —verbrechen, *n.* a high offence within a forest committed against [venison or] vert. —verordnung, *f.* an edict about forest-concerns. —verwalter, *m.* an officer appointed to keep the accounts connected with a forest. —verwaltung, *f.* the office of keeping the accounts connected with a forest. —wesen, *n.* the management of forests and every thing belonging to or connected with them. —wirthschaft, *f.* the good management of a forest, and the manner in which it is done. —wissenschaft, *f.* the science or knowledge of every thing belonging to the management of forests. —wissenschaftlich, *adj.* and *adv.* according to the good management of forests. —zeichen, *n.* a mark made with an axe on trees that are to be cut. —zins, *m.* a rent paid for the right of cutting wood in another's forest.

2. **Fórst**, *m.* [-es, *pl.* -e or Förste] V. Firste.]

Forstnagel, *m.* V. Firstnagel.

3. **Fórst**, *m.* [-es, *pl.* -e] a kind of stuff mad of silk, wool or linen.

Forsteilich, V. Forstlich.

Fórsten, *v. tr.* to provide with a forest [used only in the past participle] Ein geforsteter Mann, a person that has a share in a forest.

Förster, *m.* [s, *pl.* -] 1) an officer appointed to preserve the vert and venison within a forest, a verderer, a forester. 2) [rather unusual] a person that has a share in a forest.

Försterei, *f.* 1) the bailiwick of a ranger of a forest. 2) the habitation of a forester, verderer or ranger. 3) V. Forstamt 2).

Försterinn, *f.* a verderer's wife.

Fórstlich, *adj.* and *adv.* belonging to a forest; concerning the management of a forest. Die —e Obrigkeit, the owner or proprietor of a forest.

***Fört**, *n* [-s, *pl.* -s] (pron. Fohr or, by others, Fórt) a small fortified place, a fort or fortlet.

Fórt, [allied to vor, führen, fahren = bewegen] *adv.* 1) [noting departure, or separation, at a distance] away, off. — mit dir, away with you, off with you, go hence, depart hence, be gone, get you gone; er ist schon —, he is already gone; — mit euren Kleinen, hence with your little ones; schicke ihn — aus Frankreich, send him forth of France. 2) [noting progression or advance] forth, on. Er ging weiter —, he went further. *Fig.* *Es will mit der Sache nicht —, the business goes not on; es will mit ihm nicht —, he speeds not. 3) [in continuance, without interruption or ceasing] on. Er schläft —, he sleeps on; schreibe —, write on; ich schlief zehn Stunden in einem —, I slept ten hours together; — und —, without interruption, continually; Zwei, Drei und so —, two, three and so forth; sich im Preise — erhalten, to continue steady in price. 4) [in Scripture, noting futurity] henceforth. Und wandelten — nicht mehr mit ihm, [in Script.] and walked no more with him. 5) without delay, immediately, instantly. So — [always written sofort], immediately. 6) it is much used in composition, and denotes departure, progression or advance, and continuance.

Fórtackern, *v. intr.* and *v. tr.* to continue ploughing, to plough on.

Fortán, *adv.* 1) from that time, thenceforth. 2) for the future, henceforth.

Fórtarbeiten, *v. intr.* to work on, to continue to work. Sie mußten Tag und Nacht an den Befestigungen —, um &c., they were obliged to work at the fortifications night and day, in order to &c.

Fórtarten, *v. intr.* to propagate.

Fórtarzeneien, *v. intr.* to continue to take physic.

Fórtathmen, I. *v. intr.* to continue to breathe. II. *v. tr.* to blow away.

Fórtbacken, *ir. v. intr.* and *tr.* to bake on.

Fórtbaden, *v. intr.* to continne to bathe.

Fórtbalgen, *v. intr.* to continue to scuffle or wrestle.

Fórtbannen, *v. tr.* 1) to expulse from an[y] place by certain adjurations and ceremonies, t[o] expel by exorcism, exorcise. 2) V. Verbannen

Fórtbau, *m.* [-es, *pl.* -e] the act of con[-]tinuing to build, especially to work a mine.

Fórtbauen, *v. tr.* and *v. intr.* 1) to contin[ue] to build, to build on, [in mining] to continue th[e] working of a mine. 2) to add to a building Es wurde am rechten Flügel des Schlosses fort[-]gebaut, they added to the right wing of th[e] castle.

Fórtbaumen, *v. intr.* [with hunters] to lea[p] from tree to tree [said of squirrels, cats &c.].

Fórtbeben, *v. intr.* to continue to shake.

Fórtbegeben, *v. r.* sich —, to leave a plac[e] or station, to go off, to retire, to withdraw

Fórtbegehren, *v. intr.* 1) to continue t[o] ask. 2) to want or desire to leave a place o[r] station.

Fórtbeichten, *v. intr.* to continue to con[-]fess, to go on with one's confession.

Fórtbeißen, *ir.* I. *v. intr.* to continue t[o] bite. II. *v. tr.* to drive away by biting.

Fórtbellen, I. *v. intr.* to bark on. II. t[o] drive away by barking.

Fórtbestehen, *ir. v. intr.* to subsist, t[o] continue to exist. Der Freistaat konnte nich[t] länger —, the republic could subsist no longer wir werden nach dem Tode —, we shall con[-]tinue after death.

Fórtbeten, I. *v. intr.* to pray on. II. *v. tr.* to drive away by praying or prayers.

Fórtbetteln, I. *v. intr.* to continue beg[-]ging. II *v. r.* sich —, to beg for one's livelihood

Fórtbewegen, *v. tr.* 1) to remove [a stone &c.] Er kann sich nicht —, he is not able to mov[e] 2) to move on. Und darauf bewegte sich der Zu[g] fort, and then the procession moved on.

Fórtbieten, *ir. v. intr.* to continue to tende[r]

Fórtbinden, *ir. v. intr.* to continue to bind

Fórtbitten, 1) *ir. v. intr.* and *tr.* to continu[e] praying, to beg or pray on. 2) V. Losbitten.

Fórtblasen, *ir.* I. *v. intr.* to continue to blow to blow on. Der Wind hat die ganze Nacht fort[-]geblasen, the wind continued blowing the whol[e] night. II. *v. tr.* to remove by blowing away, t[o] blow off. 2) to continue blowing [a tune].

Fórtblättern, *v. intr.* to continue to tur[n] over the leaves of a book.

Fórtblitzen, I. *v. intr.* to continue to flash II. *v. tr. Fig.* *Er hat mich mit seinen grimmi[-]gen Blicken fortgeblitzt, he scared me away b[y] his grim looks.

Fórtblühen, *v. intr.* to continue blossom[-]ing.

Fórtbluten, *v. intr.* to continue to bleed.

Fórtbrauchen, *v. tr.* to continue the use of.

Fórtbrausen, *v. intr.* 1) to continue to roa[r] or to bluster [said of the wind]. 2) [u. w. seyn] t[o] go away with great noise.

Fórtbreiten, *v. intr.* and *tr.* to spread. *Fig.* Sich —, to propagate.

Fórtbrennen, *ir. v. intr.* and *v. tr.* to burn on

Fórtbringen, *ir. v. tr.* to carry away, to remove. Er konnte seine Papiere nicht —, he could not carry his papers along with him; das Gepäck eines Heeres —, to transport the baggage of an army; sie konnten ihn nicht *—, they could not prevail on him to go; die Ge[-]richtsdiener brachten ihn fort, the bailiffs took him away. *Fig.* to bring forward, to forward [the growth of plants &c.]. Einen —, to help any one forward; sich —, to get forward, to get one's livelihood.

Fórtbringlich, *adj.* and *adv.* that may be removed from one place to another, removable, transportable.

Fórtbringung, *f.* conveyance, transport.

Fórtbrüllen, I. *v. intr.* to bellow on. II. *v. tr.* to drive away by bellowing.

Fórtbrüten, *v. intr.* to continue brooding.

Fórtbürsten, I. *v. intr.* to brush on. II. *v. tr.* V. Wegbürsten.

Fórtbuttern, *v. intr.* to continue to churn.

Fórtdampfen, I. *v. intr.* 1) to continue to smoke or fume. 2) to pass off in vapour, to evaporate. II. *v. tr. fig.* *[in a jocose sense] to drive away by smoking.

Fórtdarben, *v. intr.* to continue in a state of want, indigence or privation.

Fórtdauer, *f.* [a state of lasting] continuance, endurance, permanence. Die — seiner Freundschaft, the continuance of his friendship; die — der Seele [nach dem Tode], the immortality of the soul.

Fórtdauern, *v. intr.* to last, to be durable, to remain in existence, to endure, to be permanent, to continue; ein —der Lärm, a continual noise.

Fórtdehnen, *v. tr.* to continue to stretch. [in music] Eine Note —, to sustain or hold out a note.

Fórtdenken, *ir.* I. *v. intr.* to continue thinking. II. *v. tr.* *to drive away in thinking. Ich wollte, daß ich diese schrecklichen Auftritte — könnte, I wish I could drive these scenes from my memory.

Fórtdienen, *v. intr.* to continue to serve.

Fórtdonnern, I. *v. imp.* to continue thundering. II. *v. tr.* **fig.* to drive away by roaring and thundering.

Fórtdrängen, *v. intr.* and *tr.* 1) to continue to press, to push. 2) to push away.

Fórtdrechseln, *v. intr.* and *tr.* to turn on.

Fórtdrehen, *v. intr.* and *tr.* V. —drechseln.

Fórtdreschen, *ir.* I. *v. intr.* to thrash on. II. *v. tr. fig.* *to drive away by beating soundly.

Fórtdrucken, *v. intr.* and *tr.* to print on.

Fórtdrücken, I. *v. intr.* to continue to press. II. *v. tr.* 1) to press on. 2) to push away. V. also Wegdrücken.

Fórtdürfen, *ir. v. intr.* to be permitted to go off.

Fórtdursten, *v. intr.* to thirst continually.

***Fórte**, *adv.* [in music] forte. *Fig.** [as a substantive, n.] Die Mathematik ist nicht sein —, mathematics are not his strong point; sein — liegt nicht im Zeichnen, drawing is not his forte.

Fortepiano, *n.* pianoforte.

Fórteilen, *v. intr.* [u. w. seyn] to hasten away.

Fórteitern, *v. intr.* to continue to discharge matter or pus, to suppurate continually.

Fórtempfinden, *ir. v. intr.* and *tr.* to continue to feel. Er fragt, ob die Seele nach dem Tode fortempfinde, he questions, whether the soul continues to feel after death; ich werde Ihre Güte stets —, I shall always be sensible of your kindness.

Fórterben, I. *v. intr.* to be transmitted from ancestors to descendents. *Fig.* Die Tugenden des Vaters erbten auf den Sohn fort, the son inherited the virtues of his father. II. *v. r.* sich —, to pass from an ancestor to an heir. *Fig.* Die Gebrechen der Eltern erben sich oft auf die Kinder fort, children often inherit the infirmities of their parents.

Fórterstrecken, *v. r.* sich —, to stretch, to extend further.

Fórterwerben, *ir. v. tr.* and *intr.* to acquire continually.

Fórterzählen, *v. intr.* and *tr.* to continue one's narration. Erzählen Sie fort, pursue your recital; lassen Sie ihn seine Geschichte —, let him continue his narration.

Fórtessen, *ir. v. intr.* to continue eating.

Fórtfahren, *ir.* I. *v. intr.* 1) [u. w. seyn] to depart in a ship or carriage. Er ist fortgefahren, he drove off. 2) [u. w. haben] to go on, to continue — zu arbeiten, to work on; — zu schreiben, to write on; er fuhr in seiner Rede oder Erzählung fort, he pursued his discourse, he prosecuted his recital; ich war, fuhr Carneades fort, noch ein Knabe, I was, pursued Carneades, yet a boy. 3) to be steadfast or constant in any course, to continue. Fahret fort, wie ihr begonnen habt, go on as you have begun. II. *v. tr.* to remove in a vehicle, or in any kind of water-craft. Holz —, to carry away [off] wood; den Schutt —, to clear away rubbish.

Fórtfasten, *v. intr.* to continue to fast.

Fórtfaulen, *v. intr.* to continue to rot.

Fórtfechten, *ir.* I. *v. intr.* to continue fighting. II. *v. tr.* to drive away by fighting.

Fórtfeiern, *v. intr.* and *tr.* to continue to celebrate.

Fórtfeilen, *v. intr.* to file on.

Fórtfeuern, I. *v. intr.* to continue firing. II. *v. tr.* to fire off or away [ammunition &c.].

Fórtfischen, *v. intr.* to continue fishing.

Fórtflattern, *v. intr.* 1) [u. w. haben] to flutter continually. 2) [u. w. seyn] to flutter away.

Fórtfliegen, *ir. v. intr.* [u. w. seyn] 1) to continue to fly. 2) to fly away. Der Vogel ist fortgeflogen, the bird has flown; *fig.* er flog [= eilte] fort, he departed swiftly.

Fórtfliehen, *ir. v. intr.* to flee, to run away.

Fórtfließen, *ir. v. intr.* [u. w. seyn] 1) to continue to flow, to flow on. Ihre Thränen fließen unaufhörlich fort, her tears flow unceasingly; die Wunde fließt noch fort, the sore is still running; *fig.* seine Rede floß reizend fort, his speech flowed charmingly on. 2) *Fig.* to pass, to be spent. Die Zeit fließt fort, time passes. 3) to flow off or away.

Fórtflößen, I. *v. intr.* to float on. II. *v. tr.* 1) to cause to be conveyed on water, to float. Holz —, to float wood. 2) to float off or away.

Fórtflöten, *v. intr.* to continue to flute. *Fig.* Die Nachtigall flötet fort, the nightingale sings continually.

Fórtfluchen, I. *intr.* to continue swearing. II. *v. tr.* to drive away by swearing.

Fórtflüchten, *v. intr.* and *r.* to flee for safety.

Fórtfluten, I. *v. intr.* to continue to flow. II. *v. tr.* to carry off on or with the flood.

Fórtfragen, *v. intr.* and *tr.* to ask on.

Fórtfressen, *ir. v. intr.* and *tr.* to eat on.

Fórtführen, *v. tr.* 1) to lead away, to carry away, to carry off, to take off. Der Wind hat meinen Hut fortgeführt, the wind has blown my hat away; er führte all sein Vieh fort, he carried away all his cattle. 2) to lead on, to carry forwards. Diese Mauer muß bis dorthin fortgeführt werden, this wall must be carried thus far; eine Linie —, to carry a line; eine Straße —, to extend a road; einen Baumgang —, to continue an alley; einen Bau —, to go on with a building. *Fig.* Gedanken sehr weit —, to carry ideas very far; einen Krieg —, to prosecute a war, to carry on war; den Handel —, to carry on trade; *seinen Staat —, to hold out one's sumptuous way of living; sein liederliches Leben —, to continue one's dissolute life.

Fórtfüllen, *v. intr.* and *tr.* to fill on.

Fórtgang, *m.* [-es] 1) endurance, continuance. Der — der Glückseligkeit, the continuance of happiness; der — eines Krieges, the process of a war. 2) a coming into actual existence or operation. Die Reise hat ihren —, the journey will take place. 3) advance, improvement. Der — in der Religion oder in Kenntnissen, an advancement in religion or knowledge; der — in den Wissenschaften, progress in learning; der Himmel gebe dieser Unternehmung guten —, may heaven speed this undertaking; welchen — hat Ihr Geschäft? how does your business go on? das Geschäft hat einen guten —, the business goes on well; die Sache hat keinen —, it does not succeed.

Fórtgeben, *ir.* I. *v. intr.* to continue to give. II. *v. tr.* to make over to another, to give away. V. Weggeben.

Fórtgehen, *ir. v. intr.* 1) to leave a place or station, to depart, to go off, to go away. Stehe auf und laß uns —, rise, and let us be going; er ist schon fortgegangen, he has gone already; gehe fort, be gone, get you gone; nun geht es fort, now we set out; *fig.* *es geht mit ihm fort [= dem Sterben zu], he is on the decline, he is dying fast; es gehen viele schlechte Säfte mit fort, a great deal of noxious humours are evacuated at the same time; der Schleim, der durch die Nase fortgeht, the pituite secerned from the nose. 2) to continue to go, to go on, to proceed. *Fig. a)* to proceed, to continue. Sie geht immer ihren Gang fort, she runs on at the same rate. *b)* to take place, to succeed.

Fórtgeigen, I. *v. intr.* and *tr.* to fiddle on. II. *v. tr.* *to drive away by fiddling.

Fórtgenießen, *ir. v. intr.* and *tr.* 1) to continue to enjoy. Lassen Sie ihn sein Glück —, let him continue in the enjoyment of his happiness. 2) to enjoy continually.

Fórtgießen, I. *v. intr.* to continue to pour. II. *v. tr.* V. Weggießen. III. *v. imp.* *to continue to rain hard. Es goß die ganze Nacht fort, the rain continued to pour the whole night.

Fórtgleiten, *ir. v. intr.* [u. w. seyn] 1) to glide or slide along. 2) to glide or slide on.

Fórtglühen, *v. intr.* to glow continually, to continue to glow.

Fórtgraben, *ir. v. intr.* 1) to dig on. *Fig.* to continue one's search. 2) to dig further.

Fórthaben, *ir. v. tr.* [in fam. lang.] 1) to continue to have one's share. Sie sollen die or Ihre monatliche Unterstützung von zwölf Gulden —, I shall continue to you your monthly allowance of twelve florins. 2) V. Abhaben 1). 3) to remove, to cause to depart. Sie möchte ihn gerne —, she would be glad to see him gone.

Fórthacken, *v. intr.* to hew on.

Fórthageln, *v. imp.* to hail on.

Fórthäkeln, I. *v. tr.* to put into an other hook. Den Faden —, [with spinners] to shift the thread to the next hook.

Fórthallen, *v. intr.* to resound continually.

Fórthalten, *ir.* 1) *v. tr.* to continue to hold, keep or have. Er hält diese Zeitungen fort, he continues to subscribe to, or to take in, these news-papers. 2) *to keep away or afar.

Fórthauen, *v. tr.* [in mining] Die reichen und milden Erze —, to hulk the lode.

Fórtheben, *ir. v. tr.* 1) to remove, to lift off. Sich —, to remove, to take one's self off; hebe Dich fort! avaunt! 2) to continue to heave.

Fórthecheln, *v. intr.* and *tr.* to hackle on.

Fórthelfen, *ir.* I. *v. intr.* 1) to assist in escaping. Einem Gefangenen —, to favour, to facilitate the escape of a prisoner. 2) to help forward, to help in getting forward. *Fig.* Einem Freunde —, to help a friend on; ich werde ihm in der Welt —, I shall forward him in the world. II. *v. r.* sich —, to gain one's subsistence; sich kümmerlich —, to make shift to live.

Fórtherrschen, *v. intr.* to continue to rule or to govern.

Fórthin and **Forthín,** *adv.* [obsolescent] V. Künftig.

Fórthinken, *v. intr.* [u. w. seyn] to limp off.

Fórtholen, I. *v. intr.* and *tr.* to continue to fetch. II. *v. tr.* to fetch off.

Fórthören, *v. intr.* and *tr.* to continue to hear, listen or attend to.

Fórthumpeln, *v. intr.* 1) [u. w. seyn] to hobble off. 2) [u. w. haben] to continue hobbling.

Fórthüpfen, *v. intr.* 1) [u. w. seyn] to hop off or away. 2) [u. w. haben] to continue hopping.

***Fortificatión,** *f.* fortification.

Fortificíren, *v. tr.* to fortify [a town &c.].

Fórtirren, *v. intr.* 1) [u. w. seyn] to stray from a place. 2) [u. w. haben] to continue in error.

***Fortíssimo,** *adv.* and [as a substantive] *n.* [in music] fortissimo.

Fórtjagen, I. *v. tr.* 1) to compel to depart, to chase away. Er hat seine Frau fortgejagt, he turned off his wife; einen Hund —, to drive away a dog; die Fliegen —, to scare away flies. 2) to dismiss from service. Einen Diener —, to turn away a servant; der Soldat wurde fortgejagt, this soldier was dismissed service; er wurde mit Schimpf und Schande vom Regimente fortgejagt, he was drummed with ignominy out of his regiment. II. *v. intr.* [u. w. seyn] to gallop away. 2) [u. w. haben] to continue hunting

Fórtkarren, I. *v. intr.* to continue to cart. II. *v. tr.* to remove by a cart, to cart away.

Fórtkegeln, *v. intr.* to bowl on.

Fórtkochen, *v. intr.* to continue cooking.

Fórtkommen, *ir. v. intr.* [u. w. seyn] 1) to get off, to escape. Der Gefangene ist glücklich fortgekommen, the prisoner got out fortunately. 2) to get forward, to proceed, to advance, to get on. Ein Weg, auf dem nicht fortzukommen ist, an impracticable road. *Fig.* *a*) to grow, to thrive [said of plants]. Bäume kommen in einem guten Boden fort, trees thrive in a good soil; diese Pflanze kommt nicht fort, wenn sie nicht begossen wird, this plant will not live, unless watered. *b*) to get one's livelihood by something. Er hat Mühe, fortzukommen, he is hard put to it for a livelihood; sich durch Arbeit sein — verschaffen, to live by one's labour; ein unternehmender Mann findet überall sein —, a man of entreprise finds the means of living everywhere.

Fórtkönnen, *ir. v. intr.* [in fam. lang.] to be able to proceed or to go on. Ich kann nicht mehr fort wie sonst, I cannot stir as I used formerly; der gejagte Fuchs kann nicht mehr fort, the hunted fox is tired or sinking.

Fórtkränkeln, Fórtkranken, *v. intr.* to remain in a low or delicate state of health.

Fórtkriechen, *ir v intr.* [u. w. seyn] to creep away, to creep off. 2) [u. w. haben] to continue creeping.

1. **Fórtkriegen,** [from kriegen = to war] *v. intr.* to continue the war.

2. **Fórtkriegen,** [from kriegen = to get] *v. tr.* to get [a thing] away, to remove.

Fórtkutschen, ‖ and ***Fortkutschieren,** *v. intr.* 1) [u. w. seyn] to ride away in a coach, to drive off. 2) [u. w. haben] to continue riding in a coach.

Fórtlachen, I. *v. intr.* to laugh on. II. *v. tr.* *to drive away by laughing or laughter.

Fórtlärmen, I. *v. intr.* to continue to be noisy. II. *v. tr.* *to drive away by making a noise.

Fórtlassen, *ir. v. tr.* to suffer to depart, to suffer to go. Einen nicht —, to keep any one from departure, to prevent any one from going; einen so angenehmen Gast läßt man nicht so bald fort, such an agreeable visitor we cannot let go so soon; sie ließen ihn nicht fort, they detained him.

‖**Fórtlauf,** *m.* [-es] the act of running away. V. Das Fortlaufen.

Fórtlaufen, *ir. v. intr.* 1) to run away, to flee; *it.* to depart privately. Wer läuft fort? sagte der sterbende Held, who runs? said the dying hero; von seinem Herrn —, to run from one's master; das Fortlaufen, a running away. 2) to extend, to lie in continued length. Der Garten läuft längs dem Flusse fort, the garden extends along the river; der Weg läuft zwischen Aeckern und Wiesen fort, the road lies between fields and meadows; ein Werk mit —den Seitenzahlen, a paged book; [in botany] eine —de Decke, [in ferns] a continuous cover. 3) to run on. *Fig.* Die Interessen laufen [immer] fort, the interests run on.

Fórtläugnen, *v. intr.* and *tr.* 1) to continue to deny. 2) Sie möchten die Unsterblichkeit der Seele —, they would set aside the immortality of the soul by their arguments. V. Wegläugnen.

Fórtläuten, Fórtlauten, I. *v. intr.* and *tr.* to continue to ring the bells. II. *v. tr.* to drive away by ringing the bells. In vielen Dörfern glauben sie noch, die Gewitter — zu können, in many villages they still believe they can dispel a thunder-storm by ringing the bells.

Fórtleben, *v. intr.* to continue to live, to live on; *it.* [as *v. tr.*] dieses Leben dürfen Sie nicht mehr — [= fortführen], you must not continue to lead such a life.

Fórtlegen, *v. intr.* and *tr.* V. Weglegen.

Fórtlehren, *v. intr.* and *tr.* to continue to teach.

Fórtleiden, *ir. v. intr.* to suffer continually.

Fórtlernen, *v. intr.* and *tr.* to continue to learn.

Fórtlesen, *ir. v. intr.* and *tr.* 1) to continue to lecture. 2) to go on reading, or to read on. Er las die ganze Nacht fort, he spent the whole night in reading.

Fórtleuchten, I. *v. intr.* to continue to shine. II. *v. tr.* to light any one to the door. *Fig.* [in common lang.] Er wird ihn —, he will turn him out of doors.

Fórtlieben, *v. intr.* and *tr.* to continue to love.

Fórtlügen, *ir. v. intr.* to continue to lie.

Fórtmachen, I. *v. r.* [in fam. lang.] Sich —, to slip away, to steal away privately, to steal off, to slink away. Er machte sich in aller Stille fort, he took French leave. II. *v. intr.* 1) to continue to make. 2) [in fam. lang.] to make haste.

1. **Fórtmahlen,** [from mahlen = to grind] *v. intr.* to continue to grind [corn &c.] or to meal.

2. **Fórtmahlen,** [from mahlen = to paint] *v. intr.* to paint on, to continue painting.

Fórtmarschiren, *v intr.* 1) to march on. 2) to march off.

Fórtmüssen, *ir. v. intr.* to be obliged to go. *Fig.* *Er mußte fort, he was obliged to go off [to die].

Fórtnähen, *v. intr.* to sew on, to continue sewing.

Fórtnehmen, *ir. v. tr.* and *intr.* 1) to take away. 2) to continue to take.

Fórtnöthigen, *v. intr.* and *tr.* 1) to compel any one to go off. 2) to continue to urge.

Fórtpacken, I. *v. intr.* to continue to pack, to pack on. II. *v. r.* [in common lang.] Sich —, to depart in haste, to pack off; packt Euch fort! get you gone, avaunt!

Fórtpeitschen, I. *v. tr.* to drive away, to expel by whipping. II. *v. intr.* to whip on, to continue to whip.

Fórtpfeifen, *ir.* I. *v. intr.* and *tr.* to continue to whistle. II. *v. tr.* to drive away or keep off by whistling or, *fig.* *, by playing badly on some wind-instrument.

Fórtpflanzen, *v. tr.* 1) to remove and plant in another place, to transplant. Bäume — [verpflanzen], to transplant trees 2) to propagate [a breed of horses or sheep &c.] Eine Sorte Fruchtbäume —, to propagate any species of fruit-tree. *Fig.* Eine Krankheit —, to spread a disease; den Schall, das Licht —, to propagate sound or light; die Luft pflanzt den Schall fort, air conveys sound; er pflanzte seine Tugenden auf seine Kinder fort, he transmitted his virtues to his children; die Lehren des Christenthums —, to propagate the doctrines of Christianism; freisinnige Grundsätze —, to propagate liberal principles or sentiments; sich —, to propagate.

Fórtpflanzung, *f.* [*pl.* -en] propagation. Die — der Thiere oder Pflanzen, des Schalles, the propagation of animals or plants, the propagation of sound; die — or das Fortpflanzen der Töne, the carriage of sounds; die — der Lichtstrahlen, the transmission of rays.

Fortpflanzungsanstalt, *f.* [die Propaganda] an institution for propagating the Christian religion.

Fórtplaudern, I. *v. intr.* to prattle on. II. *v. tr.* to drive away by prattling.

Fórtpredigen, I. *v. intr.* to continue to preach. II. *v. tr.* to drive away by preaching [badly &c.]

Fórtprügeln, I. *v. tr.* to drive away by beating soundly, to expel by cudgeling. II. *v. intr.* to cudgel on.

Fórtpumpen, I. *v. intr.* to pump on. II. *v. tr.* to remove by pumping.

Fórtraffen, I. *v. tr.* to sweep off or away, to take by a promiscuous sweep. II. *v. intr.* to continue to sweep.

Fórtrasseln, *v. intr.* 1) [u. w. seyn] to be removed rattling, to rattle away. 2) [u. w. haben] to rattle on.

Fórtrauchen, I. *v. intr.* to smoke contiually. II. *v. intr.* and *tr.* to smoke on.

Fórträumen, V. Wegräumen.

Fórtrechnen, *v. intr.* and *tr.* to continue o reckon.

Fórtreden, I. *v. intr.* to speak on. II. *v. tr.* o drive away by speaking [too much, badly &c.].

Fórtregnen, *v. imp.* to rain on. Das —, he continuance of rain.

Fórtreise, *f.* 1) departure. 2) the continance of a journey.

Fórtreisen, *v. intr.* [u. w. seyn] 1) to deart. Er reiste von London fort, he set out or e departed from London; er reiste gestern ort, he set out yesterday. 2) to continue one's urney, to continue to travel.

Fórtreißen, *ir.* I. *v. tr.* to tear away, to raw or drag along, to carry away with vionce. Das Gewässer riß die Brücke fort, the ood swept away the bridge; er riß es mit h fort, he hurried away with it; die Scheren rissen ihn fort, the bumbailiffs dragged him urriedly away, hurried him off. *Fig.* Der orn riß ihn fort, anger hurried him on. II. *intr.* 1) to tear on. 2) [u. w. seyn] to continue o be rent or torn asunder. Dieser Zeug reißt ort, the slit in this stuff gets longer.

Fórtreiten, *ir. v. intr.* [u. w. seyn] 1) to ide away. 2) to continue to ride.

Fórtrennen, *ir. v. intr.* [u. w. seyn] 1) to un off. 2) to continue to run.

Fórtrollen, I. *v. intr.* [u. w. seyn] 1) to roll ff or away. 2) to continue to roll. II. *v. tr.* 1) o roll forward. Eine Kugel —, to roll a ball.) to continue to roll.

Fórtrücken, I. *v. tr.* 1) to move away, to ove aside. Rückt Euern Stuhl fort, edge your hair away. 2) to move forward, to move on, advance. II. *v. intr.* [u. w. seyn] 1) to remove. to advance. *Fig.* In Kenntnissen —, to adnce in knowledge.

Fórtrudern, *v. intr.* 1) [u. w. seyn] to row ay. 2) [u. w. haben] to row on.

Fórtrufen, *ir.* I. *v. tr.* to call off. II. *v. intr.* call on, to continue calling.

Fórtrutschen, *v. intr.* 1) [u. w. seyn] to slide . 2) to continue to slide.

Fórtsatz, *m.* [-es, *pl.* Fortsätze] 1) V. Fortsung. 2) that which is continued; *a*) espelly in anatomy, the projecting soft end or otuberance of a bone, a process of a bone, ophysis, apophysy. Der wurmförmige —, orm-formed appendage to the blind gut; zahnähnliche —, the tooth-like process of second vertebra of the neck; der griffelmige —, the styloid process of the temporal ne. *b*) [in botany, an excrescence from the theca the mosses] apophysis.

Fórtschaffen, *v. tr.* 1) to carry or convey m one place to another, to transport. Das päck eines Heeres —, to transport the bagge of an army; in Asien schafft man die Waa auf Kameelen fort, in Asia goods are transrted on camels; Reisende —, to convey traers. 2) to send away, to dismiss. Einen Beten —, to send away a servant. 3) to do ay with, to despatch. Sie haben ihn fortgeafft [= getödtet], they have done away with n.

Fórtschaffung, *f.* the act of carrying or nveying from one place to another. Die — Wasser, transportation by water; die — n Reisenden, the conveyance of travelers. **Fortschaffungsmittel**, *n.* means of nveyance.

Fórtschelten, I. *v. intr.* and *tr.* to scold on. II. *v. tr.* to drive away by scolding.

Fórtscheren, I. *v. intr.* and *tr.* to shear on, to continue shearing. II. *v. r.* [in common lang.] sich —, to be gone; to withdraw. Schert Euch fort [as an ejaculation of mingled anger or indignation and contempt], sheer off!

Fórtscheuchen, *v. tr.* to scare away.

Fórtschicken, *v. tr.* 1) to send or send away, to dispatch. Einen Boten —, to send a messenger; einen Eigenboten —, to send a messenger express; Briefe mit der Post —, to send letters by the post. *Fig.* *Einen mit einer langen Nase —, to laugh at any one, to treat any one with derision. 2) to send away, to dismiss. Einen alten Diener —, to discard an old servant.

Fórtschieben, *ir.* I. *v. tr.* to shove away or off. Einen Tisch auf dem Boden —, to shove a table along the floor; *sich —, to take one's self off; to depart or withdraw secretly; *die Gesellschaft schob sich, Einer nach dem Andern, fort, the company went off by degrees. II. *v. intr.* to shove on; *it.* to bowl on [at nine-pins].

Fórtschießen, *ir.* I. *v. intr.* 1) [u. w. seyn] to move forward suddenly and rapidly, to shoot forward. Die Gewässer schossen fort, the flood rushed along. 2) [u. w. haben] to shoot on, to continue to shoot. II. *v. tr.* V. Abschießen 1) and 2).

Fórtschiffen, I. *v. intr.* [u. w. seyn] to set sail, to sail, to begin a voyage; to sail away. II. *v. tr.* to transport by ships.

Fórtschlafen, *ir. v. intr.* to continue sleeping, to sleep on.

Fórtschlagen, I. *v. tr.* 1) to drive away by beating. 2) to beat back [the enemy]. 3) to beat on. II. *v. intr.* 1) to beat on, to continue beating. 2) to sing on [said of nightingales]. 3) to strike on [said of clocks].

Fórtschleichen, *ir. v. intr.* [u. w. seyn] to steal away, to slink away, to sneak off. Er schlich sich fort, he slipped away.

1 **Fórtschleifen**, [from schleifen = to drag] I. *v. tr.* 1) to transport by a sled. 2) V. Fortschleppen. II. *v. intr.* to drag on.

2. **Fórtschleifen**, [from schleifen = to grind] *ir.* I. *v. tr.* to grind on [an axe, a sythe &c.]. II. *v. intr.* = fortfahren zu schleifen [auf dem Eise &c.], to continue to slide [on the ice &c.].

Fórtschlendern, *v. intr.* [u. w. seyn] 1) to go away loitering, to saunter away. 2) to loiter on. So schlendern sie fort, thus they jog on.

Fórtschlenkern, [rather vulgar] *v. tr.* to hurl away.

Fórtschleppen, *v. tr.* 1) to drag away. Sie schleppten viele Leute mit fort, they dragged away with them a great number of people; sich —, to move on slowly or heavily, to drag one's self on with difficulty. 2) to drag along. 3) to drag on.

Fórtschleudern, I. *v. tr.* to sling, fling or hurl away. Einen Stein —, to hurl a stone. II. *v. intr.* to sling, fling or hurl on.

Fórtschlummern, *v. intr.* to slumber on.

Fórtschlüpfen, *v. intr.* [u. w. seyn] to slip away.

Fórtschmausen, *v. intr.* to continue banqueting or feasting.

Fórtschmeicheln, I. *v. intr.* and *tr.* to continue to flatter. II. *v. tr.* 1) to drive away by gross flatteries. 2) to remove any one gently by flattering or coaxing.

Fórtschmelzen, I. *v. intr. ir.* 1) [u. w. seyn] to melt [away]. Der Schnee ist fortgeschmolzen, the snow has dissolved. 2) [u. w. haben] to continue to melt. II. *v. tr.* to melt on.

Fórtschmerzen, *v. intr.* to give continual pain.

Fórtschmollen, I. *v. intr.* to remain pouting. II. *v. tr.* to drive away by pouting.

Fórtschneien, *v. imp.* to continue to snow.

Fórtschnellen, I. *v. tr* 1) to send away with a jerk or fillip. 2) to fillip on. II. *v. intr.* to jump or skip away [as a grass-hopper &c.].

Fórtschrecken, *v. tr.* to scare away.

Fórtschreiben, *ir. v. intr.* and *tr.* 1) to write on. Er schrieb die ganze Nacht fort, he spent the whole night in writing. 2) to continue to compose or produce, as an author. Er schreibt noch immer fort, obschon das Alter seine Geisteskräfte geschwächt hat, he still writes on, though age has impaired his faculties.

Fórtschreien, *ir.* I. *v. tr.* to cry, bawl or squall on. II. *v. tr.* to drive away or keep off by crying, bawling or squalling.

Fórtschreiten, *ir. v. intr.* [u. w. seyn] to step forward, to go on, to proceed. Langsam —, to make a slow progress. *Fig.* Eine —de Bewegung, a progressive motion; von einem Beweise zum andern —, to proceed from one argument to another; in Kenntnissen —, to advance in learning; in der Frömmigkeit —, to improve in piety; mit dem Zeitgeiste —, to keep pace with the march of intellect; das — der Künste, the progress of arts.

Fórtschreitung, *f.* 1) motion onwards, progression. *Fig.* Die — der Wissenschaft, der Künste, oder des Geschmacks, the progressiveness of science, arts or taste. 2) [in music] a succession of sounds.

Fórtschritt, *m.* [-es, *pl.* -e] *Fig.* intellectual improvement. Sein — in den Wissenschaften, his progress in learning; sie macht —e in der Musik, she profits in music; ihre —e in ihren Studien, their proficiency in their studies; er macht —e in den Wissenschaften, he advances in learning; einer, der große —e in der Mathematik gemacht hat, one, who has made great advances in mathematics, one, who is proficient in mathematics.

Fórtschuppen, *v. tr.* [rather provincial] 1) to remove with a jerk, to jerk off. 2) to jerk on.

Fórtschwanken, *v. intr.* 1) [u. w. seyn] to stagger along. 2) [u. w. haben] to stagger on.

Fórtschwären, *ir. v. intr.* to continue to fester.

Fórtschwärmen, *v. intr.* [u. w. seyn] 1) to swarm. Die Bienen sind fortgeschwärmt, the bees swarmed. *Fig. a*) to continue to revel or to riot. *b*) to continue to indulge in enthusiastic or chimerical flights of fancy. Er schwärmt von einem Traumgebilde zum andern fort, he pursues vain or idle fancies. 2) to swarm on.

Fórtschwatzen, I. *v. intr.* to babble on, to talk on. II. *v. tr.* to drive away by babbling.

Fórtschweben, *v. intr.* [u. w. seyn] 1) to move on hovering. 2) [u. w. haben] to continue to be hanging, dangling or swinging.

Fórtschwelgen, *v. intr.* to continue to revel.

Fórtschwemmen, *v. tr.* to wash away.

Fórtschwimmen, *ir. v. intr.* [u. w. seyn] 1) to swim away. 2) to swim on.

Fórtschwirren, *v. intr.* 1) [u. w. seyn] to whir away. 2) [u. w. haben] to whir on.

Fórtsegeln, *v. intr.* [u. w. seyn] 1) to sail off or away. 2) to continue sailing.

Fórtsenden, *ir. v. tr.* to send or send away,

to dispatch. Einen Eigenboten —, to send a messenger express; Waaren —, to send goods to any place.

Fórtsetzen, *v. tr.* to move on, to place farther. Einen Baum — [more usual versetzen], to transplant a tree. *Fig.* Dieselbe Diät or Lebensordnung —, to continue the same diet; den Krieg —, to carry on war; einen Krieg —, to prosecute a war; eine Unterhandlung —, to protract a negociation; eine Erörterung —, to protract a discussion; ein Werk, Studien —, to prosecute a work, studies; Schillers Geschichte des Abfalls der Niederlande, fortgesetzt von K., Schiller's History of the Defection of the Netherlands, continued by K.; seinen Spaziergang —, to pursue one's walk; er setzte seine Reise fort, he proceeded on his journey; ein Schiff setzt seine Fahrt fort, a ship proceeds on her voyage; eine Erzählung —, to pursue a recital.

Fórtsetzer, *m.* [-s] one who continues, continuer.

Fórtsetzung, *f* [*pl.* -en] 1) carrying on to a further point. Die — eines Kriegs, einer Unternehmung, the prosecution of a war, of an undertaking. 2) that which is continued, continuation. Die — eines Buchs, the continuation of a book; die — einer Erzählung, the continuation of a story.

Fórtseufzen, I. *v. intr.* to continue sighing. II. *v. tr* to drive away by sighing or moaning.

Fórtseyn, *ir. v. intr.* to be gone, to be absent. Er ist fort, he is gone; *it.* he escaped.

Fórtsingen, *ir.* I. *v. intr.* and *tr.* to sing on. II. *v. tr* to drive away by singing [badly &c.].

Fórtsitzen, [u. w. seyn and with haben] *ir. v. intr.* to remain sitting.

Fórtsollen, *v. intr.* [chiefly in fam. lang.] to be obliged to go. Ich soll fort, they want me to have gone

Fórtspaßen, *v. intr.* to continue to jest.

Fórtspielen, *v. intr.* and *tr.* to continue to play, to play on. Das Stück wurde fortgespielt, the piece continued to be acted; sie spielten die ganze Nacht fort, they spent the whole night in gaming [gambling].

Fórtspinnen, *ir. v. intr.* and *tr.* to continue to spin, to spin on. *Fig.* Einen Gedanken —, to pursue a thought; den Lebensfaden —, to spin out, to prolong life.

Fórtspornen, *v. tr.* 1) to drive on by spurring, to spur on. 2) to continue spurring.

Fórtsprechen, *ir. v. intr.* and *tr* to speak on.

Fórtsprengen, I. *v. intr.* [u. w. seyn] to ride away at full speed, to gallop off. II. *v. tr.* 1) to continue to blow up. 2) to continue to besprinkle.

Fórtspringen, *ir. v. intr.* [u. w. seyn] 1) to leap or jump away; to run away. Der Hirsch, der von Höhe zu Höhe fortspringt, the stag that springs from height to height 2) to continue to leap or jump.

Fórtspritzen, I. *v. tr.* 1) to spout out. 2) to drive away by spirting or squirting. II. *v. intr.* 1) to continue to spout, to spout on. 2) [u. w. seyn] to escape spouting.

Fórtsprudeln, I. *v. intr.* 1) [u. w. haben] to continue to bubble. 2) [u. w. seyn] to escape bubbling. II. *v. tr.* to emit bubbling.

Fórtstechen, *v. intr.* and *ir. tr.* to continue to prick.

Fórtstecken, *v. tr.* 1) to stick or fix at a greater distance. 2) and *intr.* to continue to stick or fix.

Fortstecknagel, *m.* [in husbandry] V. Grössel.

Fórtstehen, *ir. v. intr.* [u. w. seyn and with haben] to remain standing.

Fórtstehlen, *ir.* I. *v. tr.* to steal on, to continue to steal. II. *v. r.* sich —, to withdraw privily, to slip along or away unperceived, to steal away. Von dem du dich jetzt — mußt, from whom you must now steal; er stahl sich fort, he stole away, he took French leave.

Fórtsteigen, *ir. v. intr.* [u. w. seyn] 1) to continue to mount, to mount on. || and *2) *Fig.* to strut stalk or step away.

Fórtstellen, *v. tr.* 1) to place farther; *it.* to place away or aside, to remove. ||2) to continue.

Fórtstempeln, *v. intr.* to stamp on.

Fórtsterben, *ir. v. intr.* [u. w. seyn] to die off by degrees, or one by one or one after the other.

1. **Fórtsteuern**, [from steuern = to steer] I. *v. intr.* 1) [u. w. haben] to continue to steer, to steer on. 2) [u. w. seyn] to move off or away by or in steering. II. *v. tr.* to steer on, to continue to steer [a ship &c.].

2. **Fórtsteuern**, [from steuern = to contribute] I. *v. intr.* to continue to pay taxes. II. *v. tr.* to continue to give or contribute.

Fórtstolpern, *v. intr.* [u. w. seyn] 1) to go off stumbling. 2) to stumble on.

Fórtstoßen, *ir.* I. *v. tr.* 1) to push or thrust forward or away. 2) to continue pushing, to push on. II. *v. intr.* to continue pushing.

Fórtstreiten, *ir.* I. *v. intr.* and *r.* to continue to dispute or contend in argument. II. *v. tr.* to drive away by disputing. Sie haben mich fortgestritten, they drove me away by their argumenting.

Fórtstricken, *v. intr.* and *tr.* to knit on. Sie strickte den ganzen Abend fort, she spent the whole evening in knitting.

Fórtströmen, I. *v. intr.* 1) [u. w. seyn] to stream along. 2) [u. w. haben] to continue flowing, to stream on. II. *v. tr.* to carry away by a current of water.

Fórtstürzen, *v. intr.* [u. w. seyn] to hurry or rush away.

Fórtsuchen, *v. intr.* and *tr.* to continue one's search.

Fórtsündigen, *v. intr.* to continue to sin, to continue in sin.

Fórttanzen, *v. intr.* and *tr.* 1) to continue to dance, to dance on. Sie tanzten die ganze Nacht fort, they spent the whole night in dancing. 2) [u. w. seyn] to go off dancing.

Fórttappen, I. *v. intr.* 1) [u. w. seyn] to go on groping. 2) [u. w. haben] to continue groping, to grope on. II. *v. r.* sich —, to search one's way by groping.

Fórttaumeln, *v. intr.* 1) [u. w. seyn] to go off reeling. 2) [u. w. haben] to continue to reel.

Fórtthauen, *v intr.* 1) [u. w. haben] to continue to thaw. 2) [u. w. seyn] to go off by thawing.

Fórttönen, *v. intr.* to continue to sound.

Fórttraben, *v. intr.* [u. w. seyn] 1) to trot off. 2) to continue to trot.

Fórttragen, *ir. v. tr.* 1) to bear or carry away, to carry off. 2) to continue to bear or carry, to continue to wear.

Fórttrauern, *v. intr.* to continue mourning.

Fórtträumen, *v. intr.* and *tr.* to continue dreaming.

Fórttreiben, *ir. v. tr.* 1) to drive away, to expel. 2) to drive farther, to impel. Der Dampf treibt den Wagen fort, the steam impels the waggon. 3) to drive on. *Fig.* Den Feldbau —, to carry on husbandry; ein Geschäft —, prosecute a business; er treibt es so fort, [in contempt] he still pursues the same course; treibt den verbotenen Umgang fort, he maintains the forbidden intercourse.

Fórttrieb, *m.* [-s, *pl.* -e] the act of dri[ving] forward. *Fig.* impulse.

Fórttrippeln, *v. intr.* [u. w. seyn] to trip a[way].

†**Fórttrollen**, *v. intr.* and *r.* to take one's [self] off, to be gone, to make off. V. also Abtr[ollen].

Fórttrommeln, *v. intr.* and *tr.* 1) to [drum] on. 2) to drive away by drumming.

Fórttrompeten, *v. intr.* and *tr.* 1) to [trum]pet on. 2) to drive away by trumpeting or sounding the trumpet.

Fórttrotten, I. *v. intr.* 1) to trot off. ||2) to continue to tread [grapes]. II. *v. tr.* ||to continue to tread [grapes].

Fórtüben, *v. tr.*, *intr.* and *r.* to continue to exercise [in music &c.].

*__Fortüne__, *f.* [in fam. lang.] good luck, good fortune. Er hat — gemacht [of an actor], he was successful; er hat seine — gemacht [of a man having succeeded in the world], he has made his fortune.

Fórtwachsen, *ir. v. intr.* [u. w. seyn] to continue to grow. Bäume wachsen in gutem Boden fort, trees thrive in a good soil.

Fórtwägen, *v. intr.* and *tr.* to continue to weigh.

Fórtwähren, *v. intr.* to continue, to last, to endure. Der Krieg währte fort, the war continued; eine —de Hitze, a continual heat; ein stets —der Kummer, everlasting sorrow.

Fórtwallen, *v. intr.* [u. w. seyn] 1) to walk or wander away. 2) to move gently on. 3) [u. w. haben] to continue to boil.

Fórtwalzen, 1) *v. intr.* [u. w. seyn] to walt[z] on. 2) to retire or withdraw waltzing, to walt[z] off or away.

Fórtwälzen, I. *v. tr.* to roll away, to roll forward. II. *v. intr.* to continue to roll, to roll on. III. *v. r.* sich —, to move heavily and clumsily forward, to wallow forward.

Fórtwandeln, *v. intr.* [u. w. seyn] to walk on, to walk farther.

Fórtwandern, *v. intr.* [u. w. seyn] to wander on or farther. Er wanderte fort, he departed.

||**Fórtwatscheln**, *v. intr.* [u. w. seyn] 1) to waddle away. 2) to waddle on.

Fórtwehen, I. *v. tr.* to blow away. II. *v. intr.* to blow on.

Fórtweinen, I. *v. intr.* to continue weeping, to weep on. II. *v. tr.* to drive away by weeping or shedding tears.

Fórtweisen, *ir. v. tr.* 1) to send away, to turn away. 2) [less usual] (= Fortzeigen) to show the way.

Fórtwerfen, *ir.* I. *v. tr.* to throw forward, to throw away, to cast by. II. *v. intr.* to continue to cast or throw.

Fórtwinden, *ir.* I. *v. tr.* to wind on, to continue to wreathe or twine [as a garland]. II. *v. r.* 1) to continue to wind. 2) to move on winding. 3) to have a winding direction.

Fórtwirken, *v. intr.* 1) to continue to operate. Die Arzenei wirkt noch fort, the medicine still operates; er kann noch —, he is yet able to render service; [also as a trans. verb.] er wirkte Gutes fort bis an sein Ende, he did good as long as he lived. 2) to continue to weave or to knit.

Fórtwischen, I. *v. tr.* to wipe away, to gr[...]

ay by wiping. II. *v. intr.* 1) to wipe on, to atinue wiping. 2) [u. w. seyn] [in fam. lang.] to ip away, to get off, to escape.

Fórtwollen, *v. intr.* to intend to go, to ish to go. Er wollte heute noch fort, he wantl to depart to-day.

Fórtwünschen, I. *v. tr.* to wish the remol of any person or thing. II. *v. intr.* to wish , to continue wishing.

Fórtwürfeln, *v. intr.* to continue to play dice. Sie haben die ganze Nacht fortgewürt, they spent the whole night at dice.

Fórtwurzeln, *v. intr.* 1) [u. w. seyn] to take ot. 2) [u. w. haben] to continue to take root.

Fórtzählen, *v. intr.* to count or number on.

Fórtzaubern, I. *v. tr.* to remove by a spell. *v. intr.* to continue to practice magic or rcery.

Fórtzeigen, I. *v. intr.* to continue to show. *v. tr.* to show the way to.

Fórtziehen, I. *v. intr.* [u. w. seyn] to depart th one's baggage or retinue. Ich ziehe von ndon fort, I remove from London; wann rden Sie von hier —? when are you going to ve this? sie zogen aus ihrer Heimat fort, the igrated from their native country; die Solten werden morgen —, the soldiers will rch off to-morrow; diese Vögel ziehen im rbste fort, these birds migrate in autumn. II. *tr.* to draw away or on, to draw farther. Sie gen ihn gewaltsam mit fort, they dragged n away with them.

Fórtzucht, *f.* [*pl.* -en] the continuance of a eding, propagation.

Fórtzug, *m.* [-es, *pl.* Fortzüge] removal, rching off.

Fórum, *n.* [-s] a tribunal, a court, forum. g. Einen oder etwas vor das — der öffentlen Meinung bringen or ziehen, to bring a son or thing up before the tribunal of public inion.

Fossil, *n.* [-s, *pl.* -e or -ien] fossil.

Fossil(isch), *adj.* and *adv.* fossil. —es Holz, sil wood.

Fetus, *m.* [in anatomy] fetus.

Fourage, [pron. Furahsche] *f.* [food of any d for horses] forage.

Fouragiren, [pron. Furaschihren] *v. intr.* [to et food for horses] to forage.

Fourier, [pron. Furihr] *m.* [-s, *pl.* -e] [in tary affairs] quarter-master.

Fourierschütze, *m.* an officer's servant.

Fournier, [pron. Furnihr] *n.* [-s, *pl.* -e] [with net-makers] veneer.

Fourniren, [pron. Furnihren] *v. tr.* [with net-makers] to lay thin slices or leaves of fine d on a ground of common wood, to veneer.

Fracht, *f.* [*pl.* -en] [either from fahren, or it is d to bracht-e, bringen] 1) that which is put ny thing for conveyance, that which is car- by land or by water. Die — eines Wagens, load of a waggon; die — eines Schiffes, ling, lading, freight, or cargo of a ship; e —, full freight. 2) that which constitutes ad or cargo, lading. 3) the money paid for transportation of goods [Frachtgeld], freight, iage. Nach Bezahlung der — und der Unen bleibt nur ein geringer Gewinn, after ing freight and charges, the profit is trifling. rachtbar, *adj.* and *adv.* that may be led or freighted. —brief, *m.* 1) a bill of ng, a bill of freight. 2) a bill, containing a ement of goods sent by a stage-waggon. — pfänger, *m.* consignee. —frei, *adj.* and . freight-free. —führer, *m.* one who is employed to transport goods either by land or by water. —fuhrmann, *m.* one who transports goods or heavy commodities from one place to another, a waggoner, a carrier. —gebühr, *f.* freightage. —geld, *n.* carriage, freight. —gut, *n.* the goods, merchandise conveyed on a waggon or in a ship, load, lading, cargo. —handel, *m.* carrying-trade. —lohn, *m.* V. —geld. —schiff, *n.* merchant-man. —schiffer, *m.* shipper. —straße, *f.* a road appropriated for waggons. —stück, *n.* [any thing that makes part of a load or cargo] loading. —versender, *m.* V. Frachter. —wagen, *m.* a waggon. —zettel, *m.* V. —brief.

Frachten, *v. tr.* to transport from one place to another either by waggons or by ships. Waaren nach Berlin —, to waggon goods to Berlin; Waaren nach Boston —, to ship goods to Boston; ein Schiff — [be—], to freight a ship.

Frachter, *m.* [-s, *pl.* -] freighter, consigner.

Frachtung, *f.* transport of goods by waggons or ships.

Frack, *m.* [-es, *pl.* Fräcke] [appears to be allied to the Fr. *froc* = Mönchskutte and to the Germ. Rock] 1) [not used in this sense] an upper coat, a frock. 2) a dress-coat, an evening-coat.

***Fraction**, *f.* 1) fraction, fracture. 2) division.

***Fractur**, *f.* 1) fracture. 2) [a sort of large hand-writing used for engrossing] the broken letter.

Fractur-buchstabe, *m.* V. Fractur 2). —schrift, *f.* [in printing] German text.

Frage, *f.* [*pl.* -n] [V. Fragen 1) [the act of asking] question; [at quadrille or omber] ask; [in law] die peinliche —, examination by torture, question, rack. 2) [that which is asked] question, interrogation. Eine — thun, to ask a question, to query; man hat ihm —n vorgelegt, he was interrogated; einige —n stellen, to propose some queries; die — ist, the question is; auf eine — antworten, to answer a question; es ist noch die —, ob ich gehe oder nicht, it is yet questionable, whether I go or not; da erhob sich eine — unter den Jüngern Johannis sammt den Juden über die Reinigung, [in Script.] there arose a question [dispute] between some of John's disciples and the Jews, about purifying; der in — stehende Gegenstand, the matter or point in question; das or davon ist die — nicht, that is not the question; das ist eine andere —, that is another matter. 3) [a figure of rhetoric] interrogation.

Frag-amt, *n.* advertising-office. —buch, —büchlein, *n.* [an elementary book containing a summary of principles in religion, reduced to the form of questions and answers] a catechism. —lehre, *f.* 1) catechising. 2) [a form of instruction in the principles of religion] catechism. —lehrer, *m.* catechist. —lehrig, *adj.* and *adv.* catechetical, catechistic, catechistical. —punkt, *m.* the point in question. —schüler, *m.* catechumen. —stück, *n.* 1) [in law] the matter or point in question. 2) a part of a catechism. —unterricht, *m.* V. —lehre, 2. —weise, I. *f.* catechetical method. II. *adv.* interrogatively. —wort, *n.* [a word used in asking questions] an interrogative [as, wer? was? warum? &c.]. —zeichen, *n.* [a note that marks a question] note of interrogation [?].

Fragen, [appears to be allied to the Lat. *rogare*, as also to regen &c.] *reg.* and *ir.* I. *v. tr.* and *intr.* 1) to inquire, to interrogate, to ask, to query. Warum fragest du, wie ich heiße? [in Script.] wherefore dost thou ask after my name; er ist alt genug, fraget ihn, [in Script.] he is of age, ask him; ihr fragt, warum Brutus sich gegen Cäsar erhob, you demand, why Brutus rose against Caesar; frage nach dem rechten Wege, inquire for or after the right way; er frug nach dem Wege, he inquired the way; frage nach Saulo mit Namen, von Tarsen, [in Script.] inquire for one Saul of Tarsus; seine Freunde fragten or frugen [erkundigten sich] nach ihm, his friends inquired about him; darf ich um Ihren Namen —? may I crave your name? nach dem Preise einer Waare —, to ask the price of a commodity; Einen um Rath —, to consult any one; da fragten ihn auch die Kriegsleute, und sprachen: was sollen denn wir thun? [in Script.] the soldiers also demanded of him, saying, what shall we do? Kinder — gewöhnlich viel, children are usually inquisitive. *Prov.* Wer viel fragt, bekommt viele Antworten, he that questioneth much, shall learn much; Ein or ein Narr kann mehr —, als sieben Weise beantworten, a fool may ask more questions in an hour, than a wise man can answer in seven years; [in law] einen Verbrecher peinlich —, to put a criminal to the question [to the rack]; [at quadrille or omber] ich frage, I ask. *Fig.* Nach etwas —, to be concerned about [with the prp. nach]. Meister, fragst du nichts da[r]nach, daß wir verderben, [in Script.] Master, carest thou not that we perish; nicht —d nach den Folgen, careless of consequences; ich frage nichts da[r]nach, I don't mind it; †ich frage den Henker da[r]nach, I care not a straw [pin or rush] for it. II. *v. r.* and *imp.* Es fragt sich, ob es auch wahr ist, the question is, whether it is true; es fragt sich, ob Galen je eine Leicheneröffnung mit angesehen, it is questionable whether Galen ever saw the dissection of a human body.

Fräger, *m.* [-s, *pl.* -] one who asks questions, a questioner, inquirer, interrogator. *Ein ewiger — [in anger or contempt], an inquisitive person or fellow.

Fräglich, *adj.* and *adv.* that of which is asked, in question, in debate. Die —e Sache, the matter in question; die —en Ceremonieen, the ceremonies in question.

***Fragment**, *n.* [-es, *pl.* -e] any thing apart, broken off or separated from the rest, a fragment. —e alter Schriften, fragments of ancient writings.

***Fragmentärisch**, *adj.* and *adv.* fragmentary.

Fräg[e]selig, *adj.* and *adv.* inclined to seek information by questions, inquisitive. Er hat sehr —e Kinder, his children are very inquisitive.

Fräg[e]seligkeit, *f.* inquisitiveness.

Fräg[e]spiel, *n.* [-es, *pl.* -e] 1) [a play] questions and commands. 2) [at quadrille or omber] ask.

‡**Fraischam**, [V. Fraiß] I. *adj.* and *adv.* terrible, terrific. II. *f.* terror, fear. V. Milchschorf.

‡**Fraischam-kraut**, *n.* 1) great toothwort. 2) the pansy violet or heart's ease. —rose, *f.* peony.

‡**Fraiß, Fraisch**, *f.* [allied to frieren, friesen, Frost] 1) terror, fear. 2) [in law] criminal jurisdiction. 3) the falling sickness, epilepsy.

‡**Fraiß-amt**, *n.* a court of criminal law. —fall, *m.* a criminal case. —gericht, *n.* V. —amt. —recht, *n.* V. Fraiß, 2).

***Frambasie**, *f.* the yaws [frambasia].

***Francisiren**, V. Französeln.

Franciska, [der -, or -'s] [a name of women] Frances, Fanny.

Franciskaner, *m.* [-s, *pl.* -] [one of the order of St. Francis] a franciscan, gray friar.

Franciskaner-kloster, *n.* a convent of Franciscans. —mönch, *m.* a Franciscan friar.

—nonne, *f.* Franciscan nun. —orden, *m.* the order of St. Francis of Assisi.

*Fránco, *adv.* post-paid; free of post- or other conveyance-expenses.

Fránk, [perhaps allied to frei, frech] [especially used in fam lang.] *adj.* and *adv.* frank, free; open, ingenuous, candid. Seine Fehler — bekennen, to confess one's faults frankly; etwas — verkünden, to publish a thing freely.

Fránke, Fránk, *m.* [-n and -en, *pl.* -n and -en] 1) one of the ancient Franks; *it.* a Franconian. 2) [in poetry; also in hatred or contempt] a Frenchman. 3) [a name given by the Turks, Greeks and Arabs to any of the inhabitants of the western parts of Europe] a Frank. 4) [a French silver coin of the value of nearly 28 Kreuzers or 10 pence] a franc.

Fránken, *n.* [-s] Franconia [a province in Germany].

Franken-birne, *f.* a sort of large, luscious and succulent pear. —land, *n.* 1) Franconia. 2) [sometimes, V. Franke 2] France. 3) [V. Franke 3] Franghistan. —wein, *m.* Franconian wine.

Fránkfurt, *n* [-s] Frankfort. — am Main, Frankfort upon the Main; — an der Oder, Frankfort upon the Oder; die —er Messe, the fair of Frankfort [on the Main].

*Frankiren, *v. tr.* to exempt, as a letter from the charge of postage. Einen Brief —, to pay the postage of a letter [*to frank* is only used of the privilege possessed by members of the English Parliament of franking letters]; frankirt, post-paid.

Fränkisch, *adj.* and *adv.* Francic, Franconian. —e Weine, Franconian wines [of the province of Franken in Germany]; der —e Kreis, [formerly] the circle of Franconia.

Franklinít, *m.* [-s] [a mineral] franklinite.

*Frankomanie, *f.* desire to resemble the French

Fránkreich, *n.* [-s] France.

Fránkreichisch, V. [the usual word] Französisch.

Fránse, *f.* [*pl.* -n] [Fr. *frange*, Ital. *fregio*, allied to Fries and reißen] 1) [an ornamental appendage to the borders of garments or furniture, consisting of loose threads] fringe. Mit —n besetzen, to fringe, to befringe. 2) [an open broken border] fringe.

Fransen-baum, *m.* fringe tree. —blume, *f.* [a shrub] rhacoma. —macher, *m.* fringe-maker.

Fránsen, *v. tr.* to adorn or border with fringe, to fringe, to befringe, to fimbriate.

Fránsicht, *adj.* and *adv.* resembling fringe, fringe-like.

Fránsig, *adj.* and *adv.* fringed, fringy; [in botany] fimbriate.

Fránz, [-ens, *pl.* -e] [a name of men] Francis. 2) [in composition] French.

Franz-apfel, *m.* an apple, the fruit of a dwarf tree. 1. —band, *m.* the binding of a book in calf, lettered on the back; a book thus bound. Ein Buch in Halbfranzband, a half-bound book. 2. —band, *n* a sort of silk ribbon. —baum, *m.* a dwarf tree. —birne, *f.* a pear, the fruit of a dwarf-tree. —bohne, *f.* dwarf-kidney-bean. —branntwein, *m.* French brandy, cogniac. —brod, *n.* French bread, French roll. —erbse, *f.* dwarf-pea. —fahrer, [not much used] *m.* [in sea-towns] a French merchant-man. —geld, *n.* French money. —gold, *n.* [with gold-beaters] a sort of leaf-gold. ‡—gulden, *m.* a French florin. —mann, *m.* [in jest or in contempt] a Frenchman. —männisch, *adj.* and *adv.* French. —obst, *n.* fruit of dwarf-trees. —perle, *f.* a false pearl. —scharlach, *m.* Venice scarlet. ‡—thaler, *m.* [also called Laubthaler] French dollar. —ton, *m.* [in organs] French sound. —topas, *m.* V. Rauchtopas. —wein, *m.* 1) [rather unusual] a white wine of Franconia. 2) French wine. Rother —wein, [Bordeaux Wein] claret. —weizen, *m.* cultivated polygonum or buck-wheat.

Fränzchen, *n.* [-s, *pl.* -] 1) dim. of Franz, Frank. 2) dim. of Franciska, Fanny. Unser —, our Fanny.

1. Fránze, *m.* [-n, *pl.* -n] [in jest or, chiefly, in contempt] a Frenchman.

Franzen-sitte, *f.* the manner of the French. —stamm, *m.* the French, the French race.

2. Fránze, *f.* [*pl.* -n] 1) V. Franse. 2) [in botany, a narrow sinuated membrane] the fringe.

*Franzisiren, V. Französeln.

Franziska, V. Franciska.

Franzose, *m.* [-n, *pl.* -n] 1) Frenchman. Die —n, the French. 2) *pl.* *a*) the French. *b*) [in vulgar lang.] French disease, French pox, venereal disease. V. Lustseuche. *c*) [also a distemper in cattle] murrain.

Franzosen-harz, *n.* gum guaiacum. —holz, *n.* pock-wood, guaiacum. —holzöl, *n.* oil of guaiacum. —krankheit, *f.* V. Franzosen, 2) *b* —sucht, *f.* V. Frankomanie.

Französelei, *f.* 1) a ridiculous imitation of the French manner, customs, language, and way of thinking. 2) [rather unusual] Gallicism.

Französeln, *v. intr.* 1) to imitate the manner of the French. 2) to commit Gallicisms.

†Französig, *adj.* and *adv.* affected with the venereal disease.

Französinn, *f.* 1) Frenchwoman. 2) [chiefly in fam. lang.] a French governess.

Französiren, *v. tr.* to frenchify.

Französisch, *adj.* and *adv.* 1) French. —e Waaren, French commodities; —e Weine, French wines; die —e Sprache, das —e, French; — sprechen, to speak French; sich — kleiden, to dress one's self after the French fashion; ein —es Dach, V. Dach 1; ein —er Gerber, a tawer who dresses leather after the French manner; —e Handschuhe, French gloves; —e Jagd, chase with a pack of hounds; —e Kamine, [in architecture] French fire-places; —e Kämme, small combs; die —e Kirche oder Geistlichkeit, the Gallican church or clergy; —e Ordnung, [in architecture] French order; eine —e Posaune, [in organs] French sackbut; ein —es Schloß, a rim-lock; ein —Deutsches und Deutsch—es Wörterbuch, a dictionary of the French and German languages. 2) [in vulgar lang.] affected with the venereal disease.

*Frappánt, *adj.* and *adv.* [in colloquial lang.] striking. Eine —e Aehnlichkeit, a striking resemblance.

*Frappiren, *v.* [*tr.* or rather] *imp.* [in fam. lang.] to affect vividly and suddenly with strong emotion. Es frappirte mich sehr, it struck me greatly; die plötzliche Nachricht von seinem Tode hat uns Alle sehr frappirt, the sudden news of his death affected us greatly.

Fráß, *m.* [-es, *pl.* -e] 1) the act of eating or devouring [said of an animal]. 2) also the state of eating, or of wearing or separating the parts of a substance. V. Bein—. 3) greediness of appetite, voracity, gluttony. Ein Hund, der einen guten — hat, [with hunters] a greedy dog. 4) whatever is eaten, especially whatever is eaten by animals, food. Auf den — ausgehen, [with hunters] to go in quest of food, to go in search of prey. †5) [in contempt] a bad dish. †6) [especially in students' cant] banquet, feast. Es war heute ein großer — im Goldenen Löwen, there was a great dinner at the Golden Lion. 7) an animal, that eats or that has a voracious appetite; hence in the compound word Viel—, the glutton [in the proper as well as in a fig. sense].

Fraßtrog, —zuber, *m.* a feeding-trough.

Fräßig, *adj.* and *adv.* greedy for eating, voracious. V. [the usual word] Gefräßig.

‖Frätscheln, *v. intr.* 1) V. Forscheln. 2) V. Trödeln.

‖Fratschelweib, *n.* V. Höferinn, Trödlerinn.

‖Frátt, [from fratten, allied to Fr. *frotter*, Lat. *fric*-are reiben] I. *adj.* and *adv.* fretted, galled, sore. II. *m.* [-es] gall, sore.

‖ and †Frátz, *m.* [-en, *pl.* -en] [appears to be allied to *pers*-ona &c.] 1) [in contempt] in general, a child, a brat, an ill-educated child. 2) a silly or foolish young girl.

Frátze, *f.* [*pl.* -n] [appears to be allied to the A. S. *fraced* häßlich] 1) a distorted countenance or face, grimace. —n machen or schneiden, to distort the features, to make faces. 2) a person with distorted features. 3) a caricature. 4) a silly ridiculous story.

Fratzen-bild, *n.* V. Zerrbild. —geschichte, *f.* a ridiculous and strange story. —gesicht, *n.* 1) V. Fratze, 1. 2) [in architecture, a piece of sculpture representing some grotesque form] a mask. —gestalt, *f.* a caricature. —mahler, *m.* 1) a caricaturist. 2) [in general] a coarse painter, dauber. —mahlerei, *f.* 1) painting of caricatures, caricaturing. 2) a caricature.

‖Frätzig, *adj.* and *adv.* fretted, galled, sore.

Fraú, *f.* [*pl.* -en] [very probably allied to the Fr. *bru*, the Germ. Braut (Brut), the A. S *bridd* das Junge] 1) any female grown to adult years, a woman, [eine bejahrte Frau] a matron; especially a woman who waits about the person of one of high rank, a gentlewoman [Kammer—]. 2) a married woman, the lawful consort of a man, wife, spouse; [in law] feme-covert, or femme covert; *it.* a title given to a man's wife, as — Schmidt, Mrs. Schmidt; die — Räthinn, the councillor's lady; eine — nehmen, to take a wife, to marry; eine häusliche, wirthliche —, a thrifty woman; die Bauer[s]—, a peasant's wife; die Edel—, a nobleman's lady; die Kaufmanns—, a merchant's wife. 3) a woman who governs, lady [correlative to servant or slave]; hence the female head of the family, mistress. — und Magd, mistress and maid-servant; sie ist — im Hause, she is the mistress of the house. *prov.* Wie die —, so die Magd, like mistress like maid; *it.* a title given to a princess, as Allergnädigste —, your ladyship; or, to ladies of high rank, as, die gnädige —, her ladyship, mylady; die — Gräfin, mylady countess; [V. also Frau 2] unsre —, or unsre liebe — [often written U. L. F.], [in the Roman church] our Lady, the holy Virgin; [in nunneries] a title given to nuns as distinguished from nuns not in orders; die — Aebtissinn, the lady abbess. 4) Die schöne — [a plant] a species of amaryllis or lily-daffodil [amaryllis belladonna]; unserer —en Bettstroh [a plant] lady's bedstraw. V. also Waldhaar.

Fraúchen, *n.* [-s, *pl.* -] [diminut. of Frau] little woman; *it.* a familiar term of civility or of endearment, as, sagen Sie mir doch — pray, goody, tell me!

Fraúen, *pl.* of Frau, women, ladies.

Frauen-ader, *f.* [in anatomy] the crural vein [saphaena]. —beere, *f.* a berry of the white-thorn, or hawthorn. —bild, *n.* 1) the image of a woman, especially the image of the Virgin Mary, Madona, Madonna. 2) [rather poetical] a female. Ein holdes —bild, a lovely woman, a sweet creature. —birke, *f.* V. Hangebirke. ‖—biß, *m.* V. Bathengel. —blatt, *n.* V. —münze. —blume, *f.* V

Sandbeil. || —bruder, *m.* a carmelite friar. —distel, *f.* lady's milk or lady's thistle. Die weiße —distel, V. Wegedistel. —eis, *n.* sparry gypsum, foliated or crystallized sulphate of lime, selenite. —faden, *m.* V. Sommerfaden. —feind, *m.* V. Weiberfeind. —fenchel, *m.* fennel or finckle. —fingerkraut, *n.* common bird's-foot trefoil. —fisch, *m.* V. Goldrohre. —flachs, *m.* V. Flachskraut. —glas, *n.* V —eis. Russisches —glas, muscovy glass, mica, talk, glimmer, glist, ising-glass stone. —gut, *n.* [in law] paripherna or paraphernalia. —haar, *n.* [a name of several plants] *a*) maidenhair, lady's hair. *b*) tooth-leaved maidenhair. *c*) common maidenhair. *d*) white maidenhair, wall-rue. *e*) common dodder. —handschuh, *m.* 1) a woman's glove. 2) [a plant] broad-leaved bell flower, or giant throat-wort. —hemd, *n.* shift. —herz, *n.* a woman's heart, a female heart *Fig* a tender heart. —hut, *m.* a lady's hat, a bonnet. —huth, *f.* the care of women. —käfer, *m.* [an insect] ladybird. V. also Maykäfer. —kleid, *n.* —kleidung, *f.* a female gown or garment. —kloster, *n.* a nunnery. —knecht, *m.* [in contempt] a man servilely devoted to the female sex, a dangler on women. —kraut, *n.* V —münze. —krieg, *m.* [a plant] common viper's bugloss. —lehn, *n.* V. Kunkellehn or Weiberlehn. —liebe, *f.* 1) woman's love. 2) love of women. —list, *f.* woman's tricks or cunning or art. V. Weiberlist. —lob, *n.* commendation bestowed on women or by women. —mantel, *m.* a lady's gown, or mantle, mantua, a lady's cloak. *Fig* [a plant] common lady's mantle or bearsfoot. —milch, *f.* a woman's milk. —münze, *f.* 1) [name of plants] *a*) the spear-mint. 2) costmary, alecost. —nabel, *m.* V. Nabelkraut. —orden, *m.* 1) a decoration, badge or order worn by noble-women or princesses. 2) a religious order of females. —pilz, *m.* V. Birkenschwamm. —putz, *m.* female dress or finery. —raub, *m.* a seizing and carrying away of females by force, a rape. —regierung, *f.* gynarchy, petticoat government. —rock, *m.* V. Weiberrock. —rose, *f.* V Weinrose. —saal, *m.* a saloon or room for ladies. —schneider, *m.* a ladies' habit-maker, a mantua-maker. —schuh, *m.* 1) a woman's shoe. 2) [a plant] common lady's slipper. —schuster, *m.* a woman's shoe-maker. —sinn, *m.* women's mode of thinking *Fig* feminine or delicate mind. —sleute, *pl* [in common lang.] persons of the female sex, females, women. —sperson, *f.* [mostly in law] a female. Die unverheirathete —sperson, [in law] feme-sole or femme-sole. —sommer, *m.* gossamer. —spiegel, *m.* [a name of plants] *a*) corn bell flower, corn violet, or small Venus's looking-glass. *b*) oval-leaved hedysarum. —staat, *m.* female dress or finery. —stand, *m.* 1) the state or condition of a woman. 2) the state of a married woman, [in law] coverture. 3) the place or seat in churches assigned to women. —stift, *n.* a community of women in orders, belonging to a collegiate church. —stimme, *f.* 1) female voice. 2) [in music] the highest voice. Die hohe —stimme, V. Discant. Die niedere —stimme, V. 2. Alt. —stuhl, *m.* 1) [in churches] a woman's pew. 2) [a plant] broad-leaved helleborine. —tag, *m.* 1) a festival intended to celebrate the Virgin Mary. 2) [the day of the annunciation of the holy Virgin, March 25th] lady day. —tanz, *m.* V. Kehraus. —taube, *f.* V. Turteltaube. —taufe, *f.* V. Nothtaufe. —theil, *m.* a woman's portion descending to her by law. —tracht, *f.* 1) the particular dress of women, female dress. 2) the dress of a married woman or matron. —veilchen, *n.* V. Muttervellchen. —volk, *n.* [in contempt] the female sex, womankind. —zeit, *f.* menstrual flux, courses. —zimmer, *n.* 1) *a*) a woman's apartment. *b*) a place of privacy set apart in a building for the women, harem. 2) [obsolete] a collection of women of rank, the ladies; *it.* the fair sex [in general]. 3) a woman of rank, a gentlewoman. —zwinger, *m.* [rather obsolete, except in the sense of harem] V. —zimmer, 1) *b*).

Fräulein, *n.* [-s, *pl.* - or ||-s] ‡1) a female. Und er schuf sie ein Männlein und —, [in Script.] male and female created he them. 2) [among animals one of that sex which conceives and brings forth young; more commonly das Weibchen] female. Das — aus Numidien, [a bird] the demoiselle heron. || 3) a little, also a young woman. 4) a title of any unmarried woman of the gentry, Miss; [also a title that belongs to unmarried woman of distinction or noble extraction] lady, honourable miss.

Fräulein-steuer, *f.* V. Prinzessinnsteuer. —stift, *n.* 1) a community of unmarried women of noble extraction, in orders. 2) a convent for unmarried women of noble extraction.

Fräuleinschaft, *f.* 1) the condition of an unmarried woman of distinction. 2) any number of such women united.

Fräulich, Fraulich, *adj.* and *adv.* 1) pertaining to females or women, female 2) in the manner of a woman, womanly Used in composition, as jungfräulich &c.

Frèch, [appears to be allied to regen, to the Engl. *to frisk* = herumspringen] *adj.* and *adv.* ‡1) bold, daring, courageous. 2) bold, rude, forward, impudent, transgressing the rules of decorum, saucy. — lügen, to lie impudently; ein —er Mensch, a saucy fellow; sich — benehmen, to behave one's self saucily. 3) shameless, impudent, saucy. —e Blicke, saucy looks; ein —es Auge, a saucy eye; —e Reden, licentious talking; —e Manieren, indecent manners; eine —e Geberde, an indecent gesture; eine —e Weibsperson or Dirne, an immodest female; mit —er Zutraulichkeit, with an impertinent familiarity.

Frèchheit, *f.* boldness, impudence, shamelessness, sauciness, licentiousness Die — seines Betragens, the indecency of his behaviour; die — ihrer Blicke, the immodesty or indecency of her looks.

Frèchlich, [unusual] *adv.* impudently, saucily.

*__Fregátte__, *f.* [*pl.* -n] 1) [a ship of war, of a size larger than a sloop or brig, usually having two decks, and carrying from thirty to fifty guns] a frigate. 2) a frigate-built merchant vessel. 3) [in ornithology] the man-of-war bird.

Freí, [derivation uncertain; the general sense is = körperlich nicht gebunden or gehindert] *adj.* and *adv.* 1) not being under physical restraint, free Sich — bewegen, to move freely; Fesseln hindern die —e Bewegung der Glieder, fetters constrain the limbs; einen Gefangenen — machen, to set a prisoner free, or at liberty; man hat den Gefangenen auf —en Fuß gesetzt, the prisoner was freed from arrest, was released; ein —er Durchgang, a free passage; ein —er Durchzug der Luft, a free current of air. *Fig.* *a*) [in general] not hemmed or restraint in any action. Laßt der Natur ihren —en Lauf, leave nature to her course; der Wille hat seinen —en Lauf, the will is at liberty; laßt einem eigensinnigen Kinde nicht seinen —en Willen, let not a perverse child take his own course; mache deine Seele —, give thy soul a loose; seinem Kummer —en Lauf lassen, to give a loose or a vent to one's sorrow; seinen Gedanken —en Spielraum lassen, to let loose one's thoughts, to give free scope to one's thoughts; seiner Einbildungskraft —en Lauf lassen, to give full play to one's fancy; aus —er Hand drehen, [with turners] to turn upwards; aus —er Hand zeichnen, to draw without a model; *it.* to draw out of one's own head; ein —er Pinsel, [with painters] a bold or easy manner of painting; ein — Gang, an easy gait; ein —er Anstand, easy manners. *b*) free, clear, exempt. — von Schmerz, free from pain; — von Gewissensbissen, free from remorse; — von der Kriegspflicht, free or exempt from military duty; — von Abgaben, free from taxes; — von Verantwortung, clear from responsibility; — von Schulden, clear of debts; die göttlichen Gesetze sprechen keinen von der Verbindlichkeit des Gehorsams —, the laws of God exempt no man from the obligation of obedience; von der Strafe — sprechen, to exempt or to free from punishment. In this sense it is used in composition, as, Sorgen—, free from cares; fehler—, faultless &c. *c*) not in a state of vassalage or dependence, free. Ein —er Mensch, a free-man; einen Leibeignen — geben, — lassen, — sprechen, to free, or to manumit a slave, to emancipate, to liberate a slave; einen Lehrling — sprechen, to free an apprentice; ein —es Gut besitzen, to possess a freehold estate; ein Gut — machen, to clear an estate from debt; Waaren, Güter — machen, to clear out commodities or goods at the custom-house; ein —er Staat, a free state; ein —es Volk, a free people; —e Reichsstädte, [formerly, in Germany] free cities [of the Empire], imperial cities. *d*) liberated from the government or control of parents, of a guardian or master, not dependent, free. Er ist vollkommen —, he is perfectly independent. *e*) not engaged, not bound by covenant, promise, or obligation. Sie ist noch —, she is not engaged yet; einen Soldaten — geben, to exempt a soldier from military duty. *f*) free from punishment. Einen Fehler — hingehen lassen, to pass by or to overlook a fault; einen Verbrecher — sprechen, to absolve a criminal; die Geschwornen haben den Gefangenen — gesprochen, the jury acquitted the prisoner. *g*) free from employment, not occupied. —e Stunden, leisure hours, leisure, vacant time; sind Sie heute —? are you free or disengaged to-day? den Schülern — geben, to give a holiday to pupils. *h*) free from danger of any kind. Die Meere sind —, the seas are free; — gehen, to walk about safely; *den Rücken — haben, to have one's back guarded. *i*) invested with franchises, enjoying certain immunities, free. Ein —er Hafen, a free port; die —e Jagd haben, to have a right to hunt anywhere; ein —es Haus, a privileged house; von allen Abgaben —, exempt from all duties or taxes. *k*) gratuitous, free. Er hat —en Eintritt im Theater, he has free admittance to the theatre; —en Tisch haben, to have free boarding; hundert Thaler und Alles —, a hundred dollars and bed and board; einen — halten, to defray any one's expenses; — gehalten werden, to have free quarters; einen Brief — machen, to pay the postage of a letter; *it.* to frank a letter; V. under Frankiren; ein —er Brief, a letter free of postage, a frank. *l*) [= without any special possessor] Ein Feld auf dem die Hütung — ist, common of pasture; —es Feld, [in mining] a field of which the owner is not known; in's —e fallen, [in mining] to be shut up [said of a work]. *m*) [= erlaubt] Einem etwas — geben, to dispense any one with something; es ist ihm — gegeben worden, seine Verwandte zu heirathen, he obtained a dispensation which enabled him to marry his relation; es ist ihm — gegeben worden, in der Fastenzeit Fleisch zu essen, he was permitted to eat meat in Lent. *n*) unconstrained, unrestrained, not under compulsion or control. — seyn, to be at liberty, to be free from restraint; es steht ihm —, zu thun was er will, he enjoys his free will; er hat die —e Wahl, he is free to make his own choice; *it.* he has the option; ein —es Versprechen, a free promise; etwas von or aus —en Stücken thun, to do something of one's own will, freely, spontaneously or voluntarily; einem etwas — stellen, to leave something to any one's choice or pleasure; wir stellen Ihnen dieses —, we leave this to your own option; es steht Ihnen —, zu gehen oder zu bleiben, it is optional with you to go or to stay; —e Hände haben, to be at liberty to act at one's own option. *o*) free from moral restraint. Der —e Wille, [the power of directing our own actions without restraint by necessity or fate] freewill; eine —e Handlung, a free action; — handeln, to act freely. *p*) free from undue bias or prejudice, not prejudiced. — urtheilen, to judge freely; — sprechen und schreiben, to speak and write freely; ein —er Geist, an unbiased mind; *it.* [= frei fig. *c*] a free spirit. *q*) free from scruple or reserve. — tadeln, to censure freely; seine Fehler — bekennen, to confess one's faults frankly; er sagte mir — seine Meinung, he told me his opinion with frankness; Jeder kann hier — seine Meinung sagen, every one has here the freedom to speak his mind; er sagte es — heraus, he told it unreservedly; er äußert sich zu —, he speaks his mind too freely; zu — reden, to be too lavish of one's tongue. *r*) free from a close adherence to the rules of art &c. Die —e Schreibart, a free style; der —e Satz, [in music] the composition of variegated music; eine —e Uebersetzung, a free translation; eine —e Nachahmung, a free imitation. *s*) exceeding the laws of propriety or morality, licentious. —e Reden, licentious talking; ein —es Leben, a loose manner of life; ein —es Frauenzimmer, a loose woman. 2) free from obstruction, unobstructed, open. Ein —er Platz, an open place; das —e Feld, the open field; auf —er Straße, in the open street; unter —em Himmel schlafen, to sleep in the open air; eine —e Aussicht, an open view; die —e Luft, the open air; in's —e gehen, to take the air. 3) placed in a detached situation. Einen Balken — legen, to suspend a beam by its two ends; eine — stehende Säule, an insulated column; ein — stehendes Haus, an insulated or isolated house; ein Redner, der — steht, an orator exposed to view; [in botany] ein —er Staubfaden, a loose filament. 4) giving safety or security. Ein —es Geleite, a safe-conduct; —en Zutritt bei Einem haben, to have free access to a person.

Freiacker, *m.* free ground. —**altar**, *m.* [in Catholic churches] a privileged altar. —**arche**, *f.* V. —gerinne. —**ball**, *m.* a dance or ball at a house of public resort to which no entrance is paid. Einen —ball geben, to give a ball gratis. —**bank**, *f.* 1) a moveable wooden frame on which a sculptor stretches the model to be copied. 2) [in villages] common shambles. —**bataillon**, *n.* [in military affairs] a battalion composed of volunteers. —**bau**, *m.* [in mining] In den —bau kommen, [said of a mine] to defray the expenses. —**bauer**, *m.* a peasant free of his farm. —**beuter**, *m.* 1) [formerly] [in military affairs] a volunteer. 2) freebooter, a pillager, a plunderer, a marauder. 3) a pirate, corsair. —**beuterei**, *f.* 1) freebooting, a pillaging. 2) piracy. —**beuterisch**, *adj.* and *adv.* 1) according to the manner of a freebooter. 2) piratical. Ein —beuterischer Buchdrucker (ein Nachdrucker), a piratical printer. —**bier**, *n.* 1) beer given gratis. 2) beer brewed without paying the beer-tax. —**blatt**, *n.* V. —karte. —**brauen**, *n.* the brewing of beer without paying the beer-tax. —**brauer**, *m* a brewer, who is exempt from paying the beer-tax. —**brief**, *m.* 1) a charter of manumission. 2) an instrument bestowing rights or privileges, charter. 3) a pass or passport. —**bürger**, *m.* 1) a freeman. 2) the citizen of an imperial city. 3) the citizen of a common-wealth or republic. —**bürgerlich**, *adj.* and *adv.* republican. Eine —bürgerliche Verfassung oder Regierung, a republican constitution, or government; —bürgerliche Gesinnungen, republican sentiments. —**bürgern**, *v. tr.* and *intr.* [in contempt] to republicanize. —**bürgersinn**, *m.* republicanism, civism. —**bürsche**, *f.* frank chase. —**compagnie**, *f.* [in military affairs] a company of volunteers. —**corps**, *n.* 1) partisan-corps, volunteer-corps 2) a body of freebooters. —**denker**, *m.* a latitudinarian, [in contempt] free-thinker. —**denkerei**, *f.* [in contempt] latitudinarianism. —**denkerisch**, *adj.* and *adv.* latitudinarian. —denkerische Lehren, Meinungen, latitudinarian doctrines, opinions. —**ding**, *n.* V. —gericht. —**eigen**, *adj.* and *adv.* held independent of a lord paramount, allodial (opposed to feudal). —**farbe**, *f.* a suit of winning cards. —**fechter**, [rather unusual] *m.* a privileged fencing-master. —**frau**, *f.* a baron's wife or lady, baroness, honourable Lady. —**fräulein**, *n.* an unmarried daughter of a baron, honourable Miss —**frohn**, *m.* [in law] a summoner, formerly the summoner of a secret court of criminal justice in Westphalia. —**gänger**, *m.* a soldier belonging to a partisan corps. ‖—**gast**, *m.* a journeyman of a privileged shoemaker. —**geben**, *n.* 1) the act of freeing from any obligation. 2) the suspension of the school-hours —**geboren**, *adj.* and *adv.* freeborn. —**gehorsam**, *adj.* and *adv.* voluntarily obedient. —**geist**, *m.* one who indulges freedom in thinking, a latitudinarian; (more commonly) a freethinker, an unbeliever. —**geisterei**, *f.* latitudinarianism, but especially free-thinking, unbelief. —**geisterisch**, *adj.* and *adv.* thinking at large, but especially deistical. —**geistig**, *adj.* and *adv.* not restrained by precise settled limits in opinion, indulging freedom in thinking, latitudinarian. —**gelassen**, *adj.* and *adv.* released from slavery, manumitted, emancipated. Der or die —gelassene, a freed man, a freed woman. —**gericht**, *n.* 1) a court invested with franchises. 2) V. Fehmgericht. —**gerinne**, *n.* a trench to conduct water from a mill or pond, a leat. —**gesinnt**, *adj.* and *adv.* republican. Ein —gesinnter, a republican or democrat. —**gewerbe**, *n.* a privileged trade. —**glaube**, *m.* protestantism. —**gläubig**, *adj.* and *adv.* protestant. Die —gläubigen, protestants. —**gläubigkeit**, *f.* protestantism. —**graf**, *m.* the judge of a court invested with franchises; formerly a judge of a secret criminal tribunal [Fehmgericht] in Westphalia.—**gut**, *n.* 1) any commodity exempt from duties. 2) freehold estate, allodium. 3) an estate free from any service or duty. 4) land held in free soccage, charter-land, bookland. —**hafen**, *m.* free port. —**halten**, *v. tr.* to defray. Das —halten, defrayment. —**halter**, *m.* 1) one who pays the expenses of another, defrayer. 2) the possessor of a freehold, a freeholder. —**haus**, *n.* a privileged house. —**häusler**, *m.* an inhabitant of a privileged house. —**herrschend**, *adj.* and *adv.* sovereign. —**herrscher**, *m.* a supreme lord or ruler, sovereign. —**herzig**, *adj.* and *adv.* open-hearted, frank. Junge Leute sind gewöhnlich —herzig, young persons are usually frank; seine Fehler —herzig bekennen, to confess one's faults frankly. —**hof**, *m.* 1) free farm. 2) a farm exempt from any service or duty. 3) formerly, a place of refuge, an asylum; *it.* church-yard. —**jahr**, *n.* 1) a year in which certain immunities were enjoyed. ‖2) V. Gnadenjahr. 3) [in Scripture] the year of liberty. —**karte**, *f.* [at cards] a winning card. —**kugel**, *f.* [in German popular superstition] a ball gifted with especial virtue by the Evil one. —**kux**, *m.* a share in a mine, which the miners must work gratis. —**land**, *n.* a republic or commonwealth. —**länder**, *m.* the inhabitant of a commonwealth or republic. —**ländisch**, *adj.* and *adv.* republican, democratic, democratical. —**lassung**, *f.* manumission, emancipation. —**lauf**, *m.* V. —gerinne. —**laut**, *adj.* and *adv.* [with hunters] forward either to speak or to open. Der Jäger ist —laut, a huntsman halloos too soon; der Hund ist —laut, the hound opens too soon. —**ledig**, *adj.* and *adv.* unmarried. —**lehen**, *n.* a holding of lands in fee-simple, frankfee. —**machen**, *n.* —**machung**, *f.* 1) the act of freeing or exempting. Das —machen von Waaren, the clearing of commodities at the custom-house; das —machen von Briefen, franking. V. Frankiren. 2) [in mining] the shutting up of a work. —**mann**, *m.* ‖1) a freeholder. 2) a tenant in capite or tenant in chief. —**mannlehen**, *n.* a tenure in free socage. —**markt**, *m.* a free market, a privileged market —**maurer**, *m.* a free-mason, a mason. —**maurerei**, *f.* free-masonry, masonry. —**maurergesell**, *m.* fellow-craft. —**maurergesellschaft**, *f.* the fraternity of masons. —**maurerhalle**, *f.* 1) V. —maurerloge. 2) a company of free-masons. —**maurerlehrling**, *m.* an entered apprentice. —**maurerloge**, *f.* a free-masons lodge. —**maurerorden**, *m.* the fraternity of masons. —**maurerwesen**, *n.* masonry. —**meister**, *m.* [with artificers] a privileged master. —**mündig**, *adj.* and *adv.* free-tongued, free-spoken. —**muth**, *m.* frankness, openness, ingenuousness, candour. —**müthig**, *adj.* and *adv.* frank, open, open-hearted, ingenuous, candid. Er gestand —müthig seinen Fehler, he confessed his fault frankly; —müthig seyn, to be frank. —**müthigkeit**, *f.* frankness, openness, ingenuousness, candour. Die —müthigkeit eines Geständnisses, the freeness of a confession. —**partei**, *f.* a body of freebooters. —**recht**, *n.* the right of a man to live anywhere. —**reiter**, *m.* a cavalry volunteer. —**saß**, *m.* a freeholder, yeoman. —**schein**, *m.* a license. —**schießen**, *n.* a diversion of shooting at a mark, at stated periods of the year. —**schiff**, *n.* a cartel-ship. —**schöppe**, *m.* formerly an assessor of the secret tribunal in Westphalia. V. Fehmgericht. —**schule**, *f.* free-school, charity-school. —**schüler**, *m.* a pupil taught in a free-school. —**schullehrer**, *m.* a teacher in a free-school. —**schuß**, *m.* [at a public shooting] a shot made gratis. —**schütz[e]**, *m.* 1) [in German popular superstition] a marksman who uses Freikugeln, which see. 2) a kind of archer, created by Charles VII of France in 1448. 3) sometimes, a fellow-shooter. —**singen**, *n.* [formerly with minstrels] a meeting at a singing-school where any one was at liberty to sing. —**sinn**, *m.* largeness of mind, catholicism, liberality of sentiments. —**sinnig**, *adj.* and *adv.* 1) not selfish, narrow or contracted, catholic, enlarged. Ein —sinniges Gemüth, a liberal mind; —sinnige Ansichten, liberal views; über Menschen und Dinge ein —sinniges Urtheil fällen, to judge of men and things with liberality. 2) republican. Ein —sinniger, a republican, a democrat. —**sprechen**, *n.* —**sprechung**, *f.* 1) an acquittal or sentence of a judge declaring an accused person innocent, absolution, acquittal, discharge. 2) the discharge of an apprentice. —**staat**, *m.*

common-wealth, republic. —staatsfeind, m. an enemy of republics. —stadt, f. 1) [in Hungaria] free-town. 2) [formerly, in Germany] a free city or imperial city. 3) [formerly] a city which afforded shelter and protection to fugitives; also, a city of refuge with the jews. —städtisch, adj. and adv. belonging to a free-town. —statt, —stätte, f. 1) a sanctuary, or place of refuge, franchise, asylum. 2) any place of retreat and security, asylum. —stelle, f. any situation obtained gratis in a school &c. —stuhl, m. V. —gericht. —stunde, f. leisure-hour, play-hour. —thätig, adj. and adv. V. Selbstthätig. —tisch, m. 1) free boarding. 2) board found at the public expense. —tischgänger, m. a person that boards at the public expense. —treppe, f. stairs at the outside of a building, a flight of steps [before a house], fliers. —truppen, pl. partisan-corps. —viertel, n. [in heraldry] quarter or franc quartier. —vorlesung, f. public lecture. —wasser, n. common of piscary. —willig, adj. and adv. voluntary, spontaneous. Eine —willige Handlung, a voluntary action; ein —williges Geschenk, a free gift; —willig handeln, to act spontaneously, voluntarily, freely; der —willige, [in military affairs] a volunteer. —willigkeit, f. voluntariness, spontaneousness, spontaneity. —zettel, m. 1) a license. 2) [in mining] a declaration in writing certifying that a work is shut up. —zügig, adj. and adv. exempt from a duty to be paid on removing from one country or state to another for the purpose of residence. —zügigkeit, f. the right of emigrating without paying any duty.

Freie, f. a void or open space, [in forests] a lawn.

1. **Freien**, v. tr. 1) to free, to set a liberty. 2) to invest with privileges, franchises or immunities, enfranchise.

2. **Freien**, [from the Goth. *frijon* = lieben] I. v. intr. to woo, to court, to solicit for marriage. Um ein Mädchen —, to woo a maid; Tausende — um dich, a thousand court you. *Prov.* Kurz gefreit, hat Niemand gereut, happy is the wooing that is not long adoing. *Fig.* to court, to solicit, to seek. Um ein Amt —, to solicit an office. II. v. tr. to marry. Wir wollen uns —, let us marry; nach Gelde —, to court with a view to a large dowry. *Prov.* Schnell gefreit, hat oft gereut, marry in haste, repent at leisure; he that weds before he's wise, shall die before he thrives.

Freier, m. [-s, -] a wooer, or suitor. —s Gedanken haben, or auf —s Füßen gehen, to have a mind to marry, to be looking out for a wife.

Freiersmann, m. 1) V. Freier. 2) a person employed to propose a suit of marriage.

Freierdings, adv. of one's own free will or accord, voluntarily, spontaneously.

Freierei, f. [chiefly in contempt or joke] solicitation of a woman to marriage, courtship.

Freigebig, adj. and adv. free to give, giving largely, liberal, munificent, bountiful. Ein —er Vater, a generous father; — gegen die Armen, liberal to the poor; ein —er Beschützer der Künste, a liberal patron of the arts; er ist — gegen die Armen, he gives freely to the poor; er gibt allen Menschen —, he giveth to all men liberally, generously, bounteously, or munificently; — mit Lobeserhebungen seyn, to be liberal of praise.

Freigebigkeit, f. freeness in giving, liberality, munificence, generosity, bounty, bounteousness.

Freigebung, f. V. Freigeben.

Freiheit, f. [pl. -n] the state or quality of being free; hence: 1) freedom from restraint, applicable to the body. Einen Gefangenen in — setzen, to set a prisoner at liberty, to enlarge a prisoner; sich in — setzen, to make one's escape from prison; die — wieder erlangen, to recover one's liberty. *Fig.* a) exemption from constraint, freedom from restraint. Die — von Sorgen, freedom from cares; die — von Schulden, the state of being free from debt; die — von Geschäften, freedom from occupation or business, leisure. b) freedom from restraint, applicable to the will or mind. Die natürliche — des Menschen, natural liberty; einem Leibeignen die — schenken, to free, or to manumit a slave; die persönliche —, personal freedom; die — in einem Freistaate, the liberty in a commonwealth; die bürgerliche —, civil liberty; die politische —, political liberty, the liberty of a nation; die Glaubens—, religious liberty; Grundsätze der — verbreiten, to propagate principles of liberty; — und Gleichheit der Rechte in einem Staate, liberty and equality of rights in a state; Jemandes — beschränken, to restrain any one's liberty; die — des Denkens, Schreibens, Druckens, [Denkfreiheit, Schreib- and Druckfreiheit] freedom in thinking, freedom of speech, the liberty of the press. *Prov.* — geht vor Gold und Silber, liberty is better than gold. c) [= eine freie that is leichte Manier] [with painters] die — des Pinsels, freedom of pencil. d) the power of an agent to do or forbear any particular action, according to the determination or thought of the mind, by which either is preferred to the other. Die — des Willens, the freedom of the will; die sittliche —, moral freedom; mit großer — reden, to speak one's mind very freely. e) authority or liberty given to do or forbear any act. Zu viel —, too much latitude; sich die — nehmen, etwas zu thun oder zu sagen, to take the liberty to do or to say any thing. f) liberty, privilege, exemption, immunity enjoyed by grant. Die — einer Stadt, the freedom or the privileges of a city; die — einer Messe, freedom of a fair, the privilege of holding a fair; —en ertheilen, to grant franchises; Waaren, welche mit —en versehen sind, patent commodities. 2) freedom from rules or limits, freedom of action beyond the ordinary bounds of decorum, liberty. Dieser Mahler erlaubt sich zu große —en, this painter disregards too much the rules of painting; eine dichterische —, poetic license; hüte dich vor dem, was man unschuldige —en nennt, beware of what are called innocent freedoms; Frauenzimmer sollten alle unziemliche —en zurückweisen, females should repel all improper liberties; sich einige —en mit einem Frauenzimmer herausnehmen, to take some liberties with a woman. 3) a place invested with franchises.

Freiheitsathmend, adj. and adv. aspiring after liberty. —liebend, adj. and adv. warmly attached to liberty. —sapostel, m. [mostly in a bad sense] V. —sprediger. —sbaum, m. [in the French revolution] tree of liberty. —sbrief, m. charter, patent. Der große —sbrief der Engländer, the great charter, magna charta. —sdurst, m. thirst after liberty. —sfarbe, f. [in the French revolution] white, blue and red. Die —sfarben, the three colours [white, blue and red]. —sfeind, m. an opposer to liberty. —sfieber, n. a fit of liberty. —sfreund, m. a friend, an advocate of moral and political liberty. —sgeist, m. a disposition in minds to liberty, spirit of freedom. —sgenuß, m. the enjoyment of liberty or the enjoyment of civil and religious privileges. —sgöttin, f. [in the French revolution] the goddess of liberty. —shaß, m. aversion to liberty. —shut, m. the hat of liberty. —skampf, m. struggle for liberty. —skämpfer, m. a champion for liberty. —skrieg, m. war waged and carried on for liberty, a war of independence. —slehre, f. 1) propagation of principles of liberty. 2) [in philosophy] the doctrines of the moral liberty of men. —sliebe, f. love of liberty. —slied, n. a song of liberty. —smütze, f. [in the French revolution] cap of liberty, the red cap of the Jacobins. —sprediger, m. [frequently in a bad sense] one who preaches liberty. —sschwindel, m. V. —fieber. —ssinn, m. the spirit of liberty. —ssucht, f. inordinate desire of liberty.

Freiherr, m. [-n, pl. -en] baron.

Freiherrinn, f. baroness.

Freiherrlich, adj. and adv. baronial.

Freiherrschaft, f. barony.

Freiinn, f. the unmarried daughter of a baron; it. a baroness.

Freilager, n. [-s, pl. -] V. Bivouac.

Freilagern, V. Bivouaquiren.

Freilich, [from frei] adv. 1) in truth, in fact, indeed, certainly. Werden Sie hingehen? —! shall you go there? to be sure I shall! 2) [to note concession or admission] indeed. Schiffe, — nicht so groß, aber besser bemannt, ships not so large indeed, but better manned.

Freitag, m. [from the Teutonic goddess of love *Freya*] [-es, pl. -e] Friday. Der stille [or Char-] —, Good Friday.

‡**Freitagsgröschel**, n. a small coin.

Freith[e], f. ‖1) liberty. 2) courtship. Auf die — gehen, to go a wooing.

Freithof, m. V. Freihof.

Freiung, f. [pl. -en] 1) manumission, emancipation. 2) franchise, asylum. 3) an open space in a wood, glade.

Freiwerber, m. -inn, f. a person employed to make proposals of marriage for another.

Freiwerberei, **Freiwerbung**, f. the act of proposing for another.

Fremd, [from the old *fram* = weg, Engl. *from*] adj. and adv. [formerly] remote, distant. In a more limited sense: a) belonging to another nation or country; coming from another country or place. Ein —er Prinz, a foreign prince; in einem —en Lande, in an alien land, in foreign parts; —e Völker, foreign nations; Nachrichten aus —en Ländern, foreign news; —e Waaren, foreign goods; —e Weiber [in Script.], outlandish women; eine —e Sprache, a foreign language; —e Pflanzen, exotic plants; ein —es Wort, oder ein —er Ausdruck, an exotic word or term; ein —er, an alien, a foreigner; —e aus allen Ländern Europa's, strangers from all countries of Europe; ich bin hier —, I am a stranger here; b) not belonging to our family. —e Kinder, other people's children; —e, strangers, guests; wir haben heute —e, we have company to-day; ich würde schwerlich einen —en dort finden, I should hardly find one visitor there. c) not belonging to our society or corporation. *Fig.* α) not belonging to us, belonging to others. —es Gut, other people's property; es kam in —e Hände, it came into the hands of others; sich in —e Händel mischen, to meddle with the quarrels of others; er reist unter einem —en Namen, he travels incognito; —es Licht, [with painters] false light. β) not before known, heard or seen. —e Thiere, unknown animals; dieser Gebrauch war ihnen —, this custom was strange to them; das Original war mir nicht —, I was no stranger to the original; es klang ihren Ohren neu und —, it was new and strange in their ears; *— thun gegen Einen, to cut a person; Joseph sah seine Brüder an und stellte sich — gegen sie, [in Script.] Joseph saw his brethren, but made himself strange unto them; der Herr ist mir —, the gentleman is a stranger to me; meinem Kinde ist die Welt noch —, my child is yet a stranger to the world. γ) not belonging, not connected, foreign. Die Gefühle, welche Sie äußern, sind Ihrem Herzen —, the sentiments you express are foreign to your heart. δ) odd, unusual, not according to the common way, strange. Sich — kleiden, to dress one's self oddly.

Fremd=artig, *adj.* and *adv.* 1) of a different kind or nature, unlike or dissimilar in kind, heterogeneal, heterogeneous [opposed to homogeneous]. —artige Theile, heterogeneal parts 2) extraneous. Gold von —artigen Theilen trennen, to separate gold from extraneous matter. — **artigkeit**, *f.* heterogeneity, heterogeneousness. —**geboren**, *adj.* and *adv.* born in a foreign country. —**namig**, *adj.* and *adv* having a name substituted for another, pseudonymous; without the real name. Eine —namige Flugschrift, a pseudonymous pamphlet. —**namigkeit**, *f* disguise of the real name. —**sucht**, *f.* a fondness for foreign manners, dress &c. —**süchtig**, *adj.* and *adv.* fond of foreign manners, dress &c.

Frèmde, *f.* a foreign country or place, foreign parts. In die — gehen, to go abroad, to travel [especially of German journeymen who travel for the purpose of perfecting themselves in their trade]; in der — seyn, to be abroad; aus der — kommen, to come home from travelling, to return from abroad.

Frèmdenbill, *f.* [in England] alien-bill.

Frèmdheit, *f.* 1) foreignness, strangeness; *it.* the state of being unknown. Die — eines Landes, the strangeness of a country. 2) a strange or foreign thing, especially a form of language peculiar to a foreign language, a barbarism.

Frèmdlich, *adj.* and *adv.* 1) foreign. 2) heterogeneal, heterogeneous.

Frèmdling, *m.* [-s, *pl.* -e] one who belongs to another country or place, a foreigner, a stranger, an alien. Ein — in diesem Lande, a stranger in this country; da sie nun dies Gesetz hörten, schieden sie alle —e von Israel, [in Script.] when they had heard the law, that they separated from Israel all the mixed multitude. *Fig.* Ein — in irgend einer Kunst oder Wissenschaft seyn, to be a stranger to any art or science, to be ignorant of any art or science; er ist ein — in den Rechten, he is ignorant of the law.

Fremdlings=falk, *m.* V. Wanderfalk. —**s=land**, *n.* a foreign country. —**s=recht**, *n.* the right of the king or lord of succeeding to escheats of aliens. —**s=sohn**, *m.* 1) the son of an alien. 2) a foreigner or stranger. —**s=volk**, *n.* a foreign nation.

***Frequènt**, *adj.* and *adv.* frequent, full, crowded

***Fréquentatìvum**, *n.* [-s or -ivi, *pl.* -iven or -iva] a frequentative word.

Frequentìren, *v. tr.* to frequent [a tavern, a university, a society &c.].

***Frequènz**, *f.* a crowd, a throng, a concourse. Die — [auf] dieser Universität ist gegenwärtig nicht stark or bedeutend, this university is not much frequented at present.

***Frèsco**, [the Germ. frisch] *adv.* 1) [in painting] done on fresh plaster. Die —mahlerei, [a method of painting in relief on walls, performed with water colours on fresh plaster] fresco; al— mahlen, to paint in fresco, to be a painter in fresco. 2) [in music] lively.

‖**Frèsse**, *f.* [*pl.* -n] 1) [in contempt] the chaps or mouth. 2) V. Gefräß.

Frèssen, [perhaps instead of veressen. Others compare it with the Lat. *rod*-ere or the Germ. reißen] *ir.* I. *v. tr.* 1) in general, to consume, to eat, to corrode, to consume. Der Rost frißt das Eisen, rust corrodes iron; das Feuer fraß die zwei hundert und fünfzig Männer, die das Rauchwerk opferten, [in Script.] a fire consumed the two hundred and fifty men that offered incense. *Fig.* Das Schwert soll deine jungen Löwen —, [in Script.] the sword shall devour the young lions; den wird der Hunger und die Pestilenz —, [in Script.] famine and pestilence shall devour him; † es frißt ihn der Neid, he is consumed with envy. 2) usually, to eat [said of animals]. Hunde, Pferde — dogs, horses eat; Gras —, to eat grass; dem Vieh zu — geben, to feed the cattle; Raupen — Blätter und saftige Pflanzen, caterpillars feed on leaves and succulent plants; kleine Vögel — Körner und Samen, small birds feed on grain and seeds; ein —des Pfand, an impounded animal. *Prov.* Vogel friß oder stirb, there is no other way to come off. *Fig.* [in fam. or rather vulg. lang.] Seinen Verdruß in sich —, to swallow one's vexation; sie hat einen Narren an ihm gefressen —, she dotes on him; er hat einen Narren daran ge—, he conceived an unreasonable partiality for it. 3) [in contempt] to eat voraciously, to glutonize [said of men]. — und saufen, excess in eating and drinking.

II. *v. intr.* Um sich — [= to spread by eating, corroding, &c.]. Das Feuer fraß um sich, the fire spread; der Krebs frißt um sich, a cancer eats into the flesh, spreads

Freß=bauch, *m.* [one who indulges to excess in eating] a glutton. —**begierde**, *f.* greediness, ravenousness, voracity. —**begierig**, *adj.* and *adv.* greedy voracious, ravenous. —begierig essend, eating greedily. —**fieber**, *n.* voracity of appetite from the diseased state of the stomach, bulimy. —**gier**, *f.* greediness, voracity, ravenousness. —**gierig**, *adj.* and *adv.* greedy, voracious, ravenous, gluttonous —**glocke**, *f.* [in common lang.] eating-bell, a bell rung for cattle at feeding-time. —**kober**, *m.* a meat-basket —**krankheit**, *f.* 1) V. —fieber. 2) V. Heißhunger. —**lust**, *f.* appetite for food. —**lustig**, *adj.* and *adv.* having an appetite for food. —**sack**, *m.* a meat-scrip. *Fig.* [one who indulges to excess in eating] a glutton, greedy-guts. —**spitze**, *f.* one of the palpi of insects, feeler. —**stein**, *m.* V. Höllenstein. —**sucht**, *f.* 1) voracity of appetite. 2) bulimy. —**süchtig**, *adj.* and *adv.* having a keen appetite for food. —**trog**, *m.* manger. —**wanst**, *m.* V. Freßbauch. —**wehe**, *f.* [a distemper in horses] heart-burning. —**wurzel**, *f.* [a plant] V. Zehrwurzel. —**zange**, *f.* [in entomology] pincer-shaped feeler.

Frèssen, *n.* [-s] 1) the act of eating or feeding [said of animals], or of eating voraciously or gluttonously [said of men]. *Prov.* — und Saufen macht die Aerzte reich, feasting is the physician's harvest. 2) whatever is eaten by animals; food, meat [in contempt of men]. *Fig.* † Das ist ihm ein gefundenes —, that is meat and drink for him.

Frèsser, *m.* [-s, -] 1) a great feeder [said of animals] V. also Freßbauch. 2) [a disease which occurs principally in fruit-trees] cancer.

Frèsserei, *f.* 1) excess in eating, gluttony. 2) luxury of the table, gluttony. Ihre kostbaren —en, their sumptuous gluttonies.

Frèssig, *adj.* greedy, voracious; it is used only in composition, as, Fleisch— or fressend, carnivorous.

Frèßling, *m.* [-es, *pl.* -e] V. Freßbauch.

Frètt, *n.* [-es, *pl.* -e] more commonly **Frèttchen**, **Frèttwiesel**, *n.* [-s, *pl.* -] [Fr. *furet*, perhaps allied to the Fr. *fureter* = *fouiller*, and to the Ital. *fretta* = Eile] [an animal of the weasel-kind] the ferret.

Frett=bär, *m.* a species of ferret of a brownish-grey colour. —**wiesel**, *n.* V. Frett.

‖**Frètter**, *m.* [-s, *pl.* -] V. Pfuscher.

‖**Frètzen**, **Frèren**, *v. tr.* to give food or fodder for fattening, to feed [oxen &c.].

Freùde, *f.* [*pl.* -n] [allied to froh] 1) [formerly] courage, undauntedness. Mit — in den Tod gehen, to meet death joyfully, not to be afraid of death, to dare death. 2) [the passion or emotion excited by the acquisition or expectation of good] joy, gladness, exultation, exhilaration of spirits. — über etwas empfinden, to rejoice in any thing; — an etwas haben, to take delight in any thing; Jugend und Krieg sind ohne — für ihn, youth and war are joyless to him; seine — an seinen Kindern haben, to delight in one's children; Einer, dem fremdes Unglück — macht, one that is glad at another's calamity; voller —, joyful; die übermäßige —, overjoy; sie gehorchen mit —, they obey joyfully; vor lauter — hüpfen, weinen, to leap for joy, to weep for joy; ich mache mir ein[e] — daraus, Ihnen dienen zu können, I am glad of an opportunity to oblige you; — an seinen Kindern erleben, to live to see one's children happy or well settled; Einem die — verderben †versalzen, to spoil any one's pleasure; Tage der —, gladsome days; die —n des Lebens, the pleasures of life. *Prov.* Keine Freud' ist ohne Leid, no sunshine but has some shadow; auf — folgt oft Traurigkeit, to-day we are glad, to-morrow sad; he that laughs in the morning, weeps at night; after sweet meat comes sour sauce. 3) the expression of joy, joy, gayety, mirth. Die Dächer wiederhallen von —, the roofs with joy resound. 4) the cause of joy, joy. Unsere größte —, the best of our delights; Ihr seid ja unsere Ehre und —, [in Script.] for ye are our glory and joy.

Freud=ausruf, —**los**, &c. V. Freudenausruf &c.

Freude=ausruf, *m.* V. Freudenausruf. —**bringer**, *m.* V. Freudenbringer. —**glänzend**, *adj.* and *adv.* having a cheerful countenance. —**leuchtend**, *adj.* and *adv.* lit up with mirth. —**los**, V. Freudenlos. —**n=arm**, *adj.* and *adv.* wanting joy, destitute of joy, joyless. —**n=ausruf**, *m.* a shout of joy. —**n=becher**, *m.* [in poetry] the cup of delight. —**n=bezeigung**, *f.* expression of joy or exultation. —**n=blick**, *m.* 1) a joyful look. *Fig.* fleeting joy. —**n=blume**, *f.* a flower that causes joy or pleasure. —**n=bote**, *m.* the bearer of glad tidings. —**n=botschaft**, *f.* a gladsome message. —**n=bringer**, *m.* a person or thing that causes joy. —**n=fahne**, *f.* the banner of joy. —**n=feind**, *m.* a foe to joy or mirth. —**n=fest**, *n.* a day of joy, a feast or festival, a jubilee. —**n=feuer**, *n.* a fire made as an expression of public joy or exultation, a bon-fire. —**n=geber**, *m.* one who produces joy or mirth, especially a surname of Bacchus, the god of wine. —**n=gefühl**, *n.* a sentiment of joy. —**n=genoß**, *m.* one who partakes of the same joy with another. —**n=genuß**, *m.* enjoyment of pleasure. —**n=**

sang, *m.* a song of joy; a hymn of rejoicing. —n=geschrei, *n.* words expressive of joy, an acclamation in joy, shouts of joy, cheers. Mit —, jubilant. —n=hasser, *m.* a hater of joy or mirth. —n=haus, *n.* 1) a house of joy and feasting. 2) [obsolescent] a house of lewdness and prostitution, a bawdy-house, brothel. —n=himmel, *m.* 1) heaven as the residence of joy and mirth. 2) joyfulness. —n=kleid, *n.* holiday-garment —n=kranz, *m.* a series of joyous events. —n=leben, *n.* a joyous life, merry life, or happy life. —n=leer, *adj.* and *adv.* joyless, sportless. —n=leere, *f.* joylessness. —n=lied, *n.* a song of joy. —n=los, *adj.* and *adv.* joyless —n=mädchen, *n.* a prostitute. Ein unterhaltenes —nmädchen, a kept mistress, a miss. —n=mahl, *n.* a festival entertainment. —n=meer, *n.* plenty of joy or pleasure. —n=meister, [unusual] *m.* [at courts] the director of the pleasures [maître des plaisirs.] —n=nachricht, joyous or gladsome news. —n=öl, *n.* [in Script.] oil of joy. —n=opfer, *n.* V. Dankopfer —n=pferd, *n.* a prancing horse at the funerals of princes. —n=post, *f.* glad tidings, joyous news. —n=reich, I. *adj.* and *adv.* causing great joy or pleasure. II. *n.* an empire where joy governs; [sometimes] heaven. —n=ruf, *m.* a shout of joy or exultation. Mit dreimaligem —nrufe, with three cheers. —n=saal, a poetical name of the residence of angels and blessed spirits, heaven. —n=satz, *m.* V. —nsprung. —n=schießen, *n.* a firing of guns in token of joy, feu de joie —n=schöpfer, *m.* a being that creates joy or pleasure, as, the sun. —n=schuß, *m.* a shot in token of joy. —n=selig, *adj.* and *adv.* enjoying great pleasure. —n=sonne, *f.* a source of many pleasures. —n=sprung, *m.* a leap for joy —n=stimmung, joyous humour. —n=störer, *m.* a trouble-feast, a kill-joy. —n=tag, *m.* a day of joy, a festival day, day of rejoicing. —n=tanz, *m.* a joyous dance. —n=taumel, *m.* transports of joy. —n=thräne, *f.* tear of joy. ...e vergossen —nthränen, they wept for joy. —n=todt, *adj.* and *adv.* 1) deprived of joys. dead to joy. —n=ton, *m.* a sound of joy. —n=trunk, *m.* rejoicing cup. —n=voll, *adj.* and *adv.* full of joy, joyful. Sie gehorchten —n... they obeyed joyfully —n=weib, [unusual] V. —mädchen. —n=wein, *m.* festival wine. —n=zähre, *f.* V. —nthräne. —n=zeichen, *n.* token of joy. —reich, *adj.* and *adv.* rich ...joy. —taumel, *m.* V. —ntaumel. —...nken, *adj.* and *adv.* intoxicated with joy. ...oll, *adj.* and *adv.* V. —nvoll. —weinend, *adj.* and *adv.* weeping for joy. —zitternd, *adj.* and *adv.* trembling with joy.

...reudig, *adj.* and *adv.* 1) gay, cheerful. —es Pferd, a brisk horse; die Soldaten ...en dem Feinde — entgegen, the soldiers ...ed with alacrity to meet the enemy; — ...er dem Tode entgegen, he faced death cheer...; — sterben, to die readily. 2) joyous, glad, merry, joyful. — aussehen, to look cheer... to have a cheerful or glad countenance; ... Herzens, glad of heart; nie gehorchten ...schen —er, never did men more joyfully ...; — annehmen, to accept joyfully; sie ...en ihm — zu, they heard him gladly. 3) ...g joy, joyous. Eine —e Nachricht, joyous ...; ein —er Tag, a gladsome day. 4) pleas... exhilarating, glad.

...reudigkeit, *f.* cheerfulness, alacrity.

...reuen, [V. Froh] I. *v. tr.* to make joyful, to ...den, to exhilarate. Sein Anblick freut [erfreut] ..., I am rejoiced to see him; es freuet mich, ... glad of it. II. *v. r.* sich —, to experience joy, ...joice. Es freut mich, Gelegenheit zu haben, ...em Freunde dienen zu können, I am glad of an opportunity to oblige my friend; wer sich seines Unfalls freut, wird nicht ungestraft bleiben, [in Script.] he that is glad at his calamities shall not be unpunished; laß mich nicht zu Schanden werden, daß sich meine Feinde nicht — über mich, [in Script.] let me not be ashamed, lest not mine enemies triumph over me; ich freue mich und bin fröhlich in dir, I will be glad and rejoice in thee; sich über alle Maßen —, to exult; er freute sich ungemein über den glücklichen Erfolg or des glücklichen Erfolgs seiner Pläne, he exulted in the success of his designs; ich freue mich im voraus darauf, I am pleased with the thought of it; *sich wie ein Kind —, to rejoice exceedingly.

Freund, *m* [-es, *pl.* -e] [Goth. *frijon* signifies lieben (with the original signification of approaching) of which Freund is properly the participle] one who is attached to another by affection, friend. Ein guter —, a good friend; ein vertrauter —, an intimate friend; mein alter —, an old friend of mine; sich —e machen, to get friends; sich einen zum —e machen, to win any one's friendship, to make a friend of any one; ohne —e, friendless; [in common or familiar life] er ist ein — von mir [instead of, er ist mein —], he is a friend of mine; wir wollen wieder —e seyn, let us be friends again. *Prov.* —e erkennt man in der Noth, a friend is never known till one have need; a friend in need is a friend indeed; prove thy friend, ere thou have need; es sind nicht alle —e, die Einen anlächeln, all are not friends that speak us fair; reiche Leute haben viele —e, I wot well how the world wags, he is most loved, that hath most bags; — in der Noth und hinterm Rücken, sind fürwahr zwei starke Brücken, he's a good friend that speaks well of us behind our backs; —e in der Noth gehn viele auf ein Loth, in time of prosperity friends there are plenty, in time of adversity not one among twenty; die Nacht ist Niemands —, he that runs in the night stumbles. [In a more limited sense:] *a*) a paramour. Siehe, mein —, du bist schön und lieblich, [in Script.] behold, thou art fair, my love. *b*) a person connected by consanguinity or affinity. Ein naher —, a near relation; seine —e wollten es nicht zugeben, his relatives opposed it. *c*) [one who is propitious, a favourer] friend. Ein — der Dichtkunst, a friend to poetry; ein — der Wahrheit, der Wissenschaft, a lover of truth, of science; ich bin kein — von vielem Reden, I do not like much talking. *d*) one not hostile, friend. Wer kommt so eilig in der stillen Nacht? ein —, who comes so fast in silence of the night? a friend; wer da? gut —! [in military affairs] who comes there? friend! *e*) [in commerce] a correspondent, friend. *f*) a familiar compellation. —, wie bist du hereingekommen? [in Script.] friend, how camest thou in hither?

Freund=bedürftig, *adj.* and *adv.* wanting a friend. —[e]=los, *adj.* and *adv.* friendless. —nachbarlich, *adj.* and *adv.* neighbourly, on friendly terms. —recht, *n.* a right or claim arising from relationship.

Freunden, *v. tr.* to make friends [it is used chiefly in the past participle]. Gefreundet, related.

Freundinn, *f.* 1) a female relation, kinswoman. 2) a female friend, friend. Meine —, a friend of mine. 3) a paramour, a mistress. Er hält sich eine —, he keeps a mistress.

Freundlich, *adj.* and *adv.* 1) having the disposition of a friend, expressive of kindness and friendship. Sei gut und — stets dem Menschengeschlechte, thou to mankind be good and friendly still; ein —er Mann, an affable man; ein —es Aussehen, an affable countenance; eine —e Aufnahme, a gracious reception; — antworten, to answer affably; — Einen aufnehmen, to receive any one courteously; der Gesandte wurde — aufgenommen, the envoy met with a gracious reception. —e Worte, gracious or kind words; auf eine —e Weise, in a kind way, kindly; eine —e Behandlung, a complaisant treatment; —e Manieren, sweet manners; du hast deine Magd — angesprochen, [in Script.] thou hast spoken friendly unto thy handmaid; Jemanden — grüßen lassen, to send one's kind wishes to any one. eine —e Nachricht, a fair warning; —er Leser, gentle or courteous reader 2) not hostile, friendly. 3) [what pleases] —e Blumen, pleasant flowers; ein —es Lüftchen, a friendly breeze; ein —er Anblick, a pleasant view; eine —e Gegend, a pleasing country; —es Wetter, fair weather; —e Bergarten, [in mining] the matrices of metals.

Freundlichkeit, *f.* 1) friendliness, kind condescension, graciousness, complaisance, courteousness, affability, affableness Mit — empfangen werden, to meet with a gracious reception. 2) Die — einer Lage, the pleasantness of a situation. 3) pleasing manner, exterior acts of kindness or civility.

Freundschaft, *f.* [*pl.* -en] 1) friendship. Wahre —, true friendship; die Bande der —, the bonds of friendship; sie schlossen mit einander —, they became friends; etwas aus — thun, to do something out of friendship 2) [in a general sense] good understanding, friendship, amity. In Friede und — mit der ganzen Welt leben, to be at peace and in amity with all the world. 3) relation, kindred, alliance; *it.* persons connected by consanguinity or affinity [in this sense it is seldom used among people of rank]. Er gehört zu meiner —, he is a relation of mine; er hat eine große —, he has many relations or relatives 4) favour, personal kindness, friendly aid, friendship. Einem eine — erweisen, to do any one a good office; erzeigen Sie mir die —, mit ihm darüber zu sprechen, do me the favour to mention it to him.

Freundschafts=leer, *adj.* and *adv.* without friendship. —s=band, *n.* bond of friendship. —s=bezeigung, *f.* mark, demonstration of friendship; kind and affable treatment —s=bezeigungen, friendships. —s=bund, *m.* a treaty of amity. —s=dienst, *m.* a kind act or office, good office —s=fall, *m.* [in law] a cause where friendship must be taken into account [casus pro amico]. —s=inseln, *pl* the Friendly Islands [in the South Sea]. —s=kuß, *m.* a kiss in token of friendship. —s=lied, *n.* a song in honour of friendship. —s=orden, *m.* a fraternity of friends. —s=pfand, *n.* a memorial of friendship, a token. —s=sinn, *m.* [in craniology] the organ of friendship. —s=stück, —s=stückchen, *n.* a friendly turn; [sometimes ironically] an act of malice, an ill turn. —s=trieb, *m.* a disposition to friendship, friendliness. —s=versicherung, *f.* a profession of friendship, an assurance of amity.

Freundschaftlich, *adj* and *adv.* having the disposition of a friend, friendlike, friendly, amicable. Familien, welche in —en Verhältnissen stehen, families connected in friendship; ich stehe mit ihm auf einem —en Fuße, we are on friendly terms; der Streit wurde — beigelegt, the dispute was amicably settled.

Freundschaftlichkeit, *f.* friendly disposition, friendliness, amicableness.

Frevel, [appears to be allied to froh, frei, frech. Old Germ. is fräfen = kühn] I. *m.* [-s, *pl.* -] 1) formerly, force, strength. 2) intentional injury, harm or damage done by design, mischief, wrong, transgression, trespass, offence, [in law] misdemeanour. Einen — verüben, to perpetrate a mischievous act;

— an jemand begehen, to do any one a mischief, to outrage a person; den — büßen, to atone for a misdeed; denn ihr Werk ist Mühe und in ihren Händen ist —, [in Script.] their works are works of iniquity and the act of violence is in their hands; man soll keinen — mehr hören in deinem Lande, [in Script.] violence shall no more be heard in thy land; die Erde ist voll —s, [in Script.] the earth was filled with violence. 3) mischievousness, waggery. II. *adj.* [rather in high style] malicious, mischievous. Ein freveles Beginnen, a mischievous doing.

Frevel=beweis, *m.* [in law] the visible proof of any crime [corpus delicti] ||—buße, *f.* a fine for an intentional transgression. ||—gericht, *n.* a court for trying offences and trespasses. —handlung, *f.* V. —that. —lust, *f.* a disposition to transgress; *it.* a mischievous temper, a tendency to doing mischief. —mord, *m.* an intentional murder. —muth, *m.* malicious, mischievous disposition. —richter, *m.* a judge of the court for trying offences and trespasses. —sache, *f.* an offence or trespass. —sinn, *m.* V. —muth. —that, *f.* a mischievous action, a wicked deed. ‡ and ||—vogt, *m.* V. Fiscal. —wort, *n.* wicked word.

Fréveler, Frévler, *m.* [-s] one who trespasses, a mischievous man, a trespasser, an offender.

Frévelhaft, *adj.* and *adv.* mischievous. Ein —er Mensch, a mischievous man; eine —e That, a mischievous action; — handeln, to trespass.

Frévelig, *adj.* and *adv.* V. Freventlich.

Frèveln, *v. intr.* to commit any offence or to do any act that injures another, to commit an outrage or crime. An seinem Nächsten —, to trespass against one's neighbour; frevle nicht an den Gesetzen, offer no violence to the laws.

Frèventlich, *adj.* and *adv.* with evil intention or disposition, mischievous. —e Reden, injurious talk; diese Unbild ist — begangen worden, this outrage was done mischievously.

Frèvler, *m.* [-s, *pl.* -] V. Freveler.

Freÿ, *adj.* and *adv.* [and compound words thus beginning] V. Frei &c.

Freÿa, Freía, Frígga, *f.* [V. Freien].

***Fricassé**, *n.* [-'s, *pl.* -s or -en] [in cookery, a dish of food] a fricassee.

***Fricassiren**, *v. tr.* to dress in fricassee, to fricassee. *Fig.* † Einen —, to cut any one to pieces.

***Frictiōn**, *f.* V. Reibung.

Fridrich, V. Friedrich.

Friedbrüchig, *adj.* and *adv.* V. Friedensbrüchig.

Friede or **Frieden**, *m.* [-s, *pl.* -] [seems to be allied to friedigen [in einfriedigen] = schützen, and to the Gr. φράττω] 1) a state of quiet and tranquillity; public tranquillity, that quiet, order and security, which is guarantied by the laws. Einen in Frieden lassen, to let any one alone; laßt mich in Frieden, let me be quiet; Frieden halten, to keep the peace; [in the time of private warfare] den Frieden wirken, to restore public peace; jemand in seinen Frieden nehmen, to take any one into protection. *Prov.* Wer Frieden haben will, der schweige, he that would live in peace and rest, must hear and see and say the best. 2) peace, harmony, concord. Frieden mit jemand haben, to be in peace with any one; der Frieden im Hause, domestic peace; sie lieben den Frieden, they are fond of peace and quietness; den öffentlichen Frieden stören, to violate or disturb public peace; Worte des Friedens, peaceful words; Frieden stiften, to make peace, to restore peace; die Bürger leben in Frieden und Einigkeit, the citizens live in peace and harmony; Ruhe und Frieden in einem Staate wieder herstellen, to tranquillize a state disturbed by factious or civil commotions. *Prov.* Um Frieden im Hause zu haben, muß der Mann taub und die Frau blind seyn, for domestic peace, the husband must not see, and the wife must be blind. 3) freedom from war with a foreign nation, public quiet. Frieden schließen, to conclude peace; hastig Frieden schließen, to clap up a peace; Frieden unterhandeln, to negotiate a peace; der Westphälische Frieden, the peace of Westphalia. *Prov.* Frieden ernährt, Unfrieden verzehrt, by wisdom peace, by peace plenty. 4) quietness of mind, tranquillity, calmness, peace. Der Frieden des Gewissens, quiet of conscience; großen Frieden haben, die dein Gesetz lieben, [in Script.] great peace have they that love thy law; in Frieden dahin geschieden, peace-parted; Frieden sei mit dir, fürchte dich nicht, du wirst nicht sterben, [in Script.] peace be unto thee, fear not, thou shalt not die.

Friede=fürst, —ns=fürst, *m.* the prince of peace [this name is given to Christ, in Script.]; *it.* the title of a certain Spanish minister. V. —nsfürst. —gebot, *n.* [in some courts] an injunction to keep the peace. —kauf, *m.* purchase in the lump [in order to avoid law-suits]. —los, friedlos, *adj.* and *adv.* 1) formerly, outlawed. 2) unpeaceable, quarrelsome. —machend, *adj.* and *adv.* 1) peace-making. 2) pacifying. —ns=abschluß, *m.* 1) conclusion of peace. 2) a deed containing the articles of peace. —ns=anerbieten, *n.* —ns=antrag, *m.* the offer to make peace. Friedensanerbietungen, pacific propositions. —ns=bedingung, *f.* a condition in a treaty of peace. Die —nsbedingungen, conditions of peace. —ns=bothe, *m.* a messenger of peace, the herald of peace. —ns=bothschaft, *f.* 1) an intelligence received or notice given of the restoration of peace. 2) heralds of peace. —ns=brecher, *m.* a breaker of the peace. —ns=bruch, *m.* violation of peace, breach of peace. —ns=brüchig, friedbrüchig, *adj.* and *adv.* violating peace, breaking the peace; formerly, guilty of a violation of public peace. —ns=bund, *m.* —ns=bündniß, *n.* an alliance or confederacy formed by peace or to maintain peace. —ns=congreß, *m.* a congress for making peace. —ns=einleitung, *f.* something preparatory to peace. —nseinleitungen, [Friedenspräliminarien], preliminaries of peace. —ns=engel, *m.* an angel of peace. —ns=fahne, *f.* a flag of peace. —ns=feind, *m.* an enemy to peace. —ns=fest, *n.* festivities and rejoicings at the conclusion of peace. —ns=feuer, *n.* a bonfire in honour of the restoration of peace. —ns=flagge, *f.* the white flag. Die —nsflagge ausstecken, to hang out the white flag. —ns=fürst, *m.* [in Spain] a title given lately to the famous Don Emanuel Godoi. —ns=fuß, *m.* peace-establishment. Eine Festung auf den —nsfuß setzen, to dismantle a fortress. —ns=gedanken, *pl.* peaceable thoughts, or sentiments. —ns=gericht, *n.* a court held by justices of the peace. —ns=gesandte, *m.* V —nsbothe. —ns=geschäft, *n.* negotiation for peace. —ns=hain, [in poet. lang.] *m.* a churchyard. —ns=handlung, —ns=unterhandlung, *f.* negotiation for peace. Eine —nsunterhandlung ist im Gange, a treaty of peace is on foot. —ns=instrument, *n.* a treaty of peace. —ns=kuß, *m.* [among the first Christians and in the Romish church] the kiss of peace. —ns=land, *n.* 1) a peaceful land. 2) *Fig.* heaven. —ns=marsch, *m.* a march, struck up in honour of peace. —ns=münze, *f.* a coin stamped with some device to preserve the memory of a peace. —ns=nachricht, *f.* V. —nspost. —ns=pfeife, *f.* [among the aborigines of America] the calumet. —ns=post, *f.* the news of the conclusion of peace. —ns=präliminarien, *pl.* V. —nseinleitung. —ns=predigt, *f.* a conciliatory sermon or a sermon preached in honour of the conclusion of peace. —ns=punkt, *m.* an article of peace. —ns=rech[t], *n.* the peace-making power. —ns=richter, *m.* justice of the peace. —ns=schluß, *m.* conclusion of peace, a treaty of peace. —ns=stab, *m.* the rod of peace. —ns=stifter, *m.* —ns=stifterinn, *f.* a person that pacifies, pacifier, pacificator, peace-maker. —ns=stiftung, *f.* pacification, peace-making. —ns=störer, *m.* —ns=störerinn, *f.* a person that disturbs peace, a violator of peace, disturber. —ns=störung, *f.* violation of peace, disturbance. —ns=tag, *m.* 1) a day on which peace is concluded. 2) [with journeymen] a day on which they meet. —nstage, [in poetry] halcyon-days. —ns=unterhändler, *m.* a negotiator of a treaty of peace. —ns=unterhandlung, *f.* negotiation for peace. —ns=urkunde, *f.* V. —nsinstrument. —ns=verein, *m.* V. —nscongreß. —ns=vermittelung, *f.* mediation. —ns=vermittler, *m.* mediator. —ns=vermittlerinn, *f.* mediatrix, mediatress. —ns=versammlung, *f.* V. —nscongreß. —ns=vertrag, *m.* a treaty of peace. —ns=vorschlag, *m.* a proposal for a treaty of peace. Der Feind machte —nsvorschläge, the enemy made propositions of peace, or conciliatory propositions; einer kriegführenden Macht —nsvorschläge machen, to offer pacific propositions to a belligerent power. —ns=wort, *n.* a peaceful word. —ns=zeit, *f.* time of peace. —voll, *adj.* and *adv.* peaceful.

Friedel, [-s, *pl.* -] [a familiar abbreviation for Friedrich] V. Friedrich.

‡**Frieden**, [V. Friede] *v. tr.* to guard, to secure by an inclosure, to fence. V. Einfrieden.

Friederich, V. Friedrich.

Friedfertig, *adj.* and *adv.* peaceable, pacific. Ein —er Mensch, a peaceable man; selig sind die —en, [in Script.] blessed are the peace-makers; eine —e Gemüthsstimmung, a peaceful temper; — leben, to live peaceably or quietly.

Friedfertigkeit, *f.* pacific disposition, peaceableness.

Friedhag, *m.* [-s, *pl.* -e] a fence, or hedge.

Friedhof, *m.* [-s, *pl.* -höfe] [from frieden = einhegen] churchyard, cemetery.

Friedlich, *adj.* and *adv.* 1) disposed to peace, suited to make or to restore peace. Ein —er Mensch, a peaceable man; —e Maßregeln, pacific or conciliatory measures. 2) free from war or commotion, removed from noise or tumult, peaceable. —e Zeiten, peaceable times; ein —es Leben, a quiet life; meine —e Hütte, my peaceful cottage; —regieren, to govern peaceably.

Friedlichkeit, *f.* disposition to peace, peaceableness.

Friedliebend, *adj.* and *adv.* disposed to peace. —e Nachbarn, peabeable neighbours.

Friedlos, *adj.* and *adv.* V. Friedelos.

Friedmüthig, *adj.* and *adv.* V. Friedliebend.

||**Friedpfahl**, *m.* [-s, *pl.* -pfähle] a post marking the boundary of a jurisdiction.

Friedrich, [-s, *pl.* -e] [a name of men] Frederic.

Friedrichs=pistole, *f.* [Friedrichsd'or, a gold coin of Prussia, of the value of 16 shillings] Frederic d'or. —s=salz, *n.* [in medicine] a sort of mixed salt.

Fried[e]rike [and **Frlbrike**], [-ns or der —] [a name of women] Frederica.

Friedsam, *adj.* and *adv.* 1) disposed to peace. Ein —er Mensch, a peaceable man. 2) peaceful, still, undisturbed. Die —en Begebenheiten des ländlichen Lebens, the peaceful scenes of rural life.

Friedselig, *adj.* and *adv.* V. Friedliebend.

Friedseligkeit, *f.* peacefulness.

Friedzaun, *m.* [-s, *pl.* -zäune] V. Friedhag.

Frieren, [appears to be allied to the Gr. φρίσσειν = schauern, starren] *ir.* I. *v. intr.* 1) [u. w. seyn] to be congealed by cold, to freeze. Der Branntwein friert nicht, brandy does not congeal; die Fenster —, the windows are frozen; gefrorenes Wasser, frozen water; Gefrornes, ice [for eating]. 2) [u. w. haben] to have the sensation of cold, to be cold, to shiver with cold. Mir haben die Füße gefroren, my feet were cold; —d, chill, shivering or inclined to shiver. II. *v. imp.* 1) to have the sensation of cold, to shiver with cold. Mich friert, or es friert mich, I am cold. 2) [to be of that degree of cold, at which water congeals] to freeze. Es friert nun sehr stark, it freezes now very hard.

Frieren, *n.* [-s] 1) the sensation of cold. 2) freezing, congelation. 3) a fever.

Frierpunkt, *m.* V. Gefrierpunkt.

Fries, *m.* [-es, *pl.* -e] [allied to Franse, ...tiffen] 1) [a kind of coarse woolen cloth or stuff, with a nap on one side] frieze or frize. 2) [in architecture, that part of the entablature of a column which is between the architrave and cornice] frieze or frize. 3) [in gunnery] moulding. V. Bodenfries, Hinterfries, Mittelfries.

Friesmacher, *m.* frieze-maker.

Friese, *m.* [-n, *pl.* -n] Frislander.

Friesel, *m.* [-s] [from friesen = frieren] ...disease] Der rothe —, the scarlet fever; der weiße —, [Hirsefieber] a miliary fever.

Frieselporzellane, *f.* a species of ...ry [cyprea poraria].

Friesinn, *f.* a woman of Frisland.

Friesisch, *adj.* and *adv.* pertaining to Fris...d, coming from Frisland. —e Reiter, [also ...sische Reiter, in fortification, a piece of timber ...med with wooden spikes pointed with iron, five ...ix feet long, used to defend a passage, a breach] chevaux de Frise.

...iesland, *n.* [-s] [a part of Holland] Frise, ...land.

...iesländer, *m.* —inn, *f.* V. Friese, Fries...

...iesländisch, *adj.* and *adv.* V. Friesisch.

...igga, [-'s or der -] [an ancient northern ...ns] Frea, Frigga.

...ringeisen, *n.* [-s, *pl.* -] [Wringeisen; ...dyers] wringing pole.

...ringen, *v. tr.* [wringen; with dyers] to ...g.

...isch, *adj.* and *adv.* [seems to be another ...of rasch] 1) brisk, strong, somewhat vehe...t, fresh. Ein —es Lüftchen, a fresh breeze; —er Wind, [in seamen's language] a fresh ...ze. *Fig.* *a*) brisk, lively, active. Ein —er ...ge, a lively youth; ein —es Mädchen, a ...t girl; it is sometimes used as an excla...on, or rather as a command, to move or ...eed, some verb being understood. — zu! ...ige Freunde, cheerly on! courageous ...ds; — auf! cheer up! nur — voran! bravely — zu! onwards! — zu! nur —! immer [in seamen's language] bear a hand! *b*) [just ...or performed] Er ist auf —er That ertappt worden, he was taken in the very act. 2) cool, moderately cold. Die Luft ist —, the air is cool; —e Luft schöpfen, to breathe the cool air. *Fig.* *a*) in a good state, not having lost its flavour from being long kept, not stale, being of late origin or existence, recently made or obtained. —e Waaren, fresh goods; die Austern sind nicht —, the oysters are tainted; Eier, die nicht mehr — sind, addle eggs; —e Gemüse, fresh vegetables; —e Austern, fresh oysters; —e Häringe, fresh herrings; —e Waaren, fresh goods; —es Fleisch, fresh meat [not salt]; —e Eier, new-laid or new eggs; —es Wasser, fresh water [recently from the well or spring, not warm or tepid]; —e Blumen, newly gathered flowers; — gemäht, new mown; eine —e Wunde, a green wound; —es Brod, new bread; —e Butter, fresh butter; —e Kleider, fresh clothes; —e Wäsche, clean linen; ein —es Hemd, a clean shirt or shift; ein —es Hemd anziehen, to shift; — gestoßene Butter, butter newly churned; [in metallurgy] —e Miner, liquid ores; —es Blei, V. —blei; —e Schlacken, the slag of refined metals; [in mining] —es Gestein, compact stones or rocks; —machen, to refine copper-ore with pure lead; —e Fahrten, [in mining] new ladders. *b*) not before employed, unused. —e Kohlen, [in mining] new coals; ein —es Faß anzapfen, to broach or tap a full cask; —e Pferde nehmen, to take fresh horses; —e Truppen, fresh troops. *c*) not forgotten or obliterated. Diese Geschichte ist mir in —em Andenken, the story is fresh in my mind; diese Lektüre ist mir noch in —em Andenken, that reading is still fresh in my memory. *d*) fresh, florid, ruddy, jolly. Eine —e Gesichtsfarbe, a ruddy complexion; —e Lippen, ruddy lips; ein —es Mädchen, a fresh-coloured girl; — wie eine Rose, as fresh as a rose; zwei Hirten, — wie der Morgen, two swains, fresh as the morn; — aussehen wie &c., to look freshly &c.; — und munter, healthful and gay.

Frisch-arbeit, *f.* [in metallurgy] refining or puddling. —**backen**, *n.* the privilege of baking bread on Sunday. —**bäcker**, *m.* a baker who is allowed to bake bread on Sunday. —**balg**, *m.* [in iron-works] the bellows in a finery. —**blei**, *n.* [in metallurgy] refined lead; deoxydized lead [as distinguished from litharge]. —**eisen**, *n.* 1) [in iron-works] refractory iron. 2) [in metallurgy] wrought-iron. —**esse**, *f.* [in iron-works] a finery. —**feuer**, *n.* [in iron-works] the fire in a finery. —**gestein**, *n.* [in mining] solid rocks. —**glätte** *f.* [in metallurgy] that sort of litharge which is to be deoxydized or reduced to lead. —**herd**, —**ofen**, *m.* [in iron-works] 1) a finery. 2) [in metallurgy] an inclined plane of iron in a furnace used in reducing silver by liquation. —**kienstock**, *m.* [in metallurgy] the copper which remains behind in reducing silver by liquation. —**knecht**, *m.* [in iron-works] a refiner's mate. —**machen**, *n.* [in metallurgy] liquation. —**mahlerei**, *f.* [in painting] 1) fresco. 2) a fresco-painting. —**melk**, —**milchend**, *adj.* and *adv.* [in husbandry]. Eine —milchende Kuh, a cow that lately calved. —**pfanne**, *f.* [in metallurgy] a mould for casting the loaves in liquation. —**schlacke**, *f.* the slag of refined metals. —**schmelzen**, *n.* [in metallurgy] the smelting of silver-ores which contain no lead. —**stück**, *n.* a cake of ore or a piece of black copper and lead which is formed in refining copper. —**zacken**, *m.* [in iron-works] an inclined plane of iron in a finery.

Frische, *f.* [*pl.* -n] 1) freshness. Die — der freien Luft, the freshness of the open air; die — des Morgens, the coolness of morning. *Fig.* Die — des Wassers, the freshness of water; die — der Blumen oder Pflanzen, the freshness of flowers or plants; die — der Farbe, the freshness of colour, floridness; die — der Wangen, the freshness, ruddiness of the cheeks; ihre Wangen verlieren ihre —, her cheeks their freshness lose. 2) something that refreshes, as with hunters, a springy place to which game repairs to drink.

Frischen, I. *v. tr.* 1) to refresh, to cool. Ein —der Regen, a refreshing rain; sich —, [with hunters] to drink. 2) to incite, to encourage, to cheer. 3) to improve by new touches any thing impaired. Ein gezogenes Rohr —, [with gunmakers] to new-rifle the barrel of a gun; die Hunde —, [with hunters] to purge the dogs. 4) to improve by new touches. Das Eisen —, to refine iron; die Fugen —, [with goldsmiths] to file the joints anew [in sodering]. 5) [in metallurgy] to restore or reduce to its natural state or to its metallic state. Das Blei —, to revive lead, [in modern chimistry] to deoxydize the oxyd of lead; *it.* to mix litharge or lead with copper in liquation. 6) [in mining] Eine Zeche mit Stollörtern —, to open communications between a pit and a stulm. II. *v. intr.* 1) [with hunters] to drink. ||2) —, or † frischiren [corrupted from the French *rafraichir*], to bait. 3) to pig, to farrow [said of wild swine].

Frischer, *m.* [-s, *pl.* -] [in iron-works] a refiner.

Frischerdings, *adv.* afresh, anew.

Frischling, *m.* [-es, *pl.* -e] a young wild boar of the first year, a young wild shoat. Ein übergegangener or übergelaufener —, a young wild boar of the second year.

Frischung, *f.* [*pl.* -en] 1) the act of refreshing &c. V. Frischen. 2) [with hunters] *a*) drink for dogs. *b*) a purge for dogs.

***Friseur**, [pron. Frisöhr] *m.* [-s, *pl.* -e] a hair-dresser, friseur.

***Frisiren**, *v. tr.* and *intr.* 1) to curl, to crisp, as hair, to frizzle, to dress the hair. 2) to trim [a gown with lace &c.].

Frisir-kamm, *m.* a dressing comb. —**mantel**, *m.* a cloak or cloth thrown over the shoulders whilst the hair is being dressed. —**mühle**, *f.* [with clothiers] friezing-mill. —**platte**, —**scheibe**, —**tafel**, *f.* [with clothiers] friezing-table.

Frist, *f.* [*pl.* -en] [appears to be allied to Rast] 1) a time in general. Zu aller —, at every time; in Jahres —, in the space of a year. 2) any limited time, a term. Eine Sächsische —, [in law] a term of six weeks and three days; eine doppelte Sächsische —, [in law] a term of four months; die —en verlängern, to give or to grant delay; die letzte or unerstreckliche or unversäumbare —, peremptory term. 3) prolongation of time, delay. Die zur Bezahlung einer Schuld bewilligte —, prolongation of days for payment; Einem — geben or lassen, eine Schuld zu bezahlen, to grant any one respite; einem Hinzurichtenden — gewähren or schenken, to grant or give a reprieve to a man about to be executed.

Frist-befehl, *m.* [in law] a dilatory precept. —**brief**, *m.* [in law] letter of respite. —**buch**, *n.* [in mining] a diary. —**gesuch**, *n.* [in law] a dilatory plea. —**gewährung**, *f.* V. —brief. —**mittel**, *n.* a palliative. —**tag**, *m.* day of delay, day of respite. Die —tage, [in commerce] days of grace. —**verlängerung**, *f.* prolongation of time [for the payment of a debt &c.] —**weise**, *adv.* at fixed times. —**zahlung**, *f.* a payment by instalments.

Fristen, *v. tr.* 1) to fix a certain term, to grant delay, to reprieve. 2) to put off to a distant time. Einen Tag —, to prolong a day; Einem das Leben —, to prolong a person's life; wenn Gott mir das Leben fristet, if God spare my life.

Fristung, *f.* prolongation. Die — des Lebens, the prolongation of life.

***Frisür**, *f.* [*pl.* -en] 1) hair-dressing. 2) trimming. 3) [*coiffure*] head dress. Sie haben meine or mir die — ganz in Unordnung gebracht, you have completely deranged my head-dress.

||**Fritt**, *m.* [-es, *pl.* -e] [from fritten = reiben] a gimlet.

Fritte, *f.* [*pl.* -n] [from fritten = reiben] [in glassworks, the matter of which glass is made after it has been calcined or baked in a furnace] frit. V. Glasfritte.

Fritz, [-ens or des —es, *pl.* -e] abbrev. of Friedrich. Fred Der alte —, Old Fred [so the king of Prussia, Frederic the Great, was popularly called].

Froh, [allied to frech, originally = lebhaft] *adj.* and *adv* pleased, glad, joyous, joyful cheerful. Ein —er Mensch, a joyous man; die —en Vögel, the cheerful birds. *Fig.* *a*) [= erfreut] — über unsern Sieg, joyous of our conquest; ich bin —, eine Gelegenheit gefunden zu haben &c., I am glad of having found an opportunity &c.; — gehorchen, to obey joyfully; er thut Alles mit —em Muthe, he does all cheerfully; —en Herzens, glad of heart; —, unser Leben gerettet zu haben, joyful of our life; einer Sache — werden, to enjoy a thing; des Lebens — werden, to be able to enjoy the pleasures of life; *it* to live in happiness. *b*) pleasing, causing joy or wearing the appearance of joy. Eine —e Begebenheit, a joyous or happy event; eine —e Nachricht, grateful or welcome news; ein —er Sinn, a cheerful mind; ein —es Gesicht, a glad countenance; er macht ein —es Gesicht, he looks cheerful; ein —er Tag, a gladsome day; ein —er Abend und ein —er Morgen krönte den vierten Tag, a glad evening and a glad morn crown'd the fourth day.

Froh-gefühl, *n.* pleasure of mind, gladness, gladsomeness —**gesang**, *m.* 1) a joyous song. 2) [in music] an allegro. —**müthig**, *adj.* and *adv.* gay, merry, joyous, jolly, jovial.

Frohheit, *f.* gladness, joyfulness, gladsomeness, cheerfulness.

Fröhlich, *adj.* and *adv.* 1) glad, joyous, cheerful, gay, merry, mirthful, blithe, blithesome Ein —er Jüngling, a jovial youth; ein —es Herz, a joyful heart; — aussehen, to look cheerful; die Truppen rückten — vorwärts, the troops advanced gayly, blithely, joyonsly or joyfully; Belinda lächelte und alle Welt war —, Belinda smiled and all the world was gay; soll ich meinen Most lassen, der Götter und Menschen — macht, [in Script.] should I leave my wine which cheereth God and man; seyd — über dem Abi-Melech, und er sey — über euch, [in Script.] rejoice ye in Abimelech, and let him also rejoice in you; ausgelassen —, frolicsome; — und guter Dinge seyn, to be of good cheer. 2) giving joy. —e Bothschaft, glad tidings; eine —e Nachricht, joyous news 3) expressing gladness, expressive of joy. —e Tänze oder Spiele, merry dances or plays, frolics; ländliche Spiele und —e Lieder, rural sports and jocund strains; ein —es Gesicht, a cheerful countenance.

Fröhlichkeit, *f.* 1) joyousness, joyfulness, jovialness, gayety, merriness, blithesomeness. Die — bei einem Mahle, conviviality. 2) act of pleasure, diversion. —en, sports.

Frohlocken (or **Frohlöcken**), *v. intr.* 1) to rejoice in triumph, to triumph. Ueber einen gestürzten Gegner —, to exult over a fallen adversary; frohlocke nicht über mein Elend, triumph not upon my misery; seines Glückes —, to exult at one's good luck; frohlocket dem Herrn, exult in the Lord 2) to tell triumphantly, or with exultation.

Fröhn, *m.* [-es or -en, *pl.* -e or -en] [the Goth. *frauja* signifies Herr; seems to be allied to Frau, V.] 1) a beadle or bailiff. 2) formerly, a judge.

Frohn-acker, *m.* land held in villein socage. ||—**altar**, *m.* [in the Romish church] high altar. —**amt**, *n.* 1) formerly, any public office. ||2) [in the Romish church] high or grand mass. —**arbeit**, *f.* 1) any mean personal service &c. to be performed for the lord of the fee or the landlord, socage. 2) hard work in servile occupations, ignoble toil, drudgery. —**arbeiter**, *m.* 1) a person that performs mean personal service of husbandry &c. for the lord of the fee or of the manor, socman. 2) one who labours hard in servile employments Literarische —arbeiter or —arbeiter in der Literatur, literary drudges. —**bar**, *adj.* and *adv* liable to personal service of husbandry &c. for the landlord —bare Güter, land held in villein socage; —bare Unterthanen, socmen. —**bauer**, *m.* a socager, socman, villein. —**bothe**, *m.* V. Frohn 1). —**bürger**, *m.* a citizen liable to work gratis for the town or any public establishment. —**bürgerarbeit**, *f.* clumsy work. —**dienst**, *m.* any mean personal service to be performed for the landlord either gratis or for a small recompense, average, villein socage. Gemessene —dienste, certain personal services to be performed on fixed days; ungemessene —dienste, personal services to be performed at the landlord's pleasure. —**fasten**, *n.* [in the Romish church] quarterly fasting-days, ember-fast. —**feste**, *f.* V. Fröhnerei 2). —**frei**, *adj.* and *adv.* exempt from mean personal services due to the landlord. —**freiheit**, *f.* soc. —**fuhre**, *f.* service rendered to the landlord by waggon or cart and horses. —**geld**, *n.* money paid in lieu of personal service due to the landlord, averpenny. —**gewicht**, *n.* a weight used at Augsbourg. —**gut**, *n.* land held in villein socage, socage. —**herr**, *m.* the lord to whom certain personal services are due. —**hof**, *m* a farm held in villein socage. —**knecht**, *m.* a menial liable to perform personal services in husbandry for the landlord, socager, socman. —**korn**, *n.* a reserved rent in corn paid in lieu of mean personal service due to the landlord, aver-corn. —**lehn**, *n.* fief held by villein socage, socage-tenure. —**leichnam**, *m.* [in the Romish church] Body of Christ. —**leichnamsfest**, *n.* [a festival in the Romish church] corpus Christi. —leichnams[fest]-Umzug or -Prozession, [in the Romish church] the procession on corpus Christi-day. —**leichnams-tag**, *m.* corpus Christi-day. —**leichnams-woche**, *f.* the week after Trinity-Sunday. —**loch**, *n.* V. Lohnloch. —**pfennig**, *m.* V. —geld. —**pflichtig**, *adj.* and *adv.* obliged to mean service for the landlord. —**recht**, *n.* a right or legal title to personal service which the tenant owes to the lord. —**tag**, *m.* 1) a day on which personal services of husbandry &c. are performed for the land-lord. ||2) V. —leichnamstag. —**vogt**, *m.* an overseer of persons performing personal service for the landlord. —**werk**, *n.* V. —arbeit. ||—**zins**, *m.* V. Kutscherzins.

Fröhne, *f.* [V. Frohn] [*pl.* -n] mean personal service which is performed for the land-lord or lord of the manor either gratis or for a small recompense, socage. Zur — arbeiten, to perform mean personal service for the land-lord. *Fig.* burden, duty, drudgery.

Fröhnen, I. *v. intr.* 1) to perform mean personal service for the land-lord or lord of the manor, to perform villein socage. 2) to perform service gratis, to perform free socage Einem —, to serve any one without recompense *Fig* [in contempt] Seinen Lüsten —, to indulge in sensual pleasure; Jemands Launen —, to humour a person's whims. 3) to labour in mean offices, to drudge. II *v. tr.* 1) [rather unusual] to oblige to perform mean personal service, to treat like a slave. ||2) to seize for debt &c., to distrain.

Fröhner, *m* [-s, *pl.* -] a person obliged to perform mean personal service for the lord of the manor, socager, socman. *Fig.* a drud

||**Fröhnerei**, *f.* 1) [in scorn] the act or do of performing mean personal service for lord of the manor &c.; [especially] *fig* drudger 2) public jail.

Frohsinn, *m.* [-es] a cheerful temper, dis sition or state of mind, good-humour, cheer fulness.

Frohsinnig, *adj.* and *adv.* beeing of a cheer ful temper, good-humoured, cheerful.

Frómm, [Old Scand. is *framr* = kühn u frei, Goth. *fram* = weiter, Engl. *from* = v wärts, Old Germ. *frumb* and Sw. *from* = vor Belongs perhaps to vor, Fürst, the Lat. *p pri*-mus] *adj.* and *adv.* 1) tame, peacea not wild, turbulent or refractory. Ein — Thier, a gentle beast; ein —es Pferd, a gen horse; — wie ein Lamm, as mild or gen as a lamb. *Fig.* Ein —es Schaaf, a good-natured fellow a sheep; ein —es Kin a good child; Ludwig der —e, Lewis debonair or meek 2) kind, benevolent, nignant. Du —er Gott! [as an exclama kind God! 3) godly, pious. Ein —er M a godly person, a religious man; Ei war — und gottesfürchtig, [in Script.] S was a just man and devout; ein —es a religious life; ein —es Leben leben ren, to lead a godly life; —er Weise, pi religiously; — betrachtete er das Kreu viewed the cross devoutly; *—e Wünsche, meaning, but vain wishes; ein —er B pious fraud; eine —e Miene, a devout *Prov.* Wer sich zu —en setzt, der steht auf, keep honest company, and hone shalt be. Fromm in the significations of brave, courageous, and useful is antiqua

Fromm-herzig, *adj.* and *adv.* h pious heart, devout. —**sinn**, *m.* pie ligiousness, devoutness, devotion.

Frömmelei, *f.* the assuming of a fa pearance of religion, affected piety, hy

Frömmeln, *v. intr.* to affect devout piety, to play the hypocrite. As a *v. ir* frömmelt hier, there is an air of metho

Frómmen, *v. intr.* to profit, to be of advantage. Was frommt es? what bo was frommt es Dir? what profit is it fo Das —, a profit, an advantage. Es is seinem —, it is for his benefit.

Frömmigkeit, *f* 1) the quality of tame or gentle, tameness. 2) good-nature ness. 3) kindness, benevolence. 4) piety, ness, godliness.

Frömmigkeitszünftler, *m.* tarian.

Frömmler, *m.* [-s, *pl.* -] Frömml *f.* a person who assumes an appearance a hypocrite.

Frömmling, *m.* [-es, *pl.* -e] a hy canting fellow, a pietist.

Frön, V. Frohn.

***Frónte**, *f.* [*pl.* -n] the forepart of an the part before the face. Die — eines the front of a house; **er stand vor der — seiner Truppen**, he stood in front of his troops; — **machen**, [in military affairs] to make face, to front; **das Heer, — machend gegen den Fluß**, the army fronting the river; **in —**, in front.

***Frontignac, Frontignan**, [pron. as in the French or † Frontinjack, Frontinjahn] *m.* [-s] [a species of French wine] frontinac, frontiniac.

***Frontispice** and **Frontispice** [pron. Frontispihß, or Frontispis and then *pl.* -e], *n.* [*pl.* -n] [in architecture] frontispiece.

***Fronton**, *n.* [-s, *pl.* -s] [in architecture] frontal, fronton.

Frosch, *m.* [-es, *pl.* Frösche] [perhaps allied to frisch = grün or kalt or sich schnell bewegend, of which derivations the latter seems the most probable] 1) [an amphibious animal] a frog. 2) [in farriery] *a*) lampas. *b*) barbles, barbels, barbes. 3) [a disease in children, a swelling under the tongue] ranula. 4) something prominent beyond the surrounding surface. *a*) [with coopers, the edge or brim of a cask or tub, formed by the ends of the staves] chime. V. also **Kimme**. *b*) that part of a bow or fiddle-stick on which the hairs are stretched and by which they are raised, the bearer. *c*) the sole-socket of a cloth-press. *d*) [in mining] a small piece of timber inserted in a hole by which a ladder is suspended *e*) [in carpentry] bracket. ‖ *f*) a bundle of stalks of corn.

Frosch=ader, *f.* ranular vein. —**apfel**, *m.* [a sort of apple] the reinette. —**biß**, *m.* [a plant] frogbit, the hydrocharis. —**bogen**, *m.* V. —**schnepper**. —**braten**, *m.* the roasted hind legs of a frog. —**brut**, *f.* V. —**wurm**. —**distel**, *f.* V. **Mariendistel**. —**eppich**, *m.* V. **Wassereppich**. —**fang**, *m.* the catching of frogs. —**fisch**, *m.* 1) [an animal of Surinam] frog-fish. 2) the lophius, fishing-frog, toad-fish or frog-fish. —**geier**, *m.* the honey-buzzard. —**gequäk**, *n.* croaking of frogs. —**hecht**, *m.* a species of pikes. —**jagd**, *f.* V. —**fang**. —**keule**, *f.* a hind leg of a frog. —**lache**, *f.* a puddle frequented by frogs, frog-pond. —**lattig**, *m.* [a plant] pond weed, frog-lettuce. —**leich**, *m.* the spawn of frogs. —**leichpflaster**, *n.* a plaster or salve made of frog's spawn —**löffel**, *m.* V. **Wasserwegerich**. —**öl**, *n.* [in surgery] frog-oil. —**pfeffer**, *m.* [a plant] marsh or celery-leaved crow-foot. —**quappe**, *f.* tadpole, bullhead, porwigle. —**sattel**, *m.* a saddle without a back. —**schenkel**, *m.* V. —**keule**. —**schnäpper**, *m.* a small bow for shooting frogs. —**schnecke**, *f.* a species of rock-shell [murex gyrinus] —**stein**, *m.* V. **Krötenstein** and **Schlangenauge**. —**wels**, *m.* a species of silure or sheat-fish [silurus batrachus]. —**wurm**, *m.* V. —**quappe**.

Fröschchen, ‖ **Fröschlein**, *n.* [-s, *pl.* -] [diminut. of Frosch] a little frog.

Fröschelring, *m.* [-es, *pl.* -e] [in mining] coin- or wedge-ring.

Fröschen, *v. intr.* to catch frogs.

Fröschling, *m.* [-s, *pl.* -e] V. **Frischling**.

Frost, *m.* [-es, *pl.* Fröste] [from friesen i. e. frieren] 1) [that state of temperature of the air which occasions freezing or the congelation of water] frost. **Vom —e beschädiget**, frost-bitten. *Fig.* *a*) coldness, frigidity, insensibility. **Der — des Todes**, the insensibility of death; **der — des Alters**, the frigidity of old age. *b*) want of affection, inability to excite feeling. **Ein Gedicht voller —**, a frigid poem. 2) sensation of cold in an animal body, chilliness. chill, cold. — **leiden**, to suffer cold; **der — im Fieber**, rigours. 3) frozen bodies. **Ein Pflaster für den —**, a plaster for frozen limbs.

Frost=beule, *f.* a chilblain. **Die aufgebrochene —beule**, an ulcerated chilblain, a kibe. —**bohrer**, *m.* a bore for boring holes into the frozen ground. —**geschwulst**, *f.* V. —**beule**. —**gesicht**, *n.* 1) a cold, frosty looking face. 2) *Fig.* a frosty look. —**mittel**, *n.* a remedy for frozen limbs. —**monat**, *m.* the month of December. —**pflaster**, *n.* a plaster for frozen limbs. —**punkt**, *m.* V **Eispunkt**. —**rauch**, *m.* congealed vapours in the air in frosty weather. —**salbe**, *f.* a salve for frozen limbs. —**schmetterling**, *m.* a species of butterfly [phalaena brumaria]. —**wetter**, *n.* frosty weather.

Frösteln, Fröstelн, *v. intr.* and *imp.* to be rather cold, to shiver a little with cold.

Frösten, [rather unusual] *v. intr.* and *imp.* to be cold, to shiver with cold, to be chilly. **Mich frostet**, I am cold.

Frostig, *adj.* and *adv.* 1) frosty, chilly. —**es Wetter**, frosty weather *Fig.* **Ein —er Scherz**, a cold jest; —**e Gedichte**, frigid rhymes; **ein —er Empfang**, a chill or cold reception; **einen Freund — empfangen**, to receive a friend with coldness; **der Vorschlag wurde — aufgenommen**, the proposition was coldly received. 2) susceptible of cold. **Er ist sehr —**, he is very susceptible of cold.

Fröstler, *m.* [-s, *pl.* -] a person very susceptible of cold, a chilly person.

Fröstling, [rather unusual] *m.* [-es, *pl.* -e] V. **Fröstler**. *Fig.* a cold, unfeeling person.

***Frottiren**, *v. tr.* and *intr.* to rub.

†**Frottirbürste**, *f.* flesh-brush.

Frucht, *f* [*pl.* Früchte] [probably from baren = bringen [bracht-e] 1) [in a general sense, whatever the earth produces for the nourishment of animals] fruit. **Die Früchte der Erde**, the fruits of the earth; **Gartenfrüchte**, garden-stuff; **Hülsenfrüchte**, pulse. 2) [in botany, the seed of a plant or the seed with the pericarp] fruit. **Eine falsche —**, spurious pericarp [as the cone, the spurious capsule, the spurious berry &c.] 3) [in a limited sense] grain, corn [while growing], crop. **Die — steht** or **die Früchte stehen sehr gut**, the corn has a good appearance; **die — einernten**, to reap corn. 4) the produce of trees, shrubs &c., fruit. **Früchte einmachen**, to preserve fruit; **Früchte**, fruitage. 5) the produce of animals, fruit; either the first rudiments of an animal in the womb, embryo, embryon, or the young of viviparous animals in the womb, fetus. **Die Leibes—**, the fruit of the womb; **gesegnet wird seyn die — deines Leibes**, [in Script.] blessed shall be the fruit of thy body; **eine unzeitige** or **unreife —**, abortion; hence in a more figurative sense, V. **Früchtchen**. 6) produce, proceeds. **Die Früchte eines Landgutes**, the proceeds of an estate. *Fig.* *a*) advantage, profit, good derived, fruit. — **bringen**, to profit; **das wird ihm keine Früchte bringen**, this will be of no benefit to him; **die Früchte des Fleißes**, the fruits of application or industry; [sometimes in an ill sense] **die — der Sünde**, the fruits of sin; **die Früchte der Unmäßigkeit**, the consequences of intemperance. *b*) effect, consequence, fruit. **Sie werden die — ihrer Werke essen**, [in Script.] they shall eat the fruit of their doings; **dies sind die Früchte jener unpassenden Ehen**, these are the product of those ill-mated marriages. *c*) production, that which is produced, fruit. **Die — des Gerechten ist ein Baum des Lebens**, [in Script.] the fruit of the righteous is a tree of life. ‖ *d*) moisture in the ground.

Frucht=abgabe, *f.* a tax on corn. —**acker**, *m.* a corn-field. —**ansetzen**, *n.* [in botany] the expansion of the fruit. —**ast**, *m.* a fruit-bearing branch. —**auge**, *n.* V. —**knospe**. —**balg**, *m.* [in botany, a univalvular pericarp, opening on one side longitudinally] follicle. —**band**, *n.* V. —**gehänge**. —**baum**, *m.* fruit-tree. —**baumzucht**, *f.* the culture of fruit-trees. —**beet**, *n.* V **Mistbeet**. —**behältniß**, *n.* V. —**gehäuse**. —**boden**, *m.* 1) corn-loft, granary. 2) [in botany] the receptacle [or base, by which the other parts of the fructification are connected]. **Ein einfacher —boden**, a proper or peculiar receptacle; **ein allgemeiner —boden**, a common receptacle. —**branntwein**, *m.* an ardent spirit distilled from grain. —**bringend**, *adj.* and *adv.* bearing or producing fruit, or corn, fructiferous, frugiferous **Ein —bringender Baum**, a fruit-bearing tree. *Fig.* **Gelder —bringend anlegen**, to put out money at interest. —**buche**, *f.* —**eiche**, *f.* a beech or an oak producing mast. —**erde**, *f.* fertile earth. —**erfüllt**, *adj.* and *adv.* fruitful, fertile. —**ertrag**, *m.* the proceeds of fruit or corn. —**essig**, *m.* vinegar obtained from fruit. —**feld**, *n.* a corn-field. —**garten**, *m.* 1) an orchard. 2) a kitchen-garden. —**gefilde**, *n.* fertile land. —**gehänge**, *n.* a festoon. —**gehäuse**, *n.* [in botany] the pericarp, seed-vessel. —**geländer**, *n.* an espalier. —**genießer**, *m.* usufructuary. —**genuß**, *m.* usufruct. —**gewinde**, *n.* V. —**gehänge**. —**gott**, *m.* the god of fruits, Vertumnus. —**göttinn**, *f.* 1) the goddess of agriculture, Ceres. 2) the goddess of fruits and autumn, Pomona. —**gülte**, *f.* a rent paid in corn. —**hain**, *m* a fruit-grove. —**haus**, *n.* a granary, a corn-house. —**haut**, *f.* —**häutchen**, *n.* 1) [the external covering of certain fruits or seeds of plants] husk. 2) [a cork-like wing on the top of some pericarps] the crest. —**hecke**, *f.* a thicket of fruit-shrubs. —**horn**, *n.* the horn of plenty, an emblem of abundance of fruits, cornucopia. —**hülle**, *f.* [in botany] V. —**gehäuse**. —**hülse**, *f.* [in botany] the legume. —**kasten**, *m.* a box or case for orange-trees &c. —**keim**, *m.* germ. —**kelch**, *m.* V. —**gehäuse**. —**knospe**, *f.* [in botany] gem, hibernacle. —**knoten**, *m.* [in botany, the rudiment of the fruit while yet in embryo] seed-bud, germ, ovary. —**korb**, *m.* —**körbchen**, *n.* fruit-basket. —**korn**, *n.* a grain of corn. —**kranz**, *m.* V. —**gehänge**. —**krone**, *f.* [Früchtekrone] the crown of a fruitful fruit-tree. —**lager**, *n.* [in botany] the fruit-bed [which incloses the fruit within its substance]. —**leer**, *adj.* and *adv.* fruitless. *Fig.* **Ein —leerer Versuch**, a fruitless attempt. V. —**los**. —**lese**, *f.* the gathering of fruits. —**lieferung**, *f.* a furnishing of corn. —**mahler**, *m.* a painter of fruit. —**mangel**, *m.* a dearth or scarcity of corn. —**mark**, *n.* pulp. —**markt**, *m.* corn-market. —**maß**, *n.* a measure of corn or grain. —**messer**, *n.* fruit-knife. —**muß**, *n.* stewed fruit. —**nießer**, *m.* V. —**genießer**. —**nießung**, *f.* —**nutzung**, *f.* usufruct. —**preis**, *m.* the price of corn or grain. —**reich**, *adj.* and *adv.* fertile in or abounding in corn. —**röhre**, *f.* [in botany] V. **Staubweg**. —**schnur**, *f.* V. —**gehänge**. —**schrumpf**, *m.* a loss or waste of corn [from long keeping in granaries]. —**schwanger**, *adj.* and *adv.* fruitful, fertile. —**speicher**, *m.* corn-loft. —**sperre**, *f.* a prohibition to export corn. —**stein**, *m.* [petrified fruits] carpolite. —**strauch**, *m.* a fruit-bearing shrub. —**stück**, *n.* 1) a fruit-grove. 2) [in painting] a fruit-piece. —**theure**, *f.* —**theurung**, *f.* the dearness of corn. —**tragend**, *adj.* and *adv.* fructiferous, fruitbearing, fruitful. —**wein**, *m.* cider or perry. —**wolle**, *f.* [also **das Federchen**; in botany] the down. —**zeit**, *f.* fruit-time. —**zins**, *m.* a rent paid in corn. —**zweig**, *m.* a fruitbearing branch.

Fruchtbar, *adj.* and *adv.* 1) producing fruit

or young, fructuous, fruitful. Ein —er Baum, a fruitful or prolific tree; ein —er Boden, a fruitful or fertile soil; —e Felder, rich land, fertile fields; —e Kornfelder, productive corn-fields; seid — und mehret euch, [in Script.] be fruitful and multiply; ein —es Weibchen, a prolific female; die Tauben sind sehr —, doves are very prolific; —es Holz, mastful trees; — seyn, to be fertile, to be prolific; auf eine —e Weise, fruitfully. *Fig.* Ein —er Gegenstand, a copious subject; ein —es Genie, a fertile genius; eine —e Einbildungskraft, a fertile or fecund imagination; ein —er Kopf, a prolific brain; ein Gehirn oder Geist, — an Plänen, a brain or mind teeming with schemes; — an Verbrechen, fruitful in crimes. 2) impregnating with fertility. Ein —er Regen, a fructuous rain; —e Ströme, pregnant streams; —e Witterung, fruitful weather; ein —es Jahr, a plentiful year; die sieben —en Jahre Egyptens, the seven fruitful years of Egypt; eine —e Jahrszeit, a fruitful season; — machen, to fructify, to fertilize.

Frúchtbarkeit, *f.* the state of being prolific, prolificness, fruitfulness, fertility, fecundity. Die — des Landes, the fruitfulness or productiveness of land; die — eines Bodens, the richness or fertility of a soil; die — der Felder, the fertility of fields; die — eines Thieres, the fruitfulness or fecundity of an animal. *Fig.* Die — des Verstandes, the fruitfulness of the brain; die — des Geistes, der Einbildungskraft, the fertility of genius, of fancy or imagination.

||**Frúchtbarlich,** *adv.* V. Fruchtbar.

Frúchtchen, *n.* [-s, *pl.* -] a little fruit. *Fig.* an ill-bred or ill-mannered youth. Er ist ein sauberes —, [ironically] he is a hopeful youth.

Frúchteknoten, *m.* [-s, *pl.* -] V. Fruchtknoten.

Frúchten, *v. intr.* to produce fruit. *Fig.* Was wird dies —? what purpose will this answer? mein Rath hat nichts gefruchtet, my advice has produced no effect; die angewandten Maßregeln haben etwas gefruchtet, the measures employed were effectual; zuweilen fruchtet unsere Arbeit nichts, we sometimes labour to no purpose; Arzneien, die etwas —, efficacious remedies.

Frúchtevoll, *adj.* and *adv.* rich in fruits.

Frúchtlos, *adj.* and *adv.* not bearing fruit, fruitless. Ein —er Baum, a barren tree. *Fig.* Alle Bemühungen waren —, all efforts were vain; ein —er Versuch, a fruitless attempt, an ineffectual attempt; — verschwendest du deinen Athem, you vainly waste your breath.

Frúchtlosigkeit, *f.* fruitlessness. *Fig.* Die — seiner Bemühungen, the vainness or inefficacy of his efforts.

***Fructuárius,** *m.* [- or ‡-arii, *pl.* -arien or ‡-arii] [in law] usufructuary.

Früh, [allied to the Lat. *pri*-or, *pri*-mus, and to vor, für &c.] *adj.* and *adv.* 1) happening, arriving before the usual or natural time. Ein —er Frost, an untimely frost; ein —er Schnee im Herbst, a premature fall of snow in autumn; ein —er Tod, an untimely or early death; ein —es Alter, a premature old age; die Uhr geht zu —, the clock goes too fast; er kam zu —, he came too early; warum kommt Ihr heute so —? why do you come so soon to-day? — oder spät, soon or late. 2) that comes, happens, or is done before the usual time of the day or of the year. — aufstehen, to rise early or betimes; Sie sind heute sehr — aufgestanden, you are very early up to-day; das —e Aufstehen, early rising; — Morgens, early in the morning; Morgen —, to-morrow morning; — anfangen, to begin early; der Gerichtshof versammelte sich —, the court met at an early hour; von — bis in die Nacht, from morning till night; heute —, this morning; ein —er Frühling, a forward spring; —e Blumen, forward flowers; —es Obst, early fruit; frühe[s] Gemüse, early vegetables. *Prov.* — auf und spät nieder, bringt verlorne Güter wieder, he that will thrive, must rise at five; he that has driven, may lie till seven; — zu Bett und — wieder auf, macht gesund und reich im Kauf, early to bed and early to rise, makes a man healthy, wealthy and wise.

Früh=apfel, *m.* summer-apple, hasting. —arbeit, *f.* work done early in the morning. —auf, *m.* 1) *[also Frühaufsteher] an early riser. ||2) [chiefly in a jocose sense] a child born too soon after marriage. —aufwartung, *f.* [the concurse of persons who visit a prince or great personage in the morning, das Lever] levee. —beet, *n.* [in gardening] hot-bed, shelving-bed. —birke, *f.* a variety of the common birch-tree. —birn, *f.* hasting-pear. —blume, *f.* 1) a forward flower. 2) perennial or common daisy. ||—blümel, *n.* V. —blume 2). —bohne, *f.* early bean. —erbsen, *pl.* early pease, hastings. —gebären, *n* [the act of miscarrying] abortion, abortment. —gebet, *n.* morning-prayer. —geburt, *f.* [the fetus brought forth before it is perfectly formed] a premature birth, abortion. —gerste, *f.* common barley. —gewand, *n.* V. Morgenkleid. —gewölk, *n.* easterly clouds. —glut, *f.* V. Morgenröthe. —gottesdienst, *m.* morning worship or service, matins. —hecht, *m.* a species of pike early spawning. —hopfen, *m.* hops early ripe. —kaffee, *m.* coffee taken early in the morning. —kartoffel, *f.* a sort of early potatoes. —kirsche, *f.* hasty cherry. —klug, *adj.* and *adv.* V. Altklug. —kohl, *m.* hasty cabbage. —kost, *f.* V. Frühstück. —lamm, *n.* a lamb early brought forth. —mahl, *n.* V. —stück. —messe, —mette, *f.* [in the Romish church] morning worship or service, morning prayers or songs, matins. —messer, —metter, *m.* a singer at matins. —möhre, *f.* hasty carrot. —nebel, *m.* morning mist. —obst, *n.* hasty fruit. —pfirsiche, *f.* hasting-peach. —prediger, *m.* morning preacher. —predigt, *f.* morning sermon. —regen, *m.* morning rain. —reif, *adj.* and *adv.* ripe before the proper or natural time, precocious —reife Früchte, fruits prematurely ripened; die —reifen Früchte eines Frühbeetes, the premature fruits of a hot-bed. *Fig.* Ein —reifer Verstand, an understanding prematurely ripe; ein —reifes Kind, a forward child. —reif, *m.* morning rime. —reife, *f.* precociousness, precocity, prematureness, prematurity. *Fig.* Die —reife des Verstandes, prematurity of understanding. —rettig, *m.* common garden radish. —rose, *f.* hasty rose. —roth, *n.* V. Morgenroth. *Fig.* Das —roth des Lebens, the dawn of life. —ruf, *m.* morning call. —saat, *f.* early sowing. —safran, *m.* V. Frühlingssafran. —schicht, *f.* [in mining] morning shift. —sonne, *f.* morning sun —ständchen, *n.* an entertainment of morning music given in the honour of any person. —stunde, *f.* morning hour, morning time. —thau, *m.* morning dew. —traube, *f.* hasty grape. —wach, *adj.* and *adv.* early awake. —winter, *m.* the early part of winter. —wirsing, *m.* V. Herzkohl. —zeit, *f.* 1) V. Morgenzeit. 2) *Fig.* V. Jugendzeit.

Frühe, *f.* 1) early time, morning time, dawn of the day. 2) V. Morgenröthe.

Frühestens, *adv.* earliest, soonest.

Frühjahr, *n.* [-s, *pl.* -e] V. Frühling 1, but not in the figurative sense.

Frühling, *m.* [-es, *pl.* -e] 1) [the season of the year when plants begin to vegetate and rise] the vernal season, the spring. Der blumige —, the flowery prime. *Fig.* a) [in poetry] year. Ein Mädchen, sechszehn —e alt, a girl of sixteen. b) the prime. Der — des Lebens, the spring of life; der — der Jugend, the prime of youth. 2) an animal, especially a lamb born early in the year; *it.* a child born too soon after marriage.

Frühlings=anmuth, *f.* the pleasantness of spring. *Fig.* the pleasantness of youth. —arbeit, *f.* labour done in the spring. —athem, *m.* vernal breath, vernal breeze. —baum, *m.* a young tree. —blume, *f.* 1) vernal flower. 2) common or spring whitlow-grass. —eis, *n.* ice in spring. —enzian, *m.* V. Junkerblume. —erve, *f.* spring bitter vetch. —feier, *f.* the celebration of the spring. —fieber, *n.* spring-fever. —fliege, *f.* May-fly. —gerste, *f.* spring-barley. —himmel, *m.* vernal sky. —käfer, *m.* V. [illegible]. —kleid, *n.* a garment worn in the spring, a spring dress. *Fig.* vernal bloom. —luft, *f.* vernal air. —messe, *f.* a fair in spring. —monat, *m.* one of the three spring-months, March, April, May, but chiefly the month of March. —morgen, *m.* a morning in spring. —nacht, *f.* a night in spring. —nachtgleiche, *f.* vernal equinox [opposed to the autumnal equinox]. —odem, *m.* [in poetry] V. —athem. —pflanze, *f.* vernal plant. —pracht, *f.* vernal beauty. —punkt, *m.* [in astronomy] the vernal point [where the sun ascends the North pole]. —regen, *m.* vernal rain. —reiz, *m.* youthful graces. —saat, *f.* sowing in spring. —safran, *m.* spring crocus. —schaum, *m.* V. Kukuksspeichel. —schmuck, *m.* vernal bloom. —schnee, *m.* a fall of snow in spring. —sonne, *f.* vernal sun. —sproß, *m.* spring-shoot. —sturm, *m.* vernal storm. —tag, *m.* a day in spring. —thau, *m.* vernal dew. —trieb, *m* 1) the tendency of the vegetable kingdom to shoot or sprout in spring. 2) spring-instinct, sexual propensity in spring. —trüffel, *f.* spring-truffle, white truffle. —vogel, *m.* vernal bird. —wetter, *n.* vernal weather. —wurm, *m.* —würmchen, *n.* spring-insect. —zeichen, *n.* [in astronomy] vernal sign.

Frühlingen, [unusual] *v. intr.* 1) to generate a spring. 2) to unite in sexual embrace before marriage.

Frühstück, *n.* [-s, *pl.* -e] breakfast. Ein gutes —, a good breakfast; das — einnehmen or zu sich nehmen or [less frequently] essen, to breakfast. *Fig.* † Das ist ihm ein —, he makes but a mouthful of it.

Frühstücken, I. *v. intr.* to breakfast. Noch einmahl —, to eat a second breakfast. II. *v. tr.* to take for the first meal of the day. Milch — to breakfast on milk.

Frühzeitig, *adj.* and *adv.* 1) happening before the usual or natural time. Ein —er Frost, an untimely frost; —es Obst, hasty fruit; ein —er Tod, an untimely death; —e Geburten, premature births; —e Kinder, children born before the time; Maßregeln, die man zu — nahm, measures prematurely taken. 2) *Fig.* [== early ripe or ripe before the usual course of time] premature, precocious. Ein —er Verstand, prematurity or precocity of understanding, precocious understanding.

Frühzeitigkeit, *f.* prematurity, precocity.

||**Fúcheln,** V. Fucheln.

Fuchs, *m.* [-es, *pl.* Füchse] [some derive it from the ancient Fahs = Haar, others from fa-hen = fangen. Most correctly, probably, it is allied to the North-English *faws*, Fr. *fauve* = gelb] [therefore, in general, the denomination of certain yellowish objects] 1) the fox. Ein Haufe Füchse, a sculk of foxes; Füchse jagen, to hunt foxes; der — steckt im Bau, [with hunters] the fox is kennelled or earthed; einen — aus seinem Bau treiben, to unkennel the fox; einen — prellen, to kill a fox by tossing it in a blanket; [with hunters] der — trabt, the fox is on the pad; der — rollet, the fox barks [when inclined to the sexual congress]. *Prov.* Schlau wie ein —, as cunning as a fox; ein — weiß mehr als ein Loch, he that will deceive the fox must rise betimes; ein schlafender — fängt kein Huhn, foxes when sleeping have nothing fall into their mouths; Füchse muß man mit Füchsen fangen, set a thief, to take a thief; wenn der — predigt, nehmt eure Gänse in Acht, when the fox preaches, beware of your geese; stirbt der —, so gilt der Balg, lebt er lang, so wird er alt, a certain game of forfeits. *Fig.* *a sly, cunning fellow. Ein alter —, an old fox. 2) *a*) the skin or fur of a fox. Ein Kleid mit — or Füchsen füttern, to line a garment with fox's skin. *b*) a chestnut-horse. *c*) a person with red hair. *d*) a gold coin. *Füchse haben, to have money, to be rich in money; *Füchse vorspannen, [in a bad sense] to bribe. *e*) [with dyers] Rother —, a reddish blue. 3) = Fuchsschwanz. *Fig.* *Den — streichen, to flatter any one. 4) [perhaps *Fig.*, or perhaps from some other origin] *a*) [with the students of a university] a student newly arrived at the university, a freshman. *b*) *a blunder. *c*) [at billiards] an antagonist's ball driven into the hazard without design, a lucky stroke. *d*) [in metallurgy] a lump of metal in the furnace that cannot be smelted. *e*) [in mining] Den — schleppen, to work lazily; den — mitbringen, to carry away ores. *f*) [in glassworks] the opening in the furnace, by which the fire ascends.

Fuchs-affe, *m.* a species of monkey with reddish hair. —**amber**, *m.* black amber-gris. —**balg**, *m.* the skin of a fox. —**bart**, *m.* [a plant] V. Bocksbart 3). —**bau**, *m.* kennel, earth. —**beere**, *f.* the bramble-berry. —**eisen**, *n.* a trap or gin to catch foxes, fox-trap. —**ente**, the teal. —**erde**, *f.* reddish sand. —**eule**, horned owl, long-eared owl. —**fell**, *n.* V. —balg. —**futter**, *n.* a lining of fox's skin. —**gans**, *f.* V. Erdgans. —**gebräme**, *n.* a facing of fox's skin. —**grube**, *f.* 1) the hole of a fox, kennel, earth. 2) a trap to catch foxes. —**haar**, *n.* 1) fox's hair. 2) *Fig.* red hair. —**hödlein**, *n.* [a plant] butterfly orchis. —**höhle**, —bau. —**jagd**, *f.* fox-chase, fox-hunt. —**jäger**, *m.* fox-hunter. *—**kopf**, *m.* 1) a head covered with red hair; also a person with red hair. 2) a sly, cunning fellow. —**koth**, *m.* [with hunters] the billot, fiants. —**list**, *f.* cunning, foxship. —**listig**, *adj.* and *adv.* cunning, foxish, foxlike. —**loch**, *n.* V. —bau. —**mist**, *m.* ordure of a fox, [with hunters] the billot, fiants. —**mütze**, *f.* a cap faced with fox's-skin. —**pelz**, *m.* a robe or coat furred with fox's-skin. *Fig.* *Den —pelz anziehen, to employ craft. —**prellen**, *n.* the cruel diversion of killing a fox by tossing it in a blanket. —**räude**, *f.* the scab of sheep. —**roth**, *adj.* and *adv.* having the colour of a fox, sorrel. Ein —rothes Pferd, a sorrel horse. —**scheibe**, *f.* [with furriers] three flat pieces of wood united at the top for stretching and drying the skins of foxes. —**schießen**, the shooting of foxes. —**schleppen**, *n.* [in mining] lazy working. —**schrot**, *n.* swan-shot [for fox-shooting]. —**schwanz**, *m.* 1) the tail of a fox, [with hunters, die Stange] brush. *Fig.* *Den —schwanz streichen, to flatter; einen —schwanz abgeben, to speak evil of an absent person, to backbite any one. 2) a name of several plants. *a*) fox-tail. *b*) meadow cat's-tail. *c*) common or purple willow-herb. *d*) the flower-gentle. *e*) the Italian panic grass. *f*) the common lilac. 3) [in seamen's lang.] a blockmaker's whip-saw. *—**schwänzen**, *v. intr.* to flatter. *—**schwänzer**, *m.* —**schwänzerinn**, *f.* 1) a vile flatterer. 2) back-biter, calumniator. *—**schwänzerei**, *f.* fawning, adulation, gross flattery. *—**schwänzerisch**, *adj.* and *adv.* fawning. —**schwanzgras**, *n* 1) V. —schwanz 2) *b*) 2) V. —schwanz 2) *e*). —**schwanzstreicher**, *m.* V. —schwänzer. —**schweif**, *m.* 1) the tail or brush of a fox. 2)* *Fig.* a kind of periwig. —**sucht**, *f.* the fox-evil, alopesy. —**thurm**, *m.* [in conchology] a species of whelk [buccinum turrita]. —**traube**, *f.* fox-grape. —**wurz**, *f.* V. Eisenhütchen 2). —**zimmer**, *m.* fox-yard.

Füchschen, ||**Füchslein**, *n.* [-s, *pl.* -] a little fox.

Füchselmännchen, *n.* [-s, *pl.* -] the squirrel-ape, the ring-tail maucauco.

Füchseln, I. *v. intr.* 1) to smell of a fox. 2) to hunt foxes. II. [rather unusual] *v. tr.* to treat with good humour and pleasantry or with satire, to rally.

Füchsen, *v. intr.* to smell of a fox.

Füchsen, *adj.* and *adv.* pertaining to foxes.

Füchsicht, *adj.* and *adv.* 1) fox-coloured, carroty. 2) smelling of a fox.

Füchsinn, *f.* a she-fox, vixen or bitch-fox. Die — rollt, [with hunters] the vixen goes to clicket [when inclined to the sexual congress].

Fuchtel, *f.* [*pl.* -n] [from fechten] [the word is obsolescent or, now, rather vulgar] 1) a broad sword. Einen mit der — hauen, to strike any one with the flat side of a sword. *Fig.* * and † Einen unter die — nehmen or unter der — halten, to keep any one under strict discipline. 2) chastisement with the flat side of a sword. Einem die — geben, to strike any one with the flat side of a sword.

Fuchtelklinge, *f.* [with sword-cutlers] a pliant broad sword-blade.

Fuchteln, I. *v. intr.* to brandish a sword thoughtlessly. II. *v. tr.* to strike with the flat side of a sword.

1\. **Fuder**, *n.* [-s, *pl.* -] [Low. Sax. Foer, Foder, Bohem. *Fura*, probably, therefore, from fahren] 1) cart-load, waggon-load. Ein — Holz, a load of wood. 2) a certain measure. ||*a*) a measure for meadows. Eine Wiese von zehn —, a meadow which yields ten cart-loads or waggon-loads of hay. ||*b*) [in mining] a measure for measuring ores, stones &c., generally consisting of three cart-loads. ||*c*) a dry measure for grain, containing from 36 to 72 scheffels [bushels]. *d*) a measure for wine which varies in different parts of Germany; it contains commonly 1200 bottles.

Fuderfaß, *n.* a cask or tun containing about 1200 bottles of wine.

2\. **Fuder**, *n.* [-s, *pl.* -] [= Futter] a sort of tinned iron-plate.

Fuderig, **Füderig**, *adj.* and *adv.* Ein —es Faß, a cask containing about 1200 bottles of wine; ein —er Baum, [in husbandry] a large piece of timber to be drawn by four oxen.

Fug, *m.* [-s] reason, reasonable claim, right, justice. Mit — und Recht, with authority or legal power; mit gutem —e, with good reason; ich beklage mich mit allem —e, mit gutem —e, I complain justly.

Fuge, *f.* [*pl.* -n] (from fügen) 1) the place where two bodies are united, joint, juncture; [with joiners] rabbet. Die —n an Schiffen werden mit Werg ausgestopft, the seams of ships are calked with oakum; die — zwischen zwei Steinen, [in architecture] the joining of two stones, commissures; aus den —n bringen, to put out of joint, to disjoint; hence figuratively, die Welt tritt or weicht aus ihren —n, the world is off the hinges. *Fig.* Die —n an der Hirnschale [more commonly die Nähte], the sutures or commissures of the skull. 2) *Fig.* [in music] fugue. Die einfache oder doppelte —, the simple or double fugue; eine — machen, to maintain a fugue.

Fugen-leim, *m.* [a thick odorous substance, used by bees to stop the holes and crevices in their hives, to prevent the entrance of cold air &c.] propolis. —**schnitt**, *m.* [with masons] an oblique cut on the side of a stone to fit it to another in a vault.

Fügebank, *f.* [*pl.* -bänke] [with workers in wood and coopers, a bench plane] a jointer, or shooting-plane.

Fügeblock, **Fügebock**, *m.* [-s, *pl.* -blöcke, -böcke] a wheel-wright's jack.

Fügeeisen, **Fügeisen**, *n.* [-s, *pl.* -] 1) [with coopers] the plane iron in a jointer. 2) [with glaziers] V. Fiedermesser.

Fügehobel, *m.* [-s, *pl.* -] V. Fügebank.

Fugeisen, *n.* [-s, *pl.* -] a mason's tool used in filling up commissures.

Fugen, V. Fügen.

Fügen, [allied to backen, biegen, Lat. *pag*-o (pango), Gr. πήγνυμι] I. *v. tr.* to conjoin, to connect, to join, to unite closely. Zwei Bretter an einander —, to unite two boards by a rabbet; die Faßdauben —, [with coopers] to unite the edges of staves; die Ochsen in das Joch —, to join oxen in a yoke, to yoke oxen. *Fig.* *a*) Sich in etwas —, to accommodate one's self to a thing; er fügte sich in die Umstände, he accommodated himself to circumstances; sich in die Nothwendigkeit —, to submit, to yield to necessity; sich in den Willen Gottes —, to resign one's self to the will of God; sich in jemands Launen —, to comply with a person's humour; [in music] eine Stimme, die sich in alle Abwechselungen der Töne fügt, a voice pliant to all modulations. *b*) to ordain, to dispensate, to direct. Wie Gott es füget, as God directs it. *c*) V. Hinzufügen &c. II. *v. r.* [of things, conditions] sich —, 1) to be suitable or becoming, to be proper. Das fügt sich nicht, it is not becoming. 2) to come to pass, to happen, to chance. Es fügte sich, it came to pass. 3) formerly, to betake one's self. III. [seldom used] *v. intr.* 1) Einem — (fugen), to humour any one; Einem in seinem Begehren —, to yield to any one's request. 2) to be of use. Es fügt (fugt) mir, it is of use to me. 3) to suit. Es fügt (fugt) mir, it suits me.

Fügewort, *n.* [-es, *pl.* -wörter] [in grammar] conjunction.

Fügig, *adj.* and *adv.* what occurs, what happens, used only in the compound words Gering—, Klein—.

Füglich, *adj.* and *adv.* 1) joining to another thing, fitting exactly close. 2) not causing difficulty or great labour, easy. Es kann — geschehen, it may be easily performed. 3) just to the purpose, adapted to the end proposed, convenient. Ein —er Wind, a fair wind; eine —e Antwort, a pertinent answer; er konnte es nicht — vermeiden, he could not well avoid it. 4) in conformity to law, justice or propriety. Es kann — geschehen, it may be done justly.

Füglichkeit, *f.* suitableness, fitness, pertinence, pertinency. Die — einer Rede, the pertinency of a discourse.

Füglos, *adj* and *adv.* [seldom used] unjust, unreasonable. Auf eine —e Weise, unjustly.

Fügsam, *adj.* and *adv.* 1) easily yielding to moral influence, pliant. — dem Willen des Volkes, flexible to the will of the people; ein —er Mensch, a person of a complying temper; ein —er junger Mensch, a pliable youth; ein —es Kind, an obedient child. 2) easily to be managed or handled.

Fügsamkeit, *f.* pliantness, flexibility, pliableness [of the disposition &c.].

Fügung, *f.* 1) the act of joining or uniting. 2) [the dealing of God to his creatures, the distribution of good and evil, natural or moral, in the divine government] dispensation. Die —en Gottes, the dispensations of God. 3) something effected by the providence of God, or proceeding from divine direction or superintendence. Durch eine — Gottes, by means of God's providence, providentially; einer Gefahr durch eine — des Himmels entgehen, to have a providential escape from danger. 4) the act of obeying &c. [das Sich-fügen]; obedience, submission. Die — unter den Willen Gottes, the submission to the will of God.

Fühlbar, *adj.* and *adv.* 1) [perceptible by the senses or by the mind] sensible, palpable. Ein —er Grad der Kälte, a perceptible degree of cold; eine —e Hitze, a sensible heat; auf eine —e Weise, feelingly; Einem sein Unrecht — machen, to make any one sensible of the wrong he did. 2) possessing great or nice sensibility. Ein —es Herz, a susceptible heart.

Fühlen, [seems to be allied to the A. S. *felan* = berühren, rühren, empfinden; Old Sw. *pela* signifies to touch lightly with the hand] I. *v. tr.* to feel, to touch. Einem Kranken den Puls —, or einem Kranken an den Puls —, to feel a patient's pulse; [in mining] das Gestein —, to beat rocks with a hammer for ascertaining their hardness or brittleness. *Fig.* *Einem auf den Zahn —, to feel any one's pulse, to sound any one's opinion, to try to know any one's mind. II. *v. tr.* and *intr.* to have perception by the touch, to feel. Die Feinheit eines Tuches —, to know the fineness of cloth by the feel; der Stoff fühlt sich rauh, fühlt sich glatt oder sanft [an], this stuff feels rough, or smooth or soft. *Fig.* to receive impressions by the senses or bodily organs, to be sensibly or deeply affected by, to feel. Alles was lebt, fühlt, all living creatures have perception; [proverbially] wer nicht hören will, muß —, he that is not moved by admonitions, must be moved by unpleasing sensations; Hitze oder Kälte —, to be affected by heat or cold; Schmerz —, to feel pain; Lust —, to be disposed, to be inclined; *it.* [= Wonne fühlen] to feel a delicious sensation; Linderung —, to feel relieved; einen Trieb —, to have a wish or desire; Liebe —, to be sensible of love; sein Herz fühlt Liebe und Dankbarkeit, his heart is impressed with love and gratitude; er fühlte die Schönheiten des Gedichtes nicht, he had no sense of the beauties of the poem. III. *v. r.* sich —, to have perception mentally. Wie — Sie sich? how do you feel yourself? sich müde —, to feel tired; er fühlt sich getroffen, he is conscious of having given any offence; *it.* he feels concerned by what was said; sich —, to feel one's self [to have a real and just view of one's self, or, of one's strength bodily or mental.].

Fühler, *m.* [-s, *pl.* -] 1) one who feels, feeler, or a person who possesses great sensibility. 2) an instrument used in feeling or searching, as the feelers of insects.

Fühl-faden, *m.* V. —spitze. —**farn**, *m.* [a plant] sensitive fern. —**horn**, *n.* [one of the palpi of insects] feeler. Die —hörner einer Schnecke, the horns, feelers or antennae of a snail. —**kraft**, *f.* faculty or power of perception, sensibility, feeling. —**kraut**, *n.* [Sinnpflanze, a plant of the genus mimosa] sensitive plant. —**los**, *adj.* and *adv.* not susceptible of emotion or passion, void of feeling, insensible. Ein —loses Herz, an unfeeling heart; —los bei den Leiden unsrer Mitmenschen, insensible to the sufferings of our fellow men. —**losigkeit**, *f.* want of tenderness or susceptibility of emotion and passion, insensibility. Die —losigkeit des Herzens, hardness of heart, unfeelingness. —**spitze**, *f.* [one of the palpi of insects] feeler. V. —horn.

Fühlig, *adj.* and *adv.* in composition, feeling, as Zart—.

Fühlung, *f.* V. [the usual word] Gefühl.

Fühlungslos, *adj.* and *adv.* V. Fühllos.

Fühnen, *n.* [-s] [an island in the Baltic] Funen.

Führband, *n.* [-es, *pl.* -bänder] leading-strings. V. Gängelband.

1. **Führe**, *f.* [*pl.* -n] 1) the act of carrying or conveying in a vehicle, carriage. Eine — thun, to transport something by a vehicle; it is also used in composition, as, Aus—, Ein—, Durch— &c. 2) that which carries, a vehicle, a carriage, coach, cart, or waggon. Mit eigner — reisen, to travel in one's own carriage. 3) a cart-load, a waggon-load. ||4) V. Furche.

2. ||**Führe**, *f.* [*pl.* -n] V. Fohre or Föhre.

Führen, [allied to bären = tragen, to the Lat. *ferre*, and to the Gr. φέρειν] I. *v. tr.* 1) to wear, to bear. Er führt niemals Geld bei sich or mit sich, he never carries money about him; leicht bei sich zu —, portable; ein Fluß, welcher Schlamm mit sich or bei sich führt, a muddy river; die Flüsse — trinkbares Gold mit sich, rivers run [with] potable gold; der Fluß führt Eis, the river is filled with floating ice; im Wappen —, to bear in the coat of arms; Preußen führt einen schwarzen Adler im Wappen, Prussia bears an eagle sable; er führt einen schwarzen Storch im silbernen Felde, he beareth argent a stork sable. *Fig.* Einen Namen —, to bear a name; er führt den Namen Collins, he goes under the name of Collins; einen Titel —, to have or to bear a title; etwas im Schilde —, to have some design in one's head; er führt Böses im Schilde, he devises mischief; schmutzige Reden —, to utter obscene language; zweierlei Reden —, to be double-tongued; er führt immer die Tugend im Munde, he talks always of virtue; Klage über etwas —, to complain of any thing; ein lustiges Leben —, to lead a life of gayety; sie führt ein einsames Leben, she leads a solitary life, er führte eine glückliche Ehe, he lived happily with his consort; einen guten Tisch —, to keep a good table; seidne Waaren —, to deal in silk. 2) [= handhaben] Er führt den Degen gut, he wields the sword well; den Bogen —, to handle a bow; den Pinsel gut —, to handle the pencil well; die Feder —, to handle the pen, to write, to draw up a paper. *Fig.* *Er führt eine gute Feder, he carries a good quill [he writes well]. 3) to direct the course or motion of any thing. Einen Blinden —, to lead a blind person; ein Kind an der Hand —, to guide a child by the hand, to lead a child; ein Pferd am Zaume —, to lead a horse by the bridle; ein Pferd in den Stall —, to lead a horse into the stable; Hunde am Seile —, to leash dogs; das Vieh zur Tränke —, to drive the cattle to water; die Kühe auf die Weide —, to take the cows to graze; einen Gefa[ngenen] ins Gefängniß —, to carry a prisoner to p[rison]; einen Verbrecher vor Gericht —, to bring [an] offender; in die Gefangenschaft —, to l[ead] into captivity; der Wind führte den Staub [in] die Luft, the wind raised the dust; den Wa[gen] —, to drive a carriage; einen Reisenden (= geleiten), der den Weg nicht weiß, to gui[de a] traveller who is not acquainted with the w[ay]; Einen irre —, to lead any one out of the r[ight] way, to lead any one astray, to mislead [any] one; Einen auf den rechten Weg —, to s[how] any one the right road; er führet mich zum [fri]schen Wasser, [in Script.] he leadeth me be[side] the still waters; und Judah kam gen Gilgal, [den] König über den Jordan zu —, [in Scripture] Judah came to Gilgal, to conduct the king [over] Jordan; er führte mich des Weges links, [he] directed me to the left hand road; führet sie vor uns, conduct them into our presence; sie führte mich in das Eßzimmer, she showed me into the dining-room; er führte seinen Gast in das Gesellschaftszimmer, he introduced his guest into the drawing-room; die Soldaten in die Schlacht und zum Siege —, to lead the troops to battle and to victory; das Heer —, to conduct an army, to head an army; er führte den rechten Flügel in der Schlacht von Heliopolis, he commanded the right wing at the battle of Heliopolis. *Fig.* *a*) to conduct, to carry on, to direct the concerns of. Die Geschäfte einer Familie —, to manage the affairs of a family; die Angelegenheiten eines Volkes —, to direct the affairs of a nation; die Haushaltung —, to keep the house, [in Script.] to guide the house; das Regiment or das Ruder —, to govern, to rule; er führte das Staatsruder, he was at the helm in the administration; die Aufsicht —, to superintend; er führt die Aufsicht über den Bau einer Festung, he superintends the construction of a fort; eine Rechnung —, to keep an account; die Rechnung or die Bücher —, to keep the books; einen Rechtshandel —, to carry on a suit in a court of law, to prosecute a right in a court of law; er führte meine Prozesse, he managed my law affairs; Krieg —, to carry on war, to wage war; das Wort —, to b[e] spokesman; für Einen das Wort —, to speak for another, to defend any one's cause; einen Beweis —, to hold an argument. *b*) [to [de]note the direction of an action] Er führet uns a[uf] den Pfad der Tugend, he leads us in the path of virtue; und führe uns nicht in Versuchung [the Lord's prayer] and lead us not into temptation; Einen auf das Eis —, or Einen um die Fichte —, to persuade any one to something by deceptive arts, to mislead any one; *Einen am Narrenseile —, to hold any one in hand; *Einen hinter das Licht —, to take any one in, to impose on or blind any one; Selbstprüfung kann uns zur Selbsterkenntniß —, self-examination may lead us to a knowledge of ourselves; Ruhm und Ehre — nicht immer zum Glück, fame and honours do not always render a person happy; dies führt zu nichts, this leads to nothing, to no end or conclusion; [zu] Gemüthe —, to impress on the mind, to en[force]; — Sie Ihrem Sohne die Gefahr des Müssigganges oder einer schlechten Gesellschaft zu Gemüthe, represent to your son the danger of an idle life or profligate company. 4) to form or build in a certain direction. Einen Zaun um den Garten —, to inclose the garden with a fence, to fence the garden; eine Mauer um den Hof —, to inclose a yard with walls; einen Graben um das Feld —, to ditch a field; einen Damm —, to raise a bank; einen Wall —, to raise a rampart; ein Gebäude &c. in die Höhe —, to raise a building &c.; man iese Mauer bis dorthin —, this wall must be arried thus far. 5) to have a direction towards ome place, to conduct to any place, to lead. Dieser Weg führt in die Stadt, this road leads) the town; welcher Weg führt nach Hampton? hich is the way to Hampton? 6) to carry or onvey from one place to another, either by eans of vehicles by land, or by ships in water. Waaren aus einem Lande in das andre —, to ansport goods from one country to another; Waaren aus England nach Frankreich —, to port goods from England to France; Trupp n über einen Fluß — [übersetzen], to transport oops over a river.

II. *v. intr.* [= eintragen] [in husbandry] Die ienen —, the bees convey the honey to the re.

Führer, *m.* [-s, *pl.* -] 1) a person who leads conducts, a guide, guider, leader or conctor. Der — eines Reisenden, the guide of traveller; der — einer Herde, a keeper of rds herdsman, herdman; der — eines jun a Prinzen, the governor of a young prince; : — eines Wagens, driver; der — eines hiffes, one who directs or governs a ship in r course, the steersman, a pilot, [in Script.] ternor. 2) a chief, a commander, a captain, ader 3) [with some German troops] standardrer, guidon; *it.* [mil. term] file-leader. 4) [in ural philosophy] conductor. 5) [with silkowers] the conductor of a silk-thrower's mill which the thread is conducted to the mill]. 6) [in al music] theme of a fugue.

Führerstab, *m.* a commander's staff, a ncheon.

Führerinn, *f.* a female guide, conductress. g. Die Erfahrung ist unsre beste —, experience our best guide.

Führfrohn, *f* [*pl.* -en] service rendered to landlord by waggon or cart and horses. V. ohnfuhre.

Fuhrgeräth, *n.* [-es] carriage.

Führig, *adj.* and *adv.* [with hunters] that may ied. Einen Hund — machen, to accustom a to the leash.

Fuhrknecht, *m.* [-es, *pl.* -e] 1) a driver's or er's man. 2) farming-servant.

Führling, *m.* [-es, *pl.* -e] a cask of wine t may be drawn by one horse.

Fuhrlohn, *m.* [-es] the price or expense of ying, carriage, cartage, waggonage.

Fuhrmann, *m.* [-es, *pl* Fuhrleute] 1) a goner, driver, coachman. 2) a carrier. Das werbe eines —s, the business of a carrier aggoner.

uhrmanns-herberge, *f.* carriers' inn. ittel, *m.* a carrier's frock, smock-frock. eitsche, *f* cart-whip, crop-whip —pferd, carrier's horse, cart-horse. —sprache, *f.* slang of carriers. —straße, *f.* V. Fuhrstraße. agen, *m.* a carrier's waggon. —weg, *m.* -, carriage- or waggon-road. V. Fuhrweg. wesen, *n* 1) what concerns driving and iages &c. 2) several carriages &c. together. ilitary affairs] Das —wesen bei einem Heere, waggon-train of an army. —winde, *f.* a nan's engine.

ührsattel, *m.* [-s, *pl.* -sättel] a waggoner's rrier's saddle.

ührschlitten, *m.* [-s, *pl.* -] a sledge or sled ransporting goods &c.

ührstraße, *f.* [*pl.* -n] V. Fuhrweg.

ührung, *f.* 1) the act of carrying, leading, lucting &c. V. Führen. 2) guidance, dion. Die — der öffentlichen Geschäfte, the agement of public affairs; die — Gottes, divine providence.

Fuhrwagen, *m.* [-s, *pl.* -] V. Fuhrmannswagen.

Fuhrweg, *m.* [-es, *pl.* -e] the high-way, carriage-road.

Fuhrwerk, *n.* [-es, *pl.* -e] [any thing that serves to carry or convey persons or goods, especially on wheels] carriage, vehicle. Die Kutsche ist ein sehr bequemes —, the coach is a very commodious carriage; Karren, Kutschen und anderes —, das auf Rädern läuft, carts, coaches and other vehicles that run on wheels; mit eigenem — reisen, to travel in one's own carriage; es fehlt bei dem Heere an —, the army wants carts and waggons; er nährt sich vom —e, he gets his livelihood by carrying or conveying persons or goods from one place to another.

Fuhrwesen, *n.* [-s] [any thing concerning carriages and the transportation of goods by land] amigation. Die Aufsicht über das — haben, to have the superintendence of the carriages; im Winter geht das — schwer, it is hard or difficult waggoning or carting in winter.

Fülle, *f.* [allied to voll] 1) [the state of being filled so as to leave no part vacant] fulness. *Fig.* Ich danke Ihnen aus der — meines Herzens, I thank you from the bottom of my heart. 2) abundance, plenitude. Er hat Geld die —, he has plenty of money; *er hat die Hülle und die —, he has plenty of every thing; er ist an — der Säfte krank, he is ill of plethora, of a redundancy of blood and humours; in ihm wohnet die — der Gottheit leibhaftig, [in Script.] in him dwelleth all the fulness of the Godhead bodily; die — der Gnade, the fulness of grace; ein Augenblick sollte ihn von der — der Gewalt in das Nichts des Privatstandes herunterstürzen, one moment was to plunge him from the plenitude of power into the nothingness of a private station. 3) [in cookery] V. Füllsel.

Füllen, *n.* [-s, *pl.* -] *dimin.* Füllchen [allied to the Lat. *pullus*, Gr. πῶλος, to φύω = erzeugen] [the young of the horse, ass or camel] the foal. Ein männliches —, ein Hengst—, a colt or horsecolt; ein weibliches —, ein Stuten—, a filly; ein Esels—, a foal of an ass, dieses ist das erste — dieser Stute, this is the first foal of this mare.

Füllen-garten, *m.* inclosure for foals to feed in. —stall, *m.* a stable for foals. —stute, *f.* a mare for breeding, a brood mare; *it.* a mare that has a sucking foal. —zahn, *m.* [the fore-tooth of a foal which is cast within two or three years] the milk-tooth. —zucht, *f.* the breeding and bringing up of foals

1. **Füllen** or **Fohlen**, *v. intr.* to foal.

2. **Füllen**, *v. tr.* 1) to make full, to fill. Ein Glas mit Wein —, to fill a glass with wine; füllet diesen Sack, diese Flasche, fill this sack, this bottle; sein Beutel ist immer gefüllt, his purse is always filled, well lined; sich den Magen — [= sich voll essen], to eat one's fill, to stuff or cram one's guts; seyd fruchtbar und mehret euch und füllet die Erde, [in Script.] be fruitful and multiply, and replenish the earth; der Wind füllet die Segel, the wind fills, swells the sails; einen Graben —, to fill up a ditch; gefüllte Blumen, compound or aggregate flowers; Gänse, Tauben &c. —, [in cookery] to stuff geese, pigeons &c. 2) [= schütten, gießen] to pour. Wasser in einen Krug —, to pour water into a pitcher; Bier in Flaschen —, to bottle beer.

Füll-band, *n.* [among joiners] a border of a door panel. —bier, *n.* beer with which the cask is filled up. —blatt, *n.* [among goldbeaters] empty books. —brett, *n.* [among joiners] V. Füllung 3). —dachstuhl, *m.* [in carpentry] the ridge of a roof with the rafters and girders. —eimer, *m.* [in saltworks] a pail or bucket for measuring the saltwater. —erde, *f.* 1) the earth with which the inside of a wall &c. is filled up. 2, V. Walkererde. —faß, *n.* [in mining] a vessel for measuring coals; *it* a basket for measuring coals; *it.* a basket for carrying the ore to the foundery. —gelte, *f* [in breweries] a pail or bucket with which the beer is poured out of the brewing-vat into the casks. —haare, *pl.* [among saddlers and upholsterers] hair for stuffing cushions and the like. —hals, *m.* [a large wooden tunnel by which liquor is poured into a vessel] tunnel, funnel. —horn, *n.* [emblem of abundance] the horn of plenty, cornucopia. —horngras, *n.* [a genus of plants, so called from the manner in which the flowers grow in the involucre like a horn of plenty] cornucopiae. —huhn, *n.* V. Zinshuhn. —kammer, *f.* [among sugarbakers, a large copper] a filler. —kanne, *f.* V. —gelte. —keil, *m.* [in carpentry] a wedge. —kelle, *f.* a ladle or trowel to fill with. —kleie, *f.* a certain quantity of bran which the millers take from the bakers besides the ordinary fee. —korb, *m.* [in founderies] a basket for carrying coals to the furnace —kraut, *n.* [in cookery] cabbages filled with farcemeat. —lager, *n.* [in breweries] large troughs on which the beer casks are put when filling; *it.* stilling, stand. —mund, *m.* V. Grundbau. —opfer, *n.* [in Scripture] the sacrifice of consecrations. —ort, *m.* 1) [in mining] a place where the buckets are filled. 2) [in breweries] a place where the casks are filled. 3) [among sugarbakers] a filler. —pfosten, *m.* V. Zwischenständer. —span, *m.* a thin piece of wood, steel &c., to fill up chinks with. —sparren, *m.* a principal rafter. —stange, *f.* V. Rührstange. —stein, *m.* a stone to fill up a gap in a wall with. —stückchen, *n.* [among joiners] a piece of wood to fill up a hole with. —wein, *m.* wine with which a cask is filled up. —wort, *n.* an expletive. Diese Verse sind voll —wörter, these verses abound with expletives.

Füllsel, *n.* [-s] [in cookery] stuffing, farcemeat.

Füllung, *f.* 1) the act of filling or stuffing 2) V. Füllsel. 3) a piece of board inserted between other pieces. Die —en einer Thüre, the panels or squares of a door.

Fümmelholz, *n.* [-es, *pl.* -hölzer] [with shoemakers] a piece of wood used for polishing.

Fund, *m.* [-es, *pl.* -Fünde] *dimin.* Fündchen, ||Fündlein, *n.* 1) the act of finding, the finding of something. Einen großen — thun, to find something of great value. 2) the thing found; *fig.* invention, discovery. Dieser — ist für die Wissenschaften sehr wichtig, this discovery, this invention is of great importance to science 3) [in fam. lang.] contrivance. Ein schöner —! a pretty trick!

Fund-beschwören, *n.* V. —eid. —buch, *n.* inventory. —eid, *m.* [in mining] oath of having first found out a mine. —gebühr, *f.* 1) V. —geld. 2) [in commerce] trovage, salvage. —geld, *n.* reward given to a person that has found something —grube, *f.* [in mining] a mine in which ore has been found. Die —grube strecken, to measure or survey a mine; die —grube forttragen, to dig in another place in search of ore. *Fig.* Dieses Buch ist eine reiche —grube von Gelehrsamkeit, this book is a rich source or fountain of learning, yields a rich fund of learning. —grübner, *m.* [in mining] 1) the owner of a mine. 2) he who works a mine by himself. 3) a miner. —ort, *m.* place where the mineral has been found. —recht, *n.* a right or claim arising from having found a thing; [in mining] claim of a person having found a mine, to the discovery of a mine. —register, *n.* V. —buch. —schacht, *m.* [in mining] the shaft by which a mine has first been found. —schein, *m.* a certificate of having found a thing. —schoß, *m.* V. Grundsteuer. —zahl, *f.* V. Findezahl.

*Fundament, *n.* [-es, *pl.* -e] foundation; [in architecture] basement; [in printing] V. Grund 3).

*Fundamental, *adj.* fundamental.

Fundamentalbrett, *n.* [among organbuilders] crossbar. —linie, *f.* [in the art of perspective] fundamental line. —stein, *m.* foundation stone.

*Fundation, *f.* foundation, establishment, endowment.

Fündelhaus, *n.* [-es, *pl.* -häuser] V. Findelhaus.

Fündelkind, *n.* [-es, *pl.* -er] V. Findelkind.

Fündig, *adj.* and *adv.* [in mining] V. Bauwürdig. Eine Grube, einen Gang — machen, to find or discover a mine, a lode.

*Fundiren, *v. tr.* to found, to establish.

Fündling, *m.* [-es, *pl.* -e] V. Findling.

Fünf, I. *adj.* [A. S. *fif*, Ice. *fimm*, is said to be allied to Finger, fangen] five. Die — Sinne, the five senses; es waren ihrer — or —e, they were five of them; über — Tage, five days hence; es ist — Uhr, it is five, or five o'clock; es hat schon — geschlagen, it has already struck five [o'clock]; — Viertel Ellen Tuch, a yard and a quarter of cloth; — Vierteljahr, fifteen-months; die — Bücher Mosis, the five books of Moses, the Pentateuch; eine Leier mit — Saiten, a lyre with five strings, a pentachord; — und —, je —, five and five, five at a time, by fives; — und zwanzig, five and twenty or twenty five; — und sechzig, sixty five; Geld zu — vom Hundert ausleihen, to lend out money at five per Cent. *Fig.* Er kann nicht — zählen, he knows not a from b, he can't say bo to a goose; — gerade seyn lassen, not to examine a thing closely, *prov.* to let well alone, *it.* to be too indulgent, to connive at a thing. II. 1) —, *f.* [*pl.* -e] or —e, *f.* [*pl.* -n], and —er, *m.* [-s, *pl.* -] the number or figure five; [at dice] a five or cinque. Alle — werfen, to throw all fives, two cinques; ein —er in Treff, a five of clubs. 2) —, *f.* [in piquet, a series or sequence of five, *Quinte] a quint. Eine — vom Könige, von der Dame, a quint from the king, from the queen. 3) —, *n.* [*pl.* -e] [little used] a number of five pieces.

Fünfarmig, *adj.* and *adv.* having five arms. —becherig, *adj.* [in botany] pentacapsular, quinquecapsular. —beinig, *adj.* and *adv.* having five legs, five-legged. —blatt, *n.* [in botany] V. —fingerkraut. —blätterig, *adj.* and *adv.* having five leaves, quinque-foliated, pentapetalous, pentaphyllous. Ein —blätteriger Kelch, a five-leaved calyx; eine —blätterige Hülle, a pentaphyllous involucre. —blumig, *adj.* and *adv.* bearing five flowers. [in botany] Ein —blumiger Blütenstiel, a five-flowered peduncle. —bund, *m.* a quintuple alliance. —doppelt, *adj.* fivefold, quintuple. —eck, *n.* pentagon. [in natural history] V. —strahl. —eckig, *adj.* and *adv.* having five angles or corners, pentangular, pentagonal. —eimerig, *adj.* containing five eimers [V. Eimer 2.]. —erlei, *adj.* of five different sorts. —erlei Weine, five different sorts of wine; etwas auf —erlei Art thun, to do something in five different ways or manners. —fach, *adj.* and *adv.* fivefold, quintuple. —fach zusammenlegen, to fold five times; [in botany] ein —fach geripptes Blatt, a fivenerved leaf; —fache Blätter, quinate leaves; das —fache, the quintuple; zwanzig ist das —fache von vier, twenty is the quintuple of four. —fächerig, *adj.* and *adv.* five-celled. [in botany] Eine —fächerige Kapsel, a quinquelocular capsule. —fältig, *adj.* and *adv.* V. —fach. —farbig, *adj.* and *adv.* five-coloured. —fingerfisch, *m.* [in ichthyology] the five-fingered fish, pentadactyl. —fingerig, *adj.* and *adv.* having five fingers, five-fingered. [in botany] Ein —fingeriges Blatt, a five-fingered leaf, pendactyl; ein —fingerig getheiltes Blumengefäß, quintal flower-horn. —fingerkraut, *n.* [in botany] five-leaved grass, five-leaf, cinque-foil. —flach, *n.* [in geometry] pentaedron. —flügelig, *adj.* and *adv.* having five wings, five-winged. —fuß, —füßler, *m.* [in poetry, little used instead of Pentameter] pentameter. —füßig, *adj.* and *adv.* having five feet, five-footed. Eine —füßige Bank, a bench with five legs or feet; ein —füßiger Stab, a staff five feet long; ein —füßiger Vers, a verse of five feet, a pentameter. —füßler, *m.* V. —fuß. —gericht, *n.* V. —ergericht. —gesang, *m.* [more usual, Quintett] quintetto. —getheilt, *adj.* divided into five parts, quinquepartite, five-parted; [in botany] V. —theilig. —herr, —herrscher, *m.* [one of five rulers, in whose hands the government is] pentarch, quinquevir. —herrenamt, *n.* —herrschaft, *f.* pentarchy. —herrlich, —herrschaftlich, *adj.* and *adv.* belonging or subject to a pentarchy or quinquevirate. Die —herrliche Gewalt, V. —herrschaft. —herrscher, *m.* V. —herr. —hundert, *adj.* five hundred. 5-hundertel, *n.* the five hundredth part. —hundertste, *adj.* the five hundredth. —jahr, *n.* [in ancient Rome] a space of five years, lustrum. —jährig, *adj.* and *adv.* 1) five years old. Ein —jähriges Kind, a child five years old. 2) occurring once in five years or lasting five years, quinquennial. Ein —jähriger Krieg, a war lasting five years, five year's war. —jährlich, *adj.* and *adv.* occurring once in five years, quinquennial. —jährliche Spiele zur Zeit der Römischen Kaiser, quinquennial games at the time of the Roman emperors. —kantig, *adj.* and *adv.* having five corners or angles. [in botany] Ein —kantiger Stengel, a quinquangular or pentangular stem. —kapselig, *adj.* and *adv.* [in botany] quinquecapsular, pentacapsular. —kirchen, *n.* Five-Churches [a town in Hungary]. —klang, *m.* V. Fünfte [in music]. —klappig, *adj.* and *adv.* having five valves. [in botany] Eine —klappige Samenkapsel, a quinquevalve or quinquevalvular capsule. —klauig, *adj.* [in natural history] pentisulcous. —lappig, *adj.* consisting of five lobes, five-lobed. [in botany] Ein —lappiges Blatt, a quinquelobed leaf. —mahl, *adv.* five times. —mahlig, *adj.* done or occurring five times. Ein —mahliger Versuch, an attempt or experiment five times repeated. —mann, *m.* V. —herr. —männerig, *adj.* having five husbands; [in botany] having five stamens, pentandrian. —männerige Pflanzen, pentanders. —monatig, *adj.* and *adv.* five months old; *it.* lasting five months. —monatlich, *adj.* and *adv.* occurring every five months or every fifth month. —paarig, *adj.* [in botany] having five pairs, quinquejugous. —pfünder, *m.* [in artillery] a five-pounder. —pfündig, *adj.* weighing five pounds. Eine —pfündige Kanone, V. —pfünder. —porte, —pforte, *f.* [among fishermen] a net consisting of five pieces with five openings. —reihig, *adj.* and *adv.* having five ranks or rows. Ein —reihiger Baumgang, an alley of five rows of trees, trees planted in five parallel rows. —ruderig, *adj.* and *adv.* having five seats or rows of oars. Ein —ruderiges Fahrzeug, a quinque-reme. —saitig, *adj.* and *adv.* having five strings. Ein —saitiges Instrument, a pentachord. —samig, *adj.* and *adv.* containing five seeds; [in botany] pentaspermous. —sang, *m.* V. —gesang. —satz, *m.* [in arithmetic] the rule of five. —säulig, *adj.* and *adv.* having five columns. Ein —säuliges Gebäude, a pentastyle. —schäftig, *adj.* and *adv.* 1) [among weavers] having five treadles. 2) [in architect.] consisting of, or having, five shafts [a column]. —schichtig, *adj.* and *adv.* having five layers or strata one above another. —seitig, *adj.* and *adv.* having five sides, pentagonal. V. —eckig. [in botany] Ein —seitiger Stengel, a pentagonal stem. —silbig, *adj.* and *adv.* consisting of five syllables. Ein —silbiges Wort, a word of five syllables. —spaltig, *adj.* and *adv.* [in botany] divided into five segments, five-cleft, quinquefid. Ein —spaltiges Blatt, a quinquefid leaf; ein —spaltiger Griffel, a quinquefid pistil. —spiel, *n.* [in music, more usual Quintett] a piece of music executed by five instruments or sung by five voices, quintetto. —sprachig, *adj.* and *adv.* written in five languages. —stimmig, *adj.* and *adv.* [in music] in five parts or composed for five voices. Ein —stimmiges Tonspiel [Quintett], a piece of music in five parts; ein —stimmiger Gesang [Quintett], a song executed by five voices, a vocal quintetto. —stöckig, *adj.* and *adv.* having five stories. Ein —stöckiges Haus, a house of five stories, a five storied house. —strahl, *m.* [in natural history] a sea-star of five rays. —stündig, *adj.* and *adv.* of five hours, lasting five hours. —stündlich, *adj.* and *adv.* done or occurring every five hours or every fifth hour. —tägig, *adj.* and *adv.* five days old; *it.* lasting five days. —täglich, *adj.* and *adv.* occurring every five days, or every fifth day. —tausend, *adj.* five thousand. —tausendste, *adj.* five thousandth. —thalerstück, *n.* a piece of five dollars, about nine florins, or fifteen shillings of English money. —theilig, *adj.* and *adv.* divided into five parts, five-parted, quinquepartite; [in botany] V. —spaltig. —vierein, *m.* V. —bund. —weibig, *adj.* [in botany] having five pistils, pentagynian. Die Ordnung der —weibigen Pflanzen einer Klasse, the pentagynia. —winkelig, *adj.* and *adv.* having five angles or corners, pentagonal, pentangular. [in botany] Ein —winkeliges Blatt, a quinquangular or pentangular leaf. —wöchentlich, *adj.* and *adv.* done or occurring every five weeks or every fifth week. —wöchig, *adj.* and *adv.* five weeks old; *it.* lasting five weeks. —zack, *m.* a five pronged fork. —zackig, *adj.* and *adv.* having five prongs, five-pronged. Eine —zackige Gabel, a five-pronged fork. —zählig, *adj.* V. —fach. —zähnig, *adj.* and *adv.* having five teeth, five toothed; [in botany] quinquedentate. Eine —zähnige Blütendecke, a quinquedentate perianth. —zehen, V. —zehn. —zehig, *adj.* having five toes, five-toed. —zehige Thiere, animals with five toes.

Fünfer, *m.* [-s, *pl.* -] 1) V. Fünf II. 2) a member of a body of five magistrates, quinquevir.

Fünfergericht, *n.* quinquevirate.

Fünfte, I. *adj.* fifth. Der — Tag, the fifth day; Kaiser Karl der —, the emperor Charles the fifth; das — Buch Mosis, the fifth book of Moses, Deuteronomy; zum —n Mahle, for the fifth time; zum —n, V. Fünftens. II. *f.* [in music, more usual Quinte] a fifth.

Fünft[e]halb, *adj.* four and a half. — halb Ellen, four yards and a half.

Fünftel, *n.* [-s, *pl.* -] a fifth part, a fifth. Zwei —, two fifths.

Fünftelsaft, *m.* [Quintessenz] quintessence.

Fünftens, *adv.* in the fifth place, fifthly.

Fünfzehn, [or Fünfzehen] *adj.* fifteen.

Fünfzehneck, *n.* quindecagon. —**eckig,** *adj.* [h]aving fifteen angles or corners. —**er,** *m.* the [n]umber fifteen; *it.* a piece of money. V. —kreuzer[st]ück. —**erlei,** *adj.* of fifteen different sorts. [—]**fach,** —**fältig,** *adj.* and *adv.* fifteenfold. [—]**füßig,** *adj.* and *adv.* having fifteen feet. —[j]**ährig,** *adj.* and *adv.* 1) fifteen years old. Ein [fünfzehn]jähriges Mädchen, a girl of fifteen. 2) lasting [fif]teen years. Eine —jährige Gefangenschaft, [a] fifteen years' captivity. —**jährlich,** *adj.* [an]d *adv.* done or occurring every fifteen years [or] every fifteenth year. —**kreuzerstück,** *n.* a [p]iece of money equal to fifteen kreuzers or five [pe]nce. —**löthig,** *adj.* weighing seven ounces [an]d a half. —**mahl,** *adv.* fifteen times. —**mahlig,** *adj.* done or repeated fifteen times. —[p]**fündig,** *adj.* weighing fifteen pounds, of [fif]teen pounds weight.

Fünfzehner, *m.* [-s, *pl.* -] 1) V. Fünfzehn[kr]euzerstück. 2) member of a body of fifteen [m]agistrates, quindecemvir.

Fünfzehnte, *adj.* fifteenth.

Fünfzehnt[e]halb, *adj.* fourteen and a [h]alf.

Fünfzehntel, *n.* [-s, *pl.* -] the fifteenth part, [a] fifteenth.

Fünfzehntens, *adv.* in the fifteenth place, [fif]teenthly.

Fünfzig, *adj.* fifty. Er ist — Jahre alt, he [is] fifty years old; von —en kam nicht Einer [da]von, out of fifty not one escaped; *er ist [in] den —en, he is between fifty and sixty [years [ol]d], he is fifty and odd.

Fünfzig=fach, —**fältig,** *adj.* and *adv.* [fif]ty-fold. —**jährig,** *adj.* and *adv.* 1) fifty [ye]ars old. 2) lasting fifty years. —**mahl,** *adv.* [fif]ty times. —**theil,** *n.* the fiftieth part, a fif[tie]th.

Fünfziger, *m.* [-s, *pl.* -] -**inn,** *f.* a per[so]n fifty years old. Sie ist eine —inn, she is [fif]ty [years old].

Fünfzigerlei, *adj.* of fifty different sorts.

Fünfzigste, *adj.* fiftieth.

Fünfzigstel, *n.* [-s, *pl.* -] V. Fünfzigtheil.

Fünfzigstens, *adv.* in the fiftieth place.

Fungit, *m.* [-en, *pl.* -en] [in natural history] [pe]trified sea-mushroom, spunge-stone.

Funke, *m.* [-ns, *pl.* -n] or **Funken,** *m.* [-s, [*pl.*] -, *dimin.* Fünkchen, ‖Fünklein, *n.*] [Icel. [fu]nis = Feuer] spark, sparkle, flake. Wenn [m]an glühendes Eisen hämmert, so sprüht [od]er wirft es —n, red-hot iron, when hammered, throws out sparks; —n von sich ge[ben], to emit sparks; —n aus einem Kiesel [sch]lagen, to strike, to elicit sparks out of a [flin]t. *Fig.* *Es sind einige —n or Fünkchen Geist [und] Witz in diesem Werke, there are some sparks [of] wit in this performance; er hat keinen —n, [kein] Fünkchen Verstand, keinen —n von Muth, [he] has not a spark of good sense, of courage; [es] ist kein Fünkchen Hoffnung vorhanden, there [is] not the least ray of hope. *Prov.* Aus einem [Fünk]chen —n kann ein großes Feuer werden, a [sm]all spark may kindle a great fire.

Funken=messer, *m.* an instrument for [me]asuring the force of electric sparks. —**sprü[he]nd,** *adj.* emitting, throwing out sparks.

Funkeln, *v. intr.* to sparkle, to twinkle, to [gli]tter, to glisten. Die —den Sterne, the twin[kli]ng stars; ein —der Rubin, a sparkling ruby; [sein]e Augen funkelten vor Freude, his eyes [gli]stened with joy; der Wein funkelt im Glase, [the] wine sparkles in the glass; das —, spar[kli]ng, scintillation; das — der Sterne, the [twin]klingt, scintillation of the stars.

Funkelneú or **Fúnkelneu,** *adj.* and *adv.* [in fam. or vulgar lang.] quite new, brand-new, brau-new. Funkelnagelneu, spic and span new.

Fúnken, *v. intr.* to emit sparks, to sparkle, to scintillate.

Für, *prep.* [allied to vor and führen] 1) für [obsolete = forward; now only used fig. in:] —und —, for ever and ever, continually. 2) für [denoting order] — das [or für's] Erste, Zweite &c., first, secondly, in the first place, in the second place &c.; Mann — Mann, man by man; er betrinkt sich Tag — Tag, he gets drunk day after day. 3) [denoting a more particular description of the person, thing or time one is speaking of] Ich — meine Person, — meinen Theil, liebe das nicht, as for me, I for one, for my part, I do not like it; was — Leute sind das? what people are these? was — ein Lärm ist das? or was ist das — ein Lärm? what noise is that? was — lächerliche Meinungen! what ridiculous opinions! die Handlung ist an und — sich nicht tadelnswerth, the action in itself is not blamable; er thut Alles — sich allein, he does every thing of his own accord, of his own authority; — sich leben, to live by one's self, to live a private life; er will nicht heirathen, sondern — sich bleiben, he will not marry, but remain single; — sich [in Gedanken] reden, to speak to one's self; der Schauspieler spricht es — sich [bei Seite], the actor speaks it aside; — heute ist es zu spät, for to-day it is too late; — jetzt, — dießmal, for the present, for this time; er ist — sein Lebtage, or — sein ganzes Leben, ein Krüppel, he will be a cripple for life, or for all his life; sich — beständig, or — immer, an einen Ort begeben or an einem Orte seinen Aufenthalt nehmen, to take up one's permanent residence in a place. 4) [noting a more particular relation to the subject or object of the sentence] diese Thür ist — dieses Haus zu klein, this door is too small for this house; er ist groß — sein Alter, he is tall for or of his age; er that es — die lange Weile, he did it by way of pastime, or to kill time; ein feines Gefühl — Ehre haben, to have a nice feeling or sense of honour; der Fleiß ist — den Körper nützlich, industry is beneficial to the body; die Unmäßigkeit ist — die Gesundheit schädlich, intemperance is hurtful to health; eine Guinee — eine Person bezahlen [at a dinner &c.], to pay a guinea a head; sie fürchtet — sein Leben, she fears for his life; ich fühle weder Liebe noch Haß — sie, I feel neither love nor hatred towards her; dieses Buch ist — deine Schwester bestimmt, this book is intended for thy sister; Bücher — die Jugend, books for the use of youth; — seine Kinder sorgen, to provide for one's children; ich werde — Sie thun, was ich kann, I shall do for you all I can; die Richter sind — ihn, the judges are for him; der Adel hat sich — den König erklärt, the nobility have declared for the king; es läßt sich Manches — und gegen diese Sache sagen, a great deal may be said for and against this affair, there is much to be said on both sides; ein Beweis — die Unsterblichkeit der Seele, a proof or evidence for the immortality of the soul; solche Vergnügungen sind nur — die Reichen, such pleasures or amusements are only for the rich; es ist eine große Schwachheit — einen Philosophen, it is a great weakness for a philosopher; was — Sie gut ist, ist es [darum] nicht — mich, what is good for you, is not so for me; es wird — Alle hinreichen, there will be enough for all. 5) [after some verbs, as halten, ansehen, schätzen, nehmen &c. für is used instead of the mere accusative] er hielt es — einen Schimpf, he looked upon it, he took it, considered it as an affront; er sieht es — eine Last an, he regards it as a burden; er will or möchte — reich, — gelehrt gehalten werden or gelten, he wishes to pass for rich, for learned; ich halte es — meine Pflicht, I think or take it to be my duty; ich halte es — eine große Ehre, Ihr Freund zu seyn, I look upon it as a great honour, I account it a great honour, to be your friend; ich halte es — wahr, weil Sie es sagen, I believe it to be true, since you say so; er nahm es — Ernst, he took it in earnest; er will ihn nicht — seinen Sohn erkennen, he will not acknowledge him for his son; — wen sehen Sie mich an? whom do you take me for? halten Sie es — nöthig? do you think or believe it necessary? ich halte or finde es — gut, daß Sie dieses thun, I think it advisable for you to do so; man hat mir — gewiß gesagt, I have been told for certain; ich nehme es — empfangen an, ich nehme den guten Willen — die That, I take the will for the deed, I accept of the inclination for the performance 6) [noting an equivalent substitution of persons and things] in the place of, instead of. Dieser Offizier dient — seinen Bruder, this officer serves for his brother; er hat einen Andern — sich geschickt, he has sent another in his place; ich will — Sie bezahlen, I will pay for you; ein Sachwalter ist ermächtigt, — einen Andern zu handeln, an attorney is empowered to act for another; ich stehe — ihn, ich bin — ihn Bürge, I am surety or bail for him; ein Wort — das andere setzen, to put one word instead of or for another; ich sage es Ihnen ein — alle Mahl, ein Mahl — alle Mahle, I tell you so once for all; — Bezahlung annehmen, to take in payment; er gab sein Pferd — [= um den Preis von] hundert Pfund her, he sold his horse for a hundred pounds; was bekomme ich — meine [= als Preis meiner] Mühe? what am I to have for my pains? ist dieß die Belohnung — meine Dienste? is this the reward for my services?

‡**Fürbaß,** *adv.* forward, farther.

‡ and ‖**Fürbieten,** V. Citiren 1).

Fürbitte, *f.* [*pl.* -n] prayer or petition in behalf of another, intercession. Eine — für Einen thun, einlegen, to plead in favour of any one, to intercede for any one; eine öffentliche — in der Kirche, a public prayer at church; die — der Heiligen, the intercession or mediation of the saints.

Fürbitten, V. Fürbitte thun.

Fürbitter, *m.* [-s, *pl.* -] intercessor, mediator, pleader.

Fürbitterinn, *f.* a female mediator, mediatrix, mediatress.

Fürbittschreiben, *n.* [-s, *pl.* -] a letter of intercession.

‡ and ‖**Fürbot,** *n.* [-es, *pl.* -e] V. Citation 2).

Fúrche, *f.* [*pl.* -n] [Lat. *porca;* allied to the French *percer*, from the Germ. fahren] properly any long narrow trench or channel on the surface of any thing. Die —n auf der Stirne, the furrows, wrinkles of the forehead; obgleich die Zeit manche — in dieses Gesicht gepflügt hat, though time has ploughed that face with many furrows; die —n in der Hand, the lines in the hand; [in anatomy] die —n auf der Knochenhaut, the furrows in the periosteum; [in farriery] die —n am Gaumen des Pferdes, the notches or ridges in a horse's mouth; die —n an einer Nadel, the grooves of a needle; [chiefly] a furrow made by a plough; diese —n sind nicht tief genug, these furrows are not deep enough; die letzte —, die Scheide—, the last ridge of the furrows; —n machen, ziehen, to make, to cut furrows, to furrow; *it.* a ridge of land left unploughed between furrows or at the end of a field, a balk.

Furchen-eis, *n.* ice found between the furrows. **—rain**, *m.* ridge between two furrows. **—weise**, *adv.* in furrows, like furrows.

Fúrchen, *v. tr.* to make furrows in, to furrow. Ein gleichgefurchter Acker, a field well furrowed; [in poetry] das Meer —, to plough the main, to furrow the deep; die Schiffe, die sich eine Bahn —, the ships that cleave their way; die Stirn — [in anger &c.], to knit one's brow; der Kummer furchet ihm die Stirne, sorrow furrows his brow, V. Durch—; [in botany] gefurchte Blätter, furrowed leaves.

Furchgenoß, Furchnachbar, *m.* the possessor of a field contiguous to that of another man, from which it is only separated by a balk.

Fúrcht, *f.* [Dutch *vrucht*. Dan. Frygt, appears to be allied to the Gr. φρίσσω = schaudern] fear apprehension. Eine große —, great fear, dread; die — vor dem Tode, die Todes—, the fear of death; die — vor Geistern, the fear, dread of spectres; die — Gottes, Gottes—, the fear of God, godly fear; eine knechtische —, a slavish fear; die kindliche —, filial fear, die — vor dem Mißfallen Gottes, the dread of the divine displeasure; in der — seyn, in — stehen, — haben, empfinden, to be or stand in fear, to be afraid, to fear, V. Sich fürchten; vor — erbleichen, to turn pale with fear; vor — zittern, to tremble with fear; Einen in — setzen, Einem — einjagen or machen, — bei Einem erregen, to put any one in fear, to make any one afraid, to frighten any one; in — gerathen, von — ergriffen werden, to be struck or seized with fear; ein Mann ohne —, a fearless man; Bayard, der Ritter ohne — und Tadel, Bayard, the knight without fear and reproach; Alles in — und Schrecken setzen, to carry terror every-where; Einen in — erhalten, to keep any one in awe; zwischen — und Hoffnung schweben, to fluctuate between hope and fear; aus —, überrascht or ertappt zu werden, for fear of being surprised; aus — vor einem Unfalle, for fear of any accident; aus — vor Dieben kommt er nie spät nach Hause, he never comes home late, for fear of robbers.

Fúrchtbar, I. *adj.* dreadful, formidable, frightful, terrible. Ein —er Mann, Feind, a formidable man, enemy; ein —es Ungewitter, a dreadful storm; er ist Jedermann —, he is dreaded by every body. II. *adv.* dreadfully, formidably, frightfully, terribly. SYN. V. Fürchterlich.

Fúrchtbarkeit, *f.* formidableness, dreadfulness.

Fürchten, [V. Furcht] I. *v. tr.* to fear, to be afraid of, to apprehend. Den Tod —, to fear death, to be afraid of death; wir haben Ursache, die Bestrafung unserer Sünden zu —, we have reason to fear the punishment of our sins; einen Unfall —, to fear, to apprehend an accident; Gott —, to fear God. *Prov.* Ein gebranntes Kind fürchtet das Feuer, a burnt child dreads the fire II *v. intr.* to fear, to be afraid. Ich fürchte für ihn, I fear for him; er fürchtet, entdeckt zu werden, he is afraid of being discovered; er fürchtet, die Sache möchte an den Tag kommen, he is afraid, lest the matter might come to light; es ist zu —, daß &c., it is to be feared that &c.; ich fürchte nicht, daß er es zu thun wagt, I do not fear, that he will dare to do it; er fürchtet, seine Frau möchte sterben, he fears that his wife should die. III. *v. r.* sich —, to be afraid, to stand in fear. Er fürchtet sich vor dem Zorne Gottes, he dreads the anger of God; sich vor der Strafe —, to be afraid of being punished; sich vor dem Donner —, to be afraid of thunder; er fürchtet sich vor seinem eigenen Schatten, he is afraid of his own shadow; sich vor Einem —, to be afraid of any one, to stand in fear, in awe of any one. SYN. Fürchten, Scheuen. Fürchten [originally = schauern, zittern] expresses merely the sensation excited by the apprehension of some impending evil. In Scheuen [originally = fliehen] the consequence is also implied, that one avoids the object by which the fear has been excited.

Fürchterlich, I. *adj.* terrible, dreadful, formidable, frightful. Ein —er Traum, a horrible dream; ein —er Anblick, a hideous sight or spectacle; ein —es Geschrei erheben, to raise a frightful scream, to cry out horribly; er stieß einen —en Fluch aus, he rapped out a horrible oath; eine —e That, a horrible or shocking deed, —e Gestalten, hideous forms or shapes. *Fig.* [in fam. or rather vulg. lang.] = extraordinary. Dieser Lord macht einen —en Aufwand, this lord spends a horrible deal of money, lives very expensively. II. *adv.* terribly, dreadfully, formidably, frightfully. Er schrie —, he cried horribly; es donnerte —, it thundered terribly; es regnet —, it rains as fast as it can pour, very hard. *Fig.* [in fam. or rather vulg. lang.] Es ist — schlechtes Wetter, it is terrible bad weather; er säuft —, he drinks very hard, he drinks like a fish; er ist — langweilig im Erzählen, he is terribly tedious in relating a story; sie ist — häßlich, she is horribly ugly. SYN. Fürchterlich, Furchtbar. Das Fürchterliche [the frightful] excites a more violent emotion than das Furchtbare [the fearful or dreadful]. Alexander by his military skill and the victories he obtained in consequence, was [ein furchtbarer Gegner] a formidable opponent to his enemies, and Attila by his hideous form and his cruelties that inspired every one with dread, [ein fürchterlicher Barbar] a terrible barbarian.

Fürchterlichkeit, *f.* terribleness, dreadfulness, formidableness.

Fúrchtlos, I. *adj.* free from fear, fearless, bold, courageous, intrepid, undaunted. Ein —er Krieger, a fearless, intrepid warrior. II. *adv.* without fear, fearlessly, intrepidly. Tapfere Männer setzen sich — den furchtbarsten Gefahren aus, brave men fearlessly expose themselves to the most formidable dangers.

Fúrchtlosigkeit, *f.* fearlessness, intrepidity.

Fúrchtsam, I. *adj.* 1) [as a quality of men and animals] fearful, timid, timorous Die Frauen sind von Natur —, women are naturally timorous; armselig ist der Triumph über den —en Hasen, poor is the triumph o'er the timid hare. *Fig.* *Er ist ein —er Hase, he is a chicken-hearted, faint-hearted fellow; — machen, to make afraid, to alarm, to dishearten. 2) [as a quality of a thing] cowardly, timid. Einen —en Rath geben, to give a cowardly counsel; eine —e Tugend, timid virtue; ein —es Betragen, a timid, pusillanimous conduct; eine —e Schreibart, a mean, cowardly style. II. *adv.* fearfully, timidly, timorously, cowardly. SYN. V. Schüchtern.

Fúrchtsamkeit, *f.* fearfulness, timidity, timorousness, cowardliness, faint-heartedness.

‡**Fürder**, *adv.* V. Fürbaß.

Fürderlich, Fürdern, V. Förderlich, Fördern.

‡ and ||**Fürgang**, *m.* V. Vorgang.

***Fürie**, *f.* [*pl.* -n] 1) V. Wuth. 2) a furious, turbulent woman, a fury; [in the Greek and Roman mythology] the three furies [Alecto, Megaera and Tisyphone]. 3) [in natural history] V. Fadenwurm, Tollwurm.

***Furier**, *m.* [-s, *pl.* -e] quarter-master, sergeant.

||**Furierschütz**, *m.* an officer's servant.

Fürlieb, *adv.* [it is only used with nehmen, in fam. lang.] — nehmen, mit etwas — nehmen, to be satisfied with a thing, to put up with. Mit ärmlicher Bewirthung — nehmen, to put up with poor entertainment; er ist nicht ekel, er nimmt mit Allem —, he is not nice, he puts up with any thing, makes shift with any thing

‡ and ||**Fürliebmeister**, *m.* V. Ober[...]meister.

***Furnir**, *m.* [-es, *pl.* -e] [among cabinet-makers] a thin piece of wood for veneering, inlay, veneer. V. also Einlegeholz.

Furnirhobel, *m.* a cabinet-maker's plane.

***Furniren**, *v. tr.* [among cabinet-makers] to inlay, to veneer. Furnirte Arbeit, inlaid work, marquetry.

***Furnirer**, *m.* [-s, *pl.* -] he who veneers or inlays, inlayer.

***Furrage**, [pron. Furrahsche] *f.* forage. V. also Pferdefutter.

***Furragiren**, [pron. Furraschihren] *v. intr.* [in military affairs] to forage. Das —, foraging, forage; auf's — gehen, to go a foraging.

‡**Fürschrift**, *f.* V. Vorschrift.

Fürsorge, *f.* V. Vorsorge.

Fürsorger, *m.* V. Vorsorger.

||**Fürsprach**, *m* [-s, *pl.* -e] V. Fürsprecher 1).

Fürsprache, *f.* [*pl.* -n] 1) [in law] the defence of any one or any cause by attorney. 2) V. Fürbitte.

Fürsprechen, *ir. v. intr.* V. Fürbitte th[...]

Fürsprecher, *m.* [-s, *pl.* -] 1) [in law] attorney. V. Anwalt, Sachwalter. 2) V. Fürbitter.

||**Fürspruch**, *m.* [-es] V. Fürsprache.

Fürst, *m.* [-en, *pl.* -en] [Old Germ. *furisto*, allied to für = vor] 1) a prince, a sovereign; also a member of the former German Empire or of the present German Confederation, in rank next to a duke. Kaiser, Könige, Herzoge &c. sind —en, emperors, kings, dukes &c. are princes; regierender —, reigning prince; ein unumschränkter —, a sovereign prince; ein weltlicher —, a [...] prince; er besitzt die Gunst des —en, he is in the prince's favour; *er lebt wie ein —, he lives like a prince. V. Groß—, Kur—, Landes—, Reichs—. 2) [one of the highest order of nobility] prince. Der König hat ihn zum —en gemacht, oder erhoben, the king has made him a prince, has elevated or raised him to the rank of a prince; der — Kaunitz &c., the prince of Kaunitz &c.

Fürst-abt, —bischof, *m.* [gefürsteter Abt &c.] an abbot, a bishop raised to the dignity of a prince.

Fürsten, *pl.* of Fürst.

Fürsten-apfel, *m.* a species of apple. **—bank**, *f.* the bench of princes at the diet. **—birn**, *f.* bergamot. **—braut**, *f.* 1) the bride of a prince. 2) a betrothed princess. **—brief**, *m.* letters patent conferring the dignity of prince. **—bund**, *m.* a league, alliance, or confederation of princes. Der Deutsche —bund, the German confederation. **—dienst**, *m.* employment, office in the service of a prince. **—glanz**, *m.* a princely splendour. **—größe**, *f.* princely grandeur. **—gruft**, *f.* tomb or vault of princes. **—gut**, *n.* a prince's domain. V. Kammergut, Krongut. **—haus**, *n.* 1) the palace of a prince. 2) the family of a prince, sovereign house. **—hof**, *m.* court of a prince. **—hut**, *m.* a hat or cap lined with ermine, formerly the badge of a prince; a prince's coronet. **—kind**, *n.* the child of a prince. V. Prinz. **—knecht**, *m.* the servile flatterer of a prince. **—kro**[...]

:1) a crown worn by sovereign princes. 2) [in lazonry] a prince's coronet. —leben, *n.* the ife of a prince. *Fig.* *good living. Er führt ein —leben, he lives like a prince. —lehen, *n.* a princely fee or fief. —mantel, *m.* mantle or loak of a prince as a badge of his dignity. —mäßig, *adj.* and *adv.* becoming a prince, princelike, princely. Ein —mäßiges Geschenk, princely gift; er lebt —mäßig, he lives like prince. —pracht, *f.* princely magnificence r splendour. —rath, *m.* the council of princes at the former German diet. —recht, *n.* ight or prerogative of princes. —ruf, *m.* [in nting] a signal given with the bugle-horn to adertise the prince where the chase is. —saal, *m.* hall or room where princes assemble; *it* [fig.] a rincely hall or room. —schnepfe, *f.* V Heerschnepfe, Feldschnepfe. —schule, *f.* 1) a hool or college founded by a prince 2) ollege for young princes. —sitz, *m.* residence of a prince; *it.* V. —stuhl. —sohn, . the son of a prince, a prince. —staat, *m.* V. -thum. —stamm, *m.* V. —haus 2). —stand, . 1) the condition and dignity of a prince, rinceliness. In den —stand erhoben werden, be raised or elevated to the dignity of a rince; im —stande ist man nicht immer glücklich, princes are not always happy. 2) the order f princes, as members of the former German mpire. —stuhl, *m.* the seat or chair of the rince; *fig.* V. —stand, —würde. —tag, *m.* ssembly of princes. Der Regensburger—tag, ormerly, the assembly of the princes of the empire at Ratisbon, the diet at Ratisbon. —thron, *m.* the throne of a prince. —titel, . title of a prince. —verein, *m.* V. —bund. —wort, *n.* the word, the promise of a prince. —würde, *f.* dignity of a prince.

Fürsten, *v. tr.* to make any one a prince, to ise any one to the rank or dignity of a prince. Eine gefürstete Grafschaft, a county raised to he dignity of] a principality.

Fürstenthum, *n.* [-es, *pl* -thümer] principality. [in theology] Die Fürstenthümer, [one f the nine choirs of angels] the principalities.

Fürstinn, *f.* princess, [female] sovereign.

Fürstlich, I. *adj.* 1) belonging to a prince. ie —e Würde, die —en Rechte, the dignity a prince, the rights and prerogatives of a ince; Eure —e or hoch —e Durchlaucht, your rene, most Serene Highness. 2) resembling, coming a prince, princely, prince-like. Ein —er Aufwand, a princely expense; eine —e racht, a princely magnificence; —e Tugenden, princely virtues. II. *adv.* in a princelike nner, princely. Er kleidet sich —, he dresses ke a prince.

Fürt, *f.* [*pl.* -en] [from fahren = gehen] a ace in a river or other water, where it may be ssed on foot, a ford. Die — ist gut an dieser telle the ford is good in this place; die — suchen, to search for the ford; durch eine . über den Fluß setzen, to ford a river; der luß hat dort eine —, the river is fordable ere.

‡and ‖**Fürträglich**, V. Zuträglich.

Fürtrefflich, V. Vortrefflich.

Fürwahr, *adv.* in truth, truly, indeed, forsooth certainly, verily.

Fürwitz, *m.* V. Vorwitz.

Fürwort, *n.* [-es] 1) V. Fürbitte, Empfehlung] 2) [*pl* Fürwörter] [in grammar] pronoun. n persönliches —, a personal pronoun; ein eignendes —, a possessive pronoun; die beziehenden or beziehlichen Fürwörter, the relative pronouns; ein anzeigendes or hinweisendes —, a demonstrative pronoun; ein unbestimmtes —, an indefinite pronoun; ein fragendes —, an interrogative pronoun.

†**Fürz**, *m.* [-es, *pl.* Fürze] a fart. V. Wind.

†**Fürzen, Färzen**, *v. intr.* to let a fart, to fart.

†**Fürzer**, *m.* [-s, *pl.* -] a farter.

Füsel, *m.* [-s] spirits of an inferior quality, bad brandy, bad gin.

***Füselier, Füsilier**, *m.* [-s, *pl.* -e] a fusileer.

Füselier-compagnie, *f.* —regiment, *n.* a compagny, a regiment of fusileers.

Fuß, *m.* [-es, *pl.* Füße, *dimin.* Füßchen, Füßlein, *n*] [allied to Boden, Pfote and to the Gr. πούς] 1) [the lower part of any thing that supports a body] foot. Der — einer Säule, the foot, base of a column; der — einer Bildsäule, the pedestal of a statue; der — eines Leuchters, the foot of a candlestick; am —e eines Baumes sitzen, to sit at the foot of a tree; wir kamen bald am —e der Alpen an, we soon arrived at the foot of the Alps. 2) [that limb of an animal by which it is sustained and which treads the earth in standing and walking, also that which bears some resemblance to it in shape or office] leg, foot. Die Füße einer Spinne, the legs of a spider; der — eines Pferdes, the leg or foot of a horse; der rechte —, the right foot or leg; er hat den — gebrochen, he has broken his foot or leg; die Füße eines Tisches, eines Bettes, the feet or legs of a table, of a bed; die Füße or Schenkel eines Zirkels, the legs of a pair of compasses. 3) [in the most limited sense, the lower extremity of the leg] foot. Er hat einen langen —, he has a long foot; die Zehen am —e, the toes of the foot; die Füße einer Gans, the feet of a goose; die Füße eines Raubvogels, the talons of a bird of prey; die Füße eines Papageien, the claws of a parrot; *fig.* eine Flöte mit einem A —e, [in music] a flute the lower joint of which goes down to A; zu —e reisen, to travel on foot; ein Soldat zu —, a footsoldier; die Soldaten zu —, the footsoldiers, infantry, foot; den — auf die Erde setzen, = absteigen, to alight; den — an's Land setzen, to land, to disembark; vom Kopf bis zu den Füßen, from head to foot, from top to toe; trocknen —es über einen Fluß setzen, to pass over a river dry-shod; — für —, einen — nach dem andern, foot by foot; Einem einen Stoß mit dem —e geben, to kick any one; sich Einem zu Füßen werfen, to throw one's self at any one's feet; den — in den Steigbügel setzen, to put one's foot into the stirrup; mit bloßen Füßen gehen, to walk barefoot; mit dem —e stampfen, to stamp with the feet; Einem etwas vor die Füße werfen, to throw something to any one's feet [used also in a fig. sense]; Einem auf den — treten, to tread upon any one's foot or toes; Einem auf dem —e folgen, nachgehen, nachsetzen, to follow at any one's heels, to pursue him closely; gut zu —e seyn [= ein guter —gänger seyn], to be good on one's legs, a good walker; Einen festen —es erwarten [ohne den — aus der Stelle zu setzen], to wait for any one without stirring from one's place; den Feind festen —es erwarten, to wait for the enemy resolutely; *sich auf die Füße machen, to run away, to take to one's heels, to march off, to scamper away; *nimm die Füße mit [= lauf zu], take foot in hand; keinen — aus dem Hause setzen, not to go out at all; ich werde keinen — mehr in sein Haus setzen, I shall not set foot any more in his house; auf Freiers Füßen gehen, to be looking out or about for a wife. *Fig.* Stehenden —es [= sogleich], instantly, immediately, directly; an einem Orte festen — fassen, to get a firm footing in a place; festen — halten [= nicht nachgeben], to stand one's ground; *sich mit Händen und Füßen vertheidigen or wehren, to defend one's self with might and main; Einen auf freien — setzen, to set any one at liberty, to release any one; die Gesetze, die Gefühle der Ehre und Religion mit Füßen treten, to trample under foot the laws, the sentiments of honour and religion; *er hat schon einen — im Grabe, [said of a man who is very ill] he has one foot already in the grave; am —e dieses, [of letters, accounts] at foot; *mit Einem über den — gespannt seyn, to be at variance with any one; *Einem etwas unter den — geben, to give any one advice or information of a thing secretly, to give any one a hint of a thing; es fährt, es liegt da Alles unter den Füßen herum, every thing here is in a great confusion; seinen — weiter setzen, to seek one's fortunes elsewhere; auf welchem —e stehen sie mit einander? upon what footing are they with one another? sie stehen auf einem guten —e mit einander, they are on good terms with each other; *er steht auf einem guten —e, he is in easy circumstances, he is well off; *auf einem großen —e leben, to live in great style; er weicht keinen — breit von seinen Rechten, he does not budge a foot, he does not give up or resign a particle of his rights; sein Ansehen steht auf schwachen Füßen, his authority is tottering; *dieser Brief hat Hand und —, Hände und Füße, this letter is very well written, is very good, is pertinent; *Alles, was er sagt, hat Hände und Füße, all he says is to the purpose, a propos. 4) [a measure taken from the length of a man's foot] the foot. Ein — hat zwölf Zoll, a foot has twelve inches; der zehntheilige —, the decimal foot, the foot divided into ten parts or digits; dieser Tisch ist sechs — lang, this table is six feet long; acht — ins Gevierte, eight feet square; zwanzig — lang und zehn — breit, twenty feet by ten. V. Quadratfuß, Kubikfuß, Schuh; *it.* [without a numerical word, *pl.* Fuße] etwas nach Fußen messen, to measure something by feet. *Fig.* *a*) [the proportion or standard by which any thing is measured]. Ein Gut nach dem —e der gewöhnlichen Taxe verpachten, to farm out an estate at the usual rate of rent; die Schatzung nach dem alten —e anlegen or erheben, to raise contributions at the old rate, upon the old footing. *b*) [in poetry, a certain number of syllables constituting part of a verse] foot. Die Hexameter haben sechs Füße, hexameter verses are of six feet. *c*) [in organs] higher or lower pitch of tone according to the length of the organ-pipes. Vier—ton, four feet tone. *d*) [in coinage, the proportion of weight of fine metal and alloy established by authority] standard. Die Summe von hundert Gulden im Conventions—, im Vierundzwanzigguiden—, the sum of a hundred florins in convention-money, in money of the empire. V. Münzfuß.

Fuß-angel, *f.* [an instrument with four iron spikes] a caltrop, man-trap. —arbeit, *f.* [among weavers] work done by the feet. —bad, *n.* [warm] bath for the feet, footh-bath. —ball, *m.* Das —ballspiel, foot-ball. —ballen, *m.* the ball of the foot. —bank, *f.* footstool. —becken, *n.* a basin for washing the feet. —bekleidung, *f.* any thing that is used as a covering for the feet, as stockings, slippers, shoes, boots &c. —bett, *n.* [in surgery, a hollow machine in which a broken leg is placed] a solen, a cradle. —biege, *f.* instep. —binde, *f.* [in surgery] a bandage for the feet. V. Binde 1). —blatt, *n.* 1) the sole of the foot. 2) [in botany, an American plant] Podophyllum. —boden, *m.* floor. Ein eingelegter —boden, an inlaid floor. —bodenspieker, *m.*

a kind of iron nails used in flooring. —bote, *m.* foot-messenger. —brett, *n.* footboard. —decke, *f.* 1) a coverlet for the feet 2) a carpet. V. —teppich. —dienst, *m.* service performed on foot. —eisen, *n.* 1) [a pointed piece of iron fastened to the heels of one's shoes in order to walk safely on ice] calkin, creeper. 2) a fetter. Einem —eisen anlegen, to put any one in fetters 3) V. —angel. fall, *m.* prostration. Einen —fall vor Einem thun, to prostrate one's self before any one, to throw one's self at any one's feet. —fällig, *adj.* and *adv.* prostrate. Einen —fällig um Verzeihung bitten, to implore any one's pardon on one's knees. —fessel, *f.* V. —eisen 2). —flasche, *f.* foot-stove. —förmig, *adj.* [in botany] having the shape of the foot —frohne, *f.* V. —dienst. —gang *m.* V. —pfad, —steig. —gänger, *m* —gängerinn, *f.* 1) traveller on foot, pedestrian, walker, foot-passenger. Er ist ein guter —gänger, he is a good walker. 2) footsoldier. —garde, *f.* footguards. —geschmeide, *n.* V. —eisen 2). —gesims, *n.* [in architecture] ornaments about a pedestal, in the form of a cornice. —gestell, *n.* [of a column] pedestal, stylobation. Das —gestell eines Tisches, trestle; [in hunting] das —gestell eines Habichts, the legs of a hawk. —getäfel, *n.* the inlaid work of a floor, an inlaid floor. —gicht, *f.* [Podagra] the gout [in the feet]. —gichtig, *adj.* and *adv.* [podagrisch] gouty, podagrical. Ein —gichtiger Kranker, ein —gichtiger, V. —gichtkranke. Er ist —gichtig, he has got the gout, he is subject to the gout in the feet. —gichtisch, *adj.* and *adv.* resembling the gout. —gichtkranke, *m.* [Podagrist] a person afflicted with the gout [in the feet], a gouty person. —gichtmittel, *n.* a remedy against the gout [in the feet]. —hader, *m.* a clout to clean shoes with. —hafen, *m.* 1) a pot with feet. 2) a pot for warming one's feet, a foot-stove. —haken, *m.* a pointed piece of iron, fastened to the feet and used in climbing, creeper. —halt, *m.* footing, foothold. —hammer, *m.* [among silversmiths] a hammer used to beat the bruises or dints out again. —harnisch, *m.* V. Beinharnisch. —horn, *n.* [in conchology, = Stachelschnecke] triangular whelk. —kämpfer, *m.* V. —soldat. —kissen, *n.* a cushion for the feet. —klavier, *n.* [more usual, Pedal] pedals — —kluft, *f.* V. —scheit. —knecht, *m.* ‖ 1) a forester's man or assistant. ‡ 2) V. —soldat. — knöchel, —knorren, *m.* ancle-bone, [in anatomy] malleolus. —knochen, *m.* [in anatomy] bone of the foot. —krampfig, *adj.* V. —gichtig. —krieger, *m.* V. —soldat. —kuß, *m.* the ceremony of kissing the pope's foot. — lumpen, *m.* V. —hader. —maß, *n.* 1) the measure of the foot. 2) measure by feet, a measure divided into feet. —matte, *f.* a mat for the feet. —mörser, *m.* [in artillery] a mortar of a piece with its foot. —muskel, *m.* [in anatomy] a muscle of the foot. —pfad, *m.* foot-path, foot-way. —punkt, *m.* [in astronomy, the point of the heavens directly under the place where we stand] nadir. Der —punkt ist dem Scheitelpunkt gerade entgegengesetzt, the nadir is directly opposite to the zenith. —register, *n.* pedal. —reis, *n.* [in hunting] perching-stick or roost, perch. —reise, *f.* journey on foot. —rücken, *m.* the upper part of the foot. — sack, *m.* a sack lined with fur to put the feet and legs in. —schämel, *m.* V. —bank. — scheit, *n.* [among charcoal-burners] one of the pieces of wood laid across one another at the bottom of a charcoal pile. —schelle, *f.* V. —eisen 2). —socke, *f.* a sock. —sohle, *f.* sole of the foot. —sohlenband, *n.* [in anatomy] a ligament serving to bind the bones of the sole of the foot together. —sohlenmuskel, *f.* [in anatomy] a muscle of the sole of the foot. —sohlenschlag, *m.* bastinade, bastinado. —soldat, *m.* a foot-soldier. —spiel, *n.* V. —register. —spur, *f.* mark of the foot, footing, trace, track. V. —stapfe; *it.* [among hunters] the trace, [of a deer] the foiling or slot, [of a hare] the prick, [of an otter] the seal. V. Spur, Fährte. —stab, *m.* [among carpenters] a staff one foot long, used as a measure, a foot-rule. —standbild, *n.* a pedestrian statue. —stapfe, *f.* footstep, trace, vestige. *Fig* In Jemands —stapfen treten, Jemands —stapfen nachfolgen, to tread in the steps or footsteps of any one, to follow the steps of any one, to follow or imitate any one's example. Syn. Fußstapfen, Spuren. Fußstapfen are the impression of the feet of animal bodies. Spuren are also the marks or traces of any body, without necessarily implying the impression of it in a softer. V. Spur. —steig, *m.* V. —pfad Ein erhobener —steig längs einer Landstraße hin or an beiden Seiten einer Brücke or gepflasterten Straße [Trottoir], foot-path, foot-way. —stock, *m.* 1) a narrow piece of plank, placed across a boat for the rowers to set their feet against, a stretcher. 2) V. —stab. —stoß, *m.* a thrust of the foot, a kick —strick, *m.* a snare or gin for the feet. —stricke für Pferde, shackles or locks for horses' legs. —stück, *n.* [in heraldry] the lower part of the shield. — tag, *m.* a day on which a tenant is bound to work for his landlord. —taste, *f.* pedal. — tastenspiel, *n.* V. —spiel. —teppich, *m.* carpet. —tritt, *m.* 1) a thrust of the foot, a kick. Einem einen —tritt geben, to give any one a kick, to kick any one. 2) V. Schritt. 3) V. —stapfe. 4) any thing on which one treads with the foot, footstool, step; [among weavers] a treadle Der —tritt einer Kutsche, the footboard of a coach —trittbrett, *n.* V. —brett. —tuch, *n.* 1) a piece of cloth for covering floors, floor-cloth. 2) V. —hader. —unterlage, *f.* plinth of a statue. —verblendung, *f.* the patten or base of a column. —volk, *n.* infantry, foot. —wanderung, *f.* V. —reise. —wanderungen, wanderings [on foot]. —wanne, *f.* a tub to wash the feet in. — wärmer, *m.* a foot-stove. —waschen, *n.* [in the Roman church] the act of washing the feet. —wasser, *n.* V. —bad. —weg, *m.* V. —pfad. —werk, *n.* 1) [in familiar language] the feet. Sie hat ein niedliches —werk, she has a pretty little foot. 2) any thing that serves to cover the feet, as, stockings, shoes &c. —winde, *f.* a windlass. —wurzel, *f.* [in anatomy] tarsus. —wurzelhöhle, *f.* [in anatomy] the sinus of the tarsus. —wurzelknochen, *m.* the bone of the tarsus. —wurzelschlagader, *f.* artery of the tarsus. —zehe, *f.* toe.

Füßeln, *v. intr.* [in fam. lang.] 1) to be unsteady on one's feet, to kick and jerk with one's feet 2) to touch with one's feet those of another person in order to give a sign or hint, to play with the feet.

Fußen, *v. intr.* 1) to place or fix the feet on something, to foot. 2) [among hunters, said of birds] to perch, to light. 3) to get a footing. Dieser Weg ist zu schlüpfrig, man kann nicht —, this way is too slippery, one cannot walk, one loses one's foothold. *Fig.* Auf etwas —, to rely upon something; man kann nicht darauf —, there is no relying or depending upon it.

Füßig, *adj.* and *adv.* [seldom used] having feet, footed. Ein —er Topf, a pot with feet. V. Zwei—, Drei— &c.

Füßling, *m.* [-es, *pl.* -e] the foot of a stocking.

Füstel, *m.* [-s] [in botany] fustic.

Füsti, *pl.* [in commerce] waste or damage of goods.

1. **Futter**, *n.* [-s, *pl.* -] [Old French *feultre* Ital. *fodero*; allied, perhaps, to the Lat. *vel-o* = hüllen, to Fell, Filz.] 1) *a*) [= Futteral] an outer covering, that which incloses or contains, case. V Brillen—, Flaschen—, Flöten—, Geigen—, Hut—, Kamm— &c *b*) [among shoemakers] a piece of leather to protect the boot against the spur. 2) *a*) the inner covering of any thing, as of a garment or a box, lining. Ein seidenes — [Seidenfutter], a silk lining: ein — von Pelz [Pelzfutter], a fur *lining.* *b*) [in architecture and among joiners] moulding. Das — einer Thüre, the case of a door. V. Fenster—, Thür—. *c*) [among watch-makers] the hole of the pivot, pivot-hole.

Futter-band, *n.* [among hairdressers] the caul of a wig. —barchent, *m.* a kind of fustian —brett, *n.* —diele, *f.* a board or plank to line something on the inside with [in seamen's lang.] a plank used in the ceiling of a ship. —flanell, *m.* flannel for lining. —hemd, *n.* an under-waistcoat. —holz, *n.* wood for lining or casing something. —latte *f.* [in seamen's lang.] V. —ripp. —leinwand, *f.* linen of lining. —macher, *m.* 1) one that makes stuffs for lining. 2) V. Futteralmacher. —mantel, *m.* V. —mauer. —mauer, *f.* [in architecture] the lining of a wall; [in fortifications] the lining of a bastion with masonry — ripp, *n.* [in seamen's language] a small piece of timber placed athwart-ships, a ledge — taffet, *m.* sarsenet for lining. —tuch, *n.* cloth or stuff for lining. V. 1. Futter 2) *a*). — zeug, *n.* V. —tuch.

2 **Futter**, *n.* [-s] [allied to the Low Saxon föden = ernähren] 1) [applied to that which is eaten by beasts, and only in fam. or vulgar lang. to the food of men] food, fodder, feed. Die Wiesen unseres Vaterlandes gewähren das beste — für die Schafe, the meadows of our country furnish the best feed for sheep; die Pferde starben aus Mangel an —, the horses died for want of food; Heu, Hafer und Stroh ist das beste — für die Pferde, hay, oats and straw are the best fodder for horses; dem Rindvieh — geben, to feed the cattle; das — für die Pferde, forage, das — für das Rindvieh, fodder, provender grünes, trockenes —, green, dry forage; einem Pferde körniges oder hartes — geben, to feed a horse with corn or beans; — einholen, to forage. 2) a portion of food given to a beast at a time. Die Pferde haben heute noch kein — bekommen, the horses have not yet been fed to day; wir ritten zwanzig Meilen in Einem — we rode twenty miles without baiting.

Futter-amt, *n.* forage-office. —anbau, *m.* V. —bau. —arm, *adj.* and *adv* poor in forage, destitute of forage. —bank, *f.* a chopping-board. —bau, *m.* the culture of forage. — beutel, *m.* nose-bag. —boden, *m.* hay-loft —bohne, *f.* V. Feldbohne, Pferdbohne, Saubohne. —brei, *m.* [in bee-hives] a kind of jelly at the bottom of the cells. —erbse, *f.* the hog-pea, field-pea. —fisch, *m.* 1) a fish that lives on vegetables. 2) small fish serving as food to other fish. —geld, *n.* money paid for the feed of an animal. Er hat sechs Pfund —geld für seine Pferde bezahlt, he has paid six pounds for the keep of his horses. —gerste, *f.* barley for cattle. —gewächs, —gras, *n.* grass or any green forage given to cattle. —hafer, *m.* oats for cattle. —hirse, *f.* Indian millet. — holen, *n.* the act of foraging. Er wurde beim —holen getödtet, he was killed while foraging —holer, *m.* forager. —honig, *m.* honey for feeding bees. —kammer, *f.* V. —boden. —

'asten, *m.* corn-bin. —klinge, *f.* knife of he chopping-board, chopping-knife. —knecht, *n.* hostler. —korb, *m.* a kind of basket or bag for cattle to eat out of, nose-bag. —korn, *n.* orn for cattle. —kräuter, *pl.* herbage. —abe, *f.* V. —bank. —mangel, *m.* scarcity, dearth of forage. —marschall, *m.* an officer t court whose business is to furnish the king's orses with forage. —meister, *m.* V. —marschall. —messer, *n.* V. —klinge. —metze, : a quantity of oats or corn given to a horse or a meal, a feed of oats. —netz, *n.* a net or bag or cattle to eat out of, a feeding net, nose-bag. —noth, *f.* V. —mangel. —pflanze, *f.* V. —gewächs. —pressen, *n.* V. —holen. —tresser, *m.* V. —holer. —raufe, *f.* a rack or hay or other fodder. —rehe, *f.* [in the veterinary art] the foundering of a horse. —reich, *adj.* and *adv.* abounding in forage. Diese Gegend ist —reich, this country abounds with forage. —rübe, *f.* turnip for cattle. —sack, *m.* fodder-sack, fodder-bag, nose-bag. —schneide, : V. —bank. —schneiden, *n.* V. —holen. —schneider, *m.* 1) fodder-chopper. 2) [in military affairs] V. —holer. —schreiber, *m.* clerk of the forage-office. —schwinge, *f.* a flat and shallow basket or a van to shake the oats in before they are given to the horses. —stätte, : 1) any place of feeding. 2) place where pheasants are fed. —stroh, *n.* straw to feed cattle with. —trespe, *f.* darnel for cattle. —trog, *m.* a trough for animals to eat out of. V. Trog. —wanne, *f.* V. —schwinge. —wicke, : common vetch.

Futteral, *n.* [-s, *pl.* -e] a case, covering, box or sheath.

Futteralmacher, *m.* a case-maker, boxmaker, sheath-maker.

Fütterer, *m.* [-s, *pl.* -] 1) a fodderer. 2) one that sells oats, hay, straw and other food for cattle by retail, a huckster of food for cattle.

1 **Füttern, Füttern**, [V. 1. Futter] *v. tr.* to cover any thing on the inside or outside, to line, to case. Einen Mantel mit Seide —, to line a cloak with silk; ein Kleid mit Watte —, to line or furnish a garment with wadding, to wad; einen Rock mit Pelz —, to fur a coat; Sessel mit Roßhaar —, to stuff chairs with horse-hair, V. Ausfuttern, Ausstopfen; eine Wand —, to ..., to wainscot a wall; ein Schiff inwendig mit Dielen —, to fix the planks of a ship's ceiling to the timbers; [in commerce] Waaren —, to pack bad merchandise in the middle of a ball or bundle, to adulterate goods; eine Münze —, to cover a brass-coin with a thin plate of gold or silver, to plate brass-money.

2. **Füttern, Füttern**, [V. 2. Futter] I. *v. tr.* 1) to give food to, to feed, to fodder. Wenn die Pferde arbeiten sollen, so muß man sie gut —, if horses are to work, they must be well fed; man füttert das Rindvieh ein oder zwei Mal des Tags, they fodder cattle once or twice a day; wir reisten durch, ohne [die Pferde] zu —, we passed through without baiting [the horses]; einen Vogel —, to feed a bird; man muß diesen Mann wie ein Kind —, this man must be fed like a child. 2) to give as food or fodder. Gras, Heu, Stroh &c. —, to feed with grass, hay, straw &c.; aus Mangel an Hafer müssen wir Wicken —, for want of oats we must feed with vetches. II. *v. intr.* 1) to promote growth, to nourish. Klee und Rüben ... gut, clover and turnips are very nourishing; den Pferden füttert nichts besser, als Hafer, oats are the best food for horses. 2) to take food, to eat. Die Pferde haben schon gefüttert, the horses have already baited. V. Fressen.

Das —, V. 2. Futterung 1).

1. **Fütterung**, *f.* [from 1. futtern] 1) the act of lining &c. 2) *a*) [in printing] Die — des Deckels an der Buchdruckerpresse, platen, die — des Ballenleders, the lining of the leather. *b*) [in seamen's lang.] V. Verkleidung. *c*) [in forges] V. Gestübe.

2. **Fütterung** or **Fütterung**, *f.* [from 2. futtern] 1) the act of feeding. 2) food, feed, fodder, forage. Es fehlte dem Heere an —, the army was in want of forage. 3) V. Futterholen.

Füy, Fý, *interj.* V. Pfui.

G.

G, g. 1) [the seventh letter of the alphabet] G. 2) [in music] the fifth note in the natural diatonic scale, sol. — dür, key of G major; — moll, key of G minor; der —schlüssel, the treble cliff or clef; er hat — anstatt F gegriffen, he took sol for fa.

Gaar, Gaarn, V. Gar, Garn.

***Gabbronit**, *m.* [-en, *pl.* -en] [in mineralogy] gabronite.

Gabe, *f.* [*pl.* -n] 1) any thing given. Eine — (*Dosis) Rhabarber, a dose of rhubarb; eine Arznei in mehrere —n eintheilen, to divide a medicine into several doses; [in saltworks] the quantity of saltwater furnished every week to the salt-houses; Steuern und —n [= Abgaben], taxes and imposts; er zahlt Steuern und —n, he pays scot and lot. *Fig.* any thing bestowed by the Author of our nature, gift, endowment. Diesem Menschen fehlt es nicht an —n, this man does not want talents; er ist ein Mensch von herrlichen —n, he is a man of great endowments, a man of parts; diese —n kommen von oben, these gifts come from above; er besitzt die — der Beredsamkeit, he has the gift of eloquence, [in fam. lang.] the gift of the gab; diese Frau besitzt die —, zu weinen, so oft sie will, this woman has the faculty of weeping at will; er hat die —, Jedermann zu gefallen, he has the knack of pleasing every body. 2) a donation, a present, gift. —n und Geschenke verblenden oft selbst die Weisen, gifts and presents will often blind even the wise. *Fig.* Kinder sind eine — Gottes, children are a gift or bounty of God; Brod ist eine der besten —n Gottes, bread is one of the best gifts of God. 3) [in the most limited sense] alms, charity. Einem Armen eine — geben, reichen, to bestow a charity on a poor man; diese arme Frau spricht Sie um eine milde — an, this poor woman begs charity of you. SYN. Gabe, Geschenk. Both these words signify any thing given or bestowed; but Gabe is now generally used to denote that which is given by a higher and richer person to an inferior or more needy, Geschenk that which one gives to a friend, an equal or a superior. Man macht seinem Freunde ein Geschenk, man reicht einem Bettler eine Gabe [one makes a present to one's friend, one bestows a gift or charity upon a beggar]. Thus in modern language Gabe is used to denote that which we receive from a higher being, or from one we conceive to be a higher. V. Naturgabe, Talent.

Gaben=fresser, *m.* one that takes bribes, a venal judge. —herr, *m.* [in the saltworks of Halle in Prussia] an underinspector of the salt-houses. —sammlung, *f.* a collection of alms or contributions. —verschlinger, *m.* V. —fresser.

Gäbel, *f.* [*pl.* -n, *dimin.* Gäbelchen, Gäbelein, *n.*] [allied, perhaps, to Giebel] any thing having two points or prongs and but one handle. Die — eines Baumastes, the fork or crotch of a tree; die —n or Gäbelchen an den Weinreben, tendrils or claspers [of vines]; die —n am Hirschgeweihe, the forked ends of a stag's antlers, V. —gehörn; die —, womit man ißt, table-fork; eine — mit zwei, mit drei Zinken, a two-pronged, three-pronged fork; V. Fleisch—, Mist—, Ofen—; die — einer Armbrust, the trigger of a cross-bow; die — eines Karrens, —deichsel, the shafts of a cart, thill. [in seamen's lang.] die zwei eisernen —n zur Stütze des Mastes, crotches; die — in einem Wappen, V. —stück 2).

Gabel=anker, *m.* [in seamen's lang.] small bow-anchor; [in architecture] cramp-iron, V. Schließanker. —arm, *m.* a shaft or thill [of a cart &c.]. —bäume, *pl.* or —deichsel, *f.* thills or shafts. —förmig, *adj.* and *adv.* forked, forky. Ein —förmiger Baum, a forked tree; sich —förmig theilen, to divide into two, to fork; ein Weg, der sich —förmig theilt, a road that forks; [in botany] forked; ein —förmiger Stengel, dichotomous stem; die —förmige Theilung des Hauptastes, the bifurcation of the principal bough. —frühstück, *n.* a second breakfast eaten with a knife and fork, luncheon. —fuhrwerk, *n.* V. —wagen. —gehörn, *n.* [among hunters] the forked attires of a deer. —hirsch, *m.* [among hunters] a stag or deer with forked attires. —holz, *n.* a forked piece of wood; [among waggoners] V. —deichsel; [in seamen's lang.] *a*) the standard which fastens the cutwater to the stem. *b*) knee or floor-timber placed in the fore and after-part of a ship. — —klinge, *f.* a forked blade. —kraut, *n.* [in botany] aquatic hemp; *it.* the female sweet maudlin. —kreuz, *n.* a cross in the form of a fork; [in heraldry] a pall. —maaß, *n.* an instrument for measuring the diameter of a tree. —mast, *m.* [in seamen's lang.] a forked mast. —nadel, *f.* hair-pin, hair-needle. —pferd, *n.* shaft-horse, thill-horse. —richter, *m.* [among cutlers] a piece of iron on which forks are forged. —schwanz, *m.* [in natural history] 1) a kind of night-butterfly, forked tail. 2) [a kind of humming-bird] the green humming bird with a long tail. 3) a small gosshawk. 4) the fork-tailed chaetodon. —ständig, *adj.* [in botany] dichotomous. —stange, *f.* a forked stake, pole or pale. —stich, *m.* a thrust or prick with a fork. —stiel, *m.* handle of a fork. —stück, *n.* 1) [in artillery] a piece of ordnance resting on an iron fork, a sort of swivel. 2) [in heraldry] a part of the shield in form of a desk. 3) [in seamen's lang.] V. —holz. —wagen, *m.* waggon with shafts. —zacke, *f.* the prong of a fork. —zinke, *f.* V. —zacke.

Gäbeler, *m.* [-s, *pl.* -] V. Gabelhirsch.

Gabelicht, *adj.* and *adv.* forked, forky, furcated. Ein —er Ast, a forked branch; [among hunters] ein —es Geweih, a forked attire, V. Gabelgehörn; [in mining] ein —er Gang, a load that diverges or forks.

Gäbelig, *adj.* and *adv.* forky, forked. Ein —er Baum, a forked tree; [among hunters] ein —er Hirsch, a well-branched stag.

Gäbeln, I. *v. tr.* to pierce with a fork or something resembling a fork, to take with a fork; [among hunters, said of a stag] to gore. II. *v. intr.* [in mining] to diverge, to divide into two branches, to fork.

Gäbelnbaum, *m.* [-es, *pl.* -bäume] [Abelsbeerbaum] the lote or nettle tree, lotos; [Ziegelbaum] Indian date-plum.

Gäbelung, *f.* [in mining] division into two branches, forking, furcation.

Gäbler, *m.* [-s, *pl.* -] [among hunters] V. Gabelhirsch; [in ichthyology] bullhead, cottus.

Gabriel, [-s, *pl.* -e] [a name of men] Gabriel.

Gabriele, [ns] [a name of women] Gabriela or Gabrielle.

Gäch, V. Jähe.

Gäckeln or **Gäckern**, [allied to the Lat. *cachinnor*, to kichern &c.] *v intr.* 1) ‡ to cackle, as a hen or goose. Die Hennen — wenn sie gelegt haben, hens cackle after having laid their eggs. 2) ‡ * [said of men] to prate, to prattle, to chatter, to talk in a silly manner.

Gädelbusch, *m.* [-es] [in natural history] V. Spießente.

‖**Gaden**, *m.* [-s, *pl.* -] [seems to be allied to Gatter] 1) a room, chamber, apartment. 2) a small house, a cottage. 3) story of a house. Ein Haus zu zwei, drei —, a house of two, three stories.

Gaden-diener, *m.* V. Ladendiener. —**maus**, *f.* a domestic mouse.

‖**Gädig**, *adj.* [used only in composition as] zwei—, drei—, having two, three stories.

***Gadolinit**, *m.* [-en, *pl.* -en] [in mineralogy] gadolinite.

‖**Gaffel**, *f* [*pl.* -n] [corrupted from the medio-Lat. *gabella*, and this from Gabe] 1) impost, tax, duty, excise. 2) a company of artisans or mechanics.

Gaffen, [Isl. *gap* is = Oeffnung, A. S. *geapan* = öfnen] *v. intr.* to open the mouth in wonder or surprise, to gape. Nach etwas —, to gape or stare at something; da steht er müßig und gafft, there he stands gaping in the air; die —de Menge, the gaping crowd.

Gaffer, *m.* [-s, *pl.* -] -inn, *f.* a gaper, starer.

Gagat, *n.* [-es, *pl.* -e] —**kohle**, *f.* [in mineralogy] jet.

***Gage**, *f.* [*pl* -n] salary, pay, wages.

Gäh, **Gähling**, **Gähzorn**, V. Jäh, Jähling, Jähzorn.

Gähnen, *v. intr.* 1) to open wide. Weit gähnte in der Tiefe der Abgrund, wide yawned the gulf below. 2) to yawn as through drowsiness. Wir wollen zu Bette gehen, er hat schon dreimal gegähnt, let us go to bed, he has already yawned three times; das —, the act of yawning, yawning; das — steckt an, yawning is catching.

Gähn-affe, *m.* a gaper, gaping fool, a booby. —**laut**, *m.* [in grammar] a hiatus. —**muschel**, *f.* V. Gienmuschel. —**sucht**, *f.* frequent inclination to yawn.

Gähner, *m.* [-s, *pl.* -] -inn, *f.* yawner, gaper.

Gähr, V. Gar.

Gährbottich, *m.* [-s, *pl.* -e] [in breweries] fermenting-vat.

Gähre, *f.* 1) state of fermenting, fermentation. Man muß dem Sauerteige die nöthige Zeit zur — lassen, you must give the leaven the time necessary for fermenting; die —, Göhre des Weines, the flavour of wine; dieser Wein hat die — von Burgunder, this wine has the flavour of Burgundy. 2) degree of fermenting. Dieses Brod hat zu viel —, there is too much leaven in this bread.

Gähren, *v. intr.* to ferment; [said of wine] to ferment, to work. Das —, the act of fermenting; das — des jungen Bieres, the fermentation of newly-brewed beer. *Fig.* Die gereizten Gemüther —, provoked minds ferment.

Gährkammer, *f.* [*pl.* -n] [in breweries] the room in which the beer ferments.

Gährteig, *m.* [-es, *pl* -e] leaven.

Gährung, *f.* fermentation. Es giebt drei Arten von —, die geistige, die saure und die faule, there are three kinds of fermentation, the vinous, acetous and putrefactive; die Lehre von der —, the doctrine of fermentation, zymology. *Fig.* der Staat, das Volk ist in —, the state, the people are in a ferment; die Leidenschaften in — bringen, to put the passions in a ferment; es ist etwas in —, there is some mischief brewing; es ist eine heftige — unter den Soldaten, there is a violent agitation or commotion among the soldiers, the soldiers are in violent agitation or ferment.

Gährungs-kraft, *f.* fermentative power. —**luft**, *f.* V Stickluft. —**messer**, *m.* an instrument for ascertaining the degree of fermentation, zymosimeter. —**mittel**, *n.* —**stoff**, *m.* that which causes fermentation, as yeast, barm, leaven &c., ferment.

Gailer, *m.* [-s] [among hunters = Geschröt des Fuchses] the scrotum, cods.

Gaiß, *f.* V. Geiß.

‖**Gakfen**, V. Gackeln.

***Gala**, V. Galla.

***Galaktit**, *m.* [-en, *pl.* -en] [in mineralogy] galactite.

***Galan**, *m.* [-es, *pl* -e] [in familiar or vulgar language] a gallant, a lover, a spark. Das ist ihr —, that is her lover or spark; den — machen, to play the gallant, to court the ladies.

Galander, *m.* [-s] [in natural history] 1) the weevil 2) the crested or copped lark.

***Galant**, *adj.* and *adv.* [in fam. lang.] 1) polite, genteel, courteous. Ein sehr —er Mann, a very gallant man; ein —er Herr, a fine or fashionable gentleman; sich — kleiden, to dress genteelly. 2) inclined to courtship, amorous, gallant. V. Verliebt.

***Galanterie**, *f.* [*pl.* -en] 1) politeness, elegance of manners, gentility, genteelness, gallantry. 2) amorous disposition, gallantry. 3) an amour, intrigue. 4) articles of ornament, dress and fashion, jewelry, trinkets.

Galanterie-arbeit, *f.* jewelry, ornaments, trinkets, toys. —**arbeiter**, *m.* jeweller. —**degen**, *m.* a court-sword, dress-sword. —**handel**, *m.* commerce or trade with jewelry, trinkets. —**händler**, *m.* a dealer in articles of dress, ornament and fashion, jeweller. —**händlerinn**, *f.* a milliner. —**kram**, *m.* V. —handel. —**krämer**, *m* V. —händler. —**waare**, *f.* an article of dress or ornament, a trinket, toy.

Galater, *m.* [-s, *pl.* -] [in geography] a Galatian.

Galatien, *n.* [-s] [a country in lesser Asia] Galatia.

Galaun, V. Galone.

Galban, *n.* [-es] or **Galbanum**, *n.* [-s] [in natural history] (Mutterharz) galban, galbanum.

Galeasse, *f.* [*pl.* -n] [in seamen's lang.] a heavy low-built Venetian vessel with both sails and oars, a galeas.

Galeere, *f.* [*pl.* -n] a low flat-built vessel, a galley. Einen auf die — [to hard labour in chains] schicken, zur —narbeit [to the oar] verurtheilen, to send, to condemn any one to the galleys; die Haupt—, the admiral galley, capitana; [in chimistry, a kind of distilling furnace] a galley; [in natural history] nautilus papyraceous.

Galeeren-anker, *m.* a small anchor fitted with four flukes or claws, a grapnel, grappling. —**bediente**, *m.* steward or officer having charge of the wine and water in the row-galleys. —**bursch**, *m.* V. —sklave. —**hauptmann**, *m.* captain of a galley; [in ancient Greece] a trierarch. —**ruder**, *n.* oar of a galley. —**sklave**, *m.* a galley-slave. —**stock**, *m.* a post fixed on a wharf or pier to fasten a galley to. —**vogt**, *m.* overseer of a galley. —**volk**, a crew of a galley. —**zeltstangen**, *pl.* two rails extending a loft over the sides of the canopy or poop of a galley to support the awning

Galeone, *f.* [*pl.* -n] V. Galeasse.

Galeot, *m.* [-en, *pl.* -en] V. Galeerensklave.

Galeote, *f.* [*pl.* -n] a small galley, a galliot.

Galerie, *f.* V. Gallerie.

Galgant, *m.* [-es] or —**wurzel**, *f.* [in botany] galanga.

Galgantgras, *n.* carex, cyperoides.

Galgen, *m.* [-s, *pl.* -] 1) [originally] any traverse beam. Der — an einem Schöpfbrunnen, the post of a swipe of a well; [among printers] the gallows of a printer's press, stay of the frisket, V. Lehne; [in manege] V. —mundstück; [in saltworks] a shed at the entrance of the drying-room to put salt or wood into. 2) a gallows, gibbet. Einen zum — verurtheilen, to condemn any one to the gallows, to be hanged; an den — kommen, to come to the gallows, to be hanged; ein Verbrechen, auf welchem — und Rad steht, a capital crime, a hanging-matter; es steht — und Rad darauf, it is a capital crime, geh an den —, go and be hanged; er ist dem — sehr nahe gewesen, he was within a hair's breadth of being hanged, he narrowly escaped the gallows; er schmeckt nach dem —, the gallows groans for him; er sieht aus, als ob er vom — gefallen wäre, als käme er gerade vom — her, he has a hanging look.

Galgen-amboß, *m.* an anvil with two arms or branches. —**art**, *f.* ragamuffins deserving to be hanged, thieves, rogues. —**berg**, *m.* a hill or rising ground with a gallows upon it, gallows-hill. —**bub**, —**dieb**, *m.* a fellow deserving the gallows, gallows-clapper, gallows-bird, Newgate bird. —**feld**, *n.* place where the gallows stands. —**förmig**, *adj.* and *adv.* having the form or shape of a gallows. [in heraldry] Ein —förmiges Kreuz, a potent or potencecross. —**frist**, *f.* reprieve, respite from the gallows; *fig.* * a short delay [of something disagreeable]. Eine —frist suchen, to use delays, to gain time. —**holz**, *n.* wood of a gallows or gibbet. *Prov* Er ist falsch wie —holz, he has the soul of a Judas. —**kette**, *f.* chain of the gallows or gibbet. —**leiter**, *f.* ladder of the gallows. —**männchen**, *n.* 1) [in botany] mandrake 2) [in German popular superstition, Alraun] mandrake, mandragora. —**mäßig**, *adj* and *adv.* belonging to the gallows, deserving to be hanged, patibulary. Dieser Mensch hat eine —mäßige Miene, Gesichtsbildung, this fellow has a hanging look, he looks as if he were going to be hanged; ein —mäßiger Dieb, a thief ripe for the gallows; eine —mäßige That, a hanging matter. —**mundstück**, *n.* [in manege] the sharp bit [of a horse's bridle]. —**pfeiler**, *m.* post of the gallows. —**rekel**, *m.* [in natural history, a kind of a crow] roller, V. Mandelkrähe. —**schelm**, *m.* V. —dieb. —**schwengel**, *m.* V. —dieb. ‡—**steuer**, *f.* in some countries a tax levied for the erection of a gallows and the whole administration of the criminal law. —**strick**, *m.* a rope for hanging malefactors, a halter. *Fig.* a rope-ripe, V. —dieb. —**vogel**, *m.* V. —dieb. —**werth**, *adj.* deserving the gallows. —zug, *m.* hanging feature.

Galiläa, *n.* [-'s] [in geography] Galilee [in Judea].

Galiläer, *m.* [-s, *pl.* -] -inn, *f.* Galilean.

***Galimathias,** *m.* nonsense, galimatia.

Galion[e], Galiote, V. Gallion, Galliote.

Galitzenstein, *m.* [-es, *pl.* -e] [in mineralogy] sulphate of zinc, white vitriol. Blauer —, sulphate of copper.

Galizien, *n.* [-s] 1) [province of Spain] Galicia. 2) [part of Austrian Poland] Gallicia.

Galizier, *m.* [-s, *pl.* -] -inn, *f.* a Galician or Gallician.

Galizisch, *adj.* and *adv.* Galician or Gallician.

Gall, *adj.* V. Gelt.

Gala, *f.* pomp, show, festivity, gala. In — erscheinen, to appear in one's best apparel, full-dressed, to appear in court-dress.

Galatag, *m.* gala day.

Gallapfel, *m.* [-s, *pl.* -äpfel] [a hard round excrescence on the leaves of the oaktree] gall, gall-nut. Die Galläpfel von Aleppo sind die besten, the galls from Aleppo are the best; Baumwollenzeug mit Galläpfeln färben, zubereiten, to put or steep the cotton in galls.

Gallapfel-fliege, *f.* the fly which causes the galls, gall-insect, gall-fly, cynips. —säure, *f.* [in chimistry] gallic acid. —saures Salz, gallate.

1. **Galle,** *f.* [*pl.* -n] [in the animal economy a bitter yellowish-green fluid, secreted in the glandular substance of the liver] gall, bile. Das Austreten oder Ueberlaufen, die Ergießung der —, the evacuation of the bile or gall; voll — seyn, von — überfließen, to be very bilious [used also in a figurative sense]; so bitter wie —, —n-bitter, as bitter as gall; die — eines Karpfen, the gall of a carp; [among hunters] the tail of deer, single [which is said to be the seat of the gall]. *Fig.* bitterness, rancour, spleen, anger. Das macht seine — rege, that provokes his anger; *seine — ausschütten, to vent one's passion or spleen; *die — läuft ihm über, he grows hot or angry, his passion or choler is up; ein Mensch voll —, a man full of spleen or malice; er hat keine —, it is not easy to put him into a passion, he has no gall, no resentment, no grudge; in diesem Werke ist viel —, there is much gall or bitterness in this work; eine Rede voll —, a very virulent speech.

Gallen-ader, *f.* [in anatomy] cystic vein. -behältniß, *n.* vesicle of the bile or gall, gall-bladder. —beschreibung, *f.* choladography. —bitter, *adj.* and *adv.* as bitter as gall. -blase, *f.* vesicle of the gall, gall-bladder. -blasengang, *m.* [in anatomy] cyst-hepatic duct. —blasenschlagadern, *pl.* the cystic arteries. —blasenstein, *m.* stone or calculus in the gall-bladder. —fieber, *n.* bilious fever. -fliege, *f.* V. Gallapfelfliege. —gang, *m.* biliary duct, cystic duct. Der große —gang, choledochus, or the common gall duct; die —gänge, the bilious vessels. —gefäß, bilious vessel, V. —gang. —kolik, *f.* bilious colic, cholera morbus. —krampf, *m.* V. —kolik. —krankheit, *f.* a bilious complaint, V. —sucht. —kraut, *n.* galban, galbanum. —lehre, *f.* choladology. —pulsader, *f.* biliary artery. —pulver, *n.* jalap. —stein, *m.* stone or calculus in the gall, gall-stone. —sucht, [Gallsucht] *f.* jaundice. —süchtig, [gallsüchtig] *adj.* and *adv.* [in medicine] choleric; *fig.* melancholic, atrabilarious, sullen, cross. -wespe, *f.* V. Gallapfelfliege.

2. **Galle,** *f.* [*pl.* -n] something faulty or defective. [in founderies] Die — einer Kanone, einer Glocke, honey-comb, flaw of a piece of ordnance, of a bell; [in farriery] a knot of superfluous flesh growing in the channels of a horse's mouth, barbel, barble; [among foresters] a place in a pine-tree, where the resin has gathered and made cracks in the bark.

3. **Galle,** *f.* [*pl.* -n] V. Gallapfel.

4. **Galle,** *f.* = moisture. V. Ackergalle, Glasgalle, Wassergalle.

1. **Gallen,** *v. tr.* Einen Fisch —, to take the gall out of a fish.

2. **Gallen,** *v. intr.* [among hunters] to make water, to urine, to stale.

3. **Gallen,** *v. tr.* [among dyers] to prepare with galls. Baumwollenzeug —, to put or steep cotton in galls; gegallte Seide, silk steeped in galls

Gällen, *v. intr.* 1) to utter a voice, to sound, to resound. Er schrie, daß das ganze Haus gällete, he cried that the whole house resounded; die Ohren — ihm, his ears tingle; eine —de Stimme, a shrill voice; ein —des Gelächter, a loud and boisterous laugh, a horselaugh. 2) [in mining] Das Gestein gällt, the rock reverberates, *it* it resists the miner's tool.

Galleote, V. Galeote.

Gallerie, *f.* [*pl.* -en] in general, any walk. Eine — um ein Gebäude, a gallery or corridor round a building; [in play-houses] die erste, die zweite, die dritte —, the first, the second, the third gallery; [in mining] gallery, V. Gang 4); [in fortification] a covered walk across a ditch of a town, a gallery; [in seamen's lang.] a frame like a balcony projecting from the stern or quarter of a ship, gallery; [in architecture, a long room] gallery; in der — spazieren gehen, to walk or take a walk in the gallery; die Bilder—, Gemälde—, [Bildersaal] picture gallery.

Gallertartig, *adj.* and *adv.* gelatine, gelatinous. Ein —er Saft, a gelatinous juice; das Nostoch ist —, the nostock is gelatinous.

Gallerte, *f.* [*pl.* -n] [properly something congealed] a glutinous substance obtained by decoction, jelly. Eine — von Kalbsfüßen, a jelly of calf's feet; eine — von Johannisbeeren, currant jelly; [in botany] a kind of membranous mass, tremella; [in chimistry] the gluten. V. Leimstoff.

Gallicht, *adj.* and *adv.* resembling gall or bile, bilious. Ein —er Geschmack, a bilious taste; ein —es Fieber, a bilious fever.

***Gallicismus,** *m.* [-, *pl.* -ismen] [in grammar] Gallicism.

Gallicomanie, *f.* V. Gallomanie.

Gallien, *n.* [-s] [in geography, name of ancient France] Gaul.

Gallier, *m.* [-s, *pl.* -] an inhabitant of Gaul, Gaul.

Gallig, *adj.* and *adv.* 1) [having gall] full of gall, bilious. Eine —e Person, a bilious person; *fig* ein —er Mensch, a choleric man. 2) [indicating gall or anger] choleric. Ein —es Temperament, a choleric temper; *fig.* eine —e Bemerkung, a remark full of bitterness.

Gällig, *adj.* and *adv.* [in mining] hard, solid.

***Gallimatias,** V. Galimathias.

Gallinsekt, *n.* [-es, *pl.* -en] V. Gallapfelfliege.

Gallion, *n.* [-es, *pl.* -e] the head or prow of a large ship. Das — gegen den Feind wenden, to bear towards the enemy; die Stützen des —es, the head-rails.

Gallione, *f.* [*pl.* -n] a large ship formerly used by the Spaniards in their commerce with South-America, galleon.

Gallionist, *m.* [-en, *pl.* -en] one that had a share in the trade of the Galleons that sailed to America, a Galleonist.

Galliote, *f* [*pl.* -n] a small vessel, a galiot. Eine Bombardier —, a bomb galiot, a bomb-ketch; eine Fischer—, a fishing-vessel.

Gallisch, *adj.* and *adv.* Gallic. Die —e Sprache, the Gallic tongue.

Gallivate, *f.* [*pl.* -n] a large rowing-boat used in the East-Indies.

Gallizien, V. Galizien.

Gallloch, *n.* [-es, *pl.* -löcher] [from gällen] V. Schallloch.

Gallomanie, Gallicomanie, *f.* V. Franzomanie.

Gallon, *n.* [-s, *pl.* -en] [an English liquid measure] gallon.

Gallsucht, *f.* V. Gallensucht.

Gallsüchtig, *adj.* V. Gallensüchtig.

Gallthier, *n.* [-es, *pl.* -e] V. Giltthier.

Gallus, *m.* [a name of men] Gallus.

Gallüschel, *m.* [-s] [near Naples *galluccio* signifies yellow] [in botany] V. Rehling.

Gallussäure, *f.* V. Gallapfelsäure.

Gallwatte, V. Gallivate.

Gallwespe, *f.* [*pl.* -n] **Gallwurm,** *m.* [-es, *pl.* -würmer] V. Gallapfelfliege.

Galmei, *m.* [-es, *pl.* -e] [from the Gr. *καδμία*] [in mineralogy, a kind of bituminous fossil earth, which when mixed with copper produces brass] calamine or calamin, the oxide of zinc, fossil cadmia.

Galmei-blume, *f.* or —flug, *m.* [in mineralogy, a sublimate of zinc or calamine collected in the furnace] tutty, spodium. —stein, *m.* lapis calaminaris, calamine stone.

***Galone,** *f.* [*pl.* -n] galloon, lace. V. Borte, Tresse.

***Galoniren,** *v. tr.* [mit Tressen besetzen] to lace. Eine galonirte Weste, a laced waistcoat.

Galopp, *m.* [-es, *pl.* -e] [It. *galoppo*, Fr. *galop*, allied to laufen] gallop. Ein Pferd in — setzen, to put a horse into a gallop; der starke oder gestreckte —, full gallop; ein kurzer, leichter —, short gallop, handgallop, an easy gallop, a canter; im — reiten, to go in a gallop, to gallop; — ansprengen, to fall into a gallop; im gestreckten — reiten, to ride at full gallop; *fig.* *es geht vollends im — mit ihm, he is going very fast, he has one foot in the grave.

Galoppiren, *v. intr.* to gallop. Er hat zwei Stunden lang galoppirt, he has galloped for two hours; ein Pferd — lassen, to put a horse to a gallop. Das —, the act of galloping, galloping; im — gefällt ihm dieses Pferd nicht, he does not like the gallop of this horse, the gallop of this horse does not please him.

***Galosche,** [less usual] **Galüsche,** *f.* [*pl.* -n] a shoe to be worn over another shoe to keep the foot dry, galosh, galoshe. Frauenzimmer—n, clogs.

‖**Galstrig,** *adj.* and *adv.* [ranzig] rancid, rusty. —er Speck, rusty bacon.

Galt, V. Gelt.

Galte, *f.* V. Gelte.

Galvanisch, *adj.* and *adv.* [in physics] galvanic.

Galvanisiren, *v. tr.* to galvanize.

Galvanism or —us, *m.* [-s or -sses] [a branch of the science of electricity, so called from its discoverer the Professor Galvani of Bologna] Galvanism

Gamánder, *m.* [-s] [from the Gr. and Lat. chamaedrys], **Gamánderlein**, *n.* [-s] [in botany] English treacle, Germander.

Gamásche, [or Kamasche] *f.* [*pl.* -n] gaiters, spatterdashes

***Gammarrolit**, *m.* [-en, *pl* -en] [in mineralogy] gammarolite.

Gäms, *m* [-es, *pl.* -e] [in mining] a very hard [illegible], the first rock.

Ganásse, *f.* [*pl.* -n] the nether-jaw of a horse.

Gánerbe, *m.* [-n, *pl.* -n] [gan = gemein?] [now only used in law] a co-heir, joint-heir, co-proprietor. V Miterbe.

Ganerben-gericht, *n.* a privilege of administering justice common to several persons. **—haus** or **—schloß**, *n.* a house or castle common to several persons.

Gánerbschaft, *f.* [*pl.* -en] [now only used in law] 1) property common to several persons. 2) pact, treaty or alliance of joint-heirs. 3) joint-proprietors.

Gánerbschaftlich, *adj.* and *adv.* [now only used in law] common, in common. Ein Schloß — besitzen, to possess a castle in common or in community.

Gáng, *m.* [-es, *pl.* Gänge] V. Gehen. 1) the act of going or walking, going, walk. Seinen — fördern, to mend one's pace, to go or walk faster; ein Pferd in den — bringen, to set a horse agoing. [in Scripture] erhalte meinen — auf deinen Fußsteigen, hold up my goings in thy paths; eine Maschine in den — bringen, to set a machine agoing; dieses Rad wird durch irgend etwas in seinem —e gehindert, this wheel is stopped by something; der — [or Lauf] eines Schiffes, the movement, course, headway of a ship; das Schiff ist wieder im —e, the ship is sailing again. *Fig.* Eine Meinung, ein Vorurtheil in — bringen, to spread an opinion, a prejudice; eine Mode in den — bringen, to bring a fashion in vogue; eine Sache in — setzen, to set a thing agoing, on foot; er ist sehr träge, wenn er aber einmal im —e ist, so arbeitet er mehr als ein Anderer, he is very lazy, but when he is once in, he works more than another; den — der Gerechtigkeit aufhalten or hemmen, to stop the course of justice; die Blattern sind jetzt im —e, the small-pox is very prevalent, is going about at present; Jemands Aufmerksamkeit im —e erhalten, to keep any one's attention alive, to fire any one's attention; der Sache ihren — or Lauf lassen, to let an affair or matter take its course; in vollem —e, in full activity. 2) [way or manner of walking or stepping] walk, gait. Ich kenne ihn an seinem or am —e, I know him by his gait or walk; sie hat einen edeln, majestätischen —, she has a noble, majestic gait, walk or port; er hat einen gezierten —, he has an affected walk or gait, he walks affectedly; der — eines Pferdes, the pace of a horse; dieses Pferd hat einen guten —, this horse has good action; der — dieses Pferdes ist sanft, this horse goes very easy; ein Pferd aus dem regelmäßigen —e bringen, zu einem falschen —e gewöhnen, to spoil a horse's paces. *Fig.* Jeder geht seinen —, every one has his way or manner of living or acting; er geht immer den nämlichen —, he goes on still at the old rate, he continues in his old path, he follows his old courses still; gehen Sie Ihren — fort, go on or continue as you used to do; die Sache gewinnt einen guten, schlimmen —, the affair takes a good, a bad turn; wir wollen sehen, welchen — diese Sache nehmen wird, we shall see what course or turn this affair will take, man muß den — der Geschäfte kennen, one must know the course of the business. V Geschäftsgang. im ganzen —e [Laufe, Zusammenhange] der Begebenheiten der Weltgeschichte, in the whole series of the events of history; der — des menschlichen Geistes, the turn of the human mind, *it.* the march of intellect, der — eines Gedichtes, eines Trauerspieles, the progress of a poem of a tragedy. 3) a single act of going or walking. Einen — thun, to go or run an errand, einen — [Ausgang] in die Stadt thun, to take a walk into the city, *it.* to go to town; wir wollen einen — in den Garten machen, let us take a turn in the garden; ich werde einen — zu meinem Bruder thun, I shall go and see my brother, I shall go and call upon my brother or at my brother's; das hat ihm viele Gänge, manchen sauern — gekostet, that has cost him many a weary step, man bezahlt diesem Arzte eine Guinee für jeden —, this physician is paid a guinea for every visit; [in seamen's lang.] ein — [im Laviren] a tack; [in fencing] der —, pass, passado, zwei, drei Gänge mit Einem thun, to make two three passes at any one; [in tilting] course; [in boxing] a round; [in music] einige Gänge auf dem Clavier &c. machen, to play some passages on the piano &c.; [in a mill] the act of putting the corn in the mill-hopper; das feine Mehl kommt vom zweiten —e, flour is obtained from putting the corn, when ground, once more into the mill-hopper. *Fig.* Man beobachtet alle Gänge dieses Menschen, they watch every step of this man; ich kenne seine Gänge, I know his way of acting or dealing In a more limited sense: *a*) something brought in or up by going or walking. Der — bei einem Essen, a course at table; eine Mittagsmahlzeit von drei Gängen, a dinner consisting of three courses; ein — Gras, a truss of grass. *b*) a space measured by walking; [among sportsmen] pace. Einen Hasen auf 60 Gänge schießen, to kill a hare at a distance of sixty paces. *c*) *fig.* any thing that goes. Der — einer Mühle [Mühlrad, Mühlstein], a set of stones; eine Mühle mit fünf Gängen, a mill with five stones; [among weavers, a certain number of threads] portee. 4) the place in which something or somebody can go, walk or move. Ein langer, dunkler —, a long, dark passage or alley; ein unterirdischer —, a subterraneous passage, a passage under ground; es führt ein langer — zu seinem Hause, a long avenue or alley leads to his house; seine Bude ist im vierten —e No 12, his booth or stall is in the fourth row No. 12; ein mit Linden besetzter —, ein Linden—, a limetree-walk; die Gänge in einem Garten, the walks, alleys or terraces of a garden; er weiß alle Gänge und Schliche in diesem Hause, he knows or is acquainted with every nook and corner of this house; ein langer — in einem Gebäude, längs einer Reihe Zimmer, a corridor, gallery, ein geheimer — von einem Zimmer in das andere, a secret passage from one room into another; ein bedeckter —, a covered walk, a portico, piazza; ein bedeckter — zwischen Säulen, ein Säulen—, a peristyle, *it.* a veranda; der — zwischen den Säulen und der Mauer an einem mit einem Säulen—e umgebenen Gebäude, a peridromis; [in anatomy] duct, canal; die Gänge, durch welche die Galle sich ergießt, the ducts through which the bile discharges itself, the biliary ducts; die Fettgänge, the adipose ducts; die Wassergänge des Auges, the aqueous or watery ducts of the eye; die gewundenen Gänge im Ohre, der Irr—, the labyrinth, V. Harn—, Milch—, Leber— &c.; [in mining] a metallic vein, lode; *it.* the ore; Gänge, countries; dieses Goldbergwerk hat verschiedene Gänge, this golden [illegible] has several branches; der — geht aus [illegible] Stunde, the lode does not go far; [in f[illegible]tion] die bedeckten Gänge, covered ways; [among seamen's lang.] die Gänge auf und in dem R[illegible]me [eines Schiffes], the galleries [at tennis] dedans, [among locksmiths] die Gänge an ei[ner] Schraube, the threads or grooves of a screw [among hunters] der — des Wildes, the ha[unt] [of game].

Gang-art, *f.* [in mining, the earthy, saline, or combustible substance which contains ore of metals] gang, [erroneously written] gan[gue] *it.* the ore which is between the matrix and common rock. **—erz**, *n.* [in mining] ore f[ound] in gangs. **—fisch**, *m* a sort of trout [found in] the Rhine and the lake of Constance], V. Ettiorr **—gebirge**, *n.* [in mining] a mountain containing lodes of ore **—kreuz**, *n* [among weavers] the crossing of the portee. **—pfoste**, *f.* [among carpenters] baluster. **—rad**, *n* [among carpenters] a double-wheel, wheel of a crane &c. **—säule**, *f.* column of a portico. **—schüssel**, *f.* a large dish. **—spill**, *n.* V. Spill **—stein**, *m.* V. —art. **—weise**, *adv.* [in mining] by or in lodes or veins. **—woche**, *f.* [in the Romish church] week of procession, rogation-week.

Gángbar, *adj.* and *adv.* 1) where one may go. Ein —er Weg, a practicable, passable way or road. *Fig.* Die Wasserröhren — erhalten, to keep the waterpipes in repair, in a good state. 2) passing from person to person, generally received Eine —e Münze, a current coin; falsche Münze ist nicht —, false coin is not passable, ein Wort, einen Ausdruck — machen, to bring a word, an expression in use, in vogue, to naturalize a word or an expression; eine —e Waare, a commodity that sells well, [in commerce] a leading article. 3) where one goes or pass s frequently. Eine —e Straße, a frequented road.

Gángbarkeit, *f.* Die — eines Weges, the practicable state or condition of a way, die — einer Münze, the currency of a coin; die — einer Waare, the [ready] sale of a commodity.

Gänge, *adj.* and *adv* 1) going, passing, current. *Fig.* — und gebe seyn [said of a [illegible] coin &c.], V. Gangbar 2; was nicht mehr — und gebe ist, what is no longer fashionable, what is no longer in use; das ist ihm —, he understands that well, he has great skill in that. 2) quick, active. Ein —r Hund, a swift dog.

Gängelband, *n.* [-es, *pl.* -bänder] [string by which children are supported when beginning to walk] leading strings. Ein Kind am —e führen, to lead a child in leading-strings. *Fig.* Seine Frau möchte ihn immer noch am —e führen, his wife would still keep him in leading strings; er wird sich immer am —e führen lassen, he will always be in the leading-strings. V. Führband, Leitband, Laufband.

Gängeln, *v. tr.* to lead by strings; *fig.* to manage, to control. [as a menace, in fam. or vul. lang.] oder ich wollte ihn —, daß es eine Art [illegible] or I would lead him a fine dance.

Gängelwagen, *m.* [-s, *pl.* -] [for children to learn to walk] a go-cart. V. Laufwagen, [illegible]wagen.

Gänger, *m.* [-s, *pl.* -] he that goes or walks; used in composition, as, Fuß—, a walker, traveller on foot, *it.* a footsoldier.

Gánghaft, Gánghaftig, *adj.* and *adv.* V. Gangbar 1. 2) [in mining] in lodes or veins; *it.* continuous, uninterrupted. —ige Zeche, a mine that is constantly worked; die Erze brechen —, the ores break into [illegible] veins or lodes.

Gängig, *adj.* and *adv.* 1) [used in composition, u. rück—, krebs—]. 2) [among hunters] Einen Leit- hund — machen, to train a bloodhound t the leash; ein —er Hund, a swift dog. 3) V. Gänge.

‖**Gängler**, *m.* [-s, *pl.* -] pedlar.

Gänglerwaaren, *pl.* pedlar's goods.

Gänglich, *adj.* and *adv.* V. Gangbar.

Ganiterbaum, *m.* [-es, *pl* -bäume] [a tree of the East-Indies] ganitrus.

Gänker, *m.* [-s] [a kind of longlegged spider] spinner field-spider. V Kanker.

1. **Gäns**, *f.* [*pl.* Gänse, *dimin* Gänschen, n.] [Lat. *anser*, Gr. χὴν allied to gähnen, Gr. χαίνω = schreien] the goose. Die zahme or Haus- —, tame goose; die wilde —, wild goose, eine junge —, ein Gänschen, a green or young goose gosling. *Fig* [in vulg. lang.] Er ist eine —, mit der man Alles anfangen kann, he is led by the nose like a noodle; sie ist eine dumme —, she is a silly goose, a simpleton, [in astronomy, a constellation in the milky way] anser.

Gänse-aar, —adler, *m.* [a voracious fowl of the hawkkind] a goshawk. —auge, *n.* [in commerce] a kind of coarse sack-cloth; [among printers] —augen, *pl.* [Anführungszeichen] the inverted commas, signs of quotation; eine Stelle mit —augen bezeichnen, to mark a passage with signs of quotation. ‖—backe, *f.* one half of a smoked goose. —bauch, *m* 1) [in cookery] a drawn goose [a goose ready trussed for the spit]. 2) *Fig.* a flat belly. —baum, *m.* [der gespitzte Ahorn] plane tree —blume, *f.* —blümchen, *n.* [in botany] daisy. Die große —blume, das —kraut, ox-eye, buphthalmum. —distel, *f.* [in botany] sow-thistle V. Hasenkohl —dreck, *m.* goose-dung. —dreckfarbe, *f.* gosling green. —feder, *f.* 1) goose-feather. 2) goose-quill. —fett, *n.* V. —schmalz. —fliege, *f.* a small sort of May-bug. —flügel, *m.* goose-wing. —fuß, *m.* 1) the foot of a goose. 2) [in botany] goosefoot, [among vine-dressers] —fuß or —füßer, *m.* a sort of sourish black grape; [in printing] V. —auge. —garbe, *f.* V. Gänserich 2) —gekröse, *n.* V. —klein. —habicht, *m.* V. —aar. —händler, *m.* —händlerinn, *f.* dealer in geese. —haut, *f.* the skin of a goose; *fig.* *state of the skin in shivering from cold, goose-skin. Das machte ihm eine —haut, that made him all goose-skin. —hirt, —hüter, *m* goose-herd. —kiel, *m.* goose-quill. —klein, *n.* goose-giblets. —kohl, *m.* V. —distel. —kopf, *m.* 1) the head of a goose; *fig.* a blockhead, ninny. 2) [in botany] *a*) a species of pear. *b*) stinking camomile. —koth, *m.* goose-dung. —köthig, *adj.* and *adv.* [in mining] —köthiges Erz, a rich soft gosling-green silver-ore. —kraut, *n.* a generic name of several plants. V. Gänserich 2), Gänseblume, Siebenfingerkraut, Siebenblatt, Kannenkraut. —küchlein, *n.* gosling. —laus, *f.* goose louse. —löffel, *m.* [a surgeon's instrument] goose-bill. —malve, *f.* V. —pappel. —muschel, *f.* [in conchology] a small shellfish, barnacle. —nadel, *f.* V. Stopfnadel —pappel, *f.* harewort, mallows. —pfeffer, *m.* goose-giblets dressed with a black sauce. —schmalz, *n.* goose-grease. —schwarz, *n.* V. —pfeffer. —spiel, *n.* the game of the goose. —stall, *m.* —stiege, *f.* goose-stall, goose-pen. —wein, *m.* [a jocose expression] Adam's wine, water. Er trinkt nichts als —wein, he drinks nothing but water. —zehnte, *m.* tithe of geese.

2. **Gäns**, *f.* [*pl.* Gänse, *dimin.* Gänschen, n.] [origin uncertain] any mass or lump. *a*) a large stone for columns or mills, a mill-stone. *b*) [in mining] a hard stone or rock. *c*) [in forges] pig or sow of melted iron. Die gereinigte —, [a block of iron refined and melted off for the forge or hammer] loop, bloom *d*) [in saltworks] a lump of prepared salt *e*) [in husbandry] V. Schwaden.

Gänser, Gänsert, *m.* [-s] V Gänserich 2).

Gänserich, *m* [-es, *pl.* -e] 1) [the male of fowls of the goose kind] gander. 2) [in botany] silver weed wild tansy.

Gänstaucher, *m.* [-s, *pl.* -] [in natural history] goosander, merganser.

Gänt, *m* [-es, *pl.* -e or -en] or —, *f.* [*pl.* -en] [seems to be allied to gähnen, Gr χαίνω, Lat. *cano canto* = rufen] 1) public sale, public auction, subhastation. V Versteigerung. Er stak so sehr in Schulden, daß endlich der — über ihn ausgebrochen ist, he was so deeply indebted, that at last his effects were sold to satisfy his creditors, dem —e nahe seyn, to be on the brink of having one's effects sold by public auction. 2) a meeting or concourse of creditors.

Gant-buch, *n.* inventory of the things sold by auction —haus, *n.* house or place where a public sale is held. —mann, *m.* he whose goods or effects are sold by auction. —mäßig, *adj.* and *adv.* so deeply indebted that a person's effects must be sold. ‖—meister, *m.* auctioneer. —recht, *n* law of subhastation, auction-law —rodel, *f.* V. —buch. —urtel, *n.* sentence of priority [in a meeting of creditors]. —urtelpublikation, *f.* a publication of the sentence of priority. —verkäufer, *m* V. —meister. —zeit, *f.* time when a public sale is held.

Gänten, *v. tr.* to sell by public sale or auction. V Gant, *it.* Verganten.

‡and ‖**Gänten**, *m.* [-s] a punishment somewhat resembling the pillory.

1. **Gänz**, *f.* [in forges] V. 2 Gans *c*).

2. **Gänz**, I. *adj.* [is said to come from genesen] 1) [opposed to broken or torn] entire. An diesem Fenster ist keine Scheibe mehr —, or ist keine —e Scheibe mehr, there is not one whole or entire pane of glass in this window; obgleich das Glas auf den Boden fiel, ist es doch noch —, though the glass fell to the ground, it is not broken, it is still entire or whole; dieser Tempel steht noch —, that temple is entire still; das Siegel ist noch —, the seal is still unbroken; —er Pfeffer, pepper in grains [not pounded]; —er Zimmt, cinnamon in rolls or sticks. 2) [opposed to divided] ein —es Pferd, a stone horse, an entire horse; ein —er Käse, ein —es Brod, an entire or whole cheese, an entire or whole loaf; diese Flasche ist nicht mehr —, this bottle is no longer full, has been partly emptied; eine —e Zahl, [opposed to Bruchzahl] a whole number, an integer. 3) [opposed to a part] das —e Haus durchsuchen, to search the whole house; die —e Gesellschaft fing an zu lachen, the whole company or all the company fell a laughing; ein —es Glas austrinken, das Glas — austrinken, to drink off a whole glass, to drink a glass quite off; [in mining] —es Schrot, the entire lining of the shaft or pit [in a soil which is likely to give way]; geben Sie es mir —, give me the whole, give it me all; — Rom erschrak, all Rome was terrified or alarmed; — Frankreich freute sich, all France rejoiced; die —e Welt wird darüber erstaunen, the whole world, all the world will be astonished; er schläft den —en Tag, he sleeps all day long, the whole day; ich bin ein —es Jahr in London gewesen, I was a full year in London; man ließ uns eine —e Stunde warten, they made us wait a full hour; die —e Summe beläuft sich auf &c., the whole sum amounts to &c.; ich verzeihe ihm von —em Herzen, von —er Seele, I pardon or forgive him with all my heart; ihre —e Tugend ist bloße Einfalt, all her virtue consists in mere simplicity; diese Anordnung hat meinen —en Beifall, this arrangement has my entire approbation. dazu muß ich acht —e Tage haben, I want eight whole days for it; acht —e or *—er Tage mußte ich warten, I was obliged to wait eight whole days; dieses Buch ist nicht — [nicht vollständig], this book is not complete; etwas — [vollständig] machen, to complete something, to supply what is wanting *Fig* perfect in its kind. [in familiar language] Das ist ein —er Mann, he is a clever fellow; er ist ein —er Hofmann, he is an accomplished courtier, he is quite a courtier, a perfect courtier, sie ist eine —e Tänzerinn, she is an excellent dancer, she dances in a superior manner; Sie sind ein —er Mann, daß Sie zu uns gekommen sind, it is very kind or civil of you to have come to see us; das ist ein —es Pferd, it is an excellent horse.

II. *adv.* 1) [völlig, durchaus] quite, entirely, wholly, totally — wohl, very well; — recht, quite right; er ist — zu Grunde gerichtet, he is quite, entirely, wholly ruined; — und gar verdorben, completely, entirely spoiled; — und gar nicht, not at all, by no means; sich — dem Vergnügen überlassen, to give one's self entirely up to pleasure; ich bin — der Ihrige, I am wholly, entirely yours; sein Haus ist — anders als es war, his house is quite another thing than it was, es ist ein — witziges Kind, it is a child full of wit; die Thüre ist — offen, the door is wide open; er schlug es — ab, he gave a flat refusal or denial; er läugnete es —, he denied it positively; — allein seyn, to be quite alone; das will etwas — anderes sagen or bedeuten, that signifies something very different; es ist — wahr, daß &c., it is quite true that &c.; — verändert seyn, to be entirely changed, to be quite another man; Sie haben — Recht, you are perfectly right; *it* [in composition with substantives] er ist — Freude, he is full of joy; sie ist — Schmerz, she is overwhelmed with grief; ich bin — Ohr, I am all attention. 2) [in colloquial language instead of ziemlich] tolerably, pretty. Er ist ein — artiger Herr, he is a very nice gentleman; das gefällt mir — wohl, I like it well enough; es mag ein — unterhaltendes Buch seyn, this book seems to be amusing enough; *it.* [as a mere expletive] ich erstaune —, I am perfectly or truly astonished; Sie scheinen ja — bestürzt zu seyn, why, you appear to be struck with wonder or amazement.

III. *n.* Das —e, [des —en], ein —es, [eines —en], the whole Das —e ist größer als ein Theil, the whole is greater than a part; ein —es in verschiedene Theile eintheilen, to divide a whole into several parts; ich gebe Ihnen so viel für das —e der Erbschaft, I will give you so much for the whole of the succession; es sind Fehler oder Mängel in diesem Gemälde, aber das —e, zusammengenommen, macht keinen übeln Effekt, there are some faults, defects or blemishes in that picture, but, taking it altogether, it has no bad effect; es sind einige schöne Sachen an diesem Gebäude, aber das —e taugt nichts, there are some fine pieces of architecture in this building, but the whole or ensemble is good for nothing; das kommt mich im —en auf hundert Pfund, it costs me in all a hundred pounds; er ist etwas eigensinnig, allein im —en, im —en genommen, ist er ein recht braver Mann, he is rather obstinate, but upon the whole he is a very good, a very honest man. SYN. Ganz, Vollständig, Vollkommen. A thing is said to be ganz [whole], of which simply no part is wanting; that is vollständig [complete] which is not defective, and by reason of its having no deficiency, perfectly answers its purpose or destination. Ein ganzer Anzug [an entire suit or dress] is one which is not defective in any of its parts; ein vollständiger Anzug, one that comprises every thing necessary to complete clothing, that being the object or destination of the dress. Vollkommen adds to the above, the idea of having all that is requisite to its nature or kind, and of having attained the highest degree of excellence it is capable of.

||**Ganz=hufner** or —**löhner**, *m.* a peasant or farmer possessing or holding so much land as to keep four horses or oxen. —**pacht**, *m.* and *f* a farm of which the farmer enjoys all the revenues. —**vogel**, *m.* [in natural history] thrush, fieldfare.

Gánzheit, *f.* 1) totality. Die — einer Summe, the whole or total sum, the total [of a sum]. 2) entireness, integrity.

Gänzlich, I. *adj.* whole, entire, complete. —e Dunkelheit, total darkness; in einer —en Hülflosigkeit leben, to live or to be in the utmost distress; —e Bezahlung, payment in full; sie empfing ihn in der —en Meinung, daß &c., she received him with the full persuasion or fully persuaded, that &c. II. *adv.* wholly, entirely, completely. Ich bin — der Meinung, daß &c., I am wholly or entirely of opinion, that &c.; sich — auf Jemand verlassen, to rely or depend entirely, absolutely upon any one; er ist Ihnen — gewidmet, — zugethan, he is entirely devoted to you; das feindliche Heer ist — geschlagen worden, the hostile army has been totally or completely defeated.

Gapen, *v. intr.* [in seamen's lang.] to start, to spring.

Gär, [allied to the Sw. *göra*, Icel. *giora* = machen] I *adj.* [= zubereitet, fertig] prepared, ready. Das Brod ist —, the bread is done, sufficiently baked, *it.* *the bread is all eaten up; dieser Fisch ist nicht recht —, this fish is not quite done, not done enough; das Fleisch war nur halb —, the meat was only half done [half boiled or roasted]; das Fleisch ist nicht —, the meat is underdone. [among tanners and tawers] das Leder — machen, to dress the leather; —es Leder, dressed leather; [in mining] das Eisen, das Kupfer — machen, to refine iron, copper; —es Eisen, refined iron; das —machen des Kupfers, des Eisens, the refining or refinement of copper, iron; *die Arbeit ist —, the job is over, done or finished; † ich bin noch nicht — mit ihm, I have not yet done with him.

II. *adv.* [= ganz, gänzlich] quite, entirely. Er ist mir nicht — zehn Pfund schuldig, he owes me not quite ten pounds; es sind noch nicht — vier Wochen, daß ich ihn sah, it is not yet quite four weeks since I saw him; dieser Ihr Rock ist ganz und — abgetragen, this coat of yours is entirely worn out; er ist — nicht reich, he is not at all rich, he is nothing less than rich; ist er ehrgeizig? — nicht or ganz und — nicht, is he ambitious? not at all; er weiß — nichts, ganz und — nichts von der Sache, he knows nothing at all of the matter; ich zweifle — nicht, ganz und — nicht, daß &c., I have or I make not the least doubt, but &c.; ich bin ganz und — nicht Ihrer Meinung, I am not at all of your opinion. In a more limited sense: *a*) [in familiar language] very. Ich bekomme ihn nur — selten zu sehen, I see him but very seldom; ich habe ihm — viel zu danken, I am under very great obligations to him; er ist — arm, he is very, exceedingly poor; er hat — wenig Verstand, he has but very little understanding; er ist — zu groß, he is too tall; er ist — zu neugierig, he is too curious, he is overcurious; ein — herrlicher Bissen, a most delicious morsel; es ist so — theuer, daß ich es nicht kaufen kann, it is so very dear, that I cannot afford to buy it; ich kenne ihn nur — zu gut, I know him but too well, I am but too well acquainted with him; er ist nicht — zu groß, he is not so very tall; ich bin Dir — zu gut, you have no idea how much I love you, I am so very fond of you. *b*) [emphatically for sogar, selbst] even. Er begleitete sie — nach Hause, he even went home with her, he even saw her home; vielleicht ist er — mein Vetter, perhaps he is my cousin; vielleicht gefällt er mir —, perhaps I even shall like him; so —, or auch so —, sein Name ist verhaßt, his very name is odious; ei, warum nicht —! why truly! why indeed! what an idea! er hat ihn — noch geschlagen, he has even struck him.

Gar=arbeit, *f.* [in mining = das Garmachen] refining, refinement, V. Gar I. —**aus**, *m.* and *n.* [indeclinable] [in famil. and vulg. language] utter ruin, entire ruin, finishing stroke. Einer Sache das —aus machen, to finish, to settle an affair; Einem das or den —aus machen, das or den —aus mit Einem spielen [ihn zu Grunde richten, vollends tödten], to complete any one's ruin, to undo any one to all intents and purposes, to dispatch any one; er war von Räubern verwundet worden, Andere kamen und machten ihm das —aus, he had been wounded by robbers, others came who dispatched him. —**bräter**, *m.* —**bräterinn**, *f.* a cook that sells ready-dressed meat, chiefly roast-meat, keeper of a cook-shop, victualer. —**bräterei**, *f.* a place where roast meat is sold, a cook-shop, victualling-house. —**bruch**, *m.* [among refiners] dipping the iron rod into the melting copper to see whether it is purified enough. —**brühe**, *f.* [among tanners] the substance or liquor in which the skins or hides get their last dressing. —**eisen**, *n.* [among refiners] an iron rod which from time to time is dipped into the melting copper; [in metallurgy] refined iron. —**erz**, *n.* [among refiners] ore that is roasted or burnt enough, roasted or burnt ore. —**faß**, *n.* [among tawers] dressing tub, dressing vat. —**feuer**, *n.* [among refiners] fire by which the copper is roasted. —**herd**, *m.* [among refiners] refining furnace. —**knecht**, *m.* [in mining] a refiner's man or assistant. —**koch**, *m.* —**köchinn**, *f.* cook that sells ready-dressed meat, one that keeps a cook-shop. —**könig**, *m.* [among refiners] regulus of refined copper, purified copper; *it.* copper kept melting till it is perfectly pure. —**krätze**, *f.* [among refiners] slags or scoria of refined pure copper. —**küche**, *f.* a cook shop. Eine —küche halten, to keep a cook-shop. —**kupfer**, *n.* [among refiners] refined or purified copper, melted copper. —kupferabgang beim Feinmachen des Kupfers, loss or waste in the refining or melting of copper. —**leder**, *n.* [among tawers] tawed, dressed leather. —**machen**, *n.* [among curriers] the currying or dressing of leather; [among refiners] refining, affinage. —**macher**, *m.* [among refiners] purifier or refiner of metals. —**ofen**, *m.* [among refiners] a furnace where copper is refined. —**pfanne**, *f.* a large refining pan. —**probe**, *f.* [among refiners] operation or experiment for ascertaining the quantity of pure copper contained in the ore, assay. —**salz**, *n.* [in saltworks] well-boiled salt. —**scheibe**, *f.* [among refiners] plate of refined copper. —**schlacken**, *pl.* [among refiners] V. —krätze. —**späne**, *pl.* small parcels of copper adhering to the iron-rod when dipped into the melting copper. —**stück**, *n.* [in saltworks] a piece of purified, well-boiled salt.

***Garánt**, *m.* V. Bürge.

***Garantie**, *f.* [*pl.* -en] V. Bürgschaft.

***Garantiren**, *v. intr.* and *tr.* V. Bürgen, Gewährleisten and Verbürgen.

Gárbe, *f.* [*pl.* -n, *dimin.* Gärbchen, *n.*] [Fr. *gerbe*, perhaps from *carpo*, *cerpo*, prov. zerfen = abreißen] 1) [properly something cut down] a sheaf. —n binden, to make sheaves; das Getreide in —n binden, to bind up the corn into sheaves, to sheaf the corn; die —n in Haufen legen, to heap up, to pile the sheaves; ein Haufen von zehn —n, a shock, a heap of ten sheaves of corn; *fig.* [in pyrotechnics] V. Garbenfeuer. 2) [the piece from the neck to the shoulder of an ox] a neck of beef.

Garben=band, *n.* the band of a sheaf. —**binder**, *m.* —**binderinn**, *f.* a person who ties sheaves. —**feuer**, *n.* [in pyrotechnics] a Chinese tree. —**förmig**, *adj.* and *adv.* in form of a sheaf, by sheaves. —**haufe**, *m.* a heap of sheaves. —**krähe**, *f.* [a bird] the roller. V. also Mandelkrähe. —**schichter**, *m.* he who heaps up the sheaves. —**zeh[e]nte**, *m.* tithe of sheaves.

Gärbeliren, *v. tr.* [in mining] to crush, to dash or break in pieces, to pound the ore.

Gärben, [from gar] *v. tr.* [originally probably = machen] to convert animal skins into leather, to dress. Roth —, to tan; weiß —, to taw; die gegärbten Häute vollends bereiten, to curry or dress leather; *fig.* [in vulgar language] Jemanden —, ihm die Haut, den Buckel —, to curry any one, to curry any one's hide, to thrash, to belabour any one; [among refiners] den Stahl —, to refine steel; [among engravers] die Kupferplatten —, to burnish or polish the copper-plates; [among millers] den Spelt —, to decorticate spelt or zea; das —, the currying or dressing of leather.

Gärbe=bank, *f.* [among furriers] bench for paring hides. —**baum**, *m.* [among tanners] bench or wooden leg for scraping hides, a tanner's bench. —**eisen**, *n.* [among tawers] V. Falzeisen. —**haus**, *n.* [among tanners] tan-house. V. Gärberei. *it.* V. —kammer. —**hobel**, *m.* [among coopers] a cooper's smoothing-plane. —**kammer**, *f.* a tanner's or tawer's work-shop; *it.* V. Sacristei. —**mühle**, *f.* a mill where corn is only decorticated, not ground. —**stahl**, *m.* [*Brunirstahl] burnisher, burnishing steel. —**stoff**, *m.* tannin. —**stube**, [Bähstube] *f.* the stove or hothouse where the hides are steeped in alum-water. V. Schwitzer.

Gärber, *m.* [-s, *pl.* -] a man that manufactures leather, either tanned or other leather. Der —, welcher die lohgar gemachten Häute vollends bereitet [der Lederer], currier; der Roth—, Loh—, tanner; Weiß—, tawer.

Gärber=baum, [Färberbaum] *m.* V. Essigbaum, Sumach. —**gang**, *m.* a mill where corn is only decorticated, not ground. —**geselle**, *m.* journeyman tanner or currier. —**grube**, *f.* tanpit, tan-vat. —**handwerk**, *n.* the trade of a tanner, currier. V. Gärberei 2. —**junge**, *m.* a tanner's or currier's apprentice. —**kalk**, *m.* slack-lime. —**lohe**, *f.* tan. —**messer**, *n.* a tanner's scraping-knife. V. Ausfleischmesser. —**mühle**, *f.* tanning mill [where the bark is stamped]. —**strauch**, [Färberbaum] *m.* V. Essigbaum, Sumach. —**wolle**, *f.* wool which the tawer takes off the sheepskins.

Gärberei, *f.* 1) [= das Gärben] Loh—, tanning; Weiß—, tawing. 2) the business of a tanner or currier, leather-manufacture. 3) tan-house, tan-yard.

Gärbhammer, *m* [-s, *pl.* -hämmer] [in forges] hammer by which the refined steel is forged.

Gärbherd, *m.* [-es, *pl.* -e] [in forges] refining-furnace.

Gärbottich, *m.* [-s, *pl.* -e] V. Gährbottich.

Gärbstahl, *m.* [-s, *pl.* -e] refined steel.

***Gárde**, *f.* [*pl.* -n] [Leibwache; allied to wahren, verwahren] guard. Die königliche —

the king's guard; die — zu Fuß, foot-guards; die — zu Pferd, horse-guards.

Garde-offizier, *m.* an officer of guards. —regiment, *n.* regiment of guards.

*Garderobe, *f.* [*pl.* -n] 1) wardrobe. 2) [in fam. lang.] dress, garments.

*Garderobier, [*pron.* as in the French] *m.* [-'s, *pl.* -s] keeper of the wardrobe; [among stage-players] property-man.

*Gárdian or Guárdian, [often pron. Gwardian] *m.* [-s, *pl.* -s or -e] the guardian or superior of a convent. Der Franziskaner—, the guardian of the Franciscans or Franciscan friars.

*Gardine, *f.* [*pl.* -n] curtain. Die —n vorziehen, to draw the curtains; die —n auf- or auseinander ziehen, to draw asunder, to open the curtains.

Gardinen-arm, —haken, *m.* curtain-hook. —franse, *f.* curtain-fringe. *—predigt, *f.* curtain-lecture. —ring, *m.* curtain-ring. —stange, *f.* curtain-rod. —zug, *m.* curtain-line.

*Gardíst, *m.* [-en, *pl.* -en] soldier of the guards, guards-man. Often used in composition, as Polizei—, policeman; Zoll—, custom-house officer &c.

Gárd[a]seeröl, *n.* [-s] [called after the lake of that name] [the finest sort of sweet-oil] Verona oil.

Gáre, *f.* [from gar] 1) state of being done or dressed. Die — eines Ackers, the improvement of a field; die — der Felle, Häute, the dressing of hides or skins; dieser Kohlenmeiler hat die rechte —, this charcoal-pile has burnt enough; das Kupfer hat seine —, the copper is purified or refined enough; das Erz hat seine —, the ore is roasted enough; [in saltworks] die — der Sohle, the formation of salt after having boiled enough. 2) [among tawers] Eine — Häute, twenty four skins that are tawed at a time.

Gāre, *f.* V. Gähre.

Gareiß, Gareisel, *f.* V. Karausche.

Gāren, *v. intr.* V. Gähren.

Gárgel, *m.* V. Gergel.

Gārkammer, *f.* [*pl.* -n] V. Gährkammer.

Garlei, *m.* [-es] [from the Prussian town Gardeleben; perhaps more properly from gar] name of a kind of beer brewed in Brandenburg.

Gármond, Gármondschrift, *f.* [in printing] the long primer.

Gárn, *n.* [-es, *pl.* -e] [allied to the obsolete garn = bereiten] 1) [spun threads of flax, wool &c.] yarn. — spinnen, to spin; — haspeln, abwickeln, abwinden, to wind yarn into a skein or bottom, to reel yarn; — zwirnen, to twist thread; baumwollenes —, cotton yarn; wollenes —, woolen yarn, worsted. 2) [a net of twisted threads] net. Vögel, Fische &c. in dem —e, mit dem —e fangen, to catch birds, fish &c. in a net; das — aufstellen, auswerfen, to spread the net, to cast the net; eine schöne Forelle ist in das — gegangen, a fine trout has fallen into the net, has been taken or caught in the net; [among hunters] ein —, womit Rothwild gefangen wird, buckstall; die —e, hunter's toils; *it.* the second stomach of ruminating animals. *Fig.* *In's — gehen [= sich fangen, hintergehen lassen], to bite at the hook, to be ensnared, trapped or caught; er ist mir in's — gegangen, I have caught or trapped him; sie hat ihn im —e [= in ihrer Gewalt], she has smitten him, she has him at her disposal; von Spielern ins — gelockt, inveigled by gamesters; Einen in sein — ziehen, to engage any one in one's interest.

Garn-baum, *m.* yarn-beam of the loom. —enden, *pl.* [abgeschnittene —enden] the thrums. —gabel, *f.* [among hunters] forked stake, rod to hold the net. —handel, *m.* trade in yarn. —händler, *m.* —händlerinn, *f.* a dealer in yarn. —haspel, *m.* reel, windles. —klotz, *m.* [among chandlers] a chandler's block or log. —knäuel, *m.* a bottom or clew of yarn. —leute, *pl.* people assisting in drawing the nets. —masche, *f.* net-mash. —meister, *m.* a fisherman, that fishes with great nets. —reuse, *f.* fisher's weel. —rolle, *f.* [among ropemakers] wheel, reel or winch [on which the yarn is wound up]. —sack, —schlauch, *m.* [among fishermen] a sweep-net. —spule, *f.* spool or spindle; *it.* a spindleful. —stange, *f.* V. —gabel. —stock, *m.* [among silk-weavers] a stick on which the died silk-skeins are hung up to bring them in order. —strähne, *f.* a skein of yarn. —stricker, *m.* a knitter of nets. —stück, *n.* V. —strähne. —weber, *m.* yarn-weaver. —weise, *f.* V. —haspel. —winde, *f.* yarnwindle, reel. —zug, *m.* [among fishermen] fishing with nets; *it.* the drawing of the nets.

Garnéle, *f.* [*pl.* -n] or Garnelenkrebs, [Dutch *gaerner*] *m.* [in natural history] prawn, shrimp, squill.

Gárner, *m.* V. Garnele.

*Garnisón, *f.* [*pl.* -en] garrison. V. also Besatzung 1).

Garnisonsprediger, *m.* chaplain to the garrison.

*Garnitúr, *f.* [*pl.* -en] border, trimming, garniture. V. also Besatz. Eine — Bänder, a set of ribbons; eine — Brillanten, Perlen, Granaten, a set of brilliants, pearls, granates.

Gárstig, I. *adj.* [from the ancient *gor*, Gr. σκῶρ = *dirt*] 1) dirty, nasty, filthy. —e Hände haben, to have dirty hands; ein —es Zimmer, a filthy room; —es [unreines] Wasser, nasty, muddy water; es ist ein —es Wetter, it is nasty, dirty weather, V. schmutzig; [*it.* sometimes used for ranzig] —er Speck, —e Butter, rancid bacon, rancid butter. 2) [= ungestalt, häßlich] ugly. Ein —es Gesicht, an ugly face; das ist sehr —, that is very ugly; der —e or was für ein —er Mensch! what an ugly fellow! ein —es Kleid, eine —e Perrücke, an ugly dress, an ugly wig. *Fig.* [morally ugly] er hat mir einen —en Streich gespielt, he has played me an ugly or scurvy trick; —e Handlungen, dirty, villanous, base actions; —e Reden, obscene, lewd, indecent words, foul language; er sagt gern —e Dinge, he is fond of talking bawdy; —e Bücher, obscene, bawdy books; das ist ein sehr —es Lied, that is a very obscene, smutty song. II. *adv.* 1) dirtily, nastily, filthily. 2) obscenely, bawdily. 3) *Fig.* [in fam. and in vulg. lang.] in a bad manner. Er wurde — empfangen, he was badly, shamefully received; er wurde — geprügelt, he was outrageously beaten; er hat mich — verrathen, he has vilely betrayed me.

Gárstigkeit, *f.* dirtiness, nastiness, filthiness. V. Schmutz. Die — eines Gesichtes, the ugliness of a face; die — einer Handlung, des Lasters, the vileness of an action, the ugliness of vice. V. Häßlichkeit; die — dieser Bilder, dieser Reden, the obscenity, indecency of these pictures, of this language.

Gärtchen, ||Gärtlein, [*dimin.* of Garten] *n.* [-s, *pl.* -] a little garden.

Gärteln, *v. intr.* [rather provinc.] to garden, to dress a garden. Er gärtelt gern, he is fond of gardening. Das —, gardening; er versteht das — gut, he understands gardening well.

Gárten, *m.* [-s, *pl.* Gärten] [Fr. *jardin*; Wend. *gradim* is = einzäunen; the Goth. *gards*, the Dan. Gaard signifies Haus] garden. V. Blumen—, Küchen—, Obst—. Einen — anlegen, to lay out a garden; im — arbeiten, to work in the garden; V. Gärteln.

Garten-ampfer, *m.* [in botany] patience, monk's rhubarb, garden-sorrel, spinage. —anemone, *f.* cultivated garden anemone. —anpflanzung, *f.* garden-plot. —arbeit, *f.* work in the garden, gardening. Er ist kein Freund von —arbeit, he is no great friend of gardening. —bau, *m.* 1) the cultivation of a garden, garden-tillage, horticulture. 2) the art of cultivating gardens, horticulture. Die Berliner, Fraundorfer &c. —baugesellschaft, the Berlin, Fraundorf &c. Horticultural Society. —baukunst, *f.* V. —bau 2). —beet, *n.* bed in a garden. Ein abhängig angelegtes —beet, a shelving-bed. —biene, *f.* the garden or domestic bee. —blume, *f.* garden-flower. —buch, *n.* [a work that treats of gardening] gardening-book. —cichorie, *f.* V. —wegewarte. —cypresse, *f.* garden-cypress, little cypress. —cypreßkraut, *n.* cypress-leaved Santolina. —distel, *f.* artichoke. —erbse, *f.* garden-pea. —erdbeere, *f.* garden strawberry. —erde, *f.* garden-mould. —feld, *n.* land cultivated as a garden, garden-ground, inclosure. —freund, *m.* one who is fond of gardens or gardening, a lover of gardens. —frosch, *m.* the brown garden frog. —frucht, *f.* garden-fruit. Seine —früchte verkaufen, to sell the produce of one's garden. —gemüse, *n.* vegetables, greens, garden-stuff. —geräth, *n.* gardening tools, horticultural implements. —gewächs, *n.* pot-herb, vegetable. —gewächse, *pl.* vegetables, garden-stuff. —gott, *m.* [in mythology] the God of gardens [Priapus]. —göttinn, *f.* the goddess of gardens [Flora, Pomona]. —gras, *n.* grass growing in gardens. —hammer, *m.* a gardener's hammer. —haue, *f.* a small hoe used in gardening, a weeding-hook. —haus, *n.* summer-house, garden-house. Er hat ein prächtiges —haus in die Mitte seines Gartens gebauet, he has built a splendid summerhouse in the middle of his garden; dieses —häuschen ist mit Jasmin bekleidet, this arbour or bower is covered with jasmine. —hecke, *f.* the hedge of a garden. —honig, *m.* garden honey. —hopfen, *m.* garden or cultivated hops. —huhn, *n.* a cabbage-head filled with force-meat. —hummel, *f.* garden drone. —hüter, *m.* the guard or keeper of a garden. —isop, *m.* V. Saturei. —kerbel, *m.* common or garden chervil. —kirsche, *f.* garden cherry. —klee, *m.* garden clover. —knecht, *m.* garden labourer, a gardener's servant. —kneif, *m.* V. —messer. —kraut, *n.* V. Stabwurz. —kräuter, *pl.* pot-herbs, vegetables, greens, gardenstuff. —kresse, *f.* garden cresses. —kröte, *f.* V. Feldkröte. —kümmel, *m.* garden cummin. —kunst, *f.* the art of cultivating gardens, gardening, horticulture. —land, *n.* 1) soil fit for the purposes of gardening. 2) V. —feld; *it.* V. —beet. —laube, *f.* arbour, bower. —leben, *n.* garden-life. —leiter, *f.* a ladder used in gardening, a double ladder. —lerche, *f.* garden lark, titlark. —linse, *f.* garden lentil. —lust, *f.* the pleasure of a garden or of gardening, the pleasures of a garden-life. —mark, *n.* V. Gesterie. —maßliebe, *f.* garden daisy. —meise, *f.* V. Graumeise. —meister, *m.* [in convents] a monk that has the care of the gardens. —melde, *f.* garden orach. —messer, *n.* gardening knife, pruning knife. —mohn, *m.* garden poppy. —münze, *f.* garden mint. —nelke, *f.* the cultivated garden pink or gilliflower. —nessel, *f.* garden nettle. —pappel, *f.* the garden mallows, pass-rose. —pastinake, *f.* garden parsnep. —quendel, *m.* V. —saturei. —raute, *f.* the garden rue. —recht, *n.* the right or privilege to enclose a garden, the right of enclosure. —röthling, *m.* —rothschwänzchen, *n.* [a bird] red tail. —saal, *m.* a saloon or large room in a summerhouse; *it.* an arbour or bower. —säge, *f.* V. Baumsäge. —saturei, *f.* garden savory. —scharlach, —scharlei, *m.* V. Scharlachkraut, Scharlei. —schaufel, *f.* a garden shovel. —scheere, *f.* garden shears. —schnecke, *f.* garden snail, dew snail, earth snail. V. Feldschnecke. —schnur, *f.* a gardener's line or cord. —schütze, *m.* V. —hüter. —schwamm, *m.* mushroom. —senf, *m.* cultivated mustard. —spargel, *m.* garden asparagus. —spinne, *f.* the garden spider, spinner. —thor, *n.* garden-gate. —thür[e], *f.* garden door. —walze, *f.* garden roller. —wanze, *f.* flying bug. V. Baumwanze. —wegewarte, *f.* garden succory. —werk, *n.* [—anlage] gardening, gardens, garden-plot. Es gibt schöne —werke um diese Stadt, there are fine gardens about this town. —wesen, *n.* any thing concerning gardening; gardening. —wurz, *f.* V. Stabwurz. —zaun, *m.* garden hedge or fence, garden inclosure. —zehnte, *m.* tithe of the produce of gardens. —zierrath, *m.* ornaments of a garden. —zins, *m.* garden rent.

Gärthafer, *m.* [-s] V. Stabwurz.

Gärtheil, Gärtkraut, *n.* [-s] V. Ruthenkraut.

Gärtlein, *n.* V. Gärtchen.

Gärtner, *m.* [-s, *pl.* -] gardener. Er ist ein vortrefflicher —, he is an excellent gardener. V. Baum—, Kunst— &c. *Prov* Den Bock zum — setzen, to set the fox to keep the geese.

Gärtner-kunst, *f.* art of gardening. V. Gartenkunst. —waaren, *pl.* garden-ware.

Gärtnerei, *f.* gardening, art of gardening, horticulture.

Gärtnerinn, *f.* a female gardener, a gardener's wife.

Gärwe, *f.* V. Feldkümmel.

Gärzeröl, *n.* [-s] V. Gärbseröl.

Gas, *n.* [-es, *pl.* -e] [allied to Geist, Gäscht, Gischt] [an elastic aeriform fluid] gas. Azotisches —, Stick—, azotic gas; essigsaures —, acid gas; flußsaures —, fluoric acid gas; gekohltes Wasserstoff—, carbonic hydrogen gas; kohlensaures —, carbonic acid gas; laugenartiges —, ammoniac gas; oxigenirtes, dephlogistirtes, säurendes — [or Sauerstoff—], oxigen gas; phosphorisches Wasserstoff—, phosphoric hydrogen gas; salpetersaures —, nitric gas; salzsaures —, muriatic acid.

Gas-art, *f.* a species of gas —artig, *adj.* and *adv.* of the nature or in the form of gas, gaseous. —beleuchtung, —erleuchtung, *f.* gas-light, lighting with gas. —förmig, *adj.* and *adv.* in the form of gas, gaseous. —haltig, *adj.* and *adv.* containing gas.

Gäsch, V. Gäscht.

Gäschen, *v. intr.* [V. Gas] to froth, to ferment, to foam. Das Bier gäscht, wenn es gährt, beer froths in fermentation. *Fig.* *Vor Wuth —, to foam with rage. V. Schäumen.

Gäscht, *m* [-es, *pl.* -e] [V. Gas] 1) [the bubbles caused in liquors by agitation] spume, froth, foam. 2) [the froth or flower of beer in fermentation] yeast, barm. 3) [interior motion of the constituent parts of a fluid] fermentation, effervescence.

***Gasconade**, *f.* [*pl.* -n] gasconade.

Gasconien, *n.* [-s] Gascony [in France].

Gasconier, *m.* [-s, *pl.* -] -inn, *f.* Gascon [inhabitant of Gascony].

Gasconisch, *adj.* and *adv.* Gascon. Die —e Mundart or Redensart, Gasconism.

Gase, *f.* [*pl.* -n] V. Alant.

***Gasometer**, *n.* [-s, *pl.* -] gasometer.

Gäspe, *f.* [*pl.* -n] [Sw. *gäspa* is = gähnen, allied to gaffen, to the Lat. *cavus* &c.] [in familiar language] what both hands can hold or contain, two handfuls. Eine — Haber, as much oats as both hands together can contain.

Gasse, *f.* [*pl.* -n] [from the Icel. *gasa*, to run, allied to gehen, to go, hence:] 1) any space between two things where something or somebody moves along; [in military affairs, a long space or passage between two lines or rows of soldiers] a lane. Die Soldaten bildeten eine lange —, the soldiers formed a long lane; —n laufen, in die — müssen [Spießruthen laufen], to run the gantlet or gantelope; [in husbandry] die Gassen, [in beehives] the empty space between the honeycombs; [among weavers] unequal distance of the threads of the warp; [among printers] row; die erste —, the first row. 2) [usually, a way between two rows of houses] a street, a lane; *diminut.* Gäßchen, Gäßlein, *n.* a narrow street, a lane, an alley. Eine — ohne Ausgang, Strumpf—, Sack—, a turn-again alley, a blind alley, a street or an alley that is no thoroughfare; er wohnt in der Juden—, he lives in Jews'-street; am Ende der —, at the top or bottom of the street; er that es auf öffentlicher —, he did it in the street, in the middle of the street; hören Sie den Lärm auf der —? do you hear the noise in the street? auf den —n herumlaufen, to run or saunter about the streets; die —n in einem Lager, the [streets or] lanes of a camp. *Prov.* Hans in allen —n, Jack of all trades, a busybody. Syn. Gasse, Straße. Straße [Lat. via strata] signifies originally a paved way, for with the Romans the high-roads were paved. Afterwards all the great roads in Germany came to be denominated Straßen, although not paved. In a more limited sense the word Straße is now used to denote the paved way between the houses in towns and villages. The distinction commonly made between Straße and Gasse is, that under the former are understood the long and broad ways between the houses, *streets*; under the latter the smaller and narrower, *lanes.*

Gassen-bettel, *m.* —betteln, *n.* begging about the streets. —bettler, *m.* a street beggar, common beggar. —bettlerinn, *f.* a common beggarwoman. —bube, *m.* a street-boy, blackguard-boy. —bubenstreich, *m.* a blackguard-boy's trick. —dieb, *m.* a pick-pocket, cut-purse, a common thief. —dirne, *f.* a street walker, a prostitute. †—dreck, *m.* V. —koth. —hauer, *m.* V. —lied. —hauptmann, [rather unusual] *m.* [*pl.* —hauptleute] a town or city officer of the peace, a constable. —hure, *f.* a street walker, a drab, common strumpet, a woman of the town. —junge, *m.* V. —bube. —kehren, *n.* the sweeping of the streets. —kehrer, *m.* —kehrerinn, *f.* sweeper of the streets, scavenger. —koth, *m.* dirt or mud in the streets. —kothführer, *m.* scavenger, dustman. —laterne, *f.* lamp for lighting the streets. —laufen, *n.* [a military punishment] gantlet or gantelope, running the gantlet. —lied, *n.* a vulgar ballad, such as is sung about the streets. —meister, *m.* V. —hauptmann. —mensch, *n.* V. —dirne, —hure. —pöbel, *m.* the rabble. —rinne, *f.* kennel. —scherz, *m.* blackguard joke. —schleuße, *f.* sewer in the street. —treter, *m.* lounger, idler. V. Pflastertreter. —troß, *m.* blackguards, the rabble. —vogt, *m.* V. Bettelvogt. —volk, *n.* V. —troß. —wirth, *m.* —wirthinn, *f.* a tavern-keeper. V. Schenkwirth, Schenkwirthinn. —wirthschaft, *f.* a tavern; *it.* the business of a tavern-keeper. —wirthshaus, *n.* [Bräu and Bierschenke] a tavern, alehouse, pothouse. —witz, *m.* vulgar wit, low jest.

Gast, *m.* [-es, *pl.* Gäste] [originally probably = every one who went anywhere as a stranger; it is allied to gehen, to go, provincially *goan*; it is likewise allied to the Lat. *host-is* and *hos-pes*] [in Scripture] So seyd ihr nun nicht mehr Gäste und Fremdlinge, now therefore you are no more strangers and foreigners. In a more limited sense: *a*) [in familiar language = Kunde] a customer. V. Bier—. Gäste setzen, halten, to keep an ordinary. *b*) any person entertained at the table or house of another, a guest. Sie hat heute Gäste, she has people to dine or sup with her to-day; Gäste bitten, to invite company; er hat seine Gäste gut bewirthet, he has entertained his guests, his company well, he has given a handsome entertainment to his guests; Gäste zum Abendessen erwarten, to expect guests or company to supper; alle Gäste waren sehr aufgeräumt, all the guests were in good humour; wollen Sie mein — seyn? will you dine, sup with me? seyen Sie heute mein —, dine, sup with me to-day; er hat oft Gäste, he sees a great deal of company at his house or at his table; *Prov.* ungebetene Gäste sind oft die angenehmsten, uninvited guests often are the most welcome; Sie sind mir ein willkommener —, you are very welcome, Sir; ein ungebetener —, a trencher-friend, a spunger; Jemanden zu —e laden, bitten, [in this sense Gast seems rather allied to Kost, fare] to invite any one to dinner or supper; ich speise heute nicht zu Hause, ich bin zu —e, ich gehe zu —e, I shall not dine at home to day, I am invited to dine abroad or out; sich selbst zu —e bitten [ungeladen als — kommen], to come uninvited. *c*) a person that puts up at an inn, a stranger. In diesem Gasthofe sind immer Fremde or Gäste, there are always strangers at this inn. *d*) *Fig.* [in familiar language] any person, fellow, wight. Er ist ein reicher —, he is a rich man or fellow; ein loser, schlauer —, a cunning blade; er ist ein grober —, he is a rude fellow, a clown, a churl; ein lustiger —, a merry or jolly blade or dog; [ironically] Sie sind mir ein schöner —! you are a pretty or nice fellow indeed!

Gast-becher, *m.* a large goblet to drink the guests' welcome out of. —bett, *n.* bed for a stranger. —frei, *adj.* and *adv.* hospitable. —freiheit, *f.* hospitality. Die —freiheit ausüben, to practice hospitality. —freund, *m.* a stranger enjoying the right of hospitality, a guest; *it.* a host. —freundschaft, *f.* hospitality. —freundschaftlich, *adj.* and *adv.* hospitable. —geber, *m.* host, innkeeper, landlord; master of an ordinary. —geberinn, *f.* hostess, landlady. —gebot, *n.* a rich entertainment, banquet, feast. V. Gastmahl, Gelag, Mahl, Schmaus. —gericht, *n.* V. —recht. —geschenk, *n.* present made to a stranger. —halter, *m.* V. —geber. —haus, *n.* house of entertainment; inn, hotel; V. —hof; *it.* [ein Hospital für Arme] a hospital. —herr, *m.* he who gives an entertainment, entertainer, host; *it.* V. —geber. —hof, *m.* a large inn, hotel. Im —hofe einkehren, to put up at an inn, to take one's lodging at an inn; er hat einen —hof, he keeps an inn. Syn. Gasthof, Gasthaus, Herberge, Wirthshaus. Only such houses are now called Herberge, in which travellers receive merely shelter and bed, and are intended only for the poorer classes who carry their provisions with them. If in such public houses provisions are also furnished, they are then termed Wirthshäuser. Ein Gasthof is a spacious building in which strangers or guests with their servants, horses &c. are lodged and entertained for money. Such houses are usually denominated Gasthäuser in which strangers are entertained but not lodged. —kammer, *f.* a chamber for a guest or stranger. —kleid, *n.* dress coat, dress suit. —mahl, *n.* banquet, feast, entertainment. Einem zu Ehren ein —mahl geben, halten, anstellen, to give an entertainment in any one's honour; zu einem —mahle gehen, to go to a feast or banquet. —meister, [obsolete] *m.* V. —geber; *it.* [in monasteries] brother hospitaller. —mutter, *f.* [in hospitals] the matron; *it.* [in convents] a sister who receives the poor and strangers. —ordnung, *f.* regulations for innkeepers concerning the treatment of their guests. —predigt, *f.* a sermon preached by a stranger [*i. e.* not the usual clergyman of the parish]. —recht, *n.* 1) right of hospitality. 2) [in some places] a summary way of administering justice to strangers, V. Handelsrecht, Kaufrecht. —rolle, *f.* a theatrical representation given [part performed] by a stranger. Herr N. spielt or gibt heute den Hamlet zur ersten —rolle, Mr. N. will perform the part of Hamlet for his first representation at this theatre. —stube, *f.* 1) a room for a guest or stranger. 2) the common room in an inn, coffee-room. V. Wirthsstube. —tag, *m.* a day of an entertainment or of feasting. —tisch, *m.* ordinary, table d'hôte. Am —tische essen, to dine or sup at an ordinary. —weise, *adv.* as a stranger, as a guest. —wirth, *m.* —wirthinn, *f.* V. —geber, —geberinn. —wirthschaft, *f.* 1) the keeping of an inn or hotel. 2) an inn or hotel. Er hat eine —wirthschaft errichtet, he has set up as an innkeeper. —zimmer, *n.* V. —stube 1).

‡Gästelknecht, *m.* [-es, *pl.* -e] a servant of a guild or company who invites its members to a meeting.

Gasterei, *f.* [*pl.* -en] feast, banquet, entertainment. Eine — anstellen, ausrichten, to give a great entertainment or banquet; einer — beiwohnen, to be present at a banquet, to make one at a feast.

Gastiren, *v. intr.* [in familiar language] 1) [= ein Gastmahl ausrichten, schmausen] to entertain, to give entertainments, to feast, to banquet. Er gastirt alle Tage, he feasts every day. 2) [said of an inn-keeper] to keep an inn, an ordinary. 3) to give a theatrical representation as a guest at a strange theatre.

Gastirung, *f.* V. Gasterei.

Gästung, *f.* V. Gasterei.

Gastungsrecht, [rather unusual] *n.* [right or privilege of entertaining strangers for money] right or privilege of keeping an inn.

Gát, *n.* [-es, *pl.* -e] [in seamen's language] 1) a hole [chiefly used in composition, as Hals—, Kabel—, which see]. 2) the hindpart of a ship, stern. Ein rundes —, round stern.

Gäten, [jäten] [perhaps = weiden] *v. tr.* [to free from noxious plants] to weed [a garden &c.]. Man hat schon in diesem Felde gegätet, they have already weeded this field; das Korn, Zwiebeln —, to weed corn, onions. V. Ausjäten.

Gät-gras, *n.* weeds, weedings. —hake, —haue, *f.* hoe for weeding, weed-hook, weeding-hook.

Gäter, *m.* [-s, *pl.* -] -inn, *f.* weeder.

Gätlich, I *adj.* [allied to gatten, which see] 1) commodious, suitable, convenient. 2) of middle size. Ein —er junger Mensch, a youth of middle size. II. *adv.* commodiously, conveniently, suitably. Er ist — groß, he is of middle size.

Gätte, *m.* [-n, *pl.* -n] spouse, husband, consort, mate; [said of birds, rather poet.] mate, partner. Diese Turteltaube hat ihren —n verloren, this turtle-dove has lost her mate.

Gätten, [seems to be the frequentative from gehen] I. *v. tr.* [= vereinigen, verbinden] to unite, to join. [in commerce] Waaren —, to sort goods; [among cardmakers] die Karten —, to pack the cards. II. *v. r.* sich —, to match, to couple, to pair, to copulate. V. Begatten. [in poetry] Ein freundliches Thal, wo Ruh' und Stille sich —, a pleasant valley where peace and silence reign; wo zwei Ströme sich —, where the waters of two rivers meet.

Gätter, *n.* [-s; *pl.* -] [= Gitter] [a work or frame composed of parallel or cross bars with interstices] a grate, lattice, [among tin-founders] tin cast in form of a grate; [in seamen's language, = Steuerruder] rudder, helm; [in painting, a grate or frame composed of many squares for reducing great figures to small ones or vice versa] frame. Die Umrisse einer Figur durch das — nachzeichnen, to reduce a figure by squares, to graticulate a figure.

Gatter-geld, *n.* —gulden, *m.* V. —zins. —haube, *f.* a woman's cap of silk, gold &c. in form of a net or grate. —herr, [V. —zins] *m.* a landlord that receives an additional rent over and above the quit-rent. —thor, *n.* a gate with a lattice or grate, a grated gate. —thür[e], *f.* a door with a lattice or grate, a grated door. —werk, *n.* lattice work, grate-work, trellis work. —zins, *m* [perhaps from gattern, Anglo-Saxon gaderen = einsammeln, to gather] a rent over and above the quit-rent. V. Nachzins. —zinsmann, *m.* a farmer that owes a rent over and above the quit-rent.

1. Gättern, *v. tr.* V. Gittern. [among tin-founders] Zinn —, to cast tin in form of a grate.

‖2. Gättern, [seems to be = wittern, Lat *videre* = sehen] I. *v. tr.* to gatter. II *v. intr.* [only in familiar or vulgar language] Auf etwas —, to have an eye upon something, to wait for, to watch for something.

Gätterschaft, *f.* the quality of a piece of ground being subject to paying an additional rent over and above the quitrent.

Gättinn, *f.* spouse, wife, consort; [of birds] mate.

Gattirung, *f.* [a neologism, in mineralogy] classification, the art of classifying.

Gättung, *f.* kind, genus, species, sort. Was für eine — Tuch ist das? what sort of cloth is that? er hat Zeuge von allen —en, he has stuffs of all kinds, of all sorts; es giebt verschiedene —en von Thieren, there are several kinds or species of animals; die vollkommenste — der Thiere ist der Mensch, the most perfect species of animal is man; das Thiergeschlecht begreift zwei —en, den Menschen und das Thier, the genus of animal comprehends two species, man and beast; die drei —en der Beredsamkeit, the three kinds of eloquence. V. Pflanzen—, Thier— &c. [in grammar] der —sname, [a name pertaining to the whole species] appellative name, common name; Mensch, Baum, sind —snamen, man, tree, are common names; das —swort, common noun, noun appellative; als —swort, appellatively; die verschiedenen —en der Zeitwörter, the different kinds of verbs; die thätige, die leidende —, the active, passive form; in was für einer — der Mahlerei hat sich dieser Künstler hervorgethan? in what kind of painting has this artist distinguished himself?

Gattungsmahler, *m.* a painter in a particular kind, still-life painter, genre-painter.

Gau, *m.* and *n.* [allied to the Gr. γῆ, γαῖα = Erde, Land] [-es, *pl.* -e] [the country as opposed to city] the country; *it.* a province; *it.* a district. Ehemals waren die Provinzen Deutschlands in viele —e vertheilt, formerly the provinces of Germany were divided into many districts.

Gau-ding, *n.* —gericht, *n.* a provincial court of justice, right of judicature in a certain district. —graf, *m.* a count invested with the right of judicature in a certain district; *it.* a country judge. —grafschaft, *f.* the territory of a Gaugraf. —wort, *n.* a provincial term.

Gauch, [obsolescent and provincial] *m.* [probably allied to geben in frequentative signification] [-es or -en, *pl.* -e or -en, Gäuche] 1) a beardless boy, hence a silly fellow, a ninny, a fop, gawk, buffoon. 2) the first hair of the beard, down. 3) apparition, spectre. 4) [in natural history] *a*) cantharis. *b*) the name of several birds as cuckoo, jack-daw, owl.

Gauch-bart, *m.* the first down of a man's beard, hence a young fellow, chiefly a silly young man, a ninny, gawk, V. Gauch 1); [in botany] goat's beard or salsify. —blume, *f.* common lady's smock or cuckoo flower. —brod, *n.* V. Bocksbart. —hafer, *m.* wild oats. —heil, *n.* anagallis, pimpernel, shepherd's weather-glass. —klee, *m.* V. Buchampfer.

Gauche, *f.* [*pl.* -n] [Low. Sax. Jüche, Lat. *jus*, is = Brühe] any filthy, stinking fluid. Dieses Bier ist eine wahre —, this beer is very bad, regular swipes.

Gaudieb, *m.* [gau allied to jäh = schnell] [-es, *pl.* -e] [in fam. or vulg. lang.] a cunning thief, a sharper. V. Gauner.

Gaukel, *m.* [unusual] [-s] Gaukelei, *f.* [*pl.* -en] [seems to be allied to geben] originally, a quick motion of the body; hence chiefly an odd, fanciful quick motion of the body in order to impose upon the spectator, sleight of hand, trick, legerdemain, prestigiation. Gaukeleien machen, to play tricks by sleight of hand, to juggle, to play antics; die Verwandlungen, welche die ägyptischen Magier hervorbrachten, waren bloße Gaukeleien, the changes wrought by the Egyptian magii were mere juggling tricks. *Fig.* [Schein, Trug] Das ist nur Gaukelei, that is a mere imposture.

Gaukel-bild, *n.* a fanciful vision, a phantasm; *it.* delusion, illusion. Ein holdes —bild, a sweet imagery. —blume, *f.* monkey flower, mimulus. —licht, *n.* a thin candle of bad tallow [for the use of servants]. —männchen, *n.* a small wooden figure with lead in its feet, a tumbler; [among jugglers] a puppet, a jack in a box. —possen, *pl.* ridiculous tricks, juggling-tricks, prestiges. —puppe, *f.* puppet [of a puppetshow]. —schwung, *m.* a juggler's trick. —spiegel, *m.* a mirror by which optical deceptions are practised, a conjuring mirror. —spiel, *n.* V. Gaukelei. Ein —spiel der Sinne, der Phantasie, a delusion of the senses, of fancy; ein —spiel der Hölle, a hellish delusion. —sprung, *m.* a ridiculous leap, a caper. —tanz, *m.* [a grotesque dance] pantaloon's dance, matachin. —tänzer, *m.* a grotesque dancer. —tasche, *f.* a juggler's box or pocket. Ein Stückchen aus der —tasche, a juggling-trick, legerdemain. —werk, *n.* V. Gaukelei. Das —werk der schwarzen Kunst, the illusions of the black art, of magic.

Gaukelhaft, *adj.* and *adv.* odd, ridiculous, antic, juggling; *it.* prestigious; delusive. —e Possen, juggling or legerdemain tricks; —er Prunk, delusive pomp.

Gaukelicht, *adj.* and *adv.* V. Gaukelhaft.

Gaukeln, [V. Gaukel] *v. intr.* 1) to move hastily and irregularly from place to place. Ein Irrlicht gaukelt um den Sumpf, an ignis fatuus flutters about the marsh; mit dem Lichte *herum —, to run carelessly about with the candle 2) [chiefly] to practise odd gesticulations in order to deceive the spectator, to play antics, to juggle. V. Gaukelei. Aus der Tasche —, to show juggling-tricks, to play tricks of legerdemain.

Gaukler, *m.* [-s, *pl.*-] 1) one who practises or exhibits tricks by sleight of hand, a juggler, prestigiator [in a proper as well as in a fig. sense], a conjurer, tumbler, buffoon, merry-andrew. Ein geschickter —, a clever, a dexterous juggler. 2) [in botany] monkey-flower, mimulus; [in natural history] an insect of the genus scarabaeus, tumble-dung.

Gauklerisch, *adj.* and *adv.* V. Gaukelhaft.

Gaul, *m.* [-es, *pl.* Gäule] [Lat. *caballus*] V. Pferd. [rather vulgar] horse, nag. Ein schlechter —, a sorry jade. *Prov.* Einem geschenkten — sieht man nicht in's Maul, you must not look a gift horse in the mouth. V. Acker—, Karren—.

Gaumen, *m.* [-s, *pl.* -] [perhaps allied to gähnen, gaffen, to yawn] the roof or upper part of the mouth, palate. Das kitzelt den —, that tickles or pleases the palate; die Zunge klebt mir am —, my tongue sticks to my palate.

Gaumen=beine, *pl.* [two very irregular bones which form the palate] ossa palati, bones of the palate. —**buchstabe,** *m.* a palatal. —**drüse,** *f.* palatal gland. —**sucht,** *f.* [a disease in which the patient has a perpetual and insatiable appetite for food] bulimy.

Gauner, *m.* [-s, *pl.* -] [allied to the Old Fr. *engan* = Betrug, and probably to the Low. Germ. gau = schnell] a cunning cheat, sharper, swindler, a shark, a rook. Er ist von einem alten — angeführt worden, he has been cheated or taken in by an old swindler; er ist ein Erz—, he is an arrant rogue or knave; welch ein —streich! what a rascally trick!

Gaunerei, *f.* a swindling-trick, a cheat, imposture, knavery.

Gaunern, *v. intr.* [in familiar or vulgar language = im Spiele betrügen] to cheat, to trick.

Gaupe, *f.* [*pl.* -n] [allied to Gäspe] [in architecture = Kappfenster] dormer [-window], luthern.

Gautschbret, *n.* [-es, *pl.* -er] [in papermills] pressing plank or board.

||**Gautsche,** *f.* [*pl.* -n] [allied to Kutsche, huschen] V. Schaukel.

Gautschen, *v. tr.* 1) [among papermakers] to put [the sheets] on the pressing-board. ||2) [said of children &c.] V. Schaukeln.

||**Gautscher,** *m.* [-s, *pl.* -] he that puts the sheets on the pressing-board.

*****Gavotte,** [pron. Gawotte] *f.* [*pl.* -n] [a lively dance] gavot.

*****Gaze,** *f.* [*pl.* -n] [pron. Gahs] [a very thin, slight, transparent stuff of silk or linen] gauze. Ein Schleier von — or ein —schleier, a gauze-veil.

Gazen=macher, —**weber,** *m.* gauze-maker.

Gazelle, *f.* [*pl.* -n] gazelle. V. also Antilope [Bezoarbock], Hirschziege.

Gazellenfluß, *m.* Wad-el-Gazel.

*****Gazette,** *f.* [*pl.* -n] V. Zeitung.

Ge=, an unaccented syllable that may be, but in polite language seldom is, prefixed to the infinitive mood of any verb, by omitting the terminating n or en; for instance: Geächze, Geacker, Gebeiße, Gebettel, Gebrülle &c. from ächzen, ackern, beißen &c. By means of this prefix a verb becomes a substantive of the neuter gender, wanting a plural and indicating the repetition of a thing or continuance in a particular state. It sometimes conveys also the idea of contempt. Das Geächze, das Geacker &c. = anhaltendes Aechzen, fortgesetztes Ackern, repeated and long continued groans, continual groaning, continual ploughing or tillage.

Geächt, *adj.* [in astronomy] Der —e Schein, [that aspect of two planets in which they are distant from each other the eighth part of a circle or forty five degrees] octant, octile.

Geächtet, *past. part.* of ächten. Der —e, out-law; er ist unter den —en, he is among the outlaws or proscribed.

Geäder, *n.* [-s] the veins, the venous system. Das — im menschlichen Körper, the veins of the human body; *fig.* dieses Holz, dieser Marmor hat ein sehr schönes —, this wood, this marble is very beautifully veined.

Geädert, *adj.* veiny, veined, full of veins; [in blasonry] nerved; [in mining] veined, ramified.

Geäfter, *n.* [-s] [among hunters = die Afterklauen] the edge of a deer's hoof; [of dogs] claws.

Geäß, *n.* [-es, (or Geäse, *n.* -s) *pl.* -e] 1) [among hunters = das Futter] pasture, feeding. Der Hirsch geht, zieht bei Nacht dem —e nach, the hart goes a-feeding in the night-time. 2) place or ground where the deer feed. 3) the mouth of deer. 4) lure [for a hawk].

Geäugt, *adj.* and *adv.* having eyes, eyed.

Gebäck, Gebäck, *n.* [-es, *pl.* -e] 1) V. Backwerk. 2) the quantity of bread baked at one time, a batch.

Gebacken, *past. part.* of backen. Das —e, pastry; essen Sie gern —es? do you like pastry? V. Backwerk.

Gebähn, *n.* [-es] [among hunters] dung of deer, fumet.

Gebälg, *n* [-es] [in forges] the whole of the bellows used in a forge.

Gebälge, *n.* [-s] [in vulg. lang.] V. Balgerei.

Gebälk, *n.* [-es, *pl.* -e] the beams of a house [taken collectively], timberwork. Das — an dieser Kirche, the timberwork of this church; *fig.* [in architecture, that part of the order of a column which is over the capital] entablature, entablement.

Gebämmel, Gebaumel, *n.* [-s] [in vulg. lang.] a dangling motion.

Gebände, *n.* [-s, *pl.* -] V. Gebinde.

Gebärde, *f.* [*pl.* -n] V. Geberde.

Gebären, *v. r.* [sich] V. [sich] Betragen.

Gebären, [from the old bären = tragen, Lat *fero*, Gr. φέρω] *ir. v. tr.* to bring forth. *a*) [of women] to bring forth, to give birth to, to bear. Sie hat einen Knaben, Zwillinge geboren, she has been delivered, she has been brought to bed of a boy, of twins; um welche Zeit gebar sie? at what time was she delivered? sie hat schon zwölf Kinder geboren, she has already given birth to twelve children; glücklich ist die Mutter, die ihn geboren hat, happy the mother that bore him; zur Unzeit —, fehl—, to miscarry; eine —de Frau, a woman in labour or in travail, a parturient woman; ein nach des Vaters Tode gebornes Kind, a [...]humous child; ein neugebornes Kind, a [...] born child; ein todtgebornes Kind, a [...] child; er ist blind geboren, he was born [...] ist ein geborner Deutscher, he is a nativ[e ...] many, a German by birth, or by birth a [...] er ist ein geborner Pariser, he was born in [...] he is a native of Paris; ein Geborner von [...] [Edelgeborener], noble by birth; *fig.* er i[st ...] Krieg, zur Freude geboren, he was born f[or ...] for joy; *fig.* er ist ein geborner Dichter, [Ma]ler &c., he was born a poet, a painter &[c. ...] wurde an dem und dem Tage geboren, h[e ...] born on such and such a day; alles was [gebo]ren ist, muß sterben, all that is born must d[ie ...] [seldom used but of beasts] to produce youn[g ...] bring forth, to litter V. Werfen. Lebend[ige] Thiere, viviparous animals. *c*) *Fig.* [= [...]chen] to breed, to beget, to produce, to c[...] cause. Allzugroße Freude gebiert oft K[...] a too lively joy often begets sorrow [...] Müßiggang gebiert das Laster, idleness [...] vice; ihre verirrte Phantasie gebiert t[...] Schreckbilder, her unsettled imaginatio[n ...] ates a thousand phantoms; [in Script.] die S[ünde] gebiert den Tod, sin bringeth forth death. [...] —, the bringing forth of a child, delivery, [par]turition.

Gebär=haus, *n.* a lying-in hospital [...] **mutter,** *f.* [in anatomy] womb, matrix [...] Bärmutter; die —mutterabweichung, oblic[...] of the matrix, hysteroloxy. —**stuhl,** *m.* [...] of delivery. —**zeit,** *f.* time of delivery [...] liv[...] [...]rance.

Gebärerinn, *f.* a woman in labour, [par]turient, [especially in poetry] a mother. V. [Ge]bärerinn, Wöchnerinn.

Gebäu, *n.* [-es, *pl.* -e] [mostly in poetry] Gebäude.

Gebäude, *n.* [-s, *pl.* -] 1) in general, [any] thing built. *a*) Dies Faß ist ein schönes [...] this cask is a fine piece of work; dieses Kri[egs]schiff ist ein schönes —, this man-of-war [is a] beautiful structure; [in mining] α) [an e...] by which a mine is entered] an adit; β) the [...] itself. Ein höfliches —, [containing a gr[eat deal] of ore] a rich mine; ein — auflassen, auf[geben], ihm den Rücken kehren, to abandon, to g[ive up] a mine. *b*) in the usual and more limited [sense] = Haus; a building. Ein großes, prä[chtiges] —, a large building, a splendid edifice; [dieser] Tempel ist ein schönes —, this templ[e is a] beautiful edifice; die Westminster=Abtei, [ein] ehrwürdige alte —, Westminster-Abbe[y, a] venerable old fabric; eine ägyptische [Pyra]mide ist ein mächtiges —, an Egyptian [pyra]mid is a vast pile; die öffentlichen —, the [public] buildings; ein Einsturz drohendes —, a [build]ing ready to fall; ein — aufführen, to [con]struct, to rear up, to erect a building; *fig.* [end]lich muß dieses — des Stolzes und der Ung[erech]tigkeit einstürzen, at length this ed[ifice of] pride and injustice must tumble down; [das] wankende — des spanischen Staatscred[its, the] tottering fabric of the public credit o[f Spain]. 2) [Bauart] manner of building. *Fig.* Das — einer Blume, des men[schlichen] Körpers, the structure of a flower, of [the hu]man body.

Gebauer, *n.* [-s, *pl.* -] V. [the usual] 1. Bauer.

Gebaumel, *n.* V. Gebammel.

Gebe, *adj.* what is given or given out, [...] is circulated; only used in the phrase [gang] und — seyn, to be current, to be in [...] Gange.

Gebefall, *m.* [in grammar = der dritte] *Dativ] the dative case.

Gebein, *n.* [-es, *pl.* -e] 1) [the bones of the ...tmal body collectively] the bones. [in Script.] ...r wird ihre —e zermalmen, he shall break ...heir bones; mein — hängt an meiner Haut, ...y bones cleave to my skin; dieses Schlacht...eld liegt voll —e, this field of battle is strewed ...ith bones. 2) the limbs of the human body, ...e whole body. Noch zittern mir die —e, my ...ody is still trembling all over; hier ruhen die ...-e seiner Voreltern, here rest the bones or re...ains of his ancestors; ‡seines —es ist schon ...ng nicht mehr, he has been dead and buried ...is long while. 3) [among hunters] Das — des ...irsches, a horny excrescence behind, above ...e hoofs of deer. Syn. V. Bein, Knochen.

Gebelfer, *n.* [-s] [in fam. lang.] repeated ...rking or yelping [of a young dog &c.]. *Fig.* ...s contempt, but rather vulgar] Das — der Men..., the clamour or brawling of the multitude ...mob.

Gebell, *n.* [-es] continual barking, baying. ...as fortwährende — dieser Hunde hat mich am ...chlafen gehindert, the continual barking of ...ese dogs has hindered me from sleeping.

Geben, [allied to the ancient Gaff = hohle ...nd, hollow hand; allied to Gäspe] *ir. v. tr.* 1) ...riginally = darreichen] to present for taking ...acceptance, to give. Gott gebe! God grant! ...s —, the act of giving &c.; das — der Kar...n, dealing; Einem ein Buch, Wasser, Klei...r &c. —, to give or hand any one a book, ...ter, clothes &c.; Einem etwas in die Hand —, ...put something into any one's hand; er gab es ...meine Hand, he delivered it into my hands; ...n Pferden ihr Futter —, to give the horses ...ir fodder, to feed the horses; er gab ihm die ...nd, he gave him his hand, he shook hands ...h him; Einem die Hand auf etwas — [as a ...dge], to give one's hand upon something, to ...e or pass one's word to do something; ich ...e Ihnen die Hand darauf, daß die Schuld ...ahlt werden soll, I give or pledge my word ...t the debt shall be paid; Einem einen Stuhl ...hinsetzen], to give or reach a chair to any one; ...nem ein Abendessen geben [= vorsetzen], to treat ...y one with supper; Karten —, to deal; ...ch —, to misdeal; von neuem —, to deal ...w, again; Einem gute, schlechte Karten —, ...give any one good, bad cards; wer muß —? ...wem ist das —? whose deal is it? *Fig.* *a*) ...prepare, to provide, to give. Ein Fest, eine ...ahlzeit, einen Ball —, to give a feast, an ...ertainment, a ball; ein Stück im Theater — ...führen], to play a piece in the theatre; man ...t heute Heinrich den IV., Henry the fourth ...to be played to-day; Garrick gab [spielte] ...e Rolle meisterhaft, Garrick played his part ...a masterly style. *b*) Etwas —, to be fit or ...ficient for. Dieses Holz gibt gute Balken, ...s wood is very proper for, or makes good ...ams; dieses Getreide gibt wenig Mehl, this ...n yields little flour; dieser junge Mensch ...te einen herrlichen Soldaten ge—, this young ...n would have made an excellent soldier; er ...t höchstens einen Korporal, he will be fit for ...rporal at most; dieses Stück Tuch [Leinwand] ...t kaum ein Dutzend Hemden —, this piece of ...th will hardly be sufficient for a dozen of ...rts. V. Abgeben I. 2. *c*) to place or put in a cer...n state or condition. Einen Sklaven, einen ...fangenen frei —, to set a slave, a prisoner ...e or at liberty; sich zufrieden —, to put up ...h, to be satisfied or quiet, to compose one's ...nd; er wollte sich über sein Unglück gar nicht ...rieden —, he would take no comfort, he ...uld not be comforted at all in his misfor...e or calamity; sich bloß — [eine Schwäche ...en], to lay one's self open, to expose one's ...f to; er gibt sich gar sehr bloß durch sein Benehmen, he exposes himself strangely by his conduct. *d*) to show, to teach [said of things]. Das gibt die gesunde Vernunft, common sense teaches that, that is self-evident; ihr Gesicht gibt es schon, wie gutmüthig sie ist, her very face or countenance shows or proves her good nature; der Brief gibt es, it can be seen by the letter, the letter proves it; die Sache selbst gibt es, the thing or matter speaks of itself; der Augenschein gibt es, it is obvious to every body, 't is a plain thing. *e*) Sich —, to yield, to give way [said of things and persons]. Das Tuch wird sich —, the cloth will stretch or yield; es wird sich schon —, never fear, things will be made up; es gibt sich von selbst, it is a matter of course, it follows of course; sie, er wird sich schon —, she, he will agree or conform to it in time, she, he will resign herself, himself to it. *f*) Auf Einen etwas —, or auf Einen —, to regard with submission, to attend to, to obey, to mind. Er gibt [etwas] auf seine Ermahnungen, seine Worte, he listens to his admonitions, to his words, he obeys or minds them; er gibt auf Vater und Mutter nichts, he obeys or minds neither father nor mother. *g*) *impers.* [sich ereignen] to happen, to fall out. Was gibt es? what is the matter? *es hat einen rechten Zank ge—, there has been a violent quarrel; sagen Sie mir, was es ge— hat, tell me what has been the matter; *was gibt's denn für einen Lärmen? what is all this noise for, what does this noise mean or signify? *es wird heute gewiß etwas —, there will certainly be some quarrel or row to-day; was gibt es Neues? what news? *h*) *impers.* [= da or vorhanden seyn] to exist, to be. Dort gibt es kräftige Menschen, there are stout, vigorous men there; es gibt niemand, der das nicht wüßte, there is nobody but knew that; es gab nie einen größeren Mann als ihn, there never was a greater man than he; gibt es ein schöneres Schauspiel als den Aufgang der Sonne? is there any sight more beautiful than sun-rise? einen solchen Krieg hat es noch nie ge— und wird keinen mehr —, there never was a similar war, nor will there ever be one; der Uebel, denen der Mensch ausgesetzt ist, gibt es nur zu viele, there are but too many evils, man is exposed to; ach, gibt es noch für mich ein Glück hienieden? alas, is there still some good fortune in store for me here below? es gibt gute und schlechte Menschen, there are good and bad people; es gibt nichts ungewisseres als die Zukunft, there is nothing more uncertain than the future; hier gibt es etwas zu sehen, there is something to be seen; hier gibt es etwas zu lachen, there is something to laugh at. 2) [in a more limited sense] to bestow or confer something upon any one by any action of the body. Einem eine Ohrfeige, einen Kuß —, to give any one a box on the ear, a kiss; Einem einen Tritt, einen Schlag, eine Tracht Prügel —, to give any one a kick, a blow, a good drubbing; einem Ofen zu viel Hitze —, to overheat a stove or furnace; einem Pferde die Schule —, to manage, to break a horse; einem Pferde die Sporen —, to put or set spurs to a horse; Einem einen Wink mit der Hand —, to beckon with the hand to any one; einen Wink mit dem Kopfe —, to give a nod, to nod with the head; einen Wink mit den Augen —, to wink with the eyes, to tip the wink; Einem etwas in Verwahrung —, to give any one something to keep or in keeping; Einem eine Uhr, ein Pferd auf die Probe —, to give any one a watch, a horse on trial; ein Pfand —, to give a pledge; ich habe einen Dukaten [als Angeld] darauf ge—, I have given a ducat as an earnest; er hat von seinem Gewinnste zehn Guineen den Armen ge—, he has given ten guineas of his winnings to the poor; der Kaufmann will den Zucker nicht um hundert Gulden —, the merchant will not part with his sugar for a hundred florins; ich gab es Ihnen um den Ankaufspreis, I sold it you at prime-cost; wie viel soll ich Ihnen für diesen Hut —? how much am I to give or pay you for this hat? ich kann nicht so viel dafür —, I cannot afford to give so much for it; Steuer —, to pay taxes; Einem ein Geschenk —, to make any one a present; den Bedienten ihren Lohn —, to give the servants their wages; er gibt [that is schenkt] nicht gern, he is not for giving, he is not apt to give. V. Wiedergeben, Zurückgeben. *Fig.* *a*) to let any one have something, to impart something. Einem Unterricht —, to give any one instruction, to instruct any one; Einem eine Stunde in der Musik —, to give any one a lesson in music; Einem Arbeit, Beschäftigung —, to give any one work, occupation; Einem [eine] Antwort —, to give any one an answer; Einem Nachricht —, to give any one intelligence, to send any one word, to give any one notice; Rechenschaft für etwas —, to account for a thing; Einem seine Tochter zur Frau —, to give any one one's daughter in marriage; Einem ein Amt —, to give or confer on any one an office or place; Einem ein Land zu regieren —, to give any one the government of a country; Einem freie Wahl —, to leave something to any one's choice; Einem Macht, Gewalt zu etwas —, to give any one power or authority to do something, to authorize or empower any one to do something; Einem Erlaubniß —, to give any one leave or permission; *Einem gute Worte —, to speak any one fair; Einem einen guten Rath —, to give any one a good counsel or advice; einem Kinde einen Namen —, to give a child a name; *it.* to stand godfather to a child; seine Einwilligung zu etwas —, to give one's consent to a thing; Einem sein Wort —, to give or pass one's word; Einem den Vortritt — [einräumen or lassen], to give or yield any one the precedence; einem Sklaven die Freiheit —, to give a slave freedom, to manumit a slave; Zeugniß — [ablegen], to bear witness; — Sie mir die Ehre Ihres Besuches, do me the honour to come and see me; ich gebe mir die Ehre, Ihnen zu sagen, I have the honour to tell you; ich werde mir die Ehre —, nächsten Sonntag Ihr Gast zu seyn, I shall do myself the honour of dining with you next Sunday; Einem Recht —, to allow a person to be in the right; *it.* to do any one justice; Einem Unrecht —, to blame any one; Jedermann gibt ihm Unrecht, every one thinks he is wrong, every body lays the fault upon him, or lays the blame at his door; ihm gibt man Schuld, the blame is charged upon him, the fault is laid to his charge; Einem eine Frist von acht Tagen — [verwilligen], to allow or grant any one a respite of eight days; Einem Zeit —, sich zu besinnen, to give any one time to consider; Einem Gehör —, to give ear or a hearing; einem Verbrecher Gnade — [gewähren], to grant a criminal his pardon, to pardon a criminal; Einem gewonnen Spiel —, to give up one's game as lost, to give one's game up for lost; sich Mühe —, to take pains; er gibt sich viel Mühe, englisch zu lernen, he takes great pains to learn English; *es näher — [nachgeben], to yield, to give way; Einem etwas an die Hand [= in den Sinn] —, to suggest or hint something to any one. *b*) to look upon, to consider. Sein Spiel, seinen Prozeß verloren —, to look upon one's game, one's lawsuit as lost, to give one's game, one's lawsuit for lost; ich gebe ihr höchstens zwanzig Jahre [= ich halte sie für höchstens zwanzig Jahre alt], I should take her for twenty at most; welches Alter — Sie dieser Frau? how old do you take that woman to be? ich gab diesem Kranken nicht acht Tage mehr [zu leben], I did not think, this sick man would live eight days longer; ich gebe ihm noch zwanzig Jahre [zu leben], I think he will yet live twenty years. 3) to produce, to yield. Ein Baum gibt viel, wenig Obst, a tree produces much, little fruit; dieses Land gibt guten Wein, this country produces good wine; der Kieselstein gibt Feuer, the flint gives fire; einer Gestalt eine Form —, to give a form or shape to a figure; einem Hause Luft —, to ventilate a house; Einem zu thun —, to cut out work for any one; Einem zu rathen —, to defy any one to guess; Einem zu denken —, to make any one think, to give him reason to think, to puzzle any one; Einem zu verstehen —, to give any one to understand; das wird viel zu reden —, that will furnish subject or matter for much talk; ein Aergerniß —, to give offence; das gab den Truppen Muth, that inspired the troops with courage, encouraged the troops; Gott hat ihm ausgezeichnete Talente ge—, God has endowed him with eminent talents; sich ein Ansehen — [that is sich ein Ansehen — wollen], to give one's self airs, to take airs; er versteht es, sich ein Ansehen zu —, he knows how to assume haughty airs; sich eine fromme Miene —, to assume the semblance of piety, to put on a pious air or countenance. *Fig.* to express by word of mouth or in writing. Ich will es kurz — [sagen, schreiben], I will express it in few words, I will be short; das ist sehr gut ge—, that is very well said or turned; ge— [kundgethan von der Regierung &c.] zu London, zu Wien &c. den 25. Nov. 1833, given, written, enacted in London. Vienna &c. this 25th day of Nov. 1833; ein Wort durch ein anderes — [übersetzen], to render or translate one word by another; diese Stelle kann man nicht wörtlich englisch —, this passage cannot be translated verbally into English; eine Stelle Wort für Wort wieder—, to render or translate a passage word for word; dieser Ausdruck gibt das englische Wort nicht, this expression does not render, or correspond to, the exact meaning of the English word. 4) Etwas von sich —, to send forth, to emit, to give out. Das Feuer gibt Hitze und Rauch von sich, fire emits heat and smoke; es gibt viele Blumen, die einen angenehmen Geruch von sich —, there are many flowers, that exhale or emit an agreeable scent or pleasant smell; das Instrument gibt einen melodischen Ton von sich, the instrument yields a melodious sound; eine Arzenei wieder von sich —, to vomit a medicine; der Kranke gibt Alles wieder von sich, was er ißt und trinkt, the sick man throws up or vomits all he eats and drinks. *Fig.* Seine Gedanken von sich —, to give utterance to one's thoughts, to utter or speak one's mind; er kann es nicht von sich — [= nicht deutlich erklären, was er will], he has difficulty in expressing himself, he has a bad delivery; sein Wort von sich —, to pass one's word; das Mädchen hat endlich ihr Jawort von sich ge—, at length the girl has yielded her consent.

Gèber, *m.* [-s, *pl* -] -inn, *f.* giver, donor. Gott, der — alles Guten, God, the author or dispenser of all that is good; [in Script.] einen fröhlichen — hat Gott lieb, God loveth a cheerful giver. V. Gesetz—, Rath— &c.

Gebèrde, *f.* [*pl.* -n] [from the ancient gebaren or baren = to bear, to carry; hence] 1) the manner of carrying one's self, external appearance. [rarely used in this sense] Christus ward an —n als ein Mensch erfunden, Christ was found in fashion like a man. 2) [usually =] motion of the body or limbs, expressive of sentiment or passion, gesture. Dieser Redner macht zu viele —n, this orator makes too many gestures, gesticulates too much, uses too much action; in jeder — lag Würde und Liebe, in every gesture was dignity and love; in allen ihren —n herrscht eine gewisse Anmuth, there is a certain grace in all her gestures; seine —n sind gezwungen, his gestures are affected; bäurische —n, rude manners. 3) motion of the features. Unschuld mahlt sich auf ihrer Wange, voll Anmuth ist jede —, innocence is painted on her cheeks, full of grace her every air. V. Stellung, Anstand 3). Syn. Geberde, Miene, Grimasse. Miene [from meinen] differs from Geberde [from the old (sich) gebaren = sich betragen] first, by its denoting merely voluntary and significant motions of the body, Geberden on the contrary signifying also involuntary; and also by the former being limited to the motion of the face alone. Grimasse expresses only a disagreeable distortion of the countenance from habit, affectation or insolence.

Geberden-kunde, —kunst, *f.* art of mimickry. —**macher**, *m.* gesticulator. —**spiel**, *n.* 1) pantomime, mimickry, [in ancient Greece and Rome] mime. 2) gestures, action. Das —spiel dieses Schauspielers ist voll Ausdruck, the action of this performer is very expressive. —**spieler**, *m.* a mimick, pantomime. —**sprache**, *f.* conversation by looks and gestures; mimickry, pantomime.

Gebèrden, *v.r.* sich —, to assume particular looks and gestures, to carry one's self in a particular way or manner. Er geberdete sich sehr schlecht, he carried himself very ill; sich lächerlich —, to assume ridiculous looks or gestures, to give one's self ridiculous airs; sich albern —, to behave in a silly manner, to bear one's self like a ninny; sich närrisch —, to act like a fool, to play the fool; er geberdet sich wie ein Marktschreier, he makes gestures like a mountebank, he has the gestures of a mountebank; sich ernsthaft —, to put on a serious air or countenance; er geberdet sich wie ein Besessener, he behaves like a demoniac; er würde sich entsetzlich —, wenn er es erführe, he would fly into a most violent passion, he would run mad, if he should come to know it.

Gebèrdung, *f.* the act of assuming particular looks and gestures &c.; demeanour, carriage, behaviour.

Gebèt, *n.* [*diminut.* Gebetchen, Gebetlein, *n.*] [-es, *pl.* -e] prayer. Haltet an im —e, continue in prayer; sein — thun, verrichten, to say one's prayers; dem —e beiwohnen, to attend prayer; es läutet zum —e, the bell rings for prayer; Gott im —e um etwas bitten, to ask God for something in one's prayers; ein inbrünstiges —, a fervent prayer; im —e begriffen seyn, to be at prayers; das — des Herrn, the Lord's prayer; das Kirchen—, the common prayer.

Gebets-buch, *n.* prayer-book. —**büchlein**, *n.* a small prayer-book. —**s-formel**, *f.* form of prayer. —**zeit**, *f.* time of praying.

Gebète, *n.* [-s] constant and tedious praying.

Gebètt, *n.* [-es, *pl.* -e] a bed and its furniture, bedding. Ein vollständiges —, a complete bed.

Gebèttel, *n.* [-s] continual and troublesome begging.

Gebìet, *n.* [-es, *pl.* -e] 1) [power or right of commanding] command, dominion, sway. Unter dem —e des und des Fürsten stehen, to be under the dominion of such and such a prince; sein — erstreckt sich über alle diese Provinzen, his sway or government is extended over all these provinces; er hat das — über diese Provinz bekommen, he got the jurisdiction over this province. V. Herrschaft, Botmäßigkeit. 2) territory. —chen, *n.* small territory. Dies[es] Gut liegt nicht im —e der Stadt, this [estate] does not lie within the precincts of the t[own]; sich in ein anderes — begeben, to retire or to betake one's self into another territory or country; das — dieses Cantons erstreckt sich bis [an] den Fluß, the territory of this canton exte[nds] as far as the river; ein gewisser Bezirk [eines] —es, a certain district of a territory; das Ru[ssi]sche —, the Russian territory or empire; [das] städtische —, das — einer Stadt, the precinc[ts] or jurisdiction of a town; das — eines Bisch[ofs], diocese, bishopric; das — eines Erzbisch[ofs], archbishopric; das — eines Satrapen, [sa]trapy. *Fig.* Das unermeßliche — des Welta[lls], the immeasurable extent of the universe; [das] — der Künste, the sphere or department of [the] arts; das — der Beredsamkeit, the province [of] eloquence; das gehört in das — der Philoso[phie], that belongs to philosophy, falls with[in] the verge of philosophy; das — der Gelehr[]samkeit, the republic of letters.

Gebìeten, [formerly bieten, Engl. to bid; [] Bieten] *ir. v. tr.* and *intr.* to command, to orde[r], to bid. Als Herr —, to command imperiously; Sie haben unumschränkt über mich zu —, [you] have full power over me, you may dispose of [me] as you please; er hat hier nichts zu —, he has [no] authority or command here; die Freundsch[aft] gebietet es, friendship wills, exacts or requi[res] it; meine Pflicht gebietet mir, my duty com[]mands me; Stillschweigen —, to order or im[]pose silence; Einem etwas —, to order [or] enjoin any one something; seinen Leidenschaf[ten] —, to master or curb one's passions, to ha[ve] the mastery or command over one's passio[ns,] to keep them under; seinem Zorne —, to bri[dle] or restrain one's anger; [in grammar] die —[de] Art, the imperative mood; das —, the act [of] commanding, ordering &c.

Gebìeter, *m.* [-s, *pl.* -] commander, ru[ler,] master. Jene stolzen — des Oceans, those pr[oud] rulers of the ocean; dein Herr und —, thy Lo[rd] and master.

Gebìeterinn, *f.* mistress, lady. Der [Be]diente sagte, daß seine — ausgegangen sey, [the] servant said his lady or mistress was gone [out;] Rom, welches so lange die — der Welt w[ar,] Rome, for such a length of time mistress of [the] world; endlich versprach ihm seine —, [die] — seines Herzens, es zu thun, at length [his] mistress promised him to do it.

Gebìeterisch, I. *adj.* domineering, i[m]perious. Eine —e Miene haben, to have a do[m]ineering air; einen sehr —en Ton anneh[men,] to use an imperative or peremptory tone; [—e] Worte, imperious words; [in elevated or poet[ic] diction] absolute; die —e Macht ihrer Re[ize,] the irresistible power of her charms; der — Nothwendigkeit weichen, to yield to imperi[ous] necessity. II. *adv.* imperiously, domineeri[ngly,] peremptorily. — sprechen, to speak imp[era]tively, imperiously, in an absolute tone. [Syn.] Gebieterisch, Herrisch. Gebieterisch b[espeaks] offensive behaviour towards others, arising fro[m an] overweening idea of one's own power. Such a be[ha]viour is termed herrisch when it proceeds from [an] exaggerated or misplaced notion of one's rights. [Ein] gebieterischer Ton [an imperious tone] without p[ower] creates contempt and is ridiculous; ein herrisch[es] Betragen [domineering conduct] without right [ex]cites indignation.

Gebìetiger, *m.* [-s, *pl.* -] [rarely used] Gebieter.

Gebìld, *n.* [-s] [a sort of linen] diaper

Gebìlde, *n.* [-s, *pl.* -] any thing formed, framed, an image. Die reizenden — der [Ein]bildungskraft, the delightful creations of [the] ination.

Gebinde, *n.* [-s, *pl.* -] 1) a repeated tying binding together. 2) several things tied to- ether, bundle; [in carpentry] assemblage, join- g [together]; [among bricklayers and tilers] row, nge; [among sempstresses] V. Ritze. 3) the anner of tying or binding. Auf einem Acker uß einerlei — seyn, the sheaves of a field ust be all of the same bigness, or must be all ade up uniformly; [among coopers] casks of e same size.

Gebirg[e], *n.* [-es, *pl.* -e] [V. Berg] 1) a umber of mountains collectively, a chain of ountains, a ridge of hills. Ein hohes, stei- s —, high, steep mountains; jenseits des -es, on the other side of the mountains; die renäischen —e, the Pyrenean mountains, the yrenees. 2) [in mining] gang.

Gebirgs-amsel, *f.* V. Bergamsel. — irsch, *m.* the mountain-stag. —maus, *f.* . Blichmaus, Haselmaus. —s-arten, *pl.* [in ning] kinds of stone or rocks, minerals or fos- s. Uranfängliche —s-arten, primary or prim- ive rocks; vulkanische —s-arten, volcanic cks; aufgeschwemmte —s-arten, secondary cks. V. Flötzgebirge; Uebergangs—s-arten, ansition rocks. —s-artillerie, *f.* mountain tillery. —s-beschreibung, *f.* description mountains. —s-joch, *n.* a short ridge of ountains separated from the principal chain. s-kessel, *m.* a plain closely surrounded by ountains. —s-kette, *f.* chain of mountains. s-kunde, *f.* knowledge of mountains, geog- sy. —s-paß, *m.* defile between two hills, a ountain defile. —s-pflanze, *f.* a moun- in plant. —s-rücken, *m.* the ridge of a ountain. —s-schlucht, *f.* a defile between ountains. —s-schütze, *m.* a mountain- ooter, marksman or huntsman; [especially in Pyrenees] a miquelet. —s-zug, *m.* V. —s- te.

Gebirger, *m.* [-s, *pl.* -] mountaineer, ghlander. V. Bergbewohner.

Gebirgig, *adj.* and *adv.* mountainous. Die hweiz ist sehr —, Switzerland is very moun- ous, full of mountains. V. Bergig.

Gebirgisch, *adj.* and *adv.* inhabiting the untains, living or lying in the mountains. e —en Städte, the towns situated in the untains; ein—er, a mountaineer, highlander.

Gebiß, *n.* [-sses, *pl.* -sse] 1) the instrument mastication, the teeth [applied to animals and in familiar language to persons]. Das — eines rdes, a horse's teeth; sie hat ein schönes —, has a fine set of teeth; er hat ein garstiges , he has ugly teeth, an ugly set of teeth. 2) of a bridle, bit, mouth. Das — der Wasser- se, the masticator or slavering-bit; — ohne angen, snaffle or watering-bit; — mit Stan- , canon mouth; einem Pferde das — anle- , to put the bit in the mouth of a horse, to a horse. *Fig.* Seinen Begierden Zaum und anlegen, to curb or bridle one's desires.

Gebißkettchen, *n.* the small chain of a se's bit, curb-chain.

Gebläse, *n.* [-s] the repeated blowing or nding of a wind instrument, trumpeting.

Gebläse, *n.* [-s] apparatus for blowing, lows. Das — anlassen, to set the bellows oing.

Geblättert, *adj.* [in botany] furnished with ves, leaved.

Geblöke, *n.* [-s] bleating [used of sheep]; ring or bellowing [used of cattle].

Geblümt, *adj.* adorned with flowers, flow- d, figured. —e Zeuge, flowered or figured fs; —e Handtücher, diapered towels; [in poetry] die —en Wiesen, meadows enameled with flowers; [in blasonry] flowery, flowered; die —e Einfassung eines Wappenschildes, the flowery orle.

Geblüt, *n.* [-es] 1) [Blutmasse] the whole mass and system of the blood in the animal body, blood. Dieses Kraut reinigt das —, this herb purifies the blood; gallreiches —, bilious blood; mein ganzes — [or all' mein Blut] er- starrt, wenn ich davon denke, it chills my blood, when I think of it; *das gibt kein gutes — [bet- ter Blut], that breeds no good will or friendly dispositions, V. Blut 2); chiefly *a)* [said of a wo- man with child] das — ist ihr abgegangen, she has had a loss of blood; das —, das nach der Geburt abgeht, [the natural evacuations of women in childbed after the birth of the foetus] lochia or loches. *b)* monthly courses, flowers. Sie hat ihr — verloren, her monthly courses are stop- ped or obstructed. 2) [Blutsverwandtschaft] blood. Sie sind vom nämlichen —e, they are of the same blood; zu nahe in das — heirathen, to marry too near of kin, to marry in a forbidden degree of consanguinity; von königlichem —e abstammen, to be descended or to descend from royal blood; ein Prinz vom —e, a prince of the blood.

Geborgen, [properly, *past. part.* of ber- gen] *adj.* and *adv.* sheltered, saved. Nun bin ich —, now I am safe. Syn. Geborgen, Sicher. That is said to be geborgen, which has been placed out of the danger which impended, or which has been brought into a place of safety where there is no longer any thing to be apprehended. The goods of a shipwrecked seafarer are geborgen, as soon as they are brought to land. Sicher refers to the safety or shelter in which the person or thing ge- borgen is. Kein Seefahrer, der aus dem Hafen läuft, ist sicher, daß er auch in denselben wieder einlaufen werde, no seaman who sails out of a har- bour is sure that he will run into the same again.

Gebot, *n.* [-es, *pl.* -e] 1) [from bieten, gebie- ten, to command] command, commandment, in- junction, order, precept. Die zehn —e, the ten commandments, the decalogue; gegen die —e Gottes sündigen, to sin against God's com- mandments; Einem zu —e stehen, to be at any one's command. *Prov.* Noth kennt kein —, necessity has no law. 2) the act of bidding and the sum bidden or offered, bidding, offer. Ein — auf etwas thun, to bid, to offer a sum for something; er hat ein — von zwölf tausend Gul- den auf das Haus gethan, he has offered or bid twelve thousand florins for that house; ein hohes — auf etwas thun, to bid high for a thing; das ist ein sehr annehmliches —, that is a very liberal or acceptable offer; das letzte — auf das Haus sind zwanzig tausend Gulden, the last bidding for the house is twenty thousand florins; ich habe ein höheres — gethan als er, my bid has covered his, I have bid more than he; thun Sie ein billiges —, make a reasonable offer or bid; man hat sein — angenommen, they have accepted his offer.

Gebotsbrief, *m.* a written command or order, a mandate.

Gebräme, *n.* [-s, *pl.* -] [Bräme seems to be compounded of be and Rahme] border or edge, espe- cially of fur. Das — von Zobeln, the border or edging of sable; das — von Pelz, the furred border.

Gebrannt, properly, *past. part.* of brennen, but used also as an *adj.* and *adv.* —er Stein, calcined stone; —e Mandeln, burnt almonds; —es Hirschhorn, hartshorn made by ustion.

Gebratene, *n.* [-n] roast meat. Essen sie gern —s? do you like roast meat? V. Braten.

Gebräu, *n.* [-es, *pl.* -e] V. Gebräude.

Gebrauch, *m.* [-es, *pl.* Gebräuche] 1) the act of handling or employing in any manner, use, employment. Der gute oder schlechte —, den er von seinem Reichthum macht, the good or bad use he makes of his riches; machen Sie von Ihrem Ansehen —, make use of your au- thority; ich hebe das zu künftigem —e auf, I keep this for future use; dieses Geld können Sie zu Ihrem freien —e anwenden, verwenden, you may make what use you please of this money, you may dispose of or employ this money as you like; die Jugend sollte man mit dem —e der Waffen vertraut machen, youth should be trained up to the use of arms; zum —e der Ju- gend, for the use of young persons or of youth; ich biete Ihnen den — meines Hauses an, I offer you the use of my house; Bücher können nie den — von Büchern lehren, books can never teach the use of books; ich werde von dieser Nachricht keinen — machen, I shall make no use of this intelligence; der — dieses Wortes ist selten, this word is rarely used, or made use of. 2) frequent or customary use or employ- ment of a thing, usage, practice. Der — ist der oberste Richter in lebenden Sprachen, use or usage is the umpire of living languages; dieses Wort ist nicht mehr im —e, this word is no longer in use, is obsolete; ein Wort, welches nur in der Umgangssprache im —e ist, a word only used in common conversation; er hat es im —e, alle Jahr einmal zur Ader zu lassen, he has himself bled once a year; er hat den übeln —, Gesichter zu schneiden, he has the bad habit of making [wry] faces. 3) a manner established by frequent use, custom, habitual practice. Das ist ein alter —, that is an ancient, an old custom; ein erst kürzlich eingeführter —, a newly established custom; neue Gebräu- che aufbringen, to establish or introduce new customs; sich nach den Gebräuchen eines Lan- des richten, to conform to the customs of a country; wie es der — mit sich bringt, accord- ing to custom; es ist nicht mehr der —, daß &c., it is no longer customary, to &c.; die Ge- bräuche der Kirche, die Kirchengebräuche, the rites of the church. V. Herkommen. Syn. Ge- brauch, Sitte, Gewohnheit. Sitte ex- tends to every thing internal and external in the ac- tions, or in the dress and habitation. Gewohnheit and Sitte differ from each other in this, that the lat- ter implies at the same time that the propriety or be- comingness of the usage is considered. In some coun- tries it is die Gewohnheit [the custom] to yoke two, in others four horses abreast. In this case there is no reference to the propriety. Gebrauch is the usage or custom which by common consent is observed on cer- tain occasions.

Gebrauchzettelchen, *n.* label put to medicines.

Gebrauchen, *v. tr.* to use, to make use of, to employ. Arzenei —, to take medicine or phy- sic; ich habe jenes Geld nie gebraucht, I never used that money; er gebraucht diesen Ausdruck oft, he often uses that expression, he frequently makes use of that expression; ich habe dieses Buch lange gebraucht, I have long used that book; List, Gewalt —, to use or employ cun- ning, violence; allerlei Gegenmittel —, to make use of all sorts of remedies; sich zu den Absich- ten eines Andern — lassen, to be instrumental, to be subservient to the views or designs of another; dies ist zu nichts zu —, this is an un- profitable or useless thing, it is of no use; sol- che Worte sind lange gebraucht worden, such words have long been in use; dies Wort wird selten gebraucht, this word is seldom or rarely used; ein Brille —, to use spectacles. Syn. V. Brauchen.

Gebräuchlich, *adj.* and *adv.* usual, customary, ordinary, common. Das iſt in jenem Lande ſehr —, that is very customary or common in that country; dieſes Wort iſt nicht ſehr —, this word is not often used; dieſe Redensart iſt nicht mehr —, this phrase is out of use; —e Ausdrücke, words frequently used; — werden, to grow into fashion, to grow customary. V. Gemein, Gewöhnlich, Ueblich.

Gebräuchlichkeit, *f.* usualness.

Gebräude, [-s, *pl.* -] **Gebräue**, [-s, *pl.* -] *n.* 1) what is brewed. 2) the quantity brewed at once, brewing.

Gebrauſe, *n.* [-s] a roaring noise. Das — der Wellen, der Winde, the roaring of the waves, the winds; — in den Ohren, tinkling in the ears.

Gebrech, *adj.* [in mining] fragile, brittle, soft, mellow. —es Geſtein, soft rocks.

Gebreche, *n.* [-s] 1) [das Brechen] a continued vomiting. 2) [among hunters] the snout of a wild boar. 3) [among hunters] place where wild swine have broken up the ground; the rooting-place of a wild boar.

Gebrechen, *ir. v. intr.* 1) [= mangeln, fehlen] to be wanting, to fail. [in Script.] Da nun Geld gebrach im Lande Egypten, and when money began to fail in the land of Egypt. 2) *impers.* Es gebricht an etwas, there is a want of something; woran gebricht es Ihnen? what is it you want? what are you in want of? es ſoll Ihnen an nichts —, you shall want for nothing; es gebrach an Wein, there was a want or a lack of wine; es gebricht mir an Geld, I am in want of money; wenn es ihm nicht an gutem Willen gebräche, if he did not lack good will; ſie erſetzt durch Kunſt, was ihr an natürlicher Schönheit gebricht, she supplies by art what she wants in natural beauty.

Gebrechen, *n.* [-s, *pl.* -] 1) [= Mangel] want, deficiency, scarcity, need. Das — an Lebensmitteln, the want or scarcity of provisions; — am Gelde leiden, to have a want of money, to want money. 2) [= Fehler] fault, defect, imperfection, infirmity. Ein körperliches —, a bodily defect; das ſchwere —, epilepsy; die Menſchen ſind voll —, men are full of failings or imperfections; ein Jeder hat ſeine —, every one has his faults or failings; das Alter hat mancherlei —, old age is subject to many infirmities or weaknesses; man muß die — ſeiner Freunde zu ertragen wiſſen, we must know how to bear with the faults or failings of our friends.

Gebrechlich, *adj.* fragile, frail, infirm, weak, feeble, impotent, maimed, crippled. Er hat einen —en Körper, he has a frail or crazy body; er iſt alt und —, he is old and decrepit; dieſes Spital iſt für —e Perſonen beſtimmt, this hospital is intended for infirm persons; *fig.* der Menſch iſt ein —es Weſen, man is a frail being; die Natur iſt —, nature is frail.

Gebrechlichkeit, *f.* 1) the unhealthy or unsound state of the body, infirmity. Die — des Alters, the infirmity or craziness of old age; ſeine — hinderte ihn, dem Heere ins Feld zu folgen, his sickliness hindered him from following the army into the field; *fig.* die — der menſchlichen Natur, the frailty of human nature. 2) V. Gebrechen 2). Weibliche —, infirmities or imperfections of the sex.

Gebreite, *n.* [-s] a plain, an extent of land; *it.* a field of more than four roods in breadth.

Gebrochen, *past. part.* of brechen, which see. Also used as an *adj.* and *adv.* Er iſt — [in popular language], he is ruptured. *Fig.* Ein —es Dach, a curve roof; —e Zahl, a broken number, a fraction; —e Treppe, landing place in a stair-case; eine —e Stimme, a broken voice; —es Deutſch or das Deutſche — ſprechen, to speak broken German; ein —er Accord, an arpeggio.

Gebröckel, *n.* [-s] what has been or may be broken into small pieces, friable substances, crumbs.

Gebrudel, *n.* [-s] bubbling up, spouting, gushing out.

Gebrüder, *pl* two or more several brothers. — Bethmann in Frankfurt, brothers Bethmann of Francfort.

Gebrüll, *n.* [-es] repeated bellowing, roaring. Das — der Kühe, der Ochſen, the bellowing or lowing of cows, oxen; das — des Löwen, the roaring of the lion; das — des Eſels, the braying of the ass; das — der Wellen, des Donners, the roaring of the waves, of thunder. V. Brüllen.

Gebrumme, *n.* [-s] [in fam. lang.] a murmuring or rumbling noise; *fig.* grumbling. Seine Bedienten ſind an ſein — gewöhnt, his servants are used to his grumbling. V. Brummen.

Gebrüt, *n.* [-es] brood.

Gebühr, *f.* [*p.* -en] [allied to gebären, geberden, = (ſich) benehmen] 1) that which is becoming or proper, propriety. Seine — beobachten, leiſten, to observe, to perform what is proper or due, to observe, to perform one's duty; über die — arbeiten, to work more than one's due; *it.* to work too hard, to overwork one's self; über die —, wider die — trinken, to drink immoderately, to an excess; man hat ihn über die — gelobt, they have praised or extolled him more than he deserves, beyond his desert; Jeder wurde nach Standes — bedient, every one was served according to his rank, with the respect or regard due to his rank; das iſt wider alle — [= allen Wohlſtand], that is against all decorum. 2) that which is due to a person. Um, für die — arbeiten, to work for the money due to one, for one's wages; die — für ein rechtliches oder medizinisches Bedenken, fee of consultation; dem Arzte ſeine — bezahlen, to pay the physician his fee; die —, die —en [die Steuer] bezahlen, to pay one's dues, taxes, duties, tolls, customs &c.; die Kanzlei—en, the fees of office. V. Gerichts—, Pfarr—, Schreib— &c.

Gebühren, *v. intr.* 1) [only used in the third person] to be becoming, proper, fit. Er ſprach mit ihm, wie es ſich gebühret, he spoke with him as it ought to be, in a becoming manner; er handelt ſo, wie es einem ehrlichen Manne gebühret, he acts as it becomes or behoves an honest man; er kleidet ſich, wie es ſich für ſeinen Stand gebührt, he dresses suitably to his rank or station; er bleibt länger aus, als es ſich gebührt, he makes us wait longer than he ought; es hätte ſich gebührt, daß Sie ihn eingeladen hätten, in common civility you ought to have invited him; dir gebühret es, dahin zu gehen, it would become you, it is your duty to go there; den Aelteſten gebührt es, zu ſprechen, it is the eldest that ought to speak; ſich —d betragen, to conduct one's self, to behave decently, in a becoming manner; —der Maßen, as is becoming or fit; *it.* duly; die —de Strafe leiden, to undergo the punishment due; die —de Größe haben, to have the proper or becoming size; der —de Richter, the competent judge. 2) to be due. Gib ihm, was ihm gebührt [was er mit Recht fordern kann], give him his due; Ehre, dem Ehre gebührt, honour to whom honour is due; einem Arbeiter gebührt ſein Lohn, a labourer is worthy of his reward; dieſes Amt hätte eigentlich mir gebühret, this office would have been my due; dieſe gungen — mir nicht, I do not deserve honours; [in Script.] dir, o Herr, gebühret Größe und die Majeſtät &c., thine, o Lord, the greatness and the majesty &c.; Obern die —de Ehre erweiſen, to show honour to one's superiors; er erlitt die —de Strafe, he suffered condign punish the punishment his crime deserved.

Gebührlich, I. *adj.* due, fit, proper. Ein Verhalten, a suitable, decent conduct; Ei die —e Ehre erweiſen, to show any one honour. V. Gebühren, Gebührend. II. duly, decently. Sich — betragen, to be one's self properly or decently; — von Ei ſprechen, to speak of any one as is his due iſt davon — benachrichtigt worden, he has duly advised of it.

Gebund, *n.* [-s, *pl.* Gebünde] **Gebünde** *n.* [-s, *pl.* -] V. 2. Bund, Bündel. truss, bundl Ein — Zwiebeln &c., a bunch of onions &c. ein — Stroh, Heu, a bundle, bottle or trus of straw, hay; ein — Hanf, Flachs, a torsel o hemp, flax, V. Knocke; ein — Garn, a skein o yarn; ein — Schlüſſel, a bunch of keys; ei — Reißholz, a fagot; [among bookbinders] Ge bünde, the bands for a book.

Gebündchen, **Gebündlein**, [*diminut.* o Gebund] *n.* a small bundle, a bunch.

Gebunden, *past. part.* of binden. Used als as an *adj.* and *adv.* *Fig.* —e Schreibart, metri cal style, poetry, verse; eine —e Rede, a speec in verse.

Gebündeſtahl, *m.* [-s, *pl.* -ſtähle] V Bürdeſtahl.

Gebürſch, *f.* V. Bürſche.

Geburt, *f.* [*pl.* -en] [from gebären] 1) th act of bringing forth children, parturition, de livery, travail, labour. Eine ſchmerzhafte —, painful delivery; ſie hat eine glückliche — ge habt, she has been happily delivered; ſie iſt i der — begriffen, she is in labour; ihre Mu ter ſtarb in der —, her mother died in child bed; das Kind blieb in der —, the child die immediately after its birth; eine unzeitige ode unreife —, a miscarriage, abortion. 2) the ac of coming into the world or being born, birth nativity. Die — Chriſti, the birth or nativit of Christ; gleich nach ſeiner —, directly immediately after his birth, after he was born von ſeiner — an, from his birth, from his firs coming into the world; hence Geburt = ex traction, descent, V. Abſtammung, Geſchlecht von hoher, edler, vornehmer — ſeyn, to be o noble extraction, to be high-born, to be nobl descended; er iſt von angeſehener —, he is o respectable parents; er iſt von niedriger —, h is of low extraction, meanly born or extracted of a mean or low birth; ein Mann von —, a ma of birth [= of a good family]; er iſt ein Edelman von — [* ein geborner Edelmann], he is noble or a nobleman by birth; von guter —, of ingenuous birth; nicht die —, ſondern die Geſin nungen geben dem Menſchen den wahren Adel, it is not birth but sentiments that give tru nobility to man. *Fig.* the first beginning the origin of a thing. Einen Aufruhr in der — er ſticken, to stifle an insurrection in its birth; e unterdrückte dieſe Leidenſchaft in ihrer erſten —, he restrained or repressed this passion at its very rise or birth. 3) the fruit of the womb whether it be already born or to be born yet, birth. Eine unzeitige —, an untimely birth, an abortive child, an abortion; ſich die — abtrei ben, to cause wilfully or purposely a miscarriage; *fig.* dieſes Gedicht iſt eine — ſeines Gei ſtes, this poem is a production of his genius; dieſe Narrheiten ſind —en einer zügelloſen Ein bildungskraft, these follies are the effects of an unbounded or licentious imagination; dieses Werk ist von demselben Verfasser, es ist aber eine unzeitige —, this work is by the same writer, but it is an untimely production of the brain. 4) [for weibliche Scham] a woman's private parts.

Geburts-adel, *m.* nobility of birth, inherited nobility. V. Erbadel. **—arbeit**, *f.* [which precedes the delivery] labour, travail of a woman. **—brief**, *m.* certificate of birth. **—fehler**, *m.* a fault or defect born with a person, a natural defect. **—fest**, *n.* birth-day. V. —tag. Das —fest Christi, the birth or nativity of Christ. **—geile**, *f.* [in anatomy] testicle. V. Hode. *it.* [of the female sex] ovary. V. Eierstock. **—glied**, *n.* [that part in either sex, which is the immediate instrument of generation] member of generation, natural or privy parts, genitals; [among hunters] V. Feigenblatt *b*). **—häutlein**, *n.* [in anatomy, the exterior membrane which invests the fetus in the uterus] chorion. V. Aderhäutchen. **—helfer**, *m.* a man-midwife, an accoucheur. V. also Hebarzt. **—helferinn**, *f.* mid-wife. V. also Hebamme. **—helm**, *m.* [in anatomy, a little membrane sometimes encompassing the head of a child when born] caul. **—hülfe**, *f.* the assistance given to a woman in labour, assistance rendered by a midwife or man-midwife. Die —hülfe bei widernatürlichen Geburten, embryulkia. **—jahr**, *n.* year of birth. **—land**, *n.* country, native country. **—lied**, *n.* birth-song. **—liste**, *f.* list or register of births. **—mahl**, *n.* V. Muttermahl. **—ort**, *m.* birth-place, native place. **—recht**, *n.* any right which results from descent, birth right. **—register**, *n.* [Geschlechtsregister] genealogy, pedigree **—schein**, *m.* V. —brief. **—schmerzen**, *pl.* throes or pains of child-birth, labour. In —schmerzen liegen, to be in labour. **—stadt**, *f.* native town. **—stern**, *m.* [in astrology, that degree of the ecliptic which rises above the horizon at the time of one's birth] ascendant. **—stuhl**, *m.* V. Gebärstuhl. **—stunde**, *f.* hour of birth, natal hour. **—tag**, *m* birth-day, natal day. Seinen —tag feiern, to celebrate one's birth-day or the anniversary of one's birth-day. **—tagsgedicht**, *n.* birth-day ode or poem. **—theile**, *pl.* V. —glied er). **—wehen**, *pl.* V. —schmerzen. **—zange**, *f.* [in surgery] gryphiers, forceps **—zeit**, *f.* time of a woman's delivery Eine Frau, die ihrer —zeit nahe ist, a woman near her time.

Gebürtig, *adj.* born at some place. Er ist aus Berlin —, he was born at Berlin, he is a native of Berlin; er ist aus England —, he is a native of England, he was born in England.

Gebüsch, *n.* [-es, *pl.* -e] 1) [a place overgrown with brushwood or underwood] coppice, copse, thicket. Sich in das — verstecken, to hide or conceal one's self in the thicket; in dem Garten ist ein kleines —, in dem sich viele Nachtigallen aufhalten, there is a small coppice or thicket in the garden, the retreat of many nightingales 2) single shrubs or bushes. Es steckt Wild in diesem —, there is game in these bushes.

Gebüschelt, [*past part.* of the unusual verb (sich) büscheln], *adj.* and *adv.* tufted; in bunches.

1. **Geck**, *m.* [-en, *pl.* -en] [allied to Gauch = gawk] a silly person, a fool, fop, coxcomb. Lassen Sie den alten —en schwatzen, let the old dotard talk; er ist ein unerträglicher —, he is an intolerable coxcomb or fop.

‖2. **Geck**, *m.* [-es, *pl.* -e] [origin uncertain] the suture of a calf's or sheep's skull. Den —en stechen, to open or pierce the skull of a calf or sheep. *Fig.* Einem den —en stechen, to banter a person.

3. **Geck**, *m.* [-en, *pl.* -en] **Gecko**, *m.* [-'s, *pl.* -s] [probably so called from its cry] a kind of naked lizard of India and Africa, with long legs.

Geckelkraut, *n.* [-es] [of the genus euonymus] spindle tree, prickwood. V. Spindelbaum.

Gecken, I. *v. tr.* to rally, to mock, to banter, to make a fool of, to make game of any one. II. *v. intr.* [in fam. lang.] to behave foolishly or foppishly, to play the fool or coxcomb.

Geckenhaft, *adj.* V. Geckhaft.

Geckenheil, *n.* [-s] V. Gauchheil.

Geckerei, *f.* 1) the behaviour of a fop or coxcomb, foppery, silly joke 2) mockery, raillery. — treiben, V. Gecken II.

Geckhaft, *adj.* and *adv.* foppish, foolish, silly. Dieser Mensch ist sehr —, this man is a great fool or coxcomb; —es Benehmen, foppish or foolish conduct.

Geckhaftigkeit, *f.* foppishness, silliness.

Gecko, *m.* [-'s, *pl.* -s] [in natural history] V. 3 Geck.

Geckstock, *m.* [-s, *pl.* -stöcke] swipe, brake or handle of a pump.

Gedacht, [*past part.* of denken, gedenken, which see] as an *adj.*, above-mentioned, said. Der —e Herr, the said or aforesaid gentleman.

Gedächtniß, *n.* [-sses] 1) [the retaining of past ideas in the mind] remembrance, memory. Ich habe es noch in frischem Gedächtnisse, it is still fresh in my memory; ich werde diese Wohlthat immer im Gedächtnisse behalten, I shall always preserve the memory of this benefit, I shall always bear or keep in mind this benefit; das — der Gerechten bleibet im Segen, the memory of the just is blessed; er wird in dem Gedächtnisse aller Jahrhunderte leben, he will live in the memory of all ages; bin ich noch immer in Ihrem Gedächtnisse? do you still remember me? das wird mir immer im Gedächtnisse bleiben, that will always be in my mind or memory. I shall never forget it; man hat ein Denkmahl zum Gedächtnisse dieser That errichtet, a monument has been erected in memory or in remembrance of this exploit; zum ewigen Gedächtnisse des Helden, in perpetual memory of this hero; seines Namens — stiften, to immortalize one's name, one's memory; Kaiser Karl, großwürdigsten Gedächtnisses, Emperor Charles of glorious memory; schreibseligen Gedächtnisses, of scribbling memory; das thut zu meinem Gedächtnisse, this do in remembrance of me; die Zeit wird dein — ganz ausrotten, time will blot out all remembrance of you. V. Andenken 1), Erinnerung 2). 2) [the faculty of the mind by which it retains the knowledge of past events or ideas which are past] memory, remembrance, recollection. Ein gutes, ein glückliches —, a good, a happy memory; ein starkes, treues —, a retentive memory; ein schlechtes, kurzes —, a bad, short memory; er hat kein —, es fehlt ihm an —, he has no memory; er hat viel —, aber wenig Urtheilskraft, he has a good memory, but no judgment; fassen Sie das ins —, prägen Sie das Ihrem Gedächtnisse ein, bear that in mind, imprint that on your memory; das ist mir aus dem Gedächtnisse entfallen, that has slipped out of my memory; nun kommt mir in's —, daß &c., now it occurs to my memory, that &c.; das — verlieren, um das — kommen, to lose one's memory; etwas im Gedächtnisse behalten, to keep or bear something in one's mind or memory; er hat kein — für empfangene Beleidigungen, he has no memory for, he soon forgets, the injuries or wrongs he has suffered.

Gedächtniß-bein, *n.* [in anatomy] occipital bone. **—buch**, *n.* [Gedenkbuch] memorandum book. **—fehler**, *m* fault of the memory. **—feier**, *f.* **—fest**, *n.* anniversary, commemoration Das —fest, die —feier einer Schlacht, eines Sieges begehen, to celebrate the anniversary or commemoration of a battle, of a victory. **—kraft**, *f.* the retentive power of the memory. **—kunst**, *f.* the art of memory, mnemonicks. **—mangel**, *m.* want of memory. **—münze**, *f.* medal. **—predigt**, **—rede**, *f.* sermon or speech made in commemoration or solemnization of an important or glorious event; *it.* [more particularly] funeral sermon, sermon or speech made in memory of a deceased person. **—tag**, *m.* anniversary, festive day [in commemoration of some event].

Gedackt, *adj.* covered with a lid. [only used in the following terms] [among organ-builders] Ein Register grob —er [16füßiger] Pfeifen, a register of pipes of sixteen feet; mittel— [8füßig], of eight feet; klein oder still — [4füßig], of four feet.

Gedanke, *m.* [-n, *pl.* -n] or **Gedanken**, *m.* [-s, *pl.* -] what the mind thinks or conceives, thought, idea. Ein lebhafter, feiner, kühner —, a lively, fine, bold thought; ein unreifer, unverdauter —, an immature, undigested thought; dieses Werk ist voll schöner Gedanken, this work is full of fine thoughts; seine Gedanken klar ausdrücken, to express one's thoughts clearly; sie ist mein einziger —, she is the object of all my thoughts; der — an die Liebe Gottes lindert alle Leiden, when thinking on the love of God we feel an alleviation of all our sufferings; es fallen mir allerlei Gedanken ein, all sorts of thoughts or ideas enter my mind, come into my mind or head, occur to my mind; seine Gedanken nicht beisammen haben [zerstreut seyn], to be absent, inattentive, heedless; etwas ohne Gedanken thun, to do something without thought, carelessly, thoughtlessly; das ist mir nie in die Gedanken gekommen, that never once came into my thoughts, into my head. I never thought of such a thing; sich etwas in Gedanken vorstellen, to figure to one's self something; seinen Gedanken nachhängen, *seinen Gedanken Audienz geben, to muse upon one's own thoughts, to muse, to meditate; voll Gedanken seyn, to be very thoughtful; in Gedanken seyn, in tiefen Gedanken sitzen, to be musing or pensive, to sit musing; *er ist oft mit seinen Gedanken nicht zu Hause, he is often absent [inattentive]. *Prov.* Gedanken sind zollfrei, opinions are free. In a more limited sense: *a*) [= Meinung, Ansicht] opinion. Er stand in dem Gedanken, ich hätte ihm das gesagt, he thought I had told him so; er steht in dem Gedanken, er würde sich hier besser befinden, he fancies or believes he would do better here; er macht sich den Gedanken [die Hoffnung], er werde dies Amt erhalten, he feeds or flatters his fancy with the idea or hope that he will get this office he is in hopes of getting this office; sehr hohe Gedanken von sich haben, to have a very high or lofty idea or opinion of one's own person or merit, to be self-conceited; das ist nicht Ihr —, sagen Sie mir Ihre Gedanken, that is not your opinion, tell me your thoughts, your mind; können Sie solche Gedanken von mir haben? can you entertain such an opinion, such thoughts of me? nach meinen Gedanken sollte er &c., in my opinion he ought to &c.; Jemand auf andere Gedanken bringen, to make any one change or alter his mind; ich brachte ihn auf bessere Gedanken von Ihnen, I made him conceive a more favourable opinion of you; ich möchte seine Gedanken hierüber wissen, I should like to know his thoughts, his sentiments upon this point; wir haben einerlei Gedanken, we are of the same mind or opinion; Jemand seine Gedanken eröffnen, to speak or communicate one's thoughts to any one; seine Gedanken frei heraus sagen, to speak one's mind freely. *b*) [= Vermuthung] supposition, conjecture. Wie konnten Sie doch auf die Gedanken fallen? how could such an idea enter or come into your head? how could you conceive such an idea, entertain such a thought? das bringt mich fast auf den Gedanken, daß die Sache wahr ist, that makes me almost suppose or suspect that it is true; sich arge, böse Gedanken von Einem machen, to entertain ill thoughts of any one, to conceive a bad opinion of any one; *er macht sich Gedanken hierüber, he is uneasy, he frets about it; entschlagen Sie sich dieser traurigen Gedanken, banish these melancholy thoughts out of your mind. *c*) [= Erinnerung] remembrance. Sie kommt mir unaufhörlich in die Gedanken, I have her continually present in my thoughts, I always think of her; *sich etwas aus den Gedanken schlagen, to banish or efface a thing from the memory. *d*) [= Vorhaben] design, purpose. Die Gedanken, die ich für euch habe, sind Gedanken des Friedens und nicht des Leides, [in Script.] the thoughts I think towards you, are thoughts of peace and not of evil; er hat den Gedanken, zu heirathen, aufgegeben, he has given up his intention of marrying; er geht mit dem Gedanken um, zu reisen, he projects a journey, he designs to travel, he is thinking of travelling; man hat nie den Gedanken gehabt, ihn festzusetzen, they never thought of arresting him; diese Gedanken sind mir vergangen, I have no longer any thoughts about that, I think no more of it; er war auf den Gedanken gerathen, es zu kaufen, he took a fancy to buy it; V. Einfall; [in painting] das ist keine Zeichnung, es ist ein bloßer —, that is not a drawing, it is a mere sketch or rough draught

Gedanken=bein, *n.* [in anatomy] one of the bones forming the sides and upper part of the skull, parietal bone. —dieb, *m.* plagiary. —folge, *f.* train of thought. —freiheit, *f.* V. Denkfreiheit. —leer, *adj* and *adv.* void of thought. —leere, *f.* inanity of intellect. —los, *adj.* and *adv.* unthinking, thoughtless. —lose Andacht, devotion without attention; V. —leer. —losigkeit, *f.* want of thought, thoughtlessness, inattention. Er that es aus —losigkeit, he did it inadvertently; V. —leere. —punkte, *pl.* [in grammar] points of reticence. —raub, *m.* plagiarism. —räuber, *m.* V. —dieb. —reich, *adj.* fertile or fruitful in thoughts or conceptions. —schnell, *adj.* and *adv.* as quick as thought. —späne, *pl.* detached thoughts, aphorisms. —spiel, *n.* a witty conceit, witticism. —strich, *m.* [in grammar] dash, break. —voll, *adj.* full of thought, thoughtful, pensive. —wesen, *n.* something existing merely in thought or idea.

Gedärm, *n.* [-es, *pl.* -e] or die Gedärme, *pl.* [V. Darm], all the intestines or guts of the animal body, bowels, entrails, intestines. Das — von Thieren, garbage; Schmerzen in dem —e haben, to have a pain in one's bowels; das dicke —, the great gut or large intestines; das dünne —, the small intestines; die Arzenei hat ihm ein starkes Reißen in den —en verursacht, the medicine has raked his bowels.

Gedéck, *n.* [-es, *pl.* -e] 1) [in architecture] roof. 2) a cover or a plate with a napkin, spoon, knife and fork. Bringen Sie ein — für diesen Herrn, bring a plate or cover [or a knife and fork] for this gentleman; eine Tafel von hundert —en, a table of a hundred covers. 3) the table cloth and napkins. 4) [among organ-builders] a register of covered pipes. V. Gedackt.

Gedeihen, [anciently deihen, allied to dick, Degen, tüchtig] *ir. v. intr.* [u. w. seyn] 1) [properly = dick or dicker werden, to grow thick or thicker] to grow big, to thrive. Dieses Kind isset viel, aber es gedeihet nicht dabei, this child eats a great deal, but it does not thrive; das junge Vieh gedeiht auf fetten Weiden, young cattle thrive in rich pastures; Sie müssen eine sehr gute Kost haben, denn Sie — wieder, your diet or board must be very good, for you are gathering flesh again. 2) in general, to grow. Dieser Baum gedeiht sehr, this tree is growing very fast; die Bäume — in diesem Boden nicht, trees do not thrive in this soil; der Weinstock gedeiht in diesem Lande nicht, the vine does not thrive in this country; der Kaffe gedeiht bei uns nicht, coffee does not thrive or grow in our country; das Getreide ist dieses Jahr gediehen [= gut gerathen], corn has been plentiful this year. *Fig. a*) to arise. Daraus gedeihet kein Gewinn, no gain or profit will accrue from it. *b*) to turn out. Das wird zu seiner Schande —, that will turn to his shame; das gedeihet ihm zur Ehre, zum Ruhme, that turns to his honour, to his glory. *c*) to come into a certain condition. Die Sache ist nun dahin gediehen, daß &c., the affair is now come to that point, that &c.; der Luxus ist zu einer solchen Höhe gediehen, luxury has arrived at such a height. *d*) to go on prosperously, to prosper. Seine Anschläge — nicht, his projects do not succeed; Gott hat unsere Unternehmungen — lassen, God has prospered our enterprises; alles gedeihet ihm, every thing thrives with him, he succeeds in every thing. *Prov.* Unrecht Gut gedeihet nicht, ill-gotten good never prospers, ill got, ill spent. *e*) to grow or become happy. Er ist ein schlechter Mensch, er wird nie —, he is a bad or wicked man, he will never be happy. 3) Es gedeiht Einem etwas, something increases one's bodily well-being. Grobe Kost gedeiht den Handwerkern besser, als &c, mechanics thrive better with coarse victuals or with a coarse diet, than &c.; sie ißt viel, aber es gedeiht ihr nicht, she eats a great deal, but she does not thrive. *Fig.* Das wird ihm nie — [= gelingen], he will never succeed in it; das ist ihm übel gediehen, he met with bad success.

Gedeihen, *n.* [-s] thriving, increase, profit, progress, prosperity, success. Ich wünsche Ihnen viel Segen und —, may God bless and prosper you, or I wish you all manner of blessing and prosperity; Gott gebe sein — dazu! may God grant his blessing to it! [in Script.] Gott gibt das —, God giveth the increase.

Gedeihlich, *adj.* and *adv.* tending to promote or increase, thriving. —e Speisen, nutritive food or victuals, ein —er Regen, a beneficial, fertile or productive rain. *Fig* [= heilsam, erwünscht] salutary, useful, happy, advantageous, successful. Einem alles —e Wohlergehen anwünschen, to wish any one all manner of bless and happiness; keine —e Antwort erhalten, to receive no satisfactory answer.

Gedénken, *ir. v. intr.* [V. Denken] 1) to think. Daran ist nicht zu —, we must not think of it, there is no hopes, not the least probability; ich zittere noch, wenn ich daran gedenke, I tremble yet when I think of it; gedenke meiner, think of me, remember me; *Einem etwas —, to owe any one no good will, to owe any one a spite; *ich will es ihm schon —, I'll make him pay for it; bei Menschen — ist es nicht so kalt gewesen, in the memory of man it has not been so cold; vor Menschen- fore the memory of man, time out of 2) [= erwähnen] to mention. Jemand Ehren —, to make honourable mention one; — Sie meiner in Ihrem Gebete member me in your prayers; einer Sache —, to pass a thing over in silence; besser zu —, abstractedly from that, putting the of the question, not to mention that; Streiche, die er gemacht hat, nicht zu —, mentioning other tricks he has played; unserer alten Freundschaft mit keinem gedacht, he never mentioned a syllable of former friendship; er ließ sich den gedachten Vorschlag gefallen, he acceded, agreed sented to the proposed project, to the p sition in question; oben gedachter Kauf meldet mir, the above-mentioned merchant merchant in question advises me. 3) [= to hope, to expect. — Sie Ihren Zweck reichen? do you hope or expect to attain aim? 4) [= Willens seyn] to intend, to Ich gedenke zu verreisen, I project a jo design to go upon a journey; ich gedenke ins Theater zu gehen, I have a good m go to the play to-day.

Gedenk=buch, *n.* —zettel, *n.* [D buch, Denkzettel] V. Gedächtnißbuch.

‡**Gedeyen**, V. Gedeihen.

Gedícht, *n.* [-es, *pl.* -e] [V. Dichten] 1) Erdichtung] fiction, fable. Diese Erzählun ein bloßes —, this story is a mere fictio halte das für ein —, I look upon it as a 2) [generally, a metrical composition] a piece of poetry or verses. Es sind laut they are all poems; ein — machen, verf to compose, to write a poem; er macht —chen, he writes pretty little pieces of Schillers —e, the poems of Schiller; e sches, lyrisches, dramatisches —, an epic dramatic poem; ein unzüchtiges —, smutty verses. V. Helden—, Hirten—, E

Gediegen, *adj.* and *adj.* [in mining] p gin, unmixed, native, solid. —es Gold, pure or virgin gold, silver; —es Erz, nat ein Kreuz von —em Golde [durchaus von cross of pure or massy gold. *Fig.* Er g eine —e [derbe] Antwort, he made or a sharp answer; —e [= ächte, wahre] W true, genuine wisdom; —es Verdienst, lasting merit; —er Werth, sterling —e [feste] Gesundheit, solid or sound h

Gediegenheit, *f.* solidity, purity; *it.* strength vigour, energy, pithiness. Seine Rede hät mehr — haben sollen, his speech should hav been more pithy.

Gedínge, [-s] or **Geding**, [-es, *pl.* -e] *n.* [bargain, agreement. Ein — über eine Arbe machen, to agree for the price of some wor to undertake some work by contract; er ha mit seinem Schmied wegen des Hufschlags ei — gemacht, he has contracted or made an agree ment with his blacksmith for the shoeing his horse or horses; ein — arbeiten, to wor by contract or by the job. [in mining] work task which a miner has agreed to perform sein — redlich auffahren, to perform one's tas honestly, faithfully; sein — abgeben [verbl den], to finish or work out one's task. 2) tedious bargaining, haggling.

Gedinge=arbeit, *f.* [or Gedingarbeit,] an undertaking by the great or in the gros or for a certain price, or by contract; wor or task agreed upon —buch, *n.* [in mining] book or register, in which the agreed work the miners is entered. —geld, *n.* agree price, contract price. —gezäh, *n.* [in mining] a miner's tools. —hauer, *m.* [in mining] a man hat works by the job, or by agreement. —Lohn, n. V. —geld. —Stufe, f. [in mining] a mark hewn into a rock, to show the miner how far his task goes.

Gedoppelt, [properly, *past part.* of Doppeln, which see.] *adj.* and *adv.* double. V. Doppelt. [in blazonry] Eine —e Binde, gemelles.

Gedränge, *n.* [-s] 1) [das Drängen] the act of thronging or crowding together, a thronging. Es war ein außerordentliches —, the thronging, pressure was extraordinary. 2) [a number of persons congregated and pressed together] crowd, throng, press. Sich durch das — hindurcharbeiten, to make one's way through the crowd; er warf sich mitten in das —, he threw himself into the middle of the crowd; warten wir, bis sich das — verliert, let us wait, or we had better wait, till the multitude has dispersed; in das — kommen, gerathen, to get among the crowd. *Fig.* Dem — der Stadt entweichen, to escape from the tumult or bustle of the town; mitten in dem — der Welt leben, to live in the midst of the bustle of the world; *es ist kein großes — nach dieser Waare, there is no great demand for this commodity; *es hat viel — darnach, it has a great run; *im — [in Noth] seyn, stecken, to be in a dilemma, in distress or in great straits; *er ist sehr in das — gekommen, gerathen, he is involved in great difficulties or perplexities.

Gedränge, Gedrange, [rather provincial] *adj.* pressed together, close, thronged, crowded. II. *adv.* narrowly. Wir sitzen sehr —, we sit very close.

Gedrängt, [properly, *past part.* of Drängen, which see] *adj.* and *adv.* compressed, succinct, concise. Eine —e Schreibart, a concise style; in der Genesis haben wir eine —e Erzählung der Schöpfung, in Genesis we have a concise account of the creation; die Thatsachen waren — angegeben, the facts were succinctly stated.

Gedrängtheit, *f.* conciseness. Man sollte die — nicht auf Kosten der Klarheit zu erreichen suchen, conciseness should not be studied at the expense of perspicuity.

Gedritt, *adj.* consisting of three parts, ternate, ternary. Eine —e Zahl, the ternary number, the ternary, ternion or the number three; [in astrology] der —e Schein, [the aspect of planets distant from each other 120 degrees, forming the figure of a trigon or triangle] trine, trigon; [in heraldry] ein —er Schild, a shield or field divided into three areas, a tierce or tierced escutcheon; [in commerce] —e Wechselbriefe [in dreifacher Abschrift], triple letters or bills of exchange, or bills in triplicate; [in playing at cards] ein —es haben, [in piquet] to have or hold a tierce [a sequence of three cards of the same colour].

Gedrungenheit, *f.* V. Gedrängtheit.

Gedúld, *f.* [V. Dulden] 1) patience, endurance. — haben, to have patience; —, wir sind noch nicht fertig, have patience, we have not yet done; sein Unglück mit — ertragen, to bear one's misfortune with patience, patiently; die — verlieren, to lose patience; die — verloren haben, to be out of patience; Eines — prüfen, ermüden, to try any one's patience, to wear out any one's patience; endlich war meine — erschöpft, riß mir die —, at length I lost all patience, at length I could restrain myself no longer; er wird sogleich kommen, haben Sie —, he will come directly, have or take patience; —, or einen Augenblick —, wenn ich bitten darf, pray, have patience for a moment, if you please; er hat an keinem Orte lange —, he never stays long in the same place. *Prov.* — überwindet Alles, patience overcomes all things. 2) [= Nachsicht, Langmuth] forbearance, indulgence. [in Script.] Habe — mit mir, und ich will dir alles heimzahlen, have patience with me, and I will pay thee all; — mit Einem haben, to have indulgence for any one; haben Sie — mit einem unerfahrenen Mädchen, be indulgent to an unexperienced girl; Eines — mißbrauchen, to abuse any one's forbearance; seine Gläubiger wollen noch einige Tage — mit ihm haben, his creditors will allow him some days more.

Geduldshahn, *m.* [formerly, in certain provinces of Germany] a cock which married people without children were obliged to give every year to the parson. —los, *adj.* and *adv.* without patience.

Gedúlden, *v. r.* sich —, to have patience, to bear with, to forbear. — Sie sich, es wird noch alles gut gehen, have or take patience, all will go well yet; — Sie sich nur bis um vier Uhr, do but wait, do but have patience till four o'clock; morgen muß er mich bezahlen, ich habe mich schon zu lange geduldet, to morrow he must pay me, I have waited long enough, I have forborn too long already.

Gedúldig, *adj* and *adv.* patient, forbearing, indulgent. Der —ste Mensch von der Welt, the most patient man alive; er ist bei allen Schmerzen sehr —, he bears all his pains with great patience, very patiently; Gott ist — und barmherzig, God is long-suffering and merciful; — leiden, warten, to suffer, to wait patiently; einen Schimpf — ertragen, to put up with an affront. Syn. Geduldig, Gelassen. Geduld [from dulden] denotes that quality or temper of mind which enables one to endure something disagreeable without too eagerly desiring the termination of it. He is gelassen who suppresses or moderates every violent emotion of the mind especially of a disagreeable nature. We may be gelassen, at the thought also of past or future evils; geduldig, only under present.

Gedúnsen, = Aufgedunsen, V. Aufdunsen.

Geéckt, V. Eckig.

||**Geest,** *f.* Geestland, *n.* [probably belonging to the Low Saxon gest = wüst] [in lower Saxony] dry and barren ground.

Gefahr, *f.* [*pl.* -en] [Old Germ. Fahr, Sw. *Fara*, allied to the Lat. *per*-iculum; from fahren = herbeibringen] danger, peril, hazard, risk. In — seyn, to be in danger, in jeopardy; sich in — begeben, to expose one's self to danger; der —, den —en trotzen, to brave the danger, the dangers; große — laufen, to run a great risk or danger; er lief —, verrathen zu werden, he run the risk or hazard of being betrayed; in [die] — kommen, gerathen, to be put in hazard, to be exposed to danger; es ist keine — dabei, durch den Wald zu gehen, there is no danger in passing through the forest; in — bringen, to endanger; außer — seyn, to be out of danger, to be safe; er ist nun außer aller —, [of a sick person] he is now out of all danger; der — entgehen, to escape the danger; große —en ausstehen, to go through great dangers; er schwebt, ist in —, das Leben zu verlieren, he is in danger of losing his life, he is in danger of his life; er setzte sich der — aus, den Hals zu brechen, he exposed himself to the danger of breaking his neck; auf Ihre — [hin], at your peril; ich diente ihm mit — meines Lebens, I served him at the peril or hazard of my life; er setzt sein Leben in —, he runs the risk or hazard of his life, he risks his life; etwas auf seine — und Kosten unternehmen, to undertake something at one's own peril and expense; ich will es auf die — hin thun, Euch zu mißfallen, I will do it at the peril of your displeasure; auf alle —, at all events, at all risks; in Todes— seyn, to be in danger or peril of death; Einen in — bringen, setzen, stürzen, to expose any one to danger, to bring any one into danger or peril.

Gefahrzins, *m.* rent which, when not paid at due term, forfeits the copy-hold.

Gefährde, *f.* [*pl.* -n] [V. Gefahr] danger, peril, hazard, risk; [in law] cunning, fraud, deceit, cozenage. Getreulich und sonder — [in law], faithfully and without fraud; der Eid für die —, [oath of having a just cause or of not committing an injustice wittingly] oath of integrity.

Gefährden, *v. tr.* [V. Gefahr] to expose to danger or risk, to endanger, to peril. Ich bin dabei nicht gefährdet, I risk nothing in this affair, I run no risk; sich selbst —, to expose one's self to hurt or prejudice; seine Ehre ist dabei gefährdet, his honour is at stake in this affair.

Gefähre, *n.* [-s] [in familiar language] a continual noise caused by the driving of carriages or waggons. Es ist ein beständiges — in dieser Straße, there is a continual din of carriages, or driving in this street.

Gefährlich, *adj.* and *adv.* dangerous, perilous, hazardous. Ein —er Mensch, a dangerous man; ein —er Sprung, a dangerous or perilous leap; eine —e Krankheit, a dangerous disease or illness, a mortal distemper; ein —es Unternehmen, a perilous or hazardous enterprise; die Sache ist —, it is a dangerous thing; es ist in diesem Lande — zu reisen, there is danger in travelling in this country; —e Stellen im Meer, rocks or shelves; *Sie machen es auch gar zu —, but you exaggerate the danger, you represent the danger greater than it really is; er ist — krank, he is dangerously ill.

Gefährlichkeit, *f.* 1) dangerousness, perilousness. Die — dieses Unternehmens, the dangerousness, or perilousness, of this enterprise; die — eines Ortes, the dangerous or perilous situation of a place; *it.* the dangerousness of a place [a place which threatens or brings danger, a place which is insecure (infested by robbers &c.)]. 2) [Gefahr] danger, peril, hazard. Bevorstehende —en, imminent dangers or perils. V. Fährlichkeit.

Gefährlos, *adj.* and *adv.* free from danger, without danger. Ein —er Weg, Wald, a safe road, wood, a road or wood where one may pass without any risk or danger; man kann ganz — dahin gehen, one may go thither without incurring the least danger.

Gefährlosigkeit, *f.* freedom from danger or hazard, safety. Die — eines elektrischen Versuches, the safety of an electrical experiment.

Gefährt, [from fahren = reisen, gehen, ziehen] *n.* [-es, *pl.* -e] 1) [in common language] carriage, vehicle. 2) [among hunters] V. Fährte. 3) [in mining] the track of a metallic vein or lode. Dem Gange auf das — kommen, to find out the track of the lode.

Gefährte, *m.* [-n, *pl.* -n] **Gefährtinn,** *f.* [from fahren = reisen, gehen, ziehen] 1) companion, travelling companion. Ein Waffen—, a companion in arms; Einen zum —n annehmen, to take any one for a travelling companion; seyn Sie willkommen, mein lieber, treuer —, welcome, my dear, faithful companion or comrade; er war mein — im Unglück, he was my companion or fellow in misfortune; er und seine treue Gefährtinn [Gattinn], he and his faithful spouse or consort; *fig.* die Mittelmäßigkeit ist eine Gefährtinn der

Ruhe, mediocrity is the companion of quiet. 2) [in mining] a lode running parallel to the principal lode.

Gefäll, *n.* [-es, *pl* -e] 1) the distance which a fluid body falls, fall, descent. **Dieser Fluß hat vier Fuß —**, this river has a fall of four feet, **das — der Straße beträgt hier** &c., the descent of the road is here &c; [in mining] a sloping-table on which the ore is washed, V. **Planherd**; [in geology] extent of descent, fall; [in hydraulics] the falling of the waters; **hohe —e erfordern oberschlächtige Mühlen**, waters falling from a high place require mills with troughs or channels 2) [**Gefälle** *pl.* = **Einkünfte**, *it* more generally = **Abgaben**] income, revenue; *it.* taxes, duties, dues. **Jährliche, gewisse —e**, a yearly, certain income or yearly, certain revenues; **un[be]ständige —e**, casual revenues, perquisites; **die —e bezahlen**, to pay the taxes or duties; **dies gereicht den königlichen —en zum Nachtheil**, that is prejudicial to the king's revenues.

Gefälls**einnehmer**, **—verweser**, *m.* receiver of the taxes, revenues **—kästchen**, *n.* [in mining] the trough of the sloping-table on which the ore is washed. **—wesen**, *n.* the state of the revenues or taxes, the revenues.

Gefallen, [from **fallen** = **sich schicken**] *ir. v. intr.* to please. **Sie ist nicht schön, aber sie gefällt Jedermann**, she is not handsome, but she pleases everybody; **welche von diesen Farben gefällt Ihnen am besten, am meisten?** which of these colours do you like best or most, pleases you the most? **nehmen Sie das, was Ihnen gefällt**, take that which suits your fancy; **er hat die Gabe, Jedermann zu —**, he has the knack of pleasing everybody; **dieses Benehmen gefällt mir gar nicht an Ihnen**, this conduct of yours does not please me at all; **das hat mir nie an ihm — wollen**, I could never like that in him, that never pleased me in him; **von Person hat sie mir —**, her person. her exterior pleased me: **an diesem Orte gefällt es mir am besten**, I like this place best or most; **wie hat es Ihnen in London —?** how did you like London? **das gefällt Ihnen nur so zu sagen**, you are pleased to say so; **gefällt Ihnen das?** does that please you? is that according to your liking? **es gefällt mir sehr**, I am greatly pleased with it; **setzen Sie sich, wenn es Ihnen gefällt**, sit down if you please, be pleased to sit down; **wie es Ihnen gefällt**, as you please, as you choose; **es hat dem Allmächtigen —, uns in Betrübniß zu versetzen**, it has pleased the Almighty to afflict us; **möge es Gott —, daß wir uns bald wiedersehen**, please God that we may soon meet again! **sich etwas — lassen**, to be satisfied, to be contented with something, to acquiesce, to consent to something, to comply, to put up with something; **er hat sich den Vorschlag — lassen**, he has acquiesced or consented to the proposal; **er läßt sich Alles —**, he submits to any thing, he acquiesces to whatever one desires; **das kann ich mir unmöglich — lassen**, it is impossible for me to agree to that; **er gefällt sich in Allem, was er thut**, he delights in whatever he does; **sie gefällt sich in den Huldigungen, die man ihr zollt**, she is pleased or delighted with homages paid her. SYN. **Gefallen**, **Belieben**. **Gefallen** denotes merely the pleasure which any thing causes us, without implying a wish to possess it; **Belieben**, on the contrary, that state in which we desire the possession of the object with which we are pleased.

Gefallsucht, *f.* excessive desire to please, coquetry. **Die —sucht ist nicht ihr Fehler**, coquetry is not her fault or foible. **—süchtig**, *adj.* and *adv.* overdesirous to please, coquettish. **Ein —süchtiges Frauenzimmer**, a coquettish woman.

Gefallen, *m.* [-s] pleasure, satisfaction; *it.* favour, service, obligation **— an etwas haben, finden**, to take pleasure in a thing, to be pleased or taken with a thing; **ich habe — daran**, it gives me great pleasure, it pleases me very much; **es wird mir ein großer — geschehen, wenn Sie** &c., you will do me a great favour by &c; **thun Sie, erweisen Sie mir den —, nicht mehr davon zu sprechen**, do me the favour, not to mention it any more; **thun Sie es mir zu —**, do it to please or to oblige me; **was ich dabei thue, geschieht bloß Ihnen zu —**, whatever I do in this affair, is merely to please or oblige you; **wenn Ihnen dadurch ein — geschieht, so werde ich hingehen**, if it will give you pleasure, I shall go there; **Einem zu — reden**, to speak as a person likes to hear, to flatter any one; **er redet es Euch zu —**, he says so out of complaisance to you; **ich will Ihnen hierin gern zu — seyn, leben**, I will willingly humour you in that; **nach seinem — handeln**, to do or act as one pleases or lists.

1. **Gefällig**, *adj.* and *adv.* 1) pleasing, agreeable, acceptable **Ein Gott —es** or **gott—es Opfer**, a sacrifice acceptable or agreeable to God; **diese Vase hat eine sehr —e Form**, this vase has a very pleasing shape or form; **sich bei Jedermann — machen**, to render one's self agreeable to everybody, to ingratiate one's self into everybody's favour; **—e Manieren**, easy or agreeable manners. 2) [desirous to please] complaisant, obliging, courteous. **Ein sehr —er junger Mensch**, a very obliging or polite young man; **eine —e Behandlung**, a complaisant or courteous treatment. 3) **Es ist Einem —** [**es beliebt Einem**], a person pleases to do &c. something. **Wenn es Ihnen — ist**, if you please; **ist es Ihnen —, mitzugehen?** will you go with us? are you pleased, do you choose to go with us?

2 **Gefällig**, *adj.* used in vulgar language instead of **fällig**, which see.

Gefälligkeit, *f.* 1) [desire to please] obliging disposition, complaisance, courteousness. **Sie hat viel — für ihn**, she is very complaisant to him; **haben Sie die —, mir zu sagen**, have the goodness or kindness to tell me; **er gab es aus — zu**, he consented to it out of complaisance. 2) [**Dienst, Gefallen**] favour, service. **Einem eine — erweisen**, to do any one a favour, to oblige any one; **ich danke Ihnen für alle mir erwiesene —en**, I thank you for all the favours, services, or good offices you have done me. 3) V. **Selbstgefälligkeit**.

Gefältel, *n.* [-s] [in fam. lang.] gathers, plaits, folds, puckers.

Gefangen, [past part. of **fangen**, which see] *adj.* taken prisoner, imprisoned. **Ein —er**, [as a *subst.*] a prisoner, a captive; **der, die —e**, the prisoner the captive; **die —en Könige und Prinzessinnen nebst den übrigen —en**, the captive kings and princesses together with the other prisoners; **sie führten die Weiber — mit sich fort**, they led the women captive; **Jemanden — nehmen**, to arrest, to seize any one, to take any one into custody, *it.* [in military affairs] to take any one prisoner; **Einen — legen** or **setzen**, to put any one into prison, to imprison any one; **man hält sie seit acht Tagen —**, she has been detained prisoner, she has been held or kept in custody these eight days; **er ist ein Vierteljahr lang — gesessen**, he has been imprisoned for three months; **sich — geben**, to render one's self up a prisoner; **er ist mein —er, sie ist meine —e**, he, she is my prisoner; **einen —en losgeben, loslassen**, to set a prisoner free or at liberty, to release a prisoner; **im Kriege — werden, oder zum —en gemacht werden**, to be taken prisoner, to be made prisoner of war; **man hat in dieser Schlacht wenig —e gemacht**, few prisoners were taken in this battle; **er ist —er auf sein Ehrenwort**, he is prisoner upon parole. *fig.* **seine Vernunft unter dem Gehorsam des Glaubens — nehmen**, [**sie dem Glauben unterwerfen**] to captivate one's understanding to the truths of religion. V. **Kriegsgefangener**.

Gefangens**brod**, *n.* the bread of a prisoner. **—haltung**, *f.* detention in custody, confinement. **—hüter**, *m.* one that guards the prisoners, prison-keeper. V. **—wärter**. **—nehmung**, *f.* imprisonment, seizure. **—wärter**, *m.* jailer, keeper of a prison, turnkey. **—wärterinn**, *f.* a jailer's wife.

Gefangenschaft, *f.* captivity, imprisonment, detention, confinement. **In der — leben**, to live in captivity, in bondage; **Einen aus der — loskaufen**, to redeem any one from captivity, to ransom any one; **seine langwierige — hat seinen Geist nicht niedergeschlagen**, his long imprisonment has not cast him down; **dieser Offizier ist in — gerathen**, this officer has fallen into captivity, has been made prisoner; **er war in türkische — gerathen**, he had fallen into Turkish slavery; **die babylonische —**, the Babylonian captivity.

Gefänglich, *adj.* imprisoned, captive. **Einen Verbrecher — einziehen, einbringen**, to apprehend, to imprison a criminal; **Einen — halten**, to keep any one imprisoned, to detain any one in custody; **—e Haft**, imprisonment, confinement, custody; **zur —en Haft bringen**, to put into prison, to imprison; **er sitzt immer noch in —er Haft**, he is still in prison or imprisoned.

Gefängniß, *n.* [-sses, *pl.* -sse] 1) jail, prison. **Die öffentlichen Gefängnisse**, the public prisons; **Einen in das — setzen, führen**, to put to carry any one into prison, to imprison any one; **ein finsteres, tiefes —**, a dungeon; **er sitzt im Gefängnisse**, he is in prison or imprisoned; **aus dem Gefängnisse ausbrechen**, to break prison; **Einen aus dem Gefängnisse entlassen**, to release, to discharge a prisoner. 2) [= **Gefangenschaft**] captivity, imprisonment, detention. **Ein Verbrechen mit ewigem Gefängnisse bestrafen**, to punish a crime with perpetual imprisonment. SYN. **Gefängniß**, **Kerker**. **Gefängniß** may signify any place of safe custody in which a person is held in a state of involuntary restraint. **Kerker** is the close apartment or dungeon in which a prisoner is kept confined.

Gefängnißstrafe, *f.* punishment by imprisonment. **Bei —strafe etwas verbieten**, to forbid something upon pain of imprisonment.

Gefärz, *n.* [-es] [very vulgar] a repeated or continual farting.

Gefäscht, *adj.* [in blazonry] fessy, barry.

Gefäß, *n.* [-es, *pl.* -e] [V. **Faß**.] 1) [that part of certain vessels or instruments which is held in the hand when used] handle **Das — eines Schwertes, Dolches**, the haft or hilt of a sword, of a dagger; **das — seines Degens war von Gold**, the hilt of his sword was of gold. V. **Heft, Griff, Stiel, Handhabe**. 2) [something hollow, proper for holding liquors and other things] a vessel. **Ein irdenes, hölzernes, silbernes —**, an earthen, wooden, silver vessel; **Kunst** or **Pracht—**, a vase; **hetrurische —e**, Etruscan vases; **die heiligen —e, Kirchen—e**, the holy vessels or utensils; *fig.* [in Script.] **ein — zu Ehren, zu Unehren**, a vessel to honour, to dishonour. 3) [in anatomy] any tube or canal, in which the blood and other humours are contained, secreted or circulated, a vessel. **Die [illegible]**

hatischen —e, the lymphatic vessels, the lymphatics. V. Blut—, Haar—, Milch—. 4) [among coopers] a barrel, cask.

Gefäßchen, Gefäßlein, *n.* [-s, *pl.* -] [*diminutive* of Gefäß] a small vessel.

Gefäßig, *adj.* [in anatomy and botany] vascular.

Gefäßt, [*past part.* of fassen, which see] *adj.* and *adv.* prepared, ready; *it.* collected in mind, calm. Sich — machen, to prepare one's self, to get one's self ready; sich — halten, to keep one's self ready, to be in readiness, to be prepared; er benahm sich sehr —, he behaved very calmly.

Gefäßtheit, *f.* V. Fassung 3).

Gefecht, *n.* [-es, *pl.* -e] [Low Saxon Fechte, Sw. Fegd, from fechten = (sich) bewegen] fight, battle, engagement, combat, action. Ein unvermuthetes —, a rencounter; sich in ein — einlassen, to engage in a combat; das Heer hatte sich in ein — eingelassen, ehe das Geschütz &c. the army was engaged before the cannon &c.; es kam zwischen den Truppen zu einem —e, the troops joined battle or engaged, dieses Corps hat ein — mit dem Feinde gehabt, this corps had an engagement, was engaged with the enemy; sich zum —e anschicken, to prepare for the fight or for battle; in einem —e bleiben, to be killed in action, in battle; er hat sich ... or in allen —en gut gehalten, he fought bravely in every engagement or action; es fand ein blutiges — zwischen dem beiderseitigen Vortrab Statt, a bloody engagement took place between the two vanguards; das — wieder anfangen, to re-engage; in der Hitze des —es, im hitzigsten —e, in the heat of the fight. V. ...—, Hahnen—, Stier—.

Gefechtflagge, *f.* [in seamen's language, the flag which serves as a signal for action] the flag of defiance, bloody-flag.

Gefege, *n* [-s] 1) [in familiar language] a continual sweeping and brushing. 2) that which is swept off; [among hunters] the ragged part of the deer's horns [which he sheds].

Gefeile, Gefeilsche, *n.* V. Gedinge 2).

Gefeilt, [*past part* of feilen, which see] *adj.* and *adv.* —es Gold, Silber, gold dust, silver dust. *Fig.* polite, terse. Eine —e Schreibart, a terse or polished style.

Gefenstert, V. Fenstern.

Gefiedel, *n* [-s] [in fam. and vulgar language] scraping upon a fiddle; *it.* a miserable music. Pfui, wie er kratzt! welch abscheuliches —, fie upon it, how he scrapes! what a detestable noise!

Gefieder, *n.* [-s] 1) [all the feathers of a fowl] plumage, feathers. Dieser Vogel hat ein schönes —, this bird has a fine plumage, fine feathers; das — eines Pfeiles, the feathers of an arrow; das — eines Bettes, the feathers of a bed. 2) [feathered animals] V. Geflügel.

Gefiedert, [*past part.* of fiedern, which see] *adj.* and *adv.* covered or clothed with feathers, feathered. Ein schön —es Huhn, a fowl with fine plumage; ein —er Pfeil, a feathered arrow.

Gefilde, *n.* [-s] [in the elevated or poetical style] a continuance of fields, a plain, a field. Die gesegneten — Italiens, the fertile fields or plains of Italy; ein unabsehbares —, an unbounded, immeasurable plain, or field; die — des Himmels, or die himmlischen —, the fields of heaven or the heavenly fields.

Gefingert, [*past part.* of fingern, which see] *adj.* and *adv.* [in botany] digitate, digitated. Ein —es Blatt, a digitate leaf; der —e Schotenklee, the dorychnium.

† and ‖**Gefitschel,** *n.* [-s] a continual rubbing to and fro.

Geflammt, [*past part.* of flammen, which see] *adj.* and *adv.* made in fashion of waves, watered. —er Seidenzeug, watered or tabbied silk; —es Holz, grained wood. V. Flammicht.

Geflatter, *n.* [-s] a continual flitting or fluttering.

Geflecht, *n.* [-es, *pl.* -e] any thing twisted or plaited, texture; basketwork, hurdle[-work]. Das — ihrer schönen Haare, the braids of her beautiful hair; [in anatomy] plexus, V. Ader—; [in medicine] scrophula, king's evil V. Flechte.

Gefleckt, [*past part.* of flecken, which see] *adj.* and *adv.* spotted, speckled. Der —e Tiger, the speckled or spotted tiger.

Geflötz, *n.* [-es, *pl.* -e] V. Flötz.

Geflicke, *n.* [in familiar language] botching, patching, bungling. Welch ein elendes —! what a miserable patch-work, patchery or botchery!

Geflissen, *adj.* and *adv.* diligent, industrious, earnest, attentive, studious, assiduous. V. Beflissen. — seyn, to apply one's self to something, to endeavour, to study; er ist —, alles zu entdecken, was in der Familie vorgeht, he makes it his business, his study, to discover whatever passes in the family.

Geflissenheit, *f.* diligence, assiduity, studiousness, application, endeavour. Mit großer — arbeiten, to work very sedulously, with close application.

Geflissentlich, I. *adj.* intentional, wilful. Ein —es Verbrechen, a premeditated crime. II. *adv.* intentionally, designedly, wilfully, on purpose, purposely. — etwas thun, to do something on purpose, designedly.

Geflister, *n.* [das Flistern] [in fam. language] continued whispering. Das — des Windes in den Bäumen, the whispering of the winds among the trees; es ist ein beständiges — unter ihnen, there is a continual whispering between them.

†**Gefluche,** *n.* [-s] continued swearing and cursing. Welch ein schreckliches —! what terrible oaths!

Gefluder, *n.* [-s] [in mining] V. Fluder.

Geflügel, *n.* [-s] or die —, *pl* winged animals, fowls poultry. — halten, to keep poultry. V. also Federvieh.

Geflügelt, [*past part.* of flügeln, which see] *adj.* and *adv.* winged. Die —e Schlange, der —e Fisch, das —e Pferd, the flying serpent, fish, horse.

Geflüster, *n.* V. Geflister.

Gefolge, *n.* [-s] suite, train, attendance, retinue Der König hat ein großes —, the king has a numerous retinue; er reiset mit einem kleinen —, he travels with a small retinue, with few attendants; er gehört zu dem — des Gesandten, he belongs to the ambassador's suite he is one of the ambassador's retinue; ein großes — von Kutschen, a long train or line of coaches or carriages; die zum — gehörigen Kutschen, the coaches for a prince's household; *fig.* das Laster mit seinem schadenvollen —, vice with its pernicious consequences or attendants.

Gefrage, *n* [-s] [in fam. language] continual questioning or asking. Wird Euer — kein Ende nehmen? will you never have done asking me questions or questioning me?

†**Gefräß,** *n.* [-es, *pl.* -e] 1) [= Nahrung, Speise] food, victuals [chiefly in contempt]. 2) [= der Mund, das Maul] mouth, chops, jaws. Er hat ihm Eins in's — gegeben, he has given him a slap on the chops or over the face. V Fresse.

Gefräßig, *adj.* and *adv.* [given to excessive eating; greedy for eating, used of persons and animals] gluttonous, voracious, ravenous Dieser Hund ist so —, daß er &c., this dog is so voracious, that &c.; dieser Knabe ist äußerst —, this boy is a great glutton; der Wolf ist ein —es Thier, the wolf is a voracious or ravenous animal. V. Fräßig.

Gefräßigkeit, *f.* gluttony, voracity, voraciousness.

Gefreite, *m.* [-n, *pl.* -n] [a non-commissioned officer under the corporal] lance corporal; [in ancient Greece and Rome] lancepesade.

†**Gefresse,** *n.* [-s] greedy eating, guttling, gormandizing.

Gefrierbar, *adj.* [that may be congealed or converted into ice] congealable.

Gefrieren, *ir. v. intr.* [u. w. seyn] to be congealed by cold, to freeze, to congeal. Es ist so kalt, daß der Wein im Glase gefriert, it is so very cold that the wine freezes in the glass; das Wasser gefriert bei der Kälte, water congeals by cold, cold congeals water into ice, freezes the water; dieser Teich fängt an zu —, this pond begins to freeze; der Fluß ist gefroren, the river is frozen; der Weingeist gefriert nicht, spirit of wine never freezes; es gefriert, *impers.* [u. w. haben] it freezes; es hat heute Nacht sehr stark gefroren, it froze very hard last night; das —, freezing, congelation; das Eis entsteht durch —, ice is formed by freezing or congealing; eine Flüssigkeit zum — bringen, to congeal a fluid into ice.

Gefrierpunkt, *m.* freezing-point, point of congelation.

Gefrischteisen, *n.* [-s, *pl.* -] refined iron. V. Frischen 4).

Gefrornes, *n.* [das Gefrorne] ice [for eating].

Gefüge, *n.* [-s] 1) grooves, joints [collectively]. Das — des Körpers, the construction or structure of the body; [in mining] a layer, stratum. 2) V. Schicksal.

Gefügheit, *f.* pliableness, pliancy, pliability. V Geschmeidigkeit, Biegsamkeit.

Gefügig, [less usual Gefüge] *adj.* and *adv.* pliable, flexible, pliant —es Blech, pliable or flexible tin. V. Geschmeidig. *Fig.* pliant, docile, ductile, manageable. Ein —er Mann, a man of a complying temper, *it.* a clever, dexterous man.

Gefügigkeit, *f.* pliancy, pliableness, accommodation to circumstances, concession.

1. **Gefühl,** *n* [-s, *pl.* -e] 1) [the sense of touch or feeling] feeling, touch Der Sinn, die Werkzeuge des —es, the sense, the organs of feeling; das Gesicht ist nicht über alle Theile des Körpers so verbreitet, als das —, the sense of seeing is not so diffused through all parts of the body as that of feeling; dieser Blinde kann die Farben durch das — unterscheiden, this blind man can distinguish the colours by feeling. 2) [perception by means of the sense of feeling] sensation, sensibility, feeling. Ein angenehmes, schmerzhaftes —, an agreeable, pleasurable, painful sensation; das — der Schmerzen benimmt ihm die Sprache, the sensation or acuteness of his pains deprives him of the power of speech; ein erfrornes Glied hat das — verloren, a frozen limb has lost its sensibility; er hat kein — mehr im linken Arme, there is no more feeling in his left arm. 3) [faculty or power of perception and the perceptions themselves] feeling, sense, sentiment. Er hat alles — des Elendes, or für das Elend Anderer verloren, he has lost all sense

of compassion; ein Herz, das — für Liebe und Freundschaft hat, a heart susceptible of love and friendship; dieser Mensch hat — für Ehre, this man has a sense of honour; er hat kein — für Ehre mehr, he is lost or dead to all sense of honour; sie haben kein — für die freundschaftlichsten Liebesdienste, they have no sense of the most friendly offices; nach dem —e urtheilen, to judge from one's feelings; dieser Herr ist ohne alles — der Menschlichkeit, this gentleman has no sense of humanity; theilen Sie meine —e bei dieser glücklichen Begebenheit, share my feelings, my joy on this fortunate event; er spricht in diesem Gedichte die schönsten, edelsten —e aus, he expresses in this poem the finest, the noblest sentiments; die natürlichen —e, [as between parents and children] natural sense or affection.

Gefühl-los, *adj.* and *adv.* [void of feeling] insensible, unfeeling, senseless, apathetic. Die Kälte macht die Glieder erstarren und —los, cold benumbs the limbs and renders them insensible; *fig.* ein —loser Mensch, an unfeeling man; gegen die Freuden der Liebe —los seyn, to be insensible to the pleasures of love; das —lose Grab fühlt Ihren frommen Kummer nicht, the senseless grave feels not your pious sorrow. V. Fühllos. —s-tödter, *m.* [one of a sect of mystics who maintained the principles of quietism] a quietist. —voll, *adj.* full of feeling, sensible, feeling. Ein —volles Herz, he has a feeling or sensible heart.

2. Gefühl, *n.* [-es, *pl.* -e] [corrupted from Gefell, furs, skins] [among hunters] furs in general, and the animals producing fur.

Gefühllosigkeit, *f.* [applied either to the body or the mind] want of feeling, insensibility, apathy. Die Kälte verursacht — in den Gliedern, cold causes insensibility in the limbs; die Stoiker wollten, daß die Menschen in einer gänzlichen — seyn sollten, the Stoics taught that men should be in an entire apathy. V. Fühllosigkeit.

Gefüllsel, *n.* V. Füllsel.

Gefünft, *adj.* consisting of five parts, quinary. Eine —e Zahl, a quinary number; [in astrology] der —e Schein, [the aspect of planets when distant from each other the fifth part of the zodiac, or 72 degrees] quintile; [in piquet] ein —es haben, to have or hold a quint [a set or sequence of five cards of the same colour].

Gefürstet, [*past part.* of Fürsten, which see] *adj.* and *adv.* raised to the rank of a prince or a principality, invested with the dignity of princes. Eine —e Abtey, an abby raised to the rank of a principality; ein —er Abt, an abbot raised to the rank of a prince.

Gefüße, *n.* [-s, -] [in falconry, short straps of leather tied round the legs of a hawk by which she is held on the fist] jesses. V. Falkengeschuhe.

Gegen, [allied to gehen, to go, V. gen] *prepos.* [governing the accusative and in composition with über the dative case] 1) [denoting a direction or motion towards a thing] toward, towards. Dieses Haus liegt — Norden, this house is situated towards the north; Neuhafen liegt — Osten von Neu-York, New-Haven lies toward the east or eastward from New-York; mein Fenster sieht — den Garten, my window faces the garden, looks into the garden; Einem —über sitzen, to sit opposite or over-against any one; er wohnt dem Rathhause —über, — dem Rathhause über, he lives or dwells opposite to the townhouse; sich — Morgen wenden, to turn towards the east, eastward; die Augen — den Himmel erheben, to lift up one's eyes to heaven; eine Linie, die sich — eine andere neigt, a line verging or inclining towards another. *Fig.* *a*) [noting an approach towards an end] towards, against, about. — das Ende seiner Rede, towards the end of his speech; schreibe es — das Ende der Woche, write it towards or against the end of the week; er kam — elf Uhr an, he arrived about eleven o'clock; es geschah — Mittag, it happened about noon; es geht — Morgen (= es wird bald Morgen seyn), the morning will soon dawn, day will soon break; — den Herbst werde ich zurückkommen, I shall return towards autumn; er ist — dreißig Jahre alt, he is about or near thirty years old. *b*) [noting a more particular relation of any state or action to another object] Die Liebe Gottes — die Menschen, the love of God to men or mankind; freigebig — die Armen seyn, to be liberal to the poor; undankbar — seinen Wohlthäter, ungrateful to one's benefactor; — alle Ermahnungen taub seyn, to be deaf to all admonitions; er ist voll Freundschaft — uns, he is very kind to us; er thut sehr vertraut — ihn, he is very familiar with him; Drohungen — Einen ausstoßen, to pour forth, to utter or to vent threats or menaces against any one; erwähnen Sie nichts davon — ihn, never mention any thing of it to him; er hat etwas davon — mich erwähnt, he told me something of it; sich — seine Vorgesetzten über etwas beschweren, to complain of something to one's superiors; sein Herz — einen Freund ausschütten, to open or disclose one's heart to a friend. 2) [noting a different, that is, an opposite direction] against. — den Strom schwimmen, to swim against the stream or current; — den Wind segeln, to sail against the wind; mit dem Kopfe — die Wand rennen, to run one's head against the wall. *Fig.* *a*) [noting enmity, resistance &c.] Einen Posten — den Feind behaupten, to maintain a post against the enemy; — den Feind ausziehen, to march against the enemy; — sein Unglück kämpfen, to struggle with or against one's ill fortune; ich werde Sie — Jedermann vertheidigen, I will defend you against everybody; das ist — die Ehre, die gesunde Vernunft, that is against honour, good sense, that is contrary to honour, to good sense; das ereignete sich — meine Erwartung, that happened contrary to my expectations; Alles ist — ihn, every thing is against him; eine Arznei — das Fieber, a medicine against or for the fever. *b*) [noting exchange and compensation] Ein Stück Land — ein anderes vertauschen, to exchange one piece of ground for another; wollen Sie Ihr Pferd — das meinige vertauschen? will you exchange, will you *swop horses with me? Waare — Waare, Geld — Waare geben, to barter one commodity for another, to give or pay money for a commodity; ich verkaufe es nur — baare Bezahlung, I do not sell it but for ready money; Einen — Bürgschaft losgeben, to release any one upon bail; ich wette Hundert — Eins, I'll bet a hundred to one; Sie können Ihr Geld — Quittung haben, you may have your money on giving a receipt. *c*) [in comparison of]. — die Sonne ist die Erde äußerst klein, when compared to the sun, the earth is extremely small; wie ein Tropfen Wasser — das Meer, as a drop of water in comparison with the ocean; es ist nur wenig — das, was ich Ihnen zu verdanken habe, it is but a small matter to what I owe you; und doch ist er noch glücklich — uns, and yet he is happy in comparison with us; sein Benehmen macht einen seltsamen Kontrast — seine Kleidung, his conduct and his dress form a singular contrast; eine Sache — eine andere halten, to compare one thing with or to another; alles, was sie thaten, war Frömmigkeit — dieses, all they did was piety to this. Syn. Gegen, Wider. Gegen refers merely to the situation or direction of two bodies moving towards each other; wider implies also a tendency or endeavour to exert their force against or in opposition to each other.

In composition gegen denotes opposition or reciprocity, and frequently corresponds with the English *counter*:

Gegen-abdruck, *m.* [a print taken of another fresh printed which, by being passed the press, gives the figure of the former, be[...]ted] counterproof. Einen —abdruck ab[...] einen —abdruck von einem Kupferstiche [...] Zeichnung machen, to draw a counterpr[oof], counterprove, to counterdraw. —abdr[...] —abziehen, *v. tr.* and *intr.* to coun[terdraw,] to counterprove. —absicht, *f.* oppo[site in]tention, contrary view. —abweiche[n,] *v. intr.* [in fencing] to counter-disengage. [—ab]weichung, *f.* counter-disengage. —a[...] *m.* V. —abdruck. —anklage, *f.* V — [beschul]digung. —anstalt, *f.* counter-prepa[ration,] counter-pace, counter-mine. —anstalten [ma]chen, treffen, to take contrary measures, to c[oun]ter-mine, to counter-work. —antwort[, *f.*] reply, repartee. Er gab ihm eine beißen[de] antwort, he made him a smart reply, repa[rtee;] er ist gleich mit einer —antwort da, he i[s al]ways ready with his repartee, or reply. [in] pleading] *a*) [the reply of the plaintiff to the def[endant's] plea] replication *b*) [the defendant's answer [to the] plaintiff's replication] rejoinder. Seine —an[twort] eingeben, übergeben, to rejoin, to put in [a] rejoinder. —anzeige, *f.* [in medicine, [a] symptom or occurrence in a disease which ser[ves to] direct a contrary treatment] counter-indica[tion.] —aussage, *f.* a contrary deposition. —[bat]terie, *f.* counterbattery. —bedingun[g, *f.*] reciprocal condition. —befehl, *m.* cou[nter-com]mand, counter-order. Einen —befehl g[eben,] ertheilen, to give a counter-order, to [counter]mand. —bekenntniß, *n.* 1) a count[er-ac]knowledgement or confession. 2) a reci[procal] bond or security. —beklagte, *m.* b[...] has been accused in return. —beleidi[gung,] *f.* retaliation —bericht, *m.* counter-[infor]mation, counter-statement. —besch[eini]gung, *f.* counter-attestation. V. —be[...] 2). —beschickung, *f.* compliment in r[eturn.] —beschuldigung, *f.* recrimination, [coun]ter-charge, retortion. Beschuldigungen [mit Be]schuldigungen entgegensetzen, to recrim[inate,] to retort. —besichtigung, *f.* [in law] a [re]peated inspection. —besuch, *m.* return visit, visit in return. Einem einen —besuch mach[en,] to return any one's visit; ich habe [ihm] [ei]nen —besuch abgestattet, I have returned h[is] visit. —bettungen, *pl.* [in military affairs] the counter-batteries. —beurtheilung, [*f.*] anticritique, refutation of, or reply to, a c[ri]tique or review. V. also Antikritik. —bewei[s,] *m.* proof to the contrary, counter-evidence. [—]bezauberung, *f.* counter-charm. —bezi[e]hung, *f.* —bezug, *m.* correlativeness. —bil[d,] *n.* 1) contrast. Man kann nicht wohl zwei stärk[ere] —bilder sehen, one can hardly see two perso[ns] or things that contrast with each other mo[re] strongly. 2) [opposed to Vorbild, prototype] an[ti]type. —billet, *n.* [in the theatre] count[er] ticket, a check. —blick, *m.* a reciprocal loo[k.] —bohren, *v. intr.* to counter-pierce. [V.] Bohren. —böschung, *f.* [in architecture] co[unter]span; [in fortification, the exterior talus or sl[ope] of the ditch] counter-scarp. —brief, *m.* [...] —versicherung. —buch, *n.* a book or regis[ter] kept to correct or check another account [or] register, a control. —bürge, *m.* V. [...] bürge. —christ, *m.* antichrist. —compliment, *n.* compliment in return. Er mach[te] mir ein —compliment, he returned my comp[li]ment. —copie, *f.* [among painters] a count[er-]drawing, a counter-copy. —dienst, *m.* re[...]

rocal service. —druck, m. [in physics] reac-ion. Der Druck und der —druck der flüssigen Theile im menschlichen Körper, the action and eaction of the fluid parts of the human ody. [among engravers] V. —abdruck. [in hydrau-ics] counter-pressure [in printing] V. Widerdruck. —einander, adv. towards, against, or op-osite one another; reciprocally, mutually. Sie stunden lange —einander, they were for long time standing opposite to each other; etwas —einander haben, to be upon bad rms together, to have fallen out; sie sind hr gefällig —einander, sie sind sehr freund-haftlich —einander gesinnt, they are very kind r obliging to one another; sie versprachen h Treue —einander, they promised fidelity one another, to each other; zwei Dinge —einander vertauschen, to exchange one thing r another; zwei Dinge —einander halten, ellen, to compare two things together or with ch other. [in heraldry] —einander stehend, —ander gestellt, affrontee, controntee; zwei —einander gestellte Löwen, two lions facing e another; zwei Personen —einander stel-n, [in law] to confront with one another; die ugen und die Beklagten —einander stellen, confront the witnesses with the accused. —einanderhaltung, —einanderstel-lung, f. comparison; [in law] confrontation. ie —einanderstellung der Leidenschaften, the ntrast of the passions. —einbringen, n. —schrift. —erbieten, n. offer in return. —erkenntlichkeit, f. return of an act of ndness or friendship; it. V. —geschenk. —rklärung, f. a mutual or reciprocal claration; it. a declaration in return [to the declaration of another], a denial. —hrt, f. navigation against the stream, sail-g or going up the river. —falls, adv. on e other hand, otherwise. —fenster, n. 1) window opposite another. 2) a double win-w. —finte, f. [in fencing] caveating, a unter-feint. —flammig, adj. [in heraldry] unter-flaming. —flut, f. counter-tide. —rderung, f. counter-demand, counter-im, reciprocal demand. —form, f. [in print-g] counter-plate. —freundschaft, f. re-n of friendship, mutual or reciprocal friend-p. —fuge, f. [in music] counter-fugue. —ler or —füßler, m. [one who lives on the posite side of the globe] antipode. —gabe, f. —geschenk. —gebühr, f. reciprocal due or . —gefühl, n. opposite feeling. —ge-nder, n. counter-rails —geld, n. V. —mächtniß. —gesang, m. antiphony. —ge-enk, n. present made in return. Er machte eine Uhr zum —geschenk, he presented him h a watch in return —gewalt, f. retalia-, reprisals. —gewalt brauchen, to repel force force. —gewicht, n counter-weight, nter-poise, counter-balance. Einem Körper —gewicht geben, ihm das —gewicht halten, counter-balance, to counter-poise a body; seine guten Eigenschaften halten seinen Feh-das —gewicht, his good qualities counter-ance his faults. —gewogenheit, f. mutual ciprocal affection. —gift, n. counter-poi-, antidote. Man hat ihm —gift, ein —gift eben, they have given him an antidote; als ift dienend, serving as an antidote, antido-; fig. dieses Buch ist ein —gift für gefähr-Meinungen, this book is an antidote to gerous or mischievous opinions. —gitter, ouble grating. —graben, ir. v intr. counter-dig; it. to make counter-approa-s, to counter-mine. —grund, m. an ment in opposition, counter-argument. ruß, m. reciprocal greeting, reciprocal tation; [in seamen's language] answer to, or rn of, a salute. —gunst, f. reciprocal favour. —gurt, m. [of a saddle] girth, circingle. —hall, m. repercussion of sound, echo. —halt, m. V. Widerhalt. —handschrift, f. [a mutual, written assurance] a counter-bill, counter-note. —haut, f. V. —unterlage. —hieb, m. counter-blow, counter-stroke, counter-cut. —kaiser, m. anti-emperor. —kiel, m. [in seamen's language] V. Kielschwein. —klage, f. [in law] recrimination, counter-charge. —kläger, m. —klägerinn, f. he or she that accuses the accuser of a like crime, recriminator. —klopfer, m. [in anatomy] adducent muscle of the thumb. —kritik, f. counter-critique, anti-critique. V. also —beurtheilung. ‖—lage, f. V. —vermächtniß —latte, f. [in carpentry] counter-láth. Mit —latten versehen, to counterlath. —latter, m. [a cramp or piece of iron to fasten the laths] clincher. —laufgräben, pl. counter-approaches, counter-trenches. —laut, m. V. —hall. —licht, n. [in architecture and painting] counter-light, false light. —liebe, f. return of love, mutual, reciprocal love. Er liebt ohne Hoffnung, ihre —liebe zu erhalten, he loves without hope of a return; Liebe erfordert —liebe, love requires a suitable return. —list, f. cunning opposed to cunning, counter-trick, counter-cunning. —macht, f. power opposed to power. —marke, f. a counter-ticket, a check. —marsch, m. counter-march. —masche, f. double mesh. —mauer, f. counter-mure. Mit einer —mauer versehen, to counter-mure —meinung, f. contrary opinion. —mine, f. counter-mine. —minen anlegen, —miniren, to counter-mine. —minirer, m. counter-miner. —mittel, n. remedy, antidote. Ein —mittel gegen or wider Zahnschmerzen, a remedy for the tooth-ache. —mond, V. Nebenmond. —muskel, m. [in anatomy] antagonist muscle. —nachfrage, f. V. —untersuchung. —nieten, v. tr. [= doppelt nieten] to counter-rivet. ‡—nothdurft, f. [a law-term] V. —antwort. —öffnung, f. [in surgery] counter-aperture, counter-opening. —ort, m. [in mining] an adit opposite another. —papst, m. anti-pope. —part, m. [V. Gegner] [in popular lang.] opponent, adversary, an antagonist; [in law] adverse party, opponent. —part halten, to be of a contrary opinion, to maintain or assert the contrary. —partei, f. the opposite party. Sich zur —partei schlagen, to side with the opposite party. [in law] adverse party. —patrice, f. [among letter-founders, the inner figure of a type] counter-puncheon. —pfahl, m. [in heraldry] counter-pale. —pfand, n. counter-pledge. —pfeiler, m. [V. Strebepfeiler] counter-fort, buttress, spur. Eine Mauer mit —pfeilern versehen, to prop a wall. —probe, f. assay made by a third person of different ores or minerals; [among engravers] V. —abdruck. —punkt, m. [in music] counter-point. —quittung, f. reciprocal receipt, counter-receipt. V. —schein. —rechner, m. controller. —rechnung, f. 1) counter-reckoning, bill or account made by any one to be deducted from that of another. [among bankers and merchants] discount. Rechnung und —rechnung, debit and credit. 2) [account by which that of another is checked or corrected] check-account, counter-account, control. —rede, f. 1) reply. Auf eine solche —rede war er nicht gefaßt, he was not prepared, he did not look for such a reply. [in law] counter-plea, replication. 2) contradiction. 3) excuse, apology, evasion. —register, n. counter-register, check-account, control. Ein —register halten, das —register führen, to keep a counter-register, to keep a check, to control. Das —register über die Rechnungen der Schatzkammer führen, to control the accounts of the treasury. —revolution, f. counter-revolution. —riß, m. counter-proof. —runde, f. [in military affairs] counter-round. —satz, m. in general, something opposed. Gut ist der —satz von schlimm, good is the opposite or contrary of bad; seine Handlungen stehen im —satze mit dem, was er spricht, his actions contradict his words, clash with his words, are in opposition to his words; then *a*) [in poetry, a strophe, that contradicts another] antistrophe. *b*) [words or parts of a sentence opposed to each other] antithesis. Er liebt die —sätze, he is fond of antitheses. *c*) [a whole sentence opposed to another] antithesis. *d*) [in law] V. —antwort. —schall, m. V. —hall. —schattigen, pl. [in geography, the inhabitants of the earth living on different sides from the equator] antiscians V. —wohner. —schein, m. 1) [—bekenntniß 2)] counter-receipt, counter-attestation, counter-bond or security. 2) [V. Widerschein]. Der —schein des Lichtes, des Feuers, the reflection or reverberation of light, of fire; [in painting] reflection. 3) [in astronomy, the situation of two heavenly bodies, when distant from each other 180 degrees] opposition. Wenn sich der Mond im —scheine mit der Erde befindet, when the moon is in opposition with the earth. —schenkung, f. 1) mutual or reciprocal donation. 2) a gift or present in return. —schlag, m. repercussion, rebound, counter-blow. —schmähung, f. a mutual or reciprocal invective or abuse. —schraffiren, v. tr. [among engravers] to counter-hatch; [among wood-engravers] to counter-tally. —schraffirung, f. [among engravers] counter-hatching; [among wood-engravers] countercut, counter-tally, triple-tally. —schreiben, v. intr. [in commerce] to set down wrong. —schreiber, m. one that keeps a counter-account to check that of another, controlling-clerk, controller. —schreiberei, f. controller's office. —schrift, f. an answer or reply in writing, refutation; [in law] replication, rejoinder. V. —antwort. —schritt, m. opposite or contrary act, counter-step. —schuld, f. reciprocal debt. Schuld und —schuld, debt active and passive. —schwäher, m. Er ist mein —schwäher, he is the father of my son-in-law or of my daughter-in law. —seite, f. opposite side; [of a coin] reverse. —seitig, I. adj. 1) opposite. Der —seitige Theil, the adverse or opposite party. 2) reciprocal, mutual. —seitige Neigung, Liebe, mutual or reciprocal affection, love. [in grammar] die —seitige Bedeutung der sich auf einander beziehenden Fürwörter, the reciprocity of the relatives. II. adv. mutually, reciprocally. Sich —seitig lieben, to love reciprocally or mutually. —seitigkeit, f. reciprocity. —sicherheit, f. counter-security, counter-pledge; it. mutual or reciprocal security. —siegel, n. counter-seal. Das —siegel darauf drücken, mit dem —siegel versehen, to counter-seal. —signal, n. [in seamen's language] counter-signal. —sinn, m. [sense opposite to its proper meaning] contrary sense or meaning, antiphrasis. Sie nehmen meine Worte im —sinne, you put a wrong construction upon my words; es ist hier ein —sinn in der Uebersetzung, there is a misconstruction in the translation. V. also Widersinn. —sinnig, adj. and adv. opposite to the proper meaning, preposterous. Eine Rede —sinnig erklären, to put a wrong construction upon, or to misconstrue what is said. V. also Widersinnig. —sonne, f. V. Nebensonne. —spalier, n. a hedge-row of trees or an espalier facing another, with a walk between. —spalt, m. [in surgery] contra-fissure, counter-cleft. —sparren, m. [in heraldry] counter-chevron. —spiel, n. a game directed against another. [at cards] Er hatte ein schönes —spiel [gegen mich], he had a good hand against me. *Fig.* *a*) a counter-playing, counter-shuffling. *b*) V. Widerspiel. —spieler, *m.* he that plays against another, adversary. —sprache, *f.* V. Rücksprache. —spur, *f.* [among hunters] V. Rückspur. —stand, V. Gegenstand. —stellung, *f.* 1) [in law] confrontation. 2) [in painting] contrast. ||—steuer, *f.* V. —vermächtniß [in law]. —stich, *m.* opposite thrust [in fencing]. —stimme, *f.* [in music, second part in a duet &c.] counter-part. —stimmig, *adj.* [in music] dissonent, discordant, jarring. —stolz, *m* reciprocal pride. —stoß, *m.* a counter-thrust [in fencing]. —streckung, *f.* [in surgery] contra-extension. —streich, *m.* counter-blow, blow in return; *it.* a trick played in return —strich, *m.* stroke against the grain, against the nap. —stück, *n.* [in painting] counter-part, companion. —stütze, *f.* counter-fort, spur, buttress. —tausch, *m.* counter-change, mutual change. —terrasse, *f.* counter-terrace, upper terrace. —theil, 1) *m.* [V. Gegner, —part] adverse or opposite party, opponent. 2) *n.* a thing or proposition opposite to another, contrary. Das —theil behaupten, to maintain the contrary; er thut gerade das —theil von dem, was man ihm sagt, he does just the reverse of what he is told; er ist das —theil von seinem Bruder, he is the reverse of his brother; im —theile, on the contrary. —theilig, *adj.* relating to the opposite party. —theils, *adv.* on the contrary, on the other hand. —thür, *f.* V. Vorthür. —treue, *f.* mutual or reciprocal fidelity. —trieb, *m.* V. —fahrt. Im —triebe [or dem Strome entgegen] fahren, to go up the river, against the stream. —trumm, *n.* [in mining] part of a lode opposite another. —über, *adv.* over-against, opposite. Der Stadt —über, over-against the town. —überstehend, —überliegend, opposite. V. Gegen —umwälzung, *f* counter-revolution. —unterlage, *f.* [among parchment makers] counter-summer. —unterschreiben, *ir. v tr* counter-sign. —unterschrift, *f.* counter-signature. Etwas mit seiner —unterschrift versehen, to countersign something. —untersuchung, *f.* an enquiry made by the adverse or opposite party. —unterzeichnung, *f* V. —unterschrift. —verehrung, *f.* [obsolete] V. —geschenk. —verheißung, *f.* counter-promise, reciprocal promise. —vermächtniß, *n.* reciprocal donation or legacy; [in law] a present or legacy which a husband settles on his wife in consideration of her dowry, a settlement. —verordnung, *f.* V. —befehl. —verpflichtung, *f.* counter obligation, reciprocal obligation. —verschanzung, *f.* [in military affairs] contra-vallation. —verschreibung, *f.* counter-security, reciprocal bond. —versicherung, *f.* 1) an assurance given in opposition to another. 2) [—seitige Versicherung] mutual or reciprocal assurance or security, counter-bond; [in law] V. —schein 1). —versprechen, *n.* —versprechung, *f.* counter-promise. —verweis, *m.* [—seitiger Verweis] a reciprocal reproof or rebuke, counter-check. —visite, *f.* V. —besuch. —vorstellung, *f.* [made against a demand &c.] remonstrance —vorwurf, *m.* V. —beschuldigung. —wall, *m.* [in fortification] counterscarp. —wechsel, *m.* V. Rückwechsel. —wehr, *f.* defence, resistance. Sich zur —wehr stellen, to stand upon one's defence or guard, to put one's self into a posture of defence; eine tapfere —wehr leisten, thun, to make a gallant defence, a brave resistance. —werth, *m.* equivalent. —wind, *m.* contrary, adverse or head wind. —wirkung, *f.* reaction, counter-effect. —wohner, *pl.* [in geography, those inhabitants of the earth that live at the same distance from the equator but on opposite sides] antecians. Die —wohner sind immer —schattige, aber diese sind nicht nothwendig —wohner, the antecians are always antiscians, but the latter are not necessarily antecians. —wurf, *m.* throw in return. —zärtlichkeit, *f.* mutual or reciprocal tenderness. —zauber, *m.* counter-charm. —zeichen, *n.* counter-sign, counter-signal; *it.* [in commerce, a second mark put on a bale of goods] counter-mark. —zeichnen, *v. tr.* to counter-sign; [in commerce] to counter-mark. —zeuge, *m.* counter-witness. —zeugniß, *n.* counter-evidence —zinne, *f.* [in heraldry] counter-bretesse. Mit —zinnen versehen, embattled on both sides. —zusage, *f.* V. —versprechen.

Gégend, *f.* [*pl.* -en] [allied to gegen, which see, as country to counter] 1) any space of indefinite extent towards which we direct our eyes or thoughts. Mein Stock ist in der und der — des Zimmers, my stick or cane is in such and such a part of the room; die vornehmste — einer Stadt, the principal or the most genteel part or quarter of a town; in welcher — der Stadt wohnt er? in what part of the town does he live? in welcher — [des Körpers] ist er verwundet? in what part of the body, whereabout is he wounded? [in anatomy] die — um das Herz, um die Leber, the region of the heart, of the liver; die — um den Nabel, die obere — des Bauches, the umbilical region, the epigastric region; [in astrology and geography] region; man theilt den Himmel in vier Haupt—en, the sky is divided into four regions; aus welcher — kommt der Wind? from what quarter, from what point does the wind blow? V. Himmels—, Welt—, Luft—; [in seamen's language, part of the sea where a vessel is] latitude, part of the sea under any latitude; wir begegneten ihnen in der und der —, we met them in such and such a latitude; in einer guten — vor Anker liegen, to be anchored in a good station 2) [usually] any greater or smaller part of the surface of the earth. Die umliegende —, the surrounding country, the environs; die besten Güter der —, unserer —, the best fields or estates of the country, of our part of the country; der Hagel hat nur gewisse —en getroffen, the hail has only fallen on certain tracts or districts; von einer — in die andere, from country to country; die südlichen — des Reichs, the southern parts or districts of the empire; die gemäßigten —en, the temperate regions; alle —en der Erde, all the regions of the earth; die Stadt liegt in einer schönen — am Meere, the town is situated in a fine country on the sea-side; die — um Paris, the environs of Paris; die — um die Donau, the banks of the Danube; die Sache ist in der ganzen umliegenden — [Umgegend] bekannt, the matter is known in all the country round about; hier in der —, here in the neighbourhood, in the vicinity; er kommt aus der — von Frankfurt, he comes from the neighbourhood of Frankfort; [in commerce] in unserer —, in our parts, in this place; in dortiger —, in those parts, thereabout; sich der umliegenden — [Umgegend] einer Festung versichern, to secure, to make one's self master of all the avenues of a fortress.

Gégenstand, *m.* [-es, *pl.* -stände] object. Ein angenehmer — für das Auge, a pleasant object to the sight; der — unserer Bewunderung, unseres Spottes, unserer Verachtung, the object of our admiration, raillery, contempt; er war der — des Gelächters oder Spottes der Gesellschaft, he was the laughing-stock of the company; was ist der — aller dieser geheimen Anstalten? what is the object or end of all these secret preparations? ein reizender —, a charming or delightful object; der Schall ist ein — des Gehörs, sound is an object of hearing; Glückseligkeit ist der — der Wünsche jedes Menschen, happiness is the object of every man's desires; der — seiner Liebe, seiner Seufzer &c., the object of his love, of his sighs &c.; der — einer Rede, eines Trauerspiels &c., [the thing that is treated of in a speech, tragedy &c.] the subject of a speech, of a tragedy &c.; der — einer Wissenschaft, einer Kunst, the object or subject of a science, of an art; die Wahrheit ist der — unseres Verstandes, truth is the object of our understanding.

Gegenstands-glas, *n.* [in telescopes] object-glass. V. Objectivglas. —s-punkt, *n.* [in painting] objective point.

Gégenwart, *f.* 1) [= Anwesenheit] presence. Ihre — in dieser Provinz ist nothwendig, your presence is necessary in this province; er sagte es in meiner —, in — des Königs &c., he said so in my presence or before me or before my face, in the king's presence; die wirkliche — des Leibes und des Blutes Christi, the real presence of the body and blood of Christ; [in law] in — der und der Person, in the presence of such a one; *fig.* die — des Geistes, presence of mind. 2) [the present time] the present. Dieser Mensch lebt bloß für die —, this man lives only for the present, is careless of the future 3) V. Daseyn 1).

Gégenwärtig, I. *adj.* 1) [= anwesend] present; [opposed to absent] Gott ist überall —, God is every-where, omnipresent; ich war —, als sie mit einander in Streit geriethen, I was present when they began to quarrel; bei einer Feierlichkeit — seyn, to be present at some solemnity; persönlich — seyn, to be present in person; die —en Zuschauer, the spectators present; derjenige, welcher Ihnen —es [= dieses] Schreiben [Geschenk &c.] oder Gegenwärtiges zustellen wird, he who will deliver you this letter [these presents &c.]; sey Allen durch Gegenwärtiges kund und zu wissen gethan, know all men by these presents. *Fig.* die Sache ist mir immer —, I have it always present to my thoughts, it is alwas present to my mind, I always think of it; ihm ist Alles —, every thing is present to his mind. 2) [now existing or being at this time] Die —e Zeit, the present time, [in Grammar] the present tense, the present; die —e Regierung, der —e Zustand der Dinge, the present government, the present state of things; das Gegenwärtige [die —e Zeit, Gegenwart] the present time, the present; er denkt nur an das Gegenwärtige, he thinks only of the present. II. *adv.* at present, now. — habe ich es nicht nöthig, I do not want it for the present, or at present; er befindet sich — nicht hier, he is not here at present.

Gegítter, *n.* [-s, *pl.* -] V. Gitter.

Gegíttert, [*past part.* from the unused verb gittern] *adj.* and *adv.* 1) furnished with, having bars &c. 2) [in heraldry] fretty. Ein —er Helm, a grated or crossbarred helmet.

||**Gégler**, *m.* [-s] V. Bergfink.

Gégner, *m.* [-s, *pl.* -] —inn, *f.* antagonist, adversary, opposer, opponent. Ein [illegible] ben mit einem furchtbaren — zu thun, you have to do with a terrible adversary, you have a terrible adversary to deal with; er erlegte seinen —, he killed his man or antagonist; sich zu Jemands — aufwerfen, to take party against any one.

Gegröle, *n.* [-s] disagreeable cries or noise, brawl.

Gegrúnze, *n.* [-s] [in popular language] a repeated or continual grunting.

||**Gehābe**, *adj.* and *adv.* close, tight, not leaky. Ein —s Faß, a tight cask.

Gehāben, *ir. v. r* sich —, 1) to behave [illegible] gehabt sich sehr schlecht, he conducts himself ery badly, ungentlemanlike. 2) to be in a cer-tain state of health. Sich wohl, übel —, to be well ill; gehabt Euch wohl, adieu, farewell. V. Betragen II.; Befinden II. 2).

Gehácke, *n.* [-s] [in fam. lang.] a continual hacking, chopping, mincing, hashing; *it.* a continual hoeing.

Gehäckte, *n.* [-n] hashed or minced meat, hash, mince.

Gehäge, *n.* [-s, *pl.*-] 1) [= Haag, Einzäunung] fence, hedge. Ein — um einen Garten &c. machen, to fence or to hedge in a garden &c.; wir gingen zwischen blühenden —n hin, we walked along between blooming hedges. 2) [a place inclosed or fenced in] inclosure, precinct; [among hunters] preserve for game, warren, park. V. Fasanen—, Kaninchen—, Hasen—. In fremdem — jagen, to hunt on another man's preserve, to poach, *fig.* *to encroach on another's right. *Fig.* *Einem in das — gehen, kommen, to interfere with the rights and prerogatives of another, to put one's sickle into another's harvest.

Gehäge-aufseher, *m.* forest-keeper, warrener, game-keeper. —**bereiter**, *m.* V. Jägerreiter.

Gehált, *m.* [-es, *pl* -e] 1) [that which is contained] contents of a vessel, its measure. Ein Faß von 40 Gallonen —, a cask that contains forty gallons, a cask of forty gallons; was ist der — dieses Gefäßes? how much does this vessel contain or hold? what is the capacity of this vessel? || or *sein Haus hat vielen — [viel Raum, Gelaß], his house is very spacious or roomy, there are a great many accommodations in his house. V. Inhalt. 2) [that which a body contains of other things] Der mineralische — einer Quelle, the mineral substance of a spring or well; der — der Erze, that which the ores contain of fine metals; der verordnungsmäßige — [of the coined or wrought silver], true standard [of coins]; Münzen, von gutem, von geringem —e [Korne], coins of good, of base alloy; das feinste Silber ist sechzehnlöthig an —, the finest silver is of twelve pennyweights; der innere — einer Sache, the intrinsic value or worth of a thing. *Fig.* dieses Gedicht hat keinen —, this poem has no intrinsic merit. [rather provinc.] [= der Unterhalt] entertainment, maintenance. Sein Herr gibt ihm freien —, aber keinen Lohn, his master keeps him in every thing necessary, finds him in every thing, but gives him no wages. 4) [= die Besoldung] wages, salary, pay. Bei Jemand in — stehen, to be in any one's service or pay; der — eines Beamten, the salary of an officer; der — eines Bedienten, the wages of a servant; dieser Richter hat zwölfhundert Gulden —, this judge has twelve hundred florins salary; er hat einen starken —, he has a large salary; der — eines Soldaten, the pay of a soldier. SYN. Gehalt, Besoldung, Lohn, Löhnung, Sold. Lohn denotes, in a general sense, any recompense or reward for any thing performed, good or bad; in a more limited sense, it signifies the money which a workman may justly demand for his labour. Both Löhnung and Sold signify the money or pay which a common soldier receives for his services. Besoldung is said only of the salary of persons in public offices; Gehalt also of such as are in the service of private persons.

Gehalt-leer, *adj.* and *adv.* whithout value or worth, of no value or worth. *Fig.* —leeres Geschwätz, empty talk, frothy, frivolous discourse. —**los**, *adj.* and *adv.* V. —leer. *Fig.* —lose Träumereien, chimerical reveries. —**reich**, *adj.* and *adv.* of great worth or value. Eine —reiche Rede, a pithy, nervous, expressive speech; ein —reiches Buch, a good book; eine —reiche Unternehmung, a solid undertaking or enterprise. —**s-verbesserung**, —**s-vermehrung**, —**s-zulage**, *f.* augmentation or increase of wages, of salary. —**voll**, *adj.* and *adv.* V. —reich.

Gehálten, [*past part.* of halten, which see] *adj.* 1) bound, obliged. Ich bin nicht —, das zu thun, I am not bound to do it; ich bin nicht —, Ihnen auf diese Frage zu antworten, I am not obliged to give you an answer to this question. 2) Ein gut —es Gemälde, a well-contrived picture, a picture that is in keeping; ein gut —er Charakter, a character well supported. 3) [= gesetzt, gefaßt] sober, steady, staid, grave. Auch der —ste Geist hat Augenblicke, wo &c., there are moments when even the calmest mind &c. 4) [rather unusual] [= zurückhaltend] reserved, shy. Er ist gegen Andere sehr —, he is very reserved to others. 5) [unusual] [opposed to ungehalten] V. Zufrieden.

Gehältlosigkeit, *f.* the being without worth or value. *Fig.* emptiness, frivolousness, shallowness.

Gehänge, *n.* [-s] 1) that which hangs. V. Ohr—, Uhr—. [among hunters = die Ohren eines Hundes] the ears of a dog; [in heraldry, two lines drawn across the shield from the dexter chief to the sinister base point] bend; then chiefly *a*) slope, declivity [of a hill]. Das — or Hangende [in mining], hade. *b*) [flowers, fruit, leaves &c. twisted together and hung in festoons] festoons, garlands. Ein mit —n von Blumen, von Früchten verzierter Karnieß, [in architecture] a cornice adorned with festoons. *c*) entrails of animals. Das — eines Schweines, a hog's harslet; das — eines Kalbes, a calf's pluck. V. Geschlinge. 2) [that by which a thing is suspended] a ribbon, string &c.; [among hunters] a leather-strap to which the horn is fastened, the suspender of a hunting-horn.

Geharnischt, *part.* and *adj.* [in military affairs] equipped with armour, harnessed. Ein —er Reiter, a mailed horseman, a horseman in armour; ein —es Pferd, a horse in armour.

Gehäse, *n.* [-s] [from Hase, hare] [among hunters] Das Vorder—, the fore-parts of a hare; das Hinter—, the hind parts of a hare.

Gehässig, *adj.* and *adv.* 1) [feeling hatred] hating, spiteful, full of hatred, malicious, inimical. Einem — seyn, to hate any one, to bear any one ill will, to owe any one a spite; Einem — werden, to conceive a hatred against any one, to take an aversion to any one; er legt alles auf eine —e Art aus, he interprets every thing in a malicious or malignant manner, maliciously or malignantly. 2) [deserving hatred] odious, hateful. Ein —es Laster, an odious vice; alle Sünde ist — in den Augen Gottes und guter Menschen, all sin is hateful in the sight of God and good men; sich bei Jemand — machen, to render one's self odious to any one; was ich gesagt habe, ist auf eine —e Art ausgelegt worden, what I said has been interpreted in an odious manner, or odiously.

Gehässigkeit, *f.* 1) the quality of being spiteful or malicious, ill-will, aversion. 2) the quality of exciting hatred or disgust, hatefulness, odiousness, odium.

Gehau, *n.* [-es, *pl.* -e] 1) [among foresters] the part of a forest where wood is being cut or felled; *it.* copse, coppice-wood, underwood. V. Hau. 2) a felling of trees.

Gehäuse, *n.* [-s, *pl.* -] an enclosed space, a thing in which something is contained. Das — des Obstes, the core of fruit; das — in einer welschen Nuß, the woody thick skin quartering the kernel of a walnut; V. Frucht—, Kern—, Samen—; das — einer Schnecke, the shell of a snail; das — eines Seidenwurmes, the shell, cod or ball of a silkworm; das — einer Taschenuhr, the case of a watch, watch-case; das — einer Wanduhr, Thurmuhr, the clock-frame; V. Feder—, Räder—; das — des Seecompasses, the binacle; das — einer Orgel, the case of an organ, organ-case; das — einer Windmühle, einer Treppe, the cage of a windmill, of a staircase; das — eines Degengefäßes [das Kreuz], the basket or bow of a sword-hilt.

Géhbar, *adj.* and *adv.* where one may go. Ein —er Weg, a practicable, passable way or road. V. Gangbar.

Géhbarkeit, *f.* quality or state of being practicable, or passable, practicability, practicableness [of a way &c.].

Gehéck, *n.* [-es, *pl.* -e] [chiefly among hunters] as many young as are produced at once. Ein — Küchlein, a brood or hatch of chickens.

Gehége, *n.* V. Gehäge.

Geheim, *adj.* and *adv.* [allied to Heim = Haus, house; hence = verborgen, concealed or hidden, opposed to öffentlich, bekannt, public, known] secret, clandestine, privy, private, concealed, hidden, unknown. Ein —er Ort, a secret or private place; eine —e Treppe, a private staircase, back-stairs, privy stairs; ein —er Umgang, clandestine intercourse; eine —e Zusammenkunft, a clandestine interview; in — sich erkundigen, seine Maßregeln nehmen, to inquire, to take one's measures privately, secretly; sie sehen sich nur in —, they see one another, or they meet but privately; Gott kennt unsere —sten Gedanken, God knows our inmost thoughts; die —en Artikel eines Vertrages, the secret articles of a treaty; etwas vor Einem — halten, to hide or conceal something from any one; *— gegen Einen seyn oder thun, to conceal what one is doing from any one; er hält die Sache —, he keeps the matter secret; es nagt an seinem Gemüth ein —er Gram, a secret grief preys upon his mind; die —en Lehren des Pythagoras, the esoteric doctrines of Pythagoras; —e Dinte, sympathetic ink; der —e [bildliche] Sinn der heiligen Schrift, the mystical sense of the Sacred Writings; der —e Rath, *a*) [a number of distinguished persons selected by a prince to advise him in the administration of the government] privy council, *b*) [a member of the privy council] a privy counsellor; das —e Cabinet, [the secret or select council of a prince] the cabinet of a prince; das —e Siegel, privy seal. SYN. Geheim, Heimlich. The latter is more used in ordinary life and of unimportant concerns, also of such things as one person whispers to another. Das Geheime conveys the idea of separating from the company and going aside in order to be certain of not being heard.

Geheim-bote, *m.* emissary. —**brief**, *m.* a lettre de cachet. —**buch**, *n.* a private book, secret journal. —**bund**, *m.* clandestine league, plot. —**haltung**, *f.* the act of keeping any thing secret, secrecy. —**künstler**, *m.* magician, conjuror. —**mittel**, *n.* secret remedy, arcanum. —**rath**, *m.* V. Geheim. —**schreibekunst**, *f.* [the art of writing in secret characters or cipher] cryptography, steganography. Zur —schreibekunst gehörig, cryptographical, steganographical. —**schreiber**, *m.* 1) cryptographer, steganographist. 2) private secretary [chiefly of a prince]. —**schreiberei**, *f.* 1) V. —schreibekunst, —schrift. 2) [place where a private secretary writes] secretary's office. —**schreiberstelle**, *f.* the place or office of a private secretary, secretaryship. —**schrift**, *f.* 1) a writing written in secret characters or ciphers, a cipher. 2) secret characters, cipher. **Der Schlüssel, das Alphabet zur —schrift**, the key of the cipher; **es gibt viele Arten von —schriften**, there are many kinds of ciphers. 3) [the records or papers which are preserved in archives] archives.

Geheimniß, *n.* [-sses, *pl.* -sse] 1) [a thing studiously concealed] secret. **Wer seine eigenen Geheimnisse nicht verschweigen kann, wird schwerlich die Geheimnisse Anderer bewahren**, a man who cannot keep his own secrets, will hardly keep the secrets of others; **sobald er um eine Sache weiß, so hört das — auf**, as soon as he comes to know of a thing, it ceases to be a secret; **ein — entdecken**, to discover, to find out a secret; **ein — aufdecken, verrathen, kund machen**, to disclose or divulge, to betray, to publish a secret; **in die Geheimnisse Anderer eindringen wollen**, to pry into the secrets of others; **er ist auch in dem Geheimnisse, man hat ihn auch in das — gezogen**, he is also in the secret, he has also been let into the secret; **ein — vor Einem haben**, to conceal something from any one; **Einem ein — anvertrauen**, to tell any one a secret; **ich weiß um sein —**, I know his secret; **ein — aus etwas machen**, to make a mystery of a thing; **ich mache kein — daraus**, I make no mystery or secret of it. 2) [a means or art known but by very few] secret, arcanum. **Ein — wider das Fieber**, a secret remedy for the fever; **das —, Gold zu machen**, the secret or arcanum of making gold; **die Geheimnisse der Scheidekunst**, the secrets or arcana of chimistry; **die Geheimnisse der Liebe**, the mysteries of love; [among hatters] **dem Haare das — geben** [**die Eigenschaft des Filzes ertheilen**], to felt the beaver; **die Geheimnisse der Religion, des Glaubens**, the mysteries of religion, of faith; **die Geheimnisse der Natur zu ergründen suchen**, to pry into, to study the mysteries of nature; **das —, zu gefallen, sich emporzuschwingen**, the secret of pleasing, of getting forward. 3) [= **Verborgenheit**] **Man weilet gern in des Waldes —** (**Stille, Dunkel** &c.), we love to stay in the obscurity or gloom of a forest or wood. SYN. V. **Geheim.**

Geheimniß-krämer, *m.* —**krämerinn**, *f.* [in familiar language, a person that makes a mystery of every thing] a mysterious person [in things of no importance]. —**krämerei**, *f.* mysterious conduct. —**reich**, *adj.* and *adv.* mysterious. —**voll**, *adj.* and *adv.* mysterions, mystic. **Eine —volle Stille**, a mysterious silence; **die —volle Wahrheit der Dreieinigkeit**, the mystic truth of the trinity; **—voll reden, sich —voll betragen**, to speak, to act mysteriously; **er thut sehr —voll**, he acts the mysterious man.

Geheiß, *n.* [-es] bidding, order, command. **Er that es auf — seines Herrn**, he did it by command of his master.

Gēhen, *ir.* [Sax. *gan*, D. *gaan*, Eng. *to go*, allied to the Gr. *κίω*, to the L. *eo* (feo)] I. *v. intr.* [n. w. **seyn**] 1) [denoting motion and the manner of moving] to go. **Ein Rad geht, geht nicht**, a wheel goes, does not go; **der Puls geht, geht schnell, zu langsam**, the pulse beats, is quick, is too slow; **die Uhr geht, geht vor, geht nach**, the watch goes, goes too fast, goes too slow; **der Teig fängt an zu —**, the dough is beginning to rise, to swell; **der Wagen, das Schiff geht schnell**, the carriage, the ship goes fast; **das Schiff geht fünf** [**See-**] **Meilen in einer Stunde**, the ship goes at the rate of five knots an hour; **eine Mühle geht vermittelst des Wassers**, a mill goes by water; **es geht ein starker Wind**, the wind is high, blows hard; **es geht ein kalter Wind**, the wind blows cold; **der Fluß geht mit Eis**, the river is filled with floating pieces of ice or with drifts of ice; **schnell, langsam, vorwärts oder rückwärts —**, to go or walk fast or quickly, slowly, forward, backward; **einen starken Schritt —**, to walk a good round pace, to go at a great pace; **sein Pferd geht einen guten, starken Schritt**, his horse walks well, has a good walk, **sein Pferd im Trab, im Galopp — lassen**, to put one's horse into a trot, into a gallop, to make one's horse trot, gallop; **die Kinder fangen an allein zu —, wenn sie ein Jahr alt sind**, children begin to go or walk alone at a year old; **zu Fuße —**, to go on foot; **auf den Zehen —**, to walk on tiptoe; **an Krücken —**, to walk on or with crutches; **auf Stelzen —**, to walk upon stilts (used also in a fig. sense); **irre —**, to go wrong, to go astray, to err; **spazieren —**, to go a-walking, to take a walk; **betteln —**, to go a-begging; [in contradistinction to going on horseback, in a carrriage &c.] to go on foot, to walk; **die Nacht hindurch —**, to walk all night; **es ist hier** [**man kann hier**] **nicht gut, nicht bequem —**, it is bad or not good walking here; **es ist hier sehr schlüpfrig zu —**, it is very slippery walking here; **da geht er allein, in Gedanken**, there he is walking alone, musing.

Fig. a) [to be in a certain state] **müßig —**, to be idle, to idle; **in der Irre —** [= **fehlen**], to err, to be wrong, to be mistaken, [= **verlassen seyn**] to be forsaken; [among hunters] **ein Hirsch, der hech geht**, a deer or stag that has shed its horns; **schwanger —** [= **seyn**], to go with child, to be pregnant: **die Frauen — gewöhnlich neun Monate** [viz. **schwanger**], women commonly go nine months. V. **Schwanger**; ***auf Freiers Füßen —**, to have a mind to marry, to be looking out or about for a wife; **auf bösen Wegen —**, to lead a bad, a wicked life; **nackt, barfuß, mit bloßem Kopfe —**, to go naked, bare-foot, uncovered or bare-headed; **gut gekleidet, reinlich gekleidet —**, to go in good clothes, to dress well, to be always well dressed; **in Seide und Sammt —**, to be dressed in silk and velvet; **er gehet immer in Schuhen und Strümpfen**, he always wears shoes and stockings; **er geht immer im Mantel**, he always wears a cloak.

Fig. b) [to behave, to conduct one's self] **behutsam, vorsichtig — bei einer Sache**, to proceed with prudence, circumspection in an affair; **lassen Sie mich nur —, ich will es schon in Ordnung bringen**, let me alone, or leave this affair to me, I will arrange it.

Fig. c) [to be propagated, to spread] **die Rede, das Gerücht geht**, there goes a report, the report goes or is current; **es — viele Krankheiten herum**, there are many diseases about town, it is a sickly season.

Fig. d) [denoting a certain progress or success of an affair] **dieses Geld geht, geht nicht**, this money goes or passes, is current, does not go or pass, is not current; **eine Sache geht im Schwange**, a thing is in vogue, in fashion; **ein Buch geht gut** [**ab**], a book sells well, takes; **Handel und Wandel geht nicht**, there is no trade stirring; **Alles geht gut, die Sache geht gut von Statten**, all is well, all goes well, the affair is in a fair way, goes on prosperously; **es wird Alles gut —, das wird, muß —**, all will be well, that will do, that must do or succeed; **es geht mit dieser Sache wie mit der andern**, it is with this affair as it was with the other; **es ist mir übel damit gegangen**, it went ill with me, I came badly off, I did not succeed; **es gehet ihm unglücklich mit seinen Kindern**, he is unfortunate in his children, his children are a source of much vexation to him; **es geht nur langsam mit diesen Verbesserungen**, these improvements go on but slowly; **wenn es nur nach Verdiensten ginge**, if it only went by merit, if merit alone were regarded or considered; **so geht es, wenn man unbedachtsam handelt**, this happens or comes to pass, when we act inconsiderately; **es ist mir ebenso gegangen**, it was the same with me, the same thing happened to me; **es geht ihm wie mir**, it fares with him as with me; [in popular lang.] **es ist ihr unrichtig gegangen** [= **sie hat mißgeboren**], she has miscarried; **wie geht es? wie geht es Ihnen?** how do you do? how are you? how goes it? **wie geht es mit Ihrer Gesundheit?** how is your health? how is it with your health? how are you? **es geht mir wohl, übel**, I am well, I am doing well, I am ill; **solchen Menschen kann es nicht wohl —**, such men cannot prosper; **wie wird es mir —?** what will become of me?

Fig. e) [to fit, to suit] **der Rock geht, geht gut, geht schlecht** &c., the coat fits, fits well, does not fit &c.; **diese Farbe geht nicht zu den andern**, this colour does not suit with the others.

Fig. f) [to sound] **Eine Orgel geht schön**, an organ sounds well, has a fine tone; **diese Arie geht aus A**, this air is in the key of A; **dieses Musikstück geht aus einem angenehmen Tone**, this piece of music is set in an agreeable key.

2) [with words denoting direction] **der Fluß geht um einen Berg**, the river turns or runs about a mountain; **die Mauer geht um den ganzen Garten**, the wall runs round the whole garden; **die Elbe geht durch die Stadt**, the Elbe flows through the town; **in die Höhe —**, to rise, to ascend; **der Luftballon ging gerade in die Höhe**, the air-balloon ascended in a straight line, perpendicularly; **das Korn geht in die Aehren**, the corn forms ears, shoots into ears; **der Stich ging durch die Lunge**, the thrust passed through the lungs; **es geht nichts als Galle und Blut von ihm**, he voids nothing but bilious matter and blood; **es geht Alles unverdaut von ihm**, he evacuates every thing undigested; ***er läßt Alles unter sich —**, he cannot retain any thing, every thing goes or runs through him; **entzwei —**, to fall in two, to go asunder; **in Stücke, in Trümmer —**, to fall or to go to pieces, to split; **aus einander, von einander —**, [applied to things that ought to remain entire] to cleave, to separate, [applied to persons = **scheiden**] to part, to separate; **die Gesellschaft ging um 11 Uhr aus einander**, the company broke up at eleven o'clock; **mit einander —**, [applied to men and beasts] to flock together; **Einem entgegen —**, to go to meet any one; **den kürzesten, einen und denselben Weg —**, to go or take the shortest way, one and the same way; **vorwärts, rückwärts, auf und ab —**, to go or walk forward, backward, to and fro, up and down; **voran, hinten drein —**, to go or walk on before, behind; **neben einander —**, to go or walk side by side, abreast; **essen** [**oder zu Tische**] **—, schlafen** [**oder zu Bette**] **—**, to go to dinner or supper, to go to bed; **bis an die nächste Straße —**, to go as far as the next street; **nach Hause, nach der Stadt, zur Stadt —**, to go home, to go to the town; **nach Jemand —**, to go in search of any one; **nach Wasser —**, to go for water; **über den Berg —**, to pass or cross the mountain; **über das Feld —**, to walk across the fields; **über Feld, über Land** [= **auf ein Dorf** &c.] **—**, to make an excursion into the country, to go into the country; **um die Stadt herum —**, to take a turn or a walk round the town; **in der Stadt herum —**, to walk about the town; **in den Krieg —**, to go to the war; **auf die Jagd —**, to go hunting or shooting; **in das Wasser —**, [said of a dog] to take the water; **in das Schauspiel, Theater —**, to go to the play; **in das Haus —**, to go, to step or walk into the house, to enter the house; **in den Garten —**, to go or walk

he garden; auf die Post —, to go to the post-ffice; auf die Hochzeit, den Ball —, to go to wedding, to a ball; auf einen Berg —, to scend a mountain; aus der Schule —, to go ut of school, to come from school; nicht aus em Hause —, not to stir out of the house; aus em Wege (auf die Seite) —, to go out of the ay, to draw or fall back, to step aside. to make ay, to stand out of the way; gehet mir aus m Wege, get out of my way; — Sie mir us dem Lichte, stand out of my light; geh eg da! get away, get you gone! geh deiner Wege! go about your business, get you gone! ehet mir aus den Augen! get out of my sight! ei Jemand vorbei, vorüber —, to pass by any e, durch das Thor —, to pass through the ate; über den Fluß —, to cross the river; nach aris —, to go to Paris; wir gingen gestern ach C., we walked or went to C. yesterday; zu asser, in See —, to go, to put to sea; an ord —, to go on ship-board; zu Schiffe —, embark; man kann nur zu Wasser dahin —, e cannot go there but by water; mit dem ostwagen an einen Ort —, to go or travel ywhere by the stage-coach; dieses Schiff t regelmäßig nach London, this ship goes re-larly to London; dieses Fahrzeug geht nach merica, this vessel is bound for America; in Kloster —, to enter a convent; auf Reisen, to set out upon one's travels, to take a jour-y, to travel; auf die hohe Schule —, to go college, to go to visit a university; er gt es nicht, ihm unter die Augen zu —, dares not show his face; * Einem über sei-Bücher —, to rummage any one's books library; * Einem über seinen Keller —, to al any one's wine; gegen den Feind, in Schlacht —, to go or march against the ene-y, to battle; in das Feuer —, to go into fire; Einem —, to go to any one, to step up to a rson, to approach any one, (= in sein Haus) to to see any one, to call upon any one or at y one's house; von Einem —, to leave, to sake any one; er geht viel unter die Leute, goes a great deal into society; zum Besuche, to go to pay a visit; zu Tische or Gast bei nem —, to go to dine or sup with any one.

Fig. a) (to adopt a certain way or manner of act-) Auf den Stich —, to fight a duel with swords; geraden Weg — (aufrichtig handeln), to act ndidly, to have an honest, upright way of ling, to be an upright man; er geht in Allem geraden Weg, he is an upright man in all dealings; langsam bei etwas zu Werke —, proceed slowly in an affair; Einem an die nd —, to assist, to succour, to second any, to lend any one a helping hand; der Sache den Grund —, to sift or examine the mat-thoroughly or to the bottom; an den Mi-ter —, to apply to the minister; an's Werk, die Arbeit —, to go to work, to set about a ng; mechanisch zu Werke —, to go mecha-ally to work; schwer an etwas —, to be h to do something, to set about a thing with uctance, to be persuaded with difficulty to or to undertake something; von der Arbeit (sie liegen lassen), to leave one's work or bu-ess; mit sich zu Rathe —, to deliberate, to sider; in sich —, (= Ueberlegungen anstellen; Reue empfinden) to descend or retire into one's to reflect upon one's self, *it.* to repent; nach obe —, to try to get one's livelihood; † Ei-n um das Maul —, (= ihm schmeicheln) to x, to wheedle any one; weiter dürfen Sie ein nicht — (Sie dürfen nicht mehr darin thun), must not go or proceed farther in this affair.

Fig. b) (to come into a certain state) verloren, to be lost; zu Grunde —, to go to ruin, to ruined; in die Höhe — (= aufschlagen, theuer werden), to rise in price; einer Sache verlustig —, to lose a thing; in sein Verderben —, to run into one's ruin; den Weg alles Fleisches — (sterben), to go the way of all flesh, to die; in's dreißigste Jahr —, to be going on one's thirtieth year; er geht in das achtzehnte Jahr, he is entering on his eighteenth year; über Ei-nen — (= Einen übertreffen), to surpass, to ex-cel any one; sich — lassen (= seinen Launen oder Leidenschaften folgen) to give one's self up to, to yield to one's humours or passions.

Fig. c) (denoting the relation of a state; chiefly in familiar lang.) Das geht ihm nahe, geht ihm sehr zu Herzen, that touches him to the quick, that goes near his heart, that grieves him greatly; lassen Sie es sich nicht zu sehr zu Herzen —, do not take it too much to heart, be not too much afflicted at it; das ging mir durch's Herz, durch die Seele, that touched me to the quick, struck or grieved me to the very heart, distressed me extremely; wenn Noth an Mann geht, in case of necessity, when necessity requires it; es geht Alles durch seine Hände, every thing pas-ses through his hands; es geht Alles drunter und drüber, every thing is topsy-turvy; den Schaden über sich — lassen (= auf sich nehmen), to take the damage upon one's own shoulders, upon one's self, to bear it one's self; darüber geht nichts, there is nothing beyond that, there is nothing to surpass or excel that; das geht wider den Anstand, that is against decency; er läßt viel darauf —, he spends a great deal of money; es geht dabei sehr über das Geld, den Beutel (her), it is very expensive, requires a great deal of money; es ging sehr über ihn her, he was severely lashed, censured or criti-cised; *prov.* was von Herzen gehet, gehet auch zu Herzen, what proceeds from the heart, touches the heart; geht es dir auch von Herzen? is it your earnest? do you do it cor-dially or willingly? das will mir nicht in den Kopf (or zu Kopfe, in the first sentence) —, that will never go down with me, *it.* I cannot conceive that; sobald als er ankam, ging es an ein Tanzen und Schwelgen, as soon as he arrived, they fell a dancing and rioting; als der erste Kanonenschuß ertönte, da ging es an ein Laufen, when the first cannon-shot was heard, they took to their heels.

Fig. d) Es geht um etwas, something is at stake, is put at hazard, is played for. Es geht um Geld, um nichts, um eine Flasche Wein &c., we or they are playing for money, for nothing, for a bottle of wine &c.; es geht ihm um den Kopf, his head or life is at stake.

3) (in a more limited sense) *a)* (= sich entfernen) to go away. Die Briefpost kommt und geht zwei-mal in der Woche, the mail comes and goes twice a week; ich will — (hingehen) und es ihm sagen, I will go and tell him so; wollen Sie, daß ich — (mich entfernen) soll? do you wish or want me to go away? es ist Zeit, zu —, it is time to be gone; * er hat auf diese Arznei drei-mal — müssen, this physic has made him go to stool three times or has given him three stools; geh hin in Frieden! depart in peace! lassen Sie ihn —, let him go away, * *it.* let him alone; er ist gegangen, wie er gekommen ist, he did not succeed, he had his labour for his pains; * o, — Sie! — Sie, das ist nicht möglich! oh, dear, indeed, is it possible? it is impossible! † — Sie zum Henker, zum Teufel! deuce take you, go and be hanged! go to the devil; † sein gan-zes Vermögen ist zum Teufel gegangen, all his fortune is gone to the devil, is squandered away.

b) Gehen lassen, = not to retain, to let go off. Dieser Pelz läßt die Haare —, the hair of this fur is coming off; dieser Zeug läßt die Farbe —, this stuff loses its colour, fades; † Ei-nen — lassen, to break wind backwards, to let a fart.

c) In and durch etwas gehen, = to have place or room in something. Sechs Personen — nicht in diesen Wagen, this carriage does not hold six persons; die Waaren — nicht alle in das Magazin, the warehouse does not hold all the goods; es — sechs Gläser in diese Flasche, this bottle holds or contains six glasses; *prov.* es — viele geduldige Schafe in einen Stall, if they will but accommodate themselves, every one will find a place; der Faden geht nicht durch dieses Nadelöhr, the thread cannot pass through this eye; der Tisch geht nicht durch die Thür, the table cannot pass through the door. *Fig.* Es — zwölf Stüber auf einen Schilling, a shil-ling has twelve pence; wie viel Groschen — auf einen Thaler? how many groshen has a dollar? auf ein Ries Papier — zwanzig Buch, a ream of paper has twenty quires; es — sechzehn Unzen auf ein Pfund, sixteen ounces make a pound.

d) (to reach or extend to a certain place) Das Was-ser geht ihm bis an die Kniee, the water goes up to his knees, he is in the water up to his knees; der Rock geht ihm bis auf den Fuß, his coat reaches or hangs down to his feet; der Weg geht in gerader Richtung von hier bis in das nächste Dorf, the way goes in a straight line from here to the next village; der Wald geht bis in das Gebirge, the wood goes to the moun-tains, extends as far as the mountains; diese Flinte geht achtzig Schritte weit, this gun car-ries or conveys the shot eighty paces. *Fig.* So weit muß die Lustigkeit nicht —, mirth or gaiety must not go so far; seine Liebe geht bis zur Tollheit, his love borders on madness; seine Rache ist zu weit gegangen, he has gone too far in his revenge.

e) (to be situated or directed towards) Sein Schlaf-zimmer geht nach dem Hofe, his bedroom looks out into the yard; die Thür geht auf die Straße, the door faces or fronts the street; diese Stra-ße geht (führt) nach Berlin, this road goes or leads to Berlin; dieser Weg geht nach der Stadt zu, this way leads to the town. *Fig.* Unsre Reise geht nach England, we are going or travelling to England, we are bound for England; seine Meinung ging dahin, daß &c., his opinion was, that &c; es geht gegen Morgen, gegen Abend, the morning will soon dawn, day will soon break, it is growing towards evening, evening is drawing near or on; es geht auf zehn Uhr, it turns on ten (o'clock); es geht in die vierte Wo-che, daß ich Ihnen geschrieben habe, it is more than three weeks since I wrote to you; es geht mit der Flasche zu Ende, auf die Neige, the bottle is almost emptied, there is very little left in the bottle; mit dem Kranken geht es zu Ende, the sick man is drawing near his end, lies a-dying; alle seine Wünsche — auf Frieden, all his wishes tend to, are for, peace; alle seine Reden — auf das hinaus, that's the drift of all his speeches, all his speeches come to that, aim at that, tend or drive that way; das soll wahrscheinlich auf mich —, that is probably aimed or leveled at me; das geht auf dich so gut als wie auf mich, that concerns or touches you as well as me.

II. *v. tr.* (in a few phrases) = to cause or pro-duce by walking. Sich die Füße wund —, to gall one's feet with walking; er hat sich Blasen an die Füße gegangen, he has blistered his feet by walking; *it.* as a *reflective verb.* sich müde —, to get tired or weary with walking; sie hat sich ganz müde gegangen, she is quite tired with walking. V. Ab—, Fort—, Los—, Weg— &c.

SYN. Gehen, Wandeln, Wandern, Wal-len. Gehen is said as well of beasts as of men; Wan-bein of men only, and particularly of a manner of going or walking which is unaccompanied by any labour or fatigue. V. Luſtwandeln. Wandern is said of persons travelling on foot. V. Wanderer. Wallen, which is also said of liquid bodies in motion or ebullition, signified originally gehen, to go, to move generally, and is still used in this sense, more especially in solemn style.

Gehen, *n.* [-s] V. Gang. Des —s müde ſeyn, to be tired or weary of walking; das — wird ihm ſauer, he can scarce walk, walking fatigues him greatly.

‖**Gehénd**, *adj.* and *adv.* V. Behende.

‖**Gehéndigkeit**, *f.* V. Behendigkeit.

Gehènk, *n.* [-es, *pl.* -e] V. Gehänge and Henkel.

Geheúer, *adv.* secure [especially from spirits or ghosts]. Es iſt hier nicht —, this place is haunted; *es iſt gar nicht — [= es iſt bedenklich or zweifelhaft], the thing is not clear, it is a doubtful case.

Geheúl, [-es] or **Geheúle**, [-s] *n* a continued howling; howling. Das — der Hunde, der Wölfe, the howling of the dogs, of the wolves; das — des Sturmes, der Wellen, the roaring of the tempest, of the billows; [applied to persons] cries, lamentations; das — dieſer Unglücklichen ging mir durch die Seele, the cries or lamentations of these unfortunate persons pierced my very heart.

Gehírn, *n.* [-es, *pl.* -e] 1) brain, brains. Das — von einem Kalbe, a calf's brain, V. Kalbshirn; der Schuß trieb or ſprützte ihm das — aus dem Kopfe, the shot blew his brains out; die Sonne hat ihm das — verbrannt, the sun has dried up or scorched his brains. *Fig.* *[in contempt] Ein verbranntes — haben, to have cracked brains, to be crack-brained; wenig — im Kopfe haben, to have little brains; ein leeres — haben, to be addle-brained, addle-pated; *im —e nicht wohl verwahrt, nicht richtig ſeyn, to be crack-brained, crazy; das hat ihm das — verrückt, that has turned his brain; das iſt nicht aus ſeinem —e gekommen, that did not come or proceed from his pate, that is not of his invention, not of his own growth. 2) very little used for Menſch, man, person. Dieſe wahnſinnigen —e, these frantic persons. V. Hirn.

Gehirn-balken, *m.* V. Hirnbalken. —**behälter**, *m.* brain-pan, skull. —**bruch**, *m.* V. Hirnbruch. —**haut**, *f.* —**häutlein**, *n.* membrane of the brain, meninge. —**kammer**, *f.* ventricle of the brain. —**kern**, *m.* V. Hirnbalken. —**koralle**, *f.* madrepore. Verſteinerte —koralle, V. —ſtein. —**lappen**, *pl.* lobes of the brain. —**lehre**, *f.* craniology, cranioscopy. —**los**, *adj.* and *adv.* without brain, having no brain, *fig.* without understanding, silly, brainless. —**pulsader**, *f.* artery of the brain. —**ſpalt**, *m.* fissure of the brain, V. Hirnſpalt; *it.* V. Knochenſpalt.] —**ſtein**, *m.* petrified madrepore, brain-stone.

‡ and ‖**Géhl**, *adj.* and *adv.* V. Gelb.

Gehöfte, *n.* [-s, *pl.* -] [Gehöfde] properly, the premises of a farm or the inclosure surrounded by the farm-buildings; then generally = farm. Dieſer Bezirk enthält fünfzig —, this district contains fifty farms.

Gehöhne, *n.* [-s] continual mocking, continual bantering or jeering.

Gehölz, *n.* [-es, *pl.* -e] wood, forest. Ein kleines —, a small wood, a grove; — an einem Hauſe, plantations about a house, park, V. Luſt—, Luſtwald.

Gehör, *n.* [-es, *pl.* -e] 1) [among hunters = Ohren] the ears. Das — einer Bache, the ears or lugs of a wild sow. 2) the faculty or sense of hearing. Ein gutes, ſcharfes — haben, to have a good, sharp or quick ear; ein ſchlechtes oder hartes — haben, to be dull or hard of hearing; ein muſikaliſches — haben, to have an ear for music; der Sinn des —es, the sense of hearing; das — verlieren, um das — kommen, to lose one's hearing; ein Tonkünſtler muß — [= ein gutes —] haben, a musician must have a good, a quick ear; wenn man kein — hat, ſo kann man nicht gut die Geige ſpielen lernen, if you have not a good or delicate ear, you will never learn to play well upon the violin. 3) [the state of hearing or having heard something] Etwas aus dem —e haben, to know something by hearsay; [in music] aus or nach dem —e ſpielen, to play from hearing [not from notes]. 4) [the act of hearing any one or of attending to what any one says] hearing, audience. Einem — geben [= ihn anhören], to give any one a hearing, to listen to any one; er fand ein geneigtes —, he was favourably heard; er gab mir kein —, he did not hear me; er gibt den Verläumdern kein —, he never gives ear to calumniators. 5) [= Audienz] audience. Ich machte dem Miniſter meine Aufwartung, konnte aber kein — bei ihm finden, I waited on the minister, but could not obtain a hearing; der Geſandte wurde bei dem Könige zum —e gelaſſen, verlangte, bekam —, the ambassador was admitted to an audience of the king, demanded, obtained audience; bei dem —e erſcheinen, gegenwärtig ſeyn, to attend the audience, to be present, to assist at the audience; einer Bitte — geben, to grant a request; *fig.* dem Mitleide, der Stimme der Natur — geben, to give way to one's feelings of pity or compassion, to hear the voice of nature.

Gehör-fehler, *m.* a defect in the organs of hearing. —**gang**, *m.* [in anatomy] auditory passage [in the ear], acoustic duct. —**knochen**, *m.* bone of the ear. —**kunſt**, *f.* *a)* the art of assisting the sense of hearing. *b)* acoustics. —**lähmung**, *f.* paralysis of the organs of hearing, deafness, surdity. —**lehre**, *f.* [doctrine of hearing and sound] acoustics. —**loch**, *n.* the auditory hole. —**los**, *adj.* and *adv.* wanting the sense of hearing, deaf. —**loſigkeit**, *f.* deafness, surdity. —**mangel**, *m.* the want of the sense of hearing, deafness. —**nerve**, *m.* auditory nerve. —**organ**, *n* organ of hearing. —**rohr**, *n.* acoustic instrument, ear-trumpet. —**ſaal**, *m.* audience-chamber; [in convents] parlour. —**ſchnecke**, *f.* [in anatomy, the spiral cavity of the ear] cochlea. —**ſinn**, *m.* the sense of hearing. —**tag**, *m.* day of audience [on which audience is given]. —**trichter**, *m.* V. —rohr. —**trommel**, *f.* drum of the ear, tympanum. —**weg**, *m.* V. —gang. —**werkzeug**, *n.* organ of hearing. —**zimmer**, *n.* V. —ſaal.

Gehórchen, *v. intr.* [is the frequentative verb of gehören, now obsolete in the sense [of to hear] to obey. Gott, den Geſetzen, der Obrigkeit —, to obey God, the laws, the magistrates; blindlings —, to obey implicitly; man muß ihm —, he must be obeyed; er macht, daß man ihm gehorcht, he makes himself to be obeyed; ich will, daß man mir gehorcht [or gehorche], I will be obeyed; wer — gelernt hat, wird zu befehlen wiſſen, he who has learned to obey, will know how to command; nicht —, not to obey, to disobey, to be disobedient; *fig.* alle Völker, alle Länder, die dem römiſchen Reiche gehorchten, all the nations, all the countries that were under the dominion of the Roman empire; das Meer, die Winde — Ihm, the sea, the winds yield or submit to Him. SYN. Gehorchen, Folgen. Gehorchen implies that the person who gehorcht [obeys] acts according to the will of another. One may, however, einem Andern folgen [follow another], without acknowledging any obligation to do so. Thus we say: einem Befehle gehorchen [obey a command], but, einem Beiſpiele folgen [follow an example]; the former, because we are obliged, the latter, because it pleases.

Gehören, *v. intr.* [V. Gehorchen] 1) Einem —. *a)* to be any one's property. Dieſe Häuſer — ihm, these houses belong to him; es gehört mir die Hälfte davon, half of it belongs to me; dieſes Schloß hat meinen Voreltern gehört, this castle belonged to my ancestors. *b)* to be due to any one. Dem Geſinde gehört [ſein] Lohn, wages are the due of servants, are due to servants; auf eine ſolche Frage gehört eine ſolche Antwort, such a question deserves such an answer; dieſer Titel gehört ihm nicht, this title is not his due, he does not merit this title. 2) Unter etwas —, to be subject to something. Unter ein Gericht —, to be under some jurisdiction or under the jurisdiction of some court. 3) Vor Einen or etwas —, to depend upon any one, to be submitted to any one for his decision or judgment. Die Unterſuchung or die gerichtliche Erkenntniß dieſer Sache gehört vor einen andern Richter, the cognizance of this affair belongs to another judge, this affair falls under the cognisance of another judge; das gehört nicht vor ſeinen Richterſtuhl, that is not within his jurisdiction or under his cognizance. 4) Zu etwas —, *a)* to be a part of something. Dieſe Ländereien — zu meinem Schloſſe, these lands belong to my castle; dieſer Garten hat ehemals zu dieſem Hauſe gehört, this garden was formerly an appendant to the house, formerly belonged to this house; [er] gehört zu uns, zu unſerer Familie, Geſellſchaft, he belongs to us, to our family or company, he is one of us, of our family or company; dies gehört nicht zu meinem Amte, that does not belong to my office; dieſe Einkünfte — zu meinem Amte, these revenues belong to my office; dort gehöre ich zu Hauſe, there is my home, there I am settled, there I am domiciliated; [zu] den Gelehrten —, to be one of the learned, [to] be numbered among the learned. *b)* to suit, tally with, to be suitable to, to agree. Dieſe [zwei] Handſchuhe — zuſammen, these two gloves [are] fellows; dieſe Stühle — in das Schlafzimmer, these chairs are fit or proper for, must be [put] into the bed room; wo gehört dies hin? wh[ere] is this to be put? what place does this belong to? das gehört nicht zu meinem Gegenſtande, das gehört in die Philoſophie, that has no relation to my subject, forms no part of my subject, that belongs to philosophy; dieſer Gegenſtand gehört nicht auf die Kanzel, this is [no] subject or not a proper subject for the pulpit; dieſes Wort gehört nicht hierher, this word [is] improperly used in this place or is misplaced, has no business in this place. *c)* to be necessary for. Es gehört noch Salz an die Suppe, [the] soup wants some more salt; dazu gehört Geld, that requires money; es gehört mehr dazu, den Namen des Großen zu verdienen, als [...], more is wanted or required to merit the [name] of the great, than &c.; gehört die Tugend [nicht] [or iſt die Tugend nicht erforderlich] zur Freundſchaft, ſo wird er &c., if virtue is not required to friendship, he will &c. 5) ſich —, to be [sui]table, to be becoming, proper. Ein ſolches [Be]nehmen gehört ſich für ihn nicht, such a conduct does not become him; es gehört ſich, [daß] &c., it is fit or becoming, that &c.; ſo gehört es ſich, that is the way, that is proper or as it ought to be; wie ſich's gehört und gebührt, in a becoming, proper or suitable manner, duly; es gehört ſich für einen Vater, ſeine ungehorſamen Kinder zu züchtigen, it becomes a father, it is th[e] uty of a father, to chastize his disobedient children. Syn. **Gehören, Gebühren.** Whatever necessarily forms part of, or by right belongs to another thing, is said zu **gehören** [to belong] to it. Thus. a part **gehört** [belongs] to the whole; the moon **gehört** [belongs] to the solar system &c. Whatever a person has a just claim or right to, **gehört** ihm [belongs to him]; if this claim is founded merely on his merit or worthiness, **es gebührt ihm** [it is his due].

Gehörig, I. *adj.* 1) belonging. appertaining. Die diesem Edelmanne —en Güter, the estates belonging to this lord; der zum Hause —e Garten, the garden belonging to the house; dieses Buch ist mir —, this book belongs to me, is mine; alle zu dieser Familie —en Personen, all the persons belonging to that family; was zu unserem Gegenstand nicht —e habe ich weggelassen, I omitted what had no relation to our subject, what was foreign to our subject. 2) due, proper, fit. Die —en Mittel anwenden, to employ the proper means or remedies; die —en Eigenschaften haben, to have the requisite qualities; er hat das —e Alter, dieses Amt zu bekleiden, he has the proper age to fill that office; Einem die —e Ehre erzeigen, to pay any one due honour; ein Jeder hat seinen —en Antheil erhalten, every one has received his due share; —e Verdauung, congruent digestion; in —er Form, in due form; zu —er Zeit, in due time; theilen Sie ihm das —e mit, impart or communicate to him what is necessary for him to know. II. *adv.* properly, duly, fitly. Sich — betragen, to behave in a becoming or suitable manner; tragen Sie also die Frage — vor, propose then the question in a proper manner, in due form; er ist — davon benachrichtigt worden, he has been duly informed or advised of it.

Gehörigkeit, *f.* fitness, suitableness, propriety.

Gehörn, *n.* [-es, *pl* -e] the horns [of an ox &c.]; [among hunters] attire. Das — eines Hirsches, the antlers or head of a stag. V. Geweih.

Gehörnt, [*past part.* of an unusual verb hörnen = mit Hörnern versehen] *adj.* and *adv.* horned, cornuted. [in botany] Ein —es [halbmondförmiges] Blumenblatt, a cornuted petal.

Gehórsam, *adj.* and *adv.* obedient, dutiful. Ein —er Sohn, a dutiful or duteous son; —e Unterthanen, dutiful or obedient subjects; Ihr [Dero] —er, —ster, ganz —ster Diener, [a form of politeness], your humble and obedient, your most humble and most obedient servant; [ironically and in familiar language] —er Diener! your servant, I am your servant!

Gehórsam, *m.* [-es] 1) obedience, duty, dutifulness. Kindlicher —, filial obedience; — leisten, to render or yield obedience, to be obedient, to obey; der Sohn ist seinem Vater — schuldig, the son owes obedience to his father; einem Fürsten den — aufkündigen, aufsagen, to withdraw one's allegiance from a prince; die Empörer zum — bringen, to reduce the rebels or insurgents to obedience; zum — zurückkehren, to return to one's duty or obedience; unbedingter —, implicit obedience; blinder —, a blind or passive obedience. *Prov.* — ist besser, denn [als] Opfer, obedience is better than sacrifice. ||2) [sometimes used for] a place of confinement. V. Gewahrsam.

Gehórsamen, [obsolescent] *v. intr.* to obey. V. Gehorchen.

1. **Géhre,** *f.* [*pl.* -n] [seems to be allied to kehren] 1) [among joiners &c.] oblique or diagonal direction. 2) [instrument of joiners and carpenters &c.] a bevel.

Gehre-hobel, *m.* [among joiners] an [oblique] plane for making a diagonal plane. —**holz,** —**maß,** *n* [among masons, joiners, carpenters &c.] a bevel. —**en-ziegel,** *m.* V. Gierenziegel.

2. **Géhre,** *f.* [*pl.* -n] [allied to the Lat. *cera* and κηρός] the disk or plate of wax in a beehive. honeycomb.

Géhren, *m.* [-s] [allied to the Dan. and Sw. *jern,* Engl. *iron,* Ir. *jarran* = **Eisen,** and the Gaelic *gaesum*; Engl. to *gore* is = **stechen**] a pointed instrument, as a spear, arrow, fork &c. *Fig. a*) [in architecture, a sloping plane forming an acute angle with a horizontal plane] talus or talut, slope. *b*) [a wedge-shaped or triangular piece of cloth sewed into a garment to widen it in any part] a gore. *c*) the skirt or lap of a garment. *d*) [in some provinces, a triangular piece of land] a slip, a gore.

Géhrig, *adj.* V. Schief.

Géhrung, *f.* an oblique or diagonal direction or plane.

Gehrungskolben, *m.* [among glaziers] soldering-iron.

†**Gehúdel,** *n.* [-s] a continual teazing and plaguing, drudgery; *it.* any thing done too hastily, hence any bad work, bungling piece of work.

Gehúlfe, *m* [-n, *pl.* -n] helper, assistant. Ich brauche keinen —n, um dieses zu thun, I want no one to help me to do that; der — im Amte, an assistant, a colleague, an adjunct; Einem einen —n, Einem zum —n geben, to give any one an assistant; er hat dieses Verbrechen ohne —n begangen, he has committed this crime without an accomplice.

Gehúlfinn, *f* a help-mate, partner, consort. Er und seine —, he and his help-mate, partner or wife. *Fig.* Wenn ein gründlicher Verstand eine lebhafte Einbildungskraft zur — hat, if a solid judgment is accompanied by a lively imagination.

Géhwerk, *n.* [-es, *pl.* -e] the wheel-work of a watch or clock.

Geien, *v. tr.* [in seamen's language] to brail up [the sails]. V. Aufgeien.

Geier, *m.* [-s] [Med. Lat. *gira*; it is derived from **gehren, Gier**] 1) [in natural history] *a*) the vulture, hawk. V. Bart—, Lämmer—. *Fig.* † Zum —! daß dich der —! the deuce! hol dich der —! geh zum —! deuce take you! *b*) [sometimes] a kind of swallow. V. Uferschwalbe. 2) [in forges] V. Gicht.

Geier-adler, *m.* horse-kite, carrion-kite. V. Aas—. —**eule,** *f.* owlet, madge-owlet. —**falk,** *m.* ger-falcon; *it.* merganser, goosander. —**könig,** *m.* [a vulture of South-America] the king of vultures. —**schlag,** *m.* the hunting of sea-swallows. —**stein,** *m.* [a stone found in the stomach of a vulture] vulture-stone.

Geifer, *m.* [-s] [Dutch. *zabber,* Low-Sax. **Sabbe, Sever**; seems to be allied to **Saft** &c.] [saliva, flowing or driveling from the mouth] slaver, drivel. Der — trat ihm vor den Mund, als er sprach, he foamed at the mouth, when he spoke; mit — besudeln, to defile with drivel, to slaver; der giftige — einer Schlange, eines tollen Hundes, the venomous spittle or foam of a serpent, of a mad dog; *fig.* * seinen — [Unwillen] auslassen, to fret and fume, to vent one's passion.

Geifer-bart, *m.* V. —maul. —**fisch,** *m.* bavosa raia. —**läppchen,** —**läßchen,** *n.* a slavering cloth, a bib. —**maul,** *n.* V. Geiferer. —**thierchen,** *n.* [an insect] cicada spumaria, flea locust, frog-hopper. —**tuch,** —**tüchlein,** *n.* V. —läppchen. —**wurz,** *f.* V. Seifenkraut.

Geiferer, *m.* [-s, *pl.* -] [one that slabbers or drivels] slaverer, slabberer, driveler, slabber-chops [in a proper as well as in a figurative sense].

Geiferícht, *adj.* and *adv.* [like slaver] drivel-like, slaver-like.

Geiferig, *adj.* and *adv.* containing slaver or drivel, defiled with drivel, slavered.

Geifern, *v. intr.* to drivel, to slaver, to slabber. Ein —des Kind, a slabbering child; er geifert im Reden, he sputters in speaking; vor Zorn —, to foam with rage; *fig.* —, to scold, to vent one's rage or passion, to fret and fume.

Geíge, *f.* [*pl.* -n] [appears to come from the old word **geigen** = gehen, *i. e.* sich bewegen] 1) violin, fiddle. Die —, auf der — spielen, to play on the violin or fiddle, to fiddle; ein Meister auf der — seyn, die — meisterhaft spielen, to play on the violin in a masterly manner, to be a great master of the violin; die — kratzen [schlecht spielen], to play badly on the violin, to scrape; *fig* [in familiar language] der Himmel hängt ihm voller —n, he is swimming in joy. 2) [a wooden instrument, that is put round the neck and hands of a criminal for punishment] a kind of pillory; [among comb-makers] V. Filz—.

Geigen-blatt, *n.* the finger-board of a violin. —**bogen,** *m.* bow, fiddle-stick. —**bohrer,** *m.* a drill. —**förmig,** *adj.* and *adv.* having the form or shape of a violin; [in botany] ein —förmiges Blatt, a guitar-shaped or panduraeformed leaf. —**futter,** *n* case for a violin, fiddle-case. —**hals,** *m.* neck of a violin. —**harz,** *n.* hard rosin, colophony, Spanish or Greek pitch. —**holz,** *n.* 1) any wood fit or proper for violins. 2) [in botany] an American tree, the wood of which is particularly fit to make violins of, fiddle-wood. —**holzbaum,** *m.* V. —holz 2). —**macher,** *m.* violin-maker. —**regal,** —**register,** *n.* V. —werk. —**saite,** *f.* string of a violin, fiddle-string. —**saiten-macher,** *m.* fiddle-string-maker. —**sattel,** *m.* bridge of a violin. —**schule,** *f.* a methodical arrangement of exercises to be played on the violin by beginners. —**solo,** *n.* a solo of the violin. —**spieler,** *m.* V. Geiger. —**steg,** *m.* V. —sattel. —**strich,** *m.* stroke of the fiddle-stick. —**stück,** *n.* [in music] a piece of music or a tune played on the violin; *it.* a piece written for the violin. —**stunde,** *f.* a lesson on the violin. —**ton,** *m.* the sound of a violin. —**unterricht,** *m.* V. —stunde. —**werk,** *n.* [a sort of harpsichord with a viol-stop] celestina. —**wirbel,** *m.* peg or pin of a violin, fiddle-peg. —**zug,** *m.* [a stop of any instrument imitative of the sound of a violin] violin-stop; *it.* V. —werk.

Geigen, *v. tr.* to play on the violin, to fiddle. Ein Stückchen —, to play a tune on the violin; † ich will dir etwas — [das werde ich wohl bleiben lassen], do not trust to that, don't rely or depend on it; † Einem die Wahrheit —, to tell one his own; *Prov.* wer die Wahrheit geigt, dem schlägt man den Fiedelbogen um den Kopf, he that follows truth too near the heels, shall have dirt thrown in his face; truth finds foes, where it makes none; truth must not be told at all times.

Geiger, *m.* [-s, *pl.* -] performer on the violin, violin-player, violinist, fiddler. Ein elender or schlechter —, a catgut-scraper.

Geigerchor, *m.* a band of violinplayers.

Geigereí, *f.* a continued playing on the violin, a continual fiddling or scraping.

Geil, I. *adj.* [the primary sense was probably *fat.* In the Albanian *gialpa* is = Butter] 1) [in some provinces] fat, *i. e.* fertile. Unfruchtbares Land in —e Felder umwandeln, to convert barren land into fertile fields. 2) too fat. Ein —er Erdboden, —e Pflanzen, too fat or rich a soil, plants of too luxuriant a growth, luxuriant plants; —es Fleisch, rank or rancid meat; *it.*

—es Fleisch in einer Wunde, proud flesh. *Fig.* [= wollüstig, unzüchtig] [rather vulgar] lascivious, lecherous libidinous, lustful, lewd. Ein —er Mensch, a lascivious, lecherous, lewd man; ein —es Weib, a voluptuous, wanton or lewd woman: ein —es Lied, a wanton, smutty or obscene song; —e Blicke, eine —e Stellung, lascivious, wanton, lustful looks, a lascivious posture; † er ist ein alter, —er Bock, he is an old lecher. II. *adv.* lecherously, lasciviously, lustfully, obscenely. — tanzen, to dance lasciviously, wantonly.

Geil⸗horst, *m.* [in some provinces] a place where the corn grows too rank. —**wurz**, *f.* [in botany] satyrion, V. Knabenkraut.

1. **Geile**, *f.* [*pl.* -n] [V. Geil, I. 1.] 1) [der Dünger] manure. 2) V. Geilheit.

2. **Geile**, *f.* [*pl.* -n] [allied to Kugel, and the Lat. *coleus*] testicle, stone. [among hunters] Die —n eines Hirsches, the doucets. V. Hode.

Geilen, I. *v. tr.* 1) to manure [fields &c.], to make rich or fat. 2) to castrate, to geld, to emasculate. Bäume —n, to prune, to lop trees. II. *v. intr.* 1) [unusual] to live in plenty. 2) [unusual in the fig. sense] to be wanton or lascivious. Eine —de [more usual läufige] Hündinn, a bitch at heat; die Hirsche —, the stags are rutting; *fig.* um etwas —, to sue earnestly or instantly for something, to beg something with importunity.

Geilheit, *f.* quality of being too fat or rich, rankness [said of soil]. *Fig.* Die — eines Menschen, lasciviousness, libidinousness, lewdness, wantonness, lechery, lustfulness of a man.

Geimstein, *m.* [-es] [in mining] pounded lead or silver ore.

Geiß, *f.* [*pl.* -en] [seems to come from an obsolete and only in some provinces of South Germany yet used verb geißen = gehen, *i. e.* probably, in the like manner as the Gr. αἶξ from ἀΐσσω] goat, she-goat; [among hunters] wild goat, roe. V. Ziege

Geiß⸗auge, *n.* [in botany] aegilops. —**bart**, *m.* 1) [in botany] goat-beard, goat-marjoram; *it.* the name of an eatable coral mushroom. 2) V. Bocksbart. —**baum**, *m.* white mountain maple-tree, sycomore, sycomore-tree. —**baumesche**, *f.* mountain-ash, ash-tree. —**bergerstein**, *m.* [in mineralogy] gneiss. —**blatt**, *n.* honey-suckle, woodbine. —**blatt⸗schleicher**, *m.* [in natural history] a fly that saws or cuts the honey-suckle. —**bock**, *m.* [Ziegenbock and Rehbock] he-goat, roe-buck. —**bohne**, *f.* the dung of the goats. —**brachsen** or —**brassen**, *m.* sargus [a fish of the Mediterranean]. †—**dreck**, *m.* V. —bohne. —**fell**, *n.* goat's skin. —**fuß**, *m.* 1) a goat's foot. 2) [in botany] the little wild angelica, ashweed, V. Gerich. 3) [an iron bar or crow in form of a goat's foot] handspike. [among carpenters, a stronger sort of chisel] socket-chisel. —**haar**, *n.* goat's hair. —**heerde**, *f.* a herd of goats. —**hirt**, *m.* goatherd. ‖—**hirtlein**, *n.* [a sort of pear] russeting, russeting pear. V. Rußling. —**huhn**, *n.* V. —vogel. —**hülsen**, *pl.* [a plant of the genus Ligustrum] privet, primeprint, V. Rainweide. —**käse**, *m.* goat's cheese. —**klee**, *m.* shrub-trefoil, citisus. —**kopf**, *m.* [in natural history] a sort of moor-cock or heath-cock. —**leder**, *n.* goat-skin or leather. —**lilie**, *f.* [in botany] V. —blatt. —**melker**, *m.* [in natural history] goat-sucker, goat-milker, fern-owl. —**milch**, *f.* goat's-milk. —**raute**, *f.* [a plant of the genus Galega] goat's rue. —**schaben**, *m.* [in botany] V. Alprose. —**vogel**, *m.* [in ornithology] the largest sort of curlews.

1. **Geißel**, *m.* [-s, *pl.* -] [probably allied to the Swed. *gisla* = Verhaft] [a person delivered to an enemy as a pledge] hostage. Die Stadt hat kapitulirt und — gegeben, the town has capitulated and given hostages.

2. **Geißel**, *f.* [*pl.* -n] [seems to be allied to the Goth. *gais* = Speer] [an instrument of punishment or discipline] scourge, whip. Einen mit der — hauen, to scourge, to whip, to lash any one; die — der Mönche, discipline; Einem die —n geben, to scourge, to lash any one; einem Mönche die — geben, to give the discipline. *Fig. a)* [= Züchtigung] punishment, chastisement. Diese Thorheit verdient eine neue —, this folly merits a new punishment, a new censure or lash; die — über Jemand schwingen, to censure or satirize any one severely, to lash any one. *b)* [he or that which greatly afflicts, harasses or destroys] scourge. Solche Eroberer sind —n Gottes, such conquerors are scourges of God; die Sklaverei ist eine schreckliche —, slavery is a terrible scourge. V. Strafruthe, Zuchtruthe.

Geißel⸗bruder, *m.* [one of a fanatical sect that in the thirteenth and fourteenth centuries whipped themselves in religious discipline] a flagellant. —**fahrt**, *f.* a procession of the flagellants. —**hieb**, *m.* a stroke with a whip, a lash. —**mönch**, *m.* [one of a sect of monks who at times flagellate or scourge themselves] flagellant, V. —bruder. —**ruthe**, *f.* scourge, whip. —**schnur**, *f.* the thong or braided cord of a whip, whip-lash, whip-cord. —**stiel**, *m.* handle of a whip.

Geißeler, *m.* [-s, *pl.* -] 1) one that whips or lashes, whipper, scourger. 2) V. Geißelbruder.

Geißeln, *v. tr.* to whip, to scourge, to lash. Der Apostel Paulus wurde gegeißelt, Paul, the Apostle, was scourged; einen Mönch —, to give the discipline; sich —, to scourge or whip one's self; der Löwe geißelt [schlägt] mit dem Schweife die Seiten, the lion lashes his sides with his tail; *fig.* er geißelt [plagt] seine Unterthanen bis auf's Blut, he plagues or harasses his subjects in a most cruel manner. Das —, V. Geißelung.

Geißelung, *f.* 1) the act of whipping or scourging. Die — der Mönche, discipline; die — Christi, the flagellation or whipping of Christ. 2) a picture in which the flagellation of Christ is represented.

Geißlein, [*dimin.* of Geiß] *n.* [-s, *pl.* -] kid.

Geist, *m.* [-es, *pl.* -er] [Geist is the same word with Gischt and Gäscht; its primary sense is in general *something moving, wind, breath*; now:] 1) [a fluid volatile substance that may be mixed with water and is obtained partly by fermentation, partly by distillation] spirit. Flüchtige —er, volatile spirits or liquids [that are apt to evaporate and resolve themselves into air]; feste or feuerbeständige —er, fixed spirits [that do not evaporate on simple exposure to the atmosphere]; V. Weingeist, Vitriolgeist &c.; dieser Wein hat viel —, this wine is full of spirit, is very strong. 2) [the principle animating the body] life, soul. Seinen — aufgeben, aushauchen, to give up the ghost; Vater, ich befehle meinen — in deine Hände, [in Script.] father, into thy hands I commend my spirit; der — des Menschen ist unsterblich, the soul of man or the human soul is immortal; es ist der —, der im Menschen denkt, it is the soul or mind in man that thinks; seinen — bilden, to cultivate, to improve one's mind; er hat, besitzt Gegenwart des —es, he has presence of mind; etwas im —e betrachten, to consider or to contemplate something in one's mind; seinen — mit or an etwas üben, mit etwas beschäftigen, to apply one's understanding to something. [in a more limited sense] *a)* sprighliness of temper, vivacity. Sie ist voll — und Leben, she is full of vivacity and life, she is very sprightly or gay; die —er, die Lebens—er aufwecken, to rouse one's spirits. *b)* disposition of mind. *Ich weiß, welch[-en or -es] —es Kind er ist, I know his way of thinking, it I know what to think of him. *Fig.* Der — der christlichen Liebe, des Friedens, der Rache, the spirit of charity, of peace, of revenge; der — des Widerspruchs, the spirit of contradiction: der Parthei—, party spirit; es beseelte sie Ein — des Wohlwollens und der Uneigennützigkeit, they were animated by one and the same spirit of benevolence and disinterestedness; der Buchstabe tödtet, der — aber macht lebendig [in Script.], the letter killeth, but the spirit giveth life *c)* [peculiar way of thinking and acting] Er hat seines Vaters —, he has his father's turn of mind, temper, or spirit; der — dieses Volkes, unseres Jahrhunderts ist leicht und veränderlich, the spirit of this nation, of our age is light and changeable; er hat diesen Schriftsteller nachahmen wollen, aber er hat den — desselben nicht aufgefaßt, he had a mind to imitate that author, but did not enter into the spirit of him. *Fig.* the peculiar character of a thing. Der — des Christenthums, the genius of Christianism; das ist dem —e unserer Sprache zuwider, ist gegen den — unserer Sprache, this is against the genius of our language. *d)* [in Script.] spirit [opposed to flesh]. Wandelt im —e, so werdet ihr die Lüste des Fleisches nicht vollbringen, walk in the spirit and ye shall not fulfil the lust of the flesh; das Fleisch gelüstet wider den —, the flesh lusteth against the spirit. *e)* power of thinking, vigour of intellect. Ein Mann von —, a man of parts, a man of genius; [in fam. lang.] sie hat — wie ein Engel, she is as witty as an angel; er hat einen hohen —, he is of a lofty mind [he aspires after high things], *it.* he is very proud or haughty; er hat einen lebhaften, erfinderischen —, he has a sprightly mind, an inventive head or genius; die Stärke, die Erhabenheit des Geistes, the power, the elevation of the mind; *fig.* dieses Gedicht hat vielen —, there is a great deal of sense or wit in this poem; ein starker —, a powerful mind, *it.* [chiefly in joke] a man who does not believe in the existence of spirits or spectres. *f)* a man with regard to his way of thinking. Ein großer —, a great mind or genius; ein kleiner —, a man of little wit or understanding, *it.* a narrow mind; ein starker, ein Frei—, a freethinker; ein schöner — [ein Schön—], a wit, a genius, [sometimes in contempt] witling, V. Flattergeist, Schwindelgeist. 3) [bodiless being] spirit. Gott ist ein —, God is a spirit; der unerschaffene —, the uncreated spirit; der heilige —, the Holy Ghost. [in a more limited sense] *a)* the power of this spirit. Der — Gottes, the spirit of God; die Ausgießung des heiligen —es, the pouring out of the Holy Ghost; als der — des Herrn die Propheten antrieb, when the spirit of the Lord inspired the prophets; der — [die Gabe] der Weissagung, the spirit of prophecy. *b)* [a single being of the spirit kind] Die himmlischen, die seligen —er, the heavenly, the blessed spirits [= the angels]; ein böser —, ein — der Finsterniß, evil demon or spirit, spirit of darkness; unsaubere —er, unclean spirits; [= Gespenst] apparition, spectre, spirit, ghost; es geht or läuft ein — in diesem Hause, es spuken —er in diesem Hause, this house is haunted; es geht ein — dort, there walks a spectre or ghost in that place; —er beschwören, to conjure, to raise or lay evil spirits, to exorcise; er sieht aus wie ein —, he looks like a ghost or spectre.

Geist⸗anstrengend, [properly, *pres. part.* of anstrengen, den Geist] *adj.* exerting or fatiguing the mind. —**arm**, *adj.* having little wit or understanding; [in Script.] poor in spirit —

ers-bann, m. V. —er-beschwörung. —ers-banner, m. V. —er-beschwörer. —ers-bannerei, —bannung, f. V. —er beschwörung. —ers-beherrscher, m. —ers-beherrscherinn, f. prince, princess of demons, of gnomes, of sylphs &c. —ers-beschwörer, m. one that lays ghosts or spirits, conjurer, [in the Catholic church] exorcist. —ers-beschwörung, f. conjuration of [evil] spirits, [in the Catholic church] exorcism. —ers-bild, n. phantom. —ers-erscheinung, f. apparition of spirits or of a ghost. Er hat —ers-erscheinungen, he has visions. — —ers-furcht, f. fear of spirits or spectres. —ers-fürst, m. V. —er-beherrscher. —ers-geschichte, f. a tale or story of spirits or spectres, a ghost-story. —ers-haft, adj and adv. like a ghost or spectre. —ers-herrschaft, f. empire over spirits or demons. —ers-könig, m. king of spirits or demons. —ers-lehre, f. doctrine of spirits, pneumatology. —ers-mährchen, n. V. —er-geschichte. —ers-reich, n. V. —er-welt. —ers-seher, m. one that sees ghosts and spirits, ghost-seer, visionary. —ers-seherei, f. the wild fancies of a visionary. —ers-stunde, f. hour when the ghosts and spirits are said to be abroad, midnight. —ers-welt, f. the world of spirits, intellectual world. —es-abwesend, adj. absent of mind. —es-abwesenheit, f. absence of mind. Er hat häufige —es-abwesenheiten, he is frequently absent. —es-anstrengung, f. exertion of the mind. —es-bildung, f. cultivation of the mind. Die fortschreitende —es-bildung, the march of intellect. —es-entwickelung, development of the mind. —es-freiheit, f. liberty of the mind; it. intellectual freedom. —es-freuden, pl. the pleasures of the mind. —es-frucht, f the production or product of the mind or genius. Die —es-früchte dieses Schriftstellers, the literary productions or works of this author —es-gabe, endowment of mind, talent. Ein Mann von großen —es-gaben, ohne alle —es-gaben, a man of great talents, without any talent. —es-geburt, f. a work or production of the mind. —es-gegenwart, f. presence of mind. —es-größe, f. greatness of mind, magnanimity. —es-kraft, f. 1) power of the mind, energy. Mit —es-kraft handeln, to act with energy, energetically. 2) any faculty of the soul or mind. Die —es-kräfte sind sehr verschieden, the faculties of the mind are very different. —es-schwäche, f. debility of mind, imbecility. —es-schwung, m. the flight of fancy or genius. —es-stärke, f. strength of the mind, fortitude. —es-verstörung, —es-verirrung, f. bewilderment; it. a roving or wandering of the mind, delirium. —es-werk, V. —es-geburt. —hell, adj. having great capacity, having a penetrating or quick understanding. —leer, adj. and adv. [destitute of Geist, which see] Ein —leerer Mensch, a man destitute of wit and genius, a flat, insipid fellow; ein —leeres Gesicht, a face without expression, a dull or vacant face; ein —leeres Gedicht, a poem wanting wit or genius, a dull, heavy poem. —los, adj. and adv. destitute of wit or genius, wanting spirit, spiritless, dull, insipid, without point or spirit. Ein —loser Mensch, a flat, insipid, dull man; eine —lose Unterhaltung, a dull, heavy or insipid conversation; ein —loses Gesicht, a face without expression, an unmeaning, vacant face. —reich, adj. and adv. 1) [containing a great deal of spirit] spirituous. —reicher Wein, spirituous, generous wine. 2) [possessed of genius and proceeding from genius or ingenuity] ingenious, witty, spirited. Ein —reicher Schriftsteller, an ingenious author; ein —reiches Gedicht, an ingenious, spirited poem; sie hat ein —reiches Aeußeres, eine —reiche Gesichtsbildung, she has a sprigthly, animated, expressive countenance; eine sehr —reiche Antwort, a very ingenious, witty answer or reply; er antwortete sehr —reich, he replied very ingeniously, very wittily. —voll, adj. and adv. V. —reich.

Geistig, adj. and adv. 1) [containing spirit] spirituous. Ein —er [starker] Wein, a spirituous, strong, racy, generous wine; Einem alle —en Getränke verbieten, to forbid any one all spirituous liquors; die —en Theile aus einem Körper ziehen, to extract the spirituous parts of a substance. 2) [consisting of spirit only, not material] spiritual. Ein —es Wesen, a spiritual substance or being; die —e Welt, the intellectual world. 3) [suitable to the mind, not sensual] —e Freuden, pleasures of the mind; —e Kräfte, intellectual powers or faculties; das —e Leben eines Christen, the spiritual life of a Christian. 4) little used for geistreich, which see.

Geistigkeit, f. 1) quality of being spirituous, spirituosity, spirituousness. 2) spirituality.

Geistisch, adj. and adv. having the semblance of spirit.

Geistlich, I. adj. 1) [opposed to corporeal; in this sense obsolete] spiritual. Der —e Mensch, das —e Leben, the spiritual man, spiritual life; —e Gaben, spiritual gifts. 2) [opposed to lay or temporal] spiritual, ecclesiastical. —e Lieder, —e Bücher, spiritual songs, spiritual or religious books; eine —e Person, a clerical person; die —en Güter und Einkünfte, the ecclesiastical estates and revenues; sich dem —en Stande widmen, to go into the church, to take orders; ein —er Rath, [a title among the Roman-Catholic clergy] an ecclesiastical counsellor; die —en Personen [Ordensleute], the persons belonging to a religious order, monks or nuns, the religious; in einen —en Orden treten, to enter into a religious order; [in German history] die —en und weltlichen Fürsten des Reichs, the ecclesiastic and secular princes of the empire; —e Verrichtungen, the duties or functions of a clergyman, clerical duties; —es Gericht, an ecclesiastical or spiritual [tribunal or] court; das —e Recht, [Kirchenrecht], canon-law, church-law; der —e Orden, ecclesiastical or clerical order; —er Vater, ghostly father; —e Stiftungen, religious foundations. II. adv. 1) spiritually. [in Script.] —richten, to judge spiritually; —arm seyn, to be poor in spirit. 2) like an ecclesiastic or clergyman, ecclesiastically. —gekleidet seyn, —leben, to be dressed, to live like a clergyman.

Geistliche, m. [-n, pl. -n] clerk, clergyman, ecclesiastic. Er ist ein —r, he is a clergyman, a churchman; ein anglikanischer —r or ein —r der Englischen Kirche, a clergyman of the Anglican church, a [high-] church-man; die Englischen —n, the English clergy; ein katholischer —r, a catholic priest; ein —r der presbyterianischen Kirche, a minister of the Scottish or presbyterian church; ein reformirter —r, a Calvinist pastor or minister; ein protestantischer —r, a Lutheran pastor or minister.

Geistlichkeit, f. the body of ecclesiastics, the clergy. Die — ist dort sehr geachtet, the clergy or the clergymen are greatly respected there; die Welt—, the secular clergy; die Ordens—, the regular clergy.

Geistlosigkeit, f. want of spirit, dulness, insipidity.

Geitau, n. [-es, pl. -e] [a sea-term] [a rope fastened to the aftmost leech of fore-and-aft sails to truss them up, also all ropes employed to haul up the foot, clues and leeches of other large sails, for the more readily furling of them] clue-line, clue-garnet, brail.

1. **Geiz**, m. [-es] [allied to the Dan. *gide* and the Celtic *geidziu, to desire*, as also to the Germ. Gier] 1) any eager desire. Der — nach Ruhm, the inordinate desire of renown or glory, the thirst for glory; der — nach Siegen, the thirst for or after victories. 2) [inordinate desire of gaining and possessing wealth] covetousness, avarice. Dem —e ergeben seyn, to be addicted to avarice; vom —e besessen seyn, to be possessed with avarice; schmutziger —, sordid avarice, stinginess; der — ist eine Wurzel alles Uebels, [in Script.] avarice or the love of money is the root of all evil.

†**Geiz-drache**, —hals, —hund, —kragen, —teufel, —wurm, m. [in contempt] a stingy, miserly fellow, a miser, churl, niggard, curmudgeon.

2. **Geiz**, m. [-es] [allied to the Sw. *gödsel* = excrescence] [in botany] something growing out from a plant. *a*) the tendrils or claspers of vines and other plants. *b*) the superfluous leaves of tobacco plants. *c*) superfluous and empty shoots or ears in the Indian corn.

1. **Geizen**, [V. 1. Geiz] v. intr. 1) to desire or wish for with eagerness. Nach Ehre, nach Ruhm —, to covet honour, glory. it. to be greedy of money, to be covetous, avaricious. Er mag — wie er will, so wird er doch nie reich werden, let him be ever so stingy or niggardly, he will never be rich. 2) [in a good sense] to be sparing of something. Mit der Zeit —, to be niggard of time; er geizt sehr mit seinem Lobe, he is a great niggard of his praise.

2. **Geizen**, [V. Geiz 2.] v. tr. to clear off the superfluous leaves of the tobacco plants; it. to prune the vines.

Geizig, I. adj. 1) very eager or desirous to obtain, covetous. Nach Ruhm, nach Ehre —, covetous of fame, of honour. it. [= geldgierig] greedy of money, avaricious, covetous. Ein —er Alter, a stingy, niggardly old fellow, an old miser. 2) [opposed to lavish or profuse] sparing. Die Natur ist mit ihren Gaben — gegen ihn gewesen, nature has been sparing of her gifts towards him, has not been lavish of &c. II. adv. 1) greedily. — essen, to eat greedily. it. covetously, avariciously. 2) sparingly.

Gejammer, n. [-s] wailing, lamentations.

Gejauchze, n. [-s] repeated outcries of joy and exultation, repeated shouting. Er wurde mit lautem — empfangen or aufgenommen, he was received with great huzzaing.

Gejubel, n. [-s] repeated cries of joy and exultation, shouting, shouts, rejoicings.

||**Gekampel**, n. [-s] [in fam. language] a continual disputing and quarrelling, perpetual quarrels.

Gekämpfe, n. [-s] [in familiar language] a continual fighting or combating; obstinate fight or conflict.

||**Gekauder**, n. [-s] [in fam. lang.] a continual jargon, gabble or gibberish.

Gekeife, n. [-s] [in fam. lang.] continual quarrelling, scolding or disputing. V. Gezänk.

Gekelcht, adj. and part. [in botany] having a cup.

Gekelter, n. [-s] 1) a repeated pressing of wine. 2) as much wine as is pressed at a time.

Gekitzel, n. [-s] continual tickling.

Gekläffe, n. [-s] constant barking or yelping [of young dogs]; [in fam. lang.] continual petty scolding or quarrelling; it. nonsensical talk, empty prattle, tittle-tattle.

Gekläpper, *n.* [-s] continual rattling, clacking. Das — der Zähne, the chattering of the teeth.

Geklätsche, *n.* [-s] 1) a clapping of hands, applause; *it.* the cracking or smacking of a whip &c. 2) [in fam. lang.] prattle, babble, tittle-tattle, *it.* gossip's tale or story.

Gekleint, *adj.* and *part.* —e Kohlen, [in pyrotechnics] pulverised charcoal for fireworks.

Geklimper, *n.* [-s] a constant clashing or tinkling. Das — mit Gelde, jingling of money.

Geklingel, *n.* [-s] tinkling, ringing of a bell.

Geklirre, *n.* [-s] clashing or clang [of arms].

Geklöpfe, *n.* [-s] a continual knocking.

Geknätter, *n.* [-s] crackling, crepitation.

Geknirsche, *n.* [-s] the grinding or gnashing of teeth.

Geknister, *n.* [-s] V. Geknatter.

Geköpert, *adj.* and *part.* twilled.

Gekräche, *n.* [-s] crash, continual cracking.

Gekrätz, *n.* [-es, *pl.* -e] [among workers in metal] waste matter, chippings, chips, fragments; [among goldsmiths] washings.

Gekräusel, *n.* [-s] 1) the act of curling, crisping or frizling. 2) something curled, crisped or frizzled. Das — des Haares, curled hair; das — des Hemdes, the bosom of a shirt, frill, ruffle.

Gekraut, *n.* [-es] V. Kräuterwerk.

Gekreische, *n.* [-s] continual screaming or shrieking.

Gekritzel, *n.* [-s] scribbling, scrawl. Ich kann dieses — nicht lesen, I cannot read or make out these pot-hooks.

Gekröse, *n.* [-s] [allied to Kragen, collar; in Low Sax. Kröse signifies a collar] 1) a piece of plaited linen or a kind of ruff worn by clergymen around the neck. 2) [= Busenstreif] the bosom of a shirt, frill, ruffle. 3) [a double membrane placed in the middle of the intestines] mesentery; [in medicine and physiology] epichordis. Das — eines Kalbes, eines Lammes, a calf's pluck, a lamb's pluck; das — von Gänsen, goose giblets.

Gekrös=ader, *f.* [in anatomy, a vein pertaining to the mesentery] mesaraic vein. —**blutader**, *f.* mesenteric vein. —**drüse**, *f.* mesenteric gland. —**drüsengang**, *m.* the pancreatic duct or conduct. —**entzündung**, *f.* inflammation of the mesentery, mesenteritis. —**fell**, *n.* V. —haut. —**gefäße**, *pl.* mesenteric vessels. —**geflecht**, *n.* [in anatomy] mesenteric plexus. —**haut**, *f.* mesenteric membrane, mesentery. —**mantel**, *m.* V. Gekröse 3). —**schlagader**, *f.* [in anatomy] mesenteric artery.

Gekünstel, *n.* [-s] V. Künstelei.

Geküsse, *n.* [-s] continual kissing, repeated kisses; *it.* mutual kissing.

1. **Geläch**, *n.* [-es] V. Gelächter 1).

2. **Geläch**, *n.* [-es, *pl.* -e] V. Lache, Sumpf; [among hunters] soil.

Gelächel, *n.* [-s] continual smiling.

Gelächter, *n.* [-s] 1) a fit of laughing, loud laughter. Ein —, ein lautes, schallendes — erheben, aufschlagen, to break or burst out into laughter, into a loud laugh, a horse-laugh, to laugh immoderately; es erhob sich, es entstand ein großes, ein allgemeines — in der Gesellschaft, the whole company burst out into a loud laugh. 2) [object of ridicule] laughing-stock. Der ganzen Stadt zum — werden, to become a laughing-stock to all the town; sich zum — machen, to expose one's self to ridicule or derision, to make or render one's self ridiculous; Einen zum — machen, to turn any one into ridicule, to make any one ridiculous, to ridicule any one; ich weiß sehr wohl, daß diese Heurath mich zum — der Welt machen wird, I know very well that this marriage will bring upon me the ridicule of the world.

Geladene, *m.* [-n, *pl.* -n] [one who has been invited to some repast or festival] a guest.

Gelag, *n.* [-es, *pl.* -e] 1) [in mining] layer, stratum. 2) feast, entertainment, banquet, V. Sauf—, Trink—. Bei —en ist er in seinem Elemente, banqueting, feasting is his element; —e halten, to riot, to revel; das — bezahlen or bezahlen müssen, to pay for others, *fig* *to suffer for others, to pay dear for one's rashness; in's — hineinreden, to talk at random, so speak nonsense; sie spricht in's —, her tongue runs on wheels, at random, before her wits.

Geläger, *n.* [-s] 1) the act of encamping, encampment. 2) [the place where an army or company is encamped] encampment, camp.

‡**Gelahrt**, **Gelährtheit**, V. Gelehrt, Gelehrtheit.

Gelälle, *n.* [-s] lisping, stammering [of children.]

Geländle, *n.* [-s] a tract of land; a landscape. Ein lachendes —, a smiling landscape or country. *it.* land. Das Pachtgut hat fünfhundert Morgen — [an Aeckern &c.], the farm consists of five hundred acres of land.

Geländer, *n.* [-s, *pl.* -] [a row of balusters joined by a rail] balustrade. Das — einer Treppe, einer Brücke, um einen Altar, the balustrade or rails of a stair-case, of a bridge, the railings of an altar; [in architecture, a fence or inclosure for the top of a building] a balustrade; [in gardening, lattice or woodwork to which trees &c. are trained up] espalier, trellis, V. Baum— &c.; [in seamen's lang.] die — zu beiden Seiten des Gallions eines Schiffes, the rails of the head, head-rails; die — am Hintertheile eines Schiffes, the quarter-rails.

Geländer=docke, *f.* [in architecture, a small column or pilaster used for balustrades] baluster. Die —docken des Gallions [in seamen's lang.], the rails of the head. —**fenster**, *n.* [in architecture] a window with a balcony. —**säule**, *f.* V. —docke.

Geländern, [rather unusual] *v. tr.* to encompass, inclose or adorn with rails or with a balustrade, to rail.

Gelänge, *n.* [-s] [in husbandry] a field of considerable length.

Gelangen, *v. intr.* [u. w. seyn] to arrive at, to come to, to reach. Er gelangte um 10 Uhr an das Thor, he arrived at, got to or reached the gate at ten o'clock; sein Name gelangte zu den Ohren des Königs, his name reached the ears of the king; an's Ziel, zu seinem Ziele, Zwecke —, to attain the end or purpose in view, to compass one's ends; zu einem Amte, zu Ansehen —, to arrive at, to get or obtain a place or office, to get or obtain a name, esteem or reputation; zu Reichthum —, to get or acquire riches; wann ist er zur Krone gelangt? when or what time did he arrive at the throne? zur Reife —, to come to maturity; zu einiger Vollkommenheit —, to arrive at, to attain [to] some perfection; etwas an Einen — lassen, to transmit something to any one, to get something delivered to any one; auf die Nachwelt — lassen, to transmit to posterity; eine Bittschrift an den König — lassen, to address a petition to the king.

Gelangung, *f.* the act of coming to or arriving at a place or thing. Die — zum Ziele, the attainment of one's end or purpose, success; die — zum Throne, the accession to the crown.

Geläppe, *n.* [-s] [among hunters] V. Gehänge.

Gelärm, *n.* [-es] continued noise and bustle, a tumult, uproar. Sich dem —e der Welt entziehen, to withdraw or retire from the noise of the world.

Gelaß, *m.* [-sses] 1) [= Raum] room, space. Dieses Haus hat viel —, there is a great deal of room in this house, this house is very roomy; ich habe in dieser Wohnung — genug für meine Familie, I have room enough or ample room in this lodging for my family. 2) the property left by a person at his death, succession, inheritance; [in law] mortmain.

Gelassen, I. *adj.* 1) [free from violent passions] calm, composed, moderate, temperate, tranquil, dispassionate, sedate, cool. — bleiben, to keep one's temper; er sagte mit einem —en Tone, he said with a moderate or temperate tone. 2) [particularly] patient. Ein —er Mensch, a patient person, or a person of patient temper; er bleibt bei den größten Schmerzen —, he bears or suffers patiently the greatest pains. II. *adv.* 1) calmly, sedately, quietly, coolly, temperately, moderately. Hören Sie mich — an, hear me calmly or quietly; — mit Einem reden, to speak coolly or dispassionately with any one. 2) patiently. Unterwirf dich — den unvermeidlichen Uebeln des Lebens, submit patiently to the unavoidable evils of life. S... V. Geduldig.

Gelassenheit, *f.* 1) [= Mäßigung] moderation, calmness of mind. Die — ist eine seh[r] nothwendige Tugend, moderation is a very necessary virtue; Glück oder Unglück mit — tragen, to bear prosperity or adversity with moderation; er hörte diese beleidigenden Aeußerungen mit großer —, he heard these insults with great composure, very sedately; er wurde hitzig, aber ich kam nicht aus meiner —, he flew into a passion, but I kept my temper; dem Tode mit großer — [*Resignation] entgegen gehen, to meet death with great resignation. 2) [particularly] patience. Alles mit — ertragen, to suffer and bear every thing with patience, patiently.

Gelaufe, *n.* [-s] a continual running to and fro, up and down. Diese Nacht war ein beständiges — in den Straßen, there was a continual noise of people running about in the streets last night.

Geläufig, I. *adj.* fluent, easy, ready; practised, familiar. Eine —e Hand, a current hand; eine —e Hand haben, to write with fluency, fluently; er hat eine —e Zunge, he has a voluble tongue, a great volubility or fluency of speech, he speaks very fluently; diese Sprache ist ihm so —, als seine Muttersprache, the language is as familiar to him as his mother tongue; das ist ihm —, that is easy for him, he understands that very well, that is well known to him. II. *adv.* fluently, easily, readily. Er spricht Deutsch sehr —, he speaks German very fluently.

Geläufigkeit, *f.* fluency, volubility, easiness. Die — der Zunge, the volubility of the tongue.

Gelaunt, *adj.* and *adv.* 1) inclined, disposed. Wie ist er heute —? how is he disposed to-day? in what humour or disposition is he to-day? er ist wohl or gut —, übel —, he is in good humour, he is good-humoured, he is in an ill humour, he is cross or peevish. 2) good-humoured. Er war sehr —, he was very good humoured, very gay; er war nicht —, he was out of humour.

Gelaut, *n.* [-es] [among hunters] the barking, the tongue of a dog.

Geläut, *n.* [-es, *pl.* -e] or **Geläute**, *n.* [-s, *pl.*-] 1) ringing of bells. In diesem Kloster ist ein ewiges —, there is a perpetual ringing of bells in this convent, the bells are perpetually ringing in this convent; er hört gern das — der Glocken, he is fond of hearing the bells ring, he loves a peal of bells; er zog unter dem — aller Glocken in die Stadt ein, all the bells were ringing when he entered the town; das — bezahlen, [at a funeral] to pay for tolling the bell; das — der Todtenglocken, knell; das — der Abendglocken, curfew. 2) the bells themselves. Bei dieser Kirche ist, diese Kirche hat ein schönes —, the bells of this church are very fine, sound very harmoniously; das ganze —, all the bells; das — an einem Schlitten, the bells of a sledge.

Gelb, [Lat. *gilv*-us, *galb* us, originally = flämmend] *adj.* and *adv.* yellow. —e Blumen, yellow flowers; eine —e Gesichtsfarbe, Haut haben, to have a yellow complexion, skin; —er Ocher, yellow ochre; die —e Rübe, carrot; die —e Sucht, jaundice; etwas — färben, to dye something yellow; — werden, to grow yellow, to take a yellow hue; das Korn wird —, the corn ripens; [among goldsmiths] —e Nadeln, touch-needles [used in assaying]; *fig.* * es wird mir grün und — vor den Augen, I am seized or taken with a giddiness, with a dizziness or swimming in the head, my head is swimming or turning round. V. Gold—, Oranien—.

Gelb=ammer, *f.* V. Goldammer —äu=ig, *adj.* having yellow eyes, yellow-eyed. —and, *n.* [in natural history] 1) a black sparrow with a yellow band. 2) a kind of goatchafer.) a black butterfly with yellow bands. —eere, *f.* the berry of a kind of buck-thorn that grows in the South of Europe, yellow-erry. —bein, —beinchen, *n.* a sea-fowl or kind of sand-piper with yellow legs and feet. -blätterig, *adj.* having yellow leaves. —raun, —bräunlich, *adj.* yellowish-brown. Das —braun, filemot. —brust, *f.* —brüstchen, *n.* a little bird with a yellow breast and eck, belonging to the nightingale kind. —unt, *adj.* variegated with yellow [in botany] -bunte Blätter, leaves irregularly marked ith yellow spots, variegated leaves. —erde, yellow earth; *it.* yellow colour, yellow ochre. -erz, *n.* [in mining] yellowish gold ore. —rbig, *adj.* of yellow colour, yellow coloured. -fink, *m.* yellow-hammer, V. Goldamm. —fisch, *m.* a yellowish fish. —flosser, sea-perch with yellow fins. —flügel, *m.* denomination of several birds with yellow ngs, as: the yellow water-wag-tail of America, e wit-wal of Cayenne. —fuß, *m.* V. —fs. —gar, *adj.* [among tawers] tawed or dres-d. —geblümt, *adj.* [said of stuffs] with yelw flowers. —gestreift, *adj.* with yellow ipes. —gießer, *m* brazier, brass-founder. grün, *adj.* yellowish green, gosling-green. grünlich, *adj.* yellow greenish. —holz, fustic. —kehlchen, *n.* V. —brüstchen. —hle, *f.* [in natural history] the gross-beak or wfinch of the Cape of Good Hope. —kopf, the sparrow of Bengal; *it.* the wag-tail of nada; the yellow-headed wit-wal. —körr, *pl.* V. —beere. —kupfer, *n.* yellow pper. —nase, *f.* [a kind of sandpiper] godwit. reif, *adj.* [said of corn] ripe so as to be yel-, yellow-ripe. —reife, *f.* [in husbandry] ne of perfect maturity. —roth, *adj.* yellow-red. —röthlich, *adj.* reddish-yellow. schecke, *f.* a pie-bald horse with yellow ts upon a white ground. —schild, *n.* [in ural history] yellow staphylinus or cassida. schnabel, *m.* 1) [a kind of halcyon] king-fisher. 2) [a kind of eagle] the large pygarg or pygargus. 3) V. —fink. 4) [a young unfledged bird] yellow-beak, callow-bird; *fig* * [a silly young fellow] ninny. —schnäbelig, *adj.* with a yellow beak. *Fig.* * Ein — schnäbeliger Mensch, a pert, saucy young fellow; a ninny. —schopf, *m.* [birds with a yellow crest or tuft] *a*) an American woodpecker with a yellow crest. *b*) a kind of wild duck with a yellow crest. —schwanz, *m.* any animal with a yellow tail, but chiefly the yellow-tailed perch. —specht, *m.* yellow woodpecker. —sucht, *f.* jaundice. Die —sucht bei Thieren, the yellows; ein Mittel gegen die —sucht, a remedy for the jaundice, icteric. —süchtig, *adj.* affected with the jaundice, jaundiced, icteric. —suchtwurzel, *f.* V. —wurzel. —wasser, *n.* [in medicine, a species of dropsy] ascites. —wurzel, *f.* [in botany, an Indian plant] Indian saffron, turmeric, the root of the Curcuma longa.

Gelbe, *n.* [-n] the yellow. Das — des Goldes, des Strohes &c., the yellow colour of gold, of straw &c.; dieser Zeug sticht in's —, this stuff inclines to yellow; das — im Ei, vom Ei, the yellow part of an egg, the yolk; das — an Pasteten, the eggs wherewith the pastry-cooks wash their pies over; das — sticht gegen das Blau schön ab, the yellow contrasts beautifully with the blue.

Gelben, I. *v. intr.* 1) to grow yellow, to take a yellow hue. Das Getreide gelbet schon, the corn is already ripening. 2) to part with yellow, to stain yellow. II. *v. tr.* to make or dye yellow. III. *v. r.* sich —, to grow yellow.

Gelbing, *m.* [-es, *pl.* -e] [in seamen's lang.] gallery or balcony above the helm.

Gelblich, *adj.* yellowish; [of hair] fair or light. —braun, —grün, —roth, yellowish brown, green, red.

Gelbling, *m.* [-es, *pl.* -e] V. Goldammer.

Gelblisch, *m.* [-es] [in botany] yellow water-flag.

Geld, *n.* [-es, *pl.* -er] [from gelten, to be worth] money. Bares —, ready money, money in hand, cash; er hat in barem —e bezahlt, he has paid ready money or in cash; gangbares —, good current money; schlechtes —, bad or base money; gutes —, good money; hartes, grobes, ganzes —, large money, species or specie; abgeschätztes, herabgesetztes —, reduced money; verrufenes —, cried down money; kleines —, change; haben Sie klein — bei sich? have you got any change about you? er hat kein klein —, he has no [small] change; falsches —, false coin, false money; todtes —, müßig liegendes —, money which brings or yields no interest or turns to no account, dead capital; die öffentlichen —er, the public money, the public treasure; —münzen schlagen, prägen, to stamp, to coin money; eine Summe —es, a sum of money; er hat eine schöne Summe —es bei diesem Geschäfte gewonnen, he has got a handsome sum of money by that business or concern; — im Beutel haben, to have money in one's purse; — or —er aufnehmen [entlehnen], to borrow money; *fig.* * das ist nicht mit —e zu bezahlen, that is of infinite or inestimable value, it is invaluable; Einem sein — abnehmen, [as a robber &c.] to rob any one of his money, [in gaming] to win of any one, *it.* * to trick any one out of his money; etwas zu —e machen, in's — setzen, to make money of a thing; etwas zu barem —e machen, [to sell something for ready money] to turn something into ready money or into cash; *fig.* aus Allem — machen [Nutzen ziehen], to make every thing turn to account; * *fig.* sich —, sich ein — machen, sich — verdienen, to gain or earn money; *fig.* * von seinem —e leben, to live upon one's income; *fig.* * nicht bei —e seyn [kein bares — haben], to be short of money, to be out of cash; *fig.* * nicht sehr bei —e seyn, to be low in cash, das — sehe ich dabei nicht an, ich achte dabei kein —, I do not mind or regard the money in that affair; — über — für etwas bieten, to offer a great deal of money for a thing; *fig.* * er hat sich's viel — kosten lassen, he has gone to a great expense, he has spent a great deal of money for it; man fand in seinem Hause 100 Thaler an —e, an barem —e, they found a hundred dollars in specie in his house; Einen an —e, um — strafen, to impose on one a pecuniary penalty, to fine, to mulct any one; es ist gegenwärtig kein — unter den Leuten, money is scarce at present; es ist viel falsches — im Umlauf, there is a great deal of bad money in circulation; * — und Gut haben [— und Güter haben], to be a warm, a wealthy man, to have plenty of every thing; *prov.* bar — lacht, — ist die Losung, ready money is a medicine; gutes — gegen schlechtes hingeben, [to risk one's money] to throw away good money upon bad; um bares — spielen, to play fair and for ready money, to stake money; wer — hat, hat Alles genug, money commands every thing; das ist so gut als bares —, that is as good as ready money; *fig.* * er nimmt Alles für bares —, he believes any thing one says, he is too credulous, V. Bar 3); *prov.* leicht —, leichte Waare, kupfern —, kupferne Seelenmessen, one cannot get much for little money; *fig.* † er hat — wie Heu, er mißt das — mit Scheffeln [ist sehr reich], he rolls in money; er hat —, he has a great deal of money, he is well off, he is a moneyed man; das — macht es nicht aus, money is not a cure for every sore, money alone does not make happy; bei dieser Heurath ist es nur auf das — abgesehen, money is the only thing looked to in that marriage, it is a money-match; *prov.* — regiert die Welt, money governs the world.

Geld=adel, *m.* 1) the consideration or respect money or fortune confers upon any one. 2) purchased or bought nobility. —angelegenheit, *f.* pecuniary affair. Er kam in einer —angelegenheit, in —angelegenheiten zu mir, he came to see me on money-matters; *it.* * he came to request from me a loan of money. —arm, *adj* and *adv.* poor in money, moneyless. —auflage, *f.* imposition or tax [consisting of money]. —ausgabe, *f.* expenditure in ready money, expense. —bedarf, *m.* want of money. —bedürftig, *adj.* wanting money. —begierde, *f.* inordinate desire of money, greediness, thirst for money, avarice. —begierig, *adj* greedy of money, covetous of money, avaricious —beitrag, *m.* a contribution in money. —belohnung, *f.* recompense or reward consisting of money, pecuniary reward or remuneration. —beschneider, *m.* [he who diminishes coin by paring the edge] money-clipper, V. Kipper. —besitz, *m.* possession of money. —beutel, *m.* money-bag, purse. —beutelchen, *n.* a small purse. —büchse, *f.* money-box, till. —bürge, *m.* one who is security for a sum of money. —buße, *f.* V. —strafe. —dieb, *m* money-thief. —diebstahl, *m.* money theft. —durst, *m.* [a great desire of money] thirst after money. —einnahme, *f.* receipt of money. —einnehmer, *m.* receiver of money, cashier. —erwerb, *m.* money-making. Auf —erwerb sinnen, ausgehen, to be intent on acquiring or making money. —faß, —fäßchen, *n.* a cask or barrel of money.

—foderung, *f.* 1) a demand of money, pecuniary claim or demand. —foderungen an Einen machen, to ask or demand money of any one, to dun 2) a sum of money demanded or due. *—fressend, *adj.* requiring much money, costly, expensive. —geben, *n.* paying, payment. —gefälle, *pl.* dues or revenues consisting of ready money. —geiz, *m.* avaricious desire of money, covetousness of money, avarice. —geizig, *adj.* covetous or greedy of money, avaricious. —geschäft, *n.* V. —sache. —gier, *f.* V. —begierde. —gierig, *adj.* greedy or covetous of money, avaricious. —gülte, *f.* a rent paid in money. —gürtel, *m.* a belt for holding money, a leathern money-belt. —handel, *m.* traffic in money, money-dealing, banking. —händler, *m.* money-broker; money-changer, banker, V. [the more usual words] —mäkler and —wechsler. —haufen, *m.* heap of money. —hülfe, *f.* 1) aid in money, pecuniary relief or assistance. 2) [the taxes furnished by the people to their prince] subsidy, supply. —hunger, *m.* an inordinate desire of money, greediness of money. —hungerig, *adj.* greedy of money. —jude, *m.* a Jew dealing in money; *fig.* a usurer. —kammer, *f.* a room in which money is deposited and kept, [hence] fisc, exchequer. —kästchen, *n.* a small money-box. —kasten, *m.* money-box, strong-box. —katze, *f.* V. —gürtel. —kipper, *m.* V. —beschneider. —kistchen, *n.* V. —kästchen. —kiste, *f.* money-chest, V. —kasten. —klemm, *adj.* short of money, low in cash. In diesen —klemmen Zeiten, in these times where money is so scarce. —klemme, *f.* scarcity of money; want of ready money, V. —mangel. —klumpen, *m.* V. —haufen. —körbchen, *n.* a small money-basket. —lade, *f.* money-box, till. —lehen, *n.* [Beutellehen] a tenure or fief which is acquired or held by paying money instead of knigthly services [as opposed to fiefs imposing the services of a knight]. V. also Bauerlehen. —liebe, *f.* love of money. —lieferung, *f.* supply or delivery of money; *it.* the sum delivered. —macher, *m.* coiner. —mäkler, *m.* money-broker, money-scrivener, stockbroker, exchange-broker; *it.* [sometimes, in contempt] banker. —mäklerei, *f.* traffic in money, the business of a money-scrivener. —mangel, *m.* want or scarcity of money. —männchen, *n.* [in botany] mandrake; *it.* [in German popular superstition] mandrake. —mittel, *n.* pecuniary resource, money. —muschel, *f.* [small univalvular porcelain-shell, made use of as money in India and Africa] cowries. —noth, *f.* a great scarcity or want of money, distress of money. —placker, *m.* extorter of money. —posten, *m.* sum of money due to any one. Er hat verschiedene —posten ausstehen, he has several sums of money due to him. —prägen, *n.* [the act or practice of stamping or coining money] coinage, coining. —preis, *m.* [in commerce] the course of exchange. —preisberechnung, *f.* arbitration of exchange, [calculation of the courses of exchange of different places]. —rechnung, *f.* money-account. —reich, *adj.* rich in money, moneyed. —rente, *f.* rent paid in money. —sache, *f.* pecuniary affair, money-matter. —sack, *m.* money-bag. —sammler, *m.* 1) a collector of money; *it.* tax-gatherer. 2) one who gathers money by small savings, a scraper, save-penny. —schachtel, *f.* money-box. —schaden, *m.* loss of money, pecuniary loss. †—schneider, *m.* exactor, extortioner of money. †—schneiderei, *f.* extortion of money, sharping, sharking, tricking. —schrank, *m.* money-chest, till. —schuld, *f.* debt contracted by the loan of money. —sendung, *f.* [Rimesse] remittance of money. —sorge, *f.* care caused by money. —sorte, *f.* sort of money, coin. Einen in guten, gangbaren —sorten bezahlen, to pay any one in good current coin or money. —spende, *f.* alms consisting of money. —splitternd, *adj.* requiring much money, costly, expensive. —splitterung, *f.* waste of money, great expense. —steuer, *f.* impost or contribution in money. —stock, *m* 1) poor's box. 2) (Grund—, Stamm—) fund, capital, stock. *Fig.* Der —stock eines Landes, the specie of a country. —stolz, I. *adj.* and *adv.* purseproud. II. *m.* purse-pride. —strafe, *f.* pecuniary penalty or mulct, fine, mulct; [in law] amercement. —stück, *n.* piece of money, coin. —sucht, *f.* V. —gier. —süchtig, *adj.* V. —gierig. —summe, *f.* a sum of money. —tasche, *f.* a pocket or a bag for carrying money. —tisch, *m.* 1) [in commerce] counter. 2) board or diet for which one pays. Den —tisch bei Jemand haben, to be boarded at any one's expense. —umlauf, *m.* circulation of money. —verächter, *m.* despiser, scorner of money. —verlegenheit, *f.* pecuniary embarrassment. —verleiher, *m.* money-lender. —verlust, *m.* loss of money. —verprasser, —verschwender, *m.* [one who spends money profusely or improvidently] a prodigal, a spendthrift. —verprassung, —verschwendung, *f.* prodigality, extravagance. —vortheil, *m.* pecuniary advantage or profit. —wechsel, *m.* 1) exchange of money. 2) the banking business. —wechsler, *m.* money-changer, banker. —wucher, *m.* —wucherei, *f.* usury; *it.* stockjobbing. —wucherer, *m.* usurer; *it.* jobber, stockjobber. —zulage, *f.* augmentation of any one's wages or salary, consisting of money.

Gëldern, *n.* [province of Holland] Guelderland; *it.* [the town] Guelders.

Gëlderrose, *f.* [*pl.* -n] guelder-rose, gelder-rose.

Gëldeswerth, I. *adj.* and *adv.* being worth money. II. *m.* something that will bring money, money's worth. Geld und —, money and money's worth, riches, wealth.

Gelëben, *v. intr.* [obsolescent for leben] to live. Eines Andern Gnade —, to live upon any one's charity; der Hoffnung —, to be in hopes of &c.

***Gelée**, *n.* [-'s, *pl.* -s or -en] [pronounce either Schelch or as in the French] jelly. V. Gallerte.

Gelëge, *n* [-s] [among vine-dressers] a layer or branch of vine. Diese Weine sind ursprünglich von Burgundischem —, these wines are originally of Burgundian vines. [in husbandry] small heaps of corn in the fields.

Gelëgen, I. *adj.* 1) [placed with respect to any other object] situate, situated. Ein in der Königsstraße —es Haus, a house situated in King's Street; ein wohl, schlecht —es Haus, a well, badly situated house. V. Liegen. 2) [= wohl—] well situated. Ein —es Wirthshaus, a well situated inn; ein —er Ort, a convenient place. *Fig* a) [= passend] fit, proper [applied to time]. Kommen Sie zu einer —eren Zeit, come at a more seasonable or convenient time; Sie kommen mir zu —er Zeit, you come seasonably or opportunely, † in the very nick of time; das ist eine —e Zeit, that is a proper or fit opportunity. *b*) agreeable, convenient. Es ist mir jetzt nicht —, I am not at leisure now, I am now busy; er wird kommen, wenn or wann es ihm — seyn wird, he will come, if or when he thinks proper, or if it or when will suit him; heute ist es mir nicht —, dahin zu gehen, to day I am not in the humour, not disposed, I have no mind to go there. *c*) Es ist daran —, V Liegen. II. *adv.* seasonably, opportunely. Sie kommen mir sehr —, you come very seasonably or opportunely, † in the very nick of time.

Gelëgenheit, *f.* 1) [rarely or provincially] situation of a place. V. Lage. *Fig.* [= Beschaffenheit] nature, circumstance. Nach — der Umstände, according to circumstances. 2) peculiar arrangement or disposition of a place. Alle —en eines Hauses or in einem Hause kennen, to be acquainted with, or to know every nook and corner of a house; dieses Haus hat viele —en, there are a great many accommodations in this house, this house is very commodious. *Fig.* a) [in fam. lang.] pleasure, convenience, ease. Pflegen Sie Ihrer —, use your pleasure, serve your own ease and convenience; etwas mit einer guten — thun, to do something at one's ease or convenience. *b*) [suitable time combined with other favourable circumstances] opportunity, occasion. Bei dieser — sagte er mir, he told me on this occasion; er that Alles, was er bei dieser — thun konnte, he did every thing he could on that occasion; eine günstige —, a favourable opportunity; ich hatte keine —, Baden-Baden in der Saison zu sehen, I had no opportunity of seeing Baden-Baden during the Season; eine — suchen, finden, to seek, to find an occasion or opportunity; sich der — bedienen, die — wahrnehmen, in Acht nehmen or auskaufen, ergreifen, to seize, to embrace, to take an opportunity, *prov.* to take occasion by the forelock; eine — vorbei lassen, fahren lassen, aus den Händen lassen, to let slip or pass an occasion or opportunity, to neglect or lose an opportunity; auf eine — warten, to wait for an opportunity; — zu etwas geben, to give occasion to something, to occasion something; sie haben Euch keine — zu Klagen gegeben, they have not given you any occasion of complaint; sobald es die — gibt, sich — dazu findet, as soon as the opportunity offers or presents itself, on the first opportunity; ich werde es ihm bei — zurückgeben, I shall return it to him when any opportunity offers or occurs; *prov.* — macht Diebe, opportunity makes the thief; er hat eine gute — gefunden, sich zu verheirathen, he has made a good match. *it.* means of conveying persons or things. Etwas durch eine —, mit erster — schicken, to send or forward a thing, when an opportunity offers, by the first opportunity; mit — an einen Ort reisen, to take the opportunity of going or travelling to a place; mit seiner eigenen — reisen, to travel in one's own carriage, *it.* * [in joke] to go on foot; durch welche — schicken Sie ihm das Paket? by what conveyance or carriage do you send him the parcel? die Postkutsche ist eine sichere —, the stage-coach is a sure or safe conveyance. 3) [rather provincial] any place conveniently situated or arranged. Sich eine — auf dem Lande kaufen, to buy or purchase a country-seat, or an estate in the country; es ist hier eine — [= eine Wohnung] zu vermiethen, there is a lodging or an apartment to let here; eine — [= eine Wohnung] suchen, to look out for, to seek a lodging; die — [das heimliche Gemach], the necessary house, the privy, water-closet. *Fig.* Eine — [= eine Anstellung] suchen, to seek after an office.

Gelegenheits-dichter, *m.* one that makes verses or poems on particular occasions. —gedicht, *n.* a poem upon a particular occasion, an occasional poem. —macher, *m.* a procurer, go-between, pimp. —macherinn, *f.* a procuress, go-between, bawd. V Kuppler, Kupplerinn. —predigt, *f.* a sermon on some particular occasion. —schrift, *f.* a composition written on some particular occasion; *it.* a program, programma.

Gelegenheitlich, *adj.* and *adv.* V. Gelegentlich.

Gelegentlich, *adj.* and *adv.* incidental, occasional. Ich hatte eine —e Unterredung mit ihm, I had an incidental conversation with him; ich stattete ihm einen —en Besuch ab, I occasionally paid him a visit; ich werde ihn — daran erinnern, I shall remind him of it as opportunity offers; ich erfuhr —, daß &c, I heard or learned accidentally, that &c; wenn Sie ihn — sehen sollten, so sagen Sie ihm, if you should chance to see him, tell him; thun Sie das —, do that occasionally, at leisure.

Gelehrig, *adj.* and *adv.* [easily instructed] docile, tractable. Ein —er Knabe, Kopf, a docile boy, mind; dieser Bursche ist nicht sehr —, this lad is not very docile or tractable; Hunde sind viel —er, als viele andere Thiere, dogs are much more docile than many other animals; ein —es [lenkbares] Pferd, a manageable, tractable, docile horse.

Gelehrigkeit, *f.* docility, teachableness, tractableness. Die — der Elephanten ist bemerkenswerth, the docility of elephants is remarkable.

Gelehrsam, *adj.* and *adv.* V. Gelehrig.

Gelehrsamkeit, *f.* 1) learning, erudition, scholarship. Ein Mann von großer, seltener, tiefer —, a man of great, rare, deep learning or erudition; er besitzt viel —, he is a man eminent for erudition, a man of high attainments in science and literature, a great scholar; sich — erwerben, to acquire learning. 2) science, much used in composition, as Gottes—, Rechts— &c. *it.* [rarely used] V. Gelehrigkeit.

Gelehrt, I. *adj.* 1) that has been taught. Ein —er Eid, a formal oath when the person who is to take it has been duly informed of the nature of an oath. 2) taught. Ein —er Hund, a trained dog. 3) [versed in literature and science] learned. Ein —er Mann, a learned man; eine —e Frau, a learned woman; er ist sehr — in der Geschichte, in der Mathematik, he is very learned in history, in mathematics; man hält ihn für —, he passes for a man of learning or for a learned man; eine —e Gesellschaft, a literary society; die —e Welt, the commonwealth of learning, the republic of letters, the learned world, the literati. 4) [respecting or containing learning] learned. —e Reden, learned speeches; eine —e Abhandlung, a learned treatise; —e Beschäftigungen or Arbeiten, literary occupations or labours; —e Zeitungen, Anzeigen, literary gazettes or papers, literary reviews, literary advertisements; —e Musik, a learned or elaborate composition. *Fig.* Die —e Krankheit, hypochondriac complaints, hypochondria. II. *adv.* with learning or erudition, learnedly. Er spricht sehr — davon, he speaks very learnedly of it; er hat diese Frage — besprochen, he has discussed this question learnedly; — predigen, to evince a great deal of learning in one's sermons.

Gelehrte, *m.* [-n, *pl.* -n] learned man, scholar. Eine —, a learned woman; *prov.* —n ist gut predigen, a word to the wise is enough; die —n sind nicht dieser Meinung, the learned, the men of letters or literature, the literati are not of this opinion; die englischen —n, the English literati or scholars; er ist ein großer —r, he is a great scholar. V. Gottes—, Rechts— &c.

Gelehrten-bank, *f.* 1) [particularly in the constitution of the ancient German Empire] a bench on which the learned sit. 2) the learned themselves. —feind, *m.* an enemy to learning or literature. —freund, *m.* friend or patron of learning or literature. —republik, *f.* republic of letters, commonwealth of learning. —stand, *m.* learned profession; *it.* the learned, the literati. —verein, *m.* a literary society or academy. Ein Mitglied eines —vereins, a member of a literary club or society, an academician, academist. —waare, *f.* [chiefly in joke] literary apparatus, as: books, maps &c.

Gelehrtheit, *f.* V. Gelehrsamkeit 2).

Geleier, *n.* [-s] a continual playing on the hurdy-gurdy; a continual fiddling or scraping. *Fig.* [in familiar language] a tedious, endless story; *it.* slowness, sluggishness in action. Das ist ein ewiges —, they will never have done, they are plaguy tedious.

Geleise, *n.* [-s, *pl.* -] V. Gleis.

Geleit, *n.* [-es, *pl.* e] 1) [= Begleitung] the act of accompanying a person. Er gab mir das — bis unter die Hausthüre, he waited on me, he saw me to the street-door; kann ich die Ehre haben, Ihnen das — nach Haus zu geben? can I have the honour of seeing you home? verzeihen Sie, wenn ich Ihnen nicht das — bis an die Thüre gebe, excuse me for not seeing you, or from seeing you, to the door; [in seamen's lang.] convoy; man gab den Kauffahrteischiffen zwei Kriegsschiffe zum —e mit, two ships or men-of-war were ordered to convoy the merchantmen. *Fig.* guidance. Ein solches Herz verschmäht der Sinne knechtisches —, such a heart scorns to submit servilely to the empire of the senses. 2) [the persons accompanying or attending] attendance, train, retinue. Das — bei einer Leiche, the procession of persons attending a funeral, funeral train; in —e [in Gesellschaft] reisen, to travel in company; ein Fürst hat ein großes — [= Gefolge], a prince has a numerous train or retinue. Chiefly, a train or retinue that accompanies any one for protection, escort. Unter — reisen, to travel with an escort or guard; gegenwärtig kann man ohne starkes — nicht sicher reisen, there is no travelling with safety at present without a strong escort or guard; er kam unter dem — einer Abtheilung Dragoner in Boston an, he arrived at Boston, escorted by a detachment of dragoons. 3) [protection granted to a defendant by a court of justice] safe-guard, safe-conduct; *it.* [a warrant of security given by a sovereign to protect a stranger within his territories] safe-guard, safe-conduct Der König hat ihm freies, sicheres — gegeben, the king has given him a safe-guard, safe-conduct. 4) the right of escorting travellers &c. 5) money paid for such escort. Das — bezahlen, to pay for one's escort. 6) district or territory in which any one has the right of escorting. 7) V. Geleitshaus, Geleitsamt.

Geleits-amt, *n.* 1) office which provides escorts and convoys, office of escorts and convoys. 2) office, where the money for escort and convoy is received. 3) V. —kammer. —bediente, *m.* a servant belonging to those offices. —bereiter, *m.* V. —reiter. —brief, *m.* letter of protection, passport, safe-guard, safe-conduct; [in seamen's language] a letter or warrant that allows the captain of a ship to sail under the protection of a convoy, letter of convoy. —einnahme, *f.* 1) receipt of the money paid for escort or convoy. 2) V. —geld. 3) V. —amt 2). —einnehmer, *m.* receiver of the convoy-duties. —einnehmerei, *f.* V. —amt 2). —folge, *f.* the obligation of subjects to conduct and escort travellers by order of the Sovereign. —frei, *adj.* and *adv.* exempt from the convoy-duties. —gebiet, *n.* the district or territory to which the right of convoy or escort extends. —geld, *n.* money paid for escort and convoy, convoy-duty. —gerechtigkeit, *f.* right or privilege of escorting [travellers &c.]. —grenze, *f.* boundary of the convoy. —haus, *n.* V. —amt. —herr, *m.* one to whom the right of escorts and convoy belongs. —herrlichkeit, *f.* V. —gerechtigkeit. —herrschaft, *f.* V. —herr. —kammer, *f.* [in seamen's language] board of convoy [where convoys for ships are appointed]. —leute, *pl.* people belonging to the escort or convoy; *it.* servants or officers belonging to the office of escorts or convoy. —mann, *m.* 1) [= Begleitsmann, Führer] guide, conductor. Gott sey Euer —mann! God be with you, God speed you! 2) an officer appointed to conduct travellers. —obrigkeit, *f.* V. —herr. —ordnung, *f.* regulation for convoys. —recht, *n.* V. —gerechtigkeit. —reiter, *m.* a person appointed to ride on the roads for the purpose of seeing the escort regulations attended to; *it.* an armed horseman for the protection of a convoy. —säule, *f.* a pillar or stone marking the limits of escorts. —schein, *m.* V. —zettel. —schiff, *n.* vessel of convoy. —schiffe, *pl.* convoy of men-of-war. —stätte, *f.* place where the convoy-duties are paid. —stein, *m.* V. —säule. —stelle, *f.* V. —stätte. —stern, *m.* satellite. —straße, *f.* road of escort or convoy. —tafel, *f.* table of the dues to be paid for escort and convoy. —weg, *m.* V. —straße. —zeichen, *n.* —zettel, *m.* a ticket showing the payment of the convoy-duties.

Geleiten, *v. tr.* 1) V. Begleiten. 2) [to accompany for protection] to escort, to convoy. Reisende — lassen, to escort travellers; [in military affairs] die Truppen geleiteten die Gepäckwagen, the troops convoyed the baggage waggons; [in seamen's language] Kauffahrteischiffe —, to convoy merchantmen.

1. **Geleiter**, [from leiten = to lead, to conduct] *m.* [-s, *pl.* -] conductor, guide. Gott sey dein —, God be with you, God speed you; ein guter, treuer, sicherer —, a good, faithful, sure or safe guide.

2. **Geleiter**, [from Leiter = ladder] *n.* [-s] [among hunters] the meshes of a net in form of a ladder; *it.* nets with meshes in form of a ladder.

Geleiterinn, *f.* guide, conductress.

Geleitlich, *adj* belonging to the escort or convoy. Die —e Obrigkeit, the lord who has the right of escort.

Geleitschaft, *f.* [= Gefolge] train, retinue. Er kam mit seiner ganzen —, he came with all his attendants or followers.

Geleitung, *f.* act of accompanying, conducting, escorting &c. V. Geleit.

Gelenk, [V. Lenken] *adj.* flexible, pliant, supple, limber. Dieser Taschenspieler hat sehr —e Finger, this juggler has very supple fingers; er hat einen sehr —en Körper, he is very supple in the body. *Fig.* Ein —er Geist, a pliant temper. V. Gelenkig.

Gelenk, *n.* [-es, *pl.* -e] [allied to the Sw. *länk* = the link of a chain, and to the Engl. *link*] the joining or union of two things, joint. Die —e an einer Kette, the links of a chain; [in botany, the space between two joints of a plant &c.] internode; die —e des Weinstockes, des Zuckerrohrs &c., the joints, articulations or knuckles of the vine, of the sugar-cane &c.; [among shoemakers] das — eines Schuhes, the small part of the sole before the heel; [among coppersmiths] border or edge; [among cutlers] das — eines Messers, joint of a knife; [in mining] the ear or handle of a pot, basket &c.; die —e der Finger, the joints or knuckles of the fingers; es gibt mehrere Arten von —en an dem menschlichen Körper, there are several kinds of articulations in the human body; er hat Schmerzen in den —en, he has a pain in his joints; er kann diesen Kapaunen nicht zerlegen, weil er das — nicht zu finden versteht, he cannot carve or cut up this capon, because he does not know how to find the joint; ein Glied am — ablösen, to amputate a limb in the joint or articulation; er hat sich den Arm aus dem — gefallen, he has put his arm out of joint, or he has dislocated his arm, by a fall; das Bein ist aus dem —e, the bone is dislocated or forced out of its socket; einem Pferde zwei —e vom Schweife abhauen, to cut two joints off a horse's tail; [in anatomy] freies —, [where the head of one bone is received into the shallow socket of the other] arthrodia; straffes —, [the insertion of the round end of a bone in the cup-like cavity of another] enarthrosis. V. Dreh—, Nuß—. *Fig.* [in fam. language] Dieser Mensch hat keine —e, this fellow is very awkward; er hat weder Geschick noch —, he is as stiff as a poker; he is awkward in all he does.

Gelenk=amboß, *m.* [among coppersmiths] a round anvil for making an edge or border. —**band**, *n.* [in anatomy, a ligament that surrounds every movable articulation and contains the synovia like a bag] capsular ligament. —**bein**, *n.* [in anatomy] carpus, wrist; *it.* sesamoidal bone. —**blutader**, *f.* [in anatomy] articúlar vein. —**drüse**, *f.* [in anatomy] mucilaginous gland. —**ende**, *f.* [in anatomy] the head [of a bone]. —**fläche**, *f.* [in anatomy] articular facet. —**fortsatz**, *m.* [in anatomy] cubital apophysy or apophysis. —**gang**, *m.* [in anatomy] the condyloid canal or duct. —**grube**, *f.* [in anatomy] articular foss. —**höcker**, *m.* [in anatomy] articular tubercle. —**höhle**, *f.* V. —pfanne. —**hügelchen**, *n.* [in anatomy] tubercle. —**kapsel**, *f.* [in anatomy] articular capsule. —**knopf**, *m.* condyl. —**kraut**, *n.* a sort of may-flower that grows on rocks in the North of Europe, V. Weißwurz. —**maus**, *f.* [in surgery] a gristle or cartilage that may be shoved about in the joint. —**pfanne**, *f.* articular cavity. —**ring**, *m.* hinges, turning-joint. —**saft**, *m.* synovy, synovia. —**schalig**, *adj.* [in natural history] shelly with joints, crustaceous. Die Krebse &c. sind —schalig, —schalige Thiere, crabs &c. are crustaceous. —**schlagader**, *f.* [in anatomy] articular artery. —**steifheit**, *f.* [in surgery] ancyle, ancylosis. —**steine**, *pl.* [in mineralogy] fragments of encrinite or the stone-lily. —**stück**, *n.* [the piece containing the joint; *it.* a piece of the joint] articular piece; [among shoe-makers] a piece of leather between the sole and the heel. —**theil**, *m.* part of a bone near a joint, condyl. —**wasser**, *n.* V. —saft. —**wurz**, *f.* V. —kraut, Weißwurz.

Gelénkheit, *f.* flexibility, suppleness, pliantness. V. Gelenkigkeit.

Gelénkig, *adj* and *adv.* 1) [having joints] jointed, articulated. [in botany] Eine —e Wurzel, a knuckled or articulated root; ein —er Stengel, a jointed or articulated stalk. 2) [= geschmeidig] flexible, pliant, supple, limber. —e Glieder, supple limbs, ein —er Junge, a supple, nimble lad.

Gelénkigkeit, *f.* pliantness, flexibility, suppleness, pliableness. Die — der Glieder, the suppleness of the limbs or joints; die — eines Seiltänzers, the suppleness or nimbleness of a rope dancer.

Gelénksam, *adj.* and *adv.* supple, pliant, flexible. *Fig.* V. Lenksam.

Gelénksamkeit, *f.* V. Gelenkheit, Gelenkigkeit. *Fig.* V. Lenksamkeit.

Gelérnig, *adj.* V. Gelehrig.

Geléſe, *n.* [-s] 1) [mostly in contempt] the act of reading, continual reading. Was nützt Ihr ewiges —? of what use is your perpetual reading? 2) the act of picking out and separating things; [among weavers] the separating of the threads of a warp.

Geléſen, [*past part.* of Lesen] *adj.* that is read by many. In einer unserer —sten Zeitschriften, in one of our most widely-circulated, valued or esteemed journals; er ist ein sehr —er Schriftsteller, he is a very popular or favorite author.

Geleúcht, *n.* [-es] [rather unusual] lights collectively; illumination. Das — in einem Schauspielhause, bei einem Balle, the illumination of a playhouse, of a ballroom; [in mining] the candles or lamps of the miners.

Gèlf or **Gèlft**, [-es, *pl.* -e] [from gelb] or **Gèlferz**, *n.* [-es, *pl.* -e] [in mining, a pyrite or marcasite, pregnant with silver and found in Hungary] Gelbum or Gelfum, gelft or gilft.

Gèlfern, *v. intr.* to yelp, to bark. V. Belfern.

Gelíchter, *n.* [-s] [allied to Gleich, like, equal; in contempt] kind, sort. Sie sind seines —s, they are of a piece with him, they are of the same gang; das sind Leute Eines —s, they are all of the same stamp or cast.

‡**Gelíeben**, *v. intr.* V. Belieben. Geliebt es Gott, if it please God, if God will.

Gelíebt, [*past part.* of Lieben] *adj.* beloved, dear. —er Freund, dear friend; meine —este Tochter, my dearest, my beloved daughter; der —e, the man beloved, lover; die —e, the woman beloved, mistress. [in familiar language] sweetheart; wer ist ihr —er? who is her lover? sie ist seine —e, she is his love or mistress.

||**Gelíefern**, *v. intr.* V. Gerinnen.

Gelíege, *n.* [-s] [little used] the lying; *it.* posture

Gelíegen, *v. intr.* [u. w. seyn] V. Liegen.

Gelíeger, *n.* [-s] [among hunters] V. Lager.

Gelínd, **Gelínde**, [V. Lind] I. *adj.* primarily = not hard, soft. Gelinde Haut, Hände, soft skin, hands; gelindes Leder, soft leather; gelindes Fleisch, tender flesh or meat; gelindes Kupfer, soft copper; gelinde [geschmeidige] Metalle, soft metals. *Fig.* [having a small degree of vehemence or internal strength] Gelinder Hauch, gentle breath; gelinde Aussprache eines Buchstabens, soft pronunciation of a letter; ein gelinder Wind, Regen, a gentle wind or gale, rain; das Wetter ist gelind gewesen, the weather has been mild; gelinder Frost, slight frost; gelinde Hitze, a moderate heat; gelindes Feuer, small or gentle fire; gelinde Arznei, a mild medicine or physic; ein gelinder Schmerz, a slight pain; gelinde Sitten, soft or gentle manners; *fig.* * gelinde Saiten aufziehen, to give fair words, to be submissive; sich des gelindesten Ausdruckes bedienen, to make use of, to use the mildest term; Einen mit gelinden Worten besänftigen, to appease any one with fair or civil words; er ist zu gelind gegen seine Kinder, he is too indulgent to his children; er versuchte erst die gelindesten Mittel, he first tried the fairest means; ein gelinder Verweis, eine gelinde Strafe, a mild or gentle reproof, a slight punishment; sie leben unter einer gelinden Regierung, they live under a mild or gentle government. II. *adv.* softly, gently, mildly. Es regnet gelind, it rains gently; gelind anrühren, to touch softly or gently; Einen gelind behandeln, to treat any one mildly, indulgently; einen Buchstaben gelind aussprechen, to soften the pronunciation of a letter. Syn. Gelinde, Sanft, Sachte, Leise, Gemach, Glimpflich. In the words gelinde, sanft, sachte, leise the effect denoted, is a slight touch or contact; in gemach, a slight movement. Gemach gehen, signifies not to hurry. Das Gelinde and Sanfte affects the feelings, das Leise, the hearing. Das Gelinde, from the slightness of the contact, gives merely no painful, or a less painful sensation; das Sanfte produces at the same time an agreeable one. Thus, figuratively, one would not say, gelinde, but sanfte Liebkosungen, for it is intended they should be agreeable; on the other hand one would say, gelinde Strafen, of such as are not intended to be too severe. Glimpflich implies more especially humanity and kindness.

Gelíndigkeit, *f.* softness, mildness, gentleness. Die — der Haut, the softness of the skin, die — der Luft, des Wetters, the mildness of the air, of the weather. *Fig.* Die — der Worte or Ausdrücke, the mildness, gentleness or softness of words, of expressions; die — der angewandten Mittel, the mildness of the remedies employed; die — gegen Kinder, the indulgence to children; mit — zu Werke gehen, — anwenden, to use fair means. *Prov.* Mit — richtet man viel aus, a small rain lays a great dust.

Gelíngen, [either allied to gelangen or to Glück] *ir. v. intr.* [u. w. seyn] to succeed, to prosper, to speed. Sein Plan, sein Vorhaben ist nicht gelungen, ist ihm nicht gelungen, his plan, his design did not succeed, Alles, was er unternimmt, gelingt ihm, he prospers or succeeds in all his undertakings, every thing he undertakes thrives with him; es gelingt ihm nicht, Verse zu machen, he does not succeed in making verses; es mag ihm — oder fehlschlagen, if he succeed or fail; durch die Hülfe Gottes ist es mir gelungen, with the help of God I succeeded; ein gelungenes Unternehmen, a successful enterprise; das —, success, successfulness. Syn. Gelingen, Gerathen, Einschlagen, Glücken. When exterior circumstances produce a prosperous termination, or chance favours the accomplishment of what is attempted or intended, we use glücken. When, on the contrary, the success of an undertaking proceeds from the judicious choice of the means, or depends upon our own skill or prudence, we use gelingen. Gerathen and einschlagen are said of the thing or work itself, gelingen principally of the means employed. Einschlagen implies a greater degree of uncertainty in the issue, a greater effect of chance than gerathen. A painter may say: dieses Gemählde ist mir wohl gerathen, but not: es ist gut eingeschlagen.

Gelíspel, *n.* [-s] lisp, lisping, continual lisping; *it.* whispering. Ich hörte ein — im Nebenzimmer, I heard a whispering in the adjoining room; [in poetry] das leise, sanfte — der Zephyre, the soft or gentle whispering of the zephyrs.

Gèllen, V. Gällen.

Gèllkraut, *n.* [-es, *pl.* -kräuter] bulbiferous tooth-wort. V. Schuppenwurzel.

Gelóben, *v. tr.* to promise solemnly, to vow. Etwas mit Hand und Mund —, to pledge one's faith, to pass one's word, to promise upon one's honour; Einem eine ewige Freundschaft —, to vow an eternal friendship to any one; ewige Keuschheit —, to make the vow of chastity; gelobte Enthaltsamkeit, votive abstinence; das gelobte Land, the promised land, the Holy Land; das —, the act of promising solemnly or of vowing. V. Verheißen, Versprechen, Zusagen.

Gelöbniß, *n.* [-sses, *pl.* -sse] V. Gelübde.

Gelöbung, *f.* solemn promise, vow.

Gelobungs=gemählde, *n.* a picture owed to a church &c. in some danger, a votive icture. —**s=geschenk**, —**s=stück**, *n.* a vove offering. —**tafel**, *f.* votive tablet; votive icture.

1. **Gelóck[e]**, *n.* [-es, *pl.* -] [from locken, an=ocken, to allure] the act of alluring or decoying ontinually; [among bird-catchers] decoy-bird.

2. **Gelóck**, *n* [-es] [from locken, lockig ma=en, to curl] 1) the act of curling. 2) curled air, curls, ringlets.

Gelörsch, *n.* [-es, *pl.* -e] [Welch is *clör* = och] [in mining] the lowest pit of a mine.

Gelös, *n.* [-es] [among hunters] dung, fiants.

||**Gelösen**, *v. intr.* [u. w. seyn] to get rid of a ing.

Gelöthe, *n.* [-s] soldering.

Gelöwet, *adj.* [in heraldry] Ein—er Leopard, lionne leopard.

Gèlsen, V. Gelzen.

Gèlster, V. Genster.

1. ||**Gèlt**, [from gelten, to be valid] [= nicht ahr? in familiar language] is it not so? is it not e?

2. **Gèlt**, [Dutch gelten is = verschneiden] *j.* not producing young, barren. Eine —e ih, ein —es Schaf &c. [a cow, a ewe that never s big with young or that is not big this year] barren cow, ewe; [among hunters] ein —es hier, —thier, a barren hind or doe.

Gelt=kuh, *f.* —**schaf**, —**schwein**, —**ier**, *n.* &c, a barren cow, ewe, sow, hind doe &c. —**vieh**, *n.* barren animals. —**ege**, *f.* barren goat.

Gèlte, *f.* [*pl.* -n] [allied to hohl, Kelch &c.] pail, a bucket. Eine — Wasser, a pail of ter.

1. **Gèlten**, [originally, probably = geben; th. and A. S. *gildan* is = bezahlen] *ir. v. intr.* to worth a certain sum of money. Dieses Gut t zwölftausend Gulden, this estate is worth elve thousand florins; mir gilt dieses Buch t viel [ist mir viel werth], to me this book is great value, is worth a great deal of money me; ein Dukaten gilt fünf und einen halben lden, a ducat is worth five florins and a f; die Elle von diesem Zeug gilt zwölf hillinge, the yard of this stuff costs twelve llings or this stuff sells at twelve shillings a d; was or wie viel hat der Wein gegolten? at was the price of this wine? jetzt gilt das treide [es gilt viel], corn fetches or bears a h price at present, is dear; diese beiden rde — gleich viel, these two horses are of same price or value; was gilt die Wette? much will you bet or wager? es gilt einen illing, I bet or lay you a shilling; es gilt! e! es gilt eine Wette, it is worth while to a wager; *it.* I lay a wager; *it.* we or they e laid a wager; was gilt's? how much will bet me? was gilt's, er hat es errathen? old a wager, I lay a bet, he has guessed I am sure, confident, he has guessed it. *a*) in general, to be of some worth or e, to be worth something. Verstand gilt r als Reichthum, understanding is better n riches, is preferable to riches, is above es; das Zeugniß dieses einzigen Schriftstel= gilt mehr, als das Zeugniß von hundert an= , the testimony of this single writer is of e weight, weighs more than that of a dred others; diese Münze gilt bei uns nicht, coin is not current, will not go, with us; Vertrag gilt, gilt nicht, the treaty is valid, is not valid or void or null; die meisten Stimmen —, a majority of votes carries it or prevails; diese Note gilt einen Takt, this note stands for one bar; M, als eine römische Ziffer, gilt tausend, M, as a Roman numeral, stands for a thousand; das Aß gilt elf, the ace is worth eleven, is good for eleven; das kann für keinen Beweis —, that cannot pass, cannot be admitted as a proof; das gilt nicht, that is not permitted, is not fair play; *it.* that does not count; was von dir gilt [mit Wahrheit gesagt werden kann], gilt eben nicht gerade auch von mir, what may be said of you, is not necessarily applicable to me; mir gilt der Eine so viel als der Andere, as for me, one man is as good as another, I esteem the one as much as the other; es gilt mir Alles gleich viel, das gilt mir gleich viel, it is all one, equal or indifferent to me; es gilt gleich viel, it is all one, there is no difference, it comes to the same thing; sein Wort gilt viel [hat Werth], his word is of great weight or influence; er gilt viel bei dem Minister, he is or stands in high credit or favour with the minister; das lasse ich —, that will do! well done! *it.* I grant or allow that; er fürchtet, daß man ihm diese Ausgabe in der Rechnung nicht — lassen möchte, he fears they will not allow him this expense in his bill or account; sich — or —d zu machen wissen, to set one's self off, to put one's self forward; man muß sich — or —d zu machen wissen, a man must set himself off in order to be considered; seine Rechte, Ansprüche, Reize — or —d machen, to maintain, to make good one's rights, claims, to set off one's charms; er macht das, was er weiß, — or —d, he makes the best of his knowledge; die schönen Stellen in einem Gedichte — machen [sie herausheben], to set off the beautiful passages of a poem; einen Grund — or —d machen, to lay great or much stress upon a reason, to urge or to press a reason or argument. *b*) Für etwas —, to pass or go for. Er gilt für den geschicktesten Wundarzt im Lande, he is looked upon, he passes for, he is reputed or accounted, the most skilful surgeon of the country; sie galt für die größte Schönheit ihrer Zeit, she passed for, was accounted, the greatest beauty of her time; das gilt für ausgemacht, that is taken for granted; der gute Wille gilt für die That, the will is taken for the deed or performance. *c*) to be the question, to be aimed at, to concern. Es galt ihnen Sieg oder Tod, they were to conquer or to die; es gilt Ihr Leben. es gilt Ihnen das Leben, your life is at stake, in danger or in question; [in drinking] es gilt Ihnen, I or we or they drink your health, drink to you, I or we pledge you a glass or bumper; es gilt die Gesundheit des Königs! the king's health! es gilt mir, ich sehe wohl, es soll mir —, it is aimed at me, I see it is levelled or pointed at me; diese Spötterei soll meinem Freunde —, this mockery or raillery is levelled, directed or aimed at my friend; diese Ermahnung gilt uns Allen, this admonition concerns or touches us all. *d*) to depend upon, to be required. Es gilt hier Muth, Kraft &c., it depends here on courage, strength &c., courage, strength is required here; es hat Fleiß und Mühe gegolten, it cost or required diligence and trouble; hier galt's, wer zuerst auf dem Platze war, all depended on being the first on the place; it was of the utmost, last importance, to be the first on the place; hier gilt's [i. e. Kraft, Anstrengung]! 'tis here we must prove our strength or exert ourselves! und wenn es mein Leben gilt! and though it should cost my life!

2. **Gèlten**, [V. Gelt *adj.*] *v. tr.* to castrate, to emasculate, to geld. V. Verschneiden.

Gèlter, *m.* [-s, *pl.* -] one who castrates, gelder.

Gèltling, *m.* [-es, *pl.* -e] 1) [an animal that does not produce young] barren animal; [in gardening] an onion that has been cut in such a manner as not to yield any seed. 2) a gelding, a castrated or spayed animal.

1. **Gèltung**, *f.* [in grammar] Die — eines Wortes, the acceptation, import or meaning of a word; [in music] die — einer Note, the value of a note, the proportion that a note has to another as to its duration.

2. **Gèltung**, *f.* castration, emasculation.

Gelübde, *n.* [-s, *pl.* -] [V. Geloben] 1) a solemn promise, a vow. Ich habe das — gethan, keinem Menschen mehr Geld zu leihen, I made a vow never again to lend any one money; das — der Keuschheit, der Armuth, des Gehorsams, vow of chastity, poverty and obedience; ein — thun, to make a vow; er hat das — gethan, zu fasten, zu wallfahrten, he made a vow of abstinence, of going a pilgrimage; ein — erfüllen, [in Scripture] sein — bezahlen, to fulfil, to perform, to accomplish a vow, [in Script.] to pay a vow; ein — brechen, to break or violate a vow; sich von seinem — lossprechen lassen, to get one's vow annulled. 2) [rarely used] wish, desire; the object of our wishes or hopes.

Gelübdegeschenk, *n.* V. Gelobungsgeschenk.

Gelúng, *n.* [-es, *pl.* -e] V. Geschling.

Gelúst or **Gelüst**, *n.* [-es, *pl.* -e] desire, appetite, longing. Sein — befriedigen, to satisfy one's desire, one's longing. Darum hat sie auch Gott dahin gegeben in ihrer Herzen —e [in Script.], wherefore God also gave them up to uncleanness through the lusts of their own hearts, V. Lust; das — einer schwangern Frau, a longing of a woman during her pregnancy, a woman's longing; [in medicine] pica, malacia.

Gelüsten, *v. intr.* usually *v. impers.* to long for, to lust after, to desire, to covet. Mich gelüstet darnach, I long for it, I lust after it; es gelüstet mich nach diesem Vergnügen, I desire eagerly to enjoy that pleasure; es gelüstet ihn nach Allem, was er sieht, he covets all he sees; ein Kranker läßt sich oft schädliche Dinge —, a sick man often longs for things that are bad for him or hurtful to him; Einem gelüstet nach Reichthum, dem Andern nach Ehre, the one covets riches, another honour; das Fleisch gelüstet wider den Geist [in Script.], the flesh lusteth against the spirit; daß wir uns nicht — lassen des Bösen, that we should not lust after evil things; laß dich nicht — deines Nächsten Weibes, thou shalt not covet thy neighbour's wife; er thut, was ihm gelüstet, he does whatever he likes or pleases or has a mind to do, whatever he lists; ich bin gewiß, das läßt er sich nicht —, I am sure, he never thinks of it, it never comes into his mind; er ließ es sich —, mein Nebenbuhler zu werden, he took it into his head to become my rival; das —, V. Gelust; Gelüsten nach etwas haben, to have a great desire or longing for a thing.

Gelüstern, *v. intr.* [in familiar language] V. Gelüsten.

Gelüstig, *adj.* and *adv.* V. Lüstern.

Gèlze, *f.* [*pl.* -n] [from 2. Gelten] a spayed, gelded or castrated sow.

Gèlzen, *v. tr.* to castrate, to geld, to spay. V. 2. Gelten.

Gèlzer or **Gèlter**, *m.* [-s, *pl.* -] gelder.

Gemach, [seems allied to the Low Sax. *meek* =

zahm, sanft] *adj.* and particularly *adv.* slow, gentle, soft, commodious, easy, comfortable; slowly, gently, softly, easily, comfortably. — gehen, to walk gently or slowly; der Kutscher fuhr —, the coachman drove gently or slowly; er geht — zu Werke, he manages the affair very prudently, with a great deal of circumspection; es regnet nur ganz —, it rains but very gently; das Alter nahet — heran, old age is drawing near by little and little; nur —, nicht so hitzig! but soft or softly, fair and softly! hold there! V. Gemächlich. Syn. Gemach, Langsam. Langsam denotes slowness of motion in general, gemach also conveys the idea that the body in motion uses no exertion. Langsam, therefore, may be said of the motion of all bodies, gemach only of that of persons.

Gemách, *n.* [-es, *pl.* -e or Gemächer] [probably from machen, to make, allied to *μέγαρον* or *μάγαρον*] 1) a room or apartment [chiefly a spacious or splendid one]. Die königlichen Gemächer, the royal or the king's apartments, V. Zimmer; *das heimliche —, necessary house, privy, V. Abtritt. 2) [rather unusual or provincial] story, floor. Ein viele Gemächer hohes Haus, a house of many stories. 3) V. Gemächlichkeit.

Gemachstuhl, *m.* close-stool. Auf den —stuhl gehen, to go to stool.

Gemächlich, I. *adj.* 1) [= langsam, allmählig] slow, soft, gentle. Ein —er Gang, a slow or gentle gait or walk. 2) [= bequem] commodious, easy, comfortable. Ein —es Haus, a commodious or convenient house; ein —es Leben haben, to lead an easy, agreeable life; ein —er Wagen, an easy or comfortable carriage. 3) [= indulging in ease] indolent. Ein —er, sehr —er Mensch, a man that loves his ease or conveniences; — seyn, to love one's ease. II. *adv.* 1) slowly, softly, gently. — gehen, to walk slowly or gently. 2) commodiously, easily, comfortably. — wohnen, to have a commodious or convenient lodging or habitation, to lodge comfortably or conveniently; an diesem Tische können 20 Personen — sitzen, twenty persons can be commodiously seated at this table; — leben, to live at ease. Syn. Gemächlich, Bequem. When in using the objects that surround us, we experience no trouble in the application of them, we call them bequem. A staircase is bequem, when it is neither too steep nor too narrow. Gemächlich implies that the surrounding objects do not affect us disagreeably. A chair is bequem when neither too high nor too low, and gemächlich when softly cushioned. Ein bequemer Mensch is averse from all trouble and exertion, ein gemächlicher is easily rendered uncomfortable by that which surrounds him.

Gemächlichkeit, *f.* 1) slowness. 2) the state of being convenient or commodious, commodiousness, conveniency. Mit — arbeiten, reisen, to work, to travel at one's ease, leisurely; etwas nach seiner — thun, to do something at one's convenience or leisure, at one's own time, to serve one's own ease and convenience; die — lieben, to love one's ease or conveniences; die —en eines Hauses, eines Dampfschiffes, the conveniencies or accommodations of a house, of a steam-boat. 3) [that which gives ease] accommodation, convenience. Dieses Haus hat viele —en, this house has a great many accommodations or there are a great many accommodations in this house; man kann in dieser Welt nicht alle —en haben, one cannot have every conveniency in this world; ich kann diese — sehr wohl entbehren, I can do very well without that convenience.

Gemächsam, *adj.* and *adv.* V. Gemach, Gemächlich.

Gemächsamkeit, *f.* V. Gemächlichkeit.

Gemácht, [*past part.* of machen, which see] —e Wechselbriefe, drafts ready for endorsement.

Gemächt, *n.* [-es, *pl.* -e] 1) any thing made or done, work, workmanship; *it.* creature. Denn er kennet, was für ein — wir sind [in Script.], for he knoweth our frame; Nürnberger —, Nuremberg wares or toys; [in familiar language] das ist sein —, ein elendes —, that's his work or handiwork, a miserable or wretched work or thing. 2) [= Zeugungsglied, in popular lang.] private parts [of the male sex], genitals, groin. Das — eines Pferdes, the yard of a horse.

Gemähl, *m.* [-es, -s, *pl.* -e] [is commonly derived from the old Mahl = Rede, Sw. *mal* = Rede, Versprechen; but perhaps more correctly or better from machen = verbinden, so that it was originally spelled Gemachel] [in an elevated style for Gatte] spouse, consort, husband. Er ist der — dieser Dame, he is the spouse or husband of that lady.

Gemählde, *n.* [-s, *pl.* -] painting, picture. Ein schönes —, a handsome, fine painting or picture; der Grund des —s ist zu hell, the ground of the picture is too light; die Anordnung dieses —s gefällt mir, the disposition, the grouping of this picture pleases me; ein vollendetes —, a well finished, a well executed picture; die — dieses Saales sind von Italienischen Meistern, the pictures of this room are by Italian masters; ein einfarbiges —, a brooch, monochroma, camaieu; ein — in Oel, in Wasserfarben, a picture in oil, in watercolours; ein — auf frischem Kalk or Gyps, [a painting in relief on walls with watercolours on plaster not yet dry] painting in fresco; ein Zimmer mit —n behängen, to hang or furnish a room with pictures. *Fig.* Das — des menschlichen Lebens, the picture of human life; er hat ein schönes — von seinem Glücke entworfen, he has made a fine picture of his happiness; ein getreues, lebhaftes — von den Sitten seines Zeitalters liefern, aufstellen, to give or make a faithful, lively picture or description of the manners of one's age, V. Schilderung; [in music, passages in a piece of music, in which one tries to imitate wind, thunder &c. = Ton—] imitative music.

Gemählde-ausstellung, *f.* exhibition of pictures. —freund, *m.* a lover, an amateur of pictures. —gallerie, *f.* picture gallery. —handel, *m.* trade or dealing in pictures. —händler, *m.* a dealer in pictures. —liebhaber, V. —freund. —saal, *m.* gallery of paintings, picture-gallery. —sammler, *m.* collector of pictures, of articles of vertu, V. —freund. —sammlung, *f.* collection of pictures.

Gemahlinn, *f.* [V. Gemahl] spouse, consort, wife. Der König und die Königinn, seine Gemahlinn, the king and his royal consort; wie befindet sich Ihre Frau Gemahlin? how does your lady do?

Gemahnen, *v. tr.* 1) [Einen] to remind, to put in mind. V. Erinnern. 2) *v. impers.* [= vorkommen, scheinen] to seem, to appear. Es gemahnet mich, mir, als hätte ich ihn schon gesehen, it seems or appears to me, as if I had seen him before.

Gemáng, *n.* [-es, *pl.* -e] or -futter, *n.* a mixture or different sorts of grain, meslin.

Gemangkorn, *n.* V. Mangkorn.

Gemánsche, *n* [-s] a continual paddling or puddling; *it.* hotch-potch.

Gemäntelt, *adj.* and *adv.* [in heraldry] mantled.

Gemárkung, *f.* the boundary or territory [of a town or village]. Er hat viele Morgen [...]sen in or auf unserer —, he has many ac[...] meadows within our bounds; die — Städtchens, the precincts of a small town.

Gemäsche, *n.* [-s] the meshes [of a net].

Gemäß, *n.* [-es, *pl.* -e] 1) [the instrument by which extent or dimension is ascertained] the measure. 20 Scheffel Berliner —, twenty bushels of Berlin measure. 2) [the length of a thing] measure. Das — der Sylben, the measure of the syllables.

Gemäß, I. *adj.* [according with the nature of a thing] conformable, suitable. Sein Betragen ist der Klugheit —, his conduct is conformable, is according to the rules of prudence; eine dem Gegenstand —e Sprache, language suitable to the subject; seine Schreibart [...] vollkommen seinem Charakter —, his way of writing is perfectly comformable to his character; was Sie da sagen, ist der Wahrheit —, what you are saying, is in conformity to, agree[...] with truth. II. *adv.* conformably, suitably, accordingly, agreeably, consistently. Der Be[...]schrift — handeln, to act in conformity or con[...]formably to the precept; der Natur, sei[...] Stande — leben, to live according to [the la[ws] of] nature, to one's station; dem Gegenst[and] — sprechen, to speak suitably to the subje[ct;] dem —, was Sie mir schrieben, conformabl[y] to what you wrote to me.

Gemäßheit, *f.* conformity, suitablene[ss.] Ich handelte in — der Befehle, die Sie m[ir] gaben, I acted in conformity to the orders yo[u] gave me.

Gemäßigt, [properly, *past part.* of mäßigen, which see] *adj.* and *adv.* temperate, moderate, temperately, moderately. Ein —er Himmelsstrich, a temperate climate; sich von —[en] Grundsätzen leiten lassen, to be guided by mo[derate] principles; die Gemäßigten unter [den] Papisten, the most moderate of the papists; — von etwas sprechen, to speak temperately [or] moderately of a thing.

Gemäuer, *n.* [-s, *pl.* -] 1) walls, walli[ng.] Ein altes —, a dilapidated old buildi[ng;] die Eulen nisten in altem —, in alten —[...] owls build in old decayed walls or ruins. 2) [V.] Mauerwerk.

Gemein, [allied to manch, Menge; in [...] Low Saxon mein, meen, signifies still publi[c] *adj.* and *adv.* being in plenty or abunda[nce,] common, plenty [= plentiful]. Gute Me[lo]nen sind dieses Jahr —, good melons are ple[n]tiful or common this year; Erdbeben s[ind] in Italien eine —e Sache, etwas Gemein[es,] earth-quakes are something common, are fre[]quent in Italy; diese Bäume sind bei [uns] —, these trees are common with us; [...] —sten Kräuter, the most common herbs. [In] *a more limited sense: a)* usual, ordinary, com[]mon. Nichts ist —er, als &c., there is noth[ing] more usual or common, than &c.; der —e [Lauf] der Dinge, the common or ordinary course [of] things; ein —es Jahr, a common year [of 365] days]; die —e Zeitrechnung, the common [era;] das —e Leben, common or ordinary life; [ein] Ausdruck des —en Lebens, a familiar expres[]sion or term; ein —er Ausdruck, a comm[on] expression; mit dem —en Manne zu reden, [to] speak in common or popular language; [die] —e Redeform, a common form of speech; [der] —e Menschenverstand, common sense; es [ist] die —e Meinung, it is the popular or gene[ral] opinion; das ist die —e Denkart, that is the com[]mon way of thinking; es geht die —e Rede, th[ere] is a common or current report; —es Sprich[]wort, common proverb; das —e Wesen, com[]munity, commonweal, commonwealth; [...]

-e Beste, Wohl, the public good or welfare; -e Rechte, common rights; das —e Recht, the ommon law; —e Weide [Gemeinweide], common pasture, a common; der —e Weg, common e public way or road. b) [belonging equally to more han one or to many indefinitely] common. Das ben und Gefühl sind den Menschen und Thieren —, life and sense are common to man and east; die Sonne, die Luft, die Elemente sind llen Menschen —, the sun, the air and elements re common to all men; unter Freunden ist lles —, among friends every thing is common in common; diese Freude habe ich mit Ihnen —, I have this joy in common with you; eine Klagen haben mit den Ihrigen nichts —, y complaints have nothing in common with ours; Kenntnisse — machen, to spread. diffuse, romulgate knowledge; Wahrheiten, Meinungen durch den Druck — machen, to publish to ake known truths, opinions by printing; *mit inem —e Sache machen, to associate one's lf with any one, to enter into partnership ith any one; Güter — haben, to live in mmunity of goods. c) [of little value, low in th or estimation] common, mean, vulgar. —e inge, vile, common things; diese Sache ist n zu —, this thing is too common, low or lgar for him; er hat nichts als ganz —es ng in seinem Laden, he has nothing but comn trash in his shop; dieser Mensch hat ein es Aussehen, this fellow has a low or vulgar pearance; ein sehr —er Dichter, a very orary poet; dieses Werk enthält lauter —e danken, this work contains nothing but triv, low or vulgar thoughts or ideas; —e [pöbelhafte] Ausdrücke, low or vulgar expressions, garisms; er schreibt, er spricht —, he writes, speaks in a low or vulgar manner; *sich — chen, to descend beneath one's rank or sta-, it. to debase or degrade one's self, to act anly; sich mit Jemand — machen, to make 's self too familiar with any one; sich mit echten Leuten — machen, to keep low comy; die —en Leute, der —e Mann, Haufe, bel, das —e Volk, the common people, the gar; von —er Geburt, Herkunft, of low th, of humble origin; er erhebt sich über das meine, he is above the vulgar; —e Soldaten, Gemeine, common or private soldiers, vates; ein Korporal mit 12 Gemeinen, a poral with twelve privates. Syn. Gemein, lgemein. Das Gemeine [the general] is opd to the particular, and signifies, belonging lly to more than one, or to many indefinitely; emein, relating or belonging to the whole. Eine eine Meinung, is an opinion common to many the greatest number; die allgemeine Meinung, opinion of every one without exception.

Gemein-acker, m. V. Gemeindegut. —ger, m. V. —trift. —bier, n. beer drunk ommon; it. a drinking-feast paid for in comn. —erz, n. [in mining] ordinary or comore. —feld, n. V. Gemeindegut. —geist, m. f a society] spirit of party. Es ist kein — l unter den Kaufleuten dieser Stadt, there party-spirit among the merchants of this n. b) [of a people] public spirit. Es herrscht —geist unter diesem Volke, there is no public it among this people. —gültig, adj. and generally received or valid. —gut, n. 1) nging or appertaining to all, not in a perexclusive property. [also in a fig. sense] illers Werke sind ein —gut der deutschen ion, the works of Schiller are the proy of the whole German nation. 2) V. eindegut. —herde, f. flock or herd of a munity or parish. —herrschaft, f. 1) mon jurisdiction. 2) [Mitherr] joint Lord manor. 3) joint estate or manor. —herrftlich, adj. held or possessed in common, belonging to a common jurisdiction. —hirt, m. herdsman of the parish. —holz, n. —holzung, f. a wood belonging to a community or parish. —hutung, f. V. —trift — nützig, —nützlich, adj. and adv. conducive to the public good, of public use, of common benefit. Um dieses Buch —nützig or —nützlich, —nützlicher zu machen, in order to make this book generally useful, more generally useful. —nützigkeit, f. public or general utility. —ochs, m. bull of the parish, town-bull. —ort, —platz, m. common place. V. —spruch. Sein ganzes Buch ist mit —plätzen angefüllt, his whole book is filled with common places. —satz, m. V. —ort. —schenke, f. ale-house of the parish, parish ale-house. —schießen, n. shooting-feast of the parish. —schreiber, m. clerk of the community, town-clerk, V. Stadtschreiber. —sinn, m. V. —geist. —spruch, m. V. —ort. Er endigte seine Rede mit einem —spruche über Eroberer, he finished his speech with a common-place on conquerors. —tag, m. [in Switzerland] diet. —trift, f. common pasture, common. —verständlich, adj. and adv. easy to be comprehended, intelligible to all. —verständlich predigen, so preach in an intelligible, popular manner, plainly, intelligibly. —verständlichkeit, f. general intelligibility, possibility of being understood by all. —vieh, n. cattle of the community or parish. —wald, m. a) wood belonging to a community or parish. b) wood belonging to several lords or gentlemen, joint wood. —weide, f. V. —trift. —wesen, n. [Gemeine Wesen] community, commonweal, commonwealth, —wiese, f. meadow or common of the parish. —zeche, f. [in mining] a mine worked in common; it. a mine worked by a community or parish.

Gemeinde or **Gemeine**, f. [pl. -n] 1) [the inhabitants of a village or town] community. Diese — hat viel Einwohner, this community has many inhabitants; die — versammeln, to call the community together, to assemble the community; die Vorsteher einer —, common-council; die christliche —e, the Christian communion, church; er gehört zur protestantischen —, he belongs to the protestant communion or church; die — eines Pfarrers [Kirchsprengel], parish; eine starke —, a large parish, it. a numerous congregation; wie viel —n enthält dieses Bisthum? how many parishes has this bishopric? von seiner ganzen — geliebt, loved by all his parishioners; eine geistliche —, an ecclesiastical community; eine bischöfliche —, a bishopric. V. Stadt—; it. V. —gut. 2) pl. Die Gemeinen [in England = der dritte Stand, after the Nobility and Clergy]. Das Haus der Gemeinen, [the representatives of boroughs, cities and counties in parliament] the house of Commons.

Gemeinde-backofen, m. oven belonging to a community and in which every member of the community bakes his bread. —bier, n. V. Gemeinbier. —bulle, m. V. Gemeinochs. —bürger, m. member of a community; citizen. —bürgermeister, m. mayor. —bürgerrecht, n. V. Bürgerrecht. —einkünfte, pl. the revenues of a community or parish. —esel, m. ass of a community or parish. —glied, n. member of a community; it. a parishioner. —gut, n. parish-property, parish-ground, common. —haus, n. common-hall. —holzung, f. V. Gemeinholzung. —mann, m. V. —glied. —meister, m. tax-gatherer, collector. —rath, m. magistrate or officer of a community; alderman; common-council-man; it. collectively, court of aldermen; common council. —rathspräsident, —rathsvorsteher, m. mayor. —recht, n. privilege of the parish; right of common, commonage. Jemand in das —recht aufnehmen, to admit any one to a participation of the privileges of the parish; er wurde in das —recht dieser Stadt aufgenommen, he was given the freedom of this town or city, the freedom of this town or city was bestowed on him. —schule, f. school of the community or parish, parish-school. —siegel, n. seal of the community or parish. —verrechner, m. treasurer accountant of a community. —vorsteher, m. a magistrate or officer of a community or parish. —wald, m. V. Gemeinholz. —wappen, n. the coat of arms of a community or parish.

Gemeindsherr, m. [-n, pl. -en] magistrate or officer of a community or parish, an alderman.

Gemeine, f. V. Gemeinde.

Gemeinheit, f. 1) quality or state of being common or general. Die — dieser Frucht benimmt ihrem Werthe nichts, the commonness of this fruit takes nothing from its value or worth. 2) state of being low or mean. Sich über die — seines Standes erheben, to rise above the lowness of one's station; die — des Ausdruckes, der Sprache, the vulgarity of expression, of language; das verräth die — seines Charakters, that proves the meanness of his character; eine solche — ist mir unausstehlich, I cannot bear such vulgarity, it. such a mean or pitiful action or behaviour. 3) [Gemeinde, Gemeine] community. 4) V. Gemeindegut. 5) V. Gemeintrift.

Gemeiniglich, adv. commonly, usually, ordinarily, generally. V. Gewöhnlich.

Gemeinsam, adj. and adv. V. Gemeinschaftlich.

Gemeinschaft, f. state of having any thing in common with others, mutual participation, common possession, community. Die — der Güter, the community of goods; auf die — der Güter Verzicht thun, to renounce community; in — ein Haus haben, besitzen, to have or possess a house in common, to be joint-proprietor of a house; — mit Einem machen, to associate one's self with any one, to enter into partnership with any one; sie leben mit einander in —, they have every thing in common, they live in society together; die — zwischen Seele und Leib, the union of soul and body; [in religious matters] die — Gottes, die — der Gläubigen mit Gott, the union, communion or fellowship of God, the union of the faithful with God; die — der römischen Kirche, the communion of the Romish church; von der — der Gläubigen ausgeschlossen seyn, to be cut off from the communion of the faithful, to be excommunicated; die — des Leibes und Blutes Christi, the communion of the body and blood of Christ. it. [Umgang] intercourse, familiarity. — mit Jemand haben, to have contracted a familiarity with any one, to have or hold a correspondence with any one; ich verspreche Ihnen, alle — mit ihr abzubrechen, I promise you to breack off all intercourse or correspondence with her; es war eine genaue — zwischen ihnen, they were much acquainted together; er hat keine — mit ihm, he has no intercourse or correspondence with him, he is not acquainted with him.

Gemeinschaftsdorf, n. a village that is the joint property of several lords or gentlemen; a village possessed in common.

Gemeinschaftlich, I. adj. common. Eine —e Treppe, ein —er Weg, Hof &c., a common staircase, way or road, yard; —er Feind, —e Gefahr, common enemy, common danger; die

Sache geht auf —e Kosten, the charges are born in common; eine —e Mauer zwischen zwei Häusern, partition-wall II. *adv.* in common. Ein Gut — besitzen, ein Zimmer — bewohnen, to possess an estate in common, to have a room in common; — speisen, to dine in company, to board together, to common; wir genießen die Wohlthaten der Vorsehung —, we enjoy the bounties of Providence in common. Syn. Gemeinschaftlich, Zugleich. Zugleich signifies merely happening or existing at the same time. Gemeinschaftlich implies that the efforts of many are united to effect one object.

Gemeinsglied, *n.* -mann, *m.* V. Gemeindeglied &c.

Gemèlke, *n.* [-s] a continual milking.

Geménge, *n.* [-s] 1) the act of mixing, mixture; [in husbandry] a kind of contract with a shepherd, who, instead of wages, gets a share of the profit. 2) a mingled and confused mass of ingredients, mixture, medley. Dieser Wein ist ein — von verschiedenen Ingredienzien, this wine is a mixture of different ingredients. [in chimistry] mixture [where the several ingredients are blended without an alteration of the substances]; [in mining] the mixture of different metals, alloy; [in the manufacture of glass] frit. *Fig.* Ein — von Leuten aller Stände, a mixture of people of all ranks and conditions; ein — von zerfallenen Gebäuden, a confused mass of decayed buildings.

Gemenge=büchlein, *n.* [in mining] book in which the mixture of metals is taught — **fäßlein**, *n.* [in mining] a vat or basket in which the mingled ore is carried to the furnace. — **kasten**, *m.* [among dyers] a chest in which the different kinds of blue are mixed. —**krücke**, *f.* [among dyers] stirrer. —**macher**, *m.* [among dyers] he who mixes or mingles the different colours. —**stecken**, *m.* V. —krücke. —**stoffe**, *pl.* [in chimistry] constitutive parts.

Geméngsel, *n.* [-s] confused mixture, medley, mingle-mangle, hodge-podge.

Gemèrk, *n.* [-es, *pl.* -e] mark, sign, token; [among hunters = Fährte, Spur] trace. Das — des angeschossenen Wildes, the blood of the wounded game; [in husbandry] boundary, land-mark; [in mining] a mark cut into the rock.

Gemèssen, [*past part.* of messen, which see] *adj.* and *adv.* *Fig.* precise, positive, strict. —en Befehl ertheilen, to give a positive or strict order, to order strictly or positively; sich auf das —ste ausdrücken, to express one's self with the greatest precision; ein —es Betragen, a strict, sober or sedate behaviour or conduct.

Gemèssenheit, *f.* precision, strictness.

Gemètzel, *n.* [-s] butchery, slaughter, carnage, massacre. Beide Heere stießen auf einander, und es entstand ein schreckliches —, the two armies met and made a dreadful slaughter.

Gemísch, *n.* [-es] 1) the act of mixing, mixture. 2) [a mingled mass of ingredients] mixture, medley. Dieses Getränk ist ein — von Thee, Citronensaft und Zucker, this drink is a mixture of tea, lemon-juice and sugar; ein — von Farben, a mixture of colours; [in chimistry] composition, mixture; Venezianischer Theriak ist ein — von vielen Ingredienzien, Venice treacle is a composition of a great many ingredients. *Fig.* Dieser Mensch ist ein — von Stolz und Schwäche, this man is a medley of pride and weakness; ein — von Gutem und Bösem, a mixture of good and evil.

Gèmme, *f.* [*pl.* -n] [in mineralogy] gem.

Gemórde, *n.* [-s] V. Gemetzel.

1. **Gèms**, *f.* [-en] [originated from Kamm, which see] [in mining] a kind of solid stone or rock, a kind of granite.

2. **Gèms**, *f.* [*pl.* -en] V. Gemse.

||**Gems=ballen**, *m.* V. Gemsenballen. — **bock**, *m.* the male or buck of the chamois. — **leder**, *n.* V. Gemsenleder. —**thier**, *n.* — **ziege**, *f.* the female or doe of the chamois.

Gèmse, *f.* [*pl.* -n] [probably from the ancient kam = krumm, crooked] 1) chamois. Die männliche —, the male or buck of the chamois. 2) [in mining] an instrument with two crooked prongs used for scraping, a scraper.

Gemsen=ballen, *m.* V. —kugel. — **fell**, *n.* the skin of the chamois. —**felle**, *pl.* chamois-skins. —**fuß**, *m.* foot of the chamois; [in surgery] a crooked instrument for drawing teeth, pelican. —**geier**, *m.* the vulture of the Alps. —**haar**, *n.* hair of the chamois. Zeug von —haaren, stuff made of the hair of the chamois, a kind of camlet. —**horn**, *n.* the horn of the chamois; [among organ builders] a spindle-shaped or fusiform organ-pipe. —**jagd**, *f.* the hunting of the chamois. —**jäger**, *m.* hunter of chamois, chamois-hunter. —**kraut**, *n.* V. —wurz. —**kugel**, *f.* a little ball composed of hair, found in the stomach of the chamois, aegagropile, hair-ball. —**leder**, *n.* shammy, shamoy, shamois. —lederne Handschuhe, shammy gloves. —**steiger**, *m.* V. —jäger. —**wurz**, *f.* [in botany] leopard'sbane, doronicum.

Gemüll or **Gemúlm**, *n.* [-es] waste or rejected matter of wood, stones, lime &c.; shavings or chips, rubbish. V. Mull, Mulm.

Gemúrmel, *n.* [-s] murmur, murmuring. Auf seine Rede folgte ein lautes —, his speech was followed by a loud murmuring; man hörte ein — in der ganzen Versammlung, a murmur or humming was heard in the whole assembly; *es geht ein — unter den Leuten herum, it is whispered about; das — des Wassers, the murmur of the water; das sanfte — der Bäche, der Zephyre, the soft or gentle purling of the brooks, the whispering of the zephyrs.

Gemúrre, *n.* [-s] muttering, grumbling. Es entstand ein — unter dem Volke, there arose a muttering or murmuring among the people; dieses — deutet auf nichts Gutes, these murmurs forebode nothing good; seine Bediente sind an sein —, an sein ewiges — gewöhnt, his servants are used to his grumbling, to his perpetual grumbling; *fig.* †ein altes —, an old scold, shrew or vixen.

Gemüse, *n.* [-s, *pl.* -] [V. Muß] vegetables of any sort, dressed for the table, greens. Bohnen, Erbsen sind gewöhnliche —, beans, pease are common vegetables; von —n leben, to live upon vegetables; grünes —, greens; trockenes —, pulse.

Gemüse=bau, *m.* culture of vegetables. —**garten**, *m.* kitchen-garden, V. Küchengarten. —**pflanzen**, *pl.* culinary plants, potherbs.

Gemüth, *n.* [-es, *pl.* -er] [V. Muth] 1) [the seat of affection] mind, heart, soul. Er hat ein gutes, schlimmes —, he has a good, a bad heart or mind, he is a good-natured, ill-natured man; ein hohes, ein niedriges, niederträchtiges —, a great, generous, a base soul or mind; er hat ein herrschsüchtiges —, he has a imperious spirit, he is an imperious character; dieser Mensch hat kein —, this man has no heart or feeling, no common sympathy; er ist ganz —, he is full of cordiality or feeling, he is all soul; sein — gegen Jemand ändern, to change one's disposition towards any one; sich etwas zu — ziehen, to take any thing to heart, to fret, to vex one's self about a thing; er zieht sich diese Sache sehr zu —e, this affair gives him great uneasiness, makes him very uneasy, sticks to his heart, lies heavy upon his heart; eine Wahrheit seinem —e einprägen, to imprint or impress a verity in one's mind, sein ganzes — auf etwas richten, to turn or bend all one's thoughts to or on a thing, Einem etwas zu —e führen, to lay a thing before any one, to represent a thing to any one, to remind any one of a thing; *fig.* *sich eine Flasche Wein zu —e führen [zu sich nehmen] [chiefly in jokose lang.] to drink up, to take a bottle of wine. 2) man with respect to his way of thinking, disposition, nature, temper, character. Der Stolz schleicht sich manchmal in die edelsten —er, pride will sometimes creep into the noblest minds; die aufgebrachten —er besänftigen, to appease the irritated or exasperated minds.

Gemüths=art, *f.* 1) disposition of mind, temper, humour. Dieser Mensch hat eine sanfte, eine mürrische —art, this man is of a mild, of a fretful temper; er ist von eifersüchtiger —art, he is of a jealous temper, he is naturally addicted to jealousy; die —arten dieser Kinder sind sehr verschieden, these children differ very much in their dispositions. 2) way of thinking and acting. Ein Mensch von guter, schlechter —art, a man of a good, of a bad character, a good-natured, good-tempered, an ill-natured man. — **beschaffenheit**, *f.* V. Gemüthszustand. — **besserung**, *f.* amendment of the mind or of the heart. —**bewegung**, *f.* agitation of mind, emotion. Er sprach diese Worte mit einiger —bewegung, he spoke these words with some emotion; Liebe, Haß und Furcht erzeugen verschiedene —bewegungen, love, hatred and fear cause different agitations of the soul. —**eigenheit**, *f.* peculiarity of the mind, temper [illegible] character. —**ergötzung**, *f.* amusement, refreshment of the spirits, recreation of the mind. —**erholung**, *f.* relaxation of mind. —**erquickung**, *f.* V. —ergötzung. —**fähigkeit**, *f.* faculty of the mind [in reference to the will]. —**fassung**, *f.* calmness of mind, temper. Seine —fassung verlieren, to lose one's temper; seine —fassung behalten, to keep one's temper. —**freund**, *m.* —**freundinn**, *f.* intimate, confidential friend, bosom-friend. —**freundschaft**, *f.* intimate or confidential friendship. —**gabe**, *f.* endowment or faculty of the body or of the mind. —**kraft**, *f.* power of the soul or mind [in reference to the will]. —**krank**, [illegible] distempered, ill in mind, melancholy. —**krankheit**, *f.* distemper of the mind, melancholy, dejection. —**lage**, *f.* V. —zustand. —**neigung**, *f.* inclination, bent or bias of the mind. —**regung**, *f.* V. —bewegung. —**richtung**, *f.* bias, bent of the mind. —**ruhe**, *f.* tranquillity, calmness of the mind. —**schwäche**, *f.* weakness, debility of the mind. —**stärke**, *f.* strength or force of soul. —**stimmung**, *f.* frame of mind, disposition of mind, temper. In einer heitern, muntern —stimmung sein, to be in a merry humour, to be in high-spirits. —**tugend**, *f.* virtue of the mind, natural good quality. —**unruhe**, *f.* perturbation of mind, disquietude —**verfassung**, *f.* — **zustand**, *m.* state of the mind, disposition of mind. Ich fand ihn in einem sonderbaren —zustande, I found him in a singular state of mind.

Gemüthlich, *adj.* and *adv.* 1) possessing a kind feeling or mind, a good heart, a good-humoured disposition or temper, a kind character. Die Deutschen sind ein —es Volk, the Germans are a good-natured people or nation. 2) agreeable to the inclination, according [illegible] suitable to one's inclination. Es ist mir heute nicht —, zu lesen, auszugehen, I am not in the humour, I have no mind, to read, to go out, to-day; da gehen sie ganz — mit einander spazieren, there they are walking together very good-naturedly. 3) sentimental. —e Verse, sentimental verses. 4) comfortable. Es ist hier recht —, it is very comfortable here; machen Sie es sich hier —, make yourself comfortable here, take here your ease; wir sind or befinden uns hier ganz —, we are, we feel quite comfortable here.

Gemüthlichkeit, *f.* 1) agreeableness, disposition, good-nature. 2) vague desires and sentiments.

Gen, *prep.* [V. Gegen] towards, to. Seine Hände — Himmel heben, seine Augen — Himmel richten, to lift up one's hands to heaven, to turn one's eyes to or towards heaven; [in seamen's lang.] der Wind ist Nord — West, the wind is northwest; [in poetry = nach] — Athen, — Ithaka segeln, to sail to or towards Athens, Ithaca.

Genabelt, *adj.* [in natural history] formed in the middle like a navel, umbilicate, umbilicated.

Genäge, *n.* [-s] repeated and continual sawing.

Genähe, *n.* [-s] 1) the act of sewing continually. Ihr ewiges — ist Schuld, daß &c., it is owing to her sowing perpetually, that &c. 2) that has been sewed. Das ist ein zierliches, schlechtes —, that is elegantly, badly sewed, is an elegant, a miserable needlework.

Genäsche, *n.* [-s] the act of continually eating dainties; the propensity to eat dainties, daintiness.

Genäschig, *adj.* fond of dainties, sweet things and the like, disposed to take such things by stealth; dainty, lickerish. Eine —e Katze, a thievish cat.

Genau, [allied to nahe, near, close; in lower Germany they still use nau; Anglo-Sax. *hneaw*] I. *adj.* sitting close to the body, fitting close or exactly, tight, strait. —e Schuhe, tight or strait shoes. *Fig. a)* [= vertraut] intimate, confidential. Er ist mein sehr —er Freund, he is my very intimate or confidential friend; es besteht zwischen ihnen eine —e, sehr —e Freundschaft, there is a close, a very close connection or friendship between them, they are very intimate or close friends; die Ehe ist die —este Verbindung, marriage is the strictest or closest union. b) perfect, accurate. Eine —e Untersuchung anstellen, to make a narrow search or investigation, to search minutely or narrowly; —e Rechnung ablegen, to give an exact or accurate account; ein —es Gewissen, a narrow, nice conscience. c) agreeing with a thing in its parts and circumstances. Im —en Verstande, in a strict sense, strictly speaking. d) [= ..., äußerst &c.] Der —este Preis einer Waare, the lowest price of a commodity; mit —er Noth entkommen, to escape with great difficulty or narrowly, to make a narrow escape; er ist mit —er Noth dem Galgen entgangen, he was within a hair's breadth of being hanged, he narrowly escaped the gallows. e) [= sparsam, haushältig] parsimonious, close, ... Er ist sehr —, he is very saving or parsimonious; sie ist eine —e Wirthinn, she is a saving, thrifty housewife. II. *adv.* tightly, closely. Die Thüre schließt ganz —, this door shuts very well; sein Rock liegt — an, allzu — an, his coat fits exactly or close, is too close or tight; der Frack liegt so — an, als wenn er auf den Leib gegossen wäre, this [dress-] coat fits very close. *Fig. a)* intimately. Zwei — verbundene Freunde, two friends intimately or closely united. *b)* accurately, exactly, strictly. Ich kenne diesen Herrn —, I know this gentleman very well, perfectly; erzählen Sie uns die Geschichte —, give us an exact or accurate account of the affair; etwas — untersuchen, to examine something narrowly, minutely or closely; er kennt die Umstände —, he is intimately acquainted with the circumstances; er hat den gegebenen Befehl — vollzogen, he executed with exactness or accuracy the order given him; es ist ihm — eingebunden [anbefohlen] worden, he has been strictly enjoined; sich — an eine Regel halten, to follow a rule exactly; wahre Freundschaft nimmt es nicht so —, true friendship is never so strict, so punctilious; er nimmt es damit zu —, he looks too narrowly into it, he takes it too strictly, he is too punctilious; man darf es nicht so — nehmen mit dem, was er sagt, one must not examine, what he says, too rigidly; — genommen, paßt dieses Wort nicht, strictly taken, this word is not proper; er gibt — so viel aus, als er erhält, he spends exactly or just as much as he receives; ich will Ihnen — sagen, was es kostet, I will tell you exactly what it costs. *c)* parsimoniously, savingly. — leben, to live frugally, parsimoniously; er lebt zu —, he is too saving; sich — behelfen, to live very poorly or sparingly; sehr — handeln, to stand haggling for a penny.

Genauheit, *f.* V. Genauigkeit.

Genauigkeit, *f.* 1) accuracy, precision, exactness, strictness. Etwas mit großer — untersuchen, to examine something with great exactness, very narrowly or closely; in Rechnungen und Geschäften muß man große — beobachten, we must use great exactness, we must be very exact in accounts and business; einen Befehl mit der größten — vollziehen, to execute an order with the greatest punctuality. V. Pünktlichkeit. 2) economy, closeness, parsimony. Seine — geht zu weit, he carries his economy or parsimony too far, to an excess.

*Genealog, *m.* [-en, *pl.* -en] [Geschlechtskundige] genealogist.

*Genealogie, *f.* [Geschlechtskunde] genealogy.

*Genealogisch, *adj.* and *adv.* genealogical. —e Tabellen, genealogical tables.

Genecke, *n.* [-s] continual teazing and bantering.

Genehm, *adj.* and *adv.* [from nehmen, to take] agreeable, approved of. Er thut Alles, was mir — ist, he does every thing that is agreeable to me, that pleases me; etwas — halten, to approve of, to assent to something; eine Bitte — halten, to grant a request; einen Vorschlag — halten, to agree to, to accept a proposal. V. Angenehm.

Genehmhalten, *n.* [-s] Genehmhaltung, *f.* V. Genehmigung.

Genehmigen, I. *v. tr.* to approve of, to agree, to assent to, to grant. Einen Vorschlag —, to agree to, to accept a proposal; Verträge —, to ratify treaties; ein Gesuch —, to grant a request; nicht —, to refuse; V. Genehmhalten; [in commerce] einen Wechsel —, to accept a bill of exchange. II. *v. intr.* to allow, to permit, to grant. Der Fürst hat genehmiget, daß &c, the prince has pleased to allow, that &c. SYN. Genehmigen, Zugeben, Zugestehen, Bewilligen, Einwilligen. Genehmigen conveys the idea that what another does, meets with our approbation, that it pleases us. Zugeben and zugestehen do not necessarily imply that we approve of that which we do not prevent; on the contrary, they often include the idea that it is displeasing to us. Bewilligen and einwilligen declare that we willingly grant that which another requires, and are thus distinguished from zugeben and zugestehen which express simply, that we forbear to prevent.

Genehmigung, *f.* approval, consent, assent, ratification. Ohne ihres Vaters —, without her father's consent or approbation; er hat die — der Regierung erhalten, he has obtained the consent or permission of government; die — eines Vertrags, the ratification of a treaty; [in commerce] die — eines Wechsels, the acceptance of a bill of exchange.

Geneige, *n.* [-s] 1) a continual inclining, bowing or stooping. 2) [in geometry] inclination.

Geneigen, *v. intr.* [little used] Einem —, to be favourable to any one, to favour any one.

Geneigt, *adj.* and *adv.* 1) [having an inclination or propensity to do something] inclined, disposed, propense, apt. Die Menschen sind von Natur zum Bösen —, men are naturally inclined or prone to evil; zur Tugend — seyn, to be inclined to virtue; zum Trunke — seyn, to be prone, addicted or given to drinking, to be apt to be drunk; zu gewissen Krankheiten — seyn, to be subject or predisposed to certain diseases; er ist —, vorschnell zu urtheilen, he is apt to prejudge hastily. 2) [having or bearing good-will or affection towards any one] favourable, friendly, kind. Einem — seyn, to bear any one good-will, to be well-disposed; er bezeigte sich ihm sehr —, he showed himself very favourable or friendly to him, very well affected towards him; Einem ein —es Gehör geben, to give any one a favourable hearing; einen —en Richter haben, to have a favourable judge; ich empfehle mich seinem —en Andenken, I recommend myself to his kind remembrance, to his favour; der —e Leser, the gentle, kind or courteous reader.

Geneigtheit, *f.* 1) inclination, propensity, proneness, aptness, bent, bias, disposition. Die — zum Guten, zum Bösen, disposition or propensity to good, to evil; die — zum Götzendienst, the proneness to idolatry. V. Hang, Neigung. 2) friendly disposition, friendliness, good-will, kindness. — gegen Einen empfinden, to bear one good-will, to be well affected towards any one; seine — für mich läßt mich hoffen, daß &c., his kindness to me makes me hope that &c.

*General, *m.* [-es, *pl.* -e, incorrect and provincial Generäle] 1) [commander of an army or of a division of an army] general. Alle —e der Armee, all the generals of the army; der Ober-—, the commander-in-chief, generalissimo. 2) [the chief of an order of monks] general.

General-accise, *f.* excise-general. —accisedirektor, *m.* director-general of the excise. —acciseeinnehmer, *m.* receiver-general of the excise. —adjutant, *m.* adjutant-general. —armeearzt, —armeechirurg, —armeewundarzt, *m.* physician, surgeon general of the army. —auditor, *m.* provost or judge-advocate general of the army. —baß, *m.* [in music] thorough-base; *it.* V. Grundbaß. —befahrung, *f.* [in mining] a general visit of the mines by a superior officer of the mines. —befehl, *m.* general order. —capitel, *n.* chapter general [of an order]. —commandant, *m.* commander-in-chief. —commando, *n.* the office of commander-in-chief. —commissär, *m.* commissary general. —director, *m.* director general. —feldmarschall, *m.* field-marshal general, captain general, generalissimo. —feldwachtmeister, *m.* major-general. —feldzeugmeister, *m.* master general of the ordnance, [in the Austrian army] general of the infantry. —fiscal, *m.* attorney-general. ‡—gewaltiger, *m.* [in military affairs] provost marshal of the army. —inspector, *m.* inspector general. —karte, *f.* general map [of a country]. —kasse, *f.* the treasury. —kassier, *m.* controller general of the treasury or treasurer general of the finances or exchequer. —kriegscommissär, *m.* commissary general of the army. —kriegszahlmeister, *m.* paymaster general of the army. —lieutenant, *m.* lieutenant general. —major, *m.* major general. —marsch, *m.* [a march struck up when troops are suddenly put in motion] general. Den —marsch schlagen, to beat the general. —musterung, *f.* general review. —pachter, *m.* farmer-general. —pardon, *m.* general pardon or amnesty. —post, [= Direction or = Amt] *f.* general post-office. —postmeister, *m.* postmaster general. —profos, *m.* V. —gewaltiger. —proviantmeister, *m.* master general of the provisions. —quartiermeister, *m.* quarter-master general. —schlagen, *n.* V. —marsch. —staaten, *pl.* [in the Netherlands] states general. —stab, *m.* general staff of an [the] army. —superintendent, *m.* [a dignity in the Lutheran church] superintendent general. —visitator, *m.* visitor general. —vorsteher, *m.* overseer general. Der —vorsteher einer Universität, the syndic general of a university. —wagenmeister, *m.* master general of the waggon-train. —s-würde, *f.* office and dignity of a general.

*Generalāt, *n.* [-es, *pl.* -e] 1) the office and dignity of a general, generalship. 2) the place or office of a superintendent, superintendency.

*Generālinn, *f.* general's wife or lady. Die Verfasserinn dieses Buches ist die Frau Generalinn [better, if the title must needs be added, Frau General] M., this book is by Mrs. General M.

*Generalisíren, *v. tr.* to generalize. V. Verallgemeine[r]n.

*Generalíssimus, *m.* commander in chief, generalissimo. V. Oberfeldherr.

*Generalität, *f.* the general officers of an army.

*Generālschaft, *f.* the office of a general, generalship.

*Generatiōn, *f.* generation.

*Genērisch, *adj.* and *adv.* generic, generical. V. Geschlechtlich.

Genēsen, [allied to genießen, to enjoy, and nähren, to nourish] *ir. v. intr.* [u. w. seyn] to regain health after sickness, to grow well, to recover. Er wird von seiner Krankheit, seinem Fieber nicht —, he is not likely to recover from his illness, his fever; ich hoffe, bald zu —, I hope I shall soon get well; er brauchte sehr lange, um von seiner Krankheit zu —, he was very long in recovering his health; er ist kaum von einer schweren Krankheit —, he has but just recovered from a dangerous illness; [in poetry, rather stiff] seiner Liebe —, to be cured of one's love. 2) [obsolescent] to be delivered of a child. Sie ist glücklich eines Knaben, einer Tochter —, she has been safely delivered of a boy, a daughter; das —, V. Genesung.

Genēsende, *m.* and *f.* [-n, *pl.* -n] convalescent.

Genes-haus, *n.* V. Krankenhaus. —mittel, *n.* V. Genesungsmittel.

Genēsung, *f.* restoration from sickness, recovery, convalescence. Vollkommene, gänzliche —, perfect, entire recovery; auf dem Wege der — seyn, to be in a fair way of recovery; es ist mir lieb, Sie auf dem Wege der — anzutreffen, I am happy to find you in a mending condition; mit seiner — ist es vorbei, he is past recovery, past all hope of recovery.

Genesungs-kraut, *n.* medicinal herb. V. Heilkraut. —mittel, *n.* medicine, remedy. V. Arzenei. Allgemeines —mittel, a universal medicine or remedy, a panacea, catholicon.

Genéttkatze, *f.* [*pl.* -n] [an animal of the weasel kind, less than the martin] genet.

Genf, *n.* [-s] [a town in Switzerland] Geneva.

Genfer, *m.* [-s, *pl.* -] Genferinn, *f.* inhabitant of Geneva. Die —, the Genevese or Genevois.

Genfer, Genferisch, *adj.* and *adv.* of or from or belonging to Geneva, Genevese.

Geníck, *n.* [-es, *pl.* -e] [V. Nacken] the prominent joint of the neck behind, nape; *it.* the neck. Einem einen Stich in das — geben, to give any one a stab in the nape; einem Thiere das — brechen, abstoßen, to break an animal's nape or neck; [sich] das — brechen [in falling], to break one's neck. V. Nacken.

Genick-drüse, cervical gland. —fang, *m.* [among hunters] a stab in the neck with a hanger. Einem Hirsche den —fang geben, to kill a stag by stabbing him in the neck. —fänger, *m.* [among hunters] a hanger. —fistel, *f.* [in farriery] pollevil. —mäuslein, *n.* [in anatomy] one of the three muscles of the thorax, scalenus. —schmerz, *m.* —weh, *n.* pain in the nape or neck. —schmerzen, —weh haben, to have a pain in the nape of one's neck.

Genícke, *n.* [-s] [from nicken] a continual or repeated nodding.

Genícken, *v. tr.* [from Genick] [among hunters] to stab in the neck with a hanger.

*Genie, [pron. Schenih] *n.* [-'s, *pl.* -s] [a man of superior intellectual faculties, and those faculties themselves] genius. Ein seltenes —, a rare genius; ein glückliches — ist eine Gabe der Natur, a happy genius is a gift of nature; — zur Mahlerei, zur Dichtkunst, a genius or talent for painting, for poetry; dieser Junge hat —, he is a lad of genius; *er will ein — seyn, he sets up for a wit.

Geniestreich, *m.* [in familiar language, chiefly in joke] sly, cunning trick; *it.* an extravagant trick, highflown exertion.

*Geniecorps, [pron. Schenih-kohr] *n.* [in military affairs] the corps or body of military engineers.

Geníeß, *m.* [-es] [obsolete or provinc. for Genuß] taste of a thing, enjoyment; [among hunters] the bowels and blood of the beast taken which is given to the dogs as an encouragement. Den Hunden den — geben, to give the hounds the quarry. *Fig.* *a)* profit, gain, advantage. *b)* intercourse, communion. Was hat die Gerechtigkeit für — mit der Ungerechtigkeit? [in Script.] what fellowship has righteousness with unrighteousness?

Genieß-brauch, *m.* [-es] usufruct. V. Nießbrauch, Nutznießung. —jagen, *n.* [among hunters] the first chase in autumn, the entering or blooding of hounds.

Geníeßbar, *adj.* and *adv.* fit to be taken as food or drink, eatable, drinkable. Dieses Fleisch ist nicht —, this meat is not fit to be eaten, is not eatable; dieser Wein ist sauer, er ist nicht —, this wine is sour, it is not fit to drink, is not drinkable. *Fig.* capable of being enjoyed, fit for enjoyment. Ein —es Buch, an amusing book; er ist heute gar nicht —, he is insupportable to-day.

Geníeßbarkeit, *f.* quality of being eatable or drinkable; *fig.* capability or possibility of being enjoyed.

Geníeßen, [allied to nähren] *ir. v. tr.* 1) to take as food or drink, to eat or to drink. Dieses Gericht ist wohl zu —, this dish is very eatable; dieser Wein ist nicht zu —, this wine is not fit to drink, is not drinkable; er hat seit drei Tagen nichts genossen, he has not taken or tasted any thing these three days; — Sie doch ein wenig davon, pray, taste a bit of it; [among hunters] den Hund genossen machen, to feed or reward the hound with the entrails and blood of the beast taken, to give the hound the quarry, to blood the hounds. *Fig.* to enjoy. Die or der Freuden dieses Lebens —, to enjoy the pleasures or comforts of this life; unser Vaterland genießt Ruhe or der Ruhe, our country enjoys quiet or peace; damals genoß er die or der Achtung aller rechtschaffenen Leute, at that time he enjoyed or possessed the esteem of all honest people; *it.* to have the benefit, the use of something; einen Garten, eines Gartens —, to enjoy a garden; er hat diese Pfründe 10 Jahre lang genossen, he has had the enjoyment of this benefice for ten years; glücklich sind diejenigen, welche einen guten Unterricht genossen haben, happy they that have received a good education, that have enjoyed the advantage of a good education; mein Bruder hat viele Wohlthaten bei ihm, von ihm genossen, my brother has been loaded with benefits or kindnesses at his house, he has received many acts of kindness at his hands; davon genieße ich nichts, I have no use, profit or advantage of it, it is of no use to me; *Jemand —, seines Umgangs —, to enjoy any one's company; er ist so beschäftigt, daß man ihn nicht — kann, he is so busy that one cannot have the pleasure of his company; Einen — [sich lustig über Einen machen], to laugh at any one, to make a fool of any one; *it.* *dieser Mensch ist heute nicht zu —, this man is insupportable, insufferable to-day; die Verse sind nicht zu —, these verses are very bad, are detestable, insufferable; [in popul. lang.] ein Frauenzimmer — [dessen letzte Gunst —], to enjoy a woman; [among hunters] der Jäger hat genossen [hat schon geschossen], the hunter has already shot. 2) [among hunters = riechen] [to] scent, to smell. Der Hund genießt die Fährte, the hound catches the scent or track.

Geníeßlich, *adj.* and *adv.* V. Genießbar.

Geníeßling, *m.* V. Nießling.

Geníeßung, *f.* V. Genuß.

Geniewesen, [pron. Schenihwesen] *n.* [-s] [in military affairs] any thing belonging to the act of fortification or relating to the body of military engineers.

Genīpabaum, *m.* [-s, *pl.* -bäume] [in botany] genip-tree, janipaba [a Brasilian tree].

Geníst, *n.* [-es, *pl.* -e] 1) fragments of sticks, straws, twigs and the like, serving to form a bird's nest. 2) [Gesträuch] brushwood. V. Genster.

Geníste, *f.* V. Genster.

Génitiv, *m.* [-s, *pl.* -e] [in Grammar] genitive case.

*Génius, *m.* 1) [*pl.* Genien] [a tutelary being] genius. Der gute oder böse —, the good or evil spirit or demon; der böse —, cacodemon. 2) V. Genie.

Genizabaum, V. Genipabaum.

Genōß, *m.* [-ssen, *pl.* -ssen] [Sw. *not*, ... *nauto*, probably from genießen] [frequently in a bad sense] companion, fellow, partner, confederate. V. Amtsgenoß, Bettgenoß &c.

Genóssenschaft, *f.* company, society, fel-
›wship, association, partnership. Eine gelehrte
–, a literary society; die —en der Christen,
›e assemblies of the Christians, the Christian
›cieties.

Genóssinn, *f.* a female companion or part-
er, consort.

Génsel, *m.* [-s] [in botany] purslain.

Génserich, *m.* V. Gänserich.

Génster, *m.* [-s] [probably = Geniste, from
t many little rods or twigs] [in botany] broom,
nista. Der wilde oder pfeilförmige —, ge-
sta sagittalis or genistella; der stachelige
er kleine deutsche —, green broom; spanischer
–, Spanish broom; der Färbe—, common
er's genista or broom. V. Pfriemenkraut.

Gént, *n.* [-s] [a town in Belgium] Ghent.

Génua, *n.* [-'s] [a town in Italy] Genoa.

Genuéser, *m.* [-s, *pl.* -] **Genuéserinn**, *f.*
noese.

Genuéser, Genuésisch, *adj.* and *adv.* Geese.

Genúg, [Dan. nok, Sw. *nog*, seems allied to
hen] [indeclinable] *adj.* and *adv.* enough,
ficient, sufficiently. Es ist —, ich habe —,
s enough or sufficient, it suffices, I have enough,
ave got enough; ich habe — geschrieben, gegess-
, I have written, eaten enough; er hat —
han, um seinen guten Willen zu zeigen, he has
ne enough, to show his willingness; — der
ränen, der Complimente! no more tears! let
forbear compliments or ceremonies! schon —
des Streites, we or you have disputed
ough; er ist listig —, um &c., he is subtle
cunning enough, to &c.; Sie kommen früh
, you come early enough; dazu ist er nicht
cheidt —, he is not wise enough for that; es
an Einem — [Einer or Eins ist —], one is
ficient or enough, one will do; es ist übrig
there is more than enough; ich habe übrig
, I have got plenty, more than I want; das
mir —, that is sufficient or enough for me,
n satisfied or contented with that; laß dir
— seyn, let that suffice you, be satisfied
h that; es ist nicht —, daß man es sagt,
s not enough to say so; sich selbst — seyn,
e sufficient of one's self; der Mensch ist sich
t — zu seinem eigenen Glücke, man is not
icient of himself to his own happiness; ich
e das oft — erfahren, I have experienced
t often enough; er hat es theuer — bezahlt,
as paid it dear enough; hat er Vermögen?
ig —, has he any fortune? little enough;
zu leben haben, to have a competency or
ciency; — zu arbeiten haben, to have busi-
enough, to have plenty of work; [it almost
ys follows the noun to which it refers] hundert
an sind —, um &c., a hundred men are sufficient
&c.; ich hatte nicht Zeit — dazu, I had not
enough for it; ist eine gute Erziehung
t Erbtheil —? is a good education not a
cient inheritance or patrimony? ich bin
t Kenner —, nicht — Kenner, um &c., I
not judge enough, to &c.; hier ist Geld —,
Wassers, Brotes &c., there is money enough,
r, bread enough; *it.* [it sometimes denotes a
t augmentation of the positive degree, or diminu-
delicately expressing rather less than is desired]
igh, pretty; das Wetter, so schlecht es auch
war noch günstig —, the weather, bad as
s, was yet favourable enough; er hat sich
gut — herausgezogen, he got out of the
e, he got off well enough; das ist gut —
Sie, that is good enough for you; ei!
t hübsch —, why, she is handsome enough.

enüge, *f.* state of having enough, suffi-
ciency, competency. Ich habe mein —, I have my fill; ich habe zur —, I have got enough, *it.* I have eaten enough, I am satisfied; es ist zur —, it is enough of it; ich habe zur — geschlafen, I have slept my fill; Lebensmittel zur — haben, to have provisions enough, plenty of provisions; Geld zur — haben, to have money enough, plenty of money; an alle dem habe ich kein —, all that cannot satisfy or content me. V. Genügsamkeit, Mäßigkeit. *it.* discharge of a duty, satisfaction. Dem Beleidigten — thun, to give a proper satisfaction to an injured or offended person; dem Gesetze — thun, to obey, to submit to the law; dies thut mir noch keine —, that does not yet satisfy or content me; es ist schwer, Jedermann — zu thun, zu leisten, it is hard, to satisfy, to content, to please every body; Jemandes Erwartung — leisten, thun, to answer any one's expectation; das ist eine Sache, die Ihrer Erwartung nie —, keine — thun wird, 'tis an affair that will never turn out to your satisfaction; sich selbst — thun, leisten, to satisfy or please one's self, to make one's self satisfaction.

Genügeleistung, *f.* satisfaction.

Genügen, *v. impers. intr.* to be enough or sufficient, to suffice. Mir genügt an Wenigem, a little is enough or sufficient for me, I am satisfied or content with a little; meinem Herzen kann dies nicht —, that cannot give content to my heart, cannot satisfy my heart; mir genügt schon, zu wissen, it is enough or sufficient for me to know; sich — lassen, to be satisfied or contented; wohl dem, welcher sich — läßt, welcher sich an dem, was er hat, — läßt, happy he, who is contented with what he has. *Prov.* Der ist reich genug, der sich — läßt, whoever is content, is rich; wer Allen — will, muß früh aufstehen, he had need rise betimes that would please every body; he that would please all and himself too, undertakes what he cannot do. Das —, 1) satisfaction, contentment. 2) [= Genüge] Ein — haben, to have a competence, to be satisfied; vollkommenes — thun, to give full satisfaction. *it.* rarely used for Vergnügen.

Genüglich, *adj.* and *adv.* V. Genügsam.

Genüglichkeit, *f.* V. Genügsamkeit.

Genugsam, *adj.* and *adv.* sufficient, enough. —e Stärke, sufficient strength; ein —es Auskommen haben, to have a competency or sufficiency; —e Sicherheit geben, to give sufficient security; der —e, all—e Gott, all-sufficient God; dieser Definition fehlt es an —er Deutlichkeit, this definition is not perspicuous enough; — schlafen, to sleep one's fill; es ist — bewiesen, it is sufficiently proved.

Genügsam, *adj.* and *adv.* easily satisfied, contented, frugal. — seyn, to be satisfied or content with little; ein —er Mensch, a frugal, moderate man; ein —es Herz, a contented heart; er ist sehr — in seinen Forderungen, Wünschen, he is very moderate or reasonable in his demands, desires; — leben, to live frugally.

Genugsamkeit, *f.* state of being sufficient, sufficiency.

Genügsamkeit, *f.* contentedness, frugality, moderation. — geht über Reichthum, contentment is the greatest wealth or beyond riches.

Genugthuend, *adj.* giving satisfaction; [in theology] satisfactory. Der —e Tod Jesu, the satisfactory death of Christ; —e Werke, satisfactory actions.

Genugthun, [V. Thun] *ir. v. intr.* to satisfy. Einem Gläubiger —, to satisfy a creditor; einem Beleidigten —, to give a proper satisfaction to an injured person; dem Gesetze —, to submit to, to obey the law; sich selbst —, to satisfy, to please one's self, to give one's self satisfaction; [in theology] Christus hat für unsere Sünden genuggethan, Christ has atoned for our sins.

Genugthuung, *f.* satisfaction. Einem — geben, leisten, to give any one satisfaction, to satisfy any one; einem Beleidigten — geben, to give a proper satisfaction to an injured person; Sie werden für diesen Schimpf nie eine — erhalten, you will never obtain satisfaction for this injury; ich fordere wegen der or für die Unverschämtheit Ihres Bedienten — von Ihnen, I demand or require satisfaction of you for the impudence of your man; er hat sich selbst — verschafft, he did himself justice, he righted himself; ich werde Ihnen in Ansehung Ihrer Forderungen — verschaffen, I shall satisfy you with regard to your demands; es ist eine elende —, die der Rachsüchtige nimmt, it is a wretched satisfaction that the revengeful man takes; [in theology] die — des Sohnes Gottes, [the reconciliation of men with God] the satisfactory death of the son of God, atonement; die Lehre von der —, the doctrine or tenet of atonement; die — für unsere Sünden, the atonement or expiation for our sins.

‡Genúng, V. Genug.

***Génus**, *n.* [*pl.* Genera] genus, gender.

Genúß, *m.* [-sses, *pl.* Genüsse] the act of taking as food or drink. Man muß im —sse der Speisen und Getränke mäßig seyn, we must be temperate in the use of food and drink or in eating and drinking; der — dieser Pflanze ist tödtlich, eating that plant causes death; gleich nach dem —, nach dem —sse dieses Getränkes befand er sich übel, immediately after having partaken of that drink, he was taken ill; der — des heiligen Abendmahls, the celebration of the Lord's supper, the participation of the holy sacrament, the communion. [among hunters] V. Genieß; *it.* the mere smell or scent; der — der Fährte, the scent of the track. *Fig.* enjoyment. Der — der Ruhe, der Gesundheit, the enjoyment of quiet, of health; seine Hoffnungen sind größer als seine Genüsse, his hopes are greater than his enjoyments; das gewährt mir vielen —, that affords me great pleasure, satisfaction, or enjoyment; sinnliche, geistige Genüsse, sensual, spiritual or intellectual enjoyments or pleasures; das ist ein reiner —, that is a pure or innocent pleasure or enjoyment; Alles strebte nach — und floh die Mühe, every one pursued pleasure and fled from toil. *it.* occupancy of any thing good or desirable. Den — eines Gartens haben, to have the enjoyment or use of a garden; er ist in dem vollständigen —sse seines Vermögens, he is in the full enjoyment or possession of his fortune; er besitzt dieses Gut nicht eigenthümlich, er hat nur den lebenslänglichen — davon, this estate is not his own, he only has the enjoyment, use or usufruct of it for life; der — eines Rechtes, the enjoyment of a right or privilege; ich hatte die Mühe, und er den — [Vortheil], I had the labour or toil, and he reaped or had the profit.

Genuß-jagen, *n.* V. Genießjagen. — **waaren**, *pl.* V. Verbrauchwaaren.

***Geocéntrisch**, *adj.* and *adv.* [in astronomy, having the earth for its centre or the same centre with the earth] geocentric. —e Breite, geocentric latitude.

***Geóde**, *f.* [*pl.* -n] [in mineralogy, a sort of stone with internal cavities] geode. V. Adlerstein.

***Geodesíe**, *f.* [Feldmeßkunst] the art of measuring surfaces, geodesy. Zur — gehörig, geodetic, geodetical.

*Geödisch, *adj.* and *adv.* in form or shape of a geode, geodic.

*Geognosie, *f.* [Gebirgs-, Erdkunde] geognosy.

*Geognöstisch, *adj.* and *adv.* geognostic.

*Geograph, *m.* [-en, *pl.* en] [Erdbeschreiber] geographer.

*Geographie, *f.* [*pl.* -en] [Erdbeschreibung] geography.

*Geographisch, *adj.* and *adv.* geographic, geographical. Ein —es Wörterbuch, geographical dictionary.

Geöhrt, [incorrect Geöhrt] *adj.* and *adv.* having ears, eared; [in botany] auriculate.

*Geolog, *m.* [-en, *pl.* -en] [Erdforscher, Erdkundige] geologist.

*Geologie, *f.* [*pl.* -en] [Erdkunde] geology.

*Geologisch, *adj.* and *adv.* geological.

*Geomant, *m.* [-en, *pl.* -en] [Punktirkünstler] geomancer.

*Geomantie, *f.* [*pl.* -en] [Punktirkunst] geomancy. Zur — gehörig, geomantic.

*Geometer, *m.* [-s, *pl.* -] [Meßkünstler, Feldmesser] geometer, geometrician; surveyor.

*Geometrie, *f.* [*pl.* -en] [Meßkunst, Feldmeßkunst] geometry.

*Geometrisch, *adj.* and *adv.* geometric, geometrical, geometrically. Ein —er Beweis, ein —es Verhältniß, a geometrical demonstration, a geometrical proportion; ein —er Plan or Grundriß [in optics, where the lines are drawn without the least foreshortening], geometrical draught; etwas — beweisen, to demonstrate or prove something geometrically.

Georg, *m.* [-s, *pl.* -e] [a name of men] George.

Georgenskraut, *n.* [Zahnkraut] valerian, tooth-wort. —gestirn, *n.* —planet, *m.* [in astronomy] Georgium Sidus, Uranus. —schwamm, *m.* St. George's agaric. —wurz, *f.* V. —kraut.

Georgchen, ‖Georglein, [-s, *pl.* -] *n.* [*dimin.* of Georg] Georgy.

Georgel, *n.* [-s] a continual and tedious playing upon an organ, hand-organ &c.

Georgien, *n.* [-s] [name of a country in Asia] Georgia.

Georgier, *m.* [-s, *pl.* -] —inn, *f.* an inhabitant of Georgia, a Georgian.

Georgisch, *adj.* and *adv.* Georgian.

*Geostatik, *f.* [science of the equilibrium of the earth] geostatics.

Gepaart, [*past part.* of Paaren, which see] *adj.* and *adv.* [in botany] fünffach &c. —, V. Fünfpaarig &c.

Gepäcke, *n.* [-s, *pl.* -] baggage, luggage. Das schwere — des Heeres, the heavy baggage of the army.

Gepfeife, *n.* [-s] a continual whistling or piping; [among birdcatchers] way of catching birds with a birdcall.

Gepfneisch, *n.* [-es] [among hunters] V. Genieß, Jägerrecht.

Gepickt, *adj.* and *adv.* [in architecture] vermiculated. V. Picken.

Gepipe, *n.* [-s] continual crying or pipping of chickens.

Geplacke, *n.* [-s] continual toiling, hard work, drudgery.

Geplänkel, *n.* [-s] [in military affairs] a continual skirmishing or pickeering.

Geplapper, *n.* [-s] a continual blabbing chatting, tattling, tittle-tattle.

Geplärre, *n.* [-s] continual bawling.

Geplätscher, *n.* [-s] continued purling or gurgling. Das — eines Baches, the purling of a brook; das — eines Springbrunnens, the falling noise of a fountain.

Geplätze, *n.* [-s] cracking, crash; *it.* crackling of the fire, crepitation.

Geplauder, *n.* [-s] continual talking, tattling.

Gepoche, *n.* [-s] the act of knocking repeatedly, a knocking.

Gepolter, *n* [-s] a great or thundering noise, a tumbling noise. SYN. Gepolter, Geprassel, Gerassel, Geräusch, Getöse, Getümmel. Geräusch is opposed to Stille [stillness], and signifies noise or sound of any kind generally. Silk dresses, falling rain, the wind, arms, make ein Geräusch. Ein Getöse proceeds from more violent impressions. One says: das Getöse of a waterfall, of a battle &c. Gerassel, is the noise caused by chains, carriage-wheels &c. rattling over pavement &c. Geprassel is the noise produced by the violent separation of solid bodies. Eine Mauer stürzt mit Geprassel ein [a wall falls with a crash]. Gepolter is the sound made by the falling of solid bodies. Getümmel is properly the bustle produced by a multitude of men or animals moving in a disorderly manner.

Gepräge, *n.* [-s] a mark imprinted, impression, stamp. Das — auf einer Münze, the stamp or impression on a coin; das — dieser Schaumünze hat sich gut erhalten, the type or stamp of this medal is well preserved; das — der Republik, the coinage of the Republic. *Fig.* Man erkennet das — seines Geistes auf jedem Blatte dieser Schrift, every page of this writing bears the stamp of his genius; seine Helden tragen, haben ein sonderbares —, his heroes are of a singular stamp or character.

Geprahle, *n.* [-s] boasting, bragging.

Gepränge, *n.* [-s] pomp, pageantry, show. Seinen Einzug mit großem — halten, to make one's entry with great pomp or pageantry; das — lieben, to be fond of ostentation or show; er erschien mit vielem, mit königlichem —, he made his appearance in great, royal state, with great or royal magnificence, with a numerous or royal train or retinue; Einen mit großem — begraben, to bury any one with great pomp; er thut Alles mit —, he does every thing with great pomp or pompously; *fig.* das — der Rede, the loftiness of style, lofty or pompous style. V. Leichen—, Wort—.

Geprassel, *n.* [-s] a crackling, rattling noise. Das — der Waffen, the clashing or clang of arms; das — des Feuers, the crackling of the fire; [in chimistry] das — des Salzes, the crackling or crepitation of salt [in the fire]. SYN. V. Gepolter.

Gequäke, *n.* [-s] continual croaking [of frogs].

Gerade, [allied to the Lat. *rectus*, the Germ. recht, Ice. *hratur*] *adj.* and *adv.* 1) [not deviating or crooked] straight. Eine — Linie, a straight line; ein —r Weg, a straight way or road; — Beine, straight legs; den Rücken —, sich — halten, to stand straight or upright; — gehen, to walk erect or upright; — gewachsen seyn, to have straight limbs; ein —r Gang, an erect or upright gait, *it.* a straight alley or walk; —s Wegs, in a straight course or line, directly; —s Wegs nach Paris reisen, zu Einem gehen, to travel straight or directly to Paris, to go straight to see a person; —n Weges steuern, [in seamen's lang.] to make a straight course; *fig.* —s Wegs, straight-ways, directly, immediately; [in botany] ein —r Zweig, —s Blatt, —r Stengel, a straight branch, leaf, stalk; ein —r Lichtstrahl, a direct ray [opposed to a reflected ray]; die Größe einer krummen Linie durch eine — angeben, to rectify a curve. *Fig.* Ein —r Mann, an honest, upright man; einen —n Sinn, Verstand haben, to have an upright judgment, a sound understanding; er hat ein —s Gemüth, he has a downright mind; er geht überall den —n Weg, he is an upright man in all his dealings, he has a straightforward, honest or plain way of dealing; in —r Linie von Einem abstammen, to descend in a direct line from any one; — Zahl, an even number; [illegible] — seyn lassen, not to be overstrict or rigorous, to connive at a thing; —s Verhältniß, — Proportion, a direct proportion [opposed to an inverse proportion]. 2) extending or moving directly towards a certain point; [in geometry] perpendicular. Eine — Säule, Mauer, an upright, perpendicular column, wall; diese Mauer steht nicht —, this wall is not perpendicular; [in architecture] ein —r Bogen, a straight arch; [in astronomy] die — Sphäre, the right sphere [that aspect of the heavens in which the circles of daily motion of the heavenly bodies are perpendicular to the horizon]; die — Aufsteigung eines Gestirnes, the right ascension; [in geometry] ein —r Kegel, a right cone [whose axis is perpendicular to its base]; [in seamen's language] — über dem Anker seyn, to have the anchor a-peak. *Fig.* Das — Gegentheil, [illegible] the contrary; das steht mit seinen Ansichten in —m Widerspruche, that is in direct [illegible] diametrical opposition, is directly or diametrically opposed to his views or opinions; er traf — in die Mitte, he hit or struck exactly the middle or centre; er kam —, — in demselben Augenblicke, als ich fortging, he arrived at the very moment when I went away; ich habe — so viel dafür gegeben, als ich jetzt erhalte, [illegible] gave just as much for it as I now get; ich [illegible] — so alt als er, I am just as old as he is, [illegible] are exactly of the same age; es war —, [illegible] ich wollte, it was just or exactly what I wanted; es ist mir —, als ob ich ihn schon irgendwo gesehen hätte, I have already seen him somewhere, or I am greatly mistaken; er spricht [illegible] mir —, als ob er mein Herr wäre, he speaks to me just as if he was my master; — heraus [ohne Umstände], freely, in plain terms, bluntly, without ceremonies or reserve; ich werde [illegible] — heraus sagen, daß &c., I shall tell him flatly, plainly, frankly, that &c.; nach — [written nachgerade = allmählig], by little and little, by degrees; nach — kommt die Zeit heran, wo [illegible] the time is drawing near insensibly, when [illegible] — herunter, plumb-down, perpendicularly. —

Geradesan, *adv.* 1) straight on or along. — ankommen, to approach in a direct line, to come straight along. 2) close by, hard by. Er wohnt hier —an, he lives close by, next door. —auf, *adv.* upwards in a straight line or direction. Der Weg geht den Berg —auf, the way leads straight or directly up the mountain. —aus, *adv.* straight on, straight forward. Der Weg geht immer —aus, the way leads, goes straight on. —hin, *adv.* straight on; *fig.* without consideration. Ich mochte ihm nicht — hin antworten, I did not choose to answer him rashly or inconsiderately. —machung, *f.* the making straight, straightening. Die Größebestimmung einer krummen Linie durch eine —machung, the rectification of a curve. —messer, *m.* [among carpenters and coopers] a kind of level or ruler. —richtung, *f.* V. —machung. —sinn, *m.* V. Gerad[illegible] —weg, *adv.* straight-forward, without hesitation, plainly, freely. —weg sprechen, to speak frankly, freely. —zu, *adv.* straig[illegible] on, straight-forward. **Gehen Sie —zu**, walk straight on; **dieser Weg führt —zu nach Paris**, this road leads directly to Paris. *Fig.* **Er geht in allen seinen Handlungen —zu**, he is an upright man in all his dealings, he has an honest, upright, straight-forward way of acting; **sagen Sie mir nur —zu, Sie lieben mich nicht mehr**, tell me openly, frankly, you love me no longer; ***mit Einem —zu umgehen**, to be very familiar with a person; **sich —zu an den Königwenden**, to apply directly to the king; **Waaren —zu versenden**, to forward goods directly; *it.* [in familiar language] bluntly, cavalierly, unmannerly; **er handelte sehr, zu sehr —zu**, he makes himself too familiar, he acts too cavalierly, too freely.

Gerad-lauf, *m.* a straight or direct course or motion. **Der —lauf eines Schiffes**, orthodromy. **—läufig**, *adj.* and *adv.* having a straight course, direct. [in astronomy] **Diese Planeten sind —läufig**, these planets are direct [appear to move forward in the zodiac in the direction of the signs]. **—linicht**, *adj.* and *adv.* resembling a straight line. **—linig**, *adj.* and *adv.* consisting of a right line or right lines, right lined, rectilineal, rectilinear. **Ein —liniges Dreieck, eine —linige Figur**, a rectilinear triangle, figure. **—sinn**, *m.* V. **Geradheit** [*fig.*]. **—sinnig**, *adj.* and *adv.* upright, honest, righteous.

1. **Gerāde**, [V. **Gerade**, *adj.*] *f.* quality or state of being straight. **Das Eisen in die — bringen** [**gerade richten**], to make the iron straight, to straighten it.

2. **Gerāde**, *f.* and *n.* [instead of **Geräth**, which see] [the goods which remain at the wife's disposition after her husband's death] paraphema, paraphernalia.

Gerādheit, *f.* rectitude, straightforwardness. *Fig.* [**Aufrichtigkeit**] uprightness, integrity, honesty. **Seine — geht so weit, daß &c.**, his integrity goes so far, as to &c.; **Mangel an —des Herzens**, want of righteousness or rectitude; **die — seiner Absichten**, the uprightness of his views or intentions.

Geraid, *n* [-es, *pl.* -e] V. **Gereut**.

Geräse, *n.* [-s] constant raving, violent rage, fury.

Gerässel, *n.* [-s] [continual] rattling or clanking. **Ein — von Ketten, von Waffen**, a clanking of chains, a clang or clash of arms. V. **Gepolter**.

Geräth, *n.* [-es, *pl.* -e] [from **reiten** = **bereiten**, that is **fertig machen** &c.] [collectively = **Hausrath**] goods, vessels, utensils and other appendages necessary or convenient for housekeeping, household-furniture. **Ein Haus mit kostbarem —e**, a house with splendid furniture, a house richly or splendidly furnished; **ein Zimmer mit dem nöthigen —e versehen**, to furnish a room with what is necessary; **ein mit —e versehenes Zimmer**, a furnished chamber or room; **silbernes &c. —**, vessels of silver, silver plate; **leinen** or **Linnen-, weißes —**, linen, clean linen; **das schwarze —**, foul or dirty linen; **das — eines Handwerkers**, the tools, implements of a mechanic; **das — in der Küche**, kitchen utensils; **das —** [= **Kleider**], apparel, clothes; [in Scripture] **des Mannes — soll ein Weib nicht tragen**, the woman shall not wear that which pertaineth unto a man; **das — zur Ausssteuer**, [the goods which a wife brings with her at her marriage] paraphema or paraphernalia. V. **Acker—, Bau—**.

Geräth-holz, *n.* [among foresters] timber, straight timber. **—kammer**, *f.* room where the foul linen is kept, laundry; *it.* a room for the reception of all sorts of furniture or tools, a lumberroom. **—kasten**, *m.* a chest for the reception of linen.

Gerāthen, [allied to **gerade**] *ir. v. intr.* [used with **seyn**]. 1) to come, fall or get somewhere by chance or accident. **In Eines Hände —**, to fall into any one's hands; **unter schlechte Menschen —**, to fall or get into bad company; **das ist an den rechten Mann, in gute Hände —**, that has fallen into good hands; **auf den falschen Weg —**, to lose one's way, to go astray, *fig.* to deviate, to stray from the path of duty, to err; **wir geriethen unter Räuber**, we fell in with robbers; **Einem über das Geld —**, to fall on any one's money [to take some of it]; [in Scripture] **der Geist Gottes gerieth** [**kam**] **über ihn**, the spirit of the Lord came upon him; **einander in die Haare —**, to fall together by the ears; **in Streit —**, to be engaged in a dispute or quarrel; **an einander —**, to attack or assault one another, to fall together by the ears, to go to loggerheads; **die beiden Heere geriethen an einander**, the two armies came to blows, engaged in close fight; **sie sind hart an einander —**, they had a fierce or rude encounter, they fought stoutly or obstinately, *it.* they had a violent quarrel; **von Worten geriethen sie in ein Handgemenge** [or †**kam's zu Schlägen**], from words they came to blows; **an Einen —**, [on a journey &c.] to meet with any one; **wie sind Sie an diesen Mann —?** how came you to light upon this man, to get acquainted with this man? **das Erbe ist an den Sohn —**, the inheritance or succession fell to the son; **zu etwas —**, to get or obtain something by chance or accident; **ich bin zu diesem Hause —, ich weiß nicht wie**, I got this house, or the possession of this house, I know not how; **ich bin wohlfeil dazu —**, I got it cheap, or a bargain; **auf eine irrige Meinung —**, to embrace or adopt an erroneous opinion; **ich bin auf den Gedanken —**, it came into my thoughts, into my head, it occurred to my mind, it struck me; **in einen Irrthum, Fehler —**, to make or commit an error, a fault; **auf eine Sache —**, to fall or hit upon a thing [by chance]; **er gerieth auf tausend närrische Einfälle**, a thousand foolish thoughts or ideas occurred to him, he had or lighted on a thousand foolish thoughts or ideas; **als ich das Buch aufschlug, gerieth ich auf folgende Stelle**, when I opened the book, I fell or lighted upon the following passage; **in Zorn —**, to fall into a passion, to fly into a passion, to get into a rage; **in Entzücken —**, to fall into rapture, to be transported with joy; **die Sache ist ins Stocken —**, the affair has been stopped, has come to a stand; **in Vergessenheit —**, to fall into oblivion; **in Brand —**, to catch fire; **das Haus, Dach gerieth in Brand**, the house, the roof caught fire; **in Armuth —**, to fall, to become poor, to be reduced to poverty; **in große Gefahr —**, to be exposed to great danger, to run a great risk or hazard; **in großen Schaden —**, to suffer or sustain a great loss or damage; **an den Bettelstab —**, to be reduced to beggary; [in familiar language] **den Leuten in die Mäuler, in der Leute Mäuler —**, to become the common talk of the town. 2) [= **gereichen**] to turn out, to prove. **Das wird zu Eurem Nutzen —**, that will turn out to your advantage; **das wird zum Ärgerniß —**, that will give offence; **das kann zu seinem Verderben —**, that may turn to his ruin, may prove his ruin, may ruin him. 3) to turn out well, to succeed, to prosper, to thrive. **Alles was er vornimmt, geräth ihm**, he succeeds in whatever he undertakes, every thing he undertakes prospers with him; **Obstbäume — in diesem Boden wohl**, fruit-trees thrive well in this soil; **der Wein ist heuer nicht —**, the vintage has failed, there has been little or bad wine this year; **das Korn ist dieses Jahr —, gut —**, corn has been plentiful this year; **seine Kinder wollen nicht —**, his children have bad inclinations; **wohl —e, schlecht —e Kinder**, well-bred, ill-bred children. Syn. V. **Gelingen**.

Gerāthen, [*past part.* of **Rathen**, which see] *adj.* and *adv.* advisable; *it.* useful, advantageous. **Mit dieser Summe wäre mir hinlänglich —**, that sum would answer all my wants, would do my business; **mit diesem Wörterbuche ist mir nicht —**, this dictionary is of no use to me, it will not do for me; **es wäre ihm —er** [**nützlicher**], **auf sein Vorrecht zu verzichten**, it would be more advantageous for him, to waive his privilege.

Gerathewohl, *n.* [*indeclinable*] random, chance, hazard. **Etwas auf das — thun**, to do something at random, at hazard; **etwas auf's — in Vorschlag bringen**, to propose something at random; **auf's —** [**auf gut Glück**] **herumirren**, to wander at a venture; **auf's — schießen**, to shoot at random.

Gerathschaft, *f.* V. **Geräth**.

Geräthschaften-conto, *m.* [in commerce] account of the furniture and utensils. **Geräthschafts-gut**, *n.* the furniture, movable goods, movables.

Geraufe, *n.* [-s] a scuffle, brawl or wrangle.

Geraum, *adj.* 1) spacious, wide, roomy. **Eine —e Kirche**, a spacious church. 2) [of time] long. **Es ist schon eine —e** [= **beträchtliche**] **Zeit her**, it is long, a long or great while since; **ich habe ihn seit** or **in —er Zeit nicht gesehen**, I have not seen him this great while; **eine —e Zeit vor der Gründung Roms**, long or a long space of time before the foundation of Rome; **es ereignete sich vor —er Zeit**, it happened a pretty while ago.

Geräumig, [less usual] **Geräumlich**, *adj.* and *adv.* spacious, wide, large, roomy, ample. **Ein —er Hafen**, a spacious, large port or harbour; **ein —es Zimmer, eine —e Wohnung**, a large or spacious room, a roomy mansion; **er wohnt —**, he has a great deal of room; **— sitzen**, to sit at one's ease.

Geräumigkeit, Geräumlichkeit, *f.* spaciousness, wideness, roominess. **Die — der Zimmer in einem Gebäude**, the spaciousness of the rooms in a building.

Geräumte, *n.* [-s] [among hunters] a lane or road cut through a forest. V. **Stellweg**. [in husbandry] a wood that has been made arable, or land ploughed for the first time. V. **Neuland, Neubruch**.

1. **Geräusch**, *n.* [-es] [from **rauschen**] noise, bustle. **Ein großes, ein dumpfes, ein verwirrtes —**, a great, hollow, confused noise; **macht kein —**, make no noise, do not make any noise; **das — der Wellen, der Winde**, the roaring of the waves or billows, of the winds; **das — der Bäche**, the purling or murmuring of the brooks; **das — auf einem Markte**, the noise or din of people in a market-place; **das — der Waffen**, the clashing or clang of arms; **das — der Stadt**, the bustle or hurry of the town. *Fig.* **Sich vom —e der Welt zurückziehen**, to withdraw or retire from the bustle or noise of the world; **viel —** [**Aufsehen**] **in der Welt machen**, to make a great noise in the world. Syn. V. **Gepolter**.

Geräusch-los, *adj.* and *adv.* making no noise or bustle, noiseless, without noise. **Die —losen Haine waren Zeugen unserer Liebe**, the silent groves witnessed our love. **—voll**, *adj.* and *adv.* full of noise and hustle, noisy.

fügig, *adj.* and *adv*, small, insignificant, trifling, trivial. Ein —fügiger Gegenstand, a trivial subject; ein —fügiger Grund, a frivolous reason or argument; er führte lauter —fügige Umstände an, he adduced or advanced only insignificant, trifling circumstances. —fügigkeit, *f.* 1) insignificance, unimportance, meanness. Die —fügigkeit des Preises, des Einkommens, the lowness of price, the smallness of income; die —fügigkeit eines Grundes, the futility of a reason or argument. 2) trifle, insignificant thing. —fügigkeiten haben oft einen großen Werth für Liebende, trifles often have a great value for lovers; das sind lauter—fügigkeiten, these are mere trifles. —haltig, *adj.* and *adv.* small in value, below the standard. —haltiges Gold, gold of small value, of base alloy; —haltiges Geld, bad, counterfeit money; *fig.* —haltige Gründe, Beweise, weak arguments, proofs. —haltigkeit, *f.* being below the standard, worthlessness; *fig.* futility, weakness, V. —fügigkeit. —haltung, *f.* V. —schätzung. —schätzig, I. *adj.* 1) thinking meanly of others, disdainful, contemptuous, scornful. In einem —schätzigen Tone mit Jemand sprechen, to speak with any one in a disdainful tone. 2) [esteemed lightly] mean, contemptible. —schätzige Dinge, vile, contemptible things. II. *adv.* disdainfully, scornfully, meanly, contemptibly. Jemand —schätzig empfangen, behandeln, to receive, to treat any one disdainfully or slightingly. —schätzigkeit, *f.* 1) V. —schätzung. 2) [state of being esteemed lightly] meanness, small value. —schätzung, *f.* disregard, slight, contempt. Einen mit —schätzung behandeln, to treat any one disdainfully or contemptuously, to slight any one.

Geringheit, *f.* littleness, smallness. Sehen Sie nicht auf die — des Geschenkes, sondern auf meinen guten Willen, do not mind the littleness of the gift, but my good will; die — der Geburt, the meanness, humbleness of birth; die — des Preises, lowness of price, cheapness, low price; die — des Gewichtes, deficiency of weight.

Gerinnbar, *adj.* capable of coagulating, coagulable.

Gerinne, *n.* [-s] 1) a continual running or flowing. 2) [=Rinne] a water-course, kennel, channel, gutter, pipe; [in hydraulics] das — einer Mühle, the trough or channel of a mill; das wüste —, freie —, an opening or sluice to let the water out of a mill-dam; das Stell— or Schleusen—, a trough or channel with a sluice or floodgate; [in papermills] a gutter or trough that conveys the water on the wheel.

Gerinnelt, *adj.* in form of a channel or gutter, channelled, furrowed; [in botany, having a deep longitudinal groove above and convex underneath] canaliculate, canaliculated.

Gerinnen, *ir. v. intr.* [used with seyn] to coagulate, to curdle. Das Blut gerinnt, blood coagulates or clots; die Milch fängt an zu —, the milk begins to curdle; geronnene Milch, geronnenes Blut, curdled or clotted milk, coagulated or clotted blood; ein Gift, das das Blut — macht, a poison that congeals or curdles the blood; das Lab macht die Milch —, rennet curdles the milk. V. 2. Gestehen. Das —, the act of changing from a fluid to a fixed state, concretion, coagulation, curdling.

Gerinn-baum, *m.* a tree used as a trough or channel. V. Gerinne, 2). —haue, *f.* [in mining] a hoe or pick-ax to make kennels or channels with. —senkel, *m.* [in mining] cramping-iron or hook by which a gutter or kennel is kept together. —stein, *m.* [in mining] the best sort of tin-stone pounded and washed.

Gerinnich, *n* [-es] [in salt-works] a conduit or pipe through which the saltwater passes.

Gerippe, *n.* [-s, *pl.* -] [the frame or principal parts of a thing, but without the appendages] skeleton, carcass. *a*) Das — eines Schiffes, Gebäudes, the frame-work of a ship, the carcass or shell of a building; *fig.* [the principal points or ideas of a speech, of an essay &c.] sketch, rough-draught. *b*) Das — eines thierischen Körpers, the skeleton of an animal body. In diesem Museum sieht man eine Menge —, there are a great many skeletons to be seen in that museum; ein natürliches —, a natural skeleton [when the bones are connected by the natural ligaments]; ein künstliches —, an artificial skeleton [when they are connected by wires or any foreign substance]; das ganze Schlachtfeld war noch von —n von Menschen und Pferden bedeckt, the whole field of battle was still covered with the carcasses of men and horses; *fig.* er, sie ist ein wahres —, ein wandelndes —, he, she is a mere skeleton.

Germ, *m.* [-es, *pl.* -e] [allied to Bärme, used in lower Saxony for Wärme, warmth, and to the English barm] yeast, yest, barm. Brod ohne —, unleavened bread. V. Hefen.

Germane, *m.* [-n, *pl.* -n] V. Germanier.

Germanien, *n* [-s] ancient Germany; [in poetry] modern Germany.

Germanier, *m.* [-s, *pl.* -] an ancient German. Die alten — or Germanen, the ancient Germans.

Germanisch, *adj.* and *adv.* pertaining to ancient Germany, Germanic. Das —e Recht, the Germanic law [including the German, Salic and Lombardic law].

Germanismus, *m.* [*pl.* Germanismen] Germanism.

Germen, *v. intr.* to ferment. V. Gähren.

Germer, *m.* [-s] [in botany] white sneezewort, white hellebore. V. Weiße Nießewurz.

Germig, *adj.* and *adv.* [hefig] containing yeast or barm.

Germsel, *m.* [-s] [in botany] the jack-by-the-hedge, Erysimum alliaria. V. Knoblauchskraut.

Gern, [allied to gehren, begehren, to desire] *adv.* 1) [=mit Vergnügen] with pleasure, gladly, cheerfully. Ich thue es —, I do it with pleasure; das lasse ich mir — gefallen, I gladly or cheerfully submit or consent to that, that's what I like; — oder un—, er muß es thun, he must do it whether he will or not, will he, nill he; etwas — haben, to like, to be fond of a thing, to take pleasure in a thing; so habe ich es —, das habe ich —, that is what I like; er hat, er hört es —, wenn man ihn lobt, er hört sich — loben, he loves or likes to hear himself praised, he takes pleasure in being praised; er tanzt, spielt, reitet —, he likes dancing, playing, riding, he is fond of dancing, playing, riding; er ißt — Fische, he likes fish, is fond of fish; dieses Mädchen sieht ihn —, this girl is fond of seing him, likes him; er ist überall — gesehen, he is everywhere welcome; obgleich Sie es nicht — sehen, though you do not like it; er wäre gar zu — abgereist, he wished or wanted very much to set off, he would have departed or set off with great pleasure; ich hätte es für mein Leben — [sehr —] gethan, it would have given me the greatest, the most exquisite pleasure to do it, I should have done it with the greatest pleasure; herzlich —, von Herzen — etwas thun, to do something with all one's heart; von Herzen —, with all my heart; er unternahm es nicht —, he undertook it reluctantly, unwillingly; *fig.* eine Pflanze hat — feucht, trocken &c., a plant likes a wet, a dry &c. soil; die Elephanten halten sich nicht — in kalten Ländern auf, elephants do not enjoy themselves in cold countries. 2) [=willig] without reluctance, readily, willingly. Ich glaube —, daß es nicht Ihre Absicht war, I readily believe, that is was not your intention; ich gestehe — zu, daß ich es nicht errathen hätte, I readily grant, that I should not have guessed it; dieses Pferd läßt sich nicht — beschlagen, this horse is not easy, is difficult to shoe, will never submit to being shod. 3) [= absichtlich] purposely, intentionally. Es ist — geschehen, it was done on purpose, you are welcome to it; ich habe es nicht — gethan, I did it unintentionally, without design or purpose; ich möchte nicht — mit ihm zerfallen, I should not like to fall out with him; ich möchte es — wissen, I would fain know it, I should like to know it; die Forellen halten sich — in fließendem Wasser auf, trouts love running water. 4) [= gewöhnlich, *it.* leicht] commonly, usually; *it.* easily. Wer keine Erfahrung hat, wird — betrogen, a person without experience is usually or easily deceived or taken in; dieses Holz faulet —, this wood rots easily, is apt to rot; die Flüsse treten in dieser Jahreszeit — über, the rivers commonly overflow in this season; ich pflege — früh aufzustehen, I generally rise early, I am fond of rising early; *Prov.* wer — lügt, der stiehlt, shew me a liar, and I'll shew you a thief. 5) [= immerhin, in familiar language] Lassen Sie ihn nur reden, er mag das — sagen, let him talk, he may say so, I care not. Syn. Gern, Willig. Willig [from wollen] merely excludes the notion of external force or constraint; what we do willig [willingly], we do without compulsion, it may perhaps be contrary to our inclination, yet we do it because we yield to good and sufficient reasons. Gern [from gehren, *i. e.* begehren] signifies not only that there is no compulsion, but that what we do gern, is done with pleasure.

Gern-gelehrt, *m.* [in familiar language] would-be learned, a pretender to learning. —gesehen, *n. indecl.* [in fam lang.] welcome. Einen auf ein Gericht —gesehen einladen, to invite any one with all the heart. —groß, *m.* [in fam. lang.] would-be great, a conceited fellow, a proud conceited coxcomb. —klug, *m.* [in familiar language] would-be wise. —schreiber, *m.* [in familiar language] scribbler. —witz, *m.* [in familiar language] would-be wit, pretender to wit

Geröchel, *n.* [-s] a continual rattling in the throat.

Geröhne, V. Gerönne.

Geröhrich, **Geröhricht**, *n.* [-es, *pl.* -e] 1) a place full of reeds. 2) — or Geröhre, *n.* collectively, reeds.

Geroll, *m.* [-es, *pl.* -e] [in natural history] cherry-finch. V. Kirschvogel.

Geröll, *n.* [-es, *pl.* -e] 1) a continual rolling or rumbling. 2) all sorts of things that roll or are rolled.

Geröll[e], *n.* V. Gerölle 1).

Gerönne or **Geröhne**, *n.* [-s] [among vine-dressers] the roots of vines.

Gersch, *m.* [-es] [Sax. in *Gaars* and D. *Gaars* = Gras, grass] [in botany] wild angelica.

Gerschwalbe, *f.* V. Mauerschwalbe.

Gerstammer, *f.* [*pl.* -n] [in natural history] gold hammer, yellow hammer.

Gerste, *f.* [allied to the L. Ceres, Germ Gras, V.

sch] barley. Die gemeine Frühlings—, the common spring-barley; die vierzeilige Winter—, the winter or square-barley; die türkische —, Bart—, Reis—, the sprat, battledore or Putney-barley; das ist schöne —, that is fine barley; geschälte —, peeled or hulled barley; die nackte —, naked barley; sibirische zweizeilige —, Siberian barley.

Gersten=acker, *m.* field of barley, barley-field. —ähre, *f.* ear of barley. —beize, [among tanners] preparation with barley. —bier, *n.* beer brewed of barley. —boden, *m.* 1) soil or land good for barley. 2) barley-loft. —brod, *n.* barley-bread. —brühe, *f.* barley-water. —dieb, *m.* [in popular language] the wood-sparrow. —ernte, *f.* barley-crop, barley-harvest. —feld, *n.* 1) V. —acker. 2) land or soil good for barley. —fliege, *f.* St. Mark's fly. —gras, *n.* barley-grass. —graupe, *f.* peeled barley. Feine —graupen, pearl barley. —grütze, *f.* barley-groats. —halm, *m.* culm or stalk of barley. —haufe, *m.* barley-stack, barley-rick, [in a barn] barley-mow. —kaffee, *m.* barley prepared as a surrogate of coffee; *it.* the beverage prepared from such barley, serving for coffee. —kleie, *f.* barley-bran. —korn, *n.* 1) barley-corn. 2) [in familiar language, the tenth or twelfth part of an inch] line. 3) [a weight] a grain, V. Gran. 4) [in surgery] *a)* [a tumour in the corner of the eye like a barley-corn] Aegilops, sty. *b)* a disease among hogs, V. Rankkorn. 5) [in natural history] a kind of snail with a spiral shell. —kornmuster, *n.* [among silk-weavers] *dessin à grain d'orge.* —krieche, *f.* V. —pflaume. —kuchen, *m.* barley cake. —leder, *n.* [among tanners] leather dressed with a preparation of barley. ||—mahd, *f.* barley-mow. —malz, *n.* malt, barley-malt. —mehl, *n.* barley-meal, barley-flour. —milch, *f.* [a liquor extracted from barley and sweet almonds] orgeat. —mutter, *f.* degenerated barley-corns. —pflaume, *f.* common plum, wild plum. —saat, *f.* the sowing of barley; *it.* season for sowing barley. —saft, *m.* barley-water; *it.* [in poetry and familiar language] beer. —schleim, *m.* thick barley-water, gruel made of barley. —schrot, *m.* barley-groats. —spreu, *f.* chaff of barley. —stroh, *n.* barley-straw. —trank, *m.* a decoction of barley with cinnamon and other ingredients, ptisan; *it.* beer; *it.* V. —wasser. —twalch, *m.* [a weed] darnel. tare, V. Trespe. —wasser, *n.* water in which barley has been boiled, barley-water. —wurm, *m.* V. Erdgrille. —zucker, *m.* barley-sugar [sugar boiled till it is brittle with a decoction of barley].

Gèrsten, *adj.* consisting or made of barley. —es Mehl, barley meal, barley flour; —e Kleie, barley-bran.

Gèrsten, *m.* [-s, *pl.* -] V. Gersting.

Gèrsting, *m.* [-es, *pl.* -e] a kind of cake made of barley flour, milk and eggs.

Gèrtchen, Gèrtlein, [*dimin.* of Gerte] *n.* a small switch.

Gèrte, *f.* [*pl.* -n] [probably allied to Garten and Gurt, in as much as it would be principally destined or used to bind with] switch, twig. Einem Pferde einen Hieb or Hiebe mit der — geben, to switch a horse; ein Reißigbündel mit einer — zusammenbinden, to tie a fagot with a band.

Gèrtel, *n.* [-s] or Gertelnholz, *n.* [-es] [among foresters] coppice-wood, under-wood.

Gèrtenkraut, *n.* [-es] 1) fennel-giant [of the genus ferula]. 2) southern-wood. V. Stabwurz.

Gèrtraud, Gertrūd[e], [der —, and —s or —ens] [a name of women] Gertrude.

Gertrauds=vogel, *m.* [a bird of the blackbird kind, of the size of the thrush] rock-blackbird, great red-start.

Gèrtwurz, *f.* V. Gertenkraut 2).

Gerúch, *m* [-es, *pl* Gerüche] 1) [the faculty or sense of smelling] smell. Die Nase ist das Organ des —es, the nose is the organ of smell; die Hunde haben gewöhnlich einen sehr scharfen —, dogs have generally a very acute smell, the smell of dogs is generally very acute. 2) [the quality of bodies which affects the olfactory organs] smell, scent, odour. Ein guter, übler, starker —, a good, bad, strong smell or odour; ein süßer, lieblicher, angenehmer —, a sweet, agreeable smell or scent; diese Blume hat keinen —, this flower has no smell; ich kann diesen — nicht ausstehen, I cannot bear this smell; einen lieblichen — von sich geben, verbreiten, aushauchen, to yield, to send forth or emit a sweet scent, smell or odour, to exhale an agreeable perfume; dieser Wein hat einen guten —, this wine has a fine flavour; diese Suppe hat einen brandichten —, this soup smells or tastes of burning; einen müffigen, dumpfigen — haben, to have a fusty or musty smell, to smell musty; einen — nach der See, einen See— haben, to smell of the sea, to taste of salt-water; [among hunters] der Hirsch läßt einen stärkern — zurück, als der Hase, the stag leaves a stronger scent than the hare. *Fig.* [= Ruf, reputation, where it appears to stand for Gerücht, which see] Er steht in keinem guten, in einem üblen —, he has no good name, he has a bad name; im —e der Heiligkeit sterben, to die in reputation of sanctity, to die a reputed saint.

Geruchs=kügelchen, *n.* [a dry composition of sweet smelling resins &c.] pastil. —s=nerve, *f.* [in anatomy] olfactory nerve. —s=werkzeuge, *pl.* the organs of smelling, olfactory organs.

Gerúchlos, *adj.* and *adv.* 1) destitute of the faculty or sense of smelling. 2) [yielding no smell] scentless, inodorous, without smell.

Gerúchlosigkeit, *f.* 1) quality of a person destitute of the power of smelling. 2) quality of being scentless or inodorous.

Gerücht, *n.* [-es, *pl.* -e] [allied to Ruf, reputation, and the L. *ru*-mor] rumour, report. Ein falsches —, a false rumour; es geht das —, er sey gestorben, the report goes, or is spread, it is reported or rumoured that he is dead; dieses — geht, läuft in der ganzen Stadt herum, it is a rumour, talk of the town; ein — ausbreiten, unter die Leute, in Umlauf bringen, to spread a report, to rumour something; es hat sich ein — verbreitet, the report is spread, it is rumoured or given out; es geht ein dumpfes —, it is whispered about; es ist ein bloßes —, it is a mere report or rumour; ‡ein gutes — [= einen guten Ruf] haben, to have a good report, name, reputation, character; Einen in ein böses — bringen, to defame, to slander or asperse any one's reputation or character.

Gerücke, *n.* [-s] a continual moving or removing.

Gerühen, *v. intr.* to be pleased, to vouchsafe, to deign, to condescend. Eure Majestät geruhe, may it please your majesty; Eure Majestät haben geruht, ihm zu sagen, your majesty has been pleased to tell him.

Gerühig, *adj.* and *adv.* quiet, calm, tranquil, peaceable, comfortable. Ein —es Leben führen, to lead a quiet and comfortable life. V. Ruhig.

Gerührig, *adj.* and *adv.* [in familiar language] active, lively, brisk. Dieser Alte ist noch sehr —, this old man is still very active.

Gerühsam, *adj.* and *adv.* V. Geruhig.

Gerüll[e], *n.* [-s] [from rollen, to roll] 1) loose things that come off rolling from other things, rubbish, rubble-stones; [in mining] a loose rock that crumbles by degrees. 2) [useless utensils] lumber. V. Gerümpel.

Gerúmpel, *n.* [-s] constant tumbling or rumbling. Das — eines Wagens, the jolting of a carriage; †ich fühle ein — im Magen, my belly grumbles.

Gerümpel, *n.* [-s] any thing useless and cumbersome, lumber, trash, rubbish.

Gerümpel=kammer, *f.* lumber-room. —kasten, *m.* chest or box for old tools and utensils. —markt, *m.* market where old clothes and furniture are sold, rag-fair.

Gerüst, *n.* [-es, *pl.* -e] [among builders, an assemblage or structure of timbers, boards &c., erected by the wall of a building; *it.* a temporary stage raised either for shows or spectators] scaffold, stage. Die —e wegnehmen, to remove, to take down or away the scaffolds or the scaffolding; ein — aufschlagen, to make, raise or erect a scaffold or stage; es werden für den Hof —e aufgeschlagen, stages are erecting for the court; ein fliegendes —, a flying scaffold. V. Blut—, Leichen— &c.

Gerüst=künstler, *m.* [more usual Maschinist] [in theatres] machinist. —stange, *f.* [in architecture] scaffolding-pole; —stangen, [among masons] the upper scaffolding poles, the imps.

Gerüttel, *n.* [-s] a continual shaking, jogging or jolting.

Ges, [as a *subst. n.*] [in music] G flat.

Gesäge, *n.* [-s] continual talk, talking; *it.* say, report, rumour.

Gesäge, *n.* [-s] continual sawing.

†Gesalbader, *n.* [-s] silly, trifling, dull talk, tittle-tattle; *it.* a canting discourse.

Gesalbt, [*past part.* of Salben] Der —e, ein —er, [-en, *pl.* die -en, and without the article, —e] [one consecrated to something by unction] anointed. Der —e, the anointed, the Messiah; der —e des Herrn, the Lord's anointed.

Gesäme, *n.* [-s] seeds collectively. Mit — handeln, to deal in seeds.

Gesämmel, *n.* [-s] the act of collecting or gathering; *it.* a collection, compilation [of wretched poems &c.].

Gesámmt, *adj.* and *adv.* whole, all, united, total. Die —e Dienerschaft, die —e Familie, der —e Rath, all the servants, all the family or the whole family, the whole council; seine —e Mannschaft beträgt nur 4000 Mann, all his army consists of only four thousand men; mit —er Mannschaft vorrücken, to advance with all one's forces or troops; mit —er Hand etwas thun, to do something jointly, in concert; [in feudal matters] die —e Hand, V. —belehnung; die —e Hand bekennen, to enfeoff together and jointly, to give the investiture simultaneously; die —e Lehen, V. Sterbelehen; die Gefangenen hatten —, ins —, dasselbe Schicksal, the prisoners all shared or underwent the same fate; sie haben sich — [gemeinschaftlich] verbürgt, they are bound altogether and one for all; das —e [= das Ganze] beträgt tausend Pfund, the whole, or the total amounts or comes to a thousand pounds.

Gesammt=amt, *n.* charge or office held

in common, joint office. —**belehnung**, *f.* joint enfeoffment or infeudation, simultaneous investiture. V. also gesammte Hand. —**betrag**, *m.* sum total. —**eindruck**, *m.* the impression produced by the whole. —**erbe**, *m.* heir of the whole property, sole heir. —**ertrag**, *m.* the total income, produce or profit. —**gebrauch**, *m.* 1) [gemeinschaftlicher Gebrauch] the joint or common use [of a thing]. 2) the use of the whole. —**geleit**, *n.* simultaneous escort. —**gut**, *n.* a joint estate, an estate possessed in common. —**händer**, *m.* [in feudality] one enfeoffed simultaneously with another. —**herr**, *m.* joint proprietor, joint Lord of a manor. —**herrschaft**, *f.* joint power or authority. *a*) [Herrschaft über das Ganze] the whole or undivided power or authority. *b*) [—gut] an estate or manor possessed in common, joint property of an estate or manor. *c*) V. —herr. —**kauf**, *m.* 1) common or joint purchase. 2) purchase of the whole. —**lehen**, *n.* fief held in common. —**rath**, *m.* 1) [collectively] a council whose members are elected jointly by many. 2) a member of such a council. —**regierung**, *f.* joint government, co-regency. —**richter**, *m.* common judge [of several villages &c.]. —**schrift**, *f.* a deed or document drawn up in the name of all. —**verbürgung**, *f.* bond for the whole.

Gesámmtheit, *f.* the whole quantity or amount. Die — seiner Schulden, the whole amount, the totality of his debts; die — der Bürger hat beschlossen, the citizens have resolved in a body or unanimously; *it.* V. Gesammtschaft.

Gesámmtschaft, *f.* the whole number of individuals or particulars united, the whole body, all the members of a body. Die — der Geistlichkeit, the whole body of the clergy, V. Gesammtheit; in — sich verbürgt haben, to be bound altogether and one for all.

Gesámmtschaftlich, *adj.* and *adv.* common, in common.

Gesándt, *past part.* of Senden, which see.

Gesandtposten, *m.* V. Gesandtschaftsposten.

Gesándte, *m.* [-en, *pl.* -en] ambassador, embassador, minister, envoy. Ein ordentlicher —er, an ordinary ambassador; ein außerordentlicher —er, an ambassador extraordinary; der französische —e am österreichischen Hofe, the French ambassador or minister at the Austrian court; der päpstliche —e, the nuncio, legate; der König schickte ihn als —en nach Berlin, the king sent him to Berlin on an embassy or as ambassador.

Gesándte, *f.* [*pl.* -n] V. Gesandtinn; Botinn.

Gesándtinn, *f.* ambassadress, embassadress.

Gesándtschaft, *f.* 1) [the dignity, office, charge or employment of an ambassador] embassy. Diese — ist offen, erledigt, that embassy is vacant; Einem eine — übertragen, auftragen, to charge any one with an embassy; er verrichtete, bekleidete —en in England, he was ambassador in England; während seiner —, during his embassy; der Papst hat ihn zu der — in Spanien ernannt, the pope has appointed him to the nunciature in Spain. 2) [the ambassador and his retinue] embassy, legation. Die — wurde mit großem Pompe empfangen, the embassy or legation was received with great pomp or splendour; die ganze — ist abgereist, the whole embassy or legation has departed.

Gesandtschafts-kunde, —**kunst**, *f.* diplomacy. —**posten**, *m.* the post or office of an ambassador, embassy. Er hatte verschiedene —posten bekleidet, he had been ambassador at several courts. —**prediger**, *m.* chaplain to an embassy. —**rath**, *m.* counsellor of legation. —**sekretär**, *m.* secretary to an embassy, secretary of legation. —**stelle**, *f.* V. —posten.

Gesándtschaftlich, *adj.* and *adv.* ambassadorial.

Gesáng, *m.* [-es, *pl.* Gesänge] 1) the act of singing; singing. Der — der Nachtigall, the singing or warbling of the nightingale; der klagende — der Flöte, the plaintive music or tone of the flute; angenehmer, melodischer, trauriger —, pleasing, melodious, mournful song; den Gottesdienst mit — anfangen, to begin divine service with singing; in a more limited sense: *a*) musical concord, melody. Dieses Musikstück hat wenig, keinen —, there is little, no melody in this piece of music. *b*) the art of singing. Sich auf den — legen, to apply to the art of singing. V. Kirchen— &c. *c*) [seldom, the art and practice of composing in verse] poetry. Den — lieben, to love poetry; er zeichnet sich im —e aus, he excels in poetry. 2) that which is sung. *a*) song. Ein zweistimmiger —, ein dreistimmiger —, a song in two, in three parts, a vocal duet, a trio; geistliche Gesänge, psalms, hymns; einen — anstimmen, to begin to sing a song. V. Lied, Trauer—, Triumph—. *b*) [a part or division of a large poem, answering to what in prose is called a book] canto. Ein Gedicht in 24 Gesängen, a poem in twenty-four cantos. 3) [among birdcatchers] *a*) birdcall. *b*) decoy-bird.

Gesangs-buch, *n.* book of hymns or psalms, psalm-book. —**drossel**, *f.* song-thrush. —**schwalbe**, *f.* singing-swallow. —**vogel**, *m.* singing-bird. —**weise**, I. *subst. f.* tune, melody. Eine lustige, traurige —weise, a gay, dull tune. II. [or gesangsweise] *adv.* in the manner of a song.

Gesäß, *n.* [-es, *pl.* -e] 1) [= der Hintere] the lower part of the body behind, breech, backside. Er hat ein breites —, he has large buttocks. 2) [little used, the thing on which one sits] seat. Das — eines Sessels mit Haaren ausstopfen, to stuff the seat of a chair with hair.

Gesäß-bein, *n.* [in anatomy] huckle-bone, hip-bone, ischium. —**fistel**, *f.* fistula in the fundament. —**muskel**, *f.* [in anatomy] gluteal muscle. —**schlagader**, *f.* the gluteal artery.

Gesätz, *n.* [-es, *pl.* Gesätze] a number of cases, boxes and the like inserted in each other. Ein — Schachteln, a nest of boxes.

†**Gesaufe**, *n.* [-s] continual drinking, hard, intemperate drinking.

Gesauge, *n.* [-s] 1) continual or violent sucking. 2) the dugs of animals.

Gesause, *n.* [-s] humming, whizzing. Das — des Windes, the whistling or howling of the wind; das — in den Ohren, the humming or tinkling in one's ears.

Gesäusel, *n.* [-s] murmuring, rustling. Das — des Windes, the whispering of the wind; [in poetry] des Frühlings holdes —, the gentle breezes of the spring.

Geschächt, *adj.* and *adv.* [in blasonry] V. Schachförmig.

Geschäft, *n.* [-es, *pl.* -e] 1) business, employment, occupation. Ein wichtiges, verwickeltes —, an important, intricate business or affair; dringende —e, pressing, urgent business or affairs; ein natürliches — [seine Nothdurft] verrichten, to follow the call of nature, †to do one's business; mit —en überhäuft seyn, to be overwhelmed with business, to be full of business; Einem ein — auftragen, to charge any one with a business; wer führt seine —e? who manages or carries on his business? ich kann heute nicht kommen, ich habe —e, I cannot come to-day, I have something to do; ich habe —e mit ihm, I have business, I have to do with him; sich ein — aus etwas machen, to make something one's business; häusliche —e, domestic affairs; gute, einträgliche —e machen [as a merchant], to make good, profitable or lucrative bargains, to buy or sell with profit or gain; *halsbrechende —e machen, to embark in perilous enterprises. Syn. V. Angelegenheit. 2) [not used in the plural] mercantile establishment. Ein — anfangen, to form a mercantile establishment; sein — aufgeben, to break up one's mercantile establishment, to retire from business; ein solides — [Haus], a solid house; ein ausgebreitetes, einträgliches — haben, to have an extended, lucrative trade or commerce.

Geschäfts-leben, *n.* [geschäftiges Leben] active, bustling, busy life. —**los**, *adj.* and *adv.* without business, unemployed, busiless, at leisure, disengaged. —**s-besorger**, *m.* V. —führer. —**s-besorgung**, *f.* management of affairs. —**s-erfahrung**, *f.* V. —kenntniß. —**s-führer**, *m.* [one entrusted with the business of another] a factor, agent. —sführer bei Einem seyn, to manage the affairs of any one. —**s-führung**, *f.* V. —sbesorgung. —**s-gang**, *m.* course of business; *it.* einen —sgang machen, to go somewhere on business. —**s-kenntniß**, *f.* experience, skill in business, routine. —skenntniß haben, to be versed or experienced in business. —**s-kreis**, *m.* sphere of business, department. Der —skreis eines Ministers, the department of a minister; das liegt außer meinem —skreise, that's not my province, *it.* that's none of my business. —**s-lähmung**, *f.* V. —stockung. —**s-leben**, *n.* V. —leben. —**s-leute**, *pl.* men of business. —**s-los**, *adj.* and *adv.* V. —los. —**s-mann**, *m.* man of business, a man versed or experienced in business; *it.* one employed in public affairs, an officer of state, a statesman. Der Dichter und der —smann [or Staatsmann], the poet and the statesman. —**s-sache**, *f.* business. Er ist in —ssachen nach Berlin gegangen, he has gone to Berlin on business. —**s-stockung**, *f.* stagnation of business or commerce. —**s-stube**, *f.* V. —szimmer. —**s-träger**, *m.* agent, resident; consul; chargé d'affaires. Syn. Geschäftsträger, Bevollmächtigter. The Geschäftsträger conducts or manages the affairs which are intrusted to him by another, according to the supposed will of the same, even without being expressly empowered. A Bevollmächtigter is a person invested with full power to transact any business, and especially to conclude contracts or treaties. —**s-verbindung**, *f.* commercial connection or relations. In —sverbindung mit Jemand seyn, stehen, treten, to be in, to enter into, commercial relations with any one. —**s-verkehr**, *m.* commercial intercourse. —**s-verrichter**, *m.* functionary &c., V. —sführer. —**s-zimmer**, *n.* business-room, counting-house. —**s-zweig**, *m.* branch of commerce.

Geschäftig, *adj.* and *adv.* 1) [= thätig] active, busy, bustling. Ein —es Leben führen, to lead an active, busy life; sein Eigennutz war dabei sehr —, his self-interest prompted him to, or made him very busy in, that affair. 2) [= beschäftigt] occupied, busied. Er verfügt eine Trägheit unter einer —en Miene, he conceals his idleness under an air of business; den —en machen, to affect the man of business; er zeigte sich sehr —, he showed great activity, great ardour or earnestness.

Geschäftigkeit, *f.* activity, bustling disposition.

Geschäftlosigkeit, *f.* freedom from business, leisure.

Geschämig, *adj.* and *adv.* [little used] bashful, bashfully, V. Schamhaft; *it.* V. Verschämt.

Geschaukel, *n.* [-s] swinging.

Geschehen, *ir. v. intr.* [Ice. *skedur*, allied to the L. *cad*-ere] [used with seyn] 1) [= sich ereignen] to happen, to come to pass, to befall, to chance, to fall out. Was ich fürchtete, ist —, what I dreaded, has happened or is come to pass; es geschieht alle Tage, daß &c., it happens every day that &c.; das wird nie —, that will never happen or come to pass; es ist ein Unglück —, a misfortune has happened, an accident has occurred; als die Sachen so standen, geschah es, daß &c, when matters stood thus, it happened that &c.; wenn es — sollte, daß &c., if it should happen, that &c; was auch — mag or es geschehe, was da wolle, whatever may happen, whatever may be the consequence; es kann —, daß &c., it may be, it may chance, that &c. 2) [= widerfahren, begegnen] to happen to, to befall. Es geschieht ihm Unrecht, they do him injustice, they wrong him, he is wronged; mir geschieht damit or dadurch ein großer Gefallen, they, you do me a great favour by it; es ist ihm recht —, it served him right; es soll ihm nichts [Uebles] —, he has nothing to fear, he shall get no hurt; es ist ihm zu viel —, he has been wronged; ich wußte nicht, wie mir geschah, als &c., I felt, I know not what, when &c.; wird Ihnen das wieder —? will you do so again? 3) to be done, effected or accomplished. Das kann nicht ohne große Kosten —, that cannot be executed or effected without great expense; wenn es — kann, so soll es mich freuen, I shall be very happy or overjoyed if it can be done or accomplished; es ist so gut als —, it is as good as done; dein Wille geschehe, thy will be done; *prov.* —e Dinge sind nicht zu ändern, what's done cannot be altered, it is too late to consult today about what was done yesterday; *prov.* nach —er Arbeit ist gut ruhen, repose is sweet when the work is done; alles was von meiner Seite — kann, soll —, I shall do all I can; ich kann es nicht — lassen, I cannot consent to it; allow it; ich muß es — lassen, I cannot prevent or hinder it; es geschahen von Seiten der Belagerten verschiedene Ausfälle, the besieged made several sallies; so —, Berlin den 6. Weinmonat 1834, done at Berlin, the sixth of October 1834; es ist um ihn —, he is undone, it is over with him.

1. **Gescheid**, *n.* [-es, *pl.* -e] [in some countries] a dry measure containing about two quarts.

2. **Gescheid**, *n.* [-es, *pl.* -e] or **Gescheide**, *n.* [-s, *pl.* -] [among hunters] the entrails of deer and all wild beasts, inchipin, numbles. Das — der Vögel, ropes.

Gescheid, [gescheit] [from scheiden, to separate, to divide, unterscheiden, to discern] *adj.* and *adv.* judicious, sensible, clever, prudent. Ein —er Mann, a sensible man; das ist sehr —, eine sehr —e Antwort, that is very prudent, a very judicious or sensible answer; *er ist nicht recht —, he is not in his senses, he is a little crack-brained; *ich bin mir hierin selbst nicht — genug, I do not know what to make of it, I am at my wit's end; ich kann nicht — daraus werden, I do not understand or comprehend it; *seyn Sie —, und kommen Sie mit uns, be a good boy and come along with us; er spricht sehr —, he speaks very sensibly; er geht — zu Werke, he acts prudently, he goes discreetly to work.

Gescheidheit or **Gescheitheit**, *f.* quality of being judicious &c., judiciousness, cleverness, prudence, discretion.

Geschenk, *n.* [-es, *pl.* -e] present, gift. Einem ein — geben, machen, to make any one a present, to present a gift to any one, to bestow a boon on any one; Einem ein — mit etwas machen, to make any one a present of something; ich habe es von ihm zum —e bekommen, er hat es mir zum —e gegeben, he made me a present of it, he gave it me as a present; ich habe es zum —e erhalten, I had it given me; dieser Richter nimmt gern —e, läßt sich durch —e bestechen, this judge loves presents or bribes, takes bribes; ein freiwilliges —, a free gift; *it.* the relief or charity given by the masters to travelling journeymen on their way through a town or village; *fig.* die Freundschaft ist das kostbarste — des Himmels, friendship is the most precious gift of heaven. Syn. V. Gabe.

Geschenk=geber, *m.* **—geberinn**, *f.* he or she that makes a present, donor. **—nehmer**, *m.* **—nehmerinn**, *f.* the person to whom a gift or donation is made, donee.

Gescheut, V. Gescheid.

Geschichtchen, ‖**—lein**, [*dimin.* of Geschichte] *n.* [-s, *pl.* -] a little story, a petty tale, anecdote. *Fig.* [in fam. lang.] Das ist so ein —, das ihm wenig Ehre macht, that's an affair, that does him little honour.

Geschichte, *f.* [*pl.* -n] 1) [a narrative of a fact or event] a story, narrative, tale. Eine anziehende —, an interesting story; eine merkwürdige —, a remarkable story or event; eine seltsame —, a strange story or adventure; eine wahre, erdichtete —, a true story or tale, a fictitious tale, a fiction; eine — erfinden, to invent a story; die — dieses Mannes ist sehr lehrreich, the history of this man is very instructive. *Fig.* [in fam. lang.] Es ist eine böse, verdrießliche —, 'tis a sad, vexatious or provoking affair, V. Begebenheit, Ereigniß; [in fam. lang.] Sie haben eine saubere — gemacht, you have made a fine piece of work, indeed! ich will von der ganzen — nichts wissen, I'll have nothing to do with it; was kostet die ganze —? what does the whole concern cost or come to? sie verlor die ganze — [Alles], she lost every thing or all; man erzählt viele —n von ihm, there are many stories or anecdotes circulated at his expense. 2) [a narration of events in the order in which they happened, with their causes and effects] history. Die — eines Volkes, the history of a nation; die allgemeine —, universal history; die alte, die neue —, ancient, modern history; die heilige —, sacred history; die — von England, the history of England; die — Karls des Großen, the history of Charles the great; Schillers — des dreißigjährigen Krieges, Schiller's history of the thirty years' war. V. Kirchen—, Völker—, Natur—. 3) [knowledge of facts and events] history. Die — ist eine vortreffliche Lehrmeisterinn, history is an excellent instructress, furnishes very instructive lessons.

Geschicht=buch, *n.* book of history, historical work. **—forscher**, *m.* V. —s=forscher. **—gelehrte**, *m.* one scientifically skilled in history, historian. **—gemählde**, *n.* a historical painting or picture. **—mahler**, *m.* historical painter. **—mäßig**, *adj.* and *adv.* V. Geschichtlich. **—säule**, *f.* [in architecture] historical column [on whose shaft historical facts are represented]. **—schreiber**, *m.* historian, historiographer. **—schreibung**, *f.* historiography. **—s=buch**, *n.* V. Geschichtbuch. **—s=erlernung**, *f.* study of history. **—s=erzählung**, *f.* historical narration. **—s=forscher**, *m.* he who makes historical researches, historian. **—s=forschung**, *f.* [Geschichtforschung] historical researches, the study of history. **—s=freund**, *m.* a lover of history. **—s=gelehrte**, *m.* V. Geschichtgelehrte. **—s=gemählde**, *n.* V. Geschichtgemählde. **—s=kalender**, *m.* historical almanac. **—s=kunde**, *f.* knowledge or science of history. **—s=kundig**, *adj.* and *adv.* versed in history. **—s=lehrer**, *m.* one who teaches history, lecturer on history, professor of history. **—s=tafel**, *f.* historical table. **—s=umstand**, *m.* historical circumstance. **—s=wissenschaft**, *f.* V. —skunde. **—s=zug**, *m.* historical trait, anecdote.

Geschichtlich, *adj.* and *adv.* historic, historical, historically. Ein —es Gedicht, a historical poem; —e Treue, historic fidelity or faith; — erzählen, to relate historically.

Geschick, *n.* [-es, *pl.* -e] 1) [not used in the *pl.*] fitness, suitableness, aptness, proportion. Das hat weder Art noch —, that is without fashion and proportion; das Kleid hat kein — [paßt nicht gut], the dress does not fit; eine Sache in's — bringen, to arrange, to adjust a thing; einer Sache ein — geben, to give a proper shape or form to a thing, to do a thing properly, *it.* to give a good turn to an affair; [in mining] *a*) the capability of earth or rock to produce ore. *b*) metallic vein, lode. Die —e flechten sich ineinander, the veins cross one another. 2) [not used in the *pl.*] [Fähigkeit zu etwas] faculty, skill, dexterity, address, aptitude. Viel — zu etwas haben, to have a great talent for a thing; er hat ein besonderes — dazu, he has a particular knack at it. 3) [= Schicksal] destiny, fate, lot, fatality. Ein günstiges —, a favourable destiny; ein widriges —, an adverse, fatal destiny or fortune; man kann seinem —e nicht entfliehen, there is no avoiding one's destiny; das haben Sie Ihrem guten —e zu verdanken, you owe that to your good fortune; ein besonderes — traf ihn, he met with a particular fate or destiny; es ist als ein — Gottes zu betrachten, it is to be looked upon as a providential stroke; das ist ein sonderbares —, that is a strange chance. 4) [in falconry, leashes or lunes] Ein Vogel von schlechtem —, a bird that cannot be depended upon.

Geschicke, *n.* [-s] repeated sending.

Geschicklich, [unusual] *adj.* and *adv.* V. Geschickt.

Geschicklichkeit, *f.* 1) dexterity, skill, address, cleverness, adroitness. Er beweiset in allen seinen Uebungen große —, he shows great dexterity or cleverness in all his exercises; eine Unterhandlung mit großer — führen, to conduct a negotiation with great address or skill; es fehlt ihm nicht an —, he does not want talents; mit aller seiner — ist er angeführt worden, with all his cleverness or address, he has been taken in; er hat eine große — darin, he has a great knack at it. 2) [a particular faculty] talent. Auf diese — lege ich keinen großen Werth, I set no great value upon that talent or art; dieser Hund besitzt viele —en, this dog knows many tricks.

Geschickt, [*past part.* of Schicken, which see] I. *adj.* 1) [= fähig] fit, proper, adapted, qualified. Dieses Holz ist zum Bauen nicht —, this wood is not fit or good for building; ich bin zu dieser Unternehmung nicht —, I am not qualified for that undertaking; zu Allem —, fit for any thing; ich bin heute nicht dazu — [aufgelegt], mich in einen Streit einzulassen, I am not disposed, not in the humour, to-day to engage in a dispute; Einen zu etwas — machen, to fit, to qualify any one for a thing; sich zu etwas — machen [sich zu etwas anschicken], to get ready, to prepare for something; wir waren zur Abreise —, we were ready, every thing was ready, for our departure 2) [= kenntnißreich, erfahren] learned, able, skilful, clever. Ein —er Minister, an able or clever minister; ein —er Spieler, Tänzer, a dexterous, adroit or clever gamester, dancer; ein —er Arzt, Advokat, a skilful physician, a clever lawyer; in Sprachen, in Allem — seyn, to be clever in languages, in every thing 3) [indicative of knowledge or experience] Eine —e Arbeit, an ingenious piece of work; eine —e Antwort, a clever, a sensible answer; dieser Wundarzt hat eine —e Hand, this surgeon is a skilful operator; auf eine —e Art, ingeniously, dexterously, skilfully. ||4) [= rechtzeitig] suitable, convenient, seasonable. Komme ich Ihnen um zwei Uhr zur —en Stunde? is two o'clock a convenient hour for my coming to you? er kam zu or in einem —en Zeitpunkte, he arrived at a seasonable moment. II. *adv.* 1) fitly, aptly. 2 cleverly, skilfully, dexterously. Das hat er sehr — gemacht, he has done it very cleverly; er hat sich — aus der Sache gezogen, he has come off cleverly or artfully, he has had the art to slip his neck out of the collar. ||3) seasonably, conveniently.

Geschicktheit, *f.* dexterity, skill, address. V. Geschicklichkeit 1).

Geschiebe, *n.* [-s] 1) repeated or continual shoving. 2) [in mining] rock or mineral that has been removed from its place and transported to another by violence, as by inundation &c., rubble-stones.

Geschieße, *n.* [-s] 1) continual shooting. ||2) headlong or aimless running or rushing to and fro.

Geschimpfe, *n* [-s] continual scolding or abusing, abusive language.

Geschirr, *n.* [-es, *pl.* -e] 1) [collectively, things provided as means to some end, as the tools or implements of an artisan, the furniture of a horse, of a ship &c.] apparatus. Das — eines Ackermannes, V. Ackergeräthe; das — der Pferde, the gear or harness of horses; Schiff und — der Fuhrleute, the waggon and the necessary furniture or harness of a waggoner; den Pferden das — anlegen, to harness the horses; mit eigenem —e [mit eigenen Pferden und Wagen] kommen, to come in one's own carriage; *fig.* † aus dem —e kommen, Einen aus dem —e bringen, to be confounded or abashed, to be out of countenance, to puzzle, to confound any one, to put any one out of countenance; das — eines Weberstuhles, the equipage of a loom; das — auf den Schiffen, [the rigging and apparatus of a ship] tackle; das — der Fischer, fishing-gear. 2) [= Gefäß] vessel Ein hölzernes, irdenes —, a wooden, an earthen vessel; irdenes — [= several earthen vessels together], earthenware; [in founderies] das irdene —, basin [a large earthen basin over the mould in casting statues]; silbernes und goldenes — [Tafel—], silver and gold plate; das — scheuern, reinigen, to scour, to cleanse the plates and dishes &c. V. Küchen—, Milch—, Trink—. Syn. Geschirr, Geräth, Gefäß, Faß. Geräth denotes all the different articles collectively, which are used for any purpose, of whatever kind they may be. Geschirr is a part of the Geräth, which serves one certain purpose, and usually consists of such utensils as can contain any thing. Plates, dishes &c. belong to the Tischgeschirr; knives, forks, naphins &c. to the Tischgeräth. This general definition will also apply to Pferdegeschirr. Smaller and shallower vessels are also denominated Geschirr; deeper and more capacious, Fässer and Gefäße. Formerly Faß [from fassen] signified any vessel, see Tintenfaß, Salzfaß &c.; now this word is used only for such as are made by the cooper.

Geschirr=bret, *n.* the shelves [for the plates and dishes], cup-board. —bürste, *f.* brush for cleansing the harness of horses. —geld, *n.* money paid to the lord of a manor to be exempt from performing services with a waggon and horses. —holz, *n.* wood fit or good for tools and implements of any kind. V. Nutzholz, Geräthholz. —kämme, *pl* [among silk-weavers] lams [the threads through which the warp goes as through a comb]. —kammer, *f.* room to keep saddles and horse-harnesses in, harness-room, saddle-room; *it.* V. Geräthkammer. —macher, *m.* lams-maker. —meister, *m.* a person who has the care of tools, implements, harness &c. Der —meister eines Postwagens, the guard of a mail; [in military affairs] the officer who has the care of the waggons and baggage; [in naval affairs] officer on board of ships, who has charge of the boats, sails, rigging, cordage &c., boatswain. —ordnung, *f* [among clothmakers] regulation for the quality of the cloth. —schreiber, *m.* keeper of the plate [of a prince].

Geschlacht, [in rather low style] *adj.* and *adv.* of good quality, soft, tender. —es Fleisch, tender meat; —es Holz, soft wood; —es Leder, soft leather; ein Volk — machen, to refine or polish the manners of a people, to civilize a people.

Geschlecht, *n.* [-es, *pl.* -er] [from schlagen = to divide, as the L. sexus or secus from *secare*, to divide] genus. Unter dem —e der Thiere werden zwei Gattungen begriffen, die des Menschen und die des Viehes, under the genus of animal two species are comprehended, man and beast; der Wolf gehört zu dem —e der Hunde, the wolf belongs to the genus, to the family of dogs, to the dog kind; das menschliche —, the human species or race, mankind, humankind; ein Pflanzen—, a genus or family of plants; *it.* das männliche, das weibliche — [of men, beasts and plants] the male, the female sex; das weibliche or das andere, das *schöne, das schwächere —, the female, the fair, the weaker sex, womankind, the sex; das schöne — lieben, to love the sex [women]; bei manchen Pflanzen sind die —er getrennt, in many plants the two sexes are separated [are not in one and the same plant]; [in grammar] gender; das männliche, weibliche, ungewisse or unbestimmte —, the masculine, feminine, neuter gender. *In a more limited sense: a)* [those who descend from one common progenitor] race, family. Ein zahlreiches —, a numerous race, family, progeny or offspring; Joseph war von dem Hause und —e Davids, Joseph was of the house and lineage of David; sie stammen von dem nämlichen —e, they descend from the same stock or family; er ist der letzte seines —es, he is the last of his race; von einem guten, alten, adeligen, von königlichem —e seyn, to be of a good family or house, of an ancient, noble family or race, of royal blood or extraction; dieses — brachte große Männer hervor, that race produced great men; nahe in das — heurathen, to marry a near relation; sein ganzes — bis in's vierte Glied, all his family, race or lineage [down] to the fourth generation. *b)* [all the people of the same period] generation. Das gegenwärtige —, the present generation; alle kommende —er, all the generations to come, all future or after-ages; von —e zu —e, from generation to generation.

Geschlechts=art, *f.* [in natural history] the generic character. Das ist die —art dieser Thiere, that is the generic character of these animals. —los, *adj.* and *adv.* of neither sex or gender, neuter. Eine —lose Blume, a neuter flower; ein —loses Zeitwort, Nennwort, a neuter or intransitive verb, a neuter noun. —s=adel, *m.* nobility of blood. —s=alter, *n.* [the common duration of a generation or of human life, *i. e.* thirty or thirty three years] age of man, period or duration of human life, age, generation; *it.* the whole duration of a race or family. —s=art, *f.* genus, kind or species, race. —s=baum, *m.* V. Stammbaum. —s=beschreiber, *m.* genealogist. —s=brief, *m.* a genealogical deed or writing, pedigree. —s=endung, *f.* —s=fall, *m.* [in grammar] genitive case. V. [the more usual word] Genitiv. —s=folge, *f.* succession of families or generations; in a more limited sense, a series or succession of children or descendants from the same stock, generation, genealogy, descent; *it.* V. —stamm. —s=forscher, *m.* genealogist. —s=glied, *n.* 1) the descendant or member of a family or race. 2) V. Zeugungsglied. —s=gut, *n.* entailed estate, feoffment of trust. V. Gesammtgut. —s=kunde, *f.* science of genealogy, genealogical science. —s=kundige, *m.* genealogist. —s=lehre, *f.* 1) V. —kunde. 2) [in botany] Die —s=lehre der Pflanzen, the sexual system. —s=leiter, *f.* V. —s=folge. —s=liebe, *f.* love of the sex, sexual love or inclination. —s=linie, *f.* lineage, pedigree, descent. —s=los, V. Geschlechtlos. —s=lust, *f.* carnal or sensual pleasure; *it.* V. —s=trieb. —s=name, *m.* family name, surname or sirname, patronymic name. Herakliden, Seleuciden sind —s=namen, Heraclides, Seleucides are patronymic names; [in botany] der —s=name der Pflanzen, the generic name of plants. —s=neigung, *f.* V. —liebe. —s=organ, *n.* sexual organ. —s=register, *n.* pedigree, genealogical register or table. V. —s=tafel, Stammbaum. —s=säule, *f.* [in architecture] genealogical column [on which the name, coat of arms, pedigree &c. of a family are represented]. —s=stamm, *m.* the trunk of a genealogical tree; *it.* genealogical tree, pedigree. —s=tafel, *f.* genealogical table. —s=tag, *m.* Der —s=tag einer Familie, the day of assembly of a family. —s=theil, *m.* organ of generation, genital member. Die —s=theile, the privy parts, genitals. —s=trieb, *m.* venereal desire, sexual instinct, sexual propensity. Den —s=trieb reizen, to excite the venereal desire. —s=unterschied, *m.* sexual difference. —s=urkunde, *f.* V. —s=brief. —s=verschiedenheit, *f.* difference of sex. —s=wappen, *n.* family-arms. —s=wissenschaft, *f.* V. —s=kunde. —s=wort, *n.* generic word; [in grammar] article. —s=zeichen, *n.* sexual mark, part of generation, privy parts. [in blazonry] Ohne —s=zeichen, with no sexual mark.

Geschlechter, *m.* [-s, *pl.* -] [little used; [one of patrician or noble birth or blood] patrician.

Geschlechtlich, *adj.* and *adv.* generic, generical; *it.* sexual. Der —e Name, Unterschied, the generic name, difference; eine Pflanze — untersuchen, to examine a plant with regard to its genus, generically; —e Merkmale, sexual characteristics.

Geschleif, *n.* [-es, *pl.* -e] 1) [from [illegible]

o creep, to crawl] [among hunters] the entrance nto the hole or kennel of a fox, rabbit, badger, German marmot and beaver. 2) [from schleifen, o drag] V. Geschlepp;

Geschlépp, *n* [-es, *pl.* -e] or **Geschléppe**, n. [-s, *pl.* -] what is dragged or drawn along. Das — an einem Kleide, the train of a gown. [among hunters] a bait or carrion drawn along a wood to allure beasts of prey, a drag; [in mining] V. Feldgestänge; *fig.* [in contempt] ein großes — [= Gefolge] bei sich haben, to have a numerous train, a long tail; welch ein — von Artikeln und überflüssigen Beiwörtern, what a train or string of articles and superfluous epithets.

Geschliffen, [*past part.* of Schleifen, to grind, which see] *adj.* and *adv.* polished, polite. Ein —er Mensch, ein —es Aeußere, a polite, well-bred man, a genteel appearance.

Geschlinge, *n.* [-s] 1) pluck of animals. V. Hammels—, Kalbs— &c. 2) [in architecture and gardening, something interweaved or entwined] festoon, garland. Ein Blumen—, a wreath of flowers.

Geschlitz, *n.* [-es, *pl.* -e] [in mining] an opening or narrow passage, a notch.

Geschlötter, *n.* [-s] 1) continued jogging. constant or continued knocking or shivering [from fear, cold &c.] 3) [in saltworks] [= Schlamm] thick mud or sediment in salt-pans.

Geschlúchze, *n.* [-s] continual sobbing.

Geschlúmmer, *n.* [-s] slumbering, dosing.

Geschmáck, *m.* [-es, *pl.* little used, Geschmäcke] 1) the sense of tasting, taste. Den — verlieren, to lose one's taste; einen guten, feinen, schlechten — haben, to have a good, nice, bad taste; über den — darf man nicht streiten, there is no disputing tastes. *Fig.* Die Lesung der Alten bildet den —, reading the ancients improves the taste; einen guten, richtigen, geläuterten — haben, to have a good or a just, a refined taste; das zeigt einen schlechten, verderbten — an, that proves a bad, depraved taste; — an etwas finden, to relish a thing; er hat keinen — für die Musik, die Dichtkunst &c., he has no taste or relish for music, poetry &c., he does not relish music, poetry &c.; dies ist nicht nach meinem —e, it is not to my taste or liking; das ist eine Sache des —es or das ist —ssache, that depends on taste; Einem — an etwas machen [beibringen], to inspire any one with, to give any one a taste or relish for a thing. 2) [the quality of a substance which affects the organs of taste] taste, savour [of meat &c.], flavour. Der — einer Apfelsine, the taste or flavour of an orange; gutes Wasser hat keinen —, good water has no taste; diese Frucht hat einen feinen, einen unangenehmen —, this fruit has a fine, a disagreeable flavour; dieses Bier hat einen bittern, süßen, säuerlichen —, this beer has a bitter, sweet, acid taste or flavour; dieser Kranke findet an nichts —, that sick person relishes nothing; der Wein hat den — verloren, the wine has lost its taste or flavour, is become insipid; dieser Schnupftabak hat einen moderigen — [provincial], this snuff has a musty smell; *fig.* einer Sache — abgewinnen, to get a taste for a thing. 3) *Fig.* [manner, with respect to what is pleasing] taste, style. Dieses Gemählde ist in Raphaels —, this picture is in the style of Raphael; ein in gutem —e abgefaßtes Gedicht, a poem composed in good taste; seine Kleidung ist im or nach dem besten —e, his clothes are of the best taste; in or nach dem neuesten —e, after the latest or most modern fashion; dieses Stück ist ganz in dem —e seines Jahrhunderts, this piece is quite in the taste of his age or century; eine Säule in griechischem —e, a column in the Grecian style; Gedichte in Langbeins —e, poems in the manner of Langbein; er arbeitet in einem schlechten —, he works in a bad manner or style, his manner or style is bad.

Geschmacks-los, *adj.* and *adv.* 1) destitute of the sense of tasting. Er war in seiner Krankheit —los, he had lost his taste, he had no taste during his illness; *fig.* er ist ein —loser Mensch, he is a man without any taste, *it.* he is an insipid, dull fellow. 2) [wanting the qualities which affect the organs of taste] tasteless, insipid. —lose Frucht, Brühe, tasteless or insipid fruit, broth; *fig.* —lose Bauart, Kleidung, tasteless style of building, tasteless dress; —lose Vergnügungen, tasteless or insipid pleasures or amusements. —**nerve**, *f.* [in anatomy] nervus or musculus gustatorius, nerve of gustation. —**s-empfindung**, *f.* perception of taste. —**s-kunde**, *f.* the science or knowledge of what tastes well or of what is palatable; *fig.* the science or knowledge of discerning beauty, order, congruity, proportion &c. in the fine arts and belles lettres, esthetics. —**s-lehre**, *f.* the doctrine of the beautiful and of taste, esthetics. —**s-sinn**, *m.* the sense of tasting; *fig.* taste for the beautiful. —**s-urtheil**, *n.* judgment of the beautiful or of taste. —**s-verderber**, *m.* corrupter or depraver of taste. —**s-verderbniß**, *f.* corruption or depravity of taste. —**s-wissenschaft**, *f.* V. —s-lehre. —**voll**, *adj.* and *adv.* 1) [applied to persons] possessed of good taste, tasty. Eine —volle Dame, ein —voller Schriftsteller, a tasty lady, a tasty or elegant writer. 2) [applied to things] [being in conformity to the principles of good taste] tasty, elegant, genteel. —volle Schriften, elegant writings or works; —volle Kleidung, tasty or genteel dress; —volle Möbel, tasty furniture. —**widrig**, *adj.* and *adv.* adverse to good taste, inelegant, tasteless. Ein —widriger Ausdruck, an inelegant expression.

Geschmácklich, *adj.* and *adv.* savoury, tasteful. —es Fleisch, savoury meat; —e Kräuter, tasteful herbs; — trinken &c., to drink savourily.

Geschmácklosigkeit, *f.* 1) want of the perception of taste. 2) want of taste or relish, insipidness, tastelessness. Die — einer Frucht, the tastelessness of a fruit; *fig.* die — seiner Scherze, the insipidity, flatness of his jokes; die — seines Anzuges, the tastelessness of his dress.

Geschmáckwidrigkeit, *f.* want of good taste, inelegance.

Geschmätze, *n.* [-s] 1) loud and repeated kisses or kissing, smacking. 2) noise made with the tongue and lips in eating, smacking.

Geschmaúse, *n.* [-s] banqueting, feasting.

Geschmeichel, *n.* [-s] coaxing, wheedling, flattering, caressing.

Geschmeide, *n.* [-s] [from schmieden] primarily, any thing wrought of metal, as iron rings and chains for malefactors, snuffers, watch-cases, drawing-pens, compasses &c.; now only used in the limited sense of trinkets, jewels, jewelry. Das — anlegen, to put on one's jewels; sie war ganz mit — bedeckt, she was entirely covered with ornaments.

Geschmeide-handel, *m.* the jeweler's or toyman's trade. —**händler**, *m.* dealer in jewels and trinkets, jeweler, toyman. —**kästchen**, *n.* jewel-box, casket. —**macher**, *m.* jeweler.

Geschmeidig, *adj.* and *adv.* supple, pliant, flexible, soft. —es Leder, soft, pliant or supple leather; eine —e Ruthe, a pliant rod; einen —en Körper haben, to be supple in the body, to have a supple body; —es Eisen, soft or malleable iron; das Eisen oder Wachs wird durch die Hitze —, iron or wax softens in heat; [in mining] —es Erz, ductile or malleable ore; —es Gestein, soft rocks. *Fig.* Eine —e Sprache, a [pliant or] flexible language; Einen — [nachgiebig] machen, to make any one humble, tractable, pliant; er wurde so —, daß man ihn hätte um einen Finger wickeln können, he became as supple as a glove, as pliant as a willow; ein —er Mensch, a pliant, tractable man; ein —es Gemüth, ein —er Geist, a supple, pliant, tractable temper or mind, *it.* a shifting mind; am Hofe muß man — seyn, a man must be supple or pliant at court.

Geschmeidigkeit, *f.* suppleness, pliancy, flexibility. Die — der Metalle, the ductility or malleability of the metals; die — einer Ruthe, the pliancy of a rod; die — des Charakters, the suppleness of character; die — der Zunge, the volubility of the tongue.

Geschmeiß, *n.* [-es, *pl.* -e] 1) [among hunters] the dung of birds of prey. 2) the dung or eggs of flies and butterflies, fly-blow. 3) [insects, chiefly those proceeding from the eggs of butterflies, as caterpillars &c.] vermin. *Fig.* [rather vulgar, in contempt] rabble, rascality, vermin. Ich will mit solchem —e nichts zu thun haben, I'll have nothing to do with such vermin.

Geschmiere, *n.* [-s] a continual smearing, greasing or daubing; *fig.* scribbling, scrawling, daubing.

‡**Geschmúck**, *m.* [-es, *pl.* -e] V. Schmuck.

Geschnäbel, *n.* [-s] the joining of bills, billing, as of doves. *Fig.* Das — von Verliebten, the billing or kissing of lovers.

Geschnárche, *n.* [-s] snoring.

Geschnátter, *n.* [-s] cackling of ducks or geese; *fig.* chattering, prattling.

Geschneide, *n.* [-s] 1) a continual cutting. 2) [among birdcatchers] gins or springes for catching birds. V. Dohne.

Geschnörkel, *n.* [-s] V. Schnörkelei.

Geschnüffel, *n.* [-s] continual snuffing or snuffling. *Fig.* constant scrutinizing or snuffing about.

Geschnúrre, *n.* [-s] a rattling or humming noise. Das — einer Katze, the purr of a cat; das — eines Spinnrads, the humming of a spinning-wheel.

Geschöpf, *n.* [-es, *pl.* -e] 1) any thing produced or formed, creature. Ein — der Einbildungskraft, a creature of the imagination; er ist ein neues — [in Script.], he is a new creature. 2) [particularly, any being created by God] creature. Ein lebendiges, vernünftiges —, a living, rational creature; [in familiar language = Person, person] welch' ein liebenswürdiges —! what a lovely creature! dieses — richtet ihn zu Grunde, that creature [girl or wench] ruins him; fort mit dir, häßliches —! get thee gone, ugly creature! sie ist ein allerliebstes —chen, she is a sweet little creature; *fig.* [in scorn or contempt] —e des Ministers &c., creatures of the minister &c.

Geschöß, *n.* [-sses, *pl.* -sse] 1) a missile weapon, as a dart, arrow, bolt. Ihn erreichte das tödtliche —, the deadly or fatal dart or arrow struck him. *it.* [Gewehr] a weapon or engine for shooting, fire-lock, fire-arms, V. Schießgewehr, Geschütz; [in botany] a young branch, a shoot, V. Schoß. 2) [= Stockwerk] story [of a house], floor. Ein Haus von vier Geschossen, a house of four stories. 3) [= Abgabe] scot, tax. V. Schoß.

Geschräge, *n.* [-s] a fence of pales, an enclosure with pales, paling.

Geschrei, *n.* [-es] [a loud sound uttered by the mouth of any animal, but chiefly of man] cry. Das — der Thiere, the cries of the beasts; das — des Hahnes, the crow of the cock; das — der Krähe verkündigt Regen, the croaking of the rook forebodes rain; das — des Esels, the bray of the ass; das — der Katze, the mewing of the cat; das — eines Kindes, the cries or squalls of a child; das — dieser Unglücklichen, the cries or screams of these unfortunate people; ein schrilles, schneidendes or durchdringendes —, a shrill cry or shriek; ein —, ein lautes — erheben, to raise a cry, a loud cry, to utter cries, loud cries, to cry out, to cry, shriek or scream aloud; es erhob sich, es entstand ein großes —, there arose a great cry, outcry or clamour; dieses beständige — ist sehr unangenehm, this continual clamour is very disagreeable; sein — macht mir den Kopf toll, his bawling splits my head or drives me mad. [in a more limited sense] *a*) [loud and violent complaints or urgent demands] Das — des Volkes, the clamour or cries of the people; Gott höret das — der Wittwen und Waisen, God hears the cries of the widow and the orphan. *b*) [loud and repeated talk] Viel — [viel Aufhebens, Rühmens] von etwas machen, to make much noise, a great bustle about a thing; *prov.* viel — und wenig Wolle, a great cry and little wool. *c*) [in fam. and in vulg. lang.] [a strong or loud report or rumour] Es geht ein —, it is rumoured abroad. *it.* discredit, disrepute. In das — kommen, to fall into disrepute; Einen in's — bringen, to bring any one into discredit or disrepute, to discredit, to defame any one; sie hat sich in's — gebracht, she has given room to slander; er ist im —, daß er ein Geizhals sey, he has the reputation of being a miser. V. Feld—, Freuden— &c.

Geschrill, *n.* [-es] piercing, shrill cries. Das — der Grillen, the chirping of the crickets.

Geschröt, *n.* [-es, *pl.* -e] [allied to the L. *scrotum*] the scrotum or cods [of animals, especially horses]. V. Hodensack.

||**Gescht**, V. Gäscht or Gischt.

Geschühe, *n.* [-s] cover for the feet, as shoes, boots &c. collectively; [in falconry, short straps of leather tied round the legs of a hawk, by which she is held on the fist] jesses.

Geschür, *n.* [-es] [in forges] slags, dross, scoria.

Geschütte, *n.* [-s] 1) pouring, continual pouring [down or out] 2) a heap of things thrown together; [in mining] mixed layers.

Geschütz, *n.* [-es, *pl.* -e] 1) [from schießen, to shoot] collectively, engines for shooting, cannon, ordnance, artillery. Das grobe —, the great guns, the heavy cannon, ordnance; das kleine —, the small or light artillery; das — aufführen, to erect, to raise a battery of cannon; das — ablegen (vom Gestelle), to dismount the cannon or other artillery; dieses Schiff führte sehr schweres —, this ship carried very heavy metal; das feindliche — entblößen, zum Schweigen bringen, to silence the cannon or guns of the enemy; das — vernageln, to spike the cannon or guns; das — spielen lassen, to discharge the cannon or guns; das — wurde gut bedient, the artillery has been served well; Einen unter dreimaliger Lösung des —es empfangen, to receive any one under a triple discharge of cannon; ein mit — versehenes Schiff, a vessel mounted with cannon; eine Festung mit — versehen, to furnish a fortress with artillery. 2) [in falconry] Die —e, V. Geschühe.

Geschütz-damm, *m.* V. Stückbettung. —kunst, *f.* the art of managing artillery, the art of gunnery; *it.* [die Feuerwerkskunst] pyrotechnics. —pforte, *f.* [a sea term] port-hole. —probe, *f.* trial or proof of cannons. —richtung, *f.* the levelling or pointing of a piece of ordnance. —seil, *n.* [in naval gunnery] breeching, britching. —wagen, *m.* [Munitionswagen] ammunition chest or waggon, caisson or caissoon. —wesen, *n.* artillery, gunnery. —zug, *m.* train of artillery.

Geschwächt, [*past part.* of Schwächen, which see] —e Kanonen, light pieces of ordnance, small cannons.

Geschwader, *n.* [-s, *pl.* -] [probably from the Italian *squadra, squadrone,* and this from the L. *quatuor*, four, therefore originally = Viereck, square] 1) [in military affairs, a body of cavalry] squadron [of horse]. 2) [in seamen's lang., a division of a fleet] squadron.

Geschwär, *n.* [es, *pl.* -e] V. Geschwür.

Geschwätz, *n.* [-es, *pl.* -e] idle talk, prate, babble, chattering, tittle-tattle. Er betäubte uns mit seinem —e, he stunned us with his chattering; das ist ein ewiges —, that's a perpetual chatting or gossiping; was soll dieses sinnlose —? what does this senseless prattle signify? seine Sache ist bloßes —, he is nothing but babble, he is all talk; ich kann das — der Gevatterinnen nicht ausstehen, I hate gossiping; *Einen in's — [in's Gerede, Geschrei] bringen, to bring any one upon the stage, into discredit or disrepute, to slander any one.

Geschwätze, *n.* [-s] continual talking or chatting.

Geschwätzig, *adj.* and *adv.* talkative, loquacious, garrulous. Ein —er Mensch, a talkative fellow; das —e Alter, garrulous old age; es gibt Männer, die noch —er sind, als die Weiber, some men are greater talkers than women; die Freude ist —, joy is a blab; wer kein Geheimniß bei sich behalten kann, ist ein —er Mensch, he who cannot keep a secret, is a blab or babbler.

Geschwätzigkeit, *f.* talkativeness, loquacity, garrulity; *it.* V. Geschwätz.

Geschweige, *adv.* [from schweigen, to be silent] [= weit davon] far from, much less, to say nothing of, not to mention. Ich thäte es nicht als sein Freund, — denn als [sein] Feind, I would not do it as his friend, much less as his enemy; ich habe ihn nicht gesehen, — denn angesprochen, I have not seen him, much less spoken to him, far from having spoken to him, I have not even seen him; ich kenne ihn nicht, — daß ich ihn liebte, I am so far from loving him, that I do not know him; ich fürchte mich vor seiner Freundschaft, — seiner Feindschaft, I fear his friendship, to say nothing of his enmity, or and much more his enmity.

Geschweigen, I. *v. intr.* [rather stiff] to pass over in silence, not to mention. Ich geschweige seiner andern Tugenden, I pass his other virtues over in silence, I say nothing of his other virtues; seiner übrigen Laster zu —, to say nothing of, not to mention his other vices; zu —, daß &c., I say nothing of, not to mention that &c. II. *v. tr.* to put to silence, to silence, to appease. Ein weinendes Kind —, to quiet a crying infant; mit seinem Namen — die Mütter ihre Säuglinge, with his name mothers still or hush their babes.

Geschweih, V. Schwager, Schwägerinn.

Geschwelge, *n.* [-s] a carousing, revelling, revelry, rioting.

Geschwellen, *v. intr.* [u. w. seyn] to swell. V. Schwellen.

Geschwemme, *n.* [-s] washing; *it.* [in hu. lang.] inundation; *it.* [water carelessly thrown about on a table or floor] slop, puddle.

Geschwind, I. *adj.* [probably allied to winden, to turn] quick, swift, speedy, sudden. Ein —er Hund, a fleet or swift dog; eine —e Bewegung, a quick, a rapid motion; [in music] in —er Bewegung [Allegro], allegro; ein wenig —, allegretto; sehr —, presto; er ist in Allem, was er thut, —, he is quick in all he does; ein —er Kopf, a quick mind [that conceives easily]; eine —e Antwort, a ready or prompt answer or reply; ein —er Tod, a sudden death; seine —e Abreise war Schuld daran, his sudden departure was the cause of it. II. *adv.* swiftly, quickly, fast, in haste. —gehen, to walk fast; sehr — fahren, to drive very fast; diese Taschenuhr geht zu —, this watch goes too fast; Sie sprechen zu —, you speak too quick; jenes Schiff segelt —, yonder ship sails fast; kehre — zurück, return quickly; er geht in dieser Sache sehr — zu Werke, he goes very quick in that business or affair; —! mach' —! quick! make haste! lauf' or geh' —! run quick! be quick! öffne — die Thür, open the door quickly; — fortmachen [= sich eilen], to make haste; sie hat sich — entschlossen, she has resolved promptly; ich wußte nicht, was ich — [= im Augenblick, in der Eile] sagen sollte, I did not know what to say immediately, on the spur of the moment; er ist zu — abgereist, he set off too suddenly.

Geschwind-kutsche, *f.* flying coach, *diligence. —schreibekunst, *f.* short hand writing, stenography. —schreiber, *m.* short hand writer, stenographer. —schritt, *m.* [in military affairs] quick pace. —stück, *n.* 1) a piece of cannon for quick firing. 2) [in music] allegro, presto. —wagen, *m.* V. —kutsche.

Geschwindigkeit, *f.* 1) quickness, swiftness, velocity, celerity, rapidity, speed. Die — einer Bewegung, eines Pferdes &c., the quickness or swiftness of a motion, the fleetness, celerity of a horse &c.; sie spricht mit einer solchen —, daß &c., she speaks with such volubility that &c.; diese Sache erfordert — [illegible] der Ausführung, this affair requires promptitude; ich bewundere seine —, I admire [illegible] agility; die — seiner Antwort hat mich außer Fassung gebracht, the promptness or quickness of his answer has disconcerted me; etwas in der — thun, to do something in haste, in a hurry; ich konnte den rechten Ausdruck in der — nicht finden, I could not find the proper expression in the hurry; die — des Pulsschlages, the quickness of the pulse. 2) [in physics, [illegible] affection of motion by which a body moves over a certain space in a certain time] velocity.

Geschwirr, *n.* [-s] 1) a continual chirping. 2) Das — eines Pfeils oder der Pfeile, the whizzing or whizzing sound of an arrow or several arrows collectively.

Geschwister, *n.* [-s, *pl.* -] [from Schwester] brother or sister; but generally used in the plural. Die —, the brothers or sisters, brothers and sisters; alle meine — sind gestorben, all my brothers or sisters are dead; leibliche —, brothers and sisters by the same father and mother; — von der Mutter her, brothers and sisters by the mother's side, uterine brothers and sisters; — vom Vater her, brothers and sisters by the father's side.

Geschwister-kind, *n.* cousin german, first-cousin. Sie sind —kinder, they are cousins german; er ist —kind mit meinem Vater, mit meiner Mutter, he is cousin german to my father, to my mother. —kindskind, *n.* cousin once removed. —liebe, *f.* brotherly [illegible] sisterly love.

Geschwisterlich, *adj.* and *adv.* brotherly, sisterly.

Geschworen, [*past part.* of **Schwören**, which s.]. **Der —e, ein —er** [-en, *pl.* die -en, without the article -e] [a person who for a certain judicial act or for certain judicial proceedings, has been sworn in as a judge] a sworn man; [in law] juror, ymen. **Bestochene** or **gewonnene —e zusammenbringen**, to pack a jury; **die —en** or **das —gericht**, the jury; **der Sprecher der —en**, the foreman of the jury; **ein —er bei einer Innung**, a warden in a company of tradesmen.

Geschworenen-gericht, *n.* the jury; the institution of the Jury. **—liste**, *f.* panel. **Auf die —liste setzen**, to empannel.

Geschwulst, *f.* [*pl.* **Geschwülste**] swelling, tumour. **Er hat eine — am Beine**, he has a swelling on the leg; **eine fleischichte —**, carnosity; **es ist eine — zu befürchten**, a tumefaction is to be dreaded. V. **Balg—, Luft—, Sack—**.

Geschwulstkraut, *n.* [in botany] orpine, live-long.

Geschwür, *n.* [-es, *pl.* -e] 1) sore, ulcer, aposteme, imposthume; abscess. **Ein — an der Lunge**, an ulcer in the lungs; **es hat sich dort ein — zusammengezogen, gebildet**, an aposteme or an abscess has gathered or has been formed there; **ein bösartiges, eiterndes —**, a maligo, purulent ulcer. V. **Augen—, Hals-, Nagel—** &c. 2) [in botany] exulceration.

Geschwürig, *adj.* and *adv.* V. **Schwierig**.

Gesechst, *adj.* consisting of six parts. *a*) [in astronomy] **Der —e Schein**, [the position or aspect of two planets, when distant from each other 60 degrees or two signs] the sextile position or aspect. *b*) **Das —, ein —es**, [a set or sequence of cards, as in piquet] sexte, sixieme.

Gesegnen, *v. tr.* to bless, V. [the now more usual word] **Segnen. Gott gesegne es Euch!** God bless you! much good may it do you! **Das Zeitliche, die Zeitlichkeit, die Welt —** [sterben], to depart this life, to die.

Gesell, *m.* [-en, *pl.* -en] [V. **Gesellen**] 1) [Gefährte] companion, partner, fellow. **Der Donner ist des Blitzes —**, thunder is the companion of lightning; [in mining] **die —en** [= **die Theilnehmer an einer Zeche**], the copartners or associates in a mine. V. **Diebs—, Schlaf—, ben—** &c. 2) [among mechanics] journeyman. **Er hat sechs —en in seiner Werkstatt**, he has six journeymen in his shop; **einen —en annehmen, in Arbeit nehmen**, to hire, to engage a journeyman; **zum —en gemacht werden**, to be appointed a journeyman [after having served his time]. V. **Alt—, Mit—, Schneider—** &c. [in fam. lang. = **Mensch**, fellow] **Das ist ein gefährlicher, kecker —**, that's a dangerous, bold fellow; **ein lustiger —**, a merry blade; **ein wunderbarer —**, a strange mortal, an odd fellow, a queer blade; **du bist ein undankbarer —**, you are an ungrateful fellow or rascal; **steh auf, fauler —**, get up, you lazy fellow.

Gesellen, [from the ancient **fellen**, to join] I. *v. tr.* to add as a companion, to associate. **Wir wollen noch Andere zu uns —**, let us associate others with us; **der Zufall gesellt oft Personen, die** &c., chance often joins [pairs] persons [flock &c.], who &c. II. *v. r.* **sich —**, to associate. **Sich zu Einem —** [= **mit Einem umgehen**], to associate, to keep company with any one; *it.* to join any one on the road; **sich zu liederlichen Menschen —**, to associate, to keep company with dissolute fellows; **die Menschen sollen sich —**, men ought to be sociable or companionable; [in commerce] **sich —** [= **in Gesellschaft treten**], to enter into partnership. *Prov.* **Gleich und gleich gesellt sich gern**, like loves like, birds of a feather, flock together.

Gesellen-bau, *m.* [in mining] a mine worked by several, but less than eight partners. **—braten**, *m.* a dinner or supper given by a young mechanic that has just served his time. **—jahre**, *pl.* V. **—zeit**. **—leben**, *n.* life of journeyman. **—lohn**, *m.* journeyman's wages. **—stand**, *m.* the state or condition of a journeyman. **—weise**, *adv.* as a journeyman, in quality of a journeyman. **—weise arbeiten**, to work as a journeyman. **—zeit**, *f.* the term during which a mechanic works as a journeyman, companionship.

Gesellenschaft, *f.* 1) V. **Gesellenstand**. 2) V. **Gesellenzeit**. 3) collectively, all the journeymen.

Gesellig, *adj.* and *adv.* sociable, social. **Der —e Geist**, the sociable spirit; **—e Talente**, convivial talents; **der Hund ist ein sehr —es Thier**, the dog is a very sociable animal; **er ist sehr —**, he is very sociable, companionable or good company; **—e Eigenschaften**, social qualities; **der Mensch ist ein —es Wesen**, man is a social being; **Schafe sind —e Thiere**, sheep are gregarious animals.

Geselligkeit, *f.* sociableness, sociability, socialness.

Gesellinn, *f.* female companion or partner.

Gesellmann, *m.* [-es] [among hunters] the male limehound.

Gesellschaft, *f.* 1) [the association of a number of persons either for a permanent or for a temporary purpose] society, company. **Der Mensch ist für die — geboren**, man is born for society; **die — der Menschen meiden** or **fliehen**, to shun the society of men; **ein nützliches Glied der menschlichen —**, a useful member of society; **eine — von Kaufleuten**, a company of merchants; **eine — Schauspieler**, a company of [stage-] players; **Einem — leisten**, to keep or bear any one company; **mit Einem in — reisen**, to travel in any one's company; **lassen Sie uns in — dahin gehen**, let us go thither in company or together; **werden wir die Ehre Ihrer — haben?** shall we have the honour of your company? **die — lieben**, to be fond of company. *it.* [conversation or intercourse] **Seine — ist mir lästig**, his conversation or company is troublesome or tiresome to me; **er meidet die — dieses Menschen**, he shuns the society or company of that man; **die Einsamkeit ist oft die beste —**, solitude is sometimes the best society. *it.* [the association of persons for a particular purpose] **Eine gelehrte —**, a literary or learned society; **die — Jesu**, the Society of Jesuits; **die königliche — zu London**, the Royal Society of London; **mit Jemand in — treten**, to enter into partnership with any one; **mit Jemand in — stehen**, to be in partnership with any one, to be any one's partner; **ihre — hat sich durch den Tod des Hrn. N. aufgelöst**, their partnership has been dissolved by the death of Mr. N. V. **Handlungs—, Spiel—** &c. 2) [an assemblage of persons for conversation and entertainment; a party collected by invitation or otherwise] company. **Man findet bei ihm jeden Abend —**, you find company at his house every evening; **die — kommt wöchentlich einmal zusammen**, the company or club meets once a week; **die — war zahlreich**, there was a great deal of company; **es ist — bei dem Minister** &c., there is a party or assembly at the minister's; **er gehört nicht zu unserer —**, he does not belong to our club or society; **er hat** or **sieht häufig — bei sich**, he frequently receives or sees company at his house; **sein Haus ist der Sammelplatz der guten —**, his house is the meeting place of good or fashionable company or society; **eine gemischte —**, a mixed company; **eine lustige —**, a merry set; **eine liederliche —**, a dissolute crew; **in guter, schlechter — seyn**, to be in good, bad company; **wir gehen auf's Land, wollen Sie von der — seyn?** we are going into the country, will you be of the party?

Gesellschafts-bühne, *f.* V. **—theater**. **—contract**, *m.* V. **—vertrag**. **—dame**, *f.* a female companion [**Gesellschafterinn**]; *it.* [at courts] maid of honour. **—gemählde**, *n.* a picture with human figures [opposed to a landscape]. **—glied**, *n.* a member of a society or club; [in commerce] partner, co-partner. **—handel**, *m.* trade or commerce carried on by a company of merchants. **—handlung**, *f.* partnership. **—inseln**, *pl.* Society Islands. **—lied**, *n.* a song to be sung by a company or chorus. **—mahler**, *m.* a painter of portraits or of pictures with human figures. **—rechnung, —regel**, *f.* [in arithmetic] rule of society [which teaches the distribution of a gain or loss among the members of a company according to the amount of the share of each] rule of partnership. **—spiel**, *n.* a social game, round game. **—stück**, *n.* companion [to a picture], counterpart, *pendant. V. **Gegenstück, Seitenstück**; *it.* V. **—gemählde**. **—tanz**, *m.* company dance [where more than two persons are dancing]. **—theater**, *n.* a theatre of a society of amateurs, a private theatre. **—thier**, *n.* sociable or gregarious animal. **—verderber**, *m.* a troublesome guest, trouble-feast. **—vertrag**, *m.* social contract. **—wappen**, *n.* the arms of a society or community. **—widrig**, *adj.* and *adv.* averse to society, anti-social. **—zimmer**, *n.* parlour, drawing-room, assembly-room. **Sie begaben sich in das —zimmer**, they repaired to the drawing-room; **er wurde in das —zimmer geführt**, he was ushered into the drawing-room.

Gesellschafter, *m.* [-s, *pl.* -] companion, associate. **Er ist ein guter —**, he is an agreeable companion, he is a boon companion. *it.* [in commerce] partner. V. **Handlungs—**; *it.* he who conducts the affairs or business of a company or society. V. **Geschäftsführer**.

Gesellschafterinn, *f.* female companion.

Gesellschaftlich, *adj.* and *adv.* 1) social. **Das —e Leben, —e Tugenden**, social life, social virtues; **der —e Vertrag**, social contract, V. **Gesellschaftsvertrag**. 2) sociable. V. **Gesellig**.

Gesellschaftlichkeit, *f.* sociability. V. **Geselligkeit**.

Gesenk, *n.* [-es, *pl.* -e] that which causes a thing to sink, weight; [among fishermen] leaden or iron weights at the borders of the net, sinks, leads; [among locksmiths] stamp; *it.* that which is sunk; [among vine-dressers] layer, V. **Ableger, Senker**; [in mining] a cavity, a sunk pit.

Gesenk-amboß, *m.* [among gunsmiths] an anvil with half cylindrical channels or grooves. **—hammer**, *m.* V. **Senkhammer**.

Gesenkt, [*past part.* of **Senken**, which see] *adj.* [in heraldry] abased. **Der Adler ist mit —en Flügeln abgebildet**, the eagle is represented with its wings abased.

Gesetz, *n.* [-es, *pl.* -e] *dim.* **—chen, —lein**, *n.* 1) [obsolescent] division of a song or poem, verse, strophe, stanza. **Das — eines Liedes**, the couplet or strophe of a song; **das — eines Psalmen**, the verse of a psalm; *fig.* ***ein —chen** [**ein Weilchen**] **schlafen**, to sleep a little, to take a nap. 2) [that which is established as a principle, standard or rule] law. **Die —e der Bewegung, der Bewegungslehre**, the laws of motion, of mechanics; **die —e des Magnetismus**, the laws of magnetism; sich seine Pflicht zum —e machen, to make an inviolable law of one's duty; es ist mir ein — or ich habe mir [es] zum —e gemacht, nie zu spielen, I make it a rule, never to play; die —e der Dichtkunst, der Menschlichkeit &c, the rules of poetry, the laws of humanity &c.; *Prov.* Noth hat or kennt kein —, necessity has no law. 3) [in the most limited sense, a formal rule prescribed by a superior, and particularly by the supreme power of a state] law, statute, ordinance. —e geben, to give laws; ein — bekannt machen, to promulgate a law; ein — umgehen, to elude a law; zu einem —e werden, to become, to grow into, a law; ein —aufheben, to abolish, to repeal a law; ein — halten, brechen, to keep or observe, to violate a law; Gewicht und Maß, wie sie durch — bestimmt sind, weight and measure as established by statute; —e, [nur] vom König ausgegangen, ordinances emanated by the king. *it.* collectively: das natürliche, göttliche, bürgerliche —, the natural, divine, civil law; das mosaische —, das Gesetz Moses' [in Script.], the Mosaic law [the institutions of Moses]; *it.* die Lehrer des —es [in Script.], the doctors of the law, the scribes; das ist das — und die Propheten [in Script.], this is the law and the prophets.

Gesetz-buch, *n.* code of laws. Das justinianische, theodosianische —buch, the Justinian, the Theodosian code; das peinliche [Criminal-], das bürgerliche [Civil-] —buch, the criminal code, the code of civil law. —es-entwurf, *m.* project of law, [in the English Parliament] bill. —es-kraft, *f.* force of law, legal sanction. Einer Verordnung —es-kraft geben, to give the force of law to an ordinance, to make it a law, to sanction it. —fälscher, *m.* corruptor of the laws. —gebend, *adj.* law-giving, legislative. —gebende Versammlung, Gewalt, legislative assembly or body, legislative power, legislature. —geber, *m.* law-giver, legislator. —geberinn, *f.* legislatrice. —gebung, *f.* legislation, legislative power. —gebungs-rath, *m.* legislative body. —härte, *f.* rigour of the law. —los, *adj.* and *adv.* 1) [without rule or government] anarchic, anarchical. Ein —loses Volk, ein —loser Staat, an anarchical people, state. 2) [not subject to law, unrestrained by law, without the pale of law] lawless. Jene —losen Menschen, those lawless men. —mäßig, I. *adj.* conformable to law, legal, lawful. Aus —mäßiger Ehe erzeugte Kinder, legitimate children; —mäßiger Gang einer Rechtssache, legal procedure; —mäßige Strafe, legal or lawful punishment. II. *adv.* according to law, legally lawfully; legitimately. Er kann es —mäßig fordern, he can demand it rightfully or legitimately; —mäßig verfahren, to proceed lawfully or legally. —prediger, *m.* a moral preacher, a moralizer. —predigt, *f.* a sermon, that lashes vice severely. —rolle, *f.* the scroll on which the Mosaic law was written, scroll or code of laws. —tafel, *f.* table of the law. Die —tafeln, the tables of the Mosaic law; die zwölf —tafeln der alten Römer, the twelve tables among the ancient Romans. —widrig, *adj.* and *adv.* contrary to law, illegal, unlawful. Eine —widrige Forderung, an unlawful pretension; ein —widriges Verfahren, an illegal proceeding; er wurde —widrig verhaftet, he was illegally arrested.

Gesetzlich, *adj.* and *adv.* conformable to law, legal, lawful, legitimate. —e Strafe, punishment ordained by law; eine Verordnung — machen, to give the force of law or the legal sanction to an ordinance, to sanction it; die —e Religion, positive religion, *it.* [= staatsgesetzlich, as established and sanctioned by the laws of a country] the state-religion; die —e Verunreinigung der Juden, the [legal] impurity of the Jews; — verfahren, to proceed legally.

Gesetzlichkeit, *f.* lawfulness, legality.

Gesetzlosigkeit, *f.* 1) [want of order and government] anarchy. 2) lawlessness.

Gesetzmäßigkeit, *f.* conformity to law, legality. lawfulness, legitimacy. Die — eines Verfahrens, the legality of a proceeding; die — eines Anspruches, the justice or legitimacy of a claim or pretension.

Gesetzwidrigkeit, *f.* illegality, unlawfulness.

Gesetzt, [*past part.* of Setzen, which see] *Fig.* I *adj.* 1) [= festgesetzt] established, fixed, settled Ein —er Preis, a set price; zur —en Zeit, at the time appointed. 2) [= bedächtig] steady [in manners and conduct], staid, sedate, grave. Ein —er Mann, a steady, sober man; ein —es Wesen, a sedate air. II. *adv.* supposing that, in case that. —, es wäre so, suppose it were so; —, es sey wahr, supposing it to be true.

Gesetztheit, *f.* steadiness of manners, staidness, sedateness, demureness.

Geseufze, *n.* [-s] continual sighing, groaning.

Gesicht, *n.* [-es] 1) [not used in the plural] [the faculty of seeing] sight, eye-sight. Der Sinn des —s, the sense of seeing, eye-sight; ein gutes — haben, to have a good sight, or eye-sight; ein kurzes — haben, to be short-sighted or near-sighted; mein — trägt, reicht nicht so weit, my eyes do not reach so far; das — ist ihm vergangen, er ist um das — gekommen, hat das — verloren, he has lost his sight; das — verläßt mich, my sight fails me; die Sonne scheint mir ins —, the sun shines in my eyes. 2) [perception of objects by the eye] sight, view. Etwas zu —e bekommen, to get a sight of a thing; Einen nicht aus dem —e lassen, to keep any one in sight, not to lose sight of any one; etwas aus dem —e verlieren, to lose sight of a thing; geht mir aus dem —e, get or stand out of my sight; im —e seyn or liegen, to be in view or sight; die beiden Heere standen einander im —e, the two armies were in sight of each other; wir hatten das Vorgebirge im —e, we had a sight of the promontory, we had the promontory in view; wir bekamen Land zu —e, we gained sight of land, [the] land rose before our view; dieser Zeug fällt besser ins — als der andere, this stuff has a better appearance than the other; wir lagerten uns im —e des Feindes, we encamped in sight of the enemy. 3) [*pl.* -er] [the surface of the fore-part of the head] face, countenance, visage. Ein hübsches, ein häßliches —, a handsome, an ugly face; ein breites, ein langes —, a broad, a long face; blaß im —e seyn, to be pale-faced; sein — ist mir nicht unbekannt, his face is not unknown to me; Einem ins — sehen, to look any one in the face; ich kenne ihn von —e, I know him by sight; das steht gut zu —e, that looks well; *fig.* *er sagte es ihm ins —, he told him so to his face. In a more limited sense: *a*) [cast of the features, air of the face] countenance. Ein heiteres —, a cheerful countenance; ein gemeines, alltägliches —, a common, everyday face; ein sprechendes —, an expressive countenance; er hat ein leichenblasses, todtenblasses —, he is as pale as death; ich sah es ihm am —e an, I saw it in his countenance; Einem ein saures, mürrisches — machen, to look surly, grimly, crabbedly, with an evil eye, upon any one; Einem ein freundliches — machen, to look kindly upon any one; Verzweiflung blickt ihm aus dem —e, despair is written on his countenance; sein — in Falten legen [eine ernsthafte Miene annehmen], to compose one's face, to put on a serious countenance; *ein langes — machen, to look sad, disappointed; —er machen, schneiden, to make, to pull faces; o, mache mir keine sauern —er, pray, do not make mouths at me, do not pout at me. *b*) [chiefly in fam. lang.] [the whole person with regard to physiognomy] Dieses — ist mir neu, this face is new to me; hier sind viele —er, die ich nicht kenne, here are a great many faces which I don't know; sie sieht gern neue —er, she loves to see new faces. V. Affen— &c. 4) [something to direct the vision] sight. Das — [Visir] an einem Gewehre, the sight of a gun. 5) [*pl.* Gesichte] [something imagined to be seen, though not real] vision, phantom. Ein —, —e sehen, to see a vision, visions; ein Mensch, der —e zu sehen glaubt, a visionary man; das von —en geplagte Mädchen, the visionary maid; etwas in einem —e sehen, to see something in a vision; die Propheten haben —e gehabt, the prophets had visions. Syn. V. Erscheinung.

Gesichts-achse, *f.* [an imaginary line passing through the middle of the pupil and the centre of the eye] optic or visual axis. —ausdruck, *m.* expression of the face or countenance, physiognomy. —betrug, *m.* optical illusion or deception. —bildung, *f.* cast or expression of countenance, physiognomy. Eine glückliche, edle —bildung, a happy, noble physiognomy. —blatter, *f.*, —blätterchen, *n.* pimple. —blödigkeit, *f.* dulness or dimness of sight, amblyopy. —deuter, *m.* physiognomist. —deutung, *f.* [the art of judging of men's temper by the features of the face] physiognomy. —ende, *n.* V. —kreis. —farbe, *f.* complexion. Eine röthliche, eine blasse —farbe, a ruddy, a pale complexion. —fehler, *m.* defect in the organs of seeing. —feld, *n.* V. —kreis. —fläche, *f.* the surface of the face [in anatomy] cheek-bones. —forscher, *m.* V. —deuter. —forschung, *f.* V. —deutung. —kreis, *m.* horizon. Der —kreis ist durch Berge beschränkt, the horizon is bounded or limited by mountains. [in geography, circle whose plane passes through the middle of the earth, and whose poles are the zenith and nadir] horizon. Der wahre, der astronomische —kreis, the true or astronomical horizon; der scheinbare —kreis, the sensible [apparent or visible] horizon [a lesser circle of the sphere which divides the visible part of the sphere from the invisible]; *fig.* seinen —kreis erweitern, to enlarge one's ideas, one's sphere of knowledge; das liegt außer or unter seinem —kreise, that is out of his sphere, *it.* [obsolete, provincial] [in law] that does not fall under his cognizance. —kunde, *f.* knowledge of the human countenance, physiognomy. V. —deutung. —kundige, *m.*, ein —kundiger, physiognomist. —länge, *f.* the length of the face. —linie, *f.* facial-line, lineament, feature; [in fortification] outer line or face, front; [in optics] visual line or ray [that is imagined to come from the object of the eye]. —mahler, *m.* a painter of portraits, portrait-painter. —muskel, *m.* [in anatomy] facial muscle. —nerve, *m.* 1) facial nerve. 2) optic or visual nerve. —pulsader, *f.* V. —schlagader. —punkt, *m.* 1) point of view. Das ist nicht der rechte —punkt, this is not the proper point of view or not the proper place to view a thing; *fig.* eine Sache aus dem wahren or rechten —punkte betrachten, to view a thing in its true light or aspect; von diesem —punkte aus betrachtet, ist die Aussage wichtig, in this or that point of view the evidence is important. 2) [in optics] the point of sight, the visual point. —schlagader, *f.* [in anatomy] facial artery. —schwäche, *f.* weakness or dimness

ness of sight. —seite, *f.* [in architecture] front, face [of a house]. —sinn, *m.* the sense of seeing. —strahl, *m.* [in optics] visual ray. —täuschung, *f.* V —betrug. —verdunkelung, *f.* the obscuring of the sight. —verzerrung, *f.* distortion of the face or countenance, grimace. —wahrsager, *m.* metoposcopist. —wahrsagerei, *f.* metoposcopy. —weite, *f.* the distance to which the eye reaches. —winkel, *m.* [in anatomy] facial angle; [in optics] visual or optic angle. —zug, *m.* lineament, feature. Aus Jemands —zügen auf dessen Gemüthsart schließen, to judge of any one's temper by his features; sie hat ganz die —züge ihrer Mutter, she has all the features of her mother.

Gesiebent, *adj.* consisting of seven parts, septenary. —e Zahl, septenary number; das —e, ein —es, a sequence or set of seven cards, as in piquet, a septieme.

Gesims, *n.* [-es, *pl.* -e] [perhaps from the Icel. *sima*, to adorn] [a projecture beyond the wall, column, wainscot &c] moulding, cornice. Das — an einem Kamin, mantlepiece, chimney-piece; das — an einer Thüre, an einem Fenster, door-case, window-case, window-sill; das — an einer Mauer, an einer Säulenordnung, entablature, pediment; der Kranz an dem —e, cornice, V. Karnieß; — an einem Ofen, the cornice of a stove. *it.* [in familiar language] shelf, shelves.

Gesims-glied, *n.* [in architecture] a member or part of a moulding or cornice. —hobel, *m.* [among joiners] moulding-plane, rabbet-plane —uhr, *f.* clock. V. Wanduhr.

Gesinde, *n.* [-s] [allied to senden, to send, and the ancient Sind, way] [collectively] servants, domestics; menials. All sein — fortschicken, to discharge all one's servants, all mein — ist krank, all my servants, men or people are sick. V. Hofgesinde.

Gesinde-bier, *n.* beer for the servants, small-beer. —brod, *n.* household bread, brown bread —essen, *n.* dinner, supper or victuals for the servants. —kost, *f.* food or victuals given to the servants. —lohn, *m.* servants' wages. —ordnung, *f.* regulation of servants. —saal, *m.* servants'hall. —tisch, *m.* table or board of the servants. —wein, *m.* [an indifferent or inferior quality of the] wine for the servants. —zimmer, *n.* servants'room.

Gesindel, *n.* [-s] low people, rabble, vagabonds. Jagt das — auseinander! disperse the mob or the rabble! mit solchem — will ich nichts zu thun haben, mich nicht einlassen, I'll have nothing to do with such vermin, with such vagabonds or rascalions.

Gesinge, *n.* [-s] constant singing; *it.* bad singing.

Gesinnen, *ir.* I. *v. intr.* [used with seyn] to intend, to purpose. Ich bin nicht gesonnen, Ihren Vorschlag zu willigen, it is not my intention, I do not intend or mean, I am not inclined or disposed, to acquiesce in your proposal; ich bin gesonnen, nach Paris weiter zu reisen, it is my intention, I have a good mind to proceed to Paris; wenn Sie gesonnen sind, morgen abzureisen, if you propose, if you are resolved, if you have made up your mind, to depart to-morrow; was sind Sie gesonnen, zu thun? what have you resolved upon? what is your intention? II. *v. tr.* [a term] Etwas an einen —, to require something of a person.

Gesinnt, Gesinnet, *adj.* minded, disposed, affected. Für die Regierung gut oder übel —seyn, to be well or ill affected to the government; er ist einer von den übel —en, he is one of the disaffected or discontented persons; er ist gütig, freundschaftlich gegen Sie —, he is well affected towards you, he bears you good will, he is your well-wisher; nicht gut, feindlich gegen Einen — seyn, to be ill affected towards any one, to bear him ill will, to owe him a spite, to have a grudge against him; ein treu —er Freund, a faithful friend; sie ist mütterlich gegen dieses Kind —, she has a motherly affection for this child; sie sind alle gleich —, they are all of the same mind; so bin ich —, that's my temper, disposition of mind or character; irdisch, weltlich — seyn, to be wordly-minded; er ist französisch, österreichisch —, he is attached to the French, to the Austrians, he affects the French, the Austrian party; ein königlich —er, a royalist.

Gesinnung, *f.* disposition, intention, sentiment, idea. Ich kenne seine —en gegen Sie, I know his feelings towards you; er hegt kindliche —en gegen seinen Wohlthäter, he has a filial affection for his benefactor; das war nicht meine — [Meinung, Absicht], that was not my meaning or intention; was ist Ihre —? what is your intention? what do you mean to do? in dieser Versammlung hat jeder das Recht, seine —en auszusprechen or an den Tag zu legen, in this assembly every one has the privilege of delivering his sentiments; seine — ändern, to change one's mind; diese Handlung zeugt von einer sehr edlen —, von den erhabensten —en, this action evinces or proves a very noble mind, the most exalted sentiments.

Gesippe, *n.* [-es] **Gesippschaft,** *f.* V. Sippschaft.

Gesittet, *adj.* and *adv.* 1) having certain manners, mannered. Wohl—e, übel—e Kinder, well-bred, or well-mannered, ill-bred or ill-mannered children; ein wohl—er, fein—er junger Mensch, a well-bred, well-behaved or polite youth or lad. *it.* having good manners or morals, good, moral, civilized Ein —er Mensch, a man of good manners or morals; ein —es Leben führen, to lead a good moral life; ein —es Volk, a polite people; —e [opposed to rohe, savage] Völker, civilized nations; ein Volk —, —er machen, to civilise, to refine or polish a nation. 2) [conformable to good manners] genteel, polite. Ein —es Betragen, Wesen, a genteel behaviour, genteel or polite manners. SYN. Gesittet, Sittlich, Sittsam. Gesittet refers merely to the exterior deportment; sittlich implies conformity of all our free actions with moral law. Sittsam has a special reference to that which is fit and becoming in social intercourse, in actions and discourse.

Gesittetheit, *f.* 1) politeness of manners, gentility. 2) morality. V. Sittlichkeit.

Gesittigung, Gesittung, *f.* V. Sittigung.

Gesode, *n.* [-s] V. Gesott.

†**Gesöff,** *n.* [-es] [in contempt] 1) immoderate, hard drinking, swilling. 2) the drink or liquor thus drunk, mean liquor, slop, slipslop. Welch ein schlechtes —! what a detestable swipes! V. Getränk.

Gesott, *n.* [-es] food for cattle, steeped in scalding hot water, mash. V. Siebe.

1. ‡**Gespan,** *m.* [-es, *pl.* -e] [probably from the ancient spänen = säugen, to suck; therefore = Milchbruder, foster-brother] companion, fellow, comrade, partner, assistant. V. Gehülfe.

Gespanschaft, *f.* comradeship, partnership, company. In —schaft reisen, to travel in company.

2 **Gespan,** *m.* [-es, *pl.* -e] [from the Slavonic *Ban* = Herr, master, Lord, in the Latin of the middle age *Hispanus*] [in Hungary] a palatine, count palatine.

Gespanschaft, *f.* [in Hungary] a county, palatinate.

Gespann, *n.* [-es, *pl.* -e] [a set of horses, oxen, or other beasts harnessed together to the same vehicle] team. Ein — Pferde, Ochsen &c, a team of horses, oxen &c.; dieser Pächter hat drei —e, that farmer has three teams.

Gespannt, [*past part.* of Spannen, which see] *Fig. adj* and *adv.* 1) [in fam. lang.] Mit Jemand —, über den Fuß — seyn, to have fallen out, to be at variance, on ill terms with any one. 2) [denoting a high degree of exertion] Mit —er Aufmerksamkeit zuhören, to listen with great attention, very intently; wir waren alle in der —esten Erwartung, we were all in the most anxious expectation; mit —en Blicken, with eager, with intent looks.

Gespanntheit, *f.* 1) misunderstanding, difference, disagreement. 2) state of being in attentive expectation of what is to follow.

Gesparr, *n.* [-s] [collectively] the timberwork of a roof, rafters. V. Sparrenwerk.

Gesparre, *n.* V. Gesperre.

†**Gespaße,** *n.* [-s] continual jesting or joking.

Gespe, *f.* V. Gäspe.

†**Gespeie,** *n.* [-s] continual spitting or vomiting. V. Speien.

Gespelde, *n.* V. Gespilde.

Gespenst, *n.* [-es, *pl.* -er] [from the ancient spanen, to seduce] 1) spectre, apparition, ghost, spright or spirit. Er hat ein — gesehen, he has seen a spectre; er fürchtet sich vor —ern, he is afraid of spirits; es sollen in diesem Hause —er erscheinen, umgehen, spuken, that house is said to be haunted; *er sieht aus wie ein —, he looks like a ghost, he is a mere skeleton. 2) [in natural history] *a*) [a species of Voluta, marked with reddish broad bands] spectre. *b*) ichneumon-fly.

Gespenster-erscheinung, *f.* the appearance or apparition of spirits or of a ghost. —furcht, *f.* fear of spectres. —geschichte, *f.* —geschichtchen, *n.* a ghost-story. —käfer, *m.* [a kind of grass-hopper] mantis or walking leaf. —stunde, *f.* the time when spirits or ghosts are said to walk, midnight, midnight-hour. —thier, *n.* [an animal of the genus Lemur] maki.

Gespenstisch, *adj.* and *adv.* like a spectre or ghost in appearance, ghostly.

Gesperre, *n.* [-s] 1) the act of barring or shutting; *it.* any thing that obstructs or hinders. Diese Schachteln machen viel —, these boxes take up too much room, are an encumbrance; in dieser Straße ist immer ein —, this street is always obstructed; Waaren, die ein großes — machen, cumbersome or unwieldy goods; *fig.* [rather vulgar] er gab es mir ohne vieles —, he gave it me without starting many difficulties. 2) any thing that fastens or stops, a bar. Das — eines Daches, the timberwork or rafters of a roof; das — an einem Buche, the clasps of a book, V. Schließen; das — an einer Uhr, the catch of a watch or clock; das — an einer Buchdruckerpresse, the frisket of a printing-press.

Gesperr-baum, *m.* [in ship-building, a piece of timber, used to connect the beams of a ship with her sides or timbers] knee. —macher, *m.* he who makes clasps &c., a cutler.

Gespiele, *m.* [-n, *pl.* -n] **Gespielinn**, *f.* [*pl.* -en] companion, female companion, play-mate, play-fellow. Ein einziger von den Gespielen meiner Jugend ist noch am Leben, only one of the companions of my childhood is yet alive; *fig.* Unschuld, liebliche Gespielinn des Kindes, innocence, lovely companion of the infant. *it.* a familiar friend or associate, an intimate, confidant. Seitdem ihre Gespielinn krank ist, since her confidant, companion or friend is ill.

Gespieene, *n.* [-n] that has been spewed or vomited.

Gespilde, *n.* [-s] [from spalten = theilen, to split = to divide] [law term] the right of preemption [jus retractus].

Gespinne, *n.* [-s] 1) the act of spinning; *it.* continual spinning 2) that which is spun.

Gespinnst, *n.* [-es, *pl.* -e] that which is spun and the quality of spinning. Das — an dieser Wolle ist zu grob, diese Wolle ist von zu grobem —e, the threads, yarn or spinning of this wool are, is to coarse; Wolle von feinem —e, fine-spun wool or yarn; diese Strähne sind nicht von einerlei —e, these skeins are not of the same spinning; das — des Seidenwurmes, the spinning of the silk-worm.

Gespons, *m.* and *f.* [*m.* -es or -en, *f.* -, *pl.* -e or -en] [obsolete or now only used in joke] bridegroom, bride, V. Bräutigam, Braut.

Gespött, *n.* [-s] or **Gespötte**, *n.* [-s] 1) the act of mocking or deriding, mockery, derision, raillery, banter, jeering. Sein — mit Einem, mit etwas treiben, to laugh at, to ridicule any one or a thing, to deride, to banter, to jeer any one, to make a jest of a thing; sich dem —e des Pöbels aussetzen, to expose one's self or lay one's self open to the derision or ridicule of the mob. 2) [the object of derision or ridicule]. Sich zum —e machen, to make one's self ridiculous, to make a fool of one's self, to expose one's self to be laughed at; ein — aus etwas machen, to turn something into ridicule, to make a laughing-stock of a thing; laßt uns Andern nicht zum —e dienen, let us not be a laughing-stock to others.

Gespötte, *n.* [-s] constant mocking.

Gespöttel, *n.* [-s] small or petty bantering, mockery, raillery, satire. V. Gespött.

Gespräch, *n.* [-es, *pl.* -e] discourse, conversation, dialogue. Sich mit Jemand in ein — einlassen, to enter into conversation with any one; ein — mit Jemand anknüpfen, to join conversation or discourse with any one; sie waren im —e, im vertrauten —e begriffen, they were engaged in conversation, in close or familiar conversation; ein trauliches, ein ernsthaftes —, a familiar, a serious discourse or conversation; Plato's, Lucians —e, Plato's, Lucian's Dialogues; die — des Erasmus, the colloquies of Erasmus; etwas in ein — einkleiden, to give a thing the form of a dialogue. *In a more limited sense:* *a*) [= Rede, Gerücht] report, rumour. Es gehet, es ist das allgemeine —, it is a common talk, it is generally reported. *b*) [subject of discourse] talk. Sein Abenteuer ist das — der ganzen Stadt, his adventure is the talk of the whole town.

Gesprächs-buch, *n.* book of dialogues. **—s-form**, *f.* form of a dialogue. **—stoff**, *m.* subject for conversation, topic. **—s-weise**, *adv.* in the form of a dialogue, by way of dialogue, conversation or discourse. Eine Sache —s-weise abhandeln, to treat a subject in the form of a dialogue; eine Nachricht —s-weise mittheilen, to communicate an intelligence by way of conversation.

Gesprächig, *adj.* 1) [easy of conversation] conversable, communicative, [applied to superiors] affable. Er ist sehr —, ein sehr —er Mensch [or Mann], he is very conversable or affable, a very conversable, sociable or affable man. 2) [given to much talking] talkative. Der Wein macht —, wine makes talkative.

Gesprächigkeit, *f.* 1) [readiness to converse] conversableness, affability. Seine gerühmte — ist nichts als &c., his boasted affability is nothing but &c 2) [habit of speaking much in conversation] talkativeness.

Gesprènge, *n.* [-s, *pl.* -] 1) act of blowing up with gunpowder; *it.* [in mining] pieces or fragments of rock or ore separated by gunpowder. 2) [in architecture] pent-house, concluvium.

Gesproß, *n.* [-sses] any thing that buds or shoots, young shoots or sprigs.

Gespüle, *n.* [-s] a constant washing or rinsing; *it.* dishwater, swill, hog-wash.

Gesselblume, *f.* [*pl.* -n] lesser celandine.

Gestade, *n.* [-s, *pl.* -] [from stehen, to stand] shore, bank, beach. Ein steiles, hohes —, a steep, high beach; am — dieses Flusses, See's, des Meeres, on the bank or shore of this river, on the shore or beach of this lake, of the sea; wir erblickten die — des Rheins, we perceived the banks or shores of the Rhine; längs dem — hinsegeln, to sail along the sea-shore, the coast. V. Ufer, Küste. Syn. Gestade, Ufer, Strand, Reede, Küste. Ufer is the most general denomination of the border of the sea or of a lake or river. Gestade is a part of the seashore where vessels may approach and land. Strand is a flat shore on which vessels ground or strand from the shallowness of the water, Reede a place where ships may ride securely at anchor at some distance from the shore, sheltered from the violence of the wind. Küste is used to express the land that extends along the seashore, and comprehends more than Ufer which signifies merely the border of the sea.

Gestalt, *f.* [from stellen, to put, to place] 1) form, figure, shape. Ein Kreis hat eine runde —, a circle has a round form or figure; die — des Kopfes, des Körpers, the form or shape of the head, of the body; eine Arznei in — der Pillen, a medicine in the form of pills or in pills; ein Mensch von schöner, regelmäßiger —, a man of a fine, regular shape or figure; der Engel erschien ihm unter der — eines Reisenden, the angel appeared to him in the shape or figure of a traveler; einer Sache eine neue — geben, to give a thing a new form or fashion; es fängt an, eine gute, eine bessere — zu gewinnen, it begins to assume a good, a better form; er ist schön von —, he is well-shaped, well-made; er ist ein Mann in or von meiner —, he is a man of my size or shape; das Abendmahl unter beiden —en or unter beiderlei — genießen, to receive the communion in both kinds; *it. fig.* der Sache eine — geben, to give a pleasing form or shape to a thing, to set off a thing; so hat es eine bessere —, thus it is more elegant; *it.* eine lange, hagere —, a long, thin or spare form or figure; *fig.* das war damals die — der Sachen, such was then the posture or face of affairs; die Dinge haben eine andere — gewonnen, things carry another face, bear another aspect, *the tables are turned; er führte seinen Plan folgender — aus, he executed his plan in the following manner; gleicher — [auf gleiche Weise], in the same way or manner; solcher —, in such a way or manner; er benahm sich solcher —, daß er &c., he behaved in such a manner as to &c.; welcher —? which way, in what manner, by what means, how? V. Dergestalt; nach — der Sachen, according to the circumstances. 2 [a being as endowed with form] shape. Dort saß eine fürchterliche —, there sat a formidable figure; es nahte sich eine liebliche —, a person of lovely form approached; sie erschrak vor der langen, hagern —, she started at [the] sight of the long thin figure; er sah eine — im Traume, he saw a vision in his dream; ich wollte die liebliche — umarmen, aber &c., I was going to embrace the lovely figure, but &c.

Gestaltlos, *adj.* and *adv.* 1) having no shape or form, admitting of no shape or form. 2) [without a determinate form] formless or shapeless. Eine —lose Masse, a shapeless mass; —lose Wolken, formless or shapeless clouds. 3) [wanting an agreeable shape or form] deformed, misshapen. Ein —loses Gebäude, a misshapen edifice

‡**Gestalt**, *conj.* because, as. V. Weil.

Gestalten, I. *v. tr.* to form, to shape, to fashion, to mould. Der Schädel gestaltet das Gehirn, the skull gives the brain its form or shape, forms or shapes the brain; die Natur gestaltet den Leib, nature fashions or shapes the body; die —de Kraft, the plastic virtue; er wird sie heurathen, wie sie auch gestaltet seyn möge, he will marry her, whatever may be her shape or figure; ein wohl-, ein übelgestalteter Mensch, a well shaped, well made, an ill sha[ped], ill made man; [provinc., in fam. lang.] wie ist er [ge]stalt [for gestaltet]? how is he made or sha[ped], how does he look? [in law] bei so — [for gestalteten] Sachen, so — Dingen nach, matters standing [so], such being the juncture or posture of affairs [un]der such circumstances; — [for gestalteten] S[achen] nach, according as the case requires, as shall serve. II. *v. r.* sich —, to assume or [take] a form or shape, to be formed or shaped [or] come to some shape. Ihre Brust fängt an, [sich] zu —, her breast begins to swell; das — Gestaltung. *Fig.* [in modern style] to be for[med], to appear. Ein neues, reges Leben gestaltet [sich] in or unter diesem Volke, there is a new life [and] stir in the minds and doings of this peop[le or] nation; wie die Dinge sich heutzutage gest[altet] haben, after the turn things have taken [now]-a-days; die Sache hat sich ganz anders gest[altet] als [wie] Sie mir sagten, the affair has [turned] out quite different from what you told me.

Gestaltenreich, *adj.* abounding [in] a variety of forms or figures. Die —reiche [Na]tur, nature, rich in her forms. V. Vielgestaltig.

Gestaltig, *adj.* [only used in composition] [hav]ing a certain form or shape.

Gestaltlosigkeit, *f.* 1) want of any [shape] or form. 2) [destitution of determinate or form] shapelessness. 3) [want of a pleasing [shape] or form] deformedness, deformity.

Gestaltniß, *f.* [little used] V. Beschaff[enheit], Gestaltung.

Gestaltung, *f.* 1) the act of formin[g], shaping, formation. 2) conformation, [confi]guration, form, figure. V. Bildung.

Gestammel, *n.* [-s] 1) the act of [stam]mering or stuttering, particularly a co[ntinual] stammering. 2) that is uttered or pro[nounced] stammeringly. Sein — kann Niemand [verste]hen, nobody can understand what he stam[mers].

Gestampfe, *n.* [-s] the act of stam[ping] [with the feet], a stamping or clattering [made] with the feet; *it.* a stamping or clatt[ering] sound. Wir hörten das — der Pferde, we [heard] the clattering of the horses.

Gestände, *n.* [-s, *pl.* -] [from stehen,

stand] 1) [among sportsmen] the feet of birds of prey. 2) V. Gestell.

Gestanden, [*past part.* of Stehen and Gestehen, which see] || Ein —er Mann [from stehen], a man of ripe or full, [or even] of advanced manhood; —e Milch [from 2. Gestehen], curdled milk; nur —! [from 1. Gestehen] confess now! you may as well avow!

Geständert, *adj.* [in heraldry, divided into several triangular parts of two different tinctures] gyronny.

Geständig, *adj.* confessing, having confessed Einer Sache — seyn, to confess, to acknowledge, to avow, to own a thing; er ist die Schuld nicht —, he does not confess or own the debt; er ist ihm die Schuld nicht —, he denies owing him that sum. V. 1. Gestehen.

Geständigen, *v. tr.* [law term] to own, to confess, to avow.

Geständniß, *n.* [-sses, *pl.* -sse] confession, avowal. Ein aufrichtiges, freies —, a sincere, free confession or avowal; Rousseau's Geständnisse, the Confessions of Rousseau; es erhellt aus seinem eigenen Geständnisse, it appears by his own confession; man entlockte ihm dieses —, *that confession was pumped out of him; er hat es nach Jedermanns — [Zeugniß] am besten gemacht, he has succeeded best, according to the general opinion.

Gestänge, *n.* [-s] 1) [collectively] poles joined together, an enclosure with poles or stakes, rails. Ein — um ein Feld, a fence of poles about a field. [in mining] *a*) the poles of a hydraulic engine, V. Feldgestänge; *b*) the poles on which the miners' wheelbarrows run. 2) [among hunters] V. Geweih.

Gestängesteuer, *f.* [in mining] contribution or charges for keeping a hydraulic engine in repair.

Gestank, *m.* [-s] a bad or offensive smell, stink, stench. Woher kömmt dieser —? from whence does this offensive smell, this stench proceed? einen widerlichen — von sich geben, to emit, to send forth a noisome smell or stench; *fig* [= übler Ruf] bad name; †einen — hinter sich lassen, zurücklassen, to leave a bad name behind.

Gestatten, *v. tr.* to permit, to allow, to grant. Einem seinen Willen — [rather stiff], to allow or suffer any one to do what he pleases, to let any one have his own will; ich gestatte Ihnen ein wenig Ruhe, I grant you a little repose; er gestattete ihm diese Reise nicht, he did not assent to his taking that journey, he did not allow or permit him to take that journey; wenn es die Zeit gestattet, if time permits; er braucht mehr als sein Einkommen gestattet, he spends more than his income will allow.

Gestatten, *n.* [-s] **Gestattung,** *f.* permission, allowance, consent, admission.

Gestäube, *n.* [-s] 1) rising dust. 2) coal-dust.

Gestäude, *n.* [-s] 1) [collectively] shrubs or bushes in general, shrubbery. 2) [among hunters or sportsmen, the nest of the hawk or eagle] airy or aëry.

Gesteck, *n.* V. Besteck.

1. **Gestehen,** *ir.* I. *v. tr.* to confess, to own, to acknowledge, to avow. Seinen Irrthum, seinen Fehler —, to confess, to own one's error, one's fault; wir wollen offen unsre Sünden —, let us frankly confess our sins; ich gestehe, daß ich ihm so viel Muth nicht zugetraut hätte, I admit, I grant that I did not believe him possessed of so much courage; — Sie, daß Sie Unrecht haben, confess or own yourself in the wrong; seine Liebe —, to avow one's love; [in familiar language] das gesteh' ich! das muß ich —! is it possible! indeed! who would have thought it! II. *v. r.* [obsolete and stiff] sich —, to venture, to dare. V. Unterstehen, sich —.

2. **Gestehen,** *ir. v. intr.* [u. w. seyn] [= gerinnen] to coagulate, to curdle. Das Oel gesteht, wenn man es an einem kühlen Orte aufbewahrt, oil coagulates when kept in a cool place; die Milch fängt an zu —, the milk begins to curdle; die Luft macht geschmolzenes Fett —, the air congeals melted fat; ein Gift, das das Blut in den Adern — macht, a poison that congeals the blood in the veins; gestandene Milch, curdled milk; gestandenes Blut, coagulated or clotted blood.

Gestein, *n* [-es, *pl.* -e] 1) [collectively] stones; *it.* [= Edelgestein, Edelsteine] precious stones, gems. 2) [= Steinmasse] mass of stones; [in mining] rocks, gangue. Hartes, mürbes —, hard, soft rocks; taubes, unedles —, sterile gangue [that contains no ore].

Gesteinkarte, *f.* a small card, not a court-card. **—kunde,** *f.* mineralogy. **—kundige,** *m.* mineralogist.

Gestell, *n.* [-es, *pl.* -e] 1) [that on which something stands or rests] stand, frame. Das — eines Raubvogels [among sportsmen], the feet of a bird of prey; das — eines Tisches, the frame of a table, trestle; das — eines Wagens, einer Kutsche, the frame and wheels upon which the body of a vehicle or carriage is placed; das hölzerne — einer Kutsche, the body of a coach; das — einer Windmühle, the frame or timber-work of a windmill; das — eines Pfluges, the stool or saddle of a plough. 2) any thing erected or set up. Ein — zum Trocknen der Wäsche, a horse to dry linen on; das — eines Brunnens, the curbstone or brim of a well; das — der Fischer, the net or nets of fishermen when set; [in metallurgy] das — am hohen Ofen, the basin of reception of a furnace. 3) [the place on which one stands or walks, only among sportsmen] way or lane in a forest.

Gestellmacher, *m.* wheelwright. V. Wagner.

Gesteppe, *n.* [-s] 1) the act of quilting or stitching. 2) something stitched or quilted.

Gesterig, V. Gestrig.

Gestern, [allied to the Lat adj. *hesternus*, to the Gr. χθές] *adv* yesterday. — Morgen, — früh, yesterday morning; — Abend, yesterday evening, last night; — vor acht Tagen, yesterday sennight or week; vor —, [always written vorgestern] the day before yesterday; *fig.* *wir sind erst von —, und wissen nichts, we are but of yesterday and know nothing.

Gesternt, *adj.* starred, starry. Der —e Himmel, the starry sky.

Gestichel, *n.* [-s] continued pricking; *fig.* [rather vulgar] continued sneering, V. Stichelei.

Gestick, *n.* [-es, *pl.* -e] or **Gesticke,** *n.* [-s, *pl.* -] 1) act of embroidering. 2) [the thing embroidered] embroidery.

Gestiebe, *n.* V. Gestübe.

Gestiefelt, *adj.* and *adv.* booted, in boots. Der —e Kater [nursery tale], puss in boots.

Gestielt, *adj.* furnished with a helve or stalk, helved, stalked.

Gestift, *n.* [-es, *pl.* -e] [obsolescent] [Stift] foundation, endowment.

Gestirn, *n.* [-es, *pl.* -e] 1) [collectively] the stars. Das — or die —e betrachten, beobachten, to contemplate, to observe the stars; den Lauf, die Bewegung, den Stand der —e berechnen, to calculate the course, the motion, the position of the stars. 2) [= Sternbild] constellation, asterism. Das — des Stieres, the constellation of the bull or taurus; die zwölf —e des Thierkreises, the twelve signs of the zodiac; *fig.* unter einem unglücklichen —e geboren seyn, to be born under an unlucky star or planet. 3) a single star. Die Sonne ist das schönste —, the sun is the most beautiful of the stars; das — des Tages [Sonne], der Nacht [Mond], [chiefly in a high style] the planet of the day [sun], the planet of the night [moon].

Gestirndiener, *m.* a worshipper of the sun and stars, a Sabian. **—dienst,** *m.* the worship of the sun and stars, Sabianism. **—stand,** *m.* [in astronomy] the position of the stars, constellation.

Gestirnt, *adj.* 1) furnished with a forehead. 2) V. Gesternt.

Gestirnung, *f.* V. Gestirnstand.

Gestöber, *n.* [-s, *pl.* -] a drift of dust; *it.* drizzling or drifting [of snow]. V. Schnee—, Regen—.

Gestöcke, *n.* [-s, *pl.* -] [in mining] heaped mine V. Stockwerk.

Gestolper, *n.* [-s] stumbling, tripping.

Gestopfte, *n.* [-n] V. Stopfwerk.

Gestoppel, *n.* [-s] [rather vulgar] any thing amassed or heaped up [in a disorderly manner]. Das ganze — ist keinen Dreier werth, the whole mass or heap is not worth a farthing; *fig.* [in contempt] ein — von angeführten Stellen, a collection or compilation of quoted passages.

Gestotter, *n.* [-s] stuttering, stammering.

Gestrampel, *n.* [-s] [rather provincial or vulgar] the act of kicking or stamping with the feet.

Gesträubhölzer, *pl.* props, shores, stays, supporters.

Gesträuch, *n.* [-es, *pl.* -e] 1) [collectively] shrubs, bushes, shrubbery, copse, thicket. Sich im —e verstecken, to hide one's self in the bushes or in the thicket. 2) a single shrub or bush. V. Gebüsch, Strauchwerk.

Gestreckt, [*past part.* of Strecken, which see] *adj.* In —em Laufe, Galoppe, at full gallop, at full speed.

Gestrenge, *adj.* and *adv.* obsolete for Streng, which see. Ein —r Richter, Beurtheiler, a severe judge. *it.* as a title [of honour]. —r Herr, — Frau, Sir, your worship or Lordship, Madam, your Ladyship; Eure —n, your worship, your Lordship, your Ladyship.

Gestreu, *n.* [-es] strewing. Ein — von Blumen, a strewing of flowers, flowers strewed; ein — von Asche, a train of ashes.

Gestrick, *n.* [-es, *pl.* -e] or **Gestricke,** *n.* [-s, *pl.* -] 1) knitting. 2) netting, network.

Gestrig, *adj.* of yesterday, done yesterday. Der —e Tag, die —e Nacht, yesterday, last night; die —e Zeitung, yesterday's newspaper; —en Tages, yesterday.

Gestroh, *n.* [-es] **Geströhde,** *n.* [-s] collectively, a quantity of straw. Das — für das Vieh, litter for the cattle.

Gestrudel, *n.* [-s] rising in bubbles, bubbling up, whirling; *it.* whirlpool.

Gestrunkt, *adj.* [in botany] furnished with a short and thick stalk.

Gestrüppe, *n.* [-s] [collectively] bushes and brambles.

Gestübe, *n.* [-s, *pl.* -] dust, coal-dust; [in

founderies] cement made of clay and coal-dust; *it.* the turf and earth for covering a charcoal-pile.

Gestübe-kammer, *f.* [in founderies] room or place where the cement of clay and coal-dust is made. —**pochwerk**, *n.* [in founderies] the stamper for pounding the coals for the cement. —**rand**, *m.* the border or margin of turf and earth about a charcoal-pile.

Gestüber, *n.* [-s] [among sportsmen] dung of partridges, droppings.

Gestück, *n.* [-es, *pl.* -e] a piece of ordnance, gun, cannon.

Gestühl, *n.* [-es, *pl.* -e] [rather unusual] [collectively] seats, chairs; [in a church] pews.

Gestümper, *n.* [-s] bungling, bungling piece of work, bungle.

Gestúnden, *v. tr.* [a law term] to put off, to respite. Einem die Bezahlung —, to allow any one time for payment.

Gestúndung, *f.* [a law term] delay, respite. V. Gestunden.

Gestúte, *n.* [-s, *pl.* -] [a collection of breeding-horses and mares and the place where they are kept] stud. Ein — halten, to keep a stud.

Gestüt-garten, *m.* [the place where breeding-horses and mares are kept] stud. —**haus**, *n.* the house or lodge belonging to a stud. —**hengst**, *m.* [Beschäler] stallion, stud horse. —**herr**, *m.* the owner of a stud. —**meister**, *m.* master of a stud. —**stute**, *f.* stud mare, a brood-mare. —**verwalter**, *m.* V. —meister.

Gesúch, *n.* [-es, *pl.* -e] request, petition, suit, solicitation, desire, prayer. Bewilligen Sie mein —, grant my request; Einem sein — abschlagen, to refuse any one's request or petition; das in der Bittschrift ausgesprochene — ist &c., the prayer of the petition is &c.; er ist mit seinem —e vor or vom Gericht abgewiesen worden, the court cast him out of his demand, his demand was rejected, he has been non-suited; Eurem —e bei dem Fürsten ist gewillfahrt worden, your petition to the prince has been granted; auf mein unterthänigstes —, at my most humble petition or request.

Gesúche, *n.* [-s] constant seeking or searching.

Gesúdel, *n.* [-s] scribbling, scrawling, scribble, scrawl; *it.* daubing. Ich kann dieses — nicht lesen, I cannot read this scrawl, these pot-hooks; das ist kein Gemählde, das ist ein bloßes —, this is no picture, this is a mere daub. V. Sudelei.

Gesúmm[e], *n.* [-es] or **Gesúmmse**, *n.* [-s] humming; buzzing.

Gesúmpfe, *n.* [-s, *pl.* -] bog, marsh or marshes; quagmire.

Gesúnd, [Sax. *sund*, L. *sanus*, Gr. *σάος*, Chaldee and Syriac *chasan*; primarily it signified *whole, entire*, like the E. *sound*] *adj.* and *adv.* 1) [being in a sound or healthy state] sound, healthy, healthful. —e Glieder, —er Leib, sound limbs, a sound or healthful body; an Leib und Seele —, sound in soul and body; um — zu leben, müssen wir &c., in order to be well or in good health, we must &c.; *frisch und — wieder zurück kommen, to come back safe and sound or safe and well; dieses Pferd hat sehr —e Beine, this horse has very sound legs; —es Holz, sound wood; dieser Kranke wird bald wieder — werden, this sick man will soon be restored to health, will soon recover his health; sind Sie wieder —? are you well again? die Freude hat ihn wieder — gemacht, joy has restored him to health, has cured him; in —en Tagen dachte ich nicht daran, being well or when in good health, I never thought of it; leben Sie —, bleiben Sie —! good bye, farewell! der —e Menschenverstand, die —e Vernunft, the sound or common sense, good sense, sound reason; er hat einen —en Verstand, eine —e Urtheilskraft, he is a man of sound understanding, of sound judgment. 2) [indicating health or soundness] healthful. Eine —e Gesichtsfarbe, a fresh, ruddy complexion; ein —es Aussehen haben, to look well; *fig.* eine —e Antwort, a sound, judicious, sensible answer. 3) [conducive to health] healthy, healthful, wholesome, salubrious. —e Kost, —es Wasser, wholesome, healthful diet, water; die Luft auf den Bergen ist sehr —, the air upon the mountains is very wholesome, healthful or salubrious; das ist mir nicht —, that does not suit my health, does not agree with me; *das Aderlassen war ihm sehr —, bleeding did him much good. *Fig.* *[= nützlich, heilsam] useful, wholesome. Diese Demüthigung ist ihm —, this humiliation will prove useful to him; *das ist ihm — [daran geschieht ihm recht], that serves him right.

Gesund-bad, *n.* mineral bath, spa. In ein —bad reisen, to go to a watering-place; es gibt hier vortreffliche —bäder, there are excellent mineral baths here. —**brunnen**, *m.* mineral water, mineral spring, the waters, wells. Dieses Ländchen enthält viele —brunnen, there are a great many mineral springs in this small country; den —brunnen trinken, to drink the waters, to be at the wells; er ging nach Pyrmont, um den —brunnen zu trinken, he went to Pyrmont for the benefit of the waters. —**brunnenwasser**, *n.* water from a mineral spring.

Gesúnden, *v. intr.* [u. w. seyn] to recover one's health. V. [the more usual word] Genesen.

Gesúndheit, *f.* 1) [state of being sound or healthy] soundness, health, healthiness, healthfulness. Einer guten — genießen, to enjoy a good state of health; bei guter — seyn, to be in good health; wie steht es um Ihre —? how is your health? how is it with your health? seine — wiederherstellen, wiedererlangen, to restore, to recover one's health; *fig.* die — der Seele, the health or soundness of the soul; die — des Holzes, the soundness of wood. 2) [wish of health and happiness, used chiefly in drinking] health. Zur —! [in drinking] your health! [in sneezing] God bless you! die — Eines, auf die — Eines trinken, to drink any one's health; eine —, Jemands — ausbringen, to toast any one, to drink any one's health; er brachte die folgende — aus, he gave the following toast; zuerst trank man auf die — des Königs, the king's health was drunk first; wessen — geht gegenwärtig herum? whose health is being drunk? 3) [state or qualities that promote health] wholesomeness, salubrity. Die — eines Klima's, der Luft, des Wassers, the salubrity or wholesomeness of a climate, of the air, water.

Gesundheits-amt, *n.* board of health, office of health. —**bad**, *n.* —**brunnen**, *m.* V. [the more usual words] Gesundbad, Gesundbrunnen. —**beamter**, *m.* officer of health. —**flanell**, *m.* Welsh flannel. —**glas**, *n.* a large glass out of which healths are drunk. —**göttinn**, *f.* the goddess of health, Hygeia. —**haus**, *n.* V. Genesshaus, Krankenhaus. —**lehre**, *f.* science of health. —**paß**, *m.* certificate, bill of health. —**pflege**, *f.* diet, strict regimen. —**rath**, *m.* 1) council of health, board of health. 2) one of the board of health. —**regel**, *f.* rule of health. —**schein**, *m.* V. —paß. —**schokolade**, *f.* chocolate that contains no spices and especially no vanilla. —**stein**, *m.* a polished pebble, worn by superstitious people as a preservative of health. —**taffet**, *m.* a particular kind of taffeta of a healing power or as a preservative against the effects of a cold.

Gesúndmachung, *f.* V. Heilung.

Getädel, *n.* [-s] a continued blaming, censuring or finding fault.

Getäfel, *n.* [-s] wainscot. V. Täfelwerk.

Getánze, *n.* [-s] a continual dancing.

Gethán, [*past part.* of Thun, which see] * Gesagt, —, no sooner said than done.

Getón[e], *n.* [-es] continued or repeated sounds, clang, clamour. Ueberall hörte man das — von Hörnern und Flöten, the sound of horns and flutes was heard everywhere.

Getöse, *n.* [-s] noise, din, hubbub. Das — des Donners, des Geschützes, the roar of thunder, of cannon; die Kinder machen ein —, the children make a racket; ein dumpfes —, a hollow noise; das — der Wellen, des Windes, the roaring of the billows, of the wind; *fig.* das — der Welt fliehen, to fly from the noise or bustle of the world. Syn. V. Gepolter.

Getrámpel, *n.* [-s] noise with the feet, trampling.

Getränk, *n.* [-es, *pl.* -e] drink, beverage; [in medicine] draught, potion. Nektar heißt de[r] Götter —, nectar is called the beverage of th[e] Gods; sie haben kein anderes — als Wasse[r], they have nothing to drink but water; geistig[e] —e, spirituous liquors, spirits. V. Trank. Sy[n.] Getränk, Trank, Trunk. Ein Trunk is [as] much as one can drink at once or at one draught. [Ein] Trank is any drinkable medicine, it may be useful [or] deleterious. Ein Schlaftrank is, therefore, prope[rly] speaking, a potion taken to cause sound sleep; [ein] Schlaftrunk that which is drunk before going to be[d]. Such a narcotic medicine is sometimes also called [a] Schlaftrunk, but only when privily and insidio[usly] administered in order to produce unnatural sle[ep]. Ein Getränk signifies any beverage which serves [to] quench the thirst or which is drunk on account of [its] agreeable qualities, and is thus distinguished fr[om] Trank.

Getraúen, *v. r.* sich — [to do something], [to] dare, to venture. Ich getraue mir, damit [zu] Stande zu kommen, I am sure, I shall bring [it] about, I shall accomplish it; er getraute s[ich] eine Reise zu machen, zu unternehmen, we[lche] &c., he ventured upon a journey, that &c.; — Sie sich, ihm das zu sagen? have you t[he] boldness, dare you, to tell him so? ich getra[ue] mir nicht, mit ihm davon zu sprechen, I a[m] afraid of speaking, I dare not speak with hi[m] about it.

Getreide, *n.* [-s] [from tragen = ber[vor] bringen, to bear, to produce] corn, grain. V. So[m]mer—, Winter—. Das — in die Sche[une] bringen, to house the corn; das — wird the[u]rer, the price of corn is rising; heuriges — corn of this year's growth, this year's co[rn]; das — schneiden, to cut the corn, to reap; [das] — steht gut or schön, the corn has a fair a[p]pearance, the crops [of corn] look well or p[ro]mising. V. Frucht, Korn.

Getreide-art, *f.* kind of corn or gra[in]. —**bau**, *m.* cultivation of grain, agricult[ure]; *it.* corn-land. Dieses Pachtgut hat vielen [Getreide]bau, that farm contains much corn-land. [V.] Ackerbau. —**boden**, *m.* 1) corn-land. 2) co[rn-]loft, granary. —**feld**, *n.* corn-field. —**fu[h]re**, *f.* a waggon-load of corn. —**gülte**, *f.* rent paid in corn. V. Fruchtgülte. —**hand[el]**, *m.* corn-trade. —**händler**, *m.* corn-merch[ant]. —**haufen**, *m.* heap of corn, corn-heap. —**haus**, *n.* a corn-magazine, granary. —**la[nd]**, *n.* corn-land. —**mäkler**, *m.* corn-chand[ler]

-mäklerei, *f.* dealing in corn. —markt, *m.* corn-market. —maß, *n.* a measure for corn. —mühle, *f.* corn-mill. —pacht, *m.* rent paid in corn, corn-rent. —preis, *m.* the price of corn or grain. —reich, *adj.* fertile in grain. —sack, *m.* corn sack. —sperre, *f.* prohibition to export corn, embargo on the exportation of grain. —theurung, *f.* dearness or dearth of corn. —wage, *f.* balance for weighing corn. —wagen, *m.* a waggon loaded with corn. —wucherer, *m.* V. Kornwucherer. —zehente, *m.* corn-tithes; *it.* V. —pacht. —zins, *m.* rent paid in corn, corn-rent.

Getreu, *adj.* and *adv.* 1) faithful, true. Ein seinem Herrn —er Diener, a servant faithful or true to his master; ein —er Gatte, Liebhaber, a faithful husband, a true lover; seinem Fürsten —, faithful, loyal or true to one's prince or sovereign; etwas zu —en Händen überliefern, to deliver a thing into trusty or confidential hands. [law-style] trusty. Unsern lieben —en, to our trusty and well-beloved. [in familiar language] Das ist sein or ihr —er, he is his or her intimate friend; *fig.* ein —es Gedächtniß, a faithful, retentive memory. 2) [conformable to truth] faithful, true. Eine —e Abschrift, a faithful copy or duplicate; eine —e Erzählung, Schilderung, a faithful narrative, description; ein —er Geschichtschreiber, a faithful historian.

Getreuheit, *f.* faithfulness, fidelity &c. V. Treue.

Getreulich, I. *adj.* V. Getreu. II. *adv.* faithfully, truly, honestly, loyally. Die Schlacht wurde — beschrieben, the battle was faithfully described; — und ohne Gefährde, faithfully, sincerely and without fraud.

Getriebe, *n.* [-s, *pl.* -] 1) agitation, commotion. Das — der Wellen, the agitation of the sea; *fig.* der Weise sieht das — der Menschen mit Gleichmuth, the wise man calmly views the restless or busy life of men. 2) [that by which something is put in motion] machine, machinery. Das — einer Uhr, the machinery or wheelwork, *it.* the spring of a watch or clock. *it.* [in mills] trundle, lantern; *fig.* das — menschlicher Thätigkeit, the springs of human activity. 3) [in mining, something driven] props, shores or supports. 4) [in mining] the summer or south side of a mine.

Getriebspfahl, *m.* [in mining] prop, shore or support. V. Getriebe 3). —scheibe, *f.* [among watchmakers] one of the plates between which is the wheelwork of a watch. —stab, —stock, *m.* [in mills], der —stab or —stock eines Trillings, the staff of a trundle.

Getrieben, [*past part.* of Treiben, which see] —e Arbeit [with gold- or silversmiths], embossed work.

Getrödel, *n.* [-s] slow, tedious way of doing a thing, a humming and hawing.

Getrost, I. *adj.* confident, courageous. —en Muthes seyn, to be of good heart; seyen Sie —en Muthes, die Sache wird besser ausfallen, als Sie glauben, pluck up a good heart, be of good heart, of good cheer, the affair will turn out better than you think. II. *adv.* confidently, with confidence, courageously. Sagen Sie ihm — Ihre Meinung, tell him your opinion frankly, with confidence, never fear to tell him your opinion; — sterben, to die fearlessly, courageously; dem Tode — entgegen sehen, to face death boldly, intrepidly; *fig.* wir bilden uns — ein, dann Ehre zu verdienen, wenn &c., we fondly imagine we merit honour then, when &c. III. *interj.* well! very well! never mind! cheer up! —! nur —! die Dinge werden sich ändern, never mind! cheer up! be of good heart, the things will change!

Getrösten, *v. r.* sich —, [rather stiff] to hope with confidence, to expect confidently, to be assured. Ich getröste mich der Erhörung, der Gewährung meiner Bitte, I am confident that my request will be granted me; ich kann mich keiner günstigen Antwort —, I cannot expect a favourable answer; *it.* V. Trösten.

Getrümmer, *n.* [-s] [collectively] ruins, rubbish.

Getümmel, *n* [-s] 1) tumult, bustle, turmoil, noise. Welch' ein —! what a noise, uproar or tumult! er erregte ein großes — auf der Straße, he raised a great tumult in the street; *fig.* das — der Welt, der Stadt &c., the turmoil of the world, the bustle or noise of the town. 2) [a number of persons raising a tumult] crowd, throng. Sich durch das — drängen, to squeeze one's self through the crowd. Syn. V. Gepolter.

Getüpfte, Getüpfelte, *n.* [-n] spots or dots, as on stuffs, in a miniature. V. Tupfen, Tüpfeln.

Geübt, [*past part.* of Ueben, which see] *adj.* and *adv.* exercised, versed, experienced, practised, expert, skilful. Gut —e Soldaten, well-drilled or exercised soldiers; —e Finger, Hände &c., dexterous fingers, hands &c.; ein sehr —er Wundarzt, a very experienced, expert surgeon; im Zeichnen — seyn, to be skilful in drawing; er ist ein —er Geschäftsmann, he is well versed or experienced in business; mit —em Auge, mit —er Hand, with a practised eye, with a practised hand.

Geübtheit, *f.* experience, skill, expertness, dexterity, adroitness.

Gevatter, *m.* [-s, *pl.* -] —inn, *f.* godfather, godmother, sponsor [yet it does not express this relation to the child, but either to its parents or to those who were sponsors upon the same occasion, V. Pathe], gossip. Einen zu — bitten, to ask or desire any one to be or to stand godfather to one's child; — stehen, bei einem Kind — stehen, to stand godfather or godmother to a child; er ist mein —, wir sind —, he has stood godfather to one of my children, I have stood godfather to one of his children, he and I have stood godfather together to a child; er bat alle seine —n und Nachbarn zu Gaste, he invited all his gossips and neighbours to dinner; *fig.* [in familiar and jocose language] meine Uhr, mein Ring steht —, my watch, my ring is at my uncle's, is pawned.

Gevattersbitter, *m.* a person charged to ask or desire any one to stand godfather or godmother. —brief, *m.* a letter in which a person is requested to stand sponsor to a child. —schmaus, *m.* christening feast or banquet. —schnack, *m.* the prattle of gossips, gossiping. —sleute, *pl.* persons that have stood godfather or godmother to a child. Es sind meine —sleute, they have stood godfather and godmother to my children. —smann, *m.* V. Gevatter. —streich, *m.* V. —stück 2). —stück, *n.* 1) some present, such as a cake &c. sent to the intended godfather and godmother before the christening. 2) a friendly turn or office done to a person, that has stood godfather or godmother to any one's child or children &c. *Fig.* [ironically] Das ist ein —stück, —stückchen, that's an ugly trick.

Gevatterschaft, *f.* 1) the circumstance of being sponsor to a child, and this relation to the parents of the child and to the co-sponsors, sponsorship. Das ist meine erste —, that is the first time I have stood godfather or godmother; eine — abschlagen, to refuse or decline standing godfather or godmother; seine —en kommen ihm theuer zu stehen, his relations of godfather cost him a great deal. 2) [collectively] all the godfathers and godmothers.

Geviere, *n.* [-s, *pl.* -] 1) quadripartition. 2) V. Gevierte.

Geviert, *adj.* 1) divided into four parts or consisting of four corresponding parts, quadripartite. Ein —er Schild, a quartered shield or escutcheon; ein vierfach —er Schild, a counter-quartered shield; —e Zahl [die Zahl vier], quaternary [the number four]. 2) [multiplied by itself] square or quadrate number. 3) [in astronomy] der —e Schein, quadrate, quartile, [aspect of the planets when they are distant from each other a quarter of the circle, ninety degrees].

Gevierts-elle, *f.* square or quadrate ell or yard. —fuß, *m.* square-foot. —wurzel, *f.* square root.

Gevierte, *n.* [-s, *pl.* -] square. In's — bringen, to bring into square, to square, as a stone, a beam &c.; dieser Balken hat 15 Zoll in's —, this beam is fifteen inches square; ein —s [eine Quarte], a sequence of four cards, as in the game of piquet, a quart; ich habe ein großes —s [eine Quart major], I have a quart major; [in printing, a piece of metal, used to fill the void spaces between words &c.] quadrat.

Geviertheilt, *adj.* torn into pieces by four horses, quartered. V. Viertheilen.

Gevögel, *n.* [-s] [collectively] birds, fowls. Zahmes —, poultry; wildes —, feathered game. V. Federwildbret.

Gevollmächtigen, *v. tr.* [little used] V. Bevollmächtigen.

Gewächs, *n.* [-es, *pl.* -e] 1) in general, any thing that grows or has grown; [in botany and surgery] excrescence. 2) chiefly, plant, vegetable. Jeder Baum ist ein —, every tree is a vegetable; fremde —e, exotic plants. V. Garten—, Winter— &c. 3) [not used in the plural] growth. Das ist Korn, Wein von meinem —e, that is corn, wine of my own growth; Rheinwein von gutem, von dem besten —e, Rhenish wine of good, of the best growth; jener Wein ist heuriges —, that wine is of this year's growth. 4) joint. Ein Rohr von Einem —e, a cane of one joint.

Gewächs-erde, *f.* [in gardening] mould, garden-mould. —haus, *n.* green-house, conservatory. —laugensalz, *n.* potash. —reich, I. *n.* the vegetable kingdom. II. *adj.* rich, abounding in plants or vegetables.

Gewächschen, Gewächslein, *n.* [-s, *pl.* -] [*dimin.* of Gewächs] a small plant.

Gewachsen, [*past part.* of Wachsen, which see] *adj.* adequate to. Einer Sache — seyn, to have competent power, ability or means, to be equal to a thing; wir sind diesem Unternehmen nicht —, we are not equal to that undertaking; Einem — seyn [es mit ihm aufnehmen können], to be able to cope with any one, to be a match for any one.

Gewäff, *n.* [-es] [= Waffen] 1) [unusual] weapons. 2) [among sportsmen] fangs and claws of wild beasts; the tusks or fangs [of a wild boar].

Gewahr, *adv.* sensible, perceiving, but only used in conjunction with the verb werden. Etwas — werden, to perceive or discover any thing, to become aware of any thing; wir wurden ihn von weitem —, we perceived or descried him from afar; man wird in seinem Gesichte nicht die geringste Veränderung —, one does not remark the least alteration in his face, V. Wahrnehmen; *fig.* er soll mir — werden, mit wem er es zu thun hat, I shall let him see or feel with whom he has to do.

Gewähr, *f.* [*pl.* -en] 1) [= Verwahrung] safe-keeping, charge. Etwas in seine — nehmen, etwas in seiner — haben, to take something into one's custody or charge, to have a thing in one's keeping, custody or charge; den Käufer in die — [= den Besitz] eines Gutes setzen, to put the purchaser into possession of an estate. 2) warranty, warrant, security. Für Einen — leisten, to give or be security for any one, to bail him; ich leiste Ihnen die —, daß das Pferd gesund und ohne Fehler ist, I warrant you the horse sound; ich leiste für die Wahrheit seiner Aussage —, I vouch for the truth of his deposition; ein Pfand ist die beste —, a pledge is the best security; der Verkäufer leistet die —, den Käufer in jedem Falle schadlos zu halten, the seller warrants the purchaser, to indemnify him at any rate; ohne alle — etwas kaufen, to purchase a thing without any warranty; [in law] die — leisten und angeloben [sich verbinden or verbindlich machen, die Klage fortzusetzen], to bind one's self over to prosecute; [in mining] V. —schein. 3) [in mining] *n.* [-es, *pl.* -e] land ceded or granted to a person for working a mine.

Gewähr-brief, *m.* letter of credit. —gebühr, *f.* —groschen, *m.* [in mining] fee due for the certificate of a part or share in a mine. —leistung, *f.* security given, guaranty. V. Gewähr. —mann, —smann, *m.* security, bondsman, surety. Wer einen —smann hat, der hält sich an ihn, the guaranteed claims upon the surety. *it.* [Währmann, Währbürge] voucher, authority. Gute —smänner für etwas haben, to have good vouchers for a thing; *fig.* ich habe darin den Plato &c. zum —smanne, I have the authority of Plato &c. for it. —schein, *m.* [in mining] certificate of one or several shares in a mine. —zeit, *f.* [in mining] a fixed term, during which the purchaser of a part of a mine may take possession of it.

Gewahren, *v. tr.* V. Gewahr werden.

Gewähren, I. *v. tr.* 1) Etwas, für etwas — [= etwas verbürgen], to answer for, to warrant, to engage to make good a thing. Einem seinen Schaden —, to secure any one against damage, to indemnify any one; Einem den Besitz seines Gutes —, to warrant any one the possession of his estate. 2) Etwas — [= verwilligen], to grant. Einem alles, was er verlangt, —, to grant any one all he asks; mein Wunsch ist mir gewährt worden, [also] ich bin meines Wunsches gewährt worden, I have obtained what I wished for, my wish has been fulfilled. *it.* [= versprechen, verheißen] to promise solemnly, to vow. — Sie mir ewige Verschwiegenheit, promise or vow me eternal secrecy. 3) [= ertheilen] to impart, to give. Warum hat die Natur Ihnen so viel Reize gewährt? why has nature bestowed so many charms upon you? *fig.* [= verschaffen] to afford. Die Lesung dieses Buches wird Ihnen viel Vergnügen —, [the] reading or perusing this book will afford you great pleasure; dies gewährt keinen Beweis, that affords or is no proof; Trost und Sicherheit —, to afford comfort and security. II. *v. intr.* [= Gewähr leisten, einstehen] to answer for, to warrant. Ich kann dafür nicht —, I cannot answer for it, cannot warrant it, cannot vouch for it. *it.* [= sagen, machen lassen] to let any one speak or act as he thinks proper. Da laßt uns —, leave that to us, let us arrange or settle the matter. *it.* Einen — lassen [ihm seinen Willen lassen], to let any one do as he pleases.

Gewährer, *m.* [-s, *pl.* -] [in law] bail, security.

Gewährhaber, *m.* [-s, *pl.* -] depositary, trustee.

Gewahrsam, *f.* [*pl.* -e] [a law term] 1) [= Verwahrung] custody, charge, keeping, ward. Einen in seine — nehmen, to take any one into one's custody; einen Verbrecher in sichere — bringen, to put a criminal into a safe custody; man hielt ihn in —, he was held in ward. 2) [= eine rechtliche Vorkehrung, der Vorbehalt] reservation, proviso.

Gewährschaft, *f.* V. Gewähr. — leisten, fordern, to give, to demand security.

Gewährung, *f.* 1) granting, accomplishment, attainment. Die — eines Wunsches, the accomplishment of a desire; er hat die — seiner Bitte erhalten, he had his request granted him; die — seines Gesuches, the grant of his request. 2) [the thing granted] grant.

†Gewälsch, *n.* [-es] gibberish, jargon.

Gewalt, *f.* 1) [not used in the plural] the exertion of a certain force or power. Die — des Windes, des Wassers &c., the force or power of the wind, water &c. *Fig.* Die — der Musik, the power of music; die — der Wahrheit, der Beispiele, der Verführung, the force or power of truth, of example, of seduction. 2) [not used in the plural] the employment or application of superior force. Eine Thür mit — erbrechen, to open a door with force, forcibly; — mit — vertreiben, to repel force by force; *prov.* — gehet vor Recht, might overcomes right; er entführte sie mit —, he carried her off by force; der — weichen, to submit to a superior force; Einem mit — drohen, to threaten any one to make use of force or to use forcible means; er will Alles mit — durchsetzen, he wishes to carry all by authority; etwas mit — wegnehmen, to take away something by force, forcibly; *mit aller — schreien, to cry as loud as one can, with all one's might; *mit aller — klopfen, to knock as hard as one can; *mit aller — hineinwollen, to want to enter with might and main, at any rate; mit offenbarer, ganzer —, by open force; hence frequently = Gewaltthätigkeit, violence; Einem — anthun, to do any one violence, to offer violence to any one; einem Mädchen — anthun, to ravish, to violate a girl; — schreien, to call out for help; sich selbst — anthun [= sich entleiben], to lay hands upon one's self, to do violence to one's self, to commit suicide; sich — anthun [= sich or seine Begierden zügeln], to put a restraint upon one's self, to restrain one's passions; Thun Sie sich keine — an [= handeln Sie, reden Sie frei], do not lay any restraint upon yourself, speak freely; er mußte sich — anthun, nicht zu lachen, it was with difficulty he could refrain from laughing; *fig.* einer Stelle, einem Gesetze — anthun [= sie auf eine gezwungene Art erklären], to wrest the sense of a passage or of a law; [obsolete or provincial] [in law, a refusal to appear in court when legally summoned] contumacy, contempt of court. 3) [not used in the plural] [= Macht] power, authority. Ich habe —, zu thun, was ich will, I have the power of doing what I please; das steht nicht in seiner —, that is not in his power, does not depend upon him; Einem — einräumen, geben, verleihen, to give any one power or authority, to empower, to authorize any one; er hat ihm volle — gegeben, für ihn zu handeln, he has given him full power to act for him or in his name; Einen der — berauben, to deprive any one of his power or authority, to depose any one; — über einen haben, to have power upon or with any one; ein Land unter seine — bringen, seiner — unterwerfen, to bring a country under, to subject a country to, one's dominion or power, to subdue a country; in Jemandes — seyn, to be in any one's power, at his disposal, at his mercy; eine uneingeschränkte —, absolute, unlimited, arbitrary power; die höchste, die oberste —, the supreme or sovereign power; die väterliche —, paternal power; noch in der — seines Vaters stehen, to be still dependent upon one's father; die gesetzgebende, vollziehende —, the legislative, executive power; etwas in seiner — haben, to have a thing in one's power or at one's command; die Zunge in seiner — haben, to be master of one's tongue; eine Sprache ganz in seiner — haben, to be quite master of a language, to have the mastery or command of it; sein Herz in der — haben, to have the command of one's heart, to have the mastery of or over one's passions; [in popular lang.] eine — [= viel] Geld haben, to have plenty or abundance of money. 4) [*pl.* -en] [the persons or the body exercising power or command] power, authority. Die bürgerlichen —en, the civil authorities; die gesetzgebende —, the legislative power or body; die himmlischen, die höllischen —en, the celestial, the infernal powers. V. Macht.

Gewalts-brief, *m.* [in law] 1) a power of attorney. 2) order of arrest, warrant, writ of execution. —geber, *m.* —geberinn, *f.* a person that gives a power of attorney, a constituent. —gericht, *n.* [obsolete or provincial] criminal court of justice. —haber, *m.* —haberinn, *f.* one invested with power or authority; *it.* V. Bevollmächtigter. —herr, *m.* [obsolete or provincial] a magistrate invested with criminal jurisdiction. —herrschaft, *f.* despotism. —herrscher, *m.* despot. —raub, *m.* usurpation. —räuber, *m.* usurper. —richter, *m.* [obsolete or provincial] criminal judge. —that, *f.* violent act or action, violence. —thaten ausüben, to commit acts of violence. —thäter, *m.* —thäterinn, *f.* he, she who commits acts of violence. —thätig, *adj.* and *adv.* violent. V. Gewaltsam. Ein —thätiges Verfahren, a violent proceeding; einen —thätigen Einfall in ein Land machen, to invade a country; —thätig handeln, to act violently, to use violence. —thätigkeit, *f.* violence; —thätigkeiten verüben, to commit acts of violence; etwas durch —thätigkeiten erlangen, to obtain a thing by force or violence.

Gewaltig, I. *adj.* 1) [= stark, heftig] powerful, strong, vehement, violent. Eine —e Stimme, a very loud, a powerful voice; ein —er Lärm, Sturm, Wind, a violent noise, tempest, wind; eine —e [bedeutende] Hitze, Kälte, an intense or powerful heat, cold; —e Schmerzen, violent pains. *it.* very large, very great, prodigious. Eine —e Menge Volkes, an immense crowd of people; ein —er Schatz, a vast treasure; ein —es Verbrechen, an atrocious crime; *dieser Mensch gibt sich ein —es Ansehen, that man takes very great airs, carries it mighty high; *[ironically] das ist eine —e Sache, that is a mighty affair, indeed. 2) [= mächtig] powerful, potent, mighty. Sich unter die —e Hand Gottes demüthigen, to humble one's self under the mighty hand of God; ein —er Herr, a potent or mighty Lord; ein —es Heer, a powerful army; die Gewaltigen der Erde, [in theology] the powers of the world. II. *adv.* violently, vehemently, powerfully, strongly; *it.* [mostly in familiar lang.] greatly, prodigiously, excessively. Der Wind geht or bläst —, the wind blows very hard, is very high; der Donner brüllt —, the thunder roars dreadfully; — schreien, to cry as loud as one can bawl, with might and main; er war — [= sehr] böse, he was very or extremely angry; er irrt sich —, he is egregiously mistaken; ein — großer, starker Mann, an exceedingly tall man, a powerful man; er ist — reich, he is mighty rich; Ein n — lieb haben, to have a great or violent assion for, to be excessively fond of any one.

Gewältigen, *v. tr.* [little used] 1) to get the etter of, to subdue. V. Bewältigen. [in min-g] Das Wasser —, to drain a mine, to empty of its waters; eine Zeche wieder —, to work gain a mine that had been abandoned, *it.* to pair or restore a mine. 2) — or gewaltigen tieen in etwas], to authorize or empower any se. V. Bevollmächtigen.

:**Gewältiger**, *m.* [-s] [in military affairs] ber—, General—, provost marshal of an my; *it.* V. Scharfrichter.

:**Gewältiglich**, V. Gewaltig, II.

Gewältigung, *f.* act of getting the better , of subduing. [in mining] Die — des Wassers, e draining of a mine; die — einer eingefal-nen Grube, the reparation or lining again of shaft or pit.

Gewältigungskosten, *pl.* [in mining] e expense of draining or repairing a mine.

Gewältsam, *adj.* and *adv.* forcible, vio-nt. Ein —er Tod, a violent, unnatural ath; —e Mittel brauchen, to use forcible eans, to use violence; ein Mädchen — entfüh-n, to carry off a girl by force, forcibly; — ndeln or verfahren, to use violence.

Gewältsamkeit, *f.* force, violence.

1. **Gewánd**, *f.* [provincially] V. Gewende 2).

2. **Gewánd**, *n.* [-es, *pl.* -e or Gewänder] [pro-cially Wand; A. S. *waeda* and *gewueda* is = nd and Kleid; Goth. *vactja* = kleiden] 1) any ing woven, cloth, stuff. Die Leiche in ein lei-nes — wickeln, to wrap up the corpse in a eet. 2) [= Kleidung] garment, vesture. Der hepriester zerriß sein —, the highpriest rent s garment; ihr prächtiges — erhöhte ihre eize, her splendid dress set off her charms; ir warfen alle Gewänder von uns, we threw f all our garments; [in sculpture and painting] e Gewänder, die Darstellung der Gewänder, apery; die Gewänder an diesen Figuren sind rtrefflich, the drapery of these figures is ex-llent. *Fig.* garment. Im —e der Tugend, r Wahrheit, in the garment of virtue, truth.

Gewandsbereiter, *m.* V. Tuchbereiter. fall, *m.* [in feudality] the falling or passing the best suit of clothes to the landlord, after e death of a tenant; *it.* the right of taking that it. —händler, *m.* V. Tuchhändler. —haus, cloth-hall; *it.* V. Tuchhandlung. —los, j. and *adv.* without clothes or dress. — acher, *m.* V. Tuchmacher. —recht, *n.* V. fall. —schneider, *m.* woollen draper. — hnitt, *m.* cloth-trade; *it.* the privilege of lling cloth by retail. —theil, *m.* V. —fall.

Gewánden, Gewánten, [*Drapiren] [un-al] *v. tr.* Eine Figur —, to make the drapery a figure, to clothe it.

Gewándt, *adj.* and *adv.* quick, active, nim-e, adroit, dexterous. Ein —es Pferd, a nimble rse; ein —er Arbeiter, an expeditious or ver workman; ein —er Geist, a versatile nius; eine —e Schreibart, Sprache, a free, ar, easy style, language. V. Wenden.

Gewándtheit, *f.* activity, adroitness, dexte-y, versatility. Dazu gehört —, that requires xterity; die — des Geistes, the versatility genius.

Gewárten, *v. tr.* [rather stiff] Eine or einer ache —, to expect, to look for, to hope for thing; du hast nun nichts mehr von mir zu , now you have nothing farther to expect m me; er hat seine Strafe noch zu —, he has t to expect or fear his punishment; glückli-re Zeiten —, to hope for happier or better nes.

Gewärtig, *adv.* in a state of expectation, expecting. Eine or einer Sache — seyn, V. Gewarten; etwas von Einem — seyn, to expect something from any one; [in law] Einem — seyn, to be ready to serve, to assist a person; [in feudality] Einem treu, hold und — seyn, to behave as a loyal and faithful subject.

Gewärtigen, *v. tr.* [less stiff than gewarten] to expect. V. Gewarten.

Gewäsch, *n.* [-es] prattle, nonsensical talk, gossiping.

Gewäsche, *n.* [-s] continual washing.

Gewässer, *n.* [-s, *pl.* -] a great collection of water, waters. Das — der Sündflut, the waters of the deluge; das —, die — eines Landes, the waters of a country; in diesem — or in diesen —n, in this part of the sea; die — fallen, the floods are subsiding; wohlriechende —, well scented waters. V. Wasser.

Gewätschel, *n.* [-s] waddling.

Gewébe, *n.* [-s, *pl.* -] 1) the act of weaving; *it.* the manner of weaving, texture, weft. Das — dieses Tuches ist ungleich, the weaving of this cloth is uneven; ein Schleier vom reichsten —, a veil of richest texture; ein dichtes, ein lockeres —, a close or compact, a loose texture; *fig.* das — der Adern, der Fibern &c., the plexus of the veins, fibres &c.; das künstliche — eines Blattes, the admirable contexture of a leaf. 2) any thing woven, web. Ein härenes —, hair-lace; [in anatomy] das zellichte —, cellular tissue; das — der Bienen, the cells of the bees [in a honey-comb]; *fig* [mostly in a bad sense] die ganze Geschichte ist ein — von Lügen und Falschheit, the whole story is a series or tissue of lies or forgeries and falsehood; sein ganzes Leben war ein — von schönen Handlungen, his whole life was a series of noble actions.

Gewebebaum, *m.* [among weavers] weaver's beam

Gewéhr, *n.* [-es, *pl.* -e] 1) instrument of defence and offence. *a)* [among sportsmen] Das — [= die vier größten Zähne] des wilden Schweines, the tusks or fangs of the wild boar. V. Gewäff, Gewerf. *b)* particularly = Waffe, weapon. In diesem Lande ist es verboten, — zu haben, ein — zu tragen, in this country it is forbidden, to have, to carry arms; Einen mit — versehen, to furnish any one with arms, to arm any one; zum — greifen, to take up arms; Einem das — abnehmen, to disarm any one. V. Schieß—, Seiten—. *c)* [in the most limited sense = Flinte] gun, musket, firelock. Sie warfen ihre —e weg, they threw down their muskets; [in military affairs] in's — treten, to go under arms; im —e or unter dem —e stehen, to be under arms; das — strecken, to ground arms; in's — rufen, to call to arms; das — präsentiren, to present arms; in's —! ergreift das —! to arms! schultert das —! das — auf die Schulter! shoulder arms! — hoch! recover arms! — beim Fuß! order arms! unter dem —e bleiben, to continue under arms. 2) [among hunters] persons who prevent the game from running away.

Gewehrsbude, *f.* an armourer's or gunsmith's shop. —fabrik, *f.* manufactory of arms. —gallerie, *f.* V. —saal. —gerecht, *adj* and *adv.* practised in the use of fire-arms. —händler, *m.* a dealer in fire-arms, armourer. —kammer, *f.* V. —saal. —kreuz, *n.* [a military term] a post or cross, against which the soldiers pile their arms. —magazin, *n.* magazine of arms. —mantel, *m.* [a military term] a kind of cloak or mantle, made of ticken, for covering the fire-arms of the soldiers. —manufactur, *f.* V. —fabrik. —probe, *f.* trial of fire-locks or guns. —pyramide, *f.* 1) V. —kreuz. 2) the muskets piled up in a pyramidical form, a pile of arms. —rücken, *m.* a small post, against which a soldier rests his fire-lock before a guard-house, arm-rack &c. —saal, *m.* armoury, arsenal. —schmied, *m.* armourer, gunsmith. —schmiede, *f.* V. —fabrik. —schrank, *m.* a case or closet for the safe keeping of guns or fire-arms, arm-chest.

Geweidicht, V. Weidicht.

Geweih, *n.* [-es, *pl.* -e] [probably from the ancient wigen = fechten, to fight] the horns of a deer, attire. V. Gehörn, Gestänge. Ein Hirsch, der sein — abgeworfen hat, a deer that has cast or shed his horns; das — eines zweijährigen Hirsches, the head of a pricket; — von vielen Enden, a deer's head of many antlers; der Hirsch hat ein neues — aufgesetzt, the stag has a velvet-head; [in blasonry] der Hirschkopf mit seinen —en, the head of a deer.

Geweine, *n.* [-s] continual weeping or crying.

Gewénde, *n.* [-s, *pl.* -] 1) the act of turning, turn; [in agriculture] the turning over with the plough Ein — machen, to turn the plough. 2) [= ein Stück Acker, Morgen] a landmeasure, an acre. 3) [rather provincial; as many things of the same kind as are necessary for changing] a set. Ein — Schnallen, a set of buckles; ein — Kleider, a suit of clothes; *it.* change of clothes; ein — [ein Gespann] Pferde, Ochsen &c., a set or team of horses, oxen &c. 4) [among hunters] the boughs which a deer bruises or beats down with his head in traversing thickets.

Gewéndig, *adj.* supple, pliant, active, nimble.

Gewéndigkeit, *f.* suppleness, activity, quickness, nimbleness.

Gewérbe, *n.* [-s, *pl.* -] [from werben = drehen, to turn] 1) [Gewinde] joint, hinge; *it.* [in anatomy = Gelenk] joint, articulation. 2) *Fig.* *a)* [das Anwerben] the act of enlisting or enrolling. *b)* [ein Auftrag] message, errand. Einem ein — auftragen, to charge any one with a message or errand; sein — ausrichten, to acquit one's self of, to deliver one's message or errand; was ist dein —? what is your message, what do you want? *c)* habitual occupation or business. Dieser Mensch treibt ein häßliches —, that man carries on a villanous trade; sich ein — mit etwas, aus etwas machen, to do a thing customarily, usually or habitually; er macht sich ein — daraus, sie zu verläumden, he makes it his business to calumniate or defame her; das Spiel ist sein —, gaming is his trade, or usual occupation; sie treibt mit ihrer Schönheit ein —, she makes the most of her beauty. *d)* [in the most limited sense, the business which any one follows for subsistence] trade, profession. Das — eines Schmiedes, eines Maurers &c., the trade of a smith, of a mason &c.; das — eines Advokaten, Arztes &c., the profession of a lawyer, physician &c.; was treibt er für ein —? what trade or profession does he follow or exercise? ein einträgliches —, a lucrative trade or profession. *e)* collectively, trade, commerce. Ein Land, worin das — blühet, a country, in which trade flourishes; das — liegt darnieder, trade is at a stand or dead; — und Handel gedeihen, trade and commerce prosper.

Gewerbsbein, *n.* [in anatomy, joint of the spine] vertebre, vertebra. —fleiß, *m.* industry. —fleißig, *adj.* industrious. —geld, *n.* —schoß, *m.* —steuer, *f.* tax paid for exercising any trade. —haus, *n.* V. Gewerkhaus. —recht, *n.* right or privilege of exercising a trade or profession. —schule, *f.* school of industry. Eine höhere —schule, a polytechnical school or institution.

Gewerbs-leute, *pl.* tradespeople. —**mann**, *m.* tradesman.

Gewerbsam, *adj.* and *adv.* industrious.

Gewerbsamkeit, *f.* industry.

Gewerf, *n.* [-es, *pl.* -e] [among hunters] V. Gewehr, Gewäff.

Gewerk, *n.* [-es, *pl.* -e] 1) [das Werk, die Arbeit] work. 2) [Fabrik] manufactory. 3) collectively, [Zunft, Innung, Handwerk] corporation, guild, company. Das — der Sattler, the saddlers' company. *it.* V. Gewerkschaft.

Gewerk-haus, *n.* manufactory. —**herr**, *m.* master or owner of a manufactory. —**holz**, *n.* timber. —**smann**, —**smeister**, *m.* manufacturer.

Gewerke, *m.* [-n, *pl.* -n] a workman; [in mining] miner; *it.* co-partner or co-proprietor of a mine. Die —n zusammen berufen, to call together the shareholders or co-proprietors of a mine.

Gewerken-diener, *m.* [in mining] servant or clerk to a mining company. —**kux**, *m.* share in a mine. —**probierer**, *m.* assayer to a mining company. —**schicht**, *f.* [in mining] task of a miner. —**tag**, *m.* 1) meeting-day of a tradesmens' or mechanics' company. 2) a meeting of the proprietors of a mine.

Gewerker, *m.* [-s, *pl.* -] V. Gewerksmann.

Gewerkschaft, *f.* [in mining] the co-proprietors of a mine, a mining company.

Gewerksmäßig, *adj.* and *adv.* in the manner of the manufactories.

Gewette, *n.* [-s] 1) a continual betting. 2) bet, wager. 3) V. Heer—.

1. **Gewicht**, *n.* [-es, *pl.* -e] 1) [the quantity of a body, ascertained by the balance] weight. —, das — halten [of a merchandize], to be weight; [of a ducat &c.] to be of full weight, to be weight; es hat vier Unzen an —, it weighs four ounces; Tabak, am Feuer getrocknet, verliert an —, tabacco, dried by the fire, loses weight; etwas nach dem —e kaufen, to buy a thing by the weight. 2) the nature or quality of the weight. Volles — geben, to give or sell full, honest weight, to make good weight; schwer — [a weight, of which a pound contains sixteen ounces], avoirdupois; leicht — [of which a pound contains twelve ounces], troy, troy-weight. *Fig.* Das ist eine Sache von —, von großem —, that is an affair of weight, of great or vast moment, a weighty, very weighty affair or business; es ist keine Sache von —, it is a thing of no importance; diese Gründe haben in Ihrem Munde viel mehr —, als in dem meinigen, those reasons will have much more weight, will be of much greater force in your mouth, than in mine; seine Würde gibt seinen Handlungen —, his dignity adds weight to his actions; zu viel — auf einen Traum legen, to lay too much stress upon a dream; das — in der Schreibart, energy, force of style; ein Mann von — [Ansehen, Einfluß], a man of consequence or importance. 3) [a mass of iron, lead, brass or other metal, used for ascertaining the weight of other bodies] weight. Die —e der einzelnen Staaten sind verschieden, the weights of the several states are different; das Pfund— &c., the weight of a pound &c.; ein abgezogenes, geeichtes —, standard, stamped weight; —e in Sätzen, weights in sets. *it.* any ponderous mass. Man springt besser mit —en in der Hand, a man leaps better with weights in his hand; die —e einer Uhr, eines Bratenwenders, the weights of a clock, of a kitchenjack; das — an einer Thür [Thür—], the weight of a pulley door.

Gewichts-kunst, *f.* statics. —**los**, *adj.* and *adv.* weightless. *Fig.* without influence, credit, importance &c. —**macher**, *m.* a maker of weights, balance-maker. —**s-ausschlag**, *m.* [what is beyond the due weight] overplus, surplus. —**stange**, *f.* [der Seiltänzer] a rope-dancer's pole, poy. —**stein**, *m.* stone used as a weight. Der —stein an einer Uhr, the weight of a clock; der —stein an einer Thüre, the weight of a pulley door, V. Gewicht. —**wissenschaft**, *f.* science of weighing bodies, statics. V. —kunst. —**zeichen**, *n.* [in coining] a stamp or mark impressed by the warden of the mint upon a piece of silver, showing its weight.

2. **Gewicht**, *n.* [-es, *pl.* -e] [among hunters] V. Geweih.

Gewichtig, *adj.* 1) having the just or due weight. Ein —er Dukaten, a ducat of full weight. 2) [= schwer] ponderous, weighty. Eine —e Masse, a weighty mass. *Fig.* momentous, forcible, weighty. Dieser Grund ist sehr —, this reason is very weighty.

Gewichtigkeit, *f.* ponderousness, heaviness, weightiness. *Fig.* force, importance, weightiness. Die — dieser Worte, the significancy of these words.

‡**Gewierig**, *adj.* 1) [from währen, to last] constant, lasting, durable. 2) [a law term, from gewähren, to grant] complying, favourable. Eine —e Antwort, a favourable answer.

Gewild, *n.* [-es] [among hunters] game, venison.

Gewillet or **Gewilliget**, [in law; otherwise rather stiff] *adv.* willing, disposed, ready. — seyn, to be willing or disposed, to intend, to purpose; das bin ich nicht — zu thun, I do not intend doing that, I have no mind to do that.

Gewimmel, *n.* [-s] 1) a continual and confused moving to and fro of living beings. 2) a multitude of beings in motion, a swarm, throng, crowd.

Gewimmer, *n.* [-s] whimpering, moaning.

Gewinde, *n.* [-s, *pl.* -] 1) the act of winding or twisting. 2) something wound or something that winds or turns. Ein — von Garn [Garn-Gewinde], a bottom or skein of yarn; ein — von Blumen [Blumen-Gewinde], a wreath of flowers, garland; das — am Degengefäße, the hilt of a sword; das — an einer Schraube, the worm of a screw, V. Schraubengang; das — an einer Dose &c., the joints or hinges of a snuffbox &c.; das — an den Thür- oder Fensterbändern, the ironwork or hinges of a door or window; [in seamen's language] das — an dem Steuerruder eines Schiffes, the pintles [the hooks by which the rudder hangs to the sternpost]; das — an den Masten, the top-armour. *it.* [= Verbindung, Gelenk], juncture, joint; [in anatomy] ginglymus [a species of articulation resembling a hinge]; [= verschlungene Gänge, ein Irrgewinde], labyrinth.

Gewinde-bohrer, *m.* [among carpenters] auger. —**eisen**, *n.* V. Mühleisen. —**fenster**, *n.* a window turning on hinges.

Gewinn, *m.* [-es, *pl.* -e] [V. Gewinnen] 1) the act of gaining or winning. Der — der Schlacht, the gaining of the battle; der — der [Spiel-] Partie, the winning of the game. 2) [that which is won or gained] gain, profit. Nach Abzug aller Unkosten bleibt ein reiner — von hundert Gulden, after deducting all charges there remains a net or clear profit of a hundred florins; großen — von etwas ziehen, to draw great advantages from a thing; um des —es willen, for the sake of interest, gain or lucre; um einen — von einigen Gulden würde er seinen Freund verrathen, to gain a few florins, he would betray his friend; der — bei einem Actiengeschäfte, dividend; [in mining] der — an Kupfer, Silber &c, the produce of a mine in copper, silver &c.; [in gaming or betting] winnings; wie viel beträgt Ihr — [im Spiele] how much did you win? mit seinem —e [fort]gehen, to go off with one's winnings; von seinem — leben, to live by one's winnings. *it.* [that which is obtained or offered as a reward] prize. Die —e austheilen, to distribute the prizes; die —e ausstellen [zur Schau], to exhibit the prizes; den großen or höchsten — erhalten, to get or carry the great or first prize.

Gewinn-begierde, *f.* V. —sucht. —**bringend**, *adj.* yielding or bringing profit or gain, profitable, lucrative. —**karte**, *f.* winning card. —**sucht**, *f.* greediness of gain, avarice. —**süchtig**, *adj.* and *adv.* greedy of gain, avaricious. —**süchtigkeit**, *f.* V. —sucht. —**theil**, *m.* [in commerce] dividend.

Gewinnbar, *adj.* that may be won or gained, gainable.

Gewinnen, *ir. v. tr.* and *intr.* [winnen is allied to winden, the Lat. *vinco*, the Old Fr. *vain* = Gewinn] [= erreichen] to reach, to get, to come to, to arrive at, to gain. Wir gewannen die Bresche, we gained the breach; die Spitze eines Berges —, to gain the top of a mountain; es ist schon spät, wir müssen das Dorf zu — suchen, it is already late, we must endeavour to reach or gain the village; den Vorsprung —, to get the start of any one; das freie Feld or das Freie —, to gain the open field, *fig.* to run away, to scamper away. *Fig.* a) [= sich etwas verschaffen] to get, to gain, to obtain, to acquire. Im Schweiße seines Angesichtes sein Brod —, to get or earn one's bread by the sweat of one's brow; er gewinnt seinen Unterhalt mit Abschreiben &c., he gets his livelihood by copying &c.; [in mining] Erz, das Erz —, to obtain ore, to win the ore; eine befestigte Stadt mit Gewalt — [einnehmen], to make one's self master of, to carry a fortified town by force of arms; die Oberhand — [siegen], to gain or get the better of, to gain the day; die Schlacht —, to gain or win the battle; einen Rechtsstreit —, to gain a cause; das Spiel, die Partie —, to win the game; Einem das Spiel gewonnen geben, to give up one's game as lost, to give one's game for lost; gewonnen Spiel haben [= den Vortheil haben], to have the advantage or the better of; [in seamen's language] den Wind, den Vortheil des Windes —, to gain the wind, to get to windward, to weather; Einen zum Gevatter —, to ask or to desire any one, to be or to stand godfather to one's child; Ablaß —, to gain or get indulgence; das Meisterrecht —, to be made a freeman; den Preis, Jemandes Freundschaft —, to carry the prize, to gain any one's friendship; alle Herzen, das Volk &c. —, to gain or win all hearts, the people &c.; wir müssen ihn —, we must draw or bring him over, we must win or gain him over; sie gewann den Kerkermeister, she won or brought over the jailer; Einen durch Geschenke —, to win any one by presents. *b)* [to get profit or advantage] to gain, to profit. Er hat im Handel viel gewonnen, he has gained much by trade; er gewinnt bei diesem Handel, this bargain is advantageous to him; an dieser Waare ist nicht viel zu —, that commodity will turn to little advantage or account; er hat dabei gewonnen, he was a gainer by it; im Spiele —, to win at play; von Einem im Spiele —, to win of any one; ich habe noch nie zuvor etwas von Euch gewonnen, I never won of you before; Ihre Karte hat gewonnen, your card has won; *prov.*

ie gewonnen, so zerronnen, lightly come, ghtly go; das große Loos —, to gain the pital or highest prize; die Wette —, to win e bet or wager; gewonnen haben [= den Vortheil haben], to have the advantage or the better; e gute Sache kann dadurch nur —, the good use can only gain by it; was — wir dadurch? welche Vortheile verschaffen wir uns dadurch?] hat shall we get or gain by it? what shall be the better for it? an etwas — [= darin nehmen], to obtain an increase of any thing; Deutlichkeit, an Einfluß —, to become more spicuous, to obtain greater influence or wer; unsere Freude gewinnt, wenn wir sie dern mittheilen können, our joy is enhanced communicating it to others; dieser Mann winnt sehr, wenn man ihn näher kennt, that n gains a great deal on acquaintance; bei nem — [= bei ihm in Gunst kommen], to gain in any one's favour or good will, to get o any one's good graces; er hat seit kurzem r gewonnen [= sich sehr vervollkommnet], he s much improved of late; etwas über sich [= sich zu einer Handlung mit einer gewissen strengung bestimmen], to bring one's self to a thing, to prevail on one's self; etwas r Einen —, to prevail upon any one. c) to ne into a certain state. Die Sache gewinnt ganz anderes Ansehen, eine ganz andere stalt, the thing takes quite a different turn or ect; es gewinnt das Ansehen, als wenn &c. es scheint &c.], it appears or seems as if &c; schmack an etwas —, to get a taste for a ing; die Sache gewinnt einen guten Fortgang, the thing makes great progress, succeeds ll; diese Sache hat ein glückliches Ende, einen traurigen Ausgang gewonnen, that affair taken a good end, has had a tragical issue; e Person lieb —, to take a liking to a per-, to have an affection for one; die Bäume Knospen, the trees commence to bud; das treide gewinnt schon Aehren, the corn is already shooting into ears, or forming ears; die rste hat schon Aehren gewonnen, the barley already in ear.

Gewinner, *m.* [-s, *pl.* -] —inn, *f.* gainer, ner; *it.* a winning ticket [in a lottery].

Gewinnst, Gewinst, *m.* [-es, *pl.* -e] V. winn.

Gewinsel, *n.* [-s] whining. V. Gewimer.

Gewirbel, *n* [-s] Das — der Trommeln, roll or ruffle of the drums; das — der Lerchen, the warbling of the larks; das — der Wagenräder, the whirling of the coach-wheels. V. rbeln.

Gewirk, *n.* [-es, *pl.* -e] 1) act of working weaving; *it* manner of weaving, texture. g von dichtem, lockerem —e, stuff of close or pact, of loose texture. 2) any thing woven, eb Sie erfand ein —, ihre Freier zu betrügen, she devised a web, her wooers to dece; das — der Bienen, the working of the s, honey-comb.

Gewirr, *n.* [-es] or Gewirre, *n.* [-s] 1) act of entangling, confounding or complicang. 2) entanglement, confusion, complica-. Ein — von Fäden, Haaren &c., an englement of threads, hair &c.; das — eines losses, the wards of a lock [that part of a lock, ch, corresponding to the proper key, hinders any r from opening it]. *Fig* In diesem —e von entgegengesetzten Empfindungen wußte ich nicht , in this maze or entanglement of conflicting sentiments I did not know &c.; er befindet in einem solchen —e von Geschäften, daß &c., is in such a labyrinth of affairs, he is so beset by various or manifold affairs, that &c.

Gewiß, [seems to be allied to fest, firm] I. *adj.* firm, steady, stable, sure. — stehen, to stand sure; etwas — halten, to hold a thing fast; auf dem Eise hat man keinen gewissen Tritt, on the ice one has no firm footing; ein Pferd, das einen gewissen [sichern] Gang hat, a sure-footed horse; dieser Wundarzt hat eine gewisse Hand, this surgeon has a steady hand. ein gewisser Schütze, a good marks-man; dort steht es am gewissesten, there it is safest. *Fig. a)* [zuverlässig] certain, sure, infallible, credible. Gewisse Leute haben mir es gesagt, credible people told me so; sein Geld einem gewissen Manne leihen, to lend one's money to a sure man; die Gesundheit ist kein gewisses Gut, health is not a certain or infallible good; das ist ein gewisses Zeichen, that is a sure sign. *b)* fixed, determinate, not doubtful or casual, certain, sure. Ein gewisses Einkommen haben, to have a sure or fixed income; dieses Amt ist mir —, I am sure of that office or place; ein gewisser Gewinn, a certain or sure gain or profit; er hat noch keine gewisse Lebensart [Lebensberuf, Lebensbeschäftigung], he has no determinate or settled way of living yet; keinen gewissen Wohnort haben, to have no certain abode; einen gewissen Entschluß fassen, to form an unalterable resolution; *sein Gewisses haben, to have a sure or fixed income; *um ein Gewisses einig werden, to agree for a certain price. *c)* undoubted, true, sure, certain. Diese Nachricht ist —, this news is certain, nichts ist so —, als der Tod, nothing is so certain as death; ich weiß darüber or hiervon nichts Gewisses, I know nothing certain of it; das Gewisse für das Ungewisse hingeben, to quit a certainty for an uncertainty; etwas für — annehmen, für — glauben, to take a thing for a certainty, to hold a thing as a certainty, to be sure of a thing; das ist moralisch —, that is morally true; ich weiß es —, I know it for certain, I am confident of it; man hat mir für — gesagt, daß &c, I have been told for certain, that &c.; so viel ist —, daß &c., thus much is certain, that &c. *d)* not doubting, sure. Einer Sache — seyn, to be sure, convinced or persuaded of a thing; seiner Sache — seyn, to be sure of success; ich bin —, daß er mein Freund ist, I am sure, convinced or persuaded that he is my friend; *Einen — machen [machen, daß er etwas für — hält], to make any one certain, to assure, to persuade any one of a thing, to remove all his doubts; ich that dies in der gewissen Ueberzeugung, daß &c., I did it with the full persuasion, fully persuaded that &c.; der gewissen Hoffnung leben, die gewisse Hoffnung haben, to be in great hopes. *e)* [in an indefinite sense = irgend ein, some] certain. Ich fühle ein gewisses Mißbehagen, daß &c, I feel a certain uneasiness, that &c.; ich habe davon eine gewisse Vorempfindung, I have a kind of presentiment of it; sie hat ein gewisses Etwas in ihren Benehmen, das mir sehr gefällt, there is a something in her carriage, that pleases me very much; gewisser Maßen [gewissermaßen], in a certain manner, in some measure; ein gewisser Mann hat es gesagt, a certain man has said it; ein gewisser Hr. Schmidt, a certain Mr. Smith; *it.* [in contempt] ein gewisser Mensch, den ich noch nie gesehen habe &c., a certain fellow whom I have never seen before &c.

II. *adv.* [sicherlich] certainly, surely. Das wird ihm — Vergnügen machen, that will certainly give or afford him pleasure, I am sure that will &c.; wirst du aber auch Wort halten? —, but will you keep your word? certainly, assuredly, indubitably; Sie wollten uns — überraschen, you wished no doubt to surprise us; das ist — ein Streich von ihm, that is a trick of his, I am sure or I suppose; [in familiar language = wie man sagt] Sie wollen — eine Reise machen, you are going to take a journey, I am told.

Gewissen, *n.* [-s *pl.* -] 1) the consciousness of a thing. [In Script.] Die Gottlosen werden kommen mit den — ihrer Sünden, the wicked will appear with the consciousness of their sins. *it.* the certain knowledge or consciousness of a thing &c. Ich frage Sie auf Ihr —, wissen Sie nichts davon? in conscience, upon your conscience, do you know nothing of it? er hat Alles gesagt, was er auf dem — hatte, he has told his mind without reserve. 2) [the faculty, power or principle within us, which decides on the lawfulness or unlawfulness of our own actions, affections &c.] conscience. Ein zartes —, a tender or delicate conscience; er hat kein —, he has no conscience; das — hat ihn gerührt, his conscience struck or smit him; ein nagendes or verwundetes —, a gangrened, ulcerous or wounded conscience; ein enges [= zartes] — haben, to have a delicate conscience; ein weites — haben, to be not over-srupulous; *dies kann man mit gutem — thun, one may do that with a safe conscience; *Ihr seyd —s halber dazu verbunden, you are in conscience bound to do it; das — einschläfern, to lull the conscience asleep; sein — frei machen, entledigen, to discharge one's conscience; *prov* ein gut — ist dem Haupt ein sanftes Kissen, get a good name and go to sleep; ich überlasse es Ihrem —, stelle es Ihrem — anheim, *schiebe es Ihnen in das —, I refer that to your own conscience; wider sein — handeln, to act against one's conscience, contrary to one's conviction; das habe ich nicht auf dem —, my conscience is acquitted on that score; auf mein —! [a sort of oath] in conscience, upon my conscience! die — beunruhigen, ängstigen, to trouble, to alarm the conscience. 3) [hesitation from a fear of offending or doing wrong] conscience, scruple. Sich ein — aus etwas machen, to make a conscience or scruple of a thing; er macht sich kein — daraus, zu betrügen, he makes no scruple to cheat; man muß sich ein — daraus machen, so etwas zu thun, it is matter of conscience to do such a thing.

Gewissen=los, *adj.* and *adv.* void of conscience, unconscionable, unconscientious, unprincipled, unscrupulous, without conscience Ein —loser Mensch, a man of no conscience, an unprincipled man; ein —loses Betragen, an unconscionable behaviour. —s=angst, *f.* anguish of conscience. —s=angst ausstehen, to suffer the pangs of conscience. —s=biß, *m.* qualm or sting of conscience, remorse. —s=fall, *m.* case of conscience. —s=frage, *f.* question or case of conscience Eine —s=frage lösen, to resolve a case of conscience; Einer, der —s=fragen löst, a casuist. —s=freiheit, *f.* liberty of conscience. —s=furcht, *f.* fear of remorse or conscience. —s=gericht, *n.* court of conscience. —s=heirath, *f.* a marriage of conscience [without the benediction of a priest]. —s=lehre, *f* casuistry. —s=lehrer, *m.* casuist. —s=pflicht, *f* a duty imposed by the conscience. —s=prüfung, *f.* examination of one's conscience. —s=punkt, *m* point of conscience. —s=rath, *m.* keeper of the conscience, spiritual father, confessor. —s=rüge, *f.* remorse. V. —s=biß. —s=ruhe, *f.* peace of conscience. —s=sache, *f.* matter of conscience. —s=schlaf, *m.* slumber of conscience. —s=scrupel, *m.* scruple of conscience, qualm.

—s-übung, *f.* exercise of conscience, examination of the conscience. —s-unruhe, *f.* trouble of conscience. —s-zwang, *m.* restraint of conscience, violence done to the conscience. —s-zweifel, *m.* doubt of conscience, scruple. V. —sscrupel. —s-zweifel machen, erregen, to raise scruples.

Gewissenhaft, I *adj* conscientious, religious, scrupulous. Für einen Kaufmann ist er so — als Einer, for a merchant, he is as conscientious as one can be; er ist nicht sehr — im Worthalten, he is not a very religious observer of his promise; mit der —esten Genauigkeit, with the most scrupulous exactitude. II. *adv.* conscientiously, religiously, scrupulously. — handeln, zu Werke gehen, to act or deal conscientiously; ein Versprechen — halten, to observe a promise religiously.

Gewissenhaftig, *adj.* and *adv.* V. Gewissenhaft.

Gewissenhaftigkeit, *f.* conscientiousness, scrupulousness. Er beobachtet die größte — in allen seinen Handlungen, he observes the greatest conscientiousness or scrupulousness in all his dealings.

Gewissenlosigkeit, *f.* want of principle, unscrupulousness.

Gewissermaßen, *adv.* in a certain manner, in some measure.

Gewißheit, *f.* [= Festigkeit] steadiness, steadfastness. Mit — [more usual Sicherheit] gehen, to walk with steadiness; die — der Hand, the steadiness of the hand. *Fig.* *a*) [= Zuverlässigkeit] certainty. Die — eines Versprechens, the certainty or certitude of a promise. *it.* [= Sicherheit, Unterpfand] security, surety. Wegen einer Sache — geben, to give security for a thing. *b*) exemption from failure, settled state, regularity. Die — des Einkommens, the certainty of the income; die — des Entschlusses, the firmness of a resolution. *c*) exemption from doubt, certainty. Ich weiß das mit —, I know that for certain, I am confident of it; ich bin von der — seines Todes unterrichtet, I am informed of the certainty of his death; ich wünschte wohl einige — zu haben, I would fain have some certainty; die anschauende or anschauliche —, evidence.

Gewißlich, *adv.* certainly, assuredly, surely. Das ist — wahr, that is undoubtedly true.

Gewitter, *n* [-s, *pl.* -] thunder-storm, tempest, storm. Es steigt ein — auf, a thunder-storm is gathering; es steht ein — am Himmel, we shall have a thunder-storm; das — ist vorbei, hat aufgehört, the storm has subsided, is over. *it.* [= Blitz] lightning. Das — hat in den Kirchthurm eingeschlagen, the lightning has fallen upon, has struck the church-steeple; vom — erschlagen werden, to be struck by lightning. *Fig.* Es zieht sich ein schreckliches — gegen ihn zusammen, a dreadful storm is gathering against him; das — vorüberlassen, to let the storm subside.

Gewitter-ableiter, *m.* V. Blitzableiter. —luft, *f.* heavy, sultry air prognosticating a storm, air or atmosphere impregnated with electric fluid. —nacht, *f.* 1) a stormy night. 2) darkness caused by a thunder-storm. —regen, *m.* thunder-shower. —schaden, *m.* damage caused by a thunderstorm. —schauer, *m.* V. —regen. —schwer, *adj.* —schwere Luft, air or atmosphere impregnated with electricity. —stange, *f.* V. Blitzableiter. —vogel, *m.* petrel or storm-bird. —wind, *m.* tempestuous wind. —wolke, *f.* thunder-cloud.

Gewitterhaft, *adj.* prognosticating a thunderstorm.

Gewitzel, *n.* [-s] a false display of wit, witticism.

Gewitzigt, *adj.* taught wisdom by experience. V. Witzigen.

Gewogen, [from wegen or wiegen = neigen, to bend, to incline] *adj.* and *adv.* favourable, friendly, kind. Einem — seyn, to bear any one good will, to be well-affected towards any one; er ist ihm sehr —, he is his well-wisher, his hearty friend; ich bitte Sie, mir ferner — zu bleiben, I desire you to continue me your favour; sich Jemand — machen, to gain any one's favour or good will.

Gewogenheit, *f.* affection, good will, favour, kindness. Schenken Sie mir die Ehre Ihrer ferneren —, let me have the honour to continue in your favour or friendship. *it.* a single act of kindness. Wollten Sie nicht die — haben, mir zu sagen, would not you have the kindness to tell me.

Gewohnen, *v. intr.* [u. w. seyn] [= sich etwas gewöhnen] to get accustomed or used to, to accustom, to inure one's self to. Es in einem Hause, in einem Klima —, gewohnt werden, to get accustomed or used to, to accustom one's self to a house, climate; man kann Alles —, we can use or accustom ourselves to every thing; *prov.* jung gewohnt, alt gethan, once a use and ever a custom; ich bin gewohnt, frühe aufzustehen, I am used, accustomed or wont to rise early, I am in the habit of rising early, I am an early riser; er ist der Arbeit, der Entbehrungen gewohnt, he is used, accustomed or inured to labour, to privations; der Kälte, der Hitze gewohnt seyn, to be used, inured to cold, to heat; dergleichen Betragen bin ich nicht gewohnt, I am not used to such behaviour; sie sind des Lesens nicht gewohnt, they are not in practice of reading; er ist der Plackerei schon gewohnt, drudgery has grown familiar to him; das bin ich an ihm schon gewohnt, I expect nothing better from him; that is his common practice or way; nach seiner gewohnten Art, after his usual manner; *dieser Hut ist des Regens schon gewohnt, this hat is used to rain.

Gewöhnen, I. *v. tr.* to accustom, to use, to habituate. Die Kinder muß man früh an die Arbeit —, children must be early accustomed to labour; er ist an Kälte und Hitze gewöhnt, he is inured to cold and heat; er hat sie zur Tugend gewöhnt, he has formed her to virtue; ich werde sie nach meinem eigenen Kopfe —, I shall mould her to my own idea; ein Pferd — [not very usual], to break a horse; Ochsen —, to train oxen; ein Kind —, V. Entwöhnen. II. *v. r.* sich an etwas —, to use, accustom or inure one's self to a thing. Man gewöhnt sich an Alles, there is nothing but we may accustom ourselves to; sich an den Geschmack des Tabaks —, to habituate one's self to the taste of tobacco; der Löwe gewöhnt sich an den, welcher ihn füttert, the lion familiarizes himself to, grows familiar with him that feeds him.

Gewohnheit, *f.* 1) habitual practice, custom, habit. Es ist zur — geworden, it has grown into a habit; aus — etwas thun, to do a thing by habit, habitually; es ist die — der Fürsten, so zu handeln, it is usual with princes to act so; wundern Sie sich nicht darüber, das ist so seine —, do not wonder at it, that's his common way or practice; er handelt nach seiner —, he acts according to his custom, as usual; die — des Landes bringt es so mit sich, that's the custom of the country; das ist längst aus der — gekommen, that has been long out of use; — ist die andere Natur, habit is second nature. 2) a single habit or custom. Eine schlechte — annehmen, to contract an ill habit; er hat die —, Gesichter zu schneiden, he has the habit of making faces; schlimme —en ablegen, to break one's self of ill habits or practices; gute alte —en muß man nicht ablegen, we must not lay aside good old customs; die hergebrachten —en eines Landes, the usage and customs of a country. Syn. V. Gebrauch.

Gewohnheits-recht, *n* the common law, customary law. Das —recht der Normandie, the custom or common law-book of Normandy. —sünde, *f.* habitual sin.

Gewöhnlich, I. *adj.* 1) customary, habitual, usual, ordinary. Der —e Lauf der Dinge, the ordinary course of events; auf die —e Art, in the usual manner; die —e Bedeutung eines Wortes, the usual acceptation of a word; —e Pflanzen, common plants; *ich habe über — or über mein —es [Maaß] getrunken, I have drunk more than usual; das ist unser —er Tisch, unser —es Essen, that's our daily or usual fare; *das —e [viz. Essen], daily or usual fare, commons; *mein —es ist ein Stück Rostbraten, my usual fare is a piece of roast beef; *das —e [= die monatliche Reinigung], the monthly courses, menstrual flux. 2) [in a more limited sense = mittelmäßig] inferior, ordinary, common. Der —e Schlag Menschen, the ordinary sort of men; ein —er Mensch, an ordinary fellow; dieses Buch ist eine —e Arbeit, this book is an ordinary performance. II. *adv.* customarily, usually, ordinarily, commonly. So geschieht es — mit Vorsatz, it is usually done thus on purpose; diese Jahreszeit ist — regnerisch, this season is usually or ordinarily rainy; ich trinke heute wie —, I drink to day as usual.

Gewöhnung, *f.* the act of accustoming, inuring. Die — eines Kindes, V. Entwöhnung.

Gewölbe, *n.* [-s, *pl.* -] 1) vault, arch. Der Schlußstein eines —s, the key-stone of an arch or vault. V. Kreuz—, Kugel—, Wendel—, Schnecken—. 2) a vaulted room for laying up or laying out goods, shop, ware-house, [in America] store. V. Speise—, Kaufmanns—, Waaren—. *Fig.* Das — des Himmels, the vault of heaven, the vaulted sky, the canopy of heaven.

Gewölbe-bock, *m.* a wooden arch to build vaults upon. —bogen, *m.* the arch or bending of a vault. —bruch, *m.* [in surgery] fracture of the skull. —krone, *f.* the top or crown of a vault. —pfeiler, *m.* buttress. —stein, *m.* a wedge-shaped stone. —stütze, *f.* buttress, arched buttress. —winkel, *m.* that part of a vault, which rests upon the imposts, the back of a vault.

Gewölbt, [*past part.* of Wölben, which see] *adj.* vaulted, arched.

Gewölk, *n.* [-es, *pl.* -e] collectively, clouds. Die Sonne zertheilte das —, the sun dispelled or dissipated the clouds; der Himmel ist mit —e umzogen, bedeckt, the sky is overcast, covered with clouds, is clouded; ein — von Staub [Staub—], clouds of dust.

Gewölkig, *adj.* and *adv.* cloudy. Der Himmel ist sehr —, the sky is very cloudy.

Gewölle, *n.* [-s] [from Wolle, wool] [among hunters] hair, feathers, which birds of prey swallow with the flesh and cast up again afterwards.

Gewühl, *n.* [-es] 1) the act of turning up ground, of rooting up. Die Schweine haben ein großes — auf dieser Wiese angerichtet, the swine have very much rooted this meadow. [illegible]

...ig a confused motion, bustle, stir. Es ist ein ...es — auf der Straße, daß &c., there is such tumult or crowd in the street, that &c.; das ... des Lebens, the bustle, turmoil of life.

Gewürk, n. [-es, pl. -e] V. Gewirk.

Gewürm, n. [-es, pl. -e] collectively, ...orms, reptiles. Alles —, das auf Erden kreucht ...a Script.], every creeping thing that creepeth ...pon the earth. it. vermin. *Fig.* [in contempt, ...ed of noxious human beings] Dieses schändliche ..., that base vermin or rabble.

Gewürz, n. [-es, pl. -e] 1) [those parts of ...ts which yield a spicy fragrant smell or a warm ...gent taste] aroma, spice. Dieses — ist ma...nstärkend, this spice is stomachic; Pfeffer ...d Ingwer sind sehr gewöhnliche —e, pepper ...d ginger are very common spices; der Zim...t ist ein herrliches —, cinnamon is an ex...llent aromatic; die meisten —e kommen aus ...ißen Ländern, most aromatics come from ...t countries; englisches —, all-spice, Jamaica ...pper; er handelt mit —en, he deals in spices. ...in general, any thing used in rendering food ...latable, seasoning. Salz ist ein nothwendi...—, salt is a necessary seasoning; — an Speisen thun, to spice or season the victuals; ...ist zu viel — an dieser Pastete, this pie is ... highly seasoned, to rich, too hot; diese ...chinn thut zu viel — an die Speisen, this ...k seasons too much.

...**ewürz-artig**, adj. and adv. V. Ge...rzhaft. —**beutel**, m. spice-bag. —**birne**, ... kind of aromatic pear. —**brühe**, f. spiced ...ce. —**büchse**, f. spice-box. —**fleisch**, ...agout. —**gewölbe**, n. grocer's shop. — ...**rke**, f. a pickled cucumber. —**handel**, ... trade in spices or grocery-wares. —**händ**...**l**, m. dealer in spices or grocery-wares, grocer, ...cer. —**handlung**, f. a grocer's shop. ...e —handlung haben, to keep a grocer's ...p. —**inseln**, pl. Spice Islands, Molucca ...nds. —**kram**, m. retail of spices or grocery-...es; it. grocer's shop. Einen —kram ha... V. —handlung. —**krämer**, m. a retailer ...pices or grocery-wares, retail-grocer. — ...**e**, f. spice-box. —**laden**, m. grocer's ...p. —**mühle**, f. spice-mill. —**nägelein**, ... —nelke. —**nägelkoralle**, f. a kind ...troite —**nelke**, f. clove. —**nelkenbaum**, ...clove-tree. —**nelkenöl**, n. oil of cloves. ...**eich**, adj. rich in spices, aromatic, spicy. ...**ck**, m. V. —beutel. —**schachtel**, f. V. ...**chse**. —**staude**, f. an American shrub ... aromatic umbels. —**stein**, m. aromatite, ...Wurzelstein. —**strauch**, m. calycanthus ...arolina, Carolina all-spice. —**waaren**, ...pices, grocery-wares.

...**ewürzhaft**, adj. and adj. aromatic, aro...cal, spicy. Das riecht —, that has an ...atic odour.

...**ewürzhaftigkeit**, f. state or quality of ... aromatic or spicy.

...**eyen, Geyer**, V. Geien, Geier.

...**ezäh, Gezäu** or **Gezeug**, n. [-es, pl. -e] ... to Zeug] [in mining] tools or instruments.

...**ezähkasten, Gezeugkasten**, m. chest ...e miners' tools, tool-chest.

...**ezähnt**, [past part. of Zähnen, which see] ...and adv. toothed, notched; [in botany] ...te; [in blasonry] toothed.

...**zänk**, n. [-es] or **Gezänke**, n. [-s] con... quarrelling; it. quarrel, dispute, wrangle.

...**zäu**, V. Gezäh.

...**zauder**, n. [-s] perpetual hesitation, con...l delay.

...**zeche**, n. [-s] hard drinking, carousing, drinking bout.

Gezehnt, adj. decimated.

Gezeit, f. [pl. -en] 1) [obsolete] term, fixed period. 2) ebb and flow, tide. Der — wahrnehmen, to take the opportunity of the tide, to come or get in, or go out of a harbour with the tide. 3) [in the Roman church] Die —en, the [canonical] hours [as matins and vespers].

Gezeitenbuch, n. breviary.

Gezelt, n. [-es, pl. -e] 1) tent. V. Zelt. 2) [in anatomy] the two lateral cavities of the dura mater.

Gezelt-baum, m. V. Zeltbaum —**pflock**, m. V. Zeltpflock.

Gezerre, n. [-s] pulling and hauling about.

Gezeug, n. [-es, pl. -e] 1) a tool or instrument. 2) collectively, implements or instruments; [in mining] V. Gezäh.

Gezeug-kasten, m. V. Gezähkasten [in mining], Zeugkasten —**kosten**, pl. V. Zeugkosten. —**steuer**, f. [in mining] V. Gestängesteuer. —**strecke**, f. [in mining] a tract crossed by a hydraulic engine.

Geziefer, n. [-s, pl. -] collectively, insects.

Geziefer-kenner, [more usual Entomolog] m. [one versed in the science of insects] entomologist. —**kunde**, [more usual Entomologie] f. a science of insects, entomology. —**kundige**, m. V. —kenner. —**lehre**, f. V. —kunde. —**lehrer**, m. V. —kenner. —**lehrig**, [more usual entomologisch] adj. pertaining to the science of insects, entomological.

Geziege, adj. and adv. [from zähe, tough] [in mining, used of stones, metals &c.] soft, malleable, ductile.

Geziehe, n. [-s] [vulgar] continued or violent drawing, dragging, pulling &c.

Geziemen, [probably from the ancient ziemen = scheinen, to seem] impers. I. v. intr. to be fit, becoming, suitable, proper, to become. Es geziemet Kindern, zu schweigen, wenn &c., it becomes children to be silent, children ought to be silent, when &c.; einem rechtschaffenen Mann geziemet es, die Wahrheit zu sagen, it behoves an honest man to speak truth; leben wie seinem Stande geziemet, to live suitably to one's rank or station; seinen Vorgesetzten die —de Ehre erweisen, to show due honour to one's superiors; sich —d, auf eine —de Art betragen, to conduct one's self, to behave decently, in a becoming manner. II. v. r. sich —, to be fit or becoming. Es geziemet sich nicht, seinen Vorgesetzten so zu antworten, it is not becoming to answer thus to one's superiors; wie es sich geziemet, as is fit or becoming, as is meet or proper. V. Ziemen.

Geziemlich, adj. and adv. becoming, decent, suitable.

Geziere, n. [-s] affectation, affectedness, primness. Das — dieser Dame ist mir verhaßt, I hate the affected airs of this lady.

Geziert, [past part. of Zieren, which see] adj. and adv. affected. Eine —e Dame, an affected lady; ein —es Weib, a prim woman; —e Schreibart, affected style; —es Wesen, affected or prim airs or manners, affectedness, primness; — gehen, to walk affectedly.

Gezimmer, n. [-s] 1) the act of timbering, squaring. 2) *fig.* [in contempt] constant and noisy hewing and sawing and squaring. 3) carpenter's work, timber work, V. Zimmerwerk. [in mining] Das — eines Schachtes, the lining of a shaft or pit.

Gezische, n. [-s] hissing, whissing.

Gezischel, n. [-s] the act of whispering and the thing whispered in any one's ear, whispering, whisper.

Gezitter, n. [-s] continual trembling, trepidation. Das — der Sterne im Wasser, the twinkling of stars in the water.

Gezogen, [past part. of Ziehen, which see] adj. —e Federkiele, clarified quills; eine —e Büchse, a rifled gun; —e Lichter, dipped candles; wohl—, well-bred, well-mannered.

Gezücht, n. [-es] collectively, 1) [the young hatched at once] brood. Ein — Enten, a brood of ducks. 2) race, breed. *Fig.* [in contempt, used of men of the same cast] breed, brood. Jenes heuchlerische —, that set of hypocrites.

Gezüngel, n. [-s] 1) act of playing with the tongue, billing. 2) lickerishness, daintiness.

Gezweit, adj. 1) binary. Eine —e Zahl, a binary number; [in botany] —e Blätter, bipartite leaves [that are divided into two parts to the base]. 2) V. Gedoppelt.

Gezwiefacht, adj. V. Gedoppelt.

Gezwitscher, n. [-s] the chirping or warbling [of birds].

Gezwungen, [past part. of Zwingen, which see] adj. and adv. forced, overstrained, unnatural; it. affected. —es Wesen, affected manners or airs, affectedness; — lachen, to laugh affectedly, it. to affect or force a laugh.

Gibraltarschwalbe, f. [pl. -n] swallow from the straits of Gibraltar.

1. **Gicht**, f. [pl. -en] [from gehen, to go] [in forges] 1) the terrace of the furnace. 2) the act of putting charcoals and iron-ore into the furnace 3) the quantity of char-coal and iron-ore poured into the furnace at once. 4) the mouth of the furnace.

Gicht-boden, m. [in forges] V. Gicht 1. —**brücke**, f. [in forges] V. Laufbrücke. —**bühne**, f. V. Gicht 1. —**haus**, n. [in forges] top of a furnace.

2. **Gicht**, f. [from gehen, to go] 1) [pl. -en] arthritis, gout. Die — an den Händen, the gout in the hands, chiragra; die — in den Füßen, the gout in the feet, podagra; die fliegende, laufende —, the flying or running gout; die lähmende —, the palsy or paralysis; die — in den Hüften, the gout in the hips, hip-gout, sciatica; mit der — behaftet seyn, to be diseased with the gout, to be gouty. 2) pl. —er, convulsive fits, convulsions. In —er verfallen, to fall into convulsions or into a fit; dieses Kind ist an den —ern gestorben, this child died of convulsions.

Gicht-ader, f. the sciatic vein. —**anfall**, m fit of the gout. —**artig**, adj. and adv. resembling arthritis or the gout, arthritic. —**beere**, f. black currant. —**brüchig**, adj. paralytic, palsied; [in Script.] sick of the palsy. —**brüchigkeit**, f. palsy. —**essenz**, f. gout-cordial. —**fieber**, n. arthritic fever, gout fever, paroxysm of gout. —**kolik**, f. gout in the stomach. —**körner**, pl. grains of peony. —**krank**, adj. laid up with the gout, gouty. —**kraut**, n. any plant or herb used against the gout. —**materie**, f. V. —stoff. —**mittel**, n. remedy for the gout, anti-arthritic. —**morchel**, f. V. Morchel. —**pflaster**, n. anti-arthritic plaster, diapalma. —**pille**, f. anti-arthritic pill. —**pulver**, n. anti-arthritic powder. —**rose**, f. peony, V. Pfingstrose. —**rübe**, f. V. Zaunrübe. —**schmerz**, m. arthritic pain, pain of the gout. —**stoff**, m. gouty humour or matter. —**taffet**, m. anti-arthritic taffeta. —**wasser**, n. anti-arthritic water. —

wurz, *f.* dittany, V. Diptam.

Gichterisch, *adj.* and *adv.* 1) arthritic. 2) convulsive, spasmodic. —e Bewegungen, convulsive motions; —e Zuckungen, convulsions, convulsive fits; sein ganzes Wesen zuckte —, his whole frame was convulsed.

Gichtig, *adj.* and *adv.* diseased with the gout, gouty.

Gichtisch, *adj.* and *adv.* resembling the gout or diseased with the gout, arthritic, gouty. Ein —er Mensch, a gouty person; —e Zufälle, Schmerzen, arthritic fits, pains; der —e Stoff, V. Gichtstoff.

Gickern, V. Kickern.

Giebe, *f.* [*pl.* -n] [allied to Göpel] reel, windles; [among needlemakers] a kind of reel for straightening the wire; [among clothweavers] beam of a loom.

1. **Giebel,** *m* [-s, *pl.* -] [allied to the Gr. κεφαλή, L. *caput, gibba, gibber,* G. Gipfel and Wipfel, E. *gable,* Icel. *gabl,* Goth. *gibal,* Arabic *gebal* = Berg (mountain)] 1) gable, gable-end. Der — über Thüren, Fenstern, pediment [a triangular or circular ornament over gates and windows]. 2) [in some provinces] premises.

Giebelsbruch, *m.* V. Gipfelbruch. —dach, *n.* 1) a roof with gable-ends. 2) a roof with a gable end in front. 3) pediment. —feld, *n.* [the area of a pediment] tympan, razed table. —fenster, *n* window in the gable of a house, luthern. —förmig, *adj.* and *adv.* in form of a gable; [in blasonry] pignone. —haus, *n.* a house with a gable-end. —loch, *n.* hole or opening in the gable. V. —fenster. —mauer, *f.* gable-wall. —säule, *f.* V. —spitze. —schoß, *m.* house-tax. —schwalbe, *f.* house-swallow, martin, V. Hausschwalbe. —seite, *f.* gable-side, front, frontispiece. —spieß, *m.* or —spitze, *f.* ridge or top of a gable-end; [among carpenters] king-piece, king-post [the chief beam standing perpendicularly in the middle between two rafters under the roof]. —wand, *f.* V. —mauer. —zinne, *f.* V. —spitze; *it.* acroter [a small pedestal, placed at the two extremes of pediments, serving to support the statues]. —zins, *m.* V. —schoß.

2. **Giebel,** *m.* [-s, *pl.* -] or **Gieben,** *m.* [-s, *pl.* -] [probably instead of Gilbe, on account of its yellow colour] crucian [a fish].

||**Giebigkeit,** *f.* [a law term] V. Abgabe.

Giebsen, *v. intr.* to breathe with pain, to pant.

Giekbaum, *m.* [in seamen's lang.] the mainboom of a sloop and the like vessels.

Giekbaumsegel, Giekſegel, *n.* the main-sail of a sloop &c.

Gieke, *f.* [*pl.* -n] [Sax. *ceag* = Topf, pot, E. *cag* (keg), ein kleines Faß, V. Kachel] a footstove [a case of tin or copper, within which is placed a small coal-pan, for the purpose of warming the feet].

Gien, *f.* [in seamen's language] winding-tackle [consisting of one fixed triple block and one double or triple movable block]. Der Hänger einer —, winding-tackle pendant.

Gienaffe, *m.* [-n, *pl.* -n] V. Gähnaffe.

Gienfisch, *m.* [-es, *pl.* -e] V. Gienmaul.

Gienmaul, *n.* [-s, *pl.* -e] a fish of the genus Labrus.

Gienmuschel, *f.* V. Breitmuschel.

Gier, *f.* strong desire, eagerness [frequently used in composition, as Rachgier, desire of revenge], V. Begier.

Gierde, *f.* V. Begierde.

1. **Gieren,** [V. Begehren] [rather stiff or unusual] *v. intr.* Nach etwas —, to have an inordinate desire after a thing, to long eagerly for a thing; *it.* auf etwas —, to cast a longing look on a thing.

2. **Gieren,** [allied to the Lat *gyr*-us = Kreis] *v. intr.* [in seamen's lang., to deviate from the line of her course, as a ship] to yaw. Das Schiff gieret nach der Steuerbordseite, the ship yaws to starboard.

Gierenziegel, *m.* [-s, *pl.* -] a rounded tile.

Gierfalk, *m.* V. Gerfalk.

Gierig, *adj.* and *adv.* greedy, eager, covetous. Mit —en Augen etwas betrachten, to look upon something with a covetous eye; er warf —e Blicke auf sie, he cast eager or longing looks upon her; — nach Ruhm und Ehre, greedy of glory and honour; V. Blut—, Geld—; — essen, to eat greedily; — etwas ergreifen, to seize a thing eagerly.

Gierigkeit, *f.* greediness, eagerness, avidity. Mit — essen, to eat greedily; die — im Essen, ravenousness, V. Gefräßigkeit.

Giersch, V. Gersch.

Gierschlag, *m.* the yaw [the movement by which a ship deviates from the line of her course].

Gierschwalbe, *f.* V. Mauerschwalbe.

Gierung, *f.* [in seamen's language] yaw. V. Gierschlag.

Gießen, [Sax. *geotan,* Icel. *gusa,* Gr. χέω or χύω] *ir.* I. *v. tr.* 1) [= ausgießen] to pour. Wein in ein Glas, Wasser auf die Hände —, to pour wine into a glass, water upon the hands; Wasser in den Wein —, to dilute wine with water; geschmolzenes Metall in die Form —, to pour melted metal into the mould; Wein aus einem Gefäße in ein anderes —, to pour wine from one vessel into another; Einem ein Glas Wasser in das Gesicht —, to throw or dash a glass of water into any one's face; er goß eine Tasse Thee über seine Kleider, he spilled a cup of tea over his clothes; *prov.* Oel ins Feuer gießen, to throw oil into the fire, to add fuel to the fire. 2) [= begießen] to water. Die Blumen, den Garten —, to water the flowers, the garden. *Fig.* [= reichlich mittheilen] to pour out. Ich will meinen Geist auf alles Fleisch — [in Script.], I will pour out my spirit upon all flesh. 3) [= schmelzen] to melt. Blei, Silber —, to melt lead, silver. *it.* [to form into a particular shape by pouring a liquid mass into a mould] to cast. Teller, Löffel von Silber —, to cast plates, spoons of silver; Lichter —, to mould candles; Schriften, Glocken, Kanonen —, to cast letters or types, bells, cannons; gegossenes Eisen, cast iron; gegossene Lichter, mould-candles. II. *v. r.* sich — [sich ergießen], 1) to disembogue. Unzählige Flüsse — sich in den Ozean, innumerable rivers empty themselves, disembogue into the ocean. 2) to spread abundantly. Wilde Waldströme gossen sich über die Felder, impetuous torrents overflowed the fields, or diffused their waters over the fields. III. *v. impers.* [in familiar language] Es gießt [= es regnet sehr stark], it rains as fast as it can pour, or very hard.

Gießbach, *m.* a small stream of water, collected rain, torrent. —bad, *n.* a bath consisting of hot mineral water, poured upon the diseased parts of the body, pumping. Ein —bad nehmen, gebrauchen, to be pumped. —bank, *f.* a long square bench to cast the organ pipes upon. —becken, *n.* wash-hand-basin. —beckenknorpel, *pl.* [in anatomy] arythenoides [two cartilages constituting the head of the larynx]. —blech, *n.* [among letter-founders] an iron-plate on which the overplus of the melted metal runs back into the kettle. —bogen, *m.* [in coining] a vessel in which the silver for the small coins is melted, ingot-mould. —buckel, *m.* [among chimists] melting cone. —erde, *f.* a species of earth or clay for moulds. —erz, *n.* bronze. —faß, *n.* a small cask or barrel for watering; *it.* V. —kanne. —fieber, *n.* a fever incident to persons employed in founderies. —flasche, —form, *f.* casting mould. —haus, *n.* —hütte, *f.* foundery. —kammer or Schmelzkammer, *f.* [in coining] the melting or casting room, foundery. —kanne, *f.* a watering-pot. —kannenknorpel, *pl.* [in anatomy] V. —beckenknorpel. —kasten, *m.* the rake of the plumber's table. —kelle, *f.* a ladle for melting or casting metal. —kessel, *m.* casting kettle —kopf, *m.* the rose of a watering-pot, V. 2. Brause. —krücke, *f.* V. —kasten. —kunst, *f.* art of casting metals, foundery. —lade, *f.* V. —bank. —loch, *n.* 1) the hole of a mould. 2) the funnel of a furnace. —löffel, *m.* V. —kelle. —meister, *m.* master founder. —mergel, *m.* vitrificable marl, V. —sand. —model, *n.* V. —form. —mutter, *f.* mould, matrice, V. Schriftmutter. —ofen, *m.* melting furnace. —pfanne, *f.* casting pan. —puckel, *m.* V. —buckel. —rahm, —rahmen, *m.* V. —kasten. —rinne, *f.* gutter or channel in which the melted metal runs into the mould. —röhre, *f.* the tube or pipe of a watering-pot. —sand, *m.* sand in which metals are cast, V. —mergel. —schaufel, *f.* a kind of shovel for lading out liquid bodies, scoop. —stein, *m.* 1) a porous granite found in France and used in brass-founderies. 2) sink, drain. —tafel, *f.* a table on which large mirrors are cast. —tiegel, *m.* [among wax-chandlers] wax-pot. —tisch, *m.* a table for casting. —vogel, *m.* V. Bienenhabicht. —waare, *f.* V. Gußwaare. —werk, *n.* work of cast metal. —zange, *f.* founder's pincers. —zapfen, *m.* superfluous metal at the opening or hole of the mould.

Gießer, *m.* [-s, *pl.* -] 1) a pouring utensil. *a*) a watering-pot, V. Gießkanne. *b*) [in seamen's lang., a long scoop used to wet the sides of ships or the sails] skeet. 2) founder [of metal], V. Gelb—, Glocken—, Roth—, Schrift—, Stück—, Zinn—.

Gießerlohn, *m.* a founder's wages; *it.* the money paid or stipulated for casting any thing.

Gießerei, *f.* 1) a continued casting or melting; *it.* a bad manner of casting. 2) [the house and works occupied in casting metals] foundery, V. Gießhaus, Gießhütte.

Gießung, *f.* the act of melting or casting. Die — der Metalle, the melting or fusion of metals.

Gietau, V. Geitau.

1. **Gift,** *f.* [*pl.* -en] [from geben, to give, E. gift] rarely used for Gabe, present, gift, donation. V. Mitgift.

2. **Gift,** *n.* [-es, *pl.* -e] [from geben, to give] poison. Ein geschwindes, ein langsames or schleichendes —, an active or virulent, a slow or lingering poison; mineralische, thierische, Pflanzen—e, mineral, animal, vegetable poisons; das — einer Schlange, eines Scorpions, the venom of a serpent, of a scorpion; ein tödtliches —, a deadly poison; Einem — beibringen, geben, to give or administer poison to any one; Einen mit — vergeben, to poison any one; er hat — genommen, he has taken poison, has poisoned himself; einen Pfeil mit — bestreichen, to poison an arrow. [in husbandry] mildew, V. Mehlthau; [in mining] arsenic, V. Hüttenrauch, Arsenik; [in medicine] virus, V. Pocken—, [Blattern—]. *Fig. a*) [any thing noxious to body and soul] poison. Wein ist — für diesen

kranken, wine is poison to this sick person; in seinen Schriften streut er ein gefährliches —us, his writings are filled with pernicious or noxious maxims; das — ketzerischer Meinungen, the poison of heresy. b) [in vulg. lang. it is sometimes used as a m.] spite, malice, virulence, venom. Er hat einen — auf mich, he has a great spite against me; — und Galle speien, to give vent to one's spite and malice; er hat allen seinen — ausgelassen, he has vented all his rage; ich fürchte das — seiner Feder, I fear the virulency of his pen.

Gift-abtreibend, *adj.* [in medicine] alexipharmic, alexiteric. —abtreibendes Mittel, an antidote to poison or infection, alexipharmic, alexiteric. —apfel, *m.* the fruit of the manchineel. —apfelbaum, *m.* manchineel. —arznei, *f.* 1) remedy against poison, antidote; alexipharmic, alexiteric. 2) a deadly drug, a poisoned medicine or drug. —barsch, —bars, *m.* the venomous sea-perch. —baum, *m.* 1) V. Firnißbaum. 2) [a species of Rhus or Sumach] the poison-ash, poison-tree, toxicodendron. Der javanische —baum, the upas-tree. —becher, *m.* poisoned cup or chalice, cup of poison. —beere, *f.* a poisonous berry. —bissen, *m.* a poisoned bit or morsel; *it.* a poisoned gobbet for a dog; *fig.* [among hunters] bait, V. Köder. —blase, *f.* —bläschen, *n.* a poison-bag, poison bladder [of certain animals]; *it.* the small bag in the body of the bees, that contains their sting. —bohne, *f.* a shrub of the East-Indies that bears poisonous beans, the poisonous abrus. —erz, *n.* ore containing arsenic. Weißes —erz, arsenical pyrites, arsenical iron. —esche, *f.* V. Firnißbaum, Flöhkraut. —essig, *m.* V. Pestessig. —fang, *m.* [in forges] a horizontal chimney to catch the arsenic. —fängig, *adj.* subject to be infected with contagious venom. —gewächs, *n.* a venomous herb or plant. —hahnenfuß, *m.* ranunculus palustris. —heil, *n.* salutary monk's hood, anthora. —hund, *m.* a kind of shark. —hütte, *f.* a building for the sublimation of arsenic. —kamm, *m.* the poisonous crest of a serpent. —kieß, *m.* V. Mißpickel. —kraut, *n.* venomous herb; *it.* V. Eisenhütlein, Robertskraut, Gottesgnade. —kugel, *f.* a poisoned ball or gobbet for a dog. —latwerge, *f.* electuary against poison, mithridate, theriac. —lehre, *f.* toxicology. —los, *adj.* and *adv.* void of poison, without poison. —magnet, *m.* V. Schlangenstein. —mehl, *n.* 1) [in forges] arsenical acid, white arsenic, flowers of arsenic. 2) an arsenical earth. —mischen, *n.* the act or employment of mixing up and preparing poison for destructive purposes. —mischer, *m.* —mischerinn, *f.* a person that mixes up and prepares poison for destructive purposes, poisoner, empoisoner. —mischerei, *f.* the practice of mixing poison, of poisoning. —mittel, *n.* V. —arznei. —nuß, *f.* a species of cocoa-nut reputed an alexiteric or counter-poison. —pflanze, *f.* a venomous plant. —pflaster, *n.* a plaster against poison, an alexiteric plaster. —pille, *f.* 1) a pill against poison, an alexipharmic pill. 2) a poisoned pill. —pilz, *m.* venomous or poisonous mushroom. —pulver, *n.* 1) powder against poison, alexipharmic powder. 2) a poisoned powder. —regen, *m.* V. Mehlthau. —reich, *adj.* and *adv.* containing a great deal of poison, very venomous or poisonous. —roche, *m.* poison-fish, puffin, V. Meerpfau. —schlange, *f.* venomous serpent. —schwamm, *m.* [a mushroom or fungus full of dust] puff-ball, puff; V. —pilz. —staude, *f.* a venomous shrub of Arabia. —stein, *m.* 1) stone against poison, bezoar. 2) V. Mißpickel. 3) arsenical cadmia. —sumach, *m.* V. —baum 2). —trank, *m.* a poisoned draught or potion. —tropfen, *m.* a drop of poison. —voll, *adj.* and *adv.* full of poison or venom, poisonous, venomous. *Fig.* spiteful, virulent, malignant. Eine —volle Rede, a very virulent speech. —wasser, *n.* poisoned water. —wende, *f.* swallow-wort, celandine, V. Schwalbenwurzel. —wurzel, *f.* 1) V. —wende. Die Peruanische —wurzel, contrayerva; die Virginische —wurzel, Virginian snake-root. 2) petasites, butterbur. —zahn, *m.* venom tooth. —zunge, *f.* a virulent or malignant tongue.

Giftig, *adj.* and *adv.* poisonous, venomous. —e Thiere, Pflanzen, venomous animals, poisonous plants; eine — Luft, an infected or pestilential air; der Schierlingssaft ist —, the juice of hemlock is poisonous. *Fig.* spiteful, virulent, malignant. Ein —er Mensch, a man full of spleen or malice, a spiteful, malignant man; eine —e Zunge, Rede, a virulent or malignant tongue, a virulent speech; *—werden, to grow angry, bitter or sarcastic.

Giftigkeit, *f.* quality of being poisonous, poisonousness, venomousness.

*Gigánt, *m* [en, *pl.* -en] [in mythology, one of the giants that attempted to storm heaven] Giant.

*Gigántisch, *adj.* and *adv.* gigantic, giant-like, huge. V. Riesenmäßig.

‖Gilb, V. Gelb.

Gilb-beere, *f.* V. Gelbbeere. —blume, *f.* —kraut, *n.* saw-wort [of the genus serratula]. —wurz, *f.* V. Gelbwurzel.

Gilbe, *f.* [*pl.* -n] or Gilft, *n.* [-es, *pl.* -e] 1) yellow colour, yellow substance, V. Gelbe. 2) any thing yellow. *a*) yellow ochre, iron-ochre. *b*) a yellow mineral containing silver. 3) any thing used for dying yellow, V. Genster, Färberscharte.

‖Gilben, V. Gelben.

‖Gilbicht, V. Gelblich.

Gilbig, *adj.* [in mining] yellow, V. Gelb.

Gilblichen, *n.* [-s, *pl.* -] V. 2. Giebel.

‖Gilbling, *m.* [-es, *pl.* -e] V. Goldammer.

Gilde, *f.* [*pl.* -n] [from Geld, money; primarily = a society or company, bearing the expenses in common; now generally = Zunft, Innung] corporation, guild, company. Die Bürgerschaft ist in fünf —n getheilt, the citizens or burgesses are divided into five corporations or companies; die — der Kaufleute, Schuhmacher &c., the merchants', shoemakers' company. *it.* V. Schützen—.

Gilde-bier, *n.* beer drunk at the expense of a corporation or company. —brief, *m.* V. Zunftbrief. —bruder, *m.* a member of the same corporation or company. —haus, *n.* corporation-house; *it.* [the house belonging to any individual company] hall, as: Mercers' Hall, Fishmongers' Hall &c. —meister, *m.* the head or foreman of a corporation or company.

Gilft, *n.* [-es, *pl.* -e] yellow colour, yellow substance. V. Gilbe.

Gillenstein, *m.* [-es, *pl.* -e] [in mineralogy] a greenish shist or shistus mixed with quartz, found in Switzerland.

Gilling, *f.* [*pl.* -en] [in seamen's language] counter [an arch or vault, whose upper part is terminated by the bottom of the stern]. — eines Segels, gore or goring of a sail; —en des Dahlbordes, drift-rails on the bow quarter-deck.

Gillings-hölzer or —kniee, *pl.* counter-timbers, stern-timbers.

Gimf, [Gimpf] *m.* [-es, *pl.* -e] [allied to the Gr. γόμφος = nail] [among button-makers] loop.

Gimfmühle, *f.* a spinning-mill where loops are made.

Gimpel, *m.* [-s, *pl.* -] the bull-finch, V. Blutfink, Dompfaff. *Fig.* ninny, simpleton, dunce, noodle.

Gimpf, V. Gimf.

Gingang, *m.* [-s, *pl.* -e] [a kind of striped cotton-cloth] gingham.

Ginseng, *m.* [-s] V. Kraftwurzel.

Ginst, Ginster, V. Genster.

Gipfel, *m.* [-s, *pl.* -] [allied to Giebel, gable, Wipfel, top of a tree, Gr. κεφαλή, head, and L. *caput*] the highest part of any thing, top, summit. Den — eines Berges erreichen, to gain the top, summit or peak of a mountain; das Schloß liegt auf dem — des Berges, the castle is built on the brow of the hill or mountain; die — der Bäume abhauen, to cut off the tops of the trees, to top the trees; [in botany] der — einer Blume, the apex or anther of a flower. *Fig.* pitch, pinnacle, height, top. Der —, der höchste — des Ruhmes, the pinnacle, the highest pitch of glory; das ist der — der Unverschämtheit, this is the height of impudence. Syn. Gipfel, Wipfel, Spitze. Gipfel is said of all high bodies and denotes simply the highest part, or upper extremity of them. Der Wipfel signifies the top of a tree only. Die Spitze is the acute termination of a body, or the top of any body whose sides terminate in a point.

Gipfel-bruch, *m.* [among foresters] the breaking down of the tops of the trees either by storms or great loads of snow. —reich, *adj.* and *adv.* having many tops or summits, as a mountain; *it.* having a full spreading top or crown, as a tree. —ständig, *adj.* [in botany, growing at the end of a branch or stem] terminal.

Gipfelig, *adj.* having a top or peak. Zwei—, drei—, having two, three tops or summits.

Gipfeln, *v. tr.* V. Spitzen, Zuspitzen; [in astronomy] Culminiren.

Gips, *m.* [-es, *pl.* -e] [L. *gypsum*, Gr. γύψος, primarily = Kreide, chalk] gypsum, parget, plaster-stone, gypseous earth; *it.* plaster, plaster of Paris. — brennen, to calcine gypsum; mit — überziehen, to parget, to plaster, V. Gipsen; eine Wand mit — bewerfen, to coat, plaster or parget a wall; eine Bildsäule aus —, in — bilden, to form a statue in plaster.

Gips-abdruck, —abguß, *m.* a figure formed in plaster of Paris, a plaster cast. Wir haben alle —abdrücke, —abgüsse von der Trajanssäule, we have all the figures of Trajan's pillar in plaster. —anwurf, *m.* rough-cast. —arbeit, *f.* plaster-work, plastering [of a building]; *it.* stucco-work, work in plaster of Paris. —arbeiter, *m.* 1) [one that overlays with plaster] a plasterer. 2) [one that makes figures in plaster] plasterer. —artig, *adj.* and *adv.* of the nature of gypsum, gypseous. —artige Steine, gypseous stones. —bereiter, *m.* V. —brenner. —bild, *n.* figure in plaster [of Paris] or parget. —blume, *f.* selenites, common gypseous spar. —brei, *m.* paste of gypsum or plaster of Paris. —brenner, *m.* he that calcines gypsum or makes plaster. —brennerei, *f.* house or kiln where gypsum is calcined. —bruch, *m.* gypsum or plaster-quarry. —decke, *f.* plastered ceiling, stucco-ceiling. —druse, *f.* crystallized gypsum. —erde, *f.* gypseous earth. —figur, *f.* V. —bild. —figurenhändler, *m.* image-seller. —form, *f.* mould of plaster. —gebirge, *n.* gypseous mountain. —gießer, *m.* V. Gipser 2). —grube, *f.* gypsum or plaster-quarry. —haltig, *adj.* containing gypsum. —kalk, *m.* a sort of lime prepared from gypsum, calcined gypsum. —kelle, *f.* the trowel of a plasterer. —kopf, *m.* bust in plaster of Paris. —kraut, *n.* [in botany] gypsophila. —kristall, V. —druse. —mahlerei, *f.* V. Fresco-mahlerei. —marmor, *m.* artificial marble or stucco. —mehl, *n.* flour of gypsum, powdered gypsum. —mergel, *m.* gypseous marl. —mörtel, *m.* [a fine plaster composed of lime, sand and pounded marble] stucco. —mühle, *f.* a mill for grinding or pulverising gypsum. —ofen, *m.* a kiln for burning plaster-stones. —sache, *f.* V. —bild. —sand, *m.* gypseous sand. —schaufel, *f.* a plasterer's shovel. —schläger, *m.* he that pounds or pulverises calcined gypsum. —sinter, *m.* stalactical gypsum. —spath, *m.* gypseous spar. —stein, *m.* gypseous stone. —stößer, *m.* V —schläger. —tisch, *m.* table on which the plaster is prepared. —überzug, *m.* covering or coat of plaster. —waare, *f.* any thing or figure formed in plaster. —wand, *f.* a plastered wall.

Gipsen, *v. tr.* to overlay with plaster, to parget, to plaster, as a wall, a ceiling &c. Das —, plastering.

Gipsen, Gipsern, *adj.* made of gypsum or plaster. —e Bilder, figures in plaster; eine —e Decke, a plastered ceiling.

Gipser, *m.* [-s, *pl.* -] 1) [one that overlays with plaster] plasterer. 2) [he that makes figures in plaster] plasterer.

Gipsern, V. Gipsen.

Giraffe, *f.* [*pl.* -n] [a quadruped] giraff, camelopard.

Giräll, *m.* [-es, *pl.* -e] [among gun-smiths] V. Dralle.

***Girándel**, *f.* [*pl.* -n] a branched candlestick, a girandole.

***Girasol**, *m.* [-es] [in mineralogy] girasol [a precious stone].

Girgel, V. Gergel.

***Giriren**, [most frequently pronounced dschiriren] *v. tr.* [in commerce] Einen Wechselbrief —, to circulate a bill of exchange for endorsement, to endorse a bill of exchange.

Giro, *n.* [most frequently pronounced Dschiro] — eines Wechsels, endorsement of a bill of exchange.

Girobank, *f.* bank, where business is transacted not by means of notes, but by transfer of money, bank of circulation.

Girren, *v. intr.* [allied to L. *garrio*, Gr. γαρύω or γηρύω] to coo, as pigeons or doves. *Fig.* [in poetry = zärtlich klagen &c.] to lament, to complain tenderly, to sigh. Das —, cooing; *fig.* sighing, complaining.

Girsch, V. Gersch.

Girtwurz, V. Stabwurz.

Gis, *n.* [in music] G sharp.

Gischen, V. Gäschen.

Gischt, V. Gäscht.

Gissen, *v. tr.* and *v. intr.* [in navigation] to estimate the place of a ship without any observation of the heavenly bodies. Das —, V. Gissung.

Gissung, *f.* [in navigation, V. Gissen] dead reckoning

Gitau, V. Geitau.

Gitter, *n.* [-s, *pl.* -] [‖ and †Gatter] grate, lattice, trellis. Ein eisernes —, an iron grate, iron rails or bars; das — vor einem Fenster, the grate, or lattice of a window; ein Fenster mit einem — versehen, — an ein Fenster machen, to furnish a window with bars, with a grate or lattice, to grate or lattice a window; das — vor einem Kamine, fender; das — um den Altar, the balustrade or railing round an altar. [in conchology] the reticular Lepas; [at tennis] hazard.

Gitter-bett, *n.* a bed [for children] surrounded with a railing. —blech, *n.* a grate of wire to carry things upon. —chor, *n.* [in Catholic churches, that part of the choir of a church, between the high-altar and the balustrade inclosing it] chancel. —erker, *m.* balcony. —farn, *m.* [in botany] mule-fern, hemionitis. —fenster, *n.* grated window, lattice window, trellised window; *it.* Venetian blinds. —förmig, *adj.* and *adv.* in the form of a grate or lattice. [in surgery] Der —förmige Theil eines Knochens, the spongy or porous part of a bone. —horn, *n.* [in conchology] reticulated whelk. —käfer, *m.* reticulate beetle. —schnecke, *f.* V. —horn. —schrank, *m.* wardrobe or cupboard with a grate or lattice. —schwamm, *m.* the grated spunge [a kind of mushroom]. —spath, *m.* grated spaad or spar. —stange, *f.* a bar of a grate or lattice. —stock, *m.* [among joiners] a pliant or folding rule used in lattice-work. —stuhl, *m.* a pew with a grate or lattice. —thor, *n.* a gate with a grate or lattice, a grated gate. —thür, *f.* a door with a grate or lattice, a grated door. —venus, *f.* [in conchology] reticulate Venus'shell. —walze, *f.* [in conchology] the reticulate voluta. —weise, *adv.* in form of a trellis or lattice, lattice-like. —werk, *n.* trellis-work, lattice-work. —zaun, *m.* a fence of trellis-work.

Gitterchen, ‖**Gitterlein**, [*dimin.* of Gitter] [-s, *pl.* -] *n.* a small grate or lattice.

Gitterig, *adj.* and *adv.* grated, trellised, latticed. —er Schrank, V. Gitterschrank.

Gittern, *v. tr.* to furnish with a grate or lattice, to grate, to lattice. Gegitterte Arbeit, trellis-work, lattice-work; [in blasonry] ein gegittertes Kreuz, a fretty cross; Zeuge —, to checker stuffs; gegitterter Kattun, checkered cotton.

***Glácis**, [pron. as in the French] *n.* [in fortification] glacis. V. Feldbrustwehre.

Glährke, *f.* [*pl.* -n] dab [a fish], V. Kliesche.

Gländer, V. Galander.

Glánz, *m.* [-es] [allied to Glas, gleißen, glitzen, Gr. γλαύσσω = to glitter, to shine] 1) [not used in the plural] splendour, lustre, brightness, gloss. Der — der Sonne, the lustre or glare of the sun; der — der Augen, Blumen, Farben, the brightness or brilliancy of the eyes, flowers, colours; dieser Diamant hat einen stärkern —, als der andere, this diamond has greater lustre, sparkles more than the other; dem Marmor — geben, to give a polish to marble; der — eines Zeuges, von Tuch, the gloss of a stuff, of cloth; diese Farben verlieren leicht den —, these colours are apt to fade; diese Vergoldung hat ihren — verloren, this gilding is tarnished; einem Hute, Zeuge, Felle — geben, to gloss a hat, a stuff, a skin; dem Stahle den — geben, to burnish steel; diese Perlen haben einen schönen —, these pearls are of fine water; dem Tuche den — benehmen, to take the gloss off cloth. *Fig.* splendour, magnificence. Sie erschien in dem ganzen —e ihrer Schönheit, she made her appearance in all the splendour of her beauty; er erscheint am Hofe mit mit vielem —e, he appears at court in a very splendid manner; er hält viel auf äußeren —, he is very fond of pomp or show; der — der Geburt, der Thaten, des Ruhmes, the lustre or splendour of birth, of deeds, of fame; ihr Schmuck gibt ihrer Schönheit noch mehr —, her jewels give additional lustre or brilliancy to, set off her beauty. 2) something brilliant. [in mineralogy] [*pl.* Glänze] *a*) sulphuret of lead, galena, lead-glance, schwarz-silver-ore, V. —erz, Bleiglanz. *b*) mica, glimmer, glist, muscovy-glass.

Glanz-assel, *f.* [in entomology] a sort of woodlouse [of the genus Scolopendra] —auge, *n.* the name of a large butterfly. —bank, *f.* [among hatters] glossing-bench. —blättchen, *n.* [among jewelers, a thin leaf of metal, placed under precious stones to make them appear transparent] foil. —bürste, *f.* polishing-brush. —cantille, *f.* purl, gold or silver purl. —erz, *n.* V. Glanz 2, *a*), Bleiglanz. —farbe, *f.* brilliant colour. —firniß, *m.* a glossy, brilliant varnish. —geber, *m.* V. Glänzer. —gold, *n.* V. Flittergold, Rauschgold —gras, *n.* phalaris, canary-grass. —hammer, *m.* planishing-hammer. —horn, *n.* [in conchology] waved whelk. —käfer, *m.* [in entomology] cicindela; *it.* glow-worm. —kobalt, *m.* shining cobalt-ore. —kohle, *f.* shining sea-coal, kennel-coal. —korduan, *m.* shining Morocco leather. —kugel, *f.* a polishing instrument in form of a ball, polishing-ball. —leinwand, *f.* glazed linen, buckram. —los, *adj.* and *adv.* without splendour or gloss, dull. —lose Augen, lacklustre eyes. —marmor, *m.* shining marble. —papier, *n.* glazed paper. —presse, *f.* [among cloth-makers] calender. —ruß, *m.* shining soot; *it.* lamp-black. —schetter, *m.* buckram, V. Steifleinwand. —stein, *m.* V. Spiegelstein. —taffet, *m.* lustring. —wichse, *f.* shoe-blacking.

Glänzen, I. *v. intr.* to shine, to glitter, to sparkle, to gleam, to glisten. Ihre Augen glänzten sehr lebhaft, a dazzling lustre sparkled in her eyes; wie diese Steine —! how brilliant these stones are! schon sahen wir die feindlichen Waffen —, we already saw the arms of the enemy glitter; Alles glänzt da von Gold und Silber, every thing is shining there with gold and silver; alle Sterne glänzten, all the stars sparkled or glistened; ihr ganzes Gesicht glänzt von Schminke, she is quite bright with paint; eine Thräne glänzte in ihren Augen, a tear glistened in her eyes; —de Metalle, shining, glittering, bright metals; —de Farben, brilliant colours; sie hat lebhafte und —de Augen, she has lively and sparkling eyes; in ihren Augen glänzte die Freude, joy sparkled in her eyes; —de Waffen, ein stark —der Zeug, glittering arms, a very glossy stuff; —de Lufterscheinungen, luminous meteors; *prov.* es ist nicht alles Gold, was glänzt, all is not gold that glitters. *Fig.* Die Tugend glänzt im Unglücke noch mehr, virtue shines more in adversity; sie glänzt noch mehr durch ihren Verstand, als durch ihre Schönheit, she shines still more, is still more distinguished by her understanding than by her beauty; —de Reize, dazzling charms; ein —der Verstand, sparkling wit; Wenige besitzen die Fähigkeit, in Gesellschaft zu —, few are qualified to shine in company; ein —der Ball, a splendid ball; dieses Gedicht ist voll —der Gedanken, this poem is full of brilliant thoughts; —de Tugenden, Thaten, shining, brilliant or splendid virtues, actions or achievements. II. *v. tr.* [= etwas glätten, ihm einen Glanz geben] to make smooth and shining, to gloss, to brighten. Marmor, Stahl —, to polish marble, steel; Gold, Silber, Waffen —, to burnish or furbish gold, silver, arms; Tuch, einen Zeug —, to hotpress, to gloss cloth, a stuff; das Papier —, to glaze the paper; [among hatters] einen Hut —, to gloss a hat; die Stiefel —, to blacken the boots; geglänzte Handschuhe, glazed gloves. V. Blänken. Das —, V. Glanz.

Glänz-hammer, *m.* planishing-ham-

…ber. —spath, m. V. Frauenglas. —stahl, …. a polishing or burnishing instrument, a …olisher, burnisher. —zahn, m. [a dog's or …elf's tooth used in polishing] burnisher.

Glänzer, m. [-s, pl. -] he that makes shin…g, polishes or glosses.

Glänzig, adj. [in mining] shining. Eine —e …ergart, a shining mineral.

***Glaphisch**, adj. fit or proper for sculpture, …laphic.

Glaris or **Glarus**, n. [one of the cantons of …witzerland, and the capital of that canton] Glarus, …larys.

Glarner or **Glarnisch**, adj. of or from …larus.

Glarner, m. [-s, pl. -] —inn, f. a native … inhabitant of Glarus.

Glas, n. [-es] [V. Glanz; formerly it signified …mething shining or brilliant in general; thus the an…ent Swedes called Gold (gold) *Glüs, Glaes*, and …e ancient Germans Bernstein (amber) Glas] 1) …ot used in the plural)] [a hard, brittle, transparent sub…ance] glass. —machen, blasen, to make, to blow …lass; zu — machen, to convert into glass, to vitri…; zu — werden, to become glass, to vitrify, …Verglasen; auf — mahlen, to paint upon …lass; it. auf — mahlen, auf — einbrennen, … anneal; farbiges — [as in church-windows …], stained glass; eine Tasse von — [Glas…, gläserne Tasse], a glass cup; geschliffe…s —, ground or polished glass, V. Fenster…, Spiegel— [pl. -gläser]; fossilisches —, …ssile glass; Blei läßt sich leicht in — ver…andeln, lead is easily converted into glass, …trifies easily; V. Blei—, Kupfer—, Zinn—. …ig. [= Hornhaut im Auge der Pferde] horned …nt of the eye. 2) [pl. Gläser] [any thing …de of glass] V. Arzenei—, Augen—, Brenn…, Uhren— &c. Die Gläser an einer Kut…e, the glasses or windows of a coach; das — …abla ssen, to let down the glass [of a coach]; … — zum Trinken, a drinking-glass; ein rei…s —, a clean glass; mit den Gläsern ansto…n, to touch the glasses, *to hob-nob; die …läser ausspülen, to rinse the glasses; V. …ier—, Wein—, Kelch—. *it.* [as much as a glass …ntains] a glassful, a glass. Ein — Wasser, Wein, …glass of water, wine; ein volles — trinken, … drink a bumper; kommen Sie, wir wollen … —, ein Gläschen Wein mit einander trin…, come, let us take a glass of wine together; …in — nach dem andern ausstechen, to empty …e glass after another; *er guckt gern in's … or Gläschen, he loves the bottle; *zu tief …s — gucken [= sich betrinken], to be too fa…liar with the bottle, to get tipsy or drunk.

Glas-achat, m. [a black vitreous stone re…bling the agate] Iceland agate. —achtig, adj. …—artig. —ähnlich, adj. and adv. resem…ing glass, vitreous; [in mineralogy] hyaline. …amianth, m. common asbestos. —apfel, … an apple that is apt to break, glass-apple. …arbeit, f. work in glass; it. glass-ware. Die …arbeit an einem Hause [= Fensterwerk], the …ndows of a house. —artig, adj. and adv. … [resembling glass] vitreous. 2) [capable of being …verted into glass] vitrifiable. —artigkeit, f. …ality of being vitrifiable. —asbest, m. V. …amianth. —asche, f. alkali. —auge, n. … [an artificial eye of glass or cristal] a glass …. 2) wall-eye. Ein Mensch, ein Thier mit …ugen, a wall-eyed person, animal. 3) … veterinary art] a wall-eyed horse. —äu…g, adj. and adv. wall-eyed, silver-eyed. …birne, f. a sort of pear, virgoleuse. —bla…n, n. the act or art of blowing glass. —bla…r, m. glass-blower. —blasereisen, n. … iron tube to blow the glass with] bunting-iron. —boden, m. 1) a floor of glass, glass floor. 2) the foot of a glass. —bürste, f. a glass or bottle brush. —deckel, m. 1) a cover or lid of glass, glass-cover, glass lid. 2) the cover or lid of a glass. —diamant, m. glass or spurious diamond, paste. —edelstein, m. V. —stein. —egel, m. transparent leech. —electricität, f. vitreous electricity. —erde, f. vitrifiable earth. —erz, n. [in mining] a rich, shining silver-ore. —faden, m. a glass-thread. —farbe, f. colour of glass, glass-colour. —farbig, adj. and adv. glass-coloured; [in medicine] hyaloides. —fenster, n. glass window. Ein — fenster in eine Thür setzen, to glaze a door. —feuchtigkeit, f. [in anatomy] vitreous humour, hyaloides. —flasche, f. glass bottle. —fluidum, n. [in physics] the vitreous fluid. —fluß, m. 1) [any substance or mixture, used to promote the fusion of metals or minerals] flux. 2) [painted glass imitating the colour of precious stones] V. Rubinfluß, Smaragdfluß. —form, f. a form or mould for glass-vessels. —förmig, adj. and adv. in form of a glass. —fritte, f. frit. —galle, f. 1) [a whitish salt, cast up from the materials of glass in fusion] glass-gall, vitreous salt, sandever or sandiver. 2) [that part of the glass, which sticks to the bunting-iron] bunt, knob, knot, bull's eye. —gemenge, n. V. —fritte. —geräthschaft, f. [in physics] apparatus of glass-instruments. —geschirr, n. glass utensils, glass-ware, glass; it. V. —werk. —glanz, m. vitreous or glassy splendour or lustre. —glocke, f. glass-bell. —glocken auf die Melonen setzen, sie mit —glocken bedecken, to put glass-bells upon the melons, to cover them with glass-bells. —griesig, n. broken window glass. —griff, m. [among glass makers] ferret. —grün, adj. and adv. green as glass, bottle green. —hafen, m. [among glass-makers] melting-pot, crucible. —handel, m. glass-trade. Einen —handel führen, to deal in glass. —händler, m. —händlerinn, f. dealer in glass, glass-man, glass-woman. —hart, adj. and adv. hard as glass. —haus, n. hot-house; it. conservatory, greenhouse, V. Treibhaus, Gewächshaus. —haut, f. —häutlein, n. [in anatomy] the choroid coat or tunic of the eye. —hautstaar, m. [in medicine] membranous cataract. —hell, adj. and adv. transparent as glass. —honig, m. transparent honey. —hülse, f. V. Hartriegel —hütte, f. glass-house. —igel, m. V. —egel. —kalk, m. V. —galle 1). —kasten, m. 1) a glass-chest 2) a chest or cupboard for glasses. —kirsche, f. a sort of transparent cherry, agriot. —kitt, m. a cement for joining glass. —kopf, m. [in mining] hematite. Brauner —kopf, brown hematite; rother —kopf or Blutstein, red hematite or bloodstone. —koralle, f. glass-bead, V. —perle. —korb, m. 1) a basket to pack glass in. 2) a basket full of glass. 3) a basket with several compartments to put glasses in. 4) a basket of glass, a glass-basket. Obst in niedlichen —körbchen, fruit in pretty little glass-baskets. — —körper, m. [in anatomy] V. —feuchtigkeit. —kram, m. glass trade. —krämer, m. V. —händler. —kraut, n. 1) salsola, glasswort. 2) the pellitory of the wall. 3) ficoides, V. Eiskraut. —kugel, f. glass-ball, glass-globe. —kupfererz, n. a vitreous copper-ore. —lampe, f. a sort of lamp for illuminations. —laterne, f. glass-lantern. —lava, f. hyalite. —leuchte, f. V. —laterne. —linse, f. lens [for telescopes &c.]. —machen, n. glass-making, glass-blowing. —macher, m. glass-maker, glass-blower. —macherkunst, f. the art of making glass. —mahlen, n. V. —mahlerei 1). —mahler, m. 1) painter on glass, glass-painter or stainer. 2) V. Schmelzmahler. —mahlerei, f. 1) the art of painting on glass, glass-painting, glass-staining. 2) a painting or picture on glass. 3) V. Schmelzmahlerei. —mann, m. V. —händler, —träger. —masse, f. glass-metal; it. V. —fritte. —meer, n. fig. the glassy deep. —mehl, n. glass-powder, glass-meal. —meister, m. the master or proprietor of a glass-house; it. the inspector of a glass-house. —nuth, f. groove for a window-glass. —ofen, m. [in glasshouses] glass-furnace. —paste, f. a mock jewel made of glass, paste. —perle, f. a mock pearl made of glass; glass-bead. —platte, f. a round glass-piece, a plate. —porzellan, n. transparent porcelain. —quarz, m. hyaline quartz. —rahmen, —rahm, m. a glass frame [of a looking glass &c.] —räumer, m. V. —bürste. —raute, f. pane of glass [in the shape of a lozenge], a diamond-pane. —ring, m. a glass-ring. —röhre, f. a glass tube. —salz, n. V. —galle 1). —sand, m. 1) sand proper for making glass, gravelly sand. 2) pounded or pulverized glass. —satz, m. frit. —schaum, m. V. —galle 1). —scheibe, f. pane of glass. —scherbe, f. a piece of broken glass. —schere, f. shears for cutting glass. —schleifen, n. glass-grinding. —schleifer, m. glass-grinder. —schmalz, n. 1) V. —galle 1). 2) V. —kraut 1). —schmelz, m. glass-wort, V. —kraut. —schmelzer, m. glass-melter. —schmutz, m. V. —galle 1). —schneider, m. V. —schleifer. —schörl, m. [in mining] axinite. —schrank, m. —schränkchen, n. 1) a case, cupboard or press with glass-doors. 2) a case or cupboard for holding glasses. —schürer, m. he that makes up the fire in a glass-house. —seife, f. manganese, V. Braunstein. —silbererz, n. V. —erz. —spath, m. vitreous spar, V. Flußspath. —spiel, n. the harmonical glasses, harmonica. —spinnen, n. glass-spinning. —spinner, m. glass-spinner. —stein, m. 1) [in mineralogy] Italian marble. 2) a mock jewel made of glass, V. —edelstein. —stempel, m. mark or stamp of a glass-house. —stock, m. a glass bee-hive. —streifen, m. a long and small piece of glass. —tafel, f. a glass-table, a glass-plate; it. [among glaziers] a square of glass, a pane. —theil, m. [in chimistry] the vitreous part. —thräne, f. V. —tropfen. —thür, f. glass-door. —tiegel, —topf, m. V. —hafen. —träger, m. [—mann] glass-man. —tropfen, m. [a green glass drop with a long slender tail] Rupert's drop, lacrima Batavica, V. Springglas. —vergoldung, f. 1) the gilding of glass. 2) the art of gilding glass. —waare, f. glass-ware, glass. —wand, f. a glass partition. —weide, f. V. Brechweide. —werk, n. V. —waare. Das —werk an einem Hause, V. —arbeit. —wurz, f. V. —kraut. —zähre, f. V. —tropfen. —zange, f. pincers for stretching glass, fascet. —zeolith, m. vitreous zeolite.

Glasemeister, m. V. Glasmeister.

Gläschen, ||**Gläslein**, n. [-s, pl. -] [*dim.* of Glas 2)] a small or little glass.

Gläser, m. [-s, pl. -] glazier.

Glaser-arbeit, f. glazier's work. —blei, n. glazier's lead, came. —diamant, m. glazier's diamond, emrod. —geselle, m. a journeyman glazier. —gewerk, n. V. —zunft. —handwerk, n. the trade of a glazier. —junge, m. glazier's apprentice. —meister, m. master glazier; it. [in glasshouses] V. Glasmeister. —zunft, f. glazier's company.

Gläserinn, f. a glazier's wife.

Gläserklang, m. [-es] the sound or jingling of glasses. *Fig.* Bei — und frohem Sang, with toasts and glees.

Gläserracke, f. [pl. -n] a shelf for holding glasses.

Gläsern, *adj.* and *adv.* made of glass, glassy, vitreous. —e Flaschen, glass bottles; ein —es Auge, an eye of glass or crystal, a glass or glassy eye; [in anatomy] die —e Feuchtigkeit [im Auge], vitreous or crystalline humour, hyaloides; *fig.* —es Auge, V. Glasauge.

Glasicht, *adj.* and *adv.* resembling glass, glassy, vitreous. Ein —er Körper, a glassy or vitreous body.

Gläsig, *adj.* and *adv.* consisting of glass, vitreous.

Glasiren, V. Glasuren.

Glasur, *f.* [*pl.* -en] glazing. Dem irdenen Geschirre eine — geben, to glaze the earthenware; die — der Zähne, the enamel of the teeth; [among pastry-cooks, a composition of sugar and eggs] ice; [in painting] varnish.

Glasurerde, *f.* V. Glaserde.

Glasuren, [in familiar language glasiren] *v. tr.* to glaze. Irdenes Geschirr —, to glaze earthenware; Zuckerwerk —, to ice or frost confectionary; Zeuge, Bänder —, to glaze stuffs, ribbons; glasurte Handschuhe, glazed gloves; [in painting] ein Gemählde —, to varnish or glaze a picture.

Glätscher, V. Gletscher.

Glatt, [seems to have been originally one and the same word with Glanz, and is allied to the Engl. *glad* and the L. *laetus*] I. *adj.* [opposed to rauh, rough] smooth, sleek. Etwas — machen, to smooth, to sleek, to polish a thing, V. Glätten; eine —e Oberfläche, a smooth or even surface; —e Haare, sleek hair; dieser Spiegel, dieser Marmor ist sehr —, this mirror, marble is very smooth; ein —er Zeug, a glossy stuff; ein Stück Holz — hobeln, to plane a piece of wood smooth; der Weg ist —, the way is slippery; es ist sehr — zu gehen, it is very slippery walking, V. Schlüpferig; ein —es Kinn [ohne Bart], a smooth or beardless chin; eine —e Haut, a smooth skin; ein —es Gesicht, a smooth face; [in fam. lang.] ein —es [= hübsches] Gesicht, a pretty face; ein —es [hübsches, geputztes] Mädchen, a pretty neat girl; [among tailors] mit dem Nagel — streichen, to smooth down with the nail; das Futter [eines Kleides] — anstechen, to stitch down the lining; ein —es Halstuch, a plain neckhandkerchief; —er Sammet, Atlas &c., plain velvet, satin &c.; [in botany, having a slippery surface, void of roughness] ein —er Stengel, —e Blätter, a smooth or glabrous stalk, smooth or glabrous leaves; und ihre Kehle ist —er als Oel [in Script.], and her mouth is smoother than oil. *Fig.* flattering, soothing, bland, smooth. —e [= gefällige, schmeichelhafte] Worte, fair, flattering, sweet, smooth words; Einem —e Worte geben, to speak any one fair; eine —e Zunge, a smooth tongue; ein —es Wesen, an insinuating, a polished manner or behaviour, [chiefly in a bad sense], over-refined manners. II. *adv.* smoothly, evenly, sleekly. Es geht — hinunter, it goes glibly down; — anliegen [wohl anschließen], to sit close, to fit well; diese Strümpfe liegen — an, these stockings fit very well. *Fig.* [in fam. lang. = völlig, gänzlich] quite, entirely, clean, clear. Ein Stück — abschneiden, to cut a piece clean or clear off; sie haben ihm die Haare — weggeschoren, they have shaved his head close; Alles — aufessen, to eat every thing clean up; er schlug es ihm — ab, he flatly denied it him, he gave him a flat denial; er sagte es ihm — heraus, he bluntly or roundly told him so; ich habe es — vergessen, I have quite, entirely or clean forgotten it; — weg [geradeweg], plainly, roundly, without reserve, peremptorily; — nichts [durchaus nichts], nothing at all. V. Platt.

Glatt-bärtig, *adj.* and *adv.* not having any beard, without beard, beardless. —büchse, *f.* [among sportsmen] a fowling piece [smooth-barrelled, not rifled]; —butte, *f.* a sort of flounder [a fish], halibut. —eis, *n.* [Ice with glassy and very slippery surface (after a thaw)] glazed frost. —eisen, *v. intr. impers.* to freeze after a thaw, so as to form very slippery ice. Es —eiset, it is a glazed frost. —eisen or Glätteisen, *n.* smoothing iron, polishing iron; *it.* V. Plätteisen, Plättstahl. —feile, *f.* smooth-file. —hai, *m.* the smooth dogfish. —hobel, *m.* smoothing-plane, jointer. —horn, *n.* [in conchology] smooth and glossy whelk. —rai, *m.* V. —roche. —randig, *adj.* and *adv* with smoothed angles. —roche, *m.* smooth ray. —rücken, *m.* [in natural history] 1) a sea-snail with a smooth back. 2) a fallow beetle. —schleifer, *m.* a polisher. —sohle, *f.* the smooth sole [a fish]. —züngig, *adj. fig.* smooth-tongued, glibly tongued.

Glätte, *f.* 1) [not used in the plural] [Glattheit] smoothness; *it.* slipperiness. Die — des Fußbodens, des Wassers, der Haut &c., the smoothness of the floor, water, skin &c.; dem Holze, Steine die — geben, to smooth or polish the wood, stone; die — or Glattheit der überfrorenen Straße, the slippery state of the ice-covered road. 2) [*pl.* -n] a smooth substance; [in mining] litharge. Die gelbe, weiße — [Gold—, Silber—], litharge of gold, of silver; schwarze —, black litharge; [among refiners] die — frischen [= sie wieder in Blei verwandeln], to reduce the slags of litharge to lead, V. Frischglätte, Glättfrischen.

Glätten, *v. tr.* [= glatt, glänzen machen] to smooth, to sleek, to polish, to glaze. Tuch, Leinwand —, to calender cloth, linen; geglättetes Papier, glazed paper; den Stahl, Metalle —, to polish, burnish or furbish steel, metals; silbernes Geräth — [eben schlagen], to planish plate; ein Buch —, to burnish a book. *Fig.* to free from obstruction, to make easy, to smooth. Das glättete ihm die Bahn, that smoothed his passage; die Falten auf seiner Stirne glätteten sich bei diesem Anblick, the wrinkles of his brow smoothened at this sight.

Glätten, *n.* [-s] the act of smoothing, sleeking, polishing &c.

Glätt-bein, *n.* a smooth piece of bone or ivory used for smoothing, polishing, burnisher. —eisen, V. Glatteisen. —factor, *m.* [in mining] factor or clerk for the sale of litharge. —fäßchen, *n.* a small cask or barrel for litharge. —filz, *m.* [among cardmakers, several pieces of felt sewed one upon the other for burnishing the cards] rubber. —frischen, *n.* [among refiners] reduction of litharge to lead. —gasse, *f.* [among refiners] a drain or gutter through which the litharge flows off when it separates from the silver. —glas, *n.* a smoothing or sleeking-glass. —haken, *m.* [among refiners] a hook for making a drain or gutter for the litharge. —hobel, *m.* V. Glatthobel. —holz, *n.* 1) a burnishing or sleeking-stick, a burnisher or polisher. 2) [in botany] glabraria tersa or lignum leve. —horn, *n.* [among saddlers] a smooth horn used for burnishing or polishing. —kammer, *f.* V. —stube. —keule, *f.* —kolben, *m.* a thick or blunt instrument for polishing; [among bookbinders] burnisher. —kugel, *f.* a glass-ball or globe for smoothing morocco leather. —maschine, *f.* sleeking or smoothing-machine. —mühle, *f.* [among papermakers and potters] a sleeking or smoothing-mill. —platte, *f.* [among papermakers] sleeking-stone. —schicht, *f.* [among refiners] as much litharge as separates at once from the silver. —scheibe, —schiene, *f.* [among shoemakers] sleeking-stick or tool. —stahl, *m.* a piece of steel used as a polishing instrument, burnisher, polisher. —stange, *f.* a pole with a sleeking-stone. —stein, *m.* smoothing-stone, polishing-stone, sleekstone. —stube, *f.* sleeking, smoothing or burnishing room. —tisch, *m.* a table for smoothing, sleeking or burnishing. —werkzeug, *n.* a tool for sleeking or burnishing, burnisher. —zahn, *m.* [a dog's or wolf's tooth used in polishing] burnisher.

Glätter, *m.* [-s, *pl.* -] —inn, *f.* 1) a person that smoothes, polishes &c. any thing, smoother, polisher, furbisher, planisher. V. Glätten. 2) an instrument used for smoothing, polishing &c., burnisher, V. Glättbein.

Glättermühle, *f.* V. Glättmühle.

Glattheit, *f.* V. Glätte 1).

Glättlich, *adj.* [in botany = halbglatt] half smooth, half glabrous.

Glatze, *f.* [*pl.* -n] [allied to glatt, smooth] properly, any smooth and bald surface; in a more limited sense, the bald part of the head. Eine — bekommen, to get bald. *Fig.* [in fam. lang.] bald-head, bald-pate; [in anatomy, the space between the eye-brows] glabella.

Glatz-kopf, *m.* [rather vulgar; often in joke or contempt] a bald-pated person. Jener alte —kopf, that old bald-pated fellow. —köpfig, *adj.* V. Glatzig.

Glatzig, *adj.* and *adv.* bald, bald-pated. — werden, to become bald.

Glau, [Sax. *glew*, Icel. *glü*] *adj.* and *adv.* clear, bright, V. Hell, Heiter; *fig.* V. Scharfsichtig.

Glaube, *m.* [-ns] 1) [not used in the plural] [from glauben = geloben, to promise solemnly] promise given as well as the fulfilment of a promise, faith. Treu und —n ist unter den Menschen selten, truth and faith are rare among men; etwas auf Treu und —n annehmen, to accept, to believe a thing upon any one's good faith; Treu und —n brechen, to break or violate one's faith; er hält weder Treu noch —n, he has neither honour nor honesty, he regards neither law nor gospel; ein Mann ohne Treu und —n, a man not to be trusted, or not to be relied or depended upon. 2) [not used in the plural] [from glauben = to believe] *a*) [confidence, persuasion] belief, faith, credit. —n an Einen, an etwas haben, to have faith in any one, in a thing; —n geben, beimessen, to have, to put faith in, to give credit to; das ist, das geht über allen —n, that exceeds all belief; das findet keinen —, bei Niemand —n, nobody will believe that; sich um allen —n bringen, to lose all one's credit; *der — wird ihm in die Hand kommen, experience will teach him; dazu gehört ein starker —, that is hard to be believed, that seems to be incredible; der — an Gott, an die Tugend, the belief in God, in virtue. [in theology] faith, belief. Der wahre, der falsche —, the true, the wrong belief or faith; der — ohne Werke ist todt, faith, if it has not works, is dead; stark or fest im —n seyn, to be firm in one's faith or belief; im —n wanken, to waver in faith. [in commerce = Credit] credit. Einem —n geben [= borgen], to give any one credit; —n haben, seinen —n verlieren, to have credit, to lose one's credit. *b*) [*pl.* -n, but rather unusual] [a doctrine or system of doctrines believed] religious faith, belief. Der christliche, der jüdische —, the Christian, Jewish faith or belief; der seligmachende —, the saving faith; einen —n annehmen, bekennen, to embrace, to profess a religion; den mahomedanischen —n annehmen, to turn Mahometan; seinen —n verläugnen or abschwören, to abjure one's faith, to turn apostate; die Artikel unsers —ns, the articles of er faith; vom —n abfallen, to forsake one's ith or religion, to apostatize. 3) [*pl.* -n] [= Glaubensbekenntniß] creed, symbol. Der postolische —, the Apostolic creed; den —n as Credo] herbeten, to say one's creed.

Glauben, *m.* [-s, *pl.* -] V. Glaube 2).

Glauben, *v. tr* and *intr.* [is allied to loben, merly lauben, which signified not only to give promise, but also to accept a promise] 1) to believe. *a*) Etwas —, an etwas —, [= to be convinced of the reality and truth of a thing] to believe, believe in. Eine Sache —, to believe a thing; Gespenster, Wunder —, to believe in ghosts spectres, in miracles or to have faith in iracles; an Zauberer —, to give credit to rcerers; etwas für gewiß — [= halten], to lieve a thing for certain; *etwas steif und fest , to believe a thing confidently; nicht so leicht , not to be so credulous; an Tugend, an sterblichkeit —, to believe in virtue, in immortality; an Gott —, to believe in God; *ei-* Gott —, to believe there is a God; wer glaubet und getauft wird, wird selig, wer er nicht glaubet, der wird verdammt werden Script.], he that believeth and is baptized all be saved, but he that believeth not shall be mned. *b*) Einem —, Einem etwas —, [= not doubt the truth of what a person says] to believe y one. Ich glaube es Ihnen auf Ihr Wort, I lieve you on your word; er ist ein Lügner, an glaubt ihm nicht mehr, he is a liar, he is no re believed; — Sie mir, thun Sie, was ich Ihnen sage, be advised, be ruled by me, do what I l you; das ist nicht zu —, that is not to be lieved; *er wird daran — müssen, he will be liged to believe it, experience will teach him; *er hat daran — müssen, he has been obliged submit, to buckle to it. 2) [= meinen, dafür halten] to think, to suppose, to imagine. Ich ube, daß ich es thun kann, I think I can do ich glaubte, er wäre ein ehrlicher Mann, I ought he was an honest man; es ist zu —, ß es seine Absicht war, it is to be presumed t it was his intention; sie —, daß ich im nste gesprochen habe, they suppose or believe to have spoken in earnest; wer hätte so etwas geglaubt? who would have thought of h a thing? er glaubt sich [= hält sich für] verrathen, he thinks he is betrayed; er glaubt gelehrt genug dazu, he thinks himself learned ugh for it.

Glaubens-fest, *adj.* and *adv.* firm in one's h, steady in one's religious belief. —s-fall, *m.* apostasy. —s-abtrünnige, *m.* state, renegade. —s-ähnlichkeit, *f.* logy in religious doctrines. —s-änderung, *f.* change of religion. —s-artikel, article of faith. —s-bekenner, *m.* confessor of a faith. —s-bekenntniß, *n.* 1) confession of faith 2) creed, symbol. Das apostolische —s-bekenntniß, the Apostolic creed; das sburgische —s-bekenntniß, the Angsburgh fession. —s-beschirmer, —s-beschützer, [a title of the king of England] defender of the h. —s-bote, *m.* apostle, missionary. —s-ider, *m.* V. —s-genoß —s-buch, *n.* book of h. —s-entsagung, *f.* V. —s-abfall. —s-chtling, *m.* one flying on account of his gion, refugee. —s-formel, *f.* V. —s-bekenntniß 2). —s-freiheit, *f.* religious liberty. —s-frucht, *f.* fruit of faith, that is, d works. —s-genoß, *m.* one of the same gion Wir sind —s-genossen, we confess the e faith or religion; abweichende —s-genossen, senters. —s-gericht, *n.* religious tribunal, uisition. Das spanische —s-gericht, the nish inquisition. —s-grund, *m.* 1) ar- of faith. 2) ground or foundation of faith. 3) fundamental doctrine of faith. —s-handlung, *f.* V. Autodafé. —s-held, *m.* hero or defender of the faith. —s-heuchler, *m.* religious hypocrite, canter. —s-irrthum, *m.* error or mistake in matters of faith or religion. —s-lehre, *f* 1) doctrine of faith. 2) system of religion. —s-meinung, *f.* opinion in matters of faith or religion. —s-opfer, *n.* victim of the faith. —s-partei, *f.* party in religion, religious sect —s-probe, —s-prüfung, *f.* trial in which faith is put to the test, religious ordeal. —s-punkt, *m.* point or article of faith. —s-regel, *f.* rule of faith —s-reiniger, *m* reformer of religion, religious doctrines or church institutions. —s-reinigung, *f.* reformation [of the church]. —s-richter, *m.* inquisitor. —s-sache, *f.* matter of faith or religion. —s-satz, *m.* dogma, doctrine of faith. —s-schwärmer, *m.* religious enthusiast, fanatic. —s-schwärmerei, *f.* religious enthusiasm, fanaticism. —s-scrupel, *m.* V. —s-zweifel. —s-sonderling, *m.* dissenter. —s-streit, *m.* 1) combat for the faith. 2) religious controversy. —s-streiter, *m.* V. —s-held. —verbesserer, *m* V. —s-reiniger. —s-verbesserung, *f.* V —s-reinigung. —s-verfassung, *f.* the nature, the system of faith. —s-verläugner, *m.* an apostate from the faith, a renegado. —s-verwandte, *m.* V. —s-genoß. —s-voll or —voll, *adj.* and *adv.* full of faith. —s-vorschrift, *f.* V. —s-regel. —s-werber, *m.* proselyte-maker —s-werberei, *f.* proselytism. —s-wissenschaft, *f.* theology. —s-wort, *n.* an apophthegm or short sentence of faith. —s-wuth, *f.* fanaticism [in a violent degree]. —s-wüthig, *adj.* and *adv.* fanatical [in a high degree]. —s-zunft, *f.* religious sect —s-zünftelei, *f.* sectarianism. —s-zünftler, *m.* sectarian. —s-zwang, *m.* constraint or restraint in matters of religion or worship. —s-zweifel, *m.* scruple in matters of faith or religion.

Gläuben, [obsolete, except in Scripture] V. Glauben.

Glauberit, *m.* [-s, *pl.* -e] [a mineral consisting of dry sulphate of lime and dry sulphate of soda] glauberite.

Glaubersalz, *n.* [-es, *pl.* -] Glauber-salt, sulphate of soda [a wellknown cathartic].

Glaubhaft, [Glaubhaftig] *adj.* and *adv.* worthy of belief, credible, authentic. Ein —er Mann, a credible man; —e Nachricht, —es Zeugniß, credible news, authentic or unquestionable testimony; es ist — versichert worden, daß &c., it has been credibly asserted that &c. V. Glaubwürdig, Glaublich.

Glaubhaftigkeit, *f.* worthiness of belief, credibility, authenticity. V. Glaubwürdigkeit.

Gläubig, *adj.* and *adv.* 1) believing, in compositions, as: aber—, leicht—, un— &c. 2) [professing a certain faith or religion and firmly adhering to the truth of religion] faithful. Das —e Volk, ein —es Gemüth, the faithful people, a faithful soul; der —e, ein —er, die —en, the believer, one faithful in religion, the faithful; Abraham, Vater der —en, Abraham, father of the faithful. 3) founded in faith, full of faith. Ein —es Gebet, a prayer full of faith, or trust in God.

Gläubiger, *m.* [-s, *pl.*-] creditor.

Gläubigerinn, *f.* female creditor, creditrix.

Glaublich, *adj.* and *adv.* to be believed or credited, credible. Das ist kaum —, that is hardly credible; es ist — [= wahrscheinlich], daß er kommen wird, it is probable that he will come, he is likely to come.

Glaublichkeit, *f.* credibility, probability, likelihood.

Glaubwürdig, *adj.* and *adv.* worthy of being believed, credible, authentic. —e Schriftsteller, credible or anthentic authors.

Glaubwürdigkeit, *f.* quality of being worthy of belief, credibility, authenticity.

Glauch, [allied to the Gr. γλαυκός, to glühen, Glanz &c.] *adj* ||1) bright, brilliant, smooth, polished. [in familiar language] Ein —es Gesicht, Mädchen, a pretty or smooth face, girl. 2) [in botany and mining = weißblau] bluish, greenish, sea-green. Ein —er [= tauber] Gang, a sterile vein or lode.

Glauchherd, *m.* 1) [in mining] a kind of hearth, made of boards well joined, to wash the ore upon. 2) a little airy to catch birds.

Glaukopf, *m.* [-es, *pl.* -köpfe] V. Kahlkopf.

Glede, [from laden = sammeln, to gather] *f.* [*pl.* -n] [in husbandry] a small bundle of corn [laid on the field before it is bound up into sheaves].

||**Gleich**, *n.* [-es, *pl.* -e] [in anatomy and botany] V. Gelenk.

Gleichbein, *n.* V. Gelenkbein.

Gleich, [formerly gelich, Low-Saxon liek, Eng. *like*, seems to be allied to legen, to lay, to put] 1 *adj.* and *adv.* [without any inequality or crookedness] even, level, straight. Ein —er Weg, a smooth or level way; ein —er Boden, a level or even ground; einen Weg or Spaziergang — machen, to level a road or walk; der Erde —, even or level with the ground; dem Wasser —, level with the surface of the water; — hobeln, to plane smooth, to smooth; dem Boden — machen [= abebenen], to make even or level, to level; *fig.* [= zerstören, schleifen] to lay even with the ground, to raze, to demolish; man hat die Stadt dem Erdboden — gemacht, the city has been razed to the ground; wieder — machen, to make straight again; in —er [= gerader] Linie, in a straight line; diese Straße läuft nicht —, this street is not straight; dieses Haus steht nicht —, this house stands or jets out of the row; dieser Baum ist ganz — gewachsen, this tree is quite straight; —er Faden, even, smooth thread; ein —es Rohr, ein —er Rohrstock, a cane without joints or knots; ein —er Stengel, a smooth or glabrous stalk. *Fig* *a*) [= recht, billig, seldom used] just, equitable. Ein —es Urtheil, a just or equitable judgment or decision. *b*) [of the same kind or nature] equal, like. Zu —er Zeit etwas thun [= zu einer und derselben Zeit], to do something at one and the same time; die Stadt Neapel ist die Hauptstadt des Königreichs —es Namens, Naples is the capital city of the kingdom of the same name; zwei Pflanzen —er Art, two plants of the same species or kind: sie sind von —em Alter, —en Alters, in —em Alter mit einander, they are of the same age; sie sind an Stand und Klugheit einander —, they are equal in rank and prudence; — tugendhaft oder lasterhaft seyn, to be equally virtuous or vicious; — weit auseinander liegen, to be at an equal distance from one another, to be equidistant; das ist — viel, das gilt mir —, that is the same, all one to me; ganz —e Fälle, perfectly similar cases; Personen von —en Verdiensten, persons of equal merit; ein Ei ist dem andern —, one egg is like another; er hat —e Absichten mit mir, he has the same intentions as I; —er Gestalt —er Weise, —er Maßen, in like manner, likewise; Einem —es mit —em vergelten, to render any one like for like, to be even with him; unter —en Umständen, Verhältnissen, similarly circumstanced; eine —e

Bewegung, an equal motion; ein Pferd, das einen —en Galopp geht, a horse that goes an even gallop; Einem — kommen, — seyn, to become, to be equal to, to equal any one: er kommt ihm weder an Tapferkeit noch an Tugend —, he is his equal neither in bravery nor virtue; das Gold steht mit dem Silbergelde —, in —em Werthe, gold and silver are at par [that is, no premium is given]; der Gewinn ist dem Verluste —, the gain is equivalent to the loss; eine Sache von —em Werthe, an equivalent; wenn Sie mir den —en Werth dafür geben, if you give me an equivalent for it; sich — bleiben, to be always the same, to continue the same; diese Uhr bleibt sich —, this watch has a uniform motion; die drei Winkel eines Dreieckes sind — zweien rechten, the three angles of a triangle are equal to two right angles; — weit von einander abstehende Linien, equidistant or parallel lines, parallels; Figuren von —em Umfange, isoperimetrical figures; in —e Theile theilen, to divide into equal parts or shares; die Lose bei einer Erbschaft — machen, —e Lose machen, to make the lots of a heritage equal, to make equal lots; auf —en Gewinn oder Verlust mit Einem handeln, to go halves with any one; es ist, es gilt mir Alles —, it is all the same or all one to me; *prov.* — und — gesellt sich gern, like loves like; birds of a feather flock together; er ist meines —en, he is my equal, he is upon a level with me; er ist mit ihm wie mit seines —en umgegangen, he treated him as if he was his equal; er hat seines —en nicht, seines —en finde ich nicht mehr, he has not his like, I shall not look upon his like again, he has not his equal or match; Sie können seines —en nicht finden, you cannot match him; er hält, behandelt alle —, he treats them all alike; er wird den größten Dichtern — geachtet, he ranks with the greatest poets, sich Einem — achten, to think one's self equal, not inferior to any one; Einem — kommen or seyn, to match a person, sich Einem — stellen, to put one's self upon an equality or on a par with any one; er will sich dem und dem — stellen, he pretends to be equal to such a one; er thut es den Alten —, he is equal to, he equals the ancients; Einem — [= eben so geschwind] laufen, Einem — [= eben so gut] schreiben, to run as well or as fast, to write as well, as any one; — auf spielen [at cards], to play even [without any odds]; — auf tauschen, to barter without giving any thing to boot. *c)* [= angemessen] proportionate, adequate. Die Strafe sollte dem Verbrechen — seyn, punishment should be proportionate to the crime. *d)* [= ähnlich] like, resembling. Die Tochter ist ihrer Mutter —, the daughter resembles her mother; **prov.* sie sehen einander —, wie zwei Tropfen Wasser, they are as like as two drops of water; das Bild sieht ihm sehr —, the portrait resembles him very much, is a very good likeness; das Leben ist — einer Bühne, worauf &c., life is like a stage, on which &c.; einem Waldstrome —, der &c., like a torrent, that &c.; diese Nachricht traf mich — einem Donnerschlage, I was thunder-struck at or by that news; — als ob, — als wenn, like as if, just as if, as if; — als wenn ich dazu verbunden wäre, as if I was obliged to do it.

II. *adv.* [without delay, or the intervention of time] immediately, directly, instantly, presently. — anfangs, from the first, directly at the beginning; — nachher reisten sie ab, they set out immediately after; das habe ich — gedacht, als ich es hörte, I thought so as soon as I heard it; ich sagte es ihm —, daß &c., I told him immediately, that &c.; er kam —, nachdem Sie fort waren, he came the instant you had gone; jetzt — will ich hingehen, I shall go thither forthwith, I shall directly or straight go thither; er war nicht — da, he was not there in the moment; er ist — jetzt [more usual eben jetzt] gekommen, he has just now come; es ging — Alles besser, als er angekommen war, immediately after his arrival every thing went on better; ich bin — wieder zurück, I shall return immediately; es wird — 3 Uhr schlagen, it will soon strike three o'clock, it is upon the stroke of three, V. Sogleich; [in familiar language — is frequently a mere expletive] in großen Städten ist doch — Alles anders, in large cities every thing is different; wie Sie nun — wieder zornig sind! how you have got so soon again into a rage!

III. *conj.* [in conjunction with wenn and ob, ob and wenn being sometimes omitted but understood] though, although. Wenn or ob er — arm ist, so ist er doch rechtschaffen, although he is poor, yet he is honest; wären Sie — mein Bruder! [even] though you were my brother! ist sie — nicht schön, so ist sie doch tugendhaft, if she is not handsome, she is at least virtuous; though she is not handsome, she is virtuous.

Gleich-abständig, —abstehend, *adj.* V. —entfernt. —alterig, *adj.* of the same age, coeval, contemporary. —armig, *adj.* having [two] equal arms. —artig, *adj.* and *adv.* of the same kind or nature, homogeneous. —artigkeit, *f.* homogeneousness. —bedeutend, *adj.* and *adv.* having the same sense or meaning, synonymous. Man findet selten zwei ganz —bedeutende Wörter, we rarely find two words precisely synonymous. —bein, *n.* V. Gleich and Gelenkbein. —breit, *adj.* of the same breadth. [in botany] Ein —breites Blatt, a linear leaf [which is of the same breadth throughout, except at the extremities]. —deutig, *adj.* and *adv.* V. —bedeutend. —deutigkeit, *f.* synonymy. —empfindend, *adj.* and *adv.* having common feeling, sympathetic. —empfindung, *f.* sympathy. —entfernt, *adj.* and *adv.* equally distant, equidistant. —ergestalt, —ermaßen, —erweise, *adv.* in like manner, likewise. —ewig, *adj.* and *adv.* coeternal. —falls, *adv.* likewise, also. V. Ebenfalls. —farbig, *adj.* and *adv.* of the same colour. —farbigkeit, *f.* identity or sameness of colour. —fließend, *adj.* V. —läufig. —förmig, *adj.* and *adv.* of the same form, uniform, conformable. Die Tracht der Asiaten ist —förmig, the dress of the Asiatics is uniform; eine —förmige Bewegung, Schreibart, Aufführung, a uniform motion, style, conduct; es ist dem Modell —förmig, it is conformable to the model; auf eine —förmige Art, uniformly, consistently; ein —förmig sanftes Gemüth, a uniformly mild temper; den Naturgesetzen —förmig leben, to live conformably or according to the laws of nature. Syn. Gleichförmig, Einförmig. Das Einförmige [sameness] is without variety; die Gleichförmigkeit [uniformity] gives to variety a pleasing accordance or consistency. Die Einförmigkeit tires by its continual and unvaried sameness; die Gleichförmigkeit, which consists in the conformity of all the parts, pleases. —förmigkeit, *f.* uniformity, conformity. Die —förmigkeit der Sprache, Gesinnungen &c., the uniformity of language, sentiments &c.; die —förmigkeit Ihres Gedankens mit dem meinigen, the conformity of your thought to mine. —gefühl, *n.* 1) [seldom used] conformity of sentiments. 2) sympathy. —geltend, *adj.* and *adv.* equal in value or worth, equivalent, equipollent. —geltende Ausdrücke, equivalent terms. —gesinnt, *adj.* and *adv.* 1) of the same mind, having the same sentiments as others. 2) not apt to be changeable in one's mind or opinions, consistent with one's self in respect to one's opinions. Er ist immer —gesinnt [= bleibt sich — in seinen Gesinnungen], he is ever of the same mind. —gestaltet, *adj.* having the same form or shape. —gestimmt, *adj.* tuned alike, as instruments; *fig.* congenial. —gestimmte Seelen, congenial souls, V. —gesinnt. *it.* V. Angemessen, Passend. —gewicht, *n.* equality of weight, equilibrium, equipoise, balance. Im —gewichte halten oder in's —gewicht setzen, to hold or place in equilibrium or equiponderance, to poise; das —gewicht verlieren, wiederherstellen, to lose, to reestablish the balance or equilibrium; diese Körper halten einander das —gewicht, these bodies counter-poise each other; die Lehre vom —gewichte, statics; [in seamen's lang.] das —gewicht eines Schiffes, eines Bootes, the trim or balancing of a ship, of a boat [equal disposition of the cargo of the ship, or the weight of persons or goods in a boat]; einer Galeere das rechte —gewicht geben, to trim a galley; *fig.* seinem Gegner das —gewicht halten, to cope with one's adversary; das —gewicht von Europa, the balance or balance of power of Europe; Europa im —gewichte halten, to balance Europe; das —gewicht der Gründe, the equipollency of reasons; seine guten Eigenschaften hielten seinen Fehlern das —gewicht, his good qualities counter-balanced his faults; [in painting] proportion. —gewichtslehre, *f.* statics. —gewichtspunkt, *m.* centre of gravity. —gewichtsstange, *f.* a rope-dancer's pole, a poy. —giltig, V. —gültig. —gradig, *adj.* having equal degrees. —gradige Seekarten, plane charts. —gültig, I. *adj.* 1) [= gleichgeltend] of equal value, equivalent, equipollent. [in grammar] —gültige [= bedeutende] Wörter, synonymous words; [in prosody] —gültige Silben, dubious syllables [that may be used long or short]; —gültige Handlungen, neutral or indifferent actions; mir ist es —gültig, ob &c., it is indifferent to me whether &c. 2) [feeling or exciting no interest, anxiety or care] indifferent. Wir redeten von sehr —gültigen [= unbedeutenden] Dingen, we talked of very indifferent or unimportant things; er ist mir sehr —gültig, he is very indifferent to me, I care very little about him; gegen Alles —gültig seyn, to be indifferent to, unconcerned for or about, every thing; er zeigt sich für or gegen ihre Reize —gültig, he seems not to be taken or smitten with her charms; er betrachtet Alles mit —gültigen Augen, he considers every thing with unconcerned or indifferent eyes. II. *adv.* 1) in an equal manner, equivalently. 2) indifferently, unconcernedly. Einen —gültig behandeln, aufnehmen, to treat, to receive any one coldly, indifferently. —gültigkeit, *f.* 1) equality of value. Die —gültigkeit zweier Sätze, the equipollency of two propositions. *it.* [= Unbedeutenheit, Unwichtigkeit] want of importance, insignificance, unimportance. Die —gültigkeit der Dinge an und für sich, the indifference of things in themselves. 2) [= Sorglosigkeit, Mangel an Empfindung] carelessness, unconcernedness, indifference. Seine —gültigkeit ist mir unerträglich, his indifference is unsupportable to me; man kann das Elend dieser Menschen nicht mit —gültigkeit ansehen, we cannot look upon the wretchedness of these people with indifference; nichts kann ihn aus seiner —gültigkeit [= Trägheit] bringen, nothing can rouse him from his indolence. 3) [seldom used] a thing of little or no importance, an unimportant, insignificant thing. —haltung, *f.* equal treatment of a thing or person, V. Gleich. —hoch, *adj.* of the same height; [in botany] fastigiate, fastigiated. —jährig, *adj.* and *adv.* of the same age; *it.* of the same rear. —klang, m. conformity of sound, consonance; [in music] unison. —klängig, adj. having the same sound, being in consonance. —kommend, adj. equal or equivalent to. Der dem Gewinn —kommende Verlust, the loss equivalent to the gain. —ländisch, adj. [a new word] of the same country, compatriot. —lang, adj. of the same length. —langzeitig, adj. of equal time, isochronal, isochronous. [in mechanics] —langzeitige Schwingungen, isochronal vibrations —laufen, v intr. [s. w. seyn] to be parallel. Eine —laufende Linie, parallel line. —läufig, adj. 1) having the same course. 2) parallel. 3) regular. —läufige [= regelmäßige] Zeitwörter, regular verbs. —läufigkeit, f. 1) quality of having the same course. 2) state of being parallel, parallelism. 3) regularity. —laut, m. accord of sound, homophony, consonance. Vollkommener —laut, perfect consonance; unvollkommener —laut, imperfect consonance, assonance; der —laut eines Wortes, das mehrere verschiedene Dinge bezeichnet, homonymy. —lautend, [—lautig] adj. and adv. according in sound; [in music] consonant; it. of the same tenour, of the same import. Zwei —lautende Berichte, two reports of the same tenour; die Abschrift ist mit dem Originale —lautend, the copy is conformable or correspondent with the original; —lautende Begriffe, homologous ideas. —linie, f. V. Gleicher 1). —machen, V. Gleich. —macher, m. he that makes level or even, leveller. Fig. [in the first French Revolution] leveller. —machung, f. the act of making level or even, levelling Die —machung eines Berges, the levelling of a mountain; die —machung der Lose, the equalization of the lots [of a heritage]. —maß, n. proportion, symmetry, V Ebenmaß; it. [sometimes = das Einerlei] uniformity. —mäßig, adj. and adv. 1) symmetrical, proportionate. 2) equal; it. likewise, V. Gleichfalls. —mäßigkeit, f. proportionality, V. —maß. —meßbar, adj. commensurable. —meßbarkeit, f. commensurability. —messer, m. V. Gleicher 1). —muth, m. evenness of temper or mind, equanimity. Ein großer Mann erträgt das Unglück mit —muth, a great man bears misfortunes with equanimity or calmness. —müthig, adj. and adv. equanimous. Etwas —müthig ertragen, to bear something with equanimity or calmly. —müthigkeit, f. V. —muth. —namig, adj and adv. having the same name. Ein —namiger Schriftsteller, an author of the same name; [in geometry] —namige Winkel, homologous angles; die —namigen Glieder eines Verhältnisses, the correspondent members of a proportion; [in grammar] ein —namiges Wort, a homonymous word. —namigkeit, f. identity of name; [in grammar] homonymy. —schalig, adj. [in conchology] having equal valves, equivalve. —schätzung, f. V. —haltung. —schenkelig, adj. and adv. having equal legs; [in geometry] equicrural, isosceles. Ein —schenkeliges Dreieck, an equicrural or isosceles triangle. —schwer, adj. and adv. 1) equally heavy. 2) equally difficult. —seitig, adj and adv. having equal sides, equilateral. Ein —seitiges Dreieck, an equilateral triangle. Fig. reciprocal, mutual. —seitige Freundschaft, mutual, reciprocal friendship —seitigkeit, f. equality, identity or uniformity of the sides. Fig. reciprocity, mutual return. —sinn, m. 1) synonymy [of two terms]. 2) conformity of sentiments, unanimity. 3) V. —muth. —sinnig, adj. and adv. 1) [in grammar] synonymous. 2) of one mind, unanimous. 3) V. —müthig. —stellung, f. equalization [of the shares of a succession &c.]. Die —stellung ihrer Verdienste, the comparison of their merits. —stimmig, adj. and adv. [in music] agreeing in sound, consonant, accordant. Die Tonwerkzeuge —stimmig machen, to accord or tune the instruments; diese beiden Stimmen sind nicht —stimmig, these two voices are not in unison; ein —stimmiges Concert, —stimmige Töne, a harmonious concert, harmonious sounds. Fig. congenial, unanimous. —stimmiger Beifall, unanimous applause. —stimmung, f. [in music] 1) the act of according or tuning. 2) harmony of sounds, unison, concord. Fig. concord, unanimity. Bei solcher —stimmung aller Gemüther, in such unanimity or unanimousness of all minds. —strich, m. a straight stroke or line. —theilend, adj. dividing equally. —theiler, m V Gleicher 1). —viel, adj. and adv. as much. —viel gelten, to be worth as much; es ist, gilt —viel, wer es thut, it is all one, it is no matter, never mind, who does it, V. Einerlei, —gültig, —geltend. —vielfach, adj. [in arithmetic and geometry, multiplied by the same number or quantity] equimultiple. —wage, f. V. Wasserwage. —weit, adj. and adv. equally distant, equidistant; it. parallel. Fig. Er ist —weit davon entfernt, Einem Unrecht zu thun, als &c., he is as far from doing any one wrong, as &c. —wie, conj. [= wie] as, just as, even as. Sie lieben sich —wie, or wie, Brüder, they love one another like brothers; —wie das Alter mehr Erfahrung hat, als die Jugend, so &c., as old age has more experience than youth, so &c. —winkelig, adj. having equal angles, equiangular; ein —winkeliges Dreieck, an equiangular triangle. —wirkend, adj. [in medicine] equally efficacious. —wirkende Kräfte, conspiring [cooperating] powers. —wohl, adv. and conj. nevertheless, notwithstanding, for all that, yet, however. —zeitig, adj. and adv. 1) existing or happening at the same time, contemporary, coeval. Ein —zeitiger Schriftsteller, eine —zeitige Begebenheit, a contemporary author, a contemporary event; —zeitige Geschichtschreiber, contemporary historians [who were living at the time, when any event took place]; —zeitige Schwingungen, synchronous, or isochronal vibrations; —zeitige Bewegung, simultaneous motion; die beiden Schüsse geschahen —zeitig, the two shots went off simultaneously; ein —zeitiger, a contemporary, a coeval, V. also Zeitgenoß. 2) [in prosody] dubious. —zeitige Silben, dubious syllables [that may be used long or short] —zeitigkeit, f. contemporary existence, simultaneousness, synchronism. V. —zeitig. —zeitler, [rather unusual] m. a contemporary. —zu, adv. V Geradezu.

1. Gleiche, f. 1) evenness, straightness, equality. Die — der Tage und Nächte [Tag- und Nacht—], equinox; einem Erdreich die — geben, to make a piece of ground even or level, to level it. 2) resemblance. V. Aehnlichkeit.

2 Gleiche, f. 1) [= Gelenk] joint. 2) [= Gicht] gout.

Gleichen, I. ir. v. intr. [= gleich oder ähnlich seyn] to be equal to, to equal; to be like, to resemble. Einem an Stärke —, to equal or to match any one in strength; * sie — sich wie zwei Tropfen Wasser, they are as like as two drops of water; der Weisheit mag Gold und Edelsteine nicht —, gold and precious stones are not to be compared or are not comparable to wisdom; ich möchte ihm nicht —, I should not like to resemble him, to be like him; die Kinder — gewöhnlich ihren Eltern in der Gesichtsbildung, children usually resemble their parents in features; die Mahlerei und Dichtkunst — sich sehr, painting and poetry bear a great resemblance to each other; er gleicht sich immer noch [hat sich nicht sehr verändert], he is still the same, is not changed; sie gleicht sich nicht mehr, she is not the same person, she is entirely changed; das gleicht ihm gar nicht [= sieht seiner Handlungsart nicht ähnlich], that is not at all like him. II. reg. v tr. 1) [= gleich machen] to make equal, to equal, to equalise. Der Tod gleicht alle Menschen, death equals all men; die Gewichte —, to adjust the weights to the standard, to square the weights by the standard; die Stücke in der Münze —, to size the blanks or planchets. V. Abgleichen, Ausgleichen, Eichen. 2) [= gerade, eben machen] to make even or level, to even, to level. Den Boden —, to level the ground; die Nadeln —, to straighten the needles; das Eisen —, to flat or flatten the iron Fig. Die Freude gleichte seiner Stirne Falten, joy smoothed or cleared his brow. 3) V. Vergleichen. Das —, V. Gleichung 1).

Gleicher, m [-s, pl. -] 1) [in astronomy and geography] the equator, the equinoctial, the equinoctial line, line. Wenn die Sonne im — steht, in den — tritt, so ist Tag und Nacht gleich, when the sun is in, enters the equator, the days and nights are of equal length. 2) [in forges] a workman that flattens and smooths the iron.

Gleichheit, f. 1) equality, parity. — des Maßes und Gewichtes, equality of weights and measures; die — der Personen und Stände, the equality of persons and conditions; die — der Rechte, equality of rights; Freiheit und —, liberty and equality; die — der Gemüther, der Gesinnungen, the conformity of temper, sentiments; die — der Gedanken, conformity of thoughts; es findet eine — der Gründe Statt, there is a parity of reasons; [in physics] die — der Schwere, des Druckes, equiponderance. 2) [= Aehnlichkeit] resemblance, likeness. Es ist wenig — zwischen diesem Bilde und dem Original, there is little resemblance between this picture and the original 3) [= Gleiche] straightness, evenness. Die — der Oberfläche, the evenness or equality of the surface; die — eines Baumes, the straightness of a tree.

Gleichheitszeichen, n. sign of equation (=).

Gleichniß, n. [-sses, pl. -sse] 1) image, likeness, V. [the more usual word] Ebenbild. 2) [= Vergleichung] comparison. a) simile, similitude, comparison. Jedes — hinkt, every comparison is lame; Homer ist reich an Gleichnissen, Homer is rich in similies. b) [= Gleichnißrede, Parabel] parable. Die Gleichnisse im Evangelium, the parables of the gospel; das — von den zehn Jungfrauen, the parable of the ten virgins.

Gleichnißrede, allegory, parable. —weise, adv. by way of parable or simile, parabolically, allegorically. —weise reden, to speak parabolically, to make use of parables. —wort, n. figurative expression, figure.

Gleichsam, conj. as it were, as if, like as if, almost. Das Licht ist — die Seele der Farben, light is, as it were, the soul of colours.

Gleichung, f. 1) the act of making level or equal, equalization. Die — der Abgaben, the equalization of the taxes. V Ausgleichung, Gleichmachung, Vergleichung. 2) [in algebra, a proposition asserting the equality of two quantities and expressed by the sign = between them] equation. Eine einfache —, eine — vom ersten Grad, a simple equation; eine quadratische —, eine — vom zweiten Grad, [in which the unknown quantity rises to the second degree or to two powers] a quadratic equation or an equation of the second degree; die Glieder einer —, the terms of an equation; die Wurzel einer —, the root of an equation [= the value of the unknown quantity]. 3) [in fortification, that mass of earth which serves as a parapet to the covered way, having an easy slope towards the field] glacis. 4) [in astronomy] Die — der Zeit, mean or equated time, equation [the reduction of the apparent time or motion of the sun to equable, mean or true time]. V. Sonnenzeit.

Gleichungslinie, *f.* the equinoctial line, the equator. V. Gleicher 1).

Gleis, *n.* [-es, *pl.* -e] [allied to the Gothic *laestjan*, Sax. *lithan* = gehen, to go, V. Gleiten] the track of a wheel, rut; *it.* [the space between the two wheels of a carriage] the riding-bed of a carriage. Das — halten, im —e bleiben, to follow the rut; die —e sind so tief, daß &c., the ruts are so deep that &c; aus dem —, zwischen zwei —en fahren, to drive between two ruts. *Fig.* *Im —e bleiben, to keep to, to follow the rule, not to go out of one's way, to lead a regular life; aus dem —e kommen, to go out of one's way, to be led astray; *er ist ganz aus dem —, he is quite out, quite disconcerted, out of countenance.

Gleisen, *v. intr.* to follow the rut or track.

Gleiße, *f.* [from gleißen] [in botany] 1) fool's parsley, hemlock. 2) V. Trespe.

Gleißen, *v. intr.* [= glänzen, V. Glanz] to shine, to glisten, to glitter. *Prov.* Es ist nicht Alles Gold, was gleißet, all is not gold that glistens; —d machen, to smooth, to sleek, to polish. *Fig.* to assume a false, a deceitful appearance, to play the hypocrite. —de Worte, deceitful, hypocritical words.

Gleißhammer, *m.* V. Glänzhammer. —wurm, *m.* V. Glühwurm.

Gleißling, *m* [-es, *pl.* -e] [in natural history = glänzende Wasserwanze] boat-fly, notonecta.

Gleißner, *m.* [-s, *pl.* -] dissembler, hypocrite, double-dealer, canter, canting person.

Gleißnerei, *f.* dissimulation, simulation, hypocrisy, false flattery; *it.* a hypocritical action.

Gleißnerinn, *f.* [*pl.* -en] a deceitful hypocritical woman.

Gleißnerisch, *adj.* and *adv.* dissembling, feigned, hypocritical. Er hat sie durch seinen —en Blick betrogen, he has deceived them by his hypocritical look; —e Reden, hypocritical speeches, cant.

Gleiten, [allied to leiten, to lead; Sax. *lithan* = gehen, to go; E. *to glide*] *ir. v. intr.* I. [u. w. seyn] 1) [to move smoothly and with apparent ease] to glide, to slide. Der Schlitten gleitet auf dem Eise dahin, the sledge glides or slides on the ice; ein Schiff gleitet durch das Wasser, a ship glides through the water; *fig.* gute Weine — gerne, good wines go down pleasantly. 2) [= ab—, aus—] to slip, to glide, to slide. Sein Pferd glitt auf dem Pflaster und stürzte, his horse slipt on the pavement and fell down; das Glas ist ihm aus den Händen geglitten, the glass has slipt from his hands. *Fig.* to fall into error or fault, to err. Ihr würdet wie er geglitten seyn, you would have slipped like him. II. [u. w. haben] [= schleifen, auf dem Eise] to slide. Die Kinder — gerne, children are fond of sliding; sie haben eine Stunde lang geglitten, they have slid for an hour.

Gleitbahn, *f.* a sliding-place, a slide [on the ice].

Gletscher, *m.* [-s, *pl.* -] [allied to glatt, smooth, Glas, glass &c.] [an immense mass of ice, formed in elevated vallies or on the sides of mountains] glacier, ice-mountain. Eine —reise machen, to take a journey to the glaciers.

Gletschersalz, *n.* [in chimistry] sulphate of magnesia.

Glette, V. Glätte 2).

Glied, [properly, Ge-lied, Low-Saxon and Dan. Lid; from leiten = bewegen, to move] *n.* [-es, *pl.* -er] [an extremity of the human body on account of its movableness] a limb, member. Die Arme, Hände, Finger &c. sind —er des menschlichen Körpers, the arms, hands, fingers &c are limbs or members of the human body; in allen —ern Schmerzen empfinden, to feel a pain in all one's limbs; *es liegt mir in allen —ern, I feel a certain uneasiness all over; er kann kein — rühren, he is deprived of the use of all his members; das männliche [= Zeugungs—] —, the yard, membrum virile; [in anatomy = Gelenk] joint, articulation; eines —es [= eines —es am Finger] lang, of the length of the joint of a finger. *Fig.* certain parts of a whole. *a*) Die —er einer Kette, the links of a chain. *b*) [in botany] [the space between two joints or knots] Die —er eines Halmes, the joints of a stalk. *c*) [in architecture, a subordinate part of building, as a frieze, cornice or sometimes a moulding] member. *d*) [in military affairs] rank or line [of soldiers]. Bleibt im —e, keep your ranks; aus dem —e treten, to quit one's ranks; die —er richten, stellen, to dress the ranks. *e*) [an individual of a community or society] member, fellow. Ein — der Familie, a member of the family; die —er der Kirche, the members of the church; er ist ein — des Rathes, he is a member of the council. V. Mitglied. *it.* [degree of relationship] generation. Gott suchet die Missethat der Väter heim an den Kindern bis ins dritte und vierte — [in Script.], God visits the sins of the fathers upon the children unto the third and fourth generation; mit Einem im vierten —e verwandt seyn, to be related to any one in the fourth remove or degree. *f*) Die —er eines Satzes, einer Periode, the members of a sentence, period; [in logic] die —er eines Schlusses, the terms of a syllogism; [in algebra] die —er einer Gleichung &c., the terms of an equation &c. Syn. Glied, Gliedmaß. Glieder are the limbs of animal bodies in as much as they are subordinate parts of the whole, and are capable of voluntary motion. Glieder are called Gliedmaßen in as much as they are the instruments of the soul, and subservient to its volition.

Gliedbad, *n.* a bath of a certain limb or member, a partial bath. —erband, *n.* [in anatomy] ligament. —erbau, *m.* the structure of the limbs, frame organization. *Fig.* Der —erbau einer Rede, the structure of a discourse. —erbuche, *f.* the jointed or knotty rush. —erbrand, *m.* V. Knochenbrand. —erdocke, *f.* V. —erpuppe. —erfuge, *f.* articulation. —ergeist, *m.* an antiarthritic water or liquor. —ergeschwulst, *f.* swelling of the limbs. —ergicht, *f.* V. —erkrankheit. —erhaken, *m.* [among ropemakers] a hook with several joints. —erhülse, *f.* [in botany] loment. —erkette, *f.* a chain with links [as opposed to one with rings]. —erknöchel, *pl.* [the three rows of small bones forming the fingers] phalanx. —erkoralle, *f.* jointed coral, isis. —erkrankheit, *f.* disease in the limbs or joints, articular disease, gout, arthritis, V. Gicht. —erkraut, *n.* V. —kraut. —erlahm, *adj.* and *adv.* paralytic, palsied. —erlähmung, *f.* paralysis, palsy. —erlos, V. —los. —ermann, *m.* [among painters, an image, used in contriving attitudes] layman. —erpuppe, *f.* a jointed puppet. —erreißen, *n.* violent pain in the joints or limbs, V. Gicht, —erkrankheit. —ersalbe, *f.* an antiarthritic unguent or salve. —erschmerz, *m.* pain in the joints or limbs, V. —erweh. —erschwamm, *m.* V. —schwamm. —erschwinden, *n.* growing lean, falling away, consumption. —erspannen, *n.* [in medicine] spasm, cramp, tension of the nerves or limbs. —erstärkend, *adj.* strengthening or bracing the limbs, tonic, nervine. —erwasser, *n.* V. —wasser. —erweh, *n.* pain or ache in the joints or limbs, articular disease, V. Gicht. —erwein, *m.* [wine poured over certain herbs &c. and used against the gout] antiarthritic wine. —erweise, *adv.* by joints or links; [in military affairs] by or in ranks. —erweise vorrücken, to advance in ranks. —erzucken, *n.* convulsive motion in the limbs. —erzuckung, *f.* convulsion. In —erzuckungen fallen, to fall into convulsions. —kraut, *n.* any antiarthritic herb or plant. *a*) iron-wort, Sideritis. *b*) betony. *c*) stachys, wound-wort. *d*) the white behen [a species of Cucubalus]. *e*) sweet-scented wood-roof or woodruff. —los, *adj.* and *adv.* without limbs or members. —maß, *n.* [seldom used in the singular] limb. Ein Mann von starken —maßen, a man of strong limbs, a strong-limbed man. Syn. V. Glied. —salbe, *f.* V. —ersalbe. —schwamm, *m.* [in surgery, a swelling or chronic enlargement of a joint, particularly of the knee] white swelling. —stein, *m.* [in natural history] priapolithus. —wasser, *n.* 1) [in anatomy = Gelenkwasser] synovia or synovy. Die zur Absonderung des —wassers dienenden Drüsen, the synovial glands. 2) [in surgery] ichorous humour, ichor. —wassersucht, *f.* a dropsy arising from too much synovia. —weich, *n.* [in botany] V. —kraut. —weise, *adv.* V. —erweise.

Gliederig, *adj.* furnished with joints or limbs, jointed, limbed, in composition, as: stark—, strong-limbed. V. Groß—, Grob— &c.

Gliedern, *v. tr.* to furnish with limbs or joints, to limb, to joint. Ein grob gegliederter Mensch, a large-limbed man; ein gegliederter [= organischer] Körper, an organic body; [in botany] gegliedert, jointed or knotty; *it.* [having a joint in the middle and being a little bent] geniculated; ein gegliederter Stengel, a geniculated stem or stalk; eine gegliederte Wurzel, a tuberous root. *Fig.* Ein wohl gegliederter Staatskörper, a well organized political body.

Gliederung, *f.* organization.

Gliedig, **Gliedrig**, V. Gliederig.

Gliedlich, [unusual] *adj.* relating to the member of a society.

Glime, *f.* [*pl.* -n] [in natural history] V. Engerling.

Glimmen, [allied to the Eng *to gloam*, to the Sw. *glimma* = glänzen, to shine, and to the Lat. *lumen*] *v. intr.* 1) to shine faintly, to glimmer. 2) to burn faintly. Das Feuer glimmet unter der Asche, the fire is hid, lurks under the ashes; und das —de Docht wird er nicht auslöschen [in Script.], and the smoking flax shall he not quench.

Glimmer, *m.* [-s] 1) a faint light, glimmer. 2) [in mineralogy, a mineral, consisting of thin flexible lamels or scales, having a shining surface] mica, glimmer, muscovy-glass.

Glimmererde, *f.* micaceous earth. —sand, *m.* micaceous sand. —schiefer, *m.* mica slate, micaceous shist.

Glimmerig, *adj.* and *adv.* 1) [glimmernd] shining faintly, glimmering. 2) [in mineralogy] containing glimmer, micaceous. —e Erde, —er Thon, micaceous earth, clay.

Glimmern, *v. intr.* to shine faintly, to glimmer. V. Flimmern.

Glimpf, [rather obsolete] [probably allied to linde, the L. *lenis* and *clemens*] *m.* [-es] forbearance, indulgence, mildness, softness, gentleness. Einen durch — gewinnen, to gain any one by fair means or gentleness; Einem etwas mit — verweisen, to reprove or reprimand any one gently.

Glimpflich, *adj.* and *adv.* forbearing, indulgent, mild, gentle. Ein —er Verweis, a gentle reproof. Syn. V. Gelind.

‖Glinstern, Glinzen, Glinzern, V. Glänzen.

Glinzerspath, V. Glänzspath.

Glitsche, *f.* [*pl.* -n] a sliding place, a slide. V. Gleitbahn.

Glitscheisen, *n.* [-s, *pl.* -] V. Ramme.

Glitschen, [from gleiten] *v. intr.* to slip, to slide, to glide. V. Gleiten.

Glitschig, *adj.* and *adv.* slippery. Es ist sehr — zu gehen, it is very slippery walking.

Glitzern, V. Glimmern.

Globosit, *m.* [-en, *pl.* -en] [in natural history] the petrified dolium or concha globosa.

Glöckchen, ‖Glöcklein, *n.* [-s, *pl.* -] [dimin. of Glocke] a small bell; [in botany] a bell-sh ped flower, a bell-flower. Wildes —, throat-wort, fox-glove. V. Halswurz, Akelei, Schnee—.

Glocke, [from the ancient klocken, allied to the Lat. *loqui*, Gr. λαλεῖν, Fr. *cloche*, in Picardy *cloque*] 1) [a vessel or hollow body, used for making sounds] bell. *a*) Die — [= Schelle] an or in einem Hause, the bell of or in a house; die — einer Uhr, the bell of a clock; chiefly: *b*) Die — in einer Kirche oder einem andern öffentlichen Gebäude, the bell of a church or any other public building; die —n [in einer Kirche] läuten, mit allen —n läuten, to ring the bells, to ring all the bells, to ring a peal; die —n anschlagen, to chime the be'ls; die —n läuten, schlagen an, the bells are ringing, are chiming. V. Bet—, Feuer—, Sturm—. *Fig.* [in fam. lang.] Etwas an die große — hängen, schlagen or schreiben [= etwas öffentlich bekannt machen], to make a thing public far and wide, to blaze it [abroad]; die große — läuten [= sich in einer Sache unmittelbar an den wenden, der am meisten dabei zu sagen hat], to make the person of the greatest weight speak in one's behalf; die — ist über ihn gegossen [= sein Verderben &c. ist beschlossen], his ruin is concerted or resolved upon. *c*) [= Schlaguhr] the clock which strikes. Die — hat acht geschlagen, the clock has struck eight; was ist die —? what o'clock is it? die — ist zehn Uhr, it is ten o'clock; die —n dieser Stadt gehen selten zusammen, the clocks of this town seldom agree. 2) *Fig.* any thing in form of a bell. Eine — von Glas oder Porzellan, a bell of glass or porcelain; —n auf die Melonen setzen, to put glassbells upon the melons, to cover them with glassbells; die — der Taucher [Taucher—], the diving-bell; die — der Luftpumpe, the bell of the air-pump; die — eines Hornes, einer Trompete &c., the bell of a horn, a trumpet &c.; die —n an Blumen, the bells or cups of flowers, V. Glöckchen and —nblume; [among sportsmen] a tunnel-net; [among laundresses/weatherwomen] a round [smoothing-] iron.

Glocken-apfel, *m.* a kind of apple with loose kernels. —balken, *m.* the beam that sustains a bell. —birn, *f.* bell-pear. —blume, *f.* 1) a bell-shaped flower. 2) [a genus of plants] bellflower, Campanula. —draht, *m.* the wire, by which a bell is moved, bell-wire. —förmig, *adj.* and *adv.* bell-fashioned, bell-shaped. —förmige Blumen, bell-fashioned flowers. —garn, *n.* [among sportsmen] tunnel-net. —gehäuse, *n.* V. —stube. —geläute, *n.* the ringing or chiming of bells. Er hielt unter —geläute seinen Einzug, he made his entrance, amidst a [merry] peal of bells. —getön, *n.* V. —klang. —gewicht, *n.* the weights of a clock. —gießer, *m.* bell-founder. —gut, *n.* V. —speise. —hammer, *m.* V. —klöppel; *it.* the hammer of a bell. —haus, *n.* [that part of a steeple or other building in which a bell is hung] belfry. —klang, *m.* the sound of a bell or of bells, the chiming of bells. —klöpfel, —klöppel, *m.* clapper or tongue of a bell, bell-clapper. —kolbe, *f.* V. —balken. —läuter, *m.* bell-ringer. —leiste, *f.* [in architecture] gorge or gola. —mantel, *m.* 1) [among bell-founders] coat of the bell 2) a cloak resembling a bell in shape. —maß, *n.* bell-founder's diapason [for the regulation of the size, weight &c. of bells]. —metall, *n.* V. —speise. —netz, *n.* V. —garn. —pfeffer, *m.* bell-pepper. —quast, *m.* —quästchen, *n. dim.* 1) tassel of a bell. 2) [in Sculpture] an ornament of hanging tassels in form of small bells. —rand, *m.* the edge or rim of a bell. —ring, *m.* the ring upon which the bell-clapper hangs. —saum, *m.* V. —rand. —schlag, *m.* 1) stroke of the clock. 2) the thickness of the edge of a bell, or of the rim. —schwamm, *m.* bell-mushroom. —schwengel, *m.* 1) lever to a bell. 2) V. —klöppel. —seil, *n.* rope by which a bell is rung, bell-rope. —speise, *f.* [a mixture of copper and tin] bell-metal. —spiel, *n.* chime. —spieler, *m.* chimer. —strang, *m.* V. —seil. —stube, *f.* V. —haus. —stuhl, *m.* the timber or frame which supports the bell, belfry. —tau, *n.* V. —seil. —taufe, *f.* the baptism or benediction of a bell. —thaler, *m.* a coin with the figure of a bell upon it. —thurm, *m.* steeple, belfry. —ton, *m.* V. —klang. —treter, *m.* [seldom used] V. —läuter. —weihe, *f.* the benediction or consecration of a bell. —welle, *f.* —zapfen, *m.* the ear or cannon of a bell. —zieher, *m.* V. —läuter. —zierath, *m.* V. —quast 2). —zug, *m.* 1) the ringing of a bell or of bells. 2) bell-rope. V. —seil; *it.* V. —quast 1). 3) V. —spiel.

Glöckeln, *v. intr.* [in familiar language] to ring little bells, to ring often and without necessity.

Glockenist, *m.* [-en, *pl.* -en] V. Glockenspieler.

Glöckner, *m.* [-s, *pl.* -] bell-ringer, sexton.

Glockrose, *f.* [*pl.* -n] V. Gartenpappel.

*Glorie, *f.* [*pl.* -n] 1) splendour, magnificence, glory. Er erschien in seiner ganzen —, he made his appearence in all his glory. 2) [in painting, the circle of rays surrounding the head of a figure] glory. Man mahlt die Heiligen gewöhnlich mit einer — um das Haupt, the saints are generally painted with a glory round their heads.

Glorreich, *adj.* and *adv.* glorious. Es ist eine —e That, sein Vaterland zu befreien, it is a glorious achievement to deliver one's country; — sterben, to die gloriously.

Glorwürdig, *adj.* and *adv.* worthy of glory, glorious. Kaiser Joseph, —en Andenkens, emperor Joseph of glorious memory. V. Glorreich.

*Glossarium, *n.* [-s, *pl.* Glossarien] glossary [a dictionary or vocabulary, explaining obscure or antiquated words].

Glosse, *f.* [*pl.* -n] interpretation, comment, explanation, gloss. Die — ist dunkler als der Text, the gloss or comment is more obscure than the text; Scott's —n zu der Bibel, Scott's comments on the Scriptures. V. Rand—. *Fig.* *Ueber Alles —n machen, to carp at, to find fault with, to censure every thing; *er macht über Alles —n, he is a censorious fellow.

Glossenmacher, *m.* [*Glossator] glosser, glossographer, commentator. *Fig.* a censorious person, a censurer, find-fault. Er ist ein beständiger, unerträglicher —macher, he is a perpetual, unsupportable find-fault or censor.

Glöte, Glöthe, V. Glätte 2).

†Glotze, *f.* [*pl.* -n] V. Glotzauge.

†Glotz-auge, *n.* a large staring eye, goggle-eye. —äugig, *adj.* having large staring eyes, goggle-eyed.

†Glotzen, [allied to the Gr. γλαύσσω, Ice. *gloggva*, Dan. glotte] *v. intr.* to look with large staring eyes, to stare, to goggle. V. Anglotzen.

†Glotzer, *m.* [-s, *pl.* -] he who stares at something, a starer.

Glu, V. Gluck.

‖Gluchzen, *v. intr.* V. Glucken and Schluchzen.

Gluck, *n.* 1) the voice of a hen when sitting on eggs for hatching or when calling her chickens. Die Henne macht —, —, the hen clucks. 2) [the sound of liquor when running out of a narrow-mouthed vessel] guggling or gurgling. *Er hört das —, — [Glu, Glu] der Flasche gern [= er trinkt gern], he loves the bottle.

Glück, *n.* [-es] [perhaps from Gelingen, to prosper, to succeed] 1) [a favourable or prosperous termination of any thing attempted] success. Er hat in Allem —, he succeeds in every thing, every thing he undertakes thrives with him; *weder — noch Stern haben, to be utterly unfortunate or unsuccessful; mit — krönen, to crown with success; Gott gebe — dazu, may God grant his blessing to it; jeder Vernünftige muß mir — zu diesem Versuche wünschen, every reasonable man cannot but wish me success in this attempt; Einem — zu seiner Reise wünschen, to wish any one a good journey; — zu! viel — auf den Weg! a good journey! I wish you a good journey! — auf! [a mode of salutation among miners] good speed! ich habe ihm zu seiner Heirath — gewünscht, I have given him joy upon his marriage; Ich wünsche Ihnen zu Ihrem Siege —, I congratulate you upon your victory; Einem zum neuen Jahre — wünschen, to wish any one a happy new year; ich wünsche mir — [= schätze mich glücklich], eine so gute Wahl getroffen zu haben, I congratulate myself upon having made so good a choice. 2) [a favourable chance] good luck, fortune. Es war ein —, daß Niemand im Hause war, it was lucky or fortunate that nobody was in the house; *er kann von — sagen, daß es ihm gelungen ist, it was a lucky hit for him to have succeeded; zum —e, zu allem —, kamen wir unverletzt durch, by good fortune, fortunately or luckily we escaped unhurt: zu unserm größten —e spricht er nicht gut Englisch, it is very providential for us, that he does not speak good English; es war mein —, es war ein — für mich, daß &c, it was lucky or fortunate for me, that &c.; er hat außerordentliches —, he is exceedingly lucky; es ist ihm ein großes — widerfahren, he has met with a very lucky accident; *prov.* wer das — hat, führt die Braut heim, fortune gains the bride, or luck is every thing; ich hatte das —, ihn zu sehen, I was fortunate enough to see him; I had the pleasure of seeing him; als ich das — hatte, Sie zu sprechen, when I had the honour or pleasure of speaking to you; mehr — als Verstand haben, to be more lucky than wise; er hat im Spiele kein —, he is not lucky in play; er hat im Spielen —, he plays with good luck, he is lucky in play; das hat mir — gebracht, that has brought me good luck; das — hat sich gewendet, my or his luck is gone; *es ist ein bloßes — [= ein bloßer Zufall), it is mere chance; Alles auf das — ankommen lassen, to commit every thing to chance or fortune; etwas auf gut — hin wagen, to put a thing to the venture, to take one's chance. *Fig.* chance deified, the goddess of fortune. Das — lacht or lächelt ihm, ist ihm günstig, Fortune smiles upon him, favours him, is propitious to him; das — hat ihm den Rücken gewendet, Fortune has turned her back upon him; dem — im Schoße sitzen, das Schoßkind des —es seyn, to be Fortune's favourite; das — ist blind, unbeständig, Fortune is blind, uncertain, or fickle; der Spielball des —es seyn, to be the sport of Fortune; sich dem —e anvertrauen, überlassen, to commit one's self to Fortune. 3) [an agreeable and advantageous situation] fortune, happiness. Sein — machen, to make one's fortune; seine Freundschaft war das — meines Lebens, machte das — meines Lebens aus, the happiness of my life consisted in his friendship; das — dieser Welt genießen, to enjoy the pleasures this world affords; sein — verscherzen, to trifle with one's fortune, to trifle away, to forfeit one's fortune; *prov.* Jeder ist seines [eigenen] —es Schmied, every man is the architect of his own fortune; *prov* je ärger der Schalk, je besser — [= je verwegener ein Schelm ist, desto mehr lacht ihm das —], the more knave, the better luck; hierein setzt er sein ganzes —, he puts all his happiness in that; eines vollkommenen —es genießen, to enjoy perfect happiness; im —e und Unglücke gleich groß seyn, to be equally great in prosperity and adversity.

Glücks-ball, *m.* sport of fortune. —baum, *m.* [in botany] the entire-leaved Clerodendron, Clerodendrum fortunatum [a native of India]. —bote, *m.* a messenger of good fortune. —botschaft, *f.* agreeable message or news. —bude, *f.* a shop, where goods are disposed of by lottery, lottery-shop. —budner, *m.* the man who keeps such a shop. —fall, *m.* a lucky chance or hit, a piece of good luck, a lucky incident. Es war ein bloßer —fall, daß &c., it was a mere chance, that &c. —göttinn, *f.* the goddess of fortune, Fortune. —gut, *n.* gift of fortune. —hafen, *m.* V —topf. —haube, *f.* [a little membrane sometimes encompassing the head of a child when born] caul. —jäger, *m.* V. —ritter. —kind, *n.* a child or favourite of Fortune, a lucky person. Er ist ein —kind, he is a lucky man or chap, he is the favourite of Fortune. —männchen, *n.* V. Galgenmännchen [Alraun]. —pilz, *m* *fig.* upstart. —rad, *n.* the wheel of Fortune. —ritter, *m.* an adventurer, knight-errant; *it.* a fortune-hunter, sharper, swindler. —ruthe, *f.* V. Wünschelruthe. —sohn, *m.* V. —kind. —spiel, *n.* game of hazard. —stand, *m.* 1) [= external circumstances] state of fortune or property, condition. Ich kenne seinen —stand, I am acquainted with his circumstances; er ist zu einem ansehnlichen —stande gelangt, he has acquired considerable property. 2) a happy state, state of happiness. —stern, *m.* lucky star. Er verdankt dieses seinem —sterne, und nicht seinem Verdienste, he owes that to his good fortune, not to his merit. —stoß, *m.* a lucky stroke [at billiards]. —stunde, *f.* favourable or propitious hour or moment. —topf, *m.* the vessel from which a lottery is drawn. Er hat eine Niete aus dem —topfe gezogen, he has drawn a blank. —umstände, *pl.* condition in regard to worldly estate, state of property, circumstances. Wenn man sich in angenehmen or behaglichen —umständen befindet, ist man ein Feind von Neuerungen, when men are easy in their circumstances, they are enemies to innovation. V. —stand 1) —wahn, *m.* imaginary or fancied happiness. —wechsel, *m.* change of fortune, vicissitude. Wir sind einem beständigen —wechsel ausgesetzt, we are exposed to continual vicissitudes of fortune. —wende, *f.* turn of fortune, catastrophe. —wurf, *m.* a lucky throw or hit. —zirkel, *m.* formerly, a kind of game of hazard. —zug, *m.* a lucky move [at chess and draughts]. Glücks-wunsch, *m.* wish for the welfare or happiness of any one; [in a more limited sense] congratulation. Einem seinen —wunsch abstatten, to congratulate any one, to wish any one joy. —wunschschreiben, *n.* V. —wünschungsschreiben. —wünschen, *n.* V. —wünschung. —wünscher, *m.* —wünscherinn, *f.* a person who offers congratulation, congratulator. —wünschung, *f.* V. —wunsch. —wünschungsschreiben, *n.* congratulatory letter.

Glucke, *f.* [*pl.* -n] V. Gluckhenne.

Glucken, [allied to the L. *glocire*, Gr. *γλώζω*] *v. intr.* to cluck. Die Henne glucket, the hen clucks; das —, clucking.

Gluckhenne, *f.* a hen that has chickens, a clucking-hen, V. Brüthenne; [in astronomy = Siebengestirn] Pleiads.

Glücken, [V. Glück] *v. intr.* and *imp.* [u. w. haben and seyn] to succeed, to prosper, to speed. Es glückt ihm Alles, was er unternimmt, he prospers in all his undertakings, every thing he undertakes thrives with him; endlich hat or ist es ihm geglückt, at last he succeeded, he was successful; dieser Plan glückte nicht, that design did not succeed, miscarried; es mag ihm — oder fehlschlagen, whether he succeed or fail; diese Schilderung ist ihm sehr geglückt, he has succeeded very well, he has been very successful or happy in that description. Syn. V. Gelingen.

Glücklich, I. *adj.* 1) [applied to things = günstig] successful, lucky, fortunate, prosperous, happy. Ein —es Zusammentreffen der Umstände, a fortunate concurrence of circumstances; ein —er Gedanke, ein —es Unternehmen, a happy thought, a successful enterprise; eine —e Zahl, a propitious number; ein —es Abenteuer, a lucky adventure; etwas zur —en Stunde thun, to seize the favourable moment; —er Weise, by good fortune, fortunately, luckily; ein —es Leben führen, to lead a happy life; Einem eine —e Reise wünschen, to wish any one a good journey; eine —e Wiederkunft, a safe return; ein —er Streich or Hieb [= der wenig Schaden thut], a lucky stroke; ich fand ihn in einer —en Stimmung für mich, I found him in a favourable or happy disposition for me; er hat ein —es Gedächtniß, he has a happy or excellent memory. 2) applied to persons: *a*) [meeting with good success] lucky, fortunate, successful. Er war in seinem Unternehmen —, he was successful in his enterprise; er ist im Spiele —, ist ein —er Spieler, he has good luck, he is lucky in gaming, he is a lucky gamester; der Tapfere ist gewöhnlich —, the brave man is usually fortunate; er ist der —e Mitbewerber, he is the fortunate competitor; werde ich so glücklich seyn, Sie bei mir zu sehen? shall I be so happy as to see you, shall I have the honour, the pleasure of seeing you at my lodging? *b*) [being in the enjoyment of lively sensation of pleasure] happy. — ist der, welcher &c, happy he, who or that &c.; sich — achten, schätzen, to esteem one's self happy; man ist nur in der Einbildung —, happiness consists in opinion; liebet Euch, und seyd —! love each other and be happy! II. *adv.* 1) luckily, fortunately, successfully, prosperously. Wir entrannen — der Gefahr, luckily we escaped the danger; — spielen, to play with good luck, to be lucky in gaming. 2) happily. Er lebt — mit seiner Gattinn, he lives happily with his consort.

Glückselig, or Glückselig, *adj.* and *adv.* being in a state of happiness or felicity, very happy, blessed, blissful. Ein —er Zustand, a happy condition; — ist, wer im Frieden leben kann, happy are those who can enjoy peace. V. Glücklich.

Glückseligkeit or Glückseligkeit, *f.* 1) great happiness felicity, blessedness, blissfulness. Sie setzen ihre — in die Tugend, they place felicity in virtue. 2) that which renders happy, bliss. Gesundheit und Zufriedenheit sind die größten —en auf Erden, health and content are the greatest blessings on earth.

‖Glucksen, 1) V. Glucken. 2) V. Schluchzen.

Glüh or Glüh, *adj.* [used but in compound words, V. Glühend] glowing, red-hot.

Glüh-balken, *pl.* iron bars to make the brass-plates red-hot upon. —farbe, *f.* fire colour, flame colour, glowing-red colour. —feuer, *n.* fire burning without flame, glowing fire; *it.* [in forges] V. —hitze. —hitze, *f.* [in forges] red or blood-red heat. —ofen, *m.* a furnace for making any thing red-hot. —pfanne, *f.* [in mints] an iron pan for making the silver red-hot. —rost, *m.* a grate on which any thing is made red-hot. —sand, *m.* a kind of sand-stone that does not calcine. —schachtel, *f.* [among goldbeaters] a box in which the goldleaves are made red-hot for the last time. —span, *m.* [in chimistry] V. Glühespan. —tasse, *f.* —täßchen, *n.* [in chimistry] a cupel in which gold is made red-hot. —wachs, *n.* gilders' wax [a mixture of wax, verdigrise, vitriol, red lead &c.]. —wein, *m.* mulled wine. —wind, *m.* burning wind, sirocco. —wurm, *m.* [Johanniswürmchen] a glow-worm.

Glühe, *f.* 1) state of being red-hot. 2) V. Glut. 2) [in forges] the wall sustaining the iron bars on which the brass plates are made red-hot.

Glühespan, *m.* [in chimistry] earthy magnetic iron stone, earthy oxydulated iron. V. Eisenmohr, Hammerschlag.

Glühen, [D. *gloeyen*, E. *to glow*, allied to the Ice. *glia*, Sw. *gloa* = funkeln, to sparkle, as also to glänzen and the Gr. *γλαύσσω*] I. *v. intr.* 1) to be red with heat, to glow, to be red-hot. —des Eisen, glowing or red-hot iron; eine —de Kohle, a live coal; *wie auf —den Kohlen stehen [= in einer unangenehmen Lage seyn], to be upon thorns; —de Kugeln, red-hot balls; *fig.* —de Kohlen auf das Haupt seines Feindes sammeln [= ihn durch Beweise von Wohlwollen &c. beschämen], to heap coals of fire on the head of one's enemy. 2) in general, to be very hot. Es ist hier eine —de Hitze, —d heiß, it is excessively hot here; die Sonne scheint heute —d heiß, the sun is scorching to-day; seine Hände sind —d heiß, his hands burn like fire; —der Wein, V. [the usual word] Glühwein. *Fig.* *a*) to exhibit a strong bright colour. —de Wangen, —de Farben, glowing cheeks, glowing colours; die Freude glühte [= strahlte] in ihren Augen, joy sparkled in her eyes, her eyes glistened with joy; seine Augen glühten vor Eifersucht, the fire of jealousy glared in his eyes, his eyes glowed with jealousy. *b*) to feel the heat of passion. Für Jemand —, to glow with love for any one; ein —der Eifer, a glowing, ardent zeal; —de Küsse, glowing, ardent kisses; vor Zorn, vor Rache —, to glow with anger, revenge; eine —de Einbildungskraft, an ardent, glowing imagination. II. *v. tr.* to make red-hot, as iron; *it.* = ausglühen, wärmen. Glas, Eisen —, to anneal glass, iron; geglühter Wein, V. Glühwein. *Fig.* [in poetry] Ihre schönen Augen glühten Unwillen, her beautiful eyes glowed with indignation.

Glümecke, *f.* [in botany] V. Bachbunge.

‖Glumm, [Engl. gloom, allied to Schlamm, ...hm, Lat. *limus*] *adj.* and *adv.* [applied to water] troubled, muddy. V. Trübe.

‖Glümmen or Glummen, *v. tr.* to make muddy, to muddle, as water. V. Trüben.

‖Glupen, [perhaps allied to the Gr. κλέπω, κλέπτω in the sense of doing something clandestinely] *v. intr.* [in familiar language] to look by stealth, to look with a sullen and malicious countenance. —d, V. Glupisch.

‖Glupisch, Glupsch, *adj.* and *adv.* sullen, morose, gloomy, close, saturnine, malicious.

Glut, Gluth, *f.* [*pl.* -en] a strong or violent fire or heat. Die — des Feuers or merely die —, the heat of the fire; in diesem Ofen ist eine entsetzliche —, there is a hellish fire or heat in this furnace; die — der Sonne ist unerträglich, the heat of the sun is insupportable. *it.* [= glühende Kohlen] glowing or live coals. Die — aus dem Ofen wegthun, to take the live coals out of the furnace *Fig.* vehemence of passion, ardour, glow. Die — der Andacht, the fervour of devotion; bald verlor sich seine — [= seine glühende Liebe], his ardent love, his flame soon cooled or abated.

Glut=asche, *f.* embers. —baum, *m.* [among foresters] a hollow tree, good for being reduced to coal. —deckel, *m.* cover for a fire, fire-plate. —kessel, *m.* V. —pfanne. —meer, *n.* a very large fire, a sea of fire. —messer, *m.* [an instrument for measuring the degrees of heat] pyrometer. —pfanne, *f.* a pan for holding coals, fire-pan, brasier, chafing-dish, V. Kohlpfanne. —schaufel, *f.* fire-shovel, V. Feuerschaufel. —stürze, *f.* V. —deckel. —tod, *m.* death by fire. —zange, *f.* fire-tongs, V. Feuerzange.

‖Gluten, *n.* [-s] [in natural history = Leimstoff] gluten.

Gnade, *f.* [*pl.* -n] [from nahen or neigen, therefore primarily = Geneigtheit] 1) favour, good-will, kindness, grace. Bei dem Könige in Gnaden or —n seyn, stehen, to be in the king's favour, to be in favour with the king; bei einer Dame in —n stehen, to be in the good graces of a lady; von Eines — leben, to live upon any one's charity; durch die — Gottes, durch Gottes —, by the grace of God; Wir, von Gottes —n, König von &c., We, by the grace of God, king of &c.; haben Sie die —, zu befehlen, daß &c., pray, be so kind as to command, that &c.; — vor Einem, vor Eines Augen finden [scriptural expression], to find favour in the sight or eyes of any one. 2) disposition to forgive, clemency, mercy. Zur — des Fürsten seine Zuflucht nehmen, to have recourse to the clemency or mercy of the prince; die — eines Richters anflehen, to implore the clemency of a judge; sich auf — oder Ungnade ergeben, to surrender at discretion. [in theology, the free unmerited love and favour of God, the spring and source of all the benefits men receive from him] grace. Ist's aber aus —, so ist's nicht aus Verdienst der Werke, sonst würde — nicht — seyn, and if by grace, then is it no more of works, otherwise grace is no more grace; Gott wird uns seine — angedeihen lassen, God will impart his grace to us; der — ermangeln, to want grace. 3) [any act of grace or goodwill] favour. Einem eine — erweisen, erzeigen, to grant, to do any one a favour; ich bitte Sie um diese —, ich bitte es mir zur — aus, I beg this as a favour of you; [incorrect and stiff] wann kann ich die — [= Ehre] haben, Ihnen aufzuwarten? at what time can I have the honour of waiting on you? haben Sie die —, mir zu sagen, pray, have the kindness to tell me; Einen mit —[n] überhäufen, to load any one with kindnesses or favours. 4) [remission of punishment] pardon. Einem Missethäter — angedeihen, widerfahren lassen, to pardon a malefactor; der Sieger ließ den Gefangenen — widerfahren, the conqueror gave quarter to the prisoners; er hat vom Könige — erhalten, the king has granted him his pardon, he has obtained the king's pardon; um — rufen, to cry out for mercy; *prov.* or * — für Recht ergehen lassen, to show mercy. 5) [a title used in addressing persons of noble rank] Eure —n, Ihre —n, your honour! your grace!

Gnaden=belohnung, *f.* V. —lohn. —beruf, *m.* [in theology] divine calling, vocation. —bezeigung, *f.* favour conferred upon an inferior. Einen mit —bezeigungen überhäufen, to load any one with favours. —bier, *n.* [formerly] beer of which no excise or duty is paid. —bild, *n.* [in the Catholic Church] a wonder-working image, miraculous image. —blick, *m.* a gracious or favourable look. —brief, *m.* charter, letters patent; [in military affairs] brevet. Er ist durch des Königs —brief zum Oberstlieutenant befördert worden, he has been promoted by the king's brevet to the rank of lieutenant-colonel. —brot, *n.* maintenance, derived from the favour and compassion of another. *Einem alten Diener das —brod geben, to maintain or support an old servant. —brunn, *m.* [chiefly in theology] spring, fountain of grace. —bund, *m.* [in theology] covenant of grace or mercy. —einfluß, *m.* —einwirkung, *f.* V. —wirkung. —ertheilung, *f.* V. —bezeigung, [in theology] the communication of the divine grace. —frist, *f.* reprieve, [in theology] time of grace [granted to mankind in this life for the attainment of divine favour]. †—futter, *n.* V. —brot. —gabe, *f.* any free gift or present, a gratuity; [in theology] gift of grace. —gehalt, *m.* pension. —geld, *n.* V. —gehalt. —geschenk, *n.* V. —gabe. —groschen, *m.* 1) [formerly] a medal, given by a superior to an inferior as a token of his favour. 2) [in mining] V. —steuer. —gut, *n.* 1) [in theology] a blessing, proceeding from divine grace. 2) —güter, *pl.* salt-pits granted out of favour. —hand, *f.* [in theology] the hand of God, the effect of divine grace. —heimsuchung, *f.* [in theology] perceptible manifestation of God; the effect of divine grace. —jagd, *f.* [formerly] permission granted by any one to hunt on his manor. —jahr, *n.* year of grace: *a*) during which any favour or indulgence, such as exemption from certain payments, is enjoyed, *b*) during which the widow of a clergyman or other functionary receives the salary of her husband. —kasten, *m.* [in the Roman Church] chest or trunk for the money obtained by the sale of indulgences. —kette, *f.* [formerly] a golden chain given by a prince in token of honour and favour. —kraft, *f.* [in theology] power of grace. —kraut, *n.* [in botany] hedge hyssop or water hyssop, gratiola. —lehen, *n.* a fief granted as a favour; *it.* a reversionary grant. —licht, *n.* [in theology] power of grace. —lohn, *m.* a reward obtained as a grace; [in theology] a gratuitous blessing or reward. —meister, *m.* [formerly, among tradesmen] a master received gratis. —mittel, *n.* [in theology] means of grace —ordnung, *f.* [in theology] divine ordinance of grace. —ort, *m.* [in the Catholic Church] any place where there is a miraculous image; place of pilgrimage. —pfennig, *m.* V. —groschen 1). —platz, *m.* V. —ort. —quell, *m.* V. —brunn; *fig.* [in theology] source of grace. —reich, I. *n.* [in theology] kingdom of grace. II. *adj.* and *adv.* gracious, merciful. —ruf, *m.* V. —beruf. —sache, *f.* a matter depending upon the will and pleasure of a sovereign. —schatz, *m.* V. —gut 1). —siegel, *n.* the seal, with which the paper or instrument, conferring a grant, is sealed, seal of concession. —sold, *m.* [rather unusual] pension. —söldner, *m.* [rather unusual] pensioner. —stand, *m.* [in theology] state of grace. —steuer, *f.* a charitable contribution; [in mining] subsidy towards poor miners. —stimme, *f.* [in theology] voice of grace. —stoß, *m.* the finishing blow given to persons executed, coup de grace. *Fig.* *Das hat ihm [vollends] den —stoß gegeben, that has completed his ruin. —stuhl, *m.* [among the Jews] the mercy-seat, propitiatory. —tafel, *f.* [obsolete] holy table, altar; *it.* communion. —tisch, *m.* V. —tafel; *it.* free boarding. —thron, *m.* throne of grace. —verheißung, *f.* [in theology] promise derived from divine mercy. —voll, *adj.* full of grace or mercy, merciful, gracious. —wahl, *f.* [in theology] election of grace, predestination. —wappen, *n.* coat of arms granted as a favour. —werk, *n.* [in theology] work of grace, such as redemption and sanctification. —wirkung, *f.* [in theology] effect of divine grace. —zeichen, *n.* a token of favour bestowed by a high person upon an inferior; mark of favour. —zeit, *f.* time of grace, V. —frist.

Gnaden, *v. intr.* [rarely used for gnädig seyn] to be favourable or propitious. *Gnad' uns Gott! God be propitious unto us! God have mercy upon us!

Gnädig, I. *adj.* 1) [= geneigt, wohlwollend] kind, favourable, benevolent, friendly, gracious, propitious. Er ist ein sehr —er Herr, he is a very kind or gracious master; das Schreiben des Königs war in den —sten Ausdrücken abgefaßt, the king's letter was couched in the most gracious terms; Gott sey uns —! God be propitious unto us! suche dir Gott — zu machen, try to make God propitious, to propitiate God; einen —en Blick auf Einen werfen, to cast a kind or gracious look upon any one. *it.* used as a title in addressing persons of noble rank: —er Herr! [in addressing a knight or baronet] Sir! [in addressing a nobleman] my Lord! —e Frau! [in addressing the lady of a knight or baronet] Madam! [in addressing the lady of a nobleman] my Lady! —ster Herr und Fürst! most gracious sovereign! 2) [inclined to, or indicating mercy and forgiveness] gracious, merciful, compassionate. Ein —er Richter, a merciful or clement judge; Gott ist — und barmherzig, God is gracious and merciful; sey — deinem Volke, o Herr! be merciful unto thy people, o Lord! Gott sey uns —! God have mercy upon us! ein —es Urtheil, eine —e Strafe, a mild sentence, a light, slight or mitigated punishment. *Fig.* [in familiar language = gelind] mild, gentle. Ein —er Regen [rather unusual, or used but in jest], a mild, gentle rain. II *adv.* 1) kindly, favourably, graciously, propitiously. Man empfing uns sehr —, we were received very graciously, we met with a very gracious reception. 2) mercifully, compassionately; *fig.* * [= gelinde] gently. Machen Sie es — mit mir, spare me a little, do not treat me too roughly; er ist noch — [= mit geringem Verluste] davon gekommen, he came off cheaply, tolerably well.

‡Gnädiglich, *adj.* and *adv.* V. Gnädig.

Gnarren, V. Knarren.

‖Gnatze, Gnätze, *f.* [probably from the Low-Saxon gniden = reiben, to rub] itch, mange, scab. V. Krätze.

‖Gnätzig, *adj.* and *adv.* V. Krätzig.

1. Gneiß, *n.* [-es] or Gneiße, *f.* V. Gleiße.

2. Gneiß, *m.* [-es] [from gniden = reiben, to rub] V. Krätze.

3. Gneiß, [Gneus] *m.* [-es, *pl.* -e] [allied to

Knäuel, Knauer) [in mineralogy] gneiss [a species of aggregated rock composed of quartz, feldspar and mica].

Gneißicht, *adj.* resembling gneiss.

Gneißig, *adj.* containing gneiss.

***Gnōm,** *m* [-en, *pl.* -en] [an imaginary being of the cabalists, and in popular superstition] gnome. V. Erdgeist.

***Gnōme,** *f.* [*pl* -n] a short, pithy and sententious observation, an apophthegm.

***Gnōminn,** *f* female gnome.

***Gnōmisch,** *adj.* sententious, gnomical.

***Gnōmon,** *m.* [-s] [in dialing and astronomy] gnomon V Sonnenuhrzeiger.

***Gnomōnik,** *f.* gnomonics. V. Sonnenuhrkunst.

***Gnóstiker,** *m.* [-s, *pl.* -] [in ecclesiastical history] Gnostic.

Gnū, *n.* [-es, *pl.* -e] gnu [a species of Antelope, whose form partakes of the horse, the ox and the deer].

Gnug, Gnūge, V. Genug, Genüge.

Gnúrren, V. Knurren.

Gnurrhahn, V. Knorrhahn.

‖**Góckelhahn,** *m.* [-es, *pl.* -hähne] cock. V. Hühnerhahn.

Gōdeleisen, *n.* [-s] 1) washed iron-ore. 2) forged and marked iron.

Gōding, Gōgraf, V. Gauding, Gaugraf.

‖**Gōgler,** *m* [-s, *pl.* -] V. Buchfink.

Gōhre, Gōhre, *f.* V. Gare 1) and 2. Gehre.

Gōhren, Gōhrung, V. Gehren, Gehrung.

Gōkelgut, *n.* [in mining] white vitriol [in the shape of icicles].

Gōlander, *m.* [-s, *pl.* -] V. Eisvogel.

Gōld, [probably allied to gelb, yellow; W. *gawl, galan, gole* = light, splendour; Gaelic *geal* = bright] *n.* [-es, (rarely) *pl.*-e, -er] 1) [in poetry] bright yellow colour. Das — ihrer Haare, her golden hair; das — der Aehren, the golden harvest. 2) [the well known precious metal] gold. Gediegenes or gewaschenes —, native gold; reines —, pure gold; 18karätiges —, gold of 18 carats; — in Stangen, gold in ingots; gearbeitetes —, wrought gold; gemahlenes —, water-gold, painter's gold; weißes — [Weiß—], platina; — schlagen [zu dünnen Blättchen], to beat or foliate gold; mit — überziehen, to overlay with gold, to gild; mit — einfassen, to set in gold; gezogenes —, gold-wire; geschlagenes —, beaten gold, goldleaf, leafgold; [in chimistry] salzsaures —, V. —kristall. *Prov.* V. Glänzen. 3) any thing made of gold. In diesem Pallaste glänzt Alles von — und Silber, in this palace every thing shines with gold and silver; auf — [= auf goldenem Geschirre] speisen, to eat from gold-plate. [in a more limited sense = Goldmünzen, goldcoins] Einen in — bezahlen, to pay any one in gold; ich muß — wechseln lassen, I must get one or more pieces of gold changed. *Fig.* = Geld, money. *Das ist nicht mit —e zu bezahlen, mit —e aufzuwägen [= ist unschätzbar], that is of infinite or inestimable value, is invaluable; *dieser Mensch ist nicht mit —e zu bezahlen, this man is worth his weight in gold; *prov.* eigener Herd ist —es werth, the smoke of a man's own house is better than the fire of another's; Morgenstunde hat — im Munde, early to bed and early to rise, makes a man healthy, wealthy and wise; *im —e [= im Reichthume] bis über die Ohren stecken [= sehr reich seyn], to have heaps of gold, to be well lined with gold, to roll in money; — [= Reichthum] ersetzt oft den Mangel des Verdienstes oder der Schönheit, riches often supply merit or beauty.

Goldader, *f.* 1) [in mining] vein or lode of gold. 2) [in medicine] hemorrhoidal vein. —**adergefäße,** *pl.* hemorrhoidal vessels. —**adler,** *m.* golden or royal eagle, V Königsadler. —**after,** *m.* V. Frühlingsfliege. —**ammer,** *f.* yellowhammer, V. Gelbling, Grünfink. —**amsel,** *f.* V. —drossel. —**anstrich,** *m.* 1) the act of laying on gold colour, gilding. 2) gold colour laid on. —**apfel,** *m.* 1) the golden pippin. 2) love-apple, tomato, V. Liebesapfel. —**arbeit,** *f.* 1) the working in gold. 2) any thing made of gold. —**arbeiter,** *m.* any worker in gold; [chiefly] goldsmith. —**auflösung,** *f.* 1) dissolution of gold. 2) tincture of gold, potable gold. —**auge,** *n.* 1) [a species of duck with yellow eyes] golden eye, V. Baumente. 2) [a fish] the gilthead, goldney. 3) [an insect] hemerobius. —**auszug,** *m.* [in mining and forges] the refinement of gold. —**bach,** *m.* a brook that carries gold. —**bad,** *n.* [in chimistry, the purifying of gold by antimony] the bath of gold. —**barre,** *f.* bar of gold, ingot of gold. —**barsch,** *m.* V. —börs. —**baum,** *m.* [in botany] the gold tree of Ethiopia. —**beblecht,** *adj.* covered or furnished with thin plates of gold. Ein —beblechter Lakei öffnete uns die Thüre, a servant all covered with gold opened the door to us. —**beblümt,** *adj.* embellished or embroidered with gold flowers. —**bedacht,** *adj.* furnished with a golden roof. —**bedeckt,** *adj.* covered with gold. —**begierde,** *f.* V. —gier —**belastet,** *adj.* loaded with gold. —**belaubt,** *adj.* furnished with golden leaves. —**berg,** *m.* 1) [in mining] a mountain with goldmines. 2) a heap of gold. —**bergamotte,** *f.* the golden bergamot [a pear]. —**bergwerk,** *n.* goldmine. —**berill,** *m.* chrysoberil. —**beutel,** *m.* purse full of gold. —**blatt,** *n.* [*dim.* —**blättchen,** ‖—**blättlein,** *n.*] goldleaf. —**blech,** *n.* thin plate of gold. —**blick,** *m.* [in metallurgy] the shine of gold. —**blume,** *f.* 1) a flower embroidered with gold. 2) a gold-coloured flower. 3) [in botany] V. Wucherblume, Ringelblume, Dotterblume. —**börs,** *m.* river-perch. —**börse,** *f.* V. —beutel. —**borste,** *f.* [in botany, a genus of plants] chrysitrix. —**borte,** *f.* goldlace. Ein mit —borten besetzter Rock, a goldlaced coat. —**brassen,** *m* gilthead, giltbream, [a fish] V. —fisch 2), —fohre. —**braun,** *adj.* of a chestnut colour, yellow dun. —**bruch,** *m.* V. —grube. —**buchstabe,** *m.* gilt letter. —**butte,** *f.* [a fish] plaice, V. Halbfisch, Plattfisch. —**distel,** *f.* golden thistle —**draht,** *m.* goldwire. —**drahtzieher,** *m.* goldwire drawer. —**drossel,** *f.* yellow thrush, hawfinch. —**durchwirkt,** *adj.* interweaved with gold threads. —**durst,** *m.* V. —gier. —**ecke,** *f.* 1) [a fish] surmullet. 2) [a plant] V. Ringelblume. —**eiche,** *f.* [in botany] conocarpodendron, the coniferous protea [of the Cape of Good Hope]. —**eidechse,** *f.* yellow lizard. —**erz,** *n.* gold ore. —**erzwurzel,** *f.* [a plant] ipecacuanha. —**fabrik,** *f.* a manufactory of vessels and ornaments of gold. —**faden,** *m.* gold thread. —**falb,** *adj.* and *adv.* pale gold-coloured, yellow-dun, gold-yellow. —**farbe,** *f.* gold colour. —**farben,** —**farbig,** *adj.* and *adv.* gold coloured, golden. —farbener Spießglanzschwefel, V. —schwefel. —**fasan,** *m.* goldpheasant [of China]. —**feilicht,** *n.* filings of gold, gold dust. —**finger,** *m.* the ring finger. —**fink,** *m.* goldfinch, bullfinch. —**firniß,** *m.* goldvarnish. —**fisch,** *m.* [*dim.* —**fischchen,** ‖—**fischlein,** *n*] 1) goldfish, golden fish. 2) gilthead, giltbream, goldney. 3) small river perch. —**fischer,** *m.* goldsearcher. —**fliege,** *f.* chrysomela [an insect]. —**flimmer,** *m.* small particle of gold, such as is found in the sand of rivers. —**flitter,** *m.* gold-spangle. —**fohre,** —**forelle,** *f.* 1) salmon trout. 2) V. —brassen. —**fuchs,** *m.* yellowdun horse, bright or light chestnut horse. [in familiar language] —**füchse,** *pl.* [= —stücke] goldcoins, yellow boys —**fuß,** *m.* sparrowhawk [of Hudson bay]. —**gang,** *m.* course of gold-ore in a mine, lode of gold. —**gehalt,** *m.* as much gold as is contained in any body or ore; [in mints] alloy. —**geier,** *m.* yellow vulture, V. Bartgeier, Lämmergeier. —**gelb,** *adj.* and *adv.* goldcoloured, golden. —**gelockt,** *adj.* [in poetry] with golden curls. —**geschiebe,** *n.* [in mining] gold-ore that has been removed from its place and transported to another by violence; *it.* bright grains of gold found in such ore, native gold. —**geschirr,** *n.* 1) collectively, goldplate. 2) a goldvessel. —**gewicht,** *n.* gold weight, troy weight. —**gewinn,** *m.* [in mining] the produce of a mine in gold. —**gewirkt,** *adj.* interwoven with gold threads. —**gewölk,** *n.* goldcoloured or golden clouds. —**gier,** *f.* inordinate desire of gold, greediness after, thirst for gold. —**glanz,** *m.* the splendour or lustre of gold. —**glätte,** *f.* yellow litharge chrysitis. —**gleich,** *adj.* resembling gold. —gleiches Metall, similor, pinchbeck. —**glimmer,** *m.* yellow mica. —**götze,** *m.* great wealth or riches, mammon. —**granat,** *m.* [in mineralogy] gold garnet. —**gras,** *n.* [in botany] anthoxanthum. —**gräupchen,** *n.* V. —korn. —**gries,** *m.* gold in little grains mixed with sand, V. —kies. —**grube,** *f.* goldmine, V. —bergwerk. *Fig.* Peru, diese unerschöpfliche —grube, Peru, that inexhaustible source of riches, or whose goldmines are inexhaustible; *das ist eine —grube für ihn, that is a source of riches, another Peru for him. —**grün,** *adj.* and *adv.* green with a tinge of goldcolour. —**grund,** *m.* 1) [among gilders and painters] goldsize. [among gilders] Den —grund auftragen, to wash over with egg; [in manufactures] goldground; Sammet mit einem —grunde, velvet with a goldground. 2) a valley, whose brooks carry gold; *it.* the ground or bottom of a brook or river that carries gold. —**gulden** or ‡—**gülden,** *m.* a goldflorin [formerly, a goldcoin worth about eight shillings]. —**haar,** *n.* 1) goldcoloured or golden hair. 2) [in botany] *a*) maidenhair, adiantum. *b*) [a genus of plants] goldylocks, chrysocoma. *c*) V. Goldenhaar. —**haarig,** *adj.* and *adv.* having hair of a light yellowish colour, having golden hair. —**haber,** *m.* yellow oats. —**hähnchen,** —**hähnlein,** *n.* 1) golden crested wren. 2) chrysomela, V. —fliege. 3) [in botany] the yellow windflower or anemone. —**haltig,** *adj.* containing gold, auriferous. —haltiger Sand, auriferous sand. —**handel,** *m.* goldtrade. —**harnisch,** *m.* 1) gold or gilt harness or armour. 2) [an insect] burncow, buprestis. —**haufen,** *m.* a heap of gold. —**käfer,** *m.* a beetle with goldcoloured or shining wings, rosechafer. —**kalk,** *m.* [in chimistry] 1) calcined gold, calx or oxyd of gold. 2) painter's gold, water gold. —**karausche,** *f.* crucian [a fish]. —**karpfen,** *m.* V. —fisch 2). —**kehlchen,** *n.* —**kehle,** *f.* a small bird with a yellow neck. —**kies,** *m.* gravel containing gold, auriferous gravel. —**kind,** *n.* [term of endearment] dear child, jewel, darling. —**kissen,** *n.* [in gilding] cushion. —**klumpen,** *m.* lump of gold. —**könig,** *m.* [in chimistry] regulus of antimony impregnated or imbibed with gold. —**kopf,** *m.* yellow headed grossbeak. —**korn,** —**körnchen,** —**körnlein,** *n.* small grain of gold. —**krähe,** *f.* V. Blaukrähe. —**krätze,** *f.* goldsmith's wash, washings. —**kraut,** *n.* [a plant of the genus senecio] groundsel. —**kristall,** *m.*

muriate of gold. —krone, *f.* 1) a crown of gold, goldcrown, golden diadem. 2) a goldcoin stamped with the figure of a crown. —kupfer, *n.* similor pinchbeck. —küste, *f.* [in geography, the coast of Africa where gold is found, being a part of the coast of Guinea] Gold Coast. —lachs, *m.* goldcoloured salmon. —lack, *m.* 1) goldcoloured varnish. 2) a kind of sealing-wax mixed with gold spangles. 3) wallflower. —lahn, *m.* flattened gold wire. —lahnschläger, *m.* a flatter of goldwire. —land, *n.* a country where a great deal of gold is found, gold country; *fig.* an excellent, very fertile or rich country, Utopia. —lasur, *m.* lazulite with goldcoloured spots. —lauter, *adj. fig.* as pure as gold. —leder, *n.* gilt leather. —lehm, —letten, *m.* clay containing gold, auriferous clay. —leim, *m.* chrysocalla, mountaingreen, borax, V. Berggrün. —leiste, *f.* a) a gold or gilt cornice. 2) azure beetle. —lilie, *f.* the yellow lily, yellow day-lily. —locke, *f.* a golden lock or curl. —lockig, *adj.* having golden locks or curls. —lutte, *f.* a trough or hearth for washing the pounded goldore. —macher, *m.* [one who tries to transmute metals into gold] alchymist. —macherei, —macherkunst, *f.* alchymy. —mädchen, ||—mädel, *n.* 1) [a term of endearment] dear girl, dear daughter. 2) [in fam. lang.] a very handsome girl, *very pretty lass; *it.* a very clever girl —mann, *m.*, *dim.* —männchen, ||—männlein, *n.* 1) [in German popular superstition] a sort of gnome or spirit who, at his master's or possessor's command, yields gold or wealth as often and as much as the latter chooses to have. 2) [a fam. word of endearment] dear, my dear fellow! Nein, mein —mann, —männchen, no, my dear, my love. —marder, *m.* [a reddish yellow marten of Canada] pekan. —markasit, *m.* zinc. —masse, *f.* mass of gold. —maulwurf, *m.* goldcoloured mole [without a tail]. —maus, *f.* sea-mouse, aphrodite. —merle, *f.* V. —drossel. —milz, *f.* golden saxifrage [a plant, Chrysosplenium]. —mine, *f.* goldmine. —mund, *m.* [in conchology] a shell with a gold coloured aperture or mouth. *Fig.* [a person with great oratorical power or persuasive, mellow speech or words; also as a name] Chrysostomus. —münze, *f.* a goldcoin; *it.* a gold medal. —niederschlag, *m.* [in chimistry] precipitate of gold. —pappe, *f.* —papier, *n.* gilt pasteboard, gilt paper. —platte, *f.*, —plättchen, *n.* a thin plate of gold, goldspangle. —plätten, *n.* the act of flattening goldwire. —plätter, *m.* a flatter of goldwire. —pras or —praser, *m.* [in mineralogy, a kind of green stone mixed with a bright goldcolour] Chrysoprasus, Chrysopteron. —probe, *f.* 1) [among goldsmiths] trial or test of gold, goldtest 2) [in mining, experiment for ascertaining the quantity of gold in an ore or mineral] assay. —pulver, *n.* powdered gold; [in alchymy] powder of projection. —punkt, *m.* 1) a gold or goldcoloured point or spot. 2) [in natural history] a beetle with goldcoloured spots, the burncow or buprestis with goldcoloured spots. —puppe, *f.* 1) [*dim.* —püppchen, ||—püpplein, *n*] [a term of endearment] V. —kind. 2) [in natural history] the yellow nymph, chrysalis or aurelia [of an insect]. —purpur, *m.* [in chimistry, a beautiful precipitate formed by immersing tin into a solution of gold] powder of Cassius. —quarz, *m.* quartz containing gold, auriferous quartz. —quast, *m.* —quaste, *f.* a gold tassel or tuft. —rabe, *m.* the largest species of raven with a shining plumage —regen, *m.* 1) [in pyrotechnics] goldcoloured firerain. 2) *Fig.* a liberal distribution of gold or pieces of gold, a shower of pieces of gold. —reich, *adj.* rich in gold. Ein —reicher Zeug, a rich stuff; —reiches Erz, rich ore. —reif, *m.* gold hoop or ring. —reiher, *m.* goldcoloured heron. —renette, *f.* golding. —ring, *m.* gold ring. —rose, *f* [*dim.* —röschen, ||—röslein, *n.*] little sunflower, helianthemum, V. Kirschenisop, Heidenisop. —ruthe, *f.* [in botany] golden-rod. —ruthenbaum, *m.* [a plant, the Bosea] goldenrod-tree. —safran, *m.* V. Knallgold. —salpeter, *m.* [in chimistry] nitrate of gold. —salz, *n.* [in chimistry] muriate of gold. —sammler, *m.* goldsearcher. —sand, *m.* goldsand. —schale, *f.* —schälchen, *n.* a gold cup, a small gold cup; [in chimistry] cupel. —schatz, *m.* a treasure in gold. —schaum, *m.* foliated or beaten gold, gold-leaf; *it.* tinsel. —scheiden, *v. tr.* to refine gold by separation. —scheider, *m.* goldfiner, goldrefiner. —scheidewasser, *n.* nitro-muriatic acid, aqua regalis or regia. —scheidung, *f.* parting [of gold] —schlacken, *pl.* slags of gold. —schlag, *m.* V. —blatt. —schlagader, *f.* hemorrhoidal artery. —schläger, *m.* 1) goldbeater. 2) a large hammer used in beating gold. —schlägerform, —schlägerhaut, *f.* goldbeater's skin. —schlagloth, *n.* soder used by gold and silversmiths. —schleie, *f.* goldcoloured tench [a fish]. —schlich, *m* [in mining] schlich or slich of gold [the goldore when pounded and prepared for working] —schmelzer, *m.* a melter or refiner of gold. —schmied, *m.* 1) goldsmith. 2) [in natural history] a) a black beetle with goldcoloured spots. *b*) V. —fliege. —schmiedsarbeit, *f.* goldsmith's-ware. —schmiedsgesell, *m.* journeyman goldsmith. —schmiedsinnung, *f.* goldsmiths-company. —schmiedskrätze, *f.* goldsmith's wash —schmiedskreide, *f.* chalk with which goldsmiths furbish the gold. —schmiedsladen, *m.* goldsmith's shop. —schmiedswaare, *f.* V. —schmiedsarbeit. —schmiedszeichen, *n.* punch or mark used by goldsmiths. —schrötling, *m.* [in mints] planchet of gold. —schwanz, *m.* mackerel with a yellow tail. —schwefel, *m.* [in chimistry] a combination of antimony, sulphur, and oxygen. —schwefelkies, *m.* [in mining] martial or iron pyrites mixed with gold. —seife, *f.* a place where pounded goldore is whashed. —sinter, *m.* [in mineralogy] sinter containing gold. —sohn, *m.* —söhnchen, *n.* [a term of endearment] dear boy, darling, honey, minion. —spinner, *m.* a spinner of goldthread. —stange, *f.* bar or ingot of gold. —staub, *m.* golddust. —stein, *m.* 1) a stone containing gold. 2) V. —streichstein. 3) chrysolite. 4) V. —striemer. —sternblümchen, *n.* lesser celandine. —sticker, *m.* —stickerinn, *f.* embroiderer in gold. —stickerei, *f.* embroidery in gold. —stickerkunst, *f.* the art of embroidering in gold. —stoff, *m.* goldbrocade. —streichstein, *m.* touchstone, V. Probirstein. —streifen, *m.* a stripe of gold. —streifig, *adj.* having goldstripes. —strich, *m.* [a kind of seabream] scalpe. —striemer, *m.* a purple fish with yellow streaks. —stück, *n.* 1) [little used] a piece of unwrought gold. 2) a goldcoin, V. —münze; *it.* goldmedal. 3) [in fam. lang.] V. —stoff. —stufe, *f.* a piece of goldore. —sucher, *m.* V. —sammler. —talk, *m.* [in mining] yellow talc. —teig, *m.* painter's gold, water gold. —teppich, *m.* a carpet worked with gold. —tinktur, *f.* tincture of gold, potable gold. —tinte, *f.* goldcoloured ink. —tochter, *f.* —töchterchen, *n.* [a term of endearment] dear child, dear daughter, dear girl, darling, minion, honey. —tresse, *f.* gold lace. —troddel, *f.* V. —quaste. —tropfen, *m.* a drop of melted gold. —vitriol, *m.* [in chimistry] sulphate of gold. —waare, *f.* goldsmith's ware. —wage, *f.* scales for weighing gold. *Fig.* *Seine Worte auf der —wage abwägen, to weigh one's words well —wäsche, *f.* 1) the act of washing gold, the washing of gold. 2) a place where gold is washed. —wäscher, *m.* gatherer of gold-sand, goldsearcher, goldwasher. —wasser, *n.* [a kind of brandy] goldwater, goldcordial. Danziger —wasser, Dantzic brandy. —weide, *f.* yellow willow. —wein, *m.* 1) goldcoloured wine. 2) *Fig.* [in fam. lang.] excellent wine Das ist ein —wein! that is an exquisite, a choice drop of wine! —weinstein, *m.* tartrite of gold. —werk, *n.* gilt foliage, gilding. —wespe, *f.* golden fly, yellow wasp, chrysis. —wirker, *m.* goldweaver. —wirkerei, *f.* the art of weaving gold. —wolf, *m.* 1) the common wolf. 2) the jackal. —wurm, *m.* burn-cow, buprestis; *it.* V. —maus. —wurz, —wurzel, *f.* 1) the greater celandine. 2) the mountain lily, turk's cap, martagon. —zahn, *m.* 1) [in mining] a small bar of native gold. 2) [in conchology] chrysodon. —zain, *m.* an ingot of gold. —zieher, *m.* golddrawer, V. —drahtzieher. —zopf, *m.* [in botany] V. —haar *b*).

Golden, *adj.* and *adv.* 1) [in poetry] of a bright yellow colour, shining, golden. —es Haar, —e Locken, golden hair, golden locks or curls; die —e Sonne, the golden sun; die —e Frucht, the golden fruit. 2) made or consisting of gold, golden, gold. Eine —e Kette, ein —er Ring, eine —e Uhr, a gold chain, gold ring, gold watch; ein Buch mit —em Schnitte, a book with gilt edges; ein Stock mit —em Knopf, a goldheaded cane; das —e Vließ, the golden fleece; *prov.* dem fliehenden Feinde eine —e Brücke bauen, to give a golden bridge to a flying enemy. *Fig. a*) [in fam. lang.] fine, fair, splendid. Einem —e Worte geben, to speak any one fair; —e Berge versprechen, —e Versprechungen machen, to promise whole mountains of gold. *b*) most valuable, excellent, golden. Die —e Zeit, das —e Zeitalter, the golden age; —e [= sehr glückliche] Tage, golden days; mein —es, goldiges [= liebes] Kind, V. Goldkind, Goldsohn &c.; er ist noch — gegen Jenen [rather vulgar], he is incomparably better than the other, there is no comparison between them; Georg, der —e Junge, George, the charming, excellent lad; eine —e Regel, a golden rule; die —e Zahl, [in chronology, a number showing the year of the moon's cycle] golden number; die —e Regel, [in arithmetic] the golden rule, the rule of three, or rule of proportion; die —e Ader, hemorrhoids, piles; die blinde —e Ader, the blind piles; die fließende —e Ader, the bleeding or open piles.

Goldig, *adj.* and *adv.* V. Golden.

*1. **Golf**, *m.* [-es, *pl.* -e] gulf. Der — von Venedig, the gulf of Venice; der — von Mexiko, the gulf of Mexico, V. Meerbusen.

*2. **Golf**, *m.* [-es] [Dutch *kolf*, a club or bat; Dan. *kolv*, the but-end of a gun-stock] golf [a game with ball and bat, in which he who drives the ball into a hole with the fewest strokes is the winner].

Golgas, [Galgas] *m.* printed flannel.

Golkrabe, *m.* V. Goldrabe.

||**Goll**, *m.* [-es, *pl.* -e] V. Blutfink.

Golle, *f.* [*pl.* -n] 1) a pool, puddle. 2) V. Jölle.

||**Göller**, *m.* [-s, *pl.* -] V. Grünspecht.

Golsch, [Kölsch] *m.* [-es, *pl.* -e] a kind of fustian with blue streaks.

Golse, *f.* [*pl.* -en] [a small insect] a gnat.

Golsen, Golzen, *v.tr.* to geld, V. Gelzen.

***Gondel**, *f.* [*pl.* -n] [a flat-bottomed boat used chiefly at Venice] gondola.

Gondel-artig, *adj.* in the manner of a gondola. —**fahrer**, —**führer**, —**schiffer**, *m.* gondolier.

***Gondelier, Gondolier**, *m.* [-s, *pl.* -e] gondolier.

***Gong**, *n.* [-es] gong [an instrument made of brass, of a circular form, which the Asiatics strike with a wooden mallet].

***Goniometer**, *n.* [-s, *pl.* -] [Winkelmesser] goniometer [an instrument for measuring solid angles or the inclination of planes].

***Goniometrie**, *f.* [art of measuring solid angles] goniometry.

‡ or || **Gönnegeld**, *n.* V. Angeld, Handgeld.

Gönnen, *v. tr.* [Sax. *unnan*, Sw. *unna*] 1) Einem etwas —, to be pleased with any thing happening to another, not to envy, not to grudge; ich gönne ihm sein Glück, I am rejoiced at, I am glad of his good fortune or happiness; Jedermann gönnt ihm seine Beförderung, everybody is pleased with, rejoices at, is glad of his preferment; ich gönne es ihm, I am glad for him, he has well deserved it; Einem alles Gute —, to wish any one well, to wish any one all happiness; er gönnet mir nicht das geringste Vergnügen, he grudges me every pleasure; er gönnet seinen Kindern das Brot nicht, he grudges his children the bread they eat; Jedermann gönnet ihm diese Demüthigung, every body rejoices at, is glad of his humiliation. 2) [= erlauben, vergönnen] to grant, to permit. — Sie mir einige Ruhe, grant me some repose, permit or allow me to take some repose. *it.* [mittheilen, widerfahren lassen] to give, to impart. — Sie mir die Ehre Ihres Besuches, do me the honour to come and see me; — Sie mir ferner das Glück Ihrer Freundschaft, let me have the honour to continue in your friendship.

Gönner, *m.* [-s, *pl.* -] any one who wishes the good of another, wellwisher, patron, protector. Er hat mächtige — bei Hofe, he has powerful patrons or protectors at court; dieser Fürst ist der — der Künste und Wissenschaften, this prince is the patron of the arts and sciences.

Gönnerinn, *f.* patroness, protectress.

Gönnerschaft, *f.* 1) the relation of a patron to his dependants, patronship. 2) the patrons or protectors. Er hat eine große —, he has many patrons. 3) [in familiar language] a single patron or patroness.

***Gonyometer**, *n.* V. Goniometer.

***Gonyometrie**, *f.* V. Goniometrie.

Göpel, *m.* [-s, *pl.* -] [probably from heben, to lift, therefore = Hebel, lever] [in mining] 1) a machine or gin for raising coals, water, ore &c. out of a mine, or for letting things down into a pit or mine; *it.* [in a more limited sense] a hydraulic engine moved by horses. 2) a shed built over such a machine or engine.

Göpel-herd, *m.* [in mining] round path or area in which the horse walks that sets such a machine or gin in motion. —**hund**, *m.* a long piece of wood with iron spikes or an iron chain, used as a check in such a machine. —**kette**, *f.* chain of such a gin or engine. —**knecht**, *m.* a pointed piece of iron for stopping such an engine or machine at pleasure. —**korb**, *m.* trundle or lantern of such a gin or engine. —**kreuz**, *n.* wooden cross on which the timber of such a gin rests. —**pferd**, *n.* a horse that sets and keeps such an engine in motion. —**platz**, *m.* V. —herd. —**seil**, *n.* V. —kette. —**spille**, —**spindel**, *f.* axletree of such a gin. —**steg**, *m.* V. —kreuz. —**treiber**, *m.* he that sets the engine a-going; *it.* he that drives the horses of such an engine.

Gördisch, *adj.* Gordian. Der —e Knoten, the Gordian knot.

Göre, *f.* V. Gähre, Gährung.

Görge, *m.* [-s or -ns] [in familiar language] = Georg, George, Georgy.

Görk, V. Kork.

Görl, *m.* [-es, *pl.* -e] [allied to the L. *cordula*, Kordel] a strong round twisted thread, loop.

Gorlspitzen, *pl.* loop-lace.

Görlitz, *n.* [a town in Prussian Silesia] Gorlitz. —er Leinwand, garlicks or garlix.

Gös, *n.* gos [an Indian measure of from four to five thousand paces].

Gösch or **Gösche**, *f.* [*pl.* -en, -n] flag of the bow-sprit, jack.

Göschstock, *m.* jack-staff.

†**Gösche**, *f.* [*pl.* -n] (Fr. *gosier*, throat) a large wide mouth, chops. V. Maul.

Göse, *f.* a sort of white light beer [brewed at Goslar], Goslar beer.

Göse, *m.* [-n, *pl.* -n] [Atlantfisch] gardon [a fish of the roach kind].

Göspe, *f.* V. Gäspe.

Gösse, *f.* [*pl.* -n] (from gießen, to pour) 1) the gutter stone, sink in a kitchen; [in mining] the gutter, into which a hydraulic engine discharges its water. 2) a drain, sewer, kennel.

Gossenstein, *m.* sink in a kitchen.

Göstlinger, *m.* [-s, *pl.* -] formerly, an eightpounder made use of on board of ships.

Gotha, *n.* [-s] [a town in ducal Saxony] Gotha.

Gothe, *m.* [-n, *pl.* -n] [one of an ancient Germanic tribe or nation] Goth.

Gothenburg, Götheburg, *n.* [-s] [a town in Sweden] Gothenburgh.

Gothisch, *adj.* and *adv.* [pertaining to the Goths] Gothic, Gothical. Der —e Geschmack, the Gothic taste; —e Bauart, Gothic architecture; eine Kirche im —en Geschmack, a Gothic church; —e Schrift, black-letter; ein Buch mit —er Schrift, a black-letter book.

Gothland, *n.* [-s] [a province of Sweden] Gothland, Gothia.

Gott, *m.* [-es, *pl.* Götter] [Sax. and Eng. *God*, Sw. and Dan. *gud*; seems to be allied to the Scandinavian Odin, Goth *Thiuth*, Egyptian *Theut*, Gr. Ζεύς, Lat. *Deus*] 1) [a single or individual superior spirit, god or deity] a deity, a god. Ihr Götter! [an exclamation of surprise &c.] ye gods! die heidnischen Götter, the heathen or false gods or deities; die unterirdischen Götter, the infernal gods; V. Hausgötter, Schutzgötter, Liebesgötter, Waldgötter, Wassergötter; Mars war der — des Krieges [der Kriegs—], Mars was the god of war; Romulus wurde unter die Götter versetzt, Romulus was ranked among the gods, was deified; *er ist selig wie ein —, he is or he feels as happy as a god or king. *it.* V. Abgott. Denen der Bauch ihr — ist [in Scripture], whose god is their belly; ein Geiziger macht seine Schätze zu seinem —, a covetous man makes a god of, deifies or idolizes his treasures. 2) [the eternal and infinite Spirit, the Creator and Sovereign of the Universe] God, the Supreme Being. — ist ein Geist, God is a spirit; der — der Heerschaaren, the God or Lord of hosts; mit —es Hülfe, God willing, God helping; *es gehört ihm von — und Rechtswegen, it belongs to him by rights; das ist ein Mann —es [= ein — wohlgefälliger, frommer Mann], he is a godly or righteous man; er ist or steht vor —, he is dead and gone, he is before God; die Furcht —es, the fear of God [= a holy awe or reverence of God]; das Wort —es, the word of God. *it.* as an exclamation in violent emotions of mind. —! mein —! good God! good heavens! bless me! ach —! mein Unglück! alack-a-day! Lord! what a misfortune! daß sich — erbarme! — steh' uns bei! God help us, God bless us; — sey Dank, gelobt &c.! thank God! God be praised! helf'! helf' —! [frequently used by common people as a polite utterance when another person sneezes] God bless you! — grüße Dich, grüß' Dich —! [a very familiar way of greeting] good day! how are you? — befohlen, reisen Sie, gehen Sie mit —! Adieu, good bye, God be with you, God speed you! nun, in —es Namen! well, in the name of God! wollte —! — gebe [es]! God grant it! God grant it may be so! would to God! geliebt es — [obsolete], will's —, so — will [= wenn es — gefällt]! please God, if it please God, if God please! — vergelte, belohne es Ihnen! vergelt' es —! lohn' es —! —es Lohn! God reward or bless you for it! o —, was sehe ich! my God, o Lord, what do I see! bewahre, behüte —! — bewahre, behüte! da sey — vor! God forbid, God avert! um —es Willen nicht! thun Sie es um —es Willen nicht! for God's sake, in the name of God, do not do it! um —es Willen, was machen Sie! good God, what are you doing! bei —! — weiß es! [†weiß —!] — ist mein Zeuge! [as an asseveration] by God! God knows! witness God! I swear to God! so wahr — lebt! as true as there is a God, by the living God! God is my witness! so wahr mir — helfe! so help me God! *Prov.* Wenn — will, so kräht selbst eine Art unter der Bank, when God wills, all winds bring rain; er läßt den lieben — einen guten Mann seyn [= lebt ruhig und unbesorgt], he lets matters go their own way, he lets the water take its course, Jeder für sich, — für Alle, every one for himself and God for us all.

Gott-ähnlich, *adj.* and *adv.* like or resembling God, godlike; *it.* [= herrlich, göttlich] excellent in the highest degree, divine. —**ähnlichkeit**, *f.* likeness or resemblance of God. —**begeistert**, *adj.* inspired by God or by a god. —**begünstigt**, *adj.* favoured by God or the gods. —**ergeben**, *adj.* and *adv.* resigned to the will of God, pious. —**gefällig**, *adj.* and *adv.* agreeable to God. —**geliebt**, *adj.* loved by God or the gods. —**gesandt** or —**gesendet**, *adj.* sent by God. —**geschaffen**, *adj.* created by God. —**gesegnet**, *adj.* blessed by God. —**glaube**, *m.* [Deismus] Deism. —**gleich**, *adj.* godlike, divine. —**heil**, *n.* [in botany] 1) sweet-scented cleonia [native of Portugal]. 2) self-heal, V. Braunwurz. —**längner**, *m.* V. Gotteslängner. —**los**, *adj.* and *adv.* 1) [having no reverence for God] godless, ungodly, impious, irreligious, wicked. Ein —loses Leben führen, to lead a wicked life; [in fam. lang.] ein —loses [= unartiges] Kind, a naughty child. 2) [having no belief in the existence of God] atheistical, godless. Ein —loser Mensch, an atheist; eine —lose Lehre, an atheistical doctrine. Syn. Gottloser, Sünder, Böser, Boshafter, Tückischer, Ruchloser, Verruchter. Ein Sünder is one who has voluntarily violated or disobeyed the divine law, or neglected any known duty. Ein Böser is one who intentionally wrongs or harms others. He is boshaft, who rejoices at the injury he has done to others, or at any evil which may have happened to them. Die Tücke joins to the idea of Bosheit that of secrecy and cunning. Gottlos signifies, having no reverence for God, nor respect for the divine law. Ruchlos [= ohne guten Geruch, *i. e.* Namen] is he who no longer respects either human or divine laws, and is lost to all sense of shame or honour. Verrucht is he whose pro-

sigkeit has reached such a pitch, as to be capable of evry wickedness however great or horrible. —mensch, *m.* [in theology] God and Man, God-man [an attribute of Christ]. —menschlich, *adj.* theandric. —seibeiuns, (—sei bei uns) *m.* [in popul. lang.] Old Nick, the devil. Der —seibeiuns hat ihn geholt, the devil carried him off. —selig, *adj* and *adv.* godly, pious, righteous. Ein —seliges Leben führen, to lead a godly, pious or religious life; mein Vater, [—]seligen Andenkens, my father, of blessed or happy memory. —seligkeit, *f.* godliness, piety, religiousness. Die —seligkeit ist zu allen Dingen nütze [in Scripture], godliness is profitable unto all things; übe dich in der —seligkeit, exercise thyself in godliness. —sühner, *m.* V. —versöhner. —vereinigung, *f.* union with God. —vergeß, *m.* [in botany] V. Andorn. —vergessen, [rather vulgar now] *adj.* and *adv.* unmindful of God, profane, wicked, impious, ungodly, V. —los. —vergessenheit, *f.* impiety, wickedness, V. Gottlosigkeit 1). —verhaßt, *adj.* hated by God or the gods, odious to God or the gods. —verheißen, *adj.* promised by God or the gods. —verlassen, *adj.* forsaken by God or the gods. —versöhner, *m.* the Redeemer or Saviour [an attribute of Christ]. —versöhnt, *adj.* reconciled to God. —verworfen, *adj.* rejected or abandoned by God.

Gottes-acker, *m.* burying-ground, burial-place, church-yard. —baum, *m.* the cocoa-tree. —dienst, *m.* 1) divine service, public worship, office of devotion, religious exercise. Freien —dienst haben, to have the free exercise of religion, enjoy religious liberty [= the free right of worshipping the Supreme Being according to the dictates of conscience]; der häusliche, der Privat—dienst, private exercise of religion, private worship. 2) a single act of divine service. Dem —dienste beiwohnen, to attend divine service; der —dienst ist aus or geendigt, the service is over, the church is done. —dienstlich, *adj.* 1) relating to divine service, religious. —dienstliche Handlungen, religious acts, acts of religion. 2) pious, godly, religious. —dienstlichkeit, *f.* piety, religiousness. —erde, *f.* 1) [the Earth as a creation of God] the earth. *Fig.* *Er hat auf der [weiten] —erde Niemand, der ihm or dem er angehört, he has not a soul on earth that is kindred to him, he is quite alone on earth 2) the earth of the churchyard. In —erde begraben werden, to be buried in consecrated ground, to have christian burial. —fahrt, *f.* pilgrimage. —friede, *m.* formerly, the inviolability of all persons and things belonging to divine service, God's-peace. Den —frieden brechen, to break, to violate God's peace. —furcht, *f.* the fear of God, piety, religion. —fürchtig, *adj.* and *adv.* fearing God, godly, pious —fürchtigkeit, *f.* [not to be used] piety. —gabe, *f.* 1) a gift of God. Das Brod ist eine —gabe, bread is a gift of God or Heaven. *it.* particularly, a natural gift or endowment or talent. 2) *pl* —gaben, ecclesiastical or church revenues, V. Kircheneinkünfte. —gebärerinn, *f.* the mother of our Lord, the blessed virgin Mary. —gelahrtheit or —gelehrsamkeit, *f.* divinity, theology. —geld, *n.* V. —groschen —gelehrt, *adj.* versed in the science of divinity. Der —gelehrte, theologian, divine. —gelehrtheit, *f.* V. —gelehrsamkeit. —gericht, *n.* divine judgment; chiefly, an ancient form of trial to determine guilt or innocence, ordeal. —glaube, *m.* belief in God, pious faith and reliance in the Lord. —gnade, *f.* 1) the grace or mercy of God. 2) [in botany] crane's-bill, stork's-bill. V. Storchschnabel, Giftkraut. ‡—groschen, *m.* earnest-money, earnest-penny] God's-penny [given to the poor]. —haus, *n.* house of God, place of worship, church, temple; *it.* die —häuser, convents, cloisters, abbeys. —hausleute, *pl.* [formerly] the subjects of a convent or abbey. —hauspfleger, *m.* churchwarden. —hülfe, *f.* the help of God; [in botany] the common hore-hound. —jämmerlich, *adj.* and *adv.* [in popular or vulgar language] very or exceedingly miserable. Sie prügelten ihn —jämmerlich, they thrashed him in a piteous manner. —kasten, *m.* a box in the church which contains the money, collected either for the use of the poor or for the repairs of the church, poor's-box. ||—kuh, *f.*, *dim.* —kühlein, *n.* [in entomology] lady-cow, lady-bird, or lady-bug. —lamm, *n.* 1) lamb of God [Christ]. 2) [in the Roman Church, a cake of wax stamped with the figure of a lamb, supporting the banner of a cross] agnus dei. —lästerer, *m.* —lästererinn, *f.* blasphemer. —lästerlich, *adj.* and *adv.* blasphemous. —lästern, *v. intr.* to utter blasphemy, to blaspheme. —lästerung, *f.* blasphemy. —läugner, *m* —läugnerinn, *f.* he or she that denies the existence of a God, atheist. —läugnerei, *f.* V. —läugnung. —läugnerisch, *adj.* and *adv.* atheistic, atheistical. —läugnung, *f.* atheism. —lehen, *n* [formerly] an ecclesiastical fief. —lehre, *f.* theology, divinity. —lehrer, *m.* V. —gelehrte. —lehrig, *adj.* [unusual] theological, V. Theologisch. —liebe, *f.* the love of God. —lohn, *m.* [chiefly used in popular language] God's reward, God's blessing. Habt —lohn! God reward or bless you for it! Ihr verdienet einen —lohn an mir, God will reward you for the good you do me, for your goodness to me; etwas um einen —lohn thun, to do a thing out of charity, for the love of God or for charity's sake. —mann, *m.* a godly, pious man. —mord, *m.* [the act of putting to death Jesus Christ] deicide. —mörder, *m.* deicide. —name, *m.* name of God. —natur, *f.* the nature or essence of God. ||—pfennig, *m.* V. —groschen. ||—pferd, *n.* V. Heupferd. —rathschluß, *m.* decree of God, of Heaven or of Providence. —recht, *n.* the rights, immunities or privileges of a church or convent; *it.* the ecclesiastical offices. —reich, *n.* 1) the empire of God, the universe. 2) [a state supposed to be governed by the immediate direction of God] theocracy. —sohle, *f.* a quantity of saltwater, the produce of which is destined for the poor. —sohn, *m.* 1) the son of God [Jesus Christ]. 2) V. Göttersohn. —stimme, *f.* the voice of God, divine voice. *Prov.* Volksstimme, —stimme, the voice of the people is the voice of God. —tisch, *m.* the communion-table, the Lord's supper, communion. An den —tisch, zu —tische gehen, to go to or to partake of the Lord's supper, to receive the communion, to communicate. ‡—tischrock, *m.* coat [generally a black dress-coat] worn in going to the Lord's supper. —urtheil, *n.* V. —gericht. —verächter, *m.* a contemner of God, an impious man. —verachtung, *f.* contempt of God, disrespect or irreverence towards God, impiety, irreligion. —verehrung, *f.* 1) reverence or awe of God. 2) V. —dienst. —vergessen, *adj.* —vergessenheit, *f.* V. Gottvergessen &c. —vertheidigung, *f.* the vindication of the ways of God, theodicy. —welt, *f.* the world, the earth. Diese schöne —welt, this beautiful earth; [chiefly in popular lang.] auf der —welt nichts [= durchaus nichts] zu thun haben, to have nothing at all to do; auf der —welt nichts haben, to be utterly poor or destitute.

Götter, *pl.* of Gott, which see.

Götter-ähnlich, *adj.* and *adv.* V. Gottähnlich. —bild, *n.* the image of a god. *Fig.* [in poetical style] of god-like appearance, of surpassing beauty. Sie ist ein —bild, she is an heavenly woman. —blume, *f.* [in botany] Virginian cowslip, dodecatheon. —bote, *m.* messenger of the gods, Mercury. —brod, *n.* V. —speise. —brücke, *f.* [in poetry] rainbow. —dichtung, *f.* V. 1) —lehre. 2) —fabel. —diener, *m.* worshipper of the gods. —dienst, *m.* worship of the gods. —entsprossen, *adj.* [in poetry] of divine origin. —erzeugung, *f.* the generation or descent of the gods. —erzeugungslehre, *f.* V. —geburt. —fabel, *f.* fable of the gods of the ancient pagans. —fest, *n.* banquet of the gods; *it.* banquet in honour of the gods. —geburt, *f.* [in mythology] theogony. —gericht, *n.* 1) judgment of the gods. 2) food of the gods. *Fig.* *a delicious dish. —geruch, *m.* [in botany] diosma [a native of the Cape of Good Hope]. —geschlecht, *n.* 1) the generation or race of the gods, the gods. 2) a race of men of divine origin, a divine race. —gleich, *adj.* and *adv.* V. Gottähnlich. —hand, *f.* *fig.* the will or power of the gods. —haus, *n.* [a public edifice erected in honour of some deity] temple —kraut, *n.* [in botany] ambrosia. —lehre, *f.* 1) [*Mythologie] mythology. 2) a treatise upon mythology. —mahl, *n* banquet of the gods; *it.* banquet in honour of the gods *Fig.* *a delicious banquet. —oper, *f.* 1) a mythological opera. 2) *Fig.* [in fam. lang.] an excellent opera, divine operatic music. —rath, *m.* 1) the council of the gods. 2) decree of the gods. —rathschluß, *m.* V. —rath 2). —sage, *f.* V. —fabel. —sitz, *m.* the residence of the gods, Olympus. —sohn, *m.* son of the gods. —speise, *f.* 1) the food of the gods, ambrosia; *fig.* a delicious food or dish. 2) V. —kraut. —spruch, *m.* oracle. —streit, *m.* 1) dispute, contest or combat of the gods. 2) a contest against the gods, theomachy. —tafel, *f.* table of the gods. —tisch, *m.* V. —tafel. —trank, *m.* the drink of the gods, nectar. *Fig.* *Dieser Wein ist ein —trank, this wine is a nectarian drink, is nectar. —verehrung, *f.* worship of the gods. —wein, *m.* the wine of the gods, nectar. *Fig.* *delicious wine. —wesen, *n.* every thing relating to the gods of the ancient pagans, mythology. —wohnung, *f.* habitation of the gods. —zeichen, *n.* a sign given by the gods, augury, omen. —zeit, *f.* 1) the time when the gods of the ancient pagans were worshipped, mythological time or age. 2) an exceedingly happy time, the golden age.

Götterthum, *n.* [-s] 1) the divine nature or essence, godhead, divinity 2) any thing relating to the gods of the ancient pagans, their mythology.

Gottfried, *m.* [-s, *pl.* -e] [a christian name of men] Godfrey.

Gotthard, *m.* [-s, *pl.* -e] 1) [a christian name of men] Godard. 2) [a mountain in Switzerland] Gotthard.

Gottheit, *f.* 1) the nature or essence of God, deity, divinity, godhead Die — Christi, the divinity of Jesus Christ. 2) a deity in person, a god, goddess. Die —en der Heiden, die heidnischen —en, the heathen gods or deities; die —en des Wassers, the deities of the water &c. *it.* [particularly] the Supreme Being, God. Es ist die —, die sich in uns rührt, 't is the divinity that stirs within us; die — läugnen, to deny the existence of the Supreme Being.

Gotthilf, *m.* [-s, *pl.* -e] [a christian name of men] Gotthilf.

Göttinn, *f.* a female deity, goddess. Die — der Weisheit, the goddess of wisdom. *Fig.*

[in poetry or in ecstatical language, a woman of superior charms or excellence] goddess Die —, die ich anbete, the goddess or angel whom I adore; meine — [= Geliebte] my angel, my love!

Göttlich, I. *adj.* divine, godlike. Das —e Wesen, the divine nature or essence; die —en Tugenden, the divine virtues; die —e Vorsehung, divine providence; einen —en Ursprung haben, to have a divine origin, to be of divine race, die —en Schriften [in theology], the canonical books or Scriptures; die —en Aussprüche, the oracles of God, the divine oracles; ein —er Wandel, a life conformable to God's law, a pious, godly life; Einem —e Ehre erweisen, erzeigen, to show, to render or to pay any one divine honours. *Fig.* *excellent in the highest degree. Ein —er Gedanke, eine —e Schönheit, a heavenly thought, beauty; der —e Plato, the divine Plato; ein —er Fürst, a godlike prince; eine —e Erfindung, a divine invention; ein —es Werk, a most excellent work. II. *adv.* divinely. Die — angewehten Propheten, the prophets divinely inspired; — leben, to live piously, godly. *Fig.* *most excellently, divinely. — schön, divinely fair; sie singt —, she sings most excellently, divinely.

Göttlichkeit, *f.* 1) the divine nature or essence, divinity. Die — des Wortes [Christi], the divinity of the word [of Christ]. 2) the divine origin. Die — der heiligen Schrift, the divine origin of the Scriptures.

Göttlieb, *m.* [-s, *pl.* -e] [a christian name of men] Theophilus.

Göttliebe, ||**Göttliebinn**, *f.* [a christian name of women] Theophila.

Göttlosigkeit, *f.* 1) godlessness, impiety, wickedness, ungodliness, irreligion. 2) an act of wickedness, impiety. Allerlei —en begehen, to commit all sorts of impieties.

Göttschalk, *m.* [-s, *pl.* -e] [a christian name of men] Gottshalk.

Götze, *m.* [-n, *pl.* -n] [either from Gott, or the ancient *giozan* = gießen or gesten = to form] a false deity, an idol. Den — dienen, to worship idols, to idolatrize. *Fig.* Der Geizige macht das Geld zu seinem —n, the miser makes an idol of his money; einen —n aus Einem machen, to idolize any one, to be extremely fond of, to dote on any one. Syn. V. Abgott.

Götzen-altar, *m.* the altar of an idol. —bild, *n.* the image, form or representation of a false god, idol, image. Syn. V. Abgott. —diener, *m.* —dienerinn, *f.* worshipper of idols, idolater, idolatress. —dienst, *m.* idol-worship, image-worship, idolatry. —hain, *m.* a grove conserrated to the worship of some idol. —haus, *n.* V. —tempel. —holz, *n.* V. Weißpappel. —kirche, *f.* V. —tempel. —opfer, *n.* an offering made to an idol, an idolatrous sacrifice. —pfaffe, —priester, *m.* idolatrous priest. —tempel, *m.* the temple of an idol. —wald, *m.* V. —hain.

***Goût**, *m.* [pron. as in the French] V. Geschmack.

***Gouvernánte**, *f.* [pron. Guwernante] [*pl.* -n] governess. V. Erzieherinn.

***Gouvérnement**, *n.* [pron. as in the French] [-s, *pl.* -s] government. V. also Statthalterschaft and Regierung.

***Gouverneûr**, *m.* [pron. Guwernöhr] [-s, *pl.* -e] 1) governor [of a state, town &c.]. 2) tutor, governor. V. Erzieher.

Grāb, *n.* [-es, *pl.* Gräber] [a ditch, pit or excavated place in which a dead human body is deposited] grave, tomb, sepulchre. Ein — machen, graben, to dig a grave; einen Verstorbenen zu —e tragen, to deposit a deceased man in the grave, to bury, to inter him; mit einer Leiche zu —e gehen, to attend at a funeral; eine Leiche in das — senken, legen, to inter or entomb a dead body; schon längst ruhet er im —e, it is a long time since he descended to the grave, he has been long interred or in the grave; er sieht aus, als wenn er schon im —e gelegen hätte, he looks as if he had been dug up out of his grave, he is as pale as a corpse; das — Christi, das heilige —, the sepulchre of Christ, the holy sepulchre; er nennt die Heuchler übertünchte Gräber, he calls the hypocrites whited sepulchres. *Fig. a)* death or the state of the dead. Im —e nur ist Ruh', there is no repose but in death; ein Geheimniß mit sich in's — nehmen, to take a secret into one's grave, never to divulge a secret; Einem bis zum —e, bis in's — [= bis in den Tod] getreu seyn, to be faithful to any one to the grave, till death; er steht am Rande des —es, *er hat schon einen Fuß im —e, he is on the brink of death, near death, he has one foot already in the grave; er wird seinen Vater [*noch] in's — bringen, he will cause his father's death, he will be the death of his father; in den Wellen sein — finden, to perish in the waves, to meet with a watery grave; die Nacht or die Stille des —es, the silent grave, the gloomy tomb. *b)* destruction, end, ruin. Mißtrauen ist das — der Freundschaft, distrust destroys friendship. V. Gruft, Grube.

Grab-einfassung, *f.* the enclosure of a grave or tomb —fliege, *f.* sepulchral fly. —gedanke, *m.* thought of the grave or death; *fig.* a sad, grave, gloomy thought. —gefilde, *n.* burying-ground, church-yard. —geläute, *n.* knell. —gesellschaft, *f.* a society or association, the members of which engage themselves reciprocally to the expenses of their funerals. —gerüst, *n.* [a frame in the church on which the coffin is placed, when laid in state] a funeral decoration; *it.* V. —einfassung. —gesang, *m.* [funeral] dirge. —gewölbe, *n.* vault, tomb. —hügel, *m.* a hillock or mound of earth over a grave, tomb, ||barrow. —kleid, *n.* V. Leichengewand. —kraut, *n.* wormwood. —krug, *m.* V. Aschenkrug. —legung, *f.* sepulture, burial, interment; *it.* a painting representing the sepulture of Christ. —lied, *n.* a funeral hymn, dirge. —los, *adj.* and *adv.* without a grave or tomb, graveless, tombless. —mahl, *n.* a sepulchral monument, a tomb, a sepulchre. Sie hat ihm ein prächtiges —mahl errichtet, she has erected him a magnificent or stately tomb or monument, a mausoleum. —schrift, *f.* [an inscription on a monument] epitaph. —stätte, *f.* [place in which the dead body of a human being is interred, or a place destined for that purpose] sepulchre, grave, tomb. —stein, *m.* sepulchral stone, tombstone, gravestone. —stelle, *f.* V. —stätte. —thier, *n.* the hyena. —tuch, *n.* pall; *it.* [formerly] V. Leichentuch. —zeichen, *n.* monument. V. Denkmahl.

Grabes-hügel, *m.* V. Grabhügel. —nacht, *f.* the silent grave, the gloomy tomb; *it.* death. —rand, *m.* the brink of the grave. *Fig.* Am —rande stehen, to be on the brink of death, *to have one foot in the grave. —schlummer, *m.* slumber or sleep of death. —stille, *f.* the silence or stillness of the grave. —stimme, *f.* a sepulchral voice. —tuch, *n.* V. Grabtuch.

||**Grábbeln**, V. Krabbeln.

Gráben, *m.* [-s, *pl.* Gräben] ditch, trench. Einen Acker mit einem — umgeben, to surround a field with a ditch, to ditch a field; einen — räumen, schlämmen, to cleanse a ditch; einen — ablassen, to drain a ditch; [in fortification] to saigner a moat; einen — [um ein Stück Land &c.] frisch ausschlagen, to raise up the banks of a ditch; die Gräben um eine Festung, Burg, the ditches, trenches, fosses or moats round a fortress, castle; V. Kunst—, Land—, Lauf—, Schieß—, Stadt—, Wasser—. [in mining] V. Mulde. *Fig.* *Wir sind nun über dem — [= haben die Hindernisse überstanden], now we are safe, out of danger; *sie sind entschlossen, über den — zu springen, they are resolved to hazard the leap.

Graben-absteigung, *f.* [in fortification] a narrow passage leading from the covert way to the ditch, descent. —damm, *m.* [in fortific.] dike of the cunette. —füller, *m.* *fig.* [in contempt or joke] a filler up of ditches, a soldier good enough for filling a ditch, a bad soldier. —leitung, *f.* 1) draining by ditches 2) drains, ditches. —mauer, *f.* [in fortification, the exterior talus or slope of the ditch] counterscarp. —schere, *f.* [in fortification, a kind of outwork] tenaille. —steiger, *m.* an inspector of a canal or water-course. —übergang, *m.* [in fortification] causey of fascines raised by the besiegers in a ditch. —winkel, *m.* [in fortification] angle of the ditch. —zug, *m.* 1) the digging of a ditch. 2) the direction of a ditch or canal.

Gráben, [Dan. *grave*, Engl. *to grave*, W. *crafu*; allied to the Gr. γράφειν, L. *scribere*, Germ. schreiben] *ir.* I. *v. tr.* 1) [to form or shape by cutting with a chisel or graver] to grave, to engrave, to cut, to carve. Grabe auf die zwei Steine die Namen, engrave the two stones with the names or grave the names on the two stones. *Fig.* Gott hat diese Grundsätze den Menschen in's Herz ge—, God has engraved these principles in men's minds; diese Lehre sey in dein Herz ge—, let this precept be engraved on thy mind, imprinted in or upon thy heart; meines Vaters Ermahnungen haben sich mir in das Gemüth ge—, my father's admonitions have been imprinted on my mind. 2) to excavate, to dig. Einen Brunnen —, to dig a well; er gräbt sich sein eigenes Grab, he digs his own grave; den Grund zu einem Hause —, to dig the foundation of a house; eine Grube —, to dig a pit, *fig.* *Einem eine Grube —, to lay a snare for any one; *prov.* wer Andern eine Grube gräbt, fällt selbst hinein, harm watch, harm catch. 3) [= ausgraben] to dig out, to dig. Steinkohlen, Erze —, to dig coals, ores. 4) [= eingraben] to hide, to bury. Etwas in die Erde —, to hide or bury something in the ground; sich in die Erde —, to hide one's self in the earth, to burrow, as a fox or rabbit. II. *v. intr.* 1) to grave. 2) [to work with a spade &c.] to dig. Durch einen Berg —, to dig through a mountain; — mag ich nicht, so schäme ich mich zu betteln [in Script.], I cannot dig, to beg I am ashamed. 3) nach etwas —, [to work in search of] to dig for a thing. Nach Wasser, nach Schätzen —, to dig for water, for treasures; nach Wurzeln, nach Erzen —, to dig for roots, ores, to dig roots, ores.

Grab-eisen, *n.* V. —scheit, —stichel. —meißel, *m.* V. —stichel. —schaufel, *f.* a shovel partly answering the purpose of digging. —scheit or Grabescheit, *n.* [an instrument for digging, consisting of a broad palm and a handle] spade. —stichel, *m.* [a pointed instrument for graving on hard substances] graving-tool, graver, burin.

Grabe-kelle, *f.* [a gardener's tool, somewhat like a trowel, used in taking up plants &c.] trowel. —kraut, *n.* V. Grabkraut. —land, *n.* land which is dug, instead of being ploughed.

Gräber, *m.* [-s, *pl.* -] —**inn**, *f.* 1) [one who digs] digger. V. Brunnen—, Deich—, Schanz—, Todten—. 2) [an insect] V. Aaskäfer, Todtenkäfer.

***Grace**, *f.* [pron. Grahß] V. Anmuth.

Grāchel, *f.* [*pl.* -n] V. Granne.

***Gräcisiren**, *v. tr.* to render Greek, to grecize.

***Gräcismus**, *m.* [- or ‡-mi, *pl.* -men] grecism.

***Gräcomāne**, *m.* [-n, *pl.* -n] a passionate lover or admirer of every thing Greek.

***Gräcomanie**, *f.* a passionate love or admiration of every thing Greek.

1. **Grād**, [L. *gradus*. The ancient graden or graten signifies gehen, to go] *m.* [-es, *pl.* -e] formerly, a pace, step; *it.* [in some districts] step of a staircase; in a more limited sense; *a*) [in mathematics, a division of a circle, including a three hundred and sixtieth part of its circumference] degree. Ein Winkel von 40 —, an angle of 40 degrees; jene Stadt liegt unter dem zwanzigsten — der Breite, der Länge, that city is situated in the twentieth degree of latitude, of longitude. V. Breite, Länge. *b*) [a division, space or interval, marked on a mathematical or other instrument] degree. Das Wetterglas ist auf 27 — gestiegen, the barometer has risen to the twenty seventh degree; wir haben 20 — Wärme, 5 — Kälte, we have twenty degrees of heat, five degrees of cold; einen Wärmemesser in —e abtheilen, to graduate a thermometer; die Eintheilung eines Wetterglases in —e, the graduation of a weatherglass. *Fig. a*) in general, any step or portion of progression; degree. Wir erleiden einen äußersten — der Hitze oder Kälte, we suffer an extreme degree of heat or cold; den gehörigen — des Feuers, der Hitze zu geben wissen, to know how to give fire its several degrees; es gibt —e der Tugend und des Lasters, there are degrees of virtue and vice; sie stehen noch auf dem ersten —e der Bildung, der Gesittung, they are yet in the first degree of improvement, they are yet on the first step to civilisation; in der Sprachlehre gibt es drei —e, there are three degrees in grammar; [in genealogy] ein Verwandter im dritten oder vierten —e, a relation in the third or fourth degree; [in algebra] eine Gleichung im zweiten —e, a quadratic equation, an equation of the second degree, V. Gleichung; er ist im höchsten —e glücklich, he is excessively, superlatively happy; das ist der höchste — von Unverschämtheit, that is the highest degree of insolence; den höchsten — des Ruhmes erlangen, to attain to the highest or furthest degree, to the pinnacle of glory; der — der Ehre, die Einem zukömmt, the degree of honour due to any one. *b*) [Ehrenstufe] step or degree of honour. Seinen — auf einer hohen Schule erlangen, to take one's degrees in a university; er erhielt den — eines Doctors der Rechte, he received the degree of Doctor of Laws, the degree of Doctor of Laws was conferred upon him; der — eines Hauptmannes, the rank, degree or grade of captain.

Grad=abtheilung, *f.* graduation [of a thermometer &c.]. —**bogen**, *m.* arc divided into degrees. *a*) [among seamen, an instrument, used for taking the altitude of stars about the poles] cross-staff, Jacob's staff, nocturnal. V. Viertelkreis, Sechstelkreis, Achtelkreis. *b*) protractor, transporter. V. Winkelmesser. —**buch**, *n.* [in seamen's lang.] a book containing the charts, views of coasts &c. —**eintheilung**, *f.* graduation. —**hobel**, *m.* V. Grathhobel. —**leiter**, *f.* scale. —**ring**, *m.* a graduated ring. —**sparren**, *m.* V. Grathsparren. —**wage**, *f.* spring steelyard, V. Federwage. —**weise**, *adv.* by degrees.

2. **Grād**, *m.* V. Grath.

***Gradāl**, V. Gradual.

***Gradatiōn**, *f.* 1) [in grammar] gradation. 2) [in rhetoric] climax, gradation.

***Gradīren**, *v. tr.* 1) to raise to a higher place in the scale of metals, to graduate, to refine. 2) [in chimistry] to bring fluids to a certain degree of consistency, as saltwater by evaporation, to graduate. Das —, graduation.

Gradir=eisen, *n.* [among sculptors] dented chisel. —**faß**, *n.* [in saltworks] cask or tub, into which the saltwater is led by pipes. —**haus**, *n.* [in saltworks] building for graduation, drying-house. —**herd**, *m.* the hearth on which the saltwater is graduated. —**ofen**, *m.* furnace of graduation. —**pfanne**, *f.* the pan in which the saltwater is graduated, pan of graduation. —**röhre**, *f.* pipe by which the saltwater is led into the pan or cask of graduation. —**wage**, *f.* [an instrument for measuring the specific gravity of liquors] areometer. —**wasser**, *n.* water mixed with different salts, in which goldsmiths seeth their gold. —**werk**, *n.* V. —haus.

Grādler, *m.* [-s, *pl.* -] [in melting-houses] V. Schmelzjunge.

***Graduāl**, [Gradal] *n.* [-es, *pl.* -e] [a book containing hymns and prayers] gradual, grail.

***Graduīren**, I. *v. tr.* to confer an academical degree, to graduate. II. *v. intr.* to receive an academical degree, to graduate.

***Graduīrte**, *m.* [-n, *pl.* -n] one who has received an academical degree, a graduate.

***Graduīrung**, *f.* [the act of conferring or receiving academical degrees] graduation.

Grāf, [Sax. *gerefa*, companion, fellow-traveller, as Count from the L. *comes*, companion] *m.* [-en, *pl.* -en] [a title of nobility next below a duke or prince, in some measure answering to Earl in England] count, [earl]. Ein gefürsteter —, a count raised to the rank of a prince; der König hat ihn zum —en gemacht, the king has created him a count. V. Burg—, Land—, Mark—, Pfalz— &c.

Grafen=ding, *n.* [formerly] the jurisdiction of a count. —**n=bank**, *f.* [formerly, in the German Empire] the bench of the counts. *a*) the seat where the counts of the Empire used to sit. *b*) the counts themselves. —**n=hof**, *m.* the court of a count. —**n=krone**, *f.* count's or earl's coronet. —**n=sitz**, *m.* the seat of a count; *it.* the place or residence of a count. —**n=stand**, *m.* 1) dignity of a count or earl. In den —nstand erhoben werden, to be raised to the dignity of a count or earl. 2) [collectively, all the counts of a country] order of counts or earls. —**n=tag**, *m.* [formerly] an assembly or meeting of the counts of the German empire. —**n=titel**, *m.* title of count or earl. —**n=würde**, *f.* dignity of a count or earl.

Gräfinn, *f.* [*pl.* -en] the consort of an earl or count, countess.

Gräflich, I. *adj.* belonging to a count or earl. Die —e Krone, Würde &c., count's or earl's coronet, the dignity of a count or earl. II. *adv.* in the manner of, like an earl or count. — leben, to live like a count.

Grāfschaft, *f.* [*pl.* -en] the district or territory of a count or earl, county, earldom. Die — Burgund, the county of Burgundy.

Gräll, V. Grell.

Grām, [seems to be allied to Grimm] *adv.* averse, disliking. Einem — seyn, to dislike, to hate any one, to bear any one a grudge; ich bin dem Lügen —, I hate lying or lies; ich bin mir selbst gram, daß ich &c., I am angry or displeased with myself, I hate myself for &c.; Einem — werden, to conceive a hatred, an ill-will, a grudge against any one; Esau ward dem Jacob —, Esau hated Jacob.

Grām, *m.* [-es] grief, sorrow, affliction. Vor — vergehen, sich vor — verzehren, to fall sick, to pine away with grief; der — verkürzt das Leben, grief or sorrow shortens life.

Gram=los, *adj.* and *adv.* free from grief or sorrow, sorrowless. —**sucht**, *f.* disposition to fret, to grieve, fretfulness, peevishness. —**süchtig**, *adj.* and *adv.* disposed to fret or grieve, fretful, peevish. —**voll**, *adj.* and *adv.* full of grief or sorrow, sorrowful, afflicted.

Gramatelle, *f.* [*pl.* -n] V. Garnele.

Grämelei, *f.* V. Grämlichkeit.

Grämeln, *v. intr.* to be irritated, to be displeased, to be out of humour, to be fretful or peevish, to fret.

Grämen, I. *v. tr.* to grieve, to afflict. Sein Tod grämt mich, his death grieves me. II. *v. r.* sich —, to feel pain of mind or heart, to grieve, to sorrow, to take on. Er grämt sich über or um Alles, he is afflicted, he grieves at every thing; was nützt es, sich zu —? what avails fretting? sich zu todt —, to be grieved to death, to pine away, to die with grief.

Grämhaft, **Grämig**, **Grämisch**, [in fam. lang.] V. Grämlich.

Grämler, *m.* [-s, *pl.* -] —**inn**, *f.* a morose, peevish, fretful or ill-humoured person, a saturnist.

Grämlich, *adj.* and *adv.* ill-humoured, morose, peevish, sullen, fretful, pettish. Er sieht — aus, he looks morose or peevish.

Grämlichkeit, *f.* moroseness, peevishness, sullenness, fretfulness, pettishness.

Grämling, *m.* [-es, *pl.* -e] V. Grämler.

***Grammātik**, *f.* [*pl.* -en] 1) [Sprachlehre, Sprachkunst] grammar. 2) a book treating of grammar, a grammar. Ich habe meine englische — bei Ihnen liegen gelassen, I left my English grammar with you.

***Grammātiker**, *m.* [-s, *pl.* -] [Sprachkünstler, Sprachgelehrte] grammarian.

***Grammātisch**, *adj.* and *adv.* grammatical. V. Sprachrichtig.

***Grammatist**, *m.* [-en, *pl.* -en] one who teaches grammar, grammarian; *it.* grammatist.

1. **Grān**, *m.* [-en, *pl.* -en] V. Krahn.

‖2. **Grān**, *m.* [-es, *pl.* -e] V. Knebelbart.

3. **Grān**, [L. *granum*, Fr. *grain*, E. *grain*] *m.* and *n.* [-es, *pl.* -e] or —**gewicht**, *n.* [-es, *pl.* -e] 1) [a small weight or the smallest weight, chiefly used by apothecaries] grain. Das wiegt ein Quentchen und 6 —, that weighs a drachm and six grains. 2) [also Grän] a weight of gold and silver, a grain; as a weight of gold, it is the third part of a grain, the twelfth part of a carat, the 288th part of a mark; as a weight of silver, it is the twenty fourth part of a penny weight troy and the 288th part of a mark. Dieser Dukaten ist um 2 — zu leicht, this ducat is too light by two grains.

Grän, *n.* [-es, *pl.* -e] V. Gran 2).

Granāde, *f.* V. 1) Granatapfel. 2) Granate 3).

***Granadīr**, *m.* V. Granatier.

1. **Granāt**, *m.* V. Garnele.

2. **Granāt**, *m.* [-en, *pl.* -e, or -en] [allied to the L. *granum*, the E. *grain*] 1) [in mineralogy] garnet. 2) [in botany] V. Granatapfel.

Granat=apfel, *m.* [the fruit of the pomegranate-tree] pomegranate. Der wilde —apfel, the wild pomegranate. —**apfelbaum**, *m.*

pomegranate-tree. Wilder —apfelbaum, wild pomegranate-tree, balaustine. —berg, m. a mountain containing garnets. —blüthe, f. pomegranate blossom. —branntwein, m. pomegranate brandy. —erz, n. ore containing garnets. —fluß, m. a false or factitious garnet. —kern, m. the kernel of the pomegranate. —saft, m. pomegranate-juice. —sand, m. small garnets in form of grains of sand. —schnur, f. garnet necklace. —stein, m. 1) the garnet. 2) stone or rock containing garnets. —vogel, m. chaffinch of Brazil. —wasser, n. V. —branntwein. —wein, m. V. Quittenwein.

Granate, f. [pl. -n] 1) [in mineralogy] V. 2. Granat 1). 2) [in botany] V. Granatapfel. 3) [in the art of war, a hollow ball or shell to be filled with powder, which is to be fired by means of a fusee and thrown by hand among enemies] grenade. Die — ist zerplatzt, the grenade has burst. V. Hand—.

Granat-kugel, f. [in pyrotechnics and the art of war, a kind of bomb, to be filled with grenades and gunpowder, which is to be fired by means of a fusee and thrown out of a mortar] balloon of grenades. —enbaum, m. V. Granatapfelbaum. —birne, f. [the oval-shaped fruit of an American tree] guava. —erz, n. V. Granaterz. —hagel, m. [in pyrotechnics and the art of war] a shower of grenades [small grenades which, being put into a ball of pasteboard and thrown out of a mortar, fall down like a shower of rain]. —sand, m. V. Granatsand. —tasche, f. grenade-pouch. —wein, m. V. Granatwein.

Granatier, m. [-es, pl. -e] [formerly, a soldier that threw handgrenades; now, a tall foot-soldier, wearing in many armies a high cap] grenadier.

Granatier-bataillon, n. —compagnie, f. a battalion, a company of grenadiers. —hauptmann, m. captain of grenadiers. —mütze, f. grenadier-cap. —tasche, f. grenadier-pouch; it. grenade-pouch.

Granatillholz, n. [-es] red ebony.

1. **Grand**, [allied to the E. *grind*, the Sw. *grena* = zertheilen, to separate] m. [-es, pl. -e] 1) coarse sand, gravel. 2) [in mining] clay, mixed with pounded quartz.

Grand-mehl, n. coarse flour [mixed with bran]. —ort, m. a gravelly place. —stein, m. [in mineralogy, an aggregate stone or rock, composed of quartz, feldspar and mica] granite.

2. **Grand[e]**, m. [-es, pl. -en] [in Spain, a nobleman of the first rank] grandee.

***Grandezza**, f. [the rank of a Spanish grandee] grandeeship. *Fig.* high or solemn gravity of manner.

Grandicht, **Grandig**, V. Kiesicht, Kiesig.

Grangel, m. [-s] a piece of melted copper.

Grängel, V. Kringel.

Grängewicht, n. V. 3. Gran.

***Graniren**, v. tr. to form into grains, to granulate. V. also Granuliren.

***Granit**, m. [-es, pl. -e] granite. V. also Grandstein.

Granit-artig, adj. and adv. granitic, granitical.

||**Gränitzer**, m. [-s, pl. -] a military colonist in the Austrian dominions along the frontiers of Turkey, who serves as a frontier-guard. V. also Grenzer and Grenzsoldat.

Granne, f. [pl. -n] [allied to the L. *crinis*, hair] 1) bristle [of swine]; it. cat's whiskers. 2) [in botany] the acicular or pointed leaf [of firs, pines &c.]. 3) [Achel] awn, beard [of plants].

Grannen-artig, adj. and adv. [in botany] in form or shape of an awn or beard, bearded. —los, adj. and adv. [in botany] beardless.

Grannen, v. tr. to furnish or provide with an awn or beard, bearded. Gegrannter Spelz, bearded spelt.

Grant, m. [-es] V. Kies.

***Granuliren**, v. tr. to form into grains, to granulate. V. Kornen, Körneln. Granulirtes Silber, silver in grains, granulated silver; das —, granulation.

Granze, f. wild rosemary.

Gränze, f. V. Grenze.

Grapel, m. [-s, pl. -] [allied to ||grapsen = greifen, to seize] [in mining] the eighth of a fathom, a span.

Grapels-mächtig, adj. of the breadth or length of a span, a span broad or long.

||**Grapen**, m. [-s, pl. -] an iron pot for cooking.

***Graphik**, f. the art of writing and delineating. V. Schreibekunst, Zeich[n]enkunst, Mahlerkunst.

Graphisch, adj. and adv. graphic, graphical.

***Graphit**, m. [-en, pl. -en] [carburet of iron, a substance used for pencils] graphite, black-lead, wad.

***Graphometer**, m. [-s, pl. -] [a mathematical instrument, called also semicircle] graphometer. V. Winkelmesser.

Grapp, [seems to be formed of the Fr. *râper*, to grate, to rasp; Germ. reiben] m. [-es, pl. -e] or **Grappe**, f. [pl. -n] [Färberröthe] madder. — pflanzen, bauen, to cultivate madder; feiner — [zu Pulver gestoßener —], madder in powder; geschälter —, barked madder.

Grapp-artig, adj. [in botany] resembling madder. —bereiter, m. one who prepares madder. —brühe, f. a dye made of madder. —darre, f. oven or kiln for drying madder. —färber, m. one who dyes with madder. —färberei, f. 1) the art of dying with madder. 2) the place where one dyes with madder. —mühle, f. mill for pounding madder. —pflanzung, f. [—feld, —land, n.] madder-fields. —roth, I. adj. and adv. red like madder. II. subst. n. a red made of madder. —stampfe, f. V. —mühle. —wurzel, f. the root of madder, the madder.

||**Grapse**, [V. Grapsen] f. [in vulgar lang.] 1) [an eager contest for a thing, in which one endeavours to get the thing before another] scramble. Etwas in die — [Rappse] geben, to make people scramble for a thing. 2) [in contempt for Hand] paw. Große —n haben, to have large paws.

||and†**Grapsen**, [allied to *grasp*, raffen, L. *rapere*. Gr. ἁρπάζω, to seize, to catch at] v. intr. to catch at, to snatch up, to seize.

Gras, [Sax. *graes*, *gaers*, Engl. *grass*; allied to the Sax. *growan*, Eng. *to grow*, Lat. *cresco*] n. [-es, pl. Gräser] [dim. Gräschen, ||Gräslein, n.] grass. Das — ist noch kurz, the grass is yet short; es ist sehr ungesund, sich auf das — zu legen, it is very unwholesome to lie down upon the grass; Leinwand auf das — [auf einen —platz] legen, auf dem —e bleichen, to bleach linen-cloth by laying it on the grass; ein Pferd in das — treiben, schicken, to turn a horse to grass; das Vieh geht ins —e, ist auf dem —e [= auf der Weide], the cattle is grazing; zu —, in's —gehen, to go and cut grass for the cattle, to go a-grazing; [among sportsmen] das — abfressen, V. Gräseln, Grasen. *Prov.* Es wird ihm bekommen, wie dem Hunde das — or das —fressen, he will gain nothing but vexation, he will suffer by it; *darüber ist längst — gewachsen [das ist längst vergessen], that has been long forgotten, one thinks no more of it; er hört das — wachsen, he fancies himself exceedingly wise, he is a conceited fellow; in das — beißen, to be slain, to perish in battle, to lick or bite the dust.

Gras-ährchen, n. [in botany, the calyx or corol of grasses, formed of valves embracing the seed] glume. —anger, m. a piece of ground grown over with grass, grassplot, pasture ground, green. —art, f. sort of grass. —artig, adj. [in botany] like or resembling grass, gramineous. Die —artigen Pflanzen, the gramineous plants. —bank, f. a bank or seat covered with turf. —blume, f. 1) daisy, thrift. ||2) pink. —boden, m. 1) ground where grass grows, meadow or pasture-ground, grassland. 2) V. —kammer. —bürger, m. V. Ackerbürger, Pfahlbürger. —butter, f. butter made in spring, May-butter. —esfleck, m. 1) [Grasfleck] a spot of ground overgrown with grass, grassplot. 2) a spot where grass has been cut for cattle. —es-magd, f. V. —magd. —esmücke, f. V. —mücke. —esplatz, m. V. —esfleck. —farbe, f. grasscolour. —feld, n. pasture, pasture-ground. —fleck, m. 1) a spot or stain made by grass [on a garment &c.] 2) a spot of grass, grassplot. V. —platz. —fressend, adj. herbivorous, graminivorous. —frosch, m. tree-frog, green-frog. —futter, n. food of cattle consisting of grass, pasture, herbage, grass. —fütterung, f. 1) the act of feeding cattle with grass, of soiling cattle 2) green food for beasts, grass, pasture. —garten, m. 1) an enclosed meadow. 2) orchard. —geschmack, m. taste like grass, grassy taste. —grün, adj. and adv. grass-green. —halm, m. blade or spire of grass. —hecht, m. a small pike, pickerel. —herr, m. [a fish] a kind of cod. —hirsch, m. [among hunters] a poor or lean stag. —hof, m. an enclosure or paddock near the house, for cattle to feed in. —huhn, n. [in natural history] the landrail, corncrake. V. —läufer. —hüpfer, m. grasshopper. —isop, m. wild hyssop. —junge, m. a boy or lad that tends the horses while grazing. —käfer, m. black violet chrysomela. —kammer, f. room or loft for the grass. —keim, m. the germ of the stalk [of grass]. —keimig, adj. [said of malt] sprouting or germinating in the stalks instead of the roots. —korb, m. basket for grass. —land, n. land or ground covered with grass, pasture ground, meadow-ground, grass-land. —lauch, m. porret, bladed leek. —läufer, m. land-rail, corncrake. —leber, n. [in botany] river-weed. —linde, f. lime-tree. —magd, f. a maid servant who gets grass for the cows. —mähen, v. intr. V. Mähen. —mäher, m. mower of grass; it. [in nat. hist.] V. —raupe. —metze, f. [in nat. history] dragon-fly, adder-fly. —mücke, f. warbler, hedge sparrow, petty-chaps. —nelke, f. V. Grasblume 2) and Nelke. —pappel, f. V. Gänsepappel. —pferd, n. 1) a horse that is kept on grass. 2) V. —hüpfer. —pilz, m. V. Birkenpilz. —platz, m. grassplot, green, bowling-green. —polei, m. grass-poly. —raupe, f. caterpillar found on meadows. —reich, adj. abounding with grass, rich in grass or pasture, grassy. —schmetterling, m. grass-butterfly. —schnecke, f. [a kind of snail without a shell] slug. —schnepfe, f. the common snipe. —schwiele, f. V. Schwiele. —sense, —sichel, f. scythe, sickle for cutting grass. —specht, m. V. Grünspecht. —sperling, m. V. —mücke. —stoppel, f. stubble of grass. —stück, n. V. —platz. —taffet, m. [a kind of taffeta, from the Eastindies, made of thread from certain plants] aridas. —tuch, n. a piece of packcloth, in which grass is carried. —wachs, m. V. —weide. —wagen, m. waggon for fetching grass. —webe, f. V. Sommerfaden.

—weher, *m.* land-rail. —weide, *f.* pasture, pasturage. —wittwe, *f. fig.* [in contempt or jest] an unmarried woman got with child. —wuchs, *m.* 1) the growing of grass. 2) V. —weide. Viel —wuchs haben, to have many meadows. —wurm, *m.* a caterpillar that nibbles the grass; *it.* V. Spulwurm. —wurzel, *f.* quitchgrass, dog-grass.

Gräseln, *v. intr.* [among hunters] to bite the grass, to nibble at the grass.

Gräsen, *v. intr.* 1) to feed on grass, to graze. Das Vieh —lassen, to let the cattle feed or graze, to tend the grazing cattle. 2) to cut grass. — gehen, to go a-grazing. *Fig.* [rather provincial, in vulgar lang.] Nach etwas — [= nach etwas trachten], to aspire to or after a thing, to try to get or obtain a thing. 3) to rub or touch lightly in passing, to graze. Die Kugel graste an der Mauer, the bullet grazed the wall.

Gräser, *m.* [-s, *pl.* -] —inn, *f.* 1) one that cuts and gathers grass, grasscutter. 2) [among hunters] the tongue of a stag.

Graserei, *f.* 1) act of cutting grass. 2) grass cut for fodder. 3) meadow-ground, pasture-ground, pasturage.

Gräsicht, *adj.* and *adv.* resembling grass, grassy. Ein —er Geschmack, V. Grasgeschmack.

Gräsig, *adj.* and *adv.* covered, abounding with grass, grassy. Ein —er Platz, a grassy spot or place, V. Grasplatz.

Gräslein, *n.* [-s, *pl.* -] 1) a small blade or spire of grass. 2) [among sportsmen] the traces of a stag in the grass. 3) [in natural history] V. Gräßlein.

Gräsling, *m.* [-es, *pl.* -e] 1) a small branch or sprig of a vine laid in the ground for propagation. 2) [in natural history] V. Gräßling.

Gräß, [allied either to the L. *crassus* = thick, or to grauen, Graus] *adj.* and *adv.* hideous, dreadful, horrible, shocking, disgusting. Seine grassen Blicke erschreckten mich, his ghastly looks alarmed me; der Blick der Wahnsinnigen ist —, the look of maniacs is wild; ein grasser Anblick, a hideous, shocking sight, *das war zu — [= zu stark, zu grob], that was too much, too bad. V. Gräßlich.

Grassiren, *v. intr.* [in fam. lang.] [applied to diseases] to prevail, to rage, to be spread, to be common.

Gräßlein, *n.* [-s, *pl.* -] the redpole or lesser redpole. V. Bluthänfling, Flachsfink.

Gräßlich, *adj.* and *adv.* shocking, horrible, dreadful, frightful, ghastly, hideous, atrocious. Ein —es Schauspiel, a dreadful, horrible spectacle; eine —e That, an atrocious deed; er ist — entstellt, he is dreadfully, hideously disfigured.

Gräßlichkeit, *f.* horribleness, hideousness, terribleness, atrociousness.

Gräßling, *m.* [-es, *pl.* -e] 1) [in natural history] gudgeon. 2) [in botany] ash-tree. V. Esche.

Gräsung, *f.* 1) the act of cutting grass. 2) pasture-ground, pasturage. Die Pferde in die — thun, to turn the horses out to grass.

Gräte, Gräthe, *f.* [*pl.* -n] 1) fish-bone. *Fig.* Er war spitzig, wie eine — [= er redete sehr witzig], his discourse was very biting or sarcastic; *eine — in etwas finden, V. Haar. 2) [in farriery, mangy humours or ulcers on the hind feet of horses] arrests, rat-tails, scratches or mules. V. Rattenschwanz.

Gräten=fisch, *m.* a fish with bones. —los, *adj.* without fish-bones.

Gräten, V. Grätscheln.

Gräth, [allied to the Fr. *arête*, Germ. reißen, ritzen; the ancient Swedish *grad* signifies a sword] *m.* [-es, *pl.* -e] primarily, any thing sharp or pointed, edge, ridge. Der — einer Degenklinge, eines Löffelstiels, the edge of a sword-blade, of a spoon; der — [die Spitze, der Rücken] eines Felsens, eines Gebirges, the top or ridge of a mountain. V. Rück—. [among joiners] the edge of a board that is to be let into a groove, rabbet; [among foresters] waste wood, brushwood, bavin.

Gräth=eisen, *n.* [among coopers] a knife for paring the hoops. —hobel, *m.* [among joiners] rabbet-plane. —säge, *f.* [among joiners] a saw for cutting grooves or rabbets. —sparren, *m.* [among carpenters] the corner-rafter of a hip-roof, hip. V. Lehrsparren. —thier, *n.* a shamois of a reddish colour, living on the ridges of the mountains.

Gräthe, V. Gräte.

***Grätia,** *f.* [der - or -'s] [a christian name of women] Grace.

***Grätie,** *f.* V. Grazie.

Grätig, *adj.* and *adv.* full of fishbones. Ein sehr —er Fisch, a fish full of bones. *Fig.* [in vulgar language] Geiß— [= geizig], niggardly, stingy, V. Hungerleider; *it.* er ist —, he is very irascible.

‖**Grätscheln, Grätschen,** [from the ancient graten, L. *gradior*, to go] *v. intr.* [to part the legs wide and to walk with the legs far apart] to straddle. V. Ausspreiten.

***Gratulation,** *f.* congratulation. V. Glückwunsch.

***Gratuliren,** *v. intr.* to congratulate, to wish joy. V. Glück wünschen.

‖**Grätzgarten,** *m.* [-s, *pl.* -gärten] kitchen-garden. Krätzgarten.

Grau, [Anglo-Sax. *graeg*, D. *graa*, L. *ravus*. Among the ancient Scythians *grau* signified *snow*] I. *adj.* gray, V Aschfarben, Eis—, Esel—, Rauch—, Weiß—, Hell—, Dunkel—, Schwarz—. —e Haare, gray hair; ein —es Pferd, a gray horse; die —en Mönche [Franziskanermönche], the gray friars, Franciscans; sich — kleiden, to wear gray clothes; dieser Zeug fällt or spielt in's —e, this stuff inclines to gray; er ist ganz —, his hair is quite gray; er fängt an — zu werden, he begins to grow gray-haired or hoary, his hair begins to be grizzled, *fig.* he begins to grow old; [in chimistry] der —e Nicht, spodium, tutty, V. Ofenrauch; [in familiar language] darüber lasse ich mir kein —es Haar wachsen [= bekümmere ich mich nicht], that gives or causes me no great pain or uneasiness, I will not trouble my head about that matter; *fig.* in —er [früher] Vorzeit, in remote ages or antiquity; der —e Bund, the gray league, the league of the Grisons. V. Graubünden. II. *subst. n.* [indeclinable] gray colour, gray. Syn. Grau werden, Grauen. Grau werden signifies simply to become gray, and may be used indiscriminately of any thing. Grauen is said only of the hair of men and animals, and figuratively of the day. Der Tag grauet schon [the day is beginning to dawn]; der Mensch grauet schon [the man is growing gray].

Grau=äugig, *adj.* gray-eyed. —bart, *m.* gray-beard, grizzled-beard. —blau, *adj.* gray-blue. —braun, *adj.* gray-brown. —braunsteinerz, *n.* gray oxyde of manganese. —erle, *f.* alder-tree with whitish leaves. —fink, *m.* a kind of gray finch with a yellow spot on the breast. —gelb, *adj.* gray-yellow. —golderz, *n.* black tellurium ore. —haarig, *adj.* gray-haired, hoary. —hafer, *m.* gray oats. —hänfling, *m.* gray linnet. —kehlchen, *n.* redstart or redtail with a gray throat. —kopf, *m.* 1) a gray or hoary head. 2) a gray-haired person. 3) [in natural history] a kind of hawk, kestrel, windhover, stannel. V. Wannenweiher. —meise, *f.*, *dim.* —meischen, *n.* gray titmouse. —nacken, *m.* the gray or ash-coloured sea-mew or gull. —scheckig, *adj.* marked with gray spots, grayspotted, gray-speckled. —schimmel, *m.* a gray horse; *it.* V. Grauchen. —specht, *m.* creeper of a grayish colour, V. Baumhacker. —stein, *m.* V. —werk 2). —thier, *n.* V. Grauchen. —wacke, *f.* [in mineralogy, a kind of sandstone, composed of quartz, feldspar, siliceous slate and argillite] gray wacke. —werk, *n.* 1) [among furriers] the fur of the gray or Siberian squirrel, minever. 2) [among masons] stone from the quarry [on account of its gray colour]. —werksschere, *f.* [among furriers] brake.

Graubünden, *n.* [-s] **Graubünderland,** *n.* [-es] the country of the Grisons.

Graubünder, Graubündner, *m.* [-s, *pl.* -] **Graubünd[n]erinn,** *f.* Grison.

Graubünder, Graubündisch, Graubündner, *adj.* and *adv.* of or from the Grisons, in the manner of the Grisons.

Grauchen, *n.* [-s, *pl.* -] an animal of a gray colour, particularly the ass [chiefly used in jest].

Graue, *n.* [-n] V. Grau I. and II.

‖**Gräue,** *f.* V. Grau II.

Grauel, *m.* [-s, *pl.* -] [in vulgar language] 1) V. Das Grauen. 2) V. Gräuel.

Gräuel, *m.* [-s, *pl.* -] [probably allied to raub] 1) horror, detestation, abomination. Sie haben ein — an mir [in Scripture], they abhor, abominate me. 2) an object of abomination or detestation. Er ist allen Menschen ein —, he is abhorred or detested by every body, he is the horror of all mankind; die — der Verwüstung [in Scripture], the abomination of desolation; der — der Kinder Ammons, the abomination of the children of Ammon. Syn. V. Grauen.

Gräuel=that, *f.* horrible deed, atrocious action, heinous crime. —voll, *adj.* V. Gräulich.

Graueln, Gräueln, V. Grauen 2).

Grauen, *v. intr* 1) to turn or grow gray. Sein Scheitel beginnt zu —, his head begins to grow gray, grizzled or hoary. *Fig.* to pass from darkness into light, to dawn. Als der Tag grauete, anfing zu —, when the day or morning dawned, began to dawn. Syn. V. Grau werden. 2) grauen [or grausen] *v. intr. impers.* to have an aversion to, to dislike; *it.* to be afraid of. Es grauet ihm vor der Arbeit, he has a horror of work; es grauet mir vor Fleisch, meat goes against my stomach, I have an abhorrence of meat; es grauet mir, wenn ich daran denke, it makes me shudder to think of it; ihm grauet vor Gespenstern, he is afraid of spectres.

Grauen, *n.* [-s] horror, dread, fear. Es überfiel mich ein —, I was seized with horror; man kann nicht ohne — daran denken, one cannot think of it without horror, it makes one shudder to think of it. Syn. Grauen, Gräuel, Abscheu, Grausen. Gräuel and Abscheu denote the emotion of the mind which arises from the contemplation of some great impending evil. Grauen and Grausen refer to some imminent danger or evil, and imply a high degree of fear or horror. Grausen denotes a stronger impression of fear or horror than Grauen. Things that excite Abscheu and Gräuel are also called Gräuel, so that in this signification Gräuel and Abscheu stand in the relation to one another of cause and effect.

Graùenhaft, *adj.* and *adv.* exciting horror or dread, horrible, dreadful. V. Gräulich.

†**Graùerlich, Graùserlich,** *adj.* and *adv.* horrible, dreadful. Es wird mir hier ganz —, this place strikes me with horror, makes me shudder.

Graùheit, *f.* the quality of being gray, grayness.

Graùlich or **Gräùlich,** *adj.* and *adv.* somewhat gray, grayish.

Gräùlich, *adj.* and *adv.* 1) shocking, horrible, terrible, horrid, dreadful. Eine —e That, a shocking, horrible deed; ein —er Lärm, a terrible noise; †eine —e Kälte, ein —er Verlust, an excessive cold, an enormous loss; †er verlor —, he lost enormously. 2) V. Furchtsam.

Graùpe, *f.* [*pl.* -n] [allied to reiben; the Bohemian *graupy* signifies *hail*] 1) [in mining] V. Graupelerz. 2) cupreous bismuth in grains. 3) grain deprived of its husk; peeled barley, pearl-barley. —n machen, to peel barley. V. Gersten—, Perl—, Weizen—. 4) —n or Graupeln, *pl.* sleet. Das ist kein Hagel, es sind —n, that is no hail, it is sleet.

Graupen=gang, *m.* mill for peeling barley. —**kobalt,** *m.* cobalt-ore in grains, gray cobalt. —**lasur,** *f.* V. Graupe 2). —**schleim,** *m.* barley-water. —**suppe,** *f.* barley-soup or gruel.

Graùpelerz, *n.* [-es, *pl.* -e] [in mining] small fragments of ore, pounded ore.

Graùpeln, Gräùpeln, *pl.* V. Graupe 4).

Graùpeln, Gräùpeln, *v. intr. impers.* to fall down in small fragments, to drizzle, to sleet. Es gräupelt, it sleets.

Graùs, *adj.* and *adv.* [in poetry] horrible, dreadful, V. Gräßlich. Eine —e Nacht, a dismal night.

1. **Graùs,** *m.* [-es] 1) a dismal appearance or sight, a dismal noise or tumult. In dem — der Elemente, in the terrible uproar of the elements. 2) V. Das Grauen.

2. **Graùs,** *m.* [-es] [allied to the Sw. grösen = to crush, Fr. *écraser*, E. *crash* and *crush*] rubbish, ruins; [in commerce] garbles. In Staub und — zerfallen, to fall into decay.

Graùsam, [Low Sax. and Dan. grusam, allied to the L. *crudelis*, and probably to *rudis*, Fr. *rude* and Germ. rauh, roh] I. *adj.* cruel, inhuman, barbarous. Ein —er Tyrann, a cruel tyrant; ein —er Tod, a cruel death; die —e Schöne, the cruel fair one; *fig.* [vulgar] ein —er [= heftiger] Schmerz, a cruel, violent pain; eine —e Kälte, an excessive cold; [in familiar language] der —e, die —e, the cruel man, woman; er spielt den —en [= kümmert sich nichts um die Gunst der Weiber], he acts a cruel part; sie ist nicht —, she is kind enough, *it.* she is rather lavish of her favours. II. *adv.* cruelly, inhumanly, barbarously, painfully. Er hat ihn — umbringen lassen, he has put him to a cruel death; er ist — mit ihm umgegangen, he has treated him cruelly; [vulgar] er ist — reich, he is mighty, exceedingly rich.

Graùsamkeit, *f.* [*pl.* -en] 1) cruelty, inhumanity, barbarity. Seine — befriedigen, to satisfy one's cruelty; die — des Geschickes, einer Geliebten, the cruelty of fate, of a mistress. 2) a cruel action, barbarous deed, cruelty. —en begehen, to commit acts of cruelty, cruelties.

Graùsen, *v. intr. imp.* V. Grauen 2).

Graùsen, *n.* [-s] V. Grauen.

Graùsenhaft, *adj.* and *adv.* horrible, dreadful V. Gräulich.

Graùserlich, V. Grauerlich.

***Graveùr,** [pron. Grawöhr] *m.* [-s, *pl.* -e] engraver.

***Graviren,** [pron. Grawihren] *v. tr.* and *intr.* to grave, to engrave.

Gravir=meißel, *m.* V. Grabstichel. —**zeug,** *n.* engraving-tools.

***Gravität,** *f.* seriousness, solemnity of deportment or character, gravity, V. Ernst, Ernsthaftigkeit; *it.* heaviness, weight, gravity.

***Gravitätisch,** *adj.* and *adv.* serious, solemn, grave.

***Gravitatiön,** *f.* gravitation. V. Schwerkraft.

***Gräzie,** *f.* [*pl.* -n] [beauty deified] Grace. Die drei —n, the three Graces. *Fig.* [= Anmuth] grace. Sie hat eine bezaubernde — in allem, was sie thut, she has a charming grace in all she does.

***Graziös,** *adj.* and *adv.* V. Anmuthig.

Grebe, *f.* [*pl.* -n] [from greifen] [a fowl of the genus Columbus] grebe. V. Silbertaucher.

Greep, *n.* [-es, *pl.* -e] [in seamen's language] cut-water.

Gregör, *m.* [-s, *pl.* -e] [a name of men] Gregory.

Gregoriänisch, *adj.* Gregorian. Der —e Kalender, the Gregorian calendar.

Greif, *m.* [-es, *pl.* -e] 1) [an imaginary animal, said to be generated between the lion and eagle] griffin, griffon. 2) — [or —geier, *m.*] [the largest species of fowl] condor.

Greif=geier, *m.* V. Greif 2). —**klaue,** *f.* pounce, claw, talon. —**muschel,** *f.* —**muschelstein,** *m.* V. —stein. —**pferd,** —**roß,** *n.* [*Hippogryph] hippogriff. —**schnabel,** *m.* [among dentists] a crooked instrument for drawing teeth, pelican. V. Gemsenfuß. —**stein,** *m.* [in conchology] gryphite.

Greifen, *ir.* I. *v. intr.* [Sax. gripan, Engl. *gripe*, Low-Saxon, gripe; allied to raffen, the L. *rapio* and the Gr. ἁρπάζω &c.] to stretch out the hand, to seize or lay hold of [with the hand]. Nach dem Hute —, to lay one's hand upon one's hat, to take up one's hat; an etwas —, to touch a thing; nach etwas —, to lay hold of a thing; zu den Waffen —, to take up arms; [among sportsmen] der Hund greift zur Fährte [= sucht mit der Nase am Boden], the dog noses the ground closely, catches the scent or track; seinem Gegner in den Degen —, to catch hold of, to grasp the sword of one's antagonist; er griff nach seinem Degen, he clapped or put his hand on his sword; Einem in die Haare —, to take or seize any one by the hair; zur Feder — [schreiben], to take up the pen, to put pen to paper; einem Kranken an den Puls —, to feel a patient's pulse; Einem unter das Kinn —, to chuck any one under the chin; diese Räder greifen gut in einander, the cogs of the wheels catch well, these wheels lock well into each other; der Krebs hat schon innerlich um sich gegriffen, the mortification has reached the inward parts; das Feuer griff schnell um sich, the fire spread very fast. *Fig.* In seinen eigenen Busen — [= sich selbst prüfen], to lay one's hand upon one's heart, to examine one's conscience, or one's self; Einem an die Ehre, an das Leben —, to make an attempt upon a man's honour, life; Einem an das Herz —, to attack any one in the most sensible part; Einem in's Amt —, to encroach on the office of another, V. Eingreifen; Einem unter die Arme — [= ihn unterstützen], to assist, to relieve any one, to lend any one a helping hand; zu einem Mittel —, to have recourse to an expedient; zu eine[m] Handwerke —, to choose or take up a tra[de]; zur Strafe, zum Ernste — [little used], to punis[h], to use severity; der Krieg, die Pest greift u[m] sich, the war, the plague is propagated, sprea[ds]; dieser Eroberer griff immer weiter um sich, th[e] conqueror pushed his conquests farther a[nd] farther.

II. *v. tr.* 1) [= berühren] to touch. Eine Ta[ste,] eine Saite —, to touch a key, a string; fal[sch] — [auf einem Instrumente], eine falsche Sai[te] —, to touch a wrong key or string. 2) [= ergreifen] to seize, to catch, to take hold o[f.] Man hat die Diebe gegriffen, the thieves ha[ve] been seized, taken up or apprehended; d[ie] Katze hat eine Maus gegriffen, the cat ha[s] caught a mouse; der Anker greift [= faßt i[m] Grunde], the anchor bites or holds fast; di[e] Säge kann nicht —, das Holz ist zu hart, th[e] saw cannot take any hold of the wood, it [is] too hard. *Fig.* Platz —, to take place; eine[n] Vorschlag Platz — lassen, to adopt, to accep[t] a proposal; *mit Fingern und Händen — [= kla[r] und deutlich einsehen], to see clearly or plainly; er hat ihm die Sache so deutlich gemacht, da[ß] er sie *mit Händen — kann, he has made it a[s] clear to him as the sun at noon-day, he has ex[-]plained to him the matter very well; *man kan[n] es mit Händen —, it is palpable. V. Ergreife[n,] Eingreifen. Das —, V. Griff.

Greif=bar, *adj.* and *adv.* palpable. *Fig.* —bare Dunkelheit, palpable darkness. —**brett,** *n.* V. Griffbrett 1). 2). —**holz,** *n.* [amo[ng] cloth-shearers] the wooden handle of a cloth[-]shearer's shears. —**zirkel,** *m.* [a sort of com[-]passes made with arched legs] caliber-compasse[s,] calibers or callipers. V. Taster.

Greifig, [not much used] *adj.* 1) that is ap[t] to seize or clutch. *Fig.* —e Finger haben, to b[e] light-fingered. 2) [among foresters] that whic[h] may be encompassed or spanned with the hand. Ein zwei—er Baum, a tree, two spans in cir[-]cumference. 3) liable to be laid hold of, to be stolen, tempting. V. Angreiflich.

Greifswald[e], *n.* [-s] [a town in Prussia] Gripswald.

Greinen, *v. intr.* [formerly, grinen = di[e] Zähne blöken, to shew one's teeth] [in popular lang. for weinen] to weep, to cry; *it.* V. 1. Grin[-]sen. Das —, weeping, crying.

Greiner, *m.* [-s, *pl.* -] —**inn,** *f.* one who cries or weeps, weeper; *it.* grumbler, growler.

Greis, *adj.* white or gray with age, grizzly, hoary. —es Haar, gray or hoary hair; ein —es Haupt, a hoary head; *fig.* —es [= hohes] Al[-]ter, great, advanced, old age.

1. **Greis,** *m.* [-es, *pl.* -e] [allied to grau, Fr. *gris*] a man gray with age, old man. Ein ehr[-]würdiger —, a venerable old man.

Greisenalter, Greisesalter, *n.* old age.

2. **Greis,** *m.* [-es] [probably instead of Gries] [in mining] gravel.

Greis=zwitter, *m.* tinstone.

Greisen, *v. intr.* [in poetry] to become gray-haired, to grow hoary.

Greisinn, *f.* an old woman. Eine ehrwür[-]dige —, a venerable old woman or matron.

Greißen, *v. tr.* [in mining] to cleave, to split. V. Reißen, Spalten.

Grèling, *n.* [-es, *pl.* -e] [in seamen's lang.] the smallest cable of a ship, hawser.

Grèll, *adj.* and *adv.* [perhaps allied to the Sax. *griellan*, to provoke, V. Groll] very bright, glaring, dazzling. —e Augen, piercing, glaring eyes; eine —e Farbe, a dazzling or glaring colour; —e Umrisse, hard or stiff outlines; das —e [...]

einem **Gemählde**, hardness, stiffness in a picture or tableau; eine —e Stimme, a harsh, sharp, piercing or shrill voice.

Grellheit, *f.* quality of being glaring or dazzling; hardness, stiffness, shrillness, acuteness.

Grempel, *m.* [-s] 1) (= Kram) retail trade, V. Käse—, Kleider—, Trödel. 2). V. Gerümpel. 3) V. Grempler.

Grempel-kammer, *f.* V. Gerümpelkammer. —**markt**, *m.* frippery, rag-fair. —**werk**, *n.* old goods, old furniture, old clothes, old stuff, old lumber, V. Trödelwaare.

Gremperei, *f.* V. Trödelhandel; *it.* V. Grempelwerk.

Grempler, *m.* [-s, *pl.* -] salesman, fripperer. V. Trödler.

***Grenadier**, *m.* V. Granatier.

Grendel, *m.* [-s, *pl.* -] (perhaps allied to Riegel, bolt) 1) (Riegel, Schlagbaum) bolt, bar. (chiefly) 2) — or **Grendelbaum**, *m.* the pole or beam of a plough.

Grendel-kette, *f.* the chain on the plough's beam (by means of which the plough may be set to go deeper or shallower). —**weide**, *f.* twisted osiers often used instead of the plough's chain.

1\. **Grengel**, *m.* [-s, *pl.* -] V. Grendel, Pflugbaum.

2\. **Grengel**, *m.* [-s, *pl.* -] (instead of Kringel) cracknel.

Greniß, *n.* [-sses, *pl.* -sse] the eighth part of a share in a mine.

Grensing, *m.* [-es, *pl.* -e] (in botany) 1) V. Gänserich. 2) V. Brennkraut, Hahnenfuß.

Grenze, *f.* [*pl.* -n] (allied to Rain, Rand; the Icel. *greina* signifies to separate) 1) (the extreme part of a country or any tract of land) frontier, border, boundary, limit, confine. Die natürlichen —n eines Landes, the natural frontiers or bounds of a country; die — eines Staates erweitern, to extend, enlarge, carry further the boundaries of a state; an den —n Frankreichs, on the confines of France; man empfing den Fürsten an der —, the prince was received on the frontier; über die — gehen, to pass or cross the frontier; die —n eines Gutes, the bounds or limits of an estate; die —n beziehen, to inspect the frontiers. 2) (the extreme part of any thing) extremity, limit. (in geometry) die —n eines Körpers, einer Zeichnung, the extreme points, the limits of a body, drawing. *Fig.* Die —n seiner Macht &c. überschreiten, to transgress or pass the bounds or limits of one's power; die —n der Bescheidenheit nicht überschreiten, to keep within the bounds of modesty; seinem Ehrgeize —n setzen, to set bounds to one's ambition; sein Stolz kennt keine —n, his pride knows no bounds, is unbounded. Syn. **Grenze**, **Schranke**. Grenzen and Schranken in their most general signification are thus distinguished, that Grenzen denotes simply that part which terminates a thing, or the furthest point of its extension, Schranken that which bounds or circumscribes it, or restrains its further extension. Both words are used of moral as well as of natural objects.

Grenz-acker, *m.* a field on the boundary of a district, boundary-field. —**bach**, *m.* a brook on the boundary of a district. —**baum**, *m.* a tree marking the boundary. —**befestigung**, *f.* 1) the fortification of the frontiers. 2) V. —festung. —**bereiter**, *m.* one that visits and inspects on horseback the frontiers, to prevent smuggling, visitor and inspector of the frontiers. —**bereitung**, *f.* inspection on horseback of the frontiers or boundaries. —**berichtigung**, *f.* the act of ascertaining the boundaries, the ascertainment or settlement of the boundaries or frontiers. —**besichtigung**, *f.* —**beziehung**, *f.* inspection of the frontiers or boundaries. —**bewohner**, *m.* one who dwells on the border of a country or tract of land, borderer. —**bild**, *n.* a figure or statue, marking the boundary; (among the Ancients) term. —**brücke**, *f.* bridge over a river that separates two countries. —**damm**, —**deich**, *m.* a dike marking the boundary. —**dorf**, *n.* frontier-village, border-village. —**festung**, *f.* frontier or border fortress. —**fluß**, *m.* a river marking the boundary. —**furche**, *f.* furrow marking the boundary. —**gebirge**, *n.* mountains on the frontiers of a country. —**gegend**, *f.* a frontier district. —**gemeinschaft**, *f.* contiguity, contiguousness. —**gott**, *m.* (among the Ancients) the God of boundaries, Terminus; *it.* V. —bild. —**graben**, *m.* a ditch marking the boundary. —**gut**, *n.* an estate on the boundary of a district. —**haufen**, *m.* a heap of stones or earth marking the boundary. —**haus**, *n.* a house on the frontiers of a country or on the boundary of a district. —**herr**, *m.* a proprietor or lord of a manor or land on the frontiers. —**holz**, *n.* a wood on the boundary of a district or marking the boundary. —**hügel**, *m.* 1) a hill on the frontiers. 2) V. —haufen. —**irrung**, *f.* error or dispute concerning the boundary. —**jäger**, *m.* V. —schütze. —**kette**, *f.* (in military language) a cordon (of troops). —**land**, *n.* a country or district bordering on another. —**linie**, *f.* line of demarcation, boundary-line. (used also in a fig. sense) Die —linien der Bescheidenheit, the bounds of modesty. —**los**, *adj.* and *adv.* V. Grenzenlos. —**mahl**, *n.* V. —zeichen. —**mauer**, *f.* a wall marking the boundary, boundary-wall. —**messer**, *m.* V. —scheider, Feldmesser. —**nachbar**, *m.* neighbour, borderer. —**ort**, *m.* frontier place or town, V. —stadt, —dorf. —**pfahl**, *m.* a post marking the boundary. —**platz**, *m.* V. —ort. —**punkt**, *m.* point of demarcation; *fig.* the extreme point. —**recht** or —**ens-recht**, *n.* the right of examining the boundaries. —**receß**, *m.* V. —vergleich. —**säule**, *f.* a pillar marking the boundary. —**scheide**, *f.* V. —scheidung. —**scheider**, *m.* one who, by measuring, determines the boundaries, surveyor. —**scheidung**, *f.* 1) the determination of boundaries. 2) boundary. —**schloß**, *n.* a castle on the boundary of a district, on the frontiers of a country, a border-castle. —**schnur**, *f.* V. —kette. —**schütze**, *m.* a gamekeeper who guards the boundaries of a manor. —**soldat**, *m.* a soldier serving on the frontiers; (especially) V. Granitzer or Grenzer 2). —**stadt**, *f.* frontier town. —**stein**, *m.* a stone for marking the boundary, landmark, mere-stone. —**streit**, *m.* —**streitigkeit**, *f.* contest or litigation about boundaries. —**strom**, *m.* V. —fluß. —**thierchen**, *n.* V. Aufgußthierchen. —**vergleich**, —**vertrag**, *m.* arrangement or agreement concerning boundaries, boundary-treaty. —**wall**, *m.* mound of earth or rampart marking the boundary. —**weg**, *m.* road or path marking the boundary. —**wehr** or —**wehre**, *f.* barrier. —**wildpret**, *n.* (among hunters) game that is killed on the boundary of a district, or on the frontiers of a country. —**zaun**, *m.* a hedge marking the boundary, boundary-hedge. —**zeichen**, *n.* landmark. —**zoll**, *m.* V. Wehrzoll. —**zug**, *m.* inspection of the boundaries.

Grenzen-los, *adj.* and *adv.* without bounds or limits, boundless, illimited. Der —lose Raum, boundless or infinite space; der —lose Himmel, the boundless sky; die —lose Macht Gottes, the unbounded power of God. *it.* very large, vast. Das —lose Weltmeer, the immense or vast ocean; sein Elend ist —los, his misery is extreme; ein —loser Ehrgeiz, an unbounded ambition. —**recht**, *n.* V. Grenzrecht.

Grenzen, *v. intr.* to be contiguous or adjacent to, to confine, to border on or upon. Die Türkei grenzt nördlich an Ungarn, Turkey on the north confines or borders on or upon Hungary; Großbritannien grenzt überall an das Meer, Great-Britain is surrounded or bounded on all sides by the sea; der an mein Haus —de Garten, the garden contiguous to my house. *Fig.* Seine Liebe grenzt an Narrheit, his love borders on madness; diese Meinung grenzt an Gottesleugnung, this opinion borders upon atheism. V. Angrenzen.

Grenzenlosigkeit, *f.* boundlessness, unboundedness, illimitedness.

Grenzer, *m.* [-s, *pl.* -] 1) V. Angrenzer. 2) V. Granitzer.

Greßling, V. Gräßling.

Gretchen, *n.* [*dimin.* of Grete, among common people] Madge, Meg, Peggy.

Grete, **Grethe**, *f.* [-ns] (a name of women, among common people) Margaret, Margery.

Greuel, V. Gräuel.

Greuper, *m.* [-s, *pl.* -] (in mining) ore in grains of the bigness of a walnut.

Grevelingen, *n.* [-s] (a town in Holland) Graveling.

Griebe, *f.* [*pl.* -n] (probably allied to Graupe) a crispy piece remaining of melted fat, tallow &c. greaves.

Griebs, *m.* [-es, *pl.* -e] the core of fruit.

Grieche, *m.* [-n, *pl.* -n] a native of Greece, Grecian, Greek. *Fig.* Er ist ein großer —, he is a great Grecian or Hellenist (= well versed in the Greek language &c.)

Griechenland, *n.* [-s] Greece.

Griechinn, *f.* a Greek or Grecian woman, a Greek or Grecian.

Griechisch, *adj.* and *adv.* Grecian, Greek. Ein —es Buch, a Greek book; die —e Sprache, the Greek tongue or language; die —en Schriftsteller, the Greek authors; — können, to know, to understand Greek; eine —e Wortfügung, a Grecism, Hellenism; ein —lateinisches Wörterbuch, a Greek-Latin Dictionary; das —e Feuer, the Grecian fire, Greek-fire; (in botany) —es Heu, fenugreek. Das —e, die —e Sprache, the Greek tongue, Greek; ein im —en bewanderter Gelehrter, a Greek scholar, a Hellenist, Grecian.

Griechsäule, *f.* V. Griessäule.

Griegelhuhn, *n.* [-s, -hühner] V. Birkhuhn.

Griel, *m.* [-es, *pl.* -e] V. Grasmücke.

Grieltrappe, *m.* lesser bustard.

Gries, *m.* [-es, *pl.* -e] (Sax. *greot*, E. *grit*, Sw. *grut*, Fr. *gruau*; in Lower Saxony grüsen signifies to crush or bruise) 1) coarse sand, gravel; (in medicine, small calculous concretions in the kidneys and bladder) gravel. Den — haben, to be troubled with the gravel; mit — vermischter Urin, gravelly urine. V. Blasen—, Lenden—. 2) (the coarse part of meal) grit, grits, groats. V. Grütze, Griesmehl; *it.* the dust, soil or filth severed from good spices, drugs &c., garbles.

Gries-asche, *f.* ashes made of tartar, old lees of wine. —**bart**, *m.* (in botany) wild angelica. —**brei**, thick gruel made of grits. —**docke**, *f.* (in water mills and wears) a small upright post between the corner posts of a sliding flood gate. —härig, *adj.* —härige Wolle, haird or feltered wool. —holz, *n.* 1) nephritic wood. 2) privet, prime-print, V. Hartriegel, Rainweide. —horst, *m.* a heap of coarse sand or gravel in a river collected by the force of water, isle of gravel. —huhn, *n.* sandpiper, V. Strandläufer. —kleie, *f.* bran of grits or groats. —koch, *m.* [in cookery] pie made of grits, eggs, sugar and butter. —kolik, *f.* colic occasioned by gravel in the kidneys, nephritic colic. —krampf, *m.* nephritic cramp or spasm. —kraut, *n.* [in botany] field-balm. —kuchen, *m.* a cake made of coarse flour or grits, V. —koch. —mehl, *n.* 1) the first flour obtained from grits, the finest or best flour. 2) coarse flour or meal, grits. —säule, *f.* [in watermills and wears] the corner posts of a sliding flood gate. —semmel, *f.* a small loaf or roll made of grits. —sieb, *n.* a sieve for grit. —stange, *f.* [formerly] truncheon by which an officer of arms forbade fight, warder. —stein, *m.* nephritic stone, jade. V. Nierenstein. —suppe, *f.* soup made of grits. —wärtel, *m.* [in tournaments] chief officer of arms, superintendent [of the tournament], marshal. —wasser, *n.* [in medicine] nephritic water or medicine. —werk, *n.* [in watermills] floodgate, V. —säule. —wurzel, *f.* [in botany, a plant of South America, used against the gravel] Cessampelos Pareira.

1. **Grieseln,** [allied to rieseln] I. *v. intr.* to fall into small pieces, to crumble. II. *v. tr.* to break or crush into small pieces, to crumble.

‖2. **Grieseln,** [V. Grausen] *v. intr. impers.* to shudder, to shiver. Es grieselt mich, I shudder. V. Grauen, Grausen.

Griesen, *v. tr.* to make grit.

Griesgram, *m.* [-es] [in fam. lang.] 1) ill humour, spleen. 2) grumbler, growler.

Griesgram, *adj.* and *adv.* grumbling, peevish, morose, sullen, splenetic. Er hat heute eine —e Laune, he is cross or peevish to-day.

Griesgramen, *v. intr.* to be cross, peevish, illhumoured, to fret.

Griesgrämisch, *adj.* and *adv.* V. Griesgram.

Griesicht, *adj.* and *adv.* resembling gravel. —es Mehl, coarse flour.

Griesig, *adj.* and *adv.* abounding with, consisting of gravel, gravelly; [in medicine] calculous.

Griff, [from greifen] *m.* [-es *pl.* -e] 1) the act of stretching out one's hand, of seizing or laying hold, grasp, gripe. Einen — in etwas thun, to put one's hand into a thing; einen — in den Glückstopf thun, to draw a lottery-ticket. **fig.* to try one's fortune; *etwas am or im —e haben, to know a thing by feeling, by the touch, *it.* to be a perfect dab at a thing, to have a knack at a thing; einen — auf einem Tonwerkzeuge thun, to touch an instrument, to play upon it; einen falschen — thun, to touch a wrong key or string; V. Griffbrett; *fig.* V. Handgriff; *mit listigen —en umgehen, to use tricks or shifts. 2) [as much as the hand will grasp or contain] handful; [in husbandry] V. Glebe. Ein —chen Tabak, a pinch of snuff. [among foresters] span, V. Spanne. 3) [the thing that seizes or grasps]. Die —e [= Klauen] der Raubvögel, the talons, claws, clutches of birds of prey; [vulgar for Hände] hands, clutches. Der — am Hufeisen, the toe of a horse-shoe. 4) [that part of an instrument or vessel which is held in the hand when used] handle. Die —e an einem Koffer, the handles of a trunk; der — an einem Degen, the handle or hilt of a sword; der — eines Kruges, the ear of a pitcher; [among printers] der — am Preßbengel, the wooden handle of a bar.

Griff-blatt, *n.* [in music] a leaf with figures or signs indicating the manner of playing on the flute, pianoforte &c. —brett, *n.* 1) [the board at the neck of a violin, guitar or the like] finger-board. 2) [in an organ or harpsichord] all the keys or fingerkeys. —loch, *n.* [in music] the hole [of a flute &c.]. —triebel, *m.* [among swordcutlers] driver. —winde, *f.* [among swordcutlers] a kind of reel or windle for putting the brass or silver wire about the handle of a sword.

Griffel, *m.* [-s, *pl.* -] [allied to graben, schreiben, Gr. γράφειν, L. *scribo*] a pointed instrument formerly used in writing on tables of wax, style; [among engravers] graver, style; *it* [a small wire used to point out letters to children when learning to read] fescue; *it.* a slate-pencil, V. Rechen—, Schiefer—; [in botany, the middle portion of the pistil, connecting the stigma with the germ] style, shaft.

Griffel-baum, *m.* Judas-tree, V. Salatbaum, Judasbaum. —beere, *f.* V. Preißelbeere. —förmig, *adj.* and *adv.* like a style, styliform [in anatomy] —förmiger Fortsatz or —fortsatz, *m.* styloid apophysis or process of the temporal bone. —hornzungenbein-muskel, *m.* V. —muskel. —loch, *n.* [in anatomy] stylomastoid hole. —lose, *f.* a genus of plants having neither pistils nor styles. —muskel, *m.* [in anatomy] stylo cerato-hyoideus muscle. —schlundkopfmuskel, *m.* [in anatomy] stylo-pharyngean muscle. —zungen-muskel, *m.* [in anatomy] stylo-glossus muscle.

Griffen, *v. tr.* Ein Pferd —, to shoe a horse with frost-nails, to roughshoe a horse.

Griffig, V. Greifig.

1. **Grille,** *f.* [*pl.* -n] [allied to the ancient kreien, to cry] [*dim.* Grillchen, *n.* -s, *pl.* -] 1) [an insect] cricket. 2) ophidion. 3) V. Seegrille.

Grillen-fresser, *m.* V. Madenfresser. —muschel, *f.* V. Käfermuschel.

2. **Grille,** *f.* [*pl.* -n] [allied to the Sw. *graola* = graben, to dig, hence Grille = Grübelei, close and subtile meditation] odd or capricious notion or fancy, idle thought, whim, freak, caprice, vagary. —n im Kopfe haben, to be whimsical, freakish or capricious, *it.* to have a flea in one's ear, to be restless or uneasy; —n fangen, to make almanachs for the last year, to pursue useless thoughts to be full of fancied cares; sich —n machen, to fancy one's self unhappy, to be melancholy, to trouble one's head with fancied cares; um diese —n zu vertreiben, in order to drive away this melancholy or illhumour; was für eine — ist ihm jetzt wieder in den Kopf gekommen? what whim has got possession of him now, what maggot has he now got in his head? er ist voll —n, he is full of whims, of odd or strange fancies, he is a very whimsical or capricious fellow.

Grillen-fang, *m.* useless cares, unnecessary solicitude, disposition to melancholy. —fänger, *m.* —fängerinn, *f.* a whimsical, capricious or fanciful person, a fancy-monger; a low-spirited, morose person. —fängerei, *f.* 1) fancifulness, whimsicalness, freakishness. 2) whims, maggots. —fängerisch, *adj.* V. —haft. —haft, *adj.* and *adv.* fanciful, whimsical, capricious, freakish, fantastical. —krank, *adj.* [*hypochondrisch] hypochondriac, V. Milzsüchtig. —krankheit, *f.* [*Hypochondrie] hypochondria, V. Milzsucht. —plan, *m.* whimsical, odd, ridiculous plan or design. —sucht, *f.* V. —krankheit. —süchtig, *adj.* V. —krank. —vertreiber, *m.* that drives away cares and sorrow. Wein ist häufig ein wirksamer —vertreiber, wine is frequently an efficient remedy against melancholy thoughts. —werk, *n.* [in painting] whimsical figures and scenery, grotesk or grotesque.

Grillig, V. Grillenhaft.

***Grimasse,** *f.* [*pl.* -n] [distortion of the countenance] grimace. *Fig.* Es ist nichts, als eine — [Verstellung], it is nothing else but a sham.

Grimassen-macher, *m.* —macherinn, *f.* one that makes faces or grimaces.

Grimm, *m.* [-es] [allied to gram and Grimasse. The Sw. and Sax. *grima* signifies *a mask*, as it disfigures the face] fury, rage, wrath. In — gerathen, to put one's self, to fall or fly into a passion, to become furious; voll Zorn und —, full of wrath and fury; seinen — an Einem auslassen, to vent or wreak one's passion or fury upon any one; der — wilder Thiere, the fury of wild beasts; Herr, züchtige mich nicht in deinem —e [Zorne, [in Script.], o Lord, chasten me not in thy hot displeasure.

Grimm, *adj.* and *adv.* V. Grimmig.

Grimm-darm, *m.* [in anatomy] colon. —darmsband, *n.* ligament of the colon. —darmsgegend, *f.* [in anatomy, the lateral or lumbar region, adjacent to the colon] epicolic region. —darmsgekröse, *n.* [in anatomy] mesocolon. —darmsklappe, *f.* [in anatomy] the valve of the colon. —darmsschlagader, *f.* artery of the colon. —darmszelle, *f.* cell of the colon. —enswasser, *n.* a distilled liquor used against the colic, carminative liquor or brandy.

Grimmen, *v. intr.* 1) V. Ergrimmen. 2) *v. impers.* to occasion great pain in the bowels, to gripe. Es grimmet mich, es grimmet mich im Leibe, I feel a violent griping or colic in my bowels or guts, I have got the gripes.

Grimmen, *n.* [-s] distressing pain of the bowels, colic, gripes, griping.

Grimmig, *adj.* and *adv.* wrathful, enraged, furious. Ein —es [reißendes] Thier, a furious animal, a ferocious beast or animal; ein —er Mensch, a ferocious fellow, a brute; ein —er Blick, a grim, fierce, ferocious look; — werden, to put one's self, to fly or fall into a passion, to become furious; er sieht ganz — aus, he looks quite furious; den Feind — angreifen, to fall furiously upon the enemy. *Fig.* [rather vulgar] very great, excessive. Eine —e Kälte, an excessive cold; ein —er Schmerz, an excessive pain or grief; es ist — heiß, it is exceedingly hot.

Grind, *m.* [-es, *pl.* -e] [allied to Rinde] 1) [in surgery, incrustation formed over a sore in healing] scab, scurf, V. Schorf, Rinde, Kruste. 2) itch, mange, scab, V. Erb—. Der — auf dem Kopfe, scald, V. Kopf—; der Milch—, V. Ansprung, *fig. b*); der — der Bäume, the scurf of trees, V. Räude. 3) [among hunters] the head of a stag.

Grind-hand, *f.* 1) an itchy or scabby hand. 2) [an animal resembling in form a certain plant] dead-man's head. —haube, *f.* [in surgery] a cap besmeared with a salve against the scald. —holz, *n.* [also Elsebeerbaum, Elsebeerholz] the black berry-bearing alder. —kopf, *m.* scald-head. —köpfig, *adj.* scald-headed. —kraut, *n.* any herb or plant used against the scald or itch: chiefly *a*) groundsel. *b*) scabious, V. Schwerkraut. —rabe, *m.* V. Mandelkrähe. —salbe, *f.* a salve against the scald or mange. —wurz, —wurzel, *f.* any plant, the root of which is used against the scald or itch, chiefly common or wild dock; *it.* monk's rhubarb or patience dock, V. Ampfer, Wasserampfer.

Grindicht, *adj.* resembling the scab, mange, itch or scald.

Grindig, *adj* and *adv.* diseased with the scab, mange, itch or scald, scabby, mangy, itchy.

Gringel, *m.* 1) V. Kringel. 2) V. Grendel.

Grinitsch, *m.* [-es] [in botany] common genista or broom. V. Genster.

Grinitz, V. Grünitz.

1. **Grinsen,** I. *v. intr.* [from greinen, which see] to grin, to show one's teeth. II. *v. tr.* to utter grinning.

2. **Grinsen,** *v. intr.* [in mining] to begin to melt.

Grinzen, V. 1. Grinsen.

Grishilde, *f.* [der -, or -ns] [a name of women] Grishild, Grissel, Grizel.

||**Grisseln,** V. Schauern.

Grob, [when a monosyllable Grób, when a polysyllable Gröb] *adj.* and *adv.* [probably allied to *to grow,* like the Lat. *crassus* from *cresco*; in Dutch *groven* signifies to grow strong or stout] 1) [opposed to schwach, klein] large, or gross in bulk, big, coarse. Das —e [schwere] Geschütz, the large or heavy artillery, the great guns; —es Geld [= größere Silbergeldstücke], large money; die Bezahlung geschieht in —en Münzsorten, the payment is to be made in large money [as Kronenthaler, Laubthaler &c.]; —e Späne, thick or gross shavings, —e Schrift, letters of a large size; ein —er Faden, a coarse thread; die Feder ist zu — [= macht zu dicke Striche], the pen is too broad-pointed 2) [opposed to fein] coarse. —er Sand, coarse sand, gravel —es Tuch, coarse cloth; —e Speisen. coarse food, meat or diet; —es [schwarzes] Brot, coarse, brown bread; —e Haut, rough skin; —e Gesichtszüge, coarse, gross features; —e Glieder, clumsy limbs; —e [plumpe] Hände, clums, hands; [in mining] —e Gänge or Geschicke, common or poor lodes. *Fig.* Eine —e [starke] Stimme, a deep, bass voice; —e Arbeit, rude work. *it.* rough workmanship; aus dem —en or Gröbsten arbeiten, to roughhew; das Scheren des Tuches aus dem Gröbsten, the first shearing of cloth; ein —es Gefühl, a rude or rough feeling; ohne die gröbste Sinnlichkeit, without the grossest sensuality; eine —e [plumpe] Lüge, a gross, palpable lie; ein —er Irrthum, Fehler, a gross error, fault; eine —e Sünde, a gross sin; ein —er [unmanierlicher] Mensch, a rude, uncivil, ill-mannered, clownish man, —e Sitten, coarse, rude, rough, unrefined manners; —e Sprache, rude, gross language; —e Reden, hard words, gross language; †ein —er Flegel, an insolent fellow, a churl; dieser Scherz ist zu —, this joke is too gross, too bad.

Grob-draht, *m.* coarse wire —**drähtig,** *adj.* consisting of coarse wires, threads or fibres. coarse-grained, coarse-threaded. —drähtiger Zeug, coarse stuff. —**drahtzieher,** *m.* coarse wire-drawer. —**eisen,** *n.* coarse or rough iron. —**fädig,** *adj.* coarse-threaded, coarse-fibred, coarse-grained. —**faserig,** *adj.* consisting of coarse filaments. —**feile,** *f.* coarse file, rasp. —**gestreift,** *adj.* coarsely striped. —**gliederig,** *adj.* large or strong limbed —**gran,** or —**grän,** *n.* [in commerce] grogram. —**haarig,** —**hären,** *adj.* coarse-haired. —**häutig,** *adj.* having a hard or rough skin. —**kohle,** *f.* [in mineralogy] coarse coal. —**körnig,** *adj.* coarse-grained. —**mahler,** *m.* a coarse painter, dauber. —**meißel,** *m.* V. Strammeisen. —**schmied,** *m.* 1) black-smith, V. Hufschmied. 2) [in natural history] hammer-headed shark, V. Hammerfisch. —**sinnlich,** *adj.* grossly sensual. —**speisig,** *adj.* [in mining] coarse-grained [ore].

Gröbe, *f.* V. Grobheit.

Grobheit, *f.* coarseness. Die — des Tuches, the coarseness of cloth; die — des Fadens, Drahtes &c, the coarseness of thread, wire &c. *Fig.* *a*) state of being coarse, rude, rough, gross, illmannered, uncivil. Die — der Stimme, the harshness of the voice; die — eines Fehlers, einer Lüge, the grossness of a fault, lie; die — seiner Manieren, Sitten, the coarseness of his manners, his rudeness, incivility, rusticity; seine — beleidigt Jedermann, his rudeness shocks every body. *b*) rude action or ill-mannered or uncivil expression. Eine — begehen, to commit an act of rudeness, an incivility; er hat ihm —en gesagt, he said rude things to him, he made use of injurious words, of gross language towards him.

Grobian, *m* [-s, *pl.* -e] a coarse ill-bred fellow. a rude lout, a boor.

Gröblich, I. *adj.* somewhat coarse or gross. II. *adv.* coarsely. *Fig.* grossly. Sie irren sich —, you are grossly mistaken.

Gröbs, V. Griebs.

Groden, *m.* [-s, *pl.* -] [from the Low Saxon groien = to grow] 1) a meadow on the outside of a dike. 2) grassy isle in the midst of a river.

Groll, *m.* [-es] [probably from the Sax. *griellan* = to provoke] secret, but inveterate hate or enmity, rancour, ill-will grudge, animosity. Er hegt einen — gegen ihn, he has a pique against him, he bears him a grudge, spite or ill-will; man muß keinen — im Herzen bewahren, we must not keep rancour in our hearts; ein alter —, an inveterate hatred.

1. **Grollen,** *v. intr.* to bear ill-will against. Er grollt noch immer mit mir, he bears me a grudge or spite still, has still a pique against me.

2. **Grollen,** *v. intr.* [= rollen] to roar, Der Donner grollt, the thunder roars.

Grollhaft, *adj.* rancorous, spiteful.

Gronland, *n.* [-s] [in geography] Greenland.

Grönland[s]fahrer, *m.* [in seamen's lang.] whaler.

Grönländer, *m.* [-s, *pl.* -] —**inn,** *f.* a Greenlander.

Grönländisch, *adj.* and *adv.* Greenland, Greenlandian; in the manner of the Greenlanders. Die —e Küste, the coast of Greenland.

Groot, V. Grot.

Gropp, *n.* [-en, *pl.* -en] or —**fisch,** *m.* [-es, *pl.* -e] [in lower Latin *curabus*] bullhead, miller's thumb [a fish].

Groppe, *f.* the croop or croup [of a horse]. V. Kreuz.

‡ and ||**Gröschel,** *n.* [-s, *pl.* -] a small coin, equal to about a halfpenny.

Groschen, *m.* [-s, *pl.* -] [*dim.* **Gröschchen,** ||**Gröschlein** or **Gröschel,** *n.*] [from the lower Lat. *grossus* = thick] 1) [primarily] any thick or great piece or coin, V. Gnaden—, Schau— 2) a groshen [in South Germany, a small silver-coin equal to 3 kreuzers, or 1 penny]; *it.* [in North-Germany] ein guter — or ein —Sächsisch, a groshen Saxon money [= 1 1/2 d.]; ein Preußischer — or Silbergroschen, a groshen Prussian money, a silver-groshen [= 1 1/6 d.]. *Fig.* *Es ist keinen — werth, it is not worth a farthing; *einen hübschen — Geld haben, to have a good round sum of money; *er hat einen schönen — erworben, he has gained a great deal of money.

Groschen-brod, *n.* a penny-loaf. —**stück,** *n.* a grosh[en]-piece.

Groß, *adj.* and *adv.* [Low Saxon groot, grant and grandig; L. *grandis*; Eng. *great*, probably from *to grow*] 1) tall, high. Ein —er Mann, eine —e Frau, a tall man, woman; er ist um 2 Zoll größer als wir, he is taller by two inches than we; der größte Soldat unter dem Regimente, the tallest soldier of the regiment; ein —er Baum, a tall or high tree; das Getreide ist schon *—, the corn stands already high; ein —er Berg, a high mountain; — werden [= wachsen], to grow, to grow tall; sie hat schon —e [= erwachsene] Kinder, she has already grown children; sein *größerer [= älterer] Bruder, his elder brother; *— ziehen [= erziehen], to bring up. 2) large or extended in bulk and dimensions, great, big. Ein —er Stein, a large or great stone; ein —es Land, a large or great country; ein —er Garten, eine —e Stadt, ein —es Haus, a large or great garden, city, house; dieses Feld ist 2 Morgen —, this field has two acres; ein —er Fluß, a large or great river; der Fluß wird — [= schwillt an], the river swells; ein —er Buchstabe, a capital letter; —e Schritte machen, to take large strides; —e Tagreisen machen, to travel fast, at a great rate, wie — ist die Entfernung? how great is the distance? how far is it? die —e Zehe, the great toe; —e Augen, large eyes; —e Augen machen, to stare and gape; größer machen, V. Vergrößern. 3) large in number, great. Eine —e Anzahl, Menge, a great number, quantity or multitude; eine —e Summe Geldes, a great or large sum of money; ein —es Heer, a great or numerous army; der —e Haufen [= das gemeine Volk, der Pöbel], the mass of the people, the multitude, the vulgar; ich thäte es nicht um *ein —es [= um viel Geld], I would not do it for ever so much; im —en handeln, to sell by wholesale, to be a wholesale dealer or merchant; [among hunters] die —e Jagd, V. Jagd *Fig.* Eine —e Hitze, Kälte, a great heat, cold; eine —e Freude, a great joy; eine —e Furcht, a great fear; ein —er Lärm, a great noise; ein —es Geschrei erheben, to raise a loud cry, to utter loud cries; ein —es Geschrei von etwas machen, to make a great noise, ado or bustle about a thing; eine Sache größer machen als sie ist, to exaggerate or aggravate a thing; —e Ausgaben machen, to spend a great deal of money; ein —es Verdienst, a great merit; eine —e Wahrheit, ein —er Beweis, a great truth, argument; ein —er Mann, a great man; ein —er Dichter, Geist, a great poet, genius; ein —er Spieler, a great gambler; ein —er Verbrecher, Lügner, a great criminal, liar; es ist noch eine —e Frage, ob &c. [= es ist noch sehr ungewiß, ob &c.], it is a great question whether &c.; man hat nicht *— [= viel, sonderlich] auf seine Vorstellungen geachtet, they paid little attention or regard to, they slighted his remonstrances; was ist der Mensch, daß du ihn — achtest? [in Script.] what is man, that thou shouldst magnify him? — handeln, to act nobly, with dignity; der —e Gott, the great [almighty] God; die —e [= vornehme] Welt, people of fashion, the great world, the fashionable circles; in der —en Welt leben, mit der —en Welt umgehen, to live in the great world, ein —er Herr, a great lord; die —en [= die Vornehmen], the great; die —en Spaniens, the grandees of Spain; auf —em Fuße [= vornehm] leben, to live in great style; Alexander der —e, Alexander the Great; *— thun, to carry it high, to lord it; *mit etwas — thun, sich mit etwas — machen, to boast or brag of a thing; — sprechen, to talk big, to boast, to brag.

Groß-achtbar, *adj.* [little used] highly esteemed, worthy, right honourable. —**achtel**, *n.* V. —octav. —**äderig**, *adj.* having great or large veins. —**admiral**, *m.* high admiral. —**almosenier**, —**almosenpfleger**, *m.* lord almoner, grand-almoner. —**ältern**, *pl.* grandfather and grandmother, grandparents. —**ältermutter**, *f.* great grandmother. —**ältervater**, *m.* great grandfather. —**auge**, *n.* 1) a large eye. 2) a large-eyed person. 3) [in natural history] the large-eyed seabream. —**äugig**, *adj.* large-eyed. —**backig**, *adj.* chub-cheeked. —**ballei**, *f.* chief commandery. —**bänker**, *m.* V. Bankmeister. —**base**, *f.* grand-aunt. —**baß**, *m.* double-bass. —**bauch**, *m.* —**bäuchig**, *adj.* V. Dickbauch, Dickbäuchig. —**bauer**, *m.* V. Pferdebauer. —**beerig**, *adj.* having large berries. —**bevollmächtigte**, *m.* plenipotentiary. —**binder**, *m.* cooper. —**blätterig**, *adj.* having large leaves, large-leaved. —**blech**, *n.* large iron-plate [used for pontoons]. V. Kreuzblech. —**blumig**, *adj.* having large flowers. —**botschaft**, *f.* extraordinary embassy. —**botschafter**, *m.* ambassador extraordinary. —**brüstig**, *adj.* full-breasted. —**commenthur**, *m.* chief or grand commander [of an order of knights]. —**dutzend**, *n.* twelve dozen, a gross, V. Groß, *n.* —**enkel**, *m.* great grand-son. —**enkelinn**, *f.* great grand-daughter. —**ente**, *f.* wild duck. —**fähnrich**, *m.* [formerly] standard bearer of the empire. —**falk**, *m.* saker Der männliche —falk, sakeret. —**feldherr**, *m.* [unusual] commander-in-chief —**fittig**, *m.* [in natural history] sea-swallow, V. Fregatte 3). —**fürst**, *m.* [title of the Imperial Princes of Russia] grand-duke. —**fürstenthum**, *n.* grand-dukedom. —**fürstinn**, *f.* [title of the Imperial Princesses of Russia] grand-duchess. —**fürstlich**, *adj.* and *adv.* grand-ducal. —**garn**, *n.* [among fishermen] sweepnet. —**gestalt**, *f.* V. Koloß. —**gewerk**, *n.* V. Fabrik. —**gliederig**, *adj.* large-limbed. —**günstig**, *adj.* and *adv.* [seldom used, except in ceremonious style] very favourable, gracious. —günstiger Leser! [in joke] gentle reader! —**handel**, *m.* wholesale Einen —handel führen, to sell by wholesale. —**händler**, *m.* wholesale dealer or merchant. —**handlung**, *f.* a commercial house that deals wholesale, wholesale commercial establishment; *it.* wholesale-warehouse. —**herr**, *m.* Grand Seignior. —**herrisch**, *adj.* and *adv.* like a lord, lordly. —herrisch leben, thun, to live in high style, to carry it high, to lord it. —**herrlich**, *adj.* and *adv.* pertaining to or becoming the Grand Seignior. —**herzig**, *adj.* and *adv.* magnanimous. Ein —herziger Fürst, a magnanimous prince; —herzig handeln, to act magnanimously. —**herzigkeit**, *f.* magnanimity. —**herzog**, *m.* grand-duke. —**herzoginn**, *f.* grand-duchess. —**herzoglich**, *adj.* and *adv.* grand-ducal. —**herzogthum**, *n.* 1) grand-dukedom. 2) grand-duchy. —**hofmeister**, *m.* lord steward of a prince's household. Der —hofmeister von England, the lord high steward of England. —**hörnig**, *adj.* having great horns. —**jährig**, *adj.* V. Volljährig. —**kämmerer**, —**kammerherr**, *m.* lord chamberlain. —**kanzler**, *m.* high-chancellor, lord high-chancellor. —**kind**, *n.* grand-child. —**klette**, *f.* [in botany] burdock. —**knecht**, *m.* [in husbandry] the first man-servant on a farm, foreman. —**knochig**, *adj.* having large bones, large-boned. —**komthur**, *m.* V. —commenthur. —**kopf**, *m* —**köpfig**, *adj.* V. Dickkopf, Dickköpfig. —**kopfspinner**, *m.* V. Stammraupe. —**kreuz**, *n.* grand-cross. Er ist —kreuz der Ehrenlegion, he has the grand cross of the Legion of Honour. —**küchenmeister**, *m.* [formerly] grand master of the kitchen. —**lappen**, *m.* [in natural history] the great broadlipped whelk. —**lefzig**, —**lippig**, *adj.* blubberlipped. —**mächtig**, *adj.* 1) [in ceremonious style] high and mighty. —mächtigster Herr und Kaiser! most high and mighty Lord and Emperor! 2) [rather vulg.] very great, enormous. Er trägt einen —mächtigen Hut, he wears a huge hat. —**magd**, *f.* the first servant maid on a farm. —**mama**, *f.* V. —mutter. —**marschall**, *m.* lord-marshal, lord high steward. —**maschig**, *adj.* having large meshes. —**maul**, *n.* 1) large mouth. 2) *Fig.* braggart, ranter, V. —sprecher. 3) [in conchology] Persian whelk. —**maulig**, *adj.* having a great mouth, big-mouthed; *it.* V. —lippig. —**meister**, *m.* grand master [of an order]. —**meisterschaft**, *f.* —**meisterthum**, *n.* grandmastership. —**meisterwürde**, *f.* dignity of a grand-master, V. —meisterthum. —**mögend**, *adj.* and *adv.* high and mighty, V. Hochmögend. —**mundschenk**, *m.* grand cup-bearer. —**muth**, *f.* high spirit; usually, in a more confined sense, greatness of mind, magnanimity, generosity. —**müthig**, *adj.* and *adv.* magnanimous, generous. —**müthigkeit**, *f.* V. —muth [in the more confined sense]. —**mutter**, *f.* grandmother. —**mütterlich**, *adj.* and *adv.* becoming or like a grandmother. —**nase**, *f.* great or thick nose. —**nasig**, *adj.* having a great or thick nose, bottle-nosed. —**neffe**, *m.* grand-nephew. —**nichte**, *f.* grand-niece. —**notarius**, *m.* [formerly, in Poland] V. Kronnotarius. —**octav**, *n.* 1) [in printing] large octavo, book in large-octavo. 2) Das —octav einer Orgel, the great octave, full organ. —**oheim**, *m.* great or grand-uncle. —**ohr**, *n.* 1) a great ear; *it.* a person with great or long ears. 2) [in natural history] long-eared bat. —**öhrig**, *adj.* having great or long ears, long-eared. —**papa**, *m.* [chiefly as a term of endearment or in joke] V. —vater. —**prahler**, *m.* —**prahlerei**, *f.* V. —sprecher, —sprecherei. —**prior**, *m.* grand-prior. —**profoß**, *m.* the provost marshal of an army. —**quart**, —**quartformat**, *n.* large quarto. —**referendarius**, *m.* grand referendary. —**richter**, *m.* grand-judge, chief-justice. —**schatzmeister**, *m.* grand treasurer, [in England] first Lord of the Treasury. —**schnäbler**, *m.* gross-beak [a bird]. —**schuppig**, *adj.* having large scales. —**schwertträger**, *m.* the king's sword-bearer. —**seite**, *f.* [in geometry] hypothenuse. —**siegelbewahrer**, *m.* keeper of the great-seal. —**sinn**, *m.* magnanimity, generousness, high-mindedness. —**sinnig**, *adj.* and *adv.* magnanimous, generous, high-minded. —**sohn**, *m.* grandson. —**sprechen**, *v. intr.* to talk big, to brag, to boast, to rodomontade. —**sprecher**, *m.* boaster, bragger, braggart; *it.* braggadocio, swaggerer. —**sprecherei**, *f.* 1) boasting, bragging, rodomontade, ostentation 2) a boast or brag, bravado, rodomontade. Seine Drohungen sind nichts als —sprechereien, his menaces are nothing but rodomontades. —**sprecherinn**, *f.* a boastful, bragging woman. —**sprecherisch**, *adj.* and *adv.* boastful, braggart, vainglorious, boasting, bragging, swaggering. —**städter**, *m.* inhabitant of a large city. —**stallmeister**, *m.* grand master of the horse. —**sultan**, *m.* grand sultan, grand Turk, V. —herr. —**tante**, *f.* great or grand-aunt. —**that**, *f.* great or noble achievement, exploit. *—**thuer**, *m.* —**thuerei**, *f.* —**thuerisch**, *adj.* —**thun**, *v. intr.* V. —sprecher, —sprecherei, —sprecherisch, —sprechen. —**tochter**, *f.* grand-daughter. —**traubig**, *adj.* having large grapes. —**truchseß**, *m.* [formerly, in Poland] grand-seneschal. ‡—**türk**, *m.* V. —sultan. —**uhrmacher**, *m.* clockmaker. —**urenkel**, *m.* great great grandson. —**urenkelinn**, *f.* great great grand-daughter. —**vater**, *m.* [as a term of endearment also Großväterchen, n.] grand-father; *it.* V. —vatertanz. —**väterlich**, *adj.* becoming or like a grand-father. Die —väterliche Nachsicht hat ihn verzogen or verderbt, the indulgence of his grand-father has spoiled him. —**vatersbruder**, *m.* great-uncle, V. —oheim. —**vatersschwester**, *f.* great-aunt, grand-aunt. —**vaterstuhl**, *m.* great-arm-chair or elbow-chair. —**vatertanz**, *m.* grand-father's dance [a particular dance, which is often exhibited among the middling and lower classes, at their wedding-balls;] *it.* [in general, for] an old-fashioned dance. —**vezier**, *m.* grand-vizier. —**viertel**, *n.* V. [the more usual word] —quart. —**vogt**, *m.* high-bailiff. —**vorschneider**, *m.* carver of the king's meat [formerly, an officer in the household of the king of Poland]. —**waibel**, *m.* [in Switzerland] chief sergeant or apparitor of a court of judicature. —**wanstig**, *adj.* paunch-bellied. —**weidewerk**, *n.* [among hunters] animals pursued and taken in the chace, game. —**wessir**, *m.* V. —vezier. —**würdeträger**, *m.* great dignitary.

Groß, *n.* [indeclinable] the number of twelve dozen, a gross. Ein — Brillen, a gross of spectacles.

Großbritannien, [with some authors written Großbritanien, Großbrittanien or Großbrittannien] *n.* [-s] Great-Britain.

Großbritánnier, *m.* [-s, *pl.* -] —inn, *f.* a Briton. V. Britte, Brittinn.

Großbritánnisch, *adj.* and *adv.* Britannic, British. V. Brittisch.

Größe, *f.* [*pl.* -n] 1) [seldom used in the plural] quality of being great. *a*) [extent of height] talness, height. Die — eines Menschen, the height or stature of a man; diese Kinder sind von einer —, these children are of a size; die — eines Baumes, the height of a tree. *b*) [extent of dimensions] greatness, largeness, bigness, magnitude, size, bulk. Die — der Englischen, der Deutschen Meile, the length of the English, of the German mile; die — einer Stadt, the extent or size of a town; die — eines Berges, Gebäudes, the greatness of a mountain, edifice; [in astronomy] Sterne der ersten —, stars of the first magnitude; die scheinbare — der Sonne, the apparent bigness of the sun. *Fig.* Er ist ein Narr von erster — [in fam. lang.], he is a fool of the first class; die — [= Stärke] des Geistes, the greatness or strength of genius; die — der Leidenschaft, the force, intensity or greatness of passion; die — der Tugend oder des Lasters, the greatness of virtue or vice; die — eines Verbrechens, the heinousness of a crime; wenig zu bedürfen, ist wahre —, to want little is true grandeur; die — der Seele, the greatness of mind, magnanimity, V. Seelen—; es liegt eine gewisse — in Allem, was er thut, there is something grand in whatever he does. 2) [in mathematics, any thing which can be multiplied, divided or measured] quantity. Eine stätige —, a continued quantity; eine unstätige —, a discrete quantity; positive —n, positive or affirmative quantities; negative —n, negative or privative quantities.

Größen-forscher, —**lehrer**, *m.* mathematician. —**lehre**, *f.* [*Mathematik] the science of quantity, mathematics. Die reine —lehre or Mathematik, pure mathematics; die angewandte —lehre or Mathematik, mixt mathematics. —**lehrig**, *adj.* mathematical. —**reihe**, *f.* a series of numbers or quantities.

||**Grósselbeere**, *f.* [*pl.* -n] gooseberry.

Größentheils, *adv.* in great measure, for the most part, generally. Diese Leute sind — ehr reich, most or a great part of these people are very rich.

Größern, V. Vergrößern.

Größheit, *f.* V. [the better word] Größe 1).

Grossirer, *m.* [-s, *pl.* -] V. Großhändler.

Größlich, *adj.* and *adv.* somewhat great or arge.

Größtentheils, *adv.* for the most or greatest part. V. Großentheils.

Gröt, *m.* [-es, *pl.* -e] [a coin, current in some provinces of Germany] a German groat, four German pence or Pfennige [equal to about a half-penny].

***Grotesk,** *adj.* and *adv.* [chiefly in painting] wildly formed, grotesk, grotesque. —e Figuren, grotesk figures, grotesque work; —en, whimsical figures] grotesque.

Grotesken-mahler, *m.* grotesque painter. —mahlerei, *f.* grotesque-painting. —tanz, *m.* a comic dance. —tänzer, *m.* a comic dancer.

Grótte, *f.* [*pl.* -n] [probably from the Gr. κρύπτη] grotto.

Grotten-arbeit, *f.* little stones, pebbles and shells for a grotto, work for grottoes, shell-work and the like. —arbeiter, —künstler, —macher, *m.* grotto-maker. —säule, *f.* a column ornamented with shells. —werk, *n.* V. —arbeit.

Grötzen, *m.* [-s, *pl.* -] [among furriers] the back of a fur.

***Grouppiren,** [pron. gruppihren] V. Gruppiren.

Gruasche, *f.* [in founderies] ashes of straw and stubble.

Grube, *f.* [*pl.* -n] [*dimin.* Grübchen, Grüblein, *n.* -s, *pl.* -] 1) [any cavity made by digging] pit, hole, cavity. Eine — graben, machen, to dig, make a hole or pit; in eine — fallen, to fall into a pit or hole; man fängt die wilden Thiere in —n, wild beasts are caught in pits; Grübchen spielen [among children], to play at chuck-farthing [in compositions] V. Lehm—, Mist—, Stein—, Wolfs—. [in mining = Erz—] pit, mine. *Fig.* Einem eine — graben, to lay a snare for any one; *prov.* Wer Andern eine — gräbt, fällt selbst hinein, harm watch, harm catch. *In a more limited sense* = Grab, grave, tomb. Auf der — gehen [in familiar language], to have one foot in the grave, to be at the pit's brink, on the brink of death; sie hat ihren Mann in die —e gebracht, she has been the death of her husband. 2) any cavity in a body. Das Grübchen im Kinn, the dimple in the chin; sie hat Grübchen in den Wangen, she has dimples in her cheeks. V. Herz—, Pocken—. [in anatomy] die — hinter dem Gelenkknopfe am Hinterhauptbeine, the condyloid foss of the occiput.

Gruben-arbeit, *f.* [in mining] work in the mines. —arbeiter, *m.* workman in a mine, miner. —aufstand, *m.* [in mining] report of the state of a mine. —bau, *m.* working of mines, V. —arbeit. —beil, *n.* miner's axe, pick-axe. —bericht, *m.* [in mining] V. —aufstand. —biber, *m.* a sort of beaver or castor living alone in holes. —blende, *f.* [in mining] a miner's lantern. —compaß, V. —kompaß. —ende, *n.* [among vinedressers] layer of a vine. —erz, *n.* ore from the depth of a mine. —fahren, *n.* [in mining] descent into mines. —gebäude, *n.* any entrance or passage by which a mine is entered and by which ores are obtained, as adits, shafts, pits &c. —gezäh, *n.* [miners' term] miner's tools. —holz, *n.* [in mining] timber used in or for mines, V. Holzkur. —hüter, *m.* guard or keeper of a mine. —junge, *m.* a lad assisting or helping a miner. —kittel, *m.* —kleid, *n.* miner's frock or coat. —kleine, *n.* [in mining] waste-ore. —kohle, *f.* a small charcoal burnt in a pit. —kompaß, *m.* miner's compass. —lampe, *f.* miner's lamp. —licht, *n.* miner's candle or light. —pulver, *n.* miner's powder. —scherper, *m.* V. —tscherper. —schlacke, *f.* [in forges] dross, slacks. —steiger, *m.* inspector of the miners. —tasche, *f.* a miner's pouch [in which he keeps his candle, tinder, flint and steel]. —tscherper, *m.* [miners' term] miner's knife. —wasser, *n.* water in mines. —zeug, *n.* [miners' term] miner's clothes or dress. —zug, *m.* mensuration of a mine.

Grübelei, *f.* close and subtile meditation, too great subtility or refinement in thinking; *it.* a too minute enquiry into insignificant or trifling matters.

Grübeln, I. *v. intr.* 1) to rake, to grub, to dig. [among children] — or Grübchen spielen, V. Grube 1), in der Nase —, to put one's finger into one's nose. 2) *Fig.* to enter into difficult and minute enquiries, to meditate closely, to indulge in useless and sophistical disquisitions. Ueber etwas —, to rack one's brains about a thing; er grübelt über die Sprache nach, he refines the language. II. *v. tr.* [little used] to effect or produce by close and subtile meditation. Das —, V. Grübelei.

Grübel-kopf, *m.* [in fam. lang.] V. Grübler. —krank, *adj.* troubled with the spleen, splenetic. —krankheit, *f.* melancholy, spleen, hypochondriac complaint. —nuß, *f.* thick-shelled walnut.

Grübig, *adj* full of pits, holes or scars. Der Boden or das Terrain ist sehr — hier, the ground is full of pits or holes here; ein —es [that is, ein durch Gruben entstelltes] Kinn, a pitted chin; V. Pocken—; [in botany] ein —er Pilz, a spungy mushroom.

Grübler, [Grübelkopf] *m.* [-s, *pl.* -] a person who enters into subtile and intricate inquiries, refiner.

Grüblerisch, *adj.* and *adv.* given to, indulging in close and intricate inquiries; in the manner of a Grübler.

Grübling, *m.* [-es, *pl.* -e] 1) a sort of apple with small holes or cavities in the rind, red Norman calville. 2) V. Giftschwamm. 3) V. Trüffel. 4) [a genus of plants] omphalia or omphalandria.

Grübs, V. Griebs.

Grüde, *f.* embers.

Grüden, *v. tr.* [in saltworks] to stir up [the straw-fire].

Grüdenhaus, *n.* [-es, *pl.* -häuser] ash-house.

Grüder, *m.* [-s, *pl.* -] [in saltworks] one that stirs [the straw-fire].

Grüft, *f.* [*pl.* Grüfte] [V. Grube] any cavity made by digging, pit, hole; usually, a grave and chiefly a grave with walls and an arched roof, a tomb, vault, sepulchre. Einen Leichnam in die — senken, to deposit a dead body in a vault, to entomb a dead body; die unterirdischen Grüfte zu Rom, the catacombs of Rome.

Gruftgewölbe, *n.* a vaulted tomb or sepulchre.

Grümmet, *n.* [-s] [from grün and Mahd = das Mähen, or perhaps allied to the L. *gramen*, Grame being used in Lower Saxony instead of Grummet] aftergrass, aftermath, fog.

Grummet-boden, *m.* loft for the aftermath. —butter, *f.* butter made about the latter end of summer. —erndte, *f.* crop of aftermath. —heu, *n* aftermath. —wiese, *f.* a meadow that yields a second or third crop of grass.

Grün, *adj.* and *adv.* [Icel. *graen*, Old Sax. *grene*, Eng. *green*, probably from to grow, Heb. *ruhnan*, to grow, to flourish] 1) properly, growing; hence, of the colour of herbage and plants when growing, green. Die —en Gefilde, Bäume, the verdant fields, trees; auf dem —en Rasen, on the green turf; — anmahlen, anstreichen, to paint green; im Frühlinge, wenn Alles anfängt — zu werden, in spring, when every thing begins to grow green; der —e or —ende Hain, the green or verdant grove; immer —e Bäume, evergreen trees; die —e Farbe, green colour; —e Dinte, Seide, —es Tuch, green ink, silk, cloth; die —e Insel, Palomas [a Spanish Island]; das —, V. Grün, *n.*; [in glasshouses] —e Asche, Flemish blue, *it* smalt; eine —e Hütte [in glassworks], a glasshouse, where only green glass is made; *fig.* [rather vulgar] es wird mir — und gelb vor den Augen [= es schwindelt mir], I am seized or taken with a giddiness, dizziness or swimming in the head, my head is swimming or turning round. Frequently used in compositions, as: V. Apfel—, Berg—, Blaß—, Dunkel—, Gelb—, Gras—, Lauch—, Schwarz— &c. 2) [containing its natural juices, fresh, not dry] green. Ein Stück —es Holz, a piece of green [unseasoned] wood; —e Waare [= frisches Gemüse], greens; der —e Donnerstag or —donnerstag, [perhaps from eating greens on that day] Holy Thursday, maundy Thursday; —er Stockfisch, green stockfish; [among curriers] —e Häute, raw [not tanned] hides; —es Fleisch [= not smoked or salted] raw or fresh meat; —e Steine, stones lately taken out of the quarry; *fig.* *er kann auf keinen —en Zweig kommen [= kann zu keinem Wohlstande gelangen], he cannot thrive or prosper; *er ist mir gar nicht — [= gewogen], he bears me no good-will, he has a spite or grudge against me; *sich — machen [= allzu dreist seyn], to take too much liberty, too great a latitude, to grow or be saucy or insolent. 3) [unripe, immature] green. —es Obst, green fruit; —e Erbsen, green pease; —e Trauben, green, unripe grapes.

Grün-auge, *n.* 1) a green eye. 2) [in nat. hist.] a yellow fly with green eyes. —äugig, *adj.* having green eyes, green-eyed. —bauch, *m.* [in natural history] the greenish chrysis. —beere, *f.* gooseberry. —beinchen, *n.* [in natural history] a kind of sand-piper with green legs and feet. —blau, *adj.* greenish blue. —faulbaum, *m.* evergreen privet. —fink, *m.* 1) green-finch. 2) V. —schwans. —füßchen, *n.* V. —beinchen. —füßig, *adj.* having green feet, green-footed. —gelb, *adj.* greenish yellow. [in medicine] —gelbe Galle, greenish bile. —gestreift, *adj.* having green streaks or stripes. —hänfling, *m.* V. —schwans. —holz, *n.* mountain pine. —kehlchen, *n.* [in natural history] any small bird with a green throat or breast, as the green-breasted creeper, fly-catcher &c. —kohl, *m.* green cabbage, greens. —kopf, *m.* [in natural history] thrush or blackbird with a green head. —krähe, *f.* V. Blaukrähe. —kraut, *n.* spinage and other greens, dressed for food chiefly in spring. —land, *n.* meadow-ground. —laubig, *adj.* 1) having green leaves, fresh. 2) containing green arbours. —rock, *m.* [in fam. lang, especially in jest] a man wearing a green coat or [military] uniform by or on account of his profession or employment, [particularly] a forester, a hunter, huntsman.

—rostig, *adj.* eruginous. —rüssel, *m.* green weevil. —schild, *m.* [in nat hist.] green cassida. —schlicht, *adj.* [in mining] —schlichtes Gestein, a sort of brown free-stone. —schnabel, *m.* 1) [also—schnäbler] bird with a green beak. chiefly the green-beaked bustard. 2) *Fig.* V. Gelbschnabel 3). —schwanz, *m.* any bird with a green tail, V. —fink. —schwarz, *adj.* greenish black. —span, *m.* 1) [in chimistry] verdigris. 2) [in botany] green-broom. —specht, *m.* the green woodpecker. —sperling, *m.* the greenish-black sparrow of Bahama —stein, *m.* [in mineralogy] greenstone. —streifig, *adj.* having green streaks or stripes. —wurzel, *f.* fumiter, fumatory.

Grün, *n* [-s] 1) [the colour of growing plants] green Ein schönes —, a fine green; diese Farbe sticht in's — or —e, this colour inclines to green. 2) [any thing green or verdant, as verdant grass, leaves &c.] verdure. Das — der Wiesen im Brachmonat, the verdure of the meadows in June; sich im — or —en lagern, to lie down upon the green, upon the green turf; die Pferde in das — [= auf die Weide] treiben, to put or turn the horses to grass. 3) [a substance for dying green] V. Berg—, Saft— &c. 4) V. Grüne.

Grund, *m.* [-es, *pl.* Gründe] [Sax, Dan., Sw. *grund*, D. *grond*, Russ. *grunt*, root unknown] in general, the lowest part of any thing. 1) a tract of low ground, a valley, a dale. Im —e wohnen [in Script.], to live in the valley; du lässest Brunnen quellen in den Gründen [in Scripture], thou sendest the springs into the valleys; das Dorf liegt im —e [= im Thale], the village is situated in the valley; im Neckar—e, in the valley of the Neckar. 2) [the lowest surface of any thing] bottom. Ein Glas Wein auf Einen Zug bis auf den — austrinken, to drink off or up a glass of wine at one draught; der — eines Gefäßes, the bottom of a vessel; der — eines Sees, Flusses, des Meeres, the bottom of a lake, river, of the sea; [in seamen's language] schlammiger, lehmiger, sandiger, kiesiger —, oozy, clayey, sandy, gravelly ground; zu —e gehen [said of a ship], to sink, to founder; das Schiff stößt auf den —, the ship grounds; ein Schiff in den — bohren, to send a ship to the bottom, to sink her; den — untersuchen, to sound the ground; keinen — finden, to be out of soundings; es ist — da, there is ground or sounding; es ist kein — da, there is no bottom, no sounding; guter, fester —, good anchoring-ground, weicher —, foul ground. *Fig.* *a*) bottom = ruin. Zu —e gehen, to go to ruin, to be ruined; Einen zu —e richten, to undo, to ruin any one; sich durch das Spiel zu —e richten, to ruin one's self by gaming. *b*) bottom = that which is most remote from the view. Von — meiner Seele, meines Herzens, from the bottom of my soul. heart, with all my heart; ich liebe sie von — der Seele, I love her dearly; eine Sache, die weder — noch Boden hat [= eine verwirrte Sache], a very perplexed and embarrassed case or question; einer Sache auf den — gehen, to examine or sift a matter to the bottom. 3) [the surface on which a thing rests] ground. Der — eines Zeuges, Stoffes, the ground of a stuff; der — eines blumigen Seidenzeuges, the ground of a flowered silk; Sammet mit goldenem —e, velvet with a gold ground; eine Stickerei auf weißem —e, embroidery on a white ground; [in painting, the first or original colour] ground, priming Ein leichter und durchsichtiger —, a light and transparent ground; der — zum Vergolden, gold-size, V. Kreiden—; den — auftragen, to lay on the first colour, to prime; [in blasonry] der —, the ground of a shield; [among printers] der —, the platen [of a press]; der — eines Gebäudes, the foundation of a building; den — zu einem Gebäude legen, graben, to lay, to dig the foundation of an edifice; den — zu einer Stadt legen, to found a city. *Fig.* *a*) [the beginning or basis of a thing] foundation. Cyrus hat den — zu dem Persischen Reiche gelegt, Cyrus laid the foundation of the Persian empire; den — zum Frieden legen, to lay the foundation of peace. *b*) [the original constituent parts of a thing] Er versteht diese Wissenschaft aus dem —e, he is thoroughly master of that science; von — aus [= durchaus] gut oder böse, fundamentally or thoroughly good or bad, V. —gut, —böse &c; die Furcht Gottes ist der — der Weisheit [in Script.], the fear of God is the foundation of wisdom; eine Krankheit von — aus heilen, to cure a disease radically; von — aus studiren, to study thoroughly; die ersten Gründe [Anfangsgründe] einer Wissenschaft, the elements, rudiments or first principles of a science or art. *c*) [the true or real nature of a thing] Im —e [= in der Hauptsache], at the bottom, in the main; vielleicht sprach er zu heftig, im —e aber hat er Recht, perhaps he spoke with too much warmth, but at the bottom he is right; er ist im —e ein ehrlicher Mann, he is an honest man, in the main or after all; einer Sache auf den — kommen, to examine or sift a matter to the bottom, to dive into the bottom of a matter. *d*) motive, reason. Jemandem — zu Klagen geben, to give any one an occasion of complaint; aus welchem —e hat er das gethan? from what motive has he done that? er beklagt sich mit —, he has reason or cause to complain. *e*) [the efficient cause of a thing] principle. Gott ist der —, der erste —, aller Dinge, God is the author of every thing; der — der Bewegung, the principle of motion. *f*) [principle of knowledge] Die heilige Schrift ist der — der Religion, the Scriptures are the grounds of religion; [in philosophy] der zureichende —, sufficient reason. *g*) [a reason offered in proof] argument, reason. Gute Gründe für seine Meinung anführen, to assign or alledge good reasons for one's opinion; ein entscheidender —, a decisive reason 4) [in a few instances = the surface of the earth] ground *a*) [considered with reference to its vegetative qualities] soil. Ein fruchtbarer oder unfruchtbarer —, fruitful or barren soil; ein sandiger —, a sandy or gravelly soil, V. Boden 2), Lehm—, Sand— &c. *b*) [considered with relation to property] land. estate. Auf eines Andern — und Boden bauen, to build upon an another man's ground; dieses Haus steht auf meinem — und Boden, that house stands on my ground or estate; liegende Gründe, landed property, as fields, meadows, tenements &c.; auf Englischem — und Boden, upon English ground 5) the hindmost part of some things. Der — eines Wagens, the back of a carriage. [in painting = Hintergrund] background. Der — eines Gemähldes, einer Gegend, the background of a painting, of a landscape. Used also in compositions, V. Hinter—, Vorder—. 6) the bottom of liquors, dregs, lees, grounds, V. Satz, Bodensatz.

Grund-angel, *f.* angle or fishing-line with a bullet placed a few inches from the hook, ground-angle. —anschlag, *m.* 1) estimation of the expenses of the foundation [of a building]. 2) the first estimation of the expenses of some undertaking. —artikel, *m.* principal or fundamental article [of a treaty &c.]. —balken, *m.* [in building] ground-sill, groundsel, sill, groundplate; [in watermills and wears] V. Fachbaum; [in seamen's lang.] the keel or bottom of a ship. —baß, *m.* [*Fundamentalbaß] fundamental or thorough bass. —bau, *m.* [in building] the foundation of an edifice, V. —mauer. —baum, *m.* 1) V. —balken. 2) V. Garnbaum. —bedingung, *f.* [= Hauptbedingung] principal condition. —begierde, *f.* appetency. —begriff, *m.* 1) fundamental notion or principle. 2) [in grammar] subject. —bein *n.* [in anatomy] the basilary or sphenoid bone, V. Keilbein. —besitzer, *m.* possessor of a house or landed property, landed proprietor; landlord [as opposed to the mere tenant at will]. —bestandtheil, *m.* the fundamental essence or substance. substance. —bett, *n.* [in hydraulics] the or channel of a river guarded by fascines. —birn[e], *f.* potato. —blei, *n.* [in seamen's lang.] sounding-lead, plummet —bohrer, *m.* [among masons] a boring instrument for ascertaining the nature of the ground. —bolzen, *m.* [in founderies] V. Formbolzen. —böse, *adj.* and *adv.* [chiefly in fam. lang.] fundamentally bad, thoroughly wicked. —bosheit, *f.* thorough wickedness. —brav, *adj* and *adv.* [in fam. lang.] downright, thoroughly honest or —brett, *n.* [in artillery] the bottom or side of a gun-carriage. —brief, *m.* V Erbzinsbrief, Zinsbrief. —bruch, *m.* a gap in a dike, caused by the violence of the water —brühe, *f.* V. —suppe. —buch, *n.* register of landed property, V. Lagerbuch. —damm, *m.* [in hydraulics] a dam under water, raised to obstruct a current of water. —dienst, *m.* V. Frohndienst. —ehrlich, *adj.* and *adv.* V. —brav. —eichel, *f.* ground-nut, V. Erdnuß. —eigenschaft, *f.* fundamental or essential quality. —eigenthum, *n.* landed property. —eigenthümer, *m.* —eigenthümerinn, *f.* landed proprietor, proprietress; landlord [as opposed to the tenant]. —eigenthumsrecht, *n.* exclusive right of possession of land. —eis, *n.* ground or floating-ice. Der Fluß geht mit —eis, the river is filled with floating pieces of ground-ice —eisen, *n.* [among surgeons] probe. —entwurf, *m.* sketch, V. Skizze. —erde, *f.* [in mineralogy] primitive earth. —faden, *m.* [among weavers] thread of the warp. —fähigkeit, *f.* fundamental faculty [of human nature]. —falsch, *adj.* and *adv.* fundamentally wrong, thoroughly false. —farbe, *f.* 1) primitive or original colour Gelb, Roth und Blau sind —farben, yellow, red and blue are primitive colours. 2) ground-colour [upon which others are applied], priming —faser, *f.* [in anatomy] fibril. —faul, *adj* [in fam. lang.] thoroughly, quite idle or lazy. —feld, *n.* [in painting] ground. —fest, *adj.* very fast or solid. —festes Eigenthum, landed property. —feste, *f.* foundation, basis. —feuchtigkeit, *f.* [in anatomy] radical moisture, V. Lebenssaft. —firniß, *m.* priming varnish. —fisch, *m.* V. Grundling 2). —fläche, *f.* basis, base. [in botany] Auf der —fläche aufsitzend, basilar, basilary. —fohre, —forelle, *f.* large trout. —form, *f.* primitive or principal form; [in grammar] primitive or elementary word. —gebirge, *n.* V. Ganggebirge. —geizig, *adj* and *adv.* exceedingly covetous. —geld, *n.* capital, fund, principal. *—gelehrt, *adj.* and *adv.* thorougly, very learned or erudite Ein —gelehrter Mann, a man of profound erudition —gerechtigkeit, *f.* 1) [in feudal law] seigneurial right, V. —recht 1). 2) seigneurial jurisdiction a manor in gross. —gericht, *n.* 1) V. —gerechtigkeit 2). 2) a court or tribunal deciding upon differences of territory. —gesetz, *n.* fundamental law. Die Reichs—gesetze [in the history of Germany], the pragmatic sanction. —gewalt, *f.* supreme or original power, sovereignty —gewebe, *n.* warp. —graben, *m.* a ditch serving for the foundation of a building —gut, —gütig, *adj.* and *adv.* [in fam. lang.] extremely good, kind or benign. Ein —guter Mensch, an excellent man; der —gütige Gott, od all-kind. —haar, n. [among hatters] the e soft hair of animals in winter; [among cur-ers] the root of the hair. —haken, m. a ook fastened to a long pole used for draw-g any thing from the bottom of a river &c. -hase, m. [among sportsmen] hare of the val-y. —hecht, m. a pike that keeps to the ottom of the water. —heil, n. [in botany]) V. Bauchheil. 2) St. John's wort, V. Johan-iskraut. 2) mountain parsley. —herr, m. rd of the manor; it. landlord [= landed pro-rietor in general, and also opposed to the tenant]. -herrinn, f. lady of the manor. —herr-ichkeit. —herrschaft, f. 1) manor. 2) igneurial right, V. —recht 1). 3) V. —herr, —rrinn. —heuer, f. V. —zins. —hieb, m. mong file cutters] the first and deepest cuts or rrows of a file. —hobel, m. [among joiners] a ming plane, plough. —holde, m. [in feu-d law] a villain, a vassal; it. [in general] tenant. —holz, n. V. Faulbaum. —irr-hum, m. fundamental error. —käntel, n. [in mining] discharging pipe. —karpfen, carp that keeps at the bottom of the water. -kenntniß, f. fundamental or elementary nowledge, elements, principles. —kette, f. mong weavers] fundamental warp. —ketten-aden, m. thread of the fundamental warp. -kraft, f. primitive strength or force. —ku-el, f. [in pyrotechnics] a fireball, remaining good while under water before it appears. -lade, f. [in mining] fundamental timber piece. -lage, f. 1) foundation, basis, base; [in ar-chitecture] basement; [in chimistry] radical, base. Fig. Der Glaube ist die —lage der christlichen Tugenden, faith is the foundation of Christian irtues; die —lage seines Unterrichts, the roundwork of his instruction. 2) V. —lade. -lagerholz, n. [in architecture] timber for rming a grate or frame upon piles for the upport of a building. —last, f. [in law] passive rvitude. —laut or —lauter, m. [in grammar] owel. —lauwine, f. avalanche. —legung, foundation, ground-selling. —lehre, f. 1) undamental doctrine. 2) metaphysics. —linie, 1) lowest line, first line, basis. Die —linie nes Dreiecks, the base of a triangle. 2) the utline. Die —linie entwerfen, to outline, to ketch. —los, adj. and adv. bottomless, fa-thomless. Ein —loser Schlund, Abgrund, a bot-tomless pit, abyss. it. loose, not firm or solid, marshy. Ein —loser Weg, a marshy way or road, impassable way or road. Fig. a) [= unbegrenzt] boundless. Die —lose Barmherzigkeit Gottes, the infinite, unbounded mercy of God. b) [= nicht begründet] groundless. Ein —loses Ge-rücht, eine —lose Furcht, a groundless, un-founded report, fear. —loth, n. [in seamen's language] sounding-line or lead, plummet. —mauer, f. a wall forming the foundation of building, foundation-wall; it. basement. —meinung, f. [*Hypothese] hypothesis. —mi-schung, f. mixture of the essential parts, of the elements. —muschel, f. a pelagian shell. -neigung, f. original or innate inclination propensity. —obrigkeit, f. V. —herr. —pfahl, m. [in building] pile or stake, V. —la-gerholz. —pfandbrief, —pfandschein, . [*Hypothekenschein] mortgage upon land. —pfeiler, m. V. —säule, —stütze. —pflaster, V. Estrich. —platte, f. any plate or table rving as a basis or foundation; [among printers] . Grund 3). —quelle, f. primitive source or fountain. —rebe, f. 1) [among vine-dressers] use-less branch or sprout. 2) V. Sünderkann. —rechnungsart, f. each of the four first modes or branches of arithmetic [addition, sub-traction &c.]. —recht, n. 1) right derived from the possession of ground, seigneurial right, V. Gerechtigkeit. 2) the right of building or plant-ing upon the ground of another on payment of ground-rent. —rechtlich, adj. and adv. [in fam. lang.] thoroughly, quite or very just or honest. —regel, f. fundamental rule, prin-ciple. —register, n. V. —buch. —reich, adj. [in fam. lang.] exceedingly, very rich, V. Stein-reich. —riß, m. ground plan, ichnography of a building. Fig. —riß der Erdbeschreibung, the first elements of geography. —ruhr, f. 1) V. Strandung. 2) V. Strandrecht. —saß, m. an established or fundamental proposition or principle, maxim. Ein mathematischer, phi-losophischer —saß, a mathematical, philoso-phical axiom; ein angenommener —saß, a hy-pothesis; die —säße einer Wissenschaft, Kunst, the principles of a science, art; ein —saß der Staatsklugheit, a maxim of state or politics; ein gefährlicher —saß, a dangerous maxim; rechtliche und gute —säße haben, to have honest and good principles; das ist mein —saß, that is my principle; er handelt nach —säßen, he acts consistently. —sauer, n. [among bakers] leaven preserved from one baking for the next, principal or chief leaven. —säule, f. a pillar or column supporting an edifice, supporter. Fig. Gerechtigkeit, Gesetze &c. sind die sicher-sten —säulen eines Staates, justice, laws &c. are the surest basis of a state. —schoß, m. V. —steuer. —schuld, f. mortgage upon land. —schwelle, f. V. —balken. —silbe, f. radi-cal syllable, root. —sohle, f. V. —lade. —sprache, f. [Originalsprache] original language. —spruch, m. [any passage or verse of Scripture selected by a preacher as the subject of a discourse] text. —stein, m. 1) foundation stone. Der —stein unter dem Säulenstuhle, the socle. 2) [in mills] the nether-millstone, bedder, bedetter. 3) [in mineralogy] primary or primitive rock. —stelle, f. a passage in Scripture containing a religious truth or doctrine. —steuer, f. land-tax. —stimme, f. [in music] the lowest voice, bass. —stoff, m. elementary matter, element; [in chimistry] base, radical. Fig. Der —stoff ei-nes Gedichtes, the principal subject of a poem, V. Urstoff, Uranfang. —strich, m. [in writing] the principal stroke [opposed to hair stroke]; [in painting] V. —linie 2). —stück, n. immovable, real estate. Ein schönes —stück, a fine field or estate. —stüße, f. a prop for the foundation, fundamental. —substanz, f. V. —stoff. —suppe, f. 1) [seldom used] sediment, dregs, grounds, V. Hefen Fig. Die —suppe des Volkes, the dregs of the people, the rabble. 2) [in seamen's lang.] water that is collected in the bottom of a ship, bilge-water. —takelasche, f. [in seamen's lang., the ropes and furniture belonging to anchors] ground-tackle. —tau, n. [in seamen's lang.] reliev-ing tackle. —text, m. original text. —theil, m. fundamental or essential part; [in chimistry] principle, base, V. —lage, —stoff, Urstoff. —theilung, f. division of a real estate. —ton, m. [in music] the fundamental note, root, the key-note, tonic. —trieb, m. fundamental impulse, fundamental principle of action. —übel, n. fundamental evil, the root of all evil. —ursache, f. original cause. Gott ist die —ursache aller Dinge, God is the first cause, the author of every thing. —verbes-serung, f. a thorough reformation or reform. —verdunkelung, f. [in painting] making darker the ground of a picture. —verfas-sung, f. fundamental constitution. Die —verfassung einer Gesellschaft [= ihre Statuten], the statutes of a society. —vermögen, n. 1) V. —kraft. 2) the capital, fund, stock. —ver-mögensbuch, n. register of landed property. —verpfändung, f. mortgage. —wachs, n. [in beehives] propolis, V. Stopfwachs. —wage, f. V. Wasserwage. —wägekunst, f. V. Wasser-wägekunst. —wägung, f. V. Wasserwägung. —wahrheit, f. fundamental truth, V. —saß. —wasser, n. 1) V. Horizontalwasser; [in mining] water found under ground. 2) water that breaks through a dike. —werk, n. [in watermills] the groundwork, lowerwork. —wesen, n. fundamen-tal or original substance, original being, the foun-dation and source of other beings; [in logic] sub-ject. —wissenschaft, f. fundamental science; [in philosophy, a part of the science of metaphysics] ontology. —wort, n. 1) radical or primitive word, a word from which others are derived, root. 2) V. —begriff. —zahl, f. cardinal number. —zapfen, m. floodgate of a pond. —zehnte, m. tithes paid from land. —zins, m. or —zinse, f. rent paid for lands and tenements. —zinsherr, m. the lord of the manor, landlord. —zinsmann, m. ten-ant. —zug, m. [in painting] principal line or stroke. Die —züge einer Zeichnung entwerfen, to make the sketch of a drawing, to sketch a drawing; fig. die —züge seines Charakters sind &c., the principal traits of his character are &c. —zungenmuskel, m. [in anatomy, a muscle which pulls the tongue downwards] hyo-glossus.

Gründel, m. [-s, pl. -] or **Gründel**, f. [pl. -n] 1) [a fish] groundling, gudgeon. 2) [among locksmiths] V. Grendel.

Gründen, I. v. tr. 1) V. Ergründen. 2) to lay on the ground, to ground; [in painting] to prime. Gegründete Leinwand, primed canvas; das Holz —, to prime the wood. 3) to make the foundation of a thing; [among joiners] to groove, to furrow. Ein Haus —, to lay the foundation of a house, to build a house; ein Haus auf einen Felsen, auf den Sand —, to build a house upon the rock, sand. Fig. Ein Reich — [= stiften], to lay the foundation of an empire; seine Forderungen, seine Meinung auf etwas —, to found or ground one's claims, one's opinion upon something; diese Meinung ist in der Erfahrung gegründet, this opinion is founded on, or made good by experience; ich habe gegründete Ansprüche auf Entschädigung, I have a right to demand indemnification. II. v. intr. [in seamen's lang.] to fetch bottom, to sound, to feel bottom. Tief —, [applied to water &c.] to be deep. Prov. V. Still. III. v. r. sich —, to be founded or grounded on. Alles das grün-det sich auf ein falsches Gerücht, all that is founded on a false report; dieses System grün-det sich auf &c., this system is founded or based on &c.

Grundiren, v. tr. [in painting] V. Gründen 2).

Grundirung, f. [in painting] V. Gründung 1).

Gründlich, I. adj 1) profound, thorough. Ein Mann von —er Gelehrsamkeit, a man of profound erudition; die —e Kenntniß einer Sprache, the thorough knowledge of a lan-guage; ein —er Gelehrter, Mathematiker, a profound scholar, mathematician; eine —e Heilung, a radical cure. 2) well-grounded solid. Ein —es Urtheil, a well-grounded, solid judgment; ein —er Beweis, a clear, evident proof. II. adv 1) profoundly, thoroughly, fundamentally. Er hat diesen Gegenstand — ab-gehandelt, he has treated that matter thorougly, to the bottom; er ist — geheilt worden, he has been radically cured. 2) solidly.

Gründlichkeit, f. solidity. Die — seiner Schlüsse, the solidity of his reasonings.

Gründling, m. [-es, pl. -e] 1) [among fo-resters] a knotty and crooked piece of wood. 2) [in natural history] gudgeon, groundling, V. Gründel.

Gründlingsreuse, f. bow-net, bow-wheel.

Gründlosigkeit, f. quality of being fathomless or bottomless; immense, bottomless depth [of the ocean &c.]. Die — eines Weges, the bad state of a road. *Fig.* groundlessness. Die — dieses Vorwandes, the groundlessness or futility of this pretext.

Gründung, *f.* 1) the act of laying on the ground; [in painting] the laying on of colour, priming. 2) the act of making the foundation of, or of establishing a thing, foundation. *Fig.* Die — einer Schule, einer Armenanstalt, the establishment of a school, of a mendicity institution; die — einer Stadt, eines Reiches, the foundation of a city, of an empire.

Gründungseisen, *n.* [among engravers] a scratching-knife, scraper.

Grüne, *f.* 1) the quality of being green, greenness, green colour, green. 2) green pasture. Den Pferden die — geben, to feed horses with grass. 3) [among sportsmen] green fields. 4) [in mining, seldom used] verdigris.

Grünen, *v. intr.* to become or grow green, to grow verdant; *it.* to be green, to be verdant. Im Frühlinge, wenn Alles anfängt zu —, in spring, when every thing begins to grow green; die Bäume — schon, the trees are already green; —de Bäume, verdant trees. *Fig.* *— und blühen [= im Wohlstande seyn], to flourish, to prosper.

Grünitz, *m.* [-es, *pl.* -e] 1) V. Kreuzvogel. 2) [in botany] green-broom.

Grünlich, *adj.* and *adv.* greenish. —e Galle [in medicine], eruginous bile; —blau, —gelb &c., greenish blue, greenish yellow &c.

Grünling, *m.* [-es, *pl.* -e] [in natural hist.] 1) V. Grünfink. 2) [a fish of the genus Labrus] the greenish wrasse. 3) [in botany] *a*) genista sagittalis. *b*) green agaric.

Grünzen, *v. intr.* [Lat. *grunnio*, Fr. *grogner*, Engl. *to grunt*; formerly grunzen signified *to grumble*, as well as *to cry, to weep*] to grunt. Das —, grunt, grunting.

***Gruppe**, *f.* [*pl.* -n] [especially in painting and sculpture] group. Eine — von Menschen, Thieren &c., a group of men, beasts &c.; eine — von Bäumen, a clump or cluster of trees; in —n zusammenstellen, ordnen, to group.

Gruppenweise, *adv.* by groups.

Gruppen, [more usual] ***Gruppiren**, *v. tr.* and *refl.* to group.

***Gruppiren**, V. Gruppen.

Grus, *m.* [-es] [allied to Gries, Grütze] 1) rubbish, [in commerce] garbles. 2) coarse sand, gravel, V. Gries 1).

Grussand, *m.* coarse sand, gravel.

Grüse, *f.* V. Grüne 2) and 3).

Grüseck, *m.* [-es, *pl.* -e] a kind of fish with a greenish back, greenfish.

Gruß, *m.* [-es, *pl* Grüße] salute, salutation, greeting. Den — erwiedern, to return the greeting or salutation; seinen — entbieten, melden, sagen lassen, to present one's respects, compliments, service or civilities; vermelden Sie ihm meinen besten —, my best compliments to him; tausend Grüße von mir an alle unsere Freunde, remember me in the kindest manner to all our friends; ich habe Ihnen viele Grüße auszurichten, I have a great many compliments for you; [in the Romish church] der englische —, the angelical salutation, Ave Maria. *Fig.* Er hat ihm keinen — gegeben or gegönnt [in fam. lang.], he did not pull off his hat to him, did not bow to him; [in the navy and military affairs] der —, [a discharge of cannon or of small arms &c.] salute; den — erwiedern, to return the salute.

Grußformel, *f.* form of salutation. —zeit, *f.* [among sportsmen] the time when no game is killed. V. Hegezeit.

Grüßen, [Sax. *gretan, grettan*, Eng. *to greet*, D. *groeten* or *kryten*, allied to the Fr. *crier, to cry*] *v. tr.* to address with expressions of kind wishes, to greet, to salute. — Sie ihn von mir, wenn Sie ihn sehen, give or present my respects or compliments to him, when you see him; — Sie meine Schwägerinn schönstens or recht herzlich von mir, give my love to my sister-in-law; meine Frau läßt Sie herzlich or schön or bestens —, my wife sends her love [to you]; ich grüße herzlich alle die Ihren, remember me in the kindest manner, my respects or compliments to all your family; mein Bruder läßt Sie —, my brother begs to be remembered to you; Gott grüße dich! [a familiar way of greeting] good day! how are you? *Fig.* Einen durch eine Verbeugung —, to bow to any one; Einen — [indem man den Hut abzieht], to pull off one's hat to any one; [in military and naval affairs] to salute; mit der Flagge, mit den Segeln —, to lower the colours, the top-sails by way of salute; mit Kanonenschüssen —, to salute by a discharge of cannon; Schiffe, die an einer Festung vorbeisegeln, — dieselbe, the sea salutes the land, V. Begrüßen. Das —, V. Begrüßung, Gruß.

Grütze, [allied to Grus, Gries] *f.* peeled grain, especially peeled barley and oats, grits, groats, V. Haber—, Gersten—, Buchweizen—. *Fig.* [in popular language] brains, sense, understanding. Dieser Mensch hat — im Kopfe, he has a good head-piece, he is a man of sense, of good understanding; er hat keine — im Kopfe, he is a dull, stupid fellow, he has not a grain of sense.

Grützhaber, —hafer, *m.* naked or peeled oats. —handel, *m.* trade in peeled barley and groats. —händler, *m.* —händlerinn, *f.* dealer in peeled barley and groats. —jökel, *m.* [in mineralogy] green vitriol. —kopf, *m.* stupid fellow, blockhead, V. Dummkopf. —mühle, *f.* mill for peeling grain, especially oats. —müller, *m.* maker of groats. —suppe, *f.* soup or gruel made of groats. —wurst, *f.* a sausage filled with meat and peeled barley or groats, barley-sausage.

***Gryphit**, *m.* [-en, *pl.* -en] [in mineralogy] gryphite. V. Greifstein.

Guaiácholz, *n.* [-es, *pl.* -hölzer] [in botany] lignum vitae or pockwood, Guaiacum.

***Guardein**, [pron. Gwardein] *m.* [-es, *pl.* -e] [in mints] assayer. V. also Wardein.

***Guárdian**, [pron. Gwardian] *m.* [-s, *pl.* -e] [also der Vater or Pater Guardian] the prior or superior in a Franciscan convent.

Gúbst, *f.* [*pl.* -e] the wild she-goat.

Gúcken, [Sw. tika, Scotch *kyke*] *v. intr.* [in familiar or popular language for sehen] to look, to peep. Zum Fenster hinaus —, to look out of the window. *Fig.* Das Schnupftuch guckt aus seiner or guckt ihm aus der Tasche, his handkerchief hangs out of his pocket.

Guckauge, *n.*, *dim.* —äugchen, ||—äugelein, *n.* [a jocular word for Auge] eye, peeper, sparkler. —fenster, *n.* a small window, a peeping-window. —glas, *n.* eye-glass. —kasten, *m.* raree-show. —loch, *n.* peep-hole, peeping-hole. —rohr, *n.* optic tube, telescope. ||—rübe, *f.* V. Rübe.

Gúcker, *m.* [-s, *pl.* -] 1) a person that looks or peeps. 2) V. Stern—. 3) V. Guckrohr. 4) V. Guckloch.

Gúckert, *m.* [-es, *pl.* -e] [among bakers] scraper. V. Schabeisen.

Gúckuck, V. Kuckuck.

Güdse, *f.* [*pl.* -n] a round hollow chisel, gouge.

Guhr, *f.* [*pl.* -en] [from gähren, to ferment] ||1) fermentation. 2) [in mining, a loose earthy deposit from water, found in the cavities or clefts of rocks] guhr. Metallische —en, metallic guhrs.

Gühríg, *adj.* brittle. V. Spröde.

***Guillotine**, [pron. Gilljotihne] *f.* [*pl.* -n] [an engine or machine for beheading persons at a stroke] guillotine.

***Guillotiniren**, [pron. gilljotinihren] *v. tr.* to guillotine.

Guinéa, [pron. Ginéa] *n.* [-'s] [a country in Africa] Guinea.

***Guinée**, [pron. Gineh] *f.* [*pl.* -n] [a gold coin of Great Britain of the value of 21 shillings sterling, no longer current] guinea.

***Guingan**, [pron. Gingan or *Gingang] *m.* [-s, *pl.* -e or -s] [a kind of striped cotton cloth] gingham.

***Guirlánde**, [pron. Girrlannde] *f.* [*pl.* -n] garland.

***Guitárre**, [pron. Gitarre] *f.* [*pl.* -n] guitar.

Gúlden, *m.* [-s, *pl.* -] [from Gold, this coin being originally made of this metal] a silver coin of the value of 60 kreuzers or about one shilling and eight pence sterling, a florin. Der holländische —, gilder or guilder.

Guldenzettel, *m.* a banknote of one florin.

‡**Gülden**, *m.* [-s, *pl.* -] V. Gulden.

‡**Gülden**, *adj.* V. Golden.

Güldenbaum, *m.* [in botany] the liquidamber of America. —groschen, *m.* florin, gilder. —klee, *m.* V. Leberklee. —leberkraut, *n.* [in botany] golden liverwort. —steinbrech, *m.* golden saxifrage. —wundkraut, *n.* golden-rod or Saracen's woundwort, V. Goldruthe.

Güldisch, *adj.* containing gold.

Gültbar, *adj.* and *adv.* V. Zinsbar.

Gülte, *f.* [*pl.* -n] [allied to Gilde and Gelten] an annual income, proceeding chiefly from real estates; in a more limited sense, a rent paid for lands and tenements. V. Frucht—, Geld—.

Gültbauer, *m.* —herr, *m.* —brief, *m.* —buch, *n.* V. Zinsbauer, Zinsherr, Zinsbrief, Zinsbuch.

Gülten, *v. tr.* to pay rent.

Gültig, *adj.* and *adv.* valid, legal, lawful, good in law, done in due form, authentic, binding. Ein —er Grund, a valid or good reason; diese Entschuldigung ist nicht —, this excuse won't do; ein Minderjähriger kann keinen —en Vertrag schließen, one under age cannot make a valid contract, the contract of a minor is not good in law; eine gute und —e Bürgschaft, a good and legal security; — machen, für — erklären, to make valid, to validate; die nachher erfolgte Einwilligung der Eltern hat die Heurath — gemacht, the subsequent consent of the parents has made the marriage valid; die Taufe der Ketzer ist —, baptism conferred by heretics is valid; eine —e Münze, a current coin.

Gültigen, *v. tr.* V. Gültig machen.

Gültigkeit, *f.* validity.

***Gummi**, *n.* [indeclinable] gum. Arabisches —, gum-arabic; elastisches —, gum-elastic or elastic-gum, India rubber; — Tragant, gum-tragacanth; — Kopol or Kopal, gum-copal. — gutt, — gutta, gumboge; Gambia—, gum kino; Bäume, die — ausschwitzen, gummy trees; mit — bestreichen, V. Gummiren.

Gummiartig, *adj.* of the nature of

gum, gummy, gummous. —baum, *m.* a gum tree; the arbor Chibou. —bringend, —gebend, *adj.* productive of gum, gummy. —harz, *n.* or harziges —, gum-resin, resinous gum. —lack, *m.* gumlac. —wasser, *n.* gum-water.

Gummiren, *v. tr.* to smear with gum, to gum.

Gündelkraut, *n.* [-es] [in botany] lemon thyme.

Gundelkrautrebe, *f.* ground-ivy.

Gündermann, *m.* [Gunder corrupted from Grund] [-es] [in botany] 1) ground-ivy. 2) V. Erdpfau, Kirschisop. 3) V. Erdwinde 2).

Günsel, *m.* [-s] [corrupted from the L. *consolida*] [in botany] consound, bugle, comfrey.

Gúnst, *f.* [*pl.* Günste or Gunsten, not used, except the latter form in some phrases] [from Gönnen] 1) state of mind, in which one is pleased with any thing happening to another. V. Abgunst, Mißgunst. 2) generally, favour. *a*) good-will, kindness, affection. Sich Jemands — erwerben, to gain any one's good-will or favour, to win any one's good graces; schenken Sie mir Ihre —, give me your good-will; sich um Jemands — bewerben, to court any one's favour, *to curry favour with a person; in —en stehen, to be in favour; die — des Fürsten genießen, to be in favour with the prince; zu—en einer Person, in behalf of, for the sake of, on account of a person; man hat ihm zu —en dieser edlen Handlung verziehen [rather stiff], he was pardoned in consideration of this noble deed; er hat zu Ihren —en gesprochen, he spoke in your favour, in your behalf; er hat zu—en seines jüngern Sohnes über seinen Nachlaß verfügt, he has left his estate to his younger son; das Urtheil fiel zu—en der Beklagten aus, the verdict went for the defendant; die Wahl fiel nicht zu seinen —en aus, the choice went against him. *b*) a kind act or office. Den Schuldigen verzeihen, ist eine —, to pardon the guilty is a favour; Einem eine — erweisen, erzeigen, to do, to show any one a favour; ich bitte Sie um eine —, I beg a favour of you; er ist schon lange in sie verliebt, ohne die geringste — von ihr erlangen zu können, he has been long in love with her without being able to obtain the least favour; die letzte — von einem Frauenzimmer erhalten, to obtain the last favours of a lady. *c*) leave, permission, pardon. Mit Ihrer —, mit — zu reden, zu sagen, by your favour or leave, with favour, under favour.

Gunst-bemühung, —bewerbung, *f.* endeavour to gain or win any one's favour or good-will. —bezeigung, *f.* act of kindness or good-will, favour. Einen mit —bezeigungen überhäufen, to load any one with kindness. —brief, *m.* letter of permission. —erschleichung, *f.* surreptitious obtainment of any one's favour or good-will. —schein, *m.* V. —brief.

Günstig, I. *adj.* favourable, propitious, kind, friendly, affectionate. Einem — seyn, to be favourable or propitious to any one; leih' unserem Gesuch ein —es Ohr, lend a favourable ear to our request. *Fig.* = advantageous. Das Wetter, der Wind, die Gelegenheit waren unseren Planen —, the weather, wind, occasion were propitious to, served or favoured our designs; ein —er Wind, a fair wind. II. *adv.* favourably, kindly, propitiously, advantageously. Einen — behandeln, aufnehmen &c., to treat, receive any one favourably; — auslegen, to give a friendly interpretation.

Günstling, *m.* [-es, *pl.* -e] —inn, *f.* favourite, darling, minion. Der — des Königs, the king's favourite; die —e des Glückes, the favourites or minions of fortune. V. Liebling.

Günstlingschaft, *f.* favour. Während seiner —, whilst he was in favour.

Gúrgel, *f* [*pl.* -n] [Gr. γαργαρέων, Hebrew *gargeru*, Eng. *gargle*, Fr. and Eng. *gorge*] gullet, gorge, throat. Einem die — abschneiden, to cut any one's throat; Einen an der — fassen, to take or seize any one by the throat, to throttle any one. *Fig.* *Einem das Messer an die — setzen [= Einen zu etwas zwingen], to hold a dagger to any one's throat, to force him to compliance; [in popular language] all' das Seinige durch die — jagen, to spend, waste or squander away all one's fortune by drinking or vassailing; [in vulgar language] Einem die — schmieren [= ihm Wein zu trinken geben], to moisten any one's inside, to wet his whistle.

Gurgel-abschneider, *m.* cut-throat. —ader, *f.* jugular vein. —bein, *n.* throat-bone. —hahn, *m.* [in natural history] cock of the wood. —schnitt, *m.* bronchotomy. —wasser, *n.* [in medicine] gargle.

Gúrgeln, I. *v. tr.* and *refl.* to gargle, to gargarize. II. *v. intr.* 1) to warble, to play in the throat, to quaver. 2) to emit, or to move with, a low gurgling sound. Der Bach gurgelt in seinem Felsenbette, the brook gurgles in his rocky bed.

Gúrke, *f.* [*pl.* -n] [Sw. *gurka*, Engl. *gherkin*, Fr. *courge*] [name of a plant and its fruit] cucumber. Die Blüthe der — ist gelb und glockenförmig, the flower of the cucumber is yellow and bell-shaped; eingemachte —n, pickled cucumbers, gherkins, V. Essig—, Salz—. *Fig.* [in vulgar language] Sich —n herausnehmen, to take great liberties, to grow saucy or insolent.

Gurken-beet, *n.* a bed of cucumbers. —fäßchen, *n.* barrel of gherkins. —förmig, *adj.* in form or shape of a cucumber. —kern, *m.* seed of cucumber. *—mahler, *m.* [in contempt or jest] dauber. —ranke, *f.* clasper of cucumbers. —salat, *m.* salad made of cucumbers. —same, *m.* V. —kern. —topf, *m.* a pot of gherkins; *it.* V. —fäßchen.

Gúrre, *f.* [*pl.* -n] [Ir. *garron*] a mare of mean value, a jade. *Fig.* [in contempt, of a dissolute female] a jade, wench.

Gúrren, *v. intr.* [allied to the L. *garrio*] to coo. *it.* [provincial and vulgar] Es gurrt ihm im Leibe, his belly grumbles.

Gúrt, *m.* [-es, *pl.* -e] [allied to the L. *gyrus*, the Gr. γῦρος = circle] 1) any thing small encircling another; [in architecture] plinth, V. Saum. [in artillery] Der — an einer Kanone, the clump of a gun. 2) [a broad band to fasten any thing with] Die —e an einer Bettlade, die Bett—e, the girths of a bedstead; — um den Leib, girdle or belt; den — umlegen, to put on one's girdle; die —e an einem Sattel, the girths; ein —, woran man eine Butte, einen Korb &c. trägt, strap, V. Gürtel, Bauch—, Hosen—, Leib—, Sattel— &c.

Gurt-bett, *n.* a bed with girths at the bottom. —gehenk, *n.* any thing suspended by a belt or girdle. —haken, *m.* the ring, clasp or hook of a girth, belt or girdle. —riem, *m.* the band of a girth or belt, girth-leather; [in botany] V. Eselswicke. —ring, *m.* V. —haken. —schnalle, *f.* buckle of a girth, girdle or belt. —sims, *m.* [in architecture] plinth. —werk, *n.* [in architecture] plinth of a wall.

Gürtel, *m.* [-s, *pl.* -] girdle, belt. Seinen — anlegen, to put on one's girdle; der — der Venus, the girdle, zone or cest of Venus; das Wasser geht ihm bis an den — [= bis dahin, wo der — am Leibe befestigt wird], the water comes up to his middle or waist; [in seamen's language] die —, the sheets of a sail; [in geography] zone. *Fig.* Er hat dieser Jungfrau den — gelöst, he has defloured that virgin.

Gürtel-förmig, *adj.* having the form or shape of a belt or girdle. —kette, *f.* a chain formerly worn by the ladies to hang keys &c. on, key-chain. —kraut, *n.* V. Bärlapp. —ring, *m.* the ring of a belt or girdle. —schnalle, *f.* buckle of a belt or girdle. —spange, *f.* V. —schnalle. —thier, *n.* [an inoffensive quadruped peculiar to America] armadillo, tatoo. Das —thier mit drei —n, the armadillo with three belts.

Gürten, I. *v. tr.* to gird, to girdle. Gürte dein Schwert an or um, gird on thy sword; ein Pferd —, to girth a horse. II. *v. r.* sich —, to put on one's belt or girdle.

Gürtler, *m.* [-s, *pl.* -] a maker of belts or girdles, girdler, beltmaker.

Gürtlerhandwerk, *n.* the trade of a beltmaker or girdler.

Gúß, *m.* [-sses, *pl.* Güsse] 1) the act of casting or founding metal and that which is cast. Eine Figur von Einem Gusse, a figure of one cast only or made at one cast; der — einer Glocke, the casting of a bell; ein — Buchstaben, a fount of types, font. 2) that which is poured out, gush, [in breweries] water for one brewing; *it.* a heavy fall of rain of short duration, shower. 3) place where any thing is poured, drain, sink. V. —stein, Aus—.

Guß-eisen, *n.* cast-iron; *it.* [in forges] a sow of melted iron. —form, *f.* casting-mould. —loch, *n.* the hole of a mould. —metall, *n.* cast-metal. —messing, *n.* cast-brass. —mutter, *f.* mould, matrice, V. Schriftmutter. —regen, *m.* V. Platzregen. —röhre, *f.* [in hydraulics] tube, pipe or spout of a fountain. —stahl, *m.* cast-steel. —stein, *m.* sink, drain, gutter, V. Wasserstein. —waare, *f.* cast wares, castings. —wachs, *n.* melted and purified wax. —werk, *n.* work of cast metal, V. —waare.

Gústav, *m.* [-s, *pl.* -e] [a name of men] Gustavus.

Gút, *adj.* and *adv* [Sw. *god*, Eng. *good*, Gr. ἀγαθός, probably from the old verb getzen, now ergetzen, to delight, L. *gaudere*, Gr. γηθέω] 1) [pleasing to the senses] good, pleasant, agreeable. Die Rose riecht —, the rose has a good or pleasant smell; *ein —er Geruch, a good, pleasant or agreeable smell; —er Wein, good wine; *—es [angenehmes] Wetter, fine, pleasant weather, [in mining] good, fresh air; dieses Obst ist — zu essen, this fruit is good to eat; hier ist — seyn, leben, here is good living, one lives comfortably here; *sich einen —en [= vergnügten] Tag machen, to spend a day agreeably or merrily; *es — haben, —e Tage haben, to enjoy an easy life, to live in ease and prosperity, to be well off, to be in easy circumstances; *sich —e Tage machen, to make one's self easy and comfortable, to live at ease or comfortably; — essen, to eat well or sumptuously; *einen —en Tisch führen, to keep a good table; der —e or blaue Montag, Crispin's holiday; *was gibt es —es Neues? what is the best news? is there any news stirring; —en Morgen, —en Tag, —en Abend, —e Nacht! good morning, good day, good evening, good night! *sich etwas zu —e or sich gütlich thun, to pamper one's self, to enjoy one's self; *sich auf eine Sache etwas zu —e thun [= sich daran ergetzen] [not much used in this sense], to take great pleasure in a thing, to delight in a thing, *it. fig.* to value, to pride or pique one's self upon a thing; *er thut sich auf seinen Gesang etwas zu —e, he prides himself upon his singing. *In a more restricted sense: a)* [convenient, easy, opposed to difficult or annoying] Ein —er Weg, a good way; hier geht, tanzt es sich sehr —, it is very good walking, dancing here; in diesem Wagen fährt sich's —, this is an easy carriage; es ist nicht — mit ihm zu thun zu haben, he is a hard man to deal with, 't is dangerous meddling with him; solche Gesetze sind wohl — zu geben, aber schwer zu halten or sind besser zu geben, als zu halten, it is easier to make such laws than to observe them; *Sie haben — so reden, lachen, it is easy for you to speak thus, to laugh, *it.* you may well laugh &c.; *[ironically] du hast — um Verzeihung bitten, warten &c., it is in vain for you to ask pardon, to wait. *b)* cheerful, glad. —en Muthes, —er Dinge seyn, to be of good cheer, to be merry. 2) *In a derived sense: a)* [conformable or well adapted to the end or purpose] good. Einen —en Grund legen, to lay a good foundation; —er Rath, a good advice; ein —es Gesicht haben, to have a good sight or eyesight; eine —e Nase haben, to have a good nose; er hat viel —en, natürlichen Verstand, he has much good sense; *es muß — seyn [= man muß damit zufrieden seyn], we must be satisfied with it, submit to it, buckle to it, es mag — seyn, lassen wir es — seyn, well, let that pass! —! [as an exclamation] good! well! er ist da; —! he is there; good! very good! — so! good! it is well! etwas — heißen, to approve, to sanction a thing; nicht — heißen, to disapprove; dazu ist es —, it is good for that; das ist zu nichts — [= taugt zu nichts], that is good for nothing; dieser Mann ist zu Allem —, this man is fit for any-thing; er ist — zu Fuße, he is good on his legs, a good walker; *prov.* — Ding will Weile haben, a thing done in haste is never brought to perfection; to do a thing well, requires some time; *er kam zur —en [= gelegenen] Stunde, he arrived opportunely, †in the very nick of time; dieß ist eine —e Zeit, mit ihm zu reden, this is the convenient time to speak to him; es wäre —, besser, am besten, wenn Sie warteten, you would do well to wait, you had better, best wait; das —e an [or bei] der Sache ist, daß &c., the best of the thing is, that &c.; *das war — gegeben, that was well said or spoken; *Einem etwas kurz und — [= deutlich] sagen, to tell any one roundly, plainly; *kurz und —, ich habe keine Lust, in short, I have no mind; er spricht, tanzt —, he speaks, dances well; ein —er Schauspieler, Dichter, a good actor, poet; ein — getroffenes Bild, a good likeness; mit —em Winde segeln, to sail with a fair wind; ein —es Jahr, a plentiful year; einen —en [= gesunden] Schlaf haben, to sleep soundly; das Wetter ist — zum Säen, the weather is good for sowing; das ist — für das Fieber, that is good for the fever; das wird Ihnen — thun, that will do you good; das bedeutet mir nichts —es, that forebodes me no good; es ist —, daß er kam, it is well that he came; es ist so — als geschehen, it is as good as done; es ist so — als hätte er sie schon geheurathet, he has as good as married her; er ist so — als todt, he is as good as dead; dir zu —e [= zum Vortheile], for thy benefit; das kommt uns allen zu —e, we shall all be winners by it, shall be the better for it; einen Fehler, sein Unrecht wieder — machen, to make amends for a fault, to redress the wrongs or injuries one has done to any one; Einem etwas zu —e halten, to excuse, to pardon any one; diese Arznei wird — thun, this medicine will have a good effect, will do good; *meine Augen wollen nicht mehr — thun, my eyes begin, my eye-sight begins to fail me; ein gottloser Bube, der nicht — thun will, a wicked boy, that will do no good; er hat sein Lebtage nicht — gethan, he has ever been good for nothing; diese Pflanze thut hier nicht —, this plant does not thrive here; in diesem Boden thun die Obstbäume nicht —, fruit-trees do not thrive in this soil; — stehen, sprechen or sagen für Einen, für etwas, to be bail or security for any one, to answer for, to warrant a thing; ich habe 100 Souverainsd'or bei ihm —, he owes me a hundred sovereigns; wie viel haben Sie zu —? how much is there due to you? how much do we, they &c. owe you? Einem etwas zu — schreiben, to set a thing to the credit of any one, to credit a thing to any one; das soll Ihnen zu —e gehen [= zu — geschrieben werden], that shall be credited to you; Einem [im Spiele] — geben [= vorgeben], to give any one odds; so und so viel — machen [= gewinnen], to win so and so much. *In a more limited sense: α)* not adulterated or false, real, true, pure. —es Gold, pure or fine gold; ein —er Diamant, a pure diamond; —e Tressen, real gold or silver lace. *β)* having the due or just value in commerce. —es Geld, good money; —e Creditbriefe, good letters of credit; dieses Haus, dieser Kaufmann ist — [= hat Credit], this house, this merchant is good, solvent, enjoys great credit, the credit of this house &c. is good. *γ)* maintaining a certain rank in civil life. Dieses Mädchen ist aus einer —en Familie, this girl descends from a good or respectable family; *sich zu — dünken zu etwas, to think a thing below one's self; er dünkt sich zu —, mit ihm zu reden, he disdains or scorns to speak to him; Einer ist so — wie der Andere, one is as good as the other. *b)* [having the qualities which God's law requires] good. Niemand ist —, denn der einzige Gott [in Script.], there is none good but one, that is, God; ein —er Mensch, a good, virtuous, pious man; Gott läßt seine Sonne aufgehen über —e und Böse [in Script.], God maketh his sun to rise on the evil and on the good; ein —er Geist, a good spirit or genius; er hat das —e [= die —e Eigenschaft], daß er niemals lügt, he has this good quality, never to tell a lie. *In a more limited sense: α)* not hostile, friendly, kind, amicable. Ein —er Nachbar, a good neighbour; das sind —e Leute, they are good, obliging people; im —en or in —em einen Streit beilegen, to adjust a dispute amicably; *Einem etwas in —em sagen or verweisen, to reprove any one gently; *etwas in —em [= freiwillig] thun, to do a thing of one's own accord, cheerfully, willingly; *Einem —e Worte geben, to give any one fair words, to speak him fair; er läßt weder —e noch böse Worte bei sich eingehen or statt finden, he yields or listens neither to persuasions nor threats; *prov.* ein —es Wort findet eine —e Statt, good words cost nothing; a good word is as soon said as an ill one; fair words break no bones, but foul ones many a one; sie sind sich wieder —, they are reconciled, they have made it up, they are friends again. *β)* not angry, ceasing to be offended, calm, quiet. Er ist nicht mehr so zornig, er fängt an, wieder — zu werden, he is no longer so angry, his passion begins to subside; Einen wieder — machen, to appease, to pacify any one. *γ)* kind, benevolent, affectionate. Er meint es — mit Ihnen, he is your well-wisher, wishes you well, bears you good-will; ein — gemeinter Rath, a charitable or well-meant advice; Einem —es thun, to do any one good; Böses mit —em vergelten, to render good for evil; des —en kann man nie zu viel thun, we can never do too much good; *prov.* never be weary of well-doing; —es von Einem reden, to speak well of any one, to give any one a good character; Einem — seyn, to be friendly to any one, to bear him good will, to wish him well, to like, to love him; er ist ihr von Herzen — [= liebt sie aufrichtig], he loves her heartily or sincerely; *seyn Sie doch so — [= so gefällig], und sagen Sie mir, pray, be so kind as to tell me; *wenn Sie so — seyn und es mir reichen wollen, if you will be good or kind enough to hand it me. *c)* [chiefly in familiar lang.] great or considerable, good. Sie kamen in —er Anzahl, they came in great number; er hat ein —es Stück bekommen, he has got a good, large piece; ich befinde mich ein —es Theil besser als gestern, I am or feel considerably or a good deal better than yesterday; es sind sechs —e Ellen, —e sechs Ellen, *— sechs Ellen, it is six good yards; vor einer —en Weile, a good while ago; es ist noch eine —e Strecke entfernt, it is still a good way off; eine —e Meile, a good long mile; es ist ein —es Jahr, daß ich hier gewesen bin, it is rather more than a twelvemonth that I have been here; ich muß so — [= nicht weniger] warten als er, I must wait as well as he; er ist so — Schuld als ich, it is his fault as well as mine.

Gut-achten, *n.* opinion, judgment. Ein theologisches —achten, the opinion of divines in a point of doctrine; ein ärztliches —achten, result of a consultation of physicians, medical opinions; [in commerce] das —achten eines Kaufmannes, [the advice or counsel of a merchant] parere; nach meinem —achten, in my opinion, er übt Gewalt nach —achten, he exerts a discretionary authority. **—artig**, *adj.* and *adv.* of a good sort, of a good description. —artige Kinder, well-disposed, well-minded, good-natured children; [applied to diseases] not malignant, not malign, not dangerous. **—artigkeit**, *f.* quality of being of a good sort or description &c. **—befinden**, *n.* 1) state of being well, good health. 2) V. —achten, —dünken. 3) V. —heißen. **—berath**, *m.* [in botany] water-plantain. **—denkend**, *adj* and *adv.* well-disposed, well-intentioned. **—dünken**, *n.* V. —achten. Handeln Sie nach Ihrem eignen —dünken, do as you think fit, proper or best. **—edel**, *m.* [a sort of grape] chasselas. **—erz**, *n.* [in mining] rich ore. **—fertiger**, *m.* V. Güterbestäter. **—finden**, *n.* V. —befinden 2) and 3. **—gegründet**, *adj.* well founded, solid. **—gelaunt**, *adj* and *adv.* good-humoured, in spirits. **—gesinnt**, *adj.* well-intentioned, well-disposed. **—gewicht**, *n.* [in commerce, an allowance of two pounds in every hundredweight] clough. **—gläubig**, *adj.* orthodox. **—haben**, *n.* a sum of money due to any person, credit. [in commerce] In Jemands —haben bringen, to carry to any one's credit. **—heißen**, *n.* approbation, consent. **—heißend**, *adj.* approving. **—herzig**, *adj.* good-hearted, good-natured. **—herzigkeit**, *f.* goodness of heart, good-heartedness, good-nature. **—launig**, *adj.* V. —gelaunt. **—müthig**, *adj.* V. —herzig. **—müthigkeit**, *f.* V. —herzigkeit. **—sagen**, *n.* V. Bürgschaft. **—sager**, **—sprecher**, *m.* V. Bürge. **—sagung**, *f.* V. Bürgschaft. **—that**, *f.* [the action and the thing done] a good action or deed, benefit, benefaction, V. Wohlthat. Jemand viele —thaten erweisen, to heap favours upon any one, to load any one with favours, with kindness. **—thäter**, *m.* benefactor. **—thäterinn**, *f.* benefactress, V. Wohlthäter, Wohlthäterinn. **—thätig**, *adj.* beneficent, kind, charitable, V. Wohlthätig. **—thätigkeit**, *f.* beneficence, charitableness. **—willig**, *adj.* and *adv.* 1) ready to do favours, complaisant, obliging, kind, friendly, V. Gefällig, —herzig. 2) voluntary, willing. Er that es —willig, he did it of his own accord. —**willigkeit**, *f.* 1) obligingness, complaisance, kindness, 2) willingness.

Güt, *n.* [-es, *pl.* Güter] 1) [any thing yielding profit] good, blessing. Gott ist das höchste — Aller, die ihn lieben, God is the sovereign good of all who love him; die Güter dieser Welt müssen nicht mit denen der nächsten verglichen werden, the good things of this world are not to be put in competition with those of the next; die Güter des Leibes, der Seele, the endowments of the body, of the mind; ich wollte aller Welt — nicht nehmen, ich wollte es um aller Welt — nicht thun, I would not do it for all the world, for ever so much; diese Bienen sind reich an — [Honig und Wachs], [in husbandry] these bees abound with honey and wax. 2) [particularly] property, fortune, possessions, estate. Er besitzt vieles, großes —, he is a man of large fortune, of large property; viele Güter, viel Geld und — besitzen, to possess, to enjoy great wealth; liegende Güter, lands and tenements; reich seyn an liegenden Gütern, to be rich in lands; *prov.* unrecht — gedeihet nicht, ill-gotten goods seldom thrive; Habe und — [bewegliches und unbewegliches Vermögen], movable and immovable possessions, [in law] chattels; *Hab' und — verlieren, to lose all one's fortune or property; *sich mit Leib und — verpfänden, to be bound body and goods; *— und Blut daran setzen, to hazard wealth and life. 3) a piece of land, a field, an estate. Ein wohlgebautes —, a well-cultivated estate; schöne Güter haben, to have fine estates; den Sommer auf seinem —e zubringen, to pass the summer on one's estate; ein Gütchen, Gütlein, a small estate or patrimony. V. Bauer—, Erb—, Frei—, Land—, Pacht—, Ritter—. 4) [in commerce] goods, merchandise, commodities, wares. Diese Güter sind alle verdorben, these goods are all spoiled; unten verzeichnetes —, the articles or goods noted at foot; irdenes —, earthen ware, crockery, V. Meß—, Glocken—, Stein—; bestes —, [in commerce] the best sort of tobacco in leaf. Syn. V. Habe.

Gutsteuer, *f.* property-tax, V. Vermögenssteuer.

Guts-besitzer, —**herr**, *m.* possessor or proprietor of an estate, lord of a manor. —**herrenrecht**, *n.* right of the lord of a manor. —**herrschaft**, *f.* the lord or lady of a manor. —**zwang**, *m.* power or authority of the lord of a manor over his vassals and tenants.

Güter-anschlag, *m.* apprizement or valuation of an estate, of estates. —**beschauer**, *m.* [in commerce] searcher. V. Beschauer. —**besitzer**, *m.* possessor of landed property. —**beständer**, *m.* one who hires and cultivates a farm, farmer. —**bestäter**, *m.* [*Speditor] a conveyer of goods. —**besteller**, *m.* V. —bestäter. —**gemeinschaft**, *f.* community of goods. —**handel**, *m.* commerce or trade in estates. —**kauf**, *m.* purchase of an estate or of estates. —**los**, *adj.* poor. —**masse**, *f.* the whole mass of property. —**reich**, *adj.* rich in landed property, in estates. —**schaffner**, *m.* V. —bestäter. —**stein**, *m.* V. Grenzstein. —**versender**, *m.* forwarder of goods, V. —bestäter. —**versicherung**, *f.* insurance of goods. —**wagen**, *m.* waggon [for the transportation of heavy commodities], V. Frachtwagen.

Güte, [der, die, das] V. Gut, *adj.* Die — with children, also called with the French word * die Bonne], nursery maid, governess.

Güte, *f.* 1) [little used] joy, pleasure. Sich eine — thun [= sich etwas zu gut thun], to enjoy or indulge one's self. 2) good quality of a thing, goodness. Die — des Weines, Bodens, the goodness of the wine, of the soil; die — der Luft, the healthfulness or salubrity of the air; die — seiner Grundsätze, Methode, the goodness or excellence of his principles, method; die — [= der Werth] dieser Perlen, the value of these pearls; die — des Geldes, Goldes, Silbers, the fineness of money, of gold, of silver; die — eines Handelshauses, the solidity of a mercantile house. 3) benignity of heart and acts of kindness. Ein Mensch von seltener —, a man of rare goodness or kindness; die — des Herzens, the goodness of the heart; Jemands — mißbrauchen, to abuse any one's goodness; ich werde mich seiner — gegen mich dankbar erinnern, I shall remember his goodness to me with gratitude; wollen Sie die — haben, mir zu sagen, will you be so good or kind as to tell me; er hat viel — für mich, he shows me much goodness, he is very kind to me; Einen mit —e überhäufen, to load any one with kindness; die Erde ist voll der — des Herrn [in Script.], the earth is full of the goodness of the Lord; Alles mit —, Nichts mit Gewalt, every thing by fair means and nothing by foul; den Weg der — einschlagen, to try fair means; in der — [ohne Streit or Proceß], in an amicable manner, amicably; einen Streit in der — beilegen, to make up or adjust a difference amicably; sage es in der — [= freiwillig], tell it of your own accord. [in law] accommodation. Er will nichts von —, von keiner — hören, he will not hear of any accommodation; auf dem Wege der —, amicably.

Gutheit, *f.* V. Güte 3).

Gütig, *adj.* and *adv.* good, kind, benevolent. Ein —er Fürst, a good, gracious prince; er hat ihn — [= wohlwollend] aufgenommen, he received him kindly, graciously, favourably; mit Ihrer —en Erlaubniß, by your kind leave or permission; seyen Sie so —, mir zu sagen, be so good or kind as to tell me; —er Gott! good, gracious God!

Gütigkeit, *f.* 1) V. Güte 3). 2) act of kindness. V. Gefälligkeit.

Gütlich, *adj.* and *adv.* 1) amicable. Ein —er Vergleich, an amicable adjustment, a compromise; einen Streit — beilegen, to make up or adjust a difference amicably. 2) agreeable, pleasant, in the following familiar phrases: Einem — thun, to treat a person with good things; sich — thun, to enjoy one's self; sich bei Tische — thun, to indulge in the pleasures of the table.

Gutturalbuchstabe, *m.* [-n, *pl.* -n] guttural-letter.

***Gymnasiarch**, *m.* [-en, *pl.* -en] [the governor of a school or college] gymnasiarch, head-master.

***Gymnasiast**, ***Gymnasist**, *m.* [-en, *pl.* -en] he who frequents a Gymnasium, [in general] a scholar.

***Gymnasium**, *n.* [-s, *pl.* Gymnasien] gymnasium. *a*) [somewhat less than a college and more than a grammar-school; in general] a college, school. *b*) [in antiquity] a place where athletic exercises were performed. V. also Turnplatz.

***Gymnast**, *m.* [-en, *pl.* -en] [in antiquity, teacher of gymnastics] gymnastes. V. also Turnlehrer.

***Gymnastik**, *f.* [in antiquity] gymnastic art, gymnastics. V. also Turnkunst.

***Gymnastisch**, [Gymnisch] *adj.* and *adv* gymnic, gymnastic. —e Spiele, gymnic games. V. also die Turnkunst betreffend.

***Gyps**, V. Gips.

H.

H, *n.* H. Ein großes H, a capital H; [in music, the seventh note of the natural diatonic scale] B; H dur, the key of B major.

Hä, *interj.* 1) [an expression of surprise, joy or indignation] ha, ah. 2) [when repeated, an expression of laughter] ha. Ha ha ha! ha ha ha!

Haag, *m.* [-s] [in geography] the Hague.

Haar, *n.* [-es, *pl.* -e] [*dim.* Härchen, ‖ Härlein, *n.*] [Dan. Haar, Sax. *haer*, Eng. *hair*; seems to be allied to the L. *hirtus*] 1) in general, any small filament. [in botany] Die —e einer Pflanze, the filaments, fibres, strings or hairs of a plant; die feinen —e, down; [among cloth-shearers] — und Grund, the right and wrong side, the two sides of the cloth; das Tuch aus den —en scheren, to shear the cloth for the first time, to give the first shearing to the cloth. 2) [filament growing from the skin of mammiferous animals and from some parts of the human body] hair. Einem Pferde die Mähne — für — ausraufen, to pull out a horse's mane hair for hair; die —e zwischen den Augenbraunen, the hair growing between the eye-brows; er fängt an, —e am Kinn zu bekommen, the beard begins to dawn or peep upon his chin, the down of his chin begins to appear; V. Milch—, Hasen—, Kameel—, Ziegen— &c.; das lange — am Halse eines Löwen, Pferdes, a lion's, horse's mane, V. Mähne. 3) hair of the head. Er hat nicht ein einziges —, kein Härchen auf dem Kopfe, he has not a single hair on his head; dieser Faden ist so fein als ein —, this thread is as fine as a hair; die sämmtlichen —e des Hauptes, das Haupt— or das —, the hair [of the head]; blonde, falsche —e, light, false hair; gefärbtes —, dyed hair; Einem das — or die —e schneiden, to cut any one's hair; sich die —e schneiden lassen, to get one's hair cut; Einem die —e zu kurz schneiden, to crop any one's hair too short; das — kräuseln, to curl or frizzle the hair; mit [wilde] flatternden or aufgelösten —en, with dishevelled hair; alle —e fallen mir aus, all my hair is falling off; *bei dieser Erzählung stehen Einem die —e zu Berge, this narration makes one's hair stand on end, makes one's blood run cold; *darüber laß' ich mir kein graues — wachsen, that gives or causes me no great pain or uneasiness, I shall never scratch my head for that matter; * and † einander in die —e kommen, sich an den —en herumzausen, to pull one another by the hair, to fall together by the ears, to fall or go to loggerheads; sich vor Verzweiflung die —e ausraufen, to tear one's hair for despair; Einen bei den —en herumziehen, to pull any one by the hair; [in astronomy] das — der Berenice, Coma Berenices, Berenice's Hair. *Fig* [in fam. and sometimes in vulgar lang.] †Er hat —e lassen müssen, it cost him sauce, he has been stript of his feathers, he has had the worst of it, he has been fleeced; es soll dir kein — gekrümmt werden, not a hair of thy head shall be touched, thou shalt get or receive no hurt or harm; *mit Haut und — [= ganz und gar], entirely, completely; *—e auf den Zähnen haben, to have experience, to be possessed of skill or ability, not to be a novice; es ist kein gutes — an ihm, he is a good for nothing wretch; ich frage nicht ein — darnach, I do not care a straw for it; sie hat kein — von ihrer Mutter, she does not take after her mother at all, she is not at all like her mother; auf ein — schießen, to be an excellent marksman, to hit the mark to a hair; es hängt an einem — or Härchen, the matter holds only by a thread, hangs on a thread, depends on the least accident; das macht die Sache um kein — anders, that does not alter the thing a bit; er ist um kein — besser als sie, he is not a whit better than she; er hat ein — darin gefunden, he has met with difficulties or obstacles, he has been disappointed, the thing did not answer his expectation; es fehlte nicht ein — breit daran, is was within a hair's breadth; er gibt kein — breit nach, he does not bate an inch of it; nicht ein — von seinem Rechte weichen, not to resign a particle of one's right; auf ein —, to a hair; um ein —, bei einem — [= beinahe], within an ace; bei einem — [= es fehlte gar nicht viel], wäre ich um mein Leben gekommen, I was like to have been killed, I was within a hair's breadth of being killed; †Einem in die —e wollen, to pick a quarrel with any one; †ich möchte ihm gern in die —e, my fingers itch to be at him; †sie liegen sich immer in den —en, they are ever at odds; eine Vergleichung, Auslegung &c. bei den —en herbeiziehen, to force in a comparison, an interpretation &c, to bring in a comparison &c. head and shoulders.

Haar-ader, *f.* [in anatomy] capillary vein. —aftermoos, *n.* [in botany, a moss, consisting of parallel fibres] hair-moss powder-moss. —alaun, *m.* plume-alum, V. Federalaun. —amethyst, *m.* capillary amethyst. —angel, *f.* fishing-line made of horse-hair. —aufsatz, *m.* [a kind of wig or cap of false hair] tete. —aufwickeln, *n.* [among hair-dressers] the putting hair upon pipes. —ball, —ballen, *m.* a small ball, composed of hair, found in the stomach of the chamois and other ruminant quadrupeds, aegagropile, hair-ball, V. Gemsenkugel. —band, *n.* 1) band, fillet or cord made of hair. 2) a riband for tying up the hair, hair-fillet, hair-lace. —bau, *m.* head-dress. —baum, *m.* [a shrub, native of the East-Indies] antidesma. —beere, *f.* raspberry. —beerstrauch, *m.* raspberry-bush. —beize, *f.* depilatory. —bereiter, *m.* he who prepares hair for the use of the periwig-makers. —besen, *m.* bristle-besom, hair-broom [a sort of brush]. —bett, *n.* hair-mattress. —beutel, *m.* hair-bag. *Fig.* [in fam. lang., especially in jest] Einen —beutel haben, to be a little tipsy, half-seas over; sich einen —beutel trinken, to get a little tipsy; Einem einen —beutel anhängen, to make any one tipsy, to fuddle, to intoxicate any one. —beutelperrücke, *f.* bag-wig, V. Beutelperrücke. —binde, *f.* V. —band 2). —birke, *f.* birch with capillary fibres. —bleiche, *f.* a place for bleaching hair. —bleicher, *m.* bleacher of hair, hair-bleacher. —blume, *f.* trichosanthes. —boden, *m.* [said, in jest, of a good head or crop of hair] Er hat einen dichten —boden, he has a fine head of hair. —bolzen, *m.* [in husbandry] a small anvil, on which sythes and sickles are sharpened with a hammer. —braten, *m.* [among hunters] buttock-piece of a wild boar. —breit, *adj.* of the breadth of a hair, hair-breadth, V. —dünn; [in botany] capillary. *Fig.* *Kein —breit, um kein —breit von etwas abweichen, V. Haar (3 *fig.*). —breite, *f.* hair-breadth. —bügel, *m.* hair-slide. —bürste, *f.* hair-brush. —busch, —büschel, *m.* tuft of hair. —decke, *f.* coverlet made of hair; [among brewers] hair-cloth. —dick, *adj.* of the thickness of a hair. —drossel, *f.* thrush of Carolina. —druse, *f.* crystallized fluor spar. —dünn, *adj.* as thin or fine as a hair. [in anatomy and botany] Die —dünnen Fasern, V. —faser. —eisen, *n.* [among tawers] scraper; [among hair-dressers] curling-irons, curling-tongs. —erz, *n.* ore in small filaments, capillary ore. —faden, *m.* [in botany] a kind of labiate flower, trichostema. —fall, *m.* falling off of the hair; [in medicine] fox-evil, alopecy. —farbe, *f.* 1) hair-colour, brown colour. 2) colour for dying hair, hair-dye. — —faser, *f.* —fäserchen, *n.* capillament, filament. —faserig, *adj.* [in botany] capillary. —federn, *pl.* down [of young birds]. —fein, I. *adj.* and *adv.* as fine or thin as a hair. *Fig.* exceedingly nice or subtile. Ein —feiner Unterschied, a very nice distinction. II. *n.* marsh-thread [a plant]. —fisch, *m.* [a genus of fishes] trichidion. —flechte, *f.* braid, plait or weft of hair. —flechter, *m.* one who weaves hair, hair-weaver. —förmig, *adj.* and *adv.* having the form or shape of a hair or of hairs, capilliform, hair-shaped; [in botany] capillary. —förmige Wurzeln, fibrous roots; [in mineralogy] —förmiges Erz, V. —erz. —förmigkeit, *f.* [in botany] capillary form or shape —gefäß, *n.* [in anatomy] capillary vessel. —gestirn, *n.* hair-star, V. Komet. —gold, *n.* [in mineralogy] native gold in the form or shape of hair. —gras, *n.* sealime-grass, V. Pelzgras. —gürtel, *m.* girdle made of hair, hair-girdle. —hammer, *m.* [in husbandry] a hammer used for sharpening scythes and sickles —handel, *m.* trade in hair. —händler, *m.* —händlerinn, *f.* dealer in hair, hair-merchant. —haube, *f.* periwig, wig. —hemd, *n.* hair-shirt. —holz, *n.* V. Traubenkirsche. —kalk, *m.* V. —mörtel. —kamm, *m.* comb for the hair. —kappe, *f.* V. —haube. —kies, *m.* capillary pyrites. —klauber, *m.* hair-fumbler, [a contemptible expression for a] hair-dresser or periwig-maker. *Fig.* *a finical, sophistical fellow, a fault-finder, trifler. *—klein, I. *adj.* thin, nice or minute [as a hair]. II. *adv.* to a hair. Eine Geschichte —klein erzählen, to relate a story minutely, with all the particulars. —komet, *m.* hairy comet. —kopf, *m.* head of hair, that is, the hair of females dressed without being covered. —kopfwurm, *m.* trichocephalus. —kranz, *m.* a monk's or priest's tonsure. —krause, *f.* dressed and frizzled hair, toupet or toupee. —krauser, —kräusler, *m.* hair-dresser. —kraut, *n.* V. Frauenkraut. —krone, *f.* V. —kranz; [in botany] seed-down. —kugel, *f.* V. —ball. —künstler, *m.* V. [frequently as a jocose expression] —kräusler. —kupfer, *n.* capillary native copper. —locke, *f.* lock or ringlet of hair. —los, *adj.* and *adv.* hairless, bald. Ein —loser Kopf, a bald head or pate. —mann, *m.* 1) a man dealing in hair, hair-man. 2) [among cloth-makers] cloth fulled, but not yet shorn. —mantel, *m.* dressing-gown of ladies to put on whilst having their hair dressed, combing-cloth. —matratze, *f.* hair-mattress. —mehl, *n.* hair-powder. —messer, *n.* a kind of knife for shearing, used by velvet-makers and hatters. —milbe, *f.* hair-mite, hair-worm. —moos, *n.* hair-moss. —mörtel, *m.* hair-mortar. —mütze, *f.* V. —haube. —nadel, *f.* hair-pin, hair-needle. —nest or —nestel, *n.* hair plaited and coiled together on the top. —netz, *n.* hair-net. —pastete, *f.* pie in which hair is baked. —pflanze, *f.* capillary plant. —pinsel, *m.* hair-pencil. —pomade, *f.* pomatum. —puder, *m.* —pulver, *n.* hair-powder. —putz, *m* head-dress. —putzer, *m.* [not much used] V. —kräusler. —qualle, *f* [in natural history] capillary sea-blubber. —rauser, *m.* [among tawers] wooden roller. —reiber, *m.* [among cardmakers] rubber, V. Reibeballen. —ring, *m.* a ring made of hair; *it.* a ring with hair. —röhre, *f.* [*dim.* —röhrchen, ||—röhrlein, *n.*] capillary tube. —sack, *m.* a sack or bag for hair, hair-bag; *it.* V. —beutel. —salbe, *f.* ointment for the hair, pomatum. —salz, *n.* hair-salt [a mixture of the sulphates of magnesia and iron]. —schaber, *m.* [among tawers] fleshing-knife. —schädel, *m.* scull covered with hair. —schar, *n.* [in botany] V. Bärlapp. —scharf, *adj.* and *adv.* very sharp. *Fig.* *very nice or exact. Etwas —scharf beweisen, to prove something convincingly, in a manner to leave no room for doubt; —scharf über etwas her seyn, to pursue a thing with great zeal, very ardently. —scheidel [frequently written —scheitel], *m.* the crown of the head. —schere, *f.* scissars for cutting the hair. —schlächtig, *adj.* V. Herzschlächtig. —schlag, *m.* V. Herzschlag. —schleife, *f.* 1) a braid or bow of hair. 2) a ribband or bow for adorning the hair. —schmuck, *m.* 1) the adorning of the hair. 2) ornament for the hair. 3) ornament[s] made of hair. —schmücker, *m.* —schmückerinn, *f.* [frequently in jest] hair-dresser. —schneiden, *n.* the cutting of the hair. —schnepfe, *f.* jacksnipe, juddock. —schnur, *f.* 1) string or cord of hair, hair-cord, hair-string; [in surgery] V. —seil; [among hair-dressers] V. —flechte. 2) a string of pearls &c. for adorning the hair. —schopf, *m.* tuft of hair. —schuppen, *pl.* scurf, scald-head. —schur, *f.* the shearing or cropping of the hair; *it.* tonsure. —schwanz, *m.* [in natural history] the capillary sea-star or star-fish. —schwarte, *f.* [in anatomy] pericranium, V. Schwarte. —schwefel, *m.* native or virgin sulphur or brimstone in form or shape of filaments. —seestern, *m.* [in nat. hist.] sea-suncrown. —seide, *f.* [in silk-manufactories] shoot silk, consisting of a thread of raw silk twisted round itself. —seil, *n.* V. —schnur 1); [in surgery, a few horse hairs or a twist of silk drawn through the skin] seton; [among farriers] a rowel. —seite, *f.* [among tawers] hair-side. —sieb, *n.* hair-sieve. —siebboden *m.* the bottom of a hair-sieve. —sieder, *m* he who boils hair, V. —bereiter. —silber, *n.* virgin silver in form of filaments. —sohle, *f.* sole of horsehair put into the boots or shoes —spalt, *m* [in surgery] a fracture no bigger than a hair. *—spalter, *m.* V. —klauber (*fig.*). —spieß, *m.* V. —besen. —spitze, *f.* the end or point of a hair. —stern, *m.* V. —gestirn. —strang, *m.* V. —seil; [in botany] hog's-fennel, sulphur-wort. —strich, *m.* [in calligraphy] hair-stroke. —stutz, *m.* bob-wig. —tour, *f.* V. —aufsatz. —tragend, *adj.* [in botany] capillary. —tresse, *f.* a knot or curl of hair, a tress. —trommel, *f.* [among wig-makers] a stove for drying or baking the hair. —tuch, *n.* 1) cloth made of hair, hair-cloth. 2) [in cookery] bolting-cloth, strainer. 3) V. —mantel. 4) [in commerce] a sort of shagged cloth, V. Zeltuch. —umwachsen, *adj.* grown round with hair; *it.* hairy. —verschneiden, *n.* V. —schneiden. —vitriol, *m.* native vitriol in form of filaments, trichites. —wachs, *n.* 1) V. —salbe. 2) [the tendinous extremity of the muscles] pack-wax. —weide, *f.* V. Bandweide. —weise, *adv.* hair by hair, by little and little. —wickel, *f.* a curl-paper. —wuchs, *m.* 1) growth of hair. 2) head of hair. Einen schönen —wuchs haben, to have a fine head of hair. —wulst, *m.* hair-pad. —wurm, *m.* 1) V. —milbe. 2) [in medicine] a sort of cutaneous worm, crinon, guinea-worm. 3) V. Wasserfadenwurm. —wurz, *f.* [in botany] water-lily. —wurzel, *f.* 1) the root of the hair. 2) [in botany] capillary or very fine root. —zange, *f.* [*dim.* —zängchen, ||—zänglein, *n.*] small pincers used to pluck out hairs, tweezers. —zeolith, *m.* fibrous zeolite. —zeug, *n.* 1) stuff or cloth made of hair, hair-cloth. 2) a small anvil and hammer, used to sharpen scythes and sickles. —zierde, *f.* 1) V. —putz. 2) a fine growth of hair. —zirkel, *m.* a pair of compasses with shifting points, fine compasses. —zopf, *m.* braid of hair, cue, tail, pig-tail, V. Zopf. —zotte, *f.* tuft of hair.

-zottig, *adj.* and *adv.* shaggy, shagged.

1. **Haaren** or [better] **Hären**, I. *v. tr.* V. Abhären. II. *v. intr.* to lose, shed or cast the hair. III. *v. r.* sich —, to lose or shed one's hair, to cast the hair. Dieser Pelz haaret or hären sich, the hair of this fur is coming off.

2. **Haaren**, *v. tr.* to sharpen or set a scythe or sickle [which is done by beating the edge with a hammer].

Haaricht, *adj.* and *adv.* resembling hair, hair-like, hairy, as fine or thin as hair. —es Gold, Silber, V. Haargold, Haarsilber; —gewachsenes Erz, V. Haarförmig &c.

Haarig, *adj.* and *adv.* overgrown or covered with hair, hairy. Er ist so — wie ein Bär, he is as hairy as a bear. V. Lang—, Kurz—, Kraus—. [in botany] capillary.

Håbbegierig, *adj.* V. Habsüchtig.

Håbe, *f.* 1) all one possesses, property, goods, effects. Fahrende — [= bewegliche Güter], movable goods, movables, chattels; Hab' und Gut verlieren, to lose all one's property. 2) V. Handhabe. SYN. Habe, Habseligkeit, Gut, Vermögen. Habe signifies movable, Gut immovable property. Further, Habe denotes only the material, Gut also the immaterial things which a person possesses, his rights, liberties &c. Habseligkeit signifies only the little paltry stock of goods and chattels, which constitutes the entire personal property of any one. Vermögen comprehends all the property, real and personal, which a person possesses.

Håben, [Sax. häbban, Goth. haban, D. hebben, Sw. hafva, D. haver, Eng. to have, Fr. avoir, Lat. habeo; Gr. ἅπ-τω = to touch, seems to be allied to L. capere] *ir.* I. *v. tr.* 1) to seize and hold, to take [properly, with the hand]. Da hast du Gold, here is gold for you, there, take this gold; da habt Ihr die Bücher, here are the books for you; da hast du Alles, was ich habe, there you have all I possess. *In a more confined sense: a*) to get, to obtain or procure. Dies Buch ist nicht zu —, this book is not to be had; für Geld ist Alles zu —, every thing is to be got or had for money; was [*i. e.* was für Nutzen] habe ich davon? what profit accrues to me from it? what do I get by it? ich habe nur wenig an dieser Waare, this commodity yields or brings me but small profit or gain, I get or make but small gain by this commodity. *b*) to have got or received. Ich habe einen Brief für Sie, I have [got] a letter for you; er hat Briefe von Hause, he has received letters from home; er hatte eine Ohrfeige von ihr weg, ehe er &c., she had given or hit him a box on the ear, before he &c. *Fig.* Ich habe [*i. e.* ich weiß] es von guter Hand, I have it from good hands. 2) to hold a thing by any bodily action. In der Hand —, to have or hold in the hand; — [= halten] Sie das Geld? have you the money? wir — [= halten] den Dieb, we have got the thief; bei sich —, to have about one; ich habe kein Geld bei mir, I have no money about me; Einen an or bei der Hand —, to hold any one by the hand, to hold any one's hand; er hat einen Ring am Finger, he has a ring on his finger; er hat den Hut auf [dem Kopfe], he has his hat on; er hat kein Hemd auf dem Leibe, he has no shirt on, *it. fig.* he has not a shirt to his back, is very poor. *Fig.* Einen bei der or zur Hand —, to have any one at one's disposal; etwas bei der or zur Hand —, to have a thing at hand, within reach; [in fam. lang.] da hast du es, da hast du dein Theil! there you have it, now you are in for it, that serves you right! 3) to contain. Dieses Buch hat viele Schönheiten und viele Fehler, this book has many beauties and many faults; diese Stadt hat schöne Häuser, this town has some fine houses, there are some fine houses in this town. 4) to be furnished with a thing either in body or mind, or in a bad sense, to be afflicted with a thing. Er hat viel Witz, aber keine Urtheilskraft, he has a great deal of wit, but no judgment; er hat eine vollkommene Kenntniß von dieser Sache, he is very well informed upon, has a perfect knowledge of, this matter; Jeder hat seine Fehler, every one has his failings; sie ist ein wenig schüchtern, das hat sie von ihrer Mutter, she is rather shy, she takes after her mother in that; dieselbe Krankheit —, to be affected with the same distemper; die Gicht, das Scharlachfieber —, to be ill of the gout, scarlet-fever; einen bösen Hals —, to have a sore throat; *es an den Augen —, to have sore eyes. 5) to possess [in various shades]. Viel Geld —, to have a great deal of money; ein Haus, ein Gut —, to have a house, an estate; wenig oder nichts —, to have little or nothing; *prov.* je mehr man hat, je mehr man will, the more we have, the more we want to have; *prov.* der Hab' ich ist besser als der Hätt' ich, a bird in the hand is worth two in the bush; a cottage in possession is better than a kingdom in reversion; eine Französinn zur Frau —, to have married a French woman; sie hat einen Grafen zum Manne, she has married a count, her husband is a count; * sie will ihn nicht —, [that is zum Gatten], she will not have or take him; — Sie noch einen Vater? is your father still living? wie viele Brüder — Sie? how many brothers have you? *zu leben —, to have enough to live on, to enjoy a competency or sufficiency; Geld auf Zinsen —, to have money at interest; *Einen lieb —, to love any one; ich habe das Herz nicht, es zu thun, I have not the heart to do it; etwas feil —, to have something to sell. *Fig.* to be in a certain place or in a certain relation to a thing or person. Wo — Sie Ihren Bruder, das Buch? [i. e. gelassen, hingelegt] where is your brother, the book? or where did you leave your brother, where did you put the book? Einen neben sich —, to have any one as an assistant, colleague &c.; Jemand um sich —, to have any one about one's person; *Keinen über sich —, to have no superior; den Feind vor sich —, to be in sight or view of the enemy; er ist nicht der Erste, er hatte Andere vor sich, he is not the first, others have done as much before him; wen meinst Du vor Dir zu —? [as a kind of threat] whom do you think you are speaking to? whom do you think to have to deal with? *seine Gedanken anderswo —, to be absent. 6) [= empfinden] to feel. Ekel vor etwas —, to feel disgust at a thing, to loathe, to nauseate a thing; Liebe zu etwas —, to have a liking to, a taste for a thing, to love a thing; Kummer —, to have sorrow, to be grieved or afflicted; ein großes Vergnügen an etwas —, to take great delight in a thing; *das habe ich gern, I like that, that pleases me; Hunger, Durst —, to be hungry, thirsty; ich habe nichts dawider, I have no aversion, I am not averse to it; etwas am or im Griffe, am Gefühle —, to know a thing by the touch, by feeling. 7) [= etwas — wollen] to command, to order. Ich will es so —, I will have it so; Sie haben es so — wollen, you have ordered or desired it so; *it.* [in fam. lang.] that serves you right. 8) to be in a certain state or condition. Es gut, es schlecht —, to be well off, in easy circumstances, to be badly off; ich habe einen Besuch zu machen, I have a visit to pay, I must pay a visit; er hat Ihnen Vieles zu sagen, he has a great many things to tell you; er hat zu wählen, it is his choice, he may take his choice; Sie — zu [= Sie müssen] gehorchen, you must obey; *mit Einem zu thun —, to have to deal with any one; was habt Ihr hier zu thun? what business have you got here? what's your business here? ich habe nichts dagegen [i. e. zu sagen], I have no objection; ich habe nicht weit nach Hause, [i. e. zu gehen], I have but a little way home. 9) [in the following phrases] Sein Gespött mit Einem — [= treiben], to laugh at, to ridicule, to deride, to banter, to jeer any one, to have or hold any one in derision; *er hat es keinen Hehl, he makes no secret of it; *er will es nicht Wort — [= es nicht gestehen], he will not confess it; er konnte es nicht Umgang — [rather stiff], he could not help or avoid it. II. *auxiliary verb*, to have. Ich habe gegeben, geschrieben, I have given, written; er hatte gesehen, he had seen. III. *v. r.* sich —, [= sich geberden, sich anstellen] to demean one's self, to behave. Wie er sich schlecht dabei hat! how badly or awkwardly he carries himself, how awkwardly he goes to work! wie er sich wieder einmal hat! what a singular behaviour or carriage! IV. *v. imp.* [chiefly in familiar language] Es hat keine Eile, there is no haste or hurry, the case is not urgent; es hat keine Noth [es ist nicht gefährlich], there is no fear or danger, there is nothing to be feared; damit hat es gute Wege, [= da ist nichts zu fürchten; *it.* = es eilt nicht] oh, it's all right, I am easy on that head; *it.* there is no hurry for it; [ironically] es hat sich was zu lachen! [= es ist hier kein Anlaß, zu lachen] there is nothing pleasant in that! that's no laughing matter.

Håbenichts, *m.* [*indecl.*, sometimes used in the *pl.* -e] a penniless fellow, a poor devil.

Håber, Håfer, *m.* [-s] [Sw. *hafra*, Engl. *haver*, L. *avena*, Fr. *avoine*, root uncertain] oats. Weißer, schwarzer —, white, black oats; wilder, gelblicher —, wild, yellow oats; der — auf dem Felde, standing oats; der — steht gut, the oats look well; den — mähen, to mow the oats; V. August—, Eichel—, Fahnen—, Grau—, Rauch—, Spitz—. Ein Vierling, eine Metze —, a peck of oats. *Prov.* Pferde, die den — verdienen, kriegen ihn nicht, merit seldom meets with its reward; [in fam. lang.] es ist gut — säen [= es redet Niemand in der Gesellschaft], conversation flags. *Fig.* Der — sticht ihn, [said of insolence occasioned by too much prosperity] he grows saucy, insolent, his good luck has spoiled him.

Haber-acker, *m.* field of oats. —ärnte, *f.* V. —ernte. —artig, *adj.* like or resembling oats. —artiges Gras, V. —gras. —bau, *m.* the culture of oats. —bier, *n.* beer brewed of oats. —blüthe, *f.* blossom of oats. —boden, *m.* 1) soil or land good for oats 2) oat-loft. —brei, *m.* oat-meal porridge. —brot, *n.* oatbread. —distel, *f.* oat-thistle. —ernte, *f.* crop or harvest of oats. —feld, *n.* V. —acker. —gelb, *adj.* yellow like oats. —gras, *n.* oat-grass or ciliated melic grass. —gries, *m.* —grütze, *f.* groats or grits. —griessuppe, *f.* soup of groats. —gülte, *f.* V. —zins. —gaff, *n.* V. —streu —kasten, *m.* —kiste, *f.* oat-bin. —korn, *n.* a grain or corn of oats. —kur, *f.* cure by means of water-gruel. —lattich, *m.* V. Huflattich. —malz, *n.* oatmalt —mann, *m.* [a kind of spider] field-spinner. —mark, *n.* V. —wurzel. —mehl, *n.* oatmeal. —milch, *f.* V. —wurzel. —mus, *n.* V. —brei. —nudeln, *pl. f.* vermicelli or maccaroni of Nuremberg in the form of grains of oats. —pflaume, *f.* V. —schlehe. —rohr, *n.* [= Hirtenflöte] oaten pipe, shepherd's pipe. —rose, *f.* creeping rose-bush. —rücke, *f.* V. Saatkrähe. —saat, *f.* the sowing of oats; *it.* season for sowing oats; *it.* green oats lately sprung up. —sack, *m.* a sack for oats, [in military affairs] haver-sack. —schlehe, *f.* hasty or forward sloe. —schleim, *m.* water-gruel. —schrecke, *f.* V. Heuschrecke. —seim, *m.* V. —schleim. —spreu, *f.* oats chaff. —stoppel, *f.* oatstubble. Der Wind weht über die —stoppeln, [= es fängt schon an kalt zu werden] it begins to grow cold, winter approaches. —stroh, *n.* oat-straw. —stück, *n.* a piece of ground sown with oats, a field of oats. —suppe, *f.* soup made of oatmeal. —trank, *m.* V. —schleim. —weihe, *f.* [in the Roman church] benediction of the oats. —wurzel, *f.* goat's beard, salsify. —zins, *m.* avenage.

Haberecht, [-s, *pl.* -e] *m.* [in fam. lang.] wrangler, disputer, an argumentative fellow.

Haberechten, *v. intr.* [in fam. language] to wrangle, to dispute.

Haberechterei, *f.* V. Rechthaberei.

Habesch, *n.* V. Abyssinien.

Habgier, *f.* V. Habsucht.

Habgierig, *adj.* and *adv.* V. Habsüchtig.

Habhaft, *adj.* and *adv.* in possession of, possessing. Einer Sache — werden, to get possession of a thing; man ist der Diebe — geworden, the thieves have been taken, seized or caught.

Habicht, *m.* [-s, *pl.* -e] [from haben = fangen, to catch, as the L. *accipiter*, from *accipio*] 1) hawk. 2) an esculent mushroom of a grayish colour.

Habichts-same, *m.* V. Wallsame, Weltsame. —sbinde, *f.* [in surgery] V. Sperber. —sfang, *m.* 1) the act of catching hawks. 2) V. —skorb. 3) the talon or claw of a hawk. —sfliege, *f.* a large fly of prey. —sinseln, *pl.* the Azores or Western Islands. —skorb, *m.* cage or basket for catching hawks. —skraut, *n.* hawkweed, sange. —snase, *f.* a hawk-nose, hook-nose or hooked nose, aquiline nose. —snest, *n.* a hawk's nest or airy. —snetz, *n.* a net for catching hawks. —sstein, *m.* [in mineralogy, a precious stone of the colour of the hawk] hieracites. —sstoß, *m.* [among sportsmen] V. —snetz.

*Habit, *m.* [-s] [only in familiar language] a habit, garb, dress. V. Kleid, Kleidung.

Habschaft, *f.* V. Habseligkeit.

Habselig, *adj.* and *adv.* rich, wealthy. V. Reich, Vermöglich.

Habseligkeit, *f.* [chiefly in fam. lang.] all a person has, property, fortune, goods, effects. Das ist seine ganze —, that's all he is worth, all he possesses; er hat, trägt alle seine —en bei sich, he has, carries all his substance about him; um alle seine —en kommen, to lose all one's property, one's all. Syn. V. Habe.

Habsucht, *f.* an immoderate desire of gaining and possessing wealth, avarice, covetousness, greediness.

Habsüchtig, *adj.* and *adv.* immoderately desirous of accumulating property, covetous, greedy of gain, avaricious.

Hachel, *f.* V. Achel.

Hachse, Hächse, *f.* V. Hätse.

†Hack und Mack, *m.* and *n.* [-s] tag-rag and bob-tail.

Hack, *m.* [-es, *pl.* -e] a stroke with a hoe or any other cutting instrument.

Hack-balken, *m.* [in seamen's language] V. Heckbalken. —bank, *f.* chopping-block or board. —beil, *n.* a hatchet for chopping meat, chopper. —block, *m.* chopping-block; *it.* cooper's block. —bord, —ebord, *m.* [in seam. language, the upper part of a ship's stern, which is generally ornamented with carved work] taffrail. —bret, *n.* 1) chopping-board. 2) [an instrument of music] dulcimer. —eisen, *n.* an iron instrument for chopping, chopper; [in farriery] hock or hough. —hopfen, *m.* hops that are hoed twice, cultivated hops. —klotz, *m.* V. —block. —messer, *n.* chopping-knife. —scheit, *n.* [among butchers] a cleaving-tool, cleaver; [in saltworks] V. Hackscheit. —stock, *m.*, V. —block.

1. Hacke, *f.* [*pl.* -n] 1) the act of hoeing. Einem Weinberge die erste — geben, to hoe or dress a vineyard for the first time. 2) a hatchet or axe, and chiefly a hoe or mattock. *Fig.* [in vulg. lang.] Der — einen Stiel finden [= ein Auskunftsmittel erfinnen] to find out an expedient.

2. Hacke, *f.* [*pl.* -n] heel. V. 2. Ferse, Absatz 3).

Hacken-knopf, *m.* [in botany] calligonum polygonoides. —leder, *n.* heel-piece, quarter-piece of a shoe. —schar, *f.* [in botany] good Henry, goosefoot, wild orach.

Hacken, *v. tr.* 1) to hack, to chop, to hash. Klein—, to mince; gehacktes Fleisch [Gehacktes] hashed or minced meat, hash; Holz —, to chop or cleave wood. 2) to cut or dig with a hoe, to hoe. Einen Acker, einen Weinberg —, to hoe a field, a vineyard.

Hacker, *m.* [-s, *pl.* -] one that hacks, hoes or chops. V. Holz—, Fleisch— &c.

Hackerlohn, *m.* wages paid for hoeing or chopping.

Häckerling, *m.* [-s] chopped straw [for fodder]. —schneiden, to chop straw.

Häckerlings-bank, —lade, *f.* [the machine on which straw is chopped] straw-cutter. —smühle, *f.* a mill for chopping straw. —sschneider, *m.* a person that chops straw.

Hacksch, *m.* [-es, *pl.* -en] [allied to the Eng. *hog*] boar. *Fig.* [in fam. lang.] a dirty hoggish person, an obscene fellow.

Hackschen, *v. intr.* to talk obscenely.

Häcksel, *m.* [-s] V. Häckerling.

Hadel, *f.* [*pl.* -n] [in botany] panicle.

Hadelgras, *n.* panic-grass.

Hädel, *m.* [-s] [in mineralogy] the best slich.

1. Hader, *m.* [-s, *pl.* -n] [seems to be allied to the Fr. *haillon*] rag, tatter. Syn. Hader, Lappen, Lumpen. Lappen are any little scraps of cloth or stuff, though still serviceable. Lappen are termed Lumpen when so worn or used, that they can no longer be made use of for their original purpose; when fit only for wipers, to work into paper &c. Ein Hader is a piece of stuff, which is so worn, that the threads are torn and the texture become loose.

Hader-lade, *f.* [in papermills, a trunk in which the rags are cut or chopped] cutting place. —lump, *m.* [in contempt] ragamuffin. —lumpen, *pl.* rags for making paper. —lumpenmann, *m.* rag-gatherer, rag-man. —messer, *n.* [in papermills] a great knife for cutting rags. —sammler, *m.* V. —lumpenmann. —schneider, *m.* [in papermills] an instrument, in form of a straw-cutter, for chopping rags.

2. Hader, *m.* [-s] [allied to Haß] vehement dispute, contention, quarrel, brawl, squabble, wrangle. V. Streit, Zwist, Wortwechsel, Zank. [in law] Der Eid macht allem — ein Ende, the oath puts an end to every difference.

Hader-buch, *n.* [formerly] a book in which lawsuits of little consequence were registered at Nuremberg. ‡—gericht, *n.* an inferior court of justice. —sucht, *f.* quarrelsome disposition. V. Zanksucht. —süchtig, *adj.* and *adv.* V. —haft.

Haderer, *m.* [-s, *pl.* -] 1) a quarrelsome person, wrangler, brawler, squabbler. 2) [among sportsmen] tusk of a boar.

Haderhaft, *adj.* and *adv.* quarrelsome, brawling.

Hadern, *v. intr.* to be displeased or angry; *it.* to quarrel, to squabble, to dispute or contend. Um nichts —, to dispute or wrangle about a pin's head.

1 Hafen, *m.* [-s, *pl.* Häfen] [allied to the L. *cavus*, *scapha* or the Gr. σκάφη] [a vessel more deep than broad] pot; [*dim.* Häfchen, ||Häfelchen, Häfelein, *n.*] a small pot. Ein irdener, ein eiserner —, an earthen, an iron pot. V. Fleisch—, Fuß—.

Hafen-binder, *m.* tinker. —deckel, *m.* the lid or cover of a pot. —pflanze, *f.* [in botany] calabash-tree. V. Topfbaum.

2. Hafen, *m.* [-s, *pl.* Häfen] [Sw. *hamn*, Dan. *havn*, Eng. *haven*, perhaps from haben = to halten, or Sw. *ham* = bedecken] port, harbour, haven. Ein von Natur gebildeter —, a harbour formed by nature, a natural harbour, ein künstlicher —, an artificial harbour or port, der innere —, der innere Theil des —s, the inner harbour, the basin of the harbour; in den — einlaufen, to enter a harbour, to sail into port, to put in; aus einem — auslaufen, to sail out of, to leave a port, a haven, to put to sea; einen —, die Häfen sperren, verschließen, to lay an embargo [to prevent ships from sailing out of port, or into port, or both], to blockade a port. *Fig.* a place of safety from storms or dangers, harbour, port. Er hat sich aus der Welt zurückgezogen, und ist in sicherem —, he has retired from the world and is in port; im — scheitern or Schiffbruch leiden, to be wrecked in port [= to be disappointed in an affair the very moment one thinks to be sure of success].

Hafen-anker, *m.* an anchor in a harbour, to which ships are fastened by a hawser. —aufseher, *m.* V. —meister. —bake, *f.* a beacon at the entrance of a harbour. V. Bake. —baum, *m.* bar laid across the mouth of a harbour, boom of a harbour. —damm, *m.* mole, pier of a harbour, quay. —gast, *m.* a vessel that enters a harbour and casts anchor in it. —gebühr, *f.* —geld, *n.* harbour dues, port duties. V. Ankergeld. —kette, *f.* a strong chain laid across the mouth of a harbour, boom. —leuchte, *f.* a lighthouse or beacon in or near a harbour. —meister, *m.* the overseer of a port, harbour master. —räumer, *m.* a machine for cleaning the harbour. —räumung, *f.* the cleansing of a harbour. —stadt, *f.* sea-port-town, seatown. —zoll, *m.* V. —geld.

Hafer, V. Haber.

Haferei or Havarei, *f.* [Fr. *avarie*] average.

Haff, *n.* [-s] [Dan. *Hav*, Sw. *Haf* = sea] formerly, the sea or a considerable part of it, a bay, gulf, [the Scotch word] fyrth or fryth or forth; now almost only used in: das Frische —, das Kurische — [two large bays in Prussia], the Frisch-Haff, the Kurisch-Haff.

Haff-deich, *m.* dike on the sea-side. —dorn, *m.* seabuckthorn. V. Seekreuzdorn, Sanddorn.

Hafner, † and || Häfner, *m.* [-s, *pl.* -] potter; [in some parts of Germany also for] stove-maker.

Hafner-arbeit, *f.* potter's ware, earthenware, pottery. —erde, *f.* potter's clay. —geselle, *m.* journeyman potter. —handwerk, *n.* potter's trade. —meister, *m.* master potter. —scheibe, *f.* potter's wheel. —werkstatt, *f.* potter's workhouse.

Häfnerinn, *f.* potter's wife.

1. Haft, *m.* [-es, *pl.* -en] 1) the quality of being fast or firm, hold, firmness. 2) any thing that makes fast, fastening, hook, clasp, rivet

[among glaziers] V. Haftenblei.

Hafts-dolde, *f.* bastard parsley, hedge-parsley. V. Klettenkerbel. —enblei, *n.* [among glaziers] bands, bonds [little pieces of lead with which iron rods are fastened to the panes of glass-windows]. —meißel, *m.* [among gunsmiths] a kind of chisel, socket-chisel.

2. Häft, *n.* [es, *pl.* -e] 1) [in natural hist.] ephemera, day-fly. 2) V. Heft.

3. Häft, *f.* custody, imprisonment, arrest. Jemanden zur —, in gefängliche — bringen, to put a person under arrest, to serve a writ or warrant upon any one, to secure or attach any one; in die — gerathen, to be taken into custody, to be imprisoned or arrested; einen Gefangenen seiner — entlassen, to release or discharge a prisoner.

Hafts-befehl, *m.* warrant of arrest. —beschwerde, *f.* servitude. V. Dienstbarkeit. —brief, *m.* V. —befehl. —geld, *n.* —pfennig, *m.* earnest, earnest-money, earnest-penny.

4 Häft, a termination of adjectives, from haben, haften. 1) possessing, as tugend—, possessing virtue, virtuous. 2) causing, giving, as schreck—, causing terror, terrific, nahr—, giving nourishment, nourishing, nutritious. 3) like, as schalk—, like a rogue, roguish, teufel—, like the devil, devilish.

Häftel, Häftlein, Häften, V. Heftel, Heftlein, Heften.

Häften, *v. intr.* to stick, to adhere, to hold. Dieser Nagel haftet zu fest, this nail holds too fast. *Fig.* Seine Augen hafteten auf ihr, his eyes were fixed upon her; *daran haftet es [= daran liegt das Hinderniß], there is the knot or rub; an etwas — [= hängen], to be addicted to something; er haftet so fest an seinen eigenen Meinungen, daß &c., he is so firmly attached, so wedded to his own opinions, that &c.; es haftet ihm ein Fehler an, he has one fault; es haftet nichts bei ihm, there is nothing that affects, touches or moves him; *it.* he forgets every thing, retains nothing; ein Gut, auf dem Schulden —, an estate clogged or encumbered with debts; auf seinem Gute — Hypotheken, his estate is encumbered with debts or mortgages, is mortgaged; ich hafte dafür, I warrant or answer for it, I am answerable for it; für Einen —, to be bail for, to bail any one.

Häftung, *f.* bail, surety or security.

Häg, *m.* [-es, *pl.* -e] [from hegen] 1) hedge, fence. Ein lebendiger —, a quick-set hedge or fence. 2) a bush or shrub and a place inclosed with bushes and shrubs, an enclosure, a precinct; *it.* a coppice, grove. V. Gehäge, Gehölz, Hain.

Hags-apfel, *m.* 1) [a wild sour apple] wilding, crab. 2) V. Hagebutte. —apfelbaum, wilding-tree, crab-tree. —bereiter, *m.* Hägebereiter. —eiche, *f.* evergreen oak, ilex, holm-oak. V. Steineiche, Aesche. —eichel, the fruit of the holm, acorn. —rose, *f.* briar, dog-rose.

Hägbar, *adj.* that may be enclosed or fenced in.

Hägebuche, *f.* horn-beam, yoke-elm;

Hägebuchen, *adj.* of horn-beam or yoke-elm. *Fig.* [in vulgar lang.] Ein —er [ungeschliffener] Mensch, an awkward rude fellow.

Hägebutte, *f.* [*pl.* -n] hip or hep.

Hagebutts-birne, *f.* medlar. —birnbaum, *m.* medlar-tree. —enlattwerge, rhodorrhodon. —enrose, *f.* V. Hagrose. —strauch, *m.* hip-tree, wild-briar, dog-rose. —schwamm, *m.* hairy rose-gall, bedeguar.

Hägedorn, *m.* [-es, *pl.* -e] 1) haw-thorn, white-thorn. V. Weißdorn. 2) V. Hagebuttenstrauch.

Hägedrüse, *f.* [*pl.* -n] the king's evil; *it.* testicle, stone. V. Heckdrüse.

1 Hägel, *m.* [-s] [Sw. *hagel*, Eng. *hail*, probably from the root of hack, haggle, or allied to Kugel] 1) collectively, masses of ice or frozen vapour falling from the clouds, hail. Der — hat das ganze Feld verwüstet, the hail has desolated or laid waste all the fields; daß dich der —! Blitz und —! [most vulgar oaths] damn your eyes! God blast you! *Fig.* Ein — von Schlägen, Steinen, Kugeln, Schimpfworten &c., a shower of blows, stones, balls, abuses &c. 2) small-shot. Seine Flinte war nur mit — geladen, his fowling-piece was only charged with small-shot 3) the albuminous cords which unite the yelk of the egg to the white, treadle, tread, V. Hahnentritt. Syn. Hagel, Schloßen. Hagel signifies hail, collectively; Schloßen are the individual hailstones.

Hagel-dicht, *adj.* and *adv.* as thick as hail. —gans, *f.* wild-goose. —guß, *m.* shower of hail. —korn, *n.* hail-stone; [in medicine, a disorder in the eye-lids, which consists in a tubercle like a hailstone] chalaza. —kugel, *f.* [a hollow ball, filled with small pieces of iron, bullets &c.] cartouch. V. Kartätsche. —schaden, *m.* damage done by a hail-storm. Er hat — schaden erlitten, he is a sufferer by the hail; the hail has damaged or ruined his crop. —schauer, *m.* shower of hail, hail-shower. —schlag, *m.* 1) V. —schauer. 2) V. —schaden. —schrot, *n.* slugs or shot for killing ducks. —stein, *m.* a large hail-stone. —sturm, *m.* hail-storm. —weiß, *adj.* and *adv.* [rather vulg.] as white as snow. —wetter, *n.* V. —sturm. —wolke, *f.* a hail-cloud.

2. Hägel, *m.* [-s] Jan —, or Hans —, the mob, the rabble.

Hägeln, *v. intr. impers.* to hail. Es hagelt sehr stark, it hails very hard. *Fig.* Die Pfeile hagelten auf ihn, he was covered with a shower of arrows; †es hagelte Prügel auf ihn, a shower of blows fell upon him. V. Schloßen.

Hägen, *v. impers.* [little used]] V. Behagen.

Hägen, Hegen, *v. tr.* 1) to fence, to enclose; *it.* to bar, to stop; to protect, to preserve Gehägte Waldungen, forests of defence; das Wild —, to preserve the game. V. Einhägen, *it.* V. Schützen. *Fig.* Einen bei sich — [= ihn bei sich aufnehmen] to shelter or harbour any one; *Einen — und pflegen, to take great care of any one, to treat any one with good things. 2) Ein Gericht — [= halten], to administer justice; ehemals wurden die Gerichte auf freiem Felde gehegt, formerly justice was administered in the open field. 3) [to keep or maintain in the mind with favour] to entertain, cherish, foster, harbour. Freundschaft gegen Einen —, to have a friendship for, to bear a friendship to any one; eine üble Meinung von Einem —, to entertain a bad opinion of any one; schlechte Gedanken —, to harbour evil thoughts.

Häge-bereiter, *m.* forest-keeper, game-keeper. —holz, *n.* wood or forest in defence [the trees of which must not be cut down]. ‡—mahl, *n.* an inferior court of justice, held in the open fields and deciding on contests about boundaries &c., court of the manor. V. Feldgericht. —reis, *n.* V. Laßreis. —reiter, *m.* V. —bereiter. —säule, *f.* a post or stake that shews the limits of a hunting-district. —schlag, —wald, *m.* V. —holz. —wasser, *n.* a pond or river in which it is not allowed to fish, a preserve. —weide, *f.* 1) pasture-ground in defence [on which no cattle is allowed to feed]. 2) [in botany] the water-willow, osier. —wiese, *f.* a meadow in defence [on which no cattle is allowed to feed]. —wisch, *m.* a small bundle of brushwood, or a wisp of hay or straw stuck on a pole, to indicate that a passage is stopped up. —zeit, *f.* time, when no game is killed.

Häger, *adj.* and *adv.* [Eng. *haggard*; in some districts heger is = dürr] thin, lean, lank, meager. Ein —es Gesicht, a meager face; ein sehr —er Mensch, a very thin man, a rawbone fellow; ein —er Körper, a lank or lean body. Syn. Hager, Mager. Hager (meager, haggard) refers to the form, and signifies destitute of flesh, or having little flesh. Mager (lean, thin) refers to the matter, and is the reverse of fat. One says, therefore, of a piece of lean meat, that it is mageres, but not hageres Fleisch.

Hägerfalk[e], *m.* [-en, *pl.* -en] [among sportsmen, a species of hawk] haggard.

Hägerkeit, *f.* leanness, meagerness, lankness.

Hägestolz, *m.* [-en, *pl.* -e or -en] [probably from Hag = Haus and stellen, therefore, one that stands alone as it were] an [old] bachelor.

Hagestolzenrecht, *n.* [formerly, in law] the right of confiscating the acquests or acquisitions of a deceased [old] bachelor.

Hahä, *n.* [indeclinable] [a fence or bank that interrupts an alley or walk, sunk between slopes and not perceived till approached] hawhaw.

Häher, *m.* [-s, *pl.* -] [in nat. hist.] jay. V. Birk—, Tannen—, Holz—.

1. Hähn, *m.* [-es, *pl.* -en or Hähne] [Sax. *hana*, Icel. *hane*, probably allied to the Gr. χαίνω, Germ. gähnen, L. *cano* = to open the mouth and then to cry] the male of birds, particularly of domestic or gallinaceous fowls, cock. Ein junger —, ein Hähnchen, a cockerel; ein gebratener junger —, a roasted chicken; der — tritt die Henne, the cock treads the hen; der wälsche —, Trut—, turkey-cock; V. Auer—, Birk—, Fasanen—; ein verschnittener —, a capon; der [Wetter-] — [on church-steeples &c], the weather-cock. *Fig.* [in fam. lang.] Es wird kein — darnach krähen, there will not be the least inquiry made about it, nobody will care a straw for it; der — im Korbe seyn, to be the first in company, the cock of the party or club; Einem einen rothen — auf das Haus or Dach setzen [in popular lang.], to set any one's house on fire, to fire any one's house.

2 Hähn, *m.* [-es, *pl.* -en or Hähne] [either from the Icel. and Sw. *hank* = chain or band, or *fig.* of the preceding word] 1) the cock of a gun. Den — einer Flinte spannen, to cock a gun; spannet den — ! cock your firelocks or muskets! 2) [an instrument to draw out liquor from a cask, vat &c.] cock. Den — umdrehen, to turn the cock.

3. Hähn, *m.* [-es, *pl.* -en or Hähne or Hähnen] [in metallurgy] 1) V. Herdkörner, Treibkörner. 2) V. Sprößlinge.

Hahn-balken, *m.* V. Hahnenbalken. —brei, *m.* [in white iron-plate manufactories] a paste of water, clay and coal-dust, into which the iron plates are dipped. —buche, *f.* incorrect for Hagebuche, which see. —buchen, *adj.* V. Hagebuchen. —butte, *f.* V. Hagebutte. —fisch, *m.* cock fish. —port, *n.* -en [in seamen's lang.] V. Hahnenpfoten.

Hahnen-balken, *m.* [in carpentry] collar-beam, windbeam. —bart, *m.* a cock's wattle or gills. —ei, *n.* cock's egg [a small egg, much below the usual size of hen's eggs, which by a vulgar error is supposed to have been laid by the cock]. —fuß, *m.* 1) [in botany] ranunculus. Der knollige —fuß, the bulbous ranunculus; der kriechende —fuß, ranunculus of the meadows; der gelbe —fuß, crow-foot. 2) coronopus, buck's-horn plantain, hart's-horn. 3) [in seamen's lang.] —füße, *pl.*

crow-foot. —gefecht, *n.* cock-fight. —gehäuse, *n.* [in mining and hydraulics] the box or case of metal in which the cock is. —geschrei, *n.* cock-crowing. —hode, *f.* [*dim.* ||—hödlein, *n.*] 1) a kind of small plum. 2) cornelian-cherry. 3) the red berry of the spindle-tree. 4) hep or hip. —hodenbaum, *m.* spindle-tree, prick-timber, prick-wood. —hödleinstrauch, *m.* cornelian-tree; *it.* hip-tree, wild briar, dog-rose. —hütchen, *n.* V. —hode 3). —kamm, *m.* 1) the comb of a cock, cock's comb. V. Kamm. [in anatomy] the upper or inner continuation of the ethmoid, by which it is divided into two parts. 2) [in botany] *a*) cock's comb, louse-wort, yellow rattle. *b*) rattle-grass. *c*) V. Tausendschön, Gabelkraut, Meierkraut. 3) [a shell] great scallop. —kammklee, *m.* —kämmchen, *n.* [in botany] sainfoin, cock's-head. —kampf, *m.* V. —gefecht. —kopf, *m.* the head of a cock; [in botany] V. —kammklee. —pfote, *f.*, *pl.* —pfoten, [in seamen's lang.] crow-feet of the tops. —pfötchen, *n.* V. —hode 3). —ruf, —schrei, *m.* V. —geschrei. —schritt, *m.* a cock's step, cock-stride. [in fam. lang.] Der Tag hat um einen —schritt zugenommen, the days have begun to increase or lengthen a little. —spath, *m.* [in farriery] string-halt. —sporn, *m.* cock's spur; [in botany] cock-spur. —stein, *m.* alectoria [a stone or gem sometimes found in the stomach of cocks or capons]. —tritt, *m.* 1) compression of the male fowl, tread. 2) treadle. V. Hagel 3). 3) V. —spath. —wahrsagerei, *f.* alectryomancy.

Hahnrei, *m.* [-es, *pl.* -e] [perhaps from the Ital. *cornaro*; but more probably from Hahn, as the Fr. *cocu* from *coq*] [a man whose wife is false to his bed] cuckold Einen zum — machen, to cuckold any one.

Hahnreischaft, *f.* cuckoldom.

Hai, *m.* [-es, *pl.* -e] or —fisch, *m.* [Dan. Sw. and Icel. *hay*] shark.

Haifischzähne, *pl.* shark's teeth; particulary, petrified shark's teeth, glossopetrae. —roche, *m.* [a species of ray] scate.

1. **Hain**, *m.* [-es, *pl.* -e] [instead of Hagen from hägen] [in poetry] wood, grove, thicket.

Hainbuche, *f.* V. Hagebuche. —butte, *f.* V. Hagebutte. —götze, *m.* an idol worshipped in a grove.

2. **Hain**, *m.* [-es] Freund —, a popular as well as poetical name of Death. Freund — klopft bei ihm an, he is at death's door.

Haiternessel, *f.* [*pl.* -n] V. Eiternessel.

Häkchen, *n.* [-s, *pl.* -] a little hook; [in grammar] apostrophe. *Fig.* * and † Ein — auf Jemand haben [= auf Einen erbittert seyn &c.], to bear any one a grudge, to have a spite against any one; * and † die Sache hat ein —, V. Haken.

Hakekamm, *m.* [-s] [among carpenters] the corner-rafter of a hip roof, hip. V. Lehrsparren.

Hakel, Häkel, *adj.* and *adv.* V. Häkelig, Häklig.

Häkel, *n.* [-s, *pl.* -] 1) V. Häkchen. 2) a turning tool or instrument with a crooked point.

Häkelarbeit, *f.* a species of embroidery wrought with small hooks, tambour-work. —nadel, *f.* needle used in embroidering with a tambour. —pfahl, *m.* pale of a Häkelwerk, which see. —stahl, *m.* [among turners] a crooked turning-instrument.

Häkelhufe, *f.* [*pl.* -n] V. Hakenhufe.

Häkelicht, *adj.* and *adv.* crooked, aduncous.

Häkelig, *adj.* and *adv.* full of little hooks. *Fig.* *captious, nice, ticklish, critical, difficult. Ein —er Gegenstand, a ticklish subject; eine —e Frage, a captious question; ein —er Geschmack, a nice or over-nice taste.

Häkeligkeit, *f.* quality of being full of little hooks. *Fig.* *quality or disposition of being captious, ticklish &c.; touchiness, irritability.

Häkeln, *v. tr.* & *intr.* 1) to seize and draw with little hooks; *it.* to fasten with little hooks. 2) to embroider with little hooks or with a tambour. 3) to wound with the claws or nails. *Fig.* *Sie — sich immer, they are always teazing one another.

Häkelwerk, *n.* [-es, *pl.* -e] a fence or inclosure of pales stuck across in the ground and loads of brushwood and thorns, stake-bound fence.

Haken, *m.* [-s, *pl.* -] [Sw. & Icel. *hake*, D. *haak*, Dan. *hage*, Sax. *hoc*, Eng. *hook*, allied to Ecke, Angel, L. *uncus* &c.] [*dim.* Häkchen, ||Häklein, *n.* a little hook.] in general, any thing crooked or bent; [in mining] a deviation or turning aside of a lode; usually, a hook. Hänge es an jenen —, hang it upon that hook; eine Nadel zu einem — umbiegen, to bend a pin into the form of a hook; *it.* clasp, V. Haft; [among gunsmiths] V. Hakenbüchse; der englische — [among watchmakers] scapement; [in printing] crotchet, V. Klammer; [in the manege] die —, V. Hakenzähne; [among bookbinders] clasp; [among locksmiths] picklock. Also used in compositions: V. Angel—, Brunnen—, Feuer—, Kessel—, Mist—, Nuß—, Schließ—, Schlüssel—, Thür—, Wider—, Winkel—; *it.* V. —pflug. *Fig.* * and † Die Sache hat einen —, there is a hitch in the business, there is some difficulty or mystery in it; *prov.* was ein — werden will, krümmt sich bei Zeiten, soon crooks the tree, that good grambel would be.

Hakeisen, *n.* 1) [among pewterers, a turning-tool] iron-rod. 2) the iron or share of the Hakenpflug, which see. —scheit, *n.* a strong iron bar, to which the saltpan in salthouses is fastened by its hooks. —zapfen, *m.* [among carpenters] tenon.

Hakenarmmuskel, *m.* [in anatomy] coracobrachialis. —band, *n.* [among locksmiths] that part of the iron work of doors and windows, which turns round a hinge. —bein, *n.* [in anatomy, one of the bones of the wrist] os unciforme, hooked bone. —blatt, —blech, *n.* [among locksmiths, a loop of iron or a bar or wire, bent and formed with two points, to be driven into wood to hold a book &c.] staple. —block, *m.* [in seamen's lang.] a hooked block or pulley. —bohrer, *m.* [in mining] a hooked auger. —bolzen, *m.* [in seamen's lang.] hook-bolt. —büchse, *f.* arquebuse. —eisen, *m.* V. Hakeisen. —förmig, *adj.* and *adv.* in form of a hook, hooked, aduncous. —haue, *f.* [among miners] a pick-axe or mattock used in clayey or rocky ground. —hufe, *f.* a hide or measure of land of about 15 acres. —kopf, *m.* a rope-maker's wheel. —kreuz, *n.* [in heraldry] a cross cramponnee. —lachs, *m.* the male salmon. —mörser, *m.* handmortar. —nadel, *f.* a hooked needle used to ascertain the thickness of the metal of a gun through the touch-hole. —nagel, *m.* tenter-hook. —pflug, *m.* an instrument for tilling, similar to, but more simple than the plough, hook-plough. —pulver, *n.* gunpowder for arquebuses. —rad, *n.* [among watchmakers] swing-wheel. —schar, *f.* [in husbandry] plough-share with a hook. —scheibe, *f.* [in husbandry] an iron plate with a hook, stuck on the linch-pin, in order to put a third horse to a waggon; *it.* hurter, washer. —schlüssel, *m.* hooked key, pick-lock. —schütze, *m.* arquebusier. —spieß, *m.* harping-iron, harpoon. —stock, *m.* stick with a hook. —zahn, *m.* [zähne *pl.*] [in farriery] tush [es] of a horse. —ziegel, *m.* tile with a hook.

Haken, I. *v. tr.* to seize with a hook, to hook; *it.* Einen Acker —, to till a field with the hook plough. II. *v. intr.* to catch, as a hook. *Fig.* * and † Da haket es, there's the rub or knot, there is the difficulty.

Hakicht, *adj.* and *adv.* resembling a hook, aduncous.

Hakig, *adj.* and *adv.* having hooks, hooky.

Häklig, *adj.* and *adv.* V. Häkelig.

Hakse, *f.* [*pl.* -n] [allied to Hacke] the knee-joint [especially of the hind legs in the larger animals], hock. Einem Pferde die —n abschneiden, to hamstring a horse.

1. **Halb**, [Halben, Halber] [V. Halbe.] I. *adv.* and *prep.* denoting the side or part, V. Allenthalben, Außer—, Inner—, Ober— &c. II. *Fig. prep.* [governing the genitive and always following the subst.] on account of, for reason of, for the sake of. Des Königs halben, for the sake of the king; Alters halber, on account of age; er ist Gewissens halber dazu verbunden, he is in conscience bound to do it; ich möchte es Wunders halber sehen, I should like to see it for the rarity of it. V. Derhalben, Deshalben, Meinethalben &c.

2. **Halb**, *adj.* and *adv.* [Eng., D. &. Sw. *half*, Dan. *halv*] half. Ein —es Pfund, half a pound; eine —e Stunde, half an hour; ein und ein —er Fuß, a foot and a half; es ist — Ein Uhr, it is half past twelve o' clock; um — acht, at half past seven; diese Uhr schlägt ganze und —e Stunden, this clock strikes the hours and the half-hours; hat es schon — geschlagen? has the half-hour struck? has it gone the half-hour? ein —es Hühnchen, half a chicken, one half of a chicken; ein —er Ton, half a tone, semitone, V. Halbton; ein — schwarzes und — weißes Kleid, a gown half black and half white; ein Zeug — von Wolle und — von Seide, a stuff half wool and half silk; die Centauren waren — Mensch, — Pferd, the Centaurs were half man, half horse; auf —em Wege, —en Wegs, half-way; Einem auf dem —en Wege begegnen, to meet any one half-way; das Wasser geht ihm bis an den —en Leib, the water goes up to his middle; Güter um die —e Nutzung verpachten, to let out lands on condition of receiving half the crop; der —e Mond, half moon, [in heraldry] crescent; die —e Trauer, half or second mourning; ein —er Beweis, an imperfect, half proof; es ist — wahr, it is partly true; [in seamen's lang.] ein —er Wind, quarter-wind, side-wind; er hat es nur halb gehört, he heard only half of what was said; er ist — todt, he is half dead; *fig.* *ich war — todt vor Schrecken, I was half dead for fright; Alles nur — thun, to do things by halves; [in familiar lang.] das ist weder — noch ganz or gar, it is neither good nor bad, neither the one nor the other, *prov.* neither fish nor flesh; — und —, indifferently, so so, almost, imperfectly, pretty or tolerably.

Halbabendbrod, *n.* an afternoon's luncheon, collation. —ärmel, *m.* half-sleeve. —atlas, *m.* [*Satinade] satinet. —bauer, *m.* farmer or peasant who possesses only as much land as two horses or oxen can till in a year. —bauerei, *f.* V. —pacht. —bekehrte, *m.* semi-convert. —bier, *n.* small-beer, table-beer. —bild, *n.* half-length figure, bust. —blume, *f.* [in botany] gaura. —bruder, *m.* half-brother, V. Stiefbruder. —bürtig, *adj.* half-blood. Ein —bürtiger Bruder, a brother of the half-blood. V. Stiefbruder. —*cylindrisch, *adj.* and *adv.* half or semi-cylindrical.

—damast, *m.* damask made of silk and ferret. —dornmuskel, *m.* [in anatomy] semi-spinal muscle. —dunkel, *adj.* and *adv.* — half dark, dusky. —durchsichtig, *adj.* and *adv.* semi-transparent, semi-diaphanous, semi-translucent. —e *f.* V. Hälfte. —edelstein, *m.* half precious stone [such as agate, onyx, cornelian, chalcedony and others]. —eimerig, *adj.* and *adv.* holding half an eimer. —eirund, *adj.* and *adv.* semi-ovate, half-egg-shaped; [in anatomy] das —eirunde Fenster, oval window [one of the holes in the hollow of the ear]. —eisen, *n.* [among masons] a chisel with a broad edge. —ellig, *adj.* and *adv.* of half an ell or yard. —ente, *f.* diver, Colymbus. —erbe, *m.* heir to one half of the property. —erhaben, *adj.* in bass-relief. —erhabene Arbeit, bass-relief. —fächerig, *adj.* and *adv.* [in botany] semi-locular. —fenster, *n.* [in architecture] half-window, mezzanine. —fisch, *m.* 1) flounder, halibut, [and particularly] plaice. 2) a being that is half-fish, as a mermaid. —flach, *adj.* and *adv.* half-flat. —fläche, *f.* [in painting] flat. Beim Mahlen eines Kopfes müssen die —flächen merklich seyn, when you paint a head, you should make the flat parts sensible. —flächsen, *adj.* and *adv.* half-flaxen. —flechsig, *adj.* [in anatomy] semi-tendinous. —fleck, *m.* a chip or piece of strong leather used for making the heels of shoes or boots. —flosser, *m.* [a fish] coryphaena with very short or half fins. —flug, *m.* [in heraldry] wings half expanded. —flügelig, *adj.* hemipteral. Ein —flügeliges Insekt, a hemipter. —franzband, *m.* [with bookbinders] half-bound. —franzscharlach, *m.* bastard-scarlet. —fuchs, *m.* [in nat. hist.] 1) animal partaking of the nature of the fox, but with a short tail. 2) racoon, coati. —fuderig, *adj.* holding half a fuder [V. Fuder]; [among foresters] being only of half a waggon or cart-load. —galeere, *f.* galiot. —gefiedert, *adj.* V. Fiedern. —gelehrte, *m.* one imperfectly or half-learned, half-scholar, sciolist, smatterer. Die —gelehrten, the half-learned. —geschöpf, *n.* an imperfect or mutilated creature. —geschoß, *n.* [in architecture] entre-sole, mezzanine. —geschwister, *n.* V. Stiefgeschwister. —gesell, *m.* an apprentice that has served his time, but is not yet declared a journeyman. —gesicht, *n.* the side face or half face, profile. —getreide, *n.* mongcorn, meslin. V. Mengkorn. —getrennt, *adj.* [in botany] androgynous. —gneiß, *m.* [in mineral.] half or semi-gneiss. —gott, *m.* a demi-god, demi-goddess. —gottheit, *f.* demi-god, demi-goddess. —grandstein, —granit, *n.* half-granit. —griffig, *adj.* [among foresters] V. —fuderig. —gut, *n.* pewter alloyed with lead, trifling metal. —hase, *m.* V. —kaninchen. —häutig, *adj.* [in anatomy] semi-membraneous. —hemd, *n.* [*dimin.* —hemdchen, ||—hemdlein, *n.*] waist-shirt. —holz, *n.* timber less thick than broad. —hüfener, *m.* V. —bauer. —hundert, *n.* half a hundred, number of fifty. —insel, *f.* peninsula. —invalide, *m.* a retired soldier on full pay during life. —jahr, *n.* six months, half-year. —jährig, *adj.* and *adv.* 1) lasting six months or half a year. Ein —jähriger Friede, a six months' peace. 2) six months or half a year old. Ein —jähriges Kind, a child six months old. —jährlich, *adj.* and *adv.* happening or coming every six months, half-yearly. —käfer, *m.* [in entomology] necydalis. —kaninchen, *n.* agouty, Guinea-pig. —kapaun, *m.* half-gelded cock. —kartaune, *f.* [in artillery] a half or small carronade. —kenner, *m.* sciolist, smatterer. —kenntniß, *f.* a slight, superficial knowledge, smattering. —klappe, *f.* [in botany] argemone, thorny Mexican poppy. —kreis, *m.* half-circle, semi-circle. —kreuzer, *m.* 1) [more correctly der —kreuz] secular member of the order of Malta. 2) [a coin] half-kreuzer. —kugel, *f.* hemisphere. Die östliche und die westliche —kugel, the Eastern and Western hemispheres; [in anatomy] die —kugeln des Gehirnes, the hemispheres of the brain. —kugelförmig, *adj.* and *adv.* having the figure of a hemisphere, hemispheroidal. —kugelig, *adj.* and *adv.* forming a hemisphere, hemispherical. —kugelkäfer, *m.* coccinella, lady-bird, lady-cow. —kugelrund, *adj.* semi-spherical, semi-orbicular. —kutsche, *f.* chariot. —lang, *adj.* and *adv.* having only half the usual length. —laut, I. *m.* semi-vowel. II. *adj.* and *adv.* not buite loud, low, in an under tone. —lauter, *m.* V. —laut I. —lehen, *n.* a fief leased or let on rent. —leinwand, *f.* half-linencloth. —leute, *pl.* V. —mann 2). —lind, *adj.* [among goldsmiths] —linde Feile, *f.* soft file. —lob, *n.* equivocal praise. —löhner, *m.* V. —bauer. —mann, *m.* 1) half a man, demi-man; *it.* a eunuch. 2) [*pl.* —leute] a farmer or tenant who pays half the rent in kind or the produce of land. —maßflasche, *f.* a quart bottle. —mast, *f.* [in husbandry] beechmast. —mastig, *adj* [among foresters] —mastige Hölzer, Wälder, woods, forests consisting almost entirely of beeches. —mehl, *n.* V. Mittelmehl. —meier, *m.* a farmer that possesses but half a farm, a little farmer. —mensch, *m.* a being half man half beast. *Fig.* a brutal person, a brute. —messer, *m.* [in geometry] semi-diameter radius. —metall, *n.* semi-metal [such as bismuth, zink, arsenic and others]. —mond, *m.* half-moon; [in heraldry] crescent; [in fortification] halfmoon. —mondförmig, *adj.* and *adv.* resembling in form a half moon, semilunary. [in anatomy] Die —mondförmigen Klappen, the semilunary valves. —mondschnecke, *f.* [in conchology] nerita. —mutter, *f.* V. Stiefmutter. —neue, *f.* [among sportsmen] snow that melts in the morning. —offen, *adj.* half open. Eine —offene Thüre, a door left ajar. —opal, *m.* semi-opal. —pacht, *m.* and *f.* a lease, according to which the farmer is to give to the landlord half the produce of the land. —pachter, *m.* V. —mann 2). —part, *m.* an equal share, halves. [in popular lang.] —part rufen, to cry halves; auf —part eintreten, to go halves with any one. —pfeiler, *m.* [in architecture] a short pillar at the top of a large one. —pferd, *n.* 1) [in ancient fable, a supposed monster, halfman and half horse] hippocentaur. 2) [in botany] monk's rhubarb, patience dock. —pfünder, *m.* [in artillery] a half pounder. —porphyr, *m.* half or semi-porphyry. —porzellan, *n.* mock china, delf, delft-ware. —prismatisch, *adj.* semi-prismatical. —reif, I. *m.* [in seamen's lang.] iron hoop that fastens the top-gallant mast to the top mast, iron clamp of a French cap. II. —reif, *adj.* half-ripe. —ring, *m.* a hook or ring in the form of a halfmoon to hold leaden pipes, wall-hook. —rund, *adj.* and *adv.* half round, semi-annular, semi-circular. Die —runde Feile, the halfround file. —säule, *f.* [in antiquity, a small low column with an inscription] cippus. —säure, *f.* [in chimistry] oxyd. —scharlach, *m.* half-scarlet. —schatten, *m.* [in astronomy] penumbra; [in painting] half-shade, mezzotinto. —scheid, [with some authors] —schied, *f.* the half, moiety. Zur —scheid mit einem seyn, to go halves or snacks with any one. —schlächtig, *adj.* V. —schlägig. —schlag, *m.* a mixed breed or race. —schläger, *m.* a creature of a mixed breed, a mongrel. —schlägig, *adj.* of a mixed breed, half-bred, hybrid, mongrel. —schreitig, *adj.* [in music, proceeding by semitones in succession] chromatic, semitonic. Die —schreitige Tonfolge, chromatic scale. —schule, *f.* [in manege, half terra, a terra and half corvet] mesair or mezair. —schürig, *adj.* —schürige Wolle, wool of the second shearing; *it.* wool shorn off when grown to but half its proper length. —schwester, *f.* half-sister, V. Stiefschwester, —bürtig. —sehne, *f.* [in geometry] half-sine. —seide, *f.* half silk [and half cotton or other substance]. —seiden, *adj.* made half of silk. —seidener Damast, V. —atlaß —seite, *f.* [in print.] column, V. Spalte. —silber, *n.* platina. —spänner, *m.* V. —bauer. —sparren, *m.* [in carpentry] sleeper. —städtchen, *n.* [unusual] small country-town. V. Flecken. —stich, *m.* [in seamen's lang.] V. Timmerstich. —stiefel, *m.* short boot, half-boot; *it.* [of the ancient tragic actors] buskin. —strauch, *m.* [in botany] shrub. —stündig, *adj.* and *adv.* lasting or requiring half an hour, half an hour old. —stündlich, *adj.* and *adv.* occurring every half hour, from half hour to half hour. —tägig, *adj.* lasting half a day; *fig.* short, ephemeral. —theilig, *adj.* divided into two equal parts. —tinte, *f.* [in painting] V. Mitteltinte. —todt, *adj.* half dead. —ton, *m.* [in music] semi-tone. —trauer, *f.* half or second mourning. —tuch, *n.* [*Casimir] a thin woolen cloth, cassimer. —umgedreht, *adj.* half turned. Ein —umgedrehter Cristall, [in mineralogy] a hemitrope crystal. —verdeck, *n.* 1) [in ships] half-deck. 2) [on smaller vehicles, cabriolets &c.] head, or hood. —vers, *m.* hemistich. —vetter, *m.* distant cousin or relation. —vieh, *n.* a being half beast half any thing else; *fig.* a stupid brutish person, a brute; [in husbandry] a flock of sheep, the profits of which are divided between the shepherd and Lord of the manor. —vogel, *m.* a small kind of thrush. —voll, *adj.* half-full. —wagen, *m.* a light one-horse carriage, such as a gig, cabriolet, caleche or calach. —wege, *adv.* middling, so so, indifferently. —werk, *n.* half a day's work. —wild, *adj.* half wild or savage. —wisser, *m.* —wisserinn, *f.* V. —kenner. —wisserei, *f.* a superficial or imperfect knowledge. —witz, *m.* a silly jest or wit. —wüchsig, *adj.* having but half its growth. —zeolith, *m.* prehnite. —zeug, *n.* [in papermills] the rags when cut or chopped. —zeugkasten, *m.* [in papermills] a stone or wooden trough or chest in which the chopped rags are preserved. —ziegel, *m.* a tile of but half the usual breadth. —zimmer, *n.* a room in an entresole. —zirkel, *m.* semi-circle. —zirkelförmig, *adj.* and *adv.* semi-circular.

Hälbe, *f.* 1) [originally = Seite] side. [in fam. lang.] Einen von der — ansehen, to look on any one sideways, obliquely or askance. 2) V. Hälfte.

Hälberling, *m.* [-es, *pl.* -e] an animal of a mixed breed, mongrel.

Hälbig, [unusual] I. *adj.* half, middling, tolerable. II. *adv.* pretty well, indifferently, so so.

Halbiren, *v. tr.* to divide into two parts, to halve.

Hälbling, *m.* [-es, *pl.* -e] 1) formerly, half a pfennig [about a farthing]. 2) any one that is only half or imperfectly what he ought to be, hybrid, mongrel.

Hälde, *f.* [*pl.* -n] [from the old verb halden, Low Sax. hellen = neigen, to bend] steep declivity, precipice; *it.* [in general] side of a hill; V. Berg—, Thal—; [in mining] a heap or hill of earth or stones that contain no ore; *it.* a heap of rubbish. *Fig.* †Einen auf die — setzen, to impose upon, to cheat any one.

Halen, *v. tr.* [in seamen's lang.] V. Anholen.

Hälfte, *f.* [*pl.* -n] [V. Halbe.] 1) one half, a moiety. Die — seiner Staaten, the half of his dominions; eine gute — meines Erbtheils, a full half of my inheritance; die größere —, the better half; es ist um die — zu theuer, it is too dear by half; einen Acker um die — verpachten, to let out or to lease out a field for half the crop; die Kosten zur — tragen, to bear half the expense; *mit Einem zur — gehen [in Geschäften], to go halves with any one; [in printing] die untere — des Schriftkastens, the lower case. *Fig.* [chiefly in jest] *Die — [= Ehe—], one's better half, one's rib; er hat seine theuere — verloren, he has lost his dear wife. 2) the middle. Auf der — des Weges, in the middle of the way or road, half-way; ein Gefäß bis auf die — füllen, to fill a vessel to the middle, half-full.

Hälften, *v. tr.* [little used] V. Halbiren.

Hälfter, *f.* [*pl.* -n] [*dim.* -chen, *n.*] [from halten] halter [for leading or confining a horse]. Ein Pferd an die — legen, to halter a horse. *it.* [in surgery] V. —binde; *it.* [rarely] V. Hosenträger.

Halfter-binde, *f.* a bandage to support the lower jaw. —**geld**, *n.* money or gratuity given by the purchaser of a horse to the groom of the seller. —**kette**, *f.* halter-chain. —**leine**, *f.* rope or thong with which horses are tied to the rack. —**loch**, *n.* hole through which the halter-chain is put. —**riemen**, *m.* V. —leine. —**ring**, *m.* halter ring. —**strick**, *m.* V. —leine.

Hälftern, *v. tr.* [little used] to put on a halter, to halter [a horse.]

Hälisch, *m.* [-es, *pl.* -e] [in mineralogy] native argil or alumen.

Hall, *m.* [-es, *pl.* -e] [the same word as Schall, allied to gällen] sound. Der — der Trompeten, the sound of trumpets. V. Wiederhall.

Hall-drommete, *f.* V. —horn. —**horn**, *n.* a horn or trumpet, with which the jubilee of the Jews was announced. —**jahr**, *n.* [among the Jews, every fiftieth year, in which all the slaves were liberated &c.] the year of jubilee, V. Jubeljahr. —**trompete**, *f.* V. —horn.

Halle, *f.* [*pl.* -n] [Fr. *halle*, *salle*, Sax. *healle*, Eng. *hall*, perhaps allied to the L. *aula*, the Gr. *αὐλή*] 1) any covered building, particularly a porch, vestibule; *it.* [by extension] hall; hence, a common hall. 2) stalls or shops joined to the outside of a larger edifice, as a church. 3) all the buildings of a saltwork. V. Salzwerk. 4) [in foundries] a shed for coals. 5) [in mining] V. Halde. 6) [a town in Prussian Saxony] Halle.

Hall-bursch, *m.* [from Halle = Salzkothe, salt-house] a labourer engaged in a saltwork. —**engeld**, *n.* fee due for commodities sold in the common hall of a place, marketduty. —**leute**, *pl.* people belonging to a saltwork. —**meister**, *m.* the master or proprietor of a saltwork.

***Hallelúja**, *n.* [*indeclinable*] [a Hebrew word, signifying *praise ye Jehovah*, *give praise to God*] hallelujah.

Hallen, *v. intr.* [chiefly in poetry] to sound, to resound. V. Wiederhallen.

Häller, *m.* V. Heller.

Halloh! [allied to hallen] *interj.* halloo!

Hallör[e], *m.* [-en, *pl.* -en] a man belonging to a saltwork. V. Hallbursch, Salzwerker.

†**Hallúnk[e]**, *m.* V. Halunke.

Halm, *m.* [-es, *pl.* -e or -en] [Dan., Eng. and Sw. *halm*, Sax. *healm*, L. *calamus*, Gr. *κάλαμος*] the stalk or stem of grasses, especially of corn, halm or haum.

Halm-knoten, *m.* the joint or knot of a stalk. —**lese**, *f.* gleaning. V. Aehrenlese. —**leser**, *m.* —**leserinn**, *f.* gleaner. —**motte**, *f.* a maggot or worm that pierces the stalks of corn. —**pfeife**, *f.* a pipe formed of straws, a shepherd's pipe. —**rübe**, *f.* V. Stoppelrübe. —**schneidmaschine**, *f.* a machine for cutting the stalks of corn. —**tragend**, *adj.* culmiferous.

Hälmchen, ‖**Hälmlein**, [*dim.* of Halm] *n.* [-s, *pl.* -] a little stem or stalk. [in fam. and vulgar lang.] Einem das — durch das Maul streichen [= ihm schmeicheln], to wheedle, to coax any one; — *ziehen, to draw lots.

Hals, *m.* [-es, *pl.* Hälse] [*dim.* Hälschen, *n.*] [Dan., Sw. and Icel. *hals*, L. *collum*, seems to be allied to hohl] 1) [the part of an animal's body which is between the head and the trunk] neck. Ein langer, kurzer —, a long, short neck; sie hat einen schönen, weißen —, she has a fine white neck; der — eines Pferdes, the neck of a horse; einem Vogel den — umdrehen, to wring the neck of a bird; Einem um den — fallen, to fall about any one's neck; Einen beim —e fassen, kriegen, to take or seize any one by the neck or throat, to collar any one; [in fam. lang.] er dreht dir den — um, wenn du &c. [a threat], he will break your neck, beat your brains out, if you &c.; sich den — abschneiden, to cut one's throat; er hat den — gebrochen, he has broken his neck. *Fig.* *Einem den — brechen [= ihn zu Grunde richten], to undo any one, to be the ruin of any one, to break any one's neck; er hat sich selbst den — gebrochen, he has ruined himself; das wird ihm den — brechen, that will prove his ruin; [in seamen's lang.] die Gezeit bricht den —, the flood-tide begins; Einem einen Rechtsstreit an den — werfen, to enter or bring an action against any one, to sue any one at law; Einem alles Unglück auf den — wünschen, to wish any one all manner of evil, to curse any one; sich etwas auf den — laden, über den — ziehen, to lay or draw a thing on one's neck or back, to bring a thing upon one's self; etwas am —e, auf dem —e haben, to be troubled, encumbered, pestered or plagued with a thing; er hat die Schwindsucht am —e (rather vulgar), he has fallen into, is affected with a consumption; diese Wittwe hat 5 Kinder auf dem —e (rather vulgar), this widow has five children to keep or to maintain; viele Gläubiger auf dem —e haben [rather vulgar], to be troubled with a great many creditors, to have many duns at one's heels; Einem auf dem —e sitzen, über dem —e liegen [= lästig seyn], [rather vulgar], to importune, to be troublesome to, to plague, to pester any one; Einem die Polizei über den — schicken [rather vulgar], to set the police-officers loose against any one; Einem über den — kommen [rather vulgar], to surprise any one, to come or fall upon any one suddenly or unawares; sich eine Person oder eine Sache vom —e schaffen, to rid one's self of, to get rid of a person or thing, to shake off a person or thing; bis an den — in Schulden stecken, to be over head and ears in debt; über — und Kopf, über — über Kopf, with great haste, with tumultuous hurry, precipitately, headlong. *it.* for Leben, life: Es kann ihm den — kosten, es geht ihm an den —, it may cost him his life, his head or life is at stake; mit dem —e bezahlen müssen, to pay with one's life. 2) [the interior part of the neck] throat. Er riecht aus dem —e, he has a stinking breath, his breath stinks; es steckt mir etwas im —e, something sticks in my throat; einen bösen — haben, to have a sore throat, V. —weh. *Fig.* Aus vollem —e lachen, schreien, singen, to laugh immoderately, to split one's sides with laughing; to scream or roar as loud as one can; to sing with full throat; †sich bis an den — voll essen, to cram one's belly, to stuff one's guts; †Einem den — stopfen, to stuff any one's belly [with meat and drink]; *it.* to stop any one's mouth; *bis an den — studirt haben or gelehrt seyn, to be a deep learned man, a first-rate scholar, [or ironically] to know nothing; sein Vermögen durch den — jagen, to spend, waste or squander away one's fortune by feasting; †sich den — absaufen, to kill one's self with hard drinking; †das hat er in seinen — hinein gelogen, he has lied in his throat, he is a lying rascal; [among sportsmen] — geben, to give tongue or mouth. 3) [the long slender part of many instruments and other things] neck. Der — an einer Geige und anderen Tonwerkzeugen, the neck of a violin and other musical instruments; der — einer Flasche, eines Gefäßes, the neck of a bottle, of a vessel; *fig.* *einer Flasche den — brechen, to crack a bottle; der — eines Destillirkolbens, the neck of a retort, der — an einem Sporn, the neck of a spur, der — der Harnblase, der Gebärmutter, the neck of the bladder, of the matrix; der — einer Pflanze, the neck of a plant; [in seamen's language] der — an einem Anker, the throat of an anchor; der — eines Segels, the tack of a sail; den — zusetzen, to haul down or bring aboard the tack of a sail; der — eines Knie's, the throat of a knee; der — des Stages, the eye of a stay.

Hals-ader, *f.* jugular vein or artery. —**amboß**, *m.* a brasier's anvil. —**band**, *n.* collar; *it.* [for ornament] neck-lace. Das —band eines Hundes, a dog-collar. —**bein**, *n.* collar-bone, clavicle. ‡—**berge**, *f.* gorget. —**beseh**, *m.* V. —band. —**binde**, *f.* neck-cloth, cravat, stock. —**blutader**, *f.* V. —ader. —**braten**, *m.* [am. sportsmen] the scraggy end of a deer's neck. —**bräune**, *f.* sore throat; quinsy. —**brecht**, *f.* break-neck. —**brechend**, *adj.* and *adv.* endangering the neck, attended with great risk, dangerous, perilous, hazardous. —**bruch**, *m.* the act of breaking one's neck. —**brüchig**, *adj.* [a law term] incurring the forfeiture of life, capital. —**bund**, *m.* the collar or neck-band of a shirt. ‡—**bürge**, *m.* bail or surety in a criminal cause. ‡—**bürgschaft**, *f.* security given in a criminal cause. —**dreher**, *m.* [a bird] wryneck. —**drüse**, *f.* jugular gland; [in anatomy] tonsil; [in fam. lang.] almond [of the throat]. Die —drüsen der Pferde, the vives. ‡—**eigen**, *adj.* V. Leibeigen &c. —**eisen**, *n.* 1) an iron collar which is put round the neck of criminals condemned to stand in the pillory. 2) a sort of cramp-iron, used in sluices to keep back the flood-gates. —**entzündung**, *f.* inflammation of the throat; quinsy. V. Bräune 2). —**feifel**, *f.* [a disease of horses] the vives. —**fistel**, *f.* [in surgery] fistula of the throat. —**flosser**, *m.* fish of the jugular order. —**gat**, *n.* [in ships] hole of the chess-tree. —**geflecht**, *n.* [in anatomy] plexus of the jugular veins. —**gehänge**, —**gehenk**, *n.* ornaments hung round the neck as a neck-lace. ‡—**gericht**, *n.* a criminal court of justice, criminal tribunal; *it.* the criminal jurisdiction. ‡—**gerichtsherr**, *m.* the lord of the manor, who has the right of criminal judicature; *it.* chief-justice. —**geschmeide**, *n.* V. —gehänge. —**geschwulst**, *f.* swelling or tumour of the neck or throat. [in farriery] Die —geschwulst or Bräune, strangles. —**geschwür**, *n.* an abscess of the neck.

throat; *it.* sore throat, quinsy. —**gicht**, *f.* gout in the neck or throat. —**grübchen**, *n.* pit of the nape. —**haar**, *n.* hair on the neck of certain animals, [of horses] mane. —**harnisch**, *m.* V. —stück 2). —**hemde**, *n.* a shirt or shift which only covers the neck and breast, half-shirt, waist-shirt. —**herr**, *m.* V. —gerichtsherr. —**huhn**, *n.* a fowl or hen annually paid to the lord of the manor as a token of fealty. —**joch**, *n.* a yoke which is put round the neck of oxen. —**kappe**, *f.* a monk's hood or cowl, capouch. —**kette**, *f.* chain for the neck [chiefly as an ornament], V. —gehänge. —**klammer**, *f.* V. —eisen 2). —**klampe**, *f.* [in seamen's language] chess-tree. —**klaue**, *f.* V. —eisen 2). —**knebel**, *m.* V. Knebel. —**knoten**, *m.* [in anatomy] cervical ganglion or plexus. —**koppel**, *f.* collar; *it.* V. Kummetkette. —**kragen**, *m.* cape, collar, V. Kragen. —**krankheit**, *f.* sore-throat; *it.* the quinsy, V —weh, Bräune 2); [in farriery] V. —geschwulst. —**krause**, *f.* ruff [for the neck]. —**kraut**, *n.* throat-wort, V. Kohlkraut, Waldglöcklein. —**lanzette**, *f.* pharyngotome. —**mandeln**, *pl.* [in anatomy] tonsils, almonds [of the throat]. —**muskel**, *m.* [in anatomy] cervical muscle. —**nerve**, *f.* [in anat.] cervical nerve. —**pulsader**, *f.* carotid artery. ‡—**recht**, *n.* power over life and death, V. —gericht. ‡—**richter**, *m.* V. —gerichtsherr. —**riemen**, *m.* neck-strap, V. Tragband. —**ring**, *m.* ring round the neck, collar, V. —band. —**röhre**, *f.* larynx, windpipe. —**rose**, *f.* V. Herbstrose. —**sache**, *f.* criminal cause, question of life and death, a hanging matter or business. —**schelle**, *f.* V. —eisen 1). —**schild**, *m.* —**schildlein**, *n.* [of winged insects] corcelet. —**schlag**, *m.* V. Husche. —**schlagader**, *f.* cervical artery. —**schleier**, *m.* V. Brustschleier. —**schleife**, *f.* a riband or bow for the neck. —**schloß**, *n.* V. —schnalle. —**schmuck**, *m.* ornament for the neck; V. —band, —gehänge, —kette. —**schnalle**, *f.* a clasp or buckle to a cravat or stock. —**schnur**, *f.* neck-lace, string of pearls or beads. —**schwindsucht**, *f.* quinsy. —**siele**, *f.* V. Siele. —**starre**, *f.* stiffness of the neck. *Fig.* stubbornness. —**starrig**, *adj.* and *adv.* *Fig.* stiff-necked, inflexibly obstinate, stubborn, head-strong. —**starrigkeit**, *f.* stubbornness, obstinacy. ‡—**strafe**, *f.* capital punishment, pain of death. Bei —strafe, upon pain of death. V. Todesstrafe. —**streif**, —**strich**, *m.* a small piece of lace or linen tied round the neck, tucker. —**stück**, *n.* 1) piece of the neck, neck of meat. Das —stück eines Hammels, eines Kalbes, neck of mutton, of veal. 2) Das —stück an einem Harnisch, neck-piece of an armour, gorget. —**sucht**, *f.* V. —bräune. —**talje**, *f.* [in seamen's lang.] tack-tackle. —**tuch**, *n.* [for men] neck-cloth, cravat; [for women] handkerchief for a woman's neck, neckerchief. —**verbrechen**, *n.* capital offence. —**weh**, *n.* pain in the throat, sore-throat; *it.* pain in the neck. —weh haben, to have a sore throat; *it.* to have a pain in the neck. —**wirbel**, *m.* —**wirbelbein**, *n.* [in anatomy] the cervical vertebre. —**wurz**, —**wurzel**, *f.* V. —kraut. —**zange**, *f.* the long-necked nippers of the pin-makers. —**zäpflein**, *n.* [in anatomy] uvula or top of the palate. —**zierde**, V. —schmuck.

Hälschen, ||**Hälslein**, *n.* [-s, *pl.* -] *dim.* Hals, which see.

1. **Halse**, *f.* [*pl.* -n] [among sportsmen] a dog's collar; *it.* [sometimes] a horse-collar.

2. **Halse**, *f.* [*pl.* -n] [from halen = holen, hawl] [in seamen's lang.] tack of a sail, V. Hals 3). Die —n umholen [wechseln], to change from one tack to another, to tack about; stich auf —n und Schoten, up tacks and sheets.

1. **Halsen**, [rather obsolete] *v. tr.* [Einen] to embrace any one, to jump at any one's neck.

2. **Halsen**, *v. intr.* [V. 2. Halse] [in seamen's lang.] to veer.

Halsung, *f.* V. 1. Halse.

Halt, I. *m.* [-es, *pl.* -e] 1) act of stopping, halt. — machen, to make a halt, to halt. 2) = Gehalt 2). 3) hold, support, stay, firmness, solidity. Der Pfeiler hat keinen —, the pillar has no support. II. *adv.* [in certain provinces of South-Germany, in fam. lang. for: halte ich] I believe, I suppose, methinks, perhaps, probably, rather, indeed, forsooth. Er wird — nicht kommen, I think he won't come; er weiß — nicht, daß &c., indeed, he knows not, that &c. III. *interj.* hold, stop, halt. — Kutscher! stop, coachman!

Haltbändchen, *n.* [in anatomy] a small ligament.

Haltbar, *adj.* and *adv* 1) tenable. Die Festung ist nicht —, the fortress is not tenable. *Fig.* not weak, valid. Ein —er Grund, a good or valid reason, a valid argument; diese Entschuldigung ist nicht —, this excuse won't do. 2) durable.

Haltbarkeit, *f.* 1) quality of being tenable, firmness, strength. 2) durability.

Halten, [allied to haben] *ir.* I. *v. tr.* 1) [to seize or to have seized] to hold. Ein Buch —, to hold a book; ich halte den Dieb, I hold the thief, I have got hold of him; wir — einen Apfel in der Hand oder ein Kind in den Armen, we hold an apple in the hand or a child in the arms; die Zügel gleich—, to hold the reins even; ein Pferd im Zügel or im Zaume —, to keep a good or tight hand on a horse; [in seamen's lang.] See —, to keep the sea, or to hold out in the offing. *Fig.* *a*) to fix the state or condition of a thing or person. Einen gefangen —, to keep or detain any one prisoner; eine Stadt eingeschlossen —, to keep a town in blockade; die Thüre offen —, to keep the door open; etwas unter dem Schlüssel —, etwas verschlossen, unter Riegel und Schloß —, to keep a thing under lock and key; ein Kind zur Schule — or zum Schulbesuch an—, to send a child regularly to school; seine Kinder reinlich —, to keep one's children cleanly; etwas zu Rathe —, to use a thing with economy, to husband a thing; ein Gebäude in gutem Stande —, to keep a building in repair; etwas in Ehren —, V. Ehre 3); Buch—, Rechnung —, [in commerce] to keep the books, accounts; etwas geheim —, to keep a thing a secret; Einen in Ungewißheit, in Spannung —, to keep any one in suspense; *Einen frei —, to pay for any one, to treat any one; Einen schadlos —, to indemnify any one; Waaren in einem gewissen Preise —, to keep up the price of goods; das Gesinde gut —, to use, to treat the servants well; Einen wie seinen Bruder —, to treat any one like a brother. *b*) [= veranstalten] to bring about, to hold, to keep. Einen Rath —, to hold a council; die Tage, an welchen der König Rath hält, the days when the king holds a council; die Assisen —, to hold the assizes; ein Gespräch mit Einem —, to hold a conversation, to have an interview with any one; eine Versteigerung —, to hold an auction; eine Rede —, to hold a discourse, to make a speech; eine Predigt —, to preach a sermon; Schule —, to give lessons at a school; Stunde—, to give a lesson; *it.* to do a thing in due or good time, at the time appointed; eine gute Mahlzeit —, to make, to eat a good meal; Mittagsruhe —, to take an afternoon's nap; Gottesdienst —, to perform divine service; eine Schlacht — [liefern], to give, to join battle. *c*) to fulfil, to perform, to observe, to keep. Sein Wort, sein Versprechen —, to keep one's word, one's promise; *prov.* Versprechen und — ist zweierlei, to promise and to perform are two things; sein Wort nicht —, to break one's word; die Gebote Gottes —, to keep God's commandments; die Gebote Gottes nicht —, to break the divine laws; die Fasten —, to keep Lent; Frieden —, to keep the peace; gute Ordnung —, to keep good order; *reinen Mund —, not to blab, not to divulge a thing; das Stillschweigen —, to preserve, to keep silence; †das Maul —, to hold one's tongue, to hold one's jaw; das rechte Zeitmaß [den Tact] —, to keep time; gute Wache —, to keep a strict watch; die rechte Bahn —, to follow, to keep the right way; Sie setzen 10 Pfund, ich halte sie, you lay ten pounds, I'll take them up; Eines Parthei — [auf Eines Seite seyn], to take any one's part, to side with any one; *es mit Jemanden —, to take any one's part, to be of the same opinion; — Sie es [machen Sie] wie Sie wollen, do as you please; ich pflege es so zu —, so damit zu —, such is my way or manner of doing or acting; so will ich es ge— haben, wissen, I will have it so; *er hält es mit seines Nachbars Frau, he has a [sexual] intercourse with the wife of his neighbour; *es mit dem Weine —, to stick to the wine; to prefer wine. *d*) [= unterhalten] to maintain, to keep. Pferde, einen Diener —, to keep horses, a servant; eine Kostschule —, to keep a boarding-school; Kostgänger —, to keep boarders, to board; eine Schule —, to keep a school; eine Zeitung —, to take in a newspaper, to be a subscriber to a newspaper; Freundschaft mit Jemand zu — suchen, to cultivate a person's acquaintance. *e*) to rate by judgment or opinion, to set a certain value on. Wie hoch — Sie diese Uhr? how much do you rate this watch at? how much do you ask or charge for this watch? what will you sell this watch for? Sie — sie zu hoch, zu theuer, you ask too much for it; Einen hoch —, to esteem any one highly, to make much of any one; von diesen Knaben halte ich den für den verständigsten, welcher &c., of these boys I take him to be the most intelligent, who &c.; ich halte es für wahr, weil &c., I believe it to be true, since &c.; ich — ihn für einen ehrlichen Mann, I look upon him as an honest man, I take him for an honest man; — Sie ihn für so dumm? do you think him so stupid? ich halte es für eine Ehre, I look upon it as an honour, I account it an honour; ich halte es für rathsam, zu kommen, I think it advisable to come; ich halte es für gewiß, I hold it, I take it for a certainty, I look upon it as certain; — Sie mir es zu Gnaden, [as a rather stiff expression of civility] do not take it amiss or ill; die Sadduzäer, welche —, es sey keine Auferstehung der Todten, [in Scripture] the Sadducees which say that there is no resurrection; ||er wird halt [vermuthlich] nicht kommen, probably he won't come, I don't think he will come; ||die Sache ist halt [nun einmal] so, well, now it is so. V. Halt II. *f*) Etwas auf Einen —, to esteem any one highly, to make much of any one; wenig oder nichts auf Einen —, to make little or no account of any one; er hält mehr auf sich als auf Andere, he thinks himself better than others, he is a conceited fellow. *g*) Etwas von einer Sache —, to set a certain value on a thing;

was — Sie davon? what do you think of it? 2) to check a person or thing in motion. Halt[et] den Dieb! stop thief! seinen Athem — [an sich —], to hold one's breath; Einem den Arm —, to hold any one's arm; Stiefel, welche Wasser —, boots that are water-proof; er ist so lebhaft, daß man ihn nicht — kann, he is so lively, that one cannot hold or check him; seine Thränen —, to restrain one's tears. *Fig. a*) Seinen Zorn, seine Freude —, to check or restrain one's anger, one's joy. *b*) [= stützen] to support, to hold up. Der Hals hält den Kopf, the neck supports the head. 3) [= hinhalten] *Einem ein Bein — [= stellen], to trip any one up, to trip up any one's heels; *it. fig.* to injure any one, to lay a snare for any one. 4) to move in a certain direction. Einem etwas vor das Gesicht —, to hold a thing to or before any one's face; die Arme in die Höhe —, to lift up, to raise one's arms; den Finger an die Nase —, to lay one's finger on one's nose; den Kopf gerade —, to hold or keep one's head upright, to hold up one's head; Einem eine Pistole auf die Brust —, to clap a pistol to any one's breast; ein Papier über das Feuer —, to hold a paper over the fire. 5) [= enthalten] to contain, to hold. Dieses Faß hält 2 Oxhoft, this cask holds or contains two hogsheads; die Flasche hält 2 Nößel or [starke] Schoppen, the bottle holds two pints; der Centner Erz hält so und so viel Silber, the hundredweight of ore contains so much silver. *Fig.* Der Centner hält 110 Pfund, a hundredweight has a hundred and ten pounds; ein Buch Papier hält 24 Bogen, a quire of paper has or contains 24 sheets.

II. *v. r.* sich — 1) Sich — an &c., to take or lay hold of. Wer am Ertrinken ist, sucht sich an Allem zu —, a man who is drowning, lays or catches hold of every thing, catches at every thing; *prov.* a drowning man will catch at a straw; er hielt sich an einem Aste, he caught hold of a branch. *Fig.* to stick to, to abide by, to depend upon. Ich ging zu Bette, ohne zu wissen, woran ich mich — sollte, I went to bed without knowing what to think of the matter; an wen soll ich mich —? whom am I to rely upon? *it.* whom am I to apply to? ich halte mich an sein Zeugniß, I abide by his testimony; ich werde mich deßwegen an Sie —, I shall come upon you for it; ich halte mich an seinen Rath, I stick to his advice; wir — uns an unsere Regel, we keep to our rule; — Sie sich rechts, links, keep to the right, to the left; — Sie sich zu mir, stick to me, join with me; ich halte mich zu denen, die dich fürchten, [in Scripture] I am a companion to all them that fear thee. 2) *Fig.* to carry or conduct one's self, to behave. Sich wohl —, to behave well, to do one's duty, to distinguish one's self; er hat sich in allen Treffen wohl ge—, he has behaved bravely in every action; sich ruhig —, to keep quiet; sich reinlich —, to be cleanly; *it.* to go always neat; sich in der See — [= gut], to be a good sea-boat, to be sea-worthy; to keep the sea, to hold out in the offing. *it.* *Sich — [= sich mit Erfolg vertheidigen], to maintain one's self, to resist, to hold out. Diese Festung kann sich keine 8 Tage mehr —, this fortress cannot hold out eight days longer; man kann sich gegen so überlegene Streitkräfte nicht —, one cannot stand against forces so much superior. *it.* *Sich —, [during an illness &c.] to keep a strict diet. 3) *Fig.* to continue in a good and uninjured state, to keep, to last. Aepfel, die sich —, apples that will keep; dieser Wein wird sich nicht —, this wine won't keep.

III. *v. intr.* 1) to cease to go forward, to stop. Der Kutscher mußte —, the coachman was obliged to stop; halt, Kutscher! hold or stop, coachman! die Kutsche hält vor dem Hause, the coach is at the door; wir hielten im Kaiser, we stopped or put up at the Emperor; die Truppen bekamen Befehl, zu —, the troops were ordered to halt; inne — im Studiren, mit der Arbeit, to leave off study, work; stille —, to stop, not to stir, not to resist, to submit quietly; Stand —, to stand, to resist, to be constant. 2) to be fast or firm, not to give way, to stick or adhere, to hold. Das Seil wird —, the rope will hold; dieser Nagel hält sehr fest, this nail holds very fast; das Pflaster wird nicht —, the plaster will not hold; das Eis hält [trägt], the ice bears. *Fig. a*) bei etwas — [= dabei bleiben]. Beim Winde —, [mit dem Winde segeln] to sail close to the wind, to keep the luff, to keep the wind. *b*) an etwas —, to adhere closely, to cling, to stick, to keep to a thing. Er hält an seiner Meinung, he cleaves to his opinion; er hält an diesem Glauben, he adheres to this creed; er hält an alten Gebräuchen, he keeps to old customs. *c*) auf or über etwas —, to observe a thing, to adhere to it, to insist upon, to lay a stress upon, to set a value upon. Auf Ordnung —, to maintain, to observe order; auf Wohlanständigkeit —, to preserve decency; auf die Beobachtung der Gesetze —, to watch over the observance of the laws; auf Ehre —, to stand upon the point of honour; er hält sehr auf seine Ehre, he is very jealous of his honour; auf Träume —, [= daran glauben] to believe in dreams. *d*) an sich —, to contain one's self, to refrain, to curb one's passion, to keep one's temper; *it.* to be reserved. Ich hatte Mühe, um mich zu —, I could hardly contain myself. *e*) to continue in the same uninjured state, to keep, to last. Das Wetter wird nicht —, the weather won't hold out, will change; dieses Tonwerkzeug hält den Ton nicht, this instrument does not keep in tune.

IV. *v. impers.* [in fam. lang.] Es wird hart, schwer — [= es wird Mühe kosten], it will be hard, difficult; woran hält es, daß wir nicht abreisen? what is the matter that we do not go away, what hinders or prevents our going away?

Halt-kette, *f.* V. Deichselkette, Hemmkette. —nagel, *m.* pole-bolt of a carriage. V. Schloßnagel, Schließ- or Schlußnagel. —seil, *n.* V. —tau. —statt, —stätte, *f.* 1) place of stopping, [chiefly among sportsmen] place of meeting. 2) [formerly] a place of ambush. —tau, *n.* vang of a mizen-gaff or yard. —vieh, *n.* cattle and chiefly sheep, that are wintered either for money or half the profit. —zeichen, *n.* a break, mark of suspension.

Hälter, *m.* [-s, *pl.* -] 1) a person that holds or keeps, holder, keeper, [chiefly used in composition, as Buch—, book-keeper, Gasthalter, innkeeper &c.] 2) an instrument for holding. 3) a place for holding or keeping.

Haltergeld, V. Halftergeld, Halftern.

Hälter, *m.* [-s, *pl.* -] a place in which any thing is held or kept. [in composition] Wasser—, a cistern; Fisch—, fish-box, fish-pond &c.

Hältig, *adj.* and *adv.* [in mining] containing ore [used chiefly in composition, as gold—, containing gold]; —es or hältiges Gestein, a gangue containing ore.

Haltung, *f.* 1) the act of holding. Die — der Feder, the holding of the pen. *Fig.* Die — des Landtages, eines Rathes, the session or sitting of the states, of a council; die — eines Tagebuches ist sehr nützlich, it is very useful to keep a journal or diary; die — einer Zeitung, the taking in of, or subscription to, a newspaper; die — eines Versprechens, the fulfilment, performance of a promise; [in painting] die — in einem Gemählde, the keeping of a picture; die — der Lichter und Schatten, the art of proportioning light and shade, clare-obscure. 2) manner of movement or walk, port, carriage, mien. Eine edle, majestätische —, a noble, majestic port or mien; die — eines gebildeten Mannes, the port of a gentleman; er hat keine — zu Pferde, he has no good seat on horse-back. *Fig.* Dieses Gemählde hat keine —, this picture is not in keeping. 3) that which holds or supports a thing, prop, stay, hold. Die Mauer hat keine —, the wall is not solid, has no support.

Halúnke, *m.* [-n, *pl.* -n] [perhaps allied to the Italian *allocco* = booby] raggamuffin, a scoundrel, rascal.

Hämachat or Hämachatstein, *m.* [-es] [in mineralogy] Egyptian pebble.

*Hamadryáde, *f.* [*pl.* -n] hamadryad. V. Baumnymphe.

Hamatít, *m.* [-en, *pl.* -e] hematite.

Hambrei, Hambuche, V. Hahnbrei, Hagebuche.

Hámburg, *n.* [-s] [one of the four free cities of Germany] Hamburgh, Hambro.

Hámburger, *m.* [-s, *pl.* -] Hámburgerinn, *f.* Hamburgher.

Hámburger, Hámburgisch, *adj.* of or from Hamburgh.

Hämbutte, V. Hagebutte.

Hämen, *m.* [-s, *pl.* -] [allied to the L. *hamus*, to the Sw. *haemta*, to catch] a small fishing-net fastened to a hoop and pole, hoop-net, purse-net; [among sportsmen] a tunnel-net.

Hämen or Hameln, *v. tr.* to catch in a hoop-net or tunnel-net, to tunnel.

Hämisch, *adj.* and *adv.* [perhaps allied to Hamen] insidiously malicious, spiteful or mischievous. Ein —er Mensch, a malicious man; ein —er Streich, a roguish, malicious trick; eine —e Freude, a malignant joy. Syn. Hämisch, Tückisch. Both endeavour to injure, or do evil to others in secret; but der Hämische does it that he may accomplish his purpose with the greater certainty, der Tückische, that he may escape the just punishment which awaits him if discovered. Der Tückische has generally more malice, but perhaps no wit; der Hämische is never without the latter.

Hämme, [in some provinces] I. *m.* [-n, *pl.* -n] [allied to *jambe*] 1) ham of an animal. 2) knee-joint of an animal. II. *f.* [*pl.* -n] [V. Hamme 1)] the lower and thick part of a sithe.

Hámmel, *m.* [-s, *pl.* - or Hämmel] [from the old hammen, hammeln, Sax. *hamelan* = to castrate] wether.

Hammel-braten, *m.* roast mutton. —brühe, *f.* mutton-broth. —brust, *f.* a breast of mutton. —bug, *m.* a shoulder of mutton. —fell, *n.* sheep-skin. —fett, *n.* fat or suet of sheep, mutton-suet. —fleisch, *n.* mutton. —geschlinge, *n.* sheep's pluck. —jährling, *m.* —lamm, *n.* a castrated lamb one year old. —keule, *f.* a leg of mutton. —knecht, *m.* a man that attends the sheep. —möhre, *f.* parsnip. —pelz, *m.* sheep-skin with the wool; *it.* a strip of sheep-skin with the wool. —rippchen, *pl.* mutton-chops. —schale, *f.* half a leg of mutton. —schlegel, *m.* V. —keule. —talg, *m.* V. —fett. —viertel, *n.* a quarter of mutton. —wurst, *f.* a sausage made of mutton.

Hämmeln, I. *v. tr.* to castrate male lambs or rams. V. Verschneiden. II. *v. intr.* or rather imp. [provincially], to have a too strong taste of mutton.

Hammer, *m.* [-s, *pl.* Hämmer] [Dan., Sw., Icel. and Eng. *hammer*, Sax. *hamer*; probably from the old hammeren, to mutilate, to beat] 1) hammer. *Dim.* Hämmerchen, ||Hämmerlein, *n.* [-s, *pl.*-] a little hammer. Der Kopf, Stiel des —s, the head, handle of the hammer; mit dem — schlagen, to beat with a hammer, to hammer; der — der Schmiede [Schmiedehammer], sledge-hammer; der — an einer Thüre, the knocker; V. ...ferk—, Niet—, Spitz—; †daß dich der —! the deuce! *Fig.* [in nat. hist.] hammer-oyster; [among sportsmen] der — [= die Hinterkeule] eines wilden Schweines, the hindleg, the haunch of a wild boar. 2) = Hammerwerk, a forge, iron-work. V. Blech—, Eisen—, Kupfer—.

Hammer=amboß, *m.* [among coppersmiths] anvil. —**arbeiter**, *m.* a man who works in a forge. —**auge**, *n.* V. —loch. —**axt**, *f.* a hammer with the hind end sharp and cutting; [in seamen's lang.] calking iron. —**bahn**, *f.* the flat side of a hammer. —**beil**, *n.* [in mining] hatchet; [in seamen's lang.] V. —axt. —**fisch**, *m.* the hammer-headed shark, balance-fish, zygaena or marteau. —**gerüste**, *n.* the timber-work or frame by which the forge hammer is moved. —**haue**, *f.* a hoe or mattock with a head. —**herr**, *m.* proprietor of a forge. —**hütte**, *f.* V. —werk. —**kopf**, *m.* head of a hammer. —**loch**, *n.* the eye or ear of a hammer. —**meister**, *m.* master, inspector of a forge. —**mühle**, *f.* V. —werk. —**müller**, *m.* V. —schmied. —**ordnung**, *f.* the regulation, law or statute for forges —**pfinne**, —**pinne**, *f.* the flat side of a hammer. —**pickel**, *m.* pick-axe with a head. —**rad**, *n.* wheel that lifts and keeps the forge-hammer in motion. —**schlacke**, *f.* the scales or chips, which fly from the iron when hammering. —**schlag**, *m.* 1) a stroke with a hammer. 2) V. —schlacke. —**schmied**, *m.* a smith working in a forge or foundery. —**schmiedeschlacke**, *f.* V. —schlacke. —**schmiedestahl**, *m.* V. Kuppelstahl. —**stiel**, *m.* the handle or helve of a hammer. —**strauch**, *m.* poison-berry. —**werk**, *n.* forge; foundery. —**zeichen**, *n.* a mark made by foresters on trees with a hammer.

Hämmerbar, *adj.* and *adv.*, malleable, Dehnbar.

Hämmerbarkeit, *f.* malleability.

Hämmerling, *m.* [-s, *pl.* -e] 1) [formerly] Merry Andrew, Jackpudding. ‡2) the ...rer, V. Abdecker; *it.* the executioner, jack-...ch. 3) V. Poltergeist. 4) [in nat. hist.] V. Emmerling or Goldammer.

Hämmern, *v. intr.* to move, to knock ...a hammer.

Hämmern, *v. tr.* to beat or work with the ...mer, to hammer. Auf dem Amboße —, ...beat the anvil; das Gold dünn —, to spread ... gold under the hammer; diese Metalle ...en sich —, these metals are malleable; kalt ... to harden, V. Härten.

Hammit, *m.* [-es] [in mineralogy] ammite ...ammite.

Hämmling, *m.* [-es, *pl.* -e] [allied to Ham...] a castrated creature, a eunuch.

Hämorrhoidal, *adj.* hemorrhoidal.

Hämorrhoidalkolik, *f.* hemorrhoidal ...c.

Hämorrhoiden, *pl.* hemorrhoids, the ...s.

Hamster, *m.* [-s, *pl.* -] hamster, German ...mot.

Hamster=fänger, —**gräber**, *m.* catcher of hamsters. —**fell**, *n.* a hamster's skin. —**höhle**, —**röhre**, *f.* the hole, kennel or haunt of a hamster.

Hanbutte, *f.* V. Hagebutte.

Hand, *f.* [*pl.* Hände] [*dim.* Händchen, ||Händlein, *n.* -s, *pl.*-] [Dan., Sw. and E. *hand*, allied to the L. *hendo* in *prehendo*] 1) primarily, any thing that seizes or grasps: [in falconry] die Hände der Falken, the hands [= feet] of the hawks; but chiefly, the hand in man: die rechte, die linke —, the right, the left hand; die flache — or innere —fläche, the palm; die verkehrte — or äußere or obere —fläche, the back of the hand; — über —, [in seamen's lang., the order to pull a rope quickly] hand over hand! eine — voll, a handful, er hat in beiden Händen gleiche Gewandtheit, he uses both hands with equal facility, he is ambidexter; Einem die — reichen, bieten, to stretch out, to offer one's hand to any one; Einem die — drücken, to squeeze any one's hand; sich die Hände geben, to shake hands; die Hände zusammenlegen, falten, to fold or clasp the hands; die Hände zum Himmel aufheben, gen Himmel strecken, to lift up one's hands towards heaven; die — gegen Einen aufheben, to lift up one's hand against any one; die — an den Degen legen, to lay one's hand on one's sword; *ehe man eine — umwendet, in the turning of a hand, in a trice; *die — her, die Sache ist abgemacht, the business is done, shake hands or there is my hand for it; Einem beim Schreiben die — führen, to guide or hold any one's hand when writing; Einem die Hände auflegen [ihn zu segnen], to lay hands on any one; etwas aus freier — thun [ohne Hülfe eines Werkzeuges], to do a thing by hand, with the hand merely [without the instrumentality of tools, engines &c.]; aus der — essen, to eat a short hasty meal [a hand-in-pocket eating]; — in — spazieren gehen, to walk hand in hand; von — zu —, von einer — in die andere, from hand to hand; aus einer — in die andere geben, to hand about; etwas aus den Händen legen, to lay a thing aside; in die Hände klatschen, to clap one's hands; sich mit seiner Hände Arbeit ernähren, to live by one's manual labour, by one's handiwork; mit den Händen fechten [beim Sprechen heftige Bewegungen mit den Händen machen], to gesticulate; wie ein Rasender mit Händen und Füßen um sich schlagen, to struggle like a madman with hands and feet; sich eine Person zur linken —, an die linke — antrauen lassen, to marry with the left hand; eine leichte — haben [mit Leichtigkeit etwas thun], to have an easy, light hand, to be skilled to use the hands with ease, to be handy; dieser Mahler bekömmt eine schwere —, the hand of this painter begins to grow heavy; eine gute — zum Fechten haben, to be a good hand at fencing; *prov.* eine — wäscht die andere, at court one hand will wash the other; we must help each other; one good turn deserves another; *it.* seine Hände in Unschuld waschen, to wash one's hands of a thing; *fig.* *man kann dies mit Händen greifen, that is palpable; etwas unter der — [= im Stillen] thun, to do a thing under hand, secretly, privately. 2) *Fig.* [chiefly in fam. lang.] *a*) hand, with regard to activity. Mit beiden Händen zugreifen, to seize with both hands, eagerly; freie Hände haben, to have free hands, to be free to do what one pleases, to be one's own master; gebundene Hände haben, to have one's hands bound or tied, not to be one's own master; mit vollen Händen [= reichlich] geben, to give or bestow largely, liberally, plentifully; Einem die —, hilfreiche — bieten or leisten, to lend any one a helping hand, to offer any one assistance, to aid. to assist any one; Einen auf den Händen tragen, to treat a person with great regard and honour, to make much of any one; *it.* to treat any one with tenderness, to fondle, to caress any one; die Hände brauchen, to set to work, to work diligently; — anlegen, to put the hand to work, to take in hand; ich habe ein großes Werk unter den Händen [bin damit beschäftigt], I have a great work in hand; die letzte — an ein Werk legen, to put the last hand, the finishing stroke to a work; von der — gehen, to proceed without hinderance, with facility, with ease; die Arbeit geht ihm gut von der —, he works with great facility, very dexterously; die — von Einem abziehen, to leave any one to the wide world, to forsake any one, to abandon any one to his fate; die — in etwas haben, die —, die Hände im Spiele haben, to have a hand in a thing, to have a finger in the pie; die Hände in den Schoos legen, [rather vulgar] die Hände in den Sack, in die Tasche stecken, to do nothing, to be idle, to idle; alle Hände voll zu thun haben, to have one's hands full, to be full of business; seine milde — aufthun, to be charitable; Einem die Hände versilbern, †schmieren, to grease a person's hands, to bribe a person; er hat reine Hände, his hands are clean [= he is innocent or blameless]; *prov.* treue — geht durchs ganze Land, honesty is the best policy; man muß ihm auf die Hände sehen [daß er nichts entwendet], one must have an eye upon his hands, he must be watched, lest he steal any thing; bei ihm geht alles aus der — in den Mund, he lives from hand to mouth. *b*) hand = business. Sich auf seine eigene — setzen, to set up for one's self, to begin business for one's self; [rather vulgar] auf seiner eigenen — sitzen or liegen, to have set up for one's self. *c*) hand with regard to a promise. Einem Mädchen die — geben, to lead a girl to the altar, to marry her; ihre — ist schon vergeben, versagt, her hand is already disposed of, she is already betrothed. *d*) hand with regard to possession, power or authority. Einem etwas zu —en stellen [= übergeben], to deliver any thing into any one's hand's; zu —en kommen, to arrive, to reach, to come to hands; Einem unter —en, unter die Hände geben [= anvertrauen], to commit to any one's hands, to instrust to any one; Einem etwas auf [an] die Hand geben, to give any one earnest, to pay any one money in hand; Einen an der — [zu seinen Diensten] haben, to have any one at one's disposal; etwas in den Händen [in seiner Gewalt] haben, to have a thing in one's hands or power; ich habe die Papiere in Händen, the papers are in my hands; Alles geht or läuft durch seine Hände [= muß ihm vorgelegt werden], every thing passes through his hands, must be submitted to his approbation; sein Haus aus der —, aus freier — verkaufen, to sell one's honse of one's own free will, voluntarily; die todte —, mortmain; die allgewaltige, allvermögende — Gottes, the almighty or omnipotent hand of God; sich in Jemands Händen befinden, to be in any one's hands or power; in die Hände seiner Feinde fallen, to fall into the hands of one's enemies; Andern in die Hände sehen müssen, [in Scripture] to live on others' charity or liberality. *e*) one that possesses or exerts power. Etwas aus der ersten — kaufen, to buy a thing at the first hand; ich habe dies von sehr guter —, I have it from very good hands, from good authority; er ist in gute Hände gefallen, he has fallen into good hands; das kömmt von hoher —, von hohen Händen, that comes from a person of high rank; [in the feudal system] die obere —, the paramount lord; die untere —, the vassal. *f*) hand with regard to violence. — an Einen legen, to lay hands upon, to beat any one; — an sich legen, to lay [violent] hands upon one's self, to make away with one's self. g) hand with regard to assistance given or to be given. Zur — or an die — gehen, to lend a hand, to assist; Einem mit Gelde, mit seinem Rathe an die — gehen, to assist any one with money, to give any one good advice or counsel; Einem etwas an die — geben, to furnish, to provide any one with a thing, to suggest any thing to a person. h) hand with regard to power of performance or skill. Alles, was er sagt, hat Hände und Füße, all he says is to the purpose, apropos; dieser Brief hat Hände und Füße, this letter is very well written, is very good, is pertinent. i) hand with regard to vicinity. Bei der — seyn, to be near at hand; it. to be quick or alert; etwas bei der — haben, to have a thing in readiness, at hand. it. with regard to time: vor der —, at present, just now; nach der —, afterwards, after that. k) hand-side, part. Linker — gehen, den Weg linker — einschlagen, to take to the right; Einem die rechte — geben or lassen, to give any one the right or upper hand; Einem rechter — gehen, to walk on the right hand of any one; vor der — seyn [at cards], to be eldest hand, V. Vorhand; hinter der — seyn, to be youngest hand, V. Hinterhand; es ist mir nicht zur — [= liegt nicht bequem für mich], it is not handy or convenient to me. l) hand = manner of writing. Eine schöne — schreiben, to write a fine hand; es ist Ihre —, it is your hand, handwriting or in your handwriting; geben Sie mir ein paar Worte unter or von Ihrer —, give me a note under your hand.

Hand-amboß, *m.* little anvil, hand-anvil. —anlegung, *f.* act of putting the hand to work, of setting to work; [in law] seizure, attachment —arbeit, *f.* manual labour, work of the hands, handiwork; *it.* V. —frohne. —arbeiter, *m.* handicraftsman, mechanic. —ärmel, *m.* V. —krause. —arzneikunst, *f.* surgery. —ausdruck, *m.* V. —bewegung. —ausgabe, *f.* a small, portable edition. —ballen, *m.* the ball or muscle under the thumb. —band, *n.* [in anat.] ligament of the hand. —barte, *f.* V. —beil. —baum, *m.* [in mechanics] a lever; [a sea-term] bar of the capstern. —becken, *n.* wash-hand-basin. —beil, *n.* small hatchet. —bewegung, *f.* movement or expression of the hands, gesticulation. —bewegungen machen, to gesticulate. —bibel, *f.* a portable bible, handbible. —bibliothek, *f.* a small select library. —bietung, *f. fig.* aid, succour, assistance, help. —blatt, *n.* wrist-band; *it.* ruffle. —bock, *m.* V. —ramme. —bogen, *m.* a small sort of bow for shooting, handbow. —bohne, *f.* V. Feldbohne. —bohrer, *m.* a small borer, gimlet. —breit, *adj.* and *adv.* of the breadth of a hand. —breite, *f.* a hand's breadth, handbreadth; [in botany, a lineal measure of three inches] palm. —bret, *n.* a little board with a handle, used by masons to hold the mortar upon. —brief, *m.* V. —schreiben. —briefchen, *n.* a small letter, note, billet. —buch, *n.* manual, hand-book. Ein —buch der Erdbeschreibung, a manual of geography. —büchelchen, —büchlein, *n.* a small manual, vademecum. —bücherei, [unusual] *f.* V. —bibliothek. —büchse, *f.* handgun; V. Lothbüchse. —bügel, *m.* the handle [of a firelock]. —compaß, *m.* a small compass; miner's compass. —decke, *f.* a small cover; small horsecloth. —dienst, *m.* V. —frohne. —dienster, *m.* V. —fröhner. —druck [Händedruck], *m.* shake of the hand. —eimer, *m.* pail, bucket. —eisen, *n.* handcuff, handfetter, manacle. Einem —eisen anlegen, to handcuff any one. —fackel, *f.* V. Windlicht. —fahrt, *f.* descent into a mine by means of a ladder. —faß, *n.* a vessel in which water for washing the hands is kept, a wash-hand-basin; *it.* a small, portable cask or tub. —fäustel, *m.* miner's hammer. —feile, *f.* a small file, hand-file. —fessel, *f.* V. —eisen. —fest, *adj.* and *adv.* 1) [in fam. lang.] firm in the hand, having a firm hand, stout, robust, strong. 2) [rather obsolete] being in a state of imprisonment. Einen —fest machen, to arrest or confine any one, to clap any one up in prison. 3) [sometimes] secure, sure. Einen Kauf —fest machen, to give earnest upon a bargain. —feste, *f.* [Daumenfeste] a written document, bond. —feuerspritze, *f.* a small fire-engine. —fläche, *f.* the palm of the hand. —flechse, *f.* fibre of the hand. —förmig, *adj.* and *adv.* having the shape of the hand; [in botany] palmated. —förmige Blätter, palmated leaves. —friede, *m.* [in law] security for keeping the peace. —frohne, *f.* compelled service or drudging-work performed by the hands. —fröhner, *m.* V. Frohnarbeiter; *it.* V. —arbeiter. —fußhobel, *m.* [among joiners] plough. †—gaul, *m.* V. —pferd. —gebrauch, *m.* common, convenient use. Eine Ausgabe zum —gebrauche, a portable edition. —gehörn, *n.* V. —geweih. —geld, *n.* 1) earnest-money, earnest, V. Haftgeld, Angeld; *it.* [in military affairs] enlisting-money, bounty, press-money. 2) the first money taken by a tradesman, handsel. Einem das —geld zu lösen geben, to give any one handsel. —gelenk, *n.* wrist. —gelöbniß, *n.* a promise strenghtened by the joining of hands, solemn promise. V. —pflicht, —treue. —gelte, *f.* V. Schöpfgelte. —gelübde, *n.* V. —gelöbniß. —gemein, *adj.* and *adv.* engaged in contention with the hands, fighting with the hands, coming or having come to blows, engaged in close fight. —gemeinwerden, I. *v. intr.* [u. w. seyn] to come to blows, to engage in close fight. II. *n.* close-fighting. —gemenge, *n* a fray, scuffle; *it.* obstinate fight sword in hand. Ein heftiges, blutiges —gemenge, a severe, bloody conflict; sich in das —gemenge werfen, to throw one's self into the thickest of the battle. —geschmeide, *n.* 1) ornaments for the hands or wrists, worn by ladies, bracelets. 2) *Fig.* [often in jest] V. —eisen. —gewehr, *n.* handgun, firelock; *it.* collectively, firelocks. —geweih, *n.* palmed head. —gicht, *f.* gout in the hands, chiragra. —gichtig, *adj.* and *adv.* gouty in the hands. —gift, *f.* V. —geld 1). —granate, *f.* a handgrenade. —greiflich, *adj.* and *adv. fig.* palpable, obvious, evident, manifest. —greiflich machen, to show evidently, to make evident. —griff, *m.* 1) gripe or seizure of the hand, grasp. Einen —griff thun, to lay one's hand upon, to lay hold of; [in milit. affairs] die —griffe mit dem Gewehre, the handling or wielding of arms; er hat die —griffe noch nicht recht inne or *weg, he does not well know yet how to handle the arms; —griffe ohne Commando, the manual exercise; die chemischen —griffe, manipulation. *Fig.* dexterous use of the hand, knack, dexterity. 2) handle, ear of a vessel. Der —griff eines Degens, the hilt of a sword; der —griff eines Eimers, the handle of a pail. [† or in contempt] —gucker, *m.* —guckerei, *f.* V. —wahrsager &c. —habe, *f.* V. —griff 2), Griff 4), Henkel. —haben, *v. tr.* to move with the hand, to handle. *Fig.* Die Gesetze —haben, to maintain the laws; die Gerechtigkeit —haben, to administer justice; Einen bei seinen Rechten —haben [= schützen], to support or maintain the rights of any one, to support or maintain a person in his privileges. —habung, *f.* act of handling. Die —habung der Waffen, the handling or wielding of arms; *fig.* die —habung der Gesetze, the maintaining of the laws; die —habung der Gerechtigkeit, the administration of justice. —haken, *m.* [in seamen's language] a hand-grapnel. —haspel, *m.* V. —winde. —hebe, *f.* V. —habe, —griff 2). —hoch, *adj.* and *adv.* as high as the hand is broad. —hilfe, *f.* [in manege] stay or rest upon the hand, appui. —karren, *m.* a small cart; a hand-barrow. —käse, *m* small cheese made with the hand. —kauf, *m.* 1) sale or purchase by the hand, by guess. 2) retail. 3) V. —geld 2). —klappe, *f.* V. —blatt. —klapper, *f.* castanet. —knopf, *m.* V. Hemdeknopf. —kompaß, *m.* V. —compaß. —korb, *m.* 1) hand-basket. 2) basket-hilt [of a sword &c.]. —körbchen, *n.* a small hand-basket. —krause, *f.* ruffle. —kübel, *m.* hand-pail, hand-tub. —kunst, *f.* the mechanic art. —künstig, —künstlich, *adj.* and *adv.* [*mechanisch] mechanic. —künstler, *m.* [*Mechaniker] mechanician. —kuß, *m.* the act of kissing a person's hand. Zum —kusse zugelassen werden, to be admitted to kiss the sovereign's hand. —lang, *adj.* and *adv.* as long as the hand. —langen, *v. intr.* to lend a hand, to help a man at work, to act the helper to a carpenter, bricklayer or mason and such. —langer, *m.* a helper to a workman, chiefly to a carpenter, bricklayer or mason, [of masons] hodman. —laterne, *f.* hand-lantern. —leder, *n.* hand-leather [used by shoe-makers and other mechanics]. —lehen, *n.* 1) free, hereditary fief. 2) capital fief. —leiter, *m.* —leiterin, *f.* a person that leads another by the hand, a guide; *fig.* adviser. —leitung, *f.* the leading, guiding or guidance by the hand, manuduction; *fig.* guidance, instruction. —leuchte, *f.* V. Laterne. —leuchter, *m.* a flat candlestick, hand-candlestick. —linie, *f.* line of the hand. —lohn, *m.* 1) [= Arbeitslohn, Taglohn] wages earned by manual labour. 2) [in some provinces or districts] money paid by the feoffee to the feoffer, on the granting or renewal of a lease or fief. —los, *adj.* and *adv.* without a hand, handless. —mahl, *n.* 1) a mark in the hand. 2) [formerly] promise made by the hand; *it.* engagement of marriage. —mange, *f.* V. —rolle. —mäuschen, *n.* muscle under the thumb. —messer, *n.* a convenient, handy knife; *it.* a currier's knife. —mörser, *m.* a small or hand-mortar for throwing grenades; V. —granate, Mörser. —muff, *m.* a hand-muff. —mühle, *f.* a hand-mill. —muskel, *m.* muscle of the hand. —pferd, *n.* the off-horse of a carriage, led-horse. —pflicht, *f.* obligation imposed by a promise made with joining hands. —preise, *f.* wrist-band. —presse, *f.* small press. —protzwagen, *m.* small truck-carriage. —pumpe, *f.* [in mining] a pump with a swipe. —quehle, *f.* V. —tuch. —räder, *m.* [in mining] a sieve with two handles for washing the ore. —ramme, *f.* a beetle, a rammer. —register, *n.* [in mining] the private register of the overseer. —reichung, *f. fig.* help, assistance, benevolence, charity. Den Armen —reichung thun, to relieve the poor, to give charity to the poor. —rohr, *n.* V. —büchse. —rolle, *f.* a small roller to smooth linen with. —roß, *n.* V. —pferd. —rücken, *m.* the back of the hand. —ruthe, *f.* the handle of a flail, of a whip. —säge, *f.* hand-saw. —saum, *m.* the hem of the sleeve. ||—scharwerk, *n.* V. —frohne. ||—schelle, *f.* V. —eisen. —schlag, *m.* 1) a blow or stroke with the hand. 2) the offering of the hand as a pledge of an obligation or promise. —schlag thun, den —schlag geben, to give or pledge one's word or faith, to promise solemnly by the joining of hands. —schlägel, *m.* a little mallet. ‖ and † —schmisse, *pl.* [a game] hot-cockles. ‖ or † —schmiß, *m.* a stroke in the palm of the hand. —schraube, *f.* hand-screw [an instrument of torture]; *it.* any small screw. —schraubenstock, *m.* hand-vice. —schreiben, *n.* a letter from a sovereign, not written but signed by him. Ein eigenhändiges —schreiben erhalten, to receive an autographical letter. —schrift, *f.* 1) [cast or form of writing peculiar to each hand or person] handwriting, hand. Er schreibt eine schöne —schrift [almost only to be used in familiar language], he writes a fine hand. 2) any thing written with the hand or pen, a manuscript. Es gibt in dieser Bibliothek sehr viele —schriften, there are in that library a great number of manuscripts; die —schrift ist zum Drucke fertig, the manuscript is ready for press. 3) a written obligation, bond, note under one's hand, note of hand. Ich habe ihm 100 Thaler auf seine —schrift geliehen, I have lent him a hundred dollars on his bill or note (of hand); er kann es mir nicht abläugnen, ich habe darüber eine —schrift von ihm, he cannot deny it, I have it under his hand. —schriftlich, *adj.* and *adv.* 1) written by the hand [not printed], in writing. —schriftlich besitzen, to have in manuscript. V. Schriftlich. 2) written with a person's own hand. Ein —schriftlicher Gläubiger, a creditor in virtue of a note of hand; sich —schriftlich verbinden, to bind one's self by one's own handwriting. —schuh, *m.* glove. Den —schuh hinwerfen [zu etwas herausfordern], to throw down the glove, to challenge, to defy. —schuhmacher, *m.* —schuhmacherinn, *f.* glover. —schwärmer, *m.* a small rocket thrown with the hand. —seife, *f.* soap for washing the hands, wash-ball. —sieb, *n.* a hand-sieve. —siegel, *n.* seal manual, signet. —spaten, *m.* a small spade [especially for transplanting onions]. —speiche, *f.* handspike. —spiel, *n.* 1) V. Händespiel. 2) [in an organ or harpsichord] the keys. —spieß, *m.* a little spit, on which meat is roasted, turned by the hand. —sprache, *f.* V. Fingersprache. —spritze, *f.* hand-syringe, squirt. —stein, *m.* [in mining] a little piece or chip of ore [for showing as a sample]; [in mineralogy, a stone having the shape of a hand] a palmated stone. —stock, *m.* hand-vice. —streich, *m.* V. —schlag. [in popular lang.] —streich halten, to pledge one's faith in marriage, to promise marriage. —stufe, *f.* [in mining] V. —stein. —tag, *m.* [in feudal law] day of compelled service. —taste, *f.* a stop or key. —teller, *m.* V. —fläche. —treue, *f.* promise of faith strengthened by the joining of hands. —treue abgen, —treue geben, to pledge one's faith by the joining of hands. —trommel, *f.* a tabor, taboret, timbrel. —tuch, *n.* towel. —vogel, *m.* [in falconry] a falcon that is trained to sit on the hand. —voll, *f.* a handful. *Fig.* *Eine —voll [= sehr wenige] Menschen, a handful of men. —vollweise, *adv.* by handfuls. —wagen, *m.* a double wheel-barrow. —wahrsager, *m.* [*Chiromantist] chiromancer. —wahrsagerei, *f.* [*Chiromantie] chiromancy. —wasser, *n.* water for washing the hands, Waschwasser. —weife, *f.* hand-reel. —weiser, *m.* guide; *it.* V. Wegweiser. —werk, *n.* —werker, *m.* V. Handwerk &c. [as article of its own]. —winde, *f.* a small windlass, worked by the hand. —wörterbuch, *n.* portable dictionary, pocket dictionary. —wurzel, *f.* wrist. —zeichen, *n.* the flourish or mark added to a signature; *it.* monogram. —zeichnung, *f.* a drawing or design done with a pen, pencil or crayon. —zirkel, *m.* a pair of compasses. —zuber, *m.* V. —kübel. —zug, *m.* V. Federzug. —zünder, *m.* a short linstock.

Hände-druck, *m.* —drücken, *n.* V. Handdruck. —klatschen, —klopfen, *n.* clapping of hands. Die Sängerinn wurde mit allgemeinem —klatschen empfangen, a universal clapping of hands received the fair singer at her appearance. —spiel, *n.* 1) [a game] hot-cockles. 2) movement or expression of the hands, gesticulation. —sprache, *f.* V. Fingersprache. —waschen, *n.* the washing of the hands. —werk, *n.* work of the hands, handiwork.

Händel, *m.* [-s, *pl.* Händel] [from Hand; originally any operation in which the hand is active]. 1) properly, a fray or quarrel, in which they fight with the hands; then also in a more enlarged sense, any quarrel, dispute or difference. Mit Einem Händel anfangen, Einem Händel machen, to pick up a quarrel with any one; Händel mit Einem haben, to have a quarrel, to be in a contest with any one; sich Händel über den Hals ziehen, to draw a quarrel upon one's self. *Fig.* *a)* Ein — [= ein Prozeß], a law-suit, an action; einen — (Rechts—) haben, to have a law-suit, to be at law; einen — mit Jemand anfangen, to bring or enter an action against any one, to sue any one at law. *b)* in general, any transaction, business, affair. Ein schlimmer, böser —, a bad, a sad affair; ein angelegter —, a concerted matter; ein verworrener —, an intricate business; Einen aus dem — ziehen, to bring or get any one out of trouble, out of the scrape; das ist ein anderer — [eine andere Sache], that's another thing. 2) [rather unusual in the plural] bargain, purchase. Einen — treffen, schließen, machen, to strike, to conclude, to make a bargain; mit Jemand über etwas im — stehen, to bargain, to negotiate with any one for something; den — aufsagen, aufkündigen, to break the bargain; Einem in den — fallen, ihm den — verderben, to outbid any one; sie sind —s eins geworden, they have concluded the bargain, *fig.* they have come to an agreement. *Fig.* Einem den —, den ganzen — aufsagen, to break off all commerce, connection or correspondence with any one. 3) collectively [without a plural], trade, traffick, commerce. Der innere —, inland commerce, domestic, home or inland trade; äußerer, auswärtiger —, foreign commerce or trade; der — im Großen, trade by wholesale, wholesale; der — im Kleinen, trade by retail, retail; der — mit Spezereien, mit Seide, the spice, silk trade; der — Frankreichs, the French commerce or trade; — treiben, to trade, to traffick, to carry on commerce or trade; er treibt — mit allen Arten von Waaren, he trafficks or deals in all sorts of goods; er treibt einen — mit Wolle, he deals in wool; großen — treiben, to drive a large trade; er treibt starken — nach Spanien, he carries on a great trade with Spain; der — liegt darnieder, stockt, commerce or trade languishes, is dull; der — nimmt zu und ab, trade increases and decays; den — aufgeben, verlassen, to leave off business or trade; verbotenen —, Schleich— treiben, to run, to smuggle prohibited goods, to be a smuggler; zum — gehörig, commercial. *Fig.* Sie treibt mit ihren Reizen —, she brings her charms, her beauty to market. Syn Handel, Gewerbe, Verkehr, Handlung. Gewerbe is any business which a person carries on for procuring subsistence or for profit. Der Handel is the business of exchanging commodities by barter, or the purchase and sale of goods, wares and merchandise. Verkehr is the reciprocal traffick or commerce itself. Common use also distinguishes between Handel and Handlung. The former is used to denote the business of buying and selling itself; the latter, the permanent establishment under the management of one or more persons for the purpose of carrying on that business.

Händel-kraut, *n.* V. Händleinkraut. —macher, *m.* —macherinn, *f.* a quarrelsome person; quarreler, brawler.

Handeln, [Sax. *handliah*, Eng. *handle*, Sw. *handla*, from hand, properly, to touch with the hand] I. *v. tr.* [obsolete] = behandeln, to handle, to treat. Und die Aegypter handelten uns übel [in Script.], and the Egyptians vexed us; nach ihrem Mund sollen alle Sachen gehandelt werden [in Script.], by their mouth shall every controversy and every stroke be tried; diese Sache ist nicht geschickt gehandelt worden, this affair has not been skilfully managed. II. *v. intr.* 1) to behave, to act. Gut, schlecht —, to behave or act well, ill; als ein rechtschaffener Mann —, to act or behave like an honest man; Sie haben gegen Ihr Gewissen gehandelt, you have acted against your conscience; das heißt schlecht gehandelt, that is behaving ill; gut, schlecht gegen Jemand —, to use any one well, ill, to deal, to do well, ill by any one; er hat freundschaftlich gehandelt, he has acted like a friend, has acted the part of a friend; wider Jemandes Befehl —, to act contrary to any one's order. *Fig.* [in grammar] —d, active. Ein —des Zeitwort, an active or transitive verb. 2) Von etwas —, to handle in writing or speaking, to treat of. Dieses Buch handelt von der Unsterblichkeit der Seele, this book treats of, discourses upon the immortality of the soul; dieser Brief handelt nur von gleichgültigen Dingen, this letter contains only indifferent things. 3) to negotiate, to transact business, to bargain. Wegen des Friedens —, to treat of or about the peace; um eine Uhr —, to cheapen a watch; er hat sehr genau, or *Kreuzer um Kreuzer gehandelt, he stood haggling for a penny; etwas kaufen ohne zu —, to buy a thing without bargaining or haggling; er läßt nicht —, läßt nicht mit sich —, he never asks for his goods more than he takes, he makes but one word; er läßt nicht gut mit sich —, he is hard to deal with; mit sich — lassen, to be easy, tractable, complying. 4) to deal, to trade, to traffick. Er handelt nach Indien, Spanien &c., he trades to the Indies, to Spain &c; mit Seide, Wolle —, to deal in silk, wool; im Großen und Kleinen —, to deal wholesale and retail; er handelt mit ganz Europa, he carries on trade with all Europe. III. *v. impers.* and *refl.* Es handelt sich von, the question is, the point in question is; wovon handelt es sich? what is the matter? davon handelt es sich nicht, that is not the business in hand.

Handels-angelegenheit, *f.* commercial affair or concern. —aufseher, *m.* V. Consul b). —bediente, *m.* V. —diener. —bedrückung, *f.* V. —druck. —bilanz, *f.* balance of trade. —brauch, *m.* way, custom in trade; *it.* [among bankers] usance. —brief, *m.* 1) a mercantile letter. 2) V. Kaufbrief. —buch, *n.* the book of accounts, the journal. Das große —buch, the ledger, [in courts of justice] record. —bündniß, *n.* a commercial treaty. —collegium, *n.* board of trade. —colonie, *f.* commercial colony. —diener, *m.* a merchant's clerk, a shopman. —druck, *m.* oppression, shackles of trade, a clog to trade. —entwurf, *m.* speculation. —entwürfe machen, to speculate. —fach, *n.* mercantile line. —flotte, *f.* fleet of merchantmen. —frau, *f.* tradeswoman, trading-woman, merchant's wife. —freiheit, *f.* 1) liberty of trade or commerce, free trade. 2) commercial privilege, licence for trading. —gebrauch, *m.* V. —brauch. —gehülfe, *m.* V. —diener, *it.* —genoß. —geist, *m.* commercial, mercantile spirit; *it.* the ton of merchants or tradesmen. —geiz, *m.* mercantile avarice. —genoß, *m.* [*Associé] partner in trade. —genossenschaft, *f.* V. —gesellschaft. —gericht, *n.* tribunal of commerce; *it.* board of trade. —geschäft, *n.* a commercial transaction or business. —geschäfte treiben, to trade, to traffick. —gesellschaft, *f.* trading-company, commercial society, company of merchants; *it.* partnership in trade. Die ostindische —gesellschaft, the East-India Company. —gesellschafter, *m.* V. —genoß. —gesetz, *n.* commercial law. —gesetzgebung, *f.* commercial legislation. —gewicht, *n.* avoir-dupois. —gewölbe, *n.* shop, [in America] store; *it.* a merchant's vault. —haus, *n.* mercantile house. —herr, *m.* 1) a [great] merchant. 2) the chief head of a mercantile house. —jude, *m.* a trading Jew. —kammer, *f.* board of trade. —klemme, *f.* commercial distress. —lehrling, *m.* V. Handlungslehrling. —leute, *pl.* merchants; tradesmen. —mann, *m.* merchant; tradesman; shopkeeper. —nation, *f.* V. —volk. —noth, *f.* V. —klemme. —ort, —platz, *m.* commercial, mercantile, trading place, place of trade; emporium. —rath, *m.* 1) council of commerce or trade. 2) a counsellor of commerce or trade. —recht, *n.* 1) privilege of trade, licence of trading. 2) commercial law. —reise, *f.* journey on commercial affairs. —sache, *f.* commercial affair, matter or point of trade; *it.* a lawsuit in point of commerce. —schiff, *n.* a merchant-man, a trading-vessel. —schule, *f.* mercantile school. —sicherheit, *f.* 1) capacity of being trusted, credit. 2) safety of commerce. —sorge, *f.* commercial care. —spekulation, *f.* a mercantile speculation. —sperre, *f.* prohibition of trade —staat, *m.* commercial state. —stadt, *f.* commercial, trading-town. —stand, *m.* 1) the merchants' company, the trading class, the merchants. 2) the mercantile line. —theilnehmer, *m.* V. —genoß. —unternehmung, *f.* a commercial enterprise. —verbindung, *f.* commercial association or league. —verderber, *m.* one that undersells his goods, a spoil-business, spoil-trade. —verein, *m.* commercial union; V. also —verbindung. —verfall, *m.* decay of trade. —verhältniß, *n.* commercial relation. —verkehr, *m.* commercial intercourse. —vertrag, *m.* [*Commerztraktat] a commercial treaty. —verwalter, *m.* [*Faktor] a merchant's agent, factor. —volk, *n.* commercial or trading people or nation. —weise, *f.* manner or way of acting or behaving. —wesen, *n.* any thing relating to commerce or trade. —zeichen, *n.* mark put upon goods. —zweig, *m.* branch of commerce.

Händelschaft, *f.* 1) trade, traffick, commerce. — treiben, to drive a trade, to carry on trade, to trade, to traffick. 2) the science and business of a merchant. 3) all the merchants of a place.

Händlein, *n. dim.* of Hand, which see.

Händlein-ehrenpreiß, *m.* —kraut, *n.* digitated speedwell or Veronica. —wurzel, *f.* V. Knabenkraut.

Händler, *m.* [-s, *pl.* -] **Händlerinn**, *f.* dealer, trader, trades-man, trades-woman, shop-keeper. V. Eisen—, Korn—, Obst—, Wein— &c.

Händlich, *adj.* and *adv.* 1) easily managed with the hand, easy to be handled. Dieser Hammer ist nicht —, this hammer is unwieldy, not handy or manageable; es ist mir nicht — [zur Hand], it does not lie to my hand. *it.* middling, moderate. Ein —er Stein, a stone of middling size. 2) tractable, supple, manageable. 3) [stiff] — or händlich, done with the hand. Etwas — übergeben, to deliver something with one's own hands.

Händling, *m.* [-s, *pl.* -e] [in nat. hist.] the coralloidal clavaria.

Händlung, *f.* 1) action. Eine gute oder schlechte —, a good or bad action; seine —en abmessen, to order one's actions; eine — des Glaubens, der Demuth, an act of faith, of humility; in einem dramatischen Stücke muß Einheit der — seyn, in dramatic pieces there must be unity of action; in diesem Schauspiele ist viele —, there is a great deal of incident in this play. *it.* rarely used for Aufzug, act. 2) trade, traffick, commerce. —, die — treiben, to drive a trade, to trade; die — im Großen, im Kleinen, wholesale, retail; eine — errichten, to set up in trade. 3) the profession and business of a merchant. 4) the house or shop of a merchant. Eine — errichten, anlegen, to set up a shop. Syn. V. Handel.

Handlungs-angelegenheit, *f.* V. Handelsangelegenheit. —art, *f.* V. Handelsweise. —ausdruck, *m.* a mercantile term. —bediente, *m.* V. Handelsdiener. —buch, *n.* —gesellschaft, —gesetz &c. V. Handelsbuch &c. —lehrling, *m.* apprentice to a merchant or shopkeeper. —vortheil, *m.* a secret or advantage of commerce. —wort, *n.* V. —ausdruck. —zweig, *m.* V. Handelszweig.

Händsam, *adj.* and *adv.* V. Handlich. [in seamen's lang.] Ein —er Wind, a moderate wind, favorable for sailing.

Handthieren, V. Hantiren.

Händwerk, *n.* [-es, *pl.* -e] 1) trade. Das — eines Schmieds, Zimmermanns, Schneiders, the trade of a smith, carpenter, tailor; Leute vom —e, die das — verstehen, people of the same trade, who are masters of the trade; Einem ins — greifen, to encroach upon any one's trade or profession; Einem das — legen, to forbid any one to exercise his trade or profession, *fig.* *to hinder any one from undertaking any thing. *Fig.* Der Krieg ist sein —, war is his trade; eine Sache als ein — treiben, to do a thing customarily, usually, mechanically; [in fam. lang.] ein Sachwalter, der sein — gut versteht, an attorney who is a master of his profession. das — eines Diebs, Räubers [das Diebs—, Räuber—] &c., the profession of a pickpocket, of a thief, robber &c. 2) all the persons belonging to one trade, company of tradesmen, corporate trade. Das — fordern, zusammen berufen, to call together, to assemble all the persons belonging to the same trade; das — ansprechen, grüßen, [said of a journeyman when on his travels], to apply to the masters of one's trade for relief; das — machen, to call a meeting of the masters of a trade [for settling a dispute &c.]; — or das — halten, to meet [said of a tradesmen's company]. 3) payment of a certain sum into the box of a corporate trade. Das — entrichten, to pay one's contribution to the box.

Handwerks-abgeordnete, *m.* a deputy from a corporate trade. —älteste, *m.* senior of a corporate trade. —artikel, *m.* law and statute of a trade. —brauch, *m.* custom, way or manner of tradesmen, custom of a tradesmen's company. —bursche, *m.* journeyman [especially when on his travels]. —frau, *f.* a tradesman's or handicrafts-man's wife. —gebrauch, *m.* V. —brauch. —gelehrter, *m.* one who makes a trade of science. —genoß, *m.* fellow-tradesman. —geräth, *n.* V. —zeug. —gesell, *m.* a journeyman; *it.* V. —bursche. —gruß, *m.* the salute of journeymen [when on their travels]. —herr, *m.* a magistrate who attends the meetings of any trade. —junge, *m.* apprentice. —kunde, *f.* [*Technologie] technology. —lade, *f.* a box containing the laws, records and accounts of any corporate trade; *fig.* meeting of the seniors of a corporate trade. —leute, *pl.* handicrafts-men, tradespeople, mechanics. —mann, *m.* handicrafts-man, mechanic, tradesman. —mäßig, *adj.* and *adv.* consonant to the rules of a trade. *Fig.* professional, mechanical. [often in contempt] Er treibt die Schriftstellerei ganz —mäßig, he makes nothing but a trade of his authorship. —meister, *m.* master of a trade, freeman. —neid, *m.* envy or grudge of another following the same trade, V. Brodneid. —siegel, *n.* seal of a corporate trade. —trieb, *m.* mechanical instinct. —verwandte, *m.* one of the same trade. —volk, *n.* [in contempt] trades people. —zeug, *n.* a set of tools, implements. Diese Schreinerwerkstatt ist sehr gut mit —zeug versehen, this joiner's shop is very well stocked with implements. —zunft, *f.* a tradesmen's guild or company, V. Innung, Zunft.

Händwerker, *m.* [-s, *pl.* -] handicraftsman, mechanic, tradesman.

Handwerkercompagnie, *f.* tradesmen's company.

Hänf, *m.* [-s] [the plant and name appear to be of Asiatic origin; Pers. *cannab*, L. *cannabis*, Fr. *chanvre*, Dutch and Dan. *hamp*, Eng. *hemp*] hemp. Der weibliche —, fimble hemp, V. 2 Fimmel; roher —, raw hemp; — brechen, to break or dress hemp; — ausraufen, rösten, to pull up, to steep, soak or water hemp; den — schwingen, to swingle the hemp; — hecheln, to hatchel or hackle hemp; Leinwand von —, hemp-cloth.

Hanf-acker, *m.* hemp-field, hemp-close. —bau, *m.* culture of hemp. —bereiter, *m.* —bereiterinn, *f.* hemp-dresser. —breche, *f.* brake for hemp. —brecher, *m.* hemp-beater, hemp-dresser. —darre, *f.* 1) the act of drying the hemp, dew-retting. 2) the place where it is dried. —erz, *n.* a kind of asbestus, V. Straußsteinflachs. —feld, *n.* V. —acker. —fink, *m.* V. Hänfling. —garn, *n.* hempen yarn. —hahn, *m.* the male hemp. —händler, *m.* —händlerinn, *f.* dealer in hemp. —hechel, *f.* hemp-comb, hatchel. —heede, *f.* hemp-tow. —henne, *f.* female hemp, fimble-hemp. —kamm, *m.* [among rope-makers] great hatchel. —korn, *n.* a grain of hemp, hemp-seed. —kraut, *n.* mill-mountain, purging-flax, linaria. —leinwand, *f.* hemp-cloth. —männchen, *n.* [in botany] common broom-rape, Orobanche major. —meise, *f.* coal-titmouse, V. [illegible]meise, Schwarzmeise. —mühle, *f.* mill for bruising hemp-seed. —nessel, *f.* a [illegible] nettle resembling hemp. —öl, *n.* hemp-[illegible] oil. —pflanze, *f.* V. Hanf. —reibe, *f.* a machine for rubbing the hemp, [illegible] machine, rubber. —röste, *f.* place where hemp is steeped or watered. —same, *m.* hemp-seed. —schwinge, *f.* swingle, [illegible] staff, swingling-knife. —schläger, —schwinger, *m.* hemp-beater. —stengel, *m.* [illegible] of hemp, hemp-stalk. —würger, *m.* V. —männchen.

Hänfen, *adj.* and *adv.* made of hemp, hempen. Ein —es Seil, a hempen rope; —

Leinwand, hemp-cloth.

Hänfling, *m.* [-es, *pl.* -e] linnet. Einen — abrichten, Liedchen lehren, to whistle to a linnet.

Häng, *m.* [-es] state of bending or leaning downwards, slope. Der — eines Hügels, declivity of a hill, V. Abhang. *Fig.* inclination, propensity, proneness, bent, bias. Der natürliche — zum Bösen, the natural propensity or bent to evil; er hat wenig — zum Studiren, he has little inclination to study; er hat einen starken — zum Spiele, he is too much inclined to gaming. Syn. Hang, Neigung, Trieb. Neigung signifies a leaning of the mind or will, arising from conviction or choice. Hang implies a stronger bent, and is often the effect of an insuperable natural propensity. Trieb is a natural impulse or innate propensity, and belongs also to the lower animals.

Hänge, *f.* [*pl.* -n] a loft [for a servant's bed]; *it.* [in gardening] a shelving-bed; *it.* V. Abhang. [in seamen's language] Die —n, the googings or goodings.

Hängelbank, *f.* V. Hangebank.

Hängelbirke, *f.* [*pl.* -n] weeping birch.

Hängelbirn, *f.* [*pl.* -en] a kind of pear with a long stalk. *Fig.* [vulgar, in joke] —en essen, to be hanged.

Hängeln, *v. intr.* [a sea-term] to sail from port to port, to coast.

Hängen or **Hangen**, [Eng. *to hang*, Sax. *hangan*, Icel. *hanga*, from *ha* = hoh or hoch, high; the transitive was for a long time *hahen*] *ir. v. intr.* 1) to be suspended, to hang. Der Hut hängt or hangt an einem Nagel, the hat hangs on a nail; er muß hängen [i. e. gehängt werden], he must be hanged; voll — von etwas, to be covered with, to be full of a thing. 2) [with voll] = behängt seyn mit &c. Der Baum hängt voll Aepfel, the tree is covered with, is full of apples; *fig.* *der Himmel hängt ihm voll Geigen, he is full of joy, is overjoyed, enraptured. 3) to be declivous or inclined, to slope, to hang. Sein Mantel hangt ihm bis auf den Fuß, his cloak reaches or hangs down to his feet; Ihr Kleid hängt zu viel auf eine Seite, your gown hangs too low on one side; eine —de Fläche, an inclined or sloping plane; die Mauer hangt, the wall leans or inclines; den Kopf — lassen [neigen, sinken lassen], to hang down, to hang, to bend down or incline the head; *fig.* *den Kopf, die Flügel — lassen [= muthlos werden], to become disheartened or discouraged, to despond, to droop. 4) [= fest hängen] to be fixed to a thing in a hanging posture, to adhere, cleave or cling to. Ihr Kleid blieb an den Dornen —, her gown was caught by the thorns; er blieb an einem Nagel —, he was hooked by a nail; sie hing an seinem Halse, she hung on or clung to his neck; an einander —, to hang together, to be connected, to be united. *Fig.* Eine an einander hängende Geschichte, a coherent history; er hängt ihr immer am Halse, he is always dangling about her; meine Kinder — an ihm, my children are attached to him, love him; darum wird ein Mann Vater und Mutter verlassen, und an seinem Weibe —, [in Scripture] for this cause shall a man leave father and mother and shall cleave to his wife; sein Herz hängt daran, his heart is set upon it; er hing an Allem, was sie sprach [rather high flown], he hung on all she spoke; ich weiß, woran die Sache hangt or hängt, I know where it sticks; die Sache hat lange ge—, the affair remained, was long undecided; die Sache hängt blos an ihm, the matter depends only on him; *prov.* er weiß, wo es hangt und langt, he knows the whole affair or intrigue; woran hängt [liegt] es, daß wir nicht abreisen? what is the matter that we do not go away? what hinders or prevents our going away? die Sache hängt vor Gericht [ist vor Gericht anhängig], the matter is pending, is in litispendence.

Hange-backen, *pl.* hanging cheeks. —bank, *f.* a bench fastened to a wall with hinges, so that it may be let down, hanging-bench; *it.* [in mining, place above the shaft or pit where the pails are emptied] waboard. —bauch, *m.* a belly or paunch hanging down. Er hat einen —bauch, his belly swags. —bett, *n.* V. —matte. —birke, *f.* V. Hängelbirke. —blatt, *n.* [in botany] cyanella. —brücke, *f.* V. Hängebrücke. —bohne, *f.* springe, noose or gin for catching birds, hung on bushes or trees. —eisen, *n.* any iron in which a body is hung; [among carpenters] binding joist. —haken [einer Wage], *m.* hook of suspension. —kappe, *f.* small ring of a miner's pail. —kette, *f.* V. Hängekette. —kluft, *f.* [in mining] a sloping vein or lode, V. Tagekluft. —kompaß, *m.* a kind of compass which is always hung, mariner's compass. —kutsche, *f.* a coach or carriage hung in straps. —lampe, *f.* a lamp hanging [from the ceiling]. —leuchter, *m.* a lustre, chandelier. —matte, *f.* hammock —mörser, *m.* a mortar suspended by its trunnions. —nagel, *m.* a nail that unites or holds two parts together. —pfahl, *m.* a post on which a garden-gate hangs. —riemen, *m.* a leather-strap in which any thing is suspended; chiefly, the strap in which a carriage is hung. —ring, *m.* V. —haken. —tisch, *m.* hanging-table. —wage, *f.* [in hydraulics &c.] level. —warze, *f.* a pendulous wart, acrochordon. —werk, *n.* timber-work of a roof, bridge &c., which is so joined as to hold without any pillar &c. —werksbrücke, *f.* V. —brücke.

Hängen, I. *v. tr.* 1) to hang down. Die Flügel, den Kopf —, to hang, to hang down the wings, the head; Lilien — ihre Häupter, lilies hang their heads; †das Maul —, [= mürrisch seyn] to be in the sulks, to be sulky, to sulk; [in mining] — [absolutely = das Holz in die Grube lassen], to descend the wood into the shaft or pit. *Fig.* *Den Mantel nach dem Winde —, to comply with the time or occasion, to temporize, to be a time-server. 2) to attach to something above, to suspend, to hang. Seinen Hut an einen Nagel —, to hang one's hat upon a nail; einen Mantel um sich —, to put on a cloak; etwas in die Sonne —, to hang up something in the sun, to expose something to the sun; einen Dieb, Uebelthäter —, to hang a thief, a malefactor. *Fig.* *Etwas an den Nagel —, to give over, to leave off, to lay aside, to neglect a thing; *sein Herz an etwas —, to set one's heart upon a thing; *Geld an Einen oder etwas —, to spend or squander money on a person or thing. V. Brodkorb. II. *v. r.* sich —, to hang one's self. Sich — an etwas or an Jemand, to adhere, cling or stick to a thing or person; die Reben und Hopfen — sich an die Stangen und Bäume, the vines and hops cleave to the poles and trees; der Kuchen hängt sich in der Pfanne an, the cake adheres to the pan. *Fig.* †Er hat sich an dieses Mädchen gehängt, he has attached himself to this girl; V. Anhängen, Aufhängen, Henken.

Hänge-boden, *m.* 1) a little room between two floors. 2) a printer's peel. 3) a room or loft for drying paper —brücke, *f.* suspension bridge. —bügel, *m.* a stirrup that is hung to the pommel. —bohne, *f.* V. Hangebohne. —garn, *n.* draw-net, V. Ziehgarn. —kette, *f.* drag-chain, V. Hemmkette. —muskel, *m.* [in anatomy] raiser, lifter up. —säule, *f.* a small pillar at the end of a beam, in which joists are made. —schloß, *n.* padlock. —seil, *n.* [among sportsmen] cord or line by which greyhounds are held, leash. —seilkunst, *f.* art of making chain-pumps.

Hänger, *m.* [-s, *pl.* -] 1) V. An—, Kopf—. 2) [in seamen's language] pendant. Der — am großen Maste, main-tackle pendant; der — am Fockmaste, fore-tackle pendant.

Hängfisch, *m.* [-es, *pl.* -e] stockfish.

Hanke, *f.* [*pl.* -n] [Fr. *hanche*, Eng. *haunch*, allied to Anke, the L. *ancus*, therefore something bent or curved] the hip, joint or hindquarter of a horse, haunch. Ein Pferd, das gut auf den —n sitzt, a horse that is well on his haunches.

Hankenknochen, *m.* the haunch bone.

Hanne, *f.* [*pl.* -n] [with common people, instead of Johanna] Jane.

Hannchen, *n.* [-s, *pl.* -] [*dim.* of Hanne] Jenny, Jennet.

Hannover, *n.* [-s] [town and kingdom in Germany] Hanover.

Hannoveraner, [-s, *pl.* -] *m.* **Hannoveranerinn**, *f.* Hanoverian.

Hannoverisch, [more usual] **Hannövrisch**, *adj.* and *adv.* Hanoverian.

Hans, *m.* [-ens, *pl.* -en, -e] [a nickname or contraction for Johann, John] Jack; [*dim.* Hänschen, ||Hänsel, ||Hänslein, *n.* little Jack, Jacky]. *Prov.* Was Hänschen nicht lernt, lernt — nimmermehr, an old dog will learn no tricks; *Hänschen im Keller, [an embryo or fetus] hans-en-kelder; *— ohne Sorgen, a careless, mindless fellow; *— or — Dampf in allen Gassen, a rambler, rover, busy-body, Paul Pry; *— hinter der Mauer, a coward, poltron, bully; [ironically] *die großen —en, men of importance; V. Fabel—, Prahl—, Schmal—.

Hans-graf, *m.* V. Hansgraf [from Hanse]. —narr, *m.* arrant fool, dunce, blockhead. —wurst, *m.* Jackpudding, Merry Andrew, buffoon, harlequin. Er ist wie ein —wurst gekleidet, he is dressed like a harlequin. —wurstmäßig, *adj.* and *adv.* like a buffoon or harlequin, buffoonish, buffoon-like. —wurststreich, *m.* harlequin's trick or joke, buffoonery.

Hanse, *f.* [Goth. *Hansa*, is probably allied to eins and not to be derived from An-See, near the sea] society, association, league; chiefly, the Hanseatic union. [At present, the three free towns of Luebeck, Hamburgh and Bremen are the only memorials of that confederacy and denominated Hanseatic towns].

Hansestadt, *f.* hanseatic town, Hanse-town.

Hanseat, *m.* [-en, *pl.* -en] **Hanseatinn**, *f.* a native or inhabitant of one of the Hanse towns, a Hanseate.

Hanseatisch, *adj.* and *adv.* hanseatic. Der —e Bund, the hanseatic confederacy.

Hänseln, *v. tr.* to receive into any society and to perform certain ceremonies at such a reception; to treat a new person with some ridiculous custom or ceremony; [on board of ship] to duck any one, who, for the first time, passes the equator. *Fig.* to irritate by jests and raillery, to tease, to rally any one, to make a fool of any one. Das —, [on board of ships] ducking.

Hänsel-becher, *m.* a large goblet or cup, a tumbler. —geld, *n.* [-es] novice's fees, fees of entrance, handsel. —männchen, *n.*

V. Gaukelmännchen.

Hänsgraf, *m.* [-en, *pl.* -en] [from Hanse, union] [formerly] the judge who adjusts or decides the differences arising about commerce, Hansegrave.

Hantieren and **Hanthieren**, [Icel. *handthiera*, Sw. *handtera*, allied to the Fr. *hanter*, Eng. *to haunt*] *v. tr.* and *intr.* [a little vulgar] 1) to handle, to manage, to wield. Der Stein ist zu groß, er läßt sich nicht gut —, the stone is too big for being easily managed. 2) to work with the hand, to labour, to work, to pursue an employment, to be employed, to do business. 3) to make a noise, to bustle. Das —, V. Hantierung.

Hantierer, *m.* [-s, *pl.*-] a tradesman.

Hantierung, *f.* employment, business; *it.* trade, commerce. Eine — treiben, to exercise a trade, to follow a profession; *it.* to drive a trade, to carry on a business.

Häpe, V. Hippe.

Häperig, *adj.* and *adv.* [seldom used, except in popular language] uneven, rugged. Hier geht es sich —, this way is very rugged. *Fig.* interrupted, embarrassed. †Er predigt —, he stops every moment in his sermon.

Hapern, [probably from haben, haften] *v. intr. impers.* [rather vulgar] to be interrupted or impeded by uneven or rugged ways. *Fig.* to stop, to be at a stand. Es hapert, es hapert mit der Sache, the affair is full of difficulties, does not proceed, is at a stand; woran hapert es, daß wir nicht angreifen? what is the matter that we do not attack? what hinders or prevents us from attacking; da hapert es, there it sticks, there is the knot, difficulty or point.

Häpp, **Häppen**, V. Schnapp, Schnappen.

Häppenbret, *n.* [-es, *pl.* -er] [in mining] V. Glauchherd.

Här! *interj.* V. Hott.

Härchen, **Härlein**, *n.* [-s, *pl.*-] little hair, V. Haar.

Härem, *m.* [-s *pl.* -e] [place where Eastern princes &c. confine their women] Haram.

Hären, **Hären**, V. Haaren.

Hären, *adj.* made of hair. Ein —es Sieb, a hair-sieve; ein —es Hemd, a hair-cloth, hair-shirt; ein —er Ring, a ring made of hair.

Härfe, *f.* [*pl.* -en] (Sax. *hearpe*, *earpe*, Icel. *haurpa*, Dan. *harpe*, Eng. *harp*, allied to the Gr. ἁρπάζω, the Germ. raffen, greifen] 1) the harp. Auf der — spielen, die — spielen or schlagen, to play upon the harp. In compositions, V. Spitz—, Tritt—. 2) [in conchology] Die edle —, purple-fish, purpleshell. V. also Davids—.

Harfen-klang, *m.* sound of the harp. —mädchen, *f.* an itinerant harper-girl. —muschel, *f.* harp-shell. —saite, *f.* harp-string. —schläger, *m.* —schlägerinn, *f.* —spieler, *m.* —spielerinn, *f.* harper. —schlüssel, *m.* harp-key. —spiel, *n.* play or performance on the harp. —stück, *n.* a piece of music or a tune played on the harp. —ton, *m.* V. —klang.

Härfen, *v. intr.* to play on the harp, to harp.

Härfener, **Härfer**, **Härfner**, *m.* [-s, *pl.*-]

Harfenist, *m.* [-en, *pl.* -en] harper, harpist.

Harfenett, *n.* [-s, *pl.* -e] [formerly] a little harp.

Häring, *m.* [-s, *pl.* -e] [from Heer, army, multitude, because herrings, when they migrate, move in vast shoals] herring. Frischer, grüner —, fresh herring; gesalzener, eingesalzener —, salt herring; geräucherter —, red herring, V. 2. Bückling; eingepökelter —, pickled herring; der volle —, Voll—, the hard-roed herring; der hohle —, spawned herring; —e einpacken, to barrel herrings; der fliegende —, the flying mullet.

Härings-bauch, *m.* the belly of a herring; *it.* the entrails of a herring. *Fig.* [in joke or vulgar] a thin, empty belly; *it.* a herring-gutted fellow. †—blick, *m.* the glimmering light which herrings shed when they migrate in great shoals. —brühe, *f.* 1) V. —lake. 2) [in cookery] herring-sauce. —bude, *f.* shop where herrings are sold, herring-shop. —büse, *f.* [a small vessel, used in the herring fishery] buss, herring-buss. —fang, *m.* 1) herring-fishery. 2) V. —zeit. —fänger, *m.* herring-fisher. —faß, *n.*, *dim.* —fäßchen, ||—fässel, *n.* a barrel or cask of herrings, a cag of herrings. —fischer, *m.* V. —fänger. —fischerei, *f.* V. —fang. —höke, *m.* a man that sells herrings, herring-man. —hökinn, or —frau, *f.* herring-woman. —jäger, *m.* [a sea-term] herring-smack. —könig, *m.* [a fish] red mullet. —kopf, *m.* the head of a herring. *Fig.* [in popular lang.] *Am —kopfe saugen, to live poorly or miserably. —krämer, *m.* —krämerinn, *f.* V. —höke, —frau. —lake, *f.* pickle for herring, herring-pickle. —markt, *m.* herring-market. —mewe or —meve, *f.* a kind of mew that lives on herrings. —milch, *f.* the milt or soft roe of herrings. —netz, *n.* herring-net. —öl, *n.* V. —thran. —packer, *m.* he that guts and barrels herrings, herring-packer. —pastete, *f.* herring-pie. —salat, *m.* salad of herrings, salmagundi. —salzer, *m.* one that salts the herrings, herring-salter. —schiff, *n.* V. —büse. —seele, *f.* [in vulgar language] a base, grovelling fellow. —thran, *m.* herring-oil. —tonne, *f.* V. —faß. —weib, *n.* V. —frau. —zeichen, *n.* mark on the barrels or cags of herrings. —zeit, *f.* herring-season, herring-time.

Härke, *f.* [*pl.* -n] [allied to the Eng. *rake* and *harrow*] rake.

Härken, *v. tr.* and *intr.* to rake, V. Rechen.

***Härlekin**, *m.* [-es, *pl.* -e] harlequin, Merry Andrew, Jackpudding, buffoon. V. Hanswurst.

Harlekins-jacke, *f.* harlequin's-coat. —posse, *f.* harlequin's trick or joke, buffoonery. —specht, *m.* [a bird] little speckled woodpecker. —tanz, *m.* pantaloon's dance, a kind of merry dance.

Härling, *m.* [-es, *pl.* -e] [a genus of plants] hypoxis.

Härm, *m.* [-s] [Dan., Sw. and Eng. *harm*; seems to be allied to Gram] grief, sorrow, affliction. V. Gram, Kummer. Syn. Harm, Gram, Kummer, Herzeleid. Kummer is the uneasiness or pain of mind produced by the loss of or disappointment in the expectation of any good, real or supposed, sorrow. Gram is the pain occasioned by the deeply felt loss of any highly valued good, and denotes a more violent emotion than Kummer. Harm, although originally the same word as Gram, implies a higher degree of grief. Herzeleid is the pain of mind arising from the feeling of having suffered wrong, or from the mortification of receiving evil not only undeservedly, but at the hands of those from whom we least expected it.

Harm-los, *adj.* and *adv.* 1) free from grief or sorrow, sorrowless. Ein —loses Leben führen, to lead an easy, peaceable life, a life free from sorrow. 2) inoffensive, innocent, harmless. Sie ist ein —loses Geschöpf, she is a harmless, inoffensive creature. —voll, *adj.* and *adv.* of grief or sorrow, sorrowful.

***Harmáttan**, **Harmátten**, **Harmá** *m.* [a dry easterly wind in Africa, which d vegetation] Harmattan.

Härmel, *f.* [*pl.* -n] or —kraut, *n.* raute, *f.* [in botany] harmel, wild [African]

Härmelin, *m.* V. Hermelin.

Härmen, *v. r.* sich —, to grieve [at or f to be sorrowful or afflicted. V. Grämen.

***Harmonie**, *f.* [*pl.* -n] harmony, concor [in architect.] symmetry; V. Wohlklang, Wo laut, Zusammenklang; *it. fig.* V. 2. Eintracht; [in anatomy] synarthrosis, harmony or union by straight margins.

Harmoniemesser, *m.* harmonometer.

***Harmónik**, *f.* the doctrine or science of musical sounds, harmonics.

***Harmónika**, *f.* [a musical instrument consisting of glass bells] musical glasses, harmonica.

***Harmoniren**, *v. intr.* to harmonize; to be in unison, to agree; *it.* to live in concord; *it.* to sympathize.

***Harmónisch**, *adj.* and *adv.* harmonical, harmonious. V. Wohlklingend, Uebereins or Zusammenstimmend, Einträchtig. [in anatomy] —e Knochennath, synarthrosis, harmony by straight margins; [in mathematics] —es Verhältniß, harmonical proportion.

***Harmonist**, *m.* [-en, *pl.* en] harmonist.

Härn, *m.* [-es, *pl.* -e] [seems to be one word with Urin] urine. Den — halten, to retain one's urine; den — lassen, to make water, to urine.

Harn-artig, *adj.* and *adv.* urinous. —arzt, *m.* one who pretends to state the nature of a disease by inspecting the urine, uromancer. —beschauung, *f.* inspection of urine, uroscopy; *it.* V. —beurtheilung, —wahrsagerei. —beurtheilung, *f.* the judgment formed of diseases from the inspection of the urine, urocrisia, uromancy. —blase, *f.* urinary bladder. —blasenmuskel, *m.* abductor of the urinary bladder. —brennen, *n.* a burning or scalding in the urine. —deuter, *m.* V. —arzt. —deuterei, *f.* V. —wahrsagerei. —fluß, *m.* incontinence of urine; [in medicine] diabetes. Mit dem —flusse behaftet, diabetical. —gang, *m.* urinary duct, ureter. —gangentzündung, *f.* inflammation of the ureter, ureteritis. —gefäß, *n.* urinary vessel. —geist, *m.* [in chymistry] urinous spirit. —glas, *n.* [a bottle in which urine is kept for inspection] urinal. —gucker, *m.* [in contempt] V. —arzt. —guckerei, *f.* [in contempt] V. —wahrsagerei. —haut, *f.* 1) a film which sometimes gathers on the surface of urine, pellicle of urine. 2) allantois or allantoid, V. Wursthaut. —kolben, *m.* [in chymistry, an oblong glass vessel used in making solutions] urinal. —kraut, *n.* 1) rupture-wort, herniaria. 2) toadflax, flaxweed, linaria. 3) reseda or bastard rocket. 4) V. Ackerhauhechel. —lehre, *f.* uronology. —lehrig, *adj.* uronological. —leiter, *m.* [in anatomy] V. —gang; [in surgery] V. —zapfer. —prüfung, *f.* V. —beschauung, —beurtheilung. —röhre, *f.* urethra. —röhrendrüse, *f.* gland of the urethra. —röhrenentzündung, *f.* inflammation in the urethra, urethritis. —röhrenschnitt, *m.* urethrotomy. —röhrenwulst, *m.* bulb of the urethra. —ruhr, *f.* V. —fluß. —salz, *n.* salt obtained from urine. —sand, *m.* gravel. —satz, *m.* the thick substance which generally subsides at the bottom of the urine, [in medicine] hypostasis. —säure, *f.* the uric or lithic acid, uric. —schauer, *m.* V.

—muskel. —schneller, *m.* accelerating muscle. —schnur, *f.* V. —strang. —stein, *m.* stone in the bladder, urinary calculus. —stoff, *m.* urea. —strang, *m.* [in anatomy] urachus, V. Blasenschnur. —strenge, *f.* dysury, strangury. —treibend, *adj.* and *adv.* diuretic, ischuretic, urinative. Ein —treibendes Mittel, a diuretic, ischuretic. —verhaltung, *f.* retention of urine. —verstopfung, *f.* stoppage or suppression of urine, ischury. —wahrsager, *m.* one who foretells the fortunes of persons by the inspection of their urine, caster of waters, uromancer, †piss-prophet. —wahrsagerei, *f.* uroscopy, uromancy, casting of waters. —weg, *m.* V. —gang. —winde, *f.* strangury. —zapfer, *m.* [*Catheter] [in surgery] catheter. —zwang, *m.* V. —strenge.

Harnen, *v. tr.* and *intr.* to discharge urine, to make water, to urine, to piss. Blut —, to piss blood.

Harnhaft, V. Harnartig.

Harnisch, *m.* [-es, *pl.*-e] [Fr. *harnais*, Dan. *harnesk*, Eng. *harness*, W. *harnaes*, from *harn*, that is, closely fitted, or perhaps allied to the Fr. *garnir*, the G. wahren and the Medio-Lat. *garniso* = armour.] 1) harness, armour. Den — anlegen, to put on the harness or armour. **Fig.* Einen in — jagen [= zornig machen], to put any one in a passion, to provoke any one; in — gerathen [= zornig werden], to fall into a passion, *it.* to talk of a thing with great warmth and emotion. 2) [in mining] the separating of the ore from the rock or stone. Der Gang führt einen glatten —, the ore breaks or separates easily from the rock. SYN. Harnisch, Panzer, Küraß. Harnisch signifies the whole iron, or other metal covering for the body; Panzer only that for the breast, belly and back; Küraß merely the breast-plate.

Harnisch-binde, *f.* [in surgery] V. Brustbinde. —feger, *m.* harness-cleanser. —fisch, *m.* [a fish] cuirassier, V. Panzerfisch. —haus, *n.* arsenal. —kammer, *f.* armory. —macher, *m.* armourer, harness-maker. —stein, *m.* [in mineralogy, a stone covered with a metallic crust, shining like steel] hoplitis.

***Harpax**, *m.* [-es, *pl.* -e] [chiefly in jest or contempt] an avaricious, miserly churl.

***Harpeggiren**, [pron. Harpeddschihren] *v. intr.* [in music] to arpeggiate. Das — [*das Harpeggio] the arpeggiamento, arpeggio.

***Harpune**, *f.* [*pl.*-n] harpoon, harping-iron. Die — werfen, to throw the harpoon.

***Harpuniren**, *v. tr.* to harpoon [a whale].

***Harpunirer**, *m.* [-s, *pl.*-] harpooner.

***Harpye**, *f.* [*pl.* -n] [in antiquity, a fabulous winged monster, having the face of a woman and the body of a vulture, with its feet and fingers armed with sharp claws] harpy. Die drei —n, the three harpies. *Fig.* a harpy, shrew, scold.

Harraß, *m.* [-sses, *pl.* -sse] [a stuff from the town of Arras] arras.

Harre, *f.* [in familiar language] extension of time, long run. In die — [or Länge], in length of time, at the long run; ein Geschäft, das in die — kommt, a business that lingers or goes heavily on.

Harren, *v. intr.* [seems to be allied to the Gr. *ἐκχέω*, and to hart, warten and währen] to wait, to stay, to tarry, to abide. [in Scripture] Harret auf Gott, hope in God; sieben Tage sollst du —, bis ich zu dir komme, seven days shalt thou tarry till I come to thee. SYN. Harren, Warten. Warten signifies simply to wait the arrival of some person or event. Harren joins to these above the idea of dissatisfaction; it is a disagreeable waiting for some wished-for good.

Harsch, *adj.* and *adv.* [allied to hart] harsh, rough. —e Haut, a rough or harsh skin.

Harschen, *v. intr.* [used with seyn] [little used] to grow rough, harsh or hard; *it.* to freeze.

Hart, I. *adj.* and *adv.* [Sax. *heard*, Eng. *hard*, Icel. *hardur*; is allied to warten and währen, and denoted formerly also strong, firm, great] [denoting a firmer or more compact union of the component parts and is opposed to soft] hard. —es Holz, ein —er Stein, hard wood, a hard stone; es gefriert —, it freezes hard; ein —es Bett or Lager, a hard bed; dieses Brot ist zu — gebacken, this bread is baked too hard; —e [= —gesottene] Eier, hard-boiled eggs; —es Fleisch, hard, tough meat; —es Getreide, V. Hartkorn; —es Geld [in familiar language = größeres], large money, species, specie; [in mining] —e [= frische] Schlacken, hard, rough or fresh slags; —es Blei, V. Hartblei; — machen, to make hard, to harden; — or härter werden, to become hard or harder, to harden. *it.* harsh, rough, rugged. —e Rinde, —e Haut, harsh, rough rind, skin; —es Wasser, —er Wein, hard water, hard, harsh or rough wine; —es Haar, stiff or coarse hair. *Fig.* *a*) resisting exterior impressions and apt to produce this state. Sich — halten, to inure one's self to hard or coarse fare, to all manner of fatigues &c., to deny one's self the gratification of desires; ein Kind — erziehen, not to effeminate a child, to educate or bring up a child austerely or harshly; ein —es Leben haben, to have a tough life, V. also *fig. d.* ein —es Leben führen. *b*) resisting certain moral impressions. Eine —e Stirne haben [= unverschämt seyn], to have a brazen face, to be brazen-faced, impudent; einen —en Sinn, Kopf, Nacken haben [= eigensinnig seyn], to be stubborn, obstinate; ein —es Herz, a hard, unfeeling, insensible heart; ein —er Mann, Vater, Richter, a hard, severe, rigorous, austere, hard-hearted man, father, judge; — gegen Einen seyn, to treat any one harshly, severely, roughly, rigorously. *c*) grounded in a certain insensibility of mind. Ein —es Wesen, harsh, rude manners; —e Worte, —e Ausdrücke, hard or harsh words, expressions; sie sagten sich viel —es, there passed many hard words betwixt them. *d*) difficult or attended with certain difficulties. Das Pferd trabt —, hat einen —en Trab, the horse trots hard, does not trot easily, has a hard trot; einen — Leib [Stuhlgang] haben, to be costive, to have one's bowels bound; ein —es Gehör haben, to be hard of hearing; eine —e Aussprache, a hard pronunciation; eine —e Stimme haben, to have a harsh voice, that grates the ear; —e Buchstaben [the p, t, k], hard letters; [in music] die —e Tonart [*Dur-Ton], the major tone or key; ein —es Leben führen, to lead a life full of hardships or difficulties; es sind —e Zeiten, times are hard; —e Arbeit, hard labour; —e Bedingungen, hard conditions; es wird — halten, it will be hard, difficult; ich habe es mit —er Mühe erlangt, I have obtained it with great difficulty, I had a great deal of trouble to obtain it; es kommt mich — an, es geht mir — ein, fällt mir —, it is a hard or difficult task for me; I do it with great reluctance, reluctantly. *e*) violent, rude. Ein —es Fieber, a hard fever; einen —en Sturm aushalten, to weather out a rude or violent storm; ein —er Winter, a severe, hard winter; ein —er Fall, a hard case; — anklopfen, to knock hard; ein —er Schlaf, a sound sleep, a heavy sleep; — schlafen, to sleep soundly; Einem — zusetzen, to beset any one hard; Einen — bedrängen, to press or urge any one hard; ein — bedrängtes Gemüth, an afflicted mind. *f*) not agreeing with certain rules of art, and hence: disagreeable, unpleasant, stiff, harsh, forced, unnatural. Ein —es Gleichniß, a forced simile; —e Figuren, hard figures; —e Verse, harsh verses; eine —e Schreibart, a hard, stiff, rough or rugged diction or style; eine —e Manier, ein —er Pinsel [among painters], a hard or stiff manner, a harsh pencil. II. *adv.* 1) [obsolete] strongly, very much, violently. [in Scripture] Und er schlug sie —, and he smote them hip and thigh; deß erschrak Belsazar noch härter, then was Belshazzar greatly troubled. 2) close, near. — an dem Thore wohnen, to live close or hard by the gate; — an dem Wege, close to the road.

Hart-blei, *n.* hard lead [which is obtained in refining silver]. —erz, *n.* copper-ore containing quartz. —flügelig, *adj.* [in nat. hist.] coleopteral. —flügelige Ziefern, coleopteral insects, coleopters. —gesinnt, *adj.* hard-minded, hard-hearted. —haarig, —härig, *adj.* having strong stiff hair. —häutig, *adj.* having a hard skin; *fig.* *V. —schlägig. —häutigkeit, *f.* hardness of the skin; *fig.* callousness. —herzig, *adj.* and *adv.* hard-hearted, unfeeling, cruel, inexorable. —herzigkeit, *f.* hard-heartedness. —heu, *n.* V. Johannskraut. —hobel, *m.* jack-plane. —hörig, *adj.* and *adv.* hard of hearing. Ein —höriger Mann, a deafish man. —hörigkeit, *f.* thickness or dulness of hearing. —hufig, *adj.* and *adv.* having a hard hoof. —klamm, *m.* [in mining] hard rock that does not easily break. —klemmig, [in mining] *adj.* very, extremely hard. —kopf, *m.* 1) one who has a dull, heavy understanding, a blockhead. 2) an obstinate, stubborn person. —köpfig, *adj.* and *adv.* 1) having a dull, heavy understanding. 2) stubborn, obstinate. —köpfigkeit, *f.* 1) dulness or difficulty of understanding. 2) obstinacy, stubbornness. —korn, *n.* hard grain [such as wheat, barley, rye]. —lehrig, *adj.* V. —lernig. —leibig, *adj.* and *adv.* bound in body, costive; *it. fig.* [in popular lang.] covetous, stingy. —leibigkeit, *f.* costiveness; *it. fig.* covetousness, stinginess. —lernig, *adj.* and *adv.* slow in learning. —lernigkeit, *f.* slowness in learning. —loth, *n.* hard solder. V. Schlagloth. —mäulig, *adj.* and *adv.* having a hard mouth, hard-mouthed [said of horses]; *fig.* *[said of persons] unruly, ungovernable. —mäuligkeit, *f.* state of being hard-mouthed; *fig* unruliness. —meißel, *m.* [in founderies] a sort of chisel for cutting crossways. —metall, *n.* brittle brass. —näckig, *adj.* and *adv.* *fig.* stiffnecked, stubborn, obstinate. Ein —näckiges [= hitziges] Gefecht, an obstinate fight. —näckigkeit, *f.* stubbornness, obstinacy. —riegel, *m.* [in botany] 1) privet. 2) dogwood. —rindig, *adj.* and *adv.* having a hard rind or crust. —rose, *f.* V. Eisigrose. —roth, *adj.* and *adv.* [chiefly in painting] glaring red. —schalig, *adj.* and *adv.* having a hard shell, testaceous. Die Auster ist ein —schaliges Thier, the oyster is a testaceous animal. —schälig, *adj.* and *adv.* having a hard shell or skin. —schlächtig, *adj.* and *adv.* V. Hertschlächtig. —schlägig, *adj.* and *adv.* hardened against blows, callous. —schlagloth, *n.* V. —loth. —sehnig, *adj.* and *adv.* having strong sinews or tendons, sinewy. —sinn, *m.* V. —näckigkeit. —sinnig, *adj.* and *adv.* V. —näckig. —spath, *m.* feldspar. —stich, *m.* [in forges] a ladleful of melted copper. —stück, *n.* [in forges] a piece or pig of melted copper. —werk, *n.* tutty of tin.

Hart, *f.* the name given to several woody

districts in Germany, as for instance in the Grand-Duchy of Baden, in Rhenish Bavaria. V. in general 1. Harz.

Härte, *f.* [*pl.*-n] 1) [seldom used in the *pl.*] state or quality of being hard, hardness. — ist der feste Zusammenhang der Theile der Materie, hardness is a firm cohesion of the parts of matter; die — des Fleisches, the toughness of the meat; [in metallurgy] dem Eisen, dem Stahl die — (or Härtung) geben, to temper iron, steel; dem Stahl seine — benehmen, to soften steel. *Fig.* Die — des Körpers, the state or quality of the body being inured to hardships; die — des Leibes [Stuhlganges], costiveness; die — des Herzens, the hardness of heart, hard-heartedness; Einen mit — behandeln, to treat any one harshly; die — des Winters, the rigour, severity, hardness of winter; die — der Zeiten, the hardness of the times; die — der Gesetze, the rigour of the laws; die — der Schreibart, der Verse, des Pinsels, the harshness of the style, of the verses, of the pencil; die — der Stimme, the harshness of the voice. 2) something hard. Sie hat eine — an der Brust bekommen, she has got a hard swelling in her breast. *Fig.* die —n in der Bildhauerkunst, hardnesses of sculpture; [among engravers] die —n, hatches made too hard.

Härten, *v. intr.* [used with seyn] to become hard, to harden.

Hart-pulver, *n.* [among file-cutters] powder for tempering the files. —**tonne**, *f.* a tub or trough with water for tempering red-hot steel. —**wasser**, *n.* [in forges] tempering water [made of salt-lie, of saltpetre and urine].

Härten, *v. tr.* to make hard, to harden, to endurate. Die Luft härtet Korallen, the air endurates corals; die freie Luft härtet die Steine, the open air hardens stones; das Eisen, den Stahl —, to harden, to temper iron, steel; eine gut gehärtete Klinge, a well-tempered blade.

Härtheit, *f.* V. Härte.

Härtigkeit, *f.* V. Härte.

Härtlich, *adj.* and *adv.* somewhat hard. Dieses Huhn ist —, this fowl is a little tough. *Fig.* Dieser Wein schmeckt —, this wine is somewhat hard, tart or harsh.

Härtling, *m.* [-es, *pl.* -e] 1) [in forges] hard slags or dross. 2) V. Herling.

Hartschier, *m.* V. Hatschier.

Härtung, *f.* [the act of] hardening, tempering.

1. **Härz**, *m.* [-es, *pl.* -e] [allied to *Ard-uenna* and *Hercy-nia*, and probably to the Wendish *Hord* or *Gora*, Hebrew *hor* = mountain] a chain of woody mountains in Saxony, the Hartz, the Hercynian forest.

Harz-bewohner, *m.* inhabitant of the Hartz. —**butter**, *f.* butter of the Hartz. —**dorf**, *n.* a village of the Hartz. —**gebirge**, *n.* Hercynian forest or mountains. —**gegend**, *f.* —**käse**, *m.* —**pflanze**, *f.* —**stadt**, *f.* country, cheese &c. of the Hartz. —**wald**, *m.* V. —gebirge.

2. **Härz**, *n.* [-es, *pl.* -e] [probably allied to **harren** and to the Gr. *αἱρέω* = to hold fast] rosin, rosin. Elastisches — [Feder—, Leder—], resin elastic. In compositions: V. Baum—, Fichten—, Geigen—, Oelbaum—, Pockenholz—, Schleim—, Wachholder—.

Harz-baum, *m.* a tree which yields resin, resiniferous tree, pitchtree, pinetree, gum-tree. —**eichel**, *f.* the shoot and round acorn. —**electricität**, *f.* resinous electricity. —**förmig**, *adj.* and *adv.* having the form of resin, resiniform. —**galle**, *f.* a place in pines where resin has gathered, resiniferous vessel. —**holz**, *n.* resinous wood, V. Nadelholz. —**kappe**, *f.* a jacket worn by those who scrape or gather resin. —**klee**, *m.* the bituminous clover or trefoil. —**kohle**, *f.* V. Glanzkohle. —**kuchen**, *m.* cake of the refuse of resin after the pitch has been extracted. ||and †—**lüge**, *f.* [probably corrupted, instead of Erz-lüge] a gross falsehood. —**messer**, *n.* a knife for scraping off the resin. —**meste**, *f.* a cornet of the bark of a pine-tree for gathering resin. —**pflanze**, *f.* resinous plant. —**reißen**, *n.* V. —riß 1). —**reißer**, *m.* V. —scharrer. —**riß**, *m.* 1) the act of cutting into or tapping pine-trees in order to draw out the resin, hence, crop of resin. 2) cut or incision made in a pine-tree. —**schaben**, *m.* V. —riß 1). —**schaber**, —**scharrer**, *m.* one who scrapes or gathers resin, resin-scraper, resin-gatherer. —**stein**, *m.* soapstone, steatite, steatitic talc. —**tanne**, *f.* V. —baum. —**tragend**, *adj.* resiniferous. —**wasser**, *n.* gum-water. Mit —wasser bestreichen [*gummiren], to smear with gum, to gum.

Härzen, I. *v. tr.* to scrape off or gather the resin. Einen Baum —, to scrape off or gather the resin of a tree. II. *v. intr.* to yield resin. Dieser Baum harzet, this tree exsudes resin.

Härzer or **Harzer**, *m.* [-s, *pl.* -] 1) an inhabitant of the Hartz or Hercynian forest. 2) V. Harzscharrer.

Harzicht, *adj.* and *adv.* like or resembling resin, resinous.

Harzig, *adj.* and *adv.* 1) containing resin, resinous. —e Pflanzenschleime, resinous gums. 2) smeared or soiled with resin.

***Hasardiren**, *v. tr.* and *intr.* [in colloquial language] to venture, to hazard, to risk, V. Wagen.

***Hasardspiel**, *n.* [-es, *pl.* -e] game of chance, hazard.

Häschen, *v. tr.* [seems to be allied to Haß and Hase] to catch or seize quickly or eagerly, to snatch. Einen Dieb —, to apprehend a thief; nach etwas —, to snatch at, to catch at. *Fig.* Den Augenblick —, to seize the moment; nach Gleichnissen —, to run after similes.

Häscher, *m.* [-s, *pl.* -] a thief-catcher, thief-taker, catchpoll, bum-bailiff, V. Scharwächter, Büttel.

Häschermäßig, *adj.* and *adv.* in the manner of a thiefcatcher or catchpoll, in a coarse or rough manner.

***Haschiren**, *v. tr.* [among engravers] to hatch.

***Haschirung**, *f.* [among engravers] hatching.

Hase, *m.* [-n, *pl.* -n] [Arabian *hazaz*, Sax., Eng. Dan. and Sw. *hare*, perhaps allied to the old hasen, Eng. *to hare* = to fright, V. Haschen] hare, [among sportsmen] puss. [*dim.* das Häschen, ||Häslein, a young or little hare, leveret.] Das Männchen der —n [Rammler], the male of the hare, buck-hare; der weibliche —, die Häsinn, the female hare, doe-hare; ein — im Lager, a hare on form; einen —n im Lager nach Jägersbrauch fangen, to take a hare on form; einen —n hetzen or jagen, to hunt or course a hare; einen —n auftreiben, aufjagen, to start a hare; der — duckt sich, the hare squats; furchtsam wie ein —, as fearful as a hare; V. Berg—, Feld—, Holz—, Grund—, März—, Setz—. *Prov.* Viel Hunde sind des —n Tod, a hare will be overcome by many hounds, at length one must yield to the greater number; *da liegt der — im Pfeffer, there lies the main difficulty, there it sticks, there's the rub. Der gespickte — [an instrument of torture], the larded hare; [in astronomy] hare, lepus. *Fig.* *Er ist ein —, ein furchtsamer —, he is a timid, hare-hearted fellow, a coward, poltroon.

Hasen-adler, *m.* great black eagle. —**ampfer**, *m.* V. Sauerklee. —**apfel**, *m.* V. Borsdorfer. —**art**, *f.* the nature of the hare; er ist [von] rechter —art, he is very fearful, faint-hearted. —**auge**, *n.* 1) a hare's eye. 2) [in medicine, a disease in the eyelids, when they are so inverted, or retracted that the eyes cannot be sufficiently covered by them] ectropium or ectrope, lagophthalmia. 3) [in botany] herb-bennet. —**balg**, *m.* hare's skin. *—**bange**, *adj.* and *adv.* as fearful as a hare, faint-hearted. Es ist ihm schon —bange, he is in great fear, he is afraid of his shadow. —**beize**, *f.* [in falconry] catching hares by hawks, hawking hares. —**braten**, *m.* roast hare. —**brot**, *n.* V. —ohr 3). —**fährte**, *f.* the print of a hare on the ground, prick. —**fell**, *n.* V. —balg. —**fett**, *n.* grease of a hare. *Fig.* [in vulgar language] Er hat ein wenig ins —fett getreten, he is a coxcomb or fool, harebrained. —**fleisch**, *n.* hare's flesh. —**fuß**, *m.* 1) the foot or pad of a hare. *Fig. a*) a harebrained, ridiculous fellow. *b*) a timid, hare-hearted fellow, a coward, a poltroon. 2) [a plant] harefoot. 3) [a bird] harefoot. —**füßig**, *adj.* and *adv.* *Fig. a*) playful, waggish, harebrained. *b*) cowardly, chicken-hearted, hare-hearted. —**füßigkeit**, *f.* quality of being *a*) waggish, hare-brained, *b*) cowardly. —**futter**, *n.* 1) food or meat for hares. 2) lining of hareskin. —**garn**, *n.* hare-pipe. —**gehäge**, *n.* a warren of hares. —**geier**, *m.* glede, kite. —**geil**, *n.* broom, genista. —**gras**, *n.* V. —ohr 2). —**haar**, *n.* the hair of a hare. —**haft**, *adj.* and *adv.* V. —füßig. —**hatz**, *f.* V. —hetze. —**heide**, *f.* V. —geil. —**herz**, *n.* the heart of a hare; *fig.* pusillanimity, cowardice. Ein —herz haben, to be as fearful as a hare, to be a coward. —**hetze**, *f.* V. —jagd. —**horde**, —**hürde**, *f.* trap or snare for catching hares. —**hund**, *m.* harehound, harrier. —**jagd**, *f.* hare-hunting [hare-hunting with harriers is called *hunting*, with greyhounds *coursing*]. Ein Liebhaber der —jagd, a hare-hunter. —**kasten**, *m.* a chest with holes for conveying hares alive. —**klee**, *m.* [in botany] 1) harefoot. 2) gelber —klee, kidney vetch, lady's finger, clown's wound-wort. 3) V. Buchampfer. 4) V. Schafampfer. —**klein**, *n.* hare-ragout. —**kohl**, *m.* sow-thistle, sonchus, hare's lettuce. —**kopf**, *m.* hare's head; *fig.* a silly, harebrained fellow. —**lab**, *n.* hare's rennet. —**lager**, *n.* seat or form of a hare. —**lattig**, *m.* [in botany] hare's lettuce. —**lippe**, *f.* V. —scharte. —**maul**, *n.* 1) a hare's mouth or snout; *fig.* V. —scharte. 2) small turbot. —**maus**, *f.* the rabbit of Java. —**nest**, *n.* V. —lager. —**netz**, *n.* V. —garn. —**ohr**, *n.*, *dim.* —öhrchen, ||—öhrlein, *n.* 1) hare's ear. V. also Löffel [with sportsmen]; [in printing] V. Gänsefuß. 2) [in botany] hare's-ear, Bupleurum; *it.* V. Haselöhrlein. 3) [in seamen's language] lateen sail. —**panier**, —**panner**, *n.* *fig.* [in familiar language] flight. Das —panier ergreifen, to betake one's self to one's heels, to run away. —**pappel**, *f.* hare-wort. —**pastete**, *f.* hare-pie. —**pfeffer**, *m.* V. —klein. —**pfote**, *f.* hare's foot or pad; [in botany] harefoot. —**pilz**, *m.* a sort of mushroom having the shape of a hare on form. —**scharte**, *f.* a divided upper-lip, hare-lip. —**schmalz**, *n.* V. —fett. —**schrot**, *n.* shot for hares. —**schwarz**, *n.* V. —klein. —**sprung**, *m.* 1) hare's leap, [among sportsmen] pricking, prick. 2) [among sportsmen] the hindlegs of a hare. —**spur**, *f.* V. —fährte. —**stößer**, *m.* V. —adler, —geier. —**strauch**, *m.* V. —lattig. —**zwirn**, *m.* a sort of pack-thread for making hare-pipes.

Hasel, **Häsel**, *m.* [-s, *pl.* -] V. Häsling.

Häsel, *f.* [*pl.* -n] [Ice. *harsel*, Eng. *hazel*, perhaps allied to the L. *corylus*] hazel, hazel-tree.

Hasel-busch, *m.* 1) V. Hasel. 2) a grove or copse of hazel-trees, hazel-wood. —**eiche**, *f.* a kind of oak, V. Loheiche, Traubeneiche. —**eule**, *f.* a small night-butterfly, phalaena. —**gebüsch**, *n.* V. —busch 2). —**geflügel**, *n.* [collectively = —hühner] black-game. —**gerte**, *f.* hazel-switch, hazel-rod. —**holz**, *n.* 1) the wood of the hazel. 2) V. —busch 2). —**huhn**, *n.* black-cock. —**kätzchen**, *n.* the catkin of the hazel. —**maus**, *f.* dormouse. —**nuß**, *f.* 1) hazel-nut. 2) [in conchology] rice-cowry. —**nußfarbe**, *f.* colour of the hazel-nut. —**nußöl**, *n.* V. —öl. —**nußstrauch**, *m.* V. Hasel. —**öhrlein**, *n.* the agaric of the oak; touchwood. —**öl**, *n.* oil pressed from the hazel-nut. —**ratze**, *f.* V. —maus. —**ruthe**, *f.* V. —gerte. —**staude**, *f.* —**strauch**, *m.* V. Hasel. —**wurm**, *m.* blind-worm, slow-worm. V. Blindschleiche —**wurz**, —**wurzel**, *f.* [in botany] hazel-wort.

†**Haselánt**, *m.* [-en, *pl.* -en] [in fam. lang.] jester, buffoon, droll.

Häseling, *m.* [-s, *pl.* -e] [a fish] chub, V. 1. Döbel.

†**Haseliren**, *v. intr.* V. Häseln I.

Häseln, **Häseln**, *adj.* and *adv.* of the hazel. Eine —e Ruthe, a hazel-rod, V. Haselruthe.

Häseln, [allied to Hase] [in fam. lang.] I. *v. intr.* to play, to trifle, to jest. II. *v. tr.* Einen —, to make a fool of any one, to banter, to mock any one.

Häsewitz, *m.* [-es, *pl.* -e] [in fam. lang.] a silly, ridiculous coxcomb, a harebrained fellow, V. 1. Geck.

Häsinn, *f.* V. Hase.

Häspe, **Häspe**, *f.* [*pl.* -n] [Sax. *haepse*, ing. *hasp*, seems to be allied to haben, haften, eben] the hook or joint on which a door or ate turns, hinge; *it.* the band of iron which ustains a door or window, the ironwork of a loor or window. [among locksmiths] Die —en n einem Thürpfosten, the holdfasts or staples; in mining] hook; [in artillery] a cramp-iron, V. ling—.

Häspel, *m.* [-s, *pl.* -, or Haspel, *f. pl.* -n] w. *harfwel*, seems to be allied to Wirbel and werben, werfen = to turn in a circle] a achine for winding yarn, a reel; *it.* a machine r raising great weights, a windlass, winch; [in ining] winding-engine; [in seamen's language] pstan. Den — drehen, to heave the capstan. . Drehkreuz, Hiffe, Spille, Weg—, Weife, inde.

Haspel-arm, *m.* one of the four arms of reel or windlass. —**baum**, *m.* the cylinder roller of a windlass or capstan. —**gerüst**, -**gestell**, *n.* trestle of a windlass or capstan. **habe**, *f.* the handle or winch of a reel or ndlass. —**knecht**, *m.* one that works at a ndlass or winding-engine. —**kreuz**, *n.* the ss-bars of a reel or windlass. —**pumpe**, *f.* mining] winding-engine. —**rad**, *n.* reel or ndlass in the shape of a wheel. —**stütze**, *f.* —gerüst. —**welle**, *f.* V. —baum. —**wins** , *f.* lever or handspike by which a windlass urned. —**wurz**, *f.* [in botany] V. Mäusezwie Seezwiebel. —**zieher**, *m.* V. —knecht.

Häspeler, **Häspler**, *m.* [-s, *pl.* -] —inn, eler. V. Haspelknecht.

Häspeln, *v. tr.* and *intr.* to reel. Garn —, eel yarn. *it.* to raise or hoist by means of a dlass, V. Winden. *Fig.* [in fam. lang.] Sich einer verwickelten Sache heraus— [= herziehen], to draw or wind one's self out of an icate affair. *it.* [provincially, in popular lang.] to speak too quick and indistinctly. Das —, the act of reeling [yarn] and of hoisting by means of a windlass.

Häspen, *v. tr.* to fasten with hooks, cramp-irons or hasps, to hasp.

Häsphaken, *m.* [-s, *pl.* -] hinge, V. Thürangel, Haspe.

Häspler, V. Haspeler.

Häß, *m.* [-sses] [Low Sax. Haat, Sax. *hatian*, Eng. *hate*, Sw. *hat*, Dan. *hade*, Lat. *odium* for *hodium*, Gr. κότος, probably to be deduced from heiß, Sax. *hat*, Eng. *hot*, Low Sax. heet] hate, hatred. Eingewurzelter, unversöhnlicher —, inveterate, implacable hatred; — gegen Jemand empfinden, hegen, to bear a hatred against any one; —gegen das Laster empfinden, to have a hatred for vice; einen — gegen Einen fassen, to conceive a hatred against any one; Eines — auf sich laden, sich zuziehen, to draw down, to incur the hatred of any one; aus —, out of hatred or spite; seinen — an Jemand auslassen, to wreak one's hatred upon any one.

Hässen, [V. Haß] *v. tr.* and *intr.* to hate. Seine Feinde tödtlich —, to hate one's enemies mortally, to bear a deadly hatred to one's enemies; ich haßte an ihm nur seine Laster, I hated only his vices in him. Das —, V. Haß.

Hässenswerth, **Hässenswürdig**, *adj* and *adv.* deserving hatred, to be hated, odious, hateful.

Hässer, *m.* [-s, *pl.* -] one that hates, hater. Ein — alles Guten, a hater of all good.

Hässig, V. [the usual word] Gehässig.

Häßlich, *adj.* and *adv.* [from Haß; others derive it from the old aislich = schrecklich, the Low Saxon aisen = schaudern] properly and in general, deserving hatred. 1) [in a moral respect = böse, schändlich] odious, base, wicked, vicious. Ein —er Mensch, eine —e Handlung, a base, wicked man, action; es ist nichts —er an einem Frauenzimmer als das Trinken, there is nothing more odious in a woman than drinking; es ist sehr — von Ihnen, mich so zu behandeln, it is very base, 't is a villanous thing in you to use me so; es ist eine —e Sache um das Lügen, it is an odious thing to tell lies; ein —es Wort, a hateful, obscene word; er hat mich — betrogen, he has deceived me in a villanous manner; —e Streiche, ugly tricks. 2) [in a more limited sense = widrig, unangenehm] disagreeable, unpleasant. —es Wetter, sad, dirty, nasty weather; ein —er Weg, a bad, wretched road; Sie haben einen —en Husten, you have got an ugly cough. 3) contrary to beauty, offensive to the sight, ugly. Eine —e Frau, ein —er Mann &c., an ugly woman, man; — wie der Teufel, as ugly as the devil; —e Straßen, dirty, nasty streets; er hat —e [= schmutzige] Hände, he has nasty hands; sich das Gesicht häßlich [= schmutzig] machen, to daub one's face.

Häßlichkeit, *f.* ugliness [of a person, stuff &c.] *Fig.* Die — des Lasters, einer Handlung, the ugliness of vice, of an action.

Häßling, V. Häseling.

Häst, *f.* [V. Haschen] haste, hurry, precipitation. Etwas mit —, in — thun, to do a thing in a hurry; mit — arbeiten, to use expedition. V. Eile.

Hästen, I. *v. intr.* and *impers.* Es hastet nicht, there is no hurry, V. Eilen. II. *v. r.* sich —, to be quick, to hasten, to make haste.

Hästig, *adj.* and *adv.* hasty, very quick. Sie zogen sich — zurück, they retired hastily; — trinken, to drink hastily, precipitately. *Fig.* passionate, irritable. Er ist ein —er Kopf, he is a hasty, passionate fellow.

Hästigkeit, *f.* hastiness, rashness, precipitation. *Fig.* irritability, hastiness.

Hätscheln, *v. tr.* [from haben, halten] to caress, to fondle, to coax. Ein Kind —, to fondle a child. V. Liebkosen, Verhätscheln, Verzärteln.

***Hatschier**, [-es, *pl.* -e] [Ital. *arciere*. Fr. *archer*] 1) yeoman of the imperial lifeguards at Vienna. 2) V. Trabant. 3) V. Häscher.

Hatschier-hauptmann, *m.* captain of the imperial lifeguards. —**wache**, *f.* the imperial lifeguards.

Hättstatt, *f.* V. Haltstätte.

Hätz, *f.* [*pl.* -e] or **Hätze**, *f.* [*pl.* -n] the baiting or hunting of wild beasts. *Fig.* Eine —e [Koppel] Hunde, a pack of hounds; — los! [among sportsmen] let the hounds loose! V. Bären—, Hasen—, Schweins—, Thier—.

Hatz-hund, *m.* hound. —**strick**, *m.* leash.

||**Hätze**, *f.* [*pl.* -n] [V. Atzel, Elster] magpie.

Hau, *m.* [-es, *pl.* -e] 1) the act of cutting, cut. 2) [among foresters] place where wood is being felled; *it.* copse, coppice-wood, underwood. V. Holzschlag, Schlag, Gehau.

Hau-amboß, *m.* a small square anvil for cutting files. —**bank**, *f.* chopping-board. —**beere**, *f.* 1) white hawthorn, white-thorn, V. Mehlbeere. 2) V. Elsebeere. —**block**, *m.* cutting-block, chopping block. —**degen**, *m.* 1) broadsword, cutting-sword. 2) [in familiar language] one who uses the broadsword, an experienced, brave swordsman; *it.* [in contempt] a bully, V. Eisenfresser. —**eisen**, *n.* an iron instrument for hewing or cutting. —**geld**, *n.* miner's pay or wages. —**gewehr**, *n.* a weapon for thrusting with the point and striking with the edge. —**hammer**, *m.* [in mining] V. Hammeraxt, Hammerbeil. —**hechel**, *f.* [in botany] rest-harrow, petty whin, cammock. —**holz**, *n.* 1) coppice, copse, underwood, V. Schlagholz. 2) wood fit for being felled. 3) V. —block. —**klinge**, *f.* blade of a back or broad sword. —**kloß**, *m.* V. Hackblock. —**land**, *n.* land newly ploughed [which formerly was wood]. —**meißel**, *m.* cutting-chisel. —**stempel**, *m.* punch, puncheon. —**stock**, *m.* V. —block. —**werk**, *n.* [in mining] heap of rock and ore. —**zahn**, *m.* tusk, fang. Die —zähne eines Ebers, the fangs, razors or tusks of a boar.

Haubar, *adj.* and *adv.* fit for cutting or felling.

Haubarkeit, *f.* quality of being fit for cutting or felling.

Haube, *f.* [*pl.* -n] [Low Sax. and Dan. *huve*, Sw. *hufwa*, Engl. *hood*, W. *hiof*, Fr. *coiffe*, seems to be allied to Haupt, heben, hob] 1) the upper part or covering of a thing. [in anatomy] Die —, [a little membrane sometimes encompassing the head of a child when born] caul; [in architecture] the dome, cupola or round top of a dome; die — des Chors, apsis; [in botany] glume [husk or chaff]; [with charcoal-burners] die — des Meilers, the top of the charcoal heap; [in chimistry] die — einer Retorte, the dome of a reverberatory; [with cutlers] die — eines Messers, the ferrule of a knife; [in founderies] die — [über dem Messingofen], low furnace; [among bell-founders] the crown of a bell; [in natural history] die — der Vögel, tuft or crest of feathers on the head of birds; die — einer Lerche, the tuft of a lark; [among fishermen] a drag-net, trammel. 2) a kind of cap, particularly for women, hood, coif. *Dim.* Häubchen, ||Häublein, *n.* a little cap. Das Kinderhäubchen, a child's cap; die — stecken, aufſetzen, to put on one's cap or bonnet. Fig. Seine Tochter unter die — bringen, to provide a husband for one's daughter, to marry one's daughter to &c.; unter die — kommen, to get a husband, to marry; Einem auf der — ſeyn, ſitzen, to keep a strict hand over any one, to keep any one short, to have a watchful eye upon a person; er, ſie hat mich auf der —, he, she keeps a strict eye upon me, he, she watches me closely. [in falconry, a covering for a hawk's head or eyes] hood. Dem Falken die — aufſetzen, abnehmen, to hood or hoodwink a hawk, to unhood a hawk; [among sportsmen] a sack for catching the badger in his kennel; die — der wiederkäuenden Thiere, the second stomach of ruminating animals.

Hauben-adler, *m.* the crested or tufted eagle. —band, *n.* 1) a ribbon in a woman's cap [for ornament]. 2) a ribbon to tie a cap with. —blutfink, *m.* cardinal, the gross-beak of Virginia. —colibri, *m.* crested colibri. —draht, *m.* skeleton-wire. —droſſel, *f.* the tufted or Bohemian thrush. —ente, *f.* tufted duck. —falk, *m.* crested or tufted falcon. —faſan, *m.* the tufted pheasant, the white pheasant of China; *it.* the great tufted pigeon of the Indies. —fink, *m.* the tufted red finch of the Indies, Virginia nightingale, red-bird. —flor, *m.* thin or gauze-crape. —häher, *m.* the tufted jack-daw. —handel, *m.* V. —kram. —henne, *f.* —huhn, *n.* the tufted hen or fowl. —kernbeißer, *m.* the tufted gross-beak of Ethiopia. —könig, *m.* the golden-crested wren. —kopf, *m.* V. —ſtock. —kram, *m.* a milliner's trade or shop. —krämer, *m.* man-milliner. —krämerinn, *f.* milliner. —kuckuck, *m.* the tufted cuckoo. —lerche, *f.* crested lark. —macher, *m.* cap-maker, man-milliner. —macherinn, *f.* milliner. —meiſe, *f.* tufted titmouse. —merle, *f.* crested blackbird. —nadel, *f.* minikin pin. —netz, *n.* drag-net, trammel. —papagei, *m.* tufted parrot. —perlhuhn, *n.* tufted guinea-hen. —reiher, *m.* the tufted heron. —ſchleife, *f.* a bow of ribbons. —ſpecht, *m.* the tufted green-peak. —ſteckerinn, *f.* V. —macherinn. —ſtock, *m.* a block upon which women's caps are made. —ſtreif, —ſtrich, *m.* edging or ruffle of a cap or bonnet. —taube, *f.* jacobine, ruff. —taucher, *m.* the horned or tufted grebe.

Häubeln, *v. tr.* [in falconry] to hood, to hoodwink. *Fig.* [in popular language, rather provincial] Einen —, to reprimand, to chide any one severely.

Hauben, *v. tr.* [rarely used] to put on a cap or hood; [in natural history] ein gehaubter Vogel, a crested bird. V. Häubeln.

Haubitze, *f.* [*pl.* -n] howitzer.

Haubitz-batterie, *f.* a battery of howitzers; *it.* a battery mounted with howitzers. —granate, *f.* a grenade thrown from a howitzer.

Hauch, *m.* [-es, *pl.* -e] [V. Hauchen] 1) the act of blowing or breathing, the forcible emission of breath, puff. Der — des Windes, a breath or puff of wind, a breeze, a gentle gale; das Licht mit einem —e ausblaſen, to blow the candle out at one puff; er iſt ſo ſchwach, daß ihn ein — umwerfen könnte, he is so weak that one could blow him over with a whiff; treu bis zum letzten —e des Lebens, faithful to the last gasp; das H wird mit einem —e ausgeſprochen, the h is pronounced with an aspiration, V. —buchſtabe, —laut. 2) [the air inhaled and expelled in the respiration of animals] breath. Ich fühle den ſüßen — ihres Mundes auf meiner Wange, I feel the sweet breath of her mouth on my cheek. 3) [in anatomy] V. —blatt. 4) [in medicine] plethory.

Hauch-blatt, *n.* [in anatomy] the uvula or top of the palate. —buchſtabe, *m.* aspirated letter. —forelle, *f.* the trout of the Danube. —laut, *m.* aspirated sound, aspiration. —lauter, *m.* V. —buchſtabe. —zeichen, *n.* mark of aspiration, aspirate. Das ſcharfe —zeichen, asper.

Hauchen, [Allemannic chuchen allied to the Gr. καυχ-άομαι, αὐχ-έω and εὔχ-ομαι which all signified at first only to breathe, and afterwards to speak] I. *v. intr.* to blow, forcibly to emit breath. In die Finger —, to blow one's fingers; Einem ins Geſicht —, to blow in the face of any one; der Wind haucht, the wind blows. II. *v. tr.* 1) [in grammar] to aspirate. Das H wird in dieſem Worte nicht gehaucht, the h is not aspirated in this word; gehauchte Buchſtaben, aspirated letters. 2) to inject by breathing. Leben in einen Körper —, to breathe life into a body. 3) to emit a breathing, to exhale. Die Blumen — Wohlgerüche, the flowers breathe or exhale odours or perfume. 4) *Fig.* [poetically, = athmen] to breathe. Seine Kindheit hauchte Freude, his infancy breathed joy.

Hauderer, *m.* [-s, *pl.* -] a hackney-coachman.

Haudern, *v. intr.* to drive a hackney-coach, to be a hackney-coachman.

Haue, *f.* [*pl.* -n] hoe, mattock. V. Gät—, Keil—, Reut— &c. [in mining] a wooden hammer for pounding the iron-ore.

Hauen, [Sax. *heawian*, Eng. *to hew*, D. *houwen*, old German heven = ſchneiden, to cut] *ir.* I. *v. tr.* and *intr.* 1) to strike either with a cutting or other instrument. Einen auf den Kopf —, to strike any one on the head; nach Einem —, to strike at any one; mit einem damascener Säbel haut man durch das Eiſen, a sabre of Damascus steel cuts iron; er hieb um ſich wie ein Beſeſſener, he fought, he laid about him like a madman; ich hieb es mitten durch, I cut it in two; von einander —, to cut asunder, in two; — und ſtechen [auf Hieb und Stich fechten], to cut and thrust; die Vögel — mit dem Schnabel, birds strike with the beak, peck; das wilde Schwein hat ihn ge—, the wild boar has struck him with its fangs; ein —des [=5jähriges] Schwein, a tusked or tusky boar; das Pferd haut in die Eiſen, the horse interferes or cuts. *Prov.* Es iſt weder ge— noch geſtochen, there is neither rhyme nor reason in it; man weiß nicht, ob es ge— oder geſtochen iſt, nobody knows what to make of it; *fig.* [rather vulg.] über die Schnur —, to exceed the bounds or limits, to grow licentious, to take too much liberty or too great a latitude. 2) = abhauen, to cut off. Einem einen Arm vom Leibe —, to cut off or strike off any one's arm; einen Zweig vom Baume —, to cut a branch off a tree; Gras, Holz —, to cut down grass, wood, to mow grass, to fell wood; Steine — (aus dem Steinbruch), to dig stones [from the quarry]; Erz —, to dig ore. 3) to put into a certain state or condition by cutting. Etwas in Stücke —, to cut or hew a thing in pieces; die Feinde zu Stücken, in die Pfanne, zu Fetzen —, to cut the enemies to pieces; Einen krumm und lahm —, to cut any one's arms and legs, to make a cripple of, to cripple any one; ſein Regiment iſt in Stücke ge— worden, his regiment has been put to the sword; *fig.* †Einen in die Bank —, zur Fleiſchbank — [= Einen verläumden], to backbite, to slander, to traduce, to vilify any one. 4) to cut into pieces, to cut up, to chop. Holz —, to chop wood; Fleiſch — [= aushauen], to cut up meat. 5) [to cut with an axe or other instrument for the purpose of making an even surface] to hew. S Bauholz —, to hew stones, timber; der eckig gehauene Stein, the square-hewn 6) to cause or produce by cutting. Einem Wunde in den Kopf —, to cut or wound one's head. 7) to form or shape by cutti In Stein, in Marmor —, to carve, to grave in stone, in marble; einen Namen Marmor —, to carve or engrave a name in marble; ein Bild aus Marmor —, to carve an image out of marble; Feilen —, to cut files. †8) [sometimes = ſchlagen] to beat. Einen —, to beat or whip any one; Einem (eines) hinter die Ohren —, to give one a box on the ear, to box any one's ears. II. *v. r.* ſich —. 1) to wound one's self by cutting. Sich in den Fuß, in den Schenkel —, to cut one's foot, one's thigh. 2) to fight a duel with broad-swords or sabres. 3) Sich durch etwas —, to cut one's way through. 4) [in mining] to break off, to separate.

Hauer, *m.* [-s, *pl.* -] 1) one who cuts or hews, cutter, hewer. V. Bild—, Feilen—, Fleiſch—, Holz—. [among sportsmen] [= ein fünfjähriges Schwein] a tusked wild boar [five years old]; [in mining] — or Häuer, miner. 2) a cutting instrument; [in seamen's language] cutlass; *it.* V. Haudegen; [among sportsmen] V. Hauzahn.

Hauer-arbeit, *f.* miner's work. —geld, *n.* V. —lohn. —glocke, *f.* the miner's bell. —lohn, *m.* woodcutter's wages; *it.* miner's wages. —ſteg, *m.* [in mining] a path on which the miners go to the mines.

Häuer, *m.* [-s, *pl.* -] [in mining] V. Hauer.

Häuer-glocke, —ſteg, V. Hauerglocke &

Häuern, *n.* [-s] [in seamen's lang.] the hire or pay of a sailor for a particular voyage.

Haufe, V. Haufen.

Häufeln, *v. tr.* 1) to form small heaps, to collect into small heaps. Das —, a game at cards [where as many small heaps of cards are made, as there are players.] 2) [to raise earth about plants] to hill. Die Kartoffeln —, to hill the potatoes.

Haufen, *m.* [-s, *pl.* -] or Haufe, *m.* [-ns, *pl.* -n] [*dim.* Häufchen, ‖ Häuflein, *n.*] [Dutch *hoop, hope*, Dan. *hob*, Sw. *hop*, Sax. *heape, hype*, Eng. *heap*, from heben, to raise, to lift, allied to hoch, high] 1) [in a limited sense] a heap, a pile. V. Klumpen, Kloß. Ein — Erde, Steine, a heap of earth, of stones; ein — Holz, Backſteine, a pile of wood, of bricks; ein — Schutt, a heap of rubbish, ein — Heu, a haycock, haymow; in — ſetzen, to put in a heap, to lay on a heap, to heap, to pile; Getreide in — ſchütten, to heap up corn. *Fig.* [in famil. lang.] Das koſtet ihn einen — Geld, that costs him a vast deal, a large sum of money; es liegt Alles über einem —, it is all on a heap; Einen über den — ſtoßen, werfen, to strike, to throw any one down; über den — fallen, to fall down, to tumble down, *it.* to fall to decay, to perish; er fiel über den —, he fell headlong; etwas über den — ſtoßen, to overthrow, to overturn, to subvert, to destroy any thing; das wirft alle Philoſophie über den —, that overthrows all philosophy. 2) [in a more extended sense] multitude, great number, crowd. Ein — Soldaten, a troop, a body of soldiers; ein — Volkes, a number, a crowd of people; ein — Spitzbuben, a gang of thieves: in — hereinkommen, to crowd in; wir müſſen warten, bis ſich der — verlaufen hat, we must let the crowd disperse; den — durchbrechen, to get through the crowd; ſich in den — ſtürzen, to rush into the crowd; in — zuſammengehen, to go or travel in companies; ſich in — verſammeln, to gather in crowds; in hellen —, in vast numbers, in heaps. *Fig.* Der roße —, der gemeine —, the mass of the eople, the multitude, the vulgar; sich über en gemeinen — erheben, to distinguish one's elf from the vulgar; es mit dem größten — alten, to side with the greatest or strongest arty; das kleine Häuflein der Gerechten, the mall number of the righteous.

Haufendrüsen, *pl.* [in anatomy] conglo-erate glands.

Häufen, I. *v. tr.* to collect in a heap, to eap. Papiere —, to heap papers on papers; inen Scheffel — [= gehäuft voll machen], to eap a bushel; das Salz im Maaß —, to heap he saltmeasure; ein gehäufter Scheffel, a bush-l heaped; gehäuft messen, to heap the measure; ie Erde um die Pflanzen —, to hill the plants; n botany] gehäufte Blätter, compound leaves; ehäufte Aehren, aggregate ears; gehäufte Blu-nen, aggregate flowers. *Fig.* Geschäfte auf ein-nder —, to accumulate business; Schulden —, o accumulate debts; Schätze auf Schätze —, to ccumulate treasures upon treasures; Verbre-hen auf Verbrechen —, to add one crime to nother. II. *v. r.* sich —, to accumulate, to ncrease. Sein Reichthum häuft sich von Tag zu Tag, his riches increase every day; die Zin-n häufen sich immer mehr, the interests in-rease or run on every day; es häuft sich ein nglück über das andere, one misfortune comes n the neck of an other. V. An—, Auf—.

Haufenweise, *adv.* by heaps, in heaps; *it.* n crowds, in great numbers.

Häufig, *adj.* and *adv.* crowded, thronged; *it.* bundant, copious; *it.* frequent. Die Schwal-en kommen schon —, lassen sich schon — sehen, whole flights of swallows arrive already, num-ers of swallows are seen already; der —e Ge-rauch einer Sache, the frequent use of a thing; r geht nicht — in die Kirche, he is no great equenter of churches; sie vergoß —e Thrä-n, she shed a flood of tears; dies sieht man n —sten in großen Städten, that is most fre-uently seen in great cities.

Haufwerk, *n.* [-es, *pl.* -e] [in mining] all anner of ores, stones &c. thrown together on a eap, a heap of ore; [in chimistry and mineralogy] ggregate.

Haunig, V. Haubar, Fällbar.

Hauk, *m.* [-es, *pl.* -e] [probably allied to ch, Höcker, Hügel, Scotch *heugh*] a certain eight or elevation; hence in anatomy, uvula; n the veterinary art] an excrescence in the eyes cows and horses.

Haukenblatt, *n.* V. Hauchblatt; [in bo-ny] Alexandrian laurel, hippoglossum, V. ulskraut, Zapfenkraut.

Häulein, *n.* [-s, *pl.* -] a little hoe.

Haupt, *n.* [-es, *pl.* Häupter] [*dim.* Häupt-en, ||Häuptlein, *n.*] [Low. Sax. Höved, Sax. *fod*, Icel. *hoffod*, Eng. *head*, allied to Kopf, *caput*, Gr. κεφαλή; it is to be reduced to the . *heafan, heufa*, Germ. heben, Eng. *to heave*] the highest part, the top of a thing. Das — re usual, der Kopf] des Nagels, the head of a l; eine Eiche, die ihr — bis in die Wolken ebt, an oak that raises its head into the uds; das — einer Mohnpflanze, des Kohls the head of a poppy, of a cabbage &c.; —e, am —e, zu Häupten des Bettes, at bed's head; [in heraldry] das — des Schil- das Schild—, the chief of the escutcheon; — des Laufgrabens, the head of the trench. the head of man [and sometimes of beasts]. — bedecken, to cover the head; mit ent-tem —e, bare-headed; das — neigen, to ine one's head. V. Vorder—, Hinter—. . Die Zwietracht erhob ihr fürchterliches —, ord raised her formidable head; den Feind aufs — schlagen [= gänzlich schlagen], to rout, to defeat the enemy totally. 3) *Fig.* head: *a)* instead of the whole person or animal. Die ge-krönten Häupter, the crowned heads; ein graues, ehrwürdiges — [ein ehrwürdiger Greis], a grey, venerable head, a venerable old man; er besitzt 80 Häupter [= Stücke] Rindvieh, Schweine, he possesses eighty head of cattle, of swine *b)* the principal person. Das — einer Partei, einer Secte, the head or chief of a party, of a sect; der Pabst nennt sich das — der Kirche, the pope styles himself the head of the church; die Häupter einer Stadt, the headmen, the chief or most notable men of a town; der Mann ist des Weibes —, [in Script.] the husband is the head of the wife. V. —person, Oberhaupt. In composition it expres-ses the idea of head, chief, main, principal, capital. SYN. Haupt, Kopf. Haupt denotes the head with reference to the form, Kopf with reference to the matter. Haupt is used in a higher or more solemn style. One would say: he went in bloßem Kopfe [bareheaded] in rain and snow; but, he uncovered sein ehrwürdiges Haupt [his venerable head]. Kings are called gekrönte Häupter, and not gekrönte Köpfe.

Haupt-ader, *f.* [= Kopfader] the ce-phalic vein [V. also below]. —**aderlaß**, *m.* blood-letting or phlebotomy of the head. —**arbeit**, V. Kopfarbeit and also below. —**arzenei**, *f.* cephalic medicine [for disorders in the head] [V. also below]. —**balsam**, *m.* bal-sam for the head, cephalic balsam. —**band**, *n.* V. —binde and also below. —**beschwerde**, *f.* head-ache [V. also below]. —**bild**, *n.* a bust [V. also below]. —**binde**, *f.* band or fillet for the head, head-band. Die königliche —binde, the royal diadem; [in surgery] bandage for the head [V. also below]. —**blutader**, *f.* the ce-phalic vein [V. also below]. —**bohrer**, *m.* trepan. —**brett**, *n.* the head-board of a bed, the head-piece. —**decke**, *f.* cover for the head. —**drüse**, *f.* cephalic gland [V. also below]. —**ende**, *n.* the head-piece of a bedstead. —**essenz**, *f.* cephalic essence. —**fluß**, *m.* rheu-matic affection of the head [V. also below]. —**geld**, *n.* poll-tax [V. also below]. —**geschwulst**, *f.* swelling of the head. —**gestell**, *n.* head-stall [V. also below]. —**grind**, *m.* the scab on the head, scald. —**haar**, *n.* hair of the head. —**holz**, *n.* [among carpenters] long pieces of timber that run over the heads of the pillars and join them. —**kissen**, *n.* pillow, bolster. —**kör-ner**, *pl* coriander, coriander-seed. —**krank-heit**, *f.* disease or disorder of the head [V. also below]. —**mittel**, *n.* cephalic remedy [V. also below]. —**pflaster**, *n.* cephalic plaster [V. also below]. —**pfühl**, *m.* V. —polster. —**pille**, *f.* cephalic pill. —**polster**, *n.* bol-ster, V. —kissen. —**pulver**, *n.* cephalic powder. —**putz**, *m.* V. Kopfputz. —**ring**, *m.* head-roll [V. also below]. —**salat**, *m.* lettuce which forms a head, cabbage lettuce. —**schlagader**, *f.* cepha-lic artery [V. also below]. —**schmerz**, *m.* head-ache. —**schmuck**, *m.* ornament for the head; *it.* V. Kopfputz. Der königliche —schmuck, the diadem [V. also below]. —**schur**, *f.* tonsure [V. also below]. —**seite**, *f.* the right side or face of a coin, head-side [V. also below]. —**siech**, *adj.* af-flicted with a disease of the head. —**spiritus**, *m.* cephalic spirit. —**stärkend**, *adj.* and *adv.* strengthening the head, cephalic. Ein —stär-kendes Mittel, a cephalic remedy. —**steuer**, *f.* polltax. —**stück**, *n.* 1) the headpiece of a bed. 2) V. Kopfstück [V. also below]. —**sucht**, *f.* dis-temper of the head in horses; [in medicine] alo-pesy, fox-evil. —**süchtig**, *adj.* and *adv.* afflicted with alopesy; *it.* V. —siech. —**übel**, *n.* V. Kopfkrankheit and also below. —**umlockt**, *adj.* having a locked or locky head. —**was-ser**, *n.* cephalic water. —**wassersucht**, *f.* dropsy of the head, hydrocephalus. —**weh**, *n.* V. Kopfweh. —**wirbel**, *m.* crown or top of the head. —**wunde**, *f.* wound in the head [V. also below]. —**zierde**, *f.* ornament for the head [V. also below]. —**zirkel**, *m.* glory, nimbus.

Haupt, = Hauptsächlich, Vornehmlich, Allgemein &c.

Haupt-abschied, *m.* formerly, an ab-stract or registry of the resolutions of the Impe-rial Diet, recess, V. Abschied 3). —**abschnitt**, *m.* principal section, chapter [of a book &c.]. —**absicht**, *f.* the main or principal design. —**ader**, *f.* the principal vein. Die —ader des Vorderarmes, the basilical vein, the basilic [V. also above]. —**altar**, *m.* high-altar. —**an-führer**, *m.* the principal leader or commander; commander-in-chief, V. Oberbefehlshaber. —**angelegenheit**, *f.* a principal affair, business or concern. —**angriff**, *m.* the main or princi-pal attack. —**anker**, *m.* sheet-anchor, main-anchor. —**anstifter**, *m.* the principal con-triver, plotter or instigator, the ring-leader. —**antrieb**, *m.* the principal motive. —**arbeit**, *f.* the chief or principal work [V. also above]. —**arm**, *m.* [in hydraulics] the principal pin. Der —arm eines Flusses, the principal branch or arm of a river. —**armee**, *f.* the main body of the army, the main army. —**artikel**, *m.* prin-cipal article. —**arzenei**, *f.* a principal or capital medicine, a panacea, catholicon [V. also above]. —**ast**, *m.* the principal branch. —**aufge-bot**, *n.* general levy of the people for the pur-pose of repelling an invading enemy. V. Land-sturm. —**aufstand**, *m.* the principal sedition or insurrection. —**augenmerk**, *n.* the princi-pal point, view or aim. —**balken**, *m.* 1) archi-trave. 2) principal rafter. —**band**, *n.* principal tie or band. V. Band and also above. —**baß**, *m.* [in music] fundamental base. —**bastei**, *f.* the principal bastion. —**batterie**, *f.* the greatest or most important battery. —**bau**, *m.* 1) a great, vast building. Einen —bau unternehmen, to undertake a great building, to build, to erect a great or considerable edifice. 2) the main or principal edifice or building. —**baum**, *m.* [among foresters] a full-grown, capital tree. —**be-fahrung**, *f.* [in mining] the general visiting of the mines. —**begebenheit**, *f.* a prin-cipal event or adventure. —**begriff**, *m.* principal idea, leading idea. —**bericht**, *m.* the principal report. —**beschäftigung**, *f.* principal occupation. —**beschwerde**, *f.* the chief or principal grievance [V. also above]. —**bestandtheil**, *m.* the predominant or principal ingredient or part. —**betrachtung**, *f.* principal consideration. —**betrag**, *m.* the whole sum or account, the sum total. —**be-weis**, *m.* the main or principal proof. —**bild**, *n.* V. —gemählde and also above. —**binde**, *f.* the principal fillet or bandage [V. also above]. —**bischof**, *m.* metropolitan bishop, metropoli-tan. —**bitte**, *f.* the principal prayer or re-quest. —**blutader**, *f.* the principal or greatest vein [V. also above]. —**bogen**, *m.* the chief or principal arch [of a bridge]. —**brief**, *m.* [in law] the principal document or instrument. —**buch**, *n.* 1) a capital, classical book. 2) [in commerce] ledger. —**buchstabe**, *m.* capital letter. —**damm**, *m.* the main or principal dike. —**deich**, *m.* V. —damm. —**dickicht**, *n.* the principal thicket of a forest, the thickest part of a wood. —**dichter**, *m.* a capital or great poet, a master-poet. —**drüse**, *f.* principal gland [V. also above]. —**eid**, *m.* decisory oath. —**ei-genschaft**, *f.* the principal attribute or quality. —**einfahrt**, *f.* —**eingang**, *m.* the principal gate or entry. —**endzweck**, *m.* V. —zweck. —

erbe, *m.* —erbinn, *f.* principal heir, heiress. —erzeugniß, *n.* the chief or principal product. —fabel, *f.* the fable or chief plot [of a poem &c.]. —fach, *n.* the principal study, business or province. —fahne, *f.* the principal standard, banner. —fall, *m.* 1) principal case. 2) [in feudal law] death of the lord of the manor or of a tenant. 3) right of the lord of a manor to take the best piece of the cattle when a tenant dies. —farbe, *f.* 1) principal colour. 2) V. Grundfarbe. —fehler, *m.* 1) chief, main or principal defect. 2) the greatest, capital fault. —feind, *m.* principal enemy, V. Todfeind. —festung, *f.* principal fortress. —figur, *f.* principal figure —flecken, *m.* principal borough. —flügel, *m.* principal wing. —fluß, *m.* main river [V. also above]. —frage, *f.* main or principal question. —galeere, *f.* chief galley, commander's galley. —gang, *m.* principal passage; [in mining] principal vein or lode. —gasse, *f.* principal street. —gebäude, *n.* V. —bau. —gebirge, *n.* principal mountains. —gebrechen, *n.* the main or principal defect. —gefälle, *n.* the principal dues or revenues. —gegend, *f.* principal region, cardinal point, V. —punkt. —gegenstand, *m.* main or principal object. —geld, *n.* capital stock or sum, principal [V. also above]. —geleit, *n.* main or principal convoy. —gemählde, *n.* first or principal picture or painting. —genuß, *m.* the principal enjoyment. —gericht, *n.* the principal dish. —geschäft, *n.* principal business. —geschoß, *n.* principal story of a house, first floor. —gesichtspunkt, *m.* principal point of view. —gesimse, *n.* 1) entablature. 2) cornice. —gestell, *n.* principal trestle or frame [V. also above]. —gläubiger, *m.* principal creditor. —glied, *n.* principal member. —graben, *m.* principal ditch [in fortification]. —grenze, *f.* the confines or frontiers of a kingdom or province. —grund, *m.* 1) the principal or main motive or reason. 2) the first principle, foundation, basis. Der —grund der Religion, the basis of religion. —grundpfeiler, *m.* fundamental support. —grundzins, *m.* the principal rent paid for lands and tenements —gut, *n.* 1) principal possession or estate. 2) principal or capital sum, V. —geld. —hammer, *m.* 1) principal or main hammer. 2) V. Hammerbeil. —handel, *m.* 1) principal or chief trade or commerce. 2) V. —sache. —handlung, *f.* 1) principal or main action. Ein regelmäßiges or regelrechtes Schauspiel darf keine doppelte —handlung enthalten, a regular play cannot have a double action. 2) principal trading-house, chief commercial establishment. *—hecht, *m.* a capital, extremely large pike. —heer, *n.* the main body of the army, main army. —hinderniß, *n.* main or principal obstacle. —hirsch, *m.* [among sportsmen] a stag eight years old; *it.* [in familiar language] a fine, capital stag. —huhn, *n.* V. Halshuhn. —jagd, *f.* —jagen, *n.* grand or general chase or hunting. —inhalt, *m.* general or principal contents. —karpfen, *m.* the greatest carp of a pond; *it.* *a capital carp. —karte, *f.* general map [of a country]. —kirche, *f.* principal church, cathedral, metropolitan church. —klage, *f.* the principal or chief complaint; [in law] principal action. —kläger, *m.* principal plaintiff. —knoten, *m.* *fig.* the main plot [in a play &c.]. —kohl, *m.* V. Kopfkohl. *—kopf, *m.* a capital or excellent head. —krankheit, *f.* a great, serious or dangerous illness [V. also above]. —lade, *f.* the principal box or chest of a tradesmen's company. —lager, *n.* main camp of an army, head quarters. —land, *n.* 1) mother country, main country, chief country. 2) [as opposed to islands &c.] main land, the continent [das Festland]. —last, *f.* the principal charge or burden. —laster, *n.* serious, gross vice, predominant or capital vice. —laut, *m.* consonant. —lehen, *n.* a fee held in capite or chief and of which many others hold. —lehensherr, *m.* lord paramount, head landlord —lehre, *f.* main doctrine, fundamental doctrine. —leidenschaft, *f.* the principal or predominant passion. —leiter, *f.* [in music] the fundamental scale. —leute, *pl.* V. —mann. —licht, *n.* [among painters] principal lights. —linie, *f.* 1) the principal line. 2) [in mining] Die —linie eines Ganges, the principal direction of a lode. 3) [in genealogy] direct line. —lüge, *f.* a gross lie. —lustbarkeit, *f.* principal or capital amusement. —mangel, *m.* principal defect. —mann, *m.* 1) [*pl.* —leute] captain of foot or infantry. 2) [*pl.* -leute or -männer] the chief. Der —mann einer Räuberbande, the chief of a gang of robbers or highwaymen. V. Amts-, Berg-, Schloßhauptmann &c. 3) [*pl.* -männer or -leute] [in fam. lang., with a particular accent on Haupt] a capital man. —männinn, *f.* captain's wife or lady. —mannschaft, *f.* dignity and office of a captain; *it.* jurisdiction of a captain, captaincy. —masche, *f.* a large mesh. —mast, *m.* the main-mast. —mauer, *f.* chief or principal wall, main-wall. —merkmahl, *n.* chief, main or distinctive sign, mark or character. —miethmann, *m.* principal tenant. —minengang, *m.* [in mining] principal gallery. —mittel, *n.* principal remedy; *it.* *fig.* principal means [V. also above]. —musterung, *f.* a general review. —narr, *m.* arrant fool, V. Erznarr. —neigung, *f.* chief inclination, leading propensity. —nenner, *m.* [in arithmetic] chief or general denominator. —niederlage, *f.* 1) [in commerce] a principal warehouse, store-house or magazine. 2) total defeat or overthrow. —note, *f.* V. —ton. —ort, *m.* the chief place; V —stadt. —person, *f.* the principal person or [in a play] character, head, chief. —pfahl, *m.* the principal pile or stake. —pfarre, *f.* a principal or capital benefice or living. —pfeiler, *m.* a principal pillar. —pflaster, *n.* a capital, excellent plaster [V. also above]. —pforte, *f.* the chief or great gate. —pfosten, *m.* principal post or stake. —planet, *m.* primary planet. —post, *f.* —postamt, *n.* general post-office. —posten, *m.* 1) the principal post or stake. 2) [in commercial transactions] the principal charge, sum or item [of an account or bill]. —preis, *m.* the first or great prize. —priester, *m.* cardinal. —product, *n.* 1) V. —erzeugniß. 2) [in mathematics] total produce. —punkt, *m.* principal or main point. Die vier —punkte [des Himmels], the four cardinal points. *it.* V. Augenpunkt, Gesichtspunkt. —quartier, *n.* headquarters. —quelle, *f.* chief source, headspring. —rad, *n.* the principal or main wheel. —rebell, *m.* chief, leader, or ringleader of the rebels. —rechnung, *f.* main or general account. —rechnungsart, *f.* the principal form or rule of arithmetic. Die vier —rechnungsarten, the four principal rules or operations of arithmetic. —recht, *n.* V. —fall 3). —regel, *f.* a general or principal rule. —register, *n.* 1) table of the contents of a book, index. 2) the great register or record. 3) Das —register einer Orgel, the principal register of an organ. —reif, *m.* principal hoop, trussing hoop. —reihe, *f.* 1) principal row. 2) [in heraldry] chief supported. —religion, *f.* the predominant religion [of a country]. —richtung, *f.* 1) the main, chief or principal direction, bearing or tendency of a thing, of the workings of the mind &c. 2) scaffold, scaffolding. —riegel, *m.* [in artillery] transom of a gun-carriage. —ring, *m.* the principal ring [V. also above]. —riß, *m.* 1) principal or capital chink or crack. 2) the general sketch or plan. —rolle, *f.* principal part, leading character. Die —rolle spielen, to act the principal part. —runde, *f.* [in milit. affairs] main rounds. —sache, *f.* chief matter, main point. —sänger, *m.* —sängerinn, *f.* first or principal singer, a singer of the first order. —satz, *m.* main proposition or point; *it.* leading theme; *it.* axiom. —säule, *f.* principal or capital column. —schacht, *m.* the principal shaft or pit. —schaden, *m.* the greatest or principal loss or damage; *it.* a great damage. —schanze, *f.* principal entrenchment. *—schelm, *m.* an arrant rogue or knave. —schiff, *n.* the admiral's or commodore's ship, the flag-ship. —schild, *m.* principal escutcheon. —schlacht, *f.* pitched battle, great, decisive battle. —schlagader, *f.* principal artery. Die —schlagadern, the carotid arteries [V. also above]. —schlüssel, *m.* master-key. —schmuck, *m.* chief ornament [V. also above]. —schoß, V. —geschoß. —schrift, *f.* 1) the original writing, original [of a work]. 2) the principal work or writing of an author. —schriftsteller, *m.* a principal or classical author or writer. —schuld, *f.* the capital or principal debt. Die Zinsen hat er bezahlt, aber die —schuld steht noch, he has paid the interests, but he still owes the principal. —schuldner, *m.* principal debtor. —schule, *f.* a great or central school. —schur, *f.* principal shearing [V. also above]. —schwein, *n.* [among sportsmen] a boar five years old. *Fig.* †[in contempt] a hoggish fellow. —schwierigkeit, *f.* main or principal difficulty. —segel, *n.* main sail. Die —segel, courses. —seite, *f.* the principal side. Die —seite an einem Gebäude, the front, forepart or face of a building; die —seiten einer Bastei, the faces of a bastion. [V. also above]. —sitz, *m.* principal seat or place; *it.* the seat of government, capital. —sohle, *f.* the iron shoe of the plough. —sorge, *f.* the principal care or anxiety. —spaß, *m.* a capital joke. —spieler, *m.* 1) a capital, great or passionate gambler. 2) [= Bankhalter] who holds the banque, banker. —sprache, *f.* 1) the predominant language [of a country]. 2) original language; *it.* mother-tongue. —spruch, *m.* 1) a convincing or demonstrative passage. 2) an axiom. 3) V. —urtheil. —stadt, *f.* capital city or town, metropolis, capital; *it.* Die —städte eines Landes, the principal or chief towns of a country. —städter, *m.* —städterinn, *f.* the inhabitant of the capital. —städtisch, *adj.* and *adv.* belonging or peculiar to a capital. —stamm, *m.* 1) the trunk of a tree; *it.* *fig.* V. —geld. 2) chief or principal tribe or race. —stände, *pl.* the states general or principal states of a kingdom &c. —ständer, *m.* the principal post of a partition-wall; *it.* king-post or king-piece. —stärke, *f.* chief or principal strength or force. Die —stärke des Heeres, the principal force of the army; die Geschichte ist seine *—stärke, he chiefly excels in history, history is his strong side or point, his forte. —stärkung, *f.* a corroborative medicine, a corrobo[rant]. —stein, *m.* 1) main or principal stone, [illegible] stone. 2) V. Grundstein 1). —stelle, *f.* [1)] V. Oberstelle. 2) V. —posten 1). 3) principal passage; *it.* V. —spruch 2). 4) V. Schling[illegible] —stimme, *f.* principal voice; [in music] [illegible] —stock, *m.* 1) V. —geschoß. 2) V. —[illegible] —stoff, *m.* the principal ingredient or [illegible] *Fig.* the principal subject or point, head [of a] discourse &c.] —stollen, *m.* [in mining] principal adit. —strahl, *m.* principal ray. —stra[ße], *f.* 1) principal street. 2) high-way, main [road]. —streich, *m.* 1) a capital stroke. 2) a capital trick. —streichen, *n.* [in mining] principal direction of a metallic vein or lode. —strich, *m.* fundamental line, *it.* V. Umriß. —stück, *n.* the principal piece or part, head, [V. also above]. Das —stück einer Maschine, the chief or principal piece of a machine; die —stücke in einem Wappen [in heraldry], the honorable pieces; das —stück und das Nachspiel, the play and after piece; die —stücke des christlichen Glaubens, the principal articles of [the Christian] faith; *it.* die —stücke in einem Buche, the chapters or sections of a book; erstes —stück, first chapter [V. also above]. —stuhl, *m.* V. —geld 2). —sturm, *m.* general storm or attack upon a town. —stütze, *f.* 1) the principal prop or support. *Fig.* Eine —stütze seines Thrones, a principal supporter of his throne. 2) [in geometry] the whole sine. —summe, *f.* the principal sum, the total or whole sum; *it.* V. —geld 1). —sünde, *f.* capital sin, V. Todsünde; *it.* principal sin. Das Trinken, das Fluchen ist seine —sünde, drinking, swearing is his principal sin or main fault. —tag, *m.* the principal day. —tänzer, *m.* —tänzerinn, *f.* principal dancer; *it.* the first dancer, dancer of the first order. —tau, *n.* main cable. —theil, *m.* the greatest or principal part. Der —theil eines Schiffes, the body or hull of a ship. —theilnehmer, *m.* —theilnehmerinn, *f.* the principal party concerned in a business. —thor, *n.* the principal gate. —thür, *f.* the principal door. —ton, *m.* main sound; [in music] the principal tone. —treffen, *n.* 1) V. —schlacht. 2) centre of an army. V. Mitteltreffen. —treiben, *n.* [among sportsmen] a general beating of the wood [in order to start the game]. —treppe, *f.* the great or principal staircase. —trumpf, *m.* matadore. —tugend, *f.* cardinal virtue. Menschenliebe ist eine —tugend, charity is a cardinal virtue; *it.* principal virtue. Seine —tugend ist Verschwiegenheit, his principal virtue lies in his being discreet. —übel, *n.* 1) a principal evil. 2) the greatest evil [V. also above]. —uhr, *f.* the principal clock. —umriß, *m.* principal sketch, outline or contour. —umstand, *m.* principal circumstance. —unterscheidungsmerkmahl, *n.* the distinctive character, sign or token. —unterschied, *m.* principal or essential difference. —urheber, *m.* principal author. —urkunde, *f.* principal or original document. —ursache, *f.* main or principal cause, V. —grund 1). —urtheil, *n.* principal or definitive sentence. V. Endurtheil. —ventil, *n.* V. —windklappe. —veränderung, *f.* general, principal or important change. —verbrechen, *m.* a principal or capital crime. —vergnügen, *n.* greatest or principal pleasure. —vermögen, *n.* principal fortune or property; *it.* principal, capital. —verrath, *m.* —verräther, *m.* V. Hochverrath &c. —versehen, *n.* great error, mistake, or oversight; *it.* the principal error or fault. —volk, *n.* the most numerous people; *it.* the mightiest people. —wache, —wacht, *f.* main guard, main guard house. —wahrheit, *f.* fundamental truth. —wall, *m.* principal rampart. —wand, *f.* V. —mauer. —weg, *m.* the high-way, main-road. —werk, *n.* principal or most important work. Das —werk der Orgel, the principal part or the principal stops of an organ; *it.* chief matter, main point. —wind, *m.* a wind blowing from one of the cardinal points, cardinal wind. —windklappe, the principal valve [of an organ]. —wirkung, principal effect. —wissenschaft, *f.* principal or fundamental science, V. Grundwissenschaft. —wohnung, *f.* principal habitation or residence. —wort, *n.* 1) principal, essential, energetical word. 2) [in grammar, *Substantiv] a noun substantive, noun, substantive. —wunde, dangerous wound [V. also above]. —wurf, *m.* a capital, excellent throw. —wurzel, *f.* the main or principal root, V. Pfahlwurzel. —zahl, *f.* principal number; *it.* cardinal number, V. Grundzahl. —zahlwort, *n.* a numerical word expressing a cardinal number. —zeichen, *n.* principal sign; [in astronomy] cardinal sign. —zeichnung, *f.* a capital drawing. —zeitwort, *n.* [in grammar] a principal or substantive verb. Das —zeitwort und das Hülfszeitwort, the principal verb and the auxiliary verb. —zeuge, *m.* principal witness. —ziel, *n.* the principal or main aim or end. —zierde, *f.* the principal or greatest ornament [V. also above]. —zins, *m.* principal rent. —zoll, *m.* principal toll. —zöller, *m.* chief toll-gatherer. —zug, *m.* principal stroke or feature. Die —züge in ihrem Gesichte sind regelmäßig, her principal features are regular; [in mining] der —zug eines Ganges, the principal direction of a metallic vein or lode. *Fig.* Großmuth ist der —zug seines Charakters, generosity is the principal trait of his character. —zweck, *m.* main or principal end or aim.

Häuptchen, ||Häuptlein, *n.* [-s, *pl.* -] V. Haupt.

Häuptel, *n.* [-s] [in mining] the best slich.

Häuptelkohl, *m.* [-es, *pl.* -e] cabbage which forms a head.

Häupteln, *v. intr.* to form into a head [said of certain plants, such as cabbage, lettuce].

Häuptelsalat, *m.* [-es, *pl.* -e] lettuce which forms a head, cabbage-lettuce.

Häuptenstück, *n.* [-es, *pl.* -e] V. [the usual word] Hauptstück.

||Häuptlein, V. Häuptchen.

Häuptling, *m.* [-es, *pl.* -e] principal nobleman, chief, chieftain.

Hauptlings, Häuptlings, *adv.* with the head foremost, over head, headlong.

Hauptlos, *adj.* and *adv.* headless, acephalous. *Fig. a)* destitute of a chief or leader, headless. *b)* V. Kopflos.

Hauptsächlich, *adj.* and *adv.* chief, principal, main; chiefly, principally, mainly, particularly, above all. Darauf kommt es — an, that's the main point; worauf ich — bestehe, ist &c., what I principally insist on, is &c.; das —ste, V. Hauptsache.

Haus, [-es, *pl.* Häuser] [Sax., Dan., Sw. *hus*, Eng. *house*, Croatic *kusha*, from hüten = decken, to cover] 1) [in a general sense] a cover, shelter. Das — der Schnecke, the house, cover or shell of the snail; die Schildkröte trägt ihr — auf dem Rücken, the tortoise carries its house on its back; V. Bienen—, Hühner—, Schnecken—, Tauben—, Vogel—. 2) [in a more limited sense] any building or shed. Das — des Herrn, the house of God; ein neues, ein altes —, a new, an old house; ein vierstöckiges —, a house of four stories. V. Back—, Bet—, Brau—, Garten—, Gewächs—, Schieß—. *Fig.* * Mit der Thür in's — fallen, to speak or act inadvertently, heedlessly or inconsiderately, to blurt out. 3) [in the most limited sense] a building or edifice for the habitation of man, house. Die Nomaden wohnen nicht in Häusern, the Nomads do not live in houses; ein eigenes — haben, to have a house of one's own; von — zu — gehen, to go from house to house: hence *a)* = Wohnung, habitation, lodging. Er kommt nie aus dem —e, he never goes out of doors, he never stirs abroad; er ist krank, er muß zu —e bleiben, das — hüten, he is ill, he must keep within doors, he is confined to the house; zu —e seyn, to be at home; er traf sie nicht zu —e, he found her not at home; Einen aus dem —e jagen, to turn any one out of doors; Jeder ist Herr in seinem —e, everybody is master in his own house; er ist bei uns wie zu —e, he is as it were at home with us; er hat ihm das —, sein — verboten, he has forbidden him his house; Einen in sein — aufnehmen, in's — nehmen, to shelter, to harbour, to lodge any one; der Herr, die Frau vom —e, the master, the mistress of the house, the landlord, the landlady; nach —e gehen, kommen, bringen, tragen, to go, come, bring, carry home; von —e kommen, to come from home; von —e abwesend seyn, to be from home; *prov.* — und Hof verlassen, to leave one's house and home; [in astronomy] die 12 Häuser der Sonne [= die 12 Zeichen], the twelve houses of the heavens; das — eines Planeten, the house of a planet. **Fig.* Er hätte mit allem diesem zu —e bleiben können, he might have kept all this to himself; in einer Sache zu —e seyn, to be well versed in or conversant with a thing; er ist in dieser Wissenschaft ganz zu —e, he is thoroughly master of this science; er ist mit seinen Gedanken nicht zu —e [= zerstreut], he is absent, inattentive or thoughtless; er ist nicht wohl zu —e [= nicht bei Verstande], he is not in his right senses, he is out of his wits or senses, he is crack-brained. *b)* = Heimath, one's own country, home. Einen Brief von —e bekommen, to receive a letter from home; er hat nach —e geschrieben, he has written to his friends at home; er ist in England zu —e, he is a native of England; das Rennthier ist in den nördlichsten Ländern zu —e, the reindeer inhabits the most northern countries; diese Pflanze ist nur in heißen Himmelsstrichen zu —e, this plant grows or thrives only in hot climates; er ist nirgends zu —e, he has neither house nor home, he is a vagabond. *Fig.* *Er ist ein Narr, ein Schelm von —e aus, he is an arrant fool, an arrant rogue or knave. 4) *Fig. a)* all those who dwell under the same roof, in one house. Das ganze — lief ihm zu Hülfe, the whole house ran to his assistance. *b)* all those who belong to the same family, house, family. Er wurde mit seinem ganzen —e eingeladen, he was invited with his whole family; ein gutes, ein sehr angesehenes —, a good, a very respectable house or family; er ist von gutem —e, he is of a good family; das — Oesterreich, the house of Austria; ein adeliges, ein altes —, a noble, an ancient house or family; er hat sein — emporgebracht, he has raised his family. *c)* household affairs, domestic concerns, domestic management. Sein — ist gut eingerichtet, his house is well ordered or arranged; seinem —e gut vorstehen, gut — halten, to manage one's household or domestic affairs well, to be a good housekeeper; sie hält ihrem Bruder —, she is her brother's housekeeper; sein — bestellen, to set one's house in order; bestelle dein —, denn du wirst sterben [in Scripture], set thy house in order, for thou shalt die; mit seiner Zeit gut — halten, to employ, to manage one's time well. *d)* [in commerce] a commercial or mercantile house. Angesehene Häuser in London, respectable houses in London.

Haus-älster, *f.* the domestic or common magpie. —altar, *m.* household altar. —andacht, *f.* private devotion. —anzug, *m.* V. —kleid. —apotheke, *f.* a chest of drugs or medicines kept in the house. —arbeit, *f.* work done at home or in the house. —arm, *adj.* ashamed to beg. Ein —armer, a poor man ashamed to beg, who receives charity in his house. —ärn, V. —flur. —arrest, *m.* arrest in one's house. Er hat —arrest, he is confined in his house, he is a prisoner at his house.

—arzenei, *f.* domestic medicine, family remedy. **—arzeneikasten**, *m.* V. —apotheke. **—backen**, *adj.* V. —gebacken. **—backenbrod**, *n.* V. —brod. **—bau**, **Häuserbau**, *m.* the building of a house, of houses. **—beamte**, *m.* officer of the household. **—bedarf**, *m.* the things or necessaries wanted in a house. **—bediente**, *m.* domestic servant. Die sämmtlichen —bedienten, V. —dienerschaft, —gesinde. **—besitzer**, *m.* **—besitzerinn**, *f.* owner or proprietor of a house. **—bettel**, *m.* the practice of begging from door to door. **—bettler**, *m.* **—bettlerinn**, *f.* a beggar, beggar-woman, that asks charity from door to door. **—bier**, *n.* home-brewed beer; *it.* beer for the family. **—blase**, *f.* V. Hausenblase. **—brauch**, *m.* V. —gebrauch. **—brenner**, *m.* [in nat. history] stag-beetle, the great horn-beetle or bull-fly. **—brief**, *m.* a document testifying the purchase of a house, purchase-contract of a house, V. Kaufbrief. **—brod**, *n.* household bread; *it.* V. Gesindebrod. **—buch**, *n.* book of housekeeping. **—büffel**, *m. fig.* [in popular language] Dieser Bediente ist der —büffel, that man is the drudge of the family. **—bursche**, *m.* 1) a lad or young man serving in a family, footboy. 2) a student lodging in any one's house at the university. **—capelle**, *f.* V. —kapelle. **—dieb**, *m.* **—diebinn**, *f.* a thief stealing in a dwelling-house. **—diebstahl**, *m.* a theft committed in a dwelling-house. **—diele**, *f.* V. —flur. **—dienerschaft**, *f.* all the servants of a house or family. Die —dienerschaft eines Gesandten, eines Cardinals, an ambassador's, a cardinal's household. **—drache**, *m. fig.* [in popular language] a troublesome wife, scold, shrew, termagant. **—durchsuchung**, *f.* domiciliary visitation. Man hat eine allgemeine —durchsuchung in der ganzen Stadt vorgenommen, they have searched all the houses of the town. **—ehre**, *f.* 1) the honour of the house or family. Die —ehre machen, retten, to do the honours of the house. 2) [in fam. lang., especially in jest] V. —frau 1). **—ehrn**, *m.* V. —flur. **—elster**, *f.* V. —älster. **—ente**, *f.* tame or domestic duck. **—erziehung**, *f.* private education. **—eule**, *f.* white owl, common barn-owl, church-owl. **—fliege**, *f.* house-fly. **—flur**, *f.* entrance hall of a house. **—frau**, *f.* 1) mistress of a house or family, housewife, landlady. 2) V. —hälterinn. **—freund**, *m.* **—freundinn**, *f.* friend of the house or family, intimate friend, a familiar; *it.* [frequently in jest] cavaliere servente, cicisbeo. **—friede**, **—frieden**, *m.* 1) domestic peace or tranquillity. 2) domestic security. **—gebacken**, *adj.* home-baked, baked for the use of the family. —gebackenes Brod, V. —brod. **—gebrauch**, *m.* 1) established custom of a family. 2) use in the house, domestic use or necessaries. Zum —gebrauche ist dieser Rock gut genug, this coat is good enough for the house; so viel ich für meinen —gebrauch bedarf, as much as I want for my household or family. **—gefieder**, **—geflügel**, *n.* poultry, barn-door fowl. **—geist**, *m.* familiar spirit, hobgoblin. *Fig.* Die Liebe ist ein —geist, love is a familiar. V. Kobold. **—geld**, *n.* V. —miethe 2), —zins. **—genoß**, *m.* **—genossinn**, *f.* 1) inmate of the same house. 2) lodger, V. Miethmann. 3) a person belonging to, a member of a family. 4) die —genossen: *a*) family. *b*) domestic servants, V. —gesinde. **—genossenschaft**, *f.* 1) state of living together at the same house or with the same family. 2) the inmates of the same house, family, household. 3) V. —gesinde. **—geräth**, *n.* utensils for the house, household furniture, household stuff. SYN. Hausgeräth, Möbeln. All the implements and utensils destined and requisite for housekeeping are denominated Hausgeräth. By Möbeln is generally understood such articles as are added to the interior of a house or apartment for convenience or ornament. Kitchen utensils belong to the Hausgeräth; sophas, musical instruments, pictures &c. to the Möbeln. **—geschäft**, *n.* domestic business. **—gesellschaft**, *f.* domestic society. **—gesetz**, *n.* domestic law, family law. **—gesinde**, *n.* domestic servants. **—gewand**, *n.* V. —kleid. **—gewehr**, *n.* domestic arm or weapon. **—giebel**, *m.* the gable end of a house. **—glück**, *n.* domestic happiness. **—gott**, **—götze**, *m.* household god. **—gottesdienst**, *m.* divine service performed in a private house or family, family worship, V. —andacht. **—grille**, *f.* domestic cricket. **—haft**, *f.* V. —arrest. **—hahn**, *m.* house-cock, domestic cock. **—halt**, *m.* V. —haltung. **—halten**, *v. intr.* 1) to keep house, to manage the affairs of a family. Gut —halten, to be a good manager or housekeeper, to manage the household-affairs well. Sie hält ihm —, she is his housekeeper. 2) to manage with frugality or economy, to husband, to economize. Mit seinem Einkommen —halten, to husband, to economize one's income. **—halter**, **—hälter**, *m.* 1) a man who keeps a house, householder, master of a family. 2) house-steward. Der ungerechte —halter [in Scripture], the unjust steward. 3) a good manager, economist. **—hälterinn**, *f.* 1) a woman who superintends the concerns of a family. Eine gute —hälterinn, a good housewife, a saving, thrifty woman, a good economist; sie that sich viel darauf zu gute, eine treffliche —hälterinn zu seyn, she prided herself much upon being an excellent contriver in house-keeping. 2) a female servant who has the chief care of the family, housekeeper. **—hälterisch** [hältig], *adj.* and *adv.* skilled in housekeeping, experienced in economical management, economical. Ein —hälterischer Mann, a good economist; —hälterisch leben, to live with economy, sparingly; sein Einkommen —hälterisch verwenden, to economize one's income. *Fig.* Er ist —hälterisch mit der Zeit, he husbands, employs time well. **—hältigkeit**, *f.* economy. **—haltung**, *f.* 1) the management, regulation and government of a family or the family concerns, housekeeping, economy. Sie versteht die —haltung gut, she is a good housewife. 2) family, household. Es wohnen vier —haltungen in diesem Hause, there are four families that live or lodge in that house. V. also Wirthschaft. **—haltungsbuch**, *n.* 1) book of housekeeping. 2) an economical book. **—haltungsgrundsatz**, *m.* economical principle or maxim. **—haltungskunst**, *f.* the art of housekeeping, economic art. **—haltungsregel**, *f.* rule of economy. **—haltungssache**, *f.* economical affair. **—haltungswissenschaft**, *f.* economic science, economics. **—hammel**, *m.* a wether kept in a house for fatting, house-wether; **fig.* one who keeps much at home, who hardly ever stirs out of doors, V. Stubenhocker. **—henne**, *f.* V. —huhn. **—herr**, *m.* 1) master of a house, landlord. 2) master of a family, V. —vater. **—herrenrecht**, *n.* the right of the master of a house. **—herrschaft**, *f.* 1) household government. 2) the master and mistress of the house. Die —herrschaft ist ausgegangen, the master and mistress of the house are gone out. **—hoch**, *adj.* and *adv.* as high as a house. **—hofmeister**, *m.* steward. Der —hofmeister des Königs, the comptroller of the king's household. **—huhn**, *n.* domestic hen or fowl. **—hund**, *m.* 1) [opposed to wilder Hund or Wildhund] domestic dog. 2) [a dog kept to guard the house] housedog. **—jungfer**, *f.* 1) [better: Tochter vom Hause] unmarried daughter of the house. 2) house-maid; *it.* maiden housekeeper. **—käfer**, *m.* **—käferchen**, *n.* death-watch. **—kalender**, *m.* economical almanack. **—kaninchen**, *n.* domestic rabbit. **—kanzler**, *m.* [at the court of Vienna] chancellor of the house. **—kapellan**, **—kaplan**, *m.* family-chaplain, chaplain of the house, chaplain of a domestic chapel. **—kapelle**, *f.* domestic chapel. **—kasse**, *f.* cash for household expenses. **—katze**, *f.* domestic cat. **—kauf**, *m.* purchase of a house. **—keller**, *m.* cellar of the house. **—kellner**, *m.* butler. **—kleid**, *n.* **—kleidung**, *f.* clothes worn in the house, dishabille, undress. Sie war im —kleide, she was in a dishabille or undress. **—knecht**, *m.* a man-servant that does coarse work in a house; *it.* hostler or boots [at an inn]. **—kost**, *f.* household fare. **—kreuz**, *n. Fig.* 1) domestic grief, affliction or calamity. *2) [especially in jest] a scold, shrew, termagant. **—krieg**, *m.* domestic warfare, domestic dissension. **—krone**, *f.* a crown belonging to a family, hereditary crown. **—laterne**, *f.* lantern in the entrance hall of a house. **—laub**, *n.* [in botany] house-leek, rose-root. **—lauch**, *m.* [in botany] 1) V. —laub. 2) leek. **—leben**, *n.* domestic life. **—lehrer**, *m.* family preceptor, family tutor, private tutor [in a family or house]. **—lehrerstelle**, *f.* place of a family tutor or preceptor. **—leinwand**, *f.* home-spun linen, linen-cloth for the use of a family. **—leute**, *pl.* 1) people of the house or family. 2) lodgers. 3) domestic servants. 4) V. Miethsleute. ***—lüge**, *f.* V. Nothlüge. **—mädchen**, *n.* V. Stubenmädchen. **—magd**, *f.* house-maid, maid-servant of the house, female servant of all work. **—mann**, *m.* 1) V. —genoß. 2) V. Miethsmann. **—mannskost**, *f.* V. —kost. **—marder**, a common marten. **—mark**, *n.* [in botany] spicknel. **—marschall**, *m.* the marshal of a prince's household. **—mast**, **—mastung**, *f.* stall feeding of swine. **—maus**, *f.* common or domestic mouse. **—meister**, *m.* superintendent of the household, the keeper of a nobleman's [illegible] house. **—miethe**, *f.* 1) a contract respecting a house hired or rented. Einem die —miethe aufkündigen, to give any one warning. 2) house-rent, V. also —zins. **—mittel**, *n.* household medicine, domestic remedy. **—motte**, *f.* domestic moth. **—mutter**, *f.* mother of a family. *Fig.* Sie ist eine rechte or gute —mutter, she is a good housewife. **—mütterlich**, *adj.* and *adv.* belonging to or becoming a mother of a family or a good housewife. Die —mütterlichen Pflichten, the duties of a mother of a family. **—naht**, *f.* the common or simple seam. **—ordnung**, *f.* rule of the house, domestic order. Er hält immer gute —ordnung, he always keeps good order in his house. **—orgel**, *f.* a small house-organ. **—otter**, *f.* the common or ringed snake. **—pfaffe**, *m.* [in contempt] V. —kapellan. **—plage**, *f.* a nuisance or inconvenience in a house, domestic trouble. V. —kreuz. **—plan**, *m.* 1) the plan of a house. 2) plan of housekeeping or economy. **—platz**, *m.* 1) a place or piece of ground where a house is built or may be built. 2) V. —flur. **—postille**, *f.* a book of devotion for the use of a family, postil. **—prediger**, **—priester**, V. —kaplan. **—rath**, *m.* V. —geräth. [illegible] te, **—ratze**, *f.* common or domestic rat. [illegible] **recht**, *n.* right belonging to a person [illegible] house, domestic right. Sein —recht gebrauchen, to make use of one's domestic authority. [illegible] gel, *f.* 1) rules of family-life. 2) V. —haltungsregel. **—regiment**, *n.* household government. **—riegel**, *m.* bolt of the street-door. [illegible] coat for wearing in the house. **—sache**, *f.* domestic affair; *it.* V. —haltungssache. [illegible] [obsolete, except in law] an inhabitant wh[illegible] house of his own, owner, proprietor of a house, householder. —sässig, *adj.* and *adv.* settled in a house of one's own. Alle —sässige Einwohner der Stadt, all the inhabitants of the town who have houses of their own, the householders. V. Ansässig. —schabe, *f.* stinking beetle, tenebrio. —schatz, *m.* 1) V. —lasse. 2) family-treasure. Der fürstliche —schatz, the treasure of the crown, a prince's or sovereign's own or private treasure. 3) V. —frau 1). —schlachten, *n.* the killing of sheep, pigs or cattle at home for meat. —schlächter, *m.* domestic butcher. —schlange, *f.* V. —otter. —schloß, *n.* lock of the street-door. —schlüssel, *m.* key to the street-door; *it.* key belonging to a house. —schmuck, *m.* the jewels of the crown. —schneider, *m.* tailor to a family, family tailor. —schoß, *m.* V. —steuer 1). —schule, *f.* private school. —schuster, *m.* shoemaker to a family. —schwalbe, *f.* house-swallow, domestic swallow. —schwamm, *m.* morel. —schwein, *n.* househog. —schwelle, *f.* threshold of a house. —segen, *m.* 1) domestic blessing, prosperity or happiness. 2) **Fig.* children. Das ist mein ganzer —segen, these are all my children. —setze, *f.* a plantation of vines before the house. —sorge, *f.* domestic care, care of a family. —speise, *f.* V. —kost. —sperling, *m.* house sparrow. —spinne, *f.* domestic spider. —staat, *m.* domestic republic. —stand, *m.* domestic condition, state of domestic life. In den —stand treten, to marry and establish a domestic state, to settle. —steuer, *f.* 1) tax paid for a house, house tax. 2) [in popular language] V. Hochzeitgeschenk. —streit, *m.* domestic dispute or quarrel. —stunde, *f.* 1) lesson received at home, private lesson [as opposed to school-lessons]. 2) the usual hour at which one returns home in the evening from one's club &c. Er hält seine —stunden pünktlich, he punctually keeps his hours. —suchung, *f.* examination or search of a house, domiciliary visitation. —tafel, *f.* *Fig.* a table containing the duties of domestic life. —taube, *f.* a tame or domestic pigeon, housepigeon. —tenne, *f.* V. —flur. —teufel, *m.* *Fig.* [in popular language] a contentious person in a house or family; [applied to a wife] scold, shrew, termagant. Er, sie ist ein wahrer —teufel, he, she is a real devil in his, her house. —thier, *n.* domestic animal. —thor, *n.* gate of a house. —thür, *f.* street-door, front-door. —trank, *m.* V. —trunk. —trauer, *f.* family mourning. —trauung, *f.* marriage-ceremony celebrated in a private house, nuptial ceremony performed, by special license, at a private dwelling. —trunk, *m.* family beverage; common or ordinary beverage or drink. —truppen, *pl.* a prince's household-troops. —tuch, *n.* V. —leinwand. —übel, V. —kreuz 1). —uhr, *f.* house-clock. —unke, 1) V. —otter. 2) Feldkröte. 3) *Fig.* V. —hammel, *fig.* —vater, father of the family. Ein guter —vater, a good husband, economist or manager. —verstand, common sense, good sense. —vertrag, *m.* family compact. 2) V. —brief, Miethvertrag. —verwalter, *m.* 1) house steward. 2) keeper of a nobleman's &c. house. —verwalterinn, housekeeper. —verwaltung, *f.* management of the concerns of a family. —vieh, *n.* animals or cattle belonging to a house; domestic cattle; *it.* V. —thier. —vogel, *m.* 1) V. —geflügel. 2) V. Stubenvogel. —vogt, *m.* 1) V. —verwalter 2). 2) V. Stockmeister. —vogtei, *f.* lodging or dwelling of a steward. —wanze, *f.* house-bug, domestic bug. —wasche, *f.* washing in the house. —wäsche, *f.* common or ordinary linen. —weib, *n.* 1) V. [a better word] —frau 1). 2) V. [the more usual word] —wirthinn 1). —wesen, *n.* domestic concerns, domestic affairs; *it.* family, household. Im —wesen erfahren, skilled in housewifery. —wiesel, *n.* weasel. —wirth, *m.* 1) a man who keeps or manages a house or family. Ein guter —wirth, a good manager of a house, a good economist; ein schlechter —wirth, a spendthrift. 2) master of a house, landlord, host. Auf die Gesundheit unseres gütigen —wirthes! a toast for our kind host! 3) [obsolescent] husband. —wirthinn, *f.* 1) a female manager of a house, housewife. Eine gute —wirthinn, a good housewife, manager or economist. 2) mistress of a house, landlady, hostess. Zu Ehren unserer schönen —wirthinn, in honour of our fair hostess. 3) [obsolescent] wife. —wirthschaft, *f.* domestic economy, domestic concerns, house-keeping; *it.* economics. —wurm, *m.* *Fig.* V. —hammel, *fig.* —wurz, —wurzel, *f.* 1) Die große —wurz, house-leek. 2) Die kleine —wurz, wall-pepper, the lesser house-leek. —zeuge, *m.* the inmate of a house or the member of a family who appears as a witness. —zins, *m.* house-rent. V. also —miethe 2). —zucht, *f.* domestic discipline.

Häuschen, ‖**Häuslein**, *n.* [-s, *pl.* -] [*dim.* of Haus] a little house, a small habitation, a cottage or cot. [rather provincial, = der Abtritt], a house of office, convenient or necessary house, privy.

Hausen, *v. intr.* 1) to live, to dwell. In diesem alten Schlosse — die Eulen, this old castle is the haunt of owls; man glaubt, es hause ein böser Geist in diesem Walde, this wood is thought to be haunted; diese Eheleute — nicht mit einander [in popular language], these married people do not dwell or live together; *hier werde ich nicht lange — [= bleiben], I shall not stay here long. 2) [in popular language] to keep house. Sie versteht das — gut, she is a good housewife, manager or economist; sie haust übel or schlecht, she is a bad economist; sie — gut, nicht gut mit einander, they live well, do not live well together. 3) *Fig.* to behave, to demean one's self. Arg, übel —, to proceed roughly, to make a great havoc; der Regen hat arg gehaust, the rains have done great mischief; er hauset [= tobt] wie unsinnig, he storms or rages like a madman; der Wind hauset [= tobt] fürchterlich, the wind roars or blusters dreadfully; was hauset so arg im Hofe? what makes such a noise in the yard? 4) V. Herbergen.

Hausen, *m.* [-s, *pl.* -] or —fisch, *m.* [-es, *pl.* -e] [from the Turkish word *usun* = long] common sturgeon, huso [of the genus Accipenser].

Hausen-blase, *f.* the sound or airbladder of the huso or sturgeon; hence, isinglass. —rogen, *m.* the roes of the huso or sturgeon, caviar. —stein, *m.* a calcarious concretion found in the intestines of the huso, bezoar of the huso or sturgeon.

Hausiren, [unusual] **Häusern**, *v. intr.* to go from house to house either asking alms or offering goods for sale. Ein —der Bettler, a beggar who asks charity from door to door, *it.* [in general] a vagabond, beggar; mit Waaren — or — gehen, to sell goods by carrying them about, to hawk goods about, to peddle.

Hausirer, [unusual] **Häuserer**, *m.* [-s, *pl.* -] hawker, pedlar.

Häuslein, *n.* V. Häuschen.

Häusler, *m.* [-s, *pl.* -] one who has no house of his own, but lodges in the house of another, lodger; [in law] cottager, cotter.

Häuslich, *adj.* and *adv.* 1) settled in a place or habitation. Sich wo — niederlassen, to settle in a place. 2) [belonging to the house or home, to the family] domestic. —e Angelegenheiten, domestic concerns; —e Pflichten, —es Glück, —e Ruhe, domestic duties, happiness, tranquillity. 3) skilled in domestic management, economical, frugal, thrifty.

Häuslichkeit, *f.* 1) [chiefly in familiar lang.] domesticity, domestic life. Sie hat viel Sinn für —, she is fond of a domestic life, *it.* she has good ideas of economy; wie leben Sie in Ihrer —? how do you live in your house and family-circle? er gefällt sich am besten in seiner —, he is best pleased at home, he feels most comfortable at home. 2) economy, housewifery. 3) frugality, thriftness.

Häusling, *m.* [-es, *pl.* -e] V. Häusler.

Haußen, *adv.* [provinc.] without, out of doors, abroad. V. Außen, Außerhalb.

Haut, *f.* [*pl.* Häute] [Sax. *hyd*, Eng. *hide*, L. *cut-is*, G. κύτ-ος, allied to hüten, schützen, i. e. decken, to cover, therefore, in general, a covering] skin. Die — auf der Milch, the thin skin formed on the surface of milk, cuticle of the milk; es hat sich eine — auf diesen eingemachten Sachen gebildet, a skin has been formed on these preserves; die — or Schale von Obst, the skin of fruit; die Häute or Schalen einer Zwiebel, the coats of an onion. [in anatomy] tunic, membrane, coat. Die Häute, welche die Muskeln umgeben, the membranes of the muscles; V. Bein—, Fett—, Hirn—, Schleim—, Trommel— &c. Die — eines Menschen, einer Schlange, the skin of a man, the skin or slough of a serpent; sie hat eine sehr weiße —, she has a very white skin, is of a very fair complexion; die — schauert mir, so oft ich daran denke, I shudder whenever I think of it; einem Thiere die — abziehen, abstreifen, to skin an animal; die abgezogene, abgestreifte — eines Löwen, Ochsen &c., the hide or skin of a lion, of an ox &c.; Häute bereiten, gerben, to dress, to curry a hide or skin; eine rohe, ungegerbte —, a raw, undressed hide or skin; zwischen — und Fleisch, between skin and flesh; †mit — und Haar fressen, to eat up entirely; *bis auf die — naß werden, to get thoroughly wet or drenched, wet to the skin; *mit heiler — davon kommen, to come off with a whole skin; *er ist nichts als — und Knochen, es ist nichts als — und Knochen an ihm, he is nothing but skin and bones. *Fig.* [in popular lang.] Er steckt in keiner guten —, he is sickly, he has a crazy body; ich möchte nicht in seiner — stecken, I would not be in his skin; das geht bis auf die —, that stings to the quick; Einem auf die — gehen, recht auf die — greifen, to urge, to press any one hard; ich möchte vor Freuden aus der — springen, I am ready to leap out of my skin with joy; er möchte vor Zorn aus der — fahren, he frets, he is ready to burst with anger or vexation; sich seiner — wehren, to defend one's own life; seine — wohlfeil verkaufen, seine — theuer verkaufen, to set little value upon one's life, to sell one's life dearly; mit der —, mit seiner — bezahlen, to pay with one's skin or life, to suffer death for &c.; es gilt seine —, his life is at stake; seine — selbst zu Markte tragen, to expose one's self to danger; *prov.* jeder Fuchs muß seine eigene — zu Markte tragen, every fox must pay his own skin to the flayer; die — juckt ihm nach Schlägen, he has a mind to be beat, or to have his hide curried; er ist ein Schalk in der —, eine lose —, he is a cunning blade; wieder in die alte — schlüpfen, to recommence one's former course of life; auf der faulen — liegen, to be idle, to idle; †Einem die — voll schlagen, to beat or cudgel any one soundly, to curry any one's coat; Einem die — or das Fell über die Ohren ziehen, to flay, to fleece any one; [in familiar language used for a man] eine lustige —, a jolly blade or dog; eine gute ehrliche —, a silly man. SYN. V. Balg.

Haut-ausschlag, *m.* cutaneous eruption or efflorescense, rash, V. Ausschlag 4). —beschreibung, *f.* dermography. —blutader, *f.* [in anatomy] [am Fuße] mother-vein, saphena. *—cultur, *f.* V. —pflege. —drüse, *f.* cutaneous gland. —farbe, *f.* colour of the skin, complexion. —flügel, *m.* membraneous wing. —flügelig, *adj.* having membraneous wings. Die —flügeligen Insekten, hymenoptera. —form, *f.* [among gold-beaters] mould of about a thousand leaves. —fresser, *m.* the leather-eater, dermestes. —käfer, *m.* V. —fresser. —krankheit, *f.* cutaneous disease. —lehre, *f.* dermology. —mäuschen, *n.* —muskel, *m.* [in anatomy] cutaneous muscle. —pflege, *f.* the culture of the skin. —reinigung, *f.* the cleaning of the skin. —schmiere, *f.* [in anatomy] sebaceous humour. Die Drüsen oder Bälge, in welchen die —schmiere abgesondert wird, sebaceous glands. —wurm, *m.* cutaneous worm.

Häutchen, ‖**Häutlein,** *n.* [-s, *pl.* -] [*dim.* of Haut] thin skin, cuticle, film, pellicle, membrane.

Hautbois, Hautboist, [pron. Hoboa, Hoboist] V. Hoboe, Hoboist.

Häuteln, *v. tr.* to strip off the cuticle or pellicle, to peel. Eine Ochsenzunge —, to peel or skin a neat's tongue.

Häuten, I. *v. tr.* to strip off the skin, to skin. Einen Hasen —, to skin a hare. II. *v. r.* sich —, to cast the skin. Die Schlangen und Seidenwürmer — sich, serpents and silkworms cast their sloughs or skins; seine Hand häutet sich, his hand peels.

Häuticht, *adj.* and *adv.* resembling skin, membraneous, membraniform, skinny. Ein —er Stoff, a skinny matter.

Häutig, *adj.* and *adv.* furnished with a skin, skinned; [chiefly used in composition, as] Dick—, thickskinned; *it.* consisting of membranes, membraneous; [in anatomy] —es Band, membraneous ligament; [in botany] ein —es Blatt, a membranaceous leaf.

Häutlein, V. Häutchen.

Hauung, *f.* the act of cutting or felling, V. Hauen.

Havarie, Havarei, Haverei, *f.* [mercantile term] average. Große —, gross average; kleine —, particular average. V. Haferei.

Hay, Hayfisch, Hayn, &c. V. Hai, Haifisch, Hain.

Häzel or **Hätzel,** *f.* [*pl.* -n] V. Atzel 2) and Perrücke.

He, Heh, *interj.* 1) [used in questions] Was würden Sie sagen, he? well, what should you say? *it.* [in vulgar language] he [hä]? [wie sagen Sie?] ha, what do you say? 2) [used in calling] He! he da! ho! ho there? 3) [an expression of joy] He! laßt uns lustig seyn! eigh or come, let us be merry! 4) [an expression of laughter] He, he, he! or hä, hä, hä! ha, ha, ha! V. Ha, Hi.

1. **Hebe,** *f.* 1) [from heben = to raise, to lift] [rather provincial] lifting up. In der — und Schwebe, lifted and suspended. 2) [in Scripture] V. Hebopfer.

2. **Hebe,** *f.* [in the Greek mythology] the goddess of youth, Hebe. *Fig.* [rather poetically] a beautiful young woman. *Sie ist eine wahre —, she is a perfect Hebe.

Hebel, *m.* [-s, *pl.* -] 1) lever. Die Kraft des —s, the power of the lever; der Unterstützungs- or Ruhepunkt eines —s, the fulcrum or prop, hypomochlion. 2) [among bakers = Hefe] leaven.

Hebelzeug, *n.* V. Hebezeug.

Heben, [Sax. *heavian*, Eng. *to heave*, Dan. häve, Sw. *haefwa*, allied to the Gr. ἔπω, ὑπ-τω] *ir.* I. *v. tr.* 1) [in familiar language = halten, to hold]. Etwas fest mit der Hand —, to hold a thing fast with the hand; *it.* as a *verb intrans.* Der Nagel hebt, the nail holds. 2) to raise, to heave, to lift. Eine Last —, in die Höhe —, to lift a burden; — Sie den Arm in die Höhe, raise or lift up your arm; er hat die Hand gegen seinen Vorgesetzten gehoben, he has lifted his hand against his superior; Seufzer — ihren Busen, sighs heave her bosom; Einen auf's Pferd —, to put any one on horseback; eine Dame in eine Kutsche —, to help a lady into a coach; Einen aus dem Sattel —, to throw any one off his horse, to unhorse any one, *fig.** to supplant any one; [mit einem Heber] Wein aus dem Fasse —, to draw wine out of a cask with a siphon; ein Haus — [among carpenters], to erect the timberwork of a house; ein Kind aus der Taufe —, to stand godfather or godmother to a child; einen Schatz —, to find out, to dig out a treasure; der Wind hebt den Staub, the wind raises the dust; [in printing] die Form aus der Presse —, to lift out the form; [in manege] dieses Pferd hebt gut [i. e. die Füße], this horse walks well, has a good walk. *Fig.* *a*) Es hebt mich zum Brechen, my stomach rises. *b*) Die Stimme — [= erheben], to raise the voice. *c*) Einen —, to promote any one in rank and honour, to raise any one to higher state or station; [in general] die Künste, die Gewerbthätigkeit &c. —, to encourage, to patronize the arts, industry &c. *d*) to elevate, to exalt, to rejoice. Dieser Gedanke, diese Hoffnung hebt den Geist, das Herz, that thought, that hope elevates, cheers or animates the mind, the heart. *e*) to embellish, to adorn, to set off, to relieve. Die Juwelen hoben ihre Schönheit, the jewels heightened her beauty; der Putz hebt das gute Aussehen noch mehr, dress sets off a good countenance. 3) to lift away as it were. *Fig.* *a*) Steuern, die Zölle —, to raise or levy taxes, to collect the customs. *b*) to remove, to solve. Schwierigkeiten —, to remove difficulties; Einwürfe, Zweifel —, to solve objections, doubts; einen Streit —, to settle a dispute; dies wird seine Aengstlichkeit —, that will dissipate his anxiety. II. *v. r.* sich —, 1) to move or pass upwards, to rise. Der Teig hebt sich, the dough rises. *Fig.* Der Preis von Waaren hebt sich, the price of goods rises. 2) sich weg — [= fortgehen, especially in emphatical language], to go away. Hebe dich weg von mir! get thee gone! *Fig.** Das Uebel hebt sich, the disorder gives way.

Heb-amme, *f.* midwife. —ammenkunst, *f.* midwifery, obstetrics. —ammenlohn, *m.* midwife's fee. —ammenstuhl, *m.* obstetric chair. —arm, *m.* [in mechanics] arm of a lever. —arzneikunde, *f.* the science of obstetrics. —arzneikunst, *f.* obstetrics. —arzt, *m.* V. Geburtshelfer. —eisen, *n.* V. Hebeeisen. —kunst, *f.* V. Entbindungskunst. —lade, *f.* V. Hebelade. ‡—meister, *m.* V. —arzt. —opfer, *n.* [in Scripture] heave-offering.

Hebe-arm, *m.* V. Hebarm. —balken, *m.* a beam by means of which any thing is heaved up or lifted up, lever. Die —balken einer Zugbrücke, the plyers of a drawbridge. —baum, *m.* a strong pole or staff for heaving or lifting up, lever. —bock, *m.* a sort of gin or engine for heaving; [in seamen's language] crab. V. Ziegenfuß. —baumen, *m.* V. Hebarm. —eisen, *n.* 1) iron crow, iron lever. 2) [in forges] a large poker. 3) [in surgery] elevatory, levator. —gabel, *f.* [among hunters] a forked pole, used in lifting the toils. —gerüst, *n.* V. —zeug. —kopf, *m.* V. Hebarm. —korb, *m.* a large flat basket with handles at both ends. —korn, *n.* corn taken for rent. —krahn, *m.*, —lade, *f.* a machine in the shape of a box, for lifting up heavy trees and placing them on a waggon, a crane, gin. —kunde, *f.* V. Entbindungskunst. —latte, *f.* V. Hebarm. —leiter, *f.* a machine for raising or lifting up; *it.* V. [illegible] mannswinde. —mahl, *n.* an entertainment given to builders or journeymen carpenters when they erect an edifice. —nagel, *m.* [among watchmakers] catch. —punkt, *m.* fulcrum, prop, hypomochlion. —schmaus, *m.* V. —mahl. —stange, *f.* V. —eisen. —tatze, *f.* V. Hebarm. —winde, *f.* V. —leiter. —zange, *f.* large tongs. —zänglein, *n.* [in surgery] elevatory. —zapfen, *m.* V. Hebarm. —zeug, *n.* an apparatus for raising any thing, gin, V. Hebel, Flaschenzug, Krahn, Winde, Ziegenfuß.

Heber, *m.* [-s, *pl.* -] 1) a person that raises or lifts up any thing, a raiser. 2) an instrument for raising any thing; [in mechanics] a lever, V. Hebel, Hebarm; [in surgery] elevatory, levator; [in anatomy] levator. Der — der Lippe, des Auges, the levator of the lip, of the eyelid. [in physics and hydraulics] siphon; die Schenkel eines —s, the legs of a siphon.

Heber-barometer, *n.* a barometer in the form or shape of a siphon. —förmig, *adj.* and *adv.* having the form or shape of a siphon.

Hebling, *m.* [-es, *pl.* -e] V. Hebarm.

Hebräer, *m.* [-s, *pl.* -] 1) [Hebräer as well as Jude are in the people's language often used in contempt] a Hebrew, Israelite or Jew. Der Brief Pauli an die —, the epistle of Paul to the Hebrews. 2) one skilled in the Hebrew language, hebraist. Er ist ein guter —, he is a good Hebrew scholar.

Hebräerinn, *f.* an Israelitish woman, Hebrewess, Jewess.

Hebräern, ***Hebraisiren,** *v. tr.* and *intr.* to hebraize; to make use of hebraisms. [Hebräern in popular language is often used contemptuously, to denote the manner, language or [illegible] of the Jews.]

Hebräisch, *adj.* and *adv.* Hebraic, Hebrew. Die —e Sprache, das —e, the Hebrew language or tongue, the Hebrew; die —e Grundsprache der heiligen Schrift, the Hebrew text of the holy scripture; eine der —en Sprache eigene Redensart or Wortfügung, eine —e Spracheigenheit, hebraism.

***Hebraismus,** *m.* [*pl.* Hebraismen] hebraism.

Hebriden, *pl.* the Western Isles, Hebrides. Die neuen —, [a group of islands in the South-Sea] the New Hebrides.

Hebridier, *m.* [-s, *pl.* -] Hebridierinn, *f.* a native or inhabitant of the Hebrides, a Hebridian.

Hebridisch, *adj.* and *adv.* Hebridian, in the manner of the Hebridians.

Hebung, *f.* 1) the act of raising or lifting. *Fig.* Die — [Erhebung] von Steuern, the gathering, raising or levy of taxes. 2) Die — einer Schwierigkeit, Krankheit, the removal of a difficulty, of a disease. 3) *pl.* Die —en, revenues, taxes, V. Einkünfte, Steuern. 4) elevated place. V. Erhöhung, Erhabenheit.

Hebungskammer, *f.* V. [illegible]kammer.

Hechel, *f.* [*pl.* -n] [Dutch *hekel*, Dan. *hegle*, Bohem. *hachle*, Eng. *hatchel*, allied to Haken, hook] hatchel or heckle. Den Flachs durch die — ziehen, to hatchel the flax. *Fig.* *Einen durch die — ziehen, in der — haben, tüchtig durch die — ziehen, to censure any one with severity, to criticise, satirize, to lash, † to hatchel any one, V. Durchhecheln, *fig.*

Hechel=bank, *f.* heckling-bench or hatchel-bench. —**frau**, *f.* a woman employed in hatcheling. —**kamm**, *m.* [in botany] Venus's comb, scandix. —**krämer**, *m.* one who deals in hatchels, a dealer in hatchels, seller of hatchels. —**macher**, *m.* hatchel-maker. —**mann**, *m.* 1) V. Hechler. 2) V. —krämer. —**scherz**, *m.* a biting jest, taunt. —**schrift**, *f.* a satirical writing, satire. —**stuhl**, *m.* V. —bank. —**weib**, *n.* V. —frau. —**werg**, *n.* refuse of flax or hemp, tow, hards. —**zahn**, *m.* the tooth of a hatchel.

Hecheln, *v. tr.* to hatchel [flax, hemp]. *Fig.* * Einen —, to censure or criticise any one severely, to lash, to satirize any one, V. Durchhecheln.

Hechler, *m.* [-s, *pl.* -] —**inn**, *f.* hatcheler. *Fig.* a critic, satirist, censurer.

Hechse, V. Hakse.

Hechsel, V. Häckerling.

Hecht, *m.* [-es, *pl.* -e] [Low Sax. Haked, Sax. Hacod, Eng. *hake* or *hakot*] pike [a freshwater fish] Ein kleiner —, ein Hechtchen, Hechtlein, a small pike, a jack, pickerel; ein sehr großer, starker —, a very large pike.

Hecht=angel, *f.* pike-hook. —**apfel**, *m.* a large yellow apple with red streaks, red streak apple, rambour. —**bars**, —**börs**, —**bärschling**, *m.* pike-perch. —**brühe**, *f.* 1) water in which a pike is boiled. 2) sauce for pike. —**brut**, *f.* a fry of pikes. —**grau**, *adj.* pike gray [a sort of lightgray]. —**kiefern**, *pl.* the gills of a pike. —**könig**, *m.* a yellow pike with black spots. —**kopf**, *m.* head or jowl of a pike. —**kraut**, *n.* pickerel-weed. —**reißer**, *m.* one that guts, salts and barrels pikes; a seller of pikes. —**saß**, *m.* V. —brut. —**schimmel**, *m.* a gray horse. —**s=leber**, *f.* the liver of a pike. —**s=milch**, *f.* the milt or roe of a pike. —**suppe**, *f.* V. —brühe 1). —**teich**, *m.* pond for pikes.

Heck, *n.* [-es, *pl.* -e] or **Hecke**, *f.* [*pl.* -n] [allied to Hag] 1) a fence of laths or rails. 2) [in seamen's language] the flat hindpart of a ship, the flat part of the stern, sternframe, scutcheon, V. Spiegel.

Heck=balken, *m.* [in seamen's language] great transom. —**boot**, *n.* [in seamen's language] fly-boat. —**bord**, *m.* [in seamen's lang.] tafferel of a ship. —**flagge**, *f.* naval ensign. —**stützen**, *pl.* [in seamen's language] top-timbers of the fashion-piece.

1. **Hecke**, *f.* [*pl.* -n] 1) the pairing of birds, and the act of breeding. 2) the pairing-time, the time of breeding [of birds]. 3) the place where birds are kept for breeding, breeding-cage. 4) brood, hatch, V. Brut.

2. **Hecke**, *f.* [*pl.* -n] 1) hedge, fence. Eine lebendige —, a quickset hedge; eine todte —, a dead or dry hedge, a fence [made of branches &c.] 2) V. Buschwerk, Gesträuch.

Heck=apfel, *m.* V. Heckenapfel. —**feuer**, *n.* an irregular sort of firing among soldiers, when they fire individually as they have loaded. †—**groschen**, *m.* [in popular language] a false or bad penny. †—**herberge**, *f.* hedge alehouse, hedge tavern. —**holz**, *n.* white cornelberry-tree, common privet. —**jagen**, *n.* 1) [rather provincial] hunting at unlawful seasons and on forbidden places, poaching. 2) chase where the game is driven out of bushes and hedges to certain places. —**jäger**, *m.* poacher. †—**münze**, *f.* 1) false or bad coin. 2) place where money is counterfeited. †—**münzer**, *m.* money-forger. —**pfahl**, *m.* gate post. †—**pfennig**, V. —groschen. —**schnarre**, *f.* V. Heckenschnarre.

Hecken=apfel, *m.* paradise-apple. —**baum**, *m.* hedge-row tree. —**beere**, *f.* gooseberry. —**binder**, *m.* one who makes hedges, hedger. —**feuer**, *n.* V. Heckfeuer. —**gang**, *m.* —**gäßchen**, *n.* a walk between two hedges, lane. —**holz**, *n.* V. Heckholz. —**hopfen**, *m.* wild hops. —**käfer**, *m.* may-bug. —**kerbel**, *m.* wild chervil. —**kirsche**, *f.* 1) fly honey-suckle, xylosteum. 2) bush cherry tree, dwarf cherry tree. —**rose**, *f.* dogbriar, wild rose, eglantine. —**same**, *m.* furze with rough pointy leaves, waythorn. —**scheere**, *f.* shears for clipping hedges, hedgebill, hedging-bill. ‖—**schmätzer**, *m.* V. —vogel. —**schnarre**, *f.* crake, corn-crake, land-rail. —**schneider**, *m.* clipper or dresser of hedges. —**sichel**, *f.* V. —scheere. —**springer**, *m.* V. —vogel. —**strauch**, *m.* a shrub that grows in hedges or that is proper for making hedges. —**vogel**, ‖—**wenzel**, *m.* hedge sparrow. —**wicke**, *f.* the wild vetch. —**winde**, *f.* V. Zaunwinde. ‖—**wittwe**, *f.* V. —vogel. —**zaun**, *m.* quickset-hedge.

Hecken, [allied to hegen] I. *v. tr.* to hatch, to breed, to bring forth young ones. *Fig.* Zähne —, to breed teeth. II. *v. intr.* to sit close together. Syn. Hecken, Brüten. Brüten denotes simply the sitting of the bird on its eggs in order to hatch them, to brood. Hecken comprehends also the laying of eggs, and even the pairing and nesting. In common language, therefore, Hecken is not applied to domestic fowls, which only lay eggs and hatch them without pairing and nesting.

Heck=drüse, *f.* [in surgery] an excrescence or protuberance of the throat, wen. —**groschen**, *m.* [in German popular superstition] a penny or any other coin of large size, called a breeding penny. —**lauge**, *f.* V. Mutterlauge. —**münze**, *f.* V. —groschen. —**mutter**, *f.* [in popular langular] a woman who produces many children, a very prolific woman. —**pfennig**, *m.* V. —groschen. —**thaler**, *m.* V. —groschen. —**zeit**, *f.* breeding-time of birds, V. Brutzeit, Legezeit, Paarzeit.

Hecker, Heckerling, V. Häckerling.

Heckicht, Heckig, V. Buschicht, Buschig.

Heckse, *f.* V. Kniebug, Hakse.

Hecksel, *m.* [-s, *pl.* -] V. Häckerling.

Heda! *interj.* ho there!

Hede, *f.* tow, V. Werg.

Hederich, *m.* [-s] [in botany] *a*) wild radish, V. Ackerrettig. *b*) hedge mustard. *c*) charlock, V. Ackersenf. *d*) ground ivy, V. Erdepheu. *e*) monk's rhubarb, patience-dock.

Heer, *n.* [-es, *pl.* -e] [allied to Schaar] 1) any great number, or multitude. Ein — von Zuschauern, a vast multitude of spectators; ein — von Fliegen, Mücken, a host of flies, of gnats; ein — von Heuschrecken, Raupen, an army of locusts, of caterpillars; das himmlische —, the celestial host, the angels; das wilde or wüthende —, Arthur's chase, the wild Chase; ein [ganzes] — von Zungen, a host of tongues; ein [ganzes] — von Gründen anführen, to bring a world of arguments or reasons. 2) [in a more limited sense] a body of men embodied for war, army. Ein auserlesenes —, a picked or select army; ein — aufrichten, auf die Beine bringen, to raise an army; an der Spitze des —es, at the head of the army.

Heer=arm, *m.* V. Heeresarm. —**bann**, *m.* the calling out of the people for the defence of the country, arriere-ban. —**bewegung**, *f.* V. —schwenkung. —**biene**, *f.* V. Raubbiene. —**es=arm**, *m.* an arm or column of an army. —**es=folge**, *f.* the obligation of following the army of the sovereign, V. —bann. —**es=kraft**, *f.* V. —kraft. —**es=zug**, *m.* V. —zug. —**fahne**, *f.* the great standard of an army. ‡—**fahrt**, *f.* V. Feldzug. —**flucht**, *f.* desertion. —**flüchtig**, *adj.* and *adv.* deserting or having deserted the army. —flüchtig werden, to desert [from the army or one's colours]. —**flüchtige**, *m.* deserter. —**führer**, *m.* leader of an army, commander in chief. —**fürst**, *m.* [in poetry] V. —führer. —**gans**, *f.* 1) the ash-coloured heron. 2) coot. —**gepäck**, *n.* baggage of an army. —**geräth**, *n.* the furniture of an army, equipage. —**gewette**, *n.* [formerly] the accoutrements of a fallen warrior which fell to the eldest son over and above his equal share of the inheritance; *it.* the right to such accoutrements. —**haufe**, *m.* a corps, division of an army. —**horn**, *n.* [formerly] trumpet. —**kern**, *m.* the strongest and most substantial part of an army, the choice men of the army. —**kraft**, *f.* a numerous host, army. —**kuh**, *f.* bell-cow. —**lager**, *n.* camp. —**macht**, *f.* V. —kraft. —**meister**, *m.* 1) [rarely used] V. —führer. 2) commander of an order of knights, grand master. —**meisterthum**, *n.* V. Großmeisterthum. —**moos**, *n.* horse-tail, shave-grass. —**pauke**, *f.* kettledrum. —**pauker**, *m.* kettle-drummer. —**rauch**, *m.* V. Höherauch. —**raupe**, *f.* V. Zugraupe. —**säule**, *f.* column of an army, V. Zugsäule. —**schaar**, *f.* corps or division of an army; legion. *Fig.* Der Herr der —schaaren, the lord of hosts; die himmlischen —schaaren, the celestial hosts, the angels. —**schatz**, *m.* 1) military chest. 2) [in law] fines of alienation. —**schau**, —**schauung**, *f.* review of any army. —**schild**, *m.* 1) a shield used in war. 2) dignity of a knight, knighthood. —**schnepfe**, *f.* common snipe. —**schwenkung**, *f.* evolution, manoeuvre of an army. —**spitze**, *f.* head of an army; *it.* van, vanguard. —**steuer**, *f.* war-tax, contribution. —**straße**, *f.* military road; *it.* [in general] highway, main-road. —**volk**, *n.* an army, troops. —**wagen**, *m.* a carriage or waggon belonging to an army, ammunition waggon, baggage waggon; [in astronomy] Charles's wain. —**weg**, *m.* V. —straße. —**wurm**, *m.* a collection of certain worms which hang together in clusters. —**zug**, *m.* 1) march of an army. 2) V. Feldzug. —**zwang**, *m.* V. —esfolge.

Heerd, Heerde, Heerling, V. Herd, Herde, Herling.

Hefe, *f.* [*pl.* -n] [from heben, to raise; that which has been raised by fermentation and has settled afterwards on the bottom of a vessel] yeast, barm, lees, dregs. Die — vom Weine, the dregs or lees of wine; den Wein von den —n ziehen, to draw off the wine from the lees, to rack the wine. *Fig.* Bis auf die — [= ganz] austrinken, to drink the whole, to drink all up; den Freudenbecher bis auf die — austrinken, to drink the bowl of pleasure to the dregs; er wird die — davon trinken müssen, he will be made to feel the disagreeable consequences, he must suffer for it; *auf die — kommen, auf den —n sitzen, to be reduced to extremity, to be aground; die — des Volkes, the dregs of the people. Syn. V. Abschaum.

Hefen=brod, *n.* bread made with yeast. —**kuchen**, *m.* cake made with yeast. —**stück**, *n.* —**teig**, *m.* flour formed into dough by means of yeast.

Hefficht, *adj.* and *adv.* resembling yeast or dregs, yeast-like; *it.* smelling or tasting of yeast or lees.

Hefig, *adj.* and *adv.* containing yeast, barmy, full of lees.

1. **Heft**, *n.* [-es, *pl.*-e] *dim.* —chen, ||—lein, *n.* [from haben = halten] handle, haft. Das — eines Messers, the haft of a knife; das — eines Degens, Dolches, the hilt of a sword, of a dagger; ein — an ein Messer machen, to put a knife in a haft, to haft a knife. *Fig.* Eine Sache beim —e [= auf die rechte, gehörige Art] angreifen [in fam. lang.], to go the right way to work; das — der Regierung ergreifen, to seize the reins of the state or empire; das — in Händen haben, to have the advantage, to have got the better of, *it.* to hold the reins of the state or empire.

Heft=macher, *m.* one that hafts knives. —**scharte**, *f.* the haft of the pruning-knife. [V. also below.]

2. **Heft**, *n.* [-es, *pl.* -e] [from heften = to unite] 1) several leaves or sheets of paper stitched together, book, paperbook. Die —e einer Zeitschrift, the numbers or parts of a journal or periodical. 2) an instrument for pinning or stitching any thing together, pin, hook [connected with a loop], V. Haft *m.*; [in botany] tendril of a vine, clasper.

Heft=eisen, *n.* iron-rod of glassmakers. —**faden**, *m.* a thread for stitching. —**haken**, *m.* hook of a sewing-press. —**kraut**, *n.* [in botany] lion's foot. —**lade**, *f.* [among bookbinders] sewing-press, sewing-board. —**nadel**, *f.* a long needle for sewing or stitching, stitching-needle. —**pflaster**, *n.* a plaster for fastening the remedies upon the wound, sticking-plaster. —**pulver**, *n.* agglutinative powder. —**scharte**, *f.* an osier for binding hoops. [V. also above.] —**schnur**, *f.* [among bookbinders] pack-thread. —**span**, *m.* V. —scharte. —**strick**, *m.* [in mining] a rope for tying timber &c. together.

Hefte, *f.* the act of tying the vines to their props.

1. **Heftel**, *f.* [*pl.* -n] and *n.* [-s, *pl.*-] pin, peg, hook, clasp.

Heftel=eisen, *n.* V. Hefteisen. —**macher**, *m.* V. Nadler.

2. **Heftel**, *m.* [-s, *pl.* -] [among hunters] a pole or stake to which the toils are fastened.

Hefteln, *v. tr.* to fasten by means of a peg, hook or pin.

Heften, *v. tr.* [Sw. *haefta*, Icel. *hefta*, allied to haben, Gr. ἅπ-τω, L. *ap-io, hab-eo, cap-io*] to fasten. Mit Nägeln —, to nail; er wurde an das Kreuz geheftet, he was nailed to the cross, was crucified; die Weinstöcke, die Reben —, to tie the vines to their props; mit der Nadel —, to stitch, to sew; eine Wunde —, to sew a wound together; mit weiten Stichen or verloren —, to sew with long stitches, to baste; ein Buch —, to sew or stitch a book; mit Stecknadeln —, to pin; mit Häkchen —, to hook. *Fig.* Die Augen, Gedanken auf etwas —, to fix one's eyes, one's thoughts upon a thing; die Augen starr or unverwandt auf Einen —, to have one's eyes always fixed upon any one; †Einem etwas auf den Aermel —, to pin a lie upon any one's sleeve. V. also Binden and Knüpfen.

Heftig, *adj.* and *adv.* [probably from the old hebig = great, strong, considerable] 1) forcible, violent, vehement. Ein —er Wind, a violent or boisterous wind; der Wind bläst —, the wind blows violently; ein —es Feuer, eine —e Hitze, a vehement fire, a vehement, intense heat; die Feinde machten ein —es Feuer, the enemies kept up a very brisk fire; ein —er Appetit, a ravenous appetite; —e Schmerzen, violent or smart pains; —e Begierden, vehement desires; ein —er Angriff, a violent attack; — weinen, to weep bitterly; — lachen, to break out into laughter, to burst into a loud laugh; er wurde — gerührt, he was strongly or violently affected. 2) [in a more limited sense] passionate, violent, vehement. Er ist sehr —, he is very passionate; ein —er Mann, a violent, passionate man; er ist von sehr —er Gemüthsart, he is of a very choleric disposition or temper; er wird leicht —, he takes fire presently, a little matter raises his passion; — lieben, to love passionately, vehemently; — hassen, to hate mortally; V. Auffahren[b], Aufbrausen[b], Hitzig.

Heftigkeit, *f.* violence, vehemence, impetuosity. Die — des Sturmes, the violence or vehemence of the storm; die — der Liebe, des Zornes, the vehemence of love, of anger; die — der Krankheit, the acuteness of the disease; er spricht mit —, he speaks with vehemence, passionately, vehemently; Alles, was er will, will er mit —, he is very wilful in all his desires. V. Hitze, Ungestüm.

||**Heftlein**, *n. dim.* of Heft.

||**Heftler**, *m.* [-s, *pl.*-] a rigid anabaptist.

Heftlos, *adj.* without a haft or handle.

Hege, *f.* [*pl.* -n] V. 1. Hain.

Hegen, V. Hägen.

Hege=baum, *m.* [among foresters] standel, tillar or tiller. —**reiter**, *m.* V. Hägereiter. —**zeit**, *f.* V. Hägezeit.

*__Hegira__, *f.* [pron. Hédschra] [in chronology, an epoch among the Mohamedans from which they compute time] Hegira.

Hegling, *m.* [-es, *pl.* -e] a kind of small white fish.

Heher, *m.* [-s, *pl.* -] jay. V. also Häher.

Hehl, *m. indeclin.* [V. Hehlen] concealment, secrecy. Etwas ohne — gestehen, to confess or own something without reserve or disguise, openly, frankly; ohne — sprechen, to speak frankly, openly, freely; *er hat es keinen —, he does it openly or barefaced; he does not deny it; he makes no secret of it.

Hehlen, *v. tr.* [Sax. *hecan*, Dan. häle, Eng. *to hill* (obsol. = to cover), L. *cel-are*; allied to hüllen, hohl] to conceal, V. Verhehlen.

Hehler, *m.* [-s, *pl.* -], —**inn**, *f.* concealer. Wenn es keine — gäbe, so gäbe es nicht so viele Stehler, if there were no receivers of stolen goods, there would not be so many thieves. *Prov.* Der — ist wie der Stehler, the receiver is as bad as the thief.

||**Hehlingen**, *adv.* [in popular language] under hand, in secret, secretly, stealthily.

Hehr, *adj.* and *adv.* [allied to herrlich, höher] [in poetry] holy, sacred, awful, dread, august, sublime, exalted, dignified. Heilig und — ist sein Name, holy and reverent is His name [the name of God]; —e Tugend, —e Schönheit, sublime virtue, majestic beauty. SYN. Hehr, Erhaben. Hehr implies a certain feeling of awe mingled with the idea of the sublime, which is expressed by Erhaben.

Hehr=messe, *f.* [= hohe Messe] high mass. —**rauch**, *m.* V. Höherauch.

Hehrthum, *n.* [in the catholic church] the holy sacrament.

Heida, Heisa, *interj.* [a shout of joy or exultation] huzza!

1. **Heide**, *f.* [*pl.* -n] [Sax. *haeth*, Eng. *heath*, Sw. *hed*, Dan. *hede*] heath. *a*) [in botany] heath [a plant of the genus Erica]. Ein Besen von —, a broom made of heath. *b*) a place overgrown with heath. Ueber eine große — gehen, to cross a large heath; die Lüneburger —, the heath of Lunenburg. *c*) a place overgrown with shrubs of any kind.

Heide=bereiter, *m.* forest-keeper. —**besen**, *m.* broom made of heath. —**biene**, *f.* heath-bee. —**bienkraut**, *n.* V. Kienapfel, Mutterkraut. —**blume**, *f.*, *dim.* —**blümchen**, ||—**blümlein**, *n.* 1) any flower growing on a heath, heath-flower. 2) V. Bartnelke. —**blüte**, *f.* the blossom of heath. —**busch**, *m.*, —**gebüsch**, —**gesträuch**, *n.* gorse, furze, whins. —**deich**, *m.* a dike made on moorish or fenny heaths. —**fench**, *m.* V. —**korn**. —**flachs**, *n.* flax-weed, toad-flax, purging-flax, mill-mountain. —**futter**, *n.* fodder growing on heaths. —**gebüsch**, —**gesträuch**, *n.* V. —busch. —**gries**, *m.* —**grütze**, *f.* grit or groats prepared from buckwheat. —**hahn**, *m.* grouse, moor-game. —**honig**, *m.* heath-honey. —**huhn**, *n.* grouse, moor-hen. —**knecht**, *m.* under forest-keeper. —**korn**, *n.* buckwheat. —**kraut**, *n.* 1) heath, sweetbroom. 2) berry-bearing heath. —**kresse**, *f.* wild dittander. —**land**, *n.* heath. —**lattich**, *m.* blue-coloured long-leaved lettuce. —**läufer**, *m.* V. —knecht. —**lerche**, *f.* wood-lark. —**angeld**, *n.* money paid for pasturage, V. Triftgeld. *Fig.* V. under Compositions of 2. Heide. —**n=ysop**, *m.* the dwarf cistus or little sunflower, the hedge hyssop, V. Kirschysop. —**n=meise**, *f.* tufted titmouse. —**n=reich**, *m.* 1) thlaspi or treacle-mustard. 2) — or —**n=rettig**, *m.* wild horse-radish. 3) V. —schwamm. —**n=schmuck**, *m.* saw-wort, serratula. V. Färberscharte. —**pfrieme**, *f.* broom, genista. —**rauch**, *m.* a fog rising over heaths. —**reiter**, *m.* V. —bereiter. —**rose**, *f.* heath rose. —**schaf**, *n.*, ||—**schnucke**, ||—**schmucke**, ||—**schmacke**, *f.* sheep kept on heaths. —**schwamm**, *m.* the eatable mushroom. —**schwarm**, *m.* a swarm of heath-bees. ||—**siebt**, *n.* a scythe for cutting heath. —**strecke**, *f.* a heath. —**torf**, *m.* V. Rasentorf.

2. **Heide**, *m.* [-n, *pl.*-n] [Eng. *heathen*, Icel. *heidin*, Dan. and Sw. *hedning*; probably one who lives in the country or woods, paganus] a heathen, pagan, gentile. Die Götzen der —n, the idols of the pagans. *Fig.* *Wie ein — fluchen, to swear like a trooper; er ist ärger als ein —, he is worse than a heathen.

Heiden=bekehrer, *m.* a converter of the pagans or gentiles, missionary. —**bekehrung**, *f.* the conversion of the gentiles. —**bild**, *n.* idol. —**dreck**, *m.* the first faeces of infants, meconium. *Fig.* —**geld**, *n.* [in famil. lang.] an extravagant sum of money. Das kostet mich ein —geld, that costs me a vast deal of money. —**glaube**, *m.* the belief or religion of the pagans or gentiles. —**haar**, *n.* the first hairs of an infant. —**haut**, *f.* V. —dreck. —**koth**, *m.* V. —dreck. —**land**, *n.* a country inhabited by pagans or infidels. *Fig.* —**leben**, *n.* [in fam. language] Ein —leben führen, to lead a heathenish life, to live like a heathen, to lead a dissolute, unlawful or reckless life. —**lehrer**, *m.* V. —bekehrer. —**sitte**, *f.* a heathenish custom. Nach —sitte verfahren, to act like a heathen. —**tempel**, *m.* V. Götzentempel.

Heidechse, *f.* V. Eidechse.

Heidel, *m.* [-s] V. Heidekraut.

Heidel=beere, *f.* 1) bilberry. 2) whortleberry. Die rothe —beere, the red whortleberry, V. Preiselbeere. —**beerkamm**, *m.* bilberry-comb. —**beerstaude**, *f.*, —**beerstrauch**, *m.* 1) the shrub bearing the bilberry, bilberry. 2) the shrub bearing the whortleberry, berry-bearing heath. —**blume**, *f.* the yellow aneanth. —brei, m. a pap or gruel made of groats of buckwheat. —gries, m. V. Heidegries. -hahn, m. V. Heidehahn, Birkhahn.

Heidenschaft, f. V. Heidenthum.

Heidenthum, n. [-es] 1) paganism, heathenism, gentilism. 2) the heathen or pagan nations.

Heiderich, m. V. Hederich.

Heiderling, m. [-s, pl. -e] V. Heideschwamm.

Heidicht, adj. and adv. resembling a heath.

Heidig, adj. and adv. full of heath, heathy. -es Land, heathy land.

Heidnisch, adj. and adv. heathenish, heathen, pagan. Fig. Ein —es Leben führen, -leben, to lead a heathenish life, to live like heathen.

*Heiduk, m. [-en, pl. -en] a Hungarian foot-soldier; it. [chiefly] a footman dressed in Hungarian costume and appointed to attend a carriage or sedan-chair.

Heie, f. [pl. -n] [from hauen] a heavy mallet or wooden hammer, a beetle, stamper, rammer; it. paving-beetle, a paver's rammer.

Heien, v. tr. to beat or strike with a beetle or rammer.

Heikel, Heikelig, adj. V. Häkelig.

Heil, adj. and adv. [V. Heil, n.] not hurt, sound, whole; it. restored to soundness, well, whole. *Auf —er Haut schlafen, to sleep in a whole skin; *mit —er Haut davon kommen, to come off with a whole skin, † to save one's bacon; seine Wunde wird —, ist noch nicht —, his wound is healing, is not yet healed or well; [in Scripture] sie blieben an ihrem Ort im Lager, bis sie — wurden, they abode in the camp till they were whole.

Heil, n. [-es] [Sax. hael, haelo, Dan. heel, Sw. hel and helsa, Gr. ὅλος, L. salus, allied to hohl] 1) prosperity, happiness, welfare. Das — des Staates, des Volkes, the welfare of the state, of the people; sein — in der Flucht suchen, to betake one's self to one's heels for safety; Einem alles Glück und — wünschen, to wish any one all happiness; sein — versuchen, to try one's luck, to take one's chance; das war sein —, that saved his life, it. that saved him from ruin; [in Scripture] das — der Seelen, das ewige —, eternal welfare, salvation, redemption. used as a term of salutation or congratulation, hail. — dem Könige! long live the king! — der Sonne! hail to the sun! — den Waffen des Königs! success to the arms of the king! — dem Volke, welches &c., happy the people who &c. V. —jahr. Syn. Heil, Glück. Heil refers to the wished for state, in opposition to the disagreeable. Glück applies to outward good, Heil to inward.

Heil-bringend, adj. and adv. salutary, salutiferous. V. Heilsam. —bringer, m. [little used] saver, deliverer. —geber, m., —geberinn, f. a person who brings good luck, who is the author of one's safety or happiness. —jahr, n. year of salvation, any year reckoned from the birth of Christ. —monat, m. the month in which the Saviour of mankind was born, December.

Heils-ausschuß, m. a committee of the public welfare. —glaube, m. [little used] justifying faith. —gut, n. [in theology] a blessing proceeding from divine grace. —mittel, n. [in divinity] means of grace. —ordnung, f. dispensation of divine grace, doctrine of redemption.

Heiland, m. [-es, pl. -e] [in Scripture] 1) one who saves or preserves, saviour. Darum ward er ihr —, so he was their saviour. 2) by way of distinction, Jesus Christ, the Redeemer, Saviour. Jesus Christus ist der Welt—, Jesus Christ is the Saviour of the world. V. Erlöser.

Heilbar, adj. and adv. curable. Nicht —, incurable.

Heilbarkeit, f. curability.

†Heilbock, m. [-es, pl. -böcke] [from heilen = castriren] a gelded he-goat or buck.

Heilbutt, m. [-es, pl. -en] Heilbutte, f. [pl -n] [= Hellbutte] [a fish] halibut.

Heilen, I. v. tr. [V. Heil, n.] 1) [rarely used] to make whole, to repair, to mend. [in Script.] Und er heilete den Altar des Herrn, welcher zerbrochen war, and he repaired the altar of the Lord that was broken down. 2) [generally] to heal, to cure. Einen Kranken, eine Wunde —, to cure a sick man, to heal a wound; ein —des Mittel, V. Heilmittel. Fig. to deliver, to free, to relieve. Einen von einem Irrthume —, to free or reclaim any one from an error, to undeceive, to disabuse any one; von Vorurtheilen geheilt werden, to be cured of one's prejudices; Einen von seinem Kummer —, to relieve, ease or soften any one's grief. II. v. intr. and refl. to grow well, to heal. Seine Wunde wird bald —, his wound will soon heal. Fig. Dies sind Fehler, die sich unvermerkt von selbst —, those are faults of which we break ourselves insensibly.

Heil-anstalt, f. medical establishment, hospital. —art, f. method of curing, therapeutic system. —bad, n. medical or mineral bath; it. mineral waters. Das —bad von Spaa, von Baden &c., the baths of Spaa, of Baden &c. —blatt, n. meadow-rue, thalictrum. —brunnen, m. medicinal well or spring, mineral waters. —gott, m. the God of medicine, Aesculapius. —göttinn, f. V. Gesundheitsgöttinn. —gurke, f. V. Balsamapfel. —holder, —holunder, m. dane-wort or dwarf-elder, wall-wort. V. Attich. —kraft, f. healing or sanative power, power of healing, sanativeness. Eine Arzenei ohne —kraft, a medicine of no virtue; —kräfte besitzend, medicinal. —kräftig, adj. and adv. medicinal. —kraut, n. 1) any medicinal or virtuous herb. 2) [in botany] a) chickweed, V. Gauchheil. b) bear's breech, V. Bärenklau. —kräutlein, n. the least consound or comfrey. —kunde, f. science or art of curing or healing, medical science or art, medicine, therapeutics; it. [rarely] surgery. —kundig, adj. and adv. 1) understanding the art of healing. 2) pertaining to the healing art, therapeutic. —kunst, f. V. —kunde. —künstler, m. [often used as a jocose expression] V. Arzt. —methode, f. V. —art. —mittel, n. remedy, medicine, medicament, physic. —mittellehre, f. pharmacology. —pflanze, f. V. —kraut 1). —pflaster, n. healing plaster. —plan, m. plan of healing or curing; it. V. —art. —quelle, f. medicinal spring, V. —brunnen. —salbe, f. a healing salve or ointment, balm. —schmied, m. farrier. —stätte, f. a place of cure. —stätten suchen, to seek relief in a frequent change of position [said of a sick person who experiences a certain restlessness shortly before his dissolution]. —stoff, m. a drug. —stoffskunde, —stoffslehre, f. V. —mittellehre. —trank, m. a medicinal draught, potion. —wasser, n. V. Gesundbrunnen. —wissenschaft, f. V. —kunde. —wurz, —wurzel, f. any root or plant, having a sanative power. [in botany] a) rough parsnip. b) elecampane, inula, V. Alant. c) marsh-mallow. d) tormentil, septfoil. —wurzelsaft, m. opoponax.

1. Heiler, m. [-s, pl. -] [not much used] one who heals or cures, healer, curer; physician.

2. Heiler, m. [-s, pl. -] [probably from geilen = castriren] a gelding, V. Wallach.

Heilig, adj. and adv. [from Heil] 1) [not used] salutary, wholesome. Die —e Pflanze, lavender-cotton, Santolina Chamae [Cyparissus Linnei]; das —e Holz, V. Heiligenholz. 2) properly, whole, entire or perfect in a moral sense; hence, pure in heart, free from sin and sinful affections, holy. Der —e Gott, Geist, the holy God, Ghost or Spirit; die —e Jungfrau, the blessed Virgin; der —e Paulus, Saint Paul; die —e Magdalena, Saint Magdalen; ein —er Mensch, a holy man; —e Handlungen, Gedanken, godly actions, thoughts; ein —er Trieb, a godly motion; ein —es Leben, a godly, holy life; — leben, to lead a holy life; seid —, denn ich bin — [in Script.], be ye holy, for I am holy. 3) inviolable. a) Das —e römische Reich, the holy Roman Empire; das —e Ding [= Rothlauf, in popular lang.], Saint Anthony's fire; [in anatomy] das —e Bein, os sacrum; die —e Pulsader, arteria sacra; die —e Blutader, vena sacra; ein —es Versprechen, a sacred promise; sein Wort — halten, to keep one's word sacredly; ein Geheimniß — bewahren, to keep a secret sacredly; wir schwören bei Allem, was — ist, daß &c., we swear by all that is sacred, that &c.; ein anvertrautes Gut, ein anvertrautes Geheimniß sind —e Dinge, a deposit, a secret entrusted are sacred things; ihm ist nichts —, nothing is sacred for him; die Tempel, Kirchen sind —e Oerter, temples, churches are sacred or holy places. b) [in a more limited sense, opposed to profane or to common with respect to religion or religious rites] sacred, holy. Die —e Bibel, die —e Schrift, the holy bible, the holy writ or scripture; die —en Bücher, the sacred books; der —e Vater, his Holiness [the pope]; der —e (päbstliche) Stuhl, the holy see; das —e Kollegium, the sacred College; das —e Gericht, the holy Inquisition; die —e Woche, the holy week, passion week; die —en Gefäße, the holy vessels; der —e Tisch, the holy table, altar; das —e Oel, the holy oil; die —en Mysterien des Himmels, the sacred mysteries of heaven; die —en Schriftsteller, Geschichtschreiber, the sacred writers, historians; die —e Geschichte, sacred history; der —e Abend, eve of a festival or holiday, it. Christmas eve; *der —e Christ, Christmas, it. christmas-box; das —e Abendmahl, the Lord's supper, the communion, eucharist, V. Abendmahl 2); Einen — sprechen, to saint, to canonize any one; den Sabbath — halten, to observe the sabbath sacredly. c) entitled to reverence, reverend, venerable, august. Eine —e Stille, awful silence; sein — graues Haupt flößt Ehrfurcht ein, his venerable grey head strikes with awe; die —e Unschuld, sacred innocence; ein —er Eifer, a holy zeal, it. a very eager zeal; die —e Person des Königs, the sacred person of the king.

Heilig-butt, m. —butte, f. V. Heilbutt. —heu, n. lucern. —holz, n. V. Heiligenholz. —machend, adj. sanctifying. —machende Gnade, sanctifying grace. —macher, m. sanctifier. —machung, f. sanctification. —sprechen, v. tr. to saint, to canonize. Das —sprechen, die —sprechung, canonization.

*Heilfroh, adj. [heil is here allied to the Gr. ὅλ-ος = ganz; therefore: thoroughly glad] very, quite glad, gay or contented.

Heilig, n. a hymn beginning with the word holy. Das dreimal —singen, to sing the trisagion.

1. Heilige, m. [-n, pl. -n] a saint. Eine —, a female saint; der Tag aller —n, All-Saints-day, all-hallow, all-hallows, all-saints; die —n im Himmel, des Himmels, the saints of

heaven; die Gemeinschaft der —n, the communion of saints; *fig.* * er ist ein wunderlicher —r, he is an odd or queer fellow, † a rum one.

Heiligen-bein, *n.* 1) [in anatomy] os sacrum. 2) V. —gebein. —bild, *n.* image of a saint. —blende, *f.* [little used] niche of a saint. —buch, *n.* a chronicle or register of the lives of saints, legend, legendary. —dienst, *m.* worship or adoration of the saints. *—fresser, *m.* a great hypocrite, devotee or bigot. —gebein, *n.* bones or relics of a saint. —geschichte, *f.* a legend; *it.* V. —buch. —gestalt, *f.* the figure or shape of a saint. —glanz, *m.* V. —schein. —haus, *n.*, *dim.* —häuschen, ||—häuslein, *n.* or —kapelle, *f.* chapel of a saint. —hof, *m.* a holy place, a place where a church, convent &c. stands. —holz, *n.* V. Franzosenholz. —kreuzschwester, *f.* sister of the cross. —mährchen, *n.* a tale or story of a saint, legend. —pfennig, *m.* V. Pfaffenpfennig. —pfleger, *m.* churchwarden. —schein, *m.* [Nimbus, Glorie] glory. —sohle, *f.* V. Gottessohle. —woche, *f.* the week after a great festival, octave, V. Octave.

2. Heilige, *n.* [-n] that which is holy or sacred, sacred thing or place. Das — in der Stiftshütte und im Tempel zu Jerusalem, the holy place of the tabernacle and of the temple at Jerusalem. V. Allerheiligste.

Heiligegeistwurz, *f.* angelica, lingwort, longwort.

Heiligen, *v. tr.* [from Heil] to make inviolable as it were. Die geheiligte Person des Königs, the sacred person of the king; der Zweck heiligt die Mittel nicht, the aim or end does not justify the means. *it.* particularly, in a religious sense: *a*) =weihen, to consecrate, to hallow. Eine Kirche —, to consecrate a church; Etwas Gott —, zum Dienste des Herrn —, to consecrate something to God, to the Lord. *b*) to acknowledge and honour as sacred, to sanctify. Gott —, to sanctify God; geheiliget werde dein Name, hallowed be thy name; den Sonntag —, to keep the Lord's day. *c*) to make holy, to sanctify. Die Gnade heiligt uns, the grace of God sanctifies us; die Oerter, welche Christus durch seine Gegenwart geheiliget hat, the places which Christ has sanctified by his presence.

Heiligkeit, *f.* 1) holiness, sanctity, sacredness. Die — eines Ortes, the sanctity or sacredness of a place; die — der christlichen Religion, the holiness of the christian religion; die — des Eides, the sacredness of an oath; die — Gottes, the holiness of God; in dem Geruche der — sterben, to die in reputation of sanctity, to die a reputed saint. 2) [a title of the Pope]. Es hat Seiner — gefallen, his Holiness has been pleased.

‡Heiliglich, *adv.* in a holy manner, holily, V. Heilig.

Heiligthum, *n.* [-es, *pl.* -thümer] 1) a holy place, a sanctuary. 2) a holy thing, relic. Diese Kirche ist sehr reich an Heiligthümern, this church is very rich in relics; sie verwahrt es wie ein —, she means to make a relic of it.

Heiligthum-schänder, *m.* a profaner of sacred things, a sacrilegious man, a sacrilegist. *Fig.* a fellow who profanates every thing. —sraub, *m.*, —sräuber, V. Kirchenraub, Kirchenräuber.

Heiligung, *f.* the act of making holy, sanctification. Die — des Sonntags, the keeping the Lord's day.

Heillos, *adj.* and *adv.* wicked, very bad, flagitious, profligate. Ein —er Mensch, a villanous person; eine —e That, flagitious, atrocious, villanous action; — leben, ein —es Leben führen, to lead a vicious, profligate life; seine —e Neigung zum Spiele, his baleful or dismal propensity to gaming. *Fig.* *very poor or mean, wretched, miserable. Ein —er Wein, a wretched wine.

Heillosigkeit, *f.* quality of being wicked &c., wickedness, badness, flagitiousness; *fig.* * wretchedness.

Heilsam, *adj.* and *adv.* salutary, wholesome. —e Kräuter, wholesome herbs. *Fig.* Eine —e Züchtigung, —e Gesetze, a wholesome correction, wholesome laws; —e Lehren, sound doctrines.

Heilsamkeit, *f.* salubrity, wholesomeness. Die — der Luft, der Speisen, the salubrity of the air, the wholesomeness of aliments. *Fig.* Die — von Lehren, Gesetzen, the wholesomeness of doctrines, laws.

Heilung, *f.* the act of healing or curing, cure. Dieses Mittel wird die — bewirken, this medicine will effect the cure.

Heilungs-art, *f.* V. Heilart. —mittel, *n.* V. Heilmittel.

Heim, *adv.* [perhaps from the old hemen = decken, to cover, therefore properly = Dach, roof, i. e. house, habitation; according to others from the old heimen = to inclose, to fence in] to one's own habitation or to one's own country, home.

Heim-begeben, *ir. v. r.* sich —begeben, to betake one's self home, to go or return home. —begleiten, *v. tr.* Einen —begleiten, to wait upon any one home, to see any one home. —bringen, *ir. v. tr.* to bring home. ‡ and ||—buch, *n.* a book containing the laws and regulations of a township. ||—bürge, *m.* [a sort of magistrate] clerk of a township. ||—bürgenamt, *n.*, —bürgenschaft, *f.* the office or place of such a magistrate. ||—bürgengericht, *n.*, —bürgensitzen, *n.* meeting of the magistrates or judges of a town or village in the open fields. —fahren, *ir. v. intr.* [used with seyn] to drive home, to go or ride home [in carriage or vessel]. —fahrt, *f.* return or journey home [in carriage or vessel]. —fall, *m.* [in feudal law] a passing or falling of any property or right to another person, devolution, reversion. Der —fall an den Lehensherrn, escheat. —fallen, *ir. v. intr.* [used with seyn] to fall to, to fall into the possession of, to devolve, to revert, [dem Lehensherrn] to escheat. —fällig, *adj.* and *adv.* liable to revert, devolve or escheat, revertible, escheatable. —fallsrecht, *n.* right of inheriting, right of future possession or enjoyment, reversion; *it.* [des Lehensherrn] escheatage. —führen, *v. tr.* to lead or conduct home. Eine Braut —führen, to conduct one's bride to one's house; er hat die or das reiche Fräulein N. —geführt, he married the rich Miss N. *Prov.* V. Braut. —führung, *f.* the act of leading or conducting home. Die —führung der Braut in ihre neue Wohnung, the ceremony of conducting or attending the bride to the house of her bridegroom. —gang, *m.* going or return home. *Fig.* death. —geben, *ir. v. tr.* Einem etwas —geben, 1) to give any one something [for taking it] home. 2) to give back, to return. *Fig.* [in fam. lang.] to return like for like, to retaliate. Ich werde es ihm schon —geben, I shall retaliate upon him, take my revenge upon him. —gehen, *ir. v. intr.* [u. w. seyn] to go home. *Fig.* Er ist —gegangen [zu seinen Vätern], he is gone to his long home, he is dead; [in familiar lang.] er mag mit seinem Witze —gehen, let him keep his wit to himself. —holen, *v. tr.* to fetch home, to bring home. —kehr, *f.* return home. —kehren, *v. intr.* [u. w. seyn] to return home. —kommen, *ir. v. intr.* [u. w. seyn] to come home. —krank, *adj.* having the Swiss malady, home-sick. —kunft, *f.* return home, arrival at home. —laufen, *ir. v. intr.* [u. w. seyn] to run home. —leuchten, *v. intr.* Einem —leuchten, to light any one home. *Fig.* †to refute, to snub any one; *it.* to pursue any one home with beating; *it.* to bang, to maul any one. *—machen, *v. r.* sich —machen, to go home. —recht, *n.* the right of the natives. Die Verleihung or Ertheilung des —rechtes, naturalization. —rechtsbrief, *m.* charter of naturalization. —reise, *f.* journey or voyage home. Auf der —reise begriffen seyn, to be on one's way home. —reisen, *v. intr.* [u. w. seyn] to travel home or homeward, to return home. —reiten, *ir. v. intr.* [u. w. seyn] to go or ride home on horseback. —ritt, *m.* going, riding or return home on horseback. —sagen, *v. tr.* Einem —sagen, V. [the more modern word] Entbieten; Etwas —sagen lassen, to send word or a message home. —schicken, *v. tr.* to send home. *Fig.* *Einen —schicken, to give any one a sharp answer that silences him, to nonplus any one, † to give it any one. —schlagen, *ir. v. tr.* Etwas Gekauftes —schlagen, to return or give back any thing purchased, on account of hidden damages or personal cheat. —schlagung, *f.* the annulling of a sale on account of hidden damages &c. [in law] redhibition. —sehnen, *v. r.* sich —sehnen, to long or languish for one's home. —senden, *reg.* and *ir. v. tr.* V. —schicken. —siech, *adj.* V. —krank. —stellen, *v. tr.* V. Anheimstellen]. ‡—steuer, *f.* portion, dowry. —steuergeben or —steuern, *v. tr.* to endow, to portion. —suchen, *v. tr.* Einen, 1) [now seldom used but in jest] to go and see any one at his house, to visit any one, V. Besuchen. 2) [in Scripture and in a religious sense] to send afflictions and distresses on any one to punish him for his sins or to prove him, to afflict, to visit. Gott sucht seine Auserwählte —, God visits or afflicts the elect; ich bin ein eifriger Gott, der da —sucht der Väter Missethat an den Kindern, I am a jealous God and visit the sins of the fathers upon the children; ein Land mit Krieg —suchen, to afflict or distress a country with war; diese Familie ist sehr —gesucht worden, this family has been greatly afflicted, has suffered great calamities. —suchung, *f.* 1) visit. Die —suchung Mariä, the visitation of our Lady; das Fest der —suchung Mariä, Mariä —suchung, the feast of the visitation of our Lady. 2) affliction, visitation. Was wollt ihr thun am Tage der —suchung? [in Script.] what will ye do in the day of visitation? —sucht, *f.* V. —weh. —tragen, *ir. v. tr.* to carry home. —treiben, *ir. v. tr.* to drive home. —tücke, *f.* 1) close, wily or crafty malice. 2) a wily or underhand trick. —tückisch, *adj.* and *adv.* craftily malicious, mischievous. Ein —tückischer Mensch, a malicious man; ein —tückischer Streich, V. —tücke 2); ein —tückisches Verfahren, a treacherous act or practice. —wandern, *v. intr.* [u. w. seyn] to wander home or homeward. —wärts, *adv.* homeward. —weg, *m.* way home, return home. Sie sind auf dem —wege begriffen, they are on their way home; sich auf den —weg machen, begeben, to enter upon, to set out on one's journey home. —weh, *n.* an inordinate and morbid desire of returning to one's home, the Swiss malady, homesickness; nostalgy. —weisen, *ir. v. tr.* to show home. *Fig.* to send away. —wollen, *v. intr.* to wish or want to go home. —zahlen, *v. tr.* to repay, to refund, to return. —ziehen, *ir.* I. *v. tr.* to drag home. II. *v. intr.* [u. w. seyn] to march, go, return home. —zug, *m.* march or return home. —zünden, *v. intr.* V. —leuchten.

Heimath, *f.* [*pl.* -en] home, native country

Heimaths-los, *adj.* and *adv.* without a

country or home, having no home, homeless. —**recht**, *n.* the right or privileges derived from one's being born in a certain place, domicile, home or country. Er hat sein —recht in N., he is entitled to claim N. as his home.

Heimathlich, *adj.* and *adv.* belonging to one's home or native country, native.

Heime, *f.* [*pl.* -n] *dim.* Heimchen, *n.* [-s, *pl.* -] cricket [an insect].

Heimisch, *adj.* and *adv.* belonging or relating to one's home or native country, homeborn, homebred, domestic, not foreign, not exotic. V. Einheimisch, Heimathlich. Sich in einem Hause — machen, to make one's self at home in a house.

Heimlich, *adj.* and *adv.* I. [from heim = house] 1) [little used] being in the house, domestic. —e Thiere, [= Hausthiere] [in Scripture], domestic animals. *Fig.* *a*) accustomed to the house. Ein —er [= zahmer] Vogel, a tame bird; er ist in diesem Hause —, ganz — geworden, he has made himself quite at home in that house, he has grown quite familiar or intimate in that house. *b*) [affording a feeling as if one were at home, therefore of safety, comfort &c.] free from danger and annoyance, comfortable, snug. Ein —es Häuschen, a snug or comfortable cottage; hier ist es recht —, one feels quite comfortable or at ease here; —es Wetter, fine, serene weather. II. [from the old hemen = decken, to cover] *a*) = geheim, secret, private. Ein —er Ort, a secret or private place; eine —e Treppe, a private stair-case, back-stairs, privy-stairs; das —e Gemach, house of office, convenient or necessary house, privy; die —en Theile [des Leibes], the privy parts; sie sehen sich —, they meet privately; sich — aus einer Gesellschaft entfernen, to steal away, to take French leave; er ist — hereingekommen, he came in by stealth; — unterhandeln, to negotiate underhand or privately; *— lachen, to laugh in one's sleeve; Etwas — halten, to hide or conceal something, to keep a thing secret; *— thun, to take or to assume a mysterious air. *b*) secret or private in an ill sense, clandestine. Ein —er Anschlag, a plot, a conspiracy; —e Waffen bei sich führen, to carry forbidden arms; Einem — nachstellen, to lay an ambush, to lay snares for any one; eine —e Ehe, a clandestine marriage; — zusammenkommen, to meet clandestinely; die —e Sünde, self-pollution, onanism. V. Verstohlen. Syn. V. Geheim.

Heimlichhaltung, *f.* V. Verheimlichung.

Heimlichkeit, *f.* 1) comfortableness, comfort, tranquillity. 2) secrecy, privacy. 3) a secret, V. Geheimniß.

Heimlos, *adj.* V. Heimathlos.

Heinrich, *m.* [-s, *pl.* -e] [a name of men] Henry. [in botany] Der gute —, good-henry; der böse —, mercury.

Heinrike, *f.* [*pl.* -n] [a name of women] Henriette, Harriett.

…t and ||**Heint**, V. Heute.

Heinz, *m.* [-es, *pl.* -en] 1) [*dim.* or *contraction* of Heinrich] Hal, Harry. 2) [in alchymy] der — or faule —, athanor, slow Harry, the furnace of arcana. 3) [in mining] Der — or die —enkunst, chain-pump.

Heinzenseil, *n.* 1) [in mining] the chain of the pump. 2) [in forges] the chain of the forge bellows.

Heinzelbank, *f.* 1) a form or board to cut …on, V. Schneidebank; [in husbandry] straw-cutter. 2) V. Ziehbank.

Heinzelmännchen, ||**Heinzelmännlein**, [-s, *pl.* -] [in botany] mandragora. *Fig.* [in popular superstition] V. Alraun and Galgenmännchen.

Heirath, or [more correctly] **Heurath**, *f.* [*pl.* -en] [probably from heuern = to take] marriage. Eine — zur Linken, auf die linke Hand, a left-handed marriage, a morganatical marriage; er hat eine sehr reiche — gethan, he has made a very rich match, he has married a great fortune.

Heirathsantrag, *m.* proposal or offer of marriage. —**brief**, —**contract**, *m.* V. —vertrag. —**erlaubniß**, *f.* permission of marriage, license to marry. —**fähig**, *adj.* fit to be married, marriageable. *—**gedanke**, *m.* thought or idea of marrying. Es kommen ihm —gedanken ein, er geht mit —gedanken um, he thinks of marrying, he intends to marry. —**gut**, *n.* marriage portion, dower. Ein —gut aussetzen, to constitute a portion, to make a settlement upon &c. V. Mitgabe, Mitgift. —**kuppler**, *m.* [chiefly in contempt or jest] V. —stifter. *—**lust**, *f.* inclination or mind to get married. *—**lustig**, *adj.* and *adv.* having a mind to marry. —**macher**, *m.* V. —stifter. —**punkt**, *m.* article of marriage. —**schein**, *m.* written permission of marriage, license to marry; *it.* certificate of marriage. —**spiel**, *n.* [*Mariage] [a game at cards] marriage. —**stifter**, *m.* —**stifterinn**, *f.* match-maker. —**stiftung**, *f.* the act of contriving or effecting a [union by] marriage, match-making. —**vertrag**, *m.* marriage-articles. —**verwandt**, *adj.* related or allied by marriage. —**verwandtschaft**, *f.* relation by marriage, affinity, V. Schwägerschaft. —**wappen**, *n.* armorial bearing acquired by marriage.

Heirathen, I. *v. tr.* to marry, to take in marriage. II. *v. intr.* to marry. Aus Liebe —, to marry for love; er hat reich geheirathet, he has married a fortune; unter seinem Stande —, to marry below one's self. III. *v. r.* sich —, V. Verheirathen.

Heirather, *m.* [-s, *pl.* -] one who marries.

Heisa or **Heißa**! *interj.* [exclamation of mirth, of joy &c.] hey, heyday, huzza!

||**Heisch**, V. Heiser.

Heischen, *v. tr.* [Low. Sax. *esken*, Sw. *aeska*, Eng. *to ask*, perhaps allied to the Gr. ἀξιόω] to demand, to desire, to require, to claim, to ask for, to beg. So viel für eine Waare —, to ask so much for a commodity; das Almosen —, V. Betteln.

Heischesatz, *m.* [in mathematics and philosophy] a postulatum, postulate.

Heiser, *adj.* and *adv.* hoarse. — werden, to grow hoarse; — sprechen, to speak hoarse or hoarsely.

Heiserkeit, *f.* hoarseness.

Heiß, *adj.* and *adv.* [Low. Sax. *heet*, Dan. *heed*, Sw. *het*, Sax. *hat*, Eng. *hot*, from the old Eit = Feuer, Gr. αἴθειν = to burn] hot. —es Wasser, hot or boiling water; ein —er Ofen, a hot stove; —es Wetter, hot weather; das Eisen — machen, to heat the iron; brennend, glühend —, burning hot, red-hot; siedend —, sied—, boiling, scalding hot, piping hot; der —e Erdstrich, the torrid zone; brennend —er Sand, parching sand; die Sonne scheint heute sehr —, the sun is very scorching to day; es ist mir sehr —, I am very hot; mir wird —, I grow hot; — essen, trinken, to eat, to drink hot; —e Butter, melted butter; *prov.* das Eisen schmieden, so lang es — ist, to strike the iron while it is hot, to make hay whilst the sun shines; [among shammy-dressers] die Felle — machen, to heap the hides or skins; [in forges] der Ofen geht — [= das Feuer ist verstärkt], the heat of the furnace is increased. *Fig.* —e Thränen vergießen, to cry bitterly; *Einem die Hölle — machen, to alarm any one by aggravating the matter, to make any one sweat for fear, to play the devil with any one; ein —es [= hitziges] Gefecht, a hot engagement; es war ein —er Tag für unsere Truppen, it was a hot day for our troops; *da geht es — her, there is hot or warm work; *er hat ihm diese Nachricht sied— mitgetheilt [= ohne Schonung], he blurted out that intelligence all at once to him; er hat ein —es Blut, sein Blut wird leicht —, he has hot blood, he is apt to grow hot or to fly into a passion; ein —er [brennender] Wunsch, an ardent desire; —e Liebe, Leidenschaft, ardent or violent love, passion; — lieben, to love passionately or ardently; ein —es Gebet, a fervent prayer; *hier ist ein —es Pflaster, it is very dear living here, *this is a hot place.

Heißdurst, *m.* excessive, violent thirst —**grätig**, *adj.* hard to be melted, difficult of fusion; *fig.* *refractory. —**hunger**, *m.* a ravenous or voracious appetite, canine hunger, [in medicine] bulimy. Der —hunger der Pferde, hungry evil. *Fig.* *great eagerness, ardour. —**hungerig**, *adj.* and *adv.* excessively hungry, voracious, greedy, affected with the bulimy or hungry evil; V. Gefräßig. *Fig.* *very eager or greedy. —hungerig nach etwas seyn, to have a vehement desire for, to thirst for any thing.

Heißa, V. Heisa.

Heißen, [in the northern dialects heten, old Germ. chedan, quedan = reden, Wendish *kasa* = befehlen, Russian *ukasa* = Befehl] *ir.* I. *v. tr.* 1) to name, to distinguish by a name, to call. Wie heißt man diese Pflanze? how do you call this plant? what is the name of this plant? Einen Du —, to thou any one, V. Duzen; er hat ihn einen Schurken ge—, he has called him rogue; sie wird einen Sohn gebären, deß Namen sollst Du Jesus — [in Scripture], she shall bring forth a son, and thou shalt call his name Jesus; Einen willkommen —, to bid or make any one welcome, to welcome any one; ich heiße Sie willkommen, you are welcome; *Einen kurz und lang —, to call any one names, to abuse any one; etwas gut —, to approve of, to sanction any thing, V. Billigen, Genehmigen; *das heiße ich schlafen &c., that may be called sleeping, that is sleeping; *das heiße ich einen Freund, there's a friend for you. 2) to bid, to order, to direct. Einen [or Einem] etwas thun — or —, etwas zu thun, to bid any one do a thing; thut, was man euch heißt, do as you are bid; sein Herr hat es ihn [or ihm] ge—, his master has bid him do it; er hat ihn fortgehen —, he has bid him go away, has ordered him to go away; heißet ihn hereinkommen, bid him come in; er hat ihn schweigen —, he imposed silence upon him, he bade him hold his tongue. II. *v. intr.* 1) to be called, to bear a name. Wie heißt diese Pflanze? how is this plant called? how do you call this plant? wie heißt dieser Herr? what is this gentleman's name? wie — Sie? what is your name? wie heißt dieses auf Englisch? what is this in English? what is the English of that? how is that called in English? er verdient nicht, der Sohn eines solchen Vaters zu —, he is not worthy to bear the name of such a father, to be the son of such a father; das heißt lügen, that is telling a lie, *it.* there's a lie for you. 2) to mean, to signify. Das heißt, that is, or that is to say; was soll das —? what is this meant for? what is the meaning of this? what does this mean or signify? das will wenig or nichts —, that is no great matter, 't is of little or no consequence; *ich will ihm weisen, was es heißt &c., I will show him what it is to &c.; das heißt so viel als &c., that is as much as &c., the meaning or sense of that is &c.; wissen Sie, was es heißt, Vater seyn? do you know what it is to be a father? III. *v. imp.* to be said. Hier heißt es mit Recht &c., here one may justly, one may well say &c.; damit es nicht heiße, that it may not be said; es heißt, der König will ihn zum Ritter schlagen, it is said or reported, they or people say, the king will knight him; er will sie nehmen, heißt es, he intends to marry her, as the report is.

Heiter, *adj.* and *adv.* clear, bright, serene. —e Luft, —er Himmel, serene air, sky; — werden, to clear up, to brighten. *Fig.* unruffled, calm, serene. Mit —er Stirne, with front serene; ein —er Blick, ein —es Gemüth, a serene look, mind; eine —e Unterhaltung, a sprightly, cheerful conversation; eine —e Gegend, a pleasant, sweet country. Syn. V. Hell.

Heiterkeit, *f.* serenity [of the air, sky &c.] *Fig.* Die — des Gemüths, serenity of mind or temper; nichts trübt die — seiner Tage, nothing overcasts the serenity of his life; die — eines Gespräches, the sprightliness or cheerfulness of a conversation.

Heitern, I. *v. tr.* to make serene, to serene. II. *v. r.* sich —, to clear up, to brighten. V. Aufheitern, Erheitern, Ausheitern.

Heizbar, *adj.* and *adv.* that may be heated or warmed. Ein —es Zimmer, a room with a stove or fire-place.

Heizen, *v. tr.* to heat, to make a fire [in an oven, stove, fireplace or room].

Heizer, *m.* [-s, *pl.* -], —inn, *f.* a person who heats or makes a fire [in an oven &c. or room].

Heizung, *f.* firing, fuel [fire-wood or coal].

Hèktik, Hèktisch, V. Schwindsucht, Schwindsüchtig.

Hèld, *m.* [-en, *pl.* -en] [probably from halten, = walten, i. e. to be strong; and allied to the L. *validus*] hero. *a*) [a man of distinguished valour or intrepidity in danger]. *Sich wie ein — benehmen, to behave in a heroic manner. **Fig.* Er ist ein — im Spielen, he is a great gamester; darin ist er ein ganzer —, he is quite a dab at it. *b*) the principal personage in a poem or romance] Achilles ist der — der Iliade, Achilles is the hero of the Iliad; der und der ist sein —, such a one is his hero.

Helden-alter, *n.* [the age when the heroes are supposed to have lived] heroic age. —angesicht, *n.* heroic countenance. —arm, *m.* the arm of a hero; *fig.* vigour, strength of a hero, heroic vigour. —bahn, *f.* heroic career. —blick, *m.* heroic look. —brief, *m.* heroic epistle. —buch, *n.* a heroic book, history of the exploits of heroes. —dichter, *m.* epic or heroic poet. —dichtung, *f.* 1) heroic or epic poetry. 2) V. —gedicht. —fabel, *f.* heroic fable. —gedicht, *n.* epic or heroic poem, epopee. —gedichtlich, *adj.* and *adv.* epic, heroic. V. also Episch. —geist, *m.* heroic spirit, heroism. —gesang, *m.* V. —gedicht. —geschichte, *f.* heroic story; *it.* the history of a hero. —haft, *adj.* and *adv.* V. —mäßig, —müthig. —heer, *n.* army of heroes. —herz, *n.* V. —muth. —lied, *n.* heroic song; *it.* song of heroes. —mäßig, *adj.* and *adv.* heroic, heroical, hero-like. —mäßigkeit, *f.* heroism. —miene, *f.* heroic mien or air. —muth, *m.* heroic courage or spirit, heroism. —müthig, *adj.* V. —mäßig. —oper, *f.* heroic opera. —paar, *n.* heroic pair or couple. —reich, *adj.* rich in, abounding with heroes. —ruhm, *m.* the glory of a hero or of heroes. —sänger, *m.* V. —dichter. —schar, *f.* heroic troop, a band or host of heroes. —schauspiel, *n.* V. —spiel 2). —seele, *f.* heroic soul. —sinn, *m.* V. —geist, —muth. —spiel, *n.* 1) heroic, warlike or martial game. Der Krieg ist ein —spiel, war is a game for heroes. 2) heroic play. —sprache, *f.* language of heroes, heroic language. —that, *f.* heroic deed, feat, action or exploit. —thaten verrichten, to perform [heroic] feats. —thum, *n.* V. —muth, —sinn, —mäßigkeit. —tod, *m.* heroic death. Den —tod sterben, to die as a hero; *it.* [vulgar jest] den —tod or —haft am Galgen sterben, to die game, at the gallows. —tugend, *f.* heroic virtue. —volk, *n.* heroic people or nation. —weib, *n.* a heroical woman, heroine. —zeit, *f.* heroic age, V. —alter. —zug, *m.* 1) heroic expedition, expedition of heroes. 2) heroic trait.

Hèldinn, *f.* heroine.

Hèlena, [-'s] **Helène,** [-ns, *pl.* -n] *f.* [a name of women] Helen.

Helenen-feuer, *n.* [in meteorology] Castor and Pollux [a fiery meteor which, at sea, appears sometimes adhering to a part of a ship, in the form of one, two or three balls; when one is seen alone, it is called Helena]. —kraut, *n.* V. Alant 2).

Hèlfen, *ir. v. intr.* [seldom *tr.*] (Sax. *helpan, hylpan,* D. *helpen,* Icel. *hiolpa,* Dan. *hiaelve,* Sw. *hielpa,* allied to the Gr. Ἕλπω, which originally signified heben, to heave, to lift] 1) to lend strength or means towards effecting a purpose, to help, to assist, to aid. Jemand in die Kutsche, aus der Kutsche —, to help any one into, out of the coach; Einem durch einen Fluß —, to help or assist any one in crossing a river; Einem aufstehen —, to help any one in rising, to help any one up; Einem arbeiten —, to help any one in his work; sich gegenseitig —, to help one another; *Einem davon [= zur Flucht] —, to help or assist any one in making his escape, V. Durchhelfen; helfet diesem Armen ein wenig, help that poor man a little; helft! helft! help! help! Einem in der Noth —, to help or relieve any one in distress; Einem mit seinem Credit und Beutel —, to assist any one with one's credit and purse; es war ihm nicht mehr zu — [in seiner Krankheit, seinem Unglück], he was past cure or recovery, past help; *prov.* wem nicht zu rathen ist, dem ist auch nicht zu —, he that would not hearken to a forewarning, must learn by the event; it is impossible to help or serve him who will not listen to good advice; Gott helf'! [a popular polite term used towards a person sneezing] God bless you! [to a beggar] God help you! so wahr mir Gott helfe! [as an asseveration] so help me God! hilf Gott', hilf ewiger Gott! Good God! O Lord! bless me! Arzt, hilf dir selber! physician, cure thyself! er weiß sich nicht zu —, he is at his wits' end, he is put to his last shifts; man hilft sich wie man kann, we help ourselves, we shift as well as we can; *Einem auf den rechten Weg, auf die Sprünge —, to bring any one into the right way, to put any one upon a proper scent, to show any one how to set about a thing; Einem zu seinem Glücke —, to contribute to, to forward or promote any one's good fortune; er hat mir zu meinem Unglück geholfen, he has been accessory to my misfortune; Einem zu Brod, zu einem Amte —, to put any one into a fair way of getting his livelihood, to put any one into a way to live, to procure any one a place or office; der Richter soll Jedem zu seinem Rechte —, a judge shall do justice to every one; Alles hilft zu seinem Glücke, all things conspire to make him happy, to his happiness; *Einem wieder zu seiner Gesundheit, zu seinen —, to restore any one's health, eye-sight ser Arzt hat schon Manchem ins Grab fen, this physician has already dis many a one, has sent many a one out c world; *Einem vom Fieber, von einem zesse —, to free, to deliver any one fr fever, law-suit; — Sie mir von diesem gen Menschen, deliver or rid me from troublesome man, help me to shake off importunate person or bore; Einem aus nem Irrthume —, to undeceive, to any one; *Einem aus dem Traume —, to prise any one of, to give any one a true notion or explanation of a thing; *Einem von Vermögen, von seinem Amte —, to make any one lose his fortune, his office; *Einem vom Brode — [= ihn tödten], to do any one's business, to dispatch any one. 2) to be of use or advantage, to avail. Dein Glaube hat dir geholfen [in Scripture], thy faith hath made thee whole; dieses Mittel hilft gegen das Fieber, this remedy is good for or against the fever; was wird es mir [or mich] —! what shall I be the better for it? what shall I get by it? es hilft nichts, it avails nothing, it is to no purpose; was hilft es? what boots it? ein Mittel, das hilft, an efficacious remedy; mein Rath hat nichts geholfen, my advice has had no effect, has done no good; hier hilft Alles nichts, here all efforts are vain, unavailing or useless; wenn Worte nicht —, so muß man Schläge brauchen, if words don't avail, why, then blows must! Syn. Helfen, Beistehen. Helfen signifies, to contribute strength or means; beistehen implies that the strength is spontaneously united with that of another to effect a purpose. Thus, the columns that support a building helfen (help) to bear the whole weight, but sie stehen sich nicht bei, (they do not assist each other).

Helfs-geld, *n.* V. Hülfsgeld. —rede, *f.* evasion, subterfuge, come-off, excuse, shift. —reich, *adj.* V. Hülfreich. —wurz, *f.* [in botany] the long-rooted garlic.

‡Hèlfenbein, *n.* V. Elfenbein.

Hèlfer, *m.* [-s, *pl.* -] —inn, *f.* one that helps, aids, assists, helper, aider, assistant, help, V. Gehülfe; *it.* V. Geburts—, Noth—, Mit—; der — eines Geistlichen, curate, *it.* = Diakonus, deacon; die —inn, deaconess.

Helfer-amt, *n.* the office of a deacon, deaconry, deaconship. *—s-helfer, *m.* aider, abettor, accomplice.

‡Hèlfte, *f.* V. Hälfte.

***Helice,** *f.* [*pl.* -n] [in architecture and geometry] a spiral line, helix. Zur — gehörig, helical, spiral.

***Helicit,** *m.* [-en, *pl.* -en] [a shell] helicite [fossil remains of the helix].

***Helicitisch,** *adj.* helicoid.

***Hèlikon,** *m.* [a famous mountain in Boeotia] Helicon. —erinn, *f.* female inhabitant of the Helicon, muse.

***Heliocéntrisch,** *adj.* [in astronomy] heliocentric. Der —e Ort eines Planeten, heliocentric place of a planet; —e Länge, the heliocentric longitude.

***Heliométer,** *n.* [-s, *pl.* -] [an instrument for measuring the diameter of the heavenly bodies] heliometer, astrometer.

***Helioskóp,** *n.* [-es, *pl.* -e] [a sort of telescope fitted for viewing the sun] helioscope.

***Heliothermométer,** *n.* [-s, *pl.* -] heliothermometer.

***Heliotróp,** *n.* [-es, *pl.* -e] 1) [the name of several plants] heliotrope, turnsol. 2) [in mineralogy) heliotrope, V. Sonnenauge, Katzenauge.

Hell, *adj.* and *adv.* 1) [probably allied to hallen, schallen, and gällen] not jarring or harsh, clear, shrill, piercing. Eine sehr —e Stimme, a very clear, shrill voice; die Stimme der Weiber ist —er, als die Mannsstimme, women's voices are generally more clear than men's; — sprechen, to speak with a clear voice; ein —es Gelächter, a loud laugh; *eine —e Lache aufschlagen, to set up a horse-laugh. 2) [probably allied to the Hebr. *halal*, glänzen, the Gr. ἥλιος and ἕλη] shining, luminous, bright, clear, light. Ein —es Feuer, ein —er Tag, a clear fire, day; ein —er Morgen, a light morning; —er als die Sonne, brighter than the sun; die —en Sterne, the luminous stars; der Mond scheint —, the moon shines bright; es fängt an — zu werden, it begins to be day-light, day dawns; es ist schon —er Tag, it is broad day-light; bei —em Tage, am —en Mittage, at broad noon, in plain day-light; ein —es Zimmer, a light room; es ist sehr — in dieser Kirche, this church is very light; —e Farben, light colours, V. —blau, —braun &c.; die —en Theile eines Gemähldes, the lights of a picture; eine —e [lichte] Holzung, a thin wood; —e Stelle in einem Walde, a glade. In a more limited sense: *a*) = glänzend, shining, bright. — geblänkte Waffen, bright arms; —e Augen, bright, sparkling eyes. *b*) pellucid, transparent. —es Wasser, Glas, clear water, glass; der Wein ist noch nicht —, the wine is not fine or clear yet. *Fig.* Eine Sache in ein —es Licht stellen, to place a thing in a clear light, to render it conspicuous or manifest, to make it appear as bright as noon-day; er ist ein —er Kopf, er hat einen —en Kopf, er hat einen —en or —sehenden Verstand, he has a clear understanding or judgment; er hat sehr —e Augen, einen sehr —en Blick, er sieht sehr —, he is very clear-sighted; ich sehe nicht — in dieser Sache, I do not understand this affair thoroughly, I do not see my way clearly in this matter; ich sage Ihnen die *—e Wahrheit, I tell you the plain or real truth; die —en Zwischenräume [eines Wahnsinnigen], lucid intervals. SYN. Hell, Klar, Heiter. Such bodies are said to be hell (bright), from which light either proceeds or is reflected, as: the sun, the fire, the moon &c. Bodies are called klar, which neither emit nor reflect light themselves, but which allow rays of light to pass through them. Heiter is opposed to trübe, and is das Helle, as far as it renders objects visible.

Hell≈äugig, *adj.* having bright eyes, bright-eyed. —blau, *adj.* light-blue. —braun, *adj.* light-brown. —denkend, *adj.* having a clear understanding or judgment. —dunkel, I. *adj.* half-dark, dusky. II. *n.* [in painting] clare-obscure Das —dunkel ist in diesem Gemählde gut beobachtet, the clare-obscure is supported in this piece. —farbig, *adj.* light coloured, fair. —farbige Haare, light hair. —fuchs, *m.* light-chestnut horse. —gelb, —grau, —grün, *adj.* light or bright yellow, light grey, light green. —haarig, *adj.* light-haired. —roth, *adj.* light or pale red. —sehend, *adj.* clear-sighted, perspicacious, acute. —seher, *m.* —seherinn, *f.* a magnetized person or a somnambulist, who, with the eyes shut, is said to see every thing or object and even future events. —sichtig, *adj.* clear-sighted; *fig.* perspicacious, clear-sighted. —weg, *m.* a sloping way. —weiß, *adj.* bright-white.

Hell, *n.* [-es, *pl.* -e] [in seamen's lang.] the boatswain's store-room in the forepart of a ship.

Hell≈bewahrer, *m.* boatswain. —butt, *m.*, —butte, *f.* V. Heilbutte.

Hèlle, I. *f.* 1) clearness, brightness. Die — der Stimme, eines Tones, the clearness of the voice, of a sound; die — des Tages, the open day; bei der — des Feuers lesen, to read by the fire; dieses Zimmer hat nicht — genug, this room is not light enough; die — der Augen, clearness of sight; die — fällt von oben herab, the light comes from above. 2) Eine — im Walde, a forest-glade. II. *n.* [-n] any thing light. Sie liebt das —, she is fond of light colours.

Hellebárde, Hellebárte, *f.* [*pl.* -n] [from Barte = Beil and the old barten = streiten] a halberd. Die Sergeanten beim Fußvolk trugen —n, the sergeants of foot carried halberds.

Hellebarden≈eisen, *n.* the iron or head of a halberd. —kraut, *n.* coronilla. —schaft, *m.* the shaft or pole of a halberd. —träger, *m.* halberdier.

Hèllen, I. *v. tr.* to make clear, to clarify, to impart a light colour, V. Auf—, Er—. Das Gold —, to brighten the gold. II. *v. r.* sich —, to clear up, V. Aufhellen.

***Hellène**, *m.* [-n, *pl.*-n] a native or inhabitant of Hellas, Greek, Grecian. Die —n, the Hellenes. [The term Hellene is always used in a higher style or sense than the word Grieche.]

***Hellènisch**, *adj.* and *adv.* hellenic, hellenian.

***Hellenìsm**, *m.* [-s, *pl.* -en] hellenism.

***Hellenist**, *m.* [-en, *pl.* -en] hellenist.

***Hellenistisch**, *adj.* and *adv.* hellenistic.

Hèller, *m.* [-s, *pl.* -] [probably allied to halb and the Eng. *half-penny*] the smallest copper-coin [in Germany], farthing. **Fig.* Das ist keinen — werth, that is not worth a farthing, is worth nothing; er hat nicht eines —s Werth im Vermögen, †er hat keinen blutigen or rothen —, he is not worth a farthing; bis auf den letzten —, bei — und Pfennig bezahlen, to pay the whole sum to a farthing; ich gebe keinen — dafür, I would not give a straw for it.

Heller≈arm, *adj.* [in popular lang.] excessively poor. —gewicht, *n.* V. Probirgewicht. —nadel, *f.* V. Aufsteckenadel.

Hèllsichtigkeit, *f.* clear-sightedness.

1. **Hèlm**, *m.* [-es, *pl.*-e] [Low Sax. Helft, Sax. *helf* and *hielfa*, Eng. *helve*, probably from halten] handle, helve. Der [das] — an einer Axt, the helve of an axe; der — an einem Anker, the shank of an anchor.

Helm≈holz, *n.* [in seamen's lang.] the whip-staff of a rudder, tiller. —stock, *m.* V. —holz.

2. **Hèlm**, *m.* [-es, *pl.* -e] [Sax. *helma*, Eng. *helm*, Dan. *hiaelm*, Sw. *hjelm*, Isl. *gialmar*, allied to hehlen, hohl] 1) in general, a cover or covering; [in anatomy] a child's caul. Ein mit einem — geborenes Kind, a child born with a caul upon its head; [in popular lang.] er ist mit einem — geboren [= ist ein Glückskind], he is wrapped up in his mother's smock, he is born to a good fortune. [in architecture] cupola, dome. Der — eines Brennkolbens, the upper part or helm of an alembic. 2) [in a more limited sense, the wellknown armour for the head] headpiece, cask, helmet, helm. [in heraldry] Einen — von vorn [im Wappen] führen, to bear a fronting cask or helmet.

Helm≈biene, *f.* V. Drohne. —binde, *f.* a band or bandelet belonging to a helmet. —blume, *f.* [a plant] helmet-flower. —busch, *m.* plume of the helmet, crest. —dach, *n.* a roof in the shape of a dome, cupola. —decke, *f.* [in heraldry] the ornament about a helmet, mantling. —feder, *f.* feather or plume of a helmet. —fenster, *n.* visor of a helmet. —förmig, *adj.* and *adv.* helmet-shaped. —förmige Blumen, hooded flowers, hood-flowers. —gewölbe, *n.* a vaulted roof or ceiling in the form of a cupola, V. —dach. —gitter, *n.* the bars in front of the helmet, visor. —hut, *m.* a hat in the form of a helmet. —kappe, *f.* a cap [generally made of stiff leather] in the form of a helmet, skull-cap. —kleinod, *n.* V. —schmuck. —kraut, *n.* [in botany] cassido or skull-cap, scutellaria. —lehen, *n.* noble fief or manor. —mütze, *f.* V. —kappe. —nase, *f.* the nose-piece of a helmet. —pocke, *f.* [in conchology] helmet-shell. —reif, *m.* bar of the visor. —rost, *m.* the bars of the visor or beaver. —schlange, *f.* a serpent whose head looks as if it were helmed. —schmied, *m.* helmet-maker. —schmiede, *f.* place where helmets are made and sold. —schmuck, *m.* the crest of a head-piece or helmet; V. —busch, —feder, —decke. —strauß, *m.* V. —busch. —stutz, *m.* V. —busch. —taube, *f.* crested pigeon, helmet-pigeon. —visir, *n.* the visor of a helmet. —zeichen, *n.*, —zierath, *m.* V. —schmuck.

1. **Hèlmen**, *v. tr.* to helve [an axe].

2. **Hèlmen**, *v. tr.* Einen, to furnish any one with a helmet, to helm any one; *it.* to furnish something with a crest, to crest something.

Hèlmlos, *adj.* helmless.

Helvètien, *n.* [-s] Helvetia, Switzerland. [Helvetia is particularly used in a higher style.]

Helvètier, *m.* [-s, *pl.*-], —inn, *f.* a Swiss, a Swiss woman. Die —, the Helvetii, the Swiss.

Helvètisch, *adj.* and *adv.* Helvetic. Der —e Bund, the Helvetic confederacy. V. also Eidgenossenschaft 2).

Hèmd, *n.* [-es, *pl.* -en] or **Hèmde**, *n.* [-s, *pl.* -n] [Old Germ. Hemmat, Sax. *haam*, *ham*; Fr. *chemise*, probably from hemmen = decken, to cover] Properly, any covering [for the body], V. Chor—, Futter—, Meß—, Panzer—, then chiefly, the loose garment worn next the body. Das Manns—, shirt; das Frauen —, shift; ein weißes —, a clean shirt or shift; ein beschmutztes or schwarzes —, a dirty shirt or shift; ein anderes — anziehen, das — wechseln, to change or shift one's shirt or shift; *er hat nichts als das — auf dem Leibe, er hat kein gutes — auf dem Leibe [= er ist sehr arm], he has not a shirt to his back, to put on his back; *Einen bis auf's — ausziehen, Einem nichts als das — anlassen, to strip any one to the shirt, *fig.* to strip any one of all he has, to ruin, to undo, to beggar any one, to be the ruin of any one; *prov.* das — ist mir näher, als der Rock, near is my shirt, but nearer is my skin; the smock is nearer than the petticoat; *fig.* *ich wollte lieber das — vom Leibe verkaufen, als &c., I would rather ruin myself, than &c.

Hemd≈ärmel, *m.* the sleeve of a shirt or shift, shirt-sleeve. In —ärmeln seyn, to have one's coat off, to be in one's shirt-sleeves. —kleid, *n.* a kind of loose dishabille, worn by ladies, resembling a chemise, a wrapper. —knopf, *m.* shirt-button, stud. —kragen, *m.* shirt-collar; [an Weiber—en] ruff. —krause, *f.* ruffle; *it.* frill. —nadel, *f.* shirt-pin. —preischen, *n.* wrist-band. —schlitz, *m.* the opening of a shirt or shift, placket-hole.

***Hemisphäre**, *f.* [*pl.*-n] [Erdhalbkugel] hemisphere.

***Hemistich**, [-s, *pl* -e] *m.* hemistic.

Hemmen, *v. tr.* [seems to be allied to haben and heften] to check or hinder motion, to stop. Den Lauf eines Flusses —, to arrest the course of a river; einen Wagen, ein Rad — or sperren, to stop a carriage, stop or lock a wheel; seine Thränen —, to check or restrain one's tears; —de Kraft, repressive force. *Fig.* Den Lauf der Gerechtigkeit —, to arrest or restrain the course of justice; seine Leidenschaften, seinen Zorn —, to restrain, curb or check one's passions, one's anger; eine Rede —, to interrupt a discourse. Syn. V. Aufhalten.

Hemm-fisch, *m.* [a fish which is said to attach itself to a ship and retard its motion] the sucking-fish, remora. —**gabel**, *f.* a fork for stopping a wheel. —**kette**, *f.* a chain for stopping or impeding motion, drag-chain, trigger, skid. —**schuh**, *m.* trigger.

Hemmerling, *m.* [-es, *pl.* -e] V. Goldammer.

Hemmling, *m.* [-es, *pl.* -e] [V. Hammel] a castrated creature, V. Hämmling.

Hemmung, *f.* 1) the act of checking or stopping, restraint. 2) any thing that checks or stops; [among gun-makers] catch or stay; [among watch or clock makers] escapement, scapement. Zurückspringende —, recoil-escapement; ruhende —, dead beat.

Hemmungs-spruch, *m.*, —**s-urtheil**, *n.* [der Einhaltsbefehl] a decree to suspend the execution of a former decree. Einen —sspruch zu erwirken suchen, to plead in arrest of judgment.

Hengst, *m.* [-es, *pl.* -e] [Bohem. *hynst*, Dan. and Sw. *hingst*, which is derived from the L. *hinnire* = to neigh] [a male horse not castrated] stone-horse, stallion, seed-horse, horse. Einen — legen, wallachen, to castrate, to geld a horse; den — zur Stute lassen, to let the stallion cover the mare.

Hengst-fohlen, —**füllen**, *n.* a colt. —**geld**, *n.* money paid for the use of the stallion. —**mann**, *m.* the groom who attends the stallion.

Henkel, *m.* [-s, *pl.* -] [from hängen] handle, ear, hook, eye. Der — an einem Topfe, Korbe &c., the ear or handle of a pot, basket &c.; die — einer Glocke, the ears of a bell.

Henkel-flasche, *f.*, —**gefäß**, *n.* a bottle or vessel with a handle. —**korb**, *m.* a basket with a hoop or handle. —**napf**, *m.* a porringer with an ear. —**schüssel**, *f.* a dish with ears. —**stück**, *n.* piece of money or coin with an ear, eye or ring. —**schale**, —**tasse**, *f.* cup with an ear or handle. —**topf**, *m.* a pot with a handle or ear.

Henkeln, *v. tr.* to furnish with a handle, ear, hook or eye.

Henken, I. *v. tr.* [= hängen] [formerly, in general] to hang up; [now] to put to death by suspending by the neck, to hang. Er ist verurtheilt worden, gehenkt zu werden, he has been condemned to be hanged; er wurde im Bildnisse gehenkt, he was hanged in effigy; er fürchtet sich vor dem —, he is afraid of the gallows. II. *v. r.* sich —, to hang one's self.

Henkenswerth, *adj.* deserving to be hanged. Eine Sache, die —swerth ist [more usual, eine Sache, bei der es an den Hals geht], a hanging matter.

Henker, *m.* [-s, *pl.* -] hangman, executioner, jack-ketch. Von —s Hand, unter —s Hand, durch —s Hände sterben, to die by the hand of the hangman; sein eigener — werden, to hang one's self, *fig.* to torment one's self, *it.* to ruin, to undo one's self. [in popular lang., an expression of indignation, astonishment &c.] the deuce. Der —! ei, der —! daß dich der —! das wäre des —s! oh the deuce! what, the deuce! geht zum —, packt euch zum —, hol' euch der —, deuce take you! der — hole den Narren, the deuce take the fool! das taugt den — nichts [= gar nichts], that is not worth a fig, is good for nothing; ich frage den — darnach, I do not care a straw for it; was —s, was zum — treibt er! what the deuce is he about! *Fig.* a cruel, savage fellow, a tormentor. Dieser Fürst ist der — seines Landes, seiner Unterthanen, this sovereign is the bloody tyrant of his realm, of his subjects; Pizarro war der — der Peruaner, Pizarro was the cruel destroyer of the Peruvians.

Henker-beil, *n.* the executioner's axe. —**block**, *m.* block. —**frist**, *f.* V. Galgenfrist. —**geld**, *n.*, —**lohn**, *m.* hangman's fee. —**mahl**, *n.*, —**mahlzeit**, *f.* meal before the execution, last meal of a criminal; *it. fig.* valedictory dinner or supper, parting meal. —**mäßig**, *adj.* and *adv.* hangman-like, savage, brutal. Einen —mäßig behandeln, to treat any one barbarously. —**schwert**, *n.* executioner's sword. —**s-frau**, *f.* hangman's wife; *it. fig.* a cruel, hardhearted woman. —**s-knecht**, *m.* executioner's assistant; *fig.* a cruel, bloody satellite. —**strick**, *m.* rope for hanging, halter.

Henkerei, *f.* V. Scharfrichterei.

Henkerisch, *adj.* V. Henkermäßig.

Henne, *f.* [*pl.* -n] [probably = the *she*, i. e. the female; in Icel. and Sw. *han* and *hun* is *he*, Sw. *hon* is *she*; in a more limited sense: the female of any kind of fowl, Low Sax. *hüne*, D. *hinne*, *henne*, Sax. and Dan. *henne*] V. Auer—, Birk—, Fasan—, Haselgeflügel, generally, the female of the domestic fowl, hen. Eine junge —, a young hen. V. Leg—, Gluck—, Zins—. *Prov.* V. Ei 2). [in botany] Die fette —, orpine, V. Knabenkraut.

Hennenbiß, —**darm**, *m.* V. Hühnerbiß, Hühnerdarm.

Hennegat, *n.* [-s, *pl.* -e] [in seamen's lang.] helmport.

Her, *adv.* [primitively the same as hier, and probably to be reduced to kehren, therefore turned towards as it were] 1) [in general, denoting nearness or vicinity] Rings um uns —, round about us; neben Einem — gehen, to walk at the side of any one. 2) [expressing direction from any place or time to that where we are] Kommet —, hier—! come hither or here! come this way! hin und —, to and fro, backward and forward, hither and thither; von dort —, von oben —, von unten —, from thence, from above, from below; von innen —, von hinten —, from within, from behind; von Abend —, from the west; wo—? from whence, from what part or country? wo seid Ihr —? from what country are you? what countryman are you? Ich komme weit —, von weit —, I come from afar, from a far distant place or country; ich komme vom Mittagessen —, I am coming from dinner; die Hand —! your hand! give or reach me your hand! immer —! [= kommt nur!] come on! come on! hinter Einem — seyn [= ihm nachlaufen], to run after any one, to follow any one close, to be at any one's heels, *it. fig.* *to press, to urge any one; über Einen — fallen, to fall upon any one; vom Anfange —, from the beginning; ich bin die Zeit — öfters krank gewesen, I have often been ill of late or lately; wie lange ist es —? how long is it since? how long is it ago? es ist nicht vier Tage —, it is not four days since; von undenklichen Zeiten —, from times out of mind. *Fig.* [chiefly in familiar language] Hin und — rathen, to guess this and that, to guess at random; Regel hin, Regel —! rule this way or that way, what signifies the rule, what care we for the rule! dieser Mensch ist nicht weit — [= ist von Herkunft], this man is of base, obscure extraction, *it.* is good for nothing; die ist nicht weit —, this wit is not very is very flat; dieser Zeug ist nicht weit —, this stuff is no great things; hinter Etwas — seyn, to be actually about something, to be in pursuit of any thing, to endeavour to get it; er ist immer hinter den Büchern —, he is always poring on his books.

Her-babbeln, *v. tr.* [in familiar language] to recite or repeat babbling or prattling. —**bannen**, *v. tr.* to conjure hither. Er ist wie — gebannt, he seems to be retained here by magic or enchantment. —**begeben**, *ir. v. r.* sich —begeben, to come hither. —**beichten**, *v. tr.* to own or confess; *it.* to confess one thing after the other. Er hat Alles —gebeichtet, he has confessed all. —**bekommen**, *ir. v. tr.* to get hither. Wo soll ich es —bekommen? from whence, where am I to get it? —**bemühen**, I. *v. tr.* Einen —bemühen, to trouble a person to come, to give any one the trouble to come hither. II. *v. r.* sich — bemühen, to give one's self the trouble to come hither. —**bestellen**, *v. tr.* Einen — bestellen, to appoint any one to the place where one is, to bid any one come. —**beten**, *v. tr.* to recite a prayer. Einen Rosenkranz — beten, to tell one's beads. —**betten**, *v. tr.* Einen —betten, to put up, to make a bed for any one in the place where one is. Sagt der Magd, daß man ihn da —betten soll, bid the servant to put up a bed for him here. —**beugen**, *v. tr.* to bend towards the person speaking. Er beugte sich über mich —, he leant over me. —**bewegen**, *v. tr.* and *r.* to move towards the person speaking. —**biegen**, *ir. v. intr.* to bend towards the person speaking. —**binden**, *ir. v. tr.* to bind to. Bindet ihn auf diesen Stuhl —, tie or bind him upon this chair. —**bitten**, *ir. v. tr.* to invite, to desire to come hither. —**blasen**, *ir.* I. *v. tr.* 1) to blow towards the person speaking. Der Wind bläst den Staub gegen uns —, the wind blows or drives the dust towards us. 2) [mostly with a contemptuous meaning] to play [an air or tune &c.] upon an instrument. II. *v. intr.* to blow towards the person speaking. Der Wind bläst von dieser Seite —, the wind blows from this quarter. †—**blechen**, *v. tr.* to pay down. —**blicken**, V. —sehen. —**blinken**, *v. intr.* to glitter or flash towards the person speaking. —**blinzen**, *v. intr.* to wink at or towards the person speaking. —**blitzen**, V. —blinken. —**brausen**, *v. intr.* to approach the person speaking roaring or blustering or rushing. —**breiten**, *v. tr.* to spread on the place where one is. Breiten Sie das Tuch auf den Boden —, spread or lay the cloth on the floor here. —**bringen**, *ir. v. tr.* to bring to or towards the person speaking. Dieser Beweis ist weit —gebracht, this proof is far-fetched. *Fig.* to establish as a custom or a right. Die in einem Lande —gebrachten Gewohnheiten, the ways and customs of a country; das ist bei uns so —gebracht, that is customary with us. —**brüllen**, I. *v. tr.* to utter with a bellowing voice, to vociferate, to bawl forth. II. *v. intr.* to advance towards the person speaking bellowing or roaring. —**brummen**, I. *v. tr.* to utter with a humming or murmuring voice, to mutter forth. II. *v. intr.* to approach humming or murmuring or muttering. —**buchstabiren**, *v. tr.* to spell. —**denken**, *ir.* I. *v. intr.* to think of the place where one is. II. *v. tr.* to think or fancy a person to be where we are. —**drängen**, *v. r.* sich —drängen, to press towards the place where one is. Man drängte sich um ihn —, people crowded round him. —**dringen**, *ir. v. intr.* to advance or press towards the place where one is. —**drohen**, *v. intr.* to threaten or menace rom the place where one is, stands &c.; *it.* o threaten or menace towards the person peaking. —**drücken**, *v. tr.* to press or rge towards the place where one is. —**du-deln**, *v. tr.* V. Dudeln II. 1). —**duften**, *. intr.* to emit fragrance towards the place here one is. —**dürfen**, *ir. v. intr.* to be llowed to come or go to the place where ne is. —**eilen**, *v. intr.* to hasten towards the lace where one is. —**erzählen**, *v. tr.* to reite, to relate. *Etwas an den Fingern —zu-erzählen wissen, to have a thing at one's finers' ends. —**fabeln**, *v. tr.* Etwas —fabeln, o talk nonsense. —**fahren**, *ir.* I. *v. intr.* 1) o move hastily along. Einem mit der Hand ber das Gesicht —fahren, to pass one's hand ver any one's face; hier ist die Kugel —ge-fahren, the ball has struck here; über Einen —fahren, to rush in, to fall upon any one, *fig.** o inveigh or exclaim against any one. 2) to rrive or approach in a carriage or vessel. Im-mer an der Küste —fahren, to coast along. II. *. tr.* to carry or bring near. —**fallen**, *ir. v. intr.* o fall towards the place where one is. Ein Stein fiel gegen uns —, a stone fell towards s; über Etwas, Einen —fallen, to fall upon a hing or person. *Fig.* *Ueber Einen —fallen, to oad any one with reproaches, to inveigh against ny one. —**faseln**, *v. tr.* Etwas, to talk nonense. —**feuern**, *v. intr.* to discharge firerms, to fire towards the place where one is. —**fiedeln**, V. Abfiedeln 1). —**finden**, *ir. v. tr.* nd *r.* Er konnte den Weg nicht —finden, sich icht —finden, he could not find the way, his way ither. —**flattern**, *v. intr.* to arrive or approach fluttering. —**fliegen**, *ir. v. intr.* to arrive r approach flying [as birds]. —**fließen**, *ir. v. ntr.* to flow towards the place where one is. *Fig.* to issue, to proceed, to originate, to be erived from, to flow from. Da fließen alle nsere Uebel —, all our evils flow from that; a fließen alle Wohlthaten —, from thence ome all the beneficent actions. —**flimmern**, *V.* —blinken. —**flößen**, *v. tr.* to float. Es ist —geflößtes Holz, it is floatwood. —**flöten**, *v. tr.* [rather contemptuously] to play on the flute. —**flüchten**, *v. tr., intr.* and *r.* to save a thing, ne's self by flying towards the place where ne is, to take refuge to where one is. —**fluten**, *v. intr.* to approach in high waves. —**fodern** r —**fordern**, *v. tr.* to summon, to call, to end for hither. —**fragen**, *reg.* and *ir. v. r.* sich —fragen, to find the way hither by inquiring a reat deal. —**fühlen**, *v. intr.* to feel here or ither. —**führen**, *v. tr.* to carry or bring hither. Führt mir mein Pferd —, bring me my horse; ieß ist, was mich —führt, that is what makes e come hither. —**funkeln**, *v. intr.* to emit r throw a sparkling light towards the place here one is. —**gaffen**, *v. intr.* to look hither aping. —**gang**, *m.* way or coming hither. Nach mehreren Hin- und —gängen, after going o and fro several times; er hat den Hingang ür den —gang gehabt, he has had his laour for his pains. *Fig.* Der —gang einer Sache, the way or manner in which a thing as come to pass; er hat uns den ganzen —gang der Sache erzählt, he has told us ll the details or particulars of the transction. —**geben**, *ir. v. tr.* 1) to stretch out, to each, to give to the person speaking. Geben Sie die Hand —! give me your hand! 2) to ive away, to give up, to surrender. Er gibt icht gerne —, he is not fond of giving, he is ither stingy or close-fisted; er will sein Pferd icht —geben [=verkaufen], he won't part with, on't sell his horse. *Fig.* Seinen Namen —geen, to lend one's name. —**gehen**, *ir. v. intr.*) to go, to walk, to come along. Geh —! ome along! da kömmt er —gegangen, there he comes walking or strutting along. *it.* [with über] to cover. Das Tischtuch geht nicht über den Tisch —, the cloth does not quite cover the table. *Fig.* *Ueber Etwas —gehen, to be begun suddenly and vehemently, to be set about, to be taken in hand; es wird gleich darüber —gehen, we shall fall to immediately, an attempt, a push will be made immediately; es ging über die Speisekammer —, the pantry or larder was ransacked; es geht über ihn —, his peal is rung, he is inveighed or exclaimed against; es wird bald auch über Sie —gehen, it will soon be your turn. 2) *Fig.* [chiefly in fam. lang.] to come to pass, to be done or to proceed in a certain manner. So geht es in der Welt —, this is the way of the world, so goes the world; es geht lustig —, things go on merrily; es geht ehrlich —, things are done honestly; es gehet langsam mit der Sache —, the affair or concern proceeds slowly; es geht armselig bei ihm —, he lives poorly; ein Haus, in dem es unordentlich —geht, a disorderly house; bei jenem Treffen ging es hitzig —, that was a hot engagement. —**gehören**, *v intr.* to belong to this place or hither. Dieses Buch gehöret da nicht —, that's not the place for that book; diese Frage gehöret nicht —, this question is not to the purpose. —**geifern**, *v. tr.* to utter slavering. —**geigen**, *v. tr.* [rather contemptuously] to play on the fiddle. —**geißeln**, *v. tr.* Einen, to whip any one to the place where one is. —**geleiten**, *v. tr.* to conduct or accompany hither. —**gerathen**, *ir. v. intr.* to come hither by chance. —**gießen**, *ir. v. tr.* to pour hither. —**girren**, I. *v. intr.* to coo towards the place where one is. II. *v. tr.* to utter cooing. —**glänzen**, *v. intr.* to glitter towards the person speaking. —**gleiten**, *ir. v. intr.* —**glitschen**, *v. intr.* to glide this way. —**glotzen**, *v. intr.* to look hither staring. —**greifen**, *ir. v. intr.* to touch here. —**grinsen**, *v. intr.* to look grinning this way. —**grunzen**, *v. tr.* to utter grunting or grumbling. —**gucken**, *v. intr.* V. —sehen. —**haben**, *ir. v. tr.* to have [taken] from. Wo haben Sie das —? from whence, where have you got that? wo soll ich es —haben? from whom or whence do you think I got it? —**hallen**, *v. intr.* to sound from a place to that where one is. —**halten**, *ir.* I. *v. tr.* to hold towards the person speaking, to hold out, to reach, to present, to tender. II. *v. intr.* to submit to inconvenience or punishment, to suffer, to be punished. *Mein Beutel hat schrecklich —halten müssen, they have drained me pretty sufficiently. —**hangen**, *ir. v. intr.* to hang towards the person speaking. —**hängen**, *ir. v. tr.* to hang up, to suspend here. —**heben**, *ir. v. tr.* to lift to this place or near. —**heften**, *v. tr.* to fasten, tack or pin to this place. —**heulen**, I. *v. tr.* to utter howling or crying. II. *v. intr.* to approach howling or crying. —**hinken**, *v. intr.* to approach or arrive halting or limping. —**holen**, *v. tr.* to fetch, to bring towards the person speaking. *Fig.* Dieser Beweis ist weit —geholt, this proof is far-fetched. —**horchen**, —**hören**, *v. intr.* to listen here. Horchen Sie —, come and listen. —**hüpfen**, *v. intr.* to approach or arrive skipping. —**jagen**, I. *v. tr.* to drive hither. II. *v. intr.* to ride, to run with gread speed, to gallop towards the person speaking. —**jammern**, *v. tr.* to utter with a lamentable voice. —**jauchzen**, *v. tr.* to utter joyfully or shouting. —**karren**, *v. tr.* to bring hither in carts. —**klimpern**, *v. tr.* to play badly [on the harpsichord &c.] —**klingeln**, *v. intr.* 1) to tinkle or jingle towards the person speaking. 2) to approach or arrive tinkling or jingling. —**klopfen**, *v. tr.* to knock or to rap here. —**knallen**, *v. intr.* Büchsenschüsse knallten vom Walde —, reports of guns were heard from the wood. —**knien**, *v. intr.* to kneel here. —**kommen**, I. *ir. v. intr.* to come hither, to come or draw near, to approach, to advance. Ich komme gerade vom Frühstück —, I am just coming from breakfast. *Fig.* *a*) to be customary, to be established as a custom. Ein —gekommener Gebrauch, an old, long-established custom. *b*) [= abstammen] to be descended, to be derived from. Er kommt von guten Eltern —, he descends or is descended from respectable parents. Dieß Wort kommt von keinem andern —, this word is derived from no other. *c*) to arise, to proceed, to originate. Diese Krankheit kommt von der Unmäßigkeit —, this illness proceeds from intemperance; da kömmt unser ganzes Unglück —, it is from this source that all our misfortunes flow. II. *n.* Das —kommen, coming hither, arrival. Das —kommen ist ihm verboten, they have forbidden him to come hither. *Fig.* *a*) custom, usage, precedent. Es ist so —kommens bei uns, that's customary with us; das —kommen in einem Lande, the ways and customs of a country; in diesem Lande gilt das alte —kommen, this country is governed by custom or by the common law. *b*) origin, descent, birth, extraction, family. Von geringem —kommen, of low extraction. —**kömmlich**, *adj.* and *adv.* established by ancient usage, customary, according to custom. Das —kömmliche Recht, the customary or common law. —**können**, *ir. v. intr.* to be able or permitted to come hither. —**körnen**, V. —locken. —**krächzen**, *v. tr.* to utter croaking. —**krähen**, *v. tr.* to utter crowing. —**krallen**, *v. tr.* to draw near by means of one's paws or claws. —**kriechen**, *ir. v. intr.* to crawl or creep near. *—**kriegen**, *v. tr.* V. Bekommen I. —**kritzeln**, *v. tr.* 1) to scrawl or scribble here. 2) to write something in a hurried or slovenly manner. —**krümmen**, I. *v. tr.* to crook or bend towards the person speaking. II. *v. r.* sich —krümmen, to bend, to crook or to wind this way. —**kunft**, *f.* 1) coming hither, arrival. 2) *Fig.* origin, descent, extraction, family. —**lächeln**, *v. intr.* to look smiling towards the person speaking. —**lachen**, *v. intr.* to look laughing towards the person speaking. *Fig.* Seitdem ihm das Glück von dieser Seite —lacht, since fortune smiles upon him from that quarter. —**laden**, *ir. v. tr.* 1) Einen —laden, to summon, to invite any one to this place. 2) Etwas —laden, to load or put a thing hither. —**lallen**, *v. tr.* to utter or say in a stammering or lisping manner [like children, paralysed persons &c.]. —**langen**, I. *v. intr.* 1) to be extended, to reach as far as this place. 2) V. —fühlen, —greifen. II. *v. tr.* to hand, to reach, to fetch hither. —**lassen**, *ir. v. tr.* to suffer, permit or allow to come near, to approach. —**laufen**, *ir. v. intr.* to run hither or near. Ein —gelaufener Kerl, a vagabond, an adventurer. —**legen**, *v. tr.* to put or lay hither or near. —**leiern**, *v. tr.* [in contempt] to play on the lyre. *Fig.* Eine Rede —leiern, to deliver a speech in a monotonous manner. —**leihen**, *ir. v. tr.* to lend out, V. Leihen. —**leiten**, *v. tr.* to bring or to conduct hither or near. Wasser von dem Hauptkanal —leiten, to derive water from the main channel. *Fig.* *a*) to draw, as from a root. Ein Wort —leiten, to derive a word. *b*) to draw from in reasoning, to deduce, V. Folgern; *it.* to build upon as an authority. —**leitung**, *f.* the act of leading or conducting hither or near. *Fig.* Die —leitung eines Wortes, the derivation or etymology of a word; die —leitung der Gründe, the deduction of reasons. —**lesen**, *ir. v. tr.* to rehearse, to recite, to read; *it.* to read without expression. —**leuchten**, *v. intr.* 1) to shine towards the person speaking. 2) to light here. Leuchte einmal —! bring a light hither! 3) Einem —leuchten, to carry a light before any one as far as this place, to light any one on his way hither. —liefern, *v. tr.* to deliver to this place. —locken, *v. tr.* to draw hither by persuasion, to allure, to entice hither. —lügen, *ir. v. tr.* to tell a lie or lies. —machen, I. *v. tr.* [in fam. lang.] to fix or to contrive in this place. Man muß da eine Treppe —machen, we or they must contrive a staircase there. II. **v. r.* sich —machen, to betake, to place one's self here, to come near, to approach. Sich über Etwas —machen, to set about a thing, to fall to; sich über Einen —machen, to fall upon any one, to fall foul of any one. —marsch, *m.* the march hitherward or to this place. —mögen, *ir. v. intr.* to have a mind or inclination to come hither. —murmeln, *v. tr.* to utter or say murmuring or muttering. —müssen, *ir. v. intr.* to be obliged or forced to come hither. Der Schlüssel muß —, muß wieder —, the key must be found, must be forthcoming. —nahen, V. Herannahen. —nehmen, *ir. v. tr.* to take near, to take or get from. Wo soll ich so viel Geld —nehmen? where am I to get so much money? wo nehmen Sie die Geduld —, &c.? how can you have patience &c.? den Beweis von etwas —nehmen, to draw, to deduce the proof from something. *Fig.* * Einen —nehmen, to take any one to task, to censure, to lash any one, to use any one ill, * to hawl any one over the coals, V. Mitnehmen. —neigen, I. *v. tr.* to bend or incline towards the person speaking. II. *v. r.* sich —neigen, to lean, to incline towards the person speaking. Er neigt sich auf diese Seite —, he inclines to this side. —nennen, *ir. v. tr.* to name in succession. —nöthigen, *v. tr.* Einen —nöthigen, to oblige, to force, to press any one to come hither. —packen, I. *v. tr.* to pack or put to this place. II. *v. r.* sich —packen, [in vulgar lang.] to betake, to place one's self hither, to come hither, to approach. —peitschen, *v. tr.* to drive hither by whipping, to whip hither. —pflanzen, *v. tr.* to plant here or hither. —plappern, *v. tr.* to say or recite chattering or prattling. —prügeln, *v. tr.* to cudgel or beat hither. —rauschen, *v. intr.* to come near, to approach rustling or making a noise. —rechen, *v. tr.* to rake near or hither. —rechnen, *v. tr.* to reckon up, to enumerate. —rechnung, *f.* enumeration. —recken, *v. tr.* to stretch towards the person speaking. —reden, *v. tr.* [chiefly in a contemptuous meaning] to speak, to talk. —reichen, I. *v. intr.* to extend, to reach as far as this place. II. *v. tr.* to reach, to hand, to present, to give. —reise, *f.* journey or voyage hither. —reisen, *v. intr.* to travel hither. —reißen, *ir. v. tr.* to pull near or hither. —reiten, *ir. v. intr.* to ride or come near or hither on horseback. —riechen, *ir. v. intr.* 1) to emit a smell or odour towards the person speaking. 2) to smell here. Riechen Sie einmal —! come and smell! *Fig.* †Er hat kaum —gerochen, und will &c., he is but just arrived, *it.* he is quite a new hand at this business, and presumes to &c. —ritt, *m.* coming hither on horseback, ride hither. —rollen, *v. tr.* and *intr.* to roll near or hither. —rücken, I. *v. tr.* to move or push near or hither. II. *v. intr.* to draw near, to advance, to approach. —rudern, *v. intr.* to approach or arrive rowing. —rufen, *ir. v. tr.* to call hither. Einen —rufen lassen, to send for any one. —rühren, *v. intr.* to issue or come as from a source, to proceed, to flow from, to originate, to take or have its origin. Davon rührt unser ganzes Unglück —, it is from this source that all our misfortunes flow; von wem kann dieses Gerücht —rühren? who can be the author of this report? —sagen, *v. tr.* to recite, to repeat, to rehearse. Das —sagen, recitation, rehearsal. —schaffen, *v. tr.* to move near, to produce, to procure. *Schaff' ihn her! bring him hither! * wo soll ich das Geld —schaffen? where am I to procure or get the money? —schallen, *v. intr.* to sound from a place to that where the person speaking is. —schauen, *v. intr.* V. —sehen. —scheinen, *ir. v. intr.* to shine towards the person speaking. —schenken, *v. tr.* to give away, to make a present of. †—scheren, *v. r.* sich —scheren, V. —packen II. —scheuchen, *v. tr.* to drive hither by frightening, to scare hither. —schicken, *v. tr.* to send hither. —schieben, *ir. v. tr.* to shove or push near or hither. —schießen, *ir.* I. *v. intr.* 1) [used with haben] to shoot towards the person speaking. 2) [used with seyn] to rush along, to shoot along, to run, to fly hither. II. *v. tr.* 1) to shoot hither. 2) [= hergeben] to give. Geld —schießen, to give money, to advance money; er hat die nöthigen Unkosten —geschossen, he has advanced, disbursed or laid out the necessary expenses, V. Vorschießen. —schiffen, *v. intr.* to come hither or near, to approach or arrive in a ship, to sail hither or hitherward. —schimmern, *v. intr.* V. —blinken, —scheinen. —schlagen, *ir.* I. *v. intr.* to strike here; *it.* to strike without hesitation. Schlag' —, wenn Du das Herz hast, strike, if you dare. II. *v. tr.* 1) to move hither by striking. Schlagen Sie den Ball —, send the ball hither. 2) to fix by striking. Schlagen Sie einen Nagel —, drive in a nail here. —schleichen, *ir. v. intr.* and *r.* sich —schleichen, to sneak, steal or slink near or hither. 1. —schleifen, *v. tr.* to drag near or hither. 2. —schleifen, *ir. v. intr.* to slide near or hither. —schleppen, *v. tr.* to drag near or hither. —schnattern, V. —plappern. —schreiben, *ir. v. tr.* to write hither. *Fig.* Wo schreibt sich dieser Irrthum —? whence does this error come or arise? —schreien, *ir.* I. *v. intr.* to cry towards the person speaking. II. *v. tr.* to recite, to say or tell with a loud voice. —schwanken, *v. intr.* to come near or hither tottering. —schwärmen, *v. intr.* to come near or hither in swarms. —schwatzen, *v. tr.* V. —babbeln. —segeln, *v. intr.* to sail near or hither. —sehen, *ir. v. intr.* to look this way or hither. —sehnen, *v. r.* sich —sehnen, to wish one's self hither, to long to be here. —senden, *reg.* and *ir. v. tr.* V. —schicken. —setzen, I. *v. tr.* to put near or hither. Setzen Sie das Wort hier —, put or place the word here. II. *v. r.* sich —setzen, to put or place one's self near the person speaking. —seufzen, I. *v. intr.* and *r.* sich —seufzen, to wish one's self vehemently at the place of the person speaking. II. *v. tr.* [in poetry] to sigh for, to obtain by sighing. —seyn, *ir. v. intr.* 1) to be or come from, to be native of. Niemand weiß, wo er — ist, nobody knows, where is his native place, or who he is. *Fig.* *Nicht weit — seyn, to be of little worth or value, to be good for nothing. 2) [chiefly in familiar language] über etwas — seyn, to have taken a thing in hand, to have fallen upon a thing. Die Diebe waren bereits über meine Juwelen —, the thieves were already making free with, were pocketing my jewels; über Einen — seyn, to take any one to task, to find fault with, to censure any one, to fall foul of any one; hinter Einem — seyn, to be at any one's heels, to press, to urge any one; †er ist immer hinter diesem Mädchen —, he constantly pursues that girl. —singen, *ir. v. tr.* to recite in a singing manner. —sitzen, *ir. v. intr.* to sit near or hither. Sitzen Sie — zu mir, come and sit down by me. —stammeln, *v. tr.* to utter or say stammeringly, to stammer, to lisp. —stammen, *v. intr.* to descend or be descended, to come from, to be derived, to originate. Die Franzosen stammen zum Theile von den Deutschen —, the French are partly descended from the Germans; dieses Wort stammt aus dem Griechischen —, this word is derived from the Greek. V. Abstammen. —starren, *v. intr.* to fix the eyes upon the person speaking. Sehen Sie, wie er —starrt, look, how he fixes his eyes upon us or me. —stechen, *ir. v. intr.* to thrust towards or at the person speaking. —stecken, *reg.* and *ir. v. tr.* to stick or pin here. —stehen, *ir. v. intr.* to stand, to be turned towards the person speaking. —stehlen, *ir. v. r.* sich —stehlen, V. —schleichen. —steigen, *ir v. intr.* to ascend, to mount hither; *it.* V. —kommen. —stellbar, *adj.* that may be repaired or restored, reparable. —stellen, I. *v. tr.* 1) to place or put near or hither. Stellt das Glas auf den Tisch —, put the glass upon the table here. 2) [chiefly in certain sciences, as in natural philosophy &c.] to produce, to work out by a certain procedure. Nach vielen Versuchen gelang es ihm, ein schönes Blau —zustellen, after many experiments he succeeded in producing a most beautiful blue colour. *it.* to establish, to set up. Er hat ein stattliches Gebäude —gestellt, he built, raised a stately edifice. 3) to bring back to its former state, to repair, to restore. Ein Haus wieder —stellen, to repair a house; eine Stelle in einem Schriftsteller wieder —stellen, to restore a passage in an author; den Handel, die Mannszucht wieder —stellen, to restore trade, military discipline; einen Kranken wieder —stellen, to restore a patient to health, to recover a sick person, to set any one up again; die Milchkur hat ihn wieder —gestellt, milk diet has recovered him. II. *v. r.* sich —stellen, to put or place one's self near or hither. —stellt Euch! [a phrase in exercising soldiers] as you were! —steller, *m.* V. Wiederhersteller. —stellung, *f.* reestablishment, restoration, reparation. —steuern, *v. intr.* to steer near or hither. —stieren, *v. intr.* V. —starren. —stöhnen, *v. tr.* to utter groaning. —stolpern, *v. intr.* to come near or hither, to arrive stumbling. —stoßen, *ir.* I. *v. intr.* to strike, push or thrust towards the person speaking. II. *v. tr* to thrust or push hither. —stottern, *v. tr.* to stammer out, V. —stammeln. —strahlen, *v. intr.* to emit or cast forth rays towards the person speaking. —streben, *v. intr.* to strive, to endeavour to come near or hither. —strecken, *v. tr.* to stretch out or towards the person speaking, to extend. Die Hand —strecken, to extend one's hand [to a person]. V. —recken; Geld —strecken, to advance money, V. Vorstrecken. —streichen, *ir.* I. *v. tr.* to put or spread here. II. *v. intr.* to move, pass, fly, migrate or wander hitherward. *Fig.* †Er streicht immer hinter ihr —, he is always at her heels. —streuen, *v. tr.* to strew here or hither. Man streute Blumen auf den Weg —, they strewed the way with flowers. —strich, *m.* [der Strichvögel] [among sportsmen] the coming back, the return of birds of passage. —strömen, *v. intr.* to flow with a strong course; *it.* to flow towards the person speaking. *Fig.* Die Menschen strömten von allen Seiten —, people flocked, streamed or poured hither from all quarters; Lebensmittel strömten in Fülle ins Lager —, plenty of provisions were brought into the camp. —stürmen, *v. intr.* to rush with violence towards the person speaking. —stürzen, I. *v. tr.* to throw down, to precipitate here. II. *v. intr.* and *r.* sich —stürzen, to fall or tumble with violence towards the person speaking. *Fig.* Eine Menge Unglücksfälle stürzen über mich —, a great many misfortunes or evils are poured down upon me; über Einen, Etwas —stürzen, sich —stürzen, to fall or rush upon any one or any thing. —sudeln, *v. intr.* to scribble or daub here. Wer hat auf dieses Papier —gesudelt? who has scribbled here, who has soiled this paper? —tanzen, v. intr. to come hither or near dancing. —taumeln, v intr. to come near or hither reeling or staggering. *—thun, ir. v. tr. to put, to set down here. —toben, v. intr. to come near or hither blustering, raving or raging. —tönen, V. —schallen. —tosen, V. —toben. —traben, v. intr. to come near or hither, to arrive or approach trotting. —tragen, ir. v. tr. to carry or bring hither —träger, m., —trägerinn, f. the person who carries or brings hither; fig. gossiping man or woman, gossip, tell-tale, tale-bearer. —träufeln, I. v. tr. to let fall here or hither in drops, to drip, to drop here. II. v. intr. to fall in drops, to drip, to drop towards the person speaking. —treffen, ir. v. intr. to hit or strike here. —treiben, ir. I. v. tr. to drive hither. Die Wellen trieben einen Leichnam —, the waves floated a corpse hither. II. v. intr. to float hither. —treten, ir. v. intr. to step near or hither, to approach. —triefen, v. intr. V. —träufeln II. —trillern, v. tr Ein Liedchen —trillern, to hum a tune. —trommeln, v. tr. Einen Marsch —trommeln, to beat a march on the drum. —trompeten, v. tr. to play on the trumpet. —tröpfeln, —tropfen, V. —träufeln. —wackeln, v. intr. to come near or hither waddling, to approach waddling. —wagen, v. r. sich —wagen, to dare, to venture, to come near or hither. —walzen, v. intr. to come near or hither waltzing. —wälzen, I. v. tr. to roll near or hither. II. v. r. sich —wälzen, to come near or hither, to approach rolling or wallowing. —wandeln, v. intr. to walk, travel or wander hitherward. —wanken, v. intr. to come near or hither tottering or reeling. *—watscheln, v. intr. V. —wackeln. —weg, m. way hither. —wehen, v. tr. and intr. to blow hither or hitherward. —weisen, ir. v. tr. and intr. V. —zeigen. —wenden, v. intr. to turn towards the person speaking; fig. (obsolete or ...) V. Aufwenden. —werfen, ir. I. v. tr. to throw towards the person speaking. II. v. r. sich über Einen or Etwas —werfen, to throw one's self, to fall upon any one or any thing. —wimmern, v. tr. to utter, to say, repeat or recite in a whimpering or whining tone. —winden, ir. I. v. tr. to wind or twist (thread &c.) to this place or here; it. to move near or hither by means of a windlass. II. v. r. sich —winden, to come near or hither, to approach making windings or meanders. —winken, I. v. intr. to make a sign, to beckon towards the person speaking. II. v. tr. Einen —winken, to make any one a sign to come near or hither. —winseln, v. tr. to utter, say or recite moaning or whining. —wölben, v. r. sich über etwas —wölben, to form a vault over. —wollen, ir. v. intr. to be willing, to wish or want to come hither. —wünschen, I. v. tr. Einen or Etwas —wünschen, to wish any one, any thing to be here. II. v. r. sich —wünschen, to wish one's self hither, to wish to be here. —wurf, m. a throw hitherward. —zahlen, V. —zählen. —zählen, v. tr. to enumerate, V. —zählung, f. enumeration. —zaubern, v. tr. to conjure hither. —zeichnen, v. tr. to draw, to delineate in this place. —zeigen, I. v. tr. to shew hither. II. v. intr. to point this way or hither. Zeig —! let me see! —ziehen, ir. I. v. tr. to draw or pull near or hither. II. v. intr. 1) to march hither, to approach. (to come hither in order to dwell here) to remove to this place. III. v. r. sich —ziehen, to move or march hither, to approach. —zischeln, v. tr. and intr. to whisper towards the person speaking. —zischen, I. v. intr. to hiss, to whis... towards the person speaking. II. v. tr. to utter hissing.

Heráb, adv. (from a higher place down to the person speaking, opposed to Hinab) down, from ... downwards. Den Berg —, down (from) the hill; die Wangen —, down the cheeks.

(*)Herab-begeben, ir. v. r. sich —begeben, to come down, to descend. —bemühen, I. v. tr. Einen —bemühen. II. v. r. sich —bemühen, to give any one, one's self the trouble to walk or come down, to descend. —beten, v. tr. to obtain from heaven by praying. Sie betete Segen auf ihn —, she implored heaven, to pour its blessings upon him. —beugen, I. v tr. to bend down (a bough). II. v. r. sich —beugen, to lean, to bow down, to bend downwards. —bewegen, v. tr. and r. sich —bewegen, to move down or downwards. —biegen, ir. V. —beugen. —binden, V. Abbinden. —blasen, ir. I. v. tr. to blow down. II. v. intr. to play on a wind-instrument down from an elevated place. —blicken, I. v. intr. to look down. II. v. tr. (in poetry) to express by looking down, as in contempt, pity &c. —blinken, v. intr. to glitter or twinkle down. —blitzen, I. v. intr. to flash or dart down like lightning. II. v. tr. (in poetry) to shoot or dart down. —brechen, ir. v. tr. and intr. to break down, V. Abbrechen. —bringen, ir. v. tr. to bring down; fig. to injure in wealth and prosperity. —bücken, v. r. sich —bücken, to bow down. —drängen, I. v. tr. to press or urge down. II. v. r. sich —drängen, to come down thronging, to press down. —drehen, V. Abdrehen. —dringen, ir. v. intr. to press down, to urge downwards. —drücken, v. tr. to press down. —duften, v. tr. and intr. to emit or shed fragrance down or downward. —eilen, v. intr. to hasten down. —fahren, ir. I. v. intr. to go down in carriage, to descend. II. v. tr. to carry or bring down. —fahrt, f. descent. —fallen, ir. v. intr. to fall down. —feuern, V. —schießen I. 1) and II. 1). —flattern, v. intr. to flutter down. fliegen, ir. v. intr. to fly down. —fließen, ir. v. intr. to flow down. —flimmern, v. intr. V. —blinken. —flößen, v. tr. to float down. —führen, v. tr. to lead down. —funkeln, V. —blinken. —geben, ir. I. v. tr. to give, hand or pass down. II. v. r. sich —geben, to degrade, to debase or demean one's self. V. Erniedrigen. —gehen, ir. v. intr. 1) to go or walk down, to descend. 2) to reach down. Sein Rock geht ihm bis auf die Füße —, his coat reaches or hangs down to his feet. 3) to remove from on, to come off. —gießen, ir. I. v. tr. and intr. to pour down. II. v. r. sich —gießen, to come down in torrents, to pour down. —gleiten, ir. v. intr. —glitschen, v. intr. to slide down. —häkeln, —haken, v. tr. to draw or pull down with a hook, to hook down. —hangen, ir. v. intr. to hang down. —hängen, v. tr. to hang or suspend lower down. —hauen, ir. v. tr. to cut or hew down or off, V. Abhauen. —heben, ir. v. tr. to lift or take down. —helfen, ir. v. intr. to help down, to assist in descending. —hinken, v. intr. to come down, to descend halting or limping. —holen, v. tr. to fetch, to bring down, V. —werfen, —schießen I. 1) and II. 1). —hüpfen, v. intr. to hop or jump down. —jagen, I. v. tr. to drive down. II. v. intr. to ride or run down with great speed, to gallop down. —kämmen, v. tr. 1) to comb off. 2) to comb down. —kehren, v. tr. to sweep down or off. —klettern, v. intr. to descend by means of the hands and feet, to climb down. —kollern, v. intr. to roll down. —kommen, ir. v. intr. to come down, to descend. Komm —! come or step down! Fig. to be brought low, to be lowered or reduced in cirumstances Diese Familie ist in ihren Vermögensumständen sehr —gekommen, this family has been greatly straitened in their means, greatly reduced in their circumstances. —können, ir. v. intr. to be able or allowed to walk or come down. —kriechen, ir. v. intr. to creep or crawl down. —lächeln, v. intr. to look down smiling, to smile down (upon). —langen, I. v. intr. to reach down. II. v. tr. to take down. —lassen, ir. I. v. tr. to let down, to lower. Lassen Sie Ihr Kleid —, let your gown hang down; Etwas vom Preise —lassen, V. Ablassen. II. v. r. sich —lassen, to descend. Fig. a) to humble one's self, to condescend, to stoop. Wenn er sich —läßt, mein Freund zu werden, if he condescends to become my friend; der Fürst war sehr —lassend, the prince was very condescending. b) to accommodate one's self to the capacity &c. of others. Er ist ein großer Geist, aber er läßt sich zu denjenigen —, die ihn nicht erreichen können, he is a man of superior genius, but he adapts himself to the capacity of those who are not upon a level with him. —lassung, f. act of letting down; fig. condescension, courtesy. —laufen, ir. v. intr. to run down; it. to flow from. —legen, v. tr. to lay or put lower down. —lenken, v. tr. to turn, to direct down or downwards. —leuchten, v. intr. 1) to shine down upon or from above. Der Mond leuchtet auf die Fluren —, the moon shines down upon the fields. 2) Einem die Treppe —leuchten, to light any one down stairs. —locken, v. tr. to allure, to entice to come down. *—machen, v. r. sich —machen, to come down, to descend. *—mögen, ir. v. intr. V. —wollen. *—müssen, ir. v. intr. to be obliged to come down, to descend. Er muß — (vom Pferde), he must alight. —nehmen, ir. v. tr. to take down. —nehmung, f. the act of taking down or off. Die —nehmung Christi vom Kreuze, the taking down of Christ from the cross; (in painting) eine —nehmung Christi, a picture representing Christ's being taken from the cross. —nöthigen, v. tr. Einen —nöthigen, to oblige, to press any one to come down or to descend. —packen, I. v. tr. to pack lower down. II. v. r. sich —packen, (in vulgar language) to come or get down, to descend. —prügeln, v. tr. to cause to come down by beating. *—purzeln, v. intr. to come down tumbling. —rasseln, —rauschen, v. intr. to come down, to descend, to fall rustling or making a great noise. —rechen, v. tr. to rake down. —reden, V. —sprechen. —regnen, v. intr. imp. to rain down upon. —reichen, V. —langen. —reisen, v. intr. to travel down, to descend. —reißen, ir. v. tr. to pull down. —reiten, ir. v. intr. to ride down on horseback. —rennen, ir. v. intr. to run down. —rieseln, v. intr. to purl down. —ringeln, v. r. sich —ringeln, to fall down in curls or ringlets, it. to come down winding or writhing as a snake. —rinnen, ir. v. intr. to flow or run down. —rollen, v. tr. and intr. to roll down. —rücken, v. tr. to move or put lower down. —rufen, ir. I. v. intr. to cry or call down from above. II. v. tr. to call down. —rutschen, v. intr. to glide, slide or slip down. —sagen, v. tr. to tell from above. —schaffen, v. tr. to bring down. —schallen, v. intr. to sound from above. —schauen, V. —sehen. —scheinen, ir. v. intr. to shine down from above. —scheren, I. ir. v. tr. V. Abscheren. II. v. r. reg. and ir. (vulgar) sich —scheren, V. —packen II. —schicken, v. tr. to send down. —schieben, ir. v. tr. to shove or push down. —schielen, v. intr. to look down squinting. —schießen, ir. I. v. tr. 1) to bring down by shooting, to shoot down. Er schoß ihn vom Pferde —, he shot him down from his horse. 2) to dart or shoot down.

(*) Die mit herab zusammengesetzten, hier nicht folgenden Wörter suche man bei Ab, Herunter.

(*) Such words as are compounded with herab, and are not subjoined here, are to be looked for among the compounds of Ab, Herunter.

Er schoß einen wüthenden Blick auf ihn —, he darted a furious look down upon him. II. *v. intr.* 1) to shoot or fire down from above. 2) to throw one's self, to fall, to rush down. Das Wasser schießt über die Felsen —, the water rushes down the rocks; auf einmal schoß der Falke auf die Taube —, all of a sudden the hawk made a stoop at the pigeon. —schiffen, I. *v. intr.* to come down, to descend in a ship, to sail down. II. *v. tr.* to convey down in a ship. —schimmern, V. —blinken, —scheinen. —schlagen, *ir. v. tr.* V. Abschlagen I. 1), Herunterschlagen. —schleichen, *ir. v. intr.* to sneak, steal or slink down. —schleppen, *v. tr.* to drag down. —schleudern, *v. tr.* to sling, throw or hurl down. —schlüpfen, *v. intr.* to slip, slide or steal down. —schmeißen, *ir. v. tr.* V. —werfen. —schreien, *ir. v. tr.* and *intr.* to cry down [from above]. —schreiten, *ir. v. intr.* to stride, stalk or step down. —schütteln, *v. tr.* to shake down. —schütten, *v. tr.* to pour, to empty down from above. —schwanken, *v. intr.* to come down, to descend tottering. —schweben, *v. intr.* to hover, to float down. —schwemmen, *v. tr.* to float down. —schwimmen, *ir. v. intr.* to swim down. —schwingen, *ir. v. r.* sich —schwingen, to vault, leap, jump, bound or spring down. —segeln, *v. intr.* to sail down. —sehen, *ir. v. intr.* to look down. —sehnen, *v. r.* sich —sehnen, to wish one's self down, to long to be down. —senden, *reg.* and *ir. v. tr.* V. —schicken. —senken, *v. tr.* to let down, to sink. —setzen, I. *v. tr.* to put lower down; *fig.* to reduce in rank, estimation or value, to degrade, to lower, to undervalue. Einen Offizier —setzen, to degrade an officer; das heißt einen Mann —setzen, wenn man sich weigert &c., 't is degrading, humbling or vilifying a man to refuse &c.; den Preis einer Sache —setzen, to reduce the price of a thing; die Münzen —setzen, to reduce, to cry down the money; die Steuern —setzen, to abate, to diminish the taxes; eine Sache —setzen [= verachten], to undervalue, to depreciate, to debase, to slight a thing; Jemands Verdienste —setzen, to detract from any one's merit. II. *v. r.* sich —setzen, to degrade, to debase or demean one's self. Ich werde mich nie so weit —setzen, ihn zu bitten or Freundschaft mit ihm zu schließen, I shall never stoop so low as to entreat him or to enter friendship with him. —setzung, *f.* reduction, abatement, diminution, degradation, undervaluation. —setzung der Steuern, abatement or diminution of the taxes; die —setzung des Zinsfußes, the lowering of interest. —sinken, *ir. v. intr.* to sink down or low; *fig.* to debase or degrade one's self, V. Sinken. —sprechen, *ir. v. tr.* and *intr.* to speak down from above. —sprengen, I. *v. tr.* to cause to spring down. II. *v. intr.* to ride, rush or run down, to gallop down. —springen, *ir. v. intr.* to spring, leap or jump down. —stechen, *ir.* I. *v. intr.* to make a stitch or thrust downwards. II. *v. tr.* to bring down by a thrust or by stabbing. —stecken, *v. tr.* to stick or pin lower down. —stehen, *ir. v. intr.* 1) [used with haben] to stand downwards, to hang down, to slope. 2) [used with seyn] to stand lower down, to step down. —stehlen, *ir. v. r.* sich —stehlen, V. —schleichen. —steigen, *ir. v. intr.* to descend, to come or step down. Den Berg, vom Berge —steigen, to descend the hill or mountain. —stellen, *v. tr.* to put or place lower down. —stimmen, I. *v. tr.* to tune lower. Die Saiten um einen Ton —stimmen, to lower the chords by one tone. *Fig.* Er hat die Saiten sehr —gestimmt [in fam. lang.], he has given up or abated a great deal of his first demand; er ist sehr —gestimmt, he is very dejected or low; das Alter stimmt die Leidenschaften —, old age abates, allays or cools the passions. II *v. r.* sich zu Eines Ansichten —stimmen, V. —lassen II. *fig. b*). —stoßen, *ir. v. tr.* to thrust or push down. —strahlen, V. —blinken. —strömen, *v. intr.* to flow with a strong course, to stream or pour down or downwards. *Fig.* Die Menge strömte den Berg —, the multitude poured down the mountain. —stürzen, I. *v. intr.* to fall or tumble down, to throw or precipitate one's self down. Der Falke stürzte auf das Feldhuhn —, the hawk made a stoop at the partridge. II. *v. tr.* to throw or precipitate down. III. *v. r.* sich —stürzen, to throw or precipitate one's self down. —thun, *ir. v. tr.* V. —bringen, —nehmen. —tönen, V. —schallen. —traben, *v. intr.* to trot down. —tragen, *ir. v. tr.* to bear or carry down. —träufeln, —träufen, —traufen, I. *v. tr.* to let fall down in drops, to drip. II. *v. intr.* to fall down in drops, to drip, to drop. —treiben, *ir. v. tr.* to drive down. —triefen, —tropfen, —tröpfeln, *v. intr.* V. —träufeln. —wagen, *v. r.* sich —wagen, to dare, to venture to come down, to descend. —wallen, *v. intr.* to float down. —wälzen, I. *v. tr.* to roll down. II. *v. r.* sich —wälzen, to descend rolling or wallowing. —wanken, *v. intr.* to come down, to descend tottering or reeling. —waschen, *ir. v. tr.* to wash away or off. —weisen, *ir.* I. *v. tr.* to shew down or downwards. II. *v. intr.* to point down or downwards. —werfen, *ir. v. tr.* to throw down. —winden, *ir.* I. *v. tr.* to move down or downwards by means of a windlass. II. *v. r.* sich —winden, to descend in making turnings or windings. —winken, I. *v. intr.* to make a sign, to beckon down or downwards. II. *v. tr.* to make a sign to come down. —wollen, *ir. v. intr.* to be willing, to wish or want to come down or to descend. —wünschen, I. *v. tr.* Etwas —wünschen, to wish any thing to come down or to descend. Des Himmels Segen auf Einen —wünschen, to call down Heaven's blessings upon a person. II. *v. r.* sich —wünschen, to wish one's self down, to wish to be down. —würdigen, V. —setzen. —würdigung, *f.* debasement, disparagement. —zerren, *v. tr.* to pull, drag or tug down. —ziehen, *ir.* I. *v. tr.* to draw or pull down. II. *v. intr.* to move, march or proceed down, to descend. —zischen, I. *v. intr.* to come or fall down hissing or whizzing. II. *v. tr.* to bring down by hissing. Sie zischten ihn von der Bühne —, they drove him off the stage by hissing and hooting. —zittern, *v. intr.* to fall or flow down trembling.

Herábwärts, *adv.* downwards.

*__Heráldik__, *f.* [Wappenkunst] heraldry.

Herán, *adv.* near to or towards the place where we are, hither, on, near. Nur —! come on or near, advance, approach! [in seamen's lang.] —! come along-side, come aboard! [It denotes approach and is much used in composition of verbs of motion; but these compounds being very easily understood, we only subjoin a few by way of example].

Heran-brechen, *ir. v. intr.* V. Anbrechen. —bringen, *ir. v. tr.* to bring or draw near, to approach. —eilen, *v. intr.* to hasten on or near. —fahren, *ir. v. intr.* to come on or approach in a carriage or ship; *it.* **fig.* to approach in an overhasty or precipitate manner. —fliegen, *ir. v. intr.* to approach flying, to fly near. —fließen, *ir. v. intr.* to flow towards the place where we are. —führen, *v. tr.* to lead or conduct near, to bring on or near. —kommen, *ir. v. intr.* to come on or near, to approach, to advance. Wenn die Todesstunde —kömmt, when the hour of death draws near or nigh. —kunft, *f.* coming near, approach, arrival, V. [the more usual word] Ankunft. —nahen, *v. intr.* to approach, to draw near. *Fig.* Die Stunde meiner Abreise nahet —, the hour of my departure draws near. —reifen, *v. intr.* to ripen. —rennen, *ir. v. intr.* to run near. —rücken, I. *v. tr.* to move or push near, to approach. II. *v. intr.* to draw or march near, to advance. —schleichen, *ir. v. intr.* to steal or sneak on or near. —steigen, *ir. v. intr.* to advance mounting, to ascend towards the place where we are; *it. fig.* * to strut or stalk on. —wachsen, *ir. v. intr.* to grow up, to grow tall.

Heraúf, *adv.* from a lower place towards that where we are, up, upwards. Nur —! come up! [It is much used in composition of verbs; but these compounds being easily understood, we only subjoin a few by way of example.]

Herauf-bringen, *ir. v. tr.* to bring or carry up. —dämmern, *v. intr.* to begin to peep, to dawn. Der Tag dämmerte —, the day began to peep, the day began to break or dawn. —dürfen, *ir. v. intr.* to be allowed to come up. —fahren, *ir. v. intr.* to ascend in a carriage or ship. Den Fluß —fahren, to sail up the river. —führen, *v. tr.* to lead or conduct up. —geben, *ir. v. tr.* to reach, hand or pass up [towards the place where we are]. —gehen, *ir. v. intr.* to go, walk or step up, to ascend. —helfen, *ir. v. intr.* Einem —helfen, to help any one up. Helfen Sie ihm auf diese Bank —, help or assist him in getting upon this bench. —holen, *v. tr.* to fetch up. —kommen, *ir. v. intr.* to come or get up, to ascend, to gain the top. Den Fluß —kommen, to come or sail up the river. *—können, *ir. v. intr.* to be able or allowed to come up. —rücken, I. *v. tr.* to move, push or put higher up. II. *v. intr.* to come or move nearer up. —schiffen, —segeln, *v. intr.* to sail up [the river]. —steigen, *ir. v. intr.* to come up, to mount, to ascend. [in poetry] Wann der Mond und die Sterne —steigen, when the moon and stars rise. —wachsen, *ir. v. intr.* to grow up to. —ziehen, *ir.* I. *v. tr.* to draw or pull up. II. *v. intr.* to draw or march up, to ascend. Wolken ziehen —, clouds rise.

Heraúfwärts, *adv.* upwards.

Heraús, *adv.* out of any place to that where we are, out. Er ist noch nicht zum Hause —, he has not yet come out of the house; —! come out! — damit! — mit der Sprache! out with it, speak out! — aus den Federn! get up! † — mit der Fuchtel! draw! von innen —, from within; er wohnt vorne —, he lodges in the forepart or the front of the house; frei, gerade, rund —, flatly, frankly, bluntly, without reserve. [Heraus is very much used in composition of verbs, such compounds as are not found here, are easily understood; see, however, also Hervor, Weg.]

Heraus-ackern, *v. tr.* to pluck up or root out by the plough, to plough up or out. —arbeiten, I. *v. tr.* to get out by labour or working, to work out. Etwas aus dem Gröbsten —arbeiten, to give the first form or shape to a thing, to rough-hew, to rough-work a thing. II. *v. r.* sich —arbeiten, to work one's self out of, to get out of with labour or difficulty. Ich will sehen, wie er sich aus dieser Verlegenheit —arbeiten wird, I'll see how he will extricate himself, or get out of this trouble or difficulty. —begeben, *ir. v. r.* sich —begeben, to go or step out. —beichten, *v. tr.* to confess freely or the whole truth, all that one knows. —bekommen, *ir. v. tr.* 1) to receive a balance from an account or payment, to get back in exchange. Ich bekomme noch zwei Kreuzer —, I must have two Kreutzers back again. 2) to draw out or forth, to disengage, to get out. Ich kann diesen Nagel nicht —bekommen, I cannot get this nail out. *Fig.* * Ich kann das nicht —bekommen [=erfahren, errathen], I cannot get or find that out, cannot guess that. V. —bringen. —bemühen, *v. tr.* Einen —bemühen, and *v. r.*

ſich —bemühen, to give some person, one's self the trouble to come or step out. —beſtellen, v. tr. to order to come out, to be brought out. Ich habe den Wein —beſtellt, I have ordered the wine to be brought out here. —bewegen, v. tr. and r. ſich —bewegen, to move out. —bitten, ir. v. tr. Einen —bitten, to beg, desire or ask any one to come out. —blaſen, ir. v. tr. to drive out by blowing; it. to blow out towards the place where we are. —blicken, V. —ſehen. —brauſen, I. v. intr. 1) to go or come out or forth roaring or blustering, to spout or gush out. Das Waſſer brauſt aus dem Felſen —, the water spouts or comes gushing out of the rock. 2) [applied to men &c.] to rush forth or out impetuously. 3) to express one's self violently or impetuously. II. v. tr. to utter in great heat, impetuously. —brechen, ir. I. v. tr. to break out, to force out. II. v. intr. to burst out [with impetuosity]; fig. V. Ausbrechen, Losbrechen. —brennen, ir. I. v. intr. 1) [used with haben] to burn, flame or blaze out towards the place where we are. 2) [used with ſeyn] to be consumed by fire in or from the middle or midst, or from among. II. v. tr. to take out or off by fire. —bringen, ir. v. tr. 1) to bring out [towards the place where we are]. Fig. *Kein Wort —bringen können, not to be able to utter or speak a word. 2) to draw out or forth; to get out. Den Nagel aus der Wand —bringen, to get the nail out of the wall; einen Flecken —bringen, to take or get out a stain. Fig. Eine Aufgabe —bringen, to solve a problem; ich bringe da keinen Sinn —, I cannot make out [the sense or meaning of &c.] that; er hat dieſe ſchwierige Stelle —gebracht, he has made out or discovered the sense or meaning of this difficult passage; können Sie dieſe Inſchrift —bringen? can you make out or read this inscription? durch Fragen etwas —bringen, to learn, discover, find or get out any thing by asking questions; man kann nichts aus ihm —bringen, one can get nothing out of him; ein Geheimniß —bringen, to get or find out a secret; Geld mit Gewalt von Einem —bringen, to extort money from any one; ich konnte das nie von ihm —bringen [= ihn dazu vermögen], I could never prevail upon him, or get him to do that; endlich habe ich es —gebracht, daß ich die Stelle erhielt, at length I have succeeded in obtaining the place or office. —bringung, f. extraction, discovery. —brudeln, v. intr. to come out or forth in bubbles, to bubble out. —dampfen, I. v. tr. to emit or exhale steam or vapour. II. v. intr. to pass or rise in the form of steam or vapour out of a thing. —donnern, v. tr. and intr. to utter or speak with a thundering voice, to thunder out. —drängen, I. v. tr. Einen or Etwas —drängen, to push or force out a person or thing [of its place] by pressing. II. v. r. ſich —drängen, aus der Menge, to get out of, to squeeze through the crowd. —drehen, v. tr. to wring or twist out. —dringen, ir. v. intr. to come out with violence and rapidity. Das Blut drang ihm zum Munde —, the blood gushed out of his mouth; der Feind drang aus dem Walde —, the enemy rushed out of the wood. —drücken, v. tr. to press or squeeze out. —duften, v. intr. to emit or exhale an odour towards the place where we are. —dürfen, ir. v. intr. to be allowed to come out. —eilen, v. intr. to come out hastily, to hasten out. —eitern, v. intr. to come out with the matter or pus. —fahren, ir. I. v. intr. 1) to come out suddenly, to rush, fly or burst out. Wie der Blitz zum Hauſe —fahren, to rush out of the house like lightning. Fig. Iſt es möglich? fuhr mein Freund —, is it possible? cried my friend thoughtlessly, rashly or inadvertently; es fuhr ihm ein Wort —, he slipped out or dropped a word; unbedachtſam fuhr mir dieſes Wort —, that word slipped out, before I was aware. 2) to come out in a carriage &c., ship or boat, to drive out, to sail out. II. v. tr. to convey or carry out in a carriage &c. —fallen, ir. v. intr. to fall out of a place. —finden, ir. I. v. tr. to find out, to discover. II. v. r. ſich —finden, to find one's way out. Wie ſollen wir uns aus dieſem Labyrinthe —finden? how are we to find our way out of this labyrinth? Fig. Ich finde mich nicht —, I am lost in it, I comprehend or understand nothing of the matter. —fiſchen, v. tr. to fish out or up, to take out of the water. *Fig. Wo haben Sie das —gefiſcht? where did you get, where did you pick up that? das iſt Alles, was ich aus ihm —gefiſcht [= erfahren] habe, that is all I could get out of him. —flattern, v. intr. to come out fluttering, to flutter out. —fliegen, ir. v. intr. to fly out. —fliehen, ir. v. intr. to make one's escape out of a place. —fließen, ir. v. intr. to flow or run out of a place, to issue, to emanate. Der Wein iſt —gefloſſen, the wine has run out. V. Ausfließen 1). —fluten, v. intr. to stream out in floods. —foderer, —forderer, m. challenger. —fodern, —fordern, v. tr. 1) Etwas —fordern, to demand any thing to be given up or back; Einen —fordern, to ask or demand any one to come out of a place. 2) Einen —fordern, to challenge any one, to send any one a challenge. Er ließ ihn durch einen Edelmann —fordern, he sent him a challenge by a nobleman; einen Narren muß man nicht —fordern, one must never defy a fool; ſie haben ſich auf das Brettſpiel —gefordert, they have challenged one another at backgammon; er war durch beleidigende Reden —gefordert worden, he had been provoked by offensive words. —forderung, f. challenge. —freſſen, ir. I. v. tr. to eat out of a thing. Die Ratte hat ein Stück aus dem Käſe —gefreſſen, the rat has eaten a piece out of the cheese; der Bär frißt den Honig aus den Bienenſtöcken —, the bear eats the honey out of the bee-hives. II. v. r. [if of men, in contempt] ſich —freſſen, to fatten by eating. Fig. †Sich aus der Sache —freſſen [= ziehen], to get out of the scrape, to get off. —führen, v. tr. to lead or conduct out, to bring out of a place. Führt mein Pferd —! bring out my horse! —gabe, f. 1) the act of giving back or delivering up. 2) publication of a book. Wann wird die —gabe dieſes Werkes ſtattfinden? when will this work be published? —gabeln, v. tr. to take out with a fork. —geben, ir. v. tr. 1) to reach out, to hand out of a place, to deliver up. Geben Sie mir es zum Fenſter —, give or hand it me out of the window; einen Gefangenen —geben, to give or deliver up a prisoner; er mußte Alles —geben, he was obliged to return all. 2) to pay the balance of an account, to give the change. Was wollen Sie mir —geben? what will you give me to boot? ich gebe Ihnen noch 10 Guineen —, I'll give you ten guineas to boot; Sie müſſen mir 2 Kreuzer —geben, you must give me back two kreutzers; ich kann Ihnen nicht —geben, ich habe keine Münze, I can't pay you the difference, I have no change; warum geben Sie mir nicht —? why don't you give me the change? 3) to publish, to edit [a book, a journal &c.]. Wer gibt dieſe Zeitſchrift —? who is the editor of this journal or periodical? —geber, m. editor. —gehen, ir. v. intr. to go or come out. Beim —gehen aus der Kirche, on coming out of the church. Fig. Dieſes Zimmer geht auf die Straße —, this room looks into, faces or fronts the street; dieſer Nagel geht nicht —, this nail won't come out; mit der Sprache —gehen, to speak or talk freely, frankly, openly, sincerely, plainly, roundly; gehen Sie mit der Sprache —! don't mince the matter. it. to project beyond the main body, to jut [out]. —gießen, ir. v. tr. to pour out. Aus einem Gefäße — in ein anderes gießen, to pour out of one vessel into another, to decant. —graben, ir. v. tr. to dig out or up. Einen Schatz —graben, to dig out a treasure; eine Leiche, einen Leichnam —graben, to disinter a dead body, to untomb a corpse. —greifen, ir. I. v. intr. to stretch or reach one's hand out of a place. II. v. tr. to seise or grasp and take out, to pick out. —gucken, v. intr. to look or peep out of a place. —haben, ir. v. tr. 1) to receive a balance from an account or payment, to get back in exchange. Ich muß einen Gulden —haben, I must have a florin back. 2) to draw or get out. Ich muß meinen Freund aus dem Gefängniß —haben, I must get my friend out of prison. Fig. Jetzt habe ich es —, now I have hit or guessed it. —hacken, v. tr. to dig out or up with a hoe. —häkeln, —haken, v. tr. to hook out. —halten, ir. v. tr. to hold or stretch out of a place. Er hielt mir die Hand zum Fenſter —, he reached me his hand out of the window. —hangen, ir. v. intr., —hängen, v. tr. to hang out. —hauen, ir. I. v. tr. to take out by cutting or hewing, to cut out, to hew out. Er hieb ihn mitten aus den Feinden —, he rescued him from the midst of his enemies. II. v. r. ſich —hauen, to free or disengage one's self by laying about; fig. † to get out of the scrape, to get off. —heben, ir. v. tr. to lift out, to take out. Einen Baum —heben, to grub up a tree; er hob mich aus der Kutſche —, he helped me out of the coach. Fig. to render prominent, to relieve, to set off, V. Hervorheben. —helfen, ir. v. intr. to help or assist any one in getting out of a place. Helfen Sie ihm aus dieſer Grube —, help him out of that hole or pit. *Fig. Einem —helfen, to get any one out of trouble, to bring any one off. —hetzen, v. tr. [einen Hirſch] to unharbour, rouse or dislodge [a stag]. —hinken, v. intr. to come or go out halting or limping. —holen, v. tr. to fetch out, to take out. Er holte es aus der Taſche —, he took it out of his pocket. —hüpfen, v. intr. to skip or jump out of a place. —huſten, v. tr. to cough up. Blut —huſten, to cough up, to expectorate blood. —jagen, I. v. tr. to drive or hunt out of place. II. v. intr. to ride at full speed, to gallop out of a place. —kämmen, v. tr. to take out by combing, to comb out. —kehren, v. tr. 1) to take out, to remove by sweeping or brushing, to sweep out, to brush out. 2) to turn inside out. Fig. *Das Rauhe, die rauhe Seite —kehren [= Ernſt brauchen, it. drohen], to use severity, it. to show one's teeth. —klauben, v. tr. to get out by picking, to pick out. Fig. *Den Sinn einer Stelle —klauben, to find out the sense or meaning of a passage by careful disquisition. —kleiden, I. v. tr. to dress handsomely, to trim [up]. II. v. r. ſich —kleiden, to dress, to trim one's self handsomely. —klettern, v. intr. to climb out of a place. —klopfen, v. tr. to drive or force out by beating, knocking or rapping, to beat out. Den Staub —klopfen, to beat out the dust; *Einen aus dem Bett —klopfen, to knock any one up. —klügeln, v. tr. to find out by searching closely into —kochen, V. Auskochen I. 1). —kommen, ir. v. intr. to come out or forth. Der Herr wird bald —kommen, the gentleman will soon come out; kommen Sie morgen zu uns — [auf's Land &c.], come to see us to morrow [in the country &c.]; die Kräuter kommen aus der Erde —, the herbs come, shoot or peep out of the ground; er hat das Fieber nicht mehr, ſeitdem die Blattern —gekommen ſind, his fever is gone, since the small-pox has come out. *Fig.* a) to become public, to come out. Wann wird der deutsch-englische Theil —kommen? when will the German-English part be published or come out? die Wahrheit ist endlich —gekommen, the truth has come out at last; wenn das —kömmt, if that comes to be known. b) to be found just, right, true or correct. Die Rechnung ist —gekommen, the calculation or reckoning has proved correct; die Summe kommt nicht —, the sum does not agree or answer. c) to have an effect. Das kömmt auf Eines —, that comes to the same thing, it is all the same; (ironically) das käme schön —! that would be fine, indeed! d) bei Etwas —kommen, to be got as profit or advantage. Was wird rein or netto dabei —kommen? what will be the net profits? dabei kömmt nichts —, this affair or concern is unprofitable, *it.* (= das dient zu nichts) that is of no use. —können, *ir. v. intr.* to be able to go or come out of a place. —kratzen, *v. tr.* to scratch out, to scrape out. —kriechen, *ir. v. intr.* to creep out of a place. † or ‖—kriegen, *v. tr.* V. —bekommen, —bringen. —langen, I. *v. tr.* to take or fetch out, V. —holen, —nehmen. II. *v. intr.* to pass or stretch one's hand out of a place. —lassen, *ir.* I. *v. tr.* to let out of a place. Das Vieh aus dem Stalle —lassen, to let the cattle go out of the stall; einen Gefangenen —lassen, to release a prisoner, *it.* (= entspringen lassen) to let a prisoner escape; Wein —lassen, to draw off wine. *Fig.* Seinen Zorn —lassen, to give way to, to give vent to one's anger. II. *v. r.* sich —lassen, to utter or vent one's thoughts, to express one's mind about any thing. —laufen, *ir. v. intr.* to run out of a place; *it.* V. —fließen. —lecken, *v. tr.* to get out of a thing by licking. —legen, *v. tr.* to put or lay out of a thing. —leiten, *v. tr.* to lead or to conduct out of a place. —lenken, I. *v. tr.* to turn, lead or direct out of a place. II. *v. intr.* er lenkte aus dem Wege —, he turned off or out of the way. —lesen, *ir. v. tr.* to pick out, to choose, to select. —leuchten, *v. tr.* to light any one out of a place. *—loben, *v. tr.* to cry up, to extol. —locken, *v. tr.* to allure any one to come out of a place, to draw out of a place. *Fig.* Ein Geheimniß aus Einem —locken, to draw or pump a secret out of any one; Einen —locken über etwas, to sift any one, to feel any one's pulse about any thing. —lodern, *v. intr.* to blaze out of a place. —lügen, *ir. v. tr.* Einen, and *v. r.* sich, to get any one, one's self off by telling a lie. —machen, I. *v. tr.* to get out, to take out. Nüsse —machen, to shell nuts; einen Flecken —machen, to take, get or fetch out a stain. II. *v. r.* sich —machen, (in fam. lang.) to get or stir out, to go out or abroad. Er ist so schwach, daß er sich noch nicht —machen darf, he is so weak, that he must not venture to stir out or to go abroad yet. —müssen, *ir. v. intr.* to be obliged to come out. Es muß —, was ich &c., I needs must say what I &c.; die Wahrheit muß —! the truth must come out! —nehmen, *ir. v. tr.* to take out of a place. Nehmen Sie doch — (Suppe &c.), pray, help yourself; die Besatzung aus einer Festung —nehmen, to withdraw the garrison out of a fortress, die Beine aus einem Hasen, die Gräten aus einem Fisch —nehmen, to bone a hare, a fish; einen Zahn —nehmen, to extract, to draw or pull out a tooth. **Fig.* Sich etwas —nehmen, to presume, to arrogate to one's self, to make or to be bold. Sich zu viel —nehmen, to take too much liberty or too great a latitude, to make too bold; sich —nehmen, zu sagen, to make so bold as to say; sich Freiheiten —nehmen, to take liberties; damit wir uns nicht zu viel —nehmen, lest we might presume too far. —niesen, *v. tr.* to force out by sneezing. —nöthigen, *v. tr.* to oblige, to press or urge to come out. *—packen, *v. r.* (rather vulgar) sich —packen, to get or go out of a place. Packt euch —! get ye out! —platzen, *v. intr.* to burst out. *Fig.* *Mit Etwas —platzen, to utter suddenly and incautiously, to blurt out, to pop out. —plaudern, *v. tr.* to blab out. —plumpen, V. —platzen. —pochen, *v. tr.* to force out by knocking. Ich wurde um Mitternacht —gepocht, I was knocked up at midnight. —poltern, I. *v. intr.* to fall out, to come out making a great noise or rattling. *Mit etwas —poltern, to speak or utter loudly and vehemently, to rattle out. II. *v. tr.* 1) *Einen —poltern, V. —pochen. 2) to utter or speak loudly and noisily. Schimpfworte —poltern, to belch out reproachful words or abuse. —pressen, *v. tr.* V. —drücken. *Fig.* Etwas von Einem —pressen, to extort a thing from any one. Die Folter preßte das Geständniß seines Verbrechens aus ihm —, the confession of his crime was extorted by the rack. —pressung, *f.* the act of pressing or squeezing out; *fig.* extortion. —prügeln, *v. tr.* to beat or cudgel any one out of a place. —pumpen, *v. tr.* to pump out. —putzen, I. *v. tr.* to deck [out], to decorate, to adorn, to trick out. Eine Braut —putzen, to dress up a bride; ein Zimmer —putzen, to decorate a room. II. *v. r.* sich —putzen, to dress one's self smartly, to trick one's self up. —quellen, *v. intr.* to issue forth, to spring, to gush, to spout. —quetsche, —quetschform, *f.* (among goldbeaters) mould of about a thousand leaves. —ragen, *v. intr.* V. Hervorragen. —ranken, *v. intr.* and *refl.* to spread out of a place with tendrils. —rasseln, *v. intr.* to come out rattling or clattering. —rauchen, *v. intr.* 1) to come out of a place in the form of smoke. 2) to look out of a place smoking. Zum Fenster —rauchen, to smoke out of the window. —raufen, *v. tr.* to pull out, to pluck out. Er raufte sich die Haare —, he tore his hair. —rauschen, *v. intr.* to come out rustling or making a noise. —rechen, *v. tr.* to rake out. —rechnen, *v. tr.* V. Ausrechnen. —recken, V. —strecken. —reden, I. *v. intr.* 1) to talk or speak from out of a place. 2) to speak, to talk. Frei —reden, to speak one's mind freely, to speak openly, frankly, without fear. Wie können Sie so —reden? how can you talk in such a manner? II. *v. r.* sich —reden, to exculpate one's self. —reisen, *v. intr.* to travel out of a place. —reißen, *ir.* I. *v. tr.* to tear out, to pull out. Einen Zahn —reißen, to draw a tooth; sich die Haare —reißen, to tear one's hair; Einem etwas aus der Hand —reißen, to wrest a thing from any one's hands. V. Ausreißen I. 1). *Fig.* Einen aus der Noth, der Gefahr, der Verlegenheit —reißen, to free, deliver or relieve any one from distress, danger, trouble or embarrassment. II. *v. r.* sich —reißen, to disentangle, disengage one's self. Er hat sich glücklich —gerissen, luckily he has got off or got clear; er ist so krank, daß man nicht glaubt, er werde sich —reißen, he is so ill, that it is not expected he will recover. —reiten, *ir. v. intr.* to ride out of a place (on horseback). —rennen, *ir. v. intr.* to run out of a place. —rieseln, *v. intr.* to trickle or purl out of a place. —rinnen, *ir. v. intr.* to run, leak or trickle out (of a vessel &c.). —röcheln, *v. tr.* to utter or pronounce with a rattling in one's throat. —rollen, *v. tr.* and *intr.* to roll out of a place. —rücken, I. *v. tr.* to move, push or draw out of a place. *Fig.* *Geld —rücken, to give, to advance money. II. *v. intr.* to come or march out. Das Heer rückte aus dem Lager —, the army decamped, V. Ausrücken. **Fig.* Mit Geld —rücken, to draw the purse, to pay down some money; mit der Sprache —rücken, to speak out, to speak or tell one's mind freely, plainly; rücken Sie einmal mit der Sprache —, speak the word, speak out, don't mince the matter! —rufen, *ir.* I *v. tr.* to call any one out. II. *v. intr.* to call or cry out of a place; (a military term) to cry to arms. —rupfen, *v. tr.* to pull, to pluck out. —sagen, *v. tr.* to speak out, to declare (freely). Sagen Sie ihre Gedanken frei —, utter or vent your thoughts freely. —schaffen, *v. tr.* to remove out of a place. —schallen, *v. intr.* to sound out from. —scharren, *v. tr.* V. Ausscharren I. 1). —schauen, *v. intr* to look out of a place. —schäumen, *v. intr.* to come out in the form of foam or froth. —scheinen, *ir. v. intr.* V. —schimmern. †—scheren, *v. r.* sich —scheren, V. —packen. —scheuchen, *v. tr.* to drive or scare out of a place. —schicken, I. *v. tr.* to send (out). II. *v. intr.* to send word, to send any one to fetch something, from out of a place towards another. Er hat heute nicht [zu uns] —geschickt, he did not send word [to us] to-day. —schieben, *ir. v. tr.* to shove or push out. —schießen, *ir.* I. *v. tr.* to shoot (an arrow) out of a place. II. *v. intr.* 1) to shoot or fire out of a place. 2) to come out with violence or impetuosity. Er schoß wie wüthend aus dem Hause —, he ran out of the house like a madman; eine Schlange schoß aus der Höhle —, a serpent rushed out of the hole; das Blut schoß aus der Ader —, the blood spouted or gushed from the vein. —schiffen, I. *v. intr.* to sail out of a place. II. *v. tr.* to convey out of a place, to export in a ship. —schimmern, *v. intr.* to shine or glitter out of, through or across something. —schlagen, *ir. v. tr.* to force out by beating or striking. Feuer aus einem Kieselsteine —schlagen, to strike fire out of a pebble; den Feind aus den Außenwerken —schlagen, to drive or chase the enemy from the outworks; Einem die Zähne aus dem Munde —schlagen, to beat or knock any one's teeth out; *wie viel hat er bei diesem Handel —geschlagen? how much has he got by that bargain? —schleichen, *ir. v. intr.* and *r.* sich —schleichen, to sneak or steal out of a place. —schleppen, *v. tr.* to drag out. —schlüpfen, *v. intr.* to slip out. †—schmeißen, V. —werfen. —schmücken, V. —putzen. —schneiden, *ir. v. tr.* to cut out, V. Ausschneiden 1). —schöpfen, *v. tr.* Wasser —schöpfen, to draw water out of; *it.* to scoop water out of a thing. —schreien, *ir.* I. *v. intr.* to cry out from a place. II. *v. tr.* to utter bawling. —schreiten, *ir. v. intr.* to stride or stalk out of a place. —schütteln, *v. tr.* to shake out. *Prov.* Das läßt sich nicht so aus dem Aermel —schütteln, that's not done in a trice, the matter is not so easy as you imagine. —schütten, *v. tr.* to pour or throw out of a place; *it.* to spill. —schwanken, *v. intr.* to come out reeling or tottering. —schwimmen, *ir. v. intr.* to swim out. —schwingen, *ir. v. r.* sich —schwingen, to vault, leap, jump or spring out. —schwitzen, *v. tr.* to sweat out, to exsude. —segeln, *v. intr.* to sail out. —sehen, *ir. v. intr.* to look out. —sehnen, *v. r.* sich —sehnen, to wish one's self out of a place, to long to be out. —senden, V. —schicken. —setzen, *v. tr.* to set or put out or out of doors. *Fig.* V. —streichen, Hervorheben. —seyn, *ir. v. intr.* to be out or without, to have come out. Sobald er — ist, as soon as he is out, gone out or come out; er war eben aus dem Wagen —, he had but just got out of the carriage; die Vögel sind aus dem Neste —, the birds have left their nests; wir sind noch nicht aus der schlimmen Jahreszeit —, we are not yet out of, we have not yet passed the bad season; die Pocken sind — or —gekommen, the small pox is come out; die Blumen, die Knospen sind schon weit —, the flowers, buds are already far advanced, pretty forward; der zweite Band ist —, the second volume has come out, has been published. —singen, *ir. v. tr.* and *intr.* V. Singen and Hinaussingen. —sollen, *v. intr.* to be obliged to come out. *Es soll mir —, es koste, was es wolle, I'll have or get it out, cost what it will. —spazieren, *v. intr.* to walk out. —speien, V. Ausspeien. —sperren, *v. tr.* to lock any one out. —sprechen, *ir. v. intr.* to speak. Wie können Sie so — sprechen? how can you talk in such a manner? —sprengen, I. *v. tr.* to blow out with gunpowder. II. *v. intr.* to ride out of a place at full speed, to gallop out. —springen, *ir. v. intr.* 1) to leap or jump out, to rush out, to spout or gush out. Es sprangen Funken —, sparks of fire darted or shot out; Einem in die Augen schlagen, daß das Feuer —springt, to make any one's eyes strike or flash fire. 2) to break or burst off or loose. —spritzen, *v. intr.* to spout out. Das Blut spritzte aus der Ader —, the blood spouted from the vein. —sprossen, *v. intr.* to sprout, shoot or germinate. —sprudeln, I. *v. intr.* to come out in bubbles, to bubble out. II. *v. tr.* Scheltworte, Gotteslästerungen —sprudeln, to belch out blasphemies. *—staffiren, V. —putzen. —stehen, *ir. v. intr.* 1) to stand out, to project, to jut. Dieses Haus steht zu weit auf die Straße —, this house juts out too much into the street; wie seine Augen —stehen! how his eyes project or stick out of his head; er ist so mager, daß ihm die Knochen —stehen, he is so lean that one may see his bones through his skin. 2) to come out and stand here. —stehlen, *ir.* I. *v. tr.* Einem etwas aus der Tasche &c. —stehlen, to steal any thing out of any one's pocket, to pick any one's pocket; diese Verse sind aus Milton —gestohlen, those verses are purloined or stolen from Milton. II. *v. r.* sich —stehlen, to steal, sneak or slink out of a place. —steigen, *ir. v. intr.* to get out of a place. Aus dem Wagen —steigen, to alight from the carriage; zum Fenster —steigen, to get out of the window; über die Mauer aus dem Garten —steigen, to escape or get out of the garden by climbing over the wall. —stellen, I. *v. tr.* to place or put out or without. *Fig.* II. *v. r.* sich —stellen, to prove, to show. Es stellte sich dabei heraus, daß &c., it was proved on this occasion, that &c. —stolpern, *v. intr.* to come out stumbling. —stoßen, *ir. v. tr.* to thrust or push out of a place, V. Ausstoßen II. 1). —stottern, *v. tr.* to stammer out. —strahlen, *v. intr.* to emit or cast forth rays out of a place. —strecken, *v. tr.* to stretch out [the hand &c.]. Die Zunge —strecken, to draw or thrust out one's tongue, *it.* [in order to mock any one] to loll [out] one's tongue. —streichen, *ir. v. tr.* to make smooth by passing one's hand or an instrument over a thing. Die Runzeln aus dem Papier mit dem Falzbein —streichen, to smooth the paper with the folder. **Fig.* Einen, etwas —streichen, to praise with exaggeration, to extol; Waaren —streichen, to puff goods. —streuen, *v. tr.* to strew out or abroad. —strömen, *v. intr.* to stream or pour out of a place; *Fig.* to flock out of a place. —stürmen, *v. intr.* to rush out of a place. —stürzen, I. *v. tr.* to throw or precipitate out of a place. II. *v. intr.* 1) to fall or tumble out of a place. 2) to rush out with impetuosity. III. *v. r.* sich —stürzen, to throw or precipitate one's self out of a place. —suchen, *v. tr.* to pick out, to choose, to select. —tanzen, *v. intr.* to come out dancing. —taumeln, *v. intr.* to come out reeling or staggering. —thun, *ir. v. tr.* to put forth, to take out. —toben, I. *v. tr.* to utter something with vehemence. II. *v. intr.* to come out blustering, raving or raging. —tönen, *v. intr.* V. —schallen. —traben, *v. intr.* to come out trotting, to trot out of a place. —tragen, *ir. v. tr.* to carry or bring out of a place. —treiben, *ir. v. tr.* to drive out, to expel. —treten, *ir.* I. *v. intr.* to step or come out of a place. Aus einer Gesellschaft —treten, V. Austreten. II. 3). II. *v. tr.* to press out with the feet, to tread out. —treten, *n.* [in surgery] Das —treten des Auges aus der Augenhöhle, protuberance of the eye out of its natural position, exophthalmy, V. Vorfall; das —treten des Nabels (Nabelbruch), navel rupture, exomphalos; das —treten des Blutes aus den Gefäßen, extravasation of the blood. —triefen, *v. intr.* to trickle or drip out. —trippeln, *v. intr.* to run or step lightly, to trip out of a place. —tröpfeln, —tropfen, *v. intr.* to drip, to drop out. —wachsen, *ir. v. intr.* to grow out of a place, to come out as an excrescence. —wagen, *v. r.* sich, to dare or venture to come out or forth. —wallen, *v. intr.* to boil over. —walzen, V. Auswalzen 1). —wälzen, *v. tr.* to roll out. —wandeln, —wandern, *v. intr.* to walk, travel or wander out of a place. —wanken, *v. intr.* to come out vacillating or tottering. —waschen, *ir. v. tr.* 1) to take out by washing, to wash out. Die Seife aus der Wäsche wieder —waschen, to rinse the linen. 2) to wash clean. —weichen, *v. intr.* to come out by soaking, to soak out. —werfen, *ir. v. tr.* to throw out. Den Ballast aus einem Schiffe —werfen, to discharge a ship of ballast. —wickeln, I. *v. tr.* to get out what is wound or convolved, to unwind, to disentangle, to unravel. II. *v. r.* sich —wickeln, *Fig.* to extricate one's self, to get out of difficulties &c. —winden, *ir.* I. *v. tr.* to get out by means of a windlass. II. *v. r.* sich —winden, to wind one's self out of, to extricate one's self from. —winken, I. *v. intr.* to make a sign, to beckon out of a place. II. *v. tr.* Einen —winken, to make any one a sign to come out. —wischen, I. *v. tr.* to wipe off or away. II. *v. intr. Fig.* [in fam. lang.] to slip or escape unperceived out of a place. —wohnen, *v. intr.* vorn —wohnen, to lodge towards the street, in the front of the house. —wollen, *ir. v. intr.* to wish to get out, to be disposed to come out. *Fig.* Er will mit der Sprache nicht —, he is not disposed to speak out or his mind. —wühlen, *v. tr.* to dig, grub or root out with the snout, as swine. —wünschen, I. *v. tr.* to wish any thing to be or to come out of a place. II. *v. r.* sich —wünschen, to wish one's self out of a place or situation. —würgen, *v. tr.* to eject from the stomach by straining the throat. Sein Mittagessen —würgen, to vomit one's dinner up or out. —zahlen, *v. tr.* to pay the balance of an account, to give to boot. —ziehen, *ir.* I. *v. tr.* to draw out. Den Degen aus der Scheide —ziehen, to draw the sword from the sheath or scabbard, to unsheath the sword; den Pfropf aus einer Flasche —ziehen, to uncork a bottle; einen Zahn —ziehen, to draw a tooth; eine Pflanze mit der Wurzel —ziehen, to pull a plant up by the root; die Fäden aus einem Zeuge einzeln —ziehen, to unravel a stuff thread by thread; die Ladung aus einer Flinte —ziehen, to draw the charge out of a gun; einem vernagelten Pferde den Nagel wieder —ziehen, to take out the nail that pricked a horse's foot; den Geist, das Oel aus etwas —ziehen, to extract the spirit, oil of a thing; die Besatzung aus einer Festung —ziehen, to withdraw the garrison from a fortress. *Fig.* Etwas aus einem Buche, einem Schriftsteller —ziehen, to extract something from a book, from an author; Einen aus einem schlimmen Handel —ziehen, to get any one out of trouble, to get or bring any one off. II. *v. r.* sich —ziehen, to come out of, to withdraw from. Der Feind hat sich aus der Festung —gezogen, the enemy has evacuated the fortress. *Fig.* Sich aus der Sache —ziehen, to get out of trouble, to get off, to get out of the scrape. III. *v. intr.* to come out in a train or procession, to march out; *it.* to remove. Er ist auf das Land —gezogen, he has left the town to live in the country. —zupfen, *v. tr.* to pull out, to pluck out. —zwängen, *v. tr.* to force out.

Heraúswärts, *adv.* outward, outwards.

Hèrb or **Hèrbe**, *adj.* and *adv.* [allied to the L. *acerbus*] acid, tart, sharp, astringent, bitter, harsh. Herbes Obst, acid fruit; herber Wein, tart wine. *Fig.* in a high degree unpleasant, very disagreeable, austere, bitter, harsh. Er ist von einer herben Gemüthsart, he is a sullen, austere, severe man; ein herbes Gesicht, eine herbe Miene, a grim, gruff, crabbed, sullen countenance or look; herbe Worte, bitter or hard words; ein herber Schmerz, a bitter grief.

***Herbárium**, *n.* [-s, *pl.* -rien] [a collection of dried plants] herbarium.

Hèrbe, *f.* [Herbheit, Herbigkeit] acidity, tartness, sharpness, harshness. Die — des Obstes, tartness of fruit. *Fig.* austerity, severity, harshness [of temper].

Herbéi, *adv.* [it expresses approach from a somewhat remote place] near, hither. —! —! kommt —! come here or hither, come near, approach! [Herbei is much used in composition of verbs of motion; compare also those compounded with Heran and Herzu.]

Herbei-bemühen, *v. tr.* Einen, and *refl.* sich —, to give any one, one's self the trouble to come hither or near. —bringen, *ir. v. tr.* to bring hither, near or forward, to produce [a witness]. —drängen, *v. r* sich, to come near or hither pressing or pushing. —eilen, *v. intr.* to hasten or run near or hither. —fahren, *ir.* I. *v. tr.* to carry or bring near or hither in a cart or waggon. II. *v. intr.* to come near in a carriage, to approach, to advance. —fliegen, *ir. v. intr.* to come near or hither, to approach flying, to fly near. —fließen, *ir. v. intr.* to flow towards the place where one is. —führen, *v. tr.* to lead, conduct or bring near or hither, to bring on. *Fig.* Die Uebel, welche der Krieg —führt, the evils which war brings on or along. —gehen, *ir. v. intr.* to go or walk near or hither, to approach. —hinken, *v. intr.* to come near or hither limping or halting. —holen, *v. tr.* 1) to fetch [from a remote or concealed place]. 2) *Fig.* [in seamen's lang.] to sail towards a place. Ein Eiland —holen, to endeavour to reach or make an island. —hüpfen, *v. intr.* to come near or approach hopping or skipping. —jagen, I. *v. tr.* to drive or chase near or hither. II. *v. intr.* to ride near or up at full speed, to gallop near or hither. —karren, *v. tr.* to bring, carry or convey hither or near in a cart. —kommen, *ir. v. intr.* to come on or near, to approach, to advance. —können, *ir. v. intr.* to be able to come near, to approach. —kriechen, *ir. v. intr.* to creep on or near. —kunft, *f.* coming near, approach. —lassen, *ir.* I. *v. tr.* to let any one approach or come hither. II. *v. r.* sich zu Etwas —lassen, to condescend to do a thing. —laufen, *ir. v. intr.* to run near or hither. Das Volk lief von allen Seiten —, people flocked hither from all quarters. —locken, *v. tr.* to draw, allure or entice towards the place where one is. —machen, *v. r.* sich —machen, to come near or hither, to approach. —müssen, *ir. v. intr.* to be obliged to come here or near. Das Geld muß heute —! the money must be found to day! —nahen, *v. intr.*

to approach, to draw near, to near. —**nöthigen**, *v. tr.* to oblige, to press, to urge any one to come hither, to approach. —**prügeln**, *v. tr.* to cudgel or beat near or hither. —**rasseln**, *v. intr.* to come near rattling or clattering. —**rauschen**, *v. intr.* to come near, to approach rustling. —**reiten**, *ir. v. intr.* to ride near or hither [on horseback]. —**rennen**, *ir. v. intr.* to run or hasten hither or near. —**rücken**, I. *v. tr.* to move or push near. II. *v. intr.* to draw or march near or hither, to advance. —**rufen**, *ir. v. tr.* to call hither. —**schaffen**, *v. tr.* to bring hither or near, to procure, to produce. Wenn er mir diese Summe —schafft, if he procures or finds me this sum; Beweise —schaffen, to produce or furnish proofs. —**schieben**, *ir. v. tr.* to shove or push near or hither. —**schiffen**, *v. intr.* to come hither or near, to approach in a ship, to sail hither or near. —**schleichen**, *ir. v. intr.* to sneak, steal or slink hither or near. —**schleppen**, *v. tr.* to drag near or hither; *it.* [in fam. lang.] to bring here. —**schwanken**, *v. intr.* to come near or hither tottering. —**schweben**, *v. intr.* to hover hither or near. —**schwimmen**, *ir. v. intr.* to swim hither or near. —**segeln**, *v. intr.* to sail near or hither. —**sprengen**, *v. intr.* to ride near or hither with full speed, to gallop hither or near. —**springen**, *ir. v. intr.* to run, to spring or hasten hither or near. —**stoßen**, *ir. v. tr.* to push hither or near. —**strömen**, *v. intr.* to stream or pour towards the place where we are. *Fig.* Die Menschen strömten von allen Seiten —, people flocked hither or near from all quarters. —**stürzen**, *v. intr.* to rush hither or near. —**tanzen**, *v. intr.* to come hither or near dancing. —**taumeln**, *v. intr.* to come hither or near vacillating or tottering. —**traben**, *v. intr.* to trot hither or near. —**tragen**, *ir. v. tr.* to carry, bring or bear hither or near. —**treiben**, *ir. v. tr.* to drive hither or near. —**treten**, *ir. v. intr.* to step hither or near, to approach. —**wälzen**, *v. tr.* to roll hither or near. —**wanken**, *v. intr.* to come hither or near tottering or reeling. —**wünschen**, *v. tr.* and *r.* sich —wünschen, to wish to be here or near. —**ziehen**, *ir.* I. *v. tr.* to draw or pull near or hither, to attract. Ein Unglück zieht ein anderes —, one misfortune seldom comes alone. **Fig.* Etwas an or bei den Haaren —ziehen, to bring in forcibly or unnaturally, to force in, to drag in by head and shoulders [a comparison &c.]. II. *v. intr.* to move or march hither or near. Als wir den Feind —ziehen sahen, seeing the enemy advancing towards us.

Hèrberge, *f.* [*pl.* -n] [from Heer and bergen] 1) [in general] shelter, harbour, habitation, lodging. Einem — geben, to take any one under one's roof, to lodge any one; wenn ich für diese Nacht in diesem Hause eine — fände, if I could get a lodging in this house for the night; seine — bei Jemand nehmen, to take one's lodgings, to put up at any one's house; er bat sich eine — für eine Nacht bei mir aus, he asked me for a night's lodging. 2) house of entertainment, inn, public house. In eine — einkehren, to put up at an inn; die — einer Zunft or Innung, meeting house or hall of a trades' company, house of call for journeymen. Syn. V. Gasthof.

Herbergs-mutter, *f.*, —**vater**, *m.* the hostess, the host of a house where journeymen are lodged or entertained.

Hèrbergen, I. *v. intr.* to lodge [at an inn]. II. *v. tr.* to shelter, to harbour, to lodge [any one].

Hèrberger, *m.* [-s, *pl.* -], —**inn**, *f.* one who gives shelter &c.; *it.* innkeeper, host, landlord, hostess, landlady.

||**Herbergiren**, *v. tr.*, **Herbergirer**, *m.* V. Herbergen, Herberger.

Hèrbheit, **Hèrbigkeit**, *f.* V. Herbe, *f.*

Hèrblich, *adj.* and *adv.* rather sour, acid or austere.

Hèrbst, *m.* [-es, *pl.* -e] [either allied to the Sax. *aerfwa* = erwerben, or more probably to raffen, Gr. ἅρπ-ω, L. *carpo*] 1) [the time or season of collecting the fruits of the earth] harvest, autumn. Ein kalter, regnerischer —, a cold, rainy autumn. 2) [= Weinlese, *it.* = Ernte] vintage, *it.* harvest or crop. Einen guten — machen, to make a good vintage or harvest; wir werden einen ergiebigen, halben — bekommen, we shall have a plentiful or abundant vintage, a middling crop; wenn er seinen — eingethan hat, when he has gathered in his crop.

Herbst-abend, *m.* an evening in autumn, *it.* autumnal evening. —**adonis**, *m.* [a plant] common adonis or bird's eye. —**arbeit**, *f.* labour or work done in autumn, autumn-work; *it.* labour or work at vintage or harvest time. —**aster**, *f.* autumnal aster or starwort. —**birn**, *f.* autumn-pear. —**blatt**, *n.* autumnal or yellowish leaf. —**blume**, *f.* autumnal flower, chiefly, the meadow-saffron. —**brief**, *m.* V. —faß. —**butte**, —**bütte**, *f.* a vintager's dosser [in which the grapes are gathered and carried]; *it.* a vintage-tub. —**butter**, *f.* butter made in autumn, autumn-butter. —**eis**, *n.* ice in autumn. —**feier**, *f.*, —**ferien**, *pl.* autumn holidays or vacation. —**fieber**, *n.* autumnal fever. —**frucht**, *f.* autumnal fruit. —**geschirr**, *n.* pails, casks, tubs and other vessels, used for the vintage. —**herd**, *m.* [among bird-catchers] a fowling-floor for catching birds in autumn. —**heu**, *n.* V. Grummet. —**holzung**, *f.* the cutting or fetching of wood in autumn. —**hyazinthe**, *f.* the autumnal hyacinth or purple-flower. —**laub**, *n.* leaves in autumn, autumnal or yellowish leaves. —**leute**, *pl.* vintagers, grape-gatherers. —**löwenzahn**, *m.* [a plant] autumnal dandelion. —**luft**, *f.* autumnal air. —**lust**, *f.* diversion or amusement in autumn, particularly during the vintage. —**lustbarkeit**, *f.* V. —lust. —**mäßig**, *adj.* and *adv.* suitable or agreeable to, becoming the vintage; *it.* autumnal. —**mast**, *f.* the fattening of cattle in autumn. —**messe**, *f.* a fair held in autumn. —**monat**, —**mond**, *m.* one of the three autumnal months, September, October, November, but especially the month of September. —**morchel**, *f.* autumnal morel. —**morgen**, *m.* a morning in autumn. —**nacht**, *f.* a night in autumn. —**nachtgleiche**, *f.* autumnal equinox. —**nebel**, *m.* a fog in autumn. —**obst**, *n.* fruit that ripens in autumn, late or autumnal fruit. —**ordnung**, *f.* regulation respecting the vintage. —**pflanze**, *f.* autumnal plant. —**punkt**, *m.* [in astronomy] autumnal point [at which the autumnal equinox commences]. —**reise**, *f.* a journey in autumn. —**rose**, *f.* the autumnal rose, mallow or mallows. —**saat**, *f.* sowing in autumn. —**safran**, *m.* autumnal saffron or crocus. ||—**satz**, *m.* a public notice of the day when the vintage is to begin. —**schein**, *m.* [in astronomy] autumnal aspect. —**schmaus**, *m.* a repast, banquet or feast during the vintage. —**schnee**, *m.* a fall of snow in autumn. —**sonne**, *f.* autumnal sun. —**sturm**, *m.* autumnal storm; *it.* equinoctial storm. —**stand**, *m.* [among sportsmen] haunt of the deer in autumn. —**tag**, *m.* autumnal day; *it.* a day of vintage. —**trüffel**, *f.* autumnal truffle, black or brown truffle. —**trunk**, *m.* the drink during the vintage; *it.* must which a clergyman receives from his parishioners. —**wasserbirn**, *f.* green chissel-pear. —**wetter**, *n.* autumnal weather; *it.* weather proper or good for the vintage. —**wiese**, *f.* a meadow which is only mown in autumn. —**wind**, *m.* autumnal wind. —**witterung**, *f.* V. —wetter. —**zeichen**, *n.* [in astronomy] autumnal sign of the Zodiac (Balance, Scorpion, Archer). —**zeit**, *f.* time of autumn, autumn; *it.* vintage time. —**zeitlose**, *f.* common meadow-saffron, Colchicum autumnale.

Hèrbsten, I. *v. imp.* Es herbstet schon, it is already autumnal weather. II. *v. intr.* to gather the grapes. Man wird bald —, the vintage will soon begin. *it.* to gather in corn or other crops, to reap. Das —, the vintage, *it.* harvest.

Hèrbsthaft, **Hèrbstlich**, *adj.* and *adv.* resembling autumn, autumn-like, autumnal. Die —e Luft, Nachtgleiche, the autumnal air, equinox.

Hèrbstling, *m.* [-s, *pl.* -e] any thing that is produced in autumn, as an autumnal lamb, calf &c., autumnal fruit; especially a sort of eatable mushroom, V. Brätling.

Hèrd, **Hèrd**, *m.* [-es, *pl.* -e] [from the old Germ. Herd = Erde, hence] 1) any flat place or area, destined for a particular purpose. *a*) in forges: α) the boards on which the pounded ore is washed. β) the basin into which the melted metal runs, V. Stich—. *b*) [in hydraulics, an overfall or wear for the superfluous water of a canal] waste-wear. *c*) [in mining] V. Göpelherd. *d*) the place on which fowlers catch birds, fowling-floor. *e*) [in seamen's lang.] Der — einer Blockrolle, the shell of a pulley or block. 2) [a pavement or floor of brick or stone, on which a fire is made] hearth; V. Feuer—, Koch—, Küchen—. *Fig.* house, home, fireside, hearth. Er hat weder Feuer noch —, he has neither house nor home. *Prov.* Eigener — ist Goldes werth, home is home, let it be ever so homely; für seinen eigenen — fechten, to fight for one's own habitation. *it.* V. Frisch—, Seiger—, Treibe—.

Herd-asche, *f.* 1) the ashes which gather from fuel burnt on the hearth. 2) the ashes of which the hearth of a refining-furnace is made. 3) the lead which in refining changes into litharge. —**blei**, *n.* the lead which in refining incorporates with the hearth of the furnace. —**brett**, *n.* one of the boards with which hearths are sometimes covered or lined. —**eisen**, *n.* V. —stange. —**fink**, *m.* decoy-bird. —**flut**, *f.* the slime or mire which separates when the pounded ore is washed. —**frischen**, *n.* the reducing or changing of the litharge into lead. —**gehalt**, *m.* silver contained in the lead of the hearth. —**geld**, *n.* 1) hearth-money, hearth-tax. 2) ground-rent. —**glas**, *n.* glass which in melting overflows and remains on the hearth. —**korn**, *n.*, —**körner**, *pl.* a grain of silver which sometimes settles on the border of the hearth. —**kugel**, *f.* ball by which the middle or centre of a hearth is found out. —**löffel**, *m.* an iron spoon or ladle used in assaying silver. —**platte**, *f.* iron plate covering the hearth, hearth-plate. —**probe**, *f.* assay of silver. —**recht**, *n.* 1) the right of keeping a hearth or of having a house of one's own. 2) V. —geld 1). —**schaufel**, *f.* a scraper or grater with which the hearth of a furnace is kept clean. ||—**schilling**, *m.* V. —geld 1). —**stange**, *f.* [among bakers] a baker's poker. —**stein**, *m.* a stone covering the hearth, hearth-stone. —**steuer**, *f.* V. —geld 1). —**vogel**, *m.* V. —fink. —**zins**, *m.* V. —geld 1).

Hèrde, *f.* [*pl.* -n] [Sax. *heord*, *hiord*, *hird*, Icel. and Dan. *hjord*, Eng. *herd*, allied to the old hirten = warten, to tend, Fr. *garder*] herd, flock, drove. Eine — Vieh, Ochsen, Kameele, Elephanten &c., a herd of cattle, oxen, camels, elephants &c.; eine — Schafe, Gänse &c., a flock of sheep, geese &c.; eine — Vieh, das auf den Markt geht, a drove of cattle going to market. *Fig.* Die — eines Geistlichen, the flock of a clergyman.

Herd-hammel, *m.* V. Leithammel. — **ochs**, *m.* the bull of a herd.

Hèrdenweise, *adv.* in herds; flocks or droves.

Herein, *adv.* into the place where we are, in, into. Kommen Sie hier —, come or walk in here; —! immer —! nur —! come in, walk in!

Herein-begeben, *ir. v. r.* sich —begeben, to come or walk in, to enter. —**bemühen**, *v. tr.* and *r.* Einen, sich —bemühen, to give any one, one's self the trouble to step, come or walk in. —**bestellen**, *v. tr.* to order to come in or to be brought in. —**bitten**, *ir. v. tr.* to ask or invite any one to come in. —**blicken**, *v. intr.* to look in. —**brausen**, *v. intr.* to enter blustering. —**brechen**, *ir. v. intr.* 1) to break towards the interior or inside, where the person speaking is. 2) to enter by force, to break in, to rush in. *Fig.* Ein großes Unglück brach über uns —, a great misfortune fell upon us. *it.* to set in. Die Nacht bricht —, the night draws near or on, the night is coming. V. Einbrechen. —**brennen**, *ir. v. intr.* to enter burning, to burn in upon. Wie die Sonne in dieses Zimmer — brennt! how hot the sun burns in this room! —**bringen**, *ir. v. tr.* to bring or carry in, V. Einbringen. —**drängen**, I. *v. tr.* to press or force in. II. *v. r.* sich —drängen, to throng in, to enter thronging or crowding, to press in. Die Menge drängte sich in das Zimmer —, the multitude crowded into the room. —**dringen**, *ir. v. intr.* to enter by force, to penetrate, to rush in. —**drücken**, *v. tr.* to press in. —**dürfen**, *ir. v. intr.* to be allowed to come in or to enter. —**eilen**, *v. intr.* to hasten or hurry in. —**fahren**, *ir.* I. *v. tr.* to convey, carry or bring in on a waggon. II. *v. intr.* to enter in a carriage, to drive into a place; *it.* to enter hastily or suddenly, to rush in. —**fallen**, *ir. v. intr.* to fall in, to fall into a place where we are. —**feuern**, *v. intr.* to shoot or fire into the place where we are. —**finden**, *ir. v. r.* sich —finden, to find one's way into the place where one is. —**flattern**, *v. intr.* to come in fluttering, to flutter in. —**fliehen**, *ir. v. intr.* to make one's escape, to fly into the place where we are. —**fließen**, *ir. v. intr.* to flow in. —**flüchten**, I. *v. tr.* to save by flying into the place where we are. II. *v. r.* sich —flüchten, V. —fliehen. —**führen**, *v. tr.* to lead or bring in. —**geben**, *ir. v. tr.* V. —reichen. —**gehen**, *ir. v. intr.* 1) to go in, to walk or step in, to enter. 2) to have place or room in something. Sechs Personen gehen nicht in dieses Zimmer —, this room does not hold six persons. —**gleiten**, —**glitschen**, *v. intr.* to glide, slide or slip in. *—**gucken**, *v. intr.* V. —sehen. —**hageln**, *v. intr. impers.* Es hagelt in das Zimmer —, the hail falls into the room. —**hinken**, *v. intr.* to limp or halt in. —**holen**, *v. tr.* to fetch in. —**hüpfen**, *v. intr.* to enter jumping or skipping. —**kommen**, *ir. v. intr.* to come in. —**können**, *ir. v. intr.* to be able to come in. —**kriechen**, *ir. v. intr.* to creep or crawl in. —**langen**, I. *v. intr.* to be extended, to reach in as far as this place. II. *v. tr.* to hand, reach or pass in. —**lassen**, *ir. v. tr.* to let any one come in or enter, to let in. —**laufen**, *ir. v. intr.* to run in. —**legen**, *v. tr.* to put or lay in. —**leiten**, *v. tr.* to lead or conduct in. —**leuchten**, *v. intr.* 1) to shine in towards the person speaking. 2) Einem —leuchten, to light any one in. —**locken**, *v. tr.* to draw in by persuasion or artifice, to allure or entice into the place where we are. *—**mögen**, *ir. v. intr.* to have a mind, to be willing to come in or to enter. Er mag nicht —, he won't come in. *—**müssen**, *ir. v. intr.* to be obliged to come in. —**nehmen**, *ir. v. tr.* to take in, to put in. —**nöthigen**, *v. tr.* to oblige, to urge any one to come in. —**rasseln**, *v. intr.* to enter rattling or clattering. —**rauschen**, *v. intr.* to come in, to enter rustling or making a noise. —**regnen**, *v. intr. impers.* to rain into the place where we are. —**reichen**, I. *v. tr.* to reach, hand or pass in. II. *v. intr.* V. —langen. —**reiten**, *ir. v. intr.* to come in, to enter on horseback, to ride in. —**rennen**, *ir. v. intr.* to run in, to enter precipitately. —**rinnen**, *ir. v. intr.* to run in. —**rollen**, *v. tr.* and *intr.* to roll in. —**rücken**, *v. tr.* to move or push in. —**schaffen**, *v. tr.* to bring, carry or set in. —**schauen**, *v. intr.* V. —sehen. —**scheinen**, *ir. v. intr.* to shine into the place where we are. —**schicken**, *v. tr.* to send in. —**schießen**, *ir.* I. *v. intr.* 1) to shoot or fire into the place where we are. 2) to enter hastily or suddenly, to rush in. II. *v. tr.* to shoot [an arrow &c.] into the place where we are. —**schlagen**, *v. tr.* V. Einschlagen and Schlagen. —**schleichen**, *ir. v. intr.* and *v. r.* sich —schleichen, to steal, sneak or slink in. —**schleppen**, *v. tr.* to drag in. —**sehen**, *ir. v. intr.* to look in. —**senden**, *ir. v. tr.* V. —schicken. —**seyn**, *ir. v. intr.* to have come in, to be within. —**steigen**, *ir. v. intr.* to mount into, to get in. Der Dieb ist mit einer Leiter — gestiegen, the thief entered the house by means of a ladder. —**stellen**, *v. tr.* to place or put in. —**stoßen**, *ir. v. tr.* to thrust or push in. —**strahlen**, *v. intr.* to emit or cast rays into the place where we are. —**strömen**, *v. intr.* to stream in; *fig.* to flock in. —**stürzen**, *v. intr.* and *v. r.* sich —stürzen, to fall or tumble in, to precipitate one's self, to rush into the place where we are. —**tanzen**, *v. intr.* to come in, to enter dancing. —**taumeln**, *v. intr.* to come in reeling or staggering. —**toben**, *v. intr.* to come in, to enter blustering, raving or raging. —**tragen**, *ir. v. tr.* to carry or bring in. —**treiben**, *ir. v. tr.* to drive or chase in. —**treten**, *ir. v. intr.* to step in. —**wälzen**, *v. tr.* to roll in. —**wehen**, *v. tr.* and *intr.* to blow in. —**werfen**, *ir. v. tr.* to throw in. —**winken**, *v. tr.* and *intr.* to make a sign to come in, to beckon in. *—**wollen**, *ir. v. intr.* to wish, want or be willing to come in. —**ziehen**, *ir.* I. *v. tr.* to draw or pull in. II. *v. intr.* to remove into the place where we are. —**zwängen**, *v. tr.* V. Hineinzwängen.

Hereinwärts, *adv.* towards the interior or inside where we are, inwards.

Herfür, V. Hervor.

Hèrgegen, *adv.* 1) V. Dagegen. 2) V. Hingegen.

Hèrisei, V. Kirsei.

Hèrkules, *m.* [*pl.* -sse] Hercules. Die Säulen des —, the straits of Gibraltar.

Herkules-keule, *f.* the club of Hercules. —**wurz**, *f.* the white water-lily or nenuphar.

Herkulisch, *adj.* Herculean. *Fig.* Eine —e Stärke, a herculean strength.

Hèrling, *m.* [-es, *pl.* -e] [either from herb or allied to hart] sour grapes, wild grapes.

Hèrlitze, *f.* [*pl.* -n] [either from herb or the Lat. *cornus*] 1) the cornelian cherry, cornel, V. Kornelkirsche. 2) V. Hartriegel.

Herlitzenbaum, *m.* cornel-tree, cornelian-tree.

***Hermandád**, *f.* [in Spanish = brotherhood] Hermandad.

Hèrmann, *m.* [-s, *pl.* -e] [a name of men] Herman or German.

***Hermaphrodít**, *m.* [-en, *pl.* -en] hermaphrodite, V. Zwitter.

Hèrmchen, *n.* [-s, *pl.* -] weasel.

Hèrme, *f.* [*pl.* -n] V. Hermessäule.

Hèrmel, *m.* [-s] or Hermelraute, *f.* camomile.

Hermelin, *m.* [-es, *pl.* -e] [*dim.* Hermelinchen, *n.*] 1) the ermin or ermine. 2) the fur of the ermin. Mit — gefüttert, lined with ermine; [in heraldry] ermine; ein mit — besetztes Kreuz, cross-ermine.

Hermelin-kragen, *m.* collar or cape of ermine. —**mantel**, *m.* a cloak lined with ermine.

***Hermeneútik**, *f.* hermeneutics, hermeneutic art, V. Erklärungskunst.

***Hermeneútisch**, *adj.* and *adv.* hermeneutic, hermeneutical.

Hèrmessäule, *f.* [*pl.* -n] a statue of Hermes or Mercury.

***Hermétik**, *f.* hermetic art.

***Hermétisch**, *adj.* and *adv.* hermetic, hermetical. Die —e Kunst, the hermetic art; —e Philosophie, the hermetic philosophy; das —e Siegel, the hermetic seal; ein Gefäß — siegeln, verschließen, to seal, to close a vessel hermetically.

Hèrmodattel, *f.* [*pl.* -n] hermodactyl, V. Herzwurz.

Hernách, *adv.* after, after that, afterwards. Nicht lange —, not long after; den Tag —, the next day after; ich habe es — gehört, I heard it afterwards; und — wollen wir davon reden, and then or after that we will speak of it; und —? was geschah? and then or after that? what happened?

Hernieder, *adv.* down, V. Herab, Herunter.

Herödes, *m.* Herod. *Fig.* [in popular lang.] Das danke Dir [der] —! the deuce or devil may thank you for it! Einen von — zu Pilatus [also, von Pontius zu Pilatus] schicken, to send any one from Herod to Pilate, to send any one needlessly or unnecessarily about from one to the other; *prov.* to toss any one from port to pillar.

***Heroisch**, *adj.* and *adv.* heroic, heroical. V. Heldenmüthig. Die —e Zeit, the heroic age; ein —es Gedicht, a heroic or epic poem; —e Verse, heroic verses.

***Heroismus**, *m.* heroism, V. Heldenmuth, Heldensinn.

Hèrold, *m.* [-es, *pl.* -e] [probably from the old haren = rufen, like the Gr. κήρυξ from γηρύω and the Lat. præco, from precor, i. e. sprechen] 1) herald, V. Wappen—. *Fig.* herald. Die Zeitungen sind die —e seines Ruhms, the newspapers are the heralds of his glory. V. also Verkündiger. 2) [in nat. hist.] the blue jay or jack-daw.

Herolds-amt, *n.* 1) the office of a herald, heraldship. 2) the herald's office. —**bild**, *n.*, —**figur**, *f.* heraldic figure. —**kunst**, *f.* the art of a herald, heraldic art, heraldry. —**mantel**, —**rock**, *m.* a herald's mantle or coat; *it.* a coat of arms. —**stab**, *m.* the staff of a herald, herald's staff. —**würde**, *f.* the dignity of a herald.

Hèroldinn, *f.* a female herald. Used also in a figurative sense.

***Hèros**, *m.* [*pl.* Heroen] [in pagan mythology] hero. *Fig.* a hero-like person.

Hèrr, *m.* [-n or -en, *pl.* -en] [Sax. *Hearra*, Icel., Dan. and Sw. *Herre*, L. *herus*, Fr. and Engl. *Sire* and *Sir*, seems to be allied to Hehr, Ehre and the Gr. αἴρω = to raise] 1) [the owner of any thing and he who governs or directs certain persons and things] master. Der — eines Hauses, eines

Gutes, the master of a house, the master or proprietor of an estate; dieser Bediente hat einen sehr guten —n, this servant has a very kind or good master; der — eines Rittergutes, the Lord of a manor; Cäsar, der Welt großer —, Cesar, the world's great master; der — der Heerschaaren, the Lord of hosts; der — aller —en, the Lord of lords; Jesus Christus, unser —, Jesus Christ our Lord; die Frau ist — im Hause, the wife rules the roast, wears the breeches; — über eine Sache seyn, to be master of a thing; Jeder sey — über seine Zeit, let every man be master of his time; sein eigener — seyn, to be one's own master. *Prov.* Wie der —, so der Knecht, like master, like man; *den —n spielen, to carry it high or like a lord, to lord it; sich zum —n einer Stadt machen, to make one's self master of a town; der König, unser allergnädigster —, the king, our most gracious master; mein seliger — [Gatte], my deceased husband; ein Volk, — zur See, a nation, mistress at sea; — über seine Leidenschaften seyn, to be master of one's self, to have the command or control of one's own passions; er konnte über diese Leidenschaften nicht — werden, he could not master or subdue those passions. 2) [an honorary appellation instead of Mann] gentleman. Die —en vom Unterhause, the gentlemen of the house of Commons; hier ist ein —, der Sie zu sprechen wünscht, there is a gentleman who wants to speak to you; wer ist dieser —? who is that gentleman? große —en, great lords; auf dem Fuße eines großen —n leben, to live like a lord, like a fine gentleman. *Prov.* Große —en haben lange Arme, great lords have great power; strenge —en regieren nicht lange, too great severity is of no long durance, any thing violent is not permanent; ein — von gestern, an upstart. *it.* [opposed to woman or lady in general] Die Gesellschaft bestand aus sechs —en und sechs Damen, the company consisted of six gentlemen and six ladies. 3) [a title of respect] Master (Mr.). — Jackson hat mir gesagt, Mr. Jackson told me; guten Morgen, — Schmidt! good morning, Mr. Schmidt! die —en Mediziner, the medical gentlemen; der — Graf, the earl or count; Ihr — Vater, your father; was machen Ihre —en Brüder? how do your brothers do? *it.* [in adressing men] mein —, Sir! meine —en, gentlemen! meine —en und Damen! ladies and gentlemen! hochmögende —en, your high mightinesses! gnädiger —! my Lord!

Herren-apfel, *m.* a kind of apple. —arbeit, *f.* work done for a superior lord without remuneration, V. Frohnarbeit. —arbeiter, *m.* a miner who works for certain wages. —bank, *f.* bench of the lords or knights. *—bauch, *m.* well-fed belly, V. Prälatenbauch. —befehl, *m.* V. —gebot. *—bier, *n.* good strong beer, double beer [opposed to small beer]. —bilz, *m.* V. —pilz. ||—birn, *f.* a kind of pear. —brett, *n.* [among joiners] a thin board. —brod, *n.* 1) bread for the master. 2) bread or sustenance furnished by a master. **Fig.* —brod essen, to be in service, to be a servant, to serve. —diener, *m.* 1) V. Gerichtsdiener, Rathsdiener. 2) one who crouches to the great, cringer. —dienst, *m.* service. *—dienst annehmen, in —dienst treten, to go to service. *Prov.* —dienst gehet vor Gottesdienst, a master's business requires greater regularity or exactness than divinee srvice; —dienst ist unsicher, service is no inheritance; *it.* V. Frohndienst. *—essen, *n.* a delicious meal, dainty food; *it.* a delicacy, dainty. —fastnacht, *f.* V. —sonntag. —garten, *m.* a great man's garden; *it.* the garden belonging to a manor. —gebot, *n.* the mandate of a sovereign, or the command of the lord of a manor. —gefälle, *pl.* dues payable to the lord of a manor. —geheiß, *n.* V. —gebot. —geschenk, *n.* [in saltworks] saltwater given to the clerks as a present. —gulden, *m.* V. Gatterzins. —gülte, *f.* the rents or income of an estate. —gunst, *f.* a great man's favour. *Prov.* —gunst bestehet nicht, a king's favour is no inheritance. —hand, *f.* *fig.* the power or authority of a great man, of a lord &c. *Prov.* —hand geht durch's ganze Land, the arms of the great extend everywhere, reach very far, great lords have great power. —haus, *n.* 1) residence or mansion of a lord or great man. 2) manor-house. —hof, *m.* the house of the lord of a manor, mansion, countryhouse, V. Edelhof. —hut, Herrnhut, *n.* [literally: „under the Lord's guard", the well-known establishment of the Moravian Brethren in the province of Upper-Lusatia in Saxony] Hernhut. —huter, *m.* —huterinn, *f.* [one of the religious sect, called the United Brethren] Moravian. —hutisch, *adj.* Moravian. —kirsche, *f.* cornel. —knecht, *m.* V. —diener 2). —korn, *n.* rent paid in corn. —krankheit, *f.* lord's or gentleman's disorder, *[in jest for the] gout. —kümmel, *m.* bishop's weed, ammi or amium. *—leben, *n.* easy, luxurious life. Ein —leben führen, to live like a lord, to fare sumptuously. —los, *adj.* and *adv.* 1) out of service. Ein —loser Bedienter, a servant out of place; —loses Gesindel, vagabonds, vagrants. 2) having no owner. Ein —loses Pferd, a strayed horse; eine —lose Sache, a waif; —lose Effecten, vacant effects; —lose Waaren, derelict goods. —meister, *m.* V. Heermeister. —pfarre, *f.* a living or benefice in the gift of a patron. —pilz, *m.* eatable mushroom. —recht, *n.* seigneurial or manorial right or privilege. —schenke, *f.* [rather obsolete] public house or alehouse frequented by gentlemen. —schicht, *f.* mine worked for the sovereign, royal mine. —schnepfe, *f.* common snipe. —schwamm, *m.* V. —pilz. —sitz, *m.* the country seat of a nobleman or gentleman, V. —haus. —sonntag, *m.* Shrove-Sunday. *—speise, *f.* V. —essen. —stand, *m.* 1) [the persons collectively who enjoy rank above commoners] nobility. 2) V. —stuhl. —stube, *f.* 1) the master's room. 2) V. Rathsstube. —stuhl, *m.* pew appropriated to people of quality; *it.* the pew of the lord of the manor, the squire's pew. —tafel, *f.* nobleman's or gentleman's table; *it.* the master's table. —tag, *m.* a day of rejoicing or merry-making. —tisch, *m.* V. —tafel. ||—vogel, *m.* V. Holzhäher. —wasser, *n.* a pond or fish-pond belonging to the lord of the manor. —weg, *m.* a way or passage for the lord of the manor only. —weiher, *m.* V. —wasser. —wein, *m.* very good wine, wine of an excellent flavour. —zeche, *f.* V. —schicht.

Herrchen, *n.* [-s, *pl.* -] [*dim.* of Herr] 1) little master [said of boys of noble or respectable families]. 2) [chiefly in contempt] little master, lordling. Ein süßes —, an affected beau; *it.* a whining lover; jene wohlriechenden —, those sparks.

Herrgott, *m.* [-es] [in fam. lang. for Gott] God. Unser —, der liebe —, our Lord, God almighty. [as an interjection, rather vulgar] Herrgott! Lord, †Lud!

Herrgottbärtlein, *n.* [in botany] the common knotgrass.

Herrig, *adj.* belonging to the master or to a master, V. Zwei—, Drei—, Deutsch—.

Herrinn, *f.* mistress, lady.

Herrisch, *adj.* and *adv.* 1) imperious, domineering, lordly. —e Worte, imperious words; in einem —en Tone, in a domineering tone; sein —es Wesen, his imperious, domineering or overbearing manners or demeanour. 2) V. Herrig.

||Herrlein, *n.* [-s, *pl.* -] [*dim.* of Herr] V. Herrchen.

Herrlich, *adj.* and *adv.* 1) [from Herr] belonging to a master, V. Deutsch—, Landes—, Ober— &c. 2) [probably from hehr = sublime; in old Germ. it is herlih and herro] excellent, magnificent, splendid, delicious. Ein —es Gebäude, a most beautiful, a magnificent, noble, stately edifice; ein —es Gastmahl, a sumptuous, splendid entertainment; —er Wein, excellent, delicious wine; ein —es Leben, a splendid, delicious life; — leben, —e Tage haben, to live deliciously, sumptuously or jovially; eine —e Aussicht, a delightful, charming view; ein —er Rath, an excellent counsel; wir hatten das —ste Wetter von der Welt, we had the finest weather imaginable; ein —er Sieg, a glorious victory; er ist ein —er Mensch, he is an excellent man.

Herrlichkeit, *f.* 1) magnificence, splendour, lustre, glory. Die Fürsten der Erde mit all ihrer —, the princes of the earth with all their magnificenc or pageantry; die — Gottes, the glory of God; die ewige —, eternal glory. 2) [a title of honour given to eminent persons or noblemen] excellency, lordship. Geruhen Eure —, mir zu sagen, may it please your excellency or lordship to tell me. 3) a magnificent thing. Alle diese —en konnten ihn nicht reizen, all those splendid or magnificent things could not tempt him. 4) [in fam. lang. = Freude] joy, pleasure, delight. 5) [a particular privilege of a supreme lord] Ein Gut mit allen seinen —en, an estate with all its seigneurial rights; die — [better Herrschaft] über ein Land, the sovereignty of a country; die forstteiliche —, the sovereign right over the forests. 6) V. Herrschaft 3).

Herrmann, V. Hermann.

Herrnhut, V. Herrenhut.

Herrschaft, *f.* 1) the power of governing and controling, dominion, mastery, sway. Die höchste —, supreme authority, sovereignty; Jamaika steht unter der — von Großbritannien, Jamaica is under the dominion of Great Britain; sie haben sich die — der Meere, über das Meer angemaßt, they have usurped the empire of the sea; einen König der — entsetzen, to depose a king; eine Provinz unter seine — bringen, seiner — unterwerfen, to bring a province under, to subject a province to one's dominion; nach der — der Welt streben, to aspire to, to affect the empire of the whole world; eine grausame, gelinde —, a cruel, mild domination; er übt eine despotische — über sein Gesinde aus, he exercises a despotic authority over his servants; die Frau führt die — im Hause, the wife rules the house or the roast; — über sich selbst haben, to have the command or control of one's passions, to be master of one's self. 2) a person or persons invested with power and dominion. Die — eines Landes, the sovereign of a country; die — eines Gutes, the lord or lady of a manor, V. Guts—. *it.* [opposed to Dienerschaft] master, mistress [either individually or collectively]. Er dient seiner — treu, he serves his master and mistress, his master or his mistress faithfully; ist Eure — zu Hause? is your master and mistress, your master or your mistress at home? die junge — [in a servant's expression], the young princes or princesses or the children of the master or mistress. *it.* [in general] a person of rank or quality. Welcher — gehört dieser Wagen? to whom does this carriage belong? es sind schon viele —en angekommen, many persons of rank have already arrived. [in theology, an order of angelic beings] domination. Die Mächte, die Throne und —en, powers, thrones and dominations.

3) a territory or district under the dominion of any one. In allen seinen —en fand er &c., he found in all his territories &c.; die —en, welche dieser Fürst in Deutschland besaß, the dominions which that prince possessed in Germany. [in a more limited sense] the territory of a baron over which he holds jurisdiction, barony, seigniory, lordship, manor. Er besitzt mehrere Güter und —en, he possesses several estates and baronies. *it.* V. Gerichtsbarkeit.

Herrschafts=haus, *n.* mansion, manor-house. —**name**, *m.* a name indicating power or dominion. In der Gottesgelahrtheit ist **Herr** ein —name Gottes, in divinity **Lord** is an attribute of God indicating his power or dominion. —**recht**, *n.* right of dominion or sovereignty, *it.* seigneurial right. —**wappen**, *n.* coat of arms which any one bears from his barony, seigniory or lordship.

Herrschaftlich, *adj.* and *adv.* 1) belonging to the sovereign or government. —e Einkünfte, Gebäude, the revenues of the sovereign or state, public revenues, public buildings. 2) belonging to the land of a manor. —e Gefälle, seigneurial dues; das —e Gebäude, the manor house. 3) due to the master or mistress.

Herrschen, *v. intr.* to exercise dominion, to rule, to reign, to govern. Er herrscht über einen Theil Asiens, he bears sway or dominion, he reigns or rules over a part of Asia; —de Macht, absolute power; das —de Gestirn, the reigning planet. *Fig.* Ueber die Leidenschaften —, to rule over, to subdue the passions; der Ehrgeiz herrscht in seiner Seele, ambition governs his soul; große Verschwiegenheit herrscht in ihren Rathsversammlungen, great secrecy reigns in their councils; —de Laster, reigning, predominant vices; das Fieber herrschte über einen or in einem großen Theil des Landes, the fever prevailed in a great part of the country; —de Leidenschaften, ruling, prevailing or predominant passions; eine —de Meinung, a prevalent opinion; der —de Geschmack, the reigning taste; die —de Religion, the established religion; eine —de Krankheit, a prevalent, prevailing disease; eine tiefe Stille herrschte rings umher, deep silence reigned round about. SYN. **Herrschen, Regieren.** Herrschen signifies simply to control the will and actions of others. Regieren always implies that the authority with which any one is invested, is exercised in the attainment of a good object.

Herrsch=begierde, *f.* eager desire of reigning or domineering, V. —sucht. —**begierig**, *adj.* and *adv.* desirous of reigning, V. —süchtig. —**geist**, *m.* spirit of ruling, governing or domineering. —**gewalt**, *f.* V. Herrschergewalt. —**gier**, —**sucht**, *f.* inordinate desire of ruling, governing or domineering, lust of power. —**süchtig**, *adj.* and *adv.* having or indicating an inordinate desire of ruling, governing or domineering, fond of power, imperious, domineering. Ein —süchtiger Mann, an imperious man. —**süchtigkeit**, *f.* V. —sucht. —**wuth**, *f.* tyranny. —**wüthig** or —**wütherich**, *m.* tyrant.

Herrscher, *m.* [-s, *pl.* -] ruler, governor, sovereign.

Herrscher=familie, *f.* the family of a king or reigning person, dynasty. —**geist**, V. Herrschgeist. —**gewalt**, *f.* the power of a ruler or sovereign, sovereignty; *it.* despotism.

Herz, V. Herz.

Herüber, *adv.* over to this side, across; [it denotes motion over or across a place towards the person speaking, and is much used in composition with verbs; but these compounds being easily understood, we subjoin only a few by way of example].

Herüber=bringen, *ir. v. tr.* to bring or carry over to this side. —**fahren**, *ir.* I. *v. intr.* to pass to this side. Als wir über den Rhein —fuhren, when we came across the Rhine. II. *v. tr.* to bring, transport or convey to this side. Derselbe Schiffer, welcher Sie —gefahren hat, wird Sie wieder zurückführen, the same waterman, who brought you over, will ferry you back again. —**hängen**, *ir. v. intr.* to hang or incline over to this side [on horseback]. —**reiten**, *ir. v. intr.* to ride over to this side. —**sprechen**, *ir. v. intr.* mit Einem über die Straße —sprechen, to speak across the street with any one. —**ziehen**, *ir. v. tr.* to draw or pull over to this side. *Fig.* [in popular lang.] Einen —ziehen, to cheat, to deceive any one. Er wurde schrecklich —gezogen, he was dreadfully taken in or imposed upon.

Herúm, *adv.* 1) round, about, round about. Um das Haus, um die Stadt —, round (about) the house, town; die Gegend um die Stadt — ist sehr schön, the environs of the town are very fine; der Feind hat sich der Gegend um die Festung — bemächtigt, the enemy has secured all the avenues round the fortress; rings —, rund —, round about; in der Runde, im Kreise — trinken, to drink round. 2) [denoting motion about a body towards the person speaking, opposed to **hinum**]. Er kam um die Ecke —, he turned round the corner of the street [towards the person speaking]. 3) [denoting a motion sidewards or backwards towards the person speaking]. Sie drehte den Kopf zu mir —, she turned her head to or towards me; rechts — (kehrt euch)! [a military word of command] to the right about (face)! 4) hier und dort —, here and there, in one place and another, about; *it.* hier und dort —, here and there about. An verschiedenen Oertern —, in different places; hier liegt Alles durch einander —, every thing is in confusion, in a pickle here; Papiere lagen in Menge —, a great many papers lay scattered about; er muß hier —wohnen, he must live hereabouts. *Fig.* near to in time, about. Um Christi Geburt —, about the birth of Christ; um 10 Uhr —, about 10 o'clock.

Herum=balgen, *v. r.* sich —balgen, to fight or scuffle here and there, V. Balgen. —**begeben**, *ir. v. r.* sich —begeben, to go, walk or turn round any thing; *it.* to go, step or walk to this place. Wenn Sie sich —begeben wollten, if you would come or step hither. —**beißen**, *ir. v. r.* sich —beißen, to bite, touse or worry one another [said of dogs]; *fig.* [in popular language] to wrangle, to quarrel. Die beiden Aerzte bissen sich lange —, the two doctors wrangled a long time. —**bekommen**, *ir. v. tr.* V. —bringen. —**bemühen**, *v. tr.* Einen, and *v. r.* sich —bemühen, to give any one, one's self the trouble to come, walk or turn round any thing; *it.* to come or step hither. —**betteln**, *v. intr.* to ask alms here and there, to ramble or wander about begging. Er bettelt im ganzen Lande —, he rambles or rowes over or about the whole country asking alms. —**beugen**, *v. tr.* to bend towards this side; *it.* to bend. —**bewegen**, *v. tr.* and *v. r.* sich —bewegen, to move round any thing; *it.* to move towards this place. —**biegen**, *ir.* I. *v. intr.* Um eine Straßenecke —biegen &c, to turn round the corner of a street &c. II. *v. tr.* [in popular lang.] V. —beugen. —**bieten**, *ir. v. tr.* to offer or present round or about. —**binden**, *ir. v. tr.* to tie or bind round any thing. —**bitten**, *ir. v. tr.* Einen —bitten, to ask or invite any one to come or step [round] to this place. —**blättern**, *v. intr.* to turn over the leaves of a book. Ich blätterte lange im Buche —, ohne &c., I turned over many a leaf, without &c. —**blicken**, V. —sehen. —**bringen**, *ir. v. tr.* to bring or get round any thing. Er kann den Wagen nicht um die Ecke —bringen, he cannot get the carriage round the corner. *it.* to bring hither. **Fig.* Einen —bringen, to cause or persuade any one to change his opinion or sides, to bring any one over; *it.* to persuade or engage any one to do something. —**denken**, *ir.* I. *v. intr.* to think of one after the other, to think of this and that. II. *v. tr.* sich etwas —denken, to think or suppose any thing to be round another. Wenn ich mir einen Ring um die Erde —denke, if I suppose or fancy a ring to be, if I figure to myself a ring round the earth. —**drängen**, *v. r.* sich —drängen, to press or crowd round any person or thing. —**drehen**, I. *v. tr.* 1) to turn round or about. Das Rad —drehen, to turn the wheel; die Augen im Kopfe —drehen, to roll the eyes. *Fig.* Etwas artig —drehen, to give a thing a fair, pretty or nice turn; er dreht mir die Worte im Munde —, he gives a false sense to my words, he misinterprets what I say or my words, he puts an ill construction upon my words. 2) to turn towards the person speaking. Drehen Sie den Kopf —! turn your head round! II. *v. r.* sich —drehen, to turn round or about, to whirl about. Er dreht sich auf dem Absatze —, he turns on his heel; sie drehten sich fröhlich im Ländler[tanz] —, they whirled about in the merry dance; sich die ganze Nacht im Bette — und hinumdrehen, to toss in one's bed all night. *Fig.* Um diesen Punkt dreht sich die ganze Sache —, that's the point on which every thing depends or turns, the whole affair hinges on that; um ihn dreht sich die ganze Unterhaltung —, he is the subject of the whole conversation. —**eilen**, *v. intr.* to go or turn hastily round any thing; *it.* to run hastily from one to another. —**essen**, *ir. v. intr.* Bei seinen Freunden —essen, to dine with one's friends by turns. —**fackeln**, V. Fackeln. —**fahren**, *ir. v. intr.* 1) to go round any thing in a carriage or vessel. Um die Stadt —fahren, to drive round [about] the town; um eine Insel —fahren, to sail round an island. 2) to drive or sail about any thing towards the person speaking. Fahren Sie um die Straßenecke —! drive round the corner of the street! 3) to drive or sail from place to place. Im Parke —fahren, to take a ride in the park; bei seinen Verwandten —fahren, to visit one's relations in one's carriage; [in vulgar lang.] in der Welt —fahren, to wander, roam, rove or ramble round or about the world; sie ist schon auf allen Theatern —gefahren, she has already been on all the theatres. *it.* *to lie about in confusion. Seine Papiere fahren in meinem Studirzimmer —, his papers lie about in my study; mit den Händen —fahren, to gesticulate with the hands; mit den Augen überall —fahren, to cast one's eyes everywhere. —**flattern**, *v. intr.* to flutter about. —**fliegen**, *ir. v. intr.* to fly round or about any thing; *it.* to fly here and there, to fly about. *Fig.* Seine Augen fliegen überall —, he casts his eyes everywhere. —**fließen**, *ir. v. intr.* to flow round or about any thing; *it.* to run or flow from place to place, about. —**frage**, *f.* the successive inquiry among different persons, the act of gathering or canvassing the votes. Als es zur —frage kam, when it was put to the vote. V. Umfrage. —**fragen**, *reg.* and *ir. v. intr.* to enquire successively among different persons, to enquire round, to gather the votes, to canvass. —**fuchteln**, *v. tr.* [rather vulgar] to strike or beat any one with the flat of the sword. Einander —fuchteln, to fight with swords or rapiers. —**führen**, *v. tr.* 1) to lead or conduct round or about any thing. *Fig.* Eine Mauer um einen Garten —führen, to enclose a garden with a wall. 2) to lead or conduct from place to place, about. Einen in der ganzen Stadt —führen, to lead any one all over the town; sein Pferd —führen, to walk one's horse. *Fig. Einen bei der Nase —führen, to lead any one by the nose, to amuse any one with idle promises. Ich lasse mich nicht von Ihnen an der Nase —führen, I won't be your dupe. —gaffen, v. intr. to look about gaping or staring. —gaukeln, v. intr. V. Gaukeln. —geben, ir. v. tr. to hand or pass round or about. —gehen, ir. v. intr. 1) to go, walk or turn round or about. Um die Stadt —gehen, to walk round the town; das Rad geht um seine Achse —, the wheel turns round its axis; wessen Gesundheit geht gegenwärtig —? whose health is going round at present, whose health is being drunk? der Kopf geht mir — [= ich bin schwindelig], my head turns, my head is giddy, I am giddy. Fig. Mauern, Gräben gehen um die Stadt —, walls, ditches surround the town, the town is enclosed with walls, encompassed with ditches; dieses Band geht zweimal um den Hut —, this ribbon goes or reaches twice round the hat; das geht mir im Kopfe —, that runs in my mind, that makes me uneasy; um Einen —gehen, to cajole, flatter, coax or wheedle any one. Prov. V. Brei. 2) to walk here and there, from place to place, to walk about. In der Stadt —gehen, to walk or wander about in the town; er ging zwei- oder dreimal im Zimmer —, he took two or three turns round the room, he walked twice or thrice across the room; müßig —gehen, to walk about without doing any thing, to be idle, to idle away one's time. Fig. Seine Augen überall —gehen lassen, to wander about with one's eyes, to cast one's eyes everywhere; es gehen viele Krankheiten —, there are many diseases going about, it is a sickly season; das Gerücht geht —, there goes a report, the report goes or is current. —gießen, ir. v. tr. to pour round or about. —hangen, ir. v. intr. to hang round; it. to hang here and there, without order, to hang about. —hauen, ir. v. r. sich —hauen, to fight with swords or rapiers. Die drei Angegriffenen hieben sich wacker mit ihren zehn Angreifern —, the three attacked men bravely fought their ten assailants. —hetzen, v. tr. Einen —hetzen, fig. *to play the fool with any one, to toss any one from post to pillar. —holen, v. tr. to fetch to this place. Fig. [in popular lang.] Einen —holen, a) to cause any one to change his opinion, to bring any one over, it. to reclaim any one; b) to reprimand, reprove, censure any one, to read any one a lecture, to haul any one over the coals. —horchen, v. intr. to listen here and there. —hören, v. intr. to go or walk round or about and hear what is said. —hudeln, v. tr. [in popular lang.] to harass, tease, trouble, plague any one. —hüpfen, v. intr. to leap, skip or jump about. —irren, v. intr to err or wander about, to stray about, to rove. Er irrst mit seinen Gedanken überall —, he lets his mind wander or ramble upon any subject. —jagen, I. v. tr. to drive or chase round any place; it. to drive from place to place, about. II. v. intr. to ride at full speed, to gallop round any place; it. to ride at full speed, to gallop from place to place, about. —kehren, v. tr. to turn about, to invert, to turn, to reverse, V. Umkehren. —klettern, v. intr. 1) to climb round about. 2) to climb here and there, from place to place. —klimmen, V. —klettern. —knüpfen, v. tr. to tie round or about. —kommen, ir. v. intr. 1) to come round any thing. Er kam gerade um die Ecke —, he just turned or came round the corner of the street; ich kann heute mit meinen Besuchen nicht —kommen [= fertig werden], I cannot pay all my visits to-day. 2) to come to this place or hither. 3) to come to different places. Er ist in der Welt —gekommen, he has seen the world; er ist in ganz Europa —gekommen, he has visited or seen all the countries of Europe, he has travelled all about Europe. *—kramen, v. intr. to search or rummage here and there. —kreuzen, v. intr. to cruise. —kriechen, ir. v. intr. to creep or crawl about. Der Kranke konnte kaum im Zimmer —kriechen, the sick man was hardly able to crawl about the room. —kriegen, V. —bringen. —kugeln, V. —wälzen. —lagern, v. r. sich —lagern, to lie down round or about [a tree]; it. to encamp round or about [a town]. —langen, I. v. intr. to reach round or about any thing. *Das Band langt nicht um den Hut —, the ribbon does not reach round the hat; *die Schüssel langte nicht — [= für alle Gäste], the dish did not suffice for all the guests. II. v. tr. to hand or fetch hither round any thing; it. V. —reichen. —laufen, ir. v. intr. 1) to run round. Um das Haus —laufen, to run round the house; das Rad läuft —, the wheel turns [round]. 2) to run or hasten to this place. 3) to run to and fro, from place to place, to run about, to rove, to ramble. —läufer, m., —läuferinn, f. a person who wanders or walks about without any determinate object in view, a rover, rambler, stroller, V. Landstreicher, Pflastertreter. —legen, v. tr. to put or spread round; it. to put or spread about, here and there. —lenken, v. tr. to turn round any thing; it. to turn to this way. Fig. Einen —lenken, to bring any one over to one's opinion; it. to reclaim any one. —liegen, ir. v. intr. 1) to be situated, to lie round about. Die Dörfer, welche um die Stadt —liegen, the villages situated at some distance round the town; die —liegende Gegend, the country round about, the environs, the neighbouring country; um das Haus —liegen, to lie round about the house. 2) to be here and there, scattered, dispersed. Seine Kleider liegen in meinem Zimmer —, his clothes lie about in my room; die Soldaten liegen in den Dörfern —, the soldiers are cantoned or quartered in the villages. —locken, v. tr. to draw, allure or entice to this place. —machen, I. v. tr. 1) to put or fasten round or about. 2) to plough, to turn up with the hoe, V. Umhacken. II. v. r. sich —machen, V. —begeben. —marschiren, v. intr. to march round or about; it. to march to this place. —nehmen, ir. v. tr. 1) to take or put round or about. 2) to take to this place. 3) *Fig. Einen —nehmen, a) to make a fool of, to ridicule, to deride any one; b) to reprimand, to reprove, to censure, to criticise any one. —nöthigen, v. tr. Einen —nöthigen, to oblige, press or urge any one to come to this place. —peitschen, v. tr. 1) to drive any one round any thing by whipping, to whip any one round. 2) V. Peitschen. —pflanzen, v. tr. to plant round about. —placken, —plagen, v. r. sich, to be at, or to take a great deal of pains, to labour very hard. —prügeln, v. tr. to cudgel, to drub any one. —rathen, v. intr. 1) to guess this and that, to guess at random. 2) to guess round by turns. —reichen, I. v. tr. to hand, reach or pass round or about. II. v. intr. V. —langen. —reisen, v. intr. 1) to travel round about. 2) to travel from place to place, to travel about. —reißen, ir. v. tr. 1) to tear or pull round any thing. 2) to pull or tear towards this place or backwards. 3) to pull to and fro, this way and that way. —reiten, ir. v. intr. 1) to ride round about [on horseback]. 2) to ride from place to place, to ride about [on horseback]. Er reitet immer —, he is always on horseback, he does nothing but ride about. —rennen, ir. v. intr. V. —laufen. —rollen, I. v. tr. to roll any thing; it. to roll here and there, to roll about. II. v. intr. to roll round about; it. to roll here and there, to roll about. Wie ihm die Augen im Kopfe —rollen! how his eyes roll in his head! —rücken, I. v. tr. 1) to move or push round any thing. 2) to move or push from place to place, to and fro, V. —drehen. II. v. intr. to move or draw to this place. —rühren, v. tr. to stir [about]. —rütteln, v. tr. 1) to toss about or up and down. 2) to jolt. —sagen, v. tr. to tell one after the other. —sausen, v. intr. to whistle, to whiz round or about any person or thing. —schauen, v. intr. V. —sehen. —schicken, v. tr. 1) to send round, to send about. 2) to send hither. —schiffen, v. intr. 1) to sail round about. 2) to sail from place to place, to sail about. —schlagen, ir. I. v. tr. 1) to put or throw round or about, to wrap [up]. Den Mantel um sich —schlagen, to wrap one's self up in one's cloak. 2) V. Umschlagen. 3) [in familiar language] Einen —schlagen, to beat, to cudgel any one. II. v. r. sich mit Einem —schlagen, to fight, to scuffle with any one. —schleichen, ir. v. intr. and v. r. sich —schleichen, 1) to steal or sneak round about any thing. 2) to sneak or slip along from place to place, to sneak about; it. to creap or crawl. Er ist sehr schwach, er schleicht nur —, he is very weak, he only crawls about. —schlendern, v. intr. to saunter, to loiter or lounge about. —schleppen, v. tr. 1) to drag round about any thing. 2) to drag to and fro, to drag about. †—schlingeln, v. intr. to be idle, to idle. Er schlingelt immer —, he does nothing but loiter. —schlingen, ir. I. v. tr. to wind or twine round any thing. Er schlang die Arme um sie —, he wound his arms round her, he clasped or locked her in his arms. II. v. r. sich —schlingen, to twine, to wind round or about. Der Weinstock oder Epheu schlingt sich um [die] Bäume —, the vine or ivy twines or winds about or around trees. —schmarotzen, v. intr. to go spunging from house to house, to go about spunging or acting the parasite. —schmiegen, v. r. sich —schmiegen, to cling or wind round any person or thing. —schüren, v. intr. Im Feuer —schüren, to stir or poke in the fire. —schütten, v. tr. to throw, pour or spread round about; it. to throw, pour or spread here and there, about. —schwärmen, v. intr to swarm round or about. Fig. to ramble about, to rove; it. to revel, to riot. Er schwärmt im ganzen Lande —, he roves or rambles about the whole country; wo sind or haben Sie die ganze Nacht —geschwärmt? where have you been revelling or rioting all night? —schweifen, v. intr. to move or ramble about, from place to place. [among hunters] Dieser Hirsch schweift weit —, this stag goes a feeding very far. Fig. Mit den Gedanken —schweifen, seine Gedanken —schweifen lassen, to wander about with one's thoughts. —schweifend, pres. part. and adj. wandering, vagabond, vagrant. —schwenken, I. v. tr. to move or turn round or about, to wave, to flourish. II. v. r. sich —schwenken, to move round, to turn, to wheel. Sich auf einem Fuße —schwenken, to turn upon one leg; er schwenkte sich mit dem Pferde um unsere Kutsche —, he caracoled or wheeled about our coach; [in military affairs] sich —schwenken, to wheel round. —schwimmen, ir. v. intr. 1) to swim round any thing. 2) to swim or float here and there, about. —schwingen, ir. v. tr. to swing or turn round or about. —segeln, V. —schiffen. —sehen, ir. v. intr. 1) to look behind or backwards. 2) to turn or cast one's eyes on all sides, to look about. Er sah rings —, ob &c., he looked round about to &c. —senden, ir. v. tr. V. —schicken. —setzen, v. tr. 1) to put or place round or about. 2) to put or place here and there. —seyn, ir. v. intr. [in fam. lang.] 1) to be round or about any person or thing. Die, welche um den König —

waren, they who surrounded or were about the king. V. Umgeben, Umringen. 2) to have gone, walked or turned round or about any thing. Ist er schon um die Ecke —? has he already turned round the corner? 3) to be over or past, V. Umsein. —singen, ir. v. intr. 1) to walk about singing. Auf den Straßen —singen, to sing about in the streets. 2) to sing by turns, to sing round. —sitzen, ir. v. intr. to sit round or about [the table &c.]. —spazieren, v. intr. to walk about. —spielen, v. intr. 1) to play here and there. Ich sah sie auf der Wiese —spielen, I saw them playing or at play on the meadow. 2) to play by turns or round. —sprengen, I. v. tr. 1) to sprinkle here and there, to sprinkle about. 2) [in popular lang.] to make or cause any one to run about. II. v. intr. to ride at full speed, to gallop round any thing; it. to gallop from place to place, about. —springen, ir. v. intr. 1) to spring or leap round. 2) to spring, jump, bound or leap from place to place, about. Fig. *Uebel mit Einem —springen (= ihn übel behandeln), to treat or use any one ill, to abuse any one. —spritzen, I. v. tr. 1) to spatter or sprinkle [water &c.] round any thing. 2) to spatter here and there. II. v. intr. to spout or spurt on all sides. †—stänkern, v. intr. to snuff or smell about, to search, to rummage. —stehen, ir. v. intr. 1) to stand round or about. Einer von den —stehenden sagte, one of the by-standers said. 2) to stand here and there, scattered or dispersed. Wie hier Alles —steht! what disorder or confusion every thing is in here! —stellen, v. tr. to put or place round or about; it. to put or place here and there. —steuern, v. intr. V. —schiffen. —stöbern, v. intr. V —fliegen. —stören, v. tr. and intr. to stir about, to rummage. Wer hat in meinem Kabinette —gestört? who has been rummaging in my closet? im Feuer —stören, to stir or poke the fire. —stoßen, ir. v. tr. 1) to thrust or push round. 2) to thrust or push from place to place, about. 3) to thrust or push to this side. —streichen, ir. I. v. tr. to spread or smear round any thing. Oel, Pech um etwas —streichen, to smear oil, pitch &c. round or about any thing. II. v. intr. to ramble or wander about, to rove, to range. —streichende Bettler, vagrant beggars. —streicher, m. V. Landstreicher. —streifen, v. intr. V. —streichen. —streiten, ir. v. r. sich —streiten, to dispute, to wrangle. —streuen, v. tr. 1) to strew or spread round. 2) to strew, scatter or spread here and there, about. V. Bestreuen. —stricken, v. intr. to knit round. Noch zweimal —stricken, to knit two rounds more. —suchen, v. intr. to seek or search here and there. —tanzen, v. intr. 1) to dance round or about any thing. 2) to dance up and down, to and fro, to dance about. —tasten, v. intr. to feel here and there, to grope about. —traben, v. intr. to trot round; it. to trot from place to place, to trot about. —tragen, ir. v. tr. 1) to carry or bear round. 2) to carry from place to place, about. Er trägt immer einen Dolch mit sich —, he always carries a dagger about him; Bücher [zum Verkauf] —tragen, to hawk about books. 3) to carry, bear or bring to this side. —treiben, ir. I. v. tr. 1) to turn or drive round. Das Wasser treibt die Mühlräder —, the water turns the mill-wheels. 2) to drive from place to place, to drive about. II. v. r. sich —treiben, to run from place to place, to run about, to rove, to ramble about. *Wo haben Sie sich heute —getrieben? where did you gad about or ramble to-day? er treibt sich in Kneipen —, he frequents or haunts taverns. III. v. intr. to float or swim here and there, about. —treten, ir. v. intr. 1) to step or place one's self round or about any person or thing. 2) to step or place one's self to this side. —trinken, ir. v. intr. to drink round. —trödeln, v. intr. to dally, trifle, linger or loiter about. —tummeln, I. v. tr. to move one way and the other, to put or keep in motion or action, to exercise. Ein Pferd —tummeln, to work or ride a horse, to manage a horse; *Einen —tummeln, to fatigue, harass or torment any one. II. v. r. sich —tummeln, to bustle, to stir about, to bestir one's self. —wallen, V. —wandern. —walzen, v. intr. to waltz round. —wälzen, I. v. tr. 1) to roll round. 2) to roll from place to place, to roll about. 3) to roll to this side. II. v. r. sich —wälzen, to roll round and round, to roll about; it. to wallow about [in the mire]. Fig. Sich in allen Arten von Unflätereien —wälzen, to wallow in all manner of uncleanness. —wandeln, —wandern, v. intr. 1) to walk or wander round. 2) to wander or ramble about. Er wandelt im Schlafe —, he walks in his sleep; das —wandeln im Schlafe, somnambulism. —wehen, v. tr. to blow to this side or hither. —wenden, reg. and ir. I. v. tr. 1) to turn round or about. 2) to turn to this side. II. v. r. sich —wenden, V. —drehen II. —werfen, ir. v. tr. 1) to throw round or about any thing 2) to throw here and there, to throw about. Er wirft sich beständig im Bette —, he is continually tossing or tumbling in his bed. 3) to turn quickly [one's horse]. —wickeln, v. tr. to wrap round or about. —winden, ir. v. tr. and v. r. sich —winden, to wind or twine round or about. Der Epheu windet sich um die Bäume —, the ivy winds or twines round or about trees. —wühlen, v. intr. to stir with the snout, to root or dig round or about any thing, it. here and there; fig. to rummage, V. —stören. —zanken, v. r. sich —zanken, to quarrel, dispute or wrangle with any one. Sie zankten sich lange —, they wrangled a long time. —zausen, v. tr. to touse, to pull any one from place to place, about. —zerren, v. tr. to pull, draw or haul any one round or about any thing, it. from place to place or about. —ziehen, ir. I. v. tr. 1) to draw round or about [as a circle]. Fig. Einen Graben um ein Feld —ziehen, to dig or make a ditch round a field. 2) to draw or pull from place to place, about. Einen im Zimmer —ziehen, to draw or drag any one about the room. *Fig. Einen —ziehen, to amuse any one with idle promises; er wird Sie mit der Bezahlung lange —ziehen, he will put you off for a long time before he pays you; Einen bei der Nase —ziehen, to lead any one by the nose. II. v. intr. and v. r. sich —ziehen, 1) to move or march round. Das Heer zog [sich] um die Stadt —, the army marched round the town. Fig. Ein Graben zieht sich um das Schloß —, a ditch or moat surrounds the castle; es zieht sich ein Weg um den Wald —, there is a way round the wood; ein hohes Gebirge zieht sich rings —, high mountains extend or rise all around. 2) to move to and fro, from place to place. In der Welt —ziehen, to ramble or wander about the world; —ziehende Völker, wandering or nomadic people, nomads; —ziehende Schauspieler, Bettler, strolling players, vagrant beggars. it. to remove from lodging to lodging. Er ist schon in der ganzen Stadt —gezogen, he has already lodged all over the town, in all the streets or in all parts of the town. 3) to remove to this place. Er ist zu mir —gezogen, he has removed to my house.

Herúnter, *adv.* [denoting motion or direction from a higher to a lower place towards the person speaking, V. Herab] down. Von oben —, down from above; von den Felsen —, down from the rocks; gerade —, straight down, perpendicularly; den Hut —! — mit dem Hute! hats off! — mit dem Redner! down with the orator or speaker! —vom Pferde! down from your horse, alight! —! kommt —! down! come or get down! [Words compounded with Herunter, which are not found here, may be looked for among the compounds of Herab.]

Herunter-bringen, *ir. v. tr.* to bring down, to lower. *Fig. Einen —bringen, to injure any one in health or prosperity. Diese Krankheit hat ihn sehr —gebracht, this illness has enfeebled or weakened him very much; er ist so weit —gebracht, daß er betteln muß, he is reduced to beggary. —erben, v. intr. and v. r. sich —erben, to descend from father to son as an inheritance. Es haben sich in seiner Familie einige Handschriften —geerbt, in his family some manuscripts have descended from father to son. —handeln, v tr. to beat down in bargaining. Etwas von einem Preise —handeln, to beat down the price [of any commodity]. —hangen, V. Herabhangen. *—kanzeln, V. Abkanzeln —lesen, ir. v. tr. 1) to pick off. 2) to read [a page] from top to bottom, V. Ablesen. —machen, I. v. tr. to undo, to loosen, to untie, to detach. *Fig. Einen —machen, to reprimand, revile, upbraid or taunt any one. II. v. r. sich —machen, V. Herabmachen. —reißen, ir. v. tr. to pull down or off. Fig. [in vulgar lang.] Einen —reißen, V. —machen. —schlagen, ir. I. v. tr. V. Abschlagen I. 1). II. v. intr. [vulgar] to fall or tumble down. †—schmeißen, V. —werfen. —schneiden, V. Abschneiden I 1). —setzen, V. Herabsetzen. —trennen, V. Abtrennen. —werfen, ir. v. tr. 1) to throw down from above. Er warf einen Stein —, he threw down a stone. 2) to cast off, to throw off. Aepfel —werfen, to knock down apples [with stones &c. from the tree]; das Pferd hat den Reiter —geworfen, the horse has thrown its rider. —ziehen, ir. I. v. tr. to pull or draw down or off. Den Hut —ziehen, to take off, to pull off one's hat; er zog ihm den Ring vom Finger —, he took the ring off his finger. II. v. intr. to remove to a lower story or floor. III. v. r. sich —ziehen, to move or march down, to descend. Die Truppen zogen sich in's Thal —, the troops marched or proceeded down into the valley. Fig. Der Weg zieht sich in die Ebene —, the way leads down into the plain.

Herúnterwärts, *adv.* downwards.

Hervór, *adv.* [denoting motion forward from a remote or concealed place] forth, out.

Hervor-arbeiten, I. *v tr.* to get forth by labour or working. II. v. r. sich —arbeiten, to work one's self from under any thing, to get from under or out of any thing with labour or difficulty. Er hatte viele Mühe, sich unter seinem Pferde —zuarbeiten, he had a deal of trouble to disengage himself from under his horse. —blicken, v intr. to look or peep forth or out. Die Sonne blickt durch die Wolken —, the sun is seen or peeps through the clouds. —blinken, v. intr to glitter, sparkle, shine or peep forth. —blühen, v. intr. to come or issue forth and blossom, to put forth blossoms or flowers, to bloom, to blossom. —brechen, ir. v. intr. to come or issue forth with impetuosity, to break forth. Die Feinde brachen aus dem Hinterhalte —, the enemies rushed [forth] from their ambush; die Sonne bricht aus dem Gewölk —, the sun breaks through the clouds; eine Quelle bricht aus dem Felsen —, a spring gushes or issues out of the rock. Fig. Seine Freude brach —, his joy broke forth. —bringen, ir. v. tr. to bring forth or forward. Fig. a) to produce, to generate, to beget. Jedes Thier bringt seines Gleichen —, every animal begets, brings forth or produces its like or species; Gott hat alle Dinge —gebracht, God has created all things; dieses Jahrhundert brachte geistreiche Männer —, that age produced men of genius; die verdorbene Luft bringt Krankheiten —, bad air begets or generates diseases. *b*) to utter, to pronounce, to express. Töne, Worte —bringen, to utter sounds, words. —**bringung**, *f.* the act of bringing forth, generation, production. —**dämmern**, *v. intr.* to dawn. Der Morgen dämmert —, the morning dawns. —**dampfen**, *v. intr.* to come out or forth in steam or vapour. —**drängen**, I. *v. tr.* to push or force forth or forward by pressing or crowding, to press forward. II. *v. r.* sich —drängen, to press or crowd forward. *Fig.* Er drängt sich überall —, he makes himself everywhere remarkable, he obtrudes himself everywhere. —**dringen**, *ir. v. intr* to come or issue forth with vehemence. Der Feind drang aus dem Walde —, the enemy rushed forth from the wood; die Sonne dringt durch die Wolken —, the sun breaks through the clouds; das Blut drang aus der Wunde —, the blood gushed forth from the wound. —**fliegen**, *ir. v. intr.* to fly forth or out. —**fließen**, *ir. v. intr.* to flow forth or out of. —**führen**, *v. tr.* to lead or bring forth, to bring in any one's presence. —**geben**, *ir. v. tr.* to reach or give forth. —**gehen**, *ir. v. intr.* 1) to go or come forth. Die Pflanzen gehen aus der Erde —, the plants come, shoot or peep out of the ground. *Fig.* to result, proceed, rise or spring as a consequence. Daraus gehet hervor, daß &c, hence it follows, that &c.; die Grundsätze, welche aus der Analyse —gehen, the principles that result from the analysis. 2) V. —ragen, —stehen. —**glänzen**, *v. intr.* to shine forth. *Fig.* —glänzende Eigenschaften or Talente, brilliant, shining or eminent qualities or parts. —**heben**, *ir.* I. *v. tr.* to raise above the common surface; [in painting] to relieve, to set off. Er sollte seine Figuren mehr —heben, he ought to give his figures more relief. *Fig.* to render prominent, to set off, to relieve. Das hebt ihre Schönheit noch mehr —, that heightens or sets off her beauty, gives her beauty greater lustre. II. *v. r.* sich —heben, to rise above the common surface. [in painting] Diese Figur hebt sich nicht genug —, this figure has not relief enough, does not project enough. —**keimen**, *v. intr.* to shoot forth, to germinate, to sprout. —**kommen**, *ir. v. intr.* to come forth, to come forward; *it.* to appear, to arise, to peep out. —**können**, *ir. v. intr.* to be able to come forth or out. —**kriechen**, *ir. v. intr.* to creep or crawl forth. —**langen**, *v. tr.* to draw or reach forth, to take or fetch from [under] any thing. —**lassen**, *ir. v. tr.* to let any one or any thing come forth or out. —**laufen**, *ir. v. intr.* to run forth. —**leuchten**, *v. intr.* to shine forth. *Fig.* Das macht seine Unschuld desto mehr —leuchten, that makes his innocence appear so much the brighter; seine große Seele leuchtet aus Allem —, was er thut oder spricht, his great soul shines out in every thing he does or speaks; es leuchtet aus allem diesem —, daß &c., from all that it appears, it is plain or evident, that &c.; die Größe des Schöpfers leuchtet aus allen seinen Werken —, the greatness of the creator appears or is seen in all his works. —**locken**, *v. tr.* to allure any one to come forth or out, to draw forth. —**machen**, *v. r.* sich —machen, to come forth, to make one's appearance. —**mögen**, *ir. v. intr.* to be willing, to wish or want to come forth. —**müssen**, *ir. v. intr.* to be obliged to come forth or out. —**nehmen**, *ir. v. tr.* to draw forth, to take from under any thing. —**quellen**, *ir. v. intr.* to issue forth, to spring, to gush. —**ragen**, *v. intr.* to be prominent, to project, to stand or stick out, to jut. Das —ragende Land, the jutting or projecting land; hohe Felsen ragen über das Dorf —, high rocks jut or project over, overhang the village; dieser Baum ragt zwei Schuh hoch über die Mauer —, this tree is higher than the wall by two feet; der Montblanc ragt über alle ihn umgebende Berge —, Montblanc rises above, overtops all the surrounding mountains; sie ragt eines ganzen Kopfes hoch, einen ganzen Kopf über die andern —, she is taller than the others by a whole head, she overtops the others by a whole head; [in architecture] die —ragenden Theile, the jutting parts, projections. *Fig.* Vor Andern durch seinen Muth, seine Klugheit &c. —ragen, to excel or surpass others in courage, prudence &c.; ein —ragender Charakter, a prominent character; —ragende Verdienste, eminent merits. —**ragenheit**, *f.* superiority, preeminence. —**ragung**, *f.* [in architecture] jutting-out, projecture, projection; [in anatomy] prominence, knob, protuberance. —**rauchen**, *v. intr.* to come forth or out in the form of smoke. —**rauschen**, *v. intr.* to come forth or out rustling. —**recken**, V. —strecken. —**reichen**, I. *v. tr.* to reach or hand forth. II. *v. intr.* V. —ragen. —**reißen**, *ir. v. tr.* to pull forth. —**rieseln**, *v. intr.* to purl or trickle forth or out. —**rinnen**, *ir. v. intr.* to run, leak, ooze or trickle forth or out. —**rollen**, *v. intr.* to roll forth. —**rücken**, V. Vorrücken and Rücken. —**rufen**, *ir. v. tr.* to call any one forth or out. —**schaffen**, V. —arbeiten. —**scheinen**, V. —leuchten. —**schießen**, *ir. v intr.* 1) to shoot or fire from under any thing. 2) to come or issue forth with impetuosity, to rush or gush forth; *it.* V. —keimen, —sprießen, —sprossen. —**schimmern**, V. —leuchten. —**schleichen**, *ir. v. intr.* and *v. r.* sich —schleichen, to sneak, steal or slink behind or under any thing, from or out any place. —**schleppen**, *v. tr.* to drag forth. —**schlüpfen**, *v. intr.* to slip forth or out. —**seyn**, *ir. v. intr.* to be out, to have come forth. Noch ist die Sonne nicht hinter den Bergen —, the sun has not yet appeared from behind the mountains. —**sprechen**, *ir. v. intr.* to speak from behind or under any thing. —**sprießen**, V. —sprossen. —**springen**, *ir. v. intr.* to leap or spring forth, to rush forth, to gush, to spout; [in architecture] to project, to jut, V. —ragen. —springende Winkel, saliant angles. *Fig.* to result, to proceed or to spring as a consequence. Es springt daraus —, daß &c., hence it follows, that &c.; daraus springt unser ganzes Unglück —, thence spring all our misfortunes, V. —gehen. —**spritzen**, *v. intr.* to spout forth or out. —**sprossen**, *v. intr.* to sprout or shoot forth, to germinate. —**sprudeln**, *v. intr.* to come forth or out in bubbles, to bubble forth or out. —**stechen**, *ir. v. intr.* to prick forth, through or up, to project or protrude stinging. *Fig.* to be distinguished, to excel. Diese Blume sticht durch ihre Schönheit vor allen andern —, this flower excels or surpasses all the others in beauty; dieses Werk ist gut geschrieben, aber es hat nichts —stechendes, this work is well written, but contains nothing striking; —stechende Eigenschaften, eminent, shining qualities. —**stehen**, *ir. v. intr.* V. Herausstehen, —ragen. Ein Knochen steht —, a bone sticks out; dieses Karnieß stehet nicht weit genug —, this cornice does not project enough. —**stoßen**, *ir. v. tr.* to thrust or push forth, forward. —**strahlen**, *v. intr.* to emit or cast forth rays. —**strecken**, *v. tr.* to stretch forth or out. —**strömen**, *v. intr.* to stream or pour forth; *it.* to flock forth or out. —**stürzen**, *v. intr.* and *v. r.* sich —stürzen, to precipitate one's self forward, to fall or tumble forth or out; *it.* to rush forth with impetuosity. —**suchen**, *v. tr.* to seek out, to look for any among a number. Er suchte unter seinen Papieren einen Brief —, he looked for a letter among his papers. *Fig.* Gründe, Entschuldigungen —suchen, to endeavour to find out, to seek for reasons, excuses; Händel —suchen, to seek or pick a quarrel; er sucht Alles —, um ihn zu entschuldigen, he uses his utmost endeavours, he does his utmost, he tries every means to exculpate him. —**thun**, *ir.* I. *v. tr.* to put forth. II. *v. r.* sich —thun, fig. to distinguish one's self. Sich durch seinen Muth, seine Kenntnisse —thun, to distinguish or signalize one's self by one's courage, knowledge, [V. Auszeichnen II.]. *it.* to exert one's self. —**treiben**, *ir.* I. *v. tr.* to drive forth; [in painting] V. —heben. II. *v. intr.* V. —sprossen. —**treten**, *ir. v. intr.* to step or come forth or forward. Er trat hinter der Bildsäule —, he stepped or advanced from behind the statue. *Fig.* V. —ragen. [in painting] to come out or forward. —**wachsen**, *ir. v. intr.* to grow up or out, to spring or shoot forth. —**wagen**, *v. r.* sich —wagen, to venture to come forth. —**wälzen**, *v. tr.* to roll forth. —**ziehen**, *ir. v. tr.* to draw or pull forth. Etwas unter dem Mantel —ziehen, to draw or take any thing from under one's cloak. *Fig.* to raise to eminence, to distinguish, to make eminent or known, to prefer. Einen aus dem Staube —ziehen, to raise any one from the dunghill.

Hèrwärts, *adv.* hitherward.

Hèrz, *n.* [-ens, *pl.* -en] *dim.* **Herzchen**, ||**Herzlein**, *n.* (Sax. *heort*, Eng. *heart*, Dan. *hierte*, Sw. *hjerte*, Gr. κῆρ, L. cor] 1) [the muscular viscus, situated in the thorax] the heart. Das — schlägt, the heart beats; das — klopft, pocht, the heart palpitates, throbs; er stieß ihm den Dolch durch das —, he pierced his heart with the dagger, he run his dagger through his heart; *so lange mir das — im Leibe schlägt, as long as I shall live, whilst I breathe; *er gäbe ihr das — aus dem Leibe, he would give her any thing, he would part with his life for her; ein Kind unter dem —en tragen, to be or go with child, to be pregnant, *to be in the family-way; das Kind, das sie unter dem —en trägt, the child that she bears. *Fig. a*) [the seat of the affections and passions] heart. Ein gutes, stolzes, hartes —, a good, proud, hard heart; ein steinernes, eisernes —, a heart of stone, an iron heart; sein — verhärten, to harden one's heart, sein — verschließen, to be insensible, unfeeling, hard-hearted, *it.* to keep one's own counsel; ein böses — haben, to be rotten at the core; das — erweichen, to soften the heart; ein Mensch ohne —, a man without a heart or soul, *it.* V. under *e*); *das ist ihm ein Stich in's —, gab ihm einen Stich in's —, that stabbed him to the heart, struck or grieved him to the very heart, went near his heart, touched him to the quick. *das macht mir das — schwer, that grieves my heart; *es wird mir enge um's —, my heart feels straitened, *it.* is oppressed with grief; er hat das — voll, his heart is ready to burst, ich habe das — voll von der Ungerechtigkeit, die &c., my heart swells with vexation of the injustice, which etc.; von ganzem —, von —ens Grund, von Grund des —ens etwas thun, to do any thing with all one's heart; *das liegt mir schwer auf dem —en, that lies heavy upon my heart, that sticks to my heart; *es wird mir schwach um's —, my heart faints within me; die Freude erweitert das —, joy dilates the heart; *mir ward warm um's —, dabei warm um's —, I was moved at it, touched or affected with it; *sprechen, wie es Einem um's — ist, to speak one's heart or mind [without reserve]; *ich weiß, wie es ihm um's — ist, I know what he feels, I know, by what emotions his heart is agitated; mein — sagte es mir, my heart told me so, *it.* my heart misgave me; es will ihm das — abstoßen, [in popular lang.] it will split his heart [said of a person who is bursting with impatience to give vent to his thoughts or to reveal a secret]; *das — wollte mir bei diesem Anblick springen, bersten, that sight quite melted me, my heart was ready to burst at that sight; sich etwas zu —en nehmen, to take a thing to heart, to have any thing at heart; es lag ihm am —en, he had at heart; das geht mir sehr zu —en, greift mir an's —, that touches me to the quick, goes near my heart, grieves or concerns me greatly; *er ist mir an's — gewachsen, he is grown to my heart, he is greatly endeared to me, greatly beloved by me, I love him dearly; *von —en [= sehr], very; *von —en schlecht, arm, extremely, exceedingly bad, poor; die Sprache des —ens reden, von [vom] —en weg reden, to speak feelingly, *it.* to speak cordially or sincerely, to speak one's mind; zum — sprechen, to speak to the heart, to speak in such a manner as to affect the heart; was von —en kommt or gehet, gehet auch zu —en, what proceeds from the heart, touches the heart; das war aus dem —en gesprochen, that proceeded, came or flowed from the heart. *Prov.* Weß das — voll ist, deß geht der Mund über, out of the abundance of the heart the mouth speaks; aus or mit dem —en [= innig] beten, to pray sincerely, fervently or ardently; *sein — auf der Zunge haben or tragen, to have one's heart in one's mouth, to be open-hearted, to be frank and open; *ich kann es nicht über's — bringen, es zu thun, I cannot make up my mind, I cannot bring myself, cannot find in my heart to do it; *Sie sollten sich in Ihr — hinein schämen, you ought to be ashamed of yourself. *b*) inclination, affection, love. Sein — an eine Person or Sache hängen, to set one's heart on or upon any person or thing; sie besitzt sein ganzes —, he is entirely devoted to her, she is greatly beloved by him, he loves her dearly; ein — [= Neigung, Zutrauen] zu Jemand fassen, to have an affection for any one, *it.* to repose a confidence, to put one's trust or confidence in any one; ich kann kein — zu diesem Menschen fassen, I can have no confidence in that man. *c*) secret thoughts, recesses of the mind. Man kann Niemand in's — sehen, one cannot see the bottom of people's hearts; Gott allein sieht in's —, God alone knows the bottom of our hearts; in seinem —en [insgeheim] nach etwas trachten, to try or endeavour secretly to obtain any thing; etwas auf dem —en haben, to have something heavy on one's mind, *it.* to bear a grudge for ill usage; er hat etwas auf dem —en, a secret grief preys upon his mind, *it.* he has a latent desire or wish; Einem sein ganzes — eröffnen, entdecken, to open or disclose one's heart, to unbosom one's self to any one; sie verachtet ihn in ihrem —en, she despises him in her heart; im Innersten meines —ens, in my heart's core. *d*) conscience, or sense of good or ill. Frage dein eigenes —, consult your own heart or conscience; [in Scripture] so uns unser — nicht verdammet, if our heart condemns us not. *e*) courage, spirit. Er hat —, he has courage; er ist ohne —, he wants courage; er hat kein —, he has no spirit; er hat sehr viel —, he is all courage; *[sich] ein — fassen, to take heart, to pluck up a good heart; *er bekam —, das gab ihm —, that gave him heart; wieder — fassen, to recover heart; *das — entfiel, schwand ihm, the heart or courage failed him, his heart went down to his heels; *fassen Sie sich ein —! cheer up! *f*) person or character, particularly with respect to kindness. Sich alle or Aller —en verbinden, zuwenden or gewinnen, to gain or win all hearts; ihr büßet tausend wohlgesinnte —en ein, you lose a thousand well-disposed hearts; mein —! mein —chen! [a term of endearment] my dear, my love, my dearest love! 2) [that part of the body whereabout the heart is situated] breast. Er drückte sie an sein —, he clasped her to his breast. *Fig.* the middle part or interior of certain things. Das — eines Schildes, the midst of a shield; er führt eine Lilie im —en des Schildes, he bears a flower-de-luce in the middle or centre of the shield; das — eines Baumes, the heart or core of a tree; das — eines Landes, the heart of a country; der Feind stand im —en Frankreichs, the enemy was in the heart of France; das — eines Heeres, the centre of an army; das — einer Schnalle, the catch of a buckle, chape. 3) any thing having the form or shape of a heart. Sie trägt ein goldenes —chen um den Hals, she wears a little gold heart round her neck. — [one of the suits of cards] heart. — ist Trumpf, hearts are trumps; ich spiele — aus, I lead a heart or hearts; ich habe kein —, I have no hearts. Syn. Herz, Muth. Herz denotes generally, that quality of mind which enables men to encounter danger and difficulties with firmness, or without fear or depression of spirits, intrepidity. Muth expresses that courage or fearlessness which springs from the consciousness of strength.

Herz-ader, *f.* the great artery, aorta; *it.* V. Spuader. *—allerliebst, *adj.* and *adv.* extremely amiable; *it.* very engaging, most charming, delightful. —allerliebster, *m.* [in popular language, or in jest] dearest, most beloved. —arznei, *f.* cordial medicine, cordial. —ausdehnend, *adj.* dilating the heart, heart-expanding. —balken, *m.* V. —muskel. —balsam, *m.* cordial balm, cordial. —bändel, *m.* V. —beutel. —baum, *m.* ahouai or ahovai. —beben, *n.* the trembling, quaking, quivering, palpitation of the heart. —bein, V. Hirschbein 2). —beklemmung, *f.* oppression of the heart; *fig.* pang. —beschwerung, *f.* grief, affliction, anguish, pain of the heart. —betrübt, *adj.* and *adv.* greatly afflicted, heart-sorrowing. —bettchen, ‖—bettlein, *n.* a small soft cushion or bag sometimes laid upon the breast of an infant. —beutel, *m.* [a membrane that incloses the heart] heart's purse, pericardium. —beutelwasser, *n.* the water of the pericardium, pericardian humour or liquor. —beutelwassersucht, *f.* V. —wassersucht. —bewegend, *adj.* and *adv.* heart-moving, touching, pathetic. —bewegung, *f.* motion of the heart. —blatt, *n.* 1) [in botany] a young unopened leaf in the heart or middle of a plant. *Fig.* [a term of endearment] Er, sie ist mein —blatt, —blättchen, he, she is my darling, favourite. 2) a card on which a heart or hearts are painted. 3) [in anatomy] V. Brustbein. —blume, *f.*, *dim.* —blümchen, ‖—blümlein, *n.* 1) borage. 2) white liver-wort, Parnassia. —blut, *n.* the blood of the heart, heart's-blood; *fig.* what is most precious, life, heart-blood or heart's-blood. —brand, *m.* [in medicine] lipyria. —bräune, *f.* a very malignant putrid fever, the Hungarian disease. —brechend, *adj.* and *adv.* heart-breaking, heart-rending. —bruder, *m.* V. Herzensbruder. —bube, *m.* the knave of hearts. —bündel, *m.* V. —beutel. —dame, *f.* the queen of hearts. —daus, *n.* the ace of hearts. —drücken, *n.* oppression of the heart. —drüse, *f.* [gland belonging to the heart] cardiacal gland. —durchbohrend, —durchdringend, —durchschneidend, *adj.* and *adv.* piercing the heart, heart-piercing, heart-rending —entzündung, *f.* inflammation of the heart. —erbse, *f.* heart-pea. —erfreuend, *adj.* and *adv.* heart-cheering, heart-gladdening. —erhebend, *adj.* and. *adv.* elevating the heart. —fell, *n.* V. —beutel. —fieber, *n.* 1) cardiacal fever. 2) V. Auszehrung. —finger, *m.* ring-finger. —förmig, *adj.* and. *adv.* having the form or shape of a heart, heart-shaped. —fressend, *adj.* and *adv.* preying upon the heart, heart-corroding, heart-eating. —freund, *m.* V. Herzensfreund. *—fromm, *adj.* and *adv.* having a pious, a most religious, devout heart. —geblüt, *n.* V. —blut. —geschwulst, *f.* tumour of the heart. —gespann, —gesperr, *n.* 1) heart-burn, cardialgy. 2) [in botany] mother-wort, Agripalma, cardiaca. —gewächs, *n.* scirrhus or polypus of the heart. —gras, *n.* [in botany] coronopus, buckshorn-plantain. —grube, *f.*, *dim.* —grübchen, *n.* pit of the stomach. *—gut, *adj.* and *adv.* having a good, most benevolent heart. —haut, *f.*, *dim.* —häutchen, *n.* 1) tunicle of the heart. 2) V. —beutel. —höhle, *f.* V. —kammer. —horn, *n.* V. —tute. —innig, —inniglich, *adj.* and *adv.* hearty, heart-felt. —käfer, *m fig.* V. —blatt. —kammer, *f.* [in anatomy] ventricle of the heart. —kirsche, *f.* [the black and white] heart-cherry. —kirschenbaum, *m.* heart-cherry tree. —klappe, *f.* [in anatomy] valve of the heart. —klee, *m.* wood sorrel, sour trefoil. —klopfen, *n.* palpitation, beating, throbbing of the heart. —knorpel, *m.* the sternum, V. Brustbein. —kohl, *m.* a sort of brown cole ro cabbage forming a heart. —kolbe, *f.* V. —sprosse, —stengel. —könig, *m.* the king of hearts. —kränkend, *adj.* and *adv.* heart-offending, mortifying. —kraut, *n.* 1) V. —gespann 2). 2) V. Bienenkraut. —läppchen, *n.* V. —ohr. —laub, *n.* [in architecture] leaved work or festoons in mouldings in form of a heart. —leerung, *f.* an opening or disclosing of one's heart. —lehre, *f.* [in anatomy] cardialogy. —leid, V. Herzeleid. *—lieb, I. *adj.* and *adv.* heartily beloved, very dear. II. *n.* [obsolete] sweetheart. *—liebchen, *n.* a sweetheart. Mein —liebchen, my dear, my love —liebster, *m.* [in popular lang.] lover; *it.* husband. —los, *adj.* and *adv.* 1) without a heart or soul, unfeeling, insensible. 2) without courage, heartless, spiritless, fainthearted. —losigkeit, *f.* heartlessness. —muschel, *f.* heart-shell. Die eßbare —muschel, cockle. —muskeln, *pl.* the muscles of the heart. —mutter, *f.* V. —ensmutter. —nagend, *adj.* and *adv.* preying on or gnawing the heart, heart-wounding, heart-corroding, V. —fressend. —nerve, *f.* cardiacal nerve, heart-string. —nervengeflecht, *n.* cardiacal plexus. —ohr, *n.*, *dim.* —öhrchen, *n.* auricle of the heart. —pfirsich, *m.*, —pfirsche, *f.* a kind of peach having the shape of a heart, heart-peach. —pochen, *n.* V. —klopfen. —polyp, *m.* V. —gewächs. —pulver, *n.* a cardiacal powder. —rad, *n.* the middle wheel in a clock. —röhre, *f.* [in anatomy] the aorta. —rührend, *adj.* and *adv.* heart-moving, touching, pathetic, heart-felt. —sack, *m.* V. —beutel. —same, *m.* V. —erbse. —säulen, *pl.* V. —muskeln. —schild, *m.*, *dim.* —schildchen, ‖—schildlein, *n.* [in heraldry] a small shield in the middle of the escutcheon; *it.* a shield or escutcheon in form of a heart. —schlächtig, *adj.* broken-winded [said of horses]. —schlächtigkeit, *f.* state of being broken-winded, broken-wind, shortness of breath. —schlag, *m.* 1) palpitation, beating of the heart; *it.* [in the veterinary art, a disease of sheep] shortness of breath, pursiness. 2) pluck of animals. —schneidend, *adj.* and *adv.* V. —zerschneidend. —spann, V. —gespann. —sprosse, *f.* [in botany] a sprout or shoot in the middle or heart of a plant. —stärkend, *adj.* and *adv.* invigorating, giving strength or spirits, cardiacal, cordial. Ein —stärkendes Mittel, a cordial. —stärkung, *f.* 1) invigoration, giving strength or spirits 2) invigorating or restorative remedy, a cordial. —stein, *m.* a stone having the form of a heart; [in mineralogy] a sea-urchin in a fossil state, echinites. —stelle, *f.* [in blasonry] the middle or centre of the shield. —stengel, *m* a stalk in the middle or heart of a plant. —stoß, *m.* the finishing blow given to persons executed, the coup-de-grace. *Fig.* Dieses hat ihm den [letzten] —stoß gegeben, that has completed his ruin. —tute, *f.* [in conchology] the tiger-shell. —verein, *m.* union of hearts. —wasser, *n.* V. —beutelwasser. —wassersucht, *f.* dropsy of the pericardium, hydrocardia. —weh, *n.* heart-ache, pain of the heart, cardialgy. —wunde, *f.* wound of the heart. —wurm, *m.* 1) a worm fancied to be in the heart. *Fig.* [rather high-flown or emphatically] gnawing worm in the heart or mind. 2) V. —polyp. —wurz, *f.* hermodactyl. —wurzel, *f.* tap-root, V. Pfahlwurzel, Zapfenwurzel. —zerdrückend, —zermalmend, —zerreißend, —zerschneidend, *adj.* and *adv.* heart-breaking, heart-piercing, heart-rending. —zergliederung, *f.* dissection of the heart, cardiatomy.

Herzens-bändiger, *m.* V. —zähmer. —blatt, —bube, —dame &c., V. the usual words Herzblatt, Herzbube &c. —feßler, *m.*, —feßlerinn, *f.* [in poetry] a person who captivates or enslaves every heart. —zähmer, *m.*, —zähmerinn, *f.* [in poetry] a person who subdues, conquers or captivates every heart.

Herzens-andacht, *f.* fervent devotion, elevation of the heart. —bändiger, *m.* V. Herzenszähmer. —blut, *n.* V. Herzblut. —bruder, *m.*, *dim.* —brüderchen, ||—brüderlein, *n.* a dearly beloved brother. *Fig.* [in fam. lang.] beloved friend, bosom-friend. —dieb, *m.* a person who steals or wins the heart of any one. —entzündung, *f.* V. Herzentzündung. —ergießung, *f.* V. Herzleerung. —frau, *f.* beloved woman or wife, [particularly used in addressing] my dear, good woman or wife. —freude, *f.* 1) great, lively joy; heart's joy. 2) [in botany] *a*) wood-roof. *b*) borage. —freund, *m.* beloved, intimate friend, bosom-friend, V. Busenfreund. —froh, *adj.* and *adv.* heartily, very glad, glad of heart. —gedanke, *m.* secret thought. —glaube, *m.* faith of the heart, inmost belief; [in divinity] true faith. —grund, *m.* bottom of the heart. Aus or von —grund, from the bottom of my heart, *it.* with all my heart. —güte, *f.* goodness, kindness of heart, benevolence. *—junge, *m.*, —jüngelchen, *n.* a beloved lad, an excellent lad. —junge! my dearest boy! dear lad! *—kind, *n.* beloved, charming child. —königinn, *f.* mistress who reigns in one's heart. —kummer, *m.* a secret grief. —kündiger, *m.* one that knows the heart. Gott, der —kündiger, God the searcher of hearts. —leerung, *f.* V. Herzleerung. —lust, *f.* inclination, pleasure, joy of the heart, great joy. Nach —lust, to or at one's heart's desire. *—mädchen, ||—mädel, *n.* a dearly beloved girl; *it.* a very good, charming girl. *—mann, *m.* a dearly beloved, very dear man; *it.* a very good, excellent man. —meinung, *f.* sentiment of one's heart, true, real sentiment. *Ich habe ihm meine —meinung gesagt, I have told him my mind. *—mutter, *f.* a dearly, very beloved mother. —noth, *f.* anxiety of heart, great vexation; *it.* great distress. —qual, *f.* great torment or affliction of heart. In seiner größten —qual, in the agony of his heart. —reue, *f.* sincere, heartfelt repentance, compunction, remorse, contrition. —ruhe, *f.* 1) [in anatomy] perisystole. 2) tranquillity of heart or mind, heart-ease. In größter —ruhe aß er seinen Apfel, with the utmost composure he ate his apple; ich will nach meiner —ruhe leben, I will live after my own comfort. —seufzer, *m.* a sigh coming from the bottom of one's heart; [in divinity] ejaculation, V. Stoßseufzer, Stoßgebet. —sprache, *f.* language of the heart. —trost, *m.* consolation or comfort of heart. —wunsch, *m.* desire of the heart, ardent, violent desire. Das ist sein —wunsch, that is what he desires ardently; nach —wunsch, to one's heart's desire. —wurm, *m.* V. Herzwurm. —zähmer, *m.* V. Herzenszähmer.

Hèrzeleid, *n.* [-es] [chiefly in fam. lang.] overwhelming sorrow or grief, heart-break, heart-sore, heart grief, affliction of the heart. [in popular lang.] Einem alles gebrannte — anthun, to vex, mortify or chagrin any one exceedingly; es war ein großes — für ihn, zu sehen &c., it was heart-breaking, heart-rending for him to see &c. Syn. V. Harm.

Hèrzen, *v. tr.* to press to the heart, to embrace, to hug; *it.* to caress, to fondle.

Hèrzhaft, *adj.* and *adv.* stout-hearted, courageous, bold, manly, brave. — machen, to encourage, to embolden. V. Beherzt, Muthig.

Hèrzhaftig, *adj.* and *adv.* V. Herzhaft.

Hèrzhaftigkeit, *f.* courage, V. Muth.

Hèrzig, *adj.* and *adv.* 1) [chiefly used in composition] endowed with a heart. Offen—, openhearted &c. *it.* [sometimes = gefühlvoll] feeling, sensible. 2) [in fam. lang.] dearly or tenderly beloved. Mein —es Mädchen, my dearest girl. *it.* very pretty, charming, delightful. Das ist ein —es Kind, that's a charming child; was für ein —es Kind! what a sweet little darling! —e Schuhe, very pretty shoes.

Hèrzlich, I. *adj.* and *adv.* contained in or proceeding from the heart, inward, hearty, heartfelt, cordial, loving, sincere, affectionate. Eine —e Liebe, Zuneigung, a cordial, hearty love, affection; ein —er Empfang, a cordial reception, a dearly welcome; ein —es Benehmen, affectionate manners; sie ist eine —e Freundinn, she is a warm or sincere friend; Einen — empfangen, to receive any one cordially or heartily; ich fühle eine —e Freude, I feel a heartfelt joy. II. *adv.* very, exceedingly. — gern, most willingly, with or from all one's heart; ich freue mich —, I am extremely glad, most happy; — lachen, to laugh most heartily, to split one's sides with laughing; das ist — schlecht, that is miserably bad. Syn. Herzlich, Innig. Herzlich says less than innig, it denotes merely that the expression of feeling is unfeignedly sincere; whereas innig expresses the strongest possible inward emotion.

Hèrzlichkeit, *f.* sincere affection and kindness, cordiality, sincerity.

Hèrzog, *m.* [-es, *pl.* -e] [from Heer and ziehen] duke.

Herzogs-hut, *m.* ducal hat. —krone, *f.* ducal crown or coronet. —mantel, *m.* ducal mantle. —pulver, *n.* a stomachic powder invented in France [consisting of 16 parts of sugar, one part of nutmeg and some cinnamon].

Hèrzogenbusch, *n.* [-es] [a town in Holland] Herzogenbosh.

Hèrzoginn, *f.* duchess.

Hèrzoglich, *adj.* and *adv.* ducal. Der —e Pallast, the ducal palace; — leben, to live like a duke, in the style of a duke.

Hèrzogthum, *n.* [-s, *pl.* -thümer] dukedom, dutchy.

Herzu, *adv.* [denoting approach towards the person speaking] hither, near. [This adverb is only used in composition and is the same with herbei, which see].

Hèspe, *f.* V. Haspe, Häspe.

*Hesperiden, *pl.* [in mythology] Hesperides.

*Hespèrien, *n.* the western countries [as Spain &c.]

Hèsse, *m.* [-n, *pl.* -n] a native or inhabitant of Hessia, Hessian.

Hèssel or Hèsseling, *m.* V. Häseling.

Hèssen, *n.* [-s, *pl.* -] [the name of several provinces or sovereignties in Germany] Hessen, Hesse, Hessia. Das Großherzogthum — or —-Darmstadt, the Grand-dutchy of Hesse-Darmstadt or Grand-ducal Hessia; das Kurfürstenthum — or —-Kassel, the Electorate of Hesse-Kassel, Electoral Hessia; die beiden —, both these states. Die Landgrafschaft —-Homburg, the Landgraviate of Hesse-Homburg.

Hèssisch, *adj.* and *adv.* Hessian, in the Hessian manner.

*Heterodòx, *adj.* [andersgläubig] heterodox [heretical].

*Heterodoxie, *f.* heterodoxy.

*Heterogèn, *adj.* [ungleichartig] heterogeneal, heterogeneous [unlike or dissimilar in kind].

*Heterogenität, *f.* heterogeneousness, heterogeneity.

*Heteroklìtisch, *adj.* [in grammar] heteroclitic, heteroclitical, irregular, anomalous.

*Heterophỳllisch, *adj.* [in botany = ungleichblätterig] heterophyllous.

*Heteròscii, *pl.* the Heteroscians [those inhabitants of the earth whose shadows fall one way only].

*Hethiter, *pl.* Hittites.

*Hètmann, *m.* [-s] [captain or leader of Cossacks] hetman.

Hètze, *f.* [*pl.* -n] 1) *a*) the act of hunting, coursing or baiting wild animals, hunt, chase, course. V. Bären—, Hasen—. *Fig.* [in popular lang.] In der — seyn, to be beset on all sides, to be in a fine pickle, greatly embarrassed. *b*) uproar, racket, hubbub, riot. 2) place where wild beasts are baited, baiting-place, V. Hetzbahn, Hetzgarten. 3) *a*) a pack of hounds, a hunt. *b*) [in popular lang.] a number of things or persons of the same kind, a set. Eine — Kinder, a parcel or pack of children. [4) [better Elster] magpie.

Hetz-bahn, *f.* place where wild beast are baited, baiting-place [for bulls and bears &c.]. —garten, *m.* fenced ground or park for the purpose of baiting wild beasts, *it.* V. Hetze 2). —haus, *n.* a house in which wild beasts are kept for baiting; *it.* a building in which wild beasts are baited. —hund, *m.* hound. —jagd, *f.* hunt of wild beasts. —los, *adj.* and *adv.* uncoupled. Die Hunde —los machen, to uncouple the hounds. —peitsche, *f.* hunting-whip. —platz, *m.* V. —bahn. —riemen, *m.* [a strong long line by which a courser holds his dog] leash. —schirm, *m.* a shelter [a bush or shrub] for hunting-dogs or hounds. —strick, *m.* V. —riemen. —zeit, *f.* the time or season when wild animals are fat and, therefore, are hunted, hunting-season.

Hètzen, *v. tr.* [D. hissen, hitschen, Sw. *hissa* and *hetsa*; most probably from the old hagen = jagen and eilen, V. Hatz] 1) [to pursue with hounds, as game] to hunt, to bait, to course. Einen Hirsch, Fuchs, Hasen —, to hunt a stag, fox, hare, einen Fuchs zu Tode or todt —, to hunt a fox down; einen Stier, Eber —, to bait a bull, a boar; *Einen mit Hunden aus dem Hause —, to turn or drive any one out of the house by setting the dogs on him. 2) to let loose upon, to set on or upon, as a dog. Die Hunde auf Einen, hinter Einem her —, to set the dogs upon any one. *Fig.* [in popular lang.] Die Leute an einander —, to set people against one another, to set people together by the ears; V. An—, Auf—.

Hètzer, *m.* [-s, *pl.* -] a person who baits, or one who sets on dogs. *Fig.* one that sets a person against another, instigator, inciter.

1. Heu, *n.* [-es] [Low Sax. Hau, D. *hoy*, Eng. *hay*, Icel. *hei*, probably from hauen, to cut] 1) hay. Es ist herrliches Wetter, um — zu machen, it is excellent weather for making hay. *Fig.* Alles Fleisch ist —, [in Script.] all flesh is grass. 2) [in botany] Griechisches —, fenugreek; zartes —, V. Hart—.

Heu-ärnte, *f.* V. —ernte. —barn, *m.*, V. —bucht. —baum, *m.* a large pole or beam, tied upon a load of hay, in a cart or waggon, to keep the hay down, hay-pole, hay-beam. —binder, *m.* one who makes hay into bundles or bottles. —blume, *f.* [in popular lang.] a flower that blossoms about the time when hay is made. —böden, *m.* hay-loft. —bucht, *f.* [an inclosed place in a stable for depositing hay] bay. —bühne, *f.* V. —boden. —bund, *n.*, —bündel, *n.* a bundle or bottle of hay. —ernte, *f.* hay-making, hay-harvest. —fehm, —feimen, *m.* hay-rick, hay-stack. —futter, *n.* hay-fodder. —gabel, *f.* hay-fork, pitchfork. —gewinn, *m.* [the produce of a meadow converted into hay] the crop of hay, hay-crop. Eine Meierei mit vielem —gewinn, a farm with much meadow-ground. —haufen, *m.* 1) a heap of hay, hay-rick, hay-stack. 2) a conical pile of hay in the field made for drying, hay-cock. —hechel, *f.* V. Hauhechel. —kuppe, *f.* hay-cock. —land, *n.* hay-field, meadow-ground. —leine, *f.* hay-cord [with which the hay is secured on the waggon]. —machen, *n.* hay-making. —macher, *m.*, —macherinn, *f.* 1) hay-maker. 2) —macher [in nat. hist.], V. —vogel. —macherlohn, *m.* a hay-maker's wages. —ma[h]d, *f.* 1) a meadow to be mowed 2) V. —machen. —magazin, *n.* a magazine of or for hay. —mäher, *m.* mower, hay-maker; [in nat. hist.] V. —vogel. —markt, *m.* hay-market. —messer, *n.* hay-knife. —monat, *m.* hay-month, July. —motte, *f.* hay-moth. —pferd, —pferdchen, *n.* 1) grass-hopper, locust. 2) dragon-fly. —raufe, *f.* [hay-]rack. —rechen, *m.* hay-rake. —recht, *n.* the right of converting the produce of a meadow into hay. —same, *n.* hay-seed. —scheibe, *f.* V. —haufen 2). —schein, *m.* the new-moon of July. —scheuer, *f.* hay-barn, hay-shed. —schlag, *m.* 1) V. —gewinn. 2) a meadow in defence [the grass of which must not be converted into hay]. —schober, *m.* hay-rick, hay-stack. —schoppen, *m.* shed for keeping hay, V. —scheuer. —schrecke, *f.* grass-hopper, locust, V. 1. Grille. —schreckenbaum, *m.* 1) common locust-tree, hymenaea courbaril. 2) V. Johannisbrodbaum. 3) common acacia, false acacia. 4) V. Honigerbse. —schreckengrille, *f.* V. Baumgrille. —schreckenwolke, *f.* a cloud of locusts. —seil, *n.* V. —leine. —sense, *f.* a scythe [for mowing hay]. —speicher, *m.* V. —boden. —stock, *m.* V. —schober. —vogel, *m.* bee-eater. —wage, *f.* balance for weighing hay. —wagen, *m.* a waggon for conveying hay or laden with hay, hay-waggon. —wiese, *f.* a meadow, the produce of which may be converted into hay, hay-meadow. —zehnte, *m.* tithes paid of hay. —zeit, *f.* hay-making time, hay-time.

2. Heu, *m.* [-es, *pl.* -e] [from hauen?] [a small vessel usually rigged as a sloop] hoy.

Heuchelei, *f.* hypocrisy, simulation, dissimulation. Es ist lauter—, 't is mere hypocrisy.

Heucheln, [Dan. *hykle*, Sw. *hyckla*. It probably belongs to hauchen, Allemannic chuchen, and signified at first nothing but *to speak* and afterwards: to speak otherwise than one thinks] I. *v. intr.* to feign, to dissemble, to act or play the hypocrite. Wenn ich heuchle, so &c., if I do feign or dissemble &c. II. *v. tr.* to feign, to simulate. Freude —, to counterfeit joy, to pretend to be merry; Liebe —, to feign or simulate love.

Heuchel-bube, *m.* a hypocritical villain. —buße, *f.* feigned repentance. —christ, *m.* hypocritical Christian. —freund, *m.* a deceitful, false or hollow friend —freundschaft, *f.* feigned, false friendship. —glaube, *m.* pretended faith. —kunst, *f.* the art of dissembling. —liebe, *f.* simulated, feigned love. —schein, *m.* V. Heuchelei. —that, *f.* the action of a hypocrite. —thräne, *f.* false or affected tear, crocodile tear. —werk, *n.* hypocritical doings or actions. —wort, *n.* the word or speech of a hypocrite.

Heuchelhaft, *adj.* V. Heuchlerisch.

Heuchler, *m.* [-s, *pl.* -], —inn, *f.* hypocrite, dissembler, canter. *Es [sie] ist eine Erz—inn, she is an errant hypocrite.

Heuchlerisch, *adj.* and *adv.* hypocritical. Er hat eine —e Miene, he has a hypocritical look; — reden, to cant; er ist ein —er Mensch, he is a canting fellow.

Heuen, *v. intr.* to make hay.

||1. **Heuer**, *adv.* [probably allied to the old he, ha = dieser] this year.

||2. **Heuer**, *adj.* and *adv.* [allied to kirre; the Icel. *hyr* is = zahm] 1) tame, domestic, gentle, V. Zahm. 2) V. Geheuer.

3. **Heuer**, *m.* [-s, *pl.* -] hay-maker.

||4. **Heuer**, *f.* [*pl.* -n] [Sax. hûr, Dan. hyre, from the W. *hwr*, Eng. *hire*] rent, hire; *it.* rented habitation or farm. Die — bezahlen, to pay the rent; zur — wohnen, to live in lodgings; die — aufkündigen, to give notice or warning to quit.

Heuer-acker, *m.*, —feld, *n.*, —garten, *m.* a rented field, garden &c. —kutsche, *f.*, —kutscher, *m.* V. Miethkutsche, Miethkutscher.

Heuerig, Heurig, *adj.* and *adv.* of this year, this year's.

Heuerlich, *adj.* and *adv.* that is to be rented or hired.

Heuerling, *m.* [-es, *pl.* -e] 1) [from 1. Heuer] any thing produced this year, as a lamb, fish &c. 2) [from 4. Heuer] *a*) one who rents or farms any thing, tenant. *b*) one who is hired, hireling.

Heuern, *v. tr.* [from 4. Heuer] to rent, to hire. Syn. V. Miethen.

||**Heuet**, *f.* V. Heuzeit.

Heulen, *v. intr.* [Low Sax. hulen, Eng. *to howl*, Dan. *hyle*; Sw. *ulfwa*; Icel. *ylu*, Fr. *hurler*, Lat. *ejulo*, *ululo*, Gr. ὀλολύζω, ὑλ-ακτεῖν] to howl. Die Hunde, Wölfe —, the dogs, wolves howl; *prov.* wer unter den Wölfen ist, muß mit —, who keeps company with wolves will learn to howl; you must howl when others yell; one must follow the fashion. *it.* to weep vehemently or aloud, to cry, to wail; *it.* der Sturm heulet, the tempest howls or roars. Das —, howling, roaring.

Heulkreisel, *m.* humming-top, V. Brummkreisel.

Heuler, *m.* [-s, *pl.* -] one who howls or weeps, weeper. *Fig.* [in contempt] a whining, canting fellow.

Heurath, Heurathen, V. Heirath, Heirathen.

Heurig, V. Heuerig.

Heute, [heut] *adv.* [allied to the old pronoun da, de, di = dieser, this, and Tag, day; the Gothic was *hina dag*] to-day, this day. — früh or — Morgen, — Abend, this morning, this evening; — Nacht, to-night; er wird — ankommen, he will arrive to-day or to-day he will arrive; von — an, from this day forward; *ich kenne ihn nicht erst seit —, he is an old acquaintance of mine. I have been long acquainted with him. *Fig.* Auf —, till this day; — vor acht Tagen, this day sennight or week; — über or von — über vierzehn Tage, this day fortnight; heut zu Tage, in this age, at present, now-a-days; das war früher so Sitte, aber heut zu Tage treibt man die Sache ganz anders, that was the custom formerly, but now-a-days 't is quite otherwise; — den ganzen Tag, this whole day, all to-day; zwischen — und morgen, betwixt to-day and to-morrow. *Prov.* — mir, morgen dir, to-day is ours, to-morrow may be yours, to-day me, to-morrow thee; — roth, morgen todt, to-day a man, to-morrow a mouse, to-day on a throne, to-morrow in a dungeon.

Heutig, *adj.* and *adv.* of this day. Der —e Tag, this [very] day; die —e Welt, the present age; die —en Schriftsteller, the modern authors; der —e Geschmack, the modern or present taste, the taste of the day; auf —e Art, nach der —en Art, after the present fashion or style; —es Tages [heut zu Tage], now-a-days.

***Hexaëdron**, *n.* [-s] [a regular solid body of six sides] hexaedron, a cube.

***Hexagōn**, *n.* [-s, *pl.* -e] [a figure of six sides and six angles] hexagon.

***Hexāmeter**, *m.* [-s, *pl.* -] [a verse of six feet] hexameter.

***Hexamètrisch**, *adj.* and *adv.* hexametric, hexametrical.

Hèxe, *f.* [*pl.* -n] [Sax. *haegesse*, *haegtys*, Sw. *hexa*, Eng. *hag*, Icel. *hagur* = klug] 1) witch, sorceress, hag. Er glaubt an —n, he believes in witches. *Fig.* Sie ist eine alte —, she is an old hag; kleine —! [a term of endearment] you little rogue or hussy! 2) [in nat. hist.] goat-sucker, night-jar, V. Nachtschwalbe, Milchsauger.

Hèxen, *v. intr.* to practise sorcery or witchcraft. Er kann — [in popular lang.], he is a sorcerer; um das zu errathen, muß man — können [in popular lang.], one must be a sorcerer to guess that; das Ding geht wie gehext [= sehr schnell und gut] [in popular lang.], that goes on very fast, very well. Das —, V. Hexerei.

Hexen-bann, *m.* the spell or charm of a witch or witches. —baum, *m.* the common bird-cherry-tree, V. Vogelkirschenbaum. *—brut, *f.* a brood of hags or witches. —buch, *n.* a conjuring-book. —fahrt, *f.* a fabulous expedition of the witches, said to take place once a year, in a certain night, witches' expedition. —fall, *m.* V. —proceß. —fest, *n.* nocturnal meeting or night-revelling of witches. —finger, *m.* [in mineralogy] V. Fingerstein and Donnerkeil 2). —formel, *f.* V. —spruch. —geschichte, *f.* story of witches and sorcerers. —karte, *f.* V. —spiel. —kessel, *m.* witches' caldron. —kraut, *n.* 1) enchanter's nightshade, circaea. 2) shrubby tansy. 3) fern. —kreis, *m.* magical circle or ring. —kunst, *f.* 1) magic art. 2) trick of a witch or sorcerer. —männchen, *n.* [in popular lang.] V. Alraun and Galgenmännchen. —mehl, *n.* witch-meal, vegetable sulphur. —meister, *m.* sorcerer; conjurer, necromancer. [in fam. lang.] Er ist kein großer —meister, he is no conjurer. —probe, *f.* witches' ordeal, V. Feuerprobe, Wasserprobe. —proceß, *m.* the trial of a witch or of witches —pulver, *n.* V. —mehl. —ritt, *m.* V. —fahrt. —sabbath, *m.* witches' revelling [especially, in popular belief, in the night of the first of May, on the Brocken-mountain]. —segen, *m.* conjuration, charm, spell. —spiel, *n.* [a game at cards, played with 36 cards on which are painted men of grotesk figure, two witches and two jackpuddings] magic game, magic cards. —spruch, *m.* a certain formula of words used by witches and sorcerers. —strang, *m.* [in botany] common virgin's bower, wild climbers, traveller's joy, clematis vitelba. —tanz, *m.* witches' dance. —werk, *n.* V. Hexerei. —wesen, *n.* any thing relating to witches or sorcerers.

Hèxer, *m.* [-s, *pl.*-] sorcerer, conjurer, wizard, V. Hexenmeister.

Hexerei, *f.* 1) sorcery, witchcraft. Er wurde der — angeklagt, he was accused of witchcraft. *Prov.* Geschwindigkeit ist keine —, one may play tricks by sleight of hand without being a sorcerer. 2) a trick of a witch or sorcerer.

Heyda, Heye, Heysa, V. Heida, Heie, Heisa.

Hi, [expression of subdued or chuckling, or of feminine laughter] hi, hi, hi! hi, hi, hi!

*Hiäne, *f.* [*pl.* -n] hyena, hyen, V. Grabthier.

*Hiazint or Hyacinth, *m.* [-es, *pl.* -e] [in mineralogy] hyacinth.

Hiazint-farbig, *adj.* having the colour of the hyacinth, hyacinth-coloured. —fluß, *m.* false or counterfeit hyacinth. —granat, *m.* hyacinthine garnet.

*Hiazinte or Hyacinthe, *f.* [*pl.* -n] [in botany] hyacinth.

Hiazint-aloe, *f* American Aletus, Aletris farinosa or Hyacinthus floritanus. —zwiebel, *f.* hyacinth-root.

Hie, [V. hier] *adv.* here. — und da, here and there, now and then, occasionally.

Hie-bei [hierbei], *adv.* [the accent is generally on the last syllable] hereby, by this, at this, with this. —bei ist zu bemerken, here is to be remarked or observed; —bei ist weiter nichts zu thun, here or in this affair nothing farther can be done; es bleibt —bei, es mag —bei bleiben, let it so, I agree to it; —bei blieb es, here the matter rested; —bei empfangen Sie &c., together with this, annexed or inclosed you receive &c. —durch [hierdurch], *adv.* [the accent is generally on the first syllable] 1) through this place, through here. Er wird —durch kommen, he will pass through here or this place. 2) by this, by this means. —durch werden Sie ihn noch mehr aufbringen, by so doing you will irritate him still more; —durch gab er mir zu verstehen, by this he gave me to understand. —für [hierfür], *adv* for this. —für werde ich zehn Gulden bekommen, for this I shall get or have ten florins; —für kann ich nicht, it is not my fault, I cannot help it. —gegen [hiergegen], *adv.* against this. —gegen habe ich nichts einzuwenden, I have no objection to it. —her, —hin, V. Hierher, Hierhin. —mit [hiermit], *adv.* with this, herewith. Was wollen Sie —mit sagen? what do you mean by this? —mit ist es noch nicht vorbei, this is not yet the end of the matter; —mit verdarb er Alles, with this he spoiled all. —nach [hiernach], *adv.* 1) after this. —nach strebt er, he aspires after or to this; wer fragt —nach? who cares for this? 2) by this. Richte Dich —nach, be ruled or guided by this, go by this, take your measures accordingly, V. Danach. —nächst [hiernächst], *adv.* 1) next to this. Er wohnet —nächst, he lives hard by, next door. 2) [= demnächst] presently, soon, shortly. Ich werde —nächst davon reden, I shall soon speak of it, I shall speak of it as soon as possible. —neben [hierneben], *adv.* by the side of this, near this, by here, close or hard by; *it.* besides this, with this. —nieden [hiernieden], *adv.* here beneath, here below, in this world, in this temporalness. —selbst [hierselbst], *adv.* here, in this very place. —von [hiervon], *adv.* 1) [the accent on the first syllable] of *this* thing or matter. —von weiß ich nichts, of *this* matter I know nothing; —von handelt es sich nicht, *this* is not the question. 2) [the accent on the last syllable] of this *matter*. Was denken Sie —von? what is your opinion of the matter or of it? Haben Sie —von gehört? have you heard of it? V. Davon. —wider, V. Dawider. —zu [hierzu], *adv.* 1) [the accent on the first syllable] to *this* thing. —zu kommt noch, daß &c., add to this, that &c; —zu habe ich keine Lust, to this I have no mind. 2) [the accent on the last syllable] to this *thing* or *matter*. Was sagen Sie —zu? what do you say to it? er taugt nicht —zu, he is not fit or proper for it, V. Dazu. —zwischen [hierzwischen], *adv.* 1) [the accent on the first syllable] between *this* or *these*. —zwischen ist ein großer Unterschied, between *those* two things there is a great difference. 2) [the accent on the last syllable] between these *things*. Der Raum —zwischen wäre zu groß, the intermediate space, the intermedium would be too great. V. Dazwischen.

Hieb, *m.* [-es, *pl.*-e] [from hauen] 1) the act of striking, cutting or hewing. Auf — und Stich fechten or gehen, to cut and thrust. 2) [= Schlag] blow or stroke [with an instrument]. Den — abwenden or entkräften, to ward off the blow; ich versetzte or gab ihm einen — mit dem Säbel, I gave him a cut, I cut him with the sabre; ein — mit der Axt, a cut, stroke or blow with an axe; *—e geben, to lay on blows, to beat, to cudgel; *—e bekommen, to be drubbed or thrashed, to get a drubbing; *es setzte —e, blows were dealt out, there was hard fighting; ein — mit den Zähnen, a bite; der Hund gab dem Wolfe einen — mit den Zähnen, the hound fastened the wolf; etwas auf Einen —, mit Einem —e abhauen, to cut or strike any thing off at one blow. *Prov.* Der Baum fällt nicht auf Einen —, an oak is not felled by a single blow; Rome was not built in one day. *Fig.* Einem einen — geben or versetzen, to give any one a wipe or rub. 3) a cleft, gash or notch made with an instrument, a cut. Ein leichter, tödtlicher —, a slight, a mortal cut or wound; die —e einer Feile, the cuts, strokes or furrows of a file. *Fig.* [in popular ling.] Er hat einen —, *a*) he is a little tipsy or fuddled, *b*) he is a little crack-brained. 4) [among foresters] place in a forest where wood is felled or is to be felled, V. Hau, Gehau, Schlag. 5) the right of felling wood in a forest.

Hiebwunde, *f.* a wound made with a cutting instrument [opposed to Stichwunde].

Hieber, *m.* [-s, *pl.* -] sword, back-sword, broad-sword.

Hiebig, *adj.* and *adv.* [among foresters] that may be cut or felled [in a forest], V. Haubar.

Hief, [incorrectly, but more frequently used is Hift] *m.* [-es, *pl.* -e] [allied to the Eng. *hoop*, Fr. *houpper* = to shout, to cry] the sound from a hunter's horn.

Hief-horn, *n.* hunting-horn. —riemen, *m.* the strap by which the horn is suspended. —stoß, *m.* sound or note from the horn.

Hiefe, *f.* [*pl.* -n] hep, V. Hagebutte.

Hieke, *f.* [*pl.* -n] [in mining] pyrites.

Hiel, *m.* [-es, *pl.* -e] [in seamen's lang.] the lower end of a mast, the heel [of the mast]; *it.* the after-end of a ship's keel. Der — des Kiels, the heel of the keel.

Hielen, *v. intr.* [in seamen's lang.] to heel.

Hieling, *m.* [-es, *pl.* -e] V. Hiel.

Hier, *adv.* [Sw., Dan. and Sax. *her*, Eng. *here*, originally the same with der, allied to the old hi, he = dieser] here, in this place. Er ist —, — ist er, he is here, here he is; siehe, — bin ich, behold, here am I; — ist das bewußte Haus, here is the house in question; — liegt [i. e. begraben], here lies; dieses or das Brod —, this bread here; der — beigeschlossene Brief, the inclosed letter; die — anwesenden Zeugen, the present witnesses; — ist ein Wald, dort ein Berg, here is a wood, there a mountain; so werdet ihr — [auf dieser Welt] glücklich seyn, thus you will be happy here, here below; — und da, here and there; — herum, hereabout. *Fig. a*) in this point or matter. — bin ich anderer Meinung, in this point, as to this, I am of another opinion; — irren Sie sich, in this you are mistaken. *b*) at these words. — konnte er sich des Lachens nicht enthalten, at hearing this he could not help laughing.

Hier-ab, *adv.* V. Herab, —von, —aus. —an, *adv.* 1) in this or to this place here. 2) at this, on this. —an liegt Alles, every thing turns upon this point, hinges on that; —an mag ich gar nicht denken, I won't think of it; —an erkannte ich es, by this I knew it; —an ist kein Zweifel, there is no doubt of it; —an ist viel gelegen, this is of great consequence or importance; —an kehre ich mich ganz und gar nicht, I do not care a straw for it. —auf, *adv.* 1) [the accent on the first syllable, in the beginning of a sentence or with a particular stress of voice] on or upon *this*. Ich antworte —auf, to this I reply, on this I answer; —auf müßt ihr bedacht seyn, of this you must think; —auf bestehe ich, on this I insist. 2) [the accent on the last syllable] on or upon it. Sie können sich —auf verlassen, you may depend on it. *it.* after this, after that, afterwards, then. —auf antwortete er, on or after that he replied; —auf ging er weg, after that he went away. V. Darauf. —aus, *adv.* 1) [the accent on the first syllable] out of *this* place. Man kann ihn von —aus sehen, one can see him from *this* place, from *here*; ich will ihm alle Neuigkeiten von —aus schreiben, I'll write him all the news of *this* place. 2) [the accent on the last syllable] from this, hence. —aus erhellet, daß &c., by this it appears that &c.; —aus ersehe ich, by this or hence I see; —aus ziehe ich den Schluß, hence I conclude; es wird zuletzt eine Gewohnheit —aus, at last they make a custom of it. —außen, *adv.* out here, without here. —bei, —durch, V. Hiebei, Hiedurch. —ein, *adv.* 1) [the accent on the first syllable, in the beginning of a sentence or with a particular stress of voice] into *this* place, into this. —ein gehen nicht zwei Flaschen, *this* vessel does not hold or contain two bottles; —ein will ich mich nicht mengen, in or with *this* affair I shall not meddle; —ein willige ich, *this* I consent to. 2) [the accent on the last syllable] into it. Geben Sie sich geduldig —ein, submit patiently to it. V. Darein. —für, V. Hiefür. —gegen, V. Hiegegen. —genommen, *adj.* [in commerce] taken or bought up in this place. —her, *adv.* [in the beginning of a sentence and as a demonstrative it has the accent on the first syllable, in other cases on the last] to this place, hither. Heißen Sie ihn — her kommen, bid him come hither; —her gehört jenes Buch, this is the place for that book; dies gehört nicht —her, this has no relation to, is foreign from the subject under consideration; sein Gebiet erstreckt sich bis —her, his territory extends as far as this, to this place. *it.* bis —her [=bis zu dieser Zeit], up to this time, hitherto, till now, so far. —herwärts, *adv.* hitherward. —hin, *adv.* towards this place or side, in this direction, this way. —in, —innen, *adv.* in this place, in here; *it.* herein, in this. —in wohnt er, he lives or lodges in this place here, in here; —in stimme ich mit Ihnen überein, in this, herein I agree with you. V. Darin. —mit, V. Hiemit. —nach, V. Hienach. —nächst, V. Hienächst. —neben, V. Hieneben. —nieden, V. Hienieden. —selbst, V. Hieselbst. —seyn, *n.* being here, presence. Während meines —seyns, during my sojourn or stay here. —über, *adv.* 1) [the accent on the first syllable, in the beginning of a sentence or with a particular stress of voice] over *this* place, over *this*. —über geht der Weg nach &c., over *this* [place] goes the road to &c. *Fig.* —über geht nichts, there is nothing above this, nothing is superior to this; —über habe ich mich nicht beklagt, of this I have not complained. 2) [the accent on the last syllable] over this, over it. Denken Sie —über nach, reflect on it; ich werde mit ihm —über sprechen, I shall speak to him about it. —um, *adv.* about or round this place. *fig.* about or concerning this. —unten, *adv.* below here, here below. —unter, *adv.* 1) [the accent on the first syllable, in the beginning of a sentence or with a particular stress of voice] under *this* place here, under *this* thing, under *these* things. —unter ist er verborgen, under this he is concealed. 2) [the accent on the last syllable] under this, under it. Es steckt ein Geheimniß —unter, there is a mystery hidden under this, in this; es steckt Jemand anders —unter, somebody else is concerned or has a hand in it. —von, V. Hievon. —zu, V. Hiezu. —zwischen, V. Hiezwischen.

*Hierárch, *m.* [-en, *pl.*-en] [the chief of a sacred order] hierarch.

*Hierarchie, *f.* [*pl.*-en] 1) [ecclesiastical government] hierarchy. 2) [an order of angels] hierarchy.

*Hierárchisch, *adj.* and *adv.* [belonging to ecclesiastical government] hierarchical.

*Hierocrát, *m.* [-en, *pl.*-en] V. Hierarch.

*Hierocratie, *f.* [*pl.*-en] V. Hierarchie.

*Hieroglýphe, *f.* [*pl.*-n] 1) [a mystical character or symbol used in writings and inscriptions] hieroglyph, hieroglyphic. 2) hieroglyphic writings, hieroglyphics, V. Bilderschrift.

*Hieroglýphik, *f.* hieroglyphic language, hieroglyphics. V. Bildersprache.

*Hieroglýphisch, *adj.* and *adv.* hieroglyphic, hieroglyphical, hieroglyphically.

*Hierográmm, *n.* [-es] [in antiquity, a species of sacred writings] hierogram.

*Hierogrammátisch, *adj.* and *adv.* hierogrammatic.

*Hierográph, *m.* [-en, *pl.*-en] hierographer.

*Hierographie, *f.* hierography.

*Hierománt, *m.* [-en, *pl.*-en] [in antiquity, one who divines by observing the various things offered in sacrifice] hieromant.

*Hieromantie, *f.* hieromancy.

*Hierónisch, *adj.* [in antiquity] hieronic, sacred.

*Hieronýmisch, *adj.* of the order of the Hieronomonians [so called from Saint Jerome], Hieronomonian.

*Hierónymus, *m.* [*pl.*-sse] [a name of men] Jerome.

*Hierophánt, *m.* [-en, *pl.*-en] [in antiquity, a priest who taught the mysteries and duties of religion, *it.* a priest who presided over the Eleusinian mysteries or festivals] hierophant.

*Hieroscop, *m.* [-en, *pl.*-en], —ie, *f.* V. Hieromant, Hieromantie.

Hiesig, *adj.* and *adv.* of this place or country. Die —en Einwohner, the habitants or people of this place [town, village &c.]; er ist ein —es Kind, ein —er, [in popular lang.] he is a native of this place [town, village &c.] or of this country; —es Gewächs, growth or product of this place, country or climate.

Hiez, *m.* [-es, *pl.*-e] and Hieze, *f.* [*pl.*-n] [*dim.* Hiezchen, *n.*] 1) [the fondling name of a cat, particularly in calling] puss. 2) male cat.

Hift, Hifthorn, V. Hief, Hiefhorn.

*Hilárien, *pl.* [in antiquity, a festival celebrated by the Romans in honour of the God Pan] Hilaria, V. Freudenfest.

*Hilarität, *f.* hilarity, V. Fröhlichkeit.

Hilárius, *m.* [*pl.*-sse] [a name of men] Hilary.

*Hilaród, *m.* [-en, *pl.*-en] [in antiquity, an itinerant singer and merry-andrew] hilarod[us].

Hilfe, V. Hülfe.

Hillbutte, V. Hellbutte.

‡Hilpersgriff, *m.* [-es, *pl.*-e] cunning trick, artifice, quibble.

Hiltrof, *m.* [-en, *pl.*-en] V. Birole, Goldamsel.

Hímbeere, *f.* [*pl.*-n] [either from the old Heim = Zaun, or from the old heim = hohl] raspberry. Die rothe, die weiße —, the red, the white raspberry.

Himbeer-apfel, *m.* red calville. —eis, *n.* raspberry-ice. —essig, *m.* raspberry vinegar. —gefrorene, *n.* V. —eis. —geist, *m.* spirit of raspberries. —meth, *m.* raspberry hydromel or mead. —saft, *m.* raspberry-juice. —staude, *f.*, —strauch, *m.* raspberry-bush. —wasser, *n.* raspberry-juice diluted with water. —wein, *m.* raspberry-wine.

Hímmel, *m.* [-s, *pl.*-] [probably from the old heimen = decken, to cover] 1) in general, a cover. Der — an einem Bette, the top covering, the tester of a bed; der —, welcher über der Hostie [bei Processionen] getragen wird, the canopy which is carried over the host [in processions]; der — an einer Kutsche, the roof of a coach, V. Kutschen—, Trag—. Then generally, the apparent arch or vault of air above us, the sky, the heaven. Unter freiem — schlafen, to sleep in the open air; das blaue Gewölbe des —s, the azur vault of the sky; prächtig stieg die Sonne am — auf, the sun rose or appeared majestically above the horizon; der — mit allen seinen Sternen, the firmament with all its stars; die Hebräer nahmen drei — an, the Hebrews acknowledged three heavens; *wie vom — gefallen [= sehr überrascht] seyn, to be in amaze, to be amazed; der — hängt ihm voller Geigen or Baßgeigen [in popular language], he is swimming in joy; [in Script.] die Feste des —s, the firmament; [in astronomy] der Einfluß des —s [= der Gestirne], the influence of the stars; der gesternte or gestirnte —, the starry sky; den — beobachten, to make astronomical observations. 2) [in a more limited sense, the region of the atmosphere] the sky. Ein wolkiger, trüber —, a cloudy, heavy or dark sky; ein heiterer or klarer —, a clear or serene sky; ein milder, gemäßigter —, a mild or indulgent, a temperate sky or climate; [in Script.] die Vögel des —s, the fowls of the air; der Thau des —s, the dew from heaven; das Feuer des —s, the lightning; [in painting] der — [in einem Gemählde], the sky; [in stage-scenery] der —, heavens. *Fig.* [the residence of angels and blessed spirits] heaven. In den — kommen, to get into, to come to heaven; den — erwerben or gewinnen, to win or gain paradise or heaven; seine Seele ist im —, he is dead; der Weg zum —, the way or road to heaven; [in Script.] Paulus wurde bis in den dritten — entzückt, Paul was caught up into the third heaven; ich sehe den — offen, I see the heavens opened; unser Vater, der du bist im —, our father which art in heaven; dein Wille geschehe auf Erden wie im —, thy will be done on earth as it is in heaven. *it.* the sovereign of heaven, God. Der erzürnte —, irritated heaven; der Zorn des —s, wrath of heaven; dem — sey Dank! heaven be praised! der — sey euch gnädig! heaven prosper you! *it.* *[as a threat] heaven help you! as, der Himmel sey dir gnädig, wenn er erfährt, daß &c., heaven may help you, if he should become aware, that &c.; der — weiß es! God knows! gerechter —! o heavens, good God, just heavens! um des —s willen, for heaven's sake; der — wolle das nicht! God or heaven forbid! *prov.* die Ehen werden im — geschlossen, marriages are made in heaven; [in fam. lang.] — und Erde, — und Hölle bewegen, to move heaven and earth, to turn every stone, to leave no stone unturned; zwischen — und Erde schweben, to be suspended between heaven and earth; diese Sachen sind von einander so verschieden, als der — von der Erde, these things differ as far from each other as heaven does from earth; Einen in den, bis in den — erheben [=sehr loben], to extol any one to the skies, to praise any one highly.

Himmel-an, *adv.* [in poetry] towards heaven, up to the skies, heavenward. —auf, *adv.* V. —an. —begeistert, *adj.* [in poetry] inspired by heaven, heaven-inspired. —bett, *n.* bed with a tester. —blau, I. *adj.* sky-blue, sky-coloured. II. *n.* or —bläue, *f.* sky-colour, azure. —brand, *m.* V. Wollkraut. ||—breme, *f.* V. Himbeere. —brod, *n.* the bread of heaven, manna. —dill, *f.* [a plant] V. Haarstrang. —erz, *n.* ore found at a little distance from the surface of the earth. —faden, *m.* gossamer. —fahrt, *f.* ascension into heaven [especially the visible elevation of our Saviour to heaven]. Mariä —fahrt, the Assumption of the holy virgin; der Tag, das Fest der —fahrt Christi, Mariä, the festival of Ascension, of Assumption, Ascension-day, Assumption-day. —fahrtsblume, *f.*, *dim.* —fahrtsblümchen, ||—fahrtsblümlein, *n.* the common milk-wort. —fahrtsfest, *n.* V. —fahrtstag. —fahrtsinsel, *f.* Ascension Island. —fahrtstag, *m.* Ascension-day, holy Thursday. —fahrtswoche, *f.* Ascension week. —farbe, *f.*, —farben, *adj.* V. —blau. —hoch, *adj.* and *adv.* as high as the heavens, very high, very great. —hohe Berge, mountains whose tops ascend to the skies; Einen — hoch erheben, to extol any one to the skies; *Einen —hoch bitten, to entreat, implore or conjure any one most earnestly. —reich, *n.* kingdom of heaven; [in Script.] das —reich ist nahe herbei kommen, the kingdom of heaven is at hand. *Fig.* Das ist sein —reich, that is his greatest delight or pleasure. *Prov.* Des Menschen Wille ist sein —reich, my mind to me a kingdom is. —schön, *adj.* and *adv.* [rather high-flown] most beautiful. —schreiend, *adj.* and *adv.* [often in familiar language] crying to heaven, reserved for the vengeance of the Almighty, highly wicked, highly criminal or wrong. Eine —schreiende Sünde, a crying, very great sin; eine —schreiende Ungerechtigkeit, a most revolting injustice. —segen, *m.* the blessing of heaven. —stein, *m.* sapphire. —träger, *m.* one that bears the canopy [at a procession]. —wärts, *adv.* V. —an. —weit, *adj.* and *adv.* [often in familiar lang.] remote as heaven, very distant, very wide. Diese Dinge sind —weit von einander verschieden, these things are as different as heaven and earth, as day and night; ein —weiter Unterschied, an immense difference.

Himmels-achse, *f.* the axis of the world. —**angel**, *f.* V. Weltachse, Weltpol. —**angesicht**, *n.* a heavenly countenance. —**begeisterung**, *f.* heavenly inspiration. —**bekrieger**, *m.* V. —stürmer. —**beschreibung**, *f.* description of the heavens, uranography. —**besen**, *m.* [among sailors, jocose expression for] the north-west wind. —**bett**, *n.* [the invention of the famous Dr. Graham] heavenly bed or couch. —**bewohner**, *m.* inhabitant of heaven. —**bild**, *n.* 1) a heavenly or celestial, a most beautiful figure. 2) a constellation. —**blatt**, *n.*, —**blume**, *f.* [in botany] nostock, V. also Erdblume. —**bläue**, *f.* V. Himmelbläue. —**bogen**, *m.* V. —gewölbe. —**bote**, messenger of heaven. —**brand**, *m.* V. Wollkraut. —**braut**, *f.* the spouse of heaven or God. —**breite**, *f.* astronomical latitude. —**brod**, *n.* V. Himmelbrod. —**bürger**, *m.* inhabitant or citizen of heaven, a celestial. —**duft**, *m.* [in poetry] 1) a heavenly odour. 2) V. —thau. —**faden**, *m.* V. Himmelfaden. —**feste**, *f.* the firmament. —**feuer**, *n.* lightning. *Fig.* heavenly inspiration. —**freude**, *f.* heavenly joy, celestial delight. —**frucht**, *f.* [in poetry] a heavenly, most excellent fruit. —**funke**, *m.* [in poetry] a heavenly spark. *Fig.* a heavenly thought or idea. —**gabe**, *f.* gift of heaven. —**gegend**, *f.* region or quarter of the heavens; *it.* V. —strich. —**gerste**, *f.* common or long-eared barley. —**geschöpf**, *n.* a heavenly creature. —**gewölbe**, *n.* vault of heaven, canopy of heaven, the firmament. —**gleicher**, *m.* equator. —**glück**, *n.* heavenly bliss, [celestial] beatitude. —**glut**, *f.* *fig.* V. —feuer. —**gott**, *m.* God in heaven. —**gürtel**, *m.* [in geography and astronomy] zone; *it.* V. —strich. —**haus**, *n.* V. —gewölbe; [in astrology, the station of a planet in the heavens] house. —**heer**, *n.* host of heaven, heavenly host, the celestial legions. —**höhe**, *f.* solar altitude. —**jägerinn**, *f.* the goddess of hunting, Diana. —**jungfrau**, *f.* a heavenly virgin, [particularly] a Houri. —**karte**, *f.* astronomical chart, celestial planisphere. —**kind**, *n.* a heavenly child. —**könig**, *m.* the heavenly king, king of the heavens. —**königinn**, *f.* the heavenly queen, the blessed virgin. —**korn**, *n.* V. —gerste. —**körper**, *m.* heavenly or celestial body. —**kost**, *f.* food of the Gods, ambrosia; *it.* delicious food or fare. —**kraft**, *f.* a heavenly power. —**kreis**, *m.* the celestial orb or sphere. —**kreiskugel**, *f.* [in astronomy] armillary sphere. —**kugel**, *f.* [in astronomy] celestial globe. —**kunde**, *f.* astronomy. —**länge**, *f.* astronomical longitude. —**lauf**, *m.* course or motion of the heavenly bodies. —**lehre**, *f.* uranology. —**leiter**, *f.* ladder of heaven. —**licht**, *n.* the heavenly, celestial light. Die —lichter, the luminaries [as the sun, the moon, the stars]. —**lohn**, *m.* reward of heaven, heavenly reward. —**luft**, *f.* ether. —**lust**, *f.* [in poetry] heavenly joy, celestial delight, very great joy or pleasure. —**mehl**, *n.* gypsum dissolved by the operation of the atmosphere. —**pferd**, *f.* V. Heupferd. —**pforte**, *f.* [in poetry] the gate of heaven. —**pol**, —**punkt**, *m.* the vertical point, zenith; *it.* the nadir. —**rand**, *m.* [in poetry] the horizon. —**raum**, *m.* the immense space of heaven. —**ruhe**, *f.* heavenly tranquillity. —**schlüssel**, *m.* 1) [in Script.] the key of the kingdom of heaven. 2) [in botany] and *dim.* —schlüsselchen, *n.* cowslip, primrose. —**schweiß**, *m.* V. Mehlthau. —**speise**, *f.* V. —kost. —**spur**, *f.* [among hunters] the boughs which a deer beats down with his head in traversing thickets. —**stengel**, *m.* [in botany] gentian; *it.* angelica lingwort or longwort. —**straße**, *f.* the road to heaven. —**strich**, *m.* climate. —**sturm**, *m.* the storming of heaven, the battle of the giants, gigantomachia, titanomachia. —**stürmer**, *m.* one who attempts to storm heaven, one of the titans, giant. —**thau**, *m.* the dew of heaven; *it.* manna; [in botany] Polish manna, the seed of cock's-foot-grass. —**thor**, *n.* —**thüre**, *f.* the gate, the door of heaven. —**trank**, *m.* nectar. —**wagen**, *m.* [in astronomy] Charles's wain, the great Bear. —**weg**, *m.* the way to heaven. —**weite**, *f.* the immense extent of heaven. —**wonne**, *f.* V. —freude, —lust. —**zeichen**, *n.* 1) [in astronomy] heavenly or celestial sign, one of the twelve signs of the Zodiac. 2) [among hunters] V. —spur. —**zelt**, *n.* [in poetry] V. —gewölbe. ||—**ziege**, *f.* the common snipe. —**zirkel**, *m.* a circle supposed to be drawn in the heavens; *it.* V. —kreis.

Himmeln, *v. intr.* [rather unusual] 1) [= blitzen] to lighten. 2) [= sterben] to expire, to die, to go to heaven. 3) [in jest] to have transcendental tendencies, to rove with one's thoughts or imagination in the mysteries of heaven.

Himmlisch, *adj.* and *adv.* celestial, heavenly, ethereal. Die —en Körper, the celestial bodies; die —en Zeichen, the celestial signs, the signs of the Zodiac; die —en Heerschaaren, the heavenly or celestial hosts or legions; die —en Geister, the heavenly or celestial spirits, the angels; die —en Freuden, the heavenly joys. *Fig.* supremely excellent. Pindars —e Leier, Pindar's heavenly lyre; —er Wohlklang, celestial harmony; eine —e Schönheit, a ravishing beauty.

Himpelbeere, *f.* [*pl.* -n] V. Himbeere.

Himten, *m.* [-s, *pl.* -] (a measure for corn in some provinces of North-Germany) the fourth part of a bushel, V. Vierling.

Hin, *adv.* [Low Sax. *hen*; the Icel. and Sw. *thin* is = jener; V. hier, her] (expresses motion proceeding from the person who is speaking to another place] to or towards that place, thither, thitherward. Rechts —, towards the right; nach jener Seite —, towards that side; bis zu seinem Hause —, as far as his house; längs der Mauer —, along the wall; gehen Sie dort —, go or get you thither; — damit! put it [down] there! er schleppte ihn nach dem Flusse —, he dragged him to or towards the river; — und her, — und wieder, backwards and forwards, to and fro, this way and that way, up and down, hither and thither, in all directions; — und her gehen, to walk to and fro, up and down; —und her bewegen, to move to and fro, this way and that way, backwards and forwards; sich — und her bewegen, to move, to be waved backward and forward, to oscillate, to vibrate; die —s und Herbewegung, oscillation, vibration, V Schwingung; — und wieder laufen, to run up and down, to run about. *Fig.* Etwas — und her überlegen, to consider a thing maturely on all sides, to view a thing in all its aspects, to ponder on, to agitate a thing; ich dachte — und her, und konnte kein Mittel ausfindig machen, I racked my brains, I beat my head about that affair, without finding an expedient; — und wieder, sometimes, occasionally; Mode —, Mode her, ich werde &c., in spite of fashion, what care I for the fashion I shall &c.; Freundschaft —, Freundschaft her, ich kann nicht thun, was &c., what signifies friendship? what care I for friendship, what, though you be my friend, I cannot do, what &c.; so — (= so ziemlich, mittelmäßig), so so, indifferently; ich will es auf alle Fälle — thun, I'll do it whatever falls out or happens, I'll do it at all risks; auf sein bloßes Wort — möchte ich es nicht glauben, I would not believe it on his mere word. V. —ab, —aus, —ein &c., Da—, Dort—, Immer—, Mit— &c.

Hin-arbeiten, I. *v. intr.* Auf Etwas — arbeiten, to aim or drive at any thing, to have any thing at heart. Er arbeitet nur darauf —, alle Menschen glücklich zu machen, he has no other aim or design than to make all men happy, all his efforts tend to make all men happy. II. *v. r.* sich —arbeiten, to work one's way to or towards, to get to a place with labour or difficulty. —**begeben**, *ir. v. r.* sich —begeben, to repair, to resort, to go to a place. —**betteln**, *v. r.* sich —betteln, to go to, to reach a place begging. —**binden**, *ir. v. tr.* to bind or tie to a place or thing, V. Anbinden. —**blick**, *m.* look at or towards a thing. *Fig.* Der —blick auf eine bessere Zukunft, the hope or prospect of future happiness; im —blick auf &c., in regard of &c. —**blicken**, *v. intr.* to look towards a place. —**blitzen**, *v. intr.* to flash towards. —**blühen**, *v. intr.* 1) to bloom or blossom on. 2) [in poetry] V. Verblühen. —**bringen**, *ir. v. tr.* 1) to bring, take or carry to a place. Bringe den Rock dem Schneider —, carry or take the coat to the tailor's. 2) *Fig.* to pass, to spend [one's time &c.]. Wir haben diesen Tag recht angenehm —gebracht, we have spent this day very agreeably; die Zeit unnütz or müßig —bringen, to lose, to idle away one's time; womit bringen Sie Ihre Zeit —? how do you spend your time? sie haben die Nacht mit Spielen —gebracht, they have passed the night in gaming; V. Zubringen; *it.* sein Leben or sich kümmerlich —bringen, to make just shift to live, to be hard put to it for a livelihood; *it.* sein Vermögen —bringen [= durchbringen, verschwenden], to squander away, to dissipate one's fortune; V. Durchbringen. —**brüten**, *v. intr.* to be in a state of lethargy; to brood over any thing. —**decken**, *v. tr.* Das Tischtuch —decken, to lay the cloth there; *it.* Einem [das Tischtuch] —decken, to lay the cloth for any one. —**dehnen**, I. *v. tr.* to spread or extend to or towards. II. *v. r.* sich —dehnen, to extend. Dieses Gebirge dehnt sich sehr weit —, these mountains extend very far. —**denken**, *ir.* I. *v. intr.* to think of any place, person or thing. Ich denke täglich nach Paris —, I think of Paris every day; wo denken Sie —? what do you think of? wo denken Sie — or was denken Sie [nur], so etwas or dergleichen zu thun? what's your design in doing such a thing? II. *v. tr.* to think, fancy or imagine any person or thing to be at a certain place. Wenn ich mir Sie nach London —denke, if I fancy you in London. —**deuten**, *v. intr.* to point to or at any thing or person. Mit dem Finger auf Einen —deuten, to point the finger at any one; man deutete mit dem Finger or mit Fingern auf ihn — [in a proper as well as in fig. sense], he was pointed at, V. Deuten. —**donnern**, [illegible] [in poetry] Einen —donnern, to strike, [illegible] overwhelm any one by lightning, to [illegible] any one down. —**dorren**, *v. intr.* V. [illegible]ren. —**drang**, *m.* strong impulse or de[illegible] go to or to be at a place. —**drängen**, [illegible] to press, urge or push to, towards or agai[illegible] thing. II. *v. r.* sich —drängen, to press or [illegible] or towards. Er drängt sich überall —, he [illegible] himself in everywhere. V. Drängen, [illegible]gen. —**drucken**, —**drücken**, V. Anbe[illegible] drücken. *—**dudeln**, *v. tr.* Ein Liedchen —[illegible] to hum a tune. V. Dudeln. *—**dürfen**, *ir.* [illegible] to be allowed or permitted to go there [illegible] —**eilen**, *v. intr.* to hasten thither, on [illegible] **erzählen**, *v. tr.* [in fam. lang.] to recite, [illegible] to tell. Er erzählte ihnen Etwas —, he told them a story. —fahren, *ir.* I. *v. tr.* to convey to a place in a carriage or boat. II. *v. intr.* [used with seyn] *a*) to go to a place in a carriage, ship or boat. Er ist in der Kutsche —gefahren, he went there in his coach. *b*) [in general] to go in a carriage, ship or boat. Da fährt er eben —, there he drives; längs dem Lande, der Küste —fahren, to go or coast along the shore; die Wellen fuhren über das Schiff —, the waves passed over the vessel; mit der Hand über Etwas —fahren, to pass the hand over any thing, to touch any thing swiftly or lightly with one's hand. *Fig.* *Nachlässig über Etwas —fahren, to slip over any thing, to do or perform any thing superficially, to neglect any thing; *it.* fahre —, Mitleiden! farewell pity! no more pity! *it.* to die. —fahren, *n.* or —fahrt, *f.* the act of going to a place in a carriage, ship or boat. Auf meiner —fahrt nach England, on my passage to England; [among hunters] V. —fährte. *Fig.* decease, death, demise. —fährte, *f.* [among hunters] the footing or strain [of deer]. —fall, *m.* fall. —fallen, *ir. v. intr.* to fall down. Der Länge nach —fallen, to fall all along; rücklings —fallen, to fall upon one's back or backwards; auf die Knie —fallen, to fall on one's knees; das —fallen or die —fallende Sucht [in popular lang.], epilepsy, V. Fallsucht. —fällig, *adj.* and *adv.* disposed to fall, ready to fall; falling, [in botany] deciduous, as leaf, calix &c. *Fig.* frail, weak, feeble, approaching to decay. Er ist alt und —fällig, he is old and decrepit; er ist in einem —fälligen Alter, he is worn out with old age; *it.* V. Vergänglich. —fälligkeit, *f.* frailty, weakness, craziness. Die —fälligkeiten des Alters, the infirmities of old age. —finden, *ir. v. r.* sich —finden, to find one's way to a place. Ich denke wohl mich —zufinden, I think I shall find my way thither. —fliegen, *ir. v. intr.* to fly to or towards that place; *it.* [in general] to fly along. —fliehen, *ir. v. intr.* to fly or flee to or towards a place or person for refuge or shelter; *it.* [in general] to fly along. *Fig.* Die Zeit flieht —, time passes rapidly, flies. —fließen, *ir. v. intr.* to flow to or towards that place; *it.* to flow along. Der Fluß fließt gegen Süden —, the river flows towards the south or southward; der Fluß fließt an der Stadtmauer —, the river washes the walls of the town; über Kieselsteine —fließen, to flow along over pebbles. *Fig.* Die Stunden fließen schnell —, the hours pass rapidly away, swift fly the fleeting hours. —flüchten, I. *v. tr.* to save by flying to a place. II. *v. intr.* and *v. r.* sich —flüchten, to fly or flee to or towards a person or thing for safety, to seek refuge with a person or at a place. —fluten, *v. intr.* [in poetry] to move to or towards a place in high waves. Die —flutenden Wogen, Flammen, the waving billows, flames. —fort, *adv.* henceforth, in future, V. Forthin, Künftig. —führen, *v. tr.* to lead or conduct to or towards a place. —für, ‡—füro, *adv.* V. —fort. —gaffen, *v. intr.* to stare or gape at a place or thing. —gang, *m.* the act of going to a place, way or passage thither. Der —gang und Hergang, the way there and back again; *er hat den —gang für den Hergang gehabt, he has had his labour for his pains; Christi —gang, V. Himmelfahrt. *Fig.* [in poetry] demise, decease, death, departure. —geben, *ir. v. tr.* to give to, to give away, to give up. Gib es Deinem Bruder —, give it to your brother; das würde, möchte ich um aller Welt Güter nicht —geben, I would not part with that for ever so much; sein Vermögen an Nichtswürdige —geben, to bestow one's fortune upon worthless fellows; sein Leben, sich für Jemand —geben, to sacrifice one's life for any one; sich ganz den Studien —geben, to devote one's self entirely to study. —gebung, *f.* the act of devoting, sacrificing one's self; *it.* [= *Resignation] resignation. Eine völlige —gebung in den Willen Gottes, an entire submission to the will of God. V. Ergebung. —gedenken, *ir. v. intr.* 1) to think of that place &c. 2) to intend going to a place. Wo gedenken Sie nun —? whither or where do you intend going now? V. —denken. —gegebenheit, *f.* V. Hingebung, Ergebung. —gehen, *ir. v. intr.* 1) to go to that place. Ich will —gehen, I will go there. *Fig.* [in poetry] to go to one's long home, to die. Der —gegangene, the deceased, the departed. 2) [in general] to go any where. Wo gehen Sie —? where are you going? geh' — in Frieden! depart in peace! ich weiß nicht, wo dieser Weg —geht, I know not, where this way goes or leads to. *Fig.* Wo gehen Ihre Wünsche hin? what do your wishes tend to? what are your wishes? 3) to pass. Die Zeit geht —, time passes or elapses. *Fig.* Das kann, mag so —gehen, that may be excused, one may overlook that, that is tolerable, that may pass; Etwas —gehen lassen, to pass over, not to animadvert upon any thing; es wird Dir nicht so —gehen, you shall not come off so cheaply, you shall smart or suffer for it; Etwas ungestraft —gehen lassen, to suffer any thing to pass or go unpunished; *es geht in Einem —, it may be done all at once or at the same time. —gehören, *v. intr.* to belong to that place or thither. —geißeln, *v. tr.* to scourge, whip or lash to or towards a place. —gelangen, *v. intr.* to arrive at, to come or get to a place, V. Anlangen. —geleiten, *v. tr.* to conduct or escort to a place. —gerathen, *ir. v. intr.* [in fam. lang.] to come or get to a place by chance or accident. Wo ist er —gerathen? what has become of him? V. Gerathen. —gießen, *ir. v. tr.* to pour, shed or spread there. [in poetry] Auf den Rasen —gegossen, lying or sitting gracefully or in a graceful position on the grass. —gleiten, *ir. v. intr.* to glide or slide along. Der Schlitten gleitet auf dem Eise —, the sledge slides along on the ice. *—gucken, V. —sehen. —haben, *ir. v. tr.* 1) to have put any where. Wo hast Du das Buch —? where have you put the book? 2) [in familiar lang.] to have received or got, V. Dahinhaben. —halten, *ir. v. tr.* 1) Einem Etwas —halten, to hold something towards any one. Die Hand —halten, to stretch out, to extend, to proffer one's hand. 2) *Fig.* to amuse, to put off. Einen durch schmeichelhafte Hoffnungen —halten, to amuse any one by flattering hopes, to bear any one in hand; sie haben ihn schon drei Jahre lang —gehalten, they have kept him at bay these three years. 3) to keep, to preserve, V. [better] Aufbehalten, Aufbewahren. —hangen, *ir. v. intr.* to lean, bend or hang towards a place; *fig.* to have an inclination for any person or thing. —hängen, *v. tr.* to hang up. —helfen, *ir.* I. *v. intr.* to help or assist a person in getting to a place. **Fig.* Einem —helfen, to despatch any one, to do any one's business; *it.* to complete any one's ruin. Das wird ihm vollends —helfen, that will do his business. II. *v. r.* sich [kümmerlich] —helfen, to support one's self with difficulty, to make shift to live, to struggle on. †—hocken, *v. intr.* to squat, to cower, to sit, *fig.* to be idle, to idle. —holen, *v. tr.* to fetch to a place. —jagen, I. *v. tr.* to drive or chase to or towards that place. II. *v. intr.* 1) to ride full speed, to gallop to or towards that place. Wie ein Blitz jagte er —, he galloped or flew there like lightning. 2) [in general] to go full speed. —kauern, *v. r.* sich —kauern, to cower, to crouch, to squat. —kehren, I. *v. intr.* and *v. r.* sich —kehren, to turn to or towards a place. II. *v. tr.* to sweep to or towards a place. —knien, *v. intr.* to kneel down, V. Niederknien. —kommen, *ir. v. intr.* to come or get to, to arrive at a place, to come thither or there. Ich werde —kommen, I shall come thither; ich komme nirgends —, I never go out, I see no company; er kommt häufig —, he frequently visits there; er darf —kommen, he has free access there; ein Ort, wo man nicht —kommen kann, a place not to be reached, an inaccessible place. *Fig.* Ich weiß nicht, wo sein Bruder, meine Uhr &c. —gekommen ist, I don't know what has become of his brother, of my watch &c. —können, *ir. v. intr.* to be able to go there. —kränkeln, —kranken, *v. intr.* to linger, to languish. Er kränkelt schon lange so —, he has been a long while in this lingering or languishing condition. —kriechen, *ir. v. intr.* to creep or crawl to or towards a place. —kunft, *f.* coming thither or there, arrival at &c. V. Ankunft. — —kutschen, —kutschiren, *v. intr.* to go or drive to a place in a coach. —laden, *ir. v. tr.* 1) Einen —laden, to invite, to summon any one to a place. 2) Etwas —laden, to pack or load to or on a thing. —langen, I. *v. tr.* to hand, to reach, V. —reichen. II. *v. intr.* to reach to a place; *fig.* to suffice, to be sufficient, to be adequate, V. —reichen. —lassen, *ir. v. tr.* to allow, permit or suffer any one to go or come to a place. Er will mich nicht —lassen, he won't let me go there; sich —lassen, V. Niederlassen. —lässig, *adj.* and *adv.*, —lässigkeit, *f.* V. Nachlässig, Nachlässigkeit. —lauf, *m.* the course thither; [in botany] V. Laufkraut. —laufen, *ir. v. intr.* to run thither or there, to run to a place. Laufe schnell —, make haste thither. —leben, *v. intr.* [in fam. lang.] to live, to pass one's time away. Sorglos —leben, to lead or live a careless life; in den Tag —leben, to live at random, from hand to mouth. —legen, I. *v. tr.* to put, lay or deposit in a place, to lay down, to put away. II. *v. r.* sich —legen, to lie down; *it.* to lay one's self at full length upon any thing. Ich bin sehr müde, ich will mich ein wenig *—legen, I am very tired, I'll take a little rest or repose. —lehnen, I. *v. tr.* 1) to lean against, to lean upon. Eine Stange an die Mauer —lehnen, to lean a pole against the wall. 2) V. —leiden. II. *v. r.* sich —lehnen, 1) to lean against or upon, V. Anlehnen. 2) to lean towards, to have a tendency, a bias to &c. *—leiern, I. *v. tr.* to play on the lyre or hurdy-gurdy; *fig.* to drawl, to deliver in a monotonous manner. *Ein Liedchen —leiern, to hum a tune; *Einen —leiern, to amuse any one by vain promises, to keep any one at bay. II. *v. intr. fig.* to stand fiddling or trifling, to trifle, to loiter. —leihen, *ir. v. tr.* to let, to let out, to lend, V. Ausleihen. —leiten, *v. tr.* to lead or conduct to a place. —lenken, *v. tr.* to turn to or towards a place. —lesen, *ir. v. tr.* to read any thing to any one; *it.* to read in a monotonous manner. —leuchten, *v. intr.* Einem, to light any one to a place. —liefern, *v. tr.* to furnish or deliver to a place; **fig.* Einen —liefern, to undo, to ruin any one, V. Liefern. —machen, I. *v. tr.* 1) to put, to fasten, to fix to a place. Man muß da eine Treppe —machen, a stair-case must be contrived there. 2) [in fam. lang., Etwas obenhin machen] to do a thing negligently, at random. II. *v. r.* sich —machen [in fam. lang.], to betake one's self, to resort, to go to a place. —marsch, *m.* the march thither or to that place. —marschiren, *v. intr.* to march thither or to that place. *—mögen, *ir. v. intr.* to have a mind or inclination to go thither or there. *Ich mag nicht —, I don't like to go there. —murmeln,

I. v. tr. to utter or pronounce muttering or murmuring. II. v. intr. to murmur or purl along [of a brook &c.]. —müssen, ir. v. intr. to be obliged to go thither or there. Ich muß —, I must go there. —nehmen, ir. v. tr. to take along, to take away. Fig. Gott hat ihn —genommen, God has taken him away, he is dead; er mußte dieses so —nehmen, he was obliged to put up with it, to pocket it. —neigen, I. v. intr. and v. r. sich —neigen, to incline, bend or lean towards a place. Fig. Der Sieg neigt sich auf jene Seite —, the victory inclines to that side, or begins to declare in favour of that side or party. —packen, I. v. tr. to pack or put to that place. †II. v. r. sich —packen, to betake one's self, to go to that place. —passen, v. intr. to fit, to suit. —peitschen, v. tr. to drive thither or there by whipping, to whip or lash thither. —pflanzen, v. tr. to plant thither or there. Sie pflanzten die Fahnen vor das Zelt —, they set up the colours before the tent. —raffen, v. tr. to snatch away. Fig. Der Tod rafft Alles —, death mows down all; das Fieber hat ihn —gerafft, the fever has carried him off; er wurde in der Blüthe seiner Jahre —gerafft, he was cut off in the prime of his years. —rauschen, v. intr. to move or flow along rustling or making a noise. Der Bach rauscht angenehm —, the brook purls pleasantly along. —recken, v. tr. to stretch towards, V. —halten. *—reden, v. intr. to speak or talk thoughtlessly or at random. —reichen, I. v. tr. to hold towards any one, to hand, to reach. Die Hand —reichen, to stretch out the hand; reich' es dem Herrn —, hand or reach it the gentleman. II. v. intr. to extend, to reach as far as that place. Der Strick ist zu kurz, er reicht nicht —, the rope is too short, it does not reach so far. Fig. to suffice, to be sufficient, to be adequate. Das reicht nicht —, alle Schulden damit zu bezahlen, that is not sufficient to pay all the debts. —reichend, V. Hinlänglich. —reise, f. journey or voyage thither. Meine —reise ist bezahlt, my expenses thither are defrayed. —reisen, v. intr. to travel thither. —reißen, ir. v. tr. to tear or drag along, to carry along with violence. Die Wasserfluten rissen Alles mit sich —, the flood, the torrents carried all before it, them; er riß es mit sich —, he hurried away with it. Fig. to overpower, to overcome; it. to delight, to charm, to transport. Sich von der Rachbegierde —reißen lassen, to give way to revenge; der Zorn riß ihn —, anger hurried him away; die Jugend läßt sich vom Vergnügen —reißen, youth suffers itself to be hurried away by pleasures; die Leidenschaft hat ihn —gerissen, passion has transported him; ein —reißendes Vergnügen, a transporting or ravishing pleasure; ein —reißendes Beispiel, a most tempting or seducing example; er reißt alle Gemüther durch seine Beredsamkeit —, he masters all men's minds, he wins or gains over all hearts by his eloquence; eine —reißende Rede, an admirable or charming speech. —reiten, ir. v. intr. 1) to ride thither or there [on horseback]. 2) to ride on or along [on horseback]. —rennen, ir. v. intr. to run to a place. —richten, v. tr. 1) to direct or turn to or towards a place. Er richtete seine Schritte nach N. —, he directed his steps towards N. 2) [rather unusual] to spoil, to ruin, V. Zu Grunde richten. 3) to put to death, to execute [a malefactor]. —richtung, f. 1) the act of directing &c. to &c.; of spoiling &c. 2) capital punishment, execution. —riechen, ir. v. intr. to smell at a thing. Riechen Sie einmal —! go and smell! Fig. †Er hatte kaum —gerochen [= war kaum angekommen, hatte sich kaum genähert], so &c., he had no sooner arrived or come near, than &c. —rieseln, v. intr. to purl along. —ritt, m. going there on horseback, ride thither. —rollen, v. tr. and intr. to roll to or towards a place. —rücken, I. v. tr. to move or push to another place, to remove. II. v. intr. to move, approach or advance towards a place. —rudern, I. v. intr. 1) to row to or towards that place. 2) to row on or along. II. v. tr. to transport to a place by rowing, to row to or towards. —rufen, ir. I. v. intr. to call or cry towards a place. II. v. tr. to call any one to a place. —schaffen, v. tr. to convey, to transport to a place. —schaffung, f. the act of conveying or transporting to a place, transportation, conveyance. —schaffungsmittel, n. means of transport or conveyance. —schauen, v. intr. [chiefly in poetry] to look, to cast one's eyes towards a place. —scheid, m. decease, departure, death. —scheiden, ir. v. intr. [chiefly in poetry] to decease, to depart this life, to die. Der —geschiedene, the deceased. —scheinen, ir. v. intr. to shine towards a place. †—scheren, v. r. sich —scheren, to betake one's self, to go to a place; it. to go off, to pack off. —schicken, v. tr. to send to a place. Ich habe ihn —geschickt, I have sent him there. —schieben, ir. v. tr. to shove or push to or towards a place. —schießen, ir. I. v. intr. 1) [n. w. haben] to shoot or fire to or towards a place. 2) [n. w. seyn] to move suddenly and rapidly towards a place or along, to rush along, to hasten or fly along. II. v. tr. 1) to shoot [an arrow &c.] to or towards a place. 2) [= geben] to give, to advance [money], V. Herschießen II. 2). —schiffen, I. v. intr. 1) to navigate or sail to a place. 2) to sail on or along. Am Ufer —schiffen, to coast along. II. v. tr. to convey or transport to a place by ships. —schlagen, ir. I. v. tr. 1) to move or drive to a place by striking. Schlagen Sie den Ball gegen die Wand —, send the ball towards the wall. Fig. [rather stiff] Auf welche Seite soll ich meine Augen —schlagen? to which side am I to turn or direct my eyes? 2) to fix by striking. Sie müssen da einen Nagel —schlagen, you must drive in a nail there. II. v. intr. [vulgar] V. —fallen. —schlängeln, v. r. sich —schlängeln, to wind along with a serpentine course, to serpentize along [said of a path &c.]. Ein sich —schlängelnder Fluß, a meandering river. —schleichen, ir. v. intr. and v. r. sich —schleichen, 1) to steal, slink or sneak to or towards that place or thither. 2) to steal, sneak or slink on or along. 1. —schleifen, v. tr. to drag or haul to a place or along. 2. —schleifen, ir. v. tr. [eine Kante &c.] to make an edge by grinding. —schlendern, v. intr. to go to a place or along loitering, to saunter or loiter on or along. —schleppen, v. tr. to drag to a place on or along. Fig. Sein Leben elend —schleppen, to lead a wretched, lingering life. —schleudern, v. tr. and intr. to sling or hurl to or towards a place. —schlüpfen, v. intr. to slide along, to pass lightly, to slip away. Fig. Ueber eine Sache —schlüpfen, to glance upon a thing; to touch it lightly; to slip over it. —schmachten, v. intr. [chiefly in poetry] to languish, to lead a languishing, lingering life. Im Elende —schmachten, to languish in misery. †—schmeißen, ir. v. tr. V. —werfen. —schnattern, v. tr. and intr. to utter chattering, gabbling or prattling, to chatter, to gabble, to prattle. —schreiben, ir. v. tr. and intr. 1) to write to a place. 2) to write down. Er hat es nur so in der Eile —geschrieben, he has written it in a hurry. —schütten, v. tr. to throw or pour out towards a place. —schwatzen, V. —reden. —schwimmen, ir. v. intr. 1) to swim to a place or thither. 2) to swim or float along. —schwinden, ir. v. intr. [chiefly in poetry] V. Schwinden. —schwingen, ir. I. v. tr. to swing any thing forth or towards. II. v. r. sich —schwingen, 1) to swing on or along. 2) to leap or vault to a place. —segeln, v. intr. 1) to sail to a place or thither. 2) to sail along. Längs der Küste —segeln, to coast along. —sehen, ir. v. intr. to look towards a place. —sehnen, v. r. sich —sehnen, to long to be at a place, V. Sehnen. —senden, reg. and ir. v. tr. to send to a place. V. Absenden, Abordnen. —setzen, I. v. tr. to set or put in or towards any place, to put down. Setzet das auf den Tisch —, put that down upon the table; er hat sein Haus auf einen Hügel —gesetzt [= gebaut], he has set or built his house upon a hill. II. v. r. sich —setzen, to seat one's self in any place. Ich will mich nun —setzen und schreiben, now I'll sit down to write. —seufzen, I. v. intr. 1) to sigh for a place. 2) [chiefly in poetry] to sigh on or along. Der Wind seufzt durch die Bäume —, the wind sighs or comes sighing through the trees; to pass over with a sigh or sighing noise; der Wind seufzt über die Haide —, the blast comes sighing over the heath. II. v. tr. to pass sighing [the whole night]. —seyn, ir. v. intr. [in fam. lang.] 1) to have gone to a place. Er ist —, he has gone there. 2) to be lost, to be gone, it. to be dead. Zeit und Geld, Alles ist —, time and money, all is lost or gone; †er ist —, it is over with him; V. Dahinseyn. —sinken, ir. v. intr. to sink down; it. to faint, to swoon away. —sitzen, ir. v. intr. to sit down in any place. *—sollen, v. intr. to be obliged to go to a place. Er soll —, he shall go there, it. he is to go there. —sprechen, ir. v. intr. V. —reden. —springen, ir. v. intr. to jump, leap, bound or run to or towards a place. Ich will —springen, I'll run there. —stecken, v. tr. to put to or into a place. —stehlen, ir. v. r. sich —stehlen, V. —schleichen. —stellen, v. tr. to put in a certain place, to put away, to put down. —sterben, ir. v. intr. to die, to die away. —steuern, I. v. intr. 1) to steer to a place or thither. 2) to steer along. II. v. tr. [ein Schiff] to steer towards a place. —stolpern, v. intr. 1) to go to a place stumbling. 2) to stumble and fall down. —stottern, v. tr. to stammer out. —streben, v. intr. to strive or endeavour to come to a place or to attain to, to arrive at a certain end, V. Streben. —strecken, I. v. tr. Etwas —strecken, to stretch along or out. Einen —strecken, to lay any one dead upon the spot, to kill any one. Fig. Der Tod hat ihn —gestreckt, he fell down dead. II. v. r. sich —strecken, to lay one's self down at full length [on the grass &c.] —streichen, ir. I. v. tr. to rub, stroke towards a place [away from the person speaking]; it. to spread [butter &c.] upon any thing. II. v. intr. 1) to move or pass along. Der Hase strich längs der Hecke —, the hare slipped or run along the hedge; nahe an der Erde —streichen [said of a ball, bullet &c.], to graze the earth. 2) Fig. V. Verstreichen. —strich, m. 1) a stroke towards a place. 2) departure, passage back or return of birds of passage. —strömen, I. v. intr. [chiefly in poetry] to stream towards a place or along. Fig. Die Zeit strömt schnell —, time elapses or passes quickly. II. v. tr. [chiefly in poetry] to pour out or forth. Er strömte in begeisterter Rede seine Gefühle —, he poured forth his feelings in an enthusiastic speech. —stürzen, I. v. intr. and v. r. sich —stürzen, 1) to fall, to tumble, to precipitate one's self towards a place. 2) to fall or tumble down, V. Stürzen. II. v. tr. to throw or precipitate down. —tändeln, v. tr. to pass [one's time &c.] trifling or toying. *—tanzen, v. intr. to dance off or along. —tappen, v. intr. to grope one's way to a place. —taumeln, v. intr. [in poetry] to go to a place reeling or staggering. —thauen, v. intr. to thaw, to dissolve. —thun, ir. v. tr.

to put to a place, V. —setzen, —stellen. —tosen, *v. intr.* 1) to go to, to betake one's self thither or there blustering, raving or raging. 2) to move along blustering or raging. —tönen, *v. intr.* to sound towards a place. —trachten, *v. intr.* to intend, try or endeavour to go or come thither. —tragen, *ir. v. tr.* to carry thither or there. —träger, *m.*, —trägerinn, *f.* the person who carries thither. *Fig.* Ein — und Herträger, a tell-tale, blab, V. Zwischenträger. —treiben, *ir. v. tr.* to drive to or towards a place. —treten, *ir. v. intr.* to step up to, to advance towards any person or thing. Er trat vor den König —, he stepped up to, he approached the king; es ist so finster, daß man nicht sehen kann, wo man —tritt, it is so dark that one cannot see where one treads or what one treads upon. —tritt, *m.* 1) [unusual or provincial] the act of stepping up to, approaching &c. 2) *Fig.* decease, demise, death. —tummeln, I. *v. intr.* and *v. r.* sich —tummeln, to hurry to a place bustling. II. *v. tr.* to hurry any one to a place. —wagen, *v. r.* sich —wagen, to dare or venture to go thither or there. —wallen [chiefly in poetry], —wandeln, —wandern, *v. intr.* to walk, travel or wander to or towards a place. —wanken, *v. intr.* to go to a place tottering or reeling. —wehen, *v. intr.* and *v. tr.* to blow to or towards a place. —weisen, *v. tr.* to point to, to direct to; *it.* to refer to. Einen auf den rechten Weg —weisen, to show any one the right way. —weisend, *adj.* pointing at, [in grammar] demonstrative. —weisung, *f.* reference. Unter —weisung auf &c., with reference to or in referring to &c. —welken, *v. intr.* to wither or decay, to fade away, to droop, V. Verwelken. —wenden, *reg.* and *ir.* I. *v. tr.* to turn towards a place. Die Augen irgend wo —wenden, to turn or cast one's eyes any where. II. *v. r.* sich —wenden, to turn to or towards a place. *Fig.* to have recourse to, to fly for succour to, to apply to any one. Er weiß nicht, wo er sich —wenden soll, he does not know which way to turn himself, he is put to his last shift. —werfen, *ir.* I. *v. tr.* to throw or fling down. Die Karten —werfen, to throw up the cards. *Fig.* to write down or sketch hastily. Ein Wort —werfen [= fallen lassen], to drop a word, to let fall or slip a word, to blurt it out. II. *v. r.* sich —werfen, to throw one's self down. Sich vor Einem —werfen, to cast one's self at any one's feet, to prostrate one's self before any one. —wieder, —wiederum, *adv.* 1) again, anew, once more. 2) on the other hand; in return. V. Wieder. *—wischen, *v. intr. Fig.* leicht über Etwas —wischen, to do any thing negligently or superficially; *it.* to glance at a subject, to touch lightly on it, to run it over lightly. —wissen, *ir. v. intr.* to know where to put. Ich weiß damit nirgends —, I don't know what to do with it, where to put it. *—wollen, *ir. v. intr.* to be willing, to wish, want or intend to go to that place or thither. Wo wollen Sie —? where do you intend to go? where are you going? *Fig.* Ich sehe schon, wo das, wo er — will, I see what that will come to, what he aims at, I perceive his drift. —wünschen, I. *v. tr.* Einen —wünschen, to wish any one to be at a place. II. *v. r.* sich —wünschen, to wish one's self at that place or at any place. —wurf, V. Wurf. —würgen, *v. tr.* to massacre, to butcher, to slaughter, to murder. —wurzeln, *v. intr.* to take root. *Fig.* Wie —gewurzelt, as if rooted, rivetted or nailed to the spot. —zahlen, *v. tr.* 1) to remit money, to make remittances to a place. Er hat diese Summe nach N. —gezahlt, he has remitted that sum to N. 2) to pay, to pay down. —zählen, *v. tr.* 1) V. Fortzählen. 2) to count [the money] down. —zaubern, *v. tr.* to put or place, to transport there by enchantment. —zeichnen, *v. tr.* to draw or sketch thither or there, *it.* hastily. —zeigen, *v. intr.* to point towards or at. —ziehen, *ir.* I. *v. tr.* to draw towards or to. Er zog sie zu sich —, he drew her towards him. *Fig.* Eine Sache —ziehen [= verzögern], to delay, to defer, to protract any thing. Sein Leben —ziehen, to lead a lingering life, V. —schleppen; das zieht mich zu ihm —, that attaches me to him, by that he wins my heart. II. *v. intr.* 1) to go or march, to travel along. Ziehet — in Frieden, depart in peace; schwarze Wolken zogen über uns —, black clouds passed along over our heads. 2) to go or repair to, to remove to a place. Anders wo— ziehen, to settle somewhere else, or elsewhere. —zielen, *v. intr.* 1) to aim at that place or thither. 2) [in general] to aim at a place or thing. *Fig.* Auf Etwas —zielen, to tend to, to aim at something. Ich weiß schon, wo er —zielt, I know what he aims at, what he is after, V. Abzielen. —zischeln, *v. intr.* to whisper towards. —zischen, *v. intr.* to fly along whistling or whizzing. —zug, *m.* 1) the act of going or marching to or towards a place away from the person speaking. 2) the removal of lodgings or quarters to that place. *Fig.* V. Hinscheid.

Hináb, *adv.* [denoting motion or direction from a higher place, where the person speaking is, down to a lower place, opposed to Herab, which see] down, downwards. — mit ihm! down with him! throw him down! den Strom —, down the river; den Berg, die Treppe —, down the hill, down the stairs. [Hinab is much used in composition of verbs; such compounds as are not found here, are formed in analogy with those subjoined here and with those compounded with Herab, Herunter, which see.]

Hinab-beugen, *v. tr.* to bend down [a bough &c.]. —bringen, *ir. v. tr.* to take down, to bring down. —dürfen, *v. intr.* to be allowed to go down, to descend. —erben, *v. tr.* to make over, to transfer [a right &c.] as inheritance to one's children or posterity. Dieses Recht ist von seinen Vorfahren auf ihn —geerbt, this privilege has been transmitted to him by his ancestors. —fahren, *ir.* I. *v. intr.* to go down in a carriage or boat, to descend. II. *v. tr.* to carry, bring or convey down. —fahrt, *f.* descent. —fallen, *ir. v. intr.* to fall down. —führen, *v. tr.* to lead or conduct down. —gehen, *ir. v. intr.* to go or walk down. —hangen, —hängen, *ir. v. intr.* to hang down. —kommen, *ir. v. intr.* to come down, to descend. Ich werde sogleich —kommen, I shall come down immediately. —lassen, *ir. v. tr.* 1) [in fam. lang.] to allow to go down. Lassen Sie mich in den Garten —, allow me to go down, let me go down into the garden. 2) to let down, to lower. Sie ließ sie an einem Strick —, she let them down by a cord; Wein in den Keller —lassen, to let wine down into the cellar. —rufen, *ir. v. intr.* and *v. tr.* to call down. —schlucken, *v. tr.* V. Verschlucken. —sinken, *ir. v. intr.* to sink down. —springen, *ir. v. intr.* to leap or jump down. —steigen, *ir. v. intr.* to come or step down, to descend. —trinken, *ir. v. tr.* to drink down, to swallow; *it.* V. Hinuntertrinken. —werfen, *ir. v. tr.* to throw down.

Hinábwärts, *adv.* downwards.

Hinán, *adv.* [expressing motion from the person speaking to a remote, particularly a higher place] towards a place, up to a place. Zum Himmel —, towards heaven; den Berg —, up the hill, going up the hill; muthig —! courage, advance, approach, mount!

Hinan-kommen, *ir. v. intr.* to come or get near or up, to approach, to ascend. Ich kann nicht —kommen, I cannot reach it. —steigen, *ir. v. intr.* to ascend, to mount. Den Berg —steigen, to ascend the hill.

Hinauf, *adv.* [expressing motion from the person speaking to or towards a higher place] up, upwards. Da —, dort —, up there; den Fluß —, up the river; zum Himmel —, up to heaven, towards heaven; von unten —, up from below; es sind sechs Stufen —, there are six steps up. *Fig.* Sein Geschlechtsregister geht bis zu Karl dem Großen —, his genealogical register may be traced back to the days of Charlemagne. [Hinauf is much used in composition of verbs; but these compounds being very easily understood, we only subjoin a few by way of example.]

Hinauf-arbeiten, *v. r.* sich —arbeiten, to work one's way up to, to get up to a place with labour or difficulty. [Used also in a fig. sense]. —begeben, *ir. v. r.* sich —begeben, V. —gehen. —bringen, *ir. v. tr.* to bring, take, carry or get up. —dämpfen, *v. tr.* [in seamen's lang.] Die Segel am Mastbaume —dämpfen, to clew up the sails. —fahren, *ir.* I. *v. intr.* to ascend or go up in a carriage or boat. Den Fluß —fahren, to sail up the river. II. *v. tr.* to carry or convey up. —fliegen, *ir. v. intr.* to fly up to. —führen, *v. tr.* to lead or conduct up. —gehen, *ir. v. intr.* to go or walk up, to ascend. —heben, *ir. v. tr.* to lift up, to help up. —helfen, *ir. v. intr.* Einem —helfen, to help any one up. Einem auf's Pferd —helfen, to help or assist any one in getting on horseback. —klettern, *v. intr.* to climb up. *—lassen, *ir. v. tr.* to allow any one to go up. —leuchten, *v. intr.* 1) to illumine by throwing a light upwards. 2) Einem die Treppe —leuchten, to light any one up stairs. —rücken, I. *v. tr.* to move, push or put higher up. II. *v. intr.* to advance or move higher up. —schwingen, *ir. v. r.* sich —schwingen, to leap or vault up. Er schwang sich auf das Pferd —, he leapt on horseback. *Fig.* Sich zu den höchsten Ehrenstellen —schwingen, to rise to the height or pinnacle of honours. —steigen, *ir. v. intr.* to ascend, to mount. Den Berg —steigen, to ascend the mountain. —stimmen, *v. tr.* to raise [the tone of an instrument &c.] higher, to tune up. —tragen, *ir. v. tr.* to carry up. —treiben, *ir. v. tr.* to drive up. Die Reiterei trieb den Feind den Berg —, the cavalry drove the enemy up the hill. *Fig.* Möbel bei einer Versteigerung sehr hoch —treiben, to raise very high the price of furniture by outbidding at an auction.

Hinaufwärts, *adv.* upwards. —wärts ist es weniger gefährlich als herunterwärts, it is less dangerous to get up than to come down.

Hinaus, *adv.* [expressing motion out of a place to a distance from the person speaking] out. Vorn — [in einem Hause], in the fore-part or front of the house; hinten —, in the back of the house; er wohnt hinten —, he lodges in a back-room; weit — vor die Stadt, to a great distance from the town; —! — mit ihm! get out! out with him! turn him out! dort —, out there; ich weiß nicht wo — [= ich weiß den Ausgang nicht zu finden], I don't know which way to go out, I can't find the way out, *it.* **fig.* [= ich weiß mir nicht zu helfen] I don't know which way to turn [myself], I am at my wits' end, I am put to my last shifts; jetzt, wo —? now, what are we to do? *it.* [applied to time] beyond. Ueber die Zeit — ausbleiben, to stay out beyond one's time; eine Freundschaft, die sich bis über das Grab — erstreckt, a friendship that lasts beyond the grave. [Hinaus is much used in composition of verbs; but these compounds being very easily understood, we only subjoin a few by way of example.]

Hinaus=begeben, *ir. v. r.* sich —begeben, V. —geben. —**begleiten**, *v. tr.* to accompany or see any one out of a place. —**bringen**, *ir. v. tr.* to bring or carry out. Bringen Sie ihm das Buch in den Garten —, take the book out for or to him into the garden. **Fig.* Ich glaube nicht, daß er die Sache —bringen wird, I do not think that he will be able to accomplish or to bring about his design or enterprise. —**denken**, *ir. v. intr* to think of something remote or distant. *Wo denken Sie —? what do you think of, how can you think so? *er denkt hoch —, he forms grand designs or lofty projects, he is a man of great designs, he aims at great things; *wo denkt ihr — [= hinzugehen]? where do you intend to go? —**fahren**, *ir. v. tr.* and *intr.* to go out of a place in a carriage, ship or boat. Einen Herrn zur Stadt —fahren, to drive a gentleman [in a coach] out of the town; als er zur Stadt, zum Hafen —fuhr, as he drove out of the town, as he left the harbour or sailed out of the harbour. *it.* to go beyond. Ueber ein Vorgebirge —fahren [= es hinter sich lassen], to pass beyond, to double a cape; über eine Insel —fahren, to go beyond an island; er ist mit seinem Hause drei Schuh zu weit —gefahren, he has built his house too far out [into the street &c.] by three feet. —**fallen**, *ir. v. intr.* [zum Fenster &c.] to fall out [of the window &c.]. —**fliegen**, *ir. v. intr.* to fly out of a place. —**führen**, *v. tr.* to lead or conduct out of a place. *Fig.* Eine Sache —führen, to carry any thing into complete effect, to bring about, to accomplish, to execute, to perform any thing or design [to the or its end], V. Ausführen 2). —**gehen**, *ir. v. intr.* to go or walk out of a place. Er ist —gegangen, he has gone out. *Fig.* Er ist über seinen Auftrag —gegangen [hat ihn überschritten], he has exceeded his instructions; das geht über meine Kräfte —, that is beyond, exceeds my strength; dieses Zimmer geht auf die Straße —, this room faces, fronts or looks into the street; das geht zu weit —, that juts out or projects too much; beim —gehen aus dem Schauspiele wurde er &c., as he came out of the play, he was &c. —**jagen**, *v. tr.* to chase or drive out of a place. Ich werde ihn zum Hause —jagen, I shall turn him out of doors. —**kommen**, *ir. v. intr.* to go or come out of a place. **Fig.* Es kömmt auf Eins —, this comes to the same thing, it is as broad as it is long. *—**können**, *ir. v. intr.* to be able to go out of a place. Ich kann nicht —, I can't get out. —**lassen**, *ir. v. tr.* to allow, to let any one go out. *Fig.* Eine Gelegenheit —lassen, to let go an opportunity, to let it slip. —**laufen**, *ir. v. intr.* 1) to run out of a place. 2) *Fig.* to terminate or end in a certain manner. *Es läuft Alles auf Eins —, it comes to the same [thing], 't is all one, it is as broad as it is long. —**legen**, *v. tr.* to lay or put out. —**lesen**, *ir. v. tr.* to read to the end. Ein Buch in einem Tage —lesen, to peruse, to read a book out or through in one day. —**leuchten**, *v. intr.* Einem —leuchten, to light any one out of a place. *—**machen**, *v. r.* sich —machen, V. Herausgehen. *—**müssen**, *ir. v. intr.* to be obliged to go out. *—**packen**, *v. r.* sich —packen, to get or go out of a place. Packt euch —! get ye out! —**reichen**, I. *v. intr.* to reach or extend out towards any thing. Das reicht zu weit —, that juts out or projects too far; das reicht weit —, that goes a great way; damit werde ich nicht —reichen, I shall not have enough of it, that will not be sufficient. *Fig.* Das reicht über meine Kräfte —, that is beyond, that exceeds my strength. II. *v. tr.* to stretch out of a place. Er reichte die Hand zum Fenster —, he stretched his hand out of the window. —**reiten**, *ir. v. intr.* to ride out of a place on horseback. —**rücken**, I. *v. tr.* to move or push farther out. II. *v. intr.* to move or march out. —**schaffen**, *v. tr.* to remove from out of a place. Einen zum Hause —schaffen, to turn any one out of doors. †—**scheren**, *v. r.* sich —scheren, V. —packen. —**schicken**, *v. tr.* to send out. —**schieben**, *ir. v. tr.* to push or shove out of a place. *Fig.* Etwas —schieben, V. Aufschieben, Verschieben. —**schlagen**, *ir. v. intr.* to kick. Mit dem Vorderfuße —schlagen, to strike with the fore-foot. *Fig.* to be refractory, wild, intractable, to kick against the pricks. —**schleichen**, *ir. v. intr.* and *v. r.* sich —schleichen, to sneak, steal or slink out of a place. —**schreien**, *ir. v. tr.* and *intr.* to utter with a loud voice, to call out. Er schrie Schimpfreden —, he bawled out abuses; er schrie seinen Schmerz —, he gave vent to his agony; zum Fenster —schreien, to cry or call out of the window. —**schwanken**, *v. intr.* V. —wanken. —**sehen**, *ir. v. intr.* to look out [of the window &c.]. —**setzen**, I. *v. tr.* to set or put out or out of doors. *Fig.* Weiter —setzen, to put off, to defer till a later period; das ist weit —gesetzt, that is long put off. II. *v. r.* sich —setzen, to seat or place one's self at the outer side, on the edge &c., to seat one's self out or out of doors. *Fig.* Sich über Etwas —setzen, to pass over a thing, not to mind, not to regard it; er setzt sich über das —, was man von ihm sagen kann, he is above minding what people may say of him; V. Wegsetzen. *—**seyn**, *ir. v. intr.* to have gone out. Er ist —, he has gone out; er ist auf's Land —, he has gone into the country. **Fig.* Ueber Etwas —seyn, to be above any thing; er ist über alle Scham —, he is lost to all shame; darüber bin ich —, that gives me no longer any uneasiness or concern, I don't mind that. —**singen**, *ir. v. tr.* and *intr.* to carry out or accompany singing [a corpse &c.]; *it.* to sing out loudly. —**spielen**, I. *v. tr.* 1) V. Ausspielen I. 1). 2) *Fig.* eine Sache —spielen, to protract a thing. II. *v. intr.* [in popular language] Einem —spielen, to accompany or to drive away a person playing or fiddling. —**stehlen**, *ir. v. r.* sich —stehlen, to steal or sneak out, V. —schleichen. —**stellen**, *v. tr.* V. —setzen; *it. fig.* V. —schieben, Verschieben. —**stoßen**, *ir. v. tr.* to push or drive out; to turn out of doors, V. Ausstoßen II. —**thun**, *ir. v. tr.* to put, take or turn out [or out of doors]. —**treiben**, *ir. v. tr.* to drive out, to expel. Das Vieh —treiben, to drive or lead the cattle to the pasture. **Fig.* Wie lange wird er es so —treiben? how long yet will he go on so, will he continue it so? —**wanken**, *v. intr.* to go out vacillating or tottering. —**weisen**, *ir. v. tr.* Einem den Weg zum Dorfe &c. —weisen, to show any one the way out of the village &c.; *it.* Einen —weisen, to turn any one out of a place, out of doors &c. V. —werfen. —**werfen**, *ir. v. tr.* to throw out of a place. Sie warfen ihn [zur Thüre, zum Hause] —, they turned him out of doors; wenn er die Miethe nicht bezahlt, so werde ich ihn —werfen lassen, if he does not pay his rent, I shall eject or expel him. *—**wischen**, *v. intr.* to slip out of a place. *—**wollen**, *ir. v. intr.* to wish or want to go or get out. Er will —, he wishes or wants to go or get out. **Fig. a)* Hoch —wollen, to have or form grand designs, to aim at great things; nein, mein Sohn, laß uns nicht zu hoch —wollen, no, my son, let us not soar too high. *b)* to end, to terminate in, to aim at. Wo will das —? how will that end? ich sehe schon, wo das, wo er — will, I see, what it will come to, what he aims at; wo will es endlich damit —? what will at last be the consequence of it? —**ziehen**, *ir* I. *v. tr.* 1) to draw or pull out of a place. Er zog ihn zum Zimmer —, he pulled or hauled him out of the room. 2) *Fig.* Eine Sache —ziehen, to protract a thing. II. *v. intr.* to remove. Er ist auf das Land —gezogen, he has left the town to live in the country. —**zwingen**, *ir. v. tr.* to force or oblige to go or come out.

Hinauswärts, *adv.* outwards.

Hinde, *f.* V. Hindinn.

Hinderlich, *adj.* and *adv.* hindering, impeding, embarrassing, cumbersome; troublesome. Ich will Ihnen nicht — seyn, I will be no hinderance to you; er würde Ihnen nur — seyn or fallen, he would only hinder you or be troublesome to you; er ist mir in allen meinen Absichten —, he runs counter to or he thwarts all my designs; ich werde Ihnen in Ihrem Vorhaben nicht — seyn, I will not set myself against or oppose your design; das viele Gepäcke ist einem Heere —, much baggage encumbers or clogs an army; *es geht diesen Leuten sehr —, these people live very poorly, make just shift to live.

Hindern, *v. tr.* [Sax. *hindriar*, Icel. and Sw. *hindra*, Eng. *to hinder*, from hinter, hind] to hinder, to impede, to prevent. Einen in seinen Absichten —, to obstruct, cross or thwart any one's designs; Einen an Etwas —, to hinder or prevent any one from doing any thing; er hat mich an der Fortsetzung meines Briefes gehindert, he has prevented or hindered me from continuing my letter; das hindert die Verdauung, that hinders the digestion; was hindert Euch? what hinders you? legen Sie Ihren Mantel ab, er hindert Sie nur, put off your cloak, it only encumbers you.

Hinderniß, *n.* [-sses, *pl.* -sse] hinderance, impediment, obstacle, obstruction. Das gibt or macht ein großes —, that is a great obstacle, ein — besiegen, to surmount or get the better of an obstacle; Einem ein — in den Weg legen, to throw an obstacle in any one's way; ich lege Ihrer Verheirathung kein — in den Weg, I do not oppose your marriage; —sse aus dem Wege räumen, to remove hinderances; sie werden dabei kein — finden, they will meet with no obstacle or impediment in that; das ist wieder ein neues —, that is a new difficulty or impediment again; die —sse des or eines strebenden Geistes, the trammels of rising genius.

Hinderung, *f.* V. Verhinderung and Hinderniß.

Hindinn, *f.* [Sax. *hinde*, Eng., Dan. and Sw. *hind*, seems to be allied to Kind = Geschöpf] [the female of the red deer or stag] hind, V. Hirschkuh.

Hindläufte, *f.* [*pl.* -n] [in botany] wild succory.

Hindurch, *adv.* 1) [denoting motion from the person speaking through any place or thing] through. Dort —, through that place, that way; durch den Wald —, through the wood; durch die Felder —, across the fields; durch den Leib —, through the body; sie sangen das Dorf —, they sung all the way through the village. *Fig.* [applied to time] Den ganzen Tag, die ganze Nacht —, all day, all night long; das ganze Jahr —, all the year round; ich habe die ganze Nacht — kein Auge zugethan, I did not sleep a wink all night. 2) quite through, throughout.

Hindurch=arbeiten, —**brechen**, —**bringen**, —**schiffen** &c., V. Durcharbeiten, Durchbrechen &c.

Hinein, *adv.* [expressing the direction of a motion from the person speaking into any space or place] into, in. Weit in den Wald —, far into the wood; bis in die Stadt —, into the very town, *into* the heart of the town; —! nur —! go in, step in, walk in! *Fig.* In den Tag —, at random, thoughtlessly, carelessly; in den Tag — leben, to *live* at random; in den Tag — reden, to talk at random, to talk nonsense; [in popular lang.] du solltest Dich in das Herz — schämen, you ought to be ashamed of yourself; [in vulgar lang.] das hat er in seinen Hals — gelogen, [that] he has lied in his throat, he is a lying rascal.

Hinein-arbeiten, I. *v. intr.* to work towards or into the inside. II. *v. r.* sich —arbeiten, to get into a place by exertion, to exert one's self to get into a place; *fig.* to make one's self thoroughly acquainted with any thing by constant exertion. —bauen, *v. tr.* and *intr.* to build in or into. —begeben, *ir. v. r.* sich —begeben, to go, step or walk in or into. Sich tief in den Wald —begeben, to go into the thickest part of the wood. —brausen, *v. intr.* 1) [in poetry] to rush in or into [said of wind and water]. 2) to enter furiously or with impetuosity. —bringen, *ir. v. tr.* to bring, carry, take or get in or into. **Fig.* Einem Etwas in den Kopf —bringen, to drive or beat any thing into any one's head. —denken, *ir.* I. *v. tr.* to figure to one's self one thing in another. Ich kann da keinen Sinn —denken, I can find no sense in it, I cannot make out the sense or meaning of it. II. *v. r.* sich —denken, to think or fancy one's self to be in any place. Wenn ich mich nach Amerika —denke, if I fancy myself to be in America; denken Sie sich in meine Lage —, fancy yourself in my situation; sich in eine Materie ganz —denken, to penetrate thoroughly into, to make one's self perfectly acquainted with a subject. —drängen, —dringen, —drücken, V. Eindrängen, Eindringen &c. —dürfen, *ir. v. intr.* to be allowed or permitted to go in. —eilen, *v. intr.* to hasten in or into. *—essen, *ir. v. tr.* to eat up, to swallow down. Vielerlei in sich —essen, to cram one's self with victuals. —fahren, *ir. v. intr.* o go in or into in a carriage, ship or boat. —'allen, *ir. v. intr.* to fall in or into. —flechen, V. Einflechten. —fressen, *ir.* I. *v. tr.* [vulg.] V. —essen. *Fig.* Einen Verdruß in sich —fressen, to pocket an injury or affront. II. *v. intr.* nd *v. r.* Das Scheidewasser frißt, frißt sich in as Eisen —, aqua fortis corrodes or eats into ron. —führen, *v. tr.* to lead or conduct in r into. —füllen, V. Einfüllen. —gehen, *ir.* *intr.* 1) to go, step or walk in or into, to enr. 2) In Etwas —gehen, to have place or oom in something. Die Waaren gehen nicht le in das Magazin —, the warehouse does ot hold all the goods; in dieses Gefäß gehen chs Flaschen —, this vessel holds or contains r bottles; dieser Hut geht mir nicht in den opf —, the crown of this hat does not fit my ad. **Fig.* Das geht mir nicht in den Kopf —, at will never go down with me; *it.* I cannot nceive that. —gerathen, *ir. v. intr.* V. Gethen 1). —greifen, *ir. v. intr.* to put one's nd into. *Fig.* Tief in den Beutel —greifen, lay out, to disburse or spend a great deal of mo-y; *it.* greifen Sie hierbei in Ihr eigenes Herz, think, what you would have done, thought, yourself in such a case; *it.* V. Eingreifen. —lfen, *ir. v. intr.* Einem —helfen, to help or ist any one in getting in or into. Er half ihm in Wagen —, he helped him into the carriage. heren, *v. tr.* to get in or into by witchcraft. jagen, I. *v. tr.* to drive or chase in or into. *v. intr.* to ride full speed, to gallop in or into. knüpfen, V. Einknüpfen. —können, *ir. v.* r. to be able to go or get in or into. —kriechen, *v. intr.* to creep or crawl in or into. Tief in Bett —kriechen, to cover one's self snug in 1. —lassen, *ir. v. tr.* Einen —lassen, to let any one go in or into. —lesen, *ir. v. intr.* and *v. r.* to read deep into a book &c. Haben Sie schon weit —gelesen? have you already far proceeded in your reading? *it.* sich in einen Schriftsteller —lesen, to make one's self thoroughly acquainted with an author by constant reading. —leuchten, *v. intr.* 1) to shine in or into. 2) Einem —leuchten, to light any one in or into. —locken, *v. tr* to draw, allure or entice in or into. —mischen, I. *v. tr.* to mix in. II. *v. r.* sich in Etwas —mischen, to meddle with any thing. *—mögen, *ir. v. intr.* to have a mind, to wish or want to go or get in or into. —müssen, *ir. v. intr.* to be obliged to go in or into. —nehmen, *ir. v. tr.* to take or carry in or into. Ich nahm es mit in das Haus —, I took it into the house with me. —nöthigen, *v. tr.* to oblige, press or urge any one to go or step in or into. †—prügeln, *v. tr.* to drive [any one] in or into by beating or cudgelling him; *fig.* to teach or instil by blows, to beat [a thing] into any one. —reiben, V. Einreiben. —rücken, I. *v. tr.* to move, push or shove in or into. II. *v. intr.* to enter a place in a military manner, to march in or into, V. Einrücken. *it.* Er ist zwei Ruthen in meinen Acker —gerückt, he has encroached on my field by two rods. —rufen, *ir.* I *v. intr.* to call in or into. II. *v. tr.* Einen —rufen, to call any one in. —saugen, V. Einsaugen. —schlagen, V. Einschlagen. —schleichen, *ir. v. intr.* and *v. r.* sich —schleichen, to sneak or steal into a place, V. Einschleichen. —schlürfen, V. Einschlürfen. —schmeißen, *ir. v. tr.* to fling into, V. —werfen. —senken, —sinken, —sperren, —stampfen, V. Einsenken, Einsinken &c. —stechen, *ir.* I. *v. tr.* to make by pricking or piercing. Löcher in ein Papier —stechen, to prick a paper. II. *v. intr.* to thrust a pointed instrument into any thing. Stechen Sie mit Ihrer Gabel in die Wurst —, thrust your fork into the sausage; *fig.* [in seamen's lang.] in die See —stechen, to stand for the offing, to stand out to sea. —stecken, *v. tr.* to put into, to fasten in. —stehlen, *ir. v. r.* sich —stehlen, to steal in or into. —steigen, *ir. v. intr.* to mount into, to get in. Die Diebe sind mit einer Leiter —gestiegen, the thieves entered the house by means of a ladder; in eine Grube —steigen, to descend into a pit. —stopfen, *v. tr.* V. Einstopfen. —stoßen, *ir. v. tr.* 1) to thrust, push or drive in or into. Einen Pfahl in die Erde —stoßen, to ram a pile into the earth. 2) to break by pushing or knocking. Eine Thür —stoßen, to break a door open. —stricken, —strömen, —stürmen, V. Einstricken, Einströmen &c. —stürzen, *v. intr.* and *v. r.* sich —stürzen, to throw or precipitate one's self into a place or thing. *—thun, *ir. v. tr.* to put in or into. *Fig.* Einen Blick in ein Buch &c. —thun, to cast a glance into a book &c. —tragen, *ir. v. tr.* to carry, bear or take in or into. —treiben, *ir. v. tr.* to drive in or into. —treten, V. Eintreten. —tunken, V. Eintunken. —wagen, *v. r.* sich —wagen, to dare or venture to go in or into. —werfen, *ir. v. tr.* to throw in or into. *—wollen, *ir. v. intr.* to want, wish or be willing to go or get in or into. —ziehen, *ir.* I. *v. tr.* to draw or pull in or into. *Fig.* Einen in Etwas —ziehen, to involve or entangle any one in any thing. II. *v. intr.* V. Einziehen II. —zwingen, *ir. v. tr.* to force in or into.

Hineinwärts, *adv.* V. Einwärts.

Hingegen, *conj.* on the contrary, on the other hand or side, whereas. Die Eine ist sehr schön, die Andere —, or — die Andere &c., the one is very beautiful, but the other &c.

Hinken, *v. intr.* [allied to wanken and Schenkel, the Sax. *skanku*, Sw. *skank* = Schienbein] to limp, to halt, to hobble, to be lame. Er hinkt mit dem rechten Fuße, he is lame of or in the right leg; ein —der, a lame or limping man; dieses Pferd hinkt mit einem Fuße, this horse goes lame of one foot. *Fig.* Ein —der Vers, a lame or hobbling verse; *den —den Bothen erwarten [= die Bestätigung einer schlimmen Nachricht], to wait for the lame-post, for Tom Long the carrier; der —de Bothe, fürchte ich, wird noch nachkommen, the bad news, I fear, will yet come after or are yet to come; * hier hinkt Etwas, there is a snake hid under the grass; jedes Gleichniß hinkt, every comparison is lame; *es hinkt mit ihm [= seine Sachen stehen mißlich], his affairs have taken an ill turn, he is in bad circumstances, in an unfavourable or critical condition. Das —, lameness, limping, halting.

Hinlänglich, *adj.* and *adv.* sufficient, sufficiently. Diese Summe ist nicht —, this sum does not suffice, is not sufficient; er ist — davon unterrichtet, he is sufficiently informed of it; er hat ein —es Auskommen, he has a sufficiency; ein —es Heer, um das Vaterland zu vertheidigen, an army sufficient to defend the country; —e Mittel, adequate means. SYN. Hinlänglich, Hinreichend, Genug. Hinlänglich is that which satisfies what necessity requires; hinreichend, which is fully adequate to the wants, or reasonably answers the end proposed; genug, that which satisfies desire, and has its limits only in the wishes of the person desiring.

Hinlänglichkeit, *f.* sufficiency; *it.* capacity, ability.

Hinnen, *adv.* [old and in poetry] here. Von —, from hence; lasset uns von — gehen, let us go away from here, let us depart or be gone from hence; hebe dich von —! be gone, or get [ye] gone from here! von — scheiden [= sterben], to depart this life, to die, to decease.

Hinsch, V. Hintsch.

Hinsicht, *f.* view, consideration, respect, regard, relation. In — auf ihn, with regard to him; in — auf seine Talente, with respect to his talents, as to or as for his talents; in mancher —, in many respects. V. Rücksicht.

Hinsichtlich, *adv.* [in Hinsicht] in or with respect to, with regard to, V. Rücksichtlich.

Hintan, *adv.* behind, after.

Hintan-bleiben, *ir. v. intr.* to remain behind, to lag. —fügen, *v. tr.* [better: hinzufügen] to join, to add. —setzen, *v. tr.* to put behind another thing. *Fig.* to put a smaller value upon, to slight, to neglect, to undervalue, to postpone a thing. Alle andere Rücksichten —setzen, to postpone or set aside all other considerations; seine Pflicht —setzen, to neglect one's duty, to fail in one's duty; man setzt mich —, I am slighted, I am not taken notice of. —setzung, *f.* the act of putting behind another thing; *fig.* slight, neglect. Mit —setzung seiner Ruhe, seiner Geschäfte, without any regard to, neglecting his repose, his affairs; mit —setzung der Gesetze, in contempt of, without any regard to the laws. —stehen, *ir. v. intr.* to stand behind. *Fig.* —stehen müssen, to be slighted or neglected. —stellen, V. —setzen.

Hinten, *adv.* [Sax. *hindan* and *hynan*, Goth. *hindana*, Eng. *behind*, *hind*, seems to be derived from the old Hind = jener] behind. Vorn und —, before and behind; — bleiben, to remain or stay behind, to lag; er hat ihm von — einen Stich beigebracht, he stabbed him from behind; sein Pferd ist — lahm [= kreuzlahm], his horse is lame in the back or hip, is hip-shot; sich — auf das Pferd setzen, to get up behind another on the same horse; Einen — auf's Pferd nehmen, to take a person up behind one on horseback; dieses Pferd schlägt —aus, this horse kicks; er wohnt — hinaus, he lodges or lives at the back-part, in the back of the house; das Haus hat — hinaus einen Garten, there is a garden behind the house; einen Koffer — aufbinden, to fasten or tie a trunk on behind the coach; seine Schuhe — niedertreten, to tread one's shoes down at the heel; an einen Brief — Etwas anfügen, to add something to the end of a letter; sich — anschließen [an einen Zug &c.], to join [a procession &c.] in the rear; [in military affairs] das Werk wird von — beschossen, the work is battered de-revers; [in seamen's lang.] mit gutem Winde von — her fahren or segeln, to have the wind aft, to sail with a fair wind.

Hinten=drein, —nach, *adv.* after the thing is done, afterwards, too late. Er kommt immer —drein, he is always the last, he always comes last; —nach gehen, to walk behind.

1. Hinter, [allied to hinten] I. *prep.* behind. 1) [governing the dative case, it signifies being at a place behind a person or thing either in motion or at rest] Er saß — mir, he sat behind me; er ließ mich — sich, he left me behind him; — einander gehen, to walk one after or behind the other; er hat immer eine Menge Bediente — sich her, he has always a long retinue of servants with him or a long train of servants at his heels; — Einem herlaufen, to run after, to follow, to pursue any one; den Feind — sich her haben, to have the enemy at one's heels; — dem Feinde seyn, to be at the enemies' heels, to be close at their heels, to pursue them closely; — sich herziehen, to draw or haul after or behind one; vier Wochen — einander, four weeks in succession, successively, together or running; — einander weg, all at once, without drawing breath, without interruption, uninterruptedly; — dem Hause, behind the house; — dem [or contracted: *hinter'm] Tische, behind the table; er versteckte sich — der Thüre, he hid himself behind the door; — dem Rücken, behind the back; er trat — einem Busche hervor, he stepped forth from behind a bush; [at cards] — der Hand sitzen [= die —hand haben], to be the younger hand; die Thüre — sich zumachen, to shut the door after or behind one. *Fig.* — Einem her seyn, to be at any one's heels, to be always at any one's elbow, *it.* to urge, to press any one; sie ist immer — ihren Bedienten her, she is constantly scolding [at] her servants; — einer Sache her seyn, to be actually about, to be in pursuit of any thing, to endeavour to get it; er ist schon lange — dieser Stelle her, he has hunted a long time after, he has sued or sollicited a long time for that place or situation; er ist immer — seinen Büchern her, he is always poring on his books; — der Thür Abschied nehmen, to go away privately or clandestinely, to steal away, to take French leave; — dem Berge halten, to keep one's thoughts, designs or intentions secret, to keep one's own counsel, to be close or reserved, to dissemble, to proceed with dissimulation; er hält damit — dem Berge, he won't tell his opinion or speak his mind upon that head; er hat es — den Ohren, he is a cunning fellow or blade, an arrant rogue, V. Ohr, Schelm, Kratzen, Trocken, Stecken; das hat Etwas — sich, there is a snake hid under the grass; es hat mehr — or auf sich, als man meint, it is of greater consequence or importance than one thinks; er hat es — mir, — meinem Rücken gethan, he has done it behind my back, without my knowledge. 2) [governing the accusative case, it signifies motion to a place behind any person or thing] — den [contracted: *hinter'n] Vorhang treten, to step, to hide one's self behind the curtain; — die Thür stellen, to put behind the door; — sich gehen, to go or walk backwards; — sich sehen, to look behind one or back; er kann weder — sich, noch vor sich, he can go neither backward nor forward; †Einem — die Ohren schlagen, to give any one a box on the ear, to box any one's ears. *Fig.* — Etwas kommen, to find out, to discover any thing; — Eines Sprünge kommen, to discover any one's tricks, pranks or under-hand-dealing; Einen — das [contracted: *hinter's] Licht führen, to cheat, deceive, gull, trick or defraud any one, to take any one in; sich Etwas — die Ohren schreiben, to lay any thing up in one's memory; ich werde es mir — die Ohren schreiben, I shall never forget it, I shall remember it; — sich gehen, not to succeed, to fail, to miscarry, to come to nought; die Heirath ist — sich gegangen, the match has been broken off; es will mit ihm weder — sich, noch vor sich, his affairs go neither forward nor backward, his affairs are at a stand.

II. *adj.* and *adv.* hind, hinder. Der —e Theil, the hind part or hinder part; er bewohnt den —n Theil des Hauses, he inhabits the back or back part of the house; in dem —sten Winkel, in the furthest corner; die —e Thür or die —thür, the back-door; der —e Theil des Kopfes, the hind part of the head; die —n Füße, the hind legs or feet; das —ste Glied [in military affairs], the back-side, the bringers-up; das Vorderste zu —st, das —ste zu vorderst kehren, to do every thing the wrong way or preposterously, *it.* to put a thing upside down, or topsy-turvy.

Hinter=achse, *f.* the hind axle-tree [of a waggon]. —backe, *f.* [most vulgar: Arschbacke] buttock, V. Gesäß; [in seamen's lang.] die —backen [or Billen] eines Schiffes, the buttocks of a ship. —bau, *m.* V. —gebäude. —baum, *m.* V. Garnbaum. —bein, *n.* hindleg, V. —fuß. *Fig.* Auf die —beine treten or sich auf die —beine stellen, 1) to put one's self in a posture of defence, to stand upon one's defence or guard, *it.* to shew one's teeth, 2) to retract, to recede, to flinch, *it. prov.* to slip one's neck out of the collar, V. Zurücktreten. 1. —bleiben, *ir. v. intr.* to stay or remain behind, to be left. Die —bliebenen, those left behind, the survivors, the relations or heirs of a deceased person; die —bliebene Wittwe, the relict. 2. Hinterbleiben, *Fig.* to remain undone, to be omitted, V. [the more usual word] Unterbleiben. 1. —bringen, *ir. v. tr.* Einem Etwas —bringen, to inform any one secretly of any thing; *it.* to acquaint any one with, to give any one notice of, to apprise or inform any one of a thing. Man hat es mir —bracht, I have been apprised or informed of it. 2. Hinterbringen, *ir. v. tr.* 1) to get or swallow down, V. Hinunterbringen. 2) to bring, place or put into a remote place. —bringer, *m.*, —bringerinn, *f.* one who gives intelligence or notice, who informs or apprises, informer or informant, [in contempt] tell-tale, tale-bearer. —bug, *m.* the ham, hough or hip of an animal. Ein —bug von einem Kalbe, a knuckle of veal, V. Bug. —bühne, *f.* the back-part of the stage, the background; *it.* back-garret. —castell, *n.* [in seamen's lang.] the poop [of a ship], V. —schanze; *it.* *fig.* [chiefly in jest] the posteriors, the backside. —deck, *n.* V. Verdeck. —drücken, *v. tr.* [the accent on the first syllable] 1) to press, squeeze or push behind other things. *2) to swallow with an effort, to gulp down. —ebbe, *f.* [in seamen's lang.] the end of the reflux or ebb-tide. —eisen, *n.* the hind shoe of a horse. *—essen, *ir. v. tr.* [the accent on the first syllable] V. Hinunteressen. —fährte, *f.* [among hunters] 1) the mark or impression left by the foot of an animal, trace, footing or track, [chiefly] foiling. 2) the trace, footing or track of the hindfoot. —flagge, *f.* [in seamen's lang.] flag on the poop or stern, ensign. —fleck, *m.* [among shoemakers] a piece put upon the heel of a shoe, V. Fleck II. 2). —flügel, *m.* hind wing, lower wing [of an insect]. —fries, *m.* first reinforce-ring of a gun. —führen, *v. tr.* [the accent on the first syllable] to lead or conduct behind. —fuß, *m.* hind foot [of a quadruped]. Dieses Pferd schlägt mit den —füßen aus, this horse kicks [with the hind feet]; das Pferd stellet sich auf die —füße, the horse rises or stands upon his two hind feet, prances or rears, V. Sich bäumen; *it.* [in men] the hind part of the foot, the heel; *it.* V. Plattfuß. *Fig.* Sich auf die —füße stellen, V. —bein. —gallerie, *f.* [in seamen's lang.] stern-gallery. —gang, *m.* [among hunters] the going out of a deer or other animal into the fields from the forest. —gebäude, *n.* back-building, out-house, back-house. —gebirge, *n.* the back part of a chain of mountains. —gegend, *f.* the further end, the most remote part of a landscape or country. —gehäse, *n.* [among hunters] the hind part of a hare. 1. —gehen, *ir. v. tr.* [the accent on the third syllable] Einen —gehen, to deceive, cheat, gull any one, to take any one in, to impose upon any one. Er hat seine Richter —gangen, he deceived his judges, he imposed upon them; auch die Klügsten werden bisweilen —gangen, even the most cunning are sometimes caught. 2. —gehen, *ir. v. intr.* [the accent on the first syllable] to go or walk behind or to the furthest or remotest end of a place. —gefäß, *n.* V. Hintere, Gesäß. —geschirr, *n.* the back part of a horse's harness, the breechings. —geschühe, *n.* V. —leder. —gestell, *n.* the hind stand or frame and the hind part of any stand or frame. —glied, *n.* [in logic, the second proposition of a syllogism] the minor, [in mathematics] the consequent or last term of a ratio. Das Vorderglied und das —glied eines Verhältnisses, the antecedent and consequent of a ratio. [in military affairs] the rear rank or file. —grund, *m.* background. Der —grund eines Gemähldes, the background of a picture; der —grund der Schaubühne, the background of the stage; der —grund eines Thales, the bottom of a valley; im tiefsten —grunde dieses Engthales, in the remotest recess of this glen; der —grund des Wagens, the back seat or back part of the carriage. *Fig.* Wer weiß, was in der Zeiten —grunde schlummert [= was die Zukunft uns bringen wird], who knows what events lie concealed in the womb of futurity. —gurt, *m.* [in artillery] the vent-astragal, V. Kammerband. —haar, *n.* the hair at the back part of the head. Sie kräuselt sich das —haar hübsch, she curls her hair nicely behind; sie läßt sich das —haar um den andern Tag kräuseln, she has her hind locks curled every other day. *—haben, *ir. v. intr.* [the accent on the first syllable] to have swallowed. —halt, *m.* 1) [a concealed station where troops lie in wait to attack their enemy by surprise] ambush, ambuscade. Truppen in den —halt stellen, legen, to lay troops in ambush or ambuscade, to ambush troops; in einem Walde im —halte seyn or liegen, to lie in ambush or ambuscade, to lie perdue in a wood; sie hatten sich im Walde in den —halt gelegt, they had placed themselves in ambush or ambuscade in a wood; in einen —halt gerathen, fallen, to fall into an ambuscade; sie brachen aus dem —halte hervor, they rushed forth from their ambush; im —halte lauern, to lie in wait, to be upon the catch, to lurk; *fig.* er spricht nie, ohne bei dem, was er sagt, etwas im —halte zu haben, he never speaks without some mental reservation, he never speaks his mind freely or openly. 2) those placed in ambush, ambush, ambuscade. Einen —halt bestellen, to lay an ambush. *Fig.* a snare. Einem einen —halt legen, to lay a snare for any one. 3) [in military affairs] body of reserve. *Fig.* Einen starken —halt an Jemand haben, to be under a powerful protection. 4) [in chymistry] Der —halt des Scheidewassers, that silver which is left behind with the gold in the solution with aqua fortis. —halten, *ir. v. tr.* 1) [the accent on the third syllable] to hold or keep back, to withhold. Den Lohn eines Bedienten —halten, to keep [back] the wages of a servant, V. Zurückhalten. *Fig.* Einem Etwas —halten, to conceal or hide any thing from any one; ich will euch nichts —halten, I'll keep nothing back, I'll hide or conceal nothing from you; ich habe nicht gelernt, zu —halten, I have not learned the art of dissembling. 2) [the accent on the first syllable] to hold behind any thing. —hältig [—hältisch, in popular lang.], *adj.* and *adv.* reserved, close, secret. Ein —hältiger Mensch, one who dissembles, a dissembler, a hypocrite; *it.* a very reserved man. —haltung, *f.* [the accent on the third syllable] the act of retaining or keeping, retention. —hand, *f.* 1) the back part of the hand, [in anatomy] metacarpus. 2) [in farriery] Die —hand eines Pferdes, the hind quarters of a horse. 3) [at cards] Die —hand haben, in der —hand seyn, to be the younger hand. —haupt, *n.* the back or hind part of the head, [in anatomy] occiput. —hauptsadergang, *m.* V. —hauptsblutleiter. —hauptsbein, *n.* occipital bone. —hauptsblutader, *f.* occipital vein. —hauptsblutleiter, *m.* occipital sinus. —hauptsecke, *f.* occipital angle. —hauptsmuskel, *m.* occipital muscle. —hauptsnerve, *f.* occipital nerve. —hauptsschlagader, *f.* occipital artery. —haus, *n.* V. —gebäude. —her, *adv.* after, afterwards. —her gehen, to go or walk behind; —her that es ihm leid, he was sorry for it afterwards, V. Hinter. —hof, *m.* the back court-yard, back-yard. —kammer, *f.* back-chamber or room. —kastell, *n.* V. —castell. —keule, *f.* leg [of mutton, of pork &c.], V. —viertel. —klaue, —kralle, *f.* hind paw or claw. —kopf, *m.* V. —haupt. —kriechen, *ir. v. intr.* [the accent on the first syllable] to creep or crawl behind any thing. —laden, *m.* back-shop. —lage, *f.* a thing laid up, a thing deposited, deposit, V. Unterpfand. —laß, *m.* V. Nachlaß. —lassen, *ir. v. tr.* 1) [the accent on the third syllable] to leave behind. Er hat mir bei seiner Abreise ein Andenken —lassen, he has left me a token of remembrance at his departure; ein großes Vermögen, Schulden —lassen, to leave a great fortune, debts [at one's death], to die very rich, endebted; er hat sein Vermögen testamentlich einem Neffen —lassen, he has given by will, he has left or bequeathed his property to his nephew; die —lassenen Schriften Lessings &c., the papers or writings left by Lessing &c. at his death; die —lassenen Werke eines Schriftstellers, an author's posthumous works; die —lassenen, the relations of a person deceased, the survivors or heirs; die —lassene Wittwe, the relict; die —lassenen Erben, the heirs of a person deceased. *it.* to leave an order or direction. Er hat bei seiner Abreise —lassen, daß &c., he has given or left the order or direction at his departure, that &c.; er hat dem Bedienten —lassen, daß &c., he has left word with the servant, that &c.; er hat mir —lassen, Ihnen zu sagen, he has charged me, to tell you; er hat mir —lassen, ich sollte ihm folgen, he has left word for me to follow him. 2) [the accent on the first syllable] *a*) to allow or permit any one to go behind or to a remote place. *b*) [= hinunterlassen] to let go down. Die Geschwulst in dem Schlunde läßt bei ihm nichts —, the swelling in his throat prevents him from swallowing any thing. Syn. Hinterlassen, Verlassen, Zurücklassen. Verlassen refers merely to the departure of a person or thing from the place in which it before was. Zurücklassen refers to that which one does not take with one, but which may follow. Hinterlassen differs from Zurücklassen in so far, that das Hinterlassene [what is left behind] remains there and does not follow. —lassenschaft, *f.* property left by a person deceased, V. Verlassenschaft. —last, *f.* the load behind [on a waggon]. —lastig, *adj.* and *adv.* [in seamen's lang.] ein —lastiges Schiff, a vessel too much laden or freighted behind, a vessel overladen behind or by the stern. —laterne, *f.* [in seamen's lang.] poop-lantern. —lauf, *m.* [among hunters] the hindfoot or hind-leg. —laufen, *ir. v. intr.* [the accent on the first syllable] to run behind any person or thing. —leder, *n.* [among shoemakers] the hind quarter of a shoe. Das —leder niedertreten, to tread down at the heel. —legen, *v. tr.* 1) [the accent on the third syllable] to lay up, to deposit. Eine Summe Geldes bei Jemand —legen, to deposit a sum of money in somebody's hands; ein —legtes Gut, a deposit, V. —lage. 2) [the accent on the first syllable] to lay or put behind. —leger, *m.*, —legerinn, *f.* the person who deposits any thing. —legung, *f.* the act of depositing any thing. —leib, *m.* the hind or hinder part of the body. Der —leib eines Pferdes, the hind quarters of a horse; der —leib eines Kleides, the hind or back part of the body of a gown. —leik, *n.* [in seamen's lang.] after-leech of a stay-sail. —list, *f.* a sly, insidious artifice, wile, fraud, cunning. Mit —list zu Werke gehen, to make use of wiles, fraud or cheating; Einen mit —list fangen, to catch any one by craft, stratagem or circumvention. —listen, *v. tr.* to impose upon, to circumvent, delude or cheat any one, to take a person in. —listig, *adj.* and *adv.* sly, wily, cunning, insidious, artful, deceitful. Ein —listiger Kopf, a sly, wily or deceitful fellow, a cunning blade; —listige Geschenke, Liebkosungen, insidious presents, caresses; er hat es —listig gethan, he has done it slily or craftily; er hat mich auf eine —listige Art betrogen, he has deceived or cheated me insidiously or treacherously. —listigkeit, cunningness, V. —list. —locke, *f.* a hind lock or curl. —luke, *f.* [in seamen's lang.] hatchway of the poop. —mann, *m.* he who is behind another, he who comes after another, hindman. Mein —mann drückte mich vorwärts, he who is or was behind me, pushed me forward. [in military affairs] man or soldier placed in the second or rear rank, rear-rank man, *it.* bringer-up; [at cards and other games] he who is to play immediately after another. Wer ist mein —mann? who comes or follows after me? *Fig.* [in seamen's lang.] V. Beiständer. —mast, *m.* [in seamen's lang.] the mizzen-mast, V. Besanmast. —naht, *f.* [among shoemakers] the seam on the hind quarter. —niederlaß, *m.* [among hunters] der —niederlaß einer Sau, the marks of the hind feet of a wild swine fully imprinted. —pfanne, *f.* [in salthouses] graduation-pan, V. Gradirpfanne. —pferd, *n.* thiller or thill-horse, the last horse of a team. —pforte, *f.* back-gate. [in seamen's lang.] Die —pforten, stern-ports, V. Kreuzpforten. —pfote, *f.* hind-paw, V. —klaue. —pommern, *n.* Eastern Pomerania. —quartier, *n.* [among shoemakers] hind quarter, V. —leder. *Fig.* [in popular lang., jocosely] back-side, breech, posteriors. —rad, *n.* hind-wheel. —rast, *f.* notch on the lock of a gun, V. Rast. —reihe, *f.* the last rank or file, V. —glied. *—rennen, *ir. v. intr.* [the accent on the first syllable] to run behind any person or thing, to run to a remote place. *—rücken, *v. tr.* and *intr.* [the accent on the first syllable] to move behind any person or thing or to a remote place. —saß, *m.* 1) a descendant. 2) subject, vassal. 3) V. Schutzverwandte. 4) V. Beisaß. —satz, *m.* [in logic, the third proposition of a syllogism] conclusion, V. Schlußsatz. —schanze, *f.* [in seamen's lang.] V. —castell. —schenkel, *m.* hind thigh or leg of a quadruped. —schiff, *n.* 1) ship or vessel which sails behind another. 2) the hind or hinder part of a ship, stern, poop. —schinken, *m.* ham of the hind part of a hog. —schlägel, *m.* hind quarter [particularly of a wild boar or wether]. —schlägel eines Hammels [Hammelsschlägel], quarter of mutton. —schleichen, *ir.* I. *v. tr.* [the accent on the third syllable] Einen —schleichen, to surprise any one by stealing or sneaking behind him, to creep or sneak behind any one. II. *v. intr.* [the accent on the first syllable] to steal or sneak behind any thing or away to a remote place. —schlingen, *ir. v. tr.* [the accent on the first syllable] (= hinunterschlucken) to swallow down. —schlucken, V. —schlingen. —schraube, *f.* V. Schwanzschraube. —segel, *n.* [in seamen's lang.] mizzen-sail. —seite, *f.* the back-part of any thing, back-side. —seitentakel, *n.* [in seamen's lang.] the running rigging of the mizzen-mast. —siedler, *m.* V. —saß 4). —sitz, *m.* back-seat. —spätig, *adj.* and *adv.* [among clothworkers] of unequal hair in length. —spill, *n.* [in seamen's lang.] double capstan. —sporn, *m.* [among goldbeaters] two thin iron bars which support the tinplate roll with the wire that is to be beaten. —stab, *m.* [in artillery] muzzle-astragal. —ständer, *m.* V. —stande. —ständig, *adj.* V. —stellig. —stande, *f.* [in papermills] the cleft post in which the hinder part of the swing is moved by means of a bolt. —stellen, V. —treiben. —stellig, *adj.* and *adv.* 1) insidious, treacherous. 2) [= rückständig] being in arrears, outstanding, due, owing. —stellige Schulden, outstanding debts. 3) [= rückgängig] retrogade. Etwas —stellig machen, to impede, to prevent any thing. —steven, *m.* [in seamen's lang.] stern-post. —stich, *m.* back-stitch. —streichen, *ir. v. tr.* 1) [the accent on the third syllable] to mark with an apostrophe, to apostrophize. 2) [the accent on the first syllable] to stroke or comb back or backwards [the hair &c.]. —strich [*Apostroph], *m.* apostrophe. —stube, *f.* back-room. —stück, *n.* 1) the hind or hinder piece or part of any thing. 2) [in seamen's lang., a cannon placed in a ship's stern to annoy a ship that is in pursuit of her] stern-chase. —stubel, *m.* [among locksmiths] the standing cramp-iron in the hind part of a lock. —tau, *n.* [in seamen's lang.] stern-fast. —theil, *n.* hind-part, back-part. Das —theil eines Hauses, the back, back-part or back-side of a house; das —theil eines Schiffes, the hinder part of a ship, the stern; auf das —theil [= den Hintern] fallen, to fall upon one's back-side. [among shoemakers] V. —leder, —quartier. —thor, *n.* back-gate. —thür, *f.* back-door. *Fig.* a subterfuge, shift, loop-hole, back-door. —treffen, *n.* rear of an army, body of reserve. —treiben, *ir. v. tr.* 1) [the accent on the third syllable] to drive back. *Fig.* Eine Sache —treiben, to prevent, impede, hinder, oppose or thwart any thing; er hat alle meine Absichten —trieben, he has baffled or thwarted all my designs. 2) [the accent on the first syllable] to drive behind any place or to a remote place. *—trinken, *ir. v. tr.* [the accent on the first syllable] to drink up or down. —troß, *m.* the baggage of an army. —verdeck, *n.* [in seamen's lang.] quarter-deck. —viertel, *n.* hind-quarter. Das —viertel eines Kalbes, a loin of veal; das —viertel eines Hammels, a quarter of mutton; —viertel eines Ochsen, a leg of beef. —wage, *f.* the hind spring-tree-bar of a coach or waggon. —wagen, *m.* the hind part or the hind wheels of a carriage. —wäldler, *m.* backwoods-man [in America]. —zange, *f.* the second or hind screw of a joiner's bench. —zeug, *n.* [among saddlers] crupper, *it.* breeching, V. Schwanzriemen. —ziehen, *ir.* I. *v. tr.* 1) [the accent on the third syllable] [in law]

V. Unterschlagen. 2) [the accent on the first syllable] to draw, drag or pull behind any thing or to a remote place. II. *v. intr.* [the accent on the first syllable] to remove to the backpart of a house.

2. **Hinter**, *adv.* [in familiar lang. = hinunter] down. —schlucken &c., to swallow down &c.

Hintere, *m.* [-n or Hintern, *pl.* -n] the backside, posteriors, breech. Er fiel auf den —n or Hintern, he fell upon his backside, [jocosely] upon his seat of honour; Einem einen Tritt vor den Hintern geben, to kick any one's backside or arse. *Fig.* Er gab seinem Bedienten einen Tritt vor den Hintern, he turned his servant out of doors. V. Arsch, Bürzel 3), Steiß.

Hinterhalb, *prep.* [governing the genitive case] on the hinder or farther part. —halb des Berges, on the other side of or behind the hill or mountain.

Hinterrücks, *adv.* backwards, back and from behind. —rücks fallen, to fall backwards; Einen —rücks anfallen, to attack any one from behind. *Fig* secretly, insidiously, unknown to any one. —rücks meiner, behind my back, without my knowledge.

Hinterwärts, *adv.* backwards and from behind. — sehen, to look backwards or behind one's self; Einen — anfallen, to attack any one from behind, V. Rückwärts.

||**Hintsch**, *m.* [-es] 1) shortness of breath, asthma. 2) [in botany] bitter-sweet.

Hintschkraut, *n.* V. Hintsch 2).

Hinüber, *adv.* over to that side, over, across [it is opposed to herüber, and denotes motion over or across a place away from the person speaking; it is much used in composition of verbs; but these compounds being very easily understood, we subjoin only a few by way of example].

Hinüber-bringen, *ir. v. tr.* to bring, carry, transport or convey over to that side. Etwas über den Fluß —bringen, to transport or convey any thing over or across the river. —eilen, *v. intr.* to make haste, to hasten over to that or the other side. —fahren, *ir.* I. *v. tr.* to transport or convey over to that side in a carriage, ship or boat. II. *v. intr.* to pass or cross over to that side in a carriage, ship or boat.—fahren, *n.*, —fahrt, *f.* passage over or across to that side, V. Ueberfahrt. —fliegen, *ir. v. intr.* to fly over to the other side, to that side. —fließen, *ir. v. intr.* to flow or run over to the other side, to that side. —gang, *m.* the act of going or passing over to that side. —gehen, *ir. v. intr.* to go, walk or pass over to the other side, to that side, to cross. Die Franzosen sind über die Alpen —gegangen, the French passed the Alps; nachdem ich über diesen Acker —gegangen war, after I had crossed that field; über die Straße —gehen, to cross over the street. —heben, *ir. v. tr.* Einen über einen Graben &c. —heben, to help any one over a ditch &c. by taking him up. —helfen, *ir. v. intr.* Einem —helfen, to help any one in getting over any thing or to that side; *it. fig.* *to despatch any one; Einem über die Rinne —helfen, to help any one over the gutter. —kommen, *ir. v. intr.* to get or come over to that side. —lassen, *ir. v. intr.* to let or suffer any one to go or pass over to that side. —laufen, *ir. v. intr.* to run over to that side. —reichen, I. *v. intr.* to reach or extend over to that side. II. *v. tr.* Einem Etwas —reichen, to reach or hand any thing over to any one. Er reichte ihm einen Teller über den Tisch —, he reached or handed him a plate over or across the table. —schwimmen, *ir. v. intr.* to swim over or across to that side. —setzen, I. *v. tr.* to set or put over to the other side. II. *v. intr.* to pass, get or leap over to that side. Das ganze Heer setzte über den Rhein —, the whole army crossed or passed the Rhine; er setzte über den Graben —, he leapt [over] the ditch. —springen, *ir. v. intr.* to leap or jump over to that or the other side. Ueber eine Hecke —springen, to leap [over] a hedge. —steigen, *ir. v. intr.* to mount, climb or get over any thing or to that side. —werfen, *ir. v. tr.* to throw or fling over to that side. —wollen, *ir. v. intr.* to be willing, to wish or want to go, pass or cross over to the other or that side. —ziehen, *ir.* I. *v. tr.* to draw, drag or pull over to that side. II. *v. intr.* to remove to that or the other side.

Himúm, *adv.* about, round that way; [it denotes motion about a body away from the person speaking and is opposed to Herum, which see.]

Hinúnter, *adv.* [denoting motion or direction from a higher to a lower place away from the person speaking] down. Zur Treppe —, die Treppe —, down the stairs; — mit ihm! down with him! throw him down! V. Hinab. [The compounds of Hinunter are so easily understood, that we subjoin only a few by way of example].

Hinunter-bringen, *ir. v. tr.* to bring down. —essen, *ir. v. tr.* to eat, to swallow down. —fallen, *ir. v. intr.* to fall down. —helfen, *ir. v. intr.* to help in getting down. *Fig.* *Dieser Arzt hilft vielen Kranken —, this physician dispatches a good many patients. —schlingen, —schlucken, *v. tr.* to swallow [down]. *—seyn, *ir. v. intr.* to have gone down or descended. Er ist schon —, the has already gone down; die Sonne ist —, the sun has set. —springen, *ir. v. intr.* to leap or jump down. —treiben, *ir. v. tr.* to drive down. —trinken, *v. tr.* 1) to drink, to drink up. 2) to drink down.

Hinunterwärts, *adv.* downwards, V. Hinab.

Hinweg, *m.* [-es, *pl.* -e] way to a place or thither. Ich begegnete ihm auf dem —e, I met him on my way thither; *prov.* er hat den — für den Herweg gehabt, he has had his labour for his pains.

Hinwég, *adv.* away. — von hier! away! be gone! be off! — von mir! be gone or get away from me! —, Sie Schmeichler! away, you flatterer! — mit euch! get ye gone! go your ways! hence, away! diese Bedenklichkeiten fallen nun — [weg], these scruples are now removed.

Hinweg-arbeiten, —begeben, —blasen &c., V. Wegarbeiten, Wegbegeben &c. —nehmen, *ir. v. tr.* to take away. *Fig.* Gott hat ihn —genommen, V. Hinnehmen, Wegnehmen.

Hinz, *m.* [*pl.* -e] [probably allied to the old hind = jener] [in popular lang.] 1) the same as Heinz, which see; it is also used for man in general, as in the following and similar phrases: Es kümmert mich nicht, was — oder Kunz dazu sagen wird, I don't care what people will say to it, I don't mind people's talk. 2) = Kater, male cat, tom-cat.

Hinzu, *adv.* 1) [denoting motion towards a place away from the person speaking] towards or to that place, thither. 2) [denoting increase or augmentation] to that, to it; V. Dazu.

Hinzu-bauen, *v. tr.* and *intr.* to add to a building. —begeben, *v. r.* sich, V. Hinbegeben. —bekommen, *ir. v. tr.* to receive or get besides, over and above. —bitten, *ir. v. tr.* 1) to invite to a place. 2) to invite to others. Er hat noch mehrere Freunde —gebeten, he has invited some more friends. —bringen, *ir. v. tr.* to bring to a thing, to add to it, V. Hinbringen. —denken, *ir. v. tr.* to add in one's thoughts. Sie mögen das Uebrige sich — denken, you may guess the rest. —dichten, *v. tr.* to invent and add, to forge [a part of a story &c.]. Die Wahrheit rein heraussagen, ohne Etwas — zu dichten, to tell the plain truth without adding any thing of one's own to it. —drängen, *v. r.* sich, —dringen, *ir. v. intr.* to press or crowd to or towards a place. Er drängt sich überall —, he thrusts himself in every where. —eilen, *v. intr.* to make haste, to hasten thither or there. —fügen, *v. tr.* to add. Sie müssen etwas —fügen, you must add something to it; zu einem Vertrage eine Einschränkung —fügen, to put a clause to a treaty; V. Beisetzen. —fügung, *f.* addition; [in grammar] apposition. —führen, *v. tr.* 1) to lead or conduct to or towards. 2) to lead or conduct to others. —gang, *m.* the act of going or drawing near, approach. —gehen, *ir. v. intr.* to go or advance towards or to, to approach. —gehören, *v. intr.* to belong to; to be of the party. —gießen, *ir. v. tr.* to add by pouring, to pour to something. —kommen, *ir. v. intr.* 1) to come up to, to approach, to arrive at. 2) to be added. Zu dieser Rechnung muß noch —kommen, to this account must yet be added; eine andere Schwierigkeit kam noch —, another difficulty was started; es kommt noch —, daß &c. add to it, that &c. *—können, *v. intr.* V. Hinkönnen. —kriechen, *ir. v. intr.* to creep or crawl to or towards a place, to approach creeping or crawling. —kunft, *f.* a coming to, accession. Ohne —kunft eines Menschen, without the aid or cooperation of any body; V. —thun. —lassen, V. Hinlassen. —laufen, *ir. v. intr.* to run to or towards a place, to run thither. —legen, *v. tr.* to put to it, to add. —locken, *v. tr.* to draw or entice to a place. —machen, —reiten, —rennen, —rücken, —schiffen, —schleichen, V. Hinmachen &c. —schreiben, *ir. v. tr.* to add in writing. —schreiten, *v. intr.* V. —gehen, Hingeben. —schütten, —schwimmen, V. Hinschütten, Hinschwimmen. —setzen, *v. tr.* to put any thing close to another, to add. Eine Bedingung zu einem Vertrag —setzen, to put a condition or clause to a contract; es ist unmöglich, setzte er —, it is impossible, added he; V. —fügen. —setzung, *f.* V. —fügung. —thun, *ir. v. tr.* [in fam. lang. = —fügen] to add. Das ist nicht genug, thut noch ein wenig —, that is not enough, add yet a little more. Das —thun, addition. *Fig.* Ohne Jemands —thun, without any body's aid, assistance or cooperation. —tragen, *ir. v. tr.* 1) to carry to or towards a place. 2) to carry or put any thing to another or others. —treiben, *ir. v. tr.* 1) to drive to or towards a place. 2) to drive to others. —treten, *ir. v. intr.* 1) to step up to, to approach or advance towards a place. 2) to step up to others. —tritt, *m.* the act of stepping up to, of approaching a place or person. —wagen, V. Hinwagen. —wälzen, *v. tr.* to roll towards a place or thither; to roll any thing to another or others. —wandern, V. Hinwandern. —weben, V. Einweben. —zählen, *v. tr.* to add counting or telling, to count with the rest.

Hiob, *m.* [-s, *pl.* -e] [a proper name] Job. *Fig.* Hiobs-bote, *m.* a messenger of bad news. —post, *f.* Job's post, unhappy intelligence, calamitous information. —thränen, *pl.* [in botany] Job's tears, V. Thränengras. —trost, *m.* Job's comfort. —tröster, *m.* Job's comforter.

1. **Hippe**, *f.* [*pl.* -n] [allied to kappen = schneiden] *a*) a scythe, a sickle. Man stellt den Tod mit einer — vor, Death is represented with a scythe. *b*) [in gardening] a bill, hedging-bill, pruning-bill. *c*) [among bookbinders] V. Schneidehobel.

2. **Hippe**, *f.* [*pl.* -n] [perhaps allied to the Fr. *oublie*, and to be reduced to heben] a thin hard cake made of milk, flour, eggs and sugar, a wafer. Zusammengerollte or Hohl—n, rolled wafers.

Hippen-bäcker, *m.* wafer-maker. —eisen, *n.* wafer-iron[s]. —junge, *m.* a lad that sells wafers, wafer-boy. —krämer, —träger, *m.* wafer-man.

Hippel, *f.* [*pl.* -n] V. 2. Hippe.

*Hippiatrik, *f.* farrier's art, farriery, veterinary art.

*Hippokras, *m.* [a medicinal drink composed of wine, sugar, cinnamon and other spices] hippocrass.

Hippokrates, *m.* [*pl.* -sse] [a proper name] Hippocrates *Fig.** [jocosely] physician, doctor.

Hippokratisch, *adj.* Hippocratic. [in medicine]. Ein —es Gesicht, [pale, sunken and contracted features, considered as a fatal symptom in disease] Hippocratic face.

Hippokrazien, *pl.* [in botany] Hippocratea.

*Hippolith, *m.* [-es, *pl.* -e] [in mineralogy, a stone found in the stomach or intestines of a horse] hippolith, V. Pferdestein.

Hippolyt, *m.* [-s, *pl.* -e] [a name of men] Hippolytus.

Hirn, *n.* [-es, *pl.* -e] *dim.* —chen, ||—lein, *n.* [-s, *pl.* -] [allied to the Germ. Horn, Sax. *Hyrn*] brain, brains; *dim.* the little brain, [in anatomy] cerebellum, cerebel. Einem das — einschlagen, to beat any one's brains out, V. Gehirn; [among carpenters and joiners] über —sägen, to saw obliquely, slantly or slantwise. *Fig.* [in popular lang.] the understanding Im — verrückt seyn, to be crack-brained or crazy, to have cracked brains.

Hirn-anhang, *m.* [in anatomy] hypophysis. —balken, *m.* [in anatomy, a medullary prominence in the brain which joins the two lateral parts or hemispheres of the cerebrum] corpus callosum. —balkenschlagader, *f.* artery of the corpus callosum. —beschirmer, *m.* [in surgery, an instrument, contrived to guard the brain] meningo-phylax. —blasenwurm, *m.* hydatid or hydatis of the brain. —blatt, *n.*, *dim.* —blättchen, ||—blättlein, *n.* [in anatomy, place at the top of the skull where the sutures meet] fontanel, fons pulsatilis. —blutader, *f.* vein of the brains, cerebral vein. —bohrer, *m.* trepan. —brecher, *m.* V. —reißer. —bruch, *m.* rupture, crack of the brain —brücke, *f.* V. —knoten. —brüten, *n.* [in popular language] melancholy madness. —brütig, *adj.* and *adv.* [in popular language] afflicted with melancholy madness, delirious; *it.* distracted, mad, raving. —deckel, *m.* V. —schale. —entzündung, *f.* inflammation of the brain. —fell, *n.* V. —haut. —fläche, *f.* superficies or surface of the brain. —geburt, *f.* creation of the brain, creature of the imagination, whim, fancy, chimera, phantom. —gespenst, —gespinnst, *n.* [the same as: —geburt; which see]. —gespinnstisch, *adj.* and *adv.* merely imaginary, fantastic, chimerical, V. Träumerisch. —gewebe, *n.* V. —geburt. —gewölbe, *n.* the vault of the brain, medullary vault. —grille, *f.* [in nat. hist.] 1) bastard thistle-finch, serin. 2) a kind of wood-pecker, nutjobber. 3) *Fig.* V. —geburt, —gespenst. —grundschlagader, *f.* [in anatomy] basilary artery. —haut, *f.*, *dim.* —häutchen, ||—häutlein, *n.* the skin covering the brain, membrane of the brain; [in anatomy] meninge. Die feste or obere —haut, dura mater; die untere —haut, pia mater. —hautbruch, *m.* V. —bruch —höhle, *f.* vault of the brain. —kammer, *f.* cell of the brain, V. —höhle. —kelter, *f.* [in anatomy] place in the brain where the four bloodvessels of the dura mater meet. —klappe, *f.* valve of the cerebellum. —klopfen, *n.* the beating or pulsation of the brain. —knoten, *m.* [in anatomy] annular protuberance of the brain. —krank, *adj.* and *adv.* afflicted with a distemper of the brain. **Fig.* disordered in the understanding, brain-sick, distracted, frantic. —krankheit, *f.* distemper of the brain. **Fig.* defect or disorder of the understanding, brainsickness, frenzy, V. —wuth. —kraut, *n.* [in botany] eyebright, euphrasy. V. Augentrost. —kreise, *pl.* [in anatomy, the turnings and windings of the exterior substance of the brain] epispheria. —küchlein, *n.* V. —schnitte. —lappen, *m.* [in anatomy] lobe of the brain. —lehre, *f.* craniology, cranioscopy. —los, *adj.* and *adv.* without brain, having no brain. *Fig.* without understanding, silly, brainless. Ein —loser Kopf, a hare-brained fellow, a wild head; eine —lose That, a mad deed or action. —mark, *n.* [in anatomy] medullary substance of the brain, medulla cerebri. Das verlängerte —mark, medulla oblongata or spinalis, the spinal marrow. —masse, *f.* the substance of the brain. —pfanne, *f.* V. —schale. —reißer, *m.* [in popular lang., jocose] very bad wine, heady wine. —rotz, *m.* [in farriery] the glanders. —schädel, *m.* brain-pan, skull. —schädelbein, *n.* V. —schädelknochen. —schädelbeinmark, *n.* [the medullary substance between the plates or tables of the skull] diploe, meditullium. —schädelbruch, *m.* fracture of the skull. —schädelfuge, *f.* suture of the cranium or skull. —schädelhaut, *f.* [the membrane covering the skull] pericranium. —schädelknochen, *pl.* the plates or tables of the cranium or skull. —schädellehre, *f.* V. —lehre. —schädelnaht, *f.* V. —schädelfuge. —schale, *f.* V. —schädel, Schädel. —schalenmoos, *n.* usnea, cup-thong. —scheidewände, *pl.* [in anatomy] two tables or laminae of the cranium or skull. —schlagader, *f.* artery of the brain, cerebral artery. —schnitte, *f.* a slice of bread and calf's brain. —schwiele, *f.* V. —balken. —spalt, *m.*, —spalte, *f.* [in anatomy, a foramen in the brain] vulva cerebri; *it.* V. Gehirnspalt. —spinngewebe, *n.* [a thin membrane which is spread over the brain and pia mater] arachnoid tunic, the arachnoid. —spuk, *m.* chimera, fancy, phantom, vision. —stein, *m.* [in mineralogy] encephalites. —toben, *n.* violent agitation of the brain; V. —wuth. —toll, *adj.* V. —wüthig. —trichter, *m.* [in anatomy] infundibulum cerebri, funnel of the brain. —verrückt, *adj.* [in popular lang.] V. —wüthig. —weh, [more usual: Kopfweh] *n.* head-ache. —wunde, *f.* wound or injury of the brain. —wurst, *f.* a sausage made of brains, brain-sausage, cervelas. —wuth, *f.* [in popular lang.] brain-fever, phrensy. —wüthig, *adj.* and *adv.* [in popular lang.] afflicted with the brainfever, mad, frantic, raving. —zergliederung, *f.* anatomy of the brain.

||Hirnlein, *n.* [-s, *pl.* -] *dim.* of Hirn, the little brain, cerebel or cerebellum. V. Hirn.

Hirsch, *m.* [-es, *pl.* -e] [L. Sax. Hart, Sax. *heort*, Eng. *hart*, Dan. *hiord*, Sw. *hjort*, D. *hert*, either from the old hurra = laufen, or from the old hurten = stoßen] 1) stag, hart. Der zweijährige —, brocket; ein —, der sein zweites Geweih aufgesetzt hat, a stag four years old; ein kaum jagdbarer — von 10 Enden (= ein 6 jähriger), a stag six years old; ein jagdbarer — von 10 Enden [= ein 7 jähriger], a stag seven years old; die —e sind in der Brunst or Brunft, brunften, the stags are rutting; der — tritt in die Brunft, the stag goes to rut; hören Sie die —e schreien or brüllen? do you hear the stags bray or [in rutting time] bell, troat? das Lager des —es, the lair or lodge of the stag; der — kann nicht mehr fort, the stag is at bay; der — verfehlt die Spur, [the stag puts his hindfoot beyond the forefoot] the stag overreaches. V. Damhirsch, Spießhirsch. 2) [in natural history] *a*) a kind of porcelain-shell *b*) capricorn-beetle, V. Bockkäfer.

Hirsch-baum, *m.* the stag's-horn tree, sumach, V. Gärberbaum. —bein, *n.* 1) V. —lauf. 2) [a hard cross-formed gristle at the heart of the stag] the cross of the stag, the heart-bone of the stag. —bezoar, *m.* V. —kugel. —bisam, *m.* V. —thräne. —bock, *m.* 1) the male red-deer, stag. 2) [a species of wild sheep in Africa &c.] musmon, musimon. 3) [an insect] capricorn-beetle of America, V. Holzbock —braun, *adj.* V. —farben. —brunst, —brunft, *f.* 1) the rut or rutting season of deer, V. Brunst. 2) [a kind of mushroom] morel; *it.* V. —trüffel. —brust, *f.* the breast of a stag. —bürsche, *f.* the shooting or chase of stags. —dorn, *m.* V. Kreuzdorn. —eber, *m.* the Indian hog or babyroussa. —fährte, *f.* the track or foiling of a stag. —fänger, *m.* a hanger. —farbe, *f.* fallow colour. —farben, —farbig, *adj.* and *adv.* deer-coloured, fawn-coloured, fallow. —feiste, *f.* the time or season when the stags are fat. —fink, *m.* green-finch, chloris. —fuß, *m.* V. —lauf. —futter, *n.* 1) food for deer. 2) V. —wurz. —gallerte, *f.* jelly of rasped hartshorn, hartshorn-jelly. —garn, *n.* a large net for catching stags. —garten, *m.* deer-park. —gehege, *n.* pasture, feeding or viands of deer. —geilen, *pl.* V. —hoden. —gelos, *n.* [among hunters] the dung of deer, fumets. —gerecht, *adj.* and *adv.* skilled in hunting the stag, perfect in deer-hunting. Ein —gerechter Jäger, one skilled in huntsmanship, a good huntsman. —geschrei, *n.* the braying of the stag. —geweih, *n.* the horns or head of a stag, antlers —gras, *n.* [in botany] hartshorn plantain, hartshorn. —günsel, *m.* [in botany] sweet maudlin, V. Wasserdost. —hals, *m.* a stag's neck. —haut, *f.* a stag's skin or hide. —heil, *n.* V. —wurz. —hoden, *pl.* the testicles of a stag, doucets or dowcets. —holder, —holunder, *m.* 1) the water-elder, V. Bachholder. 2) mountain elder, V. Bergholunder. —horn, *n.* 1) the horn of a stag, V. —geweih. 2) hartshorn. Geraspeltes —horn, hartshorn raspings; gebranntes —horn, burnt or calcined hartshorn. —hornbaum, *m.* V. —baum. —hörnern, *adj.* and *adv.* made or consisting of hartshorn. —hornflechte, *f.* [in botany] 1) Iceland-moss. 2) [weiße Baumflechte] the common ragged hoary lichen. —horngallerte, *f.* V. —gallerte. —horngeist, *m.* hartshorn spirit or the spirit of hartshorn. —hornkäfer, *m.* 1) the gray-coloured weevil or mite. 2) V. —käfer. —hornöl, *n.* hartshorn-oil. —hornsalz, *n.* the salt of hartshorn, hartshorn-salt. —hornzinke, *f.* small branch of a stag's head. —hund, *m.* stag-hound. —jagd, *f.*, —jagen, *n.* stag-chase, stag-hunt or hunting. —käfer, *m.* horn-beetle, stag-beetle. —kalb, *n.* fawn. —kameel, *n.* the camel of Peru, glama. —kasten, *m.* a box in which a stag is conveyed, stag-cart. —katze, *f.* V. —luchs. —keule, *f.* the haunch of a stag or deer. —klaue, *f.* V. —schale. —klee, *m.* V. —günsel, Wasserdost. —kohl, *m.* V. —mangold. —kolben, *m.* [among huntsmen] the young or little horn of a stag. —kolbenbaum, *m.* V. —baum. —kopf, *m.* a stag's head. —krankheit, *f.* [a disease in stags and horses] stag-evil, hart-evil. —kreuz, *n.* V. —bein 2). —kugel, *f.* [a calcareous concretion found in the stomach of stags] stag's bezoar. —kuh, *f.* the female of the stag, hind. —lager, *n.* the lair or lodge of a stag. —lattich, *m.* colt's-foot. V. Huflattich. —lauf, *m.* [among huntsmen] foot or leg of a stag. —leder, *n.* leather prepared from the hide or skin of a stag, buckskin. —ledern, *adj.* and *adv.* made of leather prepared from the hide of a stag, buckskin. —**lederne Handschuhe**, buckskin gloves. —**losung**, *f.* V. —geloß. —**luchs**, *m.* lynx, lusern. —**mangold**, *m.* —**melde**, *f.* lung-wort. —**möhre**, *f.* [in botany] parsnip. —**münze**, *f.* [in botany] white dittany, garden-ginger. —**netz**, *n.* V. —garn. —**niere**, *f.* stag's kidney. —**pastete**, *f.* venison-pasty. ||—**peterlein**, *n.* parsley, V. Petersilie —**plan**, *m.* [among huntsmen] place where the stags meet. —**polei**, *m.* V. —münze. —**reh**, *n.* a kind of African roebucks without beard and horns. —**ruf**, *m.* [among huntsmen] a horn to call the stags by imitating their voice. —**ruthe**, *f.* yard or pizzle of a stag. —**schale**, *f.* the edge of a stag's hoof. —**schlägel**, *m.* V. —keule. —**schröter**, *m.* stag-beetle, stag-fly. —**schuh**, *m* [among hunters] track of a stag after the rain. —**schwaden**, *m.* [among huntsmen] the single of a stag. —**schwamm**, *m.* V. —brunft 2). —trüffel. —**schwanz**, *m.* 1) V. —schwaden. 2) [in botany] danewort, dwarf-elder, wallwort. —**schweiß**, *m.* [among huntsmen] blood of the stag; *it.* blood of the stag, milk and bread given to the hounds as a reward. —**sprung**, *m.* the sole of the foot of a stag. —**stein**, *m.* V. —kugel. —**thier**, *n.* or Stier—, *m.* buffle, buffalo. —**thräne**, *f.* [a yellow matter which is engendered in the sockets of the stag's eyes; it grows hard by degrees and is used against epilepsy] lachrymae cervi. —**trüffel**, *f.* a kind of truffle, hart's or stag's truffle. —**wildbret**, *n.* 1) the stag, *it.* the hind. 2) stag-venison. —**wolf**, *m.* V. —luchs. —**wundkraut**, *n.* V. —klee. —**wurz**, *f.* 1) hartsfodder, hartwort. 2) large mountain-parsley. 3) white gentian. —**zähre**, *f.* V. —thräne. —**ziege**, *f.* the female of the musmon or musimon, V. —bock 2). —**ziemer**, *m.* 1) the back of a stag without the legs and haunches. 2) V. —ruthe. —**zunge**, *f.* 1) a stag's tongue. 2) [in botany] hartstongue. —**zungenkraut**, *n.* V. —zunge 2).

Hirschling, *m.* [-es, *pl.* -e] [in botany] V. Hirschbrunst 2).

Hirse, *f.* [*pl.* -n.] or *m.* [-ns, *pl.* -n] millet. Die Indische —, the Indian millet, millet-indian; die Italienische —, Italian pannick; wilde —, V. Blut—.

Hirsebrei, *m.*, —**fieber**, *n.* &c. V. Hirsenbrei, Hirsenfieber &c.

Hirsenacker, *m.* a field of millet, millet-field. —**bau**, *m.* the cultivation or culture of millet. —**brei**, *m.* pap or flummery made of millet, millet-pap. —**drüse**, *f.* [in anatomy, a gland resembling a millet-seed] miliary gland. —**feld**, *n.* V. —acker. —**fieber**, *n.* [a fever accompanied with an eruption like millet-seed] miliary fever. —**fink**, *m.* green-finch, chloris. —**flechte**, *f.*, —**geflecht**, *n.* miliary tetter. —**gras**, *n.* pannick-grass, millet-grass. —**grütze**, *f.* V. —brei. —**knauer**, *m.* V. —stampfer. —**korn**, *n.* 1) millet-seed. 2) a little hard pimple growing in the pores of the skin, maggot. —**körnicht**, *adj.* and *adv.* resembling millet-seeds, miliary. Die —körnichten Drüsen, V. —drüse. —**pfriemer**, *m.* [in popular lang.] one who stands upon trifles, punctilious fellow, V. Kleinigkeitskrämer. —**stampfe**, *f.* a mill for pounding millet. —**stampfer**, *m.* one who pounds millet. —**stein**, *m.* [in mineralogy, a precious stone with specks resembling millet-seeds] cenchritis. —**vogel**, *m.* V. —fink, Grünfink.

Hirt, *m.* [-en, *pl.* -en] [Sax. *heard*, *hyrde* &c. Dan. and Icel. *hyrde*, Eng. and Sc. *herd*, as in goat-herd; from the old verb hiren, hirten = wahren, warten, Fr. *garder*] [one who has the care of flocks and herds] a herdsman or herdman, a pastor, herd. Ein junger—, a swain. V. Gänse—, Kuh—, Ochsen—, Rinder—, Schaf—, Schweine—, Ziegen—. *Fig.* [in Scripture, God and Christ are denominated Hirten, shepherds] Ein guter — läßt sein Leben für seine Schafe, the good shepherd giveth his life for his sheep; der geistliche —, der —, der Seelen—, minister of the Gospel, clergyman, pastor; V. Seelen—, Seelsorger.

Hirtenamt, *n.* the charge or office of a herdsman; [chiefly] *fig.* the office of a minister of the Gospel, or pastor, pastoral office, care or duties. —**art**, *f.* pastoral manners. —**brief**, *m.* pastoral letter. —**dichtart**, *f.* pastoral or bucolic poetry. —**dichter**, *m.* a writer of pastorals, a bucolic. —**fest**, *n.* a pastoral festival. —**flöte**, *f.* 1) pastoral flute, rural, oaten pipe. 2) [in botany] star-headed water-plantain, Damasonium, V. Wasserwegerich. —**gedicht**, *n.* pastoral poem, bucolic, eclogue. Die —gedichte des Virgil und Theokrit, the bucolics or eclogues of Virgil and Theocritus; V. —gespräch. —**gericht**, *n.* V. —stab 2). —**gesang**, *m.* pastoral song, V. —gedicht. —**gespräch**, *n.* [*Ekloge] pastoral dialogue, eclogue. —**gott**, *m.* the God of shepherds, Pan. —**göttinn**, *f.* the Goddess of shepherds, Pales. —**haus**, *n.* herdsman's or shepherd's house. —**hund**, *m.* herdsman's or shepherd's dog, V. Schäferhund. —**hütte**, *f.* herdsman's or shepherd's hut. —**junge**, *m.* V. —knabe. —**kittel**, *m.*, —**kleid**, *n.* a herdsman's or shepherd's smockfrock or coat; *it.* pastoral dress or habit. —**knabe**, *m.* herdsman's or shepherd's boy. —**lager**, *n.* encampment of wandering shepherds or herdsmen. —**leben**, *n.* pastoral life. —**lied**, *n.* pastoral song. —**lohn**, *m.* wages of a herdsman or shepherd. —**los**, *adj.* and *adv.* without herdsman or shepherd; *fig.* without a chief or ruler. —**lust**, *f.* pastoral mirth or diversion. —**mädchen**, *n.* a young shepherdess; *it.* a herdsman's or shepherd's daughter. —**mäßig**, *adj.* and *adv.* suiting a herdsman or shepherd, pastoral, shepherdlike. —**pfeife**, *f.*, —**rohr**, *n.* V. —flöte. —**säckel**, *m.* V. —tasche. —**schauspiel**, *n.* pastoral. —**schutt**, *m.*, —**schütte**, *f.* corn or grain given to a herdsman or shepherd instead of his wages. —**spiel**, *n.* V. —schauspiel. —**stab**, *m.* 1) shepherd's crook or staff, pastoral staff; *fig.* [of a bishop or abbot] bishop's crosier. 2) pastoral jurisdiction. —**stand**, *m.* pastoral condition. —**stück**, *n.* pastoral. —**tasche**, *f.* 1) a herdman's or shepherd's bag, pouch or scrip. 2) [in botany] shepherd's pouch, shepherd's purse —**volk**, *n.* herdsmen or shepherds and shepherdesses; *it.* pastoral tribe, pastoral nation. —**welt**, *f.* pastoral life or manners.

Hirtenhaft, *adv.* V. Hirtenmäßig.

Hirtinn, *f.* a herdsman's wife, a shepherdess.

Hirtlich, *adj.* and *adv.* pastoral, rustic. —es Leben, pastoral life.

Hisse, *f.* [*pl.* -n] [Dan. *hisse*, Sw. *hissa*; allied to hoch, the Fr. *hausser*] [in seamen's language] a kind of windlass for raising weights and particularly for hoisting a sail, tackle.

Hisseblock, *m.* V. Blockrolle 2).

Hissen, *v. tr.* to hoist [a sail].

Hißtau, *n.* [in seamen's lang.] a rope for hoisting or lowering a sail, a halliard.

Hist! [an exclamation used by drivers or waggoners, directing their teams to pass further to the left, opposed to Hott] hoi or haw.

***Histiodromie**, *f.* the art of navigation [by means of sails], histiodromia. V. Schifffahrtskunst.

***Histörchen**, *n.* [-s, *pl.* -] a little or petty tale, story. Er hat uns ein artiges — erzählt, he has told us a pretty story; V. Geschichtchen.

***Histörie**, *f.* [*pl.* -n] 1) a story, narrative, tale. 2) history.

Historienbuch, *n.* book of history, historical book, V. Geschichtbuch. —**mahler**, *m.* V. Geschichtmahler. —**schreiber**, *m.* historian, historiographer.

***Histöriker**, *m.* [-s, *pl.* -] V. Geschichtschreiber.

***Histörisch**, *adj.* and *adv* historic, historical. —e Schreibart, historical style; ein —er Kalender, a historical almanac; — erzählen, to relate historically. V. Geschichtlich.

Hitze, *f.* [Dan. *hoede*, Sw. *heta*, Sax. *heat*, *heate*, Eng. *heat*; allied to heiß]. 1) [any accumulation of the matter of heat or caloric] heat. Die — des Feuers, der Sonne, the heat of the fire, of the sun, die — des Schmelzofens, the heat of the furnace; fließende —, welding heat, V. Schweiß—. *it.* particularly, the great warmth of the atmosphere. Eine unerträgliche —, intolerable heat; die — ist sehr groß, es ist eine große —, it is very hot weather; eine gemäßigte —, temperate heat. *Fig.* Des Tages Last und — tragen, to bear the weight and heat of the day; to fatigue one's self; to exert one's self. 2) [calorific or heating quality] Der Wein hat —, wine is warming; die Gewürze haben —, spices are hot. 3) [sensation of a high degree of warmth] Viel — haben, to have a great heat; eine innerliche —, interior heat; eine — vertreibt die andere, one heat another heat expels; die — des Fiebers, the burnings heat, height or paroxism of a fever; auf die —, in der — darf man nicht trinken, when one is hot or heated, one must not drink. *Fig.* In der — der Jugend, in the heat of youth; die jugendliche — im Zaume halten, to curb the impetuosity of youth; in der — des Gefechts, des Spieles, in the heat of the fight, of the play; in — gerathen, to grow hot, to fly into a passion; Einen in — bringen, to put any one into a great heat or passion, in der ersten —, in the first heat of passion; mit — arbeiten, to work eagerly, with eagerness; seine — mäßigen, to moderate one's ardour; die — verlieren, von der — nachlassen, to grow cool, to cool, to abate; *das Ding wird — haben [= wird schwer halten], it will be difficult; ohne — [= mit Ueberlegung], with deliberation, considerately, calmly. 4) the time when any thing is in a state of heat; [among huntsmen = Brunft] rut, rutting-time. 5) a sign of heat; *fig.* [in veterinary art, the juice distilling from the genitals of a mare in the time of her being in pride] hippomanes. 6) what is made by one heat. Eine — Brod, as much bread as is baked at one time, a baking of bread, a batch. *Fig.* Als ob sie dieselben in einer — schlügen, as if they struck them at a heat.

Hitzblase, —**blatter**, *f.*, *dim.* —**bläschen**, —**blätterchen**, *n.* a [red] pustule, pimple, wheal. —**blütig**, *adj.* and *adv.* having hot blood; *fig.* passionate, heady, hasty. —**blütigkeit**, *f.* quality of being passionate or hasty, a passionate or hasty temper, passionateness. —**butter**, *f.* melted butter. —**kopf**, *m.* *fig.* [in fam. lang.] a hot-headed, hasty or passionate man. —**köpfig**, *adj.* and *adv.* hot-headed, hot-brained, hasty, passionate. —**messer**, *m.* [an instrument for measuring the expansion of bodies by heat] pyrometer. —**messung**, *f.* the act of measuring the expansion of bodies by heat. —**mittel**, *n.* a heating remedy, a medicine of an inflammatory nature. —**monat**, *m.* that month which is generally hottest [with us, July or August].

Hitzen, *v. intr.* 1) to be hot, to experience heat. 2) to cause or give heat. Der Wein hitzt, wine heats the blood, is heating; Holzkohlen — besser als Torf, charcoal gives a greater heat than turf or peat.

Hitzig, *adj.* and *adv.* 1) causing heat. Ein —es Fieber, an inflammatory or burning fever; ein —es Getränke, —e Gewürze, heating drink, hot spices. 2) having or indicating heat. Ein —er Boden, a very fat soil; ein —es Klima, hot climate; —es Eisen, iron white with heat; *eine —e Leber haben [=gern viel trinken], to be given or addicted to drinking. *Fig.* Ein —er Kopf, a boisterous, hot, passionate or hasty spirit; *er ist — vor der Stirne, wird leicht —, he is hasty or passionate, hot-headed, he takes fire presently; eine Sache — angreifen, to undertake, to do, to apply to any thing with eagerness; *— auf Etwas seyn, to be set or bent upon any thing; Einen — verfolgen, to pursue any one eagerly or hotly; er sprach —, he spoke with great warmth, passionately; *da ging es sehr — zu, there was very warm or hot work; *nicht so —! [gemach], soft or softly, fair and softly, hold there! ein allzu—es Pferd, a horse too full of mettle; ein —es Gefecht, a hot engagement; eine —e [= läufige] Hündinn, a bitch at heat.

Hö! Hohö or **hö! hö!** *interj.* ho or hoa, ho there! holla!

1. **Hobel**, *m.* [-s, *pl.* -] [probably from hob, preter. of heben] [among tin-founders Formmantel] the top or crown of a mould. V. Mantel.

2. **Hobel**, *m.* [-s, *pl.* -] [originally Hauel, from hauen, Eng. *to hew*, Sax. *heawian*] [a joiner's] plane. V. Bank—, Beschneide—, Grund—, Hohl—, Kehl—, Scharf—, Schlicht—.

Hobel=bank, *f.* joiner's or carpenter's bench. **—binde**, *f.* [in surgery] a kind of truss. **—diamant**, *m.* glazier's diamond. **—eisen**, *n.* the iron of a plane, plane-iron. **—förmig**, *adj.* and *adv.* having the form of a plane; [in botany] hatchet-shaped. **—gehäuse**, *n.* the stock of the plane, plane-stock. **—kasten**, *m.* [among bookbinders] shaving-tub. **—klinge**, *f.* V. —eisen. **—span**, *m.*, **—späne**, *pl.* shavings [brought off by the plane]. **—spänbinde**, *f.* V. —binde. **—spanpapier**, *n.* paper made of shavings of wood.

Hobeln, *v. tr.* to plane, to smooth with a plane. *Fig.* [in popular lang.] Einen —, to polish any one; es ist ein junger Mensch, der noch sehr gehobelt werden muß, he is a young fellow that wants a great deal of polishing.

Hoboe, *f.* [*pl.* -n] hautboy. — spielen, blasen, to play on the hautboy.

Hoboist, *m.* [-en, *pl.* -en] performer on the hautboy.

Hoch, [Icel. *ha*, Sw. *ha* and *hoeg*, Sax. *heah*, Dan. *hoi*, W. *uch*, allied to heben] I. *adj.* and *adv.* 1) [opposed to low and deep.] Ein hoher Berg, Thurm, a high mountain, a lofty tower; ein hoher Baum, a high, tall or lofty tree; die höhern or höher gelegenen Theile der Erde, the higher parts of the earth; der Adler fliegt —, the eagle flies at a great height; *prov.* wer — steigt, fällt tief, the higher standing, the lower fall; *es ist mir zu — [= ich kann es nicht erreichen, *it. fig.* kann es nicht begreifen], it is too high for me, it is above my reach, I cannot reach it, *fig.* it is beyond the compass of my understanding; eine hohe Stirne, a high forehead; sie hat eine hohe Schulter, she has one shoulder higher than the other; zehn Fuß —, ten feet high; [in the military science] drei Mann —, three men in depth, three deep; hohe Absätze habend, high-heeled; [in seamen's lang.] das Meer ist —, die See geht or steigt —, the sea is rough or high, there is a heavy sea; die hohe Fluth, high-water; der Fluß geht —, the river is swelled; die hohe See, main sea, offing, sea-room; in die hohe [offene] See fahren, to stand out to sea, to stand for the offing; — or dicht beim Winde segeln, to sail near or by the wind, to sail close-hauled; [among sportsmen] der Hirsch geht — or ist — verreckt, the stag has recovered his antlers; [in forges] der hohe Ofen [Hohofen], furnace; [in mining] das hohe Gebirge, the highest part of a mountain; [am. foresters] der hohe Wald, V. —wald; [in military affairs] Gewehr —! recover arms! *Die Sonne steht —, the sun is high; *prov.* man muß nicht höher fliegen wollen, als Einem die Flügel gewachsen sind, one must not spend beyond one's means, one must not undertake things above one's abilities, no flying without wings. *Fig.* [denoting the existence of any quality of a thing in a high degree] *a*) [applied to colours =] strong, vivid, deep. Hohe Farben, high colours; ein hohes Roth, a vivid or deep red; die hohe blaue Farbe, the deep blue colour. *b*) [in music, applied to sounds, opposed to low or grave =] acute, sharp. Ein hoher Ton, a high sound or tone; ein Tonwerkzeug höher stimmen, to raise the tone of, to tune up an instrument; das Klavier um einen Ton höher stimmen, to raise the harpsichord a note higher; eine hohe Stimme, a high voice; eine zu — gestimmte Laute, a lute tuned too high; *fig.* *er spricht aus einem hohen Tone, he talks at a high rate, in a high strain, haughtily. *c*) [applied to time:] *α*) [to the time of the day] Es ist noch — am Tage, it is still high or broad day; es ist schon hoher Tag, the sun is already very high, it is already broad day-light. *β*) [to the time of life] Ein hohes Alter, an advanced age, great or old age; ein hohes Alter erreichen, to arrive at, to come to, to reach a great age; Einen — leben lassen, to drink any one's health; sie brachten ihm ein —, they drank his health. *γ*) [to the time past] Das hohe Alterthum, high antiquity; höher hinaufsteigen [ins Alterthum], to go farther back [to antiquity]. *δ*) [to the circumstances of the time] full, extreme, utmost. Es ist hohe Zeit, it is high time; es war die höchste Zeit, there was not a moment to be lost. *d*) [in business and commerce =] dear or dearer than usual. Ein hoher Preis, a high rate or price; zu hohen Preisen verkaufen, to sell dear; wie — kommt Sie dieses Buch zu stehen? how much does this book cost you or stand you in? — einkaufen, to purchase at a high rate; wie — hat er dies angerechnet? how much did he charge for that? Sie rechnen es sehr — an, you rate it very high, V. Anrechnen; — spielen, to play deep or high; der Geldkurs, die Münze steht —, cash is at a high premium, money bears great interest. *e*) [opposed to insignificant, unimportant, mean or paltry] Die höhern Wissenschaften, the upper or abstruse sciences; die höhere Geometrie, transcendental geometry; die höhern Klassen, the upper forms or classes; ein hoher Verstand, an eminent or transcendent understanding; *das ist mir zu —, that's beyond or above my reach or capacity; das höchste Gut, the supreme good, the summum bonum; hohe Worte, sublime, noble words; das Hohe [= Erhabene], the sublime; Gott ist das höchste Wesen, God is the supreme Being; ein hohes Fest, a high or solemn festival; ein hoher Tag, a high or solemn day; die hohe Woche, the holy week; die hohe Messe, das hohe Amt, V. —amt; der hohe Altar, V. —altar; [in Scripture] das hohe Lied Salomonis, Solomon's Song; die höhere Schreibart, the elevated, sublime or high style; [among huntsmen] hohes Wildbret, V. —wildbret; die hohe Jagd, the hunting of the higher sort of game, such as stags, deer, wild-boars; hoher Rang, high rank; hohe Würde, high dignity; auf einem hohen Fuße leben, to live in high or great style; Hohe und Niedere, high and low; der hohe Adel, the nobility [in England, dukes, marquesses, earls, viscounts and barons]; die hohe und niedere Geistlichkeit, the high clergy and low clergy; der hohe Priester [Hohepriester], high-priest; die hohe Pforte, the sublime Port; ein hohes Stift, V. —stift; ein höherer Richter, a superior judge; ein hohes Geschlecht, a noble, high or illustrious race or family; eine hohe [= vornehme] Person, a person of quality or distinction, of the first rank, an illustrious person; die Hohen der Welt, the high and mighty [ones]; in hoher Person [= selbst], in person; der König hat es mit eigener hoher Hand unterzeichnet, the king has signed it with his own hand; Eure Durchlaucht wollen mir die hohe Gnade erweisen, may it please your Serene Highness to do me the favour; ich habe das von hoher Hand, I have it from a high quarter; die höchste Stufe des Ruhmes, the highest pitch, the pinnacle of glory; in hohem Grade, in a high degree; in höchstem Grade übermüthig seyn, to be excessively or superlatively insolent; hohe Gerichte, V. —gericht 2); ein hohes Verbrechen, a capital crime; Etwas bei hoher Strafe verbieten, to forbid any thing under a grievous penalty; einer Sache einen hohen Werth beilegen, sie — halten, to make much of a thing; [in grammar] der höhere Grad [*Comparativ], the comparative; der höchste Grad [*Superlativ], the superlative; wenn es — kommt, auf's höchste, at most; wenn es auf's höchste kommt, when the worst comes to the worst; when all comes to all; Etwas — aufnehmen, to be strongly or sensibly affected with, to be very sensible of any thing; *Etwas — empfinden [= Etwas sehr übel nehmen], to resent highly or strongly, to take any thing very ill, in ill part; *— aufhorchen, to open both the ears, to prick up one's ears; sie ist — schwanger, she is near her reckoning, far advanced in pregnancy; *ich versichere Sie — und theuer, I assure you by all that is sacred; *— und theuer schwören, to swear by all that is sacred; *sich — versündigen, to sin grievously; — hinaus wollen, to have or form grand or lofty designs, to aim at great things; *mit seiner Waare — hinaus wollen, to overrate one's merchandise, to ask too high a price for one's merchandise; *es zu — anfangen, to undertake any thing above one's abilities, or more than one is able to perform, to begin in too high a strain, *it.* to carry it high, to be mounting a note too high; *er steht — am Brete beim Minister, he is in great favour with the minister; *es — bringen, to go far, to make one's way in the world, to make one's fortune; *er wird es nicht — bringen, he will not make his way, or push his fortune; *it.* he cannot live long; *es in einer Kunst —, auf's höchste bringen, to bring an art to a high degree, to the highest degree of perfection; — achten, schätzen, to esteem highly; ich achte die Ehre höher, als das Leben, I value honour above life; das Höchste, was ich thun kann, ist &c., the utmost I can do, is &c.; in höchster Eile, in the greatest haste or hurry. II. *adv.* in a great degree, very, highly. Ich bin — erfreut, I am very glad, most delighted; Bewegung ist für die Gesundheit höchst nöthig, exercise is highly requisite to health; diese Nachricht ist höchst wichtig, this intelligence is of the highest or utmost importance.

Hoch=achtbar, *adj.* and *adv.* highly to be respected, [an epithet of respect] honourable. —

achten, *v. tr.* 1) Etwas —achten, to esteem highly, to set a high value on something. 2) Einen —achten, to esteem, to respect any one. Er wird allgemein —geachtet, he is esteemed by every body; sich selbst —achten, to be possessed of self-estimation, *it.* to have a high opinion, to make much of one's self. —achtung, *f.* esteem, respect, regard. Einem seine —achtung bezeigen, to pay one's duty or respects to any one. —achtungsvoll, *adj.* and *adv.* respectful. Er grüßt Sie —achtungsvoll, he presents his respects to you. —adelig, *adj.* and *adv.* of very noble extraction, of the nobility, most noble. —altar, *m.* high altar. —amt, *n.* [in the Romish church] high mass, grand mass. Das —amt halten, to say high mass. —ansehnlich, *adj.* and *adv.* highly respectable. —begabt, *adj.* and *adv.* highly endowed, highly gifted. —beglückt, *adj.* and *adv.* most happy. —begünstigt, *adj.* and *adv.* highly favoured. —beherzt, *adj.* and *adv.* very courageous. —beinig, *adj.* and *adv.* high-legged, long-legged. *Fig.* [in pop. lang.] labouring under hunger and scarcity. —bejahrt, *adj.* and *adv.* stricken with years, [very] aged. —bekümmert, *adj.* and *adv.* highly concerned, grieved or afflicted. —belobt, *adj.* and *adv.* highly praised. —bemastet, *adj.* having a high or taunt mast or masts, high or taunt-masted. —berühmt, *adj.* and *adv.* highly renowned. —beschlagen, *adj.* and *adv.* [among sportsmen] big with young, near the time of bringing forth. —betagt, *adj.* and *adv.* V. —bejahrt. —betraut, *adj.* and *adv.* trusted in a high degree, very trusty. —betroffen, *adj.* and *adv.* highly astonished, perplexed or embarrassed. —betrübt, V. —bekümmert. —blau, *adj.* and *adv.* light blue, azure. —bootsmann, V. —botsmann. —bord, *n.* or —bordiges Schiff, or —bordschiff, *n.* [any vessel which is moved with sails, without oars] a high-built ship. ‡—bothe, *m.* V. Bothschafter. —botsmann, *m.* boatswain. —brüstig, *adj.* and *adv.* high-breasted. *Fig.* proud, arrogant, high-flown, conceited. —busig, *adj.* and *adv.* full-breasted. —dero, *pron.* [obsolescent for Ihr, Ihre] your. —deutsch, *adj.* and *adv.* high-German, high-Dutch. —deutschmeister, V. —meister. —dieselben, *pron.* [obsolescent for Sie] you. —edel, *adj.* and *adv.* [an epithet of address, particularly in letters] right-noble, right-worthy. —edler Herr! Eure —edeln! Sir! —edelgeboren, *adj.* and *adv.* [an epithet of address, particularly in letters] well and respectably born. —ehrwürdig, *adj.* and *adv.* [a title given to ecclesiastics] right reverend. —ehrwürdiger Herr! Eure —ehrwürden! right reverend Sir! your reverence. —eigen, *adj.* [used of high personages for Eigen] Der König hat es mit —eigener or Höchsteigener Hand unterzeichnet, the king has signed it with his own hand. —entzückt, *adj.* and *adv.* in ecstasy, ecstasied, highly enraptured, in trance. —erfahren, *adj.* and *adv.* highly experienced or skilful. —erfreut, *adj.* and *adv.* highly rejoiced, overjoyed. —erhaben, —erhoben, *adj.* and *adv.* very high or elevated, very sublime. [in sculpture] —erhobene Arbeit, alto-relievo. —erleuchtet, *adj.* and *adv.* highly enlightened. —ersprießlich, *adj.* and *adv.* highly useful, beneficial or salutary. —erstaunt, *adj.* and *adv.* greatly astonished or surprised, amazed. —erwähnt, *adj.* and *adv.* [said of high personages] above mentioned. —erzürnt, *adj.* and *adv.* highly irritated, very angry. —fahrend, *adj.* and *adv.* high-flown, lofty, haughty, imperious. —fahrt, *f.* V. Hoffahrt. —farbig, *adj.* and *adv.* high-coloured. —feierlich, *adj.* and *adv.* in a high degree solemn, most solemn. —fliegend, *adj.* and *adv.* high-flying, extravagant, enthusiastic. —fliegende Schreibart, an inflated, highflown, bombastic style; alle diese —fliegenden Plane, all those grand or lofty designs. —flieger, *m.* [in natural history, a kind of flying fish] kite-fish. —freiherrlich, *adj.* and *adv.* the same as freiherrlich, which see. —fürstlich, *adj.* and *adv.* [an epithet of address] high and princely. Eure —fürstliche Durchlaucht, Your Serene Highness. —garn, *n.* [among sportsmen] a net for catching partridges. —geachtet, *adj.* and *adv.* *part.* of —achten. —geberde, *f.* [rather high-flown] a high or lofty demeanour. —gebietend, *adj.* and *adv.* [epithet of address] high commanding, invested with high command. —gebietender Herr! dread or high and mighty lord! —gebirge, *n.* a chain of high mountains or the highest part of a chain of mountains. Schottlands —gebirge, the highlands of Scotland. —geboren, *adj.* and *adv.* [an epithet of address] high-born, right-honourable. —gebrüstet, *adj.* and *adv.* V. —brüstig. —gedacht, *adj.* and *adv.* V. —erwähnt. —geehrt, *adj.* and *adv.* [epithet of address] highly honoured. —gefärbt, V. —farbig. —gefühl, *n.* high feeling, enthusiasm. —gehörnet, *adj.* and *adv.* having high horns. —gelag, *n.* V. Gastmahl, Schmauß. —gelb, *adj.* vividly yellow. —gelehrt or ‡—gelahrt, *adj.* and *adv.* [title of address] highly learned, very learned. —gelobt, *adj.* and *adv.* [epithet of the Deity] exalted by praise, magnified, blessed. —geneigt, *adj.* and *adv.* highly favouring, gracious, most kind. —genuß, *m.* high enjoyment. —gepriesen, *adj.* and *adv.* greatly extolled or praised. —gericht, *n.* 1) place of execution, the place where the gallows are erected, the gallows. 2) [generally used in the plural, die —gerichte] high justice, high jurisdiction. 3) [among birdcatchers] gins or springes for catching birds. —gerichtsherr, *m.* the lord who is invested with high jurisdiction. —geruch, *m.* high, strong or refined smell. —gerühmt, *adj.* and *adv.* highly praised. —gesang, *m.* ode, hymn. —geschätzt, *adj.* and *adv.* much esteemed. —geschmack, *m.* 1) a strong taste. 2) *Fig.* high or refined taste. —geschürzt, *adj.* and *adv.* having one's clothes tucked up high. *Fig.* bustling, active. —gesegnet, *adj.* and *adv.* highly blessed. —gesinnt, *adj.* and *adv.* high-minded. —gestirnt, *adj.* having a high forehead. —gewild, *n.* V. —wild. —gewitter, *n.* V. Gewitter. —graf, *m.* V. Oberrichter. —gräflich, *adj.* and *adv.* the same as gräflich, which see. —grün, *adj.* and *adv.* of a vivid green. —halbgeschlagen, *adj.* [among goldbeaters] — halbgeschlagene Goldblätter, high-coloured gold-leaves. —halsig, *adj.* high or long-necked. —halten, *ir. v. tr.* V. —achten. —heilig, *adj.* and *adv.* in a high degree holy. *—her, *adv.* from above; *fig.* of noble extraction. —herzig, *adj.* and *adv.* high-minded, high-spirited, magnanimous; *it.* [rather unusual] proud, V. also —fahrend. —herzigkeit, *f.* high-mindedness, magnanimity. —holz, *n.* [among foresters] top-branches of a tree. —horn, *n.* hautboy, V. [the more usual word] Hoboe. —hornbläser, *m.* player on the hautboy, V. [the more usual word] Hoboist. —jährig, *adj.* and *adv.* V. —bejahrt. —kettig, *adj.* having an upright loom, of the high warp. —kettige Teppiche, tapestry of the high warp. —klingend, *adj.* and *adv.* loud sounding. *Fig.* —klingende Worte, Titel, high-sounding words, titles; eine —klingende Rede, a pompous speech. —kraut, *n.* [in botany] V. Dill. —land, *n.* mountainous country, high-country, high-land. Das schottische —land, the highlands of Scotland. —länder, *m.*, —länderinn, *f.* mountaineer, highlander. —lautend, *adj.* V. —klingend; [among hunters] ein —lautender Hund, a hound who cries or challenges at finding the scent of the game. —lehrer, *m.* [rather unusual] professor at a university. —lehreramt, *n.* [rather unusual] —lehrerstelle, *f.* professorship. —leuchter, *m.* [in botany] spiked willow. —lied, *n.* V. —gesang. —löblich, *adj.* and *adv.* [an epithet used in addresses to certain magistrates or authorities] very laudable, worshipful. —mahl, *n.* V. —gelag. —mastig, *adj.* V. —bemastet. —maul, *n.* a kind of salmon. —meister, *m.* grand-master. Der —meister des deutschen Ordens, der —deutschmeister, grand-master of the Teutonic order. —meisterthum, *n.* grand-masterdom. —messe, *f.* V. —amt. —mögend, *adj.* and *adv.* high puissant, high and mighty. Ihre —mögenden or —mögenheiten, their high mightinesses. —muth, *m.* 1) [obsolete] high spirits, high and noble sentiments. 2) haughtiness, arrogance, pride, superciliousness. Einem den —muth benehmen, to bring down any one's pride. *Prov.* —muth kommt vor dem Fall, pride will have a fall, pride goes before and shame follows after. —müthig, *adj.* and *adv.* haughty, arrogant, proud. Eine —müthige Miene, a haughty air, er antwortete auf eine —müthige Art, he answered haughtily or proudly; —müthig auf Etwas seyn, to be proud of, to pride one's self to a thing. **Fig.* —muthsteufel, *m.* haughty spirit. Der —muthsteufel ist in ihn gefahren, he is puffed up with pride. —nöthig, *adj.* and *adv.* highly necessary, indispensable. —nothpeinlich, *adj.* and *adv.* [little used] criminal, V. Peinlich. —pflaster, *n.* high pavement; [in Scripture] pavement. —preislich, *adj.* and *adv.* [chiefly used as an epithet in addresses to certain authorities] highly praiseworthy. —priester, *m.* highpriest, pontiff. Der römische —priester [Papst], the sovereign pontiff, the pope. —priesteramt, *n.*, —priesterthum, *n.*, —priesterwürde, *f.* pontificate. —priesterlich, *adj.* and *adv.* pontifical. —randig, *adj.* and *adv.* having a high border, edge or margin. —reister, *m.* perching-sticks, V. [illegible] —rosenroth, *adj.* and *adv.* of a bright rose colour. —roth, *adj.* and *adv.* of a vivid red colour, crimson. —rücken, *m.* V. —[illegible] —rückig, *adj.* and *adv.* high-backed. —rund, *adj.* and *adv.* [*convex] convex, V. Runderhaben. —ründe, —rundheit, *f.* [*Convexität] convexity. —sänger, *m.* he that sings the treble, V. [the more usual word] Discantsänger. —schäftig, *adj.* and *adv.* V. —kettig. —schätzbar, *adj.* and *adv.* highly estimable or valuable, highly respectable. —schätzen, *v. tr.* to esteem highly. —schenkelig, *adj.* and *adv.* having high thighs or high legs. —schneidig, *adj.* and *adv.* sharp-edged, very cutting. Ein —schneidiger Grabstichel, a triangular graver. —schule, *f.* university. —schüler, *m.* student at a university. —schulterig, *adj.* and *adv.* 1) having high shoulders, high-shouldered. 2) having one shoulder higher than the other. —schuß, *m.* [among hunters] a shot in the air, a shot that goes too high. —schwanger, *adj.* and *adv.* far advanced in pregnancy. Sie ist —schwanger, she is near her time or reckoning. —segelfisch, *m.* surgeon-fish. —selig, *adj.* and *adv.* Der —selige König, the deceased or late king. —sinn, *m.* high sentiment, enthusiasm. —sinnig, *adj.* and *adv.* high-minded, high-spirited, magnanimous. Syn. Hochsinnig, Stolz. Stolz expresses the inordinate and unreasonable conceit of our own excellence; hochsinnig, that noble self-esteem springing from the consciousness of worth which prevents a man from doing or suffering any thing which might demean him. —stämmig, *adj.* having a high stem, lofty. Ein Wald, Gehölz von —stämmigen Bäumen, ein —stämmiger Wald, V. —wald. —stift, *n.* 1) the chapter of a cathedral. 2) bishopric. Das —

stift Hildesheim, the bishopric of Hildesheim. —stiftskirche, *f.* cathedral, collegiate-church. —stimme, *f.* [in music, *Discant] treble; *it.* V. —sänger. —strebend, *adj.* high aspiring. —stück, *n.* [in cookery] chine. —teutsch, V. —deutsch. —tönend, V. —klingend. *Fig.* —trabend, *adj.* and *adv.* high-sounding, high-flown, pompous, bombastic. Ein —trabender Mensch, an ostentatious man; —trabende Worte, high-sounding words; eine —trabende Schreibart, an inflated, high-flown, bombastic style. —traber, *m.* a high-trotting horse. —verdient, *adj.* and *adv.* highly meritorious, very deserving, very worthy. —vereckt, *adj.* [among hunters] having got all the broaches or branches [said of a stag]. —vermögend, *adj* and *adv.* very mighty or potent. —vernünftig, *adj.* and *adv.* very reasonable or sensible. —verrath, *m.* high-treason. —verräther, *m.* a man guilty of high-treason. —verrätherisch, *adj.* and *adv.* treasonable. —verständig, *adj.* and *adv.* very wise or judicious. —vieh, *n.* V. Rindvieh. —wache, *f.* 1) a watch stationed on a mountain. 2) watch-fire on a mountain, beacon. —wächter, *m.* a watchman or sentry stationed on a mountain or tower. —wald, *m.* a wood of high or tall trees, of timber-trees. —warte, *f.* a watch-tower on a mountain. —weg, *m.* high-road. —weise, *adj.* and *adv.* wise in a high degree, highly or most wise [often used as an epithet in addressing certain magistrates or authorities]; *it.* [ironically] over-wise. —werth, *adj.* and *adv.* highly dear, greatly beloved. —wichtig, *adj.* and *adv.* highly important, very weighty. —wild, —wildbret, *n.* the higher sort of game, such as wild boars, stags, deer &c. —wohledel, —wohledelgeboren, *adj.* [title of address] well-born, well-descended gentle. Eure —wohledelgeboren, Your Honour. —wohlehrwürdig, *adj.* [title of address to the clergy] reverend. Eure —wohlehrwürden, reverend Sir. —wohlgeboren, *adj.* [title of address to distinguished persons] nobly born, high and noble, right honourable. Eure —wohlgeboren, right honourable Sir. —würdig, *adj.* [title of address to the higher class of the clergy] very or right reverend. Eure —würden, Your Reverence. *it.* [in the Romish church] highly venerable, sacred, holy. Das —würdigste, the host. —zuehrend, —zuverehrend, *adj.* V. —geehrt.

Höchheimer, *m.* [-s] [a very generous Rhenish wine, the produce of the vineyards of Hochheim, a village in the Duchy of Nassau, and its neighbourhood] Hock. Lassen Sie uns eine Flasche — trinken, let us drink a bottle of old Hock.

Höchlich, *adv.* highly, in a high degree. Ich bin — erfreut, I am highly rejoiced, overjoyed; sich — versündigen, to sin grievously.

Höchsel, *n.* [-s, *pl.*-] a thing put under another for the purpose of raising or heightening it.

Höchst, *superl.* of Hoch. —dieselben, —dero, —nöthig, *superl.* of Hochdieselben, Hochdero, Hochnöthig.

Höchstens, *adv.* at most, at the most. Er ist — dreißig Jahre alt, he is thirty at most; es wird Sie — fünf Gulden kosten, it will cost you five florins at most.

Höchzeit, *f.* [*pl.* -en] 1) [obsolete, in general] any time of festivity; hence formerly, a feast at court, a princely banquet. 2) [now] wedding, nuptials, nuptial festival, bridal. Die — in Kana, the marriage in Cana; am Tage seiner —, on his wedding-day; — machen, haben, halten, to celebrate one's wedding or nuptials, to marry; zur — bitten, einladen, to invite to the wedding; ich war auf der —, I was at the wedding; auf die — gehen, to go to a wedding. 3) [in familiar lang.] the company at a wedding. Die ganze — ging in das Theater, all the guests at the wedding went to the play. 4) the consummation of marriage; *it.* cohabitation, V. Beilager, Beischlaf.

Hochzeits-band, *n.* a coloured riband, such as are used to be distributed among the younger guests at a country-wedding. —bett, *n.* nuptial bed, bridal bed, V. Brautbett. —bitter, *m.*, —bitterinn, *f.* a person employed to invite people to a nuptial feast. —brief, *m.* letter of invitation to a wedding. —fackel, *f.* nuptial torch. —feier, *f.*, —fest, *n.* the celebration of nuptials, nuptial festival, nuptials. —gast, *m.* guest at a wedding. —gedicht, *n.* a nuptial song or poem, wedding-song, marriage-song, epithalamium, epithalamy. —gepränge, *n.* nuptial pomp. —gesang, *m.* V. —lied. —geschenk, *n.* [a present made on the wedding-day by the guests to the new married couple] wedding-present. —gott, *m.* Hymen, V. Ehegott. —haus, *n.* the house in which a wedding is celebrated. —kleid, *n.* nuptial or wedding-garment, wedding-gown or dress. Die —kleider, the wedding-clothes. —kosten, *pl.* the charges or expenses of a wedding. —kranz, *m.* a wreath of flowers or myrtle worn by virgins on their wedding-day, nuptial wreath or garland. —kuchen, *m.* wedding-cake, bride-cake. —kutsche, *f.* the bridal carriage which conveys the betrothed couple to church. —leute, *pl.* guests at a wedding. —lied, *n.* marriage-song, wedding-song, V. —gedicht. —mahl, *n.* wedding-feast, wedding-dinner, marriage-feast. —mäßig, *adj.* and *adv.* suitable to or becoming a wedding, as at a wedding. —mutter, *f.* a woman who furnishes the expenses of a wedding to her daughter or to another person, generally, the mother of the bride. —nacht, *f.* nuptial night, first night after marriage. —paar, *n.* V. Brautpaar. —predigt, *f.* wedding-sermon, nuptial sermon. —rede, *f.* nuptial speech. —redner, *m.* he who makes the nuptial speech. —saal, *m.* the hall or room for the wedding-feast. —schleier, *m.* the veil of the bride. —schmaus, *m.* V. —mahl. —schmuck, *m.* bridal ornaments. —spiele, *pl.* games or diversions at a wedding. —stube, *f.* V. —saal. —tag, *m.* wedding-day. —tanz, *m.* nuptial or wedding dance. —vater, *m.* a man who furnishes the expenses of a wedding to another person, generally, the father of the bride. —verse, *pl* V. —gedicht. —wagen, *m.* V. —kutsche. —wein, *m.* the wine drunk at a wedding, wedding-wine. —woche, *f.* first week after marriage, V. Flitterwoche. —zimmer, *n.* V. —stube.

Höchzeiter, *m.* [-s, *pl.*-] [now, only in popular lang.] bridegroom.

Höchzeiterinn, *f.* [now, only in popular lang.] bride.

Höchzeitlich, *adj.* and *adv.* nuptial, bridal. Ein —es Kleid, a wedding garment; — gekleidet, dressed like a person who goes to a wedding.

Höchzuehrend, &c. V. under Hoch &c.

Höck, *n.* [-es, *pl.* -e] [seems to be allied to hegen] a stable for cattle; [in seamen's lang.] *a)* a pen or cot in which sheep are inclosed on a ship's deck; *it.* hen-coop. *b)* — zu Masten, a mast pond or a place where the masts are kept in salt water in a dock-yard.

1. **Höcke**, *f.* [*pl.* -n] [allied to hoch, Höcker] 1) a heap of sheaves put together in a field. Die Garben in —n setzen, to put or set the sheaves in heaps. † and || 2) the back. Einen auf die — nehmen, to take any one on one's back; Einem die — voll schlagen, to curry any one's coat, to beat any one soundly. 3) [at backgammon] the last point of a row, the corner.

Höcken-blatt, *n.* V. Haukenblatt. —pflug, *m.* V. Hakenpflug. —spiel, *n.* [a play of children] leap-frog.

2. **Höcke**, *m.* [of the same root as 1. Höcke]. V. 2. Höcker.

†**Höckeln**, *v. tr.* to carry on the back.

†**Höcken**, I. *v. tr.* 1) to put or set in heaps. 2) Einen, to take any one upon one's back. II. *v. r.* and *intr.* 1) Auf Einen, to get upon the back of any one. Sich in einen Winkel —, to cower down in a corner. 2) to sit upon the hams or heels, to squat, to cower. *Fig.* *to be idle, to be inactive, to idle. Er hockt immer zu Hause hinter dem Ofen, he is always sitting in the chimney-corner, he never stirs from home.

Höcker, *m.* [-s, *pl.*-], **Hockerinn**, *f.* a person who puts the sheaves in heaps; [in seamen's lang.] V. Huker.

Hockerfalk, *m.* haggard or haggard-hawk.

1. **Höcker**, *m.* [-s, *pl.* -] [allied to hoch] [in general] any unevenness or inequality, as, ein Erdreich voll —, a rugged ground; then particularly a hump, hunch or ||hulch. Der — eines Kameeles, the hunch or hump of a camel; er hat einen —, he has a hump or hunch, he is hump-backed or hunch-backed. [in anatomy] knob.

Höcker-blatt, *n* V. Haukenblatt. —ochs, *m.* bison, V. Buckelochs.

2. **Höcker**, *m.*, —inn, *f.* [from the same root as 1. Höcker] huckster, hucksteress.

Höcker-frau, *f.*, —weib, *n.* V. Höckerinn.

Höckericht, *adj.* and *adv.* resembling or like a hunch or knob.

Höckerig, *adj.* and *adv.* 1) uneven, rough, rugged. Ein —er Weg, a rugged or uneven way or road; [in botany] eine —e Wurzel, a tuberous root; [in anatomy] der —e Theil der Leber, the protuberant part of the liver. *Fig.* Eine —e Schreibart, a rugged style. 2) hunch-backed, hump-backed, gibbous.

Höckern, V. Hocken.

Hocus Pocus, V. Hokus Pokus.

Höde, *f.* [*pl.* -n] [probably allied to hoch, Icel. *hatt*, Sax. hôd] testicle, stone. Die —n ausschneiden, wegschneiden, to deprive of the testicles, to castrate, to geld; die —n der Hirsche, doucets or dowcets.

Hoden-bruch, *m.* rupture of the scrotum, scrotal hernia, oscheocele, scrotocele. —förmig, *adj.* and *adv.* shaped like a testicle; [in botany] testiculate. —geschwulst, *f.* a swelling of the testicles, a venereal tumour. —haut, *f.* dartos. —kraut, *n.* fool-stones, orchis. —los, *adj.* and *adv.* without testicles, castrated. —masse, *f.* the substance or parenchyma of the testicles. —muskel, *m.* a muscle of the testicles, by which they are suspended and drawn up, cremaster. —sack, *m.* scrotum, purse. —sackförmig, *adj.* purse-shaped. —sackschlagader, *f.* artery of the scrotum. —wassergeschwulst, *f.* a tumour of the scrotum, oscheophyma.

***Hödometer**, *n.* V. Odometer.

Höf, *m.* [-es, *pl.* Höfe] [allied to Hag, haften, haben, old = einschließen] 1) that which surrounds or encompasses any thing. Der — um den Mond, die Sonne &c., halo, crown, V. Krone; der — um die Brustwarze, [the coloured circle round the nipple] areola, areole; der — um die Augen, circle. 2) [an open place, surrounded with a fence or wall] yard, court-yard; V. Bau—, Kirch—, Zimmer—. Ein Haus zwischen — und

Garten, a house between yard and garden; der — für das Federvieh, poultry-yard; V. Kloster—, Mist—, Schloß—, Vieh—. 3) [a building with a yard and the land attached to it] a farm, a grange. Ein Dorf von 20 Höfen, a village of twenty houses. *it.* a gentleman's estate or country-seat. V. Bauer—, Gast—, Herren—, Jäger—, Pfarr—, Zins—. 4) [the residence of a prince or sovereign and the persons composing his retinue or council] court. Kaiserlicher, königlicher —, imperial, royal court; an den — or nach — gehen, to go to court; die Tafel bei —e haben, to have one's board at court; bei —e etwas gelten, to be well at court; ein Befehl vom —e, an order from the court. *Fig.* Den — machen, to attempt to please by flattery and address, to make court; dem Könige den — machen, to pay or make one's court to the king; einer Dame den — machen, to court a lady, to make or pay one's addresses to a lady. 5) [little used] a [solemn] assembly or meeting; V. Gerichts—, Lehen—, Schützen—.

Hof-acker, *m.* a field or piece of ground belonging to a farm or manor. —advokat, *m.* an advocate or lawyer who has the right of pleading at the higher courts of justice, a sergeant at law. —agent, *m.* agent of the court; banker to the court. —amt, *n.* office or employment at court; office belonging to the household of the sovereign. —anwalt, *m.* V. —advokat. —apotheke, *f.* apothecary's shop attached to the court. —apotheker, *m.* apothecary to the court. —arbeit, *f.* 1) work done for the court. 2) work done for the lord of the manor, V. Frohnarbeit. —arbeiter, *m.* one who works for the court. —art, *f.* court-manner, ton of the court. —artig, *adj.* and. *adv.* courtly, in the manner of courts. —artigkeit, *f.* politeness, urbanity. —arzt, *m* physician to the court; physician in ordinary to the king &c. —bäcker, *m.* baker to the court. —bäckerei, *f.* bakery to the court. —banquier, *m.* banker to the court. —barbier, *m.* barber to the court. —bauamt, *n.* board of works [superintending the public buildings of the prince]. —bauer, *m.* a farmer or tenant subject to the lord of the manor; a serf. —beamte, *m.* a person in office about the court, an officer of a prince's household. —becker, *m.*, —beckerei, *f.* V. —bäcker &c. —bediente, *m.* a person in the service of the court, a servant employed about the court. —bedienung, *f.* service about the court. —befehl, *m.* order from the court. —befreit, *adj.* and *adv.* exempt from certain burdens by the court, privileged, patronised or protected by the court. —bescheid, *m.* resolution, decision or answer of the court. *Fig.* [ironically] a polite, but evasive answer. —bibliothek, *f.* library of the court. —bibliothekar, *m.* librarian to the court. —bier, *n.* [in popular lang.] very good beer, V. Herrenbier. —bildhauer, *m.* sculptor to the court. —böttcher, *m.* cooper to the court. —brauch, *m.* custom at court, usage of the court, court-fashion. court-etiquette. —brod, *n.* 1) bread for the court. *Fig.* —brod essen, to be in the service of the court, of a prince or sovereign. 2) [Frohnbrod] bread distributed to the socagers during socage-time. —buchdrucker, *m.* printer to the court. —buchhalter, *m.* book-keeper to the court. —buchhändler, *m.* bookseller to the court, bookseller to the king &c.; publisher in ordinary to the king &c. —burg, *f.* a castle being the palace or residence of the prince or court. Die —burg in Wien, the emperor's palace at Vienna. —capellan or —caplan, *m.* V. —kapellan. —capelle, *f.* V. —kapelle. —cavalier, *m.* a man of noble birth or rank in the service of the court, a courtier. Der erste —cavalier der Königinn, the queen's chamberlain. —ceremoniell, *n.* V. —brauch, —sitte. —commissär, *m.* a commissary appointed by the court. —commission, *f.* a commission appointed by the court. —compliment, *n.* court-compliment; *fig.* [ironically] fair empty words, court-holy-water. —conditor, *m.* V. —zuckerbäcker. —dame, *f.* 1) lady of honour to a queen or princess, court-lady. 2) [in nat. hist.] lion-puceron, V. Perlfliege. —degen, *m.* [*Galanteriedegen] dress-sword. —diener, *m.* 1) V. —bediente. 2) V. —bauer. —dienerschaft, *f.* all the persons in the service of the court, all the servants employed about the court. —dienst, *m.* 1) service performed for the court. Den —dienst haben, to be in waiting at court. 2) a place or employment at court. In —diensten stehen, to be in the service of the court, to serve or follow the court. 3) service performed for the lord of the manor. ‡—ding, *n.* V. —gericht. —drescher, *m.* one who is obliged to thrash for the lord of the manor. —einkäufer, *m.* purveyor to the court. —etat, *m.* V. —rechnung. —fähig, *adj.* and *adv.* having the right or privilege to appear, to make one's appearance at court. —faktor, *m.* factor or agent of the court. —falkenmeister, *m.* falconer to the court. —farbe, *f.* court-colour, livery. —fest, *n.* a fête or feast at court, gala-day. —fischer, *m.* fish-monger to the court. —fiskal, *m.* attorney of a court or prince. —folge, *f.* 1) the obligation of following the court. 2) V. —dienst 3). —fourier, *m.* an officer of a prince's household who provides lodgings and other accommodations for the court when travelling, court-harbinger, court-messenger. —fräulein, *n.* a maid of honour. —freiheit, *f.* 1) rights or privileges attached to the dignity of a prince. 2) an immunity or exemption enjoyed by persons belonging to the court. —freund, *m*, —freundinn, *f.* 1) a friend of the court. Er hat mehrere — freunde, he has several friends at court. 2) *Fig.* [ironically] a friend not to be depended upon, a court-friend. —freundschaft, *f.* 1) [in familiar language] friends at court. 2) *Fig.* [ironically] false friendship, court-friendship. —furier, *m.* V. —fourier. —futter, *n.* forage for the horses and cattle of the court. —futteramt, *n.* court-forage-office. —futtermeister, *m.* an officer who provides forage for the court. —futterschreiber, *m.* clerk of the court-forage-office. —gebrauch, *m.* V. —brauch. —gefolge, *n.* retinue of the court. —geräth, *n.* 1) all the utensils and implements belonging to a farm. 2) the kitchen-utensils of the court. —gericht, *n.* 1) a particular court of justice for the persons attached to the court. 2) court of agriculture. 3) a high court of judicature, superior court of justice. —gerichtsadvokat, *m.* advocate or barrister of a superior court of justice. —gerichtsassessor, —gerichtsbeisitzer, *m.* assessor of a superior court of justice. —gerichtsrath, *m.* counsellor of a superior court of justice. —gerichtsräthinn, *f.* the wife of such a counsellor. —gesinde, *n.* 1) all the persons belonging to the household of a prince or sovereign; all the persons in the service of the court. 2) the servants of the lord of a manor, of an opulent farmer &c. —gewehr, *n.* V. —wehr. —glück, *n.* fortune made at court. —gunst, *f.* court-favour. —gut, *n.* 1) domain, crown-demain, V. Kammergut. 2) demain or landed estate [opposed to a farm]. —halten, *ir. v. intr.* to keep court, to reside. —haltung, *f.* a prince's or sovereign's household, *it.* the place of residence of a sovereign prince, court. Seine —haltung an einem Orte aufschlagen, to take up one's residence at a place. —handwerker, *m.* a tradesman employed or patronised by the court. —häusler, *m.* a tenant who lives in a house belonging to the lord of the manor, for which he must do work for him. —herr, *m.* possessor of a landed estate, lord of the manor. —hieb, *m.* the reaping or cutting of corn for the lord of the manor, performed by a tenant or serf. —hörig, *adj.* and *adv.* belonging to the lord of the manor. —hund, *m.* 1) house-dog, watch-dog, mastiff. 2) a prince's dog; particularly hunting dog or hound. —jäger, *m.* huntsman or gamekeeper belonging to the court. —jägerei, *f.* 1) the body of huntsmen or gamekeepers belonging to the court. 2) the house of a huntsman or gamekeeper belonging to the court. —jägermeister, *m.* master of the chase to the prince. —jude, *m.* 1) [obsolescent] a Jew employed by the court in business, V. —faktor. 2) a Jew patronised or protected by the court. —jungfer, *f.* gentlewoman of the court. —junker, *m.* page, equerry. —kammer, *f* exchequer, exchequer-chamber. —kammerrath, *m.* counsellor of the exchequer. —kanzlei, *f.* chancery of a court. —kanzler, *m.* court-chancellor. —kapellan or —kaplan, *m.* court-chaplain; chaplain in ordinary to the king &c. —kapelle, *f.* 1) court-chapel. 2) a prince's private band, orchestra of a prince's opera. —kasse, *f.* treasury of the court. —kassenverwalter, *m.* [*—kassier], cashier or treasurer to the court. —kavalier, *m.* V. —cavalier. —keller, *m.* cellar of the court; a prince's cellar. —kellermeister, —kellner, *m.* butler to the court. —kirche, *f.* the church or chapel where the court goes to, court-chapel, V. Schloßkirche. —koch, *m.* cook to the court. —kriegsrath, *m.* 1) imperial council of war at Vienna. 2) imperial counsellor of war. —küche, *f* the prince's kitchen, *fig.* the officers of a prince's kitchen. —küchenamt, *n.* the office or officers of a prince's kitchen. —küchenmeister, *m* the master or intendant of a prince's kitchen. —küchenschreiber, *m.* the clerk of a prince's kitchen. —küfer, *m.* V. —böttcher. —kunst, *f.* art of a courtier. —künste, *pl.* court-intrigues, court-tricks. —lager, *n.* residence of the court. —lakei, *m.* footman or lackey in the service of the court. —leben, *n.* court-life. —lecker, *m.* a mean flatterer at court. —lehen, *n.* conditional fee. —leute, *pl.* people at court, courtiers. —luft, *f.* court-air. —lieferant, *m.* furnisher to the court or of the prince's household. —magd, *f.* 1) a maid-servant at court. 2) a maid-servant to the lord of the manor &c. —mahler, *m.* painter to the court; painter in ordinary to the king &c. †—manier, *f.* V. —art. —mann, [*pl.* —leute] *m.* 1) a courtier. *Fig.* a courteous, polite man, a man of elegant manners. 2) a man that must do work for the lord of the manor. —männisch, *adj* and *adv.* like a courtier, courtier-like, polite, elegant. —mark, *f.* 1) the territory or district of a manor or estate. 2) the low jurisdiction [of an estate or manor]. —marksherr, *m.* the proprietor of an estate who has the low jurisdiction. —marschall, *m.* the marshal of a prince's household. —marschallamt, *n.* 1) the office of the marshal of a prince's household. 2) the board or tribunal of the marshal of a prince's household. —mäßig, *adj.* and *adv.* in or after the manner of courts, court-like, courtly. —medikus, *m.* V. —arzt. —meier, *m.* the farmer or steward of an estate. —meister, *m.* 1) V. —meier, Meier, Schaffner, Schirrmeister. 2) V. —richter. 3) steward of a prince's household. 4) [in seamen's lang.] the steward's mate. 5) tutor, private tutor, governor. —meisterei, *f.* 1) the farmer's or steward's house. 2) [in contempt] pedagogism. —meistergehalt, *m.* the salary of a governor or tutor. —meisterinn, *f.* 1) the wife of a farmer or steward. 2) a governess. —**meisterleben**, *n.* the life of a governor or tutor. —**meisterisch**, —**meisterlich**, *adj.* and *adv.* in the manner of a governor or tutor, governor-like, tutor-like. —**meistern**, I. *v intr.* [in fam. lang.] to act as a governor or tutor. Er —meistert schon 2 Jahre, he has been a tutor these two years. II. *v. tr.* [in contempt] to tutor, to lecture, to find fault with, to criticise, to censure, to blame. Er findet immer Etwas an mir, an meinem Benehmen zu —meistern, he always finds fault with me, with my conduct; er —meistert gerne, he is fond of playing the pedant. —**meisterstelle**, *f.* the place of a governor or tutor. —**metzger**, *m.* butcher to the court. —**musikus**, *m.* musician to the court, member of the prince's private band. —**narr**, *m.* [formerly] the prince's or court's fool, the prince's jester. —**offiziant**, *m.* officer of a prince's household. —**partei**, *f.* the party of the court, the court-party. Einer von der —partei, a partisan of the court, royalist. —**platz**, *m.* V. —raum. —**postamt**, *n.* post-office of the court. —**postmeister**, *m.* postmaster to the court. —**prediger**, *m.* chaplain or preacher to the prince, chaplain in ordinary to the king &c. ||—**raithe**, *f.* V. —reite. —**ränke**, *pl.* court-intrigues. —**rath**, *m.* 1) counsellor of the court, aulic counsellor [in this signification it is a title frequently bestowed in some parts of Germany upon learned men, as professors at universities and the such]. 2) the aulic council [a court of judicature] V. Reichshofrath. 3) a member of the aulic council. —**raum**, *m.* court-yard. —**raute**, *f.* V. Stabwurz. —**rechnung**, *f.* account of expenses for a prince's household. —**recht**, *n.* 1) right belonging to a manor or estate. 2) privilege enjoyed at court. —**reite**, *f.* court-yard of a farm &c., farm-yard. —**richter**, *m.* the judge who presides at a superior court of judicature. —**rolle**, *f.* 1) a roll or register of those belonging to the lord of the manor and of their rights and privileges. 2) *Fig.* the part which any one plays at court. —**sänger**, *m.*, —**sängerinn**, *f.* a member of the prince's opera. —**schatzmeister**, *m.* treasurer of the court. —**schauspieler**, *m.*, —**schauspielerinn**, *f.* a member of a prince's theatre. —**schenk**, *m.* the king's or prince's cup-bearer. —**schlächter**, *m.* V. —metzger. —**schlosser**, *m.* locksmith to the court. —**schneider**, *m.* tailor to the court. —**schranz[e]**, *m.* a mean flatterer at court, a contemptible courtier. —**schreiber**, *m.* clerk of a superior court of justice. —**schreiner**, *m.* joiner to the court. —**sekretär**, *m.* secretary to the prince or sovereign. —**silberkammer**, *f.* a prince's or sovereign's plate-room. —**silberkämmerer**, *m.* an officer who has the care of a prince's plate. —**sitte**, *f.* court-etiquette, V. —brauch. —**sitz**, *m.* residence of the court. —**sprache**, *f.* the language of the court. *Fig.* compliments, fair empty words, court-holywater. —**staat**, *m.* 1) the state and splendour of a court. 2) household of a court, establishment of a prince, court. —**stadt**, *f.* [*Residenzstadt] a town where the court resides, residence of the court. —**statt**, *f.* 1) the place or ground where a farm or manor-house is built. 2) V. —reite. 3) residence of the court. 4) [in salt-works] a basin or reservoir of salt water. —**stätte**, *f.* 1) V. —statt 1). 2) V. —reite. —**stelle**, *f.* 1) an office or place at court. 2) [at Vienna] privy council. —**tag**, *m.* 1) V. Frohntag 1). 2) [day when a court sits to administer justice] court-day, session-day. 3) day of reception at court, levee-day, drawingroom-day, gala-day. —**tapezirer**, *m.* upholsterer to the court; upholsterer in ordinary to the king &c. —**theater**, *n.* a prince's theatre. —**thor**, *n.*, —**thür**, *f.* gate or door that opens into the court-yard. —**ton**, *m.* ton of the court. —**trauer**, *f.* court-mourning. —**trompeter**, *m.* trumpeter to the court. —**vieh**, *n.* the cattle belonging to a farm or estate. —**vogt**, *m.* steward to the lord of a manor. —**wehr**, —**wehrung**, *f.* the stock and implements belonging to a farm. —**weise**, *f.* V. —brauch. —**welt**, *f.* the court, the courtiers. —**wesen**, *n.* 1) any thing belonging or referring to the court, the affairs or management of the court. 2) [often in a bad sense] manners at court, court-fashion, court-life. —**widrig**, *adj.* and *adv.* contrary to the ways, manners or etiquette of the court. —**wirthschaft**, *f.* the administration of the housekeeping or the economy of a court. —**wort**, *n.* a polite expression, compliment. —**zirkel**, *m.* assembly or circle at court. —**zuckerbäcker**, *m.* confectioner to the court. —**zwang**, *m.* 1) compulsory service for the lord of the manor. 2) court-restraint, etiquette.

Höfelei, *f.* [in a bad sense] 1) the act of making one's court, of paying one's attendance to any one. 2) *Fig.* court-compliment, flattery.

Hofeln, *v. intr.* [in a bad sense] to make or pay one's court to any one, to court.

Höfen, [unusual] I. *v. intr.* 1) to keep court, to reside. 2) to make or pay court, to court. II. *v. tr.* to receive in one's house.

Höfener, **Höfner**, *m.* [-s, *pl.* -] 1) V. Hüfener. 2) V. Fröhner.

Hoffart or **Hoffahrt**, *f.* [from hoch and fahren] pride, arrogance, ostentation. Er ist der — ergeben, he is given up to pride or pomp. *Prov.* — und Armuth halten übel Haus, a proud mind and a beggar's purse agree not well together.

Hoffahrtsmuskel, *m.* [in anatomy, the muscle which serves to raise the eye] elevator of the eye, elevator oculi.

Hoffärtig, **Hoffährtig**, *adj.* and *adv.* proud, arrogant, haughty, ostentatious. Ein —er Mensch, a proud, ostentatious man; er geht — einher, he walks pompously; Gott widerstehet den —en, God resists the proud.

Hoffen, *v. tr.* and *intr.* [Low Sax. hapen, Sax. *hopian*, D. *hoopen*, Eng. *to hope*, Dan. *haaber*, probably allied to heben] to hope, to hope for, to expect. Er hofft, seinen Prozeß zu gewinnen, he hopes to gain his law-suit, ich hoffe auf einen glücklichen Erfolg, I hope for good success; Alles von der Güte des Fürsten —, to expect every thing from the goodness of the prince; — Sie, daß er kommen wird? do you hope he will come? hofften Sie, daß ich es thun würde? did you expect I should do it? ich hoffe nichts mehr, I have no further hopes; sie hofft noch immer, she has hopes still; es steht zu —, it is to be hoped for; es ist nichts mehr zu —, it is past hope; das will ich nimmermehr —, God forbid; ich hoffe nicht or ich hoffe es nicht, I hope not; ich hoffe auf Sie, I trust in you; ich hoffe auf Ihre Versprechungen, I confide in your promises. *Prov.* — und harren macht Manchen zum Narren, the disappointment of our hopes will often drive us to despair.

Hoffentlich, *adj.* and *adv.* to be hoped [for], as is hoped. Ein —es Glück, a piece of good fortune that may be hoped for; er wird es — thun, I hope he will do it; es wird — heute nicht regnen, it won't rain to day I hope.

Hoffer, *m.* [-s, *pl.* -] one that hopes, hoper.

Hoffnung, *f.* hope, expectation. Er machte sich — auf dieses Amt, he hoped to get, he was in hopes of getting or obtaining that office or place; seine — auf Gott setzen, to put one's hope in God; — fassen, schöpfen, bekommen, haben, to conceive, to entertain hopes, to hope; große — haben, to be in great hopes; es ist noch — vorhanden, there are hopes still; Einem — auf Etwas, zu Etwas machen, to make any one hope for a thing; *prov.* — läßt nicht zu Schanden werden, if it were not for hope, the heart would break; die — verlieren, aufgeben, fahren lassen, to lose, to give up, to abandon all hope; die or alle — ist verschwunden, dahin, it is past hope; *seine — ist zu Wasser geworden, ist in den Brunnen gefallen, his hopes have been frustrated or disappointed, have come to nought; das benimmt, raubt mir alle —, that deprives me of all hope; sich mit —en unterhalten, der — leben, to feed upon hope; Einen mit leerer — abspeisen, to sprinkle any one with court-holy-water; Eines —en täuschen, to disappoint any one's hopes; in seinen —en getäuscht werden, sich in seinen —en getäuscht sehen or finden, to be disappointed [in one's hopes]; seine Frau ist guter —, his wife is in the family way; man hat keine — mehr zu seinem Aufkommen, there is no hope of his life; das Vorgebirge der guten —, the cape of Good Hope. *Fig.* he or that which gives hope. Er ist die — der ganzen Familie, he is the hope of the whole family; die — Israels ist der Messias, the hope of Israel is the Messiah.

Hoffnungs-fülle, *f.* [in poetry] fulness of hope, great, high hopes. —**los**, *adj.* and *adv.* deprived of hope, hopeless. Er liegt —los darnieder, there is no longer any hope of his life. —**reich**, *adj.* and *adv.* V. —voll. —**voll**, *adj.* and *adv.* full of hope, hopeful. Ein —voller Sohn, a hopeful son, giving great expectations.

Hofiren, *v. tr.* and *intr.* 1) [obsolete] to keep court, to celebrate a festive occasion, to banquet; *it.* to walk with affected dignity, to strut. 2) [now, only used in jest] to make or pay one's court to a person, to court, to flatter. 3) [in popular lang.] to do one's want or business, to follow the call of nature.

Hofirer, *m.* [-s, *pl* -] one who makes court, who courts, courter.

Höfisch, *adj.* and *adv.* belonging or relating to the court, court-like, courtly. —e Sitten, courtly manners; ein —er Dichter, a flattering, courtly poet.

1. **Höflich**, *adj.* and *adv.* [either from Hof = court, like the Fr. *courtois*, *courtoisie* from *cour*, or from the obsolete Hof, Hut, Sw. *haf* = Schicklichkeit. Sw. *hofligen* = gut, good, V. 2. Höflich] courteous, civil, polite, well-bred, obliging, complaisant. Ein —er junger Mann, a polite young man; ein —es Betragen or Benehmen, courteous manners; er ist gegen Jedermann sehr —, he is very civil towards every body; — gegen die Damen seyn, to be courteous to the ladies; ich danke Ihnen —, höflichst dafür, I thank you humbly, most humbly for it.

2. **Höflich**, *adj.* and *adv.* [V. 1. Höflich] [in mining] good, middling. Eine —e Zeche, a good, rich mine; wie geht es? —, or alle —, how do you do? well, pretty well.

Höflichkeit, *f.* 1) courteousness, politeness, civility, complaisance, courtesy. Er erzeigt Fremden große —, he shows great courtesy to strangers; er hat mich mit vieler — aufgenommen, he received me very civilly or kindly, he has given me a very civil or kind reception; das ist gegen die Regeln der —, that is contrary to good manners; er besaß nicht so viel —, daß er ihn besucht hätte, he has not had the politeness to go and see him. 2) an act of civility or politeness. Einem viele —en erweisen, to show any one many civilities, to be very kind to any one; ich habe viele —en von ihm empfangen, I have received many acts of kindness at his hands; er sagte ihm viele —en, he told him many obliging things, paid him many compliments. Syn.

Höflichkeit, Lebensart, Welt. He, who shows a desire to please others and a careful attention to their wants and wishes, is called höflich. He, who prepossesses by the correctness of his behaviour, and avoidance of any thing offensive to decency or propriety, is said to have Lebensart. Welt denotes that deportment and behaviour, in the external offices and decorums of social life, which constitutes good-breeding.

Höflichkeits-bezeigung, *f.* act of civility, respect or kindness. Nach den ersten —bezeigungen, when the first compliments were over; er hat mich mit —bezeigungen überhäuft, he has heaped many civilities on me. —**brief**, *m.* a letter written merely by way of civility, a letter of ceremony or courtesy.

Höfling, *m* [-es, *pl* -e] [often used in a bad sense] courtier. V. Hofmann 1).

Höflings-brauch, *m.*, —**sitte**, *f.* manner or way of courtiers.

Höfner, *m.* V. Höfener.

Höh, *adj.* V. Hoch.

Hohes-lied *n.* [in Scripture] the Song of Solomon. —**ofen**, *m.* V. under Hoch. —**priester**, *m.* [sovereign] pontiff, V. Hochpriester.

Höhe, *f.* [*pl.* -n] 1) [the quality of being high] height, altitude. Die — eines Berges, the altitude or height of a mountain; die — eines Thurmes, the height of a tower; eine Kirche, welche 100 Fuß — hat, a church that is in height a hundred feet, that is a hundred feet high; man muß dieser Mauer mehr — geben, that wall must be raised higher; von der — des Felsens herabfallen or herabstürzen, to fall down from the top of the rock; die — eines Ortes, the altitude or height of a place; [in astronomy] die — eines Sternes, der Sonne &c., the elevation of a star, of the sun above the horizon, the altitude of a star, of the sun; die — nehmen, die — der Sonne nehmen, to take the sun's altitude; die — or die Pol—, the height or elevation of the pole, the degree of latitude; in einer — von 30 Graden, in the thirtieth degree of latitude; die — des Meeres, the offing; die — gewinnen, V. under 3), *it.* [in seamen's language] to get sea-room, to stand out for the offing; die — eines in Reih' und Glied aufgestellten Bataillons, the depth of a battalion; [in seamen's lang.] auf der — einer Insel oder einer Stadt seyn, to be off an island or town; die — von einem Vorgebirge haben, to be to windward of a cape, to weather a cape; die — des Vor- und Hinterstevens, the height of the stem and stern. *Fig.* Die — eines Tones, the height, highness, or acuteness of a tone; sie hat eine schöne —, the upper tones of her voice are good; die — des Preises, the highness of price; die — des Preises schreckte mich ab, the high price prevented me from buying it; die — des Geistes, der Gesinnungen, elevation of mind, of thoughts or ideas, an exalted mind, greatness of soul; die — des Ranges, elevation of rank, high station; mit Einem auf gleicher — stehen, to be on a level with any one. 2) [space extended upward from the surface of the earth] altitude. In die — steigen, to fly or rise high or aloft, to soar, to mount, to ascend; sich vom Bette in die — richten, to raise one's self up, to sit up in one's bed; Etwas in die — ziehen, to draw or pull any thing up, to raise a thing; den Kopf in die — werfen, to toss up the head, *it. fig.* to carry a high head; richtet den Kopf in die —, hold up your head; in die — sehen, to look up. 3) a high place. Die — gewinnen or erreichen, to gain or reach the summit [of a mountain &c.]; hier ist eine bedeutende — [Anhöhe], here is a considerable eminence; die Kunst, die —n zu messen, the art of taking or ascertaining altitudes, altimetry; auf eine — bauen, to build upon a rising ground or a hill; die Feinde besetzten die —n, the enemies occupied the heights *Fig.* Ehre sey Gott in der —! glory be to God on high, above or in heaven! von seiner — herabstürzen, to lose one's power or authority. Syn. Höhe, Hoheit. Höhe denotes simply an indefinite elevation above lower objects, and is always used comparatively, whereas Hoheit, figuratively, implies the utmost degree of elevation or excellence of any kind.

Höhen-kreis, *m.* [in astronomy, a series of circles of the spheres] a parallel of altitude, almucantar. —**lootse**, *m.* a pilot who directs a ship's course by celestial observations. —**messer**, *m.* [*Holometer] an instrument for taking or measuring altitudes, astrolabe, altimeter, holometer, pantometer; [in seamen's lang.] cross-staff, Jacob's staff, radiometer. —**messung**, *f.* act of taking or measuring altitudes, altimetry. —**rauch**, *m.* [often written Harrauch, Heerrauch] a thick yellowish, badly smelling fog [said to be caused by the burning of the moors in some parts of North-Germany]. —**verhältniß**, *n.* relation or proportion of altitude; [in music] interval. —**zirkel**, *m.* V. —kreis.

Hoheit, *f.* 1) highness, elevation. Die — des Geistes, der Seele, elevation of mind. greatness of soul; er erwiderte mit —, he replied with nobleness or nobly; die — Gottes, the greatness, highness or grandeur of God. 2) elevation in rank or power. highness, high rank. Reichthum, — und Ehre sind &c., riches, high rank and honour are &c.; in ihren verschiedenen Graden von —, in their several degrees of elevation. 3) supreme power, sovereignty, domination, dominion. Sie leben unter türkischer —, they live under the domination of the Turks; hier ist preußische —, this is the Prussian territory. 4) [a title of honour given to princes and other persons of rank] highness. Seine Königliche —, his royal highness; Seine —, der Großherr, his highness, the Grand Seignior; Ihre königliche —en, their royal highnesses. Syn. V. Höhe.

Hoheits-lästerung, *f.* the crime of high-treason, laesae majestatis crimen. —**recht**, *n.* right of sovereignty. —**rechte**, *pl.* the rights of a sovereign, [in law] regalia.

Hohl, *adj.* and *adv.* [Sax. *hol*, Eng. *hollow*, Dan. *huul*, Icel. *holur*, Gr κοῖλος, allied to the L. *coll*-um, *coel*-um, the Gr γαῦλος &c., the Fr. *houle* &c.] hollow. Ein —er Baum, a hollow tree; ein —er Zahn, a hollow tooth; [in botany] ein —er Stengel, ein —es Blatt, a fistulous stem, leaf; †es ist mir — im Magen, my belly is empty; —e Augen, Backen or Wangen, hollow eyes or eyes sunk in the head, hollow cheeks; ein — geschliffenes Glas, a concave glass, V. —glas; eine — geschliffene Klinge, V. —klinge; — ausarbeiten, — machen, to hollow; — schlagen, to emboss; eine — geprägte Denkmünze, a medal struck in creux; ein —er Weg, a hollow way or road, V. —weg; die —e Hand, the hollow of the hand; [in seamen's lang.] die —e See, the trough of the sea; die See geht —, sehr —, the sea runs high, there is heavy sea, there is a great swell on. *Fig.* Eine —e [dumpfe] Stimme, a hollow voice; jene —en Träume der Einbildungskraft, those airy or chimerical visions; ein —er Kopf, unfurnished head, empty pate.

Hohl-ader, *f.* V. —blutader. —**ast**, *m.* V. Schlangenholzbaum. —**auge**, *n.* 1) an eye sunk in the head, a hollow eye. 2) a hollow-eyed person. —**äugig**, *adj.* and *adv.* hollow-eyed. —**bäckig**, *adj.* and *adv.* hollow-cheeked. —**bau**, *m.* [in architecture] a subterranean place or passage, a vault, cellar, &c. —**beere**, *f.* V. Himbeere. —**beil**, *n.* [among joiners and carpenters] hollow adz. —**blutader**, *f.* the vena cava. Die obere —blutader, the superior vena cava; die untere —blutader, the inferior vena cava. —**bohrer**, *m.* an instrument for boring holes or making excavations, auger. —**brille**, *f.* concave spectacles. —**deichsel**, —**deißel**, *f.* V. —beil. —**docke**, *f.* [among turners] puppet, shank-mandrel. —**driller**, *m.* hollow gimblet or drill. —**drüsen**, *pl.* [in anatomy] crypts. —**eisen**, *n.* 1) hollowed iron. 2) an iron tool for making hollows, a hollow chisel, gouge. Mit einem —eisen austiefen, to scoop out with a gouge, to gouge. —**feile**, *f.* a round hollow file. —**flöte**, *f.* a pipe or flute in organs that sounds hollow. —**gang**, *m* [*Casematte] [in fortification] casemate. —**gerinne**, *n.* [in mining] a canal or water-course made of the hollow trunk of a tree. —**geschliffen**, *adj.* concave —**geschwür**, *n.* [a deep and callous ulcer] fistula. —**glas**, *n.* concave glass —**hand**, *f.* the hollow of the hand. —**häring**, *m.* shotten hering. —**hippe**, —**hippel**, *f.*, *dim.* —**hippchen**, —**hippelchen**, ‖ —**hippelein**, *n.* hollow wafer. —**hobel**, *m.* [among joiners] plough. —**kehle**, *f.* a hollow, furrow, flute, chamfer, channel, groove; [in architecture] ogee; rechte or gerade, verkehrte —kehle, upright, reversed ogee; V. Rinne. —**kehlhobel**, or —**kehlenhobel**, *m.* a plane for fluting, chamfering or grooving, a plough. —**kehlenstahl**, *m.* [among turners] a steel-tool for making grooves or chamfers, point-tool. —**kirsche**, *f.* bird-cherry. —**klinge**, *f.* hollow blade. —**kopf**, *m.* [in contempt] unfurnished head, empty pate. V. Dummkopf. —**krähe**, *f.* black wood-pecker, roller. —**kreisel**, *m.* V. Brummkreisel. —**kugel**, *f.* hollow ball. —**lauch**, *m.* leek. —**leiste**, *f.* V. —kehle. —**meißel**, *m.* hollow chisel, gouge. V. —eisen 2). —**münze**, *f.* [*Bracteat] V. Blechmünze. —**ohr**, *n.* [in conchology] large ear, Midas's ear shell, trumpet-shell —**pfeife**, —**quinte**, *f.* V. —flöte. —**ring**, *m.* hollow stand for a dish, V. Schüsselring. —**röhre**, *f.* [among turners] an iron tool for turning coarsely without smoothness. —**rund**, *adj.* [*concav] concave Ein —rundes or —rund geschliffenes Glas, a concave glass. —**ründe**, *f.* concavity. —**säule**, *f.* a hollow column. —**schleifen**, *ir. v. tr* to grind hollow. —**schnabel**, *m.* [a bird] spoon-bill, spatula. —**schnäbler**, *m.* [a bird] toucan, V. Pfefferfresser. —**schnauze**, *f.* the sword-fish, serra. —**spatel**, *m* a gardener's tool for transplanting. —**spath**, *m* hollow spar, chiastolite, macle, hohlspath. —**spiegel**, *m.* concave mirror. —**stab**, *m.* [in surgery] catheter. —**stähler**, *m.* a tool for turning round things. —**stampfer**, *m.* [among hatters] stamper —**stein**, *m.* V. —ziegel. —**stempel**, *m.* [among locksmiths] a stamp; *it.* a driver, driving-bolt —**taube**, *f.* wood pigeon. —**texel**, V —deichsel. —**treppe**, *f.* a winding stair-case, the navel or spindle of which is a thick hollow pillar —**waaren**, *pl.* [in glassworks] hollow vessels. —**wagen**, *m.* [in mining] tumbrel or tumbril —**wangig**, *adj* and *adv.* V. —backig. —**weg**, *m.* hollow way, defile, ravine. —**werk**, *n.* a roof covered with hollow or gutter tiles. —**wurz**, —**wurzel**, *f.* hollow-root, birth-wort. —**zahn**, *m.* 1) one of the middle teeth of a horse. 2) [a plant] dead nettle. —**ziegel**, *m.* hollow tile, gutter-tile —**ziegelmuschel**, *f.* imbricata concha —**zirkel**, *m.* compasses with the shanks bent outwards for the purpose of measuring hollows, spherical compasses.

Hohl, or **Holl**, *n.* [-es, *pl.* -e] [in seamen's lang.] depth of a ship or of the hold [measured from the lower-deck beams to the keel].

Hohle, *f.* V. Höhle; *it.* Höhlung, Hohlweg

Höhle, *f.* [*pl.* -n], *dim.* **Höhlchen**, *n.* [-s, *pl.* -] 1) [empty space within a body &c., any depression of surface in a body] a cavity, hollow, hole. Die —n des menschlichen Körpers, the cavities of the human body; die — in der Hand, the hollow of the hand; [in anatomy] die — an den Knochen, sinus; die — eines Löwen, a lion's den; die — des Dachses, the hole or cover of the badger; die — [der Bau] eines Fuchses, the kennel or earth of a fox; die — eines Kaninchens, the burrow of a rabbit; die — der Räuber und Diebe [eine Räuber-, eine Diebs—], the den of robbers and thieves. 2) [particularly] a cave or cavern in the earth. Die Oeffnung einer —, der Eingang zu einer —, the mouth, entrance of a cavern; in —n wohnen, to live in caves; die Baumanns—, a celebrated cavern in the Hartz mountains.

Höhlen-bewohner, *m.*, —bewohnerinn, *f.* a person who lives in a cave, troglodyte. —biene, *f.* the mining bee.

Höhlen, V. Holen.

Höhlen, *v. tr.* to hollow, to excavate. Ein gehöhlter Felsen, a hollow rock. Das —, act of making hollow, excavation.

Höhler, *m.* [-s, *pl.* -] 1) one who makes hollow or excavates, excavator. 2) a deep cellar in rocky ground, a cellar excavated in a rock.

Höhlerbier, *n.* beer kept in a very deep cellar.

Höhlern, V. Höhlen.

Hohlheit, *f.* hollowness, cavity. *Fig.* emptiness of the mind; superficiality.

Höhlig, *adj.* and *adv.* full of holes, cavities or caverns, cavernous.

Hohlunder, V. Holunder.

Höhlung, *f.* excavation, cavity, hollow. Die — einer Kugel, the concavity or hollowness of a globe; die — unter der Achsel, arm-pit, armhole, axilla.

Hohn, *m.* [-es] [old honida, Fr. *honte*, Ital. *onta*] 1) [obsolete = Schande] disgrace, shame, reproach. Denn ich muß leiden den — meiner Jugend, [in Scripture] because I did bear the reproach of my youth. 2) contumely, scorn, disdain, scoff. Einem — beweisen or zeigen, to show any one disdain; Einen mit — behandeln, to treat any one with disdain, scornfully, to sneer at any one; Einem — sprechen, to treat any one with contumelious language, to scoff, mock or jeer any one; er mußte — und Spott erdulden, he was exposed to insult and mockery. 3) object of scorn or disdain. Zum Spott und — denen, die um uns her sind, [in Scripture] a scorn and derision to them that are round about us. SYN. Hohn, Spott. The object of Spott is to render an object ridiculous, and denotes contemptuous merriment at persons or things, sportive insult or contempt. Hohn signifies that disdain or scorn, which springs from a person's opinion of the meanness of an object, and a consciousness or belief of his own superiority.

Hohn-gelächter, *n.* 1) the act of laughing in scorn, scornful laughter. 2) the object of scornful laughter. Zum —gelächter werden, to become a laughing-stock. —lache, *f.* scornful laughing, sneer, V. —gelächter. —lächeln, *v. intr.* to smile contemptuously or scornfully, to sneer. Das —lächeln, contemptuous smile, sneer. —lachen, *v. intr.* to laugh in scorn, to scoff, to mock, to sneer. Das —lachen, V. —lache. —lacher, *m.*, —lacherinn, *f.* a person who laughs to scorn, mocker, scoffer. —necken, *v. tr.* to scoff, to jeer, to mock, to treat contumeliously. Er wurde gehohnneckt, he was laughed at or made a fool of. V. Verhöhnen. —neckerei, *f.* V. Höhnerei. —rede, *f.* insulting language; *it.* irony. —schrift, *f.* V. Spottschrift. —sprecher, *m.*, —sprecherinn, *f.* scorner, scoffer, mocker.

Höhnen, *v. tr.* V. Hohnnecken.

Höhner, *m.* [-s, *pl.*] Höhnerinn, *f.* a person who scoffs or mocks, scoffer, mocker, scorner.

Höhnerei, *f.* contumelious treatment, scoffing, mockery.

Höhnisch, *adj.* and *adv.* scornful, jeering, contumelious, sneering. Eine —e Miene, a scornful air; ein —es Lächeln, a sneering smile; — lächeln, to sneer.

Höhnung, *f.* scoffing, mockery, the act of insulting.

Hohö! *interj.* [in fam. lang. an expression of wonder and indignation] oh! oh! V. Ho.

Höke, [Hoke] *m.* [-n, *pl.* -n] or Höcker, *m.* [-s *pl.* -] Hökinn, Hökerinn, *f.* [Lat. *cocio*, Sax. *hoeka*, Eng. *hawker* and *huckster*, Dan. *hoeker*, from hocken, which see] a retailer of provisions, huckster, higgler, hucksteress, V. Härings—, Käse—, Obst—, Salz—.

Höker-bann, *m.* a tax paid by hucksters. —frau, *f.* V. Hökinn. —gemäß, *adj.* and *adv.* V. —mäßig. —kram, *m.* a huckster's trade or goods. —lade, *f.* a huckster's shop. —mäßig, *adj.* and *adv.* like a huckster, in the manner of hucksters, low, bilingsgate. —salz, *n.* salt sold by retail. —waare, *f.* a huckster's goods. —weib, *n.* V. Hökinn.

Höken, [hoken] or Hökern [hokern] *v. intr.* to retail provisions, to higgle.

Höker, *m.* —inn, *f.* V. Höke and 2. Höcker.

Hökerei, *f.* a huckster's trade.

Hökerisch, *adj.* and *adv.* V. Hökermäßig.

Hökinn, *f.* V. Höke.

Hokuspokus, *m.* or Hokuspokusstreich, *m.* a juggler's trick, Hocus Pocus, thimbleriggery.

Hokuspokusmacher, *m.* a juggler, a conjuror, a Hocus Pocus, a thimblerig[ger].

Holbe, *f.* V. 1. Holm.

Hold, *adj.* and *adv.* [Sw. *huld*, Icel. *holder*, perhaps from the old hellen or heldern = neigen] 1) kind, friendly, affable, favourable. Ein —er Fürst, a gracious prince; Einem — seyn, to have an affection for any one, to bear any one good-will, to be any one's well-wisher; *er ist ihm nicht —, he does not like or love him, he bears him a grudge; Mosen waren beide, Gott und Menschen, —, [in Script.] Moses was loved both by God and men. *Fig.* —es Glück, propitious fortune; das Glück ist ihm —, fortune favours him, smiles upon him, is propitious to him. 2) attached, devoted, faithful. Seinem Herrn — und treu or —, treu und gewärtig seyn, to be faithful, trusty and loyal to one's master. 3) very lovely or beautiful. Ein —er Knabe, a lovely, sweet boy; ein —er Mund, a beautiful mouth; ein —es Lächeln, a sweet smile.

Hold-selig, *adj.* and *adv.* 1) very kind, friendly or favourable. Ein —seliger Blick, a very kind look. 2) [chiefly] most pleasing, or agreeable, lovely, sweet. Ein —seliges Lächeln, a sweet smile; ein —seliges Benehmen, a graceful deportment, graceful manners; ein —seliges Mädchen, a charming, most lovely girl. 3) beloved, highly favoured. Gegrüßet seyest du, —selige, [in Scripture] [the angel's address to Mary] hail, thou that art highly favoured. —seligkeit, *f.* 1) great kindness. 2) gracefulness, agreeableness, sweetness.

Holde, *m.* and *f.* [-n, *pl.* -n] 1) [in poetry] friend, beloved one, V. Freund, Geliebter, Freundinn, Geliebte. 2) *m.* vassal, subject.

Holder, *m.* [-s] V. Holunder.

Holder-gebackene, *n.* V. Holunderküchlein. —rose, *f.* V. Holunder 2) *d*).

Holdinn, *f.* 1) female friend, patroness, mistress, V. Freundinn, Geliebte. 2) one of the three Graces, V. Huldgöttinn.

‡Holdschaft, *f.* V. Liebschaft.

Holen, *v. tr.* [Eng. to *hale* or *haul*, Fr. *haler*, seems to be allied to wallen, *all-er*, Gr. ἑλ-κεῖν, therefore = an sich ziehen] to draw to or towards one's self. Etwas nach sich —, to draw or pull any thing along towards or after one; Athem —, to draw, take or fetch breath; einen tiefen Seufzer —, to heave or fetch a deep or profound sigh; [in mining] hol'an [den Haspel]! draw or pull! [in seamen's lang.] hol'an! haul or rouse together! den Anker zu Hause — or einholen, to heave up the anchor; unter das Ankertau —, to underrun the cable. *Fig. a*) to go and bring, to fetch. Brod, Wasser —, to fetch bread, water; lassen Sie Bier —, send for some beer; er hat den Arzt — lassen, he has sent for the physician; wenn Sie nicht kommen, so werde ich Sie —, if you do not come, I shall fetch you; die Braut heim —, to conduct one's bride to one's house; um sich Gesundheit und Heiterkeit zu —, in order to recover one's health and spirits; — und rapportiren, [said of dogs] to fetch and carry. *b*) to take away. Der Tod holet uns alle, death carries off all of us, death spares nobody; †der Henker, der Teufel hole! the devil or deuce take it! †der Henker soll ihn —! hol' ihn der Henker! deuce take him! †das hat der Teufel geholt, that is gone to the devil, is lost; er holte [sich] ein Stück Fleisch aus der Schüssel, he helped himself to or he took a piece of meat out of the dish; er holte sein Schnupftuch aus der Tasche, he took his handkerchief out of his pocket; [in popular lang.] bei ihm ist nichts zu —, there is nothing to be got from him, he is a poor devil; er hat einen Buckel voll Schläge geholt, he has been soundly drubbed; da sind nur Schläge zu —, there is nothing to be got but a drubbing; *ich habe mir einen tüchtigen Schnupfen dort geholt, I caught a very bad cold there.

Holster, *f.* [*pl.* -n] [perhaps allied to hohl, hehlen = decken, to cover] 1) holster. 2) [in conchology] pinna marina.

Holster-kappe, *f.* holster-cap. —macher, *m.* one who makes holsters, scabbard-maker. —muschel, *f.* V. Holster 2).

Holk, [Hulk] *m.* [-en, *pl.* -en] [Sax. *hulc*, Eng. *hulk*, Sw. *holk*, Gr. ὅλκας; it is generally derived from ἕλκω = ziehen, to draw, but perhaps better from hohl, which in Sw. is also *holk*] 1) [obsolete] a large, bulky or heavy ship. 2) hulk, a sheer-hulk.

Holl, *n.* [-es, *pl.* -e] [in seamen's lang.] V. 2. Hohl.

Hollbocke, *f.* V. Hohlbocke.

Holla! *interj.* holla, ho there! who is there

Holland, *n.* [-s] Holland. *Prov.* — ist in Nöthen, there is great danger or peril.

Hollander or Holländer, *m.* [-s, *pl.* -] [in seamen's lang.] V. Holländer 3).

Holländer, *m.* [-s, *pl.* -] 1) a native of Holland, Hollander, Dutchman. Der fliegende —, [a superstitious seamen's tale] the flying Dutchman. 2) a farmer who makes butter, cheese &c. after the manner of the Dutch or Hollanders. 3) [in seamen's lang., a particular turn in the bight of a rope, made to hook a tackle on] cat's paw. 4) a cylindrical papermill.

Holländerei, *f.* Dutch farm, dairy-farm.

Holländerinn, *f.* Dutch-woman.

Holländisch, *adj.* and *adv.* Dutch. —e Leinlichkeit, Dutch cleanliness; die —e Sprache, the Dutch language, the Dutch; —e Leinwand, fine linen manufactured in Holland, Holland; —er Käse, Dutch cheese; ein —er Kamin, a Dutch chimney; [in painting] die —e Schule, the Dutch school.

Hölle, *f.* [*pl.* -n] [allied to hohl, or from the Sax. *helun* = to cover] 1) [in general, any hollow or hidden place, hence] corner by the stove, chimney-corner; [and in a more limited sense, a place into which a tailor throws his shreds &c.] hell, ‡ cabbage-garden. 2) the lower regions, the place of souls after death. Es ist höher denn der Himmel, tiefer denn die —, [in Scripture] it is as high as heaven, deeper than hell. 3) the grave. Die — ist mein Haus, [in Scripture] the grave is mine house; nun muß ich zu der —n Pforten, I shall go to the gates of the grave. 4) [the place or state of punishment for the wicked after death] hell. In die — kommen, to be damned, to go to hell, in die — fahren, to descend into hell; *er hat die — an ihm verdient, he has treated him most cruelly or shamefully, so as to merit hell for it; in der Tiefe der —, in the bottom of hell; die Engel, welche sich empört haben, sind in die — gestürzt worden, the rebellious angels were cast headlong into hell. *Fig.* Dieses Haus ist eine — für mich, that house is a hell for me; *Einem die — heiß machen, to alarm any one by aggravating the matter, to make any one sweat for fear, to play the devil with any one. 5) *Fig. a)* [in poetry] the devils in hell, *it.* the damned. Die — seufzt nach ihm, hell groans for him; die — ist gegen ihn los, hell is opened to pursue him. *b)* great torment, the torments of hell. Die Bösen tragen ihre — in ihrem Herzen or Busen, the wicked bear their hell or carry their punishment about them.

Höllen-angst, *f.* the fear of hell; excessive anguish, agony, the pangs of death. Er hat —angst ausgestanden, he was in a mortal fright. *—bang, *adj.* and *adv.* impressed with excessive fear, very much afraid. Mir ward — bang, I was in great trepidation. —beherrscher, *m.* the prince or king of hell or of the infernal regions, Pluto or Satan. —brand, *m.* a fire in hell. **Fig.* one condemned to hell, a most wicked or profligate wretch, a firebrand from hell. *—braten, *m. Fig.* V. —brand. *—brut, *f.* hellish crew or brood. —bund, *m.*, —bündniß, *n.* infernal alliance. **Fig.* V. —brand. —drache, *m* the infernal dragon, the evil spirit, the devil. —fahrt, *f.* descent into hell. Die —fahrt Christi, Christ's descent into hell. —feuer, *n.* 1) the fire in hell, hell-fire. 2) *Fig.* a very violent fire, a hell-fire. —flamme, *f.* the hellish or infernal flame or fire; *it. fig.* V. —pein. —fluß, *m.* infernal river [Styx, Phlegeton, Acheron.] —fürst, *m.* the prince of hell, Satan. —geist, *m.* infernal spirit, demon. —gestalt, *f.* a hideous figure. —gestank, *m.* an infernal or hellish stench [used also figuratively in familiar language]. *—gezücht, *n.* V. —brut. —gott, *m.* the king of the infernal regions, the prince of hell, Pluto. —göttinn, *f.* [the wife of Pluto] the Goddess of hell, Proserpine. —heer, *n.* infernal army. *—heiß, *adj.* and *adv.* excessively hot, infernally hot. *—hitze, *f.* excessive or infernal heat. —hund, *m.* a dog of hell, hell-hound, Cerberus. **Fig.* an agent of hell, hell-hound. —kind, *n.* child of hell; a wicked person. —kunst, *f.* infernal art or artifice, infernal tricks. —marter, —pein, *f.* the torments, the pains of hell. **Fig.* —marter or —pein ausstehen, to suffer dreadfully or terribly. —pforte, *f* the gate of hell. —plan, *m. Fig.* an infernal or satanical plan or project. —prediger, *m.* a preacher who threatens us with eternal damnation &c. —qual, *f.* V. —pein. —rachen, *m. Fig.* the jaws of hell. —reich, *n.* infernal kingdom. —richter, *m.* judge of hell. —schmerz, *m.* excessive pain, pains of hell. —stein, *m.* [in surgery] infernal stone, caustic stone, lapis infernalis. —thor, *n.* V. —pforte. —wächter, *m.* hell-hound, Cerberus. *—wuth, *f. Fig.* an excessive or infernal rage or fury. —zopf, *m.* [in botany] duck's meat, duck-weed.

Höllisch, *adj.* and *adv.* hellish, infernal. —e Geister, infernal spirits, demons, Furies &c.; die —en Mächte, the infernal powers; die —e Schlange, der —e Feind, the evil spirit, the serpent, the devil. *[*Fig.*] —es Feuer, —er Schmerz, —er Stein, V. Höllenfeuer &c.; eine —e That, an abominable deed, a heinous crime; das ist ein —er Plan, that is a diabolical scheme; [in vulgar lang.] es ist — heiß, it is excessively hot, infernally hot; — fluchen, to swear like a trooper.

Hollúnder, V. Holunder.

1. **Hólm**, *m.* [-es, *pl.* -e] [either from halten, to hold, or from hehlen, to cover] a cross-beam, a rail.

2. **Hólm**, *m.* [-es, *pl.* -e] [Sax., Eng., Sw. and Dan. *holm*, allied to hohl or the old hol = hoch] 1) [in some districts] a hill. 2) an islet or river-isle, holm. 3) a dock-yard, V. Schiffs—, Schiffswerfte.

Holmmajor, *m.* [Hafencapitän] harbour-master, port-reeve.

***Holometer**, *n.* [-s, *pl.* -] holometer; V. Höhenmesser.

***Holothúrie**, *f.* [a kind of sea-fish full of prickles] holothuria.

Hólper, *m.* [-s, *pl* - or -n] [from the old hol = hoch] unevenness inequality, a small hillock. Ein Weg, der voller —n ist, a very uneven, rough or rugged way or road. *Fig.* shock in a carriage, jolt.

Hólpericht, *adj.* and *adv.* rugged, rough, uneven. Es geht sich hier sehr —, it is very rugged walking here. *Fig.* Eine —e Schreibart, a rugged style.

Hólperig, *adj.* and *adv.* uneven, rough, rugged. Ein —er Weg, a rough or rugged way, V. Holpericht.

‖**Hólsche**, *f.* [*pl.* -n] V. Holzschuh.

Hólterpólter, a word, used in fam. lang., to express or imitate a rattling noise, nearly the same as helter-skelter. Der Koffer fiel — die Treppe hinab, the trunk fell down the staircase with a great noise.

Holúnder, [Holder] *m.* [-s] [from hohl; the Goth. *holund* is a hollow or cave] 1) elder [a tree, Sambucus]. 2) the denomination of several other plants with hollow pithy branches. *a)* dane-wort, dwarf-elder, wall-wort, V. Attich. *b)* Spanischer —, lilac, V. Flieder. *c)* V. Drosselbeerstrauch. *d)* snow-ball, guelder-rose. *e)* common maple-tree.

Holunder-baum, *m.* elder-tree. —beere, *f.* elder-berry. —blätterwasser, *n.* water made of elder-leaves. —blüte, *f.* elder-flower. —blütessig, V. —essig. —blütwasser, *n.* elder-flower water. —büchse, *f.* a pop-gun of elder. —essig, *m.* elder-vinegar. —holz, *n.* elder-wood. —keime, *pl.* elder-buds, the tender leaves of elder. —küchlein, *n.* a small pancake with elder-berries, elder-berry fritter; *it.* elder-flowers steeped in butter and baked. —latwerge, *f.*, —muß, *n.* elder-syrup, elder-berry-jam. —röhre, *f.*, *dim.* —röhrchen, ‖—röhrlein, *n.* a tube or pipe of elder, elder-tube. —saft, *m.* elder-juice, elder-syrup. —schwamm, *m.* jew's ear, V. Judasohr. —staude, *f.*, —stock, *m.*, —strauch, *m.* elder-bush, elder-shrub. —thee, *m.* elder-tea. —traube, *f.* elder-flower as used in pancakes. —wasser, *n.* elder-water. —wein, *m.* elder-wine.

Holúnke, V. Halunke.

Hólz, *n.* [-es, *pl* Hölzer] [Low Sax., Anglo Sax and Eng. *holt*, Sw. *hult*. D. *hout*, allied to the Gr ὕλη, ὕλσ-ος, Eng. *wood*, Germ. Wald] 1) [the substance of trees] wood. Hartes, weiches, grünes, trockenes —, hard, soft, green, dry wood, ausgewittertes —, seasoned wood; dürres, abgestandenes —, fallen wood, dead wood, berghar-ziges —, bituminous or carbonated wood, sich werfendes —, wood that warps; gegrabenes —, fossil wood; unterirdisches —, wood found under the surface of the earth, fossil wood or timber, *it.* V. Erdkohle; ein Haus von —, a house made or built of wood, a wooden house; in — arbeiten, to work in wood; ein Scheit —, a log of wood, ein Meß —, a cord of wood, — machen, to cut or cleave wood for fuel; — zur Feuerung, wood-fuel; *er ist ein solcher Klotz, daß man — auf ihm hacken könnte, he is a great block-head. 2) a piece of wood. Dieses — ist nicht stark genug, this piece of wood is not strong enough; das — an einer Flinte, the stock of a fowling-piece or gun. [at the game of nine-pins] the score of what is thrown. Viel — [= viele Kegel] werfen, to carry many pins. [in Scripture] — [= Galgen] gallows, gibbet; *it.* [in Scripture] an idol, wood. V. Glatt—, Kerb—, Quer—, Strich—. 3) the branches of a tree. Dieser Baum schießt ins —, that tree shoots very much into wood. 4) a tree in regard to the nature of its wood. V. Blatter—, Blau—, Franzosen—, Gelb—, Roth—. 5) land covered with trees shrubs &c., a wood. Ein Hölzchen, a small wood, a grove. [among huntsmen] Der Jäger ziehet zu —, the huntsman goes into the wood, der Hirsch ziehet zu —, the stag approaches or enters the wood. *Prov.* V. Wald. *it.* V. Birk—, Eichen—, Feld—, Hau—, Laub—, Pfarr—, Schwarz— &c. Syn. Holz, Wald, Hain, Forst. Holz and Wald denote a large and thick collection of forest trees, a wood, a forest. Holz is used more with reference to the substance, Wald with reference to the number of the trees. Hain is a small dense wood or cluster of trees, consecrated to some deity and supposed to be hallowed by the presence of the same grove: in poetry, it is applied to any wood. Forst is a wood or forest, mostly fenced in for the preservation of the vert and venison.

Holz-abfall, *m.* [among foresters] fallen wood, small sticks. —amt, *n.* wood-office. —amianth, *m.* ligniform asbestus. —apfel, *m.* wild apple, crab, wilding. —apfelbaum, *m.* crab-tree, wilding-tree. —arbeiter, *m.* worker in wood. —arm, *adj.* and *adv.* destitute of wood, wanting wood. Ein —armes Land, a country where there is little or no wood. —art, *f.* sort of wood. Es gibt mehrere —arten, there are several sorts of wood. —artig, *adj.* and *adv.* like or resembling wood, ligniform, ligneous, woody. —asbest, *m.* V. —amianth. —asche, *f.* wood ashes. —ast, *m.* wood-branch, strong branch of a tree. —äther, *m.* V. —essigäther. —aufseher, *m.* overseer or supervisor of the wood. —aufsetzer, *m.* one who piles up wood; *it.* [in some parts of Germany] a sworn piler of wood. —auslader, *m.* one who unloads or discharges wood, discharger of wood. —auster [Baumauster] *f.* a genus of oysters in the East Indies, adhering to trees or roots. —auswäscher, *m* a sworn person who draws the floated wood on land. —axt, *f.* axe for cutting wood. —bau, *m.* 1) cultivation of wood. 2) the custruction of a house &c. of timber, timber-work, a house or building of wood. —bauer, m. a peasant who carries fire-wood to market. —beamte, m. an officer belonging to the department or standing under the control of the board of woods and forests, V. Forstbeamte. —behältniß, n. wood-house; it. [in rooms] wood-stand. —bericht, m. a forester's report. —biene, f. [a kind of bee] ligniperda. —bild, n. a wooden figure or image. —bildner, m. one who cuts figures in wood, engraver in wood. —bildnerei, f. wood-engraving, xylography. —binder, m. fagot-maker or binder. —birn, f. wild pear; it. V. Würzbirn. —birnbaum, m. wild pear-tree. —blöde, f. [among foresters] an open place in a forest, a glade, a clearing. —bock, m. 1) [a horse or wooden frame on which wood is sawed] jack, V. Sägebock. 2) [a stand in a fireplace to lay wood on] andiron, dog. 3) [an insect] a) capricorn-beetle, cerambix. b) tick, acarus. —boden, m. 1) wood-loft, V. —stall. 2) a soil for growing wood. —bohrer, m. 1) an auger, wimble or gimblet. 2) [in nat. hist.] a worm that eats into wood, ligniperda. —bräme, f. [in forestry] an underwood or coppice at the entrance of a forest, V. Vorholz. —bühne, f. V. —boden. —bund, —bündel, n. a bundle of wood, a fagot. —consumtion, f. V. —verbrauch. —deich, m. a dike lined with wood or planks. ||—deube, f. V. —diebstahl. —dicke, f. the thickness of the wood. —dieb, m., —diebinn, f. a person who steals wood in a forest, wood-thief, V. Forstfrevler. —diebstahl, m. the stealing of wood in a forest, V. Forstfrevel. ‡—ding, n. V. —gericht. —drechsler, m. turner in wood. ||—einschläger, m. V. —aufsetzer. —erbe, m. the proprietor of a wood or forest. —erbschaft, f. the ownership of a wood or forest. —erde, f. ligneous or wooden earth. —ersparniß, f. V. —sparung. —essig, m. V. —säure. —essigäther, m. pyroligneous ether. —fackel, f. a torch of pine-wood, V. Kienfackel. —fällen, n. the felling of wood. —fäller, m. [wood-]feller, wood-cutter. —fang, m. V. Floßrechen. —farbe, f. the colour of wood, wood-colour. —faser, f. fibre of wood, ligneous fibre. —fäule, —fäulniß, f. putrefaction or rottenness of wood. —feile, f. rasp, V. Raspel. —fertig, adj. is said of a charcoal-pile when it only wants covering. —feuer, n. wood-fire. —firniß, m. varnish for wooden furniture. —flöße, f. a raft for floating wood. —flößen, n. the floating of wood. —flößer, m. a man who floats wood or who works on a float or raft, rafter, floater. —förster, m. a forester to whom the care of the wood is committed but not of the game. —frei, adj. and adv. having one's wood or fuel without expense. Einen —frei halten, to find any one in wood or fuel. —fresser, m. [in nat. history] V. —bohrer 2). —frevel, m. mischief done to wood; V. Forstfrevel. —frevler, m. one who is guilty of mischievously injuring the wood, V Forstfrevler. —frohne, f. socage service, consisting in the carrying of wood. —fuhre, f. 1) the act of carrying or conveying wood. 2) a waggon for wood. 3) a waggon or cart full of wood, a cart-load of wood. —fürst, m. [in Scripture] the keeper of the king's forest. —garten, m. V. —lager. —gebund, n. V. —bund. —gedinge, n. 1) contract for a supply of wood. 2) [obsolete] V. —gericht. —gefälle, pl. revenues or proceeds of a wood or forest. —geist, m. V. —säure. —gelänge, n. [among foresters] a district destined for planting wood. —geld, n. money paid or received for wood, wood-money. —gerecht, adj. and adv. versed in the knowledge of wood; it. V, Forstgerecht. —gerechtigkeit, f. the right over a wood. —gericht, n. wood-mote, V. Forstgericht. —gewächs, n. a ligneous or woody plant. —glitsche, f. V. —rutsche. —graf, m. 1) chief forester, warden of a forest. 2) a proprietor or lord of a forest who has the jurisdiction of it. —grafschaft, f. 1) the office or dignity of a chief forester or of a warden of a forest. 2) the jurisdiction of such an officer. —gräserei, f. pasture in a wood; it. the right to such a pasture. —graupen, pl. [in mining] copper-ore in form of wood. —grund, m. a soil good for growing wood. —gründung, f. [among painters] priming on wood. —hacke, f. V. —axt. —hacker, m. 1) wood-cleaver. 2) [in nat. hist.] the creeper, woodpecker. —häher, m the roller, German parrot. —hahn, m. wood-cock. —haken, m. cramp, cramp-iron. —handel, m. wood-trade, timber-trade. —händler, m. a dealer in wood, wood-monger, wood-merchant, timber-merchant. —hape, f. V. —hippe. —hase, m. wood-hare. —hau, m. place in a forest where trees are felled, V. Gehau. —hauer, m. wood-cutter, [wood-] feller; it. V. —hacker, —spalter. —haufe[n], m. heap or pile of wood. —heher, m. V. —häher. —heie, f. V. —schlägel. —henne, f. V. —huhn. —herr, m. [in saltworks] the officer who has the care of the wood. —hippe, f. a large hedging-bill. —hof, m. 1) wood-yard, timber-yard. 2) V. —markt. —huhn, n. 1) wood-hen, it. white partridge. 2) V. Schwarzspecht. —käfer, m. V. —bock 3). —kammer, f. chamber where wood is kept, wood-chamber. —kauf, m. purchase of wood. —kirschbaum, m. wild-cherry-tree. —kirsche, f. wild cherry. —knecht, m. servant or labourer to the forester or woodkeeper. —knopf, m. a wooden button. —kohle, f. charcoal. Gegrabene or mineralische —kohle, V. Erdkohle. —krähe, f. 1) V. Hohlkrähe. 2) V. Mandelkrähe. —kur, f. the cure of a patient when he is to drink decoctions of medicinal woods. Die —kur gebrauchen, to drink decoctions of medicinal woods. —kux, m. [in mining] a share in a mine belonging to the sovereign for the wood which he grants for the use of the mine. —lack, m stick-lac. —lader, m. loader of wood. —lager, n. wood-yard, timber-yard. —land, n. wood-land. —laus, f. wood-louse. —lege, f. V. —boden 1), —bühne, —platz, —schoppen, —stall. —leger, m. V. —messer. —lerche, f. V. Heidelerche. —lese, f. the picking up or gleaning of wood. —made, f. V. —wurm. —magazin, n wood-house, a wood-magazine. —mahlerei, f. painting on wood. —mangel, m. want of wood. —mangold, m. winter-green. —mark, f. mark or boundary of a wood or forest. —märker, m. a peasant who dwells within the boundaries of a wood. —markt, m. wood-market. —maß, n. measure of wood, as a cord &c. —mast, f. 1) mast for cattle and swine, such as acorns, beech-nuts &c. 2) the feeding or fattening swine or cattle with acorns, beech-nuts &c. —mastung, f. V. —mast 2). —mehl, n. worm-dust, V. Wurmmehl. —meise, f. coal-titmouse, coal-mouse, V. Tannenmeise. —meister, m. 1) [formerly] carpenter. 2) [formerly or provincially] wood-reeve. 3) [in nat. hist.] V. —bock 3). —meß, —messen, n. the measuring of wood by the cord &c. —messer, m. a person who measures wood by the cord &c.; sworn wood-meter. —mist, m. manure consisting of the litter of fallen leaves. —muschel, [Baumsperling] f. wood-sparrow. —nagel, m. a peg. —nischel, f. V. —muschel. —nutzung, f. V. Forstnutzung. —ofen, m. [in saltworks] an oven for drying wood. —opal, m. ligniform opal, wood-opal. —ordnung, f. V. Forstordnung. —pfeife, f. V. Hohlpfeife. —platte, f. a flat piece of wood, board; it. V. —schnitt. —platz, m. V. —lager; it. V. —lege, —stall. —preis, m. price of wood. —puppe, f. a wooden puppet or doll. —raspel, f. rasp. —raum, m. wood-house. —raupe, f. V. —bohrer 2). —rechen, m. V. Floßrechen. —rechnung, f. account of wood bought and sold. —recht, n. V. Holzungsrecht. —reich, adj. and adv. abounding with wood, woody. Eine —reiche Gegend, a woody region or country; ein —reicher Meiler, V. —fertig. —richter, m. 1) V. Forstrichter. 2) [provincial] V. —messer. —ruß, m. wood-soot. —rutsche, f. a sloping slide in a forest to let down large quantities of logs or billets of wood from the top or sides of a mountain &c. —sache, f. 1) any thing made of wood. 2) V. Forstsache. —säge, f. a saw for sawing wood. —säger, m. sawyer. —same, m. wood-seed. —säure, f. pyroligneous acid. —scharre, f. a knife or other tool for scraping off the resin. —scheit, n. log or billet of wood. —scheuer, f. V. —schoppen. —schieber, m. [among bakers] oven-rake. —schiff, n. a ship laden with wood or timber; it. a ship for transporting wood or timber, timber-ship. —schlag, m. 1) the act of felling wood. 2) the right of felling wood. 3) place in a forest where trees are felled. Die —schläge ableeren or säubern, to carry away or remove the wood, to clear the premises; V. Hau, Hieb, Schlag. —schlägel, m. a beetle or mallet for driving the iron wedges into the wood. —schläger, m. V. —fäller. —schlagung, f. the act of driving piles or stakes into the ground. —schneidekunst, f. V. —bildnerei. —schneider, m. 1) one who saws and cuts wood, V. —hauer. 2) engraver in wood. —schneiderei, f. V. —bildnerei. —schneidergerüst, n. V. —bock 1). —schnepfe, f. wood-cock. —schnitt, m. wood-cut, engraving in wood. —schnitzer, m. V. —bildner. —schober, m. a large heap or pile of wood. —schoppen, m. a shed for wood, wood-house. —schragen, m. a certain measure for wood [equal to three fathoms]. —schraube, f. a screw to be fastened in wood, a wood-screw. —schreiber, m. clerk of the wood. —schreibetag, m. V. —tag. —schreier, m. V. —häher. —schuh, m. a wooden shoe. —schuhbaum, m. tupelo. —schuhmacher, m. one that makes wooden shoes. —schuppen, m. V. —schoppen. —schwarte, f. the outside of a log of wood which is cut into planks. —setzer, m. V. —aufsetzer. —sieb, n. a sieve of wood [opposed to hair-sieve &c.]. —spalter, m. wood-cleaver, V. —hacker, —hauer. —span, m. a chip or shaving of wood. —sparküche, f. V. Sparküche. —sparkunst, f. art of saving wood. —sparung, f. the saving of wood. ||—speller, m. V. —spalter. —sperling, m. V. Weidensperling. —splitter, m. splinter of wood. —stall, m. wood-house. —stätte, f. place for wood. V. —lager and —lege. —stein, m. lithoxyle, wood-stone. —steinkohle, f. bituminous wood. —stich, m. V. —schnitt. —stoß, m. pile [of wood], stake [of wood]. V. Scheiterhaufen. —stumpen, —stumpf, m. the stub of a tree, stump. —tafel, f. wooden table. —tag, m. 1) day fixed for fetching wood in the forest, wood-day. 2) day fixed for getting tickets for receiving a certain quantity of wood. —taube, f. wood-pigeon, ‡ wood-culver, ring-dove. —taxe, f. fixed price of wood. —trage, f. hand-barrow for carrying wood. —trank, m. wood-drink. —trift, f. 1) pasturage in a forest. 2) right of pasturage in a forest. —verbindung, f. V. Ständerwerk. —verbrauch, m. consumption of fire-wood. —verkauf, m. sale of wood. —verwalter, m. a person or officer who superintends the sale of wood. —verwaltung, f. board for managing the sale of wood. —**vorrath**, *m.* store of wood. —**waare**, *f.* article manufactured of wood. ||—**wädel**, *m.* time for felling wood. —**wagen**, *m.* 1) waggon laden with wood. 2) waggon for conveying wood. —**wand**, *f.* a wooden wall. —**wanze**, *f.* kermes. —**wärter**, *m.* a person appointed to attend to the wood; *it.* wood-ward. —**weg**, *m.* way in a wood. *Fig.* [jocosely, students' cant] **Auf dem —wege seyn**, to be far out of the way, to be quite on the wrong scent. —**weichsel**, *f.* V. —**kirsche**. —**weide**, *f.* pasture in the forest. —**welle**, *f.* V. —**band**. —**werk**, *n.* wood-work, timber-work. **Das —werk eines Zimmers**, wainscot, wainscoting. —**wesen**, *n.* the management of woods and every thing belonging to them, the concerns of the forest. —**wespe**, *f.* wood-wasp. —**wurm**, *m.* wood-fretter, wood-louse, wood-worm, death-watch. —**zapfen**, *m.* a wooden pin, a plug. —**zehnte**, *m.* tithes paid of wood. —**zeit**, *f.* time for felling wood. —**zettel**, *m.* a ticket for receiving a certain quantity of wood. —**zinn**, *n.* fibrous oxide of tin, wood-tin, Cornish tin-ore. —**zucht**, *f.* economy of the forest. —**zunder**, *m.* touch-wood. —**zweig**, *m.* a wood-branch.

Hölzbar, *adj.* and *adv.* that may be felled or cut down; *it.* fit for the growth of wood. **Eine Blöße wieder — machen**, to replant a clearing with trees.

Hölzen, I. *v. intr.* 1) [among hunters] to ascend a tree, to light or climb upon a tree, V. **Baumen** I. 2). 2) [among foresters] to cut, fetch, carry or collect wood. II. *v. tr.* 1) to cover with wood; [in mining] to line the shaft or pit. 2) to fill with wood. **Den Ofen —** [among bakers], to provide the oven with wood.

Hölzen, *adj.* V. **Hölzern**.

Hölzern, *adj.* and *adv.* made or consisting of wood, wooden. **Ein —es Bein**, a wooden leg; **ein —es Gefäß**, a wooden vessel. *Fig.* *a*) awkward, clumsy. **Ein —er Mensch**, an awkward fellow, a wooden person. *b*) *[applied to the taste] insipid, tasteless, flat. **Es schmeckt —**, it is flat to the taste. *c*) [applied to sounds] **Ein —er Ton**, a flat sound; **eine —e Stimme**, a harsh hollow voice.

Hölzicht, *adj.* and *adv.* like or resembling wood, ligneous, ligniform, woodlike, woody. **Eine —e Kapsel**, a woody capsule; **ein —er Rettig, eine —e Wurzel**, a stringy radish, root.

Hölzig, *adj.* and *adv.* consisting of or covered with wood, woody, wooded. **Ein —er Stengel, eine —e Wurzel**, a woody stalk, a woody root; **ein —er Hügel**, a well wooded hill, a woody hill.

Hölzung, *f.* 1) act of felling, cutting or fetching wood. 2) V. —**srecht**. 3) wood, forest. 4) V. **Holzwand**.

Holzungs-berechtigte, *m.* one who has the right or liberty of cutting or fetching wood in a forest. —**recht**, *n.* the right, privilege or liberty of cutting or fetching wood in a forest.

***Homilétik**, *f.* homiletic or pastoral theology.

***Homilétiker**, *m.* [-s, *pl.* -] teacher of homiletic theology.

***Homilétisch**, *adj.* pertaining to homiletic theology.

***Homilíe**, *f.* [*pl.*-en] homily.

Homilienschreiber, *m.* writer of homilies.

***Homocentricität**, *f.* [quality of having the same or a like centre] homocentricity.

***Homocéntrisch**, *adj.* and *adv.* homocentric.

***Homogén**, *adj.* and *adv.* [of the same kind or nature] homogeneal, homogeneous.

***Homogenität**, *f.* homogenealness, homogeneity, homogeneousness.

***Homológ, Homológisch**, *adj.* [in geometry] homologous.

***Homoným** or **Homonýmisch**, *adj.* and *adv.* homonymous.

***Homonymíe**, *f.* homonymy.

***Homöopáth**, *m.* homoeopath.

***Homöopathíe**, *f.* homoeopathy.

***Homöopáthisch**, *adj.* and *adv.* homoeopathic.

***Homophág**, *m.* [-en, *pl.* -en] one who eats raw meat or flesh.

***Homophagíe**, *f.* feeding on raw meat or flesh homophagy.

***Homophoníe**, *f.* homophony.

***Homotónisch**, *adj.* and *adv.* [in medicine] homotonous.

Hönicht, *adj.* and *adv.* sweet as honey. *Fig.* —**e Worte**, sweet, flattering words, honey words, honied words.

Hönig, *m.* and *n.* [-s] [A. Sax. *hunig*, Eng. *honey*, D. *honning*, Icel. *hunang*; the root **Hon** is probably allied to the L. *vin*-um, Gr. *οἶνος*, Germ. **Wein**] honey. **Gezeidelter —**, honey in the comb; **geseimter —**, liquid honey; **roher —**, common honey; V. **Jungfern —, Linden—, Stein—, Zucker—**; **— bauen**, to cultivate honey; **die Worte flossen ihm wie — von den Lippen**, his words were sweet as honey. *Fig.* **Der — ihrer Lippen** [= **ihr süßer Kuß**, in poetry], the nectar of her lips, her sweet kisses; *— **im Munde und Galle im Herzen führen**, to be double-hearted or false-hearted; *prov.* a honey-tongue a heart of gall; [in popular lang.] **Einem — um den Bart schmieren**, to cheat, deceive or gull any one by giving him fair words, to persuade any one by flattery or coaxing.

Honig-apfel, *m.* a sort of very sweet apple, honey-apple. —**bär**, *m.* a kind of little bear, very fond of honey. —**bau**, *m.* culture of honey. —**bauer**, *m.* one that cultivates honey, bee-master. —**baum**, *m.* a hollow tree in which bees deposit their honey. —**behältniß**, *n.* [in botany] V. —**gefäß**. —**biene**, *f.* honey-bee. —**birne**, *f.* a sort of very sweet pear, honey-pear. —**blase**, *f.* honey-bag. —**blume**, *f.* honey-flower. —**branntwein**, *m.* mead-brandy. —**brod**, *n.* V. —**schnitte**. —**brühe**, *f.* a sauce made of honey. —**dachs**, *m.* a badger of Africa, very fond of honey. —**dieb**, *m.* 1) a thief that robs the bee-hives. 2) V. —**nachtfalter**. —**dorn**, *m.*, —**erbse**, *f.* bean-tree of America; *it.* the fruit of it. —**erbsenbaum**, *m.* V. —**erbse**. —**essig**, *m.* oxymel. —**farbe**, *f.* honey-colour. —**farben**, —**farbig**, *adj.* and *adv.* honey-coloured. —**fladen**, *m.* 1) V. —**kuchen**. 2) V. —**schnitte**. 3) V. —**scheibe**. —**flecken**, *m.* a yellow spot, especially on the skin. —**fliege**, *f.* V. —**mücke**. —**gabel**, *f.* a fork for taking the honey-combs out of the hive. —**garten**, *m.* [a garden or enclosure to set bee-hives in] bee-garden. —**gefäß**, *n.* a vessel for honey or full of honey; [in botany] honey-cup, nectary. —**gehren**, *m.* V. —**scheibe**. —**gelb**, *adj.* yellow as honey, honey-coloured. —**gelte**, *f.* a pail for honey. —**gelter** [= **Einer, der Entgelt** or **Zins in Honig entrichtet**], *m.* one who pays rent in honey. —**geruch**, *m.* smell or odour of honey. —**geschmack**, *m.* taste or flavour of honey. —**geschwulst**, *f.*, —**geschwür**, *n.* [in surgery] meliceris. —**gewirk**, *n.* V. —**scheibe**. —**gras**, *n.* V. **Darrgras**. —**gülte**, *f.* V. —**zins**. —**kelch**, *m.* [in botany] V. —**gefäß**. —**klee**, *m.* melilot, sainfoin. V. **Süßklee**. —**kuchen**, *m.* 1) ginger-bread. 2) V. —**scheibe**. —**kuchenbäcker**, or —**küchler**, *m.* gingerbread-baker. —**kuckuck**, *m.* honey-guide. —**leim**, *m.* [among gilders] a glue or size made of honey and vinegar, honey-glue, honey-size. —**lese**, *f.* the collecting of honey, honey-harvest. —**lippen**, *pl.* V. —**mund**. —**loch**, *n.*, —**löcher**, *pl.* [in botany] nectareal pores. ||—**mahrte**, *f.* V. —**scheibe**. —**maul**, *n.* [in popular lang.] a person very fond of honey. —**monat**, *m.* the month in which the bees collect their honey, honey-month. —**mücke**, *f.* honey-gnat. —**mund**, *m.* [in poetry] a mouth that utters sweet or honied words; *it.* a mouth whose kisses are sweet, ambrosial mouth or lips. —**nachtfalter**, *m.* [a butterfly] honey-thief. —**öl**, *n.* [a gum of an oily nature which drops from the olive-trees in Syria] elaeomeli. —**pflaster**, *n.* [among farriers] charge. —**reich**, *adj.* and *adv.* abounding with honey. ||—**roß**, *n.* V. —**scheibe**. —**saft**, *m.* juice sweet as honey; *it.* V. —**essig**; *it.* [in botany] nectareous juice. —**sammler**, *m.*, —**sammlerinn**, *f.* a person who collects honey. —**sauger**, *m.* humming-bird, colibri. —**scheibe**, *f.* honey-comb. —**schimmel**, *m.* a white horse with honey-coloured spots. —**schmetterling**, *m.* honey-butterfly, the little Argus. —**schnitte**, *f.* a slice of bread and honey. —**schuppe**, *f.* [in botany] melliferous scale. —**seim**, *m.* honey as dropped from the comb, not clarified, virgin-honey. **Seine Worte, süßer, denn —seim** [in Scripture], his words sweeter than honey. —**stein**, *m.* honey-stone, mellite. —**stimme**, *f.* sweet voice. —**süß**, *adj.* and *adv.* sweet as honey, very sweet. —**süße Worte**, honied or honey-words. —**süße**, *f.* sweetness of honey. —**tafel**, *f.* V. —**scheibe**. —**täubling**, *m.* the red agaric. —**thau**, *m.* honey-dew. —**topf**, *m.* a pot for honey or full of honey, honey-pot. —**trank**, *m.* a drink made of honey; *it.* very sweet drink. —**umschlag**, *m.* V. —**pflaster**. —**wabe**, *f.* V. —**scheibe**. —**wasser**, *n.* simple hydromel. —**webe**, *f.* V. —**scheibe**. —**wicke**, *f.* wild chickling vetch. —**wort**, —**wörtchen**, *n.* a sweet flattering word, a honey or honied word. —**zehnte**, *m.* tithes paid of honey. —**zelle**, *f.* honey-cell. —**zins**, *m.* rent paid in honey.

Hönighaft, *adj.* V. **Honicht**.

Hönigt, *adj.* V. **Honicht**.

***Honorár**, *n.* [-es, *pl.*-e] fee, especially an author's fee.

***Honoratiören**, *pl.* [**einer Stadt, Landschaft** &c.] people of education and good-breeding, gentry.

***Honoríren**, *v. tr.* 1) [in commerce, to accept and pay when due] to honour. **Einen Wechsel —**, to honour a bill of exchange. 2) **Einen —**, to pay any one a certain fee or copy-money. 3) [in popular lang.] to do any one honour.

Hoofd, *n.* [-es, *pl.* -e] [allied to **hoch, heben**] [in seamen's lang.] 1) mole, pier. 2) a small cape, head-land or promontory, point.

Hóp or **Hópp**, *interj.* 1) [to imitate the trot of a horse] hop, hop! 2) [an exclamation used when a person or horse stumbles] holla! 3) [an exclamation of great joy, frolick and exultation, generally joined with the words **he** and **sa**] — **he**! — **sa**! hussa, heyday!

Hópfen, *m.* [-s, *pl.* -] 1) [a climbing plant] hop, hops. **Wilder —**, wild hops; **tauber** or **männlicher —**, male hops; **— bauen**, to plant or cultivate hops; **— pflücken**, to pick hops; **ein kleiner Sack —**, pocket [of hops]; **ein großer Sack —**, bag [of hops]; **dem Biere — geben**, to hop the beer; **das Bier hat zu viel —**, the beer is too much hopped. *Prov.* **Es ist — und Malz an ihm verloren**, all labour is lost on him, he is incorrigible, it is washing a blackamoor white. 2) **Der spanische —**, the Spanish marjoram.

Hopfen-acker, *m.* 1) a field or ground fit for the culture of hops. 2) hop-ground, hop-field, hop-garden, hop-yard. —**bau**, *m.* culture of hops. Den —bau treiben, to cultivate hops. —**baum**, *m.* V. —hainbuche. —**berg**, *m.* a hill where hops grow. —**blatt**, *n.* the leaf of hops. —**blüte**, *f.* the blossom of hops. —**boden**, *m.* 1) V. —acker 1). 2) loft where hops are preserved, stowage-room. —**brame**, *f.* V. —ranke. —**darre**, *f.* kiln for drying hops, hop-kiln, ||hop-oast. —**eule**, *f.* V. —nachtvogel. —**fächser**, *m.* sucker of hops. —**feld**, *n.* V. —acker 2). —**garten**, *m.* hop-garden, hop-yard. —**gärtner**, *m.* cultivator of hops. —**hainbuche**, *f.* hop-hornbeam. —**haupt**, *n.* the fruit of the female hops, flowerbud of hops. —**hefen**, *pl.* yeast, barm. —**keim**, *m.*, —**keimchen**, *n.* hop-bud. —**klee**, *m.* hop-clover. —**klette**, *f.* the greater burdock. —**korb**, *m.* [in breweries] a basket through which the beer runs when hopped. —**mehl**, *n.* dust with which the hops when ripe are overspread, mealy dew. —**nachtvogel**, *m.* hop night-butterfly. —**öl**, *n.* oil extracted from the Spanish marjoram. —**pflanze**, *f.* V. —ranke. —**pflücker**, *m.* hop-picker. —**ranke**, *f.* hop-bind, hop-vine, hop-string. —**reich**, *adj.* and *adv.* abounding with hops. —reiches Bier, well-hopped beer. —**sack**, *m.* a bag for hops or full of hops. —**salat**, *m.* salad of hops or hop-buds. —**seide**, *f.* V. Flachskraut *a*). —**seihe**, *f.* V. —korb. —**seil**, *n.* hop-string, V. —ranke. —**spargel**, *m.*, —**sprosse**, *f.* V. —keim. —**stange**, *f.* hop-pole. *Fig.* [in popular lang.] Sie ist eine wahre —stange, she is a perfect may-pole [very tall and slim]. —**stengel**, *m.* hop-bind. —**stichel**, *m.* [a pointed instrument used to make holes for planting hops] dibble. —**zapfen**, *m.* V. —haupt.

Hopfen, *v. tr.* to impregnate with hops, to hop. Das Bier —, to hop the beer.

Höpfener, Höpfner, *m.* [-s, *pl.*-] V. Hopfengärtner.

Höpp, V. Hop.

Höps, *m.* [-es, *pl.* -e] [chiefly in popular lang.] a skip, a hop, a leap, a gambol. Einen — machen, to leap, to hop, to gambol.

Hops-tanz, —**walzer**, *m.* a German dance, hop.

Höpsa, V. Hop 3).

Höpsen, *v. intr.* [allied to heben] to hop, to leap, to jump; *it.* to dance a hop.

Höpser, *m.* [-s, *pl.* -] 1) one who hops or leaps, hopper, leaper. 2) V. Hopstanz.

Hörbar, *adj.* and *adv.* that may be heard, audible.

Hörbarkeit, *f.* audibleness.

Hörche, *f.* [rather unusual] the act of listening.

Hörchen, [Sax. *heorcnian*, Eng. *to hearken*, from hören] I. *v. intr.* to hearken, to listen. Reden Sie nicht so laut, man horcht, do not speak so loud, we are overheard or somebody is listening; er horchte auf unsere Reden, he listened to what we said; horch! hear! hark! [in mining] to be upon the watch. [in poetry] Die ganze Natur horcht den harmonischen Tönen, all nature attends or listens to the harmonious sounds. II. *v. tr.* [in poetry, rather stiff] Er horchet ihre Lieder, he lists her songs.

Horch-brunnen, *m.* [in fortification] cascan. —**haus**, *n.*, *dim.* —**häuschen**, ||—**häuslein**, *n.* [in mining] [a little hut in which a miner's boy hearkens till the clock strikes for the relief. —**schwester**, *f.* listening-nun. —**winkel**, *m.* a private, secret or snug place or corner for listening.

Hörcher, *m.* [-s, *pl.* -] —**inn**, *f.* [chiefly in a bad sense] a person who listens, listener, hearkener, eaves-dropper. *Prov.* Der — an der Wand hört seine eigene Schand', listeners never hear well of themselves.

1. **Hörde**, *f.* [*pl.* -n] V. Hürde.

2. **Hörde**, *f.* [*pl.* -n] [Eng. *hord* or *horde*, D. *horde*, Tart. *horda*, *ordu*, Sax. *heord*, allied to Heerde] horde. Eine — Tartaren, a horde of Tartars; eine — Wilder, a horde, a tribe of savages; eine — Räuber, a gang of robbers.

Hordenweise, *adv.* in hordes, in troops.

***Hören**, *pl.* [in mythology, the daughters of Jupiter and Themis] Hours.

Hören, [Sax. *hyran*, Eng. *to hear*, Sw. *hoera*; it seems to be derived from Ohr, as in English to hear from ear and the L. *audio* from the Gr. οὖς] I. *v. intr.* to enjoy the sense or faculty of hearing, to hear. Gut, unvollkommen —, to hear well, imperfectly; hart —, to be hard of hearing. II. *v. tr.* and *v. intr.* 1) to perceive by the ear, to hear. Töne, Jemands Stimme —, to hear sounds, any one's voice; ich höre ihn kommen, I hear him coming; thun, als ob man Etwas nicht höre, to turn a deaf ear; es ließ sich eine Stimme —, a voice was heard; er ließ sich im Concert auf der Violine —, he played on the violin in the concert; sie wird sich heute [im Singen] — lassen, she is going to sing to-day; laß — ! let me hear: speak! was höre ich! what do I hear! ich höre von Jedermann, daß &c., I hear of every body that &c.; haben Sie etwas Neues gehört? have you heard any news? sie machen einen solchen Lärm, daß man einander nicht — kann, they make so much noise that one cannot hear the other speak; ich habe es sagen —, I have heard some people say so, I was told so; ich habe ihn nie gehört, I have never heard him [preach, read, sing &c.]; ich habe es von ihm selbst gehört, I heard him say so himself; wenn man ihn hört, so besaß mein Herr &c., according to him, my master possessed &c.; ich habe es vom — sagen [Hörensagen], I know it by hearsay; laßt mich doch ja dann und wann Etwas von euch —, pray let me hear from you now and then; die Messe —, to hear mass; bei diesem Professor habe ich die Philosophie gehört, I heard that professor read lectures on philosophy, I studied philosophy under that professor; der Richter muß beide Theile —, a judge ought to hear both parties; man hat ihn verurtheilt, ohne ihn gehört zu haben, he was condemned without being heard or without a hearing; das läßt sich —, that sounds well; *it.* there is great plausibility in what he says, you say, they say &c; diese Entschuldigung läßt sich —, this is a good, allowable or plausible excuse. 2) to attend or listen to, to mind. — Sie, welch ein Geräusch! hark, what a noise! ich sehe, Sie — nicht darauf, I see you do not attend to what is uttered. *Fig.* to take to heart what is said. Er will mich nicht —, he does not mind what I say; Gott, höre mein Gebet! God, hear my prayer! auf die Stimme des Himmels or Gottes —, to hear the voice of heaven or God. *Prov.* Wer nicht — will, muß fühlen, he who won't listen to good advice must smart for it. Das —, the act of hearing. **Fig.* Es ist ihm — und Sehen vergangen [=der Kopf hat ihm geschwindelt], he was seized with dizziness or swimming in the head.

Hör-gast, *m.* [little used for *Hospes] one who attends the lectures of a professor only for a short time, an extraordinary auditor. —**gewölbe**, *n.* V. Sprachgewölbe. —**rohr**, *n.* ear-trumpet. —**saal**, *m.* lecture-room, auditory. —**sage**, *f.* —**sagen**, *n.*, V. Hörensagen. —**stube**, *f.* V. —saal. —**trichter**, *m.* V. —rohr. —**werkzeug**, *n.* 1) = Ohr, ear. 2) acoustic instrument. —**zeuge**, *m.* ear-witness, V. Ohrenzeuge. —**zimmer**, *n.* V. —stube.

Hörensagen, *n.* [-s] hearsay. Er weiß es blos vom —, he knows it only by hearsay. *Prov.* Von — lügt man gern, they say or I heard say, is half a lie.

Hörer, *m.* [-s, *pl.* -] —**inn**, *f.* a person who hears, hearer, auditor, listener, V. Zuhörer. [in Script.] Seyd Thäter des Worts und nicht — allein, be ye doers of the word and not hearers only; [in law] ein — bei Gerichten [in some parts of Germany called Auscultator, in others Referendarius &c.], a young practitioner in law or aspirant to a legal or justice's office that attends causes or the sittings of a tribunal or board of justices for improvement.

***Horizónt**, *m.* [-es] [Gesichtskreis, Himmelsrand] horizon. *Fig.* Das ist or geht über meinen —, that's beyond my reach.

***Horizontāl**, *adj.* and *adv.* horizontal. Eine —e Sonnenuhr, a horizontal sun-dial.

Horizontal-fläche, *f.* horizontal surface. —**linie**, *f.* horizontal line. —**schuß**, *m.* V. Kernschuß. —**wage**, *f.* V. Wasserwage. —**wasser**, *n.* subterranean water, body of water under ground or below the earth's surface.

Hörn, *n.* [-es, *pl.* Hörner] [probably from the root ur = hoch, allied to the Hebrew *kereh*, L. *cornu*, Gr. κέρας, Sax. *hyrn*, *hern*, and Icel., Dan., Sw. and Eng. *horn*] 1) [in general] any thing projecting. *a*) the top or peak of a mountain, *it.* a high mountain. *b*) a cape, headland or promontory, a point. *c*) the end or extremity of a thing, corner. Die Hörner einer Mütze, the corners of a cap; die Hörner des Altares, the corners or horns of the altar; die Hörner eines Amboßes, the points or beaks of an anvil; die Hörner des Mondes, the horns of the moon; [in seamen's lang.] die Hörner der Segel, the peaks of the sails; [in mining] das — [des Haspels], the handle or winch [of the windlass]. 2) [the hard substance growing on the heads of certain animals, *it.* the feeler of an insect] horn. Die Kühe und Ziegen haben Hörner, cows and goats have horns; die Schnecken ziehen ihre Hörner ein, the snails pull or draw in their horns; die Hörner abwerfen, to shed or cast the horns. *Fig.* Das — des Heils, [in Scripture = Gott] the horn of salvation; [in fam. lang.] die Hörner einziehen, to repress one's ardour or restrain one's pride &c., to pull in the horns; Einem die Hörner bieten, to make head against any one, to bid any one defiance; sich die Hörner ablaufen, to sow one's wild oats; Etwas auf seine Hörner nehmen, to take any thing upon one's self or upon one's own shoulders, to run the risk of any thing; Hörner tragen or haben, to wear horns, to be a cuckold; sie hat ihrem Manne Hörner aufgesetzt, she has bestowed a pair of horns upon her husband, she has cuckolded or horned her husband. 3) a horned animal, used only in composition, as Ein—, Nas— &c., which see. 4) the substance of horns, horny substance, horn. Eine Tabaksdose, ein Kamm von —, a snuffbox, a comb of horn, a horn-snuffbox &c.; in — arbeiten, to work in horn; *fig.* [on account of the resemblance of the substance] das — der Pferde, Esel, a horse's or ass's hoof; [in botany] das —, horn-shaped or cornuted style. 5) a vessel or instrument made of horn, a horn, V. Trinkhorn &c. Das — des Ueberflusses, the horn of plenty, cornucopia. *it.* a wind-instrument, horn. Das — blasen, to wind or blow the horn; V. Hief—, Jäger—, Post—, Wald—. **Fig.* Mit Jemand in Ein — blasen, to act in concert with any one, to have an understanding with any one; *it. prov.* to draw the yoke together.

Horn-achat, *m.* horny agate. —**affe**, *m.* a sort of pastry-work in the shape of two horns joined. —**amboß**, *m.* bickern. —**arbeit**, *f.*

work in horn. —**arbeiter**, *m.* worker in horn; *it.* V. —bereiter. —**artig**, *adj.* and *adv.* having the nature of horn, horny. —**band**, *m.* [among bookbinders] binding in parchment or vellum. —**baum**, *m.* horn-beam, V. also Hagebuche. —**beize**, *f.* 1) maceration of horn. 2) the liquor or infusion in which horn is macerated. —**bereiter**, *m* horn-dresser. —**berg**, *m.* V. —stein. —**bläser**, *m.* one who blows or winds the horn, horn-blower, horner, [in military affairs] bugle. —**blatt**, *n.* [a plant] horn-wort. —**blei**, *n.* muriatic lead. —**blende**, *f.* [in mineral.] horn-blend. —**bock**, *m.* a ram with horns, a horned ram. —**drechsler**, —**dreher**, *m.* a turner in horn. —**durchfäule**, *f.* [in the veterinary art] hard swelling. —**erz**, *n.* horn-silver, muriate of silver. —**eule**, *f.* horned owl, horn-owl, horn-coot. —**farbe**, *f.* 1) horn-colour. 2) colour for dying horn. —**farben**, —**farbig**, *adj.* and *adv.* horn-coloured. —**fäule**, *f.* V. —durchfäule. —**feile**, *f.* a file for filing the horse's hoof. —**fels**, *m.* petrosilex. —**felsstein**, *m.* V. —stein. —**fessel**, *f.* [among hunters] strap by which the bugle is suspended. —**fisch**, *m.* horn-beak, horn-fish, gar- or gane-fish, sea-needle. —**flint**, *n.* silicious shist. —**flötz**, *n.* [in mining] a stratum or layer of blackish lime-stone, having the colour of horn. —**flügel**, *m.* elytra. —**flügelig**, *adj.* coleopteral. —**förmig**, *adj.* and *adv.* horn-shaped; [in botany] cornuted. —**frucht**, *f.* V. —same 1). —**fuß**, *m.* hoofed foot. —**füßig**, *adj.* hoofed. —**gestein**, *n.* V. —stein. —**glaserz**, *n.* V. —erz. —**gold**, *n.* the worst gold, gold of 9½ carats. —**hart**, *adj.* and *adv.* hard as horn. —**haspel**, *m.* windlass [in mining]. —**haut**, *f.* horny skin or cuticle, horny coat, callus. Die —haut des Auges, the horny coat of the eye, cornea. —**hautblatter**, *f.* V. —hautgeschwür. —**hautfistel**, *f.* fistula of the cornea. —**hautgeschwür**, *n.* an ulceration of the cornea, argema. —**häuticht**, *adj.* and *adv.* resembling a horny skin or tunicle. —**häutig**, *adj.* and *adv.* callous [in a proper as well as in a * figurative sense]. —**häutigkeit**, *f.* callousness, callosity. —**hautnagel**, *m.* [a disease of the eyes] unguis. —**hautträublein**, *n.* bothrion. —**hautvorfall**, *m.* staphyloma, staphylosis. —**hecht**, *m.* orphia. —**jagd**, *f.*, —**jagen**, *n.* chase or hunt in which the hounds are encouraged or animated by blowing the horn. —**käfer**, *m.* horn-beetle. —**kamm**, *m.* horn-comb. —**kirsche**, *f.* cornelian cherry. —**klampen**, *pl.* [in seamen's lang.] common belaying-cleats. —**klee**, *m.* sweet trefoil, bird's-foot trefoil. —**kluft**, *f.* [a certain cleft or fissure in a hoof] seam. —**klüftig**, *adj.* and *adv.* having a cleft, fissure or seam in the hoof. —**koralle**, *f.* ceratophyta. —**kraut**, *n.* the cerastium or mouse-ear chickweed. —**kuchen**, *m.* V. —affe. —**kümmel**, *m.* 1) common caraway. 2) hypecoum, V. Lappenblume. —**laterne**, *f.* horn lantern. —**leim**, *m.* very strong glue, parchment-glue or size. —**leiste**, *f.* [among joiners] a long piece of wood, a border or ledge of wood at the end of a table. —**leuchte**, *f.* V. —laterne. —**löffel**, *m.* horn-spoon. —**los**, *adj.* hornless. —**messer**, *n.* a knife for cutting horn. —**mohn**, *m.* horned poppy, glaucium. —**pflanze**, *f.* V. —koralle. —**platte**, *f.* horn-plate. —**pomeranze**, *f.* large orange, orange with a rough rind. —**presse**, *f.* a press for straightening horn, horn-press. —**quecksilber**, *n.* horn-mercury. —**raspel**, *f.* horn-rasp. —**richter**, *m.* V. —bereiter. —**salbe**, *f.* a salve for healing the seams of horses. —**same**, *m.* 1) ceratocarpus arenarius. 2) or —**samenschwamm**, *m.* ceratospermum. —**satz**, *m.* an embellishment or ornament of a bugle or hunter's horn. —**schein**, *m.* new-moon of February. —**schiefer**, *m.* horn-slate. —**schlange**, *f.* horned snake. —**schläuche**, *pl.* horn-rings [for preparing the hartshorn spirit]. —**schluß**, *m.* [in logic] dilemma. —**schnecke**, *f.* whelk, buccinum. —**schröter**, *m.* V. —käfer. —**seuche**, *f.* the horn distemper [of cattle]. —**silber**, *n.* horn-silver, muriate of silver, chlorid of silver. —**spalte**, *f.* V. —kluft. —**spaltig**, *adj.* V. —klüftig. —**späne**, *pl.* horn-shavings. —**spitze**, *f.* 1) the point of a horn. 2) tobacco-pipe-tip made of horn. —**spitzen**, *pl.* horn-tips. —**stein**, *m.* chert, horn-stone, petrosilex or rock flint. —**steinbreccie**, *f.* petrosilicious breccias. —**träger**, *m.* V. Hörnerträger. —**vieh**, *n.* horned cattle, horned beasts. —**vogel**, *m.* the hornbill; *it.* the cassiowary. —**werk**, *n.* [in fortific.] horn-work. —**wismuth**, *m.* the horned bismuth. —**zahn**, *m.* [in conchology] horned toothshell. —**zange**, *f.* large pincers for crushing horn. —**zungenmuskel**, *m.* [in anatomy] ceratoglossus.

Hörner-schall, *m.* sound of horns. Unter or mit —schall, with bugles sounding. —**schnörkel**, *m.* [in conchology] V. Thürhüter. —**schorf**, *m* [in botany] anthoceros. —**schwamm**, *m.* V. Kaulschwamm. —**träger**, *m.* a horned animal or beast. *Fig.* cuckold, cornuto.

Hörnen, *v. intr.* [unusual] to blow or wind the horn.

Hörnen, *v. tr.* to furnish with horns. Gehörntes Thier, gehörnte Eule, horned animal, horned owl; gehörnt [in botany], cornuted; der gehörnte Mond, horned moon. *Fig.* Ein gehörnter Ehemann, cuckold; [in logic] ein gehörnter Schluß, V. Hornschluß.

Hörnen [Hörnern], *adj.* and *adv.* of horn, horny, ‖ hornen. —e Arbeit, V. Hornarbeit; eine —e Tabaksdose, a horn snuffbox.

Hörnicht, *adj.* and *adv.* resembling horn, hornish, horny. —e Haut, horny or callous skin.

Hörnig, *adj.* and *adv.* consisting of horn, horny.

Hörnig, *adj.* furnished with horns. Used only in composition, as: Ein—, Zwei— &c.

Hornist, *m.* [-en, *pl.* -en] horner, bugle. V. Hornbläser.

Hörniß, *f.* [*pl.* Hornisse] [Engl. *hornet*, Sax. *hyrnet*, D. *horsel*. Either from Horn, or from the old horen = tönen] hornet.

Hornung, *m.* [-s] [from the old Hor = Koth, Sax. *horg*] February.

Hornungs-blume, *f* snow-drop. —**hecht**, *m.* a pike that spawns in February.

***Horópter**, *n.* [-s] horopter.

***Horoscóp**, *n.* [-s, *pl.* -e] horoscope.

Horst, *m* [-es, *pl.* -e or —*f. pl.* -en] [allied to Heer and the old har = hoch and *fig.* viel] 1) [obsolete] any great number or multitude, a host. 2) a bunch or tuft of grass, corn &c.; *it.* a place where grass, corn &c. grows too luxuriantly, V. Geil—. 3) a coppice, *it.* a tuft of trees, a small grove. 4) nest of a bird of prey, eyry. 5) a heap of sand or earth collected by the force of water.

Horsten, *v. intr.* [said of birds of prey] to build a nest or eyry.

Hort, *m.* [-es, *pl.* -e] [allied to hart] [in poetry] a rock; *it.* place of security, refuge, asylum. *Fig.* [applied to persons] protector, prop. Gott ist mein —, auf den ich baue, [in Scripture] God is my rock, in whom I trust.

Horte, *f.* V. Hürde.

Hosche, *f.* [*pl.* -n] a wooden box intended to convey any thing from a higher place by sliding down.

Höschen, ‖**Höslein**, *n* V. 1. and 2. Hose.

1. **Hose**, *f.* [*pl.* -n] *dim.* Höschen, ‖Höslein, *n.* [generally used in the pl.] [Fr. *chausse*, W *hos*, *hosan*, from hws, a covering, a housing] a garment covering the thighs and legs, breeches, pantaloons, trousers; [in fam. lang. or in jest] inexpressibles. Enge [= eng or dicht anliegende] or kurze —n, breeches, *it.* small clothes; weite, lange —n or Beinkleider, pantaloons; ganz weite, lange —n or Beinkleider [Pumphosen, Schifferhosen], trowsers; ein schönes Paar —n, a fine pair of breeches or trowsers; seine —n anziehen, to put on one's breeches or trowsers; die —n hinunterthun [or umkehren = seine Nothdurft verrichten, in popular lang.], to follow the call of nature, †to go backwards; V. Bade—, Pluder—, Pump—, Schlaf—, Strumpf—, Ueber—, Unter—. [in popular lang.] *Fig.* Das Herz ist ihm in die —n gefallen, his heart went down to his heels, the heart or courage failed him; sich in den Stand der geflickten —n begeben, to get married; seine Frau hat die —n an or trägt die —n, his wife wears the breeches, rules the roast.

Hosen-band, *n.* 1) a string, band or ribbon used to tie the breeches. 2) knee-band, garter. Der Orden vom —bande or vom blauen —bande, the order of the Garter. 3) [in natural history] V. Strumpfband. —**bund**, *m.* waistband. —**flicker**, *m.* mender of breeches or trowsers. *Fig.* [among hunters] a wild boar four years old. —**gurt**, *m.* —**gürtel**, *m.* V —bund. —**gurtschnalle**, *f.* waistband-buckle. —**halfter**, *f.*, —**heber**, *m.* V. —träger. —**klappe**, *f.* flap of the breeches or trowsers. —**knopf**, *m.* button of the breeches or trowsers. —**latz**, *m.* V. —klappe. —**los**, *adj.* and *adv.* destitute of breeches or trowsers, without breeches. —**nestel**, *f.* V. —band. —**sack**, *m.* V. —tasche. —**schlitz**, *m.* cod-piece. —**schnalle**, *f.* V. —gurtschnalle; *it.* V. Knieschnalle. —**schneider**, *m.* a tailor who makes breeches or trowsers, breeches-maker. —**stricker**, *m.* V. Strumpfstricker. —**tasche**, *f.* breeches-pocket. Eine kleine —tasche, fob. —**träger**, *m.* braces, suspenders, a pair of suspenders. —**zeug**, *m.* stuff for breeches or trowsers.

2. **Hose**, *f.* [*pl.* -n] *dim.* Höschen, ‖Höslein, *n.* [any thing hollow, allied to the L. *os*, Sw. *hoes* and Icel. *haus* = Hirnschädel] 1) a hollow vessel, utensil or instrument, V. Butter—. 2) [a violent discharge of water raised in a column by a whirlwind &c.] spout, water-spout.

Hosenbutter, *f.* firkin-butter, tub-butter [butter pressed into small tubs or casks and sold in them].

Höseln, I. *v. intr.* [said of bees] to bring in wax-meal. II. [unusual] *v. tr.* [ein Kind &c] to furnish with breeches or trowsers, to put into breeches &c.

Hösen, *v. tr.* V. Höseln II. *Fig.* Gehos'te Tauben, rough-footed pigeons.

Höslein, V. Höschen.

***Hóspes**, *m.* V. Hörgast.

***Hospitál**, *n.* [-es, *pl.* Hospitäler] hospital, V. Spital.

Hospital-meister, —**pfleger**, *m.* master or steward of an hospital. —**ritter**, *m.* V. Hospitaliter. —**schiff**, *n* a ship appropriated for the reception of the sick, hospital-ship.

***Hospitalíter**, *m.* [-s, *pl.* -] knight of the order of St. John, Hospitaller. V. also Johanniter-, Rhodiser- and Malteserritter.

***Hospodár**, *m.* [-es, *pl.* -e] [a title of the princes of Wallachia and Moldavia] hospodar.

***Hóstie**, *f.* [*pl.* -n] the consecrated wafer, host.

Hostienhäuslein, *n.* tabernacle.

Hott! [an exclamation of drivers, carters, wagge

ners &c. directing their teams to pass further to the right] ho! gee ho! *Fig.* [in popular lang.] **Er weiß nichts von —, noch von har**, there is no beating reason into his head, he is an ignorant fellow; **der Eine will —, der Andere har** or **hist**, they pull different ways.

Hótte, *f.* [*pl.* -n] a wooden vessel or tub to carry things in upon one's back, V. 2. **Butte**.

‡**Hótten**, *v. intr.* to go, to proceed. *Fig.* **Es will mit der Sache nicht —**, the affair does not advance or proceed.

Hottentótt, *m.* [-en, *pl.* -en] [a native of the southern extremity of Africa] Hottentot. *Fig.* [in popular lang.] a savage, brutal man.

1. †**Hótze** or **Hótzel**, *f.* [*pl.*-n] a cradle; *it.* a swing or seesaw.

2. †**Hótze** or **Hótzel**, *f.* [*pl.* -n] V. **Hutzel**.

1. †**Hótzeln** or **Hótzen**, *v. intr.* to rock [in a cradle]; *it.* to balance, to swing.

2. †**Hótzeln**, V. **Hutzeln**.

Hüb, *m.* [-es] 1) the act of lifting or raising, lift. **Eine Maschine zum — des Wassers**, an engine for raising water; [in forges] **der —**, the turn or turning half round of the water-wheel. *Fig.* [in popular lang.] **Einer Sache den — geben**, to set a thing a-going, to give it a lift. 2) the act of selecting or picking out; *it.* the thing or person selected or picked out, the best of a thing. 3) [in mining] the degree of elevation or the lift of the embolus or piston of the pump.

Hübbel, V. **Hübel**.

1. **Hübe**, *f.* V. **Hufe**.

2. **Hübe**, *f.* [*pl.* -n] [in saltworks] a tub, vessel or cask.

Hubel, *m.* [-s] or **— trog**, *m.* a trough in which the tin-ore is mixed with the dross.

Hübel or **Hübbel**, *m.* [-s, *pl.* -] [allied to **Hügel**] a little hill, hillock; [in anatomy and botany] a pimple, a little knob, a tubercle.

Hübelicht, *adj.* and *adv.* resembling hillocks and knobs, uneven, rough, knobbed.

Hübelig, *adj.* and *adv* [in botany] tuberous.

Hüben, *adv.* [in fam. lang] V. **Diesseits**.

Hübert, *m.* [-s, *pl.* -e] or **Hubèrtus**, [a name of men] Hubert, Hubertus.

Hubertsorden or **Hubertusorden**, *m.* the order of St. Hubert.

Hübsch, *adj.* and *adv.* [allied to the Sw. *hof* = **die rechte Art**, Sw. and Icel. *haefwa* = **sich schicken**] 1) [agreeable to the eye or to just taste] handsome, pretty, fine. **Ein —es Mädchen**, a pretty girl; **ein —es Haus**, a handsome house; **sie ist nicht schön, aber —**, she is not beautiful, but pretty; **sie ist — gekleidet**, she is handsomely or prettily dressed; **er tanzt —**, he dances nicely. 2) well-bred, genteel, civil. **Eine —e Aufführung**, a genteel conduct; **—e Manieren**, agreeable or genteel manners; **das ist nicht —**, that is not polite or courteous; **er benimmt sich sehr —**, he behaves very politely; [in fam. lang., in speaking to children] **geht — nach Hause**, go or walk nicely or prettily home; **sey — ruhig, liebe** or **meine Kleine**, pray, be quiet, my little dear. 3) good, proper, sufficient. **Eine —e Gelegenheit**, a good opportunity; **ein —es Vermögen**, an ample or handsome fortune; [ironically] **Sie haben da etwas —es angerichtet** or **angestellt**, you have made a fine piece of business of that.

Hübschheit, *f.* handsomeness, prettiness.

1. **Hüch**, *m.* [-es, *pl.* -e] or **Huche**, *f.* [*pl.*-n] [the name of a German river-trout] huck.

2. **Hüch**, *m.* [-es, *pl.* -e] V. **Hauk**.

Húcke, *f.* [*pl.* -n] the back, V. 1. **Höcke** 2). **Huckepack** or **—back**, *adv.* [in fam. lang.] on the back, pickback, pickapack. **Einen — pack tragen**, to carry any one pickapack.

Húckeln, *v. intr.* [allied to **hinken**] to leap or spring on one leg, to hop.

Húcken, V. **Hocken**.

Húcker, *m.* [-s, *pl.* -] 1) V. **Hocker**. 2) V. **Huker**.

Huckerscheit, *n.* [among charcoal-men] a short log of wood laid down in such a manner as to promote the draught of the air.

Hudeléi, *f.* 1) careless and hurried manner of performing any work, bungling work. 2) trouble, annoyance, vexation.

Hudeler, **Hüdler**, *m.* [-s, *pl.* -] 1) careless, bad workman, bungler. 2) one who annoys, troubles or teases.

Hüdeln, *v. tr.* [properly, to move or pull backwards and forwards, allied to **wedeln**] 1) to do a thing hastily and carelessly, to huddle, to bungle. **Eine Sache obenhin —**, to slubber over a thing or a business. 2) **Einen —**, to trouble, plague, annoy, tease or vex any one. **Das —**, V. **Hudelei**

Hüf, *m.* [-es, *pl.* -e] [Eng. *hoof*, Sax. and Sw. *hof*, Icel. *hoef*, Gr. ὁπλη, from **heben**] the hoof [of a horse &c]. **Den — eines Pferdes auswirken**, to pare a horse's hoof or foot.

Hufsbein, *n.* bone near the hoof, hoof-bone. **—beschlag**, *m.* the act of shoeing horses, shoeing; *it.* the horse-shoes, V. also **—eisen** 1). **Der —beschlag für zwei Pferde kostet jährlich viel**, the shoeing of two horses costs a great deal a year. **—eisen**, *n.* 1) horse-shoe. **Das —eisen eines Rennpferdes**, plate or racing-plate [of a race-horse]; **einem Pferde —eisen, ein —eisen auflegen, aufschlagen**, to shoe a horse; **einem Pferde die —eisen abnehmen, abreißen**, to unshoe a horse. *Fig.* [in popular lang.] **Sie hat ein —eisen verloren**, she has been blown upon, she has made a trip, she has forfeited her honour. 2) *Fig.* [in fortification] horse-shoe. **—eisendorn**, *m* punch [for opening the holes in a horse's hoof]. **—eisenkraut**, *n.* horseshoe-vetch. **—eisennase**, *f.* a kind of bat, whose nose resembles a horse-shoe. **—eisenpult**, *m.* a writing-desk in the form of a horse-shoe. **—eisensack**, *m.* a farrier's pouch, V. **Beschlagtasche**. **—eisenstab**, *m.* a small iron bar of which horse-shoes are made. **—eisentisch**, *m.* a table in the form of a horse-shoe. **—geschwür**, *n.* an ulcer or swelling on a horse's hoof. **—hammer**, *m.* a smith's shoeing-hammer. **—knotig**, *adj.* and *adv.* having many knots or swellings on the hoof. **Ein —knotiges Pferd**, a horse whose hoof is full of knots. **—kraut**, *n.* dame's violet, our lady's rose, rose of Jericho. **—lattich**, *m.* colt's foot [a plant, tussilago, Linn.]. **—nagel**, *m.* hobnail. **—nageleisen**, *n.* hobnail-mould. **—raspe**, **—raspel**, *f.* butteris. **—räumer**, *m.* horse-picker. **—schlag**, *m.* 1) the shoeing of horses, V. **—beschlag**. 2) the mark of a horse's foot, piste. 3) towing-path [by the side of canals or rivers]. 4) [from **Hufe**] V. **Hufenschlag**. **—schmied**, *m.* farrier, blacksmith. **—stempel**, *m.* [an instrument of iron or steel used for perforating holes in a horse-shoe] punch. **—tritt**, *m.* 1) the tread of a horse. 2) V. **—schlag** 2) and 3). **—wulst**, *m.* [a round bony swelling on a horse's hoof] bony hoof. **—zange**, *f.* pincers for drawing the nails out of a horse's foot or hoof. **—zwang**, *m.* defect in horses when the hoof is too narrow, the fault of being hoof-bound or narrow-heeled, narrow-heeledness. **Den —zwang bekommen**, to become hoof-bound or narrow-heeled. **—zwängig**, *adj.* and *adv.* hoof-bound, narrow-heeled.

Hüfe, *f.* [*pl.* -n] [allied to **Hof**, or perhaps from the Goth. *hoba* = plough, hence = as much land as a plough can till in a year] a measure of land [about 30 acres], hide of land.

Hufengeld, *n.* V. **—steuer**. **—gericht**, *n.* court of agriculture, V. **Feldgericht** 1); *it.* V. **Grundgericht** 2). **—groschen**, *m.* V. **—steuer**. **—gut**, *n.* a farm consisting of a hide of land. **—haber**, **—hafer**, *m.* [a quantity of oats paid by a tenant to a landlord in lieu of rent or other duty] avenage. **—meister**, *m.* a steward or clerk who receives or collects the rent paid for land. **—pfennig**, *m.* V. **—steuer**. **—recht**, *n.* the right of the landlord to take after the death of a tenant the best article of his movable goods. **—richter**, *m* village magistrate. **—schlag**, *m.* a field divided into hides; *it.* V. **Ackerfeld**. **—schoß**, *m.*, **—steuer**, *f.*, contribution levied on arable land, land-tax. **—zins**, *m.* the rent paid for land, land-rent.

Hüfen, I. *v. tr.* to furnish with a hoof or hoofs. **Gehufte Thiere**, hoofed animals. II. *v. intr.* 1) to kick out, to fling [with the hoof]. 2) to go or draw back or backwards [said of horses &c.].

Hüfener, **Hüfner**, *m.* [-s, *pl* -] a man who possesses a hide of land, V. **Halb—**, **Voll—**.

Hüfig, *adj.* and *adv.* furnished with hoofs, hoofed. **Ein —es Thier**, a hoofed animal, V. **Ein—**, **Hart—**, **Voll—** &c.

Hüfte, *f.* [*pl.* -n] [Sax. *hyppe*, *hipe*, Eng. *hip*, Dan. **Hofte**; probably allied to **Hübel**, **heben** = projecting part] hip, haunch. **Sich die — verrenken**, to dislocate or sprain one's hip; **eine hohe — haben**, to have one hip higher than the other, to be crooked; [in seamen's lang.] **die — eines Schiffes**, the quarter of a ship.

Hüftader, *f.* sciatic vein. **—bein**, *n.* hip-bone, haunch-bone; *it.* [in anatomy] coccyx or os coccygis, ischium. **—beinloch**, *n.* [in anatomy] oval hole. **—beinlochmuskel**, *m.* obturator muscle. **—beinlochnerve**, *m.* obturator nerve. **—beinlochschlagader**, *f.* obturatrix arteria. **—blatt**, *n.* V. **—bein**. **—blutader**, *f* sciatic vein. **—horn**, *n.* V. **Hiefhorn**. **—knochen**, *m.* V. **—bein**. **—lahm**, *adj.* V. **Hüftenlahm**. **—muskel**, *m.* the sciatic muscle. **—nerve**, *m.* sciatic nerve. **—pfanne**, *f.* the socket of the hip-bone. **—schlagader**, *f.* sciatic artery. **—stück**, *n.* haunch [of a slaughtered animal]. **—verrenkung**, *f* dislocation of the hip. **—weh**, *n.* pain in the hip, hip-gout, sciatic, sciatica.

Hüftenlahm, *adj.* and *adv.* having the hip dislocated, lame in the hip, hip-shot. **Ein —lahmes Pferd**, a horse whose hips are out of joint, V. **Lendenlahm**.

Hügel, *m.* [-s, *pl.* -] *dim.* **—chen**, *n.* [Sw. *hygel*, from **hoch**; Low Sax. **Hull**, Anglo-Sax. and Eng. *hill*, Sw. *hol* and *hals*, L. *collis*, Gr. κολωνός] 1) [in general] any elevation, inequality, knob, boss. **Ein kleiner — auf der Haut**, a pimple or pustule on the skin; **eine mit kleinen —n besetzte Pomeranze**, an orange with a rough rind. V. **Hübel**, **Buckel**. 2) [chiefly, a natural elevation of land] hill. **Ein kleiner —**, a hillock.

Hügelab, *adv.* down hill. **—auf**, *adv.* up hill. **—rohr**, *n.* kind of reed that grows on barren hills. **—rücken**, *m.* the ridge of a hill.

Hügelicht, *adj.* and *adv.* resembling a hill, uneven. **—er Boden**, undulating ground.

Hügelig, *adj.* and *adv.* abounding with hills, hilly. **Ein —es Land**, a hilly country.

***Hugenótt**, *m.* [-en, *pl* -en] **—inn**, *f.* [a nickname formerly given to the Protestants in France] Huguenot.

Hugenóttisch, *adj.* and *adv.* pertaining to the Huguenots, Huguenotic. **Die —e Lehre**, Huguenotism.

Hügo, *m.* [-'s or **des Hugo**] [a name of men]

Hugh.

Hüh, *interj.* [expressing horror] wheugh or whew.

Huhn, *n.* [-es, *pl.* Hühner] [allied to Hahn] 1) any fowl of the gallinaceous kind. Das welsche or indi[ani]sche —, Turkey hen; V. Birk—, Hasel—, Haus—, Reb—, Trut— &c.; [among hunters] Hühner [=Reb- or Feldhühner], partridges. 2) domestic fowl or hen. *Dim.* Das Hühnchen, ‖ Hühnlein, chicken, pullet. Die Hühner setzen, to set hens; *prov.* [in familiar language] ich habe noch ein Hühnchen mit Ihnen zu pflücken, I have a crow to pluck with you; I must have a touch with you. 3) [in cookery] Das verlorene —, hodgepodge or hotch-pot. SYN. Huhn, Henne. Huhn is the generic name. Under this denomination come: die Haushühner [domestic fowls, poultry], die welschen Hühner [turkeys], die Rebhühner [partridges] &c. Henne denotes only the female of the fowl kind, and not till it has commenced to lay eggs and breed. Till then it is still called ein Huhn or Hühnchen.

Hühner-aar, *m.* V. —geier. —**abend**, *m.* evening before a wedding, V. Polterabend. —**artig**, *adj.* and *adv.* gallinaceous. Ein —artiger Vogel, a gallinaceous fowl or bird. —**auge**, *n.* corn [on the foot]; die —augen ausschneiden, to cut the corns, V. Leichdorn. —**augenbeere**, *f.* V. Elsebeere. —**beize**, *f.* [in hunting] catching partridges by hawks, hawking at partridges. —**biß**, *m.* [in botany] 1) chickweed. 2) hen-bit, V. Vogelkraut. 3) the purging-flax, the mill-mountain. 4) sea-sandwort. 5) anagallis, pimpernel, shepherd's weatherglass. 6) berry-bearing campion. —**braten**, *m.* roast chicken or pullet. —**brühe**, *f.* broth of a fowl or pullet, chicken-broth. —**brust**, *f.* the breast of a fowl. —**darm**, *m.* [in botany] 1) hen-bit. 2) V. —biß 5). 3) the common cerastium or mouse-ear chickweed. —**dieb**, *m.* 1) a person that steals poultry. 2) weasel. 3) V. —geier. —**ei**, *n.* the egg of a hen, pullet's egg. —**fang**, *m.* the catching of partridges. —**fänger**, *m.* one who catches partridges [with a tunnel]. —**feder**, *f.* feather of a hen. —**frau**, *f.* V. —händlerinn. —**fresser**, *m.* V. —geier. *—**fricassée**, *n.* fricassee of chickens. —**fühler**, *m.* V. —taster. —**garn**, *n.* net for catching partridges, tunnel-net. —**geier**, *m.* hen-harrier, hen-harm. —**geschlecht**, *n.* the gallinaceous kind. —**geschrei**, *n.* 1) the cry of fowls; the call of partridges. 2) V. —ruf 2). —**hahn**, *m.* cock. —**hamen**, *m.* the purse in a partridge net or tunnel. —**handel**, *m.* trade in poultry. —**händler**, *m.* dealer in poultry, poulterer. —**händlerinn**, *f.* a woman who deals in poultry; *it.* a poulterer's wife. —**haus**, *n.* V. —stall. —**hirt**, *m.* V. —hüter. —**hof**, *m.* poultry-yard. —**hund**, *m.* setting-dog, spaniel, pointer. —**hüter**, *m.* one who looks after the poultry. —**klee**, —**kohl**, *m.* the mother of thyme. —**korb**, *m.* basket, coop or cage for chickens. —**lager**, *n.* the place where partridges light after being on the wing or where they have lain during the night. —**laus**, *f.* a louse infesting poultry. —**leder**, *n.* chicken-leather [a very delicate sort of leather prepared from goat's or lamb's skin]. —**leiter**, *f.* hen-roost. —**mann**, *m.* V. —händler. —**markt**, *m.* poultry-market. —**milch**, *f.* [in botany] star of Bethlehem. —**mist**, *m.* the dung of fowls or hens. —**nest**, *n.* hen's nest. —**netz**, *n.* V. —garn. —**pastete**, *f.* chicken-pie. —**raute**, *f.* veronica triphyllos. —**ruf**, *m.* 1) the cry or call of partridges. 2) bird-call, partridge-call. —**schrot**, *n.* partridge-shot. —**stall**, *m.* hen-house, hen-coop, hen-roost. —**stange**, *f.* roost, perch. —**steige**, *f.* 1) V. —korb. 2) V. —leiter. —**stopfer**, *m.* one who fattens poultry. —**taster**, *m. fig.* [in contempt] hen-groper, cotquean. —**tritt**, *m.* V. —darm. —**vögel**, *pl.* V. —geschlecht. —**vogt**, *m.* 1) a man who attends to the poultry, poultry-man. 2) a clerk or steward who receives the fowls due to the landlord and keeps an account of them. —**wärter**, *m.* V. —vogt 1). —**weh**, *n.* chin-cough, hooping-cough, V. Keichhusten. —**weib**, *n.* V. —händlerinn. —**weihe**, *f.* V. —geier. —**wurz**, —**wurzel**, *f.* bloody crane's bill. —**zehnte**, *m.* tithe of poultry. —**zeug**, *n.* V. —garn. —**zins**, *m.* rent paid in poultry. —**zucht**, *f.* the keeping of fowls, the breeding and rearing of chickens.

Hühne, *m.* V. Hüne.

Huhu, *interj.* V. Huh.

Huhu, *m.* V. Uhu.

Hui, *interj.* [Anglo-Sax. *higan* and Eng. *to hie* is = eilen, to hasten] [an exclamation to denote quickness] quick! *it.* [to mark encouragement] on, huzza! Das —, an instant, moment, trice; in einem —, in a trice.

Huk, *m.* [-es, *pl.* -e] or **Huke**, *f.* [*pl.* -n] [allied to hoch] 1) [in seamen's lang.] a cape or headland, a point. 2) a fish-hook. 3) [in anatomy] V. Hauk or Hauchblatt.

Huke, *f.* [*pl.* -n] V. 1. Höcke 3).

Huker, *m.* [-s, *pl.*] [allied to Holk, Eng. *hulk*] a Dutch vessel, hooker.

Hukerboot, *n.* a boat belonging to a hooker.

Huld, *f.* [allied to hold, which see] grace, favour, kindness. Einen mit — behandeln, to treat any one very kindly; Einem seine — schenken, to take an affection for any one, to receive any one into one's good graces; einer Dame — gewinnen, to win a lady's grace or favour; die — Gottes, the grace of God.

Huld-göttinn, *f.* [*Grazie] one of the three Graces, Grace. Die drei —göttinnen, the three Graces. *Fig.* [emphatically] a great beauty, a very beautiful woman. Die —göttinn, die ich anbete, the goddess I adore. —**reich**, —**voll**, *adj.* and *adv.* gracious, benevolent. Die Fürstinn empfing sie sehr —reich, the princess received her very graciously.

Huldigen, *v. intr.* [V. Hold and Huld] 1) Einem —, to pay one's respect or duty to any one, to do homage to any one. Eines Talenten —, to pay homage to any one's talents; seitdem er dieser Schönheit huldiget, since he is in love with, since he is the slave of that beauty; [in poetry] was den großen Ring bewohnet, huldige der Sympathie, let all those that inhabit this vast globe pay homage to sympathy. 2) [in a more limited sense] to take the oath of allegiance and fealty, to do homage. Seinem Fürsten —, to swear the oath of allegiance or to do homage to one's prince; sich von Jemand — lassen, to receive any one's oath of allegiance or homage.

Huldigung, *f.* 1) respect paid by external action, homage. Einem Frauenzimmer, einem Minister seine — darbringen, to pay one's respect or duty, to pay homage to a lady, minister &c. *Fig.* Der Wahrheit versage ich meine — nicht, I never refuse to pay homage to truth. 2) [in a more limited sense] the act of taking the oath of allegiance and fealty, homage. Die — leisten, to do homage.

Huldigungs-brief, *m.* letter of fealty or homage. —**eid**, *m.* oath of allegiance. —**feier**, *f.* the celebration of the day on which the oath of allegiance is taken. —**feierlichkeit**, *f.* the solemnities performed on the day of homage. —**fest**, *n.* V. —feier. —**groschen**, *m.* V. —münze. —**lehen**, *n.* V. Lehenwaare. —**münze**, *f.* [*—medaille] a medal struck in commemoration of the day of homage. —**pflichtig**, *adj.* and *adv.* subject to homage, homageable —**tag**, *m.* the day on which the oath of allegiance is taken, day of homage.

Huldinn, *f.* V. *Fig.* Huldgöttinn.

Huldreich, I. *adj.* V. under Huld. II. *m.* [a name of men] V. Ulrich.

Hülfe, *f.* [[seldom used in *pl.* -n] [Sax. *helpan*, *hylpan*, Sw. *hielpa*, Eng. *help*] 1) [the act or state of helping] help, assistance, aid, succour. Einem zu — eilen, to run to any one's help; — leisten, to lend a helping hand, to give help, to help, to succour; er kam mir zu — he came to my assistance; um — bitten, flehen, to ask for, to crave help or relief; Einen um — anrufen, to implore any one's help; Einen zu — rufen, to call upon any one for help or assistance; um — rufen, schreien, to call, to cry out for help; zu —! zu —! help! help! mit Gottes —, with God's help or assistance, God willing or helping; einer belagerten Stadt zu — kommen, to succour or relieve a besieged town. *Fig.* Eines Gedächtniß zu — kommen, to put any on in mind, to remind any one of a thing; er entfloh mit — der Nacht, he escaped by or under favour of the night; mit — eines Brecheisens, by the help or by means of an iron crow; [in law] die — or Hülfsvollstreckung, the execution of a judicial decree; die — thun, ergehen lassen [in law], to execute a sentence or to put a sentence in execution. 2) [the person or thing that helps or assists] help, succour. — schicken, erhalten, to send, to receive succour or succours; es war mir eine große —, it was a great help to me; Gott ist meine —, God is my help. [in the manege, what a rider makes use of to manage a horse well] aids, helps. Einem Pferde die — geben, to aid a horse.

Hülfs-begierig, *adj.* and *adv.* desirous of help or relief. —**fertig**, *adj.* and *adv.* inclined or ready to help or relieve. —**leister**, *m.*, —**leisterinn**, *f.* a person who renders assistance or brings relief. —**leistung**, *f.* act of rendering assistance or bringing help. —**los**, *adj.* and *adv.* 1) destitute of help or succour, without help or succour, helpless, succourless. Sie befindet sich in einem völlig —losen Zustande, she is in the utmost distress; Einen —los lassen, to abandon or forsake any one, to refuse any one assistance. 2) [little used] giving no help or assistance. Er sieht ihn leiden, und bleibt —los stehen, he sees him suffer without running to his help or assistance. —**losigkeit**, *f.* helplessness. —**rede**, *f.* evasion, excuse. —**reich**, *adj.* and *adv.* ready or inclined to help others, benevolent. Einem —reiche Hand leisten, to lend any one a helping hand, to bring any one help or relief, to assist, to succour any one. —**wurz**, *f.* [in botany] 1) the long-rooted garlick. 2) marsh-mallow, V. Eibisch.

Hülfs-amt, *f.* the office of an assistant or deputy. —**arm**, *m.* [in mining] an arm supporting the principal arms of a wheel. —**armee**, *f.* V. —heer. —**auflage**, *f.* [in law] warrant or order for the execution of a judicial decree. —**aussagewort**, *n.* auxiliary verb, V. [the more usual word] —zeitwort. —**band**, *n.* [in anatomy] accessory ligament. —**beamte**, *m.* assistant or associate in office, deputy. —**bedürftig**, *adj.* and *adv.* being in want of help, requiring help. Die —bedürftigen, the indigent or needy. —**bedürftigkeit**, *f.* state of being in want of help, necessity, indigence. —**bischof**, *m.* suffragan bishop, suffragan. —**bitte**, *f.* [in law] aid-prayer. —**brief**, *m.* [in law] a written order to execute the sentence of a court of justice, writ of execution. —**erbietung**, *f.* offer of help, assistance or relief. Ich nahm seine —erbietung an, I accepted his offer of assistance. —**gebot**, *n.* V. —auflage. —**geld**, *n.* 1) [in law] fee paid for an execution [in a civil cause]. 2) —gelder, *pl.* subsidies, V. —steuer. —genoß, *m.* V. Bundesgenoß. —glied, *n.* an assisting or auxiliary member or limb. —grund, *m.* [in law] subsidiary reason. —heer, *n.* auxiliary troops, forces or army. V. also —truppen. —kasse, *f.* the funds for the relief of the poor, poor-funds. —kenntniß, *f.* preliminary or auxiliary knowledge. —kirche, *f.* chapel of ease. —krieg, *m.* a war carried on by one state in succour of another, a war undertaken by an auxiliary. —laut, —lauter, *m.* [in grammar, seldom used] 1) [with some grammarians] vowel. 2) [with other grammarians] consonant. —leistung, *f.* V. Hülfleistung. —macht, *f.* allied or auxiliary power. —mittel, *n.* remedy, expedient. —nerve, *m.* accessory nerve. —note, *f.* note marking an accessory sound. —prediger, *m.* [*Diakonus] deacon. —predigeramt, *n.* office of a deacon, deaconry, deaconship. —quelle, *f.* resource, expedient. —recht, *n.* [in law] the right of putting a judicial sentence in execution. —satz, *m.* [in mathematics] lemma. —steuer, *f.* subsidy, subsidies. —stimme, *f.* [in music] obligato voice. —ton, *m.* [in music] accessory sound. —truppen, *pl.* auxiliary or subsidiary troops, auxiliaries. —vertrag, *m.* subsidiary treaty. —völker, *pl.* V. —truppen. —vollstreckung, *f.* the execution of a judiciary sentence. -wissenschaft, *f.* auxiliary or preliminary science. —wort, *n.* 1) a helping or suppletory word, an expletive. 2) V. —zeitwort. —zeitwort, *n.* auxiliary verb. Haben und seyn sind —zeitwörter, *to have* and *to be* are auxiliary verbs. —zwang, *m.* [in law] execution [in a civil cause], V. Hülfe 1).

Hülflich, *adj.* and *adv.* [obsolescent] helpful, useful, V. Hülfreich and Behülflich.

Hülk, V. Holk.

Hülle, *f.* [*pl.* -n] cover, covering, integument. Die Uebersendung und — einer Waare [in commerce], the transport and package; [in botany] involucre, involucrum; die — einer Raupe, the envelope of a caterpillar; die Raupe verliert ihre —, the caterpillar throws off its envelope. [in a more limited sense] raiment, garments; [in painting] drapery; *it.* hood or cap, V. Haube; [in poetry = dead body, corpse] remains; [in fam. lang.] die — und die Fülle haben, to have plenty of every thing. *Fig.* Die — der Nacht, the veil of night or of darkness; unter der — der Freundschaft, under the cloak or mask of friendship; er nahm ihm die — von den Augen, he opened his eyes, he dispelled the mist that was before his eyes, he undeceived or disabused him; die — fiel mir schmerzlich von den Augen, I was sadly disabused.

Hüllen, *v. tr.* [allied to hehlen] to wrap up, to muffle, to cover, to envelope; to shroud, to veil, to involve. Sich in seinen Mantel —, to wrap one's self up in one's cloak; die Erde ist in die Schatten der Nacht gehüllt, the earth is wrapt in the shades of night; die Sonne, in eine Wolke gehüllt, the sun behind a cloud; [in botany] gehüllter Blumenstiel, involucred peduncle. *Fig.* Eine Sache in Dunkel —, to perplex, entangle or make obscure any thing; die Dichter — die Wahrheit in Fabeln, poets wrap [up] truth in fables, V. Ein—, Ver—.

Hülse, *f.* [*pl.* -n] *dim.* Hülschen, ‖Hülslein, *n.* [allied to Hülle] 1) the outer covering of any thing. *a*) the skin of fruits and seeds. Die — einer Nuß, the hull of a nut; die — des Getreides, hull or glume of grain; die —n an den Weinbeeren, the skins of grapes; die —n der Erbsen, Bohnen, the husks, cods or pods of pease, of beans; Erbsen, Bohnen in der —, mit der —, pease, beans in the shell. *b*) certain hollow things which receive and hold something else: *α*) socket or hollow ring for receiving the ram-rod, *β*) cylindrical case of paper for rockets. 2) holly. SYN. Hülse, Schale, Schelfe. Schale is the external covering or shell of certain soft bodies. Schelfe is the soft rind or outer coat after it is separated. The parings or peelings of apples, potatoes, the scaly skin of the human body, &c. are Schelfen. Hülse differs from Schale, in as much as it signifies the external covering only of certain fruits and vegetables, and is always soft and flexible, Schale also that of animal bodies, and may be hard or soft. See Eierschale, Nußschale &c.

Hülsen-baum, *m.* the holm tree, holly-tree, holly. —beere, *f.* holly-berry. —frucht, *f.* leguminous plants, pulse. —früchte, *pl.* codded grains; pulse. —fruchtartig, *adj.* and *adv.* leguminous. —gewächs, *n.* leguminous plant. Die —gewächse, the legumens. —motte, *f.* phryganium, cade-worm, V. Wassermotte.

Hülsen, I. *v. tr.* 1) to furnish or cover with a husk. 2) to strip off the hull or husk, to hull, to husk, to shell. II. *v. r.* sich —, 1) to form pods, to pod. 2) to cast the husk or shell, to lose the skin, to shell. Die Erbsen — sich im Kochen, the skin of pease comes off when they are boiled.

Hülsicht, *adj.* and *adv.* resembling hulls, husks or shells, leguminous.

Hülsig, *adj.* and *adv.* having husks or shells, leguminous.

Hum, [hm] *interj.* [to express indifference or admiration] pshaw! *it.* hem, hm! hum!

***Human**, *adj.* and *adv.* humane, kind, benevolent, affable. —e Behandlung, kind treatment.

***Humaniora**, *pl.* humane learning.

***Humanisiren**, [= vermenschlichen,] *v. tr.* to humanize.

***Humanisirung**, *f.* humanising, humanisation.

***Humanist**, *m.* [-en, *pl.* -en] humanist.

***Humanistisch**, *adj.* —e Studien, humane learning.

***Humanität**, *f.* humanity, kindness, benevolence, affability.

Humanitätsstudien, *pl.* V. Humanistische Studien.

Humber, *m.* V. Hummer.

1. **Hummel**, *m.* [-s, *pl.* -] [from hummen = to hum?] bull kept for breeding.

2. **Hummel**, *f.* [*pl.* -n] [from hummen = to hum, to buzz; Sax. *humble*, Icel. *humle*] humble-bee, drone. *Fig.* [in popular lang.] Eine wilde —, a rompish girl, a romp.

Hummel-fänger, *m.* a machine before the opening of a bee-hive for catching the drones. —motte, *f.*, —schmetterling, *m.* the green sphinx with transparent wings.

3. **Hummel**, *f.* [*pl.* -n] [allied to Himmel = something high and vaulted] malt-floor.

Hummelchen, *n.* [-s, *pl.* -] a sort of bag-pipe; *it.* [in organs] thorough-base drone.

Hummeln, Hummen, *v. intr.* to hum, to buzz. V. Summen.

Hummer, *m.* [-s, *pl.* -] [Dan. and Sw. *hummer*, L. *cammarus*, Gr. κάμμαρος] 1) lobster. 2) [in seamen's lang.] sheave.

Hummer-brecher, *m.* an iron for opening lobsters. —gat, *n.* [in seamen's lang., formerly] sheave-hole. —schere, *f.* a claw of a lobster. —schiff, *n.* a boat or vessel for catching lobsters.

***Humor**, *m.* [-s] 1) [Hūmor] [moisture, chiefly the moisture or fluor of animal bodies] humour. 2) [Humōr] [general turn of mind; present disposition] humour. Sie sind heute in sehr üblem —, you are in very bad humour to-day; sein unerschöpflicher —, his inexhaustible fund of drollery.

***Humorist**, *m.* [-en, *pl.* -en] a humorist, *it.* a wag. Unsere größten —en sind Jean Paul, Hippel &c., our greatest humorists, our best humorous writers or authors are Jean Paul, Hippel &c.

***Humoristisch**, *adj.* and *adv.* humorous.

Humpe, *f.* [*pl.* -n] V. Humpen.

Humpeln, [allied to the old humpen or hammen = verschneiden] I. *v. intr.* to hobble, to limp. II. *v. tr.* to do any thing unskilfully or clumsily, to bungle, to botch.

Hümpeln, *v. tr.* V. Humpeln II.

Humpen, *m.* [-s, *pl.* -] a large vessel to drink out, a large drinking-cup; *it.* a large drinking-glass, a tumbler.

Humpler, Hümpler, *m.* [-s, *pl.* -] —inn, *f.* 1) a person that hobbles or limps. 2) a person that works badly, a bungler, botcher.

Humsen, *v. intr.* to hum, to buzz.

1. **Hund**, *m.* [-es, *pl.* -e] [Icel., Dan., Sw. and Low-Sax. *hund*, L. *canis*, Gr. κύων. It belongs to the Anglo-Sax. *huntian* or the old hunten, Eng. *to hunt* = jagen; Sw. *haenta* or Sax. *henta* is = to catch] 1) [the well-known animal] dog. Die Hündinn, female of the dog, bitch. Das Hündchen, little dog; V. Dachs—, Haus—, Hetz—, Hof—, Hühner—, Jagd—, Ketten—, Leit—, Schäfer—, Schooß—, Spür—, Wasser—, Wind—; junger —, puppy, whelp; junge —e werfen, to pup, litter or whelp; ein Wurf junger —e, a litter of whelps; einen — abrichten, to break in or train a dog; —e halten, to keep dogs; ein wüthender or toller —, a mad dog; [among hunters] die —e anfrischen, to animate the dogs with the horn and the voice; †man ist mit ihm umgegangen wie mit einem —e, they treated him like a dog, very badly; [in astronomy] der große —, canis major; der kleine —, canis minor. *Prov.* and *Fig.* [in popular lang.] Zwei —e an einem Knochen vertragen sich selten, two competitors or two rivals for the same thing seldom agree; V. Jagen; todte —e beißen nicht, when a serpent is dead, his sting hurts not; the dead have done biting; er ist so bekannt wie ein bunter —, he is known every where or by every body; der Knüttel liegt beim —e, I am or he is baulked or disappointed, I come or he comes short of my or of his design, the impediments are not to be overcome; es wird ihm bekommen wie dem —e das Grasfressen, he will gain nothing but vexation, he will suffer for it; er hat nicht, einen — aus dem Ofen zu locken, he is as poor as Job, he has nothing at all; damit kann man keinen — aus dem Ofen locken, that is of little consequence or importance, *it.* that is a mere trifle; †that's not worth three skips of a louse; er kann keinen — aus dem Ofen locken, he is good for nothing; *it.* he does not know *a* from *b*, he can't say bo to a goose, he knows nothing at all; †auf den — kommen, to be reduced to poverty and distress, to be brought low, to go to the dogs; †auf dem —e seyn, to be in a state of poverty and distress, to be ruined; *it.* to be knocked up; er muß am Ende noch —e führen, he will be reduced to great poverty at last; er geht wie ein begossener —, he goes away like a dog with his tail betwixt his legs or that has lost his tail, he sneaks off; er muß es haben, als hätte ihn ein — gebissen, he must pass it over unresented; es nimmt kein — ein Stück Brod von ihm, he is an abject, low or despicable fel-

low; am Riemchen lernen die —e Leder kauen, one never begins with great crimes, one becomes inured to vice by degrees; wenn man an den — will, so muß er Leder gefressen haben, it is an easy thing to find a stick to beat a dog; he that would hang his dog, gives out first that he is mad; den schlafenden — soll Niemand wecken, it is not good to wake a sleeping dog or lion; ein blöder — wird selten fett, bashfulness is an enemy to poverty; a close mouth catches no flies; wer mich liebt, der liebt auch meinen —, love me, love my dog; böse —e haben gemeiniglich zerzausete Ohren, snarling or brabbling dogs never want sore ears, quarrelsome curs have dirty coats; —e, die bellen, beißen nicht, barking dogs seldom bite, the greatest barkers bite not sorest; sie leben wie —e und Katzen, they agree like cats and dogs; den Letzten beißen die —e, the devil take the hindmost! einen Knüttel unter die —e werfen, to speak a word undesignedly, at hazard; V. Hase, *prov.*; *it.* [a term of reproach or contempt] —! dog! V. Blut— 2), Lumpen—. 2) [formerly, for] treasure. *Hier liegt der — begraben, that's the main or chief point, there lies the difficulty, there 's the rub.

Hunds-baum, —dachs, —dille, —flechte &c. V. Hundebaum, Hundsbaum, Hundsdachs &c. —nagel, *m.* V. Hundsleitnagel.

Hunde-arbeit, *f.*, —baum, —beerbaum, *m*, —beere, *f.* V. Hundsarbeit, Hundsbaum &c. —bellen, *n.* the barking of dogs. —bett, *n.* [in popular lang.] a wretched, miserable bed; [in mining] die Zeche liegt im —bette, the mine is at a stand. —brod, —fell, —fett, V. Hundsbrod &c. —doctor, *m.* *dog-leech. —ende, *n.* [in seamen's lang.] the eye of a cable. —fock, *f.* [in seamen's language] the halliard of the main stay-sail. —fressen, *n.* a meal or food for dogs, dog's meat. †*Fig.* a wretched, very bad meal. —führer, *m.* dog-feeder, dog-keeper. —gebell, *n.* V. —bellen. †*Fig.* —geld, *n.* a contemptible sum of money, inadequate price, a mere trifle. —geschlecht, *n.* race of dogs; *it.* the dogs. —haus, *n.*, —hütte, *f.* dog-house, dog-kennel. *Fig.* Das ist ein wahres —haus [in popular language], that's a very mean, vile or nasty habitation, that's a dog-hole; [in seamen's language, a sort of wooden porch placed over the staircase of a cabin] hood, companion. —junge, *m.* a lad who is to feed the dogs, dog-feeder. †*Fig.* a young or little rogue or rascal. —koth, *m.* V. Hundskoth. —lauch, *m.* V. Hundslauch. †*Fig.* —leben, *n.* a wretched life. Ein — leben führen, to lead a miserable life, to live like a dog. —loch, *n.* V. —haus. *Fig.* [in popular lang.] a dark prison or jail, a dungeon, black-hole. Einen in's —loch stecken or werfen, to confine or put any one in a dungeon, to clap any one up in prison, to imprison any one. *it.* a mean or dirty room or habitation or cot, a dog-hole. † and ‖*Fig.* —lose, *adj.* and *adv.* very bad or wretched. Das ist so —lose nicht, that is not so bad. —mahl, *n.*, —mahlzeit, *f. Fig.* [in popular language] a very pitiful or sorry dinner, a very wretched or paltry meal. —milch, *f.* V. Hundsmilch. —narr, *m.* [in familiar language] a man who is very fond of, who doats on dog's, dog fancier. —peitsche, *f.* dog-whip. —pint, *m.* [in seamen's lang.] pointing. —rippe, *f.* [in botany] ribwort-plantain. —scheu, *adj.* and *adv.* [in familiar language] afraid of dogs. Was macht Sie —scheu? why are you afraid of dogs? —schlag, *m.* the order for or the act of destroying dogs found in the streets [particularly during the dog-days]. —schläger, *m.* 1) killer of dogs. 2) V. —wärter. —schneider, *m.* gelder of dogs. —seiche, *f.* 1) dog's piss. 2) [in botany] V. Besenkraut. —stall, *m.* V. —haus. —steuer, *f.* 1) a tax on dogs. 2) [formerly] a tax or duty for the maintenance of the prince's dogs. *Fig.* —trab, *m.* [in familiar language] dogtrot. —wache, *f.* [in seamen's lang.] dog-watch. —wärter, *m.* dog-keeper, dog-feeder. —zeichen, *n.* a plate or collar tied round the neck of a dog.

Hunds-affe, *m.* a kind of ape or baboon with a head like a dog, cynocephalis. —apfel, *m.* mandrake, mandragora. —arbeit, *f.* 1) the act of breaking or training a dog. †*Fig.* 2) very tiresome or toilsome work or labour. —auge, *n.* 1) a dog's eye. †*Fig.* *a*) an envious or impudent look. *b*) an impudent or envious person. 2) [in botany] the great flea-bane, ploughman's spikenard, V. Ruhrkraut. —äugig, *adj.* having dog's eyes. —baum, *m.* 1) bush-cherry tree, dwarf-cherry tree, V. Heckenkirsche 2). 2) V. Vogelkirschbaum. 3) V. Faulbaum, Elsebeere. 4) V. Kreuzdorn. —beere, *f.* 1) dog berry. 2) V. Heckenkirsche 1). 3) buck-thorn-berry. 4) berry of the wayfaring-tree. —beerbaum, —beerstrauch, *m.* dogberry-tree, dogwood. —biß, *m.* 1) bite of a dog. 2) [in botany] dog's bane. —blatter, *f.* [in medicine] terminthus. —blume, *f.* V. —kamille. —blüte, *f.* V. —auge 2). —bock, *m.* the spotted capricorn. —brod, *n.* bread for dogs. †*Fig.* very bad bread; *it.* a miserable earning. —bube, *m.* V. Hundejunge. —dachs, *m.* the common badger. —dille, —distel, *f.* V. —kamille. —dreck, *m.* the dung or excrements of dogs. *Fig.* [in vulgar lang.] an entirely worthless thing or object. —fell, *n.* a dog's skin. —fett, *n.* grease of dogs. —flechte, *f.* 1) the ash-coloured ground-liverwort or lichen. 2) the green ground-liverwort with black warts. —fliege, *f.* dogfly. —fott, *m.* [a very vulgar term of reproach, considered as the most insulting affront] cowardly rascal, mean scoundrel, villain. †—fötterei, *f.* mean transaction, rascally or villanous proceeding. †—föttisch, *adj.* and *adv.* mean, rascally, cowardly; *it.* extremely disagreeable or untoward. Ein —föttischer Zufall, a very disagreeable or untoward accident. —gerecht, *adj.* understanding dogs. —gras, *n.* 1) dog's grass. 2) couch-grass. —gurke, *f.* V. —kürbiß. —haar, *n.* dog's hair. *Fig.* [in popular language] —haare auflegen, to take a hair from the same dog, *it.* to pluck another hair from the beast. —hai, *m.* the smallest species of shark, the white shark. —hode, *f.*, *dim.* —hödchen, ‖—hödlein, *n.* 1) a dog's testicle. 2) [in botany] *a*) V. —biß. *b*) orchis. —hunger, *m.* dog-appetite, canine hunger or appetite, V. Heißhunger, Ochsenhunger. —igel, *m.* the canine hedgehog. —kamille, *f.* the stinking camomile or dog's fennel. —kette, *f.* a dog's chain. —kirsche, *f.* white jalap, bryony; *it.* berry of the white bryony. —knecht, *m.* dog-feeder, dog-keeper. —knoblauch, *m.* V. —lauch. —kohl, *m.* 1) the asclepias, dog's-bane. 2) dog's mercury, cynocrambe, dog-cabbage. —kopf, *m.* 1) the head of a dog, a dog's head. 2) V. —affe. 3) a kind of shark, dog-fish. 4) tail-less bat, canis volans. 5) a serpent with a dog's head. 6) V. Leinkraut. 7) V. Löwenmaul. 8) V. Orant. —koth, *m.* V. —dreck; [in botany] the heath lousewort or red rattle. —krampf, *m.* cynic spasm. —krankheit, *f.* disease of dogs, [especially a peculiar disease in dogs] the distemper. —kraut, *n.* V. —kohl. —kuppel, *f.* a leash for leading dogs. —kürbiß, *m.* wild or squirting cucumber, V. Eselsgurke. —lattich, *m.* dandelion, piss-a-bed, swine-snout. —lauch, *m.* bear's garlic, ramsons. —laus, *f.* 1) dog-louse. 2) V. —fliege. —leder, *n.* dog's leather; dog-skin. —ledern, *adj.* made of the skin of a dog, dogskin. —loch, *n.* V. Hundeloch. —lode, *f.* the long hairs of a dog. †*Fig.* —lo den angehängt bekommen, to be severely reprimanded, vehemently chid or scolded. †*Fig.* —mager, *adj.* and *adv.* lean as a dog, very lean. —maul, *n.* the mouth of a dog; [in natural history] a kind of bat. —meise, *f.* V. Sumpfmeise, Hanfmeise. —melde, *f.* [a plant] the stinking goose-foot. —milch, *f.* milk of a bitch; [in botany] V. Eselsmilch 2). —moos, *n.* V. —flechte. †*Fig.* —müde, *adj.* and *adv.* quite tired, dog-weary. —nägelchen, *n.* V. —nelke. —nase, *f.* the nose or snout of a dog. †*Fig.* Eine —nase haben, to have a nice nose. —nelke, *f.* soapwort, saponaria. —peitsche, *f.* V. Hundepeitsche. —petersille, *f.* fool's parsley, the little hemlock. —pflaume, *f.* a sort of plum, perdrigon. —raute, *f.* dog's rue. —recht, *n.* [a part of the entrails of the beast taken, given to the hounds] hound's fee, quarry, carnage. —rippe, *f.* V. Wegebreit. —rose, *f.* dog-rose, V. Hagrose. —rübe, *f.* V. —kirsche. —ruthe, *f.* [in botany] cynomorium. —sattel, *m.* a sort of thick-haired caterpillar. —scham, *f.* [in botany] cynometra. —schirm, *m.* V. Hexschirm. —schlange, *f.* [a venomous serpent] bojobi. —schlepper, *m.* V. —läufer. —schnauze, *f.* V. —nase. —seuche, *f.* the distemper. —stall, *m.* V. Hundestall. —stern, [better Hundsstern] *m.* dog-star, Sirius; canicula or canicule. —strick, *m.* couple, leash. —tage, *pl.* dog-days. In den —tagen seyn, to be in the dog-days. —tagsfeier, *f.*, —tagsfeiertage, *pl.* the holidays or vacation of the canicular or dog-days. —tagswinde, *pl.* Etesian winds, trade-winds. —theil, *n.* V. —recht. —tod, *m.* the great yellow wolf's bane, dog's bane. —trab, *m.* dog-trot. —veilchen, *n.*, —viole, *f.* the dog's violet. —vogt, *m.* V. Hundewärter. —winde, *f.* the Virginian silk, periploca. —würger, *m.* [in botany] cynanchum or dog's bane. —wuth, *f.* canine madness, rabies canina. Stille —wuth, madness in the first stage. *Fig.* [in men] hydrophobia, V. Wasserscheu. —zäcke, *f.* V. —laus 2). —zahn, *m.* 1) dog's tooth, canine tooth; *it.* eye-tooth or dogtooth. 2) [in botany] dog's tooth. —zähnig, *adj.* having dog's teeth. —zähnige Lämmer, lambs one year old [that have yet milk-teeth]. —zern, *m.* V. Eberwurz. —zunge, *f.* 1) the tongue of a dog. 2) [in botany] *a*) hound's tongue, cynoglossum. *b*) brunella, self-heal. 3) [a fish] sole. —zwinger, *m.* a fenced place for keeping dogs, dog-yard, kennel-yard.

2. Húnd, *m.* [-es, *pl.* -e] [from the Sw. *haenta*, or the Sax. *henta* = fassen, halten] 1) [in mining] V. Göpel—. *Fig.* Den — anhängen, to rest from labour, to idle. 2) [among coopers] a tool used for putting the hoops round a cask, a cramp.

3. Húnd, *m.* [-es, *pl.* -e] [either allied to 2. Hund or to Humpen, Rumpf &c.] [in mining] a square chest with four wheels, in which the miners carry the ore, rock &c. from one place to another, miner's wheelbarrow.

Hunds-bengel, *m.* [in mining] Den —bengel stechen, to be idle, to idle. —läufer, *m.* [in mining] a miner who draws the wheel-barrow. —leitnagel, *m.* [in mining] an iron pin with barbs on its shank, rag-bolt. —nagel, *m.* V. —leitnagel.

Hündeln, *v. intr.* 1) to pup, to whelp. 2) [in popular lang.] to stink like a dog.

Húndert, [old Hunna, Goth. *hund*, *hunda*, Eng. *hundred*, W. *cant*, L. *cent-um*]. I. [a cardinal number, indeclinable] hundred. — Mann, a hundred men; vor — Jahren, a hundred years or a century ago or since. II. *n.* [-s, *pl.* -e] the number or quantity of a hundred, a hundred. Zu —en, by hundreds; zehn vom — or je

Procent, ten per cent.

Hundert-armig, *adj.* and *adv.* having a hundred arms. —**äugig**, *adj.* and *adv.* having a hundred eyes. —**blattig**, —**blätterig**, *adj.* and *adv.* having a hundred leaves, centifolious. —**fach**, —**fältig**, *adj.* and *adv.* hundred-fold, centuple. Dieſes Land trägt —fältige Früchte, gibt —fältigen Ertrag, that land yields a hundred-fold; das —fältige einer Zahl, a number centuple of another. —**füßig**, *adj.* and *adv.* having a hundred feet. —**gliederig**, —**gliedig**, *adj.* and *adv.* eine —gliederige Kette, a chain of a hundred links. —**gradig**, *adj.* and *adv.* consisting of a hundred degrees, centigrade. Ein —gradiges Thermometer, a centigrade thermometer. —**händig**, *adj.* and *adv.* having a hundred hands. —**haupt**, *n.* [in botany] eryngo, sea-holly. —**häuptig**, V. —köpfig. —**herr**, *m.* [*Centumvir] centumvir. Die —herren betreffend, centumviral. —**herrſchaft**, *f.* [*Centumvirat] centumvirate. —**jährig**, *adj.* and *adv.* a hundred years old; *it.* lasting a hundred years. Ein —jähriger Beſitz, eine —jährige Verjährung, a hundred years' possession, a centenary prescription, immemorial possession; der —jährige Kalender, the perpetual almanac. —**jährlich**, *adj.* happening every hundred years, centennial. Die —jährlichen Spiele or Feſte der Alten, the secular games of the ancients. —**kopf**, *m.* V. —haupt. —**köpfig**, *adj.* and *adv.* having a hundred heads, hundred-headed. —**mahl**, *adv.* a hundred times. —**mahlig**, *adj.* and *adv.* done or repeated a hundred times. —**mann**, *m* V. —herr. —**mäulig**, *adj.* and *adv.* having a hundred mouths. V. —züngig. —**namig**, *adj.* having a hundred names. —**opfer**, *n.* [*Hekatombe] hecatomb. —**pfünder**, *m.* [in gunnery] hundred-pounder. —**pfündig**, *adj.* of a hundred pounds. —**ſäulig**, *adj.* having a hundred columns. —**theil**, *n.* the hundredth part. —**theilig**, *adj.* and *adv.* divided into hundred parts. Ein —theiliges Thermometer, a centigrade thermometer. —**weiſe**, *adv.* by hundreds. —**züngig**, *adj.* having a hundred tongues.

Húnderte or **Húndertſte**, der, die, das, [-n, *pl.* -n] the hundredth. Sie ſind der —, you are the hundredth; der — Pfennig, the hundredth penny; **fig.* das Hundertſte in's Tauſendſte mengen, ſchwatzen or reden, vom Hundertſten auf's Tauſendſte kommen, to throw every thing into disorder or confusion, to confound all, to speak or talk without order, at random or of this and that, to skip from tree to tree.

Húndertel, [-s, *pl.* -] or **Húnderttheil**, [-s, *pl.* -e] *n.* the hundredth part.

Húndertens, [rather unusual] *adv.* in the hundredth place.

Húnderter, *m.* [-s, *pl.* -] figure containing hundreds.

Húnderterlei, *adj.* and *adv.* [indeclinable] of hundred different sorts. **Fig.* Darüber iſt — zu ſagen, a hundred different things are to be said on that point; es gibt — Gelegenheiten, there are a hundred opportunities.

Húndertſte, V. Hunderte.

Húnderttheil, V. Hundertel.

Hündinn, *f.* the female of the dog, bitch. Eine läufige —, a bitch at heat; die — iſt läufig, the bitch goes; V. Hund; [among hunters] eine — zur Zucht, a hound-bitch.

Hündiſch, *adj.* and *adv.* like a dog, doggish, currish, canine. *Fig.* [in contempt, and in popular lang.] Ein —er Neid, a churlish or currish envy; —e Unverſchämtheit, snarling or doggish impudence; man iſt — mit ihm umgegangen, they have treated him like a dog; die —en [more usual cyniſchen] Weiſen, the cynic philosophers, the Cynics.

Hüne, *m.* [-n, *pl.* -n] [perhaps allied to the Sw. *haenta* or the Sax. *henta* = fangen] a giant, V. Rieſe.

Hünen-bett, —**grab**, *n.* V. Rieſenbett, Rieſengrab. —**haft**, —**mäßig**, *adj.* and *adv.* gigantic.

Húngar or **Úngar**, *m.* [-s, *pl.* -n] Hungarian.

Húngariſch or **Úngariſch**, *adj.* and *adv.* Hungarian. —er Lederbereiter, Hungarian tanner.

Húngarn or **Úngarn**, *n.* [-s] Hungary, Hungaria.

Húnger, *m.* [-s] [V. Hungern] 1) hunger, appetite. —, großen — haben, to be hungry, very hungry; ſeinen — ſtillen, to appease one's hunger; ich ſpüre —, es kömmt mir ein — an, I feel hungry; — leiden, to suffer hunger; er kann — und Durſt beſſer ausſtehen, als Andere, he bears or endures hunger and thirst better than others; über — ſchreien, to cry with hunger; vor or für — or —s ſterben, to die with hunger, to be famished, to starve. *Prov.* — iſt der beſte Koch, hunger is the best sauce; — macht rohe Bohnen ſüß, hunger makes hard bones sweet, beans; — lehrt arbeiten, hunger will break through stonewalls; auf einem Haufen Korn über — ſchreien, to cry famine in the midst of plenty. *Fig.* violent desire. Der unerſättliche — nach Reichthum, Ehre, the insatiable desire of riches, honours, thirst after riches &c.; der — nach dem Worte des Herrn, the thirst of hearing the word of God. 2) [= Hungersnoth] famine, dearth. Es entſtand — im Lande, [in Scripture] there was a famine in the land.

Hunger-blümchen, *n.* [in botany] draba, whitlow-grass. —**blume**, *f.* yellow daisy. —**brunnen**, *m.* V. —quelle. —**geſtalt**, *f.* a famished figure or haggard person. —**harke**, *f.* a large rake or harrow, with which after the harvest the scattered ears of corn are collected on the land for the benefit of the owner, but to the prejudice of the gleaners. —**harken**, *v. intr.* to gather or collect the scattered ears of corn with such a rake. —**hocke**, *f.* a heap of sheaves which any one is allowed to house before the tithes have been levied. —**korn**, *n.* V. Mutterkorn. —**kraut**, *n.* 1) the sharp-pointed dock. 2) V. —blume. 3) pansy, heart's ease. —**kur**, *f.* a cure effected by abstinence from food. —**leider**, *m.*, —**leiderinn**, *f.* [in familiar language] a needy person that has nothing to eat, a needy wretch; *it.* a niggardly or stingy person, a niggard, miser. —**leiderei**, *f.* [in familiar language] extreme poverty or distress; *it.* niggardliness, stinginess. —**los**, *adj.* and *adv.* without hunger or appetite, wanting appetite. —**loſigkeit**, *f.* want of appetite, anorexy. —**pfarre**, *f.* a very poor parsonage, benefice or living, V. —ſtelle. —**pfote**, *f.* V. —tuch, *fig.* —**pulver**, *n.* powder against an inordinate appetite. —**quelle**, *f.* a spring which often dries up. —**rechen**, *m.* V. —harke. —**rechen**, *v. intr.* V. —harken. —**snoth**, *f.* famine, dearth. —**ſtelle**, *f.* a place or office with so small an income that the incumbent can hardly make shift to live, a very poor or paltry place or office. —**thurm**, *m.* [formerly] a tower or dungeon destined for starving any one. —**tod**, *m.* starving, dying with hunger, death caused by hunger or want of food, starvation. Den —tod ſterben, to die of hunger or starvation, to starve; ſich den —tod geben, to starve one's self with hunger. —**tuch**, *n.* black cloth with which the altars are covered in Lent. *Fig.* [in fam. lang.] Am —tuche nagen or [in vulgar lang.] die —pfoten ſaugen, to live in extreme poverty or distress. †—**wanſt**, *m.* [ironically] a swag-bellied person, fat guts.

Húngerig, *adj.* and *adv.* hungry. Ein —er Magen, a hungry stomach; ſehr or *arg — ſeyn, to be very or deadly hungry; *ich bin ſo —, daß ich die Leute anfallen möchte, I am as hungry as a wolf; ein —er [nimmerſatter] Falke, a hungry or greedy hawk; *prov.* einem —en Magen iſt nicht gut predigen, a hungry belly has no ears. **Fig.* *a*) shabby, mean, stingy. Das läßt or kömmt ſehr — heraus, that is or looks very shabby, mean or stingy; er hat ihn — bezahlt, he has paid him stingily or niggardly. *b*) longing, desirous, greedy. — nach Etwas ſeyn, thun, to be greedy of, to thirst for any thing.

Húngerigkeit, *f.* hungriness. *Fig.* [in popular language] shabbiness, meanness, stinginess.

Húngern, [Goth. and Sax. *hungrian*, Eng. *to hunger*, Sw. *hungra*; probably from the Goth. *hunjan* = verlangen] I. *v. intr.* and *impers.* to be hungry, to hunger. Ich hungere, mich hungert, es hungert mich, I am hungry; ſie werden weder — noch dürſten [in Script.], they shall not hunger nor thirst. *Fig.* to desire with great eagerness, to long for. Mich hungert darnach, I long for it; ſelig ſind, die da hungert und dürſtet nach der Gerechtigkeit [in Script.], blessed are they that hunger and thirst after righteousness. II. *v. intr.* to be without food, to fast, to starve. Er kann nicht —, he cannot endure or bear hunger; er hat oft — müſſen, he has often been obliged to fast, he has often starved; wenn mir Etwas fehlt, ſo hungere ich, when I am ill, I abstain from food. *Fig.* to be in want, to be very indigent.

Húnten, *adv.* [in popular lang., instead of = hier unten] here below, down here. — ſeyn, to be down or below.

Húnzen, [perhaps from höhnen] I. *v. impers.* [in popular lang.] Da hunzt es, there is or lies the main or chief difficulty, there is the rub. II. *v. tr.* to reprimand, to abuse, V. Aus—, Ver—.

Hüpen, *v. intr.* [among hunters] to call one's companion.

Hüpfen, *v. intr.* [Sax. *hoppan*, Eng. *to hop*, Dan. *hoppe*, Sw. *hoppo*, from heben] 1) [used with ſeyn] to hop, to skip, to jump. Mit gleichen Füßen —, to jump with the feet close; dieſer Ball iſt zu weich, er hüpft nicht, that ball is too soft, it does not bounce; ſie hüpfte vor Freude, she skipped or leapt for joy; ſein Herz hüpfte ihm vor Freude, his heart went pitapat with joy. 2) [used with haben] to jump or skip about. Die Kinder haben den ganzen Tag gehüpft, the children have been frisking or skipping all the day; die —den Inſecten, V. Hüpfer 2) *b*). Syn. Hüpfen, Springen. Hüpfen denotes merely to jump or hop upwards; ſpringen also to move with rapidity forwards.

Hüpfer, *m.* [-s, *pl.* -] 1) one that hops or skips, skipper, jumper. 2) [in nat. hist.] *a*) [a small fish of the genus Gasterosteus] stickle-back. *b*) [an insect] altica. 3) a little leap or bound, a skip.

Hürde, *f.* [*pl.* -n] [Sax. *hyrdel*, Eng. *hurdle*, allied to the L. *crates*] hurdle. Eine — von Weiden, a hurdle of osiers; — für Schafe, a pen or inclosure for sheep, fold; sheep-fold, sheep-cot, pidfold; die Schafe in die — or —n treiben, to fold or pen the sheep.

Hürden-draht, *m.* coarse iron-wire. —**gerte**, *f.* twig or osier for making hurdles. —**lager**, *n.* fold, sheep-fold, pin-fold. —**pfahl**, *m.* stake for a hurdle. —**ſchlag**, *m.* 1) the act of placing a sheep-fold on any ground; the act of folding or penning sheep. 2) the right of folding sheep, foldage. —wand, *f.*, —werk, *n.* V. Hürdung 1).

Hürden, I. *v. intr.* to place a sheepfold or pinfold. II. *v. tr.* Die Schafe —, to fold or pen the sheep; gehürdetes Land, land dunged by folding sheep on it; V. Pferchen.

Hürdung, *f.* 1) hurdle-work. 2) V. Hürdenschlag 1).

†Hure, *f.* [*pl.* -n] [probably allied to the Gr. κόρη = girl, or to the W. *huran*, from *huriaw* = to hire; now only used in low language] 1) [in general] any woman who violates chastity [eine Gefallene]. Ein Mädchen zur — machen, to debauch or deflour a girl; zur — werden, to become or be defloured or debauched; sie hat ihre Tochter selbst zur — gemacht, she has prostituted her daughter herself. 2) [in a more limited sense] a woman who prostitutes her body for hire, a harlot, prostitute, a whore, a common woman, a woman of the town, a strumpet; V. also Feildirne or feile Dirne, Metze. *Dim.* Hürchen, ||Hürlein, *n.* a little or young whore. Die öffentlichen —n in L., the common women, the women of the town in L.; den —n nachziehen, nachlaufen, to go a whore-hunting, to haunt bawdy houses. 3) [in conchology] a sort of porcelain shell. 4) [in botany] Die nackende —, the common meadow saffron; die stinkende —, the stinking goose-foot or blite.

Huren-art, *f.* 1) V. —geschlecht. 2) manners or course of life of a prostitute. —augen, *pl.* lascivious, lewd or unchaste eyes or looks. †—balg, *m.* 1) a vile prostitute, V. Hure 2). 2) a bastard child. —blick, *m.* a lascivious, lewd or unchaste look. †—bock, *m.* a lecherous man, a whoremaster. Ein alter —bock, an old lecher or fornicator. —brüche, or —brüchte, *f.* [in law] fine for fornication. —gasse, *f.* lane or street where there is a brothel or where women of the town live. —geist, *m.* unchaste or impure spirit; [in Script.] the spirit of whoredom. —geschlecht, *n.* race of whores. —gesindel, *n.* V. —pack. —gespräch, *n.* smutty or obscene discourse. —gewinn, *m.* V. —lohn. —glück, *n.* undeserved good fortune. Er hat in Allem —glück, fortune smiles upon or favours him in every thing. —handel, *m.* 1) an amorous intrigue. 2) V. —handwerk. —handwerk, *n.* the trade of a prostitute, harlotry. Sich auf das —handwerk legen, to turn prostitute, to walk the streets. —haus [*Bordell], *n.* brothel, bawdy house. †—hengst, *m.* V. —jäger. —herberge, *f.* V. —haus. —jäger, *m.* whoremonger, whoremaster, fornicator. —kind, *n.* V. Hurkind. —knecht, *m.* V. —jäger. —krankheit, *f.* venereal disease. —kraut, *n.* V. —wurz. —kuß, *m.* lewd or lascivious kiss. —leben, *n.* whorish, lewd, lascivious life, rakish life. —liebe, *f.* 1) the love of a harlot or prostitute. 2) profligate or lewd love. —lied, *n.* lascivious or bawdy song. —list, *f.* cunning trick or tricks, wile of a whore. —lohn, *m.* wages of prostitution. —maul, *n.* the mouth of a whore or other person who talks ribaldry; *it.* smutty discourse. —nest, *n.* nest or haunt of prostitutes or profligate persons, brothel, bawdy house. —pack, *n.* lewd or whorish rabble. —schmuck, *m.* whorish ornament. —sohn, *m.* a bastard, whoreson, [as a term of abuse] son of a bitch. —steuer, *f.* a tax imposed on prostitutes. —stirn, *f.* a hardened, bold, brasen or impudent front, profligate impudence. —strafe, *f.* a punishment inflicted on prostitutes; *it.* V. —brüche. —stück, —stückchen, ||—stücklein, *n.* trick of a whore, whorish trick. —thränen, *pl.* whore's tears; *it.* counterfeit tears, crocodile tears. —volk, *n.* V. —pack. —weib, *n.* a profligate or lewd woman, V. Hure 2). —wesen, *n.* harlotry, whorishness, V. —leben. —winkel, *m.* any corner or bidden place where prostitutes are to be found. In — winkel gehen, to haunt bawdy houses or stews, to go a whoring. —wirth, *m.* keeper of a brothel, a pander, pimp. —wirthinn, *f.* procuress, bawd. —wirthschaft, *f.* 1) the house or trade of a pimp or bawd. —wirthschaft treiben, to keep a bawdy-house. 2) the life of a whore or prostitute. —wurz, *f.* male fern. —zins, —zoll, *m.* V. —steuer.

Hurkind, *n.* a bastard child.

†Huren, I. *v. intr.* to whore, to commit fornication, to fornicate. Mit einer Person —, to have an illicit or criminal conversation or intercourse with any person; *prov.* — und buben, to give one's self up to all manner of debauches, to excesses of every kind. *it.* — [applied to women], to prostitute one's self, to turn or be a prostitute or woman of the town. Sie huret öffentlich, she is a common prostitute. *Fig.* — [in Scripture] to commit idolatry or fornication. II. *v. tr.* [obsolete] V. Beschlafen 2).

†Hurer, *m.* [-s, *pl.* -] whoremaster, whoremonger, fornicator. Die — und Ehebrecher wird Gott richten [in Scripture], the whoremongers and adulterers God will judge.

†Hurerei, *f.* whoring, whoredom, fornication, harlotry; [in Scripture] idolatry, fornication!

†Hürerisch, Hürisch, *adj.* and *adv.* whorish, lewd, incontinent. Ein —er Mann, ein —es Weib, a lecherous or whorish man, woman.

Hurr or **Hurre,** *adv.* [expressing a whirring noise] whirr.

Hurrah, *interj.* huzza, hurra! Unter betäubenden or donnernden —'s, amid deafening cheers or cheerings.

Hurren, *v. intr.* to whir or whirl.

Hurtig, *adj.* and *adv.* [Sw. and Dan. *hurtig*; allied to the old hurten = to push, to drive along] nimble, quick, active, agile. Gehen Sie —! go quickly! — arbeiten, to be quick at work; *mach' —! make haste! be quick! *Fig.* Ein —er Kopf, a quick mind, understanding or capacity; eine —e Antwort, a speedy answer.

Hurtigkeit, *f.* quickness, agility, activity, nimbleness. Die — der Zunge, the volubility of the tongue; die — des Körpers [rather unusual], the suppleness of the body; die — des Verstandes, the quickness or promptness of the understanding or of intellect. V. Schnelligkeit.

***Husar,** *m.* [-en, *pl.* -en] [in Hungarian = horseman] hussar.

Husaren-anzug, *m.* dress, uniform or regimentals of a hussar. —mäßig, *adj.* and *adv.* in the manner of the hussars. **Fig.* in a quick rough manner; in a dashing style. —mütze, *f.* the [fur] cap of a hussar. —oberster, *m.* colonel of hussars. —pelz, *m.* the pelisse of a hussar. —regiment, *n.* regiment of hussars. —säbel, *m.* sabre of a hussar. —sattel, *m.* saddle of a hussar. —stiefel, *pl.* boots of a hussar. —uniform, *f.* V. —anzug.

1. **Husch,** *interj.* [allied to haschen and wischen in entwischen] 1) [in fam. lang., to express a quick motion accompanied with a hissing sound] pop! quick! at once! —! da war er fort, he went in the twinkling of an eye; all at once, away he went! eins, zwei, drei.... [und] —! once, twice, thrice and away! 2) [to impose silence] be still or quiet, hush!

2. **Husch,** *m.* [-es, *pl.* -e] or **Husche,** *f.* [*pl.* -n] [in fam. or popular lang.] 1) quick and instantaneous motion; *it.* [rather provincial] a sudden and quickly passing shower of rain. 2) a box on the ear. *Fig.* [rather provincial] a sudden or unforeseen mishap. 3) [=Zeitlang] while. Es währte eine ziemliche —e, it lasted a pretty while.

Huschen, [V. 1. Husch] I. *v. intr.* to pass quickly. Er huschte in das Zimmer, he popped into the room. II. *v. tr.* [in popular lang.] to box any one's ears, to beat, to drub any one.

Hüsing, *n.* [-es, *pl.* -e] [in seamen's lang.] housing or house-line.

Huß, *interj.* [allied to hetzen, hissen] [among hunters, an exclamation, used for animating the dogs] loo! loo!

Hussah, *interj.* huzza! V. Hurrah.

Hussahen, *v. intr.* to huzza.

Hussen, Hüssen, V. Huschen.

Hussit, *m.* [-en, *pl.* -en] [a follower of John Huss] Hussite.

Hussitisch, *adj.* and *adv.* originating from or belonging to the Hussites; in the manner or after the doctrines of the Hussites.

Hüsteln, *v. intr.* to cough a little.

Husten, *v. intr.* [Low Sax. hosten, Sax. *hwostan*, Sw. *hosta*] to cough. *Fig.* [in popular lang.] Die Flöhe — hören, to have a high opinion of one's talents, a great conceit of one's self, to be very conceited. *it.* [as a verb transitive] [vulgar] Ich werde dir etwas —, you may wait for it till doom's-day, you may go to hell for it. V. Auf—, Aus—.

Husten, *m.* [-s] cough. Den — haben, bekommen, to have, to get a cough; ein trockener —, a dry cough; der blaue —, hooping-cough; schwindsüchtiger —, a hectic or *churchyard cough; krampfiger —, convulsive cough.

Husten-fieber, *n.* fever attended with cough, catarrhal fever. —kraut, *n.* colt's foot, tussilago. —kuchen, *m.*, —küchlein, *n.* cough-lozenge. —stillend, *adj.* and *adv.* good for a cough, pectoral, bechic. —wurzel, *f.* V. —kraut.

1. **Hut,** *m.* [-es, *pl.* Hüte] *dim.* Hütchen, ||Hütlein, *n.* [Low Sax. and Eng. *hood*, Dan. and Eng. *hat*, Sw. *hatt*; allied to Haut] 1) [in general] a covering for the upper part of any thing. Der — eines Kuppelthürmchens [in architecture], the top of a lantern; der — einer Abziehblase, the helm of a still; der — eines Pilzes, the cap of a mushroom; *it.* V. Finger—, Licht—. [in grammar] Das Hütchen or Hütlein, the circumflex. 2) [in a more limited sense] a covering for the head, hat; V. Feder—, Filz—, Sammet—, Stroh—. Der Kopf eines —es, the crown of a hat; der Boden eines —es, the bottom of a hat; der Rand, die Krämpe eines —es, the brim, flap, cock of a hat; ein runder —, a round hat; ein dreieckiger —, a three-cornered hat, a cocked hat. V. Bischofs—, Cardinals—, Jäger—, Kastor—, Klapp—, Kur—, Reise—, Sturm—; den — aufschlagen, aufkrämpen, to cock [up] one's hat; den — aufsetzen, to put on one's hat; den — abziehen or abnehmen, to take or pull off one's hat; den — aufbehalten, to keep one's hat on; den — herunter! off with your hat, hats off! vor Jemand den — abziehen, to pull off one's hat to any one; ohne — gehen, to go or walk bare-headed or without a hat on one's head; den — in den Kopf, in die Augen drücken, to slouch one's hat over one's eyes; den — schräg or schief aufsetzen, to cock one's hat [on one side]; diese Frauenzimmer tragen Hüte und keine Hauben, those ladies wear bonnets and no caps; [among hatters] einen — über den Stock schlagen, to give a hat its form, to shape a hat; einen alten — über den Stock schlagen, to iron an old hat, den — ausstoßen, to put the felt upon the block. *Fig.* [in fam. lang.] Viele Köpfe unter einen — bringen, to bring several people to agree, or to be all of the same opinion or mind; es fehlt ihm unter dem —e, er ist unter dem —e nicht richtig, he is a little crack-brained, deranged or

crazy; die Frau hat den —, the wife wears the breaches or rules the roast. 3) a hat-shaped thing. Ein — Zucker, loaf of sugar, V. Zuckerhut, Hutzucker.

Hut-band, *n.* hat-band. —besatz, *m.* or —besetze, *n.* the border, trimming or garniture of a hat or bonnet. —boden, *m.* bottom of a hat. —bürste, *f.* hat-brush. —eisen, *n.* an iron ring round the hat of a coachman &c. —fabrik, *f.* manufactory of hats. —feder, *f.* feather on or for a hat. —filz, *m.* felt for hats. —form, *f.* 1) the form or shape of a hat. 2) hat-block. —futter, *n.* 1) lining of a hat. 2) V. —futteral. —futteral, *n.* hat-box, hat-case. —gürtel, *m.* V. —schnur. —handel, *m.* trade in hats. —händler, *m.* one who deals in hats, dealer in hats. —kante, *f.* the edge of a hat. —kissen, *n.* a hatter's velvet-rubber. —knopf, *m.* button of a hat. —kopf, *m.* crown of a hat. —krämpe, *f.* flap, brim or cock of a hat. —kreuz, *n.* a cross-shaped frame or stand for hanging hats on. —leder, *n.* leather on the inside of a hat. —los, *adj.* and *adv.* without a hat, bare-headed. —macher, *m.*, —macherinn, *f.* hatter, hatter's wife. —macherei, *f.* V. —macherhandwerk. —machergesell, *m.* journeyman hatter. —macherhandwerk, *n.* hatter's trade. —macherinnung, *f.* hatter's company. —macherkunst, *f.* the art of making hats, hatter's trade. —machernadel, *f.* hatter's needle. —macherwerkstatt, *f.* a hatter's workshop. —manufactur, *f.* V. —fabrik. —masche, *f.* V. —schleife. —quaste, *f.* V. —troddel. —rand, *m.* brim of a hat. —rechen, *m.* a rake for hanging hats on. —ring, *m.* V. —eisen. —rose, *f.* a knot of ribbands &c. in the form of a rose for a hat; cockade. —schachtel, *f.* hat-case, hat-box; *it.* band-box. —schleife, *f.* loop to a hat; cockade. —schlinge, *f.* loop to a hat. —schnalle, *f.* buckle of a hat. —schnur, *f.* hat-string, hat-band. —spange, *f.* the clasp of a hat. —staffirer, *m.* V. —stutzer. —stock, *m.* hat-block. —stülpe, *f.* V. —krämpe. —stutzer, *m.* [formerly] a man who puts a hat into proper form and shape [which in Germany was a distinct trade from the hatter's]. —tresse, *f.* galloon or lace of a hat. —troddel, *f.* tassel of a hat. —überzug, *m.* an oil-cloth case or cover of a hat. —zeichen, *n.* a hatter's sign or mark in a hat. —zucker, *m.* loaf-sugar.

2. Hut, [Huth] *f.* 1) [not used in the *pl.*] the act of keeping or guarding; *it.* the act of tending sheep or cattle Etwas in seiner — haben, to have any thing in one's keeping, custody or charge; sie haben es in seine — gegeben, they have committed it to his keeping, they have given it him to keep; die — des Viehes, the tending of cattle; dem Schäfer den Lohn für die — bezahlen, to pay the shepherd his wages for tending the sheep. 2) [not used in the *pl.*] the place where one keeps watch or is on guard. Hier stehe ich auf meiner — [in Scripture], here I stand upon my watch; ich stelle mich auf meine — alle Nacht [in Scripture], I am set in my ward whole nights. *Fig.* Auf seiner — seyn, to be or stand upon one's guard, to observe caution; die Weisheit befiehlt, daß wir immer auf unserer — sind, it is wisdom to keep ourselves upon our guard. 3) [not used in the *pl.*] one or more persons set for a guard, watch. Nachdem sie durch die erste und andere — gegangen waren [in Scripture], when they were past the first and the second ward. 4) [*pl.* -en] a certain district or division where any one is to keep watch. Das ist nicht in meiner — geschehen, that has not happened within my district or ward. 5) [*pl.* -en] the animals committed to any one's keeping, a flock, a herd. Eine — Gänse, Schafe &c., a flock of geese, of sheep. 6) [*pl.* -en] pasture. Ein Gut mit schönen —en, an estate with fine pastures. 7) [*pl.* -en] the right of pasture.

Hut-geld, *n.* money paid for the keeping and guarding of any thing; [chiefly] shepherd's or herdsman's wages. —gerechtigkeit, *f.* right of pasture. —haus, *n.* a house to keep any thing in, a watch-house; [in mining] tool-house, V. Zechenhaus. —los, *adj.* and *adv.* [in the proper as well as in a fig. sense] not watched, not guarded. Eine —lose Herde, a flock without a shepherd or herdsman. —mann, *m.* 1) keeper. 2) herdsman. —stein, *m.* a stone marking the pasture-ground.

Hüten, [Hüthen] [Goth. *huotan*, Sax. *hydan*, Eng. *to hide*; it belongs either to the Gr. *κεύθειν* and the L. *cautus*, or to the Goth. *vitan*, the L. *videre* and the Germ. weiden] I. *v. tr.* to look to or after, to guard, to watch, to keep, to tend. Das Haus —, to have the care of the house; die Schafe, das Vieh —, to feed or tend the sheep, the cattle; die Mädchen sind schwer zu —, girls are difficult to keep; einen Gefangenen —, to watch a prisoner; Einen vor Etwas —, to keep, preserve or guard any one from any thing; ich kann ihn nicht den ganzen Tag —, I can't have my eyes upon him, I can't look after him all day long. *Fig.* Das Bett, das Zimmer, das Haus —, to keep one's bed, one's room, house, to be confined to &c. by illness. II. *v. intr.* to keep watch, to be on guard. III. *v. r.* sich —, to be cautious, to be on one's guard, to take care, to beware. Sich vor Einem, vor Etwas —, to beware of any one, of any thing; — Sie sich vor ihm, be on your guard against him, beware of him; sich vor Versehen —, to guard against mistakes; — Sie sich wohl, davon zu essen, be sure not to eat of it; er wird sich —, davon zu sprechen, he will take care not to speak of it, I am sure he won't speak of it; hüte dich vor der Ruthe! beware of the rod!

Hüt-faß, *n.* a tub or box for keeping any thing, a fish-box. —geld, *n.* V. Hutgeld.

1. Hüter, *m.* [-s, *pl.* -] —inn, *f.* V. [the usual word] Hutmacher.

2. Hüter, [Hüther] *m.* [-s, *pl.* -], —inn, *f.* a person that looks after a thing, guards and keeps it, keeper, herdsman, watch, guard. Einen zum — über Etwas setzen, to give any one the charge of, to place any one as a guard over any thing; man hat mich zum —, zur —inn der Weinberge gesetzt, they have set me as guard over the vineyards or to look after the vineyards; V. Feld—, Laden—, Thür—. [in printing, *Custos] the catchword.

Hüter-geld, *n.*, —lohn, *m.* wages given to a person who tends a herd or flock, herdsman's wages.

Huth, Hüthen, Hüther, V. Hut, Hüten, Hüter.

Hütsch, V. 2. Husch 1).

Hütsche, *f.* [*pl.* -n] footstool; [in seamen's lang.] the stretchers [of a rowing-boat].

Hütschen, *v. intr.* [allied to huschen] to glide, to slide [particularly on one's backside].

Hütte, *f.* [*pl.* -n] *dim.* Hüttchen, ‖ Hüttlein, *n.* [Low Sax. *hutte*, Sax. and Fr. *hutte*, Eng. *hut*, Dan. *hytte*, Sw. *hydda*, from the old hudan = bedecken] 1) [in general] a covered place. Ich will wohnen in deiner —n ewiglich [in Scripture], I will abide in thy tabernacle for ever; die — des Stifts, tabernacle. [in seamen's language, on men of war] — [*Campanje] poop. Die Ober —, poop-royal, top-gallant poop; *it.* die — auf einer Galeere, the canopy in the stern of a galley. V. Lauber—, Stifts—, Stroh—, Vogel—. 2) a place where any particular work or manufactory is carried on; V. Glas—, Kalk—, Pech—, Ziegel—; [particularly in mining] a forge, furnace or smelting-house, V. Blech—, Blei—, Eisen—, Gieß—; Gift—, Messing—, Schmelz—, Seiger—. 3) [a small mean habitation or dwelling] a cot, cottage, hut. Eine mit Stroh bedeckte —, a thatched cottage; die —n der Soldaten, the huts of soldiers; die Soldaten hatten kaum Zeit, —n aufzuschlagen, the soldiers had scarcely time to make huts. *Fig.* Sein Haus or seine Wohnung ist eine elende —, his house or habitation is a miserable cot or hovel.

Hütten-after, *n.* [in metallurgy] waste matter, residuum. —amt, *n.* a commission or board to superintend the furnaces belonging to a mine. —arbeit, *f.* work done in a foundery or smelting-house. —arbeiter, *m.* a man that works in a foundery or smelting-house. —bau, *m.* [a part of the art of mining] smelting and casting. —beamte, —bediente, *m.* clerk or officer of a smelting-house or foundery. —bewohner, *m.*, —bewohnerinn, *f.* one who lives in a hut or cottage, cottager. —deck *n.* [in seamen's lang.] V. Hütte 1). —faktor, *m.* the factor or overseer of a foundery or smelting-house. —gast, *m.* [in seamen's lang.] officer of the poop. —gebäude, *n.* the buildings belonging to a foundery or smelting-house. —gekrätz, *n.* V. —after. —gericht, *n.* a court that decides matters relating to mines, founderies and smelting-houses. —gezäh, —gezähe, *n.* tools or implements used in founderies or smelting-houses. —herr, *m.* the proprietor of a foundery. —hof, *m.* yard or court of a foundery or smelting-house. —hofgekrätz, *n.* V. —gekrätz. —katze, *f.* a pulmonary disorder peculiar to miners and workers in founderies and smelting-houses. —knappschaft, *f.* association or body of founders and smelters. —kosten, *pl.* expenses of smelting and casting. —kunde, *f.* art of working metals, metallurgy. —kundige, *m.* metallurgist. —leute, *pl.* workers in founderies or smelting-houses. —mann, *m.* 1) [rather stiff] inhabitant of a cottage, cottager. 2) V. —arbeiter. 3) V. —kundige. —männisch, *adj.* and *adv.* pertaining to the art of working metals or to metallurgy, metallurgic. —meister, *m.* the superintendent or overseer of a foundery or similar establishment. —nicht, —nichts, *n.* cadmia, tutty. —ordnung, *f.* regulation concerning founderies and smelting-houses. —pulver, *n.* V. —nicht. —rauch, *m.* 1) smoke that rises from a cottage or foundery. 2) [in metallurgy] a substance that separates from metals, when melting, in the shape of smoke; [this is caught and serves for the preparation of arsenic, thence] arsenical acid, white arsenic, flowers of arsenic. Gelber —rauch, orpiment; grauer —rauch, tutty; rother —rauch, realgar. —reiter, *m.* an officer [travelling on horseback] that visits and inspects founderies and smelting-houses. —schreiber, *m.* clerk or controller of a foundery or smelting-house. —siedler, *m.* [rather stiff] hermit. —steiger, *m.* an officer in founderies or smelting-houses, a surveyor or inspector of the workmen. —verwalter, *m.* director or administrator of a foundery or smelting-house. —vogt, *m.* V. —meister. —vorsteher, *m.* V. —verwalter. —wächter, *m.* a watchman in a foundery or smelting-house. —wäscher, *m.* a washer of the residuum. —werk, *n.* a foundery or smelting-house. —wesen, *n.* all affairs connected with founderies or smelting-houses. —wissenschaft, *f.* V. —kunde. —zeichen, *n.* the peculiar mark of a foundery or smelting-house. —zentner, *m.* the quintal or hundred-weight of the founderies and smelting-houses [which in Germany is generally 115 pounds]. —zinn, *n.* grain tin. V. Bergzinn.

Hütter, *m.* [-s, *pl.* -] overseer of a foundery or smelting-house.

Hüttler or **Hüttner**, *m.* [-s, *pl.* -] V. Hüttenbewohner.

Hüttlich, *adj.* and *adv.* [in poetry] conformable with or suitable to a cottage or hut. Die —e Einfalt, the simplicity of the cottage.

Hüttner or **Hüttler**, *m.* [-s, *pl.* -] V. Hüttenbewohner.

Hütung, *f.* pasture, V. Weide, Trift.

Hützel, *f.* [*pl.* -n] [probably from the provincial hutzeln = runzelig werden] a dried pear or apple [of an inferior kind].

Hutzelbrod, *n.* a kind of bread made of dry fruit and spices.

†**Hützelig**, *adj.* and *adv.* V. Runzelig.

†**Hützeln**, *v. intr.* to get wrinkles, to become wrinkled.

Huy, *interj.* [among wild-boar hunters] —! — Sau! on! hie on! *it.* V. Hui.

Húzel, V. Hutzel.

†**Húzelig**, V. Hutzelig.

(*) **Hyacinth**, **Hyäne**, &c. V. Hiazint, Hiäne &c.

*__Hyāden__, *pl.* Hyades or Hyads.

*__Hyalíth__, *m.* [-es, *pl.* -e] [in mineralogy] Hyalite, Mueller's glass.

*__Hȳder__, *f.* [*pl.* -n] water-serpent, hydra; [in mythology] hydra. Die Lernäische —, the hydra of Lerna. *Fig.* hydra. Die — des Kriegs, der Zwietracht, the hydra of war, of discord.

*__Hydrāt__, *n.* [-s, *pl.* -e] [in chimistry] hydrate.

*__Hydraúlik__, *f.* [Wasserkraftlehre] hydraulics.

*__Hydraúliker__, *m.* [-s, *pl.* -] one versed or skilled in hydraulics.

*__Hydraúlisch__, *adj.* hydraulic, hydraulical. —e Maschinen, hydraulic engines.

*__Hȳdrogēn__, *n.* [-s] [Wasserstoff] [in chimistry] hydrogen.

*__Hydrogenīrt__, *adj.* hydrogenated.

*__Hydrogrāph__, *m.* [-en, *pl.* -en] hydrographer.

*__Hydrographīe__, *f.* [Wasserbeschreibung] hydrography.

*__Hydrogrāphisch__, *adj.* hydrographic, hydrographical. —e Karten, hydrographical maps.

*__Hydrologīe__, *f.* [Wasserkunde] hydrology.

*__Hydrolōgisch__, *adj.* hydrological.

*__Hydromantīe__, *f.* hydromancy.

*__Hȳdromēter__, *n.* [-s, *pl.* -] [Wassermesser] hydrometer.

*__Hydrometrīe__, *f.* [Wassermeßkunst] hydrometry.

*__Hydropathīe__, *f.* V. Wasserheilkunde.

*__Hydrophān__, I. *adj.* hydrophanous. II. *m.* hydrophane [a variety of opal made transparent by immersion in water].

*__Hydrophobīe__, *f.* [Wasserscheu] hydrophobia, hydrophoby.

*__Hydroscōp__, *n.* [-es, *pl.* -e] [Wasseruhr] hydroscope [a kind of water-clock].

*__Hydrostātik__, *f.* [Wasserwägekunst, Wasserstandslehre] hydrostatics.

*__Hydrostātisch__, *adj.* hydrostatic, hydrostatical.

*__Hydrotéchnik__, *f.* hydraulics.

*__Hydrotéchnisch__, *adj.* hydraulic, hydraulical.

*__Hydrurét__, *n.* [-s, *pl.* -e] hydruret.

*__Hȳetometer__, *n.* [-s, *pl.* -] [Regenmesser] hydrometer, rain-gage.

(*) For words not found under Hy— look under Hi—.

Hygēa, **Hygiea**, *f.* [Gesundheitsgöttinn] the Goddess of health, Hygeia.

*__Hygiástik__, *f.* the art of preserving the health, hygiastics.

*__Hygiēne__, *f.* science of health, hygina.

*__Hygromēter__, *n.* [-s, *pl.* -] [Feuchtigkeitsmesser] hygrometer.

*__Hygrometrīe__, *f.* hygeometry.

*__Hygromētrisch__, *adj.* hygrometrical.

*__Hygroscōp__, *n.* [-es, *pl.* -e] hygroscope.

*__Hylozoíst__, *m.* [-en, *pl.* -en] [one who holds matter to be animated] holozoic.

*__Hȳmen__, [-s] 1) *m.* [Hochzeitgott] [in ancient mythology] Hymen. *Fig.* marriage, matrimony, wedding. Sich in —s Bande schmiegen, [in jest] to commit matrimony. 2) *n.* [in anatomy, the virginal membrane] hymen, V. Jungfernschloß.

*__Hymenäus__, *m.* 1) V. Hymen 1). 2) [*pl.* Hymenäen] marriage-song, wedding-song; [in the plural, also:] nuptial festivals.

*__Hymenóptern__, *pl.* [insects, having membraneous wings] hymenoptera.

*__Hȳmne__, *f.* [*pl.* -n] [a song or ode in honour of God or of some deity] hymn. Eine — auf Apollo, a hymn in honour of Apollo; das Absingen der —n, the singing of hymns, hymning.

Hymnenbuch, *n.* a collection of hymns, hymnology. —dichter, *m.* composer of hymns, hymnologist.

*__Hypállage__, *f.* [in grammar] hypallage.

*__Hypèrbel__, *f.* [*pl.* -n] 1) [in rhetoric] hyperbole. Er spricht in —n, he speaks hyperbolically, he uses hyperbole; V. Vergrößerung, Uebertreibung. 2) [in conic sections and geometry] hyperbola. V. Kegelschnitt.

Hyperbelförmig, *adj.* hyperboliform.

Hyperbōlisch, *adj.* and *adv.* 1) hyperbolic, hyperbolical, exaggerated. — sprechen, to use hyperbole, to speak hyperbolically or with exaggeration. 2) [in geometry] hyperbolic, hyperbolical.

*__Hyperboloīde__, *f.* [*pl.* -n] a hyperbolic conoid, hyperboloid.

*__Hyperborēer__, *m.* [-s, *pl.* -], —inn, *f.* [among the ancients] an inhabitant of the most northern region of the earth, hyperborean. *Fig.* [in jest] a goth; *it.* an odd fellow [in manners, costume &c.]

*__Hyperborēisch__, *adj.* and *adv.* hyperborean.

*__Hyperkritik__, *f.* [*pl.* -en] excessive rigour of criticism, hypercriticism.

*__Hýperkritiker__, *m.* [-s, *pl.* -] an over-rigid critic, hypercritic.

*__Hýperkritisch__, *adj.* and *adv.* hypercritical.

*__Hýperorthodox__, *adj.* hyperorthodox.

*__Hyperorthodoxīe__, *f.* hyperorthodoxy.

*__Hýperphysisch__, *adj.* supernatural, hyperphysical.

*__Hýpersthēn__, *n.* [-s] [a mineral] hypersthene or hyperstene, Labrador hornblend or schillerspar.

*__Hypersthenīe__, *f.* [in medicine] excess of strength.

*__Hypochónder__, *m.* [-s, *pl.* -] hypochondriac.

*__Hypochondrīe__, *f.* [Milzkrankheit, Milzsucht] hypochondriacism, hypochondriasis.

*__Hypochóndrisch__, *adj.* hypochondriac, hypochondriacal.

*__Hypochondríst__, *m.* [-en, *pl.* -en] V. Hypochonder.

*__Hypomóchlion__, *n.* [in mechanics, the fulcrum or point of suspension in a lever] hypomochlion.

*__Hypotenūse__, *f.* [*pl.* -n] [in geometry] hypotenuse.

*__Hypothecīren__, *v. tr.* [verhypotheciren] to hypothecate, to mortgage, V. Verpfänden.

*__Hypothēk__, *f.* [*pl.* -en] [Unterpfand, Verschreibung] mortgage, hypotheca.

Hypothekenbuch, *n.* a register of mortgages kept by a public officer or in a public office. —schein, *m.* [the deed] mortgage, hypotheca. —wesen, *n.* the laws and regulations relating to mortgages.

*__Hypothekārisch__, *adj.* belonging to a mortgage, hypothecary. —er [or Hypotheken-] Gläubiger, mortgagee; eine —e Schuld, a mortgage.

*__Hypothēse__, *f.* [*pl.* -n] hypothesis, supposition. V. Satz, Voraussetzung.

*__Hypothētisch__, *adj.* and *adv.* hypothetic, hypothetical, conditional. Das ist nur — wahr, that is only hypothetically true.

*__Hypotypōse__, *f.* [*pl.* -n] [in rhetoric] [Versinnlichung] hypotyposis.

*__Hȳsop__, *m.* [-s] hyssop, V. Isop.

*__Hysterīe__, or *__Hystērik__, *f.* [Mutterbeschwerung] hysterics.

*__Hystērisch__, *adj.* and *adv.* hysteric, hysterical.

*__Hysterolíth__, *m.* [-en, *pl.* -en] hysterolithes.

*__Hysteronpróteron__, *n.* [Hinterstvorderst] [a rhetorical figure] hysteron proteron.

*__Hysterotomīe__, *f.* [Kaiserschnitt] hysterotomy.

I. (the vowel)

I, **i**, [a vowel] I, i. Ein großes I, a great or capital I.

I, **Ih**, *interj.* [instead of ei or ie, which see] 1) [expressing wonder] ah, ha 2) well or what of that? — nun, es mag drum seyn, well and good, let it be so, well then it may be so.

Ībe, *f.* [*pl.* -n] or **Ibenbaum**, *m.* 1) yew, yew-tree, V. Eibe. 2) ivy, V. Epheu.

Ibenblätter, *pl.*, —laub, *n.* ivy.

Ibérien, *n.* [-s] [obsolete or in poetical lang.] Iberia.

Ībis, *m.* [*pl.* -sse] [a fowl, a native of Egypt] ibis.

Ībisch, V. Eibisch.

Ich, I. *pron.* [Sax. *ic*, Goth. and D. *ik*, Eng. *I*, Dan. *jeg*, Sw. *jag*, Icel. *eg*, L. *ego*, Gr. ἐγώ] I. — lese, I read; — Endes-Unterzeichneter erkläre, I the undersigned declare; — Unglücklicher! unhappy I! or [in fam. lang.] me! hier bin —, here I am; wer ist da? —; — bin es, who is there? I; it is I; —, der [ich] es sehe, I who see it; V. meiner, mir, mich. II. *n.* [-s] one's own person, one's self. Sein liebes —, his dear self; [in philosophy] a thinking or rational being, self; das — ist dem Nicht-— entgegengesetzt, rational beings are opposed to the corporeal world.

Íchheit, *f.* the notion I, the quality of self, self.

Íchler, [unusual] *m.* [-s, *pl.* -] V. Selbstling, Selbstsüchtige.

*__Ichneúmon__, *m.* [-s, *pl.* -e] 1) [Pharaonsratze] ichneumon. 2) ichneumon-fly.

*__Ichnogrāph__, *m.* [-en, *pl.* -en] [Grundrißzeichner] ichnographer.

*__Ichnographīe__, *f.* ichnography.

*__Ichnogrāphisch__, *adj.* and *adv.* ichnographical.

Ichsucht, *f.* V. Selbstsucht.

Ichsüchtig, *adj.* V. Selbstsüchtig.

***Ichthyographie**, *f.* [Fischbeschreibung] ichthyography.

***Ichthyolith**, *m.* [-en, *pl.* -en] fossil fish, ichthyolite, V. Fischstein.

***Ichthyolog**, *m.* [-en, *pl.* -en] ichthyologist.

***Ichthyologie**, *f.* [Fischkunde] ichthyology.

***Ichthyophag**, *m.* [-en, *pl.* -en] [Fischesser] ichthyophagist.

Ida, *f.* [-'s] [a name of women] Ida.

***Ideal**, *adj.* and *adv.* V. Idealisch.

***Ideal**, *n.* [-es, *pl.* -e] something conceived by the mind though not existing in reality, ideal image, ideal perfection. Ein — von Schönheit, an ideal beauty; ein solcher Grad von Tugend ist nur im —e vorhanden, such a degree of virtue exists in imagination or fancy only.

***Idealisch**, *adj.* and *adv.* ideal. Die —e Welt, the imaginary or ideal world; —schön, transcendentally beautiful, of a heavenly beauty.

***Idealisiren**, *v. tr.* to idealize.

***Idealism**, *m.* [-s] idealism.

***Idealist**, *m.* [-en, *pl.* -en] idealist.

***Idealistisch**, *adj.* and *adv.* Idealistical.

***Idealität**, *f.* [*pl.* -en] ideality.

***Idee**, *f.* [*pl.* -n] idea. Was für eine —! what an idea! *die — kommt mir, daß &c., it strikes me, that &c.; eine wunderliche —, a singular idea, a whim; *das ist so seine —, such is his fancy.

Ideen-lehre, *f.* ideology. —welt, *f.* the imaginary or ideal world.

***Identification, Identificirung**, *f.* [Gleichmachung] identification.

***Identificiren**, *v. tr.* to identify. Sich mit Etwas —, to identify one's self with any thing.

***Identisch**, *adj.* and *adv.* the same, identic, identical.

***Identität**, *f.* identity, identicalness.

***Ideolog**, *m.* [-en, *pl.* -en] ideologist.

***Ideologie**, *f.* [Begriffslehre] ideology.

***Ideologisch**, *adj.* ideological.

***Idiom**, *n.* [-s, *pl.* -e] idiom.

***Idiomatisch**, *adj.* idiomatic, idiomatical.

***Idiot**, *m.* [-en, *pl.* -en] idiot.

***Idiotism**, *m.* [-s, *pl.* -en] [Spracheigenheit, auch Blödsinn] idiotism; *it.* imbecility.

***Idol**, *n.* [-s, *pl.* -e] idol, V. Abgott, Götze.

Iduna, [-'s] [in the Scandinavian mythology, the goddess of immortality] Iduna.

***Idus**, *pl.* [with the ancient Romans, the 15th day March, May, July and October, the 13th of the other months] ides.

***Idylle**, *f.* [*pl.* -n] or **Idyll**, *n.* [-es, *pl.* -e] idyl, V. Hirtengedicht, Schäfergedicht.

Idyllisch, *adj.* and *adv.* idyllic, pastoral.

Iffertem, *n.* [-s] [a town in Switzerland] Yverdon.

Igel, *m.* [-s, *pl.* -] [Sax. *il, el, ile*, Icel. *igull*, ...ied to Achel, Ecke &c.] 1) hedgehog, urchin. Der junge —, hedgepig. 2) V. Egel 1).

Igel-aloe, *f.* or **Stachelaloe**, *f.* the great hedgehog aloes. —fisch, *m.* 1) hedgehog, globefish. 2) V. —schnecke. —huf, *m.* V. —s-f. —klette, *f.* the prickly parsnip, echinophora. —schnecke, *f.* sea-hedgehog, sea-urchin. —shuf, *m.* [in farriery] the crown scab. —sklee, [a plant] hedgehog. —sknospe, —skolbe, *f.*, —skopf, *m.* [in botany] 1) bur-reed. Die aufrechtstehende —sknospe &c., the great bur-reed; die schwimmende —sknospe &c., the lesser bur-reed. 2) V. Stechapfel. —skraut, *n.* wild or squirting cucumber. —stein, *m.* echinite, V. Echinit.

Igelicht, *adj.* V. Stachelig.

Ignaz, *m.* [-ens, *pl.* -e] [a name of men] Ignatius.

***Ignorant**, *m.* [-en, *pl.* -en] an ignorant.

***Ignoranz**, *f.* [Unwissenheit] ignorance [only used in contempt].

***Ignoriren**, *v. tr.* 1) [unusual] V. Nicht wissen. 2) [in familiar language] to overlook something designedly, to appear not to see or observe something.

Ihm, [the dative case of er, es]. [Low Sax. em, öme, Dan. *ham*, Eng. *him*] 1) to him, to it. Gebt ihm zu trinken, give him something to drink; sprechen Sie mit ihm, speak with or to him; ich begegnete ihm, I met him; es wird ihm nicht gelingen, he won't succeed; der Strom riß uns fort, wir konnten ihm nicht widerstehen, the current carried us away, we could not resist it. 2) [in addressing persons of the lower class] to you. Johann, ich sage Ihm, John, I tell you; von Ihm hoffe ich es zu bekommen, of you I hope to get it.

Ihn, [the accusative of er] [Sax. hine, Eng. *him*, Dan. *ham*] 1) him, it. Ich sah ihn gestern, I saw him yesterday; dieser Wein ist so sauer, daß man ihn nicht trinken kann, this wine is so sour, that one cannot drink it 2) [in addressing persons of the lower class] you. Johann, ich werde Ihn fortschicken, wenn &c., John, I will turn you away, if &c.

Ihnen, [Low Sax. ön, önen, Celtic *jem, jems*] 1) [the dative of sie, they] to them. Das gehört ihnen, that belongs to them; ich sagte ihnen, I told them; es ist ihnen gesagt worden, they have been told; Alles, was von ihnen gesagt wird, all that is said of them. 2) [the dative of Sie, with a capital letter, in addressing politely a person or several persons] to you. Wenn es Ihnen gefällig ist, if you please; was fehlt Ihnen? what is the matter with you, what ails you? ich sage Ihnen, meine Herren, I tell you, gentlemen.

1. **Ihr**, 1) [dative of the personal pronoun sie, she] *a*) to her. Geben Sie es ihr, give it [to] her; ich begegnete ihr, I met her. *b*) [in addressing a woman of the lower class] to you. Was ist Ihr denn begegnet? what has happened to you? was fehlt Ihr? what is the matter with you? 2) [plural of du] you or ye. Werdet Ihr kommen? shall you come? Ihr Götter! ye Gods! *it.* [sometimes used in addressing only one person of the lower class] Johann, seyd Ihr fertig? John, have you done?

2. **Ihr, ihre, ihr**, [possessive pronoun] 1) [belonging to one female person or thing] her. Ihr Mann und ihre Tochter, her husband and daughter; sie sucht ihre Scheere, she is looking for her scissors; ich bin von ihrer Zuneigung überzeugt, I am persuaded of her affection; sie liebt ihre Kinder, she loves her children; diese Aprikose ist reif, ihre Farbe ist sehr schön, this apricot is ripe, its colour is very fine; *it.* [in fam. lang.] nicht unsere Magd hat es gesehen, sondern unserer Nachbarinn ihre [better: die unserer Nachbarinn], not our maidservant has seen it, but our neighbour's. 2) [belonging to two or more persons of both sexes] their. Sie haben ihr Haus, ihre Häuser verkauft, they have sold their house, their houses; es ist ihre Schuld, it is their fault; *it.* [in fam. lang.] nicht unsere Kinder haben es gethan, sondern der Nachbarn ihre [better: die der Nachbarn], not our children have done it, but those of our neighbours; nicht die Geschichte der Griechen, sondern der Römer ihre [better: die der Römer], not the history of the Greeks, but that of the Romans. 3) [in the language of conversation, instead of Euer; written with a capital letter] *a*) [in addressing a single female of the lower class] your. Hat Sie Ihren Bruder gesehen? have you seen your brother? *b*) [applicable to both numbers, in addressing our equals or superiors] your. Ihr Herr Vater hat es gesagt, your father said it; gehört dies Haus Ihren Eltern, does this house belong to your parents? *it.* [in fam. lang.] yours. Das ist nicht mein Stock, sondern Ihrer [better: der Ihrige], that is not my stick, but yours. Das sind nicht meine Bücher, sondern Ihre [better: die Ihrigen], those are not my books, but yours.

Ihre, der, die, das —, V. Ihrige; *it.* V. 2. Ihr.

Ihrem, Ihren, objective cases of 2. Ihr.

Ihren, *v. tr.* [unusual] V. Ihrzen.

Ihrenthalben, —wegen, —willen, V. Ihrethalben &c.

Ihrer, 1) [genitive of the personal pronoun sie, she] of her. Die arme Frau! Niemand erbarmt sich ihrer, poor woman! nobody has compassion on her. 2) [genitive of the personal pronoun sie, they] of them. Mich jammert ihrer, I pity them; wie viel hat sie Kinder? sie hat ihrer [better: deren] vier, how many children has she? she has four; es sind ihrer sechs, there are six of them. 3) [genitive of the personal pronoun Sie, you] of you. Man hat Ihrer in Ehren gedacht, they have made honourable mention of you.

Ihrer, Ihres, objective cases of 2. Ihr.

Ihrethalben, —wegen, —willen, 1) [wegen ihrer] on her or their account, for her or their sake, in her or their behalf. 2) [with a capital letter, wegen Ihrer] on your account, for your sake.

Ihrige, der, die, das —, 1) hers. Sie findet unsern Garten schöner, als den ihrigen, she finds our garden finer than hers; die Mutter hat das Ihrige gethan, the mother has done her duty, her utmost or all she could; sie verlangt nur das Ihrige, she demands only what belongs, what is due to her or what is her due; sie hat den Ihrigen geschrieben, she has written to her parents, friends, family &c. 2) theirs. Ich habe mein Gut, meine Bücher noch, allein meine Brüder haben das ihrige, die ihrigen verkauft, I have my estate, books yet, but my brothers have sold theirs; diese Leute sind um das Ihrige gekommen, these people have lost their property. 3) [with a capital letter, in politely addressing a person or several persons] yours. Dies ist mein Hut, jenes ist der Ihrige, this is my hat, that is yours; wenn Sie ein solches Leben führen, so werden Sie das Ihrige bald durchgebracht haben, if you lead such a life, you will soon have squandered your fortune or property; thun Sie das Ihrige, do your duty or your utmost; behalten Sie das Ihrige, keep what belongs to you or what is yours; was werden die Ihrigen dazu sagen? what will your parents, friends, family &c. say to it? ich bin der Ihrige, I am yours; der, die Ihrige &c. [at the end of a letter], yours &c.

Ihro, [obsolescent, applied to persons of high rank, instead of ihr, and sometimes sein,] her, his, your. — königliche Hoheit, die Frau Großherzoginn, her royal Highness, the Grandduchess; ich habe an — Excellenz, die Frau Gräfinn, geschrieben, I have written to her Excellency the Countess; — kaiserliche Majestät [instead of Seine or Seiner, Ihre or Ihrer], His or to His, Her or to Her imperial Majesty; — [instead of Eure or Ew.] Majestät geruhen &c., please, or may it please your Majesty.

Ihrzen, [rather unusual] *v. tr.* to address a person by the pronoun Ihr.

*__Ikonograph__, *m.* [-en, *pl.* -en] iconographer.

*__Ikonographie__, *f.* [Bilderbeschreibung] iconography.

*__Ikonographisch__, *adj.* iconographic.

*__Ikonolog__, *m.* [-en, *pl.* -en] [Bilderkenner] iconologist.

*__Ikonologie__, *f.* iconology.

Iland, *n.* [-es,] V. Epheu.

Ilen, *v. tr.* [among comb-makers] to scrape off the grosser parts of ivory, horn &c.

Iler, *m.* [-s, *pl.* -] [among comb-makers] scraper.

1. ‖**Ilge**, *f.* [*pl.* -n] V. Lilie.

2. ‖**Ilge**, *m.* [-n, *pl.* -n] [in some parts of South-Germany, corrupted from Heilige] a saint. V. 1. Heilige.

*__Ilias__, **Iliade**, *f.* iliad.

*__Ilion__, **Ilium**, *n.* [-s] Ilium, Troja.

‖**Illanke**, *f.* [*pl.* -n] lavaret or trout of the Rhine.

*__Illegal__, *adj.* and *adv.* [ungesetzlich] illegal.

*__Illegalität__, *f.* [Ungesetzlichkeit] illegality.

*__Illegitim__, *adj.* and *adv.* [unrechtmäßig] illegitimate.

*__Illegitimität__, *f.* illegitimacy, illegitimation.

*__Illiberal__, *adj.* and *adv.* [ungroßmüthig; unfreisinnig] illiberal.

*__Illiberalität__, *f.* illiberality.

‖**Illing**, *m.* [-es, *pl.* -e] V. Iltis.

*__Illiquid[e]__, *adj.* not liquid [in the figurative sense, of a debt &c.]

*__Illiterat[us]__, *m.* [-en, *pl.* -en] an illiterate man.

*__Illuminat__, *m.* [-en, *pl.* -en] [one of a certain sect or secret society, founded in the year 1776 by professor Weishaupt of the then university of Ingolstadt in Bavaria, and pretending to possess extraordinary light and knowledge] illuminate. Die —en, illuminati.

*__Illumination__, *f.* [Erleuchtung or Beleuchtung] [in manifestation of joy] illumination.

*__Illuminiren__, *v. tr.* 1) to illuminate [a town &c.]. Ein Zimmer —, to light a room. 2) to colour [maps, prints &c.]. *Fig.* [in fam. lang.] Er ist illuminirt, he is flustered, tipsy, fuddled, mellow.

*__Illuminirer__, *m.* [-s, *pl.* -] —inn, *f.* a person who colours maps and prints.

*__Illusion__, *f.* [Täuschung] illusion.

*__Illusorisch__, *adj.* [täuschend] illusory.

*__Illustration__, *f.* [Erläuterung] illustration.

*__Illustrativ__, *adj.* illustrative.

*__Illustriren__, *v. tr.* 1) [erläutern] to illustrate. 2) [mit bildlichen Darstellungen, Kupferstichen, Holzschnitten &c. versehen or schmücken] to illustrate.

Ilme, *f.* [*pl.* -n] or **Ilmbaum**, *m.* elm, V. Ulme.

Ilmenholz, *n.* elm-wood.

1. **Ilse**, *f.* [*pl.* -n] [instead of Alose] alose, the shad [a fish].

2. **Ilse**, *f.* [*pl.* -n] [a name of women] Isabella, Isabel; *it.* Betty or Bess.

Iltenschnecke, *f.* [*pl.* -n] 1) [in conchology] voluta or volute. 2) [in architecture] voluta or volute.

Iltiß or **Iltis**, *m.* [-sses, *pl.* -sse] [Low Sax. Ulk, Ilk, Dan. *ilder*; either from the Eng. and Sw. *ill*, or allied to the old willwan = graben or reißen, V. Wolf] pole-cat, fitchet.

Iltisfalle, *f.* a trap for catching pole-cats.

Im, [a contraction for: in dem] — Wasser, in the water; — Sommer, Winter, in summer, in winter; — Anfang, in the beginning; — Himmel, in heaven; — Fall der Noth, in case of necessity; — [in einem] Augenblicke, in an instant, in the twinkling of an eye, in a trice; — Ganzen, upon the whole; — Falle daß &c., in case that &c.; — Trüben fischen, to fish in troubled water; — Begriffe seyn, Etwas zu thun, to be about or on the point of doing any thing; — Zorne seyn, to be in a passion; Etwas — Scherze sagen, to say any thing in jest or jestingly; — Grunde, at the bottom, in the main; — Grunde betrachtet, after all; — Gegentheile, on the contrary. V. In.

Iman, *m.* [-s, *pl.* -e] [a priest among the Mahomedans] iman or imam.

Imber, *m.* V. Ingwer.

Imbiß, *m.* [-sses, *pl.* -sse] [instead of Anbiß, as the L. *prandium* from frendeo] any short meal, breakfast, [especially] luncheon.

Imgleichen, V. Ingleichen.

Imhamen, *m.* V. Immhamen.

Imi, *n.* [V. Ahm1)] [a liquid measure, about 2 1/2 gallons] imi.

*__Imitation__, *f.* V. Nachahmung.

*__Imitiren__, V. Nachahmen.

‖**Imker**, *m.* [-s, *pl.* -] bee-master.

‖**Imkerei**, V. Bienenzucht.

Immanuel or **Emanuel**, *m.* [-s, *pl.* -e] [a name of men] Immanuel.

Immaßen, *conj.* [now only used in law, instead of in der Maße] whereas, since, because, V. Indem, Weil.

*__Immaterialität__, *f.* [Unkörperlichkeit] immateriality.

*__Immateriell__, *adj.* and *adv.* [unkörperlich] immaterial, immateriate.

*__Immatriculation__, *f.* [Einschreibung, Einzeichnung, Einverleibung] matriculation, immatriculation.

*__Immatriculiren__, *v. tr.* to enter, to enroll, to matriculate, to immatriculate. Sich — lassen, to get one's name entered [particularly in the register of a university].

*__Immatriculirt__, *adj.* matriculate. Der —e, a matriculate.

Imme, *f.* [*pl.* -n] [perhaps from bummen = sumsen] bee.

Immen-blatt, *n.* mountain-balm. —fresser, —haus, —kappe, —korb, —schwarm, —stand &c. V. Bienenfresser, Bienenhaus &c.

*__Immens__ or **Immense**, *adj.* and *adv.* [unermeßlich] [in fam. lang.] immense.

Immer, *adv.* [Low Sax. ummer, jummer, perhaps instead of je mehr, or from the Heb. *jom* = day] 1) perpetually, continually, always, ever. Gott ist — derselbe, God is always the same; sie ist — krank, she is always or continually ill; er ist — bei uns, he is always with us; noch —, still; er fürchtet sich noch — vor dem Tode, he is still afraid of dying; — und ewig, eternally, for ever and ever. 2) for the most part, almost always. Er ist — geschäftig, he is always busy. 3) on every occasion, every time. Er spricht — die Wahrheit, he always speaks the truth; er sagt — das Nämliche wieder, *es ist — die alte Leier, he says the same thing over and over, 't is the same thing over and over, 't is still the same note, he harps always on the same string; sie erblaßt —, wenn sie ihn sieht, she grows pale every time or whenever she sees him. 4) during everlasting continuance. Für —, for ever; sich für — Lebewohl sagen, to part for ever, to bid an eternal farewell. 5) with continual increase, more and more. Er wird — reicher, he grows every day richer and richer; — schlimmer, worse and worse. 6) an expletive of enforcement or emphasis. Allein es bleibt — wahr, daß &c., but it is nevertheless true, that &c; es ist — ein gewagtes Unternehmen, it is a hazardous enterprise at any rate, V. Immerhin; so reich er — seyn mag, however rich he be, though he be ever so rich, let him be ever so rich; wo es — sey, wheresoever it be; wo er nur — bleiben mag? where can he [possibly] stay so long? sobald Sie nur — können, as soon as ever you can; wie kam es —, daß &c.? pray, how did it happen, that &c.? gehen Sie — voran, do but go on before, walk on before: fahr't — zu! drive on, drive on! er mag es — hören, ich mache mir nichts daraus, let him hear it, I don't mind it, never mind, let him hear it, V. Immerhin.

Immer-dar, **—fort**, *adv.* always, constantly, continually, V. Immer. **—grün**, I. *adj.* evergreen. II. *n.* [in botany] evergreen. **—hin**, *adv.* 1) always, evermore. 2) I care not, no matter, I don't mind it. Er mag es — hin thun, he may do it for me; sey er mir — hin Feind, let him hate me as much as he pleases. 3) [as an expletive] Ein wenig ist — hin besser, als nichts, a little is still or yet better than nothing. **—kuh**, *f.* an unalienable cow, V. Eisern 1) e). **—mehr**, [or immer mehr] *adv.* 1) more and more. Die Röthe verschwindet — mehr, the redness disappears more and more. 2) [as an expletive] V. Doch, Wohl. **—während**, *adj.* and *adv.* everlasting, perpetual, continual, constant. Eine — währende Bewegung, ein — währendes Getöse, a perpetual movement, noise; — währende Sitzungen, permanent sessions; — während geschäftig seyn, to be continually or constantly busy. **—zu**, *adv.* always; *it.* [as an exclamation] forward! go on!

Immhamen, *m.* [-s, *pl.* -] [among printers] a leather-strap that catches the frame when it is opened.

Immi, V. Imi.

*__Imminent__, *adj.* [bevorstehend] imminent.

*__Immission__, *f.* [in law] seizin.

Immittelst, *conj.* in the meantime, meanwhile; V. Inzwischen, Indessen.

*__Immittiren__, *v. tr.* [in law] Einen, to vest or invest any one with, to put any one in possession.

*__Immobil__, *adj.* and *adv.* V. Unbeweglich.

*__Immobiliar-Vermögen__, *n.* [-s] V. Immobilien.

*__Immobilien__, *pl.* immovable estate, immovables.

*__Immoralisch__, *adj.* and *adv.* immoral.

*__Immoralität__, *f.* [Unsittlichkeit] immorality.

*__Immortelle__, *f.* V. Rainblume, Strohblume.

*__Immun__, [frei, steuerfrei] *adj.* free from onerous duties, free, exempt.

*__Immunität__, *f.* [Freiheit, Vorrecht] immunity, privilege.

*Impastiren, *v. tr.* 1) [among painters] Ein Gemälde —, to put several layers of paint upon a picture. 2) [among engravers] Diese Fleischpartien sind gut impastirt, this flesh is well worked up.

*Impastirung, *f.* [among painters and engravers] the act of putting several layers of paint upon a picture and of working the flesh well up; [among masons] impastation.

*Imperativ, *m.* [-s, *pl.*-e] [in grammar] the imperative mood.

*Imperatörisch, *adj.* and *adv* [gebieterisch], imperative, imperious.

*Imperfect, *n.* [-es, *pl.* -e] [in grammar] the imperfect tense.

*Imperial, *m.* [-s, *pl.* -e] 1) [a Russian gold-coin] imperial. 2) [a game at cards] imperial.

*Imperial, *adj.* [kaiserlich] imperial.

Imperial-bett, *n.* V. Himmelbett. —folio, V. —papier. —fractur, *f.* V. Kaiserschrift. —papier, *n.* paper of the largest size, imperial paper. —wasser, *n.* [a kind of brandy] imperial water.

*Imperiale, *f.* [*pl.* -n] the roof or top of a coach, imperial.

*Impersonale, *n.* [unpersönliches Zeitwort] [in grammar] an impersonal verb.

*Impertinent, *adj.* V. Unverschämt.

*Impertinenz, *f.* V. Unverschämtheit.

*Impetrant, *m.* [-en, *pl.* -en] [in law] plaintiff, V. Kläger.

*Impetrat, *m.* [in law] defendant, V. Beklagte, Verklagte.

*Impetriren, *v. tr.* [erbitten] [in law] to impetrate.

Impfen, [Sax. *impan*, Eng. *to imp*, Sw. *ympa*; from in and the D. *pote* or the Low Sax. Pate = Propfreis] *v. tr.* 1) to graft, to ingraft, to inoculate. Ein zahmes Reis auf einen Wildling —, to ingraft a natural plant upon a wild stock; V. Pfropfen. 2) [in surgery] Einen, to inoculate a person with the matter of small-pox or cow-pox. Kuhpocken —, to vaccinate.

Impf-anstalt, *f.* institution or establishment of inoculation or vaccination. —arzt, *m.* inoculator. —reis, *n.* graft, scion. —stamm, *m.* the stock which is, or is to be inoculated. —stoff, *m.* vaccine matter or infection. —wunde, *f.* a wound made for the purpose of inoculation.

Impfer, *m.* [-s, *pl.* -] 1) grafter, inoculator. 2) V. Impfarzt.

Impfling, *m.* [-es, *pl.*-e] a child that is to be or has been inoculated or vaccinated.

Impfung, *f.* 1) the act of ingrafting, inoculation. 2) [in surgery] inoculation. Die — der Kuhpocken, vaccination.

*Impingiren, *v. tr.* [rather obsolete, in law] to infringe, to transgress, to violate [the laws].

*Impliciren, *v. tr.* to implicate. Bei einer Verschwörung implicirt seyn, to be implicated in a conspiracy.

*Implorant, *m.* [-en, *pl.* -en] [in law] suitor, petitioner; *it.* plaintiff.

*Implorat, [-en, *pl.* -en] *m.* [in law] defendant.

*Imponiren, *v. intr.* Einem, to strike any one with reverence, to influence by respect, to awe, to overawe any one.

*Imposant, *adj.* commanding, imposing. Eine —e Miene, Manier, an imposing air, manner.

*Impost, *m.* [-es, *pl.* -en] 1) [a tax imposed by authority] impost. 2) [in architecture] impost, moulding.

*Imprimatur, *n.* [a licence to print any thing] imprimatur.

*Impuls, *m.* [-es, *pl.* -e] V. Antrieb 2).

In, *prep.* [Sax. *on*, W. *yn*, *en*, L. *in*, Gr. ἐν, ἐνί and εἰν, V. An]. I. [with the dative case, signifies being in a place, either in motion or at rest] in. — dem [or im] Zimmer, in the room; — Asien, — England, in Asia, in England; — or zu Paris, London, in or at Paris, London; — or zu Heidelberg, at Heidelberg; — dem Garten herumgehen, to walk about the garden; — der Hand, — den Armen halten, to hold in the hand, in the arms; — diesen Schuhen geht es sich gut, it is good walking in these shoes; — der Schule, — der Stadt seyn, to be at school, in town; was steht — diesem Briefe? what are the contents of this letter? — einiger Entfernung warten, to wait at some distance; — der Welt, in the world; mit Thränen — den Augen, with tears in one's eyes. *Fig. a)* [with reference to the object] — Gold, — Silber arbeiten, to work in gold, in silver; Einen — der Arbeit stören, to disturb any one in his work; — Gedanken vertieft seyn, to be absorbed in thought; — der Arbeit begriffen seyn, to be at work; — Sprachen geschickt seyn, to be clever in languages; — diesem, — jenem Falle, in this, in that case; im Spiele verlieren, to lose in gaming; ich lebte nur — ihr, I lived but in her. *b)* [with reference to a state] Ein Pferd im Zaume halten, to hold a horse in the reins; — Bereitschaft stehen, to be in readiness; — der Noth seyn, to be in want or distress; — Uneinigkeit mit Jemand leben, to be at variance with any one; lassen Sie mich — Ruhe, let me alone; *c)* [with reference to a means] sich — Wein, — Punsch betrinken or *übernehmen, to get drunk with wine, with punch; er dankte mir — den feurigsten Ausdrücken, he thanked me in the most ardent expressions. *d)* [with reference to a motive] Etwas — der besten Absicht thun, to do any thing with the best view or intention; — seinen eigenen Angelegenheiten reisen, to travel on one's own affairs. *e)* [with reference to time] — meiner Jugend, in my youth, when I was young; im vorigen Monat, last month; — der Nacht, in the night; um 5 Uhr — der Frühe, at five o'clock [early] in the morning; — einer Stunde reist er ab, he will set out an hour hence; — Kurzem, in a short time, shortly, soon; ich habe ihn — sechs Jahren nicht gesehen, I have not seen him these six years; — einem Augenblicke, in an instant, in the twinkling of an eye, in a trice.

II. [with the accusative case, it denotes direction or motion to a place] into. Kommen Sie — das Haus, come into the house; — die Tasche stecken, to put into the pocket; das Geld ist — ihre Hände gekommen, the money has got into their hands; — einen Brief sehen, to look into a letter; er hat sich — den Finger geschnitten, he has cut his finger; sich — den Mantel hüllen, to wrap one's self up in one's cloak; Figuren — Holz schneiden, to cut figures on wood; — Holz schneiden or stechen, to engrave on wood; — Kupfer stechen, to engrave on copper; Einem den Degen — den Leib rennen, to run any one through with one's sword; — Gold fassen, to set in gold; — die Schule, Kirche gehen, to go to school, church; — die Stadt gehen, to go into the town, to go to town; Einem ein Wort —'s Ohr sagen, to whisper a word into any one's ear; —'s Heu gehen, to go into the fields in order to make hay. *Fig. a)* [with reference to an object] — deine Hände befehl' ich meinen Geist, into thy hands I commend my spirit; — den Tag hinein leben, to live thoughtlessly, carelessly, at random; Einem — die Rede fallen, to interrupt any one; sich — eine Sache mengen, to meddle with or in a matter; sich — die Umstände schicken, to accommodate one's self to circumstances; — Jemand verliebt seyn, to be in love with a person; — Thränen ausbrechen, to burst into tears. *b)* [with reference to a state] — Armuth gerathen, to be reduced to poverty, to grow poor; — Zorn, — Entzücken gerathen, to fall into a passion, into rapture, to be transported with joy; —'s vierzigste Jahr gehen, to be going or entering on one's fortieth year. *c)* [with reference to the way or manner in which any thing is done] Blumen — einen Strauß binden, to make a nosegay; die Scene — eine Landschaft verwandeln, [in theatricals] to shift the scene into a landscape; ein Buch — mehrere Bände binden, to bind a book into several volumes. *d)* [= ungefähr] nearly, about. — die 60 Jahre alt, about sixty years old; — die 100 Fuß lang, nearly a hundred feet long. *e)* [denoting a duration of time, when you may ask bis wann? till when or what time?] [bis] tief — die Nacht hinein aufbleiben, to sit up late at night; dein ist die Herrlichkeit — Ewigkeit, thine is the glory for ever.

*Inappellabel, *adj.* [in law] eine inappellable Entscheidung, a decision from which one cannot appeal.

*Inauguralrede, *f.* [*pl.* -n] inaugural speech or address.

*Inauguralschrift, *f.* [*pl.* -en] inaugural treatise.

*Inauguration, *f.* inauguration.

*Inauguriren, *v. tr.* to inaugurate.

Inbegriff, *m.* [-es, *pl.* -e] 1) [obsolete] an enclosed space, compass. 2) that which is contained in any space, contents, tenour, purport. Ein kurzer —, a brief summary or abstract [of a book &c.], abridgement, epitome; mit —, inclusively.

Inbegriffen, *adj.* and *adv.* inclusive, inclusively.

Inbehalten, *ir. v. tr.* to keep back, to detain, V. Einbehalten.

Inbrunst, *f.* ardour, fervour. Mit — beten, to pray fervently, to pray with intenseness; mit — lieben, to love passionately or ardently.

Inbrünstig, *adj.* and *adv.* ardent, fervent. Ein —es Gebet, a fervent prayer; eine —e Liebe, an ardent or passionate love; — lieben, to love passionately or dearly. Syn. Inbrünstig, Innig. Innigkeit indicates that the passion which influences us reaches to the deepest recesses of our soul. This energy of feeling is exactly expressed by inbrünstig; innig, however, implies its presence within the soul, inbrünstig, when its violence is likewise externally visible.

Inbrünstigkeit, *f.* V. Inbrunst.

Inbürger, *m.* [-s, *pl.* -] a person who resides in the town of which he is a citizen.

*Incarceriren, *v. tr.* to incarcerate.

*Incarnat, or —roth, I. *adj.* fleshcoloured, high-red, incarnadine. II. *n.* flesh colour, carnation, incarnadine.

*Incarnation, *f.* [among painters] carnation.

*Incest, *m.* V. Blutschande.

*Incidentpunkt, *m.* V. Nebenpunkt.

*Incidentwinkel, *m.* V. Einfallswinkel.

*Incipient, *m.* [-en, *pl.* -en] beginner, apprentice.

*Incipiren, *v. intr.* to begin, to be an apprentice.

*Incisionslanzette, *f.* lancet of incision.

*Inclaviren, *v. tr.* V. Einklammern, Einschließen.

*Inclination, *f.* V. Neigung.

*Inclusive, *adj.* and *adv.* inclusive, inclusively.

*Incógnito, I. *adv.* incognito. II. *n.* incognito.

*Incompetént, *adj.* incompetent.

*Incompeténz, *f.* incompetence.

*Inconsequent, *adj.* inconsistent.

*Inconsequenz, *f.* inconsistence.

*Inconvenienz, *f.* inconvenience.

*Incorporiren, *v. tr.* to incorporate.

*Incorrect, *adj.* incorrect.

*Incorrectheit, *f.* incorrectness.

*Incrustiren, *v. tr.* to incrust.

*Inculpánt, *m.* [-en, *pl.* -en] V. Kläger.

*Inculpät, *m.* [-en, *pl.* -en] V. Beklagte.

*Inculpation, *f.* V. Anklage.

*Inculpiren, *v. tr.* V. Anklagen.

*Indecent, *adj.* and *adv.* indecent.

*Indecenz, *f.* indecency.

‖Indelt, *n.* [-es, *pl.* -e] bed-tick.

Indém, I. *conj.* 1) at the time, when, while, as. Wir waren zugegen, — er dieses sagte, we were present when he said that; — [während] ich schreibe, schläft er, while I write, he sleeps; kommen Sie, sagte er, — er mich an der Hand nahm, come, said he, taking me by the hand. 2) [denoting the means] Man brachte ihn wieder zu sich, — man ihm einen Löffel voll Wein gab, they recovered him by giving him a spoonful of wine. 3) [denoting the cause] because, since. Ich kann es nicht versprechen, — ich nicht weiß, ob &c., I cannot promise it, because I do not know, or not knowing, whether &c II. *adv.* just now, this moment, V. Sogleich.

Indéß or Indéssen, *conj.* 1) in the meantime, mean-while, while. — sie versammelt waren, while or whilst they were assembled; lesen Sie —, read in the mean-time. 2) however, nevertheless, though. Ihr Verlust ist sehr groß, — ist er nicht unersetzlich, your loss is very great, however it is not irreparable; es ist — gefährlich, mich so zu behandeln, it is dangerous though, to treat me in this manner.

Indianer, Indianisch, V. Indier, Indisch.

*Indicativ, *m.* [-s] [in grammar] the indicative mood.

Indien, *n.* [-s, *pl.* -] India, The Indies. Beide —, both the Indies; er ging nach Ost-, West—, he is gone to the East, West Indies.

Indier, *m.* [-s, *pl.* -] —inn, *f.* Indian; [in a more limited sense] a native of Hindostan.

Indig, [Indigo,] *m.* [-s] 1) indigo-plant, anil, indigo. 2) Der — or das —blau, indigo-blue, indigo; mit — färben, to dye with indigo.

Indig-bereiter, —fabrikant, *m.* manufacturer of indigo. —blau, *n.* V. — 2). —fabrik, *f.* indigo manufactory. —küpe, *f.* [among dyers] bluestone vat. —pflanze, *f.* V. Indig 1). —pflanzer, *m.* one who cultivates indigo; *it.* the proprietor of an indigo plantation. —pflanzung, *f.* indigo plantation.

*Indigenät, *n.* [-es, *pl.* -e] or —srecht, *n.* the right of a native.

Indirect, *adj.* and *adv.* indirect.

Indisch, *adj.* and *adv.* Indian. —e Leinwand, printed calico; —es Korn, Indian corn, maize; das —e Rohr, bamboo; —e Kresse, Indian cress; —es Vogelnest, [the nest of a small swallow in China &c. of most delicate taste] birds-nest.

*Indiscret, *adj.* and *adv.* indiscreet.

*Indiscretion, *f.* indiscretion.

*Individualisiren, *v. tr.* to individualize.

*Individualität, *f.* individuality.

*Individuell, *adj.* and *adv.* individual, individually.

*Individuum, *n.* [-s, *pl.* Individuen] individual.

*Indolént, *adj.* and *adv.* indolent, lazy.

*Indolénz, *f.* indolence, laziness.

*Indossát, *m.* [-en, -en] indorsee.

*Indossemént, *n.* [-es, *pl.* -e] indorsement [of a bill of exchange].

*Indossént or Indossánt, *m.* [-en, *pl.* -en] indorser.

*Indossiren, *v. tr.* Einen Wechsel —, to indorse a bill of exchange; einen Verhaftsbefehl —, to back a warrant.

*Indossirung, *f.* indorsement.

*Indulgénz, *f.* indulgence, V. Ablaß 4).

*Indúlt, *m.* [-es, *pl.* -e] 1) [in law and commerce] time allowed for payment, respite, letter of respite. 2) [in the Romish church] *a*) indulgence. *b*) indult, indulto. 3) [in Bavaria] fair.

*Industrie, *f.* industry, V. Gewerbfleiß, Betriebsamkeit.

*Industriös, *adj.* and *adv.* industrious.

Ineinánder, *adv.* into one another; confusedly. —flechten, to interlace; —fügen, to join, to mortise.

*Infallibel, *adj.* and *adv.* infallible, infallibly.

*Infallibilität, *f.* infallibility.

*Infäm, *adj.* and *adv.* infamous. *Eine —e Handlung, an atrocious deed; [in popular lang.] das ist eine —e Geschichte, this is a sad or awkward affair or business.

*Infamie, *f.* infamy.

*Infánt, *m.* [-en, *pl.* -en] [in Spain and Portugal, a prince of the royal blood] infant, infante. —inn, *f.* infanta.

*Infanterie, *f.* [Fußvolk] infantry.

*Infanterist, *m.* [-en, *pl.* -en] a footsoldier.

*Infel, or Inful, *f.* [*pl.* -n] mitre.

*Infeln or Infuliren, *v. tr.* to honour with the privilege of wearing a mitre; to adorn with a mitre, to mitre. Ein geinfelter or infulirter Abt, a mitred abbot.

*Inferiorität, *f.* [*pl.* -en] inferiority.

*Inferiren, *v. tr.* to infer.

*Infeudation, *f.* [*pl.* -en] infeudation.

*Infeudiren, V. Belehnen.

*Inficiren, *v. tr.* to infect.

*Infinitesimalrechnung, *f.* calculation or method of infinitesimals.

*Infinitiv, *m.* [-s] [in grammar] the infinitive mood.

*Infirmität, *f.* [*pl.* -en] infirmity.

*Inflammation, *f.* [*pl.* -en] inflammation.

*Inflammatorisch, *adj.* and *adv.* inflammatory.

*Inflexibel, *adj.* and *adv.* inflexible.

*Influénza, *f.* influenza.

*Information, *f.* V. Auskunft 3), Belehrung.

*Informator, *m.* [-s, *pl.* -en] V. Lehrer, Hauslehrer.

*Informiren, *v. tr.* V. Unterrichten, Belehren.

Inful, Infuliren, V. Infel, Infeln.

*Infusion, *f.* infusion.

Infusionsthierchen, *n.* infusory worm, V. Aufgußthierchen.

Ingarn, *n.* [-es, *pl.* -e] the inner smaller net.

Ingber, V. Ingwer.

Ingebäude, *n.* [-s, *pl.* -] 1) a building within the walls of a fortress. 2) the interior of a building.

Ingefieder, *n.* [-s] 1) the feathers of a bed. 2) the springs of a watch or clock.

Ingeheim, *adv.* secretly, privately, in private, V. Heimlich, Geheim.

Ingemein, V. Insgemein.

Ingemisch, *n.* [-es, *pl.* -e] V. Ingarn.

*Ingenieur, [*pron.* as in the French] *m.* [-s, *pl.* -e] engineer.

Ingenieur-korps, *n.* the body of engineers. —kunst, *f.* fortification.

Ingermánnland, *n.* [-s] [a Russian province] Ingria.

Ingleichen or Ingleichem, *conj.* [obsolescent or in law] likewise, also, as also; V. Auch, Ebenfalls, Ferner, Desgleichen II.

*Ingrediénz, *n.* [*pl.* -en] ingredient.

Ingrien, *n.* [-s] V. Ingermannland.

Ingrimm, *m.* [-es] 1) inward or sullen rage, anger or wrath. 2) violent anger or wrath.

Ingrimmig, *adj.* and *adv.* fierce. V. Grimmig.

Ingrün, *n.* [-es, *pl.* -e] [in botany] the small periwinkle.

Inguß, *m.* 1) ingot-mould, V. Einguß. 2) V. Indelt.

Ingwer, *m.* [-s] ginger. Der deutsche —, wake robin, cuckoopint or cuckoopintel, arum, V. Fieberwurzel; der gelbe —, turmeric.

Ingwer-klaue, *f.* V. —wurzel. —körner, *pl.* überzuckerte —körner, ginger-seed. —kraut, *n.* dittander, lepidium. —muß, *n.* electuary of ginger. —öl, *n.* ginger-oil. —reibe, *f.* ginger-grater. —stein, *m.* a stone resembling a race of ginger. —wurzel, *f.* race of ginger.

Inhaben, *ir. v. tr.* V. Innehaben.

Inhaber, *m.* [-s, *pl.* -] —inn, *f.* a person who holds or possesses any thing, possessor, holder. Der — eines Hauses, the possessor or proprietor of a house; der — eines Regiments, commander of a regiment, colonel; der — einer Aktie, the holder of a share, shareholder; der — eines Wechsels, the bearer of a bill of exchange

Inhafen, *m* [-s, *pl.* -häfen] V. Binnenhafen.

*Inhaftiren, *v. tr.* [in law] to put in confinement, to imprison, V. Verhaften.

*Inhaftirung, *f.* [in law] imprisonment, confinement, V. Verhaftung.

Inhalt, *m.* [-es] 1) [that which is contained] content or [generally] contents. Der — eines Fasses, the contents of a cask. *Fig.* Der — eines Buches, einer Schrift, the contents, tenour or purport of a book, of a writing; der wesentliche — [eines Briefes &c.], the substance [of a letter &c.]; der — einer Bittschrift, the suggestion of a petition; der kurze — [eines Buches &c.], the summary, abstract, abridgment, epitome or compendium [of a book &c.]. 2) [the power of containing] content or contents, capacity. Dieses Schiff hat so und so viel Tonnen —, that vessel contains so many tons or it is a vessel of so many tons; der — eines Grundstückes, the extent of a piece of ground; [in geometry] der — eines Dreiecks, Vierecks &c., the area of a triangle, square &c.

Inhalts-reich, *adj.* and *adv. Fig.* interesting, instructive. —sangabe, —anzeige, *f.* V. —sverzeichniß. —schwer, *adj.* and *adv. Fig.* containing many important things, truths &c., significative, expressive. —sverzeichniß, *n.* table of the contents [of a book], index.

Inhalten, *ir. v. tr.* and *intr.* 1) V. Einhalten, Inne halten. 2) [obsolete] V Enthalten.

*Inhibiren, *v. intr.* [in law] to inhibit.

*Inhibitorium, *n.* [-s, *pl.* -rien] [in law = Einhaltsbefehl] inhibition.

Inholz, *n.* [-es, *pl.* - hölzer] [in seamen's lang.] all the different pieces of timber forming the frame of a ship.

*Injurie, *f.* [*pl.* -n] [especially in law] offence, insult, injury, defamation. Eine schriftliche —, a libel. V. Beleidigung, Beschimpfung.

Injurien-klage, *f.*, —proceß, *m.* an action for injury or defamation.

*Injuriös, *adj.* and *adv.* [especially in law] injurious, insulting. Ein —es Betragen, insulting manners.

Inlage, *f.* V. Einlage 2).

Inland, *n.* [-es] native country. Er ist im —e weniger bekannt, als im Auslande, he is less known in his native country or at home than in foreign countries or abroad.

Inländer, *m.* [-s, *pl.* -], —inn, *f.* native of a country, [in law] indigene. Er ist ein —, sie ist eine —inn, he, she is a native of the or of this country.

Inländisch, *adj.* and *adv.* not foreign, native. —e Gewächse, Thiere, indigenous plants, animals; *it.* made in the country [not abroad]; —e Waaren, home-made goods or goods of the country.

Inliegend, *adj.* enclosed. Der —e Brief, the enclosed letter.

Inmärker, *m.* [-s, *pl.* -] V. Markgenoß.

Inne, *adv.* [Sw. *inne*, Sax. *innan*, allied to in] within. — bleiben, to stay within or at home; — halten, to keep within, at home or [applied to cattle] in the stable; sich — halten, to stay at home; mitten —, in the middle or midst. *Fig.* it denotes possession, retention, perception, and is used in the following compositions.

Inne-behalten, *ir. v. tr.* to keep, to keep back, to detain, to withhold. —haben, *ir. v. tr.* 1) to possess, to be in possession of. 2) to know. Er hat diese Sprache vollkommen —, he knows that language perfectly, he is intimately or thoroughly acquainted with that language. —halten, *ir.* I. *v. intr* to stop, to cease, to discontinue. Mit der Zahlung —halten, to stop payment. II. *v. tr.* and *r.* V. Einhalten I. 1) *Fig.* —stehen, *ir. v. intr.* to be poised or balanced. Die Wage steht —, the scales of the balance are poised or rest in equilibrium. —werden, *ir. v. intr.* to perceive, to be made conscious of. Syn. Inne werden, Merken, Gewahr werden, Wahrnehmen. A general merkt that an ambush is laid at a particular place from certain circumstances which lead him to infer it without having as yet seen it. To say that he nimmt wahr the ambush, would imply that he already sees it; wird gewahr, that he suddenly and unexpectedly discovers it; wird inne, conveys the idea that intelligence of the ambush had been given to him, but that he only gives credit to it when convinced by his own eyes.

Innen, *adv.* in the inner part, within. — und außen, within and without; von — [heraus], from within; nach — zu, towards the interior or inside, inward, inwards.

Innenwelt, *f.* the objects which are within or in our mind [as opposed to those exterior to us].

Inner, *prep.* V. Inwendig, Innerlich, Innerhalb.

Innere, *adj.* [der, die, das] interior, internal, inward, inner. Die —n Theile der Erde, the interior or internal parts of the earth; der — Hof eines Tempels &c., the inner court of a temple &c.; der — Bau des Körpers, the inward structure of the body; die innersten Gemächer, the inmost or innermost apartments; der — Handel eines Staates, the internal trade of a state; — Kraft, internal virtue; der — Werth einer Sache, the intrinsic or internal value of a thing; — Güte besteht in &c., intrinsic goodness consists in &c.; der — [engere or kleinere] Rath, the little council; der — Zustand eines Menschen, der — Mensch, the inner man; das — [beschauliche] Leben, contemplative life; die innersten Gedanken, the inmost thoughts; der — Friede, internal peace, V. Innerlich; das —, the interior or inside [of a house &c.]; das — or Innerste der Erde, the bowels or bosom of the earth; in dem Innersten des Königreichs, in the very heart of the kingdom. *Fig.* Gott allein kennt das — des menschlichen Herzens, God alone knows the inmost recesses of the heart of man.

Innerhalb, I. *adv.* on the inside, within. II. *prep.* within. *a)* [applied to place, in the inner part or on the inside of] Der Raum eines Hauses — der Mauern, the space within the walls of a house; — der Stadt, within the town; — des Laufgrabens, within the trench. *b)* [applied to time, in the compass of] — weniger Tage, within a few days.

Innerlich, *adj.* and *adv.* interior, internal, inward, intestine. Eine —e Hitze, an internal heat; eine —e Krankheit, an intestine disease; —e Eigenschaften, intrinsic qualities; —er Krieg, internal or intestine war; —e Zwistigkeiten, internal dissensions; sich — grämen, to fret inwardly; — beten, to pray mentally or inwardly. V. Innere.

Innig, *adj.* and *adv.* [Old Sw. *innig*, from in or innen] deeply felt or deeply affecting, heartfelt, cordial, hearty, fervent, ardent. Eine —e Freude, Liebe, a heartfelt joy, cordial love; der —ste Dank, the most heartfelt thanks or gratitude; ein —es Gebet, a fervent or ardent prayer; ein —er Freund, an intimate friend; eine —e Ueberzeugung, a lively persuasion; er wurde dadurch —st gerührt, he was most sensibly affected by it; sie sind — mit einander verbunden, they are intimately united; ein —er Fleiß, an intense application. Syn. V. Herzlich, Inbrünstig.

Innigkeit, *f.* quality of being heartfelt &c., cordiality, heartiness, genuine feeling, sincerity, fervour, ardour, intenseness.

Inniglich, *adj.* and *adv.* V. Innig, Herzinniglich.

Innung, *f.* [from the old verb innen = einen] an incorporated society, company [of any trade], guild, corporation; V. Gewerk 3), Handwerk 2), Gilde, Zunft. *it.* Eine — von Gelehrten, eine gelehrte —, [rather jestingly] a literary society.

Innungs-brief, *m.* act or bill of incorporation, charter. —geld, *n.* the contingent or quota of money, paid by the members of a company or corporation at certain periods. —glied, *n.* member of a company, corporation or guild. —pfennig, *m.* V. —geld. —schreiber, *m.* clerk of a company or corporation. —versammlung, *f.* meeting of a company or corporation. —verwandter, *m.* V. —glied.

*Inoculiren, *v. tr.* V. Einimpfen.

*Inquirent, *m.* [-en, *pl.* -en] the examining magistrate, ‡the inquisitor.

*Inquiriren, *v. tr.* and *intr.* to question, to interrogate, to examine [a person accused, a witness &c] officially or judicially, to try.

*Inquisit, *m.* [-en, *pl.* -en] the criminal, delinquent.

*Inquisition, *f.* 1) [obsolete or in law] judicial inquiry or examination, inquisition. 2) [a court or tribunal established for the examination of heretics] inquisition, V. Glaubensgericht, Ketzergericht.

*Inquisitor, *m.* [-s, *pl.* -en] [a member of the court of inquisition in Catholic countries] inquisitor. V. Ketzerrichter.

*Inquisitorisch, *adj.* and *adv.* inquisitorial.

Ins, [in fam. lang. for in das] into that, into it. V. In; — Besondere or —besondere, *adv.* particularly, especially, principally.

Insaß, *m.* [-ssen, *pl.* -ssen] [obsolescent or in law] inhabitant of a town &c.

Insbesondere, V. Ins and Besonders.

Inschlitt, *n.* [-es] V. Unschlitt.

Inschrift, *f.* [*pl.* -en] inscription, epigraph, V. Aufschrift, Beischrift, Ueberschrift; *it.* V. Epigramm, Sinngedicht.

Inschriftenkunde, *f.* the art of reading and explaining old inscriptions or epigraphs.

*Inscribiren, *v. tr.* V. Einschreiben [especially = to matriculate] and Eintragen *Fig. a*).

*Inscription, *f.* entering, booking, entry; matriculation.

*Insect, *n.* [-es, *pl.* -en] insect. Die Verwandlung eines —es, the metamorphosis or transformation of an insect; versteinerte —en, petrified insects, entomolites.

Insecten-kunde, —lehre, *f.* entomology. —sammler, *m.* a gatherer of insects. —sammlung, *f.* cabinet of insects.

Insel, *f.* [*pl.* -n] [L. *insula*, Eng. *isle*, *island*, Old French *isle*, probably from einzeln] island, isle. Eine kleine —, ein —chen, a little island, islet; die — Malta, the isle of Malta.

Insel-bewohner, *m.* [*Insulaner] islander. —gruppe, *f.*, —haufen, *m.* a group or cluster of isles or islands. —land, *n.* insular country; *it.* an insulated country or place. —meer, *n.* [a sea interspersed with many isles] archipelago. Das griechische —meer, the Egean sea, the Archipelago. —reich, I. *adj.* and *adv.* abounding with isles, full of isles. II. *n.* V. —staat. —staat, *m.* insular state, kingdom or empire. —stadt, *f.* a town built on an isle, an insular town or city. —volk, *n.* the inhabitants of an island, islanders.

*Inserat, *n.* [-es, *pl.* -e] inserted article, insertion.

Inseratgebühr, *f.* V. Einrücke- or Insertionsgebühr.

*Inseriren, *v. tr.* to insert [any thing in a newspaper &c.].

*Insertion, *f.* insertion.

Insertionsgebühr, *f.* V. Einrückegebühr.

Insgeheim, *adv.* privately, secretly, covertly.

Insgemein, *adv.* generally, commonly.

Insgesámmt, *adv.* all together or altogether, in a body. Sie haben sich — verbürgt, they are bound altogether and one for all. Syn. Insgesammt, Alle, Jeder. Alle implies the individual objects which belong to any kind or species, or the parts belonging to any whole. Insgesammt, or Allesammt, considers the Alle, to which a certain predicate is attributed, as united, and Jeder (each) as separate and forming a whole in itself. When at the council of Trent alle the members were assembled and Jeder had taken his place, they were insgesammt (altogether) of opinion &c. We err allesammt, only Jeder errs differently.

Insiegel, *n.* [-s, *pl.* -] [obsolete or in law] seal.

*Insignien, *pl.* badges or marks of office or honour, insignia, ensigns. Die — des Reichs, the ornaments and marks of the imperial dignity; *it.* [or Kleinodien] the jewels of the crown.

*Insinuatiōn, *f.* 1) insinuation. 2) [in law] the act of handing, delivering [a judicial decree &c.]

*Insinuiren, I. *v. tr.* 1) to intimate, hint or insinuate. 2) [in law] to hand, to deliver [a judicial decree &c.]. II. *v. r.* Sich bei Einem —, to insinuate one's self into any one's favour.

Inskünftige, *adv.* henceforth, for the future.

Insofern, I. *adv.* so far. II. *conj.* in as far as, in as much as, V. Fern.

*Insolént, *adj.* and *adv.* insolent.

*Insolénz, *f.* insolence.

*Insolvént, *adj.* insolvent.

*Insolvénz, *f.* insolvency.

Insónderheit, Insónders, *adv.* [obsolescent or in law] in particular, particularly, V. Besonders, Insbesondere.

Inspanner, *m.* [-s, *pl.* -] V. Spannnagel.

*Inspectiōn, *f.* inspection, V. Aufsicht.

*Inspéctor, *m.* [-s, *pl.* -en] inspector, V. Aufseher.

*Inspiciren, *v. tr.* and *intr.* V. Einsehen, Besichtigen, Beaufsichtigen.

*Inspiriren, *v. tr.* to inspire, V. Begeistern.

*Inspiratiōn, *f.* inspiration, V. Begeisterung.

*Installatiōn, *f.* installation.

*Installiren, *v. tr.* to install.

Inständig, *adj.* and *adv.* instant, earnest, urgent. Eine —e Bitte, an earnest or instant entreaty, suit or petition; — bitten, to entreat earnestly or instantly.

*Instánz, *f.* [*pl.* -en] a higher or lower court of judicature [considered, in gradation, one above the other]. Eine höhere —, a superior court; in letzter —, in the last resort, without further appeal.

Instehen, *ir. v. intr.* [stiff] V. Bevorstehen.

Inster, *n.* [-s] calf's pluck; *it.* entrails, tripe, guts.

Instinkt, *m.* [-es, *pl.* -e] instinct.

Instinktartig, *adj.* and *adv.* instinctive, instinctively.

*Institút, *n.* [-es, *pl.* -e] institution, establishment. [in a more limited sense] boarding-school.

*Institutiōn, *f.* institution. [in law] Die —en des Kaisers Justinian, the institutes of the emperor Justinian.

*Instructiōn, *f.* instruction, V. Anweisung, Belehrung.

*Instructiv, *adj.* and *adv.* instructive, V. Lehrreich, Belehrend.

*Instrúctor, *m.* [-s, *pl.* -en] instructor, V. Lehrer.

*Instruént, *m.* 1) [unusual] one who instructs. 2) [in law] a judicial person or judge who prepares a case for hearing or trial.

*Instruiren, *v. tr.* 1) to instruct, V. Belehren, Unterrichten. 2) Einen Prozeß —, to prepare things for a hearing or trial, V. Einleiten.

*Instrumént, *n.* [-es, *pl.* -e] 1) tool, instrument. 2) musical instrument, instrument of music. 3) [in law, a writing by which some fact is recorded for evidence or some right conveyed] instrument, document.

Instrumentenmacher, *m.* instrument-maker.

*Instrumentāl, *adj.* instrumental.

Instrumentalmusik, *f.* instrumental music.

*Insubordinatiōn, *f.* insubordination.

*Insulaner, *m.* [-s, *pl.* -] —inn, *f.* islander.

*Insultiren, *v. tr.* to insult.

*Insurgént, *m.* [-en, *pl.* -en] insurgent; [in Hungary] a militia-man.

*Insurrectiōn, *f.* insurrection.

*Integrāle, *f.* V. Integralgröße.

*Integrālgröße, *f.* Die — einer Differenzialgröße, the integral or finite quantity of which the differential is the infinitesimal.

*Integrālrechnung, *f.* integral calculus, or inverse method of fluxions.

*Integriren, *v. tr.* to integrate, to complete, to perfect. [in mathematics] Eine Differenzialgröße —, to make an integral.

*Integrität, *f.* integrity.

*Intellectuéll, *adj.* and *adv.* intellectual.

*Intelligént, *adj.* intelligent. V. the better word. Einsichtsvoll, Verständig.

*Intelligénz, *f.* intellect, judgment.

Intelligenz-blatt, *n.* [Anzeigeblatt] advertiser, intelligencer. —comptoir, *n.* intelligence-office, advertising-office.

*Intendánt, *m.* [-en, *pl.* -en] intendant.

*Intendantūr, Intendánz, *f.* [the office or function of an intendant] intendancy.

*Intensiōn, *f.* intension.

*Intensiv, *adj.* and *adv.* intensive, intensively.

*Intentiōn, *f.* intention, V. Absicht.

*Intercediren, *v. intr.* to intercede.

*Intercessiōn, *f.* intercession.

*Interdiciren, *v. tr.* to interdict, to prohibit.

*Interdíct, *n.* [-es, *pl.* -e] interdict. Ein ganzes Königreich mit einem —e belegen, to lay a whole kingdom under an interdict.

*Interessánt, *adj.* and *adv.* interesting, important. Syn. Interessant, Anziehend, Wichtig. That which is interessant does not excite in us the desire of possessing it, but merely that of enjoying and comprehending it. The Anziehende attracts by the sensible pleasure it causes in us. An object appears wichtig to our minds from the important results connected with it. Happy is he to whom wichtige pursuits are interessant; the attention he devotes to them will render the pleasures of the senses less anziehend.

*Interésse, *n.* [-s, *pl.* -n] interest, advantage. Die —n, the profit derived from money lent, interest, V. Zins. Syn. Interesse, Theilnahme. Interesse in an object is that which excites in our mind the feeling we call Theilnahme. We listen with Interesse to any one who relates the dangers he may have undergone, because the narration probably engages our attention; but we listen with Theilnahme only when we feel ourselves in some way or other attracted to the narrator. We say, hat a great, or has not the least Interesse for me, instead of, that erregt a great, or not the least Interesse. We can, however, only say that erregt, but never das hat, great Theilnahme.

Interessenrechnung, *f.* V. Zinsrechnung.

*Interessént, *m.* [-en, *pl.* -en] a party concerned in a business.

*Interessiren, I. *v. tr.* [chiefly used in familiar language] 1) to concern, affect or interest. Das interessirt mich, that is of importance or important to me. 2) Einen für Etwas —, to gain, engage or interest any one in favour of some thing. II *v. r.* Sich für Einen, für Etwas —, to interest one's self, to use one's interest in favour of any one or any thing.

*Interim, *n.* [-s] the mean time or time intervening, the interim.

Interims-bescheid, *m.* a provisional sentence. —bücher, *pl.* [in commerce] provisional books. *—minister, *m.* minister or secretary of state ad interim. —schein, *m.* provisional receipt. —wechsel, *m.* bill ad interim.

*Interimistisch, *adj.* and *adv.* provisional. in the mean-time, mean-while.

*Interjectiōn, *f.* interjection.

*Interlocút, *n.* [-es, *pl.* -e] [in law] interlocution, interlocutory sentence or decree.

*Intermézzo, [-'s, *pl.* -'s or -mezzi] *n.* interlude, by-play, a farce.

*Internúnzius, *m.* [*pl.* -zien] internuncio.

*Interpellatiōn, *f.* interpellation.

*Interpelliren, *v. tr.* to interpel.

*Interpolatiōn, *f.* interpolation.

*Interpoliren, *v. tr.* to interpolate, to foist in.

*Interpretatiōn, *f.* interpretation.

*Interpretiren, *v. tr.* to interpret.

*Interpunktiōn, *f.* punctuation.

Interpunktionszeichen, *n.* mark of punctuation.

*Interusúrium, *n.* [*pl.* -rien] [in commerce] discount for payment made before due.

*Intervāll, *m.* and *n.* [-es, *pl.* -e] [especially in music] interval.

*Intervenient, *m.* [-en, *pl.* -en] an interfering plaintiff [in a pending law-suit].

*Interveniren, *v. intr.* to intervene.

*Interventiōn, *f.* intervention.

*Intestāterbe, *m.* [-n, *pl.* -n] heir of one who dies intestate, abintestate heir, heir at law.

*Intim, *adj.* intimate.

*Intimiren, *v. tr.* [obsolescent] to intimate.

*Intimität, *f.* intimity.

*Intimus, *m.* [in fam. lang.] intimate friend, crony.

*Intolerant, *adj.* intolerant, V. Unduldsam.

*Intoleranz, *f.* intolerance.

*Intonatiōn, *f.* intonation, V. Anstimmung.

*Intoniren, *v. tr.* 1) to begin to sing, to tune. 2) to sound [a violin &c.] V. Anstimmen.

*Intrade *f.* [*pl.* -n] [in music] prelude. 2) *pl.* V. Einkünfte, Gefälle.

*Intricāt, *adj.* intricate, involved, perplexed, complicated.

*Intrigue, *f.* intrigue.

*Intriguiren, *v. intr.* to intrigue.

*Intrigánt, *adj.* and *s.* a plotting, intriguing fellow, intriguer.

*Introductiōn, *f.* introduction.

*Invalide, I. *adj.* weak, infirm, invalid. II. *m.* [-n, *pl.* -n] invalid, [especially] an invalid soldier.

Invalidenhaus, *n.* hospital for invalids.

*Invasiōn, *f.* invasion.

*Invective, *f.* [*pl.* -n] invective.

*Inventārium, *n.* [-s, *pl.* -rien] inventory.

*Inventiren, *v. tr.* to inventory. Man hat ihm inventirt, they have taken an inventory of his goods.

*Inventūr, *f.* [*pl.* -en] 1) the act of making an inventory. 2) inventory.

*Inversiōn, *f.* [in grammar] inversion.

*Investitūr, *f.* 1) investiture. 2) infeudation, enfeoffment.

*Invitatiōn, *f.* V. 2. Einladung.

*Invitiren, *v. tr.* V. 2. Einladen.

Inwärts, *adv.* inwards, V. Einwärts.

Inwendig, [chiefly in fam. or popular lang.] I. *adj.* interior, internal, inner, V. Innere. II. *adv.* within, in the inner part, in the inside.

Inwohnen, Inwohner, V. Einwohnen &c.

Inzicht, Inzucht, *f.* [in law] 1) [obsolescent] accusation, reproach. 2) [obsolescent] offence, ffront, insult, V. Injurie. 3) indication, proof. Die —en sprechen stark gegen ihn, the evidence s strong against him.

Inzwischen, *adv.* in the meanwhile, V. Indeß, Unterdessen.

Jōnien, *n.* [-s, *pl.* -] Ionia.

Jōnier, *m.* [-s, *pl.* -] —inn, *f.* Ionian.

Jōnisch, *adj* Ionic, Ionian. Die —e Mundart, der —e *Dialect, the Ionic dialect; die —en Inseln, the Ionian islands; die —e Philosophensecte, the Ionic sect [of philosophers]; [in chitecture] die —e Säulenordnung, the Ionic rder; [in music] die —e Tonart or Tonsetzung, e Ionic or Ionian mode.

*Ipecacuánha, *f.* ipecacuanha, V. Ruhrwrzel.

Iper, *f.* [*pl.* -n] elmtree, V. Ulme.

Ips, V. Gips.

Irden, *adj.* and *adv.* [from Erde] earthen. n —er Topf, an earthen pot; —e Waare, then ware, crockery.

Irdisch, *adj.* and *adv.* [from Erde] earthly, restrial. Diese —e Welt, this earthly world; e —e Liebe, an earthly love; — gesinnt, thly-minded; der —e Mensch, the terresl man; *it.* the sensual or carnal man; das , die —en Dinge, terrestrial things; das lieben, to love the earth or world, to be hly-minded.

rgend, *adv.* [perhaps from: einer Gegend] omewhere. Er muß doch —[wo] seyn, but he st be somewhere; mostly joined with: wo, her, wohin; — wo, somewhere, anywhere; woher, from some place; — wohin, some ther, to some place. 2) at any time, ever. an ich — [anders, jemahls] reich werde, if I grow rich. 3) [not much used] perhaps. wird es — nicht thun wollen, perhaps he not do it. 4) [not much used] about, nearly, ost. Es werden — dreißig seyn, there will bout thirty. 5) [unusual] now and then. 6) ed with: ein, einer, eine and etwas] any. — Buch, any book; — Einer, any one, any body; — Etwas, any thing; — ein Schriftsteller hat gesagt, some author has said; — ein Anderer muß es gethan haben, some other person must have done it; um — einer Ursache willen, for some cause or other; ist — eine Hoffnung vorhanden? is there any hope?

*Iris, *f.* 1) [in mythology, the messenger of Juno] Iris. 2) [in poetry] the rainbow, iris. 3) [the circle round the pupil of the eye] iris. 4) [in botany] the flower-de-lis or flag-flower, iris, V. Schwertlilie.

Irisch, *adj.* and *adv.* Irish.

Irland, *n.* [-s] Ireland, [in poetry] Erin.

Irländer, *m.* [-s, *pl.* -] —inn, *f.* Irishman, Irishwoman.

Irländisch, *adj.* and *adv.* Irish.

Irmen- [or Irmin-]säule, *f.* [instead of Hermansäule] [a statue representing an old warrior and worshipped by the ancient Saxons] statue of Arminius.

Irokēse, *m.* [-n, *pl.* -n] Iroquois.

Irokēsisch, *adj.* and *adv.* Iroquois, in the manner of the Iroquois.

*Ironie, *f.* [*pl.* -n] irony.

*Irōnisch, *adj.* and *adv.* ironical.

*Irrational, *adj.* [in mathematics] irrational.

Irrational-größe, *f.* irrational or incommensurable quantity. —zahl, *f.* irrational or incommensurable number.

Irre, *adj.* and *adv.* 1) out of the right way, astray. — gehen, to go astray, to mistake or lose one's way, to wander up and down, to stray; Sie gehen, Sie sind —, you have lost your way, you are out of the [right] way; ich ging im Walde —, I lost my way in the forest; Einen — führen, to lead any one astray or out of the right way; — werden, to lose one's way. 2) *Fig.* *a*) in a state of error or perplexity, confused, puzzled, having lost one's presence of mind, in a state of alarm. — seyn, to be mistaken, deceived or puzzled, to be out; Einen — führen, to guide any one into, to involve any one in error, to mislead, to puzzle, to embarrass any one; die bösen Beispiele haben ihn — geführt, bad examples have led him astray; Einen — machen, to confound, to puzzle, to distract, to disturb, to interrupt any one; *it.* to put any one out of countenance; er läßt sich nicht leicht — machen, he is not easily put out; — werden, to be disconcerted, puzzled or confounded, to be out of countenance; ich werde ganz — an ihm, I don't know what to make of him. *b*) deprived of reason, insane, delirious. Ein —r Geist, a wandering, rambling, unsettled mind; er ist —, — im Kopfe, he is crack-brained, out of his wits, distracted; — reden, to talk wildly, to rave. Syn. Irre, Unsinnig, Sinnlos, Verrückt, Wahnsinnig, Wahnwitzig. Irre is used of one whose ideas, during a state of illness, are void of any inward connexion among themselves. Unsinnig and Sinnlos indicate a deprivation of the use of the understanding and senses occasioned by any violent passion; in the Unsinnigen, however, this bereavement begins with the understanding, whence it spreads its baneful effects over the senses; with the Sinnlosen it at once stuns the senses, and thereby arrests the functions of the understanding. A person may become sinnlos from a violent blow on the head arising from the shock communicated to the organs of consciousness. Unsinnigkeit, Verrücktheit, Wahnsinn and Wahnwitz are distinguished from each other by their duration. The Unsinnige finds himself in a transitory state which vanishes with its short-lived cause, whereas the condition of the Wahnsinnigen and Wahnwitzigen is permanent. The Verrückte is distinguished from the Wahnsinnigen and Wahnwitzigen in this, that he lives in a continual waking dream. Wahnsinn implies the entire bereavement of the use of the understanding, in which a man takes that to be relly true which he merely imagines. Wahnwitz manifests itself by a profusion of ideas; but as they are unconnected and confused, they are often absurd. The Wahnwitzige is talkative, his ideas are extremely mutable; the Wahnsinnige will often continue quiet, and apparently void of thought.

Irreführer, *m.* [-s, *pl.* -] bad guide; *it.* deceiver, seducer.

Irre, *f.* [*pl.* -n] 1) the state of having lost one's way, aberration, wandering, mistaken way. In der — gehen, herumgehen, herumlaufen, to go astray, to be out of the way, to wander up and down, to stray. *Fig.* *Einen in der — herumführen, to lead any one astray. 2) [little used] maze, labyrinth.

Irren, [L. *erro*, Gr. ἐῤῥῶ] I. *v. intr.* 1) to err, to wander, to stray, to go astray, to mistake the way. In dem Walde herum —, to err, wander, rove or ramble about in the forest; ohne Heimath herum —, to wander from place to place without a settled home, to lead a vagrant life; ein —der Ritter, a knight errant. *Fig.* Seine herum —den Blicke, his wandering eyes; er irret überall mit seinen Gedanken herum, he lets his mind wander or ramble upon any subject. 2) *Fig.* to be mistaken, to be deceived. Die Gelehrtesten können —, the most learned are liable to be mistaken; *prov.* — ist menschlich, every one is liable to be mistaken, to err is human; die, welche —, or die —den zurecht weisen, to set strayed people in the right road. II. *v. tr.* 1) to lead away from the right path, to mislead, V. Irre machen. 2) Sich — lassen, to be confounded or disconcerted. Lassen Sie sich das nicht —, do not let this alarm, embarrass or confound you, be not alarmed or disquieted by it; er läßt sich in nichts —, he is never to be put out [of countenance] by any thing. 3) [chiefly in fam. lang., rather provincial] to vex, to annoy. Ihn irrt die Fliege an der Wand, he is offended at every thing, every thing annoys him. III. *v. r.* Sich —, to commit an error, to make a mistake, to mistake. Er irrt sich in seiner Rechnung, he is mistaken in his calculation; sich gröblich —, to be grievously out, to be greatly or very much mistaken, to mistake grossly; Sie — sich in seiner Person, you mistake him for another; ich habe mich in ihm geirrt, I have been mistaken in him.

Irr-beere, *f.* berry of the deadly nightshade, V. Tollbeere, Tollkirsche. —fahrt, *f.* wandering, peregrination. Die —fahrten des Ulysses, the wanderings of Ulysses. —gang, *m.* 1) [rather provincial] a straying or going out of the way, deviation, aberration. 2) labyrinth, maze [in the form of a walk]. [in anatomy] Der —gang im Ohre, labyrinth of the ear. —garten, *m.* labyrinth or maze in a garden. —gebäude, *n.* labyrinth [in the form of an edifice]. —geding, *n.* V. —leben. —geist, *m.* 1) a misguided spirit, a person under the influence of error, V. —gläubige. 2) a rover, gadabout, gadder. —gestirn, *n.* V. —stern. —gewinde, *n.* labyrinth, maze. —glaube, *m.* erroneous belief or faith, heterodoxy, V. Wahnglaube. —gläubig, *adj.* and *adv.* heterodox, heretical. Ein —gläubiger, a heretic. —gläubigkeit, *f.* heterodoxy. —haus, *n.* madhouse, bedlam, V. Narrenhaus, Tollhaus. —häusler, *m.*, —häuslerinn, *f.* a madman, madwoman, bedlamite. —kopf, *m.* a crack-brained person. —köpfig, *adj.* crack-brained. —lauf, *m.* 1) V. —gang 1). 2) wandering, peregrination. —läufer, *m.*, —läuferinn, *f.* 1) one who is gone astray, a strayed person. 2) [chiefly in contempt] rover, rambler, vagrant;

V. Sandläufer. —lehen, *n.* the reversion of the first fief that may become vacant. —lehre, *f.* erroneous doctrine, heterodoxy, heresy. —lehrer, *m.* one who professes heterodox principles, a heretic. —lehrig, *adj.* heterodox, heretical. —licht, *n.* ignis fatuus, will-with-a-wisp, jack with a lantern. [in seamen's lang.] Das —licht [an Mastbäumen &c.] lambent flame, Castor and Pollux. —pfad, *m.* V. —weg. —prediger, *m.* heterodox preacher. —rede, *f.* irrational talking, discourse or words of a raving or delirious person. —sinn, *m.* V. Wahnsinn. —sinnig, *adj.* V. Wahnsinnig. —stern, *m.* comet; *it.* planet. —wahn, *m.* erroneous notion, mistaken opinion. —weg, *m.* 1) wrong way. Auf einem —wege seyn, to have lost one's way, to be out of the right way; auf —wege gerathen, to lose one's way, to go out of one's way. *Fig.* Den —weg or auf —wege gehen, auf —wege or Abwege gerathen, to give one's self up to vice, to take to bad courses. 2) V. —gang 2). —wisch, *m.* V. —licht.

Irrenhaus, *n.* V. Irrhaus.

Irrig, *adj.* and *adv.* 1) [applied to persons] mistaken, wrong. Da sind Sie —, there you are mistaken. 2) [applied to things] erroneous, false, wrong, mistaken. Eine —e Meinung, an erroneous or mistaken opinion; —er Weise, by mistake, erroneously or falsely.

Irrsal, *n.* [-s, *pl.* -e] [obsolescent] V. Irrthum, Irrwahn, Wahn.

Irrthum, *m.* [-es, *pl.* -thümer] 1) error, mistake. Einen — begehen, in einen — verfallen, gerathen, to commit an error; Einem seinen — benehmen, aus seinem — helfen, to disabuse, to undeceive any one; Einen in — führen, to lead any one into error, to mislead any one; ein — im Rechnen, miscomputation, false reckoning; ein — in der Zeitrechnung, error in chronology, anachronism. 2) [not used in the plural] state of being in error or under a mistake, erroneousness. SYN. Irrthum, Irrung, Versehen. Irrthum indicates not only the action by which any Versehen takes place, but also the matter and nature of the erroneous judgment. Thus Irrthümer in religious balled creeds, which by some are considered as true, are false doctrines. Irrthümer are unintentionally erroneous judgments; Irrungen are undesignedly faulty actions. Versehen arise from the mistaking of the false for the true, the wrong for the right. Irrthümer are avoide by reflexion; Versehen by attention. [V. also Vorurtheil.]

Irrung, *f.* 1) error, mistake. Es ist eine — vorgegangen, an error has been committed. 2) misunderstanding, slight difference. Die —en heben, schlichten, to compose, settle, adjust or make up the differences. SYN. V. Irrthum.

1. Isabèll, *m.* [-s, *pl.* -en] a light bay horse.

2. Isabèll, *n.* [-s] or —farbe, *f.* isabella colour, isabel.

Isabell-farben, —farbig, *adj.* isabella-coloured, light bay, V. 1. Isabell.

Isabelle and Isabèlle, *f.* [Isabella's or -ns, *pl.* -n] 1) [a name of women] Isabella, Isabel. 2) [in conchology] Isabella.

Isegrimm, *m.* [-es, *pl.* -e] [either from Eisen or from the old aisen = erschrecken] 1) [an obsolete or popular name for the wolf]. 2) a peevish, surly fellow, a grumbler.

Isenkraut, *n.* [-es] V. Eisenkraut.

Island, *n.* [-es] Iceland.

Island-flechte, *f.*, —moos, *n.* Iceland-moss.

Isländer, *m.* [-s, *pl.* -], —inn, *f.* Icelander.

Isländisch, *adj.* and *adv.* Icelandic. —es Moos, V. Islandflechte.

*Isoliren, *v. tr.* to insulate. [in electrical experiments] Ein isolirter Körper, an insulated body.

Isop, *m.* [-es, *pl.* -e] or Isopen, *m.* [-s, *pl.* -] hyssop.

Isop-öl, or —enöl, *n.* hyssop-oil.

Israelít, *m.* [-en, *pl.* -en] Israelite.

Israelítisch, *adj.* and *adv.* Israelitic, Israelitish, V. Hebräisch, Jüdisch.

Isthmisch, *adj.* and *adv.* Isthmian. Die —en Spiele, the Isthmian games.

*Isthmus, *m.* isthmus, V. Landenge, Erdzunge.

Italien, *n.* [-s] Italy.

Italiéner or [less usual] Itálier, *m.* [-s, *pl.* -] —inn, *f.* Italian.

Italiénisch or [less usual] Itálisch, *adj.* Italian.

*Item, I. *adv.* [obsolete or stiff] item, also, V. Ingleichen, Deßgleichen, Ferner, Auch. [in fam. lang., jestingly] —, es hilft, after all, it is a good remedy or means, it proves good. II. *n.* an article in an account, an item.

‡Itzig, V. Jetzig.

‡Itzo, Itzt, V. Jetzt.

Ixie, *f.* [in botany] ixia.

J. [Jod]

J, [Jód] J. Ein kleines j, a small j.

Ja and já, [Icel. *jue, ja*, Sw. *ja, jo*, Sax. *gea, ia, gise*, Eng. *yes* and *yea*, from the old jaton, jeton = sagen, to say] I. *adv.* 1) [jā] [expressing affirmation or consent, opposed to no] yes. Sind Sie verheurathet? —, are you married? yes; — oder nein sagen, to say yes, yea or no; mit — oder mit Nein antworten, to answer in the affirmative or in the negative; — zu Etwas sagen, to consent, to give or to yield one's consent to any thing; er sagt zu Allem —, he is for any thing, he gives his consent to any thing, he is a very easy or complying man; Eure Rede sey —, —, nein, nein, [in Scripture] let your communication be yea, yea, nay, nay; o —, recht gern, oh yes, most willingly; —, —, so ist es, yes, yes, it is so; — wohl, — freilich, — gewiß, — wahrhaftig, — wahrlich, yes indeed, yes to be sure, yes certainly, yes truly, verily; ist er nicht gekommen? o —, is he not come? I beg your pardon, he is; ich glaube, er ist nicht dort gewesen? o —, I think he has not been there? yes he has or [in fam. lang.] but he has though; wird er es thun? ich glaube —, will he do it? I believe he will; bei — und nein, in one word; *it.* by all means, certainly. 2) [jā] [noting entreaty] pray. Versäumen Sie es doch — nicht, pray, do not neglect it; thun Sie es — nicht, be sure not to do it, do it on no account. 3) [jā] [enforcing the sense of something preceding] not only so much, but more, nay. Er hat genug, — zu viel, he has enough, nay too much; Sie haben alles das gethan, —, Sie haben noch mehr gethan, you have done all this, yes, you have done more. 4) [já] [modifying what one says; in this sense it generally is a mere expletive]. Ich sagte es Ihnen —, I told you so; es ist — nichts Unerlaubtes, why, it is not forbidden; er ist — mein Freund, why, he is my friend; Sie wissen —, daß es nicht recht ist, you know very well, that it is wrong; wenn es denn — seyn muß, if it must needs be so; er wird — doch kommen, I hope he will come. 5) [jā] indeed, certainly. Ich werde es — thun, I shall certainly do it; ich werde es — nicht sagen, I shall take care not to say so, I shall say so on no account. 6) [jā] [expressing wonder] surely, forsooth. —! ist es wahr? indeed! is it true? 7) [jā] [serving as a connecting particle] well, now. —, was ich Ihnen sagen wollte &c., now I think on it, I wished or was going to tell you &c. II. [Jā] *n.* yes. Er hat dieses — ungern gesagt, he said that yes against the grain; mit einem — beantworten, to answer in the affirmative; [in parliament] die — überwiegen, the yeas have it.

Ja-bruder, *m.* a person who says yes to every thing, who has not the courage to say no, ninny, ninny-hammer. —herr, *m.* V. Jabruder. —wort, *n.* 1) the word yes. 2) affirmation. 3) [particularly] consent or promise of marriage. Die Aeltern haben ihm ihr —wort, das —wort gegeben, her parents have given [him] their consent; sie hat ihm ihr —wort gegeben, she has consented or promised to marry him.

Jách, *adj.* and *adv.* 1) V. Jähe, Jähling, Plötzlich. 2) V. Jähzornig.

Jachzorn, *m.* V. Jähzorn.

‖Jáchern, V. Jachtern.

Jácht, *f.* [*pl.* -en] or Jáchtschiff, *n.* [-es, *pl.* -e] [a sort of quick sailing vessel] yacht.

‖Jáchtern, *v. intr.* to be merry in a noisy manner, to romp.

Jácke, *f.* [*pl.* -en] *dim.* Jäckchen, ‖Jäcklein, *n.* [Eng. *jacket*, Fr. *jaque*, Sw. *jacka*, Dan. *jakke*] jacket, jerkin. *Fig.* [in popular lang.] Einem Etwas auf die — geben, to beat or lace any one's jacket; Einem die — voll or durchschlagen, to give any one a good drubbing or banging, to beat any one soundly.

† and ‖Jáckern, I. *v. intr.* to ride fast on horseback, to gallop. II. *v. tr.* Ein Pferd müde —, to fatigue a horse by galloping.

Jácob, V. Jakob.

Jáde, *f.* [*pl.* -n] V. Bitterstein.

1. Jágd, *f.* [*pl.* -en] V. Jacht.

2. Jágd, *f.* [*pl.* -en] 1) the act of pursuing, pursuit, chase. — auf die Feinde, auf die Straßenräuber machen, to pursue the enemy, highwaymen; — auf ein Schiff machen, to give chase to a ship; *was ist das für eine —! what a noise, bustle or racket! *ist das nicht eine — um einer solchen Kleinigkeit willen! what a noise or racket about such a trifle. *Fig.* — auf Etwas machen, to hunt or run after any thing. 2) [the act or practice of pursuing wild animals for killing them] chase, hunt, hunting. Die niedere oder kleine —, the lower or lesser chase; die hohe —, the hunting of the higher sort of game, such as stags, deer &c.; die — mit Tüchern, [mit Garnen or Netzen], hunting with toils; auf die — gehen, to go a-hunting; die — hat begonnen, the hunt is up; von der — leben, to live by hunting; er ist ein Freund von der —, he is fond of field-sports; V. Bären—, Fuchs—, Hasen—, Hirsch—, Schweins—, Wolfs—. [in a more limited sense] *a*) the art or practice of the chase, huntsmanship. Er versteht sich gut auf die —, he is a good huntsman, an expert, a skilful sportsman; V. Jagdkunst, Jägerei. *b*) right of the chase, right of hunting or shooting. Die — haben, to have the right of hunting or shooting. *c*) any thing taken in hunting, game, venison. Geben sie uns von Ihrer — zu essen, let us have some of your game to eat. *d*) the huntsmen, hounds &c. Die — vorbeiziehen sehen, to see the huntsmen pass. *e*) V. —hetze.

Jagd-amt, *n.* 1) a board or office for regulating the concerns of the chase, hunting-office. 2) place of an officer employed in the hunt or chase. —anzug, *m.* V. —kleid. —bahn, *f.* V. Wildbahn. —bauer, *m.* V. —fröhner. —bediente, *m.* an officer or servant employed in the hunt or chase. —bezirk, *m.* 1) a district in which any one has the right of hunting or shooting. 2) hunting-ground. —bolzen, *m.* [in seamen's lang.] square-headed bolt. —brücke, *f.* [a bridge with a high column, that may be seen from afar] hunting-bridge. —cavalier, *m.* V. —junker —dienst, *m.* 1) V. —frohne. 2) place or office of an officer or servant employed in the chase or hunt. —edelknabe, *m.* hunting-page. —eisen, *n.* V. —spieß. —flinte, *f.* fowling-piece. —flur, *f.* 1) district within which the hunt or chase is confined. 2) V. —bezirk 2). —folge, *f.* 1) the obligation of following the lord of the manor when going a-hunting. 2) the right of pursuing wounded game into another's inclosure. 3) V. —frohne. —freund, *m.* sportsman. —frevel, *m.* offense against the laws or regulations of the chase. —frevler, *m* a person who offends against the laws or regulations of the chase. —frohne, *f.* service which the tenant is obliged to render the lord when a-hunting. —fröhner, *m.* a tenant who is bound to do certain services for the landlord when a-hunting. —garn, *n.* V. —netz. —gehäge, *n.* V. —bezirk. —geld, *n.* money paid by a tenant in order to be exempt from the services due to the landlord when going a-hunting. —geräth, *n.* V. —zeug. —gerecht, *adj.* and *adv.* skilled in the chase or in hunting. Ein —gerechter Jäger, a clever or skilful huntsman or sportsman. —gerechtigkeit, *f.* V. —recht 1). —geschichte, *f.* a hunting story, adventure or anecdote, sportsman's tale. —geschoß, *n.* any shooting-weapon used in the chase —geschrei, *n.* the hunting-cry, the cries of the huntsmen. —gewand, *n.* V. —kleid. —gezelt, *n.* V. —zelt. —gezeug, *n.* V. —zeug. —göttinn, *f.* Goddess of hunting, Diana. —grenze, *f.* the limit or boundary of a hunting-district. —halsband, *n.* hunting-collar [for hounds]. —handwerk, *n.* profession of a huntsman or gamekeeper. —haus, *n.* a hunting-box, hunting-seat, shooting-box. —hief, *m.* V. —posten. —hof, *m.* V. Jägerhof. —horn, *n.* bugle, bugle-horn, hunting-horn, V. Hiefhorn, Waldhorn. —hund, *m.* hunting-dog, sporting-dog, hound. —hut, *m.* a hat worn in hunting, hunting-hat, huntsman's hat. —junker, *m.* 1) hunting or sporting gentleman. 2) hunting-page. —kanzlei, *f.* office for regulating the concerns of the chase; hunting-office. —kette, *f.* a chain for coupling the hounds. —kleid, *n.*, —kleidung, *f.* hunting-suit. —klepper, *m.* hunting-nag. —knabe, *m.* V. —edelknabe. —kreis, *m.* V. —bezirk. —kundig, *adj.* V. —gerecht. —kunst, *f.* art and science of the chase or venery, huntsmanship, sportsmanship, sportsman's art and skill. —lager, *n.* a camp pitched for hunting. —lehen, *n.* the right of the chase bestowed as a fief. —leute, *pl.* 1) huntsmen, hunters. 2) V. —fröhner. —liebhaber, *m.* a lover of the chase, a huntsman, sportsman. —lust, *f.* 1) fondness for the chase. 2) amusement or pleasure of the chase, sport. —lustbarkeit, *f.* V. —lust 2). —lustig, *adj.* fond of hunting. —mannschaft, *f.* V. —leute. —messer, *n.* V. Weidmesser. —netz, *n.* net or toil used for the chase, hunting-net or toil. —orden, *m.* hunting-order. —ordnung, *f.* regulation for the chase. *—page, *m.* V. —edelknabe. —partie, *f.* hunting-match, hunting-party. —pferd, *n.* hunting-horse, hunter. —posten, *m.* sound or signal given with the bugle-horn. —pulver, *n.* V. Bürschpulver. —recht, *n.* 1) the right of the chase, the right of hunting or shooting. 2) regulations for the chase. 3) that part of the game taken, which is due to the lord of the manor. —rechtlich, *adj.* and *adv.* according to or concerning the right or regulations of the chase. —regal, *n.* the sovereign's exclusive right of the chase. —reiter, *m.* a huntsman on horseback. *—revier, *n.* V. —bezirk. —rock, *m.* hunting-coat. —ruf, *m.* V. —geschrei. —sache, *f.* hunting-matter, concern of the chase. —säule, *f.* a post or stake marking the confines of a hunting-district. —schiff, *n.* V. Jacht. —schlitten, *m.* V. Rennschlitten. —schloß, *n.* a house or castle used for the purposes of the chase, hunting-seat. —schreiber, *m.* a clerk or secretary employed in the affairs of the hunt or chase. —sitz, *m.* hunting-seat. —spieß, *m.* boar-spear or hunter's spear or pole. —stein, *m.* a stone that marks the confines of a hunting-district. —stock, *m.* a staff with a small fork, hunter's staff. —strick, *m.* V. Fangstrick. —stück, *n.* 1) a picture representing a piece from the chase, hunting-piece. 2) [in seamen's lang.] Die —stücke, the cannons on the prow of a man of war. —tag, *m.* hunting-day, shooting-day. —tasche, *f.* a sportsman's bag or pouch, hunting-bag. —tuch, *n.* hunting-toil or toils. —uhr, *f.* hunting-watch. —wagen, *m.* a light open carriage, hunting-carriage. —wesen, *n.* the concerns of the chase, every thing belonging or relating to hunting or shooting. —zeit, *f.* hunting- or shooting-season. —zelt, *n.* hunting-tent. —zeug, *n.* implements for the chase, hunting or chase equipage. —zink, —zinken, *m.*, —zinke, *f.* hunting-horn. —zug, *m.* a team of four horses.

Jagdbar, *adj.* and *adv.* fit for the chase, chasable, that may be hunted.

Jagdbarkeit, *f.* 1) quality of being chasable. 2) [little used] V. Jagdgerechtigkeit.

. **Jagen**, [allied to the L. *agere*, Gr. *ἄγειν*, and to wagen, that is, bewegen]. I. *v. intr.* 1) to run with great speed, to ride with great quickness, to gallop. Das Pferd ist in vollem Galoppe vorbeigejagt, the horse run by in full gallop; *wie er jagt! how he gallops along! *jaget nicht so! do not drive, run or ride so fast! *sein Puls jagt, his pulse goes pitapat. *Fig.* *Im Lesen &c. —, to read too fast, too hastily. 2) to pursue wild animals, to hunt, to follow the chase; to shoot. Er thut nichts als —, he spends all his time in hunting; mit der Flinte —, to shoot, to go shooting; es ist heute gut —, it is good hunting or shooting to-day; auf Rebhühner —, to shoot partridges; auf Löwen —, to hunt lions; dieser Hund jagt gegen den Wind, that dog runs to the wind. II. *v. tr.* 1) to drive quickly. *Sein Pferd zu Tode —, to kill one's horse by hard riding; die Gänse aus dem Garten —, to drive the geese out of the garden; Einen aus dem Hause —, to turn any one out of doors or out of the house; er hat seinen Bedienten aus dem Dienste gejagt, he has turned away his servant; *Einen von Haus und Hof —, to eject any one; in die Flucht —, to put to flight; den Feind —, to chase or pursue the enemy; Einem den Degen in den Leib —, to run one's sword into or through any one's body, to run any one through with one's sword; *er hat sich eine Kugel durch den Kopf gejagt, he has blown his brains out. *Fig.* Sein Vermögen durch die Gurgel — [in popular language], he has run through, has squandered away or wasted his estate; *Einen in Harnisch —, to put any one in a passion, to provoke, to exasperate any one. 2) to chase wild animals, to hunt. Einen Hirsch oder Hasen —, to hunt a stag or hare. 3) to take or kill the animal pursued, V. Erjagen. Das —, 1) the act of running with great speed or of galloping. *Was das für ein Rennen und — ist! what a hurry or precipitation! *Fig.* Das Rennen und — nach Glücksgütern, the eagerness or ardour with which one runs after riches. 2) the act of hunting or shooting, chase, hunt, hunting, V. Jagd. SYN. Jagen, Treiben. We treiben whatever we set in any kind of motion; we jagen only that which is set in a quick and more violent movement. Thus we say also, figuratively, the warmth of spring treibt hervor the buds on the trees, and the wind jagt hin a storm towards the mountains.

Jäger, *m.* [-s, *pl.* -], —inn, *f.* [not usual] 1) one who runs, gallops, drives too eagerly or in a headlong manner &c. 2) V. Jagdstück 2).

Jäger, *m.* [-s, *pl.* -] 1) a person who is employed in the chase, a hunter, huntsman, sportsman; *it.* a gamekeeper. *Prov.* Hungrig seyn wie ein —, to be as hungry as a hunter. 2) [in military affairs] rifleman; V. also Feldjäger 2). 3) [in seamen's lang.] a sort of quicksailing vessel, herring smack, herring buss; *it.* V. Jacht.

Jäger-bursche, *m.* huntsman's apprentice, a gamekeeper's apprentice; *it.* [in general] huntsman or gamekeeper. —buße, *f.* V. —recht 3). —garn, *n.* V. Jagdnetz. —geschoß, *n.* V. Jagdgeschoß. —haus, *n*, —hof, *m.* 1) huntsman's or gamekeeper's house or lodge. 2) V. Jagdhaus. —horn, *n.* V. Jagdhorn. —hut, *m.* hunting-hat, huntsman's cap, sportsman's cap. —junge, *m.* V. —bursche. —kleid, *n.* V. Jagdkleid. —knecht, *m.* a huntsman's or gamekeeper's man or servant. —kunst, *f.* 1) science of the chase. 2) *pl.* —künste, tricks or juggles exhibited by huntsmen or gamekeepers, sportsmen's tricks, the secret or occult arts of huntsmen. —mahlzeit, *f.* a luncheon after hunting. —mantel, *m.* a hunting-cloak. —mäßig, *adj.* and *adv.* according to the ways, manners or laws of huntsmen. —meister, *m.* master of the hunt, master of the chase [an officer]. —orden, *m.* V. Jagdorden. —recht, *n.* 1) the huntsman's or gamekeeper's fee or due. *a*) the money which the huntsman &c. is to receive for every piece of game he kills. *b*) the huntsman's part or share of the stag or deer he has killed [generally consisting in the head, the pluck &c.] 2) that part of a stag or deer which is given to the dogs, hounds' fees or reward, [in general] quarry. Den Hunden das —recht geben, to reward the dogs or hounds. 3) the penalty or forfeit incurred by offending against sportsmen's language or cant. —rüstung, *f.* hunter's equipage, sportsman's implements. —sprache, *f.* hunter's or sportsman's language or cant. —stück, *n.* the chine of a wild boar. —tasche, *f.* 1) V. Jagdtasche, Weidtasche. 2) [in conchology] pecten. —zeug, *n.* 1) V. Jagdzeug. 2) V. —rüstung. 3) Das —zeug or das einfache —zeug, the strap by which the bugle is suspended and the hanger with the belt.

Jägerei, *f.* 1) art and science of the chase, huntsmanship, sportsmanship; *it.* profession of a huntsman or gamekeeper. 2) the body of huntsmen or gamekeepers. 3) V. Jägerhaus 1).

Jägerinn, *f.* a female that hunts or follows the chase. Diana, die —, Diana, the huntress.

Jägerisch, *adj.* and *adv.* V. Jägermäßig.

Jägeteufel, *m.* [-s] 1) [in popular lang.] V. Jager 1). 2) [in botany] the perforated St. John's wort.

Jägetroß, *m.* [in seamen's lang.] a towing-line or warp made of three strands.

Jäh or **Jähe**, *adj.* and *adv.* [LowSax. *gau*, *gai*; allied to gehen, jagen] 1) exceedingly quick. — laufen, to run very fast; der —e Lauf [eines Flusses] the rapid course [of a river]. *Fig. a*) sudden. Eines —en Todes sterben, to die suddenly, to die a sudden death; ein —er Schrecken, a sudden fright, a panic fear. *b*) hasty, rash, precipitate, passionate. Ein —er Zorn, —zorn, a sudden anger, violent passion; er ist —, —zornig, he is hasty or passionate, given to anger. 2) steep, declivous, precipitous. Eine —e Klippe, a precipitous cliff. SYN. Jähe, Steil, Schroff. Each of these words is applied to an eminence, according to the different point from which it is viewed. If we are placed below, we say it is steil [related to stellen]; if above, that it is jähe [related to jagen]. We climb, therefore, a steilen rock, as we are precipitated down one that is jähe. Schroff indicates merely the perpendicular, or nearly perpendicular state of an eminence.

Jähe, *f.* 1) [chiefly in fam. lang.] great quickness or haste, precipitation. Die —, in der sie davon rannte, the great hurry, the precipitation in which she ran away. *Fig.* suddenness, hastiness. 2) steepness, declivity, precipitousness, precipice.

Jählich, V. Jäh.

Jähling, Jählings, *adv.* 1) [chiefly in fam. lang.] suddenly, precipitantly. — sterben, to die suddenly; er lief — davon, he ran away precipitantly. 2) with precipitous declivity, steeply.

‖**Jahn**, *m.* [-es, *pl.* -e] [seems to be allied to gehen, Gang] 1) empty space in a grass or corn field over which the mower has passed. Das Getreide liegt noch auf dem —e, the corn lies still in swaths, is not yet bound into sheaves. 2) felled timber laid in rows one upon another. 3) a division of the vineyard for the purpose of manuring.

Jahnen, Jähnen, V. Gähnen.

Jahr, *n.* [-es, *pl.* -e] [Low Sax. *jar*, Eng. *year*, Sax. *ger*, *gear*, perhaps allied to the L. *gyrus* = Kreis, circle, Sw. *yra*, to turn round] 1) year. Das laufende —, the present or current year; das vorige —, voriges —, last year; das künftige —, next year; Einem ein glückliches — wünschen, to wish any one a happy new year; das gemeine bürgerliche —, the civil year; das astronomische or Sonnen—, the astronomical or solar year; er wird dieses — zwanzig —e alt, he will be twenty years old this year; ein — in's andere [gerechnet], one year with another; von — zu —, from year to year; immer ein — um's or über's andere, every other year; ein gutes [= fruchtbares] —, a plentiful year, V. —gang; ein schlechtes [= unfruchtbares] —, a bad year, V. Mißjahr; —aus, —ein, year by year; *it.* throughout all the year, all the year round; einmahl im —e, once a year; das neue —, the new year; im — 1837, in the year one thousand eight hundred and thirty seven; über's —, a year hence; um ein — auf oder ab, a year more or less; — für —, alle —e, year by year, every year; es geht schon in's vierte —, daß or seit &c., it is already more than three years that or since &c.; seit — und Tag, or in — und Tag, sehe ich ihn nicht, it is already above a twelvemonth since I saw him; — und Tag [in familiar language], a long time, *it.* [in law] year and day [a year, six weeks and three days]. 2) *pl.* Die —e. *a*) [the whole duration of a being] age, years. Ein Mann von seinen —en sollte &c., a man of or in his years ought to &c.; er ist noch in seinen besten —en, he is still in the prime of his age or life; bei meinen hohen —en, in my old age; in reiferen —en, in more mature years, in the years of discretion; das giebt sich mit den —en, that will come with the years; er ist schon bei —en, he is already advanced in years, or of a certain age; zu seinen [mündigen] —en gekommen seyn, to have come to one's majority, to be of age, of full age; er ist bei seinen —en, he is of age, *it.* he is advanced in years; die —e am Baume, the age or circles of a tree; *prov.* der Verstand kommt nicht vor den —en, a man does not grow wise before he comes to his years, we shall be wise in time. *b*) old age. Ich fühle meine —e, I feel my old age. *Fig.* Laß die —e [= die alten Leute] reden [in Scripture], let the old people speak.

Jahrs-anleihe, *f.* annuity. —**arbeit**, *f.* the work or labour of a year; *it.* work paid by the year. —**arbeiter**, *m.* a workman or journeyman hired and paid by the year. —**begängniß**, *n.* V. Jahresfeier. —**buch**, *n.* [*Annalen] annual register, book of annals, chronicle. Ein —buch schreiben, to write annals; die —bücher des Tacitus, the annals of Tacitus. —**buchschreiber**, *m.* [*Annalist] a writer of annals, annalist. —**esfeier**, *f.*, —**esfest**, *n.* 1) the celebration of the anniversary, anniversary. 2) V. Neujahrsfest. —**esfeld**, *n.* a field that is ploughed and sowed every year. —**esfolge**, *f.* succession of years. Die Begebenheiten nach der —esfolge erzählen, to relate events in chronological order. —**esfrist**, *f.* time or space of a year. Innerhalb —esfrist, within a year. —**eslauf**, *m.* the course of the year. —**eslohn**, *m.* V. —lohn. —**esrechnung**, *f.*, —**estag**, *m.*, —**eszeit**, *f.* V. Jahrsrechnung &c. —**feier**, *f.* V. —esfeier. —**fünf** or —**fünft**, [the accent on the last syllable] *n.* space of five years. —**fünfzig**, [the accent on the penultima] *n.* space of fifty years. —**gang**, *m.* 1) the year with respect to fertility. Ein guter, fruchtbarer —gang, a plentiful year; Wein von diesem, von einem guten —gange, wine of this year's growth, of a good growth. 2) annual set of any publication, writing or lectures. Ein —gang Predigten, sermons for every sunday of the year. 3) V. —gewächs 1). —**gebung**, *f.* [a law term] dispensation of age [venia aetatis]. —**gedächtniß**, *n.* V. —esfeier, —esfest. —**gehalt**, *m.*, —**geld**, *n.* yearly salary or allowance; *it.* pension. —**gericht**, *n.* a court of justice held once a year, the annual or yearly assizes. —**gesell**, *m.* a journeyman hired or paid by the year. —**gewächs**, *n.* 1) a year's produce [in agriculture]. Diese Weine sind vom nämlichen —gewächse, these wines are of the same year's growth. 2) a year's shoot [in plants], annual plant. —**hundert**, [the accent on the penultima] *n.* space of a hundred years, century, age. Wir sind im 19ten —hundert, we are in the nineteenth century; die Sitten unseres —hunderts, the manners of our age. —**knecht**, *m.* a servant or man hired for a year. —**lohn**, *m.* yearly wages. —**markt**, *m.* annual fair; *it.* a fair held at fixed days of the year. —**pacht**, *m.* a lease for a number of years only, lease-hold [opposed to Erbpacht, which see]. —**pächter**, *m.* he who has a lease for a number of years only. —**rechnung**, *f.* 1) [in chronology] the manner of calculating or counting the years, era. 2) annual account. —**reihe**, *f.* a series of years. —**rente**, *f.* annual or yearly income or revenue. —**ring**, —**schuß**, *m.* V. —wuchs 1). —**sfeier**, *f.*, —**sfest**, *n.* V. —esfeier &c. —**stag**, *m.* anniversary, V. —esfest. —**sviertel**, *n.* quarter of a year, three months. —**svierteltag**, *m.* quarter-day. —**szeit**, *f.* season. Die vier —szeiten, the four seasons of the year; die schöne —szeit [Frühling] spring. —**szeitkreis**, *m.* [in astronomy and geography] colure. —**tausend**, [the accent on the penultima] *n.* space of a thousand years, millennium. —**uhr**, *f.* a clock which is only wound up once in a year. —**vier**, [the accent on the last syllable] *n.* a space of four years, *it.* olympiad. —**woche**, *f.* [in Scripture] prophetic week, consisting of seven years instead of seven days. —**wuchs**, *m.* 1) Eines Baumes, the circle of a tree which is added every year. 2) a year's shoot or sprig. —**zahl**, *f.* 1) era. Die christliche —zahl, the Christian era; die türkische —zahl, the era of the Turks, the Hegira. 2) number or date of the year. Sie haben die —zahl in Ihrem Briefe vergessen, you have forgotten the date of the year in your letter; die —zahl auf den Münzen &c., the year or date of the money or of a medal. —**zahlvers**, *m.* [*Chronogramm or *Chronostichon] chronogram. —**zehen**, or —**zehent**, [the accent on the penultima] *n.* a space of ten years. —**zeit**, *f.* V. —esfest, —stag. —**zirkel**, *m.* V. —wuchs 1).

Jahren, *v. impers.* [chiefly in fam. lang.] sich —, to arrive at the age or conclusion of one year. Es wird sich bald —, daß ich mich verheirathet habe, it will soon be a year or twelvemonth that or since I am married; es jähret sich heute, daß er starb, it is a twelvemonth to-day that he died.

Jährig, *adj.* and *adv.* a year old, lasting or having lasted a year. Ein —es Kind, a child one year old; —e Zinsen, the interest of one year; das Consulat der Römer war —, the consulship at Rome was a yearly office; eine —e Pflanze, an annual plant; heute ist es —, daß &c., it is this day a year or twelvemonth that &c.

Jährlich, *adj.* and *adv.* happening or occurring every year, yearly, annual. Sein —es Einkommen, his yearly income; — zehn Pfund Miethe bezahlen, to pay ten pounds a year rent; es geschieht —, it is done every year. — eins auch zweimal in's Theater gehen, to go to the play once or twice a year; —es Fest, —er Gedächtnißtag, V. Jahrstag.

Jährling, *m.* [-es, *pl.* -e] a young beast one year old, yearling; particularly a lamb one year old.

Jährlings-bock, —**hammel**, *m.* ram, wether one year old.

Jähzorn, *m.* 1) sudden anger, violent passion. 2) propensity to anger, cholericness.

Jähzornig, *adj.* and *adv.* given to anger, choleric, passionate, hasty. Wenn ich so — wäre wie Sie, so würden wir &c., were I as hasty as you, we should &c. Ein —er, a passionate man.

Jákal, *m.* V. Schakal.

Jákob, *m.* [-s, *pl.* -e] [a name of men] James, Jacob. Der Apostel —, or Jakobus, James, the apostle.

Jakobs-apfel, *m.* 1) a sort of apple that ripens very early [about St. James's day]. 2) a sort of potatoe that ripens very early. —**birne**, *f.* a sort of pear commonly ripe at the end of July. —**blume**, *f.* rag-wort. Die schöne —blume, purple-jacobea. —**bruder**, *m.* V. Jakobit. —**kraut**, *n.* 1) the African rag-wort [a shrub]. 2) V. —blume. —**lauch**, *m.* V. Hohllauch. —**lilie**, —**narzisse**, *f.* purple lily. —**muschel**, *f.* pecten, scallop, pilgrim. —**stab**, *m.* 1) a pilgrim's staff, Jacob's staff. 2) [nautical term] cross-staff, Jacob's staff, sea-quadrant. 3) [in astronomy] the belt of Orion. —**straße**, *f.* V. Milchstraße. —**tag**, *m.* St. James's day. —**wiese**, *f.* a meadow that is mowed but once a year about St. James's day. —**zwiebel**, *f.* V. Hohllauch.

Jákobchen, ‖**Jákoblein**, *n.* [-s, *pl.* -] [*dimin.* of Jakob] Jemmy.

Jakobéa, [-ea's or -eens, *pl.* ea's or -een] **Jakobine**, [-ns, *pl.* -n] *f.* [a name of women] Jacobine, Jaquet.

‖**Jakobi**, V. Jakobstag.

Jakobiwiese, *f.* V. Jakobswiese.

Jakobiner, *m.* [-s, *pl.* -] Jacobin. Die Grundsätze der —, jacobinism.

Jakobinermütze, *f.* the [red] Jacobin's cap, Phrygian cap.

Jakobinisch, *adj.* and *adv.* Jacobinic. —e Grundsätze, Jacobinic principles.

*Jakobinísm, *m.* [*pl.* -en] jacobinism.

Jakobít, *m.* [-en, *pl.* -en] Jacobite.

Jalápe, *f.* [in botany] jalap.

Jalappenwurzel, *f.* jalap, jalap-root.

Jálke, V. Jölle.

*Jalousie, [pron. as in the French] *f.* 1) jealousy. V. Eifersucht. 2) — or —laden, *m.* Venetian blind.

*Jámb, [Jambe], *m.* [-en, *pl.* -en] [a poetic foot ◡ —] iambic, iambus. Dieses Gedicht ist in —en geschrieben, this poem is written in iambics.

*Jámbisch, *adj.* and *adv.* iambic. —e Verse, iambic verses, iambics.

Jámmer, *m.* [-s] [V. Jammern] [grief expressed in complaints or cries] lamentation. Einen — anfangen, to begin to lament or moan. *Fig.* *a*) misery. In — und Noth seyn, stecken, to be in or to suffer extreme misery, distress or wretchedness; der — des Krieges, the miseries of war; o —! o, des —s! alas, what misery! what a pity! what a misfortune! *es ist — und Schade or —schade, daß &c., it is a great pity, a thousand pities, that &c. *b*) [little used, = fallende Sucht] falling sickness, epilepsy. *c*) a high degree of pity. Es ist ein —, zu sehen, wie &c., it moves one's pity or bowels, it is a piteous thing to see how &c.; mit — Etwas ansehen, to look upon any thing with great pity or compassion. Syn. Jammer, Klage, Wehklage. Klage [related to κλαίω and the Lat. *cla-mo*, Sw. *klaga* = sagen, to say] is the expression of every degree of pain; Jammer [related to the Lat. *gemere*] only of the highest degree. Klage shows itself by connected speech; it describes the disagreeable nature of its condition. Jammer consumes itself in sighs and groans. V. Wehklage. — V. also Bedrängniß, Drangsal, Elend, Kreuz, Leiden, Mißgeschick, Noth, Unglück, Widerwärtigkeit.

Jammer-anblick, *m.* a pitiable sight, a woeful sight. —belastet, *adj.* weighed down or oppressed with misery or misfortunes. —blick, *m.* a compassionate look; a piteous look; a woeful, pitiable or rueful look. —brief, *m.* a pitiful letter. —gebet, *n.* lamentable prayer. —gesang, *m.* song of lamentation, lamentable song. —geschrei, *n.* cry of lamentation, lamentable cries, loud wailings. —gesicht, *n.* a woeful or rueful countenance. —gestalt, *f.* a pitiable or pitiful figure. —haus, *n.* house of misery or distress. —klage, *f.* V. Wehklage. —leben, *n.* a miserable, wretched life. —lied, *n.* V. —gesang, Klaglied. —nacht, *f.* a sorrowful, mournful or woeful night. —ruf, *m.* the cry of a miserable or wretched person, lamentable cry, wail. —stand, *m.* pitiable or lamentable condition or state. V. —zustand. —tag, *m.* a mournful or woeful day, day of distress. —thal, *n. fig.* vale of misery, valley of tears, V. Thränenthal. —ton, *m.* sound of lamentation, lamentable sound, wailing sound. —voll, *adj.* and *adv.* lamentable, woeful, mournful, miserable, pitiable, wretched. Ein —voller Tag, a woeful day; —volle Zeiten, calamitous or distressful times; er sieht —voll aus, he looks miserable or wretched; eine —volle Lage, a pitiable, piteous or pitiful condition. —welt, *f.* a world full of misery; *it.* a miserable or pitiful world. —wort, *n.* word of lamentation. —zustand, *m.* piteous condition, sad plight.

Jämmerlich, *adj.* and *adv.* lamentable, miserable. Ein —es Geschrei, lamentable cries; in einer —en Lage, in a deplorable or piteous condition; ein —es Ende, a tragical end; ein —es Gesicht machen, to look dejected or miserable, *it.* [in fam. lang.] to make a wry face; er ist — ermordet worden, he has been murdered in a most horrible or barbarous manner; *er singt —, he sings pitifully; ein —er Anblick, a pitiful sight; *er hat sich — bei dieser Sache benommen, he behaved miserably in that affair; *Einen — abprügeln, to beat or thrash any one unmercifully.

Jámmern, [Sax. *geomrian*, Icel. *ymra*, L. *gemere*, allied to wimmern] I. *v. intr.* to utter lamentations, to lament, to wail, to moan, to bemoan, to bewail. Sie jammert über den Tod ihrer Kinder, she mourns for or bewails the death or loss of her children. II *v. tr.* and *impers.* to move to pity. Sie — mich, you move my pity, I take pity on you, I pity you, your condition is deplorable; sein Elend jammerte mich, his misery touched or moved me with pity or compassion; es jammert mich, ihn so unglücklich zu sehen, I am grieved, it grieves or afflicts me to see him so unhappy; ihm jammerte des Volks [in Scripture], he was moved with compassion toward the people.

‖Jáppen, *v. intr.* to gape. Nach Luft —, to gape for breath.

Ján, *m.* [-es, *pl.* -e] [at backgammon] Der große —, the right hand table; der kleine —, the left hand table.

Ján Hagel, *m.* mob, rabble, V. 2. Hagel.

*Janitschár, *m.* [-en, *pl.* -en] Janizary.

Janitscharen-aga, *m.* aga or commander of the Janizaries. —musik, *f.* Turkish music.

Jánken, *m.* [-s, *pl.* -] a disk or plate used for increasing or diminishing the heat in brass-founderies.

Jankenhaken, *m.* an iron-hook for fitting the heat-plate before the opening of the furnace.

Jänner, *m.* [-s] [or Januar, ‡Januarius] January. Im —, in the month of January.

*Jansenísm [-s] or *Jansenísmus, *m.* [doctrine of Jansen] Jansenism.

Jansenist, *m.* [-en, *pl.* -en] [a follower of Jansen] Jansenist.

Jansenístisch, *adj.* and *adv.* Jansenistical. Die —e Lehre, Jansenism.

Jansenius, *m.* Jansen [the well-known bishop of Ypres, in Flanders].

Januär, *m.* [-s, *pl.* -e] V. Jänner.

Jāpan, *n.* [-s] Japan.

Japanéser, *m.*, —inn, *f.* Japanese.

Japānisch, *adj.* and *adv.* Japanese. —e Erde, Japan-earth or catechu.

Jāse, *f.* [*pl.* -n] or Jāsen, *m.* [-s, *pl.* -] [a river-fish] the chub, cheven.

*Jasmín, *m.* [-es] jessamin or jasmine.

Jasmin-blatt, *n.* leaf of jasmine. —blüthe, *f.* jasmine flower. —laube, *f.* bower of jasmine, jessamin-bower. —öl, *n.* oil of jasmine.

Jáspachat, *m.* [-es, *pl.* -e] V. Jaspisachat.

*Jaspiren, *v. tr.* to sprinkle with divers colours, especially green and vermilion; [among bookbinders] to marble.

Jáspis, *m.* [-sses, *pl.* -sse] jasper.

Jaspis-achat, *m.* jasperated agate. —anstrich, *m.* marbling. —onyx, or Jasponyx, *m.* jasponyx.

Jäten, *v. tr.* to weed, V. Gäten, Ausgäten.

Jauche, *f.* V. Gauche.

Jauchert, Jauchart or Juchert, *n.* [-es, *pl.* -e] [allied to the L. *jugerum*, from Joch] a measure of land, acre.

Jauchzen, *v. intr.* [allied to the Gr. ἰάχω] to shout with joy, to express joy by the voice, to rejoice, to be joyful, V. Jubeln, Zujubeln.

Jauchzer, *m.* [-s, *pl.* -] exclamation of joy, shout of joy.

Jauner, *m.* [-s, *pl.* -], V. Gauner, Gaudieb.

1. Je, *interj.* 1) [expressing wonder] ah, ha; it stands also covertly for the holy name Jesus; —! Herr —! Lord, o Lord! 2) — nun, well, or what of that; — nun, meinetwegen, well and good, let it be so, well then it may be so.

2. Je, [Sw. *ae*, *ee*, *e*, Goth *aio*, Sax. *a*, *aa*, Icel. *ei*, Gr. ἀεί, V. Ewig] *adv.* I. Je, 1) ever, always. Es ist — Einer reicher, als der Andere, there are always some richer than others; — und —, constantly, always; ich habe sie — und — geliebt, I have ever loved her; von — her, at all times, always; er ist, war von — her mein Freund, he has ever been my friend, we have been friends a long time. 2) — und —, or — zuweilen, now and then, sometimes, at times. 3) [it has a distributive or partitive power, with numbers, signifying] at a time. — zwei, two and two, two at a time; — Einer um den Andern, one after another, by turns, every one or each in his turn, alternately. 4) at any time, ever. Waren Sie — in Paris? have you ever been at Paris? wenn sie — kommen sollten, if they should ever come. 5) — nachdem, according as. — nachdem sie sich benehmen werden, according as they shall behave; — nachdem die Umstände sind, es erfordern, according to circumstances. II. Je, [it is proportional before comparative degrees and connects either the two comparative members or corresponds with desto, supplying the office of the English] the. — eher, — lieber, the sooner the better; — mehr und mehr, or — länger, — mehr, the more and more; es wird mit ihm — länger, — schlimmer, he gets every day worse and worse; *prov.* — mehr man hat, — [or desto] mehr will man haben, the more one has, the more one wants to have, much would have more; *prov.* — höher der Ort, — schwerer der Fall, the higher the place, the heavier or harder the fall; ich habe sie — länger, — lieber, I love her every day more and more, or better and better; — mehr er trinkt, desto mehr hat er Durst, the more he drinks, the more thirsty he is. Syn. Je, Jemals. Jemals applies to a single point in time; je presents time to the imagination in its whole extent, indivisibility and continuance. Je seems, therefore, to have more force than jemals.

Jedánnoch, Jedénnoch, *adv.* [obsolete or in law] nevertheless, V. Jedoch, Dennoch.

Jedenfalls, *adv.* at any rate, at all events.

Jeder, jede, jedes, *pron.* [perhaps from je and der] every. — Tag, jede Woche, jedes Jahr, every day, week, year; Jedem, or einem Jeden das Seinige geben, to give every one his share or his due; — von ihnen will es haben, each of them wants to have it; auf — Seite, on each or either side; alle und jede, all and every one; an jedem Orte, every where, in every place; — spricht davon, every body speaks of it. Syn. V. Insgesammt.

Jedermann, [-s] *pron.* every one, every body, any one, any body. — weiß, daß &c., every body knows that &c; — spricht davon, all the world speaks of it.

Jedermanns-bürger, —freund, *m.* [in fam. lang.] a cosmopolite, a citizen of the world. †—hure, *f.* common prostitute.

Jedermänniglich, *adv.* [obsolete or in law] every body, all together, V. Jedermann.

Jederzeit, *adv.* at any time, always.

Jedesmahl, *adv.* 1) every time. 2) [unusual] at any time, always.

Jedesmahlig, *adj.* existing or happening at the time. Die —e Beschaffenheit der Dinge, the state or condition in which things are at the time; wie es die —en Umstände erheischen, according to circumstances, according as the case requires; der —e or jeweilige Besitzer des Hauses soll &c., he who possesses the house at the time, is to &c.

Jedóch, *conj.* yet, however, nevertheless; V. Doch, Dennoch, Indessen, Allein.

Jedweder, Jeglicher, V. Jeder.

Jelängerjelieber, *n.* [in botany] 1) honey-suckle. 2) woodbine. 3) bitter-sweet, V. Bittersüß I. 4) pansy, heart's-ease or three coloured violet.

Jelle, V. Jölle.

Jemal, ‡**Jemalen**, V. Jemals.

Jemals, *adv.* at any time, ever. Hat man — dergleichen gehört? have you ever heard the like? wenn ich — Gelegenheit finde, Ihnen zu dienen, if ever I find an opportunity of serving you; er trinkt mehr als —, he drinks more than ever. Syn. V. Je.

Jemand, [-s, or -es] [from Je and Mann] *pron.* some body, some one, any body, any one. Ist — da? is any body or any one there? who is there? es hat mir — gesagt, somebody told me; weder ich, noch — Anders, neither I nor any body else; seine Frau oder sonst — sollte &c., his wife or somebody else ought to &c; es klopft —, somebody knocks; ein gewisser —, a certain man or woman, a certain person; es ist — Fremdes, — Vornehmes ist da, some stranger, some person of quality is there; ist — so unverschämt? is there any body so impudent? kennen Sie — von dieser Gesellschaft? do you know any of that company?

Jener, jene, jenes, [old: ener] *pron. demonstrative* [referring to a distant person or thing] that. Auf — Seite des Flusses, on the other side of the river; in — Welt, in jenem Leben, in the other world, in the life to come; an jenem Tage, on that day; *it.* on the day of judgment; — Weise sagte, a certain wise man said; — Römer lachte nie, a certain Roman never laughed; zu — Zeit, at that time; dieses ist besser, als jenes, this is better than that; — Herr dort, that gentleman there or yonder; bald dieses, bald jenes, now this, now that; Jene, welche vor uns gelebt haben, those who have lived before us; — fromm, dieser gottlos, the first or the one pious, the other wicked; es ist ein Unterschied zwischen Philosophen und Weisen; jene sind nur Nachahmer dieser, there is a difference between philosophers and wise men; the former are but imitators of the latter; jene Stille, jene Ruhe ist vielleicht &c., that silence, that tranquillity is perhaps &c; [in popular lang.] daß dich dieser und —! deuce take you!

Jenner, V. Jänner.

Jenseit or **Jenseits**, *prep.* and *adv.* on the other side of, beyond. — des Berges, on the other side of the hill or mountain; — der Alpen, beyond the Alps; — des Meeres, beyond sea; von — der Donau, from beyond the Danube; die Stadt liegt —s, the town lies on the other side; diesseits und —s, on this side and the other; —s werden wir uns wiedersehen, in the other world we shall meet again. Das —s, the other world, the life to come.

Jenseitig, *adj.* being on the other or opposite side. Das —e Ufer, the opposite shore; die —en Länder, the countries on the other side of or beyond the river, mountain or mountains, sea &c; das —e Calabrien, ulterior Calabria.

Jerbóa or **Jerbúa**, *n.* [a quadruped having very short forelegs] jerboa.

***Jeremiade**, *f.* [*pl.* -n] the lamentations of Jeremiah. **Fig.* an eternal complaint or lamentation.

Jeremias, *m.* [-, *pl.* -asse] Jeremiah.

Jerusalem, *n.* [-s] Jerusalem.

Jerusalems-artischocke, *f.* Jerusalem artichoke. —**blume**, *f.* the scarlet lychnis. —**korn**, *n.* a sort of corn or rye much cultivated in the Palatinate, Egyptian rye. —**salbei**, *f.* Jerusalem sage.

Jesmin, V. [the more usual word] Jasmin.

Jesuit, [-en, *pl.* -en] or **Jesuiter**[-**Mönch**] [-s] *m.* Jesuit. *Fig.* [in contempt] a subtle canting man or fellow.

Jesuiter-collegium, *n.* college of Jesuits. —**kloster**, *n.* convent or monastery of Jesuits. —**orden**, *m.* the order of the Jesuits, or of the society of Jesus. —**pulver**, *n.* Jesuits-powder, cinchona, quinquina, Peruvian bark. —**rausch**, *m.* [in fam. lang.] einen —rausch haben, to be a little tipsy, half-seas over. —**schule**, *f.* V. —collegium. —**thee**, *m.* Mexico tea.

Jesuitisch, *adj.* and *adv.* jesuitical [in a proper as well as in a fig. sense].

Jesuitismus, *m.* jesuitism [in a proper as well as in a fig. sense].

Jesus, *m.* Jesus. — Christus, Jesus Christ.

Jesus-Christus- or **Jesuschrist-Wurzel**, *f.* [a plant] female fern.

Jetzig, [V. Jetzt] *adj.* present, now existing. Die —e Regierung, the present government; die —e Zeit, the present time; der —e Geschmack, the modern taste; nach der —en Art, after the modern fashion or style. V. Gegenwärtig, Heutig.

Jetzo, V. Jetzt.

Jetzt, [Eng. *yet*, Sax. *get*, *geta*, Bohem. *gesste*] I. *adv.* 1) at the present time, now, at present. Es ist — Zeit, it is now time or time now; was soll ich — thun? what am I to do now? eben —, gleich —, gerade —, just now, this [very] moment; gleich — wollen wir gehen, let us go immediately or instantly; für —, for the present; von — an, from this time, henceforth; bis —, till now, as yet, hitherto. 2) at one time, at another time. — hoch, — nieder, now high, now low; — dieser, — jener, now the one, then the other. V. Bald 2). 3) at that time, then. — sah er seinen Irrthum ein, then or now he was sensible of his mistake. II. *n.* Das —, [chiefly in a poetical style] the present time, the present. Syn. Jetzt, Nun. Nun is, with respect to time considered as present, what damals is for the past, and alsdann for the future; in like manner jetzt is for the present time what ehemals is for the past, and dereinst for the future.

‡**Jetzund, Jetzunder**, *adv.* V. Jetzt.

Jeweilig, *adj.* V. Jedesmahlig.

Joachim, *m.* [-s] [a name of men] Joachim.

Joch, *n.* [-es, *pl.* -e or [in popular lang.] Jöcher] [Sax. *juc*, *jeoc*, *geoc*, Eng. *yoke*, L. *jugum*, Gr. ζυγός, allied to fügen = to join] 1) [in general] any beam supporting any thing. Das — einer Brücke or Brücken—, the pillars and crossbeam supporting a bridge, the props or supports of a bridge; eine Brücke mit sechs —en, a bridge of six arches; [in mining] die — or Jöcher, the supports or props. 2) [a piece of timber fitted for receiving the necks of oxen] yoke. Die Ochsen an [in] das — spannen, to put the oxen to the yoke. *Fig.* Das — der Knechtschaft, der Sklaverei, the yoke of servitude; das — tragen, unter dem —e seyn, to wear the yoke, to be under the yoke; ein — auflegen, to impose a yoke; unter das — bringen, to bring or put under the yoke [of dominion &c.], to subjugate, to subdue; das — abwerfen, abschütteln, to shake off the yoke. 3) [something joined] *a*) Ein — Ochsen, a yoke of oxen. *Fig.* as much land as a yoke of oxen can plough in a day, a yoke of land. *b*) a chain or ridge of mountains.

Joch-bein *n.* [in anatomy] zygoma, cheek-bone, os jugale. —**beinnaht**, *f.* zygomatic suture. —**binde**, *f.* [in surgery] V. Schulterttragbinde. —**bogen**, *m.* zygomatic arch. —**fisch**, *m.* [a sort of shark] balance-fish, zygaena. —**los**, *adj.* and *adv.* [little used] free from the yoke. —**muskel**, *m.* zygomatic muscle. —**ochs**, *m.* yoke or draught-ox. —**pfahl**, *m.* a pile or stake that serves to strengthen the arch of a bridge. —**rebe**, *f.* a vine that is planted in bows. —**riemen**, *m.* yoke string or strap. —**spannung**, *f.* space between the supporters or props of a bridge. —**stier**, *m.* V. —ochs. —**träger**, *m.* crossbeam laid upon the supporters of a bridge. —**winde**, *f.* band of willow or osier used for fastening the yoke to the pole.

***Jockei**, *m.* [usually pronounced Schocken] [-s, *pl.* -e] jockey; postilion.

Jockei-hut, *m.* jockey-hat —**peitsche**, *f.* jockey-whip.

Jochart, V. Jauchert.

Jochen, V. Anjochen.

† and ||**Jodel**, *m.* [-s, *pl.* -] blackguard.

Johann, *m.* [-s, *pl.* -e] [a name of men] John.

Johanna or **Johanne**, [-a's or -ns] *f.* [a name of women] Jane, Joan. — von Arc, Joan of Arc.

Johannchen, *n.* [-s, *pl.* -] *dim.* 1) Johnny 2) [unusual, the usual word is Hannchen] Jenny, Jennet, Joan.

Johannes, *m.* John.

Johannis- [or **Johanns-**]**apfel**, *m.* John-apple, honey-apple. —**beere**, *f.* 1) currant. Die schwarze —beere, the black currant. 2) V. —beerstrauch. —**beersaft**, *m.* currant jelly. —**beerstrauch**, *m.* currant bush. —**beerwein**, *m.* currant wine. —**blume**, *f.* the great daisy, V. Maßliebe. —**blut**, *n.* scarlet grain of Poland, kermes of Poland, [Coccus Polonicus]. —**brod**, *n.* St. John's bread or carob-bean. —**brodbaum**, *m.* carob-tree. —**fest**, *n.* festival or day of St. John the Baptist, Midsummer day. —**feuer**, *n.* [a bonfire made on midsummer night] St. John's fire. —**fliege**, *f.* [a genus of insects] cantharis. —**gleimchen**, *n.* V. —käfer 1). —**gürtel**, *m.* V. —kraut. —**käfer**, *m.* 1) glowworm. 2) V. Brachkäfer. —[or **Johanns-**]**kraut**, *n.* 1) the perforated St. John's wort. 2) common worm-wood. 3) earth-moss. 4) V. Gauchheil. —**nacht**, *f.* the night of St. John's day, midsummer night. —**nuß**, *f.* St. John's nut. —**öl**, *n.* oil of the perforated St. John's wort. —**pfirsche**, *f.* early peach, midsummer peach. —**pflanze**, *f.* V. —kraut. —**roggen**, *m.* rye sowed about midsummer. —**tag**, *m.* V. —fest. —**traube**, *f.*, *dim.* —**träubchen**, or ||—**träublein**, *n.* a bunch of currants. —**wedel**, *m.* meadow-sweet, ulmaria. —**wurm**, *m.*, *dim.* —**würmchen**, ||—**würmlein**, *n.* glowworm.

Johanniter, [or —**ritter**] *m.* [-s, *pl.* -] knight of Malta or of St. John.

Johanniter-meister, —**ordensmeister**, *m.* grandmaster of the order of Malta. —

—orden, *m.* the order of the knights of St. John or of Malta. —ritter, *m.* knight of the order of St. John.

† and ‖Jökel, *m.* V. Jakob. *Fig.* a stupid fellow, blockhead.

Jökel, *m.* [-s] or —gut, *n.* [-es] [in mineralogy] native stalactical vitriol.

†Jölen, *v. intr.* to bawl, to roar.

Jölle, *f.* [*pl.* -n] [a sort of boat] the jolly or jolly-boat, yawl.

Jöll=block, *m.* [in seamen's lang.] a single block. —tau, *n.* girt-line.

Jönas, *m.* [a name of men] Jonas, Jonah.

Jonas=fisch, or —hai, *m.* common shark. —kürbis, *m.* bottle-gourd, V. Flaschenkürbis.

Jönathan, *m.* [-s, *pl.* -e] [a name of men] Jonathan. **Fig.* *a*) a very affectionate and trusty friend, Jonathan. *b*) Bruder — [a nickname for a citizen of the United States], brother Jonathan.

Jönke, Júnke, *f.* [*pl.* -n] [a kind of clumsy vessel] Chinese jonk or junk.

*Jonquille, *f.* [pron. Schongkillje] [*pl.* -n] jonquil.

Jöseph, *m.* [a name of men] Joseph.

Josephs=blume, *f.* goat's-beard, V. Wiesenbocksbart. —stab, *m.* the white double daffodil or narcissus.

Jösua, *m.* [-'s] [a name of men] Joshua.

Jöt, *n.* the letter j. *Fig.* V. Jota 2).

Jöta, *n.* 1) [name of the Greek *iota* and the Hebrew *yod*] iota. 2) **Fig.* [the least quantity assignable] jot, tittle. Es darf kein — or Jot daran fehlen, there must not be wanting a jot or tittle of it, it must be all to a tittle; er will nicht ein — von seinem Rechte fahren lassen, he will not part with a tittle of his right; nicht um ein —, not a whit, no whit.

*Journāl, *n.* [pron. Schurnahl] [-es, *pl.* -e] 1) journal, day-book. [among merchants] In's — eintragen, to enter in the journal, to journalize. 2) a newspaper.

*Joviālisch, *adj.* and *adv.* jovial, merry, joyous, gay.

Jübel, *m.* [-s] [from the L. *jubilum*] shout of joy; *it.* great rejoicing, merry-making, jubilation. Es war ein großer — in diesem Hause, there was great festivity in that house.

Jubel=braut, *f.* a woman celebrating the fiftieth year or jubilee of her marriage. —bräutigam, *m.* a man celebrating the jubilee of his marriage. —feier, *f.*, —fest, *n.* jubilee, V. —hochzeit, —jahr. —freude, *f.* great joy, loud rejoicing. —gesang, *m.* 1) song of rejoicing. 2) song of jubilee. —geschrei, *n.* shout of rejoicing, loud cheering, huzzas. —greis, *m.* an old man celebrating his jubilee. —hochzeit, *f.* jubilee of a marriage. —jahr, *n.* 1) year of jubilee. 2) [in the Romish church] a general or plenary indulgence granted by the pope every twenty-five years, jubilee. —laut, *m.* V. —geschrei. —lied, *n.* V. —gesang. —messe, *f.* jubilee mass. —münze, *f.* a coin or medal struck on some day of jubilee. —paar, *n.* a married couple celebrating the jubilee of their marriage. —prediger, —priester, *m.* a preacher or priest celebrating the jubilee of his priesthood. —predigt, *f.* jubilee sermon. —rede, *f.* jubilee speech. —sang, *m.* V. —gesang. —schmaus, *m.* jubilee feast or banquet; *it.* a feast or banquet of rejoicing. —sonntag, *m.* second sunday after Easter. —tag, *m.* day of jubilee; *it.* day of rejoicing. —ton, *m.* joyous sound, joyous accent. —voll, *adj.* rejoicing, joyful.

Jübeln, *v. intr.* to rejoice, to express joy by word and action, to shout with joy.

*Jubiläum, *n.* [-s, *pl.* -äen] jubilee, V. Jubelfest.

Juch, Júchhe, Júchhei, Júchheisa, *interj.* hurra, huzza!

Júchert, *n.* V. Jauchert.

Juchheien, *v. intr.* to huzza, to shout.

Jucht, *f.* [*pl.* -en] V. 1. Gicht 3).

Juchten, V. Juften.

† or ‖Júchzen, V. Jauchzen.

Jucken, [Low. Sax. *jöken*, D. *jeuken*; rather low] I. *v. tr.* and *impers.* to cause an uneasiness or sensation in the skin, that calls for scratching. Die Haut juckt mich, my skin itches; es juckt mich am Arme, my arm itches. II. *v. intr.* to itch. Der Kopf juckt ihm, his head itches. †*Fig.* Die Haut juckt ihm, der Buckel juckt ihm nach Schlägen, he wants a drubbing; meine Finger — mir darnach, I long to be at it, my fingers itch to be at it; die Zunge juckt ihm, he longs to speak. III. *v. r.* sich —, to scratch one's self [in order to counteract itching], V. Kratzen. Das —, itch, itching. †*Fig.* Das — nach Etwas, a constant teasing desire, itch for or after any thing.

Jücken, *v. tr.* V. Jucken III.

*Judaisiren, V. Judeln.

*Judaismus, *m.* V. Judenthum.

Jüdas, *m.* [a name of men] Judas. *Fig.* a false friend, a traitor, a Judas.

Judas=baum, *m.* Judas-tree, siliquastrum. —dorn, *m.* V. Christdorn. —gruß, *m.* a false greeting, the salutation of a traitor. —kuß, *m.* the kiss of a traitor. —ohr, *n.* [in botany] jew's ear. —schwamm, *m.* V. —ohr. —schweiß, *m.* extreme anguish.

Jüde, *m.* [-n, *pl.* -n] jew. Der ewige —, the wandering jew. **Fig.* a usurer, a miser. Er ist ein —, he is a usurer; so reich, wie ein —, as rich as a jew; [in popular lang.] —n führen, to be in an agony of fear, to be terribly afraid.

Juden=apfel, *m.* Adam's apple. —bart, *m.* the beard of a jew. —bekehrer, *m.* converter of jews. —bekehrung, *f.* conversion of the jews. —docke, *f.* V. —kirsche. —dorn, *m.* V. Christdorn. —eid, *m.* an oath taken according to the rite of the Jews. —feder, *f.* [in botany] filago. —fisch, *m.* V. Hammerfisch. —frau, *f.* the wife of a jew, a jewess. —gasse, *f.* street inhabited by jews, jewry. —gemeine, *f.* V. Judenschaft. —genoß, *m.*, —genossinn, *f.* a jewish proselyte. —gesicht, *n.* 1) a jewish physiognomy or face. 2) **Fig.* a person with a jewish or roguish face, a rogue, a knave. —harz, *n.* jew's pitch, asphaltum. —haus, *n.* the house of a jew. —heller, *m. fig.* [in popular lang.] nothing at all. Es ist keinen —heller werth, 't is not worth a farthing or a pin. —hut, *m.* 1) a jew's hat [a kind of pointed hat]. 2) [in botany] the common yellow balsam, touch-me-not. —kirchhof, *m.* a jewish churchyard. —kirsche, *f.* 1) winter-cherry, alkekengi. 2) cornelian cherry. —kopf, *m.* the head of jew, V. —gesicht. —land, *n.* country inhabited by jews, Judea, Jewry. —leim, *m.* V. —harz. —nadel, *f.* V. —stein. —nuß, *f.* V. Pimpernuß. —pech, *n.* V. —harz. —schule, *f.* 1) jewish school. 2) V. —tempel. *Fig.* [in popular language] Ein Lärm, ein Getöse, wie in einer —schule, a devilish noise, a racket, a caterwaul. —schutz, *m.* protection granted to the jews. —schutzgeld, *n.* V. —steuer. —spieß, *m. Fig.* [in popular language] Mit dem —spieße laufen, to practice usury, to be a great usurer. —sprache, *f.* jewish jargon or gibberish. —stadt, *f.* 1) town inhabited by jews, jewish town. 2) a district or quarter of a town inhabited by jews, jewish quarter, jewry. —stein, *m.* jew's stone. —steuer, *f.* duty or tribute paid by the jews [in acknowledgment of tolerance and protection granted to them]. —straße, *f.* V. —gasse. —tempel, *m.* synagogue. —viertel, *n.* V. —stadt 2). —wucher, *m.* V. —zins. —zins, *m.* 1) interest allowed to the jews. 2) *Fig.* [in popular lang.] excessive or exorbitant interest, usury. 3) V. —steuer. —zopf, *m.* [a peculiar disorder in the hair] plica polonica, V. Weichselzopf.

Judeleí or Jüdeleí, *f.* [*pl.* -en] jew-like way of acting or dealing.

Jüdeln, Jüdeln, Jüden, I. *v. intr.* 1) to act or deal like a jew, to practice usury, to act the jew or usurer. 2) to make use of hebraisms, to hebraize; *it.* to speak gibberish like a jew. II. *v. impers.* Es jüdelt hier, it smells here after jews; *it.* low jewish manners or jewish ways of acting or thinking are manifest here or in that.

Jüdenschaft, *f.* the body of the jews.

Jüdenthum, *n.* [-es] judaism.

‖ and †Jüdenzen, *v. intr.* V. Judeln.

Jüdinn, *f.* jewess.

Jüdisch, *adj.* and *adv.* jewish, judaical. Das —e Gesetz, the jewish law; das —e Land, Judea, Palestina; auf —e Art, after the jewish manner; — sprechen, to speak Hebrew; die —e Sprache, the jewish or Hebrew language; — handeln, to act like a jew; *halten Sie mich für so —? do you take me for a jew? —e Zinsen, V. Judenzins 2).

Júften, *m.* [-s, *pl.* -] or —leder, *n.* Russia leather, Muscovy hides.

Jügelbeere, *f.* [*pl.*-n] whortle-berry.

Jügend, *f.* [Low Sax. *jögd*, D. *jeugd*, Sax. *juguth*, Eng. *youth*] 1) young age, youth. Von seiner zartesten — an, from his infancy or childhood, from the cradle; in meiner —, in my youth, in my youthful days; von — an hat er &c., from his youth he has &c.; sie starb in der Blüthe ihrer —, she died in the prime, blossom or bloom of her youth; man muß der — etwas zu gut halten, young people must be excused, youth must have its time. *Fig.* Man spürt diesem Biere die — an, one feels or finds that this beer is young. 2) young persons or people. Die — unterrichten, to instruct young people; die Blüthe unserer — kam in diesem Treffen um, the flower of our young men perished in that battle. *Prov.* — hat selten Tugend, youth is hard to pass or to overcome.

Jugend=anmuth, *f.* the sweetness or gracefulness of youth. —blüthe, *f.* the bloom of youth. —fehler, *m.* fault of youth, youthful fault. —feuer, *n.* the ardour of youth. —freuden, *pl.* the pleasures or diversions of youth, youthful sports. —freund, *m.*, —freundinn, *f.* 1) a friend from one's childhood or youth. 2) a friend to young people. —gefährte, *m.*, —gefährtinn, *f.*, —genoß, *m.*, —genossinn, *f.* a companion in one's youth; *it.* playfellow. —glut, *f.* V. —hitze. —göttinn, *f.* the goddess of youth, Hebe. —hitze, *f.* the heat or ardour of youth. —jahre, *pl.* juvenile years, youthful age or days, youth. —kraft, *f.* the vigour or strength of youth. —spiel, *n.* youthful play or sport. —stärke, *f.* V. —kraft. —streich, *m.* a youthful trick, prank or frolic. —stück, *n.* V. —streich. —sünde, *f.* a youthful sin, a sin committed while young; *it.* the crime of self-pollution, onanism. —zeit, *f.* time of youth

youth. —zeitvertreib, *m.* youthful amusement or pastime.

Jügendlich, *adj.* and *adv.* youthful, juvenile. —e Gedanken, youthful thoughts; seine —en Gedichte, his juvenile poems; ein —es Gesicht, a youthful face; *er sieht noch sehr —aus, he looks still very young.

Jujúbă, *f.* [in botany] jujub.

1. † and ‖**Júks**, or **Júx**, *m.* [-es] 1) dirt. 2) small but illicit profit, small gain fraudulently obtained, V. Schmu.

2. † and ‖**Júks**, or **Júx**, *m.* [-es] [from the L. *jocus*, Eng. *joke*, allied to jauchzen] merry trick or turn, joke, lark.

1. † and ‖**Júksen** or **Júxen**, *v. intr.* to make small but illicit profit.

2. † and ‖**Júksen**, *v. intr.* V. Juchzen.

Júlchen, *n.* [-s, *pl.* -] *dim.* of Julie [a name of women] Gillet, Gill.

*__Júlep__, *m.* [-es, *pl.* -e] [in pharmacy] julap or julep.

Júli, *m.* [des Juli or Juli's] [the month of] July.

Júlia, V. Julie.

Juliáne, *f.* [-ns, *pl.* -n] [a name of women] Julian, Gillian.

Juliánisch, *adj.* Julian. Das —e Jahr, die —e Jahrrechnung, the Julian year, account.

Jülich, *n.* [-s] [a town in the Rhenish provinces of Prussia] Julich, Juliers, Giulick.

Júlie, *f.* [-ns, *pl.* -n] [a name of women] Julia, Juliet.

Július, *m.* [des Julius or ‡Julii] 1) [a name of men] Julius. 2) [the month of] July.

Julius-käfer, *m.* fullo. —pfirsich, *m.* the white nutmeg peach.

*__Júlle__, *f.* [*pl.* -n] [instead of Jölle, allied to hohl] [a kind of boat] jolly, yawl.

Júly, V. Juli.

Jumárre, *f.* [*pl.* -n] [the fabled offspring of a bull and a mare or of a stallion and a cow] jumart. V. also Maulochs.

Júng, *adj.* and *adv.* [Sax. *geong*, Sw. and Icel. *ung*, *ungr*, old Latin *junis*] young, not old. Ein —es Kind, ein —er Knabe, a young child, boy; ein —er Mann, a young man; ein —er Mensch, ein —es Bürschchen, a youth, a lad, a stripling; in meinen —en Tagen, in my youthful days, in my youth; eine —e Gans, a young goose, a gosling; eine —e Pflanze, ein —er Baum, a young plant, tree; —e Milch, new milk; der —e Mond, the new moon; — werden, to be born, to come into the world; ein Kalb, das so eben —geworden ist, a calf that has just been born; es ist etwas —es auf dem Wege [in popular and jocose lang.], she is with child or in the family way; in diesem Hause gibt es etwas —es [in popular lang.], there is a newborn child in that house. *Prov.* — gewohnt, alt gethan, that which is bred in the bone will never come out of the flesh, once a use and ever a custom. *Fig.* youthful, as in youth. Wieder — werden, to grow young again; [Einen] wieder — machen, to restore [any one] to youth; sie kleidet sich —, she dresses herself like a young woman; *diese Farbe ist zu — für sie, that colour is too young or gay for her. *it.* ignorant, having little experience, green, young. Er ist noch — in diesem Geschäfte, he is still young or green in that business. V. Jünger, Jüngste.

Jung-gesell, *m.* 1) bachelor, single man. Er ist noch —gesell, he is still single or a bachelor. 2) the youngest journeyman. —gesellenleben, *n.* the life of a bachelor. Ein —gesellenleben führen, to lead the life of a bachelor; *it.* to live a careless life; *it.* to play the rake. —gesellenschaft, *f.*, —gesellenstand, *m.* the state of being a bachelor, bachelorship. —heker, *m.* [in conchology] nerita. —meister, *m.* 1) the junior or youngest master [in a trade or tradesmen's company]. 2) [obsolescent, or in jest] the son of the master of the house, the young master. —thier, *n.* [among huntsmen] the female fawn. —werfer, *m.* [in conchology] the viviparous helix or snail-shell.

1. **Júnge**, *m.* [-n, *pl.* -n] 1) boy, lad. Er ist ein hübscher —, he is a handsome boy or lad; der kleine, liebe —! what a pretty little boy! V. Bube. 2) [= Lehr—] apprentice. Einen als —n in die Lehre geben, to apprentice any one, to bind any one as an apprentice; er hat seinen —n fortgejagt, he has turned his prentice out of doors.

Jungen-arbeit, *f.* work done by apprentices; *it.* bungling work. —jahre, *pl.* years of apprenticeship; in seinen —jahren, whilst he served his time. —leben, *n.* the life of an apprentice. —possen, *pl.* boyish tricks —steiger, *m.* [in mining] surveyor or inspector of the apprentices. —streiche, *pl.* V. —possen.

2. **Júnge**, *n.* [-n, *pl.* -n] 1) [said of men, but never used except in vulgar lang.] a young child, a little one. *Fig.* Sie hat schon ein —s [= ein uneheliches Kind] gehabt, she has had a child or a little one already. *Prov.* V. Alt. 2) a young animal. Das — eines Bären, Fuchses, cub; das — eines Löwen, the lion's whelp, das — einer Katze, kitten; — werfen, to bring forth or produce young or young ones; die —n einer Hündinn, the young ones, the puppies or whelps of a bitch.

Júngen, *v. intr.* [rather unusual] to produce or bring forth young [said of animals].

Júngenhaft, *adj.* and *adv.* boyish, unbecoming a man, improper; *it.* as if done by an apprentice, bungling. —e Arbeit, V. Jungenarbeit.

Jünger, *adj.* younger. Er ist —, als ich, he is younger than I; er ist um zehn Jahre —, als sie, he is by ten years younger than she, or he is younger than she by ten years; ein —er Sohn, a younger son; Johann Meier der —e, John Meier junior or the younger; —e Zeitungen, newspapers of a later or more recent date; wieder — werden, to grow young again.

Jünger, *m.* [-s, *pl.* -] [probably from the Lat. *jungo*] disciple, follower. Die — Christi, the disciples of Christ; *prov.* der — ist nicht über den Meister, the disciple is not above his master.

Jüngerschaft, *f.* [not much used] 1) state of being a disciple, discipleship. Während seiner —, whilst he was still a disciple. 2) all the disciples or followers of a teacher or master.

Júngfer, *f.* [*pl.* -n] [corrupted from Jungfrau] *dim.* Jüngferchen, ‖Jüngferlein, *n.* 1) virgin, maid, maiden. Sie ist noch eine —, she is still a maid or virgin; eine alte —, an old maid, *it.* [in contempt] a stale virgin. *Fig.* [a fortress that has never been taken] maiden fortress. 2) [now, the title of a young woman or girl of the middling and lower classes] Miss. — Caroline, miss Caroline; Ihre — Schwester, your sister; Ihre —n Töchter, the young ladies, your daughters; diese — ist die Schwester des &c., this young woman or lady is the sister of &c; diese —n gehen doch mit? those young women or ladies will accompany us, I hope or I suppose. V. Fräulein. 3) a waiting-woman or maid, a lady's maid or woman, chambermaid; *it.* an [unmarried] housekeeper. Geben Sie es meiner —, give it to my chambermaid, woman or housekeeper. 4) *Fig.* *a*) paving-beetle, rammer. *b*) [in nat. hist.] *α*) Venus's shell, porcelain shell. *β*) Die — or *die verfluchte —, the dragonfly, water-fly, unisets, herotrix. *γ*) Die *nackte —, meadow-saffron, V. Zeitlose; die — im Grünen, fennel flower of Crete, nigella Cretica. *c*) [in seamen's lang.] ram's block. *d*) [formerly] a block to which a prisoner was locked or forged. *e*) [formerly, in prisons] an instrument for beheading criminals, maiden. Die — küssen [formerly], to be secretly executed or beheaded in a prison. *f*) —n werfen, [to throw stones obliquely on the water so as to rebound] to make ducks and drakes. Syn. Jungfer, Jungfrau, Dirne, Magd, Mädchen. Dirne (originally any young female) is used at present only among the lowest class, unconditionally, for an unmarried female. Those who at all belong to any higher rank join an accessory notion of contempt with it. It differs from Jungfer and Jungfrau, as well with reference to age, as to the preservation of chastity. Jungfer and Jungfrau are unmarried females of any age, Dirne a young person only; the former are such as have preserved their innocence unsullied, the latter any young female. For Dirne we now use Mädchen (dimin. of Magd, which formerly signified, in general, a young female) which is distinguished from Jungfer (in a higher style Jungfrau) by indicating, in the first place, the sex, and consequently stands in contradistinction to Knabe (boy), as in Mädchenschule; and secondly unmarried females, without reference to chastity, who are still in the bloom of youth. There are old and young Jungfern. Jungfer is become a sort of title for the daughters of the middling class of citizens (whilst those of the higher class are called Fräulein), as also for respectable unmarried female servants. Magd implies a servant maid of the lowest class.

Jungfer-alaun, *m.* native alum. —antiqua, *f.* [in printing] brevier. —biene, *f.* [bee belonging to the first swarm of a hive] virgin-bee. —blei, *n.* native or virgin lead. —erde, *f.* virgin earth. —finger, *m.* ring finger. —gold, *n.* native gold, virgin-gold. —gürtel, *m.* bridal girdle. —haar, *n.* [a plant] maidenhair. —häring, *m.* herring of the first fishing. —harz, *n.* turpentine. —häutchen, *n.* [in anatomy] hymen. —honig, *m.* virgin honey. —hopfen, *m.* hops that grow the first year on the hop vines. —hund, *m.* V. Jungfernhund. —käfer, *m.* V. Marienkäfer. —kamm, *m.* V. Nadelkerbel. —kind, *n.* [in popular lang.] a bastard, natural child. —kloster, *n.*, —knecht, *m.*, —kranz, *m.*, —lecker, *m.* &c. V. Jungfernkloster &c. —magd, *f.* waiting-woman, chambermaid, V. Jungfer 3). —milch, *f.* 1) [milk which unmarried women sometimes have in their breasts] virgin's milk. 2) [a solution of gum benzoin] virginal milk, virgin's milk. —nadel, *f.* minikin. —narr, *m.* V. Jungfernnarr. —nelke, *f.* virgin-pink. —nymphe, *f.* V. Jungfer 4) *Fig.* *β*). —öl, *n.* virgin-oil. —pergament, *n.* virgin-parchment. —pflaume, *f.* maiden-plum. —quecksilber, *n.* or [in mining] —quick, *m.* virgin-mercury. —raub, *m.* rape, ravishment, [in law] abduction. —räuber, *m.* ravisher, [in law] abductor. —schloß, *n.* V. —häutchen. —schrift, —schule, *f.* V. Jungfernschrift &c. —schwarm, *m.* swarm of young bees. —schwefel, *m.* virgin-sulphur. —stand, *m.* state of a virgin or of an unmarried female. —sucht, *f.* V. Bleichsucht. —tabak, *m.* a sort of mild tobacco in Peru. —vitriol, *m.* native or virgin-vitriol. —wachs, *n.* virgin-wax. —wein, *m.* 1) unpressed wine, V. Vorlaß. 2) [a plant of the genus Clematis] Virgin's bower. V. also Waldrebe.

Jungfern-antiqua, *f.* V. Jungferantiqua. —fieber, *n.* V. —krankheit. —glas, *n.* muscovy-glass, V. Frauenglas, Marienglas. —hund, *m.* [obsolescent] lap-dog. —kloster, *n.* nunnery. —knecht, *m.* [in jest or contempt, else obsolete] a man slavishly devoted to the female sex, a dangler [after women], a beau, a fop, a spark. —**krankheit**, *f.* green-sickness, chlorosis, V. Bleichsucht —**kranz**, *m.* bridal wreath. *Fig.* or —**kränzchen**, *n.* [in popular lang.] virginity, maidenhead. —**kraut**, *n.* 1) sensitive plant, mimosa. 2) V. Bärlapp. —**lecker**, —**narr**, *m.* [in popular lang., in jest and in contempt] V. —knecht. —**rede**, *f.* [in the English parliament, the first speech of a member] maiden-speech. —**schloß**, *n.* virgin-knot, hymen, V. Jungferhäutchen. —**schrift**, *f.* [in printing] pearl. —**schule**, *f.* a school for young ladies. —**sucht**, *f.* V. —krankheit. —**volk**, *n.* [in popular lang.] the girls. —**zwinger**, *m.* V. —kloster.

Júngferlich and **Jüngferlich**, *adj.* and *adv.* V. Jungfräulich. *— thun, to play the virgin, to act or speak demurely; *sie thut gar zu —, she is too affectedly nice, too prim; *— trinken, to sip like a maiden.

Júngferschaft, *f.* virginity, maidenhead, maidenhood.

Júngfrau, *f.* [*pl.* -en] a young unmarried woman, virgin, maid. Sie ist noch eine —, she is a virgin still; die — Maria, die heilige —, the virgin Mary, the holy virgin; die — von Orleans, Joan of Arc; [in astronomy] die —, das Zeichen der —, the sign Virgo, the virgin.

Jungfrauenkloster, *n.* V. Jungfernkloster.

Júngfräulein, *n.* [-s, *pl.* -] [obsolescent] a young girl or damsel.

Júngfräulich, *adj.* and *adv.* becoming a virgin, virgin-like, virginal, maidenly. Der —e Kranz, the bridal wreath; —e Keuschheit, virginal chastity; sie beträgt sich nicht — genug, she does not behave reservedly enough.

Júngfräulichkeit, *f.* virginlike or maidenly behaviour, maidenliness.

Júngfrauschaft, *f.* virginity, maidenhead. Sie hat ihre — bewahrt, she has kept herself a virgin; einem Mädchen die — nehmen, rauben, to deprive a girl of her virginity, to deflour a girl; *it.* to violate or ravish a girl; eine ewige — geloben, das Gelübde der — ablegen, to vow perpetual chastity, to make a vow of virginity.

Júngheit, *f.* 1) [not much used] the quality of being young or new. 2) [little used] V. Jugend.

Jüngling, *m.* [-es, *pl.* -e] young man, youth, lad. Ein schöner —, a fine youth. **Fig.* Er ist kein — mehr, he is no longer young, he is advanced in years.

Jünglings-alter, *n.* the period of youth, adolescence. Er ist über das —alter hinaus, he has passed the age of youth. —**blume**, *f.* the common shrubby everlasting. —**jahre**, *pl.* years of youth, V. —alter.

Jüngst, *adv.* lately, not long ago, the other day. —verwichenen Sonntag, last sunday; — begegnete ich ihm, the other day I met him.

Jüngste, der, die, das. 1) the youngest. 2) the last. Die —n Briefe, the last letters; die —n Ereignisse, the late or most recent events; der — Tag, das — Gericht, the day of judgment, doomsday.

Jüngstens, V. Jüngst, Unlängst.

Jüngsthin, V. Jüngst, Unlängst.

Jūni, Jūnius, *m.* [des Juni or Juni's and des Junius or ‡Junii] [the month of] June.

Junikäfer, *m.* V. Johanniskäfer.

Júnke, *f.* [*pl.* -n] V. Jonke.

Júnker, *m.* [-s, *pl.* -] [from Jungherr] son of a nobleman, young nobleman, the young squire; *it.* country-gentleman, country-squire; *it.* V. Land—, Fahn—, Hof—, Jagd—, Kammer—.

Junker-birne, *f.* ognonet, onion-pear, king of summer. —**blume**, *f.* gentiana verna. —**leben**, *n.* the life of a young nobleman; the life of a country-squire.

Júnkerhaft, Júnkerisch, Júnkerlich, *adj.* and *adv.* V. Junkermäßig.

Júnkermäßig, *adj.* and *adv.* 1) [unusual] in the manner of a young nobleman &c. 2) *Fig.* cavalier, haughty, disdainful. Ein —es Betragen, a cavalier conduct; das ist ein wenig —, that is a little too free; auf —e Art, in a cavalier manner, cavalierly, peremptorily.

***Júnta**, *f.* [*pl.* Junten] Junto, Junta, council.

Júny, V. Juni.

***Júpe** or **Júppe**, *f.* [*pl.* -n] [a short close coat] juppon, jacket, V. Jacke.

Júpiter, *m.* [-s] Jupiter, Jove; [in astronomy] Jupiter.

Jupiters-bart, *m.* [in botany] Jupiter's beard. —**blume**, *f.* the umbellate campion rose, the flower of Jupiter. —**fisch**, *m.* the pike-headed or sharp-nosed whale. —**mond**, —**trabant**, *m.* satellite of Jupiter.

***Juramént**, *n.* [obsolete or in law] oath.

***Jurat**, *m.* [-s] [formerly] jurat, alderman.

***Jurato**, *adv.* [in law] upon oath.

***Juratórisch**, *adj.* and *adv.* [in law] comprising an oath, juratory.

Jürgen, *m.* [-s] [in popular lang.; corrupted from Georg] George, Georgy.

***Jūri** or **Júry**, *f.* [= Geschwornen-Gericht or die Geschwornen, members of the jury, collectively] jury. Die Mitglieder der —, the jurymen, the jurors; der Vormann or Sprecher der —, the foreman of the jury; die große, die kleine —, the grand, the petty jury.

***Juridisch**, *adj.* and *adv.* juridical. —es Kunstwort, law term; die —e Fakultät, the faculty of law.

***Jurisdictión**, *f.* jurisdiction.

***Jurisprudénz**, *f.* jurisprudence.

***Juríst**, *m.* [-en, *pl.* -en] jurisconsult, jurist, lawyer.

***Juristerei**, *f.* [in fam. lang.] pettifoggery, lawyer's tricks.

***Jurístisch**, *adj.* and *adv.* relating to the law or to the science of the law, legal, juridical, V. Juridisch.

Júrte, *f.* [*pl.* -n] [name of] the winter-habitation of the natives of Kamtschatka.

Jūry, V. Juri.

***Júst**, *adv.* [in fam. lang.] 1) just, exactly. 2) just now, but just.

***Justificatión**, *f.* [Rechtfertigung] justification.

***Justificīren**, *v. tr.* [Rechtfertigen] to justify.

Justíne, *f.* [-ns, *pl.* -n] [a name of women] Justina.

Justīnus, *m.* [a name of men] Justin.

***Justīren**, *v. tr.* to adjust. Die Schrötlinge — [in mintage], to size the planchets, blanks or pieces for coining; [in printing] to justify. Das —, the adjusting; [in printing] justification, justifying.

***Justīrer**, *m.* [-s, *pl.* -] one who adjusts or justifies, adjuster, justifier.

Justir-feile, *f.* [with type-founders] adjusting-file. —**waage**, *f.* a pair of scales [used in the mint], adjusting-balance.

***Justíz**, *f.* 1) [Gerechtigkeit] justice. 2) [Gerechtigkeitspflege or Rechtspflege] administration of the law.

Justiz-amt, —**collegium**, *n.*, —**hof**, *m.*, —**kammer**, *f.* board, chamber, council of justice. —**kommissarius**, *m.* [in Northern Germany] attorney at law. —**pflege**, *f.* administration of justice. —**rath**, *m.* counsellor of justice. —**sache**, *f.* matter of justice, legal cause. —**wesen**, *n.* any thing belonging to the administration of justice.

***Justiziarius**, *m.* justiciary, ‡justicer, V. Amtmann 1).

***Justiziariát**, *n.* the office of a justiciary.

Jütte, *f.* [*pl.* -n] [in seamen's lang.] an implement for lifting the anchor into the boat, anchor-heaver.

Juwél, *m.* [-s, *pl.* -en] or **Juwele**, *f.* [*pl.* -n] [Eng. *jewel*, Fr. *joyau*, Arab. *johar* = Edelstein, gem] a precious stone, gem, jewel; V. Geschmeide, Schmuck, Kleinod.

Juwelen-handel, *m.* the jeweller's trade or business. —**händler**, *m.*, —**händlerinn**, *f.* a person who deals in jewels, jeweller. —**käfer**, *m.* diamond beetle. —**kästchen**, *n.* case or box of or for jewels, jewel-box. —**künstler**, *m.* [unusual] jeweller. —**laden**, *m.* jeweller's shop. —**ring**, V. Demantring. —**schmuck**, *m.* a set of jewels. —**uhr**, *f.* a watch set with diamonds &c.

Juwelier, *m* [-s, *pl.* -e] jeweller.

Juwelier-arbeit, *f.* jeweller's work. —**kunst**, *f.* jeweller's trade. —**laden**, *m.* V. Juwelenladen.

Júx, Júxsen, V. Juks, Juksen.

K.

(For words not to be found under K look under C.)

K, *n.* K, k. Ein großes —, a great or capital K.

Kaa, [or Kāh] *f.* [*pl.* -en] or **Kaue**, *f.* [*pl.* -n] [allied to Kahn, Kasten, L. *cavus*] a shed, hut.

Kabácke, or **Kabache**, *f.* [*pl.* -n] a public-house or alehouse in Russia, kaback.

Kabale, *f.* V. Cabale.

***Kabáne**, *f.* [*pl.* -n] cot, cottage [originally for an Indian hut] V. Hütte.

1. ||**Kābel**, *f.* [*pl.* -n] or —, *n.* [-s, *pl.* -] [allied to the Hebr. *chebel* = Seil, and the Germ. koppeln] cable. Das — kappen, to cut the cable in the hawse; —, womit ein Schiff bei der Landung befestigt wird, seizing or lashing.

Kabel-aar or —**aring**, *f.* [a rope used in heaving the anchors] voyol. —**garn**, *n.* rope-yarn. —**gat**, *n.* the hole or room on board of a ship where the cables are kept, cable-tier. —**kleid**, *n.* the materials used for serving a cable, service. —**länge**, *f.* cable's length [120 fathom]. —**raum**, *m.* V. —gat. —**seil**, *n.* the strong rope or cable of a ferry-boat. —**stich**, *m.* V. Ankerstich. —**tanz**, *m.* a sort of sailor's dance. —**tau**, *n.* cable. —**taulänge**, *f.* V. —länge. —**weise**, *adv.* in the manner of a cable. —weise geschlagenes Tauwerk, cable-laid or shroud-laid cordage.

2. ||**Kābel**, *f.* [*pl.* -n] [allied to the Sw. *kaepp* = Stab] part, portion, share, lot.

Kabel-bier, *n.* beer brewed by the lot. —**holz**, *n.* wood that falls to a person by lot. —**weise**, *adv.* by lots. —**wiese**, *f.* a meadow assigned to one by lot.

Kabeljau, *m.* [-es, *pl.* -e] [fresh] cod or codfish.

||**Kābeln**, [V. 2. Kabel] I. *v. intr.* to draw

lots. Um etwas —, to draw or cast lots about any thing. II. *v. tr.* to distribute by lot.

‖**Kābelung**, *f.* 1) the act of drawing lots or distributing by lot. 2) share, portion, lot.

*__Kabestan__, *m.* [-es, *pl.* -e] windlass, capstan, V. Schiffswinde.

*__Kabinet__, *n.* V. Cabinet.

Kābus, *m.* **Kābuskraut**, *n.* V. Kopfkohl.

Kabūse, *f.* [*pl.* -n] 1) a small room or hut, a closet; *it.* caboose. 2) core [of an apple &c.]

*__Kachektisch__, *adj.* [in medicine] cachectic.

1. **Kachel**, *f.* [*pl.* -n] [allied to the L. *cavus* &c., V. Kaa] 1) a hollow, earthen utensil [more broad than deep]. †*Fig.* [in contempt] an old woman, an antiquated jilt. 2) a Dutch tile.

Kachel=form, *f.* a mould for making Dutch tiles. —**ofen**, *m.* a stove formed of Dutch tiles.

2. **Kachel**, *f.* [*pl.* -n] the flying bug, V. Baumwanze.

Kachelong, *m.* [-es, *pl.* -e] [in mineralogy, a variety of chalcedony] cacholong.

Kachelot, *m.* [usually pron. Kaschlott] [-es, *pl.* -e] cachalot [a cetaceous fish].

*__Kacherie__, *f.* [in medicine] cachexy.

Kacke, *f.* [Lat. *cacare*, Gr. κακκᾷν, allied to the Gr. χάω] [in popular lang.] excrement.

Kacken, I. *v. intr.* [in popular language, said of children] to go ah ah. II. *v. tr.* to barrel up [herrings].

Kackhäuschen, *n.* [in popular lang.] V. Abtritt 5).

Kackerlacker, V. Kakerlak.

*__Kadenz__, V. Cadenz.

‖**Kader**, *m.* [-s, *pl.* -] [allied to the L. *guttur*] fleshy fulness under the chin. Einen — haben, to be double-chinned.

*__Kadet__, &c., V. Cadet &c.

Käfer, *m.* [-s, *pl.* -], *dim.* —**chen**, ‖—**lein**, *n.* [Sax. *ceafor*, probably from kauen, keifen, Sax. *ceofan*] beetle, chafer.

Käfer=art, *f.* species of beetle. —**blume**, *f.* the beetle-ophris, ophris insectifera. —**ente**, *f.* the little grebe. —**gattung**, *f.* species of beetles or coleopters. —**geschlecht**, *n.* order of coleopters. —**muschel**, *f.* the multivalve lepas. —**raupe**, *f.* grub. —**schnecke**, *f.* scarabee-snail. —**schröter**, *m.* bull-bee, bull-fly. —**wurz**, *f.* the knobby-rooted fig-wort.

Kaff, *n.* [-es, *pl.* -e] [seems to be allied to the L. *cavus*] chaff.

Kaffee, *m.* [-'s] [from the Turkish *cahueh*] 1) [the berry] coffee. Den — brennen or rösten, to roast coffee. 2) [the drink] coffee. — trinken, to drink or take coffee; eine Schale or Tasse —, a cup of coffee.

Kaffee=aufsatz, *m.* V. —zeug. —**baum**, *m.* coffee-tree. —**bohne**, *f.* the berry of the coffee-tree, coffee-berry. —**braun**, *adj.* having the colour of coffee. —**brett**, *n.* coffee-board, coffee-tray. —**erbse**, *f.* dwarf pea. —**farbe**, *f.* colour of coffee. —**geräthe**, —**geschirr**, *n.* V. —zeug. —**haus**, *n.* coffee-house. —**kanne**, *f.* coffee-pot. —**kessel**, *m.* coffee-kettle. —**koch**, *m.* V. —schenk. —**lampe**, *f.* coffee-lamp. —**löffel**, *m.* tea-spoon. —**maschine**, *f.* coffee-kitchen. —**mühle**, *f.* coffee-mill. —**pauke**, *f.*, —**röscher**, *m.* V. —trommel. —**satz**, *m.* the grounds of coffee. —**schale**, *f.* cup and saucer for coffee. —**schenk**, *m.* keeper of a coffee-house, coffee-man. —**schenke**, *f.* V. —haus. —**schütter**, *m.* V. —trommel. —**schwester**, *f. Fig.* [in fam. lang., in jest] a person excessively fond of coffee. —**seihe**, *f.* V. —trichter. —**sieder**, *m.* V. —schenk. —**tasse**, *f.* coffee-dish, cup and saucer. —**teller**, *m.* plate for handing the coffee. —**tisch**, *m.* coffee-table. —**topf**, *m.* coffee-pot. —**trank**, *m.* coffee. —**trichter**, *m.* coffee-strainer, coffee-biggin. —**trommel**, *f.* a machine for roasting coffee, coffee-drum, coffee-roaster. —**wirth**, *m.* V. —schenk. —**zeug**, *n.* coffee-service, apparatus for coffee, coffee-things.

Käfich, **Käficht**, **Käfig**, *m.* [-es, *pl.* -e] [Sax. *cafa*, *cofe*, L. *cavea*, Fr. *cage*, Eng. *cage*] cage. *Fig.* [in popular lang.] prison, jail. Er sitzt im —e, he is in jail. Syn. **Käfig**, **Bauer**. Käfig [Lat. *cav-ea* related to Koben, a cabin] is commonly used to designate an inclosure, or cage, for quadrupeds, or large birds of prey; Bauer [from bauen], one for smaller singing-birds. Neither of these terms, however, are employed for an inclosure for tame animals; V. Stall, Koben, Hürde, Vogelhaus.

‖**Kafiller**, *m.* [-s, *pl.* -] [from the old killen = to flay] public flayer [of dead animals].

Kafillerei, *f.* the habitation or trade of a public flayer.

Kaftan, V. Caftan.

Kag, *m.* [-es, *pl.* -e] a Dutch sloop.

Kah, *f.* V. Kaa.

Kahl, [allied to schälen and the L. *calvus*] *adj.* and *adv.* [destitute of hair, feathers, leaves &c.] bald. Einen —en Kopf, ein —es Kinn haben, to be bald-pated, to have a beardless chin; — geschoren, shaved close; dieser Vogel ist noch ganz —, that bird is still quite callow, naked or unfledged; ein —er Rock, a threadbare, shabby coat; —e Berge, naked, sterile mountains; eine —e Gegend, a barren, open or flat country; —e Wiesen, grassless meadows; —e Bäume, bare or leafless trees; im Herbste stehen die Felder —, in autumn the fields are stripped or bare. *Fig.* *a*) not furnished with things suitable. Ein —es Schiff, an unrigged or dismantled ship; eine —e Wand, a naked or unadorned wall. *b*) paltry, poor, bad. Ein paar —e Gulden, a few paltry or †lousy florins; eine —e Ausflucht, Ausrede, Entschuldigung, a poor, sorry or shuffling subterfuge or excuse; *er ist nur sehr — bestanden, he came off but very poorly. *c*) indifferent, frigid, cold. Ein —er Mensch, a dull or heavy man, a man without energy; ein —es Lob, cold, dry or meager praise; ein —er Empfang, a cold reception. *d*) parsimonious, stingy. Eine —e Bewirthung, a poor, pitiful entertainment; *das kömmt — heraus, that is or looks very stingy. *e*) [in popular lang.] destitute of money. Er ist —, he has no money; sie haben ihn — gerupft [beim Spiele &c.], they have stripped him of all his money, they have plucked him.

Kahl=after, *m.* a kind of stickle-bag. —**bauch**, *m.* [a fish without ventral fins] apode. —**fleckig**, *adj.* having threadbare spots. —**kopf**, *m.* 1) [in popular lang., and in contempt] baldhead, baldpate; †[of a debauchee] pill-garlick. Was will da der alte —kopf? what does that old baldpated fellow want? 2) [in nat. hist.] the carrion vulture or carrion crow. —**köpfig**, *adj.* and *adv.* bald-headed, bald-pated. —**kraut**, *n.* tooth-wort, dentaria. —**rücken**, *m.* [a fish without pectoral fins] gymnotus. —**schwanz**, *m.* the needle-fish without fins.

Kahlheit, *f.* baldness [of the head, of a mountain &c.]. *Fig.* meanness, dulness, insipidity, flatness, shallowness. Die — einer Anspielung, the baldness of an allusion.

Kahm, *m.* [-es, *pl.* -en] [allied to Keim] mould gathered on liquids. — or —en bekommen, ansetzen, to become mouldy.

Kahmen, *v. intr.* to contract mould, to grow or become mouldy.

Kahmig, *adj.* and *adv.* mouldy.

Kahn, *m.* [-es, *pl.* Kähne], *dim.* **Kähnchen**, ‖**Kähnlein**, *n.* [Dan. *kane*, Sw. *kana*, Fr. *canot*, L. *canna*, allied to Kanne and the Gr. χάνειν] 1) a boat, wherry, skiff, canoe [of the North-American Indians &c.]. 2) V. Kahm.

Kahn=bein, *n.* [in anatomy] navicular or scaphoid bone. —**förmig**, *adj.* and *adv.* shaped like a boat; [in anatomy] navicular. —**geld**, *n.* ferriage, fare.

Kahnig, *adj.* V. Kahmig.

Kai, *m.* [-es, *pl.* -e] [D. *kaai*, Fr. *quai*, probably from the old kau = einschließen] 1) [not much used] coast. 2) quay or key, a mole or wharf.

Kai=geld, or —**engeld**, *n.* wharfage. —**meister**, *m.* wharfinger.

Kaien, *v. tr.* Die Raaen —, to brace the yards lengthwise.

‖**Kaiken**, *m.* [-s, *pl.* -] V. 1. Dohle.

Kaiman, *m.* [-s, *pl.* -e] the alligator, cayman.

Kaiser, *m.* [-s, *pl.* -] [from the L. *Caesar*] emperor. Der — von Oesterreich, der österreichische —, the emperor of Austria; der türkische —, the emperor of the Turks, the Turkish emperor, Grand Seignior, Sultan. *Prov.* Um des —s Bart streiten, to contend for things of no concern to us, to dispute about trifles; auf den alten — borgen, to borrow money or to contract debts without thinking of paying them.

Kaiser=apfel, *m.* a large apple of an excellent flavour. —**birne**, *f.* the white butter-pear. —**blume**, *f.* the perfoliate soapwort. ‡—**böhme**, *m.* V. —groschen. —**bohne**, *f.* a sort of bean. —**burg**, *f.* the imperial castle or palace [at Vienna]. —**geld**, *n.* imperial or Austrian money. —**groschen**, *m.* an imperial groshen [the twentieth part of a florin, about the value of a penny]. —**gulden**, *m.* the imperial florin, florin of the empire [= 2 sh. English money]. —**haus**, *n.* the imperial house or family. —**krone**, *f.* 1) an emperor's crown, imperial crown. 2) [in nat. hist.] *a*) [a plant] crown imperial. *b*) crown imperial shell. —**papier**, *n.* V. Imperialpapier. —**pflaume**, *f.* the imperial plum. —**recht**, *n.* imperial right or privilege. —**reich**, *n.* empire. —**salat**, *m.* 1) tarragon. 2) a kind of excellent salad which forms a head. —**schnitt**, *m.* [in surgery] Caesarean operation, V. Mutterschnitt. —**schrift**, *f.* [in printing] primer, great primer. —**schwamm**, *m.* V. Kaiserling 2). —**staat**, *m.* V. —reich. —**thaler**, *m.* imperial dollar [= 4 sh. English money]. —**thee**, *m.* [tea of a superior sort] imperial tea, V. also Kugelthee. —**titel**, *m.* title of emperor; imperial dignity. —**vogel**, *m.* the Numidian hen or crane. —**wahl**, *f.* election of an emperor. —**wasser**, *n.* [formerly, a kind of cordial] imperial water. —**wort**, *n.* the word or promise of an emperor. —**würde**, *f.* imperial dignity. —**wurz**, *f.* V. Meisterwurz. —**zahl**, *f.* [in chronology, a cycle of fifteen years] indiction.

Kaiserinn, *f.* empress. Die — Mutter, the empress mother, empress dowager.

Kaiserlich, *adj.* and *adv.* 1) imperial. Ihre —e Majestäten, their Imperial Majesties; die —en Truppen, the emperor's troops, the imperialists. 2) devoted to the emperor. — gesinnt seyn, to side with the imperial party, to be for the emperor, to be an imperialist. 3) like an emperor. — leben, to live like an emperor.

· **Kaiserling**, *m.* [-es, *pl.* -e] 1) [in contempt] a mean or little emperor, a would-be-emperor, a paltry imperial despot. 2) [in botany] *a*) the golden agaric. *b*) the bird's eye.

Kaiserthum, *n.* [-es, *pl.* -thümer] empire, imperial dignity.

Kaifstein, *m.* [-es, *pl.* -e] [in mineralogy] chalcedony.

Kajüte, *f.* [*pl.* -n] [Fr. *cahute*, from Kaa, Kaue = Verschlag, and Hütte] cabin [in a ship].

Kákadu, *m.* [-'s, *pl.* -e or -s] [a bird of the parrot kind] cockatoo.

Kakadukamm, *m.* [a shellfish] lepas mitella.

Kákao, V. Cacao.

Käkeln or **Käkern**, V. Gackeln.

Käken, *v. tr.* V. Kacken II.

Kákerlak, *m.* [-en, *pl.* -en] 1) [a genus of insects] moth. 2) albino, white moor or negro.

Kalamánk, **Kalamáng**, V. Calamank.

Kalánder, V. Calander.

Kálb, *n.* [-es, *pl.* Kälber] [Eng. and Sax. *calf*, Low Sax., Dan. and Sw. *kalf*, *kalv*] calf; [among hunters = Hirschkalb] fawn. Ein Kälbchen, ||ein Kälblein, a little calf; die Kuh hat ein — geworfen, the cow has calved; ein — abbinden, absetzen, abspänen, to wean a calf. *Prov.* †Die Kuh mit dem —e bekommen, to marry a girl whom another has got with child; to get the cow and the calf; †das — in's Auge schlagen, to offend any one sensibly; ein — machen [a very low expression], to vomit; *mit einem fremden —e pflügen, to profit by, to make use of the work or invention of another; †das — auslassen, to be wanton or full of waggery, to be a rake, to run riot.

Kalbsfell, *n.* 1) calf's-skin. 2) **Fig.* the drum. Dem —felle folgen, to follow the drum, to enlist for a soldier. —**fleisch**, *n.* veal. —**fleischlachs**, *m.* V. Rothlachs. —**fleischpastete**, veal-pie, forcemeat. —**fleischtalk**, *m.* carnation talc. —**leder**, *n.* calf's-leather. In —leder gebunden, bound in calf. —**ledern**, *adj.* made of calf's leather. Ein —lederner Band, a book bound in calf. —**luchs**, *m.* the great lynx.

Kalbsauge, *n.* 1) calf's-eye. †*Fig.* a large full eye, ox-eye. 2) [in botany] ox-eye, ox-eye daisy. —**bein**, *n.* V. —fuß. —**braten**, *m.* roast veal. —**bröschen**, *n.* V. —drüse. —**brühe**, *f.* calf's-broth. —**brust**, *f.* calf's-breast. —**drüse**, *f.* calf's sweetbread. —**fuß**, *m.* 1) calf's-foot. 2) [in botany] arum, wake-robin. —**gehänge**, —**gelünge**, —**geschlinge**, *n.* calf's-pluck. —**gekröse**, *n.* calf's-tripe. —**haut**, *f.* V. Kalbsfell 1). —**hirn**, *n.* calf's-brain. —**ysop**, *m.* savory, satureia. —**keule**, *f.* V. —schlägel. —**klößchen**, *n.* veal dumplings. —**kopf**, *m.* 1) calf's-head. 2) *Fig.* [in popular lang.] a stupid fellow, a blockhead. —**lab**, *n.* calf's runnet. —**luchs**, *m.* V. Kalbluchs. —**lunge**, *f.* calf's lights. —**magen**, *m.* V. Kälbermagen. —**maul**, *n.* 1) calf's mouth. 2) [in botany] calf's-snout, snap dragon. —**milch**, *f.* V. —drüse. —**nase**, *f.* [in botany] V. Löwenmaul. —**pergament**, *n.* vellum. —**schale**, half a loin of veal. —**scheibe**, *f.* fillet of veal. —**schlägel**, *m.* leg of veal. —**viertel**, quarter of a calf, quarter of veal.

Kálbe, *f.* [*pl.* -n] heifer, V. Färse.

Kálben, *v. intr.* to calve.

Kalbzeit, *f.* the season or time when the cows calve or [among hunters] when the hinds fawn.

Kälber, *pl.* of Kalb.

Kälberbraten, *m.* V. Kalbsbraten. —**esel**, —**bröschen**, *n.* V. Kalbsdrüse. —**g**, *m.* [among hunters] a stab into the breast of a deer. —**gekröse**, *n.* V. Kalbsgekröse. —**kropf**, *m.* [in botany] the wild chervil. —**magen**, *m.* calf's maw or stomach; *it.* V. Kalbslab. —**milch**, *f.* V. Kalbsmilch. —**preis**, *m.* V. Kalbsdrüse. —**schere**, *f.* V. —kropf. —**stoß**, *m.* V. Kalbsschlägel. —**tute**, *f.* [in conchology] the vituline cone. —**zahn**, *m.* 1) calf's tooth. 2) [in architecture] dentil, denticle.

†**Kälberei**, *f.* 1) waggishness, wantonness, fooling, frolic. 2) [very vulgar] vomiting.

Kälberhaft, *adj.* like a calf, calf-like. †— weinen, to cry like a sucking calf; †*it.* wanton, waggish.

Kälbern, *v. intr.* 1) V. Kalben. † 2) to frisk about in a calf-like manner, to be wanton, to romp. 3) [very low] to vomit.

||**Kälbern**, *adj.* and *adv.* relating to a calf or to veal. —es Fleisch, veal.

||**Kálch**, V. Kalk.

***Kalciniren**, *v. tr.* to calcine. Kalcinirtes Bleigelb, calcined white lead, massicot or masticot. Das —, calcination.

Kalcinirofen, *m.* annealing furnace.

Kaldaúnen, *pl.* [seems to be allied to the Gr. χολάς and to be reduced to hohl, Gr. κοῖλος] intestines, entrails, tripe, garbage. Syn. Kaldaunen, Eingeweide, Gedärme, Gekröse. Kaldaunen [related to the Gr. χολάς] is used only of slaughtered animals and in culinary, language; Eingeweide, on the contrary is said likewise of men. The Roman haruspices inspected the Eingeweide, not the Kaldaunen, of the beasts sacrificed. Kaldaunen is nearly related to Gedärme; for both signify the same parts of the animal body; the former, however, only in so far as they are prepared for food. Hence the Gedärme of fish and birds are not called Kaldaunen, but Gedärme or Eingeweide. In scientific language Gekröse is distinguished from Eingeweide and Gedärme as signifying properly only the mesentery, or fatty wrinkled skin in the middle of the Gedärme; whereas Eingeweide signify all the inner parts of the animal body, and Gedärme the canals containing the Gekröse.

Kaldaunenfett [Darmfett], *n.* suet. —**höke**, —**krämer**, *m.* tripeman. —**markt**, *m.* tripe-market, tripery. —**sieder**, *m.* V. —krämer.

***Kálekut**, V. Calecut.

Kaléndér, *m.* [-s, *pl.* -] [from the L. *calendarium*] calendar, almanack. —machen, to make almanacks, **fig.* to make almanacks for the last year, to pursue useless thoughts, to be full of fancied cares. **Fig.* Er hat einen — an sich, his body is an almanack [indicates the weather]; das steht nicht in meinem —, I know nothing of that, that is not within my sphere. Syn. Kalender, Almanach. An Almanach contains merely the Kalender for the current year, together with any remarkable events connected with it. The word Kalender, however, indicates, in general, the distribution of the days in the year.

Kalendermacher, *m.* almanack-maker. **Fig.* V. Grillenfänger. —**rechnung**, *f.* style.

Kaléndern, *v. intr.* [provincial or in popular lang.] to feast, to revel, to make merry.

***Kalésche**, *f.* [*pl.* -n] [a light open travelling-chariot or carriage] caleche, calash.

***Kalfácter**, *m.* [-s, *pl.* -] [from the L. *calefactor*] [in popular lang.] accuser, informer, delator; *it.* a fawning person.

***Kalfáctern**, *v. tr.* [in popular lang.] to denounce, to accuse, to inform against, to delate; *it.* [as a *v. intr.*] to be a fawning fellow.

Kálfater or **Kálfaterer**, *m.* [-s, *pl.* -] calker.

Kalfaterjunge, *m.* calker's mate or boy. —**werg**, *n.* oakum.

Kálfatern, *v. tr.* [probably from the old Kal = hohl and the old fatern = füttern] to calk [a ship]. Das Schiff soll kalfatert [not gekalfatert] werden, the ship ought to be calked. Das —, calking.

Kalfatbank, *f.* calker's bench or seat. —**bütte**, *f.* calker's chest. —**eisen**, *n.* calking-iron. —**hammer**, *m.* calker's hammer, calking-mallet.

Kálgen, *m.* [-s, *pl.* -] [in printing] V. Galgen.

***Káli**, *n.* [-'s, *pl.* -] kali, saltwort. Salpeter-, salz-, schwefelsaures —, nitrate, muriate, sulphate of kali.

Kaliber, *m.* V. Caliber.

***Kalif**, [-en, *pl.* -en] or **Kalife**, *m.* [-n, *pl.* -n] calif, caliph or kalif.

Kalifenwürde, *f.* the dignity of a calif, califate or caliphate.

***Kalifát**, *n.* [-es, *pl.* -e] V. Kalifenwürde.

Kalínchen, **Kalínken**, *m.* [-s, *pl.* -] or —**baum**, *m.* snow-ball, wayfaring tree, water-elder.

Kalinchenbeere, *f.* water-elder-berry.

Kálk, *m.* [-es, *pl.* -e] [Sw. and Dan. *kalk*, Eng. *chalk*, Fr. *chaux*, probably allied to the Gr. καίω = to burn] lime. — brennen, Steine zu — brennen, to burn or calcine lime, to burn stones to lime, to calcine stones; ungelöschter —, quick lime; gelöschter —, slaked lime; verwitterter —, lime slaked in the air; salpetersaurer —, nitrate of lime. V. Gips—, Leber—, Metall—, Spar—.

Kalkalabaster, *m.* calcareous alabaster. —**anstrich**, —**anwurf**, *m.* plaster [of lime]. —**arbeit**, *f.* plaster-work. —**arsenikfalz**, *n.* arseniate of lime. —**artig**, *adj.* and *adv.* calcareous. —**artigkeit**, *f.* calcareous quality or nature. —**äscher**, *m.* [among tawers] lime-pit. —**bank**, *f.* V. Löschbank. —**beschlag**, *m.* V. Mauersalz. —**beule**, *f.* a calcareous swelling. —**boden**, *m.* calcareous soil. —**borax**, *m.* borate of lime. —**brennen**, *n.* act of burning lime. —**brenner**, *m.* lime-burner. —**brennerei**, *f.* lime-kiln. —**bruch**, *m.* V. —steinbruch. —**brühe**, *f.* lime water. —**drusen**, *pl.* calcareous spar. —**erde**, *f.* calcareous earth. —**erdig**, *adj.* and *adv.* —erdiges Scheelerz, calcareous tungsten or scheelin. —**essigsalz**, *n.* acetite of lime. —**faß**, *n.* a cask, tub or trough for lime. —**fels**, *m.* calcareous rock. —**flechte**, *f.* calcareous lichen. —**flins**, *m.* tourmalin or turmalin, shorl. —**gebirge**, *n.* calcareous mountains. —**grube**, *f.* lime-pit. —**haken**, *m.* a wooden hook used in slaking lime. —**haltig**, *adj.* containing lime, limy, calciferous, calcareous. —**hütte**, *f.* lime-kiln. —**kasten**, *m.* a chest for lime; *it.* V. Löschbank. —**kelle**, *f.* trowel. —**kochsalz**, *n.* muriate of lime. —**kraut**, *n.* V. Steinkraut. —**kristall**, *m.* calcareous crystal. —**krücke**, *f.* [the rake for stirring the lime when being slaked] beater. —**kübel**, *m.* mason's bucket. —**lauge**, *f.* lie made of lime. —**leber**, *f.* sulphurate of lime. —**loch**, *n.* V. —grube. —**löscher**, *m.* one who slakes lime. —**malerei**, *f.* fresco painting. V. Fresco. —**mehl**, *n.* powdery lime. —**mergel**, *m.* calcareous marl. —**milch**, *f.* lime-water. —**mühle**, *f.* lime-mill. —**ofen**, *m.* lime-kiln. —**röse**, *f.*, —**rost**, *m.*, —**röste**, *f.* a layer of limestones and wood to be burnt to lime. —**salpeter**, *m.* calcareous nitre, nitrate of lime. —**salz**, *n.* salt exuding from walls, salt of lime. —**sand**, *m.* sand to be mixed with lime; *it.* calcareous sand. —**schaufel**, *f.* lime-shovel. —**scheel**, *m.* tungsten, scheelin. —**schiefer**, *m.* calcareous slate. —**schlot**, *m.* a large cavity in lime or chalk mountains. —**seife**, *f.* soap made of calcareous earth. —sinter, *m.* calcareous stalactite. —spath, *m.* calcareous spar. —stein, *m.* limestone. Ein derber —stein, a compact limestone. —steinbruch, *m.* limestone pit or quarry. —theil, *m.*, *dim.* —theilchen, *n.* calcareous part or particle. —tonne, *f.* V. —faß. —trog, *m.* lime-trough. —tuff, *m.* tufaceous limestone. —tünche, *f.* V. —milch. —vitriol, *m.* calcareous vitriol. —wasser, *n.* lime-water. —weinstein, *m.* tartrite of lime, calcareous tartar. —weiße, *f.* V. —milch. —wurf, *m.* the act of rough-casting or pargeting a wall, rough-casting, pargeting, rough-cast.

Kälken, *v. tr.* 1) to steep in lime-water. 2) to mix with lime, to dress or prepare with lime. Saatkorn —, to mix lime with the corn that is to be sowed; gekalktes Leder, leather dressed with lime.

Kälkicht, *adj.* and *adv.* resembling lime, limy. Der Wein schmeckt —, the wine has a limy taste.

Kälkig, *adj.* and *adv.* 1) containing lime, limy. —er Boden, limy soil. 2) smeared with lime. Sich — machen, to smear or soil one's self with lime.

***Kalkiren**, [Fr. *calquer*] *v. tr.* [in painting] to counter-draw. Das —, counter-drawing, calking.

***Kalligraph**, *m.*, —ie, *f.*, —isch, *adj.* V. Calligraph &c.

***Kálm**, *m.* [-es, *pl.* -e] [in seamen's lang.] calm.

***Kálm**, *adj.* and *adv.* calm, quiet, still.

***Kálmen**, *v. intr.* [in seamen's lang.] to be calm or quiet.

***Kalmánk**, V. Calamank.

Kalmäuser, *m.* [-s, *pl.* -] [probably from kalm = still, quiet, and the Low Sax. *musen*, Eng. *to muse*] [in fam. lang.] 1) a moping fellow, a misanthrope. 2) V. Knicker, Knauser.

Kalmäuserei, *f.* 1) mopishness, misanthropy. 2) V. Knickerei, Knauserei.

Kalmäusern, *v. intr.* 1) to be in a brown study, to muse, to mope. 2) V. Knickern, Knausern.

Kalmúck, V. Calmuck.

Kálmus, *m.* [from the L. *calamus*] sweet-smelling flag, sweet cane, sweet rush, sweet flag.

Kált, *adj.* and *adv.* [Low Sax. and Dan. *kold*, Eng. *cold*, Sax. *ceald*, Sw. *kall*, D. *koudt*, L. *gelidus*] [opposed to warm or hot] cold. —es Wetter, cold weather; die —e Zone, the frigid zone; es ist —, it is cold or cold weather; es ist — in diesem Zimmer, this room is cold; Sie wohnen hier sehr —, you have a very cold lodging here; das Eisen — schmieden, to hammer or beat the iron cold or without putting it into the fire; ein —es Bad nehmen, — baden, to take a cold bath, to bathe in cold water; die —e Pisse, strangury; ein —es Fieber, an ague; ein —er Schweiß, a cold sweat; — geschlagenes Oel, oil expressed cold; *—e Küche, cold meats or victuals; *—e Küche halten, to eat cold victuals; —e Schale, bread or fruit soaked in wine and sweetened with sugar; — werden, to grow cold; Etwas — essen, trinken, to eat, to drink any thing cold; mir ist —, ich habe —, I am cold; *es lief mir — über die Haut, *es ging mir — auf, —er Schauer ergriff mich or —e Schauer überliefen mich, I was seized with or I felt a shivering, I shivered, I shook with cold, fear &c.; *prov.* Er bläst — und warm aus einem Munde, he blames and praises one and the same thing, he speaks for and against the same thing, he blows hot and cold; das ist weder — noch warm, it is neither warm nor cold, *fig.* is good for nothing; *Einen — machen, to kill or dispatch any one, to do away with any one; ein —er Schlag, a flash of lightning or a thunderbolt that does not set on fire; der Balg bläst —, the bellows blow cold, do not blow upon the coals. *Fig.* *a*) [wanting passion, zeal, ardour or affection] indifferent, cold. Er ist —er Natur, he is of a cold constitution; ein —er Liebhaber, a cold lover; er blieb — dabei, he was unconcerned, he saw or heard it without the least emotion; ich bitte Sie, bleiben Sie —, pray, do not fly into a passion; pray, keep your temper; sie stellte sich —, she affected or feigned indifference or coldness; sie sind — gegen einander, there is a coldness between them; dieses Buch läßt den Leser —, this book makes no impression on the heart of the reader; er empfing mich sehr —, he gave me a very cold reception; er antwortete ihm —, he answered him coldly. *b*) [not moving, unaffecting] Eine —e Rede, a cold discourse; ein —er Styl, a frigid, dull style. SYN. Kalt, Frostig, Kälte, Frost. Kälte is the absence of heat in any degree; Frost only in a higher degree. We call a body kalt, when it has a less degree of warmth than our own body. Frost, however, is that degree of Kälte which freezes water. Kälte, therefore, begins to be Frost at 32° of Fahrenheit's, or at the zero point of Réaumur's thermometer. If we judge of Kälte merely from sensation, we call it Frost when it causes contraction of the skin, shivering and chattering of the teeth; V. Fieberfrost. Figuratively we call any one kalt who is deficient in warmth of sentiment. Frostig is that which excites no perceptibly agreeable feeling in others. A kalter man must necessarily be a frostiger poet; for he who is himself void of sentiment can excite none by his language in others; V. also Kaltsinnig.

Kalt=beutel, *m.* a steel-chisel for cutting iron when cold, cold-chisel. —flüssig, *adj.* and *adv.* difficult of fusion, refractory. —blüter, *m.* V. Amphibium. —blütig, *adj.* and *adv.* having cold blood, cold-blooded. *Fig.* without sensibility or feeling, cold-blooded, calm, cold. Ein —blütiger Mensch, an apathetic, cold, insensible man; —blütig handeln, to act in cold blood, without the least emotion; *it.* to act deliberately, not in a hot-headed manner, without precipitation; können Sie mich in diesem Zustande sehen, und —blütig bleiben? can you see me in this condition and be unconcerned? er bleibt —blütig in der größten Gefahr, he remains calm in the greatest danger. —blütigkeit, *f.* cold-bloodedness, calmness, coolness, composure, presence of mind, deliberateness. —bruch, *m* brittleness of iron when cold. —brüchig, *adj.* cold-short, brittle when cold; V. Bruchig, Spröde. —gierig, *adj.* sulphury. —gründig, *adj.* having a cold soil. —herzig, *adj.* and *adv.* cold hearted. —herzigkeit, *f.* cold-heartedness, insensibility. —höflich, *adj.* and *adv.* coldly civil. —meißel, *m.* V. Kaltbeutel. —schale, *f.* V. kalte Schale. —schlächter, *m.* public flayer [of dead animals]. —schlagamboß, *m.* anvil on which the copper is beaten cold or without fire. —schmied, *m.* brazier. —silber, *n.* a mixture of tartar and calcined silver. —sinn, *m.* cold disposition, coldness, indifference, insensibility. Er empfing mich mit viel —sinn, he gave me a very cold reception, received me very coldly; ihr —sinn brachte ihn zur Verzweiflung, her indifference or coldness of heart drove him to despair. —sinnig, *adj.* and *adv.* indifferent, cold. Er hörte mich —sinnig an, he listened to me with coldness or coldly; eine —sinnige Antwort, a cold or frigid answer. —sinnigkeit, *f.* V. —sinn.

Kälte, *f.* 1) coldness. Die — des Wassers, des Marmors, des Wetters, the coldness of water, of marble, of the weather. 2) cold weather or cold air, cold. Eine erstarrende —, a nipping cold or frost; die — des Klima's, der Jahrszeit, the cold of the climate, of the season; sich gegen die — verwahren, to provide against cold weather or the inclemency or rigor of the weather; die — läßt nach, the weather begins to grow mild; sich an die — gewöhnen, to inure one's self to cold; bei solcher — gehe ich nicht aus, in such cold weather as this I never go out; vor — or Frost starren, zittern, to be benumbed with cold, to tremble, shake or shiver with cold; ich vergehe fast vor —, I am almost starved with cold; eine große, durchdringende —, a great, an intense, a piercing cold. 3) *Fig* [want of ardour, emotion or affection] coldness. Er antwortete mit seiner gewöhnlichen —, he answered with his usual indifference, unconcern or coldness; Einen mit — empfangen, to receive any one coldly or with coldness, to give any one a cold reception; es herrscht eine — zwischen ihnen, there is a coldness between them.

Kälten, [unusual] *v. intr.* 1) [used with seyn] to grow cold, V. Erkalten. 2) [used with haben] to be cold.

Kälten, *v. tr.* to make cold, to chill. [in physics] —de Theile, frigorific parts.

Kälter, *m.* [-s, *pl.* -] V. Kelter.

Kältlich, *adj.* and *adv.* somewhat cold, coldish, chilly.

Kältling, [rather unusual] *m.* [-es, *pl.* -e] a cold, insensible or indifferent person.

Kalvinismus, &c. V. Calvinismus &c.

***Kalzedōn**, V. Chalzedon.

Kamāleon, V. Chamäleon.

***Kamásche**, *f.* V. Gamasche.

1\. **Kaméel**, [†Kamehl] *n.* [-es, *pl.* -e] [Hebr. *gamal*] camel. — mit einem Höcker [*Dromedar], dromedary. *Fig.* [in vulgar lang., especially students' cant] a stupid person, block-head.

Kameel=bock, *m.* the Indostan antelope. —böcklein, *n.* the black leptura or wasp-beetle. —fliege, *f.* the raphidia. —führer, *m.* V. —treiber. —garn, *n.* the hair of the Angora goat or camel goat, mohair. —haar, *n.* 1) camel's hair. 2) V. —garn. —hals, *m.* 1) camel's neck. [in nat. hist.] *a*) V. —fliege. *b*) our lady's rose. —halsfliege, *f* V. —fliege. —hären, *adj.* and *adv.* made of camel's or camel goat's hair. —härener Zeug, camelot or camlet, barracan. —hengst, *m.* the male camel. —heu, *n.* 1) sweet rush. 2) flowering rush. —kuh, *f.* female camel. —leopard, *m.* V. Silbermund. —motte, *f.* V. —spinner. —parder, *m.* camelopard, the giraff. —raupe, *f.*, —spinner, *m.* [a sort of moth] cameline. —strauß, *m.* ostrich. —stroh, *n.* V. —heu. —stute, *f.* V. —kuh. —treiber, —wärter, *m.* camel-driver. —ziege, *f.* 1) the sheep of Peru, Llama. 2) —ziege, or Kämmelziege, the Angora goat or camel-goat.

2\. **Kaméel**, *n.* [-es] [in seamen's lang., a machine for lifting ships and bearing them over a bar] camel.

3\. **Kaméel**, *n.* [-es, *pl.* -e] [in Scripture] a thick cable.

Kaméelinn, *f.* V. [the more usual word] Kameelkuh.

***Kamelót, Kamerād, Kamerāl,** &c. V. Camelot &c.

***Kamílle**, *f.* [*pl.* -n] camomile, chamomile.

Kamillen=öl, *n.* oil of camomile. —thee, *m.* camomile-tea. —trank, *m.* a decoction of camomiles, camomile-drink. —wasser, *n.* camomile-water.

Kamín, *m.* and *n.* [-es, *pl.* -e] [from the L.

caminus] 1) chimney, V. Schornstein. 2) fireplace, fireside, chimney. An dem —e, um den — herumsitzen, to sit round the fireside; ich fand das Buch auf, über dem —e, I found the book on the mantlepiece.

Kamin-bret, *n.* the frame for shutting a chimney, chimney frame. —**feger**, *m.* chimney-sweeper. —**feuer**, *n.* a fire in an open fireplace [opposed to a fire in a stove], chimney-fire. Am —feuer sitzen, to sit by the fire. —**geld**, *n.* chimney-money, hearth-money. —**geräthe**, *n.* fire or chimney utensils [as poker, tongs &c.] —**gesims**, *n.* mantle-piece. —**haken**, *m.* chimney-hook. —**mantel**, *m.* the mantle-tree of a chimney. —**platte**, *f.* the back of a chimney. —**röhre**, *f.* the funnel of a chimney; *it.* a stack of chimneys. —**rost**, *m.* grate. —**ruß**, *m.* chimney-soot; [among painters] bister. —**schirm**, *m.* fire-screen. —**sims**, *m.*, —**simse**, *f.* V. —gesims. —**stück**, *n.* a painting over a chimney, chimney-picture. —**taxe**, V. —geld. —**teppich**, *m.* hearth-rug. —**thür**, *f.* chimney-door. —**zange**, *f.* fire-tongs.

***Kamisól**, *n.* [-es, *pl.* Kamisöler] [allied to the old **heman** = decken] waistcoat; *it.* jacket.

1. **Kámm**, *m.* [-es, *pl.* Kämme] [probably allied to the Fr. *cime*, L. *cum*-ulus &c, as well as to Kopf, Giebel &c.; originally, any thing prominent or jutting] 1) a range of hills, a ridge. Es zieht sich ein langer — gegen Norden hin, there is a long ridge of hills towards the north; der — eines Gebirges, the top or ridge of a mountain. 2) [the prominent or jutting part of certain things] Der — eines Schlüssels, key-bit; der — eines Fasses, the edge or border of a cask; der — an einer Geige, Laute, the button of a violin, of a lute; der — eines Rades, the cog or tooth of a wheel; [among joiners and carpenters] der —, the manner of uniting two pieces of timber or two boards by letting them into each other, clamp; der — [von Weintrauben] the stalk where the berries hung; der — einer Schlange, the crest of a serpent; der — einer Lerche, the tuft of a lark; der — eines Pferdes, a horse's mane; der — eines Ochsen, the neck of an ox; der — einer Auster, the beard of an oyster; der — eines Helmes, the crest of a helmet; der — eines Hahns oder einer Henne, the comb of a cock or hen; dieser Hahn hat einen aufrechtstehenden —, this cock has an upright comb. *Fig.* Der — schwillt ihm [in fam. lang.], he is in a violent passion, the mustard bites his nose, he takes pepper in the nose; den — aufsetzen [in popular lang.], to bear it high, to be conceited, haughty or arrogant; †Einen über den — hauen, to bring any one a peg lower, to mortify any one's pride, to humble any one. 3) [particularly] instrument for adjusting the hair &c., comb. *dim.* ein Kämmchen, ||Kämmlein, *n.* a little comb. Ein elfenbeinerner —, an ivory comb; ein enger —, a comb with small teeth, dandruff-comb; ein weiter —, a wide-toothed comb, a horse-comb, curry-comb; [among weavers] V. —blatt; *it.* V. —litze. *Prov.* Alle über Einen — scheren, to treat or judge all alike, or in the same manner.

Kamm-artig, *adj.* and *adv.* resembling a comb. —artige Muschel, V. —muschel. —**bank**, *f.* V. —bret. —**balken**, —**baum**, *m.* [in saw-mills] the indented or notched beam or tree. —**blatt**, *n.* 1) [among weavers] reed, comb, sley, stays. 2) [in conchology] ostraco-folium. —**blume**, *f.* camomile. —**bohrer**, *m.* an auger or borer for making the holes of the cogs in cog-wheels. —**braten**, *m.* roasted ribs of beef. —**bret**, *n.* [a board or bench on which furriers comb their furs] furrier's board or bench. —**bruch**, *m.* a rupture, gap or break made by the water in the upper part of a dike. —**bürste**, *f.* comb-brush. —**dose**, *f.* V. —schachtel. —**eidechse**, *f.* iguana. —**eisen**, *n.* notching-chisel. —**farn**, *m.* flowering fern, osmunda. —**fett**, *n.* grease or fat of a horse's mane, melted horse grease. —**förmig**, *adj.* and *adv.* having the shape or form of a comb. [in botany] Der —förmige Staubbeutel, anther. —**futter**, *n.* comb-case. —**gras**, *n.* the dog's-tail grass, the cock's comb grass. —**haar**, *n.* the hair of a horse's mane. —**haken**, *m.* [in anatomy] the nape [of the neck]. —**hebel**, *m.*, —**hebelbret**, *n.* [among weavers] the balances that raise the stays. —**heuschrecke**, *f.* a kind of grasshopper or locust. —**käfer**, *m.* the great hornbeetle or bullfly. —**kraut**, *n.* the common daisy. —**lerche**, *f.* crested lark. —**litze**, *f.* the strings of yarn or the packthreads on the stays of silkweavers. —**macher**, *m.* comb-maker. —**muschel**, *f.* pecten, scallop. Versteinerte —muschel, —muschelstein, fossil pecten or scollop, pectinite. —**muskel**, *m.* muscle of the share-bone. —**pott**, *m.* V. —topf. —**rad**, *n.* cog-wheel. —**reiher**, *m.* the night-heron. —**rücken**, *m.* V. —eidechse. —**schachtel**, *f.* comb-box or comb-case. —**schaft**, *m.* shaft or staff on a silkweaver's stays. —**schale**, *f.* [in mineralogy] black slate containing but very little copper. —**scheide**, *f.* [in conchology] solen, razor, shell-fish. —**schwanz**, *m* pectinal star-fish. —**setzer**, *m.* one who makes cards for combing wool &c. —**stab**, *m.* V. —schaft. —**stein**, *m.* V. —muschel. —**stern**, *m.* V. —schwanz. —**strich**, *m.* stroke with a comb. —**stück**, *n.* a piece of beef from the neck, neck of beef. —**stürzung**, *f.* V. —bruch. —**topf**, *m.* an iron pot filled with coals for warming the combs. —**venus**, *f.* [in conchology] the cross cockle, Venus pectinata. —**wolle**, *f.* carded wool. —**zahn**, *m.* tooth of a comb. —**zwecke**, *f.* the smallest tack with a flat head.

2. **Kámm**, *m.* [-es, *pl.* Kämme] [in mining] very hard rock.

Kämmeln, *v. tr.* to card [wool].

Kämmel-kamm, *m.* a card [for combing wool]. —**thier**, *n.*, —**ziege**, *f.* V. Kameelziege 2).

Kämmelung, *f.* the act of carding [wool].

Kämmen, *v. tr.* 1) to comb [the hair], to card [wool]. Sich —, den Kopf —, to comb one's head. 2) [among carpenters] V. Kimmen.

Kämmer, *m.* [-s, *pl.*-] —**inn**, *f.* a person that combs [used chiefly in composition as Woll—, wool-comber].

Kámmer, *f.* [*pl.* -n] [allied to the Celtic *camm* = krumm, the L. and Gr. *camara*, καμάρα = a vault] chamber, room; *dim.* **Kämmerchen**, ||**Kämmerlein**, *n.* a small chamber or room. Die —n eines Fürsten, the apartments of a prince; Stube und —, sitting-room and bed-room; V. Boden—, Holz—, Milch—, Schlaf—; die — eines Mörsers, the chamber of a mortar; die — einer Mine, the chamber of a mine; [in anatomy] V. Herz—; die dunkele or finstere —, camera obscura; [at billiards] die —, the space, indicated by a line, within which the player has to strike. *Fig.* *a*) [little used] the persons or officers waiting on the prince in his apartments. *b*) the place where an assembly of civil officers, deputies &c. meet, and the assembly itself, chamber, board, office; V. Hof—, Justiz—, Rent—; die apostolische —, the apostolic chamber; die kaiserliche und des Reichs— zu Wetzlar [formerly in the German Empire], the imperial chamber of Wetzlar; die — der Abgeordneten, Deputirten, Repräsentanten, Landstände, Volksvertreter &c., the chamber of deputies, [in England] the house of commons; in die — [der Landstände] gehen, to go to the chamber [of deputies]. *c*) the board of finances, exchequer. Auf die — [der Finanzen] gehen, to go to the exchequer. *d*) domains and revenues of a prince.

Kammer-advokat, *m.* advocate or attorney of the court of exchequer or of the board of domains. —**amt**, *n.* an office at the board of finances or at the exchequer. —**anwalt**, *m.* V. —advokat. —**archiv**, *n.* archives of the exchequer &c. —**band**, *n.* [in gunnery] vent-astragal. —**beamte**, *m.* officer at the board of finances. —**becken**, *n.* chamber-pot. V. Nachttopf. —**bediente**, *m.* 1) page of a prince, valet, waiting-man. 2) V. —beamte. —**bedienung**, *f.* V. —amt. —**bezirk**, *m.* the district or circuit of the jurisdiction &c. of the court of exchequer &c. —**bote**, *m.* messenger of the exchequer &c. —**capelle**, *f.* 1) chapel for the royal, ducal &c. family only. 2) V. —musik 2). —**collegium**, *n.* board of revenues, board of domains. —**commissarius**, *m.* commissary of the exchequer &c. —**concert**, *n.* a concert played in the apartments of a prince. —**consulent**, *m.* V. —advokat. —**copist**, *m.* copyist at the exchequer &c. —**dame**, *f.* lady of the bed-chamber. —**degen**, *m.* a small sword [worn at court, on visits &c.], dress-sword. —**diener**, *m.* valet-de-chamber, waiting-man; *it.* [seldom for] page of a prince. —**dienerinn**, *f.* the wife of a valet-de-chamber. —**director**, *m.* director of the board of finances or domains or of the exchequer. —**fest**, *n.* a private feast or entertainment at court. —**fiskal**, *m.* an officer who watches over the fiscal rights and laws. —**fourier**, *m.* V. Hoffourier. —**frau**, *f.* lady's maid, waiting-woman. Eine fürstliche —frau, a [waiting-] gentlewoman of a queen, princess &c. —**fräulein**, *n.* lady of the bed-chamber, maid of honour. —**gebäude**, *n.* the building in which the board of domains or finances hold their sessions, exchequer. —**gefälle**, *pl.* the revenues of the domains of a prince &c. —**gericht**, *n.* court of the prince's chamber, supreme court of judicature, fiscal chamber. Das kaiserliche —gericht zu Wetzlar [formerly], the imperial chamber of Wetzlar. —**gerichtsbeisitzer**, *m.* an assessor of the supreme court of judicature. —**gerichtsbote**, *m.* [formerly] messenger of the imperial chamber. —**gerichtspräsident**, *m.* president of a supreme court of judicature. —**gut**, *n.* a princely domain, a public domain. —**heiduk**, *m.* a footman [in Hungarian costume] attached to the prince's person. —**heizer**, *m.* a person whose business it is to make fire in the rooms of a prince &c. —**herr**, *m.* chamberlain. —**herrinn**, *f.* the lady of a chamberlain. —**herrnschlüssel**, *m.* a small golden key worn by chamberlains as a badge of office, chamberlain's key. —**herrnstelle**, *f.* chamberlainship. —**husar**, *m.* a page [in the dress of a hussar] attending on the prince's person. —**jäger**, *m.* 1) a prince's own huntsman or gamekeeper. 2) [provincial or in popular lang., often in jest] a rat-catcher. —**jungfer**, *f.* lady's maid, waiting-woman, chambermaid. —**junker**, *m.* groom of the bedchamber. —**kasse**, *f.* the prince's coffers, exchequer, treasury. *—**kätzchen**, *n.* [in jest] lady's maid, abigail. —**knabe**, *m.* page. —**lakei**, *m.* footman or lackey attending on the prince's person. —**latte**, *f.* a prop or lath to which vines are bound. —**lehen**, *n.* a fief granted by a prince of his domains; *it.* a fief granted by the board of finances or exchequer. —**leute**, *pl.* 1) gentlemen of the bedchamber. 2) officers at the board of finances. —**mädchen**, *n.*, ‡—**magd**, *f.* lady's maid [of inferior rank], waiting maid or woman, chambermaid. —mensch, *n.* a low and obsolete word for —mädchen. —mohr, *m.* a moor or negro attending on a prince's person. —musik, *f.* 1) music performed by the band of musicians appointed for the service of a prince. 2) a band of musicians appointed for the service of a prince, a prince's private band. —musikus, *m.* a musician in the service of a prince, one of the prince's private band. —pächter, *m.* farmer of a princely or public domain. —page, *m.* page attached to the prince's person. —präsident, *m.* 1) president of the board of finances. 2) president of the chamber of deputies, [in England] the speaker. 3) V. —richter. —prokurator, *m.* attorney of the exchequer or fiscal chamber. —rath, *m.* member of the board of finances or domains, counsellor of domains or finances [often a mere title]. —richter, *m.* a judge or president of the sovereign's supreme court of judicature. —sache, *f.* V. *Cameralsache. —sänger, *m.*, —sängerinn, *f.* private singer to the king, prince &c., one of the king's &c. own vocal music-band. —schlüssel, *f.* 1) the key of a chamber or room. 2) V. —herrnschlüssel. 3) [in seamen's language] forelock of a swivel-gun. —schreiber, *m.* clerk to the board of finances or to the exchequer. —sekretär, *m.* secretary to the board of finances or domains. —spiegel, *m.* bung or stopple for a gun. —stück, *n.* a piece of ordnance for throwing large stone-balls. —stuhl, *m.* 1) arm-chair. 2) close-stool. —thür, *f.* the door of a chamber, small room or closet. —tisch, *m.* table where the officers of a prince's household eat. —ton, *m.* the lower tuning of the instruments, particularly of the organ in church music. —topf, *m.* V. —becken. —trauer, *f.* minor court-mourning [which does not extend to the whole court in its largest sense]. ‡—vogtei, *f.* V. —gut. —wagen, *m.* a long covered or vaulted waggon for a prince's luggage. —weib, *n.* [unusual] waiting-woman, chambermaid. —wesen, *n.* all that relates to the domains or the fisc, [in general] the finances. —wissenschaft, *f.* the science of finances. —zahlmeister, *m.* paymaster at the exchequer &c. —zofe, *f.* V. —jungfer.

Kämmerei, *f.* 1) the office of a chamberlain, and the persons or officers who are under the chamberlain. 2) office of finances, exchequer, and the persons belonging to it.

Kämmerer, *m.* [-s, *pl.* -] 1) a man set over any chamber or department; V. Silber—. 2) chamberlain. Der päpstliche —, the chamberlain of the pope; der Cardinal—, camerlingo [chief of the apostolic chamber]. 3) [formerly] chancellor of the exchequer; *it.* V. Kammerrath, Finanzrath 2). 4) [unusual and obsolete] V. Gerichtsverwalter.

Kämmerling, *m.* [-s, *pl.* -e] 1) chamberlain. 2) [now no longer used] valet de chamber.

Kämmertuch, *n.* [-es] [instead of Cambraituch] cambrick.

Kämmling, *m.* [-es, *pl.* -e] wool that remains in the cards after combing, waste-wool.

Kämmlingseide, *f.* floret-silk that remains in the cards after combing.

Kämp, *m.* [-en, *pl.* Kämpe] [from the L. *campus*] an enclosed piece of ground, inclosure.

Kampweide, *f.* 1) the white willow. 2) the common or black sallow.

Kämpe, *m.* [-n, *pl.* -n] 1) [obsolete] champion, V. Kämpfer, Ritter. 2) [in Northern Germany] a boar.

‖**Kampelei**, *f.* [in popular lang.] bickering, dispute, quarrel, contention in words or in petulant altercation.

‖**Kämpeln**, *v. intr.* and *v. r.* sich —, [allied to keifen] to bicker, to exchange [angry] words, to dispute, to quarrel. Sie — immer mit einander, they are continually at variance or quarreling.

Kämpf, *m.* [-es, *pl.* Kämpfe] [Sax. *camp*, Sw. *capp*, which in Icelandic signifies Kämpfer; allied to the Sw. and Icel. *kippa* = raufen] combat, fight. Der — mit Lanzen, tilt, joust; — mit Fäusten, V. Faustkampf; ein hartnäckiger, blutiger —, an obstinate, bloody combat; ein — auf Leben und Tod, a desperate fight or combat; Einen zum — fordern, herausfordern, to call any one out to a combat or contest, to challenge any one to fight; den or einen — mit Einem wagen, to engage in a contest with any one, to enter the lists with any one. *Fig.* struggle, effort. Der letzte —, der Todes—, the pangs of death, agony; im letzten —e liegen, to be in agony or at the point of death, to struggle with death; es kostet [uns] manchen —, unsere Leidenschaften zu überwinden, we must fight many a battle [with ourselves] to subdue our passions; im —e mit seinen Begierden stehen or liegen, to strive against, to withstand one's desires; das menschliche Leben ist ein beständiger —, the life of man is a continual warfare.

Kampf-begier, —begierde, *f.* eager desire to fight, longing for the combat or fight. —fertig, *adj.* and *adv.* ready for the combat, ready to fight. —gefährte, —genoß, *m.* brother in arms, companion in arms. —gesang, *m.* war-song. —geschrei, *n.* war-cry, war-whoop. —gesell, *m.* V. —gefährte. —gier, *f.* V. —begier. —gierig, *adj.* and *adv.* burning with desire to fight, longing for the combat. —hahn, *m.* 1) game-cock. 2) [in nat. hist.] ruff, V. Brausehahn. *Fig.* a wrangling, quarrelsome fellow, a wrangler, disputer or disputant. —jagen, *n.* combat of wild beasts for the amusement of great personages. —lust, *f.* V. —begier. —lustig, *adj.* V. —gierig. —platz, *m.* place of combat, field of battle; *it.* arena [for gymnastic exercises]. Sich auf den —platz wagen, to enter the lists. —preis, *m.* the prize. —recht, *n.* 1) the right of fighting with any one. 2) law of fighting. —richter, *m.* judge of the combat, umpire. —schule, *f.* gymnastic school. —spiel, *n.* gymnic game, prize-fighting; *it.* V. Turnier. —wärtel, *m.* V. Grieswärtel. —weide, *f.* V. Kampweide 2).

Kämpfen, [Sax. *campian*, Lat. *campire*, V. Kampf] I. *v. intr.* to combat, to fight. Auf Leben und Tod —, to fight desperately; Hähne mit einander — lassen, to make cocks fight, to set cocks a-fighting; um den Preis —, to fight for the prize; mit den Wellen —, to struggle with the waves; mit dem Tode — [ringen], to be in agony, to struggle with death; wider die Sünde —, to strive against sin; ich habe lange mit mir selbst gekämpft, ehe ich &c., I have been debating within myself for a long time, before I &c. II. *v. tr.* to fight. Ich habe einen guten Kampf gekämpfet [in Scripture and in a higher style], I have fought a good fight. Syn. Kämpfen, Fechten, Ringen, Streiten. When several persons mutually resist one another, they streiten together, and this may take place even by mere contradiction in words. They fechten when they endeavour to do one another bodily harm; for the aim of the Fechter is to wound his adversary. Kämpfen implies a greater exertion and expense of strength; ringen a most painful and persevering conflict, as, instead of weapons, the combatants only use their limbs, and the victory can only be won by the entire exhaustion of one or the other.

1. **Kämpfer**, *m.* [-s, *pl.* -] combatant; wrestler, prize-fighter, pugilist; champion.

2. **Kämpfer**, *m.* [-s, *pl.* -] [from Kamm = any thing jutting, or from the L. *incumba*] [in architecture] impost, moulding.

Kämpher, Kämpfer, *m.* V. Campher.

Kánapee, V. Canapee.

Kanärienſekt, &c. V. Canariensekt &c.

Kándel, *m.* [-s, *pl.* -] [allied to the L. *canalis*, Fr. *canal*] channel for water, gutter.

Kandel-baum, *m.* the lilac, pipe-tree. —beere, *f.* 1) white bryony, wayfaring-tree. 2) the berry of the white bryony &c. —blüthe, *f.* flower of the lilac. —wiede, *f.* 1) V. —beere 1). 2) V. Traubenkirsche.

Kándelzucker, *m.* [-s] [Kandel, from candiren, Ital. *candire* = zu Krystall werden] sugar-candy.

Kankel, *m.* [-s] V. Zimmet.

Känguruh, *n.* [-s, *pl.* -s or -e] kangaroo.

Kanínchen, *n.* [-s, *pl.* -] [allied to the L. *caniculus*] rabbit, cony. Das weibliche —, doe rabbit; das männliche —, buck rabbit; das — ist ein sehr fruchtbares Thier, the rabbit is a very prolific animal.

Kaninchen-bau, *m.* cony-burrow. —berg, *m.* rabbit-hill, warren, cony-warren. —eule, *f.* madge-owlet, black or grey owl. —fell, *n.* rabbit-skin. —garten, *m.*, —gehäge, *n.* warren, cony or rabbit warren. —grube, *f.* V. —bau. —hohl, *n.*, —höhle, *f.* a rabbit's hole. —jagd, *f.* the hunting of rabbits. —jäger, *m.* 1) one who hunts or catches rabbits with a ferret. 2) ferret. —wärter, *m.* keeper of a warren, warrener. —wiesel, *n.* V. —jäger 2).

1. **Kánker**, *m.* [-s, *pl.* -] [little used] spider.

Kankerstein, *m.* arachnoid.

2. **Kánker**, *m.* [-s] [L. *cancer*] [in botany] canker.

Kánne, *f.* [*pl.* -n] *dim.* Kännchen, ‖Kännlein, *n.* [Sax. *canne*, allied to the L. can-is, *can*-tharus] 1) can, tankard, pot. Er hat zu tief in die — geguckt [in popular lang.], he has drunk too much, he is flustered or tipsy; V. Gieß—, Wasser—; *it.* V. Kaffee—, Milch—, Thee—. 2) [a measure for liquids which varies in different parts of Germany] a quart. Eine — Bier, a quart or pot of beer.

Kannen-birn, *f.* V. Würzbirn. —bürste, *f.* bottle-brush. —deckel, *m.* cover or lid of a can or tankard. —gießer, *m.* pewterer. *Fig.* Ein —gießer, ein politischer —gießer or Kannegießer, a would-be politician; a person who loves to talk politics. —gießerei, *f.* [not used in the proper sense, the trade of a pewterer] talking or discussing politics. Ich bin kein Liebhaber von —gießereien, I don't like political discussions. —gießern, *v. intr.* to talk or to discuss politics. —kraut, *n.* horse-tail, shave-grass. —maß, *n.* V. Kanne 2). —öhr, *n.* the ear or handle of a tankard or pot. —pflanze, *f.* [in botany] the yellow water-lily. —träger, *m.* [in botany] bandura. —weise, *adv.* by quarts or pots. —zinn, *n.* pewter.

Kánnefaß, V. Cannefas.

Kànon, V. Canon.

***Kanonáde**, *f.* [*pl.* -n] cannonade, firing with heavy guns [in battles &c.].

Kanóne, *f.* [*pl.* -n] [Fr. *canon*, Ital. *can*[illegible] allied to the L. *can*-alis] 1) [in general] a tube. Die — am Uhrschlüssel, the tube of the key of a watch or clock; [in popular language, especially students' cant] —nstiefeln or —n, jack-boots. 2) cannon, piece of ordnance, gun. [illegible] metallene, eherne —, a brass cannon; eine eiserne —, an iron gun; eine vier-, zwölf- &c. pfündige —, a four-pounder, a twelve-pounder &c; V. Vier-, Sechs-, Acht- &c. Pfünder; eine — laden, to load or charge a cannon; eine — richten, to point or level a cannon; eine — abfeuern, losbrennen, to fire a cannon; die Heere feuerten lange mit —n gegen einander, the armies cannonaded one another a long time; ein Schiff von hundert —n, a ship of a hundred guns.

Kanonen-ball, *m.* V. —kugel. —**baum**, *m.* an American tree, the stem and boughs of which are hollow, snakewood. —**boot**, *n.* gunboat. —**bürste**, *f.* V. —wischer. —**donner**, *m.* the report of cannon. Unter —donner stieg er an's Land, he disembarked under a salute of guns. —**erreich**, *m.* V. —weite. —**fest**, *adj.* proof against cannon-shot, cannon-proof. —**feuer**, *n.* the firing or discharge of cannon. —**fieber**, *n.* [in familiar language] Er hat das —fieber, he is terribly afraid of guns or fire-arms, he is a great coward. —**gut**, *n.* metal for cannon, V. Stückgut. —**herd**, *m.* V. —wall. —**keller**, *m.* casemate, V. Stückkeller, Mordkeller. —**kugel**, *f.* cannon-ball. —**ladung**, *f.* the charge of a cannon or gun. —**lauf**, *m.* the cannon [without the carriage]. —**löffel**, *m.* [gunner's] ladle. —**metall**, *n.* V. —gut. —**pulver**, *n.* gunpowder. —**schiff**, *n.* 1) a ship mounted or furnished with guns. 2) V. —boot. —**schlag**, *m.* fusee or fuse. —**schuß**, *m.* cannon-shot. Einen —schuß weit, within a cannon-shot. —**schußweite**, *f.* the range or distance a cannon will throw a ball, cannon-shot. Innerhalb der —schußweite seyn, to be within cannon-shot. —**seil**, *n.* [in seamen's lang.] gun-tackle. —**wall**, *m.* battery. —**weite**, *f.* V. —schußweite. —**wischer**, *m.* brush for cleaning the cannon, sponge.

***Kanonier**, [-es, *pl.* -e] or † and ‡ —er, [-s, *pl.* -] *m.* cannonier.

Kanonier-kammer, *f.* [in seamen's lang.] the gun-room. —**schaluppe**, *f.* V. Kanonenboot.

***Kanoniren**, I. *v. intr.* to discharge cannon, to play with large guns, to cannonade. Man kanonirte den ganzen Tag auf einander, they cannonaded one another, they exchanged guns the whole day. II. *v. tr.* to batter with cannon-shot, to cannonade. Das —, cannonade. V. Beschießen.

Kantābria, Kantābrien, [-s] *n.* Cantabria.

Kantābrier, *m.* [-s, *pl.* -] Cantabrian.

Kantābrisch, *adj.* Cantabrian.

Kánte, *f.* [*pl.* -n] *dim.* **Käntchen**, *n.* [Celt. ant = Seite, allied to the Gr. κανθός = angle of the eye] 1) [in general but seldom used] side. *Fig.* [in fam. lang.] An allen —n, on all sides, everywhere. 2) brim, border. Die — eines Glases, the brim of a glass; die — des Tuches, the border, selvedge or fag-end of cloth; die — eines Grabens, the brink or border of a ditch. 3) corner, edge. Die — eines Steines, eines Tisches, the edge or corner of a stone, of a table; die Steine, Backsteine auf die hohe — stellen, to put or lay stones, bricks lengthways and edgeways; die — eines Spiegels, the facet of a mirror. 4) lace, V. Spitzen. Ein mit —n besetztes Kleid, a garment or dress edged with lace.

Kant-apfel, *m.* calville. —**birn**, *f.* V. Würzbirn. —**haken**, *m.* a hook by which any thing is lifted and turned, an iron-hook, cant-hook, grappling-iron. *Fig.* [in vulgar lang.] neck. Einen beim —haken kriegen, to seize any one by the neck, to arrest any one. —**horn**, *n.* [a species of snails] V. Riesenohr. —**ring**, *m.* [among carpenters] a strong iron ring with an iron hook for turning timber. —**zucker**, *m.* V. Kandelzucker.

Kanten-brett, *n.* V. Kopfbrett, Mitchbrett. —**halm**, *m.* [in botany] V. Kugelbinse. —**kleid**, *n.* a garment or gown edged with lace, a laced gown. —**kraut**, *n.* horse-tail, shave-grass. —**saum**, *m.* purl or the edging of lace. —**tuch**, *n.* 1) handkerchief with a border. 2) neck-handkerchief edged with lace. —**zwirn**, *m.* thread for lace.

Kánteln, V. Kanten 2).

Kánten, *v. tr.* 1) to form with right angles, to square [a stone &c.]. 2) to put a thing upon its edge, to turn over edge. Ein Faß —, to put a cask upon its edge, to raise or tilt a cask; einen Stein — or kanteln, to turn a stone over edge or to lay it on an edge; einen Wallfisch kanteln, to turn a whale round.

Kánter, *m.* [-s, *pl.* -] velvet-weaver's oblong frame.

Kántig, *adj.* and *adv.* having edges or corners, angular, cornered, cut out in points. Eine —e Gestalt, an angular figure; einen Stein — behauen, to square a stone.

Kantille, V. Cantille.

***Kantōn**, *m.* [-es, *pl.* -e] canton. Die Schweizer —e, the cantons of Switzerland.

***Kantoniren**, *v. intr.* to be cantonised, to lie in cantonments, in separate quarters [said of a regiment of soldiers, of a large body of troops.

***Kantonirung**, *f.* cantonment.

***Kántschu**, *m.* [-es, *pl.* -e] [a short thick whip for inflicting punishment in Russia] kantschu.

Kánzel, *f.* [*pl.* -n] [L. *cancellus*; *cancelli*, *lattices*] pulpit. Die — besteigen, to mount the pulpit; Etwas von der — verkündigen, to proclaim or publish any thing from the pulpit; [in popular lang.] Einen von der — werfen, V. Abkanzeln; Verlobte von der — abkündigen or † werfen, to proclaim the bans of marriage, to bid the bans; auf der — für Jemand bitten, to pray for any one at church.

Kanzel-andacht, *f.* devotional meditation of the clergyman in the pulpit. —**beredsamkeit**, *f.* pulpit eloquence, pulpit oratory. Er besitzt viel —beredsamkeit, he has great talents for the pulpit. —**deckel**, *m.* the roof over the pulpit. —**geschwätz**, *n.* the babble or talk of a preacher or parson, cant of the pulpit. —**himmel**, —**hut**, *m.* V. —deckel. —**lied**, *n.* the hymn during the singing of which the clergyman mounts the pulpit. —**mäßig**, *adj.* and *adv.* suited to the pulpit. —**pauker**, *m.* [low] a pulpit-thumper. —**pult**, *n.* desk on the pulpit. —**rede**, *f.* sermon. —**redner**, *m.* an eloquent preacher, pulpit orator. —**sprache**, *f.* the language or style of a preacher or clergyman, pulpitical style. —**ton**, *m.* the tone or elocution of a preacher or clergyman. Er spricht im —tone [mostly used in contempt], he speaks as if he was in the pulpit. —**tuch**, *n.* pulpit cloth. —**uhr**, *f.* hourglass [on pulpits]. —**vortrag**, *m.* delivery or elocution of a preacher or clergyman; *it.* sermon.

Kanzellei, Kanzelei, [commonly] **Kanzlei**, *f.* [*pl.* -en] [L. *cancellaria*] the house or apartment where the writing business of any board or of any court of judicature &c. is carried on or where public officers transact business, office; *it.* the persons attached to such an office; V. Reichs—, Staats—, Hof—, Kriegs— &c.; *it.* [especially] the office from which writs under the great seal and public decrees are issued, chancery [but very different from the English Chancery, which is at the same time the highest court of justice next to Parliament].

Kanzellei-archiv, *n.* archives of the chancery or of any court or public office. —**archivar[ius]**, *m.* the keeper of the archives or records of the chancery or of any court or public office. —**beamte**, *m.* an officer or clerk of the chancery or of any public office. —**bote**, *m.* messenger to the chancery &c. —**buchstabe**, *m.* a sort of large letter used for engrossing, engrossing-letter. —**decret**, *n.* decree issued by the chancery. —**diener**, *m.* a servant or beadle belonging to the chancery or to a similar office. —**direktor**, *m.* director of the chancery or of a similar office. —**gebühr**, *f.* fees of the chancery &c. —**gericht**, *n.* court of chancery. —**mäßig**, *adj.* suited to the chancery &c. Ein —mäßiges Schreiben, a letter or writing drawn up in the law-style. —**papier**, *n.* a sort of fine paper. —**rath**, *m.* counsellor of the chancery. —**register**, *n.* register of the chancery. —**registratur**, *f.* the registry of the chancery &c. —**schreiben**, *n.* a decree or writ issued by the chancery or by an other great office. —**schreiber**, *m.* chancery-clerk, clerk of the chancery. —**schrift**, *f.* engrossing-hand. —**siegel**, *n.* the great-seal; *it.* the seal of any great office. —**styl**, *m.* law-style. —**verwalter**, *m.* manager or director of the chancery or of a great office. —**verwandte**, *m.* V. —beamte.

***Kanzellist**, *m.* [-en, *pl.* -en] clerk of the chancery or of a great office.

Kánzeln, *v. tr.* V. Abkanzeln.

Kanzlei, V. Kanzellei.

Kánzler, *m.* [-s, *pl.* -] chancellor. —**inn**, *f.* wife or lady of the chancellor. — der Schatzkammer [in England, corresponding to the meaning and office of the German Finanzminister], chancellor of the exchequer; der — einer hohen Schule, the chancellor of a university, V. Groß—, Reichs—, Erz—, Kron—, Staats—, Hof—, Ordens—.

Kanzlerstelle, *f.* the office of a chancellor, chancellorship.

Kanzlist, V. Kanzellist.

***Kaolin**, *m.* [-s] [in mineralogy] kaolin.

***Káp**, *n.* V. Cap.

Kapaún, *m.* [-s, *pl.* -e] [L. *capo*, allied to kappen = to castrate] capon. *Fig.* [in fam. lang., especially in jest] a castrato, a eunuch.

Kapaunen-brühe, *f.* capon-broth. —**stein**, *m.* [a gem, superstitiously believed to be found in the stomach of cocks and capons] alectoria or lapis alectorius.

Kapaúnen, *v. tr.* to capon; *it.* [applied to men] to castrate, to emasculate. Das —, the act of caponing; *it.* [of men] castration.

Kápe, *f.* [*pl.* -n] [in seamen's lang.] mainsail.

Kapellan, &c. V. Capellan &c.

1. **Káper**, *m.* V. 2. Caper.

2. **Káper**, *f.* [*pl.* -n] caper [an acid fruit]. Wilde —, bean-caper, fabago; deutsche —, V. Dotterblume, Genster.

Kapern-brühe, *f.* caper-sauce. —**rinde**, *f.* the bark of the root of the caper-bush. —**staude**, *f.*, —**strauch**, *m.* caper-bush. —**tunke**, *f.* V. —brühe.

***Kapiren**, [low] V. Begreifen, I. 1) *fig.* *b.*)

Kapitel, *n.* V. Capitel.

Kaplán, V. Capellan.

Käppchen, *n.* [-s, *pl.* -] 1) *dim.* of Kappe, a little cap. 2) [in botany] *a*) coreopsis, the tickseed sunflower. *b*) spindle-tree or prickwood, V. Spillbaum.

Kappe, *f.* [*pl.*-n] *dim.* **Käppchen**, ‖**Käpplein**, *n.* [seems to be allied to the L. *caput* = head] 1) the upper part or covering of certain things. Die — eines Backofens, the upper or vaulted part of an oven [for baking bread]; die — einer Retorte, the dome of a retort; [among tailors &c.] a patch to be sewed on the knees of trousers, elbows of coats and heels of stockings; die — am Dreschflegel, V. Flegelkappe; die — an der Deichsel, the iron which covers the end of the pole of a carriage &c.; die — des Flintenkolbens, heel-plate; die — einer Pistole, the pommel or knob of a pistol; die — an den Pistolenholftern, holster-cap; [in fortification] bonnet; [in agriculture] die — am Getreide, the case, envelop or integument of the ears of corn; die Gerste steht in —n, the barley is not yet eared; die — einer Kanone, cap of a cannon, apron; die — einer Pumpe, the hood of a pump; [among shoemakers] die —, the piece of leather with which the toe of a shoe is lined, the toe-piece, toe-lining; *it.* V. Stulpe. 2) [a covering for the head] Die — der Mönche, a monk's hood, cowl; ein Mantel mit einer —, a cloak with a cape; die — der Weiber, a woman's hood or riding-hood, V. Regen —. 3) [chiefly, a round covering for the head] a cap. Eine wollene —, a woollen cap, V. Mütze, *it.* V. Berg—, Bienen—, Falken—. *Prov.* Einem jeden Narren gefällt seine —, every man has a fool in his sleeve; gleiche Brüder, gleiche —n, tell me with whom thou goest and I will tell thee what thou doest.

Kapp-eisen, *n.* V. Kappeneisen. —**fenster**, *n.* dormer-window. —**laken**, *n.* [in seaports] hat-money. —**loch**, *n.* V. —fenster. —**stürzung**, *f.* V. Kappensturz. —**taube**, *f.* V. Kappentaube. —**weide**, *f.* sallow-tree, willow. —**zaum**, *m.* caveson or cavesson. **Fig.* Er bedarf eines —zaumes, he wants a curb. —**ziegel**, *m.* a ridge-tile or gutter-tile.

Kappen-eisen, *n.* an iron band which covers any thing. —**förmig**, *adj.* and *adv.* having the form or shape of a hood, hood-shaped. [in botany] Ein —förmiges Blatt, a cucullate leaf. —**gras**, *n.* [in botany] zizania. —**hütlein**, *n.* [in botany] Turk's cap, the mountain-lily, martagon. —**macher**, *m.* cap-maker. —**mantel**, *m.* cloak with a cape. —**mohn**, *m.* [in botany] fumiter. —**mönch**, *m.* hooded friar, capuchin. —**muskel**, *m.* [in anatomy] trapezius or cucullaris musculus. —**nonne**, *f.* 1) hooded nun. 2) V. —taube. —**pfeffer**, *m.* guinea pepper. —**robbe**, *f.* the hooded seal. —**stiefel**, *m.* top-boot. —**sturz**, *m.* rupture or break of a dike. —**taube**, *f.* columba cucullata, jacobine. —**taucher**, *m.* Virginian seamew. —**wurm**, *m.* cucullanus.

1. **Kappen**, *v. tr.* 1) [in general] to cover. Der Hahn kappt die Henne, the cock treads the hen. 2) to furnish with a cap. Einen Strumpf —, to put a piece of linen on the heel of a stocking; Stiefel —, to top boots; einen Falken —, to hood a hawk. 3) [unusual] to strike with the cap. **Fig.* Einen —, V. Abkappen 3).

Kapphuhn, *n.* pullet.

2. **Kappen**, *v. tr.* [L. *coppare*] 1) to cut, to lop. Die Bäume —, to lop trees; [in seamen's lang.] das Ankertau —, to cut the cable in the hawse. 2) to castrate, to capon. Ein gekappter Hahn, a capon.

Kapp-hahn, *m.* capon; *it.* [in fam. lang.] an angry cock. —**messer**, *n.* cleaver.

Kapper, *m.* [-s, *pl.*-] [from kappen = to cut] whale-cutter.

Kappis, *m.* [Fr. *cabus*, from the L. *caput*] or —**kraut**, *n.* headed cabbage.

Kapriole, V. Capriole.

Kapsel, *f.* [*pl.*-n] *dim.* **Käpselchen**, *n.* [L. *capsula*, from *capio* = fassen] a case, box, cover; [in botany] capsule; V. Samenkapsel.

Kapsel-band, *n.* capsular ligament. —**beere**, —**frucht**, *f.* capsular berry, fruit. —**kunst**, *f.* [in hydraulics] forcing-pump. —**staar**, *m.* membranous cataract. —**tragend**, *adj.* capsular.

Kapselig, *adj.* [in botany] capsular. Eine zwei-, drei—e Frucht, a bicapsular, tricapsular fruit.

***Kaput[rock]**, *m.* V. 1. Capot.

***Karabalki**, *pl.* bars of silver from China, karabalki.

***Karabiner**, &c. V. Carabiner &c.

***Karacke**, *f.* V. Caracke.

***Karakter**, &c. V. Charakter &c.

***Karat**, *n.* [-es, *pl.* -e] a small weight for gold and precious stones, carat. Diese Perle wiegt so viele —e, that pearl weighs so many carats.

Karatgewicht, *n.* troy-weight.

***Karatig**, *adj.* V. Karätig.

***Karätig**, *adj.* only used in composition, as: 14 —, of fourteen carats; es giebt kein 24 —es Gold, there is no gold twenty four carats fine or of twenty four carats.

Karausche, *f.* [*pl.* -n] [Dan. *karuse*, Bohem. and Polish *karas*] the crucian [a fish].

Karauschen-fisch, —**karpfen**, *m.* bastard carp. —**wurm**, *m.* the lernaea or plague.

***Karawane**, **Karavane**, [but always pronounced Karawane] *f.* [*pl.* -n] caravan.

Karawanen-thee, *m.* tea imported from China by overland caravans to Russia and thence to other parts of Europe.

***Karawanserai**, **Karavanserai**, *f.* [- or -'s, *pl.* -s or -e] caravansary, caravanserai, khan.

***Karavelle**, *f.* V. Caravele.

Karbatsche, *f.* [*pl.* -n] [Sw. *karbas*, Pers. *kyrbac* = lederne Peitsche] [low] a whip of leather, a hunting-whip, a scourge.

Karbatschen, *v. tr.* [low] to chastise with a whip of leather &c., to whip, to lash, to scourge, V. Peitschen.

Karbe, *f.* [L. *carum*] caraway.

Karbekraut, *n.* common yarrow, V. Schafgarbe.

Karbunkel, V. Carbunkel.

†**Karch**, *m.* [-es, *pl.* Kärche] a dray; *it.* V. 2. Karren.

Karcher, *m.* [-s, *pl.* -] a drayman; *it.* V. Kärrner.

***Kardamome**, *f.* [*pl.* -n] [in botany] cardamom.

Kardätsche, *f.* [*pl.* -n] [from the Ital. *cardasso*, L. *carduus*] 1) horse-brush, curry-comb. 2) card [for combing wool], carding-comb.

Kardätschen-draht, *m.* wire used in making cards, card-wire. —**haken**, *m.* tooth or hook of a card. —**macher**, *m.* one who makes cards [for carding wool]; *it.* one who makes horse-brushes. —**tisch**, *m.* carding-table.

Kardätschen, *v. tr.* 1) to brush or curry a horse. 2) to card [wool].

Kardätscher, *m.* [-s, *pl.*-] carder.

Karde, *f.* [*pl.* -n] [from the L. *carduus*] 1) V. —ndistel. 2) Spanische —, cardoon. 3) carding-instrument, card.

Karden-distel, *f.* fuller's thistle, teasel. —**kreuzholz**, *n.* carding-frame. —**setzer**, *m.* one who puts together or arranges the teasels [for raising a nap on woollen cloth].

Kardebenedict, *n.* V. Cardobenedicten-kraut.

Kardeel, *n.* [-es, *pl.* -e] [in seamen's lang.] halser or hawser.

Kardeele, *f.* [*pl.* -n] [instead of Quardeele = Viertel, from the L. *quartus*] a cask for transporting train-oil.

Karden, *v. tr.* V. Kardätschen 2).

Kardinal, V. Cardinal.

Kardone, *f.* [*pl.* -n] cardoon, V. Karde 2).

Karduse, *f.* [*pl.* -n] [from the French *cartouche*, and this from the L. *charta*] cannon-cartridge or charge.

Kardus-kiste, *f.* a chest for cannon-cartridges. —**koker** or —**kocher**, *m.* [in seamen's lang.] a cartridge-case to carry cartridges from the ship's magazine to the men in time of battle, cartridge-box or chest. —**nadel**, *f.* needle for sewing cartridges.

Karechel, *f.* [*pl.* -n] a kind of black rook, V. Haberrücke, Saatkrähe.

Karfunkel, V. Carbunkel.

Karg, *adj.* and *adv.* [seems to be allied to gierig, and the Sw. *kara* = raffen; or perhaps from the Sax. *car* = care] parsimonious, covetous, niggardly, stingy. Mit —er Hand geben, to give sparingly or niggardly; ein —er Gesell or Filz, a miserly or stingy fellow, a miser, pinchpenny, curmudgeon. *Fig.* — mit seinem Lobe seyn, to be sparing or a niggard of one's praise; — an Worten seyn, to be scanty of words; eine —e Beschreibung, a poor description; —er Boden, steril soil.

Kargen, *v. intr.* to be parsimonious, to be penurious, to be sordidly parsimonious, to be niggardly. Er kargt an Allem, he is sordidly parsimonious in every thing.

Kargheit, *f.* stinginess, parsimony, niggardliness. *Fig.* sterility [of the soil &c.].

Kärglich, *adj.* and *adv.* sparing, parsimonious, scanty. Eine —e Mahlzeit, a poor meal. — leben, to live sparingly, poorly, pitifully, to live close, to fare but scantily; — hat ihn die Natur bedacht, nature has bestowed her gifts but niggardly on him.

Karkasse, V. Carcasse.

Karl, [-s, *pl.* -e] [a name of men] Charles. — der Große, Charlemagne.

Karls-kirsche, *f.* V. Kornelkirsche. —**vogel**, *m.* V. Blaukehlchen.

Karlovinger, *subst.* Carlovingian.

Karmin, V. Carmin.

Karnieß, *m.* [-sses, *pl.* -e] *dim.* —**chen**, *n.* [allied to the Gr. κορωνίς] [in architecture] cornice.

Karnieß-blei, *n.* [among glaziers] window-lead in the shape or form of a cornice. —**eisen**, *n.* channeling or grooving iron. —**gesimse**, *n.* an architrave crowned with a cornice, cornice-architrave. —**hobel**, *m.* [among joiners] plough. —**stahl**, *m.* a steel or chisel for turning cornices.

‖ and †**Karniffeln**, or **Karnüffeln**, *v. tr.* to beat with the fist, to pommel, to buffet, to cuff, to thump.

Kärnthen, *n.* [-s] Carinthia.

Kärnther, *m.* —**inn**, *f.* a native of Carinthia, Carinthian.

Karoline, *f.* V. 2. Carolina.

Karolinger, V. Karlovinger.

Karolingisch, *adj.* Carlovingian.

Kárpfen, *m.* [-s, *pl.* -] [Low L. *carpa, carpio*] carp [a fish]. Ein männlicher, weiblicher —, a soft-roed, hard-roed carp; einen — reißen, to draw or eviscerate a carp.

Karpfen-behälter, *m.* V. —hälter. —brut, *f.* fry of carp. —hälter, *m.* carp-pond. —karausche, *f.* V. Karausche. —könig, *m.* V. Spiegelkarpfen. —kopf, *m.* 1) jowl or head of a carp. 2) a kind of sphinx or hawk-moth. —kraut, *n.* common yarrow, V. Schafgarbe. —maul, *n.* V. —schnauze. —satz, *m.* V. —brut. —schnauze, *f.* the mouth or snout of a carp. —schwanz, *m.* V. —kopf 2). *Fig.* —sprung, *m.* somerset. —stein, *m.* [a triangular bone at the hinder part of a carp's jowl] carp-stone. —teich, —weiher, *m.* carp-pond.

***Karpie**, *f.* V. Charpie.

Karpie-bäuschlein, *n.* lint-stopple. —wälzer, *m.* [in surgery] dossil.

***Karpolíth**, *m.* [-en, *pl.* -en] [in mineralogy] carpolite.

Kárre, *f.* [*pl.* -n] [L. *carrus*, allied to *curro*, Fr. *char*; the Sw. *car* is a vessel] wheel-barrow. Einen zur — verurtheilen, Einen an die — schmieden, to condemn any one to work at fortifications &c. [with the wheel-barrow].

1. **Kárren**, *m.* [-s, *pl.* -] [probably from the old karen = schneiden] [among goldbeaters] a tool, consisting of two sharp knive-blades, for squaring the gold or silver-leaves.

2. **Kárren**, *m.* [-s, *pl.* -] [V. Karre] cart. Ein — voll Holz, a cart-load of wood; [in printing] carriage. †*Fig.* Er hat den — in den Koth geschoben, he has embroiled, entangled or perplexed the matter or affair; der — ist verfahrt, it is an intricate affair or the affair is intricate; er läßt den — stehen, he leaves the matter or all in confusion, he leaves it to others to unravel or to clear up the matter; laßt den — stehen, do not with or in this business; an einem schweren — ziehen, to be at a dead lift, to be badly off; to be in great misery or distress; noch immer an demselben — ziehen, to do still the same hard or disagreeable work, still to toil hard for a livelihood.

Karren-balken, *m.* the beam or pole of a cart. —büchse, *f.* a gun moved upon a cart or carriage; *it.* [an old name for] a cannon. —führer, *m.* V. Kärrner. —gabel, *f.* the shafts of a cart. —gaul, *m.* cart-horse. —gefangene, *m.* V. Baugefangene. —gestell, *n.* the frame of a cart. —gleis, *n.* cart-rut. —läufer, *m.* miner that draws the wheel-barrow. —rad, *n.* cart-wheel. —salbe, *f.* grease for carts &c. —schieber, *m.* a wheelbarrow-man. —schoppen, *m.* a pent-house for carts &c. —spur, *f.* V. —gleis. —strafe, *f.* the working at fortifications &c. [punishment]. —wagen, *m.* a waggon drawn by horses in file [not two abreast].

Kárren, I. *v. intr.* to draw a wheel-barrow; [in popular lang.] to drive slowly. II. *v. tr.* 1) to carry by a wheel-barrow or cart, to cart. 2) [in popular lang.] Einen über den Haufen —, to overthrow or overturn any one with a wheel-barrow or cart.

Kärrner, or **Kärner**, *m.* [-s, *pl.* -] the man who drives a cart, carter; *it.* V. Kärcher.

Kárſche, *f.* V. Karausche.

Kárst, *m.* [-es, *pl.* -e] [either from kehren to turn, or from the old karen = schneiden] a mattock; *it.* a pickaxe.

Kársten, *v. tr.* to work with the hoe or mattock, to hoe [vines &c.].

Kartätſche, *f.* [*pl.* -n] [from the Fr. *cartouche*, this from the L. *charta*] 1) cartouch, case-shot, canister-shot, grape-shot. Mit —n schießen, to fire with case-shot or grape-shot. 2) V. Karbätsche 2).

Kartätschen-büchse, *f.* case, box or canister filled with case-shot or langrel. —fasser, *m.* V. —büchse. —feuer, *n.* a discharge of case-shot. —futter, *n.* V. —büchse. —futteral, *n.* the wooden case holding the case-shot, cartouch. —kasten, *m.* chest for the cartouches filled with case-shot. —kugel, *f.* the ball in a cartouch, cartouch. —schuß, *m.* case-shot.

Kartaúne, *f.* [*pl.* -n] [probably from the L. *quartana* = Geschütz 4ter Größe] a short heavy cannon or gun, carronade. Eine ganze —, a forty eight pounder; eine halbe —, a twenty four pounder.

Kartaunenpulver, *n.* gun-powder.

Kárte, *f.* [*pl.* -n] [from the L. *charta*, Gr. χάρτης, from the verb χαράσσω = kratzen, schreiben] 1) card. *a*) visiting-card. *b*) playing-card. Ein Spiel —n, a pack of cards; die —n mischen, to shuffle; —n spielen, to play at cards; die —n abheben, to cut; die abgehobene —, breef card; die —n geben, to deal; das —ngeben, deal; wer hat —n zu geben or an wem ist das —ngeben? whose deal is it? or who is to deal? die —n falsch geben, vergeben, to misdeal; eine — verwerfen or wegwerfen, to discard, to lay out; ich habe gute —n bekommen, I have got or taken in fine cards; ich habe schlechte —n, I have no good cards; niedrige —n, small cards; die meisten —n von Einer Farbe haben, to go out with a suit, to carry a suit; die meisten —n von Einer Farbe zu kaufen suchen, to lay out for a colour; —n schlagen, to tell fortunes by or upon the cards. *Prov.* Einem in die —n sehen, schauen, gucken, to spy out any one's design; er durchschaut die —n, he is in the plot or secret; aus Einer — spielen, to act secretly in concert with any one, to collude with any one. 2) map, V. Land—; chart, V. Seeküsten—. Die — von einem Lande entwerfen, to survey a country; die — von Deutschland, the map of Germany; [a sea-term] die — stechen, pricken, to prick the chart; platte or gleichgradige —, plane chart. 3) V. Musterkarte. 4) charter. Die französische —, the French charter; die große —, [*magna charta] magna-charta.

Karten-bild, *n.* image or figure on a card. *Fig.* a bad picture or portrait. —blatt, *n.* a single card. —geld, *n.* 1) card-money [paid for the cards to the waiter or servant of the house, by those who play]. 2) stake [at cards]. —haus, *n*, *dim.* —häuschen, ‖—häuslein, *n.* a little house made of cards, a paste-board building. *Fig.* *Sein — haus ist umgeblasen, his chimerical project has been frustrated or balked. —könig, *m.* king in a pack of cards *Fig.* a mock king. —kunst, *f.* a trick played with cards. —künstler, *m.* one who plays tricks with cards; *it.* a sharper. —macher, *m.* card-maker. —macherei, *f.* [*—fabrik] manufactory of cards. —mahler, *m.* one who paints cards, limner of cards, card-painter. *Fig.* a dauber. —mahlerei, *f.* 1) the painting or limning of cards. 2) bad painting, daubing. —papier, *n.* 1) card-paper, strong paper [like that of which cards are made]. 2) the paper or envelop in which a pack of cards is wrapped. —presse, *f.* card-press. —sammlung, *f.* [*Atlas] a collection of maps, atlas. —schlagen, *n.* the act of telling fortunes by or upon the cards. —schläger, *m.*, —schlägerinn, *f.* a person who tells fortunes by or upon the cards. —spiel, *n.* 1) the playing at cards, card-playing. Er liebt das —spiel, he is fond of playing at cards or he likes to play at cards. 2) a game at cards. —spielen, *n.* V. —spiel 1). —spieler, *m.* player at cards, card-player, carder. —stamm, *m.* V. —geld 2). —stecher, *m.* an engraver of maps and charts. —stempel, *m.* 1) stamp for cards. 2) stamp on cards. 3) the act of stamping cards.

***Kartél**, V. Cartel.

Kárten, I. *v. intr.* to play at cards; *it.* to shuffle. II. *v. tr. fig.* [in fam lang.] to give a turn to a thing, to turn, to plan, to contrive. Er weiß das Spiel or es zu —, he knows how to concert measures accordingly; man muß die Sache anders —, we or they must give another turn to the matter. V. Abkarten.

Karthaúne, *f.* &c. V. Kartaune.

Karthaúſe, &c. V. Carthause &c.

Kartóffel, *f.* [*pl.* -n] [corrupted from Erdapfel] potato.

Kartoffel-acker, *m.* 1) V. —boden. 2) a field of potatoes. —anbau, —bau, *m.* culture of potatoes. —boden, *m.* soil or land good for potatoes. —branntwein, *m.* brandy made of potatoes. —brei, *m.* pap or flummery made of potatoes, mashed potatoes. —brod, *n.* bread the dough of which is mixed with potatoes. —ernte, *f.* crop or harvest of potatoes. —feld, *n.* V. —acker 2). —grube, *f.* a hole or pit in which potatoes are preserved during winter. —kloß, *m.* pudding or dumpling of potatoes. —kraut, *n.* the herb or stalks of potatoes. —mehl, *n.* potato-meal. —salat, *m.* salad made of potatoes.

Kartúſche, *f.* V. Cartouche.

Kárve, *f.* V. Kerbel.

Karyatiden, *pl.* V. Caryatiden.

Käs, *m.* [-es, *pl.* -e] [Goth. *kas* = Gefäß, allied to the Fr. *châssis*] [in papermills] the bottom of the trough.

Käſe, *m.* [-s, *pl.* -] [L. *caseus*; from the D. *kadden* = schütteln, L. *quatio*] 1) curdled milk, curd. 2) [chiefly] cheese; V. Kräuter—, Kuh—, Kümmel—, Parmer—, Schaf—, Schmier—, Schweizer—, Streich—; holländischer —, Dutch cheese; ist dieser — alt oder jung or frisch? is this cheese old or new? *Fig.* Der — der Artischocke, the bottom of an artichoke; der — eines Baumes, the clod of earth that sticks to the root of trees when they are plucked up.

Käse-blume, *f.* pasque-flower, Flora's bell. —bohrer, *m.* cheese-borer. —bude, *f.* cheese-monger's shop, V. —laden. —butter, *f.* a soft cheese which may be spread like butter, cream-cheese. —fladen, *m.* V. —kuchen. —form, *f.* cheese-mould, cheese-frame. —förmig, *adj.* having the form or shape of a cheese. —frau, *f.* 1) a woman who makes cheese 2) a woman who deals in cheese. —geld, *n.* 1) money given to servants for cheese. 2) money got by the sale of cheese. —grempel, *m.* cheese-mongery. —gülte, *f.* rent paid in cheese. —handel, *m.* trade in cheese. —händler, *m.*, —händlerinn, *f.* a person who deals in or sells cheese, cheese-monger. —haus, *n.* cheese-house. —hobel, *m.* cheese-scoop. —horde, —hürde, *f.* hurdle or crate on which cheeses are dried. —kammer, *f.* cheese-room. —kitt, *m.* a cement made of curds or cheese. —kohl, *m.* cauliflower. —korb, *m.* a basket or crate for drying cheese. —kram, *m.* V. —handel. —krämer, *m.*, —krämerinn, *f.* V. —händler &c. —kraut, *n.* savory, satureia. —kuchen, *m.* cheese-cake. —lab, *n.* runnet for making cheese, cheese-lip. —laden, *m.* cheese-monger's shop. —laib, *m.* a loaf of cheese, a whole cheese. —leim, *m.* glue made of cheese. —made, *f.* maggot found in cheese. —markt, *m.* cheese-market. —meise, *f.* titmouse. —miethe, —milbe, *f.* mite found in cheese. —mutter, *f.* the woman who superintends the making of cheeses. —napf *m.* cheese-bowl, cheese-vat; *it.* cheese-mould.

—pappel, *f.* the round-headed or dwarf mallow. —rinde, *f.* the rind or paring of cheese, cheese-paring. —*service, *n.* cheese-tray. —stecher, *m.* 1) V. —bohrer. 2) cheese-taster. —wasser, *n.* V. Molken. —wurm, *m.* V. —made. *Fig.* one who eats much cheese. —zins, *m.* V. —gülte.

Käsen, I. *v. intr.* to curd, to curdle. II. *v. tr.* to turn any thing to cheese, to make cheese of any thing.

Kaserne, *f.* V. Caserne.

Käsicht, *adj.* and *adv.* resembling cheese, cheese-like. — aussehen, to look pale or ill.

Käsig, *adj.* and *adv.* cheesy. Die —en Theile der Milch, the caseous parts of milk.

Kaspar, *m.* [-s] [a name of men] Jasper.

Kasse, *f.* [*pl.* -n] [Ital. *cassa*, Fr. *casse*, *caisse*, allied to the L. *gaza*, Germ. Katze, Goth. *kas* = Gefäß] chest, chiefly for holding money, money-box. *Fig.* *a*) ready money, cash. Bei — seyn, to be in cash. *b*) fund destined for any thing, treasure; V. Armen—, Kriegs—, Wittwen— &c. *c*) treasury. Gehen Sie zur —, und Sie werden bezahlt werden, go to the treasury and you will be paid.

Kassen-amt, *n.* the office of cashier or treasurer; *it.* treasury. —beamte, *m.* an officer of the revenue. —berauber, *m.* V. —dieb. —beraubung, *f.* V. —diebstahl. —bestand, *m.* clear amount, balance of cash. —betrug, *m.* V. —diebstahl. —betrüger, *m.* V. —dieb. —buch, *n.* cash-book. —defraudant, *m.* V. —dieb. —dieb, *m.* peculator. —diebstahl, *m.* peculation, embezzlement of public money or goods. —führer, *m.* cash-keeper, cashier, treasurer. —führung, *f.* the administration, keeping or charge of money. —geld, *n.* 1) current coin or money. 2) the money contained in a box. 3) clear amount, balance of cash. —gewicht, *n.* gold weights. —münze, *f.* V. —geld 1). —raub, *m.* V. —diebstahl. —räuber, *m.* V. —dieb. —rechnung, *f.* cash-account. —rechnungsführer, *m.* cashier. —schein, *m.* [*—billet, *n.*] a check or draft on a public treasure. —sturz, *m.* [*—revision, *f.*] the inspection or examination of any treasure or cash. —verwalter, *m.* V. —führer. —verwaltung, *f.* V. —führung.

Kassier, *m.* [-s, *pl.* -e] or —er, *m.* [-s, *pl.* -] V. Kassenführer and Cassier.

***Kastanie,** *f.* [*pl.* -n] chestnut. Die große, eßbare —, V. Marone; die wilde uneßbare —, horse-chestnut; V. Roß—, Pferde—.

Kastanien-apfel, *m.* a sort of apple. —baum, *m.* chestnut-tree. Der wilde —baum, the horse-chestnut-tree. —braun, I. *adj.* chestnut coloured, chestnut. —braune Haare, chestnut [coloured] hair. II. *n.* chestnut-colour. —eiche, *f.* Indian rose-chestnut. —haar, *n.* chestnut [coloured] hair. —holz, *n.* chestnut-wood. —land, *n.* 1) soil or land good for chestnuts. 2) a country in which there are a great many chestnut-trees. —mehl, *n.* chestnut-meal. —pflanzung, *f.* a plot of chestnut-trees, chestnut-plot. —rose, *f.* V. —eiche. —schale, *f.* the capsule of the chestnut. —stein, *m.* a chestnut-like stone. —wald, *m.*, —wäldchen, *n.* chestnut-grove, chestnut-plot.

***Kaste,** *f.* [*pl.* -n] [in the East-Indies and in ancient Egypt] cast.

Kastengeist, *m.* *Fig.* a narrow, proud and exclusive spirit of cast, of a person belonging to a certain rank or class.

Kasteien, *v. tr.* [from the L. *castigo*]. Den Leib, sich —, to inflict voluntary pain upon the body for the good of the soul, to mortify, to macerate the body. [in fam. lang. often used jocosely] Das —, V. Kasteiung. Syn. Kasteien, Züchtigen. A father züchtiget his child, a schoolmaster his perverse pupils; the repentant devotee kasteiet [mortifies] himself with fastings and by wearing a hair-shirt next his skin. Züchtigungen are reasonable when suited to the offence, to the age, sex and moral condition and character of the person chastised. Kasteiungen are, with regard to their aim, absurd and superstitious; in their execution often cruel, and in some cases, opposed to the end they have in view.

Kasteiung, *f.* [*pl.* -en] mortification, maceration [of the flesh].

Kastell, *n.* V. Castell.

Kastellan, &c. V. Castellan &c.

Kasten, *m.* [-s, *pl.* Kästen] *dim.* Kästchen, ||Kästlein, *n.* [allied to Kiste, Goth. *kas* = Gefäß] 1) [in general, a case or box containing certain things] Der — Noahs, Noah's ark; der — eines Klaviers, the case or frame of a harpsichord; [among jewellers] der — [eines Ringes], bezil, collet; [among locksmiths] der — am Schlosse, box of a lock; der — an der Orgel, organ-case; der — einer Kutsche, the body of a coach; [among clothiers] der —, frizing-frame; [among gardeners] der —, case; Pomeranzenbäume in Kästen setzen, to case orange-trees; [among hunters] V. Hirschkasten; der — or das Kästchen eines Zahnes, hole or socket of a tooth. *Fig.* [formerly, and obsolescent] fund, treasure, V. Kasse, Almosen—, Armen—, Gottes—, Stadt—. 2) [chiefly] cupboard, chest, press. In den — legen, packen or sperren, to lay up in a chest. *Fig.* [in popular lang.] Einem hinter den — gehen, kommen, to steal any one's money. *Prov.* Kisten und — voll haben, to have every thing in abundance, to have plenty of every thing. Syn. Kasten, Kiste, Koffer, Lade, Truhe. Kiste [Lat. cista] is a low chest, made either of wood or metal, with a lid, and used to keep or secure any thing in. Kasten is higher, has usually a door and can be locked. Lade or Truhe, is a chest of a peculiar form and mostly in use only among the common people. Koffer answers exactly to the English trunk.

Kasten-amt, *n.* the administration of a public fund or treasure; *it.* revenue-office, treasury. —bediente, *m.* V. —knecht. —blech, *n.* the plate that covers a lock. —deckel, *m.* the cover or lid of a chest or box. —herr, *m.* 1) [formerly] a person set over a certain fund or treasure, treasurer, cashier. 2) [obsolete or provincial] overseer of a public granary. 3) V. Almosenpfleger. ||—knecht, *m.* V. —herr 2). —kunst, *f.* V. Eimerkunst. —macher, *m.* one who makes boxes or chests, box- or chest-maker. —meister, —pfleger, *m.* V. —herr. —schiff, *n.* V. Arche 4). —schreiber, *m.* clerk at a public revenue-office. —schwand, *m.* diminution of the corn in the cornloft by drying. —stampf, *m.* [among goldsmiths and jewellers] puncheon. —verwalter, *m.* V. —herr. —vogt, *m.* 1) the patron of a convent. 2) V. —herr 2). —vogtei, *f.* the administration of the estates belonging to a convent or church.

Käster, *m.* [-s, *pl.* -] [in pipe-manufactories] he who forms the pipes, moulder.

Kästner, *m.* [-s, *pl.* -] V. Kastenherr.

***Kastor,** &c. V. Castor &c.

Kastrol, *n.* [-s, *pl.* -e] V. Casserole.

Kasuar, V. Casuar.

***Katachrese,** *f.* [*pl.* -n] [a figure in rhetoric, an abuse of a trope or of words] catachresis.

***Katafalk,** *m.* [-s, *pl.* -e] a tomb of state, a funeral decoration, catafalco.

***Katakomben,** *pl.* catacombs [subterraneous vaults for the burial of the dead].

***Katakustik,** *f.* [that part of acoustics which treats of reflected sounds] catacoustics.

***Katalepsie,** *f.* catalepsis, catalepsy, V. Starrsucht.

***Kataleptisch,** *adj.* cataleptic, V. Starrsüchtig.

***Katalog,** *m.* [-s, *pl.* -e] catalogue.

***Kataplasm,** *m.* or **Kataplasma,** *n.* [-s, *pl.* -men] poultice, cataplasm.

***Katarakt,** *m.* [-es, *pl.* -e] 1) a great fall of water over a precipice, cataract. 2) [in medicine and surgery, an opacity of the crystalline lens] cataract.

***Katarrh,** *m.* [-s, *pl.* -e] a catarrh, a cold. Ich habe mir dort einen — geholt, I caught a cold there

Katarrhalfieber, *n.* catarrhal fever.

***Katarrhalisch,** *adj.* catarrhal, catarrhous.

***Kataster, Kadaster,** *n.* [-s, *pl.* -] register of lands, [especially] the book in which the assessed taxes are entered, V. Steuerbuch.

***Katastriren, Kadastriren,** *v. tr.* to enter into the register, of lands [especially] to enter the assessed taxes in a book.

***Katastrophe,** *f.* [*pl.* -n] catastrophe or catastrophy.

Kätchen, *n.* [-s, *pl.* -] [*dim.* of Katharine] Kate, Kitty.

***Katechese,** *f.* the act of catechising.

***Katechet,** *m.* [-en, *pl.* -en] catechiser, catechist.

***Katechetik,** *f.* the Socratic or catechetical method of instruction.

***Katechetisch,** *adj.* catechetical.

***Katechisation,** *f.* the act of catechising.

***Katechisiren,** *v. tr.* to chatechise. Das —, V. Katechese.

***Katechismus,** *m.* [*pl.* -men] catechism.

***Katechumen,** *m.* [-s, *pl.* -en] catechumen.

***Kategorie,** *f.* [*pl.* -en] category.

***Kategorisch,** *adj.* and *adv.* categorical. — behaupten, to affirm categorically.

Kater, *m.* [-s, *pl.* -] male-cat, tom-cat.

Katharine, *f.* [-ns, *pl.* -n] [a name of women] Catharine.

Katharinen-alaun, *m.* alumen catinum, pot-ash. —birn, *f.* a sort of pear. —blume, *f.* 1) the common yellow toadflax. 2) the small fennel-flower. —pflaume, *f.* prunello.

***Katheder,** *m.* [-s, *pl.* -] lecturing-desk, professor's chair.

***Kathedralkirche,** *f.* [*pl.* -n] cathedral church, cathedral.

***Kathete,** *f.* [*pl.* -n] [in geometry] cathetus.

***Katheter,** *m.* [-s, *pl.* -] [in surgery] catheter.

***Katholicismus,** *m.* catholicism.

***Katholik,** *m.* [-en, *pl.* -en] —inn, *f.* a Roman-catholic.

***Katholisch,** *adj.* and *adv.* catholic, Roman catholic. Die —e Religion, the catholic religion; der —e Glauben, the catholic faith; der —e König, the catholic king [of Spain]; — werden, to embrace the catholic religion, to turn catholic; die —en Briefe, the catholic epistles.

***Katholisiren,** *v. tr.* to convert, to bring over to catholicism or the catholic creed.

***Katoptrik,** *f.* catoptrics, V. Spiegelkunst.

***Katoptrisch,** *adj.* and *adv.* catoptric, catoptrical.

Kättanker, *m.* &c. V. Katzanker &c.

Kattūn, *m.* [-es, *pl.* -e] (from the Fr. *coton*, Eng. *cotton*] stuff made of cotton, cotton-cloth, cotton, calico. Ostindischer —, printed calico.

Kattun=alabaster, *m.* alabaster of Rüdigsdorf [in Thuringia]. —binse, *f.* cotton-grass. —drucker, *m.* calico-printer. —druckerei, —fabrik, *f.* manufactory of printed calico. —erz, *n.* ore of Nagyak [in Hungary]. —form, *f.* form or mould for printing calico. —leinwand, *f.* cotton cloth, cotton, calico. —nadel, *f.* a very large pin. —papier, *n.* painted paper. —presse, *f.* calico-press. —stein, *m.* V. —alabaster. —weber, *m.* calico-maker or weaver. —weberei, *f.* manufactory of calico. —wolle, *f.* 1) cotton. 2) cotton-plant, cotton-shrub.

Kattūnen, *adj.* made of cotton, cotton. Ein —er Schlafrock, a cotton night- or dressing-gown.

Kätzbalgen, *v. r.* sich — [in fam. language], to scuffle, to wrestle, to fight.

Kätzbalger, *m.*, —inn, *f.* one who scuffles, scuffler.

Katzbalgerei, *f.* scuffle or scuffling, quarrel, wrestling.

1. **Kätze**, *f.* [probably from the old quad = übel, böse, schlimm, Ital. *cattivo*, allied to the Brittannic *quaez* = Elend] a pulmonary disorder peculiar to miners.

2. **Kätze**, *f.* [*pl.* -n] *dim.* Kätzchen, *n.* [allied to Haut, L. *cutis*, Kutte; the provincial Kotze = any thing woolly, Low L. *cotzia*] [in botany] cat-kin, cat's-tail.

3. **Kätze**, *f.* [*pl.* -n] [either allied to the L. *cos*, Germ. Kies or to quad, V. 1. Katze] brittle slate.

4. **Kätze**, *f.* [*pl.* -n] [seems to be allied to the Goth. *kas* = Gefäß, to the Germ. Kasten, Fr. *gousset*, Sw. *kudde* = a pocket] 1) a long bag for holding money, which in the shape of a girdle is fastened round the waist, money-belt, V. Geldkatze. 2) [in fortification] a cavalier.

5. **Kätze**, *f.* [*pl.* -n] [allied to the Fr. *jeter*, L. *jactare*, Sw. *kasta* = werfen, to the Goth. *kesan*, and Fr. *chasser* = treiben, as also to the Germ. haschen, Eng. to *catch*] 1) any instrument or mechanical contrivance for holding fast. *a*) [in ship-building, an interior rib, reaching from the keelson to the beams of the lower deck, to strengthen her frame] girder. *b*) [in seamen's lang.] a kedge-anchor. *c*) a large post set in the ground on a bank or in docks, to which ships are fastened, bollard. *d*) an iron hook for demolishing houses &c. *e*) a fisherman's hook. 2) any thing that drives, pushes, throws &c. or that is driven, pushed, thrown &c. *a*) catch-ball, tennis &c. V. Katzball. *b*) V. Katzschiff. *c*) swivel-gun. *d*) battering-ram. *e*) [Stripse] cat o' nine-tails.

Katz=anker, *m.* kedge-anchor. —bahn, *f.* tennis-court. —ball, *m.* 1) catch-ball, tennis-ball. 2) tennis, tennis-play. —block, *m.* [in seamen's lang.] cat-block. —haken, *m.* [in seamen's lang.] cat-hook. —löcher, *pl.* [in seamen's lang.] cat-holes. —rolle, *f.* V. —block. —schiff, *n.* [a ship from four to six hundred tons burden] cat. —sparren, —sporen, *pl.* [in seamen's lang.] riders.

6. **Kätze**, *f.* [*pl.* -n] [Fr. *chat*, D. *kat*, Eng. *cat*, L. *catus*] cat. *Dim.* Kätzchen, Kätzlein, *n.* little or young cat, kitten. Die Kätzinn, she-cat, puss; wilde —, wild cat; zahme —, Haus—, tame, domestic cat; brasilische —, carcajo; Ihre — ist trächtig, your cat with kitten; diese — mauset gut, this cat is a good mouser; *er lauert auf ihn, wie die — auf die Maus, he watches him as narrowly as a cat eyes a mouse; wie eine — schreien [miauen], to mew; *sie nascht, sie ist leckerhaft wie eine —, she is very dainty, as dainty as a cat; *sich wegschleichen wie die — vom Taubenschlage, to go away in a mist, to steal away, to take French leave; *wie die Hunde und —n leben, to agree like cat and dog; *prov.* er geht um die Sache herum, wie die — um den heißen Brei, he handles that matter like a hot iron, he goes about the bush. *Fig.* and *prov.* Eine — im Sacke kaufen, to buy a pig in a poke; die — läuft ihm den Rücken hinan, he is in great trepidation, he is alarmed or frightened; wenn die — fort ist, so tanzen die Mäuse auf dem Tische, when the cat is away, the mice play; sieht doch wohl die — den Kaiser an, a cat may look upon a king; wer wird der — die Schelle anhängen? who will bell the cat? bei Nacht sind alle —n grau, when candles are out, all cats are grey, Joan is as good as mylady in the dark; eingesperrte —n fressen keine Mäuse, a cat in mittens never caught a mouse; das ist für die — [in popular lang.], that is a mere trifle, is good for nothing.

(*) **Katzen=art**, *f.* species of the cat; *it.* the nature of cats. —artig, *adj.* and *adv.* cat-like. —artige Freundschaft, feigned, false friendship. —auge, *n.* 1) greenish-gray coloured eye. 2) a species of onyx, cat's eye. —äugig, *adj.* and *adv.* having eyes like a cat, cat-eyed. —baldrian, *m.* wild valerian. —balg, *m.* cat's skin or fur. —balsam, *m.* cat-mint, V. —münze. ‡—bart, *m.* mustaches. —bauch, *m.* [in conchology] a sort of porcelain-shell. —blei, *n.* V. —glimmer. —blume, *f.* the wood anemone. —blut, *n.* [in botany] the vervain, the holy herb. —buckel, *m.* 1) [low] the bent back of a cat. *Fig.* Einen —buckel machen, to cringe, to crouch, to fawn. †2) bow, curtsy, V. 1. Bückling. †—dreck, *m.* the excrements of a cat. —eier, *pl.* [in botany] lily of the valley, may-lily. —fell, *n.* V. —balg. —fett, *n.* grease of the wild cat. —fisch, *m.* cat-fish. —fuß, *m.* 1) V. —pfote. 2) [in botany] cat's foot. —geschrei, *n.* cry of cats, caterwauling. —gesicht, *n.* [in botany] stinking dead-nettle, galeopsis. *Fig.* [in popular lang.] a face or countenance full or expressive of cat-like propensities, malice &c., cat-like physiognomy; *it.* a face shaped round like a cat's. —glas, *n.* Muscovy glass. —glimmer, *m.* mica. —gold, *n.* yellow mica or glimmer. —grau, *adj.* gray like a cat. —igel, *m.* [in botany] water-hemp. —jammer, *m.* [in popular lang., especially students' cant] the sickness occasioned by drinking too much, crapulence. —kerbel, *m.* V. Erdrauch. —kiesel, *m.* a species of quartz. —klar, *n.* V. —glimmer. —klaue, *f.* 1) the paw of a cat. 2) [in botany] V. Trompetenblume; *it.* V. —pfötchen 1). —klee, *m.* 1) clown's wound-wort, lady's finger, kidney vetch, vulneraria rustica; *it.* hare's foot trefoil, lagopus. 2) Gelber —klee, the hop trefoil. —kopf, *m.* 1) cat's head. *Fig.* [in popular lang.] a head shaped round like a cat's. 2) [in seamen's language, a short wooden bar to be thrust into a hole of the windlass, on which to fasten the cable] norman. 3) a small mortar. —korn, *n.* the wall-barley grass, the way-bennet. —kraut, *n.* 1) V. —münze. 2) the marum germander or cat-thyme. 3) wild valerian. 4) horse-tail, shave-grass. 5) a species of hyssop. —leben, *n.* *Fig.* [in popular lang.] a tough life. Er hat ein —leben, he has nine lives, as many lives as a cat. —liebe, *f.* 1) *Fig.* false love. 2) [in botany] V. —münze. —loch, *n.* cat's hole. —luchs, *m.* a kind of white and black spotted lynx. —magen, *m.* [in botany] the corn-poppy, the corn-rose. —metall, *n.* V. —glimmer. —münze, *f.* cat-mint. —musik, *f.* *Fig.* [in popular lang.] paltry music, mock music, charivari. —öhrlein, *n.* [in botany] V. Bischofsmütze 2). —parder, *m.* the serval. —peterlein, *n.* common hemlock. —pfötchen, ‖—pfötlein, *n.* [in botany] 1) the four-leaved mimosa. 2) the red or common pimpernel, the corn pimpernel, the poor man's weather glass. 3) spindle tree, prickwood. 4) cat's foot. 5) creeping mouse-ear, pilosella. 6) V. —klee 1). —pfote, *f.* paw of a cat. —saphir, *m.* female sapphire. —scheu, I. *f.* aversion to cats. II. *adj.* afraid of cats. Er ist —scheu, he is afraid of cats or he has an aversion to cats. —schlau, *adj.* and *adv.* sly, cunning like a cat. —schlauheit, *f.* slyness or cunning of cats; *it.* cat-like slyness or cunning. —schrei, *m.* V. —geschrei. —schwanz, *m.* 1) a cat's tail. *Fig.* V. Fuchsschwanz. 2) [in botany] *a*) V. —münze. *b*) shave-grass, V. Schaftheu. *c*) [a species of reed] cat-tail or cat's-tail. —schwanzgras, *n.* the naked cupped canary-grass. †—seiche, *f.* urine of cats. —silber, *n.* cat-silver. —sprung, *m.* the leap of a cat, a cat's leap. *Fig.* [in popular lang.] Es ist nur ein —sprung dahin, it is but a short or little way thither. —stert, *m.* 1) [provincial] V. —schwanz 1). 2) [in botany] V. Kannenkraut. 3) [in seamen's lang.] rolling-hitch. —tiger, *m.* the tiger-cat. —tisch, *m.* *Fig.* [in popular language] a table in a corner. Am —tische essen, to eat alone in some corner [a punishment for children]. —traube, *f.* [in botany] mountain knot-grass, illecebra. —vogel, *m.* fly-catcher of Carolina. —wedel, *m.* V. —schwanz. —wolf, *m.* lynx. —wurzel, *f.* V. —kraut 3). —zagel, or —zahl, *m.* V. —schwanz.

(*) Sämmtliche Composita von Katze sind hier, wenn schon nicht von dem nämlichen Grundworte herkommend, dennoch zusammengestellt, um Verwirrung zu vermeiden.

(*) All the compounds of Katze, though not of the same root, are placed together, in order to avoid confusion.

Kätzchen, *n.* [-s, *pl.* -] or ‖Kätzlein, *n.* [-s, *pl.* -] *dim.* of 2. and 6. Katze. —tragend, [in botany] amentaceous.

Kätzelkraut, *n.* [-es] hare's foot trefoil, lagopus.

Kätzeln, *v. intr.* [in fam. lang.] to kitten.

Kätzen, *v. tr.* to pull down or demolish with hooks.

‖**Kätzlein**, *n.* [-s, *pl.* -] *dim.* of 2. and 6. Katze, V. Kätzchen.

Kaú or **Kaúe**, *f.* V. Kaa.

‖**Kaúchen**, *v. intr.* to squat, to cower, V. Hokken, Hucken and 2. Kauen.

Kaúdelwiede, *f.* [*pl.* -n] white bryony, wayfaring tree.

‖1. **Kaúder**, *m.* [-s] [also Kuder, perhaps from the L. *culcita*, and this from *culco*, *calco* = zusammenstopfen] 1) a distaff-full. 2) tow, V. Werg.

‖2. **Kaúder**, *m.* [-s, *pl.* -] [from kaudern = to speak unintelligibly] a turkey cock, turkey.

Kauder=wälsch, —welsch, *adj.* and *adv.* [in popular lang.] unintelligible, resembling gibberish. —wälsch sprechen or schwatzen, to speak gibberish, to speak a broken language or an odd kind of dialect, to jabber; ich verstehe sein —wälsch, sein —wälsches Geschwätz nicht, I do not understand his gibberish. —wälschen or —welschen, *v. intr.* V. —wälsch sprechen.

Kauderei, *f.* [V. 1. Kaudern] usury in trifling things.

‖1. **Kaúdern**, *v. intr.* [seems to be derived from the old heuern = miethen &c.] to higgle.

‖2. **Kaúdern**, *v. intr.* [V. 2. Kauder] to cry as a turkey. *Fig.* V. Kauderwälsch sprechen.

Kaue, *f.* [*pl.* -n] [allied to the L. *cavea*, Germ. Käfig, L. *cav-us* = hohl] 1) coop, cage. 2) a narrow partition in a stall for sheep. 3) V. Kaa.

1. **Kauen**, *v. tr.* [allied to hauen, the old kiefen = nagen, V. Kiefer] to chew, to masticate, to champ. Fleisch —, to chew meat; † *fig.* Einem Etwas in's Maul —, V. Vorkauen; ein Pferd, das an seinem Gebisse kauet, a horse that champs the bit. Das —, mastication.

Kau-gebiß, *n.* a slabbering bit. V. also Tränsgebiß. —**mittel**, *n.* [in medicine] masticatory. —**muskel**, *m.* masseter. —**pfeffer**, *m.* betel. —**zahn**, *m.* a jaw-tooth, grinder.

2. **Kauen, Kauern**, [Eng. *to cower*, allied to the Fr. *coucher*] *v. intr.* and *v. r.* sich —, to squat, to cower.

Kauer, *m.* [-s, *pl.* -] —**inn**, *f.* 1) a person who chews. 2) [in anatomy] V. Kaumuskel.

Kauern, V. 2. Kauen.

Kauf, *m.* [-es, *pl.* Käufe] [Sax. *ceap*, Icel. *kaup*] 1) the act of buying, purchase, bargain, emption. Einen — schließen, richtig machen, to make up, to conclude, to strike a bargain; er machte einen guten —, he made a good purchase; einem Andern in den — stehen, treten, fallen, to take a bargain out of another's hands, to outbid another, to interfere with another; er ist mir in den — getreten, he outbid me; Etwas durch — an sich bringen, to buy, to purchase any thing. *Prov.* [especially in law] — bricht Miethe, purchase has the preference above or before hiring or hire, rescinds a hiring-contract. 2) [an agreement or contract concerning the sale of property] bargain. Der — ist gültig, ist ungültig or gilt nichts, the bargain is valid or good in law, is null or void; einen — rückgängig machen, to make void, to annul or nullify a bargain; den — brechen, umstoßen, to break a bargain; Etwas in den — einbingen, to include any thing in the bargain; Etwas auf or in den — geben, to give any thing into the bargain. 3) the price [paid for any thing]. Bessern —es [wohlfeiler] werden, to fall in price, to grow cheaper; Sie haben dieses wohlfeilen —es bekommen, you got that very cheap; [among vine-dressers] Käufe und Schläge, the current prices of wine. **Fig.* Glauben Sie nicht, so leichten —es wegzukommen, do not think to come off so cheap; er wird es schon nähern —es geben, I am sure he will yield or submit at last. 4) the money to be paid for any thing, V. Hand—, Leib—, Reu—.

Kauf-anschlag, *m.* 1) estimate of a thing which is to be sold. 2) a bill or paper posted up to advertise the sale of any thing. —**bar**, *adj.* that is to be bought or sold, saleable, marketable. —**begierde**, *f.* a strong desire of buying or purchasing any thing. —**begierig**, *adj.* and *adv.* eager or anxious to buy. —**brief**, *m.* a document testifying the purchase of a thing, purchase-deed. —**buch**, *n.* 1) a public book in which the sales and purchases are entered. 2) [in commerce] book of accounts, journal. —**fahrer**, *m.* 1) a ship of trade, a merchantman; [in seamen's lang.] a [regular] trader. 2) the captain or owner of a merchantman. —**fahrtei**, *f.* navigation for the purpose of commerce, V. Seehandel. —**fahrteiflotte**, *f.* fleet of merchantmen. —**fahrteischiff**, *n.* ship of trade, merchantman. —**frau**, *f.* a woman engaged in trade, V. —männinn. —**geld**, *n.* 1) purchase-money. 2) earnest-money. —**gericht**, *n.* tribunal of commerce, board of trade. V. Handelsgericht. —**gier**, *f.*, —**gierig**, *adj.* V. —begierde, —begierig. —**glätte**, *f.* litharge for sale. —**gott**, *m.* the God of commerce, Mercury. —**gut**, *n.* merchandize. V. —mannsgut. —**handel**, *m.* [opposed to Tauschhandel] commerce, traffick. —**handlohn**, *m.* V. Handlohn; *it.* V. —lehen 2). —**haus**, *n.* 1) a public warehouse; *it.* custom-house. 2) a merchant's house, trading-house. 3) a house where the merchants meet. 4) a building containing shops and warehouses, bazar. —**herr**, *m.* the head of a mercantile house, great merchant. —**kontrakt**, *m.* V. —vertrag. —**laden**, *m.* merchant's shop; grocer's shop. —**lehen**, *n.* 1) a fief which after having been sold may be repurchased. 2) a duty payable by the purchaser of an estate. —**leinwand**, *f.* linen made for sale [opposed to Hausleinwand]. —**leute**, *pl.* persons buying and selling, purchasers; *it.* merchants, tradespeople, tradesmen, shopkeepers. —**lust**, *f.* inclination to buy or to purchase. —**lustig**, *adj.* and *adv.* inclined to buy. Die —lustigen, persons inclined to buy, purchasers, chapmen. —**mann**, *m.*, *pl.* —leute. 1) merchant, tradesman, shopkeeper. Ein —mann im Großen, a wholesale dealer or merchant; ein —mann im Kleinen, a retailer, a shopkeeper. 2) purchaser, customer, chapman. SYN. Kaufmann, Handelsmann, Krämer. The term Kaufmann virtually implies that the goods in which he carries on his business are bought [gekauft] by him. Handelschaft is more comprehensive than Kaufmannschaft. This seems to be the reason why a Kaufmann imagines he acquires a sort of honorable distinction by assuming also the title of Handelsmann. Krämer is a retail seller. He must therefore deal in many articles in order to obtain a quick return of the usually small capital he has to embark. —**männinn**, *f.* the wife of a merchant; *it.* any woman engaged in trade, a tradeswoman, a trading-woman. —**männisch**, *adj.* and *adv.* in the manner of a merchant, merchant-like, mercantile. —männische Ausdrücke, mercantile terms; das ist gut —männisch, that is quite in the manner of a merchant or quite merchant-like. —**mannsballen**, *m.* bale or pack of goods. —**mannsbrauch**, *m.* usage, custom or practice of or with merchants. —**mannsbuch**, *n.* book of accounts, journal. —**mannschaft**, *f.* 1) the body of merchants, society of merchants. 2) the science and business of a merchant. 3) trade, traffick, commerce. —**mannsdiener**, *m.* merchant's clerk; *it.* shopman. —**mannsfrau**, *f.* V. —männinn. —**mannsgeist**, *m.* mercantile spirit. *Fig.* a speculating or enterprising person. —**mannsgewölbe**, *n.* a merchant's shop. —**mannsgut**, *n.* merchandize. —**mannshand**, *f.* mercantile hand-writing. —**mannsjunge**, *m.* a merchant's or shopkeeper's apprentice, V. Handelslehrling. —**mannsladen**, *m.* V. —laden. —**mannsstand**, *m.* mercantile line, trade. —**mannsthaler**, *m.* [an imaginary coin] merchant's dollar. —**mannswaare**, *f.* V. —mannsgut. —**platz**, *m.* place where purchases are made, mercantile place, trading-place. —**preis**, *m.* the price for which a thing is sold. —**recht**, *n.* V. Handelsrecht. —**schilling**, *m.* 1) purchase-money. 2) earnest-money. —**schlag**, *m.* bargain. —**schoß**, *m.* fine of alienation. —**spiel**, *n.* [not much used] [*Piquet] piquet. —**stadt**, *f.* mercantile or trading town, V. —platz. —**sucht**, *f.* eager desire or inclination to buy or purchase. —**süchtig**, *adj.* eager or anxious to buy. —**vertrag**, *m.* contract concerning the sale of property. —**weise**, *adv.* V. Käuflich 2). —**zettel**, *m.* V. —anschlag 2).

Kaufen, *v. tr.* [allied to the Lat. *capio* = nehmen and to *caupo* = Kleinhändler] to buy, to purchase. Von wem haben Sie das gekauft? of whom have you bought that? auf Borg —, to buy upon trust; er hat den Garten wieder an sich gekauft, he has repurchased the garden; ich habe es um hundert Thaler gekauft, I have bought it for a hundred dollars or I have paid a hundred dollars for it; Etwas über dem Werthe, zu theuer —, to pay too highly for, to pay too much for any thing; ich habe ihm mein Pferd zu — gegeben, I have sold him my horse; [in cards] —, to take in, to exchange [cards]; wie viel — Sie? how many [cards] do you want or take? die gekauften Karten, cards exchanged or taken in; taking in; ich habe gute Karten gekauft, I have taken or got in fine cards; ich habe nichts or schlecht gekauft, I have got in scandalous cards. Das —, the act of buying or purchasing; das — geistlicher Aemter [considered as a crime], simony. SYN. Kaufen, Erkaufen, Einkaufen, Erhandeln. We kaufen what we pay money for; we erkaufen that which is acquired by purchase; we kaufen ein what is designed for use and consumption; we erhandeln what we buy when it is obtained after long bargaining about the price.

Käufer, *m.* [-s, *pl.* -] —**inn**, *f.* one who buys or purchases, buyer, purchaser, chapman, customer. Zu dieser Waare finden sich immer — or Liebhaber, this commodity sells very well, goes off very well; dieses Pferd wird leicht einen — finden, this horse will easily find a purchaser.

Käuflich, *adj.* and *adv.* 1) that may be bought. Dort sind die größten Würden —, there the greatest dignities of the state are venal. 2) by purchase. Etwas — an sich bringen, to buy, to purchase any thing; Einem eine Sache — überlassen, to sell any thing to any one.

Käuflichkeit, *f.* venality.

Käufling, *m.* [unusual] [-es, *pl.* -e] a bought or purchased child.

***Kaukasus**, *m.* Caucasus.

***Kaukasisch**, Caucasian. Die —e Race, der —e Menschenstamm, the Caucasean race.

Kaule, *f.* [*pl.* -n] ball, bullet, V. Kugel.

Kaul-arsch, *m.* 1) [provincial and very vulgar] round backside or posteriors. 2) *a*) V. —[illegible]. *b*) V. —börs. *c*) V. —frosch. —**bars**, *m.* V. —börs. —**beere**, *f.* the berry of the white bryony. —**börs**, *m.* [a fish] ruff or ruffe. —**frosch**, *m.* tadpole. —**haupt**, *n.* 1) V. —börs. 2) V. —kopf 2). —**huhn**, *n.* a hen or fowl with a roundish rump without a tail. —**kopf**, *m.* 1) V. —börs. 2) [a fish] miller's thumb. —**kröte**, *f.* tadpole. —**padde**, *f.* V. —frosch. —**quappe**, *f.* V. —börs.

Kaulicht, *adj.* and *adv.* round, globular, V. Kugelicht.

Kaum, *adv.* [Low Sax. *kum*, old Germ. kume, allied to Kummer; old Germ. kumig = traurig] 1) with difficulty, hardly, scarce or scarcely. Er kann — lesen, he can hardly read; ich kannte ihn —, I scarcely knew him; ich kann es — glauben, I can hardly believe it; er ist — der Gefahr noch entgangen or entronnen, er ist — noch entwischt, he had a very narrow escape. 2) just now, just. Wir sind — heim gekommen, we are just come in; die Sonne war — aufgegangen, als wir &c., the sun was scarce or just up, when we &c. — war „der Geist der Gesetze" erschienen, als &c., no sooner had the Spirit of Laws appeared, than &c.

Kaupelei, *f.* [in popular lang.] 1) the act of bartering or exchanging, barter. 2) cheat, imposition, tricking.

Kaupeln, *v. intr.* [allied to the L. *capio* and *caupo*, and to kaufen] to barter, to exchange.

Kaupenpflug, *m.* [-es, *pl.* -pflüge] V. Wiesenhobel.

Kaupler, *m.* [-s, *pl.* -] —**inn**, *f.* barterer.

Kausche, *f.* [*pl.* -n] [allied to the Fr. *gousse*, *gousset*, Goth. *kas* = Gefäß] [in seamen's lang.] thimble, bull's eye, traveller.

Kauscher, V. Koscher.

***Kaustik**, *f.* the art of etching.

*Käustik, *f.* the art of etching.

*Kaustisch, *adj.* and *adv.* caustic. *Fig.* Ein —er Mensch, a snappish or waspish man.

Kaute, *f.* [*pl.* -n] [allied to Kaue, Gr. καύτη] a small pit.

*Kauterisiren, *v. tr.* to cauterise.

*Kauterisation, *f.* cauterization, cautery.

Kautscher, V. Gautscher.

*Kautschuk, *n.* [-s] caouchouc. V. Federharz.

Kauz, *m.* [-es, *pl.* -e] *dim.* Käuzchen, ‖Käuzlein, *n.* [seems to be derived from kauzen, gauzen = heulen] screech-owl. *Fig.* an odd fellow. Ein wunderlicher —, a queer fellow or blade; ein durchtriebener, listiger —, a cunning blade; ein reicher —, a rich fellow.

Kauzeule, *f.* V. Schleiereule.

‖Kauzen, *v. intr.* [Low Sax. *kutsen*, Fr. *coucher*] to stoop, to duck. *Fig.* [in popular lang.] to submit.

Kaviar, *m.* [-s, *pl.* -e] caviar.

*Kawacke, *f.* amber, sea-amber, V. Bernstein.

Käy or Key, &c. V. Kai, Kei &c.

*Kazike, *m.* [-n, *pl.* -n] [king or chief among several tribes of Indians in America] Cazic or Cazique.

‡Kebsdirne, *f.* [Kebs, either from the L. *cubo*, or from the old Kebse = Magd, maid-servant, who was frequently chosen as a concubine by the master] concubine.

‡Kebsehe, *f.* [*Concubinat] concubinage.

‡Kebsfrau, *f.* V. —dirne.

‡Kebskind, *n.* [-es, *pl.* -er] bastard or natural child.

‡Kebsmann, *m.* [-es, *pl.* -männer] a man living with a woman in a state of concubinage.

‡Kebssohn, *m.* [-es, *pl.* -söhne] bastard or natural son.

‡Kebstochter, *f.* [*pl.* -töchter] bastard or natural daughter.

‡Kebsweib, *n.* [-es, *pl.* -er] V. —dirne.

Keck, *adj.* and *adv.* [allied to Queck in Quecksilber, and to be-weg-en] 1) quick, nimble. 2) [in poetry] fresh, not impaired; [in painting] lively, bright. Eine —e Farbe, a lively or bright colour. 3) active, sprightly, lively, gay. 4) fearless, bold; *it.* pert, saucy. Er ist wohl so —, or — genug, es zu thun, he is so bold as to do it; ein —er Streich, a bold stroke or attempt, a rash or daring enterprise; ein —er Mensch, an audacious man; ein —es Mädchen, a pert girl; ich bin nicht so *—, es zu sagen, I am not so bold as to say it, I dare not say it; greifet *— zu, take freely; wir müssen ihn *— machen, we must inspire him with courage or spirit, must encourage him.

Kecke, *f.* V. Keckheit.

Keckheit, *f.* boldness, daringness, assurance, pertness, sauciness.

Kecklich, *adv.* [chiefly in fam. language] boldly, without fear, without hesitation. Sagen Sie es ihm —, tell him so boldly, without fear.

Keep, *f.* [*pl.* -e] [in seamen's lang.] notch or channel.

Keering, *m.* [-es, *pl.* -e] [in seamen's lang., formerly] case of the mast.

1. Keffer, *m.* [-s] [in mineralogy] granulous tin-ore; *it.* base tin-ore.

‖2. Keffer, *m.* [-s] [probably instead of Heber] a wooden crane, pivot; [in salthouses] — or —rad, an engine or wheel turned by walking in it, a treading-wheel.

‖3. Keffer, *m.* [-s, *pl.* -] [probably allied to Koder, Käsch] a small light boat on the Elbe, skiff.

1. Kegel, *m.* [-s, *pl.* -] [allied to Kugel] 1) a body, the thickness of which decreases towards one end or extremity. Der — eines Pferdes, the shoulder-bone of a horse; [among gunsmiths] catch; [in artillery] sight [for aiming], V. Visier, Richt—; [among letter-founders] depth of a letter, V. Schrift—; [among watch- or clock-makers] fusee; [in geometry] cone. Die Achse des —s, the axis of the cone; ein gerader, senkrechter —, a right cone; ein schiefer —, a scalene cone; ein rechtwinkeliger —, a rectangular or orthogonal cone; ein stumpfwinkeliger —, an obtusangular cone; ein stumpfer —, a truncated cone. 2) kayle, pin. Ein Spiel —, a set of nine-pins; — spielen, to play at nine-pins or at skittles; die — aufsetzen, to set up the nine-pins; viel — werfen, machen, to carry or throw down a good many pins; alle neun — werfen, to tip all nine. *Prov.* Zwischen — und Kugel kommen, to be in a sad dilemma, to be between the hammer and anvil. 3) sign for an ale-house. 4) bone for making lace.

Kegel-achse, *f.* [in geometry] the axis of the cone. —ader, *f.* V. Bugader. —aufsetzer, *m.* the lad or man who sets up the nine-pins. —bahn, *f.* a place for playing at nine-pins or kayles, bowling-path, skittle-ground. —birn, *f.* a conical pear. —figur, *f.* conical figure, conoid. —fläche, *f.* conical surface. —form, *f.* conical form, conoid. —förmig, *adj.* and *adv.* conical, coniform. Eine —förmige Figur, a conic figure; [in conchology] —förmige Schnecken, turbinated shells. —geld, *n.* 1) stake at nine-pins. 2) money paid for the use of a bowling-path. —gestalt, *f.* V. —figur, —form. —käfer, *m.* beetle with a conical corcelet, cistela. —kasse, *f.* 1) box into which the money paid for the use of a bowling-path is put. 2) V. —geld 1). —kugel, *f.* bowl. ‖—leich, *n.* V. —bahn. —linicht, *adj.* and *adv.* [*parabolisch] parabolical. —linie, *f.* conic line, parabola. —linig, *adj.* and *adv.* parabolical. —platz, *m.* place for playing at nine-pins, bowling-place, skittle-ground. —schieber, *m.* player at nine-pins. —schnecke, *f.* the small rough whelk. —schnitt, *m.* conic section. —schnittlinie, *f.* [in geometry] ellipsis. —schnittlinig, *adj.* and *adv.* [*elliptisch] elliptical. —schub, *m.* 1) V. —spiel. 2) V. —platz. —schwamm, *m.* conical agaric. —spiel, *n.* the game at nine-pins. —spieler, *m.* player at nine-pins. —stand, *m.* V. —platz. —stein, *m.* conical or pointed echinite. —tragend, *adj.* coniferous. —tute, *f.* voluta, volute. —weizen, *m.* cone-wheat.

2. Kegel, *m.* [-s, *pl.* -] [derivation uncertain] bastard; only used in the [popular] phrase: Er hat weder Kind noch —, he has neither kid nor kin.

Kegeler, Kegler, *m.* [-s, *pl.* -] V. Kegelspieler.

Kegelicht, *adj.* and *adv.* conic, V. Kegelförmig. —er Käfer, V. Kegelkäfer.

Kegeln, I. *v. intr.* to play at nine-pins. II. *v. tr.* [rather unusual] to make conical, to give a conical form.

Kehlchen, *n.* [-s, *pl.* -] V. Kehle.

Kehle, *f.* [*pl.* -n] *dim.* Kehlchen, *n.* [L. *gula*, allied to hohl, Gr. κοῖλος] 1) [in general] a long cavity, a gutter, channel, flute, chamfer; [in architecture and in fortification] gorge. Die — an den Schnecken des Capitals, channel of a volute; die — eines Daches, the hollow channel between two roofs. V. Kale—. 2) throat, gorge. Eine enge, weite — haben, to have a narrow, wide throat; aus voller — lachen, to laugh immoderately, to split one's sides with laughing; sie hat eine herrliche —, she has a sweet voice or pipe; ein Laut or Ton, der aus der — kömmt, a guttural sound or note; Etwas in die unrechte — bekommen, to get any thing into the windpipe; Einen bei der — fassen, packen, to take or seize any one by the throat, to collar any one; sich die — abschneiden, to cut one's throat; Einem die — zuschnüren, to choak, to strangle any one; †sich die — schmieren, to moisten one's inside, to drink; †sein Vermögen durch die — jagen, to waste or squander away one's fortune by habitual drinking. Syn. Kehle, Gurgel, Schlund. Kehle comprehends both the windpipe and the esophagus in their whole length. The Gurgel is the entrance of the larynx, and consequently, externally, that part of the neck immediately under the chin, and, internally, that part of the Kehle which is seen on opening the mouth wide. The Schlund is the esophagus between its origin and the stomach, by means of which the food is ver-schlungen or swallowed.

Kehl-ader, *f.* jugular vein. —balken, *m.* collar-beam, top-beam, wind-beam. —bauchflosser, V. —flosser. —braten, *m.* 1) V. Halsbraten. 2) V. Kader. —bräune, *f.* V. Halsbräune. —brett, *n.* [among joiners] board for channeling the tringles or listels &c. —buchstabe, *m.* [*Gutturalbuchstabe] guttural letter. —deckel, *m.* [in anatomy] flap of the throat, epiglottis, epiglot. —deckeldrüse, *f.* gland of the epiglottis. —drüse, *f.* jugular or laryngean gland. —flosser, *m.* fish of the jugular order. —haken, *m.* [a bird] green plover. —hobel, *m.* grooving or channeling plane, plough. —holz, *n.* V. Hartriegel. —knopf, *m.* 1) [in anatomy] V. —kopf. 2) [a plant] hydrangea. —knoten, or —kopf, *m.* larynx, Adam's apple. —kopfsast, *m.* artery of the larynx. —kopfshaut, *f.* tunic of the larynx. —kopfsnerv, *m.* nerve of the larynx. —kopfsschlagader, *f.* V. —kopfsast. —kraut, *n.* 1) throat-wort, V. Halskraut. 2) Alexandrian laurel, V. Zaukenblatt. —laut, *m.* guttural sound. —lauter, *m.* V. —buchstabe. —leiste, *f.* [in architecture] talon, ogee. —linie, *f.* [in fortification] line of the gorge, demigorge. —punkt, *m.* [in fortification] the point where the two lines of the gorge meet, point of the gorge. interior polygone, the centre of a bastion. —riemen, *m.* neck-strap, throat-band. —rinne, *f.* hollow gutter, [chiefly] gutter between two roofs. —schnalle, *f.* throat-buckle. —sparren, *m.* jack-rafter. —stein, *m.* V. —ziegel. —stoß, *m.* 1) V. —leiste. 2) V. —hobel. —stück, *n.* neckpiece of an armour, gorget. —sucht, *f.* V. Halsbräune and Halsfeifel. —winkel, *m.* [in fortif.] angle of the gorge, V. —punkt. —wurz, *f.* the white waterlily, water-rose. —zäpflein, *n.* the uvula or top of the palate. —ziegel, *m.* gutter-tile.

Kehlen, *v. tr.* to hollow, to flute, to chamfer, to groove. Eine Säule —, to flute a column; einen Fisch —, to cut the throat of a fish, to draw a fish; die Häringe —, to gut the herrings.

Kehling, *m.* [-es, *pl.* -e] fresh cod or cod-fish.

Kehlung, *f.* 1) the act of hollowing, fluting, gutting &c. 2) V. Kehlhobel.

Kehr, *f.* [*pl.* -en] turn, turning, V. Heim—, Rück—, Um—, Wieder—, Zurück—.

Kehren, [allied to the Gr. γῦρος = Kreis, and κορεῖν = kehren and fegen] I. *v. intr.* Nach

Hause —, to return home, V. Zurück —. Kehrt machen [in milit. affairs], to turn or wheel round; rechtsum kehrt euch! right about face! II. *v. tr.* 1) to turn. Das Oberste zu unterst —, to put or turn a thing upside down or topsy-turvy; die Augen gen Himmel —, to turn one's eyes towards heaven; die Füße ein- or auswärts —, to turn one's toes in or out; Einem den Rücken —, to turn one's back to any one. *Fig.* Das Glück hat ihm den Rücken gekehrt, fortune has deserted him; eine Sache zum Besten —, to turn a thing well, to give it a good turn; die Sache zu seinem Besten —, to turn things to one's advantage. 2) to clean with a broom or brush, to sweep, to brush. Ein Zimmer —, to sweep a room; den Schornstein —, to sweep the chimney; seinen Hut — or bürsten, to brush one's hat. *Prov.* Kehre vor deiner Thür, sweep before your door. [in seamen's lang.] Die See —, to drag or sweep the bottom for a lost anchor or cable. III. *v. r.* Sich an Etwas —, to care for a thing, to be concerned for, to mind, to regard a thing; er kehret sich an nichts, he cares for nothing.

Kehr-ab, —aus, *m.* [a peculiar sort of dance, made use of at the conclusion of the diversion] sweep-dance. **—besen,** *m.* broom [for sweeping]. — **bürste,** *f.* clothes-brush. **—frau,** *f.* a woman who sweeps [chiefly the streets]. **—kleid,** *n.* gown with a train, V. [the more usual word] Schleppkleid. **—seite,** *f.* the reverse [of a coin &c.]. — **wieder,** *n.* blind-alley, V. also Sackgasse. — **wisch,** *m.* a mop or whisk, duster; *it.* a wisp of straw used for wiping dust or dirt. **—zehnte,** *m.* fieldrent. Den —zehnten einziehen, to collect the fieldrent. **—zehnteinnehmer, —zehntherr,** *m.* fieldrent collector. **—zehntscheuer,** *f.* the lord of the manor's barn for laying up the fieldrent. **—zeile,** *f.* a line frequently repeated.

Kehricht, *n.* [-s] sweepings. V. Schutt, Unrath.

Kehricht-faß, *n.*, **—kasten, —korb,** *m.* dust-basket. **—haufen,** *m.* heap of sweepings or dust. **—käfer,** *m.* black-beetle. **—winkel,** *m.* dust-corner.

‖ and †**Keib,** *m.* [-s] carcass, carrion. *Fig.* rascal, cheat, rogue.

Keibgeier, *m.* carrion-kite, horse-kite.

‖**Keiche,** *f.* [*pl.* -n] prison, jail.

Keichen, V. Keuchen.

Keife, Kiefe, *f.* V. Kiffe.

Keifen, *v. intr.* [originally beißen] to bark, to yelp. *Fig.* to scold, to upbraid, to chide. Syn. Keifen, Schmälen, Schelten. We keifen one who is present; but we schmälen and schelten also at the absent. We keifen sometimes from ill-humour, but we schmälen and schelten only from anger. We can schelten with a single word (V. Scheltwort). Schimpfen, however, is used in the same way (V. Schimpfwort). If we are only in a slight degree angry with any one, we can schmälen (chide) at him. It is the mildest expression of indignation.

Keifer, *m.* [-s] [seldom used] grumbler, scolder.

Keiferinn, *f.* a shrew, a scold.

Keifisch, *adj.* and *adv.* grumbling, scolding, shrewish.

Keil, *m.* [-es, *pl.* -e] *dim.* **Keilchen,** *n.* [Low Sax. *kiel*, Sw. *kil*, Wendish *kloju* = hauen, stechen, spalten] 1) [the denomination of several oblong bodies] *a)* [in artillery] coin, V. Richt—. *b)* [among printers] quoin. *c)* [in seamen's lang.] Die kleinen —e, the nuts of the anchor, V. Mast—, Schicht—, Stapel—, Vor—. *d)* [in architecture] the key-stone of a vault. *e)* Der — an Strümpfen, the clock of a stocking, V. Zwickel. *f)* [formerly, in military affairs, a body of troops drawn up in the form of a wedge] wedge. *g)* [among shoemakers] the wedge of a stretcher or last cleft in two. 2) [chiefly] wedge. Ein eiserner —, an iron wedge. *Prov.* Ein — treibt den andern, one nail drives out another; auf einen groben Klotz gehört ein grober —, a rude, unmannerly or clownish fellow must be treated rudely or roughly.

Keil-artig, *adj.* and *adv.* cuneal, V. —förmig. **—bein,** *n.* [in anatomy] the sphenoid bone. **—beinnaht,** *f.* sphenoidal suture. **—berg,** *m.* [in mining] rock in the form of a wedge. — **fäustel,** *m.* a hammer used by miners for driving in the wedges. **—förmig,** *adj.* and *adv.* wedge-shaped, cuneated. Eine —förmige Schlachtordnung, a cuneal battle-array. [in anatomy] cuneiform. [in botany] Ein — förmiges Blatt, a wedge-shaped leaf. **—fortsatz,** *m.* [in anatomy] clinoid apophysis. **—hacke,** *f.* wedge-shaped hoe or mattock. **—haken,** *m.* [a bird] curlew. **—hammer,** *m.* V. —fäustel. **—haue,** *f.* a pick axe for digging in stony ground. **—holz,** *n.* wood to be split by wedges. **—kraut,** *n.* saxifrage. **—loch,** *n.* [among joiners] the hole of a plane. **—steg,** *m.* [among printers] V. Schrägsteg. **—stein,** *m.* key-stone of a vault. **—stück,** *n.* 1) a wedge-shaped piece. 2) a piece of ordnance charged by the breech.

Keilen, I. *v. intr.* and *v. r.* sich —, to take the shape of a wedge, to become or to be wedge-shaped or cuneiform. II. *v. tr.* 1) Etwas —, to drive in or fasten any thing as a wedge or in the form of a wedge. *Fig.* [in vulgar lang.] Ein Stück Brod hinein —, to eat up eagerly, to devour a slice of bread; er kann gut —, he is a great eater, a glutton. 2) to cleave or to fasten with a wedge or with wedges, to wedge. †3) *Fig.* Einen —, to bang, to maul, to thrash any one. †4) *Fig.* [especially in students' cant] Etwas —, to buy any thing. V. Verkeilen.

Keiler, *m.* [-s, *pl.*-] wild boar.

Keim, *m.* [-es, *pl.* -e] *dim.* **Keimchen,** ‖**Keimlein,** *n.* [allied to the L. *cyma*, Gr. κῦμα, and L. *gemma* = etwas Erhabenes; according to others allied to the Gr. γεννᾷν = erzeugen, to Kind &c.] germ, first bud or shoot of a plant. Der — des Getreides, der Eichel &c., the germ of corn, of acorns &c. *Fig.* origin, first principle. Der — des Glückes, the germ of prosperity; der — der Tugend, the germ or seed of virtue.

Keim-blume, *f.* the sandy everlasting. **—hülle,** *f.* perisperm, albumen. **—monat,** *m.* blossom-month. **—voll,** *adj.* and *adv.* full of germs; *fig.* full of promise, of talents &c. **—zeit,** *f.* blossom-season, germination.

Keimen, *v. intr.* to germinate, to sprout, to bud, to shoot. *Fig.* to take a beginning, to arise, spring up. Das Wort Gottes hat in seinem Herzen gekeimt, the word of God has sprung up in his heart; —de Liebe, dawning love.

Kein, [-er, -e, -es] *adj.* [from nihein or enhein, in which en = nie, never; kein was originally = ein. Afterwards en was omitted and kein received a negative signification, like the Fr. *jamais*, from jemahls, and *personne* from the L. *persona*] 1) [formerly] some, any. [in Scripture] Habt ihr auch je Mangel gehabt? sie sprachen, nie —en, lacked ye any thing? and they said nothing. 2) not any, no; *it.* [sometimes] not a, not. Er hat —ne Kinder, he has no children; haben Sie — Geld? nein, ich habe —es, have you no money? no, I have none; das ist eine Stadt und — Dorf, that is a town and not a village; es sind —e fünfzig Mann, there are not fifty men; er darf —en Wein trinken, he must not drink wine; der Ueberwinder einer Welt ist — so großer Mann, als &c., the conqueror of a world is not so great a man as &c; dieß ist —großer Garten, this is not a large garden, this garden is not large; —er weiß, wo er ist, no one or nobody knows where he is; er ist —er der Stärksten, he is none of the strongest; ich kenne deren —en, I know none of them; sagen Sie es —em, tell it to nobody; von meinen Büchern ist —es gebunden, not one of my books is bound; —er von Beiden, neither [of them], neither the one nor the other; es mit —em halten, to be on neither side, to take neither part; er hat —e Frau und —e Kinder, he has neither wife nor children.

Keinerlei, *adj.* [indeclin.] of no sort. Auf — Weise, in no manner, in no wise or way, by no means, upon no account; — Mittel, no remedy.

Keinerseits, *adv.* on neither side.

Keineswegs, *adv.* noways, nowise, by no means, upon no account, not at all. Das war mir — angenehm, that was not at all agreeable to me; ich zweifle — daran, I have not the least doubt of it, I do not in the least doubt it.

Keinmal, *adv.* not once, never. V. Nie, Niemals. *Prov.* Einmal ist —, one act does not make a habit.

Keinseitig, *adj.* [*neutral] neutral.

Keinseitigkeit, *f.* [*Neutralität] neutrality.

Kelch, *m.* [-es, *pl.* -e] [Bohem. *kalich*, L. *calix*, Gr. κύλιξ, allied to hohl, Gr. κοῖλος, to Kehle, Kehle, Hölle &c.] 1) [in general] any thing hollow; [in botany] flower-cup, empalement, calix. 2) [chiefly] bowl, cup, chalice. Aus einem —e trinken, to drink out of a cup. *it.* communion-cup, chalice. *Fig.* Den — der Leiden trinken, leeren, to suffer great hardships, extreme misery or distress; der — der Freuden, der Trübsale, the cup of delights, of afflictions; mein Vater, ist es möglich, so gehe dieser — von mir [in Scripture], O my father, if it be possible, let this cup pass from me.

Kelch-artig, *adj.* and *adv.* having the form or shape of a cup, resembling a cup. — **blume,** *f.* calycanthus. **—deckel,** *m.* the cover of the chalice, patin. **—förmig,** *adj.* having the shape of a cup. **—futter,** *n.* the wooden case of the communion-cup or chalice. — **glas,** *n.* glass in the shape of a cup; champaign-glass; *it* large glass, tumbler. — **los,** *adj.* and *adv.* wanting a flower-cup or calix, without a cup. **—narbe,** *f.* [in botany] eye, umbril. **—schüsselchen,** *n.* V. —deckel. **—schwamm,** *m.* peziza. **—schwingel,** *m.* a sort of fescue-grass. **—teller,** *m.* V. —deckel. **—tuch,** *n.* purificatory.

‖**Keldüvel, Keelduivel,** *m.* [-s] V. [illegible]

Kelle, *f.* [*pl.* -n] [allied to Kelch] ladle; [among masons] trowel.

Keller, *m.* [-s, *pl.*-] [allied to the L. *cella*, to Höhle, and to the Gr. κοῖλος = hohl] 1) cellar. Ein gewölbter —, a vaulted cellar. V. [illegible] —, Flaschen—; *it.* V. Raths—, Stadt—. 2) [provincial or corrupted for] Kellner [which see].

Keller-assel, *f.* V. —wurm. **—beere,** *f.* V. —hals 2). **—esel,** *m.* V. —wurm. **—fenster,** *n.* cellar-light. **—geschoß,** *m.* story [of a house] under ground. **—hals,** *m.* 1) the entrance of a cellar. 2) [in botany] the common spurge olive, mezereon. **—hof,** *m.* V. Kölnhof. **—junge, —knecht,** *m.* cellar-boy, cellar-man, tapster, drawer. —

kraut, *n.* V. —hals 2). —laden, *m.* shutter of a cellar. —laus, *f.* V. —wurm. —loch, *n.* vent-hole, air-hole of a cellar. —luft, *f.* the air in a cellar. —magd, *f.* V. —mädchen. —mädchen, *n.* a female servant employed in the cellar, cellar-maid; *it.* bar-maid. —meister, *m.* the superintendent of the cellar [in a great house], butler; [in a monastery] cellarist or cellarer. —raum, *m.* part of a cellar allotted to a lodger. —ratze, —ratte, *f.* cellar-rat. *Fig.* [in popular lang., in jest or in contempt] V. Accisbedienter and Weinstecher. —recht, *n.* right or privilege of a public cellar. —schabe, *f.* V. —wurm. —schlüssel, *m.* key for the cellar, cellar-key. —schreiber, *m.* clerk or controller of a great wine- or beer-cellar. —spinne, *f.* a spider which lives in cellars. —stube, *f.*, *dim.* —stübchen, ||—stüblein, *n.* 1) the butler's room. 2) a room in a cellar. —thür, *f.* cellar-door. —wirth, *m.* landlord of a public wine- or beer-cellar. —wurm, *m.* wood-louse, milleped, tiller's louse. —wurz, *f.* the white water-lily or water-rose. —zins, *m.* cellar-rent.

Kellerei, *f.* 1) a set of cellars, cellarage [in great houses]. 2) the persons employed about a cellar. 3) V. Kellnerei.

Kellern, V. Einkellern.

Kellner, *m.* [-s, *pl.*-] 1) cellarman, butler. 2) waiter.

Kellnerei, *f.* the office or business of a butler or waiter.

Kellnerinn, *f.* V. Kellermädchen.

Kelter, *f.* [*pl.*-n] [Low Lat. *calcatorium*] 1) wine-press. 2) the building in which the wine is pressed, press-house.

Kelter=bann, *m.* 1) the privilege of a manor, according to which all the vassals belonging to it are obliged to make exclusive use of the wine-press of the lord of the manor. 2) the territory over which such a privilege extends. —baum, *m.* the beam or timber of a wine-press. —haus, *n.* the building in which the wine is pressed, press-house. —herr, *m.* the master or owner of a wine-press, chiefly of a common wine-press. —knecht, *m.* one who works at a wine-press, wine-presser, pressman. —lohn, *m.* money paid for the use of the wine-press. —meister, *m.* surveyor of a wine-press, master-pressman. —ordnung, *f.* regulation concerning the pressing of the wine. —recht, *n.* 1) the right of keeping a wine-press. 2) the fee due to the owner of a wine-press. —satz, *m.* V. —bann. —schraube, *f.* the large screw of a wine-press. —schreiber, *m.* clerk of a common wine-press. —treter, *m.* the person who treads the grapes. —wein, *m.* 1) wine extracted with a press. 2) the wine given for the use of the press. —zins, *m.* V. —lohn, —recht 2). —zuber, *m.* a tub used in a press-house.

Kelterer, *m.* [-s, *pl.* -] one who works at a wine-press, pressman, wine-presser; *it.* wine-treader.

Keltern, *v. tr.* to tread the grapes; *it.* to press the wine or grapes.

||**Kemnate**, *f.* [*pl.* -n] [Low Lat. *caminata*, from the old Kam = Stein] a stone-building; *it.* chimney.

Kempe, V. Kämpe.

Kennbar, *adj.* and *adv.* capable of being recognised, capable of being known, distinguishable, distinct. An dieser Narbe ist er —, he may be known or he is known by that scar; diese Inschrift ist noch sehr —, this inscription is still very legible; ein —er Unterschied, an obvious or conspicuous difference; ein —es Zeichen, a distinct or distinctive mark or sign.

Kennbarkeit, *f.* distinctive or characteristic mark.

Kennen, *ir. v tr.* [Sax. *cennan*, Goth. kunnan, Ion. *κοέω* for *νοέω*] to know, to be acquainted with. Einen von Gesicht, von Person —, to know any one by sight, personally; ich kenne ihn nur dem Namen nach, I know him only by name; er kannte mich an der Stimme, he knew me by my voice, ich kenne ihn nicht, und will ihn nicht —, I am not acquainted with him, nor do I desire it; die Alten kannten die Blattern nicht, the ancients knew nothing of the small pox or did not know any such thing as the small pox; wieder —, to recognize; er war so häßlich geworden, daß ich ihn nicht mehr kannte, he had become so ugly that I did not know him again; Einen — lernen, to get acquainted with any one, to make any one's acquaintance; *it.* to get acquainted with the character of any one; ich kannte ihn in Paris or ich lernte ihn in Paris —, I got acquainted with him at Paris; in diesem Hause lernte er das Spiel —, in that house he learned to game, to play [at cards, hazard &c]; er kennt die Welt nicht, he is ignorant of the world, he is a stranger in the world; er kennt sein eigenes Haus gar nicht, he is an utter stranger in his own house; Gott —, to have clear notions of God; *seine Leute —, to know whom one has to deal with; ich muß Sie meinen Freund — lehren, I must make you acquainted with my friend; er lehrte mich den Unterschied —, he taught me the difference; sich selbst — lernen, to know one's self; er kennt sich nicht mehr vor Stolz, pride blinds him; in der Leidenschaft kennt man sich nicht mehr, when we are in a passion, we do not know what we are about; wenn der Eigennutz im Spiele ist, kennt er keinen Menschen mehr, in matters of interest everybody is a stranger to him; der Ehrgeizige kennt kein Gesetz, the ambitious man respects no law; er kennt den Gegenstand or die Materie, he is knowing in that subject or matter. Syn. Kennen, Bekannt seyn [mit Etwas], Kenntniß haben [von Etwas], Bekanntschaft haben [mit Etwas oder Einem]. When I know what any thing is, I kenne it. I must however know many particulars concerning it in order to be bekannt with it. I am bekannt with a person when I keep up a friendly intercourse with him; he can, however, be bekannt to me, that is, I may know his name, abode &c., without being bekannt mit him. To have Bekanntschaft with a person of the opposite sex implies being on terms of intimate relation. V. also Kund, Kunde.

Kenn=zeichen, *n.* mark, sign, token, badge, character. Das —zeichen der Wahrheit ist &c., the characteristic of truth is &c.; [in medicine] symptom. Syn. Kennzeichen, Abzeichen, Merkmahl. Abzeichen implies every thing which renders one object perceptibly different from others; and it serves as a Kennzeichen in so far as it is a means to distinguish one thing from others. A man has an Abzeichen when he is one-eyed, when he limps &c. When it is required to render such a man recognisable, as for instance by a hand-bill, such an Abzeichen can serve as a Kennzeichen. When sailors at sea meet with sea-fowl it is a Merkmahl, or sign, of the proximity of land. V. also Anzeichen. —zeichnen, *v. tr.* [not much used] to distinguish, to mark, to characterize. —ziffer, *f.* [in mathematics] characteristic. Die —ziffer eines Logarithmen, the characteristic, index or exponent of a logarithm. —zug, *m.* a characteristic feature or trait, characteristic.

Kenner, *m.* [-s, *pl.* -] —inn, *f.* a person acquainted with the qualities of a thing, judge, connoisseur. Ein — von Alterthümern, an antiquary; ich bin kein — davon, I am no judge of it; davon ist er —, he understands that, has skill in that; er ist ein großer — von Gemählden, he is a great connoisseur in paintings; sie ist eine —inn von Perlen, she understands pearls. V. Bücher—, Münz—, Kräuter—.

Kenner=auge, *n.* the eye of a connoisseur or judge. —blick, *m.* the glance, look or view of a connoisseur. —miene, *f.* the mien, look, air of a connoisseur.

Kennerei, *f.* the skill of a pretended connoisseur, superficial knowledge, smattering.

Kennerschaft, *f.* the skill of a connoisseur, connoisseurship.

Kenntbar, Kenntlich, V. Kennbar.

Kenntniß, *f.* [*pl.* -nisse] 1) the clear perception of any thing, knowledge. Die — zukünftiger Dinge, the knowledge of future things; — von einer Sache haben, to understand any thing well, to have knowledge of any thing; er hat gar keine — davon, he has not the least notion of it; — von einer Sache nehmen, to take cognizance of any thing. 2) acquaintance with any thing, knowledge. Wie kam dieß zu Ihrer —? how came that to your knowledge? Einen von Etwas in — setzen, to impart or communicate any thing to any one. 3) skill, learning, knowledge, acquirements, attainments. Er hat eine große — von Gemählden, he understands pictures very well; er besitzt tiefe — in der Geschichte, he is a thorough adept, very conversant in history; ein Mann von vielen —en, a man of great learning; viele —e besitzen, to have great knowledge, to know much, to be a man of great acquirements or attainments; er hat eine oberflächliche — von der lateinischen Sprache, he has a smattering of the Latin tongue. Syn. V. Kunde.

Kenntniß=arm, *adj.* and *adv.* destitute of knowledge. —begierig, *adj.* and *adv.* desirous of knowledge. —los, *adj.* and *adv.* destitute of knowledge, without knowledge, ignorant. —reich, *adj.* and *adv.* full of knowledge. Er ist sehr —reich, he is a man of great learning.

Kennung, *f.* that by which any thing may be known, particularly, the mark in the tooth of a horse indicative of its age. Ein Pferd, das die — noch hat, a horse that has still the mark in his mouth; das Pferd hat die — verloren, the horse has rased.

Kenster, Kinster, *m.* [-s] [from the Lat. *genista?*] mistletoe.

Kentern, I. *v. tr.* V. Kanten 2). II. *v. intr.* [in seamen's lang.] to be overset, to overset in a squall of wind.

Kenterhaken, *m.* V. Kanthaken.

Keper, *m.* [-s] manner or way of weaving in ribs or ridges.

Kepern, *v. tr.* to weave in ribs or ridges, to quill, to twill. Der gekeperte Zeug, twilled cloth, kersey; gekeperter Barchent, nappy fustian.

Kerb, *m.* [-es, *pl.* -e] V. Kerbe.

Kerb=beil, *n.* [in seamen's lang.] a small hatchet for cutting the cables. —holz, *n.* a notched stick, tally. *Es geht bei ihm alles auf's —holz, he buys or takes every thing upon trust, upon tick. —schnitt, *m.* notch, score. —stock, *m.* V. —holz. —thier, *n.*, *dim.* —thierchen, ||—thierlein, *n.* insect [of the order hymenoptera]. —thierkenner, *m.* entomologist, V. Zieferkenner. —thierkunde, —thierlehre, *f.* entomology. —weh, *n.* [in the veterinary art] tumour or swelling in the cleft of the hoof. —zähnig, *adj.* [in botany] notched. —zettel, *m.* tally-paper, check, indented writ.

Kerbe, *f.* [*pl.*-n] *dim.* Kerbchen, ||Kerblein, *n.* [V. Kerben] notch, incision. Die — auf einem Kerbholz, the notch or score on a tally; die — an einer Armbrust, the gaffle of a cross-bow; die — an einem Pfeile, the notch of an arrow. [among farriers] Die — [am Gaumen der Pferde], notch, ridge.

Kerben-maul, *n.* [in nat. hist.] fringed tethys or sea-hare. —muschel, *f.* a kind of mytilus.

Kerbel, *m.* [-s] [L. *cerefolium*, Low Sax. *karvel*, A. Sax. *cerfille*, Fr. *cerfeuil*, Sw. *kerfwel* and *koerwel*, from kerben] chervil.

Kerbel-kern, *m.* the wild chervil. —kohl, *m.* curled cabbage. —kraut, *n.* chervil. —same, *m.* chervil-seed. —suppe, *f.* soup made of chervil, chervil-soup.

Kerben, *v. tr.* [allied to the L. *carpo*, Gr. κάρφω, V. Kerbel] to notch, to indent, to jag. [in botany] Gekerbt, notched; gekerbte Blätter, notched leaves.

Kerbig, *adj.* and *adv.* notched, jagged, indented.

Kerker, *m.* [-s, *pl.*-] [allied to the L. *carcer*, Gr. κάρκαρον, ἕρκος] prison, jail, dungeon. Ein finsterer —, a dark dungeon; Einen in den — werfen, to put any one in a dungeon, *to clap any one up in prison; Einen aus dem — ziehen, to get any one out of prison. Syn. V. Gefängniß.

Kerker-fieber, *n.* jail-fever. —haft, *f.* imprisonment, confinement in a dungeon. —meister, *m.*, —meisterinn, *f.* jailer; jailer's wife. —schmach, *f.* disgrace of imprisonment. —thurm, *m.* a tower serving as a prison, donjon, keep.

Kerkern, *v. tr.* [unusual] to imprison.

Kerkner, *m.* [-s, *pl.*-] V. [the usual word] Kerkermeister.

Kerl, *m.* [-s, *pl.* -e or -s] [originally = Mann; Sax. *ceorl* = Mann, Bauer, Ehemann, Hausvater, D. *karle* = das Männchen, Ital. *carlona* = ein gewöhnlicher Mensch] 1) [only used in familiar or popular language] [= Mann] person, man, fellow. Ein braver, ein ehrlicher —, an honest man or fellow; ein lustiger —, a merry blade or fellow, a jolly dog; ein starker, derber —, a stout blade; ein schöner —, a fine fellow or blade. 2) [in contempt and vulgar] a worthless man, a fellow. Ein gemeiner —, a base fellow; ein unverschämter —, a saucy fellow; ein pfiffiger —, a cunning dog. *it.* [very vulgar] servant. Ich will meinen — zu Ihnen schicken, I'll send my man to you.

Kerlchen, *n.* [-s, *pl.* -] [*dim.* of Kerl] a little fellow. *Er ist ein gescheidtes, ein nettes —, he is a clever, a fine fellow.

Kermes, *m. indeclin.* [from the Pers. *kirm*, L. *vermis*, Wurm] the insect from which the crimson colour is obtained, kermes. Mineralischer —, Spießglas—, kermes-mineral.

Kermes-baum, *m.* V. —eiche. —beere, *f.* 1) kermes-berry. 2) the branching phytolacca, Virginian poke, phytolacca decandra. —beersaft, *m.* V. —latwerge. —eiche, *f.* kermes-tree. —latwerge, *f.* alkermes. —scharlach, *m.* crimson. —wurm, *m.* cochineal.

1. **Kern**, *m.* [-es, *pl.* -e] [allied to Korn] 1) a cavity. Der — einer Kanone, the bore of a cannon; der — an den Pferden, *a*) V. Kennung, *b*) the furrow on the roof a horse's mouth. 2) *a*) any thing that is to make a cavity. Der — [der Geschützform], the mould within a piece of ordnance when it is cast, the core. *b*) any thing that is in a cavity, chiefly, seed of fruit, kernel, stone. Der — einer Nuß, eines Apfels, the kernel of a nut, of an apple; die —e der Weinbeeren, kernels of grapes; der — einer Kirsche, Pflaume &c., the stone of a cherry, of a plum; der — in den Melonen, the seed or kernel of a melon. 3) [in general] the interior part of a thing. Der — eines Baumes, the heart or core of a tree; der — einer Artischocke, the bottom of an artichoke; der — einer Flöte, Pfeife, fipple or stopper of a flute, of a pipe; der — des Hufes, the quick of a horse's hoof; bis auf den — lohen [among tanners], to tan thoroughly. *Fig.* the best part, choice, flower, pith, essence, substance; [but in this signification Kern is perhaps to be derived from the L. *cernere* = ausschneiden, Ital. *cerna* and Low Lat. *cernea* = Auswahl]. Der — seiner Truppen, the choice or flower of his troops; der — eines Buches, the pith of a book; den — herausziehen, to extract the marrow, main substance, quintessence.

Kern-apfel, *m.* calville. —arbeit, *f.* excellent workmanship. —ästig, *adj.* said of a tree, the branches of which grow out of the middle or heart. —ausdruck, *m.* pithy expression. —beißer, *m.* 1) hawfinch. 2) bruchus or seed-beetle, may-worm. —bohrer, *m.* the weevil or corn weevil. —branntwein, *m.* brandy made of the kernels of fruit. —brav, *adj.* and *adv.* [in fam. lang.] thoroughly honest or good. —faul, *adj.* rotten in the inside [said of wood or trees]. —fäule, —fäulniß, *f.* rottenness in the inside. —fest, *adj.* firm or solid in the inside. *Fig.* exceedingly, very firm or solid. Eine —feste Gesundheit, Körperbeschaffenheit, a very robust health, thoroughly sound constitution. —feuer, *n.* V. Centralfeuer. *Fig.* great, excellent fire. —fleisch, *n.* firm flesh, brawn; *it.* V. Brustkern. —fresser, *m.* V. —beißer 1). —frisch, *adj.* and *adv.* [in fam. lang.] very or quite fresh. —frucht, *f.* fruit with soft kernels or seeds [opposed to stone-fruit]. —gedicht, *n.* [in emphatical and in familiar language] a pithy poem, a poem full of vigour or energy. —gehäuse, *n.* the core [of an apple &c.]. —gerste, *f.* common barley. —gerte, *f.* V. Hartriegel. —geschütz, *n.* cannon the bore of which is equally wide throughout. —gesund, *adj.* sound in the inside. *Fig.* very healthy or strong, hearty. Ein —gesunder Mann, a hearty man. —gülte, *f.* rent or duty paid in corn or grain. —gut, I. *adj.* and *adv.* good, sound in the inside. *Fig.* exquisitely, thoroughly good. II. *n.* 1) choice goods, exquisite, fine goods or merchandize. 2) the essence, pith, substance. —haus, *n.* V. —gehäuse. —holz, *n.* 1) the heart of wood, the wood [distinguished from the alburnum]. 2) the best wood. 3) the pine, pine-tree. —inhalt, *m.* pithy contents; *it.* the principal or essential contents. —kraut, *n.* behen. —leder, *n.* leather of the best quality. —lehm, *m.* clay for lining the inside of a mould. —leinkraut, *n.* V. Harnkraut, Bruchkraut. —leinwand, *f.* very good, excellent linen. —los, *adj.* and *adv.* wanting a kernel or stone. *Fig.* wanting vigour or energy, feeble. —mädchen, ||—mädel, *n.* [in popular lang.] a very good girl; *it.* a handsome buxom girl or lass. —mann, *m.* [in familiar language] a very good man, excellent man; *it.* er ist ein —mann, he is every inch a man. —mehl, *n.* best flour. —milch, *f.* butter-milk. —obst, *n.* 1) V. —frucht. 2) fruit that grows on a wild stock. —raupe, *f.* a caterpillar that gnaws the heart of plants. —recht, *adj.* and *adv.* said of a cannon, the bore of which is exactly in the middle, well-bored. Eine Kanone —recht richten, to level a cannon horizontally. —reich, *adj.* full of kernels &c. —sack, *m.* a bag filled with heated kernels or fruit-stones for warming the bed. —salz, *n.* rock-salt, mineral salt. —schälig, *adj.* —schäliges Holz, wood that has circular crevices in the inside. —scheit, *n.* a very good log of wood. —schule, *f.* seed-plot, nursery for fruit-trees. —schuß, *m.* horizontal shot. Einen —schuß thun, to shoot point-blank. —schwinden, *n.* [in farriery] surbate or surbating, foundering. —sprache, *f.* pithy language. —spruch, *m.* a choice sentence, pithy sentence. —stahl, *m.* best steel. —stamm, *m.* 1) a tree grown out of a kernel. 2) an excellent, sound stem or trunk. —stechen, *n.* the act of bleeding the horse in the mouth by picking the furrows in the roof. —stein, *m.* V. Körnerstein. —stück, *n.* [among sculptors] cake. —truppen, *pl.* choice troops. —tuch, *n.* very good, excellent cloth. —volk, *n.* choice people. —waare, *f.* choice or exquisite merchandize. —weib, *n.* [in popular lang.] a very good, excellent woman or wife; *it.* a handsome buxom woman. —wein, *m.* very good, excellent wine. —wolle, *f.* the best wool that comes off the sheep's back. —wort, *n.* a pithy word, a choice word. —zug, *m.* [in fam. lang.] a famous, good, fine draught; *it. fig.* an excellent, a highly characteristic, a very original trait. —zupfen, *n.* [among hunters] distribution of the killed game or rotten flesh among the dogs.

2. **Kern**, *m.* [-es] [allied to the L. *caro*] originally = Fleisch, meat, flesh; V. Brust—.

Kernen, *v. tr.* 1) V. Auskernen. 2) to convert into globules or grains, to granulate. 3) to churn, V. Buttern.

Kernhaft, *adj.* and *adv.* strong, solid, substantial. *Fig.* pithy, energetical.

Kernicht, *adj.* and *adv.* resembling a kernel.

Kernig, *adj.* and *adv.* full of seeds or kernels. *Fig.* solid, substantial, pithy, excellent. Eine —e Sprache, a pithy language.

Kertsche, *f.* [*pl.* -n] wild plum, sloe, V. Schlehe.

Kerze, *f.* [*pl.*-n] *dim.* Kerzchen, ||Kerzlein, *n.* [allied to the L. *cera*, Fr. *cierge*, originally = Wachslicht] waxlight, taper; *it.* [in general, for] a candle. Gegossene —, mould candle; *so gerade wie eine —, as straight as a taper or as an arrow.

Kerzen-beere, *f.* [in botany] the common candleberry, myrtle, Myrica cerifera. —beerbaum, —beerstrauch, *m.* the sweet gale, willow or dutch myrtle, the bog gale. —gerade, *adj.* and *adv.* [in fam. lang.] as straight as a taper. —gießer, *m.* wax-chandler, tallow-chandler. —hell, *adj.* lighted by tapers. —krämer, *m.* chandler. —kraut, *n.* V. Königskraut. —macher, *m.* V. —gießer. —schachtel, *f.* a box for tapers or candles. —schein, *m.* light of a taper or candle. Beim —scheine lesen, to read by the light of a taper or candle. —strauch, *m.* V. —beerstrauch. —träger, *m.* [chiefly in the Romish church] taper-bearer. —weihe, *f.* [in the Romish church] the consecration of the tapers. —zieher, *m.* V. —gießer.

Kescher, *m.* [-s, *pl.*-] [probably corrupted from Häscher, Hascher] a deep purse-like net, with a hoop at the aperture, purse-net, hoop-net.

Kessel, *m.* [-s, *pl.*-] *dim.* —chen, *n.* [Low Sax. *ketel*, Dan. *kedel*, Eng. *kettle*, Bohem. *kotel*, Low Lat. *cedellus*; it seems to be allied to the L. *cat*-inus, to the Gr. κοτύλη, to Kasten, Kiste &c. Goth. *kas* = Gefäß] 1) [in general] denomination of certain hollow or excavated things. [in architecture] Der — [einer Säule], bell; [in artillery] der — [einer Kanone], the bore [of a cannon]; [among hunters] the cover of a wild boar; *it.* the burrow of a badger; [in mining] an excavation; [in hydraulics] basin [of a fountain], *it.* V. —loch 2); der — eines Abtritts, the pit of a privy; [in geography &c.] ein —, a valley surrounded on all sides by hills or mountains; [in fortification] a battery of mortars sunk in the earth, kettle. 2) [chiefly] kettle, cauldron or caldron. Der kupferne —, copper-kettle, copper; ein siedender —, a boiling copper; ein — voll Lauge, a caldronful of lie; [among apothecaries] a deep and wide pan. V. Brau—, Färbe—, Kaffee—, Milch—, Schwenk—, Wasch—, Weih—.

Kessel=asche, *f.* potash, kali. —**beere**, *f.* V. Moosbeere. —**bereiter**, *m.* brazier, coppersmith. —**besserer**, *m.* V. —flicker. —**bier**, *n.* beer brewed in small vessels in a private house, home-brewed beer. —**bombe**, *f.* a bomb thrown from a mortar. —**brauen**, *n.* the act of brewing beer in a private family; *it.* the right or privilege of brewing beer in private families. —**braun**, I. *n.* 1) the brown earth or clay with which the braziers or coppersmiths give their new kettles the brown-red colour. 2) that which flies off from the copper when hammering. II. *adj.* copper-coloured. —**büßer**, *m.* V. [the usual word] —flicker. —**fang**, *m.* [formerly] the ordeal of plunging the arm into boiling water. —**flicker**, *m.* tinker. —**flickerranzen**, —**flickersack**, *m.* a tinker's budget. —**förmig**, *adj.* having the form or shape of a kettle, kettle-shaped. —**gewölb[e]**, *n.* a vaulted roof in the form of a cupola, V. Kuppel. —**haken**, *m.* pot-hook, pot-hanger, trammel [in a chimney]. —**jagen**, *n.* 1) hunt or chase in which the game is driven into an enclosure resembling a kettle. 2) wild boar chase. —**lauf**, *m.* chamber of a mortar. —**loch**, *n.* 1) a kettle-shaped hole. 2) the deepest part of a pond [where water remains after draining]. —**macher**, *m.* V. Keßler 1). —**meister**, *m.* [among cloth-makers] he who looks to the caldron and colours. —**pauke**, *f.* kettle-drum. —**ruß**, *m.* soot that sticks to the kettles or caldrons. —**schläger**, *m.* V. Keßler. —**thal**, *n.* [in geography &c.] V. Kessel 1). —**tuch**, *n.* cloth that has been dyed in a caldron, dyed cloth.

Keßler, Kesseler, *m.* [-s, *pl.* -] 1) brazier. 2) tinker.

Keßler=arbeit, —**waare**, *f.* kettleware, brazier's ware.

Kesseln, *v. r.* sich —, to assume the form of a kettle, to form into a round excavation.

Kesser, V. Ketscher.

‖**Keste**, *f.* [*pl.* -n] [corrupted from Kastanie] 1) chestnut. 2) the wart-like or horny substance by the knee of a horse.

Kestenbaum, *m.* chestnut-tree.

Ketscher, *m.* [-s, *pl.* -] a deep purse-like net, with a hoop at the aperture, purse-net.

1. **Kette**, *f.* [*pl.* -n] [allied to the D. *kudde*, Swiss *kütt* = Heerde klein Vieh] a covey [of partridges].

2. **Kette**, *f.* [*pl.* -n] [allied to the L. *catena*, and Germ. gatten, Gatter] 1) a series, range or line of things connected. Eine — Berge, Felsen, a chain of mountains, a chain or range of rocks; eine — von Truppen, a cordon of troops. [in dancing, *chaine*] right and left all eight. Die englische — [in dancing, *chaine anglaise*], right and left. [among weavers] the warp. 2) [in a more limited sense] a chain; *dim.* **Kettchen**, ‖**Kettlein**, *n.* a little chain. Eine goldene, eiserne —, a gold, an iron chain, a chain of gold, of iron; die — an einer Uhr [Uhrkette], a watch-chain; die —, um eine Uhr anzuhängen und vor dem Verlieren &c. zu sichern, the guard of a watch; — am Hals, V. Hals—; einen Hund an die — legen, to chain a dog; Einen in —n legen, to bind any one in chains, to fetter any one; Einen von der — losmachen, to unchain any one, to free any one from his chains. V. Brust—, Draht—, Erbsen—, Halfter—, Hals—, Halt—, Hemm—, Spann—. *Fig.* *a*) [a series of things following in succession] chain, concatenation. Eine — von Unglücksfällen, a chain, train or concatenation of misfortunes. V. Verkettung. *b*) [only used in the *pl.*] bondage, slavery, chains. Diese Völker haben ihre —n zerbrochen, these nations have broken their chains; dieser Liebhaber liebt seine —n, gefällt sich in seinen —n, that lover is pleased with his chains, hugs his chains. Syn. **Kette, Fessel, Bande.** Fessel and Bande indicate the form, Ketten, on the contrary, more the material. Fessel and Bande may therefore be of several kinds; Ketten are usually of iron, though they may be of any other metal. To Fesseln belong the rings with which the hands and legs are encircled; hence we put a Kette on a dog, but men are bound with Fesseln.

Ketten=ähnlich, —**artig**, *adj.* V. —förmig. —**anker**, *pl.* moorings. —**bandwurm**, *m.* tapeworm with joints. —**baum**, *m.* a weaver's beam, roller of a weaver. —**blume**, *f.* lion's paw, tail or tooth, dandelion, piss-a-bed. —**brüche**, *pl.* [in mathematics] continued fractions. —**brücke**, *f.* chain-bridge. —**faden**, *m.* a thread of the warp. Die —fäden, the yarn of the warp. —**fisch**, *m.* a kind of ostracion or bone-fish. —**förmig**, *adj.* having the form of a chain. —**gelenk**, —**glied**, *n.* the link of a chain. —**gesang**, [*Canon] *m.* [in music] catch. —**glied**, *n.* V. —gelenk. —**hund**, *m.* a dog commonly chained up [in the court-yard &c.] for the purpose of watching, a ban-dog, watch-dog. —**koralle**, *f.* tubipore or red tubular coral. —**kugel**, *f.* chain-bullet, chain-shot. —**locke**, *f.* a chain-curl or buckle. —**los**, *adj.* unchained, unfettered. —**macher**, *m.* chain-maker. —**naht**, *f.* a seam or point resembling a chain. —**natter**, *f.* a kind of viper or adder of Carolina. —**panzer**, *m.* a coat of mail consisting of small chains. —**pumpe**, *f.* chain-pump. —**rechnung**, *f.* instrumental arithmetic. —**regel**, *f.* conjoined rule of three, chain-rule. —**reim**, *m.* a verse rhyming in the beginning and end, chained rhyme. —**ring**, *m.* 1) the link of a chain. 2) the ring at the end of a chain. —**rolle**, *f.* lace-chain, lace-warp. —**sang**, *m.* V. —gesang. —**schloß**, *n.* a chain-lock. —**schluß**, *m.* [Häufelschluß] [a logical form] sorites. —**schmied**, *m.* a smith who makes chains. —**seide**, *f.* organzine. —**stab**, *m.* the staff of a measuring-chain. —**stein**, *m.* 1) V. Rogenstein. 2) V. —koralle. —**stich**, *m.* change-stitch. —**strafe**, *f.* confinement or hard work in irons. —**toll**, *adj.* and *adv.* [in fam. language] distracted, quite mad, fit for Bedlam. —**werk**, *n.* chain-work. —**wurm**, *m.* V. —bandwurm. —**zug**, *m.* [in architecture] a sort of waved or carved work.

Kettel, *f.* [*pl.* -n] a little chain, particularly for fastening a gate or door.

Ketteln, *v. tr.* to fasten with a little chain; *it.* to join.

Ketten, *v. tr.* [V. Kette] to fasten with a chain, to chain. V. An—, Ver—. *Fig.* An Jemand gekettet seyn, to be intimately connected with, to be linked to any one; an ein Geschäft gekettet seyn, to be tied to a business.

Kettler, *m.* [-s, *pl.* -] chain-maker.

1. **Ketzer**, *m.* [-s, *pl.* -] a spindleful of yarn.

2. **Ketzer**, *m.* [-s, *pl.* -] —**inn**, *f.* [either allied to the D. *kesan* = the Lat. fornicari, Sw. *kat* = unzüchtig, unchaste; formerly an unchaste person was called a Ketzer; or ironically from the Gr. καθαρός = rein] heretic.

Ketzer=buch, *n.* a heretical book. —**eifer**, *m.* zealous persecution against or of heretics. —**gericht**, *n.* court of inquisition. —**haupt**, *n.* [*Häresiarch] heresiarch, arch-heretic, chief of a sect of heretics. —**jagd**, *f.* pursuit or persecution of heretics. —**jäger**, *m.* pursuer or persecutor of heretics. —**macher**, *m.* a bigoted man, chiefly a bigoted divine, who calls any one a heretic who differs from him in his religious opinions. —**macherei**, *f.* the passion or mania of treating like heretics all those that differ from us in religious matters. —**meister**, *m.* grand inquisitor. —**mütze**, *f.* [in Spain] a painted bonnet or cap put on the head of heretics that were to be burnt, the Sanbenito. —**richter**, *m.* [*Inquisitor] inquisitor. —**riecher**, *m.* one who believes he sees heretics every where. —**schrift**, *f.* a heretical book or writing. —**stifter**, *m.* V. —haupt. —**sucht**, *f.* V. —macherei. —**zunft**, *f.* a sect of heretics.

Ketzerei, *f.* heresy.

Ketzerisch, *adj.* and *adv.* heretical.

Ketzern, *v. tr.* [allied to the L. *caedo*, *quatio*, D. *kadden*] [in mining] to cleave with wedges.

Keubel, *m.* [-s, *pl.* -] [in mining] a sort of sieve, V. Sieb.

Keuchen, *v. intr.* [another and stronger form for hauchen] to pant, to gasp, to breathe asthmatically; *it.* [less usual] to cough. Die Damen keuchten und konnten kaum athmen, the ladies gasped and were scarcely able to respire; wenn ich fünf oder sechs Treppen hinaufgegangen bin, muß ich —, when I have gone up five or six stairs, I begin to puff and blow. Das —, the act of panting or gasping, asthmatical affection.

Keuchhusten, *m.* chin-cough, hooping-cough.

Keucher, *m.* [-s, *pl.* -] —**inn**, *f.* one who puffs and blows, who gasps or pants for breath.

Keule, *f.* [*pl.* -n] [probably allied to Kaul = Kugel] 1) [originally] any thing round. Die — eines Mörsers, pestle; [among printers] brayer; [in cookery] hind-leg of an animal, leg [of meat]; eine Hammels—, a leg of mutton. 2) [chiefly] club. Die — des Herkules, the club of Hercules. *Prov.* Jeder Schäfer lobt seine —, never seemed a prison fair or mistress foul. *Fig.* [vulgar] Eine grobe —, a coarse, rude, unmannerly woman.

Keul=förmig, *adj.*, —**schwamm**, *m.* V. Keulenförmig &c.

Keulen=förmig, *adj.* and *adv.* having the form of a club. —**lahm**, *adj.* lame in the thigh or hind-leg. —**palme**, *f.* zamia. —**schlag**, *m.* the stroke of a club. Er erlegte ihn mit Einem —schlag, he killed him with one stroke of his club. —**schwamm**, *m.* clavaria. —**wurz**, *f.* the white water-lily, water-rose.

Keulen, *v. tr.* [rather unusual] Einen —, to strike any one with a club.

Keulicht, *adj.* and *adv.* resembling a club; round, globular.

Keusch, *adj.* and *adv.* [Bohem. *cisty*, Sw. *kysk*, old Suabian kuisch, L. *castus*, allied to *caedo*, *cido* = schneiden] chaste, continent. Ein —er Jüngling, eine —e Jungfrau, a chaste youth, virgin; ein —es Herz, a pure heart; —e Begierden, Gedanken, chaste desires, thoughts; das beleidigt —e Ohren, that offends chaste ears; — leben, to live chastely or in chastity. Syn. **Keusch, Züchtig, Schamhaft, Ehrbar.** The Keusche overcomes his feelings of sensuality; the Züchtige governs his imagination, he avoids every conversation or action which can be called unzüchtig. The Schamhafte, from a natural feeling, shuns whatever is immodest. A matron is züchtig from decency, an innocent young female from modesty. Female honor has always a reference to Keuschheit as the highest virtue in woman. It is grounded on a deeper consideration of female dignity.

Keusch-baum, *m.* chaste-tree. —**kraut**, *n.* sensitive plant. —**lamm**, *n.* V. —baum. —**lammsame**, *m.* wild pepper.

Keuschheit, *f.* chastity, continence; purity. Das Gelübde der — ablegen, to make a vow of chastity.

Keutel, *m.* [-s, *pl.* -] [allied to the Low Sax. Kaut, Gr. κοίτη, L. *cav*-us = hohl] the bag in a fishing-net.

***Khan**, *m.* [-s, *pl.* -e] [in Turkey &c.] 1) [with some authors also *n.*] an inn, khan. 2) a governor, khan.

Kibitz, *m.* [-es, *pl.* -e] 1) lapwing, pewet. 2) green plover. Der schwarzbrüstige —, the black-breasted Indian plover.

Kibitz-blume, *f.* chequered fritillary. —**ei**, *n.* 1) the egg of the lapwing. 2) V. —blume.

Kicher, *f.* [*pl.* -n] or —**erbse**, *f.* [*pl.* -n] [also Zieser, from the L. *cicer*] chick-pea.

Kichern, or **Kickern**, *v. intr.* [L. *cach*-innor, Gr. κιχ-λίζω] to titter.

Kicks, *m.* [-es, *pl.* -e] a false stroke at billiards.

Kiebitz, V. Kibitz.

1. **Kiefe**, *f.* [*pl.* -n] [allied to Koffer, L. *cav*-us = hohl] 1) gill [of fish]. 2) shell [of pease].

2. **Kiefe**, *f.* [*pl.* -n] V. 1. and 2. Kiefer.

Kiefen-fuß, *m.* the water-flea. —**pricke**, *f.* —**wurm**, *m.* V. Kieferwurm.

3. **Kiefe**, *f.* V. Kiffe.

Kiefen, *v. intr.* [allied to kauen, keifen] 1) to gnaw, to chew. 2) to scold, to upbraid, to chide.

1. **Kiefer**, *f.* [*pl.* -n] [allied to Kieme, Koffer, Lat. *cav*-us = hohl] gill [of fish].

Kiefer-deckel, *m.* V. Kiemendeckel. —**wurm**, *m.* [a fish] the thorny loach.

2. **Kiefer**, *m.* [-s, *pl.* -] or *f.* [*pl.* -n] [from kauen or kiefen] jaw, jaw-bone; [in anatomy] mandible. Der obere und untere —, the upper and nether mandible, the upper and lower jaw.

Kiefer-blutader, *f.* V. —muskelblutader. —**drüse**, *f.* maxillary gland. —**fortsatz**, *m.* maxillary apophysis. —**knochen**, *m.* maxillary bone. —**muskel**, *m.* muscle of the lower jaw, maxillary muscle. —**muskelblutader**, *f.* maxillary vein. —**rand**, *m.* the superior margin of the lower jaw.

3. **Kiefer**, *f.* [*pl.* -n] or —**baum**, *m.* [according to some etymologists for Kienföhre; but it seems to be allied to the Hebr. *copher* = Pech] pine, pine-tree, pitch-tree, fir. Die schottische —, Scotch fir.

Kiefer-gehölz, *n.* a forest of pine-trees, pine-grove. —**marder**, *m.* V. Baummarder. —**pilz**, *m.* the Larch fungus. —**wald**, *m.* V. —gehölz. —**weide**, *f.* V. Dotterweide, Goldweide. —**zapfen**, *m.* cone of the pine-tree or fir.

Kiefern, *adj.* —es Holz, pine-wood.

Kieke, *f.* [*pl.* -n] [or Gieke, allied to the Sax. *ceac* [Kiek] = Topf, W. *cawg* = ein Becken] a coal-pan for warming the feet [made use of in Holland and Germany].

1. **Kiel**, *m.* [-es, *pl.* -e] [allied to Kaul = Kugel] the bulb of a plant.

2. **Kiel**, *m.* [-es, *pl.* -e] [probably referable to hohl, Gr. κοῖλος; Eng. *quill*, Dan. *kiol*] quill. Gezogene —e, Dutch quills. V. Feder—, Gänse—, Raben—, Schwan—. Die —e eines Klaviers, the quills of a harpsichord. *Fig.* [in poetry] style.

Kielbett, *n.* a bed filled with large coarse feathers.

3. **Kiel**, *m.* [-es, *pl.* -e] [Sax. *ceol*, Eng. *keel*, old Germ. chiol, Fr. *quille*] 1) keel of a ship. Der falsche, lose —, false keel; ein tiefer —, rank keel. *it.* [chiefly in poetry, for] a ship, a vessel. 2) [in botany = das Schiffchen] keel.

Kiel-bock, *m.* a ram without horns. —**flügel**, *m.* a species of snail. —**förmig**, *adj.* [in botany] keeled, carinated. —**frosch**, *m.* 1) V. Froschwurm. 2) V. Froschschnecke. —**fuge**, *f.* the rabbet or channel cut in the keel. —**gang**, *m.* [in seamen's lang.] garboard strake. —**herr**, *m.* V. Schiffer, Schiffsherr. —**holen**, *v. tr.* 1) Ein Schiff, to careen a ship. 2) Einen Matrosen [as a punishment], to keelhale or keelhaul a sailor. —**holung**, *f.* 1) careening. Eine ganze —holung, thorough careen. 2) keelhauling. —**klotz**, *m.* [in seamen's lang.] deadwood. —**kropf**, *m.* 1) a wen at the throat. 2) a child afflicted with such a wen; *it.* a changeling. —**recht**, *n.* a duty paid for a ship's entering a port or harbour for the first time, keelage. —**rücken**, *m.* a fish of the Silurus species. —**schwein**, —**schwinn**, *n.* [in seamen's lang.] keelson. —**schwimm**, *n.* V. —wasser 2). —**tau**, *n.* keel-rope. —**überzug**, *m.* false keel. —**wasser**, *n.* 1) bilge-water. 2) dead-water.

Kielen, I. *v. tr.* 1) to stick [an instrument] with quills. 2) [in seamen's lang.] Ein Schiff —, to furnish a ship with a keel. 3) V. Kielholen 1). II. *v. intr.* [of birds] to get feathers, especially the quilled or strong feathers, to become fledged.

Kielig, *adj.* furnished with quills, said of young birds which have the stems of their feathers but are otherwise unfledged.

Kieme, *f.* [*pl.* -n] [allied to the L. *cav*-us, to Koffer, Kiste &c.] gill [of a fish].

Kiemen-deckel, *m.* covering of the gills, gill-lid. —**haut**, *f.* membrane of the gills. —**öffnung**, *f.* gill-opening. —**wurm**, *m.* the lernaea or plague, sea-hare.

Kien, *m.* [-es] [Low Sax. Keen; from zünden, L. *cendo*, Sw. *kinda*] fir or pine-wood saturated with resin; resinous wood.

Kien-apfel, *m.* cone of the pine or Scotch fir, pine-cone. —**baum**, *m.* pine-tree, Scotch fir, V. 3. Kiefer. —**bohrer**, *m.* V. Borkenkäfer. —**fackel**, *f.* a torch of pine-wood. —**föhre**, *f.* V. —baum. —**fresser**, *m.* saw-fly. —**harz**, *n.* resin of pine-trees. —**holz**, *n.* pine-wood, resinous wood. —**öl**, *n.* oil obtained from pine-trees. —**post**, *f.* wild rosemary. —**ruß**, *m.* soot obtained from pine-wood and used for blacking, lamp-black. —**stock**, *m.* trunk of a pine-tree.

Kiener, *m.* [-s, *pl.* -] the man who furnishes resinous wood to forges or smelting-houses.

Kienig, *adj.* having the property of resinous wood, resinous.

||**Kiepe**, *f.* [*pl.* -n] 1) a basket to be carried on the back, back-basket, dosser. 2) a large straw-hat.

Kieper, *m.* V. Küfer, Küper and Keper.

Kiepern, V. Kepern.

Kies, *m.* [-es, *pl.* -e] [Bohem. *kyz*, L. *cos* = ein Wetzstein, V. 3. Katze] 1) gravel. Einen Gang mit — bestreuen, to gravel a walk. 2) [in mineralogy] pyrites, quarz, V. Eisen—, Kupfer—, Schwefel— &c.

Kies-ader, *f.* a vein containing gravel and especially sulphureous pyrites. —**ähnlich**, —**artig**, *adj.* resembling gravel, pyritous. —**apfel**, *m.* pyrites in balls or globules. —**bach**, *m.* a gravelly brook. —**ball**, *m.* V. —apfel. —**erde**, *f.* gravelly earth or soil. —**frucht**, *f.* V. —apfel. —**gang**, *m.* gravel-walk. —**grube**, *f.* gravel-pit. —**grund**, *m.* a gravelly bottom or soil. —**haltig**, *adj.* pyritic, pyritous, pyritiferous. —**kegel**, *m.*, —**kloß**, *m.*, —**kugel**, *f.*, —**kügelchen**, ||—**kügelein**, *n.* V. —apfel. —**lauge**, *f.* V. Cementwasser, Vitriolwasser. —**niere**, *f.* sulphureous pyrites in the shape of kidneys, pyrites in oblong globules. —**nuß**, *f.* V. —niere. —**ofen**, *m.* the oven in which the copper-ore is smelted after having been dried or roasted. —**platz**, *m.* a place or square covered with gravel, a gravelled square. —**rogen**, *m.* V. —niere, —ball. —**sand**, *m.* gravelly sand, coarse sand. —**traube**, *f.* pyrites in the shape of grapes. —**truhe**, *f.* [in hydraulics] a chest filled with gravel. —**weg**, *m.* gravelly way or walk. —**würfel**, *m.* V. —niere. —**zeche**, *f.* mine of sulphureous or arsenical pyrites. —**zimmer**, *m.* one who works alone a mine of sulphureous or arsenical pyrites.

Kiesel, *m.* [-s, *pl.* -] or —**stein**, *m.* [from Kies] pebble, pebble-stone, flint. Rheinischer — [a sort of pebble found on some parts of the shores of the Rhine, especially in the Grand-duchy of Baden, that in a polished state greatly resembles diamonds], Bristol-stone; ägyptischer —, Egyptian pebble.

Kiesel-conglomerat, *n.* V. —klumpen. —**erde**, *f.* siliceous earth. —**fels**, *m.* flinty rock. —**glas**, *n.* flint-glass. —**hart**, *adj.* and *adv.* as hard as a pebble or flint, flinty [in a proper as well as in a fig. sense]. *Er hat ein —hartes Herz, he has a flinty heart. —**klumpen**, *m.* [*Puddingstein] pudding-stone, oculatus lapis. —**mehl**, *n.* pounded pebbles, powder of pebble stones. —**sand**, —**sandstein**, *m.* coarse gravel, siliceous sandstone. —**schiefer**, *m.* siliceous shist. —**sinter**, *m.* siliceous sinter, pearl-sinter. —**spath**, [*Tremolith, *Grammatit] tremolite, amphibole, grammatite. —**stein**, *m.* V. Kiesel. —**tuff**, *m.* V. —sinter.

Kieseln, *v. intr. impers.* to hail. Es kieselt, it hails.

Kiesen, *v. tr.* [Fr. *choisir*, Sax. *ceosan*, V. Köhren] to choose, to select, V. Erkiesen. [in seamen's lang.] Einen Hafen —, to enter a port or harbour, to put into a port; die Räumde —, to put to sea, to set sail.

Kiesicht, *adj.* resembling gravel, gravelly; [in mineralogy] pyritic, pyritous.

Kiesig, *adj.* containing gravel, gravelly; [in mineralogy] pyritic, pyritous.

||1. **Kieze**, *f.* [*pl.* -n] [allied to Kiste, Kasten] a sort of hollow vessel, a small basket.

||2. **Kieze** or **Kitze**, *f.* [*pl.* -n] female cat.

||**Kiffe**, *f.* [*pl.* -n] [allied to Käfich, Koben &c.] a small miserable house, cottage or apartment.

***Kilogramm**, *n.* [-s, *pl.* -e] [a French weight] kilogram.

***Kilometer**, *n.* [-s, *pl.* -] [= 1000 metres, 5th part of a league] kilometer.

||**Kimm**, *m.* [-es] horizon.

1. **Kimme**, *f.* [*pl.* -n] [allied to the Fr. *cime*, to Kamm &c.] edge, border. Die — eines Fasses, the chimb or chime of a barrel; [in seamen's lang.] V. Kimmung.

Kimm-eisen, *n.* [among coopers] a small hatchet used in forming the bottoms of casks. —**gang**, *m.* V. Kimmplanke. —**hobel**, *m.* [among coopers] a sort of plane used in the [illegible] of barrels. —**keule**, *f.* the wooden mallet [illegible] by coopers. —**planke**, *f.* [in ship-building] [illegible] planks which cover the edge of ships [illegible]. —**weger**, *m.* [in ship-building] the thick [illegible] planks of the ship's side. —**weide**, *f.* the twigs round which the body of the basket [illegible] formed.

2 **Kimme**, *f.* [*pl.* -n] [allied to **Kammer**, **Kumpf**, L. *cym-ba*, *cub-are* &c.] notch, nick, indentation.

Kimmen, *v. tr.* 1) to notch. 2) to cut to an edge.

Kimming, **Kimmung**, *f.* [in seamen's lang.] 1) floor-heads, wrung-heads. 2) V. **Kimm.**

Kimmker, *m.* [-s, *pl.* -] V. **Böttcher.**

Kind, *n.* [-es, *pl.* -er] [Sax. *cild*, Eng. *child*, Dan. *kuld* = progeny; perhaps referable to the Sax. *cennan*, Gr. *γεννᾷν*, L. *gignere* = erzeugen] child. **Ein kleines —, ein —chen, ||—lein,** a little child, an infant, a babe, baby; **— im Mutterleibe,** embryo, foetus; ***so unschuldig seyn, wie das — im Mutterleibe,** to be as innocent as the child unborn; **ein unzeitiges —,** a child born before its time, an abortive child; **ein nachgebornes [nach dem Tode seines Vaters gebornes] —,** a posthumous child; **ein — an der Mutter Brust,** a suckling; **ein todtgebornes —,** a still-born child; **ein angenommenes —,** an adopted or adoptive child; **ein eheliches —,** a legitimate child; **ein uneheliches —,** a natural, an illegitimate child; **ein — gebären, eines —es genesen** [rather obsolete], **von einem —e entbunden werden,** to bring forth a child, to be brought to bed with a child, to be delivered of a child; **—er haben, bekommen,** to have children; **—er erzeugen,** to beget children; **sie geht mit dem —e** [in popular lang.], she is with child, she is pregnant or in the family way. *Fig.* [in fam. lang.] **Er ist ein Wiener &c. —,** he is a native of Vienna &c., he is born in Vienna; **er ist ein ächtes Londoner —,** he is a genuine or regular cockney; **die —er Gottes,** the children of God; **er ist ein — des Todes,** he is a dead man, he is lost; **er ist kein — mehr,** he is no longer a child; **er ist seiner Mutter —** [= **artet ihr nach**], he takes after his mother; **von — auf,** from a child, from childhood, V. **Kindheit; wohlan! Muth gefaßt, meine —er!** cheer up, friends! *prov.* **—er und Narren sagen die Wahrheit,** children and fools tell or speak the truth; *prov.* V. **Bad** 2); *prov.* **je lieber das —, desto schärfer die Ruthe,** or **wer sein — lieb hat, hält es strenge,** spare the rod and spoil the child; **das — bei seinem [rechten] Namen nennen,** to call every thing by its name, to speak plain; *prov.* **ein verbranntes — fürchtet das Feuer,** a burnt child dreads the fire; **auch das — im Mutterleib nicht verschonen,** to spare neither age nor sex.

Kind-bett, *n.* child-bed, lying-in, confinement. **Sie ist, liegt im —bette,** she is lying-in, in child-bed, in her confinement; **in's —bett kommen,** to be brought to bed, V. **Niederkommen, Entbunden werden; sie starb im —bette,** she died in child-bed; **aus dem —bette gehen,** to go out after lying-in, to be churched. **—betterinn**, *f.* a woman in child-bed, a woman lying-in. **—betterinnfieber**, *n.* a fever incident to women in child-bed. **—betterreinigung**, *f.* the discharges which follow child-birth, lochia. **—bettersuppe**, *f.* V. **—bettsuppe.** **—bettfieber**, *n.* V. **—betterinnfieber.** **—bettsuppe**, *f.* broth or soup for a woman in child-bed. **—taufe**, *f.* V. **Kindstaufe.**

Kindel-bier, *n.* beer drunk at a christening; *it.* christening-feast. **—markt, —tag,** *m.* V. **Kindermarkt** &c.

Kinder-alter, *n.* child's age. **—amme**, *f.* wet-nurse. **—arbeit**, *f.* the occupation or amusement of children; *it.* work for children, easy work. **—blattern**, *pl.* small-pox. **—brei**, *m.* pap. **—brut**, *f.* [in fam. language, in contempt] brats. **—dieb**, *m.* kidnapper. **—feind**, *m.* an enemy to children, one who hates children. **—flecken**, *pl.* measles. **—frau**, *f.* nurse. **—fresser**, *m.* 1) one who eats children, child-eater; [in mythology] Saturn. 2) a bugbear to frighten children. **—freund**, *m.* one who is fond of children, friend of children. **—geld**, *n.* money belonging to children, especially to minors or orphans, pupillary money. **—geschrei**, *n.* the cry, crying of children. **—glaube**, *m.* belief or faith of a child; *it.* credulity of a child. **Er hat den schönen —glauben verloren,** he lost the confiding faith or dreams of his childish years. **—händel**, *pl.* quarrel of children. **—haube**, *f.*, **—häubchen, ||—häublein**, *n.* a child's cap, biggin. **—hemd, —hemdchen, ||—hemdlein**, *n.* a child's shirt. **—husten**, *m.* hooping-cough. **—jahre**, *pl.* the years of infancy or childhood. **—kirsche**, *f.* V. **Maikirsche.** **—klapper**, *f.* a child's rattle. **—kleid, —kleidchen, ||—kleidlein**, *n.*, **—kleidung**, *f.* a child's frock, dress or garment. **—lehen**, *n.* pupillary fief. **—lehre**, *f.* instruction in the catechism. **—lehre halten,** to catechise. **—lehrer**, *m.*, **—lehrerinn**, *f.* 1) a person who teaches or instructs children. 2) catechist, catechiser. **—leicht**, *adj.* and *adv.* [in fam. lang.] very easy to be done or understood. **—liebe**, *f.* 1) the love one bears to children, love of children. 2) the love of children towards their parents, filial love. **—lied, —liedchen, ||—liedlein**, *n.* a song for children, V. **Wiegenlied.** **—los**, *adj.* and *adv.* childless, having no children, without children; bereft of one's children. **—mädchen**, *n.*, **—magd**, *f.* nursery-maid. **—mährchen, ||—mährlein**, *n.* a tale or story for children, a tale of a tub, a cock-and-bull story. **—markt**, *m.* fair before Christmas, at which Christmas-presents for children are purchased, children's fair. **—mord**, *m.* 1) child-murder, infanticide. **Der Bethlehemitische —mord,** the infanticide or slaughter of infants [ordered by Herod]. 2) [in botany] V. **Sevenbaum.** **—mörder**, *m.*, **—mörderinn**, *f.* an infanticide. **—muhme**, *f.* V. **—frau.** **—mutter**, *f.* 1) [unusual] a mother of children. 2) [in fam. lang.] a mother who is very fond of her children. 3) [rather provincial] a midwife. **—mütze**, *f.* V. **—haube.** **—narr**, *m.*, **—närrinn**, *f.* [in familiar language] a person who is excessively fond of, who doats on children. **—pech**, *n.* [in medicine] meconium. **—pfeife**, *f.* a child's whistle. **—pocken**, *pl.* small-pox. **—possen**, *pl.* childish trifles, childish tricks, fooling [in a proper as well as in a fig. sense]. V. **Kinderei.** **—pulver**, *n.* a quieting powder for infants. **—raub**, *m.* kidnapping. **—räuber**, *m.* V. **—dieb.** **—reich**, *adj.* and *adv.* having many children. **—rein**, *adj.* as pure or innocent as a child. **—rock**, *m.*, **—röckchen, ||—röcklein**, *n.* a child's frock. **—saft**, *m.* a syrup given to infants. **—schuh**, *m.* a child's shoe. *Prov.* **Die —schuhe vertreten haben,** to be no longer a child, to be past a child, to be past the spoon. **—schule**, *f.* a school for children. **—sinn**, *m.* a pure, innocent mind, a childlike candour or simplicity. **—spiel**, *n.* a child's play. ******Fig.* **Das ist ihm ein —spiel,** that's very easy for him; **es ist kein —spiel,** it is no children's play, no joking matter. **—spielwaaren**, *pl.* playthings, toys. **—spielwerk, —spielzeug**, *n.* a plaything, toy. **—spott**, *m.* sport for children, laughing-stock of children. **—sprache**, *f.* language of children, childish language. **—sterben**, *n.* [in familiar language] **starkes, häufiges —sterben,** great mortality among children. **—streich**, *m.* a childish trick, V. **Kinderei.** **—stube**, *f.* nursery. **—stuhl**, *m.*, **—stühlchen, ||—stühllein**, *n.* a [little] chair for children. **—tag**, *m.* Innocents' day. **—tand**, *m.* V. **—spielwerk.** **—taufe**, *f.* baptism of children. **—trommel**, *f.* a little drum for children. **—vogt**, *m.* a tutor. **—wagen**, *m.*, **—wägelein**, *n.* 1) a little waggon for children. 2) a go-cart. **—wärterinn**, *f.* V. **—frau.** **—welt**, *f.* 1) the life, existence or doings of children. 2) the children themselves. 3) the objects that suit children, the children's world. **—wiege**, *f.* a child's cradle. **—zucht**, *f.* education and government of children.

Kindes-alter, *n.* V. **Kinderalter.** **—beine**, *pl.* [only used in the familiar phrase:] **Von —beinen an,** from a child, from one's infancy, from the cradle. **—kind**, *n.* a child's child, grand-child. **Unsere —kinder werden davon reden,** our great grand-children, the latest posterity will speak of it. **—liebe**, *f.* filial love. **—mörder**, *m.*, **—mörderinn**, *f.* V. **Kindermörder** &c. **—noth**, *f.* V. **Kindsnoth.** **—pflicht**, *f.* filial duty. **—recht**, *n.* the right of a child, the right of filiation. **—sinn**, *m.* V. **Kindersinn.** **—statt**, *f.* **Einen an —statt annehmen, aufnehmen,** to adopt any one; **die Annahme** or **Aufnahme an —statt,** adoption. **—theil**, *m.* portion of inheritance due to each child.

Kinds-blattern, *pl.* V. **Kinderblattern.** **—brei**, *m.* V. **Kinderbrei.** **—kopf**, *m.* a child's head. ******Fig.* a childish or puerile person. **Seyen Sie kein —kopf,** don't be so childish. **—magd**, *f.* V. **Kindermagd.** **—noth**, *f.* [generally in the plural, **—nöthe**, in familiar language] labour, child-birth. **In —nöthen seyn, liegen,** to be in labour. **—pech**, *n.* V. **Kinderpech.** **—taufe**, *f.* [in familiar language] christening of a child. **Zur —taufe einladen,** to invite to the christening-feast. **—taufschmaus**, *m.* christening feast or banquet. **—theil**, *m.* V. **Kindestheil.** **—wasser**, *n.* [in medicine] the fluid of the amnios. **—zeug**, *n.* a child's clothes or apparel; *it.* V. **Wickelzeug.**

Kinden, **Kindeln**, **Kindern**, *v. intr.* 1) [unusual] to be brought to bed with, to be delivered of a child. **Sie kindet noch,** she is not yet past child-bearing. 2) to behave, to play or toy like a child.

Kinderei, *f.* childishness, puerility, childish behaviour, childish, foolish, silly trick. **—en treiben,** to play the child or fool, to trifle or fool away one's time, to be trifling.

Kindhaft, *adj.* and *adv.* V. **Kindisch.**

Kindheit, *f.* childhood, infancy. **Von meiner — an,** from my infancy, from a child. *Fig.* **In der — Roms,** in the infancy of Rome.

Kindisch, *adj.* and *adv.* childish, childlike, puerile. **—es Wesen,** childish manners, childishness; **ein —es Gesicht,** a childish face; **sie hat eine —e Freude daran,** she is delighted with it like a child; **eine —e Unterhaltung,** a puerile amusement; **sich — betragen,** to play the child, to behave childishly.

Kindlich, *adj.* and *adv.* childlike, becoming a child, filial. **Ein —er Gehorsam, eine —e Liebe,** filial obedience, love; **sie ist so —, und das macht sie so liebenswürdig,** she is so natural or unaffected, and that makes her so amiable; **—e Unschuld,** childlike innocence; **ihr habt einen —en Geist empfangen** [in Scripture], ye have received the spirit of adoption.

Kindlichkeit, *f.* childlike or filial sentiments or conduct.

Kindschaft, *f.* the relation of a child to its parents, filiation, sonship. **Die — empfangen** [in Scripture], to receive the adoption of sons.

Kink, *m.* [-es, *pl.* -e] [in seamen's language] coiling, kink.

Kinkhorn, *n.* [-s, *pl.* -hörner] [from the old

Kink = Zinke] 1) [a musical instrument] a cornet 2) [in conchology] whelk, buccinum. Versteinertes —, buccinita.

Kinn, *n.* [-es, *pl.* -e] [Sax. *cin*, Engl. *chin*, Celtic *gen*, *gana* = Wange, L. *gena*, Gr. γένυς] 1) [in general] any thing prominent. [in architecture] *a*) the brow or coping of a wall. *b*) Das — einer Dachrinne, the spout of a gutter. [in seamen's lang.] V. —back. 2) [generally] chin; *dim.* —chen, ||—lein, *n.* a little chin. Ein spitziges —, a pointed chin; das — des Pferdes, the nether jaw of a horse.

Kinn-back or —backen, *m.* [in seamen's lang.] fore-foot placed at the extremity of the keel forward. —backen, *m.* jaw or jaw-bone; [in anatomy] mandible. Zu den —backen gehörig, maxillary; der obere und untere —backen, the upper and nether mandible. —backenbein, *n.* maxillary bone. —backendrüsen, *pl.* maxillary glands. —backengrube, *f.* maxillary pit. —backenhöhle, *f.* maxillary sinus. —backenknochen, *m.* V. —backenbein. —backenzahn, *m.* jaw-tooth, cheek-tooth. —backenzwang, *m.* locked jaw, V. Mundsperre. —band, *n.* chin-cloth. —bart, *m.* beard on the chin. —grüblein, *n.* dimple in the chin. —höcker, *m.* [in anatomy] the point of the under jaw, the chin. —kette, *f.* curb. —kettenkappe, *f.* barnacles. —lade, *f.* V. —backen. —reif, *m.* V. —kette. —schlagader, *f.* artery of the chin.

Kinschwurzel, *f.* [*pl.* -n] the upright or climbing birthwort.

Kinster, *m.* V. Kenster.

Kintschelbeere, *f.* [*pl.* -n] V. Vogelkirsche.

Kippe, *f.* [*pl.* -n] [V. 1. Kippen] state of being placed on an edge, on the point of tilting. Auf der — stehen, to be on the point of falling or tilting, to be a-tilt; **fig.* to stand or be on the point of a precipice, to be on the point of perishing; *it.* of becoming bankrupt, of breaking.

Kippeln, [allied to keifen = beißen] I. *v. tr.* to cut, to clip [money]. II. *v. r.* sich — [in popular lang.] to quarrel, to wrangle.

1\. **Kippen**, [allied to the Gr. κύπτω, L. *cubo*] I. *v. intr.* 1) to move backwards and forwards, to swing. Mit dem Stuhle —, to balance one's body on a chair. 2) to be in the act or on the point of falling over or tilting; *it.* to fall or turn over. V. Auf—, Um—. II. *v. tr.* to put on the edge, to tilt. Ein Faß —, to tilt a barrel; [in seamen's lang.] den Anker —, to get the anchor up along the bow [in order to stow it to the gunnel], to stow the anchor.

Kippkarren, *m.* [-s, *pl.*-] a cart the body of which turns up or tilts, tilting-cart.

2\. **Kippen**, *v. tr.* [allied to kappen = schneiden] to cut, to clip. V. Kappen, Köpfen. — und wippen, to clip [money].

Kippgeld, *n.* clipped money; *it.* base or bad money.

Kipper, *m.* [-s, *pl.* -] — und Wipper, clipper of money.

Kippergeld, *n.* V. Kippgeld.

Kipperei, *f.* 1) the clipping of money. 2) usurious way of dealing, usury.

1\. **Kippern**, V. Kepern.

2\. **Kippern**, *v. intr.* [perhaps instead of kippern, from kaufen] to engross or forestall corn.

Kirche, *f.* [*pl.* -n] [Sax. *circe*, *circ* or *cirie*, Scotch *kirk*, Gr. κυριακόν = temple of God, or allied to the L. *circus*, Gr. ἕρκος = Einschluß] church. Eine bischöfliche —, a cathedral; eine — stiften, bauen, begaben, to found, build, endow a church. *Fig. a*) divine service. Er ist in der —, he is at church; zur or in die — gehen, to go to church; die — ist aus, the church or service is over; die Braut in die — führen, sich im Angesichte der — trauen lassen, to marry publicly; er kam unter der —, he came during divine service; vor der —, before divine service. *b*) [all those who have one creed or dogma and who use the same ritual and ceremonies] church. Die katholische or allgemeine —, the catholic or universal church; die römische und griechische —, the Roman and Greek churches; die französische —, the Gallican church; die englische —, the English or Anglican church, the [high] church of England; die reformirte —, the reformed church; die morgenländische, abendländische —, the church of the East, of the West; die jüdische —, the Jewish church; Einen wieder in den Schooß der — zurückführen, to restore any one within the pale of the church. *c*) [the body of clergy; *it.* the ecclesiastical order] church. Ich bestimmte ihn für die —, I intended him for the church. V. also Tempel.

Kirch-bau, *m.* V. Kirchenbau. —dieb, *m.* V. Kirchendieb. —dorf, *n.* village with a church. —eule, *f.* screech-owl, howlet, madge-howlet. —fahrt, *f.* 1) procession to church. 2) [obsolete] parish, V. —spiel. —frau, *f.* V. Kirchenpatroninn. —gang, *m.* 1) church-way. 2) a walk or passage in a church, aisle. 3) act of going to church [especially upon some particular occasions]. Der —gang einer Wöchnerinn, the churching of a woman after lying in. —gänger, *m.*, —gängerinn, *f.* a person who goes to church, church-goer. Ein fleißiger —gänger, a frequenter of the church. —genoß, *m.*, —genossinn, *f.* fellow parishioner. —herr, *m.* 1) V. Kirchenpatron 1). 2) [less usual for] the rector of a church. —hof, *m.* 1) the court or yard round a church. 2) church-yard, cemetery. —maus, *f.* V. Kirchenmaus. —meister, *m.* V. Kirchenälteste. —messe, *f.* a festival in commemoration of the dedication of the church, church-ale, wake, ||pattern; *it.* a fair held on such a festival. —rechnung, *f.* church-account. —schwalbe, *f.* swift, black martin. —spiel, *n.* parish; *it.* the parishioners. —spielkirche, *f.* parish-church. —spielschreiber, *m.* parish-clerk, vestry-clerk. —spielsteuer, *f.* parochial tax, parish-duty. —spielvorsteher, *m.* vestry-man. Die —spielvorsteher, vestry-men, church-wardens. —sprengel, *m.* diocese. In diesem —sprengel sind so viele —spiele, there are so many parishes in this diocese. —stand, —stuhl, *m.* V. Kirchenstand &c. —stock, *m.* church-box, poor's-box. —tag, *m.* 1) church-day. 2) V. —weihe 2). —thür, *f.* church-door. —thurm, *m.* church-steeple. —thurmspitze, *f.* the spire of a church-steeple. —vater, *m.* 1) V. Kirchenälteste, Kirchenvorsteher. 2) V. Kirchenvater 2). —weg, *m.* church-way. —weihe, *f.* 1) consecration or dedication of a church. 2) feast or festival of the consecration of a church, V. —messe. —zeit, *f.* the time or hour of divine service, church-time.

Kirchen-ablaß, *m.* indulgence [granted by the Pope or Church]. —agende, *f.* V. —buch 2). —älteste, *m.* elder of the church, church-warden, lay-elder, presbyter, vestry-man. —amt, *n.* 1) ecclesiastical office, church-office. 2) the body of vestrymen. 3) consistory. —bann, *m.* [der große —bann] excommunication; [der kleine —bann], interdict. Einen in den —bann thun, to excommunicate any one; *it.* to interdict any one; im —banne seyn, to be excommunicated or interdicted. —bau, *m.* the act of building a church, the erection or construction of a church. —baukasse, *f.* the fund appropriated for the repairs of a church. —beamte, *m.* 1) a churchman, clergyman. 2) V. —älteste. 3) V. —diener. —brauch, *m.* V. —gebrauch. —buch, *n.* 1) a book belonging to the church. 2) ritual, liturgy, agenda. 3) parochial register, church-book. —buße, *f.* penance done in the church or imposed by the church. —ceremonial, *n.* ceremonial. —ceremonie, *f.* V. —gebrauch. —convent, *m.* 1) convening or meeting of the clergymen of certain dioceses at certain fixed times. 2) V. —gericht. —dieb, *m.* V. —räuber. —diebstahl, *m.* V. —raub. —diener, *m.* 1) servant of the church. 2) sexton, V. Küster —dienst, *m.* 1) office or employment relating to the church, ecclesiastical office. 2) form of prayer, church-service, the rites of the church, liturgy. —dienstlich, *adj.* belonging or relating to divine service. —dienstliche Handlungen, religious acts, acts of religion. || or ‡—dußler, *m.* V. —knecht. —einkünfte, *pl.* the revenues of the church, of a church. —fahne, *f.* 1) [in the Romish church] a standard or banner of a church. 2) a vane. —fahnenträger, *m.* holy standard-bearer. —falk, *m.* a kind of hawk, kestrel. —fenster, *n.* church-window. —fenster von buntem Glase, oriel-window. —fest, *n.* 1) V. Kirchmesse. 2) a holiday or festival ordained by the church. —fluch, *m.* anathema, V. —bann. —freiheit, *f.* liberty or immunity of the church, ecclesiastical liberty. —friede, *m.* 1) concord or union of the members of a church. 2) V. Gottesfriede. —gänger, *m.*, —gängerinn, *f.* V. Kirchgänger. —gebäude, *n.* 1) a building belonging or attached to a church. 2) church. Diese prächtigen —gebäude, those stately churches or religious piles. —gebet, *n.* a prayer read in church, common prayer. —gebiet, *n.* [eines Bischofs] diocese. —gebot, *n.* commandment of the church. —gebrauch, *m.* ceremony or rite of the church. —gefäß, *n.* church-vessel, sacred vessel. —gehen, *n.* the [act of] going to church. —geld, *n.* 1) money or fund belonging to a church or appropriated for the repairs of a church. 2) *pl.* —gelder, the revenues of a church. —gemeinde or —gemeine, *f.* parish. —gemeinschaft, *f.* communion of the church. —gepränge, *n.* the pompous or showy ceremonies of the church. —geräth, *n.* utensils for the church, sacred vessels or utensils. —gerechtigkeit, *f.*, —gerechtsame, *pl.* immunity or privilege of a church. —gericht, *n.* ecclesiastical court, consistory. —gesang, *m.* 1) church-singing, church-music. 2) V. —lied. —geschenk, *n.* a gift or present made to a church. —geschichte, *f.* ecclesiastical history. —geschworne, *m.* V. —pfleger. —gesetz, *n.* law of the church, church-law. —gewohnheit, *f.* V. —gebrauch. —glaube, *m.* the creed or dogma of the church or of a church. —glied, *n.* the member of a church or of a communion. —gut, *n.* church-property, church-land; [—grund] glebe-land. —handbuch, *n.* V. —buch 2). —herr, *m.* V. Kirchherr. —jahr, *n.* ecclesiastical year. —kalender, *m.* the church-almanac. —kasse, *f.* V. —baukasse. —kissen, *n.* a cushion for kneeling. —knecht, *m.* a servant employed in the church, church-beadle. —kux, *m.* share in a mine belonging to a church. —lehen, *n.* 1) an ecclesiastical fief. 2) a benefice held in fief. 3) V. —satz. —lehensherr, *m.* the patron of a benefice. —lehre, *f.* doctrine of the church. —lehrer, *m.* 1) teacher of the church, V. Religionslehrer. 2) father of the church, V. —vater 2). —licht, *n.* the light or taper in a church. *Fig.* [in familiar language, frequently in jest] great teacher of the church. —lied, *n.* hymn or psalm sung in the church, church-hymn. —mantel, *m.* V. —

red. —maus, *f.* church-mouse. *Prov.* Hungerig, wie eine —maus, as hungry as a church-mouse. —musik, *f.* church-music. —nachbar, *m.*, —nachbarinn, *f.* a person who sits near us in church, neighbour in church. —ordnung, *f.* church-service, ritual, liturgy, agenda. —patron, *m.*, —patroninn, *f.* 1) patron, patroness of a benefice. 2) the guardian saint, patron, patroness. —pfleger, *m.* church-warden. —polster, *n.* V. —kissen. —postille, *f.* a book of comment on Scripture read in church. V. Postille. —propst, *m.* provost of an ecclesiastical establishment. —rath, *m.* 1) ecclesiastical council, consistory. 2) a member of the ecclesiastical council, ecclesiastical counsellor [often a mere title]. —räthlich, *adj.* belonging to the ecclesiastical council or consistory. —raub, *m.* robbery of the church, sacrilege. —räuber, *m.*, —räuberinn, *f.* a thief that robs the church, church-robber, a person guilty of sacrilege. —räuberisch, *adj.* sacrilegious. —rechnung, *f.* parish or church account. —recht, *n.* 1) privilege of the church. 2) canon-law. —rechtlich, *adj.* according to the canon-law. —regierung, *f.*, —regiment, *n.* ecclesiastical government; *it.* hierarchy. —register, *n.* V. —buch 3). —rock, *m.* cassock. —ruf, *m.* proclamation made in church, V. [the more usual word] [kirchliches] Aufgebot. —sache, *f.* ecclesiastical affair or concern. —sänger, *m.* chanter [in a church], chorister. —satz, *m.* the right of filling the ecclesiastical offices, patronage, right of presentation. —satzung, *f.* ordinance of the church. —schatz, *m.* treasure of the church. —schein, *m.* certificate from the church-register, V. Taufschein, Todtenschein, Trauschein. —schmuck, *m.* what belongs to the ornament of the church or the church-service, church-ornaments. —schutz, *m.* patronage. —siegel, *n.* the seal of a church or parish. —sitz, *m.* seat in a church, V. —stuhl. —spaltung, *f.* schism in the church. —sprache, *f.* language of the church, theological language. —staat, *m.* 1) ecclesiastical state. 2) the papal territory, the Ecclesiastical States. —stand, *m.* place in a church, V. —stuhl. —steuer, *f.* church-tax or rate; *it.* a collection or gathering of money in the church. —stock, *m.* V. Kirchstock. —strafe, *f.* ecclesiastical punishment or fine. Sich der —strafe unterwerfen, to submit to the censures of the church. —streit, *m.*, —streitigkeit, *f.* V. Religionsstreit &c. —stuhl, *m.* a pew. —tag, *m.* V. Kirchtag. —thurm, *m.* V. Kirchthurm. —vater, *m.* 1) church-warden. 2) father of the church [one of the ecclesiastical writers of the first centuries of the Christian era]. —väterkunde, *f.* V. *Patristik. —verächter, *m.* one who withdraws from an established church, separatist; *it.* one who disobeys the church-discipline. —verbesserer, *m.* reformer. —verbesserung, *f.* reformation. —verordnung, *f.* ordinance of the church. —versammlung, *f.* 1) assembly of the church, council of the church or of divines or clergymen. Die —versammlung zu Kostnitz, the council of Constance. 2) synod, [in England and Scotland] convocation. —verwalter, *m.* V. —pfleger. —visitation, *f.* visitation of a church, parochial visitation. —vogt, *m.* V. —knecht. —vorschrift, *f.* 1) V. —gesetz. 2) ritual, liturgy. 3) V. —verordnung. —vorsteher, *m.* churchwarden, V. —älteste. —weise, *f.* church-melody, V. Sangweise. —wesen, *n.* affairs of the church, ecclesiastical affairs. —zettel, *m.* 1) church-register. 2) a bill notifying the preachers on each sunday. —zierrath, *m.* V. —schmuck. —zucht, *f.* church-discipline.

Kirchlich, *adj.* and *adv.* belonging or relating to the church, ecclesiastic. Ein —es Amt, Gut, Recht &c., V. Kirchenamt, Kirchengut &c.; die —en Angelegenheiten, ecclesiastical affairs.

Kirchner, *m.* [-s, *pl.* -] clerk of the church, parish-clerk; vestry-keeper, sexton, sacristan.

||**Kirech** or **Kiree**, *m.* [-s, *pl.* -] [Polish *kireia* = great coat] a man's cloak or great coat lined with fur, fur-cloak, fur-coat.

Kirmes, **Kirmse**, *f.* [*pl.* -n] V. Kirchmesse, Kirchweihe.

Kirnen, **Kirner**, V. Körnen, Körner.

Kirrbar, *adj.* that may be allured or tamed.

Kirre, *adj.* and *adv.* [Icel. *kyrre* and Sw. *qudrr* = ruhig. Perhaps allied to the L. *cicur*] tame, familiar. Ein —r Vogel, a tame bird; — machen, to make tame or familiar, to tame. **Fig.* tractable, submissive, humble. Einen — machen, to make any one tractable, familiar or submissive; — werden, to grow tractable. SYN. Kirre, Zahm. Zahme creatures are those which live quietly with man, and are either subjected, harmless or useful to him, as fowls, ducks, horses &c. Kirre is said of such among tame animals, and particularly among birds, which instead of shunning, live, in some measure, sociably with man. The fowls in a poultry-yard are all zahm, but those brought up in a room will be so kirre as even to follow persons about.

Kirre, *f.* 1) the state of being tame or tractable. 2) —, [*pl.* -n] turtle-dove. 3) [in botany] alsine, spurrey, spergula.

1. **Kirren**, [V. Kirre] *v. tr.* to tame, to render gentle or familiar.

2. **Kirren**, [allied to girren, Gr. γηρύω; originally = to emit a sound] I. *v. intr.* to make a sound; [said of the wheels of a carriage] to creak, V. Knarren; [said of the teeth] to crunch, to gnash; [said of doves or pigeons] to coo. II. *v. tr.* to call [said of hens calling their chickens]. *Fig.* to lure, to allure, to attract. V. also Locken, Körren, Ködern.

Kirr-eule, *f.* the common owl. —hahn, *m.* [a fish] gurnard or gurnet. —mewe, *f.* a sort of mew or sea-swallow.

Kirrung, *f.* 1) the act of baiting or alluring, allurement. 2) the place where wild beasts are baited. 3) food for baiting, bait.

Kirsat, [-es] V. Kirsei.

Kirsche, *f.* [*pl.* -n] [L. *cerasum*, Pers. *keras*, probably allied to the Gr. κέρας, Korn, Kern, Hirse, and not from the town of Cerasus] cherry; V. Früh—, Mai—, Herz—, Süß—, Spät—, Weichsel—. *Prov.* Mit großen Herren ist nicht gut —n essen, those that eat cherries with great persons, will have their eyes splinted out with the stones.

Kirsch-baum, *m.* cherry-tree. —beißer, *m.* haw-finch. —blümchen, *n.* daisy. —blüte, *f.* cherry-blossom or bloom. —branntwein, *m.* cherry-brandy. —farbe, *f.* cherry-colour. —fink, *m.* V. —beißer. —garten, or —ensgarten, *m.* cherry-orchard. —geist, *m.* V. —branntwein. —gummi or —harz, *n.* gum of cherry-trees, cherry-gum. —isop, V. Heidenisop. —käfer, *m.* cherry-weevil or mite. —kern, *m.* cherry-stone or kernel. —kuchen or —enskuchen, *m.* cherry-cake. —lorbeer, —lorbeerbaum, *m.* cherry-bay, cherry-laurel. —lorbeere, *f.* fruit or berry of the cherry-laurel. —meth, *m.* hydromel or mead made with cherry-juice. —muß or —ensmuß, *n.* conserve or marmalade of cherries. —perle, *f.* a pearl of the size of a cherry. —pfirsche, *f.* or —pfirsich, *m.* cherry-peach. —pflaume or —enspflaume, *f.* the myrobolan plum. —roth, *adj.* like a red cherry in colour, cherry. —saft, *m.* cherry-juice. —schneller, *m.* V. —beißer. —stein or —enstein, *m.* cherry-stone. —stiel or —ensstiel, *m.* the stalk of a cherry. —suppe, *f.* soup made of cherries. —tarte, or —torte, *f.* cherry-tart. —vogel, *m.* V. Goldbrossel. —wäldchen, *n.* an orchard of cherry-trees. —wasser, *n.* V. —geist. —wein, *m.* wine mixed with cherry-juice; cherry-wine. —zeit or —enszeit, *f.* cherry-season.

Kirschner, *m.* V. Kürschner.

Kirsei, **Kirschei**, *m.* [-s] [from the Ital. *carisea* or Fr. *cariset*] kersey.

Kissen, *n.* [-s, *pl.* -] [Low L. *cussinus*, allied to Kutzen, Haut, Hütte, Kutte, Fr. *cotte*] cushion *Dim.* Kißchen, ||Kißlein, *n.* cushionet. Ein Kopf—, a pillow; V. Feder—, Fenster—, Kopf—, Kräuter—, Nadel—, Sattel—, Stuhl— &c.; *it.* V. Polster.

Kissen-bezug, —überzug, *m.* or —ziehe, —züge, *f.* a cover or case for a cushion or pillow.

Kiste, *f.* [*pl.* -n] [L. *cista*, Goth. *kas* = Gefäß, allied to Kasten, Pers. *kastr*] box, chest.

Kisten-deckel, *m.* the cover or lid of a chest. —holz, *n.* beech-wood for making chests. —macher, *m.* trunk-maker. —pfand, *n.* [obsolete, in law] a movable pledge.

Kister, **Kistner**, *m.* [-s, *pl.* -] V. Kistenmacher.

Kits or **Kitz**, *f.* [*pl.* -en] [a vessel with a main and mizzen-mast used as a yacht] ketch.

||**Kitschbaum**, *m.* V. Elsebeere.

Kitt, *m.* [-es, *pl.* -e] allied to Kette, from gatten = verbinden] cement. Der — der Glaser, der Schreiner, glazier's putty, joiner's putty; der — der Scheidekünstler, lute, luting.

Kitte, *f.* [*pl.* -n] 1) V. 1. Kette. 2) V. Kitt. 3) ||V. Quitte.

Kittel, *m.* [-s, *pl.* -] [allied to Kutte, Hütte &c.] frock, smock-frock [as worn by men]; bed-gown [as worn by women].

Kitten, *v. tr.* to cement; [among chimists] to lute, V. Aus—, Ver—.

1. **Kitter**, *m.* [-s, *pl.* -] cementer.

2. **Kitter**, *m.* [-s, *pl.* -] V. Zauber.

Kittern, V. Kichern.

Kitz, V. Kits.

Kitze, *f.* [*pl.* -n] *dim.* Kitzchen, ||Kitzlein, *n.* 1) a she-cat; *it.* a little cat. 2) a young goat. 3) V. Kits.

Kitzel, *m.* [-s] [Eng. ||*to kittle* and *to tickle*, Fr. *chatouiller*, L. *titillare*, seems to be allied to the Low Sax. ticken = stechen] itching, tickling, titillation. Einen — im Halse empfinden, to feel a tickling in one's throat; einen angenehmen — hervorbringen, to produce an agreeable titillation; der — der Sinne, pleasing sensations. *Fig.* [in fam. or popular lang.] longing, appetite, desire. Der — sticht ihn darnach, he has an itch after it, he longs mightily for it, he wants it sadly; er hat einen gewaltigen —, zu schreiben, zu sprechen, he has a great or violent itching to write, to talk; er hat mir den — darnach vertrieben, he has put me out of conceit with it; der — ist ihm vergangen, his longing is over.

Kitzelhusten, *m.* tickling-cough.

Kitzelig, *adj.* and *adv.* ticklish. Die Fußsohle ist ein sehr —er Theil, the sole or bottom of the foot is very ticklish. **Fig.* *a*) apt to take fire, touchy. *b*) difficult, nice, critical. Eine —e Sache, a ticklish business; ein —er Punkt, a touchy or delicate point.

Kitzeln, I. *v. tr.* to tickle, to titillate. Er kitzelt mich mit einem Strohhalme, he tickles me with a straw. *Fig.* Der Wein kitzelt den Gaumen, wine tickles the palate; die Musik kitzelt das Ohr, music pleases or gratifies the ear; er hatte durch solche Lobeserhebungen meine Ohren gekitzelt, he had tickled me with such praises; sich zum Lachen — [= gezwungen lachen], to provoke one's self to laughter; *Einen mit der Ehre —, to encourage any one upon the point of honour. II. *v. impers.* [in fam. lang.] Es kitzelt ihn, *a*) it nettles, stings, frets or vexes him, he is nettled at it, *b*) it delights him, he rejoices at it. III. *v. r.* [in fam. lang.] sich —, sich über Etwas —, to rejoice inwardly [at a thing]. Das —, V. Kitzel.

Kitzler, *m.* [-s, *pl.* -] tickler.

Klack or **Klacks,** [allied to Schlag] *interj.* [to express the sound made by the fall of a broad and soft substance] slap!

‖**Klack,** *m.* [-es, *pl.* Kläcke] [perhaps allied to Leck, Loch] [little used] cleft, fissure, chink, crack.

Kladde, *f.* [*pl.* -n] [Dutch Kladde = Schmutz] 1) waste-book, day-book. 2) first sketch or draught of a writing.

1. **Klaffen,** *v. intr.* [allied to the old klieben = spalten] to stand open, to gape, to yawn. Die Thüre, das Fenster klafft, the door, the window does not shut close, is a-jar; eine —de Wunde, a yawning wound; eine zu große Dürre macht, daß die Erde klafft, too great a drought makes the earth chink.

Klaffmuschel, *f.* the gaping wedge-shell or tellina.

2. **Klaffen,** *v. intr.* [Swed. *klaffa* = verläumden] to chatter, to clatter, V. Schwatzen, Plaudern.

Kläffen, *v. intr.* [allied to the Fr. *clapir*, *clabauder*, Sw. *glaffa*] to yelp, to bark. **Fig.* to clamour, to bawl, to chide, to scold.

Klaffer or **Kläffer,** *m.* [-s, *pl.* -] 1) a yelping dog; *it.* a hound that opens false. 2) [Klaffer] bed-talker, chatterer, V. Schwätzer; [Kläffer] a clamorous, bawling &c. person or fellow. 3) [in botany] *a*) cock's comb, lousewort. *b*) V. Bauernsenf.

Klafter, *f.* [*pl.* -n] [or *m.* -s, *pl.* -] [from klaffen = umfangen] [a measure of length containing six feet, the space to which a man may extend his arms] fathom. Eine or ein — [Brenn-] Holz, a cord of wood, a pile of fuel.

Klafter-holz, *n.* cord-wood. —**maß,** *n.* wood-measure, cord-measure. —**scheit,** *n.* a log of cord-wood. —**schlag,** *m.* the part of a forest where cord-wood is cutting. —**schläger,** *m.* wood-cleaver. —**setzer,** *m.* a sworn piler of cord-wood.

Klafterig, *adj.* containing a fathom [in composition, as zwei —, containing two fathoms].

Klaftern, *v. tr.* 1) to fathom. 2) to pile wood or other material for measurement and sale by the cord, to cord.

Klagbar, *adj.* and *adv.* accusable, actionable, that may be brought before a court of law. Eine Sache — machen, anbringen, to bring any thing before a court of law, to lay a complaint or information; [in law] — werden, to sue at law, to go to law.

Klage, *f.* [*pl.* -n] [V. Klagen] 1) complaint, lamentation. Er hat keine Ursache zur —, he has no subject of complaint; sie machten ihren —n Luft, they vented their complaints or complainings; wozu helfen alle die —n? of what use are all these lamentations? *it.* condolence; *it.* mourning; die — anlegen [obsolescent], to go into mourning; in der — gehen [obsolescent], to be in mourning, to mourn. 2) accusation, charge of an offence or crime, complaint. Eine — gegen Einen vorbringen, to prefer a complaint against any one; er führt große, bittere —n über or gegen Sie, he complains bitterly of you; [in law] suit at law, action, indictment; seine — eingeben, übergeben, vorbringen, to sue at law, to go to law; eine — gegen Einen anstellen or anhängig machen, to commence a law-suit, to bring an action against any one; eine bürgerliche, peinliche —, a civil, criminal action; eine persönliche —, a personal action; eine dingliche —, a real action; er ist mit seiner — abgewiesen worden, he has been nonsuited. SYN. V. Jammer.

Klag-endung, *f.* —**fall,** *m.* [in grammar] the accusative case. —**geschrei,** *n.* loud lament or lamentation, lamentable cries, loud wailings. —**gewand,** *n.* mourning suit or garment. —**los,** *adj.* and *adv.* 1) [little used] without complaining or complaint. 2) [at law] satisfied; indemnified. Einen —los stellen, to satisfy any one at law; to indemnify any one. —**losstellung,** *f.* satisfaction; indemnification. —**lustig,** *adj.* and *adv.* 1) litigious, quarrelsome. 2) querulous. —**punkt,** *m.*, —**rede,** *f.*, —**stimme,** *f.* V. Klagepunkt &c. —**sucht,** *f.* 1) litigiousness, quarrelsomeness, V. Streitsucht. 2) querulousness. —**süchtig,** *adj.* and *adv.* 1) querulous. 2) V. —lustig 1). —**weise,** *adv.* by way of complaint or accusation, V. Klägerisch. —**würdig,** *adj.* and *adv.* deplorable, lamentable.

Klage-bold, *m.* [in popular language] a person who is always making complaints. —**dichter,** *m.* elegiac poet. —**fall,** *m.* V. Klagendung. —**frau,** *f.* [formerly] a woman hired to lament a dead person, [hired] female-mourner. —**gedicht,** *n.*, —**gesang,** *m.* elegy. —**haus,** *n.* house of lamentation or mourning. —**laut,** *m.* V. —ton. —**lied,** *n.* 1) elegy, V. —gedicht. 2) mournful or doleful song. Die —lieder Jeremiä, the lamentations of Jeremiah. —**los,** *adj.* V. Klaglos. —**punkt,** *m.* charge. Erster, zweiter —punkt, the first, the second charge; es sind [liegen] mehrere —punkte gegen ihn [vor], there are several charges against him. —**rede,** *f.* 1) [in law] the plaintiff's complaint or pleading. 2) V. Trauerrede, Leichenrede. —**ruf,** *m.* plaintive cry, lamentation. —**sache,** *f.* law-suit. —**sänger,** *m.* V. —dichter. —**schrift,** *f.* a legal memorial containing a suit or accusation, a brief. Die zweite —schrift, replication; die dritte —schrift, surrejoinder. —**stimme,** *f.* plaintive voice. —**ton,** *m.* plaintive tone. —**weib,** *n.* V. —frau.

Klagenswerth, *adj.* and *adv.* V. Beklagenswerth.

Klägeln, *v. intr.* to be given to complaints, to be fond of complaints, to be of a querulous nature.

Klagen, [allied to the Gr. *κλαίειν* = weinen, L. *clamare* = schreien, Sw. *klaga* = sprechen] I. *v. intr.* 1) to utter expressions of grief, to lament, to complain. Er hat große Schmerzen ausgestanden, ohne zu —, he has suffered or endured great pains without moaning, lamenting or complaining; was haben Sie zu —? what ails you, what is the matter with you? where do you suffer? sie klagt sich schon mehrere Tage, she has been indisposed or ailing for several days; er klagt sich immer, he is always sickly or ailing; um einen verstorbenen Freund —, to deplore or to mourn the death of a friend or for a deceased friend; eine —de Stimme, a plaintive voice; Ihr — ist umsonst, it is in vain you lament. 2) to complain of any one or any thing. Ich habe alle Ursache, über Sie, über Ihre Aufführung zu —, I have good reason to complain of you, of your conduct; [in law] to bring an action, to sue at law; ich muß —, I must take the law or go to law, I must have recourse to the law; wider, gegen Einen —, —d gegen Einen einkommen or auftreten, to commence a law-suit, to bring an action against any one; auf Schadenersatz —, to sue for damages. II. *v. tr.* to lament, to deplore, to regret, to complain of. Einem Freunde seine Noth —, to complain of one's distress to a friend.

Kläger, *m.* [-es, *pl.* -] —**inn,** *f.* accuser, complainant, plaintiff. — seyn, als — gegen Einen erscheinen, auftreten, to be the accuser or complainant, to make one's self a party against any one; *prov.* wo kein — ist, da ist auch kein Richter, without an accuser or complainant there can be no judge.

Klägerei, *f.* disposition to complaining or continual complaining about trifles, querulousness.

Klägerisch, *adj.* and *adv.* relating to the plaintiff. Der —e Anwald, the plaintiff's attorney; eine Sache — or klageweise vorbringen, to sue at law, to go to law, to bring an action for or on account of any thing.

Kläglich, *adj.* and *adv.* 1) lamenting or complaining, plaintive, lamentable, mournful, woeful. Eine —e Stimme, a plaintive, mournful voice; —e Briefe, doleful or piteous letters; —es Geschrei, lamentable cries; — sprechen, to speak moanfully or dolefully; warum thut ihr so —? why do you complain so bitterly? 2) moving compassion, deplorable, wretched, miserable, grievous. Ein —er Fall, a deplorable, sad or grievous accident; ein —er Zustand, a deplorable condition or state; er fand mich in einem —en Zustande, he found me in a sad plight; er hat — geendet, he died in a tragical manner; das ist ein —es Machwerk, that is a wretched or miserable piece of work. V. Jämmerlich.

Kläglichkeit, *f.* state or quality of being lamentable or deplorable.

Klameien, *v. intr.* [in seamen's lang.] to stop the seams of a ship with the calking-iron.

Klameieisen, *n.* [in seamen's lang.] calking-iron.

Klamm, *adj.* and *adv.* [allied to klemmen, Sax. *clam* = ein Band] 1) tight, close, narrow. —e Schuhe, tight shoes; V. Knapp, Enge; *it.* compact, solid; —es Gold, V. —gold. 2) stiff. Die Finger werden —, the fingers grow stiff. **Fig.* oppressed about the chest, not breathing freely. Es ist mir — um das Herz, my heart is shrunk with grief, or oppressed, I am uneasy or anxious. 3) [in fam. lang.] scarce. Das Geld ist —, money is scarce.

Klamm-gällig, *adj.* [in mining] very hard or compact. —**gold,** *n.* massive gold. —**löthig,** *adj.* containing or weighing scarcely half an ounce.

Klamm, *m.* [-es, *pl.* -e] spasm in the throat.

Klammer, *f.* [*pl.* -n] [Sax. *clam*, Polish *klamra* = ein Band, V. Klamm] cramp, cramp-iron clincher; *it.* a hook; [in architecture] V. Balkenband, Strebeband; [in printing] visorium, retinaculum; [among joiners] holdfast. Eine kleine hölzerne —, [um Bilder, Wäsche &c. fest zu stecken], a peg [to fasten prints or linen to a line]; [among workers in timber] bracket. *Fig.* [in book including words] crotchet, bracket, V. Einklammern.

Klammer-erbse, *f.* sugar-pea. —**hirsch**, *m.* stag-beetle, horn-beetle, V. Hirschkäfer. —**satz**, *m.* a sentence in parenthesis. —**strauch**, *m.* [in botany] the echites.

Klámmern, *v. tr.* to hold fast with the hands, to fasten, to pinch, to crush, to squeeze, V. An—, Ein—, Um—.

Klámpe, *f* [*pl.* -n] [Eng *clamp*, allied to klamm, Klammer] clamp, clinch, holdfast, V. Krampe; [in seamen's lang.] cleat, saddle.

Klâmpern, V. Klimpern.

Klâmpner, V. Klempner.

*__Klandestine__, *f.* [*pl.* -n] [in botany] motherwort, clandestina.

Kláng, *m.* [-es, *pl.* Klänge] [L. *clangor*, V. Klingen] sound. Der — der Glocken, the sound or ringing of bells; einen — von sich geben, to make or yield a sound, to sound; [in fam. lang.] er wurde ohne — und Sang [= in der Stille] begraben, he was buried without any solemnity or privately. *Prov.* Ohne — und Gesang abziehen, to go away privately or clandestinely, to steal away, V. Ein—, Nach—, Uebel—, Wohl—, Wort—.

Klang-boden, *m.* sound-board, V. Resonanzboden. —**ente**, *f.* V. Quakente. —**gewölbe**, *n.* V. Sprachgewölbe. —**lehre**, *f.* acoustics. —**loch**, *n.* sound-hole. —**los** *adj.* soundless. —**nachahmung**, —**nachbildung**, *f.* 1) imitation of a sound. 2) [in grammar] onomatope or onomatopy. —**saal**, *m.* V. Concertsaal. —**spiel**, *n.* V. Tonspiel, Musik. —**stein**, *m.* sonorous stone. —**wort**, *n.* V. —nachahmung 2).

Klápf, I. *m.* [-es, *pl.* -e] [from klopfen] [in popular lang.] a blow given with the open hand or with something broad; *it.* the noise produced by such a blow, slap, flap, clap, clash. Einem einen — in's Gesicht geben, to give any one a slap on the face. II. *interj.* slap, bang!

Klápfen, V. Klappen.

Klápp, V. Klapf.

Klapp-bank, *f.* a folding-bench, a bench with a flap. —**boje**, *f.* buoy, V. Boje, Buke. —**bolzen**, *m.* [in seamen's lang.] preventer-bolt. —**bord**, *m.* V. Setzbord. —**handschuh**, *m.* V. Klappenhandschuh. —**holz**, *n.* clap-boards, staff-wood, staves. —**hut**, *m.* a hat with a flap, a hat that may be cocked. —**mütze**, *f.* 1) a leather-cap merely covering the top of the head; *it.* a cap with flaps, that may be turned up or down. 2) [in nat. hist.] the hooded seal or sea-calf. —**ohr**, *n.* a flap-eared horse. —**rose**, *f.* V. Klapperrose. —**stiefel**, *m.* V. Klappenstiefel. —**stuhl**, *m.* folding-chair. —**tisch**, *m.* a table with a flap, folding-table.

Kláppe, *f.* [*pl.* -n] [V. Klappen] *dim.* **Kläppchen**, ||**Kläpplein**, *n.* flap. Die — an einer Pumpe, an einem Blasebalge, the valve of a pump, of a pair of bellows; die — an einem Taubenschlage, the falling-board or trap-door of a dove-cote; die —n [an] einer Flöte oder einer Orgel, the stops or keys of a flute or organ; die — an Fagotten, Hoboen &c., reed; die —n des Herzens, the valves of the heart; —, die Fliegen zu tödten, fly-flap. *Prov.* Mit Einer — or Klatsche zwei Fliegen treffen, to kill two birds with one stone.

Klappen-handschuh, *m.* a sort of mitten with a flap at the top. —**kraut**, *n.* V. Wasserarum. —**rock**, *m.* a coat with flaps or cuffs. —**schnecke**, *f.* nerite. —**stiefel**, *m.* boot with a top, top-boot. —**ventil**, *n.* valve.

Kláppen, *v. intr.* [allied to the Gr. κολάπτω and klopfen] to make a noise as from collision, to clap, to rattle, to clatter; *it.* to strike the teeth together, to gnash; V. Klappern, Klatschen. **Fig.* to sound, well. Das klappt nicht, that does not sound well; *it.* won't do.

Klápper, *f.* [*pl.* -n] rattle. Die — am Mühlrumpfe, the clapper of a mill; V. Daumen—, — blech; [in botany] rattle, cock's comb, lousewort; *it.* thlaspi or treacle-mustard.

Klapper-apfel, *m.* calville, V. Schlotterapfel. —**baum**, *m.* cocoa-tree. —**bein**, *n.* skeleton. *Fig.* [chiefly in jest] death. —**blech**, *n.* [a musical instrument] cithern. —**büchse**, *f.* V. Klatschbüchse. —**dürr**, *adj.* [in popular lang.] exceedingly lean or meager. Er ist —dürr, he is as lean as a rake, he is a mere skeleton. —**jagd**, *f.* a chase where the game is driven towards a particular direction by means of rattles and shouting. —**mann**, *m.* 1) one provided with a rattle. 2) *Fig.* [chiefly in jest] death [represented as a skeleton whose bones rattle]. —**maul**, *n. fig.* [in popular lang.] chatterer, chatter-box. —**mühle**, *f.* 1) a clacking-mill. Ihr Mund or †Maul geht wie eine —mühle, her tongue goes like a mill-clapper or runs upon wheels. 2) *Fig.* [in popular lang.] V. —maul. —**nuß**, *f.* bladder-nut. —**rose**, *f.* common red poppy, corn-poppy. —**schlange**, *f.* rattle-snake. —**schlangenblume**, *f.*, —**schlangenkraut**, *n.*, —**schlangenwurz**, *f.* rattlesnake-root, seneca. —**schuld**, *f.* V. Klitterschuld. —**schote**, *f.* the crotalaria. —**stein**, *m.* eagle-stone, aetites.

Kláppern, *v. intr.* [from klappen] to rattle, to clack. Sehet dem Pferde nach den Füßen, ich höre, daß ein Hufeisen klappert, look at that horse's feet, I hear one of his shoes is loose; mit den Zähnen —, to chatter with one's teeth; da wird seyn Heulen und Zähn— [in Scripture], there shall be weeping and gnashing of teeth.

Kläpps, V. Klapf.

Klär, *adj.* and *adv.* [L. *clarus*, Fr. *clair*, Eng. *clear*, and *to glare* = scheinen] 1) clear, transparent, limpid, pure. —es Wasser, clear water; —e Luft, —es Glas, clear air, clear, bright, transparent glass; —er See, clear or limpid lake; den Wein — abziehen, to rack wine; — machen, V. Klären, Abklären. *it.* unmixed, pure; —er Wein, pure wine; *fig.* *Einem —en Wein einschenken, to tell any one the plain truth, to tell any one one's mind openly and freely; —es Gold, pure gold; —e Wolle, fine wool; —e Leinwand, fine linen-cloth; —e Haut, a clear skin, fair complexion. 2) [not jarring or harsh] clear. Eine —e Stimme, ein —er Ton, a clear voice, a clear sound. 3) *Fig.* *a*) not obscure, evident, apparent, manifest, clear. Ein —er Begriff, eine —e Vorstellung, a clear idea; *das ist — am or wie der Tag, that is as clear as the day, as plain as day-light; ein —er Beweis, an evident, manifest proof; Einen in's —e setzen, to set any one right, to rights; diese Sache ist mir nicht —, I do not understand this affair thoroughly, I do not see to the bottom of it; das ist Jedermann —, everybody conceives that; eine Sache in's —e setzen, — machen, to make or render any thing plain or evident, to clear up a business; sein Recht ist sonnen—, his right is a clear as the day; die Sache ist — bewiesen, the fact is clearly proved; Rechnungen — machen, to settle, to clear accounts. *b*) [free from deductions or charges] clear. Ein —er Gewinn, clear gain or profit. *c*) [in seamen's lang., not entangled, not embarrassed, unobstructed] clear. Ein Tau — machen, to clear a cable; die Riemen — machen, to ship the oars; das Tau fährt —, the cable is clear; — fahrend or — laufend, clear, rendering; eine —e Küste, a clear coast; sich — machen, to prepare, to make ready for sailing; wir sind —, we are ready for getting under sail or for setting sail. Syn. V. Hell.

Klar-äugig, *adj.* clear-eyed, clear-sighted. —**fädig**, *adj.* even-threaded, fine-spun. —**speisig**, *adj.* and *adv.* [in mining] composed of little cubes or grains, especially of lead-glance.

Klär, *m.* [-es, *pl.* e] [a sort of fine linen] lawn.

Klära, *f.* [-'s or Klarens, *pl.* -'s or Klaren] [a name of women] Clara, Claire. *Dim.* **Klärchen**, *n.* [-s, *pl.* -] little Clara. Liebes Klärchen! my dear little Clara!

Kläre, *f.* [*pl.* -n] a sort of thin broth.

Kläre, *f.* 1) clearness, brightness, purity, fineness. 2) starch, V. Stärke.

Klären, *v. tr.* [in seamen's lang.] to prepare, to make ready for service. Die Segel —, to prepare, to make ready for sailing; einen Anker —, to see an anchor clear for coming to, V. Klar.

Klären, I. *v. tr.* to clear, to clarify, to fine [any liquor]. II. *v. r.* sich —, to clarify, to grow clear or fine. Der Wein hat sich geklärt, the wine has clarified or become clear.

Klär-kessel, *m.* [in sugar-houses] the caldron or boiler in which the sugar is clarified, clarifier, second boiler. —**maschine**, *f.* [among distillers] an improved machine for the distillation of spirits.

Klärheit, *f.* 1) clearness. Die — des Kristallglases, the transparency of crystal; die — des Wassers, the clearness or limpidness of water; die — der Luft, des Himmels &c., the clearness or serenity of the air, of the sky &c., die — des Goldes, the purity or fineness of gold; die — eines Fadens, der Wolle, the fineness of a thread, of wool. *Fig.* perspicuity, luminousness, distinctness, clearness. Die — eines Grundes &c., the clearness of a reason &c. 2) [of the voice or sound] clearness. Die — der Stimme, des Tones, the clearness of the voice, of a sound.

Klarin, **Klarinétte**, V. Clarin, Clarinette.

Klariren, *v tr.* 1) [in seamen's lang.] V. Klaren and Klar. 2) to clear a ship at the custom-house.

Klärlich, *adv.* clearly, V. Klar.

Klärsel, *n.* [-s, *pl.* -] [in sugar-houses] the sugar after it comes from the clarifier or second boiler.

Klásse, **Klássiker**, **Klássisch**, V. Classe &c.

Klátsch, [probably allied to Klack] I. [the sound which is produced by the collision of two soft bodies or of a soft and a hard body] smack, slap, clash. Klitsch —! thwick thwack! II. *m.* [-es, *pl.* -e] [in popular lang.] smack, slap, clap. Er gab ihm einen — auf den Hintern, he gave him a smack on his backside.

Klatsch-büchse, *f.* pop-gun. *Fig.* [in popular lang.] V. —maul, —erinn. —**geschichte**, *f. Fig.* [in fam. lang.] babbling-story, scandalous story or report. —**gesellschaft**, *f. Fig.* [in fam. lang.] a gossiping society or company, a society of prating or gossiping persons. —**kessel**, *m.* [among sugar-refiners] the sixth boiler. —**maul**, *n. Fig.* [in popular lang.] a babbler, chatterer, chatter-box, a gossiping person. —**rose**, *f.* V. Klapperrose. —**rosenfarbig**, *adj.* crimson-red. —**taube**, *f.* V. Klatscher 2).

Klátsche, *f.* [*pl.* -n] 1) a soft and flat instrument for striking, flap, fly-flap; *prov.* V. Klappe. 2) **Fig.* a babbling and talkative person, babbler, talker; gossip.

Klátschen, I. *v. intr.* 1) to smack, to clap, to clack, to crack. Mit der Peitsche —, to crack or smack the whip; mit den Händen —, in die

Hände —, to clap one's hands, to clap; *it.* to applaud, to clap. 2) **Fig.* to talk much and idly, to chatter, to babble, to tittle-tattle, to gossip; *it.* to blab, to repeat or to relate scandalous stories. II. *v. tr.* 1) Beifall —, to express approbation by clapping the hands, to applaud, to clap. 2) **Fig.* to divulge by babbling, to babble, to blab. Syn. Klatschen, Plaudern, Schwatzen, Plappern. Plaudern is applicable to every discourse of trivial import, and which only serves as an amusement; for this reason plaudern has no definite and precise connexion. It is, in itself, neither blamable nor contemptible. All superfluous and useless talk is indicated by the word Schwatzen. Geschwätz is often annoying because it fatigues the attention uselessly; V. also Gewäsch. Klatschen is distinguished by its particular object, namely, that of relating and illiberally judging of the faults of others. Women of a low station klatschen, ladies medisiren. Plappern implies merely the moving the organs of speech and producing the sounds of words without being aware of the sense of what is uttered. Children plappern in pronouncing words connectedly without any corresponding thoughts, V. Herplappern.

Klätscher or **Klatscher**, *m.* [-s, *pl.* -] 1) V. Klatsch. 2) a sort of pigeon which makes a smacking noise with its tongue, smiter. 3) **Fig.* —, —inn, *f.* prattler, babbler, gossip. V. Klatschmaul.

Klatscherei, or **Klätscherei**, *f.* [in fam. lang.] babble, tattle, idle and mischievous talk, scandalous story or report. Gern —en machen, to love to make tales, false or bad stories, to love scandal or mischievous gossip.

Klätschhaft, *adj.* and *adv.* given to babble, busy in babbling, idly and mischievously talkative. Ein —er Mensch, V. Klatscher.

Klätschhaftigkeit, *f.* babbling disposition.

Klätze, *f.* [*pl.* -n] [instead of Glatze] 1) [in mining] a machinery without a cover or roof for breaking and pounding the ore, an uncovered or roofless stamping-mill. 2) V. Glatze.

Klauben, [also kläubeln] I. *v. tr.* to pick with the fingers, to cull. Das Erz — [in mining], to cull the ore; die Wolle —, to pick the wool. II. *v. intr.* to gnaw. An einem Knochen —, to pick a bone. **Fig.* to think closely and minutely upon a thing, to hammer at a thing. Er wird 'was daran zu — finden [in popular lang.], he will meet with many difficulties, he will find it very hard or difficult to clear that business. Einem etwas zu — geben [in popular language], to give any one a bone to pick. Syn. Klauben, Nagen. One may both klauben and nagen a bone; the latter however implies with the teeth, the former with the hands. Hence a man can do both; a dog can only nagen.

Klaube=bühne, *f.* [in mining] a board or table on which the ore is culled. —junge, *m.* the lad who culls the ore.

Klauber, **Kläubler**, *m.* [-s, *pl.*-] —inn, *f.* 1) a person employed in picking any thing; V. Klaubejunge, *Fig.* V. Wort—. 2) [a bird] nut-hatch, V. also Blauspecht, Nußhacker; *it.* V. Grauspecht.

Klauberei, *f.* [in fam. lang., especially in contempt, in a proper as well as in a fig. sense] the act of picking or culling.

Klauberig, **Klaubericht**, *n.* [-es] the refuse.

Klaue, *f.* [*pl.* -n] [allied to klieben = spalten; Sax. *clea* = Klaue and *claw* = Kralle, Haken] 1) [in general] something slit or split. [in seamen's lang.] Die —n eines Dregankers or Drachen, the flukes or claws of a grapnel or creeper; [among vinedressers] V. Gabel. 2) [chiefly the split hoof or cloven foot of oxen, swine, sheep &c., and the hooked nail of a bird or fowl] claw, talon. Die —n eines Ochsen, eines Schafes, the hoofs of an ox, of a sheep; die —n eines Raubvogels, the talons, claws or pounces of a bird of prey; *it.* the foot of beasts of prey having claws, paw; die —n eines Löwen, the claws or paws of a lion; die —n einer Katze, the paws of a cat; unter die —n einer Katze gerathen, to fall into the clutches of a cat; *it.* a horse's, mule's and ass's hoof. *Fig.* [in popular lang., in contempt = hand] In Jemand's —n seyn, to be under any one's paw, in any one's clutches; sich hüten, in Jemand's —n zu fallen, to keep out of any one's clutches; was er einmal in den —n hat, das ist verloren, what he holds or has in his clutches is lost. Syn. Klaue, Pfote, Tatze, Lauf. Pfoten are the feet of all animals; Klaue is said only of the lowest part of the feet of creatures which is cleft and furnished with horn or nails. The fore-feet of the larger animals of prey are called Tatzen. Thus we say a Bärentatze, a Löwentatze &c. We say likewise of a large dog, he strikes the little one down with his Tatze &c. The feet of some animals of game which are very swift in running are by sportsmen called Läufe, as the Lauf of a hare, of a stag &c. V. Vorderlauf, Hinterlauf.

Klauen=beschlag, *m.* the shoes or shoeing of an ox &c. —fett, *n.* grease boiled out of the feet of oxen &c. and used for burning and other purposes. —geld, *n.* V. —steuer. —hieb, *m.* a stroke with a claw. —schmalz, *n.* V. —fett. —spalt, *m.* [among hunters] slit. —steuer, *f.*, —thaler, *m.*, —zehnte, *m.* a tax paid upon cattle and chiefly oxen.

Klauel, V. Knauel.

Klauen, **Klauer**, V. Kalfatern, Kalfaterer.

Klauig, *adj.* furnished with claws or talons.

Klause, *f.* [*pl.* -n] [allied to the L. *claudo*, *clausi* &c., the Germ. schleußen, schließen; the D. *kluyse* = enger Eingang; V. Schleuße] 1) a narrow pass in a mountain, defile. 2) the habitation of a hermit, hermitage; *it.* the cell of a monk. *Fig.* [in fam. lang.] Er kommt nie aus seiner —, he never stirs out or abroad. 3) [in mining] the hole or pit into which the water runs from the buddle.

Klausenbewohner, *m.* V. Klausner.

Klausel, **Klausur**, V. Clausel, Clausur.

Klausner, *m.* [-s, *pl.*-] a recluse, a hermit, an anachorete.

Klavier, *n.* V. Clavier.

Kleback, *n.* [-s, *pl.* -e] [in sugar-houses] the moistened clay used for refining sugar in forms.

Klebe, *f.* V. Flachsseide, Flachskraut.

Kleben, [Sax. *clifan*, *cleofan*, Eng. *to cleave*, allied to the L. *glu-ten*, Gr. γλία or γλοιά] I. *v. intr.* to stick, to cleave, to cling, to adhere. Das Pech klebt an den Fingern, bleibt an den Fingern —, pitch sticks to the fingers; die Zunge klebt mir am Gaumen, my tongue sticks or cleaves to my palate. *Fig.* An der Welt, am Irdischen or Zeitlichen —, to be attached or addicted to the world, to earthly things; diese Schande bleibt ewig an ihm —, he can never efface or blot out that disgrace or ignominy, nothing will ever wash away that disgrace, that ignominy will for ever cleave to him or his name; *es bleibt nichts bei ihm —, he retains or remembers nothing, he is very forgetful; *er läßt gern Etwas an den Fingern —, he is light-fingered or nimble-fingered, he filches or steals; das Blut seiner Brüder klebt an seinen Händen, his hands are stained with the blood of his brothers; an einem Orte — bleiben, to stay or remain too long in a place. II. *v. tr.* to make to cleave or cling, to stick, V. An—, Auf—, Be—; *it.* Kleben, Kleistern, leimen, Pappen.

Kleb=auster, *f.* [a species of pholas or pierre-stone] onion-shell. —koralle, *f.* parasitic coralline. —werk, *n.* V. Klebewerk.

Klebe=blatt, *n.* [little used] an advertisement or handbill posted up. —feuer, *n.* an artificial fire which sticks to the object at which it is thrown. —garn, *n.* a net for catching larks. —gras, *n.* the common burdock. —gut, *n.* entailed property. —kraut, *n.* the name of several plants which have the quality of sticking to a thing. *a*) the lesser burdock. *b*) cleaver. *c*) hedge hen-foot or hedge-fumitory. *d*) Das blaue —kraut, procumbent. —kugel, *f.* a ball which sticks to the place where it is thrown. —läppchen, *n.* a piece of rag which sticks to a thing. *Fig.* [in fam. lang.] Einem ein —läppchen anhängen, to asperse or slander any one; *it.* to ridicule or deride any one. —laus, *f.* crab-louse. —lychnis, —nelke, *f.* the viscous catch-fly or lychnis. —netz, *n.* V. —garn. —pflaster, *n.* V. Heftpflaster. Englisches —pflaster, English court-plaister. —ranft, *n.* —ränftchen, *n.* kissing-crust. ||—roth, *n.* corrupted for Kleeroth, which see. —ruthe, *f.* lime-twig. —schrift, *f.* V. —blatt. —schwamm, *m.* the clammy agaric. —werk, *n.* 1) work consisting in the formation of loam- or clay-walls. 2) lute, V. Kitt. —wurz, *f.* V. Färberröthe. —zettel, *m.* V. —blatt.

Kleber, *m.* [-s, *pl.* -] 1) any adhesive substance. *a*) gluten. *b*) gum. 2) [in botany] Der blaue —, the procumbent asperugo, V. Klebekraut.

Kleberklee, *m.* V. Wickenklee.

Klebericht, *adj.* resembling an adhesive substance, sticky, gluish.

Kleberig, *adj.* and *adv.* adhesive, sticky, viscous, glutinous. Die Stärke ist —, starch is glutinous; —e Hände haben, to have glutinous hands, **fig.* to be light-fingered or nimble-fingered, to filch; ein —er Stoff, a sticky substance; ein —er Saft, a viscous juice; [in botany] —e Blätter, glutinous leaves.

Kleberigkeit, *f.* glutinosity, viscosity, glutinousness.

Klebrig, V. Kleberig.

Kleck, or **Klecks**, *m.* [-es, *pl.* -e] dim. Kleckschen, ||Kleckslein, [-s, *pl.*-] a [seems to be derived from legen] blot, blur. *Fig.* [in popular lang.] Einem einen — anhängen, to asperse or slander any one, to blur any one's reputation.

Kleck=buch, *n.* V. Kladde. —mahler, *m.* V. Klecker, Farbenklecker. —papier, *n.* 1) waste-paper. 2) blotting-paper. —schuld, *f.* [in fam. lang.] trifling debt; dribbling debt, dribblet.

1. **Klecken**, [V. Kleck] *v. intr.* to make blots or blurs, to write badly, to scrawl; *it.* to paint badly, to daub.

2. ||**Klecken**, [probably also from legen = hervorbringen, vermehren] *v. intr.* 1) to be profitable, to be of use, to increase, to multiply. 2) to be sufficient or enough, to be adequate. Das kleckt nicht, that is not sufficient, does not suffice, that won't do, does not answer the purpose; tausend Pfund — nicht, die er in einem Jahre verzehrt, he spends more than a thousand pounds a year.

Klecker, *m.* [-s, *pl.*-] bad pen-man, scrawler; *it.* a bad painter, dauber, V. Farben—, Pinsel—, Schmierer.

Kleckerei, *f.* 1) the act of making blots or blurs or daubing. 2) a scrawl; *it.* a daub.

Kleckig, V. Klecksig.

Kleckſen, Kleckſer, V. Klecken, Klecker.

Kleckſig, *adj.* full of blots or blurs.

Klee, *m.* [-s, *pl.* -e] [perhaps from the Old kliebenn = ſpalten] trefoil, clover. Der rothe or gemeine —, the purple trefoil, red clover; der gelbe or Hopfen—, the hop-trefoil; weißer or kriechender —, the creeping white trefoil, Dutch or white clover. V. Alpen—, Berg—, Honig—, Schnecken—, Stein— &c.

Klee-acker, *m.* field of clover or trefoil. —bau, *m.* culture of clover or trefoil. —baum, *m.* the three-leaved elm. —blatt, *n.* a leaf of trefoil. *Fig.* [in fam. lang.] a number of three, triplet. Ein —blatt wahrer Freunde, three real or true friends. —blattförmig, *adj.* having the form of a leaf of trefoil; [in heraldry] bottony. —blume, —blüte, *f.* the flower of trefoil or clover. —bube, *m.* knave of clubs. V. also Treffle- [Eicheln-] or Kreuz-Bube. —dame, *f.* queen of clubs. V. also Treffle- &c. Dame. —feld, *n.* V. —acker. —futter, *n.* clover or trefoil. —heu, *n.* hay of clover or trefoil. —könig, *m.* king of clubs. V. also Treffle- &c. König. —roth, *adj.* clover-coloured, purplish-red. —salz, *n.* or Sauer—salz, sorrel-salt. —same, *m.* seed of clover or trefoil. —sauer, *adj.* containing oxalic acid or combined with it. —saure Salze, oxalates; —saures Ammonium, oxalate of ammoniac. —säure, *f.* the oxalic acid. —staude, *f.* —strauch, *m.* the arborescent lucern. —wiese, *f.* clover or trefoil meadow. —zug, *m.* a sketch or line resembling a trefoil.

Klei, *m.* [-s, *pl.* -e] [from kleben, allied to Kleister, Klette &c.; Polish *kley* = Lehm, Bohem. *kly* = Bergharz, *klyh* = Leim] clay, loam, marl.

Klei-acker, *m.* clay-land or clayey field. —erde, *f.* clayey earth or soil. —land, *n.* V. —acker.

Kleiben, [V. Kleben] I. *v. tr.* to fasten by something glutinous or adhesive, to stick, to glue, to paste. II. *v. intr.* 1) — or mit Lehm und Stroh —, to clay or loam [a wall], to form a loam-wall or mud-wall. 2) to adhere or stick.

Kleibewerk, *n.* work consisting in the formation of loam- or clay-walls.

Kleiber, *m.* [-s, *pl.* -] a person employed in pasting, claying or loaming, in forming clay or loam walls.

Kleiberlehm, *m.* loam or clay used for covering walls.

Kleiberei, *f.* the act of forming a loam or mudwall, mud-walling.

Kleibig, V. Kleberig, Zähe.

Kleid, *n.* [-es, *pl.* -er] [from legen = decken. The old Allemannic leien = liegen is allied to the Goth. *lod hlod* = anhängen, anliegen, and to the L. *lodix* = Decke] any covering for use or ornament, tegument, cover; [in seamen's lang.] V. Segel—, Pumpen—; [in a more limited sense, generally used in the plural] clothes, garments, dress, habit. Viel auf —er verwenden, to spend a great deal of money for clothes or dress; die —er anziehen, to put on one's clothes, to dress one's self; die —er ausziehen, to take off one's clothes, to undress one's self; die abgelegten —er, cast-off clothes; *prov.* —er machen Leute, fine feathers make fine birds; das — macht den Mann nicht, it is not the cowl makes the friar, a tattered cloak may cover a good drinker; *it.* the coat and particularly dress-coat or coat and waistcoat of a man, and the gown of a woman; warum ziehen Sie Ihr neues — nicht an? why do you not put on your new coat [in speaking to a man] or gown [in addressing a woman]? ein vollständiges —, a suit of clothes, V. Amts—, Fest—, Frauen—, Kinder—, Manns—, Sommer—, Trauer—, Winter—. Syn. Kleid, Kleidung, Anzug, Gewand. Kleidung indicates not only what we use as a covering for the body but also for the head and feet. A Kleid comprehends any of the articles of clothing we are accustomed to wear. In common life we call also a coat Kleid. It is the same with the female dress; Kleid is that part of the covering of the body, in which females appear in society. An Anzug implies all we at once anziehen or put on to appear before others. A Gewand is a wide, long upper garment. It is therefore usually worn only on solemn occasions.

Kleider-barchent, *m.* fustian for clothes or lining. —baum, *m.* the American plane-tree, or large button-wood. —besen, *m.* clothes-broom, whisk. —brett, *n.* V. —rahmen. —buch, *n.* a book in which costumes are described and painted, book of costumes. —bude, *f.* a salesman's shop, a shop where clothes ready-made or old clothes are sold. —bündel, *m.* bundle of clothes. —bürste, *f.* clothes-brush. —gemach, *n.* V. —kammer. —grempel, *m.* trade or traffic in old clothes, frippery. —haken, *m.* a hook for hanging clothes on. —handel, *m.* the trade or traffick in old clothes, frippery. —händler, *m.* dealer in old clothes, clothes-seller, salesman. —haus, *n.* wardrobe-house. —hüter, *m.* V. —verwahrer. —kammer, *f.* wardrobe. —kämmerer, *m.* master of the prince's wardrobe. —kasten, *m.* chest or press for clothes, clothes-press. —kram, *m.* V. —handel. —krämer, *m.* V. —händler. —laus, *f.* a large louse. —leinwand, *f.* linen for lining. —los, *adj.* destitute of clothes, without clothes, naked. —macher, *m.* V. Schneider. Die Schneider pflegen sich heutzutage in „—macher" umzutaufen, tailors call or dub themselves habit-makers, now-a-days. —markt, *m.* a place where old clothes are exhibited for sale, rag-fair, frippery. —mode, *f.* fashion in clothes or dresses or dressing. —motte, *f.* moth. —nagel, *m.* peg [to hang clothes on]. —narr, *m.* [in fam. lang.] one who is excessively fond of fine clothes, who spends great sums for clothes. —ordnung, *f.* regulation of dress [by public authority to check extravagance], sumptuary laws or regulations. —pflock, *m.* peg [to hang clothes on]. —pracht, *f.* splendour of dress, extravagance in [the articles of] clothes. —rechen, *m.* rack [to hang clothes on]. —schabe, *f.* V. —motte. —schmuck, *m.* costly clothes or dress, fine clothes. —schrank, *m.* V. —kasten. —tracht, *f.* manner of dress, costume. —trödler, *m.* V. —händler. —verwahrer, *m.* keeper of the [prince's &c.] wardrobe. V. Garderobier. —vorrath, *m.* stock of clothes, wardrobe.

Kleiden, I. *v. tr.* [V. Kleid] 1) to furnish with the necessary covering, to cover. Eine Büchse —, to mount a gun; einen Altar, eine Kanzel —, to deck or adorn an altar, a pulpit. 2) [generally] to clothe, to dress. Die Truppen —, to clothe the soldiers; es ist ein gutes Werk, den Nackenden zu —, it is a good work to clothe the naked poor; sich —, to put on one's clothes, to dress one's self; er kleidet sich gut, he wears genteel clothes or dresses to the best advantage, he dresses well or genteelly; sich schlecht —, to dress ill or out of taste; gut gekleidet seyn, to be dressed well or genteely; V. An—, Be—. [in poetry] Die Felder haben sich in [ein] freudiges Grün gekleidet, the fields are clad in cheerful green. II. *v. intr.* and *tr.* to fit, to become. Dieser Anzug kleidet Sie sehr gut, that suit fits you very well; jener Kopfputz kleidete sie nicht gut, that head-dress did not become her.

Kleid-keule, *f.* [in seamen's lang.] serving-mallet. —span, *m.* [in seamen's lang.] serving-board.

Kleidung, *f.* 1) the act of covering. Die — einer Flinte, the mounting of a gun. 2) [generally] the act of clothing; *it.* clothes, dress, clothing; [in painting] drapery. Die — der Kriegsleute, regimental dress, uniform; eine vollständige —, a suit of clothes; aus der — schließt man auf den Mann, one judges a man by his dress; das ist keine schickliche — für Sie, that dress does not become you; in reicher —, richly clad; die —en verschiedener Nationen, the costumes of different nations.

Kleidungsstück, *n.* part of dress, article of clothing.

Kleie, *f.* [*pl.* -n] [probably from klieben = ſpalten, that is trennen] bran. Ungebeutelte —, fine bran; reine —, coarse bran.

Kleien-artig, *adj.* like bran, branny; furfuraceous. —bier, *n.* bran-beer [very bad beer, brewed from bran]. —brod, *n.* bread made of bran. —mehl, *n* grit. —stein, *m.* pot-stone. —wasser, *n.* water boiled with bran, bran-water.

Kleiig, *adj.* 1) [from Klei] clayey. 2) [from Kleie] branny.

Klein, *adj.* and *adv.* [seems to be the same as lein in diminutives. Sax. *claen* = fein, Eng. *clean* = rein] little, small. Ein —er Mann, a little or short man; ein —es Haus, a little or small house; eine —e Meile, a short mile; der —e Finger, the little finger; — schneiden, to cut into little pieces; — hacken, to chop into small pieces, to mince; — Geld, —es Geld, small money, change, half-pence; ich habe kein — Geld, I have no change; —es Schrot, small shot; —es Wasser, low water; das Wasser wird wieder — or —er, the water decreases, falls or subsides; der —e, the little boy or fellow; mein —er, my little one; meine —en, my little ones; *von — auf, from one's infancy, from a child; *das ist mein —stes, that's my youngest child; *Ihre —ste Schwester, your youngest sister; das ist ihm etwas —es, that's very easy for him; im —en verkaufen, to sell by retail; in's —e or —ere bringen, to reduce to a little or smaller compass, to abridge; im —en, in a small compass, upon a small scale; sie war im —en gemahlt, her picture was drawn in little or in miniature. *Fig.* *a*) short in duration and small in quantity or amount. Warten Sie einen —en Augenblick, wait only a short while, a moment, a minute, an instant, a little; ein —er Schlaf, a little sleep; eine —e Zeit, a little time; in einer —en Stunde werde ich wieder zurück seyn, I shall be back in less than an hour; vor einer —en Weile, a little time or while ago; eine —e Anzahl, a little or small number; ein —es Einkommen, a small revenue or income, a little or trifling income; ein — wenig, a very little; geben Sie mir ein — wenig Wein, give me a little drop of wine; [in mathematics] eine unendlich —e Größe, an infinitely small or a differential quantity. *b*) of little importance, value &c., trifling, insignificant, mean, contemptible. Ein —er König, a petty king; eine —e Sache, a small, trifling, inconsiderable matter; ein —er Verlust, a small or trifling loss; — denken, to think basely or meanly; ich habe eine —e Bitte an Sie, I have a small or little favour to ask of you; er erzählte mir alle —en Umstände der Geschichte, he told me all the particulars of the story; in's —e [Einzelne] gehen, to enter into particulars; *es geht — bei ihm her, he lives poorly, he is reduced to straits; ein —er Geist, a little mind or genius, a small, slender or shallow wit; *it.* a narrow mind or spirit. Syn. Klein, Gering, Wenig, Winzig. Klein is in general that which has no considerable size, gering that which has no great worth. Wenig is that which is not in any considerable quantity, winzig that which is of the smallest or scarcely observable size. Thus copper-coins are geringer than gold ones, even when the latter are kleiner in circumference are weniger in number, for they have less intrinsic worth and perfection.

Klein=achtel, *n.* small octavo, book in small octavo. —**äderig**, *adj.* having little veins [as marble]. —**ährig**, *adj.* having small or little ears [said of corn]. —**arbeiter**, *m.* V. —schmied. —**auge**, *n.* the sharp-toothed whale. —**äugig**, *adj.* having little or small-shaped eyes. *Fig.* [in mining] —äugiger Bleiglanz, galena or sulphuret of lead with small facets or cubes. —**asien**, *n.* Asia minor. —**bauer**, *m.* V. Halbbauer. —**beerig**, *adj.* having small or little berries. —**binder**, *m.* a cooper who makes only small tubs, pails &c. —**blätterig**, —**blättig**, *adj.* having small leaves. —**bogenform**, *f.* small folio. —**drahtzieher**, *m.* a wire-drawer who draws wire of the thickness of a quill to a great fineness. —**erz**, *n.* ore in small particles. —**fügig**, *adj.* —**fügigkeit**, *f.* V. Geringfügig &c. —**füßig**, *adj.* having little or small feet. —**geist**, *m.* a mean spirit, a narrow mind, a little mind or genius, a small or shallow wit; *it.* trifling disposition, frivolousness. —**geistig**, —**geisterisch**, *adj.* of a mean spirit, little-minded, trivial, frivolous. —**geistigkeit**, *f.* frivolousness, little-mindedness. —**gemählde**, *n.* miniature. —**gewehrfeuer**, *n.* discharge of muskets or musketry. —**gläubig**, *adj.* of little faith. —**gegliedert**, —**gliederig**, *adj.* having small limbs; *it.* having little or small links [said of a chain]. —**glöcklein**, *n.* [in botany] the waved-leaved bell-flower. —**halsig**, *adj.* having a little or short neck. —**handel**, *m.* retail. —**händler**, *m.* retailer. —**herr**, *m.* V. Stutzer. —**herzig**, *adj.* V. Engherzig. —**klieber**, *m.* [among coopers] he who cleaves the wood or staves into small pieces with wedges. —**knecht**, *m.* lower man-servant on a farm. —**kohle**, *f.* pit-coal. —**körnig**, *adj.* having small grains, V. Feinkörnig. —**krabbe**, *f.* small crab. —**laut**, *adj.* and *adv.* small or low in sound or voice. **Fig.* low-spirited, despondent. —**laut werden**, to lose courage, to despond, to be discouraged or disheartened; *it.* to lower a peg, to come a peg lower. —**mahler**, *m.* [*Miniaturmahler] miniature-painter. —**mahlerei** [*Miniaturmahlerei], *f.* art of painting in miniature. —**maschig**, *adj.* having little meshes. —**meister**, *m.* [in familiar language, chiefly in jest] fop, coxcomb, petit-maître; *it.* paltry or petty author, would-be-poet &c. —**messer**, *m.* [*Mikrometer] micrometer. —**muth**, *m.* dejection of spirit [either from sorrow or fear], despondency, pusillanimity. —**müthig**, *adj.* and *adv.* dejected in spirit, desponding, pusillanimous. —**müthig werden**, to despond, to lose courage, to become disheartened; —**müthig machen**, to discourage, to intimidate; —**müthig seyn**, to have lost all courage, to be quite cast down or dejected, to be discouraged. SYN. **Kleinmüthig, Furchtsam, Niedergeschlagen.** He who is sorrowful because he has no hope to cheer him is kleinmüthig; he who is sad because the thoughts of future ill terrify him is furchtsam, and both are niedergeschlagen in so far as their Kleinmüthigkeit and Furchtsamkeit make them sorrowful. —**müthigkeit**, *f.* V. —muth. —**rüster**, *f.* [in botany] 1) spindle-tree or prick-wood. 2) maple, maple-tree. —**schmied**, *m.* white-smith, lock-smith. —**schmiedsarbeit**, —**schmiedswaare**, *f.* iron-ware, hard wares. —**schuppig**, *adj.* having little scales. —**silber**, *n.* 1) silver-leaves, twenty five of which are in a mould. 2) platina. —**sinn**, *m.* trifling disposition, frivolousness. —**sinnig**, *adj.* and *adv.* trifling, frivolous. —**specht**, *m.* pianet. —**speisig**, *adj.* [in mining] fine-grained [ore]. —**städter**, *m.* inhabitant or citizen of a little town, cit. Solche —städter [in contempt]! such petty gentry! —**städterei**, *f.* way of acting and thinking of an inhabitant of a little town; [in contempt] low-bred or mean manners. —**städtisch**, *adj.* and *adv.* mean, low-bred, contemptible. —**uhrmacher**, *m.* watchmaker. —**vieh**, *n.* small cattle. —**weidwerk**, *n.* small game. —**ziemer**, *m.* V. Weindrossel.

Kleine, I. der, die, das —, little child, little one. Der or die liebe —! the little darling! V. Klein. II. *f.* V. Kleinheit.

Kleinen, *v. tr.* to divide or break into small parts.

Kleinheit, *f.* littleness, smallness. Die — eines Körpers, the littleness of a body.

Kleinigkeit, *f.* small matter, little matter, trifle. Er hat tausend niedliche —en in seinem Cabinette, he has a thousand pretty little things or toys in his cabinet; eine — kann ihn aufbringen, he takes umbrage at the least thing in the world; ich bitte Sie, diese — anzunehmen, pray, accept this trifle; er sieht auf —en, he stands upon trifles; das ist ihm eine —, that's very easy for him; sich mit —en abgeben, to busy one's self about trifles, to mind trifles, to trifle time away; wir sind nicht hier, um uns mit —en aufzuhalten, we are not come here to stand upon trifles, to contest for trifles, to trifle away our time; es ist eine —, it is no great matter, a mere trifle.

Kleinigkeits=geist, *m.* trifling or frivolous disposition, frivolousness. —**häscher**, —**jäger**, —**krämer**, *m.* a person that deals in or occupies himself with trifles, one who stands upon trifles, a punctilious, pedantic person. —**sucht**, *f.* V. —geist.

Kleinlich, *adj.* and *adv.* 1) rather little or small, minute. 2) paltry, mean, frivolous, trifling.

Kleinlichkeit, *f.* 1) littleness. 2) meanness, frivolousness.

Kleinod, *n.* [-es, *pl.* -e or -ien] [from klein = schön, fein and the old Od = Eigenthum] 1) something precious, a jewel, trinket. Die —ien der Krone, die Reichs—ien, the insignia of royalty, crown, scepter and other emblems; *fig.* komm, mein —, come, my jewel; die Gesundheit ist das edelste —, health is the greatest treasure; diese Provinz ist das schönste — seiner Krone, this province is the brightest gem in his crown. 2) offal of butcher's meat, such as head, pluck, entrails. 3) [in heraldry] the ornaments belonging to the helmet, such as the crest. 4) [formerly] the prize. Aber Einer erlangt das — [in Script.], but one receiveth the prize. SYN. **Kleinod, Juwel, Geschmeide.** Kleinode (Od = property, wealth) are small precious objects, whether in jewels, or in gold and silver; Juwelen are merely precious stones, and Geschmeide as an ornament of dress implies both.

Kleinodien=handel, *m.* the jeweller's trade. —**händler**, *m.* jeweller. —**kästchen**, ||—**kästlein**, *n.* jewel-box, casket, V. Schmuckkästchen.

Kleische, *f.* [*pl.* -n] [a flat fish] burt, dab.

Kleister, *m.* [-s] [allied to kleben and the L. *gluten*] paste, V. Pappe.

Kleister=aal, *m.* —**älchen**, *n.* an animalcule engendered in book-binder's paste. —**pinsel**, *m.* a pasting-brush. —**tiegel**, —**topf**, *m.* a paste-bowl, paste-pot.

Kleisterig, *adj.* and *adv.* clammy, glutinous, viscous, sticky.

Kleistern, *v. tr.* to paste.

Klemm, *adj.* and *adv.* [allied to klemmen and to Klamm, Leim] straitened, narrow, tight, V. Enge. *Fig.* [in popular lang.] Das Geld ist —, money is scarce; —e Zeiten, hard times.

Klemmchen, ||**Klemmlein**, *n.* [-s, *pl.* -] a peg to fasten prints or linen to a line.

Klemme, *f.* [*pl.* -n] 1) an instrument for compressing or pinching. *a*) pincers. *b*) a cramp, V. Zwinge. *c*) barnacles. *d*) V. Klemmchen. 2) a narrow place, a narrow pass, a defile, strait or straits. *Fig.* [in fam. or popular lang.] difficulty, dilemma, distress, want. In der — seyn, to be at a pinch; in einer großen —, recht sehr in der — seyn, to be in great straits, in a dire or sad dilemma; jetzt hat man ihn in der —, now he is caught; Einen in der — stecken lassen, to leave any one in the lurch at a pinch; Einen in die — bringen, to bring any one into a scrape. 3) V. Mundsperre. ||4) stress, force, energy.

Klemm=eisen, *n.* 1) vice-chops. 2) bit, horse-bit, curb. —**haken**, *m.* cramp-iron, cramp-hook; *it.* holdfast.

Klemmen, I. *v. tr.* [allied to the Eng. *to clam*, V. Klamm and Klemmen] to pinch, to squeeze hard and closely, to press. Diese Schuhe — mich, — mir die Füße zusammen, these shoes pinch me. II. *v. r.* Sich —, to squeeze one's self into or between; *it.* to get squeezed or pinched between two hard bodies. Ich klemmte mich zwischen die beiden Herren, I squeezed myself between these two gentlemen; ich habe mich zwischen der Thüre geklemmt, I have got my fingers pinched between the door.

Klemmig, *adj.* [in mining] hard.

Klempener, Klempner, *m.* [-s, *pl.* -] [from klempern] brasier and tinman, V. Blechner, Flaschner.

Klempener=blech, *n.* tin. —**waare**, *f.* tin-ware.

Klempern, [= klimpern] *v. intr.* to clink, to tinkle; *it.* V. Klimpern.

Kleppel &c. V. Klöppel &c.

1. **Klepper**, *m.* [-s, *pl.* -] [from the Low Sax. *kleppen* = laufen; Sax. *kleapan* = springen] 1) a swift horse, but of no high value, a nag, pad; [in contempt] a hack or hackney. 2) [vulgar] a person that runs or walks about much, rambler, rover, roamer.

Klepperdürr, *adj.* V. Klapperdürr.

2. **Klepper**, *f.* [*pl.* -n] [from the provincial kleppern = klappern] 1) V. Kinderklapper. 2) V. Klappermühle. 3) gross-beak, haw-finch.

Klette, *f.* [*pl.* -n] [allied to kleben] 1) [the rough prickly covering of the seeds of the burdock] bur. *Fig.* [in popular lang.] Sich an Einen anhängen wie eine —, to stick to any one like burs; *it.* Einem eine — anhängen, to slander any one, to cast a blur, blemish or aspersion upon any one. 2) [the plant] burdock. Die gemeine or große —, the common burdock; die kleine —, the lesser burdock. 3) V. Baumgrille 1).

Kletten=distel, *f.* the common burdock. —**gras**, *n.* V. Klebegras. —**kerbel**, *m.* 1) wild chervil. 2) bastard or hedge-parsley, caucalis. —**knopf**, —**kopf**, *m.* bur. —**kraut**, *n.* 1) V. Klette 2). 2) hemp-agrimony. 3) the lesser hound's tongue. —**specht**, *m.* V. Baumspecht. —**stange**, *f.* [among bird-catchers] the perch or pole to which the lime-twigs are fastened.

Kletten, *v. tr.* [allied to klauben] to pick, to cull [wool].

Kletterer, *m.* [-s, *pl.* -] one who climbs.

n. one who is fond of climbing, one who climbs well, climber.

Klettern, *v. intr.* [used with seyn] [provincially also klevern, allied to kleben] to climb, to clamber. Auf einen Baum —, to climb up a tree; auf einen Felsen —, to climb a rock, to scramble up a rock; an einem steilen Berg hinauf —, to climb a steep mountain. Syn. Klettern, Klimmen. Klimmen always implies a physical effort to climb higher; klettern, on the contrary, the climbing about any steep object. We can herabklettern as well as hinaufklettern, but we can never herabklimmen. Cats, monkeys, bears, wood-peckers &c. also klettern.

Kletter-eisen, *n.* climbing-iron. —fuß, *m.* a foot well adapted for climbing. —katze, *f.* **Fig.* V. Kletterer. —mast, *m.* —stange, *f.* climbing-pole.

Klettricht, *adj.* and *adv.* 1) full of burs. 2) that sticks like burs.

Klettwurz, *f.* [without a *pl.*] V. Klettendistel.

Kley, Kleye, V. Klei &c.

Klick or **Klicks,** *m.* [-es, *pl.* -e] 1. V. Kleck. 2) [in seamen's lang.] after-piece of the rudder.

||**Klicken,** *v. tr.* to throw at in small lumps, to cast any thing soft and adhesive [as mortar, mud and the like]; *it.* V. Klecken.

||**Klieben,** *ir. v. tr.* and *intr.* [Sw. *klippa* = schneiden, V. Klaue, Kloben, Kluft] to cleave, to split.

Klieb-eisen, [among coopers] cleaving iron or knife. —holz, *n.* sawed timber.

||**Kliebig,** *adj.* easily splitting, fissile.

Kliesche, V. Kleische.

***Klima,** *n.* [-s, *pl.* Klimāte] climate.

***Klimaktĕrisch,** *adj.* climacteric.

***Klimátisch,** *adj.* climatic.

Klimmen, *v. intr.* [Low Sax. klemmen, Sax. *climan* and *climban*, Eng. *to climb*, allied to klamm, Klammer] to climb. Syn. V. Klettern.

Klimmstag, *n.* V. Laufstag.

Klimperer or **Klimprer,** *m.* [-s, *pl.* -] a person who plays negligently or badly on an instrument.

Klimpern, I. *v. intr.* [allied to klempern] to jingle, to clink, to chink, to tinkle. An einem Glase —, to make a glass tinkle or jingle; er klimpert ein wenig auf dem Klaviere &c., he can play a little on the harpsichord &c. II. *v. tr.* to play negligently or badly [a tune &c.]

Kling, kling! or **Klingkling!** [imitating the repeated sound of a bell] jingle, tinkle! dingding!

Klingbar, *adj.* and *adv.* resonant, sonorous.

1. **Klinge,** *f.* [*pl.* -n] [allied to Länge, legen] blade [of a sword, knife or other cutting steel or iron instrument], V. Degen—, Messer—, Säbel—, Damaszener—, Hohl—; *it.* sword. Einen vor die — fordern, to challenge any one [to fight a duel with swords]; die Sache vor or mit der — ausmachen, to try the matter by the sword; über die — springen, to be put to the sword; über die — springen lassen, to put to the sword. *Fig.* *Bei der — bleiben, not to go from one's subject, from the matter in hand, to stick to the point.

Klingen-möhre, *f.* V. Klingelmöhre. —probe, *f.* proof or trial of a sword-blade. —schmied, *m.* blade-smith, sword-cutler. —spitze, *f.* point of the blade. —stahl, *m.* steel for making sword-blades. —stock, *m.* V. Degenstock. —waare, *f.* hard-wares, iron-ware.

2. ||**Klinge,** *f.* [allied to Länge, legen?] a long narrow valley; *it.* a ravine.

Klingel, *f.* [*pl.* -n] 1) small bell. Ziehen Sie an der —, ring the bell. 2) V. Knauel.

Klingel-beutel, *m.* a bag with a small bell, with which the church-wardens go about the church during the sermon and collect alms from the congregation, alms-bag. —beutelträger, *m.* the person whose business it is to go about with the alms-bag. —draht, *m.* the wire, fastened to a little bell, and by means of which the bell is rung. —herr, *m.* V. — beutelträger. —möhre, *f.* skirret. —quast, *m.* the tassel of a bell. —sack, *m.* V. —beutel. —schnur, *f.* the string or line of a bell.

Klingeln, *v. intr.* [from klingen] to ring or sound a small bell, to make a signal with a small bell. Es klingelt, the bell rings; an der Schelle —, to ring the bell; seinem Bedienten —, to ring [the bell] for one's servant, to call one's servant by ringing the bell; mit den Gläsern —, to jingle the glasses. Syn. V. Klingen.

Klingen, *v. intr.* [Lat. *clango*, Gr. *κλάγγω*, Eng. *to clink* and *klank*] 1) to sound, to chink. Dieses Instrument klingt gut, this instrument sounds well; das Geld klingt, the money chinks; die Gläser — lassen, to touch or jingle the glasses; hart, rauh, widrig —, to jar; die Besatzung zog mit —dem Spiele aus der Stadt, the garrison left the town, drums beating; —de Münze, gold and silver coin, ready money; wohl —d [said of the voice], sonorous, melodious; die Ohren — mir, my ears tinkle. *Fig.* Dieser Vers klingt gut, this verse sounds well; diese Handlung klingt sehr übel, this action sounds very ill. 2) to produce a sound, to tinkle, to jingle. Syn. Klingen, Klingeln. Klingen implies, in general, to yield a sound; klingeln is its diminutive and frequentative, and is therefore only said of small sounding bodies, as small bells, which yield an acute and fine tone, and which, on account of their mobility, easily iterate the sound.

Kling-adler, *m.* sea-eagle, ospray or ossifrage. —gedicht, *n.* [*Sonnett] sonnet. —klang, *m.* 1) the tinkling or jingle of a bell, of glasses &c. 2) **Fig.* bad music, or music continually repeated. 3) **Fig.* empty talk; a jingle of rhymes. —spiel, *n.* sound or play of instruments.

Klinger, *m.* [-s, *pl.* -] V. Quakente.

Klingling, V. Kling.

***Klinik,** *f.* clinical medicine.

***Kliniker,** *m.* [-s, *pl.* -] a clinical physician.

***Klinikum,** *n.* [-s, *pl.* -iken or ika] medical establishment, clinical hospital.

***Klinisch,** *adj.* and *adv.* clinic, clinical.

Klink, *m.* [-es, *pl.* -e] [in seamen's lang.] V. Klinke 2).

Klink-bolzen, *m.* [in seamen's lang.] a bolt clinched at both ends, rivet. —haken, *m.* V. Klinkenhaken. —werk, *n.* V. Klinkerwerk.

Klinke, *f.* [*pl.* -n] [allied to the Fr. *clenche*, *clinche*, *loquet*] 1) latch [of a door]. 2) [in seamen's lang.] the riveted or clinched point of a pin or bolt.

Klinken-haken, *m.* hook or staple to receive the latch. —schloß, *n.* a latch which is opened with a key.

1. **Klinken,** *v. intr.* to press upon, or to press down the latch of a door.

2. **Klinken,** *v. tr.* and *intr.* [in seamen's lang.] to clinch or rivet a pin or bolt.

1. **Klinker,** *m.* [-s, *pl.* -] [in mineralogy] clinkstone, a sort of Portland stone.

2. **Klinker,** *m.* [-s, *pl.* -n] a ship built with clincher-work; *it.* a sort of flat bottomed vessel, a Dutch clinker.

Klinker-weise, *adj.* [in seamen's lang.] Ein —weise gebautes Schiff, a ship built with clincher-work, V. 2. Klinker. —werk, *n.* [in seamen's lang.] clincher-work.

Klinop, *m.* [-s, *pl.* -e] ivy.

Klinse, *f.* [*pl.* -n] V. Ritze, Spalt.

Klipp, *m.* [-es, *pl.* -e] *dim.* —chen, ||—lein, *n.* [allied to Klapp] a snapping or knocking noise; *it.* a snap with the fingers, act of snapping the fingers.

Klipp-kanne, *f.* a wooden jug with a lid. —klapp, *n.* tick-tack. —kram, *m.* trade in toys or hardwares. —krämer, *m.* toyman, haberdasher or dealer in hardwares, pedlar. —werk, *n.* small articles of manufacture, toys.

||**Klippen,** *v. intr.* V. Klippern.

1. **Klippe,** *f.* [*pl.* -n] [from klieben, Sax. *clypan*, Sw. *klippa* = scheren, schneiden] a steep rugged rock, cliff, crag. Das Schiff scheiterte an einer —, the vessel split on or against a rock; blinde —, shelf; — vor einem Hafen, bar [at the entrance of a harbour].

Klipp-dachs, *m.* a mammifer found at the cape of Good Hope resembling the marmot. —kleber, *m.* [in natural hist.] the limpet, patella. —rose, *f.* sea-anemone.

Klippen-bock, *m.* wild goat. —dachs, *m.* V. Klippdachs. —reich, —voll, *adj.* full of cliffs or rocks. —weg, *m.* cliffy, craggy or rocky way.

2. **Klippe,** *f.* [*pl.* -n] V. Klipping.

3. **Klippe,** *f.* [*pl.* -n] a trap for catching birds, trap-cage.

Klippel, V. Klöppel.

Klipper, *m.* [-s, *pl.* -] V. Klempner.

||**Klippern,** *v. intr.* to make a noise, to click, to chink.

Klippicht, *adj.* resembling a cliff.

Klippig, *adj.* and *adv.* furnished with cliffs, full of cliffs or rocks, cliffy, craggy, rocky.

Klippfisch, *m.* [from klippen = klopfen?] 1) chaetodon. 2) dried cod-fish, stock-fish, kneeling.

||**Klipping,** *m.* [-es, *pl.* -e] [from the Sw. *klippen* = schneiden, Eng. *to clip*] triangular or square coin, obsidional coin.

||**Klippmünze,** *f.* [*pl.* -n], **Klippstück,** *n.* [-es, *pl.* -e] V. Klipping.

||**Klippschuld,** *f.* [= Kerbschuld?] [*pl.* -en] V. Kleckschuld.

||**Klippschule,** *f.* [*pl.* -n] a small school where children are taught to spell and read.

||**Klippschulmeister,** *m.* [-s, *pl.* -] master of a small spelling-school.

Klipptorf, *m.* [-s, not used in the *pl.*] hard and black turf or peat.

Klippwerk, *n.* [-es, *pl.* -e] machinery for coining small money.

Klirren, *v. intr.* [either an onomatopy or from the Gr. *ληρέω*, primitively = tönen] to clack, to click, to clink, to clatter, to clash. Die Gläser —, the glasses jingle; die Waffen —, the arms clatter or clash.

Klistier, *n.* [-es, *pl.* -e] [Gr. *κλυστήρ*, from *κλύζειν*, to wash, to cleanse] clyster.

Klistier-maschine, *f.* V. —spritze. —röhre, *f.* clyster-pipe. —spritze, *f.* syringe, clyster-pipe.

Klistieren, *v. tr.* Einen —, to administer to any one a clyster.

||**Klitsch,** *m.* [-es, *pl.* -e] noise arising from the collision of two soft bodies or of a soft and hard body, clash, V. Klatsch.

||**Klitschen,** *v. intr.* to make a clashing noise,

to produce a clashing sound, V. Klatschen.

||Klitter, m. [-s, pl. -] V. Klecks.

Klitter-buch, n. V. Kladde. —schuld, f. V. Kleckschuld.

||Klittern, V. Klecksen.

*Kloak, V. Cloak.

1. Kloben, m. [-s, pl. -] dim. Klöbchen, ||Klöblein, n. [allied to the L. globus and Klebsen] a lump, mass or bundle. Ein — Flachs, a bundle of flax.

2. Kloben, m. [-s, pl. -] dim. Klöbchen, ||Klöblein, [-s, pl. -] [from klieben = spalten] something cleft, divided or hollowed, piece or log of wood; [among lock-smiths] a) hand-vice, b) staple, c) V. Angel 2); [in mining] an instrument for pinching or holding, pincers; [in mechanics] pulley, block. Der — an einem Flaschenzuge, the block of a pulley; der — einer Wage, the handle of a balance; [among birdcatchers] a cleft stick or piece of wood to catch birds; [among watchmakers] der — des Steigerades, the potence of the balance-wheel; [among coopers] V. Reif—.

Kloben-arbeit, f. work done by the pulley. —deichsel, f. thill, shaft, V. Gabeldeichsel. —holz, n. log-wood. —macher, m. one who makes pullies. —säge, f. a large saw fixed in a square frame. —seil, n. rope for a pulley.

Kloben or Klöben, v. tr. [from klieben = spalten] to cleave, to split.

Klobeeisen, n. 1) an iron wedge. 2) — or Klöbeisen [among coopers], cleaving-iron or knife.

Klober, m. [-s, pl. -] cleaver.

Klonz, m. [-es, pl. -e] [among coopers] wedge.

Klopfe, f. [pl. -n] 1) beating, striking. Fig. †embarrassment, dilemma, straits. 2) a sheaf of corn only beaten but not clean-thrashed.

Klöpfel, m. [-s, pl. -] 1) an instrument for beating or knocking, beater, mallet, knocker, rapper, clapper, clog. Der — einer Glocke, the clapper or tongue of a bell; der — [am Halse eines Hundes], clog [put to a dog's neck]. 2) a cudgel. 3) drum-stick. 4) V. Klöppelholz.

Klöpfelring, m. the ring of the clapper of a bell.

Klöpfeln, v. intr. 1) to knock or rap softly or gently. 2) V. Klöppeln.

Klopfen, I. v. intr. [another form of klieben, Gr. κολάπτω, old Germ. clochon, V. Glocke] to knock. An die Thüre —, to knock or rap at the door; an die Wand, auf den Boden —, to knock against the wall, on the floor; Einem auf die Schulter —, to tap any one on the shoulder; fig. *auf den Busch —, V. Busch; das Herz klopft ihm, his heart goes pit-a-pat, throbs or flutters; in die Hände —, to clap one's hands, V. Klatschen; Einem auf die Backen —, to stroke or pat any one's cheeks; [in medicine] ein — der Schmerz, a throbbing or pulsative pain. II. v. tr. to beat, to strike. Den Hanf —, to beat hemp; den Staub aus einem Rocke —, to beat a coat; einen Hengst —, to twist a horse's genitals; †Einen —, to beat, bang or maul any one; †die Feinde sind geklopft worden, the enemies have been beaten, have got a banging or sound thrashing. Syn. Klopfen, Schlagen. Klopfen is used with reference to slight and playful blows, schlagen to more serious and violent ones. Klopfen any one on the fingers is an expression which has something of jesting in it; but schlagen seems to convey the idea of punishment. In sport we may klopfen a person on the cheek; but schlagen might also mean to give him a box on the ear. Whoever gives only a single blow schlägt; klopfen conveys always the motion of repeated blows. Schlagen can take place with anger and violence; klopfen usually takes place with coolness.

Klopf-brett, n. [in printing] planer. —fechter, m prize-fighter, pugilist; [in contempt] bully, hector. Ein gelehrter —fechter [chiefly in contempt], a disputant, controvertist, polemic. —fechterei, f. fighting, fight, scuffle, pugilism. Gelehrte —fechterei, literary dispute or controversy. —fisch, m. stock-fish. —garn, n. the cotton-threads of which wicks are made. —hammer, m. knocker or rapper [of a door]. —hengst, m. a castrated stallion; it. a horse not entirely castrated, rig. —holz, n. a piece of wood used for beating or knocking, beater; [in printing] V. —brett. —jagen, n. chase carried on by beating the woods. —käfer, m. death-watch, byrrhus. —keule, f. beetle, mallet. —pulver, n. vegetable sulphur, V. Herenmehl. —stein, m. stone on which shoemakers beat the leather, lap-stone.

Klöpfer, m. [-s, pl. -] 1) an instrument for knocking or beating, beater. — an der Thür, V. Klopfhammer. 2) one who beats, beater; [among hunters] beater-up. 3) [in nat. hist.] V. Holzwurm. 4) [in anatomy] V. Daumen—.

||Klöpferling, m. [-es, pl. -e] [a sort of apple] calville.

1. Klöppel, m. [-s, pl. -] [from klopfen] an instrument for knocking or beating, knocker, beater, V. Klöpfel, Knüppel, Klopfholz.

2. Klöppel, m. [-s, pl. -] [probably from knüpfen] piece of wood or bone used for making lace, lace-bone, bobbin.

Klöppel-arbeit, f. work done with the bobbin, bobbin-work; it. lace. —arbeiter, m. one who works with the bobbin; it. lace-maker. —garn, n. yarn used in making lace. —holz, n. bobbin. —kissen, n. the cushion or pad on which bobbin-work is done or lace is made. —lade, f. a box or desk on which lace is worked. —nadel, f. a needle for making lace. —pult, m. V. —lade. —sack, m. V. —kissen. —zwirn, m. thread for making lace.

1. Klöppeln, v. tr. [V. 1. Klöppel] to clog [a dog].

2. Klöppeln, v. tr. [V. 2. Klöppel] to make or weave lace.

Klöppfisch, m. V. Klopffisch.

Klöppler, m. [-s, pl. -] —inn, f. V. Klöppelarbeiter.

||Klopps, m. [-es, pl. -e] [from klopfen] piece of meat which is beaten to make it tender, steak &c.

Kloß, m. [-es, pl. Klöße] [allied to Klotz, kleben] a lump or round mass, a clod, V. Erd—; [in cookery] pudding, dumpling. Fig. [in fam. lang.] a stupid fellow, a block-head.

Klößig, adj. resembling a pudding or dumpling, doughy, sticky.

Kloster, n. [-s, pl. Klöster] [L. claustrum, from clausus, past part. of claudo = einschließen] cloister, convent, monastery. Ein — für Frauen, convent for nuns, a nunnery; in's — gehen, sich in ein — begeben, flüchten, to retire into a convent or religious order, to shut one's self up in a cloister, [applied to men] to turn monk, [applied to women] to take the veil; in ein — sperren, to confine, shut up or immure in a cloister or monastery; ein dem — entsprungener Mönch, a monk that turned his back upon his cloister, that has forsaken or renounced his order, V. Manns—, Mönchs—, Frauen—, Nonnen—. Fig. the body of monks or nuns. Das ganze — lief zusammen, all the monks or nuns run together.

Kloster-beere, f. rough-fruited gooseberry. —bewohner, m. inhabitant of a cloister or convent, a conventual, a monk or nun. —bild, n. V. Heiligenbild. —brauch, m. monastic rule, manner or custom. —bruder, m. lay-brother. —fleisch, n. [used only in popular language, fig. in] es ist ihr kein —fleisch gewachsen, she is not born for a convent or nunnery, she is not a vestal. —frau, f. nun. —gang, m. passage, piazza or peristyle of a convent, cloister. —garn, n. V. —zwirn. —garten, m. the garden of a convent or cloister. —gebäude, n. 1) the convent or cloister. 2) a building attached or belonging to a convent. —gehorsam, m. obedience or submission to the superiors in a monastery, monastic obedience. —geistliche, m. a friar, a monk. —gelehrsamkeit, f. monastic learning or erudition. —gelübde, n. the profession or the vows [of a monk or nun]. —gemeinde, —gemeine, f. 1) a parish belonging to or depending on a convent. 2) community of monks or nuns. —gericht, n., —gerichtsbarkeit, f. the jurisdiction of a convent. —gesellschaft, f. V. —gemeinde 2). —gewand, n. V. —kleid. —gewölbe, n. V. Kreuzgang. —glocke, f. the bell of a convent. —gut, n. an estate belonging to a convent. —habit, n. V. —kleid. —hof, m. the court-yard of a convent. —issop, m. [Kirchissop] church-hyssop. —jungfer, f. V. —frau. —kirche, f. the church of a convent. —kleid, n. the dress or habit of a monk or nun, monastic dress or habit. —leben, n. monastic life. —leute, pl. monks or nuns; it. the people belonging to a convent. —mauer, f. the wall of a convent. —mönch, m. friar, monk. —ordnung, f. V. —zucht. —pfeffer, m. V. Keuschbaum. —pforte, f. the gate of a convent. —rath, m. 1) the council of a convent. 2) counsellor of a convent. —schaffner, m. 1) the purveyor of a convent. 2) V. —verwalter. —schule, f. 1) a school belonging to a convent. 2) a school established in a convent, seminary. —schwester, f. 1) lay-sister. 2) V. —frau. —stand, m. the state or condition of a monk or nun, monastic state or condition. —strafe, f. claustral or monastic punishment. —thurm, m. the church-steeple of a convent. —vater, m. V. —vorsteher. —verbesserung, f. reformation of the convents. —verwalter, m. the administrator or steward of a convent. —vogt, m. the justiciary of a convent. —volk, n. [in contempt] V. —leute. —vorsteher, m. the superior of a convent or monastery. —weise, f. V. —brauch. —wenzel, m. [a bird] black-cap. —wesen, n. any thing concerning convents or monastic life. —zelle, f. cell. —zucht, f. claustral or monastic discipline. —zwang, m. claustral confinement, clausure. —zwinger, m. the space within the walls of a convent, V. —hof. —zwirn, m. sister's thread.

Klösterlich, adj. and adv. cloisteral, claustral, monastic, conventual. Das —e Leben, die —e Zucht &c., V. Klosterleben, Klosterzucht &c., — leben, to lead a monastic life.

Klotz, m. [-es, pl. Klötze] dim. Klötzchen, ||Klötzlein, n. [allied to Kloß] an unshapen mass, lump, block, trunk, stump, a lump of wood, log; [among hatters] block; [in mining] a large hammer or beetle. Fig. [in fam. lang.] idle coarse clumsy fellow. Er ist ein —, ein wahrer —, he is a loggerhead or blockhead, da steht er wie ein —, there he stands like a post, he stirs no more than a post. Prov. V. Keil.

*Klotz-augen, pl. V. Glotzauge. —erbse, f. a large round pea. —holz, n. wood in trunks or stumps. —kopf, m. stupid fellow, block-head. —köpfig, adj. very stupid. —köpfigkeit, *f.* great stupidity. —schuh, *m.* wooden shoe.

Klötzen, V. Glotzen.

Klötzig, *adj.* and *adv.* 1) blockish, coarse, clumsy. 2) clayey, sticky. —es Brod, clayey bread.

***Klúb, Klubíst**, *m.* V. Club, Clubist.

Klúcker, V. Klinker.

||**Klüfe**, *f.* [*pl.* -n] [either from kleiben = befestigen or from klieben = spalten] pin, V. Stecknadel.

Klúft, *f.* [*pl.* Klüfte] [from klieben = spalten] 1) cleft, fissure; *it.* chasm, gulf, cave, cavern. Sich in Klüften verbergen, to hide one's self in caverns; eine große —, an abyss, a bottomless pit, unfathomable depth. 2) any thing split or cleft; *it.* a pair of tongs; *it.* a pair of pincers. 3) a large fragment, large piece, lump; *it.* a log of wood. 4) [in seamen's lang.] scarf by which a jurymast is attached to the stump of a mast.

Kluft-damm, *m.* a traverse dam. —holz, *n.* log-wood.

||**Klüftig**, *adj.* full of clefts or fissures. —es Holz, cracked or shaky timber.

Klüg, [probably from the old lugen, Icel. *gloggva* = sehen] *adj.* and *adv.* 1) [having the power of discerning and judging correctly] wise, sensible. Ein —er Mann, a wise, sensible man; ein —es Kind, a sensible child; die Klügsten wurden von ihm betrogen, the most discerning or clear-sighted were deceived by him; ich bin um nichts klüger, I am nothing the wiser for it; *prov.* der Klügste gibt nach, the wisest yields or gives way; er ist mir allzu—, he is too subtle or cunning for me; er ist keiner von den Klügsten, he is none of the wisest, he is no conjurer. 2) [practically wise] prudent. Der —e, the prudent man; ein —er thut Alles mit Bedacht, a prudent man does nothing in haste or rashly; durch Schaden wird man —, bought wit is best; er ist allzu —, um zu sagen, was er denkt, he is too prudent or deep to say what he thinks; er hat — gehandelt, he has acted prudently. 3) [dictated or guided by wisdom or prudence] wise, prudent. Ein —es Betragen, a wise or prudent behaviour; ein —er Rath, a wise or prudent advice; eine —e Rede, a sensible speech. 4) understanding or comprehending a particular thing. — aus Etwas werden, to comprehend or understand a thing; ich kann nicht — daraus werden, I do not understand it, I can't make it out. 5) [in popular belief and language] [skilled in hidden arts, in magic and divination] Zum —en Manne, zur —en Frau gehen, to go to consult the magician, sorcerer or sorceress, soothsayer, ||spaeman or spaewife. 6) knowing, skilful, clever, learned. 7) having the use of one's reason, not foolish. Ich müßte nicht — seyn, wenn ich so Etwas thäte, I must have lost my senses to do any such thing; dieser Mensch ist nicht —, nicht recht —, that man is out of his wits, is not in his right wits or senses, is crackbrained, is beside himself. Syn. Klug, Weise, Verständig, Gescheut. A man who devotes himself to sensual pleasures acts neither weise, verständig nor klug; he does not act weise, for he misses the noblest aim of life; nor verständig, for he shows that he knows neither the nature nor worth of things; nor klug, since he chooses means which are injurious to his real welfare. Gescheut implies one who, schooled or aided by experience, has formed many correct and valuable rules for his conduct in life, which furnish him with a correctness of judgment and a readiness of action.

Klügeleí, *f.* cavilling, sophistry, false attempt at wisdom.

Klügeler, *m.* [-s, *pl.* -] a philosophist, caviller, sophist, wise-acre.

Klügeln, *v. intr.* to affect wisdom, to reason with affected wisdom, to search into with affected wisdom, to philosophise [said in contempt], V. Grübeln.

Klügheit, *f.* good sense, wisdom, prudence. *Prov.* — geht über Stärke, better be wise than strong; aus Gründen der —, from prudential reasons, V. Welt—, Staats—.

Klugheits-dünkel, *m.* presumption, self-sufficiency. —lehre, *f.* instruction in wisdom and prudence. —regel, *f.* rule or maxim of prudence, prudential rule.

Klügler, *m.* V. Klügeler.

Klüglich, *adv.* wisely, prudently. Etwas — einrichten, to arrange or manage any thing judiciously, wisely or prudently.

Klügling, *m.* [-es, *pl.* -e] a person of imaginary wisdom, or one who makes pretensions to great wisdom, wiseacre, a self-conceited fellow or coxcomb, V. Gernklug, Naseweis.

Klúmp, *m.* [-es, *pl.* -en or Klümpe] *dim.* Klümpchen, ||Klümplein, *n.* [Eng. *clump*, *lump*, Low Sax. Klamm, Klamp, Klump, Klunt, allied to Kloß and kleiben] a lump, clod, clot. —en Blut, clots of blood; ein — Butter, a lump of butter; [in cookery] pudding, dumpling, V. Klumpen.

Klump-eichel, *f.* V. Harzeichel. —fisch, *m.* V. Mondfisch, Mühlensteinfisch. —fuß, *m.* club-foot. —kohl, *m.* beet, V. Beete.

Klúmpen, *m.* [-s, *pl.* -] *dim.* Klümpchen, ||Klümplein, *n.* [the same as Klump] 1) mass, lump. Ein — Blei, a lump of lead; ein — Erde, a clod or lump of earth. 2) [a mass of things blended or thrown together without order] lump. Alles auf einen — werfen, to throw all on one heap; Gold, Silber, Blei &c. in Einem —, gold, silver, lead &c. in one lump. 3) [a number of things of the same kind growing or joined together] cluster. Ein — Bäume, a cluster of trees; ein — Bienen, a cluster of bees.

Klumpenbeere, *f.* the samphire of Jamaica.

Klúmpenweise, *adv.* in lumps, clods, clots or clusters.

Klúmper, *m.* [-s, *pl.* -] V. Klump.

Klumpermilch, *f.* V. Klunkermilch.

Klümperig, *adj.* and *adv.* consisting of lumps or clots, clotty, clotted. —e Milch, clotted or coagulated milk; —es Blut, clotty blood.

||**Klümpern**, *v. r.* Sich —, 1) to form into lumps, clots or clods, to clot, to agglomerate. 2) to fall or break into lumps or fragments. Dieses Brod klümpert sich, this bread crumbles.

Klúnker, *f.* [*pl.* -n] or *m.* [-s, *pl.* -] [seems to be allied to Klumpen] 1) clot of dirt sticking to one's clothes or to the wool of sheep &c. Sein Mantel ist voll —n, his cloak is quite dirty, quite bedraggled; *it.* clot of milk. 2) a tassel.

Klunker-erbse, *f.* the rose or crown pea. —kost, *f.* V. —muß. —milch, *f.* clotted or coagulated mik. —muß, *n.* clotted pudding. —wolle, *f.* V Zottelwolle.

Klúnkerig, *adj.* having clots of dirt, dirty, covered with dirt.

||**Klúnse**, *f.* [*pl.* -n] [V. Klinse] cleft, fissure, chink, gap.

Klüpfel, *m.* -s, *pl.* -] V. Klöppel.

Klüppe, *f.* [*pl.* -n] [allied to Kluft, klaffen] 1) [provinc.] [in low lang.] straits, difficulty, dilemma, pinch. Einen in der — haben, to have any one under one's paw or clutches, in one's power; wenn ich ihn jemahls in die — kriege, if ever he falls into my clutches, hands or power; er ist in der —, he is at a pinch, in great straits, V. Klemme, Enge. 2) a pinching instrument. *a*) [among farriers] barnacles. *b*) [among parchment-makers] chops. *c*) [among birdcatchers] trap, gin or noose. *d*) a pair of pincers. *e*) an instrument for twisting or tying the testicles of rams or male lambs in order to emasculate them. 3) a number of plucked birds, as larks &c.

Klüppel, V. Klöppel.

Klúppen, *v. tr.* [from klieben = schneiden] to tie or twist the testicles of rams or male lambs in order to emasculate them.

||**Klúppert**, *m.* [-s, *pl.* -e] [from kleben] a number of things joined together, cluster. Ein — Birnen, a cluster of pears.

Klúppertweise, *adv.* in clusters.

Klüse, *f.* [*pl.* -n] [allied to Klause, the L. *claudo, clausi*] [in seamen's lang.] hawse or hawse-hole.

Klüs-band, *n.* [in seamen's lang.] breast-hook nearest to the hawse-holes. —gatt, *n.* V. Klüse. —hölzer, *pl.* hawse-pieces. —loch, *n.* V. Klüse. —sack, *m.* [a bag filled with tow serving as a hawse-plug] hawse-bag. —zapfen, *m.* hawse-plug.

Klüsen, *v. intr.* [in seamen's lang.] [of a ship] to ride hawse-full.

Klútter, *f.* [*pl.* -n] [perhaps from laut] decoy-whistle, bird-call.

Klüver, *m.* [-s, *pl.* -] [in seamen's lang.] jib. Der Bügel des —s, jib-iron.

Klüver-baum, *m.* jib-boom. —fock, *m.* the fore-top stay-sail.

Klystier, *n.* V. Klistier.

Knabe, *m.* [-n, *pl.* -n] [allied to Kind] *dim.* Knäbchen, ||Knäblein, *n.* boy, lad, stripling. Sie ist von einem starken —n entbunden worden, she has been brought to bed of a fine boy; ein alter —, an old boy or bachelor; was will der alte —? what does the old fellow want? *Fig.* [a fish] V. Esche. Syn. Knabe, Junge, Bursche. Junge indicates one not yet grown up, but with reference only to sex and age. It is therefore used of those who, even among menials, are of the lowest grade and obliged to serve others. V. Pferdejunge, Küchenjunge, Lehrjunge. Knabe is a more respectable denomination than Junge. Thus we state in the annual lists of births the number of Knaben and girls. Bursche is a young man of the lower class, V. Handwerksbursche, Lehrbursche. When therefore we call a young man of higher rank a Bursche we place him on a level with youths of an inferior class.

Knaben-alter, *n.* boy's age, boyish years, boyhood —kraut, *n.* 1) fool-stones orchis. 2) V. Hanswurz. 3) Wildes —kraut, the bird's nest, ophrys nidus avis. 4) perfoliate cabbage, perfoliata. —krautmännchen, *n.* the male foolstones. —krautweibchen, *n.* female foolstones or orchis. —mäßig, *adj.* V. Knabenhaft. —schande, *f.* [*Päderastie] sodomy, pederasty, †buggery. —schänder, *m.* [*Päderast] sodomite, pederast, †bugger. —schänderei, —schändung, *f.* V —schande. —schule, *f.* school for boys. —stimme, *f.* boy's voice; [in music = *Alt] counter, counter-tenor. —streich, *m.* boy's trick, boyish trick. —traum, *m.* V. Jugendtraum. —wurz, *f.* V. —kraut 1) and 3). —zeit, *f.* boyhood.

Knäbenhaft, *adj.* and *adv.* boyish, puerile. Ein —es Betragen, boyish or puerile behaviour or manners, boyishness.

Knäbenhaftigkeit, *f.* boyishness, puerility.

Knabenschaft, *f.* 1) the state of a boy, boyhood. 2) [collectively] the boys.

Knack or **Knacks**, I. *m.* [-es, *pl.* -e] [from knicken] 1) [in popular lang.] crack, snap. Es that, gab einen —, it made a cracking noise, it gave a crack. 2) [among hunters] the boughs which a deer bruises or beats down with his head in traversing thickets. II. *interj.* crack, snap! —! da war es entzwei! crack! and it was in two or broken!

Knack=beere, *f.* strawberry. —mandel, *f.* cracking-almond, almond in the shell; V. Krachmandel. —weide, *f.* V. Knackerweide. —wurst, *f.* a sort of hard-smoked sausage [which may be broken or cracked], cervelas.

Knacke, V. Knagge.

Knacken, [= neigen; Sw. *knacka* = schlagen, *knaecka* = brechen, Eng. *to knack* = krachen] I. *v. intr.* to crack. Dieses Bett knackt, that bed cracks; mit den Fingern —, to make one's fingers snap. II. *v. tr.* to break, to crack. Nüsse —, to crack nuts; Flöhe —, to kill fleas.

Knack=Ente, *f.* [*pl.* -n] [the common or European] teal.

Knacker, *m.* [-s, *pl.* -] 1) cracking sound, crack, V. Knack. 2) instrument for breaking or cracking, cracker; nut-cracker.

Knacker=beere, *f.* V. Knackbeere. —weide, *f.* V. Brechweide, Bruchweide, Glasweide.

Knackerig, *adj.* cracking, crisp.

†**Knackern**, V. Knacken.

†**Knacks**, **Knacksen**, V. Knack, Knacken.

Knagge, *f.* [*pl.* -n] [probably from neigen = biegen] 1) knot in wood. 2) [among joiners] bracket.

Knaggen, *m.* [-s, *pl.* -] [allied to neigen = brechen, Sw. *knaecka*] a great piece of bread.

Knall, *m.* [-es, *pl.* -e] [Sw. *knall*, Sax. *cnyll* = Glockenschlag, Eng. *knell*] strong quick sound, clap, report, explosion. Der — des Donners, the clap of thunder, thunder-clap; der — von Schießgewehren, the report of fire-arms; der — einer Bombe, the bursting of a bomb; der — des Pulverthurmes war fürchterlich, the explosion of the powder-magazine was dreadful; [among hunters] — und Fall war Eins, the gun was no sooner fired than the game fell. **Fig.* — und Fall, on a sudden, suddenly; er reisete — und Fall ab, he departed all on a sudden; bei ihm ist Alles — und Fall, he does every thing with precipitation or rashness.

Knall=blei, *n.* fulminating lead. —büchse, *f.* pop-gun. —glas, *n.* V. —kügelchen. —gold, *n.* fulminating gold, saffron of gold. —hütte, *f.* 1) [obsolete] brothel, bawdy-house. 2) miserable hut, hovel. —kugel, *f.*, [generally] —kügelchen, ||—kügelein, *n.* a small hollow piece of glass which breaks with a sort of explosion; *it.* V. Springglas. —luft, *f.* phlogistic or inflammable air. —pulver, *n.* fulminating powder. —quecksilber, *n.* fulminating mercury. —silber, *n.* fulminating silver.

Knallen, [V. Knall, probably allied to schnellen] I. *v. intr.* to make a loud noise, to make a report, to crack, to fulminate. Mit der Peitsche —, to smack one's whip; diese Pistole knallt sehr stark, the report of this pistol is very loud; ein Gewehr — lassen, mit einem Gewehr — [chiefly in fam. lang.], to discharge or fire a gun. II. *v. tr.* Einen — [low], to shoot any one; †*fig.* to take any one in, to impose upon any one.

Knapp, *adj.* and *adv.* [seems to be allied to kneipen] rather less than is wanted for the purpose, scarcely sufficient, scant, scanty. Ein Kleid zu — machen, to make a coat too scant, close or tight; —e Schuhe, strait or tight shoes; *eine —e Stimmenmehrheit, a bare majority [of votes]; ein —es Maß, a scanty measure; — messen, to measure niggardly; [in seamen's lang.] der Wind ist —, the wind blows in an almost directly opposite direction; es wird — hinreichen, it will scarcely be sufficient; er war — fort, he was just gone. **Fig.* —e Zeiten, hard times; das Geld ist bei ihm —, he is short of money, money is scarce with him; er behilft sich —, es geht ihm —, es geht — bei ihm zu, he has but a scanty allowance, he is hard put to it, he can hardly make shift to live; Einen — halten, to keep any one short; wir sind — abgespeist worden, we have met with a very cold reception or entertainment.

Knapp=eule, *f.* the common owl. —sack, *m.* knapsack.

Knappe, *m.* [-n, *pl.* -n] [allied to Knabe and Knecht, and to the Eng. *knave* and *knight*] 1) [formerly] a young man, lad, boy; *it.* [in some trades] journey-man, workman, servant; V. Berg—, Mühl—, Tuch—. 2) [formerly, an attendant on a noble warrior] squire; *it.* a vassal.

Knappen, [Low Sax. knappen = klatschen, Eng. *to knap*, Sw. *knaeppa*] I. *v. intr.* [provincial, in popular lang.] 1) V. Knacken, Knistern. 2) to hobble along, to halt a little. II. *v. tr.* V. Knacken, Knappern; *it.* V. 1. Kneipen.

Knappenschaft, *f.* V. Knappschaft.

||**Knappern**, *v. tr.* [allied to the Sw. *knaeppa* = klatschen and to kneipen] to craunch or crunch, to crack, to knab, to knapple.

Knappheit, *f.* scantiness, narrowness.

Knapps, [V. Knappen] crack, snap!

Knappschaft, *f.* the body of journeymen; [in mining] the association or body of miners.

Knappschafts=älteste, *m.* the senior or foreman of the miners. —kasse, *f.* fund or money-box for poor miners. —kux, *m.* share in a mine for the benefit of the poor miners.

Knarpeln, **Knarpen**, *v. intr.* [from knarren] to crack, to crackle.

Knarpelkirsche, *f.* the red and white heart-cherry.

Knarre, *f.* [*pl.* -n] rattle [such as that of a watchman]. †*Fig.* Eine alte —, an old grumbling woman, an old scold; *it.* any thing disagreeable or troublesome.

Knarren, *v. intr.* [allied to knurren, L. *gnarro*, i. e. *narro* = sprechen; Sax. *gnyrran* = rauschen, and *gnornan* = wehklagen] to creak, to screak, to produce a creaking noise. Die Angeln dieser Thür —, the hinges of this door creak; enge Schuhe — beim Gehn, tight shoes creak in walking; der Nachtwächter knarret, the watchman springs his rattle —d reden, to speak in a shrill tone, to squeak

Knarr=ente, *f.* the gadwall or gray. —eule, *f.* V. Kirreule. —huhn, *n.* [a bird of South-America] the agami, trumpeter.

Knarricht, *adj.* resembling a creaking sound.

Knarrig, *adj.* that creaks, creaking. —e Schuhe, creaking shoes.

||**Knarzen**, *v. intr.* V. Knarren.

Knast, *m.* [-es, *pl.* -e] [seems to be the same as Knagge] knot in wood, knag guar.

Knaster, *m.* [-s, *pl.* -] 1) the best sort of tobacco, canister tobacco. 2) — or —bart, ein alter —bart [in popular lang.], a morose old fellow, old grumbler; *it.* ein alter —, an old worm-eaten book.

Knasterig, *adj.* [from Knastern] cracking, crackling.

Knastern, *v. intr.* [the same as knistern] to crackle. Ein —des Feuer, a crackling fire.

Knastig, *adj.* [from Knast] knotty [wood], knaggy, gnarly.

Knaten, V. Kneten.

Knatschen, [allied to kneten] I. *v. intr.* to paddle; *it.* V. Schmatzen. II. *v. tr.* V. Zerknittern.

Knattern, *v. intr.* V. Knastern.

Knauel or **Knäuel**, *m.* or *n.* [-s, *pl.* -] [allied to Knolle] bottom or clew [of thread &c.]. Faden auf einen — winden, to wind thread upon a bottom.

Knauelgras, *n.* V. Hundsgras.

Knaueln, **Knäueln**, *v. tr.* to form into a clew or bottom. Seide —, to wind silk into or upon a bottom.

Knauen, *v. tr.* and *intr.* to gnaw, to pick. *Fig.* Einem Etwas zu — geben, to give one a bone to pick.

Knauer, *m.* [-s] [in mining] hard rock, slate-rock. Es bäumt sich ein — auf, there appears a hard or slate-rock.

Knauf, *m.* [-es, *pl.* Knäufe] [allied to Knopf] 1) button. 2) [in architecture] the capital, head or top of a pillar. 3) the knob of a tree.

Knauf=macher, *m.* V. Knopfmacher. —nadel, *f.* pin. —stempel, *m.* [among goldsmiths] puncheon.

Knaupeln, *v. intr.* [from knauen = nagen] to pick, to gnaw, to craunch. [provincial, in popular lang.] An einem Knochen —, to pick a bone; er hat immer Etwas zu —, he has always something to nibble. *Fig.* to take great pains; to toil and moil to little purpose.

Knauser, *m.* [-s, *pl.* -], —inn, *f.* [from knauen = nagen] niggard, stingy fellow, miser, curmudgeon, pinch-penny.

Knauserei, *f.* niggardliness, stinginess, V. Knickerei.

Knauserig, *adj.* and *adv.* niggardly, miserly, stingy, V. Genau, Karg.

Knausern, *v. intr.* [V. Knauser] to play the niggard or miser, to be niggardly or stingy. Er knausert bei Allem, he is sordidly parsimonious in every thing.

Knaust, *m.* [-es] [in mining] V. 3. Gneiß.

Knaustbirn or **Knaußbirn**, *f.* the yellow musk-pear.

Knebel, *m.* [-s, *pl.* -] [the same as Knüppel, from kloppen, Low Sax. knappen] 1) a thick and short piece of wood, a short stick [serving for various purposes, as for tying across a dog's neck, a clog; or for tightening any cord or band, packing-stick], V. Knüttel. 2) a gag, V. Maul—. 3) [in botany] pearl-wort.

Knebel=bart, *m.* mustachios. Den —bart hinaufstreichen, to turn up one's mustachios. —barteisen, *n.* iron for curling the mustachios. —holz, *n.* packing-stick. —spieß, *m.* a spear with a cross-bar. —stock, *m.* V. —holz. —trense, *f.* snaffle. —wachs, *n.* wax for curling and turning up the mustachios.

Knebeler, **Knebler**, *m.* [-s, *pl.* -], —inn, *f.* 1) a person employed during the harvest in tying sheaves. 2) V. Weinschröter.

Knebeln, *v. tr.* [V. Knebel] 1) to tighten a rope or band by the aid of a stick, to tie, to bind [sheaves &c.]. Ein Tau— [in seamen's lang.], to bit a cable. 2) Einem den Mund —, to gag any one.

Knecht, *m.* [-es, *pl.* -e] [allied to Knabe] 1) [formerly] a young man, a lad. 2) [chiefly] a servant, farming servant, [and in some trades] journeyman. Ein leibeigener —, a bondman; *prov.* wie der Herr, so der —, like master, like man; Ihr unterthäniger —, your most humble servant; dieser Schuster, Fleischer hat mehrere —e [better Gesellen], that shoemaker, butcher has several journeymen. *it.* slave. Einem zum — machen, to reduce any one to servitude, to bring any one into bondage, to enslave, to enthral any one. *it.* [formerly] soldier. Er ist mit 1000 —en eingefallen, he made an invasion with a thousand men or soldiers. V. Acker—, Pferde—, Ochsen—, Haus—, Henkers—, Reit—, Stall—, Groß—, Klein—; *it.* Brau—, Schuh—. *Fig.* Ein — seiner Leidenschaften seyn, to be a slave to one's passions; wer Sünde thut, der ist der Sünde — [in Scripture], whoever committeth sin, is the servant of sin. 3) a name given to several instruments and utensils, in a manner similar to the use of the English word jack, as Stiefel—, boot-jack. Syn. Knecht, Leibeigener, Sclave. According to the present usage of language, the right of a master over a Knecht can extend only so far as to require from him that labour or service he has pledged himself to render. The Sclave is not only bound to do every kind of labour for his master, but all he has or acquires, nay even his own person is subjected to him. The Knecht and Sclave belong to the domestic establishment of their master; this is not the case with the Leibeigene. The latter has his own house, and when he has Knechte himself, is master of a family.

Knechts-arbeit, or **—s-arbeit**, *f.* the work of a servant or slave, low work, drudgery. **—dienst** or **—s-dienst**, *m.* the service of a servant or slave. **—geist** or **s-geist**, *m.* servile spirit or sentiments. **—geld**, *n.* [formerly] tax for the maintenance of the soldiers. **—gestalt**, *f.* form or figure of a servant or slave. Jesus nahm —gestalt an [in Scripture], Jesus took upon him the form of a servant. **—sinn**, *m.* servile disposition. **—stand**, *m.* servile station. **—vieh**, *n.* the sheep belonging to the shepherd's servant.

Knechterei, *f.* V. Knechtschaft.

Knechtisch, *adj.* and *adv.* servile, slavish. Eine —e Furcht, a servile or slavish fear.

Knechtlich, *adj.* and *adv.* incumbent on a servant, servile. Der —e Dienst, V. Knechtsdienst; —er Gehorsam, servile obedience.

Knechtschaft, *f.* the state or condition of a servant or slave, servitude, bondage, thraldom. Sich der — entziehen, to shake off the yoke of servitude or bondage; in — gerathen, to be reduced to slavery or bondage.

Kneif, *m.* [-es, *pl.* -e] [Sax. and Eng. *knife*, Fr. *canif*, Low. L. *canipulus*, allied to kneifen, kneipen] shoemaker's knife, cutting-knife, paring-knife, clasp-knife, a hooked knife, a pruning-knife.

Kneifen, *v. tr.* [Gr. κνίζω, κνίπτω, whence κνίψ, W. *cneifio* = scheren] to pinch, to nip. Einen in den Arm —, to pinch any one's arm; [in seamen's lang.] den Wind —, to ply to windward, to keep close to the wind. V. Kneipen.

Kneifer, Kneiper, *m.* [-s, *pl.* -] red breasted merganser or goosander.

1. **Kneipe**, *f.* [*pl.* -n] 1) instrument for pinching, pincers. †*Fig.* In der — sitzen, to be at a pinch, in great straits. 2) [in popular lang.] pinching in the bowels, griping, gripes. Die — haben, to feel the gripes or colic, to have a violent pain in one's bowe s.

2. **Kneipe**, *f.* [*pl.* -n] [probably from the old kneip or knap = klein; Sw. *nepa* = klein] a hedge-alehouse, a gin-shop, a tavern of the lowest description, a finish.

1. **Kneipen**, I. *reg.* and *ir. v. tr.* [V. Kneifen] to pinch, to nip. Meine Schuhe — mich, my shoes pinch me; die Würfel —, to cog the dice; den Wind —, V. Kneifen. II. *v. impers.* [low] Es kneipt mich im Leibe, the colic wrings me, I have a pain in my bowels. Das —, griping, gripes, V. 1. Kneipe 2).

Kneip-hahn, *m.* V. Laufkäfer. **—haken**, *m.* [in seamen's lang.] tackle-hook. **—käfer**, *m.* V. Rebenstecher. **—schröter**, *m.* stag-beetle, V. Hornschröter. **—wurm**, *m.* vine-grub. **—zange**, *f.* pincers, nippers, a pair of pincers &c.

2. **Kneipen**, *v. intr.* [in low lang., especially students' cant] to frequent low alehouses, to be a frequent visitor of, or lounger in, low taverns.

Kneipschenke, *f.* V. 2. Kneipe.

Kneiper, V. Kneifer.

Kneiß, *m.* [-es] [allied to Knauer, Knorren] V. 3. Gneiß.

Kneißeisen, *n.* tawer's paring-knife.

Kneißen, *v. tr.* [Gr. κνίζω, V. Kneifen] to take off the hair of skins, to depilate.

Knellbeere, *f.* great nightshade, belladonna.

Kneller, *m.* [-s] [low] bad tobacco.

Kneten, *v. tr.* [old Germ. cniban, chnistan = zerreiben, Low Sax. *gniden* = hin und her reiben] to knead. Den Teig —, to knead dough; den Thon —, to work clay well. *Fig.* V. Knittern II.

Knet-getriebe, *n.* kneading machine or engine. **—scheit**, *n.* kneading-beetle. **—trog**, *m.* kneading-trough.

Kneter, *m.* [-s, *pl.* -] kneader.

Knick, *m.* [-es, *pl.* -e] I. [from knicken = brechen] 1) [provincial] crack, breach, flaw. Dieses Glas hat einen —, this glass has a crack or flaw; einen — in einen Zweig machen, to break a branch. †*Fig.* Er hat einen — bekommen, his health has received an injury, has been injured or impaired. 2) [in popular lang.] the sound or noise caused by the breaking of a thing, crack. Es that einen —, it made a cracking noise, it cracked. II. [from knicken = biegen] a quickset hedge.

Knick-fang, *m.* V. Genickfang. **—fuß**, *m.* V. Knicks 2). **—holz**, *n.* brush-wood. **—lauch**, *m.* the flat-stalked garlic. **—stag**, *n.* [in seamen's lang.] preventer stay. **—weide** *f.* V. Knackerweide.

Knicken, [Sw. *knaecka* = zerbrechen, allied to neigen, L. *neco* (*nico*), *noceo* &c.] I. *v. tr.* 1) to break without an entire severance of the parts, to crack, to flaw. Ein Glas —, to crack or flaw a glass; einen Hasen — [sporting term], to break or wring off the neck of a hare. 2) to break so as to occasion a sound, to crack. Läuse —, to kill or crack lice. II. *v. intr.* 1) to burst with a sound or crack. Das Glas knickte, the glass cracked. 2) [in fam. lang.] Im Gehen, mit den Füßen, Knien —, to be weak in the joints of the knee or ancle, to bend the knee in walking, ||to be knack-kneed, in-kneed. 3) *Fig.* V. Knickern, Knausern.

Knicker, *m.* [-s, *pl.* -] pinch-penny, V. Knauser.

Knickerei, *f.* V. Knauserei.

Knickerig, *adj.* and *adv.* 1) bending the knees in walking. — gehen, to bend the knees in walking, to stagger. 2) V. Knauserig.

Knickerisch, *adj.* V. Knauserig.

Knickern, *v. intr.* 1) V. Knicken II, 2). 2) to deal in a niggardly manner, to be penurious in a bargain, to higgle; *it.* V. Knausern.

Knickig, *adj.* V. Knickerig.

Knicks, *m.* [-es, *pl.* -e] 1) V. Knick I. 1). 2) [reverence made by women] courtesy, curtsy. Einen — machen, to courtesy, to drop a courtesy.

Knicksen, *v. intr.* to courtesy.

Knie, *n.* [-s, *pl.* a dissyllable —] *dim.* **—chen**, ||**—lein**, *n.* [Goth. *kniu*, old Germ. Chniu, Gr. γόνυ, L. *genu*, allied to neigen, Icel. *hneigan*, nicken, knicken &c.] 1) knee. Die — beugen, to bend the knee; die — vor Einem beugen, to bow the knee to any one; sich auf die — niederlassen, auf die — fallen, to fall on the knees, to kneel [down]; auf den —n liegen, to be on one's knees or kneeling. **Fig.* Eine Sache über das — abbrechen, to do a thing in haste, *it.* superficially; sie sind über's — [über den Fuß] gespannt, they are at variance. 2) [in ship-building, a piece of timber in the shape of a human knee when bent] knee. Auf und niederstehende —, hanging knees; verkehrte —, dagger-knees.

Knie-band, *n.* knee-band, knee-string, garter. **—beuge**, *f.* V. —kehle. **—beugemuskel**, *m.* ham-string. **—beugen**, *n.*, **—beugung**, *f.* the act of bending the knee, genuflection, knee-tribute. **—biege**, *f.* V. —kehle. **—bohrer**, *m.* [a sea-term] V. Ochsenknie. **—bug**, *m.* hock, suffraginous flexure, V. —beuge, —kehle, Hälse. —bug von einem Kalbe, knuckle of veal. **—bügel**, *m.* a leather-cover of the knee. **—busch**, *m.* low shrub or bush; *it.* coppice or copse. **—decke**, *f.* [in a carriage] knee-boot, knee-flap. **—fall**, *m.* V. Fußfall. **—fällig**, *adj.* and *adv.* with bent or bowed knees. Einen —fällig bitten, [in a proper as well as in a fig. sense] to supplicate, to implore any one [on one's knees]. **—förmig**, *adj.* and *adv.* having the form of a knee, knee-shaped; [in botany] geniculated. **—galgen**, *m.* a gibbet or gallows consisting of a post and a traverse beam. **—gebüsch**, *n.* V. —busch. **—geige**, *f.* base-viol, violoncello. **—gelenk**, *n.* knee-joint. **—geschwulst**, *f.* windgall, vessigon. **—gicht**, *f.* gout in the knees, gonagra. **—gichtig**, *adj.* afflicted with the gout in the knees. **—gras**, *n.* V. Ackerspargel. **—gürtel**, *m.* garter. **—hoch**, *adj.* and *adv.* knee-high. **—holz**, *n.* a piece of wood bent like a knee; [in ship-building] knee, knee-timber. **—kappe**, *f.* V. —bügel. **—karbätsche**, *f.* V. —streiche. **—kehle**, *f.* the hollow part behind the knee; hough, hock. **—kehlenband**, *n.* poplitic ligament. **—kehlenmuskel**, *m.* poplitic muscle, hamstring. **—kehlennerv**, *m.* poplitic nerve. **—kehlenschlagader**, *f.* poplitic artery. **—kissen**, *n.* V. —polster. **—leder**, *n.* V. —bügel. **—polster**, *n.* hassock, cushion for kneeling. **—riemen**, *m.* garter; *it.* [among shoemakers] knee-strap. **—röhre**, *f.* tube or pipe bent as a knee. **—scheibe**, *f.* knee-pan. Die —scheibe an dem Sprunggelenke des Pferdes, stifle, stifle-joint. **—schiene**, *f.* pulley-piece. **—schnalle**, *f.* knee-buckle. **—streiche**, *f.* the finest sort of cards [for combing wool]. **—stück**, *n.* 1) V. —schiene. 2) [among painters] a painting representing the person from the head to the knees; knee-piece. **—tief**, *adj.* and *adv.* knee-deep. **—weit**, *adj.* and *adv.* having the knees far distant or much asunder, walking wide betwixt the legs.

Knien, *v. intr.* [used with seyn and haben]

to kneel, to kneel down. Einen — lassen, to make any one kneel [down]; ich bitte Sie —d um Verzeihung, I ask your pardon on my knees; [in botany] ein geknieter Stengel, a geniculated stem.

Kniese, *f.* [*pl.* -n] [in seamen's lang.] the ribs or floor-timbers of a ship.

Kniff, *m.* [-es, *pl.* -e], *dim.* —chen, ||—lein, *n.* act of pinching, pinch. **Fig.* trick, artifice, contrivance, stratagem. Syn. Kniff, Pfiff, Finte. Any device by which one tries to deceive another, and thereby gain some unfair advantage is a Kniff; a Pfiff, so far as we view its ingeniousness, and as discovering an inventive and clever mind. A Finte is such a device as consists in a lie, and which requires disguise for its execution. To make use of Kniffe is therefore disgraceful; V. also List.

Knipp, Knipps, *m.* [-es, *pl.* -e], *dim.* —chen, ||—lein, *n.* [from kneipen, V. Schnippchen] 1) snap with the finger. **Fig.* Einem einen —, ein —chen schlagen, to laugh at any one, to mock or deride any one secretly. 2) a stroke upon the fingers' ends with the ferula, a rap over the fingers' ends [a punishment in school]. —schen halten, to put out the fingers for the purpose of receiving such punishment.

Knipp-kugel, *f.*, —käulchen, —kügelchen, *n.* a marble for children to play with. —schere, *f.* small pointed scissors for cutting out paper. —tasche, *f.* a pocket with a hoop- or clasp-spring [which women hang to their side].

Knippelholz, *n.* V. Prügelholz.

Knippen, [V. Knipp] *v. intr.* to snap the fingers.

Knipps, 1) V. Knipp. 2) V. Knirps.

Knippsen, V. Knippen.

Knirps, *m* [-es, *pl.* -e] [perhaps from kneipen = abschneiden] a little fellow, a mannikin, a shrimp, a dwarfish fellow.

Knirren, V. Knarren, Knirschen.

Knirschen, [allied to knirren, knarren] I. *v. intr.* to utter a creaking or grating sound. Dieses Brod knirscht unter den Zähnen, this bread crackles under the teeth or eats gritty; mit den Zähnen —, to gnash or grind the teeth; der gefrorne Schnee knirscht unter unsern Füßen oder Schritten, the frozen snow is quite crisp under our feet or steps. II. *v. tr.* 1) to break or bruise with a creaking noise. 2) to strike together, to clash. Die Zähne —, to gnash or grind the teeth. V. Zerknirschen.

Knisterig, *adj.* and *adv.* that crackles or crepitates easily, crackling, crisp.

Knistern, [allied to the old Germ. chnistan = zerreiben, V. Kneten]. I. *v. intr.* to crackle, to crepitate. Das brennende Reißholz knistert, burning brushwood crackles; das Salz knistert im Feuer, salt crepitates in fire; ich höre eine Maus —, I hear a mouse gnawing or stirring. II. *v. tr.* to craunch, V. Zerknittern.

Knistergold, *n.* crackling or crepitating gold, tinsel.

Knittel, V. Knüttel.

Knitter, *m.* [-s, *pl.* -] an irregular fold, crease, rumple. — in Etwas machen, to rumple any thing.

Knittergold, *n.* V. Knistergold.

Knitterig, *adj.* and *adv.* full of folds, rumpled.

Knittern, [allied to knistern] I. *v. intr.* 1) [used with haben] V. Knistern. 2) [used with seyn] or sich —, to get folds or rumples, to become rumpled. II. *v. tr.* to rumple or ruffle.

Knöbbelfisch, *m.* [-es, *pl.* -e] V. Knotenfisch.

Knöbel, *m.* [-s, *pl.* -] V. Knöchel.

Knobellerche, *f.* [*pl.* -n] a kind of lark that tastes of garlick.

Knoblauch, *m.* [-es] [Knob = Knopf] garlick. Die Zwiebel des —es, clove of garlick; ein Büschel —, a bunch of garlick.

Knoblauch-birn, *f.* garlick-pear. —birnbaum, *m.* garlick-pear-tree. —braten, *m.* roast-meat seasoned with garlick. —brühe, *f.* garlick-sauce. —geruch, *m.* smell of garlick. —kraut, *n.* garlick-wild; *it.* V. Wasserlauch. —schwamm, *m.* the garlick-scented agaric. —zehe, —zinke, *f.* clove of garlick.

Knöchel, *m.* [-s, *pl.* -] [allied to Knochen] knuckle, joint [of a finger], ankle [of a foot]; [in anatomy] malleolus. *Fig.* [in fam. lang.] die.

Knöchel-band, *n.* ligament of the ankle. —bedeckung, *f.* that part of the armour which covers the ankle.

Knöchelchen, *n.* [-s, *pl.* -] [*dim.* of Knöchel and Knochen]. 1) a little knuckle or joint. 2) a little or small bone, ossicle.

Knöcheln, *v. intr.* [in fam. lang.] to play at dice.

Knochen, *m.* [-s, *pl.* -] [seems to be allied to knicken, neigen, Knie], *dim.* Knöchelchen, ||Knöchlein, *n.* bone. Der — am dicken Beine, the bone of the thigh, femur; starke — haben, stark von — seyn, to be well, large or strong limbed; in — verwandeln, to ossify; es ist nichts als Haut und — an ihm [in popular lang.], he is quite emaciated, is a mere skeleton, *it.* he is nothing but skin and bones, he is raw-boned; seine — schonen [low], to spare one's self or one's labour, to take special care of one's health; bis auf die — [die Haut] naß werden [low], to get thoroughly wet or drenched, V. Hüft—, Mark—, Röhr—, Gebein. Syn. V. Bein.

Knochen-abblätterung, *f.* exfoliation. —ansatz, *m.* epiphysis or epiphysy. —artig, —ähnlich, *adj.* and *adv.* resembling a bone, osseous, bony. —asche, *f.* ashes of bones, bone-ashes. —auswuchs, *m.* preternatural excrescence of a bone, exostosis. —band, *n.* ligament. —beschreibung, *f.* description of the bones, osteography. —brand, *m.* [a disease of cattle] mortification or gangrene of the bones. —brecher, *m.* 1) V. Beinbrech. 2) V. Beinbrecher. —bruch, *m* the fracture or disruption of a bone. —dreher, *m.* a turner in bone. —dürr, *adj.* V. Klapperdürr. —erzeugung, *f.* V. Beinerzeugung. —fäule, —fäulniß, *f.* V. Beinfäulniß. —feile, *f.* [in surgery] rugine, raspatory. —fett, *n.* 1) V. —mark. 2) fat of bones. —fisch, *m.* V. Beinfisch. —fortsatz, *m.* apophysis or apophysy. —fraß, *m.* V. —fäule. —fuge, *f.* juncture of bones. —fügung, *f.* articulation, V. Beinfügung. —gebäude, *n.* 1) system of bones. 2) V. —gerippe. —gerippe, —gerüst, *n.* skeleton. —hand, *f.* very lean hand. —hauer, *m.* butcher. *Fig.* V. —mann. —haus, *n.* V. Beinhaus. —haut, *f.*, ||—häutlein, *n.* V. Beinhaut. —kern, *m.* point of ossification. —knoten, —kopf, *m.* condyl, knot or joint. —krankheit, *f.* V. —weh. —krebs, *m.* caries. —lehre, *f.* osteology. —lehrig, *adj.* and *adv.* [*osteologisch] osteologic. —los, *adj.* and *adv.* without bones, destitute of bones, exosseous, boneless. —mann, *m.* skeleton; *fig.* [in popular language] Death. —mark, *n.* V. Beinmark. —naht, *f.* suture of the skull. —pfanne, *f.* cotyle. —platte, *f.* scale of a bone. —same, *m.* V. Beinsame. —sauer, *adj.* and *adv.* phosphorous, phosphoric. —saure Salze, phosphites; —saures Blei, phosphate of lead. —säure, *f.* phosphoric or phosphorous acid. —schlagader, *f.* artery of the bones. —schleie, *f.* [a fish] the male tench. —schwarz, *n.* V. Beinschwarz. —spalt, *m.* fissure. —splitter, *m.* splint or splinter [of a bone]. —stein, *m.* the glue-bone stone, osteocolla. —verbindung, —vereinigung, *f.* V. —fügung. —verfleischung, *f.* osteosarcosis. —versteinerung, *f.* petrifaction of bones. —weh, *n.* osteocope. —werk, *n.* 1) any thing made of bone, bone-toy. 2) a mass or heap of bones. —winde, *f.* the tuberous-rooted bindweed. —wuchs, *m.* ossification. —wurm, *m.* a disease which causes tumours on the bones of cattle. —zerlegung, *f.* dissection of the bones, osteotomy.

Knöchern, *adj.* and *adv.* made of bone, V. Beinen.

Knöchicht, *adj.* and *adv.* resembling bone, osseous, bony.

Knöchig, *adj.* and *adv.* having bones, bony.

Knöchler, *m.* [-s, *pl.* -] 1) one who plays at dice. 2) V. Knochenmann *fig.*

Knocke, *f.* [*pl.* -n] a torsel of hatcheled flax.

Knödel, *n.* [-s, *pl.* -] [= Knoten] 1) dumpling. 2) dried pear.

Knöll, *m.* [-es, *pl.* -e] V. Knollen.

Knoll-distel, *f.* the tuberous thistle. —hafer, *m.* V. Knollengras. —horn, *n.* radish-shell. —käfer, *m.* the byrrhus —lilie, *f.* mountain lily, mortagon. —rettig, *m.* common garden radish. —sucht, *f.* the knotted gout. —wicke, *f.* V. Erdnuß.

Knöllen, *v. tr.* Den Teig —, to re-knead dough.

Knöllen, *m.* [-s, *pl.* -], *dim.* Knöllchen, ||Knöllein, *n.* [Sax. *cnolle* and *hnol* = Scheitel, Ital. *zolla*] a shapeless or misshapen mass or elevation; [in surgery] a moon-calf, mole, a false conception Ein — Blut, a clot of blood; die — an thierischen Körpern, an Gewächsen, protuberances, tumours or tubercles on animal bodies, knobs or tubercles on plants; die Wurzeln vieler Gewächse sind —, the roots of many plants are tubers or tuberous. *Fig.* [low, in contempt] a clownish fellow, a boor.

Knollen-blume, *f.* bulbous crowfoot, butter-cups. —gewächs, *n.* tuberous plant. —gras, *n.* the tall oat-grass. —kraut, *n.* 1) wild licorice. 2) bladder nut-tree, bastard senna-tree. —rebe, *f.* V. —wicke. —sellerie, *m.* the turnip-rooted celery, celeriac. —stein, *m.* menilite. —wicke, *f.* tuberous-rooted glycine. —wurz, *f.* 1) V. —kraut 1) 2) the knobby-rooted fig-wort. 3) V. Erdnuß 2)

Knöllig, *adj.* and *adv.* full of clots, tubercles or knobs, clotty, knobby, tuberous. —es Blut, clotty blood; —e Wurzeln, tuberous roots.

Knöpf, *m* [-es, *pl.* Knöpfe], *dim.* Knöpfchen, ||Knöpflein, *n.* [Sw. *knapp*, Low Sax. and D. *knoop*, Sax. *cnaep*; it seems to be allied to the Isel. *gnipa* = hervorragen, V. Knauf] 1) any knob or ball fastened to another body. Der — auf einer Thurmspitze, the ball or knob on the top of a tower or steeple; der — an einem Stocke or Rohre, the head of a cane; der — auf einem Bettpfosten, the cup or ball at the top of a bedpost; der — am Degengefäße, the knob at the hilt of a sword, pommel; der — am Rappiere, the button of a foil; der — am Sattel, the pommel [of a saddle bow]; der — an einer Stecknadel, the head of a pin; der — eines Schlosses, the knob or button of a lock; der — an dem Handgriffe einer Thüre, the button of a door; der — am Bügel, the button of the reins of a bridle; der — an einem Faden &c., knot. V. Knoten. [in botany] bud, gem, button. Der — einer Rose, rose-bud. [in architecture] Der — einer Säule, V. Knauf. 2) [in cookery] Ein süßer — [*Pudding], pudding; [in anatomy] der — an einem Beine, the knob of a bone. [in seamen's lang.] *a*) a sailor's knot, hitch. *b*) [a division of the log-line which answers to half a minute as a mile does to an hour] knot. Das Schiff läuft acht Knöpfe, the ship goes or runs eight knots [= eight miles an hour]. 2) [in a more limited sense] button [used to fasten together the several parts of dress]. Seidene, goldene Knöpfe, silk, gold buttons, buttons of silk, of gold &c; zwölf Dutzend Knöpfe, a gross of buttons; machen Sie die Knöpfe an Ihrem Rocke zu, button your coat.

Knopf-baum, *m.* 1) button-tree. 2) the American button-wood. 3) the American Judas-tree, the red bud-tree. —**binse**, *f.* the clustered rush, the round-headed rush. —**draht**, *m.* wire of which the heads of pins are made. —**fabrik**, *f.* manufactory of buttons. —**form**, *f.* 1) the form or shape of a button or of buttons. 2) button-maker's borer or mould. 3) a little round plate of wood &c. which is spun over by button-makers. —**fortsatz**, *m.* [in anatomy] the condyloid apophysis. —**gießer**, *m.* founder of buttons. —**gras**, *n.* button-weed, V. Strickgras. —**grube**, *f.* [in anatomy] the fossa of the temporal bone, condyloid fossa. —**haken**, *m* button-hook, buttoner. —**hammer**, *m.* [among goldsmiths] a hammer with a rounded face. —**handel**, *m.* trade in buttons, button-trade. —**holz**, *n.* 1) V. —form 3) 2) a small board or stick for cleaning buttons. —**kraut**, *n.* the field scabious, corn-scabious. —**krötengras**, *n.* V. —binse. —**leindotter**, *m.* myagrum paniculatum. —**loch**, *n* button-hole. —**lochholz**, *n.*, —**lochschraube**, *f.* [among tailors] match. —**macher**, *m.* button-maker. —**macherarbeit**, *f.* button-ware. —**macherhandwerk**, *n.* the trade of a button-maker. —**macherwaare**, *f.* V. —macherarbeit. —**nadel**, *f.* V. Stecknadel. —**rose**, *f.* rose with a large bud. —**schere**, *f.* pinmaker's scissors. —**seide**, *f.* silk for buttons. —**spann**, *n.* [in seamen's lang.] pair of shrouds. —**spinner**, *m.* one who makes the heads of pins. —**stein**, *m.* button-stone. —**überzug**, *m.* the cover of a button.

Knöpfeln, *v. intr.* to make little knobs or knots, to knot; *it.* V. 2 Klöppeln.

Knöpfelkissen, *n.* V. Klöppelkissen.

Knöpfen, *v. tr.* to close with buttons, to button.

Knöpfstrumpf, *m.* V. [the more usual word] Gamasche.

Knöpfig, *adj.* and *adv.* full of knots, knotty.

Knöpflein, *n* [-s, *pl.* -] *dim.* of Knopf.

Knöpfleingras, *n.* dog's grass, quitch-grass, couch grass.

Knöpper, *f.* [*pl.* -n] [allied to Knopf, Knospe &c.] gall or gallnut, V. Gallapfel.

Knopper-eiche, *f.* a species of oak-tree, the winter-oak. —**eisen**, *n* square iron-bars used by nail-smiths. —**hammer**, *m.* a forge where such iron-bars are made. —**kirsche**, *f.* V. Knarpelkirsche. —**stück**, *n.* a square iron-bar used by nail-smiths.

Knöppern, *v. intr.* V. Knaupeln.

Knorpel, *m.* [-es, *pl.* -] [allied to Knopf &c.] gristle, cartilage. Der — der Nase, der Ohren, the gristle of the nose, of the ears.

Knorpel-ansatz, *m.* epiphysis. —**artig**, *adj.* and *adv.* cartilaginous, gristly. —**band**, *n.* symphysis. —**beinfügung**, *f.* synchondrosis. —**beschreibung**, *f.* chondrography. —**blume**, *f.*, —**blümchen**, ||—**blümlein**, *n.* the bastard knot-grass. —**fisch**, *m.* cartilaginous fish. —**flosse**, *f.* cartilaginous fin. —**flosser**, *m.* chondropterygious fish. —**fügung**, *f.* V. —beinfügung. —**haut**, *f.* perichondrium. —**kirsche**, *f.* V. Knarpelkirsche. —**kraut**, *n.* 1) polycnemum. 2) V. Mauerpfeffer. —**lehre**, *f.* chondrology. —**platte**, *f.* cartilaginous scale. —**ring**, *m.* annular cartilage. —**thier**, *n.* a cartilaginous animal, V. —fisch.

Knörpel, *m.* [-s, *pl.* -] the insipid stone-crop.

Knorpelicht, *adj.* and *adv.* resembling a gristle or cartilage, cartilaginous, gristly.

Knorpelig, *adj.* and *adv.* consisting of cartilage, cartilaginous, gristly. [in botany] Ein —es Blatt, a cartilaginous leaf.

Knorpeln, *v. intr.* V. Knarpeln.

Knorren, *m.* [-s, *pl.* -], *dim.* Knörrchen, ||Knörrlein, *n.* [seems to be the same as Knollen] any excrescence or protuberance. [in anatomy] Der — an den Händen, knuckle; der — an den Füßen, ankle; der — an Bäumen, knot, gnar, knar, knag, snag; dieses Stück Holz ist voller —, this piece of wood is full of knots or snags; der — an einem Rohre, the knot of a reed. *it.* V. Beule.

Knorrhahn, *m.* 1) the white-eared bustard. 2) [a fish] garnet.

Knorricht, *adj.* and *adv.* resembling a snag, knag or knot.

Knorrig, *adj.* and *adv.* knaggy, snaggy, knotty. Ein —er Baum, a snaggy or knotty tree.

Knörrkraut, *n.* [-es] the white behen.

||**Knorz**, *m.* [-es, *pl.* -e] [= Knorren] [in popular lang.] a snaggy or knotty body, a snaggy piece of wood or stick; †*fig.* V. Grobian.

||**Knorzig**, *adj.* V. Knorrig. *Fig.* Ein —er Mensch, a stunted fellow, a misshapen shrimp.

Knospe, *f.* [*pl.* -n], *dim.* Knöspchen, ||Knöspelein, *n.* [allied to Knopf] bud, gem, button. Im März sieht man —n an den Bäumen, in march we see the trees budding; die —n der Rosen, rose-buds; —n treiben, to put forth buds or gems, to bud. *Fig.* [rather poetical] a budding girl or virgin.

Knospen-beißer, *m.* vine-fretter, vine-grub. —**gras**, *n.* V Degenkraut. —**haut**, *f.*, —**häutchen**, *n.* [in botany] hymen. —**käfer**, *m.* V. —beißer. —**kranz**, *m.* a wreath or garland of flower-bearing buds. —**treibend**, *adj.* and *adv.* producing or putting forth buds. —**voll**, *adj.* and *adv.* full of buds. —**zeit**, *f.* budding season.

Knospen, *v. intr.* to put forth buds, to bud, to bourgeon. *Fig.* to be in bloom, to bud.

Knosperich, *m.* [-s] [a genus of plants] dais.

Knospern, *v. intr.* V. Knarpeln.

Knospicht, *adj* and *adv.* resembling buds, knobby.

Knospig, *adj.* and *adv.* full of buds.

Knote, *m.* [-n, *pl.* -] 1) V. Knoten. 2) [in popular language] an awkward fellow, a boor; [students' cant, in contempt] a journeyman or low mechanic.

Knöteln, *v. intr.* to make small knots, to knot.

Knoten, *m.* [-s, *pl.* -] *dim.* Knötchen, ||Knötlein, *n.* [allied to Knopf, Knollen, L. *nodus*, and to nieten. The Sw. *knota* and Icel. *hnota* = Knochen] knot. Holz voller —, wood full of knots; das Weizenstroh hat mehr — als das Haberstroh, there are more joints in wheat-straw than in the oaten; [in anatomy] der — [der Nerven], ganglion; — am Ende der Knochen, condyl. [in seamen's lang.] hitch. [in medicine] Das Podagra hat — angesetzt, the gout has formed knots, has settled in the joints; ein harter — in der Brust einer Frau, a lump or clot of milk in a woman's breast; der — am Ende eines Fadens, knot; einen — machen, knüpfen, to make or tie a knot; einen — auflösen, to untie a knot; der Gordische —, the Gordian knot. [in astronomy, the point where the orbit of a planet intersects the ecliptic] node. Absteigender —, descending node or dragon's tail; aufsteigender —, ascending node or dragon's head. *Fig.* *a*) [in fam. lang.] impediment, difficulty, intricacy. Das Ding hat einen —, there is a hitch in the business, there is some difficulty in it; da steckt der —, there lies the difficulty, there is the rub, *it* that is the main or chief point; das ist ein harter —, that is a very difficult affair or business; einen — lösen, to resolve a difficult point, to clear a difficulty; den — zerhauen, to cut the knot of the difficulty or question. *b*) Der — in einem Schauspiele or in einem Romane, the plot, knot or intrigue of a play, of a romance; den — eines Schauspiels lösen, to unravel the plot of a play; die Entwicklung des —s beginnt, wenn &c., the unravelling or winding up of the plot commences, when &c.

Knotgras, *n.* the bastard knot-grass.

Knoten-ader, *f.* the sciatic vein. —**blümchen**, ||—**blümlein**, *n.* the great spring snow-drop. —**fisch**, *m.* a kind of whale with six bunches on the back. —**fuchsschwanz**, *m.* [in botany] a kind of fox-tail grass, alopecurus geniculatus —**gras**, *n.* 1) the rough panic-grass. 2) base broad-leaved knot-grass. —**kraut**, *n.* V. —wurz. —**los**, *adj.* without knots —**lösung**, *f.* the unravelling or winding up of the plot. —**moos**, *n.* the bryum or threadmoss. —**perrücke**, *f.* tie-periwig, tie-wig. —**schürzung**, *f.* the plot [in a play &c.] —**spreu**, *f.* the chaff of linseed. —**stern**, *m.* [in conchology] the knotty sea-star. —**stock**, *m.* a knotty or snaggy stick. —**wurz**, *f.* the knobby-rooted fig-wort.

Knöterich, *m.* [-s] [from Knoten] 1) base knot-grass. 2) — or kleiner —, a kind of chickweed.

Knötig, *adj.* and *adv.* knotty. Ein —er Stock, a knotty stick; [in botany] ein —er Stengel, a geniculated stem. *Fig.* [in fam lang.] awkward, clumsy. Ein —er Mensch, an awkward fellow, a boor, a churl; —es Betragen, rude manners.

Knötigkeit, *f.* [little used] nodosity.

Knuck or **Knucks**, a sort of coarse and blunt sound as from something breaking and disjointing, V. Knack.

Knuff, *m.* [-es, *pl.* Knüffe] [low] a stroke or blow with the fist, a thump. Einem Knüffe geben, to box or thump any one.

Knüffeln, Knuffen, *v. tr.* [allied to kneipen] [low] Einen, to box or thump any one.

Knüll, *adj.* [students' cant] tipsy.

Knülle, *f.* [*pl.* -n] [allied to Knolle] a wrong fold, a rumple, pucker.

Knüllen, I. *v. tr.* to gather into small folds or wrinkles, to rumple, to pucker. II. *v. r.* sich —, to get rumples or puckers, to become rumpled.

Knulps, V. Plötze.

Knupen, *m.* [-s, *pl.* -] a skein or hank of silk.

Knüpfel, *m.* V. Klöpfel, Klöppel.

Knüpfen, Knüpfeln, *v. tr.* [from Knopf] to fasten with a knot, to tie into a knot, to tie, to bind. Einen Knoten —, to make or tie a knot; zwei Taue an einander —, to tie two ends of ropes together; ein Band —, to tie a ribbon; einen Dieb an den Galgen —, to hang a thief. *Fig.* Freundschaft mit Einem —, to knit or join friendship with any one; die Bande der Freundschaft noch fester —, to bind faster or closer the ties of friendship.

Knüppel, *m.* [-s, *pl.* -], *dim.* Knüppelchen, *n.* [allied to Knopf, Knüttel] a round and oblong piece of wood, round fagot-stick. Ein Karren voll —, a cart-load of [round] fagot-sticks. *it.* a cudgel or thick stick, V. Knüttel. *it.* a clog for a dog. Dem Hunde einen — anhängen, to tie a clog across a dog's neck, to clog a dog. *Fig.* Kleiner — [low], a short thick-set fellow.

Knüppel-band, *n.* [in seamen's lang.] strap. —brücke, *f.* a bridge made of round sticks, Swiss bridge. —damm, —weg, *m.* a road made of rows of round sticks laid broad-wise close together over marshy &c. ground or soil. —holz, *n.* wood consisting of round pieces or of round fagot-sticks. —kugel, *f.* V. Stangenkugel.

Knüppeln, *v. tr.* 1) Einen —, to beat any one with a cudgel, to cudgel any one. Er hat ihn tüchtig geknüppelt, he has belaboured him very handsomely, he has thrashed him soundly. *Fig.* to scold any one. 2) Einen Hund —, to tie a clog across a dog's neck, to clog a dog.

Knúppern, V. Knappern.

Knupper-kirsche, V. Knopperkirsche.

Knúrren, *v. intr.* [also knarren, Eng. *to gnar*, originally = tönen, allied to the Lat. *narro*, *gnarro*] to growl, to snarl. Der Hund knurrt, the dog snarls or growls; meine Gedärme — [low], es knurrt mir im Leibe, my belly grumbles. *Fig.* to grumble, to mutter, to murmur. Sie knurrt den ganzen Tag [low], she does nothing but grumble or growl all day long. Das — [im Leibe], grumbling [in the abdomen or belly]; das — eines Hundes, the growl or snarling of a dog. *Fig.* Sein beständiges —, his continual grumbling or scolding.

Knurr-hahn, *m.* 1) V. Knorrhahn. 2) sea-scorpion. —kater, *m.* *Fig.* [in popular lang.] a morose and peevish fellow, growler, a grumbler, snarler. —topf, *m.* V. —kater.

Knúrrig, *adj.* and *adv.* *Fig.* [in popular lang.] grumbling, morose, peevish.

Knúspern, V. Knistern.

Knúst, *m.* [-es, *pl.* -e] [allied to Knoten, Knopf] a crust of bread or a crusty piece of bread; *it.* V. Knaft.

Knute, *f.* [*pl.* -n] [from Knoten] [the Russian whip] knout. Einem die — geben, to flog any one with the knout.

Knuten, *v. tr.* Einen, to flog or whip any one with the knout.

Knütte, *f.* [*pl.* -n] [allied to the Fr. *nouer*, *noeud*, to nieten, V. Knoten] 1) the art of knitting. ||2) a knitting-needle.

Knüttel, *m.* [-s, *pl.* -], *dim.* Knüttelchen, *n.* V. Knüppel. *Prov.* Wenn man Vögel fangen will, muß man nicht mit —n darunter or darein werfen, to fright a bird is not the way to catch it.

Knüttel-brücke, *f.* V. Knüppelbrücke. —gedicht, *n.* a poem in doggerel verse or rhymes, doggerel. —holz, *n.* V. Knüppelholz. —reim, *m.* doggerel rhyme. —vers, *m.* doggerel verse. Die —verse, doggerel-rhymes.

Knüttelhaft, *adj.* Ein —es Gedicht, —e Verse, V. Knüttelgedicht, Knüttelvers.

Knütteln, *v. tr.* 1) V. Knüppeln. ||2) to knit [stockings &c.].

Knütten, *v. tr.* to knit.

Knütter, *m.* [-s, *pl.* -], —inn, *f.* knitter.

*__Koaks__, [pron. Kohks] V. Kohks.

Koäti, *m.* [-'s, *pl.* -] [an animal of South-America, resembling the racoon] coati, Viverra nasua [Linn.]

Koax, *n.* the sound of frogs, croaking. Die Frösche schreien —, frogs croak.

Koaxen, *v. intr.* to croak [like a frog].

Kob, *m.* [-es, *pl.* -e] 1) V. Gründling. 2) [the antelope with horns close at the base] koba.

Kobalt, *m.* [-es, *pl.* -e] [probably from the Bohem. *kow* = Erz, *kowalty* = erzhaltig] cobalt; V. Glanz—, Ruß—, Scherben—, Schlakken—.

Kobalt-bergwerk, *n.* cobalt-mine. — —beschlag, *m.* efflorescence of cobalt. —blumen, *pl.*, —blüthe, *f.* flowers of cobalt, cobalt-bloom. —druse, *f.* cobalt-crystal. —erde, *f.* indurated and friable earthy cobalt-ore, cobalt-crust. —erz, *n.* cobalt-ore. —gang, *m.* a lode of cobalt. —geist, *m.* V. 2. Kobold 1). —glanz, *m.* 1) grey cobalt. 2) white cobalt. —glas, *n.* glass of cobalt, smalt. —haltig, *adj.* and *adv.* containing cobalt, cobaltic. —haltiges Erz, V. —erz. —kalk, *m.* calcined cobalt. —klein, *n.* cobalt in small particles. —könig, *m.* V. —metall. —letten, *m.* V. —erde. —metall, *n.* regulus of cobalt. —miner, *m.* V. —erz. —mulm, *m.* V. —erde. —ocher, *m.* ochre of cobalt. —sanderz, *n.* sandy cobalt-ore. —sinter, *m.* V. —beschlag. —speise, *f.* V. —metall. —spiegel, *m.* a clear transparent cobalt-ore. —stufe, *f.* a piece of cobalt-ore. —vitriol, *m.* sulphate of cobalt. —zeche, *f.* 1) cobalt-mine. 2) the working of a cobalt-mine.

Kobaltisch, *adj.* and *adv.* 1) containing cobalt, cobaltic. 2) resembling cobalt, cobaltic.

||**Kobel**, *m.* [-s, *pl.* -] [allied to bob (from beben), Haube &c.] any thing lofty, hence, a dove-cot; *it.* a woman's head-dress. V. Taubenben—.

Kobel-ente, *f.* V. Quack- or Quackerente. —lerche, *f.*, —meise, *f.* V. Haubenlerche &c.

Koben, *m.* [-s, *pl.* -] [allied to Käfich, Koffer &c.] a small paltry or wretched habitation, hut or cabin; [in husbandry] hog-sty.

Kober, *m.* [-s, *pl.* -], [V. Koffer] *dim.* Koberchen or Köberchen, *n.* 1) a sort of basket or pannier, a dosser. *Fig.* Einen — auf dem Rücken haben [low], to be hunch- or hump-backed; [in low lang.] —kriegen, to get a good drubbing, to be soundly thrashed. 2) a wicker-basket used in catching fish.

Kober-eisen, *n.* 1) iron stolen and clandestinely sold by miners. 2) V. Roheisen. —jude, *m.* a jew pedlar. —nuß, *f.* V. Pferdenuß.

Koberling, *m.* [-es, *pl.* -e] musk-apple.

Kobern, *v. tr.* to catch [fish] in a basket. †*Fig.* Einen —, to drub or thrash any one.

Koblergut, *n.* V. Köthenergut.

1. **Kobold**, *m.* [-es, *pl.* -e] V. Kobalt.

2. **Kobold**, *m.* [-es, *pl.* -e] [allied to the Gr. κόβαλος, Low Lat. *gobelinus*] 1) goblin, hobgoblin; V. also Gespenst, Poltergeist. [in mining] gnome, pigmy, V. Berggeist. 2) [formerly] merry Andrew, jack-pudding, buffoon. 3) ||a somerset. — schießen, to make a somerset.

Koch, *m.* [-es, *pl.* Köche] 1) cook. Köchinn, *f.* woman cook, cook-maid; V. Bei—, Brat—, Gar—, Hof—, Leib—, Mund—, Schiffs—; *Prov.* V. Brei, Hunger. Es sind nicht alle Köche, welche lange Messer tragen, it is not the cowl makes the friar. 2) [something boiled] hasty pudding, raised pastry, puff-paste.

Koch-apfel, *m.*, —birn, —bohne, *f.* a sort of apples, pears, beans fit or good for boiling, boiling apple &c. —buch, *n.* cookery-book. —feuer, *n.* fire for boiling or cooking. —flott, *m.* [in seamen's lang.] kiln to supply the planks, stove. —hafen, *m.* a pot for boiling meat or vegetables &c., porridge-pot. —holz, *n.* small wood used in cooking. —junge, *m.* kitchen-boy, scullion; *it.* cook's apprentice. —kelle, *f.* V. —löffel. —kessel, *m.* a copper, boiler, seether. —kraut, *n.* vegetables for boiling, pot-herbs. —kunst, *f.* art of cookery, culinary art. Er versteht die —kunst gut, he understands cookery well. —künstler, *m.* [in jest] a master in the culinary art, a skilful cook. —löffel, *m.* pot-ladle. —löffelbret, *n.* kitchen-rack. —mairan, *m.* pot-majoram. —maschine, *f.* digester. —ofen, *m.* a stove or oven for boiling or cooking. —pfanne, *f.* sauce-pan, stew-pan. —rosine, *f.* V. Korbrosine. —salat, *m.* lettuce. —salz, *n.* kitchen-salt. —salzgeist, *m.*, —salzsäure, *f.* muriatic acid. —salzsauer, *adj.* muriatic. —salzsaures Kupfer, muriate of copper, atacamite. —schürze, *f.* kitchen-apron. —schwamm, *m.* esculent mushroom, champignon. —sgast, —smat, *m.* [in ships, the person employed to assist the ship's cook] shifter. —spumpe, *f.* [in ships] a small handpump [used for water-casks, oil-casks &c.]. —stück, *n.* piece of meat for boiling, a small piece of meat. *Fig.* Einen in —stücke zerhauen [in popular lang.], to cut any one in pieces, *it.* to lash him severely. —topf, *m.* V. —hafen. —wasser, *n.* water for the use of the kitchen. —wein, *m.* wine for the use of the kitchen. —wildpret, *n.* piece of venison for boiling. —zeug, *n.* kitchen utensils or furniture. —zucker, *m.* raw sugar, moist sugar, brown sugar.

Kochen, [Sax. *cycene*, D. *kucken*, L. *coquo*, seems to be allied to wogen = bewegen] I. *v. intr.* 1) [in general] to be in agitation or motion, to be agitated. Das Meer kocht, the sea is rough or boisterous, is agitated; die —den Wogen, the boiling waves. *Fig.* Das Blut kocht in meinen Adern, my blood boils within me or in my veins; es kocht gleich bei ihm, he is apt to fly into a passion. 2) to undergo the act of boiling, to boil. Das Wasser kocht, the water boils; —des Wasser, hot, boiling water; der Topf kocht, the pot boils; das Nachtessen kocht schon, supper is already preparing; das muß in seiner eigenen Brühe —, that must be stewed in gravy; diese Erbsen — nicht gut, these peas do not boil well. *Fig.* to be matured, to be ripened. Diese Trauben —, these grapes are ripening. II. *v. tr.* to boil. Seide &c. —, to boil silk &c.; Seife —, to make soap; [in seamen's lang.] die Planken —, to bend the planks; ein Stück Fleisch —, to boil a piece of meat; gekochtes Ochsenfleisch, boiled beef; das Fleisch ist gar zu weich gekocht, the meat is boiled to rags; sie versteht zu —, she understands cookery. *Fig.* Der Magen kocht die Speisen, the stomach digests the victuals or meats; die Sonne kocht das Obst, the sun ripens or concocts the fruit. Das —, the act of boiling or dressing meat. Er verlangt zu viel für das — dieser Speisen, he charges too much for dressing these victuals; sie versteht, sie kann das —, she understands cookery. Syn. Kochen, Sieden. Kochen, when used without any qualification, is always understood of victuals. The mistress orders what is to be gekocht when she settles what dishes shall come to table. Sieden signifies merely to heat by fire; it affords preparations of things which consist in mere heating. We sieden salt, soap, sugar, &c. Sieden implies a greater degree of heat than kochen. We say, the water boils [kocht] when its surface is slightly agitated; it siedet when it heaves in bubbles, and has attained the highest degree of heat.

Köcher, *m.* [-s, *pl.*-], **Kocherinn**, *f.* 1) a person who boils, boiler, V. Kaffeekoch, Leim—. 2) a vessel in which any thing is boiled, boiler; [chiefly] a coffee-pot.

Köcher, *m.* [-s, *pl.* -] [allied to Kas, Kachel; Finlandic *cuckare* = Beutel] 1) a long and hollow case; [chiefly] quiver. 2) the tubular coralline, V. See—.

Köcher-baum, *m.* the coral-tree of America. —**koralle**, *f.* V. — 2). —**nase**, *f.* the silver-coloured tench [a fish]. —**wurm**, *m.* the ship-worm, the ship-piercer.

Kocherei, *f.* 1) the act of boiling, cooking or dressing victuals, [chiefly] badly; *it.* [bad] cookery. 2) victuals badly dressed.

Köchinn, *f.* female cook. V. Koch.

Köcke, *f.* [*pl.*-n] V. Kag.

Köder, *m.* [-s, *pl.* -] V. Kader.

1. **Köder**, *m.* [-s, *pl.* -] [Sw. *koet*, Goth. *kiöt* = Fleisch, from kauen] bait. Den — an die Angel stecken, to put the bait to the hook or line, to bait the hook. *Fig.* allurement, enticement, temptation, lure, bait.

Köderfisch, *m.* a little fish serving as a bait.

2. **Köder**, *m.* [-s] [among shoemakers] heel-leather, heel-band.

Ködern, *v. tr.* 1) to allure by means of a bait, to bait [fish &c.]. Einen Falken —, to lure a hawk. *Fig.* Einen —, to allure, to entice any one. 2) to furnish with a bait, to bait a hook, a trap &c.].

***Köder**, *m.* V. Coder.

***Kodicill**, *n.* V. Codicill.

‖**Kofent**, *m.* [-es, *pl.* -e] [from Conventsbier] small beer.

Koffee, [obsolete] V. Kaffee.

Koffer, *m.* [-s, *pl.* -] [allied to Käfich, Koter, Lat. *cav*-us &c.] box or chest for transporting clothes &c, trunk; *dim.* Kofferchen, Kofferlein, ‖Köfferlein, *n.* little trunk or box. Syn. V. Kasten.

Koffer-deckel, *m.* the lid of a trunk. —**fisch**, *m.* trunk-fish. —**förmig**, *adj.* having the form or shape of a trunk. —**garn**, *n.* sweep-net. —**leinwand**, *f.* linen-cloth for lining trunks. —**macher**, *m.* trunk-maker. —**tuch**, *n.* V. —leinwand.

1. **Kög**, *m.* [-es, *pl.* Köge] alluvial land.

2. **Kög**, *m.* [-es, *pl.* Köge] mallet.

Kögel, *f.* [*pl.*-n] [allied to Kugel] 1) a sort of head-dress for females, cap. 2) top [of a mountain].

Kögge, *f.* [*pl.* -n] V. Kag.

Kohks, *pl.* cokes.

Kohl, *m.* [-es] [Fr. *chou*, old chol, allied to L. *olus*] 1) cabbage, cole-wort. Weißer —, white-heart cabbage; rother —, red cabbage; Blumen—, Früh—, Sommer—, Winter—; wilder —, V. Feld—. 2) Indischer —, the eatable arum, the Indian cole.

Kohl-baum, *m.* 1) V. —palme. 2) the oleander-leaved cacalia or cabbage-tree. —**blatt**, *n.* cabbage-leaf. —**distel**, *f.* the pale-flowered cnicus or water-thistle. —**eule**, *f.* 1) the white owl, barn-owl, church-owl, howlet. 2) V. —motte. —**falter**, *m.* V. —weißling. —**fresser**, *m.* V. Erdfloh. —**gänsedistel**, *f.* sow-thistle, sonchus. —**garten**, *m.* cabbage-garden, kitchen-garden. —**gärtner**, *m.*, —**gärtnerinn**, *f.* gardener who cultivates chiefly pot-herbs &c., common gardener. —**grün**, *adj.* green inclining to yellow. —**hedder**, *m.* sea-cole-wort. —**jahr**, *n.* a wet year [in which cabbages thrive well]. —**kopf**, *m.* cabbage-head. —**kraut**, *n.* headed cabbage. —**lauch**, *m.* the purple-streaked garlic. —**laus**, *f.* plant-louse. —**mangold**, *m.* the common lung-wort. —**markt**, *m.* market where greens and pot-herbs are sold. —**motte**, *f.* the moth of the cabbage-worm. —**muspflanze**, *f.* the corchorus or jew's mallow. —**palme**, *f.* cabbage-palm, cabbage-tree. —**pflanze**, *f.* cabbage-plant. —**portulak**, *m.* garden-purslain. —**rabi**, *m.* turnip-cabbage. —**raupe**, *f.* cabbage-worm. —**rose**, *f.* V. Knopfrose. —**rübe**, *f.* turnip-rooted cabbage. —**saat**, *f.* rape-seed —**samen**, *m.* cole-seed. —**schalk**, *m.* V. Schalkkohl. —**schmetterling**, *m.* V. —weißling. —**springer**, *m.* V. Grashüpfer. —**sprossen**, *pl.* cabbage or cole-sprouts. —**stengel**, *m.* cabbage-stalk. —**strunk**, *m.* V. —stengel. †*Fig.* an awkward fellow. —**weißling**, *m.* the common white butterfly. —**wurm**, *m.* 1) V. —raupe. 2) V. Engerling.

Kohle, *f.* [*pl.* -n], *dim.* Köhlchen, ‖Köhllein, *n.* [formerly any thing combustible, allied to the L. *calere*, *calor*] coal. Eine brennende, glühende —, a burning, live coal; eine todte —, a dead coal; —n brennen, Holz zu —n brennen, to make charcoal, to burn wood to charcoal, to char wood; —n brennen [as fuel], to burn coals; so schwarz wie eine —; black as a coal, coal-black; auf or über glühenden —n braten, rösten, to broil; er glüht wie eine —, he is burning hot; *prov.* wie auf glühenden —n stehen or sitzen, to be upon thorns; wenn du das thust, so wirst du feurige — auf sein Haupt sammeln [in Scripture], for in so doing thou shalt heap coals of fire on his head. [in mineralogy] sea-coal, pit-coal, V. Stein—; [in chymistry] metallische —, carbonate of copper.

Kohl-amsel, *f.* the common blackbird. —**apfel**, *m.* pome-water, pomeroy. —**bauer**, *m.* V. Kohlenbauer. —**becken**, *n.* V. Kohlenbecken. —**falk**, *m.* V. Kohlenfalk. —**feuer**, *n.* V. Kohlenfeuer. —**fisch**, *m.* the black cod-fish, coal-fish. —**fliege**, *f.* V. Kothfliege. —**fuchs**, *m.* burnt-sorrel horse. —**gehau**, —**gestübe**, —**haus**, *n.* V. Kohlengehau &c. —**holz**, *n.* V. Kohlenholz. —**knecht**, *m.* V. Kohlenknecht. —**korb**, *m.* V. Kohlenkorb. —**lösche**, *f.* V. Kohlengestübe. —**maß**, *n.* V. Kohlenmaß. —**meise**, *f.* coal-titmouse, coal-mouse. —**mund**, *m.* V. —fisch. —**pechschwarz**, *adj.* V. —schwarz. —**pfanne**, *f.* V. Kohlenpfanne. —**rabe**, *m.* V. Goldrabe. —**schreiber**, *m.* V. Kohlenschreiber. —**schwarz**, *adj.* black as a coal, very black, coal-black, jet-black. —**statt**, —**stätte**, *f.* place where charcoal is made. —**staub**, *m.* V. Kohlenstaub. —**sturz**, *m.* V. Kohlensturz. —**taube**, *f.* stock-dove, wood-pigeon. —**vögelchen**, *n.* stone-chatter.

Kohlen-arbeiter, *m.* coal-miner, collier. —**artig**, *adj.* carbonic. —**bauer**, *m.* a peasant who carries or conveys charcoals. —**becken**, *n.* chafing-dish, coal-pan. —**bergwerk**, *n.* coal-mine, coal-work, colliery. —**blende**, *f.* [in mineralogy] anthracite, anthracolite. —**boden**, *m.* V. —kammer. —**brand**, *m.* carbonization. —**brennen**, *n.* V. —brennerei 1). —**brenner**, *m.* charcoal-burner. —**brennerei**, *f.* 1) the act of charring wood, carbonization. 2) place where charcoal is made, charcoal-kiln. —**brennerhütte**, *f.* 1) charcoal-burner's hut. 2) V. —brennerei 2). —**dampf**, *m.* the smoke from charcoal. —**dämpfer**, *m.* a machine for extinguishing coals, extinguisher [for coals]. —**deckel**, *m.* a cover for fire, fire-plate. —**eiche**, *f.* black oak. —**erde**, *f.* coaly earth. —**erz**, *n.* bituminous earth, V. Branderz. —**falk**, *m.* the falcon or hawk with black or dark-brown wings. —**feuer**, *n.* a charcoal-fire, coal-fire [not a woodfire]. —**flötz**, *n.* stratum of coal. —**frau**, *f.* a charcoal-burner's or a collier's wife. —**fuchs**, *m.* 1) V. Kohlfuchs. 2) V. Köhler 2) *b*). —**führer**, *m.* V. Kohlenbauer. —**gabel**, *f.* coal-poker, coal-raker. —**gebirge**, *n* 1) mountain containing coal. 2) the stratum or bed of rock or earth over and under coal. —**gehau**, *n.* that part of a forest where wood for charcoal is felled. —**gesäuert**, V. —sauer. —**gestübe**, *n.* small-coal, slack, coal-dust; *it.* the turf or earth, with which a charcoal-pile is covered. —**glut**, *f.* burning or live coals. —**graus**, *m.* V. —gestübe. —**grube**, *f.* coal-pit. —**haken**, *m.* coal-hook. —**handel**, *m.* trade in coals, colliery [unusual]. —**händler**, *m.* coal-merchant. —**harke**, *f.* V. —kräuel. —**hau**, *m.* V. —gehau. —**haus**, *n.* coal-house. —**hieb**, *m.* V. —gehau. —**holz**, *n.* wood for charcoal. —**kammer**, *f.* coal-house, coal-room, coal-hole. —**kasten**, *m.* coal-box. —**klare**, *f.* V. —staub. —**klein**, *n.* small-coal, slack. —**knecht**, *m.* a collier's man, coal-porter; *it.* a charcoal-burner's man. —**korb**, *m.* coal-basket, coal-scuttle. ‖—**kräuel**, *m.* coal-rake. —**krücke**, *f.* coal-poker, V. —kräuel. —**kübel**, *m.* a kind of pail or tub for measuring coals. —**lösche**, *f.* V. —gestübe. —**luft**, *f.* carbonic air. —**mann**, *m.* coal-man, V. —bauer. —**maß**, *n.* coal-measure. —**meiler**, *m.* char-coal pile. —**messer**, *m.* coal-meter. —**ofen**, *m.* charcoal-kiln. —**oxydgas** or gasförmiges —**oxyd**, *n.* oxyd of carbon. —**pfanne**, *f.*, *dim.* —**pfännchen**, ‖—**pfännlein**, *n.* coal-pan; *it.* chafing-dish. —**platte**, *f.* 1) V. —deckel. 2) charcoal area. —**platz**, *m.* 1) place where charcoal is made, V. also —stätte. 2) place where coals are kept or preserved for domestic purposes. —**pulver**, *n.* pulverized coal, coal-dust. —**riß**, *m.* a sketch or plan made with charcoal. —**ruthe**, *f.* V. —krücke. —**sack**, *m.* 1) coal-sack or bag. 2) [among chymists] the hearth. —**saite**, *f.* V. —wagen. —**satz**, *m.* stratum of coals. —**sauer**, *adj.* containing carbonic acid. —saures Salz, carbonate; —saurer Kalk, —saure Schwererde &c., carbonate of lime, of barytes &c. —**säure**, *f.* carbonic acid. —**schaufel**, *f.* coal-shovel. —**schiefer**, *m.* coal-slate. —**schiff**, *n.* collier. —**schlacke**, *f.* cinders. —**schoppen**, *m.* coal-shed, coal-house. —**schreiber**, *m.* [in forges] a clerk who keeps an account of the coals. —**schütter**, *m.* 1) distributor of coals. 2) coal-scuttle. —**schwarz**, *n.* [a black colour used by painters] black of coals. —**schwelen**, *n.*, —**schweler**, *m.* V. —brennen, —brenner. —**schwemme**, *f.*, —**stätte**, *f.* V. —platz. —**speicher**, *m.* coal-house. —**staub**, *m.* coal-dust. —**stein**, *m.* V. —schiefer. —**stift**, *m.* a pencil made of charcoal. —**stoff**, *m.* carbon, pure charcoal. Wasserstoffhaltiger —stoff, carbureted hydrogen, carburet of hydrogen or bihydroguret of carbon. —**sturz**, *m.* the place where the coals are shot. —**topf**, *m.* coal-pot, fire-pot, foot-stove. —**träger**, *m.* coal-heaver [employed in colliers].

—wagen, *m.* coal-waggon. —wasserstoffgas, *n.* carbureted hydrogen gas. —weib, *n.* V. —frau. —werk, *n.* coalery, colliery, coal-pit, V. —bergwerk. —wisch, *m.* a wisp of straw or a mop used by smiths for wetting the coals. —zange, *f.* V. Feuerzange. —zeichnung, *f.* a drawing or sketch made with charcoal.

Köhlen, *v. tr.* to burn to coal or charcoal, to make charcoal, to char [wood]; [in chymistry] to carbonize. Das —, carbonization.

Köhler, *m.* [-s, *pl.* -] 1) maker of charcoal, charcoal-man, charcoal-burner. 2) [in nat. hist.] *a*) coal-fish, V. Kohlfisch. *b*) the brand-fox, V. Brandfuchs. *c*) a sort of weevil or mite.

Köhlers-börs, *m.* black-fish. —glaube, *m.* **fig.* implicit faith. —graben, *m.* V. Kohlenplatte 2). —hütte, *f.* a charcoal-burner's hut. —kraut, *n.* 1) the common club-moss. 2) the male speedwell. —lohn, *m.* the wages of a charcoal-burner.

Köhn, *m.* V. Kahm.

Köhr, Köhr, Köhren, V. Kor, Kör, Kören.

Kóje, *f.* [*pl.* -n] [allied to Kaue and to the provincial keien=liegen] 1) ||place where country-people sleep, a small sleeping-room or closet 2) [in seamen's lang.] bedplace in a cabin', berth; *it.* cabin [in a ship].

***Kokárde**, *f.* V. Cocarde.

||**Köken**, *v. intr.* to vomit, †to spew, V. †Kozzen.

Köker, *m.* [-s, *pl.* -] [allied to Kachel, Köcher] [in seamen's lang.] 1) coursey of a galley. 2) a wooden tube or case to protect any thing. Der — der Masten, the case of the mast; der — einer Pumpe, the case or covering of the tube of a pump; der — zu Karbusen, V. Karbuskoker.

Kokerstück, *n.* a cannon planted in the coursey, chase-gun.

Kokkolíth, *m.* [-s, *pl.* -en] [in mineralogy] coccolite, granuliform pyroxene.

Kökos &c., V. Cocos &c.

Kólbe, *f.* [*pl.* -n] or **Kólben**, *m.* [-s, *pl.* -] [allied to Keule, Kugel &c.] something thick and round, a knob. *a*) Die — einer Keule &c., the thick or heavy part of a club &c.; *it.* an instrument thick and longish, round at one end, club; die — or der —n eines Schießgewehrs, the butt-end of a gun or firelock; †Einen mit —n lausen, to chide or reprimand any one severely, to ring any one a peal; *it* to beat or cudgel any one; *prov.* Narren muß man mit —n lausen, fools must be loused with clubs. *b*) [among hunters] [in the *pl.*] brow-antlers, knags. *c*) [in botany] cat's tail, reed-mace. Die — des türkischen Weizens, the ear of maize. *d*) [in nat. hist.] V. Kaulbörs.

Kolbseisen, *n.* a round smoothing-iron. —weide, *f.* V. Kopfweide. —wurz, *f.* the white water-lily. —eszeit, *f.* the time when stags cast their horns, mewing-time.

Kólben, *m.* [-s, *pl.* -] V. Kolbe, —recht, Streit—. [among gun-smiths, an instrument with which the interior of a gun-barrel is polished or burnished] burnisher, or burnishing-stick; [in chymistry, *Retorte] alembic, cucurbite, retort, matrass; V. Brenn—, Destillir—; [at pallmall] the mallet; [am. glaziers] soldering-iron; [in nat. hist.] der — der Fühlhörner, the extremity or point of the antennae or feelers; [am. laundresses] V. Kolbeisen; [in gunnery] der — am Setzer, Wischer &c., the head of the rammer, spunge &c.; [in forges] loop, V. Luppe. Der — einer Pumpe, the sucker or piston of a pump; [in botany] spadix.

Kolben-ansatz, *m.* [among hunters] burs of a deer's head, cabbage. —blume, *f.* spadiceous flower. —bohrer, *m.* a borer or piercer with a conic head. —bürste, *f.* bottle-brush. —fliege, *f.* hornet. —förmig, *adj.* club-shaped, clavated. —gefäß, —glas, *n.* alembic, cucurbite, retort; *it.* a large bottle. —gras, *n.* the meadow-foxtailgrass. —hirsch, *m.* a stag or deer that has only brow-antlers or knags. —hirse, *f.* panicle or panic. —käfer, *m.* a beetle with club-shaped feelers or antennae. —moos, *n* club-moss. —recht, *n.* [formerly] right of single combat; *it.* right of private warfare, club-right. —röhre, *f.* chamber of a pump, V. Pumpenstiefel. —scheide, *f.* [in botany] spathe. —speise, *f.* [among glaziers] solder. —spiel, *n.* pallmall. —stange, *f.* pump-spear. —streich, *m.* stroke or blow with a club. —taucher, *m.* goosander, merganser. —tragend, *adj.* [in botany] spadiceous. —träger, *m.* mace-bearer. —zirkel, *m.* a pair of compasses with a club-shaped point; [among watch- or clock-makers] beam-compasses with a club-shaped point.

Kólben, I. *v. tr.* 1) to work or clean with a thick-ended instrument. [among gun-smiths] Die Seele eines Flintenlaufes —, to polish or burnish the bore of a gun-barrel. 2) to take off the thick end from any thing. Bäume —, to top or lop trees; den türkischen Weizen —, to cut off the ears of maize. II. *v. intr.* [among hunters] to get knobs or knags [said of deer].

Kólbicht, *adj.* and *adv.* resembling a club, club-shaped, clavated; [in botany] tuberous.

Kólbig, *adj.* and *adv.* having clubs, knobs or knots. —es Holz, knobby or knotty wood.

||**Kölblein**, *n.* [-s, *pl.*-] *dim.* of Kolbe.

Kölbleinkraut, *n.* 1) großes, the great burnet saxifrage. 2) kleines, burnet, garden-burnet.

Kóldergat, *n.* [-es, *pl.* -e] V. Kolderstock.

Kólderkraut, *n.* [-es, not used in the *pl.*] V. Kolmarkraut.

Kólderstock, *m.* [-es, *pl.* -stöcke] [in seamen's lang.] the whip-staff of the rudder or helm.

Kólibri, *m.* V. Colibri.

***Kolík**, *f.* [*pl.* -en] [Gr. κωλικὴ, from κῶλον = Darm] colic. Er hat die —, he is seized with a colic, the colic wrings him.

||**Kölk**, [Kulk], *n.* [-es, *pl.* -e] or **Kölke**, *f.* [*pl.* -n] a deep pool, the deepest part in a river, lake or pond.

Kolkbeere, *f.* berry of the water-elder. —rabe, *m.* V. Golbrabe.

||**Kólken**, *v. intr.* to grumble. Sein Bauch kolket, his belly grumbles.

||**Kölle** or **Kölle**, *f.* [a plant] savory.

Kollége, *m.* V. College.

Köllemisse, Köllemoder, V. Kohlfisch.

1. **Köller**, *m.* [-s] [V. 1. Kollern] [a disease of horses] staggers. *Fig.* [in popular lang.] frenzy, madness, insanity. Den — bekommen, to run mad; *it.* to fret and foam.

Kolleraber, *f.* a vein between the ears of a horse.

2. ‡**Köller**, *m.* and *n.* [-s, *pl.*-] [from the L. *collare*, Low L. *golerium*, Eng. *collar* = Kragen] *dim.* —chen, ||—lein, *n.* a neck-cloth for women, modesty-piece, tucker.

3. **Köller**, *m.* and *n.* [-s, *pl.*-] [allied to the Bohem. *kolar* = Kleid ohne Aermel, and to hohl, Gr. κοῖλος] V. Collett.

Kollerer, *m.* [-s, *pl.* -] drone.

Köllerig, *adj.* and *adv.* afflicted with the staggers. *Fig.* [in popular lang.] mad, passionate, hasty.

1. **Köllern**, *v. intr.* [allied to gällen, Gr. καλεῖν] 1) [in popular lang.] to rumble, to grumble. Es kollert mir im Bauch, my belly grumbles. 2) to make a noise like that of a turkey, to cry as a turkey. 3) [of horses] to be affected with the staggers. 4) [in popular lang.] *Fig.* to be mad or furious.

2. **Köllern**, *v. tr.* and *intr.* [allied to the Gr. κυλέω, κυλίνδω; Slavonic *kolo* = rund] to roll.

Kollét, *n.* V. Collett.

Köln, *n.* [-s] Cologn.

Köllner, *m.* [-s, *pl.* -], —inn, *f.* a native or an inhabitant of the town of Cologn.

Köllnisch, *adj.* Cologn. —e Erde, Cologn earth; —es Wasser, Cologn water.

***Kollyrít**, *m.* [-es] [in mineralogy] kollyrite.

Kólmarkraut, *n.* [-es, not used in the *pl.*] the red or common pimpernel, the corn pimpernel.

||**Kölner**, *m.* [-s, *pl.*-] a peasant who holds an estate against the payment of a ground-rent.

Kölnerhof, Kölnhof, *m.* estate held against the payment of a ground-rent.

***Kölon**, *n.* [-s] [in grammar] colon, V. Doppelpunkt.

***Kolonie**, *f.* &c. V. Colonie &c.

***Kolónne**, *f.* [*pl.* -n] V. Colonne.

***Kolophonít**, *m.* [-en] colophonite.

***Kolophónium**, *n.* [-s] V. Geigenharz, Colophonium.

***Koloquínte**, *f.* V. Coloquinte.

***Kolorít**, *n.* [-s, *pl.* -e] V. Colorit.

***Kolóß**, *m.* [-sses, *pl.* -sse] [a statue of a gigantic size] colossus. Der rhodische —, the Colossus of Rhodes. **Fig.* Er ist ein wahrer —, he is a giant.

Kolossál, Kolossálisch, Kolóssisch, *adj.* and *adv.* colossal, colossean, gigantic.

Kólschwein, Kólschwinn, *n.* [-s, *pl.* -e] keelson, V. Kielschwein.

||1. **Költer**, *m.* [-s, *pl.*-] a cover for a bed, V. Bettdecke.

2. **Költer**, *m.* [-s, *pl.* -] [L. *culter*; from the old kutten, Eng. *to cut* = schneiden] coulter, V. Pflugeisen, Pflugmesser.

***Kolúmne**, *f.* V. Colonne.

Kolumnensteg, *m.* V. Colonnenmess.

***Kolür**, V. Colur.

Kombüse, *f.* [*pl.* -n] [in ships] cook-room, cuddy.

***Komét**, *m.* [-en, *pl.* -en] 1) comet, blazing-star. Ein — mit einem Schweife, ein Schweif—, tailed comet; bärtiger, haariger —, Bart—, Haar—, bearded, hairy comet. 2) [a game at cards] comet.

Kometsartig, *adj.* comet-like. —ensystem, *n.* cometic system. —spiel, *n.* V. — 2).

***Kömiker**, *m.* [-s, *pl.* -] 1) a writer of comedies or [also in a more general sense] of farces and burlettas, comedian [unusual]. 2) an actor or player of comic parts, a comedian, a comic actor.

***Kómisch**, *adj.* and *adv.* comic, comical. —**er Dichter**, a writer of comedies, a comedian [not usual]; **ein —es Stück**, a comic piece, a comedy, a farce; **im —en Fache, im —en vorzüglich seyn**, to be very good or excellent in the comic department, to excel in comic parts. *Fig.* odd, ludicrous. droll, humorous, comical. **Eine —e Geschichte**, a comical story; **er hat sich sehr — dabei benommen**, he cut rather a ridiculous figure in the business.

***Komitát**, *n.* [-es, *pl.* -e] V. 2. **Gespanschaft.**

***Kómma**, *n.* [-s, *pl.* -s or -ta] 1) [in grammar] comma, V. **Beistrich.** 2) [in music] an enharmonic interval, comma.

***Kommandánt, Kommandiren, Kommándo**, &c. V. **Commandant** &c.

Kómmen, *ir. v. intr.* [old Goth. quiman, Sax. *cwiman*, *cuman*, allied to the Gr. κομ-ίζειν = tragen] 1) [to move towards, to advance nearer in any manner] to come. **Der Wind kommt von Westen**, the wind comes from the west; **der Wind kommt durch dieses Fenster**, the wind comes [in] through this window; [chiefly applied to persons] **er wird morgen —**, he will come to morrow; **er kommt** or **kömmt von London**, he comes from London; **komme her, kommet her!** come hither or here! **glücklich an Ort und Stelle —**, to come or arrive safe; **Einem nahe —**, to approach any one; **kommt mir nicht zu nahe!** keep your distance, keep farther off! **gegangen, geritten** &c. —, to come on foot, to come on horseback &c; **ich werde diesen Abend zu Ihnen —**, I shall come to see you this evening; **über einen Fluß —**, to pass a river; **auf die Welt —**, to come into the world, to be born; **aus der Kirche —**, to come from church; **er kommt nie in die Kirche**, he never goes to church; **er kommt oft dorthin**, he often visits there; **Einem in den Weg —**, to meet any one, *fig.* to thwart, to oppose any one; **er kommt viel unter die Menschen, unter die Leute**, he sees a great deal of company, he goes a great deal into society; **komme mir nicht wieder vor die Augen**, let me not see your face again; **nicht von der Stelle —**, not to budge or stir; **man kann nicht leicht vor den Minister —**, it is not easy to get or gain access to the minister; **wo — Sie her?** where do you come from? V. **Ab—, An—, Auf—, Aus—, Bei—, Be—, Daher—, Dahin—, Darauf—, Davon—, Durch—, Ein—, Empor—, Ent—, Fort—, Her—, Herab—, Heran—, Herauf—, Heraus—, Herbei—, Herein—, Herum—, Hervor—, Hin—, Hinab—, Hinan—, Hinaus—, Mit—, Nach—, Vor—, Weg—, Wieder—, Zu—, Zurück—, Zuvor—.** *it.* [as a circumlocution or periphrasis] **Zu Falle —** [= **fallen**], to fall, *fig.* to be ruined, *it.* to forfeit one's honour [said of single women who have been seduced]; **auf den Rücken zu liegen —**, to lie on one's back; **ich kam ihm gegenüber zu sitzen**, I sat opposite to him.

Fig. a) [applied to persons] **Einem über den Wein, über das Geld —**, to steal any one's wine, money; **Einem über seine Bücher —**, to rummage any one's books or library; **in eine Stelle —**, to get or obtain a place or office; **in den Himmel, in die Hölle —**, to get into, to come to heaven, to go to hell, to be damned; **zur Krone —**, to come to the crown; **wenn er über ein Buch kommt, so kann er** &c., whenever he gets a book into his hands, whenever he sets about or begins to read a book, he can &c.; **an Einen —** [not much used], to fall in with, to meet any one accidentally; **ich kann nicht an ihn —**, I cannot get at him; **sie kamen an einander** [in familiar language], they fell out, they quarrelled, *it.* they came to blows, they fell or went to loggerheads; **auf eine Person —**, to come to mention a person, to come to speak of a person; **jetzt komme ich darauf**, now I remember or recollect it; **wie sind Sie darauf zu reden ge—?** how came you to speak of it? **lassen Sie uns wieder auf die vorige Rede —**, let us return to or resume our former discourse; **um wieder zur Sache zu —**, to return to our subject; **Einen nicht zum Worte, zur Rede — lassen**, not to allow any one to speak, to cut any one short; **Einem gleich —**, to come up to, to equal any one; **hinter Etwas —**, to find out, to discover any thing; **in Abnahme —**, to decay, to fail, to decline; **in Hitze —**, to fly into a passion, to grow hot; **in Schweiß —**, to begin to sweat or perspire; **in der Leute Mäuler —** [in fam. lang.], to get into every body's mouth, to be made a common talk; **in Gefahr, in's Elend —**, to come into danger, to misery; **kurz von der Sache zu —**, to be short, in short; not to hold you long, to sum up all; **mit Etwas zu rechte —**, to know how to manage a thing; **ich bin wohlfeil dazu ge—**, I have got it cheap; **mit einer Sache zu Stande —, zu Ende —**, to bring any thing about or to pass, to accomplish or effect a thing, business &c.; **Einem grob —** [in popular language], to treat any one rudely or uncivilly, to be rude to any one; **so dürfen Sie mir nicht —** [in popular language], you must not speak to me or treat me in such a manner; **da — Sie mir schön** [in popular lang.], there you are in the wrong box; **kömmst du mir so, so komm' ich dir so** (vulgar)! claw me and I'll claw thee! **komm' mir nur noch einmal** (vulgar)! do it once more, or you won't do it a second time! **daraus komme ich nicht, kann ich nicht —**, I do not know what to make of that, I do not understand that; **aus diesem Manne komme ich nicht**, I do not know what to make of that man; **außer sich —, aus der Fassung —**, to be put out of countenance; **von Sinnen —**, to be deprived of one's senses; **ich bin um Alles ge—**, I have lost every thing; **von Kräften —**, to be deprived of one's strength; **wieder zu Kräften —**, to recover one's strength; **er ist in dieser Wissenschaft weit ge—**, he has made great progress in this science, he is a great proficient in this science; **er wird weit — in der Welt**, he will make his way in the world, will push his fortune; **zu kurz —**, to suffer a loss, to be a loser; **ich komme dabei zu kurz**, I am a loser by it, I am prejudiced, injured by it; **zu Etwas —**, to arrive at something, to attain to, to obtain, to get any thing; **sie ist zu einem Kinde ge—, ohne** &c. [in popular lang.], she has got a child without &c; **er kann zu nichts —**, nothing thrives with him, he succeeds in nothing; **mit solchen Mitteln kömmt man zum Zwecke**, by such means one compasses one's ends, one attains one's aim. *b)* [applied to things] **Das ist in unrechte Hände ge—**, that has fallen into the wrong hands; **die Erbschaft ist an** or **auf seinen Bruder ge—**, the inheritance fell to his brother; **in die Mode, aus der Mode —**, to grow into, out of fashion; **das ist mir aus dem Gedächtnisse ge—**, that has slipped out of my memory, I have forgotten that; **es kam zu Vorwürfen, zu Schimpfreden zwischen ihnen**, they went so far as to revile, to abuse one another; **es mag — zu was es will**, whatever may happen; **es ist mit ihm auf das Aeußerste ge—**, he is put to his last shifts; **wenn es auf's Aeußerste kommt**, when the worst comes to the worst; **wenn es hoch kömmt**, at most; **wie hoch kömmt Ihnen dieser Garten?** how much have you paid for this garden, how much did this garden cost you? **das wird Sie theuer zu stehen —**, that will cost you a vast sum of money, *it.* you will pay very dearly for it.

2) to shoot or rise above the earth, as a plant, to spring, to come, to come up. **Der Salat kommt schon**, the salad comes or comes up already. *Fig. a)* to happen, to fall out, to come to pass. **Wie** or **woher kommt es, daß** &c.? how does it happen that &c.? **wie** or [**je**] **nachdem es kömmt**, according as it falls out; **es kömmt selten ein Unglück allein**, misfortunes seldom come alone, ill-luck will seldom come single; one misfortune comes on the back of another. *b)* to arise, to proceed from. **Was soll da heraus —?** what follows from that? **alles dieses Unglück kömmt daher, weil** &c., all these misfortunes proceed from &c.; **von wem kommt diese Nachricht?** from whom does this piece of news come? **sie kömmt von guter Hand**, it comes from a good source, authority; **das kömmt nicht aus ihm** or **aus seinem Kopfe**, that is not of his own growth or invention; **das kömmt von Herzen**, that proceeds from the heart, that is sincerely meant. *c)* [= **gelangen**] to come to. **Die Reihe wird auch an Sie —**, your turn will come too; **als es an mich kam**, when it was my turn.

Kömmlich, *adj.* and *adv.* convenient, comfortable, seasonable, opportune.

***Komödiánt**, *m.* [-en, *pl.* -en] [now, chiefly in a bad sense, in contempt &c.] comedian, actor, player. **Ein wandernder —**, a strolling player, a stroller.

***Komödie**, *f.* [*pl.* -n] comedy; *it.* play.

Komödien-haus, *n.* play-house, theatre. **—schreiber**, *m.* writer of comedies, playwright.

***Kompān**, [**Kumpān**] *m.* [-s, *pl.* -e] [often in a bad sense, also much used in jest] companion, partner, associate. **Ein lustiger —**, a merry or jolly blade or fellow; **er und seine liederlichen —e**, he and his fellow-rakes.

***Kómpaß**, *m.* V. **Compaß.**

Kómpe, *m.* [-n, *pl.* -n] [obsolete] V. **Kompan.**

Kómst, *m.* [-es] [probably from the L. *compositum*] curdled milk.

Komthür, *m.* V. **Commenthur.**

Komthurei, V. **Commende.**

König, *m.* [-s, *pl.* -e] [Sax. *cyning*, *cyng*, Eng. and old Germ. *king*, Sw. *konung* and *kung*, W. *cun*, a chief, a leader] 1) [the chief or sovereign of a nation] king. **Der — von Preußen**, the king of Prussia; **im Namen des —s**, in the king's name; **Gott ist der — der —e, der — Himmels und der Erde** [in Scripture], God is the king of kings, the king of heaven and earth; **die Bücher der —e**, the books of the kings, kings. *Prov.* **—e haben lange Arme**, kings have long hands; **leben wie ein —**, to live like a king; **er ist glücklich wie ein —**, he is as happy as a king. *Fig.* **Der — des Balles**, the king of the ball; **der Löwe ist der — der Thiere, der Adler der — der Vögel**, the lion is the king of animals or quadrupeds and the eagle the king of birds; **der — im Schachspiele**, the king at chess. 2) [a card having the picture of a king] king. [at piquet] **Eine Dritte** &c. **vom — an**, a tierce from or to the king; **vierzehn —e**, fourteen by king. 3) [in chymistry] regulus.

Königs-adler, *m.* the golden eagle. **—ammer**, *f.* [a kind of bunting] emberiza regia. **—apfel**, *m.* 1) king-apple, queen-apple, pippin. 2) pine-apple. **—bann**, *m.* V. **Halsgericht.** **—binde**, *f.* [*Diadem] diadem. **—birn**, *f.* supreme pear, musk-pear. **—blau**, *n.* V. —

farbe 1). —**blume**, *f.* V. —rose. —**blut**, *n.* the blood and *fig.* the life of a king. —**burg**, *f.* the royal or the king's castle or palace. —**ehre**, *f.* V. —würde. —**eidechse**, *f.* basilisk, cockatrice. —**farbe**, *f.* 1) king's blue. 2) V. —gelb. —**fisch**, *m.* [a species of mackerel] bonito. —**fischer**, *m.* king's-fisher, halcyon. —**freund**, *m.* 1) a friend of the king. 2) royalist, loyalist. —**gelb**, *n.* king's yellow. —**gut**, *n.* royal domain; *it.* merchandize or goods belonging to the king. —**hase**, *m.* rabbit, cony. —**heher**, *m.* V. —vogel 1). —**hof**, *m.* 1) royal castle; *it.* royal domain. 2) the court of a king. —**holz**, *n.* [a wood from Brasil much esteemed by joiners] royal wood. —**karpfen**, *m.* a kind of excellent carp, rex cyprinorum. —**kerze**, *f.* [a plant] great mullen, high-taper, cow's lungwort. —**kerzenöl**, *n.* oil of mullen. —**koralle**, *f.* royal coral. —**kraut**, *n.* 1) basil, the common sweet basil. 2) V. —kerze. 3) the eupatoria or common agrimony. 4) hemp or Dutch agrimony. —**krone**, *f.* 1) royal crown. 2) [in botany] the tongue-leaved eucomis or fritillary. —**kümmel**, *m.* the common or greater bishop's weed. —**kupfer**, *n.* regúlus of copper. —**lilie**, *f.* the imperial martagon. —**mahl**, *n.* an entertainment or banquet given by a king; *it.* a princely entertainment. —**mann**, *m.* [*Royalist] royalist, loyalist. —**mantel**, *m.* [in conchology] royal mantle. —**mord**, *m.* regicide. —**mörder**, *m.*, —**mörderinn**, *f.* regicide. —**nägelein**, *n.* king's clove, caryophyllum regium. —**nuß**, *f.* V. Muskatennuß. —**papier**, *n.* royal paper, royal. —**paradiesvogel**, *m.* the king's bird, the king paradise-bird, the king of the greater birds of paradise. —**pferd**, *n.* a trammelled horse, a horse with a blaze and four white feet. —**pfirsche**, *f.* [a species of peach] the royal George. —**pflaume**, *f.* greengage. —**purpur**, *m.* the royal purple. —**ratte**, *f.* ichneumon. —**rose**, *f.* peony, V. Gichtrose. —**salat**, *m.* royal lettuce. —**säure**, *f.* V. —wasser. —**salbe**, *f.* basilicon. —**salbei**, *f.* the common large sage. —**schlange**, *f.* the buffalo snake or boiguam. —**sitz**, *m.* 1) the royal seat, the throne. 2) royal residence. —**sohn**, *m.* king's son. —**spiel**, *n.* [the name of several games] king's game or play. —**stab**, *m.* sceptre. —**stadt**, *f.* royal residence, capital of a kingdom. —**straße**, *f.* 1) the king's highway. 2) [the name given to some street in honour or remembrance of the king] king's-street. —**thron**, *m.* royal throne. —**titel**, *m.* the royal title. —**tochter**, *f.* king's daughter. —**vogel**, *m.* 1) the bird of paradise. 2) V. —paradiesvogel. —**wasser**, *n.* [in chymistry] aqua regia, nitro-muriatic acid. —**weihe**, *f.* the common kite. —**wort**, *n.* the word of a king. —**würde**, *f.* the royal dignity. —**zepter**, *m.* 1) royal sceptre. 2) [in botany] martagon. —**zucker**, *m.* double-refined sugar.

Königinn, *f.* queen. Die — von England, the queen of England; die — Mutter, the queen-mother; die verwittwete —, the dowager-queen; die — des Himmels, der Engel, the queen of heaven [Virgin Mary]. *Fig.* Die — des Balles [Ballköniginn], the queen of the ball; die — des Tages, the planet of the day, the sun; die — der Nacht, the planet of the night, the moon; die — der Bienen, queen-bee; die Rose ist die — der Blumen, the rose is the queen of flowers.

Königinnapfel, *m.* V. Königsapfel.

Königisch, *adj.* and *adv.* [rather obsolete] belonging to the king or to the royal party. Die — Gesinnten, the royalists; — gesinnt seyn, to be attached to the king.

Königlich, *adj.* and *adv.* 1) [pertaining to a king] royal, regal. Die —e Macht, the royal or regal power; die —e Würde, the royal dignity, royalty; die Zeichen der —en Würde, the emblems of royalty; die —e Würde niederlegen, to abdicate the crown; das —e Heer, the royal army; die — Gesinnten, the royalists; — gesinnt seyn, to be attached, to be loyal to the king; die —en Güter, the royal domains; die —e Familie, the royal family; —er Prinz, prince of the royal blood; die —en Brüder, the brothers of the king; Seine, Ihre —e Majestät, his, her royal majesty. 2) [becoming a king or in the manner &c. of a king] kingly. Eine —e Pracht, a kingly magnificence; er bewirthete uns — [in fam. lang.], er gab uns ein —es Mahl, he gave us a princely entertainment; er soll — begraben werden, his body will be royally interred, will be interred with kingly or princely honours; ein —es Herz haben, to have a royal heart or soul; ein —es Essen [in fam. lang.], a dish fit for a king; er lebt — [in fam. lang.], he lives like a king; das ist — [in fam. lang.], that is excellent.

Königreich, *n.* [-es, *pl.* -e] kingdom, realm. Ich würde es nicht um ein — thun [in fam. lang.], I would not do it for any thing [in the world] or for ever so much.

Königthum, *n.* [-es] royalty, kinghood [obsolete], kingship.

***Könisch**, *adj.* and *adv.* conic, conical, coniform. V. Kegelförmig.

Können, [originally the same as kennen, which see] *ir.* I. *v. intr.* 1) to be able, to have the power to do a thing. Er kann lesen, he can read; er konnte ihn beschützen, he could protect him; sie konnten es nicht bewerkstelligen, they could not bring it about; ich hätte es thun —, wenn &c., I could have done it, if &c.; wie haben Sie das sagen —? how could you say so? ich kann nichts dabei thun, I can do nothing in the business; dafür kann ich nicht, that is not my fault, I cannot help it; ich kann nicht umhin, zu bemerken, I cannot help or forbear remarking; ich kann Ihnen nicht antworten, I cannot answer you; gehen —, to be able to walk; dieses Kind kann gehen, this child can walk; ich kann nicht mehr, I am quite spent or knocked up, I can hold it out or bear it no longer; ein Pferd, das nicht mehr fort kann, a horse quite jaded, quite knocked up or tired out. 2) Seyn —, to be possible. Es kann nicht seyn, it cannot be or be done, it is impossible; es kann wohl seyn, that may be, is possible; es kann seyn, daß die Sache gelingt, it may be, it is possible that the affair will succeed, the affair may succeed. 3) to be permitted, to have the liberty to do a thing. Er kann immer kommen, he may come, let him come; Sie — ihm sagen, daß &c., you may tell him that &c.; er kann hingehen, wohin er will, he may go whither he pleases; Sie hätten fragen —, you might have asked. II. *v. tr.* to have learnt a thing, to know a thing, to be versed in a thing. Er kann von Allem Etwas, he knows a little of every thing, has a smattering of every thing; er kann verschiedene Sprachen, he knows or understands several languages; er kann nichts, he knows nothing; er kann seine Aufgabe, he knows or has learned his lesson; er kann seine Aufgabe nicht, he cannot say his lesson; Etwas auswendig —, to know any thing by heart, to have a thing by rote; sie kann kochen, she understands cookery; er kann gut reiten, he is a good horseman.

Konradskraut, *n.* [-es] the common tutsan, park-leaves.

Konstabel, *m.* [-s, *pl.* -n] 1) constable. 2) V. Constabler.

Konstanz, V. Kostnitz.

Kontor, *m.* V. Condor.

Kontör, *n.* V. Comptoir.

***Kontur**, *f.* [*pl.* -en] [especially in painting, statuary &c.] outline, contour. Die —en dieser Bildsäule sind sehr rein, the outlines of this statue are very purely done; die —en des Gebirgs, the outlines, the profile of the mountain. V. also Umriß.

Kooker, V. Koker.

***Kopal**, *m.* [-es, *pl.* -e] copal.

Kopalbaum, *m.* the lentiscus-leaved sumac. —**firniß**, *m.* copal-varnish. —**harz**, *n.* copal resin, copal.

Kopeke, *f.* [*pl.* -n] [a Russian coin, the hundredth part of a rubel] kopek.

||**Köpeln**, *v. intr.* to move backwards and forwards, to shake, to totter.

Köper, **Köpern**, V. Keper, Kepern.

Kopf, *m.* [-es, *pl.* Köpfe], *dim.* Köpfchen, ||Köpflein, *n.* [-s, *pl.* -] [allied to the L. *caput*, Ital. *capo*, Low Sax. Kop, and likewise to Schopf, Giebel, Kuppe &c.] 1) the prominent or uppermost part of a thing, top. Der — eines Berges, the top or peak of a mountain; der — des Hutes, the crown of a hat; der — einer Stecknadel, eines Nagels, eines Zirkels, the head of a pin, of a nail, of a pair of compasses; ein — Kohl, Kraut &c., a head of cabbage &c., V. Distel—, Kraut—, Mohn—, Salat— &c.; [in seamen's lang.] der — des Steuers or Steuerruders, rudder-head; der — or Köppel des Gangspills, the drumhead of the capstan; der — der Haare, root of the hair. 2) the head of men and animals. Der — eines Löwen, the head of a lion; der — eines Fisches, jowl or jole; der — eines Salmen, the jole of a salmon; ein kahler —, a bald head or pate; der — thut mir weh, schmerzt mich, I have got a headache, my head aches; dieser Wein steigt in den —, this wine affects the head, is heady; den — schütteln, to shake one's head; mit bloßem —e gehen, to go bare-headed or uncovered; mit dem —e gegen die Wand rennen, to run one's head against the wall; Einem den — abhauen, to cut off any one's head; Einem den — vor die Füße legen, to behead any one; er ist um einen — größer als ich, he is a head taller than I. Syn. V. Haupt. *Fig.* *a*) [chiefly in fam. lang.] thoughts, ideas. Man kann ihm das nicht aus dem —e bringen, one cannot beat that out of his head; es steckt ihm nichts als das im —e, he thinks of nothing but that; sich den — mit Albernheiten anfüllen, to fill one's head or brains with silly things; er hat sich in den — gesetzt, nach Amerika zu gehen, he has taken it into his head to go to America; Einem Etwas in den — setzen, to put a thing into any one's head; das kömmt nicht aus seinem —e, that is not of his own growth or invention, er hat einen steifen —, he is a headstrong, obstinate, self-willed man; nach seinem —e handeln, auf seinen — hin Etwas thun, to do a thing of one's own head, to follow one's own head or mind. *b*) [chiefly in fam. lang.] understanding, faculties of the mind. Er hat einen guten, starken —, he has a good, a clever head; er hat einen harten —, he is dull of understanding; — haben, to have sense or judgment, to have a good head or capacity; das will mir nicht in den —, I cannot conceive that, *it.* that will never go down with me; — für Etwas haben, to have a talent for any thing, er hat einen vorzüglichen —, he is a man of a superior genius or of superior talents; den — verlieren, to lose one's senses; ich weiß nicht, wo mir der — steht, my head turns round or is giddy, I do not know which way to turn myself, *it.* I am full of business, I have business of all sorts on my hands. *c)* [chiefly in familiar language] memory. Etwas im —e haben, to know any thing [by heart]; Etwas aus dem —e sagen, to say any thing without book, from memory; er kann nichts im —e behalten, he can keep nothing in his memory, can retain nothing, has a bad or treacherous memory. *d)* [chiefly in fam. language] life. Es geht ihm um den —, his life is at stake; und wenn es mir den — kostete, and if it should cost me my head, if I were to lose my head by it; ich setze meinen — zum Pfande, daß es so ist, I'll lay my life on it, I'll give you leave to cut off my head if it is not so; Sie stehen mit Ihrem —e dafür, your head will answer for it. *e)* an individual. Die Gesellschaft bestand aus 20 Köpfen, the society consisted of twenty persons; vier Morgen Landes für jeden —, four acres [of land] for every head; so viel der —, so much a head. *Prov.* Viel Köpfe, viel Sinne, so many men, so many minds; V. 1. Hut 2) *fig.* *it.* an individual with respect to his temper or faculties of mind. Er ist ein hitziger, zorniger —, he is a hasty or passionate, a hot-brained fellow, he is as hot as pepper, V. Brause—, Hitz—; er ist ein lustiger —, he is a merry blade, a jovial fellow; ein wunderlicher, seltsamer —, a whimsical, odd, singular or fantastical fellow; ein vielumfassender —, a vast genius; ein witziger, ein geistvoller —, a man of wit, of genius; ein dichterischer —, a poetical genius. V. Dumm—, Esels—, Flach—, Ochsen—, Schafs—, Starr—, Trotz— *f)* a head of cattle. Seine Herde besteht aus 20 Köpfen, his herd consists of twenty head [of cattle &c.]. *g)* [in popular lang., in the following phrases] Den — hoch tragen, den — in die Höhe tragen, to carry it high, to be haughty or proud; er hat mit dem —e durchgewollt, he threw himself into it head foremost; über Hals und —, with great haste, with tumultuous hurry, precipitately; Einen beim —e nehmen, kriegen, to seize, to arrest any one, to imprison any one; den — aus der Schlinge ziehen, to get out of trouble, out of the scrape, to get off; Einem den — bieten, to make head against, to resist any one, V. Spitze; zu —e wachsen, über den — wachsen, to grow upon any one. V. Wachsen; Einen vor den — stoßen, schlagen, to affront, to offend any one; sich auf den — stellen, to make the utmost efforts, to do one's utmost; Einem den — waschen, to reprimand severely; [reciprocally, of several] sich die Köpfe waschen, to come to blows, to fight; Einem den — zurecht bringen, setzen or rücken, to bring any one to reason, to set any one to rights; der — steht ihm nicht recht, he is not in good humour; der — steht ihm nicht darnach, he has no fancy for it, no mind to it; Einem mit einer Sache den — toll or warm machen, to beat any one's brains about a thing; machen Sie mir damit den — nicht toll! don't bother me with that! das ist ein Lärm, daß man nicht weiß, wo Einem der — steht, this is a stunning noise; Etwas im —e haben, to be a little tipsy, flustered; er ist im —e nicht richtig, he is crack-brained, crazy; der — schwindelt ihm, he is puffed up with his good fortune, his elevation has made him quite giddy, he forgets himself. 3) [Sax. *cop*, D. *kope*, Eng. *cup*, Fr. *coupe*, allied to the L. *cupa*, Germ. Kufe, L. *cavus* = hohl] *a)* Das Köpfchen or der obere Theil [einer Tasse], a cup. Das Theeköpfchen, a tea-cup. *b)* the bowl of a smoking-pipe. *c)* V. Schröpf—.

Kopf=abhacker, —abschneider, *m.* [vulgar] V. Henker, Scharfrichter. —ader, *f.* V. Hauptader. —arbeit, *f.* study, application of the mind. —arzenei, *f.* V. Hauptarzenei. —bad, *n.* bath for the head. —balsam, *m.* V. Hauptbalsam. —band, *n.* 1) band or fillet for the head, head-band, frontlet, brow-band. V. Stirnband. 2) [in anatomy] Die —bänder der Mittelhand, the ligaments of the metacarpus. —baum, *m.* the American button-wood. —bedeckung, *f.* covering for the head, as a cap, hat &c. —bein, *n.* bone of the head; [in anatomy] bone of the skull. —besteuerung, *f.* V. —geld. —binde, *f.* V. Hauptbinde. —blättchen, *n.* [in anatomy] fontanella, fons pulsatilis. —blöde, *f.* weakness of understanding, imbecillity. —bohrer, *m.* 1) [Schädelbohrer, *Trepan] trepan. 2) one who trepans, trepanner. —bolzen, *m.* a bolt with a round iron head. —brechen, *n.* beating one's head or puzzling one's brains about a thing, bothering one's mind with a thing. Bei dem Schachspiele kostet es —brechen, in playing at chess one must rack one's brains, put one's brains upon the rack; diese Arbeit braucht nicht viel —brechens, this work does not require great efforts of genius, is easy enough. —brechend, *adj.* very difficult, puzzling. —brecher, *m.* [in jest] heady wine. —bret, *n.* the head-board of a bed, the head-piece. —bürste, *f.* head-brush. —drüse, *f.* V. Hauptdrüse. —dunst, *m.* [in familiar or jocose language] inebriation, intoxication. —essenz, *f.* V. Hauptessenz. —fach, *n.* [among hatters] the capade of the crown of a hat. —fest, *adj.* immovable in one's resolutions, steady, constant. —fieber, *n.* V. Hirnwuth. —fluß, *m.* V. Hauptfluß. —förmig, *adj.* having the form or shape of a head; [in botany] capitate. —fries, *m.* the muzzle-mouldings or frieze of a cannon. —geld, *n.* poll-tax. —geschmeide, *n.* jewels or ornaments for the head, V. —putz, —schmuck. —geschwulst, *f.* swelling of the head. —gestell, *n.* V. Hauptgestell. —grind, *m.* V. Hauptgrind. —grindkraut, *n.* field or corn scabious. —haar, *n.* V. Haupthaar. —hänger, *m.*, —hängerinn, *f.* hypocritical or dull devotee. —hängerei, *f.* hypocritical or dull devotion. —haube, *f.* a woman's cap. —haut, *f.* the skin of the head. —holz, *n.* the small wood laid on the top of a charcoal pile. —hülle, *f.* any covering for the head. —joch, *n.* the head- or front-yoke. —keilbein, *n.* [in anatomy] basilar bone. —kissen, *n.* pillow, bolster. —klippel, —klöppel, *m.* V. —holz. —kohl, *m.* cabbage which forms a head, headed cabbage. —krankheit, *f.* V. Hauptkrankheit. —lattich, *m.* cabbage lettuce. —lauge, *f.* lye for washing the head; †*fig.* severe reprimand. —laus, *f.* headlouse. —leer, *adj.* brainless, silly. —los, *adj.* and *adv.* headless; *fig.* destitute of understanding or prudence, brainless, headless &c. —muskel, *m.* muscle of the head. —nadel, *f.* [an instrument to dress the hair] bodkin, crisping-pin. —nägelein, *n.* [Knopfnelke] a kind of small wild pink. —naht, *f.* suture or seam of the head. —nicken, *n.* nod of the head. —nicker, *m.* a person who nods, nodder; **fig.* a cringing fellow, a complier. —nuß, *f.* 1) †*fig.* blow on the head. 2) [in botany] coryocar nuciferum. —pein, *f.* violent or one-sided headache, megrim. —pflaster, *n.* V. Hauptpflaster. —pfühl, *m.* pillow, bolster. —platte, *f.* bald place on the head, V. also Glatze. —polei, *m.* the round-headed germander. —putz, *m.* dress or ornament for the head, head-dress. Ein modischer, lockiger —putz, a fashionable, curled head-dress. —putzer, *m.*, —putzerinn, *f.* V. [the usual word] Haarkräusler &c. —quaste, *f.* tuft or tassel for the head [of a horse]. —räude, *f.* scurf, scald-head. —reißer, *m.* [low or in jest] very bad and heady wine. —rennen, *n.* the running or tilting at the head. —riemen, *m.* the head-stall of a bridle. —ring, *m.* a pad. —salat, *m.* cabbage lettuce. —salbe, *f.* cephalic salve or unguent. —schatz, *m.* V. —geld. —scheu, *adj.* [said of a horse] shy as to the head, unwilling to suffer the head to be touched. —schlagader, *f.* the cephalic or carotid artery. —schleier, *m.* veil [for the head]. —schmerz, *m.* pain in the head. —schmerzen, *pl.* head-ache. —schmuck, *m.* ornament for the head. —schnupfen, *m.* cold in the head. —schraube, *f.* a screw with a head. —schur, *f.* V. Hauptschur. —schütteln, *n.* shaking the head. —schüttelnd, *adj.* and *adv.* shaking the head. —seite, *f.* V. Hauptseite. —stein, *m.* [in architecture] console, shoulder-piece, bracket. —steuer, *f.* poll-tax. —stoß, —streich, *m.* a stroke or blow on the head. —stück, *n.* 1) piece of the head or jowl, head-piece. 2) [in some parts of Germany] a coin of the value of about 8 pence sterling. 3) [in botany] V. —nuß 2). 4) the mouth-piece of a flute. —träger, *m.* [in anatomy] the first vertebre of the neck, atlas. —tuch, *n.* a cloth to cover the head, †kerchief. —verwirrung, *f.* confusion of or in the head. —wassersucht, *f.* water in the head, hydrocephalus. —weh, *n.* head-ache. —weide, *f.* the white willow. —werfend, *adj.* haughty, overbearing, proud. —wunde, *f.* wound in the head. —wuth, *f.* V. Hirnwuth. —zange, *f.* V. —zieher. —zeug, *n.* an ornamental cap for females. —zeugnadel, *f.* minikin-pin. —zieher, *m.* [in surgery] forceps. —zierath, *m.* ornament for the head.

Köpfen, I. *v. intr.* to form a head, to grow into a head. Der Salat köpft schon, the salad begins already to cabbage. II. *v. tr.* 1) to take off the head, to behead, to decapitate. Einen Verbrecher — [in this sense the term is rather low, V. Enthaupten], to decapitate a delinquent; die Weiden —, to top willow trees; den Tabak —, to prune tobacco. 2) to cup, V. Schröpfen.

Köpf=maschine, *f.* [an engine or machine for beheading persons at a stroke] guillotin. Mit der —maschine hinrichten, to guillotin. —weide, *f.* V. Kopfweide.

Köpfig, *adj.* and *adv.* [not much used] having a head, headed. —es Kraut, headed cabbage; [chiefly used in composition as :] zwei— &c., two-headed &c.; *Fig.* V. Köpfisch.

Köpfigkeit, *f.* [not much used] obstinacy.

Köpfisch, *adj.* and *adv.* [not much used] headstrong, capricious, obstinate.

Köpp, *m.* [-es, *pl.* -e] or Koppe, *f.* [*pl.* -n] V. Kaulquappe, Kaulhaupt.

Köppe, *f.* [*pl.* -n] [allied to Kopf, Gipfel, Kuppel] top, summit of a mountain.

Köppel, *f.* [*pl.* -n] [allied to the L. *copula*, *capere*, to heben, haben] 1) band, tie; [chiefly] tie for holding two dogs together, couple, leash. Die Hunde zur — herbeirufen, to wind or blow the horn for coupling the hounds; die — am Degen, V. Degen—, Degengehenk. 2) two things of any kind connected or linked together, couple. Eine — Hunde, a couple of dogs; eine — Windhunde, a brace of greyhounds. *it.* a collection of individuals. Eine — Jagdhunde, a pack of hounds; eine — Pferde, a string of horses [which are led to market].

it. [rarely] a number of people. 3) any district over which several persons jointly have certain rights, V. —fischerei, —huth, —jagd, —weide. 4) fenced piece of ground, enclosure.

Koppel-balken, *m.* cross-beam. —**fischerei**, *f.* fishery belonging jointly to several persons. —**genoß**, *m.* one who shares in certain rights with others. —**gerechtigkeit**, *f.* right of using a thing in common with others. —**hund**, *m.* a dog held by a leash. —**huth**, *f.* common pasture. —**jagd**, *f.* common chase. —**kette**, *f.* V. Hemmkette. —**recht**, *n.* the right of common pasture. —**riemen**, *m.* collar with which dogs are coupled, leash [for grey-hounds]. —**seil**, *n.* leash, couple. —**trift**, *f.* V. —huth. —**weide**, *f.* I. —weide, the trailing willow. II. —weide, V. —huth. —**wirthschaft**, *f.* the laying out of an estate or farm into parcels.

Köppeln, *v. tr.* 1) to tie together, to couple. 2) to fence, to enclose.

1. **Köppen**, *v. tr.* [from Koppe, Kopf] to cut off the top, to top [a tree].

2. **Köppen**, *v. intr.* [allied to the Fr. *happer*, schnappen] 1) [said of persons] to eructate, to hiccough. 2) [said of horses] to bite the crib, to have got the tick.

Koppenkette, *f.* V. Koppelkette.

Köpper, *m.* [-s, *pl.*-] crib-biter, a horse that has got the tick.

Koralle, *f.* [*pl.* -n] [from the Gr. κοράλλιον, L. *corallium*] coral. Die schwarze, die weiße —, the black, white coral; sein Kabinet enthält sehr seltene —n, he has very scarce corals in his collection.

Korall-hiazinthe, —**holz**, —**rinde**, &c., V. Korallenhiazinthe &c.

Korallen-achat, *m.* agate with red coral-like streaks, coral agate. —**artig**, *adj.* coralloid, coralloidal. —**ast**, *m.* coral-branch. —**auflösung**, *f.* 1) solution of coral. 2) tincture of coral. —**baum**, *m.* 1) coral-tree, coral-wood. 2) V. —kirschbaum. —**blume**, *f.* coralline, coralloid. —**blümchen**, ||—**blümlein**, *n.* 1) the red, common or corn pimpernel. 2) the wood-anemone. —**blüte**, *f.* V. —blume. —**drechsler**, *m.* turner in coral. —**erz**, *n.* impure mercury or quicksilver in form of coral. —**fang**, *m.* coral-fishery. —**farbig**, *adj.* rosy, coralline. —**fisch**, *m.* medusa, sea-nettle. —**fischer**, *m.* coral-diver, coral-fisher. —**fischerei**, *f.* 1) coral-fishery. 2) the right of fishing up coral. —**flechte**, *f.* white coral-seed. —**förmig**, *adj.* coralliform, coralloid. —**garn**, *n.* V. —netz. —**gewächs**, *n.* coral. —**hiazinthe**, *f.* the purple grape hyacinth. —**holz**, *n.* coral-wood. —**jaspis**, *m.* coralline jasper. —**kirschbaum**, *m.* the red-berry bearing night-shade, winter-cherry. —**krabbe**, *f.* coral crab. —**kraut**, *n.* 1) coral-plant, dwarf corallodendron [Erythrina herbacea *Linn*]. 2) V. Meerspargel. 3) St. John's wort. —**lippe**, *f.* [*fig.*; chiefly in poetry] coral or rosy lip. Ihre —lippen, her ruby-lips. —**marmor**, *m.* coralloid marble. —**moos**, *n.* 1) coral-moss, coralline. Das blasige, zellige, röhrige, gegliederte —moos, the vesiculated, celliferous, tubular, articulated coralline. 2) fever-moss. —**mund**, *m.* [*fig.*; in poetry] coral or rosy lips or mouth. —**netz**, *n.* coral net. —**niederschlag**, *m.* precipitate of coral. —**pfennig**, *m.* the small elliptic coral. —**pflanze**, *f.* 1) coral. 2) V. —kraut. —**pulver**, *n.* coral powder, pulverized coral. —**rinde**, *f.* 1) the rind of coral. 2) horn-wrack, eschara, coralloid. 3) corallite. —**roth**, *adj.* red like coral, coral. —**same**, *m.* coral-seed. —**sauger**, *m.* [a fish] syngnathus pelagicus. —**schnur**, *f.* coral neck-lace. —**schwamm**, *m.* 1) fungite. 2) the coral clavaria. —**schwarz**, *n.* black coral, antipathes, gorgonia. —**stein**, *m.* 1) corallite. 2) V. —achat. —**thier**, —**thierchen**, *n.* coralline. —**tinktur**, *f.* tincture of coral. —**weizen**, *m.* zea, spelt-corn, maize. —**winde**, *f.* articulated coralline. —**wurz**, —**wurzel**, *f.* 1) ophrys corallorhiza. 2) the common polypody. 3) the bulbiferous tooth-wort or coral-wort. —**zinke**, *f.* 1) coral-branch. 2) the trumpet-honeysuckle. —**zweig**, *m.* V. —ast, —zinke.

†**Koranzen**, *v. tr.* to chastise, to beat, to drub.

Korb, *m.* [-es, *pl.* Körbe] [old Germ. chorop, chorp, Dan. *kuro*, Low Sax. *korf*, L. *corbis*], *dim.* Körbchen, ||Körblein, [-s, *pl.*-] *n.* basket. Ein — von Binsen [Binsen—], a rush-basket; ein großer —, a hamper, pannier; der — einer Kutsche, the boot of a coach; der — an einem Säbel, the basket-hilt of a sword. *it.* the contents of a basket, as ein — Aepfel, a basket of apples. *Prov.* V. 1. Hahn *fig.* *Fig.* [in familiar language] refusal. Einen — bekommen, to meet with a refusal. V. Arbeits—, Arm—, Back—, Bienen—, Brod—, Hand—, Hühner—, Mast—, Maul—, &c.

Korb-bett, *n.* cradle [made of wicker-work]. —**feigen**, *pl.* figs which are imported in baskets or frails. —**flasche**, *f.* demijohn. —**flechter**, *m.* V. —macher. —**macher**, *m.*, —**macherinn**, *f.* basket-maker. —**macherarbeit**, *f.* basket-maker's work. —**macherhandwerk**, *n.* basket-trade. —**pfennig**, *m.* V. Schwänzelpfennig. —**rosinen**, *pl.* raisins imported in baskets. —**tabak**, *m.* V. Knaster. —**wagen**, *m.* carriage or vehicle with a body of basket-work. —**weide**, *f.* osier. —**weise**, *adv.* in or by baskets. —**wiege**, *f.* V. —bett.

Korbe, *f.* [*pl.* -n] V. Kurbel.

Korbeere, *f.* [*pl.* -n] V. Kornelle.

Korbel, V. Kerbel.

Korduan, V. Corduan.

‡**Kören**, *v. tr.* [Sw. *kora*, Icel. *kiora*, the same as kiesen, Fr. *choisir*] to choose, to pick out, to cull, V. Er—, Auser—.

Kör-gut, *n.* 1) a piece of property acquired by option. 2) an estate subject to the right of the lord of the manor's choosing the best piece of property out of the possessor's inheritance. —**herr**, *m.* 1) an officer whose business it is to inspect and taste [if necessary] the victuals brought to market. 2) an elector, V. Wahlherr. —**recht**, *n.* 1) right of election to an office. 2) the right of the lord of the manor of choosing a piece of property out of an inheritance.

***Koriander**, *m.* [-s, *pl.* -] coriander.

Koriander-korn, *n.* coriander-seed. —**schierling**, *m.* mountain-parsley. —**wasser**, *n.* coriander-water.

Korind, *n.* [-s] [in mineralogy] corundum

Korinth, *n.* [-s] [a city of Greece] Corinth.

Korinthe, *f.* [*pl.* -n] [from the fore-going word] [a small kind of dried grape, imported from the Levant] currant.

Korinthen-baum, *m.* Alpine currant-tree. —**beere**, *f.* Alpine currant.

Korinther, *m.* [-s, *pl.*-], —**inn**, *f.* Corinthian. Die Briefe Pauli an die —, the epistles of Paul to the Corinthians.

Korinthisch, *adj.* and *adv.* Corinthian. Das —e Erz, Corinthian brass; —e Ordnung, Corinthian order; das —e Kapitäl, the Corinthian capital.

‡**Körisch**, *adj.* and *adv.* fastidious, nice.

Kork, *m.* [-es, *pl.* -e] [allied to the L. *quercus* = Eiche, *cortex*, Fr. *écorce* = Rinde] 1) cork. 2) V. Bergfleisch. 3) V. See—.

Kork-artig, *adj.* and *adv.* having the nature of cork, corky, suberous. —**baum**, *m.* cork-tree, cork. —**bildner**, *m.* an artist who forms or shapes all sorts of things in cork. —**bildnerei**, *f.* the art of forming or shaping things in cork. —**bildwerk**, *n.* a figure &c. made of cork. —**eiche**, *f.* V. —baum. —**form**, *f.* model in cork. —**messer**, *n.* knife for cutting cork. —**niere**, *f.* V. Gekröse[?]. —**pfropf**, *m.* a stopple cut out of cork, a cork. —**propfenmacher**, *m.* cork-cutter. —**rüster**, *f.* the small-leaved elm. —**sauer** *adj.* and *adv.* suberic. —**säure**, *f.* suberic acid. —**schneider**, *m.* V. —bildner and —propfenmacher. —**schwamm**, *m.* the birch-agaric. —**sohle**, *f.* cork-sole. —**stöpsel**, *m.* V. —pfropf. —**ulme**, *f.* V. —rüster. —**zieher**, *m.* cork-screw.

Korken, *v. tr.* to stop [bottles &c.] with corks, to cork.

Korn, *n.* [-es, *pl.* Körner] [allied to the L. *granum*, Kern] 1) [any small hard and roundish mass] grain. Ein — Sand [Sandkorn], a grain of sand; ein — Gerste, Weizen, a corn of barley, wheat, V. Gersten—, Weizen— &c.; das Gold wird in Körnern gefunden, gold is found in grains; V. Gold—, Mohn—, Pfeffer—, Pulver—, Salz—, Sand—, Senf—, &c. [among gunsmiths] sight [upon a gun for aiming]. Einen Hirsch auf das — nehmen [among sportsmen], to take one's aim at a stag. *Fig.* Einen, Etwas auf dem —e haben [in fam. lang.], to have in one's eye, to have a design upon, to aim at a thing or person. [in mineralogy] a component part of stones and metals, grain. Dieser Stahl hat ein feines —, that steel is well refined; Steine von feinem —e, stone of a fine grain. [in coining] standard of metal, alloy. Eine Münze von gutem Schrot und —e, a coin of its full weight and due value, *fig.* ein Mann von altem Schrot und —e, a man of the old honest character, a man of the right old stamp. 2) *a)* [the seeds of wheat, rye, barley, oats &c.] corn, grain. — bauen, to cultivate corn; das — steht sehr schön, the corn looks very fine, bids very fair; das — schneiden, to cut the corn; das — auf den Speicher thun, to house the corn; türkisches —, Indian wheat, maize; V. Davids—, Heide—, Himmels—, Saat—, Sommer—, Stauden—, Winter—, &c. SYN. Korn, Getreide. Korn are the grains of seed in general; Getreide those of which bread can be made, and which are useful as an object of consumption. *b)* [the twentieth part of a scruple in apothecaries' weight] grain.

Korn-acker, *m.* a field of corn, corn-field. —**ähre**, *f.* 1) ear of corn, [chiefly] of rye. 2) [in mineralogy] spicate silver-ore. 3) [in astronomy] spica virginis. —**ährenbinde**, *f.* [in surgery] spica-bandage. —**ährenfisch**, *m.* the atherine. —**ährenkoralle**, *f.* spicate madrepore. —**ausfuhr**, *f.* exportation of corn or grain. —**bau**, *m.* cultivation of corn or grain, chiefly of rye. —**bauer**, *m.* cultivator of corn or grain, husbandman. —**beere**, *f.* cornelian-cherry, dog-berry. —**blume**, *f.* corn-flower, blue-bottle. —**blumenblau**, *adj.* V. —blumenfarben. —**blumenessig**, *m.* vinegar of blue-bottles. —**blumenfarbe**, *f.* colour of blue-bottles. —**blumenfarben**, —**blumenfarbig**, *adj.* of the colour of blue-bottles. —**blumenöl**, *n.* oil of blue-bottles. —**blumenspath**, *m.* V. Lasurstein. —**blumenwasser**, *n.* water of blue-bottles —**blüte**, *f.* 1) blossom of corn. 2) the florescence of corn. —**boden**, *m.* 1) soil for growing corn, corn-land. 2) corn-loft, granary

nary. —**brand**, *m.* blight on corn, ergot, smut. —**branntwein**, *m.* spirits distilled from grain, corn-brandy. —**büchſe**, *f.* the wooden box for granulating lead. —**dieb**, *m.* 1) one who steals corn. 2) V. —käfer. —**ernte**, *f.* crop of corn, harvest. —**fäule**, *f.* V. —brand. —**fege**, *f.* a kind of sieve or fan for cleansing the corn from the chaff, winnowing-machine. riddle. —**feld**, *n.* V. —acker. —**ferkel**, *n.* V. —hamſter. —**fink**, *m.* V. Goldammer. —**fliege**, *f.* St. Mark's fly. —**flur**, *f.* corn-fields. —**förmig**, *adj.* and *adv.* granulated, granular. —**freſſer**, *m.* any animal eating corn; [in nat. hist.] the white-winged gross-beak. —**garbe**, *f.* a sheaf of corn. —**gefilde**, *n.* corn-field; V. —acker, —flur. —**gerſte**, *f.*, —**gras**, *n.* the meadow barley-grass, the wall-barley. —**geſetze**, *pl.* laws regulating the exports and imports of corn or grain and the duties upon it, corn-laws. —**gülte**, *f.* rent or tax paid in corn. —**halm**, *m.* stalk of corn, corn-stalk. —**hamſter**, *m.* hamster. —**handel**, *m.* corn-trade. —**händler**, *m.* corn-merchant; corn-chandler. —**haufe**, *m.* heap of corn, corn-heap. —**haus**, *n.* house for keeping corn or grain, granary. —**herr**, *m.* one who is set over a public granary, overseer of a public garner. —**jahr**, *n.* a year productive in corn, corn-year. Das Jahr 18.. war ein ſehr gutes —, und Weinjahr, the year 18.. was very productive or rich in corn and wine. —**jude**, *m.* a jew who deals in corn, corn-jew; *it. fig.* a usurious dealer in corn. —**käfer**, *m.* dor-beetle, black-beetle, hedge-chafer. —**kammer**, *f.* corn-loft. —**kaſten**, *m.* 1) a large chest for keeping corn. 2) hopper, mill-hopper. 3) V. —boden 2). —**kluft**, *f.*, —**klüftchen**, *n.* tongs. —**krebs**, *m.* V. —wurm. —**kupfer**, *n.* granulated copper. —**land**, *n.* 1) a country that produces much corn, a country fertile in corn, corn-country. 2) V. —boden 1). —**leder**, *n.* granulated leather. —**lerche**, *f.* the common field lark. —**made**, *f.* V. —wurm. —**magazin**, *n.* corn-magazine, granary. —**mäkler**, *m.* corn-factor. —**mangel**, *m.* great scarcity or dearth of corn. —**markt**, *m.* corn-market, corn-fair. —**maß**, *n.* corn-measure. —**maus**, *f.* V. Feldmaus. —**mehl**, *n.* flour of corn, chiefly of rye. —**meiſter**, *m.* V. —herr. —**meſſer**, *m.* corn-meter. —**nilbe**, *f.* V. —wurm. —**mohn**, *m.* wild poppy. —**motte**, *f.* V. —wurm. —**mühle**, *f.* corn-mill. —**münze**, *f.* the corn-mint. —**mutter**, *f.* V. Mutterkorn. —**nelke**, *f.* 1) the corn-rose campion, the cockle, cockle-weed. 2) the scarlet lychnis. —**preis**, *m.* the price of corn. —**pulver**, *n.* granulated gunpowder. —**raden**, *m.* V. —nelke 1). —**ratte**, *f.* V. —hamſter. —**raupe**, *f.* V. —wurm. —**reich**, *adj.* and *adv.* 1) V. Körnerreich. 2) fertile in corn, abounding with corn. —**reuter**, *m.* V. —wurm. —**ritterſporn**, *m.* V. Ritterſporn. —**rolle**, *f.* V. —fege. —**roſe**, *f.* 1) the common poppy, corn-rose. 2) —**roſe**, *f.* or —**röslein**, *n.* V. —nelke. 3) Blaue —roſe, the field or corn scabious. —**ſchabe**, *f.* V. —wurm. —**ſchätzer**, *m.* apprizer or rater of corn. —**ſchaufel**, *f.* corn-shovel. —**ſcheuer**, barn in which corn is kept, corn-loft, granary. —**ſchinder**, *m.* V. —wucherer. —**ſchnepfe**, *f.* V. Brachſchnepfe. —**ſchreiber**, *m.* a person who keeps an account of the granary or store of corn, corn-clerk. —**ſchwertel**, *m.* corn-flag, the common red corn-flag. —**ſchwinge**, *f.* van or fan for winnowing grain, corn-van, winnowing-machine. —**ſchwinger**, a person who winnows or fans wheat &c. —**ſeihe**, *f.*, —**ſieb**, *n.* 1) V. —fege. 2) corning-sieve [for granulating gunpowder]. —**ſpeicher**, *m.* corn-loft, granary; corn-magazine. —**ſperling**, *m.* house-sparrow. —**ſperre**, *f.* V. —zuſchlag. —**ſpitze**, *f.* awn or beard of corn. —**ſtaupe**, *f.* hydatid. —**ſtein**, *m.* V. Körnerſtein. —**ſtraußgras**, *n.* V. Windhalm. —**ſtück**, *n.* piece of ground sown with corn, chiefly with rye, corn-field. —**taufe**, *f.* rogation-week. —**taxe**, *f.* rate of corn. —**vogel**, *m.* V. —wurm. —**wage**, *f.* balance for weighing corn. —**wanne**, *f.* V. —ſchwinge. —**werfer**, *m.* 1) V. —ſchwinger. ‖2) the sparrow. —**wicke**, *f.* 1) the common vetch. 2) the tufted vetch. 3) the purple coronilla. —**wiebel**, *m.* V. —wurm. —**winde**, *f.* 1) corn-bind. 2) the black bindweed. —**wolf**, *m.* 1) gryllo-talpa, palmer. 2) V. —wurm. —**wucher**, *m.* a usurious trade in corn. —**wucherer**, *m.* usurious dealer in corn. —**wurm**, *m.* [an insect destructive to the corn] corn-worm, weevil, calander. —**wut**, *f.* the red deadnettle. —**zange**, *f.* V. —kluft. —**zapfen**, *m.* V. —brand, Mutter—. —**zehente**, *m.* tithe of corn. —**zins**, *m.* V. —gülte. —**zuſchlag**, *m.* prohibition of exporting corn or grain.

Körner-baum, *m.* V. Kornelbaum. —**kraut**, *n.* V. Bruchkraut. —**lack**, *m.* seed-lac. —**leder**, *n.* grained leather, shagreen. —**milch**, *f.* emulsion. —**reich**, *adj.* and *adv.* full of corn. Eine —reiche Aehre, an ear very full of corn. —**ſcharlach**, *m.* Venice or Venetian scarlet. —**ſchild**, *m.* [in conchology] trunk-crab. —**ſtein**, *m.* granit or granite. Grauer —ſtein, granitel. —**warze**, *f.* V. Laufkäfer.

***Kórnack**, *m.* [-s, *pl.* -e] V. Elephantenführer.

Kornelle, *f.* [*pl.* -n] 1) V. Kornelbaum. 2) V. Kornelkirſche.

Kornel-baum, —**kirſchbaum**, *m.* cornel, cornelian-tree. —**kirſche**, *f.* cornelian-cherry.

Körneln, *v. tr.* 1) [to form into grains] to granulate [lead, silver, powder &c.]. 2) [to raise into small asperities, to make rough on the surface] to granulate [leather].

Körnelung, *f.* granulation.

Körnen, I *v. intr.* 1) to form corns or grains. Das Getreide fängt an zu —, the corn begins to seed, to run to seed. 2) *v. intr.* and *v. r.* ſich —, to be formed into corns or grains, to granulate. II. *v. tr.* 1) to convert into grains, to granulate, to corn. Blei, Pulver &c. —, to granulate lead, powder &c. 2) to allure by means of corn, to bait, V. Ködern. *Fig.* [in fam. lang.] to attract, to allure. Sie hat ihn richtig gekörnt, she succeeded in enticing him. Das — *a*) granulation, *b*) the act of alluring or enticing.

Körn-büchſe, *f.* V. Kornbüchſe. —**eiſen**, *n.* granulating iron. —**maſchine**, *f.* wax-chandler's sieve.

Körnicht, *adj.* and *adv.* resembling grains, grained, granulary. Die —e Flechte, the granular lichen.

Körnig, *adj.* and *adv.* consisting or full of grains, granulous, granulary. —es Baumöl, clotted oil. *it.* [in composition] grained, as grob—, coarse-grained, V. Fein—, Grob—, Klein—; [in botany] eine —e Wurzel, a granular root; [in anatomy] —e Drüſen, conglomerate glands. *Fig.* firm, compact, solid, substantial, V. Kernig; *it.* nervous, emphatic. Eine —e Schreibart, a pithy, energetic style.

Körnling, *m.* [-es, *pl.* -e] 1) [in mineralogy] granit or granite. 2) [a fish] umber, V. Aſcher.

Körnung, *f.* 1) granulation. 2) the act of alluring or enticing.

Körper, *m.* [-s, *pl.* -] *dim.* Körperchen, ‖Körperlein, *n.* [-s, *pl.* -] [Sw. *kropp*, Icel. *krof*, L. *corpus*, gen. *corpor-is*; Gr. κορμός = Rumpf, allied to the old karen, ſcheren = ſchneiden; hence primarily any detached mass or substance] 1) [matter] body. Ein leichter, ein ſchwerer —, a light, a heavy body; ein natürlicher, ein dichter —, a natural, a solid body; ein metalliſcher —, a metalline substance; ein einfacher oder vermiſchter —, a body simple or mixed; himmliſche —, celestial bodies, V. Erd—, Himmels—. 2) [the greater mass or quantity of the component parts of a thing] body. Dieſer Sirop hat nicht — genug, this sirop has not consistence enough; Wein, der viel — hat, wine of a good body, strong-bodied wine; dieſes Papier hat nicht genug —, that paper has not body enough; [chiefly in painting] eine Farbe, die — hat, a thick colour, a colour that bears a body; einer Farbe — geben, to embody, to thicken a colour. 3) [the frame of an animal] body. Ein gutgebauter —, a body well-made; aus ſeinem — eine Apotheke machen, to make an apothecary's shop of one's body; es [er, ſie] iſt ein — ohne Seele, it [he, she] is a body without a soul [= a person wanting sense]; ein entſeelter, todter —, a dead body; ein erblaßter — [in poetry], a body pale in death. 4) *Fig.* [a number of men united by one form of government or by the same occupation &c.] body. Der — or Staats—, the politic body, the body politic; der geſetzgebende —, the legislative body; die Kirche iſt ein —, deren Oberhaupt Chriſtus iſt, the church is a body, the head of which is Christ. SYN. Körper, Leib. Körper implies the body of men and animals as consisting of matter; Leib in so far as it is animated. Leib therefore is the opposite to soul, Körper to life. As soon as the human body ceases to be a fitting instrument for sensation and motion, it is no longer a Leib; it continues, however, a Körper, and a human one, as being endued with its form. The anatomist has Körper on his dissecting-table, but no Leiber.

Körper-all, *n.* V. —welt. —**anlage**, *f.* disposition of body, temperament. —**bau**, *m.* structure of the body, frame of body. Ein Mann von kräftigem —bau, a man of a robust or strong bodily texture, frame. —**beſchaffenheit**, *f.* constitution of body. Eine ſtarke, eine ſchlechte, eine ſchwache —beſchaffenheit, a strong, a bad, a weak constitution. —**bildung**, *f.* 1) the form of the human body, shape. Ein Mann von ſchöner —bildung, a man of a fine figure. 2) the improvement of the body. Tanzen und Fechten tragen zur —bildung bei, dancing and fencing render the body active and supple. —**haltung**, *f.* carriage, deportment, V. Haltung 2). —**kraft**, *f.* strength of body. —**lehre**, *f.* the doctrine of bodies, somatology. —**los**, *adj.* and *adv.* bodiless, incorporeal. —**maſſe**, *f.* 1) the mass of which a body consists. 2) [a body considered only as a great mass or bulk] bulky body. Ein Mann von ſolcher —maſſe, a man of such bulkiness. —**meſſung**, *f.* [*Stereometrie] stereometry. —**reich**, I. *adj.* and *adv.* of a good body, having much body or great consistence. II. *n.* V. —welt. —**ſtellung**, *f.* attitude. —**ſtimmung**, *f.* temperament of body, constitution. —**ſtoff**, *m.* [*Materie] matter. —**übung**, *f.* exercise of the body, gymnastic exercise. —**übungskunſt**, *f.* V. Gymnaſtik. —**übungsſpiel**, *n.* gymnic game. —**welt**, *f.* corporeal world. —**zahl**, *f.* [in mathematics] solid number.

Körperlich, *adj.* and *adv.* bodily, corporeal. —er Stoff, corporeal substance; —e Gebrechen, bodily defects; eine —e Strafe, a corporeal punishment; einen —en Eid ablegen, to take a corporeal [= solemn] oath; [in mathematics] ein —er Winkel, a solid angle.

Körperlichkeit, *f.* corporeity, materiality.

Körperschaft, *f.* corporate body, corporation.

***Korporál**, *m.* V. Corporal.

***Korsár**, *m.* V. Corsar.

Kosácke, *m.* [-n, *pl.* -n] Cossack.

Kósbeere, *f.* [*pl.* -n] V. Heidelbeere.

***Kóscher**, *adj.* and *adv.* [among Jews] not unclean, good.

‖**Kósel**, *f.* [*pl.* -n] sow.

‖**Kóseln**, *v. intr.* to farrow, to pig.

Kósen, *v. intr.* [allied to the Fr. *causer, jaser*] to talk, to converse, to chat; *it.* to caress, to make love.

Kosewort, *n.* word of endearment.

***Kosmétisch**, *adj.* beautifying, cosmetic. Ein —es Mittel, a cosmetic.

***Kósmik**, V. Kosmologie.

***Kósmisch**, *adj.* and *adv.* [in astronomy, rising or setting with the sun] cosmical. Dieser Stern geht — auf, unter, that star rises, sets cosmically.

***Kosmogonie**, *f.* [*pl.* -en] cosmogony.

***Kosmograph**, *m.* [-en, *pl.* -en] cosmographer, V. Weltbeschreiber.

***Kosmographie**, *f.* cosmography, V. Weltbeschreibung.

***Kosmográphisch**, *adj.* cosmographical, V. Weltbeschreibend.

***Kosmoláb**, *n.* [-s, *pl.* -e] cosmolabe, V. Weltmesser.

***Kosmologie**, *f.* cosmology, V. Weltlehre.

***Kosmológisch**, *adj.* and *adv.* cosmological.

***Kosmopolít**, *m.* [-en, *pl.* -en] cosmopolitan, cosmopolite, citizen of the world, V. Weltbürger.

***Kosmopolítisch**, *adj.* V. Weltbürgerlich.

***Kosmopolitísmus**, *m.* cosmopolitism, V. Weltbürgersinn.

***Kosmoráma**, *n.* [-s, *pl.*-men] V. Weltgemälde, Weltansicht.

***Kosmotheologie**, *f.* natural theology.

Kossät, *m* [-en, *pl.* -en] **Kossatengut**, *n.* V. Köthener, Köthenergut.

Kóst, *f.* [from kauen, V. Kosten] 1) food, fare, victuals. Die einfachste — ist die gesundeste, the plainest food is the most wholesome; eine gute, eine magere, eine dürftige —, a good, a slender, a stinted fare; eine nahrhafte —, a nourishing diet. 2) entertainment, board, diet. Eine gewisse Summe für — und Wohnung bezahlen, to pay a certain sum for board or diet and lodging; Einem die — geben, to give any one one's table, to board any one; ein Freund von ihm gibt ihm die —, one of his friends has him to eat with him; in die — gehen, in der — seyn, to go into board, to board somewhere; bei einem Freunde in die — gehen, to board at a friend's; bei wem gehen Sie in die —, with whom do you board? in die — geben, thun, to put out to board; freie —, free board; Einen in die — nehmen, to board any one, to give any one one's table; halbe —, half board. Syn. Kost, Speise, Zehrung. Kost comprehends more than Speise. It implies not merely that with which we appease our hunger, but also that which, according to our circumstances, we are accustomed to enjoy. He who undertakes to furnish another with Kost, binds himself to more than he who undertakes to give him Speisen. Zehrung is that which any one requires for his support while abroad, or on a journey. V. Zehrgeld.

Kost-frau, *f.* mistress of a boarding-house. —**frei**, *adj.* and *adv.* enjoying free board, that is, without expense. Er ist —frei, muß sich aber die Kleider selbst anschaffen, he pays nothing for his board, but must find himself in clothes; Einen —frei halten, to defray any one's expenses. —**gänger**, *m.*, —**gängerinn**, *f.* boarder. —gänger, —gängerinnen halten, to keep a boarding-house. —**geld**, *n* money paid for board. Er bezahlt wöchentlich zwei Thaler —geld, he pays two dollars a week for board, or he boards for two dollars a week; seinen Bedienten —geld geben, to give one's servants board-wages. —**halter**, *m.*, —**hälterinn**, *f.* a person who keeps a boarding-house. —**haus**, *n.* boarding-house. —**herr**, *m.* master of a boarding-house. —**jungfer**, *f.* a young woman boarding at any place, boarder. —**kraut**, *n.* 1) the wall hawk-weed. 2) the hawk-weed picris or yellow succory. 3) spear-mint. —**schule**, *f.* boarding-school. —**schüler**, *m.*, —**schülerinn**, *f.* boarder. —**verächter**, *m.*, —**verächterinn**, *f.* [in fam. lang.] a nice, squeamish or dainty person. Er ist kein —verächter, he is not nice in his diet, also †*fig.* in his fleshly desires. —**verständig**, *adj.* and *adv.* able to appreciate or to dress nice or dainty victuals. —**wurzel**, *f.* bear's wort.

Kóstbar, *adj.* and *adv.* 1) [= kostspielig] expensive, costly. Das Bauen ist —, building is expensive; in Paris ist es — zu leben, it is dear or expensive living at Paris. 2) valuable, precious. —e Steine, precious stones; Einen — bewirthen, to entertain any one splendidly or sumptuously; —e Möbeln, costly furniture; das schmeckt — [in popular lang.], that has an excellent or delicious taste or flavour, that is delicious. Syn. Kostbar, Köstlich, Kostspielig. Köstlich is used with reference to the intrinsic value of a thing, kostbar in so far as this value is expressed by a high price. Dishes which gratify the palate in a high degree are köstlich; they are also frequently kostbar. The difference between kostbar and kostspielig is, that the former implies Kosten, or expense, in general, the latter much and frequent expense. A building can be both kostbar and kostspielig; a lawsuit only kostspielig.

Kóstbarkeit, *f.* 1) preciousness. 2) a precious or valuable thing. —en, trinkets, jewels.

1. **Kósten**, *v. intr.* [Sw. *kosta*, Ital. *costare*, Fr. *coûter*, Bohem. *kostowati*. Pol. *kosztuje*, from the L. *constare*] to cost. Dieses Pferd hat ihn [or ihm] 100 Gulden gekostet, that horse cost him a hundred florins; der Rock kostet ihn [or ihm] zwanzig Thaler, the coat stands him in, costs him 20 dollars; ich muß es haben, es mag —, was es will, I must have it, if it cost ever so much; das Bauen kostet viel, building is very expensive or runs away with a deal of money; wie viel kostet Sie dieser Garten? how much have you paid for this garden? *Fig.* Es kostet viel Mühe &c., it costs or requires great pains; er ließ es sich viel [Geld] —, diese Stelle zu erhalten, he spent a great deal of money to obtain that place; das wird Sie das Leben, den Kopf —, that will cost you your life, your head und wenn es mich das Leben, den Kopf — sollte, were I to lose my life, my head for it; der —de Preis, prime cost, the price that a thing stands any one in. Syn. Kosten, Gelten. Gelten indicates the price with reference to the worth of the object; kosten with regard to the sum given for it. The price a seller affixes to, and demands for any object, is what the object is worth [gilt]; what the purchaser pays for it, is what it kostet.

2. **Kósten**, *v. tr.* [Goth. *kausjan*, Sax. *kostan*, L. *gustare*, from kiesen, imperf. kos, = to choose] to taste. — Sie diesen Wein, taste or try this wine. *Fig.* to feel, to experience. Ein Kind die Ruthe — lassen, to give a child the rod. Syn. Kosten, Schmecken. Kosten is to bring any thing into contact with the organs of taste to know the impression it makes on them. Schmecken is to experience and pronounce an opinion upon this impression. We need only take a small portion of any whole into the mouth to know how it tastes [schmeckt]. We therefore kosten something, or of something, when we take any small quantity into the mouth with this intention.

Kósten, *pl.* [V. 1. Kosten] expense, expenses, charges. Unnütze —, idle expenses; die — eines Krieges, the expenses of a war; sich — machen, sich in — setzen, to put one's self to great expense; auf meine —, at my expense; die — eines Processes, the costs of a lawsuit. *Fig.* Auf — seiner Ehre, at the expense of his honour; sie haben sich auf Ihre — lustig gemacht, they have laughed at you or at your expense. Syn. Kosten, Unkosten. Kosten implies merely the money expended for any object; Unkosten the expenses [Kosten] in so far as they are regarded as a loss or injury. He who loses a lawsuit calls what it has cost him Unkosten; the judge divides the Kosten between the parties concerned.

Kosten-anschlag, *m.* computation or estimation of the expenses. —**aufwand**, *m.* expense. —**ausgleichung**, *f.* compensation or balance of expenses. —**berechnung**, *f.* calculation or computation of the expenses. —**ersatz**, *m.* compensation of expenses. —**frei**, *adj.* and *adv.* free of expense. Einen —frei halten, to pay for any one. —**scheu**, I. *adj.* and *adv.* afraid of the expenses. II. *f.* the fear or dread of the expenses [of a thing]. —**verzeichniß**, *n.* a list or register of expenses.

Kóster, *m.* [-s, *pl.*-] taster, V. Vor—.

Kóstlich, *adj.* and *adv.* precious, exquisite, excellent; charming, delightful, delicious, delicate, dainty. —e Weine, delicious wines; — leben, trinken, to live, to drink delicately or daintily; —es Wetter [in familiar language], excellent, charming weather; ein —er Mensch [in familiar language], an excellent man, *it.* [ironically] a queer, odd chap, *it.* a ridiculous person. Syn. V. Kostbar.

Kóstlichkeit, *f.* 1) deliciousness, daintiness. 2) something dainty or delicious, delicacy.

Kóstnitz, [old, for Konstanz] *n.* [a town in the grand-duchy of Baden] Constance; as an *adj.*: Der —er [now, Konstanzer or Bodenr] See, the lake of Constance; die —er Kirchenversammlung, the great Council of Constance [in the XIVth century].

Kóstspielig, *adj.* and *adv.* expensive, costly. [Die] Reisen sind or [das] Reisen ist —, travelling is expensive. Syn. V. Kostbar.

Kóstspieligkeit, *f.* expensiveness, costliness.

Kōter, *m.* [-s, *pl.* -] [for Köthe-hund, V. 2. Koth] common farm-dog, cur.

1. **Kōth**, *m.* [-es] [Sax. *cwead*, D. *quad*, seems to be allied to the Gr. *χέω*, perf. *κέχοδα*, and to the Germ. Schutt, schütten, gießen, [illegible]] 1) mud, dirt, mire. In den — fallen, to fall in the mud; der Karren steckt im —e, the cart is mired; die [Land-] Straßen sind lauter —, the [high-] roads are nothing but mud; die Straßen [illegible] voller —, it is very dirty in the streets; [illegible] ihr Kleid mit — besudelt, she has dirtied her gown; bis über die Ohren mit — bespritzt [illegible], to be dirty all over. †*Fig.* Einen aus dem —e ziehen, to raise any one from the dung-hill. 2) excrement. Menschen—, excrement; der — der Thiere, dung of animals. *Prov.* Je mehr man den — rührt, desto mehr stinkt er, the more you stir, the more it will stink; wer — [illegible]

rühret or angreift, besudelt sich, touch pitch and you will be defiled.

Koth-abzucht, *f.* [*Kloak] sewer, sink, drain. —**baum**, *m.* the stinking bean trefoil. —**blech**, *n.* an iron plate covering the nave of a wheel and keeping the dirt off. —**bürste**, *f.* rubbing-brush. —**deckel**, *m.* V. —blech. —**fliege**, *f.* dung-beetle. —**führer**, *m.* V. —karrner. —**grube**, *f.* dung-pit; *it.* common sewer. —**hahn**, *m.* hoopoe or hoopoo. —**käfer**, *m.* V. Dreckkäfer. —**kärrner**, *m.* dustman. —**klumpen**, *m.* clot or lump of dirt. —**lache**, *f.* puddle; *it.* V. Mistlache. —**leitung**, *f.* V —abzucht. —**lerche**, *f.* V. Feldlerche, Haubenlerche, —mönch. —**meise**, *f.* the marsh or fen titmouse. —**meister**, *m.* V. 2. Koth. —**monat**, *m.* [*Februar] february. —**mönch**, *m.* crested lark. —**muschel**, *f.* the pool spoonshell. —**schaufel**, *f.* dirt- or mud-shovel. —**schieber**, *m.* V. Pfefferschwamm. —**schlinge**, *f.* V. Kaudelwiede. —**schlund**, *m.* V. —abzucht. —**seele**, *f.* [low] a dirty, base, pitiful, sneaking soul, mind or fellow. ||—**spritzer**, *m.* dirt splashed on any thing, splash. Ihr Mantel ist voll —spritzer, your cloak is bespattered with dirt. —**vogel**, *m.* V. —lerche. —**werk**, *n.* dirty work.

2. ||**Köth**, *n.* [-es, *pl.* -e] or **Köthe**, *f.* [*pl.*-n] [allied to Hütte, Haus, Gaden, L. *casa*; Pol. *cheta* = Schilderhaus] 1) a mean cottage or cot; [chiefly] a small house or hut where salt is made, V. Salz—. 2) a small farm.

Koth-hof, *m.* a small farm. —**hund**, *m.* V. Köter. —**knecht**, *m.* salt-boiler, V. Siedknecht, Salzsieder. —**leute**, *pl.* people engaged in a salt-work. —**meister**, *m.* the master of a salt-work, V. Siedmeister. —**pfanne**, *f.* V. Salzpfanne. —**saß**, *m.* cottager.

1. **Köthe**, V. 2 Koth.

2. **Köthe**, *f.* [*pl.*-n] [allied to Kante] 1) fetlock-joint, pastern-joint. Ein Pferd, das über die —n geschossen ist, a horse whose fetlock is crowned or swelled. 2) box, case, press.

Köthen-bein, *n.* bone of the fetlock. —**zopf**, *m.* the hair of the fetlock [of a horse].

Köthener, Köthner, *m.* [-s, *pl.* -] —**inn**, *f.* cottager, possessor of a small farm.

Köthenergut, *n.* a small farm.

Köther, *m.* [-s, *pl.* -] 1) V. Köthener. 2) V. Köter.

Kötherei, Köthnerei, *f.* a small farm.

Köthhaar, *n.* [-es, *pl.* -e] V. Köthenzopf.

Köthig, *adj.* and *adv.* dirty, muddy, miry. Ein —er Weg, eine —e Straße, a dirty way, road or street; es ist draußen sehr —, it is very dirty in the streets; — machen, to dirty.

Köthner, V. Köthener.

Köthnerei, V. Kötherei.

***Kothúrn**, *m.* [-es, *pl.* -e] buskin.

Kötscher, *m.* V. Ketscher.

1. ||**Kötze**, *f.* [*pl.* -n] or **Kötzen**, *m.* [-s, *pl.*-] [seems to be allied to Haut, Bohem. *kilze*, Wendish *koza*, and to Kutte &c.] coarse cloth, cover; *it.* thick great-coat. †*Fig.* Jemanden den —n streichen, to flatter any one meanly, to fawn upon any one.

Kotzen-sohn, *m.* bastard. —**streicher**, *m.* a mean flatterer, fawner.

2. ||**Kötze**, *f.* [*pl.* -n] [seems to be allied to the old Kot, to Kaute, 2. Koth] basket.

Kotzenträger, *m.* he who carries a basket or dosser upon the back.

|| and †**Kötzeln**, *v. tr.* Einen, to banter or jeer, to smoke any one.

Kötzen, V. 1. Kotze.

†**Kötzen**, *v. intr.* [perhaps allied to gießen, schütten, V. 1. Koth] to vomit.

†**Kötzer**, *m.* [-s, *pl.* -] —**inn**, *f.* a person who vomits; *it.* a person who coughs continually.

†**Kötzerlich**, *adj.* and *adv.* inclined to vomit, sick. Es ist mir —, I feel or am sick.

†**Kötzern**, *v. impers.* Es kotzert mich, I feel or am sick, V. Kotzerlich.

***Koupholíth**, *m.* [-en] [in mineralogy] koupholite.

Kraak, *m.* [-es, *pl.* -e] or **Kraake**, *f.* [*pl.*-n] [Fr. *caraque*] [a large ship of burden] carac.

Krábbe, *f.* [*pl.* -n] [another form of Krebs] crab, shrimp. *Fig.* [in popular lang.] *a*) a little child. Sehen Sie die kleine —? do you see the little monkey or shrimp? *b*) a little man, a dwarf, a shrimp.

Krabben-fresser, *m.* 1) the blue heron or bittern. 2) V. Kernbeißer 1). —**klaue**, *f.* [in botany] the water-aloe or freshwater-soldier. —**spinne**, *f.* the crab-spider.

1. **Krábbeln**, *v. intr.* [allied to the L. *repo*, Fr. *grimper*] to move on hands and feet, to crawl, to sprawl. In die Höhe —, to crawl up, to scramble up; ein Kind, das noch nicht — kann, a child that cannot crawl.

2. **Krábbeln**, *v. tr.* [another form of krauen = kratzen] to scratch gently, to feel, to grope; *it.* *v. impers.* Es krabbelt mich am Kopfe, my head itches, V. Krauen.

Krábber, *pl.* des Bootes, V. Bootskrabber.

||**Kräbe**, *f.* [*pl.*-n] basket, V. Korb.

Krách, *m.* [-es, *pl.* -e] [in popular language, burst of sound, loud report &c.] cracking noise, crack, crash. Ich hörte einen —, I heard a crack, or cracking noise; es that einen —, it cracked.

Krach-baum, *m.* the name of an exotic tree. —**büchse**, *f.* V. Knallbüchse. †—**dürr**, V. Klapperdürr. —**ente**, —**gans**, *f.* tadorna, vulpanser, sheldrake or borough-duck ||—**mandel**, *f.* a sweet almond with a tender shell, cracking-almond. —**schnepfe**, *f.* the lesser godwit, stone-plover. —**weide**, *f.* crack-willow.

Kráchen, I. *v. intr.* [Fr. *craquer*; allied to the Gr. *κρέκειν, κρίζειν*, to krähen, krächzen &c.] to crack, to crash. Ich hörte es —, I heard it crack; das Bett kracht, the bed cracks; wir hörten den Mast —, we heard the mast strain; mit den Fingern —, to snap one's fingers; ein Feuer, Holz, das kracht, fire, wood that crackles; der —de Donner, the burst of thunder; das Geschütz fängt an zu —, the artillery begins to thunder; hört Ihr die Kanonen —? do you hear the report of the cannon? II. *v. tr.* to break with a noise, to crack [nuts, filberts &c.].

Krácher, *m.* [-s, *pl.*-] [low] 1) one who cracks 2) V. Krach.

Krächzen, [L. *crocio*, Gr. *κρώζειν*, V. Krachen] I. *v. intr.* 1) to croak, to caw [as a raven or crow]. Eine —de Stimme, a croaking voice; er singt nicht, er krächzt, he does not sing, he croaks. *it.* to groan. Er krächzt unaufhörlich [in popular lang.], he is continually groaning. **Fig.* Ein —der Rabe, an ill-omened person, *it.* a person bringing ill news. 2) to cough and spit. II. *v. tr.* to say or sing any thing with a croaking voice.

Krächzer, *m.* [-s, *pl.*-] 1) one who croaks like a raven. †2) a croaking sound.

Kráck, I. *adv.* crack. Es macht krick —, it makes a cracking or creaking noise. II. *m.* [-es, *pl.* -e] V. Krach. ||3) raven, crow. ||4) cleft, cavern.

Krackbeere, *f.* crack-berry.

Krácke, *f.* [*pl.*-n] [probably allied to kriechen] 1) [low] a bad horse, a jade. 2) [low] an unruly, stubborn, untractable child, a young imp. 3) the tufted vetch.

Krackeel, Krackeelen, V. Krakeel &c.

||**Kräckig**, *adj.* and *adv.* full of caverns, cavernous.

Kráft, *f.* [*pl.* Kräfte] [seems to be allied to greifen; Sax. *crafian* = verlangen] strength, force, power. Thierische —, animal force or strength; anziehende, ausdehnende —, attractive, expansive force; bewegende —, moving power; anstrebende —, centripetal force; abstrebende —, centrifugal force; die Kräfte der Seele, the powers or faculties of the soul or mind; die — der Jugend, the vigour of youth; er ist in seiner vollen —, he is in his full vigour; dieser alte Mann hat noch Kräfte, that old man has still some vigour; neue Kräfte bekommen, to gather new strength, to recover one's strength; aus allen Kräften schreien, rudern &c., to cry as loud as one can, to row with might and main; das übersteigt, geht über meine Kräfte, that is above or beyond my strength; die Kräfte dieses Staates sind erschöpft, the resources of that state are exhausted; dieser Wein hat keine —, this wine has no strength, is flat; eine Brühe, die keine — hat, an unsavoury or insipid sauce; diese Speisen geben —, Kräfte, these victuals are very nourishing, nutritious or strengthening; die — einer Arzenei, the virtue of a medicine; die Kräfte der Pflanzen, the virtues of plants; die — des Magnetes, die magnetische —, the magnetic power. *Fig.* Die beste — eines Dinges, der Saft und die — eines Dinges, the quintessence of a thing, matter or substance; er sprach mit vieler —, he spoke with great force, vigour or energy; die — der Wahrheit, the force or power of truth; die — des Kolorits [in painting], the strength of colouring; der innern — nach [*intensiv], intensively; ein Urtheil in — setzen, to execute a sentence; — meines Amtes, by virtue of my office; — des Vertrages, as has been stipulated; [in] — meines Versprechens, in virtue of my promise. Syn. Kraft, Vermögen, Stärke. Kraft actually produces the effect; Vermögen is capable of producing it. Kraft is active and operative; Vermögen can become so. Stärke is a determinate, and more especially, a higher degree of Kraft. Stark is the opposite to schwach or weak; Stärke to Schwachheit. A child, even, has a certain Kraft, otherwise it could do nothing; but it has as yet no Stärke.

Kraft-anstrengung, *f.* effort. Eine letzte —anstrengung machen, to make a last effort —**arzenei**, *f.* a corroborative medicine, a corroborant, a corroborative; *it.* a powerful or efficacious medicine. —**aufwand**, *m.* employment or exertion of force or strength. Das erfordert einen großen —aufwand, that requires great efforts or vigour. —**ausdruck**, *m.* 1) indication, sign or expression of force or strength. 2) energetical, nervous, pithy term or expression. —**äußerung**, *f.* manifestation of strength or vigour. Dieß waren seine letzten —äußerungen, these were the last efforts of his energy. —**balsam**, *m.* strengthening or corroborative balm. —**brühe**, *f.* strong broth, jelly-broth. Eine durchgeseihte —brühe, cullis. —**essig**, *m.* cordial vinegar. —**farn**, *m.* the rough spleen-wort. —**fülle**, *f.* fulness of power, strength, energy, vigour. Sich mit —fülle ausdrücken, to express one's self with great force or energy; seine jugendliche —fülle, his juvenile vigour. —**gefühl**, *n.* consciousness of one's strength or vigour. —geist, *m.* 1) a mind endowed with great powers, a powerful or energetical mind. 2) a man endowed with uncommon vigour of mind, genius. —genie, *n.* V. —geist 2). *it.* [often used in a bad sense or in jest for] an over-exuberant, or an unpolished genius. —gesang, *m.* an energetical, powerful song. —kopf, *m.* V. —genie 2). —lehre, *f.* [*Dynamik] dynamics. —los, *adj.* and *adv.* 1) wanting strength, strengthless, powerless, weak, feeble. Ein —loser Mensch, a weak or feeble man, *fig.* a man without energy; —loses Mittel, ineffectual or inefficacious remedy; —lose Rede, Schreibart, a poor or weak speech, a speech without strength or energy, a poor, flagging, languid style; Einen —los machen, to weaken, enfeeble, enervate any one. 2) invalid, void, null. Ein —loser Vertrag, an invalid contract; —los machen, to invalidate, to annul. SYN. Kraftlos, Unkräftig, Schwach. A thing is unkräftig when it fails to produce an effect, whatever may be the cause of the inefficiency; kraftlos and schwach, when the cause is want of force [Kraft]. Kraftlos and schwach are used as well with reference to living as to inanimate objects; unkräftig is said only of the latter. A thing may be unkräftig for any one, and yet not be kraftlos. The kraftvollste speech will be kraftlos for one who does not attentively listen to it. The opposite to schwach is stark, as having a higher degree of force. The Schwache has no great degree of strength, but the Kraftlose has none at all. Any whole is called schwach from the fewness of its parts, and stark from their multiplicity. The whole may, therefore, be schwach though each single part is stark. An army when composed of but few men is schwach; kraftlos when exhausted by long marches and fatigue. —losigkeit, *f.* 1) feebleness, weakness, debility, languor. Eine tödtliche —losigkeit fühlen, to feel a deadly languor. *Fig.* want of energy, weakness. 2) invalidity. —mann, *m.* 1) a man of great energy. 2) and *dim.* —männchen, ||—männlein, *n.* V. [in contempt or jest] —genie. —mehl, *n.* the finest and best wheaten flour, starch-meal, starch-flour. —mensch, *m.* V. —mann and —geist 2). —milch, *f.* a strengthening beverage in the shape of milk. —mittel, *n.* 1) a strengthening medicine or drug, cordial. 2) an energetic means, a sweeping measure. —nuß, *f.*, ||—nüßlein, *n.* pistachio. —reich, *adj.* and *adv.* possessing great force or energy, energetical, vigorous. —saft, *m.* [*Extrakt] extract, essence. —sprache, *f.* 1) a strong, powerful or energetical tone or language. 2) a strong, forcible or energetical style or language. —stein, *m.* V. Kragstein. —stoß, *m.* a strong, vigorous thrust or push. —suppe, *f.*, *dim.* —süppchen, ||—süpplein, *n.* strong soup, bisk, cullis, V. —brühe. —tropfen, *pl.* essence, essential drops. —voll, *adj.* and *adv.* full of strength or force, powerful, strong, vigorous. Er hat einen —vollen Körper, he has a vigorous body; eine —volle Schreibart, a nervous, vigorous, pithy, energetical style; er drückt sich —voll aus, he expresses himself with force or energy. —wasser, *n.* a strengthening potion, cordial. —wort, *n.* a powerful, forcible, energetical word. —wurz, —wurzel, *f.* 1) ginseng. 2) leopard's bane. 3) butter-bur. 4) the dwarf viper's grass.

Kräftemesser, *m.* [an instrument for measuring the relative strength of men and animals] dynameter.

Kräftig, *adj.* and *adv.* 1) strong, powerful, vigorous, energetical. Ein —er Jüngling, a strong, vigorous youth; eine —e Stimme, a strong, powerful voice; —e Gesundheit, robust health; ein —er Ausdruck, eine —e Schreibart, an energetical, nervous, pithy expression, a nervous, pithy style. 2) imparting strength, strengthening, nourishing. —es Arzeneimittel, —e Brühe, V. Kraftarzenei, Kraftbrühe; —e Speise, nutritive food. 3) valid. Der Vertrag ist nicht —, the contract is not valid.

Kräftigen, *v. tr.* to strengthen, to confirm; V. Bekräftigen.

Kräftigkeit, *f.* efficaciousnous, vigour, energy, strength, virtue [of a remedy &c.].

Kragen, *m.* [-s, *pl.* -] [allied to ragen, hence] 1) [in general] any thing prominent or projecting. Der — einer Laute, einer Flasche &c., the neck of a lute, of a bottle &c., V. Hals 3); [in medicine] spanischer —, paraphimosis; [in seamen's lang.] der — eines Stags, the collar of a stay; die — der Masten, the coats of the masts. 2) the collar [of a coat &c.]. Der — am Hembe, shirt-collar; der — am Mantel, cape; der — am Harnische, gorget; der — eines Geistlichen, the band of a clergyman; Einen beim — fassen, to take or seize any one by the collar, to collar any one. 3) neck, throat. †Sein Vermögen durch den — jagen, to spend, waste or squander away one's fortune; †es wird ihm den — kosten, it will cost his life, he will pay for it with his life, his head or life is at stake, V. Hals.

Kragen-blume, *f.* nodding starwort. —ente, *f.* the harlequin duck, the stone-duck, the dusky and spotted duck. —huhn, *n.* the little heathcock of America. —stein, *m.* V. Krösestein 2).

Kragstein, *m.* [-es, *pl.* -e] [Krag from kragen = ragen] [in architecture] a projecting stone in the wall of a building, corbel, console, bracket, zocco, zocle.

Krähe, *f.* [*pl.* -n] [from krähen, which see] crow [especially the hooded crow or Royston crow]; V. Nebel—, Saat—. *Prov.* Es hackt keine — der andern die Augen aus, ask my fellow whether I be a thief.

Krähen-auge, *n.* 1) crow's eye. *Fig.* [a poisonous seed] nux vomica, the vomic nut, poison-nut. 2) V. Hühneraugе. —augenbaum, *m.* strychnos nux vomica. —beere, *f.* 1) crow-crake-berry. 2) whortle-berry. —dohle, *f.* V. Steindohle. —feder, *f.* a crow's feather; *it.* crow-quill [for writing]. —fuß, *m.* 1) crow's foot. *Fig.* —füße, pot-hooks, scrawled letters. —füße machen, to scrawl. 2) [in botany] *a*) buckshorn-plantain, the star of the earth, bloody crane's bill. *b*) bulbous crow-foot, creeping crow-foot. *c*) V. Schweinskresse. *d*) the slender-spiked cock's-foot panic-grass. *e*) the common clubmoss. —hütte, *f.* a hut or cottage for shooting crows. —klaue, *f.* crow's claw; [in botany] 1) V. —fuß 2) *e*). 2) the common bird's-foot trefoil. —korn, *n.* V. Mutterkorn. —roggen, *m.* V. Mutterkorn. —specht, *m.* the great black woodpecker. —zehe, *f.* water-plaintain.

Krähen, I. *v. intr.* [allied to the Gr. κρώζω, κέκραγα, Fr. *crier*, schreien] to crow. Darnach wird kein Hahn — [in popular lang.], there will not be the least enquiry made about it, nobody will care a straw for it. *it.* to croak; *it.* to laugh aloud. II. *v. tr.* to announce or proclaim crowing.

Kräher, *m.* [-s, *pl.* -] one who crows. **Fig.* a bawling or noisy man, a bawler.

Krahn, *m.* [-es, *pl.* -e] [either allied to Kranich or to Kragen] crane [machine for raising weights]. Vermittelst eines —es Waaren in die Höhe ziehen, to draw up goods with a crane; [in seamen's lang.] den Anker vor den — winden, to cat the anchor.

Krahn-balken, *m.* 1) horizontal beam or arm to a crane, peg-ladder. 2) [in seamen's lang.] cat-head. —balkenträger, *m.* supporter of the cat-head. —baum, *m.* V. —ständer. —gefälle, *pl.* the money paid for the use of a crane, cranage. —gehäuse, *n.* the frame of a crane. ‡—gerechtigkeit, *f.* V. —recht. —leiter, *f.* V. —balken 1). —meister, *m.* an officer who has the care of a crane; *it.* the proprietor of a crane. —rad, *n.* the wheel or cog-wheel of a crane. —recht, *n.* 1) right or privilege of keeping a crane, cranage. 2) the right of the sovereign of obliging vessels to unload their goods at a certain place and to pay duty for them, staple-right. —säge, *f.* pit-saw. —schreiber, *m.* the clerk of a crane [who keeps the accounts of the goods exported and imported]. —seil, *n.* rope of a crane. —ständer, *m.* upright post of the crane.

||Krähnen, [-s, *pl.* -] V. Krahn.

Krakau, *n.* [-'s] [Polish town and republic] Cracow.

Krakauer, *m.* [-s, *pl.* -], —inn, *f.* a native or inhabitant of Cracow, Cracovian.

Krakauer, Krakauisch, *adj.* and *adv.* Cracovian.

Krakeel, *m.* [-es, *pl.* -e] [allied to krähen, krächzen, Gr. κρώζω, κέκραγα] violent noise or quarrel, a great racket, uproar or row.

Krakeelen, *v. intr.* to make a great noise, to engage in a violent quarrel, to kick up a row.

Krakeeler, *m.* [-s, *pl.* -], —inn, *f.* a noisy and contentious person, a quarreller, a bawler.

Kraken, *m.* [-s, *pl.* -] a supposed enormous sea-animal, kraken.

Krakuse, *m.* [-n, *pl.* -n] a native of the [old Polish] province or district of Cracow, Cracusian.

Krakusisch, *adj.* and *adv.* in the manner of, or referring to, a Cracusian.

Krall, *m.* [-es, *pl.* -e] stroke with a claw.

Kralle, *f.* [*pl.* -n], *dim.* Krällchen, *n.* [from krauen = kratzen] claw. Die —n einer Katze, eines Vogels, the claws of a cat, of a bird. [in popular lang. =] hand. Er ist aus seinen —n entwischt, he has got out of his clutches; ich bin unter seinen —n, I am under his paw. V. Klaue 2) *fig.*

Krallenhieb, *m.* stroke with a claw.

Krallen, Krällen, I. *v. tr.* and *intr.* to scratch, pull or tear with the claws, to claw. II. *v. r.* sich —, to take hold with, to hold on by the claws.

Krallicht, *adj.* and *adv.* resembling a claw or claws.

Krallig, *adj.* and *adv.* furnished with claws.

Kram, *m.* [-es], *dim.* Krämchen, ||Krämlein, *n.* [-s, *pl.* -] [V. Kramen] 1) retail-trade. Einen — anfangen, to set up a [small] shop. V. Eisen—, Gewürz—, Käse—. 2) goods to be retailed, goods to be sold, commodities, haberdashery. Seinen — verkaufen, to sell off, to leave off business; seinen — auspacken, to unpack, to lay out one's goods; er trägt seinen — auf dem Rücken, he carries his commodities or his pack on his back. *Fig.* [in popular lang.] Das taugt nicht in meinen —, that won't do for me, does not suit me; das [illegible] in meinen —, that suits me, will do for me; that suits my purpose or turn; der [illegible] — ist nicht einen Heller werth, all those [illegible] are not worth a pin or rush; das verdirbt mir den ganzen —, that frustrates or disconcerts all my plans or schemes. 3) [more usual [illegible] or Kramladen] shop. Einen — aufschlagen, to put up a booth or stall.

Kramsbude, *f.* retail-shop; *it.* booth, stall. —diener, *m.* shop-keeper's assistant, shopman. —fenster, *n.* sky-light. —handwerk, *n.* V. Krämerhandwerk. ||—knecht, *m.* packer. —kümmel, *m.* V. Krämerkümmel. —laden, *m.* retail-shop, V. —bude. —waare, *f.* article of goods for retail, retail-commodity.

Krambámbuli, *m.* [-'s] a drink composed of brandy and sugar burnt.

Krämen, [Sax. *kryman* = to put here and there in making a noise] *v. intr.* 1) to move, to stir, to rummage. Er kramt bei seinen Büchern, unter seinen schriftlichen Sachen, he rummages his library, among his papers; was hast du da zu —? what are you about there, what business have you there? 2) [not much used] to carry on a retail-trade, to keep a [small] shop.

Krämer, *m.* [-s, *pl.* -], —inn, *f.* 1) *a*) [formerly, and still used in this sense in some parts of Germany] a merchant. *b*) retail-dealer, shopkeeper, haberdasher. V. Eisen—, Gewürz—, Käse—. Ein wandernder —, a pedlar. SYN. V. Kaufmann. 2) V. Stritze 2).

Krämer-bude, *f.* V. Krambude. —geist, *m.* [especially in contempt] a [mean] mercantile or grasping spirit. —gewicht, *n.* avoir-du-pois weight. —gilde, *f.* V. —innung. —handthierung, *f.*, —handwerk, *n.* retail-dealer's or shopkeeper's trade or business; *it.* a trade where a shop is kept. —haus, *n.* a house containing shops. —innung, *f.* corporation of merchants, merchants' guild; *it.* corporation of shopkeepers. —kümmel, *m.* 1) the small fennel-flower. 2) caraway. —land, *n.* [*fig.*, in contempt] a country of shopkeepers. —pfund, *n.* a pound avoir-du-pois. —seele, *f.* a mercenary, venal soul; *it.* V. —geist. —tand, *m.* baubles, toys. —volk, *n.* [*fig.*, in contempt] a nation of shopkeepers. —waare, *f.* a shopkeeper's or haberdasher's commodities, [especially] pedlar's ware. —wage, *f.* common scales. —zunft, *f.* V. —innung.

Kramerei, *f.* [in fam. language] rummaging, confusion, disorder.

Krämerei, *f.* retail-trade, shop-keeping. — treiben, to sell by retail, to carry on a retail-trade, to keep a shop.

Krámme, *f.* V. Krampe.

||**Krámmen**, *v. intr.* [allied to Krampe] to scratch with the claws.

Krámmetsbaum, *m.* [-es, *pl.* -bäume] juniper-tree.

Krámmetsbeere, *f.* [*pl.* -n] the juniper-berry.

Krámmetsdrossel, *f.* [*pl.* -n], **Krámmetsvogel**, *m.* [-s, *pl.* -vögel] field-fare.

Krámpe, *f.* [*pl.* -n] [allied to the Sw. *krympa* = zusammenziehen, to rümpfen, krumm] 1) cramp, cramp-iron. Die — an einem Buche, clasp of a book. 2) [among locksmiths] staple.

Krämpe, *f.* [*pl.* -n] [allied to krumm, V. Krampe] something which projects and may be turned up or down, flap or turning up of a hat. Die — seines Hutes aufschlagen, to turn up, to cock one's hat.

Krämpenschnur, *f.* the string of a hat.

Krämpel, *f.* [*pl.* -n] [probably allied to krumm, Fr. *crampon*, V. Krampe] carding-instrument, card, carding-comb.

Krämpel-bank, *f.* carding-bench. —blatt, *n.* leather-cover for cards. —kamm, *m.* carding-comb. —macher, *m.* one who makes cards [for carding wool]. —rasch, *m.* rash of carded wool. —rasche, *f.* serge of carded wool. —stück, *n.* piece of rash of carded wool.

Krämpeler, **Krämpler**, *m.* [-s, *pl.* -] one who cards wool, carder.

Krämpeln, *v. tr.* and *intr.* to pick, to comb wool, to card.

Krämpen, *v. tr.* 1) to bend, to turn up [a hat]. V. Auf—, Nieder—. 2) V. Krimpen.

Krámpf, *m.* [-es, *pl.* Krämpfe] [allied to Krampe] cramp, spasm. Er bekam im Schwimmen den —, he was seized with a cramp in swimming. V. Verzuckung, Hunds—.

Krampf-ader, *f.* enlargement or dilatation of a vein, varix, varicous vein. —aderbruch, *m.* varicocele. —aderig, *adj.* varicose. —artig, *adj.* and *adv.* spasmodic. —arzenei, *f.* V. —mittel. —distel, *f.* spear-thistle. —fisch, *m.* cramp-fish. —husten, *m.* spasmodic or convulsive cough. —kraut, *n.* V. —wurzel. —lehre, *f.* spasmology. —mittel, *n.* anti-spasmodic. —ring, *m.* a ring made of an elk's hoof [used as an anti-spasmodic]. —roche, *m.* V. —fisch. —stillend, *adj.* [*antispasmatisch] anti-spasmodic. Ein —stillendes Mittel, anti-spasmodic. —sucht, *f.* V. Kriebelkrankheit. —wurzel, *f.* the meadow-sweet, the queen of the meadows.

Krámpfen, I. *v. r.* sich —, to be contracted by spasms, to be convulsed, to have convulsive motions. II. *v. tr.* to contract convulsively, to convulse; *it.* to pain or affect with spasms, to cramp.

Krámpfhaft, *adj.* and *adv.* spasmodic, convulsive. —es Lachen, convulsive laughter; *it.* convulsions of laughter; *it.* sardonic or sardonian laughter.

Krámpfig, **Krämpfig**, *adj.* and *adv.* affected with spasm, subject to spasms.

Krämpler, V. Krämpeler.

Krámsvogel, *m.* V. Krammetsdrossel.

||**Krān**, *m.* [-es] V. Meerrettig.

Kránbeere, *f.* V. Preiselbeere.

***Kraneolōg**, [or Kraneologist] *m.* [-en, *pl.* -en] craniologist.

***Kraneologie**, *f.* [*pl.* -en] craniology.

Kránfuß, *m.* [-es, *pl.* -füße] V. Korallenschwamm

Krángeln, *v. intr.* or *v. r.* sich —, to twist.

Kränich, *m.* [-es, *pl.* -e] [allied to krähen, schreien] 1) crane. Ein junger —, a young crane. 2) [in astronomy] crane, grus. 3) *Fig.* V. Krahn.

Kranich-beere, *f.* V. Preiselbeere. —falk, *m.* hawk trained to chase cranes, crane-hawk. —fasan, *m.* pheasant like a crane, crane-pheasant. —hals, *m.* 1) crane's neck. 2) [in botany] the geranium, crane's bill. —jagd, *f.* chase of cranes. —kraut, *n.* swine's succory, hyoseris. —schnabel, *m.* 1) crane's bill. 2) [in botany] crane's bill, geranium. 3) [in surgery] crane's bill.

Kránk, *adj.* and *adv.* [perhaps allied to the provincial rahn, Low Sax. rank = dünn, thin, slender; Eng. *crank* = Windung and fallende Sucht] distempered, diseased, out of health, sick, ill. Ein —er Fuß, a diseased foot; ein —er Körper, a distempered body; der —e Theil, the affected part; bedenklich, gefährlich — seyn, to be dangerously ill; — werden, to fall sick or ill; er ist or liegt — am Fieber, he is ill or sick of a fever; sie hat eine —e Farbe, she has a sickly complexion, her complexion is very bad, she does not look well, she looks ill or sickly; vor Liebe — seyn, to be love-sick or love-stricken; sich — lachen [*fig.* in familiar language], to split one's sides with laughing. *Fig.* Am Verstande, Gemüthe — seyn, to be distempered in one's head or intellects, in mind; er ist im Gemüthe —, he is distempered in mind, dejected, melancholy; im Beutel — seyn, einen —en Beutel haben [in popular lang., in jest], to have an empty purse, to be short of money, to want money. SYN. Krank, Siech, Ungesund, Unpaß, Krankhaft. Ungesund [bodily] signifies, in general, every defect in health, including the smallest perceptible degree, and such as is unattended with any considerable pain or debility. One whose humours are in a morbid state, and who is subject to eruptions, is ungesund without being on that account krank. Krank is said of one who suffers from some particular and determinate disorder. Siech indicates the absence of health in a higher degree, by which it is distinguished from ungesund; but it is said of such whose ailments are not among those enumerated by the nosologist, but which are characterized by their own peculiar marks, crises &c.; in this it is distinguished from krank. Unpaß, or unpäßlich, is said of one who, without being krank, is not altogether quite well. Kränklich implies the being subject to various attacks from which Krankheiten may easily arise. Krankhaft means such a condition as has some resemblance to a really kranken state. We do not say a krankhafter man, but a krankhafter pulse.

Kránke, [der, die, das] a sick person, patient. Seine —n besuchen, to visit one's patients, to go one's professional rounds [said of a general practitioner or physician]; es sind viele — in diesem Spitale, there are a great many sick persons or patients in this hospital; es bessert sich mit unserem —n, our patient is getting better; wir haben ein —s [einen —en, eine —e] im Hause, we have a patient in our house; die —n wurden geheilt, the sick were healed.

Kranken-bericht, *m.* 1) the report of a physician respecting a person's health, bulletin. 2) [little used] preparation of a sick person for death. —besuch, *m.* a visit one makes or pays to a patient. Der —besuch des Arztes, the visit of the physician. —bett, *n.* the bed of a patient or sick person, sickbed. *Fig.* Auf dem —bette liegen, to keep one's bed, to be bedrid or bedridden; vom —bette wieder aufstehen, to be just recovered from an illness. —gang, *m.* [little used] 1) the gait or walk of a patient. 2) passage or gallery for patients or sick persons. —geschichte, *f.* V. Krankheitsgeschichte. —gesicht, *n.* 1) the face of a patient. 2) a sickly look or mien. —haus, *n.* a house in which somebody is ill, [chiefly] an infirmary, hospital. —hof, *m.* V. —haus. —kost, *f.* food regulated by medical rules, diet, regimen. Einen auf —kost setzen, to diet any one. —lager, *n.* V. —bett. Nach einem halbjährigen —lager, after an illness of six months, after having been bedridden for six months. —pflege, *f.* the care taken of a sick person, the attending or nursing of a patient. —saal, *m.* V. —stube. —schiff, *n.* hospital ship. —speise, *f.* food or victuals for a patient. —spital, *n.* V. —haus. —stube, *f.* sick-room. —wärter, *m.*, —wärterinn, *f.* a person attending upon a patient, nurse. —zettel, *m.* V. —bericht. —zimmer, *n.* V. —stube.

||**Kränke**, *f.* V. Fallsucht. Krieg' du die —! [a very low curse among vulgar people] God rot thee!

Kränkelei, *f.* 1) sickliness, bad state of health. 2) [seldom used] little mortification or vexation.

Kränkeln, *v. intr.* to have or to be in indifferent health, to be sickly.

Kränken, *v. intr.* to be ill, sick or indisposed.

Kränken, I. *v. tr. Fig.* 1) to injure, to wrong. Eines Ehre, Eines guten Namen —, Einen an seiner Ehre, an seinem guten Namen —, to stain or tarnish any one's honour or reputation; eines Andern Rechte —, to encroach upon any one's rights; Sie — mich, you wrong me. 2) to grieve, vex, offend or mortify. Das kränkt ihn, that hurts him; dieser Verlust muß ihn —, that loss must afflict or grieve him; sie sagten ihm Dinge, die ihn kränkten, they told him things that mortified him; er kränkte ihn auf's Allerempfindlichste, he touched, wounded him to the quick. II. *v. r.* sich — über Etwas, to be afflicted at, to grieve at or for any thing; sich vergeblich —, to afflict or torment one's self in vain. Syn. Kränken, Schmerzen. When the evil we feel is a wrong suffered by another, it schmerzt, pains us; but when it is a wrong we ourselves suffer, it kränkt, grieves us. It must pain [schmerzen] every man of kind feelings to see the innocent slandered; the latter, however, it must kränken.

Kränkhaft, *adj.* and *adv.* sickly, indisposed, crazy, morbid. —e Säfte, morbid humours. Syn. V. Krank.

Krankheit, *f.* disease, distemper, illness, malady, sickness. Englische —, the rickets; eine langwierige —, a lingering, chronical disease; in eine — fallen, to fall sick or ill. *Fig.* Die Leidenschaften sind die —en des Geistes, the passions are the maladies of the soul; eine — des Gemüthes, V. Gemüths—.

Krankheits-entscheidung, *f.* V. —wechsel. —geschichte, *f.* history of an illness. —kenner, —lehrer, *m.* pathologist. —lehre, *f.* pathology. —lehrig, *adj.* and *adv.* pathologic. —stoff, *m.* morbid matter, materia peccans. —ursachenlehre, *f.* [*Aetiologie] etiology. —wechsel, *m.* the change of a disease which indicates its event, crisis. —zeichen, *n.* symptom. —zeichenlehre, *f.* symptomatology, pathognomy. —zufall, *m.* adventitious symptom.

Kränkler, *m.* [-s, *pl.* -], —inn, *f.* a sickly person, valetudinarian.

Kränklich, *adj.* and *adv.* sickly, weakly, crazy. Ein —er Mensch, a sickly man, a valetudinarian; — aussehen, to look sickly.

Kränklichkeit, *f.* state of being sickly, sickliness, craziness.

Kränkling, *m.* [-s, *pl.* -e] a sickly person, valetudinarian.

Kränkung, *f.* vexation, mortification, grief.

Kranz, *m.* [-es, *pl.* Kränze] *dim.* Kränzchen, ||Kränzlein, *n.* [-s, *pl.* -] [allied to Krone, Kreis, L. *corona*, rund, Rand] 1) [in general] something made in the form of a circle. Der — einer Säule, the cincture, list or fillet of a column; der — eines Kastens, the cornice of a chest or cupboard; der — um ein Geländer, the capital of a balluster; der — um den Rand des Wappens, the ring about a coat of arms; der — von Leder um einen Kutschenhimmel, the cornishes or cornices of a coach; der — einer Glocke, the prim, pinch or paunch of a bell; der — an einem Betthimmel, the valances of a bed. 2) a wreath of flowers, leaves &c., garland, crown. Ein — von Lorbern &c., a wreath or crown of laurels, V. Blumen—, Epheu—, Lorber—; der — einer Braut, the wreath or crown worn by virgins on their wedding-day, bridal wreath. *Fig.* [in popular lang.] Einer Jungfrau or einem Mädchen den — rauben, to deflour a virgin or girl; sie hat ihr Kränzchen verloren, ist um den — or ihr Kränzchen gekommen, she has forfeited or lost her honour or virginity. V. Braut—, Leichen—, Myrthen—, Rosen—, Sieges—, Strahlen—, Stroh—, Trauben— &c. 3) *Fig.* Der —, das Kränzchen, [a small number of persons who meet regularly on a certain day for social or literary purposes] circle, society, club, coterie. Unser Kränzchen hat sich aufgelöst, our society or club has been dissolved; gehen Sie in das Kränzchen? do you go to the club?

Kranz-ader, *f.* coronary vein. —band, *n.* der Leber, coronary ligament of the liver. —beere, *f.* 1) V. Krammetsbeere. 2) petesia. —bein, *n.* coronal bone, V. Stirnbein. —binder, *m.*, —binderinn, *f.* V. —flechter &c. —blume, *f.* 1) flower in a wreath or garland. 2) [in botany] *a*) grielum tenuifolium. *b*) the common milk-wort. —blutader, *f.* V. —ader. —dicke, *f.* einer Glocke, the thickness of the prim or paunch of a bell. —eisen, *n.* channeling or grooving iron. —flechter, *m.*, —flechterinn, *f.* a person who makes wreaths or crowns of flowers, who weaves flowers into a wreath or garland, garland-maker. —förmig, *adj.* and *adv.* having the form of a crown or garland, coroniform. [in anatomy] Der —förmige Fortsatz, the coronoid process or apophysis. —gefäße, *pl.* [in anatomy] coronary vessels. —händler, *m.*, —händlerinn, *f.* a person who sells wreaths of flowers. —leiste, *f.* [in architecture] tringle. —los, *adj.* and *adv.* without a wreath or garland, [chiefly] without a bridal wreath. —naht, *f.* coronal suture or seam. —schlagader, *f.* coronary artery. —schlagader des Magens, stomachic coronary. —winder, *m.*, —winderinn, *f.* V. —flechter &c.

Kränzeleisen, *n.* [-s, *pl.* -] engrailing iron.

Kränzeljungfer, *f.* 1) [rather unusual] the bride. 2) V. Brautjungfer.

Kränzen, *v. tr.* 1) V. Bekränzen. 2) [among foresters] Die Bäume —, to strip off the bark of trees, to bark trees.

Kräpeln, V. Krabbeln.

1. ||**Kräpf**, *m.* [-en, *pl.* -en] or **Kräpfen**, *m.* [-s, *pl.* -] *dim.* Kräpfchen, ||Kräpflein, *n.* [-s, *pl.* -] [allied to Kropf] a kind of pastry, fritter.

2. **Kräpf**, *m.* [-en, *pl.* -en] or **Kräpfen**, *m.* [-s, *pl.* -] [allied to greifen, raffen] a hoop, cramp-iron.

Kräpp, *m.* V. Grapp.

Kräppe, *f.* [*pl.* -n] [a part of a gun-lock upon which the trigger acts] tumbler.

1. **Kräspeln**, *v. intr.* V. Knarren.

2. ||**Kräspeln**, *v. intr.* [allied to Krebs, L. *repo*, kriechen] to creep, to crawl.

Krässelbeere, *f.* [*pl.* -n] V. Kratzbeere 2).

***Kräter**, *m.* [-s, *pl.* -] crater.

|| and †**Krätschen**, *v. intr.* [allied to schreiten, L. *gradior*] to spread one's legs.

||**Krätz**, *n.* [-es] pot-herbs, greens.

Krätzgarten, *m.* V. Küchengarten, Gemüsegarten.

Krätze, *f.* [*pl.* -n] [V. Kratzen] scraper; [among clothiers] a sort of carding-instrument, card.

1. **Krätze**, *f.* [*pl.* -n] [either from the Sw. Krossa = zermalmen, or from kratzen = schaben] waste ore or metal, sweepings, scrapings, clippings. †and ||*Fig.* In die — gehen, to be lost, to be ruined, to decay, to go to waste or decay.

Krätz-frischen, *n.* the melting of the scrapings or waste metal. —kupfer, *n.* the pure copper obtained by melting the waste copper. —messing, *m.* or *n.* the clippings or cuttings of brass, V. Schrotmessing. —schlich, *m.* slick of waste ore or metal. —wäscher, *m.* washer of the waste metal or ore. —wasser, *n.* the water in which the waste metal or ore has been washed.

2. **Krätze**, *f.* [from kratzen] itch, scab.

Krätz-artig, *adj.* resembling the itch or of the nature of the itch, scabious. —heil, *n.* the common fumitory or earth-smoke. —milbe, *f.* itch-mite, hand-worm. —salbe, *f.* salve against the itch.

3. **Krätze**, *f.* [*pl.* -n] [allied to the L. *crates*, Slavon. *hroda* = Hürde, *horda* = Zaun] basket, dosser.

Krätzen, *v. tr.* and *intr.* [Fr. *gratter*, L. *radere*] 1) to scratch, to scrape. Die Hühner — in der Erde, the fowls scrape the ground; Einen —, Einen mit den Nägeln —, to scratch any one with the nails; sich im Kopfe, am Kopfe, hinter den Ohren —, to scratch one's head, *fig.* [in popular language] to be in a dilemma, to be embarrassed; mit dem Fuße —, to scrape a leg; es kratzt mich, it itches. *Fig.* Dieser Wein kratzt [in popular lang.], this wine rakes the bowels, is very bad or sour. *Prov.* Wen es juckt, der kratze sich, if any fool finds the cap fit him, let him put it on. 2) Wolle —, to card wool; auf der Geige —, to scrape upon the violin; diese Geige kratzt, this violin jars; die Feder kratzt, the pen spurts, Etwas —, to scrawl, to scribble any thing.

Kratz-beere, *f.* 1) blackberry. 2) the dewberry. 3) gooseberry. 4) the fruit of the mountain-bramble. —beerstrauch, *m.* V. Brombeerstrauch. —blech, *n.* a brass plate with square holes for polishing buttons. —brett, *n.* friezing-table. —bürste, *f.* scratching- or scrubbing-brush. —distel, *f.* fuller's thistle, teasel —eisen, *n.* scratching- or scraping-iron, scratcher, scraper. —fuß, *m.* [in fam. lang.] an awkward reverence or bow, accompanied with a scrape, scrape. Einen —fuß machen, to make or scrape a leg. —füßler, *m.* a man full of bows or scrapes. —garn, *n.* oyster-drag. —hede, *f.* waste tow. —kamm, *m.* V. Krämpel. —kelle, *f.* scraper. —kraut, *n.* the curled thistle. —platte, *f.* V. —brett. —wolle, *f.* V. Flockwolle.

Krätzer, *m.* [-s, *pl.* -] he or that which scratches, scratcher, scraper, carder.

Krätzer, *m.* [-s, *pl.* -] 1) scratching- or scraping-instrument, scraper; [among gun-smiths] worm [to unload a gun], wad-hook. 2) [in popular lang.] bad wine, wine that rakes the bowels or is acrid to the palate.

||**Krätzerei**, *f.* V. Krätz.

Krätzerig, *adj.* and *adv.* [low] —er Wein, wine that rakes the bowels, very bad or acrid wine.

Krätzgarn, *n.* [-s, *pl.* -e] **Krätzhamen**, *m.* [-s, *pl.* -] [with fishermen] drag-net.

Krätzig, *adj.* and *adv.* [properly] that which scratches or scrapes. *Fig.* [low] cross, peevish, surly, morose.

Krätzig, *adj.* and *adv.* infected with the itch, itchy, mangy, scabby.

Kräuel, *m.* [-s, *pl.* -] [from krauen] fork with crooked prongs.

1. ||**Kraueln**, *v. intr.* [allied to 2. krabbeln] to crawl, to creep, to climb.

2. **Kraueln**, *v. tr.* [from krauen] to scratch gently.

Krauen, *v. tr.* to scratch gently; *it.* to tickle.

Kraus, *adj.* and *adv.* [provincial kraus, frus

pich, L. *crisp-us*, Fr. *crépu*, allied to krumm. crisp, curled, frizzled. Der Wind macht das Wasser —, the wind ruffles or crisps the water; —e Haare, crisped or curled hair; die Neger haben —e Haare, the hair of negroes is naturally curly or is woolly; seine Haare fangen an —zu werden, his hair begins to crisp or frizzle: Tuch — machen, to nap or frieze cloth: —e Blätter, curled leaves; ein —er Busenstreif, a plaited frill; —e Franzen, fringe; ein —es Gesicht machen [in fam. lang.], to put on a sour look or grim countenance, to make a grim, dogged face, to knit one's brows; eine —e Stirn machen [in fam. lang.], to knit one's brows, to frown; bunt und — [in fam. lang.], pell-mell, biggledy-piggledy; —e Schrift [in typography], very small characters or print. *Fig.* Das ist mir zu —, that is above my reach; er macht or treibt es zu —, he carries matters too far, it is too much or bad; er ist heute in einem —en Humor or einer —en Stimmung, he is ruffled, in a ruffled or cross humour or disposition of mind to-day.

Kraus-bart, *m.* 1) a curled or crisped beard. *Fig.* a man with such a beard. 2) the coral clavaria. —beere, *f.* 1) whortleberry. 2) rough gooseberry. —distel, *f.* the curled thistle. —elster, *f.* the greater shrike, the greater butcher-bird. —haar, *n.* 1) curled or crisped hair. 2) [provincially also *m.*] V. —kopf 2). —haarig, *adj.* and *adv.* having curled or crisped hair, curly-headed. —holz, *n.* [among periwig-makers] curling-pipe or stick. Die Haare von den —hölzern abstreifen, to take the hair off the pipes. —kohl, *m.* curled or crisped cabbage or colewort. —kopf, *m.* 1) a head with curly hair, curly head, curled or frizzled head. 2) a person with curly hair. Siehst du den kleinen —kopf dort? do you see that curly-headed little fellow? —köpfig, *adj.* curly-headed. —lockig, *adj.* V. —haarig, —köpfig. —perrücke, *f.* a curled or frizzled periwig. —salat, *m.* curled lettuce. —wurz, *f.* V. —distel.

Kraúse, *f.* 1) [not much used] the quality of being crisp, curled or frizzled. Der Wind hat seinen Haaren die — benommen, the wind has uncurled his hair. 2) [*pl.* -n] something plaited, a ruff, frill, V. Busen—, Hals—, Hand—, Hemd—. *Fig.* [in fam. lang.] Sich die — zerreißen, to burst with rage, to fly into a passion.

Kraúsemünze, *f.* curled mint.

Krausemünz-öl, *n.*, —thee, *m.*, —wasser, *n.* oil, tea, water of curled mint.

Kräúsel, *n.* 1) a plaited or puckered piece of linen, a puckered frill or tucker. 2) top [a plaything for children], V. Kreisel.

Kräusel-beere, *f.* V. Krausbeere. —eisen, *n.* crisping-iron, curling-iron. —holz, *n.* V. Krausholz. —kamm, *m.* V. Frisirkamm. —mühle, *f.* V. Frisirmühle. —schnecke, *f.* top-shell, button-shell. —schneckenstein, *m.* turbinite or turbite. —werk, *n.* machinery for milling the edge of coin. —zange, *f.* crisping-pincers, curling-iron.

Kräúseler, Kräúsler, *m.* [-s, *pl.* -], —inn, *f.* hair-dresser. V. [the more usual word] Haarkräusler.

Kräúseln, *v. tr.* to make rough, to crisp, to curl. Der Wind kräuselt das Wasser, the wind crisps or ruffles the [surface of the] water; die Manschetten —, to plait ruffles; die Haare —, to curl, crisp or frizzle hair; gekräuselte Haare, curled or crisped hair; seine Haare fangen an sich zu —, his hair begins to crisp or frizzle; [among clothiers] das Tuch — [frisiren], to nap or frieze the cloth; die Münzen —, to mill coin.

Kraúsen, *v. intr.* to become crisp or curled, to curl.

Kräúsen, [not much used] I. *v. tr.* to crisp, to curl; *it.* to lay in folds, to plait. Die Stirn —, to knit one's brows, to frown. II. *v. r.* sich —, to become rough, crisp or curled. Das Wasser kräuset sich, the water curls or ripples, frets on the surface.

Kräúser, *m.* [-s, *pl.* -], —inn, *f.* [not much used] a person who dresses hair, hair-dresser; *it.* who plaits linen.

Kräúsler, *m.* V. Kräuseler.

1. Kraút, *n.* [-es] [allied to Grütze, Gries; the old kruten = zermalmen] gun-powder. — und Loth [= Pulver und Blei], powder and shot.

Kraut-horn, *n.* powder-flask, powder-horn. —kammer, *f.* [in seamen's lang.] powder-room. —laterne, *f.* [in seamen's lang.] store-room lantern. —löffel, *m.* gunner's ladle.

2. Kraút, *n.* [-es, *pl.* Kräuter] *dim.* Kräutchen, ||Kräutlein, *n.* [-s, *pl.* -] (probably from the Sax. *growan* = wachsen, Sw. *gro*, L. *cresco*, allied to the L. *gramen*] 1) [originally, any thing that grows; in this sense only used in familiar language, in the figurative and ironical phrase.] Du bist mir ein schönes Kräutchen, you are a nice fellow, you behave admirably; V. Früchtchen, Unkraut. 2) herb. Von Kräutern leben, to live upon herbs; Kräuter suchen, sammeln, to search for, to gather herbs, *it.* [= botanisiren] to herborize; er kennt die Kräuter gut, he is a clever herbalist or herborist; V. Feld—, Futterkräuter, Gartenkräuter, Heil—, Küchen-, Wundkräuter. 3) [in a more limited sense] vegetables for the kitchen. *a)* cabbage, colewort. Das weiße —, Weiß—, or —, white heart cabbages; — einmachen, to pickle cabbages. *Fig.* [low] Er muß das — fett machen, he must contribute most to it. *b)* Grünes —, spinage. *it.* [in botany] V. Glied—. 4) medicinal herb, simple, V. Heil—. *Prov.* Für den Tod ist kein —gewachsen, there is a cure for every thing but death, there is no remedy against death. *Fig.* Geduld ist ein heilsames —, patience is an excellent thing or virtue. 5) [in botany] Das Kräutchen der Geduld, the creeping mouse-ear, chick-wick, the white cerastium; geweihet —, V. Eisen—. 6) the herbaceous part of a plant, that is, the leaves and stalk [opposed to the root]. Das — an einem Gewächse abschneiden, to cut off the leaves of a plant; das — der Kartoffeln, the herb or stalks of potatoes.

Kraut-acker, *m.* cabbage-field. —artig, *adj.* and *adv.* herbaceous. Ein —artiger Stamm, an herbaceous stem. —bauer, *m.* a peasant who plants cabbages, cabbage-grower. —beet, *n.* a bed of cabbage. —biene, *f.* field or garden bee. —blatt, *n.* cabbage-leaf. —eisen, *n.* a kind of plane for cutting the cabbage for pickling. —ernte, *f.* crop of cabbage. —faß, *n.* V. —ständer. —faul, *adj.* [in mining] quite rotten. —feld, *n.* V. —acker. —garten, *m.* cabbage-garden, *it.* kitchen-garden. —gärtner, *m.* market-gardener, herbman; *it.* V. —bauer. —hacke, *f.* 1) hoe for cabbage. 2) act of hoeing cabbage. —hänfling, *m.* the lesser redpole. —haupt, *n.* head of cabbage. —hobel, *m.* V. —eisen. —holunder, or —holder, *m.* dwarf-elder, dane-wort, wall-wort. —honig, *m.* honey of the blossoms of trees &c., garden-honey. —huhn, *n.* the common lizard. —junker, *m.* [in contempt or in jest] a country-squire, a booby. —käse, *m.* cheese made with herbs or seeds. —keller, *m.* cellar for cabbage or pot-herbs. —kopf, *m.* 1) V. —haupt. 2) [in popular language] block-head. —land, *n.* V. —acker. —lerche, *f.* 1) wood-lark. 2) V. Heidelerche. —markt, *m.* cabbage-market. —messe, *f.* V. —weihe. —messer, *n.* V. —eisen. —mücke, *f.* V. —schnake. —petersilie, *f.* parsley. —pflanze, *f.* V. Kohlpflanze. —raupe, *f.* V. Kohlraupe. —reich, *adj.* abounding with cabbage. —rippe, *f.* rib of cabbage. —rübe, *f.* turnip-rooted cabbage. —salat, *m.* salad made of cabbage. —schnake, *f.* long-legs. —sellerie, *m.* the Italian or upright celery. —ständer, *m.* a tub for pickling cabbage. —stengel, —strunk, *m.* the stump or stalk of a cabbage, cabbage-stalk. —stichel, *m.* dibble. —strunk, *m.* V. —stengel. —stück, *n.* V. —acker. —suppe, *f.* soup made with cabbage. —vogel, *m.* V. —lerche; *it.* tit-lark. —weide, *f.* the herbaceous willow. —weihe, *f.* [in some parts of Germany] the festival of assumption, the assumption of the holy virgin. —wurm, *m.* V. Kohlraupe.

Kraúte, *f.* [not much used] the act of weeding.

Kraúten, *v. tr.* [not much used] to cut herbs or weeds, to weed.

Kraúter, *m.* [-s, *pl.* -] [not much used] one who weeds, weeder.

Kräúter, *m.* [-s, *pl.* -] market-gardener, herbman.

Kräúter, *pl.* of Kraut.

Kräuter-abdruck, *m.* 1) [the figure of plants in mineral substances] arborization, herborization. 2) herborized stone, phytolite. —absud, *m.* decoction of medicinal herbs or simples. —arzenei, *f.* a medicine made up of simples. —arzt, *m.* a physician who makes use of simples only. —auszug, *m.* extract of simples or medicinal plants. —bad, *n.* a bath of medicinal herbs. —bier, *n.* beer seasoned with aromatic herbs. —boden, *m.* loft for drying herbs. —brod, *n.* bread mixed with herbs. —brühe, *f.* broth seasoned with sweet herbs. —buch, *n.* herbal. —dieb, *m.* a sort of scarabaeus. —frau, *f.* herb-woman. —fressend, *adj.* eating herbs, herbivorous. —garten, *m.* herbary. —geruch, *m.* the smell of herbs. —hütte, *f.* V. Kräbenhütte. —kammer, *f.* room where herbs or simples are preserved. —käse, *m.* cheese made with herbs, green cheese. —kenner, *m.*, —kennerinn, *f.* herbalist, herborist, [in a more general sense] botanist. —kenntniß, *f.* knowledge of herbs or plants, botany. Er hat eine große —kenntniß, he is a great herbalist. —kissen, —kißchen, *n.* 1) a bag filled with certain herbs for a medicinal purpose. 2) smelling-cushion, sweet-bag. —kunde, *f.* V. —kenntniß. —kur, *f.* cure by means of herbs or simples. —lehre, *f.* botany. —lese *f.* the act of seeking or gathering herbs, herborization. —mann, *m.* a man who gathers and sells herbs, herbman. —markt, *m.* the herb-market, vegetable-market. ||—mumme, *f.* V. —bier. —mütze, *f.* a cap stuffed with certain herbs [as a supposed cure for the headache]. —reich, I. *adj.* abounding with herbs, herbous. II. *n.* vegetable kingdom. —säckchen, *n.* V. —kissen. —saft, *m.* juice of herbs, vegetable juice. —salat, *m.* a salad consisting of different herbs. —salbe, *f.* an ointment or salve of herbs. —salz, *n.* vegetable salt, tartrite of potash. —sammeln, *n.* herborization. —sammler, *m.* one who gathers herbs, herbman; herbalist. —sammlung, *f.* a collection of herbs or plants, herbal, herbarium. —suchen, *n.* V. —sammeln. —suppe, *f.* herb-soup, herb-porridge. —tabak, *m.*

tobacco made of aromatic and wholesome herbs. —**thee**, *m.* tea consisting of medicinal herbs. —**trank**, *m.* a drink or decoction of certain herbs. —**umschlag**, *m.* an epithem of medicinal herbs. —**weib**, *n.* herbwoman. —**wein**, *m.* wine seasoned with herbs. —**werk**, *n.* 1) herbage. 2) V. —**buch**. —**wissenschaft**, *f.* V. —**kenntniß**.

Kräuterich, *n.* [-es] the leaves and stalk of an herb or plant.

Kräuterig, *adj.* abounding with herbs, covered with herbs, herbous.

Kräutern, *v. intr.* to herborise, to botanize, V. Botanisiren.

Krautig, *adj.* V. Kräuterig.

Krautig, *n.* [-s] 1) V. Kräuterich. 2) V. Unkraut.

||**Kräutlein**, *n.* [-s, *pl.* -] *dim.* of Kraut.

Kräutler, *m.* [-s, *pl.* -], —**inn**, *f.* V. Kräutermann, Kräuterfrau.

||**Krautschen**, V. Krätzchen.

***Kreatur**, *f.* [*pl.* -en] 1) [obsolete for Geschöpf] creature. 2) *Fig.* [a person who is subject to the will or influence of another in a degrading degree] creature, dependent. Dieser Fürstengünstling und seine —en, this prince's favorite and his creatures.

Krebs, *m.* [-es, *pl.* -e] *dim.* Krebschen, ||Krebslein, *n.* [-s, *pl.* -] [Fr. *écrevisse*, allied to the L. *repo*, kriechen, Low. Sax. krupen, to krabbeln = sich langsam bewegen] 1) [a crustaceous fish, comprehending generally the crab, lobster, crawfish and others, but more especially denoting the] craw-fish, cray-fish, V. Fluß—, See—. †*Fig.* Einen — im Beutel haben, to be stingy. 2) [in astronomy, one of the twelve signs of the zodiac] cancer, crab. 3) [perhaps from the resemblance] *a*) [formerly] a sort of armour. *Fig.* Angethan mit dem — des Glaubens [in Scripture], putting on the breast-plate of faith. 2) [a disease] cancer. Ihre Brust ist vom —e ganz zerfressen, her breast is quite eaten away by a cancer; den — schneiden, to cut off, to extirpate a cancer; V. Bein—, Knochen—, Mutter—. *Fig.* Dieser Mißbrauch ist ein —, welcher &c., that abuse is a cancer that &c. *it.* [a disease incident to trees] canker. Dieser Baum hat den —, that tree is cankered.

Krebs-artig *adj.* and *adv.* 1) resembling or like a crab or craw-fish, cancriform. 2) [in medicine] cancerous. Ein —artiges Geschwür, a cancerous ulcer. —**auge**, *n.* crab's eye; *it.* V. —stein. —**bach**, *m.* a brook or rivulet in which crawfish are taken. —**blume**, *f.* 1) heliotrope, turnsol. 2) the Indian reed, the Indian flowering-reed. 3) the croton. 4) lion's tooth or paw, dandelion. —**brühe**, *f.* broth of pounded crawfishes or crabs. —**butter**, *f.* butter melted with pounded crabs, crabs' butter. —**distel**, *f.* the cotton or woolly thistle. —**euter**, *n.* a cow's udder stuffed with pounded crabs. —**fang**, *m.* the catching of crabs or crawfish. —**fänger**, *m.* catcher of craw-fish. —**fäule** *f.* cancer. —**förmig**, *adj.* having the form of a crab, cancriform. —**fräßig**, *adj.* V. —artig 2). —**fresser**, *m.* the blue heron or bittern. —**gang**, *m.* crab's walk, retrogade movement. **Fig.* Den —gang gehen, to go backwards instead of forwards; seine Geschäfte gehen den —gang, his business, his affairs will not prosper or is [are] going backwards. —**gängig**, *adj.* and *adv.* going or moving backwards, retrograde. **Fig.* —gängig werden, to go or fall back, to come to nought, to prove abortive. —**geschwür**, *n.* a cancerous ulcer. —**hamen**, *m.* a hoop-net for catching craw-fish. —**kascher**, —**katscher**, *m.* V. —hamen. —**koch**, *m.* puff-paste of pounded crabs. —**krabbe**, *f.* V. Kahlschwanz. —**krankheit**, *f.* cancer, V. —geschwür. —**kraut**, *n.* 1) the officinal croton, the colouring turnsol. 2) knawel. —**kreis**, *m.* the tropic of Cancer. —**leuchten**, *n.* the catching of craw-fish by means of a torch. —**linie**, *f.* V. —kreis. —**otter**, *f.* the lesser otter. —**pastete**, *f.* crab-pie. —**pflanze**, *f.* V. —blume 1). —**reuse**, *f.* bow-net, bow-weel. —**salbe**, *f.* 1) a salve or ointment of pounded crabs. 2) a salve for healing the cancer or carcinoma. —**schaden**, *m.* cancerous affection, cancer. —**schale**, *f.* shell or crust of a crawfish, lobster &c. —**scheere**, *f.* 1) claw of a crawfish, lobster or crab. 2) [in botany] water-aloes. —**schüssel**, *f.* dish of crawfish. —**spinne**, *f.* crab-spider. —**stein**, *m.* [concretion formed in the stomach of the crayfish] crab's eye. —**suppe**, *f.* soup made of pounded crabs, crab-porridge. —**vogel**, *m.* V. —fresser. —**wasser**, *n.* any piece of water which contains crayfish, V. —bach. —**weide**, *f.* osier. —**wurz**, *f.* bistort, snake-weed. —**zwirn**, *m.* the spermatic vessels of the male crawfish.

Krebsen, *v. intr.* 1) [in low lang., allied to the L. *repere* and perhaps to greifen] to grope. 2) to catch craw-fish. *Prov.* Ist es nicht gefischt, so ist es doch gekrebset, he has not quite lost his labour that has taken one fish.

Krebshaft, **Krebsicht**, *adj.* and *adv.* V. Krebsartig.

Krechente, *f.* [*pl.* -n] V. Kriechente.

||**Kreek**, *n.* [-es, *pl.* -e] creek, V. Schlupfhafen.

Kreide, *f.* [*pl.* -n] [L. *creta*, probably not from the island of Creta, but allied to the old gratten, griten, to kratzen, reißen, and to the Eng. *to write*] 1) chalk. Ein Stück —, a piece or lump of chalk; weiß wie —, white as chalk; mit — bezeichnen, to mark with chalk, to chalk. *Fig.* [in fam. lang.] Mit doppelter — schreiben, to charge too much or double, to overcharge; auf die — zehren, to eat, drink or live on credit [at an inn]; bei Einem auf der — stehen, to be in any one's books. 2) [a species of earth used by painters] crayon. Mit der — zeichnen, to draw with a crayon; schwarze —, black chalk; rothe —, red chalk; spanische —, spanish white, whiting.

Kreide-bleiweiß, *n.* white lead, ceruse. —**gebirge**, *n.* chalk-mountain. —**grube**, *f.* chalk-pit. —**grund**, *m.* V. —ngrund. —**kiesel**, *m.* flint. —**mergel**, *m.* calcareous or chalky marl. —**n-artig**, *adj.* and *adv.* resembling chalk, chalky, cretaceous. —**n-erde**, *f.* chalky earth. —**n-grund**, *m.* 1) chalky soil. 2) [among painters and gilders] white ground done over with chalk. —**n-guhr**, *f.* white guhr. —**n-krankheit**, *f.* stone-cray. —**n-mehl**, —**n-pulver**, *n.* pipe-clay. —**n-salz**, *n.* salt of chalk. —**n-säure**, *f.* V. Kohlensäure. —**n-stift**, *m.* crayon. —**n-wasser**, *n.* chalky water. —**n-weiß**, *adj.* and *adv.* white as chalk. *Fig.* [in fam. lang.] deadly pale, pale as death. Er wurde bei ihrem Anblick —nweiß, he turned quite pale at her sight. —**zeichnung**, *f.* a drawing or design done with a crayon, crayon.

Kreiden, *v. tr.* 1) to cover with chalk, to chalk. 2) to mark or write with chalk; *it.* to crayon.

Kreidicht, *adj.* and *adv.* resembling chalk, chalky, cretaceous.

Kreidig, *adj.* and *adv.* consisting of chalk, chalky, cretaceous.

Kreidling, *m.* [-es, *pl.* -e] 1) [not used] a person white as chalk, a very pale person. 2) a cretin.

Kreis, *m.* [-es, *pl.* -e] [allied to the L. *gyrus*, Gr. γῦρος] 1) [a curve line continued till it ends where it began, having all parts equally distant from a common centre] circle, round, ring. Einen — beschreiben, to describe a circle; einen — um Jemand schließen, sich in einen — um Jemand stellen, to form a circle, to place one's self in a circle round any one, to assemble round any one, to surround any one; sich in einen — stellen, to form a circle, round or ring, to form one's self into a ring; in einem —e tanzen, to dance around or in a ring; sich auf den Zehen im —e herumdrehen, to turn upon one leg; sich im —e herumbewegen, to move in the form of a circle, circularly; ein — um die Augen, um eine Wunde, a ring round the eyes, round a wound; der — um die Warzen der weiblichen Brüste, the areola; der — um die Sonne, den Mond &c., halo, V. Hof; [in astronomy and geometry] circle; V. Mittags—, Mittel—, Pol—, Thier—, Wende—; die —e einer Himmelskugel, the circles of a sphere; die —e der Planeten, the orbits of the planets. *Fig.* Den — seines Daseyns vollenden, to finish one's course; im —e seiner Familie, seiner Freunde leben, to live in the circle of one's family, of one's friends; das liegt außer dem —e seiner Einsichten, that is not within his reach or compass, that is beyond his capacity or out of his sphere; den — seiner Einsichten or Kenntnisse erweitern, to enlarge the sphere of one's knowledge; das liegt außer dem —e meiner Geschäfte, that is not within my province. 2) [the space included in a circular line] circle; [formerly] arena, the lists; der — der Erde, circle of the earth, V. Erd—; — der Welt, V. Welt—, Weltall. *it.* province, circle. Das deutsche Reich war in 10 —e getheilt, the German empire was divided into ten Circles; der ober- und niederrheinische —, the Circles of the Upper and Lower Rhine. 3) *Fig.* [an assembly surrounding the principal person, *it.* any company or assembly] circle. Ein — schöner Frauen, a circle of beautiful women or ladies. V. Zirkel. V. also Umkreis, Bezirk, Revier.

Kreis-abschied, *m.* a decree or decision formed by the members of a Circle [of the former German empire], recess of a Circle. —**älteste**, *m.* the senior or chief officer of a jurisdiction; *it.* [chiefly] rural dean. —**ältestenamt**, *n.*, —**ältestenwürde**, *f.* the office or dignity of the senior or chief officer of a jurisdiction; *it.* [chiefly] rural deanery. —**amt**, *n.* 1) [formerly] an office or charge in a Circle of the German empire. 2) [formerly] the jurisdiction of an amman of a Circle of the German empire. 3) the district or circuit of the jurisdiction of an officer of the revenues. —**amtmann**, *m.* [formerly] amman of a Circle of the German empire. —**anlage**, *f.* [formerly] the assessment or imposition of a Circle of the German empire. —**archiv**, *n.* [formerly] the archives of a Circle [of the G. E.] —**ausschreibend**, *adj.* [formerly] having the direction of a Circle [in the G. E.]. —**bahn**, *f.* circular path, orbit [of a celestial body]. Die himmlischen Körper bewegen sich nicht in —bahnen, sondern in elliptischen Bahnen, the celestial bodies do not move circularly but elliptically. —**beamte**, *m.* an officer of a certain district. —**beitrag**, *m.* 1) [formerly] quota or contingent of a Circle. 2) a quota of money &c. to be paid or contributed by a certain district. —**bewegung**, *f.* gyration, circular motion. —**bogen**, *m.* the quarter of a circle, quadrant. —**bote**, *m.* [formerly] messenger of a Circle [of the G. E.]. —**brief**, *m.* V. —schreiben. —contingent, n. V. —beitrag, —truppen 2). —director, m. director of a certain large district. —directorium, n. board for the administration of a certain large district. —drehung, f. rotation. —einnehmer, m. the receiver of the taxes &c. of a certain district. —eintheilung, f. division of a country into circles or large districts [for the purposes of administration]. —förmig, adj. and adv. [*circulär] circular, orbicular. Eine —förmige Bewegung, circular motion; [in botany] ein —förmiges Blatt, an orbicular or orbiculate leaf. —fuge, f. [in music, *Canon] V. Canon 2). —gang, m. 1) circular walk. 2) circular movement. *Fig.* Der —gang der Jahreszeiten, the revolution or vicissitude of the seasons. —gericht, n. court of justice of a circle. —gesang, m. 1) V. —fuge. 2) V. Rundgesang. —hauptmann, m. the prefect, provost or captain of a circle. —hülfe, f. [formerly] subsidies or contingent of a Circle. —kanzelei, f. the house or office of a —amt, —directorium, —gericht or —regierung. —lauf, m. V. —bahn; [in the manege] der —lauf eines Pferdes, volt; der —lauf des Blutes, circulation of the blood; *fig.* der —lauf des Geldes im Staat, the circulation of money; der —lauf der Jahreszeiten, V. —gang 2); der —lauf der Begebenheiten, the succession of events, vicissitudes of fortune. —laufend, adj. moving circularly, circular. *Fig.* [*periodisch] periodical. —linie, f. circular line. —matrikel, f. [formerly] the roll or register of a Circle [of the G. E.] in which were entered the sums which every member was obliged to contribute. —messung, f. the art of measuring circles, cyclometry. —miliz, f. [formerly] the militia of a Circle. —mühle, f. horse-mill. —nachgeordnete, m. [formerly] lieutenant-colonel of a Circle [of the G. E.]. —oberste, m. [formerly] colonel of the troops of a Circle [of the G. E.]. —rath, m. member of a —directorium or —regierung. —regierung, f. V. —directorium. —richter, m. judge of a court or tribunal of a Circle. —ritt, m. volt. —rolle, f. V. —matrikel. —schattig, adj. surrounded with a circular shade. Die —schattigen Völker, the periscii or periscians. —schluß, m. V. —abschied. —schreiben, n. 1) [formerly] a letter or missive of a Circle. 2) circular letter. —schule, f. [*Centralschule] central school. —stadt, f. principal town, capital of a circle or large district. —stand, m. [formerly] member of a Circle in the German Empire. —steuer, f. tax or contribution levied upon a circle. —tag m. [formerly] day on which the members of a Circle met; *it.* meeting of the Circle or of the Circles, diet of a Circle. —tanz, m. roundabout-dance. —truppen, pl. [formerly] 1) the militia of a Circle. 2) the troops furnished by a Circle, V. —beitrag. —verfassung, f. [formerly] constitution of a Circle. —versammlung, f. [formerly] meeting of the members of a Circle, diet of a Circle. —vierung, f. [*Quadratur des Zirkels] quadrature of the circle. —vorsteher, m. the director or president of the diet of a circle or [formerly] Circle. —wahrsagerei, f. gyromancy. —weg, m. circular way or walk. —wendung, f. the turning upon one leg. Eine —wendung machen, to turn on one leg. [in the manege] volt. —zerrbild, n. anamorphosis. —zugeordnete, m. [formerly] deputy of a Circle of the German empire.

Kreischen, v. intr. [allied to the old krelen = schreien, krähen] 1) to cry with a shrill voice, to scream, to shriek, to screech, to squall, [in general] to call with a loud voice [said, chiefly, of females]. Eine —de Stimme, a shrill voice; um Hilfe —, to cry or call aloud for help. 2) to make a shrill noise, to creak loudly.

Kreisel, m. [-s, pl. -] [from Kreis] 1) any thing which moves in a circular manner, [chiefly] a top [with which children play]. Den — treiben, to spin or whip a top. 2) [in nat. hist.] top-shell, button-shell, trochus. 3) [in the veterinary art] V. Drehkrankheit.

Kreisel-bohrer, m. drill. —förmig, adj. and adv. formed or shaped like a top; [in botany] turbinate, turbinated. —klee, m. the snail medic. —koralle, f. turbinated madrepore. —peitsche, f. lash to whip a top. —rad, n. [in modern mechanics] tourbine. —schnäbler, m. [a variety of the domestic pigeon] turbit. —schnecke, f. V. — 2). —schneckenstein, m. trochite. —spiel, n. 1) the act of spinning or whipping a top. 2) a kind of game at ninepins in which the pins are beaten down with a top. —wind, m. whirlwind.

Kreiseln, I. v. intr. and v. r. sich —, to turn with a circular motion, to turn about, to whirl. An dem Orte, wo man das Wasser [sich] — sieht, ist ein Abgrund, in that place where you see the water turn about, there is a gulf. II. v. intr. to spin or whip a top.

Kreisen, I. v. intr. to go or move in a circle. Um Etwas —, to turn round any thing; der Mond kreiset um die Erde, the moon turns round the earth; die Zeit kreiset, time returns or revolves. *it.* [among hunters] to walk round a forest and search for game. II. v. tr. 1) to make or describe a circle; *it* to make circular. 2) [in mining] to pound the ore. III. v. r. sich —, to turn or move in a circle or circularly, to turn about or round.

Kreisling, m. [-es, pl. -e] the pinheaded or dwarf agaric.

Kreißen, v. intr. [allied to kreischen, schreien] to be in labour, to travail. Im — liegen, to be in labour.

Kreiß-wasser, n. a beverage for women in labour.

Kreißer, m. [-s, pl. -] V. Murrkopf. —inn, f. a woman in labour.

||**Krellen, Krelen**, V. Krallen, Kratzen.

Kremmling m. [-es, pl. -e] the green agaric, agaricus virescens.

Krempe, Krempel, V. Krämpe.

Krendel, V. Brendel.

Krengel, V. Kringel.

*__Kreosot__, n. [-s] [in medicine] creosot.

*__Krepine__, f. [pl. -n] a little hanging ornament in fringe, bob.

*__Krepiren__, v. intr. [vulgar] to die [said only of animals].

Krepp, m. [-es, pl. -e] 1) double crape. 2) frizzed or frizzled hair.

Krepp-flor, m. crape. —macher, —weber, m. crape-maker or weaver.

Kreppen, v. tr. [not much used] to crape, V. Kraus machen.

1. **Kresse**, f. [pl. -n] [allied to the L. *cresco* = wachsen] cress, cresses. Die breitblätterige —, spanische —, pepperwort, Spanish cress; die schmalblätterige or wilde —, bushy pepperwort; die unvollkommene —, the wild cress; die indische —, Indian cress; V. Berg—, Bitter—, Brunn—, Spring—, Wiesen—, Winter—.

Kreß-same, m. seed of cresses. —salat, m. salad of cresses.

2. **Kresse**, f. [pl. -n] [a fish] gudgeon, V. Gründling.

||**Kreßler**, m. [-s, pl. -] the land-rail.

Kreßling, m. [-es, pl. -e] 1) the pepper agaric or mushroom. 2) [a fish] gudgeon.

||*__Krethi und *Plethi__, [in popular lang.] a motley crew or mob, a crowd pell-mell gathered.

Kreuz, n. [-es, pl. -e] [Sw. *kryss, kors*, Pers. *cruse*, Armen. *croax*, L. *crux*, allied to schräg and Krücke, referable to ragen, regen] 1) [in general, any thing prominent or projecting, hence:] *a*) [in mining] the iron pin of the Göpel [which see] *b*) [the broad part at the end of the backbone or spine] the small of the back, the reins or loins [in the human species]. Das — thut mir weh, ich habe Schmerzen im —e, I have a pain in my reins or loins; er strengte sich so gewaltig an, daß er das — zerbrach, he overstrained himself so much that he broke his back; sich das — verrenken, to strain or sprain one's hip or chine; das — der Thiere, the hind-quarter, crup or rump of animals; dieses Pferd hat ein schönes —, that horse has a fine croup; ein Pferd, das auf dem —e trägt, a horse that carries double; das Pferd hat viel Vermögen im —e, the horse has a strong back; Sie werden ihm das — brechen, you will break his back. 2) *dim.* —chen, ||—lein, n. [-s, pl. -] [two pieces placed across each other] cross. Ein rechtwinkeliges —, a rectangular cross; ein schräges, geschobenes or Andreas—, an oblique or St. Andrew's cross, [in heraldry] saltier; Etwas in's — legen, setzen, to put or set any thing cross-wise or across; zwei in's — übereinander gelegte Hölzer, two pieces of wood laid or placed across each other; die Arme, die Füße über das — legen, to cross the arms, the legs; Etwas mit einem —chen bezeichnen, to mark any thing with a little cross; in's — segeln, to ply off and on, to tack, to laveer; in's — laufen, to lie across or crosswise, to cross one another, to intersect; [in fam. lang.] in's — und in die Quere, — und Quer, die — und die Quere, in all directions. Das — [in astronomy, four stars in the southern hemisphere, in the form of a cross] crosier; [in heraldry] cross, croslet; *it.* [a suit of cards] clubs. Ein — ausspielen, to play or lead a club. [in seamen's lang.] crown, V. Anker—. Brasset die Raaen in's —, square the yards. [in coining, the right side of money stamped with a cross] cross; [in music] sharp, diesis. Eine Note mit einem —e bezeichnen, to mark a note with a sharp; vor dieser Note steht ein —, this note is marked with a sharp, is sharp. 3) [a gibbet, particularly that on which our Saviour suffered] cross. Einen zum Tode am —e verdammen, to condemn any one to die on the cross, to be crucified; Einen an's — binden, heften, schlagen, to fasten or nail any one to the cross. *it.* [a monument with a cross upon it, to excite devotion] cross. Ein hölzernes, steinernes —, a wooden, stone cross; vor dem —e niederfallen, sich niederwerfen, to prostrate one's self at the foot of the cross or crucifix; ein — an einen Ort setzen, an einem Orte aufrichten, to set up, to erect, to plant a cross in a place. *Fig.* Am —e stehen [in popular language], to be in distress, to be at a pinch; zum —e kriechen [in popular language], to humble one's self, to submit; das Zeichen des —es, the sign of the cross; das Zeichen des —es, das — machen, ein — schlagen, to describe the figure of a cross, to make the sign of the cross, to cross one's self. *Fig.* [in fam. lang.] Das — vor Einem, vor Etwas machen, to hold in detestation, to abominate, to detest, to abhor, to hate any one or any thing; das — nehmen, to engage in the holy war or crusade, to take the cross; das — predigen, to exhort to take the cross, to preach the crusade. 4) *Fig.* [in popular lang.] Das —, vexation, affliction, sorrow, tribulation, misfortune. Er hat in seinem Leben viel — ausgestanden, he has had many crosses in his life;

ein böses Weib ist ein großes —, a bad wife is a great misfortune; er hat mir viel — gemacht, he has caused me much sorrow or affliction.

Kreuz-abnahme, —abnehmung, *f.* 1) the act of taking Christ off or down from the cross. 2) a picture representing the act of taking Christ down from the cross, the descent from the cross. —arm, *m.* the bar of a cross, cross-bar. —axt, *f.* twibil. —band, *n.* [in anatomy] cross-ligament; [among carpenters] a cross piece of timber, cross-bar. Unter —band versenden [Zeitungen, Druckschriften &c.], to send sous-bande [daily papers, periodicals &c.]. —batterie, *f.* cross-battery. —baum, *m.* 1) V. Wunderbaum. 2) V. Maßholder. —beere, *f.* 1) the berry of the buckthorn, yellow berry. 2) V. Stachelbeere. 3) V. Kratzbeere. —beerstrauch, *m.* V. —dorn. —bein, *n.* [in anatomy] os sacrum. —beinig, *adj.* cross-legged. —berg, *m.* mountain of the cross, calvary. —bild, *n.* crucifix. —bindsel, *n.* [in seamen's lang.] seizing snake. —blatt, *n.* V. —kraut 2). —blech, *n.* the strongest iron-plate. —blume, *f.* 1) common milk-wort. 2) V. Gottheil. 3) V. Knabenkraut. 4) V. Gewürzstaude. 5) V. —kraut. —blümchen, *n.* the bird's eye. —bock, *m.* a trestle on which wood is sawed for fuel, sawing-jack. —bogen, *m.* ogive. —bogenstellung, *f.* cross arch. —bramraa, *f.* the yard of the mizen top-gallant-sail. —bramsegel, *n.* mizen top-gallant-sail. —brav, *adj.* and *adv.* [in popular lang.] thoroughly honest or good. —bruder, *m.* 1) a man wearing the sign of the cross, crusader. 2) [in fam. lang.] fellow-sufferer, V. Unglücksgefährte. —bube, *m.* knave of clubs. —dame, *f.* queen of clubs. —distel, *f.* V. Eberwurz. —dorn, *m.* 1) [among locksmiths] the stem of a lock. 2) [in nat. hist.] *a*) buckthorn. *b*) barberry. *c*) boxthorn. —dukaten, *m.* a Hungarian ducat stamped with the figure of a cross. —ente, *f.* V. Eisente. —enzian, *m.* the crosswort gentian. —erhöhung, *f.* 1) the setting up or erecting of a cross. 2) holy-cross day. —fahne, *f.* banner or standard having the form of a cross and used in churches; *it.* the banner or standard of the cross. —fahrer, *m.* 1) a person or a ship that cruises, cruiser; privateer. 2) [formerly] a person engaged in a crusade, crusader. —fahrt, *f.* 1) cruise. 2) crusade. 3) pilgrimage, procession with the cross and banner. —fahrtwoche, *f.* V. —woche. —feuer, *n.* cross-fire. —flüchtig, *adj.* and *adv.* avoiding the cross, shunning the duties of a religious life. —förmig, *adj.* and *adv.* having the form of a cross, cross-shaped; [in botany] cruciform. Eine —förmige Blumenkrone, a cruciform corol; [in surgery] —förmiger Schnitt, crucial incision. —fuchs, *m.* the arctic or cross-fox. —fuß, *m.* 1) a stand in the form of a cross. 2) square foot, V. Geviertfuß. —gang, *m.* 1) procession with the cross. 2) cross-walk, cross-passage; *it.* cloister. —gasse, *f.* 1) cross-street. 2) street of the cross. —gericht, *n.* [formerly] ordeal of the cross. —gestell, *n.* a trestle or stand in the form of a cross. —gewebe, —gewirk, *n.* crossing. —gewölbe, *n.* a cross vault. —groschen, —gulden, *m.* [formerly, in some parts of Germany] a groshen, a florin stamped with the figure of a cross. —gurt, *m.* the cross girth, girth of the saddle. —halfter, *f.* cross-halter. —hammer, *m.* a hammer in the form of a cross, cross-hammer. —haspel, *m.* 1) [in mining] windlass. 2) [in printing] cross. —herr, *m.* V. —ritter. —hieb, *m.* 1) a cut passing across or in the form of a cross. 2) [among file-cutters] cross cut or stroke. —holz, *n.* 1) a piece of wood crossing another at right angles, cross-wood; [in seamen's lang.] kevel. 2) [in botany] *a*) wood of the buckthorn; *it.* buckthorn. *b*) agalloch, agallochum. —käfer, *m.* 1) V. Speckkäfer. 2) V. Maikäfer. 3) V. Erbsenkäfer. —kanker, *m.* V. —spinne. —käse, *m.* a sort of cheese made in Suabia in the form of a cross. —kirche, *f.* 1) a church built in the form of a cross. 2) a church consecrated to the holy cross. —klampe, *f.* [in seamen's lang.] common belaying-cleat. —kloster, *n.* a convent built in the form of a cross. —kluft, *f.* [in mining] a branch that crosses a vein, V. Querkluft. —knochen, *m.* V. —bein. —knoten, *m.* 1) a double knot. 2) [in anatomy] ganglion of the os sacrum. —könig, *m.* king of clubs. —kopf, *m.* 1) [in popular language] a good head, a person of abilities. 2) [term of abuse, against Roman-Catholics] a follower or partisan of the Pope or the tenets of the Romish Church, a person popishly inclined, a popish man. —kraut, *n.* 1) groundsel. Das gemeine —kraut, the common groundsel; das große —kraut, the common rag-wort, V. Jakobskraut. 2) the crucianella or petty madder. 3) cross-wort. 4) the hedge-mustard. 5) the caper-spurge. —kristall, *m.* cruciform crystal. —kröte, *f.* V. Unke. —lahm, *adj.* and *adv.* lame in the back or hip, hip-shot; V. Hüftenlahm. Ein Pferd —lahm machen, to break a horse's back. —maß, *n.* 1) a surveyor's rule or square. 2) [in printing] prototype. —meise, *f.* V. Tannenmeise, Waldmeise. —meißel, *m.* [among locksmiths, a kind of chisel] carp's tongue. —muskel, *m.* [der breite], the sacrolumbaris muscle. —nagel, *m.* a nail with a cross on its head, cross-nail. —naht, *f.* a seam made with cross stitches. —nessel, *f.* the water figwort. —orden, *m.* the order of the cross. —pfad, *m.* cross-path. —pfennig, *m.* a small coin [farthing] with a cross on it. —pflanze, *f.* 1) V. —kraut. 2) V. Gottheil. —pforte, *f.* [in seamen's lang.] stern-port. —predigt, *f.* exhortation to take the cross. —punkt, *m.* the point at which two lines cross each other, intersection. —qualle, *f.* the cross medusa. —ranke, *f.* the cross vine. —raute, *f.* the common rue. —riemen, *m.* [a strap upon the back of a horse near the tail] crupper. —ritter, *m.* knight of the cross, knight of Malta. —ruthe, *f.* a square rood. —salbei, *m.* the small sage. —scheide, *f.* V. Meßscheibe. —schenkel, *m.* [eines Rades] the cross-bar of a watch-wheel. —schiff, *n.* a ship that cruises, cruiser. —schlag, *m.* a stroke forming a cross. —schmerzen, *pl.* pain in the back or loins. —schnabel, *m.* cross-beak, V. —vogel. —schnitt, *m.* [in surgery] crucial incision. —schraffirung, *f.* counter-hatching. —schraube, *f.* cross screw. —schuh, *m.* V. —fuß. —schule, *f.* 1) a name borne by several establishments for public education in Germany, as the —schule at Leipzig, at Dresden &c. 2) school of affliction, misfortunes, adversity. —schwester, *f.* a person subject to great affliction or adversity; *it.* a companion in misery, fellow-sufferer. —segel, *n.* the mizen top-sail. —spinne, *f.* the cross-spider, the hazel spider. —sprung, *m.* a cross caper. —stab, *m.* 1) a staff with a cross on it. 2) [among weavers] a crossing stick or staff, coat-staff. —stange, *f.* V. —stenge. —stein, *m.* 1) a stone having the form or shape of a cross. 2) cross-stone, harmotome, staurolite. —stenge, *f.* [in seamen's lang.] mizen top-mast. —stengenstag, *n.* the mizen top-stay. —stengenstagsegel, *n.* the mizen top-stay-sail. —stich, *m.* cross-stitch. —stock, *m.* the stone-frame of a window; *it.* [in general, for] a window. —straße, *f.* V. —gasse. —tag, *m.* rogation-day, crouchmas-day. —tanne, *f.* V. Weißtanne. —thaler, *m.* a dollar with a cross upon it. —tragend, *adj.* bearing the cross, cruciferous. —träger, *m.* cross-bearer; *fig.* [in familiar language] an afflicted man; *it.* [in familiar language] a willing sufferer. Er ist ein geduldiger —träger, he is resigned or patient in his afflictions. —verband, *m.* the dressing of a wound in form of a cross. —vogel, *m.* cross-beak, cross-bill, V. —schnabel. —webung, *f.* crossing. —wechsel, *m.* [among hunters] the going across of a deer. —weg, *m.* cross-way. —weh, *n.* V. —schmerzen. —weise, *adj.* in the form of a cross, cross-wise, across. Die Wege gehen —weise übereinander, durchschneiden sich —weise, the ways cross one another; —weise übereinander gehen, liegen, to lie across, to cross or intersect one another; er hatte die Arme —weise übereinander gelegt, his arms were folded across; die Füße, die Arme —weise übereinander legen, to cross one's legs, arms. —winde, *f.* V. —haspel. —woche, *f.* rogation-week. —wurz, *f.* 1) V. —kraut. 2) rampion. 3) V. —enzian. 4) the common buckbean or marsh-trefoil. —zeichen, *n.* the sign of the cross. Das —zeichen annehmen, to take the cross. —zoll, *m.* square inch. —zug, *m.* 1) procession with the cross. 2) crusade. 3) cruise. Einen glücklichen —zug machen, to make a lucky cruise; dieses Schiff ist auf einen —zug ausgefahren, that ship is gone on a cruise.

Kreuzestod, *m.* death on the cross.

Kreuzen, I. *v. intr.* and *v. r.* sich —, 1) to lie across, to cross one another. Wege, welche —, or sich —, ways that cross one another. *Fig.* Tausend Entwürfe — [sich] in seiner Seele, a thousand projects pass in his mind or agitate his mind; ihre Meinungen — sich, their opinions clash. 2) to cruise. Ihre Schiffe — im Kanale, their ships cruise in the Channel. II. *v. tr.* to lay one body across another, to cross. III. *v. r.* sich —, to cross one's self, to make the sign of the cross. V. Bekreuzen, II.

Kreuzer, *m.* [-s, *pl.* -] 1) [a small coin, originally with a cross upon it] kreutzer [worth the third part of a penny English money]. 2) cruiser; privateer.

Kreuzigen, I. *v. tr.* to crucify. Sie kreuzigten den Sohn Gottes, they crucified the son of God. *Fig.* Sein Fleisch —, to mortify or crucify one's flesh; mit Jesu Christo gekreuziget seyn, to be crucified with Christ. II. *v. r.* sich —, V. Kreuzen, III.

Kreuzigung, *f.* crucifixion. *Fig.* Die — des Fleisches, the mortification of the flesh.

1. **Kribbeln**, *v. intr.* and *v. impers.* [probably allied to greifen, L. *repere*, kriechen] to crawl about like insects, to move in a confused multitude, to swarm. Da kribbelt es Raupen &c. [in fam. lang.], there is a number of caterpillars crawling about.

2. **Kribbeln**, [allied to krabbeln, kratzen] I. *v. tr.* to scratch or rub gently. *Fig.* Der Senf kribbelt in der Nase, the mustard bites one's nose; das kribbelt ihn im Kopfe [in popular lang.], that makes him uneasy or angry, that irritates or frets him. II. *v. intr.* and *v. impers.* to feel a sensation like that of a crawling insect, to tickle. Es kribbelt mich in der Nase, my nose itches; es kribbelt mich in der ganzen Hand, I feel a pricking or stinging in my hand.

Kribbelkopf, *m.* [in popular lang.] irritable or passionate person. —köpfig, *adj.* and *adv.* [in popular lang.] irritable, irascible. —krankheit, —sucht, *f.* a malady called by physicians Raphania.

Krick, V. Krack.

Krickelei, *f.* [in popular lang.] 1) moroseness 2) a delicate, nice, difficult business or affair.

Krickeln, *v. intr.* [allied to the Low Sax. krikelen = zanken] [in popular lang.] to be morose, peevish, captious, punctilious.

Krickelkopf, *m.* V. Krickler.

Krickler, *m.* [-s, *pl.* -] [in popular lang.] a morose, peevish person, a captious or punctilious man.

Kricklich, *adj.* and *adv.* [in popular lang.] 1) morose, peevish, captious, punctilious. 2) delicate, nice, difficult.

Kriebeln, V. Kribbeln.

Kriebelkrankheit, *f.* V. Kribbelkrankheit.

‖**Krieben**, *m.* [-s, *pl.* -] V. Lendenbraten.

Griebs, V. Griebs.

Kriech, *n.* [-es, *pl.* -e] [perhaps from the old greina = theilen] [in seamen's language] cut-water.

Krieche, *f.* [*pl.* -n] 1) V. Kriechente. 2) a sort of small round plum, wild plum.

Kriechenbaum, *m.* wild plum-tree.

Kriechen, *ir. v. intr.* [seems only to be another form of regen] to creep. Der Epheu kriecht am Boden hin, ivy creeps along the ground; die Schlangen, die Würmer —, serpents, worms creep or crawl; ein —des Thier, a creeping animal; auf allen Vieren —, to creep or go upon all fours; im Zimmer herum —, to creep or crawl about the room; in alle Winkel —, to creep or get into every corner; in's Bett — [in fam. lang.], to creep or get into bed; hinter den Ofen — [in fam. lang.], to get or to hide one's self behind the stove; in's Gefängniß — müssen [in popular language], to be clapped up, to be put in a prison, to be imprisoned; diese Küchlein sind erst eben aus den Eiern gekrochen, those chickens have just been hatched. *Fig.* V. Kreuz, 3) *fig.*; vor den Ministern —, to cringe or crouch to the ministers; ein —der Mensch, eine —de Seele, a cringing fellow or creature; ein —des Betragen, a servile, low, groveling, mean behaviour.

Kriech-bohne, *f.* dwarf kidney-bean. —ente, *f.* teal. —erbse, *f.* dwarf pea. —mücke, *f.* gnat. —röhre, *f.* a kind of pipe coralline. —rose, *f.* the white dog-rose. —säule, *f.* V. Griechsäule. —weide, *f.* the creeping willow.

Kriecher, *m.* [-s, *pl.* -], —inn, *f.* 1) a cringing, crouching, servile, sneaking person, cringer. 2) a scraping-iron.

Kriecherei, *f.* 1) a servile, groveling, sneaking conduct. 2) a servile, mean or groveling action.

Kriechling, *m.* [-es, *pl.* -e] V. Krieche 2).

Krieg, *m.* [-es, *pl.* -e] [commonly derived from the Sw. and Dan. *krig* = schreien, Fr. *cri* = Schrei, Gr. κράζω, κέκραγα, krakeelen; but the old Werre (Fr. *guerre*, Eng. *war*) from wirren and Wig from wegen (= bewegen) render the derivation from regen very probable] war; V. Angriffs—, Vertheidigungs—, Hülfs—. Der — wird bald ausbrechen, war will soon break out; sich zum —e rüsten, to prepare for war; in den — gehen, ziehen, to go to war, to take the field; den — in das Herz des Landes spielen, to transfer the war into the heart of the country; ein Land mit — überziehen, to invade a country; — mit Jemand führen, to make or wage war upon any one; im —e begriffen seyn, to be at war; sein Heil im —e versuchen, to seek or try one's fortune in war; der kleine —, combats between detachments and small parties, skirmishes; ein innerlicher — [Bürgerkrieg], an intestine or civil war; der heilige —, the holy war; der dreißigjährige —, the thirty years' war, V. Land—, See—. *Fig.* contention, contest, quarrel, litigation. Der — der Elemente, the conflict, strife or warring of the elements; Erde und Meer schienen mit einander — zu führen, the earth and sea seemed to be at war; wir werden deßhalb keinen — mit einander anfangen [in fam. lang.], we shall not contend or quarrel about that; woher kommt Streit und — unter euch [in Scripture]? from whence come wars and fightings among you? V. Feder—.

Kriegs-fertig, *adj.* and *adv.* prepared for war; *it.* inclined to war, warlike. Sie sind allezeit —fertig, they are always ready for war. —führend, *adj.* and *adv.* waging war, carrying on war, belligerent. Die —führenden Mächte, the belligerent powers. —gewohnt, *adj.* inured to war.

Kriegs[or Krieges]-adel, *m.* military nobility, [with certain Eastern nations] warrior-cast. —anführer, *m.* leader in war, commander, chief. —angelegenheit, *f.* military affair or matter. —anstalt, *f.* 1) V. —rüstung 1). 2) military institution or school. 3) hospital for disabled soldiers. —artikel, *m.* article of war, V. —gesetz. —aufruf, *m.* summons to take up arms for the defense of the country, appeal to arms. —baukunst, *f.* [the art or science of fortifying places] fortification, military architecture. —baumeister, *m.* military architect, engineer. —beamte, *m.* a person who has some employment in the army though not a soldier, commissary, such as a military lawyer and judge surgeon, quarter-master &c. —bedarf, *m.* warlike stores, ammunition. —bedienung, *f.* a military charge or office. —bediente, *m.* V. —beamte. —bedürfniß, *n.* V. —bedarf. —befehlshaber, *m.* chief, general, commander of the army. Der oberste -befehlshaber, the commander-in-chief. —befestigung, *f.* [in law, the trial of a cause by putting in the plaintiff's declaration and the defendant's answer] contestation. —begebenheit, *f.* a military event. —blut, *n.* blood shed in war. —brauch, *m.* V. —gebrauch. —bühne, *f.* V. —schauplatz. —camerad, *m.* brother in arms, [especially among officers] brother-officer. V. —gefährte. —casse, *f.* V. —kasse. —collegium, *n.* war-office. —commissär, *— commissarius, *m.* military commissary. — commissariat, *n.* commissariat of war. — dienst, *m.* 1) military service. —dienste nehmen, —in dienste treten, to enter the army, to enter or enlist one's self a soldier, to turn soldier; —dienste thun, in —diensten stehen, to bear arms, to serve in the army; in preußischen —diensten stehen or seyn, to serve in the Prussian army; er hat 20 Jahre —dienste gethan, he has borne arms or he has served twenty years, he has been twenty years in the service; er thut schon 10 Jahre —dienste, he has borne arms or served these ten years. 2) a military charge, office or employment. —drangsal, *n.* distress, hardship, horrors of war. —drommete, *f.* [in poetry] the martial trumpet. —ehren, *pl.* military honours. —eid, *m.* military oath. — empörung, *f.* revolt or insurrection of the army, mutiny. —entwurf, *m.* plan of military operations. —erfahren, *adj.* and *adv.* experienced or skilled in war or in the military art. Ein großer, —erfahrener Held, a great captain. —erfahrenheit, —erfahrung, *f.* experience or skill in war or military affairs. —erklärung, *f.* declaration of war. —eröffnung, *f.* the beginning of hostilities, opening of the campaign. —erwerbniß, *n.* acquisition made in or by war. —fach, *n.* 1) war department. 2) military art or science, V. —kunst, —wissenschaft. —fackel, *f.* [*fig.*] torch or flame of war. Er hat die —fackel angezündet, he has kindled the war. —fall, *m.* case of war; *it.* military event. Im —falle, in case of war, if war should break out. —fernglas, —fernrohr, *n.* polemoscope. —feuer, *n.* [*fig.*] flame of war. Das —feuer brach von Neuem aus, the war was kindled again. —feuerkunst, *f.* military pyrotechnics, gunnery. — flamme, *f.* V. —feuer. —flotte, *f.* fleet, navy. —freund, *m.* 1) a friend or lover of war. 2) brother in arms. —freundschaft, *f.* friendship made during a war. —fuhre, *f.* carriage or conveyance required in war. — fuß, *m.* war-establishment. —gebrauch, *m.* usage of war. —gefahr, *f.* 1) danger attending war. 2) danger or fear of an approaching war. Sie sind in beständiger —gefahr, they are continually threatened with war. —gefährte, *m.* companion in arms, fellow-soldier, brother-officer. —gefangen, *adj.* taken in war. —gefangene, *m.* prisoner of war. Die —gefangenen auswechseln, to exchange prisoners [of war]. —gefangenschaft, *f.* state of a prisoner of war. In —gefangenschaft gerathen, to fall into the hands of the enemy, to be made prisoner of war. —geist, *m.* warlike or martial spirit. — gelehrsamkeit, *f.* 1) erudition in the military art. 2) the military art or science. —gelehrt, *adj.* skilled in the art of war or in military affairs. —geleite, *f.* a military escort. —genoß, *m.* V. —gefährte. —gepäck, *n.* 1) the baggage of an army. 2) the equipage of a soldier. —geräth, *n.*, —geräthschaft, *f.* the equipage of an army, military equipage. —gericht, *n.* 1) military tribunal, council of war, court martial. —gericht halten, to hold a council of war or a court martial; —gericht über Einen halten, to try any one before a court martial. 2) the officers composing a court martial. —gesang, *m.* a military, warlike or martial song or chorus. —geschichte, *f.* 1) history of a war or of wars. 2) a military tale or story. —geschick, *n.* chances or vicissitudes of war. —geschrei, *n.* 1) shout or yell of war, warhoop. 2) strong rumour of war. 3) watchword or rallying word. —geschwader, *n.* 1) a squadron or body of troops. 2) a detachment of ships of war, a squadron. ‡—geselle, *m.* V. —gefährte. —gesetz, *n.* military code, [especially] articles of war. —getöse, *n.* the din of war. —getümmel, *n.* tumult of war. —gewalt, *f.* 1) military force or strength. 2) military authority or power. —gewerbe, *n.* V. —handwerk. —gezelt, *n.* V. —zelt. —glück, *n.* fortune of war, chance of war or arms. Das —glück ist veränderlich, the chance of arms is uncertain. —glut, *f.* V. —feuer. — gott, *m.* the God of war, Mars. —göttinn, *f.* Goddess of war, Bellona, Minerva. —gurgel, *f.* 1) rough voice of a fierce soldier. 2) *Fig.* a rude and fierce soldier or warrior. — händel, *pl.* the affairs of war, military affairs. —handwerk, *n.* profession of war, military profession. —haufen, *m.* a body of troops. —haupt, *n.* V. —befehlshaber. ‡— hauptmann, *m.* captain. —heer, *n.* army. —held, *m.* warlike hero, a great warrior. — heldinn, *f.* a warlike heroine, a female warrior, a warrioress, an amazon. —herold, *m.* herald of arms. —herr, *m.* the sovereign, in his quality of supreme chief of the military forces. —hospital, *n.* military hospital. —hülfe, *f.* 1) auxiliary troops. 2) subsidies. —jahr, *n.* year of war. Nach 30 —jahren, after thirty years of war. —kammer, *f.* military or war department. —kanzlei, *f.* war-office. —karte, *f.* military map. —kasse, *f.* military chest. —kassier, *m.* V. —zahlmeister. —kette, *f.* [*Cordon] military cordon. —keule, *f.* [in botany] V. Keulenschwamm. —kleid, *n.* military habit, soldier's clothes, uniform, [an officer's] regimentals. —**knecht**, *m.* [obsolete or in emphatic lang.] soldier. —**kosten**, *pl.* expenses of war. —**kunde**, *f.* military knowledge, tactics. —**kundig**, *adj.* skilled in the military art or in tactics. —**kunst**, *f.* art of war, military art or science; *it.* V. —list. —**lager**, *n.* camp. —**last**, *f.* burden of war. —**läufte**, *pl.* time or events of war. —**leben**, *n.* a military life. —**leute**, *pl.* military men, soldiers. —**lied**, *n.* war-song, soldier's song. V. also —gesang. —**list**, *f.* stratagem. —**liste**, *f.* 1) list or roll of the troops. Sich in die —liste einschreiben lassen, to enlist or enter one's self as a soldier. 2) account or register of the expenses of war. —**listig**, *adj.* fertile in stratagems. —**losung**, *f.* watch-word. —**macht**, *f.* 1) belligerent power. 2) military power, army, forces. Eine —macht auf die Beine bringen, to raise an army or troops; —macht zu Land, zu Wasser, land-forces, naval forces. —**manier**, *f.* V. —gebrauch. —**mann**, *m.* military man, warrior, soldier. Ein gemeiner —mann, a private. —**mannschaft**, *f.* soldiers, soldiery, troops, army. —**mantel**, *m.* military cloak. —**minister**, *m.* minister of war. —**ministerium**, *n.* war-office. —**noth**, *f.* distress, calamity of war. ‡—**nothdurft**, *f.* V. —bedarf. —**obere**, *m.* officer. ‡—**oberste**, *m.* superior officer, colonel. —**ordnung**, *f.* military regulation or discipline. —**perspectiv**, *n.* V. —fernrohr. ||—**pfleger**, *m.* [in law] one without whose knowledge and advice a female is not allowed to transact any legal business. —**pflicht**, *f.* 1) military duty. 2) military oath. Die —pflicht leisten, V. [under Fahne] zur Fahne schwören. 3) the obligation to bear arms, to serve. —**pflichtig**, *adj.* and *adv.* subject to bear arms or serve in the army. Die —pflichtigen, the conscripts. — —**pflichtigkeit**, *f.* V. —pflicht 3). —**platz**, *m.* a fortified town, a place of arms. —**posaune**, *f.* V. —drommete. —**rath**, *m.* 1) council of war. 2) a session or deliberation of the council of war. 3) [member of the war-department] counsellor of war. —**recht**, *n.* 1) law of war, military law, articles of war. 2) [obsolete] court martial, V. —gericht. —**regel**, *f.* V. —ordnung. —**regierung**, *f.* military government, stratocracy. —**richter**, *m.* 1) member of a council of war; *it.* V. —rath 3). 2) [Auditor] the military lawyer and judge in military cases. Der oberste —richter [Generalauditor], provost-marshal, judge advocate general. —**roß**, *n.* battle-horse. —**rotte**, *f.* a body or detachment of troops. —**ruf**, *m.* 1) V. —aufruf. 2) military reputation, fame or renown. —**ruhm**, *m.* military glory. —**rüstung**, *f.* 1) preparation for war, war-like preparation. 2) a warrior's apparel, armour, panoply. —**sache**, *f.* affair or matter of or concerning war. —**sänger**, *m.* [formerly] bard. —**satt**, *adj.* weary of war. —**schaar**, *f.* a body of soldiers or troops; *it.* [not much used] a regiment. —**schaden**, *m.* 1) damage done in or by war. 2) duty or tax levied to defray the expenses of, or damage done by, war. —**schauplatz**, *m.* theatre or seat of war. —**schiff**, *n.* ship of war, man of war. —**schiffvogel**, *m.* 1) sea-swallow. 2) albatros. —**schuld**, *f.* debt occasioned by war. ‡—**schuldheiß**, *m.* legal officer attached to the army who assists at courts martial, judge-advocate. —**schule**, *f.* school of war, military school. —**sekretär**, *m.* secretary of war. —**sold**, *m.* pay. —**spiel**, *n.* 1) war considered as a play. 2) the name of several games, as at billiards, war. —**spielmann**, —**spieler**, *m.* [not much used] musician of a regiment. —**sprache**, *f.* military language or expression or terms. —**staat**, *m.* a military state or power. —**stand**, *m.* 1) military profession. 2) war-establishment. —**steuer**, *f.* 1) war-tax. 2) contribution. V. Brandschatzung. —**strafe**, *f.* military punishment. —**straße**, *f.* military road [also = Etappenstraße]. —**testament**, *n.* military testament. —**that**, *f.* military exploit, achievement or feat. —**übung**, *f.* military exercise, manoeuvre. —**unkosten**, *pl.* V. —kosten. —**unruhen**, *pl.* 1) troubles of war. 2) V. —empörung. —**verfassung**, *f.* military constitution. —**verheerung**, *f.* desolation or devastation caused by war. —**verpflegungsamt**, *n.* commissariat of war. —**verständig**, *adj.* V. —kundig. —**vogel**, *m.* V. Seidenschwanz. ||—**vogt**, *m.* V. —pfleger. —**volk**, *n.* 1) [rather obsolete] soldiers, soldiery. 2) —volk or better —völker, troops, forces. ||—**vormund**, *m.* V. —pfleger. —**vorrath**, *m.* military stores, provision and ammunition. —**waffe**, *f.* arms used in war. —**wagen**, *m.* [formerly] war-chariot, V. Streitwagen. —**wehr**, *f.* V. —waffe. —**wesen**, *n.* 1) military concerns, military system. 2) V. —kunst. —**wissenschaft**, *f.* military science. —**zahlamt**, *n.* army pay-office. —**zahlmeister**, *m.* army paymaster, paymaster of the forces. —**zeit**, *f.* time of war. —**zelt**, *n.* tent in war or in or for a campaign. —**zeug**, *n.* V. Feldgeräth 2), Heergeräth, [especially] ordnance. —**zeugamt**, —**zeugdirectorium**, —**zeugkollegium**, *n.* board of ordnance. —**zierath**, *f.* military ornament. —**zögling**, *m.* military pupil. —**zucht**, *f.* military discipline. V. Mannszucht. —**zug**, *m.* military expedition, campaign. —**zwang**, *m.* 1) [obsolete] military execution. 2) military subordination.

1. ||**Kriegen**, *v. tr.* [allied to ragen, regen, recken] 1) to lay hold of, to seize. Einen beim Kopfe —, to take any one by the head, *it.* to apprehend, to arrest, to seize any one; es ist mir zu hoch, ich kann es nicht —, it is too high, I cannot reach it; endlich hat man die Diebe gekriegt, at last the thieves have been taken. 2) to get, to obtain, to receive. Seinen Theil —, to get one's part; eine Stelle —, to obtain a place; eine Krankheit —, to get or catch a distemper; Briefe —, to receive letters; wir werden Gäste —, we shall have some guests; es ist nichts zu —, there is nothing to be had; Schläge —, to get blows.

2. **Kriegen**, *v. intr.* [from Krieg] to wage war, to war; *it.* to contend. Mit einander —, to be at war [with each other]; die —den Mächte, the belligerent powers.

Krieger, *m.* [-s, *pl.* -], —**inn**, *f.* warrior. V. Kriegsheld. *Fig.* — in Füllerei [in Script.], men of strength to mingle strong drink.

Krieger-haft, *adj.* like or resembling a warrior or soldier, warrior-like, soldier-like, fit for a warrior or soldier, becoming a warrior or soldier. —**mäßig**, *adj.* and *adv.* becoming a warrior. —**stand**, *m.* 1) military profession. 2) the body or cast of soldiers or warriors.

Kriegerisch, *adj.* and *adv.* warlike, martial, military. Ein —es Ansehen or Aussehen, a martial or warlike appearance; —e Musik, martial music; ein —es Volk, a martial or warlike people or nation.

Kriekente, *f.* [*pl.* -n] V. Kriechente.

Krimm, *f.* Crimea.

||**Krimmen**, I. *v. tr.* [seems to be allied to kribbeln, Gr. χρίμπτω] to scratch or rub gently, to tickle. II. *v. impers.* to itch. Es krimmt mich im Halse, my throat itches. *it.* to gripe. Es krimmt mich im Bauche, the colic wrings me, I have a griping in the bowels. V. Grimmen 2).

Krimpe, *f.* [V. Krimpen] shrinking [of cloth &c.]. [among tailors] Das Tuch ist nicht in der — gewesen, the cloth has not been wetted.

Krimpelspiel, *n.* [-s] [a game at cards] gleek.

Krimpen, *v. intr.* [allied to schrumpfen, Krampf] I. *v. intr.* to shrink [as cloth]. [in seamen's lang.] V. Auf—. II. *v. tr.* to wet or sponge [cloth].

Kringel, *m.* [-s, *pl.* -] or *f.* [*pl.* -n] [allied to Ring] a bun or cake formed in the shape of a knot, twisted bun, twist; *it.* a cracknel.

Krinitz, *m.* [-es, *pl.* -e] V. Kreuzvogel.

Krinne, *f.* [*pl.* -n] [= Rinne] notch, channel, cranny.

Krippe, *f.* [*pl.* -n] *dim.* —**chen**, —**lein**, *n.* [-s, *pl.* -] [Sw. *krubba*, Low Lat. *grupia*, probably allied to Grube, Gruft] 1) manger, crib. 2) [in hydraulics] *a*) a fence of pales. *b*) a dike or dam. *c*) a sort of hedge, hurdlework.

Krippen-beißen, *n.* the act of biting the manger. —**beißer**, *m.* a horse which has a trick of biting the manger, V. Kopper. *Fig.* [in popular lang.] *a*) Ein alter —beißer, an old worn-out fellow. *b*) a morose, grumbling, snappish fellow. —**beißig** or —**bissig**, *adj.* [of a horse] apt to bite the manger. *Fig.* [in popular lang.] morose, grumbling, snappish. —**knecht**, *m.* a man who makes fagots for dams or dikes, fagot-maker. —**reiter**, *m.* a person who contrives to keep his horse at the manger of others by riding to his different acquaintances, a parasite, a parasitical country-squire. —**setzer**, *m.* V. —beißer. —**werk**, *n.* starling of a bridge.

Kripper, *m.* [-s, *pl.* -] [a bird] the foolish bunting.

***Krise**, *f.* [*pl.* -n] crisis.

Krispeln, *v. tr.* [allied to the L. *crispus*, kraus] Leder —, to work leather in grain, to pommel a hide on the flesh-side.

Krispelholz, *n.* pommel.

Krist, *m.* &c. V. [the correctly spelt word] Christ &c.

***Kristall** or **Krystall**, *m.* [-es, *pl.* -e] 1) [in chymistry and mineralogy] crystal. Mineralischer or mineralischer —, mineral crystal; dieser Körper bildet —e, setzet —e an, schießt in —e an or schießt an, this body crystalizes; die Salze zu —en anschießen lassen, to crystalize salts; isländischer —, Iceland crystal. 2) factitious crystal, crystal-glass, crystal. Hell wie —, clear or transparent as crystal, crystaline; ein Leuchter von —, a crystal candlestick; [in poetry] der — des Wassers, the lucidity, limpidness, or transparency of water.

Kristall-achat, *m.* V. Eisachat. —**apfel**, *m.* a species of etite or eagle-stone. —**beschreiber**, *m.* V. —lehrer. —**beschreibung**, *f.* crystalography. —**blüte**, *f.* flowers of crystal. —**born**, *m.* [especially in poetry] crystaline or crystal spring or fountain. —**dose**, *f.* a crystal snuff-box. —**druse**, *f.* cluster or group of crystals. —**erz-zinn**, *n.* grain-tin. —**fluß**, *m.* 1) coloured crystal. 2) [in poetry] crystal-stream or river. —**form**, *f.* form of crystal, crystaline form. —**glas**, *n.* 1) factitious crystal, crystal-glass, crystal. Das venetianische —glas, Venice crystal. 2) a crystal-glass. —**grube**, *f.* V. —kluft. —**gucker**, *m.* [in popular belief] one who attempts to tell the fortunes of a person by looking into a crystal mirror, crystalomancer. —**guckerei**, *f.* divination by looking into a crystal mirror, crystalomancy. —**hell**, *adj.* and *adv.* clear or transparent as crystal, crystaline. Ein —heller Himmel, a crystaline, very transparent or transparently blue, sky; —helles Wasser, crystal or crystaline water. —**himmel**, *m.* [astronomy] crystaline heaven. —**kapsel**, *f.* [in anatomy] crystaline capsule. —kluft, *f.* crystal-mine. —knopf, *m.* a crystal button. —kraut, *n.* V. Eiskraut. —kugel, *f.* 1) a crystal ball. 2) a species of etite or eagle-stone. —kunde, —lehre, *f.* crystalography. —lehrer, *m.* crystalographer. —leuchter, *m.* a crystal candlestick. —linse, *f.* [in anatomy] crystaline humour, crystaline lens. —quelle, *f.* V. —born. —rose, *f.* V. —kugel. —saft, *m.* V. —linse. —schneider, *m.* crystal-cutter or engraver on crystal. —seher, *m.* crystalomancer. —spiegel, *m.* crystal mirror; *it.* [in crystalomancy] magic mirror [of crystal]. —staar, *m.* membranous cataract. —stecher, *m.* V. —schneider. —waare, *f.* any thing made of crystal, crystal ware. —wahrsagerei, *f.* crystalomancy.

Kristállbar, *adj.* and *adv.* that may be crystalized, crystalisable. Das Salz ist —, salt crystalizes or is susceptible of crystalisation.

Kristállbarkeit, *f.* quality of being crystalisable.

Kristállen, I. *adj.* and *adv.* 1) consisting of or resembling crystal, crystaline, crystal. 2) V. Kristallhell. II. *v. tr.* V. Kristallisiren.

***Kristallisatión,** *f.* crystalization *a*) [the act or process of crystalizing]; *b*) [a crystalized body].

Kristállisch, [*Kristallinisch] *adj.* and *adv.* 1) having the form of crystal, like crystal, crystal-form, crystaline. 2) clear as crystal. Die —e Feuchtigkeit im Auge, the crystaline humour.

***Kristallisíren,** *v. tr.* and *intr.* to crystalize. Kristallisirte Körper, crystalized bodies, crystalizations; sich — [= zu Kristallen bilden or anschießen], to crystalize.

***Kritérium,** *n.* [standard of judging] criterion.

***Kritík,** *f.* [*pl.* -en] 1) [the art of judging with propriety of the beauties and faults of a literary performance &c.] criticism, critique, critic. Die Regeln der —, the rules of criticism. 2) [a critical examination of the merits of a performance] critique, critic, [critical] review. Addison schrieb eine — über das verlorne Paradies, Addison wrote a critique on paradise lost; er schrieb eine sehr günstige — über dieses Werk, seine — dieses Werkes fiel sehr günstig aus, he reviewed this work very favourably.

Kritikáster, *m.* [-s, *pl.*-] V. Krittler.

Krítiker, *m.* [-s, *pl.* -] critic, [in literary matters, also] reviewer, V. Kunstrichter.

Krítisch, *adj.* and *adv.* 1) [relating to criticism] critic, critical. Eine —e Abhandlung, a critical dissertation; eine —e Zeitschrift, a [critical] review; ein Werk — untersuchen, to examine a work critically; er hat diesen Schriftsteller or sein Buch — or literarisch todt gemacht [in fam. lang.], he cut this author or his book thoroughly or sadly up. 2) [pertaining to a crisis] critical, decisive, important. Ein —er Zeitpunkt, a critical time or moment; [in medicine] der —e Tag, the critical day.

***Kritisíren,** *v. tr.* to criticise. Ein Werk —, to criticise a work; er kritisirt alle meine Handlungen [in fam. lang.], he criticises, censures all my actions, he finds fault with all I do.

Kritteléi, *f.* minute or frivolous criticism, finding constantly fault.

Kritteln, *v. intr.* [seems to be allied to the Icel. *kretta* = widersprechen, D. *kryten* = kreischen, schreien] to criticise minutely or frivolously, to find constantly fault with. Er krittelt über Alles, he finds fault with every thing, he is a censorious fellow, he carps at every thing.

Kríttler, *m.* [-s, *pl.*-] constant fault-finder, over-nice critic.

Kríttlich, *adj.* and *adv.* 1) captious, exceptious, carping, punctilious, nice. — seyn, V. Kritteln. 2) difficult, nice. —e Arbeit, irksome, tedious work.

Kritzeléi, *f.* scrawling, scrawl.

Krítzelig, *adj.* and *adv.* making or resembling pot-hooks. Diese Feder schreibt —, this pen grates or spurts; — schreiben, to scrawl, to scribble.

Krítzeln, [another form of kratzen] *v. tr.* and *intr.* to scratch, to scrawl, to scribble.

Krítzler, *m.* [-s, *pl.* -], —inn, *f.* scrawler, scribbler.

Kröbs, V. Griebs.

Kröck, *m.* [-es] tufted vetch.

***Krokodíll,** *n.* and *m.* [-es, *pl.* -e] crocodile. Das Amerikanische —, the American crocodile, alligator, cayman.

Krokodill=birn, *f.* 1) the fruit of the avigato or avocado, alligator-pear. 2) or —birnbaum, *m.* alligator pear, avigato. —blatt, *n.* umbellated sainfoin or hedysarum. —eier, *pl.* crocodile's eggs. —thränen, *pl.* crocodile tears, false affected tears.

1. **Kröllen, Krölzen,** *v. intr.* to cry as a gor-cock or moor-cock.

2. ||**Kröllen,** I. *v. intr.* to curdle, coagulate or curl in hot water. II. *v. tr.* to coagulate or crisp in hot water, to scald.

Kroll=blume, *f.* [in botany] medeola. —erbse, *f.* a scalded pea. —hecht, *m.* [in cookery] a pike dressed and served up with the tail in the mouth. —lilie, *f.* V. Berglilie. —quappe, *f.* V. Ulmerquappe.

Krönchen, ||**Krönlein,** *n.* [-s, *pl.*-] [*dim.* of Krone] 1) a small crown. 2) [in botany] corollet, corollule.

Króne, *f.* [*pl.* -n] [allied to the L. *corona*, Gr. κορώνη; W. *crwnn* or *cren* and Irish *cruin* = rund] 1) [the prominent and circular part of a thing or a prominent border surrounding a thing circularly] crown, circle; [in architecture] crowning; [in botany] *a*) corol, V. Blumen—, *b*) [the margin of a radiated compound flower] corona, *c*) V. Krönchen 2); die — eines Baumes, the top or crown of a tree; die — eines Priesters, the shaven crown of a priest. [in popular language] Die —, the top or crown of the head; *it.* the head. Er hat Etwas in der — [in popular language], he is a little tipsy, flustered, muddled; die — am Hirschgeweih, the crown of a stag's head; die — eines Zahnes, corona; [among jewellers] die — eines geschliffenen Diamantes, the crown of a rose-diamond. [in optics] halo or luminous circle around the sun, moon &c., corona. 2) [ornament worn by kings &c.] crown. Eine — von Blumen &c., a crown of flowers; kaiserliche, königliche —, imperial, regal crown; päpstliche or dreifache —, the papal or triple crown, tiara. *Fig.* Einem Werke die — aufsetzen, to crown a work; diese berühmte That setzte allen andern die — auf, that famous action crowned all the rest; sie ist die — ihres Geschlechtes, she is the best or pink of her sex; er ist die — meiner Freunde, he is the best of my friends. 3) *Fig.* regal power or dignity. Zur — gelangen, to come to the crown; nach der — streben, to aspire to the crown; auf die — Verzicht thun, to renounce the crown. 4) *Fig.* state, power, kingdom. Die — England, the crown of England; die drei nordischen —n, the three northern crowns or powers. 5) [a coin stamped with the figure of a crown] crown. Die französische —, French crown, French dollar; die englische —, English crown, V. Kronenthaler.

Kron=amt, *n.* an office or charge of the crown [chiefly in the former kingdom of Poland]. —armee, *f.* V. —heer. —beamte, *m.* officer of the crown. —beere, *f.* V. Heidelbeere. —bewerber, *m.* [*—prätendent] pretender to the crown. —blatt, *n.* [in botany] petal. —blume, *f.* fritillary. —bolzen, *m.* [formerly] a bolt or arrow the point of which has the form of a crown, a quarrel. —einkünfte, *pl.* the revenues of the crown. —eisen, *n.* best sort of iron [marked with a crown]. —erbe, *m.* heir to the crown, V. —prinz. —erbse, *f.* V. —enerbse. —feldherr, *m.* commander in chief [chiefly in the former kingdom of Poland]. —fleisch, *n.* [among butchers] midriff, diaphragm. —förmig, *adj.* and *adv.* having the form of a crown, coroniform. [in anatomy] Der —förmige Fortsatz [im Unterkiefer], coronoid process. —gehörn, *n.* small branching horns in the form of a crown on a stag's head, trochings, palmer, palmatory, crown of a stag's head. —gesims, *n.* cornice. —glas, *n.* V. —englas. —großfeldherr, *m.* [especially in ancient Poland] the commander in chief, generalissimo of the crown. —gut, *n.* royal domain, crown-land, crown-demesne. —heer, *n.* army of the crown, king's army [not much used]; *it.* [formerly] army of the kingdom of Poland. —hirsch, *m.* a stag with trochings or with a crown. —kanzler, *m.* *a*) [in ancient Poland], *b*) [in England] Lord [high] Chancellor. —lehen, *n.* fief of the crown. —leuchter, *m.* chandelier, lustre. —lychnis, *f.* [in botany] lychnis coronata. —marschall, *m.* fieldmarshall [of the crown]. —naht, *f.* coronal suture, V. Kranznaht. —notarius, *m.* prothonotary. —papier, *n.* crown-paper. —prinz, *m.* prince royal, crown-prince, V. —erbe. —prinzessinn, *f.* princess royal, crown-princess. —prinzlich, *adj.* and *adv.* belonging to, becoming a prince royal. Der —prinzliche Palast, the palace of the prince royal. —rad, *n.* crown-wheel, swing-wheel, canting-wheel. —raden, *m.* [in botany] the common or red rose campion. —rasch, *m.* best or superior cloth rash. —sarsche, *f.* a kind of serge. —sbeere, *f.* whortleberry. —schatzmeister, *m.* treasurer of the crown. —schenke, *m.* [formerly] king's cup-bearer. —schnepfe, *f.* V. Brachschnepfe. —steuer, *f.*, —thaler, *m.* V. —en=steuer, —en=thaler. —truppen, *pl.* [not much used] troops or forces of the crown, V. —heer. —vogel, *m.* V. —entaube. —werk, *n.* [in fortification] crown-work. —wicke, *f.* the coronilla. —windblume, *f.* the garden anemone. —zahn, *m.* V. Augenzahn, Hundszahn.

Kronen=anemone, *f.* the garden anemone. —antritt, *m.* accession to the crown. —artig, *adj.* and *adv.* in form of a crown, resembling a crown, crown-like; [in botany] petaloid. —backe, *f.* V. —taube. —band, *n.* coronary ligament. —bein, *n.* [in farriery] coronal bone. —blatt, *n.* V. Kronblatt. —blech, *n.* finest iron-plate [marked with the figure of a crown]. —erbse, *f.* umbellate pea. —fortsatz, *m.* coronoid process. —glas, *n.* crown-glass. —gold, *n.* gold of eighteen carats. —jasmin, *m.* the syringa or mock-orange, pipe-tree. —klee, *m.* 1) the common hedysarum or French honeysuckle. 2) medicago coronata. —kraut, *n.* 1) the prickly drypis. 2) a sort of glasswort or saltwort, salsola kali. —lage, *f.* [in botany] foliation. —los, *adj.* and *adv.* having no crown, deprived of the crown; [in botany] having no coral, apetalous.

—naht, *f.* V. Kronnaht. —nessel, *f.* the sea-pudding, cat actinia. —räuber, *m.* usurper of the throne or crown. —schötchen, *n.* V. —wicke. —steuer, *f.* [formerly, especially in France] donative to the king on his accession or coronation. —taube, *f.* crowned pigeon. —thaler, *m.* [in the South of Germany = 4 sh. 6 d. English] a [crown-] dollar. —tragend, *adj.* wearing a crown. —träger, *m.* crowned head. —tute, *f.* crown-imperial-shell. —wicke, *f.* coronilla.

Krönen, *v. tr.* 1) to crown, to wreath[e]. Mit Lorbeer gekrönt, wreathed or crowned with laurel; einen Dichter —, to crown a poet. *Fig.* Du hast ihn mit Ruhm und Ehre gekrönt, thou hast crowned him with glory and honour; ein rühmlicher Tod krönte seine Heldenthaten, a glorious death crowned his exploits; die Tugend —, to crown virtue; das Ende krönet das Werk, the end crowns the work; ein gekrönter Ehemann [in fam. lang., in jest], a cuckold. 2) [to invest with a crown] to crown. Einen König, Kaiser —, to crown a king, an emperor; ein gekröntes Haupt, a crowned head.

Kronsbeere, *f.* V. Preiselbeere.

Krönung, *f.* coronation.

Krönungs-feier, *f.* the ceremony or celebration of the coronation. —feierlichkeit, *f.* solemnity of the coronation. —fest, *n.* V. —feier. —münze, *f.* a coin or medal [struck] in commemoration of the coronation. —ort, *m.* place of coronation. —tag, *m.* coronation-day.

Kroos, *n.* [-es] sea-weed.

†**Kröpel**, *m.* [-s, *pl.* -] [allied to the Low Sax. kruven = kriechen] [vulgar and provincial] a small mean thing, V. Krüppel.

Kröpel-bau, *m.* a vicious way or method of working a mine. —haft, *adj.* and *adv.* V. Krüppelhaft.

Kropf, *m.* [-es, *pl.* Kröpfe] [appears to be allied to Krapf = etwas Gekrümmtes] *dim.* Kröpfchen, ||Kröpflein, *n.* [-s, *pl.* -] 1) crop, craw [of a bird]. Dieser Vogel hat einen vollen —, this bird has its crop full. †*Fig.* Er hat sich den — recht voll gestopft, he has stuffed well. 2) wen [at the throat]. 3) [in botany] excrescence. 4) [in the veterinary art] a tumour or bladder under the jaws of cattle filled with air and water. 5) Der — eines Schiffes, head or bow of a ship.

Kropf-artig, *adj.* and *adv.* of the nature of a wen, scrofulous. Eine —artige Geschwulst, a scrofulous tumour. —bein, *n.* V. Kehlkopf. —blume, *f.* [in botany] erinus. —eidechse, *f.* a sort of lizard [lacerta strumosa, Linn.]. —eisen, *n.* [among masons] an iron tool to raise or heave large stones with. —ente, *f.* morillon. —felge, *f.* felly of the cog-wheel. —fisch, *m.* ostracion. —gans, *f.* pelican. —gerste, *f.* the wall-barleygrass. —klette, *f.* the common burdock. —mensch, *m.* V. Cretin. —mittel, *n.* a remedy for wens. —natter, *f.* adder of Egypt [coluber haje, Linn.]. —salamander, *m.* V. —eidechse. —salat, *m.* V. Kopfsalat. —taube, *f.* V. Kröpfer 2). —vogel, *m.* 1) V. —gans. 2) bittern or bittour. —wage, *f.* [in seamen's language] breast-hooks or fore-hooks. —wurz, —wurzel, *f.* 1) the knotty-rooted figwort. 2) common fern. 3) V. —klette.

Kröpfen, I. *v. tr.* 1) to bend rectangularly. 2) to cram [birds &c.] †Einen —, to cram or stuff any one with meat. II. *v. intr.* [said of birds of prey] to eat. III. *v. r.* sich —, [said of pigeons] to pout.

Kröpfer, *m.* [-s, *pl.* -] 1) one who crams [birds &c.]. 2) [in nat. hist.] cropper-pigeon.

Kröpficht, *adj.* V. Kropfartig.

1. **Kröpfig**, *adj.* and *adv.* 1) afflicted with a wen [at the throat]. 2) bent rectangularly.

2. **Kröpfig**, *adj.* and *adv.* [allied to the Low Sax. kruven = kriechen] short, stunted.

Kröß, *n.* [-es, *pl.* -e] V. Gekröse.

||**Kröschen**, *v. intr.* V. Kreischen.

Kröse, *f.* [*pl.* -n] [among coopers] 1) notch. 2) notching-tool, V. Gergel.

Krösestein, *m.* [-es, *pl.* -e] 1) the star-coral. 2) [a sort of gypsum] compact sulphate of lime.

Kröte, *f.* [*pl.* -n] [perhaps allied to schreiten (kreiten) as the Fr. *crapaud* is allied to the L. *repo*; Low Sax. kruven = kriechen] 1) toad. *Fig.* [in popular lang.] Er ist eine häßliche —, he is an ugly toad; giftig werden, wie eine —, to swell like a toad; er ist so giftig, wie eine —, he is full of malice or spite. 2) an offensive tumour in animals.

Kröten-auge, *n.* 1) V. —stein. 2) V. Vergißmeinnicht. —balsam, *m.* V. —münze. —bilz, *m.* V. —pilz. —binse, *f.* toadrush. —biß, *m.* [in botany] V. Froschbiß. —blatt, *n.* [in botany] *a*) the water-dock. *b*) the curled dock. —dille, *f.* the stinking camomile. —distel, *f.* the small meadow-rue. —fisch, *m.* toad-fish. —flachs, *m.* toad-flax. —fuß, *m.* the slender spiked cock's foot panic grass. —gallusschel, *f.* V. —pilz. —gerippe, *n.* conferva. —gift, *n.* the spit of a toad. —gras, *n.* 1) the soft rush. 2) V. —binse. 3) V. —fuß. —hai, *m.* angel-fish, scate. —käfer, *m.* V. Goldkäfer. —kraut, *n.* 1) ragwort. 2) V. Lungenkraut. 3) V. Waldnessel. 4) V. Traubenkraut. —loch, *n.* V. —nest. —melde, *f.* the thorn-apple. —münze, *f.* the water-mint. —nessel, *f.* V. —kraut 3). —nest, *n.* a low swampy place full of toads. ||—petersilein, *n.* common hemlock. —pilz, *m.* the egg agaric. —schwamm, *m.* V. Mistschwamm. —stein, *m.* toad-stone.

Krücke, *f.* [*pl.* -n] [allied to the Lat. *crux*, Kreuz, probably from ragen], *dim.* Krückchen, ||Krücklein, *n.* [-s, *pl.* -] 1) any thing crooked or hooked; [among organ-builders] spring. Die — an einer Geige, peg of a violin. *it.* a tool for scraping or drawing any thing away [such as mud, rubbish and the like], mud-scraper; *it.* a hooked peg, pick-lock; *it.* forked stick. V. Kalk—, Ofen—, Pech—, Schlamm—. 2) a crutch. An —n gehen, to walk or go with or on crutches. Syn. Krücke, Stab. A Stab is sufficient for him who wishes to save himself from falling; a Krücke is necessary for him who cannot move his body forward by his feet alone. The Krücke must therefore be curved at its upper end, that the weight of the body, whether by means of the hand, or under the arm, may rest upon it.

Krücken-blatt, *n.* the flat piece or board at the end of a scraper. —förmig, *adj.* having the form of a crutch; [in blazonry] potence. —stiel, *m.* the handle of a scraper. —stock, *m.* 1) a stick in form of a crutch. 2) a crutch.

Krückel, *n.* [-s, *pl.* -] [*dim.* of Krücke] 1) a small scraper. 2) V. 2. Dietrich. 3) a wrong fold [in cloth &c.]

Krück-Elster, *f.* [*pl.* -n] lanner, shrike.

Krücken, I. *v. intr.* to walk with or on crutches. II. *v. tr.* to draw away or remove with a scraping instrument; *it.* to cleanse with such an instrument.

Krück-Ente, *f.* [*pl.* -n] teal.

Krüden, *m.* [-s] [in botany] V. Hahnenkamm 2).

Krug, *m.* [-es, *pl.* Krüge], *dim.* Krügchen, ||Krüglein, *n.* [-s, *pl.* -] [Fr. *cruche*, Sw. *kruka*, D. *kruik*, *kroes*, allied to the Fr. *creux* = hohl, Gr. κρωσσός = Wassergefäß] 1) pitcher, stone-bottle, mug, jug. Ein — voll Oel, a bottle of oil; Wein in Krüge füllen, to put wine into stone-bottles, jugs or pitchers; ein — Selterser [||Selzer-] Wasser, a stone-bottle of water of Selters. *Prov.* Der — geht so lange zu Wasser, bis er bricht, the pitcher goes so often to the well that it comes home broken at last. V. Bier—, Oel—, Wein—. 2) [in North-Germany] ale-house, public-house.

Krug-bier, *n.* beer in stone-bottles or jugs. —bürste, *f.* [stone-] bottle-brush. —fiedler, *m.* V. Bierfiedler. —förmig, *adj.* having the form of a pitcher; [in botany] urceolate. —gerechtigkeit, *f.* right or privilege of keeping a public-house. —wirbel, *m.* V. Räderthierchen.

Krüger, *m.* [-s, *pl.* -] ale-house keeper, public-house keeper. —inn, *f.* ale-house-keeper's wife; *it.* a woman who keeps an ale-house.

||**Krülle**, *f.* [*pl.* -n] curl. V. Haarlocke.

||**Krüllen**, or **Krüllen**, *v. tr.* V. Kräuseln.

Krull-erbse, *f.* V. Krollerbse. —farn, *m.* true maidenhair. —lilie, *f.* the mountain-lily, martagon, Turk's cap. —weizen, *m.* spelt. —wolle, *f.* Danish wool.

Krume, *f.* [*pl.* -n] [from the Sax. *cramman* or Low Sax. *cruman* = zerreiben] *dim.* Krümchen, ||Krümlein, Krümel, Krümelchen, *n.* [-s, *pl.* -] 1) crum[b]. Essen Sie gern die —? do you like the crum? 2) a small piece, a little bit. Es ist kein Krümchen davon vorhanden, there is not the least crumb, bit &c. of it; ein Krümchen Salz, a little grain of salt.

Krümelig *adj.* and *adv.* crummy.

Krümeln, I. *v. intr.* to fall into crums, to crumble. II. *v. tr.* to convert into crums, to crumble.

Krümel-sauer, *n.* [among bakers] leaven preserved in crums.

1. **Krümen**, *v. tr.* V. Krümeln. II.

2. **Krümen**, *v. intr.* [probably allied to the old Sw. *gro*, Eng. *to grow* = wachsen, or to grün] to put forth the young blades or shoots [of corn].

Krumm, *adj.* and *adv.* [allied to Krampf, krimpen, schrumpfen, Eng. *crome* or *crow* = Haken] crooked, curved, bent. Eine —e Linie, a curve line, a curve; ein —er Pfad, a winding or crooked path; der —e Lauf eines Flusses, the winding course of a river; die —en Windungen einer Schlange, the writhing folds of a serpent; eine Nadel — biegen, to bend a needle; dieser Baum fängt an — zu werden, this tree begins to grow crooked; dieses Holz wird —, this wood warps; ein —es Maul, a wry mouth; eine —e Nase, a crooked nose; dieser Mensch ist —, that man has crooked or bandy legs, *it.* that man is crook-backed, a cripple; —e Finger haben, to have crooked fingers, *fig.* to be light-fingered; er wird alt und fängt an — und gebückt zu gehen, he grows old and begins to stoop; Sie werden mit der Zeit ganz — werden, you will be quite crooked in time; Einen — schließen, to chain any one in a crooked position; — schreiben, not to write straight, to write up and down; †Einen — und lahm schlagen, hauen, to bang any one soundly, to thrash or maul any one unmercifully, to beat any one to a cripple, to cripple any one. *Fig.* —e Sprünge machen [in popular lang.], to use shifts; —e Wege [in [illegible] language], indirect ways; mit Etwas — herum kommen [in popular lang.], to beat about the bush; Einen — ansehen [in popular lang.], to look askew upon any one, to look at any one with an ill eye.

Krumm-ästig, *adj.* having crooked boughs. —bein, *n.* a crooked leg; *it.* a person having a crooked leg, polt-foot. —beinig, *adj.* having crooked legs, bandy-legged. Ein —beiniges Pferd, a crook-legged horse. —buckel, *m.* a crooked or bent back; †*it.* a crook-backed person, crook-back. —darm, *m.* [in anatomy] ileum intestinum. —darm-ader, *f.* iliac blood-vessel. —flächig, *adj.* having a crooked or curved surface. —fuß, *m.*, —füßig, *adj.* V. —bein, —beinig. —gängig, *adj.* full of windings and turnings, anfractuous. —gehörnt, *adj.* having crooked horns. —geschnäbelt, *adj.* having a crooked bill. —hals, *m.* a wry neck; †*it.* a wry-necked person. —halsig, *adj.* wry-necked. —hecht, *m.* V. Krollhecht. —holz, *n.* 1) a crooked or curved piece of wood; [in ship-building] rib. 2) a wheelwright, cartwright. —holzbaum, *m.* the mountain pine-tree, the wild mountain pine. —holzkiefer, *f.* V. —holzbaum. —horn, *n.* 1) a crooked horn. 2) an animal with crooked horns. —hörnig, *adj.* V. —gehörnt. —kiefer, *m.* [a fish] cyprinus aspius. —linig, *adj.* curvilinear. †—maul, *n.* wry-mouth. †—mäulig, *adj.* wry-mouthed. —nase, *f.* crooked nose. —nasig, *adj.* having a crooked nose. —schenkelig, *adj.* having crooked thighs. —schnabel, *m.* 1) a crooked bill. 2) [a bird] cross-bill, scooper. —schnäbelig, *adj.* having a crooked bill. —stab, *m.* crook; *it.* crosier. —stabträger, *m.* crosier-bearer. —stampfer, *m.* [among hatters] stamper. —stroh, *n.* crumpled straw, litter. —zange, *f.* crooked tongs. —zirkel, *m.* cylindrical or spherical compasses, V. Dickzirkel.

Krümme, *f.* 1) crookedness, curvity, curvature. Die — eines Weges, the anfractuousness of a way. 2) [*pl.* -n] turning or winding. Der Fluß hat viele —n, the river has many turnings or windings; ein Weg voll —n, a way full of windings and turnings, an anfractuous way. V. Krümmung.

Krümmen, I. *v. tr.* to crook, to bend, to curve Eine Nadel —, to bend a needle; gekrümmte Beine, crooked or bandy legs; der gekrümmte Lauf eines Flusses, the crooked or winding course of a river. II. *v. r.* sich —, to bend, to become crooked. Dieser Balken fängt an sich zu —, that beam begins to bend; Holz, das sich krümmt, wood that warps; jener Mann fängt an sich zu — [not much used], that man begins to stoop; sich unter der Last —, to bend or sink under the load; eine Straße, ein Fluß krümmt sich, a road, a river winds or serpentizes. *Prov.* Auch der kleinste Wurm krümmt sich, wenn er getreten wird, the least worm turns again if you tread upon it. *Fig.* Sich vor Jemand —, to cringe or crouch to any one, to humble one's self before another.

Krümmung, *f.* [*pl.* -en] 1) the act of bending &c. 2) V. Krümme.

Krümpen, V. Krimpen.

Krünitz, *m.* [-es, *pl.* -e] cross-bill, V. Kreuzschnabel.

||**Krünkel**, *n.* [-s, *pl.* -] a fold, wrinkle.

||**Krünkelig**, *adj.* full of folds or wrinkles, wrinkled.

Krüppel, *m.* [-s, *pl.* -] [Sw. *krympling*, Dan. *krypling*, allied to the Icel. *crypen* = to move crooked, Low Sax. krupen = kriechen] cripple. Einen zum — machen, to deprive any one of the use of his limbs, to maim, to cripple any one; zum — werden, to be crippled. *Fig.* [in pop. lang.] a little shrimp. Syn. Krüppel, Lahm, Hinkend. When a limb is rendered useless by any natural defect, the limb and the person are lahm; he who is lahm in the feet, hinkt. A Krüppel is one whose hands or feet, or whole body, have not that completeness and natural form which is requisite for their beauty and ready use. He who has no arms or feet, is not lahm and hinkend, but a Krüppel. He who has crooked feet, but does not limp, may be called a Krüppel, but not lahm.

Krüppel-baum, *m.* a stunted tree, a dwarf-tree. —busch, *m.* a stunted or dwarfish bush or shrub. —spill, *n.* [in seamen's lang.] crab.

Krüppelei, *f.* [low] drudgery, toilsome work.

Krüppelhaft, *adj.* and *adv.* maimed, lame, disabled, crippled.

Krüppelig, *adj.* and *adv.* maimed, lame, disabled, crippled. Ein —er Mensch, a cripple; ein —er Baum, a stunted tree, dwarf-tree.

Krüse, *f.* [*pl.* -n] 1) V. Krause. 2) V. Krug.

Krüspel, Krüspeln, V. Knorpel, Knorpeln.

Krüspig, *adj.* V. Kraus.

Krüste, *f.* [*pl.* -n] [L. *crusta*, Fr. *croûte*, Low Sax. *korste*, allied to the L. *cortex* = Kork] *dim.* Krüstchen, ||Krüstlein, *n.* [-s, *pl.* -] crust. Die — des Brodes, einer Pastete, the crust of bread, of a pie; geben Sie ihm das Krüstchen, give him the crust; eine — von Weinstein, a crust of tartar; sein Körper ist Eine —, he is all over scab or scurf.

Krüstig, *adj.* and *adv.* crusty.

Krütze, *f.* [*pl.* -n] V. Krücke.

***Kryolith**, *m.* [-es, *pl.* -e] cryolite.

***Krypto**, secret, occult, hidden [in composition, as:]

Krypto-calvinist, *m.* a clandestine calvinist. —gamie, *f.* [in botany] cryptogamy. —gamisch, *adj.* cryptogamian. —gamist, *m.* a cryptogamian plant. —graphie, *f.* cryptography. —graphisch, *adj.* cryptographical. —leucitlava, *f.* cryptoleucite.

***Krystáll**, V. Kristall.

Kubébe, *f.* V. Cubebe.

Kubel, *f.* [*pl.* -n] jaw of a pig or hog.

Kübel, *m.* [-s, *pl.* -] *dim.* Kübelchen, *n.* [-s, *pl.* -] [Gr. κύπελλον and σκύφος = Becher, Lat. *cupa*, Kufe, allied to the L. *cavus*, *scapha* &c.] bucket, pail, tub. Mit einem — Wasser aus dem Flusse schöpfen, to draw water out of the river with a bucket or pail. V. Kalk—, Melk—, Milch—, Rühr—, Speiß—, Wasch—. [in gardening] case, box Pomeranzenbäume in — setzen, to case orange-trees.

Kübelharz, *n.* officinal resin.

Kubik, Kubisch, V. Cubik, Cubisch &c.

Kübler, *m.* [-s, *pl.* -] cooper, V. Böttcher, Faßbinder.

Küche, *f.* [*pl.* -n] *dim.* Küchelchen, ||Küchlein, *n.* [from kochen] 1) kitchen. Das bringt Etwas in die —, *fig.*, that helps to make the pot boil; sie ist durch die — gelaufen, she understands cookery a little; †des Teufels —, *fig.*, hell; †in des Teufels — kommen, *fig.*, to get into a great scrape or into the wrong box. 2) *Fig.* *a*) the art of dressing victuals, cookery. Die — verstehen, to understand cookery, V. Kochkunst. *b*) what is dressed for the table. Kalte —, cold meat or victuals; die — bestellen, besorgen, to dress the meat or victuals, to cook, to provide for the dinner or supper; er liebt eine gute —, geht nur der guten — nach, he loves good or nice eating, he frequents no houses but where a good table is kept. *c*) [collectively] the people belonging to the kitchen.

Küchen-amt, *n.* 1) office in a great person's kitchen. 2) all the persons belonging to a great man's kitchen. —arbeit, *f.* kitchen-work. —ausdruck, *m.* expression or term used in cookery. —bediente, *m.* a man employed about the kitchen. Die sämmtlichen —bedienten, all the persons employed in a great man's kitchen. —bret, *n.* kitchen-shelf. —dienst, *m.* V. —amt 1). —feuer, *n.* kitchen-fire. —garten, *m.* kitchen-garden. —gärtner, *m.* gardener who cultivates pot-herbs &c., kitchen-gardener. —geräth, *n.*, —geräthschaft, *f.* kitchen-furniture, kitchen-utensils. —geschirr, *n.* kitchen-furniture, V. —geräth. —gesinde, *n.* the persons employed in a great man's kitchen. —gewächs, *n.* vegetables for the kitchen, pot-herbs, greens &c. —hader, *m.* V. —lumpen. —handtuch, *n.* V. —tuch. —herd, *m.* hearth in the kitchen. —holz, *n.* small wood for the kitchen, kitchen-wood. —junge, *m.* kitchen-boy, scullion. —kammer, *f.* pantry, larder. —knabe, *m.* [not used] V. —junge. —knecht, *m.* man employed in the kitchen. —kräuter, *pl.* kitchen-herbs, pot-herbs. —latein, *n.* bad Latin [such as was spoken in the kitchens of monasteries] dog-Latin. —leben, *n.* life of a cook. —licht, *n.* kitchen-candle, candle for the kitchen or for the servants. —löffel, *m.* V. Kochlöffel. —lumpen, *m.* a dish-clout. —mädchen, *n.*, —magd, *f.* kitchen-maid, cook-maid. —maß, *n.* [formerly] measure of flour at Leipzig. —mäßig, *adj.* and *adv.* fit for the kitchen, smelling of the kitchen. —mäßiges Latein, V. —latein. —meister, *m.* master of the kitchen [an office in great establishments]. ‡ or †—mensch, *n.* kitchen-wench. —messer, *n.* kitchen-knife. —muschel, *f.* common or edible muscle. —obst, *n.* fruit for boiling or baking, boiling or baking fruit. —pflanze, *f.* V. —gewächs. —salz, *n.* kitchen-salt. —schelle, *f.* [in botany] pasque-flower. —schilling, *m.* [in popular lang.] whip-breech. —schlüssel, *m.* kitchen-key. —schrank, *m.* press or cupboard in a kitchen, meat-safe, larder. —schreiber, *m.* clerk of the kitchen [in a prince's or other great person's household]. —schürze, *f.* kitchen-apron. —schwalbe, *f.* martin, martlet. —schwamm, *m.* eatable mushroom. —sieb, *n.* kitchen-sieve. —sprache, *f.* bad language, gibberish, jargon. —stück, *n.* a painting representing [the interior &c. of] a kitchen. —thür, *f.* kitchen-door. —tisch, *m.* kitchen-table, dresser. —tuch, *n.* kitchen-towel. —wagen, *m.* a vehicle to convey provisions or stores for the kitchen [in a prince's &c. household]. —zettel, *m.* bill of fare. —zeug, *n.* kitchen-linen. —zucker, *m.* brown sugar, moist sugar, cassonade.

Kuchen, *m.* [-s, *pl.* -] [from kochen = backen] cake; *dim.* ein Küchlein or Küchelchen, [-s, *pl.* -] a small cake; V. Apfel—, Asch—, Brod—, Hochzeit—, Honig—, Käse—, Kirsch—, Mohn—, Opfer—, Pflaumen— &c.

Kuchen-bäcker, *m.* pastry-cook. —bäckerei, *f.* pastry trade, *it.* pie-house. —bret, *n.* the board on which a cake is put into the oven, cake-board. —eisen, *n.* wafer-iron. —form, *f.* 1) the form of a cake. 2) mould for making cakes. —förmig, *adj.* and *adv.* having the form of a cake. —pfanne, *f.* cake-pan. —rad, —rädchen, *n.* jagging-iron. —schieber, *m.* peel. —teig, *m.* paste or dough for cakes.

1. ||Küchlein, *n.* [-s, *pl.*-] *dimin.* of Kücher.

2. Küchlein, *n.* [-s, *pl.*-] 1) *dimin.* of Kuchen. 2) chicken.

Küchler, *m.* [-s, *pl.*] V. Kuchenbäcker.

Kücken, &c. V. Gucken &c.

Kuckuck, *m.* [-s, *pl.* -e] [Fr. *coucou*, Gr. *κόκκυξ*, Sw. *gök*, Sax. *gaec*, *geac*, probably so called from its note] 1) cuckoo. Das Geschrei, der Ruf des —s, the note of the cuckoo. *Prov.* Der — ruft seinen eigenen Namen aus, he betrays himself; *it.* †the pot calls the kettle black; the kiln calls the oven burn-house; er wird den — nicht wieder rufen hören, he won't live to see the summer; [in popular language] daß dich der — ! deuce take you! 2) [in botany] the pyramidal or mountain bugle. Blauer —, the common or meadow bugle, middle consound.

Kuckucks-ammer, *f.* the babbling warbler. —blume, *f.* 1) cuckoo-flower. 2) V. Feldkresse, Wiesenkresse. 3) the man orchis. —brod, *n.*, — klee, *m.*, — kohl, *m.* wood-sorrel, cuckoo-sorrel. —pfeife, *f.* a pipe imitating the note or call of the cuckoo. —schiefer, *m.* a species of slate of a bluish colour with red spots. —speichel, *m.* 1) cuckoo-spittle. 2) V. —blume 1). —stein, *m.* V. —schiefer.

Kuder, *m.* [-s, *pl.* -] [an other form of Kater] 1) the male of the wild cat. ||2) V. Steinmarder.

Kudern, *v. intr.* V. Krollen.

1. Kufe, *f.* [*pl.* -n] *dim.* Küfchen or Kufchen, *n.* [-s, *pl.*-] [perhaps allied to heben, schieben] one of the curved pieces of wood that form a sledge, cheek of a sledge.

2. Kufe, *f.* [*pl.* -n] *dim.* Küfchen or Kufchen, *it.* ||Küflein, *n.* [-s, *pl.* -]. [L. *cupa*, another form of Kübel, Küpe, allied to Koffer, Kober &c.] 1) a large tub, a vat. Eine — binden, to hoop a tub; eine —voll, a tub-full, a vat-full; V. Beiz—, Wein—, Zeug—. 2) a large beer-barrel. 3) [in conchology] the snipe, snipe-bill.

Kufen-bier, *n.* march-beer. —gewölbe, *n.* V. Tonnengewölbe.

Küfer, *m.* [-s, *pl.*-] cooper.

Küfer-handwerk, *n.* cooper's trade. —knecht, *m.* journeyman cooper.

Kuffe, *f.* [*pl.* -n] or Kuffschiff, *n.* a kind of vessel with a main-mast and mizen-mast.

Küffer, *m.* V. Koffer.

||Küflein, *n*, *dim.* of 2. Kufe.

Küfner, *m.* V. Küfer.

Kugel, *f.* [*pl.* -n] *dim.* Kügelchen, ||Kügelein, *n.* [-s, *pl.*-] [Sw. and Pol. *kulu*, allied to kollern &c.] [in general] something rounded. *a*) [in anatomy] Die — eines Beines, the rounded head or extremity of a bone; sich die — ausfallen, to dislocate one's arm &c. by a fall; die — einrenken, to set a bone into joint. *b*) a round body, a ball, globe, sphere. Eine — zum Billardspielen, a ball to play at billiards; eine — zum Wählen, ballot; die Erde ist eine —, the earth is a ball or globe; —n und Kegel, bowls and nine pins. [in botany] tubercle; [in nat. hist.] V. —thier. *c*) a ball of iron or lead, a bullet. —n wechseln, to fight with pistols; Einen auf —n herausfordern, to challenge any one to fight with pistols; sich eine — vor den Kopf schießen, to blow one's brains out; eine 24 pfündige —, a ball or bullet of four-and-twenty pounds, a four-and-twenty pounder; eine glühende —, a red-hot ball.

Kugel-abschnitt, *m.* V. —schnitt. —achse, *f.* the axis of the sphere. —armbrust, *f.* a cross-bow for shooting bullets, stone-bow. —back, *n.* [on board of men-of-war] shot-locker. —bahn, *f.* V. Kegelbahn. —band, *n.* V. Kapselband. —baum, *m.* a tree lopped in form of a ball. —becher, *m.* a roundish cup or goblet. —binse, *f.* the round-headed rush. —blume, *f.* 1) the common globularia or blue daisy. 2) the globe-flower, globe-ranunculus. —büchse, *f.* a rifle-gun. —dicke, *f.* caliber. —distel, *f.* the globe thistle. —dreiecksiehre, *f.* spherical trigonometry. —fisch, *m.* orb-fish, orbis. —flasche, *f.* a round-bellied bottle. —flechte, *f.* round-headed coralline lichen. —form, *f.* 1) spherical form, sphericalness. 2) a mould for casting balls or bullets. —förmig, *adj.* and *adv.* globular, spherical, orbicular. —frei, *adj.* and *adv.* musket-proof. —fuß, *m.* [among joiners] a foot in form of a ball. —futter, *n.* a patch of cloth or leather, commonly greased, in which the bullets for a riflegun are wrapped. —gerade, *adj.* and *adv.* [among gunsmiths &c.] very straight, quite equal. —gestalt, *f.* V. —form 1). —gewölbe, *n.* a hemispherical vault. —gießer, *m.* 1) caster of balls or bullets. 2) V. —form 2). —gleich, *adj.* V. —gerade. —größe, *f.* V. —dicke. —haufen, *m.* a pile of balls or bullets. —haupt, *n.* V. Kaulbörs. —karte, *f.* planisphere. —kasten, *m.* an inclosed place in an arsenal where the balls or bullets are kept. —knopf, *m.* 1) [among gunsmiths] the tool for turning the cavity of a mould for casting bullets. 2) V. Knopfbaum. —kreisel, *m.* V. Brummkreisel. —lack, *m.* artificial lac. —lehr, *n.* shot-gage. —loch, *n.* V. —sack. —loos, *n.* balloting. Das —loos ziehen, to ballot. —losung, *f.* balloting. —maß, *n.* V. —lehr. —maßliebe, *f.* V. —blume 1). —messer, *m.* spherometer. —narzisse, *f.* globular daffodil. —pflaster, *n.* V. —futter. —plan, *m.* bowling-ground, bowling-green, V. also Kegelbahn. —platz, *m.* 1) V. the foregoing word. 2) V. —kasten. —probe, *f.* V. —lehr. —quarz, *m.* globulous quarz. —recke, *f.* shot-garland, shot-locker. —regen, *m.* a shower of balls or bullets. —ring, *m.* a ring without a bezil. —rund, *adj.* and *adv.* round as a ball, spherical, globular. **Fig.* [of a stumpy and very thick or fat person] fat and round, [of a horse] sleek. —ründe, *f.* sphericalness, sphericity. —saat, *f.* V. —regen. —sack, *m.* the hazard in a billiard-table. —scheibe, *f.* [in nat. hist.] ascidia quadradentata. —schnapper, *m.* V. —armbrust. —schnecke, *f.* spherical sea-shell or conch. —schnitt, *m.* spherical section, segment of a sphere. —schwamm, *m.* puff-ball, puff, puffin, fuzz-ball. —spiegel, *m.* spherical mirror. —spiel, *n.* V. Ballspiel. —spinne, *f.* V. Kreuzspinne. —thier, —thierchen, *n.* globe-animal, volvox. —[n]wagen, *m.* ammunition waggon, caisson. —wahl, *f.* V. —loos; [in botany] V. —schwamm. —winkel, *m.* spherical angle. —wurm, *m.* V. —thier. —zange, *f.* V. —zieher 2). —zieher, *m.* 1) a spiral instrument for drawing out a bullet, worm. 2) [in surgery] forceps. —zirkel, *m.* V. —schnitt.

Kugelicht, *adj.* and *adv.* resembling a ball, round, globular.

Kugelig, *adj.* and *adv.* having the form of a ball, globular, spherical, orbicular. —e Körper, spherical bodies. V. Kugelförmig, Kugelrund.

Kugeln, I. *v. intr.* 1) to roll like a ball. 2) to bowl. 3) to ballot. II. *v. tr.* 1) to roll [a ball]. Sich auf dem Rasen —, to roll upon the grass or turf. 2) to make any thing round or spherical, to round.

Kugelung, *f.* balloting, ballot.

Kuh, *f.* [*pl.* Kühe] [Sax. *cu*, Sw. and Isel. *ko*, Russ. *kua*, Sanscrit *go*, Pers. *ghau*] cow. Eine junge —, heifer; blinde — spielen, V. Blind. *Prov.* Bei Nacht sind alle Kühe schwarz, when candles are out, all cats are grey; †Joan is as good as my Lady in the dark; er sieht es an, wie die — das neue Thor, he stands gaping at it like a simpleton.

Kuh-auge, *n.* 1) a cow's eye. *Fig.* a large full eye, ox-eye. 2) [in botany] V. —dill. —bauch, *m.* *Fig.* hanging belly. —blatter, *f.* V. —pocke. —blume, *f.* 1) V. Dotterblume. 2) dandelion, †piss-a-bed. 3) the ox-eye daisy. —brücke, *f.* V. Kühbrücke. —butter, *f.* butter made of cow's milk. —dill, *m.*, —dille, *f.* 1) the corn camomile. 2) the stinking camomile. —dreck, *m.* V. —fladen. —dung, *m.* V. —mist. —euter, *n.* cow's udder. —fladen, *m.* cow-dung, neat's dung. —fladenöl, *n.* the spirit of all-flower water. —fladenwasser, *n.* all-flower water. —fleisch, *n.* cow's flesh, cow's meat. —fuß, *m.* *Fig.* an iron crow. —futter, *n.* food or fodder for cows. —glocke, *f.* a bell for a cow. —haar, *n.* cow's hair. —haaren, *adj.* of cow's hair. —häckig, *adj.* V. Engbeinig. —hamen, *m.* the collar of a cow, by which it is fastened to the manger. —haut, *f.* the hide of a cow. *Fig.* [in pop. lang.] Das läßt sich nicht auf eine —haut schreiben, there is so much to be said on that subject that I shall never have done. —hirt, *m.*, —hirtinn, *f.* cow-herd, neat-herd. —horn, *n.* 1) cow's horn; *it.* [a wind-instrument] the horn of the cow-herd. 2) [in botany] fenugreek. —kalb, *n.* female calf. —käse, *m.* cheese made of cow's milk. —koth, *m.* V. —fladen. —kraut, *n.* 1) the perfoliate soap-wort. 2) V. —wurzel. —leder, *n.* neat's leather. —ledern, *adj.* of neat's leather. —maul, *n.* cow's mouth. —melker, *m.*, —melkerinn, *f.* one who milks the cows, milker, dairy-man, dairy-maid. —milbe, *f.* tick. —milch, *f.* cow's milk. —mist, *m.* cow's dung. —molken, *pl.* whey of cow's milk. —pacht, *m.* V. Viehpacht. —pastinak, *f.* cow-parsnip. —peterlein, *n.* cow-weed. —pocken, *pl.* cow-pox. Einem Kinde die —pocken einimpfen, to inoculate a child with the cow-pox, to vaccinate a child. —pockenarzt, *m.* inoculator of the cow-pox. —pockengift, *n.* vaccine matter or virus. —pockenimpfung, *f.* vaccination. —pockenmaterie, *f.*, —pockenstoff, *m.* vaccine matter, ichor, virus or lymph. —reigen, —reihen, *m.* [especially in Switzerland] cow-call, ranz-des-vaches. —sauger, *m.* the nocturnal goat-sucker, the churn-owl. —schelle, *f.* 1) V. —glocke. 2) V. Meereichel. —schwanz, *m.* cow's tail. —stall, *m.* cow-house. —stelze, *f.* the yellow wagtail [motacilla boarula Linn.]. —weide, *f.* cow-pasture. —weizen, *m.* 1) cow-wheat. 2) V. Lolch. —wurzel, *f.* 1) the annual mercury. 2) V. Fieberwurzel 1). —zehente, *m.* V. Milchzehente.

Küh-brücke, *f.* [in seamen's lang.] spare deck or orlop. —füßig, *adj.* V. Engbeinig. —haar, *n*, —hirt, *m.* &c., V. Kuhhaar &c. —ruhe, *f.* or —unter, *n.* a shady place where cows are driven during the greatest heat.

Küher, *m.*, —inn, *f.* V. Kuhhirt, Kuhhirtinn.

Küherei, *f.* V. Schweizerei.

Kühl, *adj.* and *adv.* [Sax. *col*, Eng. *cool*, allied to kalt] cool. Die Luft ist —, es geht eine —e Luft, the air is cool, it blows a cool breeze; ein —er Morgen, a cool morning; ein —es Zimmer, a cool room; den Punsch — werden lassen, to let the punch cool; — werden, to grow cool, to cool; *fig.* to lose the heat of excitement or passion, to cool.

Kühl=böse, *f.* [in breweries] cooling-vat or tub, cooler. —**eimer**, *m.*, —**faß**, *n.* cooling-pail or cask, cooler; [in chymistry] refrigeratory. —**gefäß**, *n.* cooling-vessel, cooler. —**kessel**, *m.* cooling-kettle, cooler. —**mittel**, *n.* cooling remedy, refrigerant. —**ofen**, *m.* [in glass-houses] cooling-furnace. —**pfanne**, *f.* cooling pan, cooler. —**pflaster**, *n.* cooling-plaster. —**salbe**, *f.* cooling-salve. —**schiff**, *n.* V. —böse. —**schlange**, *f.* serpentine worm of a still, serpentine. —**stock**, *m.* cooler. —**trank**, *m.* cooling-drink, julep. —**trense**, *f.* mastigadour. —**trog**, *m.* cooling-trough. —**wanne**, *f.* cooling-fan, a utensil for cooling liquor. —**wisch**, *m.* a whisk for sprinkling water, V. Löschwisch.

Kühle, *f.* 1) coolness, cool. Die — des Morgens, der Luft, the cool of the morning, the coolness, freshness of the air; in der — spazieren gehen, to walk in the cool; in der — reisen, to travel in the cool of the day. *Fig.* want of ardour, emotion or affection, coldness, coolness. Einen Plan mit — fassen, to form a design coolly. 2) [in seamen's lang.] gale, breeze. Eine durchgehende —, a settled wind; frische —, loom-gale; eine kleine —, schlaffe —, a light or small gale or breeze; labbere —, steady breeze; steife —, a hard, strong or stiff gale. 3) [in breweries] V. Kühlböse.

Kühlen, I. *v. intr.* and *v. r* sich —, 1) to grow cool, to cool. Etwas — lassen, to let any thing cool; [in seamen's lang.] der Wind kühlet, the wind freshens. 2) to be cool. II. *v. tr.* to make cool, to cool. Den Wein —, to cool wine; —de Mittel, cooling remedies, refrigerants, refrigeratives. **Fig.* Seinen Muth or sein Müthchen an Einem —, to wreak one's anger upon any one. III. *v. r.* sich —, to grow cooler, to cool. Das Wetter fängt an, sich zu —, the weather begins to cool.

Kühlig, *adj.* and *adv.* coolish.

Kühling, *m.* [-es, *pl* -e] 1) [a fish] cyprinus idus. 2) V. Meergrundel. 3) V. Schafpilz.

Kühlung, *f.* 1) act of cooling. 2) coolness, cool, cool air, cool state of the atmosphere. Die — der Nacht, the cool of the night; in der — gehen, to walk in the cool. 3) a fresh breeze, V. Kühle 2). 4) [in poetry] cool water, a cool brook &c.

Kühn, *adj.* and *adv.* [probably from können] bold, hardy, daring. — wie ein Löwe, bold as a lion; eine —e Unternehmung, a bold enterprise. *Fig.* Ein —er Ausdruck, eine —e Figur, a bold expression, figure. Syn. V. Dreist.

Kühnmuth, *m.* courage, bravery, intrepidity, boldness.

Kühnheit, *f.* 1) boldness. Verzeihen Sie meine —, pardon my presumption. *Fig.* — des Styls, der Ausdrücke &c., boldness of style, of expressions &c. 2) a bold, daring action or enterprise.

Kühnlich, *adv.* boldly.

Kuhr, Kühr, Kühren, V. Kur &c.

Kuks, V. Kux.

Kukuk, V. Kuckuck.

Kukumer, *f.* [*pl.* -n] V. Gurke.

Kullern, V. Kollern.

Kumm, Kumme, *f.* [*pl.* -n] V. 2. Kumpf.

Kümmel, *m.* [-s] [Lat. *cuminum*, Gr. *κύμινον*, Sax. *cymen*, Sw. *kumen*, Hebr. *kamón*] 1) cumin. 2) caraway, common caraway. 3) the small fennel-flower. 4) Römischer —, the French lavender. 5) the field-fennel-flower. 6) wild thyme.

Kümmel=branntwein, *m.* caraway-brandy. —**brod**, *n.* bread with caraway-seeds in it. —**brühe**, *f.* broth made with caraway-seeds. —**käse**, *m.* cheese with caraway-seeds. —**öl**, *n.* caraway-oil. —**suppe**, *f.* soup made with caraway-seeds. —**wasser**, *n.* caraway-water.

1. **Kummer**, *m.* [-s] [allied to Kamm, Lat. *cumulus*, Sw. *kummel*] rubbish. Den — wegschaffen, to carry off, to take away the rubbish. V. Schutt.

2. **Kummer**, *m.* [-s] [probably from the old kamen = nehmen, allied to kommen, Gr. *κομίζειν*] [obsolete, except in law] seizure, sequestration. Jemands Güter mit — belegen, to distrain, to attach any one's goods, to make an attachment of any one's goods.

3. **Kummer**, *m.* [-s] [allied to the old quimen = wimmern] 1) [obsolete] groans. 2) *Fig. a)* grief, sorrow, affliction, vexation. Der — verkürzt das Leben, grief or sorrow shortens life; — haben, to be distressed, to fret; in — leben, to live in sorrow, to lead a sorrowful life; das macht ihm vielen —, that causes him much sorrow, great uneasiness or vexation; er macht sich über Alles —, he makes himself uneasy, he afflicts himself, he frets about every thing, he grieves at or for the least thing; vor —, aus — sterben, to grieve, to pine one's self to death, to die of a broken heart; in diesen Tagen des —s, in those days of sorrow or affliction; das ist mein geringster —, that is the least of my cares, my least concern. *b)* want, poverty. Hunger und — leiden [proverbially], to be in extreme distress, want or penury. Syn. V. Harm.

Kummer=antlitz, *n.* sorrowful face or countenance. —**frei**, *adj.* V. —los 1). —**krank**, *adj.* and *adv.* ill or sick with sorrow or grief. —**los**, *adj.* and *adv.* 1) free from sorrow, tranquil, easy. 2) [= unbekümmert] careless, thoughtless. —**miene**, *f.* V. —antlitz. —**seufzer**, *m.* a sorrowful sigh. —**tag**, *m.* a sorrowful day, day of affliction. *Fig.* [in seamen's lang.] —tage, fish-days, days of abstinence, banian days. —**voll**, *adj.* and *adv.* sorrowful, distressful. Ein —volles Leben führen, to lead a sorrowful life.

Kümmerer, *m.* [-s, *pl.* -] 1) [in law, obsolete] a person whose goods have been distrained or seized. 2) [among hunters] a stag wounded in the dowcets.

Kümmerhaft, *adj.* and *adv.* labouring under grief and vexation, grieved, afflicted, sorrowful.

Kümmerlich, *adj.* and *adv.* distressed, needy, destitute, scanty, pitiful. — leben, sich — helfen, to have but a scanty allowance, to be hard put to it for a livelihood, to live poorly or miserably; *it.* [obsolete] sorrowful.

Kümmerlichkeit, *f.* misery, distress, penury.

Kümmerling, *m.* [-es, *pl.* -e] cucumber, V. Gurke.

Kümmerlingskraut, *n.* dill, anethum, V. Dill.

1. **Kümmern**, *v. tr.* [in law] V. Be—, Ver—.

2. **Kümmern**, I. *v. tr.* and *impers.* to grieve, to vex, to give concern; *it.* to regard, to concern. Seine Lage kümmert mich, I am grieved at his situation, his situation grieves or afflicts me; das kümmert mich nicht, I do not care for that, that is nothing to me; es kümmert ihn wenig, [sich] seine Freunde zu erhalten, he does not mind keeping up his acquaintances; was kümmert Euch das? what is that to you? what need you care for that? what interest can you take in that? II. *v. r.* sich —, 1) to be concerned, to mind, to care for. Sich um nichts —, to care for nothing; er kümmert sich um Alles, he meddles with every thing. 2) to grieve, to sorrow. Sich zu Tode —, to pine one's self to death, to grieve to death.

Kümmerniß, *f.* [*pl.* -nisse] [obsolete] grief, sorrow.

Kummet, [Kummt] *n.* [-es, *pl.* -e] [Pol. *chomato*, Eng. *hame*, perhaps allied to hemmen] horse-collar, hame.

Kummet=decke, *f.* the leathern cover of a horse-collar or hame. —**fell**, *n.* V. —decke. —**horn**, *n.* the haum. —**kappe**, *f.* V. —decke. —**kette**, *f.* great iron-rings by which the thill-horse is fastened to the cart, thill-tugs, fastening-chain. —**macher**, *m.* harness-maker. —**pferd**, *n.* a draught-horse.

Kummkarren, *m.* V. Kippkarren.

Kumpan, *m.* V. Kompan.

Kumpe, *m.* V. Kompe.

Kumpen, *m.* [-s, *pl.* -] V. 2. Kumpf.

1. **Kumpf**, *m.* [-es, *pl.* -e] [seems to be allied to Kopf] [in mills] nut.

2. **Kumpf** or **Kumm** [-es, *pl.* -e] or **Kumpen**, *m.* [-s, *pl.* -] or **Kumme**, *f.* [*pl.* -n] [allied to the L. *cymba* = Kahn, *cumera* = Kasten] 1) a deep utensil, a basin, a bowl, a terrine. V. Spül—. 2) a deep place in a river; a pond, lake or cistern. 3) the box or body of a cart. 4) [in mining] V. Pochtrog.

Kumpfnase, *f.* snub-nose.

Kumst, V. Komst.

Kund, *adj.* and *adv.* known. Das ist mir nicht —, that has not come within my knowledge; Einem Etwas — machen or thun, to acquaint any one with any thing, to advise or inform one of any thing; es wurde nichts von dieser Verhandlung —, nothing of that transaction transpired; — werden, to come to light, to get abroad; — und zu wissen sey hiermit, or — sey hiemit Jedermann, know all men by these presents. Syn. Kund, Bekannt. Kund indicates knowledge obtained from without; bekannt has reference to that derived through the understanding. A stranger makes himself kund, known, when he mentions his name; but we make a pupil in geometry bekannt with the properties of a circle, triangle &c. We therefore make facts and events kund, and doctrines bekannt.

Kundbar, *adj.* and *adv.* known, notorious. Etwas — machen, to publish, to divulge any thing; eine —e Sache, a notorious thing, an affair manifest to the world.

Kundbarkeit, *f.* notoriety.

1. **Kunde**, *f.* 1) knowledge, information, intelligence. Ich hatte gar keine — davon, I had not the least knowledge of it; er zog — hierüber ein, he got information about it; die — verbreitete sich schnell, the intelligence, the report spread rapidly; — von Etwas nehmen, to take notice of any thing. 2) V. Erd—, Geschichts—, Kräuter—, Natur—, Pflanzen—, Stern—. Syn. Kunde, Kenntnisse. Kunde implies a knowledge of facts or events; Kenntnisse, what we know in general, whether doctrines or facts. The Kunde of former ages is the Kenntnisse of ancient events. Of scientific objects we have Kenntnisse, but no Kunde.

Kundelos, *adj.* and *adv.* having no knowledge, being a stranger in any thing.

2. **Kunde**, *m.* [-n, *pl.* -n] die — or **Kundinn**, *f.* 1) [obsolete] *a)* informer, witness, V. Zeuge. *b)* acquaintance. 2) [generally] customer, [less used] chapman, chap-woman. Viele —n haben, to have a great many customers, [said of a physician] to have much practice; Einem

—n zuweisen, verschaffen, to help any one to customers; sie ist mein — or meine —, she is a customer of mine. *Fig.* [in popular lang.] Ein wunderlicher —, a queer chap.

Kundenbrod, *n.* household-bread.

Künden, *v. intr.* [rather stiff] 1) to become known, to come to light. Es kundete schon gestern, daß &c., it was reported or given out, the report was spread yesterday already, that &c. 2) to be known or notorious.

Künden, *v. tr.* V. Ankünden.

Künder, *m.* [-s, *pl.*-] [little used] V. Ver—; *it.* V. Herold.

Kündig, *adj.* and *adv.* 1) acquainted with or informed of a thing, experienced, skilled. Einer Sache — seyn, to be informed of, acquainted with any thing, to know any thing; ein der Sache or in dieser Sache —er Mann, a man versed or experienced in that business; ich bin dieses Spieles —, I know this game; der Wege und Stege — seyn, to be well acquainted with, to know well the roads or ways; vieler Sprachen — seyn, to be master of many languages, to know many languages. 2) V. Erd—, Geschichts—, Natur—, Pflanzen—, Stern—. Syn. Kundig, Erfahren, Geübt, Versucht. The Kundige confines his knowledge merely to facts and physical objects, and consequently to that of individual things; the Erfahrene raises this knowledge to general truths, and draws from what he has seen and heard universal propositions and rules, from which he judges of other similar facts. A good pilot is kundig, acquainted with the coast and rocks in his own neighbourhood, but this does not make him an erfahrenen navigator. He who possesses a knowledge of any thing, is kundig of it; he who has acquired an expertness in a thing, is geübt; and he who has entered upon undertakings and overcome difficulties and dangers, is versucht. Good pilots are kundig, acquainted with the coasts and rocks; clever archivists are geübt in the reading of ancient records; versuchte warriors have endured much and been often exposed to danger.

Kündig, *adj.* and *adv.* known, notorious, manifest. —werden, to become public or notorious, to get abroad; und — or kündlich groß ist das gottselige Geheimniß [in Scripture], and without controversy great is the mystery of godliness.

Kündigen, *v. tr.* to make known, to publish, V. Ab—, An—, Auf—, Ver—.

Kündigkeit, *f.* experience, skill, knowledge.

Kündigkeit, *f.* notoriety.

Kündleute, *pl.* customers. V. Kundmann.

Kündlich, V. Kündig.

Kündmachung, *f.* publication, declaration. [in law] Die — eines Spruches, the intimation of a sentence; feierliche — eines Gesetzes &c., promulgation of a law &c.; die — seiner Gesinnungen, the manifestation of his sentiments.

Kündmann, *m.* [-es, *pl.* -leute] customer, chapman, V. 2. Kunde 2).

Kündschaft, *f.* 1) custom [in trade], customers. Sie sind zu theuer, Sie werden meine — nicht bekommen, you are too dear, you shall not have my custom; eine starke — haben, to have a great many customers, [applied to artificers or tradespeople &c.] to have a great deal of work, [applied to a physician] to have much practice; gute und wohlfeile Waare verschafft einem Laden —, good and cheap wares bring customers to a shop; dieses Gerücht hat der — dieses Ladens geschadet, that rumour has made this shop lose its custom. 2) knowledge, experience, acquaintance; information, intelligence. — von einer Sache haben, to have knowledge of, to be acquainted with, to be informed of any thing; sich auf — legen, — einziehen, to seek, to get intelligence, to explore, to make inquiry; auf — ausgehen, to go out for intelligence or information, to go out to reconnoitre [in military affairs], to spy; auf — seyn, to be out to reconnoitre; nachdem wir von dem Lager des Feindes — eingezogen hatten, after having reconnoitred the enemy's camp. 3) testimony, testimonial [of a workman or journeyman].

Kündschaften, *v. intr.* to seek or get information or intelligence, to make inquiry, to spy; [in military affairs] to reconnoitre.

Kündschafter, *m.* [-s, *pl.* -], —inn, *f.* a person employed in obtaining intelligence, scout, spy, prier, informer.

‡**Künft**, *f.* arrival. Die — Christi, advent.

Kunft-fest, *n.* first sunday in advent. —sonntag, *m.* sunday in advent. —zeit, *f.* time in advent, advent season.

Künftig, *adj.* and *adv.* [from kommen] future, to come. —e Zeit, time to come, the future; die —en Geschlechter, the generations to come; ihr —er Gatte or [in popular language] ihr —er, her spouse that is to be, her intended; seine —e Gattinn or [in popular lang.] seine —e, his wife that is to be, his intended; das —e Leben, the future state, futurity; —e Dinge vorhersagen, to foretel what is to come; der —e Monat, next month; in's —e, in future, for the future, henceforth, henceforward; — können Sie es machen or halten, wie Sie wollen, henceforth you may do as you please.

Künftighin, *adv.* in future, for the future, henceforth, hereafter.

Künftigkeit, *f.* futurity.

Kunigúnde, *f.* [der — or —ns] [a name of women] Cunegund.

Kunigundenkraut, *n.* 1) the common eupatorium or hemp-agrimony. 2) V. Zweizahn.

Künkel, *f.* [*pl.* -n] [seems to be allied to the L. *conus* and to Kegel] 1) distaff. Eine — anlegen, to dress a distaff, V. Spinnrocken. 2) [provincial] *Fig.* spinning room or company.

Kunkel-adel, *m.* [in law] maternal nobility. —band, *n.*, —brief, *m.* V. Rockenband &c. —lehen, *n.* [in law] petticoat-hold.

Kuno, *m.* [-s] [a name of men] Cuno, Kuno.

Kunst, *f.* [*pl.* Künste] [from können] 1) [in general, any skill or dexterity, but chiefly the dexterity or power of performing any thing according to certain rules] art, skill. Die — vervollkommnet die Natur, art improves nature; die Erzeugnisse der Natur und die Werke der —, the productions of nature and the works of art; hiebei ist mehr Natur, als —, there is more of nature than of art in that; versuchen Sie Ihre —, try your skill; die — zu mahlen, Häuser zu bauen &c., the art of painting, of building; viel — in allen Leibesübungen zeigen, to exhibit much or great skill or dexterity in all bodily exercises; die — zu gefallen, the art of pleasing; [in fam. lang.] das ist keine —, that is easy enough, one needs not be a conjurer to do that. 2) [a system of rules serving to facilitate the performance of certain actions] art. Gemeine, handwerkmäßige Künste, mechanic arts; V. Buchdrucker—, Drechsler—, Orgelbauer—, Schreib— &c.; die freien Künste, the liberal arts; Magister der freien Künste, master of arts, M. A. or A. M.; die Fakultät der freien Künste, faculty of arts; die schönen Künste, the fine arts; ein Kenner der —, a connoisseur; der Geschmack an den schönen Künsten, taste for the fine arts, [und Naturseltenheiten] virtu; die schwarze —, *a*) [in pop. superstition] the black art, necromancy, witch-craft, *b*) [among engravers] mezzotinto; das Seiltanzen ist eine brodlose —, rope-dancing is an unprofitable art or profession. 3) trick, legerdemain, slight of hand. Künste mit Karten machen, to show tricks with cards. *Fig.* Er ist mit seinen Künsten am Ende, he is at his wits' end. 4) a work of art, a piece of machinery, [especially] an artificial waterwork, water-machine, hydraulic engine. Eine — abschützen, to stop a waterwork by a floodgate.

Kunst-adel, *m.* 1) the nobility which the arts confer upon any one. 2) the sublime of an art. —akademie, *f.* academy of [the] fine arts. —anlage, *f.* 1) talent for an art or for the arts. 2) pleasure-ground, park. Die neuen —anlagen or Anlagen bei C., the new walks and plantations or pleasure-grounds near C. —arbeit, *f.* a piece of work executed with art or skill, work of art. —arbeiter, *m.* V. Künstler. —ausdruck, *m.* a technical term. —ausstellung, *f.* exhibition of works of art. —beflissen, *adj.* and *adv.* giving the chief part of one's time and attention to the arts or to any art. Der —beflissene, student of the arts or of any art. —beflissenheit, *f.* application to the arts or to any art. —beruf, *m.* vocation or talent for the fine arts. —beschreibung, *f.* description of works of art. —betriebsam, *adj.* and *adv.* actively occupied in exercising a particular art or [higher] trade. —betriebsamkeit, *f.* the active employment in the exercise of an art or [higher] trade, V. Industrie. —cabinet, *n.* V. —kammer. —drechsler, —dreher, *m.* a turner who makes fine articles, a turner in ivory. —eifer, *m.* 1) zeal for the arts or for any art. Den —eifer erregen, to promote or encourage the arts. 2) the enthusiasm of an artist or for the arts. —erfahren, *adj.* and *adv.* experienced, skilled or versed in the arts or in any art. —erfahrene Männer, —erfahrene, connoisseurs, the learned. —erfahrenheit, *f.* experience or skill in any art or in the arts. —erfahrung, *f.* V. —erfahrenheit. —erfindung, *f.* 1) invention of any art. 2) ingenious invention. —erzeugniß, *n.* [*—produkt] production of art. —fähig, *adj.* and *adv.* having talent for the arts or for any art. —fähigkeit, *f.* talent for any art or for the arts. —färber, *m.* V. Schönfärber. —fechter, *m.* V. Fechtmeister. —fertig, *adj.* and *adv.* V. —erfahren. —fertigkeit, *f.* 1) great skill or dexterity in any art. 2) skill or dexterity acquired by practice. —feuer, *n.* fire-work. —feuerwerker, *m.* fire-master, fire-worker, pyrotechnist. —findig, *adj.* ingenious, inventive. —fleiß, *m.* industry in the exercise of any art, V. Industrie. —fluß, *m.* artificial river, canal. —freund, *m.*, —freundinn, *f.* a person who has a taste for the arts or for objects of virtu, a lover of the arts, an amateur. —gabe, *f.* V. —fähigkeit. —gärtner, *m.* a professed gardener, horticulturist. —gärtnerei, *f.* the higher branches of gardening or horticulture. —gebäude, *n.* an ingenious building, an edifice built with a great deal of art. —gebilde, *n.* V. —werk. —gefühl, *n.* 1) taste or sensibility for the arts. 2) the good taste or tact of an artist. —geheimniß, *n.* secret of any art. —geist, *m.* [*—genie] genius of an artist. —gemäß, *adj.* and *adv.* conformable, consonant or according to the rules of art. —genoß, *m.*, —genossinn, *f.* a person of the same art or trade, fellow-artist. —genossenschaft, *f.* 1) state of being a fellow-artist. 2) body of artists, the artists who exercise the same art collectively. —geräth, *n.*, —geräthschaft, *f.* the tools or implements of an artist. —gerecht, *adj.* and *adv.* correct as to the rules of art, V. —gemäß. —geschichte, *f.* history of the arts or of any particular art. —geschichtlich, *adj.* and *adv.* pertaining to the history of the arts. —geschwür, *n.* V. [in the healing art] V. Fontanell. —gesellschaft, *f.* V. —genossenschaft. —gestänge, *n.* [in mining] the poles of a hydraulic engine. —getriebe, *n.* machine, works of a machine. —gewebe, *n.* texture or web full of, or made with great art or skill. —gewerbe, *n.* a trade requiring art. —gewerk, *n.* a manufactory. —gezeug, *n.* 1) V. —getriebe. 2) hydraulic engine. —graben, *m.* canal; *it.* aqueduct, conduit. —griff, *m.* dexterity in the exercise of any art, habitual facility, *knack. *Fig.* trick, artifice. Mit —griffen umgehen, to use artifices. —halle, *f.* hall or saloon for works of art, museum. —handel, *m.* trade in works of art. —händler, *m.* dealer in works of art or virtu, [especially] picture-dealer, print-seller. —handlung, *f.* shop where works of art are sold, repository of arts. —höhle, *f.* artificial cavern, grotto. —jünger, *m.*, —jüngerinn, *f.* a beginner in some art, [frequently, in a more peculiar sense] a lucky or proficient beginner in some art, *it.* [in a quite particular sense] a young actor or player, a young actress, as, ein hoffnungsvoller —jünger, an actor that promises well. —kammer, *f.* a room in which works of art are collected, cabinet of curiosities. Die —kammern zu Dresden, the [picture] galleries of Dresden. —kämmerer, *m.* [obsolescent] inspector or director of a cabinet of curiosities &c. —kenner, *m.* connoisseur. —kenntniß, *f.* knowledge of the arts. —kniff, *m.* cunning trick, artifice, V. Kniff. —lehre, *f.* [*Technologie] technology. —liebend, *adj.* and *adv.* loving the arts. —liebhaber, *m.*, —liebhaberinn, *f.* lover of the arts or of objects of virtu, amateur. —liebhaberei, *f.* inclination, taste for the arts. —los, *adj.* and *adv.* 1) artless, simple, unaffected. Eine —lose Erzählung, an artless tale. 2) destitute of art, wanting art. —losigkeit, *f.* 1) artlessness, simplicity, unaffectedness. 2) want of art. —mäßig, *adj.* and *adv.* consonant to the rules of art, *it.* technical. —mäßigkeit, *f.* conformity to the rules of art. —meister, *m.* 1) [rather unusual] a great or perfect master in one's art or trade. 2) a person skilled in the construction of water-works. —mittel, *n.* an artificial remedy. —neid, *m.* envy of artists or of persons following the same trade. —pfeifer, *m.* musician of the town. —rad, *n.* a wheel of a water-work. —recht, *adj.* and *adv.* V. —gerecht. —redner, *m.* [*Rhetor] rhetorician. —rednerisch, *adj.* and *adv.* [*rhetorisch] rhetorical. —regel, *f.* rule of art. —reich, *adj.* and *adv.* excelling in art, skilful, ingenious. Ein —reicher Sänger, an excellent or eminent singer; ein —reiches Werk, an ingenious work; eine —reiche Hand, a skilful hand. —reiter, *m.*, —reiterinn, *f.* 1) [not much used] a very clever horseman. 2) [popularly called englischer Reiter] a man or woman who exhibits at public places and for payment feats of horsemanship, an equestrian performer [as for instance Ducrow's troop at Astley's in London &c.]. —richter, *m.*, —richterinn, *f.* a person who judges of the productions of art, especially of the fine arts, a critic. V. Kritiker. —richterei, *f.* minute or frivolous criticism, bad criticism. —richterlich, *adj.* and *adv.* suited to a critic, critical; *it.* according to the rules of art. Eine —richterliche Abhandlung, a critical dissertation. —richtern, *v. intr.* to play the critic, to criticise. —richtig, *adj.* and *adv.* correct as to the rules of art. —richtigkeit, *f.* V. —mäßigkeit. —ring, *m.* the ring of a hydraulic engine. —sache, *f.* work of art, artificial curiosity. —sammlung, *f.* collection of works of art, of virtu or of artificial curiosities. —schacht, *m.* the shaft or pit of a hydraulic engine. —schatz, *m.* precious collection of works of art or of virtu. —schreiner, *m.* cabinet-maker. —schule, *f.* school or academy of arts. —silber, *n.* artificial silver. —sinn, *m.* disposition or talent for the arts. —spiegel, *m.* optic mirror. —spiel, *n.* game of skill. —sprache, *f.* technical language; *it.* peculiar terms used in describing productions of the fine arts. —springer, *m.* tumbler, vaulter. —sprung, *m.* the leap of a tumbler or vaulter. —stange, *f.* pole of a hydraulic engine. —stecher, *m.* [*Graveur] engraver. —straße, *f.* [*Chaussee] road made by art, high-road. —strom, *m.* V. —fluß. —stück, *n.* 1) V. —arbeit. 2) curious performance, slight of hand, trick, legerdemain. —stücke mit Karten machen, to show tricks with cards. —stürmerei, *f.* [*Vandalismus] vandalism. —tischler, *m.* V. —schreiner. —trieb, *m.* mechanical instinct of certain animals; *it.* [of men] the inward impulse towards the fine arts. —verächter, *m.* one who despises or hates the arts, despiser of the arts. —verein, *m.* a society or association formed for promoting the fine arts, [modern term] art-union. —verstand, *m.* knowledge of the arts. —verständig, *adj.* and *adv.* understanding any particular art. —verständige, *m.* a person skilled in any art or competent to judge in any art. Den Schaden durch —verständige schätzen lassen, to get the injury estimated by a jury of artists. —versuch, *m.* essay in any art. —verwandte, *m.* V. —genoß. —weg, *m.* V. [the more usual word] —straße. —weise, *f.* the particular habit of an artist [as, for instance, of a painter, in managing colours, lights and shades], manner. —welt, *f.* empire of the arts. —werk, *n.* work of art. —widrig, *adj.* and *adv.* contrary to the rules of art. —widrigkeit, *f.* quality or state of being contrary to the rules of art. —wort, *n.* technical term. —wörteln, *v. intr.* to affect to make use of technical terms. —zeiger, *m.* a guide [who shows and explains curiosities], cicerone. —zeug, *n.* 1) water-work, hydraulic engine. 2) apparatus belonging to a water-work or requisite for the construction of a water-work.

Künstelei, *f.* 1) artificial effort or refinement. 2) something artificial or affected. Das Betragen des Heuchlers ist lauter —, the behaviour of the hypocrite is all affectation.

Künsteln, *v. tr.* [mostly in a bad sense] 1) to bestow much art upon a thing, to produce with art and labour, to refine upon a thing. Alles Gekünstelte beleidigt den guten Geschmack, any thing that has been too much refined upon or that is affected, mannered or not natural, offends good taste; ein gekünsteltes Gemälde, a mannered or affected picture; ein gekünstelter Anzug, an affected dress; es liegt etwas Gekünsteltes in Allem, was er thut, he is full of affectation in every thing. 2) to imitate by efforts of art. Eine gekünstelte Schönheit, artificial, borrowed beauty [more indebted to art than nature]; gekünsteltes Gold, sophisticated gold; ein gekünstelter Ausdruck, a coined or made word or expression.

Künstig, *adj.* and *adv.* 1) V. Künstlich. 2) V. Bau—, Scheide— &c.

Künstler, *m.* [-s, *pl.* -], —inn, *f.* artist. Er ist einer unserer besten —, sie ist eine unserer besten —innen, he, she is one of our best artists; [in fam. lang.] er ist ein rechter —, ein Tausend—, he is a very cunning man, he is truly a conjurer, he is a man skilled in many different things.

Künstlerart, *f.* manner or way of artists. —grille, *f.* whim or fancy of an artist. —hand, *f.* a skilful hand. Das kömmt von —händen, that comes from a skilful hand, is done in a fine workmanlike manner. —leben, *n.* the life of an artist. —neid, *m.* V. Kunstneid. —ruhm, *m.* the glory of an artist. —sinn, *m.* taste or talent for the arts. —stolz, *m.* pride of an artist. —verein, *m.* society or association of artists; *it.* [less used] academy [of arts]. —weise, *f.* V. —art.

Künstlerei, *f.* V. Künstelei.

Künstlerisch, *adj.* and *adv.* fit for, belonging to an artist. Eine —e Aufgabe, a task or problem for an artist.

Künstlich, *adj.* and *adv.* 1) made or contrived with art or skill, artificial, ingenious. Dieser Körper bewegt sich —, that body moves artificially or by art; das ist — gemacht, that is skilfully, ingeniously made or contrived; ein —er Tanz, a dance arranged with art; eine —e Hand, a skilful hand, V. Künstlerhand. *Fig.* Er hat sich auf eine —e Art herausgezogen, he came or got off very ingeniously or cunningly; er hat es durch —e Mittel erhalten, he has obtained it by artful, cunning or crafty means; —e Ausflüchte, artful, clever or cunning subterfuges. 2) not natural, factitious, artificial. —er Wein, made wine; —er Zinnober, —er Stein, factitious cinnabar, stone; —e Zähne, false teeth; eine —e Schönheit, V. Künsteln 2); —es Gold, V. Künsteln 2); das —e Jahr, der —e Tag, artificial year [of 365 days and about 6 hours], artificial day [of 24 hours]. 3) [not used in the better style of speaking or writing] clever, dexterous, skilful. Ein —er Mann, a very clever or ingenious man.

Künstlichkeit, *f.* 1) quality of being made or contrived with art or skill. Die — dieser Maschine besteht &c., the ingenuity of the mechanism or construction of this machine consists &c. 2) a thing made with art or skill or skilfully. 3) something artificial or affected.

Kunterbunt, *adj.* and *adv.* [in popular lang.] confused, in great confusion, higgledy-piggledy, topsy-turvy, helter-skelter.

1. **Kunz**, *m.* [-es, *pl.* -e] 1) [a name of men for Conrad] Conrad. *Prov.* Es sey or er heiße Hinz oder —, let him be who he will, whoever he be; er fällt drein, wie — in die Nüsse, he sets about it tooth and nail, with might and main. 2) V. Kater.

‖2. **Kunz**, *m.* [-es, *pl.* -e] [also Kuntsch, allied to the Wend. *kunta*] V. 3. Eber.

‖3. **Kunz**, *m.* [-es, *pl.* -e] V. Hagebutte.

Küpe, *f.* [*pl.* -n] [L. *cupa*, allied to Kübel, Koffer &c.] a large tub, a vat, V. 2. Kufe; [among dyers] a copper or boiler, [chiefly] blue vat.

Küpenblau, *adj.* that has been dyed blue in the vat.

Küper, Küpern, V. Keper, Kepern.

Küper, *m.* [-s, *pl.* -] V. Küfer.

Küperspieker, *m.* a nail an inch and a half long.

Kupfer, *n.* [-s, *pl.* -] [from the L. *cuprum*] 1) copper. Rothes —, red copper; gelbes —, yellow copper, brass; das — gar machen, to refine, to purify copper; Gefäße von —, vessels of copper; in — stechen, to engrave on copper; in — arbeiten, to work in copper. 2) a copper-vessel or the copper-vessels, coppers. 3) copper-coin, copper. 4) [a printed representation from an engraved plate] print, copperplate, engraving. Ein Buch, ein Werk mit —n, a book with prints, an illustrated work, V. —stich. 5) [in popular lang., jestingly] pimples in the face. Er hat viel — im Gesichte, handelt mit —, his face is full of pimples, he is a fiery-faced or red-faced, copper-nosed fellow, his face hangs out a red flag.

Kupfer-abschnitzel, pl. und Feilicht, copper clippings and filings. —ader, f. [in mining] a vein or lode of copper or copper-ore. —arbeit, f. work done in copper; any thing made of copper. —arsenik, m. arseniate of copper. —artig, adj. and adv. of the nature of copper, like copper, copperish, coppery. —asche, f. copper-ashes. —atlas, m. V. —blüte. —auflösung, f. solution of copper. —bergwerk, n. copper-mine. —blatt, n. copper-plate, V. —stich. —blau, n. V. Bergblau 1). —blech, n. plate or sheet of copper. —bleche [for covering the roofs of spires, for coppering ships], copper-sheathings; ein Schiff mit —blech beschlagen, to cover or sheathe a ship with sheets of copper, to copper a ship. —blick, m. [in metallurgy] the shine of copper. —blumen, pl. flowers of copper. —blüte, f. capillary red copper-ore. —boden, adj. Ein —es Schiff, a copper-bottomed ship. —brand, m. black copper-ore. —braun, n. 1) scales which fly off from copper when hammering. 2) —braun or —bräune, f. brownish-red copper-ore. —brot, n. regulus of copper. —buch, n. [rather unusual] a book full of prints or engravings. —draht, m. copper-wire. —druck, m. 1) the act of taking prints or impressions from copper-plates. 2) copper-plate, print. —drucker, m. printer of copper-plates. —druckerei, f. 1) the business of a printer of copper-plates, copper-plate printing. 2) the office or establishment where copper-plates are printed. —druckerfarbe, f. lamp-black. —druckerpresse, f. rolling-press. —druse, f. copper-druse, copper-crystal. —erz, n. copper-ore. —fahlerz, n. fallow copper-ore. —farbe, f. colour of copper, copper-colour. —farben, —farbig, adj. copper-coloured. —farbiges Gesicht, V. —gesicht. —federerz, n. V. —blüte. —feil, n; —feile, f, —feilicht, n. copper-filings. —frischofen, m. [in metallurgy] a finery. —gang, m. gangue of copper, lode of copper. —gehalt, m. quantity of copper contained in any substance. —geist, m. spirit of copper. —gelb, n. brittle brass, yellow copper. —geld, n. copper-coin, copper. V. also V. —münze. —geräth, —geschirr, n. vessels or utensils made of copper, copper-vessels &c. —gesicht, n. [in fam. lang.] face full of red pimples, copper face. —gilbe, f. a metallic earth containing yellow copper. —glanz, m. 1) brightness of copper. 2) V. —glas. —glas, n. grey or black copper-ore. —gold, n. a mixture of gold and copper, similor. —grün, I. adj. and adv. eruginous. II. n. 1) eruginous colour. 2) [in mineralogy] a) oxyd of copper. b) mountain-green. c) V. Grünspan 1). —halt, m. V. —gehalt. —haltig, adj. and adv. containing copper, copperish, coppery. —hammer, m. 1) a particular hammer for beating copper. 2) copper-mill, copper-work. —hammerschlag, m. 1) scales that fly off the copper in hammering. 2) V. —asche. —handel, m. 1) trade in copper. 2) trade in prints or copper-plates. —händler, m. 1) dealer in copper. 2) dealer in prints or copper-plates, V. [the more usual word] —stichhändler. —handlung, f. 1) V. —handel. 2) shop in which copper is sold; it. in which prints are sold, print-shop or picture-shop. —hiefe, f. mountain-green in globules, cupreous yellow pyrites. —kalk, m. oxyd of copper. —kies, m. V. —hiefe. —könig, m. regulus of copper. —kram, m. V. —handel. —krämer, m. V. —händler. —lachs, m. fresh salmon. —laden, m. V. —handlung 2). —lasur, f. V. Bergblau 1). —markasit, m. V. —kies. —moos, n. native copper. —münze, f. copper-coin. —nase, f. [in popular lang.] a nose full of red pimples, copper-nose. —nickel, m. copper-nickel. —ocher, m. copper-oker. —ofen, m. furnace for melting copper. —öl, n. a solution of acetate of copper or of oxyd of copper in oil of turpentine, oil of copper. —phosphorsäure, f. phosphate of copper. —platte, f. a plate of copper, copper-plate; it. [= a large print] copper-plate. —presse, f. press for copper-plates, rolling-press. —probe, f. assay of copper-ore [to know how much copper it contains]. —quelle, f. a source or spring containing copperas. —rauch, m. 1) V. —ruß. 2) vitriolic earth, copperas. —rost, m. 1) rust of copper, copper-rust. 2) V. —grün II. 2. —roth, I. adj. and adv. V. —farben. II. n. 1) copper-colour. 2) red oxyd of copper. —röthe, f. 1) V. —roth II. 2) native or virgin copper. —ruß, m. a substance which separates from copper when melting, in the shape of smoke. —salpeter, m. nitrate of copper. —salz, n. acetate of copper. —sammlung, f. collection of prints or engravings. —sanderz, n. sandy or gravelly mountain-green. —schiefer, m. cupriferous slate. —schlacke, f. slag of copper. —schlag, m. V. —hammerschlag 1). —schläger, m. V. —schmied. —schlich, n. V. —braun. —schlich, m. [in metallurgy] slich of copper. —schmied, m. copper-smith, brazier. —schmiede, f. a brazier's or copper-smith's shop. —schröter, m. instrument for cutting copper, chisel. —schwärze, f. black oxyd of copper. —späne, pl. filings or chips of copper. *—spiritus, m. V. —geist. —stecher, m. engraver on copper. —stecherei, [better] —stecherkunst, f. art of engraving on copper. —stein, m. a stone containing copper. —stich, m. engraving [on copper], copper-plate, print. —stichhändler, m. dealer in copper-plates, print-seller. —stufe, f. piece or fragment of copper-ore. —tafel, f. V. —stich. —thaler, m. a Swedish copper-dollar [of the value of about four pence]. —vitriol, m. blue vitriol. —waare, f. brazier's-ware. —wasser, n. 1) sulphate of copper. 2) copperas. —weißerz, n. white copper-ore. —werk, n. 1) book of engravings or prints; [especially] a large or expensive illustrated work. 2) copper-work. —wolle, f. V. Haarkupfer. —zeche, f. V. —bergwerk. —zuschlag, m. [in metallurgy] flux of copper.

Küpferchen, n. [-s, pl. -] [dim. of Kupfer] small print or engraving, [often in contempt] a small, paltry or valueless print or engraving.

Küpfericht, adj. and adv. resembling or like copper, coppery. Fig. Ein —es Gesicht [in fam. lang.], a face full of red pimples, a copper face.

Küpferig, adj. and adv. containing copper, coppery, V. Kupferhaltig.

||Küpferlein, V. Küpferchen.

Küpfern, v. tr. [ein Schiff —] to copper [a ship]. Ein gekupfertes Schiff, a copper-bottomed ship.

Küpfern, adj. and adv. made of copper. Ein —es Dach, a copper-roof.

Kuppe, f. [pl. -n] dim. Küppchen, ||Küpplein, n. [-s, pl. -] [allied to Kopf] the round or blunt point of a thing, [chiefly] the top of a mountain, summit; it. the head of a nail.

Kupp-meise, f. the crested tit-mouse. —nagel, m. hob-nail.

1. Kuppel, f. [pl. -n] [Ital. cupola, Fr. coupole, allied to Kuppe, Kopf, bob] cupola, dome. Gedrückte —, a diminished or surbased dome; in die Höhe or über sich steigende —, surmounted dome.

Kuppeldach, n. a roof shaped as a dome.

2. Kuppel, f. [pl. -n] V. Koppel.

Kuppel-bändig, adj. and adv. [among hunters] trained or accustomed to walk in the leash. —hund, m. V. Koppelhund. —pelz, m. [in fam. lang.] a reward given to a person who has brought about a marriage or match.

Kuppelei, f. 1) [in fam. lang.] act and practice of promoting marriage or of making a match, match-making. 2) act and practice of promoting illicit intercourse, of pimping or procuring.

Kuppeln, I. v. tr. to couple [dogs], to join, to unite. Gekuppelte Bildsäulen, grouped or coupled statues. Fig. [in fam. lang.] to form or promote a connexion between persons of two sexes, to promote marriage, to marry, to make a match. Sie will mir eine Frau —, she will procure me a wife. II. v. intr to promote illicit intercourse, to procure, to pimp.

||Kuppen, v. tr. [allied to kappen] to cut short, to clip. Einen Baum —, to top or lop a tree; die Nägel an den Fingern —, to cut one's nails.

Kuppig, adj. having a top. —e Meise, V. Kuppmeise.

Kuppler, m. [-s, pl. -], —inn, f. 1) a person who tries to bring about marriages or to make matches, match-maker. 2) [in a bad sense] procurer, procuress, pander, pimp, go-between.

Kupplerhandwerk, n. V. Kuppelei.

||Küppse, f. V. Kuppe.

1. Kur, V. Cur.

Kurschmied, m. a blacksmith skilled in, and exercising the veterinary art, the care of horses &c.

2. Kur or Kür, f. [pl. -en] 1) [obsolete] choice, option. 2) [formerly] the dignity of an elector in the German empire, electoral dignity. 3) the territory of an Elector, electorate.

Kur-erbe, m. heir to an electorate, electoral prince. —fürst, m. [prince] elector [in the former German Empire]. —fürstenbank, f. bench of the electors [at the diet of the former German Empire]. —fürstenrath, m. electoral college. —fürstentag, m. meeting of the electors. —fürstenthum, n. electorate. —fürstenverein, m. union or confederation of the electors. —fürstinn, f. electress. —fürstlich, adj. and adv. electoral. —haus, n. electoral house. —hut, m. electoral crown. —lande, —länder, pl. electoral dominions. —mantel, m. the cloak of an elector, electoral cloak. —prinz, m. [the eldest son of a prince-elector] electoral prince. —prinzessinn, f. [the consort of a prince-elector's eldest son] electoral princess. —schwert, n. [formerly] the sword of the electoral house of Saxony. —würde, f. electoral dignity.

†Kuranzen, V. Koranzen.

*Küraß, m. [-sses, pl. -sse] [Fr. cuirasse, most probably from cuir = Leder] cuirass. Syn. V. Harnisch.

Küraßreiter, m. V. Kürassier.

Kürassier, m. [-es, pl. -e] cuirassier.

Kürassierregiment, n. regiment of cuirassiers.

Kurbe, Kurbel, f. [pl. -n] [from the old kurben = biegen; L. curvus = krumm] a curved or crooked handle, winch, windlass. Die — an einer Kaffeemühle, the handle of a coffee-mill.

Kurbelspieß, m. 1) a turnspit with a handle. 2) a spear with a cross-bar for stabbing the wild boar.

Kürbiß, *m.* [-ſſes, *pl.* -ſſe] [Pers. *corbos*, L. *cucurbita*, allied to the L. *curvus* = krumm, V. Kurbe] 1) gourd, pumpion, pumpkin. Langer, flaſchenförmiger —, bottle-gourd V. Birn—, Flaſchen—, Warzen—. 2) Aethiopiſcher ſaurer —, V. Affenbaum.

Kürbiß-apfel, *m.* a sort of boiling-apple. **—art**, *f.* species of gourd. Die —arten, cucurbitaceous plants. **—artig**, *adj.* cucurbitaceous. **—baum**, *m.* 1) gourd-tree, calabash-tree. 2) V. Affenbaum. **—birn**, *f.* V. Pfundbirn. **—brei**, *m.* gourd-pap. **—flaſche**, *f.* gourd-bottle. **—förmig**, *adj.* and *adv.* having the form of a gourd. —förmige Pflanze, cucurbitaceous plant. **—frucht**, *f.* gourd. **—kern**, *m.* seed of a gourd, gourd-kernel or seed. **—kirſche**, *f.* V. Schwarzwurz. **—wurm**, *m.* a broad worm resembling the seed of a gourd that breeds in the human intestines, cucurbitinus lubricus.

Kürbs, *m.* [-es, *pl.* -e] V. Kürbiß.

*__Küren__, *v. tr.* V. [the usual word] Curiren or Heilen.

Küren, *v. tr.* [obsolete] to choose, to select.

*__Kuriös__, *adj.* and *adv.* [in fam. or pop. lang.] 1) [obsolescent] curious, prying [in a bad sense]. 2) singular, odd.

*__Kuriosität__, *f.* 1) [obsolescent] curiosity [in a bad sense]. 2) [*pl.* -en] curiosity, rarity.

Küriſch, *adj.* and *adv.* V. Kurländiſch. Das —e Haff [name of a gulf on the northern coast of Prussia], the Curish Haff.

Kurland, *n.* [-s] Courland.

Kurländer, *m.* [-s, *pl.* -], **—inn**, *f.* a native or an inhabitant of Courland.

Kurländiſch, *adj.* and *adv.* of Courland, belonging to Courland or its natives or inhabitants, in the manner of the latter.

‖**Kurre**, *f.* [*pl.* -n] [allied to knurren] turkey-hen, V. Pute.

Kurrhahn, *m.* V. Birkhahn.

‖**Kurrig**, V. Kirre.

Kürſchner, *m* [-s, *pl.* -] furrier, V. Pelzhändler, Rauchhändler.

Kürſchner-arbeit, *f.* fur-work. **—gare**, *f.* the dressing of furs. **—handwerk**, *n.* furrier's trade. **—innung**, *f.* furrier's company or guild. **—laden**, *m.* furrier's shop. **—meiſter**, *m.* master furrier. **—naht**, *f.* furrier's seam, round seam. **—waare**, *f.* furs and skins.

Kürſchnerei, *f.* V. Kürſchnerhandwerk.

Kurz, *adj.* and *adv.* [L. *curtus*, allied to (the old) koren, kerben = ſchneiden] short. Ein —er Stock, ein —er Mantel, a short stick, a short cloak; ſie hat ihr Kleid kürzer gemacht, she has made her gown shorter; einen Stock um einen Schuh kürzer machen, to shorten a stick one foot; dieſe Steigbügel ſind um ein Loch zu —, these stirrups are too short by one hole; —e Haare, short or cropped hair; er iſt dick und —, he is thick and short; Einen um eine Spanne, um einen Kopf kürzer machen [in fam. language], to cut any one's head off; der kürzeſte Weg, the shortest cut, the nearest way; wenden Sie ſich an den Miniſter, das iſt das Kürzeſte, der kürzeſte Weg, apply to the minister, that is the shortest way; eine Sache — und klein ſchlagen [in familiar language], to break a thing into a thousand pieces; ein —es Geſicht haben, to be short-sighted, or near-sighted; Einen — halten [in fam. lang.], to keep any one short or under, to keep a strict hand over any one; [among hunters] —es Wildbret, the testicles of a stag, the dowcets; —e Brühe, broth or soup not thin or watery, but of a certain consistency; —e Waare, hardware, haberdashery. *Fig.* Den Kürzern ziehen, to have or get the worst, to be a loser, to be worsted or overpowered; zu — kommen, to be a loser, to lose; ich komme dabei zu —, I am a loser by it; Sie werden dabei nicht zu — kommen, you will lose nothing by it, you will not be the worse for it; es geſchieht ihm nicht zu — [in familiar language], he loses nothing by it, he is not the worse for it; Einem zu — thun [in fam. language], to wrong, to prejudice any one; meine Zeit iſt —, I have little time or leisure; jene Friſt iſt zu —, that term is too short; ein Wechſelbrief auf —e Sicht, a bill of exchange at short sight; im Winter ſind die Tage —, the days are short in winter; eine —e Dauer, a short duration; vor —er Zeit, vor —em, a sort time ago, lately, not long ago; in —er Zeit, in —em, in a little or short time, ere long, soon, shortly; — vorher, a little while or time before; — nachher or — hernach, — darnach, — darauf, a little while or time afterwards; über lang oder —, über — oder lang [in fam lang.], some time or other, sooner or later; eine —e Sylbe, a short syllable; ein —es Gedächtniß, a short memory; —en Athem haben, to be short-winded, to have short breath; Etwas — machen, to shorten, to compress, to abridge any thing; *it.* to cut short; um es — zu machen, to be short, to make short work of it, to sum up all; man kann ſich nicht kürzer faſſen, one cannot express one's self more succinctly, briefly or concisely, one cannot be shorter; — in ſeinen Antworten ſeyn, to give short answers; erklären Sie es mir — und deutlich, explain it to me briefly and plainly; eine —e Rede, a short speech; — von der Sache zu reden [in fam. lang.], to be short, to cut it short, to make it short; — abbrechen, to cut it short; Einen — abfertigen [in fam. lang.], to dismiss any one with a short answer, to be short with any one, to dismiss any one abruptly; — und gut [in fam. lang.], without circumlocution, plainly; in a word, in short; — und gut, — um, ich will es nicht [in fam. lang.], in short, I won't have it; ſeine Baarſchaft iſt — beiſammen [in fam. lang.], he is short of money.

Kurz-ährig, *adj.* having short ears [said of corn]. **—angebunden**, *adj.* and *adv.* [in familiar language] irritable, choleric, irascible, hot-brained. —angebunden ſeyn, to grow easily angry, to be hot-brained, to be short with any one. **—arm**, *m.* 1) a short arm. 2) a person having a short arm or short arms. **—armig**, *adj.* having short arms. **—athemig**, *adj.* short-winded, asthmatic. **—behangen**, *adj.* [among hunters] having short ears. **—bein**, *n.* 1) a short leg. 2) [in familiar language, frequently in jest] a person having a short leg or short legs. 3) [in natural history, a genus of lizards, the efts] seps. **—beinig**, *adj.* having short legs, breviped. **—blühend**, *adj.* not blowing or blossoming long; [in poetry] short-lived. **—boſſeln**, *n.* short bowls. **—flügelig**, *adj.* short-winged. **—fuß**, *m.* 1) a short foot. 2) [in familiar language, often in jest] a person having a short foot or short feet. **—füßig**, *adj.* having short feet. **—gefaßt**, *adj.* concise, succinct, pithy. **—gefeſſelt**, *adj.* [in farriery] short-jointed. **—geſchwänzt**, *adj.* having a short tail. **—gewehr**, *n.* sergeant's halberd. **—haarig**, *adj.* having short hair. **—hals**, *m.* 1) a short neck. 2) [in familiar language] a person having a short neck, a short-necked person. **—halſig**, *adj.* having a short-neck, short-necked. **—kopf**, *m.* [rather unusual] a choleric, irritable, hot-brained fellow. **—naſig**, *adj.* having a short nose, snub-nosed. **—ohr**, *n.* 1) a short ear. 2) *a*) a person having short ears. *Fig.* [in contempt] a crop-eared fellow. *b*) an animal having short ears, [of a horse] V. Stutzohr **—öhrig**, **—geöhrt**, *adj.* having short ears. *Fig.* [in contempt] crop-eared. Solch' ein —öhriger Puritaner! such a crop-eared Puritan! **—rock**, *m.* 1) a short coat or gown. 2) [in fam. language] a person wearing a short coat or gown. **—röckig**, *adj.* having or wearing a short coat or gown. **—roth**, *adj.* V. Kleeroth. **—ſchreibekunſt**, *f.* short-hand, short-hand-writing, stenography, brachygraphy. V. also [the more usual words] Geſchwindſchreibekunſt, Stenographie **—ſchreiber**, *m.* [the more usual word is Geſchwindſchreiber or Stenograph] short-hand-writer, stenographer. **—ſchub**, *m.* short bowls; V. —boſſeln. **—ſchwanz** *m.* 1) a short tail. 2) V. Krabbe. **—ſchwänzig**, **—ſchweifig**, *adj.* having a short tail, short-tailed. **—ſichtig**, *adj.* and *adv.* short-sighted, near-sighted; *fig.* not able to look far into futurity, of limited intellect, short-sighted. **—ſichtigkeit**, *f.* short-sightedness, [*it fig.*]. **—ſilbig**, *adj.* and *adv.* having a short syllable or short syllables. Ein —ſilbiges Wort, a word consisting of short syllables. *Fig.* Ein —ſilbiger Menſch, a man of few words, who speaks little; er iſt —ſilbig in ſeinen Antworten, he gives short answers. **—ſilbigkeit**, *f. fig.* V. Einſilbigkeit. **—ſinn**, *m.* limited intellect. **—ſtämmig**, *adj.* 1) having a short stem or trunk. 2) dwarfish, stumpy. **—ſtängelig**, *adj.* having a short stalk. **—ſtiel**, *m* 1) a short stalk. 2) [a sort of apple] shank-apple, short-shank, short-start. **—ſtielig**, *adj.* having a short stalk. **—tönig**, *adj.* of a short sound, short. Eine —tönige Silbe, a short syllable. **—tönigkeit**, *f* shortness [of a syllable]. **—um**, *adv.* [in fam language] 1) without making a circuit. Er kehrte or machte —um, he turned short. 2) in few words, without circumlocution, briefly, in short. **—waare**, *f.* hardware, haberdashery. **—waarenhändler**, *m.* dealer in hardware, haberdasher. **—weil[e]**, *f.* pastime, merriment, mirth, joke, fun Das iſt eine —weile für Kinder, that is an amusement or pastime for children; wenn Ihnen das —weile macht, if that amuses you; ſeine —weile mit Einem haben, to banter, to jeer any one, to make sport, a fool of any one; Etwas aus —weile thun, to do any thing out of joke or fun. Syn. Kurzweil[e], Zeitvertreib, Unterhaltung. Kurzweil[e] implies only a merry and joking pastime, or such as excites laughter; Zeitvertreib consists in light occupations which dispel tedium, and amuse: they may, however, be of a serious description. Unterhaltung is both useful and instructive. The vulgar require from the stage kurzweilige jests; the idler looks for Zeitvertreib, the man of taste for Unterhaltung which may instruct his mind and improve his heart **—weilen**, I. *v. intr.* to be merry, to joke, to divert one's self. II. *v. tr.* Einen, to amuse, to entertain any one by joking &c Sich —weilen, to amuse, to divert one's self. **—weilig**, *adj.* and *adv.* merry, jocose, diverting, facetious, funny. Ein —weiliger Menſch, a facetious, waggish, funny fellow. **—wierig**, *adj.* and *adv.* [rather unusual] of short duration. **—wildbret**, *n.* the testicles of a stag, the dowcets.

Kürze, *f.* 1) shortness. Die — des Weges, the shortness of the way or distance. *Fig.* Die — der Zeit, des Lebens, the shortness of time, of life; in der — Etwas erzählen, to relate any thing briefly, in few words, concisely; sich der — befleißigen, to study brevity; [in popular lang.] es soll ihm keine — geschehen, he shall not be a loser by it, the worse for it; sich selbst — thun [in popular language], to hurt or wrong one's self, to be one's own enemy. 2) short space of time. In der —, shortly, in a little while, soon.

Kürzen, I. *v. tr.* to shorten, V. Ab—, Ver—. *Fig.* Einem Arbeiter den Lohn —, to lessen, diminish or abridge the wages of a workman, V. Schmälern; sein Leben —, to shorten one's life; die Zeit —, to make time pass quickly; Einem die Zeit —, to amuse, entertain, divert any one; sich die Zeit —, to amuse one's self. II. *v. refl.* sich —, to become short or shorter, to shorten.

Kürzlich, *adv.* 1) not long ago, lately. Ich habe ihn — gesehen, I have seen him lately or I saw him the other day. 2) [little used] in a little while, shortly, soon. 3) in few words, briefly, shortly, concisely.

Kürzung, *f.* abbreviation, abridgment.

Kürzungszeichen, *n.* sign of abbreviation, apostrophe.

Kuschen, *v. intr.* [Fr. *coucher*] to crouch, to lie down [said of dogs]. *Fig.* [vulgar of persons] to submit, to be quiet.

Kuß, *m.* [-sses, *pl.* Küsse] [V. Küssen], *dim.* Küßchen, ||Küßlein, *n.* [-s, *pl.* -] kiss, buss. Einen — erwiedern, to return a kiss; einen — rauben, sich einen — nehmen, to steal a kiss; der or ein Judas— [in fam. lang.], treacherous kiss, Judas' kiss; Einem einen — zuwerfen, to kiss one's hand to any one. *Prov.* Einen — in Ehren kann Niemand wehren, an innocent kiss is allowed. V. Schmatz.

Kuß-hand, *f.* act of kissing one's own hand in salutation of another person. Einem eine —hand zuwerfen [chiefly said of or with children], to kiss one's own hand in salutation to another person; gib dem Herrn eine —hand [said to children, chiefly], kiss the gentleman's hand. —**mahl**, *n.* red spot or mark of a kiss. —**mund**, *m.* a mouth made for kissing; *it.* [in pop. lang.] a kiss on the mouth.

Küssen, *v. tr.* [Gr. κύειν, Fut. κύσειν, seems to be allied to κίω, L. *cio*, and to have signified primarily: sich hinbewegen gegen Einen; hence] 1) to touch. Ein sanfter Wind küßte die Blumen [in poetry], a gentle wind kissed the flowers; die Erde, den Staub —, to fall down, to fall on the ground, to be thrown on the ground, to be felled to the ground. 2) [to salute with the lips] to kiss. Einen auf den Mund, auf die Wange, or Einem den Mund &c. —, to kiss any one's mouth, cheek; Einem die Hand — [not Einen auf die Hand —], to kiss any one's hand; ich sah, wie sie einander küßten, I saw them kiss each other or one another; sie — einander beständig, they are always kissing or billing. 3) to snatch up by kissing. Die Thränen von den Wangen —, to kiss the tears from the cheeks. Syn. Küssen, Herzen. We herzen only from love, we küssen, however, also from reverence. We herzen those we embrace, but other parts, as the hand, or foot, may be geküßt. Inanimate objects may be geküßt, our own species only we can herzen.

Küßlich, Küßlich, *adj.* and *adv.* [in poetry] made for kissing, tempting to kiss. Ein —er Mund, V. Kußmund.

Küste, *f.* [*pl.* -n] [Fr. *côte*, allied to the L. *costa* = Rippe, Fr. *côté* = Seite] coast, sea-shore. Die Englischen —n, the English coasts; eine gefährliche —, a dangerous or perilous coast; platte und offene —, a flat shore; längs der — hinfahren, hinsegeln, to coast along, to sail along the coast or shore; an der — stranden or scheitern, to run a-shore or a-ground, to wreck on the coast. Syn. V. Gestade.

Küsten-bewahrer, *m.* a ship to guard the coast, cruiser, guard-coast. —**bewohner**, *m.* inhabitant of the coast or coasts. —**fahrer**, *m.* 1) one who sails near the shore, coaster. 2) coasting-vessel, coaster. —**fahrerei**, —**fahrt**, *f.* navigation along the coast, coasting. —**fluß**, *m.* a small river rising on or near the coast. —**handel**, *m.* coasting-trade. —**insel**, *f.* a small island near the coast. —**jäger**, *m.* 1) a hunter on the coast. 2) V. Strandhähnlein. —**kenntniß**, *f.* knowledge of the coasts. —**land**, *n.* country near the sea-shore, coast. Frankreich hat mehr als 500 Stunden —land, or hat eine —strecke von mehr als &c., France has a coast of above five hundred leagues. —**lootse**, *m.* coasting-pilot. —**strecke**, *f.* V. —land. —**wache**, *f.* watch on a coast; coast-guard, the [armed] coast-service.

Küster, *m.* [-s, *pl.* -], —**inn**, *f.* clerk of a church; sacristan; sexton; the wife of the sacristan.

Küster-amt, *n.*, —**dienst**, *m.* V. Küsterei 2). —**wohnung**, *f.* V. Küsterei 1).

Küsterei, *f.* 1) house or dwelling of the sexton or sacristan. 2) the office of a sexton, sextonship.

||**Küter**, *m.* [-s, *pl.* -] [from kutten] a butcher employed for killing animals in the houses of others, house-butcher, private butcher.

Kutsche, *f.* [*pl.* -n] [probably from the Fr. *coche* or Ital. *cocchio*, Engl. *coach*; allied to Koth = Hütte, to Kutte &c., hence any thing hollow] 1) coach; *dim.* Kütschchen, ||Kütschlein, *n.* [-s, *pl.* -] a little coach. Eine zweisitzige —, a chariot; viersitzige —, a double-seated coach; V. Lehn—, Mieth—, Staats—; eine sechsspännige —, a coach and six; — und Pferde halten, to keep one's coach; in der — fahren, to ride in a coach; in die — steigen, to step or get into the coach; aus der — aussteigen, to get out of the coach, to alight. 2) [at billiards] mass. 3) [in gardening] hot-bed.

Kutsch-baum, *m.* coach-beam, carriage-beam. —**beschlag**, *m.* 1) iron-work of a coach. 2) V. —futter 1). —**bock**, *m.* coach-box, coachman's or driver's seat. —**boden**, *m.* the boot of a coach; *it.* bottom of a coach. —**feder**, *f.* the spring of a coach. —**fenster**, *n.* coach-window or glass. —**futter**, *n.* 1) the lining of a coach. 2) cover or housing of a coach. —**gaul**, *m.* V. —pferd. —**geschirr**, *n.* harness or trappings for coach-horses. —**gestell**, *n.* the carriage of a coach. —**haus**, *n.* coach-house. —**himmel**, *m.* coach-top. —**kasten**, *m.* 1) the body of a coach. 2) chest or trunk in a coach. —**kissen**, *n.* cushion or squab of a coach. —**kiste**, *f.* V. —kasten 2). —**macher**, *m.* coach-maker. —**pferd**, *n.* coach-horse. —**polster**, *n.* bolster, cushion or pad of a coach. —**quast**, *m.* tassel of a coach. —**rad**, *n.* coach-wheel. *—**remise**, *f.* V. —haus. —**riemen**, *m.* main-brace of a coach. —**schlag**, *m.* coach-door. —**steuer**, *f.* tax upon carriages. —**thür**, *f.* V. —schlag. —**tritt**, *m.* step of a coach; *it.* foot-board of a coach-box.

Kutschen-baum, *m.*, —**bock**, *m.* &c. V. Kutschbaum &c.

Kutschen, *v. intr.* [in fam. lang.] 1) to ride in a coach. 2) to drive a coach.

Kutscher, *m.* [-s, *pl.* -] coachman, V. Leib—, Mieth—, Post—.

Kutscher-lohn, *m.* 1) the wages of a coach-man. 2) coach-hire. —**sitz**, *m.* [Kutschsitz] box; [behind for the servant or groom, when the master himself drives] dickey.

Kutschiren, *v. intr.* V. Kutschen.

Kütt, Kütten, V. Kitt, Kitten.

Kutte, *f.* [*pl.* -n] [Low Lat. *cotta*, Fr. *cotte* = Weiberrock; allied to Hütte, Haut] cowl, capoch. Die — anlegen, to turn monk; die — ablegen, to forsake, to renounce one's order; Einen in eine — stecken [in fam. lang.], to make any one turn monk or friar.

Kutten-geier, *m.* king of vultures. —**mönch**, *m.* capuchin-friar.

Kuttel, *f.* [*pl.* -n] [Low Sax. *küt* = Gedärme, Sw. *kött* = Fleisch] 1) chitterling, tripe: V. Eingeweide. 2) [in nat. hist.] V. Schiffs—.

Kuttel-bank, *f.* tripe-house, tripe-shop. —**fisch**, *m.* the cuttle-fish, sepia. —**flecke**, *f.* chitterlings dressed for eating. —**hof**, *m.* [rather provincial] butcher's yard, slaughtering-yard, shambles. —**kraut**, *n.* 1) wild thyme, serpillum. 2) Welsches —kraut, mother of thyme. —**markt**, *m.* tripe-market, tripery.

||**Kutten**, *v. intr.* [Engl. *to cut*, allied to the L. *caedo* and *cudo*] 1) to dig, to cut. 2) V. Ein—.

Kutter, *m.* [-s, *pl.* -] [a vessel] cutter.

Kuttler, *m.* [-s, *pl.* -], —**inn**, *f.* tripe-man, tripe-woman.

Kutz, *interj.* [in fam. lang.] cat! cat!

Kütz, *m.* [-es, *pl.* -e] [allied to Kitze] kid.

Kutze, *f.* [*pl.* -n] or **Kutzen**, *m.* [-s, *pl.* -] [another form of Kotzen] a coarse cover or coverlet. †Einem den —n streichen, V. 1. Kotze.

†**Kutzenstreicher**, *m.* V. Kotzenstreicher.

Kützel, Kützeln, V. Kitzel, Kitzeln.

Kux, *m.* [-es, *pl.* -e] [Boh. *kukus*, *kus* = ein Theil, probably from the old katten, katsen = schneiden] [formerly] any share in a thing; now, share in a mine. Einen — kaufen, to buy a share of a mine.

Kuxkränzler, *m.* broker who sells shares in a mine.

Kybitz, *m.* V. Kibitz.

End of the first Volume.

Lightning Source UK Ltd.
Milton Keynes UK
UKHW021623030219
336610UK00007B/718/P

9 780365 20153